SUGGESTIONS FOR FAST, EFFECTIVE USE OF THE INDEX

1. PLEASE **READ THE FOREWORD** TO THE INDEX WHICH APPEARS IN THIS VOLUME.

2. STOP AND THINK ABOUT YOUR SUBJECT; TAKE A MOMENT TO **SELECT THE TERMS MOST DESCRIPTIVE OF YOUR RESEARCH SUBJECT.** IT HELPS TO SELECT THE PRINCIPAL SUBJECT RATHER THAN THE SECONDARY SUBJECT AND TO LOOK FOR NOUNS RATHER THAN ADJECTIVES.

3. IF YOU KNOW THE SHORT TITLE OR THE POPULAR NAME OF A STATUTE, YOU MAY CONSULT THE **SHORT TITLE/POPULAR NAME INDEX**, WHICH IMMEDIATE-LY PRECEDES THE GENERAL INDEX. ALSO PRECEDING THE GENERAL INDEX IS THE **EXECUTIVE AGENCY INDEX**, WHICH CONTAINS REFERENCES TO THE STATUTORY AND CONSTITUTIONAL PROVISIONS CREATING THE AGENCIES.

4. IF YOUR SEARCH DOES NOT LEAD YOU TO THE CODE SECTION SOUGHT, OR IF YOU HAVE QUESTIONS ABOUT OR SUGGESTIONS FOR THE INDEX, PLEASE FEEL WELCOME TO **CONTACT THE INDEXERS.** THE INDEXERS MAY BE REACHED DIRECTLY BY THE FOLLOWING METHODS: **TOLL-FREE INDEX NUMBER, 1-800-897-7922,** BETWEEN 8:00 AM AND 4:30 PM, EASTERN TIME ZONE; **FAX NUMBER 1-434-972-7686; INTERNET E-MAIL** ADDRESSED TO **lng-cho-indexing@lexisnexis.com.**

GENERAL STATUTES OF NORTH CAROLINA

ANNOTATED

Volume 20
2011 INDEX
A to I

INDEX TO GENERAL LAWS OF NORTH CAROLINA
ENACTED BY THE GENERAL ASSEMBLY

Prepared under the Supervision of
THE LEGISLATIVE SERVICES OFFICE OF THE GENERAL ASSEMBLY
OF THE STATE OF NORTH CAROLINA
by
The Editorial Staff of the Publisher

LexisNexis®

4657728

ISBN 978-1-4224-8674-0

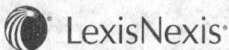 LexisNexis·

Matthew Bender & Company, Inc.
701 E. Water Street, Charlottesville, VA 22902-5389
www.lexisnexis.com

Customer Service: 1-800-833-9844

Foreword to the Indexes

Purpose–The purpose of this Foreword is to communicate to index users some of the characteristics of this particular index and also to provide insight into the way in which the Indexing staff tried to translate the years of contactwith index users into a useful, efficient, and easy-to-use index. You know how to use an index; this Foreword and the suggestions for using the index are offered to aid in the effective use of this particular index.

Coverage–Each section of the General Statutes of North Carolina through legislation enacted during the 2011 Session, and each provision of the Constitutions of North Carolina and the United States has been thoroughly examined and covered in the index. Also included in the index is coverage of court rules of the state courts; the text of these rules appears in the soft-bound "Annotated Rules of North Carolina."

Special Indexes–Also contained in this index, at the beginning of the first index volume, are an updated index of executive agencies, containing references to the statutory and constitutional provisions creating them, and an updated combined index of short titles and popular names of legislation.

Citations–Statutory provisions are referred to in the index by section number (e.g., §48-10-101), including when indicated, subsections (e.g., §20-141(h)). The constitutions are identified by abbreviations, a table of which follows this Foreword.

Philosophy–The index is a combination of two approaches to indexing, topical and descriptive word. LexisNexis® undertook this dual approach in order to provide index users with the advantages of each approach; the addition of thousands of descriptive main headings to a topical framework combines the access provided by the descriptive word approach and the organization and consistency of terminology provided by the topical approach. The result is a user-friendly and manageable index.

Cross References–Users sometimes question the necessity or desirability of cross references ("see" lines) in indexes. Cross references are used to keep indexes to a manageable size by reducing the amount of repetition of treatment under different headings. To make cross references even more useful and efficient, LexisNexis® has taken the following steps.

Double Jumps–"Double jump" cross references, which are cross references to other cross references, have been avoided.

Three Section Rule–Cross references have been used only to direct users to index entries covering three or more sections.

Group Section References–Group section references, which cite the user to the principal statutory treatment of a subject, have been attached to many of our cross references; this provides the user with the option to go immediately to the code for the cited material.

Main headings–Main headings were derived from the language of the General Statutes of North Carolina, from the phraseology commonly used in the courts of North Carolina and terminology commonly used in the legal profession. In addition, an effort was made to employ phrases commonly applied to General Statutes sections, such as frequently used nonlegal terms.

Communication with the Indexers-LexisNexis® solicits your help in keeping this index as useful as possible. You may communicate with Indexing regarding any matter concerning the Index such as suggestions for improvements to the Index or the inability to locate a particular section in the Index by **toll-free telephone number (1-800-897-7922),** by **Internet E-mail (lng-cho-indexing@lexisnexis.com)** or by **fax (1-434-972-7686).** All suggestions, questions or comments receive serious consideration. For all other non-Index questions and comments or to place orders, **Customer Service** may be reached by **toll-free telephone number (1-800-833-9844)** or by **toll-free fax (1-800-828-8341).**

Scope of Index–The general index does not attempt to cover each topic in the vast field of law but refers only to those materials contained in the General Statutes. A thorough knowledge of the format and terminology of the General Statutes contributes to the efficient use of this index as a guide to subject matter.

Suggestions–LexisNexis® offers a few suggestions for efficient use of this index. Creating an index involves communicating with index users by anticipating where index users might look. It is hoped that these examples suggest to index users how the Indexers went about this process of anticipation and thus improve the communication between the Indexers and index users.

(1) *Gain familiarity with the contents of the General Statutes and the index.* Although it is not a predicate to using the index successfully, knowledge of the arrangement, terminology, topical treatment, analyses and reference system of both the General Statutes and the index is conducive to the efficient use of the index.

(2) *Consult the principal subject and not the secondary subject.* Thus, for motor vehicle registration, look under **MOTOR VEHICLE REGISTRATION** and not under **REGISTRATION;** for drivers' licenses, look under **DRIVERS' LICENSES** and not under **MOTOR VEHICLES;** for attorneys' fees, look under **ATTORNEYS' FEES** and not under **FEES.**

(3) *Search under commonly used phrases or terms of art.* Thus, for wrongful death, look under **WRONGFUL DEATH** and not under **DEATH;** for declaratory judgments, look under **DECLARATORY JUDGMENTS** and not under **JUDGMENTS**.

(4) *Look under specific areas of law and not under broad areas of law.* Thus, for life insurance, look under **LIFE INSURANCE** and not under **INSURANCE;** for nonprofit corporations, look under **NONPROFIT CORPORATIONS** and not under **CORPORATIONS.**

(5) *Consult the most pertinent subject.* Thus, for depositions, look under **DEPOSITIONS** and not under **EVIDENCE** or **TESTIMONY** or **WITNESSES;** for sales by executors and administrators, look under **EXECUTORS AND ADMINISTRATORS** and not under **WILLS** or **DESCENT AND DISTRIBUTION** or **INTESTATE SUCCESSION.**

(6) *Consult allied or related headings.* If your search under one heading is to no avail, try a related heading. Thus, if a search under the heading **PEACE OFFICERS** is fruitless, try **POLICE** or **HIGHWAY PATROL** or other related headings. Each section has itemized entries, but perhaps they appear under headings that may not have initially occurred to you.

(7) *Use descriptive words or phrases to aid in your search.* If you have trouble expressing your search topically, use descriptive words or phrases. Thus, if it does not occur to you to search under concealment of merchandise in mercantile establishments for the crime of concealing unpurchased merchandise, look under **SHOPLIFTING;** if you want the provisions covering a motor vehicle manufacturer's duty as to new automobiles that cannot be repaired after a reasonable number of attempts, the index provides the option of looking under **LEMON LAW;** if public safety telephone service does not come to mind, try **911 SYSTEM.**

(8) *Begin your search with "starting point" headings.* "Starting point" headings are collections of entries or cross references that can provide assistance in getting a search started by exposing the index user to a diverse sampling of statutory terminology, which could suggest to the user other headings to consult. Although there is no formal list of "starting point" headings, the following have proven to be useful for that purpose: **DEFINED TERMS** (entries for all defined terms); **PRISON TERMS** (entries for each offense that carries a prison term); **CRIMINAL LAW AND PROCEDURE** (direction to all criminal offenses); **MISDEMEANORS** (all misdemeanor offenses); **FELONIES** (all felony offenses); **FINES** (all offenses carrying a fine); **BOARDS AND COMMISSIONS** (lists of all boards and commissions).

(9) *Use cross references.* Pay close attention to and make full use of the index cross references. An index cross reference is a direction, using the word "See", to the index user to go to another part of the index to find treatment. There are two types of cross references, external and internal. External cross references direct index users to another main heading. Thus, "**AERONAUTICS. Aircraft.** See AIRCRAFT" directs the index user from the main heading **AERONAUTICS** to the main heading **AIRCRAFT.** Internal cross references direct index users from one subheading within a main heading to another subheading within that same main heading. Thus, under the main heading **MOTOR VEHICLE EQUIPMENT,** "**Seat belts.** See within this heading 'Safety belts.'" directs the index user from the subheading **Seat belts** to the subheading **Safety belts.**

(10) *Keep in touch.* Let LexisNexis® know how you like the index. Contact the Indexers directly as indicated above under **Communication with the Indexers** if you have questions about or suggestions for the index.

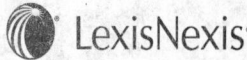

Table of Abbreviations

AdmissPrac Rule................................Rules Governing Admission to the Practice of Law

Amd...Amendment

AppProc Rule...................................North Carolina Rules of Appellate Procedure

Appx ....Appendix

Arbitration Rule...............................Rules for Court-Ordered Arbitration in North Carolina

Art ....Article

Bar Rule ....Rules and Regulations of the North Carolina State Bar

CEA ....Canons of Ethics for Arbitrators

ChildhoodVaccine Rule ....Rules of the Industrial Commission Relating to North Carolina Childhood Vaccine-Related Injury

CJE Rule ....Rules of Continuing Judicial Education

CLE Reg ....Regulations Governing Continuing Legal Education

CustodyVisit Rule ....Custody and Visitation Mediation in North Carolina

DisputeRes Comm Rule......................Rules for the Dispute Resolution Commission

FarmMediation Rule ....Prelitigation Farm Nuisance Mediation Program

ICDeathBenefits Rule ....Rules of the Industrial Commission Relating to the Law-Enforcement Officers', Firemen's, Rescue Squad Workers' and Civil Air Patrol Members' Death Benefits Act

ICManagedCare Rule.........................North Carolina Industrial Commission Rules for Managed Care Organizations

ICMediated Settlmt Rule ....Mediated Settlement and Neutral Evaluation Conferences Rules of the North Carolina Industrial Commission

ICRehabProf Rule ....North Carolina Industrial Commission Rules for Utilization of Rehabilitation Professionals in Workers' Compensation Claims

ICTortClaim Rule..............................Rules of the Industrial Commission Relating to Tort Claims

ICWorkComp Form ....Workers' Compensation Rules of the North Carolina Industrial Commission Official Forms

ICWorkComp Rule ....Workers' Compensation Rules of the North Carolina Industrial Commis-

IDS Rule ....Rules for Indigent Defense Services

IndigCounsel ....Rules and Regulations Relating to the Appointment of Counsel for Indigent Defendants in Certain Criminal Cases

JudCond Canon ....Code of Judicial Conduct

JudStdsComm Rule.............................Rules of the Judicial Standards Commission

JudStdsComm SupCtReview Rule ....Rules for Supreme Court Review of Recommendations of the Judicial Standards Commission

MediationDistCrimCt Rule ....Rules Implementing Mediation in Matters Pending in District Criminal Court

MLG ....Medico-Legal Guidelines

NC Const ....Constitution of North Carolina

ProfCond Rule ....Rules of Professional Conduct of the North Carolina State Bar

SettlmtEquitDistrib Rule ....Rules Implementing Settlement Procedures in Equitable Distribution and Other Family Financial Cases

SPCM Rule ....Standards of Professional Conduct for Mediators

SupCtLibrary Rule ....North Carolina Supreme Court Library Rules

SuperCtMediatedSettlemt Rule...........Rules Implementing Statewide Mediated Settlement Conferences in Superior Court Civil Actions

SuperCt Rule.......................................General Rules of Practice for the Superior and District Courts

US Const ....Constitution of the United States

**The court rules appear in the softbound "Annotated Rules of North Carolina."
The constitutions appear in Volume 19.**

Executive Agency Index

A

ADMINISTRATIVE RULES REVIEW COMMISSION, §143B-30.1.

ADVISORY COMMISSION FOR NORTH CAROLINA STATE MUSEUM OF NATURAL SCIENCES, §143B-344.18.

ADVISORY COMMISSION ON MILITARY AFFAIRS, §127C-1.

ADVISORY COUNCIL ON CANCER COORDINATION AND CONTROL, §130A-33.50.

ADVISORY COUNCIL ON THE EASTERN BAND OF THE CHEROKEE, §143B-411.1.

AFRICAN-AMERICAN HERITAGE COMMISSION, §143B-135.

AGENCY FOR PUBLIC TELECOMMUNICATIONS, §143B-426.9.

AGRICULTURAL HALL OF FAME, §106-568.13.

AGRICULTURE FINANCE AUTHORITY, §122D-4.

AIR CARGO AUTHORITY, §63A-3.

AIR QUALITY COUNCIL, §143B-317.

ALARM SYSTEMS LICENSING BOARD, §74D-4.

ALCOHOLIC BEVERAGE CONTROL COMMISSION, §18B-200.
Tribal alcoholic beverage control commission, §18B-112.

ALCOHOLISM RESEARCH AUTHORITY, §122C-431.

AMERICA'S FOUR HUNDREDTH ANNIVERSARY COMMITTEE, §143B-85.

ANIMAL HEALTH DIVISION OF THE NORTH CAROLINA DEPARTMENT OF AGRICULTURE, §19A-22.

APPRAISAL BOARD, §93E-1-5.

APPRENTICESHIP COUNCIL, §94-2.

ARTS COUNCIL, §143B-87.

ARTS SOCIETY, INCORPORATED, §143B-89.

ATLANTIC STATES MARINE FISHERIES COMMISSION, §113-252.

AUCTIONEERS COMMISSION, §85B-3.

AWARDS COMMITTEE, §143B-83.

B

BICYCLE COMMITTEE, §136-71.13.

BOARD FOR LICENSING OF GEOLOGISTS, §89E-4.

BOARD FOR LICENSING OF SOIL SCIENTISTS, §89F-4.

BOARD OF AGRICULTURE, §106-2.

BOARD OF ARCHITECTURE, §83A-2.

BOARD OF ATHLETIC TRAINER EXAMINERS, §90-524.

BOARD OF BOILER AND PRESSURE VESSEL RULES, §95-69.13.

BOARD OF CERTIFIED PUBLIC ACCOUNTANT EXAMINERS, §93-12.

BOARD OF CORRECTION, §143B-715.

BOARD OF DIETETICS/NUTRITION, §90-353.

BOARD OF ELECTROLYSIS EXAMINERS, §88A-5.

BOARD OF EMPLOYEE ASSISTANCE PROFESSIONALS, §90-501.

BOARD OF EXAMINERS FOR SPEECH AND LANGUAGE PATHOLOGISTS AND AUDIOLOGISTS, §90-303.

BOARD OF FUNERAL SERVICE, §90-210.18A.

BOARD OF GOVERNORS OF THE UNIVERSITY OF NORTH CAROLINA, §116-3.

BOARD OF LANDSCAPE ARCHITECTS, §89A-3.

BOARD OF LAW EXAMINERS, §84-24.

BOARD OF LICENSED PROFESSIONAL COUNSELORS, §90-333.

BOARD OF MASSAGE AND BODYWORK THERAPY, §90-625.

BOARD OF NURSING, §90-171.21.

BOARD OF OCCUPATIONAL THERAPY, §90-270.68.

BOARD OF PHARMACY, §90-85.6.

BOARD OF PHYSICAL THERAPY EXAMINERS, §90-270.25.

BOARD OF PODIATRY EXAMINERS FOR THE STATE OF NORTH CAROLINA, §90-202.4(a).

BOARD OF TRANSPORTATION, §143B-350.

BOARD OF TRUSTEES FOR RETIREMENT SYSTEM FOR TEACHERS AND STATE EMPLOYEES, §135-6.

BOARD OF TRUSTEES OF THE NORTH CAROLINA FIREMEN'S AND RESCUE SQUAD WORKERS' PENSION FUND, §58-86-5.

BOARD OF TRUSTEES OF THE NORTH CAROLINA MUSEUM OF ART, §140-5.13.

BOARD OF TRUSTEES OF THE STATE HEALTH PLAN FOR TEACHERS AND STATE EMPLOYEES, §135-44.

BOILER SAFETY BUREAU, §95-69.12.

BOXING ADVISORY COMMISSION, §143-652.2.

1

BRAIN INJURY ADVISORY COUNCIL, §143B-216.65.

BUILDING CODE COUNCIL, §143-136.

BUREAU OF MINES, §113-26.1.

C

CAPE FEAR NAVIGATION AND PILOTAGE COMMISSION, §76A-1.

CAPITAL PLANNING COMMISSION, §143B-373.

CEMETERY COMMISSION, §§65-49 to 65-54.

CENTER FOR MISSING PERSONS, §143B-1010.

CHILD CARE COMMISSION, §143B-168.4.

CIVIL AIR PATROL SECTION, §143B-272.73A.

COASTAL RESOURCES ADVISORY COUNCIL, §113A-105.

COASTAL RESOURCES COMMISSION, §113A-104.

CODE OFFICIALS QUALIFICATION BOARD, §143-151.9.

COMMISSION FOR MENTAL HEALTH, DEVELOPMENTAL DISABILITIES AND SUBSTANCE ABUSE SERVICES, §143B-147.

COMMISSION FOR PUBLIC HEALTH, §130A-29.

COMMISSION FOR THE BLIND, §143B-157.

COMMISSION OF ANATOMY, §130A-33.30.

COMMISSION ON AGRICULTURE, FORESTRY AND SEAFOOD AWARENESS, §120-150.

COMMISSION ON CHILDREN WITH SPECIAL HEALTH CARE NEEDS, §143-682.

COMMISSION ON INDIGENT DEFENSE SERVICES, §7A-498.4.

COMMISSION ON SCHOOL TECHNOLOGY, §115C-102.5.

COMMISSION TO STUDY THE CARE OF THE AGED AND HANDICAPPED, §143-279.

COMMITTEE ON INAUGURAL CEREMONIES, §143-533.

COMMUNITY COLLEGES SYSTEM OFFICE, §115D-3.

COMMUNITY DEVELOPMENT COUNCIL, §143B-437.1.

COMMUNITY OF BUTNER PLANNING COMMISSION, §122C-402.

COMMUNITY PENALTIES BOARD, §7A-775.

CONSUMER AND ADVOCACY ADVISORY COMMITTEE FOR THE BLIND, §143B-163.

CORRECTION ENTERPRISES.
Division of correction enterprises, §148-131.

COUNCIL FOR THE DEAF AND THE HARD OF HEARING, §143B-216.31.

COUNCIL FOR WOMEN, §143B-393.

COUNCIL OF INTERNAL AUDITING, §143-747.

COUNCIL OF STATE GOVERNMENTS, §143-186.

COUNCIL ON DEVELOPMENTAL DISABILITIES, §143B-177.

COUNCIL ON SICKLE CELL SYNDROME, §130A-131.2.

COUNCIL ON THE HOLOCAUST, §143A-48.1.

COURTS COMMISSION, §7A-506.

CREDIT UNION COMMISSION, §143B-439.

CREDIT UNION DIVISION, §54-109.10.

CREMATORY AUTHORITY, §90-210.122.

CRIME CONTROL DIVISION, §143B-1103.

CRIME VICTIMS' COMPENSATION COMMISSION, §15B-3.

CRIMINAL JUSTICE EDUCATION AND TRAINING STANDARDS COMMISSION, §17C-3.

CRIMINAL JUSTICE INFORMATION NETWORK GOVERNING BOARD, §143-661.

CROP IMPROVEMENT ASSOCIATION, §106-273.

D

DEPARTMENT OF ADMINISTRATION, §§143-335, 143B-366.

DEPARTMENT OF AGRICULTURE AND CONSUMER SERVICES, §§106-2, 143A-56.

DEPARTMENT OF COMMERCE, §143B-427.

DEPARTMENT OF CULTURAL RESOURCES, §§121-3, 143B-49.

DEPARTMENT OF ENVIRONMENT AND NATURAL RESOURCES, §143B-279.1.

DEPARTMENT OF HEALTH AND HUMAN SERVICES, §143B-136.1.

DEPARTMENT OF INSURANCE, §§58-2-1, 143A-73.

DEPARTMENT OF JUSTICE, §§114-1, 143A-49.

DEPARTMENT OF LABOR, §143A-67.

DEPARTMENT OF PUBLIC INSTRUCTION, §143A-44.1.

DEPARTMENT OF PUBLIC SAFETY, §143B-600.

DEPARTMENT OF REVENUE, §143B-217.

DEPARTMENT OF STATE AUDITOR, §143A-24.

DEPARTMENT OF STATE TREASURER, §143A-30.

DEPARTMENT OF THE SECRETARY OF STATE, §143A-19.

DEPARTMENT OF TRANSPORTATION, §143B-345.

DIVISION OF ADULT CORRECTION, §143B-700.

DIVISION OF AERONAUTICS, §143B-355.

DIVISION OF AGING, §143B-181.1.

DIVISION OF CORRECTION ENTERPRISES, §148-131.

DIVISION OF CRIMINAL STATISTICS, §114-10.

DIVISION OF EMERGENCY MANAGEMENT, §143B-1000.

DIVISION OF JUVENILE JUSTICE, §143B-800.

DIVISION OF LAW ENFORCEMENT, §143B-600.

DIVISION OF LEGISLATIVE DRAFTING AND CODIFICATION OF STATUTES, §114-9.

DIVISION OF MOTOR VEHICLES OF THE DEPARTMENT OF TRANSPORTATION, §20-1.

DIVISION OF NORTH CAROLINA AQUARIUMS, §143B-289.40.

DIVISION OF PUBLICATIONS, §147-54.1.

DIVISION OF SERVICES FOR THE DEAF AND THE HARD OF HEARING, §143B-216.33.

DIVISION OF WASTE MANAGEMENT, §130a-291.

DOMESTIC VIOLENCE COMMISSION, §143B-394.15.

E

ECONOMIC DEVELOPMENT BOARD, §143B-434.

ECONOMIC INVESTMENT COMMITTEE.
Job development investment grant program, §143B-437.48.

EDENTON HISTORICAL COMMISSION, §143B-95.

EDUCATION CABINET, §116C-1.

ELEVATOR AND AMUSEMENT DEVICE DIVISION, §95-110.4.

EMERGENCY MEDICAL SERVICES ADVISORY COUNCIL, §143-510(a).

EMPLOYMENT SECURITY DIVISION OF NORTH CAROLINA, §96-3.

ENERGY POLICY COUNCIL, §113B-2.

ENVIRONMENTAL MANAGEMENT COMMISSION, §143B-282.

EXECUTIVE MANSION FINE ARTS COMMITTEE, §143B-79.

F

FALLS LAKE WATERSHED ASSOCIATION, §77-140.

FARMWORKER COUNCIL, §143B-426.25.

FEDERAL TAX REFORM ALLOCATION COMMITTEE, §143-433.7.

FINANCIAL LITERACY COUNCIL, §114-50.

FORENSIC SCIENCE ADVISORY BOARD, §114-16.1.

FORESTRY COUNCIL, §143A-66.1.

G

GASOLINE AND OIL INSPECTION BOARD, §119-26.

GENERAL STATUTES COMMISSION, §164-12.

GEOGRAPHIC INFORMATION COORDINATING COUNCIL, §143-725.

GLOBAL TRANSPARK AUTHORITY, §63A-3.

GOVERNOR'S ADVISORY COUNCIL ON AGING, §143B-180.

GOVERNOR'S COUNCIL ON EMPLOYMENT OF THE HANDICAPPED, §143-283.1.

GOVERNOR'S CRIME COMMISSION, §143B-1100.

GOVERNOR'S JOBS FOR VETERANS COMMITTEE, §143B-420.

GOVERNOR'S MANAGEMENT COUNCIL, §143B-426.22.

GRASSROOTS ARTS PROGRAM, §143B-121.

GREEN BUSINESS FUND ADVISORY COMMITTEE, §143B-437.5.

GRIEVANCE RESOLUTION BOARD, §148-118.6.

H

HEALTH AND WELLNESS TRUST FUND COMMISSION, §147-86.32.

HIGH ROCK LAKE MARINE COMMISSION, §77-51.

HISTORICAL COMMISSION, §143B-62.

HISTORIC BATH COMMISSION, §143B-99.

HISTORIC HILLSBOROUGH COMMISSION, §143B-103.

HISTORIC MURFREESBORO COMMISSION, §143B-107.

HOME INSPECTOR LICENSURE BOARD, §143-151.46.

HOUSING FINANCE AGENCY, §122A-4.

HUMAN RELATIONS COMMISSION, §7A-761.

I

INDIAN HOUSING AUTHORITY, §157-66.

INDUSTRIAL COMMISSION, §97-77.

INFORMATION TECHNOLOGY SERVICES OFFICE, §§147-33.75 to 147-33.104A.

INNOCENCE INQUIRY COMMISSION, §15A-1462.

INSURANCE GUARANTY ASSOCIATION, §58-48-25.

INSURANCE UNDERWRITING ASSOCIATION, §58-45-10.

INTERAGENCY COORDINATING COUNCIL FOR CHILDREN FROM BIRTH TO FIVE WITH DISABILITIES AND THEIR FAMILIES, §143B-179.5.

INTERNSHIP COUNCIL, §143B-417.

INTERPRETER AND TRANSLITERATOR LICENSING BOARD, §90D-5.

INTERSTATE COMMISSION FOR JUVENILES, §7B-4001.

IRRIGATION CONTRACTORS' LICENSING BOARD, §89G-4.

J

JOHN MOTLEY MOREHEAD MEMORIAL COMMISSION, §143B-111.

JUDICIAL STANDARDS COMMISSION, §7A-374.1.

JUSTICE ACADEMY, §17D-2.

JUSTUS-WARREN HEART DISEASE AND STROKE PREVENTION COUNCIL, §143B-216.60.

JUVENILE CRIME PREVENTION COUNCILS, §143B-845.

JUVENILE JUSTICE, OFFICE OF, §147-33.30.

L

LAKE LURE MARINE COMMISSION, §77-80.

LAKE WYLIE MARINE COMMISSION, §77-30.

LAND CONSERVATION AND LAND DEVELOPMENT BUREAU, §54-49.

LAND POLICY COUNCIL, §113A-153.

LANDSCAPE CONTRACTORS' REGISTRATION BOARD, §89D-4(a).

LIBRARY AGENCY OF STATE. Department of cultural resources, §125-1.

LOCAL GOVERNMENT COMMISSION, §159-3.

LOCKSMITH LICENSING BOARD, §74F-5.

M

MANUFACTURED HOUSING BOARD, §143-143.10.

MARINE FISHERIES COMMISSION, §143B-289.51.

MARRIAGE AND FAMILY THERAPY LICENSURE BOARD, §90-270.49.

MARTIN LUTHER KING, JR. COMMISSION, §143B-426.34A.

MEDICAL BOARD, §90-2.

MEDICAL CARE COMMISSION, §143B-165.

MINING COMMISSION, §143B-290.

MINORITY HEALTH ADVISORY COUNCIL, §130A-33.43.

MOREHEAD CITY NAVIGATION AND PILOTAGE COMMISSION, §76A-31.

MOTOR VEHICLE DEALERS' ADVISORY BOARD, §20-305.4.

MOTOR VEHICLE REINSURANCE FACILITY, §58-37-5.

MOUNTAIN ISLAND LAKE MARINE COMMISSION, §77-70.

MOUNTAIN RESOURCES COMMISSION, §153B-3.

N

NONGAME WILDLIFE ADVISORY COMMITTEE, §113-335.

NURSING SCHOLARS COMMISSION, §90-171.60.

O

OCCUPATIONAL SAFETY AND HEALTH REVIEW COMMISSION, §95-135.

OFFICE OF ADMINISTRATIVE HEARINGS, §7A-750.

OFFICE OF COORDINATOR OF SERVICES FOR VICTIMS OF SEXUAL ASSAULT, §143B-394.1.

OFFICE OF ENVIRONMENTAL EDUCATION AND PUBLIC AFFAIRS, §143B-285.22.

OFFICE OF INDIGENT DEFENSE SERVICES, §7A-498.2.

OFFICE OF INFORMATION TECHNOLOGY SERVICES, §§147-33.75 to 147-33.104A.

OFFICE OF INTERNAL AUDITOR. Department of health and human services, §143B-216.50.

OFFICE OF LOCAL GOVERNMENT ADVOCACY, §143-506.14.

OFFICE OF OCCUPATIONAL SAFETY AND HEALTH, §95-133.

OFFICE OF POLICY AND PLANNING. Department of health and human services, §143B-216.70.

OFFICE OF STATE COMPTROLLER, §143B-426.36.

OFFICE OF STATE PERSONNEL, §126-3.

OFFICE OF WOMEN'S HEALTH, §130A-131.25.

P

PARKS AND RECREATION AUTHORITY, §143B-313.1.

PERFUSION ADVISORY COMMITTEE, §90-684.

PESTICIDE BOARD, §143-436.

PIEDMONT TRIAD RESEARCH INSTITUTE, §116-250.

PLANT CONSERVATION BOARD, §106-202.14(a).

POSTAL HISTORY COMMISSION, §143-675.

POST-RELEASE SUPERVISION AND PAROLE COMMISSION, §143B-720.

PRIVATE PROTECTIVE SERVICES BOARD, §74C-4.

PROFESSIONAL ADVISORY COMMITTEE, §143B-161.

PROPERTY TAX COMMISSION, §105-288(b).

PSYCHOLOGY BOARD, §90-270.6.

PUBLIC EMPLOYEE DEFERRED COMPENSATION PLAN. Board of trustees, §143B-426.24.

PUBLIC HEALTH STUDY COMMISSION, §120-195.

PUBLIC LIBRARIAN CERTIFICATION COMMISSION, §143B-67.

PUBLIC LIVESTOCK MARKET ADVISORY BOARD, §106-407.1.

PUBLIC RADIO ADVISORY COMMITTEE, §143B-426.12.

R

RADIATION PROTECTION AGENCY.
Department of environment and natural resources, §104E-6.

RADIATION PROTECTION COMMISSION, §104E-7.

RAIL COUNCIL, §143B-362.

RATE BUREAU, §58-36-1.

REAL ESTATE COMMISSION, §93A-3.

RECREATIONAL THERAPY LICENSURE BOARD, §90C-23.

RESPIRATORY CARE BOARD, §90-649.

RIVER BASINS ADVISORY COMMISSIONS, §77-111.

ROANOKE ISLAND COMMISSION, §143B-131.1.

ROANOKE ISLAND HISTORICAL ASSOCIATION, §143B-92.

ROANOKE RIVER BASIN ADVISORY COMMITTEE, §77-103.

ROANOKE RIVER BASIN BI-STATE COMMISSION, §77-91.

RURAL ELECTRIFICATION AUTHORITY, §117-1.

S

SCIENCE AND TECHNOLOGY RESEARCH CENTER, §143B-442.

SEAFOOD INDUSTRIAL PARK AUTHORITY, §113-315.25.

SEDIMENTATION CONTROL COMMISSION, §143B-299(a).
Department of the environment and natural resources, §143B-298.

SELF-INSURANCE SECURITY ASSOCIATION, §97-131.

SENIOR TAR HEEL LEGISLATURE, §143B-181.55.

SENTENCING AND POLICY ADVISORY COMMISSION, §164-35.

SHERIFFS' EDUCATION AND TRAINING STANDARDS COMMISSION, §17E-3.

SMALL BUSINESS CONTRACTORS AUTHORITY, §143B-472.102.

SOCIAL SERVICES COMMISSION, §143B-153.

SOCIAL WORK CERTIFICATION AND LICENSURE BOARD, §90B-5.

SOIL AND WATER CONSERVATION COMMISSION, §106-840.

SOUTHERN GROWTH POLICIES BOARD, §143-492.

SOUTHERN STATES ENERGY BOARD, §104D-1.

SPECIAL PROSECUTION DIVISION, §114-11.6.

STATE ADVISORY COUNCIL ON OCCUPATIONAL SAFETY AND HEALTH, §95-134.

STATE AGENCY FOR FEDERAL SURPLUS PROPERTY.
Department of administration, §143-64.1.

STATE BAR, §84-15.

STATE BOARD OF BARBER EXAMINERS, §86A-4.

STATE BOARD OF CHIROPRACTIC EXAMINERS, §90-139.

STATE BOARD OF COMMUNITY COLLEGES, §115D-2.1.

STATE BOARD OF COSMETIC ART EXAMINERS, §88B-3.

STATE BOARD OF DENTAL EXAMINERS, §90-22.

STATE BOARD OF EDUCATION, §115C-10.

STATE BOARD OF ELECTIONS, §163-19.

STATE BOARD OF ENVIRONMENTAL HEALTH SPECIALISTS EXAMINERS, §90A-50.

STATE BOARD OF EXAMINERS FOR NURSING HOME ADMINISTRATORS, §90-277.

STATE BOARD OF EXAMINERS IN OPTOMETRY, §90-116.

STATE BOARD OF EXAMINERS OF ELECTRICAL CONTRACTORS, §87-39.

STATE BOARD OF EXAMINERS OF FEE-BASED PRACTICING PASTORAL COUNSELORS, §90-385.

STATE BOARD OF EXAMINERS OF PLUMBING AND HEATING CONTRACTORS, §87-16.

STATE BOARD OF OPTICIANS, §90-238.

STATE BOARD OF REFRIGERATION EXAMINERS, §87-52.

STATE BOARD OF REGISTRATION FOR FORESTERS, §89B-3(a).

STATE BOARD OF REGISTRATION FOR PROFESSIONAL ENGINEERS AND LAND SURVEYORS, §89C-4.

STATE BUILDING COMMISSION, §143-135.25.

STATE BUREAU OF INVESTIGATION, §114-12.

STATE CAPITAL POLICE DIVISION, §143B-900.

STATE CHILD FATALITY REVIEW TEAM, 143B-150.20.

STATE COMMISSION OF INDIAN AFFAIRS, §143B-404.

STATE COMMUNITY CORRECTIONS ADVISORY BOARD, §143B-1158.

STATE EDUCATION ASSISTANCE AUTHORITY, §116-203.

STATE EDUCATION COMMISSION, §§116C-2, 143-261.

STATE ETHICS COMMISSION, §138A-6.

STATE FIRE AND RESCUE COMMISSION, §58-78-1.

STATE HEARING AID DEALERS AND FITTERS BOARD, §93D-3.

STATE HIGHWAY PATROL, §20-184.

STATE JUDICIAL COUNCIL, §7A-409.

STATE LABORATORY OF PUBLIC HEALTH, §130A-88.

STATE LIBRARY COMMISSION, §143B-90.

STATE LICENSING BOARD FOR GENERAL CONTRACTORS, §87-2.

STATE MARKETING AUTHORITY, §106-529.

STATE PERSONNEL COMMISSION, §126-2.

STATE SURPLUS PROPERTY AGENCY. Department of administration, §143-64.01.

STATE YOUTH ADVISORY COUNCIL, §143B-385.

STATE YOUTH COUNCIL, §143B-387.

STRUCTURAL PEST CONTROL COMMITTEE, §106-65.23.

STRUCTURAL PEST CONTROL DIVISION OF DEPARTMENT OF AGRICULTURE, §106-65.23.

STUDY COMMISSION ON AGING, §120-180.

SUBSTANCE ABUSE PROFESSIONALS CERTIFICATION BOARD, §90-113.32.

SUSTAINABLE COMMUNITIES TASK FORCE, §143B-344.35.

SUSTAINABLE LOCAL FOOD ADVISORY COUNCIL, §106-830.

SYMPHONY SOCIETY, INC., §143B-94.

T

TEXTBOOK COMMISSION, §115C-87.

TOBACCO TRUST FUND COMMISSION, §143-715.

TRAILS COMMITTEE, §143B-333.

TRAVEL AND TOURISM BOARD, §143B-434.1.

TRIBAL ALCOHOLIC BEVERAGE CONTROL COMMISSION, §18B-112.

TRYON'S PALACE COMMISSION, §143B-71.

TURNPIKE AUTHORITY, §136-89.182.

U

U.S.S. NORTH CAROLINA BATTLESHIP COMMISSION, §143B-73.

UTILITIES COMMISSION, §62-10.

UWHARRIE REGIONAL RESOURCES COMMISSION, §153C-3.

V

VESSEL COMMITTEE OF WILDLIFE RESOURCES COMMISSION, §75A-3.

VETERANS' AFFAIRS COMMISSION, §143B-399.

VETERANS' MEMORIAL COMMISSION, §143B-133.

VETERINARY MEDICAL BOARD, §90-182.

W

WAGE AND HOUR DIVISION, §95-25.17.

WATER POLLUTION CONTROL SYSTEM OPERATORS CERTIFICATION COMMISSION, §143B-300.

WATER TREATMENT FACILITY OPERATORS BOARD OF CERTIFICATION, §90A-21.

WELL CONTRACTORS CERTIFICATION COMMISSION, §143B-301.10.

WESTERN NORTH CAROLINA PUBLIC LANDS COUNCIL, §143B-324.1.

WILDLIFE RESOURCES COMMISSION, §143-240.

Z

ZOOLOGICAL AUTHORITY, §143-177.

ZOOLOGICAL PARK COUNCIL, §143B-335.

Short Title/Popular Name Index

A

ABANDONMENT ACT, §§14-322 to 14-326.1.

ABC LAW, §§18B-100 to 18B-1119.

ABC STORES, §§18B-800 to 18B-807.

ABORTION, §§14-44 to 14-46.
Woman's right to know act, §90-21.80.

ABSENTEE VOTING ACT, §§163-226 to 163-239.

ABUSED, NEGLECTED OR EXPLOITED DISABLED ADULT ACT, §108A-99.

ACCESS TO CIVIL JUSTICE ACT, §§7A-474.1 to 7A-474.5.

ACCIDENT-TRAUMA VICTIM IDENTIFICATION
Carolyn Sonzogni Act, §90-600.

ACCOUNTANTS' ACT, §§93-1 to 93-13.

ACTUARIAL NOTE ACT, §§120-112 to 120-114.

ACUPUNCTURE PRACTICE ACT, §§90-450 to 90-459.

ADMINISTRATION DEPARTMENT ACT, §143-334.

ADMINISTRATIVE PROCEDURE ACT, §§150B-1 to 150B-52.

ADULT CARE HOME RESIDENTS' BILL OF RIGHTS, §§131D-19 to 131D-34.

ADULT PROTECTION ACT, §§108A-99 to 108A-111.

ADVERTISING CONTROL ACT, §§136-126 to 136-140.

AEDIN'S LAW
Regulation of animal exhibitions, §106-520.3A.

AERONAUTICS ACT, §§63-1 to 63-89.

AFDC, §§108A-27 to 108A-39.1.

AFTER-BORN CHILD ACT, §31-5.5.

AGRICULTURAL DEVELOPMENT ACT, §106-580.

AGRICULTURAL DEVELOPMENT AND FARMLAND PRESERVATION ENABLING ACT, §106-735.

AGRICULTURAL FINANCE ACT, §122D-1.

AGRICULTURAL LIMING MATERIALS AND LANDPLASTER ACT, §106-92.1.

AGRICULTURE EXTENSION SERVICE
Agriculture development act, §§106-580 to 106-587.

AID TO FAMILIES WITH DEPENDENT CHILDREN ACT, §§108A-27 to 108A-39.1.

AIR AND WATER QUALITY REPORTING ACT, §§143-215.63 to 143-215.69.

AIR AND WATER RESOURCES ACT, §§143-211 to 143-215.74I.

AIRCRAFT LABOR AND STORAGE LIENS, §§44A-50 to 44A-90.

AIR POLLUTION CONTROL, §§143-215.103 to 143-215.114C.

AIRPORT DEVELOPMENT ACT, §§63-65 to 63-73.

AIRPORT DISTRICTS ACT, §63-78.

AIRPORT ZONING
Model airport zoning act, §63-37.

ALARM SYSTEMS LICENSING ACT, §74D-1.

ALCOHOLIC BEVERAGE CONTROL, §§18B-100 to 18B-1119.

ALIEN PROPERTY ACT, §§64-1 to 64-5.

ALIEN RECIPROCAL INHERITANCE ACT, §§64-3 to 64-5.

ALIMONY ACT, §§50-16.1A to 50-17.

AMBER ALERT SYSTEM, §143B-272.71.

AMBULATORY SURGICAL FACILITY LICENSURE ACT, §§131E-145 to 131E-152.

AMUSEMENT DEVICE SAFETY ACT OF NORTH CAROLINA, §95-111.1.

AMY JACKSON LAW, §§14-208.5 to 14-208.32.

ANATOMICAL GIFT ACT, §130A-412.3.

ANIMAL WELFARE ACT, §19A-20.

ANNEXATION ACT, §§160A-29 to 160A-58.28.

ANNUITY DISCLOSURE ACT, §58-60-120.

ANTI-BLACKLISTING ACT, §14-355.

ANTI-CLOSED SHOP ACT, §§95-78 to 95-84.

ANTI-DEFICIENCY JUDGMENT ACT, §45-21.38.

ANTIFREEZE LAW OF 1975, §106-579.1.

ANTILAPSE ACT, §31-42.

ANTI-MONOPOLY ACT, §§75-1 to 75-35.

ANTI-SLOT MACHINE ACT, §§14-304 to 14-309.1.

ANTITRUST ACT, §§75-1 to 75-35.

ANTI-VANDALISM ACT, §1-538.1.

APPALACHIAN TRAILS SYSTEM ACT, §113A-72.

APPORTIONMENT ACT, §§120-1 to 120-2.2.

APPRAISERS ACT, §§93E-1-1 to 93E-1-14.

AQUACULTURE DEVELOPMENT ACT, §106-757.

AQUATIC WEED CONTROL ACT OF 1991, §113A-220.

ARBITRATION
Revised uniform arbitration act, §1-569.31.

ARBITRATION ACT
International commercial arbitration and conciliation act, §1-567.30.

ARBITRATION OF LABOR DISPUTES, §§95-36.1 to 95-36.9.

ARCHAEOLOGICAL RECORD PROGRAM, §70-46.

ARCHAEOLOGICAL RESOURCES PROTECTION ACT, §70-10.

ARCHITECTS LICENSING ACT, §§83A-1 to 83A-17.

ARCHIVES AND HISTORY ACT, §121-1.

ARMORY ACT, §§127A-161 to 127A-169.

ARREST WITHOUT WARRANT, §§15A-401 to 15A-406.

ARTIFICIAL INSEMINATION, §§49A-1, 90-187.10.

ARTWORK ON CONSIGNMENT, §§25C-1 to 25C-5.

ASSET PROTECTION ACT, §58-13-1.

ASSIGNED RISK, §20-279.21.

ASSIGNMENT OF PUPILS ACT, §§115C-364 to 115C-372.

ASSISTED LIVING ADMINISTRATORS, §§90-288.10 to 90-288.20.

ASSOCIATE SAFETY PROFESSIONALS (ASP), §§90-671 to 90-674.

ASSUMED BUSINESS NAME ACT, §§66-68 to 66-71.

ATHLETE AGENTS
Uniform athlete agent act, §78C-85.

ATHLETIC TRAINERS LICENSING ACT, §90-522.

ATLANTIC STATES MARINE FISHERIES COMPACT ACT, §§113-252 to 113-258.

ATTACHMENT ACT, §§1-440.1 to 1-440.46.

ATTENDANCE OF WITNESSES FROM WITHOUT STATE IN CRIMINAL PROCEEDINGS ACT, §15A-816.

AUTOPSIES, §§130A-398 to 130A-401.

B

BABY DROP OFF, §14-322.3.

BACKGROUND INVESTIGATIONS, §§114-19.1 to 114-19.15.

BAD CHECK, §§14-106 to 14-107.1.

BALANCED GROWTH POLICY ACT, §§143-506.6 to 143-506.14.

BALLOON PAYMENTS, §25A-34.

BANG'S DISEASE ACT, §§106-388 to 106-398.

BANK BRANCH ACT, §53-62.

BANK DEPOSITS AND COLLECTIONS
Uniform commercial code-bank deposits and collections, §25-4-101.

BANK DEPOSITS AND COLLECTIONS-UNIFORM COMMERCIAL CODE, §§25-4-101 to 25-4-504.

BANK HOLDING COMPANY ACT OF 1984, §53-225.

BANKING LAW, §§53-1 to 53-208.

BAR ACT, §§84-15 to 84-38.

BARBER ACT, §§86A-1 to 86A-26.

BARBITURATE AND STIMULANT DRUGS ACT, §§90-86 to 90-113.8.

BASEBALL PARK DISTRICT, §§160C-1, 160C-2.

BASTARDY ACT, §§49-1 to 49-17.

BATTLE ACT, §41-10.

BEE AND HONEY ACT OF 1977, §§106-634 to 106-644.

BEST EVIDENCE RULE
Uniform photographic copies of business and public records as evidence act, §8-45.4.

BETTERMENTS ACT, §§1-340 to 1-351.

BICYCLE AND BIKEWAY ACT OF 1974, §§136-71.6 to 136-71.13.

BILL OF RIGHTS FOR ADULT DAY CARE HOME RESIDENTS, §§131D-19 to 131D-34.

BIOLOGICAL ORGANISM ACT, §106-65.42.

BIOLOGICS LAW OF 1981, §106-707.

BLACKLISTING ACT, §14-355.

BLUE LAWS, §160A-191.

BLUE SKY LAW
North Carolina securities act, §78A-1.

BOATING SAFETY ACT, §§75A-1 to 75A-19.

BOAT TITLING ACT, §§75A-32 to 75A-49.

BOILER AND PRESSURE VESSEL ACT, §§95-69.8 to 95-69.20.

BOILER AND PRESSURE VESSEL ACT OF NORTH CAROLINA, §95-69.8.

BOLL WEEVIL ERADICATION ACT, §106-65.67.

BORROWING ACT FOR LIMITATIONS, §1-21.

BRAIN DEATH ACT, §§90-320 to 90-323.

BRANCH BANK ACT, §53-62.

BREAKING AND ENTERING, §14-54.

BREATH TESTS, §§20-16.2, 20-139.1.

BRIDGE LOAD LIMIT ACT, §136-72.

BROADCAST DEFAMATION ACT, §§99-1 to 99-5.

BROWN-BAGGING ACT, §18B-301.

BROWNFIELDS PROPERTY REUSE ACT OF 1997, §130A-310.30.

BRUCELLOSIS ACT, §§106-388 to 106-398.

BUCKET SHOP, §§16-3 to 16-6.

BUDGET ACT, §§143-1 to 143-34.7.

BUDGET AND FISCAL CONTROL ACT FOR LOCAL GOVERNMENT, §§159-7 to 159-41.

BUGGING, §14-155.

BUILDING CODE, §§143-136 to 143-143.3.

BUILDING CONTRACT ACT, §§143-128 to 143-135.8.

BULK TRANSFERS-UNIFORM COMMERCIAL CODE, §§25-6-101 to 25-6-111.

BUREAU OF INVESTIGATION
Background investigations, §§114-19.1 to 114-19.15.

BURGLARY, §§14-51 to 14-57.

BURGLARY TOOLS ACT, §14-55.

BUSINESS CORPORATION ACT, §55-1-01.

BUSINESS ENERGY IMPROVEMENT PROGRAM, §§143-345.16 to 143-345.18.

BUSINESS TAX CREDIT, §§105-129.15 to 105-129.19.

BUSINESS UNDER ASSUMED NAME ACT, §§66-68 to 66-71.

C

CAMPAIGN CONTRIBUTIONS AND EXPENDITURES, §§163-278.6 to 163-278.40I.

CAMPUS POLICE ACT, §§74G-1 to 74G-12.

CAPITAL FACILITIES FINANCING ACT, §§159D-1 to 159D-57.

CAPITAL IMPROVEMENT PLANNING ACT, §§143-34.40 to 143-34.45.

CAPITAL ISSUES LAW
North Carolina securities act, §78A-1.

CARDIAC REHABILITATION CERTIFICATION PROGRAM, §§131E-165 to 131E-170.

CAROLYN SONZOGNI ACT, §90-600.

CARRIER ACT, §§62-259 to 62-279.

CARTWAY ACT, §§136-69, 136-70.

CAVE PROTECTION ACT, §§14-159.20 to 14-159.23.

CDL
Commercial driver's license act, §20-37.10.

CEMETERY ACT, §65-46.

CENTENNIAL CAMPUS AND HORACE WILLIAMS CAMPUS FINANCING ACT, §§116-198.31 to 116-198.40.

CERTIFICATES OF TITLES, §§20-50 to 20-71.1.

CERTIFIED PUBLIC ACCOUNTANTS ACT, §§93-1 to 93-13.

CERTIFIED SAFETY PROFESSIONALS (CSP), §§90-671 to 90-674.

CHANGE OF VENUE ACT, §1-83.

CHARITABLE REMAINDER TRUST ADMINISTRATION ACT, §36C-4B-1.

CHARTER SCHOOLS, §§115C-238.29A to 115C-238.29J.

CHATTEL MORTGAGE RECORDATION ACT, §47-20.

CHEMICAL TESTS FOR INTOXICATION OF DRIVERS ACT, §20-139.1.

CHILD BICYCLE SAFETY ACT, §20-171.6.

CHILD CUSTODY AND SUPPORT ACT, §§50-13.1 to 50-13.12.

CHILD CUSTODY JURISDICTION AND ENFORCEMENT ACT, §§50A-101 to 50A-317.

CHILD PLACEMENT COMPACT, §§110-57.1 to 110-57.7.

CHILDREN'S SUPPORT ACT FOR ILLEGITIMATE CHILDREN, §§49-1 to 49-9.

CHILD SUPPORT ENFORCEMENT, §§110-128 to 110-142.2.

CHURCH SCHOOLS, §§115C-547 to 115C-554.

CIGARETTE TAX, §§105-113.5 to 105-113.33.

CITIZEN'S ARREST, §§15A-404, 15A-405.

CITY-COUNTY CONSOLIDATION ACT, §§160B-1 to 160B-21.

CIVIL PROCEDURE ACT, §§1-1 to 1-601.

CIVIL RIGHTS, INTERFERENCE WITH, §99D-1.

CLEAN COASTAL WATER AND VESSEL ACT, §§77-125 to 77-132.

CLOSED SHOP ACT, §§95-78 to 95-84.

CLOSING-OUT SALES ACT, §§66-76 to 66-83.

COASTAL AREA MANAGEMENT ACT OF 1974, §113A-100.

COLOR OF TITLE, §§1-38, 98-8.

COMMERCIAL BANKING LAW, §§53-1 to 53-208.

COMMERCIAL CODE, §25-1-101.

COMMERCIAL DRIVERS' LICENSE ACT, §20-37.10.

COMMERCIAL FEED LAW OF 1973, §106-284.30.

COMMERCIAL FERTILIZER LAW, §106-655.

COMMERCIAL FISHERMEN'S HULL INSURANCE, PROTECTION AND INDEMNITY CLUB ACT, §58-20-1.

COMMERCIAL REAL ESTATE BROKER LIEN ACT, §44A-24.1.

COMMODITIES ACT, §§78D-1 to 78D-33.

COMMON TRUST FUND ACT, §53-163.9.

COMMUNITY ACTION PARTNERSHIP ACT, §108B-21.

COMMUNITY COLLEGE FACILITIES GENERAL OBLIGATION FINANCE ACT, §116D-41.

COMMUNITY COLLEGES, §§115D-1 to 115D-81.

COMMUNITY CONSERVATION ASSISTANCE PROGRAM, §143-215.74M.

COMMUNITY PROPERTY
Uniform disposition of community property rights at death act, §31C-12.

COMMUNITY SCHOOLS ACT, §§115C-203 to 115C-209.

COMMUNITY THIRD PARTY TRUSTS/POOLED TRUSTS ACT
Benefiting persons with severe chronic disabilities, §36D-1.

COMMUNITY TRUSTS FOR PERSONS WITH SEVERE CHRONIC DISABILITIES, §§36D-1 to 36D-11.

COMPANY POLICE ACT, §74E-1.

COMPENSATING USE TAX ACT, §§105-164.1 to 105-164.44D.

COMPETENCY ACT FOR CRIMINAL DEFENDANTS, §8-54.

COMPULSORY ATTENDANCE ACT, §§115C-378 to 115C-383.

COMPULSORY INSURANCE ACT, §§20-309 to 20-319.

COMPULSORY MEAT INSPECTION ACT, §§106-549.15 to 106-549.28.

COMPULSORY POULTRY INSPECTION ACT, §§106-549.49 to 106-549.69.

CONCEALED WEAPONS, §14-269.

CONDEMNATION ACT, §§40A-1 to 40A-70.

CONDOMINIUM ACT, §§47C-1-101 to 47C-4-120.

CONDOMINIUMS
Unit ownership act, §47A-1.

CONFIDENTIALITY OF LEGISLATIVE COMMUNICATIONS, §§120-129 to 120-134.

CONFORMITY ACT FOR JUDGMENTS, §1-237.

CONNOR ACT, §47-18.

CONSERVATION AND HISTORIC PRESERVATION AGREEMENTS ACT, §121-34.

CONSOLIDATED CITY-COUNTY ACT OF 1973, §160B-1.

CONSOLIDATED JUDICIAL RETIREMENT ACT, §135-50.

CONSPIRACY TO VIOLATE CIVIL RIGHTS, §99D-1.

CONSUMER AND CONSUMER INFORMATION PRIVACY ACT, §58-39-1.

CONSUMER FINANCE ACT, §53-164.

CONTINUING CRIMINAL ENTERPRISE, §14-7.20.

CONTRIBUTING TO THE DELINQUENCY OF MINORS, §14-316.1.

CONTRIBUTION AMONG TORT-FEASORS
Uniform act, §1B-1.
Uniform contribution among tort-feasors act, §1B-1.

CONTRIBUTIONS TO POLITICAL CAMPAIGNS, §§163-278.6 to 163-278.40I.

CONTROLLED SUBSTANCES ACT, §90-86.

CONTROLLED SUBSTANCES REPORTING SYSTEM ACT, §§90-113.70 to 90-113.76.

CONTROL SHARE ACQUISITION ACT, §55-9A-01.

COOPERATIVE INNOVATION HIGH SCHOOL PROGRAMS, §§115C-238.50 to 115C-238.55.

COOPERATIVE MARKETING ACT, §54-130.

CORNEAL TISSUE REMOVAL, §130A-391.

CORPORATE OFFICERS INDEMNIFICATION ACT, §§55-8-50 to 55-8-58.

CORPORATE TAKEOVERS, §§75E-1 to 75E-9.

CORPORATION INCOME TAX ACT, §105-130.
S corporation income tax act, §§105-131 to 105-131.8.

CORRECTION ENTERPRISE FUND, §148-130.

CORRECTION ENTERPRISES, §§148-128 to 148-134.

CORRECTIONS COMPACT, §148-119.

COSMETIC ART ACT, §88B-1.

COTTON WAREHOUSE ACT, §106-451.6.

COUNTY-CITY CONSOLIDATION ACT, §§160B-1 to 160B-15.

COUNTY LAND TRANSFER TAX ACT, §§105-600 to 105-604.

COUNTY SERVICE DISTRICT ACT OF 1973, §§153A-300 to 153A-310.

COURTS-MARTIAL, §§127A-47 to 127A-61.

COVENTRY ACT, §§14-30, 14-30.1.

CREDIT CARD INSURANCE ACT, §58-3-145.

CREDIT MONITORING SERVICES ACT, §75-133.

CREDIT REPAIR SERVICES ACT, §66-220.

CREDIT UNION ACT, §§54-109.1 to 54-110.10.

CREMATION, §130A-388.

CREMATORY ACT, §§90-210.40 to 90-210.54, 90-210.120.

CRIME AGAINST NATURE, §14-177.

CRIME VICTIMS COMPENSATION ACT, §15B-1.

CRIME VICTIMS FINANCIAL RECOVERY ASSISTANCE ACT, §§15B-30 to 15B-37.

CRIME VICTIMS RIGHTS ACT, §§15A-830 to 15A-841.

CRIMINAL EXTRADITION ACT, §15A-750.

CRIMINAL HISTORY RECORD CHECKS, §§114-19.1 to 114-19.15.

CRIMINAL JUSTICE PARTNERSHIP ACT, §§143B-273 to 143B-273.19.

CRIMINAL PROCEDURE ACT, §§15A-101 to 15A-2012.

CUSTODIAL TRUST ACT, §33B-21.

CUSTODY AND SUPPORT OF CHILDREN ACT, §§50-13.1 to 50-13.12.

CUSTOMER INFORMATION SAFEGUARDS ACT, §§58-39-1, 58-39-130 to 58-39-165.

D

DAIRY STABILIZATION AND GROWTH PROGRAM, §§106-812 to 106-815.

DAM SAFETY LAW OF 1967, §143-215.23.

DARFUR
Sudan (Darfur) divestment act, §§147-86.41 to 147-86.49.

DEATH BENEFITS ACT, §§143-166.1 to 143-166.7.

DEATH BY WRONGFUL ACT, §28A-18-2.

DECLARATORY JUDGMENTS ACT, §1-267.

DEFAMATION ACT, §§99-1 to 99-5.

DEFAULTED STUDENT LOAN RECOVERY ACT, §§105B-1 to 105B-4.

DEFENSE OF PUBLIC SCHOOL EMPLOYEES, §§143-300.13 to 143-300.18.

DEFENSE OF STATE EMPLOYEES, §§143-300.2 to 143-300.10.

DEFERRED PROSECUTION, §15A-1341.

DEFICIENCY JUDGMENT ACT, §45-21.38.

DEMURRER TO THE EVIDENCE ACT, §15-173.

DENTAL HYGIENE ACT, §§90-221 to 90-233.1.

DENTAL PEER REVIEW PROTECTION ACT, §90-48.7.

DEPARTMENT OF ADMINISTRATION ACT, §143-334.

DEPOSITIONS, §§8-74 to 8-83.

DESCENT AND DISTRIBUTION ACT, §§29-1 to 29-30.

DIETETICS/NUTRITION PRACTICE ACT, §§90-350 to 90-369.

DISABILITY INCOME PLAN OF NORTH CAROLINA, §135-100.

DISASTER SERVICE VOLUNTEER LEAVE, §166A-30.

DISCARDED COMPUTER EQUIPMENT MANAGEMENT ACT, §§130A-309.90 to 130A-309.98.

DISSENT FROM WILL ACT, §§30-1 to 30-3.

DISTRIBUTION LAW, §§29-1 to 29-30.

DIVORCE ACT, §§50-2 to 50-22.

DNA DATABASE AND DATABANK ACT OF 1993, §15A-266.

DOCUMENTS OF TITLE, §§25-7-101 to 25-7-603. Uniform commercial code-documents of title, §25-7-101.

DO NOT CALL LAW, §§75-100 to 75-105.

DOOR CLOSING ACT, §45-21.38.

DRAG RACING, §20-141.3.

DRAM SHOP LIABILITY, §18B-305.

DRINKING WATER ACT, §130A-311.

DRIVER'S LICENSE ACT, §20-5. Commercial driver's license act, §20-37.10.

DRIVER'S LICENSE COMPACT, §20-4.21.

DRIVER TRAINING SCHOOL LICENSING LAW, §§20-320 to 20-328.

DRUG AND COSMETIC ACT, §§106-120 to 106-145.12.

DRUG PARAPHERNALIA ACT, §90-113.20.

DRUG PARAPHERNALIA CONTROL ACT OF 2009, §§90-113.80 to 90-113.84.

DRUGS North Carolina controlled substances act, §§90-86 to 90-113.8.

DRUG TESTING REGULATION, §§95-230 to 95-235.

DRUG TREATMENT COURT ACT OF 1995, §7A-790.

DRUNKEN DRIVING, §§20-138.1 to 20-139.1, 20-179.

DRY-CLEANING SOLVENT CLEANUP ACT OF 1997, §§143-215.104A to 143-215.104U.

DRY-CLEANING SOLVENT TAX, §§105-187.30 to 105-187.34.

DURABLE POWER OF ATTORNEY, §§32A-8 to 32A-14.

E

ECOSYSTEM ENHANCEMENT PROGRAM, §§143-214.8 to 143-214.13.

EDUCATIONAL PERSONNEL QUALIFICATIONS ACT, §§115C-349 to 115C-358.

EDUCATION COMPACT, §115C-104.

EGG LAW, §106-245.13.

ELECTION LAWS, §§163-1 to 163-321.

ELECTRIC MEMBERSHIP CORPORATIONS ACT, §§117-6 to 117-26.

ELECTROLYSIS PRACTICE ACT, §88A-1.

ELECTRONIC NOTARY PUBLIC ACT, §10B-38.

ELEVATOR SAFETY ACT OF NORTH CAROLINA, §95-110.1.

EMANCIPATION OF MARRIED PERSONS, §52-2.

EMANCIPATION OF MINORS, §§7B-3500 to 7B-3509.

EMERGENCY INTERIM LOCAL GOVERNMENT EXECUTIVE SUCCESSION ACT OF 1959, §162B-5.

EMERGENCY MANAGEMENT ACT OF 1977, §166A-1.

EMERGENCY MANAGEMENT ASSISTANCE COMPACT, §166A-40.

EMERGENCY MEDICAL SERVICES ACT OF 1973, §§143-507 to 143-517.

EMERGENCY PROGRAM TO REDUCE HOME FORECLOSURES ACT, §§45-100 to 45-107.

EMERGENCY WAR POWERS ACT, §147-33.1.

EMINENT DOMAIN ACT, §§40A-1 to 40A-70.

EMPLOYEES' RETIREMENT SYSTEM ACT FOR LOCAL GOVERNMENTS, §§128-21 to 128-38.2.

EMPLOYMENT AND TRAINING ACT OF 1985, §§143B-438.1 to 143B-438.6.

EMPLOYMENT PREFERENCE FOR VETERANS, §§126-80 to 126-83, 128-15.

EMPLOYMENT SECURITY LAW, §96-1.

E-NC INITIATIVE, §§143B-437.44 to 143B-437.47.

ENDANGERED WILDLIFE LAW, §§113-331 to 113-337.

ENERGY CONSERVATION FINANCE ACT, §142-60.

ENERGY LOAN FUND, 143B-437.14.

ENERGY POLICY ACT, §62-2.

ENERGY POLICY ACT OF 1975, §§113B-1 to 113B-24.

ENGINEERING AND LAND SURVEYING ACT, §89C-1.

ENTERPRISE CORPORATION ACT, §53A-35.

ENVIRONMENTAL COMPACT ACT OF 1971, §113A-21.

ENVIRONMENTAL EDUCATION AND PUBLIC AFFAIRS, OFFICE OF, §143B-285.20.

ENVIRONMENTAL EDUCATION AND PUBLIC AFFAIRS ACT, §§143B-285.20 to 143B-285.25.

ENVIRONMENTAL POLICY ACT OF 1971, §113A-1.

EQUAL EMPLOYMENT OPPORTUNITY, §§126-16 to 126-39.

EQUAL EMPLOYMENT PRACTICES ACT, §143-422.1.

EQUINE ACTIVITY LIABILITY, §§99E-1 to 99E-3.

EQUINE INFECTIOUS ANEMIA, §§106-405.15 to 106-405.20.

EROSION CONTROL
Sedimentation pollution control act of 1973, §§113A-50 to 113A-66.

ESCHEAT LAW, §§116B-1 to 116B-4.

ETHEN'S LAW
Unborn victims of violence act, §§14-23.1 to 14-23.8.

ETHICS
State ethics commission, §§138A-6 to 138A-15.
State government ethics act, §§138A-1 to 138A-45.

ETHICS, LEGISLATIVE ACT, §§120-85 to 120-106.

ETHNIC HATE CRIMES, §14-401.14.

EVIDENCE RULES, §Rules 101 to §1102.

EXECUTIVE BUDGET ACT, §§143-1 to 143-34.7.

EXECUTIVE ORGANIZATION ACT OF 1971, §143A-1.

EXECUTIVE ORGANIZATION ACT OF 1973, §143B-1.

EXPUNGEMENT OF CRIMINAL RECORDS, §§15A-145 to 15A-148.

EXTRADITION ACT, §15A-750.

EYEWITNESS IDENTIFICATION REFORM ACT, §15A-284.50.

F

FACILITY AUTHORITY ACT, §160A-480.1.

FAIR HOUSING ACT, §§41A-1 to 41A-10.

FALSE ADVERTISEMENT ACT, §§66-76 to 66-83.

FALSE CLAIMS ACT, §1-605.

FAMILY LAW ARBITRATION ACT, §50-41.

FAMILY PRESERVATION ACT, §§143B-150.5 to 143B-150.9.

FAMILY PURPOSE DOCTRINE, §75A-10.1.

FAMILY SUPPORT ACT, §52C-1-100.

FAMILY THERAPY LICENSURE ACT, §§90-270.45 to 90-270.62.

FARM AND HOME DEVELOPMENT PROGRAM
Agriculture development act, §§106-580 to 106-587.

FEDERAL LIEN REGISTRATION ACT, §44-68.10.

FEDERAL WATER RESOURCES DEVELOPMENT LAW OF 1969, §143-215.38.

FEE-BASED PRACTICING PASTORAL COUNSELOR CERTIFICATION ACT, §§90-380 to 90-396.

FEED LAW OF 1973, §106-284.30.

FELONY FIREARMS ACT, §§14-415.1 to 14-415.4.

FELONY SENTENCING, §§15A-1340.13 to 15A-1340.17.

FERTILIZER LAW, §§106-655 to 106-677.

FICTITIOUS NAME ACT, §§66-68 to 66-71.

FIDUCIARIES ACT, §32-1.

FIDUCIARY POWERS
Renunciation of property and renunciation of fiduciary powers act, §31B-7.

FINANCIAL PRIVACY ACT, §53B-1.

FINANCIAL RESPONSIBILITY ACT OF 1953, §20-279.39.

FINANCIAL RESPONSIBILITY ACT OF 1957, §§20-309 to 20-319.

FINANCIAL TRANSACTION CARD CRIME ACT, §§14-113.8 to 14-113.17.

FIREMEN'S AND RESCUE SQUAD WORKERS' PENSION FUND, §§58-86-1 to 58-86-91.

FIRE-SAFETY STANDARD AND FIREFIGHTER PROTECTION ACT, §58-92-1.

FIRE SALES ACT, §§66-76 to 66-83.

FIRST IN AMERICA INNOVATIVE EDUCATION ACT, §116C-4.

FIRST ONE-CENT LOCAL GOVERNMENT SALES AND USE TAX ACT, §§105-463 to 105-474.

FIRST ONE-HALF CENT LOCAL GOVERNMENT SALES AND USE TAX, §105-480.

FISCAL INFORMATION ACT FOR LOCAL GOVERNMENT, §§120-30.41 to 120-30.49.

FISHERIES LAW, §§113-127 to 113-316.

FISHERMAN'S ECONOMIC DEVELOPMENT ACT, §113-315.15.

FISH FARMING
Aquaculture development act, §§106-756 to 106-764.

FLANAGAN ACT, §§14-304 to 14-309.1.

FOOD, DRUG AND COSMETIC ACT, §106-120.

FOOD STAMP PROGRAM, §§108A-1 to 108A-3.

FORECLOSURE ACT FOR TAX LIENS, §§105-374, 105-375.

FOREIGN INSURANCE COMPANIES ACT, §§58-16-1 to 58-16-55.

FOREIGN JUDGMENTS
North Carolina uniform foreign-country
    money judgments recognition act, §1C-1850.
Uniform enforcement of foreign judgments act,
    §1C-1701.

FOREIGN LEGAL CONSULTANTS, §§84A-1 to
84A-8.

FOREIGN-MONEY CLAIMS
North Carolina foreign-money claims act,
    §1C-1834.

FOREST DEVELOPMENT ACT, §106-1010.

FOREST FIRE PROTECTION COMPACT,
    §§113-60.11 to 113-60.15.

FOREST PRODUCT ASSESSMENT ACT,
    §106-1025.

FRANCHISE TAX ACT, §§105-114 to 105-129.

FRAUDS, STATUTE OF, §§22-1 to 22-4.

FRAUDULENT TRANSFERS ACT, §39-23.12.

FUEL USE TAX ACT FOR TRUCKERS,
    §§105-449.37 to 105-449.57.

FUNDS TRANSFERS
Uniform commercial code-funds transfers,
    §25-4A-101.

**FUNDS TRANSFERS-UNIFORM
    COMMERCIAL CODE**, §§25-4A-101 to
    25-4A-507.

G

GAMBLING LAW, §§14-292 to 14-309.1.

GAS CONSERVATION ACT, §§113-381 to 113-415.

GASOLINE AND OIL INSPECTION ACT,
    §§119-14 to 119-47.

**GENERAL ASSEMBLY APPORTIONMENT
    ACT**, §§120-1 to 120-2.2.

GENETIC IDENTIFICATION, §§15A-266 to
15A-270.

GEOLOGISTS LICENSING ACT, §89E-1.

GIFTED STUDENTS, §§115C-150.5 to 115C-150.8.

GIFTS TO MINORS
Uniform transfers to minors act, §§33A-1 to
33A-24.

GIFT TAXES, §§105-188 to 105-197.1.

GLOBAL TRANSPARK AUTHORITY ACT,
    §63A-1.

GLUE SNIFFING ACT, §§90-113.8A to 90-113.14.

GOING OUT OF BUSINESS SALES, §§66-76 to
66-83.

GOOD FUNDS SETTLEMENT ACT, §45A-1.

GOOD NEIGHBOR COUNCIL ACT, §§143B-391,
143B-392.

GOOD SAMARITAN ACT, §§20-166, 90-21.14.

GOVERNMENT COMPETITION ACT OF 1998,
    §§143-701 to 143-709.

**GOVERNMENT EMPLOYEES INTERCHANGE
    ACT**, §§126-51 to 126-58.

**GOVERNMENT SALE OF MERCHANDISE
    ACT**, §66-58.

**GOVERNOR'S COUNCIL ON EMPLOYMENT
    OF THE HANDICAPPED ACT**, §143-283.1.

GREEN BUSINESS FUND, §§143B-437.4 to
143B-437.8.

GROUP LIFE INSURANCE ACT, §§58-58-135 to
58-58-165.

GUARDIANSHIP FOR VETERANS, §§34-1 to
34-18.

H

HABEAS CORPUS, §§17-1 to 17-46.

HABITUAL FELONS, §§14-7.1 to 14-7.6.
Violent habitual felons, §§14-7.7 to 14-7.12.

**HANDICAPPED EMPLOYMENT COUNCIL
    ACT**, §§143-283.1 to 143-283.8.

HATE CRIMES, §14-401.14.

**HAZARDOUS CHEMICALS RIGHT TO KNOW
    ACT**, §95-173.

**HAZARDOUS MATERIALS EMERGENCY
    RESPONSE ACT**, §166A-20.

**HAZARDOUS RECREATION PARKS SAFETY
    AND LIABILITY**, §§99E-21 to 99E-25.

HAZARDOUS SUBSTANCES CONTROL ACT,
    §§143-215.75 to 143-215.104.

**HAZARDOUS WASTE MANAGEMENT
    COMMISSION ACT OF 1989**, §§130B-1 to
    130B-24.

HEALTH CARE FACILITIES FINANCE ACT,
    §131A-1.

HEALTH CARE POWERS OF ATTORNEY,
    §§32A-15 to 32A-26.

**HEALTH CARE PURCHASING ALLIANCE
    ACT**, §§143-621 to 143-636.

HEALTH CHOICE FOR CHILDREN
Health insurance program for children,
    §§135-47 to 135-47.3.

HEALTH INFORMATION EXCHANGE ACT,
    §90-413.1.

**HEALTH INSURANCE PROGRAM FOR
    CHILDREN ACT OF 1998**, §§108A-70.18 to
    108A-70.28.

**HEALTH MAINTENANCE ORGANIZATION
    ACT OF 1979**, §58-67-1.

HEATING CONTRACTORS' LICENSE ACT,
    §§87-16 to 87-27.1.

HIGHER EDUCATION BONDS
Community colleges facilities finance,
    §§116D-41 to 116D-49.
Financing capital facilities, §§116D-6 to 116D-13.

HIGH SPEED CHASES, §20-145.

HIGH-VOLTAGE LINE SAFETY ACT, §§95-229.5
to 95-229.13.

HIGHWAY PATROL, §§20-184 to 20-196.4.

HIGHWAY RELOCATION ASSISTANCE ACT,
    §§133-5 to 133-18.

HIGHWAY USE TAX, §§105-187.1 to 105-187.11.

**HISTORIC AND NATURE PRESERVE
    DEDICATION ACT**, §§143-260.6 to
    143-260.10G.

HIT AND RUN DRIVING, §20-166.

HITCHHIKING, §20-175.

HOG CHOLERA CONTROL ACT, §§106-316.1 to 106-316.4.

HOLDING OVER, §42-26.

HOME CARE AGENCY LICENSURE ACT, §§131E-135 to 131E-143.

HOME CARE CLIENTS' BILL OF RIGHTS, §§131E-144.1 to 131E-144.7.

HOME INSPECTOR LICENSURE ACT, §143-151.43.

HOME SCHOOLS, §§115C-563 to 115C-565.

HONEY ACT, §§106-634 to 106-644.

HORSE INDUSTRY PROMOTION ACT, §106-820.

HOSPICE LICENSURE ACT, §§131E-200 to 131E-207.

HOSPITAL, MEDICAL AND DENTAL SERVICE CORPORATION READABLE INSURANCE CERTIFICATES ACT, §58-66-1.

HOSPITAL AUTHORITIES ACT, §§131E-15 to 131E-34.

HOSPITAL DISTRICT ACT, §§131E-40 to 131E-47.

HOSPITAL LICENSURE ACT, §§131E-75 to 131E-99.

HOSPITAL PROVIDER ASSESSMENT ACT, §108A-120.

HOTCHPOT, §§29-23 to 29-29.

HOUSEBREAKING, §§14-51 to 14-57.

HOUSEHOLD CLEANERS ACT, §§66-85 to 66-88.

HOUSING AUTHORITIES LAW, §§157-1 to 157-39.8.

HOUSING FINANCE AGENCY ACT, §122A-1.

HOUSING TRUST AND OIL OVERCHARGE ACT, §122E-1.

HULL INSURANCE
Commercial fishermen's hull insurance protection and indemnity club act, §58-20-1.

HUMAN BURIAL AND HUMAN SKELETAL REMAINS PROTECTION ACT, §§70-26 to 70-40.

HUMAN SERVICE AND VOLUNTEER TRANSPORTATION
Remove barriers to coordinating act, §§62-289.1 to 62-289.7.

HUNTING OR FISHING ON POSTED PROPERTY, §§113-281 to 113-287.

I

IDENTIFICATION BADGES FOR HEALTH CARE PRACTITIONERS, §90-640.

IDENTITY FRAUD, §14-100.1.

IDENTITY THEFT, §§14-113.20 to 14-113.25.

IDENTITY THEFT PROTECTION ACT, §§75-60 to 75-65.

ILLEGITIMATE CHILDREN'S LEGITIMATION LAW, §§49-10 to 49-13.1.

IMMUNIZATION, §§130A-152 to 130A-157.

IMPAIRED DRIVING, §§20-138.1 to 20-139.1.

IMPEACHMENT, §§123-1 to 123-13.

IMPLIED CONSENT ACT, §20-16.2.

INACTIVE HAZARDOUS SITES RESPONSE ACT OF 1987, §130A-310.13.

INCOME AND PRINCIPAL ACT, §§37-16 to 37-40.

INCOME TAX, §§105-130 to 105-163.44.

INCOME TAX ACT FOR ESTATES, TRUSTS AND BENEFICIARIES, §105-160.

INCOME TAX WITHHOLDING ACT, §§105-163.1 to 105-163.24.

INDEMNIFICATION ACT FOR CORPORATE OFFICERS, §§55-8-50 to 55-8-58.

INDIGENT DEFENSE SERVICES, §§7A-450 to 7A-458.

INDIVIDUAL INCOME TAX ACT, §105-133.

INDUSTRIAL AND POLLUTION CONTROL FACILITIES FINANCING ACT, §§159C-1, 159D-1 to 159D-27.

INJUNCTION ACT, §§1-485 to 1-500.

INMATE LABOR ACT, §§148-26 to 148-49.

INSOLVENT DEBTORS ACT, §§23-23 to 23-38.

INSTITUTIONAL FUNDS
Uniform prudent management of institutional funds act, §36E-1.

INSURABLE INTEREST ACT, §§58-58-70 to 58-58-90.

INSURANCE GUARANTY ASSOCIATION ACT, §58-48-1.

INSURANCE HOLDING COMPANY SYSTEM REGULATORY ACT, §§58-19-1 to 58-19-70.

INSURANCE INFORMATION AND PRIVACY PROTECTION ACT, §§58-39-1 to 58-39-76.

INSURANCE LAW, §58-1-1.

INSURANCE REGULATORY REFORM ACT, §58-41-1.

INSURERS FALSE ADVERTISING PROCESS ACT, §§58-29-1 to 58-29-25.

INTERCHANGE OF GOVERNMENTAL EMPLOYEES ACT OF 1977, §126-51.

INTEREST ACT, §§24-1 to 24-17.

INTERFERENCE WITH CIVIL RIGHTS, §99D-1.

INTERNATIONAL BANKING ACT, §53-232.1.

INTERNATIONAL COMMERCIAL ARBITRATION AND CONCILIATION ACT, §1-567.30.

INTERPRETER AND TRANSLITERATOR LICENSURE ACT, §90D-1.

INTERSTATE AGREEMENT ON DETAINERS, §§15A-761 to 15A-767.

INTERSTATE BANKING ACT, §53-209.

INTERSTATE BRANCH BANKING, §§53-224.9 to 53-224.31.

INTERSTATE COMPACT FOR ADULT OFFENDER SUPERVISION, §148-65.4.

INTERSTATE COMPACT FOR JUVENILES, §7B-4000.

INTERSTATE COMPACT ON JUVENILES, §§7B-2800 to 7B-2827.

INTERSTATE COMPACT ON THE PLACEMENT OF JUVENILES, §§7B-3800 to 7B-3806.

INTERSTATE CORRECTIONS COMPACT, §148-119.

INTERSTATE DEPOSITIONS AND DISCOVERY ACT, §1F-1.

INTERSTATE FAMILY SUPPORT ACT, §52C-1-100.

INTERSTATE INSURANCE PRODUCT REGULATION COMPACT ACT, §§58-91-1 to 58-91-80.

INTERSTATE WILDLIFE VIOLATOR COMPACT, §113-300.5.

INTESTATE SUCCESSION ACT, §29-1.

INVESTMENT ADVISERS ACT, §78C-1.

INVESTMENT SECURITIES, §§25-8-101 to 25-8-511.
Uniform commercial code-investment securities, §25-8-101.

J

JACOB BATTLE ACT, §41-10.

JOB DEVELOPMENT INVESTMENT GRANT PROGRAM, §§143B-437.44 to 143B-437.56.

JOB MAINTENANCE AND CAPITAL DEVELOPMENT FUND, §143-437.11.

JOINT MUNICIPAL ELECTRIC POWER AND ENERGY ACT, §159B-1.

JOY RIDING, §14-72.2.

JUDGMENT CONFORMITY ACT, §1-237.

JUDICIAL DEPARTMENT ACT OF 1965, §7A-1.

JUDICIAL RETIREMENT ACT, §§135-50 to 135-75.1.

JUNKYARD CONTROL ACT, §§136-141 to 136-155.

JUVENILE CODE, §§7B-100 to 7B-3806.

K

KAITLYN'S LAW, §110-102.1A.

KICKBACKS, §§58-27-5, 95-47.6, 95-47.24.

KIDNAPPING ACT, §§14-39 to 14-43.3.

KU KLUX KLAN, §§14-12.2 to 14-12.15.

L

LABELING OF HOUSEHOLD CLEANERS ACT, §§66-85 to 66-88.

LABOR DISPUTES ARBITRATION ACT, §§95-36.1 to 95-36.9.

LABORERS' LIEN LAW, §§44A-1 to 44A-6.1.

LABOR OF PRISONERS ACT, §§148-26 to 148-49.

LAND CONTRACTS REGISTRATION ACT, §§47-17 to 47-36.

LANDLORD AND TENANT ACT, §§42-1 to 42-76.

LAND POLICY ACT OF 1974, §113A-150.

LAND TITLE REGISTRATION ACT, §§43-1 to 43-64.

LAPSED LEGACY ACT, §31-42.

LAW-ENFORCEMENT OFFICERS, FIREMEN, RESCUE SQUAD WORKERS AND CIVIL AIR PATROL MEMBERS
Death benefit act, §§143-166.1 to 143-166.7.

LAW ON THE PROTECTION OF MINORS FROM HARMFUL MATERIALS, §19-9.

LEAD POISONING IN CHILDREN, §§130A-131.5 to 130A-131.9G.

LEAKING PETROLEUM UNDERGROUND STORAGE TANK CLEANUP ACT OF 1988, §143-215.94L.

LEARNER'S PERMITS, §§20-7, 20-11, 20-30.

LEASES
Uniform commercial code-leases, §25-2A-101.

LEASES-UNIFORM COMMERCIAL CODE, §§25-2A-101 to 25-2A-532.

LEGISLATIVE APPORTIONMENT ACT, §§120-1 to 120-2.2.

LEGISLATIVE ETHICS ACT, §§120-85 to 120-106.

LEGITIMATION OF ILLEGITIMATE CHILDREN, §§49-10 to 49-13.1.

LEMON LAW, §§20-351 to 20-351.10.

LESSER INCLUDED OFFENSES, §§15-169, 15-170, 20-140.

LETTERS OF CREDIT, §§25-5-101 to 25-5-117.
Uniform commercial code-letters of credit, §25-5-101.

LIBEL AND SLANDER ACT, §§99-1 to 99-5.

LIBRARY COMPACT, §§125-12 to 125-17.

LICENSE TAX ACT, §§105-33 to 105-102.6.

LICENSURE ACT FOR SPEECH AND LANGUAGE PATHOLOGISTS AND AUDIOLOGISTS, §§90-292 to 90-307.

LIEN LAW, §§44A-1 to 44A-35.

LIFE AND HEALTH INSURANCE GUARANTY ASSOCIATION ACT, §58-62-2.

LIFE INSURANCE ACT FOR GROUP INSURANCE, §§58-58-135 to 58-58-165.

LIFE INSURANCE DISCLOSURE ACT, §58-60-1.

LIFE INSURANCE STANDARD NONFORFEITURE LAW, §58-58-55.

LIFE INSURANCE STANDARD VALUATION LAW, §58-58-50.

LIMING MATERIALS AND LANDPLASTER ACT, §106-92.1.

LIMITATION OF ACTIONS FOR CIVIL CASES, §§1-15 to 1-56.

LIMITATION OF ACTIONS FOR MISDEMEANORS, §15-1.

LIMITED LIABILITY COMPANY ACT, §57C-1-01.

LIMITED PARTNERSHIPS
Revised uniform limited partnership act, §59-101.

LIQUOR LAW, §§18B-100 to 18B-1119.

LIS PENDENS ACT, §§1-116 to 1-120.2.

LITTLE FTC ACT, §75-1.1.

LITTLE SMITH ACT FOR SUBVERSIVE ACTIVITIES, §§14-11 to 14-12.1.

LIVESTOCK DEALER LICENSING ACT, §106-418.15.

LIVESTOCK LAW, §§68-15 to 68-46.

LIVESTOCK MARKETS, §§106-406 to 106-418.

LIVESTOCK PROMPT PAY LAW, §106-418.1.

LIVING WILLS ACT, §§90-320 to 90-323.

LOAD LIMIT FOR BRIDGES, §136-72.

LOBBYING, §§93B-6, 120-47.1 to 120-47.11.

LOCAL GOVERNMENT BOND ACT, §159-43.

LOCAL GOVERNMENT BUDGET AND FISCAL CONTROL ACT, §159-7.

LOCAL GOVERNMENT EXECUTIVE SUCCESSION ACT, §§162B-5 to 162B-13.

LOCAL GOVERNMENT FINANCE ACT, §159-1.

LOCAL GOVERNMENT FISCAL INFORMATION ACT, §120-30.41.

LOCAL GOVERNMENT PUBLIC TRANSPORTATION SALES TAX ACT, §105-506.

LOCAL GOVERNMENT RETIREMENT SYSTEM ACT, §§128-21 to 128-38.2.

LOCAL GOVERNMENT RISK POOL ACT, §58-23-1.

LOCAL GOVERNMENTS ACT, §§160A-1 to 160A-588.

LOCAL GOVERNMENT SALES AND USE TAX
First one-cent local government sales and use tax act, §§105-463 to 105-474.
First one-half cent local government sales and use tax act, §§105-480 to 105-487.
Second one-half cent local government sales and use tax act, §§105-495 to 105-502.
Third one-half cent local government sales and use tax act, §§105-515 to 105-521.

LOCAL GOVERNMENT SALES AND USE TAX FOR BEACH NOURISHMENT, §105-525.

LOCAL IMPROVEMENT ACT, §§160A-216 to 160A-238.

LOCAL OPTION ELECTIONS
Alcoholic beverage elections, §§18B-600 to 18B-605.

LOCKSMITH LICENSING ACT, §§74F-1 to 74F-18.

LONDON LIBEL ACT, §§99-1 to 99-5.

LONG-TERM CARE INSURANCE ACT, §58-55-1.

LONG-TERM CARE PARTNERSHIPS, §§58-55-55 to 58-55-80.

LOOTING, §§14-288.1 to 14-288.20.

LORD CAMPBELL'S ACT, §28A-18-2.

LOSE CONTROL, LOSE LICENSE, §20-11.

LOTTERY ACT, §§14-289 to 14-291.2.

LOW-INCOME HOUSING TAX CREDIT, §§105-129.40 to 105-129.45.

LOW-LEVEL RADIOACTIVE WASTE MANAGEMENT AUTHORITY ACT OF 1987, §§104G-1 to 104G-23.

LYNCHING, §§114-15, 162-23.

M

MACHINE GUN ACT, §14-409.

MACHINERY ACT, §105-271.

MANUFACTURED HOMES STANDARDS CODE ACT, §§143-144 to 143-151.5.

MARINE FISHERIES COMPACT, §§113-252 to 113-258.

MARKETABLE TITLE ACT, §§47B-1 to 47B-9.

MARKETING ASSOCIATIONS
Cooperative marketing act, §54-130.

MARRIAGE AND FAMILY THERAPY LICENSURE ACT, §90-270.45.

MARRIED PERSON'S ACT, §§52-1 to 52-12.

MARRIED PERSONS' EMANCIPATION ACT, §52-2.

MARTIN ACT, §52-2.

MASON ACT FOR NONSUIT, §15-173.

MASSAGE AND BODYWORK PRACTICE ACT, §§90-620 to 90-636.

MASSAGE PARLORS, §§14-202.10 to 14-202.12.

MASS GATHERINGS, §§130A-251 to 130A-258.

MATERNITY HOMES, §131D-1.

MAXIMUM HOUR LAW, §§95-25.1 to 95-25.25.

MEAT INSPECTION ACT, §§106-549.15 to 106-549.28.

MECHANICS' AND MATERIALMEN'S LIEN, §§44A-7 to 44A-24.

MEDICAID, §§108A-54 to 108A-70.5.

MEDICAL ASSISTANCE PROVIDER FALSE CLAIMS ACT, §§108A-70.10 to 108A-70.16.

MEDICAL CARE DATA ACT, §§131E-214 to 131E-214.4.

MEDICAL EXAMINERS ACT, §§130A-377 to 130A-395.

MEDICAL MALPRACTICE, §§90-21.11 to 90-21.14.

MEDICAL PRACTICE ACT, §§90-1 to 90-18.5.

MEDICATION AIDE REGISTRY, §§131E-114.2, 131E-270.

MEMBERSHIP CAMPING ACT, §66-230.

MENTAL HEALTH, DEVELOPMENTAL DISABILITIES, AND SUBSTANCE ABUSE ACT OF 1985, §122C-1.

MERIT SYSTEM ACT, §§126-1 to 126-79.

METHAMPHETAMINE LAB PREVENTION ACT of 2005, §§90-113.50 to 90-113.60.

METROPOLITAN SEWERAGE DISTRICTS ACT, §162A-64.

METROPOLITAN WATER DISTRICTS ACT, §162A-31.

M.I.A., §§28B-1 to 28B-10.

MIDWIFERY PRACTICE ACT, §§90-178.1 to 90-178.7.

MIGRANT HOUSING ACT OF NORTH CAROLINA, §95-222.

MILEAGE ACT, §§20-340 to 20-350.

MILITARY AND OVERSEAS VOTERS Uniform act, §163-258.1.

MILK CONTROL ACT, §§106-266.6 to 106-266.19.

MINE SAFETY AND HEALTH ACT OF NORTH CAROLINA, §74-24.1.

MINING ACT OF 1971, §§74-46 to 74-68.

MINING COMPACT, §§74-37, 74-38.

MINOR VETERANS ENABLING ACT, §165-12.

MISDEMEANOR SENTENCING, §§15A-1340.20 to 15A-1340.23.

MISSING IN ACTION Absentees in military service, §§28B-1 to 28B-10.

MISTRIAL, §§15A-1061 to 15A-1065.

MODEL AIRPORT ZONING ACT, §63-37.

MODEL PAYMENT AND PERFORMANCE BOND, §§44A-25 to 44A-35.

MONEY TRANSMITTERS ACT, §§53-192 to 53-208.30.

MONOPOLIES ACT, §§75-1 to 75-35.

MORTGAGE ACT, §§45-4 to 45-80.

MORTUARY TABLES, §§8-46, 8-47.

MOTION PICTURE FAIR COMPETITION ACT, §§75C-1 to 75C-5.

MOTIONS TO SUPPRESS, §§15A-971 to 15A-980.

MOTORBUS ACT, §§62-259 to 62-279.

MOTOR CARRIER SAFETY REGULATION UNIT, §§20-376 to 20-397.

MOTOR FUEL MARKETING ACT, §75-80.

MOTOR TRAFFIC LAW, §§20-138.1 to 20-171.

MOTOR VEHICLE ACT OF 1937, §§20-39 to 20-183.

MOTOR VEHICLE CERTIFICATES OF TITLE, §§20-50 to 20-71.1.

MOTOR VEHICLE DEALERS AND MANUFACTURERS LICENSING LAW, §§20-285 to 20-308.2.

MOTOR VEHICLE REGISTRATION, §§20-50 to 20-71.1.

MOTOR VEHICLE REPAIR ACT, §20-354.

MOTOR VEHICLE SAFETY AND FINANCIAL RESPONSIBILITY ACT OF 1953, §20-279.39.

MOTOR VOTERS, §163-82.19.

MOUNTAIN RESOURCES PLANNING ACT, §153B-1.

MOUNTAIN RIDGE PROTECTION ACT OF 1983, §113A-205.

MOUTH HYGIENE ACT, §§90-221 to 90-233.1.

MOVERS, §§20-356 to 20-372.

MULTISTATE TRUST INSTITUTIONS ACT, §§53-302 to 53-329.

MUNICIPAL CORPORATIONS ACT, §§160A-1 to 160A-588.

MUNICIPAL ELECTION LAW, §§163-279 to 163-306.

MUNICIPAL EMPLOYEES' RETIREMENT SYSTEM ACT, §§128-21 to 128-38.2.

MUNICIPAL FINANCE ACT, §§159-1 to 159-200.

MUNICIPAL HOSPITAL ACT, §131E-5.

MUNICIPAL SERVICE DISTRICT ACT OF 1973, §160A-535.

MURDER, §§14-17, 14-18.

N

NARCOTICS North Carolina controlled substances act, §§90-86 to 90-113.8.

NATIONAL CRIME PREVENTION AND PRIVACY COMPACT, §114-19.50.

NATIONAL GUARD MUTUAL ASSISTANCE COMPACT, §§127A-175 to 127A-184.

NATIONAL GUARD TUITION ASSISTANCE ACT OF 1975, §116-209.50.

NATURAL AND SCENIC RIVERS ACT OF 1971, §113A-30.

NATURE AND HISTORIC PRESERVE DEDICATION ACT, §143-260.6.

NATURE PRESERVES ACT, §113A-164.1.

NC GREEN BUSINESS FUND, §§143B-437.4 to 143B-437.8.

NEGOTIABLE INSTRUMENTS Uniform commercial code-negotiable instruments, §25-3-101.

NEGOTIABLE INSTRUMENTS-UNIFORM COMMERCIAL CODE, §§25-3-101 to 25-3-605.

NEW MOTOR VEHICLES WARRANTIES ACT, §§20-351 to 20-351.10.

NIMBLE DIVIDEND LAW, §55-6-40.

911 EMERGENCY TELEPHONE SYSTEM Public safety telephone act, §§62A-1 to 62A-12.

NO CALL LAW, §§75-100 to 75-105.

NONFORFEITURE ACT FOR LIFE INSURANCE, §58-58-55.

NONFORFEITURE FOR INDIVIDUAL DEFERRED ANNUITIES, §§58-58-60, 58-58-61.

NONPROFIT ASSOCIATIONS Uniform unincorporated nonprofit association act, §59B-1.

NONPROFIT CORPORATIONS ACT, §55A-1-01.

NONPUBLIC SCHOOLS, §§115C-547 to 115C-565.

NONSUIT ACT FOR CRIMINAL CASES, §15-173.

NONSUPPORT ACT, §§14-322 to 14-326.1.

NORTH CAROLINA ACT TO REMOVE BARRIERS TO COORDINATING HUMAN SERVICE AND VOLUNTEER TRANSPORTATION ACT, §62-289.1.

NORTH CAROLINA AGRICULTURAL FINANCE ACT, §122D-1.

NORTH CAROLINA AGRICULTURAL LIMING MATERIALS AND LANDPLASTER ACT, §106-92.1.

NORTH CAROLINA AMBER ALERT SYSTEM, §143B-272.71.

NORTH CAROLINA ANTIFREEZE LAW OF 1975, §106-579.1.

NORTH CAROLINA APPALACHIAN TRAILS SYSTEM ACT, §113A-72.

NORTH CAROLINA ARCHAEOLOGICAL RECORD PROGRAM, §70-46.

NORTH CAROLINA ARCHIVES AND HISTORY ACT, §121-1.

NORTH CAROLINA BEE AND HONEY ACT OF 1977, §§106-634 to 106-644.

NORTH CAROLINA BIOLOGICAL ORGANISM ACT, §106-65.42.

NORTH CAROLINA BIOLOGICS LAW OF 1981, §106-707.

NORTH CAROLINA BUSINESS CORPORATION ACT, §55-1-01.

NORTH CAROLINA CAPITAL FACILITIES FINANCING ACT, §§159D-1 to 159D-57.

NORTH CAROLINA CEMETERY ACT, §65-46.

NORTH CAROLINA COMMERCIAL FEED LAW OF 1973, §106-284.30.

NORTH CAROLINA COMMERCIAL FERTILIZER LAW, §106-655.

NORTH CAROLINA COMMUNITY THIRD PARTY TRUSTS/POOLED TRUSTS ACT
Persons with severe chronic disabilities, §36D-1.

NORTH CAROLINA COMMUNITY TRUSTS FOR PERSONS WITH SEVERE CHRONIC DISABILITIES, §§36D-1 to 36D-11.

NORTH CAROLINA CONSUMER FINANCE ACT, §53-164.

NORTH CAROLINA CONTROLLED SUBSTANCES ACT, §90-86.

NORTH CAROLINA CONTROLLED SUBSTANCES REPORTING SYSTEM ACT, §§90-113.70 to 90-113.76.

NORTH CAROLINA CONTROL SHARE ACQUISITION ACT, §55-9A-01.

NORTH CAROLINA COSMETIC ART ACT, §88B-1.

NORTH CAROLINA COTTON WAREHOUSE ACT, §106-451.6.

NORTH CAROLINA CREMATORY ACT, §90-210.120.

NORTH CAROLINA DRINKING WATER ACT, §130A-311.

NORTH CAROLINA DRUG PARAPHERNALIA ACT, §90-113.20.

NORTH CAROLINA DRUG TREATMENT COURT ACT OF 1995, §7A-790.

NORTH CAROLINA EGG LAW, §106-245.13.

NORTH CAROLINA EMERGENCY MANAGEMENT ACT OF 1977, §166A-1.

NORTH CAROLINA EMERGENCY WAR POWERS ACT, §147-33.1.

NORTH CAROLINA ENERGY POLICY ACT OF 1975, §§113B-1 to 113B-24.

NORTH CAROLINA ENGINEERING AND LAND SURVEYING ACT, §89C-1.

NORTH CAROLINA ENTERPRISE CORPORATION ACT, §53A-35.

NORTH CAROLINA ENVIRONMENTAL POLICY ACT OF 1971, §113A-1.

NORTH CAROLINA FAMILY LAW ARBITRATION ACT, §50-41.

NORTH CAROLINA FINANCIAL PRIVACY ACT, §53B-1.

NORTH CAROLINA FOOD, DRUG AND COSMETIC ACT, §106-120.

NORTH CAROLINA FOREIGN-MONEY CLAIMS ACT, §1C-1834.

NORTH CAROLINA GEOLOGISTS LICENSING ACT, §89E-1.

NORTH CAROLINA GLOBAL TRANSPARK AUTHORITY ACT, §63A-1.

NORTH CAROLINA GOVERNMENT COMPETITION ACT OF 1998, §§143-701 to 143-709.

NORTH CAROLINA HAZARDOUS MATERIALS EMERGENCY RESPONSE ACT, §166A-20.

NORTH CAROLINA HEALTH CHOICE FOR CHILDREN
Health insurance program for children, §§135-47 to 135-47.3.

NORTH CAROLINA HOME INSPECTOR LICENSURE ACT, §143-151.43.

NORTH CAROLINA HOUSING FINANCE AGENCY ACT, §122A-1.

NORTH CAROLINA HOUSING TRUST AND OIL OVERCHARGE ACT, §122E-1.

NORTH CAROLINA INDUSTRIAL AND POLLUTION CONTROL FACILITIES FINANCING ACT, §159D-1.

NORTH CAROLINA INTERCHANGE OF GOVERNMENTAL EMPLOYEES ACT OF 1977, §126-51.

NORTH CAROLINA INTERNATIONAL COMMERCIAL ARBITRATION AND CONCILIATION ACT, §1-567.30.

NORTH CAROLINA INVESTMENT ADVISERS ACT, §78C-1.

NORTH CAROLINA LAW ON THE PROTECTION OF MINORS FROM HARMFUL MATERIALS, §19-9.

NORTH CAROLINA LIFE AND HEALTH INSURANCE GUARANTY ASSOCIATION ACT, §58-62-2.

NORTH CAROLINA LIMITED LIABILITY COMPANY ACT, §57C-1-01.

NORTH CAROLINA LIVESTOCK PROMPT PAY LAW, §106-418.1.

NORTH CAROLINA MASSAGE AND BODYWORK THERAPY PRACTICE ACT, §§90-620 to 90-636.

NORTH CAROLINA METROPOLITAN SEWERAGE DISTRICTS ACT, §162A-64.

NORTH CAROLINA MOTOR VEHICLE REPAIR ACT, §20-354.

NORTH CAROLINA NEW ORGANIZATIONAL VISION AWARD (NC NOVA) SPECIAL LICENSURE DESIGNATION, §§131E-154.12 to 131E-154.14.

NORTH CAROLINA NONPROFIT CORPORATIONS ACT, §55A-1-01.

NORTH CAROLINA OCCUPATIONAL THERAPY PRACTICE ACT, §90-270.65.

NORTH CAROLINA PERSONS WITH DISABILITIES PROTECTION ACT, §§168A-1 to 168A-12.

NORTH CAROLINA PERSONS WITH DISABILITIES PROTECTION LAW, §168-1.

NORTH CAROLINA PESTICIDE LAW OF 1971, §143-434.

NORTH CAROLINA PLANNED COMMUNITY ACT, §§47F-1-101 to 47F-3-120.

NORTH CAROLINA POULTRY PRODUCTS INSPECTION ACT, §106-549.49.

NORTH CAROLINA PROFESSIONAL EMPLOYER ORGANIZATION ACT, §58-89-1.

NORTH CAROLINA PROJECT DEVELOPMENT FINANCING ACT, §159-101.

NORTH CAROLINA PUBLIC TRANSPORTATION AUTHORITIES ACT, §160A-575.

NORTH CAROLINA RACIAL JUSTICE ACT, §§15A-2010 to 15A-2012.

NORTH CAROLINA RADIATION PROTECTION ACT, §104E-1.

NORTH CAROLINA RECREATIONAL THERAPY LICENSURE ACT, §§90C-20 to 90C-37.

NORTH CAROLINA REGIONAL RECIPROCAL SAVINGS AND LOAN ACQUISITION ACT, §54B-48.1.

NORTH CAROLINA RULES OF EVIDENCE, §8C-1.

NORTH CAROLINA RURAL INTERNET ACCESS AUTHORITY ACT, §§143B-437.40 to 143B-437.43.

NORTH CAROLINA RURAL REDEVELOPMENT AUTHORITY ACT, §§143B-437.20 to 143B-437.33.

NORTH CAROLINA SALES AND USE TAX ACT, §105-164.1.

NORTH CAROLINA SCRAP TIRE DISPOSAL ACT, §130A-309.51.

NORTH CAROLINA'S EASTERN REGION ACT, §§158-30 to 158-42.

NORTH CAROLINA SECURE AND FAIR ENFORCEMENT (S.A.F.E.) MORTGAGE LICENSING ACT, §53-244.010.

NORTH CAROLINA SECURITIES ACT, §78A-1.

NORTH CAROLINA SEED LAW OF 1963, §106-277.1.

NORTH CAROLINA SHAREHOLDER PROTECTION ACT, §55-9-01.

NORTH CAROLINA SILVER ALERT SYSTEM, §143B-272.72.

NORTH CAROLINA SMALL EMPLOYER GROUP HEALTH COVERAGE REFORM ACT, §58-50-100.

NORTH CAROLINA SOIL ADDITIVES ACT OF 1977, §106-50.28.

NORTH CAROLINA SOIL SCIENTIST LICENSING ACT, §89F-1.

NORTH CAROLINA SPECIAL AIRPORT DISTRICTS ACT, §63-78.

NORTH CAROLINA STATE BUILDING CODE, §143-138.

NORTH CAROLINA STATE LOTTERY ACT, §18C-101.

NORTH CAROLINA TIME SHARE ACT, §93A-39.

NORTH CAROLINA TOXIC VAPORS ACT, §90-113.8A.

NORTH CAROLINA TRAILS SYSTEM ACT, §113A-83.

NORTH CAROLINA UNCLAIMED PROPERTY ACT, §§116B-51 to 116B-80.

NORTH CAROLINA UNIFORM FOREIGN-COUNTRY MONEY JUDGMENTS RECOGNITION ACT, §1C-1850.

NORTH CAROLINA UNIFORM INTERSTATE DEPOSITIONS AND DISCOVERY ACT, §1F-1.

NORTH CAROLINA UNIFORM PARTNERSHIP ACT, §59-31.

NORTH CAROLINA UNIFORM PRUDENT INVESTOR ACT, §36C-9-907.

NORTH CAROLINA UNIFORM TRUST CODE, §§36C-1-101 to 36C-11-1106.

NORTH CAROLINA VACATION RENTAL ACT, §§42A-1 to 42A-36.

NORTH CAROLINA VETERINARY PRACTICE ACT, §90-180.

NORTH CAROLINA WATER AND SEWER AUTHORITIES ACT, §162A-1.

NORTH CAROLINA WELL CONSTRUCTION ACT, §87-83.

NORTH CAROLINA WELL CONTRACTORS CERTIFICATION ACT, §87-98.1.

NORTH CAROLINA WORKERS' COMPENSATION ACT, §97-1.

NOTARY PUBLIC ACT, §10B-1.

NURSE LICENSURE COMPACT, §§90-171.80 to 90-171.94.

NURSES AIDES REGISTRY ACT, §90-171.55.

NURSING HOME ADMINISTRATOR ACT, §90-275.1.

NURSING HOME LICENSURE ACT, §§131E-100 to 131E-131.

NURSING HOME PATIENTS' BILL OF RIGHTS, §§131E-115 to 131E-131.

NURSING POOL LICENSURE ACT, §§131E-154.1 to 131E-154.8.

NURSING PRACTICE ACT, §§90-171.19 to 90-171.53.

NUTRITION/DIETETICS PRACTICE ACT, §90-350.

O

OCCUPATIONAL DISEASE ACT, §§97-52 to 97-76.

OCCUPATIONAL LICENSING ACT, §§105-33 to 105-113.

OCCUPATIONAL SAFETY AND HEALTH ACT OF NORTH CAROLINA, §95-126.

OCCUPATIONAL THERAPY PRACTICE ACT, §90-270.65.

ODOMETER ALTERATION
Vehicle mileage act, §§20-340 to 20-350.

OIL AND GAS CONSERVATION ACT, §113-381.

OIL AND GASOLINE INSPECTION ACT, §§119-14 to 119-47.

OIL POLLUTION AND HAZARDOUS SUBSTANCES CONTROL ACT OF 1978, §143-215.75.

ONE-QUARTER CENT COUNTY SALES AND USE TAX ACT, §105-535.

OPEN BURNING LAW, §§113-60.21 to 113-60.31.

OPEN MEETINGS ACT, §§143-318.9 to 143-318.18.

OPTOMETRY ACT, §§90-114 to 90-127.3.

OSTEOPATHY ACT, §§90-129 to 90-138.

OUTDOOR ADVERTISING CONTROL ACT, §§136-126 to 136-140.

OUT-OF-STATE PAROLEE SUPERVISION ACT, §§148-65.1 to 148-65.3.

OVERHEAD HIGH-VOLTAGE LINE SAFETY ACT, §§95-229.5 to 95-229.13.

P

PALMISTRY, §14-401.5.

PARAPHERNALIA ACT, §§90-113.20 to 90-113.24.

PARDONS, §§147-21 to 147-25, NC Const Art III §5, US Const Art II §2.

PARENTAL RESPONSIBILITY ACT, §1-538.1.

PARK COMMISSION ACT, §143-258.

PARKING AUTHORITIES LAW, §160A-550.

PAROCHIAL SCHOOLS, §§115C-547 to 115C-554.

PAROLE ACT, §§148-52.1 to 148-64.

PARTNERSHIP ACT, §59-31.

PARTY LINES, §14-401.8.

PASSWORDS, §14-12.4.

PATERNITY ACT, §§49-1 to 49-17.

PATIENTS' BILL OF RIGHTS FOR NURSING HOME PATIENTS, §§131E-115 to 131E-131.

PAWNBROKERS AND CASH CONVERTERS MODERNIZATION ACT OF 1989, §91A-1.

PAYABLE ON DEATH ACCOUNTS, §§54-109.57, 54B-130.

PAYMENT BOND, §§44A-25 to 44A-35.

PAYMENT INTO COURT, §§1-508 to 1-510.

PEDERASTY, §14-202.1.

PEEPING TOM, §14-202.

PEREMPTORY CHALLENGES, §§9-19 to 9-21.

PERFORMANCE BOND, §§44A-25 to 44A-35.

PERJURY, §§14-209 to 14-211.

PERPETUITIES
Uniform statutory rule against perpetuities, §41-20.

PERSONAL PROPERTY LIEN ACT, §§44A-1 to 44A-6.1.

PERSONNEL SYSTEM ACT, §§126-1 to 126-88.

PERSONS WITH DISABILITIES PROTECTION LAW, §168-1.

PEST CONTROL
Structural pest control act of North Carolina of 1955, §§106-65.22 to 106-65.41.

PEST CONTROL COMPACT, §§106-65.55 to 106-65.61.

PESTICIDE LAW OF 1971, §143-434.

PET ADMITTANCE TO HOTEL ROOMS, §72-7.1.

PHARMACY PRACTICE ACT, §§90-85.2 to 90-85.41.

PHRENOLOGY, §14-401.5.

PHYSICALLY HANDICAPPED ACT FOR SECOND INJURY, §97-35.

PHYSICAL THERAPY PRACTICE ACT, §§90-270.24 to 90-270.39.

PICKETING, §14-225.1.

PIPELINES, §62-50.

PLANNED COMMUNITY ACT, §§47F-1-101 to 47F-3-120.

PLANT PROTECTION AND CONSERVATION ACT, §§106-202.12 to 106-202.22.

PLUMBING AND HEATING CONTRACTORS ACT, §§87-16 to 87-27.1.

PODIATRY ACT, §§90-202.2 to 90-202.14.

POINTS SCHEDULE, §20-16.

POLICE PURSUIT, §20-145.

POLITICAL ACTIVITY OF STATE EMPLOYEES ACT, §§126-13 to 126-15.1.

POLITICAL CAMPAIGN CONTRIBUTIONS, §§163-278.6 to 163-278.40I.

PORK PROMOTION ASSESSMENT ACT, §106-790.

PORTABLE CONSUMER ELECTRONIC DEVICES INSURANCE, §§58-44A-1 to 58-44A-25.

POSTED PROPERTY
Hunting and fishing, §§113-281 to 113-287.

POSTMORTEM MEDICAL EXAMINERS ACT, §§130A-377 to 130A-395.

POST-TOWING PROCEDURES, §§20-219.9 to 20-219.14.

POULTRY INDUSTRY ACT, §§106-539 to 106-549.

POULTRY PRODUCTS INSPECTION ACT, §106-549.49.

POUR-OVER TRUST ACT, §31-47.

POWELL ACT, §§136-41.1 to 136-41.3.

PRACTICE OF MEDICINE ACT, §§90-1 to 90-21.

PREJUDGMENT ATTACHMENT ACT, §§1-440.1 to 1-440.46.

PREMARITAL AGREEMENT ACT, §52B-1.

PREMIUM TAX
Taxes upon insurance companies, §§105-228.3 to 105-228.10.

PRESENTENCE REPORTS, §§15A-1332, 15A-1333.

PRESIDENTIAL PREFERENCE PRIMARY ACT, §163-213.1.

PRICE GOUGING DURING STATE OF DISASTER, §§75-37, 75-37.1.

PRIMARY ELECTION LAWS, §§163-104 to 163-115, 163-119.

PRIMARY FOREST PRODUCT ASSESSMENT ACT, §113A-189.

PRINCIPAL AND INCOME ACT, §37A-1-101.

PRISONERS OF WAR
Absentees in military service, §§28B-1 to 28B-10.

PRISON LABOR ACT, §§148-26 to 148-49.

PRIVATE CAPITAL FACILITIES FINANCE ACT, §159D-35.

PRIVATE EDUCATIONAL FACILITIES FINANCE ACT, §§115E-1 to 115E-23.

PRIVATE PROTECTIVE SERVICES ACT, §§74C-1 to 74C-33.

PRIVATE SCHOOLS ACT, §§115C-547 to 115C-565.

PRIVILEGED COMMUNICATIONS ACT, §§8-53 to 8-53.5.

PROBATION, §§15A-1341 to 15A-1347.

PRODUCTS LIABILITY ACT, §§99B-1 to 99B-11.

PROFESSIONAL CORPORATION ACT, §55B-1.

PROFESSIONAL EMPLOYER ORGANIZATION ACT, §58-89-1.

PROJECT DEVELOPMENT FINANCING ACT, §159-101.

PROMPT PAY LAW, §§106-418.1 to 106-418.7.

PROPERTY RECORDATION ACT, §§47-17 to 47-36.

PROPERTY TAXES
Machinery act, §§105-271 to 105-395.1.

PROPRIETARY SCHOOLS ACT, §§115D-87 to 115D-97.

PROSECUTION BONDS, §§1-109 to 1-112.

PROSTITUTION, §§14-203 to 14-208.

PROTECTION OF THE ABUSED, NEGLECTED OR EXPLOITED DISABLED ADULT ACT, §108A-99.

PRUDENT INVESTOR ACT, §36C-9-907.

PRUDENT MANAGEMENT OF INSTITUTIONAL FUNDS ACT, §36E-1.

PSYCHOLOGY PRACTICE ACT, §90-270.1.

PSYCHOTHERAPY PATIENT/CLIENT SEXUAL EXPLOITATION ACT, §§90-21.41 to 90-21.48.

PUBLIC ACCOUNTANTS LAW, §§93-1 to 93-13.

PUBLIC ASSISTANCE ACT, §§108A-24 to 108A-70.5.

PUBLIC BUILDING CONTRACTS ACT, §§143-128 to 143-135.8.

PUBLIC HEALTH AUTHORITIES ACT, §§130A-45 to 130A-45.11.

PUBLIC HEALTH LAW, §§130A-1 to 130A-460.

PUBLIC HOSPITAL PERSONNEL ACT, §§131E-257 to 131E-257.2.

PUBLIC SAFETY TELEPHONE ACT, §§62A-1 to 62A-12.

PUBLIC SCHOOL ACT, §§115C-1 to 115C-546.2.

PUBLIC TRANSPORTATION AUTHORITIES ACT, §160A-575.
Regional public transportation authorities act, §§160A-600 to 160A-625.

PUBLIC UTILITIES ACT, §62-1.

PUBLIC UTILITIES COMMISSION ACT, §§62-10 to 62-98.

PUBLIC UTILITIES COMMISSION PROCEDURE ACT, §§62-60 to 62-82.

PUBLIC WORKS ACT, §§133-1 to 133-33.

PUBLIC WORKS EMINENT DOMAIN LAW, §§40A-40 to 40A-56.

PURCHASE MONEY MORTGAGE ACT, §45-21.38.

PURE FOOD ACT, §§106-120 to 106-145.12.

Q

QUALIFIED BUSINESS INVESTMENT TAX CREDIT, §§105-163.010 to 105-163.015.

QUARRIES AND MINES ACT, §§74-24.1 to 74-68.

QUASHING INDICTMENTS, §§15-153, 15-155.

QUIETING TITLE ACT, §41-10.

R

RABIES, §§130A-184 to 130A-200.

RACIAL JUSTICE ACT, §§15A-2010 to 15A-2012.

RACING ON STREETS AND HIGHWAYS, §20-141.3.

RACKETEER INFLUENCED AND CORRUPT ORGANIZATIONS ACT (RICO), §75D-1.

RADIATION PROTECTION ACT, §104E-1.

RADIO DEFAMATION ACT, §§99-1 to 99-5.

RAPE ACT, §§14-27.1 to 14-27.10.

READABLE INSURANCE POLICIES ACT, §58-38-1.

REAL ESTATE APPRAISERS ACT, §§93E-1-1 to 93E-1-14.

REAL ESTATE LICENSE LAW, §§93A-1 to 93A-59.

REAL PROPERTY ACQUISITIONS POLICIES ACT, §§133-5 to 133-18.

REAL PROPERTY ELECTRONIC RECORDING ACT, §47-16.1.

REAL PROPERTY LIEN ACT, §§44A-7 to 44A-24.

REAL PROPERTY MARKETABLE TITLE ACT, §§47B-1 to 47B-9.

RECIPROCAL INHERITANCE ACT, §§64-3 to 64-5.

RECIPROCAL INTERSTATE BANKING ACT, §53-209.

RECKLESS DRIVING, §20-140.

RECORDATION ACT, §§47-17 to 47-36.

RECORDS AS EVIDENCE
Uniform photographic copies of business and public records as evidence act, §8-45.4.

RECREATIONAL THERAPY LICENSURE ACT, §§90C-20 to 90C-37.

RECREATIONAL TRESPASS, §§14-159.6, 113A-95.

RECREATION ENABLING LAW, §§160A-350 to 160A-356.

REDEVELOPMENT LAW, §§160A-500 to 160A-526.

REFUND ANTICIPATION LOAN ACT, §§53-245 to 53-254.

REFUNDING BOND ACT, §142-29.1.

REGIONAL NATURAL GAS DISTRICT ACT, §160A-660.

REGIONAL PUBLIC TRANSPORTATION AUTHORITY ACT, §160A-600.

REGIONAL RECIPROCAL SAVINGS AND LOAN ACQUISITION ACT, §54B-48.1.

REGIONAL SEWAGE DISPOSAL PLANNING ACT OF 1971, §162A-26.

REGIONAL TRANSIT AUTHORITY VEHICLE RENTAL TAX, §§105-550 to 105-555.

REGIONAL TRANSPORTATION AUTHORITY ACT, §160A-630.

REGIONAL WATER SUPPLY PLANNING ACT OF 1971, §162A-20.

REGISTERED PUBLIC OBLIGATIONS ACT, §159E-1.

REGISTERS OF DEEDS SUPPLEMENTAL PENSION FUND ACT OF 1987, §161-50.

REGISTRATION ACT, §§47-17 to 47-36.

REGISTRATION ACT FOR MAKERS OF MORTGAGES AND DEEDS OF TRUST, §§53-233 to 53-242.

REGISTRATION ACT FOR MOTOR VEHICLES, §§20-50 to 20-71.1.

REGISTRATION OF TRADEMARKS ACT, §§80-1 to 80-14.

REGISTRATION OF VOTERS ACT, §§163-82.1 to 163-82.26.

RELIGIOUS SCHOOLS, §§115C-547 to 115C-554.

RELOCATION ASSISTANCE
Uniform relocation assistance and real property acquisition policies act, §§133-5 to 133-18.

REMOVAL FROM OFFICE ACT, §§128-16 to 128-20.

RENT-A-COPS, §§74E-1 to 74E-13.

RENUNCIATION OF PROPERTY AND RENUNCIATION OF FIDUCIARY POWERS ACT, §31B-7.

RESCUE WORKERS' PENSION FUND ACT, §§58-86-1 to 58-86-91.

RESIDENTIAL MORTGAGE FRAUD ACT, §14-118.10.

RESIDENTIAL PROPERTY DISCLOSURE ACT, §§47E-1 to 47E-10.

RESPIRATORY CARE PRACTICE ACT, §§90-646 to 90-665.

RETAIL INSTALLMENT SALES ACT, §§25A-1 to 25A-45.

RETALIATORY EMPLOYMENT DISCRIMINATION, §§95-240 to 95-245.

RETIREMENT SYSTEM ACTUARIAL NOTE ACT, §§120-112 to 120-114.

RETIREMENT SYSTEM FOR COUNTIES, CITIES AND TOWNS ACT, §§128-21 to 128-38.4.

RETIREMENT SYSTEM FOR TEACHERS AND STATE EMPLOYEES, §§135-1 to 135-18.7.

REVENUE ACT, §§105-1 to 105-270.

REVENUE BOND ACT, §§159-80 to 159-97.

REVERSE MORTGAGE ACT, §53-255.

REVISED UNIFORM ANATOMICAL GIFT ACT, §130A-412.3.

REVISED UNIFORM ARBITRATION ACT, §1-569.31.

REVISED UNIFORM LIMITED PARTNERSHIP ACT, §59-101.

RICO ACT, §75D-1.

RIDESHARING, §§136-44.21 to 136-44.26.

RIGHT-OF-WAY, §§20-155 to 20-158.1.

RIGHT TO NATURAL DEATH, §§32A-15 to 32A-26, 90-320 to 90-323.

RIGHT TO WORK LAW, §§95-78 to 95-84.

ROAD ACT, §§136-4 to 136-155.

ROADWAY CORRIDOR OFFICIAL MAP ACT, §§136-44.50 to 136-44.53.

ROLLER SKATING RINK SAFETY AND LIABILITY, §§99E-10 to 99E-14.

RULE AGAINST PERPETUITIES
Uniform statutory rule, §41-20.

RULES OF EVIDENCE, §8C-1, §Rules 101 to §1102.

RULES OF THE ROAD, §§20-138.1 to 20-171.

RURAL DEVELOPMENT PROGRAM
Agriculture development act, §§106-580 to 106-587.

RURAL ELECTRIFICATION ACT, §§117-1 to 117-5.

RURAL INTERNET ACCESS AUTHORITY ACT, §§143B-437.40 to 143B-437.43.

RURAL TELEPHONE ACT, §§117-29 to 117-35.

S

SAFECRACKING, §14-89.1.

SAFE HAVEN FOR INFANTS, §14-322.3.

SAFETY AND FINANCIAL RESPONSIBILITY ACT OF 1953, §§20-279.1 to 20-279.39.

SAFETY PROFESSIONALS, §§90-671 to 90-674.

SALES
Uniform commercial code-sales, §25-2-101.

SALES AND USE TAX ACT, §105-164.1.

SALES-UNIFORM COMMERCIAL CODE, §§25-2-101 to 25-2-725.

SALVAGE TITLES, §§20-71.2 to 20-71.4.

SAVINGS AND LOAN ASSOCIATIONS, §54B-1.

SAVINGS AND LOAN INTERSTATE BRANCH ACT, §§54B-265 to 54B-278.

SAVINGS BANK INTERSTATE BRANCH ACT, §§54C-199 to 54C-212.

SAVINGS BANKS, §§54C-1 to 54C-212.

SCENIC RIVERS SYSTEM ACT, §§113A-30 to 113A-44.

SCHOOL-BASED MANAGEMENT AND ACCOUNTABILITY PROGRAM, §§115C-105.20 to 115C-105.39.

SCHOOL BUDGET AND FISCAL CONTROL ACT, §§115C-422 to 115C-452.

SCHOOL BUSES, §§115C-239 to 115C-262.

S CORPORATION INCOME TAX ACT, §105-131.

SCRAP TIRE DISPOSAL ACT, §130A-309.51.

SCRAP TIRE DISPOSAL TAX, §§105-187.15 to 105-187.19.

SEARCH WARRANT ACT, §§15A-241 to 15A-259.

SECOND INJURY ACT, §97-35.

SECOND ONE-HALF CENT LOCAL GOVERNMENT SALES AND USE TAX ACT, §105-495.

SECRET SOCIETIES PROHIBITION ACT, §§14-12.2 to 14-12.15.

SECURE AND FAIR ENFORCEMENT (S.A.F.E.) MORTGAGE LICENSING ACT, §53-244.010.

SECURED TRANSACTIONS, §§25-9-100 to 25-9-709.
Uniform commercial code-secured transactions, §25-9-101.

SECURITIES ACT, §78A-1.

SEDIMENTATION POLLUTION CONTROL ACT OF 1973, §113A-50.

SEED LAW OF 1963, §106-277.1.

SELF-SERVICE STORAGE FACILITIES LIENS, §§44A-40 to 44A-46.

SENTENCE SUSPENSION ACT, §§15A-1341 to 15A-1347.

SENTENCING SERVICES PROGRAM, §7A-770.

SERVICE DISTRICT ACT FOR MUNICIPALITIES, §§160A-535 to 160A-544.

SETOFF DEBT COLLECTION ACT, §§105A-1 to 105A-16.

SEWAGE DISPOSAL PLANNING ACT, §§162A-26 to 162A-30.

SEWER AUTHORITIES ACT, §§162A-1 to 162A-19.

SEXUAL OFFENDER REGISTRATION PROGRAM, §§14-208.5 to 14-208.13.

SHAREHOLDER PROTECTION ACT, §§55-9-01 to 55-9-05.

SHAREHOLDER'S APPRAISAL ACT, §§55-13-30, 55-13-31.

SHELLEY'S CASE, §39-1.1.

SHERIFFS' SUPPLEMENTAL PENSION FUND ACT OF 1985, §143-166.80.

SHOP BOOK RULE, §§8-42 to 8-44.

SHOPLIFTING ACT, §14-72.1.

SILVER ALERT SYSTEM, §143B-272.72.

SINGLE ACT LAW FOR FOREIGN CORPORATIONS, §§55-15-01 to 55-15-33.

SLANDER ACT, §§99-1 to 99-5.

SLAYER ACT, §§31A-3 to 31A-12.1.

SLOT MACHINE ACT, §§14-304 to 14-309.1.

SMALL BUSINESS CONTRACTORS, §§143B-472.100 to 143B-472.112.

SMALL EMPLOYER GROUP HEALTH COVERAGE REFORM ACT, §58-50-100.

SMALL FACE AMOUNT LIFE INSURANCE DISCLOSURE ACT, §58-60-90.

SMALL LOANS ACT, §§53-164 to 53-191.

SMOKING IN PUBLIC PLACES, §§130A-491 to 130A-498, 143-595 to 143-601.

SOCIAL SERVICES ACT, §§108A-1 to 108A-11.

SOCIAL WORKER CERTIFICATION AND LICENSURE ACT, §90B-1.

SOFT DRINK TAX ACT, §§105-113.41 to 105-113.64.

SOIL ADDITIVES ACT OF 1977, §106-50.28.

SOIL AND WATER CONSERVATION DISTRICTS LAW, §§139-1 to 139-57.

SOIL SCIENTIST LICENSING ACT, §89F-1.

SOLID WASTE MANAGEMENT ACT OF 1989, §130A-309.01.

SOLID WASTE MANAGEMENT LOAN PROGRAM AND LOCAL GOVERNMENT SPECIAL OBLIGATION BOND ACT, §159I-1.

SOUTHEASTERN INTERSTATE FOREST FIRE PROTECTION COMPACT, §§113-60.11 to 113-60.15.

SOUTHEAST INTERSTATE LOW-LEVEL RADIOACTIVE WASTE MANAGEMENT COMPACT, §§104F-1 to 104F-5.

SOUTHERN GROWTH POLICIES AGREEMENT ACT, §§143-490 to 143-506.

SOUTHERN STATES ENERGY COMPACT, §§104D-1 to 104D-5.

SPECIAL AIRPORT DISTRICTS ACT, §63-78.

SPECIAL ASSESSMENTS ACT, §§160A-216 to 160A-238.

SPECIAL EDUCATION, §§115C-106 to 115C-145.

SPEECH AND LANGUAGE PATHOLOGISTS AND AUDIOLOGISTS LICENSURE ACT, §§90-292 to 90-307.

SPEED, §§20-141 to 20-141.3, 20-144, 20-145.

SPEEDY TRIAL ACT, §15-10.

STANDARD NONFORFEITURE LAW FOR INDIVIDUAL DEFERRED ANNUITIES, §§58-58-60, 58-58-61.

STANDARD NONFORFEITURE LAW FOR LIFE INSURANCE, §58-58-55.

STANDARD VALUATION LAW FOR LIFE INSURANCE, §58-58-50.

STATE AND LOCAL GOVERNMENT REVENUE BOND ACT, §159-80.

STATE BAR ACT, §§84-15 to 84-38.

STATE BUDGET ACT, §§143C-1-1 to 143C-10-3.

STATE CAPITAL FACILITIES FINANCE ACT, §142-80.

STATE COLLEGES ACT, §§116-31 to 116-40.5.

STATE-COUNTY CRIMINAL JUSTICE PARTNERSHIP ACT, §§143B-273 to 143B-273.19.

STATE EMPLOYEE INCENTIVE BONUS PROGRAM, §§143-345.20 to 143-345.25.

STATE EMPLOYEES' POLITICAL ACTIVITY ACT, §§126-13 to 126-15.1.

STATE EMPLOYEE'S RETIREMENT ACT, §§135-1 to 135-18.7.

STATE ENERGY CONSERVATION FINANCE ACT, §142-60.

STATE ETHICS COMMISSION, §§138A-6 to 138A-15.

STATE FAIR HOUSING ACT, §§41A-1 to 41A-10.

STATE GOVERNMENTAL ACCOUNTABILITY AND INTERNAL CONTROL ACT, §§143D-1 to 143D-12.

STATE GOVERNMENT ETHICS ACT, §138A-1.

STATE HIGHWAY PATROL, §§20-184 to 20-196.4.

STATE LOTTERY ACT, §18C-101.

STATE NATURE AND HISTORIC PRESERVE DEDICATION ACT, §143-260.6.

STATE PARKS ACT, §§113-44.7 to 113-44.15.

STATE PERSONNEL SYSTEM ACT, §§126-1 to 126-88.

STATE PSYCHIATRIC HOSPITAL FINANCE ACT, §§142-100 to 142-113.

STATE REFUNDING BOND ACT, §142-29.1.

STATE TRUST COMPANY CHARTER ACT, §§53-330 to 53-365.

STATE VETERANS HOME ACT, §165-45.

STATEWIDE PRIMARY ACT, §§163-104 to 163-115, 163-119.

STATUTE OF FRAUDS, §§22-1 to 22-4.

STATUTE OF FRAUDS FOR SALES OF GOODS, §25-1-206.

STATUTE OF LIMITATIONS FOR CIVIL CASES, §§1-15 to 1-56.

STATUTE OF LIMITATIONS FOR MISDEMEANORS, §15-1.

STATUTE OF USES, §41-7.

STATUTORY SHORT FORM POWER OF ATTORNEY, §§32A-1 to 32A-3.

STERILIZATION ACT, §§35-36 to 35-50.

STERILIZATION OPERATION ACT, §§90-271 to 90-275.

STIMULANT DRUGS ACT, §§90-86 to 90-113.8.

STOCK LAW, §§68-15 to 68-46.

STOP AND FRISK ACT, §15A-255.

STRAWBERRY ASSESSMENT ACT, §106-781.

STREAMLINED SALES AND USE TAX AGREEMENT
Uniform sales and use tax administration act, §§105-164.42A to 105-164.42L.

STREET AND HIGHWAY ACT, §§136-4 to 136-155.

STRUCTURAL PEST CONTROL ACT OF NORTH CAROLINA OF 1955, §106-65.22.

STRUCTURED SENTENCING, §§15A-1340.10 to 15A-1340.23.

STRUCTURED SETTLEMENT PROTECTION ACT, §1-543.10.

STUDENT LOANS
Defaulted student loan recovery act, §§105B-1 to 105B-4.

STUDIES ACT OF 1995, §§14-415.10 to 14-415.23.

SUBDIVISIONS, CITIES, §§160A-371 to 160A-376.

SUBDIVISIONS, COUNTIES, §§153A-330 to 153A-335.

SUBSTANCE ABUSE PROFESSIONALS CERTIFICATION ACT, §§90-113.30 to 90-113.46.

SUBVERSIVE ACTIVITIES ACT, §§14-11 to 14-12.1.

SUDAN (DARFUR) DIVESTMENT ACT, §§147-86.41 to 147-86.49.

SUITABILITY IN ANNUITY TRANSACTIONS ACT, §58-60-150.

SUMMER SCHOOLS, §§115C-232, 115C-233.

SUNDAY CLOSING ACT, §160A-191.

SUNDAY HUNTING ACT, §103-2.

SUNSHINE LAW, §§143-318.9 to 143-318.18.

SUPERFUND PROGRAM, §§130A-310.20 to 130A-310.23.

SUPPLEMENTAL PROCEEDINGS LAW, §§1-352 to 1-368.

SUPPLEMENTAL RETIREMENT INCOME ACT OF 1984, §135-90.

SUPPORT ACT, §§52C-1-100 to 52C-9-902.

SUPPORT AND CUSTODY OF CHILDREN ACT, §§50-13.1 to 50-13.12.

SUPPORT OF CHILDREN OF PARENTS NOT MARRIED TO EACH OTHER, §49-1.

SUPPRESSION MOTIONS, §§15A-971 to 15A-980.

SURPLUS LINES ACT, §58-21-1.

SURVIVAL LAW, §28A-18-1.

SUSPENSION OF SENTENCE, §§15A-1341 to 15A-1347.

SWEEPSTAKES, §§14-289 to 14-291.2.

SWINE FARM SITING ACT, §106-800.

T

TATTOOS, §130A-283.

TAX INCENTIVES FOR NEW AND EXPANDING BUSINESSES, §§105-129.2 to 105-129.11.

TAX LIEN FORECLOSURE ACT, §§105-374, 105-375.

TAX MACHINERY ACT, §§105-271 to 105-395.1.

TEACHERS' RETIREMENT ACT, §§135-1 to 135-18.7.

TELEPHONE RECORDS PRIVACY PROTECTION ACT, §§14-113.30 to 14-113.33.

TEMPORARY LARCENY, §14-72.2.

TENANT SECURITY DEPOSIT ACT, §§42-50 to 42-56.

TENDER OFFER DISCLOSURE ACT, §§78B-1 to 78B-11.

TENNESSEE VALLEY AUTHORITY, §§105-258, 105-458 to 105-462.

TENTATIVE TRUSTS, §28A-15-10.

TENURE, §§115C-304, 115C-325.

TEST TUBE BABIES, §49A-1.

THE HEALTH INSURANCE PROGRAM FOR CHILDREN ACT OF 1998, §§108A-70.18 to 108A-70.28.

THIRD ONE-HALF CENT LOCAL GOVERNMENT SALES AND USE TAX ACT, §§105-515 to 105-521.

TIME SHARE ACT, §93A-39.

TOBACCO PRODUCTS TAX ACT, §105-113.2.

TOBACCO RESERVE FUND AND ESCROW COMPLIANCE, §§66-290 to 66-294.1.

TOBACCO TRUST FUND, §§143-715 to 143-723.

TOLLING ACT, §1-21.

TORRENS TITLE REGISTRATION ACT, §§43-1 to 43-64.

TORT CLAIMS ACT, §§143-291 to 143-300.1A.

TOXIC VAPORS ACT, §90-113.8A.

TRADEMARK REGISTRATION ACT, §§80-1 to 80-14.

TRADE SECRETS PROTECTION ACT, §§66-152 to 66-157.

TRAFFIC LAWS, §§20-138.1 to 20-171.

TRAILS SYSTEM ACT, §113A-83.
Appalachian trails system act, §§113A-72 to 113A-77.

TRAINING WAGE, §95-25.3A.

TRANSFER ON DEATH (TOD) SECURITY REGISTRATION ACT, §41-50.

TRANSFERS TO MINORS
Uniform transfers to minors act, §§33A-1 to 33A-24.

TRANSPORTATION AUTHORITIES
Public transportation authorities act, §§160A-575 to 160A-588.
Regional public transportation authorities act, §§160A-600 to 160A-627.
Regional transportation authority act, §§160A-630 to 160A-651.

TRAVEL AND TOURISM POLICY ACT, §143B-434.2.

TREATMENT FOR EFFECTIVE COMMUNITY SUPERVISION ACT OF 2011, §143B-272.80.

TRESPASS, §§14-127 to 14-163.1.

TRESPASS ACT, §113A-95.

TRESPASSER RESPONSIBILITY ACT, §38B-1.

TRUANCY, §§115C-378 to 115C-383.

TRUCK ACT, §§62-259 to 62-279.

TRUCKERS' FUEL USE TAX ACT, §§105-449.37 to 105-449.57.

TRUST CODE, §36C-1-101.

TRUSTEES' POWERS ACT, §§32-25 to 32-28.

TRUTH IN MUSIC ADVERTISING ACT, §75-125.

TUITION, §§116-143 to 116-144.

T.V.A., §§105-258, 105-458 to 105-462.

U

U.C.C., §25-1-101.

UMSTEAD ACT FOR GOVERNMENT SALE OF MERCHANDISE, §66-58.

UNAUTHORIZED DOMESTIC INSURERS ACT, §§58-14-1 to 58-14-15.

UNAUTHORIZED INSURERS FALSE ADVERTISING PROCESS ACT, §58-29-25.

UNAUTHORIZED INSURERS PROCESS ACT, §58-16-35.

UNBORN VICTIMS OF VIOLENCE ACT/ETHEN'S LAW, §§14-23.1 to 14-23.8.

UNCLAIMED PROPERTY ACT, §§116B-51 to 116B-80.

UNDERGROUND DAMAGE PREVENTION ACT, §87-100.

UNEMPLOYMENT COMPENSATION Employment security law, §§96-1 to 96-35.

UNIFORM ACT FOR OUT-OF-STATE PAROLEE SUPERVISION, §148-65.2.

UNIFORM ACT TO SECURE THE ATTENDANCE OF WITNESSES FROM WITHOUT A STATE IN CRIMINAL PROCEEDINGS, §15A-816.

UNIFORM ATHLETE AGENT ACT, §78C-85.

UNIFORM BOILER AND PRESSURE VESSEL ACT OF NORTH CAROLINA, §95-69.8.

UNIFORM BOLL WEEVIL ERADICATION ACT, §106-65.67.

UNIFORM CHILD CUSTODY JURISDICTION AND ENFORCEMENT ACT, §§50A-101 to 50A-317.

UNIFORM COMMERCIAL CODE, §25-1-101.

UNIFORM COMMERCIAL CODE-BANK DEPOSITS AND COLLECTIONS, §25-4-101.

UNIFORM COMMERCIAL CODE-BULK TRANSFERS, §§25-6-101 to 25-6-111.

UNIFORM COMMERCIAL CODE-DOCUMENTS OF TITLE, §25-7-101.

UNIFORM COMMERCIAL CODE-FUNDS TRANSFERS, §25-4A-101.

UNIFORM COMMERCIAL CODE-GENERAL PROVISIONS, §25-1-101.

UNIFORM COMMERCIAL CODE-INVESTMENT SECURITIES, §25-8-101.

UNIFORM COMMERCIAL CODE-LEASES, §25-2A-101.

UNIFORM COMMERCIAL CODE-LETTERS OF CREDIT, §25-5-101.

UNIFORM COMMERCIAL CODE-NEGOTIABLE INSTRUMENTS, §25-3-101.

UNIFORM COMMERCIAL CODE-SALES, §25-2-101.

UNIFORM COMMERCIAL CODE-SECURED TRANSACTIONS, §25-9-101.

UNIFORM COMMON TRUST FUND ACT, §53-163.9.

UNIFORM CONTRIBUTION AMONG TORT-FEASORS ACT, §1B-1.

UNIFORM CRIMINAL EXTRADITION ACT, §15A-750.

UNIFORM CUSTODIAL TRUST ACT, §33B-21.

UNIFORM DECLARATORY JUDGMENT ACT, §1-267.

UNIFORM DISPOSITION OF COMMUNITY PROPERTY RIGHTS AT DEATH ACT, §31C-12.

UNIFORM DRIVER'S LICENSE ACT, §20-5.

UNIFORM ELECTRONIC TRANSACTIONS ACT, §§66-311 to 66-327.

UNIFORM ENFORCEMENT OF FOREIGN JUDGMENT ACT, §1C-1701.

UNIFORM FEDERAL LIEN REGISTRATION ACT, §44-68.10.

UNIFORM FIDUCIARIES ACT, §32-1.

UNIFORM FOREIGN-COUNTRY MONEY JUDGMENTS RECOGNITION ACT, §1C-1850.

UNIFORM FRAUDULENT TRANSFERS ACT, §39-23.12.

UNIFORM INTERSTATE DEPOSITIONS AND DISCOVERY ACT, §1F-1.

UNIFORM INTERSTATE FAMILY SUPPORT ACT, §52C-1-100.

UNIFORM LIMITED PARTNERSHIP ACT Revised act, §59-101.

UNIFORM MILITARY AND OVERSEAS VOTERS ACT, §163-258.1.

UNIFORM PARTNERSHIP ACT, §59-31.

UNIFORM PHOTOGRAPHIC COPIES OF BUSINESS AND PUBLIC RECORDS AS EVIDENCE ACT, §8-45.4.

UNIFORM PREMARITAL AGREEMENT ACT, §52B-1.

UNIFORM PRINCIPAL AND INCOME ACT, §37A-1-101.

UNIFORM PRUDENT INVESTOR ACT, §36C-9-907.

UNIFORM PRUDENT MANAGEMENT OF INSTITUTIONAL FUNDS ACT, §36E-1.

UNIFORM REAL PROPERTY ELECTRONIC RECORDING ACT, §47-16.1.

UNIFORM RELOCATION ASSISTANCE AND REAL PROPERTY ACQUISITION POLICIES ACT, §133-5.

UNIFORM SALES AND USE TAX ADMINISTRATION ACT, §105-164.42A.

UNIFORM SIMULTANEOUS DEATH ACT, §28A-24-7.

UNIFORM STANDARDS FOR MANUFACTURED HOMES ACT, §§143-144 to 143-151.5.

UNIFORM STATUTORY RULE AGAINST
PERPETUITIES, §41-20.

UNIFORM TRANSFER ON DEATH (TOD)
SECURITY REGISTRATION ACT, §41-50.

UNIFORM TRANSFERS TO MINORS ACT,
§§33A-1 to 33A-24.

UNIFORM TRUST CODE, §36C-1-101.

UNIFORM UNINCORPORATED NONPROFIT
ASSOCIATION ACT, §59B-1.

UNIFORM VENDOR AND PURCHASER RISK
ACT, §39-37.

UNION SHOP ACT, §§95-78 to 95-84.

UNIT OWNERSHIP ACT, §47A-1.

UNIVERSITY IMPROVEMENT GENERAL
OBLIGATION BONDS FINANCE ACT,
§116D-6.

UNIVERSITY OF NORTH CAROLINA, §§116-1
to 116-44.8.

UNMARKED HUMAN BURIAL AND HUMAN
SKELETAL REMAINS PROTECTION ACT,
§70-26.

URBAN REDEVELOPMENT LAW, §160A-500.

USE TAX ACT, §§105-164.1 to 105-164.44D.

USURY ACT, §24-2.

UTILITIES ACT, §§62-1 to 62-333.

UTILITIES COMMISSION ACTS, §§62-10 to
62-98.

UTILITIES COMMISSION PROCEDURE ACT,
§§62-60 to 62-82.

UWHARRIE REGIONAL RESOURCES ACT,
§§153C-1 to 153C-4.

V

VACATION RENTAL ACT, §§42A-1 to 42A-36.

VAPORS ACT, §§90-113.8A to 90-113.14.

VARSER ACT, §1-500.

VEGETABLE PLANT LAW, §106-284.14.

VEHICLE EQUIPMENT SAFETY COMPACT,
§§20-183.13 to 20-183.21.

VEHICLE FINANCIAL RESPONSIBILITY ACT
OF 1957, §§20-309 to 20-319.

VEHICLE MILEAGE ACT, §§20-340 to 20-350.

VENDOR AND PURCHASER RISK ACT, §39-37.

VENUE FOR CIVIL CASES, §§1-76 to 1-87.

VENUE FOR CRIMINAL CASES, §§15A-131 to
15A-136.

VESSEL TITLING ACT, §75A-32.

VETERANS' AFFAIRS ACT, §§165-1 to 165-44.

VETERANS' ENABLING ACT FOR MINORS,
§§165-12 to 165-16.

VETERANS' GUARDIANSHIP ACT, §§34-1 to
34-18.

VETERANS HOME ACT, §165-45.

VETERANS' PREFERENCE, §§126-80 to 126-83,
128-15.

VETERANS' RECREATION AUTHORITIES
LAW, §165-23.

VETERINARY PRACTICE ACT, §90-180.

VIATICAL SETTLEMENTS ACT, §58-58-200.

VIRGINIA-NORTH CAROLINA INTERSTATE
HIGH-SPEED RAIL COMPACT, §§136-220 to
136-222.

VITAL STATISTICS PROGRAM, §§130A-90 to
130A-121.

VOCATIONAL AND TECHNICAL EDUCATION,
§§115C-151 to 115C-169.

VOLUNTARY STERILIZATION LAW, §§90-271 to
90-275.

VOTER REGISTRATION ACT, §§163-82.1 to
163-82.26.

VOTING TRUST ACT, §§55-7-30, 55-7-31.

W

WAGE AND HOUR ACT, §95-25.1.

WAREHOUSE RECEIPTS, BILLS OF LADING
AND OTHER DOCUMENTS OF TITLE,
§§26-7-101 to 25-7-603.

WAR POWERS ACT, §§147-33.1 to 147-33.6.

WATER AND AIR QUALITY REPORTING ACT
OF 1971, §143-215.63.

WATER AND AIR RESOURCES ACT, §§143-211
to 143-215.74I.

WATER AND SEWAGE FACILITIES ACT,
§§153A-283 to 153A-288.

WATER AND SEWER AUTHORITIES ACT,
§162A-1.

WATERCRAFT SAFETY ACT, §§75A-1 to 75A-19.

WATERED STOCK ACT, §§55-6-21, 55-6-22.

WATER RESOURCES DEVELOPMENT
PROJECTS FOR FEDERAL WATER
RESOURCES, §§143-215.38 to 143-215.43.

WATER SUPPLY PLANNING ACT, §§162A-20 to
162A-25.

WATER USE ACT OF 1967, §143-215.11.

WEAPONS OF MASS DEATH AND
DESTRUCTION, §§14-288.21 to 14-288.24.

WEATHERIZATION ASSISTANCE PROGRAM,
§108A-70.30.

WEIGHTS AND MEASURES ACT OF 1975,
§§81A-1 to 81A-88.

WELL CONSTRUCTION ACT, §87-83.

WELL CONTRACTORS CERTIFICATION ACT,
§87-98.1.

WELL DRILLER REGISTRATION ACT,
§143-355.

WHISTLEBLOWER PROTECTION
Protection for reporting improper government
activities, §§126-84 to 126-88.
Retaliatory employment discrimination,
§§95-240 to 95-245.

WHITE CANE LAW, §§20-175.1 to 20-175.3, 168-5.

WHITE GOODS, §§130A-309.80 to 130A-309.86.

WILDLIFE RESOURCES LAW, §§143-237 to 143-254.2.

WILLARD ACT FOR FOREIGN INSURANCE COMPANIES, §§58-16-1 to 58-16-55.

WILLS ACT, §§31-1 to 31-47.

WILLS REVOCATION ACT, §§31-5.1 to 31-5.8.

WIND POWER TAX CREDIT, §§105-130.31, 105-151.9.

WIRELESS TELECOMMUNICATIONS FACILITIES, §§153A-349.50 to 153A-349.53.

WIRETAPPING ACT, §14-155.

WITHHOLDING, §§105-163.1 to 105-163.24.

WITNESS ACT, §§8-49 to 8-58.1.

WOMAN'S RIGHT TO KNOW ACT, §90-21.80.

WORKERS' COMPENSATION ACT, §97-1.

WORKPLACE VIOLENCE PREVENTION
Civil no-contact orders, §§95-260 to 95-271.

WORTHLESS CHECK, §§14-106 to 14-107.1.

WRONGFUL DEATH ACT, §28A-18-2.

Z

ZONING, COUNTIES, §§153A-340 to 153A-348.

ZONING, MUNICIPALITIES, §§160A-381 to 160A-392.

ZONING ACT FOR AIRPORTS, §§63-30 to 63-37.1.

General Index

A

AARON'S ROD.
Taking wild plants from land of another,
§14-129.

ABANDONED AND NEGLECTED
CEMETERIES, §§65-85 to 65-113.
See CEMETERIES.

ABANDONED CHILDREN.
Acts barring rights of parents, §31A-2.
Baby drop off, §14-322.3.
Child abuse, exceptions, §§14-318.2, 14-318.4(c).
Birth of abandoned children.
Establishing facts relating to birth, §130A-107.
Child abuse.
Exceptions, §§14-318.2, 14-318.4.
Termination of parental rights proceedings.
Generally, §§7B-1100 to 7B-1114.
See TERMINATION OF PARENTAL RIGHTS.
Willful neglect or refusal to provide adequate
support, §14-322.

ABANDONED, IDLE OR UNUSED PROPERTY.
Environmental contamination.
Brownfields property reuse act of 1997,
§§130A-310.30 to 130A-310.40.
See BROWNFIELDS PROPERTY REUSE.
Unclaimed property generally, §§116B-51 to
116B-80.
See UNCLAIMED PROPERTY.

ABANDONED MANUFACTURED HOMES.
Identification, deconstruction, recycling,
disposal, §§130A-309.111 to 130A-309.118.
See MANUFACTURED HOMES.

ABANDONED MOTOR VEHICLES, §§20-137.6 to
20-137.14.
Accident involving parked or unattended
vehicle.
Report to owner, §20-166.1(c).
Accumulation of abandoned vehicles.
Prevention, §20-137.6.
Antique vehicles.
Exemption from provisions, §20-137.14.
Automobile graveyards defined, §136-143.
Contracts for disposal.
Authority of secretary, §20-137.12.
Public areas used for collection areas, §20-137.12.
Definitions, §20-137.7.
Demolishers.
Defined, §20-137.7.
Duties on purchasing or acquiring, §20-137.11.
Derelict vehicles.
Defined, §20-137.7.
Disabled vehicles.
Parking or leaving standing on highways,
§20-161(a).
Warning lights, display, trucks, §20-161(c).
Enclosed vehicles.
Exemption from provisions, §20-137.14.
Exceptions from provisions, §20-137.14.
Immunity.
No liability for removal, §20-137.13.

ABANDONED MOTOR VEHICLES —Cont'd
Law enforcement officers.
Agent of owner or operator for removal,
§20-161(d), (e).
Duties, §20-114.
Legislative declaration, §20-137.6.
Lienholders.
Identification, §20-137.10(d).
Municipalities.
Removal and disposal of junked and abandoned
vehicles, §160A-303.
Abandoned junked vehicles, §160A-303.2.
Notice.
Sale, §20-137.10(c) to (d1).
Tagging of vehicles, §20-137.10(a), (c).
Owner's identity undetermined, §20-137.10(d).
Parking or leaving standing on highways.
Clear to approaching drivers, §20-161(b).
Disabled vehicles, §20-161(a), (a1).
Warning lights, display, trucks, §20-161(c).
Removal and storage.
Agent of owner or operator for removal.
Law enforcement officer deemed, §20-161(d),
(e).
Controlled access highway, §20-161(f).
Costs, liability of owner, §20-161(g).
Speed limit posted 45 miles per hour or greater,
§20-161(a1).
Private parking lots.
Removal of unauthorized vehicles, §20-219.2.
Private property.
Removal from, §§20-137.9, 20-219.2.
Provision for credit if new license purchased,
§20-100.
Purpose of provisions, §20-137.6.
Regulation, restraint and prohibition,
§153A-132.2.
Removal, disposal or storage, §§20-137.9,
20-137.13, 153A-132.
Agent of owner or operator for removal.
Law enforcement officer deemed, §20-161(d), (e).
Cities and towns, §§160A-303, 160A-303.2.
Coastal area counties.
Service districts to provide, §153A-301(b), (c).
Controlled access highway, §20-161(f).
Costs, liability of owner, §20-161(g).
No liability for, §20-137.13.
Private property, §20-137.9.
Unauthorized vehicle, §20-219.2.
Reports.
Duties of peace officers, §20-114(c).
Rules and regulations.
Adoption, §20-137.8.
Sale.
Authority of secretary, §20-137.12.
Notice, §20-137.10(c), (d).
When not required, §20-137.10(d1).
Salvage yards.
Defined, §20-137.7.
Secretary of department of transportation to
regulate, §20-137.8.
Tags.
Defined, §20-137.7.

1

ABANDONED MOTOR VEHICLES —Cont'd
Tags —Cont'd
Effect, §20-137.10(c).
Generally, §20-137.10(a).
Title.
Vesting in state, §20-137.11.
Towing.
Removal generally, §§20-137.9, 20-137.13,
153A-132.
Towing generally.
See TOWING OF VEHICLES.
Value.
Abandoned vehicles valued in excess of one
hundred dollars, §20-137.10(d).
Abandoned vehicles valued less than one hundred
dollars, §20-137.10(d1).
Appraisal or determination.
Authority of officers, §20-137.10(e).
Warning lights, display, trucks.
Disabled vehicles.
Parking or leaving standing on highways,
§20-161(c).

ABANDONMENT.
Acts barring rights of spouse, §31A-1(a).
Aid to families with dependent children.
Reports to district attorneys, §15-155.2.
Attorneys at law.
Entrusted property, ProfCond Rule 1.15-2.
Birth of abandoned children.
Establishing facts relating to birth, §130A-107.
Cartways, §136-70.
Cemeteries, §§65-85 to 65-113.
See CEMETERIES.
Children and minors.
See ABANDONED CHILDREN.
Child support.
Child support enforcement program generally,
§§110-128 to 110-142.2.
See CHILD SUPPORT.
Willful neglect or refusal to provide adequate
support, §14-322.
Cruelty to animals, §14-361.1.
Disposition of property.
Seized, confiscated or unclaimed property, §§15-11
to 15-17.
Unclaimed property generally, §§116B-51 to
116B-80.
See UNCLAIMED PROPERTY.
Divorce.
Grounds for divorce, §50-7.
Ejectment of residential tenant.
Personal property of tenant abandoned.
Delivery of property to custody of nonprofit
organization, §42-25.9.
Highways, roads and streets.
Cartways, tramways or railways, §136-70.
Controlled-access facilities, §136-89.50.
Dedicated road or street deemed abandoned if not
used within fifteen years, §136-96.
Municipality keeping open and assuming
responsibility.
Roads within one mile of corporate limits,
§§136-55.1(b), 136-63(b).
Notice, §136-55.1(a).
Request to abandon or change.
Board of county commissioners, §136-63(a).
Husband and wife.
Acts barring rights of spouse, §31A-1(a).
Competency of spouse as witness against other,
§8-57(b).

ABANDONMENT —Cont'd
Husband and wife —Cont'd
Guardian's sale of abandoned incompetent
spouse's estate, §35A-1306.
Willful abandonment, §14-322.
Junked motor vehicles, §§153A-132, 153A-132.2.
Lost instruments and records.
See LOST INSTRUMENTS AND RECORDS.
Manufactured homes.
Identification, deconstruction, recycling, disposal,
§§130A-309.111 to 130A-309.118.
See MANUFACTURED HOMES.
Motor vehicles.
Generally, §§20-137.6 to 20-137.14.
See ABANDONED MOTOR VEHICLES.
Navigable waters, structures, removal,
§76-40(c).
Oil and gas wells, §113-395.
Public utility franchises.
Service, §62-118.
Railroad easements and rights of way.
Presumption, §§1-44.1, 1-44.2(a), (b).
Refrigerators, §14-318.1.
Repair business.
Disposal of unclaimed property, §66-67.1.
Seized, confiscated or unclaimed property.
Disposition generally, §§15-11 to 15-17.
Six month abandonment period.
Failure or refusal to provide adequate support,
§14-322.1.
Willful abandonment, §14-322.1.
Unclaimed property generally, §§116B-51 to
116B-80.
See UNCLAIMED PROPERTY.
Veterinarians.
Abandoned animals, §90-187.7.
Water or sewer utility service.
Service, §62-118(b), (c).
Welfare recipients, investigations, §15-155.2.

ABATEMENT.
Lead poisoning hazards, §130A-131.9C.
Nuisances.
General provisions, §§19-1 to 19-8.3.
See NUISANCES.
Offenses against public morals, §§19-1 to 19-20.
See NUISANCES.

ABATEMENT, REVIVAL AND SURVIVAL.
Collaborative law procedures.
Equitable distribution, §50-79.
Death before limitation expires.
Action by or against personal representative or
collector, §1-22.
Death, insanity or incompetency of party.
Abatement unless continued by proper party,
§1A-1 Rule 25(c).
No abatement after verdict, §1A-1 Rule 25(g).
Death of receiver of corporation.
Continuance against successor or against
corporation in case of new receiver, §1A-1
Rule 25(e).
Equitable distribution, §50-20(l).
Collaborative law procedures, §50-79.
Executors and administrators.
Death before limitation expires.
Action by or against personal representative or
collector, §1-22.
Presentation of claims.
Substitution of personal representative to
constitute, §28A-19-1(c).
Rights of action surviving decedent, §28A-18-1.

ABATEMENT, REVIVAL AND SURVIVAL
—Cont'd
Executors and administrators —Cont'd
Wrongful death, §28A-18-2.
Incompetency or insanity of party.
Action not to abate by reason of, §1A-1 Rule 25(b).
Investment advisers.
Civil liabilities for violations, §78C-38(c).
Public officers.
Death or separation from office.
Successor automatically substituted as party,
§1A-1 Rule 25(f).
Securities regulation.
Civil liabilities, §78A-56(e).
Support of illegitimate children.
Death of mother not bar to proceeding, §49-5.

ABATTOIRS.
Biological residues in animals, §§106-549.81 to
106-549.89.
Meat inspection requirements, §§106-549.15 to
106-549.28.
Poultry products inspection, §§106-549.49 to
106-549.69.
Rendering plants and rendering operations,
§§106-168.1 to 106-168.16.

ABC ACT.
See ALCOHOLIC BEVERAGES.

ABC BOARDS, §§18B-700 to 18B-706.
ABC stores, §§18B-800 to 18B-808.
See ABC STORES.
Accounting system, §§18B-205(b), 18B-702(l).
Accounts, §18B-205(a).
Annual independent audit, §18B-702(s).
Appointment.
City boards, §18B-700(b).
County boards, §18B-700(c).
Improper influence by commission, §18B-704(a).
Merged boards, §18B-703(b).
Appropriations, §18B-702(g).
Interim appropriations.
Delayed in adopting budget, §18B-702(i).
Obligations, incurring, §18B-702(m).
Transfer of money from appropriations,
§18B-702(h).
Audits, §§18B-205(c), 18B-702(s).
Compliance with performance standards.
Regular or special audits, §18B-705(a).
Bill, invoice, claim against board, §18B-702(n).
Approval required.
Board approval, §18B-702(o).
Finance officer, §18B-702(n).
Checks or drafts signed by finance officer,
§18B-702(p).
Payment, compliance statement, signature of
finance officer, §18B-702(q).
Bond.
Members, general managers, finance officers,
§18B-700(i).
Borrowing money, §18B-702(r).
Budget.
Adoption, §18B-702(g).
Delay, interim budget, §18B-702(i).
All money received and expended included in,
§18B-702(c).
Amendments, §18B-702(h).
Annual balanced budget.
Duty to operate under, §18B-702(c).
Appropriations, §18B-702(g).
Interim appropriations, §18B-702(i).

ABC BOARDS —Cont'd
Budget —Cont'd
Appropriations —Cont'd
Obligations, incurring, §18B-702(m).
Transfer of money from appropriations,
§18B-702(h).
Budget message, submission, §18B-702(d).
Budget officer, §18B-702(b).
Copy for public inspection, §18B-702(e).
Directions and limitations.
Adopting budget, §18B-702(g).
Fiscal year, §18B-702(c).
Hearing, §18B-702(f).
Notice, publication, §18B-702(e).
Interim budget, §18B-702(i).
News media.
Copy made available for, §18B-702(e).
Notice of hearing.
Publication, §18B-702(e).
Obligations, incurring, §18B-702(m).
Preparation, §18B-702(d).
Publication.
Statement budget submitted, notice of hearing,
§18B-702(e).
Public inspection, §18B-702(e).
Submission, §18B-702(d).
Statement budget submitted.
Publication, §18B-702(e).
Transfer of money from appropriations,
§18B-702(h).
Working capital funds.
Working capital defined, established by
commission, §18B-702(g).
Business with which associated.
Defined, §18B-201(g).
Chairman, §18B-700(a).
Vacancy, §18B-700(e).
Checks or drafts.
Signed by finance officer, §18B-702(p).
Closure of local ABC system.
Failure to meet performance standards,
§18B-705(c).
Insolvent system, §18B-801(d).
Purchases from another board by mixed beverage
permittees, §18B-203(a).
Compensation of board members, §18B-700(g).
Different level, change.
Notification, report required, §18B-700(g).
Nonmonetary compensation or benefits.
Authorization required, §18B-700(g).
Compliance with commission rules.
Duty, §18B-701(b).
Failure to comply.
Removal, §18B-701(b).
Composition, §18B-700(a).
Confidential information.
Improper use, disclosure, §18B-201(j).
Conflicts of interest, §18B-201.
Penalties, §18B-700(h).
**Contract for enforcement of ABC laws with
local board.**
Conviction prohibiting, §18B-202.
**Contract or agreement evidencing obligation
incurred.**
Compliance certificate, §18B-702(m).
Corporate body.
Transacting business as, §18B-702(a).
Customer-friendly, modern, efficient stores.
Promoting, mission, §18B-700(a1).
Debts.
City or county not obligated, §18B-702(r).

ABC BOARDS —Cont'd
Defense of employees and officers.
Counties, §160A-167.
Deposits, §18B-702(t).
Disbursements, §18B-702(n), (o).
Checks or drafts signed by finance officer, §18B-702(p).
Distribution of revenue, §18B-805.
Payment, compliance statement, signature of finance officer, §18B-702(q).
Discharge of members.
Conviction of crime, §18B-202.
Disclosure of conflict of interest.
Duty, §18B-201(k).
Duties, §18B-701(b).
Annual balanced budget.
Operation under, §18B-702(c).
Embezzlement by members and employees, §18B-702(w).
Ethics.
Code of ethics.
Adoption of policy containing, §18B-706(a).
Education of members, requirement, §18B-706(b).
Model ethic policy for boards.
Commission to develop, §18B-706(c).
Family members.
Dealing for, §18B-201(c).
Employing immediate family members.
Restrictions, immediate family defined, §18B-700(k).
Finance officer.
Bill, invoice, claim against board.
Approval required, §18B-702(n).
Payment, compliance statement, signature of finance officer, §18B-702(q).
Checks or drafts signed by, §18B-702(p).
Defined, §18B-101.
Designation, §18B-702(j).
Duties and powers, §18B-702(k).
False certificate, §18B-702(v).
Obligations incurred.
Signature required, §18B-702(m).
Financial benefit.
Use of position on board for purposes of, §18B-201(f), (i).
Business with which associated.
Defined, §18B-201(g).
Disclosure of conflict, §18B-201(k).
Exceptions, §18B-201(h).
Financial condition.
Statement of.
Duty of finance officer to file, §18B-702(k).
Financial interest in commercial alcoholic beverage enterprise.
Restrictions, §18B-201(a).
Financial operations, §18B-702.
Local acts preempted, §18B-702(x).
Violations, penalties, §18B-702(v).
Fiscal control rules.
Adoption by commission, compliance required, §18B-702(u).
Fiscal year.
Budget purposes, §18B-702(c).
General manager.
Bond, §18B-700(i).
Budget officer, §18B-702(b).
Defined, §18B-101.
Finance officer.
Good cause shown, §18B-702(j).
Salary, §18B-700(g1).

ABC BOARDS —Cont'd
Gifts to members, law regulating, §18B-201(d), (i).
Immunity of members from civil liability.
Limited immunity, §18B-700(j).
Improper influence by commission.
Appointment of board members, §18B-704(a).
Incurring obligations, §18B-702(m).
Violations by members or employees, liability, §18B-702(v).
Insolvency of local ABC system.
Closing system, §18B-801(d).
Purchases from another board by mixed beverage permittees, §18B-203(a).
Investments, §18B-702(t).
Joint store operation, §18B-703(h).
Local acts preempted, §18B-700(j).
Financial operations, §18B-702(x).
Performance standards, §18B-705(d).
Removal of members and employees, §18B-704(j).
Malfeasance by members and employees, §18B-702(w).
Merger of local operations.
Appointment of merged board, §18B-703(b).
Conditions for merger, §18B-703(a).
Dissolution, §18B-703(e).
Distribution of profits, §18B-703(c).
Failure to meet performance standards, §18B-705(c).
Jurisdiction of enforcement officials, §18B-703(d).
Negotiation of details, §18B-703(f).
Operation to follow general law, §18B-703(g).
Mission, §18B-700(a1).
Nepotism, §18B-700(k).
Number of members, §18B-700(a).
Obligations, incurring, §18B-702(m).
Violations by members or employees, liability, §18B-702(v).
Officers, §18B-501.
Performance improvement plans, §18B-705(b).
Performance standards.
Compliance by boards.
Commission to ensure, §18B-705(a).
Methods used for ensuring, §18B-705(a).
Establishing, commission rules and regulations, §18B-203(a).
Compliance with rules, duty, §18B-701(b).
Failing to meet.
Remedies, §18B-705(c).
Local acts preempted, §18B-705(d).
Notice of intent to take action.
Failing to meet standards, §18B-705(c).
Performance improvement plans, §18B-705(b).
Powers, §18B-701(a).
Public authority.
Not considered, §18B-702(a).
Qualifications, §18B-700(d).
Removal of members and employees, §18B-700(f).
Appeal, §18B-704(h).
Authority of commission, §18B-704(g).
Causes, §18B-704(c).
Conviction of crime, §18B-202.
Failure to comply with commission rules, §18B-701(b).
Findings of fact.
Commission to provide, §18B-704(d).
Hearing, §18B-704(e).
De novo, standard of review, §18B-704(f).
Notice of availability provided, §18B-704(d).
Procedure, §18B-704(f).

ABC BOARDS —Cont'd
Removal of members and employees —Cont'd
Hearing —Cont'd
Request, §18B-704(e).
Time for holding, §18B-704(f).
Local acts preempted, §18B-704(j).
Process, §18B-704(d).
Purpose of provisions, §18B-704(b).
Stay of action.
Request for hearing, §18B-704(e).
Termination of employees for personnel reasons.
Provisions not to replace, §18B-704(i).
Vote required, §18B-704(f).
Reports, §18B-205(a).
Audit report, §18B-702(s).
Revenue, distribution, §18B-805.
Salary for board employees, §18B-700(g1).
Sales of liquor.
Controlling, responsibility, mission, §18B-700(a1).
Security interest.
Pledge, §18B-702(r).
Self-dealing, §18B-201(b).
Termination of employees for personnel reasons.
Removal provisions not to replace, §18B-704(i).
Terms of office, §18B-700(a).
Training requirements.
Mandatory training.
Establishing, commission rules and regulations, §18B-203(a).
Compliance with rules, duty, §18B-701(b).
Travel allowance, per diem, §18B-700(g2).
Use of position on board for financial benefit, §18B-201(f), (i).
Business with which associated.
Defined, §18B-201(g).
Disclosure of conflict, §18B-201(k).
Exceptions, §18B-201(h).
Vacancy, §18B-700(e).
Working capital funds.
Working capital defined, established by commission, §18B-702(g).

ABC COMMISSION.
See ALCOHOLIC BEVERAGE CONTROL COMMISSION.

ABC LICENSES.
Local licenses, §§105-113.77 to 105-113.79.
Permits generally.
See ABC PERMITS.

ABC OFFICERS.
Alcohol law enforcement agencies, §18B-500.
Disposition of seized beverages, §18B-503.
Forfeitures, §18B-504.
Inspection of licensed premises, §18B-502.
Local ABC enforcement officers, §18B-501.
Accountability to appointing authority and commission.
Enforcement reports, §18B-501(f1).
Appointment by local boards, §18B-501(a).
Arrest authority, §18B-501(b).
Assisting other local agencies, §18B-501(b).
Assisting state and federal enforcement, §18B-501(e).
Contractors who hire officers with other agencies, §18B-501(f).
Contracts with other law enforcement agencies.
Alternative to hiring local officers, §18B-501(f).
Designation as ABC officers, §18B-501(a).
Discharge, §18B-501(g).

ABC OFFICERS —Cont'd
Local ABC enforcement officers —Cont'd
Enforcement agreements.
Contracts with other law enforcement agencies.
Alternative to hiring local officers, §18B-501(f).
Finance officer, §18B-702.
General manager, §18B-700.
Investigatory and enforcement authority, §18B-501(b).
Local option elections.
Small resort town ABC elections, §18B-600(e5).
Pursuit outside normal territorial jurisdiction, §18B-501(c).
Subject matter jurisdiction, §18B-501(b).
Territorial jurisdiction, §18B-501(c).
Restitution to law enforcement agency, §18B-505.

ABC PERMITS.
ABC stores, §18B-603.
Administrative procedure act.
Applicability, §18B-906(a).
Exception on location of hearing, §18B-906(b).
Adult establishments or other sexually oriented businesses.
Local government regulation not preempted, §18B-904(g).
Alcoholic beverages generally.
See ALCOHOLIC BEVERAGES.
Applications.
False information, §18B-902(c).
Form, §18B-902(a).
Automatic expiration.
Change in ownership, §18B-903(c).
Bottlers.
Authorization, §18B-1110(a).
Commercial permit, §18B-1100.
Fee, §18B-902(d).
Breweries.
Authorization, §18B-1104.
Commercial permit, §18B-1100.
Fee, §18B-902(d).
Power to issue, §18B-1001.
Brew on premises.
Fee, §18B-902(d).
Issuance, §18B-1001.
Brown-bagging permit, §18B-1001.
Fee, §18B-902(d).
Business not operating.
Automatic expiration, §18B-904(c).
Change in management, §18B-903(d).
Change in ownership.
Automatic expiration, §18B-903(c).
Cider and vinegar manufacturers.
Commercial permit, §18B-1100.
Effect of permit, §18B-1114.2.
Fee, §18B-902(d).
Commercial permits, §18B-1100.
Commercial transportation.
Permit required, §18B-1115.
Cooking schools, §18B-1000.
Sales at cooking schools, §18B-1006(g).
Corporations.
Person to qualify, §18B-900(c).
Culinary permit, §18B-1001.
Duration, §18B-903(a).
Fee, §18B-902(d).
Direct shipments into state.
Out-of-state retailer and wholesalers.
Wholesalers permit, §18B-102.1.

ABC PERMITS —Cont'd
Distilleries.
  Authorized acts, §18B-1105(a).
  Commercial permit, §18B-1100.
  Fee, §18B-902(d).
  Fuel alcohol, §18B-1105(b).
Drugs.
  Prohibited on licensed premises, §18B-1005(a).
Duration, §18B-903(a).
  Change in ownership.
    Automatic expiration, §18B-903(c).
Elections.
  Permits not dependent on elections, §18B-603(f).
Expiration.
  Change in ownership.
    Automatic expiration, §18B-903(c).
Facsimile permits, §18B-1006(e).
Failure to surrender permit, §18B-1006(f).
False permits, §18B-1006(e).
Fees, §18B-902(d).
  Disposition, §18B-902(g).
  Duplicate, §18B-903(f).
  Name change.
    Issuance of new permit, §18B-903(g).
  Nonrefundable, §18B-902(f).
  Registration of persons holding permits,
    §18B-903(b1).
  Renewal, §18B-903(b).
Firm, association or general partnership.
  Person to qualify, §18B-900(c).
Fortified wine permit.
  Duration, §18B-903(a).
Fortified winery permit.
  Authorization, §18B-1102.
  Commercial permit, §18B-1100.
  Fee, §18B-902(d).
Fuel alcohol permit.
  Commercial permit, §18B-1100.
  Fee, §18B-902(d).
Guest room cabinet permit.
  Fee, §18B-902(d).
Hearings.
  Location, §18B-906(b).
  Recommendations.
    Testimony by designated local official,
      §18B-904(f).
Investigations.
  Prerequisite to issuance, §18B-902(b).
Issuance.
  Authority of commission, §18B-901(d).
  Commercial permits.
    Types authorized, §18B-1100.
  Commission, §18B-900(a).
  Factors to be considered, §18B-901(c).
  Investigations prior to issuance, §18B-902(b).
  Notice, §18B-904(d).
  Notice to local government, §18B-901(b).
  Places eligible, §18B-1001.
  Temporary permits, §18B-905.
  Who issues, §18B-901(a).
  Who permit issued to, §18B-904(a).
Keg or kegs of malt beverages.
  Purchase-transportation permit, §18B-403.1.
Kinds of permits, §18B-1001.
  Fees, §18B-902(d).
Limited liability companies.
  Person to qualify for permits, §18B-900(c).
Limited partnerships.
  Person to qualify, §18B-900(c).
Limited winery permit.
  Commercial permit, §18B-1100.

ABC PERMITS —Cont'd
Limited winery permit —Cont'd
  Fee, §18B-902(d).
  Free tasting samples, §18B-1103(b).
  Special qualification, §18B-1103(a).
Liquor importer/bottler permit.
  Authorizations, §18B-1105.1.
Location no longer suitable.
  Suspension or revocation of permit, §18B-904(e).
Lost permits.
  Issuance of duplicates, §18B-903(f).
**Major league professional sports teams with
    suites available for sale or leas.**
  Special occasion permit to sports facility occupied
    by.
  Patrons authorized to make available alcoholic
    beverages in suites, §18B-1006(p).
Malt beverages.
  Importers, §18B-1108.
    Commercial permit, §18B-1100.
    Fee, §18B-902(d).
  Keg or kegs of malt beverages.
    Purchase-transportation permit, §18B-403.1.
  Nonresident vendor, §18B-1113.
  Off-premises malt beverage permit, §18B-1001.
  On-premises malt beverage permit, §18B-1001.
  Special event permit, §18B-1100.
    Authorization, §18B-1114.5.
    Fee, §18B-902(d).
  Tasting permit, §18B-1001.
    Fee, §18B-902(d).
  Wholesalers, §18B-1109(a).
    Commercial permit, §18B-1100.
    Fee, §18B-902(d).
Mixed beverage permits, §18B-1001.
  Additional requirements, §18B-1007.
  Fee, §18B-902(d).
  Hotels and restaurants.
    National historic landmark district,
      §18B-1006(n).
  Plan to collect and recycle containers.
    Submitted with application, §§18B-902(h),
      18B-903(b2).
  Recycling requirement, §18B-1006.1.
  Temporary permit, §18B-1007(d).
Name change.
  Issuance of new permit, §18B-903(g).
National historic landmark district.
  Mixed beverages permit.
    Hotels and restaurants.
      Issuance of permits in certain counties,
        §18B-1006(n).
Nonresident malt beverage vendor permit.
  Commercial permit, §18B-1100.
  Fee, §18B-902(d).
Nonresident wine vendor permit.
  Commercial permit, §18B-1100.
  Fee, §18B-902(d).
Nontransferable, §18B-903(e).
Notice.
  Issuance, §18B-904(d).
    Notice to local government, §18B-901(b).
Off-premises fortified wine permit, §18B-1001.
  Fee, §18B-902(d).
Off-premises malt beverage permit, §18B-1001.
  Duration, §18B-903(a).
  Fee, §18B-902(d).
Off-premises unfortified wine permit,
  §18B-1001.
  Fee, §18B-902(d).
One-time permits, §18B-1002.

ABC PERMITS —Cont'd
On-premises fortified wine permit, §18B-1001.
Fee, §18B-902(d).
Plan to collect and recycle containers.
Submitted with application, §§18B-902(h),
18B-903(b2).
Recycling requirement, §18B-1006.1.
On-premises malt beverage permit, §18B-1001.
Duration, §18B-903(a).
Fee, §18B-902(d).
Plan to collect and recycle containers.
Submitted with application, §§18B-902(h),
18B-903(b2).
Recycling requirement, §18B-1006.1.
On-premises unfortified wine permit,
§18B-1001.
Fee, §18B-902(d).
Plan to collect and recycle containers.
Submitted with application, §§18B-902(h),
18B-903(b2).
Recycling requirement, §18B-1006.1.
Out of state purchases.
Suspension or revocation, §18B-104(a), (d), (e).
Owner of business or management company.
Permit issued to, §18B-904(a).
Partnerships.
Person to qualify, §18B-900(c).
Permits based on existing permits, §18B-603(h).
Places eligible, §18B-1001.
Posting, §18B-904(b).
Private clubs.
Residential private clubs, §18B-1006(k).
Purchase-transportation permits, §§18B-403 to
18B-405.
Purchasing in greater amounts than allowed,
§18B-303(c).
Qualifications for permits.
Convention centers, §18B-900(e).
Conviction defined, §18B-900(b).
Discretion of commission, §18B-901(d).
Manager of off-premises establishment,
§18B-900(d).
Requirements, §18B-900(a).
Who must qualify, §18B-900(c).
Recreation districts, §18B-1006(j).
Recyclable beverage containers.
Plan for collection and recycling.
Mixed beverage and on-premises applicants to
prepare and submit with application,
§§18B-902(h), 18B-903(b2).
Registration of persons holding, §18B-903(b1).
Renewal, §18B-903(b).
Responsibilities of permittees.
Employees, §18B-1003(b).
Certain employees prohibited, §18B-1003(c).
Financial responsibility, §18B-1003(d).
Premises, §18B-1003(a).
Retail business.
Purchase only from wholesalers with business in
state and proper permit, §18B-1006(h).
Rules and regulations.
Retail permits, §18B-1008.
Salesmen.
Authorized acts, §18B-1111(a).
Commercial permit, §18B-1100.
Duration, §18B-1111(c).
Fee, §18B-902(d).
Persons required to obtain, §18B-1111(b).
Term, §18B-1111(c).
Schools.
Business located on property of public school,
§18B-1006(a).

ABC PERMITS —Cont'd
Sole proprietorships.
Person associated with business to qualify,
§18B-900(c).
Special ABC areas.
Elections, §18B-603(f2).
Special occasion permit, §18B-1001.
Fee, §18B-902(d).
Limited special occasion permit, §18B-1001.
Duration, §18B-903(a).
Fee, §18B-902(d).
Special one-time permit.
Administrative procedure, §18B-1002(d).
Conditions of permit, §18B-1002(c).
Duration, §18B-903(a).
Fee, §18B-902(d).
Intent of section, §18B-1002(b).
Kinds of permits, §18B-1002(a).
Spirituous liquor tasting permit, §18B-1001.
Fee, §18B-902(d).
Sports clubs, §18B-1006(k).
Sale of malt beverages, unfortified wine or mixed
beverages and operation of ABC system
allowed in six cities and counties.
Issuance of permits to sports clubs throughout
county, §18B-603(h).
Stadiums.
In-stand sales, §18B-1009.
Hours of sale, §18B-1006(q).
Supervision of business.
Permittee or manger, §§18B-1005.1(b),
18B-1005(b).
Surrender.
Change in ownership.
Automatic expiration, §18B-903(c).
Failure to surrender, §18B-1006(f).
Suspension or revocation.
Administrative penalties, §18B-104(a).
Business or location no longer suitable,
§18B-904(e).
Conviction of permittee or permittee's employee of
certain violations, §18B-904(e).
Effect on other permits, §18B-104(e).
Summary suspension or revocation.
Violation by business in urban redevelopment
area, §18B-904(e).
Urban redevelopment areas.
Violation of sales restrictions, §18B-904(e).
Wine distribution agreements.
Violations of article, §18B-1207(c).
Temporary permits, §18B-905.
Term, §18B-903(a).
Transferability, §18B-903(e).
Unfortified wine permit.
Duration, §18B-903(a).
Unfortified winery permit.
Authorization, §18B-1101.
Commercial permit, §18B-1100.
Fee, §18B-902(d).
Universities and colleges.
Permit for business on campus, §18B-1006(a).
Viticulture/oenology course authorization,
§18B-1114.4.
Vendor representative.
Authorized acts, §18B-1112(a).
Commercial permit, §18B-1100.
Fee, §18B-902(d).
Number of permits, §18B-1112(b).
Viticulture/oenology course authorization.
Generally, §18B-1114.4(a).
Limitations on issuance, §18B-1114.4(b).

ABC PERMITS —Cont'd
Viticulture/oenology course authorization
  —Cont'd
  Manufacture of wines, §18B-1114.4(b).
  Winery.
    Holder not deemed to be, §18B-1114.4(d).
  Winery special event permits, §18B-1114.4(c).
  Authorization, §18B-1114.1(a).
Wholesalers.
  Direct shipments into state.
    Out-of-state retailer and wholesalers,
      §18B-102.1.
  Malt beverages, §18B-1109(a).
  Restrictions on sales by wholesalers to retail
    permittees, §18B-1006(h).
  Supplier's financial interest in wholesaler,
    §18B-1119.
  Wine, §18B-1107(a).
Wine importer, §18B-1106(a).
  Commercial permit, §18B-1100.
  Fee, §18B-902(d).
  Primary American source of supply.
    Sale to wholesalers, §18B-1106(c).
Winemaking on premises permit, §18B-1001.
  Fee, §18B-902(d).
Wine producer permit, §18B-902(d).
  Authorization, §18B-1114.3(a).
  Commercial permit, §18B-1100.
  Limitation on total gallons sold annually,
    §18B-1114.3(b).
  Wine producer defined, §18B-1000.
Wineries.
  Commercial permits, §18B-1100.
  Fortified wineries, §18B-1102.
  Limited wineries.
    Free tasting samples, §18B-1103(b).
    Special qualifications, §18B-1103(a).
  Special event permit.
    Authorization, §18B-1114.1(a).
    Fee, §18B-902(d).
    Jurisdictions permit valid, §18B-1114.1(b).
  Special show permit, §18B-1114.1(a).
    Commercial permit, §18B-1100.
    Limitation, §18B-1114.1(b).
  Unfortified wineries, §18B-1101.
  Viticulture/oenology course authorization.
    Holder not deemed to be winery, §18B-1114.4(d).
  Wine distribution agreements.
    Violations of article.
      Suspension or revocation of winery permit,
        §18B-1207(c).
Wine shipper packager permit, §18B-1001.3.
  Fee, §18B-902(d).
Wine shipper permit.
  Direct shipments into state.
    Application, authorization, §18B-1001.1(a).
    Manner of making, §18B-1001.1(c).
    Quarterly summary of shipped wine,
      §18B-1001.2(a).
    Registration of permittee, §18B-1001.2(a).
    Rules, adoption, §18B-1001.2(b).
    State jurisdiction, permittee subject to,
      §18B-1001.1(d).
    Wholesaler in state, appointment,
      §18B-1001.1(b).
Wine shop permits, §§18B-902(d), 18B-1001.
  Renewal, §18B-903(b).
Wine tasting permit, §§18B-902, 18B-1001(d).
Wine wholesaler, §18B-1107(a).
  Commercial permit, §18B-1100.
  Fee, §18B-902(d).

ABC STORES, §§18B-800 to 18B-808.
ABC boards, §§18B-700 to 18B-706.
Alcoholic beverages generally.
  See ALCOHOLIC BEVERAGES.
Alcoholism funds, §18B-805(h).
Boards.
  Local ABC board, §§18B-700 to 18B-706.
Bond.
  Employees, §18B-803(c).
  Manager, §18B-803(b).
Closing of stores.
  Grounds, §18B-801(c).
  Insolvent ABC system, §18B-801(d).
  State of emergency, §18B-110.
Consumption at ABC store, §18B-301(e), (f).
Damaged alcoholic beverages.
  Sale.
    Not owned by local board, §18B-806(b).
    Owned by local board, §18B-806(a).
    Procedure, §18B-806(c).
    Records, §18B-806(d).
Days of operation, §18B-802(b).
Display of spirits distilled in North Carolina,
    §18B-800(e).
Distribution of revenue.
  Cities and counties, §18B-805(e).
  Gross receipts defined, §18B-805(a).
  Mixed beverage profit shared, §18B-805(f).
  Primary distribution, §18B-805(b).
  Quarterly distributions, §18B-805(g).
  Statutory distributions, §18B-805(c).
  Sale at less than uniform price, §18B-805(i).
Elections.
  City elections, §18B-600(d).
  Form of ballot, §18B-602(g).
  Mixed beverage election held simultaneously,
    §18B-603(d2).
  Permits.
    Effect of election on issuance, §18B-603(c).
    Not dependent on election, §18B-603(f).
  Ski resort, §18B-600(e2).
Expenditures of alcoholism funds, §18B-805(h).
Hours of operation, §18B-802(a).
Insolvent system.
  Closing of stores, §18B-801(d).
Joint store operation, §18B-703(h).
Local ABC boards.
  See ABC BOARDS.
Local ABC enforcement officers.
  Accountability, enforcement reports, §18B-501(f1).
  Appointment, §18B-501(a).
  Assisting other local agencies, §18B-501(d).
  Assisting state and federal enforcement,
    §18B-501(e).
  Contracts with other agencies.
    Alternative to hiring local officers, §18B-501(f).
  Discharge, §18B-501(g).
  Jurisdiction, §18B-501(b), (c).
Location of stores, §18B-801(b).
  Municipal objection to proposed location,
    §18B-801(b1).
Manager, §18B-803(a), (b).
  Bond, §18B-803(b).
  Local acts preempted, §18B-803(c).
Merger of local operations.
  Board for merged system, §18B-703.
Municipal objection to proposed location,
    §18B-801(b1).
North Carolina distilled spirits.
  Display, §18B-800(d).
Number of stores, §18B-801(a).

ABC STORES —Cont'd
Permits.
Effect of election on issuance, §18B-603(c).
Permits not dependent on elections, §18B-603(f).
Powers of local ABC board, §18B-701(a).
Pregnancy, warning signs, display.
Dangers of consumption during pregnancy,
§18B-808(a), (b).
Rules and regulations, §18B-807.
Sales.
Commission approval, §18B-800(c).
Damaged alcoholic beverages, §18B-806.
Distilled in North Carolina.
Display of spirits, §18B-800(e).
Spirituous liquor, §18B-800(a).
Sundays and holidays, §18B-802(b).
Wine, §18B-800(b).
Sales price.
Fortified wine, §18B-804(c).
Spirituous liquor, §18B-804(b).
Spirituous liquor.
Approval of sale, §18B-800(c).
Price, §18B-804(b).
Sold only in ABC stores, §18B-800(a).
Uniform price, §18B-804(a).
State of emergency.
Governor closing, §18B-110.
Sundays and holiday sales, §18B-802(b).
Time of operation, §18B-802(a).
Uniform price of spirituous liquor, §18B-804(a).
Wine.
Sale of fortified wine, §18B-800(b).
Working capital, §18B-805(d).

ABDUCTION.
AMBER alert system.
Child abduction, §143B-1021.
Kidnapping and abduction, §§14-39 to 14-41.
See KIDNAPPING.

ABORTION, §§14-44 to 14-46.
Certification.
Fitness of institutions, §14-45.1(a).
Concealing birth of child, §14-46.
Consent.
Legal counsel for indigent persons, §7A-451(a).
Parental or judicial consent, §§90-21.6 to 90-21.10.
Woman's right to know act.
Informed consent required, §90-21.82.
Department of health and human services.
Reports.
Certification of fitness of health care
institutions, §14-45.1(a).
Statistical summary reports concerning medical
and demographic characteristics of
abortions, §14-45.1(c).
**Destroying unborn child by using drugs or
instruments,** §14-44.
First twenty weeks of woman's pregnancy,
§14-45.1(a).
Health care institutions.
Certification of fitness, §14-45.1(a).
Requirement to perform abortion, §14-45.1(f).
Health insurance.
State health plan for teachers and state
employees.
Coverage mandate, §135-48.50.
Health of woman gravely impaired, §14-45.1(b).
Injunctions.
Obstruction of abortion clinic, §14-277.4(d).
Woman's right to know act.
Civil remedies, §90-21.88(b).

ABORTION —Cont'd
Injuring pregnant woman by using drugs,
§14-45.
Legal services programs.
Limitations on eligible cases, §7A-474.3(c).
Life of woman threatened, §14-45.1(b).
Use of state funds for abortion.
Exception to prohibition, §143C-6-5.5.
Minors.
Parental or judicial consent for abortion, §§90-21.6
to 90-21.10.
Woman's right to know act.
Informed consent from minor and adult giving
consent, §90-21.87.
Real-time view of unborn child.
Unemancipated minors, §90-21.85(c).
Miscarriages.
Using drugs or instruments to produce
miscarriage, §14-45.
Obstruction of abortion clinics, §14-277.4.
Parental or judicial consent for abortion,
§§90-21.6 to 90-21.10.
Definitions, §90-21.6.
District court jurisdiction, §7B-200(a).
Medical emergency exception, §90-21.9.
Parental consent required, §90-21.7(a).
Medical emergency exception, §90-21.9.
Waiver of requirement, §90-21.8.
Petition by pregnant minor, §90-21.7(b).
Petition by pregnant minor on own behalf.
Waiver of parental consent requirement,
§90-21.7(b).
Violations, misdemeanor, §90-21.10.
Waiver of parental consent requirement.
Appeal by minor, §90-21.8(h).
Availability inapplicability to unemancipated
minor seeking treatment in state,
§90-21.8(a).
Confidentiality, §90-21.8(d).
Costs not required of minors, §90-21.8(i).
Findings necessary, §90-21.8(e).
Hearing, §90-21.8(d).
Participation by minor, §90-21.8(c).
Petition by pregnant minor, §90-21.7(b).
Assistance by court, §90-21.8(b).
Precedence of proceedings over pending matters,
§90-21.8(d).
Summons or notice not served upon parent,
guardian, etc., upon request of petitioner,
§90-21.8(g).
Written findings of fact and conclusions of law,
§90-21.8(f).
Woman's right to know act.
Informed consent from minor and adult giving
consent, §90-21.87.
Real-time view of unborn child.
Unemancipated minors, §90-21.85(c).
Physicians and surgeons.
Producing abortion contrary to law.
Denial, annulment, suspension or revocation of
license, §90-14(a).
Refusal of physician to perform, §14-45.1(e).
Remains of terminated pregnancies.
Manner of disposition, §130A-131.10.
State funds used for.
Prohibition, exceptions, §143C-6-5.5.
**State health plan for teachers and state
employees.**
Coverage mandate, §135-48.50.
Statistical summary reports.
Medical and demographic characteristics of
abortions, §14-45.1(c).

ABORTION —Cont'd
Unborn victims of violence act/Ethen's law.
Acts not prosecuted, §14-23.7.
Woman's right to know act, §§90-21.80 to
90-21.92.
Abortion compelled by medical emergency,
§90-21.86.
Anonymity of woman in court proceedings,
§90-21.89.
Assurance of informed consent, §90-21.90.
Voluntariness of consent, §90-21.91.
Citation of act, §90-21.80.
Civil remedies.
Attorneys' fees and costs, §90-21.88(c).
Injunction, §90-21.88(b).
Privacy protection in court proceedings,
§90-21.89.
Right of action for damages, §90-21.88(a).
Consent required, §90-21.82.
Assurance of informed consent, §90-21.90.
Voluntariness of consent, §90-21.91.
Minor upon whom abortion performed,
§90-21.87.
Construction of statutory provisions.
Severability, §90-21.92.
Definitions, §90-21.81.
Information to be provided, §90-21.82.
Physical presence of woman and in language
she understands, §90-21.90(a).
Woman unable to read.
Materials to be read to her, §90-21.90(b).
Internet web site to be maintained by department,
§90-21.84.
Printed materials to be available on web site,
§90-21.83.
Medical emergency procedures, §90-21.86.
Printed materials to be available on web site,
§90-21.83(a).
Available at no cost from department,
§90-21.83(c).
Legibility, readability, etc., §90-21.83(b).
Privacy protection in court proceedings, §90-21.89.
Real-time view of unborn child.
Averting of eyes or refusal to listen to
explanation, §90-21.85(b).
Certification of woman as to opportunity to
view, §90-21.85(a).
Duties of technician and physician, §90-21.85(a).
Unemancipated minors, §90-21.85(c).
Severability of statutory provisions, §90-21.92.
Title of act, §90-21.80.
Voluntariness of informed consent, §90-21.91.
Written certification of informed consent,
§90-21.82.
Assurance of informed consent, §90-21.90.

ABORTION CLINICS.
Certification of facilities.
Fee authorized, §131E-269.
New facilities.
Initial licensure fees, §131E-272.
Obstruction of health care facility, §14-277.4.
Access to or egress from, §14-277.4(a).
Exemptions, §14-277.4(h).
Felony offense.
Habitual offenders, §14-277.4(c).
Free speech not abridged, §14-277.4(e).
"Health care facility" defined, §14-277.4(f).
"Health care services" defined, §14-277.4(g).
Injunctive relief, §14-277.4(d).
Misdemeanor offense, §14-277.4(c).

ABORTION CLINICS —Cont'd
Obstruction of health care facility —Cont'd
Personal injury, §14-277.4(b).
Picketing right not abridged, §14-277.4(e).
**Weapons at demonstrations at private health
care facilities, §14-277.2.**

ABSCONDING DEBTORS.
Arrest, §1-355.
Attachment, grounds, §1-440.3.

ABSCONDING JUVENILES.
Interstate compact on juveniles, §§7B-2800 to
7B-2827.
See INTERSTATE COMPACT ON JUVENILES.
**Taking juvenile into temporary custody
without court order, §7B-1900.**
Transporting to nearest secure custody facility,
§7B-1901(c).

ABSENCE FROM RESIDENCE.
Death not presumed by mere absence,
§28C-1(a).
Estates of missing persons, §§28C-1 to 28C-22.
See MISSING PERSONS.

ABSENCE FROM SCHOOL.
Compulsory attendance law, §§115C-378 to
115C-383.
See COMPULSORY SCHOOL ATTENDANCE.

ABSENTEE BALLOTS, §§163-226 to 163-239.
**Alternative procedures for requesting
application and voting, §163-227.2(a).**
Application procedure, §163-227.2(b).
Disapproval of application, §163-227.2(d).
Furnishing voter with ballot, instruction sheets,
entry of name in register, §163-227.2(c).
Office hours for receipt of applications.
Counties running modified full-time office,
§163-227.2(f).
One or more sites in counties for applying for and
casting ballots, §163-227.2(g).
Plan of implementation, adoption, §163-227.2(g).
Relocation of voter within county.
Effect, §163-227.2(e2).
Safekeeping of application, §163-227.2(d).
Voting procedure, §163-227.2(e).
Applications for.
Absence for sickness or physical disability,
§163-230.1(a1).
Alternate procedures, §163-227.2.
Completed applications and ballots.
Container-return envelope, §163-230.1(b).
Invalid written requests, §163-230.2(b).
Method of requesting ballots, §163-230.2.
Military absentee voting.
Certified list of approved applications,
§163-251(a) to (c).
Military and overseas voters, §163-258.7.
Primary elections.
Second primary, §163-227.1.
Register of applications, §163-228.
Retention, §163-233.
Simultaneous issuance of ballots with application,
§163-230.1(a).
Valid written requests, §163-230.2(a).
**Candidate witnessing absentee ballots of
nonrelative.**
Misdemeanor, §163-237(b1).
Certified list of executed absentee ballots.
Received on day before election, §163-232.
Received on or after election day.
Challenges, §163-232.1(c).

ABSENTEE BALLOTS —Cont'd
Certified list of executed absentee ballots
  —Cont'd
  Received on or after election day —Cont'd
    Mailing of copies to board of elections,
      §163-232.1(c).
    Military and overseas ballots, §163-232.1(b).
    Posting of lists, §163-232.1(c).
    Preparation of list, §163-232.1(a).
    Retention of lists, §163-232.1(d).
Challenge of voters.
  Burden of proof, §163-89(c).
  Hearing, §163-89(e).
  Separate challenge to each ballot, §163-89(c).
  Signing of challenge, §163-89(c).
  Time for challenge, §163-89(a).
  To whom challenge addressed, §163-89(d).
  Who may challenge, §163-89(b).
Container-return envelopes.
  Application on, §163-229(b).
  Delivery to applicant, §163-230.1(a2).
Counting.
  County boards of elections, §163-234.
County boards of elections.
  Certified list of executed absentee ballots.
    Received on day before election, §163-232.
    Received on or after election day, §163-232.1.
  Counting of absentee ballots by, §163-234.
  Duties, §163-236.
  Military and overseas voters.
    Absentee voting at office of board of elections,
      §163-255.
    Certified list of executed absentee ballots.
      Ballots received on or after election day,
        §163-232.1(b).
    Electronic notice of election, §163-258.16.
  Required meeting of county board, §163-230.1(c1).
  Retention of applications, §163-233.
  Violations by.
    Penalties, §163-236.
Curtained or private area for marking ballot.
  One stop voting sites, §163-227.2(i).
Date ballots available for voting, §163-227.3(a).
Definition of "near relative," §163-230.1(f).
Delaying ballots pending appeal, §163-227.3(a).
Election defined, §163-226(c).
False statements, §163-237(a), (b).
Felonies, §163-226.3(a).
Fire district elections.
  Ballots not permitted, §163-226(b).
Forgery, §163-237(c).
Fraud, §163-237(c).
In-person registration.
  Voting by retrievable absentee ballot,
    §163-82.6A(c).
In-person voting for person previously
  registered by mail, §163-166.12(a).
Instruction sheets, §163-229(c).
Issuance.
  Delivery of absentee ballots and container-return
    envelope to applicant, §163-230.1(a2).
  Simultaneous issuance with application,
    §163-230.1(a).
List.
  Executed absentee ballots.
    Received on day before election, §163-232.
    Received on or after election day, §163-232.1.
Military absentee voting.
  Applicability of provisions.
    Inapplicable to persons after change of status,
      §163-253.

ABSENTEE BALLOTS —Cont'd
Military absentee voting —Cont'd
  Applications for absentee ballots.
    Certified list of approved applications,
      §163-251(a) to (c).
  Challenges.
    Hearing by county board of elections,
      §163-251(d).
  Change of status.
    Provisions inapplicable after, §163-253.
  Counting ballots, §163-251(d).
  County boards of elections.
    Absentee voting at office of board of elections,
      §163-255.
  Day of primary or election.
    Registration and voting on, §163-254.
  Disqualified because of change in residence or
    conviction, §163-253.
  List of applicants to whom ballots have been
    issued.
    Distribution, §163-251(b).
    List constitutes registration, §163-251(c).
    Preparation, §163-251(a).
  Office of board of elections.
    Absentee voting at, §163-255.
  Primary or election day.
    Registration and voting on, §163-254.
  Proof of military status.
    Presenting if requested, §163-253.
  State board of elections.
    Duties generally, §163-256(b).
    Rules and regulations, §163-256(a).
Military and overseas voters, §§163-258.1 to
  163-258.31.
  Address of last place of residence.
    Assigning overseas voters to precincts,
      §163-258.5.
  Applicability of provisions.
    Effect on voting provisions generally, §163-239.
  Applications.
    Arrival after transmission of ballots and ballot
      materials, §163-258.9(c).
    Confirmation of receipt, §163-258.14.
    Covered voters not registered to vote in state,
      §163-258.7(b).
    Covered voters registered to vote in state,
      §163-258.7(a).
    Declaration accompanying federal write-in
      absentee ballot.
      Use to apply, §163-258.7(d).
    Electronic transmission system.
      Capable to receive, §163-258.7(c).
      Standing request for electronic delivery of
        application.
        Request by voter providing electronic mail
          address, §163-258.15(b).
    Federal postcard application, §163-258.7(a), (b).
    Methods, §163-258.7(a), (b).
    Regular application method.
      Use by covered voters registered to vote in
        state, §163-258.7(a).
    Standing request for electronic delivery of
      application.
      Request by voter providing electronic mail
        address, §163-258.15(b).
    Timely receipt, §163-258.8.
    Valid request, §163-258.8.
  Authentication not required, §163-258.17(b).
  Casting ballots.
    Timeliness, §163-258.10.

ABSENTEE BALLOTS —Cont'd
Military and overseas voters —Cont'd
  Casting ballots —Cont'd
    Using federal write-in absentee ballot,
      §163-258.11.
  Certified list of executed absentee ballots.
    Ballots received on or after election day,
      §163-232.1(b).
    Calling names of voter listed and marking
      voting square, §163-258.26(b).
    Disposition, time, §163-258.26a§163-232.1(b).
    Execution of certificate, form,
      §163-258.26a§163-232.1(a).
    List constitutes precinct registration,
      §§163-232.1(c), 163-258.26(a).
    Preparation of list, §163-258.26(a).
  Challenging.
    Person already recorded as voting in election,
      §163-258.26(b).
  Change of status.
    Inapplicability of article, §163-258.27.
    Registration under article remains valid,
      §163-258.27.
  Confirmation of receipt of application and voted
    ballot, §163-258.14.
  Construction of act.
    Electronic signatures in global and national
      commerce act.
      Effect of article on, §163-258.20.
    Uniformity of application and construction,
      §163-258.19.
  Counting, §163-232.1(d).
  Covered voter defined, §163-258.2.
  Declaration.
    Ballot to include and be accompanied by,
      §163-258.13.
    Form and content.
      State board of elections to prescribe,
        §163-258.4(e).
  Definitions, §163-258.2.
  Delivery of ballot to address specified.
    Timeliness, §163-258.12(a).
  Effect of provisions, §163-239.
  Elections covered by act, §163-258.3.
  Electronic free access system.
    Confirmation of receipt of application and voted
      ballot, §163-258.14.
  Electronic mail address requested from each
    covered voter, §163-258.15(a).
    Not public record, §163-258.15(a).
    Standing request for electronic delivery of
      application.
      Request by voter providing electronic mail
        address, §163-258.15(b).
    Use for official communications only,
      §163-258.15(a).
  Electronic notice of election.
    Certified candidates and ballot measures.
      Update of notice to include, §163-258.16(c).
    Copy.
      Covered voter may request, §163-258.16(b).
    County board of elections web site.
      Update of notice available on, §163-258.16(d).
    Time for preparation, §163-258.16(a).
  Electronic signatures in global and national
    commerce act.
    Effect of article on, §163-258.20.
  Electronic transmission system.
    Applications.
      Capable to receive, §163-258.7(c).

ABSENTEE BALLOTS —Cont'd
Military and overseas voters —Cont'd
  Electronic transmission system —Cont'd
    Applications —Cont'd
      Standing request for electronic delivery of
        application.
        Request by voter providing electronic mail
          address, §163-258.15(b).
    Ballots and ballot material sent to voter by,
      §163-258.9(b).
    State board of elections to establish,
      §163-258.4(c).
    Voter registration.
      Capable to receive, §163-258.6(c).
  Emergency rules prescribing special procedures or
    requirements, §163-258.31.
  Failure to satisfy nonessential requirement.
    Document not invalidated, §163-258.17(a).
  Federal or state office election.
    Elections covered by act, §163-258.3.
  Federal postcard application.
    Using to apply, §163-258.7(a), (b).
  Federal write-in absentee ballot.
    Using to vote, §163-258.11.
  Information regarding voter registration and
    casting ballots.
    State board of elections to make available,
      §163-258.4(b).
    Single office responsible for, §163-258.30(b).
  Informing appropriate election official that voter
    is covered voter, §163-258.7(e).
  Injunction or other equitable relief, §163-258.18.
  Late postmark on timely received ballot.
    Ballot not rejected, §163-258.12(b).
  Local elections.
    Elections covered by act, §163-258.3.
  Material misrepresentation of fact in completing
    document grounds for perjury conviction.
    Declaration accompanying ballot, §163-258.13.
  Military-overseas ballots.
    Certified list of executed absentee ballots.
      Received on or after election day,
        §163-232.1(b).
    Defined, §163-258.2.
  Mistake or omission.
    Document not invalidated, §163-258.17(a).
  Nonessential requirement.
    Failure to satisfy.
      Document not invalidated, §163-258.17(a).
  Notice.
    Electronic notice, §163-258.16.
  Official responsible for implementation.
    State board of elections, §163-258.4(a).
  Overseas voter defined, §163-258.2.
  Precinct of address of last place of residence.
    Assigning overseas voters, §163-258.5.
  Registration of voters.
    Change of status of covered voter registering
      under article.
      Validity of registration, §163-258.27.
    Declaration accompanying federal write-in
      absentee ballot.
      Method used to register, §163-258.6(b).
    Electronic transmission system.
      Capability to accept registration method,
        §163-258.6(c).
    Federal postcard application.
      Method used to register, §163-258.6(a).
    Methods, §163-258.6.
    Receipt of registration prior to election.
      Time, §163-258.6(d).

ABSENTEE BALLOTS —Cont'd
Military and overseas voters —Cont'd
Registration of voters —Cont'd
Registration in person including day of election or primary, §163-258.28.
Rules and regulations, §163-258.30(a).
Emergency rules, §163-258.31.
Short title.
Uniform military and overseas voters act, §163-258.1.
Standardized absentee voting materials.
State board of elections to develop, §163-258.4(d).
State ballot measure.
Elections covered by act, §163-258.3.
Timely receipt of ballot, §163-258.12(a), (b).
Transmission of ballots and ballot materials to covered voters.
Applications arriving after transmission, §163-258.9(c).
Electronic transmission system, §163-258.9(b).
Timeliness, §163-258.8(a).
Uniformed service defined, §163-258.2.
Uniformed-service voter defined, §163-258.2.
Uniformity of application and construction, §163-258.19.
Uniform military and overseas voters act.
Short title, §163-258.1.
Voting at office of board of elections, §163-258.29.
Voting in person on day of election, §163-258.28.
Misdemeanors.
County boards of elections.
Violations by, §163-236.
Prohibited acts, §163-237.
Municipal elections, §§163-226.2, 163-302.
One stop voting.
Challenge entered against voter, §163-227.2(h).
Procedure, §163-227.2.
Requirements for approval, §163-227.2(g1).
Penalties.
County boards of elections.
Violations by, §163-236.
General penalty, §163-237(d).
Prohibited acts, §§163-226.3(a), 163-237.
Persons previously registered by mail who have not voted for federal office.
Exemptions, §163-166.12(d).
Identification proof submitted by voter.
County board to note, §163-166.12(b1).
Voting when identification numbers not matched, §163-166.12(b2).
In-person voting, §163-166.12(a).
Mail-in absentee voting, §163-166.12(b).
Provisional voting, §163-166.12(c).
Primary elections, §163-226.1.
Reduction of time by which absentee ballots required to be printed and distributed, §163-22(k).
Second primary.
Applications for absentee ballots, §163-227.1.
Providing of ballots, §163-227.3(b).
Prohibited acts, §§163-226.3(a), 163-237.
Investigation and prosecution by boards of elections, §163-226.3(b).
Qualifications of voters.
Primary elections, §163-226.1.
Register of absentee ballot applications and ballots issued, §163-228.
Regular official ballots, §163-229(a).
Return of ballots, §163-230.1(c).

ABSENTEE BALLOTS —Cont'd
Sickness or disability to last calendar year.
Application to constitute request for ballot in all primaries and elections during year, §163-226(a2).
State board of elections.
Duties generally, §163-256(b).
Method of requesting ballots.
Rules and regulations, §163-230.2(c).
Military absentee voting.
Rules and regulations, §163-256(a).
Providing absentee ballots, §163-227.3.
Report of violations to district attorneys, §163-238.
Rules and regulations, §163-230.1(e).
Single office responsible for procedures, §163-256(b).
Violations of provisions.
Investigation and prosecution, §163-226.3(b).
Violations of provisions.
Investigations by boards of elections, §163-226.3(b).
Prohibited acts generally, §§163-226.3(a), 163-237.
Reports of violations to district attorneys, §163-238.
Voting procedures, §§163-227.2(e), 163-231(a).
Transmitting executed ballots to chairman of county boards of elections, §163-231(b).
Voting system with retrievable ballots.
One stop voting procedure, §163-227.2(e1).
Who may vote absentee, §163-226(a).
Withdrawal of absentee ballots not allowed, §163-233.1.

ABSENTEE INSURANCE FUND.
Missing persons, §28C-19.

ABSENTEES.
Estates of missing persons, §§28C-1 to 28C-22.
See MISSING PERSONS.
Military service, §§28B-1 to 28B-10.
Presumption of death, §28C-1.
Service of process.
Alternative methods.
Party that cannot be served or found within state, §1A-1 Rule 4(j).

ABSENTEES IN MILITARY SERVICE, §§28B-1 to 28B-10.
Complaint.
Hearing, §28B-3(b).
Notice of hearing, §28B-3(a).
Defined, §28B-1.
Evidence.
Transfer of property valued at less than $5,000.
Court order authorizing transfer, §28B-9(c).
Transfer of property valued at more than $5,000.
Court order authorizing transfer, §28B-10.
Guardian ad litem.
Appointment by court, §28B-3(c).
Hearings.
Transfer of property valued at more than $5,000, §28B-10(c).
Husband and wife.
Transfer of property valued at less than $5,000.
Application to superior court, §28B-9(a).
Transfer of property valued at more than $5,000, §28B-10.
Receivers.
Appointment.
Action for appointment, §28B-2(a).
Order of appointment, §28B-4(a).

ABSENTEES IN MILITARY SERVICE —Cont'd
Receivers —Cont'd
Appointment —Cont'd
Spouses or next of kin, §28B-4(b).
Bonds, §28B-5(a).
Complaints.
Contents, §28B-2(b).
Death of absentee.
Termination of receivership, §28B-8(b).
Inventory, filing, §28B-5(b).
Final inventory.
Termination of receivership, §28B-8(c).
Limitation of action.
Actions against receiver, §28B-8(d).
Maintenance and support of dependents, §28B-6.
Misconduct.
Report of clerk, §28B-5(b).
Modification.
Addition or subtraction from statutory powers of
receiver, §28B-6(b).
Order of appointment, §28B-4.
Powers and duties, §28B-6(a).
Removal, §28B-7(b).
Resignation, §28B-7(a).
Termination.
Death of absentee, §28B-8(b).
Filing of final inventory, §28B-8(c).
Final accounting, §28B-8(c).
Order of court, §28B-8(a).
Release from duties, §28B-8(d).
Transfer of property.
Order of court, §28B-9(b).
Evidence of validity of proceedings, §28B-9(c).
Property valued at less than $5,000.
Application.
Form, §28B-9(a).
Property valued at more than $5,000, §28B-10(a)
to (g).
Summary procedure.
Property valued at more than $5,000,
§28B-10(a) to (g).

ABSENT PARENTS.
Child support enforcement program generally,
§§110-128 to 110-142.2.
See CHILD SUPPORT.

ABSENT WITNESSES.
Depositions, use in court proceedings, §1A-1
Rule 32(a).

ABSOLUTE DIVORCE.
See DIVORCE.

ABSTRACTS.
Evidence.
Certified copies of abstracts of grants, §§8-6, 8-7.
Recording of certified copies, §8-8.
Validation, §8-9.
Property taxes, §§105-309 to 105-311.

ABUSE.
Abused, neglected or dependent juveniles,
§§7B-100 to 7B-1414.
See CHILD ABUSE, NEGLECT OR
DEPENDENCY.
Disabled adults, §§108A-99 to 108A-111.
See ABUSED, NEGLECTED OR EXPLOITED
DISABLED ADULTS.
Domestic violence.
See DOMESTIC VIOLENCE.
Patient abuse, §14-32.2.

**ABUSED, NEGLECTED OR EXPLOITED
DISABLED ADULTS, §§108A-99 to 108A-111.**
Abuse.
Criminal offense, §14-32.3(a).
Defined, §108A-101(a).
Director to notify district attorney, §108A-109.
Appeals.
Motion in the cause.
Review of orders issued pursuant to provisions,
§108A-107.
Caretaker.
Defined, §§14-32.3(d), 108A-101(b).
Interference with provision of protective services.
Injunction, §108A-104(b).
Citation of act.
Short title, §108A-99.
County directors of social services.
Cooperation with, §108A-103(b).
Definition of "director,"§108A-101(c).
Duties on receiving reports, §§108A-14,
108A-103(a), (d).
Medical evaluations.
Contracts for providing, §108A-103(c).
Notification to district attorney of abuse,
§108A-109.
Definitions, §108A-101.
Disabled adults defined, §§14-32.3(d),
108A-101(d), (e).
District courts.
Defined, §108A-101(f).
Domestic setting.
Defined, §14-32.3(d).
Elder adult defined, §14-32.3(d).
Emergency services.
Defined, §108A-101(h).
Emergency defined, §108A-101(g).
Entry of premises without adult's consent,
§108A-106(e).
Inspection of adult's financial records.
Order, §108A-106(f).
Order for, §108A-106(a), (b).
Petition for, §108A-106(c).
Immunity of petitioner, §108A-106(g).
Notice of filing, §108A-106(d).
Essential services.
Defined, §108A-101(i).
Payment for, §108A-108.
Exploitation defined, §108A-101(j).
Funding of protective services, §108A-110.
Immunity, §108A-102(c).
Indigent defined, §108A-101(k).
Legislative intent, §108A-100.
Motion in the cause.
Review of orders issued pursuant to provisions,
§108A-107.
Neglect.
Criminal offense, §14-32.3(b).
Defined, §108A-101(m).
Payment for essential services, §108A-108.
Protective services.
Caretaker.
Interference with provision of protective
services.
Injunction, §108A-104(b).
Consent to provide, §108A-104(a).
Withdrawal, §108A-104(c).
Defined, §108A-101(n).
Funding, §108A-110.
Lack of capacity to consent.
Defined, §108A-101(l).

ABUSED, NEGLECTED OR EXPLOITED DISABLED ADULTS —Cont'd
Protective services —Cont'd
Lack of capacity to consent —Cont'd
Effect of determination of lack of capacity to consent, §108A-105(d).
Guardian ad litem, §108A-105(b).
Notice of hearing, §108A-105(b).
Order authorizing, §108A-105(c).
Petition, §108A-105(a).
Purpose of act, §108A-100.
Reports.
Content, §108A-102(b).
Director to notify district attorney, §108A-109.
Duty to report, §108A-102(a).
Immunity, §108A-102(c).
Short title of act, §108A-99.
Standards, adoption, §108A-111.

ABUSE OF PATIENTS.
Physical abuse unlawful, §14-32.2(a).
Criminal process, issuance, request of attorney general, §14-32.2(g).
Defenses, §14-32.2(f).
Definitions, §14-32.2(c) to (e1).
Provisions not to supersede other offenses, §14-32.2(h).
Punishment, §14-32.2(b).

ACADEMIC CREDIT OR DEGREE OBTAINED BY FRAUDULENT MEANS, §14-118.2.

ACCELERATION.
Commercial code.
Leases.
Consumer leases.
Option to accelerate at will, §25-2A-109(2).
Option to accelerate at will, §25-1-309.
High cost home loans, §24-1.1E(b).

ACCEPTANCE.
Funds transfers, UCC.
Payment order, §25-4A-209.
Leases, UCC, §25-2A-515.
Acceptance of part of unit acceptance of entire unit, §25-2A-515(2).
Accessions, goods becoming, §25-2A-310.
Damages.
Lessors' damages for noncompliance, §25-2A-528.
Default.
Burden of establishing, §25-2A-516.
Notice, §25-2A-516.
Effect, §25-2A-516.
Firm offers, §25-2A-205.
Generally, §25-2A-206.
Nonconforming goods or delivery of goods, §25-2A-509.
Revocation, §25-2A-517.
Damages, §25-2A-519.
Justifiable revocation, §25-2A-517.
Lessors' rights and remedies, §25-2A-508.
Wrongful revocation, §25-2A-523.
Sales, UCC.
Breach after acceptance.
Burden of establishing, §25-2-607(4).
Buyer's damages, §25-2-714.
Documents deliverable on acceptance, §25-2-514.
Effect of acceptance, §25-2-607.
Generally, §25-2-606.
Improper delivery.
Buyer's rights, §25-2-601.
Installment contracts, §25-2-612.

ACCEPTANCE —Cont'd
Sales, UCC —Cont'd
Nonacceptance.
Seller's damages, §25-2-708.
Revocation in whole or in part, §25-2-608.
Service of process.
Personal jurisdiction by, §1A-1 Rule 4(j5).

ACCESSIONS.
Leases, UCC, §§25-2A-103(2), 25-2A-310.
Secured transactions.
Perfection and priority of security interests, §25-9-335.

ACCESSORIES.
Generally.
See ACCOMPLICES AND ACCESSORIES.

ACCESS TO CIVIL JUSTICE ACT.
General provisions, §§7A-474.1 to 7A-474.5.
See LEGAL SERVICES PROGRAMS.

ACCESS TO JUDICIAL PROCEEDINGS AND RECORDS, §1-72.1.

ACCIDENT AND HEALTH INSURANCE.
Generally.
See HEALTH INSURANCE.

ACCIDENT INVESTIGATORS.
Safety professionals, §§90-671 to 90-674.

ACCIDENTS.
Aircraft.
Liability determination, §63-15.
Amusement devices, §95-111.10.
Boats.
Death, injury or disappearance.
Filing of report, §75A-11(b).
Notice to law enforcement agency, §75A-11(c).
Boilers.
Investigations, §95-69.11.
Elevators, §95-110.9.
Landlord and tenant.
Liability for accidental damage, §42-10.
Liquefied petroleum gases.
Limitations on liability, §119-60.
Mine accidents.
Bureau of mines, §113-26.1.
Defined, §74-24.2.
Mine safety and health, §§74-24.1 to 74-24.20.
See MINE SAFETY AND HEALTH.
Powers of commissioner of labor, §74-24.7(c) to (e).
Reporting, §74-24.13.
Motor carriers.
Reports not to be used as evidence, §62-274.
Motor vehicles.
Generally.
See MOTOR VEHICLE ACCIDENTS.
Public utilities.
Investigation by commission, §62-41.
Safety professionals, §§90-671 to 90-674.
School buses.
Claims for death or injury to pupil, §§115C-257 to 115C-259.
See SCHOOL BUSES.
Winter sports safety and accidents, §§99C-1 to 99C-5.
Workers' compensation.
Compensation from other states, §97-36.
Death resulting, compensation, §97-38.
Generally, §§97-1 to 97-101.1.
See WORKERS' COMPENSATION.
Notice to employer, §§97-22, 97-23.

ACCIDENTS —Cont'd
Workers' compensation —Cont'd
Reports, §97-92.

**ACCIDENT-TRAUMA VICTIM
 IDENTIFICATION,** §§90-600 to 90-604.
Body information tags.
Contents, §90-604(b).
Use, §90-604(a).
Citation of article, §90-600.
Next of kin.
Timely notification, §90-603.
Organ donors.
Routine search for information, §90-602.
Personal effects search.
Definitions, §90-602(a).
Immunity for good faith compliance, §90-602(d),
 (e).
Sanctions against hospitals, §90-602(d).
Scope of search, §90-602(c).
Who may search, §90-602(a1), (a2).
Policy of state, §90-601.
Purpose of article, §90-601.
Search of driver record, §90-602(b).
Short title, §90-600.

ACCOMMODATION ENDORSER.
Joinder of debtor by surety.
Surety defined to include, §26-12(a).
Surety's recovery on obligation paid.
Surety defined to include, §26-3.1.

ACCOMMODATION MAKER.
Joinder of debtor by surety.
Surety defined to include, §26-12(a).
Surety's recovery on obligation paid.
Surety defined to include, §26-3.1(b).

ACCOMPLICES AND ACCESSORIES.
After the fact accessories, §14-7.
**Alcoholic beverage sale to or purchase by
 minors,** §18B-302(c).
Fines and other penalties, §18B-302.1(b), (c).
Before the fact accessories, §14-5.2.
Collections out of state of employee earnings.
Resident as aider, §95-74.
Continuing criminal enterprise, §14-7.20.
Egg act violations, §106-245.27(a).
Escape.
Aiding or assisting.
 Class 1 misdemeanor, §148-45(d).
Conveying messages to convicts and other
 prisoners, §14-258.
Use of deadly weapon, §14-258.2.
Futures contracts, §16-4.
Habeas corpus.
Concealing party entitled to writ, §17-28.
Larceny, §14-70.
Prisoner injuries.
Inflicting or assisting in infliction of self injury to
 prisoner resulting in incapacity, §148-46.1.
Prostitution, §14-204.
Punishment of accessories.
After the fact accessories, §14-7.
Before the fact accessories, §14-5.2.

ACCORD AND SATISFACTION.
**Advance payments to person claiming bodily
 injury,** §1-540.3.
Affirmative defense, §1A-1 Rule 8(c).
Commercial code general provisions.
Performance or acceptance under reservation of
 rights, §25-1-308(c).

ACCORD AND SATISFACTION —Cont'd
Motor vehicle accident settlements, §1-540.2.
Negotiable instruments.
Use of instrument, §25-3-311.
Receipt of less sum discharge.
Agreement, §1-540.
Secured transactions.
Assignment to satisfy preexisting obligation,
 inapplicability, §25-9-109(d).
Collateral accepted in full or partial satisfaction of
 obligation, §§25-9-620 to 25-9-622.

ACCOUNTABILITY.
**State governmental accountability and
 internal control act,** §§143D-1 to 143D-12.
See STATE GOVERNMENTAL
 ACCOUNTABILITY AND INTERNAL
 CONTROL ACT.

ACCOUNTANTS, §§93-1 to 93-13.
Age.
Minimum age, §93-2.
Assistants.
Certification not required, §93-9.
Board of examiners, §93-12.
Confidentiality of records, §93-12.2.
Business under assumed name.
Partnerships, exemption, §66-68(e).
Certificates of qualification.
Assistants need not be certified, §93-9.
Issuance, §93-12.
Reciprocity, §93-10.
Required, §§93-3 to 93-6.
Revocation or suspension, §93-12.
Child support enforcement.
Forfeiture of licensing privilege, §50-13.12.
Civil penalties, §93-12.
Confidentiality records of board, §93-12.2.
Corporations.
Practice through corporate form.
 Prohibition, §93-8.
Professional corporations generally, §§55B-1 to
 55B-16.
 See PROFESSIONAL CORPORATIONS.
Use of title "certified public accountant," §93-5.
Definitions, §93-1(a).
Disciplinary action, §93-12.
Education.
Continuing education.
 Powers of board of examiners as to, §93-12.
Qualifications of applicants for examination,
 §93-12.
Examinations.
Powers and duties of board as to, §93-12.
Qualifications of applicants, §93-12.
 New requirements.
  Effect, §93-12.1.
Fees, §93-12.
Fiduciaries.
Employment and compensation.
 Powers which may be incorporated by reference
  in trust instrument, §32-27.
Immunity.
Insurance companies.
 Annual audited financial reports.
  Adverse financial condition reports by CPA,
   §58-10-225(b).
Insurance companies.
Annual audited financial reports.
 Generally, §§58-10-185 to 58-10-285.
 See INSURANCE COMPANIES.

ACCOUNTANTS —Cont'd
Licenses.
Statewide license for privilege of practicing.
Firm or corporation.
Not issued in name of, §105-41(e).
License not authorization to practice, §105-41(i).
Not transferable, §105-41(a).
Personal privilege licenses, §105-41(e).
Required, §105-41(a).
Tax for each license, §105-41(a).
Amount, §105-41(c).
Counties and cities levying, prohibition, §105-41(h).
Exemptions, §105-41(b).
License taxes.
Statewide license for privilege of practicing, §105-41.
Nonresidents.
Certificates of qualification.
Persons certified in other states, §93-10(a), (b).
Out-of-state firms, §93-10(c).
Partnerships.
Use of title "certified public accountant,"§93-4.
Peer review.
Board of examiners, §93-12.
Practice of law.
Prohibited, §93-1(b).
Professional corporations.
Generally, §§55B-1 to 55B-16.
See PROFESSIONAL CORPORATIONS.
Public accountants defined, §93-1(a).
Public officers and employees.
Accountancy provisions not applicable to, §93-11.
Public practice of accountancy.
Cooperation, §93-8.
Defined, §93-1(a).
Prohibited practice, §93-6.
Qualifications, §§93-2, 93-12.
Reciprocity.
Certification, §93-10.
Records.
Board of examiners, §93-12.
Referees meetings.
Statement of account by, §1A-1 Rule 53(f).
Registration.
Required, §93-6.
Rules for registration, §93-12.
Reports.
Board of examiners.
Annual report to governor, §93-12.
Peer review, §93-12.
Rules and regulations.
Board of examiners, §93-12.
Peer review.
Authority of board to adopt, §93-12.
Rules of professional conduct.
Power of board to adopt, §93-12.
Title.
Misleading titles.
Prohibited, §93-6.
Use of titles, §93-4.
Corporations, §93-5.
Individuals, §93-3.
Violations of provisions, §93-13.

ACCOUNTS AND ACCOUNTING.
ABC boards.
Accounting system, §§18B-205(b), 18B-702(l).
Accounts, §18B-205(a).
Absentees in military service.
Termination of receivership.
Final accounting, §28B-8(c).

ACCOUNTS AND ACCOUNTING —Cont'd
Accountants, §§93-1 to 93-13.
See ACCOUNTANTS.
Agricultural finance authority, §122D-18(a).
Alcoholic beverages.
Required accounts and systems, §18B-205(a), (b).
Assignments for benefit of creditors.
Final account in twelve months, §23-11.
Quarterly accounts, §23-11.
Trustee of deed of trust to account for property coming into hands, §23-2.
Attorneys at law.
Deposit of funds, ProfCond Rule 1.15-2.
Records and accountings, ProfCond Rule 1.15-3.
Banks.
False entries in banking accounts.
Felony, §53-130.
Savings banks.
Deposit accounts, §54C-164.
Generally accepted accounting principles, §54C-161.
Joint accounts, §54C-165.
Personal agency accounts, §54C-167.
Statement of account from bank to depositor.
Final adjustment if not objected to within five years, §53-75.
Depositor not relieved from exercising diligence to errors, §53-76.
Rendering annually or on request, §53-75.
Bedding law account, §106-65.104.
Book accounts, evidence.
Accounts under $10, §8-42.
Copies, §8-44.
Executors or administrators to approve, §8-43.
Book debt oath.
Administrators, §11-11.
Form of oath, §11-11.
Boxing revenue account, §143-655(c).
Certified public accountants, §§93-1 to 93-13.
See ACCOUNTANTS.
Clean water management trust fund.
Established, §143-15.3B(a).
Collection agencies.
Application of funds where there is debtor-creditor relationship, §58-70-85.
Furnishing acknowledgment of account, §58-70-60(a).
Remittance trust account, §58-70-65(a) to (c).
Return of accounts.
Request by creditor, §58-70-75.
Termination of permit, §58-70-80.
Collegiate and cultural attraction plate account, §20-79.7(b).
Commerce department.
Industrial development fund.
Utility account, §143B-437.01(b1).
Common trusts funds.
Court accounting, §53-163.6.
Community colleges, §115D-58.5.
Community third party or pooled trusts.
Final disbursement and accounting.
Trustee of medicaid pooled trust, §36D-11(a).
Statements provided, §36D-5(a).
Constitution of the United States.
Receipts and expenditures of public money.
Publication of statement and account, US Const Art I §9.
Contracts for deed.
Periodic statements of account, §47H-5.
Corporations.
Accounting records, §55-16-01(b).

ACCOUNTS AND ACCOUNTING —Cont'd
Court process.
Collection of accounts.
Simulation of court process in connection with collection, §14-118.1.
CPAs, §§93-1 to 93-13.
See ACCOUNTANTS.
Current accounts.
Accrual of action to recover balance due, §1-31.
Custodial trusts.
Accounting by custodial trustee, §33B-15.
Establishment of checking, savings or other accounts, §33B-9(c).
Decedents' estates.
Collectors.
Duty to file inventories, accounts and other reports, §28A-11-3(a).
Settlement of accounts, §28A-11-4(b).
General provisions, §§28A-21-1 to 28A-21-6.
See EXECUTORS AND ADMINISTRATORS.
Inventories, §§28A-20-1 to 28A-20-4.
See DECEDENTS' ESTATES.
Default judgments.
Clerk to ascertain interest upon default judgment on account, §24-6.
Detectives.
Collection of claims, accounts, etc., by detective.
Misdemeanor offense for detective to collect, §14-401.2.
Drainage districts.
Filing account of expenses, §156-77.
Durable power of attorney.
Incapacity or incompetency of principal.
Filing annual and final accounts, §32A-11(b).
Ecosystem restoration fund, §143-214.12(c).
Receipts and disbursements, §143-214.13.
Evidence.
Book accounts.
Copies of book accounts in documentary evidence, §8-44.
Documentary evidence of book accounts under $60, §8-42.
Executors and administrators to approve book accounts, §8-43.
Documentary evidence.
Itemized and verified accounts, §8-45.
Executors and administrators.
Book accounts.
Proved by personal representative, §8-43.
Generally, §§28A-21-1 to 28A-21-6.
See EXECUTORS AND ADMINISTRATORS.
Facility authorities.
Fiscal accountability, §160A-480.3(f).
Fiduciaries.
Personal accounts.
Deposit in fiduciary's personal account, §32-10.
Firefighters' relief fund.
Disbursement of funds by trustees.
Account of moneys received and disbursed to be kept, §58-84-40(a) to (d).
Fiscal year, §147-85.
Fraud.
Court process in connection with collection of account.
Simulation of court process, §14-118.1.
Guardians.
Generally, §§35A-1260 to 35A-1269.
See GUARDIAN AND WARD.
Highway patrol.
Oversized and hazardous shipment escort fee.
Escort fee account, §20-196.4(d).

ACCOUNTS AND ACCOUNTING —Cont'd
Housing authorities and projects.
Local government finance.
Special provisions pertaining to public housing authorities, §159-42(f).
Systems as part of city or county accounting system, §157-4.2.
Housing trust fund.
Separate accounts, §122E-5(c).
Incompetence, restoration.
Filing an approval of final accounts from guardian, §35A-1130(e).
Judicial sales.
Private sale.
Filing of account, §1-339.40(a), (b).
Public sale.
Filing of account, §1-339.31(a).
Local ABC boards.
Accounting system, §§18B-205(b), 18B-702(l).
Accounts, §18B-205(a).
Local development.
Expenditures, §158-7.2.
Local government finance, §§159-1 to 159-188.
See LOCAL GOVERNMENT FINANCE.
Manufactured home dealers.
Escrow or trust accounts.
Accounting by dealer, §143-143.53.
Marine fisheries commission.
Examination of accounts and books by state auditor, §113-257.
Missing persons.
Limitations on accounting, §28C-14.
Mortgage bankers, brokers and servicers.
Escrow accounts, §53-244.105(d).
Mortgage broker duties, §53-244.109.
Mortgage servicer duties, §53-244.110.
Prohibited acts, §53-244.111.
Trust accounts, §53-244.105(d).
Mortgages and deeds of trust.
Sales under power of sale.
Clerk to audit account and record, §45-21.33(b).
Trustees of deed of trust.
Assignment of benefit of creditors.
Accounting of property, §23-2.
Motor carriers, §62-269.
Mutual, open and current account.
Action upon, §1-31.
Naval militia.
Accounting officer, §127A-71.
Rendition of accounts, §127A-72.
Oil pollution and hazardous substances discharges.
Expenses of agencies for removal, §143-215.86(e).
Open accounts.
Accrual of action to recover balance due, §1-31.
Partnerships.
Formal account, right of partners, §59-52.
Surviving partners.
Compelling accounting, §59-83.
Duty to account and settle, §59-82.
Power of attorney.
Durable power of attorney.
Incapacity or incompetency of principal.
Filing annual and final accounts, §32A-11(b).
Principal and income act.
Allocation of receipts during administration of trust.
Separate accounting for business and other activities, §37A-4-403.
Prisons and prisoners.
Trustee for estate of debtor, §23-20.

ACCOUNTS AND ACCOUNTING —Cont'd
Public warehousemen.
Books of account, §66-39.
Referees meetings.
Statement of accounts, §1A-1 Rule 53(f).
Rescue squad workers' relief fund, §58-88-15.
Retail installment sales.
Statement of account.
Additional statements, §25A-35(b).
Annual statement, §25A-35(a).
Income tax purposes, information request for.
Seller to provide such information, §25A-35(c).
Savings banks.
Deposit accounts, §54C-164.
Generally accepted accounting principles,
§54C-161.
Joint accounts, §54C-165.
Personal agency accounts, §54C-167.
Schools.
Accounting system, §115C-440.
Annual independent audit, §115C-447.
Budgetary accounting for appropriations,
§115C-441.
Septage management account, §130A-291.1(e3).
Small claim actions.
Form of complaint on account, §7A-232.
Small estates.
Savings accounts.
Collection of property by affidavits.
Transfer of ownership rights on presentation
of affidavit, §28A-25-1(c).
Soil and water conservation districts.
Annual audit, §139-7.
Solid waste management.
Regional solid waste management authorities.
Fiscal accountability, §153A-428(a).
Southern growth policies agreement.
Board, §143-497(d), (e), (f).
Spay/neuter account, §19A-62.
Distributions to counties and cities, §19A-64.
Eligibility for distributions, §19A-63.
Special proceedings.
Commissioner of sale to account, §1-406.
Special registration plate account, §20-79.7(b),
(c).
State departments and agencies.
Expenditures for departments and institutions,
§143-154.
Fiscal year, §147-85.
Investigations and audits, §143-157.
Statewide accounts receivable program,
§§147-86.20 to 147-86.27.
State emergency response account, §166A-6.02.
State treasurer.
Fiscal year, §147-85.
Office of treasurer declared office of deposit and
disbursement, §147-74.
Pool accounts for local government unemployment
compensation, §147-86.1.
Separate funds.
Accounts of funds kept separate, §147-82.
Statewide accounts receivable program.
State departments and agencies, §§147-86.20 to
147-86.27.
See STATEWIDE ACCOUNTS RECEIVABLE
PROGRAM.
Superior courts.
Clerks of court.
Fees and other receipts, §7A-108.
Transfers to minors.
Accounting by and determination of liability of
custodian, §33A-19.

ACCOUNTS AND ACCOUNTING —Cont'd
Trust companies.
Seizure by commissioner.
Administration of accounts, §53-383(c).
Trustees of deed of trust.
Assignment for benefit of creditors.
Accounting of property coming into hands,
§23-2.
Trusts and trustees.
Class in esse.
Sale of property held by, §41-11.1(l).
Common trusts funds.
Court accounting, §53-163.6.
Judicial proceedings involving trusts.
Accounting to clerk, §36C-2-208.
Trustee of a testamentary trust, §36C-2-209.
Unemployment compensation.
Training and employment account, §96-6.1(b).
Utilities commission.
Power to establish system of accounts, §62-35(a).
Veterans' guardianship act.
Filing accounts, §34-10.
Failure to file, §34-11.
Cause for removal, §34-11.
Hearing on accounts, §34-10.
Wastewater treatment.
Certification of water pollution control system
operator.
Establishment of water pollution control system
account, §90A-42(b).
Water and air resources.
Department of environment and natural
resources.
Accounts established within, §143-215.3A(a) to
(b1).
Wildlife conservation account, §143-247.2.
Year.
Fiscal year, §147-85.

ACCOUNTS RECEIVABLE.
Statewide accounts receivable program.
State departments and agencies, §§147-86.20 to
147-86.27.
See STATEWIDE ACCOUNTS RECEIVABLE
PROGRAM.

ACCRUAL OF ACTIONS.
Actions generally.
See ACTIONS.
**Action upon mutual, open and current
account,** §1-31.
Fraud or mistake, relief on ground of, §1-52.
Limitation of actions generally.
See LIMITATION OF ACTIONS.
**Personal injury or physical damage to
claimant's property,** §1-52.
Wrongful death actions, §1-53.

ACCRUAL OF INTEREST.
Time from which interest runs, §24-3.

ACETYLENE HEADLAMPS.
**Vehicles eligible for historic vehicle owner
special registration,** §20-132.

ACID-FREE (ALKALINE) PAPER.
**State publications of historical and enduring
value.**
Compliance with requirement, monitoring,
§125-11.13(b).
Designation of publications on annual basis,
§125-11.13(a), (b).
Identification that publication printed on
permanent paper, §125-11.13(a).

ACID-FREE (ALKALINE) PAPER —Cont'd
State publications of historical and enduring value —Cont'd
Notice to agencies responsible for publishing designated titles, §125-11.13(b).
Report as to titles designated for printing on alkaline paper, §125-11.13(c).
Required to be printed on, §§125-11.13(a), 143-170.5.
Responsibility of agency to print on alkaline paper, §125-11.13(b).

ACIDS.
Malicious throwing, §14-30.1.
Municipal regulation of corrosive substances, §160A-183.

ACKNOWLEDGMENTS.
Banks.
Stockholders, officers or directors, §47-93.
Building and loan associations.
Officers or stockholders, §47-94.
Child support agreement.
Filing fees, §110-134.
Paternity acknowledged, §110-132.
Clerk of superior court.
Party, validation, §47-106.
Seal of clerk omitted, validation, §47-53.1.
Clerk's certificate.
Form.
Upon probate by justice of peace or magistrate, §47-44.
Upon probate by nonresident official without seal, §47-45.
Clerk's seal omitted, §47-86.
Clerks without seals, §47-99.
Commissioners of the United States.
Validation of instruments acknowledged before, §47-108.12.
Conditional sales or leases of railroad property, §47-24.
Consuls.
Probate of deeds before consular or agents of the United States, §47-91.
Consuls general, §47-83.
Vice-consuls and vice-consuls general, §47-84.
Conveyances.
Certification of correctness.
Failure of register of deeds to certify.
Validation of registration, §47-50.1.
Defective acknowledgment on old instruments validated, §47-52.
Corporations.
Admission to record of certain corporate deeds declared valid, §47-108.1.
By president and attested by treasurer under corporate seal, §47-70.
Forms for probate of deeds and other conveyances, §47-41.01(b), (c).
Interested corporations.
Probates before officer, §47-63.
Probates before officers, stockholders or directors of corporations prior to January 1, 1945, §47-64.
Proof of corporate articles before officer authorized to probate, §47-75.
Validation of corporate deeds containing error and acknowledgment, §47-97.1.
Curative statutes.
See CURATIVE ACTS AND STATUTES.
Deeds, §47-17.
Certification of correctness.
Failure of register of deeds to certify.
Validation of registration, §47-50.1.

ACKNOWLEDGMENTS —Cont'd
Deeds —Cont'd
Corporations.
Forms for probate of deeds and other conveyances, §47-41.01(b), (c).
Defective acknowledgment on old deeds validated, §47-52.
Defective certification or adjudication of clerk, etc., admitting to registration, §47-49.
Defined, §10B-3.
Deputy clerks.
Before deputy clerks of courts of other states, §47-79.
Validation of acts, §47-108.7.
Division of motor vehicles.
Power to acknowledge signatures, §20-42(a).
Durable power of attorney.
Substitution of attorney-in-fact, §32A-12(b).
Electronic signature or record, §66-321.
Federal, foreign or sister state officials authorized to take, §47-2.
Fee for taking acknowledgment, §161-10(a).
Fee of magistrate for proving, §7A-309.
Forms.
Acknowledgment by grantor, §47-38.
Husband's and wife's or other grantor's acknowledgment before same officer, §47-38.
Clerk's certificate.
Upon probate by justice of peace or magistrate, §47-44.
Upon probate by nonresident official without seal, §47-45.
Husband's and wife's or other grantor's acknowledgment before same officer, §47-40.
Power of attorney.
Certificate of acknowledgment of instrument executed by attorney in fact, §47-43.
Grantors.
Form, §47-38.
Husband's and wife's or other grantor's acknowledgment before same officer, §47-38.
Handwriting.
Proof of handwriting of maker refusing to acknowledge, §47-57.
Husband and wife.
Absence of wife does not affect deed as to husband, §39-9.
Before different officers, §39-8.
Before same officer.
Form, §47-40.
Different times and places, §39-8.
Fraud.
Certain conveyances not affected by fraud, §39-11.
Order immaterial, §39-8.
Powers of attorney.
Acknowledgment of spouse of grantor unnecessary, §39-12.
Leases, §47-17.
Liens.
Discharge of lien.
Filing acknowledgments, §44-48.
Limitation of actions.
Party to obligation, co-obligor or guarantor.
Effect of acknowledgment by, §1-27(a).
Marriage settlements and other contracts, §47-25.
Military officers.
Validation of instrunments acknowledged by officers of certain ranks, §47-2.1.

ACKNOWLEDGMENTS —Cont'd
Nonprofit associations.
Agent for service of process.
Signature and acknowledgment of appointment, §59B-11(c).
Notarial certificate.
Acknowledgment of principal acting in own right or representative capacity.
Form, §10B-41(a).
Requirements for acceptance, §10B-40(b).
When printed or typed name of notary not required, §10B-41(c).
Notaries public.
Acknowledgment omitting seal of notary.
Validation, §47-53.1.
Authority to perform, §10B-20(a).
Electronic notaries, §10B-115.
Electronic notaries.
Authority to perform, §10B-115.
Fee charged, §10B-118.
Fee charged, §10B-31.
Electronic notaries, §10B-118.
Powers.
Underage notaries, §47-108.
Taken by recommissioned notary who failed to take oath.
Validation, §10B-71.
Partnerships.
Limitation of actions.
Effect of acknowledgment by partner, §59-39.1.
Paternity.
Child support agreement, §110-132.
Filing fee, §110-134.
Power of attorney.
Durable power of attorney.
Substitution of attorney-in-fact, §32A-12(b).
Execution and acknowledgment of instrument, §47-43.1.
Certificate of acknowledgment of instrument executed by attorney in fact.
Form, §47-43.
Prior certificates, §47-48.
Railroad equipment or rolling stock.
Sale, lease or loan on condition title remain in vendor, lessor or bailor until paid for, §47-24.
Registers of deeds.
Fee for taking acknowledgment, §161-10(a).
Savings and loan associations.
Officer or stockholder in association, §47-94.
Seal of clerk or notary omitted.
Validation, §47-53.1.
Secured transactions.
Filing office.
Filing of written record, §25-9-523(a).
Timeliness of acknowledgment, §25-9-523(e).
Perfection of security interests.
Possession by secured party to perfect, §25-9-313(f), (g).
Self authentication of acknowledged documents, §8C-1 Rule 902.
State officers authorized to proof or acknowledge instruments, §47-1.
Superior courts.
Clerks of court.
Authority of clerk to take acknowledgment, §7A-103.
Trademarks.
Assignment of registration.
Acknowledgment as prima facie evidence, §80-6(d).

ACKNOWLEDGMENTS —Cont'd
Uniform unincorporated nonprofit association act.
Agent for service of process.
Signature and acknowledgment of appointment, §59B-11(c).
Who authorized to take, §47-2.

ACQUIRED IMMUNE DEFICIENCY SYNDROME.
See AIDS AND HIV.

ACTIONS.
Abandoned manufactured homes.
Identification, deconstruction, recycling, disposal.
Recovery of disposal costs incurred by county for, §130A-309.114(c).
Abortion.
Woman's right to know act.
Attorneys' fees and costs, §90-21.88(c).
Privacy protection in court proceedings, §90-21.89.
Right of action for damages, §90-21.88(a).
Absentees in military service.
Receivers.
Powers to bring and defend actions, §28B-6.
Release from duties, limitation of actions, §28B-8.
Access to civil justice act, §§7A-474.1 to 7A-474.5.
See LEGAL SERVICES PROGRAMS.
Access to judicial proceeding or record.
Effect of provision on other laws, §1-72.1(f).
Effect of provision on other types of relief, §1-72.1(g).
Motion to determine, §1-72.1(a).
Procedures upon filing of motion, §1-72.1(b).
Ruling on motion, §1-72.1(c).
Sealing of document or testimony, §1-72.1(d).
Service of motion, §1-72.1(b).
Status of movant, §1-72.1(a).
Access to public records.
Compelling, §132-9.
Accrual of actions, §1-15.
Adoption.
Failure to disclose nonidentifying information.
Civil action for equitable or monetary relief, §48-10-104.
Unauthorized disclosure of identifying information.
Civil action for equitable or monetary relief, §48-10-105(d).
Visitation of adopted grandchild.
Action by biological grandparent, §50-13.2A.
Adult care homes.
Residents' bill of rights, §131D-28.
Collection of penalty for violation, §131D-34(g).
Instituting civil actions, §131D-28.
Agricultural finance authority.
Power to sue and be sued, §122D-6.
Agriculture fees and taxes.
Suits to prevent collection prohibited, §106-9.6.
Agritourism activity liability, §§99E-30 to 99E-32.
Air pollution control.
Failure to pay penalties, §143-215.114A(f).
Alarm systems licensing.
Licensee's failure to pay penalties, §74D-11(e).
Proof of licensure by alarm system business.
Required to maintain action, §74D-14.
Alienation of affection, §52-13.
Limitation of action, §52-13(b).

ACTIONS —Cont'd
Alienation of affection —Cont'd
Natural person as party, §52-13(c).
Permanent physical separation of spouse,
§52-13(a).
Aliens.
Suits against state, US Const Amd 11.
Alimony.
Maintenance of certain actions as independent
actions, §50-19(a).
Separate action during pendency, §50-19(b).
Without action, §50-16.10.
Ancient minerals claims.
Extinguished in certain counties, §§1-42.1 to
1-42.9.
Appeals.
See APPEALS.
Apportionment or redistricting.
State legislative or congressional districts.
Challenge to plan, §§1-81.1, 1-267.1, 120-2.3 to
120-2.5.
Three-judge panel, §1-267.1.
Arbitration and award.
Statewide court-ordered nonbinding arbitration in
certain civil actions.
Amount in controversy, §7A-37.1(c).
Arbitrators.
Immunity as judges from civil liability for
official conduct, §7A-37.1(e).
Fees, §7A-37.1(c1).
Findings of general assembly, §7A-37.1(a).
Implementation of procedure, §7A-37.1(d).
Supreme court.
Adoption of rules, §7A-37.1(b).
Supervising implementation and operation,
§7A-37.1(b).
Architects.
Civil penalty for violations of provisions,
§83A-16(b), (c).
Associations.
Suits by or against unincorporated associations,
§1-69.1(a).
Uniform unincorporated nonprofit association act,
§59B-7(e).
Association participation in official proceedings,
§59B-8(a).
Change in members or management, effect,
§59B-12.
Judgment or order against association, §59B-9.
Standing to assert claim, §59B-8(b).
Venue, §59B-13.
Athlete agents.
Civil remedies against for violations, §78C-100.
Attorney general.
Duties of attorney general as to civil litigation,
§114-6.
Attorneys at law.
Unauthorized practice of law.
Actions by private persons damaged by
unauthorized practice, §84-10.1.
Bailments.
Trespass committed during existence of bailment,
§99A-1.
Boat liens.
Action to regain possession of vessel, §44A-6.1(a).
Bond.
Action on bond generally, §§58-76-1 to 58-76-30.
See BONDS, SURETY.
Limitation of actions, §§1-50(a), 1-52.
Model payment and performance bond, §44A-27.
Prosecution bonds, §§1-109 to 1-112.

ACTIONS —Cont'd
Bond —Cont'd
Satisfaction.
Defendant may plead satisfaction, §1-60.
Budget of state.
Civil liability for violations, §143C-10-2.
Non-state entities receiving state funds.
Actions to recover state funds, §143C-6-22(c).
Business trusts.
Authority to sue and be sued, §39-45.
Business under assumed name.
Recovery in civil action not prevented for
violations, §66-71(b).
Cable television.
State franchising of cable television service.
Forfeiture of franchise, §66-354(b).
PEG channel availability and use.
Action to compel compliance, §66-357(g).
Theft, §14-118.5.
Campaign contributions and expenditures.
Civil remedies other than penalties,
§163-278.34(c).
District attorney, notifying and consulting with,
§163-278.34(f).
Collection of penalty, §163-278.34(e).
Late filing penalty, §163-278.34(a1).
Carriers.
Joinder of causes of action, §62-205.
Lost or damaged goods.
Generally, §§62-203, 62-204.
Rights against prior carrier, §62-206.
Change of venue, §§1-83 to 1-87.
Charitable solicitation.
Enforcement actions, §§131F-23(c), 131F-24.
Charitable trusts.
Enforcement of trust by settlor, §36C-4-405.1(a),
(b).
**Child care provider criminal history record
check.**
Disagreement with department's decision,
§110-90.2(d).
Child custody or visitation, §§50-13.1, 50-13.5.
Attorneys' fees, §50-13.6.
**Childhood vaccine-related injury
compensation.**
Right of state to bring action, §130A-430(a).
Child labor violations.
Civil penalty, §95-25.23(b).
Child support, §§50-13.4, 50-13.5.
Attorneys' fees, §50-13.6.
Independent actions for divorce.
Maintenance of certain actions as independent
actions permissible, §50-19.
Chop shops.
Private actions, §14-72.7(d).
Civil no-contact orders.
Workplace violence prevention, §§95-260 to
95-271.
See WORKPLACE VIOLENCE PREVENTION.
Civil rights, interference with, §99D-1(b) to (c).
Claim and delivery of personal property.
Recovery of personal property, §1-230.
Claims against the state.
False claims act, §1-608.
Generally, §§1-605 to 1-631.
See FALSE CLAIMS ACT.
Liability, §1-607.
Procedure generally, §1-615.
Retaliation for lawful acts done to prevent
violations.
Private right of action, §1-613.

ACTIONS —Cont'd
Claims against the state —Cont'd
False claims act —Cont'd
State proceeding with action brought by private person, §1-609.
Statute of limitations, §1-615(a).
Class actions, §1A-1 Rule 23(a).
Tax refunds, §105-241.18.
Class in esse.
Special proceeding to sell, lease or mortgage property held by.
Membership subject to increase by persons not in esse, §41-11.1.
Coal and petroleum suppliers.
Stocks of coals and petroleum fuel capacity, §143-345.14(e).
Collection agencies.
Civil liability for violations, §58-70-130.
Special requirements in actions by agency plaintiffs, §§58-70-145 to 58-70-155.
Commercial real estate broker lien act.
Enforcement of lien, §44A-24.8.
Complaint, parties, §44A-24.9.
Costs, §44A-24.12.
Commissioner of banks.
Nonliability to suit, §53-94.
Power to sue and defend, §53-94.
Commodities, §78D-22(a).
Community college board of trustees.
Tort actions against, §115D-58.12(b), (c), (d).
Community college construction contract claim.
Contract completed, contractor dissatisfied with director's decision, §143-135.6(c).
Condominiums.
Breach of warranty.
Limitation of action, §47C-4-116.
Tort or contract liability.
Owners' association and declarant, §47C-3-111.
Consolidated city-county act.
Assumption of debt.
Action to set aside referendum, §160B-19(i).
Constitution of North Carolina.
Civil cases.
Jury trial, NC Const Art I §25.
Form of action, NC Const Art IV §13.
Constitution of the United States.
Actions to which United States a party, US Const Art III §2.
Contracts for deed.
Title requirements for executing contract.
Violations, purchaser's remedies, §47G-6(c).
Violations of chapter, purchaser's remedies, §47G-8.
Contracts with forum selection provisions.
Void as against public policy, §22B-3.
Contracts to improve real property, §22B-2.
Contribution among joint tort-feasors, §§1B-1 to 1B-7.
Enforcement, §1B-3.
Release or covenant not to sue, §1B-4.
Controlled substance examination and screening of employees.
Recovery of civil penalty imposed, §95-234(b).
Corporations.
Actions against directors of public corporations, §55-7-48.
Derivative actions, §§1A-1 Rule 23(b), 55-7-40 to 55-7-49.
Drainage.
Payment of bonds authorized, §156-53.

ACTIONS —Cont'd
Corporations —Cont'd
Foreign corporations.
Failure to obtain certificate of authority, §55-15-02(a).
Indemnification.
Business corporations, §§55-8-50 to 55-8-58.
Nonprofit corporations, §§55A-8-50 to 55A-8-58.
Nonprofit corporations.
Corporations already in existence, §55A-17-03(b).
Creditors action against member, §55A-6-24.
Derivative actions, §55A-7-40.
Judicial dissolution, §§55A-14-30 to 55A-14-33.
Power to sue and be sued, §55A-3-02(a).
Voluntary dissolution.
Claims against dissolved corporations, §55A-14-09(a).
Savings provisions, §55-17-03(b).
Costs.
General provisions, §§6-1 to 6-62.
See COSTS.
Counties.
Damages.
Suits against counties involving governmental functions, §153A-435(a), (b).
Defense of employees and officers, §160A-167.
Delinquent officials.
Retention of county funds.
Citizen to recover funds, §128-10.
Inspection departments.
Failure to take corrective action, §153A-368.
Outdoor advertising.
Regulation of nonconforming off-premises outdoor advertising.
Payment of monetary compensation for removal.
Determination, §153A-143(f).
Riparian owners.
Venue for actions, §153A-288.
Special assessments for critical infrastructure needs.
Challenge of validity of assessment, §153A-210.3(c).
County alcoholic beverage control board.
Defense of employees and officers, §160A-167.
Credit device fraud.
Civil action for damages, §14-113.6(c).
Credit unions.
Power to sue and be sued, §54-109.21.
Crime victims.
Compensation.
Claimant's action for damages.
Notice to commission, attorney general's duties, §15B-16(c).
Recovery of profits or funds, §15B-34(a).
Commission, responsibilities of, §15B-34(c).
Criminal acts.
Civil actions seeking to recover damages.
Statutes of limitation and repose, §1-15.1.
Criminal conversation, §52-13.
Limitation of action, §52-13(b).
Natural person as party, §52-13(c).
Permanent physical separation of spouse, §52-13(a).
Criminal street gangs.
Civil actions based on conduct.
Effect of conviction for criminal gang activity, §14-50.26.
Cruelty to animals.
Civil remedies, §§19A-1 to 19A-4.

ACTIONS —Cont'd
Dam safety law.
Civil penalties, §143-215.36(b).
Debt buyer plaintiffs filing.
Attachments to complaint required, §58-70-150.
Debt collectors.
Liability in private actions, §75-56(b).
Debtors.
Joint and several debtors, §§1-113, 1-114.
Decedents' estates.
Collectors for estates.
Power to maintain and defend actions,
§28A-11-3(a).
Federal estate tax and generation-skipping tax
referenced.
Construction of formula provisions in trusts.
Proceeding to determine settlor's intention,
§36C-1-113(d).
Construction of formula provisions in wills.
Proceeding to determine settlor's intention,
§31-46.1(d).
Powers of personal representatives or fiduciaries,
§28A-13-3(a).
Recovery of estate property, §28A-15-12(a1) to (d).
Survival of actions, §28A-18-1(a).
Actions in favor of decedent which do not
survive, §28A-18-1(b).
Transfers or conveyances by decedent to defraud
creditors.
Actions by personal representative to recover,
§28A-15-10.
Declaratory judgments, §§1-253 to 1-267.
See DECLARATORY JUDGMENTS.
Defamation.
See DEFAMATION.
Definitions.
Civil action, §1-6.
Criminal action, §1-5.
Generally, §1-2.
Kinds of actions, §1-4.
Special proceedings, §1-3.
Department of health and human services.
Costs to be paid by persons admitted to
institutions, §§143-117 to 143-127.1.
See HEALTH AND HUMAN SERVICES
DEPARTMENT.
**Derivative actions, §§1A-1 Rule 23(b), 55-7-40 to
55-7-49.**
Disabled persons.
Civil actions for discriminatory practices,
§§168A-11, 168A-12.
**Discharge of employee for lawful use of lawful
products during nonworking hours,**
§95-28.2(e).
Discrimination in business.
Enforcement of provisions, §75B-4.
Dismissal, discontinuance and nonsuit.
See DISMISSAL, DISCONTINUANCE AND
NONSUIT.
Divorce.
General provisions.
See DIVORCE.
Dogs.
Dangerous dogs.
Strict liability.
Injuries or property damage, §67-4.4.
Domestic violence.
Institution of civil action, §50B-2(a).
Who may institute, §50B-2(a).
Drainage corporations.
Payment of bonds authorized, §156-53.
Payment of bonds enforced, §156-53.

ACTIONS —Cont'd
Drainage districts.
Bondholder's remedy, §156-99.
Dredging permits, §113-229.
Droughts.
Local government failure to implement
conservation measures.
Unpaid penalties, recovery, §143-355.6(c3).
Drugs law violations.
Employing or intentionally using minor to commit
drug law violations, §90-95.5.
Dry-cleaning solvent cleanup.
Collection of unpaid civil penalties,
§143-215.104P(f).
Reimbursement for cost of remediation of
uncertified site, §143-215.104O(b), (c).
Education of children with disabilities.
Civil action by party without right to appeal or
person aggrieved by review officer's decision,
§115C-109.9(d).
Elections.
State board of elections.
Authority to assist in litigation, §163-25.
**Electrical materials, devices, appliances and
equipment sales, §66-27.01.**
Electrologists.
Reports of violations of chapter.
Immunity from suit, §88A-23.
Venue for actions brought under chapter,
§88A-22(b).
**Electronic filing of pleadings and other
documents, §7A-49.5.**
Electronic surveillance.
Civil cause of action for violation of article.
Damages authorized, §15A-296.
Emancipation of juvenile.
Generally, §§7B-3500 to 7B-3509.
See EMANCIPATION.
Right to sue and be sued as adult, §7B-3507.
Embezzlement.
Civil liability, §1-538.2(a) to (d).
Eminent domain.
Generally.
See EMINENT DOMAIN.
Employee assistance professionals.
Civil action to enforce article, §90-506(a).
Employee drug screening.
Recovery of civil penalty imposed, §95-234(b).
Employee theft, §1-538.2(a) to (d).
**Employer discrimination for lawful use of
lawful products during nonworking hours,**
§95-28.2(e).
Employment security.
Claims for benefits, §96-15.
Equine activity liability.
Limiting and preventing liability generally,
§§99E-1 to 99E-3.
Established legal services programs.
Access to civil justice act, §§7A-474.1 to 7A-474.5.
Excise stamp tax.
Recoverable by action, §105-228.33.
Execution sales.
Defective title.
Remedy of purchaser against defendant, §1-323.
Executors and administrators.
Generally.
See EXECUTORS AND ADMINISTRATORS.
Expedited evictions.
Defendants to action, §42-62(b).
Nature of cause of action of landlord, §42-60.
Standard of proof, §42-61.

ACTIONS —Cont'd
Expedited evictions —Cont'd
Who may bring action, §42-62(a).
Expenses of litigation.
See COSTS.
Facility authorities.
Powers of authority, §160A-480.4.
Facsimile solicitations.
Unsolicited facsimiles, §75-118(a).
Costs and fees, §75-118(b).
Federal remedies not affected, §75-118(d).
Venue, §75-118(c).
Fair housing, §41A-7(h) to (k).
False claims act.
False or fraudulent claims against the state,
§1-608.
Generally, §§1-605 to 1-631.
See FALSE CLAIMS ACT.
Liability, §1-607.
Procedure generally, §1-615.
Retaliation for lawful acts done to prevent
violations.
Private right of action, §1-613.
State proceeding with action brought by private
person, §1-609.
Statute of limitations, §1-615(a).
False pretenses and cheats.
Civil liability for obtaining property by,
§1-538.2(a) to (d).
**Federal estate tax and generation-skipping tax
referenced.**
Construction of formula provisions in trusts.
Proceeding to determine settlor's intention,
§36C-1-113(d).
Construction of formula provisions in wills.
Proceeding to determine settlor's intention,
§31-46.1(d).
Felony, forfeiture of gain, §14-2.3(b).
Fiduciaries.
Claims against estate or trust.
Powers which may be incorporated by reference
in trust instrument, §32-27.
**Fire-safety standard and firefighter protection
act.**
Civil actions for violations, §58-92-30(f).
Foreign-country money judgments.
Recognition.
Raising issue in original matter, §1C-1855(a).
Statute of limitation, §1C-1858.
Forfeiture of gain from felony, §14-2.3(b).
Forms of action.
Civil actions, NC Const Art IV §13.
One form of action, §1A-1 Rule 2.
Forum selection.
Contracts with forum selection provisions.
Void and unenforceable, §22B-3.
Contracts to improve real property, §22B-2.
Freedom of information.
Compelling disclosure of public records, §132-9.
Frivolous actions.
Inmates presenting frivolous complaints.
Court determination, dismissal, §1-110(b).
Gain from felony, forfeiture, §14-2.3(b).
Grain dealers.
Action on bond, §106-605(b).
Guardian's powers.
Administering incompetent's estate, §35A-1251.
Administering minor ward's estate, §35A-1252.
Hazardous materials emergency response.
Action for recovery of costs, §166A-27.
Response of emergency medical personnel, costs,
§130A-20.01.

ACTIONS —Cont'd
Health.
Forfeiture of money or property unlawfully
acquired, §130A-28.
Recovery of money or property, §130A-27.
Health benefit plans.
Negligent decisions of plan providers, §§90-21.50
to 90-21.56.
See HEALTH CARE LIABILITY.
Health care facilities.
Certificate of public advantage.
Decisions on issuing or allowing to remain in
effect, §131E-192.10(a) to (d).
Highways, roads and streets.
Condemnation, §§136-103 to 136-121.1.
See HIGHWAYS, ROADS AND STREETS.
County public roads incorporated into state
highway system.
No court action against board of transportation,
§136-59.
Home foreclosure rescue scams, §75-122.
Housing authorities and projects.
Remedies of obligee, §§157-18 to 157-22.
Husband and wife.
Quieting title, §41-10.
Torts between husband and wife, §52-5.
Acts arising outside state, §52-5.1.
Identity theft, §1-539.2C.
Illegitimate children, support.
When prosecution may be commenced, §49-4.
Indigent persons.
Access to civil justice act, §§7A-474.1 to 7A-474.5.
See LEGAL SERVICES PROGRAMS.
Affidavit that person unable to advance court
costs.
Required to sue as indigent, §1-110(a).
Courts may authorize person to sue as indigent,
§1-110(a).
Criteria for meeting status as indigent, §1-110(a).
Dismissal of case and charge of court costs.
Allegations in affidavit untrue, §1-110(a).
Inmates filing pro se motion to proceed as
indigent, §1-110(b).
Complaint frivolous, determination by court,
dismissal, §1-110(b).
Insurance.
Agents.
Soliciting agent represents the company,
§58-58-30.
Unauthorized insurers.
Soliciting, negotiating or selling insurance for,
§58-33-95(b).
Brokers.
Unauthorized insurers.
Soliciting, negotiating or selling insurance for,
§58-33-95(b).
Consumer and customer information privacy.
Action by individual for violations, §58-39-105.
Deposits held in trust by commissioner or
treasurer.
Foreign or alien insurance companies.
Enforcing or terminating trust, §58-5-90(c).
False statement to procure or deny benefit of
policy or certificate, §58-2-161(b).
Foreign or alien insurance company deposit liens,
§58-5-70.
Fraud.
False statement to procure or deny benefit of
policy or certificate, §58-2-161(b).
Interstate insurance product regulation compact.
Enforcement, §58-91-40(d).

ACTIONS —Cont'd
Insurance —Cont'd
Interstate insurance product regulation compact
—Cont'd
Indemnification, immunity, and defense of
commission, §58-91-25(e).
Limited representatives.
Unauthorized insurers.
Soliciting, negotiating or selling insurance for,
§58-33-95(b).
Policies or contracts.
Conditions or stipulations.
Court or jurisdiction for bringing action or
suit.
Prohibited, §58-3-35(a).
Prohibited conditions or stipulations void,
§58-3-35(c).
Time for bringing action or suit.
Less than period prescribed by law,
prohibited, §58-3-35(b).
Soliciting agent represents the company,
§58-58-30.
Supervision, rehabilitation and liquidation of
insurers.
Rehabilitation.
Actions by and against rehabilitator,
§58-30-90.
Surplus lines insurer.
Actions against, §58-21-100.
Unauthorized insurers, §58-28-15.
Transacting business.
Action for violations instituted by attorney
general, §58-28-13(k).
**Interlocal agreements concerning economic
development.**
Binding effect, action to specifically enforce,
§158-7.4(c).
International banking.
Actions against international banking
corporations, §53-232.7.
Interstate family support.
Minor parent, §52C-3-302.
Inverse condemnation, §40A-51.
Investment advisers.
Civil liabilities for violations, §78C-38.
Jail keepers causing injuries to prisoners,
§162-55.
Joint and several debtors, §§1-113, 1-114.
**Journalist's qualified privilege against
disclosure in any legal proceeding, §8-53.11.**
Judgments and decrees.
Declaratory judgments, §§1-253 to 1-267.
See DECLARATORY JUDGMENTS.
Foreign-country money judgments.
Recognition.
Raising issue in original matter, §1C-1855(a).
Statute of limitation, §1C-1858.
Generally.
See JUDGMENTS AND DECREES.
Limitation of actions.
Periods prescribed generally, §1-46.
Ten-year limitation, §1-47.
Judicial sales.
Party to action by purchaser, §1-62.
Jurisdiction generally, §§1-75.1 to 1-75.12.
See JURISDICTION.
**Jury duty, discharge of employee called to
serve, §9-32(b), (c).**
Kinds of actions, §1-4.
Landlord and tenant.
Expedited evictions, §§42-60 to 42-62.

ACTIONS —Cont'd
Landlord and tenant —Cont'd
Lien on crops.
Disputes between parties, §42-17.
Residential rental agreements.
Rights and remedies enforceable by civil action,
§42-44(a).
Security deposit, recovery, §42-55.
**Law enforcement peer support group
counselor's privilege, §8-53.10.**
**Leave for parent involved in school, discharge
of employee, §95-28.3(c).**
Legal expense funds for elected officials,
§§163-278.300 to 163-278.320.
See LEGAL EXPENSE FUNDS FOR ELECTED
OFFICIALS.
Legal services of North Carolina, Inc.
Access to civil justice act, §§7A-474.1 to 7A-474.5.
See LEGAL SERVICES PROGRAMS.
Libel and slander.
Generally.
See DEFAMATION.
Liens.
Commercial real estate broker lien act.
Enforcement of lien, §44A-24.8.
Complaint, parties, §44A-24.9.
Costs, §44A-24.12.
Failure to commence action for enforcement.
Discharge of liens, §44-48.
Mechanics, laborers and materialmen dealing
with owner.
Enforcement of lien, §44A-13(a).
Possessory liens on personal property.
Action to regain possession of motor vehicle or
vessel, §44A-6.1(a).
Immediate possession of property.
Action by owner or person dealing with lienor,
§44A-4(a).
Motor vehicles or vessels.
Action to regain possession, §44A-6.1.
Storage charges.
Action on debt, §44A-4(a).
Limitation of actions.
See LIMITATION OF ACTIONS.
Limited liability companies.
Derivative actions by members, §57C-8-01.
Foreign limited liability companies.
Certificate of authority required to maintain
action or proceeding in court, §57C-7-03(a).
Members as parties to proceedings by or against
company, §57C-3-30(b).
Mergers, effect on pending proceedings,
§57C-9A-23(a).
Limited partnerships.
Suits by or against, §1-69.1(a).
Liquefied petroleum gas dealers.
Liability limitations, §119-62.
Lis pendens, §§1-116 to 1-120.2.
Litigation expenses.
See COSTS.
Livestock prompt pay law.
Failure of payment, §106-418.6.
Local boards of education.
Against board.
Burden of proof on complaining party,
§115C-44(b).
Order or action of board presumed correct,
§115C-44(b).
Breach of bond by treasurer of county school fund.
County commissioners to institute action,
§115C-44(a).

ACTIONS —Cont'd

Local boards of education —Cont'd

Defense of members and employees, §115C-43(a) to (c).

Recovery of money or property due board.

Board to institute action, §115C-44(a).

Tort or negligence action against board, §115C-42.

Local governmental employees' retirement system.

Deficiency in payment of benefits.

Commencement of action, §128-27(i).

Local government finance.

Bond issues.

Enforcement of contract of sale, §159-133.

Funding and refunding bonds.

Costs of actions validating bonds, §159-75.

Testing validity of funding or refunding bonds, §159-74.

Setting aside supplemental tax referendum, §159-97(d).

Local government officers and employees.

Defense of civil actions or proceedings, §160A-167.

Local governments.

Notice of claims against local units of government, §1-539.16.

Manufactured home manufacturers, dealers, salespersons or set-up contractors.

Buyer's action for violations, §143-143.12(c), (d).

Mediation.

Superior court civil cases.

Mediated settlement conferences, §7A-38.1.

Rules implementing,

SuperCtMediatedSettlemt Rules 1 to 15.

Medicaid.

False claims by providers, §§108A-70.12, 108A-70.13.

Objection to or failing to comply with civil investigative demand, §108A-70.14(i).

Medical expenses at issue.

Testimony of injured party as to medical expenses, §8-58.1.

Medical payments programs administered under chapter 130A.

Assignment to state of rights to third party benefits, §130A-13(a) to (d).

Mental health area authorities.

Defense of agents, employees and board members, §122C-153(a) to (d).

Waiver of governmental tort immunity.

Purchase of liability insurance, §122C-152(a) to (f).

Methamphetamine watch program.

Immunity from civil and criminal liability.

Good faith actions, §114-43.

Metropolitan sewerage districts.

Inclusion of additional political subdivision or unincorporated areas.

Limitation on action to set aside, §162A-68(f).

Militia.

Recovery of organization owned property, §127A-118.

Milk and milk products.

Milk distributors.

Liens on tangible and intangible assets, §44-69.3(e).

Sanitation violations.

Action to recover amount assessed as civil penalty, §130A-22(a).

Missing persons.

Receivers.

Power to bring or defend suits, §28C-8.

ACTIONS —Cont'd

Monopolies and restraint of trade.

Attorney general.

Mandatory order.

Action to obtain, §75-14.

Prosecution of civil actions generally, §75-15.

Attorneys' fees, §75-16.1.

Limitation of actions, §75-16.2.

Right of action by person injured, §75-16.

Mortgages and deeds of trust.

Consumer home loans.

Enforcement of section, §24-10.2(e).

Debt collection and servicing.

Remedies of borrower, §45-94.

Foreclosures.

Attacking certain foreclosures on ground trustee was agent, etc., of owner of debt.

Limitation of time for attacking, §45-21.39(a).

Reverse mortgages.

Actions by borrowers for damages, §53-271(d).

Trustee neither necessary or proper party, §45-45.3(c), (d).

Motion picture fair competition.

Enforcement of provisions, §75C-5.

Motor fuel marketing violations, §75-86.

Motor vehicle dealers, §20-308.1.

Motor vehicle liability insurance.

Uninsured and underinsured policy provisions, §20-279.21(b).

Motor vehicle repairs.

Remedies for violation of article, §20-354.9.

Motor vehicles.

Chop shops.

Private actions, §14-72.7(d).

Odometer violations, §20-348(b).

Limitation of actions, §20-348(b).

Possessory liens on personal property.

Action to regain possession, §44A-6.1(a).

Sublease and loan assumption arranging, §20-106.2(f).

Uninsured motorists, §20-279.21(b).

Mountain ridge protection.

Civil action against persons alleged in violation, §113A-211(b).

Municipalities.

Civil penalty, recovery, §160A-175(c).

Defense of employees and officers, §160A-167.

Effect of chapter upon prior laws, §160A-2.

Joint municipal electric power and energy act.

Bond issues.

Venue for actions relating to bonds or security for bonds, §159B-37.

Remedies of bondholders, §159B-19.

Notice of claims against local units of government, §1-539.16.

Outdoor advertising.

Regulation of nonconforming off-premises outdoor advertising.

Payment of monetary compensation.

Determination of compensation, §160A-199(f).

Power to sue and be sued, §160A-11.

Public officers.

Retention of funds of town by delinquent official.

Citizen to recover funds, §128-10.

Solar collectors, limitations on regulating.

Civil actions, §160A-201(d).

Zoning or unified development ordinance.

Validity, limitation of actions, §160A-364.1.

ACTIONS —Cont'd
Natural and scenic rivers system violations,
   §113A-42(a).
Negotiable instruments.
   Accrual of actions, §25-3-118.
   Limitation of actions, §25-3-118.
Nonprofit associations.
   Suits by or against, §1-69.1(a).
   Uniform unincorporated nonprofit association act,
      §59B-7(e).
      Association participation in official proceedings,
         §59B-8(a).
      Change in members or management, effect,
         §59B-12.
      Judgment or order against association, §59B-9.
      Standing to assert claim, §59B-8(b).
      Venue, §59B-13.
Nonprofit corporations.
   Corporations already in existence, §55A-17-03(b).
   Creditors action against member, §55A-6-24.
   Derivative actions, §55A-7-40.
   Judicial dissolution, §§55A-14-30 to 55A-14-33.
   Power to sue and be sued, §55A-3-02(a).
   Removal of director by judicial proceeding,
      §55A-8-10.
   Unlawful loans or distributions by directors,
      §55A-8-33.
   Voluntary dissolution.
      Claims against dissolved corporations,
         §55A-14-09(a).
Nonsuits.
   See DISMISSAL, DISCONTINUANCE AND
      NONSUIT.
Nuisances.
   Abatement generally.
      See NUISANCES.
Nursing homes.
   Administrative penalty, recovering, §131E-129(f).
   Medical directors of licensed homes.
      Limitation on liability, §90-21.18.
   Patient's bill of rights, §131E-123.
Odometer violations with intent to defraud,
   §20-348(b).
Oil and gas conservation.
   Department of environment and natural
      resources.
      Suits by department, §113-399.
   Landowner protection.
      Compensation for damages, §113-421(c).
         Provisions limiting access to court void and
            unenforceable, §113-421(d).
**Oil pollution and hazardous substances
   control.**
   Offshore oil and gas activities, §§143-215.94DD(b),
      (c), 143-215.94FF(b), (c).
   Removal of oil discharges.
      Limitation on liability of persons engaged in,
         §143-215.93A.
One form of action, §1A-1 Rule 2.
**Option to purchase contracts executed with
   residential lease agreements.**
   Violations.
      Option purchaser's remedies, §47G-7.
Ordinances.
   Recovery of civil penalty, §160A-175(c).
Parental authority over juvenile.
   Enforcement of parental authority, juvenile
      leaving home and refusing to return,
      §7B-3404.

ACTIONS —Cont'd
Parent and child.
   Malicious or willful destruction of property by
      minors.
      Action for recovery of damages from parents,
         §1-538.1.
   Negligent supervision of minor.
      Right of educational entity to recover against
         parents, §1-538.3.
Parking authorities.
   Allegations required in actions against authority,
      §160A-563.
Parties.
   See PARTIES.
Partition, §§46-1 to 46-44.
   See PARTITION.
Partnerships.
   Dissolution and winding up.
      Accrual of actions, §59-73.
   Parties to suits by or against partnerships,
      §1-69.1(a).
Paternity.
   Generally.
      See PATERNITY.
Pawnbrokers and cash converters.
   Bond, §91A-14.
Perpetuation of testimony, §1A-1 Rule 27(c).
Personal property.
   Interference with property rights.
      Recovery of damages, §99A-1.
   Recovery of personal property, §1-230.
Pesticides.
   Power of board to institute action in superior
      court, §143-461.
Planned community act.
   Tort and contract liability.
      Association and lot owners, §47F-3-111.
Pleadings.
   See PLEADINGS.
Principals or teachers.
   Allowance of counsel fees and costs in certain
      cases, §6-21.4.
Prisoners.
   Limitation of actions.
      Persons under disability on January 1, 1976 as
         result of being imprisoned.
         When statute commences to run, §1-17(a1).
   Pro se motion to proceed as indigent, §1-110(b).
      Frivolous complaint, determination by court,
         dismissal, §1-110(b).
Private personnel services.
   Overstated earnings expectations from employers.
      Fees reimbursement from employers due to,
         §95-47.3A(e).
Products liability, §§99B-1 to 99B-11.
Profit from felony, forfeiture, §14-2.3(b).
Prosecution bonds, §§1-109 to 1-112.
   Indigent, suit as, §1-110(a).
   Land actions.
      Defendant's bond for costs, §1-111.
         Plaintiff not entitled to recover, certification
            by attorney.
            Bond not required, §1-112(a).
         Summary ejectment.
            Bond not required, §1-112(b).
         Unable to give bond, not worth amount,
            affidavit by defendant.
            Bond not required, §1-112(a).
   Plaintiff's bond for costs, §1-109.
   Prisoners.
      Pro se motion to proceed as indigent, §1-110(b).

ACTIONS —Cont'd

Psychotherapy patient/client sexual exploitation act, §90-21.42.

Public contracts.

Adjustment and resolution of state construction contract claim.

Civil action by contractor on portion of claim denied, §143-135.3(d).

Contractors action on behalf of subcontractor, §143-134.2.

Public lands.

Attorney general, §§146-69, 146-70.

Grants.

Vacation of grants, §146-61.

State action, §146-63.

Institution of actions by state, §146-70.

Pending entries, §146-38.

Service of process on state in land actions, §146-69.

Public officers and employees.

Action to try title to office.

Quo warranto, §§1-514 to 1-532.

See QUO WARRANTO.

Counsel.

Employment of counsel in cases where state is interested, §147-17.

Describing party by official title rather than by name, §1A-1 Rule 25(f).

Improper government activities.

Reporting.

Civil actions for injunctive relief or remedies, §126-86.

Retention of funds of county or town by delinquent official.

Citizen to recover funds, §128-10.

Public records.

Compelling disclosure, §132-9.

Public warehousemen.

Bonds, surety.

Injured person may sue on bond, §66-37.

Quieting title, §41-10.

Quo warranto.

General provisions, §§1-514 to 1-532.

See QUO WARRANTO.

Radiation protection.

Expenses of state and local agencies, §104E-17.

Real estate brokers.

Commercial real estate lien.

Enforcement, §44A-24.8.

Complaint, parties, §44A-24.9.

Costs, §44A-24.12.

Real property.

Contracts to improve real property.

Provisions making contract subject to laws of another state.

Void as against public policy, §22B-2.

Defendant's bond for costs and damages in land actions, §§1-111, 1-112(a), (b).

Marketable title.

Prima facie evidence of title ownership, §47B-2(d).

Quieting title, §41-10.

Receivers.

Powers of receivers of corporations, §1-507.2.

Recorded device.

Owner's action, §14-436.

Relief from judgment or order, §1A-1 Rule 60(b).

Religious societies.

Power of trustees to sue and be sued, §61-2.

Remainders, reversions and executory interests.

Grantees of reversion and assigns of lease have reciprocal rights under covenants, §42-8.

ACTIONS —Cont'd

Rental referral agencies.

Damages from violations of provisions.

Action for damages, §66-146(a).

Action on bond, §66-145(c).

Repairs, remedies for violating article, §20-354.9.

Repeal of statute.

Actions not affected, §12-2.

Rescue squads.

Defense of employees or officers in civil or criminal actions, §160A-167.

Retaliatory employment discrimination, §95-243.

Right-to-sue letter, §95-242(a) to (c).

Retirement system for teachers and state employees.

Payment of benefits.

Commencement of actions, §135-5(n).

Right of access to judicial proceeding or record.

Appeal of ruling, §1-72.1(e).

Effect of provision on other laws, §1-72.1(f).

Effect of provision on other types of relief, §1-72.1(g).

Motion to determine, §1-72.1(a).

Procedures upon filing of motion, §1-72.1(b).

Ruling on motion, §1-72.1(c).

Sealing of document or testimony, §1-72.1(d).

Service of motion, §1-72.1(b).

Status of movant, §1-72.1(a).

Roller skating rink safety and liability, §§99E-10 to 99E-14.

Sale of merchandise by governmental units.

Aggrieved parties, actions by, §66-58(m).

Sales and use tax.

Overcollections by seller.

Cause of action against seller, notice required, §105-164.11(c).

Sales commission, §66-192(a).

Frivolous actions.

Liability, §66-192(b).

Savings banks.

Involuntary liquidation.

Commencement by attorney general, §54C-83(l).

School employees.

Defense of board of education members and employees, §115C-43(a) to (c).

Secondary action by shareholders, §1A-1 Rule 23(b).

Securities regulation.

Civil liabilities generally, §78A-56.

Manipulation of market, §78A-56(b1).

Shoplifting.

Civil liability, §1-538.2(a) to (d).

Skateboarding, inline skating and freestyle bicycling.

Assumption of inherent risks, limitation on liability, §§99E-21 to 99E-25.

Skier safety and skiing accidents, §§99C-1 to 99C-5.

Small claim actions, §§7A-210 to 7A-232.

See SMALL CLAIMS.

Soil and water conservation districts.

Invalidity of expenditures, §139-8.1(d).

Land-use regulations.

Enforcement, §§139-10, 139-11.

Special education.

Children with disabilities.

Civil action by party without right to appeal or person aggrieved by review officer's decision, §115C-109.9(d).

ACTIONS —Cont'd
State departments and agencies.
Deposit in unlawful depository.
Recovery of deposit, §147-80.
Executive organization act of 1973.
Pending actions and proceedings, §143B-19.
State treasurer.
Deposits in unlawful depository.
Recovery, §147-80.
May demand and sue for money and property of
state, §147-71.
Statutes of limitation.
See LIMITATION OF ACTIONS.
Strawberry plant sellers.
Collection of assessment owed association,
§106-785(d).
**Sublease of motor vehicles and loan
assumption arranging.**
Violations of provisions, §20-106.2(f).
Surety's recovery on obligation paid.
No assignment necessary, §26-3.1(a).
Construction of term "surety,"§26-3.1(b).
Taxation.
Class actions.
Refund of tax paid, §105-241.18.
Unconstitutional statute, §1A-1 Rule 23(d).
Constitutional challenge of tax statute,
§105-241.17.
Exclusivity of remedy, §105-241.19.
Extraterritorial authority to enforce payment,
§105-269.
Precedence over other civil actions, §105-246.
Property taxes.
Foreclosure of tax lien.
Action in nature of action to foreclose
mortgage, §105-374.
Public utilities.
Action for recovery of tax, §105-344.
Recovery of taxes by taxpayers, §105-381(c), (d).
Recovery of taxes, §105-243.
Refund of tax paid.
Class actions, §105-241.18.
Unconstitutional statute, §1A-1 Rule 23(d).
Suits in other state to enforce collection,
§105-269(a).
Teachers or principals.
Allowance of counsel fees and costs in certain
cases, §6-21.4.
Telephone solicitations.
Action by subscriber for violation, §75-105.
Theft by employees, §1-538.2(a) to (d).
Time share violations.
Right of action by person injured by, §93A-55.
Title.
Quieting title, §41-10.
Torrens system registration.
Adverse claims.
Limitation of action, §43-19.
Assurance fund.
Action for indemnity, §43-50.
Trade secrets.
Misappropriation.
Limitation of actions, §66-157.
Preservation of secrecy by court, §66-156.
Right of action, §66-153.
Transfer fee covenants.
Recording, liability, §39A-3(b).
Transportation department.
Enforcement of causes of action, §136-18.
Trespass.
Marketable title.
Prima facie evidence of title ownership,
§47B-2(d).

ACTIONS —Cont'd
Trust companies.
Liability of directors for violation of provisions.
Action by shareholder, §53-356(b).
Power of commissioner to bring actions, §53-413.
Trusts and trustees.
Attorneys' fees and costs, §36C-10-1004.
Breach of trust, §§36C-10-1001 to 36C-10-1009.
Charitable trusts.
Enforcement of trust by settlor, §36C-4-405.1(a),
(b).
Compensation of trustee.
Additional compensation allowed by court,
§36C-7-708.
Enforcement and defense of claims.
Duty of trustee, §36C-8-811.
Powers of trustee, §36C-8-816.
Exculpatory term relieving trustee of liability.
Enforceability, §36C-10-1008.
Federal estate tax and generation-skipping tax
referenced in trust.
Construction of formula provisions.
Proceeding to determine settlor's intention,
§36C-1-113(d).
Judicial proceedings involving trusts, §§36C-2-201
to 36C-2-209.
Limitation on trustee's personal liability,
§36C-10-1010.
Removal of trustee, §36C-7-705.
Revocable trusts.
Contesting validity, limitation of action,
§36C-6-604(a).
Termination, modification, combination or division
of trust, §36C-4-410.
Unauthorized practice of law.
Actions by private persons damaged by
unauthorized practice, §84-10.1.
Unclaimed property act.
By another state on behalf of state, §116B-76(d).
Enforcement of chapter by treasurer, §116B-75(a).
Establishment of claim to property, §116B-68.
Limitation of action, proceeding by treasurer to
enforce provisions, §116B-71(b).
On behalf of another state, §116B-76(c).
Underground storage tank leak cleanup.
Actions for fund reimbursement, §143-215.94G.
Groundwater protection loan fund.
Default or violation of loan agreement,
§143-215.94P(e).
Injunctive relief, §143-215.94Y.
Recovery of unpaid civil penalties by attorney
general, §143-215.94W(f).
Unemployment compensation.
Claims for benefits, §96-15.
Uniform contribution among tort-feasors,
§§1B-1 to 1B-6.
**Unincorporated associations, organizations,
etc.**
Suits by or against, §1-69.1(a).
Uniform unincorporated nonprofit association act,
§59B-7(e).
Association participation in official proceedings,
§59B-8(a).
Change in members or management, effect,
§59B-12.
Judgment or order against association, §59B-9.
Standing to assert claim, §59B-8(b).
Venue, §59B-13.
**Uninsured and underinsured policy
provisions,** §20-279.21(b).

ACTIONS —Cont'd
Unit ownership.
Common interests, §47A-26.
Exhaustion of remedies against association,
§47A-26.
Service of process on designated agent, §47A-26.
University of North Carolina.
Nuclear reactors.
Damage or personal property arising from
construction or operation of, §116-40.2.
Self-insurance.
Defense of suits or actions against covered
persons, §116-220(d).
Unsolicited facsimiles, §75-118(a).
Costs and fees, §75-118(b).
Federal remedies not affected, §75-118(d).
Venue, §75-118(c).
Urban redevelopment.
Obligee of commission, §160A-518.
Venue.
General provisions, §§1-76 to 1-87.
See VENUE.
Vessel liens.
Action to regain possession, §44A-6.1(a).
Veterans' recreation authorities.
Power to sue and be sued, §165-31.
Viatical settlements, §58-58-290(b).
Victims of crime.
Recovery of profits or funds, §15B-34(a).
Commission, responsibilities of, §15B-34(c).
Visitation.
Action or proceeding for custody or visitation,
§50-13.1.
Adopted grandchild, §50-13.2A.
Wages.
Recovery of unpaid wages, §95-25.22.
Water and air resources.
Civil penalties, §143-215.6A(g).
Water and sewer authorities.
Riparian owners.
Actions against authority by, §162A-18.
Wine distribution agreements.
Venue of actions under article, §18B-1207(d).
Violations of article by winery, §18B-1207(a).
Winter sports safety and accidents, §§99C-1 to
99C-5.
Witnesses.
Arrest in civil cases.
Exemptions, §8-64.
Fees of witnesses, §6-53.
Hearing impaired.
Appointment of interpreters authorized, §8B-2.
Women's credit rights.
Enforcement of article, §25B-3(a).
Workers' compensation.
Fines and penalties.
Collection by industrial commission, §97-101.
Insurance or proof of financial ability to pay
benefits.
Actions against employers failing to comply
with provisions, §97-95.
Workplace violence prevention.
Civil no-contact orders, §§95-260 to 95-271.
See WORKPLACE VIOLENCE PREVENTION.
Wrongful death.
Cause of action permitted, §28A-18-2.

ACTION TO PERPETUATE TESTIMONY, §1A-1
Rule 27(c).

ACTIVITY BUSES.
Defects, §115C-248(d).

ACTIVITY BUSES —Cont'd
Defined, §20-4.01.
Inspection, §115C-248(d).
Maximum speed, §20-218(b), (c).
Operating after consuming alcohol, §20-138.2B.
Proper use.
Policy adopted by local boards, §115C-247.
Purchase by local boards of education,
§§115C-47, 115C-247.
Stopping at railroad grade crossings,
§20-142.3(a).

ACTORS.
Children and minors.
Artistic and creative services and talent agency
contracts, §§48A-11 to 48A-18.
Youth employment exemption, §95-25.5(g).
Wage and hour act.
Exemptions, §95-25.14(a).

ACTS.
Coded bill drafting, §120-20.1.
Francis X. Martin.
Collection of private acts.
Evidence, §8-2.
General laws.
Defined, NC Const Art XIV §3.
Style of the acts, NC Const Art II §21.
When acts take effect, §120-20.

ACTS BARRING PROPERTY RIGHTS.
Adultery, §31A-1(a).
Killing decedent generally, §§31A-3 to 31A-15.
See SLAYER ACT.

ACTS BARRING RIGHTS OF PARENTS,
§31A-2.

ACTUARIES.
Insurance.
Property and casualty actuarial opinions,
§§58-10-150 to 58-10-175.
See CASUALTY INSURANCE.
Insurance commissioner hiring qualifications,
§58-2-171.
Legislative actuarial notes.
Amendments in law relative to retirement system,
§120-114.
Citation of act, §120-112.
Generally, §120-114.
Research division of legislative services
commission.
Duties, §120-113.
Functions, §120-113.
Title of article, §120-112.
**Local governmental employees' retirement
system.**
Board of trustees.
Duties of actuary, §128-28(m) to (p).
Mortality tables, §§8-46, 8-47.
Retirement system for general assembly.
Actuarial notes, §§120-112 to 120-114.
**Retirement system for teachers and state
employees.**
Board of trustees to keep actuarial data,
§135-6(h).
Definition of actuarial equivalent, §135-53.
Duties of actuary, §135-6(l) to (o).
Small employer group health coverage.
Certification, §58-50-130(f).
**State health plan for teachers and state
employees.**
Actuarial valuation of retired employees' health
benefits, §135-48.12.

ACUPUNCTURE.
Activities prohibited, §90-456.
Child support enforcement.
  Forfeiture of licensing privilege, §50-13.12.
Chiropractors.
  Exemption from licensing, §90-452(b).
Continuing education.
  Audits of licensees, §90-457.1(d).
  Definition of "continuing education
    unit,"§90-457.1(c).
  Failure to comply, §90-457.1(e).
  Hours set by board, §90-457.1(b).
  License renewal requirement, §90-457.1(a).
  Requests for extension of time to complete,
    §90-457.1(f).
Definitions, §90-451.
Display of license, §90-458.
Exemptions.
  Practice of acupuncture, §90-452(b).
Fees, §90-457.
Felony convictions.
  Forfeiture of license, §15A-1331A.
Identification badges required, §90-640.
Legislative declaration.
  Purpose of, §90-450.
Licenses.
  Continuing education requirement, §90-457.1(a).
  Display, §90-458.
  Expired licenses, §90-455(e).
  Fees, §90-457.
  Forfeiture.
    Felony convictions, §15A-1331A.
  Inactive license, §90-455(c).
  Initial license, §90-455(a).
  Lapsed licenses, §90-455(f).
  Renewal, §90-455(b).
    Expired licenses, §90-455(e).
    Fee, §90-457.
    Suspended licenses, §90-455(d).
  Suspended licenses, §90-455(d).
Licensing board.
  Compensation of members, §90-453(d).
  Duties, §90-454.
  Meetings, §90-453(c).
  Membership, §90-453(a).
  Powers, §90-454.
  Terms of members, §90-453(b).
Names.
  Use of title, §90-458.
Physicians and surgeons.
  Exemption from licensing, §90-452(b).
Practice of acupuncture.
  Defined, §90-451.
  Exemptions, §90-452(b).
  Unlawful acts, §90-452(a).
Prohibited activities, §90-456.
Purpose of article, §90-450.
Reimbursements by third-party, §90-459.
Students practicing acupuncture.
  Exemption from licensure, §90-452(b).
Third-party reimbursements, §90-459.
Titles.
  Use, §90-458.

AD DAMNUM CLAUSE.
Pleadings, §1A-1 Rule 8.

ADDICTION.
Alcoholism research authority, §§122C-431 to
  122C-433.
Basic education program.
  Alcohol and drug education program,
    §115C-81(a3).

ADDICTION —Cont'd
Chemical dependency.
  See CHEMICAL DEPENDENCY.
Chiropractors.
  Grounds for disciplinary action, §90-154(b).
**Discharge, discipline, etc., of employee failing
    to comply with employer's requirements,**
    §95-28.2(b).
Drug treatment courts, §§7A-790 to 7A-801.
  See DRUG TREATMENT COURTS.
Incompetence, determination of, §§35A-1101 to
  35A-1116.
  See INCOMPETENCY.
**Lawyers and judges impaired by substance
    abuse or addiction.**
  Lawyer assistance program, Bar Rules D.0601 to
    D.0623.
  See LAWYERS ASSISTANCE PROGRAM.
Physicians and surgeons.
  Grounds for denial, revocation or suspension of
    license, §90-14(a).
  Referral of physician to state medical society
    physician health and effectiveness committee,
    §90-14(b).
Substance abuse counselors, §§90-113.30 to
  90-113.46A.
  See SUBSTANCE ABUSE PROFESSIONALS.
Substance abuse generally.
  See MENTAL HEALTH, DEVELOPMENTAL
    DISABILITY, SUBSTANCE ABUSE.
Work first program recipients of assistance.
  Treatment required, drug testing, §108A-29.1.

**ADDITIONAL TIME AFTER SERVICE BY
  MAIL,** §§1-593, 1A-1 Rule 6(e).

ADDITIVES.
Color additives.
  Food, drug and cosmetic act, §§106-129 to
    106-137.
Gasoline tax.
  Defined, §105-449.60.

ADDRESS CONFIDENTIALITY PROGRAM,
  §§15C-1 to 15C-13.
Acceptance of designated address.
  Duty of state agencies, §15C-8(b).
Application to participate, §15C-4(a) to (c).
  Assistance for applicants, §15C-10(a).
  Falsifying application information, §15C-6.
Assistance for applicants, §15C-10(a).
Authorization card, §15C-4(d), (e).
Boards of elections.
  Substitute address, use by, §15C-8(e).
Cancellation of certification of participant,
  §15C-7(a) to (c).
Certification of eligibility, §15C-10(b).
**Change of address or telephone number of
  participant.**
  Notification of attorney general, §15C-5(b).
Change of name of participant.
  Notification of attorney general, §15C-5(a).
Definitions, §15C-2.
Disclosure of address, §15C-9(a), (c).
  Notification, §15C-9(b).
  Prohibited acts, §15C-9(d), (e).
  Penalties, §15C-9(f).
Established, §15C-3.
Falsifying application information, §15C-6.
Immunities, §15C-11.
Letter of certification of eligibility, §15C-10(b).

ADDRESS CONFIDENTIALITY PROGRAM
—Cont'd
Marriage licenses.
Form of license for program participant, §51-16.1.
Public schools.
Actual address and telephone number of
participants confidential, §115C-402(f).
Students, use of substitute address, §115C-366(g).
Use of substitute address by administrative units,
§15C-8(i).
Purpose of provisions, §15C-1.
**Records or documents pertaining to
participant, §15C-7(d).**
Registers of deeds.
Substitute address, use by, §15C-8(h).
**Requesting state agencies to use substitute
address.**
Responsibility of participant, §15C-8(a).
Rulemaking, §15C-12.
State lottery.
Confidentiality of prize winners, §18C-132(k).
Substitute address.
Agencies of North Carolina.
Use by, §15C-8(a) to (d).
Attorney general to designate, §15C-3.
Boards of elections.
Use by, §15C-8(e).
Cessation of participation in program.
Notification to persons who use substitute
address, §15C-7(e).
Elections.
Use by boards of elections, §15C-8(e).
Public record.
Not deemed to be, §15C-8(j).
Registers of deeds.
Use by, §15C-8(h).
School administrative units.
Use by, §15C-8(i).
Students, use of, §115C-366(g).
Taxation.
Use for purposes of, §15C-8(f), (g).
Taxation.
Substitute address.
Use for purposes of, §15C-8(f), (g).
Time.
Additional time for participants, §§1A-1 Rule 6(f),
15C-13.
Waiver from requirements.
Request by state agencies, submission, §15C-8(c).
Acceptance or denial by attorney general,
§15C-8(d).

ADDRESSING ENVELOPES.
**Work-at-home solicitations, advertising
restrictions, §75-31.**

ADET SCHOOLS.
Limited driving privilege, §20-179.3(g2).
Restoration of license after conviction.
Impaired driving conviction.
Condition of probation, §20-179(g) to (k).
Obtaining certificate of completion, §20-17.6(c).

ADJOURNMENT.
Clerks of court, §7A-103.
Congress, US Const Art I §§5, 7, Art II §3.
Sheriffs.
Superior courts.
Court adjourned by sheriff when judge not
present, §7A-96.
Superior courts.
Sheriff to adjourn court when judge not present,
§7A-96.

ADJUDICATION OF INCOMPETENCY,
§§35A-1101 to 35A-1116.
See INCOMPETENCY.

ADJUDICATORY HEARINGS.
Abused, neglected or dependent juveniles,
§§7B-801 to 7B-808.
Delinquent and undisciplined juvenile actions,
§§7B-2403 to 7B-2412.

ADJUSTABLE INTEREST RATES.
Equity lines of credit, §24-1.2A(a).

ADJUSTERS.
Debt adjusters, §§14-423 to 14-426.
Insurance adjusters.
Generally.
See INSURANCE ADJUSTERS.
Public adjusters, §§58-33A-1 to 58-33A-95.
See INSURANCE ADJUSTERS.

ADJUTANT GENERAL, §§127A-19, 127A-20.
Administrative and operational matters.
Relationships of adjutant general, §127A-20.
Appointment, §127A-19.
**Assistant adjutant general for air national
guard.**
Appointment, §127A-19.
**Assistant adjutant general for army national
guard.**
Appointment, §127A-19.
Deputy adjutant general.
Appointment, §127A-19.
Military head of militia, §127A-19.
Qualifications, §127A-19.
Staff members and other personnel, §127A-19.

ADMINISTRATION DEPARTMENT.
Allocation of property and space.
Rules governing, §143-342.
Capital facilities finance act.
Generally, §§142-80 to 142-101.
See CAPITAL FACILITIES FINANCE ACT.
Capital planning commission.
Appointment, §143B-374(a).
Clerical and other services, §143B-374(b).
Composition, §143B-374(a).
Creation, §143B-373(a).
Duties, §143B-373(a), (d).
Ex officio members, §143B-374(a).
Expenses, §143B-374(b).
Information to be provided to, §143B-373(b), (c).
Meetings, §143B-374(b).
Powers and duties, §143B-373(a), (d).
Public lands.
State governmental complex, §146-22.1.
Quorum, §143B-374(b).
Records.
Turned over to department of administration,
§143B-374(b).
Citation of article, §143-334.
Coal and petroleum suppliers.
Authority to collect data, §143-345.14(a).
Civil enforcement, §143-345.14(e).
Confidentiality of information, §143-345.14(f).
Definitions, §143-345.14(b), (f).
Refusal to supply data, §143-345.14(d).
Rulemaking authority, §143-345.14(c).
Stocks of coals and petroleum fuel capacity.
Reporting requirements, §143-345.13.
Contingency and emergency fund.
Use for construction and repair of public
buildings, §143-345.3.

ADMINISTRATION DEPARTMENT —Cont'd
Costs.
Publications.
Statement of cost, §143-170.1.
Courier.
Evidence.
Chain of custody, §8-103.
Court of appeals.
Providing adequate quarters for court, §7A-19(b).
Creation, §§143-335, 143B-366.
Definitions, §143-336.
Publications, §143-169.2.
Stocks of coal and petroleum fuels, §143-345.14(b), (f).
Disorderly conduct in buildings, §143-345.2.
Domestic violence commission, §§143B-394.15, 143B-394.16.
Duties, §§143-341, 143B-367, 143B-368.
Functions, §143B-368(a).
Energy loan fund, §§143B-437.14 to 143B-437.16.
Established, §143B-366.
Executive mansion.
Authority of department of administration not affected, §143-415.
Farmworker council, §§143B-426.25, 143B-426.26.
Fees.
Use of state-owned office space by self-supporting agencies, §143-342.1.
Flags.
Official "prisoner of war/missing in action" flag.
State capitol.
Department authorized to fly on certain holidays, §143-345.9.
Functions of department, §143B-368(a).
Funds.
Contingency and emergency fund.
Use for construction and repair of public buildings, §143-345.3.
Future public buildings.
Program for location and construction, §143-345.5.
General services division.
Addition to administrative department, §143-343.
Governor's management council, §§143B-426.22, 143B-426.23.
Clerical services report, §143B-426.23.
Creation, §143B-426.22(a).
Within department of administration, §143B-426.22(a).
Meetings, §143B-426.23.
Membership, §143B-426.22(a).
Powers and duties, §143B-426.22(b).
Reports.
Annual report, §143B-426.23.
Head of department, §143B-369.
Highways, roads and streets.
Test drilling or boring.
Filing record of results with secretary of administration, §136-102.3.
Historically underutilized businesses, statewide uniform certification.
Authority of secretary, §143-48.4(a).
Input from other departments, §143-48.4(b).
Minority business purposes.
Use of businesses listed in database required, §143-48.4(c).
Internship council.
Clerical services, §143B-418.
Compensation, §143B-418.
Creation, §143B-417.
Duties, §143B-417.

ADMINISTRATION DEPARTMENT —Cont'd
Internship council —Cont'd
Members, §143B-418.
Powers and duties, §143B-417.
Quorum, §143B-418.
Selection of members, §143B-418.
Mailing lists.
Updating, §143-169.1.
Certification, §143-169.1(a).
Name, §143B-366.
North Carolina state art society.
Authorization to provide space for art society, §140-12.
Office space.
Fees for use of state-owned office space by self-supporting agencies, §143-342.1.
Pistols, revolvers, shotguns or rifles.
Sale to local government, law enforcement agency or state, §143-63.1(b).
Destruction of unsold weapons, §143-63.1(c).
Powers and duties, §§143-341, 143B-367, 143B-368.
Functions, §143B-368(a).
Property.
Surplus property of state.
State agency.
Federal surplus property, §§143-64.1 to 143-64.5.
General provisions, §§143-64.01 to 143-64.06.
Transfer of property, §143-344(b).
Saving clause, §143-345.
Supervision of governor, §143-344(c).
Publications.
Administrative review procedures for public documents, §143-170.2(c).
State departments and agencies.
Failure to comply with provisions, §143-170.3(a), (b).
Cost of public documents.
Reduction in printing budget for failure to comply with section, §143-170.1(a3).
Statement of cost, §143-170.1(a), (a1), (b).
Definitions, §143-169.2.
Limitations upon, §143-169.
Mailing lists.
Updating, §143-169.1.
North Carolina purchase directory, §143-345.8.
Procedures manuals for public documents, §143-170.2.
Administrative office of the courts, §143-170.4.
Alkaline paper.
Designated public documents to be printed on, §143-170.5.
Consultation with certain state departments and agencies, §143-170.2(a).
Guidelines.
Final guidelines, §143-170.2(b), (d1).
Initial guidelines, §143-170.2(a).
Production elements for public documents, §143-170.2(a).
Reporting requirements.
Failure to comply with provisions, §143-170.3(a), (b).
Recycling and reuse requirements.
Applicability, §143-169(c).
Statement that document printed on recycled paper, §143-170.1(a2).
Statement of cost of public documents, §143-170.1(a), (a1), (b).
Public buildings and grounds.
Construction and repair of public buildings.
Use of contingency and emergency fund, §143-345.3.

ADMINISTRATION DEPARTMENT —Cont'd
Public buildings and grounds —Cont'd
Disorderly conduct in and injury to public
buildings and grounds, §143-345.2.
Future public buildings.
Program for location and construction,
§143-345.5.
Program for location and construction of future
public buildings, §143-345.5.
Raleigh.
Moore and Nash squares and other public lots,
§143-345.4.
Secretary powers and duties, §143-340.
Western residence of the governor.
Repair and reconstruction, §143-345.7.
Public lands, §§146-1 to 146-83.
See PUBLIC LANDS.
Records transfer, §143-344(b).
Saving clause, §143-345.
Supervision of governor, §143-344(c).
Reports.
Conciseness, §143-168.
Farmworker council, §143B-426.26(b).
Governor's management council.
Annual report, §143B-426.23.
Publications.
State departments and agencies.
Failure to comply with reporting
requirements, §§143-170.3, 143-170.4.
Rules and regulations.
Allocation of property and space, §143-342.
Governor shall adopt, §143-345.1.
Sale of merchandise by governmental units.
Exception to prohibition, §66-58(b).
Saving clause.
Transfer of functions, §143-345.
School buses.
Purchase through department, §115C-249(g).
Science and technology.
Board of science and technology, §§143B-472.80,
143B-472.81.
Secretary.
Duties, §143-340.
Head of department, §143B-369.
Highways, roads and streets.
Test drilling or boring.
Filing record of results with secretary,
§136-102.3.
License plate.
Special plate, number, §20-79.5.
Powers, §143-340.
Public lands.
Service of process on state in land actions,
§146-69.
Self-supporting agencies using state-owned
office space.
Fees, §143-342.1.
Short title, §143-334.
State energy office.
Guaranteed energy savings contracts.
Evaluation of use by state agencies.
Adoption of rules for evaluation,
§143-64.17F(b).
Recommendations as to savings, §143-64.17F(c).
State veterans home.
Administration and operation, §165-46.
Surplus property of state.
State agency.
Federal surplus property, §§143-64.1 to
143-64.5.
General provisions, §§143-64.01 to 143-64.06.

ADMINISTRATION DEPARTMENT —Cont'd
Transfer of functions, §143-344(b).
Saving clause, §143-345.
Supervision of governor, §143-344(c).
Veterans affairs department.
Transfer to department of administration,
§143A-96.1.
Veterans homes.
Operation and administration, §165-46.
Youth councils.
Compensation of members, §143B-386.
Creation, §143B-385.
Duties, §143B-385.
Local youth council.
Purposes, §143B-388.
Members, §143B-386.
Powers and duties, §143B-385.
Purposes, §143B-388.
Quorum, §143B-386.
Selection of members, §143B-386.
State youth council.
Established, §143B-387.
Powers and duties, §143B-387.

ADMINISTRATION OF ESTATES.
Decedents' estates.
See DECEDENTS' ESTATES.
Executors and administrators.
See EXECUTORS AND ADMINISTRATORS.
Mentally ill and developmentally disabled,
§7A-307.
Principal and income act.
General provisions, §§37A-1-101 to 37A-6-602.
See PRINCIPAL AND INCOME ACT.
Trusts and trustees.
General provisions, §§36C-1-101 to 36C-11-1106.
See TRUSTS AND TRUSTEES.

ADMINISTRATIVE CODE AND REGISTRY.
Publication generally, §§150B-21.17 to
150B-21.25.
See PUBLICATION OF ADMINISTRATIVE
CODE AND REGISTER.
Rebuttable presumption rule adopted.
Entry in administrative code, §150B-21.9(a1).

ADMINISTRATIVE HEARINGS, OFFICE OF,
§§7A-750 to 7A-760.
Administrative law judges.
Additional judges, §7A-753.
Appointment, §7A-753.
Availability to exempt agencies, §7A-758.
Expenses.
Reimbursement, §7A-755.
Temporary judges, §7A-757.
Longevity pay, §7A-751(b).
Number, §7A-760(a).
Oaths, §7A-754.
Power to administer oaths, §7A-756.
Private practice of law, §7A-754.
Qualifications, §7A-754.
Reimbursement for expenses, §7A-755.
Removal from office, §7A-754.
Salary, §7A-751(b).
Senior judge.
Designation by chief judge, §7A-752.
Performance of duties of chief judge.
Chief judge absent or unable to serve,
§7A-752.
Specialization, §7A-753.
Subpoenas, §7A-756.
Temporary judges, §7A-757.

ADMINISTRATIVE HEARINGS, OFFICE OF
—Cont'd
Age discrimination in employment.
  Deferral agency, §7A-759(b1).
Chief administrative law judge.
  Absence or unable to serve.
    Senior judge to perform duties, §7A-752.
  Appointment, §7A-752.
  Head of office, §7A-751(a).
  Longevity pay, §7A-751(a).
  Rules review committee.
    Designation of director and staff, §7A-760(b).
  Salary, §7A-751(a).
  State personnel act.
    Exempt from provisions, §7A-760(a).
  Term, §7A-752.
Creation, §7A-750.
Deferral agency, §7A-759(a) to (i).
  Confidentiality, §7A-759(g).
  Contested cases, §7A-759(d), (e).
  Contracts to serve as deferral agency, §7A-759(b).
  Designation, §7A-759(a).
  Federal authority not limited, §7A-759(h).
  Investigations, §7A-759(c).
  Monetary compliance with settlement or
    compromise, §7A-759(f).
Duties, §7A-750.
E.E.O.C. actions.
  Deferral agency, §7A-759(b1).
Enforcement of powers, §7A-756.
Exempt agencies, §7A-758.
  Availability of administrative law judges to,
    §7A-758.
Expenses reimbursed, §7A-755.
Head of office.
  Chief administrative law judge, §7A-751(a).
Municipalities.
  Availability of administrative law judges to,
    §7A-758.
**Number of employees and administrative law
  judges, §7A-760(a).**
Oaths, §§7A-754, 7A-756, 7A-759(c).
Political subdivisions.
  Availability of administrative law judges to,
    §7A-758.
Purpose, §7A-750.
**Qualifications of administrative law judges,
  §7A-754.**
Reimbursement of expenses, §7A-755.
Removal of administrative law judges, §7A-754.
Rules review committee.
  Director and staff.
    Designated by chief administrative law judge,
      §7A-760(b).
Salary.
  Administrative law judges, §7A-751(b).
  Chief administrative law judge, §7A-751(a).
Senior judge.
  Designation by chief judge, §7A-752.
  Performance of duties of chief judge.
    Chief judge absent or unable to serve, §7A-752.
**Specialization of administrative law judges,
  §7A-753.**
Standards of conduct, §7A-754.
State personnel act.
  Employees subject to, §7A-760(a).
Status, §7A-750.
Subpoena issuance, §7A-756.
Subpoenas, §7A-756.
Temporary judges, §7A-757.

ADMINISTRATIVE LAW JUDGES, §150B-40(e).
**Administrative procedure generally, §§150B-1
  to 150B-52.**
  See ADMINISTRATIVE PROCEDURE.
Assignment, §150B-32(a).
Decisions, §150B-34(a).
  Applicability of provisions, §150B-34(d).
Disqualification, §150B-32(b), (c).
Ex parte communications.
  Prohibited, §150B-35.
Judgment on the pleadings.
  Authority to grant, §150B-34(e).
**Office of administrative hearings, §§7A-750 to
  7A-760.**
  See ADMINISTRATIVE HEARINGS, OFFICE OF.
Powers, §150B-33(b).
Preponderance of evidence.
  Case decision based on, §150B-34(a).
Stays, §150B-33(a).
Summary judgment.
  Authority to grant, §150B-34(e).

ADMINISTRATIVE OFFICE OF THE COURTS,
  §§7A-340 to 7A-346.
**Abused, neglected or dependent juvenile
  actions.**
  Guardian ad litem program to provide services,
    §§7B-1200 to 7B-1204.
  Permanency mediation program.
    Establishment, §7B-202.
Advance sheets.
  Contracting for printing of advance sheets,
    §7A-6(b).
  Designation of commercial advance sheets as
    official reports, §7A-6(b1).
  Furnishing of advance sheets, §7A-6(c).
  Sale of advance sheets, §7A-6(b).
    Remittance of proceeds of sale, §7A-6(b).
Appellate division reports.
  Distribution of copies, §7A-343.1.
Assistant director.
  Appointment, §7A-342.
  Compensation, §7A-342.
  Duties, §7A-345.
Bad checks.
  Collection of fees and restitution, §14-107.2(a1),
    (d).
  Reporting worthless check collection, §7A-346.2.
  Worthless checks collection program.
    Collection of worthless checks fund, §7A-308(c).
    Fees, superior court clerks, §7A-308(c).
Budget of state.
  Development of recommended budget.
    Judicial branch estimate, §143C-3-2.
Child abuse, neglect and dependency.
  Guardian ad litem program to provide services,
    §§7B-1200 to 7B-1204.
  Permanency mediation program.
    Establishment, §7B-202.
Contracts.
  Assistant clerks.
    Local government funding, §7A-102(g).
  Deputy clerks.
    Local government funding, §7A-102(g).
  Judicial secretaries.
    Local government funding, §7A-44.1(d).
Copies.
  Appellate division reports.
    Distribution of copies, §7A-343.1.
Courts commission.
  Ex officio member, §7A-507.

ADMINISTRATIVE OFFICE OF THE COURTS
—Cont'd

Credit card, charge cards or debit cards.
Payment of fees and costs by.
Contract with vendor, duty of director, §7A-343.

Deaf and hearing-impaired interpreters.
Policies and procedures for appointment and
payment.
Duty of director, §7A-343.

Director.
Appointment, §7A-341.
Assistant clerks.
Local funding assistance, §7A-102(f).
Compensation, §7A-341.
Deputy clerks.
Local funding assistance, §7A-102(f).
Duties, §7A-343.
Judicial secretaries.
Local funding assistance, §7A-44.1(c).
Service equivalent to service as superior court
judge, §7A-341.
Supervision of office, §7A-340.
Voting rights act of 1965.
Duties as to, §§120-30.9C, 120-30.9H.

Disability.
Retirement on account of total and permanent
disability, §7A-55.
Applicability of provisions, §7A-56.

District attorneys, temporary assistance to,
§7A-64.

DNA database and databank.
Expungement of DNA records.
Automated procedure to facilitate.
Study, report, §15A-266.5(d).

Drug treatment courts, §§7A-790 to 7A-801.
See DRUG TREATMENT COURTS.

Duties of director, §7A-343.

Elections.
Submission of acts to United States attorney
general, §120-30.9C.

**Electronic access to superior court records in
clerks office.**
Contracts to provide public, §7A-109(d), (e).

Electronic filing in courts statewide.
Contract with vendor to provide, §7A-49.5(c).
Establishment and operation of systems and
services.
Duty of director, §7A-343.

Employees.
Appointment, §7A-342.
Compensation, §7A-342.
Health and safety programs.
Authority of administrative office to establish,
§143-589.

Establishment, §7A-340.

Expungement of criminal records.
Confidential files, §15A-146(c).
Disclosure.
Courts or persons to whom disclosure allowed,
§15A-151(a).
Duty of office to maintain, §15A-151(a).
DNA records.
Automated procedure to facilitate.
Study, report, §15A-266.5(d).
Notification to AOC, §15A-150(a).

Family court fee, §7A-314.1(a).
Reduction, procedure, §7A-314.1(b).

Foreign language interpreters.
Policies and procedures for appointment and
payment.
Duty of director, §7A-343.

ADMINISTRATIVE OFFICE OF THE COURTS
—Cont'd

Guardian ad litem program.
Providing services to abused, neglected or
dependent juveniles, §§7B-1200 to 7B-1204.

**Identification cards for judicial department
employees.**
Duty of director to issue, §7A-343.

Impaired driving integrated data system.
Information maintained in office's database,
§7A-346.3.
Report by office, §7A-346.3.

Implied consent offense procedures.
Forms, adoption, §20-38.4(b).

Indigent defense services.
Budgeting process, §7A-498.2(e).
Clerical support, §7A-498.2(c).

**Information to be furnished to administrative
officer,** §7A-346.

Innocence inquiry commission.
Administrative support.
Office to provide, §15A-1462(b).

Internal audit division, §7A-343.
Audit work papers, drafts, other audit documents.
Availability, restrictions, §7A-343.4(b).
Duty to maintain, §7A-343.4(b).
Definitions, §7A-343.5.
Internal auditing defined, §7A-343.5.
Rules governing, §7A-343.4(c).
Standards for internal audits, §7A-343.4(a).

Law clerks.
Salaries of law clerks set by administrative officer,
§7A-7(a).

**Magistrates performing duties outside county
of residence during emergency.**
Assignment and compensation, policies and
procedures.
Director of administrative office of courts to
prescribe, §7A-343.

Motor vehicle license plates.
Special license plate issuable to director,
§20-79.4(b).

Office of guardian ad litem services.
Established within administrative office of the
courts, §7B-1200.

Officers, §7A-340.

**Per-mile reimbursement for transportation by
privately owned vehicles,** §7A-343.

Reports.
Annual report on work of judicial department.
Direction to prepare and submit, §7A-343.
Appellate division reports.
Distribution of copies, §7A-343.1.
Contracting for printing of reports, §7A-6(b).
Designation of commercial reports as official
report, §7A-6(b1).
Legislative reporting.
Local government services contracts,
§7A-346.2(a).
Worthless check collection, §7A-346.2(b).
Sale of reports, §7A-6(b).
Remittance of proceeds of sale, §7A-6(b).

Research assistants.
Salaries of research assistants set by
administrative officer, §7A-7(a).

Retirement.
Age requirements, §7A-51(a) to (e).
Applicability of provisions, §7A-56.
Compensation for retirement, §7A-51(a) to (e).
Applicability of provisions, §7A-56.

ADMINISTRATIVE OFFICE OF THE COURTS
—Cont'd
Retirement —Cont'd
On account of total and permanent disability,
§7A-55.
Applicability of provisions, §7A-56.
Service requirements, §7A-51(a) to (e).
Applicability of provisions, §7A-56.
Safety and health programs for employees.
Authority to establish, §143-589.
Secretaries.
Determination of number and salaries of
secretary, §7A-7(b).
Sentencing services act, §§7A-770 to 7A-777.
See SENTENCING SERVICES.
Setoff debt collection, §§105A-1 to 105A-16.
See SETOFF DEBT COLLECTION.
Stenographers.
Determination of number and salaries of
stenographers, §7A-7(b).
Supervision of office, §7A-340.
Temporary assistance to district attorneys,
§7A-64.
Total and permanent disability.
Retirement on account of, §7A-55.
Applicability of provisions, §7A-56.

ADMINISTRATIVE PROCEDURE, §§150B-1 to
150B-52.
Administrative code.
Publication generally, §§150B-21.17 to
150B-21.25.
Rebuttable presumption rule adopted.
Entry in administrative code, §150B-21.9(a1).
Administrative hearings, office of, §§7A-750 to
7A-759. See within this heading, "Office of
administrative hearings."
Administrative law judge.
Defined, §150B-2.
Agencies.
Defined, §150B-2.
Alcoholic beverages.
Applicability, §18B-906.
Ambulatory surgical facilities.
Adverse action on licenses.
Applicability of provisions, §131E-148(b).
American Recovery and Reinvestment Act
implementation.
Rulemaking, §150B-21.1B(b).
Answers.
Hearings, §150B-38(d).
Appeals, §§150B-43 to 150B-52.
Appeal of right directly to appellate division,
AppProc Rules 18, 20.
Appellate division, §150B-52.
Appeal of right directly to appellate division,
AppProc Rules 18, 20.
Contested tax cases, §150B-45(a).
Evidence.
New evidence, §150B-49.
Intervention.
Motion to intervene, §150B-46.
Judgment on the pleadings.
Reviewing decision allowing, §150B-51(d).
Jury.
Review by court without jury, §150B-50.
Manner of seeking review, §150B-45(a).
New evidence, §150B-49.
Petitions.
Contents, §150B-46.
Copies served on all parties, §150B-46.

ADMINISTRATIVE PROCEDURE —Cont'd
Appeals —Cont'd
Petitions —Cont'd
Time for filing petition, §150B-45(a).
Power of court in disposing of case, §150B-51(d).
Procedure for seeking, §150B-45.
Records, §150B-47.
Contents, §150B-47.
Costs, §150B-47.
Filing with clerk of superior court, §150B-47.
Review by court without jury, §150B-50.
Right to judicial review, §150B-43.
Scope of review, §150B-51(c).
Service of process.
Copies of petition served on all parties,
§150B-46.
Standard of review, §150B-51(b).
Stays, §150B-48.
Obtaining stay of court's decision, §150B-52.
Summary judgment.
Reviewing decision allowing, §150B-51(d).
Waiver, §150B-45(b).
Applicability of provisions.
Exemptions, §150B-1(c) to (f).
Assisted living administrators, applicability,
§90-288.18(b).
Banks.
Hearings.
Special provisions, §§150B-38 to 150B-42.
Cardiac rehabilitation certification program.
Adverse action on certificates, §131E-168(b).
Code.
Publication generally, §§150B-21.17 to
150B-21.25.
Codifier of rules.
Defined, §150B-2.
Publication of code and register.
Copies of register and code.
Distribution of free copies, §150B-21.24.
North Carolina administrative code.
Authority to revise form of rules,
§150B-21.20(a).
Duties, §150B-21.18.
Effect of codifier's revision of rule,
§150B-21.20(b).
North Carolina register.
Duties, §150B-21.17.
Commission.
Defined, §150B-2.
Community colleges.
Construction contract claims.
Adjustment and resolution, §143-135.6(a) to (f).
Consolidation.
Hearings, §150B-26.
Contested cases.
Children's health insurance program.
Review of decisions, §108A-70.29.
Commencement, §150B-23(a).
Time for filing petition, §150B-23(f).
Defined, §150B-2.
Exemptions, §150B-1(e).
Filing fee.
Amount of fee, §150B-23.2(a).
Indigency waiver, §150B-23.2(d).
Payment methods, §150B-23.2(c).
Refund.
State losing party, §150B-23.2(d).
Time for collecting, §150B-23.2(b).
Final decision or order, §150B-34.
Hearings.
Generally, §§150B-22 to 150B-42. See within
this heading, "Hearings."

ADMINISTRATIVE PROCEDURE —Cont'd
Contested cases —Cont'd
Judgment on the pleadings.
Authority of judge to grant, §150B-34(e).
Reviewing decision allowing, §150B-51(d).
Medicaid contested case procedures.
Appeals by recipients, §108A-70.9A.
Generally, §108A-70.9B.
Informal review by department, §108A-70.9C.
Prehearing statement, filing, §150B-23(a2).
Preponderance of evidence.
Case decided on, §150B-34(a).
Settlement through informal procedures,
§150B-22.
Summary judgment.
Authority of judge to grant, §150B-34(e).
Reviewing decision allowing, §150B-51(d).
Declaratory rulings.
Binding effect, §150B-4(a).
Changing ruling, §150B-4(a).
Denial of request.
Judicial review, §150B-4(a1).
Failure to timely issue.
Deemed denial, judicial review, §150B-4(a1).
Issuance upon request, §150B-4(a).
Procedure for requesting prescribed in agency
rules, §150B-4(a).
Response by agency to request, §150B-4(a1).
Time for responding to request, §150B-4(a1).
Written ruling on merits, issuance, time,
§150B-4(a1).
Definitions, §150B-2.
Depositions, §150B-39(a).
Hearings, §§150B-28(a), 150B-39(a).
Subpoenas.
Witness fees, §150B-39(c).
Discovery, §150B-39(b).
Hearings, §150B-39(a).
Subpoenas.
Witness fees, §150B-39(c).
Educational agencies.
Subject to administrative procedure act, §115C-2.
Elections.
Precinct boundaries.
Exemption of state board of elections,
§163-132.5B.
Evidence.
Appeals.
New evidence, §150B-49.
Dying declarations, §8-51.1.
Hearings, §150B-41(a), (b).
Opportunity to present evidence, §§150B-25(c),
150B-40(a).
Rules of evidence, §150B-29(a), (b).
Subpoenas, §§150B-27, 150B-39(c).
Exempt agencies' rules.
Duty to submit rule for inclusion in
administrative code, §150B-21.21(b).
Publication of code and register, §150B-21.21(c).
Exemptions.
Contested case provisions, §150B-1(e).
Full exemptions, §150B-1(c).
Rule making, §150B-1(d).
University of North Carolina, §150B-1(f).
Fees.
Contested case filing fees, §150B-23.2.
Copies of register and code, §150B-21.25.
Subpoenas.
Witness fees, §150B-39(c).

ADMINISTRATIVE PROCEDURE —Cont'd
Foreign corporations.
Nonprofit corporations.
Revocation of certificates of authority.
Inapplicability of administrative procedure
act, §55A-15-33.
Health maintenance organizations, §58-67-155.
Hearings, §§150B-22 to 150B-42.
Absence of party.
Proceeding with hearing in absence of party,
§§150B-25(a), 150B-40(a).
Administrative law judges, §150B-40(e).
Assignment, §150B-32(a).
Decisions, §150B-34.
Disqualification, §150B-32(b), (c).
Ex parte communications.
Prohibited, §150B-35.
Office of administrative hearings.
See ADMINISTRATIVE HEARINGS, OFFICE
OF.
Powers, §150B-33(b).
Stays, §150B-33(a).
Answers, §150B-38(d).
Arguments.
Opportunity to present, §150B-25(c).
Banks.
Special provisions, §§150B-38 to 150B-42.
Consolidation, §150B-26.
Contested tax cases, §150B-31.1.
Applicability, §150B-31.1(a).
Confidentiality, §150B-31.1(e).
Law enforcement agency reports, admissibility,
§150B-31.1(d).
Simplification of procedures, §150B-31.1(b).
Venue, §150B-31.1(c).
Decisions.
Failure to timely make.
Court order compelling action, justification,
§150B-44.
Final decision, §150B-42(a).
Unreasonable delay of decision.
Court order compelling action, right to seek,
§150B-44.
Depositions, §150B-28(a).
Evidence, §150B-41(a), (b).
Opportunity to present evidence, §§150B-25(c),
150B-40(a).
Rules of evidence, §150B-29(a), (b).
Subpoenas, §§150B-27, 150B-39(c).
Ex parte communications, §150B-40(d).
Prohibited, §150B-35.
Final decision, §150B-42(a).
Findings of fact.
Final decision, §150B-42(a).
Informal procedures.
Settlement of contested cases, §150B-22.
Insurance.
Department of insurance and commissioner of
insurance.
Special provisions, §§150B-38 to 150B-42.
Interpreters.
General provisions.
See INTERPRETERS.
Intervention, §§150B-23(d), 150B-38(f).
Judgment on the pleadings.
Authority of judge to grant, §150B-34(e).
Reviewing decision allowing, §150B-51(d).
Licenses.
Occupational licensing agencies.
Special provisions, §§150B-38 to 150B-42.

ADMINISTRATIVE PROCEDURE —Cont'd
Hearings —Cont'd
  Notice, §§150B-23(b), (c), 150B-38(b), (c).
    Official notice, §§150B-30, 150B-41(d).
  Office of administrative hearings, §§7A-750 to
    7A-759. See within this heading, "Office of
    administrative hearings."
  Official notice, §§150B-30, 150B-41(d).
  Open to public, §§150B-23(e), 150B-38(e).
  Opportunity for hearing to be provided,
    §150B-23(a).
  Presiding officer, §150B-40(b), (c).
  Records.
    Official record, §§150B-37(a), 150B-42(b).
      Forwarding copy to agency, §150B-37(c).
      Transcript, §§150B-37(b), 150B-42(c).
  Scope of provisions.
    Special provisions, §150B-38(a).
  Special education petitions, §150B-22.1(a).
    Administrative law judge.
      Qualifications, §150B-22.1(b).
    Definition of "IDEA,"§150B-22.1(c).
  Stipulations, §§150B-31(a), 150B-41(c).
    Disposition of contested case by stipulation,
      §150B-31(b).
  Subpoenas, §150B-27.
  Summary judgment.
    Authority of judge to grant, §150B-34(e).
    Reviewing decision allowing, §150B-51(d).
  Tax cases, §150B-31.1.
  Venue, §150B-24(a).
    Waiver of objection to venue, §150B-24(b).
  Witnesses.
    Cross-examination, §§150B-25(d), 150B-40(a).
    Subpoenas, §§150B-27, 150B-39(c).
Hospitals.
  Licenses.
    Adverse action on licenses, §131E-78(a) to (c1).
    Denial or revocation of license, §131E-78(a).
Insurance.
  Hearings.
    Department of insurance and commissioner of
      insurance.
      Special provisions, §§150B-38 to 150B-42.
Interpleader and intervention.
  Appeals.
    Motion to intervene, §150B-46.
  Hearings.
    Motion to intervene, §§150B-23(d), 150B-38(f).
Joint hearings, §150B-38(g).
Judgment on the pleadings.
  Authority of judge to grant, §150B-34(e).
  Reviewing decision allowing, §150B-51(d).
Judicial or official notice.
  Publication of code and register.
    Effect of inclusion of rule in code, §150B-21.22.
Judicial review, §§150B-43 to 150B-52. See within
  this heading, "Appeals."
Jury.
  Appeals.
    Review by court without jury, §150B-50.
Licenses.
  Application of provisions, §150B-3(d).
  Defined, §150B-2.
  Expiration, §150B-3(a).
  Hearings.
    Occupational licensing agencies.
      Special provisions, §§150B-38 to 150B-42.
    Hospitals, §131E-78(a) to (c1).
  Licensing defined, §150B-2.

ADMINISTRATIVE PROCEDURE —Cont'd
Licenses —Cont'd
  Notice.
    Suspension, revocation or cancellation of
      license, §150B-3(b).
  Nursing homes, §131E-103(b).
  Occupational licenses.
    Defined, §150B-2.
  Special provisions, §150B-3.
  Suspension.
    Notice, §150B-3(b).
    Summary suspension, §150B-3(c).
Mediated settlement conferences.
  Attendance, §150B-23.1(d).
  Costs, §150B-23.1(i).
  Definitions, §150B-23.1(b).
  Immunity, §150B-23.1(h).
  Inadmissibility of negotiations, §150B-23.1(j).
  Mediators, §150B-23.1(e).
  Order by administrative law judge, §150B-23.1(c).
  Purpose of section, §150B-23.1(a).
  Right to hearing, §150B-23.1(k).
  Sanctions, §150B-23.1(f).
  Standards, §150B-23.1(g).
Mine safety and health standards.
  Procedure utilized for adoption and promulgation,
    §74-24.4(b).
Nonprofit corporations.
  Administrative dissolution by secretary of state.
    Inapplicability of administrative procedure act,
      §55A-14-24.
  Foreign corporations.
    Revocation of certificates of authority.
      Inapplicability of administrative procedure
        act, §55A-15-33.
Notice.
  Hearings, §§150B-21.2(e), 150B-23(b), (c),
    150B-38(b), (c).
    Official notice, §§150B-30, 150B-41(d).
  Licenses.
    Suspension, revocation or cancellation,
      §150B-3(b).
Nursing homes.
  Adverse action on licenses, §131E-103(b).
Occupational licensing agency.
  Defined, §150B-2.
Office of administrative hearings, §§7A-750 to
  7A-760.
  Administrative law judges.
    Longevity pay, §7A-751(b).
    Number, §7A-760(a).
    Salary, §7A-751(b).
    Senior judge.
      Designation by chief judge, §7A-752.
      Performance of duties of chief judge.
        Chief judge absent or unable to serve,
          §7A-752.
  Age discrimination in employment.
    Deferral agency, §7A-759(b1).
  Appointment of administrative law judges,
    §7A-753.
  Chief administrative law judge.
    Absence or unable to serve.
      Senior judge to perform duties, §7A-752.
    Appointment, §7A-752.
    Head of office, §7A-751(a).
    Longevity pay, §7A-751(a).
    Rules review committee.
      Designation of director and staff, §7A-760(b).
    Salary, §7A-751(a).

ADMINISTRATIVE PROCEDURE —Cont'd
Office of administrative hearings —Cont'd
Chief administrative law judge —Cont'd
State personnel act.
Exempt from provisions, §7A-760(a).
Term, §7A-752.
Civil rights division.
Investigating charges, authority, §7A-759(c1).
Creation, §7A-750.
Deferral agency.
Broad construction of provisions, §7A-759(i).
Confidentiality, §7A-759(g).
Contested cases, §7A-759(d), (e).
Contracts to serve as deferral agency, §7A-759(b).
Designation, §7A-759(a).
Federal authority not limited, §7A-759(h).
Investigations, §7A-759(c).
Monetary compliance with settlement or compromise, §7A-759(f).
Duties, §7A-750.
E.E.O.C. actions.
Deferral agency, §7A-759(b1).
Enforcement of powers, §7A-756.
Exempt agencies.
Availability of administrative law judges to, §7A-758.
Expenses reimbursed, §7A-755.
Head of office.
Chief administrative law judge, §7A-751(a).
Municipalities.
Availability of administrative law judges to, §7A-758.
Number of employees and administrative law judges, §7A-760(a).
Oath administration, §7A-756.
Deferral agency, §7A-759(c).
Oaths and affirmations, §7A-759(c).
Oaths of administrative law judges, §7A-754.
Political subdivisions.
Availability of administrative law judges to, §7A-758.
Purpose, §7A-750.
Qualifications of administrative law judges, §7A-754.
Reimbursement of expenses, §7A-755.
Removal of administrative law judges, §7A-754.
Rules review committee.
Director and staff.
Designated by chief administrative law judge, §7A-760(b).
Salary.
Administrative law judges, §7A-751(b).
Chief administrative law judge, §7A-751(a).
Senior judge.
Designation by chief judge, §7A-752.
Performance of duties of chief judge.
Chief judge absent or unable to serve, §7A-752.
Specialization of administrative law judges, §7A-753.
Standards of conduct, §7A-754.
State personnel act.
Employees subject to, §7A-760(a).
Status, §7A-750.
Subpoena issuance, §7A-756.
Temporary administrative law judges, §7A-757.
Parties.
Defined, §150B-2.
Petitions.
Appeals.
Time for filing petition, §150B-45(a).

ADMINISTRATIVE PROCEDURE —Cont'd
Petitions —Cont'd
Contents, §150B-46.
Copies served on all parties, §150B-46.
Policy of state, §150B-1(a).
Prehearing statement.
Contested case, §150B-23(a2).
Property insurance.
Mediation of emergency or disaster claims.
Administrative procedure act applicability, §58-44-120.
Publication of administrative code and register, §§150B-21.17 to 150B-21.25.
See PUBLICATION OF ADMINISTRATIVE CODE AND REGISTER.
Purpose of provisions, §150B-1(b).
Records.
Appeals, §150B-47.
Hearings.
Official record, §§150B-37, 150B-42(b), (c).
Residence.
Defined, §150B-2.
Rulemaking procedure.
Abolition of part or all of agency.
Transfer of agency's duties.
Effect on rule, §150B-21.7.
Administrative code.
Publication, §§150B-21.17 to 150B-21.25.
Rebuttable presumption rule adopted.
Entry in administrative code, §150B-21.9(a1).
American Recovery and Reinvestment Act implementation.
Adoption of rule, §150B-21.1B(b).
Entry of rule into code, §150B-21.1B(c).
Expiration date of rule, §150B-21.1B(d).
Expiration date of temporary rule, §150B-21.1B(e).
Purpose of provision, §150B-21.1B(a).
Review of determinations regarding temporary rules, §150B-21.1B(f).
Review of written objections, §150B-21.1B(c).
Annual review by agency, §150B-19.1(b).
Burden upon persons required to comply.
Reduction, §150B-19.1(a).
Changes.
Permanent rules.
Response to commission objection, §150B-21.12(c).
Clear and unambiguous manner.
Rules written in, requirement, §150B-19.1(a).
Conduct of hearings, §150B-38(h).
Coordination of rules adopted.
Overlapping policies and programs of agencies, §150B-19.1(d).
Coordinators.
Agencies to designate rulemaking coordinators, §150B-21(a).
Duties of rulemaking coordinators, §150B-21(b) to (e).
Cost-effective, §150B-19.1(a).
Cumulative effect of rules adopted.
Agency to consider, §150B-19.1(a).
Definitions.
Substantial economic impact, §150B-21.4(b1).
Economic impact.
Alternative considered if substantial impact, §150B-19.1(f).
Effective dates.
Day of adjournment defined, §150B-21.3(d).
Delayed effective dates, §150B-21.3(b1).
Executive order exception, §150B-21.3(c).

ADMINISTRATIVE PROCEDURE —Cont'd
Rulemaking procedure —Cont'd
Effective dates —Cont'd
Fee increase or new fee established,
§150B-21.3(c1).
Legislative day defined, §150B-21.3(d).
Objections to adoption, §150B-21.3(b2).
OSHA standard, §150B-21.3(e).
Permanent rules, §150B-21.3(b).
Technical change, §150B-21.3(f).
Temporary and emergency rules, §150B-21.3(a).
Emergency rules.
American Recovery and Reinvestment Act
implementation, §150B-21.1B.
Declaratory judgment.
Standing to file for, §150B-21.1A(c).
Department of health and humans services.
When agency may adopt, §150B-21.1A(a).
Effective date, §§150B-21.1A(d), 150B-21.3(a).
Expiration, §150B-21.1A(d).
Publication, §150B-21.1A(e).
Review, §§150B-21.1A(b), 150B-21.8(a).
Standing to file for declaratory judgment,
§150B-21.1A(c).
When agency may adopt, §150B-21.1A(a).
Environmental rules.
Agencies authorized to implement and enforce
state and federal environmental laws,
§150B-19.3(b).
Imposing more restrictive standard, limitation,
or requirement than federal law,
§150B-19.3(a).
Executive order exception.
Effective dates, §150B-21.3(c).
Exemptions, §150B-18.
Existing rules, review.
Public comment, tracking agency progress.
Single web portal for, §150B-19.2(b).
Rules modification and improvement procedure,
§150B-19.2(a).
Federal law.
Rules to implement, required for compliance.
Duty of agency proposing rule, §150B-19.1(g).
Fee increase or new fee established.
Effective dates, §150B-21.3(c1).
Fiscal notes on rules.
Content, §150B-21.4(b2).
Erroneous note, §150B-21.4(c).
Local funds, §150B-21.4(b).
Review, §150B-19.1(e).
State funds, §150B-21.4(a).
Substantial economic impact, §150B-21.4(b1).
Judicial review.
Permanent rule returned by commission,
§150B-21.8(d).
Limitations on what can be adopted as a rule,
§150B-19.
Local governments.
Rules affecting, §§150B-21.26 to 150B-21.28.
Notice of proposed rules.
Information posted on web site when notice
submitted, §150B-19.1(c).
Objections to adoption, §150B-21.3(b2).
Commission objection, §150B-21.12.
OSHA standard.
Effective dates, §150B-21.3(e).
Notice and hearing not required, §150B-21.5(c).
Overlapping policies and programs of agencies.
Coordination of rules adopted, §150B-19.1(d).
Permanent rules.
Actions prior to adopting, §150B-21.2(a).

ADMINISTRATIVE PROCEDURE —Cont'd
Rulemaking procedure —Cont'd
Permanent rules —Cont'd
Adoption of proposed rule, §150B-21.2(g).
Amendment of rule.
Notice and hearing not required,
§150B-21.5(a).
Review by commission, scope, §150B-21.8(c).
Approval by commission, §§150B-21.10,
150B-21.11.
Changes.
Response to commission objection,
§150B-21.12(c).
Comments, §150B-21.2(f).
Accepting at public hearing, §150B-21.2(e).
Differs substantially from text of proposed rule.
Defined, §150B-21.2(g).
Rule not adopted, §150B-21.2(g).
Effective dates, §150B-21.3(b).
Executive order exception, §150B-21.3(c).
OSHA standard, §150B-21.3(e).
Technical change, §150B-21.3(f).
Explanation as to why rule adopted,
§150B-21.2(h).
Extending period for review.
Public hearing on rule, §150B-21.14.
Fiscal notes, §150B-21.4(a) to (c).
Judicial review.
Rule returned by commission, §150B-21.8(d).
Mailing list of persons requesting notice,
§150B-21.2(d).
Notice of public hearing, §150B-21.2(e).
Rescheduled hearing, §150B-21.2(e).
Notice of rulemaking.
When not required, §150B-21.5.
Notice of text, §150B-21.2(c).
Objection by commission.
Action, §150B-21.12(a).
Changes, §150B-21.12(c).
Return of rule, §150B-21.12(d).
Time limit, §150B-21.12(b).
OSHA standard.
Effective dates, §150B-21.3(e).
Procedure when approved, §150B-21.11.
Public hearing, §150B-21.2(e).
Notice, §150B-21.2(e).
Rescheduled.
Notice, §150B-21.2(e).
Public hearing for rule where review period has
been extended, §150B-21.14.
Public hearing on proposed rule.
When not required, §150B-21.5.
Record of proceeding, §150B-21.2(i).
Repeal of rule.
Notice and hearing not required,
§150B-21.5(b).
Return of rule to agency.
Objection by commission, §150B-21.12(d).
Review by commission, §150B-21.8(b).
Action on rule, §150B-21.10.
Amendment, scope, §150B-21.8(c).
Approval procedures, §150B-21.11.
Extending period for review, §150B-21.13.
Time limit, §150B-21.9(b).
Timetable for review.
Extension of time, §150B-21.13.
Public hearing on rule where time for
review has been extended, §150B-21.14.
Steps for adopting, §150B-21.2(a).
Technical change.
Effective dates, §150B-21.3(f).

ADMINISTRATIVE PROCEDURE —Cont'd
Rulemaking procedure —Cont'd
Petitioning agencies to adopt rules.
  Denial of petition.
    Procedure, §150B-20(c), (d).
  Generally, §150B-20(a).
  Granting or denying petition.
    Generally, §150B-20(b).
Policy, guideline, interpretative statement.
  Enforcement, adoption in accordance with
    article required, §150B-18.
Principles when developing and drafting rules,
  §150B-19.1(a).
Publication of code and register, §§150B-21.17 to
  150B-21.25.
Rebuttable presumption.
  Rule adopted, entry in administrative code,
    §150B-21.9(a1).
Reference to material.
  Incorporation of material and rule by reference,
    §150B-21.6.
Register.
  Publication, §§150B-21.17 to 150B-21.25.
Repeal of law authorizing agency to adopt rule.
  Effect, §150B-21.7.
Restrictions on what can be adopted as a rule,
  §150B-19.
Review by agency.
  Annual review, §150B-19.1(b).
Review by commission.
  Criteria, determining whether rule meets,
    §150B-21.9(a).
  Emergency rules, §150B-21.8(a).
  Scope, amendment to permanent rule,
    §150B-21.8(c).
  Standards for review, §150B-21.9(a).
  Temporary and permanent rules, §150B-21.8(b).
  Time limit, §150B-21.9(b).
Review of existing rules.
  Public comment, tracking agency progress.
    Single web portal for, §150B-19.2(b).
  Rules modification and improvement procedure,
    §150B-19.2(a).
Rulemaking coordinators.
  Agencies to designate, §150B-21(a).
  Duties, §150B-21(b) to (e).
Rules affecting local governments.
  Minimizing effects of rules on local budgets,
    §150B-21.27.
  Office of state budget and management.
    Duties, §150B-21.28.
    Preliminary review by, §150B-21.26(a).
    Scope, §150B-21.26(b).
Rules review commission, §§143B-30.1 to
  143B-30.4.
  Appointment, §143B-30.1(a).
  Compensation, §143B-30.1(d).
  Composition, §143B-30.1(a).
  Computer access to North Carolina
    administrative code, §143B-30.1(f).
  Creation, §143B-30.1(a).
  Employees.
    Assignments, §143B-30.1(e).
  Expenses, §143B-30.1(d).
  Independent agency, §143B-30.1(c).
  Meetings, §143B-30.1(c).
  Number of members, §143B-30.1(a).
  Procedures and forms in submitting rules.
    Commission to prescribe, §143B-30.1(f).
  Quorum, §143B-30.1(c).

ADMINISTRATIVE PROCEDURE —Cont'd
Rulemaking procedure —Cont'd
Rules review commission —Cont'd
  Terms, §143B-30.1(a).
    Expiration, §143B-30.1(b).
  Vacancies, §143B-30.1(a).
    Resignation, dismissal, ineligibility, etc.,
      §143B-30.1(c).
Scope of article, §150B-18.
State building code.
  Notice and hearing not required, §150B-21.5(d).
Technical change.
  Effective dates, §150B-21.3(f).
Temporary rules.
  Comments on proposed rule.
    Acceptance of written comments, time period,
      §150B-21.1(a3).
  Declaratory judgment.
    Rule returned to agency, §150B-21.1(b2), (c1).
  Effective date, §§150B-21.1(d), 150B-21.3(a).
  Expiration, §150B-21.1(d).
  Findings of need for rule, written statement,
    §150B-21.1(a4).
    Statement not meeting criteria,
      §150B-21.1(b1) to (b3).
    Supplementation, §150B-21.1(b1).
  Notice of intent to adopt and of public hearing,
    §150B-21.1(a3).
  Publication, §150B-21.1(a3), (e).
  Public hearing, §150B-21.1(a3).
  Recent act, change, regulation or order.
    Defined, waiver 210 day requirement,
      §150B-21.1(a2).
  Review, §§150B-21.1(b), 150B-21.8(b).
  Rule not entered into code, §150B-21.1(b3).
  Standing to file action for declaratory judgment,
    §150B-21.1(c).
  When agency may adopt, §150B-21.1(a).
Unnecessary, unduly burdensome, inconsistent
  rules.
  Annual review to identify, repeal, §150B-19.1(b).
Validity of rules, §150B-18.
  Erroneous fiscal note.
    Effect, §150B-21.4(c).
Rules and regulations defined, §150B-2.
Service of process.
Appeals.
  Copies of petition served on all parties,
    §150B-46.
State bar rules.
Publication of code and register, §150B-21.21(a),
  (c).
Stays.
Appeals.
  Administrative decision, §§150B-48, 150B-52.
Hearings, §150B-33(a).
Stipulations.
Hearings, §§150B-31(a), (b), 150B-41(c).
Subpoenas, §150B-39(c).
Hearings, §§150B-27, 150B-39(c).
Witnesses.
  Fees, §150B-39(c).
Substantial evidence.
Defined, §150B-2.
Summary judgment.
Authority of judge to grant, §150B-34(e).
Taxation.
Contested tax cases.
  Appeals, procedure for seeking review,
    §150B-45(a).
  Hearings, §150B-31.1.

ADMINISTRATIVE PROCEDURE —Cont'd
Turnpike authority.
Exemptions, §136-89.194(h).
University of North Carolina.
Exemption, §150B-1(f).
Unreasonable delay of decision.
Court order compelling action, right to seek,
§150B-44.
Venue.
Hearings, §150B-24.
Contested tax cases, §150B-31.1(c).
Waiver.
Appeals, §150B-45(b).
Hearings.
Venue.
Waiver of objection to venue, §150B-24(b).
Witnesses.
Hearings.
Cross-examination, §§150B-25(d), 150B-40(a).
Subpoenas, §§150B-27, 150B-39(c).
Subpoenas.
Fees, §150B-39(c).

**ADMINISTRATIVE SEARCH AND
INSPECTION WARRANTS,** §15-27.2.
**Nonresidential buildings that fail to meet
minimum standards.**
Investigations, §160A-439(b).
Wildlife protectors, securing, §113-302.1(c).

ADMINISTRATIVE SUBPOENA.
False claims act violations.
Civil investigative demand, §1-614.

**ADMINISTRATOR OF SAVINGS INSTITUTION
DIVISION.**
Savings and loan associations.
Generally.
See SAVINGS AND LOAN ASSOCIATIONS.
Savings banks.
Generally.
See SAVINGS BANKS.

ADMINISTRATORS.
See EXECUTORS AND ADMINISTRATORS.

ADMIRALTY.
Constitution of the United States, US Const Art
I §8.
Jurisdiction of courts, US Const Art III §2.

ADMISSION FEES.
Privilege tax on gross receipts.
Live entertainment, §105-37.1.

ADMISSIONS.
Adultery.
Admissibility of admission or confession as
evidence, §14-184.
Compromise and settlement.
Advance or partial payments.
Not to constitute admission of liability,
§1-540.3(a).
Motor vehicle collisions or accidents.
Settlement of property damage claims not to
constitute admission of liability, §1-540.2.
**Contents of writings, recordings and
photographs,** §8C-1 Rule 1007.
Delinquent and undisciplined juvenile actions.
In-custody admission, §7B-2101(b).
When admissions by juvenile accepted by court.
Determination factual basis for admission,
§7B-2407(c).
Determination that admission product of
informed choice, §7B-2407(b).

ADMISSIONS —Cont'd
Delinquent and undisciplined juvenile actions
—Cont'd
When admissions by juvenile accepted by court
—Cont'd
Duties of court before accepting, §7B-2407(a).
Fornication.
Admissibility of admission or confession as
evidence, §14-184.
Gambling contracts, §16-2.
Garnishment.
Garnishee, §1-440.28(a) to (g).
Limitation of actions.
Party to obligation, co-obligor or guarantor.
Effect of admission by, §1-27(a).
Medical malpractice.
Arbitration of negligent health claims,
§90-21.63(c).
Partnerships.
Bound by admission of partner, §59-41.
Limitation of actions.
Effect of admission by partner, §59-39.1.
Payment into court.
Defendant ordered to satisfy admitted sum,
§1-510.
**Pre-trial conference to consider possibility of
obtaining,** §1A-1 Rule 16(a).
Proof of service.
Written admission of defendant, §1-75.10(a).
Request for admission, §§1A-1 Rule 26(a), 1A-1
Rule 36(a).
Answer, §1A-1 Rule 36(a).
Effect of admission, §1A-1 Rule 36(b).
Expenses on failure to admit, §1A-1 Rule 37(c).
Statements against interest.
Hearsay exception, §8C-1 Rule 804(b).

ADMISSION TO THE BAR.
See ATTORNEYS AT LAW.

ADMONITION.
Attorney discipline.
Imposition of discipline, Bar Rule B.0123.
Issuance by grievance committee, Bar Rule
B.0113.

ADOPT-A-HIGHWAY PROGRAM, §136-140.1.

ADOPTION, §§48-1-101 to 48-10-105.
Abused, neglected or dependent juveniles.
Periodic review hearings as to placement.
Custody removed from parent, permanency
plan, §7B-906.
Surrender of juvenile for adoption, agency plan
for placement, §7B-909.
Termination of parental rights, permanent
placement plan, §7B-908.
Action, §50-13.2A.
Failure to disclose nonidentifying information.
Civil action for equitable or monetary relief,
§48-10-104.
Unauthorized disclosure of identifying
information.
Civil action for equitable or monetary relief,
§48-10-105(d).
Visitation of adopted grandchild, §50-13.2A.
Adoptee.
Defined, §48-1-101.
Adoption facilitator.
Defined, §48-1-101.
Adoptive homes.
Regulation of agencies receiving or placing
children in, §§131D-10.1 to 131D-10.9.
See CHILD PLACING AGENCIES.

ADOPTION —Cont'd
Adults.
Applicability of article, §48-5-100.
Consent.
Contents, §48-5-102(b).
Persons from whom consent required, §48-5-102(a).
Revocation, §48-5-102(d).
Spouse of petitioner in stepparent adoption, §48-5-102(c).
Defined, §48-1-101.
Incompetent adults.
Consent of guardian, §48-5-103(a), (b).
Guardian ad litem to investigate and report to court, §48-5-103(c).
Petition for adoption.
Married prospective adoptive parent.
Joinder of both spouses, §48-5-101(b).
Who may file, §48-5-101(a).
Advertising.
Desire to adopt, §48-10-101(b1).
Unauthorized persons, misdemeanor, §48-10-101(b), (c).
Affidavit of parentage.
Agency placements, §48-3-206(b).
Contents, §48-3-206(a).
Execution, §48-3-206(a).
Filing with petition for adoption, §48-2-305.
Agencies.
Defined, §48-1-101.
Agency placements.
Acquisition of legal and physical custody of minor, §48-3-203(a).
Adoption of minors, §48-3-201.
Affidavit of parentage, §48-3-205(b).
Confidential intermediary.
Child placing agency acting as.
Authorized disclosures, §48-9-109.
Obtaining and sharing information, §48-9-104(b).
Defined, §48-1-101.
Consent withheld contrary to best interest of minor.
Court order dispensing with consent, §48-3-603(b).
Criminal history investigation, §48-3-203(d1).
Custody of minor pending adoption decree.
Legal custody with agency, §48-3-502(a).
Petition by agency for full legal and physical custody, §48-3-502(b).
Execution of consent, §48-3-605(d).
Identifying information.
Release by agency, §§48-3-203(f), 48-9-109.
Investigation required, §48-3-203(d1).
Notice to parent when adoption decree issued, §48-3-203(c).
Parties by whom consent required, §48-3-601.
Preplacement assessments.
Selection of prospective adoptive parent, §48-3-203(d).
Promulgation of rules by social services commission, §48-3-203(e).
Recruitment of adoptive parents, §48-3-204.
Relinquishment of one parent sufficient for placement for adoption, §48-3-201(d).
Schedule of fees or expenses charged.
Statements of services to prospective adoptive parents, §48-3-203(b).
Statement of services provided to prospective adoptive parents, §48-3-203(b).
Time for execution of consent, §48-3-604.

ADOPTION —Cont'd
Alien adoptees.
Contents of decree of adoption, §48-2-606(b).
Alleged father of minor adoptee, no notice given.
Court to give notice, §48-2-404.
Appeals.
Consent of parent or guardian obtained by fraud or duress, §48-2-607(c).
Procedure, notice, §48-2-607(b).
Prohibited grounds for appeals, §48-2-607(a).
Relinquishment of parent or guardian obtained by fraud or duress, §48-2-607(c).
Statute of limitations.
Action for damages against adoptee or adoptive parent for fraud or duress, §48-2-607(c).
Unfavorable preplacement assessments, §48-3-308(a).
Appearances.
Hearing on petition to adopt adult, §48-2-605(b).
Assistance for adoptive parents.
Interstate compact on adoption and medical assistance, §§7B-3900 to 7B-3906.
Attorneys at law.
Attorneys specializing in family law.
Certification standards, Bar Rules D.2401 to D.2407.
Representation of adoptee, §48-2-201(b).
Representation of parents, §48-2-201(a).
Attorneys' fees.
Revocation of consent.
Fees awarded to person who revoked upon non-return of minor, §48-3-608(c).
Revocation of relinquishment.
Failure to return minor, §48-3-706(b).
Background information provided to prospective adoptive parents, §48-3-205.
Best interest of adoptee.
Standard of proof for hearings on petition, §48-2-603.
Biological parents.
Consent of biological father, §48-2-206.
Bringing or sending juvenile into state for purposes of placement for adoption.
Applicability of article, §7B-3705.
Bond required for person, agency, etc., bringing juvenile into state, §7B-3701.
Consent of department of health and human services, §7B-3700(a).
Definitions, §7B-3704.
Misdemeanor for violating provisions, §7B-3703.
Responsibility for care and training of juvenile, §7B-3700(b).
Burden of proof.
Hearing on petition, §48-2-603(a).
Adoption of adult, §48-2-605(b).
Certificate of identification for individual of foreign birth, §130A-108(a).
Readoption in state, §130A-108(b).
Children and minors.
Abused, neglected or dependent juveniles.
Periodic review hearings as to placement.
Custody removed from parent, permanency plan, §7B-906.
Surrender of juvenile for adoption, agency plan for placement, §7B-909.
Termination of parental rights, permanent placement plan, §7B-908.
Affidavit of parentage, §48-3-206.
Agency placements generally. See within this heading, "Agency placements."

ADOPTION —Cont'd
Children and minors —Cont'd
Applicability of article to stepparents, §48-3-100.
Child, defined, §48-1-101.
Consent.
 Generally. See within this heading, "Consent."
 Required for direct placement of minor,
  §48-3-201(b).
Consequences of consent to adopt minor,
 §48-3-607.
Custody.
 Denial of petition to adopt, §48-2-604(c).
 Execution of consent, §48-3-607(b).
 Failure to consent, §50-13.2(d).
 Minor in health care facility.
  Authorization to transfer custody to agency,
   §48-3-402.
  Definitions, §48-3-401.
 Pending adoption decree, §§48-3-501, 48-3-502.
 Visitation of adopted grandchild.
  Action by biological grandparent, §50-13.2A.
Denial of petition to adopt minor, §48-2-604(c).
Direct placements generally. See within this
 heading, "Direct placements."
Disclosure of background information.
 Forms to collect information, §48-3-205(d).
 General information provided to prospective
  adoptive parents, §48-3-205(a).
 Preservation of health information by agency,
  §48-3-205(c).
 Use against provider in pending civil or
  criminal actions prohibited, §48-3-205(b).
Dismissal of petition, §48-2-604(a).
 Notice and hearing, §48-2-604(b).
Interstate placements, §48-3-207.
Married and emancipated minors, adoption of,
 §48-5-100.
Notice to alleged father of minor adoptee,
 §48-2-404.
Placement of minors for adoption, §48-3-201.
Recruitment of adoptive parents.
 Cooperation between agencies, §48-3-204(c).
 Photo-listing service, §48-3-204(b).
 Rules for agencies to follow, §48-3-204(a).
Relinquishment generally. See within this
 heading, "Relinquishment."
Revocation of consent to adoption of minor,
 §§48-3-607 to 48-3-609.
Stepparent's adoption of minor.
 General provisions. See within this heading,
  "Stepparents."
Transfer of custody from health care facility.
 Attending practitioner, defined, §48-3-401.
 Authorization for transfer of minor to agency.
  Duration of authorization, §48-3-402(b).
 Health care facility, defined, §48-3-401.
Who may place minors for adoption, §48-3-201(a).
Child support.
Consequences of consent by parent to adoption,
 §48-3-607(c).
Duty of former parent to make past-due
 payments.
 Effect of decree of adoption, §48-1-106(c).
Collateral agreements to consent.
Enforceability, effect on consent, §48-3-610.
Confidential intermediary.
Authorized disclosures, §48-9-109.
Certificate of death.
 Copy upon request, §130A-93.
Defined, §48-1-101.
Obtaining and sharing information, §48-9-104(b).

ADOPTION —Cont'd
Confidential intermediary —Cont'd
Person subject of search deceased.
 Delivery of death certificate to person
  requesting services, §48-9-104(d).
Release of identifying information, §48-9-104(b).
Confidentiality.
Criminal history record check.
 Prospective parent.
  Privileged information, §48-3-309(f).
Proceedings generally, §48-2-203.
Records.
 General provisions, §§48-9-101 to 48-9-109. See
  within this heading, "Records."
Conflicts resolved in favor of minors,
 §48-1-100(c).
Consent.
Adult adoptions.
 Contents, §48-5-102(b).
 Persons from whom consent required,
  §48-5-102(a).
 Revocation, §48-5-102(d).
 Spouse of petitioner in stepparent adoption,
  §48-5-102(c).
Agency placements, §48-3-601.
 Consent withheld contrary to best interest of
  minor.
  Court order dispensing with consent,
   §48-3-603(b).
 Execution of consent by agency, §48-3-605(d).
 Time for execution of consent, §48-3-604(d).
Biological father.
 Applicability of court decision, §48-2-206(i).
 Computation of time, §48-2-206(g).
 Hearings, §48-2-206(d).
 Jurisdiction, §48-2-206(f).
 Notice of intent to place for adoption,
  §48-2-206(a).
  Contents, §48-2-206(b).
  Failure to respond, §48-2-206(c).
 Service of process, §48-2-206(e).
 Transfers and appeals, §48-2-206(h).
Bringing juvenile into state or taking or sending
 juvenile out of state for purposes of
 placement, §§7B-3700 to 7B-3705.
Collateral agreements, effect on consent,
 §48-3-610.
Consequences, §48-3-607.
Contents, mandatory provisions, §48-3-606.
Court order dispensing with consent in certain
 situations, §48-3-603(b).
Custody of minor upon revocation, §48-3-608(c).
Custody of minor upon voiding of consent,
 §48-3-609(b).
Direct placements, §§48-3-201(b), 48-3-601.
Dismissal of adoption proceeding upon voiding of
 consent, §48-3-609(c).
Effect, §48-3-607.
Execution.
 Agencies, §48-3-605(d).
 Timing, §48-3-604(d).
 Contents, mandatory provisions, §48-3-606.
 Foreign execution, §48-3-605(e).
 General provisions, §48-3-605(c).
 Guardian, timing, §48-3-604(c).
 Indian children, §48-3-605(f).
 Man whose consent is require, timing,
  §48-3-604(a).
 Minor twelve years of age or older, timing,
  §48-3-604(e).
 Mother, timing, §48-3-604(b).

ADOPTION —Cont'd
Consent —Cont'd
Execution —Cont'd
Parent or guardian of minor, §48-3-605(a).
Parent under age of eighteen, §48-3-605(b).
Failure to respond to notice of filing.
Consent not required, §48-2-207(a).
Final and irrevocable, §48-3-607(a).
Foreign consent, §48-3-605(e).
Fraud or duress in obtaining consent of parent or guardian.
Statute of limitations for appeal, §48-2-607(c).
General provisions, §§48-3-601, 48-3-603.
Guardian ad litem for incompetent parents, §48-3-602.
Hearings to determine if consent required, §48-2-207(b).
Proceeding after determination, §48-2-207(c).
Incompetent parents, §48-3-602.
Inheritance, succession, insurance, child support and other benefits or claims.
Minors, §48-3-607(c).
Irrevocable consent.
Second consent to adoption by same adoptive parents, §48-3-608(e).
Legal and physical custody in prospective adoptive parent, §48-3-607(b).
Mandatory contents, §48-3-606.
Minor age twelve or older.
Consent required, §48-3-601.
Court order dispensing with consent, §48-3-603(b).
Time for execution, §48-3-604(e).
Persons whose consent not required, §48-3-603.
Failure to respond to notice of filing, §48-2-207(a).
Hearings to determine if consent required, §48-2-207(b), (d).
Persons whose consent required, §48-3-601.
Hearings to determine if consent required, §48-2-207(b), (c).
Readoption after stepparent adoption.
Adoptee, §48-6-102(d).
Adoptee's parent who was spouse of adoptive parent, §48-6-102(g).
Adoptive parent, §48-6-102(f).
Guardian of minor adoptee, §48-6-102(h).
Petitioner's spouse, §48-6-102(e).
Who must execute consent, §48-6-102(c).
Revocation of consent.
Adoption cannot proceed without another consent, §48-3-608(d).
Attorneys' fees to person who revoked upon non-return of minor, §48-3-608(c).
Custody of minor, §48-3-608(c).
Direct placement, §48-3-608(b).
Generally, §48-3-608(a).
Second consent by same adoptive parents.
Irrevocable, §48-3-608(e).
Stepparent's adoption of stepchild, §48-4-102.
Timing of execution, §48-3-604.
Void, §48-3-609(a).
Custody of minor, §48-3-609(b).
Dismissal of adoption proceeding, §48-3-609(c).
Construction of chapter, §48-1-100(c).
Liberally construed generally, §48-1-100(d).
Criminal history record checks.
Criminal history defined, §48-1-101.

ADOPTION —Cont'd
Criminal history record checks —Cont'd
Mandatory preplacement criminal checks of prospective adoptive parents of minor in custody or placement responsibility of county department of social services.
Department of justice.
Duties, §48-3-309(c).
Performance of check by, §48-3-309(h).
Forms, §48-3-309(d).
Negligence in carrying out provisions.
No liability for, §48-3-309(g).
Notification of results, §48-3-309(e).
Privileged information, §48-3-309(f).
Responsibility of department, §48-3-309(a).
Unfavorable preplacement assessment, §48-3-309(b).
Parents seeking to adopt minor in custody of county department of social services, §114-19.7.
Preplacement assessments, §48-3-303(d).
Minor in custody or placement responsibility of county department of social services.
Mandatory preplacement criminal checks of prospective adoptive parents, §48-3-309.
Prospective adoptive parents, §114-19.3(d).
Criminal law and procedure.
Prohibited placement activities, §48-10-101.
Unauthorized disclosure of identifying information, §48-10-105.
Unlawful payments related to adoption, §48-10-102.
Damages.
Failure to disclose nonidentifying information.
Civil action for monetary relief, §48-10-104.
Unauthorized disclosure of information.
Civil action for monetary relief, §48-10-105.
Death of joint petitioner pending final decree, §48-2-204.
Decedents' estates.
Inheritance rights of child subject to adoption.
Consequences of consent by parent to adoption, §48-3-607(c).
Intestate succession, §29-17.
Share of after-adopted children, §28A-22-2.
Decree of adoption.
Alien adoptees, §48-2-606(b).
Biological grandparents' rights, effect, §48-1-106(f).
Child support arrearage of former parent not terminated, §48-1-106(c).
Contents, §48-2-606(a).
Former parent of adoptee not to be named on decree, §48-2-606(c).
Former parents' rights, effect, §48-1-106(c).
Inheritance rights of adoptee, §48-1-106(b).
Instruments transferring ownership, language of kinship included in instrument.
Effect of decree, §48-1-106(e).
Legal effect, §48-1-106(a).
Omission of information from petition, effect on decree, §48-2-306(b).
Parent and child relationship established, §48-1-106(b).
Recognition of foreign decrees, §48-2-205.
Restoration of original certificate if decree set aside, §48-9-108.
Rights of biological grandparents, §48-1-106(f).
Rights of former parents, §48-1-106(c).
Stepparent adoption or readoption.
Effect on relationship between child and stepparent's spouse, §48-1-106.

ADOPTION —Cont'd
Definitions, §48-1-101.
Direct placements.
  Custody of minor pending adoption decree,
    §48-3-501.
  Information regarding prospective adoptive parent
    provided to parent or guardian, §48-3-202(b).
  Minor placed with relative, preplacement
    assessment not required, §48-3-301(b).
  Persons whose consent required, §48-3-601.
  Preplacement assessments.
    Provided to parent or guardian, §48-3-202(b).
  Recruitment of adoptive parents, §48-3-204.
  Revocation of consent, §48-3-608(b).
  Selection of prospective adoptive parent,
    §48-3-202(a).
  Violation of preplacement assessment
    requirements, §48-3-301(c).
Disclosure of confidential information.
  General provisions, §§48-9-101 to 48-9-109. See
    within this heading, "Records."
Dismissal of petition, §48-2-604(a).
  Consent becomes void, §48-3-609(c).
  Notice and hearing, §48-2-604(b).
Dispositional hearing on petition.
  Disclosure of fees and charges, §48-2-602.
  Extension of time for hearing, §48-2-601(c).
  No contest to petition, §48-2-601(a).
  Procedure generally, §48-2-603.
  Time for hearing, §48-2-601(b).
  Transfer of proceeding to district court.
    Issue of fact or defense raised before clerk,
      §48-2-601(a1).
Division.
  Defined, §48-1-101.
Divorce.
  Visitation of adopted grandchild.
    Action by biological grandparent, §50-13.2A.
Duress in execution of notice waiver,
  §48-2-406(c).
Failure to disclose nonidentifying information,
  §48-10-104.
Fees.
  Agency placements.
    Schedule of fees included in statement of
      services, §48-3-203(b).
  Dispositional hearing on petition.
    Disclosure of fees and charges, §48-2-602.
  Lawful payments related to adoption.
    Agency fees and charges, §48-10-103(e).
  Preplacement assessments, §48-3-304.
  Report to court, §48-2-504.
  Unlawful payments related to adoption,
    §48-10-102(a).
Felonies.
  Unlawful payments related to adoption.
    Subsequent violations, §48-10-102(b).
Fines.
  Unlawful payments related to adoption,
    §48-10-102(b).
Foreign adoption decrees, recognition,
  §48-2-205.
Foreign birth.
  Certificate of identification for individual of
    foreign birth, §130A-108.
Former parent adoption, §§48-6-100 to 48-6-102.
  See within this heading, "Readoption."
Former parents of adoptees.
  Child support arrearage not terminated by
    adoption decree, §48-1-106(c).

ADOPTION —Cont'd
Former parents of adoptees —Cont'd
  Name prohibited on decree of adoption,
    §48-2-606(c).
Foster care and adoption assistance payments,
  §§108A-48 to 108A-50.
Foster homes.
  Control over child caring facilities, §§110-45 to
    110-48.
  Foster care and adoption assistance payments,
    §§108A-48 to 108A-50.
Fraud in execution of notice waiver,
  §48-2-406(c).
Grandparent visitation, §48-1-106(f).
  Actions, §50-13.2A.
Guardian ad litem.
  Adoption of incompetent adults.
    Investigation and report to court, §48-5-103(c).
  Consent execution for incompetent parents,
    §48-3-602.
  Representation of adoptee, §48-2-201(b).
Guardians.
  Adoption of incompetent adults.
    Consent, §48-5-103(a), (b).
  Appointment for minor child.
    Consent not required from parent, §48-3-603(a).
  Defined, §48-1-101.
  Execution of consent, time, §48-3-604(c).
  Relinquishment of child generally. See within this
    heading, "Relinquishment."
Hearings.
  Confidentiality of hearings, §48-2-203.
  Dispositional hearing on uncontested petition,
    §48-2-601.
  Petition for adoption of adult.
    Appearance of parties, §48-2-605(a).
    Burden of proof, §48-2-605(b).
    Procedure generally, §48-2-605(b).
  Petition for adoption of minor.
    Continuance of hearing on court's motion,
      §48-2-603(c).
    Procedure generally, §48-2-603.
    Sanctions for violations of chapter, §48-2-603(b).
    Standard of proof, §48-2-603(a).
Hearsay exception.
  Statement of personal or family history, §§8C-1
    Rule 803, 8C-1 Rule 804.
Husband and wife.
  Death of joint petitioner pending final decree,
    §48-2-204.
  Prohibition on adoption, §48-1-103.
  Spouse of petitioner must join in petition,
    §48-2-301(b).
Identification of adoptees.
  Confidentiality of records generally, §§48-9-101 to
    48-9-109. See within this heading, "Records."
Income tax credit for adoption expenses.
  Amount, §105-151.32(a).
  Reduction of amount, §105-151.32(b).
  Repeal of provision, §105-151.32(c).
Indians.
  Adoptee subject to Indian child welfare act,
    §48-1-108.
  Execution of consent, §48-3-605(f).
**Information provided to prospective adoptive
  parents,** §48-3-205.
Inheritance rights.
  Consequences of consent by parent to adoption,
    §48-3-607(c).
  Effect of decree of adoption, §48-1-106(b), (e).

ADOPTION —Cont'd
Injunctions.
Prohibited placement activities, §48-10-101(d).
Unauthorized disclosure of information,
§48-10-105(c).
Unlawful payments related to adoption,
§48-10-102(c).
Interstate compact on adoption and medical assistance, §§7B-3900 to 7B-3906.
Administrator, appointment by secretary of health and human services, §7B-3906.
Authorization to secretary of health and human services, §7B-3902.
Definitions, §7B-3901.
Federal government payment provisions, inclusion in compact, §7B-3905.
General assembly advice to enter into compact, §7B-3900(b).
Medical assistance certification of child with special needs, §7B-3904(a).
Applicability of provisions, §7B-3904(c).
Entitlement of holder of certificate, §7B-3904(b).
Provisions required to be included in compact, §7B-3903(a).
Provision that may be included in compact, §7B-3903(b).
Purposes and legislative findings, §7B-3900(a).
Interstate compact on the placement of children, §§7B-3800 to 7B-3806.
Interstate placements, §48-3-207.
Intestate succession, §29-17.
Consequences of consent by parent to adoption, §48-3-607(c).
Jurisdiction.
Adoptee also subject of pending proceeding in district court.
Jurisdiction of district court, §48-2-102(b).
Foreign court exercising jurisdiction, §48-2-100(c).
Requirements, §48-2-100(b).
Superior court, §48-2-100(a).
Jury trial.
No right to jury, §48-2-202.
Lawful payments related to adoption, §48-10-103.
Legal custody.
Defined, §48-1-101.
Legislative intent, §48-1-100(a).
Liberal construction of chapter, §48-1-100(d).
Limitation of actions.
Action for damages against adoptee or adoptive parent for fraud or duress in obtaining consent, §48-2-607(c).
Medical assistance for children of adoptive parents.
Interstate compact on adoption and medical assistance, §§7B-3900 to 7B-3906.
Minors.
Adoption of minors generally. See within this heading, "Children and minors."
Defined, §48-1-101.
Misdemeanors.
Prohibited placement activities, §48-10-101.
Unauthorized disclosure of identifying information, §48-10-105.
Unlawful payments related to adoption, §48-10-102(b).
Motion for release of information.
Protection of adoptee or public, §48-9-105.
Name.
Former parents' names not to be listed on decree, §48-2-606(c).

ADOPTION —Cont'd
Name —Cont'd
Name of adoptee after adoption, §48-1-105.
Notice.
Agency placements, §48-3-203(c).
Clerk of court to give notice of proceedings, §48-2-403.
Consent of person not required, rights in proceeding, §48-2-405.
Court to give notice to alleged father, §48-2-404.
Dismissal of petition to adopt minor, §48-2-604(b).
Filing of petition.
Adoption of adult, §48-2-401(d).
Adoption of minor, §48-2-401(c).
Failure to respond.
Consent not required, §48-2-207(a).
Generally, §48-2-401(b).
Time for filing response, §48-2-401(f).
Identity of biological parent cannot be ascertained, §48-2-402(b).
Motion for release of information.
Notice of hearings, §48-9-105(b).
Relinquishment, §48-3-706(a).
Service of process, §48-2-402(a).
Time for serving notice of petition, §48-2-401(a).
Unknown biological parent, §48-2-402(b).
Waiver.
Effect on person who executes waiver, §48-2-406(b).
Motion to set aside for fraud or duress, §48-2-406(c).
Procedure, §48-2-406(a).
Who is entitled to notice, §48-2-401(e).
Other rights of adoptee not divested by decree, §48-1-107.
Parental consent.
Biological father, §48-2-206.
Parent and child.
Adoption by former parent, §§48-6-100 to 48-6-102.
Definition of "parent," §48-1-102.
Execution of consent, §48-3-605.
Relinquishment of minors generally. See within this heading, "Relinquishment."
Parties.
Defined, §48-1-101.
Payments related to adoption.
Agency fees, §48-10-103(e).
Contingent on placement for adoption, prohibited, §48-10-103(c).
Lawful payments generally, §48-10-103(a).
Preplacement assessment, §48-10-103(b).
Recovery of payment.
Receipt by person with fraudulent intent to prevent adoption from being completed, §48-10-103(d).
Sliding scale fees by agency.
Authorized, §48-10-103.
Unlawful payments, §48-10-102(a).
Persons entitled to notice, consent not required.
Rights in adoption proceedings, §48-2-405.
Persons who may adopt, §48-1-103.
Persons who may be adopted, §48-1-104.
Petition for adoption.
Additional documents to be filed, §48-2-305.
Adults.
Hearing on petition to adopt adult, §48-2-605.
Caption, §48-2-303.
Contents, §48-2-304(a).
Adoption of adult, §48-2-304(e).

ADOPTION —Cont'd
Petition for adoption —Cont'd
Contents —Cont'd
Adoption of minor, §48-2-304(b) to (d).
Death of joint petitioner pending final decree,
§48-2-204.
Denial of petition to adopt minor, §48-2-604(c).
Dispositional hearing, §48-2-603.
Uncontested petition, §48-2-601.
Documents to be filed with, §48-2-305.
Filing concurrently with petition to terminate
parental rights, §48-2-302(c).
Filing of additional information, §48-2-306(a).
Form of caption, §48-2-303.
Granting.
Sanctions for violations of chapter, §48-2-603(b).
Hearing on petition, §48-2-603.
Joinder.
Readoption after stepparent adoption.
Joinder of petitioner's spouse, §48-6-102(b).
Spouse of petitioner, §48-2-301(b).
Unmarried petitioner, §48-2-301(c).
Joint petition between spouses.
Death of joint petitioner pending final decree,
§48-2-204.
Jurisdiction, §48-2-100.
Notice, §48-2-401.
Omission of information, effect on decree,
§48-2-306(b).
Placement requirement, §48-2-301(a).
Preplacement assessment not complete.
Affidavit of explanation attached to petition,
§48-3-307(b).
Readoption after stepparent adoption.
Joinder of petitioner's spouse, §48-6-102(b).
Spouse of petitioner must join in petition,
§48-2-301(b).
Standard petition promulgated by department,
§48-2-304(f).
Stepparent's adoption of stepchild, §48-4-101.
Termination of parental rights.
Petitions filed concurrently, §48-2-302(c).
Time of filing, §48-2-302(a).
Failure to file timely, §48-2-302(b).
Filing concurrently with petition to terminate
parental rights, §48-2-302(c).
Unmarried prospective adoptive parent.
Joinder by others prohibited, §48-2-301(c).
Venue, §48-2-101.
Who may file, §48-2-301(a).
Physical custody.
Defined, §48-1-101.
Placement.
Defined, §48-1-101.
Placement assessments.
Fees for preparation.
Agreement, §48-3-304(a).
Authority to charge fee, §48-3-304(a).
Maximum fees, basis for, §48-3-304(c).
Review by court, §48-3-304(b).
Waiver, unable to pay, §48-3-304(c).
Time for completing, §48-3-303(d).
**Placement for adoption by unauthorized
persons.**
Misdemeanor, §48-10-101(a), (c).
Placement of children.
Control over child caring facilities, §§110-45 to
110-48.
Foster care and adoption assistance payments,
§§108A-48 to 108A-50.

ADOPTION —Cont'd
Preplacement assessments.
Adoption of minors, §48-3-301(a).
Agency assessment of individual, §48-3-302(d).
Agency placements.
Selection of prospective adoptive parent,
§48-3-203(d).
Agency refusal to conduct.
Assessment prepared by county department of
social services, §48-3-302(e).
Contents of report, §48-3-303(c).
Copies of favorable assessments, §48-3-306.
Copy of assessments retained by agency,
§48-3-305(b).
Copy sent to subjects of assessment, §48-3-305(a).
Criminal record check, §48-3-303(d).
Minor in custody or placement responsibility of
county department of social services.
Mandatory preplacement criminal checks of
prospective adoptive parents, §48-3-309.
Defined, §48-1-101.
Delivery of copy to parent or guardian who placed
minor for adoption.
Certificate to be filed by prospective adoptive
parent, §48-3-307(c).
Determination of suitability to be adoptive parent.
Assessment to include factors in support of
determination, §48-3-303(f).
Determination of unsuitability to be adoptive
parent.
Assessment to state specific concerns,
§48-3-303(g).
Filing of original assessment with division,
§48-3-305(a).
Direct placement for adoption of minor.
Information provided about prospective adoptive
parents, §48-3-202(b).
Placement made in violation of section,
§48-3-301(c).
Placement with relative of minor.
Assessment not required, §48-3-301(b).
Favorable assessment.
Copies to be provided, §48-3-306.
Filing of petition before assessment complete,
§48-3-307(b).
Filing with adoption petition, §48-2-305.
Lawful payments related to adoption,
§48-10-103(b).
Multiple assessments.
Request by prospective adoptive parents,
§48-3-302(c).
Personal interview requirement, §48-3-303(b).
Petition for adoption filed before assessment
complete, §48-3-307(b).
Placement occurring before assessment complete,
§48-3-307(a).
Prepared in other states, §48-1-109(b).
Requested by prospective adoptive parent.
Agency refusal to conduct.
Assessment prepared by county department of
social services, §48-3-302(e).
Direct placements in violation of section,
§48-3-301(c).
Multiple assessments, §48-3-302(c).
Permissibility of request generally, §48-3-302(a).
Selection of prospective adoptee not required,
§48-3-302(b).
Review of information obtained, §48-3-303(e).
Rules established by social services commission,
§48-3-303(i).

ADOPTION —Cont'd
Preplacement assessments —Cont'd
Sources of information, assessment to contain list, §48-3-303(h).
Time for completion, §48-3-302(a).
Unfavorable assessment.
Not public records, §48-3-308(e).
Response filed with division, §48-3-308(b) to (e).
Action to be taken by county department of social services, §48-3-308(d).
Authority of division to take action, §48-3-308(c).
Review procedure, §48-3-308(a).
Who may prepare, §48-1-109(a).
Prohibited activities in placement, §48-10-101.
Property interest contingent on family relationship with former family divested by decree, §48-1-107.
Purpose of chapter, §48-1-100(b).
Readoption.
Adoptee adopted by stepparent.
Consent, §48-6-102(c) to (h).
Joinder in petition by petitioner's spouse, §48-6-102(b).
Permissibility, §48-6-102(a).
Applicability of article, §48-6-100.
Applicability of other articles, §48-6-101.
Custody orders already existing.
No effect, §48-6-102(j).
Effect on relationship between child and parent, §48-1-106(d).
Relationship between adoptee and parent who was married to adoptive parent.
Not affected by adoption under this section, §48-6-102(i).
Recognition of foreign adoption decrees, §48-2-205.
Records.
Adoption or name change of minor, §48-9-102(f).
Authorized disclosures, §48-9-109.
Birth certificates.
Motion for release of information may be accompanied by request for birth certificate, §48-9-105(d).
New birth certificate.
Adoption by stepparent, §48-9-107(b).
Adoption of adult, §48-9-107(a).
Adoption of minor, §48-9-107(a).
Copies to adoptee's new family, §48-9-107(c).
Issuance only by state registrar, §48-9-107(d).
Reference to adoption on certificate prohibited, §48-9-107(a).
Removal of original birth certificate from records, §48-9-107(d).
Reports of adoptions from other states, §48-9-107(e).
Original birth certificate of adoptee.
Release by state registrar, §48-9-106.
Release of original certificate by state registrar, §48-9-106.
Removal from records upon decree, §48-9-107(d).
Removal of original certificate from register of deeds, §48-9-107(d).
Restoration of original certificate if decree set aside, §48-9-108.
Restoration upon setting aside of adoption decree, §48-9-108.
Sealing of original birth certificate, §48-9-107(c).
Clerk of superior court to file records with division.
Priority, §48-9-102(d).

ADOPTION —Cont'd
Records —Cont'd
Confidential nature generally, §48-9-102(a).
Copy of final order, §48-9-102(g).
Defined, §48-9-101(a).
Disclosures authorized, §48-9-109.
Failure to disclose nonidentifying information, §48-10-104.
Filing by clerk of superior court with division, §48-9-102(d).
Inspection after final decree of adoption.
Prohibited generally, §48-9-102(c).
Inspection during adoption proceeding, §48-9-102(b).
Motion for release of information.
Determining factors of cause for release, §48-9-105(c).
Notice of hearings, §48-9-105(b).
Original birth certificate of adoptee.
Request for release authorized with filing of motion, §48-9-105(d).
Protection of adoptee or public, §48-9-105(a).
Service of process, §48-9-105(b).
Order of name change, §48-9-102(g).
Permanently indexed and filed, §48-9-102(e).
Release of identifying information.
Agency placement adoption, §§48-3-203(f), 48-9-109.
Confidential intermediaries, §48-9-104(b).
Family member defined, §48-9-104(c).
Person subject of search deceased.
Death certificate delivered to person requesting services, §48-9-104(d).
Prohibited, §48-9-104(a).
Protection of adoptee or public, §48-9-105.
Unauthorized disclosure, §48-10-105.
Release of nonidentifying health-related information.
Agency release to former parent or sibling, §48-9-103(f).
Court release to adoptee or adoptive parent, §48-9-103(e).
Express provisions for confidentiality, §48-9-103(c).
Failure to disclose, §48-10-104.
Omission of identifying information, §48-9-103(c).
Procedure for verifying identity of requester, §48-9-103(g).
Protection of adoptee or public.
Motion for release of information not otherwise obtainable, §48-9-105.
Request to agency, §48-9-103(b).
Request to court, §48-9-103(b).
Request to state registrar of vital statistics prohibited, §48-9-103(h).
Review of denial, §48-9-103(d).
Unauthorized disclosure, §48-10-105.
Who may request, §48-9-103(a).
Report of adoption or name change of minor, §48-9-102(f).
Sealed, permanently retained, §48-9-102(c).
Statistical research.
Disclosure not resulting in identification of adoptee authorized, §48-9-109.
Unauthorized disclosure of information, §48-10-105.
Generally, §48-10-105(a).
Misdemeanor, §48-10-105(b).
Relinquishment.
Agency acceptance of relinquishment, §48-3-702(b), (c).

ADOPTION —Cont'd
Relinquishment —Cont'd
Agency placement of minors for adoption,
　§48-3-201(c).
　Relinquishment from one parent sufficient,
　　§48-3-201(d).
Contents, mandatory provisions, §48-3-703(a).
Contents, optional provisions, §48-3-704.
Custody of minor upon execution, §48-3-705(b).
Custody of minor upon revocation, §48-3-706(b).
Defined, §48-1-101.
Dismissal of proceeding upon voiding of
　relinquishment, §48-3-707(c), (d).
Effect, §48-3-705(a).
General procedures, §48-3-702.
Guardian relinquishment of guardianship powers,
　§48-3-701(a).
　Timing of execution, §48-3-701(c).
Irrevocable second relinquishment, §48-3-706(d).
Mandatory contents, §48-3-703(a).
Optional contents, §48-3-704.
Parental relinquishment of rights, §48-3-701(a).
　Timing of execution, §48-3-701(b).
Procedures generally, §48-3-702(a).
Revocation.
　Adoption cannot proceed until other
　　relinquishment obtained, §48-3-706(c).
　Condition precedent, §48-3-707(b).
　Custody of minor, §48-3-706(b).
　Procedure, §48-3-706(a).
　Second relinquishment irrevocable,
　　§48-3-706(d).
Termination of rights, §48-3-705(c).
　Certain rights not terminated until
　　relinquishment filed, §48-3-705(d).
Timing of execution, §48-3-701(b), (c).
Void, §48-3-707(a).
　Dismissal of adoption proceeding, §48-3-707(c),
　　(d).
Reports.
Adoption or name change of adult, §48-9-102(a).
Adoption or name change of minor, §48-9-102(f).
Copies of report to court, §48-2-503(c).
Exceptions to requirement, §48-2-501(d).
Fee for preparing.
　Agreement, §48-2-504(a).
　Application of fees collected, §48-2-504(c).
　Court may charge petitioner, §48-2-504(a).
　Maximum fees.
　　Basis for, §48-2-504(c).
　Review by court, §48-2-504(b).
　Waiver of fees.
　　Unable to pay, §48-2-504(c).
Filing of report to court, §48-2-503.
Interim report.
　Specific concerns identified by agency,
　　§48-2-503(b).
Order for report to court, §§48-1-109(c),
　48-2-501(a).
　Adoption petition and additional documents
　　provided to preparer, §48-2-501(c).
　Preparation, agency responsibility, §48-2-501(b).
Preparation of report to court.
　Adoption of rules to implement provisions,
　　§48-2-502(c).
　Contents, §48-2-502(b).
　Fees, §48-2-504.
　Procedure, §48-2-502(a).
Preplacement assessments generally. See within
　this heading, "Preplacement assessments."
"Report to the court" defined, §48-1-101.

ADOPTION —Cont'd
Reports —Cont'd
Stepparent adoptions, §48-2-501(d).
Supplemental report.
　Specific concern identified by agency,
　　§48-2-503(b1).
Time for filing report to court, §48-2-503(a).
Revocation of consent, §§48-3-607 to 48-3-609.
Rights of adoptee.
Vested property interest not divested by decree,
　§48-1-107.
Service of process.
Agency placements.
　Petition to terminate parental rights filed
　　instead of serving notice, §48-2-402(c).
Filing of proof of service, §48-2-407.
Identity of biological parent cannot be
　ascertained, §48-2-402(b).
Motion for release of information, §48-9-105(b).
Notice of filing of petition, §48-2-402(a).
Proof of service, §48-2-407.
Unknown biological parent, §48-2-402(b).
Solicitation of adoptees for adoption.
Unauthorized persons, §48-10-101(a).
Specific performance.
Failure to disclose nonidentifying information.
　Civil action for equitable relief, §48-10-104.
State health plan for teachers and state
　employees.
Coverage of adopted child, §135-48.42(b).
　Effective date of coverage, §135-48.43(c).
Statute of limitations.
Action for damages against adoptee or adoptive
　parent.
　Fraud or duress in obtaining consent,
　　§48-2-607(c).
Stepparents.
Applicability of articles on adoption of minors,
　§§48-3-100, 48-4-100.
Consent to adoption of stepchild, §48-4-102.
　Execution by adoptee, §48-4-103(e).
　Execution by guardian of minor stepchild,
　　§48-4-103(c).
　Execution by stepchild's parent who is not a
　　spouse of stepparent, §48-4-103(b).
　Execution by stepparent's spouse, §48-4-103(a).
　Final and irrevocable, §48-4-103(d).
Defined, §48-1-101.
Effect on relationship between child and parent
　who is spouse of stepparent, §48-1-106(d).
Petition for adoption.
　Who may file, §48-4-101.
Report to court.
　Exception to requirement, §48-2-501(d).
Visitation rights of biological grandparents.
　Previously existing rights not terminated,
　　§48-4-105(a).
　Right to petition not affected by article,
　　§48-4-105(b).
Who may file petition, §48-4-101.
Summons to commence proceedings.
Filing not necessary, §48-2-401(g).
Taking and sending child out of state for
　purposes of placement.
Applicability of article, §7B-3705.
Consent of department of health and human
　services required, §7B-3702.
Definitions, §7B-3704.
Misdemeanor for violating provisions, §7B-3703.
Termination of parental rights.
Agency placements.
　Legal and physical custody of minor with
　　agency, §48-3-203(a).

ADOPTION —Cont'd
Termination of parental rights —Cont'd
Agency placements —Cont'd
Petition to terminate filed instead of serving notice, §48-2-402(c).
Certified copy of order to be filed with adoption petition, §48-2-305.
Consent not required from persons whose rights terminated, §48-3-603(a).
Generally, §§7B-1100 to 7B-1114.
See TERMINATION OF PARENTAL RIGHTS.
Irrevocable consent or relinquishment of child to county for adoption.
Termination as condition precedent to adoption, §7B-1111(a).
Jurisdiction of clerks of superior court, §7B-1101.
Permanent placement review hearing.
Cancellation, placement for adoption prior to review, §7B-908(e).
Person filing adoption petition, right to file petition or motion, intervention, right, §7B-1103(a), (b).
Petition for adoption filed concurrently with petition to terminate parental rights, §48-2-302(c).
Selection of adoptive parents, §7B-1112.1.
Time.
Notice of proceedings by clerk of court, §48-2-403.
Petition for adoption, time for filing, §48-2-302.
Placement assessments, completing, §48-3-303(a).
Transfer of custody from health care facility.
Authorization to transfer minor to agency, §48-3-402(a).
Unauthorized disclosure of information.
Civil action for equitable or monetary relief, §48-10-105(d).
Injunctions, §48-10-105(c).
Unknown biological parent.
Notice and service of process, §48-2-402(b).
Unlawful payments related to adoption, §48-10-102.
Venue.
Petition for adoption, §48-2-101.
Transfer, stay or dismissal for improper venue, §48-2-102(a).
Waiver of notice, §48-2-406.
Who may adopt, §48-1-103.
Who may be adopted, §48-1-104.
Wills.
After-born or after-adopted children, §§31-5.5, 31-5.5(a) to (c).

ADOPTIVE HOMES.
Regulation of agencies receiving or placing children in, §§131D-10.1 to 131D-10.9.
See CHILD PLACING AGENCIES.

ADULT ABUSE, NEGLECT AND EXPLOITATION, §§108A-99 to 108A-111.
See ABUSED, NEGLECTED OR EXPLOITED DISABLED ADULTS.

ADULT CARE HOME MEDICATION AIDES.
Examination for individuals seeking employment as, §131D-4.5B(c).
Fee for certification as, §131D-4.5.
Infection control, injection safe practices, glucose monitoring.
In-service training program, §131D-4.5B(a).
In-service training program, §131D-4.5B(a).
Registry, §§131E-114.2, 131E-270.

ADULT CARE HOME MEDICATION AIDES —Cont'd
Staff performing medication aide duties.
Requirements, §131D-4.5B(b).

ADULT CARE HOMES, §§131D-2.1 to 131D-2.18.
Abuse, neglect, exploitation.
Resident's right to be free of, §131D-21.
Actions.
Residents' bill of rights.
Collection of penalty for violation, §131D-34(g).
Instituting civil actions, §131D-28.
Administrative hearings.
Contesting penalty, §131D-34(e).
Administrative penalties, §131D-34.
Administrators of facilities.
Certification, law governing, §131D-2.18(a).
Directory of administrators.
Department to keep, §131D-2.13(b).
Residents' bill of rights.
Implementation of provisions, §131D-25.
Admission of new residents.
Resident assessment on admission, §131D-2.15.
Suspension, §131D-2.7(d).
Failure to carry out resident assessment responsibilities, §131D-2.15(c).
Adult care home resident discharge team.
Assisting in finding placement for discharged resident, §131D-4.8(e).
Defined, §131D-2.1.
Meetings, §131D-4.8(f).
Adult home specialists.
County departments of social services.
Training requirements, §131D-2.12(a), (b).
Alzheimer's disease.
Special care units.
Disclosure of information, §131D-8(a), (b).
Applicability, §131D-8(d).
Definition of "special care unit,"§131D-8(e).
License renewal.
Examination of disclosures for accuracy, §131D-8(c).
Antitrust, antikickback or safe harbor law.
Not superseded, §131D-2.17(a).
Assessment of residents on admission.
Assessment instrument.
Use, training, §131D-2.15(a).
Corrective action plan.
Failure to carry out responsibilities, §131D-2.15(c).
Failure to carry out responsibilities, §131D-2.15(c).
Required, §131D-2.15(a).
Review by department, §131D-2.15(b).
Time requirement, §131D-2.15(a).
Use of assessment, §131D-2.15(a).
Assistance granted to persons in adult care homes.
State-county special assistance, §§108A-40 to 108A-47.1.
See SOCIAL SERVICES.
Audits, §131D-4.2(f).
Bill of rights.
Actions.
Instituting civil action, §131D-28.
Address and telephone number of section responsible for enforcement, §131D-24(b).
Administrator of facility.
Implementation of provisions, §131D-25.
Civil actions.
Institution of action, §131D-28.

ADULT CARE HOMES —Cont'd
Bill of rights —Cont'd
Community advisory committees.
  Appointment, §131D-31(b).
    Minimum qualifications for appointment,
      §131D-31(g).
  Establishment, §131D-31(b).
  Functions of committees, §131D-32(a) to (j).
  Joint nursing and adult care home community
    advisory committees, §131D-31(c).
  Minimum qualifications for appointment,
    §131D-31(g).
  Officers, §131D-31(f).
  Privileged communications, §131D-31(i).
  Purpose, §131D-31(a).
  Terms of office, §131D-31(d).
  Training, §131D-31(h).
  Vacancies, §131D-31(e).
Compliance with provisions.
  Insuring compliance, §131D-26(c).
Confidentiality of information, §131D-27.
Copy of declaration of residents' rights.
  Posting requirements, §131D-24(a).
Declaration of residents' rights, §131D-21.
  Copy of declaration, §131D-24(a).
Definitions, §131D-20.
Disclosure of medical records to private peer
  review committee, §131D-21.1.
Enforcement of provisions.
  Address and telephone number of section
    responsible for enforcement, §131D-24(b).
  Responsibility for enforcement, §131D-26(a).
Enumeration of rights, §131D-21.
Fiduciaries.
  Transfer of management responsibilities,
    §131D-22.
Guardians.
  Transfer of management responsibilities,
    §131D-22.
Implementation of provisions, §131D-25.
Investigations.
  Violations of provisions, §131D-26(a1), (b).
Legislative intent, §131D-19.
Licenses.
  Revocation of facilities license for violations of
    provisions, §131D-29.
Notice to resident, §131D-24.
No waiver of rights, §131D-23.
Peer review, §131D-21.1.
Penalties, §131D-34.
Telephone number of section responsible for
  enforcement, §131D-24(b).
Transfer of management responsibilities,
  §131D-22.
Violations of provisions.
  Investigations, §131D-26(a1), (b).
  Reporting number of substantiated violations,
    §131D-26(d).
Waiver of rights.
  No waiver, §131D-23.
**Capital expenditure used for renovating or
  replacing.**
Exemption from certificate of need review,
  §131E-184(e).
Change in ownership.
Fees, fines and penalties outstanding.
  New license not issued, §131D-2.4(f).
Charges for services.
Resident's right to statement of, §131D-21.
Civil penalties, §131D-34.

ADULT CARE HOMES —Cont'd
Combined homes.
Rules for operation, law governing, §131D-2.18(c).
Commission for public health.
Immunization of employees and residents.
  Rules, adoption, §131D-9(f).
Communicable diseases.
Guidelines for reporting suspected outbreaks,
  §131D-4.4B.
HIV, hepatitis, other bloodborne pathogens.
  Infection prevention, §131D-4.4A.
Medication aides.
  In-service training, infection control,
    §131D-4.5B.
Supervisors.
  Infection control training, §131D-4.5C.
Community activities.
Resident's right to participate, §131D-21.
Community advisory committees.
Hindering or interfering with duties.
  Prohibited in order to maintain license,
    §131D-2.4(e).
Complaint hotline number.
Posting requirements, §131D-2.13(c).
Compliance history provider file, §131E-266.
Compliance history review.
Prior to licensing, §131D-2.4(b).
Confidentiality of information.
Death of resident.
  Reporting, §131D-34.1(d).
Quality assurance, medical, or peer review
  committees, proceedings and records,
  §131D-21.2(b).
Residents' bill of rights, §§131D-21, 131D-27.
Unauthorized disclosure.
  Policies and procedures to ensure, §131D-2.14.
Construction projects and plans.
Review.
  Fee charged by department of health and
    human services, §131E-267(f).
Contesting penalties imposed, §131D-34(e).
Contract agency.
Criminal history records check.
  Requirement, §131D-40(a1).
County departments of social services.
Adult home specialists.
  Training requirements, §131D-2.12(a), (b).
Monitoring homes, §131D-2.11(b).
Review of performance, §131D-2.11(c).
County's share of costs, §143B-139.5.
**Criminal history record checks for providers
  and employees,** §§114-19.3, 114-19.10,
  131D-40.
Criminal penalty.
Operation without license, §131D-2.6(b).
Day care programs, §131D-6.
Death of resident.
Confidentiality, §131D-34.1(d).
Notification to department, §131D-34.1(a).
  Duties of department upon receipt of,
    §131D-34.1(b), (c).
Standard reporting format, §131D-34.1(e).
Deficiencies.
Informal dispute resolution, §131D-2.11(a2).
Definitions, §§131D-2.1, 131E-101, 131E-231.
Delay of enforcement action.
Informal dispute resolution not complete.
  Prohibited, §131D-2.11(a2).
Department of Health and Human Services.
Construction projects and plans.
  Review.
    Fee charged, §131E-267(f).

ADULT CARE HOMES —Cont'd
Department of Health and Human Services
  —Cont'd
Share of costs, §143B-139.5.
Discharge of residents.
Adult care home resident discharge team.
  Assisting in finding placement for resident,
    §131D-4.8(e).
  Defined, §131D-2.1.
  Meetings, §131D-4.8(f).
Appeal, §131D-4.8(c), (d).
  Resident to remain in facility until issuance of
    decision, §131D-4.8(g).
Hearing unit.
  Appeal to, §131D-4.8(c), (d).
  Defined, §131D-2.1.
Individual to receive notice on behalf of resident.
  Identifying, §131D-4.8(b).
Notice, §131D-4.8(b).
Reasons for initiating, §131D-4.8(a).
Resident's rights, §131D-21.
Disclosure of information to department,
  §131D-2.14.
Dispute resolution.
Deficiencies found during inspection,
  §131D-2.11(a2).
Emergencies.
Waiver of rules for certain homes providing
  shelter or service during disaster or
  emergency, §131D-7(a).
  Definition of "emergency management
    agency,"§131D-7(b).
Employees.
Criminal history record checks.
  Action on positive check, §131D-40(b).
  Conditional employment, §131D-40(f).
  Immunity from liability, §131D-40(g).
  Limited immunity, §131D-40(c).
  Penalty for furnishing false information,
    §131D-40(e).
  Relevant offenses, §131D-40(d).
  Required for certain employees, §131D-40(a).
Immunization, §131D-9.
Enforcement of provisions, §131D-4.2(g).
Evaluation of residents.
Persons in need of medical and nursing care,
  §131E-106.
Evidence.
Temporary management.
  Hearing on petition for appointment of
    temporary manager, §131E-233(b).
Exceptions from licensure, §131D-2.3.
**False information, omission of information on
  license application.**
Civil penalty, §131D-34(d1).
Fiduciaries.
Bill of rights.
  Transfer of management responsibilities,
    §131D-22.
General assembly.
Residents' bill of rights.
  Legislative intent, §131D-19.
Guardians.
Bill of rights.
  Transfer of management responsibilities,
    §131D-22.
Health care professional registry.
Compliance, law governing, §131D-2.18(b).
Health facilities personnel registry, §131E-256.
**HIV, hepatitis B and C, other bloodborne
  pathogens.**
Infection prevention requirements, §131D-4.4A(a),
  (b).

ADULT CARE HOMES —Cont'd
Hospice care in assisted living residence,
  §131D-2.2(c).
Immunity.
Persons interviewed during inspection,
  §131D-2.14.
Immunization of residents and employees.
Definition of "employee,"§131D-9(g).
Determination of individual's status, §131D-9(d).
Documentation, §131D-9(c).
Notification of requirement, §131D-9(b), (b1).
Requirement, §131D-9(a).
  Exceptions, §131D-9(e).
Rules, §131D-9(f).
Infection prevention.
Adult care home staff.
  Defined, §131D-4.4A(a).
Guidelines for reporting suspected communicable
  disease outbreaks, §131D-4.4B.
Medication aides.
  In-service training, §131D-4.5B.
Requirements, time limit, §131D-4.4A(b).
Supervisors.
  Infection control training, §131D-4.5C.
Informal dispute resolution.
Deficiencies found during inspection,
  §131D-2.11(a2).
Injunctions.
Operation without license.
  Action by department, §131D-2.6(a).
Inspections, §§131D-2.11(a), 131E-105.
Immunity of persons interviewed, §131D-2.14.
Informal dispute resolution.
  Deficiencies found, §131D-2.11(a2).
Refusal to allow.
  Civil penalty, §131D-34(d).
Resident assessments.
  Review by department as part of inspection,
    §131D-2.15(b).
Waiver of annual inspection, §131D-2.11(a1).
Intent of legislature, §131D-4.1.
Investigations.
Death of resident within seven days of use of
  physical restraint, §131D-34.1(c).
Residents' bill of rights.
  Violations of provisions to be investigated,
    §131D-26(a1), (b).
Legislative intent, §131D-4.1.
Licensure.
Change in ownership.
  Fees, fines and penalties outstanding.
    New license not issued, §131D-2.4(f).
Community advisory committees.
  Hindering or interfering with duties.
    Prohibited in order to maintain license,
      §131D-2.4(e).
Compliance history review.
  Prior to licensing, §131D-2.4(b).
Definitions, §131E-101.
Department to license, §131D-2.4(a).
Enforcement of provisions, §131D-4.3(c).
Exceptions, §131D-2.3.
Facilities not currently licensed.
  Issuance of license, duration, §131D-2.4(a).
False information, omission of information on
  application.
  Civil penalty, §131D-34(d1).
Fees, §131D-2.5(a).
  Initial fees for new facilities, §131E-272.
Inspection of licensed facilities, §131D-2.11(a).
  Immunity of persons interviewed, §131D-2.14.

ADULT CARE HOMES —Cont'd
Licensure —Cont'd
Inspection of licensed facilities —Cont'd
Informal dispute resolution.
Deficiencies found, §131D-2.11(a2).
Resident assessments.
Review by department as part of inspection,
§131D-2.15(b).
Waiver of annual inspection, §131D-2.11(a1).
Monitoring for licensure compliance,
§131D-2.11(a).
County departments of social services,
§131D-2.11(b).
Review of performance, §131D-2.11(c).
NC NOVA special licensure designation,
§§131E-154.12 to 131E-154.14.
New facilities.
Initial Licensure fee, §131E-272.
Operation without license.
Legal action by department, §131D-2.6.
Prior violations by applicants.
No license issued, §131D-2.4(c).
Provisional license.
Downgrade to, §131D-2.7(a).
Issuance of new license, time period,
§131D-2.4(c).
Renewals, §131D-2.4(d).
Residents' bill of rights.
Revocation of license, §131D-29.
Revocation, §131D-2.7(b).
Issuance of new license, time period,
§131D-2.4(c).
Residents' bill of rights.
Notification of, §131D-21.
Violations, §131D-29.
Special care units, §131D-4.6(b), (c).
Suspension.
Summary suspension, §131D-2.7(c).
Issuance of new license, time period,
§131D-2.4(c).
Type A or type B violations.
Issuance of new license, time period,
§131D-2.4(c).
Long-term care ombudsman program,
§§143B-181.15 to 143B-181.25.
See LONG-TERM CARE OMBUDSMAN.
Mail.
Resident's right to send and receive, §131D-21.
Management.
Temporary management, §131D-35.
Medical care commission.
Powers, §§131D-4.5, 143B-165.
Medication aides.
Examination for individuals seeking employment
as, §131D-4.5B(c).
Fee for certification as, §131D-4.5.
Infection control, injection safe practices, glucose
monitoring.
In-service training program, §131D-4.5B(a).
In-service training program, §131D-4.5B(a).
Registry, §§131E-114.2, 131E-270.
Staff performing medication aide duties.
Requirements, §131D-4.5B(b).
Monitoring for licensure compliance,
§131D-2.11(a).
County departments of social services,
§131D-2.11(b).
Review of performance, §131D-2.11(c).
Multiunit assisted housing with services.
Conditions or care needs.
Persons not to be cared for, §131D-2.2(b).

ADULT CARE HOMES —Cont'd
Multiunit assisted housing with services
—Cont'd
Defined, §131D-2.1.
Fees charged registered program, §131D-2.5(b).
Persons not to be cared for, §131D-2.2(b).
NC NOVA special licensure designation,
§§131E-154.12 to 131E-154.14.
Change in ownership, §131E-154.14(g).
Confidentiality of information submitted by
applicants, §131E-154.14(c).
Definitions, §131E-154.13.
Duration of designation, §131E-154.14(g).
Establishment of program, §131E-154.14(a).
Issuance of documentation, §131E-154.14(e).
Time period, §131E-154.14(f).
Purpose of provisions, §131E-154.12(b).
Reapplication intervals, §131E-154.14(d).
Rules to implement, §131E-154.14(b).
Title of provisions, §131E-154.12(a).
Notice.
Discharge of residents, §131D-4.8(b).
Residents' bill of rights.
Notice to resident, §131D-24.
Nursing care.
Evaluation of residents, §131E-106.
Nursing homes.
General provisions.
See NURSING HOMES.
Patients' bill of rights, §§131E-115 to 131E-131.
See NURSING HOMES.
**Obtaining services from providers other than
housing managers.**
Right to obtain services at resident's own expense,
§131D-2.2(d).
Operation without license.
Action for injunction or other process.
Authority of department, §131D-2.6(a).
Procedure, §131D-2.6(d).
Criminal penalty, §131D-2.6(b).
Hindering secretary's performance of duty.
Procedure, §131D-2.6(c).
Penalties, §131D-34.
Persons not to be cared for, §131D-2.2(a).
Petition for contested case.
Contesting penalty, filing, time, §131D-34(e).
Physical restraint.
Investigations.
Death of resident within seven days of use,
§131D-34.1(c).
Report on use, §131D-2.13(e).
Placement for discharged resident.
Adult care home resident discharge teams,
§§131D-2.1, 131D-4.8(e), (f).
Privacy.
Resident's rights to, §131D-21.
Provider file.
Department to establish and maintain,
§131D-2.13(d).
**Quality assurance, medical, or peer review
committees.**
Confidentiality of proceedings and records,
immunity from discovery, §131D-21.2(b).
Immunity, §131D-21.2(a).
Rate adjustments.
Report documentation used, §131D-4.2(h).
Rating certificates.
Basis for rating, §131D-10(a).
Initial ratings, §131D-10(b).
Display of rating certificates, §131D-10(d).
Penalties, effect on rating, §131D-10(c).

ADULT CARE HOMES —Cont'd

Records.
Peer review, §§131D-21.1, 131D-21.2(b).
Provider file.
Department to establish and maintain,
§131D-2.13(d).
Quality assurance, medical, or peer review
committee.
Confidentiality of records, immunity from
discovery, §131D-21.2(b).
Review by department, §131D-2.14.

Remedies.
Residents' bill of rights, §131D-34.
Reporting number of substantiated violations,
§131D-26(d).

Reports, §131D-4.2(a).
Communicable disease outbreaks.
Guidelines for reporting, §131D-4.4B.
Costs, §131D-4.2(b).
First report due date, §131D-4.2(e).
Exemptions, §131D-4.2(d).
Physical restraint.
Use, §131D-2.13(e).
Suspension of admissions to facilities.
Failure to submit annual report, §131D-4.2(g).

Resident assessment, §131D-2.15.

Resident's records.
Review by department, §131D-2.14.

Restraints.
Resident's right to be free of, §131D-21.

Room ventilation and temperature.
Monitoring, enforcement of rules, department
duties, §131D-2.13(a).

Rules and regulations, §§131D-2.16, 131E-104.
Adoption as emergency rules, §131D-4.3(b).
Adoption by social services commission,
§131D-4.3(a).
Immunization of residents and employees,
§131D-9(f).
Medical care commission, §131D-4.5.

Safety.
Minimum requirements, §131D-4.4(a).

Security of personal possessions.
Resident's right to, §131D-21.

Services provided.
Resident's rights to statement of, §131D-21.

Severability of provisions, §131D-2.17(b).

Smoking prohibited within, §§131D-4.4(b),
131E-114.3(a).
Administrative penalty, §§131D-4.4(d),
131E-114.3(c).
Duties of owner, manager and operator of adult
care home, §§131D-4.4(c), 131E-114.3(b).

Social, political, religious resources.
Resident's right to participate, §131D-21.

Special care units.
Cost reports, §131D-4.2(a), (b).
Defined, §131D-4.6(a).
Licensing, §131D-4.6(b), (c).

Specialist fund, §131D-4.7.

Staffing requirements, §131D-4.3(a).

Suspension of admissions, §131D-2.7(d).
Failure to carry out resident assessment
responsibilities, §131D-2.15(c).
Failure to submit annual report, §131D-4.2(g).

Telephone.
Resident's right of access to, §131D-21.

Temporary management, §131D-35.
Accounting after termination, §131E-244(a).
Appointment of manager.
Alternatives, §131E-235(a), (b).

ADULT CARE HOMES —Cont'd

Temporary management —Cont'd
Appointment of manager —Cont'd
Grounds, §§131E-233(c), 131E-234.
Procedures, §131E-233(a), (b).
Candidates for temporary manager, §131E-237.
Compensation of temporary manager, §131E-236.
Conditions on return to owner, §131E-243(d).
Conflict of laws, §131E-246.
Contingency fund.
Department may maintain, §131E-242(a).
Funds provided for management, court order,
§131E-242(b).
Reallocation, §131E-242(c).
Continuing need, review, §131E-243(a).
Correction of deficiencies in excess of $1,000.
Correction without prior approval,
§131E-239(d).
Written plan submitted by manager,
§131E-239(a).
Hearing on plan, §131E-239(c).
Service of copy upon department and
respondent, §131E-239(b).
Definitions, §131E-231.
Expenses of management.
Accounting after termination, §131E-244(a).
Deficiencies, liability, §131E-244(b).
Lien for reasonable costs, §131E-244(c).
Notice, §131E-244(f).
Priority, §131E-244(d).
Recording, §131E-244(e).
Reasonableness, petition to determine,
§131E-244(b).
Repayment over time, §131E-244(b).
Findings of legislature, §131E-230.
Leases, mortgages and contracts by respondent.
Manager not required to honor, §131E-241(a).
Real estate or goods necessary for continued
operation.
Application to court to set compensation for,
§131E-241(b), (c).
Liability for payment for goods and services,
§131E-240(a).
Action to enforce liability, §131E-240(b).
Deposit of amounts received, §131E-240(a).
Omission to pay respondent for payment to
manager, §131E-240(c).
Receipt given for payment, §131E-240(a).
Lien for reasonable costs, §131E-244(c) to (f).
Obligations of licensee, §131E-245.
Payment for goods or services.
Liability for, §131E-240(a) to (c).
Petition, §131E-232.
Powers and duties of temporary manager,
§131E-238.
Preexisting leases, mortgages and contracts.
Avoidance, §131E-241(a) to (c).
Removal or remedying conditions.
Alternative to appointment of temporary
manager, §131E-235(a), (b).
Replacement of manager, mismanagement,
§131E-243(b).
Termination, court order, §131E-243(c).
Accounting by manager after, §131E-244(a).

Transfer from facility.
Resident's rights, §131D-21.

Unlicensed operation.
Legal action by department, §131D-2.6.

Violations and penalties.
Actions to collect penalties, §131D-34(g).

ADULT CARE HOMES —Cont'd
Violations and penalties —Cont'd
Civil penalty.
Factors considered in determining, §131D-34(c), (c1).
Proceeds remitted to state treasurer for deposit in accordance with state law, §131D-34(i).
Recommendations to department, submission, time, §131D-34(c2).
Repeat violations, §131D-34(a).
Type A1 violation, §131D-34(a).
Type A2 violation, §131D-34(a).
Type B violation, §131D-34(a).
Classification of violations, §131D-34(a).
Commencement of penalty imposed, §131D-34(f).
Contesting penalties, §131D-34(e).
Penalty review committee.
Review of penalties assessed, §131D-34(h).
Plan of correction.
Type A1 violation, §131D-34(a).
Type A2 violation, §131D-34(a).
Type B violation, §131D-34(a).
Plan of protection.
Type A1 violation, §131D-34(a).
Type A2 violation, §131D-34(a).
Type B violation, §131D-34(a).
Recommendations as to penalty.
Submission to department, time, §131D-34(c2).
Repeat violations, §131D-34(a).
Staff training in lieu of assessing penalty, §131D-34(g1).
Type A1 violations, §131D-34(a).
Type A2 violations, §131D-34(a).
Type B violations, §131D-34(a).
Waiver of annual state inspection, §131D-2.11(a1).

ADULT DAY CARE PROGRAMS.
Alzheimer's disease.
Disclosure requirements for programs offering special care services for persons with, §131D-6(b1) to (b4).
Civil penalty for violations, §131D-6(c).
Defined, §131D-6(b).
Exempt programs, §131D-6(d).
Harming or willfully neglecting person under care, §131D-6(c1).
Inspection and certification, §131D-6(b).
Policy of state, §131D-6(a).
Rules to protect health, safety and welfare, §131D-6(b).
Transportation for participants, §131D-6(a).

ADULT EDUCATION.
Entitlement to attend, §115C-231(c).
Free tuition.
Persons 18 years of age or older not having completed high school, §115C-231(b).
No adult left behind initiative.
Workforce development commission.
Agencies included in, §143B-438.14(a).
Community based nonprofit organizations.
Including, §143B-438.14(a).
Contracts to carry out components, §143B-438.14(c).
Duty to initiate, §143B-438.14(a).
Evening-weekend certificate and degree programs, §143B-438.14(b).
Goals, §143B-438.14(b).
Increase in residents earning associate degrees, §143B-438.14(b).

ADULT EDUCATION —Cont'd
No adult left behind initiative —Cont'd
Workforce development commission —Cont'd
Reporting on details of implementation, §143B-438.14(d).
Organization and administration of program, §115C-231(a).
Removal or prohibiting enrollment.
Persons having attained age of 21 years, §115C-231(c).

ADULTERATION.
Antifreeze.
Deemed to be adulterated, §106-579.5.
Commercial feed.
Deemed to be adulterated, §106-284.38.
Flour, cornmeal and grain, §§106-621 to 106-628.
Food, drug and cosmetic act, §§106-120 to 106-145.
See FOOD, DRUG AND COSMETIC ACT.
Gasoline and oil inspection.
Products offered for sale, §119-35.
Grains, §§106-621 to 106-628.
See GRAIN ADULTERATION.
Health.
Embargo of adulterated or misbranded food, §130A-21(a) to (e).
Meat inspection.
Defined, §106-549.15.
Examinations and inspection before slaughter, §106-549.17.
Exemptions, §106-549.27(e).
Motor vehicles.
Antifreeze.
Deemed to be adulterated, §106-579.5.
Poultry inspection.
Ante mortem inspections, §106-549.53(a).
Condemnation, §106-549.53(c).
Defined, §106-549.51.
Enforcement, §106-549.58(b).
Exemptions, §106-549.62(f).
Soil additives act, §§106-50.28 to 106-50.41.

ADULTERY, §14-184.
Acts barring rights of spouse, §31A-1(a).
Admissibility of admission or confession as evidence, §14-184.
Divorce.
Grounds for divorce, §50-7.
Domestic violence.
Effect upon prosecuting for violation of section 14-184 or other offense against public morals, §50B-8.
Parties as witnesses, §8-50(a).

ADULT ESTABLISHMENTS.
ABC permits.
Local government regulation of adult establishments or other sexually oriented businesses.
Provisions not deemed to preempt, §18B-904(g).
Adult bookstores.
Defined, §14-202.10.
Adult live entertainment.
Defined, §14-202.10.
Adult mini motion picture theaters.
Defined, §14-202.10.
Restrictions on occupancy of viewing booths, §14-202.11(b).
Adult motion picture theaters.
Defined, §14-202.10.

ADULT ESTABLISHMENTS —Cont'd
Definitions, §14-202.10.
Person, §14-202.12.
Local regulation, §14-202.11(c).
Massage business defined, §14-202.10.
Massage defined, §14-202.10.
Nuisances.
Offenses against public morals.
Abatement generally, §§19-1 to 19-8.3.
See NUISANCES.
Restrictions as to adult establishments,
§14-202.11(a).
Penalty for violation of provisions, §14-202.12.
Sexually oriented devices.
Defined, §14-202.10.
Specified anatomical area defined, §14-202.10.
Specified sexual activities, §14-202.10.

ADULT HIGH SCHOOL DIPLOMAS.
World War II veterans.
Powers of board of education, §115C-12.

ADULT PROTECTION ACT, §§108A-99 to
108A-111.
See ABUSED, NEGLECTED OR EXPLOITED
DISABLED ADULTS.

ADULTS.
Abused, neglected or exploited disabled adults,
§§108A-99 to 108A-111.
See ABUSED, NEGLECTED OR EXPLOITED
DISABLED ADULTS.
Adoption, §§48-5-100 to 48-5-103.
See ADOPTION.
Adult care homes.
Generally.
See ADULT CARE HOMES.
Education.
General provisions, §115C-231.
Health.
Establishment of program, §130A-223(a), (b).

AD VALOREM TAXES.
Oil, gas and mineral interest severed or
separated from surface fee.
Listing to be effective against surface fee holder,
creditors, purchasers, heirs or assigns,
§§1-42.1 to 1-42.9.
Property taxes.
Generally.
See PROPERTY TAXES.
Sales and use tax.
See SALES AND USE TAX.

ADVANCE DIRECTIVES FOR HEALTH CARE.
Do not resuscitate orders, §90-21.17.
Health care power of attorney.
Combined with or incorporated into, §32A-26.
Generally, §§32A-15 to 32A-26.
See HEALTH CARE POWERS OF ATTORNEY.
Living wills.
Right to natural death generally, §§90-320 to
90-323.
Registry, §§130A-465 to 130A-471.

ADVANCE HEALTH CARE DIRECTIVE
REGISTRY, §§130A-465 to 130A-471.
Access to registry, §130A-469.
Documents to be registered, §130A-466(a).
Effect of registration, §130A-468(d).
Establishment, §130A-465.
Fee for filing, §130A-466(e).
Amount, §130A-470(a).
Subject to audit, §130A-470(c).

ADVANCE HEALTH CARE DIRECTIVE
REGISTRY —Cont'd
File number and password, §130A-468(a).
Access to registry, §130A-469.
Immunities, §130A-471.
Limitation of liability, §130A-471.
Notarization of documents, §130A-466(b).
Original document returned to person who
filed, §130A-468(b).
Reproduction entered into database,
§130A-468(a).
Return address required, §130A-466(d).
Revocation of registered document,
§130A-468(c).
Unregistered documents, validity, §130A-467.
Voluntary contributions of funds, §130A-470(b).
Who may file, §130A-466(c).

ADVANCEMENTS.
Agriculture.
Landlord's lien on crops for rents, §42-15.
Death of advancee before intestate donor,
§29-27.
Defined, §29-2.
Effect, §29-25.
Future advancements, §§29-23 to 29-29.
Generally, §29-23.
Gift inter vivos.
Presumption of gift, §29-24.
Guardians.
Parties to proceedings, §35A-1324.
Housing authorities and projects.
Municipal cooperation and aid.
Advances and donations by city and
municipality, §157-43.
Intestate succession.
General provisions, §§29-23 to 29-29.
See INTESTATE SUCCESSION.
Inventory.
Failure to give inventory, §29-28.
Landlord and tenant.
Agricultural tenancies.
Lien on crops, §42-15.
Mental health and developmental disabilities.
Surplus income and advancements, §§35A-1321 to
35A-1330.
Mortgages and deeds of trust.
Advances and future obligations, §§45-67 to 45-74.
Nonprofit corporations.
Directors.
Notice to members, §55A-16-21.
Obtaining advances under promise to work
and pay for, §14-104.
Obtaining advances under written promise to
pay from designated property, §14-105.
Release by advancee, §29-29.
Sharecroppers.
Landlord failing to make advance, §14-359.
Receiving advance with intent to defraud,
§§14-358, 14-359.
Taking into account and computation at
estate, §29-23.
Valuation.
Determination, §29-26.

ADVANCE PAYMENTS TO PERSONS
CLAIMING BODILY INJURIES, §1-540.3.

ADVANCES.
Contract rates and fees, §24-1.1.
Powers of fiduciaries incorporated by
reference, §32-27.

ADVANCES —Cont'd
Savings and loan association interest rates,
§24-1.4.
State opt-out for federal preemptions,
§24-2.3(a), (b).

**ADVANCES AND FUTURE OBLIGATIONS,
INSTRUMENTS TO SECURE,** §§45-67 to
45-74.
Article not exclusive, §45-74.
Definitions, §45-67.
Discharge of record of instrument, §45-73.
**Fluctuation of obligations within maximum
amount,** §45-69.
Instruments to secure equity lines of credit.
Future advances statute not to apply, §45-83.
Priority of security instrument, §45-70(a).
Balance of obligation secured exceeds amount
secured, §45-70(a1).
Electric or gas utility obligations, §45-70(d).
Electric or telephone membership corporation
obligations, §45-70(d).
Insurance, taxes, assessment incurred by secured
creditor, §45-70(c).
Probate and registration.
Termination of future optional advances, §45-72.
Requirements, §45-68.
Applicability, §45-68.
Satisfaction of security instrument, §45-71.
Security instruments.
Defined, §45-67.
Satisfaction, §45-71.
Termination of future optional advances,
§45-72(a).

ADVANCE SHEETS.
Administrative officer of the courts.
Designation of commercial advance sheets as
official reports, §7A-6(b1).
Furnishing advance sheets without charge,
§7A-6(c).
Sale of advance sheets, §7A-6(b).
Printing.
Contracting for printing of advance sheets by
administrative officer of the courts, §7A-6(b).
Sales.
Administrative officer of the courts to sell,
§7A-6(b).

ADVERSE POSSESSION.
Boundaries.
Color of title.
Known and visible lines and boundaries, §1-38.
Canals.
No title by possession of right of way, §1-44.
Color of title, §1-38.
Seven years' possession under color of title, §1-38.
Commissioner's deeds in judicial sales.
Constitute color of title, §1-38(a).
Definitions.
Public trust rights, §1-45.1.
Entry on land.
Action must be commenced within one year after
entry, §1-41.
**Evidence of seven years possession under
color of title,** §1-38(b).
Highways.
No title by possession of public ways, §1-45.
Turnpike companies.
No title by possession of right of way, §1-44.
Landlord and tenant.
Tenant's possession is landlord's, §1-43.

ADVERSE POSSESSION —Cont'd
Maps recorded prior to October 1, 1973.
Qualified as if certified, §1-38(c).
Marriage.
Disability of marriage, §1-18.
Mineral rights.
Severance of surface and subsurface rights, §1-42.
Persons under disability.
Seven years possession under color of title.
Possession perpetual bar against, §1-38(a).
Possession follows legal title, §1-42.
Presumptions.
Effect of record chain of title, §1-42.
Railroad right of way.
Abandonment, §1-44.1.
Title presumed out of state, §1-36.
Public trust rights.
Defined, §1-45.1.
No adverse possession of property subject to,
§1-45.1.
Public ways.
No title by possession of public ways, §1-45.
Railroads.
Abandonment of right of way.
Presumption, §1-44.1.
No title by possession of right of way, §1-44.
Record chain of title.
Prima facie evidence of possession, §1-42.
Right of way.
No title by possession of right of way, §1-44.
Railroad right of way.
Presumption of abandonment, §1-44.1.
Seizing within twenty years necessary, §1-39.
Seven years possession under color of title.
Entry or action against possessor barred, §1-38(a).
State of North Carolina.
Title against state, §1-35.
Validity of possession against claimants under
state, §1-37.
Title against state, §1-35.
Title conclusively deemed out of state, §1-36.
Torrens system registration.
No right by adverse possession, §43-21.
Trustee's deeds in foreclosure.
Constitute color of title, §1-38(a).
Twenty year limitation, §1-40.
Seizing within twenty years necessary, §1-39.

ADVERTISING.
Adoption.
Desire to adopt, §48-10-101(b1).
Unauthorized persons, misdemeanor,
§48-10-101(b), (c).
Affidavit of publication.
Legal advertising, §§1-598, 1-600(a).
Prima facie evidence, §1-600(b).
Alcoholic beverages.
Authority of commission to make rules,
§18B-105(b).
Compliance with rules of commission,
§18B-105(a).
Architects.
Rules and regulations prohibiting.
Board not to adopt, §83A-6(b).
Attorneys at law, ProfCond Rule 7.2.
Communications of fields of practice, ProfCond
Rule 7.4.
Dramatization depicting fictional situation,
ProfCond Rule 7.1.
False or misleading communications concerning
services, ProfCond Rule 7.1.

ADVERTISING —Cont'd
Auctions and auctioneers.
Misleading or untruthful advertising.
Grounds for suspension or revocation of license, §85B-8(a).
Bids and bidding.
Public building contracts, §143-131(a).
Billboards.
Blue Ridge parkway.
Control of outdoor advertising, §§113A-165 to 113A-170.
Churches or schools.
Obstructing view at entrance, §136-102.
Outdoor advertising generally, §§136-126 to 136-140.
See OUTDOOR ADVERTISING.
Transportation department reporting requirements, §136-12.1.
Blue Ridge parkway.
Control of outdoor advertising, §§113A-165 to 113A-170.
Cemeteries.
Perpetual care fund.
Requirements for advertising, §65-63.
Chiropractors.
False or misleading advertisement, grounds for disciplinary actions, §90-154(b).
Free or reduced rate service.
Notice to patient, §90-154.1(b).
Cities.
Outdoor advertising.
Regulation of nonconforming off-premises outdoor advertising, §160A-199.
Closing-out sales.
Advertising sale contrary to provisions, §66-81.
False advertisements, §66-82.
Consumer finance act.
False or misleading statements, §53-183.
Continuing care retirement communities.
Marketing by unlicensed providers, §58-64-5(a).
Counties.
Outdoor advertising.
Regulation of nonconforming off-premises outdoor advertising, §153A-143.
Deceptive and fraudulent advertising, §14-117.
Defacing or destroying advertisements, §14-385.
Department of administration.
Purchases and contracts through department.
Competitive bidding procedure, §143-52.
Setting of benchmarks, §143-53.1(a).
Use of American Recovery and Reinvestment Act funds, §143-53.1(b).
Diamonds.
Unfair trade practices in diamond industry, §66-74.
Drug paraphernalia, §90-113.24(a), (b).
Eggs.
Designation in block letters, §106-245.20.
Elections.
Candidate-specific communications, §§163-278.110 to 163-278.113.
Charges, §163-278.18(a), (b).
Disclosure requirements for media advertisements, §§163-278.39 to 163-278.39C.
Mass mailings and telephone banks.
Candidate-specific communications, §§163-278.110 to 163-278.113.
Electrologists.
Board of electrologist examiners.
Powers to regulate, §88A-6.

ADVERTISING —Cont'd
Electronic surveillance devices.
Felony, §15A-288(a2).
Employee assistance professionals.
Representation as licensed professional, §90-508.
Ethics.
Misuse of public office.
Use of public position for private gain, §138A-31(b), (c).
False advertising.
Attorneys at law, ProfCond Rule 7.1.
Auctioneers.
Grounds for suspension or revocation of license, §85B-8(a).
Chiropractors.
Grounds for disciplinary actions, §90-154(b).
Closing-out sales, §66-82.
Advertising sale contrary to provisions, §66-81.
Consumer finance act.
False or misleading statements, §53-183.
Deceptive and fraudulent advertising, §14-117.
Food, drug and cosmetic act, §§106-122, 106-138(a), (b).
Geographical location.
Deceptive representation in telephone directory, print advertisement or Internet, §75-42.
Hatcheries and chick dealers, §106-545.
Health maintenance organizations, §58-67-65(a).
Insurance unfair trade practices, §58-63-15.
Live music performance or production.
Truth in music advertising act, §§75-125 to 75-128.
Lubricating oils.
Sale of lubricants different from advertised name prohibited, §119-8.
Unauthorized insurers false advertising process act, §§58-29-1 to 58-29-25.
See UNAUTHORIZED INSURERS.
Food, drug and cosmetic act.
Definitions and general consideration, §106-121.
False advertising, §§106-122, 106-138(a), (b).
Violations made misdemeanor, §106-124(c).
Free insurance as inducement to purchase goods or services, §§66-380 to 66-382.
Funeral service.
Defined, §90-210.20(a).
Gasoline prices.
Drawing or pumping fuel by purchaser himself, §14-117.2(a), (b).
Geographical location.
Deceptive representation in telephone directory, print advertisement or Internet, §75-42.
Hatcheries and chick dealers.
False advertising, §106-545.
Health maintenance organizations.
False or misleading advertising, §58-67-65(a).
Solicitation of enrollees.
Not deemed validation of law relating to advertising by health professionals, §58-67-170(b).
Injuring advertisements, §14-384.
Insurance.
Free insurance as inducement to purchase goods or services, §§66-380 to 66-382.
Interstate insurance product regulation compact, generally, §§58-91-1 to 58-91-80.
See INTERSTATE INSURANCE PRODUCT REGULATION COMPACT.
Medicare supplement insurance.
Filing requirements for advertising, §58-54-35.

ADVERTISING —Cont'd
Insurance —Cont'd
Third party administrators.
Approval, §58-56-21.
Unauthorized insurers.
Domestic companies, §58-14-10.
Cease and desist orders, §58-14-15.
False advertising process act.
Generally, §§58-29-1 to 58-29-25.
See UNAUTHORIZED INSURERS.
Unfair trade practices.
False advertising, §58-63-15.
Viatical life insurance settlements, §58-58-260.
Contract securities, §78A-14.
Workers' compensation self-insurance.
Third-party administrators and service
companies.
Approval of advertising, §58-47-175.
Irrigation contractors.
Advertising or other use of designation, §89G-2.
Job listing services.
Identification of self by service, §95-47.26(a).
Prerequisites, §95-47.26(b).
Term "no fee" not to be used, §95-47.26(d).
Judicial sales, §1-595.
Public sale.
Posting and publishing notices of sale of real
property, §1-339.17(a) to (e).
Posting notice of sale of personal property,
§1-339.18(a), (b).
Time for beginning advertisement, §1-339.16.
**Law enforcement officers' association
publications.**
Soliciting advertisements for publications,
§14-401.10.
Legal advertising.
Affidavit of publication, §§1-598, 1-600(a).
Prima facie evidence, §1-600(b).
Charges, §1-596.
Evidence of publication in newspaper.
Proof of publication of notice in newspaper
prima facie evidence, §1-600(b).
Sworn statement prima facie evidence of
qualification, §1-598.
Judicial sales, §1-595.
Newspapers.
Affidavit of publication, §§1-598, 1-600(a).
Prima facie evidence, §1-600(b).
Charges, §1-596.
No qualified newspaper in county, §§1-597,
1-599.
Proof of publication of notice in newspaper,
§1-600(a).
Method of proof not exclusive, §1-600(c).
Prima facie evidence, §1-600(b).
Requisites for newspaper publication, §1-597.
Applicability of provisions, §1-599.
Sworn statement prima facie evidence of
qualification, §1-598.
Public sales, §1-595.
Rates and charges.
Newspapers, §1-596.
Sales.
Public sales, §1-595.
Validation.
Certain legal advertisements validated, §1-601.
Liquid fuels.
Sale of fuels different from advertised name
prohibited, §119-8.
Live music performance or production.
Truth in music advertising act, §§75-125 to
75-128.

ADVERTISING —Cont'd
Locksmiths, §74F-12(b).
Lotteries.
Misdemeanor offense of advertising lotteries,
§14-289.
State lottery, §18C-130(e).
Lubricating oils.
Sale of lubricants different from advertised name
prohibited, §119-8.
Mattresses and bedding tags.
Advertising prohibited, §106-65.99(d).
Medicare supplement insurance.
Filing requirements for advertising, §58-54-35.
Membership camping, §66-242.
Misuse of public office.
Use of public position for private gain,
§138A-31(a).
Mortgage bankers, brokers and servicers.
Advertising materials.
Mortgage broker duties, §53-244.109.
Prohibited acts, §53-244.111.
Motor courts, rates and charges, §§72-50 to
72-52.
Motor vehicle dealers.
Coercing or attempting to coerce dealer to
participate voluntarily in advertising
campaign, §20-305.
Name of licensee to appear, §20-290(c).
Motor vehicle manufacturers.
False or misleading advertising, §20-305.
Name of licensee to appear, §20-290(c).
Motor vehicle servicing or repairing.
Private passenger vehicles.
Truthful advertisements of costs, §66-285.
Newspapers.
Legal advertising.
Affidavit of publication, §§1-598, 1-600(a).
Prima facie evidence, §1-600(b).
Charges, §1-596.
No qualified newspaper in county, §§1-597,
1-599.
Proof of publication of notice in newspaper,
§1-600(a).
Method of proof not exclusive, §1-600(c).
Prima facie evidence, §1-600(b).
Requisites for newspaper publication, §1-597.
Applicability of provisions, §1-599.
Sworn statement prima facie evidence of
qualification, §1-598.
Validation of certain advertisements, §1-601.
Unfair competitive practices.
Applicability of provisions to publications,
§75-1.1.
Notaries public.
Expert on immigration matters, prohibition,
§10B-20(j).
In language other than English.
Notice included, requirement, §10B-20(i).
Nurses.
Loans.
Consolidation of information on existing
scholarships and loan programs,
§90-171.50.
Salary levels, job opportunities, refresher courses
and license renewal requirements.
Developing publicity on, §90-171.53.
Nursing home administrators.
Fraudulent, misleading or deceptive advertising.
Grounds for revocation or suspension of license,
§90-285.1.

ADVERTISING —Cont'd
Obscenity.
Literature and exhibitions.
Advertising or otherwise promoting sale of obscene material, §14-190.1(f).
Opticians.
Certain advertising as grounds for revocation or suspension of license, §90-249(b).
Outdoor advertising.
Blue Ridge parkway.
Control of advertising on parkway, §§113A-165 to 113A-170.
Cities.
Regulation of nonconforming off-premises outdoor advertising, §160A-199.
Counties.
Regulation of nonconforming off-premises outdoor advertising, §153A-143.
General provisions, §§136-126 to 136-140.
See OUTDOOR ADVERTISING.
Scenic highways, state and national parks and historic areas.
Advertising adjacent to park.
Limitations, §136-129.2(a) to (c).
Podiatrists.
False advertising as grounds for suspension or revocation of license, §90-202.8(a).
Political advertising.
Candidate-specific communications, §§163-278.110 to 163-278.113.
Charges, §163-278.18(a), (b).
Disclosure requirements for media advertisements, §§163-278.39 to 163-278.39C.
Mass mailings and telephone banks.
Candidate-specific communications, §§163-278.110 to 163-278.113.
Posting.
Unlawful posting of advertisements.
Criminal trespass, §14-145.
Preneed funeral contracts and funds.
False or misleading advertising.
Refusal to issue or renew, suspension or revocation of license, §90-210.69(c).
Prepaid legal services plans.
State bar approval prohibited, Bar Rule E.0304.
Private personnel services, §95-47.6.
Private protective services.
Unlicensed persons, §74C-16(c).
Prizes.
Representation of eligibility to win a prize, §75-33.
Representation of winning a prize, §75-32.
Professional counselors.
Persons claiming exemption from licensure, §90-332.1(b).
Professional employer organizations, §58-89A-80(d).
Public building contracts.
Procedure for letting of public contracts, §143-131.
Radio and television.
Unfair competitive practices.
Applicability of provisions to broadcasts, §75-1.1.
Real estate brokers and salespersons.
License required, §93A-1.
Rental vehicles.
Advertising and sales practices, §§66-200 to 66-207.
Representation of being specially selected, §75-34.
Representation of eligibility to win a prize, §75-33.

ADVERTISING —Cont'd
Representation of winning a prize, §75-32.
Retail installment sales, §25A-2(e).
Retirement communities or facilities.
Certified retirement community program, §143B-437.101(a).
Sale of prints by art dealers, §25C-11(a).
Sales and use tax.
Advertisement to absorb tax unlawful, §105-164.9.
Savings banks.
False or misleading advertising, §54C-64.
Scenic highways, state and national parks and historic areas.
Outdoor advertising adjacent to park.
Limitations, §136-129.2(a) to (c).
Speech and language pathologists and audiologists.
False or misleading advertising, §§90-301A, 90-304(b).
State lottery, §18C-130(e).
Structural pest control.
Name of company shown on license and identification card, §106-65.31(b3).
Time shares.
Exchange programs.
Statement to be included, §93A-48(d).
Prizes, §93A-46.
Tourist camps and homes.
Rate advertisements, §§72-50 to 72-52.
Trespass.
Posting of advertisements.
Unlawful posting, §14-145.
Truth in advertisement.
Cost of service or repair of private passenger vehicles, §66-285.
Unfair competitive practices.
Applicability of provisions, §75-1.1.
Viatical life insurance settlements, §58-58-260.
Contract securities, §78A-14.
"Wholesale.."
Use of term "wholesale,"§75-29(a) to (c).
Work-at-home solicitations, §75-31.
Workers' compensation.
Self-insurance.
Third-party administrators and service companies.
Approval of advertising, §58-47-175.

ADVERTISING CONTROL ACT, §§136-126 to 136-140.
See OUTDOOR ADVERTISING.

ADVISORY JURY, §1A-1 Rule 39(c).

AED.
Automated external defibrillator, §90-21.15.

AEDIN'S LAW.
Animal exhibitions, regulation, §106-520.3A.

AERONAUTICS.
Aircraft.
See AIRCRAFT.
Airports.
See AIRPORTS.

AERONAUTICS ADMINISTRATION.
Rules and regulations.
Enforcement, §63-47.

AERONAUTICS DIVISION, §143B-355.

AFDC.
Work first program generally, §§108A-27 to 108A-39.
See WORK FIRST PROGRAM.

AFFIDAVITS.
Advertising.
Legal advertising.
Affidavit of publication, §§1-598, 1-600(a).
Prima facie evidence, §1-600(b).
Aliens.
Verification of work authorization.
Violations, consequences.
First violation, §64-31(a).
Failure to file affidavit, §64-31(b).
Appeal bonds.
Justification assurance, §1-286.
Arrest in civil cases.
Plaintiff, §1-411.
Copy to defendant, §1-414.
Counter affidavits, §1-418.
Assignments for benefit of creditors.
Petition for assignment, §23-13.
Attachment.
Amendment, §1-440.11(c), (d).
Bonds, §1-440.8(b).
Complaint.
Verified complaint use as affidavit, §1-440.11(b).
Discharge upon giving bonds, §1-440.39(b).
Dissolution of order, §1-440.36(c).
Filing.
Judge to require, §1-440.5(c).
Motion by plaintiff to sell remaining debts and
evidences of indebtedness, §1-440.46(b).
Requirements, §1-440.11(a).
Sheriffs.
Sale of debts and other evidences of
indebtedness, §1-440.46(b).
Attorney disciplinary proceedings.
Consent to disbarment, Bar Rule B.0117.
Disbarred or suspended attorney to show
compliance with order, Bar Rule B.0124.
Grievance reduced to affidavit form, Bar Rule
B.0111.
Resignation while under investigation, Bar Rule
B.0117.
Attorneys at law.
Continuing legal education.
General compliance procedures, CLE Reg 8.
Bail bondsmen and runners.
Affidavits filed with clerk of court, §58-71-140(d).
Bonds, surety.
Mortgage in lieu of bond.
Value of property required, §58-74-30.
**Campaign contribution and expenditure
statements and reports.**
Certified as true and correct, §163-278.32.
False certification knowing information to be
untrue, criminal penalty, §163-278.27(a1).
Change of venue.
Application for removal, §1-85.
Child support.
Acknowledgment of paternity in agreement to
support, §110-132(a).
Setting aside affidavit of parentage by trial
court, §110-132(a1), (a2).
Claim and delivery, §1-473.
Third parties.
Property claimed by third person, §1-482.
CLE compliance, Bar Rule D.1608.
Color of title under destroyed instrument,
§98-8.
Commercial drivers' licenses.
Applicant for license with P or S endorsement.
Person not on state or national sex offender
registries, §20-37.14A(b).
False affidavit, criminal penalty,
§20-37.14A(c).

AFFIDAVITS —Cont'd
Concealed handgun permit.
Renewal.
Permittee remains qualified, §14-415.16(b).
Contempt.
Civil contempt.
Order or notice, §5A-23(a).
Proceeding initiated on motion of aggrieved
party, §5A-23(a1).
Continuing legal education compliance, Bar
Rule D.1608.
Credits upon judgments, §1-242.
Criminal procedure.
Depositions of nonattending witness, §8-74.
Expungement of records.
First offenders not over age of 21.
Filing of petition.
Drug offenses, §15A-145.2(a).
Toxic vapors offenses, §15A-145.3(a).
First offenders under age of 18.
Filing of petition, §15A-145(a).
Gang offenses, §§14-50.30(a), 15A-145.1(a).
Misdemeanor conviction 15 years prior to filing
petition.
Affidavits filed with petition, §15A-145(d1).
Motion for appropriate relief.
Supporting affidavits, §15A-1420(b).
Motion to suppress evidence.
Pretrial motion in superior court.
Affidavit supporting motion, §15A-977(a).
Nontestimonial identification orders, §15A-273.
Criminal street gangs.
Expungement of records.
First offenders under age of 18.
Filing of petition, §14-50.30(a).
Decedents' estates.
Debts and claims.
Right of personal representative to require
affidavit of claimant, §28A-19-2(b).
Deeds.
Errors in registered instruments.
Corrective affidavit and notice, §47-36.1.
Unregistered deeds prior to January, 1920, §47-19.
Default judgment, §1A-1 Rule 55(a).
Devisavit vel non.
Witness to will as evidence, §31-35.
District attorneys, removal, §7A-66.
Drivers' licenses.
False affidavits.
Perjury, §20-31.
Durable power of attorney.
Statement by attorney-in-fact of no actual
knowledge of termination of power by
revocation.
Conclusive proof of nonrevocation or
nontermination of power, §32A-13(c).
**Equitable distribution of marital and divisible
property.**
Inventory affidavit, §50-21(a).
Executors and administrators.
Domiciliary administration.
Payment of debt and delivery of property
without ancillary administration,
§28A-26-2(a).
Limited personal representatives.
Final accounting, §28A-21-2.2.
Expungement of criminal records.
First offenders not over age of 21.
Drug offenses.
Affidavits filed with petition, §15A-145.2(a).

AFFIDAVITS —Cont'd
Expungement of criminal records —Cont'd
First offenders not over age of 21 —Cont'd
Toxic vapors offenses.
Affidavits filed with application,
§15A-145.3(a).
First offenders under age of 18.
Affidavits filed with petition, §15A-145(a).
Gang offenses, §§14-50.30(a), 15A-145.1(a).
Nonviolent felony offenses, §15A-145.4(c).
Misdemeanor conviction 15 years prior to filing
petition.
Affidavits filed with petition, §15A-145(d1).
False affidavit.
Perjury, §20-112.
Foreign judgments.
Affidavit stating judgment final and unsatisfied,
§1C-1703(a).
Foreign-money claims.
Enforcement of judgment, §1C-1826(i).
Seizure or restraint of assets, §1C-1830(d).
Foresters.
Consulting foresters.
Affidavit of compliance with provisions,
§89B-14(b).
Funeral service.
Good moral character of license applicant,
§90-210.26.
Impaired driving.
Chemical analysis of blood.
Refusal to submit to analysis.
Law enforcement officer's affidavit,
§20-16.2(c1).
Chemical analyst's affidavit.
Admissibility without further authentication or
testimony of analyst, §20-139.1(e1), (e2).
Incompetence, determination of.
Notice and petition mailed to respondent's next of
kin.
Proof of mailing or acceptance, §35A-1109.
Indigent persons.
Small claims actions.
Appeals, §7A-228(b1).
Suing as indigent, §1-110(a).
In forma pauperis appeals, §1-288.
Injunctions.
Preliminary injunction, §1-485.
Insurance companies.
Affidavit of company president or other chief
officer.
Compliance with insurance law.
Required to do business, §58-2-150.
Landlord and tenant.
Execution of judgments for possession more than
thirty days old, §42-36.1A.
Land titles or family history, §47-1.
Larceny.
Mutilation, larceny or destruction of public
records and papers, §14-76.
Legal advertising.
Affidavit of publication, §§1-598, 1-600(a).
Prima facie evidence, §1-600(b).
Letters testamentary and of administration.
Application, §28A-6-1.
Lis pendens notice, §1-119(a).
Lost instruments and records.
Petitions and motions.
Facts stated to be verified by affidavit of
petitioner, §98-14.
**Lost note or other indebtedness secured by
mortgage, deed of trust, other instrument.**
Form of affidavit, §47-46.3.

AFFIDAVITS —Cont'd
Magistrates.
Verification of pleadings.
Power of magistrate to take affidavit for
verification, §7A-292.
**Manufactured home permanently attached to
real property,** §47-20.6.
**Manufactured home qualifying as real
property.**
Surrender of title certificate.
Affidavit of qualification by owner, §20-109.2(b).
Marriage certificates.
Delayed issuance, §51-21.
Marriage license.
Issuance to applicant unable to appear, §51-8.2.
**Mental health, developmental disabilities and
substance abuse.**
Involuntary commitment.
Petition and affidavit before clerk or magistrate,
§122C-261.
Substance abuser, §122C-281.
Mortgages and deeds of trust.
Lost note or other indebtedness secured by.
Form of affidavit, §47-46.3.
Motion for appropriate relief, §15A-1420(b).
Motions supported by affidavits.
Affidavit served with motion, §1A-1 Rule 6(d).
Motor vehicles.
False affidavit.
Perjury, §20-112.
Licenses.
False affidavits.
Perjury, §20-31.
Municipal parking violations.
Rented or leased vehicles.
Responsibility of owner, §160A-301(e).
Traffic control photographic system.
Evidence exempting owner from liability,
§160A-300.1(c).
New trial.
Motion.
Time for serving affidavits, §1A-1 Rule 59(c).
Nonprofit associations.
Uniform unincorporated nonprofit association act.
Property held by association.
Statement of authority to transfer, §59B-6(c),
(d).
Optometrists.
Persons in practice before passage of statute,
§90-119.
Partition sales.
Notice.
Certification and affidavit of notice, §46-28(b).
Paternity.
Acknowledging paternity, §130A-101(f).
Perjury.
Punishment for perjury, §14-209.
Probate of wills.
Compelling production of will, §28A-2A-4.
Examination of witnesses by, §28A-2A-16.
What shown on application for probate,
§28A-2A-5.
Proof of service of process, §1-75.10(a).
Prosecution bonds.
Land actions.
Defendant unable to give, not worth amount.
Bond not required, §1-112(a).
Publication.
Legal advertising.
Affidavit of publication, §§1-598, 1-600(a).
Prima facie evidence, §1-600(b).

AFFIDAVITS —Cont'd
Publication —Cont'd
Service by.
　Proof of service, §1-75.10(a).
Public contracts.
Minority business participation goals.
　Good faith efforts required.
　　Affidavit submitted with bid, §143-128.2(c).
Public works.
Regulation of contractors.
　Noncollusion affidavits, §133-30.
　Perjury in affidavit, §133-31.
Registered instruments.
Errors.
　Corrective affidavit and notice, §47-36.1.
Removal for fair trial, §1-85.
Search warrants, §§15A-244, 15A-245(a).
Self-proved wills, §31-11.6(b), (c).
Service of process.
Mail in foreign country, §1A-1 Rule 4(j3).
Motions supported by affidavits.
　Affidavits served with motions, §1A-1 Rule 6(d).
Proof of service, §1-75.10(a).
　Designated delivery service, §1A-1 Rule 4(j2).
　Registered or certified mail, §1A-1 Rule 4(j2).
　Signature confirmation, §§1-75.10(a), 1A-1 Rule 4(j2).
Signature confirmation.
Proof of service, §§1-75.10(a), 1A-1 Rule 4(j2).
Small claims actions.
Indigents desiring to appeal, §7A-228(b1).
Small estates.
Collection of property by affidavit.
　See SMALL ESTATES.
State officers aithorized to prove or acknowledge, §47-1.
Summary judgment, §1A-1 Rule 56(c), (e) to (g).
Claimant, §1A-1 Rule 56(a).
Defending party, §1A-1 Rule 56(b).
Service, §1A-1 Rule 56(c).
Superior court clerks, removal, §7A-105.
Supplemental proceedings.
Debtors earnings necessary for family support, §1-362.
Ordering debtor or judgment debtor to appear at specified time and place to answer, §1-360.
Temporary restraining order without notice, §1A-1 Rule 65(b).
Time for, §§1-593, 1A-1 Rule 6(d).
Toll collection on turnpike projects.
Contesting liability for unpaid toll.
　Informal review, §136-89.218(a).
Payment of toll required.
　Vehicle in care, custody and control of another, §136-89.212.
Torrens system registration.
Adverse claims existing at initial registry, §43-19.
Tort claims against state departments and agencies.
Claimant to provide affidavit, §143-297.
Demurrer or other pleading to affidavit, §143-297.
Trust companies.
Directors.
　Affidavit of acceptance, §53-352(b).
Seizure by commissioner.
　Action following full settlement, §53-393.
　Claims against company.
　　Notice of rejection by commissioner, §53-387.
　　Notice regarding presentation of claims, §53-386.

AFFIDAVITS —Cont'd
Uniform unincorporated nonprofit association act.
Property held by association.
　Statement of authority to transfer, §59B-6(c), (d).
Usurpation office.
Arrest and bail of defendants, §1-519.
Utilities commission.
Use of affidavits in proceedings, §62-68.
Verification of pleadings, §§1-148, 1A-1 Rule 11(b), (c).
Wage and hour act.
Power of commissioner of labor to take affidavits, §95-25.16(b).
Wills.
Self-proved wills, §31-11.6(b), (c).

AFFIRMATIONS.
Defined, §10B-3.
Generally.
See OATHS OR AFFIRMATIONS.
In lieu of oath, §11-4.
Perjury, §§14-209 to 14-211.

AFFIRMATIVE DEFENSES.
See DEFENSES.

AFFRAYS.
Aggravated affrays.
Punishment for misdemeanor affrays, §14-33(b), (c).
　Factors determining classification of offense, §14-33(b), (c).
　Habitual misdemeanor assault, §14-33.2.
Arrest without warrant, §15A-401.
Misdemeanor affrays, §14-33(b), (c).
Habitual misdemeanor assault, §14-33.2.
Self-defense.
Evidence of former threats upon plea of self-defense, §14-33.1.
Simple affray, §14-33(a).
Punishment for misdemeanor affrays, §14-33(a).

AFRICAN-AMERICAN HERITAGE COMMISSION.
Chair, §143B-135(e).
Compensation, §143B-135(g).
Composition, §143B-135(b).
Creation, §143B-135(a).
Duties, §143B-135(a).
Meetings, §143B-135(f).
Officers, §143B-135(e).
Quorum, §143B-135(f).
Removal, §143B-135(d).
Terms, §143B-135(b).
Vacancies, §143B-135(c).
Vice-chair, §143B-135(e).

AFTER-ACQUIRED PROPERTY.
Registration of instrument containing after-acquired property clause.
Definitions, §47-20.5(a), (b).
Effectiveness, §47-20.5(c).
Indexing by register of deeds, §47-20.5(f).
Instruments creating security interest made by public utilities, §47-20.5(h).
Notice of extension registered in lieu of instrument, §47-20.5(d).
　Operation, §47-20.5(e).
Required to pass title against lien creditors or purchasers for consideration, §47-20.5(g).
Secured transactions.
Security interest in after-acquired property, §25-9-204(a), (b).

AFTER-ADOPTED CHILDREN.
Will not revoked by, §31-5.5(a) to (c).

AFTERBORN CHILDREN.
Children's allowance, when entitled, §30-17.
Estates.
Taking of property by deed or writings, §41-5.
Intestate succession generally, §29-9.
Wills, §31-5.5(a) to (c).

AGE.
Accountants.
Minimum age, §93-2.
Adult education, §115C-231.
Alarm system business.
Licensing requirement, §74D-2(d).
Bail bondsmen and runners.
Licenses.
Minimum age, §58-71-50(b).
Blood donations.
Persons under 18 years selling.
Unlawful, §130A-412.31.
Sixteen year olds, §130A-412.31.
Bus drivers.
Age limits for public passenger-carrying vehicles, §20-10.
Capital punishment.
Mitigating circumstances.
Age of defendant, §15A-2000(f).
Commercial drivers' licenses.
Minimum age, §20-9(a).
Congress.
Representatives, US Const Art I §2.
Senators, US Const Art I §3.
Credit union members.
Minimum age to hold office, §54-109.31(e).
Minimum age to vote at meetings, §54-109.31(d).
Deeds.
Married persons under eighteen made competent as to certain transactions, §39-13.2.
District courts.
Twenty-fifth judicial district judges.
Validation of official acts performed after mandatory retirement age, §7A-4.21.
Drivers' licenses.
Minimum age for drivers' licenses, §20-9(a).
Elections.
Qualifications of voters.
Minimum age, §163-55(a).
Right to vote.
Not to be abridged on account of age, US Const Amd 26.
Persons eighteen years of age, US Const Amd 26.
Executors and administrators.
Persons disqualified to serve, §28A-4-2.
Farm tractors.
Minimum age for operation, §20-10.
Fireworks.
Display operator's permit.
Requirement, §58-28A-3(b).
Funeral service.
Qualifications for licenses, §90-210.25(a).
Hearing aid dealers and fitters.
Qualifications for license, §93D-5(a).
Implements of husbandry.
Minimum age for operation, §20-10.
Jurors.
Qualifications to serve as, §9-3.

AGE —Cont'd
Justices or judges of general court of justice.
Age limit for service as, §7A-4.20.
Marriage.
Capacity, §51-2.
Minors, §48A-2.
Mopeds.
Minimum age for operation, §20-10.1.
Mortality tables.
Evidence, §§8-46, 8-47.
Motor vehicle insurance.
Discriminatory practices, §58-3-25(a).
Nursing home administrators.
Qualifications, §90-278.
Occupational licensing board.
Requirements for licensure, §93B-9.
Opticians.
Minimum age, §90-237.
President of the United States, US Const Art II §1.
Private protective services.
Licenses.
Qualification, §74C-8(d).
Probate and registration.
Acknowledgments before notaries under age, §47-108.
Public passenger-carrying vehicles.
Age limits for drivers, §20-10.
Public schools.
Admission requirements, §115C-364(a), (b).
Adult education, §115C-231.
Compulsory attendance.
Children required to attend, §115C-378.
Evidence of child's age.
Birth certificates prima facie evidence, §130A-109.
Secondary proof, §130A-109.
Free tuition, §115C-1.
Kindergartens.
Age of eligibility for enrollment, §115C-81(f).
Teachers.
Minimum age, §115C-295(a).
Rape indictments.
Victim female child under age of 13, §15-144.1(b).
Retirement system for teachers and state employees.
Local board of education to provide age, §115C-47.
School bus drivers.
Minimum age, §20-218(a).
Sexual offense indictments.
Victim 13 years of age or less, §15-144.2(b).
Sheriffs.
Minimum age, §162-2.
Sterilization.
Persons over eighteen.
Operation lawful upon request, §90-271.
Persons under eighteen.
Married persons.
Operation lawful upon request, §90-271.
Unmarried persons, §90-272.
Teachers.
Minimum age, §115C-295(a).
Tobacco products, §14-313.
Vice-president, US Const Amd 12.

AGED PERSONS.
See SENIOR CITIZENS.

AGED RECORDS.
Inspection of public records, §132-6(f).

AGE LIMIT FOR JUSTICES AND JUDGES, §7A-4.20.

Validation of certain actions of district court judges of twenty fifth judicial district performed after mandatory retirement, §7A-4.21.

AGENCIES AND DEPARTMENTS.
See STATE DEPARTMENTS AND AGENCIES.

AGENCY FOR PUBLIC TELECOMMUNICATIONS, §§143B-426.8 to 143B-426.20.
See PUBLIC TELECOMMUNICATIONS, AGENCY FOR.

AGENTS.
ABC law enforcement agents, §18B-500.
ABC officers, local, §18B-501.
Alarm system businesses.
Qualifying agents.
Designation, §74D-2(c).
Anatomical gifts.
Gifts of body or body part of decedent, §130A-412.11(a).
Gifts prior to donor's death, §130A-412.6.
Athlete agents, §§78C-85 to 78C-105.
See ATHLETE AGENTS.
Attorneys at law.
Agent of lawyers' or judges' association.
Duty of confidentiality when acting as, ProfCond Rule 1.6.
Banks.
Personal agency accounts.
Generally, §53-146.3.
Bonds, surety.
Actions on bonds.
Evidence against principal admissible against sureties, §58-76-25.
Indemnity bonds to state maximum liability and period of liability, §66-65.
Collection of debts or accounts.
Simulation of court process in connection with collection, §14-118.1.
Commissions to sales representatives, §§66-190 to 66-193.
Community colleges.
Negligence of agents.
Waiver of governmental immunity by act of obtaining liability insurance, §115D-24.
Compensation.
Powers which may be incorporated by reference in trust instrument, §32-27.
Trustees and other fiduciaries, §§32-53 to 32-62.
See FIDUCIARIES.
Consent to health care for minors.
Parent authorizing agent to consent, §§32A-28 to 32A-34.
Corporations.
Embezzlement.
Receipt of property by virtue of office or employment, §14-90.
Indemnification generally.
Business corporations, §§55-8-50 to 55-8-58.
Nonprofit corporations, §§55A-8-50 to 55A-8-58.
Misconduct in private office.
Malfeasance of corporation agents, §14-254(a).
Oaths, §11-5.
Registered agent.
Business corporations.
Foreign corporations, §55-15-07.

AGENTS —Cont'd
Corporations —Cont'd
Registered agent —Cont'd
Nonprofit corporations, §55A-5-01.
Foreign corporations, §55A-15-07.
Credit unions.
Personal agency accounts.
Generally, §54-109.63.
Deeds.
Execution of deed dated before 1835.
Evidence of due execution, §8-13.
Torrens system registration.
Instruments describing party as agent not to operate as notice, §§43-63, 43-64.
Disclosure of real parties.
Person trading as "agent" to disclose, §66-72.
Eggs.
Act of agent as that of principal, §106-245.28.
Embezzlement.
Receipt of property by virtue of office or employment, §14-90.
Employers and employees.
Violating duties owed employers.
Influencing agents in violating duties, §14-353.
Witness required to give self-incriminating evidence, §14-354.
No suit or prosecution to be founded thereon, §14-354.
Fiduciaries generally.
See FIDUCIARIES.
Futures contracts, §16-4.
Health care for minors.
Parent authorizing agent to consent, §§32A-28 to 32A-34.
Health maintenance organizations.
Licensing, §58-67-90.
Hospital authorities.
Corporate agents, §131E-23(b).
Exercise of powers through agents, §131E-23(b).
Hospital, medical and dental service corporations.
Licenses, §58-65-115.
Associations to transact business through licensed agents only, §58-65-120.
Required, §58-65-120.
Insurance agents generally.
See INSURANCE AGENTS.
Limited liability companies.
Agency law to apply under chapter, §57C-10-03(c).
Agency power of managers, §57C-3-23.
Delegation of authority by managers, §57C-3-24(c).
Insurance purchased on behalf of agent, §57C-3-32(c).
Registered office and registered agent, §57C-2-40.
Lobbyists.
Generally, §§120C-100 to 120C-800.
See LOBBYISTS AND LOBBYING.
Lotteries.
Acting as agent for lotteries, §14-291.
Managing general insurance agents, §§58-34-2 to 58-34-15.
Marketing and branding farm products.
Power to employ agents and assistants, §106-186.
Missing persons.
When agent's acts binding on estates, §28C-21.
Mortgages and deeds of trust.
Appointment of agency.
Agency to sell under power may be appointed by parol or writing, §45-7.

AGENTS —Cont'd
Mortgages and deeds of trust —Cont'd
Foreclosures.
Attacking foreclosures on ground trustee was
agent, etc., of owner of debt, §45-21.39(a).
Sales under power of sale.
Trustee agent of owner of debt.
Validation of foreclosure sale, §45-21.47.
Negotiable instruments.
Authorized signature of represented person,
§25-3-402(a) to (c).
Partnerships.
Applicability of law of agency, §59-34(c).
Partner as agent of partnership as to partnership
business, §59-39(a).
Partner by estoppel.
Agent of persons consenting to representation,
§59-46(b).
Plant pests.
Inspections authorized, §106-422.
Powers of attorney.
Powers conferred by statutory short form.
Employment of agents, §32A-2.
**Powers of fiduciaries generally, §§32-25 to
32-27.**
Private protective services.
Qualifying agents.
Designation, §74C-8(c).
Rendering plants and rendering operations.
Authority of agents of licensee, §106-168.11.
Representation and binding of others.
Persons representing and binding others,
§§36C-3-301 to 36C-3-305.
Residential property disclosure act.
Duty of agent to inform owner of rights and
obligations, §47E-8.
Liability of agent for owner's refusal to provide
disclosure statement, §47E-8.
**Sales representative commissions, §§66-190 to
66-193.**
Savings and loan associations.
Personal agency accounts.
Generally, §54B-139.
Service of process.
Process agents.
Appointment by agency of state, §1A-1 Rule 4(j).
Sports agents, §§78C-85 to 78C-105.
See ATHLETE AGENTS.
State departments and agencies.
Identification cards for field agents or deputies of
state departments, §128-14.
Structural pest control.
Designation of resident agent, §106-65.30(b).
Torrens system registration.
Instruments describing party as agent not to
operate as notice, §§43-63, 43-64.
**Trader or merchant transacting business with
addition of words agent.**
Disclosure of name of principal or partner by sign
placed conspicuously in place of business,
§66-72.
Transfer agents.
Security transfers.
See FIDUCIARIES.
Trust and trustees.
Distribution of estates to nonresident trustees.
Appointment of process agent required,
§28A-22-4.
Uniform fiduciaries act, §§32-1 to 32-13.
See FIDUCIARIES.

AGE OF MAJORITY.
Age of minor, §48A-2.

AGGRAVATED SENTENCING.
Allowing, §15A-1340.16(b).
Bifurcated trials, §15A-1340.16(a1).
Felony structured sentencing, §15A-1340.16.
Intention to seek.
Contents, §15A-924(a).
Impaired driving.
Sentencing hearing.
Determining existence of aggravating factors,
§20-179.
List of factors, §15A-1340.16(d).
Pleading, §15A-1340.16(a).
Prior records, §15A-1340.16(a).
Procedure, §15A-1340.16(a2), (a3), (a5).
Written findings, §15A-1340.16(c).

AGGRAVATING CIRCUMSTANCES.
Attorney disciplinary proceedings.
Imposition of discipline, Bar Rule B.0114.
Capital felonies, §15A-2000(e).
Impaired driving.
Sentencing hearing.
Determining existence of aggravating factors,
§20-179.

AGGRESSIVE DRIVING.
Elements of offense, §20-141.6(a).
Misdemeanor, §20-141.6(c).
Proof of offense, §20-141.6(b).
Reckless driving as lesser included offense,
§20-141.6(d).

AGRARIAN GROWTH ZONES.
Defined, §143B-437.010(a).
Determination, §143B-437.010(b).
Property partially within zone,
§143B-437.010(c).
Publication of list, §143B-437.010(b).

AGREEMENTS OF CHILD SUPPORT, §110-133.
**Acknowledgment of paternity in agreement to
support,** §110-132.
Filing of affirmations, acknowledgments, etc.,
§110-134.

**AGRICULTURAL CONSERVATION
EASEMENTS.**
**Agricultural development and farmland
preservation trust fund committee,**
§106-744(g) to (i).
Applicability of section, §106-744(d).
Authority of county.
Acquisition by purchase of qualifying farmland,
§106-744(a).
Construction of section, §106-744(d).
Countywide farmland protection plan,
§106-744(e), (f).
Defined, §106-744(b).
**North Carolina agricultural development and
farmland preservation trust fund.**
Distribution of money in fund, §106-744(c1).
County match, §106-744(c2).
Established, use, §106-744(c).
Rules, adoption by commissioner, §106-744(c3).

**AGRICULTURAL DEVELOPMENT, §§106-580 to
106-587.**
Agricultural extension service.
Cooperation of departments and agencies with
service, §106-583.
Appropriations.
By counties, §106-585.

AGRICULTURAL DEVELOPMENT —Cont'd
Appropriations —Cont'd
Local appropriations, §106-587.
Authority granted by article supplementary,
§106-586.
Citation of act, §106-580.
Congress.
Funds made available by congress, §106-585.
Cooperation of departments and agencies with
agricultural extension service, §106-583.
Counties.
Appropriations by counties, §106-585.
Local appropriations, §106-587.
Utilizing facilities for installing and promoting
programs, §106-582.
Declaration of intent, §106-581.
Declaration of policy, §106-583.
Definitions, §106-581.1.
Funds made available by congress, §106-585.
Intent of article, §106-581.
Municipalities.
Local appropriations, §106-587.
Policy declaration, §106-583.
Programs.
Counties authorized to utilize facilities for
installing and promoting, §106-582.
Purpose of article, §106-581.
Research facilities.
Maximum use of existing facilities, §106-584.
Short title, §106-580.
State departments and agencies.
Cooperation with agricultural extension service,
§106-583.
Supplementary grant of authority by article,
§106-586.
Title of article, §106-580.

AGRICULTURAL DEVELOPMENT AND
FARMLAND PRESERVATION ENABLING
ACT, §§106-735 to 106-744.
See FARMLAND PRESERVATION.

AGRICULTURAL DEVELOPMENT AND
FARMLAND TRUST FUND, §106-744(c) to
(c3).

AGRICULTURAL DISTRICTS.
Voluntary agricultural districts.
Agricultural development and farmland
preservation enabling act generally,
§§106-735 to 106-744.
See FARMLAND PRESERVATION.

AGRICULTURAL EXTENSION SERVICE.
Agricultural development generally, §§106-580
to 106-587.
See AGRICULTURAL DEVELOPMENT.
Workers' compensation.
Employee defined, §97-2.

AGRICULTURAL FAIRS.
See FAIRS.

AGRICULTURAL FARM WORKERS.
See MIGRANT FARM WORKERS.

AGRICULTURAL FEES AND TAXES.
Assessment procedure.
Authority of commissioner of agriculture,
§106-9.3(f), (g).
Finality of assessment, §106-9.3(d).
Hearing requested by objecting taxpayer,
§106-9.3(c).
Interest rate, §106-9.3(e).

AGRICULTURAL FEES AND TAXES —Cont'd
Assessment procedure —Cont'd
Limitation of actions, §106-9.3(a).
Notice to taxpayer, §106-9.3(b).
Delivery of notice, §106-9.3(b).
Time period for assessment, §106-9.3(e).
Delinquent taxes.
Attachment.
Collection of delinquent taxes, §106-9.4(b).
Collection of delinquent taxes.
Certificate of particulars, §106-9.4(c).
Choses in action, §106-9.4(b).
Cumulative nature of remedies, §106-9.4(d).
Intangible personal property, §106-9.4(b).
Order issued by commissioner of agriculture,
§106-9.4(a).
Other remedies, §106-9.4(d).
Suits to prevent collection prohibited, §106-9.6.
Cumulative nature of remedies, §106-9.4(d).
Garnishment.
Collection of delinquent taxes, §106-9.4(b).
Order issued by commissioner of agriculture,
§106-9.4(a).
Other remedies, §106-9.4(d).
Eastern North Carolina agricultural center
fund, §106-6.2(a).
Noncompliance cases.
Determination of amount due by commissioner,
§106-9.2(c).
Overpayment.
Refund of overpayment, §106-9.5.
Payment under protest.
Recovery of fee or tax so paid, §106-9.6.
Preventing collection.
Suits prohibited, §106-9.6.
Property taxes.
Agricultural, horticultural and forestland,
§§105-277.2 to 105-277.7.
Exemptions, §105-275.
Reduced valuation.
Certain farm products classified for taxation at,
§105-277.01.
Protest payments.
Recovery of fee or tax so paid, §106-9.6.
Records.
Examination of records, §106-9.2(b).
Noncompliance cases.
Determination of amount due by commissioner,
§106-9.2(c).
Required of persons paying fees or taxes to
commissioner or department, §106-9.2(a).
Recovery of tax.
Payment under protest, §106-9.6.
Refund of overpayment, §106-9.5.
Reports.
Noncompliance cases.
Determination of amount due by commissioner,
§106-9.2(c).
Required of persons paying fees or taxes to
commissioner or department, §106-9.2(a).
Southeastern North Carolina agricultural
center fund, §106-6.2(b).
Suits to prevent collection prohibited, §106-9.6.

AGRICULTURAL FESTIVALS.
Winery special event permit authorization,
§18B-1114.1.

AGRICULTURAL FINANCE AUTHORITY,
§§122D-1 to 122D-23.
Accounts and accounting, §122D-18(a).

AGRICULTURAL FINANCE AUTHORITY
—Cont'd
Actions.
Power to sue and be sued, §122D-6.
Appointment of members, §122D-4(b) to (d).
Audits, §122D-18(b).
Bond issues, §122D-10.
Authorized, §122D-10(a), (i).
Coupon bonds, §122D-10(g).
Covenant of state, §122D-15.
Definition of "bonds" or "notes,"§122D-3.
Deposits.
Bonds as security for public deposits, §122D-17.
Interim receipts or temporary bonds, §122D-10(h).
Investments.
Bonds as legal investment, §122D-17.
Pledge.
Statutory pledge, §122D-11.
Powers of authority, §122D-6.
Proceeds.
Trust funds, §122D-16(a).
Purchase of bonds by authority, §122D-13.
Refunding bonds, §122D-12.
Sale of bonds, §122D-10(c), (e), (f).
Signatures on bonds, §122D-10(d).
Taxation.
Exemption from taxes, §122D-14.
Terms and conditions of bonds, §122D-10(b), (c).
Chairman.
Election, §122D-5(a).
Citation of act.
Short title, §122D-1.
Composition, §122D-4(b).
Construction and interpretation.
Liberal construction of provisions, §122D-20.
Severability of provisions, §122D-22.
Contracts.
Experts and consultants.
Employment on contractual basis, §122D-5(d).
Power to contract, §122D-6.
Creation, §122D-4(a).
Definitions, §122D-3.
Domicile of authority, §122D-4(e).
Duties.
Delegation, §122D-4(i).
Executive director, §122D-5(b), (c).
Expenses of members, §122D-4(g).
Experts and consultants.
Employment on contractual basis, §122D-5(d).
Findings of legislature, §122D-2(a) to (c).
General fund.
Termination of authority.
Deposits of assets in, §122D-21.
Immunities, §122D-23.
Insurance.
Agricultural loans, §122D-9.
Investments.
Bond issues.
Legal investments, §122D-17.
Moneys of authority.
Authorized investments, §122D-16(a).
Legislative findings and declarations, §122D-2(a) to (c).
Lending institutions.
Defined, §122D-3.
Loans.
Agricultural loans.
Defined, §122D-3.
Insurance, §122D-9.
Powers of authority, §122D-6.

AGRICULTURAL FINANCE AUTHORITY
—Cont'd
Loans —Cont'd
Agricultural loans —Cont'd
Purchases and sales of agricultural loans, §122D-7.
Insurance of agricultural loans.
Agreements, §122D-9(d).
Amount, §122D-9(b).
Authorized, §122D-9(a).
Default.
What constitutes, §122D-9(c).
Maximum aggregate value of agricultural loans insured, §122D-9(e).
Lending institutions.
Loans to, §122D-8.
Powers of authority, §122D-6.
Meetings, §122D-4(h).
Powers, §122D-6.
Delegation, §122D-4(i).
Quorum, §122D-4(f).
Reports.
Annual report to governor and general assembly, §122D-18(a).
Severability of provisions, §122D-22.
Short title of act, §122D-1.
State departments and agencies.
Cooperation of state agencies, §122D-19.
Taxation.
Exemption from taxes, §122D-14.
Termination of authority, §122D-21.
Terms of members, §122D-4(c).
Trust funds, §122D-16(a).
Vacancies.
Filling, §122D-4(d).
Vice-chairman.
Election, §122D-5(a).

AGRICULTURAL HALL OF FAME, §§106-568.13 to 106-568.17.
Acceptance of awards, §106-568.17.
Admission of candidates, §106-568.16.
Board of directors, §106-568.14.
Terms, §106-568.15.
Candidates.
Admission, §106-568.16.
Control of hall of fame, §106-568.14.
Creation, §106-568.13.
Display of awards, §106-568.17.
Established, §106-568.13.
State agency designation, §106-568.13.
Supervision of hall of fame, §106-568.14.
Terms of directors, §106-568.15.
Transfer to department of agriculture and consumer services, §143A-61.

AGRICULTURAL LIMING MATERIALS AND LANDPLASTER.
Limestone, marl and landplaster, §§106-92.1 to 106-92.17.
See LIMESTONE, MARL AND LANDPLASTER.

AGRICULTURAL OPERATION NUISANCE LIABILITY.
Declaration of policy, §106-700.

AGRICULTURAL PRODUCTS PROMOTION, §§106-550 to 106-568.
Activities deemed not illegal or in restraint of trade, §106-552.
Applicability of provisions.
Tobacco excluded, §106-550.

AGRICULTURAL PRODUCTS PROMOTION
  —Cont'd
Assessments.
  Alternative method for collection, §106-564.1.
    Cattle-related assessments, §106-564.3.
    Further alternative method, §106-564.2.
    Sweet potatoes, §106-564.4.
  Amount and basis of proposed assessment, §106-557.
  Cattle-related assessments.
    Alternative method for collection, §106-564.3.
  Collection of assessments, §106-564.
    Alternative method of collection, §§106-564.1 to 106-564.4.
    Further alternative method for collection, §106-564.2.
  Continuance of assessments approved at prior referendum, §106-566.
  Custody and use of funds, §106-564.
  Dissatisfaction with assessments, §106-567.
  Effect of more than one-third vote against assessment, §106-560.
  Effect of two-third vote for assessment, §106-561.
  Financial statement.
    Publication by treasurer of agency, §106-568.
  Financing program of production, use and sale, §106-553.
  Growers and producers on question of assessments, §106-556.
  Maximum assessment, §106-557.
  Publication of financial statement by treasurer of agency, §106-568.
    Bond required, §106-568.
  Purpose of assessment, §106-557.
  Refund.
    Milk product assessments, §106-567.1.
    Time for demanding, §106-567.
  Rights of farmers dissatisfied with assessment, §106-567.
  Sweet potato-related assessments.
    Alternative method for collection, §106-564.4.
  Time for demanding refund, §106-567.
  Treasurer of agency.
    Publication of financial statement, §106-568.
Associations deemed not illegal or in restraint of trade, §106-552.
Ballot by mail.
  Alternative method of conducting referendum, §106-557.1(a).
  Applicability of provisions, §106-557.1(b).
Board of agriculture.
  Application to board for authorization of referendum, §106-554.
  Action by board, §106-555.
Citation of federal act, §106-551.
Cotton promotion association.
  Special referendum provisions, §106-559.
County agents.
  Notice of referendum, §106-562.
Declaration of policy, §106-550.
Designation of federal law, §106-551.
Farmers' rights.
  Dissatisfaction with assessments, §106-567.
Farm organizations.
  Notice of referendum, §106-562.
Federal agricultural marketing act, §106-551.
Federal assessment programs.
  Official state board, §106-555.1.
    Subsequent referenda not required, §106-555.1.
Growers.
  Conduct of referendum among growers on question of assessments, §106-556.

AGRICULTURAL PRODUCTS PROMOTION
  —Cont'd
Meetings deemed not illegal or in restraint of trade, §106-552.
Milk products.
  Referendum.
    Basis of vote, §106-559.1.
    Supervision, §106-563.1.
  Refund of assessment, §106-567.1.
Policy declaration, §106-550.
Producers.
  Conduct of referendum among producers on question of assessments, §106-556.
Publications.
  Financial statement by treasurer of agency, §106-568.
Referendum.
  Alternative method of conducting, §106-557.1(a).
    Mail ballot, §106-557.1(a).
      Applicability of provisions, §106-557.1(b).
  Amount and basis of proposed assessment, §106-557.
  Application to board of agriculture for authorization, §106-554.
    Action by board, §106-555.
  Area or statewide basis, §106-559.
  Arrangements for holding referendum, §106-563.
  Continuance of assessments approved at prior referendum, §106-566.
  Declaration of results, §106-563.
  Effect of more than one-third vote against assessment, §106-560.
  Effect of two-thirds vote for assessment, §106-561.
  Eligibility for participation, §106-559.
  Expenses in connection therewith, §106-558.
  Financing program of production, use and sale, §106-553.
  Growers and producers on question of assessments, §106-556.
  Management of referendum, §106-558.
  Milk product assessment.
    Basis of vote, §106-559.1.
    Supervision of referendum, §106-563.1.
  Notice of referendum, §106-557.
  Notice to farm organizations and county agents, §106-562.
  Preparation and distribution of ballots, §106-563.
  Question to be submitted, §106-559.
  Regulations as to referendum, §106-562.
  Special provisions for cotton promotion association, §106-559.
  Subsequent referendum, §106-565.
Restraint of trade.
  Associations, meetings or activities deemed not in restraint of trade, §106-552.
Strawberries or strawberry plants excluded from article, §106-550.
Subsequent referendum, §106-565.
Surety bond.
  Assessments.
    Publication of financial statement by treasurer of agency, §106-568.
Tobacco excluded from article, §106-550.

AGRICULTURAL RESEARCH, §§106-568.1 to 106-568.12.
Assessments.
  Collection of assessment, §106-568.8(a).
  Continuation of assessment, §106-568.10.
  Dissatisfaction with assessments.
    Refunds to farmers, §106-568.9.

AGRICULTURAL RESEARCH —Cont'd
Assessments —Cont'd
Effect of more than one-third vote against
assessment, §106-568.11.
Effect of two-thirds vote in favor of assessment,
§106-568.12.
Levy of assessment.
When assessment shall and shall not be levied,
§106-568.5.
Policy as to assessment, §106-568.2.
Promotion of agricultural research and
dissemination of findings, §106-568.2.
Purposes for assessment, §106-568.6.
Refunds to farmers dissatisfied with assessment,
§106-568.9.
Remittance, §106-568.8(b).
Statement of amount of proposed assessment,
§106-568.6.
When assessment shall and shall not be levied,
§106-568.5.
Board of agriculture.
Petition for referendum.
Action of board, §106-568.3(a).
Development act.
Maximum use of existing research facilities,
§106-584.
Disposition of assessment, §106-568.8(a).
Report of receipts and disbursements,
§106-568.8(a), (b).
Notice of referendum.
Promotion of agricultural research and
dissemination of findings, §106-568.6.
**Promotion of agricultural research and
dissemination of findings.**
Declaration of policy, §106-568.1.
Joint action of farmers, §106-568.1.
Policy declaration, §106-568.1.
Referendum.
Announcements prior to referendum, §106-568.4.
Arrangements for poll holders, §106-568.7.
By whom referendum to be managed, §106-568.4.
Canvass and announcement of results, §106-568.7.
Continuation of assessment, §106-568.10.
Declaration of results, §106-568.7.
Effect of more than one-third vote against
assessment, §106-568.11.
Effect of two-thirds vote in favor of assessment,
§106-568.12.
Management of referendum, §106-568.4.
Notice of referendum, §106-568.6.
Petition for referendum.
Action of board of agriculture, §106-568.3(a).
Policy as to referendum, §106-568.2.
Preparation and distribution of ballots,
§106-568.7.
Promotion of agricultural research and
dissemination of findings, §106-568.2.
Regulations as to referendum, §106-568.6.
Subsequent referendum, §106-568.10.
Regulations as to referendum.
Promotion of agricultural research and
dissemination of findings, §106-568.6.
Reports.
Receipts and disbursements of assessment,
§106-568.8(a), (b).
Tobacco research commission, §106-568.3(b).

AGRICULTURAL SEEDS.
Defined, §106-277.2.
Inspection, §106-277.21.
Labels, §106-277.10.

AGRICULTURAL SEEDS —Cont'd
Sampling and testing, §106-277.21.
Seeds generally, §§106-277 to 106-277.34.
See SEEDS.
Unlawful acts, §106-277.9.

AGRICULTURAL SPREADER VEHICLES.
Defined, §20-51.
Vehicle registration and titling requirements.
Exemption, §20-51.

AGRICULTURAL TOURISM SIGNS,
§106-22.5(a).
Qualification of agricultural facility for,
§106-22.5(b).

**AGRICULTURAL WATER RESOURCES
ASSISTANCE PROGRAM,** §139-60.

AGRICULTURE.
Adams act.
Experiment stations.
Legislative assent to act, §106-23.
Adulteration of grains, §§106-621 to 106-628.
See GRAIN ADULTERATION.
Advances.
Landlord's lien on crops for rents, §42-15.
Agricultural conservation easements, §106-744.
**Agricultural development and farmland
preservation enabling act,** §§106-735 to
106-744.
See FARMLAND PRESERVATION.
**Agricultural development and farmland
preservation trust fund committee,**
§106-744(g) to (i).
Agricultural spreader vehicles.
Defined, §20-51.
Vehicle registration and titling requirements.
Exemption, §20-51.
Agritourism activity liability, §§99E-30 to
99E-32.
Animal exhibitions.
Regulation, §106-520.3A.
Animals.
Generally.
See ANIMALS.
Animal waste management, §§143-215.10A to
143-215.10M.
See ANIMAL WASTE MANAGEMENT.
Animal waste management system operators,
§§90A-47 to 90A-47.6.
See ANIMAL WASTE MANAGEMENT SYSTEM
OPERATORS.
Apiaries.
See BEES AND HONEY.
Aquaculture development, §§106-756 to 106-764.
Auction of livestock.
Livestock markets.
Generally, §§106-406 to 106-418.
See LIVESTOCK MARKETS.
Prompt pay law, §§106-418.1 to 106-418.7A.
See LIVESTOCK MARKETS.
Bees and honey.
See BEES AND HONEY.
Biological organism act, §§106-65.42 to
106-65.49.
See BIOLOGICAL ORGANISM ACT.
Biologics.
General provisions, §§106-707 to 106-715.
See BIOLOGICS.
Board of agriculture.
See AGRICULTURE BOARD.
Boll weevil eradication, §§106-65.67 to 106-65.78.

AGRICULTURE —Cont'd
Chickens.
  Eggs.
    See EGGS.
Cigarettes.
  See CIGARETTES AND TOBACCO PRODUCTS.
Commercial feed.
  General provisions, §§106-284.30 to 106-284.46.
    See FEED.
Commercial fertilizers, §§106-655 to 106-677.
  See FERTILIZERS.
Commissioner of agriculture.
  See AGRICULTURE COMMISSIONER.
Commission on agriculture and forestry
    awareness, §§120-150 to 120-154.
  Advisory committee, §120-151.
  Appointment, §120-150.
  Creation, §120-150.
  Duties.
    Generally, §120-154.
  Expenses.
    Subsistence and travel expenses, §120-152.
  Facilities, §120-153.
  Qualifications of members, §120-150.
  Reports, §120-154.
  Staff, §120-153.
  Terms of office, §120-150.
  Travel expenses, §120-152.
Commodities.
  Generally, §§78D-1 to 78D-33.
    See COMMODITIES.
Compost, §130A-309.11.
  State procurement, §130A-309.14(f).
  Stormwater control best management practices
    and process water treatment processes.
    Composting operations, §143-214.7A.
Conservation easements.
  Agricultural conservation easements, §106-744.
Constitution of North Carolina.
  Capital projects for agriculture.
    Authorization for creation of agency to issue
      revenue bonds, NC Const Art V §11.
  Commissioner of agriculture.
    Acting commissioner, NC Const Art III §7.
    Compensation and allowances, NC Const Art III
      §9.
  Council of state.
    Membership, NC Const Art III §8.
    Duties, NC Const Art III §7.
    Elective officers, NC Const Art III §7.
  Incapacity.
    Determination, NC Const Art III §7.
  Interim commissioner, NC Const Art III §7.
  Vacancies.
    Filling, NC Const Art III §7.
Consumer protection.
  Records of sales of farm products.
    Dated sales confirmation slips inapplicable to
      consumers, §106-202.6(b).
Cooperative associations.
  Authorized purposes, §§54-111, 54-124.
Cotton.
  Generally.
    See COTTON.
Cotton warehouses, §§106-451.6 to 106-451.28,
  106-451.40 to 106-451.44.
  See COTTON WAREHOUSES.
County planning and zoning.
  Property used for farm purposes.
    Regulations affecting, §153A-340(b), (j).

AGRICULTURE —Cont'd
Countywide farmland protection plans,
  §106-744(e), (f).
Crops.
  General provisions.
    See CROPS.
Crop seed improvement board, §§106-269 to
  106-276.
  Department of agriculture and consumer services.
    Transfer to department, §143A-64.
Dairies and dairy products.
  Dairy stabilization and growth program,
    §§106-812 to 106-815.
  Ice cream plants, creameries and cheese factories.
    Inspections generally, §§106-246 to 106-255.
      See ICE CREAM PLANTS, CREAMERIES
        AND CHEESE FACTORIES.
  Production, distribution, inspection, grading and
    testing generally, §§106-267 to 106-268.1.
    See MILK AND MILK PRODUCTS.
Damage to commodities or production
    systems.
  Definitions, §1-539.2B(c).
  Double damage liability, §1-539.2B(a).
  Valuation, §1-539.2B(b).
Decedents' estates.
  Continuation of farming operations, §§28A-13-3,
    28A-13-4.
  Crops of deceased persons, §28A-15-1.
Definitions.
  Development act, §106-581.1.
  Nuisance liability of agricultural and forestry
    operations, §106-701(b), (b1).
Department of agriculture and consumer
    services.
  See AGRICULTURE AND CONSUMER
    SERVICES DEPARTMENT.
Development act generally, §§106-580 to
  106-587.
  See AGRICULTURAL DEVELOPMENT.
Drainage, §§156-1 to 156-141.
  See DRAINAGE.
Drainage districts, §§156-54 to 156-138.4.
  See DRAINAGE DISTRICTS.
Easements.
  Agricultural conservation easements, §106-744.
Eggs, §§106-245.13 to 106-245.28.
  See EGGS.
Emblements.
  In lieu of emblements, farm lessee holds out year,
    with rents apportioned, §42-7.
Equine activity liability, §§99E-1 to 99E-3.
Executors and administrators.
  Continuation of farming operations, §28A-13-4.
    Powers of personal representative, §28A-13-3(a).
  Crops.
    Ungathered at death of deceased person,
      §28A-15-1(d).
Exemption from creditors' claims.
  Crops and animals, §1C-1601(a).
Experiment stations.
  Legislative assent to Adams act, §106-23.
Extension service.
  Agricultural development generally, §§106-580 to
    106-587.
    See AGRICULTURAL DEVELOPMENT.
Fairs, §§106-502 to 106-520.7.
  See FAIRS.
Farm credit administration.
  Banks.
    Obligations of agencies supervised by.
      Investments in, §53-44.1.

AGRICULTURE —Cont'd
Farm credit administration —Cont'd
Banks —Cont'd
Obligations of agencies supervised by —Cont'd
Securities for deposit of public funds,
§53-43.1.
Farm equipment.
Age for operation, §20-10.
Certificate of title exemptions, §20-51.
Defined, §20-4.01.
Driver's license exemptions, §20-8.
Identification marks, removing, defacing, etc.,
§14-401.4.
Registration exemptions, §20-51.
Farmland preservation, §§113A-240, 113A-241.
Agricultural development and farmland
preservation enabling act, §§106-735 to
106-744.
See FARMLAND PRESERVATION.
Farm machinery franchises, §§66-180 to 66-188.
Farm machinery tax credit.
Property taxes paid on, §105-151.21.
Farm name registration, §§80-33 to 80-39.
Farm nuisance dispute mediation, §7A-38.3,
FarmMediation Rules 1 to 10.
Farm operations commission.
Sale of merchandise by governmental units.
Exception to prohibition, §66-58(b).
Farm tractors.
Age for operation, §20-10.
Certificate of title exemptions, §20-51.
Defined, §20-4.01.
Driver's license exemptions, §20-8.
Registration exemptions, §20-51.
Tires, §20-122(c), (d).
Farmworker council, §§143B-426.25,
143B-426.26.
Feed.
Advisory service.
Establishment of pilot program, §106-21.1.
Fee for test samples, §106-21.1.
Commercial feed, §§106-284.30 to 106-284.46.
See FEED.
Fees.
Feed advisory service.
Test samples, §106-21.1.
Generally.
See AGRICULTURAL FEES AND TAXES.
Fertilizers.
Commercial fertilizers, §§106-655 to 106-677.
See FERTILIZERS.
Soil additives act, §§106-50.28 to 106-50.41.
See SOIL ADDITIVES ACT.
Finance authority.
Agricultural finance authority, §§122D-1 to
122D-23.
See AGRICULTURAL FINANCE AUTHORITY.
Food bank information and referral service.
Maintenance by department of agriculture and
consumer services, §106-21.2.
Food, drug and cosmetic act, §§106-120 to
106-145.
See FOOD, DRUG AND COSMETIC ACT.
Fruit handlers unfair practices, §§106-496 to
106-501.
See FRUIT HANDLERS UNFAIR PRACTICES.
Funds.
Eastern North Carolina agricultural center fund,
§106-6.2(a).
Southeastern North Carolina agricultural center
fund, §106-6.2(b).

AGRICULTURE —Cont'd
Gasoline and oil inspection board.
Department of agriculture and consumer services.
Transfer to department, §143A-62.
Gleaning.
Exemption from civil liability for farmers
permitting, §106-706.
Grain dealers, §§106-601 to 106-615.
See GRAIN DEALERS.
Hall of fame, §§106-568.13 to 106-568.17.
Honey.
See BEES AND HONEY.
Housing authorities and projects.
Housing applications by farmers, §157-39.
Rural housing projects, §157-38.
Housing standards for migrant farm workers,
§§95-222 to 95-229.1.
**Ice cream plants, creameries and cheese
factories.**
Inspections generally, §§106-246 to 106-255.
See ICE CREAM PLANTS, CREAMERIES AND
CHEESE FACTORIES.
Income tax credit.
Farm machinery.
Property taxes paid on, §105-151.21.
Insurance.
Farmowners' policies.
Ice, snow or sleet damage, §58-44-55.
Judicial sales.
Private sale of farm commodities or produce
authorized, §1-339.34(a).
Landlord and tenant.
Emblements.
In lieu of emblements, farm lessee holds out
year, with rents apportioned, §42-7.
Holding out year in lieu of emblements, farm
lessee holds out year, with rents apportioned,
§42-7.
Landlord's lien on crops, §§42-15 to 42-25.
Termination.
Rights of tenant on termination, §42-7.
Terms of agricultural tenancies in certain
counties, §42-23.
Turpentine and lightwood leases, §42-24.
Landplaster.
Limestone, marl and landplaster, §§106-92.1 to
106-92.17.
See LIMESTONE, MARL AND
LANDPLASTER.
Liens.
Effective period for liens on peanuts, cotton and
grains, §44-69.1.
Landlord's lien on crops, §§42-15 to 42-25.
Leaf tobacco.
Effective period for tobacco sold in auction
warehouses, §44-69.
Secured transactions.
Collateral, disposition.
Rights of secured party, §25-9-315(a).
Crops.
Priority of security interests in, §25-9-334(i).
Production money security interests,
§25-9-324.1.
Production-money crops.
Defined, §25-9-102(a).
Status of security interest in,
§25-9-103.1(a).
Production-money obligation.
Application of payments, §25-9-103.1(b).
Defined, §25-9-102(a).

AGRICULTURE —Cont'd
Liens —Cont'd
Secured transactions —Cont'd
Crops —Cont'd
Production-money security interests.
Burden of establishing status,
§25-9-103.1(d).
Continuation of status, §25-9-103.1(c).
Status, §25-9-103.1(a).
Production of crops.
Defined, §25-9-102(a).
Default.
Time of default, §25-9-606.
Perfection and priority.
Buyers receiving delivery.
Interests that take priority over or take free
of agricultural lien, §25-9-317(a).
Choice of law governing agricultural liens,
§25-9-302.
Filed financing statement providing certain
incorrect information.
Priority of agricultural lien perfected by,
§25-9-338.
Filing.
Assigned perfected interests need not be
refiled, §25-9-310(c).
When filing not required to perfect lien,
§25-9-310(b).
When required to perfect lien, §25-9-310(a).
Interests that take priority over or take free
of agricultural lien, §25-9-317(a).
Law governing, §25-9-302.
Lessees receiving delivery.
Interests that take priority over or take free
of agricultural lien, §25-9-317(c).
Multiple conflicting interests in same
collateral.
Other UCC provisions governing,
§25-9-322(f).
Proceeds and supporting obligations, time
of perfection, §25-9-322(b).
Rules governing priority, §25-9-322(a), (g).
When perfected, §25-9-308(b).
Light-traffic road weight and load limitations.
Exceptions, §20-118(c).
Limestone, §§106-92.1 to 106-92.17.
See LIMESTONE, MARL AND LANDPLASTER.
Livestock brands, §§80-45 to 80-66.
See LIVESTOCK BRANDS.
Livestock dealer licensing, §§106-418.8 to
106-418.16.
See LIVESTOCK DEALER LICENSING.
Livestock diseases.
Brucellosis, §§106-388 to 106-398.
See BRUCELLOSIS.
Cattle tick, §§106-351 to 106-363.
See CATTLE TICK.
Compensation for killing diseased animals,
§§106-323 to 106-335.
See LIVESTOCK DISEASES.
Control of livestock diseases generally, §§106-400
to 106-405.
See LIVESTOCK DISEASES.
Equine infectious anemia, §§106-405.15 to
106-405.20.
Generally, §§106-304 to 106-307.7.
See LIVESTOCK DISEASES.
Hog cholera, §§106-310 to 106-322.3.
See HOG CHOLERA.
Tuberculosis, §§106-336 to 106-350.
See TUBERCULOSIS IN LIVESTOCK.

AGRICULTURE —Cont'd
Livestock markets.
Generally, §§106-406 to 106-418.
See LIVESTOCK MARKETS.
Prompt pay law, §§106-418.1 to 106-418.7A.
See LIVESTOCK MARKETS.
Marketing and branding farm products,
§§106-185 to 106-196.
See FARM PRODUCTS MARKETING AND
BRANDING.
Marketing associations, §§54-129 to 54-166.
See MARKETING ASSOCIATIONS.
Marketing authority, §§106-528 to 106-534.
See MARKETING AUTHORITY.
Marl.
Limestone, marl and landplaster, §§106-92.1 to
106-92.17.
See LIMESTONE, MARL AND
LANDPLASTER.
Meat inspections, §§106-549.15 to 106-549.39.
See MEAT INSPECTIONS.
Mediation of farm nuisance disputes, §7A-38.3,
FarmMediation Rules 1 to 10.
Migrant farm workers.
See MIGRANT FARM WORKERS.
Milk and milk products.
Ice cream plants, creameries and cheese factories.
Inspections generally, §§106-246 to 106-255.
See ICE CREAM PLANTS, CREAMERIES
AND CHEESE FACTORIES.
Production, distribution, inspection, grading and
testing generally, §§106-267 to 106-268.1.
See MILK AND MILK PRODUCTS.
Regulation of milk and cream generally.
See MILK AND MILK PRODUCTS.
Motor carrier safety regulation unit.
Exemptions from certain requirements,
§20-381(b).
Nonpoint source pollution control program.
Agriculture cost share program, §§106-850 to
106-852.
**North Carolina sustainable local food advisory
council,** §§106-830 to 106-833.
**North Carolina wine and grape growers
council,** §143B-437.91.
**Nuisance liability of agricultural and forestry
operations.**
Agricultural operation defined, §106-701(b).
Changed conditions in locality, §106-701(a).
Applicability of provisions, §106-701(c).
Construction of provisions, §106-701(e).
Declaration of policy, §106-700.
Farm nuisance dispute mediation, §7A-38.3,
FarmMediation Rules 1 to 10.
Forest operation defined, §106-701(b1).
Legislative determination, §106-700.
Local ordinances affected, §106-701(d).
Policy declaration, §106-700.
Purpose of article, §106-700.
Nutrient offset credits.
Purchase to offset nutrient loadings of surface
waters, §143-214.26.
Occupational safety and health.
Citations.
Contesting citations, §95-137(b).
Standards.
Promulgation, §95-131(g).
Organic products.
Certification.
Standards, guidelines and policies, §106-22.3(a).

AGRICULTURE —Cont'd
Organic products —Cont'd
  Organic food production act.
    Compliance with, §106-22.3(b).
Pest control.
  Biological organism act, §§106-65.42 to 106-65.49.
  Boll weevil eradication, §§106-65.67 to 106-65.78.
  Compact, §§106-65.55 to 106-65.61.
  Structural pest control, §§106-65.22 to 106-65.41.
Plant pests, §§106-419 to 106-423.1.
Plant protection and conservation, §§106-202.12
    to 106-202.22.
  See PLANT PROTECTION AND
    CONSERVATION.
Poultry generally.
  See POULTRY AND POULTRY PRODUCTS.
Poultry products inspections, §§106-549.49 to
    106-549.69.
  See POULTRY PRODUCTS INSPECTIONS.
Preservation of farmland, §§106-735 to 106-744.
  See FARMLAND PRESERVATION.
Prisons and prisoners.
  Employment of prisoners, §148-26(d).
**Promotion of use and sale of agricultural
    products,** §§106-550 to 106-568.
  See AGRICULTURAL PRODUCTS PROMOTION.
Prompt pay law.
  Livestock, §§106-418.1 to 106-418.7A.
    See LIVESTOCK MARKETS.
Property taxes.
  Agricultural, horticultural and forestland,
    §§105-277.2 to 105-277.7.
    See PROPERTY TAXES.
Pulverized limestone and marl, §§106-92.1 to
    106-92.17.
  See LIMESTONE, MARL AND LANDPLASTER.
Records of dated farm products sales.
  Dated sales confirmation slips, §106-202.6(a).
  Inapplicable to consumers, §106-202.6(b).
Rendering plants and rendering operations,
    §§106-168.1 to 106-168.16.
  See RENDERING PLANTS AND RENDERING
    OPERATIONS.
Rents.
  In lieu of emblements, farm lessee holds out year,
    with rents apportioned, §42-7.
  Terms of agricultural tenancies in certain
    counties, §42-23.
Research, §§106-568.1 to 106-568.12.
  See AGRICULTURAL RESEARCH.
Runoff.
  Composting operations.
    Stormwater control best management practices
      and process water treatment processes,
      §143-214.7A.
  Nonpoint source pollution control program.
    Agriculture cost share program, §§106-850 to
      106-852.
  Water supply watershed protection.
    Local and statewide standards.
      Requirements as to agriculture and
        silviculture activities, §143-214.5(d1).
Sales and use tax.
  Exemptions, §105-164.13.
Searches and seizures.
  Lien on crops.
    Unlawful seizure by landlord, §42-22.
Seed board, §§106-277.31 to 106-277.33.
Seeds, §§106-269 to 106-284.22.
  See SEEDS.

AGRICULTURE —Cont'd
Slaughterhouses generally.
  See SLAUGHTERHOUSES.
Soil additives act, §§106-50.28 to 106-50.41.
  See SOIL ADDITIVES ACT.
Soil and water conservation districts, §§139-1
    to 139-57.
  See SOIL AND WATER CONSERVATION
    DISTRICTS.
Southern dairy compact, §§106-810, 106-811.
State farm operations commission.
  Sale of merchandise by governmental units.
    Exception to prohibition, §66-58(b).
State farms, §106-22.1.
States.
  Cooperation of federal and state governments.
    Legislative assent to Adams act for experiment
      station, §106-23.
Structural pest control, §§106-65.22 to 106-65.41.
  See STRUCTURAL PEST CONTROL.
Sustainable local food advisory council,
    §§106-830 to 106-833.
Swine farms, §§106-800 to 106-806.
  See HOGS, PIGS AND SWINE.
Taxation.
  Generally.
    See AGRICULTURAL FEES AND TAXES.
Tobacco.
  Cigarettes and tobacco products.
    See CIGARETTES AND TOBACCO
      PRODUCTS.
Tobacco research commission, §106-568.3(b).
Tobacco trust fund commission, §§143-715 to
    143-723.
  See TOBACCO TRUST FUND COMMISSION.
Tourism.
  Agricultural tourism signs, §106-22.5.
Transportation department.
  Seed planted by department of transportation.
    Approval by department of agriculture and
      consumer services, §136-18.2.
Unfair practices by fruit handlers, §§106-496 to
    106-501.
  See FRUIT HANDLERS UNFAIR PRACTICES.
United States.
  Cooperation of federal and state governments.
    Legislative assent to Adams act for experiment
      station, §106-23.
  Promotion of use and sale of agricultural
    products.
    Federal agricultural marketing act, §106-551.
University of North Carolina.
  Agricultural research stations.
    Control by board of governors, §116-39.
Vegetable handlers unfair practices, §§106-496
    to 106-501.
  See VEGETABLE HANDLERS' UNFAIR
    PRACTICES.
Vegetable plant law, §§106-284.14 to 106-284.22.
  See VEGETABLE PLANT LAW.
Vocational and technical education.
  Acquisition of land for instructional programs,
    §115C-163.
Wage and hour act.
  Exemptions from wage and hour act, §95-25.14(a).
Warehouses.
  Cotton warehouses, §§106-451.6 to 106-451.28,
    106-451.40 to 106-451.44.
  See COTTON WAREHOUSES.
Waste management, §§143-215.10A to
    143-215.10M.
  See ANIMAL WASTE MANAGEMENT.

AGRICULTURE —Cont'd
Water and air resources, §§143-211 to 143-215.9C.
See WATER AND AIR RESOURCES.
Water pollution control.
Nonpoint source pollution control program.
Agriculture cost share program, §§106-850 to 106-852.
Water resources assistance program, §139-60.
Water supply watershed protection.
Local and statewide standards.
Requirements as to agriculture and silviculture activities, §143-214.5(d1).
Wine and grape growers council, §143B-437.91.
Workers' compensation.
Farm laborers.
Exceptions to provisions, §97-13(b).
Sellers of agricultural products.
Exceptions to provisions, §97-13(d).

AGRICULTURE AND CONSUMER SERVICES DEPARTMENT.
Adulteration of grains.
Generally, §§106-621 to 106-628.
See GRAIN ADULTERATION.
Agricultural development and farmland preservation enabling act.
Administration of provisions, §106-735(c).
Agricultural hall of fame.
Transfer to department, §143A-61.
Animal health division.
Animal welfare section, §§19A-22, 19A-25.
Antifreeze.
Registration generally, §§106-579.1 to 106-579.14.
See ANTIFREEZE.
Aquaculture development.
Generally, §§106-756 to 106-764.
See AQUACULTURE DEVELOPMENT.
Lead agency, powers and duties, §106-759.
Bees and honey.
Generally, §§106-634 to 106-644.
See BEES AND HONEY.
Biologics.
Generally, §§106-707 to 106-715.
See BIOLOGICS.
Board of agriculture.
Transfer to department, §143A-59.
Boll weevil eradication.
Generally, §§106-65.67 to 106-65.78.
See BOLL WEEVIL ERADICATION.
Brucellosis.
Generally, §§106-388 to 106-398.
See BRUCELLOSIS.
Cattle tick.
Eradication generally, §§106-351 to 106-363.
See CATTLE TICK.
Collection and publication of information.
Classification as to prevent identification of information received from individual farm operators, §106-24.1.
Relating to agriculture, §106-24(a).
Relating to water use, §106-24(b).
Commercial feed law.
Generally, §§106-284.30 to 106-284.46.
See FEED.
Commercial fertilizers.
Generally, §§106-655 to 106-677.
See FERTILIZERS.
Commissioner of agriculture.
Transfer of powers and duties to department, §143A-58.

AGRICULTURE AND CONSUMER SERVICES DEPARTMENT —Cont'd
Confidentiality of information collected and published, §106-24.1.
Cooperation with United States department of agriculture, §106-24.
Cotton grower's organization, §§106-65.84 to 106-65.91.
See COTTON GROWER'S ORGANIZATION.
Cotton warehouses.
Generally, §§106-451.6 to 106-451.28, 106-451.40 to 106-451.44.
See COTTON WAREHOUSES.
Counties.
Forest protection and development.
Cooperation between counties and state, §106-906.
Creation, §143A-56.
Crop seed improvement board.
Transfer to department, §143A-64.
Distribution of food, surplus commodities and agricultural products.
Contracts and agreements with federal government, §143-64.5.
Division of forest resources.
Designated as emergency response agency, §166A-18.
Egg law.
Generally, §§106-245.13 to 106-245.28.
See EGGS.
Egg promotion tax.
Generally, §§106-245.30 to 106-245.39.
See EGG PROMOTION TAX.
Endangered plant species.
Conservation and protection generally, §§106-202.12 to 106-202.22.
See PLANT PROTECTION AND CONSERVATION.
Equine infectious anemia.
Generally, §§106-405.15 to 106-405.20.
See EQUINE INFECTIOUS ANEMIA.
Established, §106-2.
Euthanasia technicians, certification.
Criminal background check, §114-19.29.
Extension service.
Agricultural development generally, §§106-580 to 106-587.
See AGRICULTURAL DEVELOPMENT.
Farmed deer.
Production and sale, §§106-549.97, 106-549.98.
Farmland preservation.
Agricultural development and farmland preservation enabling act.
Administration of provisions, §106-735(c).
Feed advisory service, §106-21.1.
Feeding garbage to swine.
Generally, §§106-405.1 to 106-405.9.
See FEEDING GARBAGE TO SWINE.
Fees, §106-6.1(a).
Fees and taxes paid to department generally.
See AGRICULTURAL FEES AND TAXES.
Food bank information and referral service, §106-21.2.
Food defense.
Protection from intentional contamination, §130A-481.
Food, drug and cosmetic act.
Generally, §§106-120 to 106-145.
See FOOD, DRUG AND COSMETIC ACT.
Food embargoes.
Notice to department, §130A-21(a).

AGRICULTURE AND CONSUMER SERVICES DEPARTMENT —Cont'd

Forest fires.
Powers and duties, §106-895(a), (b).

Forest maintenance, forest fire prevention, reforestation, preservation of forests.
Department to have charge of work, §143A-65.1.

Forest rangers.
Appointment, §106-896.

Forestry council.
Created in department, §143A-66.1.
Generally, §§143A-66.1 to 143A-66.3.

Gasoline and oil inspection board.
Transfer to department, §143A-62.

Grain dealers.
Generally, §§106-601 to 106-615.
See GRAIN DEALERS.

Hog cholera.
Generally, §§106-310 to 106-322.3.
See HOG CHOLERA.

Ice cream plants, creameries and cheese factories.
Inspections generally, §§106-246 to 106-255.
See ICE CREAM PLANTS, CREAMERIES AND CHEESE FACTORIES.

Land conservation and land development bureau, §54-49.

Limestone, marl and landplaster.
Generally, §§106-92.1 to 106-92.17.
See LIMESTONE, MARL AND LANDPLASTER.

Livestock dealer licensing.
Generally, §§106-418.8 to 106-418.16.
See LIVESTOCK DEALER LICENSING.

Livestock diseases.
Brucellosis generally, §§106-388 to 106-398.
See BRUCELLOSIS.
Cattle tick, §§106-351 to 106-363.
See CATTLE TICK.
Compensation for killing diseased animals, §§106-323 to 106-335.
See LIVESTOCK DISEASES.
Equine infectious anemia, §§106-405.15 to 106-405.20.
See EQUINE INFECTIOUS ANEMIA.
Generally, §§106-304 to 106-307.7.
See LIVESTOCK DISEASES.
Hog cholera generally, §§106-310 to 106-322.3.
See HOG CHOLERA.
Tuberculosis generally, §§106-336 to 106-350.
See TUBERCULOSIS IN LIVESTOCK.

Marketing and branding farm products.
Generally, §§106-185 to 106-196.
See FARM PRODUCTS MARKETING AND BRANDING.

Meat inspections.
Generally, §§106-549.15 to 106-549.39.
See MEAT INSPECTIONS.

Milk and milk products.
Production, distribution, inspection, grading and testing generally, §§106-267 to 106-268.1.
See MILK AND MILK PRODUCTS.
Sanitation, §§106-266.33, 106-266.34.

Pest control compact.
Filing of bylaws and amendments with department, §106-65.57.

Plant conservation scientific committee.
Creation within department, §106-202.17.

Plant protection and conservation.
Generally, §§106-202.12 to 106-202.22.
See PLANT PROTECTION AND CONSERVATION.

AGRICULTURE AND CONSUMER SERVICES DEPARTMENT —Cont'd

Pork.
Promotion assessments, §§106-790 to 106-796.
See PORK PROMOTION ASSESSMENTS.

Poultry and poultry products.
Generally.
See POULTRY AND POULTRY PRODUCTS.

Poultry products inspection.
Generally, §§106-549.49 to 106-549.69.
See POULTRY PRODUCTS INSPECTIONS.

Prescription drug distributors.
Wholesale distributors generally, §§106-145.1 to 106-145.13.
See WHOLESALE PRESCRIPTION DRUG DISTRIBUTORS.

Public livestock market advisory board.
Transfer to department, §143A-65.

Public livestock markets generally, §§106-406 to 106-418.
See LIVESTOCK MARKETS.

Quail.
Production and sale of pen-raised quail.
Regulation by department, §106-549.94(a).

Records and reports required of persons paying fees or taxes to, §106-9.2.

Rendering plants and rendering operations, §§106-168.1 to 106-168.16.
See RENDERING PLANTS AND RENDERING OPERATIONS.

Research.
Generally, §§106-568.1 to 106-568.12.
See AGRICULTURAL RESEARCH.

Rest areas.
Promotion of North Carolina farm products, §136-89.59A.

Rural rehabilitation corporation.
Transfer to department, §143A-63.

Sale of merchandise by governmental units.
Exceptions to prohibition, §66-58(c).

Seed law, §§106-269 to 106-284.22.
See SEEDS.

Serums, viruses, vaccines, biologics and other products for control of animal diseases.
Purchase for resale, §106-307.1.

Soil additives act, §§106-50.28 to 106-50.41.
See SOIL ADDITIVES ACT.

Soil and water conservation account, §106-844.

Soil and water conservation commission, §§106-840 to 106-844.

Soil and water conservation districts, §§139-1 to 139-57.
See SOIL AND WATER CONSERVATION DISTRICTS.

State farm program.
Management for department, §106-22.1.

State forests and state recreation forests.
Acquisition and control.
Appropriations, budget designation, §106-875.
Generally, §§106-870 to 106-887.
See STATE FORESTS.
Charge of, §143A-65.1.

Strawberries.
Assessments generally, §§106-781 to 106-786.
See STRAWBERRIES.

Structural pest control division, §106-65.23(a).
Transfer to department, §143A-60.

Structural pest control generally, §§106-65.22 to 106-65.41.
See STRUCTURAL PEST CONTROL.

AGRICULTURE AND CONSUMER SERVICES DEPARTMENT —Cont'd
Surplus food, commodities and agricultural products.
　Distribution under contracts and agreements with federal government, §143-64.5.
Transportation department.
　Seed planted by transportation department.
　　Approval by department of agriculture and consumer services, §136-18.2.
Tuberculosis in livestock.
　Generally, §§106-336 to 106-350.
　　See TUBERCULOSIS IN LIVESTOCK.
Vegetable plant law.
　Generally, §§106-284.14 to 106-284.22.
　　See VEGETABLE PLANT LAW.
Wholesale prescription drug distributors.
　Generally, §§106-145.1 to 106-145.13.
　　See WHOLESALE PRESCRIPTION DRUG DISTRIBUTORS.

AGRICULTURE AND FORESTRY AWARENESS, COMMISSION ON, §§120-150 to 120-154.

AGRICULTURE BOARD.
Appointment of members, §106-2.
Biological organism act.
　General provisions, §§106-65.42 to 106-65.49.
　　See BIOLOGICAL ORGANISM ACT.
Biologics.
　Definition of "board,"§106-708.
　Rules and regulations, §106-709.
Chairman, §106-2.
Commercial fertilizers.
　Authority to make rules and regulations, §106-673.
　General provisions, §§106-655 to 106-677.
　　See FERTILIZERS.
Commissioner of agriculture.
　Joint duties of commissioner and board, §106-22.
Composition, §106-2.
Cotton warehouses.
　Generally, §§106-451.6 to 106-451.28, 106-451.40 to 106-451.44.
　　See COTTON WAREHOUSES.
Fees.
　Generally, §106-6.1(a).
Food, drugs and cosmetics.
　Generally, §§106-120 to 106-145.
　　See FOOD, DRUG AND COSMETIC ACT.
　Regulations of board, §106-139.
　Standards of quality.
　　Establishment of reasonable standards, §106-128.
Investigations.
　Marketing and branding farm products, §106-187.
Limestone, marl and landplaster.
　Authority of board to make rules and regulations, §106-92.16.
Liquefied petroleum gases.
　Power to set minimum standards, §119-55.
Livestock.
　Prompt pay law.
　　Authority of board, §106-418.7.
　Public livestock markets.
　　Revocation of permit by board, §106-407.2.
Llamas as livestock.
　Rules adopted by board to refer to llamas as livestock, §106-22.4.
Marketing and branding farm products.
　Investigating marketing of products, §106-187.

AGRICULTURE BOARD —Cont'd
Mattresses and bedding.
　General provisions, §§106-65.95 to 106-65.107.
Meat inspection.
　Sanitary conditions of establishments.
　　Rules and regulations prescribed by board, §106-549.22.
Meetings of board, §106-4.
Membership, §106-2.
Milk and milk products.
　Ice cream plants, creameries and cheese factories.
　　Tests by board, §106-250.
　Production, distribution, inspection, grading and testing generally, §§106-267 to 106-268.1.
　　See MILK AND MILK PRODUCTS.
Plant pests.
　Agents of board.
　　Inspection, §106-422.
　Regulations.
　　Authority of board to adopt, §106-420.
Powers and duties.
　Commissioner of agriculture.
　　Joint duties of commissioner and board, §106-22.
　Joint duties of commissioner and board, §106-22.
Promotion of use and sale of agricultural products.
　Application to board for authorization of referendum, §106-554.
　Action by board on application, §106-555.
Prompt pay law.
　Authority of board, §106-418.7.
Research.
　Promotion of agricultural research and dissemination of findings.
　　Action of board on petition for referendum, §106-568.3(a).
State fair.
　Constructing and financing facilities and improvements for fair, §106-503.1.
　Operation of state fair, §106-503(a).
Terms of office, §106-2.
Transfer of powers and duties to department, §143A-59.
Vacancies in board, §106-2.
Weights and measures.
　Establishment of standards, §81A-4.

AGRICULTURE COMMISSIONER.
Acting officers, NC Const Art III §7.
Bees and honey, §§106-634 to 106-644.
　See BEES AND HONEY.
Biological organism act.
　Definition of commissioner, §106-65.44.
　Enforcement of article, §106-65.46.
　General provisions, §§106-65.42 to 106-65.49.
　　See BIOLOGICAL ORGANISM ACT.
Board of agriculture.
　Joint duties of commissioner and board, §106-22.
Boll weevil eradication.
　Generally, §§106-65.67 to 106-65.78.
　　See BOLL WEEVIL ERADICATION.
Cigarettes and tobacco products.
　Leaf tobacco sales, §§106-461 to 106-465.
　　See LEAF TOBACCO SALES.
Commercial feed.
　Enforcing official, §106-284.32.
　General provisions, §§106-284.30 to 106-284.46.
　　See FEED.
Commercial fertilizers.
　Administration of article, §106-658.

AGRICULTURE COMMISSIONER —Cont'd

Commercial fertilizers —Cont'd

Analysis.
Duty of commissioner to make analysis, §106-662.
General provisions, §§106-655 to 106-677.
See FERTILIZERS.
Inspections.
Duty of commissioner to inspect, §106-662(a).
Samples.
Duty of commissioner to sample, §106-662(a).
Testing.
Duty of commissioner to test, §106-662(a).

Compensation and allowances, NC Const Art III §9.

Cotton warehouses.
Generally, §§106-451.6 to 106-451.28, 106-451.40 to 106-451.44.
See COTTON WAREHOUSES.

Council of state.
Membership, NC Const Art III §8.

Department of agriculture and consumer services.
Transfer of powers and duties to department, §143A-58.

Eggs.
Definitions in egg law, §106-245.14.
Power of commissioner, §106-245.23.
Sanitary conditions.
Approval of method by commissioner, §106-245.22(a).

Election, §106-10.
Date of election, §163-1(a).
Vacancy in office, §163-8.

Elective officers, NC Const Art III §7.

Fairs.
Supervision of fairs, §106-520.3.

Fees and taxes paid to commissioner generally.
See AGRICULTURAL FEES AND TAXES.

Food, drugs and cosmetics.
Enforcement of article.
Further powers of commissioner, §106-140.
Report of minor violations in discretion of commissioner, §106-127.
Violations of article.
Report of minor violations in discretion of commissioner, §106-127.

Fruits.
Unfair practices by handlers of fruits.
Additional powers of commissioner to enforce article, §106-500.
Approval of contracts between handlers and producers, §106-499.

Gasoline and oil inspection.
Administration by commissioner of agriculture, §119-23.

Grain.
Adulteration of grains.
Definition of commissioner, §106-621.
General provisions, §§106-621 to 106-628.
Sign furnished by commissioner, §106-624.

Grain dealers.
Authority to investigate, §106-612.
Definition of commissioner, §106-601(b).
General provisions, §§106-601 to 106-615.
See GRAIN DEALERS.

Incapacity.
Determination, NC Const Art III §7.

Interim officers, NC Const Art III §7.

AGRICULTURE COMMISSIONER —Cont'd

License plate.
Special plate, number, §20-79.5.

Limestone, marl and landplaster.
Sale of agricultural liming materials and landplaster.
Appeals from assessments and orders of commissioner, §106-92.13.

Liquefied petroleum gases.
Administration of article, §119-57.

Livestock.
Prompt pay law.
Authority of commissioner, §106-418.7.
Duties of commissioner, §106-418.4.
Public livestock markets.
Permits from commissioner for operation of markets, §106-406.
Transportation of livestock.
Establishment of regulations for transportation, §106-14.

Longevity pay, §106-10.

Lubricating oils.
Inspection duties devolve upon commissioner, §119-6.

Mattresses and bedding.
General provisions, §§106-65.95 to 106-65.107.

Meat inspection.
Powers of commissioner.
Additional powers, §106-549.36(a), (b).
Refusal of commissioner to inspect and certify meat, §106-549.30.

Milk and milk products.
Records and reports of milk distributors and processors.
Powers of commissioner, §106-262.

Natural History Museum.
Advisory commission.
Member of commission, §143B-344.18.

Pests.
Declaring wild animal or bird, §113-300.2.

Plant law.
Interference with commissioner, etc., or other violation a misdemeanor, §106-284.20.

Poultry products inspections.
Definition of commissioner, §106-549.51.
Limiting entry of products to establishment, §106-549.63.
Powers of commissioner, §106-549.68(a) to (c).
Registration of poultry products brokers, renderers or animal food manufacturers, §106-549.58(c).

Powers and duties, §143A-57, NC Const Art III §7.
Egg law, §106-245.23.
Food, drugs and cosmetics.
Further powers of commissioner for enforcement of article, §106-140.
Joint duties of commissioner and board, §106-22.
Milk or milk products.
Records and reports of distributors and processors, §106-262.
Prompt pay law, §106-418.4.
Rendering plants and rendering operations.
Receipt of application for license, §106-168.5.
Transfer to department, §143A-58.

Prompt pay law.
Authority of commissioner, §106-418.7.
Duties of commissioner, §106-418.4.

Records and reports required of persons paying fees or taxes to commissioner, §106-9.2.

AGRICULTURE COMMISSIONER —Cont'd
Rendering plants and rendering operations.
  Application for license.
    Duties of commissioner upon receipt of
      application, §106-168.5.
  Rules and regulations.
    Authority to adopt, §106-168.12.
Rules and regulations.
  Transportation of livestock, §106-14.
Salary, §106-11.
  Longevity pay, §106-11.
Seeds.
  Administration of article, §106-277.14.
  Enforcement of article, §106-277.14.
  General provisions, §§106-277 to 106-277.34.
    See SEEDS.
Soil additives act, §§106-50.28 to 106-50.41.
  See SOIL ADDITIVES ACT.
Succession to office of governor, §147-11.1(b).
Term of office, §§106-10, 163-1(a).
Transportation of livestock.
  Establishment of regulations, §106-14.
Vacancy in office.
  Filling, §§106-10, 163-8, NC Const Art III §7.
Vegetables.
  Unfair practices by handlers of vegetables.
    Additional powers of commissioner to enforce
      article, §106-500.
    Approval of contracts between handlers and
      producers, §106-499.
Weights and measures.
  See WEIGHTS AND MEASURES.

AGRICULTURE COST SHARE PROGRAM.
Nonpoint source pollution control program,
  §§106-850 to 106-852.

AGRITOURISM ACTIVITY LIABILITY, §§99E-30
  to 99E-32.
Agritourism activity.
  Defined, §99E-30.
Agritourism professional.
  Defined, §99E-30.
Definitions, §99E-30.
Injury or death of participant.
  Limitation on legal liability of professional,
    §99E-31(a).
    Exceptions, §99E-31(b), (c).
    In addition to other limitation, §99E-31(d).
Signs containing warning notice.
  Failure to comply.
    Invoking immunity prohibited, §99E-32(c).
  Form of notice requirements, §99E-32(b).
  Posting and maintaining required, §99E-32(a).
  Requirements, §99E-32(a).

AHOSKIE, TOWN OF.
Room occupancy tax.
  Uniform provisions.
    Authorized to levy, §160A-215(g).
    Generally, §160A-215.
Satellite annexation.
  Limitation on area of satellite corporate limits,
    inapplicability, §160A-58.1(b).

AIDING AND ABETTING.
Accessories.
  After the fact, §14-7.
  Before the fact, §14-5.2.
Alcoholic beverages.
  Sale to or purchase by underage persons,
    §18B-302(c).
  Fines and other penalties, §18B-302.1(b), (c).

AIDING AND ABETTING —Cont'd
Bigamy, §14-183.
Concealing birth of child, §14-46.
Concealment of death, §14-401.22(b).
Eggs.
  Violations of egg act.
    Persons punishable as principals, §106-245.27.
Futures contracts, §16-4.
Habeas corpus.
  Concealing party entitled to writ, §17-28.
Hazing, §14-35.
Impaired driving.
  Punishment, §20-179(f1).
Interstate commerce.
  Earnings of employees in interstate commerce.
    Collections out of state to avoid exemptions.
      Resident not to abet collection out of state,
        §95-74.
Larceny, §14-70.
Marriage licenses.
  Obtaining license by false pretenses, §51-15.
Minors purchasing or possessing alcohol,
  §§18B-302.1(b), (c), 18B-302(c).
Prisons and prisoners.
  Aiding in prisoner self-injury resulting in
    incapacity, §148-46.1.
  Conveying messages to convicts and other
    prisoners, §14-258.
  Use of deadly weapon during escape, §14-258.2.
Prostitution.
  Acts abetting prostitution unlawful, §14-204.
Public officers and employees.
  Misuse of confidential information, §14-234.1.
Underage drinking, §18B-302(c).
  Fines and other penalties, §18B-302.1(b), (c).
Worthless checks, §14-107(b).

AIDS AND HIV.
Adult care home.
  Infection prevention requirements, §131D-4.4A.
Anatomical gifts.
  Information for potential donors, §130A-148(b).
  Laboratory tests for AIDS virus infection.
    Immunity of facility or institution,
      §130A-148(e).
    Required, §130A-148(c), (d).
Arrest.
  Initial appearance before magistrate.
    Detention for communicable diseases,
      §15A-534.3.
Blood donors.
  Information for potential donors, §130A-148(b).
  Laboratory tests for AIDS virus infection.
    Immunity of facility or institution,
      §130A-148(e).
    Required, §130A-148(c).
Confidentiality.
  Records identifying person who has AIDS virus
    infection, §130A-143.
Defendants accused of offense involving
  vaginal, anal or oral intercourse.
  Testing.
    Request by victim for testing, §15A-615(a).
    Defendant in custody of division of adult
      correction, §15A-615(c).
    Order requiring.
      District attorney to petition court,
        §15A-615(b).
      Findings required, §15A-615(b).
Different treatment for individual with AIDS.
  Not unlawful, §130A-148(j).

AIDS AND HIV —Cont'd
Foster care and adoption assistance.
Rate of payments.
HIV foster care and adoption assistance,
§108A-49.1(c).
**Handling dead body of person infected with
HIV.**
Notification to person handling, §130A-395(a), (c).
Laboratory tests for AIDS virus infection,
§130A-148(i).
Blood transfusion.
Immunity of facility or institution,
§130A-148(e).
Information for potential donors, §130A-148(b).
Testing required, §130A-148(c).
Consent.
Organ or tissue transplant, §130A-148(d).
When not required, §130A-148(f).
Notification of results, §130A-148(g).
Organ or tissue transplant.
Immunity of facility or institution,
§130A-148(e).
Information for potential donors, §130A-148(b).
Testing required, §130A-148(d).
Protection of public health.
Commission may authorize or require tests
when necessary to protect, §130A-148(h).
Rules establishing standards, §130A-148(a).
Semen, §130A-148(b), (c), (e).
Public schools.
Prevention of sexually transmitted diseases.
Health education, §115C-81(e1).
**Referral of individual with AIDS to another
provider or facility.**
Not unlawful, §130A-148(j).
Release of confidential information.
Records identifying person who has AIDS virus
infection.
Circumstances, §130A-143.
**Treating individual with AIDS differently than
individual without AIDS.**
Not unlawful, §130A-148(j).

**AID TO FAMILIES WITH DEPENDENT
CHILDREN.**
District attorneys, reports to, §§15-155.1 to
15-155.3.
Setoff debt collection, §§105A-1 to 105A-16.
See SETOFF DEBT COLLECTION.
Work first program generally, §§108A-27 to
108A-39.
See WORK FIRST PROGRAM.

AIR AND WATER QUALITY REPORTING ACT,
§§143-215.63 to 143-215.69.

AIR BAGS.
Unlawful installation or reinstallation,
§20-136.2.

AIR CARGO AIRPORT AUTHORITY ACT,
§§63A-1 to 63A-25.
See GLOBAL TRANSPARK AUTHORITY.

AIR CARGO AIRPORT FACILITIES.
North Carolina's eastern region, §§158-30 to
158-42.
See NORTH CAROLINA'S EASTERN REGION.

AIR CARRIERS.
Alcoholic beverages for use in air commerce,
§18B-107.
Exemption from wage and hour act,
§95-25.14(c).

AIR CARRIERS —Cont'd
Property taxes.
Public service corporations.
Generally, §§105-333 to 105-344.
See PROPERTY TAXES.
Sales and use tax.
Interstate air couriers or carriers.
Definitions, §105-164.3.
**Tax incentives for new and expanding
businesses.**
Creating jobs credit.
Constructing or planning to construct hub,
§105-129.8(d).
Interstate air carriers.
Sunset provisions, §105-129.2A(a1).
Investment in machinery or equipment.
Constructing or planning to construct hub,
§105-129.9(e).

AIR-CLEANING DEVICES.
Corporate franchise tax.
Deducted reserves, §105-122(d).
Deductible liabilities, §105-122(b).

AIR CONDITIONERS.
Chlorofluorocarbon refrigerants, §§130A-309.80
to 130A-309.87.
Energy star qualified products.
Sales and use tax holiday, §105-164.13D(a).
Evaporator coils or condensers.
Person delivering to secondary metals recycler.
Receipt, fingerprint, §66-11(b).
Purchase limitations.
Secondary metals recyclers, §66-11(d).
Public assistance.
Weatherization assistance program, §108A-70.30.

AIR CONDITIONING CONTRACTORS.
**Plumbing, heating and fire sprinkler
contractors.**
Generally, §§87-16 to 87-27.1.
See PLUMBING, HEATING AND FIRE
SPRINKLER CONTRACTORS.

AIR CONDITIONING INSPECTORS.
County inspection departments.
Generally, §§153A-350 to 153A-375.
See COUNTY INSPECTION DEPARTMENTS.

AIRCRAFT.
Accidents.
Collision of aircraft.
Liability, §63-15.
Use of aircraft to discover certain motor vehicle
violations.
Primarily for accident prevention, §20-196.2.
Acrobatic flying.
Penalty, §63-18.
Aeronautics instructors.
Defined, §63-1(a).
Air instruction.
Defined, §63-1(a).
Airmen.
Defined, §63-1(a).
Alcoholic beverages.
Forfeiture generally, §18B-504.
Use in air commerce, §18B-107(a), (b).
Antique airplanes.
Property tax assessment.
Antique airplane defined, §105-277.12(a).
Designated special class of property for
assessment, §105-277.12(b).

AIRCRAFT —Cont'd

Bailment, lease or rental of vehicle or draft animals.
Protection of bailor against bailee's acts, §§14-165 to 14-169.
See BAILMENTS.

Burglary.
Breaking or entering into or breaking out of aircraft, §14-56.

Collision of aircraft.
Liability.
Determination, §63-15.

Commercial fishing.
Spotter planes in commercial fishing operations.
Coastal and estuarine commercial fishing licenses, §113-171.1(d).

Construction, design and airworthiness.
Conformity to federal standards, §63-22.

Construction of provisions, §63-1(b).

Contracts entered into while in.
Jurisdiction, §63-17.

Damages.
Forced landing, §63-13.

Definitions, §63-1(a).

Department of transportation.
Management and use of aircraft.
Priority of uses, §136-102.9.
Rates charged for use, §136-102.9.

Disabled persons.
Right to use of public conveyances, §168-3.

Discharge of barreled weapon or firearm into.
While occupied or in operation, §14-34.1(a) to (c).

Division of motor vehicles.
Additional airplanes.
Purchase, §20-3.1.

Dropping objects.
Penalty, §63-18.

Drugs.
Forfeiture of conveyances used in controlled substances violations.
Generally, §§90-112, 90-112.1.
Operation of aircraft while impaired, §§63-27, 63-28.

Federal license, §63-20.
Possession and exhibition of license certificates, §63-21.
Violations of provisions, §63-23.

Flying under the influence, §63-27.
Infliction of serious bodily injury, §63-28.

Highway patrol.
Use of aircraft to discover certain motor vehicle violations, §20-196.2.

Hunting from, §113-291.1(b).

Impaired operation.
Chemical analysis, §63-27(d).
Defense precluded, §63-27(b).
Infliction of serious bodily injury.
Defense precluded, §63-28(b).
Felony, §63-28(d).
Offense, §63-28(a).
Pleading, §63-28(c).
Misdemeanor, §63-27(e).
Offense, §63-27(a).
Pleading, §63-27(c).

Intoxication.
Operation of aircraft while impaired, §§63-27, 63-28.

Joyriding, §14-72.2.

Jurisdiction.
Contracts, §63-17.

AIRCRAFT —Cont'd

Jurisdiction —Cont'd
Crimes and torts, §63-16.
State jurisdiction retained, §63-24.

Labor and storage liens, §§44A-50 to 44A-90.
See AIRCRAFT LABOR AND STORAGE LIENS.

Larceny.
Motor-propelled conveyances used in committing larceny and similar crimes.
Seizure and forfeiture of conveyances, §14-86.1.
Taking of aircraft, §63-25.
Unauthorized use of motor-propelled conveyance, §14-72.2.

Laser devices.
Pointing at aircraft.
Criminal penalty, §14-280.2(a).
Definitions, §14-280.2(b).
Inapplicability of section, §14-280.2(c).

Lawfulness of flight, §63-13.

Liens.
Aircraft labor and storage liens, §§44A-50 to 44A-90.
See AIRCRAFT LABOR AND STORAGE LIENS.

Mental disability or infirmity of pilot.
Report and testimony by physician, immunity, §90-21.20A(a), (b).

Navigable air space.
Defined, §63-1(a).

Obstructing takeoff and landing operations, §63-37.1.

Operation of aircraft.
Defined, §63-1(a).
Impaired persons, §§63-27, 63-28.
Qualifications of operators, §63-20.

Overflights.
Municipal regulation, §160A-180.

Ownership of space, §63-12.

Peace officers.
Enforcement of provisions, §63-45.
Regulations of civil aeronautics administration, §63-47.

Pesticide applicator licenses, §§143-452 to 143-459.

Physical disability or infirmity, pilots.
Report by physician, immunity, §90-21.20A(a).
Testimony by physician, immunity, §90-21.20A(b).

Physician's report or testimony.
Pilot's physical disability or infirmity.
Immunity of physician for making report, §90-21.20A(a), (b).

Real property.
Landing on lands or waters of another, §63-13.
Ownership of space, §63-12.

Registration of aircraft.
Federal registration, §§63-22, 63-23.

Restricted areas.
Defined, §63-1(a).

Sales and use tax.
Periodic rental payments.
Souring payments, §105-164.4B(b).
Rate of tax, §105-164.4(a).
Refunds.
Aviation fuel, passenger plane maximum, §105-164.14(a1).
Economic incentive refunds, §105-164.14A(a).
Industrial facilities refunds, §105-164.14B(a).

Sovereignty in space, §63-11.

Special use airspaces.
Applications, §63-91.

AIRCRAFT —Cont'd
Special use airspaces —Cont'd
Approval.
Notification to federal aviation administration,
§63-92(a).
Legislative declaration.
Public purpose, §63-90.
Public purpose declared, §63-90.
Rejection.
Notification to federal aviation administration,
§63-92(b).
Review of applications, §63-91.
State airways.
Defined, §63-1(a).
State of North Carolina.
Jurisdiction.
Contracts, §63-17.
Crimes and torts, §§63-16, 63-24.
Sovereignty in space, §63-11.
Takeoff and landing operations.
Illegal obstructing, §63-37.1.
Taking of aircraft, §63-25.
Tampering with aircraft, §63-26.
Torts.
Jurisdiction, §63-16.
State jurisdiction retained, §63-24.
Transportation department.
Management and use of aircraft.
Priority of uses, §136-102.9.
Rates charged for use, §136-102.9.
Trick or acrobatic flying, §63-18.
Wage and hour act.
Exemption as to employees of air carriers,
§95-25.14(c).

**AIRCRAFT FACILITY PROPERTY TAX
CREDIT,** §105-129.12.

AIRCRAFT LABOR AND STORAGE LIENS,
§§44A-50 to 44A-90.
Definitions, §44A-50.
Enforcement of lien by sale, §44A-85.
Fees, §44A-80.
Notice of lien.
Contents of notice, §44A-60(b).
Expiration of lien unless notice filed, §44A-60(a).
Filing of notice by clerk of court, §44A-65.
Form of notice, §44A-60(d).
Sworn to or affirmed, and subscribed by the
lienor, §44A-60(c).
Persons entitled to, §44A-55.
Priority of lien on aircraft, §44A-70.
Termination of lien on aircraft, §44A-75.
Title of purchaser, §44A-90.

AIR PISTOLS.
Firearms generally.
See FIREARMS AND OTHER WEAPONS.
Minors.
Permitting young children to use dangerous
weapons.
Whether air pistol deemed dangerous firearm,
§14-316(b).
**Possessing or carrying on campus or other
educational property,** §14-269.2.

AIR POLLUTION.
Action for failure to pay civil penalty,
§143-215.114A(f).
Administration of air quality program.
Department of natural resources and community
development, §143-215.106.

AIR POLLUTION —Cont'd
Animal waste management, §§143-215.10A to
143-215.10M.
See ANIMAL WASTE MANAGEMENT.
**Asbestos NESHAP for demolition and
renovation.**
Local air pollution control programs,
§130A-452(a), (b).
Assessments.
Title V program.
Assessment of program implementation fees,
§143-215.106A.
Attorney general.
Civil action for failure to pay penalties,
§143-215.114A(f).
Bonds, surety.
Compliance bonds.
Special orders, §143-215.110(e).
Cities regulating or restricting emissions,
§160A-185.
Civil penalties.
Amount, §143-215.114A(c).
Coal-fired generating units.
Emissions of oxides of nitrogen and sulfur
dioxide by investor-owned utilities,
§143-215.114A(b1).
Contested case petitions.
Filing, §143-215.114A(d).
Continuing violations, §143-215.114A(b), (b1).
Disposition of proceeds, §143-215.114A(h).
Enforcement procedures generally, §143-215.114A.
Failure to pay.
Civil action, §143-215.114A(f).
Grounds for imposition, §143-215.114A(a).
Notice of assessment, §143-215.114A(d).
Remission request, §143-215.114A(e).
Coal-fired generating units.
Emissions of oxides of nitrogen and sulfur dioxide
by investor-owned utilities, §143-215.107D.
Civil penalties for violations, §143-215.114A(b1).
Compliance with provisions, §143-215.107D(f),
(g).
Criminal penalties for violations,
§143-215.114B(f) to (h).
Definitions, §143-215.107D(a).
Environmental compliance costs, accelerated
recovery, §62-133.6(b).
Adjustments or reductions in rate base,
§62-133.6(e), (f).
Amortization, §62-133.6(b).
Compliance plans, filing, §62-133.6(c).
Defined, §62-133.6(a).
Emissions limitations, statement by utilities
subject to, §62-133.6(i), (j).
Enforcement of utility compliance,
§62-133.6(h).
Final agency action not subject to review,
§62-133.6(k).
Hearing to review compliance costs,
§62-133.6(d).
Market based rates and services, authority to
implement, §62-133.6(g).
Rate base to remain unchanged, §62-133.6(e).
Permits to include certain conditions,
§143-215.107D(h).
Prohibited acts, §143-215.107D(b) to (e).
Statements by utility, §143-215.107D(j).
Voluntary agreement to transfer to state certain
emissions allowances, §143-215.107D(i).
Complex sources.
Construction or modification.
Approval or disapproval of environmental
management commission, §143-215.109(b).

AIR POLLUTION —Cont'd
Complex sources —Cont'd
Control by commission, §143-215.109.
Comprehensive plan or plans for prevention, abatement and control of air pollution, §143-215.107(a).
Consent orders.
Public notice and review, §143-215.110(a1).
Corporate franchise tax.
Deducted reserves, §105-122(d).
Deductible liabilities, §105-122(b).
Counties.
Local air pollution control programs authorized, §143-215.112.
Criminal penalties, enforcement procedures.
Actual knowledge, circumstantial evidence, §143-215.114B(c).
Coal-fired generating units.
Emissions of nitrogen and sulfur dioxide by investor-owned utilities, §143-215.114B(f) to (h).
Defenses, affirmative defense and bars to prosecutions, applicability, §143-215.114B(e).
False statements, certifications or representation, §143-215.114B(i).
Knowingly or willfully, state of mind not found, §143-215.114B(d).
Person defined, §143-215.114B(a).
Previous federal conviction, no proceeding based on, §143-215.114B(b).
Declaration of policy, §143-215.105.
Definitions, §143-215.105.
Coal-fired generating units.
Emissions of oxides of nitrogen and sulfur dioxide by investor-owned utilities, §143-215.107D(a).
Department of natural resources and community development.
Administration of program, §143-215.106.
Dry-cleaning equipment not using hazardous substances.
Business and energy tax credits, §105-129.16C(a) to (d).
Dry-cleaning solvent cleanup fund.
Transfer of sales and use taxes to fund, §105-164.44E.
Dumping toxic substances, §14-284.2.
Enforcement procedures, §§143-215.114A to 143-215.114C.
Injunctive relief, §143-215.114C.
Engineers certifying application for permit.
Expedited review of applications, §143-215.108(h).
Environmental management commission.
Auxiliary powers, §143-215.111.
Complex sources.
Adoption and development of rules and regulations, §143-215.109(a).
Approval or disapproval of construction or modification, §143-215.109(b).
Enforcement procedures, §§143-215.114A to 143-215.114C.
General powers, §143-215.111.
Local air pollution control programs, §143-215.112.
Permits.
Generally, §143-215.108.
Powers.
General powers, §143-215.111.
Special orders, §143-215.110.
Supervision of programs, §143-215.106.

AIR POLLUTION —Cont'd
Environmental policy act, §§113A-1 to 113A-13.
See ENVIRONMENTAL POLICY ACT.
Expedited review of permit applications certified by professional engineer, §143-215.108(h).
Fees.
Title V program.
Assessment of implementation fees, §143-215.106A.
Fires and fire protection.
Open burning regulated, §§106-944, 106-946.
Industrial and pollution control facilities financing.
Industrial and pollution control facilities financing act, §§159C-1 to 159C-27.
See INDUSTRIAL AND POLLUTION CONTROL FACILITIES FINANCING.
North Carolina capital facilities financing act.
North Carolina industrial and pollution control facilities financing act, §§159D-1 to 159D-27.
See INDUSTRIAL AND POLLUTION CONTROL FACILITIES FINANCING.
Injunctions.
Enforcement procedures, §143-215.114C.
Investigations.
Permits, §143-215.108(d).
Limitation of actions.
Civil action for failure to pay penalties, §143-215.114A(f).
Local air pollution control programs.
Asbestos NESHAP for demolition and renovation, §130A-452(a), (b).
Certification by environmental management commission, §143-215.112(b).
Environmental management commission.
Oversight and supervision, §143-215.112(a).
Establishment.
Certification by commission required, §143-215.112(b).
Counties and municipalities may establish with approval of commission, §143-215.112(c).
Finance, §143-215.112(d1).
Hearings.
Circumstances under which commission may hold, §143-215.112(e).
Judicial review of final administrative decisions, §143-215.112(d2).
Misdemeanors, §143-215.112(d).
Oversight and supervision by commission, §143-215.112(a).
Rules and regulations.
Violations constitute misdemeanors, §143-215.112(d).
Motor vehicles emission control.
Enforcement of provisions, §20-128.1(c).
Inspections generally.
See MOTOR VEHICLE INSPECTIONS.
Requirements generally, §§20-128.1(a), 20-128(c).
Exception for pollution reduction modifications, §20-128(d).
Safety inspections, scope, §20-183.3(a).
Standards.
Rules and regulations, §20-128.2(a).
Violations of provisions.
Penalty, §20-128.1(d).
Time for bringing vehicle into conformity with provisions, §20-128.1(b).
Municipalities.
Emission of pollutants.
Prohibited, §160A-185.

AIR POLLUTION —Cont'd
Municipalities —Cont'd
Local air pollution control programs authorized,
§143-215.112.
New facilities.
Construction of containment source, equipment or
cleaning device.
Activities allowed prior to obtaining permit,
§143-215.108A(a).
Permit required, §143-215.108A(a).
Nitrogen oxides.
Investor-owned utilities.
Emissions by coal-fired generating units owned
or operated by, §143-215.107D.
Statewide goals for reduction, report,
§143-215.107B.
Notice.
Civil penalties.
Assessment, §143-215.114A(d).
Title V program.
Assessment of implementation fees,
§143-215.106A(a).
Open burning regulated, §§106-944, 106-946.
Orders.
Special orders, §143-215.110.
Permits.
Activities requiring permits, §143-215.108(a).
Alteration or expansion of existing facilities.
Modification of permit, §143-215.108A(b) to (j).
Changes without requiring revision.
Adoption of rules, §143-215.108(a1).
Contested cases.
Filing of petition, §143-215.108(e).
Expedited review of applications certified by
professional engineer, §143-215.108(h).
Investigations, §143-215.108(d).
Modification, §143-215.108(a2).
Alteration or expansion of existing facilities,
§143-215.108A(b) to (j).
New facilities, §143-215.108A(a).
Powers of commission, §143-215.108(c).
Purposes of section.
Actions upon applications to effectuate,
§143-215.108(b).
Reduction of emission of air contaminants.
Submission of written description of current and
projected plans, §143-215.108(g).
Required.
Activities requiring permits, §143-215.108(a).
Review of applications other than those certified
by professional engineers, §143-215.108(i).
Term, §143-215.108(d1).
Title V program.
Assessment of program implementation fees,
§143-215.106A.
Zoning or subdivision ordinances.
Request to local government to determine
applicability, §143-215.108(f).
Petitions.
Civil penalties.
Contested cases, §143-215.114A(d).
Permits.
Contested cases, §143-215.108(e).
Policy declaration, §143-215.105.
Rules and regulations.
Complex sources.
Adoption and development of rules and
regulations by commission, §143-215.109(a).
Smoking.
See SMOKING.

AIR POLLUTION —Cont'd
Solid waste management.
General provisions, §§130A-290 to 130A-305.
See SOLID WASTE MANAGEMENT.
Sources of air pollution.
Complex sources, §143-215.109.
Construction or modification, §143-215.109(b).
Control generally, §143-215.108.
Special orders.
Compliance bonds, §143-215.110(e).
Effect of compliance, §143-215.110(d).
Issuance, §143-215.110(a).
Procedure, §143-215.110(b).
Standards and classifications.
Criteria for standards, §143-215.107(b).
Duty to prepare and develop comprehensive plan
or plans for prevention, abatement and
control of air pollution, §143-215.107(a).
**State plans to reduce emissions from
job-related travel.**
Alternative-fueled or low emission vehicles,
purchase by state, §143-215.107C(a) to (c).
Plan for private sector employees,
§143-215.107C(e).
Plan for state employees, §143-215.107C(d).
Sulfur dioxide (SO2).
Investor-owned utilities.
Emissions by coal-fired generating units owned
or operated by, §143-215.107D.
Superior courts.
Civil penalties.
Civil action for failure to pay, §143-215.114A(f).
Supervision of program.
Environmental management commission to review
and supervise program, §143-215.106.
**Title V program assessment of implementation
fees,** §143-215.106A(a).
Notices of assessments, §143-215.106A(a).
Reduction.
Fee becoming due and payable during fiscal
year permit holder paid assessment,
§143-215.106A(c).
Schedule of assessments, §143-215.106A(b).
Transportation projects.
Planning regionally significant transportation
projects, §136-202.
Venue.
Civil action for failure to pay penalties,
§143-215.114A(f).
Violations.
Enforcement procedures, §§143-215.114A to
143-215.114C.
Water and air quality reporting, §§143-215.63 to
143-215.69.
See WATER AND AIR QUALITY REPORTING.
Water and air resources, §§143-211 to
143-215.9C.
See WATER AND AIR RESOURCES.
Zoning permits.
Applicability of zoning or subdivision ordinance.
Request to local government to determine,
§143-215.108(f).

AIR POLLUTION EPISODES.
Open burning prohibited statewide, §106-944.

AIRPORT AUTHORITIES.
Borrowing money, §159-210.
Sales and use tax refunds, §105-164.14(c).
Security interest.
Entering into contracts creating, §160A-20.

AIRPORT AUTHORITIES —Cont'd
Smoking in public places.
  Local government regulation of smoking,
    §130A-498.

AIRPORT BOARDS OR COMMISSIONS.
Security interest.
  Entering into contracts creating, §160A-20.

AIRPORT DEVELOPMENT ACT.
State aid, §§63-65 to 63-73.
  See AIRPORTS.

AIRPORTS.
Air cargo airports and related facilities.
  North Carolina's eastern region, §§158-30 to
    158-42.
    See NORTH CAROLINA'S EASTERN REGION.
Air navigation facilities.
  Defined, §63-1(a).
Air schools.
  Defined, §63-1(a).
Alcoholic beverages.
  Mixed beverages.
    Effect of election on permit issuance,
      §18B-603(e).
Appropriations.
  Municipal airports, §63-8.
  State aid.
    Sources of funds, §§63-68, 63-69.
  Transportation department.
    Continuing aviation appropriations, §§136-16.4,
      136-16.5.
Construction and interpretation.
  Singular and plural, §63-1(b).
Contracts.
  Transportation department.
    Airport construction, repair, etc., §63-73.
Counties.
  Establishment of airport, §63-3.
  Public enterprises.
    Operating, financing and fixing rates,
      §§153A-274 to 153A-280.
Definitions, §63-1(a).
  Special airport districts, §63-79.
Disorderly conduct, §14-275.1.
Federal aid.
  Acceptance, §§63-70, 63-71(a).
  Department of transportation.
    Powers as to, §63-71.
Global TransPark authority.
  General provisions, §§63A-1 to 63A-25.
    See GLOBAL TRANSPARK AUTHORITY.
Highways, roads and streets.
  Connection of airports with state highway system.
    Powers of department of transportation,
      §136-18.
Jurisdiction.
  Municipal jurisdiction exclusive, §63-58.
Legislative declaration.
  Airports a public purpose, §63-50.
Local development.
  North Carolina's eastern region, §§158-30 to
    158-42.
    See NORTH CAROLINA'S EASTERN REGION.
Misdemeanors.
  Obstructing takeoff and landing operations,
    §63-37.1.
  Zoning violations, §63-35.
Municipal airports, §§63-1 to 63-9.
  Acquisition of property, §63-49(a) to (d).
    Sites, §§63-5, 63-6.

AIRPORTS —Cont'd
Municipal airports —Cont'd
  Acquisition of property —Cont'd
    Validation of prior acquisitions, §63-51.
  Appropriations, §63-8.
  Cities.
    Establishment by cities.
      Authorized, §63-2.
  Counties.
    Establishment by counties, §63-3.
    Powers of municipalities granted to counties,
      §63-57(b).
    Purpose of provisions declared county purposes,
      §63-57(a).
  Eminent domain, §§63-5, 63-6, 63-49(b).
    Joint operation of airports, §63-56(h).
  Establishment.
    Cities and towns authorized to establish, §63-2.
    Counties authorized to establish, §63-3.
    Joint airports.
      Establishment by cities, towns and counties,
        §63-4.
  Existing airports.
    Powers of governing bodies as to, §63-7.
  Federal aid, §63-54.
    Acceptance, §63-54(a).
    Compliance with federal regulations, §63-54(b),
      (c).
  Fees.
    Establishment for existing airports, §63-7.
  Gift or devise.
    Acquisition of property by, §63-6.
  Joint airports established by cities, towns and
    counties, §63-4.
  Joint operation of airports, §63-56.
    Agreements, §63-56(b), (c).
      Specific performance, §63-56(k).
    Authorized, §63-56(a).
    Board.
      Composition, §63-56(d), (l).
      Generally, §63-56(d) to (f), (l) to (n).
      Officers, §63-56(e).
      Powers and duties, §63-56(d), (f), (m).
    Cessation of use of facilities for aeronautical
      purposes, §63-56(o).
    Eminent domain, §63-56(h).
    Expansion or enlargement of facilities,
      §63-56(p).
    Funds.
      Joint fund, §63-56(i), (j).
    Ordinances, §63-56(g).
    Water and sewer systems.
      Operation, §63-56(q).
  Jurisdiction.
    Municipal jurisdiction exclusive, §63-58.
  Legislative declaration.
    Airports a public purpose, §63-50.
  Powers of municipalities operating airports,
    §63-53.
    Airports on public waters and reclaimed land,
      §63-55(a), (b).
    Powers declared granted to counties, §63-57(b).
  Property taxes.
    Authorized purposes, §160A-209(c).
  Public purpose.
    Airports declared public purpose, §63-5.
  Reclaimed land, §63-55(a), (b).
  Regulation of aircraft overflights, §160A-180.
  Rules and regulations.
    Powers of municipalities operating airports,
      §63-53.

AIRPORTS —Cont'd
Municipal airports —Cont'd
Severability of provisions, §63-9.
Towns.
Establishment by towns, §63-2.
Trees and other vegetation.
Encroachment upon airport protection privileges prohibited, §63-49(d).
Waters.
Airports on public waters, §63-55(a), (b).
Municipalities.
Public enterprises generally, §§160A-311 to 160A-328.
See MUNICIPAL UTILITIES.
Peace officer enforcement of provisions, §§63-45, 63-47.
Powers of general assembly as to airport facilities, NC Const Art V §13.
Protection privileges.
Acquisition by municipalities, §63-49(c).
Defined, §63-1(a).
Encroachments upon.
Prohibited, §63-49(d).
Rural airports.
State aid.
Sources of funds, §63-68.
Special airport districts, §§63-78 to 63-89.
Advances, §63-88.
Aeronautical facilities.
Defined, §63-79.
Bond issues.
Elections, §63-87.
Powers of districts, §§63-83, 63-84.
Taxes for supplementing airport revenue bond projects, §§63-85, 159-97(i).
Citation of act.
Short title, §63-78.
Conflict of laws.
Inconsistent laws declared inapplicable, §63-89.
Contracts.
Powers of districts, §63-83.
Creation, §63-80.
Action to set aside.
Limitation of actions, §63-80(e).
Advances for preliminary expenses, §63-88.
Election, §63-80(c).
Hearing.
Notice, §63-80(b).
Limitation of actions.
Actions to set aside creation, §63-80(e).
Notices, §63-80(d).
Hearing, §63-80(b).
Resolution of governing body, §63-80(a).
Definitions, §63-79.
District board.
Appointment of members, §63-81(a).
Composition, §63-81(a).
Defined, §63-79.
Inclusion of additional units of local government.
Appointment of new members, §63-82(e).
Meetings, §63-81(b).
Notice, §63-81(b).
Oath of office of members, §63-81(a).
Officers.
Election, §63-81(c).
Quorum, §63-81(b).
Vacancies, §63-81(a).
Elections.
Bond elections, §63-87.
Creation of district, §63-80(c).

AIRPORTS —Cont'd
Special airport districts —Cont'd
Eminent domain.
Powers of districts, §63-83.
Fiscal impact of bills, resolutions or rules.
Local government fiscal information, §§120-30.41 to 120-30.49.
Inclusion of additional units of local government, §63-82.
Actions to set aside inclusion, §63-82(d).
Annexation by participating unit of local government.
Effect, §63-82(f).
Limitation of actions.
Actions to set aside inclusion, §63-82(d).
New members of district board.
Appointment, §63-82(e).
Procedure generally, §63-82(a) to (c).
Limitation of actions.
Actions to set aside creation, §63-80(e).
Actions to set aside inclusion of additional units of local government, §63-82(d).
Notice.
Creation of district, §63-80(d).
Hearing, §63-80(b).
District board.
Meetings, §63-81(b).
Powers of districts, §63-83.
Seals and sealed instruments.
Power to adopt official seal, §63-83.
Taxation.
Levy and collection of taxes generally, §63-86.
Levy for supplementing airport revenue bond project, §§63-85, 159-97(i).
Powers of districts, §63-83.
Rate of tax.
Determination by district board, §63-86.
Title of act.
Short title, §63-78.
State aid.
Acceptance authorized, §63-70.
Activities eligible, §63-67.
Amount.
Limitations, §63-68.
Appropriations.
Source of funds, §§63-68, 63-69.
Conditions, §63-68.
Department of transportation.
Powers of department as to, §§63-65, 63-66.
Eligibility.
Activities eligible, §63-67.
Limitations, §63-68.
Rural airports, §63-68.
Source of funds, §§63-68, 63-69.
Traffic signs and traffic control devices.
Uniform signs and devices.
Exemption as to informational and directional signs, §136-30(d).
Transportation department.
Agent of public agency which applies for federal aid, §63-71(b).
Appropriations.
Continuing aviation appropriations, §§136-16.4, 136-16.5.
Connection of state airports with public highway system, §136-18.
Contracts.
Airport construction, repair, etc., §63-73.
Federal aid.
Powers as to, §63-71.
Operation of airports by department, §63-72.

AIRPORTS —Cont'd
Transportation department —Cont'd
Powers, §§63-65, 63-66, 63-71, 63-72.
Public highway system.
Connection of state airports with system.
Powers of department, §136-18.
State aid.
Powers of department as to, §§63-65, 63-66.
Transportation system defined, §136-5.1.
Transportation system.
Defined, §136-5.1.
Trespass upon airport property, §63-26.1(b).
Unlawful, §63-26.1(a).
Waters and watercourses.
Municipal airports.
Airports on public waters and reclaimed land,
§63-55(a), (b).
Zoning, §§63-30 to 63-37.1.
Air cargo airport authority.
Political subdivision not to adopt regulation in
violation, §63-31(f).
Air rights.
Acquisition, §63-36.
Board of appeals.
Appeals to board, §63-33(c).
Composition, §63-33(c).
Judicial review, §63-34.
Copies of papers may be returned, §63-34(c).
Costs, §63-34(e).
Petition, §63-34(a).
Proceedings not stayed, §63-34(b).
Restraining order, granting, §63-34(b).
Meetings, §63-33(c).
Powers, §63-33(c).
Citation of act.
Short title, §63-37.
Eminent domain.
Acquisition of air rights, §63-36.
Enforcement of act, §63-35.
General zoning ordinances.
Effect, §63-31(b).
Hearings.
Adoption of zoning regulations, §63-33(a).
Injunctions.
Violations of provisions, §63-35.
Joint boards, §63-31(c).
Legislative declaration, §63-30.
Misdemeanors.
Violations of provisions, §63-35.
Notice.
Hearing on adoption of zoning regulations,
§63-33(a).
Penalties.
Violations of provisions, §63-35.
Permits, §63-32(a).
Obstruction marking and lighting may be
required, §63-32(c).
Regulations.
Administrative agency, §63-33(b).
Adoption.
Authorized, §63-31(a).
Procedure, §63-33(a).
Area affected by, §63-31(d).
Restrictions on, §63-31(e).
Title of act.
Short title, §63-37.
Variances, §63-32(b).
Obstruction marking and lighting may be
required, §63-32(c).
Violations of provisions.
Injunctions, §63-35.

AIRPORTS —Cont'd
Zoning —Cont'd
Violations of provisions —Cont'd
Penalties, §63-35.

AIR RESOURCES ACT, §§143-211 to 143-215.9C.
See WATER AND AIR RESOURCES.

AIR RIFLES.
Firearms generally.
See FIREARMS AND OTHER WEAPONS.
Minors.
Permitting young children to use dangerous
firearms.
Whether air rifle deemed dangerous firearm,
§14-316(b).
**Possessing or carrying on campus or other
educational property, §14-269.2.**

AIRSPACE.
Special use airspaces, §§63-90 to 63-92.

ALAMANCE COUNTY.
Agricultural tendencies in certain counties.
Terms of, §42-23.
Ambulance services.
Attachment or garnishment and lien for,
§§44-51.4 to 44-51.8.
Obtaining ambulance services without intending
to pay, §14-111.2.
Requesting ambulance falsely, §14-111.3.
Board of county commissioners.
Filling vacancies on board, §153A-27.1.
**Condemnation or acquisition of land by local
government unit outside county.**
Consent of board of commissioners necessary,
§153A-15.
Coroner elected as nominee of political party.
Filling vacancy in office, §152-1.
**Cropper or tenant neglecting or refusing to
perform terms of contract without just
cause.**
Forfeiture of right of possession to premises,
§42-27.
Dog collars.
Unlawful removal of electronic dog collars,
§14-401.17.
Dogs used in hunting.
Regulation by wildlife resources commission,
§113-291.5(a).
On-premises unfortified wine licenses.
Discretion to decline to issue, §105-113.71(b).
Registration of deeds.
Tax certification, no delinquent taxes due,
§161-31(b).
School property.
Acquisition and improvement, §153A-158.1.
Sheriff.
Vacancy, performance of duties until vacancy
filled, §162-5.1.
Small city mixed beverage elections.
Inapplicability of subsection to, §18B-600(e1).

ALARMS.
Fire alarms.
Giving false alarm, §14-286.
Molesting alarms, §14-286.

**ALARM SYSTEMS LICENSING, §§74D-1 to
74D-14.**
Action by alarm system business.
Proof of licensure required to maintain, §74D-14.
Action for failure to pay civil penalty,
§74D-11(e).

ALARM SYSTEMS LICENSING —Cont'd

Age requirement for licensing, §74D-2(d).

Alarm system business defined, §74D-2(a).

Alarm system education fund.
  Created as special fund, §74D-30(a).
  Fees deposited into fund, §74D-30(c).
  Investment of money in fund, §74D-30(d).
  Uses, §74D-30(d).

Appeals.
  Suspension or revocation of license, §74D-10(b).

Apprenticeship registration permit.
  Duration, §74D-8.1(b).
  Issuance, §74D-8.1(a).
  Restrictions on holder, §74D-8.1(c).

Assignment of license.
  Prohibited, §74D-7(b).

Attorney general.
  Investigative powers, §74D-5.2.

Board.
  Appointment of members, §74D-4(c), (d).
  Chairman, §74D-4(f).
  Compensation of members, §74D-4(e).
  Composition, §74D-4(b).
  Director, §74D-5.1.
  Established, §74D-4(a).
  Exclusive jurisdiction, §74D-11(c).
  Expenses of members.
    Reimbursement, §74D-4(e).
  Hearings, §74D-5(b).
  Meetings, §74D-4(g).
  Powers, §74D-5(a).
  Quorum, §74D-4(g).
  Removal of members, §74D-4(d).
  Space, physical facilities and services provided by
    state agency.
    Payment to state agency, §74D-4(h).
  Terms of members, §74D-4(c).
  Vacancies.
    Filling, §74D-4(d).

Branch offices, §74D-7(d).
  Notification requirements to board, §74D-7(d).

Citation of act.
  Short title, §74D-1.

Confidentiality.
  Criminal background check, §74D-2.1(b).
  Home address, telephone number of licensee,
    license applicant, spouse, children, parents,
    §74D-2(f).
  Investigations by attorney generally, §74D-5.2.

**Contract for sale, installation or service of
    alarm system.**
  Unlicensed or unregistered persons.
    Contract void, §§74D-11(f), 74D-14.

Criminal background checks.
  Applicants for license or registration.
    Authorization to conduct, §74D-2.1(a).
    Fingerprints of new applicants, §74D-2.1(a).
  Confidentiality, §74D-2.1(b).

Denial of license.
  Grounds, §74D-6.

Employee registration, §74D-8(a).
  Registration card, §74D-8(c), (d).
  Termination of employment.
    Notice, §74D-8(b).

Examinations.
  Board may require, §74D-2(e).

Exemptions from provisions, §74D-3.

Fees, §74D-7(e).
  Alarm system education fund.
    Deposited into fund, §74D-30(c).
  Transfer of certain fees, §74D-13.

ALARM SYSTEMS LICENSING —Cont'd

Fingerprints.
  Criminal background checks.
    Applicants for license or registration,
      §74D-2.1(a).

Form of license, §74D-7(a).

Fraud.
  Conviction of crime involving fraud.
    Grounds for denial of license, §74D-6.

Funds.
  Transfer of funds, §74D-13.

Good moral character and temperate habits.
  License requirement, §74D-2(d).
  Prima facie evidence applicant does not possess,
    §74D-2(d).

Hearings.
  Board, §74D-5(b).

**Home address, telephone number of licensee,
    license applicant, spouse, children,
    parents.**
  Confidentiality, §74D-2(f).

Injunctions, §74D-11(a).

Invalidity of provisions.
  Severability, §74D-12.

Investigations.
  Attorney general, §74D-5.2.
    Confidentiality, §74D-5.2.
    Report, release to licensee, §74D-5.2.
  Powers of board, §74D-5(a).

Liability insurance.
  Cancellation of policy, §74D-9(e).
  Certificate of insurance to be maintained on file,
    §74D-9(f).
  Requirements, §74D-9(d).

Local governments.
  Permits.
    Requirement by ordinance, §74D-11(c).

Misdemeanors, §74D-11(b).

Name of licensee.
  Engaging in business under, §74D-7(c).
  License to state, §74D-7(a).

Penalties.
  Civil penalties in lieu of suspension or revocation
    of license, §74D-11(d).
  Violations of provisions, §74D-11(b).

Qualifying agents.
  Business entities engaging in alarm system
    business.
    Designation, §74D-2(c).

Registration.
  Denial of registration, §74D-6.
  Employees of licensees, §74D-8.

Required, §74D-2(a).
  Exceptions, §74D-3.

Rules and regulations.
  Powers of board, §74D-5(a).
  Violations as grounds for suspension or revocation
    of license, §74D-10(a).

Separate license.
  Department or division of business entity,
    §74D-2(a).

Severability of provisions, §74D-12.

Subpoenas.
  Powers of board, §74D-5(a).

Suspension or revocation of license.
  Appeal, §74D-10(b).
  Civil penalties in lieu of, §74D-11(d).
  Grounds, §74D-10(a).
  Powers of board generally, §74D-5(a).

Term of license, §74D-7(b).

ALARM SYSTEMS LICENSING —Cont'd
Title of act.
Short title, §74D-1.
Unlicensed or unregistered persons.
Contract for sale, installation or service of alarm system.
Contract void, §§74D-11(f), 74D-14.

ALBEMARLE.
All-terrain vehicles.
Use by employees on certain highways, §20-171.24.
Traffic control photographic systems, §160A-300.1(d).

ALBEMARLE POTATO FESTIVAL.
Official state Irish potato festival, §145-30.

ALBEMARLE SOUND.
Obstructions.
Lumbermen to remove, §76-42.

ALCOHOL AND DRUG EDUCATION PROGRAM.
Basic education program, §115C-81(a3).

ALCOHOL AND DRUG EDUCATION TRAFFIC SCHOOLS.
Limited driving privilege.
Driving for other than work-related purposes, §20-179.3(g2).
Restoration of license.
Impaired driving.
Condition of probation, §20-179(g) to (k).
Minors.
Impaired driving or driving after consuming alcohol or drugs.
Requirement for obtaining certificate of completion, §20-17.6(c).

ALCOHOLIC BEVERAGE CONTROL BOARDS.
See ABC BOARDS.

ALCOHOLIC BEVERAGE CONTROL COMMISSION.
ABC commission fund, §18B-208(b).
Advertising, rules.
Authority to promulgate, §18B-105(b).
Appointment, §18B-200(b).
Bond issues, §18B-208(a).
Chairman.
Salary, §18B-200(a).
Compensation, §18B-200(a).
Composition, §18B-200(a).
Conflicts of interest.
Dealing for family members, §18B-201(c).
Financial interest restricted, §18B-201(a).
Gifts, §18B-201(c).
Self-dealing, §18B-201(b).
State government ethics act.
Applicable provisions, §18B-201(e).
Creation, §18B-200(a).
Discharge of members.
Conviction of crime, §18B-202.
Employees, employment, authority, §18B-200(d).
Enforcement division.
Transfer to department of public safety, §143A-243.
Ethics.
Requirements for local boards.
Model policy, development, §18B-706(c).
State government ethics act.
Applicable provisions, §18B-201(e).
Family members.
Dealing for, §18B-201(c).

ALCOHOLIC BEVERAGE CONTROL COMMISSION —Cont'd
Financial interest restricted, §18B-201(a).
Financial operations of local boards.
Rules, adoption, compliance required, §18B-702(u).
Fiscal control rules for local boards.
Adoption, compliance required, §18B-702(u).
Improper influence.
Appointment of local board members, §18B-704(a).
Insolvency or closure of local ABC system.
Purchases from another board by mixed beverage permittees, §18B-203(a).
License plates.
Special plate, number, §20-79.5.
Native Americans.
Tribal alcoholic beverage control, §18B-112.
Orders.
Service of orders, §18B-500(d).
Performance standards for local board.
Establishing, rules and regulations, §18B-203(a).
Powers.
General provisions, §18B-203(a).
Implied powers, §18B-203(b).
Pregnancy, consumption during.
Signs warning of dangers.
Distribution and posting, §§18B-203(a), 18B-808.
Primary American source of supply of wine.
Wine importers and nonresident vendors.
Recognition, §18B-203(a).
Removal of local board members and employees, §18B-704.
Self-dealing, §18B-201(b).
Service of orders, §18B-500(d).
Special fund, §18B-208(b).
State government ethics act.
Applicable provisions, §18B-201(e).
State warehouse, §18B-204.
Training requirements for local board.
Mandatory training.
Establishing, rules and regulations, §18B-203(a).
Tribal alcoholic beverage control, §18B-112.
Vacancies in office.
Filling, §18B-200(c).

ALCOHOLIC BEVERAGE CONTROL PERMITS.
Generally.
See ABC PERMITS.

ALCOHOLIC BEVERAGE LICENSES.
ABC permits generally.
See ABC PERMITS.
Local licenses, §§105-113.77 to 105-113.79.

ALCOHOLIC BEVERAGES.
ABC boards, local, §§18B-700 to 18B-706.
See ABC BOARDS.
ABC commission.
See ALCOHOLIC BEVERAGE CONTROL COMMISSION.
ABC commission fund, §18B-208(b).
ABC stores, §§18B-800 to 18B-808.
See ABC STORES.
Accounts and accounting.
Required, §18B-205(a), (b).
Administrative procedure act.
Applicability, §18B-906(a).
Exception on hearing location, §18B-906(b).
Exception on new evidence, §18B-906(c).

ALCOHOLIC BEVERAGES —Cont'd
Advertising.
Authority of commission, §18B-105(b).
Compliance with rules of commission,
§18B-105(a).
Aiding and abetting.
Sale to or purchase by underage persons,
§§18B-302.1(b), (c), 18B-302(c).
Aircraft.
Impaired operation, §63-27.
Infliction of serious bodily injury, §63-28.
Airports and airplanes.
Forfeiture generally, §18B-504.
Mixed beverages.
Effect of elections on issuance of permits,
§18B-603(e).
Use in air commerce.
Purchase and storage, §18B-107(a).
Sale, §18B-107(b).
Alcoholic beverage control commission.
See ALCOHOLIC BEVERAGE CONTROL
COMMISSION.
Alcoholism research authority, §§122C-431 to
122C-433.
Alcohol law enforcement.
Agents for law enforcement, §18B-500.
Contracts with other law enforcement agencies.
Alternative to hiring local enforcement officers,
§18B-501(f).
Department of public safety.
Alcohol law enforcement agents.
Appointment by secretary, §18B-500.
Alcohol law enforcement section.
Defined, §18B-101.
Discharge for conviction of crime, §18B-202.
Transfer to department, §143A-243.
Forfeitures, §18B-504.
Inspection of licensed premises, §18B-502.
Local ABC officers, §18B-501.
Restitution to law enforcement agency, §18B-505.
Seized beverages.
Disposition, §18B-503.
Alcohol screening tests.
See ALCOHOL SCREENING TEST.
Alcohol treatment center.
Joint security force, §122C-421(a), (b).
Alcohol vaporizing devices, §90-113.10A.
Amounts that may be purchased.
Kegged malt beverages, §18B-303(a).
Liquor and fortified wine, §18B-303(a).
Malt beverages, §18B-303(a).
Purchase-transportation permit.
Purchasing in grater amounts, §18B-303(c).
Unfortified wine, §18B-303(a).
Unlawful purchases in greater amounts,
§18B-303(b).
Without permit, §18B-303(a).
Amusement device operators.
Operating device equipment under the influence.
Prohibition, §95-111.11(b).
Applications for permits, §18B-902.
Athletic contests.
Publicly displaying fortified wine, spirituous
liquor or mixed beverages at athletic contests,
§18B-301(f).
Audits.
Local ABC boards, §18B-205(c).
Local ABC stores, §18B-205(c).
State warehouse, §18B-204.
Ball parks.
In-stand sales, §18B-1009.
Hours of sale, §18B-1006(q).

ALCOHOLIC BEVERAGES —Cont'd
Beer.
Definition of "malt beverage,"§18B-101.
Malt beverages generally. See within this
heading, "Malt beverages."
Beer franchises, §§18B-1300 to 18B-1308.
See BEER FRANCHISES.
Beverage containers.
Recycling requirements for certain permit holders,
§18B-1006.1.
Disposal of in landfills or by incineration.
Prohibited, §130A-309.10(f3).
Plan to collect and recycle submitted with
application, §§18B-902(h), 18B-903(b2).
Bingo games.
Sale or consumption, §18B-308.
Boards.
Local ABC boards.
See ABC BOARDS.
Boating under the influence, §75A-10(b), (b1).
Bootlegging, §18B-304.
Unauthorized substances taxes, §§105-113.105 to
105-113.113.
See UNAUTHORIZED SUBSTANCES TAXES.
Bottlers.
Distribution agreements, §18B-1110(b).
Permits.
Authorization, §18B-1110(a).
Commercial permit, §18B-1100.
Brown-bagging permit, §§18B-301, 18B-1001.
Budgets.
Local ABC boards, §18B-702.
Burden of proof.
Compensation for injury caused by sales to
underage persons, §18B-122.
Change in management.
New manager employed.
Substitution of manager, submission, fee,
§18B-903(d).
Change in ownership of establishment.
Automatic expiration of permit, surrender,
§18B-903(c).
Charities.
Furnishing alcoholic beverages to inmates of
charitable institutions, §14-258.1(b).
**Chemical analysis of impairing substances in
blood generally.**
See IMPAIRED DRIVING.
Child labor restrictions.
Licensed premises, §95-25.5(j).
Cider.
Commercial permit, manufacturers, §18B-1100.
Exemption from alcoholic beverage provisions,
§18B-103.
Clean, well-lighted and orderly premises.
Permittee's responsibilities, §18B-1003(a).
Closing local ABC system.
Grounds, §18B-801(c).
Insolvency, §18B-801(d).
Commercial transportation, §18B-1115.
Commercial vehicles.
Operating a commercial vehicle after consuming
alcohol, §20-138.2A.
Odor of alcohol.
Evidentiary effect, §20-138.2A(b1).
Screening test for alcohol, §20-138.2A(b2).
Operating while possessing alcoholic beverages,
§20-138.2C.
**Commission for mental health, developmental
disabilities and substance abuse services,**
§§143B-147 to 143B-150.

ALCOHOLIC BEVERAGES —Cont'd
Community service.
Minors.
Aiding and abetting sale to or purchase by underage persons.
Fines and other penalties, §18B-302.1(b), (c).
Sales to.
Fines and other penalties, §18B-302.1(a), (c).
Community theatre.
Defined, §18B-1000.
Compensation for injury caused by sales to underage persons, §§18B-120 to 18B-129.
Burden of proof, §18B-122.
Claims for relief.
Creation, §18B-121.
Exception, §18B-125.
Limitation on damages, §18B-123.
Clerk of superior court.
Duties, §18B-127.
Common-law rights not abridged, §18B-128.
Definitions, §18B-120.
Evidence.
Admissibility, §18B-122.
Exemptions from article, §18B-125.
Holding of documents.
No liability for holding, §18B-129.
Joint and several liability, §18B-124.
Limitation of actions, §18B-126.
Limitation on damages, §18B-123.
Refusal to sell.
No liability, §18B-129.
Statute of limitations, §18B-126.
Superior court.
Duty of clerk, §18B-127.
Complimentary alcoholic beverages.
Air carriers serving, §18B-107(b).
Conduct on licensed premises, §18B-1005.
Prohibited conduct, §§18B-1005.1(a), (c), 18B-1005(a).
Supervision, §§18B-1005.1(b), 18B-1005(b).
Conflicts of interest.
Alcoholic beverage control commission, §18B-201.
Local ABC boards, §18B-201.
Penalties, §18B-700(h).
Wholesalers.
Supplier's financial interest in wholesaler, §18B-1119.
Congressionally chartered veterans organizations.
Defined, §18B-1000.
Constitution of the United States, US Const Amds 18, 21.
Construction of chapter, §18B-100.
Consumption.
Bingo games, §18B-308.
Fortified wine and spirituous liquor.
Restrictions, §18B-301(d).
Where lawful, §18B-301(d).
Hours of consumption, §18B-1004(a).
Malt beverages and unfortified wine.
General provisions, §18B-300(a).
Off-premises establishments, §18B-300(b).
Ordinances.
Property owned or occupied by city or county, §18B-300(c).
Minors.
Prohibition, §18B-302(b).
Consumption not authorized by permits, §18B-1006(d).
Misdemeanor, violation by 19 or 20 year olds, §18B-302(i).

ALCOHOLIC BEVERAGES —Cont'd
Controlled-drinking programs.
Department of health and human services, §20-139.1(g).
Controlled substances.
Prohibited on licensed premises, §18B-1005(a).
Convention center.
Defined, §18B-1000.
Cooking school.
Defined, §18B-1000.
Permits, §18B-1001.
Restrictions on sales at cooking schools, §18B-1006(g).
Counties.
Confinement facilities.
Furnishing alcoholic beverages to inmates, §14-258.1.
Licenses.
Beer and wine retail licenses, §105-113.78.
Local ABC boards.
See ABC BOARDS.
Local option elections, §18B-600(b).
Favorable county vote.
Effect on city, §18B-604(b).
Negative county vote.
Effect on city, §18B-604(c).
Ordinances.
Consumption.
Malt beverages and unfortified wine, §18B-300(c).
Restriction on adoption, §18B-100.
Regulation of places of amusement, §153A-135.
County boards of alcoholic control.
Defense of employees and officers, §160A-167.
Criminal offenses, criminal procedure.
County alcoholic beverage control act.
Defense of employees and officers in civil or criminal actions, §160A-167.
Direct shipments into state, §18B-102.1(e).
Forfeitures.
Disposition after trial, §18B-504(e).
Owner unavailable for criminal trial, §18B-504(i).
Return of property when no charge is made, §18B-504(j).
Seizure of property, §18B-504(c).
Imports and exports.
Unauthorized imports and exports, §18B-102(b).
Interference with inspections, §18B-502(b).
Law enforcement agents.
Subject-matter jurisdiction, §18B-500(b).
Local ABC officers.
Subject-matter jurisdiction, §18B-501(b).
Territorial jurisdiction, §18B-501(c).
Manufacturers.
Unauthorized manufacture, §18B-102(b).
Second unlawful manufacturing offense, §18B-307(c).
Minors.
Aiding and abetting sale to and purchase by underage persons, §18B-302(c).
Fines and other penalties, §18B-302.1(b), (c).
Consumption.
Violation by 19 or 20 year olds, §18B-302(i).
Purchase or possession, §18B-302(b), (i).
Violation by 19 or 20 year olds, §18B-302(i).
Open container law, §20-138.7(e).
Unlawful transportation, §18B-401(a).
Poisonous beverages, trafficking in, transporting or possessing, §14-329.

ALCOHOLIC BEVERAGES —Cont'd
Criminal offenses, criminal procedure —Cont'd
Possession.
Unlawful possession, §18B-102(b).
Sales.
Unauthorized sales, §18B-102(b).
Searches and seizures.
Disposition after trial of seized alcoholic
beverages, §18B-503(c).
Holding seized alcoholic beverages for
administrative hearings, §18B-503(d).
Sale proceeds from disposition of seized
alcoholic beverages, §18B-503(f).
Tax violations, punishment, §105-113.73.
Transportation.
Open container violations, §18B-401(a).
Unauthorized transportation, §18B-102(b).
Damaged alcoholic beverage sales, §18B-806.
Definitions, §18B-101.
ABC stores.
Gross receipts, §18B-805(a).
Beer franchises, §18B-1301.
Compensation for injury caused by sales to
underage persons, §18B-120.
Malt beverage, §18B-101.
Oceangoing vessel, §18B-106(b).
Permits.
Conviction, §18B-900(b).
Retail activities, §18B-1000.
Transportation.
Passenger area of a motor vehicle, §18B-401(c).
Wine distribution agreements, §18B-1201.
Denatured alcohol.
Exemption from alcoholic beverage provisions,
§18B-103.
Dentists.
Exemption from chapter, §18B-103.
Department of public safety.
Alcohol law enforcement agents.
Appointment by secretary, §18B-500.
Alcohol law enforcement section.
Defined, §18B-101.
Transfer to department, §143A-243.
Direct shipments into state.
Armed forces installations, §18B-109(b).
Indian country lands, §18B-109(b).
Out-of-state retailers or wholesalers.
Wholesaler's permit required, §18B-102.1(a).
Cease and desist orders, violations, issuance,
§18B-102.1(b).
Criminal penalty for violation, §18B-102.1(e).
Presumptive evidence of intent to violate
provision, §18B-102.1(b).
Producers holding permit from bureau of
alcohol, tobacco and firearms.
Illegal shipments, notice to bureau,
§18B-102.1(d).
Inapplicability of provisions, §18B-102.1(c).
Prohibited, §18B-109(a).
Wine purchased while visiting winery premises,
§18B-109(d).
Wine shipper permittees, §§18B-109(c),
18B-1001.1, 18B-1001.2.
Disabled persons.
Refusal to sell not to be discriminatory,
§18B-305(c).
Disasters.
Prohibitions and restrictions during state of
emergency.
County powers, §14-288.13.
Municipal powers, §14-288.12.

ALCOHOLIC BEVERAGES —Cont'd
Discrimination.
Refusal to sell not to be discriminatory,
§18B-305(c).
Tribal alcoholic beverage control.
Discrimination against non-Indians, prohibition,
§18B-112(g).
Disorderly conduct.
Prohibited on licensed premises, §18B-1005(a).
Disposition of seized beverages, §§18B-503,
18B-504.
Distilleries.
Display of spirits distilled in North Carolina in
ABC stores, §18B-800(e).
Permits.
Authorized acts, §18B-1105(a).
Commercial permits, §18B-1100.
Fuel alcohol, §18B-1105(b).
Spirituous liquor tasting permit, §18B-1001.
Fee, §18B-902(d).
Searches and seizures.
Disposition of seized, confiscated or unclaimed
property.
Provisions not applicable to whiskey
distilleries, §15-17.
Divorce.
Excessive use.
Grounds for divorce, §50-7.
Drivers' licenses.
Issuance to habitual drunkards, §20-9(c).
Revocation or suspension.
Mental incompetents, alcoholics and habitual
users, §20-17.1.
Underage purchasers of alcohol, §20-17.3.
Driving by person less than 21 years old after
consuming alcohol or drugs, §20-138.3.
Driving by provisional licensee after
consuming alcohol.
Restoration of license after conviction, §20-17.6.
Driving instruction.
Impaired instruction or supervision, §20-12.1(a),
(b).
Driving under the influence.
Generally.
See IMPAIRED DRIVING.
Drugs.
Prohibited on licensed premises, §18B-1005(a).
Drunk driving.
Generally.
See IMPAIRED DRIVING.
Eating establishment.
Defined, §18B-1000.
Education.
Alcohol addicted children.
Appropriate education provided for.
Policy of state to insure, §115C-149.
Children with special needs.
Alcohol addicted children excluded from
article, §115C-149.
Policy of state, §115C-149.
State board of education to adopt rules,
§115C-150.
Elections, §§18B-600 to 18B-605.
See LOCAL OPTION ELECTIONS.
Emergencies.
Powers of governor, §18B-110.
Prohibitions and restrictions during state of
emergency.
County powers, §14-288.13.
Municipal powers, §14-288.12.

ALCOHOLIC BEVERAGES —Cont'd
Employees of permittees.
  Actions of employees.
    Permittee's responsibility, §18B-1003(b).
  Prohibited employment.
    Certain persons, §18B-1003(c).
Employer discrimination for lawful use of lawful products during nonworking hours, §95-28.2.
Enforcement of ABC laws.
  Agents for law enforcement, §18B-500.
  Alcoholic beverage control commission.
    See ALCOHOLIC BEVERAGE CONTROL COMMISSION.
  Contracts with other law enforcement agencies.
    Alternative to hiring local enforcement officers, §18B-501(f).
  Department of public safety.
    Alcohol law enforcement agents.
      Appointment by secretary, §18B-500.
    Alcohol law enforcement section.
      Defined, §18B-101.
      Discharge for conviction of crime, §18B-202.
      Transfer to department, §143A-243.
  Enforcement agreements.
    Contract by local ABC boards with other law enforcement agencies, §18B-501(f).
  Forfeitures, §18B-504.
  Inspection of licensed premises, §18B-502.
  Local ABC board, §§18B-700 to 18B-706.
    See ABC BOARDS.
  Local ABC enforcement officers, §18B-501.
  Restitution to law enforcement agency, §18B-505.
  Seized beverages.
    Disposition, §18B-503.
Ethyl alcohol.
  Exemption from alcoholic beverage provisions, §18B-103.
Evidence.
  Compensation for injury caused by sales to underage persons.
    Admissibility, §18B-122.
  Possession for purpose of sale.
    Prima facie evidence.
      Possession by person not permitted to possess, §18B-304(b).
Exclusive outlets.
  "Giving things of value" defined, §18B-1116(c).
  Prohibited, §18B-1116(a).
    Exemptions, §18B-1116(b).
Exemptions from chapter, §18B-103.
  Exclusive outlets.
    Prohibited, §18B-1116(b).
Fake ID used to purchase.
  Sale to or purchase by underage persons, §18B-302(e).
  Conviction report to division, §18B-302(g).
Fighting.
  Prohibited on licensed premises, §18B-1005(a).
Financial operations.
  Local ABC boards, §18B-702.
Financial responsibility.
  Permittees, §18B-1003(d).
Firearms and other weapons.
  Alcohol remaining in body or blood.
    Carrying concealed handgun prohibited, §14-415.11(c2).
  Carrying concealed handgun while consuming.
    Prohibited, §14-415.11(c2).
  Establishments where alcoholic beverages are sold and consumed.
    Carrying weapons into establishments, §14-269.3(a), (b).

ALCOHOLIC BEVERAGES —Cont'd
Flavor extracts.
  Exemption from alcoholic beverage provisions, §18B-103.
Flying under the influence, §63-27.
  Infliction of serious bodily injury, §63-28.
Food business.
  Defined, §18B-1000.
  Urban redevelopment area location.
    Sales of beverages, §18B-309.
      ABC permit suspension or revocation for violation, §18B-904(e).
Food, drug and cosmetic act.
  Foods deemed to be adulterated, §106-129.
Forfeiture.
  Custody until trial, §18B-504(d).
  Defendant unavailable, §18B-504(i).
  Disposition.
    After trial, §18B-504(e).
    Manner of disposition, §18B-504(f).
  Exemptions from forfeiture, §18B-504(b).
  Innocent parties.
    Protection of interest, §18B-504(h).
  Property subject to forfeiture, §18B-504(a).
  Return of property.
    Innocent parties, §18B-504(h).
    When no charges made, §18B-504(j).
  Sales.
    Disposition of forfeited property, §18B-504(f).
    Proceeds of sale, §18B-504(g).
  Seizure of property, §18B-504(c).
  Unavailability of defendant, §18B-504(i).
Fortified wine.
  Consumption, §18B-301(d).
  Defined, §18B-101.
  Possession, §18B-301.
  Transportation.
    Holder of permit for retail sales, §18B-405.
Fraudulent use of identification to purchase, §18B-302(e).
  Allowing use of identification, §18B-302(f).
  Conviction report to division, §18B-302(g).
Fuel alcohol.
  Distilleries.
    Permits, §18B-1105(b).
Gambling.
  Allowing gambling in houses of public entertainment, §14-293.
  Prohibited on licensed premises, §18B-1005(a).
Hearing officers.
  Appointment, §18B-200(d).
Home brewing.
  Making wines and malt beverages for private use, §18B-306.
Hospitals.
  Exemption from provisions, §18B-103.
Hospitals for mentally disordered.
  Furnishing to inmates, §14-258.1(b).
Hotel.
  Defined, §18B-1000.
Hours for sale and consumption, §18B-1004.
  ABC stores, §18B-802.
Hours of sale.
  Ball parks and stadiums.
    In-stand sales, §18B-1006(q).
  Sunday hours, §18B-1004(c).
Identification documents used to purchase.
  Allowing use of identification, §18B-302(f).
    Conviction report to division, §18B-302(g).
  Failure to show proper identification.
    Refusal to sell or furnish beverages.
      No liability, §18B-129(a).

ALCOHOLIC BEVERAGES —Cont'd
Identification documents used to purchase
—Cont'd
Fraudulent use of identification, §18B-302(e).
Conviction report to division, §18B-302(g).
Holding customer's ID in attempt to determine
age.
No liability, §18B-129(b).
Illicit mixed beverages or spirituous liquors.
Unauthorized substances taxes, §§105-113.105 to
105-113.113.
See UNAUTHORIZED SUBSTANCES TAXES.
Immunity of permittee, agent or employees.
Failure to show proper identification.
Refusal to sell, §18B-129(a).
Holding customer's ID while attempting to
determine age, §18B-129(b).
Impaired driving.
Generally.
See IMPAIRED DRIVING.
Implied warranty of merchantability.
Sale of goods, UCC, §25-2-314.
Imports and exports.
Denatured alcohol.
Exemption from provisions, §18B-103.
Liquor importer/bottler permit, §18B-1105.1.
Malt beverages.
Authorization of permit, §18B-1108.
Unauthorized imports and exports prohibited,
§18B-102(a).
Violation a misdemeanor, §18B-102(b).
Wine.
Distribution agreements, §18B-1106(b).
Permits, §18B-1106(a).
Primary American source of supply of wine.
Recognition of importer as, §18B-203(a).
Sales to wholesalers by importer permittee,
§18B-1106(c).
Inhalants.
Alcohol vaporizing devices, §90-113.10A.
Insolvency of local ABC system.
Closing, §18B-801(d).
Inspections.
Authority to inspect licensed premises,
§18B-502(a).
Interference with inspections, §18B-502(b).
State warehouse.
Private warehouses, §18B-204(b).
In-stand sales at ball parks or stadiums,
§18B-1009.
Hours of sale, §18B-1006(q).
Instruction on driving vehicle.
Impaired instruction or supervision, §20-12.1(a),
(b).
Intent of chapter, §18B-100.
Interstate interchange economic development
zones.
Permit for businesses, §18B-1006(m).
Intoxicated persons.
Sales to, §18B-305(a).
Intoxication in public, §§14-443 to 14-447.
Investigations.
Expenses.
Restitution, §18B-505.
Law enforcement agents, §18B-500.
Local ABC officers, §18B-501.
Permits.
Prior to issuance, §18B-902(b).
Restitution.
Expenses, §18B-505.
Joint store operation, §18B-703(h).

ALCOHOLIC BEVERAGES —Cont'd
Jurisdiction.
Law enforcement agents, §18B-500.
Local ABC officers, §18B-501.
Kegs.
Malt beverages.
Amounts that may be purchased, §18B-303(a).
Defined, §18B-101.
Purchase-transportation permit, off-premises
consumption.
Copy.
Purchaser and permittee to keep,
§18B-403.1(d).
Retention by off-premises permittee, time
period, §18B-403.1(b).
Display to law enforcement.
Duty of purchaser, §18B-403.1(d).
Form adopted by commission, §18B-403.1(c).
Issuance by off-premises permittee,
§18B-403.1(b).
Purchase from store named on permit,
§18B-403.1(d).
Required to purchase and transport for
off-premises consumption, §18B-403.1(a).
Warning to permittee, first violation,
§18B-403.1(e).
Law enforcement agents.
Appointment, §18B-500(a).
Discharge, §18B-500(e).
Jurisdiction.
Subject matter jurisdiction, §18B-500(b).
Territorial jurisdiction, §18B-500(c).
Service of process.
Orders of commission, §18B-500(d).
Subject matter jurisdiction, §18B-500(b).
Territorial jurisdiction, §18B-500(c).
Licenses.
Local licenses.
City beer and wine retail licenses,
§105-113.77(a).
City wholesaler license, §105-113.79.
County beer and wine retail licenses,
§105-113.78.
Suspension or revocation of permit.
Effect on licenses, §18B-104(d).
Local ABC boards, §§18B-700 to 18B-706.
See ABC BOARDS.
Local ABC enforcement officers.
Accountability, enforcement reports, §18B-501(f).
Appointment, §18B-501(a).
Assisting other local agencies, §18B-501(d).
Assisting state and federal enforcement,
§18B-501(e).
Contracts with other agencies.
Alternative to hiring local officers, §18B-501(f).
Discharge, §18B-501(g).
Jurisdiction.
Subject matter jurisdiction, §18B-501(b).
Territorial jurisdiction, §18B-501(c).
Local ABC systems.
Boards, §§18B-700 to 18B-706.
See ABC BOARDS.
Enforcement officers, §18B-501.
Stores, §§18B-800 to 18B-808.
See ABC STORES.
Local option elections, §§18B-600 to 18B-605.
See LOCAL OPTION ELECTIONS.
Lockers.
Private clubs, §18B-1006(b).
Lottery law.
Defined, §18B-101.

ALCOHOLIC BEVERAGES —Cont'd
Lottery law —Cont'd
Enforcement by alcohol law enforcement agents, §18B-500(b).
Magistrates.
Powers in cases involving alcohol offenses, §7A-273.
Mailing alcoholic beverages from outside state, §18B-109(a).
Major league professional sports teams with suites available for sale or lease.
Special occasion permit issued to sports facility occupied by.
Patron of suites authorized to furnish alcoholic beverages.
Hosting reception, parties or other special occasions, §18B-1006(p).
Malt beverages.
Amounts that may be purchased, §18B-303(a).
Beer franchises generally, §§18B-1300 to 18B-1308.
See BEER FRANCHISES.
Breweries.
Authorization permit, §18B-1104.
Power to issue, §18B-1001.
Commercial permits, §18B-1100.
Consumption, §18B-300.
Defined, §18B-101.
Elections.
Determination of results, §18B-602(b).
Effect, §18B-604.
Issuance of permits, §18B-603(a).
Form of ballot, §18B-602(e).
Subsequent elections, §18B-602(c).
Hours for sale, §18B-1004.
Importers.
Permits.
Authorization, §18B-1108.
Kegs.
Amounts that may be purchased, §18B-303(a).
Defined, §18B-101.
Purchase-transportation permit, off-premises consumption.
Copy.
Purchaser and permittee to keep, §18B-403.1(d).
Retention by off-premises permittee, time period, §18B-403.1(b).
Display to law enforcement.
Duty of purchaser, §18B-403.1(d).
Form adopted by commission, §18B-403.1(c).
Issuance by off-premises permittee, §18B-403.1(b).
Purchase from store named on permit, §18B-403.1(d).
Required to purchase and transport for off-premises consumption, §18B-403.1(a).
Warning to permittee, first violation, §18B-403.1(e).
Making for private use, §18B-306.
Permits.
Commercial permits, §18B-1100.
Elections.
Effect on issuance of permits, §18B-603(a).
Fees, §18B-902(d).
Off-premises permit, §18B-1001.
On-premises permit, §18B-1001.
Special event permit, §18B-1100.
Authorization, §18B-1114.5.
Fees, §18B-902(d).

ALCOHOLIC BEVERAGES —Cont'd
Malt beverages —Cont'd
Permits —Cont'd
Tasting permit, §18B-1001.
Fees, §18B-902(d).
Rail line agents.
Sale and delivery to, §18B-108.
Recycling containers.
Plan for collection and recycling.
Submission by on-premises permit applicant, §§18B-902(h), 18B-903(b2).
Tastings on premises, §18B-1001.
Transportation.
Holder of permit for retail sales, §18B-405.
Vendors.
Nonresident vendors.
Authorization of permit, §18B-1113.
Wholesalers.
Beer franchises generally, §§18B-1300 to 18B-1308.
See BEER FRANCHISES.
Permits.
Authorization, §18B-1109(a).
Management of establishment.
Change in manager.
Substitution of manager, submission, §18B-903(d).
Manufacturers.
Cider.
Commercial permits, §18B-1100.
Exemption from provisions, §18B-103.
Private use.
Wines and malt beverages, §18B-306.
Second offense of manufacturing, §18B-307(c).
Unauthorized manufacture prohibited, §18B-102(a).
Violation a misdemeanor, §18B-102(b).
Unlawful manufacturing, §18B-307(a), (b).
Vinegar.
Commercial permits, §18B-1100.
Exemption from provisions, §18B-103.
Wines and malt beverages.
Private use, §18B-306.
Merchantability, implied warranty.
Sale of goods, UCC, §25-2-314.
Merger of local operations.
Cities and counties, board for merged system, §18B-703.
Military affairs.
Direct shipment of beverages into state.
Armed forces installations, §18B-109(b).
Minors.
Alcoholism.
Consent of minor to treatment, §90-21.5(a).
Consumption.
Alcohol screening test.
Authority of law enforcement to require, §18B-302(j).
Evidence in court or administrative proceeding.
Results, refusal to submit to, §18B-302(j).
Exempt activities, §18B-302(k).
Prohibition, §18B-302(b).
Exempt activities, §18B-302(k).
Misdemeanor, violation by 19 and 20 year olds, §18B-302(i).
Conviction reports.
Sent to division of motor vehicles, §18B-302(g).
Defenses.
Sales to, §18B-302(d).

ALCOHOLIC BEVERAGES —Cont'd
Minors —Cont'd
Driving after consuming alcohol.
  Restoration of driver's license after conviction,
    §20-17.6.
Driving by person less than 21 years old after
  consuming alcohol or drugs, §20-138.3.
Employment of youth by person holding ABC
  permits, §95-25.5(j).
Fines and other penalties, §18B-302.1.
Fraudulent use of identification to purchase,
  §18B-302(e).
  Allowing use, §18B-302(f).
Giving to.
  Conviction report sent to division of motor
    vehicles, §18B-302(g).
  Fines and other penalties, §18B-302.1(a).
  Prohibited, §18B-302(a1).
Handling in course of employment, §18B-302(h).
Purchase or possession.
  Aiding and abetting, §18B-302(c).
  Conviction reports to division of motor vehicles,
    §18B-302(g).
  Driver's license.
    Allowing use of license, §18B-302(f).
    Fraudulent use, §18B-302(e).
    Revocation for underage purchase of alcohol,
      §20-17.3.
  Fraudulent use of identification.
    Allowing use, §18B-302(f).
  Nineteen or twenty year olds, §18B-302(i).
  Prohibited, §18B-302(b), (i).
Sales to.
  Aiding and abetting, §18B-302(c).
  Conviction report sent to division of motor
    vehicles, §18B-302(g).
  Defense to violation of subsection, §18B-302(d).
  Fines and other penalties, §18B-302.1(a), (b).
  Fraudulent use of identification to purchase,
    §18B-302(e).
  Prohibited, §18B-302(a).
Mixed beverages.
Airports.
  Elections.
    Effect of election on issuance of permit,
      §18B-603(e).
Defined, §18B-101.
Elections.
  ABC store election held simultaneously,
    §18B-603(d2).
  Airports.
    Effect of election on issuance of permits,
      §18B-603(e).
  City elections, §18B-600(e).
    Small city elections, §18B-600(e1).
  Form of ballot, §18B-602(h).
  Permits.
    Effect of election on issuance, §18B-603(d).
    Three cities within county approving.
    When county may approve mixed beverage
      sales throughout county, §18B-603(d1).
Handling of bottles.
  Restrictions, §18B-1007(b).
Hours for sale, §18B-1004.
Insolvency or closure of local ABC system.
  Purchase by permittees from another ABC
    board, §18B-203.
Permits, §18B-1001.
  Additional requirements for permittees,
    §18B-1007.

ALCOHOLIC BEVERAGES —Cont'd
Mixed beverages —Cont'd
Permits —Cont'd
  Elections.
    Effect of elections on issuance, §18B-603(d).
    Airports, §18B-603(e).
  Hotels and restaurants in national historic
    landmark district, §18B-1006(n).
  Temporary permit for new permittee to continue
    business at same location, §18B-1007(d).
Price list.
  Available to customers, §18B-1007(c).
Purchases.
  Designated ABC store, §18B-1007(a).
    City mixed beverage permittees, §18B-600(e).
      Smaller city mixed beverage permittees,
        §18B-600(e1).
    Ski resort permittees, §18B-600(e2).
    Small resort town permittees, §18B-600(e5).
    Small town mixed beverage permittees,
      §18B-600(e3).
  Insolvency or closure of local ABC system.
    Purchase from another ABC board, §18B-203.
Recycling containers.
  Plan for collection and recycling.
    Submission by mixed beverage permit
      applicant, §§18B-902(h), 18B-903(b2).
Transportation.
  Permits, §18B-404.
Moonshining, §18B-307.
Unauthorized substances taxes, §§105-113.105 to
  105-113.113.
See UNAUTHORIZED SUBSTANCES TAXES.
Motor vehicles.
Chemical analysis of impairing substances in
  blood generally.
See IMPAIRED DRIVING.
Commercial vehicle, operating after consuming
  alcohol, §20-138.2A.
  Odor of alcohol.
    Evidentiary effect, §20-138.2A(b1).
    Screening test for alcohol, §20-138.2A(b2).
Confiscation.
  Vehicles used in illegal transportation.
    Reports by officers, §20-114(c).
Habitual drunkards.
  Issuance of drivers' licenses prohibited, §20-9(c).
Impaired driving generally.
See IMPAIRED DRIVING.
Impaired instruction or supervision, §20-12.1(a),
  (b).
Manner of transportation, §18B-401.
Minors.
  Drivers' licenses.
    Revocation for underage purchases, §20-17.3.
    Use of fraudulent license to purchase,
      §18B-302.
Open bottle violations, §18B-401(a).
  Mandatory revocation of driver's license,
    §20-17(a).
  Period of suspension or revocation, §20-19(g1).
Motor vehicles defined, §20-138.7(a3).
Ordinances regulating, §18B-300(c).
Possession or consumption of alcoholic beverage
  in passenger compartment, §20-138.7(a1).
  Exceptions, §20-138.7(a2).
Transporting open container in passenger area
  and while driver consuming alcohol,
    §20-138.7.
  Alcoholic beverage defined, §20-138.7(f).
  General offense, §20-138.7(a).

ALCOHOLIC BEVERAGES —Cont'd
Motor vehicles —Cont'd
Open bottle violations —Cont'd
Transporting open container in passenger area
and while driver consuming alcohol
—Cont'd
Implied consent law, offense subject to,
§20-138.7(b).
Implied driving offense also charged,
§20-138.7(e).
Limited driving privilege, §20-138.7(h).
Misdemeanor for violating, §20-138.7(e).
Motor vehicle defined, §20-138.7(a3).
Odor insufficient to prove alcohol remaining
in driver body, §20-138.7(c).
Open container defined, §20-138.7(f).
Passenger area of motor vehicle defined,
§20-138.7(f).
Pleading in prosecution for violation,
§20-138.7(g).
Possession or consumption in passenger
compartment, §20-138.7(a1), (a2).
Screening test, §20-138.7(d).
School bus, operating after consuming alcohol,
§20-138.2B.
Municipalities.
Confinement facilities.
Furnishing alcoholic beverages to inmates,
§14-258.1.
Licenses.
City beer and wine retail licenses,
§105-113.77(a).
City wholesaler license, §105-113.79.
Local ABC boards.
See ABC BOARDS.
Local option elections generally, §§18B-600 to
18B-605.
See LOCAL OPTION ELECTIONS.
Location of ABC store within corporate limits.
Objection to location by governing body,
§18B-801(b1).
Ordinances.
Consumption.
Malt beverages and unfortified wine,
§18B-300(c).
Restriction on ordinances, §18B-100.
National origin.
Refusal to sell not to be discriminatory,
§18B-305(c).
Native Americans.
Direct shipments into state.
Indian country lands, §18B-109(b).
Tribal alcoholic beverage control.
Appeal of actions of tribal control commission,
§18B-112(h).
Applicability of provisions, §18B-112(a).
Authority of state control commission,
§18B-112(f).
Commission to be established, §18B-112(d).
Compliance with certain provisions required,
§18B-112(b).
Conflicts of law, §18B-112(j).
Discrimination against non-Indians, prohibition,
§18B-112(g).
Failure of tribe to comply with state laws,
§18B-112(i).
Fines and penalties paid to commission,
§18B-112(h).
Rules of state control commission to be adopted,
§18B-112(e).

ALCOHOLIC BEVERAGES —Cont'd
Native Americans —Cont'd
Tribal alcoholic beverage control —Cont'd
Sale of approved alcoholic beverages only,
§18B-112(c).
Nonresidents.
Direct shipments into state.
Out-of-state retailers and wholesalers,
§18B-102.1.
Malt beverage vendor.
Permit.
Authorization, §18B-1113.
Restrictions on sale by nonresident vendors,
§18B-1118.
Wine vendors.
Authorization of permit, §18B-1114.
North Carolina distilled spirits.
Display of spirits in ABC stores, §18B-800(d).
Nuisances.
Offenses against public morals.
Abatement generally, §§19-1 to 19-8.3.
See NUISANCES.
Oceangoing ships.
Use on, §18B-106.
Off-premises establishment.
Consumption.
Malt beverages and unfortified wine,
§18B-300(b).
Open container law, §18B-401(a).
Mandatory revocation of driver's license,
§20-17(a).
Period of suspension or revocation, §20-19(g1).
Manner of transportation, §18B-401(a).
Ordinances regulating open containers,
§18B-300(c).
Transporting open container in passenger area
and while driver consuming alcohol.
Alcohol beverage defined, §20-138.7(f).
General offense, §20-138.7(a).
Implied consent law, offense subject to,
§20-138.7(b).
Implied driving offense also charged,
§20-138.7(e).
Limited driving privilege, §20-138.7(h).
Misdemeanor for violation, §20-138.7(e).
Motor vehicle defined, §20-138.7(a3).
Odor on breath of driver insufficient to prove
alcohol remaining in body, §20-138.7(c).
Open container defined, §20-138.7(f).
Passenger area of vehicle defined, §20-138.7(f).
Pleading in prosecution, §20-138.7(g).
Possession or consumption in passenger
compartment, §20-138.7(a1), (a2).
Screening test, §20-138.7(d).
**Operating a commercial vehicle after
consuming alcohol,** §20-138.2A.
Odor of alcohol.
Evidentiary effect, §20-138.2A(b1).
Screening test for alcohol, §20-138.2A(b2).
**Operating a school bus, school activity bus, or
child care vehicle after consuming alcohol,**
§20-138.2B.
Odor of alcohol.
Evidentiary effect, §20-138.2B(b1).
Screening for alcohol, §20-138.2B(b2).
Ordinances.
Consumption.
Malt beverages and unfortified wine,
§18B-300(c).
Restrictions on ordinances, §18B-100.

ALCOHOLIC BEVERAGES —Cont'd
Out-of-state purchases.
Limitation, §18B-402.
Transportation, §18B-402.
Out-of-state retailers and wholesalers.
Direct shipments into state, §18B-102.1.
Ownership of establishment, change.
Automatic expiration of permit, surrender,
§18B-903(c).
Penalties.
Administrative penalties, §18B-104.
Compromise, §18B-104(b).
Disposition, §18B-104(c).
Permits.
See ABC PERMITS.
Pharmaceutical products.
Exemption from provisions, §18B-103.
Physicians and surgeons.
Exemption from chapter, §18B-103.
Poisons.
Manufacture of poisonous liquors, §14-329(a).
Trafficking in, transporting or possessing
poisonous liquors, §14-329(b) to (d).
Possession.
Evidence.
Possession for purpose of sale.
Possession by person not permitted to
possess, §18B-304(b).
Fortified wine and spirituous liquor.
Amount, §18B-301(b).
Incident to sale, §18B-301(e).
Possession at home, §18B-301(a).
Special occasions, §18B-301(c).
Unlawful possession or use, §18B-301(f).
Malt beverages and unfortified wine.
General provisions, §18B-300(a).
Sales.
Possession for purpose of sale, §18B-304(a).
Unauthorized possession prohibited, §18B-102(a).
Violation a misdemeanor, §18B-102(b).
Unlawful possession or consumption.
Possession not authorized by permits,
§18B-1006(d).
Pregnancy, consumption during.
Signs warning of dangers.
Design, size, contents, §18B-808(c).
Development, §18B-808(b).
Display, ABC stores, §18B-808(a), (d).
Distribution and posting, §18B-203(a).
Fee, §18B-808(b).
Premises.
Defined, §18B-101.
Permittee's responsibilities, §18B-1003(a).
Primary American source of supply of wine.
Wine importers and nonresident vendors.
Recognition, §18B-203(a).
Sales by importer permittee to wholesalers,
§18B-1106(c).
Sales by nonresident wine vendors, §18B-1114.
Prisons and prisoners.
Employees.
Use of intoxicants, narcotic drugs or profanity,
§148-23.
Furnishing alcoholic beverages to inmates,
§14-258.1(b).
Private club.
Defined, §18B-1000.
Lockers, §18B-1006(b).
Permits.
Residential private clubs, §18B-1006(k).

ALCOHOLIC BEVERAGES —Cont'd
**Private use, making wines and malt beverages
for,** §18B-306.
Property.
Allowing property to be used for manufacture of
beverage, §18B-307(a).
Prostitution.
Prohibited on licensed premises, §18B-1005(a).
Public intoxication, §§14-443 to 14-447.
Public schools.
Alcohol addicted children.
Appropriate education provided for.
Policy of state to insure, §115C-149.
Children with special needs.
Excluded from provisions of article,
§115C-149.
Policy of state, §115C-149.
State board of education to adopt rules,
§115C-150.
Basic education program.
Alcohol and drug education program,
§115C-81(a3).
Instruction in dangers of harmful or illegal
drugs, including alcohol, §115C-81(c).
Discipline of students.
Driving eligibility certificate.
Effect of disciplinary action for enumerated
student conduct, §20-11(n1).
Property owned or leased by local board of
education and used for school purposes.
Possession and consumption of fortified wine
and spirituous liquor upon, §18B-301(f).
Purchases.
Amount purchased, §18B-303(a).
Greater amounts, §18B-303(c).
Unlawful purchases, §18B-303(b).
Exclusive outlets.
"Giving things of value" defined, §18B-1116(c).
Prohibited, §18B-1116(a).
Exemptions, §18B-1116(b).
Malt beverages and unfortified wine.
General provisions, §18B-300(a).
Minors, prohibition, §18B-302(b), (i).
Mixed beverages.
Designated ABC store, §18B-1007(a).
City mixed beverage permittees, §18B-600(e).
Smaller city mixed beverage permittees,
§18B-600(e1).
Ski resort permittees, §18B-600(e2).
Small resort town permittees, §18B-600(e5).
Small town mixed beverage permittees,
§18B-600(e3).
Insolvency or closure of local ABC system.
Purchase from another ABC board by
permittees, §18B-203.
Out of state purchases.
Transportation, §18B-402.
Purchase-transportation permits, §§18B-403 to
18B-405.
Purchasing in greater amounts than allowed,
§18B-303(c).
Purpose of chapter, §18B-100.
Racial minorities.
Refusal to sell not to be discriminatory,
§18B-305(c).
Raffles.
Sale or consumption, §18B-308.
Railroads.
Local option elections.
Passenger terminus locations, §18B-600(h).

ALCOHOLIC BEVERAGES —Cont'd
Railroads —Cont'd
Malt beverages and wine.
Sale and delivery to rail line agents, §18B-108.
Operating trains and streetcars while intoxicated,
§14-281.
Sale on trains, §18B-108.
Recreation districts.
Permits, §18B-1006(j).
**Recycling requirements for certain permit
holders.**
Beverage containers, §18B-1006.1.
Disposal of in landfills or by incineration.
Prohibited, §130A-309.10(f3).
Plan to collect and recycle submitted with
application, §§18B-902(h), 18B-903(b2).
Refusal to sell, discretion for seller,
§18B-305(b).
Religion.
Sacramental wine.
Exemption from provisions, §18B-103.
Religious discrimination.
Refusal to sell not to be discriminatory,
§18B-305(c).
Reports.
Required reports, §18B-205(a).
Research.
Manufacture, possession, consumption for
purposes of.
Exemption from provisions, §18B-103.
Residential private club.
Defined, §18B-1000.
Responsibilities of permittees, §18B-1003.
Restaurant.
Defined, §18B-1000.
Restitution.
Expenses of investigation, §18B-505.
Retail business.
Defined, §18B-1000.
Purchase from wholesalers with business in state
and proper permit, §18B-1006(h).
Riots and civil disorders.
Prohibitions and restrictions during state of
emergency.
County powers, §14-288.13.
Roller skating rink operators.
Duty to prohibit sale or use, §99E-11.
Rules and regulations.
ABC stores.
Promulgation, §18B-807.
Advertising.
Authority of commission, §18B-105(b).
Effective date.
Promulgation by commission, §18B-207.
Permits.
Retail permits.
Promulgation by commission, §18B-1008.
Promulgation.
Authority of commission, §18B-207.
Ships and shipping.
Use on oceangoing ships, §18B-106(c).
State warehouse.
Promulgation, §18B-204(d).
Sacramental wine.
Exemption from provisions, §18B-103.
Salaries.
Commission.
Chairman, §18B-200(a).
Sales.
ABC stores, 18B-800 to §18B-808.
See ABC STORES.

ALCOHOLIC BEVERAGES —Cont'd
Sales —Cont'd
Aviation.
Use in air commerce, §18B-107(b).
Ball parks or stadiums.
In-stand sales, §18B-1009.
Hours of sale, §18B-1006(q).
Bingo games, §18B-308.
Cider.
Exemption from provisions, §18B-103.
Damaged alcoholic beverages, §18B-806.
Defined, §18B-101.
Discretion for seller, §18B-305(b).
Discriminatory refusals prohibited, §18B-305(c).
Distilled in North Carolina.
Display of spirits in ABC stores, §18B-800(e).
Exclusive outlets.
"Giving things of value" defined, §18B-1116(c).
Prohibited, §18B-1116(a).
Exemptions, §18B-1116(b).
Fraudulent use of identification to purchase,
§18B-302(e).
Hours of sale, §18B-1004(a).
Applicability of section, §18B-1004(e).
Ball parks and stadiums.
In stand sales, §18B-1006(q).
Exemption from section, §18B-1004(e).
Local option, §18B-1004(d).
Sunday hours, §18B-1004(c).
Implied warranty of merchantability, §25-2-314.
In-stand sales.
Ball parks or stadiums, §18B-1009.
Hours of sale, §18B-1006(q).
Intoxicated persons, §18B-305(a).
Minors.
Prohibited sales, §18B-302.
Nonresidents.
Restrictions on sales by nonresident vendors,
§18B-1118.
Nontaxpaid alcoholic beverages, §18B-111.
Out-of-state purchases.
Limitation, §18B-402.
Possession for purpose of sale.
Prima facie evidence.
Possession by person not permitted to
possess, §18B-304(b).
Unlawful possession, §18B-304(a).
Rail line agents.
Malt beverages and wine.
Sale and delivery to, §18B-108.
Refusal to sell.
Discretion for seller, §18B-305(b).
Discriminatory refusals prohibited, §18B-305(c).
Salesmen.
Permits, §18B-1111.
Seized alcoholic beverages, §§18B-503, 18B-504.
Trains, §18B-108.
Unauthorized sales prohibited, §18B-102(a).
Violation a misdemeanor, §18B-102(b).
Urban redevelopment areas.
Sales within, §18B-309.
ABC permit suspension or revocation for
violation, §18B-904(e).
Vinegar.
Exemption from provisions, §18B-103.
When sales stop.
Effect of election, §18B-604(f).
Wine.
List of approved wines, §18B-1006(c).
Sales and use tax.
Rate of tax on sale of spirituous liquor other than
mixed beverages, §105-164.4(a).

ALCOHOLIC BEVERAGES —Cont'd
Sales and use tax —Cont'd
Refunds, inapplicability, §105-164.14(d1).
School buses.
Operating after consuming alcohol, §20-138.2B.
Odor of alcohol.
Evidentiary effect, §20-138.2B(b1).
Screening for alcohol, §20-138.2B(b2).
Schools.
Discipline of students.
Driving eligibility certificate.
Effect of disciplinary action for enumerated
student conduct, §20-11(n1).
Permits.
Business located on campus, §18B-1006(a).
Property owned or leased by local board of
education and used for school purposes.
Possession and consumption of fortified wine
and spirituous liquor upon, §18B-301(f).
Searches and seizures.
Disposition of seized alcoholic beverages,
§§18B-503, 18B-504.
Whiskey distilleries.
Disposition of seized, confiscated or unclaimed
property.
Provisions not to apply to whiskey distilleries,
§15-17.
Secured transactions.
Wholesalers.
Security interest of supplier in inventory or
property of wholesaler, §18B-1119(c).
Sexual discrimination.
Refusal to sell not to be discriminatory,
§18B-305(c).
Sexually explicit conduct.
Prohibited on licensed premises, §18B-1005.1(a).
Exceptions, §18B-1005.1(c).
Ships and shipping.
Commercial transportation.
Malt beverages and wine, §18B-1115(f).
Use on oceangoing ships.
Delivery permitted, §18B-106(a).
"Oceangoing vessel" defined, §18B-106(b).
Promulgation of rules and regulations,
§18B-106(c).
Special education.
Alcohol addicted children excluded from provisions
of article, §115C-149.
Spirituous liquor.
ABC stores.
See ABC STORES.
Consumption, §18B-301.
Defined, §18B-101.
Display of spirits distilled in North Carolina,
§18B-800(d).
Liquor importer/bottler permit.
Authorizations, §18B-1105.1.
Possession, §18B-301.
Tasting permit, §18B-1001.
Conditions for conducting consumer tastings,
§18B-1001.
Fee, §18B-902(d).
Liability for violations, §18B-1001.
No charge to consumers, §18B-1001.
Transportation.
Commercial transportation, §18B-1115.
Sports clubs.
Defined, §18B-1000.

ALCOHOLIC BEVERAGES —Cont'd
Sports clubs —Cont'd
Permits, §18B-1006(k).
Sale of malt beverages, unfortified wine, or
mixed beverages and operation of ABC
system allowed in six cities and counties.
Issuance of permits to sports clubs
throughout county, §18B-603(h).
Stadiums.
In-stand sales, §18B-1009.
Hours of sale, §18B-1006(q).
Standards for alcoholic beverages.
Authority to establish, §18B-206(a).
Effective date, §18B-206(b).
Testing, §18B-206(c).
State of emergency.
Powers of governor, §18B-110.
Prohibitions and restrictions during.
County powers, §14-288.13.
Municipal powers, §14-288.12.
State warehouse.
Audits, §18B-204(b).
Commercial transportation, §18B-1115(g).
Contracts.
Private warehouses, §18B-204(a).
Inspections, §18B-204(b).
Private warehouses.
Contracting for private warehouses,
§18B-204(a).
Emergency operation, §18B-204(c).
Temporary operation, §18B-204(c).
Rules and regulations.
Promulgation, §18B-204(d).
Transportation by state warehouse carrier,
§18B-1115(g).
Storage.
Warehouse receipts.
Storage under government bond, §25-7-201(b).
Sundays.
Hours of sale, §18B-1004(c).
Supervision of licensed premises.
Permittee or manager, §§18B-1005.1(b),
18B-1005(b).
Taxation.
General provisions.
See ALCOHOLIC BEVERAGES TAX.
Local license taxes, §§105-113.77 to 105-113.79.
Nontaxpaid alcoholic beverages.
Defined, §18B-101.
Possession, transportation or sale, §18B-111.
Unauthorized substances taxes, §§105-113.105 to
105-113.113.
See UNAUTHORIZED SUBSTANCES TAXES.
Taxicabs.
Transportation of alcoholic beverages,
§18B-401(b).
Time.
Hours for sale and consumption, §18B-1004.
Tour boats.
Permits.
Restrictions on sales on tour boats,
§18B-1006(i).
Restrictions on sales on tour boats, §18B-1006(i).
Tourism ABC establishment.
Defined, §18B-101.
Transportation.
Alcoholic beverages purchased out of state,
§18B-402.
Amounts that may be transported, §18B-400.
Transportation in greater amounts, §18B-406.

ALCOHOLIC BEVERAGES —Cont'd
Transportation —Cont'd
Commercial transportation.
  Boats.
    Malt beverages and wine, §18B-1115(f).
  Common carriers, §18B-1115(c).
  Motor vehicle carriers, §18B-1115(d).
  Permit.
    Required, §18B-1115.
  Spirituous liquor, §18B-1115(e).
  State warehouse carrier, §18B-1115(g).
  When transportation legal, §18B-1115(b).
  Wine.
    Boats, §18B-1115.
Definitions.
  Passenger area of a motor vehicle, §18B-401(c).
Direct shipment into state, §18B-109.
Excess amounts, §18B-406.
Limitation upon out-of-state purchases, §18B-402.
Malt beverages and unfortified or fortified wines.
  Transportation by permittee, §18B-405.
Manner of transportation.
  Open container, §18B-401(a).
    Mandatory revocation of license, §20-17(a).
    Ordinances regulating, §18B-300(c).
    Transporting open container in passenger
      area of vehicle and while driver
      consuming alcohol, §20-138.7.
  Taxis, §18B-401(b).
Nontaxpaid alcoholic beverages, §18B-111.
Open container, §18B-401(a).
  Mandatory revocation of driver's license,
    §20-17(a).
  Open container in passenger area of vehicle and
    while driver consuming alcohol, §20-138.7.
  Ordinances regulating, §18B-300(c).
Out of state purchases, §18B-402.
Purchase-transportation permits.
  Amount authorized to purchase and transport,
    §18B-403(a).
  Commercial transportation, §18B-1115.
  Display, §18B-403(e).
  Disqualifications of applicant, §18B-403(c).
  Form, §18B-403(d).
  Issuance, §18B-403(b).
    Disqualifications of applicant, §18B-403(c).
    Mixed beverage permits, §18B-404(b).
  Malt beverages and unfortified or fortified wine.
    Transportation by permittee, §18B-405.
  Mixed beverage permits.
    Designated employee, §18B-404(a).
    Designated stores, §18B-404(c).
    Issuance, §18B-404(b).
    Size of bottles, §18B-404(d).
  Purchasing in greater amounts than allowed,
    §18B-303(c).
  Restrictions on permit, §18B-403(e).
  Special occasions, §18B-403(g).
  Time permit valid, §18B-403(f).
Taxis.
  Restrictions, §18B-401(b).
Unauthorized transportation prohibited,
  §18B-102(a), (b).
Unlawful transportation.
  Excess amounts, §18B-406.
Tribal alcoholic beverage control, §18B-112.
Unfortified wine.
Consumption, §18B-300.
Permits.
  Elections.
    Effect of election on issuance, §18B-603(b).

ALCOHOLIC BEVERAGES —Cont'd
Unfortified wine —Cont'd
Transportation.
  Holder of permit for retail sales, §18B-405.
Unincorporated areas.
Defined, §18B-101.
Universities and colleges.
Permits.
  Business located on campus, §18B-1006(a).
  Viticulture/oenology course authorization,
    §18B-1114.4.
Urban redevelopment designated areas.
Percentage of total alcohol sales to total business
  sales, §18B-309(a).
Investigation and report by commission,
  §18B-309(b).
Records required of business, filing
  requirements, §18B-309(c).
Vendors.
Malt beverages.
  Nonresident vendor.
    Authorization, §18B-1113.
    Restrictions on sales by nonresident vendor,
      §18B-1118.
  Representatives.
    Permits.
      Authorization, §18B-1112.
Wine vendors.
  Nonresident vendor.
    Authorization of permit, §18B-1114.
    Restrictions on sale by nonresident vendor,
      §18B-1118.
Vinegar.
Commercial permit, manufacturers, §18B-1100.
Exemption from alcoholic beverage provisions,
  §18B-103.
Violation of chapter.
Discharge of employees, §18B-202.
Viticulture/oenology courses.
Authorization, §18B-1114.4.
Warehouse receipts.
Storage under government bond, §25-7-201(b).
Warehouses.
Bonds.
  Issuance by commission, §18B-208(a).
State warehouse, §18B-204.
Warranties.
Implied warranty of merchantability, §25-2-314.
Wholesalers.
Beer franchises generally, §§18B-1300 to
  18B-1308.
  See BEER FRANCHISES.
Permits.
  Malt beverages.
    Authorization, §18B-1109(a).
  Restrictions on sales by wholesalers to retail
    permittees, §18B-1006(h).
  Supplier's financial interest in wholesaler.
    Generally, §18B-1119.
  Wine.
    Authorization, §18B-1107(a).
Suppliers.
  Financial interest in wholesaler.
    Financial assistance to proposed purchasers,
      §18B-1119(a), (b).
    Security interest in inventory or property of
      wholesaler, §18B-1119(c).
Wine.
  Distribution agreements, §18B-1107(b).
  Permits.
    Authorization, §18B-1107(a).

ALCOHOLIC BEVERAGES —Cont'd
Wholesalers —Cont'd
Wine —Cont'd
Sources of wine received by wholesalers,
§18B-1107(a).
Wine generally.
See WINE.
Winemaking on premises.
Permit, §18B-1001.
Fee, §18B-902(d).
Wine producer.
Defined, §18B-1000.
Permit, §18B-902(d).
Authorization, §18B-1114.3(a).
Commercial permit, §18B-1100.
Limitation on total gallons sold annually,
§18B-1114.3(b).
Wine shipper packagers.
Direct shipments into state, §18B-1001.1(c).
Permit, §18B-1001.3.
Fee, §18B-902(d).
Wine shippers.
Direct shipments into state, §18B-109(c).
Manner of making, §18B-1001.1(c).
Permit.
Application authorization, §18B-1001.1(a).
Quarterly summary of shipped wine,
§18B-1001.2(a).
Registration, §18B-1001.2(a).
Rules, adoption, §18B-1001.2(b).
Sales and use tax.
Collection responsibility, §105-164.8(b).
Subject to state jurisdiction, §18B-1001.1(d).
Wholesaler in state, appointment,
§18B-1001.1(b).
Wine tasting, §18B-1001.
Wine vendor.
Nonresident vendor, §18B-1114.
Witnesses.
Illicit sale.
Testimony enforced in certain criminal
investigations, §8-55.
Immunity of witness, §8-55.
Workers' compensation.
Impairment by use of alcohol.
Rebuttable presumption, §97-12.
No compensation payable.
Injury or death caused by intoxication, §97-12.
Zero tolerance law.
Driving by person less than 21 years old after
consuming alcohol or drugs, §20-138.3.

ALCOHOLIC BEVERAGES TAX.
Applicability of tax, §105-113.68(b).
Bonds, surety.
Nonresident vendors, §105-113.86(b).
Wholesalers and importers, §105-113.86(a).
Definitions, §105-113.68(a).
Excise tax on beer, wine and liquor,
§§105-113.80 to 105-113.87.
Discount.
Expenses incurred in preparing reports and
records, §105-113.85.
Distribution of part of beer and wine taxes.
City defined, §105-113.82(f).
County in which ABC stores established by
petition, §105-113.82(c).
Local revenue.
Governor may not reduce distribution,
§105-113.82(d).
Method of distribution, §105-113.82(a1).

ALCOHOLIC BEVERAGES TAX —Cont'd
Excise tax on beer, wine and liquor —Cont'd
Distribution of part of beer and wine taxes
—Cont'd
Municipality incorporated on or after January 1,
2000, §105-113.82(h).
Percentages of net amount distributed,
§105-113.82(a).
Population estimates, §105-113.82(e).
Time of distribution, §105-113.82(d).
Use of funds for any public purpose,
§105-113.82(g).
Exemptions.
Armed forces, sales to, §105-113.82(c).
Free tasting, §105-113.82(e).
Major disasters.
Beverages rendered unsalable by,
§105-113.82(a).
Out-of-sate sales, §105-113.82(d).
Expenses incurred in preparing reports and
records.
Discount, §105-113.85.
Monthly reports, §105-113.84.
Payment.
Beer and wine tax, §105-113.83(b).
Liquor tax, §105-113.83(a).
Railroad sales, §105-113.83(c).
Railroad sales.
Monthly reports, §105-113.83(c).
Rate of tax.
Beer, §105-113.80(a).
Liquor, §105-113.80(c).
Wine, §105-113.80(b).
Refund for tax paid on sacramental wine,
§105-113.87(a), (b).
Sacramental wine.
Refunds, §105-113.87(a), (b).
Licenses.
Counties.
Beer and wine retail licenses, §105-113.78.
Local exceptions, §105-113.71(b).
Refusal to issue, §105-113.71(a).
Defined, §105-113.68(a).
Duration, §105-113.70(b).
Effect of license, §105-113.69.
Exclusive license, §105-113.70(d).
Issuance, §105-113.70(a).
License tax, §105-113.69.
Municipalities.
City beer and wine retail licenses.
Additional license, tax on, §105-113.77(b).
Amount, §105-113.77(a).
City wholesaler license, §105-113.79.
Local exceptions, §105-113.71(b).
Refusal to issue, §105-113.71(a).
Other applicable administrative provisions,
§105-113.89.
Qualifications of licensee, §105-113.70(a).
Records.
Requirements, §105-113.88.
Transfers, §105-113.70(c).
Malt beverages.
Defined, §105-113.68(a).
Misdemeanors.
Violations, §105-113.73.
Spirituous liquors.
Defined, §105-113.68(a).
Wine.
Fortified wine.
Defined, §105-113.68(a).

ALCOHOLIC BEVERAGES TAX —Cont'd
Wine —Cont'd
Unfortified wine.
Defined, §105-113.68(a).

ALCOHOLISM.
Basic education program.
Alcohol and drug education program,
§115C-81(a3).
Chemical dependency.
See CHEMICAL DEPENDENCY.
Chiropractors.
Grounds for disciplinary action, §90-154(b).
**Discharge, discipline, etc., of employee failing
to comply with employer's requirements,**
§95-28.2(b).
Drug treatment courts, §§7A-790 to 7A-801.
See DRUG TREATMENT COURTS.
Grants.
Research authority.
Application for grants, §122C-433(a), (b).
Incompetence, determination of, §§35A-1101 to
35A-1116.
See INCOMPETENCY.
**Lawyers and judges impaired by substance
abuse or addiction.**
Lawyer assistance program, Bar Rules D.0601 to
D.0623.
See LAWYERS ASSISTANCE PROGRAM.
Physicians and surgeons.
Grounds for denial, revocation or suspension of
license, §90-14(a).
Referral of physician to state medical society
physician health and effectiveness committee,
§90-14(b).
Prisons and prisoners.
Substance abuse programs.
See PRISONS AND PRISONERS.
Research authority, §§122C-431 to 122C-433.
Specialty hospitals.
Alcohol detoxification programs, §131E-65.
Substance abuse counselors, §§90-113.30 to
90-113.46A.
See SUBSTANCE ABUSE PROFESSIONALS.
Substance abuse generally.
See MENTAL HEALTH, DEVELOPMENTAL
DISABILITY, SUBSTANCE ABUSE.
Work First program recipients of assistance.
Treatment required, drug testing, §108A-29.1.

ALCOHOLISM RESEARCH AUTHORITY,
§§122C-431 to 122C-433.
Appointment of members, §122C-431(a).
Authorized to receive and expend funds,
§122C-432.
Chairman, §122C-431(b).
Composition, §122C-431(a).
Creation of alcoholism research authority,
§122C-431(a).
Executive secretary, §122C-431(b).
Expenditures.
Authorized to receive and expend funds,
§122C-432.
Expenses of members, §122C-431(b).
Funds.
Authority to receive and expend funds, §122C-432.
Grants.
Application for grant, §122C-433(a), (b).
Rules and regulations.
Promulgation, §122C-433.
Terms of office, §122C-431(a).
Vacancies in office, §122C-431(a).

ALCOHOLISM RESEARCH AUTHORITY
—Cont'd
Vice-chairman, §122C-431(b).

ALCOHOL LAW ENFORCEMENT AGENTS,
§18B-500.
Appointment by secretary of public safety,
§18B-500(a).
Arrest authority, §18B-500(b).
Controlled substances act, enforcement,
§18B-500(b).
Department of public safety.
Alcohol law enforcement section.
Defined, §18B-101.
Transfer to department, §143A-243.
Designation, §18B-500(a).
Discharge, §18B-500(e).
Forfeitures, §18B-504.
Inspections of licensed premises, §18B-502.
Investigatory and enforcement actions,
§18B-500(b).
Local ABC officers, §18B-501.
Lottery laws, enforcement of, §18B-500(b).
Reserve agents.
Workers' compensation.
Considered division employees for, §18B-500(a).
**Resignation as alcohol law-enforcement
agents,** §18B-500(a).
Restitution to law enforcement agency,
§18B-505.
Seized beverages.
Disposition, §18B-503.
Service of commission order, §18B-500(b).
**State officer with jurisdiction throughout
state,** §18B-500(c).
Subject matter jurisdiction, §18B-500(b).
Territorial jurisdiction, §18B-500(c).
Workers' compensation.
Reserve agents.
Considered division employees for, §18B-500(a).

ALCOHOL OR DRUG ABUSE.
Basic education program.
Alcohol and drug education program,
§115C-81(a3).
Chemical dependency.
See CHEMICAL DEPENDENCY.
**Discharge, discipline, etc., of employee failing
to comply with employer's requirements,**
§95-28.2(b).
Drug treatment courts, §§7A-790 to 7A-801.
See DRUG TREATMENT COURTS.
Incompetence, determination of, §§35A-1101 to
35A-1116.
See INCOMPETENCY.
**Lawyers and judges impaired by substance
abuse or addiction.**
Lawyer assistance program, Bar Rules D.0601 to
D.0623.
See LAWYERS ASSISTANCE PROGRAM.
Substance abuse counselors, §§90-113.30 to
90-113.46A.
See SUBSTANCE ABUSE PROFESSIONALS.
Substance abuse generally.
See MENTAL HEALTH, DEVELOPMENTAL
DISABILITY, SUBSTANCE ABUSE.
Work first program recipients of assistance.
Treatment required, drug testing, §108A-29.1.

ALCOHOL REHABILITATION CENTER.
Joint security force, §122C-421(a), (b).

ALCOHOL SCREENING TEST.
Commercial vehicle drivers.
Operating a commercial vehicle after consuming alcohol, §20-138.2A(b2).
Driver of vehicle, §20-16.3.
Limited driving privileges.
Use of results or fact of refusal to take screening, §20-179.3(j).
Minor suspected of consuming alcohol, §18B-302(j).
Driving by person less than 21 after consuming alcohol or drugs, §20-138.3(b2).
Open container law violations.
Evidence in determining whether alcohol present in driver's body, §20-138.7(d).
School bus drivers.
Operating a school bus, school activity bus, or child care vehicle after consuming alcohol, §20-138.2B(b2).

ALCOHOL, TOBACCO AND FIREARMS LAWS.
Agents authorized to enforce criminal laws, §15A-406.

ALCOHOL VAPORIZING DEVICES, §90-113.10A.

ALDERMEN, BOARDS OF.
Generally.
See CITY COUNCILS.

ALEXANDER COUNTY.
Ambulance service, attachment or garnishment and lien for, §§44-51.4 to 44-51.8.
Board of county commissioners.
Filling vacancies on board, §153A-27.1.
Cropper or tenant neglecting or refusing to perform terms of contract without just cause.
Forfeiture of right of possession to premises, §42-27.
Maps in special proceedings, recording and photographing copies, §47-32.
On-premises unfortified wine licenses.
Discretion to decline to issue, §105-113.71(b).
Registration of deeds.
Tax certification, no delinquent taxes due, §161-31(b).
School property.
Acquisition and improvement, §153A-158.1.
Sheriff.
Vacancy, performance of duties until vacancy filled, §162-5.1.
Special school tax, election to abolish.
Number of petitions required, §115C-505.
Tax elections for industrial development purposes, §§158-16 to 158-24.

ALFALFA.
Weights and measures.
Standard weights and measures, §81A-42.

ALIAS.
Orders of attachment, §1-440.13(b).
Sex offender and public notification registration.
Alias person using at time of conviction. Statement required, §14-208.7(b).

ALIAS SUMMONS, §1A-1 Rule 4(d).
Discontinuance for failure to issue within time specified, §1A-1 Rule 4(e).
Docketing, §1A-1 Rule 4(g).

ALIAS SUMMONS —Cont'd
Judgments based on summons erroneously designated validated, §1-217.1.

ALIENATION OF AFFECTION, §52-13.
Limitation of action, §52-13(b).
Natural person as party, §52-13(c).
Permanent physical separation of spouse, §52-13(a).

ALIEN INSURANCE COMPANIES.
Generally.
See FOREIGN OR ALIEN INSURANCE COMPANIES.

ALIEN PROPERTY ACT, §§64-1 to 64-5.

ALIENS.
Actions.
Suits against state, US Const Amd 11.
Adoption of persons born outside United States, §48-2-606(b).
Congress.
Eligibility to be representative, US Const Art I §2.
Contracts to purchase or sell real property.
Validation, §64-2.
Conveyance of real property.
Right, §64-1.
Deeds.
Certified copies made by United States alien property custodian.
Evidence, §47-34.
Registration allowed, §47-33.
Drivers' licenses.
Cancellation.
Legal presence of licensee in country no longer authorized, §20-15(a).
Limited duration license.
Expiration, §20-7(f).
Issuance to applicant in country under valid visa, §20-7(s).
Issuance to applicant presenting documentation demonstrating legal presence, §20-7(s).
Escheat in absence of reciprocity.
Personal property, §64-4.
E-Verify program to verify work authorization of newly hired employees.
Counties.
Duty to register and participate, §153A-99.1.
Definition of E-Verify, §64-25.
Employers to use, §64-26(a).
Seasonal temporary employee exception to requirement, §64-26(c).
Violations, consequences, §§64-31 to 64-33.
Municipalities.
Duty to register and participate, §160A-169.1.
Records.
Preservation of E-Verify forms, §64-26(b).
State departments, agencies, etc.
Verification of legal status after hiring new employees, §126-7.1(f).
Verification of work authorization generally, §§64-25 to 64-38.
Fair housing, §§41A-1 to 41A-10.
See FAIR HOUSING.
Intestate succession, §29-11.
Jails.
Citizenship status of prisoners, §162-62.
Limitation of actions.
War.
Effect on limitation period, §1-34.
Mental health, developmental disabilities and substance abuse.
Proceedings, §122C-344.

ALIENS —Cont'd
Naturalization, US Const Art I §§8, 9.
Parole.
  Early conditional release to ICE.
    Arrest authority, §148-64.1(d).
    Discretionary nature of release, §148-64.1(b).
    Eligibility, §148-64.1(a).
    Return of inmate to corrections department,
      §148-64.1(b1).
    Revocation of release, §148-64.1(e).
      Ineligibility for future release, §148-64.1(f).
    Unlawful reentry as violation of release,
      §148-64.1(c).
Personal property.
  Reciprocal rights, §64-3.
    Burden of proof, §64-5.
    Escheat in absence of reciprocity, §64-4.
Personnel system.
  Verification of legal status to work in United
    States, §126-7.1(f).
President of the United States.
  Ineligible for presidency, US Const Art II §1.
Psychologists.
  Licensure of foreign graduates, §90-270.11(c).
Real property.
  Contracts.
    Validation, §64-2.
  Information as to foreign ownership of real
    property.
    Secretary of state to collect, §64-1.1.
  Right to hold and convey, §64-1.
Reciprocal rights, §64-3.
  Burden of proof, §64-5.
  Escheat in absence of reciprocity, §64-4.
Registration cards.
  False or fraudulent, §14-100.1.
Seasonal temporary employees.
  Verification of work authorization.
    E-Verify.
      Exception to requirement, §64-26(c).
Secretary of state.
  Information as to foreign ownership of real
    property.
    Secretary of state to collect, §64-1.1.
State agencies, departments, etc.
  Verification of legal status to work in United
    States, §126-7.1(f).
Suits against state, US Const Amd 11.
Unemployment compensation.
  Eligibility for benefits, §96-13(f).
  Employment.
    Exclusion of services performed by, §96-8.
United States alien property custodian.
  Certified copies of deeds made by.
    Evidence, §47-34.
    Registration, §47-33.
Validation.
  Contracts to purchase or sell real property, §64-2.
Verification of work authorization, §§64-25 to
  64-38.
  Anonymous complaints, §64-28(a).
  Appeal of orders, §64-36.
  Complaints.
    Anonymous complaints, §64-28(a).
    False and frivolous complaints.
      Criminal offense, §64-28(b).
    Filing, §64-28(a).
    Forms.
      Contents, §64-27(b).
      Design and promulgation, §64-27(a).
    Hearings, §64-30.

ALIENS —Cont'd
Verification of work authorization —Cont'd
  Complaints —Cont'd
    Investigation of complaints, §64-29(a).
      Certain categories of complaints not
        investigated, §64-29(b).
      Federal government verification exclusive
        method of determining authorization,
        §64-35.
      State bureau of investigation assistance in
        investigating, §64-29(c).
      Subpoenas for production of documents in aid
        of investigation, §64-29(d).
    Process following complaint, §64-30.
  Counties.
    E-Verify.
      Duty to register and participate, §153A-99.1.
  Definitions, §64-25.
  Employ.
    Defined, §64-25.
  Employees.
    Defined, §64-25.
  Employers.
    Defined, §64-25.
  E-Verify.
    Counties.
      Duty to register and participate, §153A-99.1.
    Defined, §64-25.
    Employers to use, §64-26(a).
      Seasonal temporary employee exception to
        requirement, §64-26(c).
      Violations, consequences, §§64-31 to 64-33.
    Municipalities.
      Duty to register and participate, §160A-169.1.
    Records.
      Preservation of E-Verify forms, §64-26(b).
    Seasonal temporary employees.
      Exception to requirement, §64-26(c).
    State departments, agencies, etc.
      Verification of legal status after hiring new
        employees, §126-7.1(f).
  Labor commissioner.
    Appeal of orders, §64-36.
    Complaint forms, §64-27.
    Definition of commissioner, §64-25.
    Filing complaints with commissioner, §64-28(a).
    Independent determination of authorization.
      Prohibited, §64-35.
    Investigation of complaints, §64-29(a), (b).
      Federal government verification exclusive
        method of determining authorization,
        §64-35.
      Law enforcement assistance, §64-29(c).
      Subpoenas for production of documents,
        §64-29(d).
    Rulemaking to implement provisions, §64-37.
    Violations, consequences.
      Copies of orders.
        Retention, §64-34.
      Duties of commissioner, §§64-31 to 64-33.
  Municipalities.
    E-Verify.
      Duty to register and participate, §160A-169.1.
  Notice of presence of unauthorized alien, §64-30.
  Rulemaking to implement provisions, §64-37.
  State departments, agencies, etc.
    Verification of legal status after hiring new
      employees, §126-7.1(f).
  Statutory construction.
    Employers not to be required to violate federal
      or state law, §64-38.

ALIENS —Cont'd
Verification of work authorization —Cont'd
Unauthorized aliens.
Defined, §64-25.
Notice of presence of unauthorized alien,
§64-30.
Violations, consequences.
Copies of orders.
Retention, §64-34.
First violation.
Affidavit, §64-31(a).
Failure to file, §64-31(b).
Second violation, §64-32.
Third and subsequent violations, §64-33.
Work authorization.
Verification of work authorization, §§64-25 to
64-38.
Workers' compensation, §97-38.

ALIMONY.
See DIVORCE.

ALIMONY PENDENTE LITE.
**Absolute divorce not to affect rights of spouse
to,** §50-11(c).

ALKALI.
Malicious throwing, §14-30.1.
Municipalities.
Regulation of corrosive substances, §160A-183.

ALKALINE PAPER.
**State publications of historical and enduring
value.**
Compliance with requirement, monitoring,
§125-11.13(b).
Designation of publications on annual basis,
§125-11.13(a), (b).
Identification that publication printed on
permanent paper, §125-11.13(a).
Notice to agencies responsible for publishing
designated titles, §125-11.13(b).
Report as to titles designated for printing on
alkaline paper, §125-11.13(c).
Required to be printed on, §§125-11.13(a),
143-170.5.
Responsibility of agency to print on alkaline
paper, §125-11.13(b).

ALLEGHANY COUNTY.
**Ambulance service, attachment or
garnishment and lien for,** §§44-51.4 to
44-51.8.
**Blank or master forms of mortgages, deeds of
trust, etc.**
Indexing and recording, inapplicability of
provisions, §47-21.
Board of county commissioners.
Filling vacancies on board, §153A-27.1.
**Condemnation or acquisition of land by local
government unit outside county.**
Consent of board of commissioners necessary,
§153A-15.
Coroner elected as nominee of political party.
Filling vacancy in office, §152-1.
Counties generally.
See COUNTIES.
**County boards of education elected on
partisan basis.**
Vacancies in office, §115C-37.1.
**Cropper or tenant refusing to perform terms
of contract.**
Forfeiture of right of possession to premises,
§42-27.

ALLEGHANY COUNTY —Cont'd
Game laws, local acts not repealed,
§113-133.1(e).
**Maps in special proceedings, recording of
photographic copies,** §47-32.
Violation as misdemeanor, inapplicability of
provisions, §47-32.2.
Oil, gas or mineral claims.
Certain ancient claims extinguished, preservation,
procedure, §1-42.3(a) to (d).
Room occupancy taxes.
Uniform provisions, §153A-155.
School property.
Acquisition and improvement, §153A-158.1.
Sheriff.
Vacancy, performance of duties until vacancy
filled, §162-5.1.
Tax sales, notices by publication validated.
Inapplicability of provisions, §47-108.24.

ALLEYS.
Judicial sales.
Dedication of real property subdivided for sale,
§1-339.9(b).
Littering, §14-399.
No title by possession of public ways, §1-45.
Poisons.
Putting poisonous foodstuffs, etc., in certain public
places prohibited, §14-401.
Right of way.
Left turns into, §20-155(b).
Pedestrians, §20-173(c).
Vehicles emerging from or entering highway from,
§20-156(a).
Secret societies.
Wearing masks, hoods, etc., on public ways,
§14-12.7.

ALLIGATORS.
Feeding unlawful, §113-291.11.
**Propagation and production of American
alligators.**
Facility requirements, §106-763.1(b).
License required, §106-763.1(a).
Untagged or undocumented alligators possessed
by facility operator, §106-763.1(c).

ALL-TERRAIN VEHICLES.
Age restrictions.
Exceptions, §20-171.15(e).
Helmet and eye protection requirements for
minors, §20-171.19(a1).
Persons less than eight years of age,
§20-171.15(a).
Persons less than sixteen years of age,
§20-171.15(c), (d).
Persons less than twelve years of age,
§20-171.15(b).
Prohibited acts by sellers, §20-171.17.
Amusement device safety.
Amusement device defined as not including,
§95-111.3(a).
Applicability of provisions.
Exceptions.
Farming operations, §20-171.22(a).
Hunting or trapping, §20-171.22(b).
Ocean beach area, operating on, §20-171.22(c).
Careless or reckless operation, §20-171.19(d).
County and municipal employees.
Use on certain highways, §20-171.24(a) to (e).
Applicable counties and municipalities,
§20-171.24(f).

ALL-TERRAIN VEHICLES —Cont'd
Defined, §20-4.01.
Disabled sportsmen.
Use to transverse public roadways while hunting
  or fishing, §20-171.26(a).
  Lights and horn, required equipment,
    §20-171.26(c).
  Membership in disabled sportsmen program and
    hunting or fishing license.
    Evidence of carried by person operating
      vehicle, §20-171.26(e).
  Operation of vehicles, laws governing,
    §20-171.26(b).
  Speed limit, §20-171.26(d).
**Electric service employee engaged in power
    line inspection.**
  Head protection and eye protection.
    Required while operating all-terrain vehicle,
      §20-171.19(a2).
Equipment requirements, §20-171.18.
  Natural gas utilities operating on highways and
    rights of way, §20-171.25(c).
Eye protection required, §20-171.19(a).
  Electric service employee engaged in power line
    inspection, §20-171.19(a2).
  Minors, §20-171.19(a1).
Farming operations.
  Applicability of provisions, §20-171.22(a).
Headlights, §20-171.19(g).
  Vehicles operated by disabled sportsmen,
    §20-171.26(c).
Helmets required, §20-171.19(a).
  Electric service employee engaged in power line
    inspection, §20-171.19(a2).
  Minors, §20-171.19(a1).
Highways, roads and streets.
  Natural gas utilities operating vehicles on,
    §20-171.25.
  Operation on, prohibition, §20-171.19(e).
    Interstate or limited-access highways,
      §20-171.19(f).
Hunting or trapping.
  Applicability of provisions, §20-171.22(b).
Impaired driving, §20-171.19(c).
Interstate highways.
  Operation on prohibited, §20-171.19(f).
**Law enforcement officers and fire, rescue and
    emergency medical services.**
  Use on certain highways, §20-171.23(a) to (f).
Lights.
  Headlamps and tail lamps, §20-171.19(g).
  Natural gas utilities operating, §20-171.25(c).
  Vehicles operated by disabled sportsmen,
    §20-171.26(c).
Limited-access highways.
  Operation on prohibited, §20-171.19(f).
Natural gas utilities operating.
  Permitted on public highways and rights-of-way.
    Applicability of provision, §20-171.25(b).
    Equipment requirements, §20-171.25(c).
    Operator to carry official company identification,
      §20-171.25(e).
    Scope of permission, §20-171.25(a).
    Speed limits, §20-171.25(d).
Ocean beach area, operating on.
  Applicability of provisions, §20-171.22(c).
Operation, §§20-171.15 to 20-171.22.
  Age restrictions, §20-171.15.
    Prohibited acts by sellers, §20-171.17.
  Application of provisions, §20-171.22.

ALL-TERRAIN VEHICLES —Cont'd
Operation —Cont'd
  Equipment requirements, §20-171.18.
    Natural gas utilities operating on public
      highways and rights-of-way, §20-171.25(c).
    Natural gas utilities operating on public highways
      and rights-of-way, §20-171.25.
  Passengers, §20-171.16.
  Penalties for violations, §20-171.21.
  Prohibited acts by owners and operators,
    §20-171.19.
  Safety training certificate, §20-171.20.
  Vehicles operated by disabled sportsmen,
    §20-171.26(b).
Owners.
  Authorizing operation contrary to law,
    §20-171.19(b).
Passengers, §20-171.16.
Penalties for violations, §20-171.21.
Safety training certificate, §20-171.20.
Sellers, prohibited acts by, §20-171.17.
Tail lights, §20-171.19(g).
  Vehicles operated by disabled sportsmen,
    §20-171.26(c).
**Trespass to land on motorized all terrain
    vehicle,** §14-159.3.
Utility easements.
  Operating vehicle upon after being forbidden to do
    so, §14-134.2.

ALPACAS.
Llamas classified as livestock.
  Definition of llama including, §106-22.4.

ALPHA AND BETA PARTICLES.
Radiation protection act generally, §§104E-1 to
    104E-29.
  See RADIATION PROTECTION.

ALTERATION OF JUDGMENT.
Motions, §1A-1 Rule 59(e).

ALTERNATIVE CLAIMS OR DEFENSES, §1A-1
    Rule 8(e).
Joinder of claims, §1A-1 Rule 18(a).

ALTERNATIVE DISPUTE RESOLUTION.
Arbitration.
  Family law arbitration generally, §§50-41 to
    50-62.
  See FAMILY LAW ARBITRATION.
  Generally.
    See ARBITRATION.
  Revised uniform arbitration act, §§1-569.1 to
    1-569.31.
    See ARBITRATION.
Collaborative law proceedings, §50-78.
Community mediation centers, §7A-38.5.
  Negotiation not discoverable or admissible in
    evidence, §8-110.
Education of children with disabilities.
  Mediation of disputes, §115C-109.4.
Mediated settlement conferences.
  Court ordered mediated settlement conferences,
    SuperCtMediatedSettlemt Rules 1 to 15.
  See MEDIATED SETTLEMENT
    CONFERENCES.
Mediation.
  Generally.
    See MEDIATION.
Persons with disabilities.
  Public service discrimination cases, §168A-10.1.
Special education.
  Education of children with disabilities.
    Mediation of disputes, §115C-109.4.

ALTERNATIVE FUEL, §§105-449.130 to
105-449.139.
Bond or letter of credit.
Required as condition of obtaining and keeping
licenses.
Amount, §105-449.133(b).
Persons required to have bond, §105-449.133(a).
Bulk end-users.
Bond or letter of credit required as condition of
license, §105-449.133.
Defined, §105-449.130.
Informational return, §105-449.138(a).
Liability for tax, §105-449.137(a).
Marking of storage facility, §105-449.138(b).
Persons required to have license, §§105-449.131,
105-449.139.
Storage facilities.
Marking, §105-449.138(b).
Definitions, §105-449.130.
Due date of tax.
Change by licensee, §105-449.135(b).
Energy credit and banking act.
Alternative fuel revolving fund, §143-58.5.
Participation by state departments, institutions
and agencies.
Purchase of alternative fuels, §143-58.4.
Imposition of tax, §105-449.136.
Informational return.
Bulk end-users and retailers, §105-449.138(a).
Inspection, §§119-14 to 119-47.
See GASOLINE AND OIL INSPECTION.
Liability for tax imposed, §105-449.137(a).
Licenses.
Application for, §105-449.132.
Bond or letter of credit as condition of obtaining
and keeping.
Amount, §105-449.133(b).
Persons required to have bond, §105-449.133(a).
Denial or cancellation, §105-449.134.
Issuance, §105-449.135(a).
Notification of changes, §105-449.135(b).
Persons required to have license, §105-449.131.
Liquid alternative fuel, tax imposed,
§105-449.136.
List of providers, §105-449.139(c).
Notice.
Changes by licensee, §105-449.135(b).
Offenses, §105-449.139(b).
Payment of tax, §105-449.137(b).
Providers.
Bond or letter of credit as condition of license,
§105-449.133.
Liability for tax, §105-449.137(a).
Persons required to have license, §105-449.139.
Providers of alternative fuel.
Defined, §105-449.130.
List, §105-449.139(c).
Persons required to have license, §105-449.131.
Records kept by license holders,
§105-449.139(a).
Retailers.
Bond or letter of credit required as condition of
license, §105-449.133.
Defined, §105-449.130.
Informational return, §105-449.138(a).
Liability for tax, §105-449.137(a).
Marking of storage facility, §105-449.138(b).
Persons required to have license, §105-449.131.
Storage facilities.
Marking, §105-449.138(b).

ALTERNATIVE FUEL —Cont'd
Return.
Informational return.
Bulk end-users and retailers, §105-449.138(a).
Storage facilities.
Marking by bulk end-users or retailers,
§105-449.138(b).
Tax at motor fuel rate imposed, §105-449.136.
Violation, §105-449.139(b).

ALTERNATIVE FUEL VEHICLES.
Energy credit and banking act.
Participation by state departments, institutions
and agencies.
Purchase, §143-58.4.
Special license plates, §20-79.4(b).
State goal to purchase new or replacement
vehicles, §143-215.107C(b).
Alternative fueled vehicle defined,
§143-215.107C(a).
Report on progress, §143-215.107C(c).

ALTERNATIVE LEARNING PROGRAMS AND
ALTERNATIVE SCHOOLS.
Driving eligibility certificate.
Effect of disciplinary action for enumerated
student conduct, §20-11(n1).
Establishment.
Development of rules and policies.
Local boards of education, §115C-47.
Proposals to establish, §115C-105.47A(a).
Submission, §115C-105.47A(b).
Placement of at-risk or disruptive students.
Determination of support services and
intervention strategies, §115C-105.48(b).
Document procedures used to identify student
prior to referring student, §115C-105.48(a).
Reasons for referring student, school to provide,
§115C-105.48(a).
Student records, providing alternative schools,
§115C-105.48(a).

ALUMINUM CANS.
Incineration, disposal by prohibited,
§130A-309.10(f1).
Landfills, disposal in prohibited,
§130A-309.10(f).

ALZHEIMER'S DISEASE.
Adult care homes.
Special care units.
Disclosure of information, §131D-8(a), (b).
Adult day care programs.
Disclosure requirements for programs offering
special care services for persons with,
§131D-6(b1) to (b4).
Long-term care insurance.
Coverage for, §58-55-35(b).
Silver alert system.
Missing persons suffering from dementia, other
cognitive impairment, §143B-1022.

AMATEUR RADIO ANTENNAS.
Zoning regulations.
Municipal planning and regulation of
development.
Accommodation of amateur radio antennas,
§160A-383.3.
Reasonable accommodation, §153A-341.2.

AMATEUR RADIO OPERATORS.
Specialized license plates, §20-79.4(b).

AMATEUR SPORTS.
Athletics generally.
See ATHLETICS.

AMATEUR SPORTS —Cont'd
Limited food establishment.
Preparing and serving food in conjunction with
events.
Defined, §130A-247.
Permits, issuance, §130A-248(a4).
Sanitation, rules governing, adoption,
§130A-248(a4).
State games.
Insurance.
Liability insurance coverage required,
§143-299.3(b).
State departments and agencies.
Motor vehicles.
No liability for damages, §143-299.3(b).

AMBASSADORS.
Constitution of the United States, US Const Art
II §§2, 3, Art III §2.
Probate and registration.
Authorized to take probate, §47-2.

AMBER ALERT SYSTEM, §143B-1021.
Abduction of child.
Emergency alert program, §143B-1021(e).
Criteria for dissemination of information,
§143B-1021(b).
Duty to develop and maintain.
Center for missing persons, §143B-1016.
Emergency alert program.
Abduction of child, §143B-1021(e).
Established within center for missing persons,
§143B-1021(a).
Funding, §143B-1021(f).
**Overhead permanent changeable message
boards,** §143B-1021(d).
Statewide implementation.
Procedures and guidelines, adoption,
§143B-1021(c).
**Statewide system for rapid dissemination of
information.**
Purpose, §143B-1021(a).
Training materials.
Development, §143B-1021(c).

AMBER LIGHTS.
Use on certain vehicles, §20-130.2.

AMBULANCES.
Approach of ambulance.
Duties of motorists, §20-157(a).
Assault on emergency personnel, §14-288.9.
Attachment.
Liens.
County or city ambulance services, §§44-51.4 to
44-51.8.
Automated external defibrillator (AED),
§90-21.15.
Controlled access roads.
Means of emergency access required, §20-158.3.
Counties.
County or city ambulance service lien, §§44-51.4
to 44-51.8.
EMS services in fire protection districts,
§153A-309(a), (b).
Health services, §153A-250.
Making false ambulance request, §14-111.3.
Obtaining ambulance services without intending
to pay, §§14-111.1, 14-111.2.
Named counties, §14-111.2.
Service districts, §§153A-300 to 153A-310.
**Criminal background checks of EMS
personnel,** §114-19.21.

AMBULANCES —Cont'd
Crossing median of divided highway.
When permitted, §20-140.3.
Emergency medical services, §§143-507 to
143-519.
See EMERGENCY MEDICAL SERVICES.
Emergency medical technicians.
Offenses against.
Aggravating factor in sentencing, §15A-1340.16.
False pretenses and cheats.
Making false ambulance request, §§14-111.3,
14-286.1.
Obtaining ambulance services without intending
to pay, §§14-111.1, 14-111.2.
Named counties, §14-111.2.
Franchises.
County ambulance services, §153A-250.
Garnishment.
Liens.
County or city ambulance service, §§44-51.4 to
44-51.8.
Health insurance coverage for services.
State health plan for teachers and state
employees.
Payments for county or city services,
§135-48.57.
Horns and warning devices, §20-125(b).
Liens.
County or city ambulance service.
Attachment or garnishment.
Collection authorization, §44-51.4.
Counties to which article applicable, §44-51.8.
Discharging lien, §44-51.7.
Filing, §44-51.6.
General lien for service, §44-51.5.
Recoveries for personal injuries, §44-49.
Attorneys' fees, §44-50.
Charges, §44-50.
Creation of lien, §44-49.
Disputed claims to be settled before payments,
§44-51.
Evidence, §44-50.
Limit on recovery, §44-50.
Receiving person charged with duty of retaining
fund, §44-50.
Services by county or municipality.
Discharge, §44-51.3.
Filing, §44-51.2.
Real property of recipient, §44-51.1.
Lights.
Electronically modulated headlamps, §20-130(d).
Red lights.
Exception to prohibition, §20-130.1(b).
Limitation of actions.
County or city ambulance services.
Enforcement of lien for, §44-51.1.
Move over law.
Approach of ambulance, §20-157(a).
Parked or standing on roadway and giving
warning signal, §20-157(f).
Municipal property taxes.
Authorized purposes, §160A-209(c).
**Obtaining ambulance services without
intending to pay,** §§14-111.1, 14-111.2.
Named counties, §14-111.2.
**Parked or standing on roadway and giving
warning signal.**
Duties of driver approaching, §20-157(f).
Penalty for violations, §20-157(g).
Property damage, §20-157(h).
Serious injury or death, §20-157(i).

AMBULANCES —Cont'd
Parking within 100 feet of ambulance,
§20-157(e).
Penalty for violation, §20-157(g).
Property damage, §20-157(h).
Serious injury or death, causing, §20-157(i).
Personnel.
Offenses against.
Aggravating factor in sentencing, §15A-1340.16.
Red lights, §20-130.1(b).
Regulation of emergency medical services,
§§131E-155 to 131E-161.
See EMERGENCY MEDICAL SERVICES.
Requesting ambulance falsely, §§14-111.3,
14-286.1.
Right-of-way, §20-156(b).
Sanitary districts.
Corporate powers of sanitary district board,
§130A-55.
Sirens.
Vehicles on which authorized, §20-125(b).
Speeding.
When speed limits not applicable, §20-145.
**State health plan for teachers and state
employees.**
Payments for county or city ambulance services,
§135-48.57.
Traffic lights.
Preempting.
Local authority to permit, §20-169.
Window tinting exceptions, §20-127(c).

AMBULATORY SURGICAL FACILITIES,
§§131E-145 to 131E-152.
Abuse and neglect of patients, §14-32.2.
Administrative regulations.
Adverse action on licenses, §131E-148(b).
Certificates of need, §§131E-175 to 130E-191.1.
See HEALTH CARE FACILITIES.
Construction projects.
Review of projects and plans.
Fee charged by department of health and
human services, §131-267(d).
Definitions.
Licensing of facilities, §131E-146.
Hiring nurses.
Verification of licensure status, §90-171.43A(a),
(b).
Injunctions.
Hindering secretary's performance of duties,
§131E-152(b).
Operation without license, §131E-152(a).
Procedure, §131E-152(c).
Licenses.
Adverse action on licenses, §131E-148(a), (b).
Applications for licenses, §131E-147(b).
Renewal application, §131E-147(c).
Assignability of license, §131E-147(d).
Definitions, §131E-146.
Denial of license, §131E-148(a).
Applicability of provisions, §131E-148(b).
Development of standards, §131E-145(b).
Enforcement of standards, §§131E-145(b),
131E-149(b).
Establishment of standards, §131E-145(b).
Injunctive relief, §131E-152(a) to (c).
Inspections, §131E-150(a), (b).
Issuance, §131E-147(d).
Penalties for violation of provisions, §131E-151.
Posting of license on premises, §131E-147(e).
Purpose of part, §131E-145(b).

AMBULATORY SURGICAL FACILITIES
—Cont'd
Licenses —Cont'd
Renewal of license, §131E-147(c).
Required, §131E-147(a).
Revocation of license, §131E-148(a).
Applicability of provisions, §131E-148(b).
Rules and regulations, §131E-149(a).
Enforcement, §131E-149(b).
Suspension of license, §131E-148(a).
Applicability of provisions, §131E-148(b).
Title of part.
Ambulatory surgical facility licensure act,
§131E-145(a).
Transferability of license, §131E-147(d).
Violations of provisions.
Penalties, §131E-151.
Medical care commission.
Defined, §131E-146.
Nurses, hiring.
Verification of licensure status, §90-171.43A(a),
(b).
Obstruction of health care facility, §14-277.4.

AMBUSHING.
Secret assault, §14-31.

AMENDED STATUTES.
Construction and interpretation, §12-4.

AMENDING PLEADING, §1A-1 Rule 15(a) to (d).

AMENDMENT OF JUDGMENT.
Motions, §1A-1 Rule 59(e).

AMERICAN ALLIGATORS.
Propagation and production, §106-763.1.

**AMERICAN EX-PRISONERS OF WAR
HIGHWAY,** §136-102.1.

AMERICAN FAMILY DAY.
Designation, §103-7.

AMERICAN HISTORY.
Basic education program.
Founding principles, §115C-81(g).

AMERICAN HOLLY.
**Taking, etc., of certain wild plants from land of
another,** §14-129.

AMERICAN INDIANS.
See NATIVE AMERICANS.

AMERICAN LEGION.
Emblem.
Commercialization of American Legion emblem,
§14-395.
Wearing by nonmembers, §14-395.
Junior or youth baseball.
Certification of birth dates furnished to veterans'
organizations, §130A-120.
Property taxes.
Exclusion of real and personal property, §105-275.

**AMERICAN RECOVERY AND REINVESTMENT
ACT.**
**Attorneys' fee in action regarding claim,
dispute or protest.**
Prohibition, §6-19.1(b).
Implementation.
Rulemaking procedure, §150B-21.1B.
**Purchases and contracts through department
of administration.**
Use of American Recovery and Reinvestment Act
funds, §143-53.1(b).

AMERICAN REVOLUTION BICENTENNIAL COMMISSION.
Department of cultural resources.
Transfer of commission to department, §143B-51.

AMERICAN SIGN LANGUAGE.
Certification of teachers, §115C-81.3(b).
Community colleges.
Sign language instruction, §115D-5(r).
High school modern foreign language, §115C-81.3(a).

AMERICA'S FOUR HUNDREDTH ANNIVERSARY COMMITTEE, §§143B-85, 143B-86.

AMICUS CURIAE BRIEFS.
Appeals, AppProc Rule 28(i).

AMMUNITION.
Dealers.
Door lock exemption permit, §§58-79-22, 143-143.4.
Furnishing bullets to inmates of charitable, mental or penal institutions, §14-258.1.
Persons subject to domestic violence orders.
Surrender and disposal of firearms.
Emergency or ex parte order, §50B-3.1.
Products liability lawsuits involving, §99B-11.
Teflon-coated bullets.
Manufacture sale, purchase or possession unlawful, §14-34.3(a).
Inapplicability of provisions, §14-34.3(b).
Misdemeanor, §14-34.3(c).

AMNESTY.
Attorney disciplinary amnesty in illicit drug use cases, Bar Rule B.0130.
Underground petroleum storage tank leak cleanup.
Reports of suspected discharge or release.
Limited amnesty, §143-215.94F.

AMOUNT IN CONTROVERSY.
District courts.
Proper division for trial of civil actions.
Determination by amount in controversy, §7A-243.
Small claims actions in district courts, §7A-210.
Statewide court-ordered-nonbinding arbitration in certain cases, §7A-37.1.
Superior courts.
Proper division for trial of civil actions.
Determination by amount in controversy, §7A-243.

AMPHETAMINES.
Controlled substances generally.
See DRUGS AND CONTROLLED SUBSTANCES.
Methamphetamine watch program.
Immunity from civil and criminal liability.
Good faith actions, §114-43.
Precursor chemicals.
Possession or distribution with intent to manufacture, §90-95(d1).
List of chemicals to which subsection applies, §90-95(d2).
Schedule II controlled substances, §90-90(c).
Trafficking, §90-95(h).

AMPLIFIED SPEECH REGULATION BY CITIES, §160A-184.

AMPUTATION.
Podiatry.
Amputation of entire foot excluded from definition, §90-202.2(a).

AMPUTATION —Cont'd
Podiatry —Cont'd
Podiatrist to perform at licensed hospital, §90-202.2(b).
Workers' compensation.
Computation of compensation for amputation, ICWorkComp Rule 405.

AMUSEMENT DEVICE SAFETY, §§95-111.1 to 95-111.18.
Accidents.
Investigations, §95-111.10(b).
Removing of damaged parts, §95-111.10(d).
Reports.
Required, §95-111.10(a).
Use or moving of device, §95-111.10(c).
Alcohol or other impairing substance.
Operating device equipment under the influence.
Prohibition, §95-111.11(b).
Applicability of article, §95-111.2(a).
Attorney general.
Representing department of labor, §95-111.15.
Certificate of operation.
Liability insurance required, §95-111.12(b).
Required, §95-111.7(a).
Suspension, revocation or refusal to issue or renew.
Appeals, §95-111.6(c).
Operation of device after revocation or refusal to issue certificate, §95-111.7(c).
Violations of article or rules and regulations, §95-111.6(b).
Citation of article, §95-111.1(a).
Civil penalties, §95-111.13(a) to (e).
Administrative proceeding.
Final determination, §95-111.13(g).
Copy of final order, filing, §95-111.13(h).
Exception to determination.
Time for taking, §95-111.13(g).
Factors considered, §95-111.13(f).
Finality of determination, §95-111.13(g).
Commissioner of labor.
Powers and duties, §95-111.4.
Compliance with article and rules and regulations, §95-111.7(b).
Confidentiality.
Trade secrets, §95-111.17.
Construction of article and rules and regulations, §95-111.18.
Criminal penalties, §95-111.13(i).
Death resulting from violation.
Criminal penalty, §95-111.13(i).
Definitions, §95-111.3(a) to (h).
Department of labor.
Elevator and amusement device division, §95-110.4.
Entrance to amusement device.
Authority of owner or operator to deny, §95-111.14.
Exemptions from article, §95-111.2(b).
Federal laws.
Agreements to enforce, §95-111.16.
Findings of general assembly, §95-111.1(b).
Inspection.
Pre-opening inspection and test, §95-111.5(a) to (c).
Intent of article, §95-111.1(c).
Liability insurance.
Amount, §95-111.12(a).
Proof of insurance, §95-111.12(c).
Required, §95-111.12(a), (b).

AMUSEMENT DEVICE SAFETY —Cont'd
Liability insurance —Cont'd
Waterslides.
Notification to commission of personal injuries involving, §95-111.12(d).
Location.
Notice, §95-111.8.
Noncomplying devices.
Stopping or limiting use, §95-111.6(a).
Notice.
Location notice, §95-111.8.
Operators.
In attendance at all times, §95-111.11(a).
Operating device equipment under the influence.
Prohibition, §95-111.11(b).
Operating more than one device.
Restrictions, §95-111.11(a).
Qualifications, §95-111.11(a).
Pre-opening inspection and test, §95-111.5(a) to (c).
Reports.
Accidents, §95-111.10(a).
Rules and regulations.
Adoption, §95-111.4.
Construction, §95-111.18.
Severability of article, §95-111.18.
Short title, §95-111.1(a).
Tests.
Pre-opening inspection and test, §95-111.5(a) to (c).
Trade secrets.
Confidentiality, §95-111.17.
Unsafe device.
Operation of, §95-111.9.
Violations of article.
Civil penalties, criminal penalties, §95-111.13.
Waterslides.
Defined, §95-111.3(h).
Insurance.
Liability insurance, §95-111.12(a).

AMUSEMENT LICENSING AND LICENSE TAXES.
Amusement or entertainment not otherwise taxed.
Cities may levy but counties may not, §105-37.1(d).
Charities.
Exemption, §105-40.
Educational purposes.
Exemption, §105-40.
Exemptions from tax, §105-40.
Live entertainment, §105-37.1.
Religious societies.
License taxes.
Exemption, §105-40.

AMUSEMENT OR ENTERTAINMENT NOT OTHERWISE TAXED.
License tax by city but not county, §105-37.1(d).
Privilege tax on gross receipts, admission fee charged, §105-37.1.
Rate and payment, §105-37.1(b).

AMUSEMENT PARKS.
Amusement device safety generally, §§95-111.1 to 95-111.18.
See AMUSEMENT DEVICE SAFETY.

AMUSEMENTS.
Amusement device safety, §§95-111.1 to 95-111.18.

AMUSEMENTS —Cont'd
Counties.
Regulation of places of amusement, §153A-135.
Disabled persons.
Right to use of places of public amusement, §168-3.
Licensing, license taxes.
Exhibiting performance, show or exhibition, §105-37.1.
Municipalities.
Regulating and licensing businesses, etc., §§160A-181, 160A-194.
Video gaming machines, §§14-306, 14-306.1A, 14-306.2, 14-306.4.

AMY JACKSON LAW.
Sex offender and public protection registration generally, §§14-208.5 to 14-208.32.
See SEX OFFENDER AND PUBLIC PROTECTION REGISTRATION.

ANABOLIC STEROIDS.
Controlled substances.
Generally, §§90-86 to 90-113.8.
See DRUGS AND CONTROLLED SUBSTANCES.
Schedule III, §90-91(k).
Unauthorized substances taxes, §§105-113.105 to 105-113.113.
See UNAUTHORIZED SUBSTANCES TAXES.

ANACONDA.
Regulation of large constricting snakes.
Generally, §§14-416 to 14-422.
See REPTILES.

ANALINGUS.
Rape.
See RAPE.

ANALYTICAL SERVICES BUSINESSES.
Sales and use tax.
Economic incentive refunds, §105-164.14A(a).

ANATOMICAL GIFTS, §§130A-412.3 to 130A-412.33.
Acceptance of gift, when unauthorized, §130A-412.13(j).
Advance health care directive registry, §§130A-465 to 130A-471.
AIDS.
Information for potential donors, §130A-148(b).
Laboratory tests for AIDS virus infection.
Immunity of facility or institution, §130A-148(e).
Required, §130A-148(c), (d).
Amendment of gift.
Body or body part of decedent, §130A-412.12(a), (b).
Falsification of document, §130A-412.19.
Parent of minor after minor's death, §130A-412.10(g), (h).
Person other than donor precluded from taking certain actions, §130A-412.10(a) to (f).
Prior to donor's death.
Method of amending, §130A-412.8(a), (d), (e).
Applicability of provisions, §130A-412.5.
Bar to action by other persons, §130A-412.10(a).
Blood donations.
Persons under 18 years selling.
Unlawful, §130A-412.31.
Sixteen year olds donating, §130A-412.31.

ANATOMICAL GIFTS —Cont'd
Body or body part of decedent.
Method of making gift, §130A-412.12(a).
Who may make gift, §130A-412.11.
Consent for organ or tissue donation in order of priority established.
Duties of federally designated organ procurement organization, §130A-412.33(c).
Defacement or obliteration of document, §130A-412.19.
Definitions, §130A-412.4.
Delivery of document during lifetime of donor.
Not required, §130A-412.15(a).
Discretion and sensitivity with respect to beliefs of families and potential donors.
Federally designated organ procurement organization to encourage, §130A-412.33(d).
Donor cards.
Availability at division of motor vehicles offices, §20-7.3.
Donor registry, §130A-412.22.
Organ procurement organizations' rights and duties, §130A-412.16(a).
Effect of gift.
Bar to action by other persons, §130A-412.10(a).
Effect of refusal, §130A-412.9(d).
Embalming or funeral service for gift of entire body.
Rights of recipients, §130A-412.16(h).
Evaluation of donation potential.
Duty of federally designated organ procurement organization, §130A-412.33(a).
Examination and copying of document, §130A-412.15(b).
Falsification of document, §130A-412.19.
Fees for removal, processing, storage, etc.
Authorization for, §130A-412.18(b).
Financial liability for cost related to evaluation of suitability of donor's organ or tissue.
Family of person whose organ or tissue to be donated not liable, §130A-412.32(c).
Hospitals.
Federally designated organ procurement organizations and tissue banks.
Access to patient's medical records, §130A-412.32(b).
Written agreement with addresses, requirements of provisions, §130A-412.32(e).
Hold harmless provision.
Hospital made party to action arising out of failure of federally designated organ procurement organization, §130A-412.33(f).
Medical records.
Access by federally designated organ procurement organization and tissue bank.
Deceased patient's medical records, §130A-412.32(d).
Protocols for organ procurement, §130A-412.32(a).
Immunity of hospitals and hospital personnel in good faith compliance, §130A-412.32(g).
Requirements not to exceed protocol provisions of Title XI of social security act, §130A-412.32(f).
Signed statement with federally designated organ procurement organization, §130A-412.32(a).
Human tissue donation programs, §§130A-413, 130A-415.
Immunities from liability, §130A-412.20(a) to (c).

ANATOMICAL GIFTS —Cont'd
Law governing validity of document, §130A-412.21(a), (b).
Legislative declaration.
Use of tissue declared service, §130A-412.30.
Liability, §130A-412.30.
License to give trust fund, §§20-7.4 to 20-7.6.
Medical examiners.
Cooperation with procurement organization, §130A-412.23(a), (d).
Defined, §130A-412.23(d).
Interference of recovery of body part with postmortem examination, §130A-412.23(e).
Limitations on authorization of removal or donation of body parts, §130A-412.23(c).
Medicolegal examination of donor.
Authorized to conduct, §130A-412.24(b).
Expeditious provision of requested information to examiner, §130A-412.24(c).
Postmortem examination conducted in manner and time period compatible with preservation, §130A-412.23(b).
Release of personal identifying information of decedent and postmortem examination results upon request of procurement organization, §130A-412.24(a).
Removal of body part before postmortem examination.
Record describing condition of body part sent to examiner, §130A-412.23(f).
Medical records.
Access by federally designated organ procurement organizations and tissue banks.
Hospitals to provide, §130A-412.32(b).
Medical suitability examination of part donated, §130A-412.16(c) to (e).
Method of making gift.
Body or body part of decedent, §130A-412.12(a).
Prior to donor's death, §130A-412.7(a), (b).
Negligence.
Liability, §130A-412.30.
Objection to gift of body or body part of decedent, §130A-412.11(b), (c).
Options of organ or tissue donation and option to decline.
Families of potential organ donors made aware of by federally designated organ procurement organization, §130A-412.33(b).
Organ procurement organizations.
Coordination agreements with hospitals, §130A-412.17.
Recipients of gift, §130A-412.13(a), (c), (g), (h).
Rights and duties, §130A-412.16.
Penalties for violations.
Falsification, defacement, etc., of document, §130A-412.19.
Sale or purchase of parts, §130A-412.18(a).
Personal effects search of accident trauma victims, §90-602.
Physicians, participation in removal or transplant of part, §130A-412.16(i), (j).
Presumption of validity, §130A-412.21(c).
Prior to donor's death.
Amendment or revocation of gift.
Method of amendment or revocation, §130A-412.8(a), (c), (d), (e).
Method of making gift, §130A-412.7(a), (b).
Person other than donor precluded from taking certain actions, §130A-412.10(a) to (f).
Refusal to make gift.
Amendment or revocation of refusal, §130A-412.9(c).

ANATOMICAL GIFTS —Cont'd
Prior to donor's death —Cont'd
Refusal to make gift —Cont'd
Methods of making refusal, §130A-412.9(a).
Who may make gift, §130A-412.6.
Privileged and confidential information.
Hospital and patient information, interviews,
reports, etc., §130A-412.33(e).
Purpose of gift.
Priority of recipients, §130A-412.13(b) to (i).
Recipients of gift, §130A-412.13.
Rights superior to all others regarding part
donated, §130A-412.16(h).
Recording of wishes of decedent.
Method of making gift of body or body part of
decedent, §130A-412.12(a).
Refusal to make gift, §130A-412.9.
Examination and copying of document,
§130A-412.15(b).
Revocation of refusal by parent of minor after
minor's death, §130A-412.10(g), (h).
Registry of donors, §130A-412.22.
Organ procurement organizations' rights and
duties, §130A-412.16(a).
Revocation of gift.
Body or body part of decedent, §130A-412.12(a) to
(c).
Falsification of document, §130A-412.19.
Parent of minor after minor's death,
§130A-412.10(g), (h).
Person other than donor precluded from taking
certain actions, §130A-412.10(a) to (f).
Prior to donor's death.
Methods of revocation, §130A-412.8(a), (c), (d),
(e).
Sale or purchase of parts, §130A-412.18(a).
Search of donor registry.
Rights and duties of procurement organizations,
§130A-412.16(a).
Search of individual for document of gift,
§130A-412.14.
Personal effects search of accident trauma
victims, §90-602.
Short title.
Revised uniform anatomical gift act, §130A-412.3.
Standard of care, §130A-412.30.
Unclaimed bodies.
Exemption of body for which deceased has made
anatomical gift, §130A-415(f).
Use of gift, §130A-412.13(b) to (k).
Use of tissue declared a service, §130A-412.30.
Validity of document.
Presumption and law governing, §130A-412.21.
Warranties.
No liability in warranty, §130A-412.30.
Who may make gift.
Body or body part of decedent, §130A-412.11.
Prior to donor's death, §130A-412.6.
Wills.
Amendment or revocation of gift prior to donor's
death, §130A-412.8(e).
Invalidation of will after donor's death, effect,
§130A-412.7(d).
Method of making gift prior to donor's death,
§130A-412.7(a).
Refusal of gift, §130A-412.9(a).

**ANATOMIC PATHOLOGY SERVICES, BILLING
FOR.**
Communication of requirements to licensees,
§90-701(k).

**ANATOMIC PATHOLOGY SERVICES, BILLING
FOR** —Cont'd
Contract terms.
Disclosure not required, §90-701(e).
Defined, §90-701(e).
Dentist billing for services.
Disclosure required, §90-701(a).
Penalty for violations, §90-701(i).
License revocation or suspension, §90-701(j).
Exemptions, §90-701(d), (g).
Hospital billing for services.
Disclosure required, §90-701(b).
Penalty for violations, §90-701(i).
License revocation or suspension, §90-701(j).
License revocation or suspension.
Violations of provisions, §90-701(j).
Misdemeanor.
Violations of provisions, §90-701(i).
**Name and address of laboratory performing
services.**
Required on bill, §90-701(c).
Penalty for violations, §90-701(i).
Physician billing for services.
Disclosure required, §90-701(a).
Penalty for violations, §90-701(i).
License revocation or suspension, §90-701(j).
Podiatrist billing for services.
Disclosure required, §90-701(a).
Penalty for violations, §90-701(i).
License revocation or suspension, §90-701(j).
Second medical opinions.
Services of more than one laboratory not
prohibited, §90-701(h).
Violations of provisions.
License revocation or suspension, §90-701(j).
Misdemeanors, §90-701(i).

ANATOMY COMMISSION.
Appointments, §130A-33.31(a), (b).
Autopsies.
Unclaimed bodies.
Consent of commission, §130A-415(d).
Board of anatomy.
References to former board in testamentary
dispositions, §130A-33.32.
Chairman, §130A-33.31(d).
Clerical and other services, §130A-33.31(g).
Creation, §130A-33.30.
Duties, §130A-33.30.
Meetings, §130A-33.31(f).
Members, §130A-33.31(a).
Powers and duties, §130A-33.30.
Quorum, §130A-33.31(e).
Removal of members, §130A-33.31(c).
Terms, §130A-33.31(a).
Testamentary dispositions.
References to former board of anatomy,
§130A-33.32.
Unclaimed bodies.
Adoption of rules, §130A-416.
Autopsies.
Consent of commission, §130A-415(d).
Consent of commission for autopsy, §130A-415(d).
Notification to commission, §130A-415(a), (g), (i).
Minors in custody of county at time of death,
§130A-415(g).
Vacancies, §130A-33.31(b).

ANCESTRAL PROPERTY.
Intestate succession.
Distinction between ancestral and nonancestral
property abolished, §29-3.

ANCESTRY.
Hearsay exception.
Records of religious organizations, §8C-1 Rule
803.
Statement of personal or family history, §8C-1
Rule 804(b).

**ANCIENT AND ARABIC ORDER NOBLES OF
THE MYSTIC SHRINE.**
Property tax exclusion, §105-275.

ANCIENT DOCUMENTS.
Authentication and identification of evidence,
§8C-1 Rule 901(b).
Hearsay exception, §8C-1 Rule 803.

**ANCIENT EGYPTIAN ORDER NOBLES OF
THE MYSTIC SHRINE.**
Property tax exclusion, §105-275.

ANCILLARY ADMINISTRATION, §§28A-26-1 to
28A-26-9.
Assets.
Assets in jurisdiction outside state subject to
ancillary administration, §28A-26-1.
Nonresident decedents.
Assets subject to claims, allowances, etc.,
§28A-26-8(a).
Remission of surplus assets, §28A-26-9.
Bonds, surety.
Personal representatives granted ancillary letters,
§28A-26-4(a).
Claims.
Certain claims binding, §28A-26-8(b).
Limitation on presentation, §28A-26-8(c).
Payment, §28A-26-8(d).
Duties of personal representatives in ancillary
administration, §28A-26-8.
Foreign corporations.
Authority to act as ancillary personal
representative, §28A-26-3(a).
General provisions, §28A-26-1.
Granting ancillary letters, §28A-26-3(a).
Bond for personal representatives, §28A-26-4.
Nonexistence of domiciliary personal
representative, §28A-26-3(b).
No ancillary administrator within ninety days.
Payment of debt and delivery of property to
nonresident domiciliary, §28A-26-2(c).
Nonresident decedents.
Assets subject to claims, etc., §28A-26-8(a).
Payment of debt and delivery of property
without ancillary administration in state,
§28A-26-2.

ANESTHESIA.
Dentists.
Anesthesia and parenteral sedation, §90-29(b).
Standards for general anesthesia and
parenteral sedation.
Board of dental examiners to establish by
regulation, §90-30.1.
Podiatry.
Administration of anesthetic other than local
excluded from definitions, §90-202.2(a).

ANESTHESIOLOGISTS.
Professional corporations.
Formation authorized, §55B-14(c).

ANGIER, TOWN OF.
Satellite annexation.
Limitation on area of satellite corporate limits,
inapplicability, §160A-58.1(b).

ANIMAL AUCTIONS.
Livestock markets.
Generally, §§106-406 to 106-418.
See LIVESTOCK MARKETS.
Prompt pay law, §§106-418.1 to 106-418.7A.
See LIVESTOCK MARKETS.
Public auctions.
Defined, §19A-23.
Licensing, §19A-28.
Changes in ownership, management, etc.,
§19A-31.
Fees, §19A-28.
Operation without license, §19A-33.
Refusal, suspension or revocation, §19A-32.
Transfer prohibited, §19A-31.
Standards of care.
Adoption by board, §19A-24(a).

ANIMAL BAITING, §14-362.1.
Dog baiting, §14-362.2.

ANIMAL CONTROL OFFICERS.
County appointment authorized, §67-30.
Impoundment of dogs and cats, §130A-192.
Powers and duties of county dog warden,
§67-31.

ANIMAL CRUELTY.
See CRUELTY TO ANIMALS.

ANIMAL CRUELTY INVESTIGATORS.
Appointment, §19A-45(a).
Badges, §19A-45(b).
Care of seized animals, §19A-47.
Complaints.
Filing, §19A-46(a), (c).
Costs of proceedings, §19A-46(d).
Educational requirements, §19A-49.
Expenses.
Reimbursement, §19A-45(d).
Forcible entry.
Order by district court judge, §19A-46(e).
Interference with investigator.
Penalty, §19A-48.
Oath of office, §19A-45(c).
Powers, §19A-46(a), (b).
Removal from office, §§19A-45(b), 19A-49.
Seizure of animal.
Care of seized animals, §19A-47.
Magistrate's order, §19A-46(a).
Execution of order, §19A-46(b), (c).
Terms of office, §19A-45(b).

ANIMAL DEALERS.
Defined, §19A-23.
Licensing, §19A-29.
Change in ownership, management, etc., §19A-31.
Fees, §19A-28.
Operation without license, §19A-33.
Refusal, suspension or revocation, §19A-30.
Appeals, §19A-32.
Transfer prohibited, §19A-31.

ANIMAL-DRAWN VEHICLE.
Traffic laws apply, §20-171.

ANIMAL EXHIBITIONS.
Aedin's law.
Cites as, §106-520.3A(a).
Attorney general.
Representation of department in actions and
proceedings.
Duty, §106-520.3A(g).
Civil penalty for violation, §106-520.3A(f).

ANIMAL EXHIBITIONS —Cont'd
Definitions, §106-520.3A(b).
Health risks.
Education outreach, §106-520.3A(e).
Operation permit.
Required, inspection required, suspension or
revocation, §106-520.3A(c).
Purpose of section, §106-520.3A(a).
Rules concerning operation.
Adoption by commissioner, requirements,
§106-520.3A(d).

ANIMAL FEED.
Feed generally, §§106-284.30 to 106-284.46.
See FEED.
Raw milk dispensed as animal feed,
§106-266.35.

ANIMAL FIGHTING, §14-362.1.
Cockfighting, §14-362.
Dog fighting, §14-362.2.
Care of animals subjected to illegal treatment,
§19A-70.

ANIMAL INSURANCE.
Mandatory or voluntary risk sharing plans.
See MANDATORY OR VOLUNTARY RISK
SHARING PLANS.
Types of insurance authorized, §58-7-15.

ANIMAL RESEARCH FACILITIES.
Interference with, §14-159.2.

ANIMALS.
Animal cruelty investigators, §§19A-45 to
19A-49.
Animal exhibitions.
Regulation, §106-520.3A.
Animal shelters.
See ANIMAL SHELTERS.
Assistance animals.
Assaulting, §14-163.1.
Auctions.
Licensing public auctions, §§19A-28 to 19A-33.
Livestock markets.
Generally, §§106-406 to 106-418.
See LIVESTOCK MARKETS.
Prompt pay law, §§106-418.1 to 106-418.7A.
See LIVESTOCK MARKETS.
Public auctions defined, §19A-23.
Standards of care for public auctions.
Adoption by board, §19A-24(a).
Bailments.
Vehicles and draft animals, §§14-165 to 14-169.
Bang's disease, §§106-388 to 106-398.
See BRUCELLOSIS.
Bears.
Protection of black bears, §§19A-10 to 19A-14.
Biological residues in animals, §§106-549.81 to
106-549.89.
See BIOLOGICAL RESIDUES IN ANIMALS.
Biologics.
General provisions, §§106-707 to 106-715.
See BIOLOGICS.
Black bears.
Protection, §§19A-10 to 19A-14.
Brands.
Livestock generally, §§80-45 to 80-66.
See LIVESTOCK BRANDS.
Brucellosis, §§106-388 to 106-398.
See BRUCELLOSIS.
Care of animals subjected to illegal treatment,
§19A-70.

ANIMALS —Cont'd
Cats.
See CATS.
Cattle tick, §§106-351 to 106-363.
See CATTLE TICK.
Counties.
Abuse of animals.
Prohibition, §153A-127.
Dangerous animals.
Possession or harboring of dangerous animals.
Regulation, §153A-131.
Licenses.
Taxation, §153A-153.
Shelters.
Establishing, standards, §153A-442.
Taxation, §153A-153.
Criminal interference with animal research,
§14-159.2.
Cruelty to animals.
General provisions.
See CRUELTY TO ANIMALS.
Investigators, §§19A-45 to 19A-49.
Dangerous animals.
Possession or harboring.
Regulation by counties, §153A-131.
Dangerous dogs, §§67-4.1 to 67-4.5.
Dead animals.
Dead domesticated animals.
Disposition of, §106-403.
Transportation department.
Removal of dead animals.
Powers of department, §136-18.
Dealers.
Livestock dealer licensing generally, §§106-418.8
to 106-418.16.
See LIVESTOCK DEALER LICENSING.
Definitions, §19A-1.
Dangerous dogs, §67-4.1(a).
Welfare Act, §19A-23.
Discharge of oil or hazardous substances.
Liability for damages to animal life,
§143-215.90(a) to (c).
Dogs.
See DOGS.
Equine infectious anemia, §§106-405.15 to
106-405.20.
Euthanasia, §19A-24.
Defined, §19A-23.
Exemption from creditors' claims, §1C-1601(a).
False pretenses and cheats.
Pedigree of animals.
Obtaining property by false representation of
pedigree, §14-102.
Registration of animals.
Obtaining certificate of registration by false
representation, §14-103.
Fish and fishing.
See FISH AND FISHING.
Guide dogs, §§168-4.2 to 168-4.6.
Hog cholera, §§106-310 to 106-322.3.
See HOG CHOLERA.
Horses.
General provisions.
See HORSES.
Hotels, inns and other transient lodging
places.
Admitting to rooms, §72-7.1.
Hunting and wildlife.
See HUNTING AND WILDLIFE.
Impoundment.
Animals not wearing rabies vaccination tags,
§130A-192.

ANIMALS —Cont'd
Impoundment —Cont'd
Leashing or restraining ordinances.
Dogs and cats in violations, §130A-192(b).
Livestock running at large, §§68-17 to 68-24.
See LIVESTOCK RUNNING AT LARGE.
Surrendered dogs and cats by owners,
§130A-192(b).
Interference with animal research, §14-159.2(c).
Kennels.
See KENNELS.
Landlord and tenant.
Tenant security deposit act.
Pet deposits, §42-53.
Larceny.
Animals subject to larceny, §14-84.
Horses, mules, swine, cattle or dogs, §14-81.
Temporary purposes, §14-82.
Law enforcement animals.
Assaulting, §14-163.1.
Leases, UCC.
Unborn young.
Definition of "goods,"§25-2A-103(1).
Identification, §25-2A-217.
Liens.
Boarding animals.
Possessory liens on personal property.
Persons entitled to, §44A-2(c).
Livestock.
Brands, §§80-45 to 80-66.
See LIVESTOCK BRANDS.
Brucellosis, §§106-388 to 106-398.
See BRUCELLOSIS.
Cattle tick, §§106-351 to 106-363.
See CATTLE TICK.
Compensation for killing diseased animals,
§§106-323 to 106-335.
See LIVESTOCK DISEASES.
Control of livestock diseases generally, §§106-400
to 106-405.
See LIVESTOCK DISEASES.
Dealer licensing, §§106-418.8 to 106-418.16.
See LIVESTOCK DEALER LICENSING.
Diseases generally, §§106-304 to 106-307.7.
See LIVESTOCK DISEASES.
Equine infectious anemia, §§106-405.15 to
106-405.20.
Generally.
See LIVESTOCK.
Hog cholera, §§106-310 to 106-322.3.
See HOG CHOLERA.
Impoundment of animals running at large,
§§68-17 to 68-24.
See LIVESTOCK RUNNING AT LARGE.
Markets.
Generally, §§106-406 to 106-418.
See LIVESTOCK MARKETS.
Prompt pay law, §§106-418.1 to 106-418.7A.
See LIVESTOCK MARKETS.
Quarantine.
See LIVESTOCK DISEASES.
Tuberculosis, §§106-336 to 106-350.
See TUBERCULOSIS IN LIVESTOCK.
Meat inspections, §§106-549.15 to 106-549.39.
See MEAT INSPECTIONS.
Milk and milk products.
Ice cream plants, creameries and cheese factories.
Animals prohibited, §106-246.
Motor vehicles.
Applicability of traffic laws to persons riding
animals or driving animal-drawn vehicles,
§20-171.

ANIMALS —Cont'd
Motor vehicles —Cont'd
Passing horses or other draft animals.
Reasonable care, §20-216.
Municipalities.
Abuse of animals.
Define and prohibit abuse of animals,
§160A-182.
Animal shelters.
Establishment, standards, §160A-493.
Dangerous animals.
Possession or harboring, §160A-187.
Domestic animals.
Regulation, §160A-186.
Taxation.
License tax, §160A-212.
Oaths.
Animal cruelty investigators, §19A-45(c).
Pedigree of animals.
Obtaining property by false representation of
pedigree, §14-102.
Pet shops.
See PET SHOPS.
Poultry generally.
See POULTRY AND POULTRY PRODUCTS.
Poultry products inspections, §§106-549.49 to
106-549.69.
See POULTRY PRODUCTS INSPECTIONS.
Prompt pay law.
Livestock, §§106-418.1 to 106-418.7A.
See LIVESTOCK MARKETS.
Quarantine of livestock with diseases
generally.
See LIVESTOCK DISEASES.
Rabies.
General provisions, §§130A-184 to 130A-201.
See RABIES.
Registration of animals.
Obtaining certificate of registration by false
representation, §14-103.
Rendering plants and rendering operations
generally, §§106-168.1 to 106-168.16.
See RENDERING PLANTS AND RENDERING
OPERATIONS.
Reports.
Spay/neuter program.
Animal shelters receiving state or local funding,
§19A-65.
Research.
Criminal interference, §14-159.2.
Restitution.
Interference with animal research.
Conditions of probation, §14-159.2(d).
Interpretation of provisions, §14-159.2(e).
Sale of goods, UCC.
Identification of goods, §25-2-501(1).
Sale of unborn animals, §25-2-501.
Definition of goods, §25-2-105(1).
Identification of goods, §25-2-501(1).
Sale of meat of diseased animals.
Regulation of sale, §14-342.
Shelters.
Counties.
Establishing, standards, §153A-442.
Municipalities.
Establishment, standards, §160A-493.
Slaughterhouses generally.
See SLAUGHTERHOUSES.
Spay/neuter program, §§19A-60 to 19A-66.
Account, §19A-62.
Application for reimbursement, §19A-64(b).

ANIMALS —Cont'd
Spay/neuter program —Cont'd
Account —Cont'd
Counties or cities.
Distributions to, §19A-64.
Eligibility for distributions, §19A-63(a).
Notification of available funding, §19A-66.
Creation, §19A-62(a).
Distributions to counties and cities, §19A-64.
Eligibility for distributions, §19A-63.
Low-income persons.
Eligibility for distributions, §19A-63(a).
Defined, §19A-63(b).
Proof establishing eligibility, rules, §19A-63(c).
Notification of available funding, §19A-66.
Priorities for distribution, §19A-64(c).
Reimbursable costs, §19A-64(a).
Report, §19A-62(c).
Sources of funding, §19A-62(a).
Uses, §19A-62(b).
Components, §19A-61.
Education program, §19A-61.
Establishment, §19A-61.
Legislative findings, §19A-60.
Local programs, assistance, §19A-61.
Low-income persons.
Eligibility for distributions from account, §19A-63.
Purpose, §19A-60.
Reports.
Animal shelters receiving state or local funding, §19A-65.
Taxation.
Counties may levy animal tax, §153A-153.
Traffic laws.
Applicability to persons riding animals or driving animal-drawn vehicles, §20-171.
Trusts and trustees.
Care of animal alive during settlor's lifetime.
Creation, termination, enforcement, use of property, §36C-4-408.
Veterinarians.
General provisions, §§90-179 to 90-187.15.
See VETERINARIANS.
Wildlife.
Hunting and wildlife.
See HUNTING AND WILDLIFE.

ANIMAL SHELTERS.
Care of animals subjected to illegal treatment.
Deposit by defendant of funds necessary for.
Petition by shelter requesting, §19A-70.
Certificate of registration, §19A-26.
Refusal, suspension or revocation, §19A-30.
Appeals, §19A-32.
Counties.
Establishing, standards, §153A-442.
Euthanasia, §19A-24.
Sodium pentobarbital and other drugs for euthanasia of animals.
Registration for purpose of obtaining and using, §90-101(a2).
Impoundment of animals.
Leashing or restraining ordinances.
Dogs and cats in violation, §130A-192(b).
Rabies vaccination tags.
Animals not wearing, §130A-192.
Surrendered dogs and cats by owners, §130A-192(b).

ANIMAL SHELTERS —Cont'd
Municipalities.
Establishment, standards, §160A-493.
Spay/neuter program, §§19A-60 to 19A-66.
Report required on receiving funding, §19A-65.
Standards of care.
Adoption by board, §19A-24(a).

ANIMALS RUNNING AT LARGE.
Dogs.
Dangerous dog going beyond owner's property without leash or muzzle, §67-4.2(a).
Female dogs in heat, §67-2.
Nighttime, §67-12.
Sheep-killing dogs, §67-3.
Wildlife management areas.
Impoundment of unmuzzled dogs running at large, §67-14.1(b) to (e).
Impoundment.
Livestock, §§68-17 to 68-24.
See LIVESTOCK RUNNING AT LARGE.
Livestock generally.
See LIVESTOCK RUNNING AT LARGE.

ANIMAL WASTE MANAGEMENT, §§143-215.10A to 143-215.10M.
Action on permit application, §143-215.10C(c).
Application for permit, contents, §143-215.10C(d).
Bird operations, §143-215.10C(f).
Certification of animal waste management system operators, §§90A-47 to 90A-47.6.
Construction and design of system, §143-215.10C(b).
County planning and zoning.
Swine farms served by animal waste management systems, §153A-340(b).
Definitions, §143-215.10B.
Discharge of waste, publication of notice or press release, §143-215.10C(h).
Dry litter poultry facility.
Animal waste management plan, §143-215.10C(f1).
Application for permit, §143-215.10C(a1).
Fees, §143-215.10G(a) to (c).
Permits, §143-215.3D(a).
Inspections, §143-215.10F.
Notice of discharge, §143-215.10C(h).
Permit requirement, §143-215.10C(a).
Violation points system applicable to swine farms, §143-215.6E.
Plan requirements, §143-215.10C(e).
Press release, discharge, §143-215.10C(h).
Property taxes.
Special classes of property excluded from tax base, §105-275.
Publication of notice of discharge, §143-215.10C(h).
Public livestock markets.
Permit holders, exemption from requirements, §143-215.10C(i).
Purpose of act, §143-215.10A.
Reports.
Contents, §143-215.10M(a).
Itemization of information, §143-215.10M(b).
Review of operations.
Conflicts of interest, §143-215.10D(c).
Reporting procedure, §143-215.10D(a).
Requirement, §143-215.10D(b).
Swine farms, performance standards.
Anaerobic lagoons and sprayfield systems prohibited.
Definitions, §143-215.10I(a).

ANIMAL WASTE MANAGEMENT —Cont'd
Swine farms, performance standards —Cont'd
Anaerobic lagoons and sprayfield systems
prohibited —Cont'd
Performance standards as prerequisite to
issuance of permit, §143-215.10I(b).
Swine integrators.
Definitions, §143-215.10H(a).
Disclosure of violations, §143-215.10H(d).
Notice of termination or new relationship,
§143-215.10H(c).
Registration.
Required, §143-215.10H(b).
Technology development, §143-215.10C(g).
**Violation points system applicable to swine
farms.**
Appeals process to be provided for, §143-215.6E(c).
Determinations in developing, §143-215.6E(b).
Development, §143-215.6E(a).
Provisions of system, §143-215.6E(a).
Violations requiring immediate notification.
Federal employees, §143-215.10E(b).
State employees, §143-215.10E(a).

**ANIMAL WASTE MANAGEMENT SYSTEM
OPERATORS,** §§90A-47 to 90A-47.6.
Certification program.
Operators in charge, §90A-47.3(a).
Certification required, §90A-47.2(a).
Contracts.
Reports, §90A-47.2(b).
Definitions, §90A-47.1(a), (b).
Enforcement.
Rules, §90A-47.6.
Examinations, §90A-47.3(b).
Fees.
Certification, §90A-47.4(a).
Renewal fee, §90A-47.4(b).
Fines.
Willful violations, §90A-47.5(b).
Goals, §90A-47.
Operators in charge.
Certification program, §90A-47.3(a).
Contracts with more than one owner,
§90A-47.2(b).
Qualifications for certification, §90A-47.2(a).
Training program, §90A-47.3(b).
Purpose of part, §90A-47.
Renewal of certificate, §90A-47.4(b).
Reports.
Operators in charge contracting with more than
one owner, §90A-47.2(b).
Revocation of certificate, §90A-47.5(a).
Rules, §90A-47.6.
Suspension of certification, §90A-47.5(a).
Training program.
Operators in charge, §90A-47.3(b).

ANIMAL WELFARE, §§19A-20 to 19A-41.
Animal shelters.
Certificates of registration.
Duration, §19A-26.
Refusal, suspension or revocation, §19A-30.
Appeals, §19A-32.
Required, §19A-26.
Defined, §19A-23.
Sodium pentobarbital and other drugs for
euthanasia of animals.
Registration for purpose of obtaining and using,
§90-101(a2).
Spay/neuter program, §§19A-60 to 19A-66.
Reports required on receiving funding, §19A-65.

ANIMAL WELFARE —Cont'd
Animal shelters —Cont'd
Standards of care.
Board of agriculture to adopt, §19A-24(a).
Appeals.
Denial, suspension or revocation of license or
certificate, §19A-32.
Applicability of provisions, §19A-37.
Exemptions, §§19A-37, 19A-39.
Assessment of civil penalty, §19A-40.
Attorney general.
Representation of department of agriculture and
consumer services, §19A-41.
Auctions.
Defined, §19A-23.
Licenses.
Change in ownership, management or operation
of business, §19A-31.
Fees, §19A-28.
Penalty for operation without license, §19A-33.
Refusal, suspension or revocation, §§19A-30,
19A-32.
Required, §19A-28.
Transfer prohibited, §19A-31.
Standards of care at public auctions.
Board of agriculture to adopt, §19A-24(a).
Boarding kennel.
Defined, §19A-23.
License.
Change in ownership, management or operation
of business, §19A-31.
Fee, §19A-28.
Penalty for operation without license, §19A-33.
Refusal, suspension or revocation, §§19A-30,
19A-32.
Required, §19A-28.
Transfer prohibited, §19A-31.
Standards of care.
Board of agriculture to adopt, §19A-24(a).
Board of agriculture.
Euthanasia.
Procedures, §19A-24(a).
Technicians performing.
Certification, rules, §19A-24(b).
Hearings, §19A-32.
Refusal, suspension or revocation of certificate
or license, §19A-30.
Standards of care.
Adoption, §19A-24(a).
Care of animals subjected to illegal treatment,
§19A-70.
Citation of act.
Short title, §19A-20.
Civil penalty, §19A-40.
Cruelty to animals.
See CRUELTY TO ANIMALS.
Dealers.
Defined, §19A-23.
Licenses.
Change in ownership, management or operation
of business, §19A-31.
Fees, §19A-29.
Penalty for acting as dealer without license,
§19A-34.
Refusal, suspension or revocation, §19A-30.
Appeals, §19A-32.
Required, §19A-29.
Transfer prohibited, §19A-31.
Definitions, §19A-23.

ANIMAL WELFARE —Cont'd
Department of agriculture and consumer services.
Animal health division.
Animal welfare section, §19A-22.
Employees, §19A-25.
Investigations, §19A-25.
Dog wardens.
Violations of provisions by, §19A-36.
Euthanasia.
Defined, §19A-23.
Gas method approved.
Rules, requirements, §19A-24(a).
Methods allowed, §19A-24(a).
Procedures for euthanasia, §19A-24(a).
Rules, adoption, §19A-24(a).
Sodium pentobarbital and other drugs for euthanasia of animals.
Animal shelters.
Registration for purpose of obtaining and using, §90-101(a2).
Technicians performing euthanasia.
Certification, rules, §19A-24(b).
Denial, revocation, suspension, §19A-24(c).
Fingerprints, providing, criminal background check, §19A-24(d).
Criminal background check, §114-19.29.
Training for person participating in process.
Mandatory training, §19A-24(a).
Fees for licenses, §§19A-27 to 19A-29.
Use of fees, §19A-38.
Hearings, §19A-32.
Refusal, suspension or revocation of certificate or license, §19A-30.
Hunting dogs.
Training establishments.
Inapplicability of provisions, §19A-39.
Injunctions.
Cruelty to animals.
Preliminary injunction, §19A-3.
Investigations.
Director of animal welfare section, §19A-22.
Legislative declaration.
Purposes of act, §19A-21.
Misdemeanors.
Acting as dealer without license, §19A-34.
Dog wardens.
Violations of provisions by, §19A-36.
Failure to adequately care for animals, §19A-35.
Operation of pet shop, kennel or auction without license, §19A-33.
Pet shops.
Defined, §19A-23.
Licenses, §19A-27.
Change in ownership, management or operation of business, §19A-31.
Fee, §19A-27.
Penalty for operation without license, §19A-33.
Refusal, suspension or revocation, §19A-30.
Appeals, §19A-32.
Required, §19A-27.
Transfer prohibited, §19A-31.
Standards of care.
Board of agriculture to adopt, §19A-24(a).
Preliminary injunction.
Cruelty to animals, §19A-3.
Purposes of act, §19A-21.
Records of purchase and sales.
Requiring licensees and certificate holders to keep.
Power of board of agriculture, §19A-24(a).

ANIMAL WELFARE —Cont'd
Research facilities.
Defined, §19A-23.
Exemptions from provisions, §19A-37.
Right of entry.
Director of animal welfare section, §19A-25.
Title of act.
Short title, §19A-20.
Transportation of animals.
Manner of transporting to and from licensed premises.
Adoption by board of agriculture, §19A-24(a).
Use of fees for enforcing and administering article, §19A-38.

ANNE CARTER LEE GRAVE SITE.
Maintenance of grave, §136-44.

ANNEXATION.
Annexation agreements.
Approval, §160A-58.23.
Authority not granted by part, §160A-58.26.
Authorized, §160A-58.23.
Binding on parties, §160A-58.27(a).
Contents, §160A-58.24(a).
Definitions, §160A-58.22.
Duration, §160A-58.23.
Effect, §160A-58.25.
Effect of part on prior local acts, §160A-58.28.
Execution, §160A-58.23.
Hearings, §160A-58.24(c).
Modification, §160A-58.24(d).
Notice, §160A-58.24(b).
Part grants no annexation authority, §160A-58.26.
Prohibiting city from annexing into area.
Petition to annex area, §160A-58.27(i).
Purpose of part, §160A-58.21.
Scope of part, §160A-58.21.
Termination, §160A-58.24(d), (f).
Territorial limits, §160A-58.24(e).
Violation.
Relief from, §160A-58.27(a) to (i).
Violations, §160A-58.25.
Annexation by petition of property owners, §160A-31(a), (b1).
Annexing ordinance.
Authority to pass, effective date, §160A-31(d), (d1).
Area deemed contiguous, §160A-31(f).
Authority of municipality to adopt or petition.
Legal interest in property required, §160A-31(i).
Capital costs.
Extension of water and sewer lines.
Determination, §160A-31(d2).
Certifying sufficiency, §160A-31(c).
Debts, laws, ordinances, regulations of municipality.
Persons and property subject to, §160A-31(e).
Distressed areas, §160A-31(j).
Form of petition, §160A-31(k).
Form, §160A-31(b), (b2), (k).
Investigation of sufficiency, §160A-31(c).
Municipal services provided, §160A-31(d3).
Municipal taxes.
Real and personal property subject to, §160A-31(e).
Poverty threshold.
Determining if required number of households meet, §160A-31(l).
Public hearing, §160A-31(d).
Notice, publication, §160A-31(c).
Signed by property owners, §160A-31(a).

ANNEXATION —Cont'd
Annexation by petition of property owners
—Cont'd
Statement as to establishment of vested rights in
property subject to petition, §160A-31(g).
Water and sewer lines.
Capital costs to extend.
Determination, §160A-31(d2).
Annexation of noncontiguous areas.
Assumption of debt.
Rural fire departments, §160A-58.2A(a).
Exemption from section, §160A-58.2A(c).
Payments, calculation, §160A-58.2A(b).
Schedule for payment, §160A-58.2A(d).
Authority, §160A-58.1(a).
Definitions, §160A-58.
Extraterritorial powers, §160A-58.4.
Hearing, §160A-58.2.
Ordinances.
Annexed area subject to city taxes and debts,
§160A-58.3.
Petition for annexation, §160A-58.1(a).
Contents, §160A-58.1(c).
Form, §160A-58.1(c).
Resolution in lieu of petition.
Property owned by municipality,
§160A-58.7(a).
Signatures required, §160A-58.1(a).
Statement by petitioners concerning vesting
rights, §160A-58.1(d).
Powers.
Extraterritorial powers, §160A-58.4.
Primary corporate limits.
Defined, §160A-58.
Transition from satellite to primary limits,
§160A-58.6.
Property owned by municipality.
Property not owned by city or city has no legal
interest.
Annexation prohibited, §160A-58.7(b).
Resolution in lieu of petition, §160A-58.7(a).
Public hearing, notice, publication,
§160A-58.7(a).
Recordation, §160A-58.8.
Reports, §160A-58.8.
Satellite corporate limits.
Defined, §160A-58.
Transition from satellite to primary limits,
§160A-58.6.
Standards.
Annexing area not meeting standards,
§160A-58.1(b2).
Inapplicability of certain standard to specified
cities and towns, §160A-58.1(b).
Noncontiguous areas proposed for annexation,
§160A-58.1(b).
Taxation.
Annexed area subject to city taxes and debts,
§160A-58.3.
Water and sewer rates.
Special rates, §160A-58.5.
Assumption of debt.
Rural fire departments, §160A-31.1(a).
Exemption from section, §160A-31.1(c).
Payment.
Calculation, §160A-31.1(b).
Schedule, §160A-31.1(d).
Camp Butner hospital.
Annexation of territory extending into Camp
Butner reservation, §122C-410(a).

ANNEXATION —Cont'd
City prohibited from annexing area.
Petition seeking permission to annex,
§160A-58.27(i).
County service districts.
Authority, findings required, §153A-303(a).
By petition of owners, §153A-303(b).
County research and production service districts.
Removal of territory from.
Applicability of general annexation law to
removed territory, §153A-314.1(d).
Effective date of resolution, §153A-303(f).
Fire protection district.
Chapter 69 district annexing, §153A-304.2(a),
(b).
Municipality annexing all or part of district,
§153A-304.1(a) to (d).
Hearing on resolution, §153A-303(e).
Law enforcement service district.
Annexation of portion of district by
municipality.
Tax reduction and refund, §153A-304.4.
Notice of hearing, §153A-303(e).
Report, §153A-303(d).
Required provision or maintenance of services,
§153A-305(b).
Sanitary districts within city limits, §153A-303(c).
Definitions.
Municipalities initiating annexation, §160A-58.51.
Development financing district.
District established by county, §159-107(e).
Economic development and training districts.
County extending district, §153A-317.14.
Effective date of certain annexation
ordinances.
Ordinances adopted from January 1, 1987 to
August 3, 1987, §160A-58.9.
Ordinances adopted under Article 4A of Chapter
160A, §160A-58.9A(a), (b).
Applicability of provisions, §160A-58.9A(c).
Elections.
Registration of voters in areas proposed for
incorporation or annexation, §163-288.2.
Firemen's and rescue squad workers' pension
fund.
Firemen whose residence is annexed by a city.
Monthly pensions upon retirement, §58-86-55.
Fire protection district.
Municipality annexing all or part of district,
§153A-304.1(a) to (d).
Fire protection in annexed area.
Rural fire departments.
Annexation initiated by municipality.
Contract to provide, §160A-58.57.
Local acts.
Effect of part on prior local acts, §160A-58.28.
Map of annexed area.
Recordation, §160A-29.
Metropolitan sewerage districts.
Inclusion of additional political subdivision or
unincorporated areas.
Annexation of area lying outside district not
construed as inclusion, §162A-68(h).
Municipalities initiating annexation,
§§160A-58.50 to 160A-58.63.
Adjacent to or contiguous to municipality's
boundaries.
Requirement of area to be annexed,
§160A-58.54(a).
Annexation ordinance, §160A-58.55(h).
Amendment.
Area subject to appeals, §160A-58.60(i).

ANNEXATION —Cont'd
Municipalities initiating annexation —Cont'd
Annexation ordinance —Cont'd
Effect, §160A-58.55(j).
Extension of duration.
Petition seeking review, §160A-58.60(j).
Petition to deny, §160A-58.55(i).
Recording, §160A-61.
Appeals by property owners.
Amendment of annexation ordinance,
§160A-58.60(i).
Applicability, §160A-60(k).
Claim for property tax revenue loss.
Assertion by municipality prohibited,
§160A-60(l).
Costs charged to municipality.
Final order against, §160A-60(n).
Extension of annexation ordinance,
§160A-58.60(j).
Grounds, §160A-58.60(a).
Petition seeking review in superior court.
Consolidation of petitions, §160A-58.60(d).
Content requirements, §160A-58.60(b).
Duty of municipality upon receipt of petition,
time, §160A-58.60(c).
Filing, time, §160A-58.60(a).
Service of copies, §160A-58.60(b).
Procedure for conducting review, §160A-58.60(f).
Remedies allowed, §160A-58.60(g).
Scope of review, §160A-58.60(f).
Settlement, §160A-60(m).
Stay of operation of annexation ordinance.
Application for, §160A-58.60(e).
Who may appeal, §160A-60(h).
Authority to annex, §160A-58.52.
Authorized expenditures, §160A-62.
Combined notice of public informational meeting,
public hearing, opportunity for water and
sewer, §160A-58.55(d).
Contract with private firms to collect solid waste,
§160A-58.59.
Contract with rural fire department to provide fire
protection.
Appeal to local government commission.
Good faith offer not made, §160A-58.57(g), (h).
Judicial review, §§160A-58.57(i),
160A-58.60.
Duty of municipality to make good faith effort
to negotiate, §160A-58.57(a).
Good faith offers, §160A-58.57(b) to (d).
First responder services, §160A-58.57(e).
No obligation to enter into contract,
§160A-58.57(f).
Stay of operation of annexation ordinance.
Request pending outcome of review,
§160A-58.57(g).
Criteria for area to be annexed, §160A-58.54(a).
Definitions, §160A-58.51.
Bona fide farm purposes, §160A-58.54(c).
Property, §160A-58.54(c).
Solid waste collection.
Private firm providing collection services,
§160A-58.59(i).
Denial of annexation ordinance.
Petition, §160A-58.55(i).
Effect of annexation ordinance, §160A-58.55(j).
Expenditures authorized, §160A-62.
Failure to provide services.
Remedies, §160A-58.55(n).
Fire protection to annexed area.
Contract with rural fire department to provide,
§160A-58.57.

ANNEXATION —Cont'd
Municipalities initiating annexation —Cont'd
Fixing new boundaries, requirements,
§160A-58.54(b).
Mandamus.
Failure to provide services, §160A-58.55(n).
Map of annexed area.
Recording, §160A-61.
Methods used for population and land estimates,
§160A-63.
Petition by property owner seeking review,
§160A-58.60.
Plans to provide services.
Amendment, changing, §160A-58.55(h).
Duty to make prior to public hearing,
§160A-58.53.
Failure to provide services, remedies,
§160A-58.55(n).
Policy of state, §160A-58.50.
Population and land estimates, §160A-63.
Power to annex, §160A-58.52.
Prerequisites, §160A-58.53.
Procedure, §160A-58.55.
Public hearing, §160A-58.55(g).
Combined notice, §160A-58.55(d).
Resolution of intent to fix date, time,
§160A-58.55(c).
Public informational meeting, §160A-58.55(f).
Action prior to, §160A-58.55(e).
Combined notice, §160A-58.55(d).
Resolution of intent to fix date, time,
§160A-58.55(c).
Recording with register of deeds.
Map and copy of ordinance, §160A-61.
Report on plans to provide services.
Duty to make prior to public hearing,
§160A-58.53.
Reports to local government commission,
§160A-58.55(o).
Resident population requirements, §160A-58.54(a).
Resolution of consideration.
Mailing to property owners, time,
§160A-58.55(b).
Map or description of area required,
§160A-58.55(b).
Notice, §160A-58.55(b).
Required, duration, §160A-58.55(a).
Resolution of intent to proceed.
Adoption required, time, §160A-58.55(c).
Rural fire department.
Assumption of proportionate share of fire
department debt, §160A-58.58(a), (b).
Contract to provide fire protection, §160A-58.57.
Simultaneous annexation proceedings,
§160A-58.55(m).
Solid waste collection.
Private firm providing collection services.
Contract with firm to provide services.
Amount paid by municipality,
§160A-58.59(d).
Appeal, no contract offered, §160A-58.59(g).
Duty of municipality, §160A-58.59(a).
Provisions municipality may require,
§160A-58.59(c).
Definitions, §160A-58.59(i).
Duty of municipality, §160A-58.59(a).
Economic loss.
Duty of municipality to pay firm,
§160A-58.59(a).
Notice of resolution of intent to annex.
Duty to provide firms, §160A-58.59(b).

ANNEXATION —Cont'd
Municipalities initiating annexation —Cont'd
Solid waste collection —Cont'd
Private firm providing collection services
—Cont'd
Notice that firm provides services,
§160A-58.59(a2).
Other arrangements satisfactory to parties.
Duty of municipality, §160A-58.59(a).
Qualifications of firm for options,
§160A-58.59(a1).
Statement by municipality.
Prior to public hearing, information required,
§160A-58.53.
State policy, §160A-58.50.
Surveys.
Expenditures authorized, §160A-62.
Total area to be annexed.
Requirements, §160A-58.54(a).
Urban purposes, area developed for.
Determining, §160A-58.54(b).
Requirement for area annexed, §160A-58.54(a).
Water and sewer services.
Application to participate in system,
§160A-58.56(d).
At no cost other than periodic user fees.
Defined, §160A-58.56(h).
Average installation of a connection for a
residential lot.
Defined, §160A-58.56(h).
Charge for installation, §160A-58.56(d), (e).
Construction of lines.
Expenditures authorized, §160A-62.
Extension of time to provide.
Failure to timely provide not fault of
municipality, §160A-58.56(g).
Installation, §160A-58.56(f).
Maintenance and repair of connection lines,
§160A-58.56(f).
Opportunity to obtain.
Offering property owners prior to adoption of
annexation ordinance, §160A-58.56(b).
Time for completing, §160A-58.56(c).
Public water or sewer system defined,
§160A-58.56(a).
Requesting.
Combined notice, §160A-58.55(d).
Required to provide, §160A-58.56(a).
Time for providing, §160A-58.56(a).
Title to connection lines, §160A-58.56(f).
Personal property.
Tax liability of newly annexed territory,
§160A-58.10.
Petition.
Agreement prohibiting city from annexing into
area.
Permission to annex, §160A-58.27(i).
Annexation by petition, §160A-31.
Violations of part or agreement.
Review of action by city, §160A-58.27(a) to (i).
Population of five thousand or more.
Expenditures.
Authorized, §160A-52.
Recordation.
Annexation recorded, §160A-51.
Property tax liability of newly annexed
territory, §160A-58.10.
Recordation, §§160A-51, 160A-90(a).
Agreements with person having freehold interest
in annexed property, §160A-90(b).
Maps and election results, §160A-29.

ANNEXATION —Cont'd
Recordation —Cont'd
Municipalities initiating annexation.
Map of annexed area, copy of ordinance,
§160A-61.
Referendum on question of extension.
Election results recorded, §160A-29.
Regional sports authorities, §160A-479.17.
Right of entry.
Surveys of proposed new areas, §160A-30.
Rural fire departments.
Annexation initiated by municipality.
Assumption of proportionate share of fire
department debt, §160A-58.58.
Contract to provide fire protection in annexed
area, §160A-58.57.
Rural fire protection districts.
Annexation by municipality furnishing fire
protection, §69-25.15.
Sanitary district and municipality extending
simultaneously, §130A-70(a) to (h).
Sanitary districts.
Extension of district, §130A-69.
Satellite annexation in conjunction with municipal
annexation, §130A-70.1.
Satellite annexation.
Annexation of noncontiguous areas, §§160A-58.1
to 160A-58.8.
Surveys of proposed new areas, §160A-30.
Taxation.
Applicability of section, §160A-58.10(a).
Law enforcement service district.
Annexation of portion of district by
municipality.
Tax reduction and refund, §153A-304.4.
Property tax liability for newly annexed territory,
§160A-58.10.
Prorated taxes, §160A-58.10(b).
Taxes in subsequent fiscal years, §160A-58.10(c).
Transfer of tax records, §160A-58.10(d).
Violation of part or agreement.
Petition seeking review of action by city,
§160A-58.27(a).
Appeal from final decision of superior court,
§160A-58.27(g).
Conducted by court without jury,
§160A-58.27(d).
Date for review, court to fix, §160A-58.27(d).
Finding that city in violation.
Relief granted by court, §160A-58.27(f).
Finding that city not in violation.
Affirmance of action, §160A-58.27(f).
Oral argument, briefs, evidence, §160A-58.27(d).
Ordinance deemed amended, §160A-58.27(h).
Respondent, information supplied, duty,
§160A-58.27(c).
Service of copies, §160A-58.27(b).
Stay of operation of ordinance, granting or
denying, §160A-58.27(e).
Wills.
Executors and administrators.
Powers and duties, §28A-13-8.

ANNUAL AUDITED FINANCIAL REPORTS.
Insurance companies.
Generally, §§58-10-185 to 58-10-265.
See INSURANCE COMPANIES.

ANNUAL CHARGE FOR REVOLVING CREDIT
PLANS, §24-11(a).
Disclosure requirements for charge cards,
§24-11.2(b).

ANNUAL CHARGE FOR REVOLVING CREDIT PLANS —Cont'd
Disclosure requirements for credit cards, §24-11.1(b).

ANNUITIES.
Application of annuitant or proposed owner.
Individual annuity contract, §58-58-146(a).
Copies, §58-58-146(a).
Authorized, §58-7-15.
Charitable gift annuities.
Authorized, §58-3-6(a).
Business of insurance.
Issuance not to constitute engaging in, §58-3-6(e).
Definition of "educational institution,"§58-3-6(f).
Enforcement of provisions by insurance department, §58-3-6(d).
Information to be made available to insurance commissioner, §58-3-6(c).
Notice to insurance department, §58-3-6(b).
Death benefits.
Surrender fees on, §58-58-147.
Decedents' estates.
Killing decedents.
Additional liability for annuity company, §31A-11(c).
Proceeds payable to slayer, §31A-11(a).
Disclosure required, §§58-60-120 to 58-60-145.
See ANNUITY DISCLOSURE.
Funding agreements.
Insurers authorized to write life insurance and annuities, §58-7-16.
Group annuity contracts, §58-58-145(a).
Assignment of interest in, §58-58-155.
Certificates.
Contents, §58-58-145(b).
Issuance, §58-58-145(b).
Non-applicability of provisions, §58-58-145(d).
Provision in contract regarding, §58-58-145(c).
Individual annuity contracts.
Application of annuitant or proposed owners, §58-58-146.
Interstate insurance product regulation compact, §§58-91-1 to 58-91-80.
See INTERSTATE INSURANCE PRODUCT REGULATION COMPACT.
Killing decedents.
Additional liability for annuity companies, §31A-11(c).
Proceeds payable to slayer, §31A-11(a).
Life insurance generally.
See LIFE INSURANCE.
Local governmental employees' retirement system, §128-30.
Mortality tables.
Worth of annuities.
Establishing present worth, §8-47.
Principal and income act.
Deferred compensation, annuities, similar payment.
Allocation, §37A-4-409.
Insurance policies.
Allocation of receipts not normally apportioned during administration of trust, §37A-4-407(a) to (c).
Public officers and employees, §§147-9.2 to 147-9.4.
Rates.
Exemption from applicability of rating provisions, §58-40-15.

ANNUITIES —Cont'd
Renunciation, §31B-1(a).
Renunciation of succession, §31B-1.
Retirement system for teachers and state employees.
Annuity reserve fund, §135-8(c).
Merger with pension reserve fund into pension accumulation fund, §135-8(g).
Annuity savings fund, §135-8(b).
Transfer of credits from local governmental employees' retirement system, §135-18.1(b).
Definitions, §135-1.
Merger of annuity reserve fund and pension reserve fund into pension accumulation fund, §135-8(g).
State institutions of higher education.
Optional retirement program.
Underwriting program by purchase of annuity contracts, §135-5.1(a).
School employees.
Annuity contracts, §115C-341.
Custodial accounts in lieu of, §115C-341.
Senior specific certification and professional designations.
Use of fraudulent marketing practice in solicitation, sale or purchase of product.
Rules to protect consumers, §58-63-75.
Solicitation, §§58-60-120 to 58-60-145.
See ANNUITY DISCLOSURE.
Standard nonforfeiture law for deferred annuities, §58-58-61.
Cash surrender value, §58-58-61(h).
Effective date, §58-58-61(o).
Inapplicability of section, §58-58-61(b).
Interest rates used in determining minimum amounts, §58-58-61(e).
Lapse of time considerations, §58-58-61(l).
Limited death benefits, disclosure, §58-58-61(k).
Maturity date, §58-58-61(j).
Minimum values, §58-58-61(d).
Paid-up annuity benefits, §58-58-61(i).
Present value, §58-58-61(f), (g).
Proration of values, §58-58-61(m).
Required contract provision, §58-58-61(c).
Rules, §58-58-61(n).
Title of law, §58-58-61(a).
Standard provisions, §58-58-23.
Suitability in annuity transactions, §§58-60-150 to 58-60-180.
Applicability of act, §58-60-155(b).
Exemptions, §58-60-160.
Citation of act, §58-60-150.
Corrective action.
Order of commissioner to take, §58-60-175(a).
Reduction or elimination of penalty if taken, §58-60-175(b).
Definitions, §58-60-165.
Exemptions from act, §58-60-160.
Purpose of act, §58-60-155(a).
Recommendations.
Defined, §58-60-165.
Duties of insurers and insurance producers, §58-60-170(a), (b).
Exceptions, §58-60-170(c).
National Association of Securities Dealers conduct rules.
Compliance with, §58-60-170(h).
System to supervise recommendations of insurance producers, §58-60-170(e) to (g).
Records, §58-60-180(a).
How maintained, §58-60-180(b).

ANNUITIES —Cont'd
Suitability in annuity transactions —Cont'd
Title of act, §58-60-150.
Unfair methods of competition.
Violations as, §58-60-175(c).
Surrender fees on death benefits, §58-58-147.
Teachers.
Annuities and deferred compensation, §§147-9.2 to 147-9.4.
Third-party administrators.
Generally, §§58-56-2 to 58-56-66.
See THIRD-PARTY ADMINISTRATORS.
Transfers to minors.
Creating custodial property and effecting transfer, §33A-9.
Custodian investing in, §33A-12.
University of North Carolina.
Purchase of annuity or retirement income contracts for faculty members, officers and employees, §116-17.
Custodial accounts in lieu of, §116-17.
Worth of annuities.
Mortality tables.
Establishing present worth of annuities, §8-47.

ANNUITY DISCLOSURE, §§58-60-120 to 58-60-145.
Applicability, §58-60-125(b), (c).
Buyer's guide.
Defined, §58-60-130.
Standards, §58-60-135(b).
Face-to-face meetings, §58-60-135(a).
Free-look period, §58-60-135(c).
Definitions, §58-60-130.
Disclosure documents.
Contents, §58-60-140.
Defined, §58-60-130.
Standards, §58-60-135(b).
Face-to-face meetings, §58-60-135(a).
Free-look period, §58-60-135(c).
Purpose, §58-60-125(a).
Report to contract owners, §58-60-145.
Short title, §58-60-120.

ANNULMENT OF MARRIAGE.
Action for child custody or support, procedure, §50-13.5.
Acts barring rights of spouse, §31A-1(a).
Appearances.
Failure of defendant to appear in action.
Notice of trial not required, §50-10(b).
Child born of voidable or bigamous marriage legitimate, §50-11.1.
Complaints.
Material facts deemed denied by defendant, §50-10(a).
District courts.
Proper division for trial of civil actions, §7A-244.
Fraudulent misrepresentation as to age in obtaining license for marriage, §51-2(c).
Grounds for annulment.
Void and voidable marriages, §51-3.
Guardians.
Incompetent spouses.
Attorney-in-fact may commence, defend or maintain actions, §50-22.
Incompetent spouses.
Actions on behalf of, §50-22.
Judgments.
Material facts found by judge or jury.
Judgment not given in favor of plaintiff until, §50-10(a).

ANNULMENT OF MARRIAGE —Cont'd
Jurisdiction in rem or quasi in rem, §1-75.8.
Jury trial or trial before judge without jury.
Determination, §50-10(c).
Material facts found by judge or jury.
Judgment not given in favor of plaintiff until, §50-10(a).
Material facts found by judge or jury.
Genuine issue of material fact.
Determination, §50-10(d).
Judgment not given in favor of plaintiff until, §50-10(a).
Material facts in complaint deemed denied by defendant, §50-10(a).
Notice.
Failure of defendant to appear in action.
Notice of trial not required, §50-10(b).
Reference by consent, §1A-1 Rule 53(a).
Registration, §130A-111.
Summary judgment.
When summary judgment provisions applicable, §50-10(d).
Trial.
Jury trial or trial before judge without jury.
Determination, §50-10(c).
Notice of trial.
Failure of defendant to appear in action.
Notice not required, §50-10(b).
Vital statistics.
Registration of annulments, §130A-111.
Void and voidable marriages, §51-3.
What marriages may be declared void, §§50-4, 51-3.
Wills.
Revocation by annulment, §31-5.4.
Revival, §31-5.4.

ANONYMOUS COMMUNICATIONS AND PUBLICATIONS.
Libelous articles by newspapers or broadcasts by radio and television, §99-3.
Threatening letters, §14-394.

ANSON COUNTY.
Agricultural tendencies in certain counties.
Terms of, §42-23.
Ambulance service.
Attachment or garnishment and lien for, §§44-51.4 to 44-51.8.
Obtaining ambulance services without intending to pay, §14-111.2.
Condemnation or acquisition of land by local government unit outside county.
Consent of board of commissioners necessary, §153A-15.
Counties generally.
See COUNTIES.
Cropper or tenant refusing to perform terms of contract.
Forfeiture of right of possession to premises, §42-27.
Dangerous firearm use by young children, permitting.
Air rifles, air pistols and bb guns not dangerous firearm, §14-316(b).
Deeds in Anson.
Evidence of records of deeds, §8-26.
Dog collars.
Unlawful removal of electronic dog collars, §14-401.17.
Dogs used in hunting.
Regulation by wildlife resources commission, §113-291.5(a).

ANSON COUNTY —Cont'd
Game laws, local acts not repealed,
§113-133.1(e).
Officers compensated from fees.
Statement to be rendered, §128-13.
Oil, gas or mineral claims.
Certain ancient claims extinguished, preservation,
procedure, §1-42.1(a) to (d).
Registration of deeds.
Tax certification, no delinquent taxes due,
§161-31(b).
**Room occupancy tax levied by county, uniform
provisions,** §153A-155.
School property.
Acquisition and improvement, §153A-158.1.
Special school tax, election to abolish.
Petition required, §115C-505.
Wills in Anson.
Evidence of records of wills, §8-26.

ANSONVILLE.
All-terrain vehicles.
Use by employees on certain highways,
§20-171.24.

ANSWERS, §1A-1 Rule 7(a).
Administrative procedure.
Hearings, §150B-38(b).
Attorney disciplinary proceedings, Bar Rule
B.0114.
Cases removed to United States district court.
Time for filing upon remand to state court, §1A-1
Rule 12(a).
Crossclaims, §1A-1 Rule 7(a).
Defenses, §1A-1 Rule 8(b).
Affirmative defenses, §1A-1 Rule 8(c).
Denials.
Failure to deny.
Effect, §1A-1 Rule 8(d).
Form, §1A-1 Rule 8(b).
Discipline of attorneys, Bar Rule B.0114.
Emancipation of juvenile.
Time for filing, §7B-3502.
Eminent domain.
Private condemnors.
Petitions.
Answer to petition, §40A-25.
Public condemnors, §40A-45(a).
Determination of issues raised, §40A-42(d).
Failure to answer, §40A-46.
Reply to answer, §40A-45(b).
Service of answer, §40A-45(b).
Time for filing answer, §40A-46.
Expedited evictions.
Time for filing, §42-68.
Forms, §1A-1 Rule 84.
Highways, roads and streets.
Condemnation, §§136-106, 136-107.
Interrogatories, §1A-1 Rule 33(a).
**Interrogatories to discover assets of judgment
debtors,** §1-352.1.
Inverse condemnation, §40A-51(a).
Judicial standards commission proceedings,
JudStdsComm Rule 13.
Amendment, JudStdsComm Rule 16.
Libel and slander.
Proof of matter charged or mitigating
circumstances, §1A-1 Rule 9(i).
Payment into court.
Admissions.
Defendant ordered to satisfy admitted sum,
§1-510.

ANSWERS —Cont'd
Quo warranto.
Defendant undertaking before answer, §1-523.
Judgment by default and inquiry on failure of
defendant to give bond, §1-525.
Request for admission, §1A-1 Rule 36(a).
Small claims actions, §7A-218.
Assigned actions, §7A-220.
Special proceedings.
Contested proceedings, §1-394.
Termination of parental rights proceedings,
§7B-1108.
Failure of respondent to answer, §7B-1107.
Time for filing.
Summons to notify respondent, §7B-1106(a).
Third party answer, §1A-1 Rule 7(a).
Time for serving, §1A-1 Rule 12(a).
When presented, §1A-1 Rule 12(a).

ANTE LITEM NOTICE.
**Local acts not to require notice to local unit of
government of claim,** §1-539.16.

ANTENNAS.
Amateur radio antennas.
Zoning regulations, reasonable accommodation,
§153A-341.2.
Municipal planning and regulation of
development, §160A-383.3.
Wireless telecommunications facilities,
§§153A-349.50 to 153A-349.53.

ANTENUPTIAL AGREEMENTS.
Uniform premarital agreements act, §§52B-1 to
52B-11.
See PREMARITAL AGREEMENTS.

ANTHRAX.
Mass death and destruction weapons.
Nuclear, biological or chemical weapons,
§§14-288.21 to 14-288.24.
See WEAPONS OF MASS DEATH AND
DESTRUCTION.
Nuclear, biological or chemical agents.
Terrorist incident using, §§130A-475 to 130A-479.
See TERRORIST INCIDENT USING
NUCLEAR, BIOLOGICAL OR CHEMICAL
AGENTS.

ANTIBIOTICS.
Biological residues in animals, §§106-549.81 to
106-549.89.
See BIOLOGICAL RESIDUES IN ANIMALS.
Food, drug and cosmetic act.
Drugs deemed misbranded, §106-134.

ANTIBLACKLISTING ACT, §14-355.

ANTICIPATION NOTES.
Bond issues.
Local government finance.
General provisions, §§159-160 to 159-165.
See LOCAL GOVERNMENT FINANCE.
Housing finance agency, §122A-8.

ANTICIPATORY REPUDIATION.
Leases, UCC, §25-2A-402.
Retraction, §25-2A-403.
Sales, UCC, §25-2-610.
Retraction, §25-2-611.

ANTICLOSED SHOP ACT, §§95-78 to 95-84.
See EMPLOYMENT RELATIONS.

ANTIDEFICIENCY JUDGMENT ACT, §45-21.38.

ANTIFREEZE, §§106-579.1 to 106-579.14.
Administration of article.
  Commissioner of agriculture to administer,
    §106-579.7(b).
Adulteration.
  Deemed adulterated, §106-579.5.
Analysis.
  Reporting results of examination, §106-579.8.
Appeals.
  Judicial review of acts, orders or rulings,
    §106-579.12(e).
Board of agriculture.
  Defined, §106-579.3.
  Exclusive jurisdiction, §106-579.14.
Commissioner of agriculture.
  Administration of article, §106-579.7(b).
  Defined, §106-579.3.
  Exclusive jurisdiction, §106-579.14.
Condemnation.
  Enforcement of article, §106-579.10(b).
Court orders.
  Reports summarizing court orders, §106-579.13(b).
Decrees.
  Reports summarizing decrees, §106-579.13(b).
Definitions, §106-579.3.
District attorneys.
  Instituting and prosecuting proceedings,
    §106-579.12(c).
Enforcement of article.
  Condemnation orders, §106-579.10(b).
  Seizure of antifreeze, §106-579.10(b).
  "Stop sale" orders, §106-579.10(a).
  "Withdrawal from distribution" orders,
    §106-579.10(a).
  Supplying distribution data, §106-579.10(d).
Evidence.
  Copy of analysis administered as evidence,
    §106-579.10(c).
Fees.
  Inspection fee, §106-579.4.
  License fee, §106-579.4.
Incineration, disposal by prohibited,
    §130A-309.10(f1).
Injunctions, §106-579.12(d).
Inorganic salts.
  Antifreeze solutions compounded with.
    Manufacture or sale prohibited, §66-66.
Inspections.
  Authorized, §106-579.8.
  Fee, §106-579.4.
  Sampling and analysis, §106-579.8.
Judgments.
  Reports summarizing judgments, §106-579.13(b).
Judicial review of acts, orders or rulings,
    §106-579.12(e).
Jurisdiction.
  Exclusive jurisdiction vested in board and
    commissioner, §106-579.14.
Landfills, disposal in prohibited,
    §130A-309.10(f).
Licenses.
  Application for license.
    Confidential formula information, §106-579.11.
    Furnishing statement of formula or contents of
      antifreeze, §106-579.11.
      Confidential formula information,
        §106-579.11.
  Cancellation of license, §106-579.4.
  Fee, §106-579.4.
  Issuance, §106-579.4.

ANTIFREEZE —Cont'd
**List of brands and classes or types of
    antifreeze.**
  Publishing or furnishing list, §106-579.13(a).
Misbranding.
  Deemed misbranded, §106-579.6.
Misdemeanors.
  Manufacture or sale of antifreeze solutions
    compounded with inorganic salts or petroleum
    distillates, §66-66.
Notice.
  Repeal of existing regulation, §106-579.7(a).
  Warning notice for minor violations,
    §106-579.12(b).
Open containers.
  Placing in public places, §14-401.
Petroleum distillates.
  Antifreeze solutions compounded with.
    Manufacture or sale prohibited, §66-66.
Prohibited acts, §106-579.9.
Publications.
  Dissemination of certain information,
    §106-579.13(c).
  List of brands and classes or types of antifreeze,
    §106-579.13(a).
  Report summarizing judgments, decrees and court
    orders, §106-579.13(b).
Purpose of article, §106-579.2.
Registration.
  Application for registration, §106-579.4.
    Modifying application, §106-579.4.
  Refusal to register, §106-579.4.
Reports.
  Sampling and analysis, §106-579.8.
  Summarization of judgments, decrees and court
    orders, §106-579.13(b).
Rules and regulations.
  Execution of rules or regulations, §106-579.7(b).
  Issuance, amendment or repeal of any rule or
    regulation, §106-579.7(a).
  Notice to repeal existing regulation, §106-579.7(a).
Sampling and analysis.
  Evidentiary value of copy of analysis,
    §106-579.10(c).
  Reporting results of examination, §106-579.8.
Seizure of article.
  Enforcement of article, §106-579.10(b).
Short title, §106-579.1.
"Stop sale" orders.
  Enforcement of article, §106-579.10(a).
Temporary restraining orders.
  Violations of article, §106-579.12(d).
Title of article, §106-579.1.
Uniformity of requirements, §106-579.2.
Unlawful acts, §106-579.9.
Violations of article.
  Continuing violations constitutes separate
    violation, §106-579.12(a).
  Instituting proceedings, §106-579.12(c).
  Minor violations.
    Notice of warning, §106-579.12(b).
  Preliminary or permanent injunctions,
    §106-579.12(d).
  Prosecution of violations, §106-579.12(c).
  Temporary restraining orders, §106-579.12(d).
"Withdrawal from distribution" orders.
  Enforcement of article, §106-579.10(a).
  Supplying distribution data, §106-579.10(d).

ANTILAPSE STATUTE.
Generally, §31-42.

ANTI-PYRAMID STATUTE, §14-291.2.

ANTIQUE AIRPLANES.
Property tax assessment.
Antique airplane defined, §105-277.12(a).
Designated special class of property for
assessment, §105-277.12(b).

ANTIQUE FIREARMS.
Defined, §§14-402(c), 14-409.11(a).
Exclusions from definition, §14-409.11(b).
Felons.
Unlawful to purchase, own, possess, care or
control firearms or weapons of mass death
and destruction.
Inapplicability, §14-415.1(a).
Permit or license to sell pistols.
Inapplicability of provisions to, §14-402(b).

ANTIQUE SLOT MACHINES.
**Defense in prosecution for possession of slot
machine,** §14-309.1.

ANTIQUE VEHICLES.
Abandoned and derelict motor vehicles.
Exemption from provisions, §20-137.14.
Dealers.
Temporary supplemental license.
Off-premises sales, §20-292.1.
Historic vehicle owner special registration,
§20-132.
Property taxes.
Defined, §105-330.9(a).
Special class, assessment, §105-330.9(b).
Special plates, §20-79.4(b).

ANTIQUE WEAPONS.
Mass death and destruction weapons.
Applicability of section, §14-288.8.

ANTITRUST.
**Cooperative agreements among physicians or
between physician, hospital or other
person.**
Immunity from scrutiny of federal and state
antitrust laws, §§90-21.26(a), 90-21.36(a).
Federal or state antitrust laws defined,
§90-21.25.
Firearms and other weapons.
Unlawful for felon to possess.
Inapplicability of antitrust violations,
§14-415.1(e).
Monopolies and restraint of trade, §§75-1 to
75-42.
See MONOPOLIES AND RESTRAINT OF
TRADE.
Motor fuel marketing generally, §§75-80 to
75-90.
See MOTOR FUEL MARKETING.

APARTMENTS.
Landlord and tenant.
General provisions.
See LANDLORD AND TENANT.
Liens.
Possessory liens on personal property.
Persons entitled to lien, §44A-2(e).
Unit ownership, §§47A-1 to 47A-28.
See UNIT OWNERSHIP.

APEX, CITY OF.
Accessory building of bona fide farm.
Building code exemption.
Zoning ordinance, §160A-360(k).

APEX, CITY OF —Cont'd
Satellite annexation.
Limitation on area of satellite corporate limits,
inapplicability, §160A-58.1(b).

APIARIES.
Bees and honey.
See BEES AND HONEY.

APOTHECARIES.
Pharmacists and pharmacy.
See PHARMACISTS AND PHARMACIES.

APPALACHIAN STATE UNIVERSITY.
University of North Carolina.
Constituent institution of university of North
Carolina, §116-4.
Traffic and parking.
Specific provisions applicable to Appalachian
state university, §116-44.5.

APPALACHIAN TRAILS SYSTEM, §§113A-72 to
113A-77.
Acquisition of rights of way and lands,
§113A-76.
Manner of acquiring, §113A-76.
**Administration of lands acquired by state
outside of boundaries,** §113A-75(e).
Appropriations.
Expenditures authorized, §113A-77.
Citation of article, §113A-72.
Connecting or side trails, §113A-74.
Coordination with national trails system act,
§113A-74.
**Conveyance of land acquired within certain
distance of right-of-way to forest service,**
§113A-75(d).
**Cooperation and assistance of board of
transportation,** §113A-75(c).
County inspection department permits.
Environmental compliance requirements for
land-disturbing activity, §153A-357(d).
**Due consideration to conservation of
environment, advice and assistance from
local governments and organizations,**
§113A-75(b).
Expenditures.
Authorization, §113A-77.
Legislative declaration, §113A-73.
Motor vehicles.
Use regulated, §113A-75(g).
Policy, §113A-73(a).
Purpose, §113A-73(b).
Real property.
Acquisition, §113A-76.
Regulations, establishing, §113A-75(f).
Rights of way.
Acquisition, §113A-76.
Cooperation with federal agencies to develop,
§113A-75(a).
Short title, §113A-72.
Title, §113A-72.

APPEAL BONDS.
Appeal of right, AppProc Rule 17(a).
Appeal to appellate division, §1-270.
Cap on amount.
Judgment directing payment of money.
Noncompensatory damages of $25,000,000 or
more, §1-289(b), (c).
Certiorari, §1-269.
**Discretionary review of court of appeals
determination,** AppProc Rule 17(b).
Before court of appeals determination, AppProc
Rule 17(c).

APPEAL BONDS —Cont'd
Health care facilities.
Certificates of need.
Appeal of final decision by department,
§131E-188(b1).
In forma pauperis, §1-288, AppProc Rule 17(d).
Injunctions.
Restraining orders and injunctions in effect
pending appeals, §1-500.
Judgment directing payment of money, stay,
§1-289(a).
Amount of bond, determination, §1-289(a2).
Cap on bond amount, noncompensatory damages
of $25,000,000 or more, §1-289(b), (c).
Deposit into court in lieu of, §1-289(a1).
Dismissal of appeal, failure to give bond,
§1-289(a1).
Perishable property, sale, proceeds deposited or
invested, §1-289(a1).
Justification of sureties, §1-286.
**Physician or surgeon review of revocation or
suspension of license,** §90-14.9(a).
Medical board not required to give, §90-14.11(a).
Quo warranto, §1-529.
Recordari, §1-269.
Record on appeal.
Undertaking as part of record, §1-297.
Security for costs, AppProc Rule 6.
Stays.
Fiduciaries.
Security limited for, §1-294.
Judgment directing conveyance, §1-291.
Judgment directing payment of money, §1-289(a).
Amount of bond, determination, §1-289(a2).
Cap on bond amount, noncompensatory
damages of $25,000,000 or more, §1-289(b),
(c).
Deposit into court in lieu of, §1-289(a1).
Dismissal of appeal, failure to give bond,
§1-289(a1).
Perishable property, sale, proceeds deposited or
invested, §1-289(a1).
Judgment for personal property, §1-290.
Judgment for real property, §1-292.
Service of undertaking on appellee, §1-295.
Undertaking in one or more instruments, §1-295.
Supersedeas, §1-269.
Undertaking on appeal, §1-285(a).
Exception as to state, city, county, local board of
education or an officer or agency thereof,
§1-285(b).
Justification of sureties, §1-286.

APPEALS.
ABC boards.
Removal of members and employees, §18B-704(h).
Abortion.
Parental or judicial consent to abortion.
Waiver of parental consent requirement,
§90-21.8(h).
**Abused, neglected or dependent juvenile
actions.**
Final order of court.
Disposition pending appeal, §7B-1003.
Modification of original order after affirmation
by appellate court, §7B-1004.
Notice to preserve right to appeal.
Permanency planning, §7B-507(c).
Permanency planning.
Notice to preserve right to appeal, §7B-507(c).
Proper parties, §7B-1002.

APPEALS —Cont'd
**Abused, neglected or dependent juvenile
actions** —Cont'd
Final order of court —Cont'd
Right of appeal, §7B-1001.
Permanency planning.
Notice to preserve right to appeal order,
§7B-507(c).
Proper parties.
Final order of court, §7B-1002.
Right of appeal.
Final order of court, §7B-1001.
Access to judicial proceeding or record.
Ruling on motion, appeal of, §1-72.1(e).
Accident and health insurance.
Utilization review.
Noncertification, §58-50-61(j) to (l).
Administrative boards and agencies.
Appeal of right directly to appellate division,
AppProc Rule 18(a).
Extension of time for taking action, AppProc
Rule 18(f).
Notice of appeal.
Filing and serving, time, AppProc Rule 18(b).
Record on appeal.
Additional materials, AppProc Rule 18(e).
Composition, AppProc Rule 18(c).
Settling the record, AppProc Rule 18(d).
Time and method for taking, AppProc Rule
18(b).
Declaratory ruling.
Denial, §150B-4(a1).
General provisions, §§150B-43 to 150B-52.
See ADMINISTRATIVE PROCEDURE.
Miscellaneous provision governing agency appeals,
AppProc 20.
Superior courts.
Proper division for review or appeal of
administrative agency decisions,
§7A-250(a).
Administrative rules.
Permanent rules.
Judicial review.
Rule returned by commission, §150B-21.8(d).
Adoption.
Consent of parent or guardian obtained by fraud
or duress, §48-2-607(c).
Procedure, notice, §48-2-607(b).
Prohibited grounds for appeals, §48-2-607(a).
Relinquishment of parent or guardian obtained by
fraud or duress, §48-2-607(c).
Unfavorable preplacement assessments,
§48-3-308(a).
Adult care homes.
Discharge of residents, §131D-4.8(c).
Affirmance of judgment.
Power of court, §1-297.
Agriculture.
Marketing and branding of farm products.
Classification of farm products, §106-191.
Air pollution control.
Local air pollution control programs.
Judicial review of final administrative decisions,
§143-215.112(d2).
Airports.
Zoning.
Board of appeals, §63-33(c).
Judicial review of board, §63-34.
Alarm systems licensing.
Suspension or revocation of license, §74D-10(b).

APPEALS —Cont'd
Alcoholic beverages.
Tribal alcoholic beverage control.
Appeal of actions of tribal control commission, §18B-112(h).
Aliens.
Verification of work authorization.
Labor commissioner.
Appeal of orders, §64-36.
Amicus curiae briefs, AppProc Rule 28(i).
Annexation.
Municipalities initiating annexation.
Contract with private firm to provide solid waste collection.
No contract offered, §160A-58.59(g).
Contract with rural fire department to provide fire protection.
Good faith offer not made, §160A-58.57(g) to (i).
Petition by property owner seeking review, §160A-58.60.
Antifreeze.
Judicial review of acts, orders or rulings, §106-579.12(e).
Appeal information statement.
Adoption by court of appeals, AppProc Rule 41(a).
Completion, filing, time, AppProc Rule 41(b).
Mail, filing by, AppProc Rule 41(b).
Purpose, AppProc Rule 41(a).
Appeal of right from administrative agencies, boards, commissions to appellate division, AppProc Rules 18, 20.
Appeal of right from court of appeals to supreme court, §7A-30, AppProc Rule 14.
Appeal bond, AppProc Rule 17.
Briefs.
Copies, AppProc Rule 14(d).
Filing and serving.
Failure, AppProc Rule 14(d).
Time, AppProc Rule 14(d).
Constitutional questions.
Appeal presenting.
Content of notice, AppProc Rule 14(b).
Dissent in court of appeals.
Appeal based on.
Content of notice, AppProc Rule 14(b).
Docketing, AppProc Rule 14(c).
How taken, AppProc Rule 14(a).
Notice of appeal.
Content, AppProc Rule 14(b).
Filing and serving.
Time, AppProc Rule 14(a).
Record on appeal.
Composition, transmission, copies, AppProc Rule 14(c).
Scope of review, AppProc Rule 16.
Apportionment and redistricting.
Action challenging state legislative or congressional plan.
Direct appeal to supreme court, §120-2.5.
Arbitration, §1-569.28(a), (b).
Preaward ruling by arbitrators.
Appealability of arbitrator's ruling, §1-569.18(b), (c).
Attorneys at law.
Admission to practice, AdmissPrac Rules .1401 to .1405.
Agreements of counsel.
Recognition, AppProc Rule 33(c).
Appearance, AppProc Rule 33(a).

APPEALS —Cont'd
Attorneys at law —Cont'd
Counsel of record.
Appearance, AppProc Rule 33(a).
Entry of attorney as, AppProc Rule 33(a).
Disciplinary proceedings, §84-28(h).
Electronically filed documents.
Signature.
More than one attorney listed as attorney for parties, AppProc Rule 33(b).
From board of law examiners, §84-24.
Out-of-state attorneys.
Limited practice, AppProc Rule 33(d).
Secure leave periods.
Authorization, AppProc Rule 33.1(a).
Designation, AppProc Rule 33.1(c).
Content, AppProc Rule 33.1(d).
When to file, AppProc Rule 33.1(f).
Where to file, AppProc Rule 33.1(e).
Length, AppProc Rule 33.1(b).
Number, AppProc Rule 33.1(b).
Purpose, AppProc Rule 33.1(a).
Signature and address on papers, AppProc Appx B.
Specialization.
Denial of certification or continued certification, Bar Rules D.1805, D.1806.
Bail.
Bond forfeiture.
Release from final judgment, §15A-544.8(f).
Setting aside, §15A-544.5(h).
Correction of errors by appellate division.
Authority of court to act pending appeal, §15A-1453(a).
Bank commissioner.
Branch banking, interstate, §53-224.30.
Orders appealed to commission.
Appellate review panel, §53-92(d).
Banking commission.
Final orders of, §53-92(d).
Banks.
Bank holding companies.
Decisions of commissioner, §53-231.
International banking.
Commissioner's decisions, §53-232.17.
Regional reciprocal banking.
Decisions of commissioner, §53-215.
Trust terminated on insolvency of trustee bank.
Appointment of new trustee, §53-29.
Beach area essential property insurance.
Insurance underwriting association.
Plan of operation.
Orders of commission with respect to plan, §58-45-30(c).
Biological residues in animals.
Detention or quarantine of animal, animal product or feed, §106-549.83.
Blind persons.
Aid to the blind.
Denial of application for aid, §111-16.
Boat liens.
Action to regain possession of vessel.
Appeal to district court for trial de novo, §44A-6.1(b).
Bonds, surety.
Amount of bond, determination, §1-289(a2).
Appeal of right to supreme court, AppProc Rule 17(a).
Appeal to appellate division, §1-270.
Cap on amount of bond.
Noncompensatory damages of $25,000,000 or more awarded, §1-289(b), (c).

APPEALS —Cont'd
Bonds, surety —Cont'd
Certiorari, §1-269.
Discretionary review of court of appeals
determination, AppProc Rule 17(b).
Before determination, AppProc Rule 17(c).
Health care facilities.
Certificates of need.
Appeal of final decision by department,
§131E-188(b1).
In forma pauperis, §1-288, AppProc Rule 17(d).
Injunctions.
Restraining orders and injunctions in effect
pending appeals, §1-500.
Judgment directing payment of money, §1-289(a).
Cap on amount, noncompensatory damages of
$25,000,000 or more, §1-289(b), (c).
Justification of sureties, §1-286.
Physician or surgeon review of revocation or
suspension of license, §90-14.9(a).
Medical board not required to give, §90-14.11(a).
Quo warranto, §1-529.
Recordari, §1-269.
Record on appeal.
Undertakings as part of record, §1-297.
Security for costs, AppProc Rule 6.
Stays.
Fiduciaries.
Security limited for, §1-294.
Judgment directing conveyance, §1-291.
Judgment directing payment of money,
§1-289(a).
Cap on amount, noncompensatory damages of
$25,000,000 or more, §1-289(b), (c).
Judgment for personal property, §1-290.
Judgment for real property, §1-292.
Service of undertaking on appellee, §1-295.
Undertaking in one or more instruments,
§1-295.
Supersedeas, §1-269.
Undertaking on appeal, §1-285(a).
Exception as to state, city, county, local board of
education or an officer or agency thereof,
§1-285(b).
Justification of sureties, §1-286.
Boundaries.
Special proceeding to establish boundaries.
Appeal to session, §38-3(b).
Briefs.
Additional authorities.
Memorandum, AppProc Rule 28(g).
Additional issues.
Appellee's brief, AppProc Rule 28(c).
Amicus curiae briefs, AppProc Rule 28(i).
Appeal of right from court of appeals to supreme
court, AppProc Rule 14(d).
Appellant's brief.
Appendixes.
When not required, AppProc Rule 28(d).
When required, AppProc Rule 28(d).
Content, AppProc Rule 28(b).
Appellee's brief.
Additional issues, presentation, AppProc Rule
28(c).
Content, AppProc Rule 28(c).
Appendixes.
Verbatim portion of transcripts, AppProc Rule
28(d).
Arrangement of content, AppProc Appx E.
Case submitted for decision on written briefs,
AppProc Rule 30(d).

APPEALS —Cont'd
Briefs —Cont'd
Content, AppProc Appx E.
Appellant's brief, AppProc Rule 28(b).
Appellee's brief, AppProc Rule 28(c).
Copies.
Appeal of right from court of appeals to
supreme court, AppProc Rule 14(d).
Clerk to reproduce and distribute, AppProc Rule
13(b).
Discretionary review on certification by supreme
court, AppProc Rule 15(g).
Death penalty cases.
Filing and serving, AppProc Rule 13(a).
Discretionary review on certification by supreme
court, AppProc Rule 15(g).
Filing and serving.
Failure, consequences, AppProc Rule 13(c).
Appeal of right from court of appeals to
supreme court, AppProc Rule 14(d).
Discretionary review on certification by
supreme court, AppProc Rule 15(g).
Time, AppProc Rule 13(a).
Appeal of right from court of appeals to
supreme court, AppProc Rule 14(d).
Discretionary review on certification by
supreme court, AppProc Rule 15(g).
Rehearing.
Petition granted, AppProc Rule 31(d).
Reply briefs, AppProc Rule 28(h).
Function, AppProc Rule 28(a).
Identity of persons under age of 18.
Protection, AppProc Rule 28(a).
Indexes, AppProc Appx B.
Joinder of multiple parties, AppProc Rule 28(f).
Juvenile matters, AppProc Rule 3.1(c).
Identity of persons under age of 18.
Protection, AppProc Rule 28(a).
No-merit briefs, AppProc Rule 3.1(d).
Length limitations.
Briefs filed in court of appeals, AppProc Rule
28(j).
Memorandum.
Additional authorities, AppProc Rule 28(g).
Order of arrangement, AppProc Appx E.
Page limitations.
Briefs filed in court of appeals, AppProc Rule
28(j).
Record on appeal.
References to, AppProc Rule 28(e).
Rehearing.
Petition granted, AppProc Rule 31(d).
Reply briefs, AppProc Rule 28(h).
Time.
Filing and serving, AppProc Rule 13(a).
Appeal of right from court of appeals to
supreme court, AppProc Rule 14(d).
Discretionary review on certification by
supreme court, AppProc Rule 15(g).
Rehearing.
Petition granted, AppProc Rule 31(d).
Reply briefs, AppProc Rule 28(h).
Unpublished opinions.
Citation, AppProc Rule 30(e).
Verbatim portion of transcripts.
Appendixes, AppProc Rule 28(d).
Word count limitations.
Briefs filed in court of appeals, AppProc Rule
28(j).
Brownfields property reuse.
Decision by department as to whether or not to
enter into agreement, §130A-310.36.

APPEALS —Cont'd

Building code council, §143-141.

Building codes.
Alternative designs and construction, §143-140.1.
Door lock exemptions.
Revocation of permit, §143-143.4(f).

Calendaring cases for hearing, AppProc Rule 29(b).

Capital punishment.
Automatic review of judgment and sentence, §15A-2000(d).
Direct appeal to supreme court.
Death sentences included in superior court judgments, §7A-27(a).
Indigent persons.
Representation of indigent persons, §7A-451(b) to (e).
Appellate appointments, IndigCounsel Model Plan Art VIII §8.2.
New trial.
Notice of new trial, §15-193.
Prisoner taken to place of trial when new trial granted, §15-195.
Notice of appeals, §15-189.
Notice of reprieve or new trial, §15-193.

Cap on amount of bond to stay execution.
Judgment directing payment of money.
Noncompensatory damages of $25,000,000 or more, §1-289(b), (c).

Caption of documents.
Format, style, AppProc Appx B.

Certificate of determination of appeal.
Procedure after determination, §1-298.

Certification of cause for discretionary review by supreme court, §7A-31, AppProc Rule 15.

Certiorari.
See CERTIORARI.

Change of name.
Denial of request, §101-5(f).

Child abuse, neglect or dependency.
Central registry and responsible individuals list.
Judicial review, §§7B-320, 7B-324.

Child custody jurisdiction and enforcement, §50A-314.

Child custody order enforcement pending appeal.
Enforcement by civil contempt proceedings, §50-13.3(a).

Childhood vaccine-related injury compensation.
Decisions of commission, §130A-428(c).

Children's health insurance program.
Benefits eligibility, §108A-70.26(c).
Review of decisions, §108A-70.29.

Child support.
Enforcement pending appeal.
Civil contempt, §50-13.4(f).
Expedited process.
Orders of child support hearing officer, §50-38.

Civil actions or special proceedings.
How and when taken, AppProc Rule 3.

Claim and delivery.
Issuance or refusal to issue order to sheriff, §1-474(a).

Clerks of court.
In forma pauperis.
Fees of clerk, §1-288.
Oath and bond.
Duty to take and give, AppProc Rule 39(a).
Office hours, AppProc Rule 39(a).
Records kept, AppProc Rule 39(b).

APPEALS —Cont'd

Clerks of court —Cont'd
Superior court clerks.
Civil actions, §1-301.1.
Estate matters, §1-301.3.
Special proceedings, §1-301.2.

Coastal area management.
Denial of permits, §113A-123.

Collection agencies.
Denial of permit, §58-70-30.

Commercial feed.
Judicial review of act, orders or rulings, §106-284.44(e).

Commercial vehicles, disqualification from driving.
Testing positive in a drug or alcohol test, §20-37.20B.

Concealed handgun permit.
Denial, revocation or nonrenewal of permit, §§14-415.15(c), 14-415.18(a).

Consolidation of appeals, AppProc 40.

Constitution of North Carolina.
Court of appeals.
Jurisdiction, NC Const Art IV §12.
Right of appeals from certain decisions directly to supreme court, §7A-30.
Jurisdiction of the general court of justice, NC Const Art IV §12.
Supreme court.
Jurisdiction, NC Const Art IV §12.

Constitution of the United States.
Court of appeals decisions.
Right of direct appeal from certain decisions, §7A-30.
Review of facts tried by jury, US Const Amd 7.

Consumer finance act.
Commission may review rules, orders or acts of commissioner, §53-188.

Contempt.
Civil contempt, §5A-24.
Criminal contempt, §5A-17.
Juveniles.
Direct contempt, finding of, §5A-32(g).

Continuing legal education board of trustee decisions, Bar Rule D.1610.

Cooperative agreements among physicians or between physician, hospital or other person.
Judicial action as to certificates of public advantage, §90-21.33.

Corporations.
Administrative dissolution of business corporation.
Denial of reinstatement, §55-14-23.
Foreign corporations.
Revocation of certificate of authority, §55-15-32.
Refusal of secretary of state to file documents, §55D-16.

Costs, §6-33, AppProc Rule 35.
Discretion of appellate court in recovery of cost, §6-33.
Dismissal.
Taxing, AppProc Rule 35(a).
Execution to collect in appellate courts, AppProc Rule 35(d).
Federal courts.
State costs on appeals to federal courts, §6-17.
Generally, §6-33.
Judgment affirmed or reversed, AppProc Rule 35(a).

APPEALS —Cont'd
Costs —Cont'd
Magistrates.
 Recovery of cost, §6-33.
Mandate of court.
 Direction as to, AppProc Rule 35(b).
Prosecution bonds.
 Sureties on bonds liable for costs, §6-3.
Schedule of fees and costs, AppProc Appx F.
Security for costs.
 Appeal bond, AppProc Rule 17.
 Appellant required to provide, AppProc Rule
   6(a).
 Criminal appeals.
   No security required, AppProc Rule 6(e).
 Dismissal.
   Failure to file, defect in security, AppProc
     Rule 6(d).
 Filed with record on appeal, AppProc Rule 6(c).
 In forma pauperis appeals, AppProc Rule 6(b).
 Taxable in trial tribunals, AppProc Rule 35(c).
 To whom allowed, AppProc Rule 35(a).
Counties.
Bonds, surety.
 Exception as to, §1-285(b).
Inspection departments.
 General appeal to commissioner of insurance,
   §153A-374.
 Orders to take corrective action, §153A-370.
 Stop orders, §153A-361.
Planning and zoning.
 Board of adjustment, §153A-345(b).
 Certiorari, appeals to superior court, §153A-349.
Special assessments.
 General court of justice, §153A-197.
Court of appeals, §§7A-16 to 7A-21.
 See COURT OF APPEALS.
Courts-martial for national guard, §127A-62.
Credit unions.
Suspension and conservation.
 Decisions of administrator, §54-109.92(k).
**Criminal justice education and training
   standards commission.**
Denial, suspension or revocation of certification,
   §17C-11(b).
Criminal procedure.
Appellate division.
 Certiorari, §15A-1444(e), (g).
 Correction of errors, §§15A-1441 to 15A-1453.
Briefs.
 Death penalty cases.
   Filing and serving, AppProc Rule 13(a).
Burden of proof.
 Prejudicial error, §15A-1443(a).
Capital punishment.
 Automatic review, §15A-2000(d).
 Briefs.
   Filing and serving in death penalty cases,
     AppProc Rule 13(a).
 Direct review by supreme court, §7A-27(a).
 New trial.
   Notice, §15-193.
   Taking prisoner to place of new trial, §15-195.
 Notice of appeal, §15-189.
 Reprieve.
   Notice, §15-193.
Certiorari, §15A-1444(e), (g).
 Correction of errors by appellate division,
   §15A-1448(c).

APPEALS —Cont'd
Criminal procedure —Cont'd
Correction of errors by appellate division,
   §§15A-1441 to 15A-1453.
 Affirmance of sentence, §15A-1447(e).
   Duties of clerk of superior court upon,
     §15A-1452(b).
 Ancillary actions during appeal, §15A-1453.
 Authorized, §15A-1441.
 Bail.
   Authority of court to act pending appeal,
     §15A-1453(a).
 Capital cases, §15A-1441.
 Certiorari, §15A-1448(c).
 Compliance with directive of appellate court.
   Duties of clerk of superior court, §15A-1452.
 Double jeopardy.
   When charges must be dismissed with
     prejudice, §15A-1447(g).
 Grounds, §15A-1442.
 Jurisdiction, §15A-1448(a).
 Lack of jurisdiction on part of trial court.
   Errors which may be reviewed even though
     no objection, exception or motion made,
     §15A-1446(d).
 Motion for appropriate relief, §15A-1453(b).
 New trial.
   Duties of clerk of superior court upon order of
     new trial, §15A-1452(c).
   Relief available upon appeal, §15A-1447(a).
 Notice of appeal, §15A-1448(b).
   Time for, §15A-1448(a).
 Prejudice to defendant.
   Burden of showing prejudice, §15A-1443(a).
   Grounds for correction of errors generally,
     §15A-1442.
   No prejudice by granting of relief which
     defendant has sought, §15A-1443(c).
   When prejudice exists, §15A-1443(a), (b).
 Preservation of right to appeal, §15A-1446(a).
   Errors subject to review even though no
     objection, exception or motion made,
     §15A-1446(d).
   Waiver of right to assert error upon appeal.
     Failure to make appropriate and timely
       motion or objection, §15A-1446(b).
 Procedures, §15A-1444(d).
 Relief available upon appeal, §15A-1447.
 Reversal.
   Relief available upon appeal, §15A-1447(b),
     (c).
 Security for costs not required, §15A-1449.
 Sentencing.
   Relief available upon appeal, §15A-1447(d),
     (f).
 State may appeal, §15A-1445(a).
   Order granting motion to suppress,
     §15A-1445(b).
 Stays, §15A-1451(a).
   No stay when state appeals, §15A-1451(b).
 Time for entry of appeal, §15A-1448(a).
 Waiver of right to assert error upon appeal.
   Failure to make appropriate and timely
     motion or objections, §15A-1446(b).
 Withdrawal of appeal, §15A-1450.
   Order to be entered by clerk of superior court,
     §15A-1452(a).
 Right to appeal not waived, §15A-1448(a).
Cost on appeal, §6-33.
Defined, §15A-101.

APPEALS —Cont'd
Criminal procedure —Cont'd
District courts, §7A-290.
Appeal by defendant from, §15A-1431(b).
Compliance with judgment no bar,
§15A-1431(d).
Notice of appeal, §15A-1431(c).
Appeal after compliance with judgment,
§15A-1431(d).
Pretrial release.
Order remains in effect pending appeal,
§15A-1431(e).
Procedure, §15A-1444(c).
Stays, §15A-1431(f1).
Withdrawal of appeal, §15A-1431(c), (g).
After calendaring case, §15A-1431(h).
Appeal by state from, §15A-1432(a).
Affirmance of judgment of district court,
§15A-1432(e).
Hearing on motion, §15A-1432(c).
Motion, §15A-1432(b).
Remand to district court for further
proceedings, §15A-1432(d).
Bail bond status, §7A-290.
Notice of appeal, §7A-290.
Appeal by defendant from district court,
§15A-1431(c), (d).
Evidence.
Insufficiency of evidence to prove crime charged.
Preserving issue for appeal at trial, AppProc
Rule 10(a).
How and when taken in criminal cases, AppProc
Rule 4.
Identity of persons under age of 18.
Protection.
Juvenile victims of sexual offenses, AppProc
Rule 4(e).
Impaired driving, implied consent offenses,
§20-38.7.
Insufficiency of evidence to prove crime charged.
Preserving issue for appeal at trial, AppProc
Rule 10(a).
Juvenile victims of sexual offenses.
Protection of identity, AppProc Rule 4(e).
Magistrates.
Appeal by defendant from, §15A-1431(a).
Compliance with judgment no bar,
§15A-1431(d).
Notice of appeal, §15A-1431(c).
Appeal after compliance with judgment,
§15A-1431(d).
Pretrial release.
Order remains in effect pending appeal,
§15A-1431(e).
Procedure, §15A-1444(b).
Stays, §15A-1431(f1).
Withdrawal of appeal, §15A-1431(c), (g).
After calendaring case, §15A-1431(h).
Cost on appeal, §6-33.
Motion for appropriate relief.
Correction of errors by appellate division.
Ancillary actions during appeal, §15A-1453(b).
Denial of motion.
No effect on right to assert error upon appeal,
§15A-1422(e).
Finality of decision, §15A-1422(f).
Making of motion not prerequisite to asserting
error on appeal, §15A-1422(a).
Motion in appellate division, §15A-1418.
Motion may be made and acted on regardless of
notice of appeal, §15A-1414(c).

APPEALS —Cont'd
Criminal procedure —Cont'd
Motion for appropriate relief —Cont'd
Ruling of court subject to review, §15A-1444(f).
Ruling on motion, §15A-1422(b) to (d).
Motion to suppress evidence.
Order denying motion, §15A-979(b).
Order granting motion, §15A-979(c).
Notice of appeal.
Content, AppProc Rule 4(b).
Filing and serving, time, AppProc Rule 4(a).
Manner of serving, AppProc Rule 4(c).
Oral notice, giving at trial, AppProc Rule 4(a).
Plea bargaining.
Noncompliance with provisions.
Limitation on collateral attack on conviction,
§15A-1027.
Prejudicial error.
Burden of proof, §15A-1443(a).
Constitutional error, §15A-1443(b).
Defined, §15A-1443(a).
Preservation of right to appeal.
Post-trial motions.
Not prerequisite to assertion of error on
appeal, §15A-1446(c).
Prosecutorial appeal, §15A-1445.
Appeal by state from district court, §15A-1432.
Rehearing.
Petition not entertained in criminal cases,
AppProc Rule 31 (g).
Relief from errors, §15A-1401.
Restitution to victims of crime.
Effect of appeal of conviction upon which order
based, §15A-1340.38(d).
Right of appeal, §15A-1444(a), (a1), (a2).
Security for costs not required, AppProc Rule 6(e).
State of North Carolina.
Correction of errors by appellate division.
Appeal by state, §15A-1445(a).
Order granting motion to suppress,
§15A-1445(b).
Stays.
No stay when state appeals, §15A-1451(b).
District courts.
Appeal by state from, §15A-1432.
Stays.
Correction of errors by appellate division,
§15A-1451(a).
No stay when state appeals, §15A-1451(b).
Pending appeal, AppProc Rule 8(b).
Sufficiency of evidence.
Reviewable on appeal regardless of whether
motion made during trial, §15A-1227(d).
Time.
Notice of appeal.
Filing and serving, AppProc Rule 4(a).
To which appellate court appeal addressed,
AppProc Rule 4(d).
Transcript.
Ordering, AppProc Rule 7(a).
Production, AppProc Rule 7(b).
Trial de novo, NC Const Art IV §12.
Withdrawal of appeal, AppProc Rule 37(d).
Damages.
Frivolous appeals.
Sanction imposed, AppProc Rule 34(b).
Dam safety law.
Applications for construction, §143-215.33.
Death of party.
Substitution, AppProc Rule 38(a).
Public officer, AppProc Rule 38(c).

APPEALS —Cont'd
Decedents' estates.
Estate proceedings.
Applicable provisions, §28A-2-9(a), (c).
Special proceedings.
Applicable provisions, §28A-2-9(b), (c).
Declaratory judgments.
Review, §1-258.
Deeds and other registered instrument.
Errors in registration.
Petition to corrected, §47-36.
Delinquent and undisciplined juvenile actions.
County appeal, limitations, §7B-2604(c).
Disposition after appeal, §7B-2606.
Disposition pending appeal, §7B-2605.
Parties, §7B-2604(a).
Right to appeal, §7B-2602.
Transfer decision, §7B-2603.
State appeal, limitations, §7B-2604(b).
Department of environment and natural resources.
Final orders and decisions of secretary.
Right of appeal to court of appeals, §7A-29(a).
Department of health and human services.
Final orders and decisions.
Right of appeal to court of appeals, §7A-29(a).
Depositions pending appeal, §1A-1 Rule 27(b).
Directed verdict.
Action on motion, §1A-1 Rule 50(b).
Discipline of public school students.
Long-term suspension, §115C-390.8.
Discretionary review on certification by supreme court.
Appeal bond, AppProc Rule 17.
Appellant, appellee defined, AppProc Rule 15(i).
Authorization, §7A-31(a).
Briefs.
Copies, AppProc Rule 15(g).
Filing and service, AppProc Rule 15(g).
Failure, consequences, AppProc Rule 15(g).
Case certified before court of appeals determination.
Authorization, §7A-31(b).
Briefs, filing, service, AppProc Rule 15(g).
Case certified for review of court of appeals determination.
Authorization, §7A-31(c).
Briefs, filing, service, AppProc Rule 15(g).
Certification.
After determination by court of appeals, §7A-31(c).
Before determination by court of appeals, §7A-31(b).
Determination, orders, filing, service, AppProc Rule 15(e).
Effect, §7A-31(a).
Procedure prescribed by rule of court, §7A-31(d).
Docketing of appeal, AppProc Rule 15(e).
Interlocutory orders by court of appeals, AppProc Rule 15(h).
Petition, AppProc Rule 15(a).
Content, AppProc Rule 15(c).
Filing and service, AppProc Rule 15(b).
Form, AppProc Appx D.
Response.
Filing and serving, AppProc Rule 15(d).
Time.
Filing and service, AppProc Rule 15(b).
Response, AppProc Rule 15(d).
Record on appeal.
Composition, filing, copies, AppProc Rule 15(f).

APPEALS —Cont'd
Discretionary review on certification by supreme court —Cont'd
Scope of review, AppProc Rule 16.
Dismissal.
Appeal bond to stay execution on money judgment.
Failure to give bond, §1-289(a).
Briefs.
Failure to file, AppProc Rule 13(c).
Appeal of right from court of appeals to supreme court, AppProc Rule 14(d).
Discretionary review on certification by supreme court, AppProc Rule 15(g).
Costs.
Taxing, AppProc Rule 35(a).
Failure of appellant to take timely action, AppProc Rule 25(a).
Frivolous appeals.
Sanction imposed, AppProc Rule 34(b).
Security for costs.
Failure file, defect in security, AppProc Rule 6(d).
District attorneys, removal from office, §7A-66.
District courts.
Appeal from judge, §1-277(a).
Clerk to judge, §7A-251(b).
Costs in civil action, §7A-305(b), (c).
Costs in criminal actions, §7A-304(b).
Determination, §7A-304(d).
Criminal procedure, §7A-290.
Appeal by defendant, §15A-1431.
Appeal by state, §15A-1432.
Entry of orders under rules.
Trial judges, AppProc Rule 36.
Final judgment of court in civil action.
Direct appeal to court of appeals, §7A-27(c).
Game commission rulings.
Heard in district court division, §7A-250(c).
Interlocutory orders.
Direct appeal to court of appeals, §7A-27(d).
Liens.
Possessory liens on personal property.
Action to regain possession of motor vehicle or vessel.
Appeal to district court for trial de novo, §44A-6.1(b).
Procedure after determination of appeal, §1-298.
Settling record on appeal.
Power of trial judge, §1-283.
Small claim actions.
Indigent persons, §7A-228(b1).
Jury trial on appeal, §7A-230.
Priority of judgment when appeal taken, §7A-226.
Stay of execution on appeal, §7A-227.
Trial de novo, §7A-228(a).
Dismissal of appeal, §7A-228(c).
How appeal perfected, §7A-228(b).
Oral notice of appeal, §7A-228(a).
Perfection of appeal, §7A-228(b).
Procedure generally, §7A-229.
DNA evidence preservation.
Order to dispose of evidence prior to time period of expiration, §15A-268(f).
DNA testing after conviction.
Motion by defendant.
Appeal of denial, §15A-270.1.
Docket entry of stay, §1-293.
Docketing appeal, AppProc Rule 12(b).
Appeal of right from court of appeals to supreme court, AppProc Rule 14(c).

APPEALS —Cont'd
Docketing appeal —Cont'd
Discretionary review on certification by supreme court, AppProc Rule 15(e).
Dogs.
Dangerous dogs.
Determination that dog is potentially dangerous dog, §67-4.1(c).
Double jeopardy.
Correction of errors by appellate division.
When charges must be dismissed with prejudice, §15A-1447(g).
Drainage.
Canals.
Right to drain into canal, §156-10.
Petitions.
Agreement for construction, §156-29.
Drainage districts.
Acquiring title for purpose of easements or rights-of-way, §156-70.1.
Bonds, surety, §156-66.
Construction of drainage law, §156-135.
Easements, §156-70.1.
Hearings.
Final hearings, §156-75.
Improvement, renovation, enlargement and extension of canals, structures and boundaries, §§156-93.2, 156-93.3.
Notice, §156-70.1.
Publication in case of unknown owners, §156-58.
Public or private ways.
Maintenance of drainage across, §156-88.
Railroads.
Drainage across railroads, §156-90.
Right of appeal, §156-66.
Rights of way, §156-70.1.
Drivers' licenses.
Denial, cancellation, etc., §20-25.
Disqualification from driving commercial vehicle for testing positive in a drug or alcohol test, §20-37.20B.
Drugs.
Controlled substances.
Judicial review of drug commission, §90-113.2.
Drug treatment court probation.
Revocation, §7A-271(f).
Dry-cleaning solvent cleanup, §143-215.104S.
Education.
Budget dispute between board of education and board of county commissioners.
Procedure for resolution, §115C-431(c) to (e).
Education programs at residential schools.
Decisions of school personnel.
Appeals to secretary, §143B-146.14.
Employees.
Repayment of money owed to state.
Delinquent employees, §143-554(a).
Local boards of education.
Appeals to local boards, §115C-45(c).
Appeals to superior court, §115C-45(c).
Special education.
Children with disabilities.
Review of hearing officer's decision, §115C-109.9.
Elections.
Contributions and expenditures in political campaigns.
State board of elections.
Appeals from board, §163-278.26.
Protest of election.
Appeal of decision to state board, §163-182.11.

APPEALS —Cont'd
Elections —Cont'd
Protest of election —Cont'd
Appeal of decision to superior court, §163-182.14(a), (b).
Appeal to general assembly or house thereof, §163-182.14(c).
Attorneys' fees not to be awarded against state board of elections, §163-182.14(d).
State board of elections.
Appeal of right to court of appeals, §7A-29(a).
Voter registration.
Denial of registration, §163-82.18.
Electronic filing, AppProc Rule 26(a).
Service of process by electronic means, AppProc Rule 26(c).
Electronic surveillance.
Order granting motion to suppress, §15A-294(h).
Elevator safety act.
Convictions for violation of article, §95-110.10.
Emancipation of juvenile, §7B-3508.
Eminent domain, §40A-13.
Conservation easements.
Condemnation of property encumbered by, §40A-85.
Private condemnors, §40A-28(c).
Jury trial, §40A-29.
Employer safety and health program.
Penalties, §95-256(c).
Engineers and land surveyors.
Disciplinary action.
Judicial review, §89C-22(d).
Error.
Cross-assignment of error, §1-271.
Writs of error abolished, §1-268.
Evidence.
Exceptions, §1-186(b).
Exceptions.
Decisions on matters of law, §1-186(a).
Evidence, §1-186(b).
Executors and administrators.
Resignation, §28A-10-6.
Revocation of letters, §28A-9-4.
Failure of appellant to take timely action, AppProc Rule 25(a).
Failure to comply with rules of appellate procedure, AppProc Rule 25(b).
Fair housing commission, §41A-7(m).
Felony guilty or no contest pleas in district court.
Appeals authorized, §15A-1029.1(b).
Fertilizers.
Commercial fertilizers.
Assessments of penalties, orders or rulings, §106-670.
Filing of papers, AppProc Rule 26(a).
Closing of document, AppProc Rule 26(g).
Courts always deemed open for, AppProc Rule 39(a).
Form, AppProc Rule 26(g).
Format, AppProc Appx B, AppProc Rule 26(g).
Index, AppProc Rule 26(g).
Paper size, AppProc Rule 26(g).
Style, AppProc Appx B.
Time, computation, extension, AppProc Rule 27.
Findings by court.
Review on appeal, §1A-1 Rule 52(c).
Fish and fisheries resources.
Dredging permits, §113-229.
Food and nutrition services, §108A-79(h).

APPEALS —Cont'd
Forests and forestry.
Protection and development corporations, §106-985.
Form and format of papers filed, AppProc Appx B, AppProc Rule 26(g).
Forma pauperis, §1-288.
Forms, AppProc Appx D.
Frivolous appeals.
Juvenile code.
No-merit briefs, AppProc Rule 3.1(d).
Sanctions, AppProc Rule 34(b).
Grounds, AppProc Rule 34(a).
Remand to trial division to determine, AppProc Rule 34(c).
Hearing on determination, AppProc Rule 34(d).
Game commission rulings.
Heard in district court division, §7A-250(c).
General assembly.
Investigating committees.
Appeal from denial of right to be heard, §120-18.
General court of justice.
Appellate division, NC Const Art IV §5.
Geologists.
Judicial review of final agency decision, §89E-20(c).
Grade crossings.
Elimination or safeguarding of crossings.
Procedure for appeal, §136-20(g).
Guardians.
Determination of incompetence.
Orders of clerk, §35A-1115.
Sterilization of mentally ill or retarded ward.
Mentally necessity, appeal of clerk's order, §35A-1245(f).
Health, §130A-24.
Applicability of provisions to actions taken by department of environment and natural resources, §130A-24(e).
Decisions of local boards of health, §130A-24(d).
Interpretation and enforcement of rules.
Adopted by commission, §130A-24(a).
Adopted by local board of health, §130A-24(b).
Petition for contested case, §130A-24(a1).
Local boards of health.
Hearings, §130A-24(c).
Procedure, §130A-24.
Health care facilities.
Certificates of need.
Administrative and judicial review, §131E-188.
Health care liability.
Exhaustion of administrative remedies and appeals, §90-21.54.
Health Choice.
Provider requirements, §108C-12.
Highways, roads and streets.
Cartways, church roads or mill roads.
Special proceeding for establishment, alteration or discontinuance.
Procedure for appeal, §136-68.
Condemnation proceedings.
Right of appeal, §136-119.
County public roads incorporated into state highway system.
Filing of complaints, §136-64.
Drainage of highway.
Judgment of commissioners.
Right to appeal, §136-23.
Highway use tax, §105-187.10(c).

APPEALS —Cont'd
Hospitals.
Certificate of need law.
Administrative and judicial review, §131E-188.
Licenses.
Adverse action on licenses, §131E-78(c1).
Denial or revocation of license.
Judicial review, §131E-78(c1).
Housemovers.
Revocation of license for unsafe practices, §20-374(b).
Housing authorities and projects.
Eminent domain.
Certificate of convenience and necessity.
Issuance, §157-28.
How and when taken.
Civil actions or special proceedings, AppProc Rule 3.
Criminal cases, AppProc Rule 4.
Juvenile matters, AppProc Rule 3.1.
Identity of persons under age of 18.
Protection.
Appeal information statement, AppProc Rule 41(b).
Briefs, AppProc Rule 28(a).
Form, AppProc Appx D.
Juvenile matters, AppProc Rules 3.1(b), 3(b).
Juvenile victims of sexual offenses, AppProc Rule 4(e).
Motions in appellate courts, AppProc Rule 37(c).
Oral argument, AppProc Rule 30(a).
Impaired driving, implied consent offenses, §20-38.7.
Sentence imposed.
Jury trial on aggravated factors, §20-179(a1), (a2).
Incompetence, determination of.
Order adjudicating incompetence, §35A-1115.
Indexes.
Format, style, AppProc Appx B.
Industrial commission.
Awards, §97-86.
Interest on awards after hearing, §97-86.2.
Payment of award pending appeal in certain cases, §97-86.1.
Court of appeals.
Review of final orders, §7A-250(b).
Insurers.
Expenses of appeals brought by insurers, §97-88.
Right of appeal from industrial commission to court of appeals, §7A-29(a).
Tort claim rules.
Appeal to court of appeals, ICTortClaim Rules T401 to T404.
Appeal to full commission, ICTortClaim Rules T301 to T310.
In forma pauperis, §1-288.
Appeal bond, AppProc Rule 17(d).
Infractions.
Review of disposition by superior court, §15A-1115.
Appeal of district court decision, §15A-1115(a).
Review of infractions originally disposed of in superior court, §15A-1115(b).
Injunctions.
Injunction pending appeal, §1A-1 Rule 62(c).
Restraining orders and injunctions in effect pending appeals, §1-500.
Bonds, surety, §1-500.

APPEALS —Cont'd

Insufficiency of evidence to prove crime charged.

Preserving issue for appeal at trial, AppProc Rule 10(a).

Insurance.

Accident and health insurance.

Utilization review.

Noncertification, §58-50-61(j) to (l).

Beach area property essential property insurance.

Commissioner to superior court, §58-45-50.

Commissioner's orders and decisions.

Appeal from supreme court, §58-2-75(d).

Credit insurance, §58-57-75.

Direct right of appeal to court of appeals, §7A-29(a).

Jurisdiction of trial judge, §58-2-75(c).

Motor vehicle reinsurance facility, §58-37-65(f).

Orders with respect to plan of operation, §58-37-40(d).

Petition, §58-2-75(a).

Place of hearing.

Change, §58-2-75(b).

Post assessment insurance guaranty association, §58-48-45(c).

Rates, §§58-2-80, 58-2-85, 58-2-90, 58-40-105(b).

Stays.

Commencement of proceedings not to operate as stay, §58-2-75(e).

Transcript of hearing.

Commissioner to provide, §58-2-75(b).

Unauthorized insurers.

Domestic companies, §58-14-15.

Credit insurance.

Orders of commissioner, §58-57-75.

Fair access to insurance requirements, §58-46-30.

Holding companies.

Orders of commissioner, §58-19-70(a).

Interstate insurance product regulation compact.

Product approval, denial, §58-91-55(a).

Post-assessment insurance guaranty association.

Appeals to commissioner, §58-48-42.

Commissioner.

Judicial review, §58-48-45(c).

Rate bureau, §58-36-35.

Administration review, §58-36-85.

Commissioner of insurance.

Appeals from orders of commissioner, §58-36-25.

Motor vehicle insurance.

Termination review, §58-36-85(d) to (g).

Rates.

Orders and decisions of commissioner, §§58-2-80, 58-2-85, 58-2-90, 58-40-105(b).

Unauthorized insurers.

Cease and desist orders, §58-28-20(e).

Domestic companies.

Judicial review of orders of commissioner, §58-14-15.

Unfair trade practices.

Cease and desist orders.

Judicial review, §58-63-35.

Undefined practices.

Judicial review by intervenor, §58-63-45.

Insurance consumer and customer information privacy.

Final order of commissioner, §58-39-100.

Insurance underwriting association.

Plan of operation.

Orders of commission with respect to plan, §58-45-30(c).

APPEALS —Cont'd

Interlocutory orders.

Review on appeal from judgment, §1-278.

Interlocutory orders by court of appeals.

Discretionary review on certification by supreme court, AppProc Rule 15(h).

International commercial arbitration and conciliation, §1-567.67(a), (b).

Investment advisers.

Judicial review of orders, §78C-29(a), (b).

Issues on appeal.

Insufficiency of evidence to prove crime charged.

Preserving issue at trial, AppProc Rule 10(a).

Jury charge or omission.

Making basis of issue presented on appeal, AppProc Rule 10(a).

Preserving during trial, AppProc Rule 10(a).

Proposed issues.

Appellant's proposed issues, stating, AppProc Rule 10(b).

Appellee's proposed issues.

Alternative basis in law for supporting judgment, order, determination, AppProc Rule 10(c).

Request, objection, motion.

Presenting during trial, ruling upon, obtaining. Preserving issues at trial, AppProc Rule 10(a).

Joinder of actions.

Consolidation of appeals, AppProc 40.

Joinder of parties on appeal.

Appellants, AppProc Rule 5(a).

Appellees, AppProc Rule 5(b).

Briefs, AppProc Rule 28(f).

Procedure after joinder, AppProc Rule 5(c).

Service of process on joint appellants and appellees, AppProc Rule 26(e).

Judgments and orders not in session.

Orders for perfecting appeal.

Clerk authorized to make, §1-281.

Judicial standards commission proceedings.

Hearing panels decision.

Proceedings in supreme court, JudStdsComm Rule 26.

Junkyard control.

Final decisions of secretary of transportation, §136-149.1.

Jurisdiction.

Adverse ruling as to jurisdiction.

Right of immediate appeal, §1-277(b).

Rules of appellate procedure do not extend jurisdiction of appellate courts, AppProc Rule 1(c).

Stay of proceedings to permit trial in foreign jurisdiction.

Review of rulings on motion, §1-75.12(c).

Jury charge or omission.

Making basis of issue presented on appeal, AppProc Rule 10(a).

Juvenile code.

Abused, neglected or dependent juvenile actions, §§7B-1001 to 7B-1004.

Briefs, AppProc Rule 3.1(c).

No-merit briefs, AppProc Rule 3.1(d).

Delinquent and undisciplined juvenile actions, §§7B-2602 to 7B-2606.

Expedited filings, AppProc Rule 3.1(c).

Frivolous appeals.

No-merit briefs, AppProc Rule 3.1(d).

How and when taken, AppProc 3.1.

APPEALS —Cont'd
Juvenile code —Cont'd
Identity of persons under age of 18.
  Protection in juvenile matters, AppProc Rules 3.1(b), 3(b).
    Appeal information statement, AppProc Rule 41(b).
    Briefs, AppProc Rule 28(a).
    Form, AppProc Appx D.
    Motions in appellate courts, AppProc Rule 37(c).
    Oral argument, AppProc Rule 30(a).
Notice of appeal.
  Filing and serving in juvenile matters, AppProc 3.1(a).
Priority over other cases, AppProc Rule 3.1(e).
Record on appeal, AppProc Rule 3.1(c).
Transcripts, AppProc Rule 3.1(c).
Landlord and tenant.
Lien on crops.
  Tenant's undertaking on continuance or appeal, §42-18.
Summary ejectment.
  Appeal to district court, §42-32.
Surety on crops.
  Landlord, §42-19.
  Tenant, §42-18.
Law-enforcement officers.
Salary continuation plan.
  Determination of cause and extent of incapacity, §143-166.19.
Liens.
Action to regain possession of motor vehicle or vessel.
  Involuntary relinquishment of possession by lienor, §44A-6.1(a).
Limestone, marl and landplaster.
Assessments and orders of commissioner of agriculture, §106-92.13.
Limited liability companies.
Revocation of certificate of authority of foreign limited liability companies, §57C-7-14(b).
Lobbying.
Reports.
  Decision of secretary of state regarding, §120C-401(g).
Local ABC boards.
Removal of members and employees, §18B-704(h).
Local government finance.
Executive committee to commission, §159-4(b).
Magistrates.
Cost on appeal, §6-33.
Criminal procedure, §§15A-1431, 15A-1444.
Removal of magistrate, §7A-173(d).
Trial de novo on appeal, NC Const Art IV §12.
Mail.
Filing by, AppProc Rule 26(a).
  Appeal information statement, AppProc Rule 41(b).
Service by, AppProc Rule 26(c).
  Additional time after service by, AppProc Rule 27(b).
Mandates of court, AppProc Rule 32(a).
Costs.
  Direction as to, AppProc Rule 35(b).
Issuance, AppProc Rule 32(a).
Time, AppProc Rule 32(b).
Meat inspection.
Enforcement against condemned meat, §106-549.32(a).

APPEALS —Cont'd
Medicaid, §§108A-70.9A to 108A-70.9C.
Appeals by recipients.
  Applicability of provisions, §108A-70.9A(b).
  Definitions, §108A-70.9A(a).
  Final decision, §108A-70.9A(f).
  Form for appeal request, §108A-70.9A(e).
  Notice of adverse determination and right to appeal, §108A-70.9A(c).
  Request for hearing, §108A-70.9A(d).
Contested case procedures.
  Applicability of provisions, §108A-70.9B(a).
  Burden of proof, §108A-70.9B(d).
  Decision of administrative law judge, §108A-70.9B(g).
  Informal review by department, §108A-70.9C.
  Issues to be heard, §108A-70.9B(f).
  Mediation, §108A-70.9B(c).
  New evidence, submission, §108A-70.9B(e).
  Notice of hearing, §108A-70.9B(b).
  Simplified procedure, §108A-70.9B(b).
Hospital provider assessments, §108A-123(e).
Informal review by department, §108A-70.9C.
Provider requirements, §108C-12.
Medical malpractice.
Arbitration of negligent health claims.
  Appeal of decision of arbitrator, §90-21.68.
Mental health, developmental disability, substance abuse, etc.
Appeals panel, §122C-151.4.
Area authorities.
  Appeals panel, §122C-151.4.
  Procedure for appeal by, §122C-151.2(c).
  Right of appeal, §122C-151.2(a), (b).
County programs.
  Appeals panel, §122C-151.4.
  Procedure for appeal by, §122C-151.2(c).
  Right of appeal, §122C-151.2(a), (b).
Facilities.
  Licenses.
    Adverse action on license, §122C-24.
Involuntary commitment.
  District court hearing, §122C-272.
    Substance abusers, §122C-288.
Surplus income and advancements.
  Mental health and retardation, §35A-1328.
Mines and minerals.
Decisions on mine safety, §74-24.10(a).
Modification of safety and health standards, §74-24.5.
Permits, §§74-51, 74-61.
Modification of judgment.
Powers of court, §1-297.
Money transmitters.
Rules review by commission, §53-208.27(b).
Mortgages and deeds of trust.
Reverse mortgages.
  Commissioner's decisions, §53-272.
Sales under power of sale, §45-21.16(e).
Motion for appropriate relief, §15A-1422.
Motions in appellate courts.
Affidavits, briefs or other papers supporting.
  Filing, AppProc Rule 37(a).
Application for order or other relief made by motion, AppProc Rule 37(a).
Determination, AppProc Rule 37(b).
Filing and serving.
  Time, AppProc Rule 37(a).
    Response, AppProc Rule 37(a).
Identity of persons under age of 18.
  Protection, AppProc Rule 37(c).

APPEALS —Cont'd
Motions in appellate courts —Cont'd
  Response.
    Filing and serving, time, AppProc Rule 37(a).
  Time.
    Filing and serving, AppProc Rule 37(a).
    Response, AppProc Rule 37(a).
Motor clubs and associations.
  Judicial review of commissioner of insurance,
    §58-69-25.
**Motor vehicle dealers' and manufacturers'
  licenses.**
  Actions of commissioner, §20-300.
Motor vehicle inspections.
  Licenses to perform inspections.
    Denial, revocation or suspension, or assessment
      of civil penalty, §20-183.8G(g).
Motor vehicle violations.
  Civil penalty assessed, §20-178.1.
Moving companies.
  Revocation of license for unsafe practices,
    §20-374(b).
Municipalities.
  Assessments.
    Appeal to general court of justice, §160A-230.
  Bonds, surety.
    Undertaking on appeal.
      Exception as to, §1-285(b).
  Building inspection, §160A-434.
  Streets.
    Building setback lines.
      Appeals by property owners for variance or
        modification, §160A-306(c).
  Subdivisions, decisions on subdivision plats,
    §160A-377.
  Zoning.
    Boards of adjustment, §160A-388.
    Certiorari to superior court, §160A-393.
Mutual burial associations.
  Dispute over liability for benefits, §90-210.102.
  Revocation of license or authority, §90-210.94.
Names.
  Change of name.
    Denial of request, §101-5(f).
National guard.
  Courts-martial, §127A-62.
Nonprofit corporations.
  Denial of reinstatement following administrative
    dissolution by secretary of state,
    §55A-14-23(b) to (d).
  Foreign corporations.
    Revocation of certificate of authority,
      §55A-15-32.
North Carolina rules of appellate procedure.
  Title of rules, AppProc Rule 1(a).
Notice.
  Abused, neglected or dependent juvenile actions,
    §7B-1001(b), (c).
    Permanency planning.
      Notice to preserve right to appeal order,
        §7B-507(c).
  Appeal of right from court of appeals to supreme
    court, AppProc Rule 14(a), (b).
  Appeal of right from final administrative agency
    determination, AppProc Rule 18(b).
  Content, AppProc Rule 3(d).
    Appeal of right from court of appeals to
      supreme court, AppProc Rule 14(b).
    Criminal cases, AppProc Rule 4(b).
  Criminal procedure.
    Content, AppProc Rule 4(b).

APPEALS —Cont'd
Notice —Cont'd
  Criminal procedure —Cont'd
    Correction of errors by appellate division,
      §15A-1448(a), (b).
    District courts, §7A-290.
      Appeal by defendant from, §15A-1431(c), (d).
    Filing and serving, time, AppProc Rule 4(a).
      Manner of serving, AppProc Rule 4(c).
    Magistrates.
      Appeal by defendant from, §15A-1431(c), (d).
    Oral notice, giving at trial, AppProc Rule 4(a).
  Delinquent and undisciplined juvenile actions,
    §7B-2602.
    Appeal of order transferring jurisdiction of
      juvenile to superior court, §7B-2603(a).
  Docketing appeal, AppProc Rule 12(b).
  Filing.
    Appeal in civil action or special proceeding
      taken by, AppProc Rule 3(a).
    Appeal of right from court of appeals to
      supreme court, AppProc Rule 14(a).
    Appeal of right from final administrative agency
      determination, AppProc Rule 18(b).
    Criminal cases, AppProc Rule 4(a).
    Juvenile matters, AppProc 3.1(a).
    Time for filing and serving, AppProc Rule 3(c).
  Forms, AppProc Appx D.
  Juvenile matters.
    Filing and serving, AppProc 3.1(a).
  Manner of service, AppProc Rule 3(e).
    Criminal cases, AppProc Rule 4(c).
  Physician or surgeon review of revocation or
    suspension of license, §90-14.9(a).
  Rehearing.
    Petition granted, AppProc Rule 31(d).
  Small claims actions, §7A-228.
  Time and manner for giving notice.
    Appeal to appellate division in civil actions and
      special proceedings, §1-279.1.
  Time for filing and serving, AppProc Rule 3(c).
    Appeal of right from court of appeals to
      supreme court, AppProc Rule 14(a).
    Appeal of right from final administrative agency
      determination, AppProc Rule 18(b).
    Criminal cases, AppProc Rule 4(a).
  Utilities commission decisions, §62-90(a), (b).
  Withdrawal of appeal, AppProc Rule 37(d), (e).
Occupational safety and health.
  Judicial review of administrative decisions,
    §95-141.
Oil and gas conservation.
  Hearings before department, §113-401.
    Application for court review, §113-403.
    Effect of pendency of judicial review, §113-406.
**Oil pollution and hazardous substances
  control.**
  Civil penalties.
    Time for filing petition, §143-215.88A(a).
  Damages.
    Contesting liability for damage to public
      resources.
      Time for filing petition, §143-215.90(b).
Open for filing papers.
  Courts always deemed open for, AppProc Rule
    39(a).
Opinions of appellate courts.
  Unpublished opinions, AppProc Rule 30(e).
Oral argument.
  Appellee not heard.
    Failure to file brief, AppProc Rule 13(c).
      Appeal of right from court of appeals to
        supreme court, AppProc Rule 14(d).

APPEALS —Cont'd
Oral argument —Cont'd
Appellee not heard —Cont'd
Failure to file brief —Cont'd
Discretionary review on certification by
supreme court, AppProc Rule 15(g).
Case submitted for decision on written briefs,
AppProc Rule 30(d).
Content, AppProc Rule 30(a).
Failure of counsel to appear, AppProc Rule 30(c).
Identity of persons under age of 18.
Protection, AppProc Rule 30(a).
Numerous counsel.
Time allowed, AppProc Rule 30(b).
Opening and concluding.
Appellant entitled, AppProc Rule 30(a).
Order of argument, AppProc Rule 30(a).
Pre-argument review.
Decision without oral argument, AppProc Rule
30(f).
Rehearing.
Petition granted.
Notice of time and place, AppProc Rule 31(d).
Time allowed, AppProc Rule 30(b).
Unpublished opinions.
Citation, AppProc Rule 30(e).
Outdoor advertising.
Final decisions of secretary of transportation,
§136-134.1.
Vegetation, cutting or removal, §136-133.3.
Parental authority over juvenile.
Civil action to enforce, juvenile leaving home and
refusing to return, §7B-3404.
Parties.
Abused, neglected or dependent juvenile actions.
Proper parties to appeal final order, §7B-1002.
Joinder, AppProc Rule 5.
Briefs, AppProc Rule 28(f).
Substitution.
Death of party, AppProc Rule 38(a).
Other than death of party, AppProc Rule 38(b).
Public officers.
Death, resignation, ceases to hold office,
AppProc Rule 38(c).
Who may appeal, §1-271.
Partition.
Report of commissioners.
Order of confirmation, §46-19(c).
Passenger tramways.
Commission of labor order, §95-123.
Perpetuation of testimony.
Depositions, §1A-1 Rule 27(b).
Personnel system.
Grievances and disciplinary action, §§126-34 to
126-41.
Veteran believing preference not received.
Appeals directly to state personnel commission,
§126-82(d).
Pesticide dealers and manufacturers.
Denial, suspension or revocation of license,
§143-451(b).
Petition for discretionary review, AppProc Rule
15.
Pharmacy audit rights.
Appeals process, §90-85.51.
Physicians and surgeons.
Medical malpractice.
Arbitration of negligent health claims, appeal of
decision of arbitrator, §90-21.68.
Revocation or suspension of license.
Appeal bond, §90-14.9(a).
Medical board not required to give bond,
§90-14.11(a).

APPEALS —Cont'd
Physicians and surgeons —Cont'd
Revocation or suspension of license —Cont'd
Notice of appeal, §90-14.9(a).
Parties who may appeal from decision of
superior court, §90-14.11(a).
Scope of review, §90-14.10.
Stay of medical board decision, §90-14.9(b).
Stay of superior court decisions, §90-14.11(b).
Podiatrists.
Denial, revocation or suspension of license,
§90-202.8(c).
Pollution control.
Applicability of article.
Additional methods, §159C-24.
Environmental documents.
Administrative and judicial review, §113A-13.
Environmental policy act.
Review of agency actions involving major
adverse changes or conflicts, §113A-5.
Powers of attorney.
Gifts.
Court order authorizing gift, §32A-14.11.
Preneed funeral contracts and funds.
Judicial review, §90-210.69(e).
Preserving issues on appeal, AppProc Rule 10.
Prisons and prisoners.
Release pending appeal, §15A-1353(e).
Private protective services.
Licenses.
Suspension or revocation, §74C-12(b).
Probation.
Post-trial relief from judgment of probation,
§15A-1342(f).
Revocation of probation or imposition of special
probation upon violation, §15A-1347.
Property tax commission.
Right of appeal from commission to court of
appeals, §7A-29(a).
Property taxes.
Agricultural, horticultural and forestland.
Present use value.
Decision on qualification or appraisal of
property, §105-277.4(b1).
Collection of taxes.
Delayed pending appeal, §105-378(d).
Motor vehicles.
Special committee for motor vehicle appeals,
§105-325.1.
Personal property.
Value, situs or taxability, §105-317.1(c).
Power of board of equalization to hear,
§105-322(g).
Proprietary schools.
Suspension, revocation or refusal of license,
§115D-93(b).
Prosecution bonds.
Liability for costs.
Sureties on prosecution bonds liable, §6-3.
Public lands.
Allocated state lands.
Right of appeal to governor and council of state,
§146-31.
Public officers.
Death, resignation, ceases to hold office.
Substitution of party, AppProc Rule 38(c).
Public schools.
Assignment of students to schools.
Decision denying reassignment, §115C-370.
Education of children with disabilities.
Review of hearing officer's decision,
§115C-109.9.

APPEALS —Cont'd
Public schools —Cont'd
Student disciplinary measures, §115C-392.
Teachers.
Dismissal or demotion, §115C-325(n).
Public utilities commission decisions, §§62-90
to 62-98.
Court of appeals.
Review of final orders, §7A-250(b).
Purchases and contracts through department
of administration.
Law applicable to printing supreme court reports
not affected, §143-62.
Quo warranto, §1-529.
Bonds of parties, §1-529.
Radiation protection.
Denial, suspension or revocation of licenses,
§104E-13(c).
Radioactive wastes.
Privilege license tax on radioactive and hazardous
waste facilities.
Appeals of tax rate to board, §160A-211.1(c).
Recordari.
Authorized, §1-269.
Bonds, surety, §1-269.
Issuance as substitute for appeal, §1-269.
Record on appeal.
See RECORD ON APPEAL.
Registered instrument.
Errors in registration.
Petition to corrected, §47-36.
Rehearing.
Briefs.
Petition granted, AppProc Rule 31 (d).
Criminal cases.
Petition not entertained, AppProc Rule 31 (g).
Petition.
Certificate of non-interested attorneys, AppProc
Rule 31 (a).
Content, AppProc Rule 31(a).
Determination, AppProc Rule 31 (c).
Filing.
Time, AppProc Rule 31(a).
Notice that petition granted, AppProc Rule 31
(d).
Procedure when petition granted, AppProc Rule
31 (d).
To which court addressed, AppProc Rule 31 (b).
Stay of execution.
Obtaining when petition filed, AppProc Rule 31
(e).
Waiver of right to petition.
Appeal from court of appeals, AppProc Rule 31
(f).
Restitution.
Effect of appeal of conviction upon which order
based, §15A-1340.38(d).
Reversal or modification of judgment.
Court may make restitution, §1-297.
Reversal of judgment.
Powers of court, §1-297.
Right to appeal.
Appeal from courts of trial divisions, §7A-27.
Appeal from superior or district court judge,
§1-277(a).
Immediate appeal, §1-277(b).
Jurisdictional rulings.
Right of immediate appeal from adverse ruling,
§1-277(b).
Who may appeal, §1-271.

APPEALS —Cont'd
Rules of administrative agency.
Permanent rules.
Judicial review.
Rule returned by commission, §150B-21.8(d).
Rural fire departments.
Annexation initiated by municipality.
Contract to provide fire protection.
Good faith offer not made, §160A-58.57(g) to
(i).
Sanctions.
Failure to comply with rules of appellate
procedure, AppProc Rule 25(b).
Savings and loan associations.
Branch offices.
Final decision on application, §54B-22(j).
Cease and desist orders.
Judicial review, §54B-71.
Fines.
Judicial review, §54B-71.
Incorporation.
Final decision of commission, §54B-16.
Interstate branches.
Agency decision, §54B-277.
Supervisory control of associations, §54B-68(b),
(d).
Savings banks.
Branch offices.
Applications for permission to establish.
Final decision of commissioner of banks on,
§54C-23(g).
Cease and desist orders.
Judicial review, §54C-84.
Fines.
Judicial review, §54C-84.
Incorporation.
Application to organize savings bank.
Final decision of commission, §54C-16.
Interstate branch banks.
Commissioner of banks' decisions, §54C-211.
School employee injured during episode of
violence.
Entitlement to salary and other benefits.
Appeal of board of education decision,
§115C-338(c).
Scope of review of decisions of court of
appeals.
Appellant, appellee defined, AppProc Rule 15(c).
Dissent in court of appeals.
Appeal based solely upon, AppProc Rule 15(b).
How determined, AppProc Rule 15(a).
Limited to issues stated in notice or petition,
exceptions, AppProc Rule 15(a).
Scope of rules of appellate procedure, AppProc
Rule 1(b).
Secretary of environment and natural
resources.
Final orders and decisions.
Right of appeal to court of appeals, §7A-29(a).
Secured transactions.
Filing office.
Refusal to accept record or cancellation of
record, §25-9-520(e).
Securities regulation.
Cease and desist orders, §78A-47(b).
Judicial review of administrator's orders,
§78A-48(a).
Cease and desist orders, §78A-47(b).
Not to operate as stay, §78A-48(b).
Saving provision, §78A-65(e).
Security for costs, AppProc Rule 6.

APPEALS —Cont'd
Seeds.
Licensing of dealers.
Revocation or refusal of license for cause,
§106-277.19.
Stop-sale orders.
Right of appeal, §106-277.22.
Sentencing.
Release pending appeal, §15A-1353(e).
Resentencing after appellate review, §15A-1335.
Service of process.
Briefs.
Time for filing and serving, AppProc Rule 13(a).
Discretionary review on certification by
supreme court, AppProc Rule 15(g).
Reply briefs, AppProc Rule 28(h).
Copies served on all parties, AppProc Rule 26(b).
Electronic means, AppProc Rule 26(c).
Joint appellants and appellees, AppProc Rule
26(e).
Mail, AppProc Rule 26(c).
Additional time after service by, AppProc Rule
27(b).
Manner of service, AppProc Rule 26(c).
Motions in appellate courts.
Filing and serving.
Time, AppProc Rule 37(a).
Notice of appeal.
Appeal of right from court of appeals to
supreme court, AppProc Rule 14(a).
Criminal cases, AppProc Rule 4(a), (c).
Juvenile matters, AppProc 3.1(a).
Manner of service, AppProc Rule 3(e).
Criminal cases, AppProc Rule 4(c).
Time for filing and serving, AppProc Rule 3(c).
Appeal of right from court of appeals to
supreme court, AppProc Rule 14(a).
Criminal cases, AppProc Rule 4(a).
Petition for review.
Discretionary review on certification by supreme
court, AppProc Rule 15(b).
Response, AppProc Rule 15(d).
Proof of service, AppProc Rule 26(d).
Stays.
Bonds, surety.
Service of undertaking on appellee, §1-295.
Time.
Computation, extension, AppProc Rule 27.
Sessions and sittings of courts, AppProc Rule
29(a).
Setoff debt collection act.
Actions taken at hearings, §105A-9.
Sex offenses assistance program for victims.
Forensic medical examinations.
Appeal of denial of claim for assistance,
§143B-1200(g).
**Sheriffs' education and training standards
commission.**
Denial, suspension or revocation of certificate,
§17E-9(b).
Social services.
Adult protection.
Motion in the cause.
Review of orders issued pursuant to
provisions, §108A-107.
Applicability of certain provisions, §108A-73.
Conflict of laws, §108A-79(l).
Food and nutrition services, §108A-79(h).
Judicial review, §108A-79(k).
Right of appeal, §108A-79(a).

APPEALS —Cont'd
Social services —Cont'd
Termination or modification of assistance.
Further appeal to department, §108A-79(g).
Hearing, §108A-79(i), (j).
Hearings, §108A-79(d), (e).
Decision, §108A-79(f).
Notice of action and right to appeal,
§108A-79(b), (c).
Right of appeal, §108A-79(a).
Solid waste management.
Hazardous waste facilities.
Preempting local ordinance, §130A-293(e).
Municipalities initiating annexation.
Contract with private firm to provide solid
waste collection.
No contract offered, §160A-58.59(g).
Special education.
Children with disabilities.
Review of hearing officer's decision,
§115C-109.9.
Special proceedings.
Manner and time for giving notice of appeals,
§1-279.1.
Surveys ordered by clerk, §1-408.1.
Undertaking on appeal, §1-285.
State bar.
Right of appeal from North Carolina state bar to
court of appeals, §7A-29(a).
State departments and agencies.
Attorneys' fees.
Parties appeals or defending against agency
decision, §6-19.1(a).
Bonds, surety.
Exception as to state agencies, §1-285(b).
Decisions of administrative agencies.
Final judgment of superior court upon review of
decision.
Appeals of right from superior courts to court
of appeals, §7A-27(b).
Right of appeal from certain administrative
agencies to court of appeals, §7A-29(a).
State institutions.
Damage of personal property, §143-127.6.
State of North Carolina.
Criminal law and procedure.
Appeals by state.
Correction of errors, §15A-1445(a), (b).
From district court, §15A-1432.
Stay, §15A-1451(b).
Exception as to state, §1-285(b).
Stays, §1A-1 Rule 62(d).
Appeal to appellate division, §1-270.
Attachment.
Orders dissolving or modifying, §1-440.38.
Bonds, surety.
Judgment directing conveyance, §1-291.
Judgment directing payment of money,
§1-289(a).
Cap on amount, noncompensatory damages of
$25,000,000 or more, §1-289(b), (c).
Judgment for personal property, §1-290.
Judgment for real property, §1-292.
Security limited for fiduciaries, §1-294.
Service of undertaking on appellee, §1-295.
Undertaking in one or more instruments,
§1-295.
Cap on amount of bond to stay execution.
Noncompensatory damages of $25,000,000 or
more awarded, §1-289(b), (c).
Docket entry of stay, §1-293.

APPEALS —Cont'd

Stays —Cont'd

Fiduciaries.

Security limited for fiduciaries, §1-294.

Incompetence, determination of.

Order adjudicating incompetence, §35A-1115.

Judgment directing conveyance, §1-291.

Judgment directing payment of money, §1-289(a).

Cap on amount, noncompensatory damages of $25,000,000 or more, §1-289(b), (c).

Judgment for personal property, §1-290.

Judgment for real property, §1-292.

Judgment not vacated by stay, §1-296.

Pending appeal.

Civil cases, AppProc Rule 8(a).

Criminal cases, AppProc Rule 8(b).

Physician or surgeon review of revocation or suspension of license, §90-14.9(b).

Superior court decisions, §90-14.11(b).

Power of appellate court not limited, §1A-1 Rule 62(f).

Rehearing.

Obtain when petition filed, AppProc Rule 31 (e).

Scope of stay, §1-294.

Service of process.

Bonds, surety.

Service of undertaking on appellee, §1-295.

Small claims actions, §7A-227.

Substitution of parties, AppProc Rule 38.

Superior courts.

Administrative agency decision.

Proper division for review or appeal of decisions, §7A-250(a).

Appeal from judge, §1-277(a).

Clerks entering appeals, §§1-301.1 to 1-301.3.

Clerk to judge, §7A-251(a).

Costs in criminal actions.

Determination, §7A-304(d).

Criminal actions.

Correction of errors in appellate division.

General provisions, §§15A-1441 to 15A-1453.

Procedure after determination of appeal, §1-298.

Settling record on appeal.

Power of trial judge, §1-283.

Trial judges.

Entry of orders under rules, AppProc Rule 36.

Supersedeas.

Authorized, §1-269.

Bonds, surety, §1-269.

Issuance to suspend execution, §1-269.

Supreme court of North Carolina.

Appeal of right from court of appeals, §7A-30, AppProc Rule 14.

Supreme court of the United States.

Costs of state on appeals, §6-17.

Surviving spouses.

Year's allowance.

Assignment, §30-23.

Suspension or variance of rules of appellate procedure, AppProc Rule 2.

Taxation.

Collection of taxes.

Attachment or garnishment, §105-242(b).

Jeopardy assessment and collection, §105-241.23(c).

Review of denial of refund or assessment.

Final determination, judicial review, §105-241.16.

Time.

Attorneys at law.

Secure leave periods.

Designation, filing, AppProc Rule 33.1(f).

APPEALS —Cont'd

Time —Cont'd

Briefs.

Filing and serving, AppProc Rule 13(a).

Appeal of right from court of appeals to supreme court, AppProc Rule 14(d).

Rehearing.

Petition granted, AppProc Rule 31(d).

Reply briefs, AppProc Rule 28(h).

Computation, AppProc Rule 27(a).

Criminal cases.

Correction of errors by appellate division, §15A-1448(a).

Filing and serving notice, AppProc Rule 4(a).

Extensions.

Administrative boards and agencies.

Appeal of right directly to appellate division, AppProc Rule 18(f).

Motions, AppProc Rule 27(c), (d).

Failure of appellant to take timely action, AppProc Rule 25(a).

Filing record on appeal, AppProc Rule 12(a).

Juvenile matters.

Expedited filings, AppProc Rule 3.1(c).

Mail.

Additional time after service by, AppProc Rule 27(b).

Mandates of court.

Issuance, AppProc Rule 32(b).

Motions in appellate courts.

Filing and serving, AppProc Rule 37(a).

Notice of appeal.

Filing and serving, AppProc Rule 3(c).

Appeal of right from court of appeals to supreme court, AppProc Rule 14(a).

Appeal of right from final administrative agency determination, AppProc Rule 18(b).

Criminal cases, AppProc Rule 4(a).

Oral argument.

Time allowed, AppProc Rule 30(b).

Petition for review.

Discretionary review on certification by supreme court.

Filing and service, AppProc Rule 15(b).

Response, AppProc Rule 15(d).

Rehearing.

Briefs.

Petition granted, AppProc Rule 31(d).

Determination, AppProc Rule 31(c).

Petition.

Filing, AppProc Rule 31(a).

Settling record on appeal, AppProc Rule 11.

Taking by written notice.

Appeals to appellate division in civil actions and in special proceedings, §1-279.1.

Time tables for appeals, AppProc Appx A.

Transcripts.

Ordering, production, delivery, AppProc Rule 7.

Torrens system registration.

Report of examiners.

Exceptions to report, §43-11(c).

Tort claims against state departments and agencies.

Appeal to court of appeals, ICTortClaim Rules T401 to T404.

Appeal to full commission, ICTortClaim Rules T301 to T310.

Cost, §143-291.1.

Court of appeals, §143-293.

Supersedeas, §143-294.

APPEALS —Cont'd
Tort claims against state departments and agencies —Cont'd
Full commission, §143-292.
Transcript copies, §143-291.1.
Rules of industrial commission.
Appeals to court of appeals, ICTortClaim Rules T401 to T404.
Appeals to full commission, ICTortClaim Rules T301 to T310.
Supersedeas.
Appeal to court of appeals to act as supersedeas, §143-294.
Toxic substance identification complaints.
Judicial review of commission orders, §95-195(d).
Traffic violations.
Civil penalty assessed, §20-178.1.
Transcripts.
Briefs.
Appendixes.
Verbatim portion of transcript, AppProc Rule 28(d).
Civil cases.
Ordering, AppProc Rule 7(a).
Production, AppProc Rule 7(b).
Contract for transcription of proceedings.
Civil cases, AppProc Rule 7(a).
Criminal cases.
Ordering, AppProc Rule 7(a).
Production, AppProc Rule 7(b).
Delivery of completed transcript, AppProc Rule 7(b).
Juvenile matters, AppProc Rule 3.1(c).
Ordering, AppProc Rule 7(a).
Production, AppProc Rule 7(b).
Trial tribunal.
Defined, AppProc Rule 1(d).
Entry of orders by trial judges.
Death, incapacity, absence of authorized judge, AppProc Rule 36(b).
Rules not specifying particular judge, AppProc Rule 36(a).
Trust companies.
Hearings.
Appeal of decisions generally, §53-412(d).
Venue, §53-412(e).
Trusts and trustees.
Appeal of clerk's decision, §36C-2-203(e).
Turnpike authority.
Toll collection on turnpike projects.
Open road tolls.
Contesting liability for unpaid toll, §136-89.218(c).
Underpasses or overpasses.
Elimination or safeguarding of inadequate underpasses or overpasses.
Procedure for appeal, §136-20(g).
Unemployment compensation.
Board of review for appeals policies and procedures, §96-4(b).
Hearing to determine status, rights and liabilities of employers and employing units.
Appeal of board decisions, §96-4(q), (r).
Claims for benefits, §96-15(c) to (i).
Hearing of disputed claims.
Denial of motion to quash subpoena, §96-4(l).
United States.
Costs of state on appeals to federal courts, §6-17.
Unpublished opinions of appellate courts,
AppProc Rule 30(e).

APPEALS —Cont'd
Uranium exploration.
Administrative review of decisions of department, §74-85.
Judicial review of decisions of department, §74-85.
Utilities commission.
Court of appeals.
Review of final orders, §7A-250(b).
Vacation rentals.
Expedited evictions, §42A-25.
Vessel liens.
Action to regain possession, §44A-6.1(b).
Waiver.
Failure to make motion or objection, §15A-1446(b).
Water and air resources.
Abatement of existing pollution.
Special orders, §143-215.2(a).
Hearings.
Judicial review, §143-215.5(a).
Judicial review of actions under article, §143-215.5(a).
Permit applications, §143-215.5(b).
Use of water resources.
Capacity use areas, §143-215.13.
Waters and watercourses.
Withdrawing, diverting or obtaining water.
Surface water transfers.
Review of decision on certificate, §143-215.22L(o).
Withdrawal of appeal.
Civil cases, AppProc Rule 37(e).
Criminal cases, AppProc Rule 37(d).
Notice, AppProc Rule 37(d), (e).
Other parties not effected, AppProc Rule 37(f).
Workers' compensation.
Administrative decisions appealed, ICWorkComp Rule 703.
Appeal to court of appeals, ICWorkComp Rule 702.
Awards, §97-86.
Interest on awards after hearing, §97-86.2.
Judgment on award.
Decision as to certificate of accrued arrearages, §97-87(c).
Payment of award pending appeal in certain cases, §97-86.1.
Commission appeals, ICWorkComp Rule 701.
Insurers.
Expenses of appeals brought by insurers, §97-88.
Remand from appellate courts, ICWorkComp Rule 702A.
Work First program.
Mismanagement of assistance, appointment of personal representative, §108A-37(c).
Program of temporary public assistance for purposes of appeal, §108A-27.15(b).
Writs.
Writs of error abolished, §1-268.
Year's allowance.
Assignment in superior court.
Judgment and order for commissioners.
Appeal from judgment, §30-31.1.

APPEARANCES.
Abused, neglected or dependent juvenile actions.
Failure of parent, guardian, etc., personally served to appear, §7B-407.

APPEARANCES —Cont'd

Adoption.

Hearing on petition to adopt adult, §48-2-605(b).

Annulment of marriage.

Failure of defendant to appear in action.

Notice of trial not required, §50-10(b).

Bail.

Failure to appear, §15A-543(a).

Imposition of conditions of pretrial release.

Prior failure to appear and answer charges, §15A-534(d1).

Penalties, §15A-543(b), (c).

Closed-circuit television.

First appearance before district court judge, §15A-601.

Corporations.

Organizations generally.

Appearance by counsel or agent, §15A-773(b).

Delinquent and undisciplined juvenile actions.

Failure of parent, guardian or custodian to appear.

Contempt, §§7B-1805(b), (c), 7B-1806.

First appearance of juvenile for felony cases, §7B-1808.

Parent, guardian or custodian to attend hearings, §7B-2700.

Excusing appearance, §7B-2700.

District courts.

Attorneys at law.

Withdrawal of appearance, SuperCt Rule 16.

First appearance before district court judge, §§15A-601 to 15A-606.

Divorce.

Failure of defendant to appear in action.

Notice of trial not required, §50-10(b).

Executors and administrators.

Actions against personal representatives or collectors.

Service on or appearance of one binds all, §28A-18-4.

Failure to appear.

Abused, neglected or dependent juvenile actions, §7B-407.

Delinquent and undisciplined juvenile actions.

Contempt of parent, guardian or custodian for failure to appear, §§7B-1805(b), (c), 7B-1806.

Dismissal with leave when defendant fails to appear and cannot readily be found, §15A-932.

Divorce or annulment, notice of trial not required, §50-10(b).

Garnishees, §1-440.27.

Motor vehicle offenses.

Court to report failure to appear, §20-24.2.

Revocation of drivers' license, §20-24.1.

Penalties, §15A-543.

Referees meetings, §1A-1 Rule 53(f).

Service of pleadings and other papers on party in default not required, §1A-1 Rule 5(a).

Small claims actions.

Appeals, §7A-228(c).

First appearance before district court judge.

Charges.

Defendant to be informed of charges against him, §15A-605.

Sufficiency.

Determination, §15A-604(a).

Proceedings on finding of insufficiency, §15A-604(b).

APPEARANCES —Cont'd

First appearance before district court judge —Cont'd

Clerk of court.

When clerk may conduct appearance, §15A-601(e).

Closed-circuit television, §15A-601.

Consolidation of proceedings, §15A-601(b).

Continuance, §15A-601(d).

Charges found to be insufficient, §15A-604(b).

Determination whether defendant had retained or been assigned counsel, §15A-603(a).

Generally, §15A-601(a).

Indigent persons.

Determination whether defendant has been assigned counsel.

Duty of judge, §15A-603(a).

Proceedings when defendant asserts indigence and desires counsel, §15A-603(c).

Right to be furnished counsel.

Defendant to be informed by judge, §15A-603(b).

Information to be given defendant, §§15A-602, 15A-603, 15A-605.

Initial appearance.

Consolidation of proceedings, §15A-601(b).

Probable cause hearing.

Attorneys at law.

Defendant to be informed of right to counsel, §15A-606(e).

Continuance, §15A-606(f).

Scheduling by judge, §15A-606(a), (d).

Waiver, §15A-606(a).

After first appearance, §15A-606(g).

Evidence not to be admitted in trial, §15A-606(b).

Proceedings on, §15A-606(c).

Required, §15A-601(a).

Right to counsel.

Defendant to be informed by judge, §15A-603(b), (d).

Self-incrimination.

Warning of right against self-incrimination, §15A-602.

Sufficiency of charge.

Determination, §15A-604(a).

Procedure if insufficient, §15A-604(b).

Time for, §15A-601(c).

Waiver not allowed, §15A-601(d).

Waiver of representation by counsel, §15A-603(e).

First appearance before magistrate, §15A-511.

Audio and video transmission.

Conducting of proceeding by, §15A-511(a1).

Bail.

Release, §15A-511(e).

Communicable disease.

Detention of defendant, §15A-534.3.

First appearance before district court judge.

Consolidation and proceedings, §15A-601(b).

Generally, §15A-511(a).

Impaired drivers.

Administration of test, §15A-534.2(d).

Compliance with provisions, §15A-534.2.

Conditions for release, §15A-534.2(c).

Detention in custody, §15A-534.2.

Implied consent offenses, §20-38.4.

Officers other than magistrates.

Authority to conduct initial appearance, §15A-511(f).

Probable cause.

Arrest without warrant.

Determination of probable cause, §15A-511(c).

APPEARANCES —Cont'd

First appearance before magistrate —Cont'd

Statement by magistrate, §15A-511(b).

Warrant.

    Procedure when arrest is pursuant to warrant, §15A-511(d).

Warrantless arrest.

    Procedure on, §15A-511(c).

Garnishees.

Failure to appear, §1-440.27.

Impaired driving, implied consent offenses.

Initial appearance before magistrate, §20-38.4.

Infractions.

Appearance bonds, §15A-1113(c).

Failure to appear to answer charge.

    No order for arrest, §15A-1116(b).

Jurisdiction.

Grounds for personal jurisdiction without service of summons, §1-75.7.

Judgment against nonappearing defendant.

    Proof of jurisdiction, §1-75.11.

Organizations.

Appearance by counsel or agent, §15A-773(b).

Securing attendance of organizations as defendants, §15A-773.

Parental authority over juvenile.

Order directing juvenile to appear before court.

    Juvenile leaving home and refusing to return, §7B-3404.

Partnerships.

Organizations generally.

    Appearance by counsel or agent, §15A-773(b).

Personal jurisdiction without service of summons.

General appearance in action, §1-75.7.

Real estate appraisal board.

Enforcement of chapter, §93E-1-13(b).

Referees meetings.

Failure to appear, §1A-1 Rule 53(f).

Service of pleadings and other papers, §1A-1 Rule 5(a).

Superior courts.

Attorneys at law.

    Withdrawal of appearance, SuperCt Rule 16.

Two-way audio and video transmissions, §15A-601(a1), (a2).

Waiver.

Defendant may execute written waiver and plead not guilty, §15A-1011(d), (e).

APPELLATE COURTS PRINTING AND COMPUTER OPERATIONS FUND, §7A-343.3.

APPELLATE DEFENDER.

Appointment by commission, §7A-498.8(a).

Appointment of assistants and staff, §7A-498.8(c).

Consultation on capital cases, §7A-498.8(b).

Continuing legal education, §7A-498.8(b).

Counsel of record in capital cases, §7A-498.8(b).

Federal capital cases, §7A-498.8(b).

Funding, §7A-498.8(d).

Indigent defense services.

Capital cases.

    Appointment, compensation eligibility, IDS Rules 2B.1 to 2B.4.

        Standards for, IDS Appxs 2B.1 to 2B.3.

Non-capital criminal and non-criminal cases.

    Appointment, compensation eligibility, IDS Rules 3.1 to 3.7.

Legal representation, §7A-498.8(b).

APPELLATE DEFENDER —Cont'd

Maintenance of clearinghouse, §7A-498.8(b).

Recruitment of appointed counsel, §7A-498.8(b).

APPELLATE DIVISION OF GENERAL COURT OF JUSTICE.

Advance sheets.

Contracting for printing by administrative officer of the court, §7A-6(b).

Designation of commercial advance sheets as official reports, §7A-6(b1).

    Furnishing without charge, §7A-6(c).

    Sale to general public, §7A-6(b).

        Remittance of proceeds, §7A-6(b).

Appellate division reports.

Distribution of copies, §7A-343.1.

Court of appeals.

See COURT OF APPEALS.

Distribution of appellate division reports, §7A-343.1.

Division within general court of justice, §7A-4.

Judicial conduct.

Authority of supreme court to prescribe standards, §7A-10.1.

Law clerks.

Justices or judges entitled to services of one clerk, §7A-7(a).

Salaries of clerks, §7A-7(a).

Organization, §7A-5.

Reporters.

Appointment by supreme court, §7A-6(a).

Duties, §7A-6(a).

Salary, §7A-6(a).

Reports.

Contracting for printing of reports by administrative officer of the courts, §7A-6(b).

Designation of commercial reports as official reports, §7A-6(b1).

Sale of reports to general public, §7A-6(b).

    Remittance of proceeds of sales, §7A-6(b).

Research assistants.

Justice or judges entitled to services of one research assistant, §7A-7(a).

Salaries of research assistants, §7A-7(a).

Rules of practice and procedure.

Supreme court to prescribe rules, §7A-33.

Secretaries.

Determination of number and salaries of secretaries, §7A-7(b).

Stenographers.

Determination of number and salaries of stenographers, §7A-7(b).

Supreme court.

See SUPREME COURT OF NORTH CAROLINA.

APPELLATE DIVISION REPORTS.

Distribution of copies, §7A-343.1.

APPENDICITIS.

Food, drug and cosmetic act.

False advertising of drug or device, §106-138(b).

APPLES.

Dried apples.

Standard weight and measure, §81A-42.

Immature apples.

Grade standards, requirements for maturity, adoption, §106-189.2(a).

Criminal penalty for violating, §106-189.2(b).

Marketing and branding farm products.

Generally, §§106-185 to 106-196.

    See FARM PRODUCTS MARKETING AND BRANDING.

APPLES —Cont'd
Promotion of use and sale of agricultural products.
Generally, §§106-550 to 106-568.
See AGRICULTURAL PRODUCTS PROMOTION.
Unfair practices.
Practices by handlers, §§106-496 to 106-501.
See FRUIT HANDLERS UNFAIR PRACTICES.

APPLE SEEDS.
Standard weight and measure, §81A-42.

APPLIANCES.
Bailment, lease or rental of vehicle or draft animal.
Protection of bailor against bailee's acts, §§14-165 to 14-169.
See BAILMENTS.
Electric appliance sales.
Actions.
Enforcement of provisions, §66-27.01.
Compliance with provisions required, §66-23.
Evidence.
Acceptable listings as to safety of goods, §66-25.
Identification marks.
Removal, alteration, changing or defacement.
Prohibited, §66-24.
Required, §66-24.
Installation.
Legal responsibility for proper installation unaffected, §66-26.
Liability.
Effect of provisions, §66-26.
Merchantability.
Acceptable listings as to safety of goods, §66-25.
Safety.
Acceptable listings as to safety of goods, §66-25.
Testing.
Acceptable listings as to safety of goods, §66-25.
Violations of provisions, §66-27.
Exemption from creditors' claims, §1C-1601(a).
Interfering with gas, electric and steam appliances.
Criminal trespass, §14-151.

APPLICATORS OF PESTICIDES, §§143-452 to 143-459.
See PESTICIDE APPLICATORS.

APPOINTMENT OF COUNSEL FOR INDIGENT PERSONS.
Abused, neglected or dependent juvenile actions.
Appointment for parent, §7B-602.
Notice in summons of right to counsel and appointment information, §7B-406(b).
Payment of court-appointed counsel, §7B-603(a) to (b).
Delinquent and undisciplined juvenile actions, §7B-2000(a).
Payment, §7B-2002.
Presumption of indigence, §7B-2000(b).
Secure or nonsecure custody hearings.
Appointment of counsel for juvenile, §7B-1906(c).
Summons to notify parent of right, §7B-1805(b).
Fees for preparation of copies.
Not chargeable to attorney appointed to represent indigent at state expense, §7A-308(b1).
Innocence claim inquiry.
Formal inquiry, §15A-1467(b).

APPOINTMENT OF COUNSEL FOR INDIGENT PERSONS —Cont'd
Innocence claim inquiry —Cont'd
Judicial review by three-judge panel, §15A-1469(e).
Interstate compact on juvenile.
Return of escapees or absconders, §7B-2805(c).
Mental health, developmental disability, substance abuse.
Involuntary commitment.
Substance abuser's commitment hearing, §122C-286(d).
Representation of indigent persons.
General provisions, §§7A-450 to 7A-458.
See INDIGENT DEFENSE SERVICES.
Indigent defense services act, §§7A-498 to 7A-498.8.
See INDIGENT DEFENSE SERVICES.
Indigent services rules, IDS Rules 1.1 to 3.7.
See INDIGENT DEFENSE SERVICES.
Model plan, IndigCounsel Model Plan Arts I to X.
See INDIGENT DEFENSE SERVICES.
Termination of parental rights proceedings.
Adjudicatory hearing, parents, §7B-1109(b).
Parent's right to counsel and appointment of counsel, §7B-1101.1(a).

APPOINTMENT TO PUBLIC OFFICE.
Notice, §143-47.7.
Definitions, §143-47.6.
Per diem compensation and travel allowances, §143-47.9.

APPORTIONMENT.
Action challenging plans apportioning state legislature and congressional districts.
Appeal to supreme court.
Direct appeal, §120-2.5.
Contents of judgments invalidating plan, requirements, §120-2.3.
Filed in Wake county superior court, §1-81.1(b).
Opportunity given general assembly to remedy defects, §120-2.4.
Three-judge panel, §1-267.1(a).
Appointment of two additional judges to panel, §1-267.1(b).
Copy of complaint.
Service on senior resident judge, §1-267.1(b).
Decision, §1-267.1(c).
Disqualification of judge.
Replacement, appointment, §1-267.1(b).
Former member of general assembly.
Prohibited from setting, §1-267.1(b).
Majority of court prevails, §1-267.1(c).
Organization, §1-267.1(b).
Presiding judge, §1-267.1(b).
Required to enter order or judgment affecting act of assembly, §1-267.1(c).
Venue in Wake county superior court, §1-81.1(a).
Attorney general.
Approval of act, amending, deleting, adding to, modifying or repealing plan.
Duty to seek, §120-30.9B(b).
Failure to seek, §120-30.9B(b).
Congress, US Const Art I §§2, 3, Amds 14, 17.
Drainage.
Expenses for repairs, §156-11.
General assembly.
Dividing precincts.
Compliance with federal law, §120-2.2(c).
Prohibited, §120-2.2(a).

APPORTIONMENT —Cont'd

General assembly —Cont'd

Dividing precincts —Cont'd

Rejection based upon federal law, §120-2.2(a), (b).

House of representatives, §120-2(a) to (d), NC Const Art II §5.

Senate, §120-1(a) to (d), NC Const Art II §3.

Severability of apportionment acts, §120-2.1.

Municipalities.

Council.

Electoral districts, §160A-23(b).

Redistricting after federal decennial census, §160A-23.1.

APPRAISAL MANAGEMENT COMPANIES.

Real estate appraisal management companies, §§93E-2-1 to 93E-2-11.

See REAL ESTATE APPRAISAL MANAGEMENT COMPANIES.

APPRAISALS AND APPRAISERS.

Chattel mortgages.

Insurance companies.

Investments, §58-7-180(c).

Commissioner of banks.

Appraisal of assets of doubtful value, §53-112.

Compensation for killing diseased livestock.

Cattle affected with Bang's disease and tuberculosis, §106-324.

Report of appraisal, §106-326.

Glanders affected animals, §106-325.

Report of appraisal of cattle affected with Bang's disease and tuberculosis, §106-326.

Corporations.

Appraisal rights generally, §§55-13-01 to 55-13-40.

See CORPORATIONS.

Conversion of domestic corporation to different business entity.

Appraisal rights, §55-11A-13(a), (b).

Merger or share exchange.

Appraisal rights, §55-11-06(a), (b).

Nonprofit corporations.

Mergers with unincorporated entities.

Appraisal rights, §55-11-10(e).

Reorganization of organization.

Shares, appraisal rights, §55-10-03(e).

Decedents' estates.

Employment, §28A-20-4.

Eminent domain.

Right of entry prior to condemnation, §40A-11.

Fiduciaries.

Employment and compensation of appraisers.

Powers which may be incorporated by reference in trust instrument, §32-27.

Homestead exemption.

Costs.

Laying off homestead and exemption, §6-28.

Reassessment of homestead, §6-29.

Insurance companies.

Chattel mortgages.

Investments, §58-7-180(c).

Valuation.

Assets of doubtful value, §58-7-197(c).

Real property, §58-7-193(d).

Mortgage bankers, brokers and servicers.

Appraisers and appraisal services.

Prohibited acts, §53-244.111.

Mortgages and deeds of trust.

Appraisal by financial institution employee.

Fee charge authorized, §24-10(h).

APPRAISALS AND APPRAISERS —Cont'd

Motor vehicle damage appraisers generally.

See MOTOR VEHICLE DAMAGE APPRAISERS.

Motor vehicle liability insurance.

Appraisers selected by insurer and insured.

Dispute as to fair market value of vehicle before and after loss, §20-279.21(d1).

Nonprofit corporations.

Mergers.

Unincorporated entities.

Appraisal rights, §55-11-10(e).

Property taxes.

See PROPERTY TAXES.

Public lands.

State allocated lands.

Acquisitions, §146-22.2(a), (b).

Real estate appraisal management companies, §§93E-2-1 to 93E-2-11.

See REAL ESTATE APPRAISAL MANAGEMENT COMPANIES.

Real estate appraisers, §§93E-1-1 to 93E-1-14.

See REAL ESTATE APPRAISERS.

Savings and loan associations.

Holding companies.

Reorganization of ownership.

Appraisal rights, §54B-261(a1).

Savings banks.

Stock savings banks.

Reorganization.

Appraisal rights, §54C-195(b).

Trust companies.

Mergers, share exchanges or asset transfers.

Appraisal rights, §53-362.

APPRENTICESHIP, §§94-1 to 94-12.

Alarm systems licensing.

Apprenticeship registration permit, §74D-8.1.

Apprenticeship agreements.

Approval by director, §94-8.

Contents, §94-7.

Defined, §94-5(a).

Director of apprenticeship.

Approval of agreements, §94-8.

Rotation of employment.

Agreements may provide for, §94-9.

Signatures, §94-8.

Terms, §94-7.

Apprenticeship committees.

Appointment, §94-5(b).

Defined, §94-5(a).

Functions, §94-5(c).

Sponsors.

Functions, §94-5(c).

Apprenticeship council.

Appointment of members, §94-2.

Chairman.

Appointment, §94-2.

Compensation of members, §94-2.

Composition, §94-2.

Director of apprenticeship.

Confirmation of appointment of director, §94-3.

Duties, §94-2.

Meetings, §94-2.

Number of members, §94-2.

Qualifications of members, §94-2.

Reports, §94-2.

Terms of members, §94-2.

Transfer to department of labor, §143A-71.

Apprenticeship programs.

Defined, §94-5(a).

APPRENTICESHIP —Cont'd
Apprenticeship programs —Cont'd
Sponsors.
Defined, §94-5(a).
Barbers, §86A-24.
Collective agreements between employers and employees.
Apprenticeship provisions not invalidated, §94-11.
Definitions, §§94-5(a), 94-6.
Director of apprenticeship.
Appointment, §94-3.
Apprenticeship agreements.
Approval of agreements, §94-8.
Apprenticeship council.
Confirmation of appointment of director, §94-3.
Duties, §94-4.
Powers, §94-4.
Fees, §94-12.
Hearing aid dealers and fitters.
Registration, §93D-9.
Legislative declaration.
Purposes of provisions, §94-1.
Locksmiths, §74F-7.1.
Exemptions from provisions, §74F-16.
Minimum wage, §95-25.3(b).
Opticians.
Provisions not to apply to apprentices, §90-236.
Qualifications for admission on basis of apprenticeship, §90-240(a), (f).
Registration of apprentices, §90-243.
Purposes of provisions, §94-1.
Reports.
Apprenticeship council, §94-2.
Rotation of employment, §94-9.
Signatures.
Apprenticeship agreements, §94-8.

APPROPRIATE RELIEF, MOTION FOR.
Generally, §§15A-1411 to 15A-1422.
See MOTION FOR APPROPRIATE RELIEF.

APPROPRIATIONS.
ABC boards, §18B-702(g).
Agriculture.
Development act, §§106-585, 106-587.
Airports.
Municipal airports, §63-8.
State aid.
Sources of funds, §§63-68, 63-69.
Transportation department.
Continuing aviation appropriations, §§136-16.4, 136-16.5.
Archives and history.
Department of cultural resources.
Responsibility for administering appropriations for grants-in-aid, §121-12.1.
Expending appropriations for grants-in-aid, §121-12.2.
Armories.
Supplementing available funds authorized, §127A-167.
Unexpended portion of state appropriation, §127A-169.
Art.
Promotion of arts, §143-407.
Aviation.
Continuing appropriation to department of transportation, §136-16.4.
Beaufort and Morehead railroad company.
Continuing appropriation, §136-16.6(c).
Bentonville Battlefield fund.
Appropriation of money credited, §121-7.5(c).

APPROPRIATIONS —Cont'd
Black Mountain advancement center for women.
General assembly not obligated to appropriate funds, §143B-269(h).
Blind persons.
Aid to the blind.
County appropriations, §111-17.
Budget of state.
Capital improvement projects.
Reversion of appropriation, §143C-8-11(a).
Committee report construed with act, §143C-5-5.
Compliance with budget.
Chapter and appropriations acts, §143C-6-7(a).
Deadline for enactment, §143C-5-4.
Deficit avoidance methods, §143C-6-2(a).
Highway appropriations, §143C-6-11.
Introduction of appropriations bills.
Exceptions to ordering rules, §143C-5-2.
Order of enactment, §143C-5-2.
Rule of procedure, §143C-5-1.
Statement of funds availability, §143C-5-3.
Nonprofit corporations, §143C-6-21.
Repairs and renovations reserve account.
Appropriation required to expend, §143C-4-3(c).
Required, §143C-1-1(b).
Reversion of unencumbered funds, §143C-1-2(b).
Savings reserve account.
Appropriation required to expend, §143C-4-2(b).
Withdrawal of funds from state treasury, §143C-1-2(a).
Building code.
Code officials qualification board, §143-151.20.
Community colleges.
Financial support.
Elections on questions of appropriations, §§115D-33 to 115D-37.
Congress, US Const Art I §§7, 9.
Constitution of the United States, US Const Art I §9.
Army, US Const Art I §8.
Revenue bills, US Const Art I §7.
Counties.
Agricultural development act, §§106-585, 106-587.
Beach erosion control, §153A-438.
Cemeteries.
Abandoned and neglected cemeteries.
County care of rural cemeteries, §65-112.
Economic development commissions, §158-12.
Health services.
Counties may appropriate revenues, §153A-248(a).
Ordinances, §153A-248(b).
Hurricanes.
Flood and hurricane protection works, §153A-438.
Inspection departments.
Financial support, §153A-354.
Private entities.
Appropriation of money to private entity to carry out public purpose, §153A-449.
State highway fund.
Allocation of funds, §136-41.1(a) to (c).
Annual appropriation out of fund, §136-41.1(a).
Contracts for maintenance, etc., of streets, §136-41.3.
Eligible municipalities, §§136-41.1(b), 136-41.2(a) to (c).
Incorporated since January 1, 1945, §136-41.2(d).
Excess accumulation of funds, §136-41.3.

APPROPRIATIONS —Cont'd
Counties —Cont'd
State highway fund —Cont'd
Nature of funds distributed, §136-41.1(d).
Records and annual statement, §136-41.3.
Use of funds, §136-41.3.
Western North Carolina Development Association, Inc., §153A-447(a), (b).
County boards of elections.
Boards of county commissioners to make appropriations for, §163-37.
Crime victims compensation.
Compensation payable.
Available to extent general assembly appropriates funds, §15B-25.
Cultural resources department.
Promotion of arts, §143-407.
Education.
School districts.
Allocation by purpose, function or project.
Discretion of county commissioners, §115C-429(b).
Basic education program.
Supplemental nature of funds appropriated for program, §115C-81.1.
Budget, §§115C-425 to 115C-434.
Capital outlay appropriations by county.
Inadequacy of county appropriation, petition by board of education, §115C-440.1(c).
Report on by local government commission, §115C-440.1(a), (b).
Capital outlay fund.
Included in fund, §115C-426(f).
Commissioners to determine amount appropriated, §115C-429(b).
County appropriations.
Allocation to local administrative units, §115C-437.
Apportionment among local school administrative units, §115C-430.
Dispute between board of education and county commissioners.
Procedure for resolution, §115C-431.
Driver education, §115C-216.
Local current expense fund.
Included in fund, §115C-426(e).
Other funds.
Included in funds, §115C-426(g).
State public school fund.
Included in fund, §115C-426(d).
Transfer of funds appropriated, §115C-433(c).
Emergencies, amendment of budget, §115C-433(d).
Elections.
County boards of elections.
Boards of county commissioner to make appropriations for, §163-37.
Energy.
Southern states energy compact.
Supplementary agreements ineffective until funds appropriated, §104D-4.
Fire departments.
State volunteer fire department.
Local appropriations, §58-80-55.
Firefighters' relief fund.
State appropriation, §§58-85-10, 58-85-15, 58-85-25.
Firemen's and rescue squad workers' pension fund.
Administrative expenses of fund, §58-86-20.
Fire protection grant fund, §58-85A-1(c).

APPROPRIATIONS —Cont'd
General assembly.
Legislative research commission.
Payment of expenses from appropriations, §120-30.18.
Highways, roads and streets.
Congestion relief and intermodal transportation 21st century fund.
Appropriations to fund, §§136-255, 136-256.
Primary, secondary and urban road systems, §136-44.2.
Reports to appropriations committees of general assembly, §136-44.2B.
Special appropriations for highway construction, §136-44.2C.
Transportation department, §143C-6-11.
Historic districts and landmarks, §160A-400.12.
Hospital authorities, §131E-30.
Housing finance agency.
Authorization to accept appropriated moneys, §122A-18.
Receipt, administration and compliance with conditions and requirements of appropriation.
General power of agency, §122A-5.
Inaugural ceremonies committee.
Payments from appropriations, §143-539.
Interlocal cooperation.
Joint agencies, §160A-462(b).
Internal improvements.
State deemed shareholder in corporation accepting appropriation, §124-2.
Libraries.
Interstate library compact, §125-12 Art IX.
Public library service.
State policy as to public library service.
Annual appropriation therefore, §125-7.
Livestock.
Combating animal and fowl diseases, §106-308.
Disposition of surplus funds, §106-309.
Tuberculosis.
Counties to appropriate funds for eradication of tuberculosis, §106-343.
Amount of appropriation, §106-346.
Local ABC boards, §18B-702(g).
Local development.
Authorized activities.
Approval of appropriations, §158-7.1(c).
Economic development agreements, terms, §158-7.1(h).
Economic development commissions.
Localities, §158-12.
Encouragement of developments, §158-7.1.
Limitation on appropriations and expenditures, §158-7.1(f).
Local government budget and fiscal control acts.
Applicability, §158-7.1(e).
Local governments.
Open space.
Acquisition, §160A-406.
Parks and recreation, §160A-353.
Project development financing debt instruments.
Appropriations agreements, §159-111(e).
Mental health, developmental disabilities and substance abuse.
Area authorities, §§122C-147, 122C-147.1.
Militia.
Support of militia.
Local appropriations, §127A-138(a).
Municipalities.
Agricultural development act.
Local appropriations, §106-587.

APPROPRIATIONS —Cont'd
Municipalities —Cont'd
Continuing contracts.
Appropriation of sufficient funds, §160A-17.
Contract with and appropriating money to private entities.
Authorization, §160A-20.1.
Local development.
Economic development commissions, §158-12.
Public safety.
Resources to protect public.
Appropriations under contract with state, §160A-289.1.
State highway fund.
Allocation of funds, §136-41.1(a) to (c).
Annual appropriation out of fund, §136-41.1(a).
Contracts for maintenance, etc., of streets, §136-41.3.
Eligible municipalities, §§136-41.1(b), 136-41.2(a) to (c).
Incorporated since January 1, 1945, §136-41.2(d).
Excess accumulation of funds, §136-41.3.
Ineligibility for funds, §136-41.2B.
Nature of funds distributed, §136-41.1(d).
Records and annual statement, §136-41.3.
Small municipalities, accumulation of allocations, §136-41.3.
Use of funds, §136-41.3.
Election regarding allocated funds, use of funds, §136-41.4.
North Carolina center for nursing.
State budget support, §90-171.72.
North Carolina railroad.
Continuing appropriations, §136-16.6(a), (b).
Nurses.
North Carolina center for nursing.
State budget support, §90-171.72.
Occupational safety and health.
Commissioner of labor.
Request for sufficient appropriations, §95-150.
Parks and recreation.
Local governments, §160A-353.
Post-war reserve fund, §§143-191 to 143-194.
Public officers and employees.
Diversion of appropriations to state institutions, §143-114.
Public transportation.
Transportation department.
Continuing appropriations for public transportation, §§136-16.8, 136-16.9.
Railroads.
Transportation department.
Continuing rail appropriations, §§136-16.6(a) to (c), 136-16.7.
Regional planning commissions, §153A-396.
Regional sports authorities, §160A-479.9(a).
School districts.
Allocation by purpose, function or project.
Discretion of county commissioners, §115C-429(b).
Basic education program.
Supplemental nature of funds appropriated for program, §115C-81.1.
Budget, §§115C-425 to 115C-434.
Capital outlay appropriations by county.
Inadequacy of county appropriation, petition by board of education, §115C-440.1(c).
Report on by local government commission, §115C-440.1(a), (b).

APPROPRIATIONS —Cont'd
School districts —Cont'd
Capital outlay fund.
Included in fund, §115C-426(f).
Commissioners to determine amount appropriated, §115C-429(b).
County appropriations.
Allocation to local administrative units, §115C-437.
Apportionment among local school administrative units, §115C-430.
Dispute between board of education and county commissioners.
Procedure for resolution, §115C-431.
Driver education, §115C-216.
Local current expense fund.
Included in fund, §115C-426(e).
Other funds.
Included in funds, §115C-426(g).
State public school fund.
Included in fund, §115C-426(d).
Transfer of funds appropriated, §115C-433(c).
Emergencies, amendment of budget, §115C-433(d).
Solid waste management.
Regional solid waste management authorities.
State and local governments, §153A-428(b).
State debt, §§142-1 to 142-29.7.
State-owned railroad company.
Continuing appropriations, §136-16.6(a), (b).
State treasurer.
Short-term notes in emergencies.
Authorization to make, §147-70.
Superior court judges.
Hiring of secretaries, §7A-44.1(b).
Transportation department.
Allocations by department chief financial officer to eliminate overdraft, §136-16.10.
Aviation.
Continuing aviation appropriations, §136-16.4.
Purposes, §136-16.5.
Highway appropriations, §143C-6-11.
Public transportation.
Continuing appropriations for, §136-16.8.
Purposes, §136-16.9.
Rail appropriations.
Continuing rail appropriations, §136-16.6(a) to (c).
Purposes, §136-16.7.
Reports to appropriations committees of general assembly, §136-44.2B.
United States, US Const Art I §9.
University of North Carolina.
Carryforward of funds not used in fiscal year, §116-30.3(e).
Constituent institutions.
Special responsibility constituent institutions, §116-30.2(a).
Reversions, §116-30.3(a).
School of science and mathematics, §116-30.2(b).
Distinguished professors endowment trust fund, §116-41.18(c).
Excess receipts, availability, §116-30.3A.
General fund for operation of university.
Receipt by president, administration, powers and responsibilities, §116-14(b1), (b2).
Urban redevelopment.
Municipalities may appropriate funds to commission, §160A-520.
Veterans, §165-9.

APPROPRIATIONS —Cont'd
Vocational and technical education.
State funds, §115C-156.
Weights and measures.
Funds for administration of act, §81A-6.

**AQUACULTURE DEVELOPMENT, §§106-756 to
106-764.**
Alligators.
Propagation and production of American
alligators, §106-763.1.
American alligators.
Propagation and production, §106-763.1.
Citation of article.
Short title, §106-757.
**Damage to agricultural commodities or
production systems.**
Definitions, §1-539.2B(c).
Double damage liability, §1-539.2B(a).
Valuation, §1-539.2B(b).
Definitions, §106-758.
**Department of agriculture and consumer
services.**
Lead agency, §106-759(a).
Powers and duties, §106-759(b).
Findings of legislature, §106-756.
Fish disease management.
Development and implementation of plans,
§106-762(a).
Release of fish, §106-762(b).
Fish hatcheries and production facilities.
Aquarium or ornamental trade in fish,
§106-761(h).
Commercial catchout facilities, §106-761(e).
Holding pond/tank permit, §106-761(f).
Hybrid striped bass, §106-761(c).
Licenses, §106-761(d).
Revocation, §106-761(c).
Possession of species other than those listed,
§106-761(g).
Registration, §106-761(a).
Species subject to section, §106-761(b).
Fish passage, §106-763(a).
Legislative findings and purpose, §106-756.
Natural watercourses.
Blocking, §106-763(a).
Penalties.
Violation of act, §106-764.
Purpose of article, §106-756.
Residual stream flow, §106-763(b).
**Robbing or injuring hatchery or other
aquaculture operation, §113-269(g).**
Shellfish leases.
Water column leases for aquaculture, §113-202.1.
Title of article.
Short title, §106-757.
Violation of provisions, §106-764.

AQUARIUMS.
**North Carolina aquariums, §§143B-289.40 to
143B-289.44.**
See NORTH CAROLINA AQUARIUMS.

**AQUATIC WEED CONTROL, §§113A-220 to
113A-227.**
Citation of article, §113A-220.
County service districts, §153A-301(e).
Definitions, §113A-221.
Injunctions.
Violation of article, §113A-226(b).
Noxious aquatic weeds.
Areas of state, §113A-222(b).

AQUATIC WEED CONTROL —Cont'd
Noxious aquatic weeds —Cont'd
Commissioner of agriculture.
Powers, §113A-224(a), (b).
Control, removal or destruction.
Compliance with applicable federal and state
laws, §113A-223(d).
Cost-efficiency and effectiveness, §113A-223(c).
Secretary, §113A-223(b).
Defined, §113A-221.
Designation, §113A-222(a).
Modification or withdrawal, §113A-222(d).
Rules, §113A-222(c).
Importation, sale, etc.
Regulation by commissioner, §113A-224(a), (b).
Secretary.
Powers and duties.
Generally, §113A-223(a).
State departments and agencies.
Cooperation with secretary, §113A-225.
Penalties.
Violation of article, §113A-226(a).
Rules and regulations.
Adoption, §113A-227.
Secretary.
Defined, §113A-221.
Powers and duties.
Generally, §113A-223(a).
Short title of article, §113A-220.
State departments and agencies.
Cooperation with secretary, §113A-225.
Violation of article.
Injunctions, §113A-226(b).
Penalties, §113A-226(a).

ARBITRATION, §§1-569.1 to 1-569.31.
Actions subject to arbitration, Arbitration Rule
1.
Exceptions, Arbitration Rule 1.
Affirmative defense, pleading, §1A-1 Rule 8(c).
Agreements to arbitrate.
Arbitration by agreement, Arbitration Rule 1.
Case or controversy, §1-569.6(b).
Challenge to proceedings, §1-569.6(d).
Conditions precedent, §1-569.6(c).
Effect of, §1-569.4.
Nonwaivable provisions, §1-569.4(c).
Prohibitions, §1-569.4(b).
Validity of, §1-569.6(a).
Waiver or varying provision of act, §1-569.4(a).
Nonwaivable provisions, §1-569.4(b), (c).
Amount in issue.
Maximum amount, Arbitration Rule 1.
Exceptions, Arbitration Rule 1.
Excessive claims, Arbitration Rule 1.
Appeals, §1-569.28(a), (b).
Preaward ruling by arbitrators.
Appealability of arbitrator's ruling, §1-569.18(b),
(c).
Applicability of article, §1-569.3(a) to (c).
Applicability of rules, Arbitration Rules 1, 9.
Arbitrators.
Appointment, §1-569.11.
Canons of ethics for arbitrators. See within this
heading, "Ethics."
Conflicts of interest, §§1-569.11(b), 1-569.12.
Continuing duty to disclosure, §1-569.12(b).
Defined, §1-569.1.
Disclosure requirements, §1-569.12.
Disqualification, Arbitration Rule 2.
Eligibility of arbitrators, Arbitration Rule 2.

ARBITRATION —Cont'd
Arbitrators —Cont'd
Ex parte communications with arbitrator.
  Prohibited, Arbitration Rule 3.
Expenses.
  Payment, §1-569.21(d).
  Rules for court-ordered arbitration, Arbitration
    Rule 2.
Fees.
  Payment, §1-569.21(d).
  Rules for court-ordered arbitration, Arbitration
    Rule 2.
Immunity from civil liability, §1-569.14(a).
Impartiality, disclosure of, §1-569.12(a).
Loss of immunity, §1-569.14(c).
Method of appointment, §1-569.11(a).
Motor vehicle accidents.
  Immunity prohibited, §1-569.14(f).
Nature of immunity, §1-569.14(b).
Oath of office.
  Rules for court-ordered arbitration, Arbitration
    Rule 2.
Objections to appointment.
  Conflicts of interest, §1-569.12(c).
Panel of arbitrators.
  Action by majority, §1-569.13.
Presumption of impartiality, §§1-569.12(e),
  1-569.23(a).
Replacement, §§1-569.7, 1-569.15(d), Arbitration
  Rule 2.
Selection of arbitrators, Arbitration Rule 2.
Service as neutral arbitrator, §1-569.11.
Statewide court-ordered nonbinding arbitration in
  certain civil actions.
  Immunity as judges from civil liability for
    official conduct, §7A-37.1(e).
Testimony as witness, §1-569.14(d).
Attorneys at law.
Attorneys representation at hearings, Arbitration
  Rule 3.
Former arbitrators.
  Conflict of interest, ProfCond Rule 1.12.
Lawyers serving as third-party neutrals, ProfCond
  Rule 2.4.
Representation by lawyer, §1-569.16.
Attorneys' fees.
Civil action against arbitrator, §1-569.14(e).
Client assistance committee, Bar Rules D.0701 to
  D.0704.
Model plan for district bar, Bar Rules D.0801 to
  D.0808.
Awards.
Contested judicial proceedings.
  Court submission to arbitrator, §1-569.20(d).
Copies.
  Delivery to parties, Arbitration Rule 4.
Correction of award, §1-569.24.
Filing of award, Arbitration Rule 4.
Findings of fact and conclusions of law.
  Not required, Arbitration Rule 4.
Judgment on award, §1-569.25.
Modification or correction of award, §1-569.24.
  Change by arbitrator, §1-569.20(a).
  Grounds, §1-569.20(a).
  Notice to parties, §1-569.20(b).
  Other provisions applicable to, §1-569.20(e).
Notice to parties.
  Modification or correction of award,
    §1-569.20(b).
  Objection to motion to modify award,
    §1-569.20(d).

ARBITRATION —Cont'd
Awards —Cont'd
Opinions supporting award.
  Not required, Arbitration Rule 4.
Preaward ruling by arbitrators.
  Incorporation into award, §1-569.18(a).
Record of award, §1-569.19(a).
Scope of award, Arbitration Rule 4.
Signature of arbitrators.
  Rules for court-ordered arbitration, Arbitration
    Rule 4.
Time limit for award, §1-569.19(b).
Vacating award.
  Conflicts of interest of arbitrator, §1-569.12(d).
  Contested judicial proceedings, §1-569.23.
  Failure to follow established procedures,
    §1-569.12(f).
  Motion to vacate award, §1-569.23.
Writing.
  Award to be in writing, Arbitration Rule 4.
Child support or custody.
Family law arbitration generally, §§50-41 to
  50-62.
See FAMILY LAW ARBITRATION.
Citation of act, §1-569.31.
Civil actions.
Application for judicial relief, §1-569.5.
Venue, §1-569.27.
Collaborative law proceedings.
Alternative dispute resolution permitted, §50-78.
Commencement of proceedings, §1-569.9.
Waiver of objections, §1-569.9(b).
Conduct of hearing, §1-569.7(d).
Conferences.
Arbitrator's discretion, §1-569.15(a).
Confidentiality of information.
Canons of ethics for arbitrators.
  Faithfulness to relationship of trust and
    confidentiality inherent in office, CEA Rule
    6.
Confirmation of award, §1-569.22.
Contested judicial proceedings, §1-569.22.
Modification or correction of award, §1-569.24(b).
Motion to vacate award.
  Denial of motion as confirmation, §1-569.23(d).
Conflicts of interest.
Arbitrators, §§1-569.11(b), 1-569.12.
Canons of ethics for arbitrators.
  Disclosures required, CEA Rule 2.
Vacating award.
  Conflicts of interest of arbitrator, §1-569.12(d).
Consolidation of separate arbitration
  proceedings, §1-569.10.
Construction of act.
Applicability of article, §1-569.3(a) to (c).
Federal electronic signatures in global and
  national commerce act.
  Relationship to federal act, §1-569.30.
Short title, §1-569.31.
Uniformity of application and construction,
  §1-569.29.
Contempt of arbitration proceedings,
  §1-569.17(h).
Contested judicial proceedings, §§1-569.22 to
  1-569.25.
Confirmation of award, §1-569.22.
Court submission of award to arbitrator,
  §1-569.20(d).
Litigation expenses, §1-569.25(c).
Modification or correction of award, §1-569.24.
Vacating award, §§1-569.12(e), 1-569.23.

ARBITRATION —Cont'd
Contracts with forum selection provisions.
  Void and against public policy, §22B-3.
    Contracts to improve real property, §22B-2.
Costs, Arbitration Rule 7.
  Judgment on award, §1-569.25(b).
  Payment of fees and expenses of arbitrator and
    other expenses, §1-569.21(d).
Counties.
  Outdoor advertising.
    Regulation of nonconforming off-premises
      outdoor advertising.
      Relocating and reconstructing outdoor
        advertising, §153A-143(i).
Courts.
  Extent of intervention, §1-567.35.
  International commercial arbitration.
    Applications to superior court, §1-567.66.
    Extent of court intervention, §1-567.35.
Damages.
  Additional remedies, §1-569.21(c).
  Award by arbitrator, §1-569.21(b).
  Exemplary relief, §1-569.21(a).
  Grounds for awarding, §1-569.21(b).
  Payment of arbitrator's expenses, §1-569.21.
  Punitive damages, §1-569.21(a), (e).
Decedents' estates.
  Disputed claims, §28A-19-15.
Definitions, §1-569.1.
  Court.
    Rules of court-ordered arbitration, Arbitration
      Rule 8.
  International commercial arbitration,
    §1-567.32(a).
  Arbitration agreement, §1-567.37(a).
Delegation of nonjudicial functions by court,
  Arbitration Rule 8.
Depositions.
  Discovery permitted, §1-569.17(b).
Designation of actions by court, Arbitration Rule
  8.
Discovery.
  Grounds for permitting, §1-569.17(c).
  Issuance of process, §1-569.17(d).
Divorce.
  Family law arbitration generally, §§50-41 to
    50-62.
    See FAMILY LAW ARBITRATION.
Effective date of rules.
  Applicability to cases filed on or after, Arbitration
    Rule 9.
Employers and employees.
  Conciliation service, §§95-32 to 95-36.
  Voluntary arbitration of labor disputes, §§95-36.1
    to 95-36.9.
Ethics.
  Canons of ethics for arbitrators.
    Appointment by one party.
      Ethical considerations relating to arbitrators
        appointed by one party, CEA Rule 7.
    Choice of law, CEA Rule 8.
    Communications with parties.
      Avoidance of impropriety or appearance of the
        propriety, CEA Rule 3.
    Conflicts of interest.
      Disclosures, CEA Rule 2.
    Decision-making in just, independent and
      deliberate manner, CEA Rule 5.
    Diligence.
      Conducting proceedings diligently, CEA Rule
        4.

ARBITRATION —Cont'd
Ethics —Cont'd
  Canons of ethics for arbitrators —Cont'd
    Fairness of arbitration process.
      Conducting proceedings fairly, CEA Rule 4.
      Upholding, CEA Rule 1.
    Integrity of arbitration process.
      Upholding, CEA Rule 1.
    Professional responsibility principles.
      Canons subject to, CEA Rule 8.
    Relationship of trust and confidentiality
      inherent in office.
      Faithfulness to, CEA Rule 6.
Evidence.
  Compelling attendance of witnesses, §1-569.17(a).
  Depositions permitted, §1-569.17(b).
  Exhibits.
    Copies admissible, Arbitration Rule 3.
  Law of evidence used as guide, Arbitration Rule 3.
  Presentation of case, §1-569.7(c).
  Rules of evidence.
    Applicability to proceedings, §1-569.7(f).
    Inapplicability, exception, §1-569.15(e).
  Trial de novo.
    No evidence of arbitration admissible,
      Arbitration Rule 5.
Executors and administrators.
  Referral of disputed claim, §28A-19-15.
Exemption and withdrawal from arbitration,
  Arbitration Rule 1.
Family law arbitration generally, §§50-41 to
  50-62.
  See FAMILY LAW ARBITRATION.
Fees.
  Payment of fees and expenses of arbitrator,
    §1-569.21(d).
  Trial de novo.
    Filing fee, Arbitration Rule 5.
  Witnesses fees, §1-569.17(f).
Forms, Arbitration Rule 8.
Forum selection.
  Contracts with forum selection provisions.
    Void and unenforceable, §22B-3.
      Contracts to improve real property, §22B-2.
Guardian's powers in administering
  incompetent's estate, §35A-1251.
Guardian's powers in administering minor
  ward's estate, §35A-1252.
Hearings, §1-569.15(c).
  Adjournment.
    Setting date, §1-569.15(c).
  Attorneys at law.
    Right to representation by attorney, Arbitration
      Rule 3.
  Conclusion of hearing, Arbitration Rule 3.
  Conduct of hearing, §1-569.7(d).
  Date.
    Advancement by agreement, Arbitration Rule 8.
    Setting, Arbitration Rule 8.
  Evidence.
    Exhibits.
      Copies admissible, Arbitration Rule 3.
    Law of evidence used as guide, Arbitration Rule
      3.
  Exhibits.
    Copies admissible, Arbitration Rule 3.
  Ex parte communications with arbitrator.
    Prohibited, Arbitration Rule 3.
  Failure to appear, Arbitration Rule 3.
  Indigent persons.
    Proceedings in forma pauperis, Arbitration Rule
      3.

ARBITRATION —Cont'd
Hearings —Cont'd
Limits, Arbitration Rule 3.
Motions, Arbitration Rule 3.
Notice, Arbitration Rule 8.
Pre-hearing exchange of information, Arbitration
Rule 3.
Presence at hearing, Arbitration Rule 3.
Record of testimony and evidence.
No record of hearing made, Arbitration Rule 3.
Rights of parties, §1-569.15(d).
Scheduled by court, Arbitration Rule 3.
Subpoenas, Arbitration Rule 3.
Time for.
Advancement of date by agreement, Arbitration
Rule 8.
Setting date, §1-569.15(c), Arbitration Rule 8.
Witnesses, Arbitration Rule 3.
Subpoenas, Arbitration Rule 3.
Immunities.
Arbitrators, §1-569.14(a).
State court-ordered nonbinding arbitration in
certain civil actions.
Arbitrators.
Immunity as judges from civil liability for
official conduct, §7A-37.1(e).
Indigent persons.
Hearings.
Proceedings in forma pauperis, Arbitration Rule
3.
Initiation of arbitration, §1-569.9.
Injunctions.
Motion to compel arbitration, §1-569.7(a).
Insurance companies.
Annual audited financial reports.
Annual audit by certified public accountant.
Disputes, §58-10-210(c).
**International commercial arbitration and
conciliation,** §§1-567.30 to 1-567.87.
See INTERNATIONAL COMMERCIAL
ARBITRATION AND CONCILIATION.
Judgment on award.
Costs, §1-569.25(b).
Recordation, docketing and enforcement,
§1-569.25(a).
Rules for court-ordered arbitration, Arbitration
Rule 6.
Jurisdiction.
Exclusive jurisdiction, §1-569.26(b).
Subject-matter jurisdiction, §1-569.26(a).
Labor disputes.
Conciliation service and mediation, §§95-32 to
95-36.
See LABOR DISPUTES.
Voluntary arbitration, §§95-36.1 to 95-36.9.
See LABOR DISPUTES.
Law firm disputes.
State bar rules for arbitration of internal
disputes, Bar Rules E.0401 to E.0410.
Marriage.
Family law arbitration generally, §§50-41 to
50-62.
See FAMILY LAW ARBITRATION.
Mediation generally.
See MEDIATION.
Medical negligence.
Arbitration of negligent health claims, §§90-21.60
to 90-21.69.
See MEDICAL MALPRACTICE.
Modification or correction of award, §1-569.24.
Change by arbitrator, §1-569.20(a).

ARBITRATION —Cont'd
Modification or correction of award —Cont'd
Criteria, §1-569.24(a).
Grant deemed confirmation, §1-569.24(b).
Grounds, §1-569.20(a).
Joinder of motions, §1-569.24(c).
Notice to parties, §1-569.20(b).
Other provisions applicable to, §1-569.20(e).
Motions.
Application for judicial relief, §1-569.5(a).
Notice of initial motion, §1-569.5(b).
Service of motion, §1-569.5(b).
Enforceability of agreement, §1-569.7(c).
Modification or correction of award.
Joinder of motions, §1-569.24(c).
Motion to compel arbitration, §1-569.7(a).
Order of court.
Court action pending, §1-569.7(e).
Judicial discretion, §1-569.7(d).
Provisional remedies, §1-569.8(a).
Stay of proceedings, §1-569.7(f), (g).
Summary disposition, §1-569.7(b).
Vacating award, §1-569.23.
Municipalities.
Outdoor advertising.
Regulation of nonconforming off-premises
outdoor advertising.
Relocation and reconstruction of sign.
Resolution of disputes, §160A-199(i).
Nonbinding arbitration in certain civil actions.
Statewide court-ordered.
Amount in controversy.
Limitations on, §7A-37.1(c).
Arbitrators.
Immunity as judges from civil liability for
official conduct, §7A-37.1(e).
Fees, §7A-37.1(c1).
Findings of general assembly, §7A-37.1(a).
Implementation of procedure, §7A-37.1(d).
Supreme court.
Adoption of rules, §7A-37.1(b).
Supervising implementation and operation,
§7A-37.1(b).
Notice, Arbitration Rule 8.
Awards.
Modification or correction of award,
§1-569.20(c).
Objection to motion to modify award,
§1-569.20(d).
Effective notice, §1-569.2(a).
Hearings.
Rules for court-ordered arbitration, Arbitration
Rule 8.
Motions.
Notice of initial motion, §1-569.5(b).
Receipt of notice, §1-569.2(c).
What constitutes, §1-569.2(b).
Nurse licensure compact, §90-171.92.
Oaths.
Arbitrators, Arbitration Rule 2.
Objections to proceedings.
Waiver of, §1-569.9(b).
Panel of arbitrators.
Action by majority, §1-569.13.
Partnerships.
Power of partner to submit partnership to
arbitration, §59-39(c).
Preaward ruling by arbitrators.
Appealability of arbitrator's ruling, §1-569.18(b),
(c).
Incorporation into award, §1-569.18(a).

ARBITRATION —Cont'd
Preaward ruling by arbitrators —Cont'd
Judicial enforcement, §1-569.18.
Protective orders.
Issuance by arbitrator, §1-569.17(e).
Provisional remedies, §1-569.8(b).
Interim awards, §1-569.8(b).
Issuance by arbitrator, §1-569.8(b).
Order of court, §1-569.8(a).
Service of process.
Service of subpoenas in civil action, §1-569.17(a).
Signatures.
Award.
Arbitrators' signatures, Arbitration Rule 4.
State boundaries, §§141-3, 141-4.
Statewide court-ordered nonbinding arbitration in certain civil actions.
Amount in controversy.
Limitation on, §7A-37.1(c).
Arbitrators.
Immunity.
Same immunity as judges from civil liability for official conduct, §7A-37.1(e).
Fees, §7A-37.1(c1).
Findings of general assembly, §7A-37.1(a).
Implementation of procedure, §7A-37.1(d).
Supreme court.
Adoption of rules governing procedure, §7A-37.1(b).
Implementation and operation.
Supervising, §7A-37.1(b).
Stay of proceedings, §1-569.7(f), (g).
Subpoenas, Arbitration Rule 3.
Summary disposition.
Authority of arbitrator, §1-569.15(b).
Motions, §1-569.7(b).
Supreme court.
Statewide court-ordered nonbinding arbitration in certain civil actions.
Adoption of rules, §7A-37.1(b).
Supervising implementation and operation, §7A-37.1(b).
Termination of action by agreement before judgment.
Rules for court-ordered arbitration, Arbitration Rule 6.
Title of act, §1-569.31.
Trial de novo.
Costs following trial de novo, Arbitration Rule 7.
Demand for.
Filing, Arbitration Rule 5.
Fee, Arbitration Rule 5.
Service on parties, Arbitration Rule 5.
Evidence.
No evidence of arbitration admissible, Arbitration Rule 5.
Fees.
Filing fee, Arbitration Rule 5.
Judicial immunity, Arbitration Rule 5.
Jury.
No reference to arbitration in presence of jury, Arbitration Rule 5.
Reference to arbitration in presence of jury.
Prohibited, Arbitration Rule 5.
Right to, Arbitration Rule 5.
Witnesses.
Arbitrator not to be called as witness, Arbitration Rule 5.
Trusts and trustees.
Fees, costs and expenses.
Awarding against assets of trust, §36C-10-1004.

ARBITRATION —Cont'd
Vacating award.
Conflicts of interest of arbitrator, §1-569.12(d).
Contested judicial proceedings, §§1-569.12(e), 1-569.23.
Failure to follow established procedures, §1-569.12(f).
Motion to vacate award.
Denial of motion as confirmation, §1-569.23(d).
Filing requirements, §1-569.23(b).
Grounds, §1-569.23(a).
Rehearing, §1-569.23(c).
Waiver of rights.
Effect of provisional remedies, §1-569.8(c).
Wastewater systems.
Certification of contractors and inspectors.
Complaints, §90A-81(b).
Witnesses.
Compelling testimony, §1-569.17(a).
Deposition of witness, §1-569.17(b).
Fees for attending arbitration proceedings, §1-569.17(f).
Hearings, Arbitration Rule 3.
Subpoenas, Arbitration Rule 3.
Subpoenas, Arbitration Rule 3.

ARBORETUM.
Western North Carolina arboretum, §§116-240 to 116-244.
See WESTERN NORTH CAROLINA ARBORETUM.

ARBOR WEEK.
Designation, §103-6.

ARCHAEOLOGICAL RECORD, §§70-46 to 70-52.
Archaeological investigations.
Defined, §70-48.
Permits.
Application, §70-51(a).
Criminal record checks.
Applicants for permits or licenses, §§70-13.1, 114-19.17.
Issuance, §70-51(b).
Notice, §70-51(d).
Suspension, §70-51(e).
Terms, conditions or limitations, §70-51(c).
Archaeological resource.
Defined, §70-48.
Citation of article, §70-46.
Contents, §70-49(b).
Definitions, §70-48.
Establishment, §70-49(b).
Findings of general assembly, §70-47.
Program.
Defined, §70-48.
Establishment, §70-49(a).
Purposes, §70-49(a).
Voluntary participation, §70-49(a).
Purpose of article, §70-47.
Removal of resource from record, §70-49(c).
Rules and regulations.
Adoption, §70-52.
Short title of article, §70-46.
Site steward program.
Administration, §70-50.
Establishment, §70-50.
State archaeologist.
Defined, §70-48.

ARCHAEOLOGICAL RESOURCES PROTECTION, §§70-10 to 70-20.
Archaeological investigations.
Defined, §70-12.

**ARCHAEOLOGICAL RESOURCES
PROTECTION** —Cont'd
Archaeological investigations —Cont'd
Permits.
Applications, §70-13(a).
Criminal record checks of applicants,
§§70-13.1(b), (c), 114-19.17.
Definitions, §70-13.1(a).
Issuance.
Findings required, §70-13(b).
Required, §70-15(a), (b).
Terms, conditions or limitations, §70-13(c).
Religious or cultural sites.
Procedure when permit may result in harm
to, §70-13(d).
Suspension or revocation, §70-13(e).
Citation of act.
Short title, §70-10.
Confidentiality of information, §70-18.
Definitions, §70-12.
Department of cultural resources.
Cooperation with private individuals, §70-19.
Delegation of responsibilities, §70-20.
Forfeitures.
Violations of provisions, §70-17.
Highways, roads and streets.
Objects on highway right-of-way, §136-42.1.
Historical commission.
Rules and regulations, §70-14.
Indians.
Permits for archaeological investigations.
Procedure when permit may harm cultural or
religious site, §70-13(d).
Legislative findings, §70-11(a).
Penalties.
Violations of provisions, §70-15(c).
Civil penalties, §70-16.
Permits.
Archaeological investigations, §70-13.
Private individuals.
Cooperation with, §70-19.
Purpose of provisions, §70-11(b).
Rights of way.
Objects on highway right-of-way, §136-42.1.
Rules and regulations.
Historical commission, §70-14.
Short title of act, §70-10.
Title of act.
Short title, §70-10.
Underwater archaeological sites.
Salvage of abandoned shipwrecks and other
underwater sites, §§121-22 to 121-28.
**Unmarked human burial and human skeletal
remains, §§70-26 to 70-40.**
See UNMARKED HUMAN BURIAL AND
SKELETAL REMAINS PROTECTION.
Violations of provisions.
Forfeitures, §70-17.
Penalties, §70-15(c).
Civil penalties, §70-16.
Separate offense for each day on which violation
occurs, §70-15(d).

ARCHITECTS.
Actions.
Civil penalty for violations of provisions,
§83A-16(b), (c).
Advertising.
Rules and regulations prohibiting.
Board not to adopt, §83A-6(b).

ARCHITECTS —Cont'd
Board.
Administration of provisions, §83A-2(a).
Appointment of members, §83A-2(b).
Bonds, surety.
Treasurer, §83A-2(c).
Composition, §83A-2(b).
Defined, §83A-1.
Disciplinary actions, §83A-14.
Expenses of members, §83A-3(a).
Fees, §83A-4.
Finances, §83A-3(b).
Injunctions.
Power to seek, §83A-17.
Meetings, §83A-2(c).
Number of members, §83A-2(b).
Officers, §83A-2(c).
Quorums, §83A-2(c).
Records, §83A-5(a).
Roster, §83A-5(b).
Rules and regulations.
Administrative procedure act.
Applicability, §83A-6(c).
Powers generally, §83A-6(a), (b).
Seal, §83A-5(c).
Vacancies, §83A-2(b).
Child support enforcement.
Forfeiture of licensing privilege, §50-13.12.
Civil penalty, §83A-16(a).
Actions to recover, §83A-16(b), (c).
Condominium plats or plans.
Certification, §47C-2-109.
Conflicts of interest.
Public works.
Employment of architects when interested in
use of materials prohibited, §133-1.
Construction.
Exemptions from provisions as to architects,
§83A-13(c).
Contractors.
Exemptions from provisions as to architects,
§83A-13(b).
Corporations.
Corporate certificate, §83A-3.
Corporate practice, §83A-8.
Professional corporations generally, §§55B-1 to
55B-16.
See PROFESSIONAL CORPORATIONS.
Definitions, §83A-1.
Disasters.
Qualified immunity for volunteers during a
disaster, §83A-13.1(a) to (d).
Disciplinary actions, §83A-14.
Emergencies.
Qualified immunity during an emergency,
§83A-13.1(a) to (d).
Engineers.
Exemption of architectural work incidental to
engineering project, §83A-13(a).
Examinations.
Licensing by examination, §83A-7(a).
Exemptions from provisions, §83A-13(a) to (e).
Fees.
Board, §83A-4.
Felony convictions.
Forfeiture of license, §15A-1331A.
Injunctions, §83A-17.
Landscape architects.
General provisions, §§89A-1 to 89A-8.
See LANDSCAPE ARCHITECTS.

ARCHITECTS —Cont'd
Licenses.
Corporate certificate.
Application for, §83A-8(a).
Defined, §83A-1.
Reciprocity, §83A-8(b).
Subject to rules and regulations of board,
§83A-8(c).
Denial.
Grounds, §83A-15.
Examinations, §83A-7(a).
Qualification requirements, §83A-7(a).
Expiration, §83A-11.
Forfeiture.
Felony convictions, §15A-1331A.
Reciprocity, §83A-7(b).
Corporate certificates, §83A-8(b).
Renewal, §83A-11.
Fees, §83A-4.
Required, §83A-12.
Statewide license for privilege of practicing.
Firm or corporation.
Not issued in name of, §105-41(e).
License not authorization to practice, §105-41(i).
Not transferable, §105-41(a).
Personal privilege licenses, §105-41(e).
Required, §105-41(a).
Tax for each license, §105-41(a).
Counties and cities levying, prohibition,
§105-41(h).
Exemptions, §105-41(b).
Suspension or revocation.
Grounds, §83A-15.
License taxes.
Statewide license for privilege of practicing,
§105-41.
Limitation of actions.
Real property improvements.
Recovery of damages for defective or unsafe
conditions, §1-50(a).
Misdemeanors.
Violations of provisions, §83A-16(a).
Motor vehicles.
Volunteer architects during an emergency or
disaster.
Inapplicability of qualified immunity,
§83A-13.1(c).
Partnerships.
Practice of architecture, §83A-9.
Practice of architecture.
Corporate practice.
Defined, §83A-1.
Qualification for, §83A-8.
Partnership practice, §83A-9.
Prohibited practice, §83A-12.
Professional corporations, §55B-14(a).
Generally, §§55B-1 to 55B-16.
See PROFESSIONAL CORPORATIONS.
Public buildings and grounds.
Bids and bidding.
Architectural, engineering and surveying
services, §§143-64.31 to 143-64.34.
Certain buildings involving public funds to be
designed, etc., by architect, §133-1.1.
Public works.
Bids and bidding.
Architectural, engineering and surveying
services, §§143-64.31 to 143-64.34.
Buildings involving expenditure of public funds.
Certain buildings involving public funds to be
designed, etc., by architect, §133-1.1.

ARCHITECTS —Cont'd
Public works —Cont'd
Employment of architects when interested in use
of materials prohibited, §133-1.
Relocation assistance, §§133-5 to 133-18.
Qualified immunity.
Volunteers during a disaster or emergency,
§83A-13.1(a) to (d).
Reciprocity.
Licensing by reciprocity, §83A-7(b).
Corporate certificates, §83A-8(b).
Records.
Board, §83A-5(a).
Roster, §83A-5(b).
Rules and regulations.
Administrative procedure act.
Applicability, §83A-6(c).
Powers of board generally, §83A-6(a), (b).
Seals and sealed instruments.
Board, §83A-5(c).
Confidential information.
Records submitted for project approval
revealing, §132-1.2.
Professional seals, §83A-10.
Signatures.
Plans or specifications under exemptions,
§83A-13(e).
Subcontractors.
Payments to for improvements upon real property,
§§22C-1 to 22C-6.
Unit ownership.
Plans of buildings.
Certificate of architects, §47A-15(a).
Violations of provisions.
Injunction, §83A-17.
Penalties, §83A-16(a).
Civil penalty, §83A-16(a).
Actions to recover, §83A-16(b), (c).

ARCHITECTURE.
Promotion of arts, §§143-403 to 143-407.1.

ARCHIVES AND HISTORY.
**Advisory commission for state museum of
natural history,** §§143B-344.18 to
143B-344.23.
Alkaline (acid-free) paper.
Historical publications.
Printing state publications of historical value
on, §§125-11.13(a) to (c), 143-170.5.
Appropriations.
Department of cultural resources.
Responsibility for administering appropriations
for grants-in-aid, §121-12.1.
Expending appropriations for grants-in-aid,
§121-12.2.
Archaeological resources protection, §§70-10 to
70-20.
See ARCHAEOLOGICAL RESOURCES
PROTECTION.
**Artifacts owned by state and in custody or
curated by office of archives and history.**
Selling, trading or loaning by department,
§121-7(a).
Bentonville Battlefield fund, §121-7.5.
Budget requests.
Preparation of budget requests.
Procedures for preparing, §121-12.2.
Cemeteries.
Historic preservation program.
Abandoned cemeteries, §121-8(g).
Citation of act, §121-1.

ARCHIVES AND HISTORY —Cont'd
Colonial North Carolina.
Historical publications, §121-6(c).
Conservation and historic preservation agreements, §§121-34 to 121-42.
Corporations.
Outdoor historical dramas, §143-204.8.
Counties.
Historic preservation program.
Cooperation with local governments, §121-8(e).
Historic properties.
Acquisition, maintenance, etc., of property.
Procedures where assistance extended to counties, §121-11.
Definitions, §121-2.
Department of cultural resources.
Archival and historical agency of state, §121-3.
Artifacts owned by state and in custody of office of archives and history.
Selling, trading or placing on permanent loan, §121-7(a).
Budget requests.
Procedures for preparing budget requests, §121-12.2.
Defined, §121-2.
Duties.
Enumerated, §121-4.
Grants-in-aid.
Expending appropriations, §121-12.2.
Responsibility for administering appropriations, §121-12.1.
Museum of history.
Maintenance and administration of museum by department, §121-7(a).
Powers.
Enumerated, §121-4.
Transfer of commission to department, §143B-51.
Tryon's Palace, §§121-14 to 121-21.1.
Division.
General assembly.
Retention of books, records, etc., §120-37(f).
General assembly.
Retention of books, records, etc., by office of archives and history, §120-37(f).
Governor.
Historical publications.
Editing and publishing of official messages and other papers of governor, §121-6(b).
Portrait of governor.
Acquisition of portrait during term of office, §121-13.
Security of historic properties.
Designated employees commissioned special peace officers by governor, §121-10(a).
Grants.
Department of cultural resources, §121-12.1.
Responsibility for administering appropriations for grants-in-aid, §121-12.1.
Expending appropriations for grants-in-aid, §121-12.2.
Historical publications, §121-6.
Alkaline (acid-free) paper.
Printing state publications of historical value on, §§125-11.13(a) to (c), 143-170.5.
Historic preservation and conservation agreements, §§121-34 to 121-42.
Historic preservation program, §121-8.
Defined, §121-2.
Historic properties.
See HISTORIC PROPERTIES.

ARCHIVES AND HISTORY —Cont'd
Murfreesboro historical commission, §§143B-107 to 143B-110.
Museums.
Administration, §121-7.
Branches established, §121-7.
Defined, §121-2.
Maintenance, §121-7.
Maritime museum.
Disposition of artifacts, §121-7.1.
Natural History Museum.
Advisory commission, §§143B-344.18 to 143B-344.23.
Nonstate owners of history museums.
Procedures where assistance extended, §121-11.
North Carolina museum of forestry.
Satellite museum of state museum of natural sciences, §143B-344.23.
Records, §121-7(b).
State aid.
Criteria for state aid to historical museums, §121-12(c1).
Titles to artifacts, §121-7(c), (d).
Name.
Archival and historical agency, §121-3.
Natural History Museum.
Advisory commission, §§143B-344.18 to 143B-344.23.
Nature and historic preserves, §§143-260.6 to 143-260.10F.
North Carolina register of historic places, §121-4.1.
Outdoor historical dramas.
Allotments to outdoor historical dramas.
Audits, §143-204.8(d).
Authorization, §143-204.8(a).
Definition, §143-204.8(c).
Guidelines for approval, §143-204.8(b).
Amusement tax exemptions, §105-40.
Wage and hour act.
Exemptions, §95-25.14(a).
Youth employment, §95-25.5(h).
Youth employment.
Exemptions from certain provisions, §95-25.5(h).
Portrait of governor.
Acquisition of portrait during term of office, §121-13.
Public records.
Assistance to public officers, §121-5(c).
Defined, §121-2.
Designation of state archival agency, §121-5(a).
Destruction of records regulated, §121-5(b).
Funding of program, §121-5(e).
Fees collected by registers of deeds and remitted to state treasurer, §161-11.5.
Preservation of permanently valuable records, §121-5(d).
Public officers.
Assistance to officers, §121-5(c).
Regulation of destruction of records, §121-5(b).
State archival agency designated, §121-5(a).
Register of historic places, §121-4.1.
Salvage of abandoned shipwrecks and other underwater sites, §§121-22 to 121-28.
Short title, §121-1.
State aid.
Department of cultural resources.
Responsibility for administering appropriations for grants-in-aid, §121-12.1.
Expending appropriations for grants-in-aid, §121-12.2.

ARCHIVES AND HISTORY —Cont'd
State aid —Cont'd
Historical commission.
Criteria for state aid to historical museums, §121-12(c1).
Criteria for state aid to historic properties, §121-12.
State archives.
Larceny of records, §14-72(b).
Mutilation or defacement of records, §14-76.1.
State historical records advisory board.
Composition, §121-5.1(a).
Meeting, §121-5.1(f).
Per diem and travel expenses, §121-5.1(d).
Primary duties, §121-5.1(b).
Removal of members for good cause, §121-5.1(c).
State coordinator, appointment, §121-5.1(e).
Title.
Museums.
Archives, §121-7(c), (d).
Tryon's Palace and Tryon's Palace commission, §§121-14 to 121-21.1.
See TRYON'S PALACE.

ARENAS.
ABC permits.
Special occasion permit to sport facility occupied by major league professional sports team.
Patrons of suites available for sale or lease.
Authority to provide alcoholic beverages for receptions, parties or other occasions, §18B-1006(p).
Facility authorities.
Seating at regional facility arena, §160A-480.7.
Smoking in public places.
Applicability of article to local government, §143-601.
Certain indoor arenas, §143-599.
Nonsmoking areas in state-controlled buildings, §143-597.

ARGUMENT OF COUNSEL.
Court's control of argument, §7A-97.
Criminal proceedings.
Abusive, personal experiences, personal belief as to truth or falsity of evidence, matters outside record.
Argument prohibited, §15A-1230(a).
Length, number and order, law governing, §15A-1230(b).
Position or conclusion as to issue.
Argument permitted, §15A-1230(a).
Opening and concluding arguments, SuperCt Rule 10.

ARMED FORCES.
Generally.
See MILITARY.
Military property, care of, §§127A-125 to 127A-131.
See MILITARY PROPERTY, CARE OF.
Militia.
Generally.
See MILITIA.
Naval militia, §§127A-67 to 127A-74.
See NAVAL MILITIA.
State defense militia, §§127A-80, 127A-81.
Unorganized militia, §§127A-87 to 127A-91.
See UNORGANIZED MILITIA.
Missing in action.
Estates of absentees in military service, §§28B-1 to 28B-10.
See ABSENTEES IN MILITARY SERVICE.

ARMED FORCES —Cont'd
National guard.
General provisions.
See NATIONAL GUARD.
Naval militia, §§127A-67 to 127A-74.
See NAVAL MILITIA.
Pay of militia, §§127A-105 to 127A-111.
See MILITIA.
Prisoners of war.
Estates of absentees in military service, §§28B-1 to 28B-10.
See ABSENTEES IN MILITARY SERVICE.
State defense militia, §§127A-80, 127A-81.
Unorganized militia, §§127A-87 to 127A-91.
See UNORGANIZED MILITIA.
Veterans.
General provisions.
See VETERANS.

ARMED ROBBERY, §14-87(a).
Conveyances used in committing robbery.
Seizure and forfeitures, §14-86.1.
DNA sample for DNA analysis.
Obtaining upon arrest for, §15A-266.3A.

ARMORED CARS.
Private protective services generally, §§74C-1 to 74C-30.
See PRIVATE PROTECTIVE SERVICES.

ARMORIES, §§127A-161 to 127A-169.
Acquisition of land by US to be added to military bases, §104-7.
Alcoholic beverage permits.
Civic center defined to include, §18B-1000.
Mixed beverage permit.
Kind of permit that may be issued, §18B-1001.
Recycling requirement, §18B-1006.1.
On-premises fortified wine permit.
Kind of permit that may be issued, §18B-1001.
Recycling requirement, §18B-1006.1.
On-premises malt beverage permit.
Kind of permit that may be issued, §18B-1001.
Recycling requirement, §18B-1006.1.
On-premises unfortified wine permit.
Kind of permit that may be issued, §18B-1001.
Recycling requirement, §18B-1006.1.
Appropriations.
Supplementing available funds authorized, §127A-167.
Unexpended portion of state appropriation, §127A-169.
Contracts.
Department of public safety.
Making contracts, etc., §127A-164.
Conveyances.
Counties and municipalities may lease, convey or acquire property for use as armory, §127A-165.
Prior conveyances validated, §127A-166.
Validation of prior conveyances, §127A-166.
Counties.
Lease, conveyance or acquisition of property for use as armory, §127A-165.
Local financial support, §127A-168.
Definitions, §127A-161.
Department of public safety.
Defined, §127A-161.
Powers.
Acquisition of land, §127A-164.
Contracts.
Making contracts, etc., §127A-164.

ARMORIES —Cont'd
Department of public safety —Cont'd
Powers —Cont'd
Enumerated, §127A-163.
Specified, §127A-163.
Fostering development of armories and facilities, §127A-162.
Leases.
Counties and municipalities may lease, convey or acquire property for use as armory, §127A-165.
Local financial support, §127A-168.
Municipalities.
Lease, conveyance or acquisition of property for use as armory, §127A-165.
Local financial support, §127A-168.

ARMOR-PIERCING BULLETS.
Teflon-coated bullets.
Manufacture, sale, purchase or possession, §14-34.3.

ARMS.
Workers' compensation.
Loss of arms.
Permanent total disability.
Qualification for, lifetime compensation, §97-29(d).
Rates of compensation, ICWorkComp Rule 405.

ARMY.
Absentees in military service.
Estates of absentees, §§28B-1 to 28B-10.
See ABSENTEES IN MILITARY SERVICE.
Generally.
See MILITARY.
Guardian and ward.
Veterans' guardianship act, §§34-1 to 34-18.
See VETERANS' GUARDIANSHIP ACT.
Veterans.
General provisions.
See VETERANS.

ARRAIGNMENT.
Audio and visual transmission, conducting by.
Noncapital cases, §15A-941(b), (c).
Charges.
Read to defendant or summarized, §15A-941(a).
Closed circuit television, §15A-941.
Failure of defendant to plead.
Fact recorded, tried as if pleading not guilty, §15A-941(a).
Generally, §15A-941.
Order of proceedings in jury trial, §15A-1221(a).
Request for arraignment in accordance with section.
Defendant required to file, time for filing, failure to file, §15A-941(d).
Right to counsel, §15A-942.
Superior court.
Not guilty plea.
Effect, §15A-943(b).
Optional calendaring, §15A-944.
Required calendaring, §15A-943(a), (c).
Waiver, §15A-945.
Written request for arraignment, §15A-941(d).
Right to counsel, §15A-942.

ARREST.
Alimony.
Remedy available, §50-16.7(d).
Arson.
Power of attorney general, §58-79-5.

ARREST —Cont'd
Assistance by private persons.
Authority, §15A-405(a).
Benefits to private persons, §15A-405(b).
Liability.
Freedom of private person from, §15A-405(a).
Request by officer, §15A-405(a).
Avoiding arrest.
Aggravating factors in sentencing, §15A-1340.16.
Bail bondsmen and runners.
Surrender of defendant by surety.
Arrest of defendant for purpose of surrender, §58-71-30.
Bank examiners.
Power to make arrest, §53-121.
Campus police officers, §§74E-6(d), 74G-6(b).
Territorial jurisdiction of officer to make arrest.
Immediate and continuous flight, §15A-402(f).
Capitol police.
Powers, §143B-900(d).
Territorial jurisdiction, §143B-900(d).
Child support enforcement.
Remedy of arrest available, §50-13.4(f).
Citizens' arrest, §§15A-404, 15A-405.
Recapture of escaped prisoners, §148-40.
Civil cases, §§1-409 to 1-439.
See ARREST IN CIVIL CASES.
Clerks of court.
Warrant for arrest.
Clerk may issue, §15A-304(f).
Commitment to detention facility pending trial, §15A-521.
Congress.
Privilege from, US Const Art I §6.
Cost, nonpayment, §6-48.
Costs in criminal actions in superior or district courts, §7A-304(a).
County officers outside territory.
Felonies, §15A-402(e).
Court of appeals.
Warrant for arrest.
Judges may issue, §15A-304(f).
Criminal contempt.
Custody of person charged with criminal contempt, §5A-16(b).
Deaf or hearing impaired person.
Interpreter, officer to procure, §8B-2(d).
Debt collectors.
Representing that nonpayment may result in arrest, §75-51.
Debtor leaving state or concealing himself, §1-355.
Definitions.
Order for arrest, §15A-305(a).
Warrant for arrest, §15A-304(a).
Diabetes.
Police assistance to persons arrested while unconscious or semiconscious, §15A-503.
District courts.
Costs in criminal actions, §7A-304(a).
Warrants for arrest.
Judges may issue, §15A-304(f).
DNA sample for DNA analysis.
Required upon arrest for certain offenses, §§15A-266.3A, 15A-502.1.
Dog wardens.
Power of arrest, §67-31.
Domestic violence.
Violation of order, §50B-4(b).
Duties upon arrest, §§15A-401(c), 15A-501.

ARREST —Cont'd

Elections.

County boards of elections.

Power to maintain order, §163-34.

Offenses by voters.

Election officers to cause violators to be arrested, §163-273(b).

Precinct election officials.

Power to maintain order, §163-48.

State board of elections.

Power to maintain order, §163-24.

Electronic recording of custodial interrogations.

Admissibility as evidence, §15A-211(e).

Admission of other statements not precluded, §15A-211(g).

Applicability, §15A-211(b).

Definitions, §15A-211(c).

Destruction of recording, §15A-211(h).

Purpose of provisions, §15A-211(a).

Remedies for noncompliance, §15A-211(f).

When required, §15A-211(d).

Entry on private premises or vehicle, §15A-401(e).

Environment and natural resources.

Special peace officers.

Arrest powers, §113-28.2.

Epilepsy.

Police assistance to persons arrested while unconscious or semiconscious, §15A-503.

Escape.

Persons escaped from penal institutions, §162-35.

Prevention of escape, use of force, §15A-401(d).

Executions.

Debtor leaving state or concealing self, §1-355.

Expungement of criminal records.

See EXPUNGEMENT OF RECORDS.

Extradition, §§15A-721 to 15A-750.

Fugitives from other states, §§15A-728, 15A-729.

Arrest prior to requisition, §15A-733.

Confinement in jail when necessary, §15A-732.

Rights of accused person, §§15A-730, 15A-731.

Warrantless arrest, §15A-734.

Warrant of arrest, §15A-741.

Execution, §§15A-728, 15A-729.

Issuance, §15A-727.

Federal law enforcement officers.

Assistance in enforcing criminal laws in state, §15A-406.

Fingerprints.

Person arrested, §15A-502(a).

Exceptions, §15A-502(b), (c).

Law-enforcement agencies.

Forwarding of fingerprints to, §15A-502(e).

Fish and wildlife inspectors and protectors.

Arrest without warrant, §113-136(d).

Search on arrest, §113-137(a).

Service of arrest warrant, §113-136(e).

Fleeing or attempting to elude arrest or apprehension.

Police chases, speed limit not applicable, §20-145.

Speeding, §20-141.5.

Force.

Use of deadly force to resist arrest, §15A-401(f).

Investigations of use of deadly force by law enforcement officers, §147-90.

Use of force in arrest, §15A-401(d), (e).

Forest law-enforcement officers.

Powers, §106-900.

General assembly.

Duty and privilege of members.

Protection from arrest, §120-9.

ARREST —Cont'd

Highway patrol, §§20-49, 20-188.

Historic property.

Special police, powers, §121-10(b).

Homicide detentions.

Electronic recording of custodial interrogations, §15A-211.

Hot pursuit.

Campus police officers.

Immediate and continuous flight, §15A-402(f).

Company police.

Power to make arrest, §74E-6.

County and city officers.

Immediate and continuous flight, §15A-402(d).

Officers from other states, §15A-403.

How arrest made, §15A-401(c).

Identification as peace officer.

Requirement upon making arrest, §15A-401(c).

Impaired driving, implied consent offenses.

Authority of officers investigating implied consent offense, §20-38.2.

Initial appearance before magistrate, §15A-534.2.

Information as to arrest public record, §132-1.4(c).

Information to arrested person.

Requirements upon making arrest, §§15A-401(c), 15A-501.

Infractions.

Detention of person charged, §15A-1113(b).

Territorial jurisdiction, §15A-1113(d).

Failure to appear to answer charge.

No order for arrest, §15A-1116(b).

Initial appearance before magistrate.

Audio and video transmission.

Conducting of proceeding by, §15A-511(a1).

Bail.

Release, §15A-511(e).

Communicable disease.

Detention of defendant, §15A-534.3.

First appearance before district court judge.

Consolidation of proceedings, §15A-601(b).

Generally, §15A-511(a).

Impaired drivers.

Administration of test, §15A-534.2(d).

Compliance with provisions, §15A-534.2.

Conditions for release, §15A-534.2(c).

Detention in custody, §15A-534.2.

Officers other than magistrates.

Authority to conduct initial appearance, §15A-511(f).

Probable cause.

Arrest without warrant.

Determination of probable cause, §15A-511(c).

Statement by magistrate, §15A-511(b).

Warrant.

Procedure when arrest is pursuant to warrant, §15A-511(d).

Warrantless arrest.

Procedure on, §15A-511(c).

Insurance commissioner powers, §58-2-50.

Interpreter for deaf or hearing impaired person.

Officer to procure, §8B-2(d).

Judicial officer.

Taking person arrested before, §15A-501.

Magistrates.

Initial appearance before magistrate, §15A-511.

Impaired driver, §15A-534.2.

Warrants for arrest.

Issuance, §15A-304(f).

ARREST —Cont'd
Mental health facilities.
State facilities.
Special policemen, §122C-183.
Militia.
Power of arrest in certain emergencies,
§127A-149.
Minors.
Arrest of adult supervising minor children.
Care of minor children, §15A-401(g).
Notification of parent or guardian, §15A-505(a),
(b).
Notification of principal of school, §15A-505(c).
Photographs and fingerprints.
Not authorized for juveniles, §15A-502(c).
Motor vehicle offenses.
Authority of state highway patrol, §20-188.
Lights.
Violations of provisions.
Time to bring lamps into conformance with
requirements, §20-133(b).
Nonresidents, reciprocal provisions, §§20-4.18 to
20-4.20.
Photographs and fingerprints.
Not authorized for misdemeanors under motor
vehicles provisions, §15A-502(b).
Police authority of division, §20-49.
Offense in presence of officer.
Arrest without warrant, §15A-401(b).
Offense out of presence of officer.
Arrest without warrant, §15A-401(b).
Officers from other states, §15A-403(a).
Applicability of provisions, §15A-403(c).
Hearing before judicial officer, §15A-403(b).
Unlawful arrest by officers, §14-43.1.
Order for arrest.
Criminal process generally, §15A-301.
Defined, §15A-305(a).
Delivery, execution and service of criminal
process, §15A-301.
Indictment.
Copy of indictment, §15A-305(c).
Issuance, §15A-305(b).
Who may issue, §15A-305(d).
Service and execution of criminal process,
§15A-301.
Statement of cause and order, §15A-305(c).
Parole.
Violations of parole, §15A-1376(a).
Photography.
Person arrested, §15A-502(a).
Exceptions, §15A-502(b), (c).
Intoxication.
Photographs for purpose of showing,
§15A-502(d).
Law-enforcement agencies.
Forwarding of photographs to, §15A-502(e).
Procedure for taking photo, §15A-502(b1).
Police officers from other states.
Unlawful arrest, §14-43.1.
Preliminary examinations, §15A-521.
Preventing arrest.
Aggravating factors in sentencing, §15A-1340.16.
Prisons and prisoners.
Debtor and creditor.
Discharge of insolvent prisoners.
Persons taken in arrest proceedings, §23-29.
Private persons.
Assistance to law-enforcement officers.
Benefits to private person, §15A-405(b).
Request by officer, §15A-405(a).

ARREST —Cont'd
Private persons —Cont'd
Authority, §15A-405(a).
Detention of offenders.
Authorized, §15A-404(a), (b).
Manner of detention, §15A-404(c).
Period of detention, §15A-404(d).
Surrender of offender to officer, §15A-404(e).
Liability.
Freedom from, §15A-405(a).
Privilege from arrest.
Congress, US Const Art I §6.
Probable cause.
Arrest by officer without warrant, §15A-401(b).
Initial appearance before magistrate.
Arrest without warrant.
Determination of probable cause, §15A-511(c).
Warrant for arrest.
Showing of probable cause, §15A-304(d).
Probation.
Probation officers, §15-205.
Violation of probation, §15A-1345(a).
Public record.
Information as to arrest public record, §132-1.4(c).
Recapture of escaped prisoners, §148-40.
Reptiles.
Regulated reptiles.
Violations of provisions, §14-420.
Requirements upon making arrest,
§§15A-401(c), 15A-501.
Resisting arrest.
Aggravating factors in sentencing, §15A-1340.16.
Obstruction of justice for assisting officers in
performance of duties, §14-223.
Use of deadly weapon or deadly force to resist
arrest, §15A-401(f).
Investigations of use of deadly force by law
enforcement officers, §147-90.
Return of released person.
Immunity of officer, §15A-504(b), (c).
Lack of probable cause for arrest, §15A-504(a), (c).
Revenue law enforcement agents, §105-236.1(b).
Rewards.
Information leading to arrest and conviction.
Governor may offer rewards, §15-53.1.
Right of entry.
Entry on private premises or vehicle, §15A-401(e).
Right to counsel.
Peace officers to advise person arrested of right to
counsel, §15A-501.
**Sealing by court order to withhold public
record,** §132-1.4(k).
**Sex offender and public protection
registration.**
Failure to register, §14-208.11(a1).
Shoplifting.
Detention or arrest of suspect.
Liability for detention, malicious prosecution,
false imprisonment or false arrest,
§§14-72.1, 14-72(d).
Speeding to elude arrest, §20-141.5.
Superior courts.
Costs in criminal actions, §7A-304(a).
Warrant for arrest.
Judges may issue, §15A-304(f).
Supplemental proceedings.
Debtor leaving state or concealing self, §1-355.
Supreme court.
Warrant for arrest.
Justices may issue, §15A-304(f).

ARREST —Cont'd
Territorial jurisdiction of officers to make arrest.
  Campus police officers.
    Immediate and continuous flight, §15A-402(f).
  City officers, §15A-402(b).
    Immediate and continuous flight, §15A-402(d).
    Outside territory, §15A-402(c).
  County officers, §15A-402(b).
    Immediate and continuous flight, §15A-402(d).
    Outside territory.
      Felonies, §15A-402(e).
  Implied consent offenses.
    Authority of officers investigating, §20-38.2.
  State officers, §15A-402(a).
  Transportation of persons in custody, §15A-402(c).
Unconscious or semiconscious persons.
  Assistance to persons arrested while unconscious
    or semiconscious, §15A-503(a), (b).
  Cost of medical care, §15A-503(c).
Unlawful arrest by officers from other states,
    §14-43.1.
Warrantless arrest.
  Extradition of fugitives from other states,
    §15A-734.
Warrants.
  Amendment.
    Criminal warrants may be amended to show
      ownership of property, §15-24.1.
  Arrest by officer pursuant to warrant,
    §15A-401(a).
  Arrest by officer without warrant, §15A-401(b).
  Contents, §15A-304(c) to (e).
  Courts-martial of national guard.
    Power to issue, §127A-56.
  Criminal process generally, §15A-301.
  Criminal summons.
    Enforcement, §15A-303(e).
  Defined, §15A-304(a).
  District court judges.
    Power of judge to issue arrest warrants,
      §7A-291.
  Execution, delivery and service of criminal
    process, §15A-301.
  Extradition.
    Fugitives from other states, §15A-741.
      Execution, §§15A-728, 15A-729.
      Issuance, §15A-727.
  Initial appearance before magistrate.
    Procedure when arrest is pursuant to warrant,
      §15A-511(d).
  Issuance, §15A-304(b).
    Who may issue, §15A-304(f).
  Law enforcement officers.
    Power of officer to issue arrest warrant.
      Termination of power upon establishment of
        district court, §7A-274.
  Magistrates.
    Power of magistrate to issue arrest warrant in
      criminal action, §7A-273.
  Mayors.
    Power of mayor to issue arrest warrant.
      Termination of power upon establishment of
        district court, §7A-274.
  Mental health facilities.
    State facilities.
      Special policemen, §122C-183.
  Order for arrest, §15A-304(e).
  Peace officers.
    Arrest pursuant to warrant, §15A-401(a).
    Arrest without warrant, §15A-401(b).

ARREST —Cont'd
Warrants —Cont'd
  Probable cause.
    Showing of probable cause, §15A-304(d).
  Public records, §132-1.4(k).
  Service of criminal process generally, §15A-301.
  Statement of the crime, §15A-304(c).
Weights and measures.
  Powers of commissioner of agriculture, §81A-16.
Wildlife protectors.
  Arrest without warrant, §113-136(d).
  Search on arrest, §113-137(a).
  Service of arrest warrants, §113-136(e).
Witnesses.
  Civil cases.
    Exemption from arrest, §8-64.
  Criminal cases.
    Material witnesses.
      Order of arrest, §15A-803(g).
    Witnesses from without state.
      Exemption from arrest, §15A-814.

ARREST IN CIVIL CASES.
Affidavit by plaintiff, §1-411.
  Copy to defendant, §1-414.
  Counter affidavits, §1-418.
Attorneys at law.
  Indigent persons.
    Right to counsel, §1-413.
Bail.
  Civil cases.
    See BAIL.
Bonds, surety.
  Order for arrest.
    Undertaking before order, §1-412.
Cases in which arrest allowed, §1-410.
Concealment.
  Cases in which arrest allowed, §1-410.
Congress.
  Privilege from arrest, US Const Art I §6.
Contempt.
  Exclusive nature of provisions.
    Exception as to contempt, §1-409.
Copies of affidavit and order to defendant,
    §1-414.
Debtor leaving state or concealing self, §1-355.
  Debtor removing or disposing property with intent
    to defraud creditors.
    Cases in which arrest allowed, §1-410.
Embezzlement.
  Cases in which arrest allowed, §1-410.
Exclusive nature of provisions, §1-409.
  Exception as to contempt, §1-409.
Execution against the person, §1-311.
  Form of execution, §1-313.
Fraud.
  Cases in which arrest allowed, §1-410.
Habeas corpus.
  Party held in execution not to be discharged,
    §17-36.
Indigent persons.
  Order for arrest.
    Information to be included in order, §1-413.
Jury.
  Petit jury.
    Exemption from civil arrest, §9-16.
Motion to vacate order, §1-417.
Order for arrest, §1-411.
  Copy to defendant, §1-414.
  Execution of order, §1-415.
  Form, §1-413.

ARREST IN CIVIL CASES —Cont'd
Order for arrest —Cont'd
Issuance, §1-413.
Motion to vacate, §1-417.
Jury trial on, §1-417.
Return, §1-413.
Undertaking before order, §1-412.
Vacation of order.
Failure to serve, §1-416.
Privilege from arrest.
Congress, US Const Art I §6.
Quo warranto.
Defendant usurping office, §1-519.
Scope of provisions.
Cases in which arrest allowed, §1-410.
Seduction.
Cases in which arrest allowed, §1-410.
Supplemental proceedings.
Debtor leaving state or concealing self, §1-355.
Torts.
Cases in which arrest allowed, §1-410.
Usurpation of office.
Defendant usurping office, §1-519.
Witnesses.
Attendance of witnesses.
Exemption from civil arrest, §8-64.

ARREST OF JUDGMENT.
Prosecuting witness, §6-49.
Relief now available by motion for appropriate relief, §15A-1411(c).

ARREST WARRANTS.
See ARREST.

ARSENALS.
Acquisition of land by US to be added to military bases, §104-7.

ARSENIC.
Highway pavement markings.
Arsenic content in glass beads contained in paint used to mark highways, §136-30.2.
Pesticides.
Coloration or discoloration required, §143-443(a).

ARSENIC-TREATED WOOD.
School classrooms and playground equipment.
Duty of local boards to address, §115C-47.
Duty of state board of education, §115C-12.

ARSON.
Arrest.
Power of attorney general, §58-79-5.
Attempts to commit crime.
Burning or attempting to burn buildings not covered by other provisions, §14-67.1.
Barges, §14-63.
Barns, §14-62.
Bridges, §14-61.
Buildings.
Defined, §14-58.1.
Not covered by other provisions.
Burning or attempting to burn, §14-67.1.
Public buildings.
Bureau of investigation.
Authority over, §114-15.
Burning certain public buildings, §14-59.
Bureau of investigation.
Investigations of misuse of state property, §114-15.1.
Public buildings.
Authority over, §114-15.

ARSON —Cont'd
Capital punishment.
Aggravating circumstances.
Capital punishment in commission of arson, §15A-2000(e).
Crimes punishable by death, NC Const Art XI §2.
Chapels, §§14-49(b1), 14-62.2.
Churches, §§14-49(b1), 14-62.2.
Coach houses, §14-62.
Construction.
Burning of building or structure in process of construction, §14-62.1.
Cotton ginhouses, §14-64.
Definitions.
Building, §14-58.1.
House, §14-58.1.
Destructive devices.
Making false report concerning devices, §14-69.1.
DNA sample for DNA analysis.
Obtaining upon arrest for, §15A-266.3A.
Dwelling houses.
Fraudulently setting fire, §14-65.
Educational institution buildings, §14-60.
Emergency medical technicians.
Serious injury to, §14-69.3.
False bomb or other device.
False reports concerning destructive devices, §14-69.1(a).
Definition of "report,"§14-69.1(e).
Public buildings, §14-69.1(c).
Restitution, §14-69.1(d).
Perpetrating hoax by use of bomb or device, §14-69.2(a).
Public building, §14-69.2(c).
Restitution, §14-69.1(d).
Ferries, §14-63.
Fire-engine houses, §14-61.
Firefighters.
Serious injury to, §14-69.3.
Fire investigations and inspection of premises, §§58-79-1 to 58-79-45.
First degree, §14-58.
Fraudulently setting dwelling on fire, §14-65.
Ginhouses, §14-64.
Granaries, §14-62.
Hoaxes.
False bombs or other devices, §14-69.2.
House.
Defined, §14-58.1.
Fraudulently burning dwelling, §14-65.
Manufactured-type house, §14-58.2.
Insurance.
Burning of personal property, §14-66.
Dwelling house fraudulently set fire to, §14-65.
Investigations.
Failure of officers to investigate incendiary fires, §14-69.
Manufactured-type house, §14-58.2.
Masjids, §14-49(b1).
Meeting houses, §14-62.2.
Mills, §14-62.
Mobile homes, §14-58.2.
Mosques, §14-49(b1).
Murder committed during commission of felony.
First degree murder, §14-17.
Outhouses, §14-62.
Personal property, §14-66.
Property owners.
Compliance with orders of public authorities.
Failure of owner to comply with orders, §14-68.

ARSON —Cont'd
Public authorities.
Compliance with orders of public authorities.
Failure of owner of property to comply with
orders, §14-68.
Public buildings and grounds, §14-59.
Punishment for arson, §14-58.
Recreational trailer home, §14-58.2.
Rescue-squad building, §14-61.
Schoolhouses, §14-60.
Second degree, §14-58.
Shops, §14-62.
Stables, §14-62.
State capitol, §14-59.
Synagogues, §14-49(b1).
Tobacco houses, §14-64.
Toll bridges, §14-61.
Warehouses, §14-62.
Watercraft, §14-63.

ART.
Arts council, §§143B-87, 143B-88.
Artwork on consignment, §§25C-1 to 25C-5.
Composer-laureate for state.
Appointment, §143-407.1(a), (b).
Consignments.
Artwork on consignment, §§25C-1 to 25C-5.
Cultural resources department, §§143-403 to
143-415.
See CULTURAL RESOURCES DEPARTMENT.
Definitions, §143-403.
Sale of prints, §25C-10.
Executive mansion fine arts committee,
§§143B-79, 143B-80.
Grassroots arts program, §§143B-121 to
143B-125.
Local governments.
Powers as to museums and arts programs,
§160A-488.
Municipalities.
Powers as to museums and arts programs,
§160A-488.
Property taxes.
Authorized purposes, §160A-209(c).
North Carolina museum of art, §§140-5.12 to
140-5.16.
North Carolina state art society, §§140-12 to
140-14, 143B-89.
Promotion of arts, §§143-403 to 143-407.1.
Sale of fine prints, §§25C-10 to 25C-16.
State art museum, §§140-5.12 to 140-5.16.
Theft or destruction of art.
Property of public museums or galleries, §14-398.
**University of North Carolina School of the
Arts,** §§116-63 to 116-69.1.
See UNIVERSITY OF NORTH CAROLINA
SCHOOL OF THE ARTS.

ART DEALERS.
Artwork on consignment.
Creditors may not reach works, §25C-4.
Defined, §25C-1.
Interest of dealer who accepts work, §25C-2.
Status of works subsequently purchased by dealer
from own account, §25C-3.
Sale of prints, §§25C-10 to 25C-16.
Disclosure requirement, §25C-14.
General prohibitions, §25C-11.
Rights and liabilities not inclusive, §25C-15.

ARTERIOSCLEROSIS.
Food, drug and cosmetic act.
Drug or device, false advertising, §106-138(b).

ARTHRITIS PROGRAM, §130A-222(a).

ARTICLES OF INCORPORATION.
Amendment, §§55-10-01 to 55-10-09.
Defined, §55-1-40.
Filing, §55-2-03.
Nonprofit corporations.
Amendment, §§55A-10-01 to 55A-10-07.
Conclusive proof of incorporation, §55A-2-03(b).
Contents, §55A-2-02(a), (b).
Existence begins when articles filed, §55A-2-03(a).
Powers of corporation need not be set forth,
§55A-2-02(c).
Restated articles, §55A-10-06.
Regional transportation authorities.
Included in resolution creating, requirements,
§160A-633(b).
Statutory powers need not be set out, §§55-2-02,
55-3-02.
Trust companies.
Contents, §53-332(a).
Noncorporate entities, §53-332(b).
Signature, §53-332(a).

ARTIFICIAL COLORING.
Food, drug and cosmetic act.
Foods deemed misbranded, §106-130.

ARTIFICIAL FLAVORING.
Food, drug and cosmetic act.
Foods deemed misbranded, §106-130.

ARTIFICIAL INSEMINATION.
Status of child born, §49A-1.

ARTIFICIAL INSEMINATION OF ANIMALS.
Veterinarians.
Exemption from provisions regulating
veterinarians, §90-187.10.

ARTIFICIAL LIMBS.
Sales and use tax.
Exemption, §105-164.13.

ARTISAN BAKERIES.
Sales and use tax exemption.
Bakery items sold by, §105-164.13B(a).

**ARTISTIC AND CREATIVE SERVICES
CONTRACTS.**
Minors, §§48A-11 to 48A-16.

ARTISTIC ORGANIZATIONS.
Solicitation of contributions, §§131F-1 to
131F-33.
See CHARITABLE SOLICITATION.

ARTS COUNCIL, §§143B-87, 143B-88.
Compensation of members, §143B-88.
Creation, §143B-87.
Department of cultural resources.
Transfer of commission to department, §143B-51.
Duties, §143B-87.
Members, §143B-88.
Powers, §143B-87.
Quorum, §143B-88.
Selection of members, §143B-88.

ARTS FESTIVALS.
Amusement license taxes.
Exemption, §105-40.

ARTS, PROMOTION OF.
Appropriations, §143-407.
Cultural resources department.
Duties, §143-406.

ARTS, PROMOTION OF —Cont'd
Cultural resources department —Cont'd
Executive Mansion.
Authority of administration department not
affected, §143-415.
Powers of department, §143-411.
Purpose of provisions, §143-410.
Definitions, §143-403.
Funds, §143-407.
Gifts.
Acceptance by cultural resources department,
§143-407.
Reports.
Submission of biennial report to governor,
§143-406.

ARTWORK ON CONSIGNMENT, §§25C-1 to
25C-5.
Art dealers.
Acceptance of works of fine art on consignment.
Interest of art dealer who accepts, §25C-2.
Creditors of art dealer may not reach works of
fine art on consignment with art dealer,
§25C-4.
Defined, §25C-1.
Subsequent purchase of work of fine art for own
account.
Status of works of fine art subsequently
purchased, §25C-3.
Debts.
Art dealers.
Creditors of art dealer may not reach works of
fine art on consignment with art dealer,
§25C-4.
Definitions, §25C-1.
Insurance.
Provisions as to insurable interest.
Not affected, §25C-5.
Risk of loss.
Provisions not affected, §25C-5.
Works of fine art.
Acceptance on consignment.
Interest of art dealer who accepts, §25C-2.
Defined, §25C-1.
Subsequent purchase by art dealer for own
account.
Status of works of fine art subsequently
purchased, §25C-3.

ASBESTOS HAZARD MANAGEMENT,
§§130A-444 to 130A-451.
Accreditation of persons performing
management.
Exemptions, §130A-447(c).
Fee, §130A-448(a).
Required, §130A-447(a).
Temporary accreditation, §130A-447(b).
Administrative penalties, §130A-22(b1), (b2).
Asbestos NESHAP for demolition and
renovation.
Local air pollution programs.
Adoption and enforcement, §130A-452(a), (b).
Definitions, §130A-444.
Demolition.
Permit fee where removal part of, §130A-450.
Exposure standards.
Public areas, §130A-446.
Fees.
Removal permits, §130A-450.
Local air pollution programs.
Asbestos NESHAP for demolition and renovation.
Adoption and enforcement, §130A-452(a), (b).

ASBESTOS HAZARD MANAGEMENT —Cont'd
Penalties.
Administrative penalties, §130A-22(b1), (b2).
Permits.
Material removal permits, §130A-449.
Removal permits.
Fees, §130A-450.
Public areas.
Exposure standards, §130A-446.
Removal.
Permits, §130A-449.
Fees, §130A-450.
Renovation.
Permit fee where removal part of, §130A-450.
Rules and regulations.
Adoption, §130A-451.
Schools.
Inspection, §130A-445.
School management plans.
Rules and regulations, §130A-445.
Training courses.
Approval, fee, §130A-448(b).

ASBESTOSIS.
Workers' compensation.
Defined, §97-62.
Disability or death from.
Compensation, §97-61.6.
Disablement defined, §97-54.
Discontinued benefits.
Claims for further benefits, §97-66.
Exposure deemed injurious, §97-57.
First examination of and report on employee,
§§97-61.1, 97-61.2.
General provisions of act to control benefits,
§97-64.
Hearings on reports, §§97-61.1, 97-61.5, 97-61.6.
Injurious exposure.
Period necessary, §97-63.
Occupational diseases enumerated, §97-53.
Occupational diseases generally.
See WORKERS' COMPENSATION.
Rates of compensation, §§97-61.5(b), 97-61.6.
Reduction of rate where tuberculosis developed,
§97-65.
Removal from hazardous condition.
Compensation upon.
Waiver of right to compensation as alternative
to forced change of occupation, §97-61.7.
Removal from hazardous occupation.
Compensation upon, §97-61.5(b).
Second examination and report, §97-61.3.
Third examination and report, §97-61.4.

ASHEBORO MUNICIPAL AIRPORT.
Location of North Carolina aviation hall of
fame and North Carolina aviation museum,
§145-21.

ASHE COUNTY.
Acquisition of property, power, §153A-158.1(a).
Agricultural tendencies in certain counties.
Terms of, §42-23.
Ambulances.
Obtaining ambulance services without intending
to pay, §14-111.2.
Requesting ambulance falsely, §14-111.3.
Ambulance service.
Attachment or garnishment and lien for,
§§44-51.4 to 44-51.8.
Blank or master forms of mortgages, deeds of
trust, etc.
Indexing and recording, inapplicability of
provisions, §47-21.

ASHE COUNTY —Cont'd
Condemnation or acquisition of land by local government unit outside county.
Consent of board of commissioners necessary, §153A-15.
Counties generally.
See COUNTIES.
Cropper or tenant refusing to perform terms of contract.
Forfeiture of right of possession to premises, §42-27.
Game laws, local acts not repealed, §113-133.1(e).
Maps in special proceedings, recording of photographic copies, §47-32.
Violation as misdemeanor, inapplicability of provisions, §47-32.2.
Oil, gas or mineral interest separated from surface fee, extinguished, title in surface fee holder.
Failure to list property for tax purposes for 10 years prior to January 1, 1977, §1-42.4(a) to (d).
Protection of interest against surface fee, §1-42.4(b), (d).
On-premises unfortified wine licenses.
Discretion to decline to issue, §105-113.71(b).
Probates and registration orders before clerks of inferior courts.
Validation, §47-59.
Real estate mortgage loans.
Interest, commissions and repayment, §45-43.
School property.
Acquisition and improvement, §153A-158.1.

ASHEVILLE.
Land-use development incentives.
Reduction of energy consumption, §160A-383.4.

ASPHALT.
Disposal of demolition debris consisting of used asphalt, §130A-294(m).

ASSAULT AND BATTERY.
Acid or alkali, malicious throwing, §14-30.1.
Aggravated assault and battery.
Habitual misdemeanor assault, §14-33.2.
Punishment for misdemeanor assaults, §14-33(b), (c).
Factors determining classification of offense, §14-33(b), (c).
Arrest without warrant, §15A-401.
Blind persons, §14-32.1.
Castration, §§14-28, 14-29.
Children as victims.
Bail, §15A-534.4.
Costs.
Allowance of costs to defendant, §6-19.
Allowance of costs to plaintiff, §6-18.
Crossing county lines.
Assault in one county, death in another, §15-130.
Crossing state lines.
Assault in this state, death in another, §15-131.
Deadly weapons.
See ASSAULT WITH DEADLY WEAPON.
Defenses.
Plea of self-defense.
Evidence of former threats upon plea, §14-33.1.
Detention facilities.
Person employed at state or local detention facility.
Assault on, §14-34.7(b).
Infliction of physical injury, punishment, §14-34.7(c).

ASSAULT AND BATTERY —Cont'd
Disabled persons, §14-32.1.
Aggravated assault, §14-32.1(e).
Definition of handicapped person, §14-32.1(a).
DNA sample.
Required upon conviction for assaulting, §15A-266.4.
Simple assault, §14-32.1(f).
DNA sample for DNA analysis.
Obtaining upon arrest for certain offenses, §§15A-266.3A, 15A-266.4.
Domestic violence, §§50B-1 to 50B-9.
See DOMESTIC VIOLENCE.
Emergency personnel.
Assault or affray upon while discharging duties, §14-34.6(a).
Infliction of bodily injury, §14-34.6(b).
Use of deadly weapons other than firearms, §14-34.6(b).
Use of firearms, §14-34.6(c).
Assault with firearm upon, §14-34.2.
Riots and civil disorders, §14-288.9.
Endangering executive, legislative or court officers.
Applicability of article, §14-16.9.
Assault on executive, legislative or court officers, §14-16.6.
Definitions, §14-16.10.
Inflicting serious bodily injury, §14-16.6(c).
Officers-elect to be covered, §14-16.9.
Threats against officers, §14-16.7.
Mailing threatening letters or documents, §14-16.7(b).
No requirement of receipt of threat, §14-16.8.
Serious bodily injury, §14-16.7(a).
Use of deadly weapons, §14-16.6(b).
Violent attacks against persons or dwellings, §14-16.6(a).
Evidence.
Plea of self-defense.
Evidence of former threats upon plea, §14-33.1.
Felonious assault with deadly weapon, §14-32.
Firearms.
Detention facilities.
Person employed at state or local detention facility.
Assault with firearm upon in performance of duties, §14-34.5(b).
Emergency medical services personnel.
Assault with firearm upon, §§14-34.2, 14-34.6(c).
Firemen.
Assault with firearm upon fireman, §14-34.2.
Habitual misdemeanor assault, §14-33.2.
Law enforcement officers.
Assault with firearm upon law enforcement officer, §14-34.2.
Assault with firearm upon law enforcement officer in performance of duties, §14-34.5(a).
Pointing gun at person, §14-34.
Probation or parole officers.
Assault with firearm upon while in performance of duties, §14-34.5(a).
Firefighters.
Assault or affray on.
Class F felony.
Using firearm, §14-34.6(c).
Class H felony.
Inflicting serious bodily injury or using deadly weapon other than firearm, §14-34.6(b).
Class I felony, §14-34.6(a).
Habitual misdemeanor assault, §14-33.2.

ASSAULT AND BATTERY —Cont'd
Hearing impaired.
Assault upon handicapped persons, §14-32.1.
Lesser included offenses.
Conviction of assault, when included in charge;
§15-169.
Limitation of actions, §1-52.
Maliciously assaulting in secret manner,
§14-31.
Mentally ill.
Assault upon handicapped persons, §14-32.1.
Minors.
Bail, §15A-534.4.
Inflicting serious injury or using deadly weapon in
presence of minor, §14-33(d).
Misdemeanor assaults, batteries and affrays,
§14-33(b), (c).
Habitual misdemeanor assault, §14-33.2.
Motor vehicle assault.
Mandatory revocation of license, §20-17(a).
Occupational safety and health.
Assaulting or killing person engaged in inspection,
investigative or law-enforcement functions.
Criminal liability, §95-139(f).
Patient abuse, §14-32.2.
Police.
Assault on a law enforcement officer, §14-34.7(a).
Infliction of physical injury, punishment,
§14-34.7(c).
Probation or parole officers.
Assault on, §14-34.7(a).
Infliction of physical injury, punishment,
§14-34.7(c).
Public school property.
Principals to report offenses occurring on school
property, §115C-288(g).
Rape.
See RAPE.
Riots and civil disorders.
Assault on emergency personnel, §14-288.9.
Secret manner.
Maliciously assaulting in secret manner, §14-31.
Self-defense.
Evidence of former threats upon plea of
self-defense, §14-33.1.
Serious bodily injury.
Assault inflicting, §14-32.4(a).
Sex offenses generally.
See SEX OFFENSES.
Sexual battery.
Elements of offense, §14-27.5A(a).
Punishment, §14-27.5A(b).
Simple assault and battery, §14-33(a).
Strangulation, §14-32.4(b).
Threats.
See THREATS.
Unborn child.
Assault inflicting serious bodily injury on unborn
child, §14-23.5(a).
Class F felony, §14-23.5(c).
Serious bodily harm defined, §14-23.5(b).
Battery on unborn child, §14-23.6(a).
Class A1 misdemeanor, §14-23.6(b).
Venue.
Assault in one county, death in another, §15-130.
Assault in this state, death in another, §15-131.
Warrantless arrest, §15A-401.

ASSAULT WITH DEADLY WEAPON.
Custodial interrogations, electronic recording,
§15A-211.

ASSAULT WITH DEADLY WEAPON —Cont'd
Detention facilities.
Person employed at state or local detention
facility.
Assault with firearm upon in performance of
duties, §14-34.5(b).
Disabled persons.
Assaults upon, §14-32.1.
Emergency medical services.
Personnel assaulted with deadly weapon,
§§14-34.2, 14-34.6(b).
Firefighters.
Assault or affray on using deadly weapon or
firearm, §14-34.6.
Fire protection.
Firemen assaulted with deadly weapon, §14-34.2.
Highway patrol.
Law enforcement officer assaulted with deadly
weapon, §14-34.2.
Inflicting serious injury.
Punishment for felonious assault, §14-32(b).
Intent to kill.
Punishment for felonious assault, §14-32(a), (b).
Law enforcement officers.
Assault with deadly weapon upon law
enforcement officer, §14-34.2.
Assault with firearm upon law enforcement officer
in performance of duties, §14-34.5(a).
Probation or parole officers.
Assault with firearm upon in performance of
duties, §14-34.5(a).
Punishment for felonious assault.
Inflicting serious injury, §14-32(b).
Intent to kill and inflict serious injury, §14-32(a),
(c).

ASSAULT WITH MOTOR VEHICLE.
Mandatory revocation of license, §20-17(a).

ASSEMBLY.
Firearms and other weapons.
Carrying into assemblies, §14-269.3(a).
Mass gatherings, §§130A-251 to 130A-258.
See MASS GATHERINGS.
Right to assembly, NC Const Art I §12, US Const
Amd 1.

ASSES.
Brands generally, §§80-45 to 80-66.
See LIVESTOCK BRANDS.
Equine infectious anemia, §§106-405.15 to
106-405.20.

ASSESSMENT COMPANIES, §§58-11-1 to
58-11-35.
Advance assessments.
Requirements, §58-11-20.
Bylaws.
Contracts must accord with, §58-11-5.
Filing of copies, §58-11-1.
Charters.
Contracts must accord with, §58-11-5.
Filing of copies, §58-11-1.
Contracts.
Conformance with charter and bylaws required,
§58-11-5.
Deposit requirements, §58-11-20.
Foreign assessment companies, §58-11-25.
Revocation for noncompliance, §58-11-30.
Foreign companies.
Deposits by, §58-11-25.
Mutual life insurance companies.
Assessments prohibited, §58-11-35.

ASSESSMENT COMPANIES —Cont'd
Policies.
"Assessment plan" to be printed on, §58-11-10.
Revocation for noncompliance, §58-11-15.
Conformance with charter and bylaws required, §58-11-5.
Revocation of authority to do business, §§58-11-15, 58-11-30.

ASSESSMENTS.
Agricultural fees and taxes.
Procedure, §106-9.3.
Agricultural products promotion.
See AGRICULTURAL PRODUCTS PROMOTION.
Agricultural research.
See AGRICULTURAL RESEARCH.
Air pollution control.
Title V program.
Assessment of program implementation fees, §143-215.106A.
Banks.
Impairment of capital, §53-42.
Banks and consumer finance licensees.
Operating and maintaining office of commissioner of banks, §53-122(a), (e), (f).
Cigarettes and tobacco products.
Promotion of sale and use of tobacco.
See TOBACCO SALES.
Coastal fishery and seafood industry promotion, §§113-315.4 to 113-315.8.
Condominium owners' associations.
Common expenses, §47C-3-115.
Lien for assessment, §47C-3-116.
Conservation and historic preservation agreements.
Assessment of land or improvements subject to agreement, §121-40.
Cotton grower's organization, §§106-65.88, 106-65.90.
County water and sewer districts.
Special assessments authorized, §162A-92.
Drainage.
Deficiencies.
Supplemental assessments to make up deficiencies, §156-22.
Jurors.
Vacancy appointments of assessment jurors, §156-22.
Liens.
Drainage assessments declared liens, §156-21.
Petitions.
Agreement for construction.
Viewers, §156-28.
Subsequent owners bound, §156-14.
Supplemental assessment to make up deficiencies, §156-22.
Vacancy appointments of assessment jurors, §156-22.
Drainage corporations, §156-42.
Canals already constructed, §156-43.
Payment of dues entitles to use of canal, §156-46.
Penalty for nonpayment of assessments, §156-51.
Shareholders to pay assessments, §156-45.
Drainage districts, §§156-54 to 156-138.4.
See DRAINAGE DISTRICTS.
Fiduciaries.
Establishing and maintaining reserves.
Powers which may be incorporated by reference in trust instrument, §32-27.
Fraternal orders.
Collection, §58-25-15.

ASSESSMENTS —Cont'd
Fraternal orders —Cont'd
Funds derived from, §58-25-10.
Horse industry promotion, §§106-823 to 106-825.
Jurisdiction.
Personal jurisdiction.
Grounds, §1-75.4.
Life and health insurance guaranty association, §58-62-41.
Limestone, marl and landplaster.
Sale of agricultural liming materials and landplaster.
Appeals from assessments and orders of commissioner of agriculture, §106-92.13.
Marketing authority.
Exemptions, §106-534.
Medicaid.
Hospital provider assessments, §§108A-120 to 108A-127.
See MEDICAID.
Mortgages and deeds of trust.
Reverse mortgages.
Contractual provisions for payment, §53-261.
Mutual insurance companies, §§58-8-40 to 58-8-55.
Nature preserves.
Land subject to permanent dedication agreement, §113A-164.11.
Oil and gas conservation.
Taxation, §113-387.
Collection, §113-388.
Planned community act.
Common expenses, §§47F-3-115, 47F-3-116.
Pork promotion assessment, §§106-790 to 106-796.
Primary forest product assessment act, §§106-1025 to 106-1032.
See FOREST PRODUCTS ASSESSMENT.
Sanitary districts.
Levy of tax, §130A-62(a) to (d).
Seafood industry and coastal fishery promotion, §§113-315.4 to 113-315.8.
Social security.
Coverage of governmental employees under title II of social security act.
Contribution fund, §135-24(f).
Strawberries, §§106-781 to 106-786.
Street light assessments, §153A-206.
Taxation.
Generally.
See TAXATION.
Income tax.
Generally.
See INCOME TAX.
Property taxes.
Generally.
See PROPERTY TAXES.
Trust companies, §53-368.

ASSESSORS.
Generally.
See COUNTY ASSESSORS.
Magistrates.
Appointment of assessors by magistrate.
Fees of assessors, §7A-310.

ASSET-BACKED SECURITIES FACILITATION.
Definitions, §53-425.
Exceptions to provisions, §53-426(b).
Waiver of equity of redemption, §53-426(a).

ASSETS OF JUDGMENT DEBTORS.
Discovery.
Additional method, §1-352.2.

ASSETS OF JUDGMENT DEBTORS —Cont'd
Discovery —Cont'd
   Generally, §§1-352 to 1-368.
     See SUPPLEMENTAL PROCEEDINGS.
   Interrogatories to discover assets generally,
     §1-352.1.
   Supplemental proceedings generally, §§1-352 to
     1-368.
     See EXECUTIONS.

ASSIGNED RISK INSURANCE.
Workers' compensation.
   Rate bureau.
     Duties, §58-36-1.

ASSIGNMENT OF CASES FOR TRIAL, §1A-1
   Rule 40(a).

ASSIGNMENT OF PUPILS ACT, §§115C-364 to
   115C-372.
See SCHOOLS AND EDUCATION.

ASSIGNMENT OF THING IN ACTION.
**Action by assignee without prejudice to setoff
or defense existing,** §1-57.

ASSIGNMENTS.
**Action by assignee on assignment of thing in
action.**
   Action without prejudice to setoff or other defense,
     §1-57.
Assignments for benefit of creditors.
   See ASSIGNMENTS FOR BENEFIT OF
     CREDITORS.
Child support.
   Public assistance.
     Acceptance of assistance constitutes assignment
       of support rights to state or county,
       §110-137.
   Unemployment compensation benefits, §110-136.2.
   Wages, §110-136.1.
Claims against the state, §143B-426.40A.
Consumer finance act.
   Earnings.
     Prohibited, §53-180(b).
Contracts.
   Real property pledged as security, §47-17.2.
Conveyances.
   Real property pledged as security, §47-17.2.
Cost.
   Liability of assignee for cost, §6-32.
Default, secured obligation assigned.
   Secured transactions.
     Rights and duties of secondary obligors,
       §25-9-618.
Financing statements.
   Secured party of right.
     Powers assigned, §25-9-514.
**Firemen's and rescue squad workers' pension
fund.**
   Rights nonassignable, §58-86-90.
Issues.
   Probate and registration.
     Assignment of leases, rents, issues or profits,
       §47-20(b) to (e).
Judgments.
   Docketing.
     Entry on judgment docket, §1-246.
   Recordation.
     Photographic process, §1-239.1.
   Signing.
     Required, §1-246.
     Witnessing, §1-246.

ASSIGNMENTS —Cont'd
Leases, rents, issues or profits.
   Registration, §47-20(b) to (e).
Leases, UCC, §25-2A-303.
**Limited liability company membership
interest,** §57C-5-02.
   Right of assignee to become member, §57C-5-04.
Lotteries.
   State lottery.
     Certificates of authority, §18C-143(b).
     Contracts with lottery game retailers, §18C-140.
     Prizes.
       Right to prize not assignable, §18C-132(h).
**Mechanics, laborers and materialmen dealing
with owner.**
   Claim of lien.
     Notice of assignment of claim, §44A-12(e).
**Medical payments programs administered
under chapter 130A.**
   Assignment to state of rights to third party
     benefits, §130A-13(a) to (d).
Mortgage bankers, brokers and servicers.
   Mortgage servicer duties, §53-244.110.
Mortgages and deeds of trust.
   Real property pledged as security, §47-17.2.
Parties.
   Assignees, §1-57.
Partner's interest in partnership, §59-57(a).
   Rights of assignee in case of dissolution, §59-57(b).
**Partner's right in specific partnership
property,** §59-55(b).
Preneed funeral contracts and funds,
   §90-210.68(b), (c), (e).
Probate and registration, §47-1.
   Leases, rents, issues or profits, §47-20(b) to (e).
Renunciation of property or interest.
   Bar to right to renounce, §31B-4(a).
Sale of goods, UCC.
   Rights of buyer and seller, §25-2-210.
Secured transactions.
   Assignment of perfected interest.
     Refiling not needed to perfect, §25-9-310(c).
   Inapplicability of article, §25-9-109(d).
   Real property pledged as security, §47-17.2.
   Third party rights, §§25-9-401 to 25-9-409.
State lottery.
   Certificates of authority, §18C-143(b).
   Contracts with lottery game retailers, §18C-140.
   Prizes.
     Right to prize not assignable, §18C-132(h).
**State officers authorized to prove or
acknowledge,** §47-1.
Surety's recovery on obligation paid.
   No assignment necessary, §26-3.1(a).
   Construction of term "surety,"§26-3.1(b).
Surviving spouses.
   Year's allowance, §§30-19 to 30-31.2.
     See SURVIVING SPOUSES.
Tobacco manufacturer escrow funds.
   Assignment of rights to state, §143C-9-5.
Trademarks.
   Registration, §80-6.
Trust beneficiary's assignee.
   Attachment of distributions for beneficiary's
     benefit, §36C-5-501(a).
   Exceptions, §36C-5-501(b).
   Mandatory distribution overdue, §36C-5-506.
   Spendthrift provisions, §§36C-5-502, 36C-5-503.
Wages.
   Acceptance by employer of assignment.
     Employer not responsible until, §95-31.

ASSIGNMENTS —Cont'd
Wages —Cont'd
Child support, §110-136.1.
Consumer finance act.
Assignment of earnings prohibited, §53-180(b).
Usurious loans, §14-391.
Year's allowance, §§30-19 to 30-31.2.
See SURVIVING SPOUSES.

ASSIGNMENTS FOR BENEFIT OF CREDITORS.
Accounts and accounting.
Final account in twelve months, §23-11.
Quarterly accounts, §23-11.
Affidavits.
Petition for assignment, §23-13.
Appointment of trustees.
Insolvent trustee.
Substitute appointed, §23-5.
Order of appointment, §23-15.
Removal of trustee upon petition of creditors.
Substitute appointed, §23-6.
Substitute for incompetent trustee appointed in special proceedings, §23-4.
Bankruptcy and insolvency.
Insolvent trustee, §23-5.
Bonds, surety.
Release of insolvent upon giving bond, §23-40.
Substituted trustee to give bond, §23-7.
Surrender of principal.
Surety may surrender, §23-41.
Trustees.
Insolvent trustee removed unless bond given, §23-5.
Claims.
Creditors to file verified claims with clerk, §23-9.
Clerks of court.
Notice of petition.
Clerk to give, §23-14.
Discharge, §23-16.
Opposition.
Suggestion of fraud by opposing creditor, §23-17.
Execution of assignment.
Debts mature on executions, §23-1.
Executors and administrators.
Summary revocation of letters testamentary and of administration, §28A-9-2.
False swearing as to verified claims filed with clerk, §23-9.
Fraud.
Judgment of fraud by opposing creditor, §23-17.
Superior or district court to try issue, §23-39.
Fraudulent conveyances.
Trustee to recover property conveyed fraudulently, §23-3.
Limited liability companies.
Cessation of membership, §57C-3-02.
Misdemeanors.
Filing of verified claims by creditors with clerk.
False swearing, §23-9.
Trustees.
Violations of duties generally, §23-12.
Notice.
Petition.
Clerk to give notice of petition, §23-14.
Orders.
Discharge of insolvent, §23-15.
Terms and effect of order, §23-16.
Trustees.
Appointment, §23-15.

ASSIGNMENTS FOR BENEFIT OF CREDITORS —Cont'd
Payments.
Trustees.
Priority of payments by trustee, §23-10.
Perishable property.
Sale within ten days of registration, §23-8.
Petitions, §23-13.
Notice.
Clerk to give notice of petition, §23-14.
Preferences.
No preferences, §23-1.
Trustee to recover property fraudulently conveyed, §23-3.
Priority of payments by trustee, §23-10.
Sales.
Perishable property.
Sale within ten days of registration, §23-8.
Schedule of property.
Filing by trustee, §23-2.
Trust companies.
Seizure by commissioner.
Directors' resolution to place control under commissioner, §53-378.
Trustees.
Accounts quarterly, §23-11.
Appointment.
Order of appointment, §23-15.
Fraudulent conveyances.
Recovery of property fraudulently conveyed, §23-3.
Incompetent trustees.
Substitute appointed in special proceedings, §23-4.
Insolvent trustee removed unless bond given, §23-5.
Substitute appointed, §23-5.
Misdemeanors.
Violations of duties generally, §23-12.
Payments.
Priority of payments by trustee, §23-10.
Powers.
Generally, §23-44.
Removal upon petition of creditors.
Substitute appointed, §23-6.
Schedule of property to be filed by trustee, §23-2.
Substitute trustees.
Bonds, surety, §23-7.
Incompetent trustees, §23-4.
Removal of trustee on petition of creditors, §23-6.
Uniform fiduciaries act generally, §§32-1 to 32-13.
See FIDUCIARIES.
Verified claims filed by creditor with clerk, §23-9.
Violation of trustee duty, §23-12.

ASSISTANCE ANIMALS.
Assaulting.
Civil remedies not affected, §14-163.1(g).
Harm, causing.
Criminal penalty, §14-163.1(c).
Harm defined, §14-163.1(a).
Killing willfully, §14-163.1(a1).
Restitution by persons convicted of violation, §14-163.1(d1).
Self-defense affirmative defense, §14-163.1(f).
Serious harm, causing.
Criminal penalty, §14-163.1(b).
Serious harm defined, §14-163.1(a).

ASSISTANCE ANIMALS —Cont'd
Assaulting —Cont'd
Taunting, teasing, harassing, delaying or
    obstructing.
    Criminal penalty, §14-163.1(d).
Veterinarians, inapplicability of section to,
    §14-163.1(e).
Blind pedestrians.
Rights and privileges without guide dog,
    §20-175.3.
**Common carrier fares for blind person
    accompanied by,** §62-144(b).
Defined, §14-163.1(a).
Donation of service animal for training,
    §168-4.6.
Prohibited acts, §168-4.5.
Registration of service animal, §168-4.3.
Responsibility for service animal, §168-4.4.
Right to be accompanied by service animal,
    §168-4.2.
Penalty for depriving of right, §168-4.5.
Tags, §168-4.2(a).
Trainers.
Right to be accompanied by service animal,
    §168-4.2(b).
Training of service animal, §168-4.3.
Donation, §168-4.6.

ASSISTANT PRINCIPALS.
Dismissal.
Low-performing schools, §115C-325(q).

ASSISTED LIVING ADMINISTRATORS,
    §§90-288.10 to 90-288.20.
Administrative procedures, applicability,
    §90-288.18(b).
Adverse actions on certificates, §90-288.18.
Applicability, §90-288.12(b).
Certification.
Administrative procedures, applicability,
    §90-288.18(b).
Adverse actions, §90-288.18.
Amendments, authority, §90-288.18(a).
Contents, §90-288.15(a).
Expiration, §90-288.15(b).
Fees, §90-288.15A.
Issuance, §90-288.15(a).
Lost, destroyed or mutilated certificates,
    §90-288.15(c).
Posting of certificates, §90-288.17.
Practicing without certificate, §90-288.20.
Procedures, §90-288.14.
Qualifications, §90-288.14.
Recall, suspension or revocation, §90-288.18(a).
Reciprocity, §90-288.16.
Renewal, §90-288.15(b).
    Fee, §90-288.15A.
Replacement certificates, §90-288.15(c).
Required, §90-288.12(a).
Validity of certificate, §90-288.12(a).
Citation of act, §90-288.10.
Criminal penalty.
Practicing without certificate, §90-288.20.
Defined terms, §90-288.13.
Exemptions, §90-288.12(b).
Findings, §90-288.11.
Posting of certificates, §90-288.17.
Preceptors.
Defined, §90-288.13.
Purpose of act, §90-288.11.
Qualifications, §90-288.14.
Reciprocity, §90-288.16.

ASSISTED LIVING ADMINISTRATORS —Cont'd
Reports, §90-288.19.
Title of act, §90-288.10.
Validity of certificate, §90-288.12(a).

**ASSISTED LIVING HOME MEDICATION
    AIDES.**
Fee for certification as, §131D-4.5.
Medication aide registry, §§131E-114.2,
    131E-270.

ASSISTED LIVING HOUSING.
Generally.
See ADULT CARE HOMES.

ASSOCIATE SAFETY PROFESSIONALS (ASP),
    §§90-671 to 90-674.

ASSOCIATIONS.
Agriculture products promotion.
Meetings, activities or associations deemed not in
    restraint of trade, §106-552.
Automobile dealers.
Declaratory and injunctive relief, §20-308.1(d).
Averment of capacity, §1A-1 Rule 84.
Building and loan associations.
See SAVINGS AND LOAN ASSOCIATIONS.
**Burning of unincorporated association's
    buildings,** §14-61.
Cemetery associations or corporations, §§65-16
    to 65-17.1.
Class actions.
Secondary action by members, §1A-1 Rule 23(b).
Community colleges.
Trustee association regions.
    Division of regions, §115D-62.
Cooperative associations, §§54-111 to 54-128.
See COOPERATIVE ASSOCIATIONS.
Declaratory judgments.
Word "person" construed as including
    unincorporated association or society, §1-265.
Deeds and other conveyances.
Forms for probate executed by corporation.
    Applicability to unincorporated associations,
        §47-41.01(e).
Depositions, use in court proceedings, §1A-1
    Rule 32(a).
Deposition upon oral examination, §1A-1 Rule
    30(b).
Health maintenance organizations, §§58-67-1 to
    58-67-185.
See HEALTH MAINTENANCE
    ORGANIZATIONS.
Interrogatories to parties, §1A-1 Rule 33(a).
Land and loan associations, §§54-45 to 54-73.
See LAND AND LOAN ASSOCIATIONS.
**Life and health insurance guaranty
    association,** §§58-62-2 to 58-62-95.
See LIFE AND HEALTH INSURANCE
    GUARANTY ASSOCIATION.
Lloyds insurance associations, §58-17-1.
Marketing associations, §§54-129 to 54-166.
See MARKETING ASSOCIATIONS.
Motor clubs and associations, §§58-69-2 to
    58-69-60.
See MOTOR CLUBS AND ASSOCIATIONS.
Mutual burial associations, §§90-210.80 to
    90-210.107.
See MUTUAL BURIAL ASSOCIATIONS.
Political contributions.
Prohibited acts, §163-278.19.
**Post assessment insurance guaranty
    association,** §§58-48-1 to 58-48-130.
See POST ASSESSMENT INSURANCE
    GUARANTY ASSOCIATION.

ASSOCIATIONS —Cont'd
Real estate appraisers.
   License or certificate not issued to, §93E-1-3(a).
   Use of term licensed real estate appraiser or
      certified real estate appraiser, prohibited,
      §93E-1-3.1(c).
**Real property conveyances by voluntary
   organizations and associations.**
   Prior deeds validated, §59B-15(b).
   Trustees.
      Effect as to conveyances by trustees, §59B-15(a).
Religious societies, §§61-1 to 61-7.
Restraint of trade.
   Promotion of use and sale of agricultural
      products.
      Meetings, activities or associations deemed not
         in restraint of trade, §106-552.
Roanoke Island historical association,
   §§143-199 to 143-202.
Savings and loan associations.
   See SAVINGS AND LOAN ASSOCIATIONS.
**Secondary actions by members, §1A-1 Rule
   23(b).**
Seeds.
   North Carolina crop improvement association,
      §106-273.
Service of process.
   Personal jurisdiction.
      Manner of service to exercise, §1A-1 Rule 4(j).
Social security.
   Coverage of governmental employees under title II
      of social security act.
      Transfers from state to certain association
         service, §135-27.
Unincorporated associations.
   Declaratory judgments.
      Word "person" construed, §1-265.
   Judgments and decrees.
      Binding effect of judgments against
         associations, §1-69.1(a).
   Property tax abstracts.
      Content requirements, §105-309(b).
   Secondary action by members, §1A-1 Rule 23(b).
   Service of process.
      Personal jurisdiction, manner of service, §1A-1
         Rule 4(j).
   Suit by or against, §1-69.1(a).
   Uniform unincorporated nonprofit association act,
      §§59B-1 to 59B-15.
      See UNINCORPORATED ASSOCIATIONS.

ASSUMED NAMES.
Boxing under fictitious or assumed name,
   §143-655(b).
Business under assumed name, §§66-68 to 66-71.
   Accountants.
      Partnerships engaged in practice of certified
         public accountancy.
         Exemption from provisions, §66-68(e).
   Actions.
      Violations of provisions.
         Recovery in civil action not prevented,
            §66-71(b).
   Certificates.
      Copy.
         Prima facie evidence, §66-69.1.
      Filing required, §66-68(a).
         Exceptions, §66-68(d), (e).
      Index of certificates.
         Register of deeds to keep, §66-69.
         Transfer of assumed name, §66-69.

ASSUMED NAMES —Cont'd
Business under assumed name —Cont'd
   Certificates —Cont'd
      Index of certificates —Cont'd
         Withdrawal of assumed name, §66-69.
      Signing, §66-68(b).
      Transfer of assumed name, §66-68(f).
         Index, §66-69.
      Withdrawal of assumed name, §66-68(f).
         Index, §66-69.
   Evidence.
      Copy of certificate prima facie evidence,
         §66-69.1.
   Misdemeanors.
      Violations of provisions, §66-71(a).
   Partnerships.
      Public accountancy.
         Exemption of partnerships engaged in
            practice of certified public accountancy,
            §66-68(e).
      Withdrawal of partner or new partner.
         New certificate, §66-68(c).
   Transfer of assumed name, §66-68(f).
   Violations of provisions.
      Penalties, §66-71(a).
      Recovery in civil action not prevented,
         §66-71(b).
   Withdrawal of assumed name, §66-68(f).
Defendant sued in fictitious name.
   Amendment of pleading or proceeding upon
      discovery of true name, §1-166.
**Hotels, inns and other transient lodging
   places.**
   Registration of guests to be in true name, §72-30.
Insurance producers.
   Commissioner notified, §58-33-83.
Optometrists.
   Practicing under other than own name, §90-125.
Partnerships.
   Applicability of "assumed name" statute,
      §59-84.1(a).
**Plumbing, heating and fire sprinkler
   contractors.**
   Licenses.
      Issuance in trade name, §87-26(c) to (e).
Professional employer organizations.
   Fictitious or assumed name.
      Conducting business under, §58-89A-80(a).

ASSUMPTION OF LOANS.
Sublease and loan assumption arranging.
   Motor vehicles, §20-106.2.

ASSUMPTION OF RISK.
Affirmative defense, pleading, §1A-1 Rule 8(c).
Minor employed to commit drug violation.
   Doctrine defense to civil liability, §90-95.5.
Roller skaters and spectators.
   Obvious and necessary inherent risks, §99E-12.
   Defense to suit against operator, §99E-14.
**Skateboarding, inline skating and freestyle
   bicycling, §99E-24.**
Skiing competitions, §99C-4.

ASSUMPTION REINSURANCE, §§58-10-20 to
   58-10-65.
See REINSURANCE.

ASTHMA.
**Students with asthma or students subject to
   anaphylactic reactions.**
   Possession and self-administration of medication.
      Backup medication to be provided,
         §115C-375.2(c).

ASTHMA —Cont'd
Students with asthma or students subject to anaphylactic reactions —Cont'd
Possession and self-administration of medication —Cont'd
Demonstration of skill level to use, §115C-375.2(b).
Disciplinary action, §115C-375.2(e).
Generally, §115C-375.2(a).
Immunity from liability, §115C-375.2(g).
Information kept on file, §115C-375.2(d).
Renewal of permission annually, §115C-375.2(f).

ASYLUM.
Extradition.
No immunity from other criminal prosecution while in this state, §15A-748.

ATHLETE AGENTS, §§78C-85 to 78C-105.
Action by education institution against agent or student-athlete, §78C-100(a).
Damages, §78C-100(b).
Discovery of violation, accrual of action, §78C-100(c).
Rights, remedies or defenses not limited, §78C-100(e).
Several and joint liability, §78C-100(d).
Administrative penalty, §78C-101.
Agency contracts.
Cancellation by student-athlete.
Consequences, §78C-96(c).
Notice of cancellation, §78C-96(a).
Waiver of right, §78C-96(b).
Defined, §78C-86.
Notice by student-athlete of existence of contract.
To athletic director, §78C-95(b).
To educational institution, §78C-95(a).
Prohibited conduct, §78C-98(a).
Provisions required, §78C-94(b).
Record of contract, providing student-athlete, §78C-94(e).
Registration requirements.
Contract in violation void, §78C-88(d).
Requirements, §78C-94(a).
Voidable, nonconforming contracts, §78C-94(d).
Waiver of attorney client privilege, §78C-94(c), (f).
Warning to student-athlete as to consequences of signing, §78C-94(c).
Attorney-client privilege.
Waiver of attorney client privilege.
Records maintained by agent, §78C-97(c).
Signing agency contract, §78C-94(c), (f).
Attorneys licensed and resident of state.
Acting without certificate of registration, §78C-88(c).
Child support enforcement.
Forfeiture of licensing privilege, §50-13.12.
Suspension or revocation of license, §110-142.1.
Civil penalty, §78C-101.
Civil remedies, §78C-100.
Criminal penalties, §78C-99.
Damages.
Action by education institution against agent or student-athlete, §78C-100(b).
Definitions, §78C-86.
Electronic records and signature.
Law governing, §78C-103.
Fees.
Registration, §78C-93.
Felony convictions.
Forfeiture of certificate, §15A-1331A.

ATHLETE AGENTS —Cont'd
Nonresidents agents acting as agent in state.
Secretary of state.
Agent for service of process, §78C-87(a).
Notice by student-athlete of cancellation of agency contract, §78C-96(a).
Notice by student-athlete of existence of agency contract.
To athletic director, §78C-95.
Prohibited conduct, §78C-98(a), (b).
Civil remedies, §78C-100.
Criminal penalties, §78C-99.
Records required to be maintained, §78C-97(a).
Attorney-client privilege waived, §78C-97(c).
Open to public inspection, §78C-97(b).
Prohibited conduct, §78C-98(b).
Registration.
Acting without certificate.
Attorneys licensed and resident of state, §78C-88(c).
When permitted, §78C-88(b).
Agency contract resulting from conduct in violation of provisions.
Void, §78C-88(d).
Application, §78C-89(a).
Copy of application in lieu of.
Agent registered in another state, §78C-89(b).
Public record, §§78C-89(c), 78C-90(g).
Renewal, §78C-90(d), (e).
Duration, §78C-90(f).
Fees, §78C-93.
Forfeiture of certificate.
Felony convictions, §15A-1331A.
Issuance of certificate, §78C-90(a).
Prohibited conduct, §78C-98(b).
Refusal to issue certificate, §78C-90(b).
Consideration in making determination, §78C-90(c).
Renewal, §78C-90(d), (e).
Required to act as agent in state, §78C-88(a).
Suspension, revocation or refusal to renew.
Authority of secretary, §78C-91(a).
Notice and opportunity for hearing required, §78C-91(b).
Temporary registration, §78C-92.
Rules, adoption, §78C-105.
Service of process.
Secretary of state.
Agent for service of process.
Appointed for nonresident athlete agents, §78C-87(a).
Severability of provisions, §78C-104.
Subpoenas.
Secretary of state, authority to issue, §78C-87(b).
Uniform athlete agents act.
Article cited as, §78C-85.
Uniformity of application and construction, §78C-102.

ATHLETIC CLUBS.
Prepaid entertainment contracts, §§66-118 to 66-125.

ATHLETICS.
Alcoholic beverages.
Publicly displaying fortified wine, spirituous liquor or mixed beverages at athletic contests, §18B-301(f).
Assault and battery.
Evidence of threats upon plea of self defense, §14-33.1.
Sports officials, §14-33.

ATHLETICS —Cont'd
Bonuses.
Not forbidden, §14-379.
Boxing, §§143-651 to 143-658.
See BOXING.
Bribery.
Acceptance of bribes by players, managers, etc.,
§14-374.
Completion of offenses, §14-375.
Definition of bribe, §14-376.
Elements of offense of bribery of players,
managers, etc., §14-373.
Community colleges.
Intercollegiate athletics program.
Use of state funds, tuition or student aid to
create or operate.
Prohibited, §115D-43.
Compensation.
Extra compensation not forbidden, §14-379.
**First aid or emergency treatment, liability
limitation.**
Services provided by volunteer health care
provider.
Services deemed not to be a normal and
ordinary course of provider's business or
profession, §90-21.14(b).
Intentionally losing contests, §14-377.
Leave of state employees.
Paid leave for certain athletic competition,
§126-8.1.
Limited food establishment.
Preparing and serving food in conjunction with
amateur sporting events.
Defined, §130A-247.
Permits, issuance, §130A-248(a4).
Sanitation, rules governing, adoption,
§130A-248(a4).
Limiting margin of victory or defeat, §14-377.
Official state sport.
Stock car racing, §145-36.
Schools.
Concussions and head injuries.
Concussion defined, §115C-12.
Information sheet.
Signing required to participate, §115C-12.
Removal of student exhibiting signs or
symptoms from activity, §115C-12.
Written clearance.
Required for student to resume activity,
§115C-12.
Eligibility rules for interscholastic athletic
competition.
Adoption by state board, §115C-12.
Emergency action plan to deal with serious
injuries.
Each school to adopt, §115C-12.
Transfer by student for athletic participation
purposes, §115C-366(f).
**Throwing, dropping, etc., objects at sporting
events.**
Offenses against the public safety, §14-281.1.
Venue.
Protection of athletic contests.
Proper venue of prosecutions under article,
§14-378.

ATHLETIC TRAINERS.
Board of examiners.
Compensation, §90-524(f).
Composition and terms, §90-524(b).

ATHLETIC TRAINERS —Cont'd
Board of examiners —Cont'd
Contributions.
Acceptance, §90-526(b).
Creation, §90-524(a).
Duties, §90-525.
Expenses, §90-534(a).
Fees, §90-534(b).
Funds.
Custody and use, §90-526(a).
Meetings, §90-524(h).
Officers, §90-524(g).
Powers, §90-525.
Qualifications, §90-524(c).
Removal of members, §90-524(e).
Vacancies, §90-524(d).
Citation of article, §90-522(a).
Continuing education.
Renewal of license, §90-533(a) to (c).
Definitions, §90-523.
Actively engaged, §90-530(b).
Disciplinary actions.
Complaints, §90-539.
Grounds, §90-536(a).
Sanctions, §90-536(b).
Expenses, §90-534(a).
Funds.
Custody and use of, §90-526(a).
Identification badges required, §90-640.
Immunities.
Good faith reports of misconduct or incapacity,
§90-539.
Injunctions.
Illegal practices, §90-537.
Licenses.
Applications, §90-528(a).
Continuing education, §90-533(a) to (c).
Examination.
Licensure without examination, §90-530(a).
Exemptions, §90-527(b).
Issuance, §90-528(c).
Trainers previously certified, §90-529.
Lapse, §90-532.
Person engaged in practice prior to effective date
of article, §90-530(a).
Qualifications of applicant, §90-528(b).
Reciprocity, §90-531.
Renewal, §90-532.
Continuing education, §90-533(a) to (c).
Required, §90-527(a).
Trainers previously certified, §90-529.
Misdemeanors, §90-538.
Purpose of article, §90-522(b).
Reciprocity.
Licenses, §90-531.
Reimbursements.
Third-party reimbursements, §90-540.
Schools.
Hiring by school units, §90-535.
Third-party reimbursements, §90-540.
Violations, §90-538.
Penalties, §90-538.

ATLANTIC BEACH.
All-terrain vehicles.
Use by employees on certain highways,
§20-171.24.
Eminent domain.
Exercise of power, purposes, modified provisions,
§40A-3(b1).

ATLANTIC BEACH —Cont'd
Eminent domain —Cont'd
Vesting of title and right to possession,
§40A-42(a).
**Ordinances to regulate and control swimming,
personal watercraft operation, surfing and
littering in Atlantic Ocean,** §160A-176.2.

ATLANTIC OCEAN.
Jurisdiction over marine fisheries resources.
Marine fisheries commission, §113-134.1.
Municipalities.
Ordinances effective in beach towns, §160A-176.1.
**Ordinances to regulate and control swimming,
personal watercraft operation, surfing and
littering in Atlantic Ocean,** §§160A-176.1,
160A-176.2.

**ATLANTIC STATES MARINE FISHERIES
COMPACT AND COMMISSION,** §§113-251 to
113-258.

ATM CARDS.
Financial transaction card crime act, §§14-113.8
to 14-113.17.
See FINANCIAL TRANSACTION CARDS.

ATMS, §53-62(d1).

A TOAST TO NORTH CAROLINA.
State toast, §149-2.

**ATOMIC ENERGY, RADIOACTIVITY AND
IONIZING RADIATION.**
Confidentiality.
Disclosure authorization, §104E-29(b).
Protection of information, §104E-29(a).
Criminal penalties for violation, §104E-29(c).
Counties.
Privileged license taxes.
Low-level radioactive and hazardous waste
facilities, §153A-152.1(a) to (c).
Regulation of radioactive substances, §153A-128.
Definitions.
Dumping of radioactive material, §14-284.2.
Radiation protection, §104E-5.
Dumping of radioactive material.
Definitions, §14-284.2(b) to (d).
Elements of offense, §14-284.2(a).
Penalty for willful violations, §14-284.2(a).
Dumping of toxic substances.
Willful violations of provisions, §14-284.2(a).
**Fees for facilities producing electricity in
state,** §166A-6.1(a), (b).
Mass death and destruction weapons.
Manufacture, assembly, etc., §14-288.8.
Nuclear, biological or chemical weapons,
§§14-288.21 to 14-288.24.
See WEAPONS OF MASS DEATH AND
DESTRUCTION.
Municipalities.
Regulation of radioactive substances, §160A-183.
Property insurance.
Nuclear reaction, nuclear radiation or radioactive
contamination.
Optional policy provisions as to loss or damage
from, §58-44-25.
Radiation protection act.
Generally, §§104E-1 to 104E-29.
See RADIATION PROTECTION.
Radioactive waste.
See RADIOACTIVE WASTE.
Spent nuclear fuel.
Transportation of spent nuclear fuel, §20-167.1.

**ATOMIC ENERGY, RADIOACTIVITY AND
IONIZING RADIATION** —Cont'd
Taxation.
Property taxes.
Exemptions.
Special nuclear materials, §105-275.
Transportation of spent nuclear fuel, §20-167.1.
University of North Carolina.
Damage or personal injury arising from
construction or operation of nuclear reactors.
Actions, §116-40.2.
Insurance in connection with construction or
operation of nuclear reactors.
Authorization to purchase, §116-40.2.
Water and air resources.
Prohibited discharges, §143-214.2(a).

AT-RISK STUDENTS.
Extended services programs, §§115C-238.30 to
115C-238.33.
Based on needs assessments of children,
§115C-238.31(c).
Collaboratively based programs, §115C-238.31(d).
Community-based locations, §115C-238.31(d).
Goals and expected outcomes based on needs
assessment, §115C-238.32(b).
Implementation of services, §115C-238.31(a).
Integrated with existing classroom and school
activities, §115C-238.31(c).
Intent of general assembly, §115C-238.30.
Model plans developed by state board,
§115C-238.33(a).
Needs assessment, §115C-238.32(a).
Purposes, §115C-238.30.
School based programs, §115C-238.31(d).
Target of programs, §115C-238.31(b).

ATTACHMENT.
Affidavits.
Amendment, §1-440.11(c), (d).
Complaint.
Verified complaint used as affidavit,
§1-440.11(b).
Filing.
Judge to require, §1-440.5(c).
Requirements, §1-440.11(a).
Sheriffs.
Sale of debts and other evidences of
indebtedness, §1-440.46(b).
Agriculture.
Delinquent fees and taxes.
Collection of delinquent fees and taxes,
§106-9.4(b).
Alimony.
Remedies available, §50-16.7(e).
Ambulances.
County or city ambulance services, §§44-51.4 to
44-51.8.
Ancillary proceedings, §1-440.1(a).
**Authority to fix and determine procedural
details.**
Court of proper jurisdiction, §1-440.9.
Bank deposits and collections.
When item subject to legal process, §25-4-303(a).
Bills of lading.
Attachment of goods covered by a negotiable
document, §25-7-602.
Blind persons.
Aid to the blind.
Payment of awards.
Exemption from attachment, §111-18.

ATTACHMENT —Cont'd

Bonds, surety.
Actions on bond.
Defenses.
Certain defenses disallowed, §1-440.8(d).
Affidavit of surety, §1-440.8(b).
Amount of bond, §1-440.10.
Approval by court.
Bonds subject to, §1-440.8(c).
Conditions of bond, §1-440.10.
Discharge of attachment upon giving bond.
Amount of bond, §1-440.39(b).
Effect, §1-440.39(c), (d).
Motion for, §1-440.39(a).
Execution of bonds, §1-440.8(a).
Filing.
Judge to require, §1-440.5(c).
Increased or new bond.
Order to furnish, §§1-440.40(a), 1-440.42(a).
Failure to comply, §1-440.42(c).
Objections to bond or surety.
Defendant, §1-440.40(b).
Plaintiff, §1-440.42(a), (b).
Recovery on bond.
When defendant prevails in principal action,
§1-440.45(c).
When plaintiff prevails in principal action,
§1-440.46(d).
Requirements, §1-440.10.
Stay of order dissolving or modifying.
Plaintiff's bond, §1-440.38.

Child support.
Enforcement of support.
Remedy available, §50-13.4(f).

Corporations.
Grounds for attachment, §1-440.3.

Death of defendant after levy, §1-440.34.

Discharge of attachment upon giving bond.
Amount of bond, §1-440.39(b).
Effect, §1-440.39(c), (d).
Motion for, §1-440.39(a).

**Dissolution, dismissal or setting aside of
attachment.**
Proceedings after, §1-440.45(a), (b).

Dissolution of attachment.
Failure to serve summons or give notice by
publication within time, §1-440.7(b).
Jury trial, §1-440.36(c).
Motion for, §1-440.36(a).
Hearing of motion, §1-440.36(b), (c).
Remedies of third person claiming attached
property or interest therein, §1-440.43.
Service of process.
Noncompliance with time limit, §1-440.7(b).
Stay of order dissolving order of attachment,
§1-440.38.

Documents of title.
Attachment of goods covered by a negotiable
document, §25-7-602.

Exemption of property from creditor claims.
See EXEMPTION OF PROPERTY FROM
CREDITOR CLAIMS.

Family law arbitration, §50-44(c).

Federal liens.
Certificate of nonattachment, §44-68.14(b), (c).

**Firemen's and rescue squad workers' pension
fund.**
Exemption of pensions from attachment,
§58-86-90.

Fraternal benefit societies.
Benefits subject to attachment, §58-24-85.

ATTACHMENT —Cont'd

Funds transfers, UCC.
Creditor process served on receiving bank,
§25-4A-502.

Garnishment.
See GARNISHMENT.

Grounds for attachment, §1-440.3.

Habeas corpus.
County may be called on to aid execution, §17-22.
Failure to obey writ, §17-16.
Refusal of attachment.
Liability of judge refusing attachment, §17-17.
Sheriffs.
Attachment against sheriff to be directed to
coroner, §17-18.
Order of discharge.
Compelling obedience, §17-23.

Injunctions.
Transfer of certificate of stock, §1-440.19(c).
Transfer of negotiable warehouse receipts,
§1-440.20(b).

**Insurer supervision, rehabilitation and
liquidation.**
Attachment prohibited during pendency of
liquidation proceeding, §58-30-295.

Intent to defraud creditors.
Grounds for attachment, §1-440.3.

Judgments.
Jurisdiction required for rendering personal
judgment against defendant, §1-440.1(b).
Procedure after judgment.
When defendant prevails in principal action,
§1-440.45(a), (b).
When plaintiff prevails in principal action,
§1-440.46.
Sale of attached property before judgment,
§1-440.44.
Satisfaction of judgment.
When plaintiff prevails in principal action,
§1-440.46(a).
Satisfaction of plaintiff's claim.
Rendering judgment providing for application of
attached property to, §1-440.1(c).

Jurisdiction.
In rem or quasi in rem jurisdiction.
Grounds, §1-75.8.
Required for rendering personal judgment against
defendant, §1-440.1(b).

Jury.
Dissolution of order of attachment.
Jury trial of motion, §1-440.36(c).

Legislative retirement system.
Exemption from attachment, §120-4.29.

Levy.
Death of defendant after levy, §1-440.34.
Goods in warehouses, §1-440.20(a).
Order of attachment.
Delivery of copy of order to defendant not
required, §1-440.15(c).
Methods of execution generally, §1-440.15(a).
Personal property.
Levy upon personal property before real
property, §1-440.15(b).
Tangible personal property in defendant's
possession, §1-440.18.
Real property.
Docketing levy, §1-440.17(b).
How levy made, §1-440.17(a).
Levy on personal property before real property,
§1-440.15(b).
Stock in corporation, §1-440.19.

ATTACHMENT —Cont'd

Liens.

County or city ambulance service, §§44-51.4 to 44-51.8.

Death of defendant after levy, §1-440.34(b).

Mechanics, laborers and materialmen dealing with owner.

Remedy available to lien claimant, §44A-15.

Priority of liens, §1-440.33(f), (g).

When lien of attachment begins, §1-440.33(a) to (e).

Lis pendens.

Docketing notice of attachment upon lis pendens docket, §§1-116(a), 1-440.33(a).

When notice of suit required to be filed, §§1-116, 1-116(a).

Municipalities.

Remedies for collecting taxes, §160A-207.

Nature of attachment, §1-440.1(a) to (c).

Nonresidents.

Grounds for attachment, §1-440.3.

Notice.

Order of attachment.

Filing in county where real property of defendant located, §1-440.33(a).

Publication.

Issuance of notice of order when no personal service, §1-440.14(a) to (c).

Order of attachment.

Additional orders of attachment at time of original order, §1-440.13(a).

Alias and pluries orders, §1-440.13(b).

Contents, §1-440.12(a).

Dissolution of order, §1-440.36.

Execution.

Methods, §1-440.15(a).

Return, §1-440.16(a) to (c).

Form, §1-440.12(a).

Issuance.

By whom issued, §1-440.5(a).

Time for, §§1-440.5(b), 1-440.6(a), (b).

Levy.

Delivery of copy of order to defendant not required, §1-440.15(c).

Methods of execution generally, §1-440.15(a).

Modification of order, §1-440.37.

Remedies of third person claiming attached property or interest therein, §1-440.43.

Stay of order modifying order of attachment, §1-440.38.

More than one order issued.

Priority of liens, §1-440.33(c) to (e).

Notice.

Filing in county where real property of defendant located, §1-440.33(a).

Publication.

Notice of issuance when no personal service, §1-440.14(a) to (c).

Publication.

Notice of issuance when no personal service, §1-440.14(a) to (c).

Return after execution, §1-440.16(a).

Garnishee process issued, §1-440.16(b).

No levy made, §1-440.16(c).

Return date.

Order not to contain, §1-440.12(b).

Personal property.

Levy upon personal property before real property, §1-440.15(b).

Levy upon tangible personal property in defendant's possession, §1-440.18.

ATTACHMENT —Cont'd

Powers of court.

Procedural details, §1-440.9.

Procedural details, statute fails to make definite provision.

Authority of court to fix procedural details, §1-440.9.

Property subject to attachment, §1-440.4.

Property taxes, §§105-366, 105-368.

Publication.

Issuance of notice of order when no personal service.

Original order issued after publication, §1-440.14(b).

Service by publication subsequent to issuance of order, §1-440.14(a).

No newspaper published in county where action pending, §1-440.14(c).

Real property.

Docketing levy, §1-440.17(b).

How levy made, §1-440.17(a).

Levy upon personal property before real property. Not required, §1-440.15(b).

Lien.

Attachment when levy docketed and indexed, §1-440.33(b).

Notice of issuance of order of attachment.

Filing in county where real property of defendant located, §1-440.33(a).

Remedies.

Remedies of defendant not exclusive, §1-440.41.

Third person claiming attached property or interest therein, §1-440.43.

Residue of attached property or proceeds thereof.

Delivery to defendant after judgment and costs paid, §1-440.46(e).

Retirement system for teachers and state employees.

Exemption from attachment, §135-9.

Return.

Sheriff's return, §1-440.16(a) to (c).

Sales.

Sale of attached property before judgment, §1-440.44.

Proceeds.

Disposition, §1-440.44(b).

When sheriff to apply for authority to sell property, §1-440.44(a).

Satisfaction of judgment.

When plaintiff prevails in principal action, §1-440.46(a).

Sales and use tax.

Delinquent taxes, §105-164.39.

Scope of provisions.

Actions in which attachment may be had, §1-440.2.

Grounds for attachment, §1-440.3.

Property subject to attachment, §1-440.4.

Secured transactions.

Security interest attachment.

Financial asset.

Security interest arising in purchase or delivery of, §25-9-206.

Payment against delivery transactions, §25-9-206(c), (d).

Purchase through securities intermediary, §25-9-206(a), (b).

Service of process.

Publication.

Notice of issuance of order of attachment where no personal service, §1-440.14(a) to (c).

ATTACHMENT —Cont'd
Service of process —Cont'd
Publication —Cont'd
Time for service by publication, §1-440.7(a).
Time for, §1-440.7(a).
Dissolution of attachment for noncompliance, §1-440.7(b).
Shares of stock.
Levy on stock in corporation, §1-440.19(a), (b).
Plaintiff prevailing in principal actions, §1-440.46(c).
Sale of stock.
Certificate of sale, §1-440.46(c).
Transfer of certificate of stock.
Restraining order or injunction, §1-440.19(c).
Sheriffs.
Affidavits.
Sale of debts and other evidences of indebtedness, §1-440.46(b).
Care of attached property.
Expenses, §1-440.35.
Liability, §1-440.35.
Residue of attached property or proceeds thereof.
Delivery to defendant after judgment and costs paid, §1-440.46(e).
Return, §1-440.16(a) to (c).
Sale of attached property before judgment.
Proceeds.
Retention by sheriff, §1-440.44(b).
When sheriff to apply for authority to sell property, §1-440.44(a).
Satisfaction of judgment.
Duties as to, §1-440.46(a) to (c).
Stay of order dissolving or modifying order or attachment, §1-440.38.
Support and maintenance.
Actions in which attachment may be had, §1-440.2.
Taxation.
Collection of taxes, §105-242(b).
Compliance of garnishee, §105-242.1(b).
Exempt property, §105-242(e).
Notice, §105-242.1(a).
Electronic notice, §105-242.1(a1).
Release from liability, §105-242.1(c).
Property taxes, §§105-366, 105-368.
Third parties.
Remedies of third person claiming attached property or interest therein, §1-440.43.
Warehouse receipts.
Attachment of goods covered by a negotiable document, §25-7-602.
Transfer of negotiable warehouse receipt.
Restraining order or injunction, §1-440.20(b).
Warehouses.
Levy on goods in warehouses, §1-440.20(a).
Plaintiff prevailing in principal actions, §1-440.46(c).
ATTAINDER.
Bill of attainder.
Constitutional provisions, US Const Art I §§9, 10, Art III §3.
ATTEMPTS TO COMMIT CRIME.
Arson.
Burning or attempting to burn buildings not covered by other provisions, §14-67.1.
Bribery of horse show judges or officials, §14-380.2.
Drugs.
Controlled substances, §90-98.

ATTEMPTS TO COMMIT CRIME —Cont'd
Felonies, punishment for, §14-2.5.
Lesser included offenses.
Conviction for attempt, §15-170.
Malicious use of explosive or incendiary.
Property occupied by persons, §14-49.1.
Misdemeanors, punishment for, §14-2.5.
Robbery.
Common law robbery, §14-87.1.
Use of firearms or weapons in robbery, §14-87(a).
ATTENDANCE AT PUBLIC SCHOOLS.
Compulsory attendance law, §§115C-378 to 115C-383.
See COMPULSORY SCHOOL ATTENDANCE.
ATTENDANCE OF DEFENDANT.
Securing attendance of criminal defendants confined in institutions within state, §15A-711.
ATTENDANCE OF WITNESSES.
Securing attendance in criminal proceedings.
Out-of-state witnesses, §§15A-811 to 15A-816.
Prisoners as witnesses, §§15A-821 to 15A-823.
ATTESTATION.
Banking corporations.
Deeds and conveyances executed by corporations and attested by secretary or cashier.
Validated, §47-42(b), (c).
Coroner's inquest.
Stenography transcript of proceedings, §152-7.
Corporate conveyances.
Filing corporations.
Validation of certain conveyances of foreign dissolved corporations, §47-108.6.
Defined, §10B-3.
Elections.
Registration of voters.
Contents of application form, §§163-82.4, 163-82.20.
Federal liens.
Execution of certificate, §44-68.13.
North Carolina's eastern region.
Incorporation of region.
County clerk's attestation of resolution, §§158-8.5, 158-33.
Oaths.
How attested.
May be self-proved, §31-11.6.
Proof of attested instrument for registration.
Certificate of officer taking proof, §47-13.1.
Form.
Instrument proved by signature of maker, §47-43.3.
Instrument proved by signature of subscribing witness, §47-43.4.
Instrument proved by subscribing witness, §47-43.2.
Handwriting, §47-12.1(a), (b).
Subscribing witnesses, §47-12.
Certificate of officer taking proof.
Form, §47-43.2.
Instrument proved by signature of witness, §47-43.4.
Grantee or beneficiary incompetent as, §47-12.2.
Public lands.
Conveyance of state land, §146-75.
Self-authentication of public documents, §8C-1 Rule 901.
Wills, §31-3.3.

ATTESTED WRITTEN WILL, §31-3.3.
Manner of probate, §28A-2A-8.

ATTORNEY-CLIENT PRIVILEGE.
Client-lawyer confidentiality, ProfCond Rule 1.6.
Medical board proceedings.
Provision of information to subject of proceedings.
Exceptions, §90-16(d).
Waiver.
Athlete agency contracts.
Records maintained by agent, §78C-97(c).
Student-athlete signing, §78C-94(c), (f).
Motion for appropriate relief, §15A-1415(e).

ATTORNEY DISCIPLINARY PROCEEDINGS.
See ATTORNEYS AT LAW.

ATTORNEY GENERAL.
Acting officers, NC Const Art III §7.
Actions.
Duties of attorney general as to civil litigation,
§114-6.
Additional clerical help, §114-5.
Address confidentiality program.
General provisions, §§15C-1 to 15C-13.
See ADDRESS CONFIDENTIALITY
PROGRAM.
Air pollution control.
Civil penalties.
Civil action for failure to pay, §143-215.114A(f).
Alarm systems licensing.
Investigative powers, §74D-5.2.
Amusements.
Amusement device safety.
Representing department of labor, §95-111.15.
Animal exhibition operators.
Representation of department in actions and
proceedings against.
Duty, §106-520.3A(g).
Animal welfare.
Representation of department of agriculture and
consumer services, §19A-41.
Apportionment or reapportionment.
Act, amending, deleting, adding to, modifying or
repealing plan.
Approval, duty to seek, failure, §120-30.9B(b).
Arson.
Powers as to arrest and prosecution, §58-79-5.
Assistants.
Assignments, §114-4.
Authority to appoint staff, §114-4.
Compensation, §114-4.
State insurance department.
Assignment to department, §114-4.2A.
Attorney general interns, §114-8.1.
Attorneys at law.
Impracticability of representing state entity.
Advice to governor to employ outside counsel,
§147-17.
Auctions and auctioneers.
Enforcement of provisions.
Commission entitled to services of attorney
general, §85B-9(c).
Biologics.
Prosecution of violations.
Concurrent jurisdiction with district attorneys,
§106-714(a).
Boards and commissions.
Charges for legal services to state boards and
commissions, §114-8.2.
Boundaries of state.
Jurisdiction over territory within state, §141-6(c).

ATTORNEY GENERAL —Cont'd
Campus police.
Custodian of records of program, §74G-5(a).
Fees, §74G-12.
Immunity for acts and omissions in carrying out
provisions, §74G-11.
Powers as to, §74G-4.
**Charges for legal services to state boards and
commissions,** §114-8.2.
Charitable solicitation.
Civil action to enforce chapter, §131F-24(a).
Investigations by, §131F-24(b).
Voluntary compliance.
Termination of investigation or enforcement
action, §131F-24(c).
Charitable trusts.
Qualified beneficiaries.
Treatment as, §36C-1-110.
Civil investigative demand.
Medicaid.
False claims by providers, §108A-70.14.
Civil litigation.
Duties as to, §114-6.
Clerical help.
Additional assistants, §114-5.
Common law.
Powers at common law, §114-1.1.
Company police.
Fees, §74E-12.
Powers, §74E-4.
Records.
Legal custodian, §74E-5.
Compensation and allowances, NC Const Art III
§9.
**Contracts exceeding one million dollars,
review,** §114-8.3(a).
Board for licensing of geologists, §89E-5(e).
Building codes, contracting for examination to
certify code enforcement officials,
§143-151.16(d).
Correction department.
Public contracts, §143-134(b).
Global transpark authority.
Contracts for supplies, materials, printing,
equipment, §63A-24.
Medicaid.
Contracts generally, §108A-55(b).
Purchases and contracts through department of
administration, §143-48.1(c).
North Carolina center for applied textile
technology at Gaston College, §115D-67.4.
Purchases through department of administration.
Generally, §143-52.2.
Medicaid, §143-48.1(c).
Soil scientists board of licensing, §89F-5(d).
State bar, §84-23(d).
Transportation department.
Public contracts, §143-134(b).
Research and experimental work, §136-28.1(h).
Trust companies.
Conservatorship, §53-401.
Foreign offices.
Agreements with bank supervisory agencies,
§53-326(d).
Out-of-state institutions.
Agreements with bank supervisory agencies,
§53-320(d).
Seizure by commissioner.
Employment of professionals, §53-391.
Turnpike authority.
Public contracting provisions, §136-89.194(g).

ATTORNEY GENERAL —Cont'd
Controlled substances reporting system.
Department to inform of unusual prescribing
patterns, §90-113.74(e).
Control share acquisitions.
Investigative and regulatory powers, §75E-3.
**Cooperative agreements among physicians or
between physician, hospital or other
person.**
Authority, §90-21.35.
Copy of report submitted to attorney general,
§90-21.32(a).
Defined, §90-21.25.
Objection to issuance of certificate of public
advantage, §90-21.29.
Review after issuance of certificate of public
advantage, §90-21.31.
Suit to authorize cancellation of certificate,
§90-21.33(c).
Council of state.
Membership, NC Const Art III §8.
Credit monitoring services act.
Required disclosure.
Enforcement, §75-135(c).
Crime victims compensation.
Action by claimant for damages.
Duty after notice from commission, §15B-16(c).
Asserting rights of fund or commission.
Authorization, §15B-16(f).
Representation of state, §15B-5.
**Criminal justice education and training
standards commission.**
Chairman, §17C-5(a).
Custody of books, §17C-7(b).
Staff assistant, §17C-7(a).
Dam safety law.
Civil penalties.
Action to recover, §143-215.36(b).
Injunctive relief, §143-215.36(c).
Declaratory judgments.
Party to proceedings involving constitutionality,
§1-260.
Department of commerce.
Energy division.
Employment of attorney for, §114-4.2D.
**Department of health and human services
actions to recover costs of care.**
Prosecution of actions by attorney general,
§143-124.
Department of public safety.
Division of adult correction.
Rules and regulations, forms and instructions.
Filing with, §143B-702.
Department of transportation.
Assistant attorneys general.
Legal assistance for department of
transportation, §114-4.2.
Deputies.
Authority to designate, §114-4.4.
Disabled persons.
Designation of attorney specializing in law of the
handicapped, §114-4.2F.
Discrimination in business.
Enforcement of provisions.
Actions, §75B-4.
District attorneys.
Consulting and advising prosecutors.
Duties of attorney general, §114-2.
Division of adult correction.
Rules and regulations, forms and instructions.
Filing with, §143B-702.

ATTORNEY GENERAL —Cont'd
Domestic violence-related homicides.
Reporting and database system, §114-2.7.
Dry-cleaning solvent cleanup.
Institution of civil action to collect civil penalty,
§143-215.104P(f).
Duties, NC Const Art III §7.
Civil litigation, §114-6.
Department of justice, §114-2.
Devotion of full time to duties, §114-3.
Economic and community development.
Energy division of department.
Employment of attorney for division, §114-4.2D.
Elections.
Date of election, §163-1(a).
Elective officers, NC Const Art III §7.
Vacancy in office.
Election to fill, §163-8.
Voting rights act of 1965.
Duties under, §§120-30.9H, 120-30.9I.
Electronic surveillance generally, §§15A-286 to
15A-298.
See ELECTRONIC SURVEILLANCE.
Elevators.
Representing department of labor, §95-110.12.
Energy efficiency program.
Assignment of attorney for, §114-4.2D.
Energy policy council.
Assignment of attorney for, §114-4.2D.
Engineers and land surveyors.
Legal advisor to board, §89C-23.
Execution sales.
Notification of attorney general, §1-339.55.
False claims act.
Civil action, §1-608(a).
Retention of portion of damages recovered,
§1-608(c).
Civil investigative demand.
Administrative subpoena, §1-614.
Investigations, §1-608(a).
Reports, §1-617(b).
Rules, adoption, §1-618.
Fire investigations.
Authorized investigations, §58-79-1.
Forest fires.
Deputy investigators, §58-79-25.
Powers of attorney general, §§58-79-5, 58-79-10.
Right of entry, §58-79-10.
Subpoenas, §58-79-10.
Contempt for failure to comply, §58-79-15.
Witnesses, powers as to, §58-79-10.
Fish and fisheries resources.
Attorney for agencies, §113-131(d).
Foreign limited liability companies.
Action to restrain violations, §57C-7-13.
Foreign or alien insurance companies.
Actions to enforce compliance with provisions,
§58-16-50.
General assembly.
Opinion on questions of law.
Duties of attorney general, §114-2.
Geologists.
Legal advisor to board, §89E-24.
Governor.
Succession to office of governor, §147-11.1(b).
Highways, roads and streets.
Condemnation proceedings.
Employment of outside counsel, §136-103.1.
Homicides.
Domestic violence-related homicides.
Reporting and database system, §114-2.7.

ATTORNEY GENERAL —Cont'd
Hospital, medical and dental service
corporations.
Conversion.
Enforcement authority, §§58-65-132(d),
58-65-133(d).
Foundation to receive fair market value of
corporation.
Approval of determination of fair market
value, §58-65-133(h).
Hospitals.
University of North Carolina hospital at Chapel
Hill.
Employment of attorney for hospital, §114-4.2B.
Hunting and wildlife.
Attorney for agency, §113-131(d).
Identify theft.
Investigation of complaints, §14-113.23.
Incapacity.
Determination, NC Const Art III §7.
Incompetence, determination of.
Representation of petitioner on appeal by
respondent to appellate division, §35A-1115.
Interim officers, NC Const Art III §7.
Interns, §114-8.1.
Irrigation contractors licensing board,
§89G-4(g).
Job development investment grant program.
Approval of agreements, §143B-437.57(b).
Job maintenance and capital development
fund.
Grant agreement, duties, §143B-437.012(j).
Judgments.
Consent judgments.
State departments and agencies.
Approval, §114-2.2(a) to (c).
Justice department.
Actions.
Duties of attorney general as to civil litigation,
§114-6.
Assistants.
Assignments, §114-4.
Assignment to state insurance department,
§114-4.2A.
Authority to appoint, §114-4.
Compensation, §114-4.
Legal assistance for department of
transportation, §114-4.2.
Boards and commissions.
Charges for legal services to state boards and
commissions, §114-8.2.
Charges for legal services, §114-8.2.
Civil litigation.
Duties as to, §114-6.
Clerical assistants.
Additional clerical help, §114-5.
Client state entities to reimburse department for
costs and expenses, §114-8.2.
Creation of department under supervision of
attorney general, §114-1.
Crime laboratory ombudsman, §114-16.2.
Criminal justice standards division.
Administrative duties and responsibilities,
§17C-9(c).
Created, §17C-9(a).
Director.
Appointment by attorney general, §17C-9(b).
Deputies.
Authority to designate, §114-4.4.
Disabled persons.
Designation of attorney specializing in law of
the handicapped, §114-4.2F.

ATTORNEY GENERAL —Cont'd
Justice department —Cont'd
Duties, §114-2.
Devotion of full time to duties, §114-3.
Forensic science advisory board, §114-16.1.
General assembly.
Legislative assistance from department,
§114-8.4.
General provisions, §§114-1 to 114-20.1.
See JUSTICE DEPARTMENT.
Real estate commission.
Employment of attorney, §114-4.2C.
Reimbursement to department for costs and
expenses, §114-8.2.
Salary, §114-7.
Longevity pay, §114-7.
Special prosecution division.
Duties, §114-11.6.
Established, §114-11.6.
Supervision and direction of attorney general,
§114-1.
University of North Carolina hospital at Chapel
Hill.
Employment of attorney, §114-4.2B.
Labor.
Enforcement of rules and regulations, §95-13.
Landscape contractors.
Services to board, §89D-4(e).
License plate.
Special plate, number, §20-79.5.
Limited liability companies.
Foreign limited liability companies.
Actions by, §57C-7-13.
Interrogatories by secretary of state disclosing
violations.
Certification to attorney general for actions,
§57C-1-31.
Limited liability partnerships.
Foreign limited liability partnerships.
Action to restrain from transacting business,
§59-94.
Lobbying.
Complaints involving state ethics commission
members.
Referral to, investigation, forwarding to district
attorney, §120C-603(b).
Local governmental employees' retirement
system.
Board of trustees.
Legal advisor of board, §128-28(k).
Local government finance.
Legal advisor to commission, §159-3(d).
Offending officers.
Quo warranto proceedings, §159-182.
Marine fisheries commission.
Legal services, §143B-289.54(l).
Master settlement agreement.
Cigarette and tobacco products manufacturers.
Duties as to enforcing against nonparticipating
members, §105-113.4C.
Medicaid.
False claims by providers.
Authority to investigate, institute proceedings,
etc., §108A-70.13(a).
Civil investigative demand, §108A-70.14.
Report by Medicaid fraud control unit, §114-2.5A.
Review of contracts exceeding one million dollars,
§108A-55(b).
Mines and minerals.
Safety and health.
Legal representation of department of labor,
§74-24.18.

ATTORNEY GENERAL —Cont'd
Monopolies and restraint of trade, §§75-9 to
75-15.
Mortgage debt collection and servicing.
Enforcement of provisions, §45-94.
New motor vehicles warranties act.
Civil action by, §20-351.6.
Nonprofit corporations.
Exercise of corporate franchises not granted.
Authority of attorney general, §55A-3-05.
Mergers.
Limitations of charitable or religious
corporations.
Notice and approval, §55A-11-02(a), (b), (c).
**North Carolina center for applied textile
technology at Gaston College.**
Contracts exceeding one million dollars, review,
§115D-67.4.
**Nuisances against public morals, action to
abate,** §19-2.1.
Oaths.
Form of oaths of office, §11-11.
Occupational safety and health.
Legal representation of department of labor,
§95-142.
Offshore oil and gas activities.
Removal of prohibited discharges.
Referral of unexplained discharges to state and
federal law enforcement agencies,
§143-215.94EE(b).
Pesticides.
Board may call upon attorney general for advice,
§143-461.
Post-secondary education.
Nonpublic post-secondary educational institutions.
Licensing.
Enforcement authority of attorney general,
§116-15(j).
Powers.
Address confidentiality program.
Rulemaking, §15C-12.
Common-law powers, §114-1.1.
Justice department.
Transfer of powers to department, §§143A-49.1,
143A-50.
Practice of law.
Authorization to practice in North Carolina.
Prerequisite to appointment or election, NC
Const Art III §7.
Preclearance.
Voting rights act of 1965.
Duties under, §§120-30.9H, 120-30.9I.
Price gouging during state of disaster.
Seller not in violation.
Statement issued by attorney general,
§75-38(b).
Private protective services.
Appointment of director, §74C-6.
Firearms training.
Certified trainers.
Establishment of training program,
§74C-13(l).
Unarmed security guards.
Establishment of training program,
§74C-13(m).
Investigative powers, §74C-7.
Prosecution of violations, §74C-17(b).

ATTORNEY GENERAL —Cont'd
Private protective services —Cont'd
Training.
Certified trainers.
Establishment of training program,
§74C-13(l).
Unarmed security guards.
Establishment of training program,
§74C-13(m).
Public lands.
Grants.
Vacation of grants.
State action, §146-63.
Institution of actions by state, §146-70.
Service of process on state in land actions,
§146-69.
Public officers and employees.
Defense of state employees.
Compromise and settlement of claims,
§143-300.6(b).
Public utilities.
Actions against to recover penalties, institution
and prosecutions, §62-312.
Utilities commission.
Participation in commission proceedings,
§62-20.
Witnesses.
Expert witnesses.
Power to employ, §62-20.
Qualifications, NC Const Art III §7.
Quo warranto, §159-182.
Action by attorney general.
Complaint of private party, §1-515.
Grounds, §1-515.
Own information.
Action upon, §1-515.
**Racketeer influenced and corrupt
organizations.**
Civil remedies instituted by, §75D-8(b).
Real estate commission.
Employment of attorney for commission,
§114-4.2C.
Services to board, §93A-3(e).
**Reports of domestic violence-related
homicides,** §114-2.7.
**Retirement system for teachers and state
employees.**
Legal advisor to board of trustees, §135-6(j).
Roanoke Island commission.
Assignment of legal counsel to commission,
§143B-131.7.
Salaries, §114-7.
Longevity pay, §114-7.
Savings banks.
Involuntary liquidation.
Commencement of action by attorney general,
§54C-83(l).
School bus accidents.
Claims, authority to pay, §115C-257.
Defense of claim by attorney general,
§143-300.1(d).
Duties of attorney general, §143-300.1(b).
Service of process.
Personal jurisdiction.
Service on local public bodies, §1A-1 Rule 4(j).
Service on state or agency thereof, §1A-1 Rule
4(j).

ATTORNEY GENERAL —Cont'd
Setoff debt collection, §§105A-1 to 105A-16.
See SETOFF DEBT COLLECTION.
Settlement or resolution of litigation or
potential litigation.
Agreements entered into by state or state
department, agency, etc.
Report as to payments received and terms or
conditions of payment, §114-2.5(a).
Attorney general's authority to negotiate
settlement of cases not affected,
§114-2.5(b).
Report on agreements, §114-2.4(b).
Review of agreements, §114-2.4(a).
Report on pending lawsuits in which state is a
party, §114-2.6.
Shareholder protection act.
Investigative and regulatory powers, §75E-3.
Sheriffs education and training standards
commission.
Custody of records, §17E-5(b).
Staff assistance, §17E-5(a).
Soil scientists.
Legal advisor to board for licensing, §89F-24.
Special prosecution division.
Duties, §114-11.6.
Established, §114-11.6.
State auditor.
Comparing warrants drawn by auditor.
Duties of attorney general, §114-2.
State banking commission.
Staff attorney as full time legal assistant to
commission, §53-96.
State boundaries.
Jurisdiction over territory within state, §141-6(c).
State debt.
Payment of moneys received for debts due state.
Duties of attorney general, §114-2.
State departments and agencies.
Collection of money owed to agencies,
§147-86.11(e).
Consent judgments.
Approval, §114-2.2(a) to (c).
Counsel for departments, agencies and
institutions, §147-17(b).
Private counsel.
Employment.
Permission from attorney general, §114-2.3.
Private investigators.
Consent of attorney for use of, §114-15.2.
Representation of departments, agencies and
institutions, §114-2.
Settlement or resolution of litigation or potential
litigation.
Report by attorney general as to payment
received and terms or conditions of
payment, §114-2.5(a).
Report on agreements, §114-2.4(b).
Review of terms of proposed agreements,
§114-2.4(a).
State treasurer.
Deposits in unlawful depositories.
Recovery, §147-80.
Structured settlement agreements.
Standing to raise issues relating to transfer,
§1-543.14(d).
Sudan (Darfur) divestment act.
Enforcement, §147-86.49.
Telephone solicitations.
Do not call registry.
Bill insert informing subscriber of existence.
Drafting, §75-102(m).

ATTORNEY GENERAL —Cont'd
Telephone solicitations —Cont'd
Do not call registry —Cont'd
Providing and maintaining.
Federal registry not ready for use, §75-102(n).
Investigation of violations, action for civil
penalties, §75-105(a).
Term of office, §163-1(a).
Textbooks.
Contracts with publishers.
Advice from and suits by attorney general,
§115C-93.
Tobacco escrow compliance.
Duties, §66-294.1.
Generally, §§66-292 to 66-294.1.
Torrens system registration.
Rules of practice prescribed by attorney general,
§43-3.
Tort claims against state departments and
agencies.
Duty of attorney general, §143-298.
Trusts and trustees.
Charitable trusts.
Notice of judicial proceedings, §36C-2-205(i).
Qualified beneficiaries.
Treated as, §36C-1-110.
Unauthorized insurers.
Transacting business.
Action for violations instituted by attorney
general, §58-28-13(k).
Underground petroleum storage tank leak
cleanup.
Injunctive relief, §143-215.94Y.
Institution of actions to recover civil penalties,
§143-215.94W(f).
Underground storage tanks.
Leaking petroleum cleanup.
Groundwater protection loan fund.
Default or violation of loan agreement,
§143-215.94P(e).
University of North Carolina.
Self-insurance.
Defense of actions or suits against covered
persons, §116-220(d).
Vacancy in office, NC Const Art III §7.
Filling, §163-8.
Voting rights act of 1965.
Duties under, §§120-30.9H, 120-30.9I.
Wage and hour act.
Representation of department of labor, §95-25.18.
Warrants for payment of money.
Comparing warrants drawn by state auditor.
Duties of attorney general, §114-2.
Water and air resources.
Civil penalties.
Failure to pay.
Institution of civil actions, §143-215.6A(g).
Wells.
Construction.
Injunctive relief.
Institution of actions, §87-95.

ATTORNEY GENERAL OF UNITED STATES.
Voting rights act of 1965.
Submissions to attorney general of United States,
§§120-30.9A to 120-30.9I.

ATTORNEYS AT LAW.
Abused, neglected or dependent juvenile
actions.
Attorney advocate.
Appointment when guardian ad litem
nonattorney, standing, §7B-601.

ATTORNEYS AT LAW —Cont'd
Abused, neglected or dependent juvenile actions —Cont'd
Local guardian ad litem program, conflict of interest.
Appointment of district bar member, §7B-1202.
Notice in summons of right to counsel and appointment information, §7B-406(b).
Parent's right to counsel, §7B-602.
Payment of court-appointed counsel, §7B-603(a) to (c).
Accounts.
Deposit of funds, ProfCond Rule 1.15-2.
Records and accountings, ProfCond Rule 1.15-3.
Addiction.
Lawyer assistance program, Bar Rules D.0601 to D.0623.
See LAWYERS ASSISTANCE PROGRAM.
Administrative committee.
Continuing legal education hearings before committee, rules governing, Bar Rules D.1001 to D.1011.
Failure to pay membership fees or costs, Bar Rule D.0903.
Compliance after suspension, Bar Rule D.0904.
Reinstatement from inactive status, Bar Rule D.0902.
Transfer to inactive status, Bar Rule D.0901.
Admission to practice, Bar Rule C.0103.
Appeals.
From board of law examiners, §84-24.
Jurisdiction.
Wake county superior court, AdmissPrac Rule .1404.
Notice, AdmissPrac Rule .1402.
Records, AdmissPrac Rule .1403.
Right of appeal, AdmissPrac Rule .1401.
Supreme court.
Appeal from superior court to, AdmissPrac Rule .1405.
Wake county superior court, AdmissPrac Rule .1404.
Appeal to supreme court from, AdmissPrac Rule .1405.
Bar candidate committee, AdmissPrac Rule .0604.
Bar examinations, Bar Rule C.0102.
Board of law examiners.
Powers, §84-24.
Dates, AdmissPrac Rule .0902.
Fees.
Review of written bar examination, AdmissPrac Rule .1002.
Frequency, AdmissPrac Rule .0901.
Passing score, AdmissPrac Rule .0904.
Review of written bar examinations.
Board representative, AdmissPrac Rule .1005.
Fees, AdmissPrac Rule .1002.
Generally, AdmissPrac Rule .1001.
Multistate bar examination.
No provision for review, AdmissPrac Rule .1003.
Scores.
Release, AdmissPrac Rule .1004.
Subject matter, AdmissPrac Rule .0903.
Written examinations, AdmissPrac Rule .0901.
Board of law examiners, §§84-24 to 84-26, AdmissPrac Rules .0101 to .0103.
Address, AdmissPrac Rule .0101.
Approval of rules and regulations, Bar Rule C.0104.
Chair, §84-24, AdmissPrac Rule .0103.

ATTORNEYS AT LAW —Cont'd
Admission to practice —Cont'd
Board of law examiners —Cont'd
Compensation of members, §84-26.
Composition, §84-24.
Creation, §84-24.
Executive secretary.
Board may employ, §84-24.
Expenses of members, §84-26.
Membership, AdmissPrac Rule .0103.
Number of members, AdmissPrac Rule .0103.
Office hours, AdmissPrac Rule .0101.
Powers, §84-24.
Prescription of applicant fees, §84-25.
Purpose, AdmissPrac Rule .0102.
Subpoena and summons, power, §84-24.
Teachers in law schools.
Ineligibility to be members, §84-24.
Terms, §84-24.
Burden of proof.
Good moral character, AdmissPrac Rule .0601.
Comity applicants, AdmissPrac Rule .0203.
Interim permits, AdmissPrac Rule .1301.
Licenses, AdmissPrac Rule .1301.
Qualifications, AdmissPrac Rule .0502.
Compliance with rules.
Required, AdmissPrac Rule .0201.
Continuances.
Hearings, AdmissPrac Rule .1204.
Criminal record check, §84-24.
Definitions, AdmissPrac Rule .0202.
Depositions.
Board of law examiners.
Election, Bar Rule C.0101.
Executive secretary, AdmissPrac Rule .0103.
Use in hearings, AdmissPrac Rule .1206.
Education.
General education requirement, AdmissPrac Rule .0701.
Legal education requirement, AdmissPrac Rule .0702.
False statements, failure to disclose, ProfCond Rule 8.1.
Fees.
Bar examinations.
Review of written bar examinations, AdmissPrac Rule .1002.
Comity applicants, AdmissPrac Rule .0502.
General applicants, AdmissPrac Rule .0404.
Late filing fee, AdmissPrac Rule .0403.
Refund of fees, AdmissPrac Rule .0405.
Nonpayment, AdmissPrac Rule .0206.
Fingerprinting applicants, §84-24.
General applicants, AdmissPrac Rule .0203.
Deadline for filing application, AdmissPrac Rule .0403.
Fees, AdmissPrac Rule .0404.
Late filing fee, AdmissPrac Rule .0403.
Refund of fees, AdmissPrac Rule .0405.
Form of application, AdmissPrac Rule .0402.
How to apply, AdmissPrac Rule .0401.
Licenses.
Issuance, AdmissPrac Rule .1302.
Lists, AdmissPrac Rule .0204.
Qualifications, AdmissPrac Rule .0501.
Good moral character.
Burden of proof, AdmissPrac Rule .0601.
Requirements, AdmissPrac Rules .0501, .0502.
Hearings, AdmissPrac Rule .1201.
Applicants, AdmissPrac Rule .0205.
Conduct of hearings, AdmissPrac Rule .1203.

ATTORNEYS AT LAW —Cont'd
Admission to practice —Cont'd
Hearings —Cont'd
Continuances, AdmissPrac Rule .1204.
Discovery, AdmissPrac Rule .1206.
Notice, AdmissPrac Rule .1202.
Request by applicant for hearing de novo,
AdmissPrac Rule .1203.
Protest of applications, AdmissPrac Rule .0804.
Reopening of case, AdmissPrac Rule .1207.
Subpoenas, AdmissPrac Rule .1205.
Information concerning applicant, AdmissPrac
Rule .0602.
Failure to disclose, AdmissPrac Rule .0603.
Inherent powers of courts unaffected, §84-36.
Jurisdiction.
Appeals.
Wake county superior court, AdmissPrac Rule
.1404.
Law schools.
Requirement of degree from approved law
schools, Bar Rule C.0105.
Licenses, Bar Rules C.0102, C.0103.
Comity applicants, AdmissPrac Rule .1301.
General applicant, AdmissPrac Rule .1302.
Notice.
Hearings, AdmissPrac Rule .1202.
Request by applicant for hearing de novo,
AdmissPrac Rule .1203.
Oath, Bar Rule C.0103.
Protest of application.
Format, AdmissPrac Rule .0802.
Hearing, AdmissPrac Rule .0804.
Nature of protest, AdmissPrac Rule .0801.
Notice to applicant, AdmissPrac Rule .0803.
Refusal by board on own motion to license,
AdmissPrac Rule .0805.
Withdrawal by applicant.
Right to withdraw, AdmissPrac Rule .0803.
Qualifications, AdmissPrac Rules .0501, .0502.
Requirement of degree from approved law
schools, Bar Rule C.0105.
Re-application, AdmissPrac Rule .0605.
Rules and regulations.
Power of board of law examiners, §84-24.
Subpoenas.
Power of board, AdmissPrac Rule .1205.
Supreme court.
Appeal from superior court to, AdmissPrac Rule
.1405.
Wake county superior court.
Appeals, AdmissPrac Rule .1404.
Appeal to supreme court from, AdmissPrac
Rule .1405.
Admonition.
Attorney discipline.
Imposition of discipline, Bar Rule B.0123.
Issuance by grievance committee, Bar Rule
B.0113.
Adoption.
Representation of adoptee, §48-2-201(b).
Representation of parents, §48-2-201(a).
Advertising.
Targeted communication, ProfCond Rule 7.3.
Affidavits.
Continuing legal education.
General compliance procedures, CLE Reg 8.
Disbarred or suspended attorney to show
compliance with provisions of order, Bar Rule
B.0124.

ATTORNEYS AT LAW —Cont'd
"Ambulance chasing."
Prohibited acts, §84-38.
Amnesty in elicit drug use cases, Bar Rule
B.0130.
Annual state bar membership fees.
Suspension for nonpayment of dues, Bar Rule
D.0903.
Compliance after suspension, Bar Rule D.0904.
Appeals.
Admission to practice of law, AdmissPrac Rules
.1401 to .1405.
Agreements of counsel.
Recognition, AppProc Rule 33(c).
Appearance, AppProc Rule 33(a).
Counsel of record.
Appearance, AppProc Rule 33(a).
Entry of attorney as, AppProc Rule 33(a).
Disciplinary proceedings, §84-28(h).
Electronically filed documents.
Signature.
More than one attorney listed as attorney for
parties, AppProc Rule 33(b).
From board of law examiners, §84-24.
Out-of-state attorneys.
Limited practice, AppProc Rule 33(d).
Secure leave periods.
Authorization, AppProc Rule 33.1(a).
Designation, AppProc Rule 33.1(c).
Content, AppProc Rule 33.1(d).
When to file, AppProc Rule 33.1(f).
Where to file, AppProc Rule 33.1(e).
Length, AppProc Rule 33.1(b).
Number, AppProc Rule 33.1(b).
Purpose, AppProc Rule 33.1(a).
Signature and address on papers, AppProc Appx
B.
Specialization.
Denial of certification or continued certification,
Bar Rules D.1805, D.1806.
Appearances.
Authority.
Filing or producing if requested, §84-11.
Employment contract.
Filing or producing if requested, §84-11.
Evidence of attorney-client relationship.
Filing or producing if requested, §84-11.
First appearance before district court judge,
§15A-603.
Retainer agreement.
Filing or producing if requested, §84-11.
Withdrawal, SuperCt Rule 16.
Appointment of counsel.
Abused, neglected or dependent juvenile actions,
§§7B-602, 7B-603.
Attorney disappearance, death or transfer to
disability inactive status.
Protection of clients' interests, Bar Rule B.0122.
Delinquent and undisciplined juvenile actions,
§§7B-1906(c), 7B-2000, 7B-2002.
Fees for preparation of copies.
Not chargeable to attorney appointed to
represent indigent at state expense,
§7A-308(b1).
Indigent defense services act, §§7A-498 to
7A-498.8.
See INDIGENT DEFENSE SERVICES.
Indigent services rules, IDS Rules 1.1 to 3.7.
See INDIGENT DEFENSE SERVICES.
Innocence claim inquiry.
Formal inquiry.
Advice of counsel, indigency, appointment,
§15A-1467(b).

ATTORNEYS AT LAW —Cont'd

Appointment of counsel —Cont'd

Innocence claim inquiry —Cont'd

Judicial review by three-judge panel, §15A-1469(e).

Interstate compact on juvenile.

Return of escapees or absconders, §7B-2805(c).

Mental health, developmental disability, substance abuse.

Involuntary commitment.

Substance abuser's commitment hearing, §122C-286(d).

Representation of indigent person generally, §§7A-450 to 7A-458.

See INDIGENT DEFENSE SERVICES.

Termination of parental rights proceeding, §7B-1109(b).

Parent's right to counsel and appointment of counsel, §7B-1101.1(a).

Arbitration.

Representation by lawyer, §1-569.16.

Arbitration and award.

Fee disputes.

Client assistance committee, Bar Rules D.0701 to D.0704.

Model plan for district bar, Bar Rules D.0801 to D.0808.

Hearings.

Right to representation by attorney, Arbitration Rule 3.

Internal law firm disputes, Arbitration Rule 3, Bar Rules E.0401 to E.0410.

Arguments in trials in superior court.

Court's control, §7A-97.

Arraignment.

Right to counsel, §15A-942.

Arrest.

Right to counsel.

Peace officers to advise person arrested of right to counsel, §15A-501.

Arrest in civil cases.

Indigent persons.

Right to counsel, §1-413.

Athlete agents.

Acting without certificate of registration.

Attorneys licensed and resident of state, §78C-88(c).

Attorney-client privilege.

Client-lawyer confidentiality, ProfCond Rule 1.6.

Waiver.

Athlete agency contracts.

Records maintained by agent, §78C-97(c).

Student-athlete signing, §78C-94(c), (f).

Motion for appropriate relief, §15A-1415(e).

Audits.

Lawyers trust accounts, Bar Rule B.0128.

Authorized practice committee.

Procedures to prevent and restrain unauthorized practice of law, Bar Rules D.0201 to D.0207.

Chairpersons' powers and duties, Bar Rule D.0205.

Counsel's powers and duties, Bar Rule D.0207.

Definitions, Bar Rule D.0203.

Generally, Bar Rule D.0202.

Powers and duties of committee.

Generally, Bar Rule D.0206.

Purposes for establishing, Bar Rule D.0201.

State bar councils' powers and duties, Bar Rule D.0204.

Bail bondsmen and runners.

Prohibited from becoming sureties or runners, §§15A-541(a), 58-71-105.

ATTORNEYS AT LAW —Cont'd

Bank accounts.

Deposit of funds, ProfCond Rule 1.15-2.

Records and accountings, ProfCond Rule 1.15-3.

Bank directive.

Lawyer maintaining trust or fiduciary accounts, ProfCond Rule 1.15-2.

Bank receipts.

Record requirements, ProfCond Rule 1.15-3.

Bankruptcy and insolvency.

Appearance for creditor in insolvency proceedings.

Unlawful for anyone except attorney, §84-9.

Bankruptcy law specialty, Bar Rules D.2201 to D.2207.

Applicability of other requirements, Bar Rule D.2207.

Certification standards, Bar Rule D.2205.

Continuing legal education, Bar Rule D.2205.

Continued certification, Bar Rule D.2206.

Definition of specialty, Bar Rule D.2202.

Establishment of specialty field, Bar Rule D.2201.

Examination for specialty, Bar Rule D.2205.

Peer review, Bar Rule D.2205.

Continued certification, Bar Rule D.2206.

Plan of legal specialization, applicability of provisions, Bar Rule D.2204.

Recognition of specialist, Bar Rule D.2203.

Suspension or revocation of certification.

Continued certification, Bar Rule D.2206.

Bank statements.

Record requirements, ProfCond Rule 1.15-3.

Bar examinations, AdmissPrac Rules .0901 to .1005.

Blind persons.

Aid to the blind.

Lending North Carolina reports to blind lawyers, §111-29.

Board of law examiners, §§84-24 to 84-26, AdmissPrac Rules .0101 to .0103.

Address, AdmissPrac Rule .0101.

Approval of rules and regulations, Bar Rule C.0104.

Chair, §84-24, AdmissPrac Rule .0103.

Compensation of members, §84-26.

Composition, §84-24.

Creation, §84-24.

Executive secretary.

Board may employ, §84-24.

Expenses of members, §84-26.

Membership, AdmissPrac Rule .0103.

Number of members, AdmissPrac Rule .0103.

Office hours, AdmissPrac Rule .0101.

Powers, §84-24.

Prescription of applicant fees, §84-25.

Purpose, AdmissPrac Rule .0102.

Subpoena and summons, power, §84-24.

Teachers in law schools.

Ineligibility to be members, §84-24.

Terms, §84-24.

Business transactions with clients.

Conflict of interest, ProfCond Rule 1.8.

Candidates for judicial office.

Compliance with code of judicial conduct, ProfCond Rule 8.2.

False statements regarding, ProfCond Rule 8.2.

Censure.

Imposition of discipline, Bar Rule B.0123.

Issuance by grievance committee, Bar Rule B.0113.

Checks.

Canceled checks, copies.

Record requirements, ProfCond Rule 1.15-3.

ATTORNEYS AT LAW —Cont'd
Child support.
Procedure to insure payment.
Appointment to represent party support payment owed, §50-13.9(f).
List of attorneys willing to undertake representation, §50-13.9(e).
Choice of law.
Disciplinary authority of North Carolina, ProfCond Rule 8.5.
CLE. See within this heading, "Continuing legal education."
Client-lawyer confidentiality, ProfCond Rule 1.6.
Client security fund, Bar Rules D.1401 to D.1420.
Appropriate uses of fund, Bar Rule D.1416.
Audit of accounts, Bar Rule D.1413.
Authority to establish fund, Bar Rule D.1402.
Board of trustees.
Annual report, Bar Rule D.1415.
Appointment and removal of members, Bar Rule D.1406.
Chairperson, appointment, Bar Rule D.1410.
Lay participation, Bar Rule D.1405.
Meetings, Bar Rule D.1414.
Operational responsibility of fund, Bar Rule D.1403.
Size of board, Bar Rule D.1404.
Succession, Bar Rule D.1409.
Term of office, Bar Rule D.1407.
Staggered terms, Bar Rule D.1408.
Vice-chairperson, appointment, Bar Rule D.1411.
Definitions, Bar Rule D.1401.
Disbursement of funds, Bar Rule D.1413.
Investment criteria, Bar Rule D.1413.
Jurisdiction of state bar, Bar Rule D.1402.
Maintenance of accounts, Bar Rule D.1413.
Purposes, Bar Rule D.1401.
Reimbursement applications, Bar Rule D.1417.
Processing, Bar Rule D.1418.
Source of funds, Bar Rule D.1412.
Subrogation for reimbursement, Bar Rule D.1419.
Supreme court, authority reserved by, Bar Rule D.1420.
Uses of fund, Bar Rule D.1416.
Clients' interests protected.
Appointment of counsel when attorney disappears, dies or transferred to disability inactive status, Bar Rule B.0122.
Clients to be notified by disbarred or suspended member, Bar Rule B.0124.
Collection agencies.
Practice of law by collection agencies, §58-70-120.
Shared office space, §58-70-125.
Committees, CLE Reg 1.
Communications.
Concerning lawyer's services, ProfCond Rule 7.1.
Fields of practice, ProfCond Rule 7.4.
With clients, ProfCond Rule 1.4.
Fees and expenses, ProfCond Rule 1.5.
With judge or jurors.
Ex parte communications, ProfCond Rule 3.5.
With person represented by counsel, ProfCond Rule 4.2.
Compliance after suspension for failure to pay fees, Bar Rule D.0904.
Concurrent conflict of interest, ProfCond Rule 1.7.
Specific rules, ProfCond Rule 1.8.
Conference between attorney and prisoner.
Secret listening, §§14-227.1, 14-227.3.

ATTORNEYS AT LAW —Cont'd
Confidential information.
IOLTA accounts.
Defined, disclosure, restrictions, ProfCond Rule 1.15-4.
Confidentiality of information, ProfCond Rule 1.6.
Confidential government information.
Lawyer acquiring as public officer or employees.
Representing client with interest adverse to information, ProfCond Rule 1.11.
Defined, ProfCond Rule 1.0.
Discussions with prospective clients, ProfCond Rule 1.18.
Conflicts of interest.
Current clients, ProfCond Rule 1.7.
Specific rules, ProfCond Rule 1.8.
Former clients.
Duties to, ProfCond Rule 1.9.
Former judges, arbitrators, mediators or other third party neutrals, ProfCond Rule 1.12.
Government officers and employees.
Special conflicts, former and current officers and employees, ProfCond Rule 1.11.
Imputation, ProfCond Rule 1.10.
Lawyer as witness, ProfCond Rule 3.7.
Prospective clients, matters with, ProfCond Rule 1.18.
Sale or purchase of practice, notice, ProfCond Rule 1.17.
Consent.
Informed consent.
Aggregate settlement or agreement for two or more clients, ProfCond Rule 1.8.
Communicating with client when client's consent required, ProfCond Rule 1.4.
Defined, ProfCond Rule 1.0.
Consent to disbarment, Bar Rule B.0117.
Constitution of North Carolina.
Rights of accused to counsel, NC Const Art I §23.
Constitution of the United States.
Right to counsel, US Const Amd 6.
Consultants.
Foreign legal consultants, §§84A-1 to 84A-8, Bar Rules F.0101 to F.0113.
Administrative committee recommendations, Bar Rule F.0107.
Adoption of rules, §84A-8.
Appeals, Bar Rule F.0108.
Applications, Bar Rule F.0101.
Denial, Bar Rule F.0113.
Fees, Bar Rule F.0111.
Forms, Bar Rule F.0102.
Audits, §84A-5.
Board of law examiners.
Delegation of duties by state bar, §84A-7.
Certificate of registration, §84A-2.
Application, §84A-2(a).
Accompanying documents, §84A-2(d).
Fee, §84A-2(c).
Photograph of applicant, §84A-2(b).
Evidence of applicant's application, qualifications, etc., §84A-2(e).
Good moral character of applicant, §84A-3(c).
Issuance of certificate, §84A-3(b).
Failure to satisfy all provisions, §84A-3(d).
Review by North Carolina state bar, §84A-3(a).
Committee recommendations, Bar Rule F.0107.
Delegation of duties by state bar, §84A-7.
Duties, §84A-5.

ATTORNEYS AT LAW —Cont'd
Consultants —Cont'd
Foreign legal consultants —Cont'd
Failure to disclose, Bar Rule F.0105.
Fees.
Certificate of registration, §84A-2(c).
Duties of consultant, §84A-5.
Foreign country.
Defined, §84A-1.
Good moral character of applicant.
Certificate of registration, §84A-3(c).
Hearings, Bar Rule F.0109.
Investigations, Bar Rule F.0106.
Licenses, §84A-1.
Examinations, §84A-1(b).
Issuance, §84A-1(a).
Moral character and general fitness.
Burden of proof, Bar Rule F.0104.
Permanent record, Bar Rule F.0112.
Prohibited activities, §84A-4(b).
Public records, §84A-2(f).
Reciprocity, §84A-2(g).
Requirements for applicants, Bar Rule F.0103.
Review and order of council, Bar Rule F.0110.
Rules and regulations.
Adoption of rules, §84A-8.
Scope of practice, §84A-4.
Service of process, §84A-6.
Written legal advice.
Jurisdiction other than admitted to practice in, §84A-4(c).
Contempt.
Clerks of court.
Certification of orders, §84-36.1.
Disciplinary hearing commission of state bar.
Power to hold in contempt, §84-28.1(b1).
Suspended or disbarred attorney failing to comply with obligations, Bar Rule B.0124.
Contingent fees and contingent fee agreements, ProfCond Rule 1.5.
Continuing legal education, Bar Rules D.1501 to D.1610.
Accreditation of prerecorded and live programs, Bar Rule D.1604.
Accreditation of sponsors and programs, Bar Rule D.1520.
Accreditation standards, Bar Rule D.1519.
Accredited sponsors, Bar Rule D.1603.
Application requirements, CLE Reg 3.
Adoption of regulations for program, Bar Rule D.1527.
Affidavit of compliance, Bar Rule D.1608.
Agency appeals, CLE Reg 10.
Announcement of approval of courses by accredited sponsors, Bar Rule D.1602.
Annual report by members of state bar, Bar Rule D.1522.
Appeals, Bar Rule D.1610.
Approval of courses, Bar Rule D.1602.
Attendee fee, Bar Rule D.1606.
Computation, CLE Reg 6.
Audit of accounts, Bar Rule D.1513.
Authority for agency appeals, CLE Reg 10.
Bankruptcy law specialty, Bar Rule D.2205.
Continued certification, Bar Rule D.2206.
Bar examiner of board of law examiners, credit earned through service, Bar Rule D.1607.
Bar review/refresher courses, approval, Bar Rule D.1602, CLE Reg 2.
Board of continuing legal education.
Annual report, Bar Rule D.1515.

ATTORNEYS AT LAW —Cont'd
Continuing legal education —Cont'd
Board of continuing legal education —Cont'd
Appointment and removal of members, Bar Rule D.1506.
Chairperson, appointment, Bar Rule D.1510.
Referral of matters to board by grievance committee.
Failure of respondent in disciplinary proceeding to practice sound office management, Bar Rule B.0112.
Broadcast programs, Bar Rule D.1604.
Compliance procedures, CLE Reg 8.
Computation of credit, Bar Rule D.1605.
Hours, CLE Reg 5.
Computer-based CLE, accreditation, Bar Rule D.1611.
Course materials, approval, Bar Rule D.1602.
Course requirements.
Accreditation of video or other audiovisual programs, CLE Reg 4.
General course approval, CLE Reg 2.
Credit hours, Bar Rule D.1521.
Computation, CLE Reg 5.
Criminal law specialty, Bar Rule D.2505.
Continued certification, Bar Rule D.2506.
Defined, Bar Rule D.1601.
Definitions, Bar Rules D.1501, D.1601.
Disabilities, substitute programs for attorneys with, Bar Rule D.1607.
Disbursement of funds, Bar Rule D.1513.
Effective date of rules governing administration of program, Bar Rule D.1526.
Estate planning and probate law specialty, Bar Rule D.2305.
Continued certification, Bar Rule D.2306.
Executive committee, Bar Rule D.1601.
Exemptions from continuing education requirement, Bar Rule D.1517.
Facilities to be provided by sponsors, Bar Rule D.1602.
Family law specialty, Bar Rule D.2405.
Continued certification, Bar Rule D.2406.
Fees, Bar Rule D.1606.
Attendee's fees.
Computation, CLE Reg 6.
Reinstatement fee, CLE Reg 9.
Review of fees, CLE Reg 6.
Sponsors.
Computation, CLE Reg 6.
Uniform application, CLE Reg 6.
Funding for program, Bar Rule D.1512.
General compliance procedures, Bar Rule D.1608.
General course approval, Bar Rule D.1602.
Hearings before administrative committee of state bar, Bar Rules D.1001 to D.1011.
Hearing generally, Bar Rule D.1006.
Hearing panel, Bar Rule D.1007.
Notice of hearing, Bar Rule D.1005.
Purposes of regulations, Bar Rule D.1001.
Referral from board of continuing legal education, Bar Rule D.1003.
Reinstatement hearing, Bar Rule D.1009.
Report by committee to council, Bar Rule D.1011.
Report by panel to committee, Bar Rule D.1010.
Review of recommendation of hearing panel, Bar Rule D.1002.
Suspension hearing, Bar Rule D.1008.
Time of hearing, Bar Rule D.1004.
Hours required, Bar Rule D.1518.

ATTORNEYS AT LAW —Cont'd
Continuing legal education —Cont'd
Immigration law specialty, Bar Rules D.2601 to D.2607.
In-house CLE and self-study, approval, Bar Rule D.1602.
Ceneral course approval, CLE Reg 2.
Investment criteria for funds, Bar Rule D.1513.
Jurisdiction.
Jurisdiction and authority, Bar Rule D.1502.
Law school courses, approval, Bar Rule D.1602, CLE Reg 2.
Lay participation, Bar Rule D.1505.
Maintenance of accounts, Bar Rule D.1513.
Meetings, Bar Rule D.1414.
Noncompliance procedures, Bar Rule D.1609, CLE Reg 9.
Noncompliance with requirement, Bar Rule D.1523.
Nonlegal educational activities, approval, Bar Rule D.1602.
Nonresidents.
Operational responsibility, Bar Rule D.1503.
Operational responsibility.
Other committees, Bar Rule D.1601.
Penalty for late filing of affidavit of compliance, Bar Rule D.1608.
Powers and duties, Bar Rule D.1516.
Prerecorded and live programs, accreditation of, Bar Rule D.1604.
Procedures.
Compliance, CLE Reg 8.
Noncompliance, CLE Reg 9.
Review of board decision, CLE Reg 10.
Program, Bar Rule D.1518.
Purposes of rules, Bar Rule D.1501.
Quorum, Bar Rule D.1601.
Real property law specialty, Bar Rule D.2105.
Continued certification, Bar Rule D.2106.
Records of sponsors, Bar Rule D.1602.
Reinstatement after suspension for noncompliance, Bar Rule D.1524.
Reinstatement fee, Bar Rule D.1609.
Revenues applied to expense of administration, Bar Rule D.1513.
Rules concerning administration, Bar Rules D.1601 to D.1610.
Rules governing administration of program, Bar Rules D.1501 to D.1527.
Scope of rules governing administration of program, Bar Rule D.1517.
Size of board, Bar Rule D.1504.
Simultaneous broadcast, prerecorded material, computer-based CLE, Bar Rule D.1604.
Source of funds for program, Bar Rule D.1512.
Special cases and exemptions, Bar Rule D.1607, CLE Reg 7.
Specialization certification, rules governing accreditation, Bar Rules D.1901 to D.1908.
Accreditation of courses, Bar Rule D.1906.
Accreditation of sponsor, Bar Rule D.1907.
Computation of hours of instruction, Bar Rule D.1904.
Definitions, Bar Rule D.1902.
General provisions, Bar Rule D.1901.
Lecture-type CLE activities, Bar Rule D.1903.
Alternatives to course instruction, Bar Rule D.1905.
Showing by applicants, Bar Rule D.1908.
Sponsor fee, Bar Rule D.1606.

ATTORNEYS AT LAW —Cont'd
Continuing legal education —Cont'd
Sponsors.
Accredited sponsors.
Application requirements, CLE Reg 3.
Substitute compliance, Bar Rule D.1607.
Succession in office, Bar Rule D.1509.
Suspension for noncompliance, Bar Rule D.1523.
Term of office, Bar Rule D.1507.
Staggered terms, Bar Rule D.1508.
Vice-chairman, appointment, Bar Rule D.1511.
Videotape programs, accreditation, CLE Reg 4.
Contracts.
Contingent fee agreements, ProfCond Rule 1.5.
Restriction on practice, ProfCond Rule 5.6.
Conviction of criminal offense.
Clerks of court.
Certification of orders, §84-36.1.
Corporations.
Practice of law.
Attorney retained or employed by corporation, §84-5(b).
Nonprofit corporations.
Indigent legal services by, §84-5.1.
Professional corporations, regulations for practicing law, Bar Rules D.0101 to D.0106.
Prohibition as to practice of law by corporation, §84-5(a).
Violations of provisions.
Misdemeanor, §84-8(a).
Professional corporations generally, §§55B-1 to 55B-16.
See PROFESSIONAL CORPORATIONS.
Receivers.
Counsel fees, §1-507.9.
Costs.
Failure to file complaint on time.
Attorney liable for cost, §84-12.
County attorneys, §153A-114.
Court appointed counsel.
Abused, neglected or dependent juvenile actions, §§7B-602, 7B-603.
Delinquent and undisciplined juvenile actions, §§7B-1906(c), 7B-2000, 7B-2002.
Fees for preparation of copies.
Not chargeable to attorney appointed to represent indigent at state expense, §7A-308(b1).
Indigent defense services act, §§7A-498 to 7A-498.8.
See INDIGENT DEFENSE SERVICES.
Indigent services rules, IDS Rules 1.1 to 3.7.
See INDIGENT DEFENSE SERVICES.
Interstate compact on juvenile.
Return of escapees or absconders, §7B-2805(c).
Mental health, developmental disability, substance abuse.
Involuntary commitment.
Substance abuser's commitment hearing, §122C-286(d).
Representation of indigent persons generally, §§7A-450 to 7A-458.
See INDIGENT DEFENSE SERVICES.
Termination of parental rights proceeding, §7B-1109(b).
Parent's right to counsel and appointment of counsel, §7B-1101.1(a).
Credit unions.
Selection of attorneys to handle loan-closing proceedings, §54-109.18.

ATTORNEYS AT LAW —Cont'd
Criminal case records.
Records to identify attorney representing
defendant, §7A-109.2(a).
Criminal conduct.
Client engaging in, remedial measures, ProfCond
Rule 3.3.
Lawyer not to counsel client to engage in,
ProfCond Rule 1.2.
Criminal conviction, guilty or no contest pleas.
Disciplinary order, §84-28(d).
Stay of order pending outcome of appeal,
§84-28(d1).
Criminal history record checks.
Applicants for admission to practice, §84-24.
Criminal law and procedure.
Abiding by client's decision, ProfCond Rule 1.2.
Appearance.
Recordation.
Requirement that clerk record entry,
§15A-142.
When entry of attorney in criminal proceeding
occurs, §15A-141.
Appointment of counsel.
Indigent defense services act, §§7A-498 to
7A-498.8.
See INDIGENT DEFENSE SERVICES.
Representation of indigent persons generally.
See INDIGENT DEFENSE SERVICES.
Arraignment.
Right to counsel, §15A-942.
Arrest.
Right to counsel, §15A-501.
Conference between attorney and prisoner, secret
listening, §§14-227.1, 14-227.3.
Contingent fees, charging prohibited, ProfCond
Rule 1.5.
Counsel for accused, US Const Amd 6.
Criminal case records.
Records to identify attorney representing
defendant, §7A-109.2(a).
Defendant representing himself.
Standby counsel, §15A-1243.
Entry of attorney in criminal proceeding.
General entry.
Attorney making general entry obligated to
represent defendant at all subsequent
stages, §15A-143.
Recordation.
Requirement that clerk record entry,
§15A-142.
When entry of attorney occurs, §15A-141.
Meritorious claims and contentions, ProfCond
Rule 3.1.
Motion for appropriate relief.
Appointment of counsel for indigent defendant,
§15A-1421.
Nontestimonial identification.
Right to counsel, §15A-279.
Pleas.
Aid of counsel, §15A-1012(a).
Probable cause hearings.
Defendant to be advised of right to counsel,
§15A-606(e).
Determination whether right to counsel waived,
§15A-611(c).
Representation of state and defendant,
§15A-611(a).
Probation revocation hearings.
Right to counsel, §15A-1345(e).

ATTORNEYS AT LAW —Cont'd
Criminal law and procedure —Cont'd
Prosecutors, special responsibilities, ProfCond
Rule 3.8.
Right to counsel generally, §15-4, NC Const Art I
§23, US Const Amd 6.
Waiver of counsel.
Indigent persons, §7A-457.
Withdrawal of attorney with permission of court,
§15A-144.
Criminal law specialty, Bar Rules D.2501 to
D.2509.
Applicability of other requirements, Bar Rule
D.2507.
Certification standards, Bar Rule D.2505.
Continuing legal education, Bar Rule D.2505.
Continued certification, Bar Rule D.2506.
Definition of specialty, Bar Rule D.2502.
Establishment of specialty field, Bar Rule D.2501.
Examination for specialty, Bar Rule D.2505.
Juvenile delinquency law specialist.
Recognition as specialist, Bar Rule D.2503.
Standards for certification, Bar Rule D.2508.
Continuing certification, Bar Rule D.2509.
Subspecialty, Bar Rule D.2502.
Lapse of certification, Bar Rule D.2506.
Peer review, Bar Rule D.2505.
Plan of legal specialization.
Applicability of provisions, Bar Rule D.2504.
Recognition of specialist, Bar Rule D.2503.
Suspension or revocation of certificate.
Continued certification, Bar Rule D.2506.
Damages.
Fraudulent practice.
Liability of attorney in double damages, §84-13.
Death.
Appointment of counsel to protect clients'
interests, Bar Rule B.0122.
Debtor and creditor.
Appearance for creditor in insolvency and certain
other proceedings.
Unlawful for anyone except attorney, §84-9.
Declining representation, ProfCond Rule 1.16.
Dedicated trust account.
Defined, ProfCond Rule 1.15-1.
Deposit of trust funds in, ProfCond Rule 1.15-2.
Defense of public school employees.
Employee's obligation for attorney fees,
§143-300.17.
Defense of state employees.
See PUBLIC OFFICERS AND EMPLOYEES.
Definitions.
Admission to practice, AdmissPrac Rule .0202.
Discipline and disability rules of state bar, Bar
Rule B.0103.
Practice of law, §84-2.1.
State bar.
Judicial districts, §84-19.
Delinquent and undisciplined juvenile actions.
Appointment of counsel for juvenile generally,
§7B-2000(a).
Payment, §7B-2002.
Presumption of indigence, §7B-2000(b).
Right to counsel, §7B-2000(a).
Secure or nonsecure custody hearings.
Appointment of counsel for juvenile,
determining if juvenile retained counsel,
§7B-1906(c).
Summons to notify parent of right to counsel and
appointment of counsel, §7B-1805(b).
Deposit of fiduciary funds, ProfCond Rule 1.15-2.

ATTORNEYS AT LAW —Cont'd
Deposit of trust funds, ProfCond Rule 1.15-2.
Deposits.
State bar.
Securing of deposits, §84-34.1.
Diligence in representation, ProfCond Rule 1.3.
Diminished capacity.
Client with, ProfCond Rule 1.14.
Direct contact with prospective clients,
ProfCond Rule 7.3.
Disability, CLE substitute program, Bar Rule
D.1607.
Disability proceedings.
Address of record, Bar Rule B.0126.
Appointment of counsel to protect clients'
interests when attorney transferred to
disability inactive status, Bar Rule B.0122.
Chairperson of hearing commission, powers and
duties, Bar Rule B.0108.
Clerks of court.
Certification of orders, §84-36.1.
Confidentiality, Bar Rule B.0129.
Counsel's powers and duties, Bar Rule B.0107.
Defendant alleges disability in disciplinary
proceeding, Bar Rule B.0118.
Definitions, Bar Rule B.0103.
Evidence, preservation, Bar Rule B.0118.
Fees and costs, Bar Rule B.0118.
Final determination of incapacity or disability.
Entry upon judgment docket of superior court,
Bar Rule B.0123.
Hearing committee's powers and duties, Bar Rule
B.0109.
Hearings, Bar Rule B.0118.
Initiation of hearing by hearing committee, Bar
Rule B.0118.
Involuntary commitment of member, proceedings,
Bar Rule B.0118.
Judicial declaration of incompetence of a member,
proceedings, Bar Rule B.0118.
Petition for reinstatement after transfer to
disability inactive status, Bar Rule B.0125.
Proceedings initiated by state bar, Bar Rule
B.0118.
Protection of clients' interests when attorney
transferred to disability inactive status, Bar
Rule B.0122.
Appointment of counsel, Bar Rule B.0122.
Reinstatement after transfer to disability inactive
status, Bar Rule B.0125.
Secretary's powers and duties, Bar Rule B.0110.
State bar council's powers and duties, Bar Rule
B.0104.
Disappearance of attorney.
Appointment of counsel to protect clients'
interests, Bar Rule B.0122.
Disaster response plan of the state bar, Bar
Rules D.0301 to D.0303.
Disaster response team, Bar Rule D.0301.
General policy and objectives, Bar Rule D.0302.
Report on results, Bar Rule D.0303.
Disbarment, §84-28(c).
Consent to disbarment, Bar Rule B.0117.
Employing as legal clerk or assistant, ProfCond
Rule 5.5.
Forfeiture of license.
Felony convictions, §15A-1331A.
Imposition of discipline, Bar Rule B.0123.
Obligations of disbarred attorney, Bar Rule
B.0124.
Reinstatement, Bar Rule B.0125.

ATTORNEYS AT LAW —Cont'd
Disbarment —Cont'd
Resignation while under investigation, order
disbarring member, Bar Rule B.0117.
Restoration of license, §84-28(c).
Disciplinary proceedings.
Action on grievance.
Notice to complainant, Bar Rule B.0121.
Notice to member, Bar Rule B.0120.
Address of record, Bar Rule B.0126.
Administration of reciprocal discipline, Bar Rule
B.0116.
Admissions.
Prehearing conference for purposes of obtaining,
Bar Rule B.0114.
Admonition.
Imposition of discipline, Bar Rule B.0123.
Issuance by grievance committee, Bar Rule
B.0113.
Affidavit consenting to disbarment, Bar Rule
B.0117.
Affidavit form, grievances, Bar Rule B.0111.
Affidavit stating member's desire to resign, Bar
Rule B.0117.
Aggravating factors in imposing discipline, Bar
Rule B.0114.
Amendment of judgments, Bar Rule B.0114.
Amnesty in elicit drug use cases, Bar Rule
B.0130.
Answer.
Filing by defendant, Bar Rule B.0114.
Appeals, §84-28(h).
Appearance by defendant in his or her own behalf.
Filing of proof of delivery of copy, Bar Rule
B.0114.
Appearance by defendant represented by counsel.
Filing by counsel of proof of delivery of copy,
Bar Rule B.0114.
Audit of trust accounts, investigative subpoenas,
Bar Rule B.0128.
Censure.
Imposition of discipline, Bar Rule B.0123.
Issuance by grievance committee, Bar Rule
B.0113.
Public censure, §84-28(c).
Chairperson of grievance committee, powers and
duties, Bar Rule B.0105.
Proceedings before committee, Bar Rule B.0113.
Chairperson of hearing commission, powers and
duties, Bar Rule B.0108.
Clerks of court.
Certification of orders, §84-36.1.
Complaint.
Amendments, Bar Rule B.0113.
Content requirements, Bar Rule B.0114.
Filing, Bar Rule B.0114.
Issuance, Bar Rule B.0113.
Service, Bar Rule B.0114.
Concurrent jurisdiction of state bar and courts,
Bar Rule B.0102.
Conference prior to hearing for obtaining
admissions or narrowing issues, Bar Rule
B.0114.
Confidentiality, Bar Rule B.0129.
Documents, papers, etc, of state bar, staff,
counsel, etc, §84-32.1(a), (b).
Evidence brought forward in hearing
considered public record, §84-32.1(c).
Lawyer assistance program records not
considered public, §84-32.1(d).
Consent orders after trial, Bar Rule B.0114.

ATTORNEYS AT LAW —Cont'd
Disciplinary proceedings —Cont'd
Consent to disbarment, Bar Rule B.0117.
Continuance of hearing, Bar Rule B.0114.
Convening grievance to consider grievance, Bar
    Rule B.0112.
Conviction in criminal case, effect of finding of
    guilt, Bar Rule B.0115.
Counsel's powers and duties, Bar Rule B.0107.
Courts.
    Enforcement of powers of council, §84-28(i), (j).
Criminal conviction, guilty or no contest pleas,
    §84-28(d).
    Stay of order pending outcome of appeal,
        §84-28(d1).
Default.
    Failure to file answer, Bar Rule B.0114.
    Order imposing discipline, Bar Rule B.0114.
Definitions, Bar Rule B.0103.
Depositions.
    Investigations of professional misconduct,
        §84-29.
Disability alleged by defendant in disciplinary
    proceeding, Bar Rule B.0118.
Disbarment, §84-28(c).
    Consent to, Bar Rule B.0117.
    Imposition of discipline, Bar Rule B.0123.
    Obligations of disbarred attorney, Bar Rule
        B.0124.
    Reinstatement, §84-32(d), Bar Rule B.0125.
    Resignation while under investigation, order
        debarring member, Bar Rule B.0117.
    Restoration of license, §84-32(c).
Disciplinary authority of North Carolina.
    Choice of law, ProfCond Rule 8.5.
    Lawyer admitted to practice in state subject to,
        ProfCond Rule 8.5.
Discovery, Bar Rule B.0114.
Dismissal.
    Notice of action, Bar Rule B.0120.
Dispositional alternatives, §84-28(c).
Disqualification of member of council or hearing
    commission due to interest, Bar Rule B.0127.
District bars not to conduct separate proceedings,
    Bar Rule B.0102.
District grievance committees, Bar Rules B.0201
    to B.0207.
    Acknowledgment of receipt of grievance from
        state bar, Bar Rule B.0204.
    Appearances by complainants and respondents
        at meetings, Bar Rule B.0203.
    Appointment of members, Bar Rule B.0201.
    Assignment of grievance to investigating
        member, Bar Rule B.0204.
    Assistance in questions, Bar Rule B.0206.
    Authority, Bar Rule B.0202.
    Confidentiality of meetings, Bar Rule B.0203.
    Conflicts of interest, Bar Rule B.0207.
    Creation, Bar Rule B.0201.
    Decision reports, Bar Rule B.0204.
    Deliberations by committee, Bar Rule B.0204.
    Fee disputes, grievances involving, Bar Rule
        B.0202.
    Filing grievances with committees, Bar Rules
        B.0202, B.0204.
    Form letters, Bar Rules B.0208 to B.0217.
    Investigation of grievance, Bar Rule B.0204.
    Judicial districts eligible to form, Bar Rule
        B.0201.
    Jurisdiction and authority, Bar Rule B.0202.

ATTORNEYS AT LAW —Cont'd
Disciplinary proceedings —Cont'd
District grievance committees —Cont'd
    Letter of notice to respondent attorney and
        responses, Bar Rule B.0204.
    Meetings, Bar Rule B.0203.
    Missing attorneys, Bar Rule B.0206.
    Notice of meetings, Bar Rule B.0203.
    Notice to state bar of locally filed grievances,
        Bar Rule B.0204.
    Organization, Bar Rule B.0201.
    Procedure upon institution of grievance, Bar
        Rule B.0204.
    Quorum for meetings, Bar Rule B.0203.
    Recordkeeping, Bar Rule B.0204.
    Referral of grievances to committees, Bar Rule
        B.0202.
    Report of committee's decision, Bar Rule
        B.0204.
    Rules of the state bar, committees subject to,
        Bar Rule B.0202.
Drug use cases, amnesty, Bar Rule B.0130.
Enforcement of powers, Bar Rule B.0119.
Evidence, §84-29.
    Confidentiality of documents, papers, etc, of
        state bar, staff, counsel, etc.
    Considering evidence brought forward in
        hearing as public record, §84-32.1(c).
    Formal hearings, Bar Rule B.0114.
    Imposition of discipline, Bar Rule B.0114.
    Record of evidence, §84-32(a).
Failure to employ sound office management
    techniques.
    Referral of case to board of continuing legal
        education, Bar Rule B.0112.
False statements, failure to disclose, ProfCond
    Rule 8.1.
Federal courts, administration of reciprocal
    discipline, Bar Rule B.0116.
Felony convictions.
    Forfeiture of license, §15A-1331A.
Filing of grievance, Bar Rule B.0111.
Formal hearing, Bar Rule B.0114.
Form grievance to be in, Bar Rule B.0111.
Form letters, district grievance committees, Bar
    Rules B.0208 to B.0217.
    Letter of notice to respondent attorney, Bar
        Rule B.0216.
    Letter to complainant acknowledging grievance,
        Bar Rule B.0213.
    Letter to complainant from investigating
        attorney, Bar Rule B.0215.
    Letter to complainant/respondent where district
        grievance committee recommends finding of
        no probable cause, Bar Rule B.0210.
    Letter to complainant where district committee
        recommends finding of probable cause, Bar
        Rule B.0212.
    Letter to complainant where local grievance
        alleges fee dispute only, Bar Rule B.0208.
    Letter to complainant where local grievance
        alleges fee dispute with other violations,
        Bar Rule B.0209.
    Letter to investigating attorney assigning
        grievance, Bar Rule B.0214.
    Letter to respondent where district grievance
        committee recommends finding of probable
        cause, Bar Rule B.0211.
    Letter transmitting completed file to North
        Carolina state bar, Bar Rule B.0217.

ATTORNEYS AT LAW —Cont'd
Disciplinary proceedings —Cont'd
Grievance committee.
Powers and duties, Bar Rule B.0106.
Grounds for discipline, §84-28(b).
Guilt in criminal case, effect of finding, Bar Rule B.0115.
Hearing commission, §84-28.1.
Appointment of members, §84-28.1(a).
Compensation of members, §84-28.1(c).
Composition, §84-28.1(a).
Contempt.
Power to hold in contempt, §84-28.1(b1).
Number of members, §84-28.1(a).
Powers, §84-28.1(b), (b1).
Hearing committee, designation, Bar Rule B.0114.
Hearing committee's powers and duties, Bar Rule B.0109.
Immunity from suit.
Persons immune, §84-28.2.
Imposition of discipline, Bar Rule B.0123.
Inactive status.
Transfer to inactive status for mental incompetence or physical disability, §84-28(g).
Inherent powers of courts unaffected, §84-36.
Initial determination, Bar Rule B.0112.
Injunctions.
Practice of law by attorney, §84-28(f).
Interim report of council concerning grievance, Bar Rule B.0112.
Investigations.
Initial determination, Bar Rule B.0112.
Investigators, §84-31.
Judgment or order, relief from, Bar Rule B.0114.
Judgments, §84-32(a).
Amendment, Bar Rule B.0114.
Judicial district grievance committees, rules governing, Bar Rules B.0201 to B.0207.
Form letters, Bar Rules B.0208 to B.0217.
Jurisdiction of council, §84-28(a).
Letter of caution.
Issuance by grievance committee, Bar Rule B.0113.
Letter of notice sent to respondent, Bar Rule B.0112.
Letter of warning.
Issuance by grievance committee, Bar Rule B.0113.
Lifting stay of suspension with conditions, Bar Rule B.0114.
Mitigating factors in imposing discipline, Bar Rule B.0114.
Motion to lift stay of suspension, Bar Rule B.0114.
New trial, Bar Rule B.0114.
Notice of findings of incapacity or disability, Bar Rule B.0123.
Notice of imposition of discipline, Bar Rule B.0123.
Notice to complainant of action, Bar Rule B.0121.
Notice to member of action or dismissal, Bar Rule B.0120.
Obligations of disbarred or suspended attorneys, Bar Rule B.0124.
Open hearings, Bar Rule B.0114.
Other jurisdictions.
Effect of disciplinary proceedings in, §84-28(e).
Petition for reinstatement after disbarment or suspension, Bar Rule B.0125.
Post-trial motions, Bar Rule B.0114.
Prehearing conferences, Bar Rule B.0114.

ATTORNEYS AT LAW —Cont'd
Disciplinary proceedings —Cont'd
Preliminary hearings held by grievance committee.
Quorum and vote required for finding probable cause, Bar Rule B.0113.
Pretrial motions.
Hearing and disposing of, Bar Rule B.0114.
Probable cause determination by grievance committee, Bar Rule B.0113.
Procedure at formal hearings, Bar Rule B.0114.
Procedure for discipline, Bar Rule B.0102.
Procedure on reciprocal discipline, Bar Rule B.0116.
Proceedings before grievance committee, Bar Rule B.0113.
Production of books, papers and other documents.
Subpoena issued at formal hearings, Bar Rule B.0114.
Subpoena issued in proceedings before grievance committee, Bar Rule B.0113.
Subpoena to compel during initial determination, Bar Rule B.0112.
Prosecutor.
Appointment, §84-31.
Purposes of discipline for misconduct, Bar Rule B.0101.
Reciprocal discipline, Bar Rule B.0116.
Record at formal hearings, Bar Rule B.0114.
Record of proceedings, §84-32(a).
Referral of case to board of continuing legal education.
Respondent failing to employ sound office management, Bar Rule B.0112.
Refusal to obey lawful orders.
Enforcement of powers, Bar Rule B.0119.
Reinstatement after disbarment or suspension, §84-32(d), Bar Rule B.0125.
Relief from judgment or order, Bar Rule B.0114.
Reprimand.
Imposition of discipline, Bar Rule B.0123.
Issuance by grievance committee, Bar Rule B.0113.
Private reprimand, §84-28(c).
Resignation while under investigation, Bar Rule B.0117.
Rights of accused person, §84-30.
Rules of civil procedure.
Pleadings and proceedings to conform to, Bar Rule B.0114.
Secretary's powers and duties, Bar Rule B.0110.
Service of complaints and other documents or papers, Bar Rule B.0114.
Settlement of case.
Meeting of parties prior to hearing, Bar Rule B.0114.
Size of papers presented to commission for filing, Bar Rule B.0114.
State bar council's powers and duties, Bar Rule B.0104.
Stay of period of suspension, Bar Rule B.0114.
Stipulation of issues, facts or matters of law.
Meeting of parties prior to hearing, Bar Rule B.0114.
Subpoenas.
Issuance at formal hearings, Bar Rule B.0114.
Issuance by chairperson of grievance committee during initial determination, Bar Rule B.0112.
Issuance in proceedings before grievance committee, Bar Rule B.0113.

ATTORNEYS AT LAW —Cont'd
Disciplinary proceedings —Cont'd
Surrender of license.
Voluntary surrender, §84-32(b).
While under investigation, Bar Rule B.0117.
Suspension, §84-28(c), (d).
Imposition of discipline, Bar Rule B.0123.
Obligation of suspended attorney, Bar Rule B.0124.
Reinstatement, §84-32(d), Bar Rule B.0125.
Restoration of license, §84-32(c).
Stay of period of suspension with conditions, Bar Rule B.0114.
Time for filing answer, Bar Rule B.0114.
Time for scheduling hearing, Bar Rule B.0114.
Trust account, audit.
Investigative subpoena, Bar Rule B.0128.
Witnesses, §84-29.
Rights of accused person as to, §84-30.
Subpoena compelling attendance in proceedings before grievance committee, Bar Rule B.0113.
Subpoenas to compel attendance during initial determination, Bar Rule B.0112.
Subpoena to compel attendance at formal hearing, Bar Rule B.0114.
Disclosure of confidential information, ProfCond Rule 1.6.
Discovery.
Frivolous discovery, ProfCond Rule 3.4.
Dispute as to fees.
Lawyer responsibilities, ProfCond Rule 1.5.
Disputed monies.
Deposit with clerk of court, §93A-12.
Disqualification.
Former judge, clerk, arbitrator, mediator or third party neutral, ProfCond Rule 1.12.
Imputed disqualification.
Principles of, ProfCond Rule 1.10.
Public officers and employees.
Special conflicts, former and current officers and employees, ProfCond Rule 1.11.
District courts.
Courtroom decorum, SuperCt Rule 12.
Scheduling conflicts.
Guidelines for resolving, SuperCt Rule 3.1.
Withdrawal of appearance, SuperCt Rule 16.
District grievance committees, rules governing, Bar Rules B.0201 to B.0207.
Form letters, Bar Rules B.0208 to B.0217.
Division of fees, ProfCond Rule 1.5.
Lawyer or firm sharing fees with nonlawyer, ProfCond Rule 5.4.
Drug use.
Disciplinary amnesty in elicit drug use cases, Bar Rule B.0130.
Electronic contact with prospective clients, ProfCond Rule 7.3.
Employment agreements.
Restriction on practice, ProfCond Rule 5.6.
Employment security.
Representation of parties to proceedings before division, §96-17(b).
Representation of state and department in civil actions, §96-7(a).
Entrusted property, ProfCond Rule 1.15-2.
Defined, ProfCond Rule 1.15-1.
Equity line of credit.
Future advances.
Notice regarding, form, §45-82.3(f).

ATTORNEYS AT LAW —Cont'd
Equity line of credit —Cont'd
Request to terminate made by attorney.
Notice to borrower, form, §45-82.2(d).
Estate planning and probate law specialty, Bar Rules D.2301 to D.2307.
Applicability of other requirements, Bar Rule D.2307.
Certification standards, Bar Rule D.2305.
Continued certification standards, Bar Rule D.2306.
Continuing legal education, Bar Rule D.2305.
Definition of specialty, Bar Rule D.2302.
Establishment of specialty field, Bar Rule D.2301.
Examination for specialty, Bar Rule D.2305.
Peer review, Bar Rule D.2305.
Plan of legal specialization, applicability of provisions, Bar Rule D.2304.
Recognition of specialist, Bar Rule D.2303.
Ethics opinions and ethics advisories, Bar Rules D.0101 to D.0104.
Definitions, Bar Rule D.0101.
Ethics, Bar Rule D.0103.
Ethics opinions and decisions, Bar Rule D.0104.
Requests, Bar Rule D.0102.
Evidence.
Altering, destroying or concealing, ProfCond Rule 3.4.
Disciplinary proceedings.
Confidentiality of documents, papers, etc, of state bar, staff, counsel, etc.
Considering evidence brought forward in hearing as public record, §84-32.1(c).
False evidence offered, ProfCond Rule 3.3.
Obstructing party's access to, ProfCond Rule 3.4.
Prohibited acts as to opposing party and counsel, ProfCond Rule 3.4.
Excessive fees and expenses.
Charging client prohibited, factors in determining, ProfCond Rule 1.5.
Executions.
Execution against the person.
Indigent defendants.
Appointment of counsel, §1-311.
Executors and administrators.
Counsel fees allowable to attorneys serving as representatives, §28A-23-4.
Employing attorneys.
Powers of personal representatives and fiduciaries, §28A-13-3(a).
Ex parte communications with judge or jurors, ProfCond Rule 3.5.
Ex parte proceedings.
Information to tribunal, ProfCond Rule 3.3.
Expediting litigation, ProfCond Rule 3.2.
Extrajudicial statements, ProfCond Rule 3.6.
Fairness to opposing party and counsel, ProfCond Rule 3.4.
False communications concerning services, ProfCond Rule 7.1.
False evidence offered, ProfCond Rule 3.3.
False or misleading statements.
Bar admission, disciplinary matters, ProfCond Rule 8.1.
Communications concerning services, ProfCond Rule 7.1.
Regarding judges or candidates for judicial office, ProfCond Rule 8.2.
To third persons, ProfCond Rule 4.1.
To tribunal, ProfCond Rule 3.3.
Family law arbitration, §50-48.

ATTORNEYS AT LAW —Cont'd
Family law specialty, Bar Rules D.2401 to
D.2407.
 Applicability of other requirements, Bar Rule
  D.2407.
 Certification standards, Bar Rule D.2405.
 Continued certification standards, Bar Rule
  D.2406.
 Continuing legal education, Bar Rule D.2405.
 Definition of specialty, Bar Rule D.2402.
 Establishment of specialty field, Bar Rule D.2401.
 Peer review, Bar Rule D.2405.
 Plan of legal specialization, applicability of
  provisions, Bar Rule D.2404.
 Recognition of specialist, Bar Rule D.2403.
Fee arbitration, model plan for district bar,
 Bar Rules D.0801 to D.0808.
 Appointment of committee on fee arbitration
  members, Bar Rule D.0801.
 Chairperson of committee, Bar Rule D.0802.
 Decision of arbitrators, Bar Rule D.0806.
 Enforcement of decisions of arbitrators, Bar Rule
  D.0807.
 Jurisdiction of committee, Bar Rule D.0803.
 Proceedings.
  Generally, Bar Rule D.0805.
 Recordkeeping by coordinator of fee arbitration,
  Bar Rule D.0808.
 Request for arbitration, processing, Bar Rule
  D.0804.
Fees generally.
 See ATTORNEYS' FEES.
Fiduciaries.
 Counsel fees allowed attorneys serving as
  fiduciaries, §32-61.
 Employment and compensation.
  Powers which may be incorporated by reference
   in trust instrument, §32-27.
Fiduciary funds.
 Defined, ProfCond Rule 1.15-1.
 Deposit, ProfCond Rule 1.15-2.
Financial assistance to client, ProfCond Rule 1.8.
Fingerprinting.
 Applicants for admission to practice, §84-24.
Firm names and letterheads, ProfCond Rule 7.5.
Foreign legal consultants. See within this
 heading, "Consultants."
Forfeiture.
 Contingent fee.
  Charging in criminal or civil forfeiture
   proceeding, ProfCond Rule 1.5.
Former clients.
 Duties to, ProfCond Rule 1.9.
Form letters involving disciplinary matters.
 District grievance committees, Bar Rules B.0208
  to B.0217.
Fraud.
 Client engaging in fraudulent conduct, remedial
  measures, ProfCond Rule 3.3.
 Defined, ProfCond Rule 1.0.
 Lawyer not to counsel client to engage in
  fraudulent conduct, ProfCond Rule 1.2.
 Liability for fraudulent practice.
  Double damages, §84-13.
Frivolous claims and contentions, ProfCond
 Rule 3.1.
Frivolous discovery, ProfCond Rule 3.4.
General trust account.
 Defined, ProfCond Rule 1.15-1.
 Deposit of trust funds in, ProfCond Rule 1.15-2.

ATTORNEYS AT LAW —Cont'd
Gift from client.
 Soliciting, ProfCond Rule 1.8.
Government officers and employees.
 Action as public official, ProfCond Rule 6.6.
 Conflict of interest.
  Special conflicts, former and current officers and
   employees, ProfCond Rule 1.11.
Guardian ad litem.
 Discharge and appointment.
  Attorney as guardian ad litem, §35A-1107(a),
   (b).
Immigration law specialty, Bar Rules D.2601 to
 D.2607.
Impairment.
 Lawyer assistance program, Bar Rules D.0601 to
  D.0623.
 See LAWYERS ASSISTANCE PROGRAM.
Impeachment.
 Accused entitled to counsel, §123-9.
Implied authorization to take action, ProfCond
 Rule 1.2.
 Disclosure of confidential informations, ProfCond
  Rule 1.6.
Imputation of conflict of interest, ProfCond Rule
 1.10.
Imputed disqualification.
 Principles of, ProfCond Rule 1.10.
Inactive status.
 Reinstatement from, Bar Rule D.0902.
 Transfer to, Bar Rule D.0901.
Incompetence, determination of.
 Attorney as guardian ad litem, §35A-1107(a), (b).
 Right to counsel, §35A-1107(a).
Incompetence, restoration.
 Right to counsel, §35A-1130(c).
Indigent persons.
 Access to civil justice act, §§7A-474.1 to 7A-474.5.
  See LEGAL SERVICES PROGRAMS.
 Class action unpaid residuals.
  Payment to indigent person's attorney fund and
   state bar for civil legal services to indigents,
   §1-267.10(b).
 Fees for preparation of copies.
  Not chargeable to attorney appointed to
   represent indigent at state expense,
   §7A-308(b1).
 Indigent defense services act, §§7A-498 to
  7A-498.8.
  See INDIGENT DEFENSE SERVICES.
 Innocence claim inquiry.
  Appointment of counsel.
   Formal inquiry, §15A-1467(b).
   Judicial review by three-judge panel,
    §15A-1469(e).
 Representation of indigent persons generally.
  See INDIGENT DEFENSE SERVICES.
Industrial commission.
 Utilization of rehabilitation professionals and
  workers' compensation claims, ICRehabProf
  Rule VII.
**Industrial commission mediated settlement
 conferences.**
 Attendance, ICMediatedSettlmt Rule 4(a).
Influencing judge or juror, ProfCond Rule 3.5.
Innocence claim inquiry.
 Formal inquiry.
  Advice of counsel, indigency, appointment,
   §15A-1467(b).
 Judicial review by three-judge panel.
  Indigent persons.
   Appointment of counsel, relief from costs,
    §15A-1469(e).

ATTORNEYS AT LAW —Cont'd
Interest on lawyer's trust accounts, ProfCond
  Rule 1.15-4.
  Rules governing administration of plan, Bar Rules
    D.1301 to D.1316.
Interest on trust or fiduciary accounts,
  ProfCond Rule 1.15-2.
**International commercial arbitration and
  conciliation.**
  Representation by attorney, §1-567.48(b).
  Conciliation proceedings, §1-567.79.
**Interstate and international law firm
  registration,** Bar Rules E.0201 to E.0206.
  Certificate, Bar Rule E.0204.
  Conditions, Bar Rule E.0202.
  Effect, Bar Rule E.0205.
  Fee, Bar Rule E.0203.
  Nonrenewal of registration, Bar Rule E.0206.
  Required, Bar Rule E.0201.
IOLTA, ProfCond Rule 1.15-4.
  Rules governing administration of plan, Bar Rules
    D.1301 to D.1316.
Judges.
  Ex parte communications with, ProfCond Rule
    3.5.
  False statements regarding, ProfCond Rule 8.2.
  Former judges.
    Conflict of interest, ProfCond Rule 1.12.
  Influencing, ProfCond Rule 3.5.
Judgments.
  Attorney in action not to probate papers therein.
    Final judgments in which documents verified in
      violation of section.
      Validation of certain documents verified by
        attorneys, §47-8.1.
**Judicial district grievance committees, rules
  governing,** Bar Rules B.0201 to B.0207.
  Form letters, Bar Rules B.0208 to B.0217.
Jury.
  Argument of counsel, §7A-97.
    Court's control of argument, §7A-97.
  Communicating with after discharge, ProfCond
    Rule 3.5.
  Ex parte communications with, ProfCond Rule
    3.5.
  Influencing, ProfCond Rule 3.5.
Juvenile code.
  Custody hearings.
    Determining need for continued secure or
      nonsecure custody.
      Right to counsel at hearing, §7B-506.
Juvenile delinquency law specialist.
  Recognition as specialist, Bar Rule D.2503.
  Standards for certification, Bar Rule D.2508.
    Continuing certification, Bar Rule D.2509.
  Subspecialty, criminal law specialist, Bar Rule
    D.2502.
Knowledge and skill.
  Competent representation, ProfCond Rule 1.1.
Land examiners.
  Torrens system registration, §§43-4, 43-5.
Law firms.
  Arbitration of internal disputes, Bar Rules E.0401
    to E.0410.
    Administration of program, Bar Rule E.0404.
    Authority to adopt amendments and
      regulations, Bar Rule E.0410.
    Confidentiality, Bar Rule E.0409.
    Expenses and fees of arbitrators, Bar Rule
      E.0408.
    Jurisdiction, Bar Rule E.0403.

ATTORNEYS AT LAW —Cont'd
Law firms —Cont'd
  Arbitration of internal disputes —Cont'd
    List of arbitrators, Bar Rule E.0406.
    Purposes of state bar rules, Bar Rule E.0401.
    Selection of arbitrators, Bar Rule E.0407.
    Submission to arbitration, Bar Rule E.0402.
    Uniform arbitration act to govern procedures,
      Bar Rule E.0405.
    Voluntary program, Bar Rule E.0402.
  Defined, ProfCond Rule 1.0.
  Fee sharing with nonlawyer, ProfCond Rule 5.4.
  Forming partnership with nonlawyer, ProfCond
    Rule 5.4.
  Imputation of conflict of interest, ProfCond Rule
    1.10.
  Names and letterheads, ProfCond Rule 7.5.
  Nonlawyer assistants, responsibilities, ProfCond
    Rule 5.3.
  Professional corporation or association.
    Practice in, ProfCond Rule 5.4.
  Professional corporations and professional limited
    liability companies practicing law,
    regulations, Bar Rules E.0101 to E.0106.
  Professional independence of lawyer, ProfCond
    Rule 5.4.
  Registration of interstate law firms, Bar Rules
    E.0201 to E.0206.
  Responsibilities of partners, managers and
    supervisory lawyers, ProfCond Rule 5.1.
  Restriction on practice, ProfCond Rule 5.6.
  State bar.
    Interstate and international law firm
      registration, Bar Rules E.0201 to E.0206.
  Subordinate lawyer, responsibilities, ProfCond
    Rule 5.2.
  Unauthorized practice of law, ProfCond Rule 5.5.
**Law students, rules governing practical
  training,** Bar Rules C.0201 to C.0207.
  Activities permitted by students, Bar Rule C.0206.
  Certification as legal intern, Bar Rule C.0204.
  Definitions, Bar Rule C.0202.
  Eligibility to engage in activities permitted, Bar
    Rule C.0203.
  Form of withdrawal of dean's certificate, Bar Rule
    C.0204.
  Purposes, Bar Rule C.0201.
  Supervising attorneys, Bar Rule C.0205.
  Use of student's name, Bar Rule C.0207.
Lawyer referral service.
  Participation, ProfCond Rule 7.2.
Lawyer's trust accounts.
  Audit.
    By investigative subpoena, Bar Rule B.0128.
  Interest on lawyer's trust accounts (IOLTA).
    Audit of accounts, Bar Rule D.1313.
    Disbursement of funds, Bar Rule D.1313.
    Funding for program, Bar Rule D.1312.
    Investment criteria, Bar Rule D.1313.
    IOLTA board of trustees, Bar Rules D.1301 to
      D.1316.
      Annual report of board, Bar Rule D.1315.
      Appointment and removal of members, Bar
        Rule D.1306.
      Chairperson, appointment, Bar Rule D.1310.
      Funding for program carried out by board,
        Bar Rule D.1312.
      Jurisdiction and authority of board, Bar Rule
        D.1302.
      Lay participation, Bar Rule D.1305.
      Meetings of board, Bar Rule D.1314.

ATTORNEYS AT LAW —Cont'd
Lawyer's trust accounts —Cont'd
Interest on lawyer's trust accounts (IOLTA)
—Cont'd
IOLTA board of trustees —Cont'd
Purposes of board, Bar Rule D.1301.
Responsibility for operating program of board,
Bar Rule D.1303.
Severability of provisions, Bar Rule D.1316.
Size of board, Bar Rule D.1304.
Staggered terms, Bar Rule D.1308.
Succession in office, Bar Rule D.1309.
Terms of office, Bar Rule D.1307.
Vice-chairperson, appointment, Bar Rule
D.1311.
Maintenance of accounts, Bar Rule D.1313.
Legal ethics, procedures for ruling on
questions, Bar Rules D.0101 to D.0104.
Legal knowledge and skill.
Competent representation, ProfCond Rule 1.1.
Legal services organizations.
Limited legal services programs, ProfCond Rule
6.5.
Membership in, ProfCond Rule 6.3.
Legal services provided by law students.
Rules governing, Bar Rules C.0201 to C.0207.
Letterheads.
Law firm names and letterheads, ProfCond Rule
7.5.
Letter of warning.
Issuance by grievance committee, Bar Rule
B.0113.
Letters of caution.
Issuance by grievance committee, Bar Rule
B.0113.
Licenses.
Forfeiture of license.
Felony convictions, §15A-1331A.
Inherent powers of courts unaffected, §84-36.
Issuance, Bar Rules C.0102, C.0103.
Comity applicants, AdmissPrac Rule .1301.
General applicants, AdmissPrac Rule .1302.
Restoration of license ordered.
Duty of board of law examiners to issue, §84-24.
Statewide license for privilege of practicing.
Firm or corporation.
Not issued in name of, §105-41(e).
License not authorization to practice, §105-41(i).
Not transferable, §105-41(a).
Personal privilege licenses, §105-41(e).
Required, §105-41(a).
Tax for each license, §105-41(a).
Counties and cities levying, prohibition,
§105-41(h).
Exemptions, §105-41(b).
Surrender while under investigation, Bar Rule
B.0117.
License taxes.
Statewide license for privilege of practicing,
§105-41.
Limited legal services programs, ProfCond Rule
6.5.
Limited liability companies.
Professional limited liability companies,
regulations for practicing law, Bar Rules
E.0101 to E.0106.
Limiting liability.
Prospective agreement limiting lawyer's liability.
Prohibition, ProfCond Rule 1.8.
Limiting scope of representation, ProfCond Rule
1.2.

ATTORNEYS AT LAW —Cont'd
List of attorneys.
Secretary of revenue.
Clerk of superior court to furnish list to
secretary, §7A-110.
Literary or media rights.
Negotiating agreement with client, ProfCond Rule
1.8.
Lobbying.
Lawyer holding public office, ProfCond Rule 6.6.
Local government finance.
Bond issues.
Contract involving legal services, §159-131.
Employment of bond attorneys, §159-123(e), (f).
Malpractice.
Agreement limiting lawyer's liability or settling
claim, ProfCond Rule 1.8.
Failure to file complaint on time.
Attorney liable for cost, §84-12.
Fraudulent practice.
Liability of attorney in double damages, §84-13.
Professional liability insurance.
Certificate of coverage provided by bar
members, Bar Rule A.0204.
Mediation.
Former mediators.
Conflict of interest, ProfCond Rule 1.12.
Lawyers serving as third-party neutrals, ProfCond
Rule 2.4.
Medicolegal guidelines for attorney-physician
relationship, MLG Rules 1 to 6.
Mental health, developmental disabilities and
substance abuse.
Involuntary commitment.
District court hearing.
Discharge of counsel.
Substance abusers, §122C-289.
Duty of assigned counsel.
Substance abusers, §122C-289.
Representation of state's interest,
§122C-268(b).
Respondent's right to counsel, §122C-268(d).
Lawyer assistance program, Bar Rules D.0601 to
D.0623.
See LAWYERS ASSISTANCE PROGRAM.
Rights of clients.
24-hour facilities.
Contact and consultation with legal counsel,
§122C-62(a).
Release of information to attorney, §122C-53(i).
Special counsel to represent the respondent and
the state.
Employment, §122C-270.
Misappropriation of entrusted property.
Duty to report, ProfCond Rule 1.15-2.
Misconduct, ProfCond Rule 8.4.
Disciplinary rules of state bar generally, Bar
Rules B.0101 to B.0217. See within this
heading, "Disciplinary proceedings."
Reporting, ProfCond Rule 8.3.
Misdemeanors.
Practice of law by disqualified persons, §84-2.
Solicitation of retainer or contract for legal
services, §84-38.
Unauthorized practice of law, §84-8(a).
Motions.
Out-of-state attorneys.
Motion for admission to practice law in state,
§84-4.1.
Municipalities.
Defense of employees and officers, §160A-167.

ATTORNEYS AT LAW —Cont'd
Municipalities —Cont'd
Voting rights act of 1965.
Publications in North Carolina register,
§120-30.9H.
Submission of charges to United States attorney
general by municipal attorney, §120-30.9F.
Nonresidents.
Out-of-state attorneys.
Admission to practice law, §84-4.1.
Nontestimonial identification.
Right to counsel, §15A-279(d).
Oaths.
Admission to practice of law, §84-1.
Attorney in action not to probate papers therein.
Validation of certain documents verified by
attorneys, §47-8.1.
Form of oaths of office, §11-11.
Obstructing party's access to evidence,
ProfCond Rule 3.4.
Opposing party and counsel.
Fairness to, ProfCond Rule 3.4.
Organization as client.
Representing, ProfCond Rule 1.13.
Out-of-state attorneys.
Practice of law.
Admission to practice, §84-4.1.
Summary revocation of permission, §84-4.2.
Parole.
Indigent parolees.
Entitlement to counsel, §148-62.1.
Partnerships.
Fee sharing with non-lawyer, ProfCond Rule 5.4.
Firm names and letterheads, ProfCond Rule 7.5.
Forming partnership with non-lawyer, ProfCond
Rule 5.4.
Imputation of conflict of interest, ProfCond Rule
1.10.
Non-lawyer assistants, responsibilities, ProfCond
Rule 5.3.
Professional independence of lawyer, ProfCond
Rule 5.4.
Responsibilities of partners, managers and
supervisory lawyers, ProfCond Rule 5.1.
Restriction on practice, ProfCond Rule 5.6.
Subordinate lawyer, responsibilities, ProfCond
Rule 5.2.
Unauthorized practice of law, ProfCond Rule 5.5.
Pleading, signing and verifying, §1A-1 Rule 11.
Practice of law.
Accountants.
Engaging in practice of law prohibited, §93-1(b).
Collection agencies.
Unauthorized practice of law, §58-70-120.
Corporations.
Attorney retained or employed by corporation,
§84-5(b).
Nonprofit corporations.
Indigent legal services by, §84-5.1.
Prohibition as to practice of law by corporation,
§84-5(a).
Violations of provisions.
Misdemeanor, §84-8(a).
Defined, §84-2.1.
Disqualification of certain persons, §84-2.
Foreclosures.
Fee for conducting foreclosures.
Prohibited to all except licensed attorneys,
§84-6.
Inherent powers of courts unaffected, §84-36.
Oath on admission to practice, §84-1.

ATTORNEYS AT LAW —Cont'd
Practice of law —Cont'd
Out-of-state attorneys.
Admission to practice, §84-4.1.
Summary revocation of permission, §84-4.2.
Professional corporations and professional limited
liability companies.
Regulations for practicing law, Bar Rules
E.0101 to E.0106.
Pro hac vice, §84-4.1.
State bar.
Persons other than members of state prohibited
from practicing law, §84-4.
Unauthorized practice.
Actions by private persons damaged by
unauthorized practice, §84-10.1.
Actions by state bar, §84-37(a).
Additional nature of provisions, §84-37(e).
Advisory opinions, §84-37(f).
Injunction, §84-37(b).
Plaintiff may examine adverse party,
§84-37(d).
Venue, §84-37(c).
Appearance for creditor in insolvency and
certain other proceedings by anyone except
attorney, §84-9.
Authorized practice committee procedures, Bar
Rules D.0201 to D.0207.
Collection agencies, §58-70-120.
Disqualified persons, §84-2.
Exceptions, §84-7.1.
Fees derived from unauthorized practice.
Collection prohibited, §84-8(b).
Foreclosures.
Fee for conducting foreclosures.
Prohibited to all except licensed attorneys,
§84-6.
Indictments.
Duty of district attorneys to indict persons
upon receipt of information of violation,
§84-7.
Injunctions, §84-37(b).
District attorneys to bring injunction
proceedings upon application, §84-7.
Internship by law students for government
agencies.
Exception, §84-7.1.
Investigation by state bar, §84-37(a).
Legal clinics of law schools.
Exception, §84-7.1.
Misdemeanor, §84-8(a).
Persons other than members of state bar, §84-4.
Prepaid legal services plans, Bar Rules E.0301 to
E.0309.
Advertising of state bar approval prohibited, Bar
Rule E.0304.
Amendments, filing requirement, Bar Rule
E.0303.
Annual registration, Bar Rule E.0305.
Index of registered plans, Bar Rule E.0307.
Jurisdiction of state bar, Bar Rule E.0309.
Registration fee, Bar Rule E.0306.
Registration required, Bar Rule E.0301.
Registration site, Bar Rule E.0302.
State bar may not approve or disapprove plans,
Bar Rule E.0308.
Prepaid or group legal services plans.
Participation, ProfCond Rule 7.3.
Prisoner and attorney conference.
Secret listening, §§14-227.1, 14-227.3.

ATTORNEYS AT LAW —Cont'd

Probate and registration.
Attorney in action not to probate papers therein.
Validation of certain documents verified by
attorneys, §47-8.1.

Probate law specialty.
Certification standards for estate planning and
probate law specialty, Bar Rules D.2301 to
D.2307.

Probation.
Revocation hearing.
Right to counsel, §15A-1345(e).

Pro bono work.
Legal services provided by law students, Bar
Rules C.0201 to C.0207.

Professional conduct.
Abandoned property.
Entrusted property, ProfCond Rule 1.15-2.
Accounts.
Deposit of funds, ProfCond Rule 1.15-2.
Records and accountings, ProfCond Rule 1.15-3.
Actions impliedly authorized.
Disclosure of confidential information, ProfCond
Rule 1.6.
Lawyer may take, ProfCond Rule 1.2.
Admission to bar.
False statements, failure to disclose, ProfCond
Rule 8.1.
Adverse interest to client.
Acquiring, conflict of interest, ProfCond Rule
1.8.
Advertising, ProfCond Rule 7.2.
Communications of fields of practice, ProfCond
Rule 7.4.
Dramatization depicting fictional situation,
ProfCond Rule 7.1.
False or misleading communications concerning
services, ProfCond Rule 7.1.
Targeted communications, ProfCond Rule 7.3.
Advisor, ProfCond Rule 2.1.
Agent of lawyers' or judges' association.
Duty of confidentiality when acting as,
ProfCond Rule 1.6.
Aggregate settlement or agreement.
Two or more clients, ProfCond Rule 1.8.
Agreements restricting practice, ProfCond Rule
5.6.
Allocation of authority between client and lawyer,
ProfCond Rule 1.2.
Arbitrators.
Former arbitrators.
Conflict of interest, ProfCond Rule 1.12.
Lawyers serving as third-party neutrals,
ProfCond Rule 2.4.
Attorney-client privilege.
Client-lawyer confidentiality, ProfCond Rule
1.6.
Audit by state bar, ProfCond Rule 1.15-3.
Bank accounts.
Deposit of funds, ProfCond Rule 1.15-2.
Records and accountings, ProfCond Rule 1.15-3.
Bank directive.
Lawyer maintaining trust or fiduciary accounts,
ProfCond Rule 1.15-2.
Bank receipts.
Record requirements, ProfCond Rule 1.15-3.
Bank statements.
Record requirements, ProfCond Rule 1.15-3.
Bar admission.
False statements, failure to disclose, ProfCond
Rule 8.1.

ATTORNEYS AT LAW —Cont'd

Professional conduct —Cont'd
Business transactions with clients.
Conflict of interest, ProfCond Rule 1.8.
Canceled checks.
Record requirements, ProfCond Rule 1.15-3.
Candidates for judicial office.
Compliance with code of judicial conduct,
ProfCond Rule 8.2.
False statements regarding, ProfCond Rule 8.2.
Candor toward tribunal, ProfCond Rule 3.3.
Capacity of client diminished, ProfCond Rule 1.14.
Checks.
Canceled checks, copies.
Record requirements, ProfCond Rule 1.15-3.
Choice of law.
Disciplinary authority of North Carolina,
ProfCond Rule 8.5.
Client-lawyer confidentiality, ProfCond Rule 1.6.
Client's decisions.
Lawyer to abide by, ProfCond Rule 1.2.
Client with diminished capacity, ProfCond Rule
1.14.
Communications concerning lawyer's services,
ProfCond Rule 7.1.
Communications of fields of practice, ProfCond
Rule 7.4.
Communications with clients, ProfCond Rule 1.4.
Fees and expenses, ProfCond Rule 1.5.
Communications with judge or jurors.
Ex parte communications, ProfCond Rule 3.5.
Communications with person represented by
counsel, ProfCond Rule 4.2.
Compensation.
Acceptance of compensation from other than
client, ProfCond Rule 1.8.
Fees and expenses, ProfCond Rule 1.5.
Law firm.
Fee sharing with non-lawyer, ProfCond Rule
5.4.
Sale or purchase of practice.
Increase in fees, ProfCond Rule 1.17.
Competence to handle legal matter, ProfCond
Rule 1.1.
Concurrent conflict of interest, ProfCond Rule 1.7.
Specific rules, ProfCond Rule 1.8.
Confidential information, ProfCond Rule 1.6.
Confidential government information.
Lawyer acquiring as public officer or
employees.
Representing client with interest adverse to
information, ProfCond Rule 1.11.
Defined, ProfCond Rule 1.0.
Discussions with prospective clients, ProfCond
Rule 1.18.
IOLTA accounts.
Defined, disclosure, restrictions, ProfCond
Rule 1.15-4.
Confirmed in writing.
Defined, ProfCond Rule 1.0.
Conflict of interest.
Current clients, ProfCond Rule 1.7.
Specific rules, ProfCond Rule 1.8.
Former clients.
Duties to, ProfCond Rule 1.9.
Former judges, arbitrators, mediators or other
third party neutrals, ProfCond Rule 1.12.
Government officers and employees.
Special conflicts, former and current officers
and employees, ProfCond Rule 1.11.
Imputation, ProfCond Rule 1.10.

ATTORNEYS AT LAW —Cont'd
Professional conduct —Cont'd
Conflict of interest —Cont'd
Lawyer as witness, ProfCond Rule 3.7.
Prospective clients, matters with, ProfCond Rule 1.18.
Sale or purchase of practice, notice, ProfCond Rule 1.17.
Consent.
Informed consent.
Aggregate settlement or agreement for two or more clients, ProfCond Rule 1.8.
Communicating with client when client's consent required, ProfCond Rule 1.4.
Defined, ProfCond Rule 1.0.
Consultations with client, ProfCond Rule 1.4.
Contingent fees and contingent fee agreements, ProfCond Rule 1.5.
Contracts.
Contingent fee agreements, ProfCond Rule 1.5.
Restriction on practice, ProfCond Rule 5.6.
Criminal cases.
Abiding by client's decision, ProfCond Rule 1.2.
Contingent fees, charging prohibited, ProfCond Rule 1.5.
Meritorious claims and contentions, ProfCond Rule 3.1.
Prosecutors, special responsibilities, ProfCond Rule 3.8.
Criminal conduct.
Client engaging in, remedial measures, ProfCond Rule 3.3.
Lawyer not to counsel client to engage in, ProfCond Rule 1.2.
Dealing with unrepresented person, ProfCond Rule 4.3.
Decisions of client.
Lawyer to abide by, ProfCond Rule 1.2.
Declining representation, ProfCond Rule 1.16.
Dedicated trust account.
Defined, ProfCond Rule 1.15-1.
Deposit of trust funds in, ProfCond Rule 1.15-2.
Definitions, ProfCond Rule 1.0.
Law-related services, ProfCond Rule 5.7.
Prepaid legal services plan or group services plan, ProfCond Rule 7.3.
Prospective client, ProfCond Rule 1.18.
Safekeeping property, ProfCond Rule 1.15-1.
Sexual relations with clients, ProfCond Rule 1.19.
Deposit of fiduciary funds, ProfCond Rule 1.15-2.
Deposit of trust funds, ProfCond Rule 1.15-2.
Deposit slips.
Record requirements, ProfCond Rule 1.15-3.
Diligence in representation, ProfCond Rule 1.3.
Diminished capacity.
Client with, ProfCond Rule 1.14.
Direct contact with prospective clients, ProfCond Rule 7.3.
Disbarred attorney.
Employing as legal clerk or assistant, ProfCond Rule 5.5.
Disciplinary authority of North Carolina.
Choice of law, ProfCond Rule 8.5.
Lawyer admitted to practice in state subject to, ProfCond Rule 8.5.
Disciplinary matters.
False statements, failure to disclose, ProfCond Rule 8.1.
Disclosure of confidential information, ProfCond Rule 1.6.

ATTORNEYS AT LAW —Cont'd
Professional conduct —Cont'd
Discovery.
Frivolous discovery, ProfCond Rule 3.4.
Dispute as to fees.
Lawyer responsibilities, ProfCond Rule 1.5.
Disqualification.
Former judge, clerk, arbitrator, mediator or third party neutral, ProfCond Rule 1.12.
Imputed disqualification.
Principles of, ProfCond Rule 1.10.
Public officers and employees.
Special conflicts, former and current officers and employees, ProfCond Rule 1.11.
Disrupting tribunal, ProfCond Rule 3.5.
Division of fees, ProfCond Rule 1.5.
Lawyer or firm sharing fees with nonlawyer, ProfCond Rule 5.4.
Dramatization depicting fictional situation, ProfCond Rule 7.1.
Elections.
Lawyer candidate for judicial office.
Compliance with Code of Judicial Conduct, ProfCond Rule 8.2.
Electronic contact with prospective clients, ProfCond Rule 7.3.
Employment agreements.
Restriction on practice, ProfCond Rule 5.6.
Entity as client.
Representing organization, ProfCond Rule 1.13.
Entrusted property, ProfCond Rule 1.15-2.
Defined, ProfCond Rule 1.15-1.
Evaluation for use by third parties, ProfCond Rule 2.3.
Evidence.
Altering, destroying or concealing, ProfCond Rule 3.4.
False evidence offered, ProfCond Rule 3.3.
Obstructing party's access to, ProfCond Rule 3.4.
Prohibited acts as to opposing party and counsel, ProfCond Rule 3.4.
Excessive fees and expenses.
Charging client prohibited, factors in determining, ProfCond Rule 1.5.
Ex parte communications with judge or jurors, ProfCond Rule 3.5.
Ex parte proceedings.
Information to tribunal, ProfCond Rule 3.3.
Expediting litigation, ProfCond Rule 3.2.
Explaining matter to client, ProfCond Rule 1.4.
Extrajudicial statements, ProfCond Rule 3.6.
Fairness to opposing party and counsel, ProfCond Rule 3.4.
False communications concerning services, ProfCond Rule 7.1.
False evidence offered, ProfCond Rule 3.3.
False or misleading statements.
Bar admission, disciplinary matters, ProfCond Rule 8.1.
Communications concerning services, ProfCond Rule 7.1.
Regarding judges or candidates for judicial office, ProfCond Rule 8.2.
To third persons, ProfCond Rule 4.1.
To tribunal, ProfCond Rule 3.3.
Fees and expenses, ProfCond Rule 1.5.
Acceptance of compensation from other than client, ProfCond Rule 1.8.
Law firm.
Fee sharing with non-lawyer, ProfCond Rule 5.4.

ATTORNEYS AT LAW —Cont'd
Professional conduct —Cont'd
Fees and expenses —Cont'd
Sale or purchase of practice, increase, ProfCond Rule 1.17.
Fiduciary funds.
Defined, ProfCond Rule 1.15-1.
Deposit, ProfCond Rule 1.15-2.
Financial assistance to client, ProfCond Rule 1.8.
Firm.
Defined, ProfCond Rule 1.0.
Fee sharing with non-lawyer, ProfCond Rule 5.4.
Forming partnership with non-lawyer, ProfCond Rule 5.4.
Imputation of conflict of interest, ProfCond Rule 1.10.
Names and letterheads, ProfCond Rule 7.5.
Non-lawyer assistants, responsibilities, ProfCond Rule 5.3.
Professional corporation or association.
Practice in, ProfCond Rule 5.4.
Professional independence of lawyer, ProfCond Rule 5.4.
Responsibilities of partners, managers and supervisory lawyers, ProfCond Rule 5.1.
Restriction on practice, ProfCond Rule 5.6.
Subordinate lawyer, responsibilities, ProfCond Rule 5.2.
Unauthorized practice of law, ProfCond Rule 5.5.
Firm names and letterheads, ProfCond Rule 7.5.
Forfeiture.
Contingent fee.
Charging in criminal or civil forfeiture proceeding, ProfCond Rule 1.5.
Former clients.
Duties to, ProfCond Rule 1.9.
Former judges, arbitrators, mediators or other third party neutrals.
Conflict of interest, ProfCond Rule 1.12.
Fraud.
Client engaging in fraudulent conduct, remedial measures, ProfCond Rule 3.3.
Defined, ProfCond Rule 1.0.
Lawyer not to counsel client to engage in fraudulent conduct, ProfCond Rule 1.2.
Frivolous claims and contentions, ProfCond Rule 3.1.
Frivolous discovery, ProfCond Rule 3.4.
General trust account.
Defined, ProfCond Rule 1.15-1.
Deposit of trust funds in, ProfCond Rule 1.15-2.
Gift from client.
Soliciting, ProfCond Rule 1.8.
Government officers and employees.
Action as public official, ProfCond Rule 6.6.
Conflict of interest.
Special conflicts, former and current officers and employees, ProfCond Rule 1.11.
Impartiality and decorum of tribunal.
Respecting, ProfCond Rule 3.5.
Implied authorization to take action, ProfCond Rule 1.2.
Disclosure of confidential informations, ProfCond Rule 1.6.
Imputation of conflict of interest, ProfCond Rule 1.10.
Imputed disqualification.
Principles of, ProfCond Rule 1.10.
Inadvertent receipt of writing, ProfCond Rule 4.4.

ATTORNEYS AT LAW —Cont'd
Professional conduct —Cont'd
Independent professional judgment.
Lawyer to exercise, ProfCond Rule 2.1.
Influencing judge or juror, ProfCond Rule 3.5.
Informed consent.
Aggregate settlement or agreement for two or more clients, ProfCond Rule 1.8.
Communicating with client when client's consent required, ProfCond Rule 1.4.
Defined, ProfCond Rule 1.0.
Informing client as to status of matter, ProfCond Rule 1.4.
In-person contact with prospective clients, ProfCond Rule 7.3.
Interest on lawyers' trust accounts, ProfCond Rule 1.15-4.
Interest on trust or fiduciary accounts, ProfCond Rule 1.15-2.
Iolta, ProfCond Rule 1.15-4.
Judges.
Ex parte communications with, ProfCond Rule 3.5.
False statements regarding, ProfCond Rule 8.2.
Former judges.
Conflict of interest, ProfCond Rule 1.12.
Influencing, ProfCond Rule 3.5.
Jurors.
Communicating with after discharge, ProfCond Rule 3.5.
Ex parte communications with, ProfCond Rule 3.5.
Influencing, ProfCond Rule 3.5.
Jury trial.
Waiver in criminal case.
Abiding by client's decision, ProfCond Rule 1.2.
Knowingly.
Defined, ProfCond Rule 1.0.
Knowledge and skill.
Competent representation, ProfCond Rule 1.1.
Law firm.
Defined, ProfCond Rule 1.0.
Fee sharing with non-lawyer, ProfCond Rule 5.4.
Forming partnership with non-lawyer, ProfCond Rule 5.4.
Imputation of conflict of interest, ProfCond Rule 1.10.
Names and letterheads, ProfCond Rule 7.5.
Non-lawyer assistants, responsibilities, ProfCond Rule 5.3.
Professional corporation or association.
Practice in, ProfCond Rule 5.4.
Professional independence of lawyer, ProfCond Rule 5.4.
Responsibilities of partners, managers and supervisory lawyers, ProfCond Rule 5.1.
Restriction on practice, ProfCond Rule 5.6.
Subordinate lawyer, responsibilities, ProfCond Rule 5.2.
Unauthorized practice of law, ProfCond Rule 5.5.
Law reform activities affecting client's interest, ProfCond Rule 6.4.
Law-related services.
Responsibilities regarding, ProfCond Rule 5.7.
Lawyer referral service.
Participation, ProfCond Rule 7.2.
Lawyer's or judge's assistance programs.
Confidentiality when lawyer acting as agent for, ProfCond Rule 1.6.

ATTORNEYS AT LAW —Cont'd
Professional conduct —Cont'd
Legal entity as client.
Representing, ProfCond Rule 1.13.
Legal knowledge and skill.
Competent representation, ProfCond Rule 1.1.
Legal services organizations.
Limited legal services programs, ProfCond Rule 6.5.
Membership in, ProfCond Rule 6.3.
Letterheads.
Firm names and letterheads, ProfCond Rule 7.5.
Limited legal services programs, ProfCond Rule 6.5.
Limiting liability.
Prospective agreement limiting lawyer's liability.
Prohibition, ProfCond Rule 1.8.
Limiting scope of representation, ProfCond Rule 1.2.
Literary or media rights.
Negotiating agreement with client, ProfCond Rule 1.8.
Lobbying.
Lawyer holding public office, ProfCond Rule 6.6.
Malpractice.
Agreement limiting lawyer's liability or settling claim, ProfCond Rule 1.8.
Mediators.
Former mediators.
Conflict of interest, ProfCond Rule 1.12.
Lawyers serving as third-party neutrals, ProfCond Rule 2.4.
Mental impairment.
Client with diminished capacity, ProfCond Rule 1.14.
Meritorious claims and contentions, ProfCond Rule 3.1.
Minority.
Client with diminished capacity, ProfCond Rule 1.14.
Misappropriation of entrusted property.
Duty to report, ProfCond Rule 1.15-2.
Misconduct, ProfCond Rule 8.4.
Reporting, ProfCond Rule 8.3.
Names.
Firm names and letterheads, ProfCond Rule 7.5.
Nonlawyers in law firms.
Responsibility for, ProfCond Rule 5.3.
Notice of sale or purchase of practice, ProfCond Rule 1.17.
Obstructing party's access to evidence, ProfCond Rule 3.4.
Opposing party and counsel.
Fairness to, ProfCond Rule 3.4.
Organization as client.
Representing, ProfCond Rule 1.13.
Partnerships.
Fee sharing with non-lawyer, ProfCond Rule 5.4.
Firm names and letterheads, ProfCond Rule 7.5.
Forming partnership with non-lawyer, ProfCond Rule 5.4.
Imputation of conflict of interest, ProfCond Rule 1.10.
Non-lawyer assistants, responsibilities, ProfCond Rule 5.3.
Partner defined, ProfCond Rule 1.0.

ATTORNEYS AT LAW —Cont'd
Professional conduct —Cont'd
Partnerships —Cont'd
Professional independence of lawyer, ProfCond Rule 5.4.
Responsibilities of partners, managers and supervisory lawyers, ProfCond Rule 5.1.
Restriction on practice, ProfCond Rule 5.6.
Subordinate lawyer, responsibilities, ProfCond Rule 5.2.
Unauthorized practice of law, ProfCond Rule 5.5.
Person represented by counsel.
Communications with, ProfCond Rule 4.2.
Plea in criminal case.
Abiding by client's decision, ProfCond Rule 1.2.
Political, economic, social or moral views of client.
Representation not endorsement, ProfCond Rule 1.2.
Preamble, ProfCond Rule 0.1.
Prepaid or group legal services plans.
Participation, ProfCond Rule 7.3.
Professional corporation or association.
Practice in, ProfCond Rule 5.4.
Professional judgment.
Independent professional judgment, ProfCond Rule 2.1.
Lawyer may exercise, ProfCond Rule 1.2.
Professional misconduct, ProfCond Rule 8.4.
Reporting, ProfCond Rule 8.3.
Prompt representation, ProfCond Rule 1.3.
Proprietary interest in cause action.
Acquiring, ProfCond Rule 1.8.
Prosecutors.
Special responsibilities, ProfCond Rule 3.8.
Prospective clients.
Direct contact with, ProfCond Rule 7.3.
Duties to, ProfCond Rule 1.18.
Protective action.
Client with diminished capacity, ProfCond Rule 1.14.
Publicity during trial, ProfCond Rule 3.6.
Public officers and employees.
Action as public official, ProfCond Rule 6.6.
Conflict of interest.
Special conflicts, former and current officers and employees, ProfCond Rule 1.11.
Purchase of practice, ProfCond Rule 1.17.
Reasonable.
Defined, ProfCond Rule 1.0.
Reasonable belief.
Defined, ProfCond Rule 1.0.
Reasonable diligence and promptness in representation, ProfCond Rule 1.3.
Reasonably should know.
Defined, ProfCond Rule 1.0.
Records and accountings, ProfCond Rule 1.15-3.
Referral service.
Participation, ProfCond Rule 7.2.
Reform activities affecting client's interest, ProfCond Rule 6.4.
Reporting professional misconduct, ProfCond Rule 8.3.
Requests for information.
Compliance with client's reasonable request, ProfCond Rule 1.4.
Respect for third persons rights, ProfCond Rule 4.4.
Restriction on practice, ProfCond Rule 5.6.
Safekeeping property, ProfCond Rule 1.15.
Definitions, ProfCond Rule 1.15-1.

ATTORNEYS AT LAW —Cont'd
Professional conduct —Cont'd
Safekeeping property —Cont'd
General rules, ProfCond Rule 1.15-2.
Interest on lawyers' trust accounts, ProfCond
Rule 1.15-4.
Records and accounting, ProfCond Rule 1.15-3.
Sale of practice, ProfCond Rule 1.17.
Scope of representation, ProfCond Rule 1.2.
Organization as client, ProfCond Rule 1.13.
Scope of rules, ProfCond Rule 0.2.
Screened.
Defined, ProfCond Rule 1.0.
Securities.
Holding in fiduciary account, ProfCond Rule
1.15-2.
Segregation of lawyer's funds, ProfCond Rule
1.15-2.
Settlements.
Abiding by client's decision, ProfCond Rule 1.2.
Aggregate settlement for two or more clients,
ProfCond Rule 1.8.
Sexual relations with clients, ProfCond Rule 1.19.
Sharing fees with nonlawyer, ProfCond Rule 5.4.
Soliciting professional employment, ProfCond Rule
7.3.
Advertising, ProfCond Rule 7.2.
Communications of fields of practice, ProfCond
Rule 7.4.
Specialists.
Communications of fields of practice, ProfCond
Rule 7.4.
Stock.
Holding, identification, ProfCond Rule 1.15-2.
Substantial.
Defined, ProfCond Rule 1.0.
Suspended attorney.
Employing as legal clerk or assistant, ProfCond
Rule 5.5.
Tampering with evidence, ProfCond Rule 3.4.
Targeted communications, ProfCond Rule 7.3.
Telephone contact with prospective clients,
ProfCond Rule 7.3.
Terminating representation, ProfCond Rule 1.16.
Terminology, ProfCond Rule 1.0.
Third parties.
Communications with persons represented by
counsel, ProfCond Rule 4.2.
Dealing with unrepresented person, ProfCond
Rule 4.3.
Evaluation for use by, ProfCond Rule 2.3.
Respect for third persons rights, ProfCond Rule
4.4.
Truthfulness to third persons, ProfCond Rule
4.1.
Third-party neutrals.
Former neutrals.
Conflict of interest, ProfCond Rule 1.12.
Lawyers serving as, ProfCond Rule 2.4.
Thoroughness and preparation.
Competent representation, ProfCond Rule 1.1.
Trial publicity, ProfCond Rule 3.6.
Tribunal.
Defined, ProfCond Rule 1.0.
Trust funds.
Accounting, ProfCond Rule 1.15-3.
Defined, ProfCond Rule 1.15-1.
Deposit, ProfCond Rule 1.15-2.
Interest on lawyers' trust accounts, ProfCond
Rule 1.15-4.

ATTORNEYS AT LAW —Cont'd
Professional conduct —Cont'd
Trust funds —Cont'd
Quarterly reconciliation of accounts, ProfCond
Rule 1.15-3.
Truthfulness in statements to others, ProfCond
Rule 4.1.
Unauthorized practice of law, ProfCond Rule 5.5.
Unclaimed entrusted property, ProfCond Rule
1.15-2.
Unrepresented persons.
Dealing with, ProfCond Rule 4.3.
Violation of rules of professional conduct.
Acts constituting professional misconduct,
ProfCond Rule 8.4.
Lawyer in firm.
Nonlawyer's violations, ProfCond Rule 5.3.
Responsibility for other lawyer's violations,
ProfCond Rule 5.1.
Reporting professional misconduct, ProfCond
Rule 8.3.
Waiver of jury trial in criminal case.
Abiding by client's decision, ProfCond Rule 1.2.
Withdrawal from representation, ProfCond Rule
1.16.
Witness.
Lawyer as, ProfCond Rule 3.7.
Writing.
Contingent fee agreements, required, ProfCond
Rule 1.5.
Defined, ProfCond Rule 1.0.
Inadvertent receipt of writing, ProfCond Rule
4.4.
Written communications.
Direct contact with prospective clients,
ProfCond Rule 7.3.
Professional corporations.
Practice in, ProfCond Rule 5.4.
Professional counselors.
Exemption from licensure, §90-332.1(a).
Professional judgment.
Independent professional judgment, ProfCond
Rule 2.1.
Lawyer may exercise, ProfCond Rule 1.2.
Professional liability insurance.
Certificate of coverage.
State bar members to provide, Bar Rule
A.0204.
Professional limited liability companies.
Regulations for practicing law, Bar Rules E.0101
to E.0106.
Additional information furnished state bar, Bar
Rule E.0105.
Administration of regulations, Bar Rule E.0105.
Appeal to state bar council, Bar Rule E.0105.
Application for certificate of registration.
Form, Bar Rule E.0106.
Application for renewal of certificate of
registration.
Form, Bar Rule E.0106.
Articles of amendment, merger and dissolution.
Filing with secretary of state bar, Bar Rule
E.0105.
Authority of state bar to adopt regulations, Bar
Rule E.0101.
Authority over professional matters, Bar Rule
E.0104.
Certificate of registration.
Form, Bar Rule E.0106.
Certification by council of North Carolina state
bar.
Form, Bar Rule E.0106.

ATTORNEYS AT LAW —Cont'd
Professional limited liability companies
  —Cont'd
  Regulations for practicing law —Cont'd
    Deceased or retired member's name may be
      retained in name of company, Bar Rule
      E.0102.
    Definitions, Bar Rule E.0101.
    Disqualified member's name not to appear in
      company's name, Bar Rule E.0102.
    Disqualified person not to receive income, Bar
      Rule E.0104.
    Expiration of certificate of registration, Bar
      Rule E.0103.
    Filing fees, Bar Rule E.0105.
    Forms, Bar Rule E.0106.
    Management, Bar Rule E.0104.
    Member becoming judge or official, name
      appearing in company name.
      Change of company name, Bar Rule E.0102.
    Name of company, Bar Rule E.0102.
    Records of state bar, Bar Rule E.0105.
    Registration, Bar Rule E.0103.
    Registration fees, Bar Rule E.0103.
    Renewal of certificate of registration, Bar Rule
      E.0103.
    Supplementation of statutory law, Bar Rule
      E.0101.
    Trade name allowed, Bar Rule E.0102.
    Words professional limited liability company to
      appear in name, Bar Rule E.0102.
Professional misconduct, ProfCond Rule 8.4.
  Reporting, ProfCond Rule 8.3.
Pro hac vice.
  Practice of law, §84-4.1.
Prompt representation, ProfCond Rule 1.3.
Proprietary interest in cause action.
  Acquiring, ProfCond Rule 1.8.
Prosecuting attorneys.
  See DISTRICT ATTORNEYS.
Prospective clients.
  Direct contact with, ProfCond Rule 7.3.
  Duties to, ProfCond Rule 1.18.
Publicity during trial, ProfCond Rule 3.6.
Purchase of practice, ProfCond Rule 1.17.
Real estate settlement agents' trust or escrow
  accounts.
  Interest earned paid to state bar, §45A-9.
Real property law specialty, Bar Rules D.2101 to
  D.2107.
  Applicability of other requirements, Bar Rule
    D.2107.
  Certification standards, Bar Rule D.2105.
    Continued certification, Bar Rule D.2106.
  Continuing legal education, Bar Rule D.2105.
    Continued certification, Bar Rule D.2106.
  Definition of specialty, Bar Rule D.2102.
  Establishment of specialty field, Bar Rule D.2101.
  Examination, Bar Rule D.2105.
  Peer review, Bar Rule D.2105.
    Continued certification, Bar Rule D.2106.
  Plan of legal specialization, applicability of
    provisions, Bar Rule D.2104.
  Recognition as specialist, Bar Rule D.2103.
  Standards for certification, Bar Rule D.2105.
  Standards for continued certification, Bar Rule
    D.2106.
  Suspension or revocation of certification.
    Continued certification, Bar Rule D.2106.
Reasonable diligence and promptness in
  representation, ProfCond Rule 1.3.

ATTORNEYS AT LAW —Cont'd
Records, ProfCond Rule 1.15-3.
  Public records.
    Confidential communications by legal counsel to
      public board or agency, §132-1.1.
    Trial preparation material, §132-1.9.
Referral service.
  Participation, ProfCond Rule 7.2.
Refrigeration contractors.
  Board of examiners.
    Power to retain counsel, §87-61.1(b).
Reinstatement after disbarment, suspension or
  transfer to disability in active status, Bar
  Rule B.0125.
Reinstatement after suspension for failure to
  comply with continuing legal education
  rules.
  Reinstatement hearing before administrative
    committee of state bar, Bar Rule D.1009.
Reinstatement from inactive status, Bar Rule
  D.0902.
Reporting professional misconduct, ProfCond
  Rule 8.3.
Representation of indigent persons generally.
  See INDIGENT DEFENSE SERVICES.
Reprimand.
  Imposition of discipline, Bar Rule B.0123.
  Issuance by grievance committee, Bar Rule
    B.0113.
Resignation while under investigation, Bar
  Rule B.0117.
Restoration of license ordered.
  Duty of board of law examiners to issue, §84-24.
Restriction on practice, ProfCond Rule 5.6.
Retail installment sales.
  Fees.
    Provisions included in provisions, §25A-21.
Rules for continuing legal education. See within
  this heading, "Continuing legal education."
Rules governing admission to practice of law.
  See within this heading, "Admission to
  practice."
Rules of professional conduct, ProfCond Rules
  1.0 to 8.5. See within this heading, "Professional
  conduct."
Safekeeping property, ProfCond Rule 1.15.
  Definitions, ProfCond Rule 1.15-1.
  General rules, ProfCond Rule 1.15-2.
  Interest on lawyers' trust accounts, ProfCond Rule
    1.15-4.
  Records and accounting, ProfCond Rule 1.15-3.
Sale of practice, ProfCond Rule 1.17.
Savings and loan associations.
  Legal services in connection with loans, §54B-165.
Scheduling conflicts.
  Guidelines for resolving.
    District and superior courts, SuperCt Rule 3.1.
Scope of representation, ProfCond Rule 1.2.
  Organization as client, ProfCond Rule 1.13.
Secret listening.
  Conference between prisoner and his attorney,
    §14-227.1(a).
    Admissibility as evidence, §14-227.1(b).
    Violations made misdemeanors, §14-227.3.
Securities.
  Holding in fiduciary account, ProfCond Rule
    1.15-2.
Segregation of lawyer's funds, ProfCond Rule
  1.15-2.
Settlements.
  Abiding by client's decision, ProfCond Rule 1.2.

ATTORNEYS AT LAW —Cont'd
Settlements —Cont'd
Aggregate settlement for two or more clients,
ProfCond Rule 1.8.
Sexual relations with clients, ProfCond Rule
1.19.
Sharing fees with nonlawyer, ProfCond Rule 5.4.
Sheriffs.
Practicing attorneys disqualified for office, §162-2.
Signing discovery requests, responses, etc.,
§1A-1 Rule 26(g).
Signing pleadings, §1A-1 Rule 11.
Social services.
Special county attorneys for social service
matters, §§108A-16 to 108A-18.
Solicitation of clients, §84-38.
Soliciting professional employment, ProfCond
Rule 7.3.
Advertising, ProfCond Rule 7.2.
Communications of fields of practice, ProfCond
Rule 7.4.
Solicitors.
See DISTRICT ATTORNEYS.
Specialists.
Communications of fields of practice, ProfCond
Rule 7.4.
Specialization, Bar Rules D.1701 to D.2709.
Appeal to state bar council, Bar Rule D.1804.
Appeal to Wake county superior court, Bar Rule
D.1805.
Applicant not in compliance with certification
standards, Bar Rule D.1801.
Applications incomplete, Bar Rule D.1801.
Areas of specialty, Bar Rule D.1725.
Audit of accounts maintained, Bar Rule D.1713.
Bankruptcy law specialty, Bar Rules D.2201 to
D.2207.
Board of legal specialization.
Annual report, Bar Rule D.1715.
Appointment and removal of members, Bar
Rule D.1706.
Chairperson, appointment, Bar Rule D.1710.
Hearing and appeal rules, Bar Rules D.1801 to
D.1806.
Jurisdiction and authority, Bar Rule D.1702.
Lay participation, Bar Rule D.1705.
Meetings, Bar Rule D.1714.
Operational responsibility, Bar Rule D.1703.
Powers and duties, Bar Rule D.1716.
Size of board, Bar Rule D.1704.
Succession in office, Bar Rule D.1709.
Term of office, Bar Rule D.1707.
Staggered terms, Bar Rule D.1708.
Vice-chairperson, appointment, Bar Rule
D.1711.
Certification of specialists.
Denial of continued certification, Bar Rule
D.1802.
Establishment of additional standards, Bar Rule
D.1722.
Hearing and appeal on denial of certification or
continued certification, Bar Rule D.1724.
Minimum standards for continued certification,
Bar Rules D.1720, D.1721.
Suspension or revocation of certification, Bar
Rule D.1723.
Procedure, Bar Rule D.1803.
Continuing legal education, accreditation
standards, Bar Rules D.1901 to D.1908.
Accreditation of courses, Bar Rule D.1906.
Accreditation of sponsors, Bar Rule D.1907.

ATTORNEYS AT LAW —Cont'd
Specialization —Cont'd
Continuing legal education, accreditation
standards —Cont'd
Alternatives to lecture-type CLE course
instruction, Bar Rule D.1905.
Applicants to make satisfactory showing of
requisite number of hours, Bar Rule
D.1901.
Computation of hours of instruction, Bar Rule
D.1904.
Definitions, Bar Rule D.1902.
Lecture-type CLE activities, Bar Rule D.1903.
Lecture-type CLE course instruction.
Alternatives, Bar Rule D.1905.
Showing by applicants, Bar Rule D.1908.
Criminal law specialty, certification standards,
Bar Rules D.2501 to D.2509.
Dependent certifying organizations, rules for
approval, Bar Rules D.2001 to D.2006.
Application procedure, Bar Rule D.2005.
Effect of approval, Bar Rule D.2006.
Factors considered, Bar Rule D.2003.
Policy statement as to guidelines, Bar Rule
D.2001.
Procedure generally, Bar Rule D.2002.
Standards for approval, Bar Rule D.2004.
Disbursement of funds, Bar Rule D.1713.
Establishment of additional standards for
certification, Bar Rule D.1722.
Estate planning and probate law specialty, Bar
Rules D.2301 to D.2307.
Examination for specialty.
Failure of written examination, Bar Rule
D.1801.
Family law specialty, certification standards, Bar
Rules D.2401 to D.2407.
Funding for program, Bar Rule D.1712.
Hearing and appeal on denial of certification or
continued certification, Bar Rule D.1724.
Appeal to state bar council, Bar Rule D.1804.
Applications incomplete or applicant not in
compliance with certification standards, Bar
Rule D.1801.
Denial of continued certification, Bar Rule
D.1802.
Expenses related to, Bar Rule D.1806.
Failure of written examination, Bar Rule
D.1801.
Judicial review of state bar council decisions,
Bar Rule D.1805.
Notices, Bar Rule D.1806.
Suspension or revocation of certification, Bar
Rule D.1803.
Investment criteria of funds, Bar Rule D.1713.
Judicial review of state bar council decisions, Bar
Rule D.1805.
Limitations imposed on specialists, Bar Rule
D.1718.
Maintenance of accounts, Bar Rule D.1713.
Minimum standards for certification, Bar Rule
D.1720.
Continued certification, Bar Rule D.1721.
Petition for review by board.
Application rejected by specialty committee, Bar
Rule D.1801.
Previous decisions approving standards
reaffirmed, Bar Rule D.1726.
Privileges conferred on specialists, Bar Rule
D.1718.

ATTORNEYS AT LAW —Cont'd
Specialization —Cont'd
Purposes of plan of certified legal specialization, Bar Rule D.1701.
Reaffirmance of previous decisions approving standards, Bar Rule D.1726.
Real property law specialty, certification standards, Bar Rules D.2101 to D.2107.
Source of funds for program, Bar Rule D.1712.
Specialty committees, Bar Rule D.1719.
Review of incomplete applications and applications not in compliance, Bar Rule D.1801.
Suspension or revocation of certification, Bar Rule D.1723.
Procedure, Bar Rule D.1803.
Workers' compensation law, Bar Rules D.2700 to D.2707.
State bar.
Active members, §84-16, Bar Rule A.0201.
Administrative suspensions, Bar Rule A.0201.
Admission to practice.
Rules governing admission to practice of law. See within this heading, "Admission to practice."
Agency of state, §84-15.
Annual meeting, §84-33, Bar Rule A.0501.
Council to provide suitable program for, Bar Rule A.0105.
Reports made to, Bar Rule A.0106.
Annual membership fees, Bar Rule A.0203.
Compliance after suspension for failure to pay fees, Bar Rule D.0904.
Failure to pay membership fees, Bar Rule D.0903.
Appeals.
Right of appeal from state bar to court of appeals, §7A-29(a).
Appointment of counsel for indigent defendants in certain criminal cases.
Model plan for appointment, Bar Rules D.0501 to D.0510.
Rules and regulations relating to, Bar Rules D.0401 to D.0406.
Approval of bylaws, Bar Rule A.0901.
Arbitration of internal law firm disputes, Bar Rules E.0401 to E.0410.
Bankruptcy law specialty, Bar Rules D.2201 to D.2207.
Bar examination.
Fees of applicants, §84-25.
Board of continuing legal education.
Referral of matters to board by grievance committee, Bar Rule B.0112.
Rules concerning administration of program, Bar Rules D.1601 to D.1610.
Rules governing administration of program, Bar Rules D.1501 to D.1527.
Board of law examiners.
Compensation of members, §84-26.
Expenses of members, §84-26.
Prescription of applicant fees, §84-25.
Board of legal specialization.
Bankruptcy law specialty, certification standards, Bar Rules D.2201 to D.2207.
Continuing legal education, rules concerning accreditation, Bar Rules D.1901 to D.1908.
Criminal law specialty, certification standards, Bar Rules D.2501 to D.2509.
Estate planning and probate law specialty, certification standards, Bar Rules D.2301 to D.2307.

ATTORNEYS AT LAW —Cont'd
State bar —Cont'd
Board of legal specialization —Cont'd
Family law specialty, certification standards, Bar Rules D.2401 to D.2407.
Hearing and appeal rules, Bar Rules D.1801 to D.1806.
Independent certified organization, rules for approval, Bar Rules D.2001 to D.2006.
Plan of legal specialization, Bar Rules D.1701 to D.1726.
Real property law specialty, certification standards, Bar Rules D.2101 to D.2107.
Workers' compensation law specialty, certification standards, Bar Rules D.2700 to D.2707.
Bylaws, Bar Rule A.0901.
Model bylaws, Bar Rules A.1001 to A.1013.
Amendment, Bar Rule A.1012.
Annual membership fee, Bar Rule A.1006.
Authority and purpose, Bar Rule A.1002.
Board of directors, Bar Rule A.1011.
Committees, Bar Rule A.1010.
Counselor, Bar Rule A.1005.
District bar finances, Bar Rule A.1008.
Meetings, Bar Rule A.1007.
Membership, Bar Rule A.1003.
Name, Bar Rule A.1001.
Officers, Bar Rule A.1004.
Prohibited activities, Bar Rule A.1009.
Classes of membership, Bar Rule A.0201.
Classification or division of work under appropriate sections and committees, Bar Rule A.0102.
CLE, Bar Rules D.1501 to D.1610.
Specialization certification, rules governing accreditation, Bar Rules D.1900 to D.1908.
Client assistance committee, Bar Rules D.0701 to D.0704.
Client security fund board of trustees.
Rules governing administration of fund, Bar Rules D.1401 to D.1420.
Code of professional conduct. See within this heading, "Professional conduct."
Committee on consumer protection.
Procedures for committee, Bar Rules D.0201 to D.0207.
Committee on grievances.
Judicial district grievance committees, rules governing, Bar Rules B.0201 to B.0207.
Form letters, Bar Rules B.0208 to B.0217.
Powers and duties in disciplinary matters, Bar Rule B.0106.
Powers and duties of chairperson of committee in disciplinary matters, Bar Rule B.0105.
Committee on indigent appointments, Bar Rule D.0504.
Committee on membership and fees.
Continuing legal education hearings before committee, rules governing, Bar Rules D.1001 to D.1011.
Procedures for, Bar Rules D.0901 to D.0904.
Committees generally, §84-22.
Compensation of officers, Bar Rule A.0401.
Confidentiality of documents, papers, etc, involving discipline, §84-32.1(a).
Evidence brought forward in hearing considered public record, §84-32.1(c).
Lawyer assistance program records not considered public, §84-32.1(d).

ATTORNEYS AT LAW —Cont'd
State bar —Cont'd

Continuing legal education, Bar Rules D.1501 to D.1610.
  Specialization certification, rules governing accreditation, Bar Rules D.1901 to D.1908.
Cooperation with local bar association committees, Bar Rule A.0103.
Corporations.
  Regulations for professional corporations practicing law, Bar Rules E.0101 to E.0106.
Council.
  Appointment of councilors, §84-18(b).
  Compensation of councilors, §84-20.
  Composition, §84-17.
  Contracts for supplies, materials, services, printing, equipment.
    Audit of contractor's records.
      Standard provision, §84-23(d).
    Cost plus percentage of cost agreement or contract.
      Prohibited, §84-23(d).
    Submitted to attorney general for review, §84-23(d).
  Courts commission.
    Representative of council to be ex officio member, §7A-507.
  Discipline and disability matters, powers and duties, Bar Rule B.0104.
  Election and appointment of councilors, §84-18(b), Bar Rules A.0801 to A.0806.
  Geographical rotation or division of representation by district bar, Bar Rule A.0806.
  Indigent persons.
    Representation of indigent persons.
      Implementing regulations by council, §7A-451(d).
  Number of members, §84-17.
  Per diem and mileage, §84-20.
  Powers, §84-23.
  Property, powers as to, §84-23(d).
  Publication of official journal, §84-23(c).
  Public members, §84-17.
    Term of office, §84-18(c).
  Quorum at meeting, Bar Rule A.0604.
  Regular meetings, Bar Rule A.0601.
  Rules and regulations.
    Adoption, §84-21(a).
    Indigent persons.
      Representation of indigent persons, §7A-451(d).
    Promulgation, §84-21(b).
    Rulemaking authority, §84-23(a).
  Special meetings, Bar Rule A.0602.
    Notice of call, Bar Rule A.0603.
  Subpoena power, §84-23(b).
  Terms of councilors, §84-18(a).
    Public members, §84-18(c).
  Travel and subsistence expenses, §84-20.
  Vacancies, Bar Rule A.0805.
Court of appeals.
  Appeals of right for state bar, §7A-29(a).
Courts inherent powers unaffected, §84-36.
Creation, §84-15.
Criminal law specialty, certification standards, Bar Rules D.2501 to D.2509.
Definitions.
  Judicial districts, §84-19.
Deposits.
  Securing, §84-34.1.

ATTORNEYS AT LAW —Cont'd
State bar —Cont'd

Disability inactive members, Bar Rule A.0201.
Disability rules generally, Bar Rules B.0101 to B.0217. See within this heading, "Disability proceedings."
Disaster response plan, Bar Rules D.0301 to D.0303.
  Disaster response team, Bar Rule D.0301.
  General policies and objectives, Bar Rule D.0302.
  Reports on results, Bar Rule D.0303.
Disciplinary rules generally, Bar Rules B.0101 to B.0217. See within this heading, "Disciplinary proceedings."
Disciplinary suspension/disbarments.
  Category of inactive members, Bar Rule A.0201.
District bars.
  Membership fees, §84-18.1(b).
District court judges.
  Selection of nominees, Bar Rule A.1013.
District grievance committees, rules governing, Bar Rules B.0201 to B.0207.
  Form letters, Bar Rules B.0208 to B.0217.
Domestic violence victim assistance act.
  Funding, §7A-474.19.
Duties of officers, Bar Rules A.0401 to A.0404.
Election of councilors.
  Mail elections, Bar Rule A.0804.
  Nominations, Bar Rule A.0802.
  Notice, Bar Rule A.0802.
  Purposes of rules, Bar Rule A.0801.
  Vacancies, Bar Rule A.0805.
  Voting procedure, Bar Rule A.0803.
  When election held, Bar Rule A.0802.
Election of officers, Bar Rule A.0304.
  Nominating committee, Bar Rule A.0305.
Eligibility for office, Bar Rule A.0302.
Enumeration of officers, Bar Rule A.0301.
Estate planning and probate law specialty, certification standards, Bar Rules D.2301 to D.2307.
Ethics opinions and ethics advisories, Bar Rules D.0101 to D.0104.
Family law specialty, certification standards, Bar Rules D.2401 to D.2407.
Fee arbitration committee.
  Model plan for district bar fee obligation, Bar Rules D.0801 to D.0808.
Fees.
  Annual membership fees, Bar Rule A.0203.
Filing papers under rules and regulations, Bar Rule A.1201.
Form letters involving disciplinary matters, district grievance committees, Bar Rules B.0208 to B.0217.
Geographical rotation or division of representation of district bar, Bar Rule A.0806.
Immediate past president.
  Duties, Bar Rule A.0403.
Inactive members, §84-16, Bar Rule A.0201.
Inactive status.
  Reinstatement from, Bar Rule D.0902.
    Fee, §84-34.2.
  Transfer to, Bar Rule D.0901.
Indigent defendants.
  Appointment of counsel in certain criminal cases.
    Model plan for appointment, Bar Rules D.0501 to D.0510.

ATTORNEYS AT LAW —Cont'd
State bar —Cont'd
Indigent defendants —Cont'd
Appointment of counsel in certain criminal
cases —Cont'd
Rules and regulations relating to, Bar Rules
D.0401 to D.0406.
Interstate and international law firm registration,
Bar Rules E.0201 to E.0206.
IOLTA board of trustees.
Rules governing administration of plan, Bar
Rules D.1301 to D.1316.
Judicial district grievance committees, rules
governing, Bar Rules B.0201 to B.0207.
Form letters, Bar Rules B.0208 to B.0217.
Judicial districts.
Defined, §84-19.
Organization of judicial district bars, Bar Rules
A.0902, A.0903.
Law students, rules governing practical training,
Bar Rules C.0201 to C.0207.
Legal ethics, procedures for ruling on questions of,
Bar Rules D.0101 to D.0104.
Limited liability companies.
Regulations for professional limited liability
companies practicing law, Bar Rules E.0101
to E.0106.
Local bar associations.
Savings clause as to, §84-35.
Meetings of council.
Quorum, Bar Rule A.0604.
Regular meetings, Bar Rule A.0601.
Special meetings, Bar Rule A.0602.
Notice of call, Bar Rule A.0603.
Meetings of state bar.
Annual meeting, Bar Rule A.0501.
Annual program provided by council, Bar
Rule A.0105.
Reports made, Bar Rule A.0106.
Notice of meetings, Bar Rules A.0501, A.0502.
How given, Bar Rule A.0503.
Parliamentary rules, Bar Rule A.0505.
Quorum, Bar Rule A.0504.
Special meetings, Bar Rule A.0502.
Membership, §84-18.1(a), Bar Rule A.0201.
Annual membership fees, Bar Rule A.0203.
Failure to pay, Bar Rules D.0903, D.0904.
Fees, §84-34.
Active members, §84-16.
District bars, §84-18.1(b).
Failure to pay, Bar Rule D.0903.
Compliance after suspension, Bar Rule
D.0904.
Specific statutory authority for certain fees,
§84-34.2.
List of members, §84-34.
Privileges, §84-16.
Records of state bar, Bar Rule A.0202.
Register of members, Bar Rule A.0202.
Waiving or rebating annual membership fee,
Bar Rule A.0203.
Model bylaws, Bar Rules A.1001 to A.1013.
Amendments, Bar Rule A.1012.
Annual membership fee, Bar Rule A.1006.
Authority and purpose, Bar Rule A.1002.
Board of directors, Bar Rule A.1011.
Committees, Bar Rule A.1010.
Counselor, Bar Rule A.1005.
District bar finances, Bar Rule A.1008.
Meetings, Bar Rule A.1007.
Membership, Bar Rule A.1003.

ATTORNEYS AT LAW —Cont'd
State bar —Cont'd
Model bylaws —Cont'd
Name, Bar Rule A.1001.
Officers, Bar Rule A.1004.
Prohibited activities, Bar Rule A.1009.
Nominating committee appointed to nominate
candidates, Bar Rule A.0305.
North Carolina bar association.
Savings clause as to, §84-35.
Notice of call of special meeting of council, Bar
Rule A.0603.
Notice of election of councilors, Bar Rule A.0802.
Notice of meetings of state bar, Bar Rules A.0501
to A.0503.
Office of state bar, Bar Rule A.1101.
Officers, §84-22.
Compensation, Bar Rule A.0401.
Election, Bar Rule A.0304.
Nominating committee, Bar Rule A.0305.
Enumerated, Bar Rule A.0301.
Immediate past president's duties, Bar Rule
A.0403.
Need not be members of council at time of
election, Bar Rule A.0302.
President elect duties, Bar Rule A.0403.
President's duties, Bar Rule A.0402.
Removal, Bar Rule A.0307.
Secretary's duties, Bar Rule A.0404.
Succession upon vacancy, Bar Rule A.0306.
Term of office, Bar Rule A.0303.
Vacancies, Bar Rule A.0306.
Vice-president duties, Bar Rule A.0403.
Organization of local bar associations encouraged
and fostered, Bar Rule A.0104.
Paralegals.
Continuing education, Bar Rule G.0201.
Accreditation standards, Bar Rule G.0202.
Fees, Bar Rule G.0204.
General course approval, Bar Rule G.0203.
Hours of instruction, computation, Bar Rule
G.0205.
Plan for certification.
Administration and distribution of funds, Bar
Rule G.0112.
Alternative qualification period, Bar Rule
G.0119.
Audit, Bar Rule G.0112.
Board of paralegal certification.
Appointment, nomination, vacancies,
removal, Bar Rule G.0105.
Chairperson, Bar Rule G.0109.
Established, jurisdiction, Bar Rule G.0102.
Meetings, Bar Rule G.0113.
Number of members, composition, Bar Rule
G.0104.
Operational responsibility, Bar Rule
G.0103.
Powers and duties, Bar Rule G.0115.
Report on activities, Bar Rule G.0114.
Succession, Bar Rule G.0108.
Term, Bar Rules G.0106, G.0107.
Vice-chairperson, Bar Rule G.0110.
Certification committee, Bar Rule G.0118.
Continued qualification, evidence of, Bar Rule
G.0120.
Education requirements, Bar Rule G.0119.
Examination, Bar Rule G.0119.
Funding, Bar Rule G.0111.
Investment of funds, Bar Rule G.0112.

ATTORNEYS AT LAW —Cont'd

State bar —Cont'd

Paralegals —Cont'd

Plan for certification —Cont'd

Lapse, suspension or revocation of certification, Bar Rule G.0121.

Hearing and appeal, right, Bar Rule G.0122.

Privileges and responsibilities of lawyers not altered, Bar Rule G.0117.

Purpose, Bar Rule G.0101.

Retention of jurisdiction by council, Bar Rule G.0116.

Standards for certification, Bar Rule G.0119.

Continued certification, Bar Rule G.0120.

Term of certification, Bar Rule G.0120.

Parliamentary rules at meetings of state bar, Bar Rule A.0505.

Positive action for lawyers (PALS) committee.

Disciplinary amnesty in elicit drug use cases, Bar Rule B.0130.

Practice of law.

Persons other than members of state bar prohibited from practicing law, §84-4.

Prepaid legal services, §84-23.1.

Additional nature of provisions, §84-23.1(a).

Insurance.

When subject to regulation under insurance provisions, §84-23.1(d).

Registration of plans, §84-23.1(b1).

Administrative fee, §84-23.1(b2).

Rules governing, Bar Rules E.0301 to E.0309.

President.

Duties, Bar Rule A.0402.

President-elect duties, Bar Rule A.0403.

Professional corporations.

Regulations for practicing law, Bar Rules E.0101 to E.0106.

Professional liability insurance.

Certificate of coverage, member to provide, Bar Rule A.0204.

Professional limited liability companies.

Regulations for practicing law, Bar Rules E.0101 to E.0106.

Publication of notice of meetings of state bar, Bar Rule A.0503.

Purpose of state bar, Bar Rule A.0101.

Quorum at meeting of council, Bar Rule A.0604.

Quorum for meetings of state bar, Bar Rule A.0504.

Real property law specialty, certification standards, Bar Rules D.2101 to D.2107.

Records of state bar membership, Bar Rule A.0202.

Register of members, Bar Rule A.0202.

Regular meetings of council, Bar Rule A.0601.

Removal from office, Bar Rule A.0307.

Reports made to annual meeting, Bar Rule A.0106.

Retired/nonpracticing members.

Category of inactive member, Bar Rule A.0201.

Rules of professional conduct, ProfCond Rules 1.0 to 8.5. See within this heading, "Professional conduct."

Seal, form and custody, Bar Rule A.1301.

Secretary.

Discipline and disability matters, powers and duties, Bar Rule B.0110.

Duties, Bar Rule A.0404.

Serving papers under rules and regulations, Bar Rule A.1201.

ATTORNEYS AT LAW —Cont'd

State bar —Cont'd

Specialization of lawyers.

Bankruptcy law specialty, certification standards, Bar Rules D.2201 to D.2207.

Continuing legal education, rules governing accreditation, Bar Rules D.1901 to D.1908.

Criminal law specialty, certification standards, Bar Rules D.2501 to D.2509.

Estate planning and probate law specialty, certification standards, Bar Rules D.2301 to D.2307.

Family law specialty, certification standards, Bar Rules D.2401 to D.2407.

Hearing and appeal rules of legal specialization, Bar Rules D.1801 to D.1806.

Independent certified organizations, rules for approval, Bar Rules D.2001 to D.2006.

Plan of legal specialization, Bar Rules D.1701 to D.1726.

Real property law specialty, certification standards, Bar Rules D.2101 to D.2107.

Special meetings of council, §84-33, Bar Rule A.0602.

Notice of call, Bar Rule A.0603.

Special meetings of state bar, Bar Rule A.0502.

Standing committees and boards, Bar Rule A.0701.

Succession to office upon vacancy, Bar Rule A.0306.

Term of office, Bar Rule A.0303.

Training of law students, rules governing, Bar Rules C.0201 to C.0207.

Unauthorized practice.

Actions, §84-37(a).

Additional nature of provisions, §84-37(e).

Advisory opinions, §84-37(f).

Injunction, §84-37(b).

Plaintiff may examine adverse party, §84-37(d).

Venue, §84-37(c).

Investigation, §84-37(a).

Vacancies in office, Bar Rule A.0306.

Vacancies on council, Bar Rule A.0805.

Vice-president duties, Bar Rule A.0403.

Waiver for rebating annual membership fee, Bar Rule A.0203.

Workers' compensation law specialty, certification standards, Bar Rules D.2700 to D.2707.

State departments and agencies.

Employment of special counsel to represent departments, officers, agencies, etc, §147-17(a).

Allocation of authority between counsel and state client, §147-17(d).

Final decision making authority.

Designation of counsel with, §147-17(d).

Payment, §147-17(c).

Use limited, §114-2.3.

Stock.

Holding, identification, ProfCond Rule 1.15-2.

Substance abuse.

Lawyer assistance program, Bar Rules D.0601 to D.0623.

See LAWYERS ASSISTANCE PROGRAM.

Superior courts.

Courtroom decorum, SuperCt Rule 12.

List of attorneys furnished to secretary of revenue.

Clerk to furnish list, §7A-110.

ATTORNEYS AT LAW —Cont'd

Superior courts —Cont'd

Scheduling conflicts.

Guidelines for resolving, SuperCt Rule 3.1.

Secure leave periods for attorneys, SuperCt Rule 26.

Withdrawal of appearance, SuperCt Rule 16.

Surrender of license while under investigation, Bar Rule B.0117.

Suspension.

Continuing legal education hearings before administrative committee, Bar Rule D.1008.

Employing as legal clerk or assistant, ProfCond Rule 5.5.

Failure to pay membership fees, Bar Rule D.0902.

Imposition of discipline, Bar Rule B.0123.

Obligations of suspended attorney, Bar Rule B.0124.

Reinstatement after suspension, Bar Rule B.0125.

Tampering with evidence, ProfCond Rule 3.4.

Targeted communications.

Direct contact with prospective clients, ProfCond Rule 7.3.

Terminating representation, ProfCond Rule 1.16.

Termination of parental rights.

Adjudicatory hearing, appointment for indigent parents, §7B-1109(b).

Appointment to assist nonattorney guardian ad litem, §7B-1108(b).

Indigent defense services act, §§7A-498 to 7A-498.8.

See INDIGENT DEFENSE SERVICES.

Termination of parental rights proceeding.

Parent's right to counsel and appointment of counsel, §7B-1101.1(a).

Third parties.

Communications with persons represented by counsel, ProfCond Rule 4.2.

Dealing with unrepresented person, ProfCond Rule 4.3.

Evaluation for use by, ProfCond Rule 2.3.

Respect for third persons rights, ProfCond Rule 4.4.

Truthfulness to third persons, ProfCond Rule 4.1.

Third-party neutrals.

Former neutrals.

Conflict of interest, ProfCond Rule 1.12.

Lawyers serving as, ProfCond Rule 2.4.

Training of law students, rules governing, Bar Rules C.0201 to C.0207.

Trial preparation material.

Public records.

Definitions, §132-1.9(h).

During legal proceedings, §132-1.9(d).

Effect of disclosure, §132-1.9(f).

Following legal proceedings, §132-1.9(e).

Preparation in anticipation of legal proceedings, §132-1.9(c).

Right to deny access, §132-1.9(b).

Scope of provision, §132-1.9(a).

Work-products that are not public records, §132-1.9(g).

Trial publicity, ProfCond Rule 3.6.

Trust accounts of lawyers.

Audit by investigative subpoena, Bar Rule B.0128.

Interest on lawyer's trust accounts (IOLTA).

Rules governing administration of plan, Bar Rules D.1301 to D.1316.

Trust funds.

Accounting, ProfCond Rule 1.15-3.

Defined, ProfCond Rule 1.15-1.

ATTORNEYS AT LAW —Cont'd

Trust funds —Cont'd

Deposit, ProfCond Rule 1.15-2.

Interest on lawyers' trust accounts, ProfCond Rule 1.15-4.

Quarterly reconciliation of accounts, ProfCond Rule 1.15-3.

Truthfulness in statements to others, ProfCond Rule 4.1.

Unauthorized practice of law, ProfCond Rule 5.5.

Actions by private persons damaged by unauthorized practice, §84-10.1.

Actions by state bar, §84-37(a).

Additional nature of provisions, §84-37(e).

Advisory opinions, §84-37(f).

Injunction, §84-37(b).

Plaintiff may examine adverse party, §84-37(d).

Venue, §84-37(c).

Appearance for creditor in insolvency and certain other proceedings by anyone except attorney, §84-9.

Authorized practice committee procedures, Bar Rules D.0201 to D.0207.

Collection agencies, §58-70-120.

Disqualified persons, §84-2.

Exceptions, §84-7.1.

Fees derived from unauthorized practice.

Collection prohibited, §84-8(b).

Foreclosures.

Fee for conducting foreclosures.

Prohibited to all except licensed attorneys, §84-6.

Indictments.

Duty of district attorneys to indict persons upon receipt of information of violation, §84-7.

Injunctions, §84-37(b).

District attorneys to bring injunction proceedings upon application, §84-7.

Internship by law students for government agencies.

Exception, §84-7.1.

Investigation by state bar, §84-37(a).

Legal clinics of law schools.

Exception, §84-7.1.

Misdemeanor, §84-8(a).

Notaries not licensed attorneys.

Prohibition on rendering services constituting, §10B-20(k).

Persons other than members of state bar, §84-4.

Unclaimed entrusted property, ProfCond Rule 1.15-2.

Unemployment compensation.

Representation of parties to proceedings before division, §96-17(b).

Representation of state and department in civil actions, §96-7(a).

Unrepresented persons.

Dealing with, ProfCond Rule 4.3.

Verifying pleadings, §1A-1 Rule 11.

Waiver of counsel.

Indigent persons, §7A-457.

Withdrawal from representation, ProfCond Rule 1.16.

Collaborative law proceedings, §50-76(c).

Obligations of disbarred or suspended attorney, Bar Rule B.0124.

Withdrawal of appearance, SuperCt Rule 16.

Witness.

Lawyer as, ProfCond Rule 3.7.

ATTORNEYS AT LAW —Cont'd

Workers' compensation law specialty, Bar Rules D.2700 to D.2707.

Work product.
Collaborative law proceedings.
Privilege, inadmissible, §50-77(a), (b).
Scope of discovery, §1A-1 Rule 26(b).

Written communications.
Direct contact with prospective clients, ProfCond Rule 7.3.

ATTORNEYS' FEES, ProfCond Rule 1.5.

Abortion.
Woman's right to know act.
Civil action, §90-21.88(c).

Abused, neglected or dependent juvenile actions.
Payment of court-appointed counsel, §7B-603(a) to (c).

Acceptance of compensation from other than client, ProfCond Rule 1.8.

Access to public records.
Compelling disclosure, §132-9(b) to (e).

Administration of estates, §7A-307(c).

Admissions.
Failure of party to admit, §1A-1 Rule 37(c).

Adoption.
Revocation of consent.
Fees awarded to person who revoked upon non-return of minor, §48-3-608(c).
Revocation of relinquishment.
Failure to return minor to person who revoked, §48-3-706(b).

Agency decisions.
Parties appealing or defending, §6-19.1(a).

Alimony.
Actions, §50-16.4.

Allowance of counsel fees as part of costs in certain cases, §6-21.1.

American recovery and reinvestment act.
Civil actions regarding, claims, disputes, protests. Prohibition, §6-19.1(b).

Annexation.
Municipalities initiating.
Appeals, §160A-58.60(n).

Appeals.
Costs generally, AppProc Rule 35.

Arbitration of disputes.
Client assistance committee, Bar Rules D.0701 to D.0704.
Model plan for district bar, Bar Rules D.0801 to D.0808.

Arbitrators.
Civil action against arbitrator, §1-569.14(e).

Automobile dealers.
Actions by, §20-308.1(b).

Bonds, surety.
Model payment and performance bonds.
Suits under provisions, §44A-35.

Business combinations or control share acquisitions unlawful, §75E-4.

Business contracts, reciprocal fees, §6-21.7.

Business corporations.
Derivative actions, §55-7-46.
Inspection of records by shareholders.
Court-ordered inspection, §55-16-04(c).

Business opportunity sales violations.
Action for recovery of damages, §66-100(b).

Cases involving principals or teachers, §6-21.4.

Chattel mortgages.
Attorneys' fees in addition to interest, §6-21.2.

ATTORNEYS' FEES —Cont'd

Child custody.
Action or proceeding for custody or visitation, §50-13.6.

Childhood vaccine-related injury compensation, ChildhoodVaccin Rule 203.

Child support.
Action for support of minor child, §50-13.6.
Income withholding.
Computation of amount to be withheld, §110-136.6(a).
Limitations on amount withheld, §110-136.6(b).
Relief from order based on nonpaternity.
Bad faith attempts to gain relief, §50-13.13(g).

City acting outside scope of authority.
Successful challenge, §6-21.6.

Civil rights, interference with, §99D-1(b), (b1).

Commercial real estate broker lien act.
Action to enforce lien, §44A-24.12.

Condominium assessment lien, §47C-3-116(e), (e1).

Condominium law violations, §47C-4-117.

Condominium owners' associations and declarant.
Declarant liable to association, §47C-3-111(d).

Consumer finance act.
Loan agreement not to provide for payment by borrower, §53-180(e).

Contingent fees and contingent fee agreements, ProfCond Rule 1.5.

Contracts.
Reciprocal fees in business contracts, §6-21.7.

County acting outside scope of authority.
Successful challenge, §6-21.6.

Credit device fraud.
Telecommunication services, §14-113.6(c).

Credit repair service violations, actions to recover damages, §66-225(a).

Credit rights of married women.
Actions to enforce articles, §25B-3(a).

Debt buyers.
Party's obligation to pay for services rendered. Material furnished court, §6-21.2.

Defense of public school employees.
Employee's obligation for attorney fees, §143-300.17.

Delinquent and undisciplined juvenile actions.
Court appointed attorney, §7B-2002.

Depositions.
Failure of party to attend, §1A-1 Rule 37(d).
Oral examination.
Failure to attend or serve subpoena, §1A-1 Rule 30(g).

Derivative actions.
Payment, §55-7-46.

Disclosure of public records.
Action to compel, §132-9(b) to (e).

Discount buying club violations, action to recover damages, §66-136(a).

Discovery conference.
Failure to participate, §1A-1 Rule 37(g).

Discovery, failure to comply with order, §1A-1 Rule 37(b).

Discovery, motion compelling.
Granting or denying, §1A-1 Rule 37(a).

Discrimination against employees for lawful use of lawful products during nonworking hours.
Civil actions for violations, §95-28.2(e).

Division of fees, ProfCond Rule 1.5.
Lawyer or firm sharing fees with nonlawyer, ProfCond Rule 5.4.

ATTORNEYS' FEES —Cont'd
Divorce.
Barred by separation agreement or premarital
agreement provisions, §50-16.6(b).
Custody and support of minor children, §50-13.6.
Domestic violence, §50B-3(a).
Drainage district petitions, §§156-60, 156-61.
Dry-cleaning solvent cleanup.
Remediation of uncertified sites.
Civil action for reimbursement cost,
§143-215.104O(c).
Elections.
Protest of election.
Attorneys' fees not to be awarded against state
board of elections, §163-182.14(d).
Elective share of surviving spouse.
Expenses including attorneys' fees.
Apportionment, §30-3.4(h).
Electronic surveillance.
Civil action for violation of article, §15A-296(a).
Eminent domain.
Appointment of attorney for unknown parties,
§40A-32.
Petitioner abandoning condemnation proceeding
taxed with fee for respondent's attorney,
§1-209.1.
Right of entry prior to condemnation.
Recovery for damages resulting, §40A-11.
**Employee's use of lawful products during
nonworking hours.**
Actions brought pursuant to section, §95-28.2(e),
(f).
Evidence of indebtedness.
Attorneys' fees and notes, etc., in addition to
interest, §6-21.2.
Excessive fees and expenses.
Charging client prohibited, factors in determining,
ProfCond Rule 1.5.
Execution sales.
Special proceeding to determine ownership of
surplus, §1-339.71(d).
Executors and administrators.
Counsel fees allowable to attorneys serving as
representatives, §28A-23-4.
False claims act civil actions.
Award to qui tam plaintiff, §1-610(d).
Defendant prevailing party, §1-610(g).
Fee arbitration, model plan for district bar,
Bar Rules D.0801 to D.0808.
Fiduciaries.
Counsel fees allowed attorneys serving as
fiduciaries, §32-61.
Freedom of information.
Compelling disclosure of public records, §132-9(b)
to (e).
Frivolous actions.
Cases involving principals or teachers, §6-21.4.
Punitive damages, §1D-45.
Funds transfers.
Improper execution or failure to execute payment
order, §25-4A-305(e).
Grievances involving fee disputes.
Jurisdiction and authority of district grievance
committees, Bar Rule B.0202.
Guardians.
Procedure to compel accounting, §35A-1265(a).
Incompetence, determination of, §35A-1116(a).
Court-appointed counsel, §35A-1116(b).
Indigent person representation, §7A-452(b).
Fixing of counsel fees, §7A-458.

ATTORNEYS' FEES —Cont'd
Inspection of land or documents.
Failure to respond to request, §1A-1 Rule 37(d).
Insurance.
Allowance of counsel fees as part of costs in
certain cases.
Basis for and amount of fees, §6-21.1(a).
Order of judge, findings of fact required,
§6-21.1(b).
**Insurance consumer and customer information
privacy.**
Action by individual for violations, §58-39-105(c).
**International commercial arbitration and
conciliation.**
Awarding, order of costs, §1-567.61(h).
Interrogatories.
Failure of party to serve answers, §1A-1 Rule
37(d).
Interstate family support, §52C-3-312(b).
Law firm.
Fee sharing with non-lawyer, ProfCond Rule 5.4.
Leases, UCC.
Unconscionable lease contracts or clauses,
§25-2A-108(4).
Letters of credit.
Damages for wrongful dishonor or breach,
§25-5-111(e).
Liens.
Past-due child support, §44-50.
Possessory liens on personal property.
Enforcement of lien by sale.
Noncompliance, §44A-4(g).
Recoveries for personal injuries.
Enforcement of lien rights, §44-50.1(a) to (c).
**Limited liability company derivative actions
by members,** §57C-8-01(e).
Actions brought by reasonable cause, §57C-8-01(f).
Limited partnerships.
Derivative actions, §59-1004.
**Mediated settlement conferences or other
settlement procedures in district court.**
Actions involving equitable distribution, alimony
or support.
Monetary sanction for failure of party to attend
mediated settlement conference,
§7A-38.4A(e).
Medical malpractice.
Arbitration of negligent health claims,
§90-21.65(e).
**Membership camping contract violations,
purchaser's remedies,** §66-247(a).
Model plan for district bar fee arbitration, Bar
Rules D.0801 to D.0808.
Monopolies and restraints of trade, §75-16.1.
Mortgages and deeds of trust.
Consumer home loans.
Actions under provisions, §24-10.2(f).
Debt collection and servicing.
Remedies of borrower, §45-94.
Foreclosure, §84-6.
Reverse mortgages.
Actions by borrowers for damages, §53-271(d).
Motion picture fair competition violations,
§75C-5.
**Motor fuel marketing violations, private
actions,** §75-86.
Motor vehicle captive finance sources.
Civil actions for violations, §20-308.21(b).
Motor vehicle repairs.
Remedies for violation of article, §20-354.9.

ATTORNEYS' FEES —Cont'd
Motor vehicles.
New motor vehicle warranties act, §20-351.8.
Sublease and loan assumption arranging.
Violations of provisions, §20-106.2(f).
Mountain ridge protection.
Civil action against persons alleged in violation,
§113A-211(b).
New motor vehicles warranties act, §20-351.8.
Nonjustifiable cases, §6-21.5.
Nuisances against public morals.
Actions abating, §19-8.
Defendant's expenses incurred in defending
actions, §19-2.1.
Lien on real and personal property, §19-6.
**Oil pollution and hazardous substances
control.**
Offshore oil and gas activities, §143-215.94CC(c).
**Outpatient involuntary commitment
proceedings, §7A-451.1.**
Personal injury suits.
Basis for and amount of fees, §6-21.1(a).
Order of judge, findings of fact required,
§6-21.1(b).
Planned community act.
Assessments for common expenses.
Foreclosure of lien for assessments,
§47F-3-116(e), (e1), (e2).
Declaration limits on attorneys' fees, §47F-3-120.
Pork promotion assessments.
Recovery of unpaid assessments, §106-790.
**Post assessment insurance guaranty
association.**
Right to recover, §58-48-50(a1).
**Prepaid entertainment contracts, actions for
damages, §66-125(a).**
**Principals of schools, allowance in cases
involving, §6-21.4.**
Property damage suits.
Basis for and amount of fees, §6-21.1(a).
Order of judge, findings of fact required,
§6-21.1(b).
**Psychotherapy patient/client sexual
exploitation act, §90-21.43.**
Public meetings.
Declaratory relief for violations of provisions.
Assessment and award, §143-318.16B.
Public officers and employees.
Improper government activities.
Reporting, §126-87.
Public records.
Compelling disclosure, §132-9(b) to (e).
Punitive damages.
Frivolous or malicious actions, §1D-45.
Quo warranto.
Appropriation of public funds to pay, §1-521.
Real estate brokers.
Commercial real estate lien.
Action to enforce lien, §44A-24.12.
Receivers of corporations.
Counsel fees, §1-507.9.
Reciprocal fees in business contracts.
Amount of fees permissible, §6-21.7(b), (f).
Consumer contracts, effect of provisions,
§6-21.7(e).
Definitions, §6-21.7(a).
Determination of reasonable fees, §6-21.7(c).
Nonapplicability of certain presumptions or
amounts awarded in other cases, §6-21.7(d).
Insurance contracts, effect of provisions,
§6-21.7(g).

ATTORNEYS' FEES —Cont'd
Reciprocal fees in business contracts —Cont'd
Nonapplicability of certain presumptions or
amounts awarded in other cases, §6-21.7(d).
Sales contracts, effect of provisions, §6-21.7(e).
Validity of contract provisions, §6-21.7(b).
**Rental referral agency violations, action to
recover damages, §66-146(a).**
Requests for admission, failure to admit, §1A-1
Rule 37(c).
Retail installment sales.
Fee provisions included, §25A-21.
**Retaliatory employment discrimination,
§95-243(c).**
Returned checks, §6-21.3(b).
Sale of prints by art dealers.
Wrongful refusal to repay purchaser, §25C-15(b).
Sale or purchase of practice.
Increase in fees, ProfCond Rule 1.17.
Sales commissions.
Civil actions, §66-192(a).
Frivolous actions, §66-192(b).
Sharing fees with nonlawyer, ProfCond Rule 5.4.
Shoplifting and theft by employees.
Civil liability, §1-538.2(a).
Solar collectors.
Municipal ordinances.
Limitations on regulating solar collectors.
Civil actions, §160A-201(d).
State departments and agencies.
Defending actions arising from activities of state
employees, §147-17.
Structured settlement agreements.
Violation of provisions, §1-543.15(b).
Summary judgment.
Affidavits made in bad faith, §1A-1 Rule 56(g).
Teachers, allowance in cases involving, §6-21.4.
Telephone solicitations.
Action for violation, awarding, §75-105(d).
**Trade secrets, claim of misappropriation,
§66-154(d).**
Transfer fee covenants.
Recording, liability, §39A-3(b).
Trusts and trustees.
Awarding in proceeding involving trust,
§36C-10-1004.
Unauthorized practice of law.
Fees derived from unauthorized practice.
Collection prohibited, §84-8(b).
Underground storage tanks.
Leaking petroleum cleanup.
Actions for fund reimbursement,
§143-215.94G(e).
Groundwater protection loan fund.
Civil action for default or violation of loan
agreement, §143-215.94P(e).
**Vehicle mileage act violations, private civil
actions, §20-348(a).**
Visitation.
Action or proceeding for custody or visitation,
§50-13.6.
Vocational rehabilitation.
Subrogation.
Payment of fees based upon established fee
schedule, §143-547(a).
Workers' compensation.
Approval by industrial commission, §97-90(a).
Determination of reasonableness of fee,
§97-90(c).
Filing agreement for fee or compensation,
§97-90(c).

ATTORNEYS' FEES —Cont'd
Workers' compensation —Cont'd
Approval by industrial commission —Cont'd
Receipt of fees not approved by commission,
§97-90(b).
Industrial commission hearings, §97-88.1.

ATTORNEYS IN FACT.
Powers of attorney.
Advance instruction for mental health treatment,
§§122C-71 to 122C-77.
See MENTAL HEALTH, DEVELOPMENTAL
DISABILITY, SUBSTANCE ABUSE.
General provisions, §§32A-1 to 32A-14.
See POWER OF ATTORNEY.
Health care powers of attorney, §§32A-15 to
32A-26.
See HEALTH CARE POWERS OF ATTORNEY.
Renunciation of succession, §31B-1.
Service of process on partnerships.
Personal jurisdiction, manner of service, §1A-1
Rule 4(j).

ATTORNMENT.
Unnecessary on conveyance or reversions, etc.,
§42-2.

ATTRACTIVE NUISANCE DOCTRINE.
Child trespasser.
Harm caused by artificial condition on property.
Child trespasser defined, §38B-4.
Liability of possessor of property, §38B-3.

ATV'S.
See ALL-TERRAIN VEHICLES.

AUCTIONS AND AUCTIONEERS, §§85B-1 to
85B-9.
Advertising.
Misleading or untruthful advertising.
Grounds for suspension or revocation of license,
§85B-8(a).
Agreement with owner of property.
Required for auction, §85B-7(a).
Animals, public auctions.
Defined, §19A-23.
Licenses.
Change in ownership, management or operation
of business, §19A-31.
Fees, §19A-28.
Penalty for operation without license, §19A-33.
Refusal, suspension or revocation, §§19A-30,
19A-32.
Required, §19A-28.
Transfer prohibited, §19A-31.
Applicability of provisions, §85B-2.
Exceptions, §85B-2.
Apprentice auctioneers.
Licenses.
Applications, §85B-4(c).
Fees, §85B-6.
Forfeiture.
Felony convictions, §15A-1331A.
Qualifications for license, §85B-4(b).
Required, §85B-4(a).
Supervisor of apprentice, §85B-4(c1).
Attorney general.
Enforcement of provisions.
Commission entitled to services of attorney
general, §85B-9(c).
Auctioneer recovery fund.
Failure to make required contribution.
Grounds for suspension or revocation of license,
§85B-8(a).

AUCTIONS AND AUCTIONEERS —Cont'd
Auctioneer recovery fund —Cont'd
Fee to be included in fund, §85B-4.1(a).
Investments, §85B-4.1.
Licenses.
Contribution to fund as prerequisite to license,
§85B-4(f).
Payments from fund.
Application to commission, §85B-4.2.
Hearings, §85B-4.3.
Attorneys' fees, §85B-4.7.
Automatic suspension of license, §85B-4.8.
Board directing payment, §85B-4.6.
Compromise of claim, §85B-4.6.
Determination of small claims without prior
judicial determination, §85B-4.5.
Disciplinary action against licensee, §85B-4.12.
Grounds, §85B-4.2.
Limitations, §85B-4.7.
Notice, §85B-4.2.
Persons ineligible to recovery from, §85B-4.11.
Proof of conversion and other fraudulent act,
§85B-4.4.
Pro rata distribution, §85B-4.7.
Repayment to fund, §85B-4.8.
Disciplinary action against licensee,
§85B-4.12.
Required showings, §85B-4.3.
Response and defense by commission,
§85B-4.4.
Small claims.
Determination without prior judicial
determination, §85B-4.5.
Subrogation of rights, §85B-4.9.
Persons ineligible to recovery from, §85B-4.11.
Sources of funding, §85B-4.1(a).
License fees, §85B-4(g).
Nonresidents.
License fees, §85B-5.
Use of funds, §85B-4.1(c).
Waiver of rights, §85B-4.10.
Charities.
Exemptions from auction provisions, §85B-2.
Child support enforcement.
Forfeiture of licensing privilege, §50-13.12.
Clients' funds.
Handling, §85B-7.1.
Commercial code.
Sale by auction, §25-2-328.
Commission.
Appointment of members, §85B-3(a).
Attorneys at law.
Employment of attorney to assist in
enforcement, §85B-9(c).
Chairman, §85B-3(e).
Compensation, §85B-3(g).
Duties, §85B-3.1(a).
Employees, §85B-3(c).
Hearings, §85B-8(e).
Investigations, §85B-8(e).
Number of members, §85B-3(a).
Public member, §85B-3(b).
Purchase of equipment and supplies, §85B-3.1(d).
Qualifications of members, §85B-3(b).
Real property, powers, §85B-3.1(c).
Terms of members, §85B-3(a).
Vacancies, §85B-3(a).
Vote required for actions, §85B-3(d).
Conduct of auction, §85B-7.
Continuing education.
License renewal, §85B-4(e1).

AUCTIONS AND AUCTIONEERS —Cont'd
Corporations.
Licenses, §85B-4(g).
Criminal history record checks.
Applicants for auctioneer license, §§85B-3.2,
114-19.8.
Decedents' estates.
Sales in settlement of decedents' estates.
Exemptions from auction provisions, §85B-2.
Definitions, §85B-1.
Electronic auction service.
State surplus property.
Sale or disposal by, §143-64.03(d).
Escrow accounts, §85B-7.1.
Exemptions from provisions, §85B-2.
Fees.
Auctioneer recovery fund.
Fee to be included in fund, §85B-4.1(a).
Licenses, §85B-6.
Felony convictions.
Forfeiture of license, §15A-1331A.
Fines.
Civil penalties.
Imposition by commission, §85B-3.1(b).
Hearings.
Commission, §85B-8(e).
Injunctions.
Violations of provisions, §85B-9(b).
Investigations.
Commission, §85B-8(e).
Judicial sales.
Exemptions from auction provisions, §85B-2.
Licenses.
Applications, §85B-4(c), (d).
Apprentice auctioneers.
Applications, §85B-4(c).
Fees, §85B-6.
Qualifications for license, §85B-4(b).
Required, §85B-4(a).
Supervisor of apprentice, §85B-4(c1).
Auctioneer recovery fund.
Contribution to fund as prerequisite to license,
§85B-4(f).
Availability at auction, §85B-7(c).
Corporations, §85B-4(g).
Criminal history record checks of applicants,
§114-19.8.
Definitions, §85B-3.2(a).
Denial of license, §85B-3.2(d), (e).
Disposition of fees collected, §85B-3.2(g).
Duties of commission, §85B-3.2(b).
Release of information, §85B-3.2(c).
Review of information by applicant, §85B-3.2(f).
Denial.
Grounds, §85B-8(a).
Fees, §85B-6.
List of licensees.
Publication, §85B-4(h).
Local governments.
Charging fees or requiring licenses prohibited,
§85B-6.
Nonresidents, §85B-5.
Partnerships, §85B-4(g).
Qualifications for licensure, §85B-4(b), (d).
Reciprocity, §85B-5.
Renewal, §85B-4(e), (e1).
Required, §85B-4(a).
Suspension or revocation, §85B-8(e).
Applying for license, §85B-8(f).
Felony convictions, §15A-1331A.

AUCTIONS AND AUCTIONEERS —Cont'd
Licenses —Cont'd
Suspension or revocation —Cont'd
Grounds, §85B-8(a).
Payments from auctioneer recovery fund,
§85B-4.8.
Livestock markets.
Exemptions from auction provisions, §85B-2.
Generally, §§106-406 to 106-418.
See LIVESTOCK MARKETS.
Prompt pay law, §§106-418.1 to 106-418.7A.
See LIVESTOCK MARKETS.
Local governments.
Licenses.
Charging fees or requiring licenses prohibited,
§85B-6.
Misdemeanors.
Violations of provisions, §85B-9(a).
Motor vehicle repairs.
Applicability of repair provisions to work done for
motor vehicle auctions, §20-354.1.
Motor vehicles.
Exemptions from auction provisions, §85B-2.
Municipalities.
Public auction of real or personal property,
§160A-270.
Nonresidents.
Licenses, §85B-5.
Partnerships.
Licenses, §85B-4(g).
Prompt pay law.
Livestock, §§106-418.1 to 106-418.7A.
See LIVESTOCK MARKETS.
Public schools.
Sale of school property, §115C-518.
Reciprocity.
Licenses, §85B-5.
Records.
Auctioneer to maintain records, §85B-7(b), (d).
Religious societies.
Exemptions from auction provisions, §85B-2.
State surplus property.
Electronic auction service.
Sale or disposal by, §143-64.03(d).
Subrogation.
Auctioneer recovery fund.
Payments from fund, §85B-4.9.
Tobacco.
Exemptions from auction provisions, §85B-2.
Liens.
Effective period for lien on leaf tobacco sold in
auction warehouse, §44-69.
Trust accounts, §85B-7.1.
Violations of provisions.
Grounds for suspension or revocation of license,
§85B-8(a).
Injunctions, §85B-9(b).
Misdemeanors, §85B-9(a).
Waiver.
Auctioneer recovery fund.
Failure to comply with chapter.
Waiver of right, §85B-4.10.

AUDIO-CASSETTE TAPE TEXTBOOKS.
**Textbook contracts to include clause granting
state board of education license to
produce, §115C-90.**

AUDIOLOGISTS.
General provisions, §§90-292 to 90-307.
See SPEECH AND LANGUAGE PATHOLOGISTS
AND AUDIOLOGISTS.

AUDIOLOGISTS —Cont'd
Hearing aids.
Health insurance.
Medical necessity determination, utilization review, §58-3-285(c).
Required coverage, §58-3-285(a).
Professional corporations.
Formation authorized, §55B-14(c).
Self-referrals, §§90-405 to 90-408.

AUDIO RECORDINGS.
Autopsies.
Photographs, video or audio recordings of autopsy, §§130A-389.1, 132-1.8.
Piracy.
See RECORD AND TAPE PIRACY.
Secret listening.
Electronic surveillance, §§15A-286 to 15A-298.
See ELECTRONIC SURVEILLANCE.

AUDIO TRANSMISSION.
Pretrial release.
Conduct of proceedings, §15A-532(b), (c).

AUDIOVISUAL RECORDING DEVICES.
Unlawful use in motion picture theater, §14-440.1.

AUDITORIUMS.
Alcoholic beverage permits.
Mixed beverage permit.
Kind of permit that may be issued, §18B-1001.
Recycling requirement, §18B-1006.1.
On-premises fortified wine permit.
Kind of permit that may be issued, §18B-1001.
Recycling requirement, §18B-1006.1.
On-premises malt beverage permit.
Kind of permit that may be issued, §18B-1001.
Recycling requirement, §18B-1006.1.
On-premises unfortied wine permit.
Kind of permit that may be issued, §18B-1001.
Recycling requirement, §18B-1006.1.
Municipalities.
Power to establish and support, §160A-489.
Smoking in public places.
Applicability of article to local government, §143-601.
Nonsmoking areas in state-controlled buildings, §143-597.

AUDITS AND AUDITORS.
ABC boards, §§18B-205(c), 18B-702(s).
Compliance with performance standards.
Regular or special audits conducted, §18B-705(a).
Administrative office of the courts.
Internal audits division.
Standards, report, work papers, §7A-343.2.
Advance health care directive registry.
Fee for filing, §130A-470(c).
Agricultural finance authority, §122D-18(b).
Alcoholic beverages.
Local ABC boards, §18B-205(c).
State warehouse.
Private warehouses, §18B-204(b).
Attorneys at law.
Audit by state bar, ProfCond Rule 1.15-3.
Lawyers trust accounts, Bar Rule B.0128.
Beach area essential property insurance.
Insurance underwriting association.
Audit, §58-45-65.1.

AUDITS AND AUDITORS —Cont'd
Board for licensing of geologists.
Contracts for supplies, materials, printing, equipment, contractual services.
Audit of contractor's records.
Standard clause, §89E-5(e).
Boards and commissions.
Occupational licensing boards, §93B-4.
Settlement of affairs of certain inoperative boards and agencies, §143-272.
Budget of state.
Audit by state auditor, request for, §143C-2-1(c).
Grant funds.
Audit oversight, §143C-6-23(g).
Capital facilities finance agency.
Private capital facilities finance act.
Annual audit of books and accounts, §159D-53.
Commissioner of banks.
Confidentiality of official records, §53-99.
Community colleges, §§115D-56.16, 147-64.6(a).
Community third party or pooled trusts.
Annual audits, §36D-5(b).
Court of appeals.
Clerk of court.
Financial accounts of clerk audited, §7A-20(b).
Credit unions.
Supervisory committee, §54-109.49.
Department of health and human services.
Office of internal auditor, §§143B-216.50, 143B-216.51.
Department of public safety.
Division of adult correction.
On-site post audits of prisons, staffing audits, §143B-709(a).
Division of adult correction.
On-site post audits of prisons, staffing audits, §143B-709(a).
Executors and administrators.
Employment of auditors.
Powers of personal representatives, §28A-13-3(a).
Fish and fisheries resources.
Promotion of coastal fisheries and seafood industry, §113-315.9.
Seafood industrial park authority.
Oversight of state auditor, §113-315.35.
Foreign legal consultants, §84A-5.
Gasoline tax, §105-449.121(b).
Global transpark authority.
Contracts for supplies, materials, printing, equipment.
Audit of contractors records.
Standard provision, §63A-24.
Health care facilities.
Finance act.
Books and accounts to be audited, §131A-19.
Hospital authorities.
Reports to be filed, §131E-29.
Housing authorities and projects.
Local government finance.
Special provisions pertaining to public housing authorities, §159-42(g).
Insurance.
Annual audited financial reports.
Generally, §§58-10-185 to 58-10-265.
See INSURANCE COMPANIES.
Financial statements.
CPA audits, §58-2-205.
Health insurance risk pool, §58-50-235.
Interstate insurance product regulation compact.
Commission, §58-91-60(f).

AUDITS AND AUDITORS —Cont'd
Insurance —Cont'd
Supervision, rehabilitation and liquidation of insurers.
External audit of receiver's books, §58-30-255.
Insurance underwriting association.
Audit, §58-45-65.1.
Job development investment grant program.
Records of recipient, §143B-437.58(c).
Judicial sales.
Public sale.
Accounts and reports of commissioner or trustee, §1-339.31(b).
Local ABC boards, §§18B-205(c), 18B-702(s).
Compliance with performance standards.
Regular or special audits conducted, §18B-705(a).
Local development.
Industrial development commission.
Bureau.
Annual audit, §158-23.
Local government finance, §159-34.
Nonprofit corporation receiving public funds, §159-40(a) to (d).
Lottery.
Operation of lottery, §18C-122.
State lottery commission, §18C-116.
Manufactured home dealers.
Escrow or trust accounts, §143-143.54.
Medicaid and Health Choice provider requirements.
Audits, extrapolation of results, §108C-5(i) to (s).
Provider requirements, §108C-11.
Medicaid contracts.
Standard provision for audit of contractor records, §108A-55(b).
Mental health, developmental disability, substance abuse.
Area authorities, §122C-144.1(c).
Motor carrier safety regulation unit.
Department of public safety.
Audit of motor carriers for compliance, §20-379.
Motor vehicle registration.
International registration plan.
Audit of vehicle registrations under, §20-91.
Mutual burial associations.
Assessment by board of funeral service, §90-210.81.
911 system.
Board, §62A-50.
Nonprofit corporation receiving public funds, §159-40(a) to (d).
North Carolina state art society.
Operations of society.
Subject to oversight of state auditor, §140-13.
North Carolina symphony society.
Operations of society.
Subject to oversight of state auditor, §140-8.
North Carolina transportation museum special fund.
Audit, §121-7.6(d).
Nurses.
Board of nursing.
Funds, §90-171.25.
Oaths.
Form of oath, §11-11.
Occupational licensing boards, §93B-4.
Outdoor historical dramas.
State auditor to audit, §143-204.8(d).

AUDITS AND AUDITORS —Cont'd
Pharmacists and pharmacies.
Audit rights, §§90-85.50 to 90-85.53.
Appeals process.
Copy of audit findings to plan sponsor after appeal, §90-85.51(c).
Dismissal of unsubstantiated portion of audit, §90-85.51(b).
Mandatory establishment, §90-85.51(a).
Applicability of provisions, §90-85.53.
Definitions, §90-85.50(a).
Enumeration of rights, §90-85.50(b).
Recoupment of disputed funds.
Charge or assessment, §90-85.52(c).
Contractually agreed responsible party as payee, §90-85.52(b).
Time for, §90-85.52(a).
Piped natural gas tax, §105-187.46(b).
Prisons.
Division of adult correction.
On-site post audits of prisons, staffing audits, §143B-709(a).
Public schools.
Annual independent audit, §115C-447.
Public utilities.
Utilities commission, §62-37(b).
Recreational therapy licensure board, §90C-25.
Rescue squad workers' relief fund, §58-88-15.
River basins advisory commissions, §77-115(b).
Roanoke river basin bi-state commission.
Accounts and records, §77-96(c).
Savings banks.
Dissolution.
Involuntary liquidation.
Final distribution, §54C-83(p).
Examinations by commissioner of banks.
Extended audit, §54C-56(a).
Payment of expenses, §54C-56.
Service corporations, §54C-144(c).
Soil scientists board of licensing.
Contracts for supplies, materials, printing, services.
Audit of contractor's records.
Standard provision, §89F-5(d).
Southern growth policies agreement.
Board.
Compliance with audit or inspection laws, §143-497(f).
State auditor.
General provisions, §§147-64.1 to 147-64.14.
See STATE AUDITOR.
State bar.
Contracts for supplies, materials, services, printing, equipment.
Audit of contractor's records.
Standard provision, §84-23(d).
State departments and agencies.
Internal auditing requirements, §§143-745 to 143-747.
Settlement of affairs of certain inoperative boards and agencies.
Affairs of board or agency, §143-272.
State health plan for teachers and state employees.
Oversight of state auditor, §135-48.28.
State lottery.
Commission, §18C-116.
Operation of lottery, §18C-122.
Records of contractors.
Standard provision in contracts awarded by commission, §18C-150.

AUDITS AND AUDITORS —Cont'd
Strawberry plant sellers, §106-785(c).
Superior courts.
Clerks of court.
Accounting for fees and other receipts, §7A-108.
Supreme court.
Financial accounts of the clerk of supreme court,
§7A-11.
Third-party administrators' operations.
Insurers' responsibilities, §58-56-26(c).
Tobacco trust fund commission.
State auditor to conduct, §143-723.
Transportation department.
Operations of department.
Subject to oversight of state auditor, §136-10.
Turnpike authority, §136-89.186.
Unit ownership.
Annual audit of records, §47A-20.
University of North Carolina.
Functions and programs.
Internal auditors.
Access to records, data or other information,
§116-40.7(b).
Confidentiality of audit work papers,
exceptions, §116-40.7(c).
Independent reviews and analysis,
§116-40.7(a).
Retention of reports and records, §116-40.7(c).
Special responsibility institutions, §116-30.8.
Wastewater systems.
Certification of contractors and inspectors.
Board, §90A-75(d).

AULANDER, CITY OF.
On-premises unfortified wine licenses.
Discretion to decline to issue, §105-113.71(b).

AUNTS.
Intestate succession.
Distribution.
Among uncles and aunts and their lineal
descendants, §29-16(c).

**AUTHENTICATION AND IDENTIFICATION OF
EVIDENCE.**
Copies of official records, §1A-1 Rule 44(a).
General provisions, §8C-1 Rule 901(a).
Illustration of examples, §8C-1 Rule 901(b).
Self-authentication, §8C-1 Rule 902.
Subscribing witness.
Testimony not necessary to authenticate, §8C-1
Rule 903.

**AUTHENTICATION OF COPY OF OFFICIAL
RECORD,** §1A-1 Rule 44(a).

AUTHENTICATION OF DOCUMENTS.
Certificates of authentication.
Authority of secretary of state, §66-270.
Definitions, §66-271.
Issuance of certificate, §66-272.
Limitation on authority of secretary, §66-274(c).
Non-certifiable documents, §66-274(b).
Other methods of authentication, §66-275.
Prerequisites to authentication, §66-273.
Purpose of certificate precluding issuance,
§66-274(a).

AUTHORITIES.
Agricultural finance authority, §§122D-1 to
122D-23.
See AGRICULTURAL FINANCE AUTHORITY.
Alcoholism research authority, §§122C-431 to
122C-433.

AUTHORITIES —Cont'd
Capital projects for industry.
Authorities may issue bonds, NC Const Art V §9.
Community colleges.
Tax-levying authorities, §§115D-32(a), 115D-33(a).
Constitution of North Carolina.
Bond issues to finance capital projects for
industry, NC Const Art V §9.
Crematory authority, §90-210.122.
Education assistance authority, §§116-201 to
116-209.40.
See EDUCATION ASSISTANCE AUTHORITY.
Electrification.
Rural electrification authority, §§117-1 to 117-5.
Eminent domain.
Power of eminent domain, §40A-3(c).
Energy conservation loan authority.
Housing finance agency, §§122A-5.3, 122A-6.1.
Facility authorities, §§160A-480.1 to 160A-480.15.
See FACILITY AUTHORITIES.
Global TransPark authority, §§63A-1 to 63A-25.
See GLOBAL TRANSPARK AUTHORITY.
Hospital authorities, §§131E-15 to 131E-33.
See HOSPITAL AUTHORITIES.
Housing authorities and projects, §§157-1 to
157-70.
See HOUSING AUTHORITIES AND PROJECTS.
Housing finance agency.
Energy conservation loan authority, §§122A-5.3,
122A-6.1.
Mortgage insurance authority, §122A-5.2.
Mortgage insurance authority, §122A-5.2.
Parking authorities, §§160A-550 to 160A-565.
Parks and recreation authority, §§143B-313.1,
143B-313.2.
Public health authorities, §§130A-45 to
130A-45.13.
See PUBLIC HEALTH AUTHORITIES.
Public transportation authorities.
General provisions, §§160A-575 to 160A-588.
See PUBLIC TRANSPORTATION
AUTHORITIES.
Regional public transportation authority,
§§160A-600 to 160A-627.
See REGIONAL PUBLIC TRANSPORTATION
AUTHORITY.
Regional sports authorities, §§160A-479 to
160A-479.17.
See REGIONAL SPORTS AUTHORITIES.
Regional transportation authorities, §§160A-630
to 160A-651.
See REGIONAL TRANSPORTATION
AUTHORITIES.
Rural electrification authority, §§117-1 to 117-5.
**Sale, lease or exchange of property between
governmental units.**
Action taken by governmental unit, §160A-274(c).
Authority, §160A-274(b).
Governmental unit defined, §160A-274(a).
Seafood industrial park authority, §§113-315.25
to 113-315.39.
See SEAFOOD INDUSTRIAL PARK
AUTHORITY.
Small business contractor authority.
See SMALL BUSINESS CONTRACTORS.
Solid waste management.
Regional solid waste management authorities,
§§153A-421 to 153A-432.
See REGIONAL SOLID WASTE
MANAGEMENT AUTHORITIES.

AUTHORITIES —Cont'd
Tennessee Valley Authority.
Taxation, §§105-458 to 105-462.
Turnpike authority, §§136-89.180 to 136-89.218.
See TURNPIKE AUTHORITY.
Veterans' recreation authorities, §§165-23 to
165-38.
See VETERANS' RECREATION AUTHORITIES.
Water and sewer authorities, §§162A-1 to
162A-19.
See WATER AND SEWER AUTHORITIES.

AUTISM.
Defined, §35A-1101.
Determination of incompetence, §§35A-1101 to
35A-1116.
See INCOMPETENCY.

**AUTOMATED CAMERA OR VIDEO
RECORDING SYSTEM.**
School buses.
Failure to stop for bus receiving or discharging
passengers.
Use in detecting and prosecuting violation,
§20-217(h).

**AUTOMATED EXTERNAL DEFIBRILLATORS
(AED),** §90-21.15.
Definitions, §90-21.15(b).
Immunity from liability, §90-21.15(d) to (f).
Products liability claims, §90-21.15(f).
Public policy, §90-21.15(a).
Seller's notification requirements, §90-21.15(g).
Use of device construed, §90-21.15(c).

AUTOMATED TELEPHONE SYSTEMS.
State government agency systems.
Minimization of number of menus, §143-162.1.

AUTOMATED TELLER MACHINES, §53-62(d1).
Cards, §§14-113.8 to 14-113.17.
See FINANCIAL TRANSACTION CARDS.

**AUTOMATIC DIALING AND RECORDED
MESSAGE PLAYERS.**
Circumstances allowing, §75-104(b).
Restriction, §75-104(a).

**AUTOMATIC RENEWAL CLAUSES IN
CONSUMER CONTRACTS.**
Disclosures required, §75-41(a), (b).
Exceptions to provisions, §75-41(c), (d).
Violations of provisions.
Clause void and unenforceable, §75-41(e).

AUTOMATIC STAY TO ENFORCE JUDGMENT,
§1A-1 Rule 62(a).

AUTOMATIC WEAPONS.
Mass death and destruction weapons.
Manufacture, assembly, etc., §14-288.8.

AUTOMOBILE ACCIDENTS.
See MOTOR VEHICLE ACCIDENTS.

AUTOMOBILE DEALERS' LICENSE ACT,
§§20-285 to 20-308.22.
See MOTOR VEHICLE DEALERS.

**AUTOMOBILE MANUFACTURERS' LICENSE
ACT,** §§20-285 to 20-308.22.
See MOTOR VEHICLE MANUFACTURERS.

AUTOMOBILE MECHANICS.
Motor vehicle mechanic and storage liens.
Assignment of actions to enforce to magistrates,
§7A-211.1.

AUTOMOBILE REPAIR FACILITIES.
Motor vehicle repairs generally, §§20-354 to
20-354.9.
See MOTOR VEHICLE REPAIRS.

AUTOMOBILES.
Abandoned and derelict motor vehicles,
§§20-137.6 to 20-137.14.
See ABANDONED MOTOR VEHICLES.
Accidents.
See MOTOR VEHICLE ACCIDENTS.
Clubs and associations, §§58-69-2 to 58-69-60.
See MOTOR CLUBS AND ASSOCIATIONS.
Commissioner.
See MOTOR VEHICLES COMMISSIONER.
Damage appraisers.
See MOTOR VEHICLE DAMAGE APPRAISERS.
Dealers.
See MOTOR VEHICLE DEALERS.
Division.
See MOTOR VEHICLES DIVISION.
Drivers' licenses.
Commercial drivers' licenses, §§20-37.10 to
20-37.23.
See COMMERCIAL DRIVERS' LICENSES.
Generally.
See DRIVERS' LICENSES.
Drunk driving.
See IMPAIRED DRIVING.
Equipment.
See MOTOR VEHICLE EQUIPMENT.
Financial responsibility, §§20-279.1 to 20-284.
See MOTOR VEHICLE FINANCIAL
RESPONSIBILITY.
Generally.
See MOTOR VEHICLES.
Impaired driving.
See IMPAIRED DRIVING.
Inspections, §§20-183.2 to 20-183.8G.
See MOTOR VEHICLE INSPECTIONS.
Insurance.
See MOTOR VEHICLE INSURANCE.
Lemon law, §§20-351 to 20-351.10.
See LEMON LAW.
License plates.
See LICENSE PLATES.
Manufacturers.
See MOTOR VEHICLE MANUFACTURERS.
New motor vehicles warranty act, §§20-351 to
20-351.10.
See LEMON LAW.
Odometers, §§20-340 to 20-350.
See ODOMETERS.
Railroad grade crossings, §§20-142.1 to 20-142.5.
See RAILROAD GRADE CROSSINGS.
Reckless driving.
See RECKLESS DRIVING.
Registration.
See MOTOR VEHICLE REGISTRATION.
Rentals.
See RENTAL VEHICLES.
Service agreement companies, §§66-370, 66-372,
66-373.
See MOTOR VEHICLE SERVICE AGREEMENT
COMPANIES.
Size, weight and loads.
See MOTOR VEHICLE SIZE, WEIGHT AND
LOADS.
Speed.
See SPEED RESTRICTIONS AND VIOLATIONS.

AUTOMOBILES —Cont'd
Stolen vehicles.
  See STOLEN PROPERTY.
Taxicabs.
  See TAXICABS.
Tires.
  See TIRES.
Titling.
  See MOTOR VEHICLE TITLING.
Towing.
  See TOWING OF VEHICLES.
Traffic lights.
  See TRAFFIC LIGHTS.
Traffic regulations.
  See TRAFFIC REGULATIONS.
Traffic tickets.
  See TRAFFIC TICKETS.
Trailers.
  See TRAILERS.

AUTOMOBILE THEFT REWARD SERVICE.
Motor clubs and associations, §58-69-2.

AUTOPSIES.
Authorization.
  Who may authorize, §130A-398.
Fees.
  Medical examiners, §130A-389(a).
Homicide investigations, §15-7.
Inmates of certain public institutions,
    §130A-399.
  Written consent required, §130A-400.
Medical examiners, §130A-389.
  Performance of autopsies or other pathological
    examinations, §130A-389(a), (b).
  Postmortem medicolegal examinations and
    services generally, §§130A-377 to 130A-395.
    See MEDICAL EXAMINERS.
  Reports.
    Autopsies performed pursuant to next of kin
      request, §130A-389(d).
    Requests by next of kin for autopsy, §130A-389(b),
      (c).
  When autopsies or other pathological
    examinations to be performed, §130A-389(a),
    (b).
Medical schools.
  Postmortem examinations in medical schools,
    §130A-401.
  Written consent required, §130A-400.
Photographs, video or audio recordings of
    autopsy.
  Applicability of provisions, §130A-389.1(f).
  Confidentiality, §132-1.8.
  Inspection, §130A-389.1(a).
  Special proceedings.
    Notice of commencement, §130A-389.1(e).
    Show cause upon denial, §130A-389.1(d).
  Unlawful disclosure, §130A-389.1(c).
  Unlawful possession, §130A-389.1(h).
  Who may obtain.
    Private individuals, §130A-389.1(c).
    Public officers and employees, §130A-389.1(b).
  Willful violations, §130A-389.1(g).
Postmortem medicolegal examinations and
    services generally, §§130A-377 to 130A-395.
  See MEDICAL EXAMINERS.
Reports.
  Medical examiners, §130A-389(a), (d).
Right to perform autopsy.
  Limitation on right, §130A-398.

AUTOPSIES —Cont'd
Unclaimed bodies.
  Consent of commission of anatomy, §130A-415(d).
Who may authorize, §130A-398.
Workers' compensation.
  Right to require in case of death, §97-27(c).

AUTO RACING EVENTS.
Alcoholic beverage permit to recreation
    district, §18B-1006(j).

AUTREFOIS, ACQUIT OR CONVICT.
Double jeopardy.
  See DOUBLE JEOPARDY.

AUXILIARY POLICE, §160A-283.
City authorized to organize, §160A-282(a).
Workers' compensation benefits, §160A-282(b),
    (c).

AVD.
Alcohol vaporizing devices, §90-113.10A.

AVERAGE WEEKLY WAGES.
Workers' compensation.
  Defined, §97-2.
  Partial disability, §97-30.
  Total incapacity, §97-29.

AVERASBORO, TOWNSHIP OF.
Room occupancy tax levied by county, uniform
    provisions, §153A-155.

AVERY COUNTY.
Acquisition of property, power, §153A-158.1(a).
Blank or master forms of mortgages, deeds of
    trust, etc.
  Indexing and recording, inapplicability of
    provisions, §47-21.
Board of county commissioners.
  Filling vacancies on board, §153A-27.1.
Coroner elected as nominee of political party.
  Filling vacancy in office, §152-1.
Counties generally.
  See COUNTIES.
Dog collars.
  Unlawful removal of electronic dog collars,
    §14-401.17.
Game laws, local acts not repealed,
    §113-133.1(e).
Housing authority commissioners.
  Tenant serving as commissioner, exemption from
    provision of law allowing, §157-5.
Oil, gas or mineral interest, extinguished, title
    in surface fee holder, §1-42.5(a) to (d).
  Protection of interest from surface fee holder,
    §1-42.5(b), (d).
On-premises unfortified wine licenses.
  Discretion to decline to issue, §105-113.71(b).
Room occupancy tax levied by municipalities
    in county.
  Uniform provisions.
    Generally, §160A-215.
    Municipalities authorized to levy, §160A-215(g).
School property.
  Acquisition and improvement, §153A-158.1.
Sheriff.
  Vacancy, performance of duties until vacancy
    filled, §162-5.1.
Small city mixed beverage elections.
  Inapplicability of subsection to, §18B-600(e1).
Western North Carolina Development
    Association, Inc.
  Appropriation of funds to, §153A-447(a), (b).

AVIATION.
Aircraft.
See AIRCRAFT.
Airports.
See AIRPORTS.
Aviation hall of fame.
Official location, §145-21.
Continuing appropriation to department of transportation, §136-16.4.
North Carolina aviation museum.
Official location, §145-21.

AVIATION GASOLINE.
Gasoline tax.
Defined, §105-449.60.

AVIATION HALL OF FAME.
Official location, §145-21.

AVIATION MAINTENANCE TECHNICIANS.
Motor vehicle license plates, §20-79.4(b).

AWARDS.
Agriculture.
Hall of fame.
Acceptance of awards, §106-568.17.
Annual award to native living outside state, §140A-3.
Design, §140A-1.
Established, §140A-1.
Expenses, §140A-6.
Fields of recognition, §140A-2.
Form, §140A-1.
Funds.
Expenses of administration, §140A-6.
Nonresidents.
Annual award to native living outside state, §140A-3.
Periods covered, §140A-2.
Recipients.
Selection for awards, §140A-5.
Arbitration and awards.
Generally.
See ARBITRATION.
International commercial arbitration and conciliation generally, §§1-567.30 to 1-567.87.
See INTERNATIONAL COMMERCIAL ARBITRATION AND CONCILIATION.
National guard.
Authority to wear medals, ribbons and other awards, §127A-46.
Creation of additional awards, §127A-45.5A.
Design of additional awards, §127A-45.5A.
Meritorious civilian service award, §127A-45.5.
Outstanding unit award, §127A-45.2A.
State active duty award, §127A-45.
State awards system, §§140A-1 to 140A-6.

AWARDS COMMITTEE.
Appointment, §143B-84.
Compensation, §143B-84.
Creation, §143B-83.
Department of cultural resources.
Transfer of committee to department, §143B-51.
Duties.
Generally, §143B-83.
Members, §143B-84.
Powers and duties.
Generally, §143B-83.
Quorum, §143B-84.
Selection of members, §143B-84.

AYDEN, TOWN OF.
Ayden collard festival.
State collard festival, §145-27.

AYDEN, TOWN OF —Cont'd
Satellite annexation.
Limitation on area of satellite corporate limits, inapplicability, §160A-58.1(b).

AZALEAS.
Trespass.
Taking, etc., of certain wild plants from land of another, §14-129.

B

BABCOCK TESTS.
Milk and milk products.
Scales and weights, §106-267.5.

BABY CHICKS.
Disposing of as pets or novelties forbidden, §14-363.1.
Sales and use tax.
Exemption, §105-164.13.

BABY DROP OFF LAW.
Abandonment of child, §14-322.3.
Child abuse or neglect exceptions, §§14-318.2, 14-318.4.
Temporary custody without court order.
Authorized persons, §7B-500(b).
Immunity, §7B-500(e).
Individual's responsibilities, §7B-500(c), (d).
Inquiries of parents, §7B-500(c), (d).
Notification, §7B-500(c), (d).
Voluntarily delivered to individual, §7B-500(d).
Termination of parental rights, grounds, §7B-1111(a).

BABYSITTERS.
Wage and hour act.
Exemptions from wage and hour act, §95-25.14(a).

BABY SITTING SERVICES.
Sex offender providing.
Prohibition, §14-321.1(b).
Baby sitting service defined, §14-321.1(a).
Criminal penalty, §14-321.1(c).

BACKGROUND CHECKS.
Generally.
See CRIMINAL HISTORY RECORD CHECKS.

BACKING OF VEHICLE.
Movement to be safe and without interfering with traffic, §20-154.

BACK PAY.
False claims act.
Retaliation for lawful acts done to prevent violations.
Private right of action, §1-613.
Local governmental employees' retirement system.
Retroactive or additional contributions.
Back pay cases, §128-30(b2).
Retaliatory employment discrimination civil actions.
Award to employee, §95-243(c).
Retirement system for teachers and state employees.
Retroactive or additional contributions.
Back pay cases, §135-8(b2).

BAD CHECKS.
Applicability of provisions.
Prima facie evidence in worthless check cases, §14-107.1(b).

228 GENERAL INDEX

BAD CHECKS —Cont'd

Boating safety.
Vessel agents, §75A-5.2(g).

Collection program.
Administrative office of the courts, §14-107.2(a1), (d).
Check passer and check taker defined, §14-107.2(a).
Community mediation center.
Establishment of program, assistance, fee for services, charging, §14-107.2(b1).
District attorney may establish, §14-107.2(b).
Eligibility criteria, district attorney may establish, §14-107.2(b).
Participation, check passer not prosecuted, §14-107.2(c).
Remitting fee and providing restitution.
Procedures established by administrative office of the courts, §14-107.2(d).

Construing word "credit," §14-107(c).

Costs.
Remedies for returned check, §6-21.3(b).

Credit defined, §14-107(c).

Damages.
Remedies for returned check, §6-21.3(a), (d).

Defenses.
Affirmative defense, §6-21.3(c).

Definitions.
Credit, §14-107(c).
Prima facie evidence in worthless check cases, §14-107.1(a).

Delivery of check or draft to acceptor by mail or delivery other than in person.
Prima facie evidence in worthless check cases.
Applicability of provisions, §14-107.1(c).

Demand letter.
Form, §6-21.3(a2).

Dishonor.
Introduction of check or draft as evidence of fact of dishonor, §14-107.1(e).

Drawing, making, uttering or issuing and delivering, unlawful, §14-107(a).
Soliciting or aiding and abetting, §14-107(b).

Identified check passer, §14-107.1(d).

Magistrates.
Powers in worthless check cases, §7A-273.

Mail.
Delivery of check or draft to acceptor by mail.
Prima facie evidence in worthless check cases, §14-107.1(c).

Motor vehicle dealers or manufacturers.
Highway use taxes.
Submitting bad check in payment of taxes collected by licensee.
Suspension or revocation of license, §20-294.

Motor vehicle fees or taxes, §20-178.

Notification letter.
Form, §6-21.3(a1).

Obtaining property in return for worthless check, draft or order, §14-106.

Prima facie evidence in worthless check cases, §14-107.1.
Affidavit of employee of bank or depository, §14-107.1(f).
Applicability of provisions, §14-107.1(b), (c).
Conditions making provisions applicable, §14-107.1(b), (c).
Definitions, §14-107.1(a).
Dishonor of check or draft, §14-107.1(e).
Identifying check passer, §14-107.1(d).

BAD CHECKS —Cont'd

Processing fees, payment, judge may order, §14-107(e).

Punishment for worthless checks, §14-107(d).

Remedies, §6-21.3.

Restitution, judge may order, §14-107(e).

Returned checks.
Remedies, §6-21.3.

Services charges, payment, judge may order, §14-107(e).

Taxation.
Penalty for bad checks in payment, §105-236(a).
Property taxes.
Payment of taxes.
Penalty, §105-357(b).
Waiver of penalty, §105-358(a).

Worthless checks collection program.
Collection of worthless checks fund, §7A-308(c).
Fees, superior court clerks, §7A-308(c).

BAD FAITH.

Abused, neglected or exploited disabled adults.
Immunity from civil or criminal liability for reporting.
Effect of bad faith or malicious purpose report, §108A-102.

Airports.
Zoning board of appeals.
Judicial review of agency decision, §63-34.

Arson.
Fire incident reports, §58-79-45(a).

Attorneys' fees.
Oil pollution and hazardous substance control.
Award of attorneys' fees to prevailing defendant, §143-215.94CC.
Trade secrets.
Awarding attorneys' fees in misappropriation actions, §66-154(d).

Auctions and auctioneers.
Disciplinary actions against licensee.
Dishonest or bad faith conduct as grounds, §85B-8.

Bank deposits and collections.
Damages.
Measure of damages, §25-4-103(e).

Best evidence rule.
Lost or destroyed originals.
When original document not required, §8C-1 Rule 1004.

Corporations.
Mailing financial statements to shareholders.
Failure to timely file, §55-16-20(c).

Cost where executor, administrator, trustee or person authorized by statute a party, §6-31.

Damages.
Bank deposits and collections.
Measure of damages, §25-4-103(e).

Decedents' estates.
Claims against the estate.
Pleading statute of limitations, §28A-19-11.

Depositions upon oral examination.
Motion to terminate or limit, §1A-1 Rule 30(b).

Emergency management personnel.
Governmental immunity, §166A-14.

Fiduciaries.
Negotiable instruments.
Checks drawn payable to third persons, §32-6.
Checks payable to fiduciary, §32-7.
Deposit in fiduciary's personal account.
Check drawn by fiduciary upon account, §32-10.

BAD FAITH —Cont'd
Fiduciaries —Cont'd
Negotiable instruments —Cont'd
Deposit in name of fiduciary, §32-8.
Deposit in name of principal.
Check drawn upon account of principal and
bank by fiduciary, §32-9.
Deposit in names of two or more trustees.
Checks drawn upon trust account, §32-11.
Transfer of negotiable instruments, §32-5.
Trust and trustees.
Powers which may be incorporated by reference
in trust agreement in absence of bad faith,
§32-27.
Fire incident reports, §58-79-45(a).
Fraud.
Insurance fraud.
Immunity from liability for reporting,
§58-2-160(a), (b).
Governmental immunity.
Emergency management personnel, §166A-14.
Health care benefits providers.
Multiple employer welfare arrangements.
Qualifications for licensure, §58-49-40.
Insurance companies.
Cessations of business.
Liability for statements or communications
made in bad faith, §§58-41-40, 58-41-40(a).
Insurance fraud.
Immunity from liability for reporting fraud,
§58-2-160(a), (b).
Insurance market assistance program.
Good faith immunity from operation of programs,
§58-40-135.
Mechanics' and materialmen' liens.
Dealings with one other than owner.
Priority of lien, §44A-22.
Motor vehicle insurance.
Reinsurance facility.
Information to policyholder upon cession,
§58-37-25(c).
Safe driver incentive plan.
Furnishing statement or information in bad
faith, §58-36-65(f).
Municipalities.
Warranted deeds.
Effect of fraud, malice or bad faith on
immunity, §160A-275.
Negotiable instruments.
Fiduciaries.
Checks drawn payable to third persons, §32-6.
Checks payable to fiduciary, §32-7.
Deposit in fiduciary's personal account.
Check drawn by fiduciary upon account,
§32-10.
Deposit in name of fiduciary, §32-8.
Deposit in name of principal.
Check drawn upon account of principal and
bank by fiduciary, §32-9.
Deposit in names of two or more trustees.
Checks drawn upon trust account, §32-11.
Transfer by fiduciary, §32-5.
Oil pollution and hazardous substance control.
Attorneys' fees.
Award of attorneys' fees to prevailing defendant,
§143-215.94CC.
Open meetings of public bodies.
Additional remedies for violations of article,
§143-318.16A(c).
**Partnerships, knowledge of fact within
meaning of article.**
Knowledge of other facts as in circumstances to
show bad faith, §59-33(a).

BAD FAITH —Cont'd
Statute of limitations.
Decedents' estates.
Pleading statute of limitations, §28A-19-11.
**Summary judgment affidavits made in bad
faith,** §1A-1 Rule 56(g).
Trade secrets.
Attorneys' fees.
Awarding attorneys' fees in misappropriation
actions, §66-154(d).
Trust and trustees.
Powers which may be incorporated by reference in
trust agreement in absence of bad faith,
§32-27.
Warranted deeds.
Municipalities.
Effect of fraud, malice or bad faith on
immunity, §160A-275.

BADGES.
Company police, §74E-7.
Fraternal orders.
Unauthorized wearing, §58-25-70.

BADIN LAKE.
Uwharrie regional resources act, §§153C-1 to
153C-4.

BAGELS.
Sales and use tax exemption.
Bakery items sold by artisan bakeries,
§105-164.13B(a).

BAGGAGE.
Carriers.
Careful handling, §62-202.
Checks, §62-203.
Sale of unclaimed baggage, §62-209.
**Emergency operating authority granted to
duly licensed owner of vehicle or vehicles,**
§62-265.
Hotels.
Liability for loss, §72-2.
Fire loss, §72-4.

BAGGAGE CHECKS, §62-203(d), (e).

BAGS.
Plastic bags.
Retail outlet providing.
Plastic bag management.
Counties containing barrier islands,
§§130A-309.120 to 130A-309.125.
Recyclable material, requirements,
§130A-309.10(c).

BA'HAI.
Marriage, §51-1.

BAIL.
Alimony.
Remedy available, §50-16.7(d).
Appeals.
Correction of errors by appellate division.
Authority of court to act pending appeal,
§15A-1453(a).
Appearance.
Failure to appear, §15A-543(a).
Imposing conditions on pretrial release,
§15A-534(d1).
Penalties, §15A-543(b), (c).
Appearance bond.
Failure to appear and answer on prior occasions.
Secured appearance bond required, no
conditions set, §15A-534(d1).

BAIL —Cont'd
Appearance bond —Cont'd
Pretrial release.
Condition imposed, §15A-534(a).
Arrest in civil cases.
Action on sheriff's bond.
Where judgment recovered against sheriff,
§1-432.
Allowance of bail, §1-425.
Amendment of process or pleading.
Bail not discharged, §1-439.
Authorized, §1-419.
Bail may arrest defendant, §1-435.
Bail not discharged by amendment of process or
pleading, §1-439.
Death of defendant.
Bail exonerated, §1-433.
Defendant in jail.
Sheriff may take bail, §1-430.
Defendants undertaking, §1-420.
Delivery of defendants undertaking to clerks,
§1-421.
Deposit in lieu of bail, §1-426.
Application of deposit to plaintiff's judgment,
§1-429.
Authorized, §§1-419, 1-426.
Bail substituted for deposit, §1-428.
Certificate of deposit, §1-426.
Judgment.
Deposit applied to plaintiff's judgment,
§1-429.
Payment of deposit into court, §1-427.
Sheriff.
Liability on sheriff's bond, §1-427.
Payment of deposit into court, §1-427.
Substitution of bail for deposit, §1-428.
Discharge of defendant, §1-419.
Examination of bail, §1-424.
Exception to bail.
New bail, §1-422.
Notice, §1-421.
Notice of justification, §1-422.
Exoneration of bail, §1-433.
Imprisonment of defendant.
Bail exonerated, §1-433.
Justification of bail, §1-424.
Liability of bail to sheriff, §1-437.
Motion, proceedings against bail, §1-436.
Motion to reduce bail, §1-417.
New bail, §1-422.
Notice by plaintiff of not accepting bail, §1-421.
Notice to plaintiff of justification, §1-422.
Proceedings against bail by motion, §1-436.
Qualification of bail, §1-423.
Quo warranto.
Defendant usurping office, §1-519.
Sheriff.
Bonds, surety.
Liability on bond, §§1-427, 1-432.
Defendant in jail.
Sheriff may take bail, §1-430.
Substitute for deposit, §1-428.
Surrender of defendant, §1-434.
When bail to pay costs, §1-438.
When sheriff liable as bail, §1-431.
Attorney prohibited from becoming surety,
§15A-541(a).
Bail bond.
Defined, §15A-531.
Bail bondsmen and runners, §§58-71-1 to
58-71-195.
See BAIL BONDSMEN AND RUNNERS.

BAIL —Cont'd
Breach of condition.
Forfeiture, §§15A-544.1 to 15A-544.8.
Surrender of principal, §15A-540.
Capias.
Bond of prisoner committed on capias in civil
action, §162-32.
Capital punishment.
Discretion of judge as to pretrial release,
§15A-533(c).
Child support.
Enforcement of support.
Remedy of arrest and bail available, §50-13.4(f).
Illegitimate children.
Continuance, surety of person accused of being
father, §49-5.
Child victims.
Violent crimes against, §15A-534.4.
Community penalties program.
Remission of bail bond if defendant sentenced to
community or intermediate punishment,
§15A-547.1.
Concealed handgun permit.
Proceedings pending for disqualifying crime.
Grounds for denial of permit, §14-415.12(b).
Conditions, §15A-534.
Controlled substance offenses.
Presumptions concerning conditions,
§15A-533(d).
Determination.
Judicial officers may determine, §15A-532(a).
Electronic monitoring.
County fee to cover costs of monitoring,
§7A-313.1.
Interference with devices, §14-226.3.
Excessive bail, NC Const Art I §27, US Const
Amd 8.
Pretrial release, §15A-534(a).
Release after conviction in superior court.
Determination, §15A-536(b), (c).
Evidence to be considered, §15A-536(f).
Right to have conditions determined, §15A-533(b).
Surrender of principal by surety.
After breach of condition, §15A-540(b).
Going off the bond before breach, §15A-540(a).
New conditions of pretrial release, §15A-540(c).
Contempt.
Power of court to punish for contempt not
affected, §15A-546.
Controlled substance offenses.
Conditions of pretrial release.
Presumptions concerning conditions in
controlled substance cases, §15A-533(d).
Methamphetamine manufacturing, §15A-534.6.
Costs.
Civil cases.
When bail to pay costs, §1-438.
Pretrial release services in district or superior
courts, §7A-304(a).
Several actions on one recognizance.
Allowance of costs to defendant, §6-19.
Allowance of costs to plaintiff, §6-18.
Courts-martial of national guard.
Pretrial confinement.
Provisions applicable, §127A-54(b).
Criminal contempt.
Custody of person charged with criminal
contempt, §5A-16(b).
**Defendant sentenced to community or
intermediate punishment.**
Remission of bail bond, §15A-547.1.

BAIL —Cont'd
Definitions, §15A-531.
Delinquent and undisciplined juvenile actions.
Pretrial release of delinquent juvenile.
Transferring jurisdiction of juvenile to superior court, §§7B-2204, 7B-2603(b).
Deposit in lieu of bail.
Civil cases, §§1-419, 1-426 to 1-429.
District courts.
Criminal actions.
Status of bail bond, §7A-290.
Judges of district court.
Power to set bail, §7A-291.
DNA sample.
Collection as condition of pretrial release, §15A-534.
Domestic violence, §15A-534.1(a).
Retention of defendant in custody without action.
Time limitation, §15A-534.1(b).
Effecting release.
Persons authorized, §15A-537(a).
Duties of person effecting release, §15A-537(b).
Powers of law-enforcement or custodial officers, §15A-537(c).
Electronic monitoring as condition of bond or pretrial release.
County fee to cover costs of monitoring, §7A-313.1.
Interference with electronic monitoring devices, §14-226.3.
Evidence, rules of.
Inapplicability, §8C-1 Rule 1101(b).
Excessive bail.
Liability as bail, §1-437.
Action on sheriff's bond, §1-432.
Liability on sheriff's bond, §1-427.
Payment of deposit into court, §1-427.
When liable, §1-431.
Surrender of defendant.
Bail exonerated, §1-433.
Bail may arrest defendant, §1-435.
Surrender of defendant.
Detention of defendant, §1-434.
Usurpation of office.
Defendant usurping office, §1-519.
Written undertaking, §1-420.
Delivery to clerk, §1-421.
Exoneration.
Civil cases, §§1-433, 1-434.
Extradition, §§15A-736, 15A-738.
Fugitives from other states, §15A-735.
Failure to appear.
Imposition of conditions on pretrial release.
Prior failure to appear and answer charges, §15A-534(d1).
Penalty, §15A-543.
Felonies.
Failure to appear, §15A-543(b).
Fingerprints.
Collection as condition of pretrial release, §15A-534.
Forfeiture, §§15A-544.1 to 15A-544.8.
Contents of forfeiture, §15A-544.3(b).
Entry of forfeiture, §15A-544.3(a).
Final judgment, §15A-544.6.
Docketing as civil judgment, §15A-544.7(a).
Execution, §15A-544.7(c), (d).
Lien of judgment, §15A-544.7(b).
No final judgment after forfeiture set aside, §15A-544.5(g).
Relief from final judgment of forfeiture, §15A-544.8.

BAIL —Cont'd
Forfeiture —Cont'd
Identifying information on bond, §15A-544.2(a).
Effect of release on bond that does not contain, §15A-544.2(b).
Jurisdiction, §15A-544.1.
Notice of forfeiture, §15A-544.4(a), (c).
Mailing, §15A-544.4(b), (d), (e).
Relief from final judgment of forfeiture.
Appeals, §15A-544.8(f).
Exclusive nature of relief, §15A-544.8(a).
Finality of judgment as to other parties not affected, §15A-544.8(e).
Procedure, §15A-544.8(c), (d).
Reasons, §15A-544.8(b).
Setting aside forfeiture.
Appeals, §15A-544.5(h).
Exclusive nature of relief, §15A-544.5(a).
Failure to appear stricken, procedure, §15A-544.5(c).
Final judgment of forfeiture set aside, §15A-544.5(g).
Motion procedure, §15A-544.5(d), (e).
One motion per forfeiture, §15A-544.5(e).
Procedure, §15A-544.5(c) to (e).
Prohibited in certain circumstances, §15A-544.5(f).
Reasons, §15A-544.5(b).
Restrictions, §15A-544.5(e) to (g).
Fugitives from other states awaiting extradition, §15A-735.
Guaranteed arrest bond certificates issued by motor clubs.
Acceptance in lieu of cash bail or other bond, §58-69-55(a).
Forfeiture and enforcement, applicable provisions, §58-69-55(b).
Surety company becoming surety with respect to.
Filing undertaking, amount, §58-69-50(a).
Form of undertaking, §58-69-50(b).
Habeas corpus.
Right of habeas corpus not abridged, §15A-547.
When party bailed or remanded, §17-35.
Hearings.
Source of money or property posted, §15A-539(b).
House arrest with electronic monitoring.
Pretrial release.
Condition imposed, §15A-534(a).
Impaired driving offense.
Order to abstain from alcohol consumption.
Pretrial release order, §15A-534(i).
Initial appearance before magistrate.
Release on bail, §15A-511(e).
Law enforcement officers.
Power of officer to set bail.
Termination of power upon establishment of district court, §7A-274.
Limitation of actions.
Action against bail, §1-52.
Mayors.
Power of mayor to set bail.
Termination of power upon establishment of district court, §7A-274.
Mental health, developmental disability, substance abuse.
Involuntary commitment.
Escape and commission of crime after escape or while resident of facility.
Pretrial release denied, §122C-254(a).
Misdemeanors.
Failure to appear, §15A-543(c).

BAIL —Cont'd
Misdemeanors —Cont'd
  False qualification by surety, §15A-542(b).
  Surety.
    Persons prohibited from becoming surety.
      Violation of provisions, §15A-541(b).
Mortgage in lieu of bond.
  Recognizance for appearance in criminal
    proceeding, §58-74-5.
  Required for recognizance in criminal proceeding.
    Cancellation of mortgage in such proceedings,
      §58-74-10.
Motor clubs and associations.
  Bail or cash appearance bond service, §58-69-2.
  Guaranteed arrest bond certificates issued by
    motor clubs, §58-69-50.
National guard.
  Courts-martial.
    Pretrial confinement.
      Provisions applicable, §127A-54(b).
Obligor.
  Effect of bail bond upon, §15A-534(h).
Orders.
  Modification.
    Motion of person detained, §15A-538(a).
    Motion of prosecutor, §15A-539(a).
    Substitution of surety, §15A-538(b).
  Pretrial release, §15A-534(d).
    Impaired driving offense.
      Order to abstain from alcohol consumption,
        §15A-534(i).
    Modification of orders, §15A-534(e).
      Evidence to be considered, §15A-534(g).
    Revocation of order, §15A-534(f).
      Evidence to be considered, §15A-534(g).
  Release after conviction in superior court,
    §15A-536(d).
    Modification or revocation of order, §15A-536(e).
      Evidence to be considered, §15A-536(f).
Peace officers.
  Power of peace officer to set bail.
    Termination of power upon establishment of
      district court, §7A-274.
  Prohibited from becoming surety, §15A-541(a).
Postrial release.
  Guilt established and defendant awaiting
    sentence or appeal.
    Authority of court to release, §15A-536(a).
    Conditions imposed, required, factors,
      §15A-536(b), (c).
    Evidence considered by judge, §15A-536(f).
    Modification or revocation of order, §15A-536(e).
    Order by judge authorizing release,
      §15A-536(d).
Pretrial release.
  Audio and video transmissions.
    Conduct of proceedings, §15A-532(b), (c).
  Capital cases.
    Discretion of judge, §15A-533(c).
  Closed-circuit television.
    Conduct of proceedings, §15A-532(b), (c).
  Conditions.
    Assurance of appearance and no unreasonable
      risk of harm to community, §15A-533(e).
    Controlled substance offenses.
      Presumptions concerning conditions,
        §15A-533(d).
    Criminal history report for defendant.
      Domestic violence offenses, §15A-534.1(a).
    Determination.
      Conditions which must be imposed,
        §15A-534(a), (b).

BAIL —Cont'd
Pretrial release —Cont'd
  Conditions —Cont'd
    Determination —Cont'd
      Evidence to be considered, §15A-534(g).
      Factors, §15A-534(c).
      Felony defendant currently on probation for
        prior offense, §15A-534(d2).
      Judicial officers may determine, §15A-532(a).
      Right to have conditions determined in
        noncapital cases, §15A-533(b).
    Domestic violence offenses.
      Criminal history report for defendant,
        §15A-534.1(a).
    Electronic monitoring.
      County fee to cover costs of monitoring,
        §7A-313.1.
      Interference with devices, §14-226.3.
    Impaired driving offense.
      Order to abstain from alcohol consumption,
        §15A-534(i).
    Prior failure of defendant to appear and answer
      charges, §15A-534(d1).
    Sex offenses and crimes of violence against child
      victims, §15A-534.4(a).
    Waiver of conditions, §15A-534.4(b).
  Delinquent and undisciplined juvenile actions.
    Transferring jurisdiction to superior court,
      §§7B-2204, 7B-2603(b).
  Domestic violence, §15A-534.1(a).
    Retention of defendant in custody without
      action, time limitation, §15A-534.1(b).
  Electronic monitoring as condition.
    County fee to cover costs of monitoring,
      §7A-313.1.
    Interference with devices, §14-226.3.
  Failure to appear and answer on prior occasions,
    §15A-534(d1).
  Impaired driving offense.
    Order to abstain from alcohol consumption,
      §15A-534(i).
  Mental health, developmental disability,
    substance abuse.
    Involuntary commitment.
      Escape and commission of crime after escape
        or while resident of facility.
        Pretrial release denied, §122C-254(a).
  Noncapital cases, §15A-532(b).
  Orders, §15A-534(d).
    Modification, §15A-534(e).
      Evidence to be considered, §15A-534(g).
    Revocation, §15A-534(f).
      Evidence to be considered, §15A-534(g).
  Persons committed to mental health facility,
    §15A-533(a).
  Policies.
    Issuance, §15A-535(a), (b).
  Public health.
    Denial to protect, §15A-534.5.
  Restrictions on travel, associations, conduct or
    place of abode.
    Prior failure of defendant to appear and answer
      charges, §15A-534(d1).
  Secured appearance bond.
    Prior failure of defendant to appear and answer
      charges, §15A-534(d1).
  Sex offenses and crimes of violence against child
    victims, §15A-534.4.
  Two or more failures to appear and answer on
    prior occasions, §15A-534(d1).

BAIL —Cont'd
Pretrial release —Cont'd
Two-way audio and video transmissions.
Conduct of proceedings, §15A-532(b), (c).
Prisons and prisoners.
Discharge of insolvent prisoners.
Persons taken in bail proceedings, §23-29.
Probation.
Violation of probation.
Bail following arrest, §15A-1345(b), (b1).
Probation officers.
Prohibited from becoming surety, §15A-541(a).
Public health.
Detention to protect, §15A-534.5.
Quo warranto.
Defendant usurping office, §1-519.
Right to bail.
Noncapital offenses.
Right to have conditions of pretrial release
determined, §15A-533(b).
Rules of evidence.
Inapplicability, §8C-1 Rule 1101(b).
Runners.
Bail bondsmen and runners, §§58-71-1 to
58-71-195.
See BAIL BONDSMEN AND RUNNERS.
Sex offenders.
Post-release supervision.
Arrest for violation.
Bail following arrest when releasee is sex
offender, §15A-1368.6(b1).
Sexual offenses, §15A-534.4.
Sheriffs.
Bond of prisoner committed on capias in civil
action, §162-32.
Civil cases.
Defendant in jail.
Sheriff may take bail, §1-430.
Liability on bond, §§1-427, 1-432.
Prohibited from becoming surety, §15A-541(a).
Source of money or property posted,
§15A-539(b).
Superior courts.
Pretrial release.
Policies.
Issuance, §15A-535(a), (b).
Release after conviction.
Authorized, §15A-536(a).
Conditions.
Determination, §15A-536(b), (c).
Evidence to be considered, §15A-536(f).
Order, §15A-536(d).
Modification or revocation, §15A-536(e).
Evidence to be considered, §15A-536(f).
Surety.
Defined, §15A-531.
False qualification by surety, §15A-542(a).
Penalty, §15A-542(b).
Persons prohibited from becoming sureties,
§15A-541(a).
Penalty for violation, §15A-541(b).
Surrender of principal.
After breach of condition, §15A-540(b).
Going off the bond before breach, §15A-540(a).
New conditions of pretrial release, §15A-540(c).
Surrender of principal.
Breach of condition, §15A-540.

**BAIL BONDSMEN AND RUNNERS, §§58-71-1 to
58-71-195.**
Accommodation bondsmen.
Defined, §58-71-1.

BAIL BONDSMEN AND RUNNERS —Cont'd
Affidavit filed with commissioner.
Appointment of bondsman, §58-71-141(a).
Affidavits filed with clerk of court,
§58-71-140(d).
Age.
Licenses.
Minimum age, §58-71-50(b).
Amount of bail bond.
Limit on amount of bond to be written by
professional bondsman, §58-71-175.
Appointment of bondsman.
Affidavit filed with commissioner, §58-71-141(a).
Former insurer defined, §58-71-141(c).
Rules, §58-71-141(b).
Arrest.
Surrender of defendant by surety.
Arrest of defendant for purpose of surrender,
§58-71-30.
Attorneys at law.
Prohibited from becoming sureties or runners,
§58-71-105.
Bankruptcy and insolvency.
Notice of receivership, §58-71-81.
Breach of undertaking.
Surrender of defendant, §§58-71-20, 58-71-25.
Arrest of defendant, §58-71-30.
Child support enforcement.
Forfeiture of licensing privilege, §50-13.12.
Licenses, suspension or revocation, §58-71-80(a).
Collateral.
Receipts for, §58-71-100.
Commissioner of insurance.
Administration of provisions, §58-71-5(a).
Deposit of securities.
Disposal, authority, §58-71-151.
Master trust, §58-71-151.
Evidence of commissioners' actions, §58-71-5(b).
Examinations, §58-71-170.
Rules and regulations, §58-71-5(a).
Confidentiality of information.
Criminal history record checks, §58-71-51(b).
Runners.
Notice of termination of appointment,
§58-71-125.
Surety bondsmen.
Notice of termination of appointment,
§58-71-115(c).
Conflict of laws, §58-71-195.
Continuing education, §58-71-71(b), (c).
Failure to comply with requirements,
§58-71-71(e).
Contracts.
Transfer of business, §58-71-122.
Criminal history record check.
Applicants for license, §58-71-50(a).
Authorization, §58-71-51(a).
Confidentiality of information, §58-71-51(b).
Procedure, §58-71-51(a).
Renewal in even numbered years, §58-71-75(c).
Death of bail bondsman, §58-71-121.
Defects not to invalidate undertakings,
§58-71-10(a).
Definitions, §58-71-1.
Deposit of securities.
Disposal by commissioner, §58-71-151.
Local requirements prohibited, §58-71-190.
Master trust, §58-71-151.
Professional bondsmen.
Deficiencies.
Deposit of additional securities, §58-71-160(a).

BAIL BONDSMEN AND RUNNERS —Cont'd
Deposit of securities —Cont'd
Professional bondsmen —Cont'd
Deficiencies —Cont'd
Failure to give notice, §58-71-160(b).
Disposition of securities.
Power of attorney.
Bondsman to furnish with securities, §58-71-155.
Required, §58-71-145.
Trust, securities held in, §58-71-151.
Release and cancellation of undertaking.
Deposit for defendant admitted to bail authorizes, §58-71-135.
Substituting bail by sureties for deposit, §58-71-130.
Discontinuance of business.
Cancellation of license, §58-71-120.
Drug violations.
Misdemeanors.
Denial of license, §58-71-80(b2).
Revocation, refusal to renew license, §58-71-80(b1).
Education.
Approval of courses, §58-71-71(d).
Continuing education, §58-71-71(b), (c).
Failure to comply with requirements, §58-71-71(e).
False representation that requirements met, §58-71-71(e).
Exemptions, §58-71-71(c).
Qualifications of instructors, §58-71-72(a), (b).
Requirements, §58-71-71(a), (b).
Rules and regulations, §58-71-71(f).
Employment of staff for office duties, §58-71-40(e).
Evidence.
Commissioners' actions, §58-71-5(b).
Examinations.
Commissioner of insurance, §58-71-170.
Educational requirements for taking, §58-71-71(a).
Licenses, §58-71-70.
Fees, §58-71-70.
Fees.
Deposit of securities.
Master trust, §58-71-151.
Disposition, §58-71-180.
Licenses, §58-71-55.
Examinations, §58-71-70.
Renewal, §58-71-75(d).
Dual license holding, §58-71-82.
Felonies.
Conviction of felony.
Grounds for denial, suspension, revocation or refusal to renew license, §§15A-1331(a), 58-71-80(b).
Reports.
Knowingly and willfully falsifying, §58-71-165.
Fingerprints.
Criminal history record checks.
License applicants to furnish commission.
Renewal in even numbered years, §58-71-75(b).
First-year licensees, §58-71-41(a) to (e).
Defined, §58-71-1.
Exceptions to provisions, §58-71-41(e).
Inability to become employed.
Affidavit, §58-71-41(d).
Notice of completing supervision, §58-71-41(b).
Supervision, §58-71-41(a), (b).

BAIL BONDSMEN AND RUNNERS —Cont'd
First-year licensees —Cont'd
Termination of contract or employment.
Notification to commissioner, §58-71-41(c).
Suspension, revocation or refusal to renew license, §58-71-80(c).
Forfeiture of bail.
Procedure, §58-71-35(a).
Remission of judgment, §58-71-35(b).
Fraud.
Grounds for denial, suspension, revocation or refusal to renew license, §58-71-80(a).
Hearings.
Licenses.
Denial, suspension, revocation or refusal to renew, §58-71-85(b).
Source of bail.
Rights unaffected, §15A-539(c).
Identification cards, §58-71-40(d).
Incapacitated or incompetence of bail bondsman, §58-71-121.
Jailers.
Prohibited from becoming sureties or runners, §58-71-105.
Licenses.
Applications, §58-71-40(b).
Criminal history record check on applicants, §§58-71-50(a), 58-71-51.
Renewal.
Even numbered years, §58-71-75(c).
Reapplication, §58-71-40(c).
Renewal.
Even numbered years, §58-71-75(a), (b).
Runners.
Contents of application for runner's license, §58-71-65.
Disclosure of prior licensure as professional bondsman or runner, §58-71-65.
Endorsement by bail bondsman, §58-71-65.
Cancellation of license.
Discontinuance of business, §58-71-120.
Criminal history record check.
Applicants for license, §§58-71-50(a), 58-71-51.
Renewal.
Even numbered years, §58-71-75(c).
Denial, suspension, revocation or refusal to renew, §58-71-85(a).
Conviction of felony, §58-71-80(b).
Dual license holding, §58-71-82.
Felony convictions, §15A-1331A.
First-year licensee whose employment or contract terminated, §58-71-80(c).
Grounds, §58-71-80(a).
Hearing, §58-71-85(b).
Misdemeanor drug violations, §58-71-80(b1), (b2).
Notice, §58-71-85(b).
Discontinuance of business.
Cancellation of license, §58-71-120.
Dual license holding, §58-71-82.
Examinations, §58-71-70.
Eligibility after application, time, §58-71-70.
Fees, §58-71-70.
Notice of time and place, time, §58-71-70.
Subsequent exam after failure, time, §58-71-70.
Unable to complete within time limit, §58-71-70.
Fees, §58-71-55.
Examinations, §58-71-70.
Renewal, §58-71-75(d).
Dual license holding, §58-71-82.
First-year licensees, §58-71-41(a) to (e).

BAIL BONDSMEN AND RUNNERS —Cont'd

Licenses —Cont'd

Identification cards, §58-71-40(d).

Individual natural persons only, §58-71-40(a).

Investigation of applicant, §58-71-40(b).

Local licenses prohibited, §58-71-190.

Monetary penalty for violations, §58-2-70(a), (c), (d), (g).

Qualifications, §58-71-50(b).

Registration, §58-71-140(a) to (c).

Renewal, §58-71-45.

  Applications.

    Even numbered years, §58-71-75(a), (b).

  Criminal history record check.

    Even numbered years, §58-71-75(c).

  Date, §58-71-75(a).

  Dual license holding, §58-71-82.

  Fee, §58-71-75(d).

  Refusal to renew, §§58-71-80 to 58-71-85.

  Required, §58-71-75(a).

Required, §58-71-40(a).

Resident of state.

  Requirement, §58-71-50(b).

    Proof of residency, §58-71-50(c).

Restitution for violations, §58-2-70(e), (f), (g).

Runners.

  Applications.

    Contents of application for runner's license, §58-71-65.

    Disclosure of prior licensure as professional bondsman or runner, §58-71-65.

    Endorsement by bail bondsman, §58-71-65.

  Cancellation, §58-71-45.

  Qualifications, §58-71-50(b).

  Registration, §58-71-140(c).

  Required, §58-71-40(a).

Surrender, §58-2-65.

Suspension or revocation, §§58-71-80 to 58-71-85.

  Applicable provisions, §58-2-70(h).

  Child support enforcement, §58-71-80(a).

  Criminal convictions, §§15A-1331A, 58-2-60(b).

  Notice and hearing, §58-2-70(b).

Term of license, §58-71-45.

Transfer of business, §58-71-122.

Limit on amount of bond to be written by professional bondsman, §58-71-175.

Local governments.

Duplication of regulations prohibited, §58-71-190.

Misdemeanors.

Drug violations.

  Denial of license, §58-71-80(b2).

  Revocation or refusal to renew license, §58-71-80(b1).

Violations of provisions, §58-71-185.

Modification of bail.

Rights unaffected, §15A-539(c).

Notice.

Bankruptcy.

  Notice of receivership, §58-71-81.

First-year licensees.

  Completion of supervision, §58-71-41(b).

Licenses.

  Denial, suspension, revocation or refusal to renew, §58-71-85(b).

Runners.

  Appointments and terminations, §58-71-125.

Surety bondsmen.

  Appointments and terminations, §58-71-115.

Obligors.

Defined, §58-71-1.

Office staff, license exemption, §58-71-40(e).

BAIL BONDSMEN AND RUNNERS —Cont'd

Parole or probation officers.

Prohibited from becoming sureties or runners, §58-71-105.

Payment of bond.

Deferral, §58-71-167(a), (b).

Peace officers.

Prohibited from becoming sureties or runners, §58-71-105.

Penalties.

Violations of provisions, §58-71-185.

Personation of law-enforcement officer, §58-71-95.

Powers of attorney.

Deposit of securities by professional bondsmen.

  Bondsmen to furnish power of attorney with securities, §58-71-155.

Premiums.

Payments.

  Deferral, §58-71-167(a), (b).

Professional bondsmen.

Defined, §58-71-1.

Deposit of securities.

  Deficiencies.

    Deposit of additional securities, §58-71-160(a).

    Failure to give notice, §58-71-160(b).

  Disposition of securities.

    Power of attorney.

      Bondsman to furnish with securities, §58-71-155.

  Required, §58-71-145.

Examination, §58-71-170(a).

Licenses.

  Generally. See within this heading, "Licenses."

Reports, §58-71-165.

Rebates.

Prohibited practices, §58-71-95.

Receipts for collateral, §58-71-100(a).

Records.

Separate from records of other businesses, §58-71-168.

Reduction in bond.

No return of premium, §58-71-16.

Registration.

Licenses and power of appointment, §58-71-140(a) to (c).

Statewide electronic bondsmen registry, §58-71-140(e).

Reports.

Professional bondsmen, §58-71-165.

Runners.

  Bail bondsman to annually report runners, §58-71-125.

Surety bondsmen.

  Insurers to annually report surety bondsmen, §58-71-115.

Resident of state.

Applicants for license.

  Requirement, §58-71-50(b).

  Proof of residency, §58-71-50(c).

Rules and regulations.

Commissioner of insurance, §58-71-5(a).

Educational requirements, §58-71-71(f).

Runners.

Defined, §58-71-1.

Eligibility to be runner, §58-71-125.

Licenses.

  Applications.

    Contents of application for runner's license, §58-71-65.

BAIL BONDSMEN AND RUNNERS —Cont'd
Runners —Cont'd
Licenses —Cont'd
Applications —Cont'd
Disclosure of prior licensure as professional
bondsman or runner, §58-71-65.
Endorsement by bail bondsman, §58-71-65.
Cancellation, §58-71-45.
General provisions. See within this heading,
"Licenses."
Qualifications, §58-71-50(b).
Registration, §58-71-140(c).
Required, §58-71-40(a).
Notice.
Appointments and terminations, §58-71-125.
Persons prohibited from becoming runners,
§58-71-105.
Reports.
Bail bondsman to annually report runner,
§58-71-125.
Security deposits. See within this heading,
"Deposit of securities."
Shared trust accounts, §58-71-100(b).
Sheriffs.
Prohibited from becoming sureties or runners,
§58-71-105.
Signatures.
Bonds not to be signed in blank, §58-71-110.
Countersigning.
Authority given only to licensed employees,
§58-71-110.
Solicitation.
Prohibited practices, §58-71-95.
Statewide electronic bondsmen registry,
§58-71-140(e).
Sureties.
Appointment.
Notice, §58-71-115(a).
Defined, §58-71-1.
Examination, §58-71-170(b).
Insurers to annually report surety bondsmen,
§58-71-115.
Liability not affected by agreement or lack of
qualifications, §58-71-10(b).
Notice.
Appointments and terminations, §58-71-115.
Persons prohibited from becoming sureties,
§58-71-105.
Prerequisites, §58-71-15.
Qualifications, §58-71-15.
Reduction in bond.
No return of premium, §58-71-16.
Registration of power of appointment,
§58-71-140(b).
Surrender of defendant by surety, §§58-71-20 to
58-71-30.
Termination of appointment.
Notice, §58-71-115(b).
Surrender of defendant by surety.
Arrest of defendant for purpose of surrender,
§58-71-30.
Authorized, §58-71-20.
Procedure, §58-71-25.
Return of premium.
When not required, §58-71-20.
Term of licenses, §58-71-45.
Transfer of business, §58-71-122.
Trust accounts, §58-71-100(b).
Violations of provisions.
Grounds for denial, suspension, revocation or
refusal to renew license, §58-71-80(a).

BAIL BONDSMEN AND RUNNERS —Cont'd
Violations of provisions —Cont'd
Penalties, §58-71-185.
Prohibited practices, §58-71-95.

BAIL EXONERATED.
Arrest in civil cases, §1-433.
Surrender of defendant, §1-434.

BAILMENTS.
Artwork on consignment, §§25C-1 to 25C-5.
Civil action for interference with property.
Trespass committed during existence of bailment,
§99A-1.
Embezzlement.
Master and servant.
Larceny by servant or employee, §14-74.
Receipt of property by bailee by virtue of office or
employment, §14-90.
Hired property.
Conversion, §14-168.1.
Prima facie evidence of intent, §14-168.3.
Trucks, automobile or other motor vehicles,
§14-168.5(a).
Definitions, §14-168.2.
Failure to return, §14-167.
Hiring with intent to defraud, §14-168.
Malicious or willful injury to, §14-165.
Protection of bailor against acts of bailee.
Violations made misdemeanors, §14-169.
Subletting hired property, §14-166.
Leases, UCC.
Risk of loss passing to lessee.
Goods held by bailee and delivered without
being moved, §25-2A-219(2).
Motor vehicle repairs.
Exceeding estimate.
Shop not to retain vehicle for refusal to pay
excessive charges, §20-354.5(d).
Options to purchase.
Failing to return rented property on which there
is purchase option, §14-168.4.
Sales, UCC.
Seller's remedy of stoppage of delivery in transit,
§25-2-705.
Subletting of hired property, §14-166.
Hiring with intent to defraud, §14-168.
**Trespass committed during existence of
bailment.**
Civil action for interference with property, §99A-1.
**Vehicles and draft animals, protection of
bailor against bailee's act,** §§14-165 to
14-169.
Attorney in fact.
Conversion by attorney in fact, §14-168.1.
Bailee.
Conversion by bailee, §14-168.1.
Conversion.
Bailees, lessees, tenants or attorneys in fact,
§14-168.1.
Prima facie evidence of intent to convert.
Property other than motor vehicle, §14-168.3.
Truck, automobile or other motor vehicle,
§14-168.5(a).
Truck, automobile or other motor vehicle.
Demand for return, §14-168.5(b).
Prima facie evidence of intent to convert,
§14-168.5(a).
Definitions, §14-168.2.
Failure to return hired property, §14-167.
Report of failure to return hired motor vehicles,
§20-102.2.

BAILMENTS —Cont'd
Vehicles and draft animals, protection of bailor against bailee's act —Cont'd
Fraud.
Hiring with intent to defraud, §14-168.
Lessee.
Conversion by lessee, §14-168.1.
Malicious or willful injury to hired personal property, §14-165.
Options to purchase.
Failing to return rented property on which there is purchase option.
Intent to commit crime, presumption, §14-168.4(b).
Misdemeanor, §14-168.4(a).
Prosecution of violations, §14-168.4(c).
Subletting of hired property, §14-166.
Tenant.
Conversion by tenant, §14-168.1.
Violations made misdemeanors, §14-169.
Willful injury to hired personal property, §14-165.

BAIL OR CASH APPEARANCE BOND SERVICE.
Motor clubs and associations, §58-69-2.

BAITING ANIMALS, §14-362.1.
Black bears.
Placing food products as bait in area with open season for black bears, §113-294(r).
Dog baiting, §14-362.2.

BAKERY ITEMS.
Sales and use tax exemption.
Sales by artisan bakery, §105-164.13B(a).

BALANCED GROWTH POLICY ACT,
§§143-506.6 to 143-506.13.
Citation of article, §143-506.6.
Citizen participation.
Governor to establish process of citizen participation, §143-506.11.
Cooperation of agencies.
Endorsement by general assembly, §143-506.9.
Declaration of policy, §143-506.8.
Governor.
Citizen participation.
Governor to establish process, §143-506.11.
Designation of growth centers, §143-506.10.
Growth centers.
Designation, §143-506.10.
Legislative declaration, §§143-506.7, 143-506.8.
Partnerships.
Implementation of a state-local partnership, §143-506.13.
Policy areas.
Delineation of program area guidelines, §143-506.12.
Program area guidelines.
Delineation, §143-506.12.
Purposes, §143-506.7.
Policy areas, §143-506.12.
State departments and agencies.
Cooperation of agencies encouraged by general assembly, §143-506.9.
State-local partnership.
Implementation, §143-506.13.
Title, §143-506.6.

BALD EAGLES.
Unlawfully taking, possessing, etc., §113-294(l).

BALD HEAD ISLAND.
Eminent domain.
Vesting of title and right to possession, §40A-42(a).

BALLISTIC KNIVES.
Possession and sale, §14-269.6(a), (b).

BALLOON PAYMENTS.
High cost home loans, §24-1.1E(b).
Home loans for term in excess of six months, §24-1.1A(a).
Retail installment sales, §25A-34.

BALLOON RACES.
Winery special event permit authorization, §18B-1114.1.

BALLOT COUNTERS, §163-43.

BALLOTS.
Absentee ballots.
Generally, §§163-226 to 163-239.
See ABSENTEE BALLOTS.
Generally.
See ELECTIONS.

BALL PARKS.
In-stand sales of alcoholic beverages, §18B-1009.
Hours of sale, §18B-1006(q).

BANG'S DISEASE, §§106-388 to 106-398.
See BRUCELLOSIS.

BANK BILLS.
Limitation of actions not affecting actions to enforce payment, §1-32.

BANK BRANCH ACT, §53-62.

BANK DEPOSITS AND COLLECTIONS,
§§25-4-101 to 25-4-504.
Account.
Defined, §25-4-104(a).
Afternoon.
Defined, §25-4-104(a).
Agents.
Agency status of collecting banks, §25-4-201(a).
Alteration of instruments.
Customer's duty to discover and report, §25-4-406.
Applicability of article, §25-4-102(a).
Attachment and garnishment.
When item subject to legal process, §25-4-303(a).
Banking day.
Defined, §25-4-104(a).
Branch or separate offices deemed separate bank, §25-4-106.
Burden of proof.
Stop payment order.
Burden of proof of loss, §25-4-403(c).
Care.
Certain action constituting ordinary care, §25-4-103(c).
Citation of article, §25-4-101.
Clearinghouse.
Defined, §25-4-104(a).
Effect, §25-4-103(b).
Collection by depositary and collecting banks.
Action.
When action seasonable, §25-4-202(b).
Agency status.
Item indorsed "pay any bank,"§25-4-201(b).
Presumption and duration of agency status of collecting banks, §25-4-201(a).
Provisional status of credits, §25-4-201(a).
Bills of lading.
Warranties of collecting bank as to documents, §25-7-508.
Charge-back.
Right of charge-back, §25-4-212(a) to (f).

BANK DEPOSITS AND COLLECTIONS —Cont'd
Collection by depositary and collecting banks
—Cont'd
Delayed, §25-4-108(a), (b).
Direct return, §25-4-212(a) to (f).
Documents of title.
Warranties of collecting bank as to documents,
§25-7-508.
Duration of agency status of collecting banks,
§25-4-201(a).
Holder in due course.
When bank gives value for purposes of holder in
due course, §25-4-209.
Indorsements.
Missing indorsement, §25-4-205.
Insolvency, §25-4-214(a) to (d).
Instructions.
Effect of instructions, §25-4-203.
Liability for insolvency, neglect, etc., §25-4-202(c).
Methods of sending and presenting, §25-4-204(a),
(b).
Payment.
Deposit of money.
Availability, §25-4-213(f).
When deposit becomes final, §25-4-213(e).
Final payment of item by payor bank,
§25-4-213(a).
Liability of bank, §25-4-213(d).
Provisional debits and credits.
When provisional debits and credits become
final, §25-4-213(b), (c).
Suspends payment.
Defined, §25-4-104(a).
When provisional debits and credits become
final, §25-4-213(b), (c).
Preference, §25-4-214(a) to (d).
Presentment.
By notice of item not payable by, through or at
bank, §25-4-210(a).
Liability of secondary parties, §25-4-210(b).
Method of sending and presenting, §25-4-204(a),
(b).
Refund.
Right of refund, §25-4-212(a) to (f).
Responsibility for collection or return,
§25-4-202(a).
Security interests.
Accompanying documents and proceeds,
§25-4-208(a).
Credit given, §25-4-208(b).
Final settlement, §25-4-208(c).
Sending and presenting.
By notice of item not payable by, through or at
bank, §25-4-210(a).
Liability of secondary parties, §25-4-210(b).
Direct to payor bank, §25-4-204(c).
Methods for sending and presenting,
§25-4-204(a), (b).
Settlement by bank.
Final settlement, §25-4-211(d).
Medium of settlement, §25-4-211(a).
Midnight deadline, §25-4-211(c).
Time of settlement, §25-4-211(a).
Status.
Agency status.
Presumption and duration of agency status of
collecting banks, §25-4-201(a).
Provisional status of credits, §25-4-201(a).
Transfer between banks, §25-4-206.
Value.
When bank gives value for purposes of holder in
due course, §25-4-209.

BANK DEPOSITS AND COLLECTIONS —Cont'd
Collection by depositary and collecting banks
—Cont'd
Warehouse receipts.
Warranties of collecting bank as to receipts,
§25-7-508.
Warranties.
Documents of title.
Warranties of collecting bank as to receipts
and bills, §25-7-508.
When action seasonable, §25-4-202(b).
When provisional debits and credits become final,
§25-4-213(b), (c).
Liability of banks, §25-4-213(d).
Withdrawal.
When certain credits become available for
withdrawal, §25-4-213(e).
Collection of documentary drafts.
Definition of documentary draft, §25-4-104(a).
Dishonor.
Duty to notify customer of dishonor, §25-4-501.
Referee in case of need, §25-4-503.
Report of reasons for dishonor, §25-4-503.
Handling of documentary drafts, §25-4-501.
"On arrival" drafts.
Presentment, §25-4-502.
Presentment.
Duty to send for presentment, §25-4-501.
"On arrival" drafts, §25-4-502.
Responsibility of presenting bank for documents
and goods, §25-4-503.
Privilege of presenting bank to deal with goods,
§25-4-504(a).
Security interest for expenses, §25-4-504(b).
Referee, §25-4-503.
Responsibility of presenting bank for documents
and goods, §25-4-503.
Security interest for expenses, §25-4-504(b).
Commercial code general provisions, §§25-1-101
to 25-1-310.
See COMMERCIAL CODE.
Conflict of laws.
Liability of bank, §25-4-102(b).
Contributory negligence.
Unauthorized signature or alteration,
§25-4-406(c), (d).
Customer.
Defined, §25-4-104(a).
Damages.
Certain action constituting ordinary care,
§25-4-103(e).
Limitation by agreements, §25-4-103(a).
Measure of damages, §25-4-103(e).
Definitions.
Agreement for electronic presentment,
§25-4-110(a).
Article 1 general definitions.
Applicability, §25-4-104(d).
Banks generally, §25-4-105.
Collecting bank, §§25-4-105, 25-4-105.1(c).
Depositary bank, §25-4-105.
Generally, §25-4-104(a).
Intermediary bank, §25-4-105.
Other definitions applying to article, §25-4-104(b),
(c).
Payable at bank, §25-4-105.1(b).
Payable through bank, §25-4-105.1(a).
Payor banks, §25-4-105.
Presenting bank, §25-4-105.
Remitting bank, §25-4-105.
Delays, §25-4-108(a), (b).

BANK DEPOSITS AND COLLECTIONS —Cont'd

Depositary and collecting banks.

Collection by. See within this heading, "Collection by depositary and collecting banks."

Defined, §25-4-105.

Documentary drafts.

Collection. See within this heading, "Collection of documentary drafts."

Defined, §25-4-104(a).

Draft.

Defined, §25-4-104(a).

Executions.

When item subject to legal process, §25-4-303(a).

Federal reserve regulations.

Effect, §25-4-103(b).

Forgery.

Customer's duty to discover and report, §25-4-406.

Intermediary bank.

Defined, §25-4-105.

Item.

Defined, §25-4-104(a).

Limitation of actions, §25-4-111.

Negligence.

Unauthorized signature or alteration, §25-4-406(c), (d).

Payment.

Properly payable.

Defined, §25-4-104(a).

Suspends payment.

Defined, §25-4-104(a).

Payor banks.

Alteration of instruments.

Customer's duty to discover and report unauthorized alteration, §25-4-406.

Attachment and garnishment.

When item subject to legal process, §25-4-303(a).

Certifying items.

Order in which items may be certified, §25-4-303(b).

Charging items.

Order in which items may be charged, §25-4-303(b).

Clearinghouse.

Defined, §25-4-104(a).

Collection by depositary and collecting banks.

Final payment of item by payor bank, §25-4-213(a).

Sending direct to payor bank, §25-4-204(c).

Suspension of payments, §25-4-214(a) to (d).

Customer relationship.

Customer's duty to discover and report unauthorized signature or alteration, §25-4-406.

Customer's right to stop payment, §25-4-403(a).

Burden of proof of loss, §25-4-403(c).

Oral stop payment order, §25-4-403(b).

Death of customer, §25-4-405(a), (b).

Controlling provisions, §25-4-405(c).

Definition of customer, §25-4-104(a).

Dishonor.

Liability to customer for wrongful dishonor, §25-4-402(a).

Damages, §25-4-402(b).

Time for determining account insufficiency, §25-4-402(c).

Improper payment.

Bank's right to subrogation on improper payment, §25-4-407.

Incompetence of customer, §25-4-405(a), (b).

Controlling provisions, §25-4-405(c).

BANK DEPOSITS AND COLLECTIONS —Cont'd

Payor banks —Cont'd

Customer relationship —Cont'd

No obligation to pay check more than six months old, §25-4-404.

Stop payment order.

Bank's right to subrogation on improper payment, §25-4-407.

Customer's right to stop payment, §25-4-403(a).

Oral order, §25-4-403(b).

Subrogation.

Bank's right to subrogation on improper payment, §25-4-407.

When bank may charge customer's account, §25-4-401(a) to (d).

Customer not liable, §25-4-401(b).

Wrongful dishonor.

Bank's liability to customer, §25-4-402(a).

Damages, §25-4-402(b).

Death of customer, §25-4-405(a), (b).

Controlling provisions, §25-4-405(c).

Defined, §25-4-105.

Delays, §25-4-108(a), (b).

Responsibility for late return of item, §25-4-302(a).

Defenses, §25-4-302(b).

Dishonor.

Liability to customer for wrongful dishonor, §25-4-402(a).

Damages, §25-4-402(b).

Time of dishonor, §25-4-301(c).

Executions.

When items subject to legal process, §25-4-303(a).

Forgery.

Customer's duty to discover and report, §25-4-406.

Incompetence of customer, §25-4-405(a), (b).

Controlling provisions, §25-4-405(c).

Late return of item.

Responsibility, §25-4-302(a).

Defenses, §25-4-302(b).

Legal process.

When items subject to legal process, §25-4-303(a).

Notice.

When items subject to notice, §25-4-303(a).

Order in which items may be charged or certified, §25-4-303(b).

Payment.

Definition of suspending payment, §25-4-104(a).

Final payment, §25-4-213(a).

Improper payment.

Bank's right to subrogation on improper payment, §25-4-407.

No obligation to pay check more than six months old, §25-4-404.

Recovery of payment by return of items, §25-4-301(b).

Posting.

Deferred posting, §25-4-301(a).

Recovery of payment by return of items, §25-4-301(b).

Responsibility for late return of item, §25-4-302(a).

Defenses, §25-4-302(b).

Return of items.

Recovery of payment by return of items, §25-4-301(b).

When item deemed return, §25-4-301(d).

BANK DEPOSITS AND COLLECTIONS —Cont'd
Payor banks —Cont'd
  Setoff.
    When items subject to setoff, §25-4-303(a).
  Signature.
    Unauthorized signature.
      Customer's duty to discover and report,
        §25-4-406.
  Stopping payment.
    Bank's right to subrogation on improper
      payment, §25-4-407.
    Burden of proof of loss, §25-4-403(c).
    Customer's right, §25-4-403(a).
    Duration of order, §25-4-403(b).
    When items subject to stop-order, §25-4-303(a).
  Subrogation.
    Right to subrogation on improper payment,
      §25-4-407.
  Suspension of payments, §25-4-214(a) to (d).
    Defined, §25-4-104(a).
  Time of dishonor, §25-4-301(c).
  Unauthorized signature or alteration.
    Customer's duty to discover and report,
      §25-4-406.
  When bank may charge customer's account,
    §25-4-401(a) to (d).
    Customer not liable, §25-4-401(b).
  When items subject to notice, stop-order, legal
    process or setoff, §25-4-303(a).
  Wrongful dishonor.
    Liability to customer, §25-4-402(a).
    Damages, §25-4-402(b).
Posting.
  Deferred posting, §25-4-301(a).
Presenting banks.
  Defined, §25-4-105.
  Electronic presentment, §25-4-110(a).
    Presentment notice, §25-4-110(b), (c).
Presumptions.
  Agency status of collecting banks, §25-4-201(a).
  Provisional status of credits, §25-4-201(a).
Procedure.
  Specification or approval of, §25-4-103(d).
Receipt of items.
  Time of receipt, §25-4-107(a), (b).
Remitting bank.
  Defined, §25-4-105.
Secured transactions.
  Collecting bank.
    Security interest of collecting bank in items,
      accompanying documents and proceeds,
      §25-4-208(a).
    Credit given, §25-4-208(b).
    Final settlement, §25-4-208(c).
  Collection of documentary drafts.
    Privilege of presenting bank to deal with goods.
      Security interest for expenses, §25-4-504(b).
Setoffs.
  When items subject to setoff, §25-4-303(a).
Settle.
  Defined, §25-4-104(a).
Short title of article, §25-4-101.
Statute of limitations, §25-4-111.
Stopping payment.
  Bank's right to subrogation on improper payment,
    §25-4-407.
  Burden of proof of loss, §25-4-403(c).
  Customer's right, §25-4-403(a).
  Duration of order, §25-4-403(b).
  When items subject to stop-order, §25-4-303(a).

BANK DEPOSITS AND COLLECTIONS —Cont'd
Time.
  Afternoon.
    Defined, §25-4-104(a).
  Collection by depositary and collecting banks.
    Finality of deposit of money, §25-4-213(e).
      Availability, §25-4-213(f).
    Finality of provisional debits and credits,
      §25-4-213(b), (c).
  Delays, §25-4-108(a), (b).
  Midnight deadline.
    Defined, §25-4-104(a).
  Receipt of items, §25-4-107(a), (b).
  Time of dishonor, §25-4-301(c).
  When action seasonable, §25-4-202(b).
Unauthorized signature or alteration.
  Customer's duty to discover and report, §25-4-406.
Variation of article by agreement, §25-4-103(a).
Warranties.
  Encoding warranties, §25-4-207.2(a).
    Damages, §25-4-207.2(c).
  Presentment warranties, §25-4-207.1(a).
    Accrual of cause of action, §25-4-207.1(f).
    Breach of warranty claim, §25-4-207.1(d).
    Damages, §25-4-207.1(b).
    Defenses, §25-4-207.1(c).
    Disclaimers, §25-4-207.1(e).
  Retention warranties, §25-4-207.2(b).
    Damages, §25-4-207.2(c).
  Transfer warranties, §25-4-207(a).
    Accrual of cause of action, §25-4-207(e).
    Damages, §25-4-207(c).
    Disclaimers, §25-4-207(d).
    Dishonored items, §25-4-207(b).
When action seasonable, §25-4-202(b).
Withdrawal.
  When certain credits become available for
    withdrawal, §25-4-213(e).

BANK EXAMINERS, §§53-117 to 53-123.
Appointment, §53-117(a).
Arrest.
  Power to make arrest, §53-121.
Bribery.
  Accepting bribes, §§14-233, 53-124.
Commissioner of banks.
  Appointment of bank examiners, §53-117(a).
Confidentiality of information.
  Disclosure, §53-125.
Examination of banks.
  Duties generally, §53-118.
  Refusal to be examined.
    Taking possession of and liquidating banks,
      §53-118.
  Reports which commissioner of banks is
    authorized to accept as part of examination,
    §53-117(c), (d).
  Rules and regulations as to, §53-117(b).
Felonies.
  Bribery.
    Keeping or accepting bribe or gratuity, §53-124.
  False reports, §53-124.
Loans.
  Prohibited loans or gratuities, §53-126.
Misconduct in public office.
  Bribes.
    Accepting bribes, §14-233.
  Reports.
    Making of false report by bank examiners,
      §14-233.

BANK EXAMINERS —Cont'd
Misdemeanors.
  Disclosing confidential information, §53-125.
Oaths.
  Power to administer, §53-120.
Reports, §53-123.
  False reports, §§14-233, 53-124.
Rules and regulations.
  Examination of banks, §53-117(b).
State banking commission.
  Rules and regulations.
    Examination of banks, §53-117(b).
Witnesses.
  Power to summon, §53-120.

BANK HOLDING COMPANIES, §§53-225 to
  53-232.
Acquisitions.
  Commercial banks, §53-17.1(e), (f).
  Criteria, §53-227.1(a).
    No criteria in state where company has
      principal place of business, §53-227.1(b).
Appeals.
  Decisions of commissioner, §53-231.
Citation of article, §53-225(a).
Commissioner.
  Appeal of commissioner's decision, §53-231.
  Rules and regulations, §53-230.
Criteria for certain bank holding company
  acquisitions, §53-227.1.
Definitions, §53-226.
Dividends.
  Income tax.
    Adjustment to expenses related to,
      §105-130.6A(c), (e), (f), (h).
Fees.
  Registration, §53-232.
Income tax.
  Dividends.
    Adjustment to expenses related to,
      §105-130.6A(c), (e), (f), (h).
Reciprocal interstate banking, §§53-209 to
  53-218.
  See RECIPROCAL INTERSTATE BANKING.
Registration.
  Fees, §53-232.
  Forms, §53-227.
  Required, §53-227.
Rules and regulations.
  Promulgation by commissioner, §53-230.
Scope of act, §53-225(d).
Short title of article, §53-225(a).
Violation of banking laws.
  Cease and desist orders.
    Issuance, §53-228.
  Penalties, §53-228.

BANKING CARDS.
Credit cards.
  See CREDIT CARDS.
Financial transaction card crimes, §§14-113.8 to
  14-113.17.
  See FINANCIAL TRANSACTION CARDS.

BANKING COMMISSION.
Administrative orders of commissioner.
  Penalties for violations.
    Imposition of civil money penalties,
      §53-107.2(b).
  Review by banking commission, §53-107.2(a).
Appeals from final orders, §53-92(d).
Appointment, §53-92(b).

BANKING COMMISSION —Cont'd
Bank examiners.
  Rules and regulations.
    Examination of banks, §53-117(b).
Borrowing public.
  Appointment as members, §53-92(b).
Branch banks.
  Review of actions of commissioner, §53-62(f).
Chairman.
  State treasurer, §53-92(c).
Commissioner of banks.
  Commission bound by requirements imposed on
    commissioner as to certain matters, §53-92.1.
  Executive director, §53-92(c).
  Generally, §§53-92 to 53-116.
    See BANKS COMMISSIONER.
  Orders appealed to commission.
    Appellate review panel, §53-92(d).
  Powers of commissioner.
    Exercise of powers under supervision of banking
      commission, §53-95.
  Review of exercise of powers, duties and functions,
    §53-92(d).
Compensation, §53-92(b).
Conflicts of interest.
  Interest in financial institution, restriction,
    §53-92(b), (c).
Executive director.
  Commissioner of banks, §53-92(c).
Incorporation.
  Review of actions of commissioner, §53-4.
Interest in financial institution, restriction,
  §53-92(b), (c).
International banking.
  Rules and regulations, §53-232.15.
Legal assistance.
  Attorney on staff of attorney general, §53-96.
Limited service facilities.
  Review of actions of commissioner, §53-62(f).
Meetings, §53-92(c).
Number of members, §53-92(b).
Powers.
  Generally, §§53-92, 53-114.
Practical bankers.
  Appointment as members, §53-92(b).
Quorum, §53-92(c).
Rules and regulations, §53-115(a).
  Additional nature of rule-making authority,
    §53-115(b).
  Books, accounts and records of banks, §53-110(a).
    Classification and retention of records,
      §53-110(b).
  Industrial banks, §53-144.
  International banking, §53-232.15.
State treasurer.
  Chairman, §53-92(c).
  Ex officio member, §53-92(b).
Supervision of common trust funds, §53-163.7.

BANKING COMMISSIONER.
Commissioner of banks.
  Generally, §§53-92 to 53-116.
    See BANKS COMMISSIONER.

BANKRUPTCY AND INSOLVENCY.
Alcoholic beverage ownership acquired
  through.
  Special one-time permit issued, §18B-1002(a).
Assets.
  Liens.
    Wages for two months' lien on assets, §44-5.1.

BANKRUPTCY AND INSOLVENCY —Cont'd

Assignments for benefit of creditors.
Insolvent trustee, §23-5.

Attorney appearance for creditor in insolvency proceedings.
Unlawful for anyone except attorney, §84-9.

Attorneys specializing in bankruptcy law.
Certification standards, Bar Rules D.2201 to D.2207.

Bail bondsmen and runners.
Notice of receivership, §58-71-81.

Banks.
Defined, §53-1.
Deposits.
Receiving deposits in insolvent banks, §53-132.
Dissolution and liquidation.
Receivers.
Statute relating to receivers applicable to insolvent banks, §53-22.
Records.
Destruction of records of liquidation insolvent banks, §53-24.
Trusts terminated on insolvency of trustee bank, §§53-25 to 53-32.
Investigations.
General or special investigations of insolvent banks, §53-100.
Receivers.
Statute relating to receivers applicable to insolvent banks, §53-22.
Trust terminated on insolvency of trustee bank, §§53-25 to 53-32.
When commissioner of banks may take charge, §§53-19, 53-20(a).

Beach area essential property insurance.
Insurance underwriting association.
Insolvent insurers.
Nonrecoupable assessments, §58-45-85.

Congress.
Powers of congress, US Const Art I §8.

Consolidated city-county act.
Authority of counties, cities, towns and villages to avail themselves of bankruptcy law, §23-48.

Constitution of the United States.
Powers of congress, US Const Art I §8.

Corporations.
Receivers generally, §§1-507.1 to 1-507.11.
See CORPORATIONS.

Counties.
Authority to avail themselves of bankruptcy law, §23-48.

Credit unions.
Suspension and conservation, §54-109.92.

Deed of trust covering property in bankruptcy.
Trustee neither necessary or proper party, §45-45.3(c).

Discharge as affirmative defense, pleading,
§1A-1 Rule 8(c).

Discharge of insolvent prisoners.
Generally.
See DISCHARGE OF INSOLVENT PRISONERS.

Employment security.
Lack of work caused by employer.
Eligibility for benefits, §96-14.

Exemptions provided by federal bankruptcy code.
Inapplicable to residents of state, §1C-1601(f).

Exempt property generally.
See EXEMPTION OF PROPERTY FROM CREDITOR CLAIMS.

BANKRUPTCY AND INSOLVENCY —Cont'd

Homestead exemptions.
See HOMESTEAD EXEMPTIONS.

Jeopardy.
Unlawful to solicit claims of creditors in proceedings, §23-46.
Misdemeanor, §23-47.

Judgments.
Cancellation of judgments discharged through bankruptcy proceedings, §1-245.

Leases, UCC.
Lessee's rights to goods on lessor's insolvency, §25-2A-522.

Liens.
Wages for two months.
Lien on employer's assets, §44-5.1.

Limited liability companies.
Cessation of membership, §57C-3-02.

Local improvement districts.
Authority to avail themselves of bankruptcy law, §23-48.

Manufactured home manufacturers, dealers, salespersons or set-up contractors.
Filing for protection, notification, §143-143.11A(d).

Misdemeanors.
Solicitation of claims of creditors in proceedings, §§23-46, 23-47.

Money transmitters.
Extraordinary reports required, §53-208.13(a).
Permissible investments.
Held in trust during bankruptcy of licensee, §53-208.6(b).
Surety bond.
Proceeds held in trust, §53-208.8(e).

Mortgages and deeds of trust.
Sales under power of sale.
Procedure upon lifting of automatic bankruptcy stay, §45-21.22(c).
Trustee in deed of trust neither necessary or proper party, §45-45.3(c).

Motor vehicle reinsurance facility members,
§58-37-15.

Municipalities.
Authority to avail themselves of bankruptcy law, §23-48.

Partnerships.
Defined, §59-32.
Dissolution and winding up, §§59-61, 59-70.

Prisoners.
Generally.
See DISCHARGE OF INSOLVENT PRISONERS.

Probate and registration.
Recording bankruptcy records, §47-29.

Provider sponsored organizations.
Continuation of benefits, §131E-300.
Covered services offered to beneficiaries, §131E-301(a).
Allocations by division, §131E-301(b), (c).
Hold harmless agreements, §131E-299(a), (c).
Protection against insolvency.
Deposits, §131E-298(a).
Failure to comply with net worth requirements.
Appropriate action by division, §131E-298(b).
Plan, §131E-298(c).
Special deposit, §131E-299(b), (c).

Receivers generally, §§1-501 to 1-507.11.
See RECEIVERS.

Recording of bankruptcy records, §47-29.

Reinsurance.
Ceding insurer, §58-7-30.

BANKRUPTCY AND INSOLVENCY —Cont'd
Sale of goods, UCC.
Buyer's right to goods on seller's insolvency, §25-2-502.
Promise to revive debt of bankruptcy.
Statute of frauds, §22-4.
Sales and use tax.
Taxpayer going into bankruptcy.
Tax constitutes prior lien, §105-164.37.
School districts.
Authority to avail themselves of provisions of bankruptcy law, §23-48.
Solicitation.
Unlawful to solicit claims of creditors in proceedings, §23-46.
Misdemeanor, §23-47.
Statute of frauds.
Revival of debt of bankruptcy, §22-4.
Taxing districts.
Authority to avail themselves of bankruptcy law, §23-48.
Towns.
Authority to avail themselves of bankruptcy law, §23-48.
Trespass on land.
Insolvency of defendant.
When allegation of insolvency unnecessary, §1-486.
Trust institutions acting as fiduciary.
Revocation of license to do business, §53-163.
Trusts and trustees.
Bankruptcy or insolvency of trustee.
Personal obligations of trustee.
Trust property not subject to, §36C-5-507.
Unemployment compensation.
Lack of work caused by employer.
Eligibility for benefits, §96-14.
Villages.
Authority to avail themselves of bankruptcy law, §23-48.

BANKRUPTCY LAW SPECIALTY.
Certification standards, Bar Rules D.2201 to D.2207.

BANKS, §§53-1 to 53-158.1.
Abandoned property.
Disposition of unclaimed property generally, §§116B-51 to 116B-80.
See UNCLAIMED PROPERTY.
Acceptances.
Definition of "trade acceptance,"§53-55.
Generally, §53-56.
Loans.
When acceptance considered direct loan to drawer, §53-56.
Restrictions, §53-56.
Accounts and accounting.
False entries in banking accounts, §53-130.
Statement of account from bank to depositor.
Deemed final adjustment if not objected to within five years, §53-75.
Depositor not relieved from exercising diligence to errors, §53-76.
Rendering annually or on request, §53-75.
Worthless checks, §14-107.
Acknowledgments.
Stockholders, officers or directors, §47-93.
Acquisitions.
State associations.
Supervisory acquisitions, §53-17.1.

BANKS —Cont'd
Administrative procedure.
Hearings.
Special provisions, §§150B-38 to 150B-42.
Agents.
Personal agency accounts.
Generally, §53-146.3.
Appraisal fees.
Loans secured by real property, §24-10(h).
Assessments.
Expenses of operating office of commissioner of banks, §53-122.
Impairment of capital, §53-42.
Assets.
Appraisal of assets of doubtful value, §53-112.
Conservatorship, §§53-148 to 53-158.1.
Misrepresenting assets and liability of banks, §53-130.
Uncollectible assets.
Writing off, §53-91.1.
Automated teller machines or banking facilities, §53-62(d1).
Bank bills.
Limitation of action not affecting actions to enforce payment, §1-32.
Bank examiners, §§53-117 to 53-123.
See BANK EXAMINERS.
Bank holding companies.
Generally, §§53-225 to 53-232.
See BANK HOLDING COMPANIES.
Reciprocal interstate banking act generally, §§53-209 to 53-218.
See RECIPROCAL INTERSTATE BANKING.
Banking commission.
See BANKING COMMISSION.
Bonds, surety.
Dissolution and liquidation.
Commissioner of banks.
Taking possession, §53-20(h).
Employees, §53-90.
Officers, §53-90.
Branch banks.
Authorized, §53-62(b).
Capital requirements for establishment, §53-62(c).
Commissioner of banks.
Approval of establishment, §53-62(b).
Capital requirements, §53-62(c).
Review of commissioner's actions by state banking commission, §53-62(f).
Definition of "branch,"§53-1.
Discontinuance, §53-62(e).
Industrial banks.
Power to establish, §53-141.
Interstate banking, §§53-224.9 to 53-224.31.
See BRANCH BANKS.
Limited service facilities.
Conversion of limited service facility to branch, §53-62(d).
Loan committee, §53-78.
Officers, §53-62(c).
Operation, §53-62(c).
School thrift or savings plan.
Acceptance of deposits not construed as establishment or operation of branch, §53-43.6(b).
State banking commission.
Review of actions of commissioner, §53-62(f).
Bribery.
Directors or officers accepting fees or gifts.
Prohibited, §53-86.

BANKS —Cont'd
Bribery —Cont'd
  Loans or gratuities to commissioner of banks or
      bank examiners.
    Prohibited, §53-126.
Building and loan associations.
  See SAVINGS AND LOAN ASSOCIATIONS.
Business paper.
  Acceptance generally, §53-56.
  Defined, §53-55.
Campaign contributions and expenditures.
  Loan proceeds from financial institution,
      §163-278.15(b).
  Exceptions to prohibitions, §163-278.19(a2).
Certificates of deposit.
  Unlawful issuance, §53-63.
Certificates of incorporation, §§53-2 to 53-5.
Charters.
  Approval, §53-17.1(c).
  Authorization, §53-17.1(a).
  Bank holding companies, §53-17.1(e), (f).
  Date of applicability of provisions, §53-17.1(i).
  Effect of charter on commercial bank, §53-17.1(g).
  Eligible state associations, §53-17.1(b).
  Governing provisions, §53-17.1(d).
  Prerequisites to commencement of business,
      §53-17.1(h).
Checks.
  Bad checks generally.
    See BAD CHECKS.
  False certification of check.
    Penalty, §53-131.
  Fees on remittances covering checks.
    Prohibited, §53-70.
  Payable in exchange, §53-71.
    Exemptions.
      Checks in payment of obligations due state
          and federal government, §53-73.
  Remittances covering checks.
    Fees not to be charged, §53-70.
Child support enforcement.
  Location of absent parents.
    Information to be provided, §110-139(d).
Clearinghouse certificates.
  State banking commissioner may require or
      permit, §53-114.
Clerks of court.
  Superior court.
    Deposit of money held by clerk, §7A-112.1.
Closed accounts.
  Worthless checks, §14-107.
Closed banks.
  Reopening effect upon certain contracts, §53-38.
Collection agencies.
  Not included in definition of "collection
      agency,"§58-70-15(c).
Collections.
  Bank deposits and collections generally,
      §§25-4-101 to 25-4-504.
    See BANK DEPOSITS AND COLLECTIONS.
Commencement of business.
  Payment of capital stock as prerequisite, §53-6.
    Surplus fund, §53-39.
  Statement as prerequisite, §53-7.
  Time for, §53-5.
  Transactions preliminary to, §53-9.
  When authorized, §53-8.
**Commercial loan commitments to be in
    writing,** §22-5.
Commercial paper.
  Acceptances.
    Generally, §53-56.

BANKS —Cont'd
Commercial paper —Cont'd
  Branch or separate offices deemed separate bank,
      §25-4-106.
  Defined, §53-55.
  Instructions.
    Effect of instructions, §25-4-203.
Commissioner of banks, §§53-92 to 53-116.
  See BANKS COMMISSIONER.
Confidential records.
  Compliance review documents, §53-99.1(b).
  Regulatory rating prepared by bank
      commissioner, §53-99(d).
Conservatorship, §§53-148 to 53-158.1.
  Appointment of conservator, §53-148.
  Creditors.
    Special funds for paying creditors ratably,
        §53-151.
  Deposits.
    New deposits, §53-151.
      Segregation of recent deposits not effective
          after bank turned back to officers,
          §53-153.
    Rate of organization on agreement of depositors
        and stockholders, §53-152.
    Segregation of new deposits, §53-151.
      Not effective after bank turned back to
          officers, §53-153.
    Special funds for paying depositors ratably,
        §53-151.
  Dissolution and liquidation.
    Naming of conservator not liquidation, §53-158.
  Duties of conservator, §53-148.
  Embezzlement and misapplication of funds.
    Applicability of general provisions to
        conservator, §53-157.
  Examination of bank, §53-149.
  Expenses of conservator, §53-148.
  Liquidation.
    Naming of conservator not liquidation, §53-158.
  Notice.
    Turning bank back to officers, §53-153.
  Powers of conservator, §53-148.
  Preferred stock provisions, scope, §53-158.1.
  Reorganization on agreement of depositors and
      stockholders, §53-152.
  Rights and liabilities of conservator.
    Applicability of certain general provisions,
        §53-157.
  Salary of conservator, §53-148.
  Termination of conservatorship, §53-150.
  Turning bank back to officers.
    Notice, §53-153.
    Segregation of recent deposits not effective
        after, §53-153.
Consolidated banks.
  Authority to consolidate, §53-12(a).
  Deemed one bank, §53-13.
  Investigation by commission, §53-12(a).
  Notice, publication, §53-12(a).
  Procedure, §53-12(a).
  Proceedings of directors and stockholders.
    Certified copies, filing, §53-12(a).
  State banks or trust companies with national
      banks, §53-16.
  Subsidiaries, §53-12(b).
  Substitution as executor or trustee under will,
      §28A-2A-12.
Consumer finance act, §§53-164 to 53-191.
  See CONSUMER FINANCE ACT.

BANKS —Cont'd
Conversions.
Bank to stock association, §54B-46.
 Actions subject to review, §54B-46(d).
 Applicability of provisions, §54B-46(a).
 Approval by stockholders, §54B-46(g).
 Authority of resulting stock association,
  §54B-46(h).
 Board approval as prerequisite, §54B-46(b).
 Conditions, §54B-46(e).
 Effect of conversion, §54B-46(i).
 Plan of conversion, §54B-46(c).
 Submission of plan to stockholders, §54B-46(f).
Savings association to state bank.
 Application to convert, §53-17.2(b).
 Authority, §53-17.2(a).
 Conditions to be met for approval, §53-17.2(e).
 Effect, §53-17.2(i).
 Plan of conversion, §53-17.2(c).
  Approval by stockholders or members,
   §53-17.2(g).
  Submission to stockholders or members,
   §53-17.2(f).
 Resulting bank.
  Authorization by commissioner, §53-17.2(h).
  Continuation of former institution, §53-17.2(i).
 Review of action taken by commissioner,
  §53-17.2(d).
 Rules, promulgation, §53-17.2(d).
 Supervising and monitoring process, §53-17.2(f).
 Transactions included in term conversion,
  §53-17.2(a).
**Cooperative associations generally, §§54-111 to
 54-128.**
See COOPERATIVE ASSOCIATIONS.
Copies.
Records, §§53-110(b), 53-113.
Corporations.
International banking.
 Applicability of business corporation act,
  §53-232.5.
Corporations law.
General corporation law to apply, §53-135.
Creation.
Incorporation, §§53-2 to 53-17.2.
Credit cards.
General provisions.
 See CREDIT CARDS.
Credit unions, §§54-109.1 to 54-110.10.
See CREDIT UNIONS.
Customer-bank communications terminals.
Establishment off premises, §53-62(d1).
Damages.
Directors.
 Liability, §53-82.
Days of operation, §53-77.1A.
Deeds and conveyances.
Validation.
 Deeds executed by nonresident bank,
  §47-108.16.
 Secretary or cashier attesting, §47-42(b), (c).
Defamation.
Willfully and maliciously making derogatory
 reports, §53-128.
Definitions, §53-1.
Acceptances.
 Trade acceptance, §53-55.
Bank holding companies, §53-226.
Capital, §53-62(a).
Cash, §53-51(b).
Commercial or business paper, §53-55.

BANKS —Cont'd
Definitions —Cont'd
Emergency suspension of business, §53-77.3(a).
Federal reserve system, §53-61(a).
Financial privacy, §53B-2.
Industrial banks, §53-136.
International banking, §53-232.2(a).
Regional reciprocal banking, §53-210.
Reserve, §53-51(a).
Shareholder, §53-108.
Term "stock" to include preferred stock, §53-156.
Deposit insurance.
Securing through FDIC or successor corporation.
 Powers in securing, §53-9.1(b).
 Required to engage in business, §53-9.1(a).
Depositories.
Directors.
 Designation by directors, §53-84.
Industrial banks.
 Designation, §53-142.
Deposits.
Bank deposits and collections generally,
 §§25-4-101 to 25-4-504.
 See BANK DEPOSITS AND COLLECTIONS.
Certificate of deposit.
 Unlawful issuance, §53-63.
Clerks of superior courts.
 Deposit of money held by clerk, §7A-112.1.
Collateral required as security for deposits.
 Debentures issued by secretary of housing and
  urban development or federal housing
  administration, §53-45(d).
Collection of taxes.
 Bank deposits subject to attachment or
  garnishment, §105-242(b).
 Exempt property, §105-242(e).
Conservatorship.
 New deposits, §53-151.
  Segregation of recent deposits not effective
   after bank turned back to officers,
   §53-153.
 Rate of organization on agreement of depositors
  and stockholders, §53-152.
 Segregation of new deposits, §53-151.
  Not effective after bank turned back to
   officers, §53-153.
 Special funds for paying depositors ratably,
  §53-151.
Demand deposits.
 Defined, §53-1.
 Deposits payable on demand, §53-65.
Dissolution and liquidation.
 Commissioner taking possession.
  Unlocated depositor, §53-20(x).
 Voluntary liquidation.
  Unclaimed deposits, §53-18.
Failure to meet deposit demands.
 Commissioner not to take over banks failing to
  meet, §53-116.
Insolvency.
 Receiving deposits in insolvent banks, §53-132.
Insurance, §53-9.1.
Joint deposits, §§41-2.1, 53-146 to 53-146.3.
Minors.
 Operating deposit account in name of minor,
  §53-43.5(a).
Payable on death accounts, §§54-109.57A,
 54B-130A.
 Savings banks, §54C-166.1.
Payable on demand, §53-65.

BANKS —Cont'd
Deposits —Cont'd
School thrift or savings plan, §53-43.6(a).
  Branch acceptance of deposits in furtherance of
    plan not construed as establishment,
    §53-43.6(b).
Secured transactions.
  Security interests in deposit accounts.
    Perfection and priority, §§25-9-304, 25-9-327.
    Rights of banks, §25-9-341.
    Rights of banks, control agreements,
      §25-9-342.
    Set-off or recoupment, §25-9-340.
    Transfer of funds, §25-9-332(b).
Securities for deposit of public funds.
  Obligations of agencies supervised by farm
    credit administration, §53-43.1.
  Obligations of agencies supervised by federal
    home loan bank board, §53-43.2.
Solicitation of deposits.
  Prohibited.
    Consumer finance act, §53-180(j).
State and state officials.
  Statements showing deposits of, §53-68.
Statement of account from bank to depositor.
  Deemed final adjustment if not objected to
    within five years, §53-75.
    Depositor not relieved from exercising
      diligence as to errors, §53-76.
  Rendering annually or on request, §53-75.
Superior court clerks.
  Deposit of money held by clerk, §7A-112.1.
Survivorship in bank deposit created by written
  agreement, §41-2.1.
Time deposits.
  Defined, §53-1.
Unclaimed property generally, §§116B-51 to
  116B-80.
  See UNCLAIMED PROPERTY.
Directors.
Acceptance of fees and gifts prohibited, §53-86.
Acknowledgments taken by director, §47-93.
Appointment of advisory directors, §53-91.3(b).
Depositories.
  Designation by directors, §53-84.
Dissolution and liquidation.
  Placing assets and business under control of
    commissioner.
    Resolution of majority of directors, §53-20(b).
Dividends.
  Power to declare dividends, §§53-87, 53-87.1.
Election, §53-67.
Embezzlement or misapplication of funds,
  §53-129.
Examining committee, §53-83.
Executive committee, §53-78.
  Minutes of meetings, §53-79.
Liability, §53-82.
Limitation of action to recover penalty or
  forfeiture imposed, §1-33.
Meetings, §53-67.
  Minutes, §53-79.
Number of directors, §53-67.
  Additional directorships.
    Stockholders may authorize, §53-67.
Oath of office, §53-81.
Penalty or forfeiture imposed by statute.
  Limitation of actions, §1-33.
Powers, §53-67.
Probates before directors, §47-92.
Qualifications, §53-80.

BANKS —Cont'd
Directors —Cont'd
References to, §53-91.3(a).
Removal of directors.
  Commissioner may require, §53-119.
Reports.
  Changes in directors, §53-42.1(d).
Stockholders.
  Book of shareholders.
    Directors to provide, §53-85.
  Election of directors, §53-67.
Terms of office, §53-67.
Disposition of unclaimed property generally,
  §§116B-51 to 116B-80.
  See UNCLAIMED PROPERTY.
Dissolution and liquidation, §§53-18 to 53-36.
Commissioner taking possession.
  Accountants and other experts.
    Employment, §53-20(o).
  Applicability of provisions, §53-20(v).
  Attorneys at law.
    Employment of local attorneys, §53-20(o).
  Bond, surety, §53-20(h).
  Claims against bank.
    Action on claims, §53-20(k).
    Lists of claims presented, §53-20(l).
    Notice and time for filing claims, §53-20(j).
    Powers and duties as to, §53-20(g).
    Rejection of claims, §53-20(k).
  Compensation of commissioner, §53-20(t).
  Deposits.
    Funds collected, §53-20(n).
    Unlocated depositor, §53-20(x).
  Directors may act by resolution, §53-20(b).
  Dividends.
    Declaration, §53-20(m).
    Unclaimed dividends held in trust, §53-20(p).
  Exclusive method of liquidation, §53-20(u).
  Failure to meet deposit demands.
    Commissioner not to take over banks failing
      to meet, §53-116.
  Injunction, §53-20(f).
  Inventory, §53-20(i).
  Liquidation by commissioner of all banks in
    receivership required, §53-20(w).
  Notices, §53-20(c), (d).
    Answer to notice, §53-20(f).
    Claims, §53-20(j), (k).
  Remedy by bank for seizure, §53-20(f).
  Reopening of closed banks, §§53-37, 53-38.
  Report, §53-20(q).
    Annual report, §53-20(s).
    Report to secretary of state concerning certain
      matters relative to liquidation of closed
      banks, §53-36.
  Resumption of business.
    Permission, §53-20(e).
  Settlement.
    Action by commissioner after full settlement,
      §53-20(r).
  When authorized, §§53-19, 53-20(d).
Conservatorship.
  Naming of conservator not liquidation, §53-158.
Deeds of trusts.
  Validation.
    Acts of officers of insolvent banks as trustees
      in deeds of trust, §53-33.
  Foreclosures and executions of deeds by
    commissioner of banks, §53-35.
  Sales by commissioner of banks under deeds
    of trust giving banks power of sale,
    §53-34.

BANKS —Cont'd
Dissolution and liquidation —Cont'd
Deposits.
 Commissioner of banks.
  Taking possession.
   Unlocated depositor, §53-20(x).
 Voluntary liquidation.
  Unclaimed deposits, §53-18.
Directors.
 Placing assets and business under control of
  commissioner.
 Resolution of majority of directors, §53-20(b).
Dividends.
 Commissioner taking possession.
  Declaration of dividends, §53-20(m).
  Unclaimed dividends held in trust, §53-20(p).
 Voluntary liquidation.
  Unclaimed dividends, §53-18.
Injunctions.
 Taking possession by commissioner, §53-20(f).
Insolvency.
 Receivers.
  Statute relating to receivers applicable to
   insolvent banks, §53-22.
 Records.
  Destruction of records of liquidated insolvent
   banks, §53-24.
 Trust terminated on insolvency of trustee bank,
  §§53-25 to 53-32.
 When commissioner of banks may take charge,
  §§53-19, 53-20(a).
Notice.
 Commissioner taking possession, §53-20(c), (d).
  Answer to notice, §53-20(f).
  Claims, §53-20(j), (k).
Publication.
 Report by commissioner to secretary of state
  concerning certain matters relative to
  liquidation of closed banks, §53-36.
Receivers.
 Commissioner of banks.
  Liquidation by commissioner of all banks in
   receivership required, §53-20(w).
 Statutes relating to receivers.
  Applicability to insolvent banks, §53-22.
Records.
 Destruction of records of liquidated insolvent
  banks, §53-24.
 Disposition of books and records, §53-23.
Reopening of closed banks.
 Conditions under which banks may reopen,
  §53-37.
 Contracts.
  Certain contracts not affected, §53-38.
 When authorized, §53-37.
Sale of stock of defunct banks validated, §53-21.
Taking possession by commissioner of banks,
 §§53-19, 53-20.
Trust terminated on insolvency of trustee bank.
 Additional remedy, §53-32.
 Appeals.
  Appointment of new trustee, §53-29.
 Appointment of new trustee.
  Additional remedy, §53-32.
  Appeal from order, §53-29.
  Applicability of petition and all instruments
   involved, §53-31.
  Final order.
   Registration, §53-30.
  Hearing where objection made, §53-29.
  No objection made, §53-28.

BANKS —Cont'd
Dissolution and liquidation —Cont'd
Trust terminated on insolvency of trustee bank
 —Cont'd
 Appointment of new trustee —Cont'd
  Petition, §§53-26, 53-27.
  Registration of final order, §53-30.
 Generally, §53-25.
 Objection to new trustee.
  Appointment where no objection made,
   §53-28.
  Hearing where objection made, §53-29.
 Petition for new trustee, §53-26.
  Applicability to all instruments involved,
   §53-31.
  Contents, §53-27.
  Notice.
   Publication, §§53-26, 53-27.
Voluntary liquidation, §53-18.
Dividends.
Declaration of dividends, §53-87.
Directors.
 Power to declare dividends, §53-87.
Dissolution and liquidation.
 Commissioner taking possession.
  Declaration of dividends, §53-20(m).
 Voluntary liquidation.
  Unclaimed dividends, §53-18.
Generally, §§53-87, 53-87.1.
Preferred stock, §53-155.
 Issuance to the United States Treasury,
  §53-87.1(a), (b).
Requirements for declaration of dividends, §53-87.
Surplus.
 Use of surplus, §53-88.
Drafts.
Negotiable instruments.
 Generally, §§25-3-101 to 25-3-605.
 See NEGOTIABLE INSTRUMENTS.
Embezzlement.
Conservators, §53-157.
Prohibited acts, §53-129.
Emergency suspension of business.
Authorization, §53-77.3(b).
Construction and interpretation, §53-77.3(d).
Definitions, §53-77.3(a).
Legal holiday for certain purposes, §53-77.3(c).
Employees.
Acceptance fees and gifts prohibited, §53-86.
Bonds, surety, §53-90.
Embezzlement or misapplication of funds,
 §53-129.
Overdraft liability, §53-89.
Removal of employees.
 Commissioner may require, §53-119.
Share purchase and option plans, §53-43.3.
Equity line of credit.
Future advances.
 Notice regarding, form, §45-82.3(f).
Request to terminate made by.
 Notice to borrower, form, §45-82.2(d).
Evidence.
Records.
 Certified copies, §53-113.
Examiners.
Generally, §§53-117 to 53-123.
See BANK EXAMINERS.
Executors and administrators.
Stockholder.
 Not liable as, §53-40.

BANKS —Cont'd
Farm credit administration.
Investments in obligations of agencies supervised
by, §53-44.1.
Obligations of agencies supervised by.
Securities for deposit of public funds, §53-43.1.
Federal deposit insurance corporation.
Deposit insurance, §53-9.1.
Federal home loan bank board.
Investment in obligations of agencies supervised
by, §53-44.2.
Obligations of agencies supervised by.
Securities for deposit of public funds, §53-43.2.
Federal reserve system.
Definitions, §53-61(a).
Membership in federal reserve bank, §53-61(b).
Compliance with reserve requirements required,
§53-61(c).
Powers vested by federal act, §53-61(c).
Supervision and examination of bank, §53-61(e).
Reserve requirements.
Compliance, §53-61(d).
Members of system, §53-50(b).
Savings banks.
Authority to join federal reserve bank,
§54C-177.
Fees.
Checks.
Remittances covering checks.
No fees to be charged, §53-70.
Directors.
Acceptance prohibited, §53-86.
Officers.
Acceptance prohibited, §53-86.
Operating and maintaining office of commissioner
of banks, assessment, §53-122(a), (e), (f).
Out-of-state, state banks.
Branch banking in North Carolina.
Supervisory and examination fees,
§53-224.24(d).
Felonies.
Deposits.
Insolvent banks.
Receiving deposits, §53-132.
Embezzlement or misapplication of funds,
§53-129.
False certification of check, §53-131.
False entries in banking accounts, §53-130.
Misrepresenting assets and liabilities of banks,
§53-130.
Fiduciary capacity, acting in.
Deposit in name of fiduciary.
Bank authorized to pay amount of deposit,
§32-8.
Merger or consolidation.
Fiduciary powers and liabilities of banks or
trust, §53-17.
Stockholder.
Not liable as, §53-40.
Trust institutions, §§53-158.10 to 53-163.2.
See TRUST COMPANIES.
Finance companies.
Consumer finance act, §§53-164 to 53-191.
See CONSUMER FINANCE ACT.
Financial records privacy, §§53B-1 to 53B-10.
See FINANCIAL RECORDS PRIVACY.
Financial transaction cards.
General provisions, §§14-113.8 to 14-113.17.
See FINANCIAL TRANSACTION CARDS.
Forgery.
Notes, checks and other securities, §14-119.
Connecting genuine parts, §14-125.

BANKS —Cont'd
Governor.
Holidays.
Power to proclaim banking holidays, §53-77.
Guardians.
Deposit of ward's money held by applicant for
letters, §35A-1232(b) to (d).
Stockholder.
Not subject to liability as, §53-40.
Holding companies.
Generally, §§53-225 to 53-232.
See BANK HOLDING COMPANIES.
Reciprocal interstate banking act generally,
§§53-209 to 53-218.
See RECIPROCAL INTERSTATE BANKING.
Holidays.
Emergency suspension of business.
Legal holiday for certain purposes, §53-77.3(c).
Governor empowered to proclaim banking
holidays, §53-77.
Opening for transactions on holidays not required,
§53-54.
Savings banks, §54C-175.
Hours of business, §53-77.1A.
Transactions not performed during banking hours,
§53-54.
Income tax.
Refund anticipation loans, §§53-245 to 53-254.
See INCOME TAX.
Incompetency of customer.
Authority as payor or as collecting bank.
Controlling provisions, §25-4-405(c).
Incorporation.
Certificate of incorporation.
Acknowledgment, §53-3.
Certification, §53-5.
Contents, §53-2.
Evidentiary effect, §53-5.
Filing, §53-3.
Industrial banks, §53-137.
Issuance, §53-4.
Recordation, §53-5.
Refusal.
Grounds, §53-4.
Signing, §53-3.
Commencement of business.
Payment of capital stock as prerequisite, §53-6.
Surplus fund, §53-39.
Statement as prerequisite, §53-7.
Time for, §53-5.
Transactions preliminary to, §53-9.
When authorized, §53-8.
Examination of proposed bank, §53-4.
General corporation law to apply, §53-135.
How incorporated, §53-2.
Industrial banks, §53-137.
Certificate of incorporation.
Contents, §53-137.
Number of incorporators, §53-137.
Number of incorporators, §53-2.
Review of actions by commission, §53-4.
State banking commission.
Review of actions of commissioner, §53-4.
Industrial banks, §§53-136 to 53-145.
See INDUSTRIAL BANKS.
Injunctions.
Dissolution and liquidation.
Taking possession by commissioner, §53-20(f).
Insolvency.
Defined, §53-1.

BANKS —Cont'd
Insolvency —Cont'd
Deposits.
Receiving deposits in insolvent banks, §53-132.
Dissolution and liquidation.
Receivers.
Statute relating to receivers applicable to
insolvent banks, §53-22.
Records.
Destruction of records of liquidated insolvent
banks, §53-24.
Trust terminated on insolvency of trustee bank,
§§53-25 to 53-32.
When commissioner of banks may take charge,
§§53-19, 53-20(a).
Investigations.
General or special investigations of insolvent
banks, §53-100.
Receivers.
Statute relating to receivers applicable to
insolvent banks, §53-22.
Trust terminated on insolvency of trustee bank,
§§53-25 to 53-32.
Insurance.
Deposit insurance, §53-9.1.
Insurance companies.
Disclosure of regulatory rating prepared by bank
commissioner, §53-99(d).
Insurance premium financing.
Exemption from license requirement, §58-35-10(a).
International banking, §§53-232.1 to 53-232.17.
See INTERNATIONAL BANKING.
Interstate banking.
Branch banks, §§53-224.9 to 53-224.31.
See BRANCH BANKS.
Investigations.
Insolvent banks.
General or special investigations, §53-100.
Official communications relating to, §53-109.
Investments.
Bonds guaranteed by United States, §53-44(a).
Fiduciaries.
Bonds deemed cash in settlements by
fiduciaries, §53-44(c).
Security for loans and deposits, §53-44(b).
Capital stock or other securities of financial
institution, §53-47(a).
Farm credit administration.
Obligations of agencies supervised by, §53-44.1.
Farm loan bonds, §53-60.
Federal home loan bank board.
Obligations of agencies supervised by, §53-44.2.
Federal housing administration, secretary of
housing and urban development or veterans
administrations, securities approved by.
Insured mortgages and obligations of national
mortgage associations and federal home
loan banks, §53-45(a).
Financial institution's capital stock or other
securities, §53-47(a).
Industrial banks.
Limitations.
Applicability of general provisions, §53-143.
International banking.
Restrictions on international banking
corporations, §53-232.11(b).
Limitations on investments.
Securities, §53-46.
Suspension of limitation, §53-49.
Mutual funds, §53-46.1.
Powers generally, §53-43.

BANKS —Cont'd
Investments —Cont'd
Protection of bank from loss.
Investment in corporation, partnership, firm or
company, §53-47(b).
Stock or assets of other business.
Completion of investment, time for, §53-47(e).
Discrimination against nonbanks, prohibition,
§53-47(d).
Disposal of stock exceeding limitations,
§53-47(f).
Monitoring impact on bank, §53-47(f).
Other financial institutions, §53-47(a).
Without limitation, certain circumstance,
§53-47(b).
Subsidiaries.
Investing in without limitation, §53-47(b).
Unimpaired capital fund in stock or assets of
other businesses, §53-47(c).
Investment securities.
Dealing in investment securities.
Engaging in business not authorized, §53-43.
Joint accounts.
Additions.
Effect, §53-146.1(c).
Common law provisions, applicability,
§53-146.1(a1).
Establishment, §53-146.1(a).
Estate tax provisions not repealed, §53-146.1(b).
Section not deemed exclusive, §53-146.1(a1).
Withdrawals.
Effect, §53-146.1(c).
Joint deposits, §§41-2.1, 53-146 to 53-146.3.
Deposits in two names, §53-146.
Joint accounts.
Generally, §53-146.1.
Payable on death accounts, §§53-146.2A,
54-109.57A, 54B-130A.
Savings banks, §54C-166.1.
Personal agency accounts.
Generally, §53-146.3.
Right of survivorship, §41-2.1.
Larceny.
Choses in action, §14-75.
**Lead-based paint presence on property or
other health-related issues.**
Providing financial assistance, §130A-131.9F.
Licenses.
International banking corporations, §§53-232.8,
53-232.9.
Taxation, §105-102.3.
Limitation of actions.
Actions against bank directors or stockholders,
§1-33.
Actions to enforce payment of bank bills.
Limitations not applicable to, §1-32.
Limited service facilities.
Approval of establishment, §53-62(b).
Authorized, §53-62(b).
Branch banks.
Conversion of limited service facility to branch,
§53-62(d).
Commissioner of banks.
Approval of establishment, §53-62(b).
Review of commissioner's actions by state
banking commissioner, §53-62(f).
Defined, §53-1.
Discontinuance of operation, §53-62(d).
Notice.
Discontinuance of operation, §53-62(d).

BANKS —Cont'd
Limited service facilities —Cont'd
Operation, §53-62(c).
Discontinuance, §53-62(d).
State banking commission.
Review of actions of commissioner, §53-62(f).
Liquidation. See within this heading, "Dissolution and liquidation."
Loan committee, §53-78.
Minutes of meetings, §53-79.
Loans.
Acceptances.
When acceptance considered direct loan to drawer, §53-56.
Bank examiners.
Prohibited loans or gratuities, §53-126.
Commercial loan commitments to be in writing, §22-5.
Commissioner of banks.
Prohibited loans or gratuities, §53-126.
Consumer finance act.
General provisions, §§53-164 to 53-191.
See CONSUMER FINANCE ACT.
Federal housing administration, secretary of housing and urban development or veterans administrations, securities approved by.
Credit insurance, eligibility for, §53-45(c).
General laws not applicable, §53-45(d).
Insured or guaranteed loans, §53-45(b).
General powers, §53-43.
Income tax.
Refund anticipation loans, §§53-245 to 53-254.
See INCOME TAX.
Industrial banks.
Limitations.
Applicability of general provisions, §53-143.
Powers generally, §53-141.
Limitations.
Suspension of limitations, §53-49.
Total loans and extension of credit to one person, §53-48(a), (b).
Person defined, §53-48(d).
Things not considered money borrow, §53-48(c).
Officers.
Loans to executive officers, §53-91.2.
Refund anticipation loans, §§53-245 to 53-254.
See INCOME TAX.
Reports.
Loan secured by ten percent or more of voting stock, §53-42.1(b).
Contents of report, §53-42.1(b).
Stock of bank or parent holding company, secured by.
Purchase of or to carry stock, prohibition, §53-64(b).
Unlawful, §53-64(a).
Total loans and extension of credit to one person.
Limitations, §53-48.
Mentally ill.
Incompetency of customer.
Authority of payor or collecting bank, §25-4-405(a), (b).
Merger and consolidation.
Authority to consolidate, §53-12(a).
Conditions for interstate merger prior to June 1, 1997, §53-224.21.
Deemed one bank, §53-13.
Fiduciary powers and liabilities of banks and trust companies merging or transferring assets and liabilities, §53-17.

BANKS —Cont'd
Merger and consolidation —Cont'd
Interstate bank mergers.
North Carolina state banks.
Establishment of out-of-state branches by merger, §53-224.18.
Out-of-state banks.
Establishing of North Carolina state branches by merger, §53-224.19.
Purpose of law, §53-224.17.
Investigation by commission, §53-12(a).
National banks.
Merger or consolidation of state banks or trust companies with, §53-16.
North Carolina state banks.
Powers of branches resulting from merger, §53-224.22(b).
Notice and filing requirements, §53-224.20.
Notice, publication, §53-12(a).
Out-of-state banks.
Powers of branches resulting from merger, §53-224.22(a).
Procedure, §53-12(a).
Proceedings of directors and stockholders.
Certified copies, filing, §53-12(a).
Savings banks, §§54C-35 to 54C-40.
Subsidiaries, §53-12(b).
Surviving bank.
Vesting of property and rights of several companies into surviving company, §53-13.
Microfilm.
Records, §53-110(b).
Minors.
Deposits.
Operating deposit account in name of minor, §53-43.5(a).
Safe-deposit boxes.
Leasing or renting to minors, §53-43.5(b), (c).
Misdemeanors.
Acceptance of fees or gifts by directors, officers or employees, §53-86.
Bank examiners.
Disclosing confidential information, §53-125.
Deposits.
Certificate of deposit.
Unlawful issuance, §53-63.
Derogatory reports.
Willfully and maliciously making, §53-128.
Loans or gratuities to commissioner of banks or bank examiners, §53-126.
Names.
Unlawful use of "bank," "banking" or "trust" incorporate name, §53-127(d).
Offenses generally, §53-134.
Money transmitters, §§53-208.1 to 53-208.30.
See MONEY TRANSMITTERS.
Mortgage bankers, brokers and servicers, §§53-244.010 to 53-244.121.
See MORTGAGE BANKERS, BROKERS AND SERVICERS.
Mortgages and deeds of trust.
Dissolution and liquidation.
Validation.
Acts of officers of insolvent banks as trustees in deeds of trust, §53-33.
Foreclosures and executions of deeds by commissioner of banks, §53-35.
Sales by commissioner of banks under mortgages and deeds of trust giving banks power of sale, §53-34.
Mortgages held by banks, §45-44.

BANKS —Cont'd
Mortgages and deeds of trust —Cont'd
Powers generally, §53-43.
Reverse mortgages, §§53-255 to 53-272.
See REVERSE MORTGAGES.
Mutual funds.
Investments, §53-46.1.
Names.
Certificate of incorporation to set forth, §53-2.
Industrial banks.
Certificate of incorporation to set forth, §53-137.
Corporate title, §53-138.
Misleading names.
Grounds for refusal for certificate of
incorporation, §53-4.
Unlawful use of "banks," "banking," "banker" or
"trust company" in nonbanking entity name.
Action to enjoin, §53-127(e).
Remedies not exclusive, §53-127(f).
National banks.
Conversion, consolidation or merger of state banks
with.
Authorized, §53-16(a).
Effect, §53-16(b), (e).
Shareholders.
Approval, §53-16(a).
Dissenting shareholders' rights, §53-16(c).
Shares.
Value as debt of resulting national bank,
§53-16(d).
Negotiable instruments.
Generally, §§25-3-101 to 25-3-605.
See NEGOTIABLE INSTRUMENTS.
Newspapers.
Reports of banks to commissioner.
Publication of summary of report, §53-105.
Special report, §53-106.
Nonbanking affiliates.
Commissioner of banks.
Examination, §53-104.1.
**Nonbanking entity using terms indicating
bank or trust company business.**
Unlawful use, §53-127.
Nonresidents.
Validation of deeds executed by nonresident
banks, §47-108.16.
Notice.
Administrative orders of commissioner.
Hearings on, §53-107.1(b).
Branch banks, interstate banking.
Branch banks resulting from interstate merger,
§53-224.20.
Notice of subsequent merger or other change in
control, §53-224.28.
Conservatorship.
Turning bank back to officers, §53-153.
Dissolution and liquidation.
Commissioner taking possession, §53-20(c), (d).
Answer to notice, §53-20(f).
Claims, §53-20(j), (k).
Impairment of capital, §53-42.
Limited service facilities.
Discontinuance of operation, §53-62(d).
Regional bank holding companies.
Acquisition by.
Publication by commissioner of notice of
intent to acquire, §53-211(d).
Reserves.
Deficiency in reserve fund, §53-50(c).
Stock and stockholders.
Impairment of capital, §53-42.

BANKS —Cont'd
Notice —Cont'd
Stock and stockholders —Cont'd
Sale of stock if subscription unpaid, §53-41.
Oaths.
Directors.
Oath of office, §53-81.
Officers, §§53-78 to 53-91.3.
Acceptance of gifts or fees prohibited, §53-86.
Acknowledgments taken by officer, §47-93.
Bonds, surety, §53-90.
Directors. See within this heading, "Directors."
Embezzlement or misapplication of funds,
§53-129.
Executive officers.
Loans to, §53-91.2.
Overdraft liability, §53-89.
Removal of officers.
Commissioner may require, §53-119.
Reports.
Changes in executive officers, §53-42.1(d).
Share purchase and option plans, §53-43.3.
**Off-premises customer-bank communications
terminals,** §53-62(d1).
Out-of-state branch banks.
Generally, §§53-224.9 to 53-224.31.
See BRANCH BANKS.
Overdrafts.
Payment by officer or employee, §53-89.
Payable on death (POD) accounts.
Change to account, not affecting status,
§53-146.2A(c).
Establishment, §53-146.2A(a).
Estate tax laws, effect, §53-146.2A(d).
Incidents of account, §53-146.2A(a).
Interest and incidents, §53-146.2A(a).
Savings banks, §54C-166.1.
Section not deemed exclusive, §53-146.2A(b).
Penalties, §§53-124 to 53-146.3.
Administrative orders of commissioner.
Civil money penalties, §§53-107.1(d),
53-107.2(b).
Advertising larger amount of capital stock than
actually paid in, §53-133.
Deposits.
Insolvent bank receiving, §53-132.
Embezzlement or misapplication of funds,
§53-129.
Failure of bank to make report to commissioner,
§53-107.
False certification of check, §53-131.
False entries in banking accounts, §53-130.
Loans or gratuities to bank examiners or
commissioner of banks, §53-126.
Misrepresenting assets and liabilities of banks,
§53-130.
Names.
Unlawful use of "bank," "banking" or "trust
company" in corporate name.
Injunction, §53-127(e).
Remedies not exclusive, §53-127(f).
Personal agency accounts.
Establishment, §53-146.3(a), (c).
Effect, §53-146.3(d).
Survivorship, §53-146.3(b).
Point-of-sale terminals, §53-62(d1).
Powers.
Generally, §53-43.
Practical banker.
Defined, §53-1.

BANKS —Cont'd
Preferred stock, §§53-154 to 53-156.
Conservatorship.
Scope of preferred stock provisions, §53-158.1.
Privacy of financial records.
Generally, §§53B-1 to 53B-10.
See FINANCIAL RECORDS PRIVACY.
Private banker.
Acting as private banker, §14-401.7.
Probate and registration.
Probate before stockholders or directors in
banking corporations, §§47-10, 47-92.
Validation of deeds and conveyances.
Attestation by secretary or cashier, §47-42(b),
(c).
Nonresident banks, §47-108.16.
Promissory notes.
Discount and negotiation.
Powers of banks generally, §53-43.
Publication.
Conservatorship.
Notice of turning bank back to officers, §53-153.
Reports of banks to commissioner.
Summary of report, §53-105.
Special report, §53-106.
Public officers and employees.
Deposits.
Statements showing deposits of state officials,
§53-68.
Real property.
Powers as to, §53-43.
Receivers.
Dissolution and liquidation.
Commissioner of banks.
Liquidation by commissioner of all banks in
receivership required, §53-20(w).
Statutes relating to receivers.
Applicability to insolvent banks, §53-22.
Insolvency.
Statute relating to receivers applicable to
insolvent banks, §53-22.
Reciprocal interstate banking, §§53-209 to
53-218.
See RECIPROCAL INTERSTATE BANKING.
Records.
Copies, §53-110(b).
Evidence.
Certified copies, §53-113.
Disposition, §53-110(b).
Dissolution and liquidation.
Destruction of records of liquidated insolvent
banks, §53-24.
Disposition of books and records, §53-23.
Evidence.
Certified copies, §53-113.
Reproduction, §53-110(b).
Retention, §53-110(b).
Refund anticipation loans, §§53-245 to 53-254.
See INCOME TAX.
Reopening of closed banks, §§53-37, 53-38.
Reorganization, §53-14.
Reports, §53-105.
Change in executive officers, §53-42.1(d).
Changes in control, §53-42.1(a).
Directors.
Changes in directors, §53-42.1(d).
Dissolution and liquidation.
Commissioner taking possession, §53-20(q), (s).
Failure to make report, §53-107.
Loan secured by ten percent or more of voting
stock, §53-42.1(b).

BANKS —Cont'd
Reports —Cont'd
Out-of-state bank with branch in North Carolina,
§53-224.24.
Special reports, §53-106.
Summary of report.
Publication, §53-105.
Reserves.
Deficiency in reserve fund.
Notice to commissioner of banks, §53-50(c).
Defined, §53-51(a).
Falling below legal requirement.
Powers and duties of commissioner of banks,
§53-111.
Notice.
Deficiency in reserve fund, §53-50(c).
Requirement of reserve fund, §53-50(a), (b).
Reverse mortgages, §§53-255 to 53-272.
See REVERSE MORTGAGES.
Safe-deposit boxes.
Abandoned property.
Unpaid rentals.
Delivery of contents to state treasurer,
§53-43.7(c), (d).
Minors.
Leasing or renting to minors, §53-43.5(b), (c).
Unpaid rentals.
Abandoned property.
Delivery of contents to state treasurer,
§53-43.7(c), (d).
Notice, §53-43.7(c).
Opening of box, §53-43.7(a).
Destruction of items of little apparent value,
§53-43.7(b).
Notice, §53-43.7(a).
Printing of provisions on contracts for rental of
safe-deposit boxes, §53-43.7(f).
Salaries.
Commissioner of banks, §53-96.
Employees of the office of the banks
commissioner.
Exemptions from classification and
compensation rules.
Purpose of exemptions, §53-96.1(b).
Savings and loan associations.
Conversion.
Bank to stock association, §54B-46.
General provisions, §§54B-1 to 54B-278.
See SAVINGS AND LOAN ASSOCIATIONS.
Investments.
Deposits in banks, §54B-185.
Merger of banks and associations, §54B-47.
Sale of loans to banks, §54B-161.
Savings banks, §§54C-1 to 54C-212.
See SAVINGS BANKS.
School thrift or savings plan.
Authorized, §53-43.6(a).
Branches.
Acceptance of deposits in furtherance of plan
not construed as establishment, §53-43.6(b).
Secured transactions.
Rights of banks.
Control agreement.
Refusal to enter into or disclose existence of,
§25-9-342.
Security interests in deposit accounts.
Control agreements.
Rights of banks with respect to agreements,
§25-9-342.
Perfection and priority.
Law governing, §25-9-304.

BANKS —Cont'd
Secured transactions —Cont'd
Security interests in deposit accounts —Cont'd
Perfection and priority —Cont'd
Rules of priority, §25-9-327.
Rights and duties of banks, §25-9-341.
Set-off or recoupment, §25-9-340.
Transfer of funds from deposit account, §25-9-332(b).
Securities.
Asset-backed securities facilitation, §§53-425, 53-426.
Dealing in securities on commission.
Taxed as private banker, §14-401.7.
Security broker.
When deemed security broker, §14-401.7.
Shares and shareholders, §§53-39 to 53-42.1.
Acknowledgments, §47-93.
Advertising larger amount of capital stock than actually paid in, §53-133.
Authorized but unissued stock, §53-10(b).
Book of stockholders, §53-85.
Capital notes, issuance, §53-43.4.
Consolidation, approval, §53-12(a).
Debentures, issuance, §53-43.4.
Decrease of capital stock, §53-11.
Definitions.
Shareholder, §53-108.
Term "stock" to include preferred stock, §53-156.
Directors.
Book of shareholders provided by, §53-85.
Election of directors, §53-67.
Qualifications of directors.
Stock ownership, §53-80.
Dissolution and liquidation.
Preferred stock, §53-155.
Sale of stock of defunct banks validated, §53-21.
Use of surplus, §53-88.
Voluntary liquidation, §§53-18, 53-87.
Employee share purchase and option plans, §53-43.3.
Fiduciaries not personally liable, §53-40.
Forfeiture or penalty imposed.
Limitation of actions, §1-33.
Impairment of capital, §53-42.
Assessments, §53-42.
Increase of capital stock.
Authorized, §53-10(a).
Unissued stock, §53-10(b).
Industrial banks.
Amount of authorized capital stock, §53-139.
Certificate of incorporation to set forth, §53-137.
Sale of capital stock, §53-140.
Investment in stock.
Limitations, §53-47.
Suspension of limitation, §53-49.
List of shareholders, §53-108.
Loans secured by banks own stock or stock of holding company, §53-64.
Merger and consolidation, approval, §53-12(a).
National banks.
Conversion, consolidation or merger of state banks or trust companies with, §53-16.
Notice.
Impairment of capital, §53-42.
Sale of stock if subscription unpaid, §53-41.
Officers' share purchase and option plans, §53-43.3.
Payment of capital stock, §53-6.
Surplus fund, §53-39.

BANKS —Cont'd
Shares and shareholders —Cont'd
Preferred stock.
Approval by commissioner, §53-154.
Authorized, §53-154.
Conservatorship.
Scope of preferred stock provisions, §53-158.1.
Dividends, §53-155.
Issuance, §53-154.
Rights and liabilities of preferred stockholders, §53-155.
Term "stock" to include preferred stock, §53-156.
Preferred stock issued to the United States Treasury.
Dividends, §53-87.1(a), (b).
Probates before stockholders, §47-92.
Purchase of own shares or shares of parent holding company, §53-64(c).
Reorganization, approval, §53-14.
Subscription unpaid, stock sold, §53-41.
Surplus converted into capital stock, §53-88.
Small loan companies, §§53-164 to 53-191.
See CONSUMER FINANCE ACT.
State banking commission, §53-92(b) to (d).
See BANKING COMMISSION.
State of North Carolina.
Checks payable in exchange.
Exemption of checks for obligations due state, §53-73.
Deposits.
Statements showing deposits of state and state officials, §53-68.
Stockbroker.
Acting as stockbroker, §14-401.7.
Supervisory acquisitions.
State associations, §53-17.1.
Surplus.
Converted into capital stock, §53-88.
Defined, §53-1.
Dividends.
Use of surplus, §53-88.
Use of surplus, §53-88.
Surplus fund.
Commencement of business.
Payment of capital stock as prerequisite, §53-39.
Survivorship.
Bank deposits created by written agreement, §41-2.1.
Joint deposits, §53-146.
Personal agency accounts, §53-146.3(b).
Suspension of business.
Emergencies, §53-77.3.
Taxation.
Collection of taxes.
Bank deposits subject to attachment or garnishment, §105-242(b).
Exempt property, §105-242(e).
License taxes, §105-102.3.
Terms indicating business bank or trust company.
Unlawful use by nonbanking entity.
Definitions, §53-127(a).
Restrictions on use, §53-127(b).
Exceptions, §53-127(c).
Penalty for violations, §53-127(d).
Totten trust.
Payable on death accounts, §§54-109.57A, 54B-130A.
Savings banks, §54C-166.1.

BANKS —Cont'd
Trust companies and interstate trust business, §§53-301 to 53-424.
See TRUST COMPANIES.
Trusts and trustees.
Deposits.
In name of two or more trustees, §32-11.
Dissolution and liquidation.
Trust terminated on insolvency of trustee bank, §§53-25 to 53-32.
Stockholder.
Not personally liable as, §53-40.
Unclaimed property generally, §§116B-51 to 116B-80.
See UNCLAIMED PROPERTY.
Uncollectible assets.
Writing off, §53-91.1.
Uniform commercial code.
Bank deposits and collections, §§25-4-101 to 25-4-504.
See BANK DEPOSITS AND COLLECTIONS.
United States.
Checks payable in exchange.
Exemptions of checks in payment of obligations due federal government, §53-73.
Federal reserve system, §53-61.
Validation.
Dissolution and liquidation, §§53-33 to 53-35.
Transactions not performed during banking hours, §53-54.
Wills.
Probate of wills.
Substitution of consolidated bank as executor or trustee under will, §28A-2A-12.

BANKS COMMISSIONER, §§53-92 to 53-116.
Actions.
Nonliability to suit, §53-94.
Power to sue and defend, §53-94.
Administrative orders.
Civil money penalties for violations, §§53-107.1(d), 53-107.2(b).
Hearings.
Notice and opportunity for hearing, §53-107.1(b).
Powers of commissioner, §53-107.1(a), (c).
Review by banking commission, §53-107.2(a).
Appeals.
Branch banking, interstate, §53-224.30.
Appointment, §53-92(a).
Assessments for operating office, §53-122.
Assets.
Appraisal of assets of doubtful value, §53-112.
Attorneys at law.
Employment of counsel to prosecute offenses, §53-134.
Bank examiners.
Appointment of bank examiners, §53-117(a).
Branch banks.
Approval of establishment, §53-62(b).
Capital requirements, §53-62(c).
Interstate banks.
Appeal of commissioner's decisions, §53-224.30.
Approval by commissioner, §53-224.15.
Interstate branching by merger, §53-224.18.
Cooperative agreements, §53-224.24(c).
Enforcement of law, §53-224.25.
Examination of branches, §53-224.24(a).
Rulemaking authority, §53-224.26.
Review of commissioner's actions by state banking commission, §53-62(f).

BANKS COMMISSIONER —Cont'd
Cease and desist orders.
Administrative orders generally, §§53-107.1, 53-107.2.
Clerical help, §53-101.
Confidentiality of records, §§53-99(b), 53-120(c), (e).
Conservatorship.
Appointment of conservator, §53-148.
Examination of bank, §53-149.
Termination of conservatorship, §53-150.
Consumer finance act generally, §§53-164 to 53-191.
See CONSUMER FINANCE ACT.
Deputy commissioner, §53-93.1(b).
Appointment, §53-93.1(b).
Chief, §53-93.1(a).
Powers, §53-93.1(b).
Directors of banks.
Removal of directors.
Commissioner may require, §53-119.
Dissolution and liquidation.
Deeds of trust.
Validation of certain acts of commissioner as to, §§53-34, 53-35.
Taking possession.
Accountants and other experts.
Employment, §53-20(o).
Applicability of provisions, §53-20(v).
Attorneys at law.
Employment of local attorneys, §53-20(o).
Bond, surety, §53-20(h).
Claims against bank.
Lists of claims presented, §53-20(l).
Notice and time for filing claims, §53-20(j).
Powers and duties as to, §53-20(g).
Rejection of claims, §53-20(k).
Compensation of commissioner, §53-20(t).
Debts and claims.
Action on claims, §53-20(k).
Lists of claims presented, §53-20(l).
Notice and time for filing claims, §53-20(j).
Powers and duties as to, §53-20(g).
Rejection of claims, §53-20(k).
Deposits.
Deposit of funds collected, §53-20(n).
Unlocated depositor, §53-20(x).
Directors may act by resolution, §53-20(b).
Dividends.
Declaration, §53-20(m).
Unclaimed dividends held in trust, §53-20(p).
Exclusive method of liquidation, §53-20(u).
Failure to meet deposit demands.
Commissioner not to take over banks failing to meet, §53-116.
Injunction, §53-20(f).
Inventory, §53-20(i).
Notices, §53-20(c), (d).
Answer to notice, §53-20(f).
Claims, §53-20(j), (k).
Receivership.
Liquidation by commissioner of all banks in receivership required, §53-20(w).
Remedy by bank for seizure, §53-20(f).
Reopening of closed banks, §§53-37, 53-38.
Report, §53-20(q).
Annual report, §53-20(s).
Report to secretary of state concerning certain matters relative to liquidation of closed banks, §53-36.

BANKS COMMISSIONER —Cont'd
Dissolution and liquidation —Cont'd
Taking possession —Cont'd
Resumption of business.
Permission, §53-20(e).
Settlement.
Action by commissioner after full settlement,
§53-20(r).
When authorized, §§53-19, 53-20(a).
Voluntary liquidation.
Approval, §53-18.
Duties.
Generally, §§53-93, 53-104.
**Emergency program to reduce home
foreclosures.**
Extension of filing dates for appropriate loans,
§45-105.
State home foreclosure prevention project and
fund, §45-104.
Employees of banks.
Removal of employees.
Commissioner may require, §53-119.
**Employees of the office of the banks
commissioner.**
Exemptions from classification and compensation
rules.
Purpose of exemptions, §53-96.1(b).
Executive director.
State banking commission, §53-92(c).
Fees and assessments for operating office.
Banks, §53-122(a).
Collection annually or in installments, §53-122(f).
Consumer finance licensees, §53-122(a).
Expenses not to exceed fees collected, §53-122(d).
Processing applications or proceedings, §53-122(b).
Reduction.
Estimated fees and assessments exceed
operating costs, §53-122(e).
Special assessments, §53-122(a).
Incorporation.
Examination of proposed bank, §53-4.
Review of actions by commission, §53-4.
Industrial banks.
Supervision by, §53-144.
International banking.
Appeal of commissioner's decisions, §53-232.17.
Cease and desist orders, §53-232.16.
Definition of "commissioner,"§53-232.2(a).
International representative offices.
Review of operations, §53-232.14(c).
Investigations.
Insolvent banks, §53-100.
Official communications relating to, §53-109.
Legal assistance, §53-96.
Limited service facilities.
Approval of establishment, §53-62(b).
Review of commissioner's actions by state banking
commissioner, §53-62(f).
Loans.
Prohibited loans or gratuities, §53-126.
Money transmitters.
Generally, §§53-208.1 to 53-208.30.
See MONEY TRANSMITTERS.
Mortgage bankers, brokers and servicers.
Generally, §§53-244.010 to 53-244.121.
See MORTGAGE BANKERS, BROKERS AND
SERVICERS.
Mortgage debt collection and servicing.
Enforcement of provisions, §45-94.
Mortgage foreclosure prevention.
Emergency program to reduce home foreclosures.
Extension of filing dates for appropriate loans,
§45-105.

BANKS COMMISSIONER —Cont'd
Mortgage foreclosure prevention —Cont'd
Emergency program to reduce home foreclosures
—Cont'd
State home foreclosure prevention project and
fund, §45-104.
Nonbanking affiliates.
Examination, §53-104.1.
Officers of banks.
Removal of officers.
Commissioner may require, §53-119.
Offices, §53-102.
Official communications, §53-109.
Orders.
Administrative orders, §§53-107.1, 53-107.2.
Powers.
Actions, §53-94.
Examination of nonbanking affiliate, §53-104.1.
Exercise under supervision of banking
commission, §53-95.
Generally, §53-93.
Investigations of insolvent banks, §53-100.
Offices, powers as to, §53-102.
Supervision of banks, §53-104.
Prosecution of offenses against banking laws,
§53-134.
Records.
Confidentiality of certain records, §§53-99(b),
53-120(c), (e).
Generally, §53-99(a).
Reports.
Banks to report to commissioner, §53-105.
Failure to make report.
Notice of violation, §53-107.
Penalty, §53-107.
Publication of summary of report, §53-105.
Special reports, §53-106.
Special reports, §53-106.
Reserves below legal requirement.
Powers and duties of commissioner, §53-111.
Reverse mortgages generally, §§53-255 to
53-272.
See REVERSE MORTGAGES.
**Review of exercise of powers, duties and
functions.**
State banking commission, §53-92(d).
Salary, §53-96.
Employees of the office of the banks commissioner.
Exemptions from classification and
compensation rules.
Purpose of exemptions, §53-96.1(b).
Savings and loan associations.
Annual statements of associations, §54B-76.
Cease and desist orders, §54B-59.
Confidentiality of information, §54B-63.
Conflicts of interest, §54B-62.
Deputy commissioner.
Powers and duties, §54B-54(a), (b).
Dividends.
Approval required, §54B-43.
Duties, §54B-52.
Examination and investigation, §§54B-56 to
54B-58.
Fees.
Supervision and examination fees, §54B-57(a).
Holding companies.
Supervision by, §54B-262.
Incorporation applications.
Consideration, §54B-11.
Criteria for recommendation of approval,
§54B-12.

BANKS COMMISSIONER —Cont'd
Savings and loan associations —Cont'd
Jurisdiction, §54B-67.
Liquidation of associations.
Involuntary liquidation, §54B-70.
Lists of stockholders.
Filing in office of commissioner, §54B-21.
Loans.
Collateral.
Test appraisal of collateral, §54B-61.
Granting to commissioner prohibited, §54B-62(a).
Rule-making power of commissioner, §54B-155.
Mergers, §54B-246.
Mutual and stock associations.
Simultaneous conversion/mergers, §54B-37.1.
Oaths.
Power to administer, §54B-60(a).
Powers generally, §54B-52.
Records.
Access to books and records of associations, §54B-60(a).
Regional reciprocal savings and loan acquisition.
Appeals of decisions, §54B-48.7.
Removal of directors, officers and employees, §54B-69.
Service corporations, §54B-194.
Subpoena power, §54B-60(a), (b).
Failure to comply with subpoena, §54B-60(c).
Supervisory consolidations, §54B-44.
Supervisory control, §54B-68.
Supervisory conversions, §54B-44.
Supervisory mergers, §54B-44.
Withdrawable accounts.
Holding withdrawable accounts permitted, §54B-62(c).
Witnesses.
Powers as to, §54B-60(a).
Seal of office, §53-98.
Secretarial help, §53-101.
State banking commission.
Commission bound by requirements imposed on commissioner as to certain matters, §53-92.1.
Executive director, §53-92(c).
Powers of commissioner.
Exercise of powers under supervision of banking commission, §53-95.
Review of exercise of powers, duties and functions, §53-92(d).
State home foreclosure prevention project and fund, §45-104.
Stock.
Authorized but unissued stock.
Approval of commissioner, §53-10(b).
Decrease of capital stock.
Approval by commissioner, §53-11.
Preferred stock.
Approval of issuance, §53-154.
Subpoenas.
Administrative orders.
Powers in connection with, §53-107.1(c).
Investigations of insolvent banks, §53-100.
Supervision of banks, §53-104.
Taking possession, §§53-19, 53-20.
Tellers' windows.
Approval of establishment, §53-62(b).
Term of office, §53-92(a).
Trust companies and interstate trust business.
Generally, §§53-301 to 53-424.
See TRUST COMPANIES.
Vacancy, §53-92(a).

BANKS COMMISSIONER —Cont'd
Witness fees.
Employees of office used as witness, §53-122(c).
BANK SERVICES CARDS.
Credit cards.
See CREDIT CARDS.
Financial transaction card crimes, §§14-113.8 to 14-113.17.
See FINANCIAL TRANSACTION CARDS.
BANQUETS.
Utility commission members attending banquets sponsored by public utilities, §62-327.
BAPTISMAL CERTIFICATES.
Hearsay exceptions, §8C-1 Rule 803.
BAR ASSOCIATION.
Court commission.
Ex officio member, §7A-507.
State bar, §§84-15 to 84-38.
See ATTORNEYS AT LAW.
BARBERS, §§86A-1 to 86A-27.
Apprenticeship, §86A-24.
Examinations, §86A-24(a).
Retaking.
Requirement, §86A-24(c).
Supervision of apprentices.
Required, §86A-24(b).
Board of barber examiners.
Appointment of members, §86A-4(a), (b).
Bonds, surety.
Executive secretary, §86A-6.
Civil penalties.
Generally, §86A-27(a) to (d).
Compensation of members, §86A-7(a).
Composition, §86A-4(a).
Costs.
Disciplinary costs, §86A-27(d).
Duties, §86A-5(a).
Employees, §86A-7(b).
Executive secretary, §86A-6.
Duties, §86A-6.
Expenses of members, §86A-7(a).
Inspections, §86A-15(b).
Number of members, §86A-4(a).
Office, §86A-6.
Officers, §86A-6.
Powers, §86A-5(a).
Public-at-large member, §86A-4(d).
Qualifications of members, §86A-4(a).
Record of proceedings, §86A-21.
Removal of members, §86A-4(c).
Reports.
Annual report to governor, §86A-7(e).
Right of entry.
Inspections, §86A-15(b).
Rules and regulations, §86A-5(b).
Seal, §86A-6.
Terms of members, §86A-4(a).
Bonds, surety.
Schools.
Guaranty bond required for approval, §86A-22.
Certificates of registration.
Criteria for issuance, §86A-10.
Data on registrants.
Board to keep, §86A-21.
Denial, §§86A-18, 86A-19.
Display, §86A-16.
Expiration, §86A-17(a).
Restoration, §86A-17(b).

BARBERS —Cont'd
Certificates of registration —Cont'd
Issuance, §86A-10.
Qualifications, §86A-3.
Reciprocity, §86A-12.
Effect, §86A-12(c).
Qualifications of applicants, §86A-12(a).
Waiver of certain qualifications, §86A-12(b).
Renewal, §86A-17(a), (c).
Required, §86A-1.
Suspension or revocation, §§86A-18, 86A-19.
Felony convictions, §15A-1331A.
Practicing during period of suspension or
revocation.
Penalty, §86A-20.
Temporary permits.
Graduates of barber schools, §86A-11(a).
Persons licensed in other state, §86A-11(c), (d).
Persons whose licenses expired, §86A-11(b).
Child support enforcement.
Forfeiture of licensing privilege, §50-13.12.
City privilege license tax.
Barbershops or beauty salons, §160A-211(b).
Civil penalties, §86A-27(a) to (d).
Client's home.
Practicing barbering in out of medical necessity,
§86A-15(c).
Cosmetic art.
Exemptions from barbering provisions, §86A-14.
Costs.
Disciplinary costs, §86A-27(d).
Definitions.
Practice of barbering.
What constitutes, §86A-2.
Equipment and instruments.
Requirements, §86A-15(a).
Examinations.
Applications, §86A-8.
Apprenticeship, §86A-24(a).
Retaking.
Requirement, §86A-24(c).
Fees, §86A-25.
Payment required, §86A-8.
Frequency, §86A-9.
Instructors, §86A-23(a).
Applications for, §86A-23(b).
Qualifications for certificate of registration,
§86A-3.
Times and places, §86A-9.
Exemptions from provisions, §86A-14.
Members of same family, §86A-26.
Family members.
Exemption from provisions, §86A-26.
Fees.
Examinations, §86A-25.
Payment required, §86A-8.
Generally, §86A-25.
Felony convictions.
Disqualification for certificate or permit, §86A-18.
Forfeiture of license, §15A-1331A.
Fraud.
Prohibited acts, §86A-20.
Injunctions.
Illegal practice, §86A-20.1.
Inspections, §86A-15(b).
Instructors, §86A-23.
Certificates, §86A-23.
Examinations, §86A-23(a).
Applications for, §86A-23(b).
Intoxication.
Disqualifications for certificates or permits,
§86A-18.

BARBERS —Cont'd
Military.
Exemptions from barbering provisions, §86A-14.
Misdemeanors.
Prohibited acts, §86A-20.
Municipalities.
Privilege license tax.
Barbershops or beauty salons, §160A-211(b).
Nurses.
Exemptions from barbering provisions, §86A-14.
Practice of barbering.
What constitutes, §86A-2.
Prohibited acts, §86A-20.
Reciprocal licensing, §86A-12.
Effect of reciprocity, §86A-12(c).
Qualifications of applicants, §86A-12(a).
Waiver of certain qualifications, §86A-12(b).
Reports.
Board of barber examiners.
Annual report to governor, §86A-7(e).
Right of entry.
Board of barber examiners.
Inspections, §86A-15(b).
Rules and regulations.
Sanitary rules and regulations, §86A-15(a).
Schools, §86A-22.
Sanitary rules and regulations, §86A-15(a).
Violations.
Disqualifications for certificates or permits,
§86A-18.
Schools.
Approval by board, §86A-22.
Attendance at approved school.
Qualifications for certificate of registration,
§86A-3.
Bonds, surety.
Guaranty bond required for approval, §86A-22.
Permits, §86A-13.
Applications, §86A-13.
Denial, §§86A-18, 86A-19.
Display, §86A-16.
Fees, §86A-25.
Renewal, §86A-13(b).
Required, §86A-1.
Suspension or revocation, §§86A-18, 86A-19.
Requirements, §86A-22.
Rules and regulations, §86A-22.
Shops.
Permits, §86A-13.
Applications, §86A-13(a).
Display, §86A-16.
Fees, §86A-25.
Renewal, §86A-13(b).
Required, §86A-1.
Suspension or revocation, §§86A-18, 86A-19.
Violations of provisions.
Prohibited acts, §86A-20.

BARBITAL.
Schedule II controlled substance, §90-92(a).

BARBITURATES.
Controlled substances generally, §§90-86 to
90-113.8.
See DRUGS AND CONTROLLED SUBSTANCES.
**Driver's license not to be issued to habitual
user,** §20-9(c).

BARBITURIC ACID.
Food, drug and cosmetic act.
Drugs deemed misbranded, §106-134.

BAR EXAMINATION, AdmissPrac Rules .0901 to
.1005.

BARGES.
Burning of barges, §14-63.

BARLEY.
Adulteration of grains.
Generally, §§106-621 to 106-628.
See GRAIN ADULTERATION.
Grain dealers.
Generally, §§106-601 to 106-615.
See GRAIN DEALERS.
Standard weight and measure, §81A-42.

BARNS.
Burning of barn, §14-62.

BARRELS.
Trucks of leaf tobacco in barrels.
Load to be securely fastened, §20-120.

BARROOMS.
ABC permits generally.
See ABC PERMITS.
Gaming.
Allowing gambling in houses of public
entertainment, §14-293.
Minors.
Permitting minors to enter barrooms, §14-317.
Smoking prohibited.
Restaurants and bars, exceptions, §§130A-496,
130A-497.

BAR TO PROPERTY RIGHTS.
Killing decedent generally, §§31A-3 to 31A-15.
See SLAYER ACT.

**BAR TO RIGHT TO RENOUNCE PROPERTY
OR INTEREST,** §31B-4(a).

BASEBALL.
Athletic contests generally.
See ATHLETICS.
Junior or youth baseball.
Certification of birth dates furnished to veterans'
organizations, §130A-120.

BASIC EDUCATION PROGRAM, §115C-81.

**BASINWIDE WATER QUALITY MANAGEMENT
PLANS,** §143-215.8B.

BASKETBALL.
Athletic contests generally.
See ATHLETICS.

BASTARDY.
**Illegitimate children, support, legitimation,
civil actions regarding,** §§49-1 to 49-17.
See CHILDREN BORN OUT OF WEDLOCK.
Paternity.
Proceedings to establish generally.
See PATERNITY.

BATH HISTORICAL COMMISSION, §§143B-99
to 143B-102.
Appointments, §143B-102.
Compensation of members, §143B-102.
Creation, §143B-99.
Department of cultural resources.
Transfer of commission to department, §143B-51.
Duties, §143B-99.
Exemption from provisions, §143B-100.
Members, §143B-102.
Powers and duties, §143B-99.
Quorum, §143B-102.
Reports, §143B-101.

BATH HISTORICAL COMMISSION —Cont'd
Selection of members, §143B-102.
Status, §143B-100.

BATHROOMS.
See RESTROOMS.

BATTERED WIVES.
See DOMESTIC VIOLENCE.

BATTERIES.
Lead-acid batteries, §§130A-309.70 to
130A-309.73.
Incineration, disposal by prohibited,
§§130A-309.10(f1), 130A-309.70(a), (b).
Civil penalty for violation, §130A-309.70(c).
Inspection of retailers, §130A-309.73(a).
Landfills, disposal in prohibited, §§130A-309.10(f),
130A-309.70(a), (b).
Civil penalty for violation, §130A-309.70(c).
Persons not selling.
Not prohibited from collecting and recycling,
§130A-309.73(b).
Retailers.
Acceptance for recycling required,
§130A-309.71(a).
Posting of notice, §130A-309.71(b).
Civil penalty for failure to post,
§130A-309.71(c).
Inspection.
Authorized, §130A-309.73(a).
Warning to person for noncompliance.
Issuance by department, §130A-309.73(a).
Wholesalers.
Acceptance for recycling required,
§130A-309.72(a).
Civil penalties for violations, §130A-309.72(b).

BATTERY.
See ASSAULT AND BATTERY.

BATTLE ACT.
Quieting title, §41-10.

BATTLE OF THE FORMS.
Sale of goods, UCC.
Additional terms in acceptance or confirmation,
§25-2-207.

BATTLESHIP COMMISSION, §§143B-73 to
143B-74.3.

BAWDY HOUSES.
Abatement of nuisances against public morals,
§§19-1 to 19-8.3.
See NUISANCES.
Bad character of inmates and frequenters.
Prima facie evidence, §14-188(a).
Definitions.
Keeper, §14-188.
Keeper.
Defined, §14-188.
Misdemeanor offense, §14-188(b).

BB GUNS.
County regulation, §153A-130.
Firearms and other weapons generally.
See FIREARMS AND OTHER WEAPONS.
Municipal regulation, §160A-190.
**Permitting young children to use dangerous
firearms.**
Whether BB gun deemed dangerous firearm,
§14-316(b).
**Possessing or carrying on campus or other
educational property,** §14-269.2.

BEACH ACCESS PROGRAM, §§113A-134.1 to 113A-134.3.

Acquisition, improvement and maintenance of system, §113A-134.3(a).

Administration of program, §113A-134.2(a).

Coordination of state and local programs, §113A-134.3(b).

Creation of program, §113A-134.2(a).

Definitions, §113A-134.2(b).

Funding of program, §113A-134.3(c).

Legislative findings, §113A-134.1(a), (b).

Priorities, §113A-134.3.

Purposes, §§113A-134.1(a), (b), 113A-134.2(a).

Standards, §113A-134.3.

BEACH AREA ESSENTIAL PROPERTY INSURANCE, §§58-45-1 to 58-45-96.

Appeals, §58-45-50(a).
Commissioner to superior court, §58-45-50.
Costs of recording and transcribing, §58-45-50(b).
Denial of policy, §58-45-35(c).
Proposed order, submitting, §58-45-50(b).
Statement of case and evidence.
Appellant and appellee to file, §58-45-50(b).

Commissioner.
Appeal from commissioner to superior court, §58-45-50.
Appeals from acts of association, §58-45-50.
Examination of affairs of association, §58-45-70.
Immunity of commissioner from liability, §58-45-60.
Plan of operation of association, §58-45-30(a) to (f).
Action on, §58-45-30.
Rules and regulations, §58-45-75.

Definitions, §§58-45-5, 58-45-6.
Plan of operation defined, §58-45-30(f).

Homeowners' insurance policy.
Insurance underwriting association.
Issuance, §58-45-35(b1).

Homeowners' rate filings.
Publication in North Carolina register, §58-45-15.

Insurance underwriting association.
Accumulated surplus.
Removal from association, use for other than expressed purposes.
Prohibition, §58-45-25(b2).
Retained, use, §58-45-25(b1).
Agent.
Authority to temporarily bind coverage, §58-45-35(d).
Insurance agent not deemed agent of association, §58-45-35(d).
Appeals from acts of association, §58-45-50.
Applications to association for coverage, §58-45-35(a).
Assessments against insolvent insurers, §58-45-85(a).
Audit, §58-45-65.1.
Board of directors.
Temporary board of directors, §58-45-20.
Catastrophe recovery charge.
Authorizing member companies to impose, §58-45-47(c).
Defined, §58-45-5.
Duration, §58-45-47(g).
Excess collections remitted to association, §58-45-47(g).
Identified to policyholders, §58-45-47(d).
Recalculation, adjustment, §58-45-47(f).
Report by association, §58-45-47(e).

BEACH AREA ESSENTIAL PROPERTY INSURANCE —Cont'd

Insurance underwriting association —Cont'd
Ceding of insurance to association by members, §58-45-40.
Commercial property.
Coverage limits, §58-45-41(a).
Composition, §58-45-10.
Confidential information identifying policyholders.
Disclosure, consent required, §58-45-95.
Coverage limits, §58-45-41(a).
Contents of habitational property, §58-45-41(b).
Excess coverage, §58-45-41(c).
Creation, §58-45-10.
Credits for policyholders, schedule.
Mitigation and construction features, §58-45-45(e).
Credit to member insurers, §58-45-25(b).
Applied to nonrecoupable assessment, §58-45-25(b).
Deferral of nonrecoupable assessments.
Insolvent insurers, §58-45-85(b).
Deficit event.
Catastrophe recovery charge.
Authorizing member companies to impose, §58-45-47(c).
Defined, §58-45-5.
Duration, §58-45-47(g).
Excess collections remitted to association, §58-45-47(g).
Identified to policyholders, §58-45-47(d).
Recalculation, adjustment, §58-45-47(f).
Report by association, §58-45-47(e).
Financing arrangements.
Authority to enter into, §58-45-47(h).
Means of financing deficit.
Determination by association, §58-45-47(c).
Nonrecoupable assessment issued upon members, §58-45-47(a).
Maximum amount, §58-45-47(a).
Notice of deficit given commissioner, §58-45-47(b).
Disclose of information concerning association, §58-45-95.
Dissolution, §58-45-96.
Examination by commissioner, §58-45-70.
Excess coverage.
Property value exceeds coverage limits, §58-45-41(c).
Exemption from taxation, §58-45-1(c).
Geographical territories for rating purposes, §58-36-10.
Habitational property.
Coverage limits, §58-45-41(a).
Contents, §58-45-41(b).
Homeowners' coverage.
Amount.
Report by member companies, §58-45-71.
Homeowners' insurance policy.
Issuance, §58-45-35(b1).
Identification of policyholder.
Disclosure of confidential information, consent required, §58-45-95.
Immunity from liability, §58-45-60.
Insolvent insurers.
Assessment against, §58-45-85(a).
Deferral of nonrecoupable assessments, §58-45-85(b).
Inspections.
Reports made available, §58-45-55.

BEACH AREA ESSENTIAL PROPERTY
     INSURANCE —Cont'd
Insurance underwriting association —Cont'd
   Installment plan for premium payments,
     §58-45-45(f).
   Losses and expenses exceeding funding,
     §58-45-47.
   Losses, reinsurance costs, operating expenses.
     Accumulated surplus used to pay, §58-45-25(b1).
   Meetings.
     Open meetings act, §58-45-90.
   Membership, §58-45-10.
     Ceding of insurance to association by members,
       §58-45-40.
   Mitigation and construction features.
     Credits for policyholders, schedule, §58-45-45(e).
   Open meetings act, §58-45-90.
   Participation in nonrecoupable assessments.
     Certification of member's participation,
       §58-45-5.
     Credit received by insurers applied to
       assessment, §58-45-25(b).
     Insurer's participation, §58-45-25(a).
     Nonrecoupable assessment defined, §58-45-5.
     Required of each member, §58-45-25(a).
   Plan of operation.
     Amendments, §58-45-30(c).
     Appeals.
       Orders of commission with respect to plan,
         §58-45-30(c).
     Approval, §58-45-30(b).
     Defined, §58-45-30(f).
     Homeowners' insurance policy defined,
       §58-45-30(d).
     Manufacturing risks coverage, §58-45-30(e).
     Principal residence policies, §58-45-30(d).
     Submission to commissioner, §§58-45-20,
       58-45-30(a).
   Policies.
     Issuance, §58-45-35(b).
     Temporary binders of insurance, §58-45-36.
       Authority of agents, §58-45-35(d).
   Powers, §58-45-15.
   Public availability of information concerning
     association, §58-45-95.
   Rates, rating plans, rate rules and forms.
     Appeal procedures, §58-45-45(d).
     Credits for policyholders, schedule.
       Mitigation and construction features,
         §58-45-45(e).
     Deductible for named storm losses,
       §58-45-45(a2).
     Filing, §58-45-45(b), (d).
     Homeowners' insurance surcharge,
       §58-45-45(a1).
     Installment plan for premium payments,
       §58-45-45(f).
     Named storm loss deductible, §58-45-45(a2).
     North Carolina rate bureau rates plus
       surcharge, §58-45-45(a1).
     Rate requirements, §58-45-45(a).
     Schedule of credits for policyholders.
       Mitigation and construction features,
         §58-45-45(e).
     Separate policies of windstorm and hail
       insurance.
       Filings with commissioner, §58-45-45(b).
     Surcharges, §58-45-45(a1).
     Wind and hail coverage surcharge,
       §58-45-45(a1).

BEACH AREA ESSENTIAL PROPERTY
     INSURANCE —Cont'd
Insurance underwriting association —Cont'd
   Reinsurance.
     Purchase.
       Association to consider every year,
         §58-45-45(g).
   Reports.
     Annual report to commissioner, §58-45-65.
     Catastrophe recovery charge, §58-45-47(e).
     Inspections by or on behalf of association.
       Reports to be made available, §58-45-55.
     Member companies, §58-45-71.
   Reserves.
     Unearned premiums, losses, and loss expenses.
       Association shall make provisions for,
         §58-45-46.
   Successor organization created, §58-45-96.
   Take out program.
     Use by association, §58-45-25(c).
   Tax exemption, §58-45-1(c).
   Temporary binders of insurance, §58-45-36.
     Authority of agents, §58-45-35(d).
   Unearned premium, loss, and loss expense
     reserves.
     Association shall make provisions for,
       §58-45-46.
   Wind, storm or hail insurance, §58-45-35(e).
Legislative declarations, §58-45-1.
Market of last resort.
   Legislative declaration, §58-45-1(b).
Mitigation and construction features.
   Schedule of credits to policyholders based on,
     §58-36-15(d1).
Plan of operation of association, §58-45-30(a) to
   (f).
Premium taxes.
   Payment through association, §58-45-80.
Purpose of provisions, §58-45-1(a).
Reinsurance.
   Powers of association, §58-45-15.
Reports.
   Association to file annual report with
     commissioner, §58-45-65.
   Inspections by or on behalf of association.
     Availability of reports, §58-45-55.
   Insurance underwriting association.
     Catastrophe recovery charge, §58-45-47(e).
   Member companies, §58-45-71.
Rules and regulations.
   Commissioner may promulgate, §58-45-75.

BEACH BINGO.
Applicability of bingo article to, §14-309.14.

BEACH EROSION CONTROL.
Counties.
   Service districts, §§153A-300 to 153A-310.
   Special assessments.
     Authority to make, §153A-185.
     Generally, §§153A-185 to 153A-210.7.
       See SPECIAL ASSESSMENTS BY
         COUNTIES.
**Local government sales and use tax for beach
   nourishment,** §§105-525 to 105-531.
   Administration of taxes, §105-529.
   Applicability of article, §105-526.
   Definitions, §105-527.
   Distribution, §105-531(a).
   Expiration, §105-530.
   Levy of one percent tax, §105-528.
   Short title, §105-525.

BEACH EROSION CONTROL —Cont'd
Local government sales and use tax for beach nourishment —Cont'd
Use, §105-531(b).
Municipalities.
Assessments.
Authority to make assessments for beach erosion control, §160A-238.
Powers in connection with, §160A-491.
Property taxes.
Authorized purposes, §160A-209(c).
Service districts.
Purposes for establishing, §160A-536(a).

BEACHES.
Access program, §§113A-134.1 to 113A-134.3.
Adverse possession of property subject to public trust rights.
No adverse possession, §1-45.1.
All-terrain vehicles.
Operating on ocean beach area, §20-171.22(c).
Beach nourishment.
Local government sales and use tax, §§105-525 to 105-531.
Clean coastal water and vessel act, §§77-125 to 77-132.
See CLEAN COASTAL WATER AND VESSEL ACT.
Coastal area management.
General provisions.
See COASTAL AREA MANAGEMENT.
Erosion protection.
Special assessments by counties, §§153A-185 to 153A-210.7.
See SPECIAL ASSESSMENTS BY COUNTIES.
Hurricane flood protection and beach erosion control project revolving fund, §143-215.62.
Income tax credit.
Donations of real property for public beach access or use, §105-151.12.
Littering, §14-399.
Management plan, §§113A-134.11, 113A-134.12.
Municipalities.
Erosion control.
Assessments, authority, §160A-238.
Powers in connection with, §160A-491.
Property taxes.
Authorized purposes, §160A-209(c).
Service districts.
Purposes for establishing, §160A-536(a).
Ocean beaches.
Public trust rights in, §77-20(d), (e).
Offshore oil and gas activities, §§143-215.94AA to 143-215.94JJ.
See OFFSHORE OIL AND GAS ACTIVITIES.
Oil or hazardous substances discharges, §§143-215.83 to 143-215.94.
See OIL OR HAZARDOUS SUBSTANCES DISCHARGES.
Ordinances.
Beach towns, §§160A-176.1, 160A-176.2.
Plastic bag management.
Retailers.
Counties containing barrier islands, §§130A-309.120 to 130A-309.125.
Property insurance.
Essential property insurance, §§58-45-1 to 58-45-96.
See BEACH AREA ESSENTIAL PROPERTY INSURANCE.

BEACHES —Cont'd
Public trust rights.
No adverse possession, §1-45.1.
Ocean beaches, §77-20(d), (e).
Sales and use tax for beach nourishment.
Local government, §§105-525 to 105-531.
Special assessments by counties.
Erosion protection, §§153A-185 to 153A-210.7.
See SPECIAL ASSESSMENTS BY COUNTIES.
Water quality of coastal fishing waters.
Monitoring, §113-221.3(a), (b).

BEACH MANAGEMENT PLAN, §§113A-134.11, 113A-134.12.

BEACONS.
Displaying false lights on seashore, §14-282.
Interfering with, §76-58.
Rafts to exercise care in passing, §76-57.

BEAGLES.
Field trials for beagles.
Hunting license exemption, §113-276(k).

BEAM INDICATORS.
Motor vehicle headlamp requirements, §20-131(a).

BEANS.
Standard weight and measures, §81A-42.

BEARS.
Black bears.
Captivity licenses.
Applicability to, §113-272.5(f).
Protection, §§19A-10 to 19A-14.
Dogs.
Injuring or killing bear on wildlife management areas, killing dogs, §67-14.1(a).
Hunting and wildlife generally.
See HUNTING AND WILDLIFE.
Open seasons, §113-291.7.
Protection of black bears.
Enclosure.
Prohibited except as provided, §19A-10.
Enforcement of provisions, §19A-14.
Exemptions from provisions, §19A-11.
Forfeiture of bear held on July 1, 1975, §19A-12.
Misdemeanors, §19A-13.
Peace officers.
Enforcement of provisions, §19A-14.
Penalties, §19A-13.
Placing food products as bait in areas with open season on black bears, §113-294(r).
Purchase.
Prohibited except as provided, §19A-10.
Sale.
Prohibited except as provided, §19A-10.
Surrender of bear held on July 1, 1975, §19A-12.
Violations of provisions.
Penalty, §19A-13.
Zoos.
Exemption from provisions, §19A-11.
Regulation of taking, §113-291.7.
Sale of parts prohibited, §113-291.3(b).
Unlawfully taking, possessing, transporting, etc., §113-294(c1).

BEAUFORT AND MOREHEAD RAILROAD COMPANY.
Appropriations.
Continuing appropriation, §136-16.6(c).

BEAUFORT COUNTY.
Ambulances.
Attachment or garnishment and lien for, §§44-51.4 to 44-51.8.

BEAUFORT COUNTY —Cont'd

Ambulances —Cont'd

Obtaining ambulance services without intending
to pay, §14-111.2.

**Blank or master forms of mortgages, deeds of
trust, etc.**

Indexing and recording, inapplicability of
provisions, §47-21.

Board of county commissioners.

Filling vacancies on board, §153A-27.1.

Coroner elected as nominee of political party.

Filling vacancy in office, §152-1.

Counties generally.

See COUNTIES.

**Cropper or tenant refusing to perform terms
of contract.**

Forfeiture of right of possession to premises,
§42-27.

Dog collars.

Unlawful removal of electronic dog collars,
§14-401.17.

Game laws, local acts not repealed,
§113-133.1(e).

Grants in navigable waters, registration,
§113-205(a).

Housing authority commissioners.

Tenant as commissioner, exemption from provision
of law allowing, §157-5.

Low-income housing tax credits.

Qualified building eligible for credit,
§105-129.41(c).

**Maps in special proceedings, recording of
photographic copies,** §47-32.

Violation as misdemeanor, inapplicability of
provisions, §47-32.2.

North Carolina's northeast commission,
§§158-8.2 to 158-8.8.

Open fires in high hazard counties.

Applicability of provisions, §106-942(a).

Ground clearing fires, special permit required,
§106-942(c).

Woodland fires, permits required, §106-942(b).

**Probate and registration orders before clerks
of inferior courts validated,** §47-59.

Registration of deeds.

Tax certification, no delinquent taxes due,
§161-31(b).

Sheriff.

Vacancy, performance of duties until vacancy
filled, §162-5.1.

Special school tax, election to abolish.

Petition required, §115C-505.

Tax sales, notices by publication validated.

Inapplicability of provisions, §47-108.24.

BEAUTIFICATION DISTRICTS.

**Alcoholic beverage elections, places eligible to
hold,** §18B-600(g).

BEAUTY SALONS.

City privilege license taxes, §160A-211(b).

Cosmetic art generally, §§88B-1 to 88B-29.

See COSMETIC ART.

BEAVER.

Beaver damage control advisory boards,
§113-291.10.

**Control of beaver damage on private and
public lands.**

Beaver damage control advisory board.

Development of statewide program to control
beaver damage, §113-291.10(b).

BEAVER —Cont'd

**Control of beaver damage on private and
public lands** —Cont'd

Beaver damage control advisory board —Cont'd

Established, §113-291.10(a).

Implementation of program, advisory capacity
to wildlife resources commission,
§113-291.10(b).

Membership, §113-291.10(a).

Conflict with other provisions, section prevails,
§113-291.10(e).

Implementation of program developed by advisory
board.

Wildlife resources commission to implement,
§113-291.10(c).

Notification to county of wish to participate.

Counties volunteering to participate,
§113-291.10(f).

Snares, use when trapping beaver pursuant to
damage control program, §113-291.10(d).

Depredation permits.

Landowner's property damaged or destroyed,
§113-291.9(f).

Use or sale of beaver parts taken under,
§113-291.9(b).

Hunting and wildlife.

General provisions.

See HUNTING AND WILDLIFE.

Landowner's property damaged or destroyed.

Taking without depredation permit, §113-291.9(f).

Open season for taking with firearms,
§113-291.9(a).

Sales.

Beaver parts taken under depredation permits,
§113-291.9(b).

Snares, §113-291.9(d).

Use when trapping pursuant to beaver damage
control program, §113-291.10(d).

Trapping.

Use of snares when trapping, §113-291.9(d).

Trapping pursuant to beaver damage control
program, §113-291.10(d).

Use of trap number 330 of connibear type,
§§113-291.6(d), 113-291.9(c).

**Unlawfully selling, possessing for sale or
buying,** §113-294(f).

BED AND BREAKFAST ESTABLISHMENTS.

Defined, §130A-247.

Defrauding innkeeper, §14-110.

Sanitation of food and lodging establishments.

Exemption from provisions, §130A-250.

**Sanitation of private homes offering
accommodations as.**

Adoption, §130A-248(a2), (a3).

Variance from rules adopted, §130A-248(a5).

BEDDING.

Mattresses and bedding.

General provisions, §§106-65.95 to 106-65.107.

BEDROOMS.

**Secretly peeping into room occupied by
another person,** §14-202.

BEECH MOUNTAIN.

Room occupancy tax.

Uniform provisions.

Authorized to levy, §160A-215(g).

Generally, §160A-215.

BEEF.

Standard weight and measure, §81A-42.

BEER.
Definition of "malt beverage,"§18B-101.
Excise tax, §§105-113.80 to 105-113.87.
Franchises, §§18B-1300 to 18B-1308.
Kegs.
  Amounts that may be purchased, §18B-303(a).
  Defined, §18B-101.
  Purchase-transportation permit, off-premises
    consumption.
    Copy.
      Purchaser and permittee to keep,
        §18B-403.1(d).
      Retention by off-premises permittee, time
        period, §18B-403.1(b).
    Display to law enforcement.
      Duty of purchaser, §18B-403.1(d).
    Form adopted by commission, §18B-403.1(c).
    Issuance by off-premises permittee,
      §18B-403.1(b).
    Purchase from store named on permit,
      §18B-403.1(d).
    Required to purchase and transport for
      off-premises consumption, §18B-403.1(a).
    Warning to permittee, first violation,
      §18B-403.1(e).
  Secondary metals recyclers.
    Purchase limitations, §66-11(d).
Malt beverages generally.
  See ALCOHOLIC BEVERAGES.
Oceangoing ships.
  Alcoholic beverages for use on, §18B-106.

BEER FRANCHISES, §§18B-1300 to 18B-1308.
Agreement.
  Alteration of provisions of article by parties.
    Prohibited, §18B-1308.
  Existence of franchise agreement.
    When deemed to exist, §18B-1302(b).
  Filing of distribution agreement, §18B-1303(a).
  Nature of franchise agreement, §18B-1302(a).
  Price maintenance.
    Prohibited, §18B-1303(c).
  Provisions of article as part of all agreements,
    §18B-1308.
  Termination.
    Good cause.
      Absence of good cause, §18B-1305(d).
      Notice of cause, §18B-1305(b).
      Termination for cause without advance notice,
        §18B-1305(c).
      What constitutes, §18B-1305(a).
    Notice of cause, §18B-1305(b).
    Termination for cause without advance notice,
      §18B-1305(c).
    Wrongful termination.
      Damages, §18B-1306(b).
      Injunctive relief, §18B-1306(a).
Coercion.
  Prohibited acts by suppliers, §18B-1304.
Damages.
  Transfer of wholesaler's business.
    Disapproval or prevention of transfer,
      §18B-1307(c).
  Wrongful termination of agreement, §18B-1306(b).
Definitions, §18B-1301.
Discrimination.
  Prohibited, §18B-1303(b).
Injunctions.
  Wrongful termination of agreement, §18B-1306(a).
Legislative declaration.
  Purpose of provisions, §18B-1300.

BEER FRANCHISES —Cont'd
Purpose of provisions, §18B-1300.
Suppliers.
  Defined, §18B-1301.
  Prohibited acts, §18B-1304.
Transfer of wholesaler's business.
  Approval of certain transfers, §18B-1307(b), (c).
  Damages for disapproval or prevention of transfer,
    §18B-1307(c).
  Death.
    Right of transfer to designated family member
      upon, §18B-1307(a).
Wholesalers.
  Defined, §18B-1301.
  Discrimination.
    Prohibited, §18B-1303(b).
  Remedies for wrongful termination of agreement,
    §18B-1306.
  Transfer of wholesaler's business.
    Approval of certain transfers, §18B-1307(b), (c).
    Damages for disapproval or prevention of
      transfer, §18B-1307(c).
    Death.
      Right of transfer to designated family
        member upon, §18B-1307(a).

BEES AND HONEY, §§106-634 to 106-644.
Administration of article.
  Designation of persons to administer, §106-643.
Apiary defined, §106-635.
Bees defined, §106-635.
Beeyard defined, §106-635.
Board.
  Authority to accept donations, gifts or grants,
    §106-637.
  Contracts.
    Authority to enter into contracts, §106-637.
  Defined, §106-635.
  Regulations.
    Authority of board to adopt, §106-638.
Boll weevil eradication.
  Authority to regulate honeybee colonies in
    elimination zones and other areas,
    §106-65.76.
Brazilian or African bee, §106-635.
Colonies.
  Defined, §106-635.
  Minimum standards for colony strength, §106-638.
Comb defined, §106-635.
Commercial beekeeper, §106-635.
Commissioner.
  Defined, §106-635.
  Diseases.
    Authority of commissioner to protect industry
      from diseases and disorders, §106-640.
    Giving false information to commissioner,
      §106-641.
  Duties, §106-636.
  Emergency action by commissioner, §106-642.
  Powers, §106-635.
Contracts.
  Authority of board to enter into contracts,
    §106-637.
Declaration of policy, §106-634.
Definitions, §106-625.
Diseases.
  Authority of commissioner to protect industry
    from diseases, §106-640.
    Giving false information to commissioner,
      §106-641.
  Defined, §106-635.

BEES AND HONEY —Cont'd
Diseases —Cont'd
Minimum standards for disease tolerance levels, §106-638.
Moveable frame hives, §106-641.
Regulations for control and prevention, §106-639.
Disorders.
Authority of commissioner to protect industry from diseases and disorders, §106-640.
Defined, §106-635.
Moveable frame hives, §106-641.
Regulations for control and prevention, §106-639.
Donations.
Authority of board to accept, §106-637.
Duties of commissioner, §106-636.
Emergencies.
Action by commissioner, §106-642.
Exposed defined, §106-635.
General assembly.
Legislative declaration, §106-634.
Gifts.
Authority of board to accept, §106-637.
Grants.
Authority of board to accept, §106-637.
Health certificates.
Defined, §106-635.
Issuance, §106-641.
Hives.
Defined, §106-635.
Moveable frame hives.
Inspection for disease or disorder, §106-641.
Honeybees defined, §106-635.
Honey defined, §106-635.
Honeyflow defined, §106-635.
Honey plants defined, §106-635.
Infested or infected defined, §106-635.
Inspections.
Conduct of inspections and other activities, §106-643.
Moveable frame hives.
Inspection for disease or disorder, §106-641.
Penalties for preventing inspection, §106-644(a), (b).
Legislative declarations, §106-634.
Marketing associations, §§54-129 to 54-166.
See MARKETING ASSOCIATIONS.
Moveable frame hives.
Defined, §106-635.
Diseases, §106-641.
Disorders, §106-641.
Inspection for disease or disorder, §106-641.
Penalties.
Violations of provisions, §106-644(a), (b).
Permits.
Defined, §106-635.
Moving permits.
Issuance, §106-641.
Selling bees, §106-639.1.
Policy declaration, §106-634.
Registration.
Adoption of regulations for registration of honeybees, §106-641.
Rules and regulations.
Authority of board to adopt regulations, §106-638.
Control and prevention of diseases and disorders, §106-639.
Sales.
Permit to sell bees, §106-639.1.
Symptomless carrier defined, §106-635.
Violations of article.
Penalties, §106-644(a), (b).

BEETS.
Standard weight and measure, §81A-42.

BEGGING.
False representation of physical disability.
Obtaining money by, §14-113.
Persons standing upon highway or street, §20-175(b).
Regulation.
Counties, §153A-126.
Municipalities, §160A-179.

BELMONT.
All-terrain vehicles.
Use by employees on certain highways, §20-171.24.
Room occupancy tax.
Uniform provisions.
Authorized to levy, §160A-215(g).
Generally, §160A-215.
Satellite annexation.
Limitation on area of satellite corporate limits, inapplicability, §160A-58.1(b).

BELOW-COST SALES.
Motor fuels, §75-82.

BENCH TRIAL.
Trial of issues by court, §1A-1 Rule 39(b).

BENEVOLENT AND PROTECTIVE ORDER OF ELKS.
Property taxes.
Exclusion, §105-275.

BENEVOLENT ASSOCIATIONS.
Property taxes.
Exemption of real and personal property, §105-278.7.

BENNETT PLACE MEMORIAL COMMISSION.
Department of cultural resources.
Transfer of commission to department, §143B-51.

BENSON.
Room occupancy tax.
Uniform provisions.
Authorized to levy, §160A-215(g).
Generally, §160A-215.
Satellite annexation.
Limitation on area of satellite corporate limits, inapplicability, §160A-58.1(b).

BENTONVILLE BATTLEFIELD FUND.
Appropriation of money credited, §121-7.5(c).
Creation, §121-7.5(a).
Receipts credited to fund, §121-7.5(b).

BENZINE.
Household cleaners labeling, §§66-85 to 66-88.

BEQUESTS.
Wills generally.
See WILLS.

BERMUDA RUN.
Room occupancy tax.
Uniform provisions.
Authorized to levy, §160A-215(g).
Generally, §160A-215.

BERNARD ALLEN MEMORIAL EMERGENCY DRINKING WATER FUND, §87-98.

BERRIES.
Promotion of use and sale of agricultural products.
Generally, §§106-550 to 106-568.
See AGRICULTURAL PRODUCTS PROMOTION.

BERRIES —Cont'd
State berries, §145-18(b), (c).

BERTIE COUNTY.
Condemnation or acquisition of land by local government unit outside county.
Consent of board of commissioners necessary, §153A-15.
Cropper or tenant refusing to perform terms of contract.
Forfeiture of right of possession to premises, §42-27.
Game laws, local acts not repealed, §113-133.1(e).
Grants in navigable waters, registration, §113-205(a).
Housing authority commissioners.
Tenant as commissioner, exemption from provision of law allowing, §157-5.
Low-income housing tax credits.
Qualified building eligible for credit, §105-129.41(c).
Multi-county water conservation and infrastructure district.
Generally, §158-15.1.
North Carolina's northeast commission, §§158-8.2 to 158-8.8.
Officers compensated from fees.
Statement to be rendered, §128-13.
Probate and registration orders before clerks or inferior courts validated, §47-59.
Registration of deeds.
Tax certification, no delinquent taxes due, §161-31(b).
Wastewater systems.
Innovative septic tank systems.
Ordinance billing fee as property tax, §130A-343.1(c).

BEST EVIDENCE RULE.
Contents of writings, recordings and photographs, §§8C-1 Rule 1001 to 8C-1 Rule 1008.
Admission of party, §8C-1 Rule 1007.
Collateral matters, §8C-1 Rule 1004.
Definitions, §8C-1 Rule 1001.
Duplicates, admissibility, §8C-1 Rule 1003.
Functions of court and jury, §8C-1 Rule 1008.
Lost or destroyed originals, §8C-1 Rule 1004.
Not obtainable original, §8C-1 Rule 1004.
Opponent possesses original, §8C-1 Rule 1004.
Original, requirement, §8C-1 Rule 1002.
Public records, §8C-1 Rule 1005.
Summaries, §8C-1 Rule 1006.
Copies of destroyed records, §98-1.
Copies of official records.
Authentication, §1A-1 Rule 44(a).
Proof of official record.
Authentication of copy, §1A-1 Rule 44(a).
Lack of record, proof of, §1A-1 Rule 44(b).

BEST INTEREST OF CHILD.
Child custody, §50-13.2(a).
Parent presumed to know, §35A-1225(a).
Termination of parental rights.
Determination, §7B-1110.

BETTERMENTS, §§1-340 to 1-351.
Assessment of damages.
Annual value of land and waste charged against defendant, §1-341.
Execution suspended for, §1-340.
Value of improvements estimated, §1-342.

BETTERMENTS —Cont'd
Assessment of damages —Cont'd
Value of premises without improvements.
Estimate, §1-346.
Disabilities.
Procedure where plaintiff is under disability, §1-349.
Election by plaintiff that defendant take premises, §1-347.
Eviction of defendant.
Recovery from plaintiff, §1-350.
Executions.
Suspension of execution for assessment, §1-340.
Judgments, §1-344.
Jury.
Verdict, §1-344.
Liens, §1-344.
Life estates.
Life tenant recovers from remainderman, §1-345.
Mentally ill.
Procedure where plaintiff is under disability, §1-349.
Minors.
Procedure where plaintiff is under disability, §1-349.
Mortgages and deeds of trust.
Provisions not applicable to suit by mortgagee, §1-351.
Payments to court, §1-348.
Petitions.
Claimant, §1-340.
Property taxes.
Increase or decrease of real property appraised value in years a reappraisal not made.
Reasons for making increase or decrease, §105-287(b).
Rents.
Improvements to balance rents, §1-343.
Sales.
Default.
Land sold on default, §1-348.

BETTING.
Elections.
Bet or wager on election, §163-274(a).
Futures contracts, §§16-3 to 16-6.
Generally.
See GAMBLING.
Lotteries, §§14-291 to 14-291.2.
Racing vehicles on streets and highways, §20-141.3(c).

BEVERAGE CONTAINER DEPOSITS.
Sales and use tax.
Exemption, §105-164.13.

BEVERAGES.
Alcoholic beverages.
See ALCOHOLIC BEVERAGES.
High-calcium foods and beverages.
Local boards of education.
Preference in purchasing contracts, §115C-264.1(a), (b).
Implied warranty of merchantability.
Sale of goods, UCC, §25-2-314.
Juice and bottled water.
Contracts for sale of.
Educational institutions to competitively bid, §143-64.
Milk and milk products.
Production, distribution, inspection, grading and testing generally, §§106-267 to 106-268.1.
See MILK AND MILK PRODUCTS.

BEVERAGES —Cont'd
Warranties.
 Implied warranty of merchantability, §25-2-314.

BEYOND REASONABLE DOUBT.
Delinquent and undisciplined juvenile actions.
 Quantum of proof where petition alleges
  delinquency, §7B-2409.

BFP.
 See BONA FIDE PURCHASERS.

BIBLES.
Administration of oath upon Holy Scriptures,
 §11-2.
Hearsay exception, family records, §8C-1 Rule
 803.
Sales and use tax.
 Exemption, §105-164.13.

BIBLE SCHOOLS.
Child care facilities.
 Schools conducted during vacation periods not
  included in term, §110-86.

BICYCLE AND BIKEWAY ACT, §§136-71.6 to
 136-71.12.
Citation of article, §136-71.6.
Coordination of program, §136-71.9.
Definitions, §136-71.7.
Designation of bikeways, §136-71.11.
Development of program, §136-71.
Duties, §136-71.10.
Functions of department.
 Duties generally, §136-71.10.
Funds, §136-71.12.
General assembly.
 Authorization of funds, §136-71.12.
How article cited, §136-71.6.
Legislative findings, §136-71.8.
Program development, §136-71.9.
Public roads.
 Designation of bikeways, §136-71.11.

BICYCLE RACING, §20-171.2.

BICYCLES.
Alleys, building entrances, private roads or
 driveways.
 Driver emerging from or entering to yield to
  person on bicycle, §20-173(c).
Amusement device safety.
 Amusement device defined as not including,
  §95-111.3(a).
Bicycle and bikeway act, §§136-71.6 to 136-71.12.
 See BICYCLE AND BIKEWAY ACT.
Child bicycle safety act, §§20-171.6 to 20-171.9.
 Article known and cited as, §20-171.6.
 Civil fine assessed parent or guardian found
  responsible, §20-171.9(d).
 Definitions, §20-171.8.
 Infraction for violation, §20-171.9(d).
 Legislative findings and declaration, §20-171.7(a).
 Negligence or liability not assessed for violation,
  §20-171.9(c).
 Passenger on bicycle, requirements, §20-171.9(b).
 Protective bicycle helmet.
  Wearing while riding roadway, bicycle path,
   required, §20-171.9(a).
 Purposes of article, §20-171.7(b).
 Restraining seat for small children.
  Requirement to be passenger, §20-171.9(b).
 Short title of act, §20-171.6.
 Subsequent purchase of helmet or restraining
  seat.
 Waiver of fine for violation, §20-171.9(e).

BICYCLES —Cont'd
Definitions, §20-171.1.
Freestyle bicycling.
 Assumption of risks, limitation on liability,
  §§99E-21 to 99E-25.
General penalty provisions, penalty not
 specified.
 Infractions, §20-176(a).
  Maximum penalty authorized, §20-176(b).
 Misdemeanors, §20-176(a).
  Class 2 misdemeanors, §20-176(c).
  Imprisonment for certain violations, limitation,
   §20-176(c1).
 Negligence per se, determining.
  Crimes and infractions treated identically,
   §20-176(d).
Lamps.
 Requirements, §20-129(e).
North Carolina trails system.
 Bicycles, use of trails.
  Game or hunting lands, §113A-87.1(e).
  Hiking and walking, land also open to,
   §113A-87.1(d).
  Records of lands made open to, §113A-87.1(c).
  Restrictions or removal from use, §113A-87.1(b).
  Usage agreement, §113A-87.1(a).
 Transportation system defined, §136-5.1.
Racing.
 Approved racing events, §20-171.2(b).
  Exemptions from compliance with traffic laws,
   §20-171.2(c).
 Highways.
  Prohibited generally, §20-171.2(a).
   Exception as to approved racing events,
    §20-171.2(b).
Searches and seizures.
 Unclaimed bicycles.
  Advertisement and sale or donation, §15-12(b).

BIDS AND BIDDING.
Advisory budget commission.
 Certain purchases exempted from provisions of
  articles, §§143-56, 143-57.
 Rules.
  Covering certain purposes, §143-60.
Architectural, engineering and surveying
 services.
 Public building contracts, §§143-64.31 to
  143-64.34.
Community-based corrections programs.
 Contracts with service providers, §143-272.86.
Drainage districts.
 Construction of improvements, §156-84.
Facility authorities.
 Construction contracts, §160A-480.6.
Highways, roads and streets.
 Letting of contracts to bidders after
  advertisement, §136-28.1(a) to (k).
Judicial sales.
 Upset bids.
  See JUDICIAL SALES.
Motion pictures.
 Fair competition, §§75C-1 to 75C-5.
North Carolina purchase directory, §143-345.8.
Public contracts.
 Architectural, engineering and surveying services,
  §§143-64.31 to 143-64.34.
 Generally, §§143-128 to 143-135.9.
  See PUBLIC CONTRACTS.
Public works.
 Regulation of contractors.
  List of bidders, §133-33.

BIDS AND BIDDING —Cont'd
Public works —Cont'd
Regulation of contractors —Cont'd
Suspension from bidding, §133-27.
Purchase directory.
North Carolina purchase directory, §143-345.8.
Purchases and contracts through department of administration, §§143-48 to 143-64.
See PURCHASES THROUGH DEPARTMENT OF ADMINISTRATION.
Sanitary districts.
Plan for accomplishing objective of district, §130A-63(b).
State departments and agencies.
Consultant services.
Architectural, engineering and surveying services, §§143-64.31 to 143-64.34.
General provisions, §§143-64.20 to 143-64.24.
State lottery.
Contracts for purchase of services, supplies, equipment, §18C-151.
Unclaimed property.
Public sale of abandoned property by treasurer, §116B-65.
Upset bids.
See JUDICIAL SALES.

BIENNIAL STATE OF ENVIRONMENT REPORT, §143B-279.5.

BIFURCATED TRIAL.
Enhanced sentencing.
Aggravating factors, §15A-1340.16(a1).
Impaired driving.
Appeal to superior court.
Aggravated factors, §20-179(a1), (a2).
Punitive damages, §1D-30.

BIGAMY, §14-183.
Acts barring rights of spouse, §31A-1(a).
Children born of voidable marriage legitimate, §50-11.1.
Competency of witnesses.
Husband and wife, §8-57(b).
Marriage void, §51-3.

BILLBOARDS.
Alcoholic beverage advertising, §18B-105(b).
Blue Ridge parkway.
Control of outdoor advertising, §§113A-165 to 113A-170.
Cities.
Regulation of nonconforming off-premises outdoor advertising, §160A-199.
Counties.
Regulation of nonconforming off-premises outdoor advertising, §153A-143.
Obstructing view at entrance to school, church or public institution, §136-102(a), (b).
Outdoor advertising control act, §§136-126 to 136-140.
See OUTDOOR ADVERTISING.
Scenic highways, state and national parks and historic areas.
Outdoor advertising adjacent to park.
Limitations, §136-129.2(a) to (c).
Transportation department.
Legislative reporting requirements, §136-12.1.

BILLIARDS.
Counties.
Regulation of places of amusement, §153A-135.
Minors.
Permitting minors to enter billiard rooms, §14-317.

BILLIARDS —Cont'd
Municipalities.
Regulation of pool and billiard halls, §160A-181.

BILL OF PARTICULARS, §1A-1 Rule 84.
Criminal procedure, §15A-925.
Motion for more definite statement, §1A-1 Rule 12(e).

BILL OF RIGHTS.
Adult care homes, §§131D-19 to 131D-34.
See ADULT CARE HOMES.
Basic education program in public schools.
Civil literacy, §115C-81(g).
Constitution of North Carolina.
Declaration of rights, NC Const Art I §§1 to 37.
Constitution of the United States, US Const Amds 1 to 10.
Nursing homes.
Patients' bill of rights, §§131E-115 to 131E-131.
See NURSING HOMES.

BILLS AND NOTES.
Negotiable instruments.
General provisions, §§25-3-101 to 25-3-605.
See NEGOTIABLE INSTRUMENTS.

BILLS BY GAS AND ELECTRIC LIGHT COMPANIES.
Reading of meter to be shown on bill, §66-9.

BILLS OF ATTAINDER.
Constitutional provisions, US Const Art I §§9, 10, Art III §3.

BILLS OF COSTS.
Attachment execution for unpaid costs, §6-4.

BILLS OF EXCHANGE.
Commercial paper generally.
See NEGOTIABLE INSTRUMENTS.
Costs.
Several suits or actions on one instrument.
Allowance of costs to defendant, §6-19.
Allowance of costs to plaintiff, §6-18.
Default judgments.
Clerk to ascertain interest upon default judgment on bill of exchange, §24-6.
Fiduciaries drawing, §32-7.
Payable to third persons, §32-6.
Forgery, §14-122.
Selling of certain forged securities, §14-121.
Larceny of choses in action, §14-75.
Negotiable instruments generally.
See NEGOTIABLE INSTRUMENTS.
Powers of attorney.
Powers conferred by statutory short form, §32A-2.

BILLS OF GENERAL ASSEMBLY.
Action on bills, NC Const Art II §22.
Approval of bills, §120-29.1.
Coded bill drafting.
Act in law defined, §120-20.1(c).
Applicability of section, §120-20.1(d).
Deleted material and added material only changes, §120-20.1(b1).
New section, subsection or subdivision added, §120-20.1(b2).
Struck through or underlined material, §120-20.1(a), (b).
Enrolling clerk.
Deposit of original bills and resolutions enrolled for application, §120-33(f).
Duties, §120-33.
Presenting true ratified copies, §120-33(d) to (d2).

BILLS OF GENERAL ASSEMBLY —Cont'd
Enrolling clerk —Cont'd
Proofreading bills, §120-33(c).
Ratification of enrolled bills, §120-33(a).
Substituting corresponding Arabic numerals for
written words, §120-33(b).
Typewritten bills, §120-33(c).
Governor's approval of bill, §120-29.1(a).
Calculation of time for approval, §120-29.1(d).
Failure to take action on bill, §120-29.1(b).
Objections, §120-29.1(c).
Veto, NC Const Art II §22, Art III §5.
Local government fiscal information act,
§§120-30.41 to 120-30.49.
Local, private and special legislation, NC Const
Art II §24.
Reconvening of legislature, NC Const Art II §22,
Art III §5.
Request that session not be held, §120-6.1(a).
Form of request, §120-6.1(b).
Revenue bills, NC Const Art II §23.
**Signing by presiding officers of both houses
required,** NC Const Art II §22.
Style of acts, NC Const Art II §21.
Three readings required, NC Const Art II §22.
Veto by governor, NC Const Art II §22, Art III §5.
Voting rights act of 1965.
Submission of changes to United States attorney
general, §§120-30.9A to 120-30.9I.
When acts take effect, §120-20.

BILLS OF INDICTMENT.
General provisions, §§15-144 to 15-155.
See INDICTMENTS.

BILLS OF LADING.
Actions by or against carriers.
Evidence, §8-41.
**Alcoholic beverages transported by motor
carriers,** §18B-1115(d).
Counterfeiting, §21-42.
Documents of title.
Uniform commercial code, §§25-7-101 to 25-7-603.
See DOCUMENTS OF TITLE.
Evidence.
Actions by or against carriers, §8-41.
False bills, issuing, §21-42.
Forgery, §21-42.
Gasoline and oil transporters.
Required to have in possession, §119-42.
**Receiving property for transportation in
interstate commerce.**
Issuance by carrier, §62-203(a).
Suretyship.
Indorser not guarantor for other parties,
§25-7-505.
Uttering, §21-42.

BILLS OF SALE.
Execution sales, §1-339.62.
Judicial sales.
Person holding public sale may execute and
deliver, §1-339.23(c).
Private sale of personal property, §1-339.39.
Sale under execution, §1-315(b).

BINDERS.
**Lenders engaged in mortgage or deed of trust
loans.**
Acceptance or denial of temporary insurance
contracts, §58-3-140.
Motor vehicle insurance, §20-279.21(k).
Property insurance policies, §58-44-20.

BINGO.
Alcoholic beverage sale or consumption,
§18B-308.
Beach bingo.
Applicability of article, §14-309.14.
Conduct of bingo game, §14-309.5.
Certain property, §14-309.7(d).
Charitable or nonprofit causes.
Purposes of conduct of bingo, §14-309.5(a).
Limit on number of sessions, §14-309.8.
Payment of member of organization to conduct
game, §14-309.7(c).
Penalties for violations, §14-309.5(b).
Public sessions, §14-309.13.
Responsibility of special committee, §14-309.10.
Definitions, §14-309.6.
Exempt organization.
Defined, §14-309.6.
False information in audit, §14-309.11(c).
Licenses.
Applications, §14-309.7(a).
Contents, §14-309.7(b).
Fee, §14-309.7(a).
Limit on number of sessions, §14-309.8.
Permits.
Single occasion permit, §14-309.7(e).
Prizes.
Maximum, §14-309.9(a).
Applicability of section, §14-309.9(c).
Proceeds.
Audit, §14-309.11(b).
False information, §14-309.11(c).
Deposit, §14-309.11(a).
False information in audit, §14-309.11(c).
Use, §14-309.11(a).
Public sessions, §14-309.13.
Raffles.
Not to be conducted in conjunction with bingo,
§14-309.15(e).
Records.
Open for inspection, §14-309.11(d).
Single occasion permit, §14-309.7(e).
Video bingo.
Ban on new machines, regulation of existing
machines, §§14-306.1A, 14-306.4.
Violations, §14-309.12.

BIODIESEL FUEL.
Business and energy tax credits.
Biodiesel producers, §105-129.16F.
Gasoline tax.
Biodiesel provider.
Defined, §105-449.60.
Renewable fuel facility construction tax credit,
§105-129.16D.

BIOLOGICAL AGENTS.
Mass death and destruction weapons.
Nuclear, biological or chemical weapons,
§§14-288.21 to 14-288.24.
See WEAPONS OF MASS DEATH AND
DESTRUCTION.
Murder as a result of the use of, §14-17.
Prohibited discharges into air or water,
§143-214.2(a).
**Terrorist incident using nuclear, biological or
chemical agents,** §§130A-475 to 130A-479.
See TERRORIST INCIDENT USING NUCLEAR,
BIOLOGICAL OR CHEMICAL AGENTS.

BIOLOGICAL AGENTS REGISTRY, §130A-479.
Confidentiality of information, §130A-479(e).

BIOLOGICAL AGENTS REGISTRY —Cont'd
Definitions, §130A-479(b).
Generally, §130A-479(a).
Penalty for violations, §130A-479(f).
Reports, §130A-479(d).
Rules, §130A-479(c).

BIOLOGICAL ORGANISM ACT, §§106-65.42 to
    106-65.49.
Article not applicable in certain cases,
    §106-65.49.
Authority under other statutes not abrogated,
    §106-65.47.
Board of agriculture.
    Adoption of regulations, §106-65.45.
    Defined, §106-65.44.
    Further authority of board, §106-65.46.
Commissioner of agriculture.
    Defined, §106-65.44.
    Enforcement of article, §106-65.46.
Criminal penalties, §106-65.48.
Definitions, §106-65.44.
Division of entomology.
    Defined, §106-65.44.
Enforcement of article, §106-65.46.
Environmental protection.
    Purpose of article, §106-65.43.
Intergovernmental cooperation.
    Memoranda of understanding, §106-65.47.
Memoranda of understanding.
    Intergovernmental cooperation, §106-65.47.
Purpose of article, §106-65.43.
Short title, §106-65.42.
States.
    Memoranda of understanding, §106-65.47.
Title of article, §106-65.42.
United States.
    Memoranda of understanding, §106-65.47.
Violation of law or regulations, §106-65.48.

BIOLOGICAL RESIDUES IN ANIMALS,
    §§106-549.81 to 106-549.89.
Animal defined, §106-549.81.
Animal feed defined, §106-549.81.
Animal produce defined, §106-549.81.
Appellate review.
    Detention or quarantine, §106-549.83.
Bond.
    Preservation or disposition of animal, animal
        product or feed, §106-549.83.
Burden of proof.
    Content of biological residue, §106-549.82.
Civil penalties, §106-549.89.
Definitions, §106-549.81.
Detention of animal, animal product or feed,
    §106-549.82.
    Movement of contaminated animals forbidden,
        §106-549.84(a).
Fines, §106-549.89.
Inspections.
    Examining facilities, inventory, etc., §106-549.85.
Investigations.
    Discovering violations of article, §106-549.86.
Movement of contaminated animals forbidden,
    §106-549.84(a), (b).
Penalties for violations of provisions.
    Civil penalties, §106-549.89.
    Fines, §106-549.89.
Quarantine of animal, animal product or feed,
    §106-549.82.
    Movement of contaminated animals forbidden,
        §106-549.84(a).

BIOLOGICAL RESIDUES IN ANIMALS —Cont'd
Records.
    Examining and/or copying records, §106-549.85.
Right of entry.
    Inspection of facilities, inventory, etc.,
        §106-549.85.
Rules and regulations.
    Promulgation of, §106-549.87.
Violations of article.
    Investigations to discover violation, §106-549.86.
    Misdemeanors, §106-549.88.
        Civil penalties, §106-549.89.
        Fines, §106-549.89.

BIOLOGICS, §§106-707 to 106-715.
Attorney general.
    Prosecution of violations, §106-714(a).
Board of agriculture.
    Definition of "board,"§106-708.
    Rules and regulations, §106-709.
Definitions, §106-708.
District attorneys.
    Prosecution of violations, §106-714(a).
Fines, §106-715.
Injunctions, §106-714(b).
License to produce.
    Applications, §106-710(c).
        Inspection of establishment applying,
            §106-710(b).
    Fees, §106-710(d).
    Issuance, §106-710(d).
    Renewal, §106-710(d).
    Required, §106-710(a).
    Revocation or suspension, §106-711.
Penalties.
    Civil penalties, §106-715.
Purpose of law, §106-707.
Registration.
    Application for registration.
        Information to accompany, §106-712(b).
    Generally, §106-712(a).
    Revocation or suspension, §106-713.
Short title of law, §106-707.
Violations of provisions.
    Injunctions, §106-714(b).
    Penalties, §106-714(a).
        Civil penalties, §106-715.
        Fines, §106-715.

BIOMASS RESOURCES.
Business and energy tax credits, §§105-129.15 to
    105-129.19.

BIOMETRIC DATA.
Identify theft generally, §§14-113.20 to 14-113.25.

BIOMETRIC IDENTIFICATION.
Alcoholic beverage sales to or purchase by
    underage persons.
    Use of biometric identification system,
        §18B-302(d).

BIOPROCESSING INDUSTRIES.
Sales and use tax industrial facilities refunds,
    §105-164.14B(a).

BIOTERRORISM.
First responder vaccination program.
    First responders exposed to infectious diseases
        when deployed to disaster locations,
        §130A-485.
Nuclear, biological or chemical agents.
    Terrorist incident using, §§130A-475 to 130A-479.
    See TERRORIST INCIDENT USING
        NUCLEAR, BIOLOGICAL OR CHEMICAL
        AGENTS.

BIRD-FOOT VIOLET.
Taking, etc., of certain wild plants from land of another, §14-129.

BIRDS.
Animals generally.
See ANIMALS.
Animal waste management, §§143-215.10A to 143-215.10M.
See ANIMAL WASTE MANAGEMENT.
Cardinal.
State bird, §145-2.
Certificate of registration.
Obtaining by false representation, §14-103.
Cruelty to animals.
See CRUELTY TO ANIMALS.
Hunting generally.
See HUNTING AND WILDLIFE.
Migratory game birds.
Hunting.
Federal law observed.
Methods of taking, §113-291.1(f), (f1).
Shooting hours, bag limits and seasons, §113-291.2(a).
Managed hunts, §113-291.2(a).
Unlawfully taking, possessing or transporting, §113-294(m).
Municipalities.
Sanctuaries, §160A-188.
Poultry generally.
See POULTRY AND POULTRY PRODUCTS.
Poultry products inspections, §§106-549.49 to 106-549.69.
See POULTRY PRODUCTS INSPECTIONS.

BIRTH CERTIFICATES.
Admission for first time to school.
Certified copy required, §115C-364(c).
Adoption.
Confidentiality of records generally, §§48-9-101 to 48-9-109.
See ADOPTION.
Affidavit of paternity.
Listing declaring father on certificate and presumption as natural father, §130A-101(f).
Age of child registering for school.
Prima facie evidence, §130A-109.
Amendment of birth certificate, §130A-118(a).
Fee, §130A-118(d).
Certificate of identification.
Birth of unknown parentage, §130A-107.
Foreign births, §130A-108.
Children born out of wedlock, §130A-101(f).
Affidavit acknowledging paternity.
Listing declaring father on certificate and presumption as natural father, §130A-101(f).
Child support.
Relief from order based on nonpaternity.
Modification of birth certificate, §50-13.13(h).
Contents, §130A-102.
Copies, §130A-93(d).
Health and medical information contained in, §130A-93(e).
New certificates, §130A-93(f).
Duties of local registrars, §130A-97.
Establishing fact of birth by person without certificate, §130A-106(a) to (c).
Evidentiary value, §§130A-104(d), 130A-109.
Fee for registering or amending, copies, §161-10(a).

BIRTH CERTIFICATES —Cont'd
Felonies and misdemeanors.
Generally, §130A-26A(a), (b).
Filing of birth certificate, §130A-101.
Health and medical information contained in.
Copies, §130A-93(e).
Illegitimate children judicially determined.
Furnishing facts as to paternity, §130A-119.
Irregular registration of birth certificates.
Validation of registration, §130A-105.
Legitimation.
Names entered upon birth certificates, §130A-101(f).
New certificate upon legitimation, §§49-12.1, 49-13.
Local registrar's duties, §130A-97.
Name of husband entered on certificate, §130A-101(e).
New certificates, §130A-118(b), (c), (e).
Copies, §130A-93(f).
Fee, §130A-118(d).
Filing, §130A-118(e).
Paternity of illegitimate children judicially determined.
Furnishing facts as to paternity, §130A-119.
Putative father's name entered on certificate, §130A-101(e).
Registers of deeds.
Copies to be forwarded by local registrars, §130A-97.
Registration of birth certificate, §130A-101.
More than five days and less than one year after birth, §130A-103.
One year or more after birth, §130A-104.
Social security numbers.
Parents to provide, §130A-101(g).
Stillbirth.
Certificate of birth resulting in, §130A-114(d).
Surname of child, §130A-101(e).
Validation of irregular registration of birth certificates, §130A-105.
Vital records generally, §§130A-90 to 130A-121.
See VITAL STATISTICS.
Where parentage cannot be established.
Certificate as identification in lieu of birth certificate, §130A-107.
Without certificate.
Establishing fact of birth by person without certificate, §130A-106(a), (c).
Cumulative nature of provisions, §130A-106(a), (c).

BIRTH CONTROL.
Health benefit plan coverage.
Prescription contraceptive drugs and devices and outpatient contraceptive services, §58-3-178.
Small employer group health coverage.
Contraceptive drugs and devices, §58-50-155(a).
Sterilization.
See STERILIZATION.
Surgical interruption of vas deferens or fallopian tubes.
Operation lawful upon request of married person or person over 18, §90-271.
No liability for nonnegligent performance of operation, §90-274.

BIRTH DEFECTS MONITORING PROGRAM.
Birth defect defined, §130A-131.16(b).
Confidentiality of information, §130A-131.17(a).
Persons other than authorized program staff, §130A-131.17(b).

BIRTH DEFECTS MONITORING PROGRAM
—Cont'd
Confidentiality of information —Cont'd
Record of all persons given access to information, §130A-131.17(d).
Contacting case subjects, §130A-131.17(c).
Established, §130A-131.16(a).
Program defined, §130A-131.16(b).
Review of medical records, §130A-131.16(c).
Civil or, §130A-131.16(d).
Statistical compilations, §130A-131.17(e).

BIRTHS.
Abandoned children.
Establishing facts relating to birth, §130A-107.
Abortion generally.
See ABORTION.
Birth certificates.
See BIRTH CERTIFICATES.
Concealing birth of child, §14-46.
Defects.
Monitoring program, §§130A-131.16, 130A-131.17.
Hearsay exception.
Records of religious organizations, §8C-1 Rule 803.
Statement of personal or family history, §8C-1 Rule 804(b).
Vital statistics.
General provisions, §§130A-90 to 130A-121.
See VITAL STATISTICS.

BISHOPS.
See CLERGY.

BISON.
Inspections, §106-549.39.
Meat inspections, §§106-549.15 to 106-549.39.
See MEAT INSPECTIONS.

BITCH DOGS.
Permitting at large, §67-2.

BLACK BEARS.
Captivity licenses.
Applicability to, §113-272.5(f).
Placing food products as bait in area with open season for black bears, §113-294(r).
Protection, §§19A-10 to 19A-14.

BLACKBERRIES.
Standard weights and measures, §81A-42.

BLACKJACKS.
Carrying weapons on campus or other educational property, §14-269.2(d), (e).
Weapons generally.
See FIREARMS AND OTHER WEAPONS.

BLACKLISTING.
Antiblacklisting act, §14-355.

BLACKMAIL, §14-118.

BLACK MOUNTAIN ADVANCEMENT CENTER FOR WOMEN.
Description of grounds, §143B-269(b).
Educational and vocational training for inmates, §143B-269(f).
Established, §143B-269(a).
General assembly not obligated to appropriate funds, §143B-269(h).
Inmates, §143B-269(c).
Training.
Educational and vocational training, §143B-269(f).
Transfer, §143B-269(d).

BLACK MOUNTAIN ADVANCEMENT CENTER FOR WOMEN —Cont'd
Inmates —Cont'd
Work release, §143B-269(g).
Joint security force, §122C-421(a), (b).
Medical services and food services contracts, §143B-269(e).
Work release, §143B-269(g).

BLACK PEOPLE.
Discrimination.
See DISCRIMINATION.
Racial minorities generally.
See RACIAL MINORITIES.

BLADENBORO, TOWN OF.
Satellite annexation.
Limitation on area of satellite corporate limits, inapplicability, §160A-58.1(b).

BLADEN COUNTY.
Acquisition of property, power, §153A-158.1(a).
Agricultural tendencies in certain counties.
Terms of, §42-23.
Ambulance service.
Attachment or garnishment and lien for, §§44-51.4 to 44-51.8.
Blank or master forms of mortgages, deeds of trust, etc.
Indexing and recording, inapplicability of provisions, §47-21.
Condemnation or acquisition of land by local government unit outside county.
Consent of board of commissioners necessary, §153A-15.
Counties generally.
See COUNTIES.
Cropper or tenant refusing to perform terms of contract.
Forfeiture of right of possession to premises, §42-27.
Game laws, local acts not repealed, §113-133.1(e).
Grants in navigable waters, registration, §113-205(a).
Low-income housing tax credits.
Qualified building eligible for credit, §105-129.41(c).
Officers compensated from fees.
Statement to be rendered, §128-13.
Open fires in high hazard counties.
Applicability of section, §106-942(a).
Ground clearing activities, special permit required, §106-942(c).
Woodland fires, permit required, §106-942(b).
Records in Bladen.
Copies of lost records, §8-33.
School property.
Acquisition and improvement, §153A-158.1.
Southeastern North Carolina regional economic development commission, §§158-8.3 to 158-8.8.

BLANK CARTRIDGE PISTOLS.
Sale, §14-407.1.

BLANKET ACCIDENT AND HEALTH INSURANCE, §58-51-75.
Approval of policy form, §58-51-85.

BLANKET BONDS.
Clerks of superior courts, §7A-107.

BLAZE ORANGE.
Hunters wearing hunter orange material, §113-291.8(a) to (c).

BLENDED FUEL TAX.
Gasoline tax generally, §§105-449.60 to
    105-449.126.
    See GASOLINE TAX.

BLIGHTED AREAS.
Defined, §160A-503.
Urban redevelopment, §§160A-500 to 160A-526.
    See URBAN REDEVELOPMENT.

BLIND AND VISUALLY IMPAIRED.
Aid to the blind.
    Administration of assistance, §111-13.
    Alternate sources of income, §111-21.
    Appeals.
        Denial of application for aid, §111-16.
    Application for aid, §111-14.
        Denial of application, §111-16.
        Notice requirements, §111-16.
    Appropriations by counties, §111-17.
    Attachment.
        Payment of awards exempt from attachment,
            §111-18.
    Attorneys at law.
        Lending North Carolina reports to blind
            lawyers, §111-29.
    Awards.
        Change in condition.
            Reopening awards upon change, §111-20.
        Death of recipient, §111-18.1(a).
        Exemption from execution, attachment or
            garnishment, §111-18.
        Notice of award, §111-16.
        Payment of award, §111-18.
            Death of recipient, §111-18.1(a).
        Reopening upon change in condition, §111-20.
    Beneficiaries not deemed paupers, §111-22.
    Business operations.
        Authority to conduct certain operations,
            §111-27.1.
    Cash payment service.
        Death of recipient, §111-18.1(b).
    Commission for the blind.
        Denial of application for aid.
            Appeal to commission, §111-16.
        Rules and regulations, §111-13.
    Counties.
        Appropriations by counties, §111-17.
        Intercounty transfer of recipients, §111-19.
    Court reports.
        Lending North Carolina reports to blind
            lawyers, §111-29.
    Department of health and human services.
        Conducting certain business operations,
            §111-27.1.
        Cooperation with federal government in
            rehabilitation of blind and visually
            impaired, §111-28.1.
        Federal grants.
            Authority to receive, §111-28.
        Promoting employment of needy blind persons,
            §111-27.
        State grants.
            Authority to receive, §111-28.
    Director of social services.
        Authority of director, §111-35.
    Direct relief, §111-6.
        Matching of federal funds, §111-6.
    Disqualifications for relief, §111-21.
    Eligibility for relief, §111-15.
    Employment of needy blind persons.
        Promoting employment, §111-27.

BLIND AND VISUALLY IMPAIRED —Cont'd
Aid to the blind —Cont'd
    Employment of needy blind persons —Cont'd
        Vending stands on public property, §111-27.
    Estimating of number of needy blind persons,
        §111-17.
    Evidence.
        Personal representatives for certain recipients
            of aid.
            Findings not competent as evidence in other
                proceedings, §111-32.
    Executions.
        Payment of awards exempt from execution,
            §111-18.
    Federal aid.
        Acceptance of aid, §111-25.
        Authority of department of health and human
            services to receive, §111-28.
        Grants affording maximum aid, §111-29.
        Grants from federal government, §111-24.
        Matching federal funds, §111-6.
        Termination of aid, §111-26.
        Use of aid, §111-25.
    Fraud in obtaining assistance, §111-23.
    Funds.
        Expenditure of equalizing funds, §111-29.
        Source of funds, §111-17.
    Garnishment.
        Payment of awards exempt from garnishment,
            §111-18.
    Grants.
        Federal aid, §111-24.
            Affording maximum aid, §111-29.
    Information concerning blind persons.
        Use of information, §111-28.
    Intercounty transfer of recipients, §111-19.
    Investigations.
        Application for aid, §111-14.
    Minors.
        Personal representatives for certain recipients
            of aid.
            Affecting provisions for payments for minors,
                §111-33.
    Misrepresentation or fraud in obtaining
        assistance, §111-23.
    Notice, §111-16.
    Objective standards for qualifications of personnel,
        §111-13.
    Paupers.
        Beneficiaries not deemed paupers, §111-22.
    Payment of monthly relief, §111-17.
    Personal representatives for certain recipients of
        aid, §111-30.
        Courts for purposes of article, §111-31.
        Findings not competent as evidence in other
            proceedings, §111-32.
        Minors.
            Affecting provisions for payments for minors,
                §111-33.
    Personnel.
        Objective standards for qualifications of
            personnel, §111-13.
    Public assistance.
        Death of recipient of cash payment service,
            §111-18.1(b).
    Qualifications for eligibility for relief, §111-15.
    Records.
        Personal representatives for certain recipients
            of aid.
            Adoption as courts, §111-31.

BLIND AND VISUALLY IMPAIRED —Cont'd
Aid to the blind —Cont'd
  Retirement benefits.
    Vending-stand operators, §111-27.2.
  Rules and regulations.
    Commission for the blind to make, §111-13.
  Social services.
    Authority of director, §111-35.
  Source of funds, §111-17.
  State aid.
    Authority of department of health and human
      services to receive, §111-28.
  Transfer of recipients.
    Intercounty transfer, §111-19.
  United States.
    Cooperation with federal departments or
      agencies, §111-24.
    Department of health and human services
      authorized to cooperate with federal
      government, §111-28.1.
  Vending stands on public property.
    Operation of vending facilities on state
      property, §§111-41 to 111-47.
    Promoting employment of needy blind persons,
      §111-27.
    Retirement benefits for operators, §111-27.2.
Assault on handicapped persons, §14-32.1.
  DNA sample.
    Required upon conviction, §15A-266.4.
Assistance granted to persons in adult care
    homes.
  State-county special assistance, §§108A-40 to
    108A-47.1.
  See SOCIAL SERVICES.
Coin-operated vending machines.
  Installation of machines, §111-43.
Commission for the blind.
  Aid to the blind.
    Appeal to the commission for denial of
      application for aid, §111-16.
    Rules and regulations made by commission,
      §111-13.
  Appointments, §143B-158(b).
    Officers, §143B-160.
  Blind persons, majority of commission members,
    §143B-158(c).
  Care of the aged and handicapped.
    Study, §§143-279 to 143-283.
  Chairperson, §§143B-158(d), 143B-160.
  Clerical and other services, §143B-158(j).
  Consumer and advocacy advisory committee for
    the blind, §§143B-163, 143B-164.
  Creation, §143B-157.
  Duties, §143B-157.
  Establishment, §143B-157.
  Financial interest of member, §143B-158(g).
  Meetings.
    Regular and special meetings, §143B-159.
  Number of members, representatives of state
    programs, §143B-158(a).
  Officers, §143B-160.
  Per diem, travel and subsistence expenses,
    §143B-158(h).
  Powers and duties, §143B-157.
  Professional advisory committee.
    Compensation, §143B-162.
    Creation, §143B-161.
    Members, §143B-162.
    Powers and duties, §143B-161.
    Quorum, §143B-162.
    Selection, §143B-162.

BLIND AND VISUALLY IMPAIRED —Cont'd
Commission for the blind —Cont'd
  Quorum, §143B-158(i).
  Removal by governor, §143B-158(g).
  Special meetings, §143B-159.
  Terms, consecutive terms, §143B-158(e), (f).
  Vice-chairman, §143B-160.
Common carrier fares.
  Blind person accompanied by guide dog,
    §62-144(b).
Community-based support groups.
  In-home services, §111-7.
Consumer and advocacy advisory committee
    for the blind.
  Applicability of provisions, §143B-163(d).
  Chairman, §143B-164(b).
  Clerical services, §143B-164(e).
  Compensation, §143B-164(f).
  Creation, §143B-163(a).
  Meetings.
    Regular and special meetings, §143B-164(d).
  Members, §143B-164(a).
  Powers and duties, §143B-163(b), (c).
  Quorum, §143B-164(c).
  Shifts in budget items, §143B-163(e).
  Special meetings, §143B-164(d).
Contributions for particular facilities.
  Acceptance of contributions authorized, §111-12.1.
  Rules and regulations as to receiving and
    expending contributions, §111-12.3.
  Treating contributions as state funds to match
    federal funds, §111-12.2.
Definitions, §111-11.
  Operation of highway vending facilities, §111-49(a)
    to (c).
  Operation of vending facilities on state property,
    §111-42(a) to (d).
Department of health and human services.
  Aid to the blind, §§111-27 to 111-28.1. See within
    this heading, "Aid to the blind."
  Operation of highway vending facilities.
    Preference to blind persons.
      Responsibility of department, §111-48.
  Operation of vending facilities on state property.
    Locations for vending facilities.
      Duty to inform department, §111-45.
    Preference to blind persons.
      Responsibility of department, §111-41.
Deposit with or transferred to state treasurer.
  Disposition of funds, §111-12.6.
Education of blind children.
  Governor Morehead school.
    State school for sight impaired children,
      §§143B-164.10 to 143B-164.18.
    See GOVERNOR MOREHEAD SCHOOL.
Elections.
  Assistance to voters, §163-166.8.
Eye examinations.
  Aid to the blind.
    Application for aid, §111-14.
    Arranging for examination of eyes, §111-8.
    Medical and surgical treatment, §111-8.
False representation as to physical disability.
  Obtaining money by, §14-113.
    Rehabilitation center for the blind and visually
      impaired.
      Authority to receive federal grants-in-aid,
        §111-6.1.
Governor Morehead school.
  State school for sight impaired children,
    §§143B-164.10 to 143B-164.18.
  See GOVERNOR MOREHEAD SCHOOL.

BLIND AND VISUALLY IMPAIRED —Cont'd
Governor's council on the employment of the handicapped, §§143-283.1 to 143-283.8.
Guide dogs.
Common carrier fares.
Blind persons accompanied by, §62-144(b).
Pedestrians' rights and privileges without guide dog, §20-175.3.
Service animals generally, §§168-4.2 to 168-4.6.
Signal for blind persons crossing streets, §20-175.2.
In-home services, §111-7.
Insurance on motor vehicles.
Discriminatory practices prohibited, §58-3-25(b).
License tax for privilege to practice profession.
Exemption, §105-41(b).
Mattresses and bedding.
Exemptions for blind persons.
Bedding manufactured, sanitized or renovated by nonprofit agency for the blind, §106-65.106(a).
Medical and surgical treatment.
Arranging for examination of eyes.
Securing and paying for treatment, §111-8.
Motor vehicle insurance.
Discriminatory practices prohibited, §58-3-25(b).
Nonprofit work centers for the blind and severely disabled.
Public contracts.
Purchases from, §143-129.5.
Purchases through department of administration.
Agency procurement of goods directly from center, §143-48.2(a).
Agency procurement of services directly from center, §143-48.2(b).
Bids or making offers by center, §143-48.2(c).
Procurement program, §143-48.2(b).
Operation of highway vending facilities.
Contracts, §111-50(a).
Definitions, §111-48.
Preference to visually handicapped persons, §111-48.
Current operators, §111-51.
Priority for specific line vendors, §111-51.
Profits.
Deposits, §111-52.
Use, §111-52.
Rules and regulations, §111-50(c).
Operation of vending facilities on state property.
Applicability of article.
Exclusions, §111-47(a), (b).
Coin-operated vending machines.
Installation of machines, §111-43.
Definitions, §111-42(a) to (d).
Exclusions from article, §111-47(a), (b).
Installation of coin-operated vending machines, §111-43.
Location provided by state agency, §111-44.
Duties to inform department of health and human services, §111-45.
North Carolina aquariums contracting for food or vending services.
Authority to contract not withstanding provisions of article, §111-47.1(a).
Existing contracts not altered, §111-47.1(b).
Preference to visually handicapped persons, §111-41.
Responsibility of department of health and human services, §111-41.

BLIND AND VISUALLY IMPAIRED —Cont'd
Operation of vending facilities on state property —Cont'd
Services provided by state agency, §111-44.
Those other than blind persons, §111-46.
Visually handicapped.
Facilities operated by those other than blind persons, §111-46.
Pedestrians.
Guide dogs.
Signal for blind persons crossing streets, §20-175.2.
Rights and privileges of blind persons without white cane or guide dog, §20-175.3.
Rights of way, §20-175.2.
White canes.
Public use by other than blind persons, §20-175.1.
Signal for blind persons crossing streets, §20-175.2.
Private contributions.
Acceptance of contributions for particular facilities authorized, §111-12.1.
Rules and regulations as to receiving and expending contributions, §111-12.3.
Treating contributions as state funds to match federal funds, §111-12.2.
Professional advisory committee, §§143B-161, 143B-162.
Public contracts.
Nonprofit work centers for the blind and severely disabled.
Purchases from, §143-129.5.
Register of blind in state.
Facts to be described, §111-4(a).
Maintenance of complete register, §111-4(a).
Reports of examinations by physicians and optometrists, §111-4(b).
Rehabilitation center for the blind and visually impaired.
Established, §111-6.1.
Federal aid.
Authority to receive grants-in-aid, §111-6.1.
Grants.
Authority to receive federal grants-in-aid, §111-6.1.
Intent of center, §111-6.1.
Operation of center, §111-6.1.
Purposes of center, §111-6.1.
Rules and regulations, §111-6.1.
Rehabilitative services to visually impaired persons.
Jurisdiction of certain divisions within department of health and human services, §111-11.1.
Reserve and operating capital fund.
Expending funds, §111-12.5.
Retaining funds, §111-12.5.
Retirement system for teachers and state employees.
Enrollment of blind or visually handicapped employees, §135-16.1(a) to (c).
Sale of merchandise by governmental units.
Exceptions, §66-58(b), (c).
Sales and use tax.
Exemption of sales by blind persons, §105-164.13.
Sales by training schools and workshops.
Distribution and sale of products, §111-6.
School for sight impaired children.
Governor Morehead school, §§143B-164.10 to 143B-164.18.
See GOVERNOR MOREHEAD SCHOOL.

BLIND AND VISUALLY IMPAIRED —Cont'd
Seeing-eye dogs.
Assaulting assistance animals, §14-163.1.
Common carrier fares for blind persons
accompanied by, §62-144(b).
Pedestrians rights and privileges without guide
dog, §20-175.3.
Service animals generally, §§168-4.2 to 168-4.6.
Signal for blind persons crossing street, §20-175.2.
State treasurer.
Funds deposited with or transferred to state
treasurer.
Disposition of funds, §111-12.6.
Teachers.
Blind teachers not to be discriminated against,
§115C-299(b).
Training schools and workshops, §111-6.
Special educational opportunities outside state,
§111-6.
Vending facilities.
Operation of highway vending facilities, §§111-48
to 111-52.
Operation of vending facilities on state property,
§§111-41 to 111-47.
Visually impaired persons defined, §111-11.
Voting.
Assistance to voters, §163-166.8.
White canes.
Public use by other than blind persons prohibited,
§20-175.1.
Signal for blind persons crossing streets,
§20-175.2.
Workers' compensation.
Loss of vision.
Rates of compensation, §97-31.
Workshops.
Training schools and workshops, §111-6.

BLIND BIDDING FOR FIRST RUN MOTION PICTURES, §75C-3.

BLOCK GRANTS.
Budget of state.
Director to submit plans, §143C-7-2(a).
Information to be included, §143C-7-2(b).
Department of administration duties and powers, §143-341.

BLOOD BANKS.
AIDS.
Information for potential donors, §130A-148(b).
Laboratory tests for AIDS virus infection,
§130A-148(c), (e).
Anatomical gifts generally, §§130A-412.3 to 130A-412.33.
See ANATOMICAL GIFTS.
Applicability of provisions.
Limitations, §90-220.14.
Hepatitis.
Selection of donors.
Risk of transmission of agents that may cause
hepatitis to be minimized, §90-220.13.
Supervision by licensed physician required, §90-220.12.
Umbilical cord stem cells and blood banking.
Free educational information provided on
department web site, §130A-128.1.

BLOOD DONORS.
Anatomical gifts.
General provisions, §§130A-412.3 to 130A-412.33.
See ANATOMICAL GIFTS.

BLOOD DONORS —Cont'd
Persons under 18 years selling.
Unlawful, §130A-412.31.
Selection of donors.
Risk of disease transmission to be minimized,
§90-220.13.
Sixteen year olds donating blood, §130A-412.31.

BLOOD GROUPS.
Physical examination of persons, §1A-1 Rule 35(a).

BLOOD POISON.
Food, drug and cosmetic act.
Drug or device, false advertising, §106-138(b).

BLOODROOT.
Taking, etc., of certain wild plants from land of another, §14-129.

BLOOD TESTS AND SAMPLES.
Competency of blood tests, §8-50.1.
Discovery in criminal cases.
Disclosure of results by defendant, §15A-905.
DNA analysis, §§15A-266 to 15A-270.
See DNA.
Impaired driving.
Chemical analysis of impairing substances in
blood.
Generally.
See IMPAIRED DRIVING.
Livestock.
Brucellosis, §106-390.
Nontestimonial identification.
Delinquent and undisciplined juvenile actions,
§§7B-2103 to 7B-2109.
Generally, §§15A-271 to 15A-282.
See IDENTIFICATION.
Paternity, actions to establish, §49-14(d).
Competency of blood tests, §8-50.1.
Expedited procedures to establish paternity in
IV-D cases, §110-132.2.

BLOWING ROCK.
Room occupancy tax.
Uniform provisions.
Authorized to levy, §160A-215(g).
Generally, §160A-215.

BLUEBERRY.
Official berry of state, §145-18(c).

BLUE DOGBANE.
Taking, etc., of certain wild plants from land of another, §14-129.

BLUE LIGHTS.
Use on vehicles prohibited, §20-130.1(c).
Specially constructed vehicles used in shows,
exhibitions, parades.
Inoperable blue light on vehicle, inapplicability
of prohibition, §20-130.1(c1).

BLUE RIDGE PARKWAY.
Control of outdoor advertising, §§113A-165 to 113A-170.
Advertisements prohibited within one thousand
feet of center line, §113A-165.
Billboards.
Existing billboards, §113A-167.
Center line.
Advertisements prohibited within one thousand
feet, §113A-165.
Condemnation procedure, §113A-169.
Existing billboards, §113A-167.
Injunctions, §113A-170.

BLUE RIDGE PARKWAY —Cont'd
Control of outdoor advertising —Cont'd
Misdemeanor, §113A-170.
Rules and regulations.
Adoption, §113A-166.
Secretary of environment and natural resources.
Rules at option, §113A-166.
Unlawful advertising.
Removal, etc., §113A-168.
Western North Carolina public lands council,
§§143B-324.1 to 143B-324.3.

BLUE SKY LAW.
Securities regulation.
General provisions, §§78A-1 to 78A-66.
See SECURITIES.

BLUE STAR MEMORIAL HIGHWAY, §136-102.1.

BOARDING HOUSES.
Hotels and other lodging places.
See HOTELS AND OTHER LODGING PLACES.

BOARD OF ALDERMEN.
Generally.
See CITY COUNCILS.

BOARD OF AWARDS, §143-52.1.

BOARD OF CORRECTION.
Department of public safety, §143B-715.

BOARD OF DIRECTORS.
Corporations generally.
See CORPORATIONS.
Nonprofit corporations.
See NONPROFIT CORPORATIONS.

BOARD OF EDUCATION.
Local boards of education generally.
See LOCAL BOARDS OF EDUCATION.
State board of education.
See STATE BOARD OF EDUCATION.

BOARD OF LAW EXAMINERS.
Address, AdmissPrac Rule .0101.
Appeals from board, §84-24.
Approval of rules and regulations, Bar Rule
C.0104.
Chair, §84-24, AdmissPrac Rule .0103.
Compensation of members, §84-26.
Composition, §84-24.
Creation, §84-24.
Executive secretary.
Board may employ, §84-24.
Expenses of members, §84-26.
Membership, AdmissPrac Rule .0103.
Number of members, AdmissPrac Rule .0103.
Office hours, AdmissPrac Rule .0101.
Powers, §84-24.
Prescription of applicant fees, §84-25.
Purpose, AdmissPrac Rule .0102.
Subpoena and summons, power, §84-24.
Teachers in law schools.
Ineligibility to be members, §84-24.
Terms, §84-24.

BOARDS AND COMMISSIONS.
Accountants.
Board of examiners, §93-12.
Administrative rules review commission,
§§143B-30.1 to 143B-30.4.
Advisory budget commission.
See BUDGETS.
Advisory commission for state museum of
natural history, §§143B-344.18 to
143B-344.23.

BOARDS AND COMMISSIONS —Cont'd
African-American heritage commission,
§143B-135.
Agricultural, horticultural and forestland.
Special classification for property taxes purposes.
Use-value advisory board, §105-277.7.
Agriculture and forestry awareness,
commission on, §§120-150 to 120-154.
Agriculture, board of.
See AGRICULTURE BOARD.
Alarm systems licensing board, §§74D-4 to
74D-5.1.
Alcoholic beverages.
Commission.
See ALCOHOLIC BEVERAGE CONTROL
COMMISSION.
Local ABC boards.
See ABC BOARDS.
Tribal alcoholic beverage control commission,
§18B-112(d).
Allowances officials conditioned on filing of
notice, §143-47.9.
Anatomy commission, §§130A-33.30 to
130A-33.32.
Appeal of right from administrative agencies,
boards, commission to appellate division,
AppProc Rules 18, 20.
Architects.
Board, §§83A-1 to 83A-6.
Assets.
Settlement of affairs of certain inoperative boards
and agencies.
Conversion and allocation of assets, §143-268.
Delivery to secretary of administration,
§143-267.
Attorney general.
Charges for legal services to state boards and
commissions, §114-8.2.
Attorneys at law.
Board of continuing legal education.
See ATTORNEYS AT LAW.
Board of law examiners, §§84-24 to 84-26,
AdmissPrac Rules .0101 to .0103.
Auctioneer's commission, §85B-3.
Audits and auditing.
Occupational licensing boards, §93B-4.
Settlement of affairs of certain inoperative boards
and agencies, §143-272.
Banking commission.
See BANKING COMMISSION.
Barbers.
Board of barber examiners, §§86A-4 to 86A-7.
Bath historical commission, §§143B-99 to
143B-102.
Battleship commission, §§143B-73 to 143B-74.3.
Beaver damage control advisory board,
§113-291.10.
Bees and honey, §§106-635, 106-637, 106-638.
Blind persons.
Commission for the blind, §§143B-157 to
143B-160.
Boilers.
Board of boiler and pressure vessel rules,
§95-69.13.
Building codes.
Code officials' qualification board.
See BUILDING CODES.
Building commission, §§143-135.25 to 143-135.28.
Cape Fear river navigation and pilotage
commission, §§76A-1 to 76A-25.

BOARDS AND COMMISSIONS —Cont'd

Capital planning commission, §§143B-373, 143B-374.

Cemeteries.
Commission, §§65-48 to 65-54.

Child care commission, §§110-86, 110-88, 143B-168.4, 143B-168.5.

Children with special health care needs commission, §§143-682 to 143-684.

Chiropractors.
Board of examiners, §§90-139 to 90-142.

Cigarettes and tobacco products.
Tobacco boards of trade, §106-465.

Coastal resources commission, §113A-104.

Commission to study the care of the aged and handicapped, §§143-279 to 143-283.

Community appearance commissions, §§160A-451 to 160A-455.

Community colleges.
State board.
See COMMUNITY COLLEGES.

Community corrections.
State community corrections advisory board, §143B-1157.

Compensation for services.
Per diem, subsistence and travel allowances, §138-5(a) to (f).

Compensation to officers conditioned on filing of notice, §143-47.9.

Congressional districts.
Appointment of members from each district, statute requiring.
Extra position due to congressional redistricting, §143B-13(f2).
Residency lost due to congressional redistricting, §143B-13(f1).
Two or members from same district due to congressional redistricting, §143B-13(f).

Consolidated human services boards.
See CONSOLIDATED HUMAN SERVICES AGENCY.

Constitutional amendments publication commission, §§147-54.8 to 147-54.10.

Cosmetic art.
Board of cosmetic art.
See COSMETIC ART.

Counties.
Boards of commissioners.
See COUNTY BOARDS OF COMMISSIONERS.

Courts commission, §§7A-506 to 7A-510.

Creation.
Writing required, §147-16.2(d).

Credit unions.
Commission, §143B-439.

Crime commission.
Governor's crime commission, §§143B-1100 to 143B-1102.

Crime victims compensation commission, §15B-3.

Criminal justice information network governing board, §§143-660 to 143-664.

Crop seed improvement board, §143A-64.

Definitions.
Fees and charges by agencies, §12-3.1(b).
Notice of appointments to public office, §143-47.6.
Occupational licensing boards, §93B-1.

Dental hygienists.
Board of dental examiners, §§90-222, 90-223.

Dentists.
Board of dental examiners.
See DENTISTS AND DENTISTRY.

BOARDS AND COMMISSIONS —Cont'd

Department of public safety.
Board of correction, §143B-715.

Department of transportation disadvantaged minority-owned and women-owned business program.
Joint legislative commission on, §§120-275 to 120-279.

Dietitians and nutritionists.
North Carolina board of dietetics/nutrition, §§90-352 to 90-356.

Disabled persons.
Commission to study the care of the aged and handicapped, §§143-279 to 143-283.

Discrimination against lawful use of lawful products during nonworking hours, §95-28.2.

Dispute resolution commission.
Court ordered mediated settlement conferences in superior court civil actions.
Regulation of mediators and other neutrals, §7A-38.2(b) to (k).

Domestic violence commission, §§143B-394.15, 143B-394.16.

Drainage district commission, §§156-79 to 156-93.1.

Drug commission, §§143B-147 to 143B-150.

Economic development board, §§143B-434 to 143B-437.

Economic development commissions, §§158-8 to 158-15.

Economic development plan, §143B-434.01(a).

Edenton historical commission, §§143B-95 to 143B-98.

Education.
Education commission, §§143-261 to 143-266.
Local boards of education, §§115C-35 to 115C-51.
See LOCAL BOARDS OF EDUCATION.
School technology commission, §§115C-102.5 to 115C-102.7.
State board of education.
Generally.
See STATE BOARD OF EDUCATION.
State board of higher education.
Powers and duties, §116-158.
State education commission, §§143-261 to 143-266.
See EDUCATION COMMISSION.
Teaching fellows commission, §§115C-363.22, 115C-363.23.

Elections.
County boards of elections, §§163-30 to 163-37.
See COUNTY BOARDS OF ELECTIONS.
State board of elections generally, §§163-19 to 163-28.
See STATE BOARD OF ELECTIONS.

Electrical contractors.
Board of examiners, §§87-39 to 87-42.

Electrologists.
Board of electrolysis examiners, §§88A-5 to 88A-8.

Engineers.
Board of examiners, §§89C-4 to 89C-12.

Environmental health specialists.
Board of examiners, §§90A-50 to 90A-59.

Environmental management commission, §§143B-282 to 143B-285.

Environmental review commission, §§120-70.41 to 120-70.47.

Ethics.
State ethics commission, §§138A-6 to 138A-15.

BOARDS AND COMMISSIONS —Cont'd
Expiration of board or commission created by governor or other state officials.
Constitutional elective officers creating, §147-16.2(b).
Executive branch officials creating, §147-16.2(c).
Executive order of governor creating, §147-16.2(a).
Fees and charges.
Agencies establishing fees and charges by rule, §12-3.1(a), (c).
Definitions, §12-3.1(b).
Consultation with joint legislative commission on governmental operations, §12-3.1(a), (a1).
Fire and rescue commission, §§58-78-1 to 58-78-20.
First flight centennial commission, §§143-640 to 143-643.
Forensic science advisory board, §114-16.1.
Foresters.
Board of registration, §§89B-3 to 89B-8.
Funeral service.
Board of funeral service, §§90-210.18A to 90-210.29B.
Gasoline and oil inspection board, §119-26.
Gender based appointments.
Appointing members to statutorily created decision making or regulatory entities.
Appointments to reflect proportion that gender represents in population of state, §143-157.1(a).
Report by appointing authority of number of appointments of each gender, §143-157.1(b).
Local government reporting, §143-157.1(d).
State reporting, §143-157.1(c).
General assembly.
Appointments, §120-121.
Employees and consultants.
Legislative commissions and committees.
Contracting for employment and consultant services, §120-32.02(a) to (c).
Environmental review commission, §§120-70.41 to 120-70.47.
Grants, contributions and loans.
Legislative commissions and committees.
Applying for, receiving and accepting, §120-32.03(a), (b).
Joint legislative commission on governmental operation, §§120-71 to 120-79.
Legislative research commission, §§120-30.10 to 120-30.18.
Legislative services commission, §§120-31 to 120-36.22.
Reports for state institutions and departments, §120-12.
Service by general assembly members, §120-123.
General contractors.
Board, §§87-2 to 87-8, 87-9.1.
General statutes commission, §§164-12 to 164-19.
See GENERAL STATUTES COMMISSION.
Geologists.
Board for licensing geologists, §§89E-4, 89E-5.
Global TransPark development commission, §§158-35, 158-36.
Governor's crime commission, §§143B-1100 to 143B-1102.
Grievance resolution board.
Prisoners' grievance procedure, §§148-118.6 to 148-118.9.
Hazardous waste management commission.
See HAZARDOUS WASTE MANAGEMENT.

BOARDS AND COMMISSIONS —Cont'd
Hearing aid dealers and fitters.
Board, §93D-3.
High Rock lake marine commission, §§77-50 to 77-58.
Hillsborough historical commission, §§143B-103 to 143B-106.
Historical commission, §§143B-62 to 143B-65.
Historic Bath commission, §§143B-99 to 143B-102.
Home inspectors.
Licensure board, §§143-151.43 to 143-151.64.
Human relations commission, §§7A-761, 143B-392.
Indians.
Commission of Indian affairs, §§143B-404 to 143B-411.
Indigent defense services.
Commission on, §§7A-498.4, 7A-498.5.
Industrial commission.
Generally.
See INDUSTRIAL COMMISSION.
Industrial development commission, §§158-21 to 158-24.
Innocence inquiry commission.
Generally, §§15A-1460 to 15A-1475.
See INNOCENCE CLAIM INQUIRY.
Interstate commission for juveniles, §7B-4001.
Irrigation contractors licensing board, §89G-4.
John Motley Morehead memorial commission, §§143B-111 to 143B-115.
Joint legislative commission on governmental operation, §§120-71 to 120-79.
Judicial standards commission, §§7A-374.1 to 7A-378.
Jury commissions, §9-1.
Justice department.
Forensic science advisory board, §114-16.1.
Rules review commission, §§143B-30.1 to 143B-30.4.
Lake Lure marine commission, §§77-80 to 77-88.
See LAKE LURE MARINE COMMISSION.
Lake Wylie marine commission, §§77-30 to 77-38.
Landscape architects.
Board, §89A-3.
Landscape contractors.
Board, §89D-4.
Land surveyors.
Board of examiners, §§89C-4 to 89C-12.
See ENGINEERS.
Legislative appointments to boards and commissions, §120-121(d).
Bill enactment required, §120-121(a).
Conflicts of interest.
Service by members of general assembly on certain boards and commissions, §120-123.
Contents of bills, §120-121(c).
Multiple appointments, §120-121(b).
Service by members of general assembly on certain boards and commissions, §120-123.
Vacancies in appointments, §120-122.
Legislative research commission, §§120-30.10 to 120-30.18.
See LEGISLATIVE RESEARCH COMMISSION.
Legislative services commission, §§120-31 to 120-36.22.
Liability insurance commission, §§58-32-1 to 58-32-30.
See LIABILITY INSURANCE COMMISSION.

BOARDS AND COMMISSIONS —Cont'd
Libraries and librarians.
Public librarian certification commission,
§§143B-67 to 143B-70.
State library commission, §§143B-90, 143B-91.
License plates.
Special plate, number, §20-79.5.
License to give trust fund commission, §§20-7.5,
20-7.6.
Limitation of actions.
Settlement of affairs of certain inoperative boards
and agencies.
Claims settlement, §143-270.
Livestock market advisory board, §106-407.1.
Lobbying for legislative action.
Liaison personnel.
Designating, §§120C-500, 120C-501.
Local government finance commission.
See LOCAL GOVERNMENT FINANCE.
Local governments commission, §128-12.
Locksmith licensing board, §74F-5.
Lodging expenses, §138-5(a) to (f).
Lottery.
North Carolina state lottery commission,
§§18C-110 to 18C-116.
Manufactured housing board, §143-143.10.
Marine fisheries commission, §§143B-289.50 to
143B-289.61.
See MARINE FISHERIES COMMISSION.
Marine fisheries compact commission,
§§113-254 to 113-257.
Marriage and family therapists.
Board, §§90-270.49 to 90-270.51.
Martin Luther King, Jr., commission,
§§143B-426.34A, 143B-426.34B.
Massage and bodywork therapy.
Board of massage and bodywork therapy,
§§90-625 to 90-628.
See MASSAGE AND BODYWORK THERAPY.
Medical board, §§90-2 to 90-8.
See MEDICAL BOARD.
Medical care commission, §§143B-165 to
143B-168.
Meetings.
Legislative commissions, committees and standing
subcommittees, §143-318.14A.
Meetings of public bodies generally, §§143-318.9
to 143-318.18.
See MEETINGS.
**Mental health, developmental disabilities and
substance abuse services commission,**
§§143B-147 to 143B-150.
See MENTAL HEALTH, DEVELOPMENTAL
DISABILITY, SUBSTANCE ABUSE.
Metropolitan sewerage districts.
District boards, §§162A-65 to 162A-67.
Metropolitan water districts.
District board, §§162A-32 to 162A-34.
Midwives.
Joint subcommittee of medical board and board of
nursing, §§90-178.4, 90-178.7.
Military affairs.
Advisory commission on military affairs, §§127C-1
to 127C-4.
Mining commission, §§143B-290 to 143B-293.
**Morehead City navigation and pilotage
commission,** §§76A-31 to 76A-54.
See MOREHEAD CITY NAVIGATION AND
PILOTAGE COMMISSION.
Motor vehicle dealers advisory board,
§20-305.4.

BOARDS AND COMMISSIONS —Cont'd
Mountain Island lake marine commission,
§§77-70 to 77-78.
See MOUNTAIN ISLAND LAKE.
Mountain resources planning commission,
§153B-3.
Municipal zoning adjustment boards,
§160A-388.
Murfreesboro historical commission,
§§143B-107 to 143B-110.
**Natural History Museum Advisory
Commission,** §§143B-344.18 to 143B-344.23.
NC Openbook.
Web sites of government entities, required links,
§143C-2-5(c).
North Carolina's northeast commission,
§§158-8.2 to 158-8.8.
North Carolina state lottery commission,
§§18C-110 to 18C-116.
Notice and record of appointment.
Filing, contents, §143-47.7.
Nurses.
Board of nursing, §§90-171.20 to 90-171.27.
Nursing home administrators.
Board of examiners, §§90-277 to 90-285.1.
Nutritionists and dietitians.
North Carolina board of dietetics/nutrition,
§§90-352 to 90-356.
Occupational licensing boards.
General provisions, §§93B-1 to 93B-16.
See OCCUPATIONAL LICENSING BOARDS.
Occupational safety and health commission,
§95-135.
Occupational therapists board, §§90-270.68,
90-270.69.
Official appearance commission, §§160A-451 to
160A-455.
Officials qualification board, §143-151.8.
**On-site wastewater contractors and inspectors
certification board,** §90A-73.
Opticians.
Board, §§90-238, 90-239.
Optometrists.
Board of examiners, §§90-116 to 90-122.
Pastoral counselors.
Fee-based practicing pastoral counselors.
State board of examiners, §90-385.
Per diem, subsistence and travel allowances.
Applicability of schedules, §138-5(b).
Convention registration fees, §138-5(a).
Per diem, amount, §138-5(a).
Members whose salaries paid from state funds,
§138-5(f).
Subsistence expenses, amount, §138-5(a).
Documentation of actual lodging expenses,
required, §138-5(d).
General assembly members, §138-5(f).
Travel expenses, amount, §138-5(a).
General assembly members, §138-5(f).
Out-of-state travel, §138-5(e).
Personnel system.
Commission, §§126-2, 126-4.
Pesticide board generally, §§143-434 to
143-470.1.
See PESTICIDE BOARD.
Pharmacists and pharmacies.
Board of pharmacy, §§90-85.6 to 90-85.13.
Physical therapists.
Board of examiners, §§90-270.24 to 90-270.39.
Plant protection and conservation board,
§§106-202.12 to 106-202.15.

BOARDS AND COMMISSIONS —Cont'd
Plumbing, heating and fire sprinkler contractors.
Board, §§87-16 to 87-20.
Podiatrists.
Board of podiatry examiners, §90-202.4.
Postal history commission, §§143-675 to 143-679.
Post-release supervision and parole commission, §§143B-720, 143B-721.
Prisons and prisoners.
Grievance resolution board.
Administrative remedy procedure generally, §§148-118.1 to 148-118.9.
Private protective services board, §§74C-4 to 74C-6.
Property tax commission.
See PROPERTY TAX COMMISSION.
Property taxes.
Agricultural, horticultural and forestland.
Special classification for property taxes purposes.
Use-value advisory board, §105-277.7.
Proprietary schools.
State board, §115D-89.1.
Public health.
Commission for public health.
See HEALTH AND HUMAN SERVICES DEPARTMENT.
Public librarian certification commission, §§143B-67 to 143B-70.
Public records, §§132-1 to 132-10.
See RECORDS.
Purchases through department of administration.
Board of awards, §143-52.1.
Radiation protection.
Commission, §§104E-7, 104E-8.
Real estate commission, §93A-3.
Records.
Public records, §§132-1 to 132-10.
See RECORDS.
Settlement of affairs of certain inoperative boards and agencies.
Official records turned over to department of cultural resources, §143-268.
Redevelopment commission, §§160A-504 to 160A-512.
Refrigeration contractors.
Board of examiners, §§87-52 to 87-56.
Regional planning commissions, §§153A-391 to 153A-398.
Regional response team advisory committee.
Hazardous materials emergency response, §166A-26.
Reports.
From state institutions and departments to general assembly, §120-12.
Respiratory care board, §§90-649 to 90-652.
River basins advisory commissions, §§77-110 to 77-118.
See RIVER BASINS ADVISORY COMMISSIONS.
Roanoke Island commission, §§143B-131.1 to 143B-131.10.
Roanoke river basin bi-state commission, §§77-90 to 77-99.
Rules review commission, §§143B-30.1 to 143B-30.4.
Salaries.
Exceptions to provisions, §138-7.
Moving expenses of state employees, §138-8.

BOARDS AND COMMISSIONS —Cont'd
Sale, lease or exchange of property between governmental units.
Action taken by governmental unit, §160A-274(c).
Authority, §160A-274(b).
Governmental unit defined, §160A-274(a).
Sanitary districts.
Boards, §§130A-50 to 130A-56.
Science and technology.
Board of science and technology, §§143B-472.80, 143B-472.81.
Secretary of state.
Appointments, §147-36.
Sedimentation control commission, §§113A-54 to 113A-56, 143B-298, 143B-299.
Seed board, §§106-277.31 to 106-277.33.
Seeds.
Board of crop seed improvement, §§106-269 to 106-276.
Senior citizens.
Commission to study the care of the aged and handicapped, §§143-279 to 143-283.
Sentencing and policy advisory commission, §§164-35 to 164-49.
See NORTH CAROLINA SENTENCING AND POLICY ADVISORY COMMISSION.
Service of process.
Personal jurisdiction.
Manner of service, §1A-1 Rule 4(j).
Process agent, appointment, §1A-1 Rule 4(j).
Settlement of affairs of certain inoperative boards and agencies.
Allocation of certain assets to state agency or department, §143-268.
Audits.
Affairs of board or agency, §143-272.
Payment for audit and other expenses, §143-272.
Claims.
Certification to state treasurer, §143-271.
Escheat of balance to University of North Carolina, §143-271.
Payment, §143-271.
Statement of claims against board of agency, §143-270.
Conversion of certain assets into cash, §143-268.
Delivery of certain assets to secretary of administration, §143-267.
Deposit of funds by state treasurer, §143-269.
Escheat of balance to University of North Carolina, §143-271.
Limitation of actions.
Claims against board of agency, §143-270.
Official records turned over to department of cultural resources, §143-268.
Release and payment of funds to state treasurer, §143-267.
Sheriffs' education and training standards commission.
General provisions, §§17E-1 to 17E-12.
Social services commission, §§143B-153 to 143B-156.
Social workers.
Certification and licensure board, §§90B-3 to 90B-6.
Soil and water conservation commission, §§106-840 to 106-844.
Soil scientists.
Board for licensing, §§89F-4, 89F-5.
Southeastern North Carolina regional economic development commission, §§158-8.3 to 158-8.8.

BOARDS AND COMMISSIONS —Cont'd

Southern dairy compact commission, §106-811.

Southern growth policies agreement board,
§§143-492 to 143-497.

Southern states energy compact board,
§§104D-1 to 104D-5.

Speech and language pathologists and
audiologists.
Board of examiners, §90-303.

State banking commission.
See BANKING COMMISSION.

State board of pensions, §143A-29.

State education commission, §§143-261 to
143-266.

State ethics commission, §§138A-6 to 138A-15.

State farms operation commission, §66-58.

State fire and rescue commission, §§58-78-1 to
58-78-20.
See FIRE AND RESCUE COMMISSION.

State health plan for teachers and state
employees.
Board of trustees, §§135-48.20 to 135-48.22.

State library commission, §§143B-90, 143B-91.

State lottery commission, §§18C-110 to 18C-116.

Subsistence expenses, §138-5(a) to (f).

Supplemental retirement income plan.
Supplemental board of trustees, §135-96.

Teaching fellows commission, §§115C-363.22 to
115C-363.23A.

Textbook commission, §§115C-87, 115C-88.

Tobacco boards of trade.
Membership, §106-465.
Organization, §106-465.

Tobacco research commission, §106-568.3.

Tobacco trust fund.
General provisions, §§143-715 to 143-723.
See TOBACCO TRUST FUND COMMISSION.

Transportation board.
See TRANSPORTATION BOARD.

Travel and tourism board, §143B-434.1.

Travel expenses, §138-5(a) to (f).

Tribal alcoholic beverage control commission,
§18B-112(d).

Tryon Palace commission, §§143B-71, 143B-72.

Universities and colleges.
State board of higher education.
Powers and duties, §116-158.

University of North Carolina.
Board of governors.
See UNIVERSITY OF NORTH CAROLINA.
Constituent institutions.
Boards of trustees, §§116-31 to 116-33.
See UNIVERSITY OF NORTH CAROLINA.

Urban redevelopment commission.
See URBAN REDEVELOPMENT.

Use-value advisory board.
Agricultural, horticultural and forestland.
Special classification for property taxes
purposes, §105-277.7.

U.S.S. North Carolina battleship commission,
§§143B-73 to 143B-74.3.

Utilities commission.
Generally, §§62-10 to 62-98.
See UTILITIES COMMISSION.

Uwharrie regional resources act, §153C-3.

Veterans commission, §§143B-399 to 143B-401.

Veterans employment priority.
Priority in employment assistance for United
States armed forces veterans, §§165-44.1 to
165-44.6.

BOARDS AND COMMISSIONS —Cont'd

Veterans' memorial commission, §§143B-133,
143B-133.1.

Veterinarians.
Board, §§90-181 to 90-186.

Virginia-North Carolina interstate high-speed
rail compact commission, §136-222.

War manpower commission, §135-16.

Water infrastructure.
State water infrastructure commission, §§159G-65
to 159G-67.

Water pollution control.
System operators certification commission,
§§143B-300 to 143B-301.1.

Water treatment facility operators.
Board of certification, §§90A-21 to 90A-28.

Web sites.
NC Openbook.
Web sites of government entities, required links,
§143C-2-5(c).

Welfare.
Board of public welfare, NC Const Art XI §4.

Well contractor certification commission,
§§143B-301.10 to 143B-301.12.

Western North Carolina regional economic
development commission, §§158-8.2 to
158-8.8.

Wildlife resources commissions, §§143-237 to
143-254.5.
See WILDLIFE RESOURCES COMMISSION.

Workforce development boards, local,
§143B-438.11.

Workforce development commission,
§143B-438.10.

Writing required to create, §147-16.2(d).

Zoning.
Municipalities.
Adjustment boards, §160A-388.

BOARDS OF CITY COMMISSIONERS.
Generally.
See CITY COUNCILS.

BOARDS OF COUNTY COMMISSIONERS.
Generally.
See COUNTY BOARDS OF COMMISSIONERS.

BOARDS OF ELECTIONS.
County boards of elections generally, §§163-30
to 163-37.
See COUNTY BOARDS OF ELECTIONS.

Political activities by board members and
employees, §§163-38 to 163-40.1.

State board of elections generally, §§163-19 to
163-28.
See STATE BOARD OF ELECTIONS.

BOATING SAFETY, §§75A-1 to 75A-26.
See BOATS AND OTHER SMALL WATERCRAFT.

BOATING UNDER THE INFLUENCE,
§75A-10(b), (b1).

BOATS AND OTHER SMALL WATERCRAFT,
§§75A-1 to 75A-26.

Accidents.
Duties of others on board, §75A-11(d).
Notice to law enforcement agency, §75A-11(c).
Rendering assistance, §75A-11(a).
Report, filing, §75A-11(b).

Alcoholic beverages.
Forfeiture generally, §18B-504.
Operation of boat or manipulation of water skis
while intoxicated, §75A-10(b), (b1).

BOATS AND OTHER SMALL WATERCRAFT
—Cont'd

Alcoholic beverages —Cont'd
Transporting.
Malt beverages and wine, §18B-1115(f).
Use on oceangoing ships, §18B-106.
Boating safety education.
Required to operate motorboats, §75A-16.2(a).
Certification card or proof person in compliance.
Presentation to law enforcement upon
request, §75A-16.2(b).
Personal water craft.
Operators subject to more specific provisions,
§75A-16.2(e).
Person deemed in compliance, §75A-16.2(b).
Preemption of local regulation, §75A-16.2(d).
Violations.
Infraction, no penalty, court costs assessed,
§75A-16.2(c).
Proof of compliance presented in court,
conviction prohibited, §75A-16.2(c).
Boating under the influence, §75A-10(b), (b1).
Breaking or entering into or breaking out of,
§14-56.
Bridges.
Fastening to, §136-80.
Burning, §14-63.
Certificate of title, §§75A-32 to 75A-49. See within
this heading, "Titling."
Clean coastal water and vessel act, §§77-125 to
77-132.
See CLEAN COASTAL WATER AND VESSEL
ACT.
Commercial fishing boats.
Defined, §75A-5.1(b).
Identification numbers.
False information, §75A-5.1(d).
Renewal of number, §75A-5.1(a), (c).
Muffling devices.
Exemption from provisions, §75A-9(b).
Courses of instruction.
Certification card, §75A-16.1(d).
Commission conduct of training, §75A-16.1(c).
Designation of authorized instructors,
§75A-16.1(b).
Fraudulent acts, §75A-16.1(f).
Rules for, §75A-16.1(e).
Statewide system, §75A-16.1(a).
Dealers.
Operation of watercraft by.
Rules and regulations, §75A-19.
Death, injury or disappearance resulting from
occurrence.
Filing of report, §75A-11(b).
Notice to law enforcement agency, §75A-11(c).
Definitions, §75A-2.
Commercial fishing boats, §75A-5.1(b).
Department of transportation.
Insuring vessels operated by department,
§136-82.1.
Disabled persons.
Right to use of public conveyances, §168-3.
Discharge of firearm into.
While occupied or in operation, §14-34.1(a) to (c).
Discharges of oil or hazardous substances,
§§143-215.83 to 143-215.94.
See OIL OR HAZARDOUS SUBSTANCES
DISCHARGES.
Diver's flag, §75A-13.1.
Drugs.
Forfeiture, §§90-112, 90-112.1.

BOATS AND OTHER SMALL WATERCRAFT
—Cont'd

Drugs —Cont'd
Operation while under the influence, §75A-10(b),
(b1).
Duties and import taxes.
Vessels traveling between states, US Const Art I
§9.
Enforcement of provisions.
Flashing blue light, use of, §75A-17(c).
Law enforcement officers, §75A-17(a).
Siren, use of, §75A-17(d).
Slowing for no-wake zones, §75A-17(f).
Stopping when directed by law enforcement,
§75A-17(e).
Wildlife resources commission, §75A-3(a).
Agreement to enforce, §75A-17(b).
Funds for enforcement, §75A-3(c).
Evidence.
Proof of ownership of vessel, §75A-10.2.
Family purpose doctrine.
Applicability of doctrine, §75A-10.1.
Forfeiture, §18B-504.
Controlled substances, §§90-112, 90-112.1.
Hazardous waste.
Storage, §143-214.2B.
Heads.
Marine toilets, §75A-6(o).
Hunting from vessels, §§113-291.1(b), 113-294(g).
Identification numbers, §§75A-5, 75A-7.
Applications, §75A-5(a).
Change of address of owner of vessel.
Notification to wildlife resources commission,
§75A-5(j).
Change of ownership, §75A-5(c).
Display, §75A-5(a).
Other numbers, §75A-5(k).
Exemptions from requirement, §75A-7(a).
Federal overall systems of identification
numbering.
Conformity with, §75A-5(d).
Fees.
Application fee, §75A-5(a).
Change of ownership of vessel, §75A-5(c).
Renewal fee, §75A-5(h).
Government-owned vessels.
Permanent certificate of number, §75A-7(c).
Voluntary numbering, §75A-7(b).
Lifeboats.
Exemption from requirement, §75A-7(a).
Period of numbering, §75A-5(a), (g).
Reciprocity, §75A-5(b).
Records.
Public records, §75A-5(f).
Renewal, §75A-5(h).
Required, §75A-4.
Exemptions, §75A-7(a).
Transfer of interest in vessels.
Notification to wildlife resources commission,
§75A-5(i).
Unauthorized numbers, §75A-5(k).
Impaired operation.
Operation while intoxicated, §75A-10(b), (b1).
Intoxication.
Operation while intoxicated, §75A-10(b), (b1).
Lake Norman no-wake zone, §75A-14.1.
Legislative declaration, §75A-1.
Lifeboats.
Identification number exemption, §75A-7(a).
Life preservers, etc.
Personal watercraft, §75A-13.3(d).

BOATS AND OTHER SMALL WATERCRAFT
—Cont'd
Life preservers, etc —Cont'd
Requirements, §75A-6(n).
Lights.
Displaying false lights on seashore, §14-282.
Motorboats, §75A-6(n).
Litter.
Depositing or discharging, §75A-10(c).
Medical waste, §75A-10(d), (e).
Local water safety committees.
Administrative and staff services, §75A-26(d).
Authorized, §75A-26(a).
Duties of members, §75A-26(g).
Existing organizations or committees, §75A-26(c).
Expenses of members, §75A-26(d).
Meetings, §75A-26(b), (f).
Notification of sponsorship or withdrawal of
sponsorship, §75A-26(e).
Selection of members, §75A-26(b).
Magistrates.
Boating offenses, powers, §7A-273.
Manufacturers.
Operation of watercraft by.
Rules and regulations, §75A-19.
Marine sanitation devices.
Defined, §77-125.
Pumpout dates.
Records to be kept by owners or operators of
vessel with, §77-128(a).
Violations, criminal penalty, §77-128(b).
Medical waste.
Depositing or discharging, §75A-10(d), (e).
Motorboats.
Boating safety education.
Required to operate, §75A-16.2.
Classification, §75A-6(a).
Defined, §75A-2.
Equipment.
Federal boat safety act of 1971.
Conformance with, §75A-6(m).
Generally, §75A-6.
Muffling devices, §75A-9.
Permission for operation of vessel.
Compliance as prerequisite, §75A-6(l).
Length.
Classification, §75A-6(a).
Life preservers, etc., §75A-6(n).
Lights, §75A-6(n).
Muffling devices, §75A-9.
Muffling devices, §75A-9.
Navigation rules.
Compliance with, §75A-6.1(a).
Enforcement, §75A-6.1(b).
Violations, §75A-6.1(c).
Negligence.
Operation in reckless or negligent manner,
§75A-10(a).
No-wake zones.
Lake Norman no-wake zone, §75A-14.1.
Temporary waiver of enforcement, §75A-14.2.
Obstructing passage in rivers or creeks, §77-12.
Personal floatation devices.
Personal watercraft, §75A-13.3(d).
Requirements, §75A-6(n).
Personal watercraft.
Defined, §75A-13.3(a).
Following too closely, §75A-13.3(e).
Lanyard-type engine cut-off device.
Requirement, §75A-13.3(d).
Liability insurance of liveries, §75A-13.3(c2).

BOATS AND OTHER SMALL WATERCRAFT
—Cont'd
Personal watercraft —Cont'd
Local governments, marine commission or lake
authorities.
Regulation, authorization, §75A-13.3(h).
Minors operating, §75A-13.3(b), (b1).
Leasing, hiring or renting to, §75A-13.3(c).
Narrow channel.
Defined, §75A-13.3(f1).
No-wake speed, operating at greater speed,
§75A-13.3(a1).
No-wake speed.
Operating at speed greater than in certain
areas, prohibition, §75A-13.3(a1).
Performers engaged in professional exhibition.
Inapplicable of provisions, §75A-13.3(f).
Personal floatation device.
Requirement, §75A-13.3(d).
Reasonable and prudent operation.
Requirement, §75A-13.3(e).
Reckless operation, §75A-13.3(e).
Regulation of operation, §75A-13.3.
Renting to public.
Liability insurance requirements, §75A-13.3(c1).
Persons under 16 years of age, §75A-13.3(c).
Safety equipment requirements, §75A-13.3(d).
Sunset and sunrise.
Operating at any time between prohibited,
§75A-13.3(a).
Swerving at last moment to avoid collision,
§75A-13.3(e).
Towing another, §75A-13.3(d1).
Wake jumping, §75A-13.3(e).
Weaving through congested traffic, §75A-13.3(e).
Policy of state.
Legislative declaration, §75A-1.
Ports authority, §§136-260 to 136-275.
Possessory liens on personal property.
Action to regain possession of vessel.
Involuntary relinquishment of possession by
lienor, §44A-6.1(a).
Appeal to district court for trial de novo,
§44A-6.1(b).
General provisions, §§44A-1 to 44A-6.1.
Vessel defined, §44A-1.
Proof of ownership, §75A-10.2(a), (b).
Records.
Title, §75A-38(a).
Regatta or race.
Muffling devices.
Exceptions to requirements, §75A-9(c).
Registration.
Prima facie evidence of ownership, §75A-49.
Rules affecting general public.
Notification, §113-301.1.
Rules and regulations.
Agencies which may apply for rules, §75A-15(b).
Courses of instruction, §75A-16.1(e).
Effect of rules, §75A-15(d).
Electric generating facilities, §75A-15(e).
Navigation rules, §75A-6.1(a) to (c).
Operation of watercraft by manufacturers,
dealers, etc., §75A-19.
Scope of rules, §75A-15(a).
Special regulations, §75A-15.
United States aids to navigation system.
Rules implementing, §75A-15(c).
Sales and use tax.
Rate of tax, §105-164.4(a).

BOATS AND OTHER SMALL WATERCRAFT
—Cont'd
Seizure and forfeiture of conveyances used in committing larceny and similar crimes, §14-86.1.

Shad boat.
State historical boat, §145-11.

Ships and shipping.
See SHIPS AND SHIPPING.

Skin and scuba divers.
Diver's flag, §75A-13.1.
Description, §75A-13.1(b).
Duties of operators of vessels as to, §75A-13.1(c).
Required, §75A-13.1(a).
Violations of provisions, §75A-13.1(d).

State parks and state lakes.
Operation and use rules, §113-35(c).

Surfboards.
Hours for surfboarding, §75A-13(c).
Manipulation in reckless or negligent manner, §75A-10(a).
Manipulation while intoxicated or under influence of drugs, §75A-10(b).
Requirements for vessels towing, §75A-13(a), (b), (d).
Exceptions, §75A-13(c).

Titling, §§75A-32 to 75A-49.
Applicability of definitions, §75A-33.
Certificate of title, §§75A-32 to 75A-49.
Application.
Contents, §75A-35(a), (b).
Form, §75A-35(b).
Who may apply for, §75A-34(a).
Change of address.
Notice by owner, §75A-36.
Duplicate certificates, §75A-39.
Duration, §75A-37(a).
Evidence, §75A-37(a).
Fees, §75A-38(b).
Leases, UCC.
Leases applicable to certificate of title statute, §25-2A-104(1).
Levy of execution, §75A-48.
Lost, stolen, etc.
Certificate, §75A-39.
Security interest, §75A-40.
Filing, §75A-43.
Legal holder subject to security interest, §75A-45.
Notice of interest, §75A-42.
Priority shown on certificate, §75A-44.
Release, §75A-46.
Subsequently created interest, §75A-41.
Surrender of certificate when interest paid, §75A-47.
Transfer, §75A-37(b).
Change of address.
Notice by owner, §75A-36.
Citation of article, §75A-32.
Commission.
Authority of employee, §75A-34(b).
Definitions, §75A-33.
Evidence.
Certificate of title.
Prima facie evidence of ownership, §75A-37(a).
Execution.
Levy, §75A-48.
Records, §75A-38(a).

BOATS AND OTHER SMALL WATERCRAFT
—Cont'd
Titling —Cont'd
Registration.
Prima facie evidence of ownership, §75A-49.
Security interest, §§75A-40 to 75A-47.
Certificate of title to show, §75A-40.
Filing, §75A-43.
Interest subsequently created, §75A-41.
Legal holder subject to interest, §75A-45.
Notice of interest, §75A-42.
Priority of interest shown on certificate, §75A-44.
Release, §75A-46.
Surrender when security interest paid, §75A-47.
Short title of article, §75A-32.
Transfer of title, §75A-37(b).
Fees, §75A-38(b).

Toilets.
Marine sanitation devices.
Defined, §77-125.
Pumpout dates.
Records to be kept by owners or operators of vessel with, §77-128(a).
Violations, criminal penalty, §77-128(b).
Marine toilets, §75A-6(o).
Pumpout facilities and services at marinas.
Clean coastal water and vessel act, §§77-125 to 77-132.
See CLEAN COASTAL WATER AND VESSEL ACT.

Torts.
Family purpose doctrine.
Applicability, §75A-10.1.

Tour boats.
Alcoholic beverage permits, §18B-1006(i).

Trailers.
Vehicles transporting.
Motor vehicle size, weight and loads, §20-116(m).

Trespass.
Removing boats, §14-162.

United States agencies.
Furnishing information.
Duty of wildlife resources commission, §75A-12.

United States aids to navigation system.
Adoption, §75A-15(c).

Unmooring or turning adrift, §14-162.

Vessel agents.
Compensation, §75A-5.2(c).
Conducting transactions by different methods, §75A-5.2(b).
Eligible persons, §75A-5.2(a).
Prohibited acts, criminal penalties, §75A-5.2(h).
Purpose, §75A-5.2(a).
Returned checks or drafts by, §75A-5.2(g).
Rules regarding disciplinary and other actions, §75A-5.2(e).
Rules regarding qualifications and duties, §75A-5.2(d).
Termination of authority, exemption from certain administrative law provisions, §75A-5.2(f).

Vessel liveries.
Compliance with provisions.
Prerequisite to rental of vessels, §75A-8.
Equipment.
Duty to equip rented vessels as required, §75A-8.
Personal watercraft rentals.
Liability insurance requirements, §75A-13.3(c2).

Vessels defined, §75A-2.

BOATS AND OTHER SMALL WATERCRAFT
—Cont'd
Waste.
Storage of waste on vessels, §143-214.2B.
Water skis.
Hours for water skiing, §75A-13(b).
Manipulation in reckless or negligent manner,
§75A-10(a).
Manipulation while intoxicated or under influence
of drugs, §75A-10(b).
Personal watercraft.
Towing person on water skis, §75A-13.3(d1).
Requirements for vessels towing, §75A-13(a), (b),
(d).
Exceptions, §75A-13(c).
Wildlife protectors jurisdiction, §113-136(c).
Wildlife resources commission.
Administration and enforcement of provisions,
§75A-3(a).
Funding, §75A-3(c).
Information.
Furnishing to agencies of United States,
§75A-12.
Motorboat committee, §75A-3(b).

BOAT TITLING, §§75A-32 to 75A-49.
See BOATS AND OTHER SMALL WATERCRAFT.

BOBCATS.
Rabies emergencies.
Plan to reduce threat of rabies exposure to
humans and domestic animals, §130A-201.
Rabies emergency for particular county.
Plan to reduce exposure to humans and domestic
animals, §113-291.2(a1).
Sale of parts, §113-291.3(b).

BODIES.
See DEAD BODIES.

BODYGUARDS.
Generally, §§74C-1 to 74C-30.
See PRIVATE PROTECTIVE SERVICES.

BODY MEASUREMENTS.
Nontestimonial identification, §§15A-271 to
15A-282.
See IDENTIFICATION.

BODY PIERCING.
Children and minors.
Without consent of parents, §14-400(b).

BODY SHOPS.
Repair of motor vehicles, §§20-354 to 20-354.9.
See MOTOR VEHICLE REPAIRS.

BODYWORK THERAPY, §§90-620 to 90-636.
See MASSAGE AND BODYWORK THERAPY.

BOILER AND MACHINERY INSURANCE,
§58-7-15.
Mandatory or voluntary risk sharing plans.
See MANDATORY OR VOLUNTARY RISK
SHARING PLANS.

BOILER ROOM OPERATIONS.
Telephone rooms, securities regulation,
§78A-11.
Criminal penalties, §78A-57(a) to (a4).

BOILERS, §§95-69.8 to 95-69.20.
Accident investigations, §95-69.11.
Appeals.
Civil penalties, §95-69.19(d).
Applicability of provisions, §95-69.10(a).
Exceptions, §95-69.10(b) to (g).

BOILERS —Cont'd
Board of boiler and pressure vessel rules.
Chair, §95-69.13(a).
Composition, §95-69.13(a).
Creation, §95-69.13(a).
Definition of "board,"§95-69.9(a).
Duties, §95-69.13(b).
Expenses of members, §95-69.13(c).
Meetings, §95-69.13(b).
Number of members, §95-69.13(a).
Qualifications of members, §95-69.13(a).
Terms of members, §95-69.13(a).
Building code.
Enforcement of code, §143-139(c).
Chief inspector.
Appointment, §95-69.12.
Defined, §95-69.9(b1).
Citation of act.
Short title, §95-69.8.
Civil penalties.
Amounts, §95-69.19(a), (b).
Appeals, §95-69.19(d).
Factors considered, §95-69.19(c).
Filing of final order, effect, §95-69.19(e).
Commissioner of labor.
Accident investigations, §95-69.11.
Definition of "commissioner,"§95-69.9(c).
Duties, §95-69.11.
Injunctions, §95-69.11.
Noncomplying devices.
Orders to stop or limit use, §95-69.17(a).
Powers, §95-69.11.
Rules and regulations, §95-69.14.
Powers and duties of commissioner, §95-69.11.
Subpoenas, §95-69.11.
Definitions, §95-69.9.
Deputy inspector.
Defined, §95-69.9(d1).
Exemptions from provisions, §95-69.10(b) to (g).
Hot water heaters, §§66-27.1 to 66-27.4.
Injunctions, §95-69.11.
Inspections.
Certificates, §95-69.16.
Definition of "inspection certificate,"§95-69.9(e).
Noncompliance with provisions, §95-69.18(b).
Penalty for violation, §95-69.19(a).
Operation after nonissuance or revocation of
certificate, §95-69.18(c).
Penalty for violation, §95-69.19(b).
Operation without valid inspection certificate,
§95-69.18(a).
Penalty for violation, §95-69.19(a).
Refusal to issue or renew certificate,
§95-69.17(b).
Judicial review, §95-69.17(c).
Operation after nonissuance of certificate,
§95-69.18(c).
Penalty for violation, §95-69.19(b).
Suspension or revocation of certificate,
§95-69.17(b).
Judicial review, §95-69.17(c).
Operation after revocation of certificate,
§95-69.18(c).
Penalty for violation, §95-69.19(b).
Fees.
Assessment and collection, §95-107.
Disposition, §95-108.
Powers and duties of commissioner, §95-69.11.
Required, §95-69.16.
Inspectors.
Classification of inspectors, §95-69.15(a).

BOILERS —Cont'd
Inspectors —Cont'd
Commissions, §95-69.15(b).
Definition of "inspector's
commission,"§95-69.9(f).
Deputy inspector.
Defined, §95-69.9(d1).
Misrepresentation of self as inspector.
Penalty, §95-69.20(a).
Misdemeanors.
False statements, §95-69.20(b).
Misrepresentation of self as inspector,
§95-69.20(a).
Noncomplying devices.
Orders to stop or limit use, §95-69.17(a).
Operation.
After nonissuance or revocation of inspection
certificate, §95-69.18(c).
Noncompliance with provisions, §95-69.18(b).
Penalties for violations, §95-69.19(a), (b).
Without valid inspection certificate, §95-69.18(a).
Pressure vessels.
Defined, §95-69.9(g).
Safety bureau.
Establishment, §95-69.12.
Subpoenas, §95-69.11.
Tampering with boilers, §14-153.
Title of act.
Short title, §95-69.8.

BOILING SPRINGS.
Room occupancy tax.
Uniform provisions.
Authorized to levy, §160A-215(g).
Generally, §160A-215.

BOLL WEEVIL ERADICATION, §§106-65.67 to
106-65.78.
Bees and honey.
Authority to regulate honeybee colonies in
elimination zones and other areas,
§106-65.76.
Certificates.
Defined, §106-65.69.
Citation of act, §106-65.67.
Commissioner of agriculture.
Defined, §106-65.69.
Cooperative programs.
Authorized, §106-65.70.
Cotton.
Authority to prohibit planting of cotton,
§106-65.74.
Defined, §106-65.69.
Elimination zones.
Destruction and treatment of cotton in zones,
§106-65.75.
When compensation payable, §106-65.75.
Participation in eradication program.
Authority to require participation, §106-65.74.
Criminal penalties.
Violations of provisions, §106-65.78(a), (b).
Declaration of policy, §106-65.68.
Definitions, §106-65.69.
Elimination zones.
Cotton.
Destruction and treatment of cotton in zones,
§106-65.75.
When compensation payable, §106-65.75.
Designation, §106-65.74.
Honeybee colonies.
Authority to regulate, §106-65.76.

BOLL WEEVIL ERADICATION —Cont'd
Elimination zones —Cont'd
Pasturage.
Authority to regulate, §106-65.76.
Right of entry, §106-65.76.
Entry of premises.
Eradication activities, §106-65.71.
Inspections, §106-65.71.
Forged or counterfeited documents.
Criminal penalties, §106-65.78(a).
Host.
Defined, §106-65.69.
Infested.
Defined, §106-65.69.
Inspections.
Entry of premises, §106-65.71.
Moving regulated article into state.
Criminal penalties, §106-65.78(b).
Participation in eradication program.
Authority to require participation, §106-65.74.
Pasturage.
Elimination zones.
Authority to regulate pasturage, §106-65.76.
Permits.
Defined, §106-65.69.
Policy declaration, §106-65.68.
Purpose of article, §106-65.68.
Quarantine.
Regulations governing quarantining, §106-65.73.
Regulated article.
Defined, §106-65.69.
Reports.
Information contained in report, §106-65.72.
Right of entry.
Authority to regulate entry in elimination zones
and other areas, §106-65.76.
Eradication activities, §106-65.71.
Inspections, §106-65.71.
Rules and regulations.
Authority to adopt, §106-65.77.
Quarantining, §106-65.73.
Short title, §106-65.67.
States.
Cooperative programs authorized, §106-65.70.
United States.
Cooperative programs authorized, §106-65.70.
Violations of provisions.
Criminal penalties, §106-65.78(a), (b).

BOMBS.
Burglary with explosives, §14-57.
Campus or other educational property.
Possessing or carrying on, §14-269.2.
Civil disorders.
Certain weapons at civil disorders, §14-288.20.
Exploding, §14-283.
Explosives generally.
See EXPLOSIVES.
Keeping for sale or selling without license,
§14-284.
Mass death and destruction weapons.
Manufacture, assembly, etc., §14-288.8.
Nuclear, biological or chemical weapons,
§§14-288.21 to 14-288.24.
See WEAPONS OF MASS DEATH AND
DESTRUCTION.
Minors detonating in schools.
Parental liability for damages, §1-538.3.
Regulation of sale of explosives, §14-284.1.
Weapons generally.
See FIREARMS AND OTHER WEAPONS.

BOMB SCARES.
Drivers' licenses.
Revocation or suspension of license.
Minors, §20-13.2(c2).
False reports concerning destructive device.
Destructive device located in any building or
vehicle, §14-69.1(a).
Destructive device located in public building,
§14-69.1(c).
Report defined, §14-69.1(d).
Restitution, costs and consequential damages,
ordering, §14-69.1(d).
General assembly.
Evacuation of state legislative buildings and
grounds, §120-32.1A.
Hoax by use of false bomb or other device,
§14-69.2(a).
Public buildings, §14-69.2(c).
Restitution, costs and consequential damages,
ordering, §14-69.2(d).
Parental liability for disruption.
Minors causing in schools, §1-538.3.

BONA FIDE PURCHASERS.
Conveyances.
Husband and wife.
Certain conveyances not affected by fraud,
§39-11.
Registration necessary to pass title as against
creditors and bona fide purchasers, §47-18.
**Execution against property of judgment
debtor not lien on personal property as
against,** §1-313.
Investment securities.
Enforcement of completed or altered instrument,
§25-8-206.
Judgments and decrees.
Title not affected when judgment set aside,
§1-108.
Notice of pending litigation.
Filing to be effective against, §1-116(d).
Partition.
Impeachment of commissioner's report.
Purchases not affected, §46-19(a).
Title not affected when judgment set aside,
§1-108.
Sale of goods, UCC.
Title acquired by bona fide purchasers,
§25-2-403(1).
Simultaneous death.
Protection of purchasers for value, §28A-24-8(b).

BOND FOR TITLE.
Contracts for deed, §§47H-1 to 47H-8.
See CONTRACTS FOR DEED.

BOND ISSUES.
Agricultural finance authority, §§122D-10 to
122D-17.
Definition of "bonds" or "notes,"§122D-3.
Powers of authority, §122D-6.
Airports.
Special airport districts, §§63-83, 63-84, 63-87.
Alcoholic beverages commission, §18B-208(a).
Banks.
Investments, §§53-44 to 53-46.
Capital appreciation bonds.
Local government finance.
Authorization.
Future acts, §159-100(c).
Local government bond act, §159-100(b).
Revenue bond act, §159-100(a).

BOND ISSUES —Cont'd
Capital appreciation bonds —Cont'd
Local government finance —Cont'd
Calculating principal, §159-99(b).
Defined, §159-99(a).
Terms and conditions, §159-99(c).
State authority to issue, §142-15.3(b).
Provisions governing, §142-15.3(a).
Capital facilities finance act.
Special indebtedness generally, §§142-80 to
142-101.
See CAPITAL FACILITIES FINANCE ACT.
Community colleges.
Financial support.
Elections on question of issuance, §115D-36.
Previously established institutions, §115D-34(b).
Local financial support of institutions.
Authority to issue bonds and notes, §115D-38.
Consolidated city-county act, §§160B-13 to
160B-15.
Constitution of North Carolina.
Capital projects for industry.
Authorities may be created, NC Const Art V §9.
General assembly.
Actions on revenue bills, NC Const Art II §23.
Health care facilities.
Authorized, NC Const Art V §8.
Higher education facilities.
Authorized, NC Const Art V §12.
Hospitals, NC Const Art V §8.
Seaport and airport facilities.
Authorized powers as to, NC Const Art V §13.
Corporations.
Drainage, §§156-52, 156-53.
Interest.
Sale below par permitted, §24-2.
Payment of bonds enforced, §156-53.
Costs.
Several suits on one instrument.
Allowance of costs to defendant, §6-19.
Allowance of costs to plaintiff, §6-18.
Counties.
Critical infrastructure needs.
Special assessments for, §153A-210.6.
Highways, roads and streets.
Prohibition of local road bonds, §136-98(b).
Local government bond act.
General provisions, §§159-43 to 159-78.
See LOCAL GOVERNMENT FINANCE.
Local government revenue bond act.
General provisions, §§159-80 to 159-97.
See LOCAL GOVERNMENT FINANCE.
Relocation of county seat.
Procedures if county votes to relocate, §159-67.
Savings banks.
Investment in county obligations, §54C-137.
School bonds.
Election required, §115C-501(f).
Service districts.
Authorization, §153A-308.
County service districts, §153A-308.
County water and sewer districts.
Authorized, §162A-90.
Critical infrastructure needs.
Revenue bonds to finance projects.
Cities.
Authorization to issue, §160A-239.6(a).
Modification of authority of city,
§160A-239.6(b).
Counties, §153A-210.6.

BOND ISSUES —Cont'd
Drainage.
Corporations, §§156-52, 156-53.
Payment of bonds authorized, §156-53.
Educational institutions.
Private capital facilities finance act.
Institutions for higher education and
elementary and secondary education,
§§159D-35 to 159D-57.
See CAPITAL FACILITIES FINANCE
AGENCY.
Electric membership corporations, §117-21.
Covenants or agreements for security of bonds,
§117-22.
Purchase and cancellation of bonds, §117-23.
Specific grant of power, §117-18.
Embezzlement, §14-90.
Facility authorities, §§160A-480.8 to 160A-480.14.
Powers of authority, §160A-480.4.
Fairs.
State fair.
Constructing and financing facilities and
improvements for fair, §106-503.1(a).
Fiduciaries.
Investments.
Powers which may be incorporated by reference
in trust instrument, §32-27.
Fish and fisheries resources.
Seafood industrial park authority, §113-315.31.
Forests and forestry.
Protection and development corporations.
Issuance of securities restricted, §106-987.
Forgery, §14-122.
Selling of certain forged securities, §14-121.
General assembly.
Requirements for passage of revenue bills, NC
Const Art II §23.
Governor.
Council of state.
Duties performed by other officers, §142-9.
Health care facilities.
Authority to finance by bond, NC Const Art V §8.
Health care facility financing generally,
§§131A-1 to 131A-25.
See HEALTH CARE FACILITY FINANCING.
Highways, roads and streets.
GARVEE bonds.
Issuance of grant anticipation revenue vehicles
to finance federal-aid highway projects,
§136-18.
Distribution of funds derived from,
§136-17.2A(i).
Hospital authorities.
Definition of bonds, §131E-16.
Exemption from taxation, §131E-28(c).
Revenue bonds and notes, §131E-26(a), (b).
Hospitals.
Authority to finance by bond issue, NC Const Art
V §8.
Housing authorities and projects.
See HOUSING AUTHORITIES AND PROJECTS.
Housing finance agency.
See HOUSING FINANCE AGENCY.
Income tax.
Exemption from federal income taxation.
Registered public obligations act.
Generally, §§159E-1 to 159E-15.
See REGISTERED PUBLIC
OBLIGATIONS.
Purpose of act, §159E-3(a), (b).

BOND ISSUES —Cont'd
Income tax —Cont'd
Federal tax reform allocation committee,
§§143-433.6 to 143-433.9.
**Industrial and pollution control facilities
financing.**
Industrial and pollution control facilities financing
act, §§159C-1 to 159C-27.
See INDUSTRIAL AND POLLUTION
CONTROL FACILITIES FINANCING.
North Carolina capital facilities financing act.
North Carolina industrial and pollution control
facilities financing act, §§159D-1 to
159D-27.
See INDUSTRIAL AND POLLUTION
CONTROL FACILITIES FINANCING.
Industry.
Capital projects for industry.
County may create authorities to issue bonds,
NC Const Art V §9.
Interest.
Corporate bonds may be sold below par, §24-2.
Refunding bonds.
State debt, §§142-29.6(a), 142-29.7.
**Interest rate swap agreements for
governmental units,** §§159-193 to 159-200.
See SWAP AGREEMENTS.
Investment securities, §§25-8-101 to 25-8-511.
See INVESTMENT SECURITIES.
Joint municipal electric power and energy.
See JOINT MUNICIPAL ELECTRIC POWER
AND ENERGY ACT.
Land and loan associations.
Powers, §54-53.
Larceny of choses in action, §14-75.
Local government bond act.
General provisions, §§159-43 to 159-78.
See LOCAL GOVERNMENT FINANCE.
Local government revenue bond act.
General provisions, §§159-80 to 159-97.
See LOCAL GOVERNMENT FINANCE.
Metropolitan sewerage districts, §§162A-69,
162A-70.
Metropolitan water districts, §§162A-36(a),
162A-37.
Mosquito control districts.
Power to issue bonds, §130A-357.
Municipal hospitals.
Power of municipality to issue, §131E-7(a).
Sale to nonprofit corporation.
General obligation or revenue bonds
outstanding.
Escrow fund, placement of money in by
corporation, §131E-8(b).
Municipalities.
Joint municipal electric power and energy.
See JOINT MUNICIPAL ELECTRIC POWER
AND ENERGY ACT.
Local government bond act.
General provisions, §§159-43 to 159-78.
See LOCAL GOVERNMENT FINANCE.
Local government revenue bond act.
General provisions, §§159-80 to 159-97.
See LOCAL GOVERNMENT FINANCE.
Sinking funds.
Local government finance, §§159-1 to 159-188.
See LOCAL GOVERNMENT FINANCE.
Municipal service districts, §160A-543.
Parking authorities, §§160A-556, 160A-560 to
160A-562.

BOND ISSUES —Cont'd
Ports and harbors.
Constitution of North Carolina.
Seaport and airport facilities, NC Const Art V
§13.
Ports authority, §136-265.
Special user projects.
Generally, §136-266.
Powers of attorney.
Powers conferred by statutory short form, §32A-2.
Private activity bonds.
Federal tax reform allocation committee.
Composition, §143-433.7.
Duties, §143-433.8.
Established, §143-433.7.
Formulas for allocation, §143-433.9.
Legislative findings, §143-433.6(a) to (d).
Private educational facilities finance.
Authorized, NC Const Art V §12.
Private nonprofit educational institutions.
Private capital facilities finance act.
Institutions for higher education and
elementary and secondary education,
§§159D-35 to 159D-57.
See CAPITAL FACILITIES FINANCE
AGENCY.
**Project development financing debt
instruments.**
Local governmental units, §§159-101 to 159-113.
See LOCAL GOVERNMENT FINANCE.
Public schools.
Merged school administrative units consisting of
one entire county and part of second county.
Issuance, §115C-513(a), (b).
Qualified school construction bonds, §115C-489.5.
Qualified zone academy bonds, §§115C-489.5,
115C-489.6.
School districts, §§115C-481 to 115C-484.
See SCHOOL DISTRICTS AND
ADMINISTRATIVE UNITS.
Public utilities.
Securities regulation.
Generally, §§62-160 to 62-171.
See PUBLIC UTILITY SECURITIES.
Railroads.
Powers of railroad corporations, §136-190.
Refunding bonds.
Local government finance.
See LOCAL GOVERNMENT FINANCE.
State debt, §§142-29.1 to 142-29.7.
See STATE DEBT.
Regional natural gas districts, §160A-673.
Regional sports authorities, §160A-479.12.
Taxation.
Exemption on interest of bonds,
§160A-479.14(c).
Regional transportation authorities, §160A-647.
Registered public obligations, §§159E-1 to
159E-15.
See REGISTERED PUBLIC OBLIGATIONS.
Sanitary districts, §130A-61.
Validation of bonds, §130A-77.
Tax levy for validated bonds, §130A-78.
Savings and loan associations.
Investments.
County obligations, §54B-188.
Fannie Mae obligations, §54B-187.
Federal home loan bank obligations, §54C-134.
Municipal obligations, §54B-188.
North Carolina obligations, §54B-183.
United States obligations, §54B-182.

BOND ISSUES —Cont'd
Savings and loan associations —Cont'd
Loans.
Security, §54B-151(d).
State associations, powers, §54B-77(b).
Savings banks.
Investments.
County obligations, §54C-137.
Federal government-sponsored enterprise
obligations, §54C-136.
Municipal obligations, §54C-137.
North Carolina obligations, §54C-133.
United States obligations, §54C-132.
Stock savings banks.
Power to issue bonds, §54C-146(b).
School districts.
General provisions, §§115C-481 to 115C-484.
See SCHOOL DISTRICTS AND
ADMINISTRATIVE UNITS.
Securities regulation.
General provisions, §§78A-1 to 78A-66.
See SECURITIES.
Sinking funds.
Local government finance, §§159-1 to 159-188.
See LOCAL GOVERNMENT FINANCE.
Soil and water conservation districts.
Watershed improvement works or projects,
§139-49(a) to (g).
Solid waste management.
Local governments.
Solid waste management loans and special
obligation bonds, §§159I-1 to 159I-30.
See SOLID WASTE MANAGEMENT LOANS
AND SPECIAL OBLIGATION BONDS.
Regional solid waste management authorities.
Revenue bonds and notes.
Advances, §153A-432.
Issuance, §153A-431.
State capital facilities finance act.
Special indebtedness generally, §§142-80 to
142-101.
See CAPITAL FACILITIES FINANCE ACT.
State debt, §§142-1 to 142-29.7.
See STATE DEBT.
State departments and agencies.
Amount of bonds, §143-163.
Covenants in resolutions authorizing bonds,
§143-165.
Federal aid.
Acceptance of federal loans and grants.
Permitted, §143-164.
Financing of certain public undertakings,
§143-163.
Governor.
Approval by governor and council of state,
§143-165.
Security, §§143-163, 143-165.
Terms, §143-163.
State education assistance authority.
General provisions.
See EDUCATION ASSISTANCE AUTHORITY.
Local road bonds.
Prohibition, §136-98(b).
Taxation.
Exemption of state bonds, §§142-12, 142-17.
Continuation of state tax exemptions, §142-12.1.
Federal taxation of interest income on state or
local bonds on issuance thereof.
Effect, §142-12.1.

BOND ISSUES —Cont'd
Transportation department.
 GARVEE bonds.
  Issuance of grant anticipation revenue vehicles
   to finance federal-aid highway projects,
   §136-18.
   Distribution of funds derived from,
    §136-17.2A(i).
Trust companies.
 Investment in bonds, §53-342.
Turnpike authority.
 Revenue bonds.
  See TURNPIKE AUTHORITY.
Unclaimed property generally, §§116B-51 to
  116B-80.
 See UNCLAIMED PROPERTY.
Universities and colleges.
 Private capital facilities finance act.
  Institutions for higher education and
   elementary and secondary education,
   §§159D-35 to 159D-57.
   See CAPITAL FACILITIES FINANCE
    AGENCY.
University of North Carolina.
 See UNIVERSITY OF NORTH CAROLINA.
Urban redevelopment.
 Definition of "bonds,"§160A-503.
 Liability on bonds.
  Limitations on, §160A-516(b).
 Powers of redevelopment commission, §§160A-512,
  160A-516(a), 160A-517.
 Presumptions as to issuance, §160A-516(f).
 Rights of obligees of commission, §§160A-517(b),
  160A-518.
 Sale of bonds, §160A-516(d).
  Private sale, §160A-516(g).
 Security.
  Powers of redevelopment commission as to
   securing bonds, §160A-517(a).
 Signatures on bonds, §160A-516(e).
Usury.
 Corporate bonds may be sold below par, §24-2.
Water and sewer authorities.
 Bondholder's remedies, §162A-12.
 Power of authority, §162A-6(a).
 Refunding bonds.
  Generally, §162A-13.
  Power to issue, §162A-13.
 Revenue bonds.
  Power to issue, §162A-8.
  Remedies of bondholders, §162A-12.
 Trust funds.
  Moneys received deemed trust funds, §162A-11.

BONDS, SURETY.
ABC boards.
 Members, general managers, finance officers,
  §18B-700(i).
ABC stores.
 Employees, §18B-803(c).
 Managers, §18B-803(b).
Absentees in military service.
 Receivers.
  Required, §28B-5(a).
Actions, §§58-76-1 to 58-76-30.
 Complaint shows party interest, §58-76-10.
  Election to sue officer individually, §58-76-10.
 Damages.
  Officer unlawfully detaining money liable,
   §58-76-20.

BONDS, SURETY —Cont'd
Actions —Cont'd
 Debts.
  Officer liable for negligence in collecting,
   §58-76-30.
 Destroyed bonds, §98-9.
 Election of rights of remedies.
  Suing officer individually, §58-76-10.
 Evidence against principal admissible against
  sureties, §58-76-25.
 Liability and right of action on official bonds,
  §58-76-5.
  Summary remedy on bond, §58-76-15.
 Limitation of actions, §§1-50(a), 1-52.
 Model payment and performance bond, §44A-27.
 Negligence in collecting debt, §58-76-30.
 Payable to court officer.
  Suit in name of state, §58-76-1.
 Principals.
  Evidence against principal admissible against
   sureties, §58-76-25.
 Satisfaction.
  Defendant may plead satisfaction, §1-60.
 State of North Carolina.
  Bonds in actions payable to court officer.
   Suit in name of state, §58-76-1.
 Summary remedy on official bonds, §58-76-15.
 Surety's recovery on obligation paid.
  No assignment necessary, §26-3.1(a).
   Construction of term "surety,"§26-3.1(b).
 Unlawfully detaining money, §58-76-20.
Administrators, §§28A-8-1 to 28A-8-6.
Agents.
 Indemnity bonds to state maximum liability and
  period of liability, §66-65.
Agriculture.
 Promotion of use and sale of agricultural
  products.
  Publication of financial statement by treasurer
   of agency, §106-568.
Air pollution control.
 Compliance bonds.
  Special orders, §143-215.110(e).
Alcoholic beverage control boards.
 Members, general managers, finance officers,
  §18B-700(i).
Alcoholic beverage control stores.
 Employees, §18B-803(c).
 Managers, §18B-803(b).
Alcoholic beverages tax.
 Nonresident vendors, §105-113.86(b).
 Wholesalers and importers, §105-113.86(a).
Alimony.
 Bond for costs unnecessary, §50-2.
 Securing payment, §50-16.7(b).
Alternative fuel.
 Bond required as condition of obtaining and
  keeping licenses, §105-449.133.
Appeals.
 See APPEAL BONDS.
Architects.
 Board.
  Treasurer, §83A-2(c).
Arrest in civil cases.
 Bail.
  See BAIL.
 Order for arrest.
  Undertaking before order, §1-412.
Assignments.
 Surety's recovery on obligation paid.
  No assignment necessary, §26-3.1(a).
   Construction of term "surety,"§26-3.1(b).

BONDS, SURETY —Cont'd
Assignments for benefit of creditors.
Release of insolvent upon giving bond, §23-40.
Substituted trustee to give bond, §23-7.
Surrender of principal.
Surety may surrender, §23-41.
Trustees.
Insolvent trustee removed unless bond given, §23-5.
Attachment.
See ATTACHMENT.
Attorneys' fees.
Model payment and performance bonds.
Suits under provisions, §44A-35.
Bail.
See BAIL.
Bail bondsmen and runners, §§58-71-1 to 58-71-195.
See BAIL BONDSMEN AND RUNNERS.
Banks.
Dissolution and liquidation.
Commissioner of banks.
Taking possession, §53-20(h).
Employees, §53-90.
Officers, §53-90.
Barber schools.
Guaranty bond required for approval, §86A-22.
Bills of lading.
Indorser not guarantor for other parties, §25-7-505.
Biological residues in animals.
Preservation or disposition of animal, animal product or feed.
Posting of bond required, §106-549.83.
Blanket bonds.
Clerks of superior courts, §7A-107.
Boxing promoter's license, §143-654(c).
Building codes.
Manufactured buildings, structures or components.
Securing permits to erect modular buildings, §143-139.1(a).
Business opportunity sales.
Filing of copies with secretary of state, §66-97(c).
Requirements, §66-96.
Caveat to will.
Costs, §31-33(d).
Cemeteries.
Abandoned and neglected cemeteries.
Money for maintenance and preservation.
Clerk of superior court, §65-95.
Certiorari, §1-269.
Charitable solicitations.
Solicitors, §131F-16(d).
Child placement.
Bringing or sending child into state for purposes of placement or adoption.
Person, agency, association, etc., bringing child into state, §7B-3701.
Child support.
Payments secured by bond, §50-13.4(f).
Claim and delivery.
Defendant's undertaking for replevy, §1-478.
Qualification and justification of defendant's surety, §1-479.
Plaintiff's undertaking, §1-475.
Exceptions to undertaking, §1-477.
Sheriffs.
Liability for sufficiency of sureties, §§1-477, 1-479.

BONDS, SURETY —Cont'd
Claim and delivery —Cont'd
Third parties.
Property claimed by third person, §1-482.
Clerk of board of county commissioners.
Approval of official bonds.
Recording votes approving bond, §58-72-55.
Closing-out sales.
Required for license, §66-77(b).
Collection agencies.
Amount, §58-70-20.
Permit applications, §58-70-5(e).
Prerequisite to issuance of permit, §58-70-20.
Commercial code.
Definition of surety, §25-1-201(b)(40).
Documents of title.
Indorser not guarantor for other parties, §25-7-505.
Commodities.
Official action under chapter.
Administrator not required to post, §78D-23(b).
Community colleges.
Investment of idle cash, §115D-58.10.
Compliance bonds.
Execution sales.
Upset bids on real property, §1-339.64(b).
Judicial sales.
Upset bid on real property at public sales, §1-339.25(b).
Mortgages and deeds of trust.
Compliance bond in case of upset bids on real property, §45-21.27.
Condition of official bonds, §58-72-10.
Continuing care facilities.
Rehabilitation of facilities.
Refusal or vacation of orders, §58-64-45(g).
Contracts.
Principal and surety distinguished in judgment and execution, §26-1.
Contribution among sureties, §26-5.
Coroners.
Certified copies as evidence, §152-4.
Execution, §152-3.
Official bonds of county officers generally, §§58-72-1 to 58-72-70.
See OFFICIAL BONDS OF COUNTY OFFICERS.
Registration, §152-4.
Cosmetic art.
Private cosmetic art schools, §88B-17.
Costs.
Defendant's liability in criminal actions.
Confession of judgment, §6-47.
Bond given to secure fine and cost, §6-47.
Several suits on one instrument.
Allowance of costs to defendant, §6-19.
Allowance of costs to plaintiff, §6-18.
Cotton warehouses, §106-451.11(a).
Action on bond by person injured, §106-451.12.
Inspectors, §106-451.25.
Registration, §106-451.42(b).
Counties.
When county may pay premiums on official bonds, §58-72-15.
County commissioners.
Clerk of board.
Approval of official bonds.
Recording votes approving bond, §58-72-55.
Official bonds.
Liability of commissioner as surety, §58-72-60.
Record of board conclusive as to facts stated, §58-72-65.

BONDS, SURETY —Cont'd
County commissioners —Cont'd
Official bonds —Cont'd
Vacancy declared.
Judge to file statement of proceedings with commissioners, §58-72-45.
Surety companies.
Clerk to notify county commissioners of condition of company, §58-73-10.
County officers.
Official bonds generally, §§58-72-1 to 58-72-70.
See OFFICIAL BONDS OF COUNTY OFFICERS.
Court of appeals.
Clerk of court, §7A-20(a).
Credit repair services, §66-222.
Credit unions.
Blanket fidelity bond.
Purchase by board of directors, §54-109.44.
Generally, §54-109.11.
Custodial trustees, §33B-14.
Damages.
Actions on bonds.
Officer unlawfully detaining money liable for damages, §58-76-20.
Debtor and creditor.
Joinder of debtor by surety, §26-12(a), (b).
Notice to creditor to take action, §§26-7 to 26-9.
Decedents' estates.
Collectors, §28A-11-2.
Debts and claims.
Distribution of estate despite contingent or unliquidated claim.
Bond of heirs and devisees, §28A-19-5.
Default judgments.
Plaintiff, §1A-1 Rule 55(c).
Definitions.
Model payment and performance bond, §44A-25.
"Surety," §26-3.1(b).
Deposit in lieu of bond.
Cash or securities deposited in lieu of bond, §58-75-1.
Deposits.
State funds, §147-79.
Discount buying clubs, §66-135.
Divorce.
Bonds for costs unnecessary, §50-2.
Documents of title.
Indorser not guarantor for other parties, §25-7-505.
Drainage.
Petitions.
Agreement for construction, §156-26(d).
Drainage districts.
Amount of penalty, §156-57.
Appeals, §156-66.
Construction of improvements.
Contractors, §156-84.
Penalties.
Amount of penalty, §156-57.
Petitions.
Filing with petition, §156-57.
Treasurer, §156-81.1.
Dropout prevention grants.
Nonprofit organizations receiving.
Contract requiring fidelity bonding, §115C-64.8.
Election of rights and remedies.
Actions on bonds.
Suing officer individually, §58-76-10.
Elective share of surviving spouse.
Responsible person, §30-3.5(e).

BONDS, SURETY —Cont'd
Electrical contractors.
Board of examiners.
Secretary-treasurer, §87-40.
Energy conservation.
Guaranteed energy savings contracts, §143-64.17B(c), (d).
Engineers and land surveyors.
Board of examiners.
Executive director, §89C-9.
Examinations.
Annual examination of official bonds, §58-72-20.
Executions.
Debtor leaving state or concealing self, §1-355.
Execution sales.
Special proceedings to determine ownership of surplus.
Transfer of proceedings to civil issue docket of superior court, §1-339.71(c).
Upset bid on real property.
Compliance bond, §1-339.64(b).
Forthcoming bond for personal property, §§1-318 to 1-320.
Principal and surety distinguished in judgment and execution, §26-1.
Principal liable on execution before surety, §26-2.
Stay of execution.
Dissenting surety not liable to surety on stay of execution, §26-6.
Executors and administrators.
See EXECUTORS AND ADMINISTRATORS.
Federal estate tax apportionment.
Distribution before final apportionment.
Distributee to provide security for tax liability, §28A-27-7.
Fiduciaries.
Surety companies.
Expense of fiduciary bond charged to fund, §58-73-35.
Firefighters' relief fund.
Treasurer of state firemen's association.
State appropriation.
Bond to be given by treasurer, §58-85-10.
Trustees.
Treasurer of board of trustees, §58-84-30.
Fish and fisheries resources.
Promotion of coastal fisheries and seafood industry.
Financial officers, §113-315.9(a), (b).
Foresters.
Board of registration.
Secretary, §89B-7.
Forfeitures.
Failure of surety companies to pay judgment is forfeiture, §58-73-25.
Forthcoming bond for personal property, §1-318.
Procedure on giving bond, §1-319.
Subsequent levies, §1-319.
Summary remedy, §1-320.
Fraternal benefit societies.
Organization.
Filing with articles of incorporation, §58-24-45(b).
Fruits.
Unfair trade practices by handlers of fruits.
Required bond, §106-498.
Garnishment.
Garnishee retaining possession, §1-440.32(b).
Gasoline and oil inspection.
Cancellation of license, §119-19.

BONDS, SURETY —Cont'd
Gasoline and oil inspection —Cont'd
Inspectors to be bonded, §119-25.
Gasoline tax.
Failure to file replacement bond or additional
    bond, §105-449.120(a).
Required as condition of obtaining and keeping
    certain licenses, §105-449.72.
Grain dealers.
Application for license, §§106-604, 106-605.
Guardians.
Action on bond.
    Persons injured by breach of condition,
        §35A-1234.
    Relief of endangered guardians, §35A-1237.
    Several wards with estate in common,
        §35A-1235.
Adjusting guardian's bond.
    Authority of clerks of superior court,
        §35A-1203(c).
Approval, §35A-1230.
Breach of condition.
    Action on bond by person issued by, §35A-1234.
Clerk.
    Approval, §35A-1230.
    Liability of official bond, §35A-1238.
    Recording, §35A-1231(a).
    Reduced penalty, §35A-1233.
    Renewal of bond.
        Duties of clerk upon failure to renew,
            §35A-1236.
Common wards for one guardian, §35A-1235.
Conditions of bond, §35A-1231(a).
Deposited or invested money, ward's estate
    including.
    Exclusion when computing amount of bond,
        §35A-1232(a).
Disinterested public agents.
    Health and human services bond, §35A-1239.
Health and human services bond, §35A-1239.
Increase on sale of realty or personal property,
    §35A-1231(b).
Judicial sale, holding, §1-339.10(b), (c).
Limitation of action against surety, §1-52.
Nonresident guardian, §35A-1230.
Penalty.
    Reduction by clerk, §35A-1233.
Public guardian, §35A-1271.
Real property.
    Increase on sale of realty, §35A-1231(b).
Recording, §35A-1231(a).
Renewal, §35A-1236.
    Failure to renew, §35A-1236.
Required, §35A-1230.
Standby guardians for minor children, §35A-1380.
Sureties.
    Relief of endangered sureties, §35A-1237.
Terms of bond, §35A-1231(a).
Health care facilities.
Certificates of need.
    Administrative review, §131E-188(a1).
    Appeal of final decision by department,
        §131E-188(b1).
Hearing aid dealers and fitters.
Board.
    Secretary-treasurer, §93D-3(d).
Historic properties.
Special peace officers to be bonded, §121-10(c).
Home inspectors, §143-151.58(b).
Housemovers.
In addition to insurance coverages required,
    §20-359.1(d).

BONDS, SURETY —Cont'd
Illegitimacy.
Support of illegitimate children.
    Bond for future appearance of defendant, §49-9.
Industrial development commission, §158-21.
Infractions.
Appearance bonds, §15A-1113(c).
Injunctions, §1A-1 Rule 65(c).
Appeals.
    Restraining orders and injunctions in effect
        pending appeals, §1-500.
Insurance.
Reciprocal insurance.
    Domestic reciprocals.
        Attorney's bond, §§58-15-105, 58-15-110.
Supervision, rehabilitation and liquidation of
    insurers.
    Claims of surety, §58-30-210.
    Commissioner and deputies.
        Responsibility on official bonds, §58-30-30.
Insurance adjusters.
Public adjusters, §58-33A-50.
Insurance brokers, §58-33-30(f).
Insurance premium financing.
Licensees, §58-35-15(a).
Interest.
Default judgments.
    Clerk to ascertain interest, §24-6.
Penal bonds.
    Exceptions to contract rate, §24-5(a).
    Legal rate from date of entry of judgment,
        §24-5(a1).
Investment advisers, §78C-17(e).
Irrigation contractors, §89G-6(a).
Job listing services.
Licensure requirement, §95-47.22(b).
Required, §95-47.24.
Judges.
Official bonds.
    Vacancy declared.
        Statement of proceedings filed with
            commissioners, §58-72-45.
Judgments.
Cancellation as to surety, §26-11.
Failure of surety companies to pay judgment,
    §58-73-25.
Principal and surety distinguished in judgment
    and execution, §26-1.
Judicial sales.
Bond of person holding sale, §1-339.10.
Upset bid on real property at public sales,
    §1-339.25(b).
Justification of sureties.
Official bonds, §58-72-30.
    Compelling justification before judge.
        Effect of failure.
            Successor bonded, §58-72-40.
    Considered debts and liabilities, §58-72-40.
    Oath required, §58-72-30.
    Successor bonded, §58-72-40.
**Kerosene distributors, suppliers and terminal
    operators.**
License requirement, §119-15.3.
Landlord and tenant.
Summary ejectment.
    Payment to stay execution of judgment,
        §§42-34.1(b), 42-34(b) to (c1).
    Undertaking to stay order of execution.
        Form of undertaking, §42-34(d).
Tenant security deposit act.
    Landlord may furnish bond from insurance
        company, §42-50.

BONDS, SURETY —Cont'd
Limitation of actions.
Bail.
Action against bail, §1-52.
Fiduciaries, §1-50(a).
Action against surety, §1-52.
Model payment and performance bond.
Actions on payment bonds, §44A-28(b).
Personal representatives, §1-50(a).
Action against surety, §1-52.
Public officers and employees, §1-52.
Liquefied petroleum gases.
Dealers.
Bond as substitute for liability insurance,
§119-56.
Livestock markets.
Required bonds of operators of public livestock
markets, §106-407.
Loan brokers.
Requirements as to bond or trust account,
§66-108(a).
Noncompliance misdemeanor, §66-108(b).
Local governments.
Finance.
Blanket performance bond, §159-29(c).
Finance officer's bond, §159-29(a).
Individuals handling money, §159-29(b).
Lost instruments and records.
Action on destroyed bond, §98-9.
Lotteries.
State lottery.
Retailers.
Bonds or letters of credit, furnishing,
§18C-143(c).
Magistrates, §7A-174.
**Manufactured home manufacturers, dealers,
salespersons or set-up contractors,**
§143-143.12.
Mass gatherings.
Provisional permit.
Forfeiture of bond, §130A-256(d).
Performance bond or other surety to be filed,
§130A-255(a).
**Mechanics, laborers and materialmen dealing
with owner.**
Deposit of bond and satisfaction of lien.
Discharge of record lien, §44A-16(a).
Medical board secretary, §90-7.
Membership camping.
Nondisturbance agreement.
Surety bond in lieu of agreement, §66-246.
Military property sales facilities, §127B-4(c).
Militia.
Property and fiscal officer of North Carolina,
§127A-22(c).
Mines and minerals.
Forfeiture, §§74-56(d), 74-59.
Generally, §74-54.
Permits, §§74-51, 74-54.
Bond required, §74-50(c).
Modifications, §74-52(d).
Release, §74-56(c).
Missing persons.
Temporary, §28C-3.
Mobile homes and trailers.
Approval by board, §143-143.12.
Model payment and performance bonds,
§§44A-25 to 44A-35.
Money transmitters.
Licenses, §53-208.8.

BONDS, SURETY —Cont'd
Mortgage bankers, brokers and servicers.
Surety bond requirement, §53-244.103(b).
Replacement bond, §53-244.103(c).
Summary reinstatement of bond requirement,
§53-244.103(e).
Waiver of bond requirement, §53-244.103(d).
Mortgage in lieu of bond, §§58-74-1 to 58-74-35.
Affidavit of value of property required, §58-74-30.
Civil cases.
Prosecuting or defending civil case, §58-74-25.
Clerk of superior court.
Depositing mortgage with register of deeds,
§58-74-20.
Executing mortgage on real estate of value of
required bond, §58-74-1.
Official bonds, §58-74-1.
Recognizance for appearance in criminal
proceeding, §58-74-5.
Cancellation of mortgage in such proceedings,
§58-74-10.
Register of deeds.
Clerk of court may give surety by mortgage
deposited with register, §58-74-20.
Security of costs or fine in criminal action,
§58-74-5.
Cancellation of mortgage in such proceedings,
§58-74-10.
Special proceedings.
Prosecuting or defending special proceeding,
§58-74-25.
Statute.
Validating statute, §58-74-15.
Validating statute, §58-74-15.
Value of property required.
Affidavit of value, §58-74-30.
When additional security required, §58-74-35.
When additional security required, §58-74-35.
Motor carriers.
Joinder of surety prohibited, §62-274.
Road tax on carriers using fuel purchased outside
state.
Refunds to motor carriers who give bond,
§105-449.40.
Security for protection of public, §62-268.
Motor clubs and associations.
Prerequisite to issuance of license, §58-69-10.
**Motor vehicle dealers' or manufacturers'
licenses,** §20-288(e).
Cancellation by surety, §20-288(f).
Refusal to renew, §20-288(g).
Motor vehicle license plate contractors,
§20-63.01.
Motor vehicles.
Actions against company executing, §20-279.24(b).
Authorized surety companies, §20-279.24(a).
Brokers, §62-263(e).
Cancellation of surety, §20-279.29.
Financial responsibility.
Proof of financial responsibility, §§20-279.18,
20-279.24.
Methods, §20-279.18.
Real estate, §20-279.24(a).
Municipalities.
Cemetery trustees.
Secretary and treasurers, §160A-349.2.
Order of abatement, §160A-175(e).
Solicitation campaigns.
Adequate bond posted to protect public from
fraud, §160A-178.

BONDS, SURETY —Cont'd
Mutual burial associations.
Secretary or secretary-treasurer, §90-210.95.
Navigation and pilotage.
Pilots, §76-45.
Cape Fear river, §76A-5(e).
Nonpublic post-secondary educational institutions.
Licensing.
Guaranty bond required of applicant, §116-15(f1).
Notice.
Surety companies.
Clerk to notify county commissioners of condition of company, §58-73-10.
Surety, indorser or guarantor may notify creditor to take action, §26-7(a).
Applicability of provisions, §26-7(d).
Effect of failure of creditor to take action.
Discharge of parties, §26-9(a).
Separate notice of co-sureties, co-indorsers or co-guarantors, §26-9(c).
Waiver of defense provisions, §26-9(b).
Evidence of notice, §26-8(c).
Extent of notice, §26-7(b).
Holder or owner of obligation to disclose other sureties, indorsers and guarantors, etc., §26-7(c).
Method of notice, §26-8(a).
Return of service, §26-8(b).
Nuisances.
Abatement.
Offenses against public morals.
Preliminary injunction, §19-2.1.
Nurses.
Nurses aides registry, §90-171.55(b).
Nurses aides registry, §90-171.55(b).
Oaths.
Justification of sureties on official bonds, §58-72-30.
Official bonds of county officers generally, §§58-72-1 to 58-72-70.
See OFFICIAL BONDS OF COUNTY OFFICERS.
Oil and gas conservation.
Hearings before department.
Stay bond, §113-407.
Persons drilling for oil or gas to register and furnish bond, §113-378.
Violations, §113-380.
Ordinances.
Enforcement of ordinances.
Unlawful use of real property, §160A-175(e).
Parties.
Satisfaction.
Defendant may plead satisfaction, §1-60.
Partnerships.
Surviving partners, §§59-74, 59-75.
Purchase by surviving partner, §59-81(c).
Pawnbrokers and cash converters, §91A-14.
Payment bonds.
Model payment and performance bonds generally, §§44A-25 to 44A-35.
See PAYMENT AND PERFORMANCE BONDS.
Penal bonds, interest, §24-5(a), (a1).
Performance bonds.
Model payment and performance bonds generally, §§44A-25 to 44A-35.
See PAYMENT AND PERFORMANCE BONDS.
Pesticides.
Licenses.
Financial responsibility of licensees, §143-467(a), (b).

BONDS, SURETY —Cont'd
Pesticides —Cont'd
Rules and regulations, §143-467(c).
Physicians and surgeons.
Revocation or suspension of license.
Appeal bond, §90-14.9(a).
Medical board not required to give, §90-14.11(a).
Pilots.
Navigation and pilotage.
Cape Fear river, §76A-5(e).
Pleadings.
Surety companies.
Not to plead ultra vires, §58-73-20.
Post-secondary educational institutions.
Nonpublic institutions.
Licensing.
Guaranty bond required of applicant, §116-15(f1).
Precious metal dealers.
Permits.
Bond or trust account required, §66-168.
Preliminary injunctions, §1A-1 Rule 65(c).
Premiums on bonds.
Official bonds.
When county may pay premiums, §58-72-15.
Prepaid entertainment contracts, §66-124.
Records, §66-124.1.
Principal and agent.
Actions on bonds.
Evidence against principal admissible against sureties, §58-76-25.
Death of principal.
Subrogation of surety paying debt, §26-4.
Distinguish between surety and principal in judgment and execution, §26-1.
Liability on execution before surety, §26-2.
Remedies of surety against principal.
Summary remedy of surety, §26-3.
Prisons and prisoners.
Persons authorized to collect or receive moneys, §148-2(a).
Private personnel services.
Licensees, §95-47.2(j).
Private protective services, §74C-10.
Professional counselors.
Injunctive relief.
Board not required to post bond, §90-342.
Professional employer organizations.
Surety bond filed by applicant for license, §58-89A-50.
Proprietary schools.
Guaranty bond.
Operating school without bond, §115D-96.
Required for school's license to operate, §115D-95.
Prosecution bonds, §§1-109 to 1-112.
Indigent, suit as, §1-110(a).
Land actions.
Defendant's bond for costs, §1-111.
Plaintiff not entitled to recover, certification by attorney.
Bond not required, §1-112(a).
Summary ejectment.
Bond not required, §1-112(b).
Unable to give bond, not worth amount, affidavit by defendant.
Bond not required, §1-112(a).
Plaintiff's bond for costs, §1-109.
Prisoners.
Pro se motion to proceed as indigent, §1-110(a), (b).

BONDS, SURETY —Cont'd
Public building contracts.
Bid bond in lieu of cash deposits, §143-129(b).
Performance bonds, §143-129(c).
Procurement from particular surety, agent,
    producer or broker.
    Officer or employee requiring prohibited,
        §58-31-66.
Public officers and employees.
Acting as officer before qualifying as such,
    §14-229.
Actions on bonds.
    Venue, §1-78.
Official bonds.
    County officers generally, §§58-72-1 to 58-72-70.
      See OFFICIAL BONDS OF COUNTY
        OFFICERS.
    On presentation of proper bond officer to be
      inducted, §58-73-30.
Penalty for officer acting without bond, §58-72-5.
Retention of funds of county or town by
    delinquent official.
    Citizen to recover funds, §128-10.
Surety companies.
    State officers may be bonded in surety company,
      §58-73-1.
Public schools.
School finance officer and other officers, employees
    and agents, §115C-442(a) to (c).
Public utilities.
Generally, §62-64.
Rates.
    Temporary rates, §62-135(c).
Quo warranto.
Action by private person with leave, §1-516.
    Leave withdrawn and action dismissed for
      insufficient bond, §1-518.
    Solvent sureties required, §1-517.
Appeals, §1-529.
Defendant's undertaking before answer, §1-523.
    Judgment by default and inquiry on failure of
      defendant to give bond, §1-525.
Radiation protection.
Security for emergency response and perpetual
    maintenance costs, §104E-18(a).
Powers of commission as to, §104E-18(b).
Real estate brokers and salespersons.
Private real estate schools, §93A-36.
Real property.
Defendant's bond for costs and damages in land
    actions, §§1-111, 1-112(a), (b).
Warranties.
    Required for certain warranties, §58-1-20(b).
Receivers, §1-504.
Applicant for receiver.
    Furnishing bond to adverse party, §1-502.1.
Receivers of corporations, §1-507.2.
Refusal of appointment on bond being given,
    §1-503.
Recordari, §1-269.
Records.
Approval of official bonds.
    Clerk records vote approving bond, §58-72-55.
Register of deeds, §161-4(a).
Mortgage in lieu of bond.
    Clerk of court may give surety by mortgage
      deposited with register, §58-74-20.
Official bonds of county officers generally,
    §§58-72-1 to 58-72-70.
    See OFFICIAL BONDS OF COUNTY
      OFFICERS.

BONDS, SURETY —Cont'd
Register of deeds —Cont'd
Vacancies in office.
    Assistant or deputy register of deeds holding
      over, §161-4(b).
Rental referral agencies, §66-145(b).
Actions on bond, §66-145(c).
Restraining orders, §1A-1 Rule 65(c).
**Retirement system for teachers and state
    employees.**
Management of funds.
    Personal profit or acting as surety prohibited,
      §135-7(e).
Savings and loan associations.
Blanket indemnity bond, §54B-109(a).
Collection agents, §54B-109(b).
Examination by commissioner, §54B-109(e).
Unauthorized investments.
    Indemnity bond, §54B-109(c), (d).
Savings banks.
Blanket indemnity bond, §54C-109(a).
Collection agents, §54C-109(b).
Securities regulation.
Dealers and salesmen, §78A-37(d).
Service of process.
Habeas corpus ad testificandum.
    Applicant to give bond, §17-44.
Model payment and performance bond.
    Service of notice, §44A-27(c).
Surety, indorser or guarantor may notify creditor
    to take action.
    Method of notice, §26-8(a).
Sheriffs.
Boards of county commissioners.
    Duties as to bond of sheriff, §§162-9, 162-10.
Generally, §162-8.
Liability of surety, §162-12.
Official bonds of county officers generally,
    §§58-72-1 to 58-72-70.
    See OFFICIAL BONDS OF COUNTY
      OFFICERS.
Small business contractors.
Bonding assistance, §143B-472.107.
    Conditions, §143B-472.108.
    Small business surety bond fund,
      §143B-472.106.
    Surety bonding line, §143B-472.109.
Soil and water conservation districts.
Board of supervisors, §139-7.
Solicitors of contributions, §131F-16(d).
Special proceedings.
Commissioners.
    Sale of property, §§1-407 to 1-407.2.
Mortgage in lieu of bond.
    Prosecuting or defending special proceeding,
      §58-74-25.
State lottery.
Retailers.
    Bonds or letters of credit, furnishing,
      §18C-143(c).
State treasurer.
Depositories, §147-78.
State funds, §147-79.
Stay of execution.
Dissenting surety not liable to surety on stay of
    execution, §26-6.
Subrogation.
Surety paying debt of deceased principal
    subrogated, §26-4.
Summary remedy of surety, §26-3.
Summary remedy on official bond, §58-76-15.

BONDS, SURETY —Cont'd
Superior courts.
Clerks of court, §7A-107.
Employees of office of clerk, §7A-107.
Mortgage in lieu of bond.
Depositing mortgage with register of deeds, §58-74-20.
Supersedeas.
Issuance to suspend execution, §1-269.
Supreme court.
Clerk of the supreme court to be bonded, §7A-11.
Surety companies, §§58-73-1 to 58-73-35.
See SURETY COMPANIES.
Surveyors of counties.
Official bonds of county officers generally, §§58-72-1 to 58-72-70.
See OFFICIAL BONDS OF COUNTY OFFICERS.
Telephonic sellers.
Gift or prize, §66-263.
Terms of official bonds, §58-72-10.
Tobacco products tax.
Dealers.
Wholesale dealer or retail dealer, §105-113.38.
Transfers to minors.
Custodians, §33A-15(c).
Treasurers of counties.
Official bonds of county officers generally, §§58-72-1 to 58-72-70.
See OFFICIAL BONDS OF COUNTY OFFICERS.
Trust companies.
Directors.
Surety and indemnity bond, §53-358(a), (b).
Seizure by commissioner, §53-384.
Injunction of action by commissioner, §53-382(a).
Trusts and trustees.
Class in esse.
Sale of property held by, §41-11.1(d).
Trustee's bond, §36C-7-702.
Tryon's Palace.
Financial officer and treasurer designated by commission to disburse funds and property, §121-20(a).
Ultra vires.
Surety companies not to plead ultra vires, §58-73-20.
Universities and colleges.
Nonpublic post-secondary educational institutions.
Licensing.
Guaranty bond required of applicant, §116-15(f1).
Uranium exploration permits, §§74-78 to 74-81, 74-83.
Vegetables.
Unfair practices by handlers of vegetables.
Required bond, §106-498.
Veterans' guardianship act.
Guardians.
Separate bond for each appointment, §34-4.
Warehouses.
Public warehousemen, §66-36.
Injured person may sue on bond, §66-37.
Warehouse receipts.
Indorser not guarantor for other parties, §25-7-505.
Warranties.
Real property.
Required for certain warranty, §58-1-20(b).

BONDS, SURETY —Cont'd
Water and sewer companies.
Required, §62-110.3.
Water supply and waterworks.
Water and sewer companies.
Required, §62-110.3.
Wills.
Caveat to wills.
See WILLS.
Executors and administrators.
Executing will without giving bond, §28A-26-4.
Workers' compensation.
Self-insurance.
Employer groups, §58-47-90(e), (f).
Self-insurers.
Deposits with commissioner.
Individual self-insurers excluded from association aggregate security systems, §97-185.
Licensure.
Deposit of securities or surety bond by applicants, §97-170(e).

BONE DISEASE.
Food, drug and cosmetic act.
Drug or device, false advertising, §106-138(b).

BONE MASS MEASUREMENT.
Diagnosis and evaluation of osteoporosis and low bone mass.
Health benefit plan coverage, §58-3-174.

BONUSES FOR COST SAVINGS SUGGESTIONS OR INNOVATIONS.
State employee suggestion program (NC-Thinks), §§143-345.20 to 143-345.25.

BOOK ACCOUNTS.
Shop-book rule, §§8-42 to 8-44.

BOOK CLUBS.
Discount buying clubs generally, §§66-131 to 66-137.
See DISCOUNT BUYING CLUBS.

BOOKMAKING.
Gambling and betting contracts.
Prohibited, §§16-1, 16-2.
Gambling generally.
See GAMBLING.
Organized crime.
RICO generally, §§75D-1 to 75D-14.
See RACKETEER INFLUENCED AND CORRUPT ORGANIZATIONS (RICO).

BOOK OF ORDERS APPOINTING RECEIVERS OF JUDGMENT DEBTORS.
Clerk of court to file and record appointment, §1-364.

BOOKS.
Exemption from creditors' claims, §1C-1601(a).

BOONE.
Room occupancy tax.
Uniform provisions.
Authorized to levy, §160A-215(g).
Generally, §160A-215.

BOOTLEGGING, §18B-304.
Unauthorized substances taxes, §§105-113.105 to 105-113.113.
See UNAUTHORIZED SUBSTANCES TAXES.

BORROWING MONEY.
Airport authorities, §159-210.

BORROWING MONEY —Cont'd
Bond issues.
See BOND ISSUES.
Consolidated city-county act.
Authorized, §160B-13.
Debt limitations, §160B-15.
Credit unions.
Powers of credit unions generally, §54-109.21.
Electric membership corporations.
Specific grant of power, §117-18.
Fairs.
State fair.
Constructing and financing facilities and
improvements, §106-503.1(a).
Hospital authorities.
Contracts with federal government, §131E-27.
Housing finance agency.
General power of agency, §122A-5.
Loans.
See LOANS.
Local government finance.
Regulation, NC Const Art V §4.
Mosquito control districts.
Corporate powers of board of commissioners,
§130A-355.
Railroads.
Powers of railroad corporations, §136-190.
Savings and loan associations.
Mutual deposit guaranty associations.
Powers of associations, §54B-244(b).
Power to borrow money, §54B-162.
Savings banks.
Power to borrow money, §54C-176.
State debt.
See STATE DEBT.

BOTTLED WATER.
Contracts for sale of.
Educational institutions to competitively bid,
§143-64.

BOTTLER PERMIT.
Authorization, §18B-1110.
Distribution agreements, §18B-1110(b).

BOTTLES.
Containers generally.
See CONTAINERS.
Polluting bottles.
Unlawful to pollute bottles used for beverages,
§14-288.

BOUNCED CHECKS.
Bad checks generally.
See BAD CHECKS.

BOUNDARIES.
Adverse possession.
Color of title.
Known and visible lines and boundaries, §1-38.
Annexation.
Extension of corporate limits generally, §§160A-29
to 160A-58.90.
See ANNEXATION.
Coastal lands.
Seaward boundary.
High water mark, §77-20(a) to (e).
Condominiums.
Relocation of boundaries between adjoining units,
§47C-2-112.
Units, §47C-2-102.
Declaration amendment changing,
§47C-2-117(d).

BOUNDARIES —Cont'd
Constitution of North Carolina.
State boundaries, NC Const Art XIV §2.
Conveyances.
Use of word adjoining instead of words bounded
by, §39-2.
Coordinate system.
Use in descriptions, §102-6.
Counties, §§153A-17 to 153A-22.
Criminal trespass.
Landmarks.
Removing, altering or defacing landmarks,
§14-147.
Drainage districts.
Establishment, §156-65.
Extension, §156-93.3.
Existing districts may act together, §156-93.7.
Election precincts, §§163-132.3 to 163-132.5F.
**Establishing boundaries and interest where
conveyance and copy lost, §98-3.**
Fires and fire protection.
Rural fire protection districts.
Changes in area of district, §69-25.11.
**Hearsay exception, reputation concerning,
§8C-1 Rule 803.**
Hospital authorities.
Creation of authority, §131E-17(a) to (c).
Housing authorities and projects.
Area of operation, §157-39.1(a) to (c).
Land boundary corners.
Use of coordinate system in description, §102-6.
Landmarks.
Removing, altering or defacing landmarks.
Criminal trespass, §14-147.
Lost instruments and records.
Establishing boundaries where conveyance and
copy lost, §98-3.
Metropolitan sewerage districts.
Description, §162A-65(b).
Metropolitan water districts.
Description, §162A-32(b).
Municipalities.
Corporate limits.
General provisions, §§160A-21 to 160A-58.28.
See MUNICIPALITIES.
Sanitary district and municipality extending
boundaries simultaneously, §130A-70(a) to
(h).
Parking authorities.
Coterminous with boundaries of city, §160A-552.
Petitions.
Special proceeding to establish, §38-3(a).
Public health authorities.
Operating facilities outside territorial limits,
§130A-45.6.
Public lands.
Allocated state lands, §§146-33, 146-34.
Grants.
Correction of grants.
Change of county line before grant issued or
registered, §146-47.
Public schools.
Special taxing districts.
Superintendents to furnish boundaries,
§115C-500.
**Referees, compulsory reference, §1A-1 Rule
53(a).**
Sanitary districts, §130A-49(a).
Extension of boundaries.
Municipality and district extending boundaries
simultaneously, §130A-70(a) to (h).

BOUNDARIES —Cont'd
Sanitary districts —Cont'd
Extension of boundaries —Cont'd
Validation of extension, §130A-75(a), (b).
Industrial villages.
Status within boundaries of district,
§130A-49(b).
Seaward boundary of coastal lands.
High water mark, §77-20(a) to (e).
Special proceeding to establish, §§38-1 to 38-4.
Appeals, §38-3(b).
Authorized, §38-1.
Disputed boundaries.
Surveys, §38-4(a).
Hearing, §38-3(a).
Judgments.
Survey after judgment, §38-3(c).
Notice.
Appeals, §38-3(b).
Occupation sufficient ownership, §38-2.
Petition, §38-3(a).
Procedure, §38-3(d).
Summons.
Failure to answer, §38-3(a).
Issuance by clerk, §38-3(a).
Surveys.
After final judgment, §38-3(c).
Appointment of surveyor, §38-4(b).
Calling surveyors as witnesses, §38-4(c).
Disputed boundaries, §38-4(a).
Fees for surveyors, §38-4(d).
Order by clerk, §38-3(a).
Venue, §38-1.
Witnesses.
Surveyors, §38-4(c).
State boundaries, §§141-1 to 141-8, NC Const Art
XIV §2.
Subdivisions.
Control corners.
Use to fix boundaries prima facie evidence of
correct method, §39-32.4.
Summons and process.
Special proceeding to establish boundaries,
§38-3(a).
Townships, §153A-19(a) to (c).
Transportation engineering divisions.
Designation of boundaries by department,
§136-14.1.
Trees and timber.
Unlawful cutting or removal of timber as result of
misrepresentation of property lines,
§1-539.1(c).
Trespass.
Criminal trespass.
Removing, altering or defacing landmarks,
§14-147.
Veterans' recreation authorities, §165-26.

BOUNTY HUNTERS.
Governor authorized to employ, §15-53.

BOW HUNTING.
Method of taking wild animals or wild birds,
§113-291.1(a).
Nongame fish.
Taking in inland and joint fishing waters,
§113-275(k).

BOWIE KNIVES.
Carrying concealed weapons, §14-269.
Confiscation and disposition, §14-269.1.

BOWIE KNIVES —Cont'd
Possessing and carrying on educational
property, §14-269.2.
Sale to minor, §14-315.
Weapons generally.
See FIREARMS AND OTHER WEAPONS.

BOWLING ALLEYS.
Child care facilities.
Drop-in or short-term child care not included in
term child care, §110-86.

BOXES.
Flat trucks loaded with.
Load to be securely fastened, §20-120.

BOXING, §§143-651 to 143-658.
Advisory commission.
Compensation, §143-652.2(e).
Creation, §143-652.2(a).
Meetings, §143-652.2(c).
Members, §143-652.2(a).
Review of rules and regulations, §143-652.2(d).
Staff assistance, §143-652.2(f).
Term of appointment, §143-652.2(g).
Vacancies, §143-652.2(b).
Alcohol law enforcement section.
Regulation of boxing, rules, authority to issue,
§143-652.1.
Athletic contests generally.
See ATHLETICS.
Bond.
Promoters, §143-654(c).
Civil penalties, §143-658(a).
Contract requirements, §143-656.
Corporation or partnership.
Manger's or promoter's license issued to,
§143-654(b).
Criminal penalties, §143-658(b).
Definitions, §143-651.
Fees.
Admission, §143-655(b1).
Licenses, §143-655(a).
Permits, §143-655(b).
Fictitious or assumed names.
Persons may not participate under, §143-654(b).
Financial arrangements, §143-656.
Injunctions, §143-658(c).
Licenses.
Bond for promoter's license, §143-654(c).
Fees, §143-655(a).
Generally, §143-654(b).
Required, §143-654(a).
Permits.
Fees, §143-655(b).
Promoters.
Required, §143-654(a).
Valid for single match, §143-654(d).
Promoters.
Bond for license, §143-654(c).
Permits.
Fees, §143-655(b).
Valid for single match, §143-654(d).
Rules regulating boxing, §143-652.1.
Sanctioned amateur matches, §143-657.1.
State boxing revenue account, §143-655(c).
Unarmed combat matches prohibited, §143-653.

BOXING REVENUE ACCOUNT, §143-655(c).

BOYCOTTS.
Insurance.
Unfair trade practices.
Prohibited acts, §58-63-15.

BPOL TAXES.
License taxes generally, §§105-33 to 105-109.
See LICENSE TAXES.

BRAILLE.
Textbook contracts to include clause granting state board of education license to produce, §115C-90.

BRAIN DEATH.
Defined, §90-323.
Right to natural death generally, §§90-320 to 90-323.
See RIGHT TO NATURAL DEATH.
Use as sole basis for determination of death, §90-323.

BRAIN INJURIES.
Brain injury advisory council, §§143B-216.65, 143B-216.66.
Chair, §143B-216.66(c).
Clerical and other assistance, §143B-216.66(f).
Duties, §143B-216.65.
Established, §143B-216.65.
Meetings, quorum, §143B-216.66(d).
Members, terms, vacancies, expenses, §143B-216.66(a), (b), (e).
Interscholastic athletic activities.
Concussions and head injuries, §115C-12.
Workers' compensation.
Brain or closed head injury.
Permanent total disability.
Qualification for, lifetime compensation, §97-29(d).

BRAKE LININGS.
Type and brand to be approved by commissioner of motor vehicles, §20-124(h).

BRAKES.
All-terrain vehicles, §20-171.18.
Hydraulic brake fluid.
Restrictions on sale, §20-124(h).
Linings.
Approved brake lining, §20-124(h).
Motorcycles and motor-driven cycles, §20-124(d).
Repair of motor vehicles, §§20-354 to 20-354.9.
See MOTOR VEHICLE REPAIRS.
Requirements generally, §20-124(a), (c).
Safety inspections.
Scope of inspections, §20-183.3(a).
Sales.
Restrictions, §20-124(h).
Trailers.
Inapplicability of provisions.
Trailers used by farmers, §20-124(g).
Requirements, §20-124(f).
Semitrailer attached to truck tractor.
Requirements, §20-124(e), (e1).
Trucks.
Requirements for motor trucks, §20-124(e), (e1).
Truck tractors.
Requirements, §20-124(e), (e1).
Violations of restriction on sales, §20-124(h).

BRAN.
Standard weights and measures, §81A-42.

BRANCH BANKS.
Authorized, §53-62(b).
Capital requirements for establishment, §53-62(c).
Commissioner of banks.
Approval of establishment, §53-62(b).
Capital requirements, §53-62(c).

BRANCH BANKS —Cont'd
Commissioner of banks —Cont'd
Review of commissioner's actions by state banking commission, §53-62(f).
Definition of "branch,"§53-1.
Discontinuance, §53-62(e).
Industrial banks.
Power to establish, §53-141.
Interstate banking, §§53-224.9 to 53-224.31.
Acquisition of a branch, §53-224.13.
Conditions for acquiring and maintaining, §53-224.14(b), (c).
Conditions for approval, §53-224.15.
Notice of desire to acquire and maintain, §53-224.14(a).
Additional branches, §53-224.27.
Appeal of commissioner's decisions, §53-224.30.
Bank mergers, §§53-224.17 to 53-224.22.
Closing of branches, §53-224.29.
Cooperative agreements, §53-224.24(c).
Definitions, §53-224.9.
De novo banks, §53-224.12.
Conditions for approval, §53-224.15.
Conditions for establishing and maintaining, §53-224.14(b), (c).
Notice of desire to establish and maintain, §53-224.14.
Enforcement of laws, §53-224.25.
Examination of out-of-state, state bank branches, §53-224.24(a).
Fees to be paid by out-of-state, state banks, §53-224.24(d).
North Carolina state banks in other states.
Application process, §53-224.11(b).
Authorized, §53-224.11(a).
Notice of subsequent merger or other change in control, §53-224.28.
Periodic reports of out-of-state, state banks, §53-224.24(b).
Powers of North Carolina state banks doing business in other states, §53-224.16(b).
Powers of out-of-state banks, §53-224.16(a).
Purpose of law, §53-224.10.
Rulemaking authority, §53-224.26.
Savings and loan associations, §§54B-265 to 54B-278.
See SAVINGS AND LOAN ASSOCIATIONS.
Savings banks, §§54C-199 to ?54C-212.
See SAVINGS BANKS.
Severability of supervisory provisions, §53-224.31.
Supervisory authority.
Applicability, §53-224.23.
Generally, §§53-224.24 to 53-224.31.
Interstate bank mergers.
Conditions for interstate merger prior to June 1, 1997, §53-224.21.
North Carolina state banks.
Establishing of out-of-state branches by merger, §53-224.18.
Powers of branches resulting from merger, §53-224.22(b).
Notice and filing requirements, §53-224.20.
Out-of-state banks.
Establishing of North Carolina state branches by merger, §53-224.19.
Powers of branches resulting from merger, §53-224.22(a).
Purpose of law, §53-224.17.
Limited service facilities.
Conversion of limited service facility to branch, §53-62(d).

BRANCH BANKS —Cont'd
Loan committee, §53-78.
Officers, §53-62(c).
Operation, §53-62(c).
Out-of-state branch banks, §§53-224.9 to
53-224.31. See within this heading, "Interstate
banking."
School thrift or savings plan.
Acceptance of deposits not construed as
establishment or operation of branch,
§53-43.6(b).
State banking commission.
Review of actions of commissioner, §53-62(f).

BRANDISHING.
Habitual misdemeanor assault, §14-33.2.
Pointing firearm at person, §14-34.

BRANDS AND MARKS.
Farm products.
Marketing and branding farm products, §§106-185
to 106-196.
See FARM PRODUCTS MARKETING AND
BRANDING.
Fertilizers.
Registration of brands, §106-660.
Gold, §80-40.
Articles of gold plate, §80-42.
Violations of provisions.
Misdemeanors, §80-44.
Greases.
Juggling mark prohibited, §119-10.
Mixing different brands for sale under standard
trade name prohibited, §119-11.
Health.
Embargo of adulterated or misbranded food,
§130A-21(a) to (e).
Labels generally.
See LABELS.
Limestone, marl and landplaster.
Sale of agricultural liming materials and
landplaster.
Registration of brands by distributors,
§106-92.7.
Liquid fuels.
Juggling trademark prohibited, §119-10.
Mixing different brands for sale under standard
trade name prohibited, §119-11.
Livestock generally, §§80-45 to 80-66.
See LIVESTOCK BRANDS.
Lubricating oils.
Display of brand or trade name of lubricating oil,
§119-2.
Imitation of standard equipment prohibited,
§119-9.
Juggling mark prohibited, §119-10.
Misrepresentation of brands for sale, §119-3.
Mixing different brands for sale under standard
trade name prohibited, §119-11.
Secretary of state.
Duties as to, §147-36.
Silver, §80-41.
Articles of silver plate, §80-43.
Violations of provisions.
Misdemeanors, §80-44.
Timber marks, §§80-15 to 80-23.
See TIMBER MARKS.
Trademarks.
See TRADEMARKS.

BRASS.
Dealing in regulated, §66-11.

BRASS KNUCKLES.
Carrying concealed weapons, §14-269.
Confiscation, §14-269.1.
Possessing or carrying on educational
property, §14-269.2.
Sale to minor, §14-315.
Weapons generally.
See FIREARMS AND OTHER WEAPONS.

BREACH OF THE PEACE.
Assault and battery.
See ASSAULT AND BATTERY.
Disorderly conduct, §§14-132, 14-275.1, 143-345.2.
Nuisances.
Offenses against public morals.
Abatement generally, §§19-1 to 19-8.3.
See NUISANCES.
Riots and civil disorders, §§14-288.1 to
14-288.20.
See RIOTS AND CIVIL DISORDERS.
Secured transactions.
Default.
Agreements as to rights and duties inapplicable
to breach of the peace, §25-9-603(b).
Repossession.
No sanctioning of breach of the peace,
§25-9-609(b).

BREAD.
Sales and use tax exemption.
Bakery items sold by artisan bakeries,
§105-164.13B(a).

BREAKFASTS.
Utility commission members attending public
breakfasts sponsored by public utilities,
§62-327.

BREAKING AND ENTERING.
Alarm systems licensing, §§74D-1 to 74D-14.
See ALARM SYSTEMS LICENSING.
Buildings, §14-54.
Place of religious worship.
Criminal penalty, §14-54.1(a).
Defined, §14-54.1(b).
Burglary generally, §§14-51 to 14-57.
See BURGLARY.
Coin or currency operated machine, §14-56.1.
Defensive force.
Protection of home, workplace, motor vehicle,
§14-51.2.
DNA sample for DNA analysis.
Obtaining upon arrest for certain offenses,
§15A-266.3A.
Executing officer may break and enter
premises, §15A-251.
Habitual breaking and entering status offense,
§§14-7.25 to 14-7.31.
Charging person with status offense, §14-7.28(a).
Definitions, §14-7.25.
Evidence of prior convictions, §14-7.29.
Felony breaking and entering offenses.
Breaking and entering defined, §14-7.25.
Inapplicability of article, §14-7.26.
Indictments.
Requirements, §14-7.28(b).
Separate indictments, §14-7.28(a).
Judgment, §14-7.30(c).
Offenses committed before person 18 years of age.
Not to constitute more than one felony,
§14-7.26.
Pardon extended for breaking and entering
offense.
Not to constitute felony offense, §14-7.26.

BREAKING AND ENTERING —Cont'd
Habitual breaking and entering status offense —Cont'd
Persons who may be charged with, §14-7.26.
Presenting charge of status offender to jury, §14-7.30(a), (b).
Proving prior convictions, §14-7.29.
Punishment, §14-7.27.
Sentencing.
Class B felon, §14-7.31(a).
Commencement, §14-7.31(b).
Consecutive sentence, §14-7.31(b).
Determining prior record level, §14-7.31(b).
Habitual felons or violent habitual felons statutes.
Conviction not considered for sentencing under, §14-7.31(c).
Punishment, §14-7.27.
Separately charged with breaking and entering and status offense, §14-7.28(a).
Status offender defined, §14-7.25.
Trial of breaking and entering offense, §14-7.30(a).
Jails.
Intent to injure prisoners, §14-221.
Motor vehicles.
Preparation to commit breaking and entering into motor vehicle.
Criminal penalty, §14-56.4(d).
Definitions, §14-56.4(a).
Inapplicability to certain persons, §14-56.4(e).
Master key, manipulative key or other lock-picking device or hot wiring device.
Buying, selling or transferring, §14-56.4(c).
Possession with intent to commit felony, larceny or unauthorized use, §14-56.4(b).
Prevention of felonies.
Authorized, §15-43.
Protection of home, workplace, motor vehicle.
Defensive force, §14-51.2.
Railroad cars, motor vehicles, aircraft, etc., §14-56.

BREAKING OUT OF DWELLING HOUSE, §14-53.

BREAST CANCER.
Accident and health insurance.
Mammograms.
Coverage, §58-51-57.
Cancer patient navigation program.
Breast and cervical cancer control program, §130A-216.
Health maintenance organizations, coverage.
Mammograms, §58-67-76.
Hospital, medical and dental services corporations.
Mammograms.
Coverage, §58-65-92.
Mammograms.
Accident and health insurance.
Coverage, §58-51-57.
Accreditation of facilities performing, §143B-165.
Health maintenance organizations, coverage, §58-67-76.
Hospital, medical and dental services corporations.
Coverage, §58-65-92.
Small employer group health coverage, §58-50-155(a).
Mastectomy.
Post-mastectomy inpatient care coverage.
Health benefit plans, §58-3-168.

BREAST CANCER —Cont'd
Reconstructive breast surgery.
Small employer group health coverage, §58-50-155(a).
State health plan for teachers and state employees.
Coverage mandate, §135-48.50.
Reconstructive breast surgery resulting from mastectomy.
Accident and health insurance coverage, §58-51-62.
Health maintenance organizations, coverage, §58-67-79.
Hospital, medical and dental services corporations, coverage, §58-65-96.

BREAST FEEDING.
Not indecent exposure, §14-190.9(b).

BREATHALYZERS.
Arrest.
Used as condition of release, §15A-534.2.
Impaired driving generally.
See IMPAIRED DRIVING.
Required for certain drivers, §20-16.3.

BREWERIES.
Commercial permits, §18B-1100.
Consumption on premises.
Authorization of brewery permit, §18B-1104.
Exclusive outlets, §18B-1116(a).
On-premises malt beverage permit.
Kind of permit that may be issued, §18B-1001.
Recycling requirement, §18B-1006.1.
Permit authorization, §18B-1104.
Sale of breweries malt beverages.
Authorization of brewery permits, §18B-1104.
Vendor representative permit.
Authorization, §18B-1112.

BRIBERY.
Athletic contests.
Players, managers, etc, §14-373.
Acceptance of bribe, §14-374.
Completion of offenses, §14-375.
Completion of offenses, §14-375.
Definition of bribe, §14-376.
Bank directors or officers.
Accepting fees or gifts, §53-86.
Bank examiners.
Accepting bribe, §§14-233, 53-124.
Bank loans or gratuities to, §53-126.
Commercial bribery, §14-353.
Commissioner of banks.
Bank loans or gratuities to, §53-126.
Constitution of the United States, US Const Art II §4.
Department of administration.
Purchases and contracts to department.
Acceptance of bribes, §143-63.
Election officers, §163-275.
Electrologists.
Disciplinary actions, §88A-21(a).
Electronic surveillance orders, §15A-290(b).
Employees violating duties owed employers, §14-353.
General assembly.
Legislative ethics act, §120-86(a).
Horse show judges or officials.
Attempts at bribery to be reported, §14-380.2.
Definition of "bribe," §14-380.3.
Printing provisions of article in horse show schedules, §14-380.4.

BRIBERY —Cont'd
Horse show judges or officials —Cont'd
Protection of horse shows, §14-380.1.
Jurors, §14-220.
Lobbyists or principals offering or giving gifts without corrupt intent.
Statutes not violated, §120C-303(c) to (e).
Meat inspectors, §106-549.26.
Medicaid providers.
Activities inapplicable, §108A-63(i).
Construction of provisions in relation to federal statute, §108A-63(j).
Offering or paying, §108A-63(h).
Soliciting or receiving, §108A-63(g).
Misuse of public office.
Gifts to influence discharge of public duties, §138A-32(a), (i).
Offering bribes, §14-218.
Public officers and employees.
Bribery of officials, §14-217.
Purchases and contracts through department of administration.
Acceptance of bribes, §143-63.
Real estate appraisers.
By real estate appraisal management companies, §93E-2-7(a).
Utilities commission.
Gifts to members, employees or staff, §62-327.
Vice-president of the United States, US Const Art II §4.

BRIDGES.
Burning public bridge, §14-61.
Construction guidelines, §136-44.7D.
Counties.
Authorizing bridges over navigable waters, §153A-243.
Fishing from bridges.
Regulation or prohibition, §153A-242.
Criminal trespass.
Injuring bridges, §14-146.
Destroying, breaking, tearing down, etc., §14-146.
Drainage districts.
Control and repairs, §156-92.
Maintenance of drainage, §156-88.
Draws in bridges.
Commissioners for opening and clearing streams, §77-10.
Railroad companies to provide draws, §136-78.
Eminent domain.
By whom right may be exercised, §40A-3(a).
Environmental policy act.
Replacement program for bridges, §136-76.1(b).
Fastening vessels to bridges misdemeanor, §136-80.
Firefighting equipment used in responding to fire emergency.
Exceeding posted bridge limitation prohibited, §20-118.4(b).
Fishing from bridges.
Counties regulating, §153A-242.
Municipalities.
Power to prohibit or regulate, §160A-302.1.
Signs on bridges, §136-102.5.
Footways.
Maintenance of footways by department of transportation, §136-81.
Herbert C. Bonner bridge replacement project.
Contract for accelerated construction, §136-89.183B(a).

BRIDGES —Cont'd
Herbert C. Bonner bridge replacement project —Cont'd
Report by department, §136-89.183B(c).
Termini location, §136-89.183B(b).
Hurricane evacuation standard for construction projects, §136-102.7.
Hydraulics for flood waters.
Construction guidelines, §136-44.7D.
Load limits for bridges.
Determination of safe load-carrying capacity, §136-72.
Penalty for violations of provisions, §136-72.
Local, private and special legislation prohibited, NC Const Art II §24.
Monuments and memorials.
Historical commission.
Approval before acceptance by state, §100-3.
Motor vehicle speed limitations, §20-144.
Municipalities.
Fishing from bridges.
Power to prohibit or regulate, §160A-302.1.
Parks and recreation.
Toll bridges.
Private operation in public parks, §100-16.
Privately owned bridges, construction and maintenance.
State highway or road right of way.
Use and encroachment, §136-18.
Railroads.
Companies to provide draws, §136-78.
Replacement program.
Completion of program, §136-76.1(a).
Environmental policies.
Applicability of act to bridge replacement program, §136-76.1(b).
Initiation, §136-76.1(a).
Removal of bridges not replaced, §136-76.1(a).
Ships and shipping.
Fastening vessels to bridges misdemeanor, §136-80.
Signs.
Fishing bridges, §136-102.5.
Speed limitations, §20-144.
Toll bridges.
Authority of county commissioners with regard to toll bridges, §136-88.
Burning of certain bridges, §14-61.
Mid-Currituck bridge project, §136-89.183A.
Owners of toll bridges not under supervision of department of transportation.
Rights and liabilities of owners, §136-88.
Private operation in parks, §100-16.
Public toll roads and bridges.
Turnpike authority, §§136-89.180 to 136-89.218.
See TURNPIKE AUTHORITY.
Transportation department.
Disposal of debris, §136-97(b).
Maintenance of footways, §136-81.
Vessels.
Fastening vessels to bridges misdemeanor, §136-80.
Yadkin river bridge replacement project.
Contract for accelerated construction, §136-89.183C(a).
Proximity and termini, §136-89.183C(b).

BRIDGETON.
Satellite annexation.
Limitation on area of satellite corporate limits, inapplicability, §160A-58.1(b).

BRIEFS.
Appeals.
Additional authorities.
  Memorandum, AppProc Rule 28(g).
Additional issues.
  Appellee's brief, AppProc Rule 28(c).
Amicus curiae briefs, AppProc Rule 28(i).
Appeal of right from court of appeals to supreme
    court, AppProc Rule 14(d).
Appellant's brief.
  Appendixes.
    When not required, AppProc Rule 28(d).
    When required, AppProc Rule 28(d).
  Content, AppProc Rule 28(b).
Appellee's brief.
  Additional issues, AppProc Rule 28(c).
  Content, AppProc Rule 28(c).
Appendixes.
  Verbatim portion of transcript, AppProc Rule
    28(d).
Arrangement, AppProc Appx E.
Case submitted for decision on written briefs,
    AppProc Rule 30(d).
Content, AppProc Appx E.
  Appellant's brief, AppProc Rule 28(b).
  Appellee's brief, AppProc Rule 28(c).
Copies.
  Appeal of right from court of appeals to
    supreme court, AppProc Rule 14(d).
  Clerk to reproduce and distribute, AppProc Rule
    13(b).
Death penalty cases.
  Filing and serving, time, AppProc Rule 13(a).
Filing and serving.
  Failure, consequences, AppProc Rule 13(c).
  Appeal of right from court of appeals to
    supreme court, AppProc Rule 14(d).
  Time, AppProc Rule 13(a).
    Appeal of right from court of appeals to
      supreme court, AppProc Rule 14(d).
  Rehearing.
    Petition granted, AppProc Rule 31(d).
  Reply briefs, AppProc Rule 28(h).
Function, AppProc Rule 28(a).
Identity of persons under age of 18.
  Protection, AppProc Rule 28(a).
Indexes, AppProc Appx B.
Joinder of multiple parties, AppProc Rule 28(f).
Juvenile matters, AppProc Rule 3.1(c).
  Identity of persons under age of 18.
    Protection, AppProc Rule 28(a).
Length limitations.
  Briefs filed in court of appeals, AppProc Rule
    28(j).
Memorandum.
  Additional authorities, AppProc Rule 28(g).
Order of arrangement, AppProc Appx E.
Page limitations.
  Briefs filed in court of appeals, AppProc Rule
    28(j).
Record on appeal.
  References to, AppProc Rule 28(e).
Rehearing.
  Petition granted, AppProc Rule 31(d).
Reply briefs, AppProc Rule 28(h).
Time.
  Filing and serving, AppProc Rule 13(a).
    Appeal of right from court of appeals to
      supreme court, AppProc Rule 14(d).
    Rehearing.
      Petition granted, AppProc Rule 31(d).

BRIEFS —Cont'd
Appeals —Cont'd
Time —Cont'd
  Filing and serving —Cont'd
    Reply briefs, AppProc Rule 28(h).
Type style, type size.
  Briefs filed in court of appeals, AppProc Rule
    28(j).
Unpublished opinions.
  Citation, AppProc Rule 30(e).
Verbatim portion of transcript.
  Appendixes, AppProc Rule 28(d).
Word count limitations.
  Briefs filed in court of appeals, AppProc Rule
    28(j).
Filing and service.
Dispositive motions.
  Briefs in support or opposition, §1A-1 Rule
    5(a1).
Motions seeking final determination.
Service of briefs in support or opposition, §1A-1
    Rule 5(a1).
Utilities commission proceedings.
Exceptions to recommended decision or order,
    §62-78(b).
Proposed findings of fact and conclusions of law
    prior to decision or order, §62-78(a).
Workers' compensation appeals, ICWorkComp
  Rule 701.

BRIGHT'S DISEASE.
Food, drug and cosmetic act.
Drug or device, false advertising, §106-138(b).

BROADBAND COMMUNICATIONS.
Broadband service providers.
Voice grade communication services, §62-113(c).
Cities providing communications services,
  §§160A-340 to 160A-340.6.
See MUNICIPAL UTILITIES.
Poles, ducts, conduits controlled by
  municipality or membership corporation.
Request to utilize, §62-350.
Transportation department.
Powers of department, §136-18.

BROADCAST DEFAMATION ACT, §§99-1 to
  99-5.
See DEFAMATION.

BROADCASTERS AND BROADCASTING.
Alcoholic beverage advertising, §18B-105(b).
Contempt.
Criminal contempt.
  Basis for holding in contempt, §5A-11(b).
Court orders prohibiting publication or
  broadcast of reports of open court
  proceedings or public records, §7A-276.1.
Journalist's qualified privilege, §8-53.11.
Libel and slander.
See DEFAMATION.
Radio.
See RADIO.
Television.
See TELEVISION.

BROADCAST JOURNALISTS.
Journalist's qualified privilege against
  disclosure in any legal proceeding,
  §8-53.11(b).
Definitions, §8-53.11(a).
Eyewitness observation of criminal or tortuous
    conduct, no privilege, §8-53.11(d).

BROADCAST JOURNALISTS —Cont'd
Journalist's qualified privilege against disclosure in any legal proceeding —Cont'd
Order to compel disclosure, notice to journalist and hearing, §8-53.11(c).
Overcoming privilege, person seeking to compel disclosure, §8-53.11(c).

BROKERS.
Cemetery brokers.
Defined, §65-48.
Licenses, §65-57.
Commodities.
General provisions, §§78D-1 to 78D-33.
See COMMODITIES.
Insurance brokers generally.
See INSURANCE BROKERS.
Loan brokers, §§66-106 to 66-112.
Mortgage bankers, brokers and servicers, §§53-244.010 to 53-244.121.
See MORTGAGE BANKERS, BROKERS AND SERVICERS.
Motor carriers.
Bonds, surety, §62-263(e).
Licenses, §62-263.
Utilities commission.
Regulation of brokers, §62-261.
Pawnbrokers and cash converters, §§91A-1 to 91A-14.
See PAWNBROKERS AND CASH CONVERTERS.
Real estate brokers, §§93A-1 to 93A-38.
See REAL ESTATE BROKERS.
Stockbrokers.
Acting as stockbroker, §14-401.7.

BROKERS' LIENS.
Secured transactions, §25-9-206(a), (b).

BRONZE.
Dealing in regulated, §66-11.

BROOMCORN.
Standard weight and measure, §81A-42.

BROTHELS.
Abatement of nuisances against public morals, §§19-1 to 19-8.3.
See NUISANCES.
Keeping a disorderly or bawdy house, §14-188.
Prostitution.
Generally, §§14-203 to 14-208.
See PROSTITUTION.

BROUGHTON HOSPITAL.
Joint security force, §122C-430.

BROWN-BAGGING ACT, §18B-301.

BROWN-BAGGING PERMIT, §18B-1001.
Fee, §18B-902(d).

BROWNFIELDS PROPERTY REUSE, §§130A-310.30 to 130A-310.40.
Additional remediation of property.
Prospective buyer or other person completing remediation or redevelopment required, §130A-310.33(c).
Appeals.
Decision by department as to whether or not to enter into agreement, §130A-310.36.
Brownfields agreement defined, §130A-310.31(b).
Brownfields property or Brownfields site defined, §130A-310.31(b).
Brownfields property reuse act implementation account, §130A-310.38.
Fees imposed credited to, §130A-310.39(b).

BROWNFIELDS PROPERTY REUSE —Cont'd
Brownfields property reuse act of 1997.
Short title, §130A-310.30.
Cancellation of notice of Brownfields property, §130A-310.35(e).
Comment period during public meeting.
Department to take into account, §130A-310.34(d).
Construction of provisions, §130A-310.37(a).
Deed when Brownfields property sold, lease, conveyed or transferred, §130A-310.35(d).
Definitions, §130A-310.31(a), (b).
Description of Brownfields property.
Brownfields agreement to contain, §130A-310.32(c).
Enforcement of land-use restriction, §130A-310.35(f).
Entry into Brownfields agreement, §130A-310.32.
Environmental assessment conducted on Brownfields property.
Person conducting not potentially responsible person, §130A-310.33(b).
Environmental contamination defined, §130A-310.31(b).
Failure to comply with Brownfields agreement.
Violation of provisions, §130A-310.32(d).
Federal priorities list.
Department not to enter into Brownfields agreement for sites listed, §130A-310.37(c).
Fees.
Credit to Brownfields property reuse act implementation account, §130A-310.39(b).
Failure to pay fees, §130A-310.39(c).
Schedule of fees to be collected, §130A-310.39(a).
Immunity of state, agencies, officers, employees or agents, §130A-310.37(b).
Information provided by prospective developer, §130A-310.32(a).
Interest.
Unpaid fees, §130A-310.39(c).
Land-use restrictions.
Enforcement, §130A-310.32(a).
Liability for remediation to current standards, §130A-310.33(c).
Reliance on negotiating Brownfields agreement, §130A-310.32(b).
Liability for remediation of areas of contaminants identified in Brownfields agreement.
Limitation on liability, §130A-310.33(a).
Liens.
Unpaid fees, §130A-310.39(c).
National priorities list.
Department not to enter into Brownfields agreement for sites listed, §130A-310.37(c).
Noncompliance with Brownfields agreement.
Violation of provisions, §130A-310.32(d).
Notice of Brownfields property, §130A-310.35(a).
Applicability of provisions, §130A-310.35(g).
Cancellation, §130A-310.35(e).
Filing copy in register of deeds office, §130A-310.35(b).
Recording, §47-29.1(c).
Notice of intent to redevelop Brownfields property, §130A-310.34(a).
Publication, §130A-310.34(b).
Notice to public and community by prospective developer desiring to enter into Brownfields agreement, §130A-310.34(a).

BROWNFIELDS PROPERTY REUSE —Cont'd
Persons to whom liability protection applies,
    §130A-310.33(a).
Property taxes.
    Definitions, §105-277.13(b).
    Qualifying improvements, §105-277.13(a).
    Table of percentage of appraised value,
        §105-277.13(c).
Publication of notice of intent to redevelop
    Brownfields property, §130A-310.34(b).
Public meeting on Brownfields agreement,
    §130A-310.34(c).
    Comment received during.
        Taken into consideration by department,
            §130A-310.34(d).
Recording notice of Brownfields property,
    §§47-29.1(c), 130A-310.35(b), (c).
Register of deeds.
    Filing copy of notice of Brownfields property in
        office of register of deeds, §130A-310.35(b).
    Recording notice of Brownfields property,
        §130A-310.35(c).
Remedial standards based on land-use
    restrictions.
    Brownfields agreement may provide for,
        §130A-310.32(b).
Reports by department to environmental
    review commission, §130A-310.40.
Statement of remediation activities to be
    included in Brownfields agreement,
    §130A-310.32(c).
Summary of notice of intent to redevelop
    Brownfields property, §130A-310.34(a).
Violation of provisions.
    Failure to comply with Brownfields agreement,
        §130A-310.32(d).

BRUCELLOSIS, §§106-388 to 106-398.
Blood sample testing, §106-390.
    Compulsory testing of animals, §106-393.
Brands.
    Diseased animals to be branded and quarantined,
        §106-390.
Compensation for killing diseased animals.
    Appraisal of cattle affected with Bang's disease,
        §106-324.
        Report of appraisal, §106-326.
    Generally, §§106-323 to 106-335.
        See LIVESTOCK DISEASES.
    Marketing of cattle affected with Bang's disease,
        §106-327.
Compulsory testing, §§106-393, 106-395.
    Blood sample testing, §106-390.
Control and eradication of brucellosis.
    Cooperation with United States department of
        agriculture, §106-389.
Control of livestock diseases generally,
    §§106-400 to 106-405.
    See LIVESTOCK DISEASES.
County boards of commissioners.
    Cooperation of county boards, §106-394.
Defined, §106-389.
Duties of state veterinarian, §106-393.
Liability of vendors.
    Civil liability, §106-391.
Livestock diseases generally, §§106-304 to
    106-307.7.
    See LIVESTOCK DISEASES.
Misdemeanors.
    Sale of animals known to be infected or under
        quarantine, §106-398.

BRUCELLOSIS —Cont'd
Misdemeanors —Cont'd
    Violations made misdemeanor, §106-397.
Program for vaccination, §106-389.
    Sale, etc., of vaccine, §106-389.
Quarantine, §§106-388, 106-390.
    Duties of state veterinarian, §106-393.
Rules and regulations.
    Authority to promulgate and enforce, §106-396.
Sale of diseased animals, §106-390.
    Civil liability of vendors, §106-391.
    Nonresident sales, §106-392.
    Punishment for sale, §106-398.
    Removal of identification marks, §106-390.
State veterinarian.
    Duties, §106-393.
    Quarantine of animals, §106-393.
United States department of agriculture.
    Cooperation with department in control and
        eradication of brucellosis, §106-389.
Vaccination.
    Program for vaccination, §106-389.
    Sale, etc., of vaccine, §106-389.
Violations made misdemeanor, §106-397.

BRUNSWICK COUNTY.
Acquisition of property, power, §153A-158.1(a).
Agricultural tenancies in certain counties.
    Terms of, §42-23.
Ambulance service.
    Attachment or garnishment and lien for,
        §§44-51.4 to 44-51.8.
Board of county commissioners.
    Filling vacancies on board, §153A-27.1.
Condemnation or acquisition of land by local
    government unit outside county.
    Consent of board of commissioners necessary,
        §153A-15.
Coroner elected as nominee of political party.
    Filling vacancy in office, §152-1.
Counties generally.
    See COUNTIES.
County boards of education elected on
    partisan basis.
    Vacancies in office, §115C-37.1.
Cropper or tenant refusing to perform terms
    of contract.
    Forfeiture of right of possession to premises,
        §42-27.
Dog collars.
    Unlawful removal of electronic dog collars,
        §14-401.17.
Game laws, local acts not repealed,
    §113-133.1(e).
Grants in navigable waters, registration,
    §113-205(a).
Low-income housing tax credits.
    Qualified building eligible for credit,
        §105-129.41(c).
Maps in special proceedings, recording of
    photographic copies, §47-32.
Registration of deeds.
    Tax certification, no delinquent taxes due,
        §161-31(b).
Room occupancy tax levied by county, uniform
    provision, §153A-155.
Room occupancy tax levied by municipalities
    in county.
    Uniform provisions.
        Generally, §160A-215.
        Municipalities authorized to levy, §160A-215(g).

BRUNSWICK COUNTY —Cont'd
School property.
Acquisition and improvement, §153A-158.1.
Sheriff.
Vacancy, performance of duties until vacancy
filled, §162-5.1.
**Southeastern North Carolina regional
economic development commission,**
§§158-8.3 to 158-8.8.
**Swimming, surfing and littering in Atlantic
Ocean.**
City ordinances effective in Atlantic Ocean,
§160A-176.1.
Wills.
Evidence.
Records of wills in Brunswick, §8-27.

BRUSH FIRES.
Criminal trespass.
Setting fire to grass, brushlands and woodlands,
§14-136.

BUCKET SHOP ACT.
Futures contracts, §§16-3 to 16-6.
Securities regulation, §§78A-1 to 78A-66.
See SECURITIES.

BUCK SPRINGS.
Transportation department.
Maintenance of grounds at home of Nathaniel
Macon, §136-44.

BUCKWHEAT.
Standard weight and measure, §81A-42.

BUDGETS.
ABC boards, §18B-702.
Cemeteries.
Commission.
Annual budget, §65-54.
Community colleges.
See COMMUNITY COLLEGES.
Condominium owners' associations.
Summary provided, meeting to ratify,
§47C-3-103(c).
Director of the budget.
See STATE BUDGET.
District health departments.
Dissolution of department.
Distribution of budgetary surplus, §130A-38(d).
Education.
Public school budgets, §§115C-425 to 115C-434.
See SCHOOL DISTRICTS AND
ADMINISTRATIVE UNITS.
Energy.
Southern states energy compact.
Submission of budgets of board, §104D-3.
Governor.
Duties of governor, NC Const Art III §5.
Highways, roads and streets.
State primary, secondary and urban road systems,
§136-44.2.
Historical and archaeological properties.
Allotment and expenditure of funds, §143B-53.1.
Housing authorities and projects.
Local government finance.
Special provisions pertaining to public housing
authorities, §159-42(c).
System as part of city or county system, §157-4.2.
Indigent defense services, office of, §7A-498.2(d),
(e).
Industrial development commission.
Bureau.
Furnishing county commissioners with proposed
budget, §158-22.

BUDGETS —Cont'd
Joint municipal electric power and energy act.
Balanced budget, §159-41(a) to (f).
Local ABC boards, §18B-702.
**Local government budget and fiscal control
act,** §§159-7 to 159-42.
See LOCAL GOVERNMENT FINANCE.
**Mental health, developmental disability,
substance abuse.**
Area authorities, §122C-144.1(a).
Occupational safety and health.
Commissioner of labor to submit to general
assembly, §95-150.
Office of information technology services,
§147-33.88(a).
Performance budgeting.
Community colleges, §115D-31.3.
Public schools.
Generally, §§115C-425 to 115C-434.
See SCHOOL DISTRICTS AND
ADMINISTRATIVE UNITS.
River basins advisory commissions, §77-115(a).
Sanitary districts.
Annual budget, §130A-62(a).
Operation under annual budget, §130A-62(a).
School budget generally, §§115C-425 to
115C-434.
See SCHOOL DISTRICTS AND
ADMINISTRATIVE UNITS.
Southern growth policies agreement.
Board, §143-497.
State budget, §§143C-1-1 to 143C-10-3.
See STATE BUDGET.
State debt, §§142-1 to 142-29.7.
See STATE DEBT.
State treasurer.
Director of the budget, §147-84.
State veterans home.
Annual budget, §165-55(b).
University of North Carolina.
Duties of board of governors, §116-11.
Energy conservation savings, §116-30.3B.
Urban redevelopment.
Commission budgeting and accounting systems as
part of municipality budgeting accounting
systems, §160A-505.1.

BUGGERY.
Rape.
See RAPE.
Sex offenses generally.
See SEX OFFENSES.

BUGGIES.
**Bailment, lease or rental of vehicle or draft
animals.**
Protection of bailor against bailee's acts, §§14-165
to 14-169.
See BAILMENTS.
Traffic laws apply to animal-drawn vehicles,
§20-171.

BUGGING.
Electronic eavesdropping, §§14-227.1 to 14-227.3.

BUILDING AND LOAN ASSOCIATIONS.
Acknowledgments.
Officers or stockholders, §47-94.
Collection agencies.
Not included in definition of "collection
agency," §58-70-15(c).
Mortgages and deeds of trust.
Mortgages held by associations, §45-44.

BUILDING AND LOAN ASSOCIATIONS —Cont'd

Mortgages and deeds of trust —Cont'd
Probate before stockholders in association, §47-9.
Officers.
Acknowledgment and registration by officer, §47-94.
Probate before stockholders in association, §47-9.
Savings and loan associations, §§54B-1 to 54B-278.
See SAVINGS AND LOAN ASSOCIATIONS.
Small estates.
Transfer of ownership rights by presentation of affidavit, §28A-25-1(c).
Stockholders.
Acknowledgment and registration, §47-94.

BUILDING CODES, §§143-136 to 143-143.5.

Adoption of North Carolina state building code, §143-138(a).
Standards to be followed, §143-138(c).
Alternative designs and construction.
Appeals regarding, §143-140.1.
Amendments to code, §143-138(d).
Applicability of article, §143-143.
Appropriations.
Code officials qualification board, §143-151.20.
Boilers.
Enforcement of building code, §143-139(c).
Bonds, surety.
Manufactured buildings, structures or components.
Securing permits to erect modular buildings, §143-139.1(a).
Building code council.
Adoption and preparation of state code, §143-138(a).
Amendment of state code, §143-138(d).
Appeals.
Further appeals to courts, §143-141(d).
Interpretations of code, §143-141(b).
Method of appeal, §143-141(a).
Variations of code, §143-141(c).
Committees, §143-137(a).
Compensation, §143-136(b).
Creation, §143-136(a).
Duties.
Further duties of council, §143-142(a), (b).
Enforcement agencies.
Recommending changes in enforcement procedures, §143-142(b).
Expenses, §143-136(b).
First meeting, §143-137(a).
Fiscal affairs, §143-137(d).
Manufactured buildings, structures or components.
Certification, §143-139.1(a).
Meetings.
First meeting, §143-137(a).
Regular meetings, §143-137(b).
Membership, §143-136(a).
Organization, §143-137(a).
Per diem, §143-136(b).
Recommending statutory changes, §143-142(a).
Revision committees, §143-137(a).
Rules and regulations, §143-137(a).
Staff, §143-137(c).
Terms, §143-136(a).
Business occupancy buildings.
Special safety to life requirements applicable to existing high-rise buildings.
Inapplicability of provisions to, §143-138(j).

BUILDING CODES —Cont'd

Carbon monoxide detectors, §143-138(b2).
Certificates for code enforcement officials.
Actions under section, §143-151.17(c).
Administration, §143-151.19.
Clerical and staff services, §143-151.19(a).
Contents, §143-151.19(d).
Continuing education.
Professional development program, §143-151.13A.
County electrical inspectors, §143-151.13(e).
Denial, §143-151.17(d).
Duplicate certificates, §143-151.19(e).
Examinations, §143-151.13(a).
Contracts.
Review of contract exceeding one million dollars, §143-151.16(d).
Fees, §143-151.16(d).
Fees, §143-151.16(a).
Examinations, §143-151.16(d).
Indian tribe employing officials to enforce codes.
Applicability of provisions to federally recognized tribe, §143-151.17(e).
Injunctions, §143-151.18.
Investigations, §143-151.17(b).
Issuance, §143-151.13(f).
Reissuance by board, §143-151.15.
Penalties, §143-151.18.
Performance levels, §143-151.13(b).
Probationary or temporary certificates, §143-151.13(d).
Professional development program.
Board may establish, §143-151.13A(b).
Credit hours required, §143-151.13A(b), (c).
Evidence of completion, §143-151.13A(b).
Extension of time to comply, §143-151.13A(e).
Officials defined, §143-151.13A(a).
Purpose, §143-151.13A(b).
Reactivation or limited certificate, §143-151.13A(d).
Rules, adoption, §143-151.13A(f).
Records of names and addresses of officials, §143-151.19(c).
Reissuance by board, §143-151.15.
Renewal, §143-151.16(b).
Professional development program, §143-151.13A.
When examination required, §143-151.16(c).
Required, §143-151.13(a).
Return of certificate to board, §143-151.15.
Rules and regulations.
Certified copies, §143-151.19(b).
Suspension, revocation or refusal to grant.
Grounds, §143-151.17(a).
Tenure, §143-151.13(c).
Violations, §143-151.18.
Certificates for occupancy.
Electric service, §143-139.2(b).
Applicability of provisions, §143-139.2(c).
Certification of manufactured buildings, structures or components, §143-139.1(a).
Child care facilities.
Mandatory standards for licensing, §110-91.
Cisterns, provisions regarding, §143-138(b12).
Classes for various trades affected by state building code, §143-138.1.
Code officials qualification board.
Appointments, §143-151.9(b).
Appropriations, §143-151.20(b).
Chairman, §143-151.11(a).

BUILDING CODES —Cont'd
Code officials qualification board —Cont'd
Code enforcement.
Defined, §143-151.8(a).
Comity, §143-151.14.
Compensation, §143-151.10.
Definitions, §143-151.8.
Donations.
Acceptance by board, §143-151.20(a).
Duties, §143-151.12.
Established, §143-151.9(a).
Expenses, §143-151.10.
Fees.
Certificates for code enforcement officials.
Schedule of fees, §143-151.16(a).
Disposition, §143-151.21.
Gifts.
Acceptance by board, §143-151.20(a).
Grants.
Board may provide, §143-151.20(b).
Local inspection departments.
Defined, §143-151.8(a).
Meetings, §143-151.11(c).
Members, §143-151.9(a).
Population.
Determination, §143-151.8(b).
Powers, §143-151.12.
Reciprocity, §143-151.14.
Reports.
Submission, §143-151.11(d).
Rules and regulations.
Promulgation, §143-151.12.
Salaries, §143-151.10.
Standards.
Generally, §143-151.13.
Terms, §143-151.9(b).
Vacancies, §143-151.9(c).
Vice-chairman, §143-151.11(b).
Construction and interpretation.
Existing laws.
Effect of article upon existing laws, §143-143.
Contents of state building code, §143-138(b).
Definitions.
Code officials qualification board, §143-151.8.
Electric wiring of houses, buildings and
structures.
Definition of building, §143-143.2.
Distribution of state code, §143-138(g).
Door lock exemption permits.
Businesses applicable, §143-143.4(a).
Conditions for permit, §143-143.4(b).
Definitions, §143-143.4(g).
Filing of permit, §143-143.4(c).
Implementation rules, §143-143.4(i).
Inspections by insurance department,
§143-143.4(d).
Penalty for violation of provisions, §143-143.4(h).
Revocation of permit, §143-143.4(e).
Appeal of decision, §143-143.4(f).
Effect of state code upon local codes,
§143-138(e).
Electric service.
Certificates for occupancy, §143-139.2(b).
Applicability of provisions, §143-139.2(c).
Insulation requirements, §143-139.2(a), (b).
Applicability of provisions, §143-139.2(c).
Wiring of houses, buildings and structures.
Requirements, §143-143.2.
Elevators.
Enforcement of building code, §143-139(d).

BUILDING CODES —Cont'd
Elevators —Cont'd
Special safety to life requirements applicable to
existing high-rise buildings.
Requirements for buildings, §143-138(i).
Emergency electrical power supply.
Special safety to life requirements applicable to
existing high-rise buildings.
Requirements for buildings, §143-138(i).
Enforcement.
Boilers, §143-139(c).
Elevators, §143-139(d).
General building regulations, §143-139(b).
Procedural requirements, §143-139(a).
Remedies, §143-139(b1).
State buildings, §143-139(e).
Enforcement agencies.
Building code council.
Recommending changes in enforcement
procedures, §143-142(b).
Hearings.
Questions under building code, §143-140.
Exemption from permit requirement,
§143-138(b5), (b6).
Existing laws.
Effect of article upon existing laws, §143-143.
Exit requirements.
Special safety to life requirements applicable to
existing high-rise buildings.
Requirements for buildings, §143-138(i).
Fair housing.
Unlawful discriminatory housing practices
provisions.
Inapplicability to code provisions applicable to
handicapped, §41A-6(d).
Family care home.
Defined, §143-138(k).
Farm buildings, exemptions, §143-138(b4).
Accessory building of bona fide farm.
Municipal zoning ordinance exemption,
§160A-360(k).
Fees.
Code officials qualification board.
Certificates for code enforcement officials,
§143-151.16.
Disposition, §143-151.21.
Fertilizer, equipment for storage or handling.
Exemption from provisions, §143-138(b8).
Fire alarm systems.
Special safety to life requirements applicable to
existing high-rise buildings.
Requirements for buildings, §143-138(i).
Fire prevention code provisions, §143-138(b1).
Fire protection of electrical conductors.
Special safety to life requirements applicable to
existing high-rise buildings.
Requirements for class III buildings,
§143-138(i).
Fire stopping for vertical shafts.
Special safety to life requirements applicable to
existing high-rise buildings.
Requirements for buildings, §143-138(i).
Fuel, equipment for storage or handling.
Exemption from provisions, §143-138(b8).
Gas pumps.
Ethanol blends dispensing equipment, §143-143.6.
General building regulations.
Enforcement, §143-139(b).
Hearings.
Enforcement agencies.
Questions under building code, §143-140.

BUILDING CODES —Cont'd

High-rise buildings to be provided with safety to life facilities, §143-138(i).

Industrial machinery.
Exemption from provisions, §143-138(b9).

Injunctions.
Code officials qualification board.
Certificates for code enforcement officials, §143-151.18.

Inspections.
Local inspection departments.
Code officials qualification board.
Defined, §143-151.8(a).
State buildings, §143-139(e).

Instructional classes for various trades affected by state building code, §143-138.1.

Insulation and energy utilization standards.
Applicability of provisions, §143-139.2(c).
Electric service, §143-139.2(a), (b).
Applicability of provisions, §143-139.2(c).
Electric wiring of houses, buildings and structures, §143-143.2.
Enforcement, §143-139.2(a).

Judicial notice, §143-138(l).

Life requirements for existing high-rise buildings, §143-138(i).

Liquefied petroleum gas.
Residential structures.
Inspection of liquefied petroleum gas piping systems for, §143-139.3.

Local codes, effect of state code upon, §143-138(e).

Local inspection departments.
Code officials qualification board.
Defined, §143-151.8(a).

Locking mechanisms for seclusion rooms in schools, §143-138(b11).

Manufactured buildings, structures and components.
Agencies offering testing, evaluation, inspection and certification.
Rules for approving, adoption, §143-139.1(a).
Bonds, surety.
Securing permits to erect modular buildings, §143-139.1(a).
Building code council.
Certification, §143-139.1(a).
Certification, §143-139.1(a).
Eave projection, standards, §143-139.1(b).
Exterior wall, standards, §143-139.1(b).
Foundations, standards, §143-139.1(b).
Labels and seals.
Evidence of approval, §143-139.1(a).
Minimum standards, §143-139.1(b).
Roof pitch, standards, §143-139.1(b).
Siding and roofing materials, standards, §143-139.1(b).
Testing, evaluation, inspection and certification, §143-139.1(a).
Unlicensed persons erecting.
Rules, adoption, §143-139.1(a).

Manufactured homes generally, §§143-144 to 143-151.5.
See MANUFACTURED HOMES.

Misdemeanors.
Violation of state code, §143-138(b).

Nonbusiness occupancy building built prior to adoption of 1953 code.
Compliance with certain provisions by December 31, 2006 required, §143-138(j1).

North Carolina state building code, §143-138.

BUILDING CODES —Cont'd

Permit exemptions, §143-138(b5), (b6).

Preparation of North Carolina state building code, §143-138(a).

Pressurized fans.
Special safety to life requirements applicable to existing high-rise buildings.
Requirements for class II buildings, §143-138(i).

Publication of code, §143-138(g).

Public buildings and grounds.
Enforcement in state buildings, §143-139(e).

References to other rules of special types, §143-138(b7).

Refuge areas required in class III high-rise buildings.
Special safety to life requirements applicable to existing high-rise buildings, §143-138(i).

Reports.
Code officials qualification board, §143-151.11.

Rulemaking procedure.
Notice and rule-making hearing not required.
State building code, §150B-21.5(d).

School buildings.
Locking mechanisms for seclusion rooms in schools, §143-138(b11).

Smoke compartmentation for institutional buildings.
Special safety to life requirements applicable to existing high-rise buildings.
Requirements for buildings, §143-138(f).

Smoke detectors.
Business occupancy buildings, §143-138(j).
Special safety to life requirements applicable to existing high-rise buildings.
Requirements for buildings, §143-138(i).

Smoke venting in class III high-rise buildings.
Special safety to life requirements applicable to existing high-rise buildings, §143-138(i).

Special safety to life requirements applicable to existing high-rise buildings, §143-138(i).

Specific activities and functions of state code.
Enumeration, §143-138(b).

Sprinkler systems.
Special safety to life requirements applicable to existing high-rise buildings.
Requirements for class III buildings, §143-138(i).

Standards to be followed in adopting state code, §143-138(c).

State building code, §143-138.

State buildings.
Applicability of county or municipal building code, §143-135.1(a), (c).
Enforcement agencies, §143-139(e).

Toilets.
Shopping malls.
Horizontal travel distance for access, §143-143.5.
Temporary toilet facilities at construction sites.
Requirements, §143-143.3(a).
Standards to be established, §143-143.3(b).

Type of building or structure regulated, §143-138(b3).

Violations of state code, §143-138(h).

Voice communication system.
Special safety to life requirements applicable to existing high-rise buildings.
Requirements for buildings, §143-138(i).

Water heater efficiency requirements, §143-138(b10).

BUILDING COMMISSION, §§143-135.25 to 143-135.28.
Appointment of members, §143-135.25(c).
Capital improvement project.
Defined, §143-135.27.
Chairman.
Election, §143-135.25(c).
Compensation, §143-135.25(e).
Composition, §143-135.25(c).
Conflicts of interest.
Interested members not to participate in authorization of contract, §143-135.28.
Creation, §143-135.25(a).
Department of administration.
Created within, §143-135.25(a).
Designer.
Final selection.
Duty as to, §143-135.26.
Exception, §143-135.26.
Duties, §143-135.26.
Expenses.
Reimbursement for travel and subsistence, §143-135.25(e).
Meetings, §143-135.25(d).
Memorandum of understanding, §143-135.26.
Number of members, §143-135.25(c).
Powers, §143-135.26.
Staff.
Provided by state construction office, §143-135.25(b).
State construction office.
Director.
Qualifications, §143-135.25(b).
Staff provided by, §143-135.25(b).
Terms, §143-135.25(c).
Vacancies, §143-135.25(c).

BUILDING CONTRACTORS.
Electrical contractors.
Generally, §§87-39 to 87-51.
See ELECTRICAL CONTRACTORS.
General contractors.
Generally, §§87-1 to 87-15.4.
See GENERAL CONTRACTORS.
Irrigation contractors, §§89G-1 to 89G-13.
See IRRIGATION CONTRACTORS.
Plumbing, heating and fire sprinkler contractors.
Generally, §§87-16 to 87-27.1.
See PLUMBING, HEATING AND FIRE SPRINKLER CONTRACTORS.
Refrigeration contractors, §§87-52 to 87-64.1.
See REFRIGERATION CONTRACTORS.

BUILDING ENTRANCES.
Right of way.
Vehicle about to enter or cross, §20-156(a).

BUILDING INSPECTIONS AND INSPECTORS.
County inspection departments, §§153A-350 to 153A-375.
See COUNTY INSPECTION DEPARTMENTS.
Filing of lis pendens by cities and counties in certain cases, §1-120.2.
Municipal building inspection, §§160A-411 to 160A-439.
See MUNICIPAL BUILDING INSPECTION.

BUILDINGS.
Allocated state lands.
Acquisition.
Buildings having historic, architectural or cultural significance, §146-23.1.

BUILDINGS —Cont'd
Allocated state lands —Cont'd
Acquisition —Cont'd
Energy efficiency standards, §146-23.2(a), (b).
Arson.
Defined, §14-58.1.
General provisions, §§14-58 to 14-69.2.
Not covered by other provisions.
Burning or attempting to burn, §14-67.1.
Public buildings.
Bureau of investigation.
Authority, §114-15.
Burning certain public buildings, §14-59.
Burglary, §§14-51 to 14-57.
Child care facilities.
Mandatory standards, §110-91.
Claim and delivery.
Property concealed in buildings, §1-480.
Code, §§143-136 to 143-143.5.
See BUILDING CODES.
Community colleges.
Fire and casualty insurance on institutional buildings and contents, §115D-58.11(a) to (c).
Public building contracts.
Construction contract claims.
Adjustment and resolution, §143-135.6.
Concealed property in buildings.
Claim for delivery of personal property, §1-480.
Condemnation of unsafe buildings.
Municipalities generally, §§160A-411 to 160A-439.
See MUNICIPAL BUILDING INSPECTION.
Condominium act, §§47C-1-101 to 47C-4-120.
See CONDOMINIUMS.
Construction indemnity agreements invalid, §22B-1.
Counties.
Care and use of county property, §153A-169.
Damages.
Rewards for information, §153A-446.
Defined, §153A-350.
Failure of owner to comply with orders of public authorities, §14-68.
Inspection departments, §§153A-350 to 153A-375.
See COUNTY INSPECTION DEPARTMENTS.
Joint buildings, §153A-164.
Planning and zoning.
Applicability of provisions, §153A-347.
Repair, closing or demolition of nonresidential buildings, §153A-372.1.
Sites of county buildings, §153A-169.
Discharge of barreled weapon or firearm into.
While occupied or in operation, §14-34.1(a) to (c).
Disorderly conduct.
Public buildings and facilities.
Trespasses to land and fixtures, §14-132.
Eminent domain.
Removal of structures on condemned land, §40A-9.
Energy efficiency standards.
Allocated state lands.
Acquisition, §146-23.2(a), (b).
Energy-efficient buildings.
Performance standards for sustainable, §§143-135.35 to 143-135.40.
See PUBLIC BUILDINGS AND GROUNDS.
Evacuation of public buildings.
Governor may order in emergency, §14-288.19(a).
Penalty for willful refusal to leave, §14-288.19(b).
Fluorescent lights and thermostats containing mercury.
Demolition of building containing.
Removal and recycling, §130A-310.61.

BUILDINGS —Cont'd
General assembly.
State legislative building.
Official name, §129-12.1.
Hospital authorities.
Subject to building laws, ordinances and
regulations, §131E-25.
Housing authorities and projects.
Applicability of building laws, §157-13.
General provisions, §§157-1 to 157-70.
See HOUSING AUTHORITIES AND
PROJECTS.
Indemnity agreements.
Construction indemnity agreements invalid,
§22B-1.
Joint tenants and tenants in common.
Dismantling portion of building.
Damages, §1-539.2.
Mountain ridge construction.
Certain building prohibited, §113A-209(a) to (c).
Mountain ridge protection.
Existing buildings, §113A-210.
Municipalities.
Building inspection, §§160A-411 to 160A-439.
See MUNICIPAL BUILDING INSPECTION.
Generally.
See MUNICIPALITIES.
Nuisances.
Abatement.
Offenses against public morals, §§19-1 to 19-8.3.
See NUISANCES.
Party walls, §1-539.2.
Ports authority.
Removal of buildings, §136-268.
Public building contracts.
Architectural, engineering and surveying services,
§§143-64.31 to 143-64.34.
See PUBLIC CONTRACTS.
Generally, §§143-128 to 143-135.9.
See PUBLIC CONTRACTS.
Public buildings.
Burning of certain public buildings, §14-59.
General provisions.
See PUBLIC BUILDINGS AND GROUNDS.
Public lands.
Allocated state lands.
Severance approval delegation, §146-35.
Public officers and employees.
Failure of owner to comply with orders of public
authorities, §14-68.
Public works.
General provisions, §§133-1 to 133-4.1.
See PUBLIC WORKS.
School buildings and property.
Generally, §§115C-517 to 115C-530.
See SCHOOL BUILDINGS AND PROPERTY.
State legislative building.
Designation, §129-12.1.
Official name, §129-12.1.
State prison system.
Additional facilities.
Authorized, §148-37(a).
Structural pest control, §§106-65.22 to 106-65.41.
See STRUCTURAL PEST CONTROL.
Subversion.
Use of public buildings, §14-11.
Transportation department.
Acquisition of buildings, §136-19.3.
Trespass.
Injuring buildings, §14-159.

BUILDINGS —Cont'd
Trespass —Cont'd
Public buildings and facilities.
Disorderly conduct in and injuries to buildings
and facilities, §14-132.
Unit ownership, §§47A-1 to 47A-28.
See UNIT OWNERSHIP.
**Unsafe building, condemnation, correction of
defects,** §§160A-411 to 160A-439.
See MUNICIPAL BUILDING INSPECTION.
Veterans' recreation authorities.
Projects subject to building laws, §165-32.
Wildlife resources commission.
Transfer, §143-248.

BUILDING TRADES TRAINING.
Vocational and technical education generally,
§§115C-151 to 115C-169.
See VOCATIONAL AND TECHNICAL
EDUCATION.

BULBS.
**Promotion of use and sale of agricultural
products.**
Generally, §§106-550 to 106-568.
See AGRICULTURAL PRODUCTS
PROMOTION.

BULLDOZERS.
Mechanical breakdown service agreement,
§66-374.

BULLET-PROOF VESTS.
**Defendant wearing or having in possession
during commission of felony.**
Enhanced sentence, §15A-1340.16C(a).
Burden of proof, §15A-1340.16C(d).
Exceptions, §15A-1340.16C(b1), (e).
Indictments or informations, §15A-1340.16C(c).

BULLETS.
**Furnishing bullets to inmates of charitable,
mental or penal institutions,** §14-258.1.
**Products liability lawsuits involving
ammunition,** §99B-11.
Teflon-coated bullets.
Manufacture, sale, purchase or possession,
§14-34.3.

BULLYING.
Cyber-bullying, §14-458.1.
Public schools.
Bullying and harassing behavior, §§115C-407.15
to 115C-407.18.

BUNCOMBE COUNTY.
Alcohol detoxification program.
Facility not to be removed from county without
prior approval of general assembly, §131E-65.
Ambulances.
Attachment or garnishment and lien for,
§§44-51.4 to 44-51.8.
Obtaining services without intending to pay,
§14-111.1.
Requesting ambulance falsely, §14-111.3.
Board of county commissioners.
Filling vacancies on board, §153A-27.1.
**Condemnation or acquisition of land by local
government unit outside county.**
Consent of board of commissioners necessary,
§153A-15.
Coroner elected as nominee of political party.
Filling vacancy in office, §152-1.
Counties generally.
See COUNTIES.

BUNCOMBE COUNTY —Cont'd
Dog collars.
Unlawful removal of electronic dog collars,
§14-401.17.
Game laws, local acts not repealed,
§113-133.1(e).
Oil, gas or mineral claims.
Certain ancient claims extinguished, preservation,
procedure, §1-42.1(a) to (d).
**Probates and registration orders before clerks
of inferior courts validated,** §47-59.
Real estate mortgage loans.
Interest, commissions and repayment, §45-43.
Registration of deeds.
Tax certification, no delinquent taxes due,
§161-31(b).
**Room occupancy tax levied by county, uniform
provisions,** §153A-155.
Sheriff.
Vacancy, performance of duties until vacancy
filled, §162-5.1.
Special police officers, joint security force,
§122C-421(a).
Special school tax, election to abolish.
Petition required, §115C-505.
**Western North Carolina Development
Association, Inc.**
Appropriation of funds to, §153A-447(a), (b).
**Western North Carolina regional economic
development commission,** §§158-8.1 to
158-8.8.

BUOYS.
Interfering with, §76-58.
Rafts to exercise care in passing, §76-57.

BUPRENORPHINE.
**Prescribing or dispensing for treatment of
opiate dependence.**
Registration of physicians, §90-101(a1).

BURDEN OF PROOF.
**Abused, neglected or dependent juvenile
actions.**
Adjudicatory hearing, §7B-805.
Nonsecure custody hearings, §7B-506(b).
Responsible individuals list, placement on,
§7B-805.
Adoption.
Hearing on petition to adopt adult, §48-2-605(b).
Hearings on petition for adoption, §48-2-603(a).
Alcoholic beverages.
Compensation for injury caused by sales to
underage persons, §18B-122.
Attorney discipline.
Reinstatement after disbarment, Bar Rule B.0125.
Bail.
Refusal of money or property offered, §15A-539(b).
Bank deposits and collections.
Stop payment order.
Burden of proof of loss, §25-4-403(c).
Biological residues in animals.
Content of biological residue, §106-549.82.
Bullet-proof vests.
Defendant wearing or having in possession during
commission of felony.
Enhanced sentence, §15A-1340.16C(d).
Business and energy tax credit.
Eligibility and amount of credit, §105-129.18.
Capital punishment.
Death penalty for mentally retarded defendants
prohibited.
Defendant's burden, §15A-2005(a), (c), (f).

BURDEN OF PROOF —Cont'd
**Certificate of relief from collateral
consequences, criminal procedure.**
Conditions for issuance, §15A-173.2(b).
Just cause for revocation or modification,
§15A-173.4(b).
Child support.
Setting aside affidavit of parentage by trial court,
§110-132(a2).
Civil actions and proceedings.
Presumptions, §8C-1 Rule 301.
Claims against the state.
False claims act.
Civil actions for violations, §1-615(c).
Commercial code general provisions.
Option to accelerate at will.
Burden of establishing lack of good faith,
§25-1-309.
Commercial paper.
Order to stop payment.
Burden of proof of loss, §25-4-403(c).
**Common carriers duty to transport freight
within reasonable time.**
Delay in shipping, §62-200(c).
Contempt.
Civil contempt.
Proceeding initiated on motion of aggrieved
party, §5A-23(a1).
Contributory negligence, §1-139.
Controlled substances.
Exemptions or exceptions, §90-113.1(a).
Registration or order form, §90-113.1(b).
**Credit repair service violations, actions for
damages.**
Proving exemption or exception, §66-225(d).
Criminal investigation information records.
Preventing disclosure of information considered
public record, §132-1.4(e).
**Death penalty for mentally retarded
defendants prohibited.**
Defendant's burden, §15A-2005(a), (c), (f).
Death penalty, race as basis of judgment,
§15A-2011(c).
Delinquent and undisciplined juvenile actions.
Adjudicatory hearing, §7B-2409.
Prior adjudication of delinquent.
Delinquency history level determination,
§7B-2507(f).
Secure or nonsecure custody hearing, §7B-1906(d).
Discharge of employee called to jury duty.
Action for damages, §9-32(b).
Elections.
Challenge to candidacy, §163-127.5(a), (b).
Employment security.
Benefits, §96-14.
Claims for benefits.
Witnesses.
Discharge, demotion or intimidation,
§96-15.1(b).
Enhanced sentence.
Aggravating factors, §15A-1340.16(a).
Bullet-proof vests.
Defendant wearing or having in possession
during commission of felony,
§15A-1340.16C(d).
Firearms or deadly weapons.
Use or display during commission of felony,
§15A-1340.16A(e).
Methamphetamine manufacture.
Serious injury inflicted upon law enforcement or
emergency personnel, §15A-1340.16D(c).

BURDEN OF PROOF —Cont'd
Expedited evictions.
Affirmative defense to subsequent action for
complete eviction, §42-64(b).
Civil causes of action, §42-61.
Exemption from complete eviction where grounds
established, §42-64(c).
False claims act.
False or fraudulent claims against the state.
Civil actions for violations, §1-615(c).
Firearms or deadly weapons.
Bar to possession due to mental commitment.
Restoration process to remove bar,
§122C-54.1(c).
Use or display during commission of felony.
Enhanced sentence, §15A-1340.16A(e).
Foreign judgments.
Motion for enforcement of foreign judgment,
§1C-1705(b).
Recognition of foreign-country moneys judgments.
Burden of establishing applicability of article,
§1C-1852(c).
Burden of establishing nonrecognition,
§1C-1853(f) to (g).
Health Choice.
Provider requirements.
Appeal of adverse determinations, §108C-12(d).
Impaired driving.
Sentencing hearing.
Aggravating or mitigating factors, existence,
§20-179(a).
Evidentiary standards, §20-179(o).
Infractions, §15A-1114(f).
**International commercial arbitration and
conciliation.**
Tribunal conducting proceeding, §1-567.49(b).
Investment advisers.
Civil or administrative proceedings, §78C-40.
Judicial standards commission.
Disciplinary hearing, JudStdsComm Rule 18.
Leases, UCC.
Default of lessor.
Burden of establishing default after acceptance
of goods, §25-2A-516.
Legitimation of illegitimate children.
Legitimation where mother married, §49-12.1(b).
Life imprisonment without parole.
Second or subsequent conviction of class B1
felony, §15A-1340.16B(e).
Livestock markets.
Transportation, sale, etc., of diseased livestock.
Burden of proving health, §106-414.
Local boards of education.
Actions against board, §115C-44(b).
Medicaid.
Contested case procedures, §108A-70.9B(d).
False claims by providers.
Civil actions, §108A-70.13(c).
Provider requirements.
Appeal of adverse determinations, §108C-12(d).
Medical malpractice.
Standard of health care, §90-21.12(a).
Emergency medical condition, treatment of,
§90-21.12(b).
**Mental health, developmental disability,
substance abuse.**
Involuntary commitment.
Hearing following automatic commitment,
§122C-268.1(i).
Substance abuser's commitment hearing,
§122C-286(h).

BURDEN OF PROOF —Cont'd
**Mental health, developmental disability,
substance abuse** —Cont'd
Weapons.
Bar to possession due to mental commitment.
Restoration process to remove bar,
§122C-54.1(c).
Methamphetamine manufacture.
Serious injury inflicted upon law enforcement or
emergency personnel.
Enhanced sentence, §15A-1340.16D(c).
Mitigating factors, §15A-1340.16(a).
Monopolies and restraint of trade.
Unfair methods of competition, acts and practices.
Party claiming exemption from prohibition,
§75-1.1(d).
Motion for appropriate relief.
Denial.
Defendant's burden of proof, §15A-1419(b), (c).
Ordinances, §160A-79(c).
Partition sales.
Sale in lieu of partition.
Order for sale, §46-22(d).
Paternity, civil action to establish, §49-14(b).
Setting aside orders of paternity, §49-4(h).
Prejudice to defendant, §15A-1443(a).
Presumptions.
See PRESUMPTIONS.
Products liability.
Claims based on inadequate design or
formulation, §99B-6(a).
Claims based on inadequate warning or
instruction, §99B-5(a).
Products liability lawsuits involving firearms,
§99B-11(b).
Property taxes.
Listing property.
Timely filing of abstract, §105-311(c).
Punitive damages.
Aggravating factors, §1D-15(b).
Sale of goods, UCC.
Burden of establishing breach after acceptance,
§25-2-607(4).
Sales and use tax.
Certificate of exemption accepted by seller from
purchaser.
Sale not retail sale, §105-164.28(a).
Secured transactions.
Purchase-money security interest.
Non-consumer goods, §25-9-103(g).
Securities regulation.
Exemptions.
Burden of proving exemption on person
claiming it, §78A-18(b).
Simultaneous death.
Evidence of death, §28A-24-7.
120-hour survivorship requirement, §28A-24-2(a).
Co-owners with rights of survivorship,
§28A-24-3.
Victim survival of slayer, overcoming presumption,
§28A-24-5.
**Tax incentives for new and expanding
businesses.**
Eligibility for credit and amount of credit,
§105-129.7(a).
Telephonic sellers.
Exemptions or exceptions, §66-266(e).
Termination of parental rights proceedings.
Adjudicatory hearing, §7B-1109(f).
Establishing grounds for terminating, §7B-1111(b).

BURDEN OF PROOF —Cont'd
Tort claims against state departments and agencies.
Contributory negligence, §143-299.1.
Trade secrets.
Misappropriation, §66-155.
Unclaimed property act.
Existence and amount of property and abandonment, §116B-58.
Unemployment compensation.
Benefits, §96-14.
Claims for benefits.
Witnesses.
Discharge, demotion or intimidation, §96-15.1(b).
Utilities commission.
Proceedings instituted by commission, §62-75.
Water resources.
Capacity use areas, §143-215.15(f).
Waters and watercourses.
Withdrawing, diverting or obtaining water.
Surface water transfers.
Final determination on certificate issuance.
Burden of proof and findings required, §143-215.22L(m).
Wine distribution agreements.
Amendment, termination, cancellation or nonrenewal.
Good cause, §18B-1205(c).
Workers' compensation.
Person claiming exemption or forfeiture, §97-12.

BUREAU OF ALCOHOL, TOBACCO AND FIREARMS.
Agents authorized to enforce criminal laws, §15A-406.

BUREAU OF INVESTIGATION, §§114-12 to 114-20.1.
Abuse, neglect or dependency of juvenile.
Report by director upon finding evidence of sexual abuse in child care facility, §7B-307(c).
Aliens.
Verification of work authorization.
Investigation of complaints.
Law enforcement assistance in investigation, §64-29(c).
Background investigations, §§114-19.01 to 114-19.50.
Child care providers.
Criminal record checks, §114-19.5.
Education.
Criminal record checks of school personnel, §114-19.2.
Fees for performance.
Conducted for purposes other than administration of criminal justice, §114-19.1(a).
Foster parents.
Criminal record check, §114-19.4.
Positions must be confirmed by general assembly, §114-15(a).
Priority in processing, §114-19.1(c).
Providers of treatment for or services to children, the elderly, mental health patients, the sick and the disabled.
Criminal record checks, §114-19.3.
Rights to receive records of bureau.
Not enlarged, §114-19.1(d).
Central prison identification bureau.
Transfer of activities to new bureau, §114-18.

BUREAU OF INVESTIGATION —Cont'd
Child sexual abuse in child care.
Investigation, §114-15.3.
Clinical facilities, §114-16.
Computers, electronic mail or Internet.
Crimes authorized to investigate, §114-15(b1).
Concealed handgun permit.
Copy of permit sent to, information available on statewide system, §14-415.17.
Submission of fingerprints to FBI for records check, §14-415.13(b).
Created, §114-12.
Crimes authorized to investigate, §114-15(a), (b), (b1).
Criminal justice information network governing board, §§143-660 to 143-664.
Criminal statistics.
Duties, §114-19(a).
Reception and collection, §114-18.
Criminologists.
Employment, §114-16.
Delinquent or undisciplined juvenile actions.
Fingerprinting or photographing juveniles.
Proper format for transfer to bureau, §7B-2102(c).
Director.
Appointment by attorney general, §114-13.
Assistants, §114-13.
Duties, §114-14.
Mileage payments, §114-15(d).
Powers, §114-14.
Salary, §114-13.
DNA database and databank.
Administered by SBI, §15A-266.3.
Annual report, §15A-266.5(c).
Expungement of records.
Charges dismissed on appeal or pardon of innocence granted, §15A-148(b).
Generally, §§15A-266 to 15A-266.12.
See DNA.
Materials, supplies, envelopes for obtaining samples.
Duty to provide, §15A-266.6(c).
Procedures, adoption, §15A-266.7.
Duties, §114-12.
Election fraud.
Investigation, §114-15(a).
Electronic surveillance generally, §§15A-286 to 15A-298.
See ELECTRONIC SURVEILLANCE.
Evidence.
Availability to district attorneys, §114-15(c).
Expungement of criminal records.
Charges dismissed or person found not guilty or not responsible.
Law enforcement agencies ordered to expunge records, §15A-146(b).
As result of identity theft, §15A-147(c).
DNA records, §15A-148(b).
Notification to SBI, §15A-150(c).
Pardon or innocence granted, §15A-149(b).
Fees.
Performance of certain background investigations, §114-19.1(a).
Fingerprinting.
Records, §114-18.
Firearms.
Surplus weapons.
Sale, trade or disposal, §143-63.1(d).
Fires and fire prevention.
Investigations.
Attorney general acting through bureau, §58-79-1.

BUREAU OF INVESTIGATION —Cont'd

Forensic science advisory board, §114-16.1.

Gaming.
Investigation of gaming law violations, §114-15(a).

General assembly.
Background investigation of person who must be confirmed by legislative action.
Requests to bureau of investigation, §120-19.4A.

Governor.
Services subject to call of governor, §114-15(a).

Impaired driving.
Blood or urine tests results.
Admissibility, rules of procedure, adoption, §20-139.1(c2).

Laboratory and clinical facilities, §114-16.
Forensic science advisory board, §114-16.1.
State crime laboratory ombudsman, §114-16.2.

List of crimes authorized to investigate, §114-15(a), (b).

Local law enforcement officers.
Cooperation, §114-17.

Lotteries.
Investigation of lottery law violations, §114-15(a).

Lynchings.
Investigation, §114-15(a).

Methamphetamine laboratories.
Report on number of laboratories discovered each year, §90-113.64.

Mileage.
Director and assistants, §114-15(d).

Misuse of state property.
Reports of department heads, §114-15.1.

Mob violence.
Investigations of, §114-15(a).

Personnel.
Transfer, §114-14.1.

Photography.
Records, §114-18.

Police.
Cooperation of local enforcement officers, §114-17.

Powers, §114-12.

Protection of public officials.
Authority to provide protection, §114-20.
Designation of areas for protection of public officials, §114-20.1(a).
Promulgation of rules and regulations governing ingress to or egress from buildings, §114-20.1(b).

Pseudoephedrine products.
Study and report by bureau of investigation.
Use of products to make methamphetamine, §114-19.01.

Public buildings and grounds.
Arson, damage or theft, §114-15.

Public lands.
Investigation of cases involving misuse of state property, §114-15.1.

Public utilities.
Employment applications.
Criminal history record from state bureau of investigation, §62-333.

Radio system.
State system available to bureau, §114-16.

Records.
Availability to district attorneys, §114-15(c).
Expungement of criminal records.
Charges dismissed or person found not guilty or not responsible.
Law enforcement agencies ordered to expunge records, §15A-146(b).
As result of identity theft, §15A-147(c).

BUREAU OF INVESTIGATION —Cont'd

Records —Cont'd
Expungement of criminal records —Cont'd
DNA records, §15A-148(b).
Pardon or innocence granted, §15A-149(b).
Photographing and fingerprinting records, §114-18.

Reports.
DNA database and databank.
Annual report, §15A-266.5(c).
Methamphetamine laboratories.
Report on number of laboratories discovered each year, §90-113.64.
Violations of criminal statutes involving misuse of state property, §114-15.1.

Social security fraud.
Investigations, authority, §114-15(a).

State crime laboratory ombudsman, §114-16.2.

State radio system.
Availability to bureau, §114-16.

Transfer of personnel, §114-14.1.

Transfer to department, §143A-51.

Waste discharges.
Referral by secretary for review, §143-215.6B(k).

Witnesses.
Fees, §114-15(d).

BUREAU OF LICENSE AND THEFT.

Division of motor vehicles.
Seized vehicles, custody, disposition, §20-49.3.
Specially constructed vehicles.
Inoperable vehicles, title.
Verification as substantially assembled, §20-53.1(b).
Vehicle verification.
Certain out-of-state vehicles, specially constructed vehicles.
Required for issuance of title, §20-53(e).

BURGAW.

All-terrain vehicles.
Use by employees on certain highways, §20-171.24.

Room occupancy tax.
Uniform provisions.
Authorized to levy, §160A-215(g).
Generally, §160A-215.

Satellite annexation.
Limitation on area of satellite corporate limits, inapplicability, §160A-58.1(b).

BURGLAR ALARMS.

Alarm systems licensing, §§74D-1 to 74D-14.
See ALARM SYSTEMS LICENSING.

Private protective services generally, §§74C-1 to 74C-30.
See PRIVATE PROTECTIVE SERVICES.

BURGLARY, §§14-51 to 14-57.

Airplanes.
Breaking or entering into or breaking out of aircraft, §14-56.

Boats.
Breaking or entering into or breaking out of boats or other watercraft, §14-56.

Breaking or entering buildings.
Definition of "building,"§14-54(c).
Felony offenses, §14-54(a).
Generally, §14-54.
Misdemeanor offenses, §14-54(b).

Breaking out of dwelling, §14-53.

Building that is place of religious worship.
Criminal penalty, §14-54.1(a).

BURGLARY —Cont'd
Building that is place of religious worship
—Cont'd
Defined, §14-54.1(b).
Capital punishment.
Aggravating circumstances.
Capital felony in commission of burglary, §15A-2000(e).
Crimes punishable by death, NC Const Art XI §2.
Coin-operated machines.
Breaking into or forcibly opening, §14-56.1.
Damaging or destroying machine, §14-56.2.
Defensive force.
Protection of home, workplace, motor vehicle, §14-51.2.
Definitions.
Buildings.
Breaking or entering buildings, §14-54(c).
First degree burglary, §14-51.
Second degree burglary, §14-51.
DNA sample for DNA analysis.
Obtaining upon arrest for certain offenses, §15A-266.3A.
Dwelling houses.
Breaking out of dwelling house, §14-53.
Explosives.
Use of explosives in burglary, §14-57.
Firearms and other weapons.
Preparation to commit burglary or other housebreaking, §14-55.
First degree burglary, §§14-51, 14-52.
Habitual breaking and entering status offense, §§14-7.25 to 14-7.31.
See BREAKING AND ENTERING.
Implements of housebreaking.
Preparation to commit burglary or other housebreakings, §14-55.
Mobile homes.
Breaking or entering into or breaking out of trailers, §14-56.
Motor vehicles.
Breaking or entering into or breaking out of vehicles, §14-56.
Preparation to commit breaking and entering into motor vehicle.
Criminal penalty, §14-56.4(d).
Definitions, §14-56.4(a).
Inapplicability to certain persons, §14-56.4(e).
Master key, manipulative key or other lock-picking device or hot wiring device.
Buying, selling or transferring, §14-56.4(c).
Possession with intent to commit felony, larceny or unauthorized use, §14-56.4(b).
Murder during commission, §14-17.
Paper currency machines.
Breaking into machine, §14-56.3.
Preparation to commit burglary or other housebreakings, §14-55.
Prior convictions of breaking and entering.
Habitual breaking and entering status offense, §§14-7.25 to 14-7.31.
See BREAKING AND ENTERING.
Protection of home, workplace, motor vehicle.
Defensive force, §14-51.2.
Punishment for burglary, §14-52.
Mandatory period of incarceration, §14-52.
Railroad cars.
Breaking or entering into or breaking out of cars, §14-56.
Second degree burglary, §§14-51, 14-52.
Explosives used in burglary, §14-57.

BURGLARY —Cont'd
Slot machines.
Breaking into or forcibly opening, §14-56.1.
Trailers.
Breaking or entering into or breaking out of trailers, §14-56.
Watercraft.
Breaking or entering into or breaking out of boats or other watercraft, §14-56.

BURGLARY AND THEFT INSURANCE, §58-7-15.
Mandatory or voluntary risk sharing plans.
See MANDATORY OR VOLUNTARY RISK SHARING PLANS.

BURGLARY TOOLS.
Preparation to commit burglary, §14-55.

BURIAL.
Animals.
Disposition of dead domesticated animals, §106-403.
Burial at sea, §§130A-113(b), 130A-388(b).
Certification and duties of medical examiners, §130A-388(b).
Cemeteries.
General provisions.
See CEMETERIES.
Cremation.
General provisions, §§90-210.120 to 90-210.135.
See CREMATION.
Decedents' estates.
Funeral and burial expenses deemed obligation of estate, §28A-19-8.
Discrimination.
Burial without regard to race or color, §65-72(a).
Violations of provisions misdemeanors, §65-72(b).
Disposition of remains of terminated pregnancies, §130A-131.10.
Executors and administrators.
Carrying out burial arrangements prior to appointment, §28A-13-1.
Exemption of burial plot from creditors' claims, §1C-1601(a).
Franchise tax.
Mutual burial associations, §105-121.1.
Funeral service.
General provisions, §§90-210.18A to 90-210.29B.
See FUNERAL SERVICES PROVIDERS.
Hog cholera.
Burial of hogs and other livestock dying in transit, §106-319.
Burial of hogs dying natural death, §106-310.
Identification of bodies before burial or cremation, §90-210.29A.
Medical examiners.
Postmortem medicolegal examinations and services.
Burial at sea.
Certification and duties of medical examiners, §130A-388(b).
When examiner's permission necessary before burial, §130A-388(a), (b).
Minimum burial depth, §65-77.
Preneed funeral contracts and funds, §§90-210.60 to 90-210.73.
See PRENEED FUNERAL CONTRACTS AND FUNDS.
Property taxes.
Real property set aside for burial.
Exemption, §105-278.2(a).

BURIAL —Cont'd
Property taxes —Cont'd
Real property set aside for burial —Cont'd
Real property defined, §105-278.2(c).
Special class, designation, assessment,
§105-278.2(b).
Racial minorities.
Burial without regard to race or color, §65-72(a).
Violations of provisions misdemeanors,
§65-72(b).
Sales and use tax.
Exemption of funeral expenses, §105-164.13.
Maintenance and repair of ingress and egress to
burial grounds.
Powers of department, §136-18.
**Unmarked human burial and human skeletal
remains protection, §§70-26 to 70-40.**
See UNMARKED HUMAN BURIAL AND
SKELETAL REMAINS PROTECTION.
Veterans' cemeteries.
Days for burial, §65-44.
Workers' compensation.
Expenses of burial, §97-38.

BURIAL ASSOCIATIONS.
**Mutual burial associations, §§90-210.80 to
90-210.107.**
See MUTUAL BURIAL ASSOCIATIONS.

BURIAL AT SEA, §§130A-113(b), 130A-388(b).

BURKE COUNTY.
Ambulance service.
Attachment or garnishment and lien for,
§§44-51.4 to 44-51.8.
Board of county commissioners.
Filling vacancies on board, §153A-27.1.
**Condemnation or acquisition of land by local
government unit outside county.**
Consent of board of commissioners necessary,
§153A-15.
Copies of grants in Burke.
Admission into evidence, §8-10.
Coroner elected as nominee of political party.
Filling vacancy in office, §152-1.
Counties generally.
See COUNTIES.
**Cropper or tenant refusing to perform terms
of contract.**
Forfeiture of right of possession to premises,
§42-27.
Dog collars.
Unlawful removal of electronic dog collars,
§14-401.17.
**Game laws, local acts not repealed,
§113-133.1(e).**
Housing authority commissioners.
Tenant as commissioner, exemption from provision
of law allowing, §157-5.
Oil, gas or mineral claims.
Certain ancient claims extinguished, preservation,
procedure, §1-42.3(a) to (d).
Registration of deeds.
Tax certification, no delinquent taxes due,
§161-31(b).
**Room occupancy tax levied by county, uniform
provision, §153A-155.**
School property.
Acquisition and improvement, §153A-158.1.
Sheriff.
Vacancy, performance of duties until vacancy
filled, §162-5.1.

BURKE COUNTY —Cont'd
Small city mixed beverage elections.
Inapplicability of provisions to, §18B-600(e1).
**Tax elections for industrial development
purposes, §§158-16 to 158-24.**
**Western North Carolina Development
Association, Inc.**
Appropriation of funds to, §153A-447(a), (b).

BURLAP.
**Dealers of scrap, salvage or surplus, failure to
keep records of purchases, §66-10(b).**

BURNING.
Arson.
See ARSON.
Boats and barges, §14-63.
Bridges and buildings, §14-61.
Building under construction, §14-62.1.
**Churches and other places of worship,
§§14-49(b1), 14-62.2.**
Dwelling.
Arson.
See ARSON.
Fraudulently setting fire, §14-65.
Fires and fire prevention generally.
See FIRES AND FIRE PREVENTION.
Forest fires.
See FOREST FIRES.
Ginhouses and tobacco houses, §14-64.
**Mobile, manufactured or trailer homes,
§14-58.2.**
Personal property, §14-66.
Public building, §14-59.
School or education buildings, §14-60.
Timber.
Damages for unlawful burning, §1-539.1(a).
Will.
Revocation of written will, §31-5.1.

BUS COMPANIES.
Certificates of authority, §62-262.1.
Fees, §62-300.
Charter service rates, fares and charges.
Exempt from regulations, §62-146.1(j).
**Complaints about rates, fares, charges, etc.,
§62-146.1(h).**
Defined, §62-3.
Discontinuance or reduction in service.
Certificate or permit.
Inapplicability of provisions to bus companies,
§62-262.2(e).
Granting permission, §62-262.2(c).
Hearings.
Determination with or without public hearing,
§62-262.2(d).
Notice to be given, §62-262.2(a).
Objections to granting permission, §62-262.2(b).
Petitions for permission, §62-262.2(a).
**Fare, just and reasonable rates, fares and
charges.**
Establishment pursuant to this section,
§62-146.1(i).
**Fixed service, petition for new or revised
rates, fares or charges, §62-146.1(d).**
Franchises.
Fixed routes, franchise to specify, §62-113(b).
**Hearings on proposed new or revised rates,
fares or charges, §62-146.1(e).**
Interlining of passengers, §62-146.1(b).
**Investigation, suspension, etc., of proposed
new revised rates, fares or charges,
§62-146.1(g).**

BUS COMPANIES —Cont'd
Joint rates between companies, §62-146.1(c).
Policy of state, §62-259.1.
Proof of financial responsibility, §62-268.
Rates, §62-146.1.
Revenue levels authorized by utilities commission, §62-146.1(f).
Safe and adequate service, equipment and facilities.
Duty to provide, §62-146.1(a).
Service, §62-146.1.
Discontinuance or reduction, §62-262.2.

BUSES.
Disabled persons.
Right to use of public conveyances, §168-3.
Disorderly conduct at bus station, §14-275.1.
Drivers.
Age limits for public passenger-carrying vehicles, §20-10.
Length.
Passenger buses owned and operated by local governments, §20-116(l).
Lights.
Additional lighting equipment required on certain vehicles, §20-129.1.
Motor carriers generally, §§62-259 to 62-280.1.
See MOTOR CARRIERS.
Motor vehicle license plates.
Permanent license plates for city-owned buses or trolleys, §20-84(b).
Nonprofit activity buses.
Railroad grade crossings.
Stopping at, §20-142.3(a).
Violation of speed limit, §20-218.2.
Property taxes.
Public service corporations.
Generally, §§105-333 to 105-344.
See PROPERTY TAXES.
Railroad grade crossings.
Activity buses.
Stopping at crossings, §20-142.3(a).
Rearview mirrors.
Requirements, §20-117.1(a).
Registration.
Common carriers of passengers.
Fees, §20-87.
Interchange of buses with nonresident common carriers, §20-87.1.
Repair of motor vehicles, §§20-354 to 20-354.9.
See MOTOR VEHICLE REPAIRS.
School buses.
Generally.
See SCHOOL BUSES.
Sex offenders.
Unlawful to drive commercial passenger vehicle or school bus without appropriate license or while disqualified, §20-27.1.
Speed limits.
Nonprofit activity buses, §20-218.2.
School buses, §20-218(b).
Penalty for violation, §20-218(c).
Stations.
Disorderly conduct at bus station, §14-275.1.
Transitway lanes, §20-146.2(a1).
Transportation system defined, §136-5.1.
Width, §20-116(k).
Window tinting exception for hire passenger vehicles, §20-127(c).

BUSHELS.
Standard weights and measures, §81A-42.

BUSINESS AND ENERGY TAX CREDITS, §§105-129.15 to 105-129.19.
Biodiesel producers.
Qualifying credit, §105-129.16F(a).
Sunset provision, §105-129.16F(b).
Burden of proving eligibility and amount, §105-129.19.
Cap on credit, §105-129.17(b).
Carryforwards.
Claimed against franchise or income tax, §105-129.17(a).
Definitions, §105-129.15.
Dry-cleaning equipment not using hazardous substances, §105-129.16C(a) to (d).
Election of tax against which credit claimed, §105-129.17(a).
Franchise tax.
Election of tax against which credit claimed, §105-129.17(a).
Income tax.
Election of tax against which credit claimed, §105-129.17(a).
Information required to supplied secretary of revenue, §105-129.18.
Renewable energy property facilities.
Amount of credit, §105-129.16I(a).
Installments, §105-129.16I(b).
Termination of credit, §105-129.16I(c).
Renewable energy property investment, §105-129.16A(a).
Ceiling on credit, §105-129.16A(c).
Donations to nonprofit organization or governmental unit to acquire renewable energy property.
Credit generally, §105-129.16H(a).
No double benefit, §105-129.16H(c).
Records of donations, §105-129.16H(b).
Double credit not allowed, §105-129.16A(d).
Expiration, property sold, taken out of service, etc., §105-129.16A(b).
Nonresidential property ceiling, §105-129.16A(c).
Public funds used, credit not allowed, §105-129.16A(a).
Residential property ceiling, §105-129.16A(c).
Sunset, §105-129.16A(e).
Renewable fuel facilities construction credit.
Dispensing credit, §105-129.16D(a).
No double credit, §105-129.16D(c).
Production credit, §105-129.16D(b).
Sunset, §105-129.16D(d).
Reports, §105-129.19.
Small business employee health benefits, §105-129.16E.
Allocation, §105-129.16E(b).
Definitions, §105-129.16E(c).
Qualifying credit, §105-129.16E(a).
Sunset provision, §105-129.16E(d).
Work opportunity tax credit, §105-129.16G.

BUSINESS AND INDUSTRIAL EXPANSION.
Site development grants, §143B-437.02.

BUSINESS COMBINATIONS.
Chapter not to supersede, restrict or limit other applicable laws, §75E-7.
Civil penalties for unlawful activities, §75E-5.
Cumulative effect of remedies for unlawful activities, §75E-6.
Investigative and regulatory powers of attorney general, §75E-3.
Nonresidents deemed to appoint secretary of state as agent for service, §75E-8.

BUSINESS COMBINATIONS —Cont'd
Preventing or restraining violations, attorney general, §75E-4.
Private action by person injured, §75E-4.
Saving clause as to provisions of chapter, §75E-9.
Unlawful activities, §75E-2.

BUSINESS CONTRACTS.
Reciprocal attorneys' fees in business contracts, §6-21.7.

BUSINESS CORPORATIONS.
Generally, §§55-1-01 to 55-17-05.
See CORPORATIONS.

BUSINESS COURT JUDGES.
Complex business cases.
Special superior court judges.
Designation to hear and decide cases, §7A-45.3.

BUSINESS DISCRIMINATION, §§75B-1 to 75B-7.
Actions not prohibited, §75B-3.
Chapter not exclusive, §75B-7.
Contracts void, §75B-6.
Definitions, §75B-1.
Enforcement of chapter, §75B-4.
Prohibited, §75B-2.
Remedies cumulative, §75B-5.

BUSINESS INVESTMENT TAX CREDIT.
Qualified business investments, §§105-163.010 to 105-163.015.

BUSINESS LICENSES.
Clearinghouse for license information.
Department of commerce.
Authorized to establish, §143B-431(e).
License information service.
Department of commerce.
Authorized to establish, §143B-431(e).
Municipal regulations, §160A-194.
Occupational licensing boards generally, §§93B-1 to 93B-16.
See OCCUPATIONAL LICENSING BOARDS.

BUSINESS LICENSE TAXES.
Generally, §§105-33 to 105-109.
See LICENSE TAXES.

BUSINESS NECESSITY.
Fair housing violation, §41A-5(a).

BUSINESS OPPORTUNITY SALES, §§66-94 to 66-100.
Bonds, surety.
Filing of copies with secretary of state, §66-97(c).
Requirements, §66-96.
Contracts.
Provisions, §66-99(b).
Voiding of contract.
Remedy of purchaser, §66-100(a).
Written contracts required, §66-99(a).
Damages.
Remedy of purchaser, §66-100(b).
Definition of "business opportunity,"§66-94.
Disclosure statement.
Contents, §66-95.
Filing with secretary of state, §66-97(a).
Failure to file.
Misdemeanor, §66-97(e).
Fee, §66-97(a).
Uniform statements, §66-97(d).
Required, §66-95.
Injunctions.
Violations of provisions, §66-100(c).

BUSINESS OPPORTUNITY SALES —Cont'd
Misrepresentations.
Prohibited acts, §66-98.
Prohibited acts, §66-98.
Remedies of purchasers.
Additional nature of remedies, §66-100(d).
Generally, §66-100(a) to (e).
Responsible sellers exemption.
Information to be filed with secretary of state, §66-94.1(c).
Qualifications, §66-94.1(a), (b).
Secretary of state.
Bonds, surety.
Filing with secretary, §66-97(c).
Disclosure statement.
Filing with secretary of state, §66-97(a).
Uniform statements, §66-97(d).
Responsible sellers exemption.
Filing information with secretary, §66-94.1(b).
Service of process.
Appointment of secretary as attorney to receive process, §66-97(b).
Service of process.
Appointment of secretary of state as attorney to receive process.
Seller to file consent, §66-97(b).
Trademarks.
Prohibited acts, §66-98.
Trust accounts.
When required, §66-96.
Violations of provisions.
Remedies of purchaser, §66-100(a) to (e).
Additional nature of remedies, §66-100(d).
Unfair practices, §66-100(e).

BUSINESS PROPERTY INVESTMENT TAX CREDIT.
Business and energy tax credits generally, §§105-129.15 to 105-129.19.

BUSINESS RECORDS.
Collection agencies.
Entry of default or summary judgment against debtor.
Evidence to establish amount and nature of debt, §58-70-155(b).
Hearsay exceptions.
Records of regularly conducted activity, §8C-1 Rule 803.
Absence of entry in records, §8C-1 Rule 803.
Interrogatories, option to produce, §1A-1 Rule 33(c).

BUSINESS RETENTION AND EXPANSION.
One North Carolina fund, §§143B-437.70 to 143B-437.74.
See ONE NORTH CAROLINA FUND.

BUSINESS TAX INCENTIVES.
Business and energy tax credits, §§105-129.15 to 105-129.19.
Tax incentives for new and expanding businesses, §§105-129.2 to 105-129.13.
See TAX INCENTIVES FOR NEW AND EXPANDING BUSINESSES.

BUSINESS, TRADE AND CORRESPONDENCE SCHOOLS.
National guard.
Tuition assistance, §§116-209.50 to 116-209.55.
Private schools.
General provisions.
See PRIVATE AND PAROCHIAL SCHOOLS.

BUSINESS, TRADE AND CORRESPONDENCE SCHOOLS —Cont'd

Proprietary schools, §§115D-87 to 115D-97.
See PROPRIETARY SCHOOLS.

Vocational and technical education, §§115C-151 to 115C-169.
See VOCATIONAL AND TECHNICAL EDUCATION.

BUSINESS TRUSTS.
Actions.
Authority to sue and be sued, §39-45.
Deeds and other conveyances, §39-46(a), (b).
Applicability of law for conveyances by corporations, §47-41.02.
Construction of provisions, §39-46(c), (d).
Forms for probate executed by corporation.
Applicability to business trusts, §47-41.01(e).
Prior deeds validated, §39-47.
Definition, §39-44.
Real property.
Authority to acquire and hold, §39-45.
Conveyances, §39-46(a), (b).
Construction of provisions, §39-46(c), (d).
Title vested, §39-46(a).

BUSINESS UNDER ASSUMED NAME.
Accountants.
Partnerships engaged in practice of certified public accountancy.
Exemption from provisions, §66-68(e).
Actions.
Violations of provisions.
Recovery in civil action not prevented, §66-71(b).
Certificates.
Copy.
Prima facie evidence, §66-69.1.
Filing required, §66-68(a).
Exceptions, §66-68(d).
Index of certificates.
Register of deeds to keep, §66-69.
Transfer of assumed name, §66-69.
Withdrawal of assumed name, §66-69.
Signing, §66-68(b).
Transfer of assumed name, §66-68(f).
Index, §66-69.
Withdrawal of assumed name, §66-68(f).
Index, §66-69.
Evidence.
Copy of certificate prima facie evidence, §66-69.1.
Partnerships.
Public accountancy.
Exemption of partnerships engaged in practice of certified public accountancy, §66-68(e).
Withdrawal of partner or new partner.
New certificate, §66-68(c).
Transfer of assumed name, §66-68(f).
Violations of provisions.
Penalties, §66-71(a).
Recovery in civil action not prevented, §66-71(b).
Withdrawal of assumed name, §66-68(f).

BUS STATIONS.
Disorderly conduct at bus station, §14-275.1.
Eminent domain.
By whom right may be exercised, §40A-3(a).

BUTNER ADVISORY COUNCIL, §§122C-413, 122C-413.1.

BUTTER AND EGG LOTTERY.
Selling numbers tickets, §14-291.1.

BUTTERFLY BALLOTS.
Use prohibited, §163-165.4B.

BUY BACKS.
Business opportunity sales, §§66-94 to 66-100.
See BUSINESS OPPORTUNITY SALES.

BUYING AND SELLING PUBLIC OFFICES, §14-228.

BYLAWS.
Community third party or pooled trusts.
Adoption, filing, §36D-4(d).
Conference of clerks of superior court, §7A-806(d).
Corporations, §55-2-06.
Amendment, §§55-10-20, 55-10-22.
Emergency bylaws, §55-2-07.
Nonprofit corporations, §55A-2-06.
Amendment, §§55A-10-20, 55A-10-21.
Emergency bylaws, §55A-2-07.
Mutual burial associations.
Operation in noncompliance with, §90-210.88.
Requirements, §90-210.81.

BYSTANDERS.
Trials.
Exclusion in rape cases, §15-166.

C

CABARRUS COUNTY.
Acquisition of property, power, §153A-158.1(a).
Ambulance service.
Attachment or garnishment and lien for, §§44-51.4 to 44-51.8.
Obtaining ambulance services without intending to pay, §14-111.2.
Requesting ambulance falsely, §14-111.3.
Board of county commissioners.
Filling vacancies on board, §153A-27.1.
Condemnation or acquisition of land by local government unit outside county.
Consent of board of commissioners necessary, §153A-15.
Coroner elected as nominee of political party.
Filling vacancy in office, §152-1.
Cropper or tenant refusing to perform terms of contract.
Forfeiture of right of possession to premises, §42-27.
Land-use development incentives.
Reduction of energy consumption, §160A-383.4.
Motor vehicle emission inspections.
Counties inspections required to be performed in, §143-215.107A(c).
Officers compensated from fees.
Statement to be rendered, §128-13.
Registration of deeds.
Tax certification, no delinquent taxes due, §161-31(b).
Room occupancy tax levied by county, uniform provisions, §153A-155.
School property.
Acquisition and improvement, §153A-158.1.
Sheriff.
Vacancy, performance of duties until vacancy filled, §162-5.1.
Tax sales, notices by publication validated.
Inapplicability of provisions, §47-108.24.
Wild plants, taking of certain plants from land of another.
Inapplicability of provisions, §14-129.

CABBAGE.
Standard weights and measures, §81A-42.

CABLE CAR.
Passenger tramways, §§95-116 to 95-125.
See TRAMWAYS.

CABLE TELEVISION.
Automatic dialing and recorded message players.
Circumstances allowing, §75-104(b).
Electioneering communications.
Disclosures, prohibited sources.
Mass mailings and telephone banks.
Candidate-specific communications, §§163-278.110 to 163-278.113.
Environmental document for constructing, maintaining or removal of lines.
Not required for lines across right of way of street or highway, §113A-12.
Municipalities.
Cities providing communications services, §§160A-340 to 160A-340.6.
See MUNICIPAL UTILITIES.
Public enterprises generally, §§160A-311 to 160A-328.
See MUNICIPAL UTILITIES.
Overhead high-voltage line safety.
Exemption from act, §95-229.11(a).
Sales and use tax.
Cable service defined, §105-164.3.
Distribution of part of tax to counties and cities.
Video programing service.
City changes, §105-164.44I(h).
Distribution, §105-164.44I(a).
Ineligible cities, §105-164.44I(i).
Late information, §105-164.44I(f).
Nature, §105-164.44I(j).
Population determination, §105-164.44I(g).
Subsequent distribution, §105-164.44I(d).
Supplemental PEG channel support, §§105-164.44I(b), 105-164.44J.
2006-2007 fiscal year distribution, §105-164.44I(c).
Use of proceeds, §105-164.44I(e).
Rate of tax, §105-164.4(a).
State franchising of cable television service, §§66-350 to 66-360.
Annual service report, §66-353.
Authority, §66-351(a).
Award of franchise, §66-351(b).
Complaints by customers, §66-356(c).
Definitions, §66-350.
Discrimination against service area residents, §66-356(a).
Existing local agreements.
Effect of provisions, §66-355(a).
Termination, §66-355(b).
Extension of service area, §66-352(c).
FCC standards of customer service, compliance, §66-356(b).
Filing procedures, §66-354(a).
Forfeiture of franchise.
Failure to file notices, §66-354(b).
No build-out requirements, §66-356(d).
Notice of change of ownership, §66-354(a).
Notice of franchise, §66-352(a).
Failure to file, §66-354(b).
Notice of service for service area, §66-352(b).
Failure to file, §66-354(b).
PEG channels.
Availability and use.
Action to compel compliance, §66-357(g).

CABLE TELEVISION —Cont'd
State franchising of cable television service —Cont'd
PEG channels —Cont'd
Availability and use —Cont'd
Additional channels, §66-357(d).
Applicability of provisions, §66-357(a).
Locality request to service provider, §66-357(b).
Number of initial channels, §66-357(c).
Programming requirements, §66-357(d).
Reprogramming, §66-357(e).
Responsibility for operation and content, §66-357(f).
Time for providing upon request, §66-357(b).
Distribution of part of sales and use tax to counties and cities.
Supplemental PEG channel support, §§105-164.44I(b), 105-164.44J.
Transmission.
Methods, §66-358(a).
Signal standards, §66-358(b).
Public buildings, service for, §66-360.
Report by franchise holder, §66-353.
Report to revenue laws study committee, §66-356(e).
Scope of franchise awarded, §66-351(b).
Secretary of state authority, §66-351(a).
Successors in interest.
Notice of change of ownership, §66-354(a).
Termination of existing agreement, §66-355(b).
Time for providing service following notice, §66-352(b).
Withdrawal of notice, §66-352(d).
Theft of service, §14-118.5.
Actual damages not prerequisite to civil actions, §14-118.5(d).
Applicability of provisions, §14-118.5(e).
Charges for cable television service.
Avoiding lawful charge by use of instruments, apparatus, etc., §14-118.5(a).
Civil penalties, §14-118.5(c).
Facilities or equipment of cable television company.
Rearranging, tampering, etc., of facilities or equipment of company, §14-118.5(a).
Prima facie evidence, §14-118.5(e).
Refusal to provide service to alleged violators, §14-118.5(g).
Sale, distribution, etc., of converters, decoders, etc., §14-118.5(b).
Satellite dish or antenna, §14-118.5(f).
Winning prizes.
Representation of eligibility broadcast by, §75-33(c).

CADAVERS.
Anatomical gifts, §§130A-412.3 to 130A-412.33.
See ANATOMICAL GIFTS.
General provisions.
See DEAD BODIES.

CAFES.
Alcoholic beverage permits.
Eating establishment defined to include, §18B-1000.
Off-premises malt beverage permit.
Kind of permit that may be issued, §18B-1001.
On-premises malt beverage permit.
Kind of permit that may be issued to, §18B-1001.
Recycling requirement, §18B-1006.1.

CAFES —Cont'd
Alcoholic beverage permits —Cont'd
On-premises unfortified wine permit.
Kind of permit that may issued, §18B-1001.
Recycling requirement, §18B-1006.1.
Special occasion permit.
Kind of permit that may be issued, §18B-1001.

CAFETERIA PLANS.
Community colleges.
Flexible compensation plan, §115D-25.2.
University of North Carolina.
Flexible compensation plans, §116-17.2.

CAFETERIAS.
Alcoholic beverage permits.
Eating establishment defined to include,
§18B-1000.
Off-premises malt beverage permits.
Kind of permit that may be issued, §18B-1001.
On-premises malt beverage permit.
Kind of permit that may be issued to,
§18B-1001.
Recycling requirement, §18B-1006.1.
On-premises unfortified wine permit.
Kind of permit that may be issued, §18B-1001.
Recycling requirement, §18B-1006.1.
Special occasion permit.
Kind of permit that may be issued, §18B-1001.
Governmental units operating, §66-58(a).
Public schools operating, §66-58(c).
State legislative building, operation in,
§66-58(c).

CAKES.
Sales and use tax exemption.
Bakery items sold by artisan bakeries,
§105-164.13B(a).

CALABASH.
Ordinances to regulate and control swimming,
personal watercraft operation, surfing and
littering in Atlantic Ocean, §160A-176.2.
Satellite annexation.
Limitation on area of satellite corporate limits,
inapplicability, §160A-58.1(b).

CALCIUM.
High-calcium foods and beverages.
Local boards of education.
Preference in purchasing contracts,
§115C-264.1(a), (b).

CALCIUM CHLORIDE.
Antifreeze solutions compounded with,
prohibited, §66-66.

CALDWELL COUNTY.
Ambulances.
Attachment or garnishment and lien for,
§§44-51.4 to 44-51.8.
Obtaining ambulance services without intending
to pay, §14-111.2.
Board of county commissioners.
Filling vacancies on board, §153A-27.1.
Condemnation or acquisition of land by local
government unit outside county.
Consent of board of commissioners necessary,
§153A-15.
Coroner elected as nominee of political party.
Filling vacancy in office, §152-1.
Counties generally.
See COUNTIES.

CALDWELL COUNTY —Cont'd
Dangerous firearm use by young children,
permitting.
Air rifles, air pistols and BB guns not dangerous
firearm, §14-316(b).
Dog collars.
Unlawful removal of electronic dog collars,
§14-401.17.
Foxes, open season for taking with firearms,
§113-291.4A(a), (b).
Game laws, local acts not repealed,
§113-133.1(e).
Housing authority commissioners.
Tenant as commissioner, exemption from provision
of law allowing, §157-5.
Oil, gas or mineral claims.
Certain ancient claims extinguished, preservation,
procedure, §1-42.3(a) to (d).
Real estate mortgage loans.
Interest, commissions and repayment, §45-43.
School property.
Acquisition and improvement, §153A-158.1.
Sheriff.
Vacancy, performance of duties until vacancy
filled, §162-5.1.
Small city mixed beverage elections.
Inapplicability of provisions to, §18B-600(e1).

CALENDARING OF ACTIONS FOR TRIAL,
§1A-1 Rule 40(a).
Criminal law and procedure.
Calendaring by district attorney for
administrative purposes, §15A-941(e).
Superior courts, criminal case docketing, §7A-49.4.
Evidence.
Proof of dates.
Clerk's calendar may be used, §8-48(a).

CALL BEFORE YOU DIG.
Underground damage prevention.
Generally, §§87-100 to 87-114.
See UNDERGROUND DAMAGE
PREVENTION.

CALLER ID.
Exception from trace device regulations,
§15A-261.
Telephone solicitations.
Solicitor blocking or circumventing, prohibition,
§75-102(h).

CALLIGRAPHY.
Artwork on consignment, §§25C-1 to 25C-5.
Sale of prints, §§25C-10 to 25C-16.

CAM.
Impaired driving.
Condition of probation.
Defendants subjection to level one or two
punishments, §20-179(h1), (h3).
Order to abstain from alcohol consumption.
Condition of pretrial release, §15A-534(i).
Regulations for continuous alcohol monitoring
systems.
Division of adult correction, §15A-1343.3.

CAMDEN COUNTY.
Ambulance service.
Attachment or garnishment and lien for,
§§44-51.4 to 44-51.8.
Obtained without intending to pay, §14-111.2.
Requesting ambulance falsely, §14-111.3.
Blank or master forms of mortgages, deeds of
trust, etc.
Indexing and recording, inapplicability of
provisions, §47-21.

CAMDEN COUNTY —Cont'd

Condemnation or acquisition of land by local government unit outside county.

Consent of board of commissioners necessary, §153A-15.

Cropper or tenant refusing to perform terms of contract.

Forfeiture of right of possession to premises, §42-27.

Dog collars.

Unlawful removal of electronic dog collars, §14-401.17.

Game laws, local acts not repealed, §113-133.1(e).

Grants in navigable waters, registration, §113-205(a).

Housing.

Tenant as commissioner, exemption from provision of law allowing, §157-5.

Maps in special proceedings, recording of photographic copies, §47-32.

Violation as misdemeanor, inapplicability of provisions, §47-32.2.

North Carolina's northeast commission, §§158-8.2 to 158-8.8.

Open fires, §106-942.

Applicability of provisions, §106-942(a).

Ground clearing activities, special permit required, §106-942(c).

Woodland fires, permit required, §106-942(b).

Registration of deeds.

Tax certification, no delinquent taxes due, §161-31(b).

School property.

Acquisition and improvement, §153A-158.1.

Tax sales, notices by publication validated.

Inapplicability of provisions, §47-108.24.

Wastewater systems.

Innovative septic tank systems.

Ordinance billing fee as property tax, §130A-343.1(c).

CAMERAS.

Digital cameras.

Portable consumer electronic devices insurance.

Claims handling, adjuster licenses, §58-33-27.

Generally, §§58-44A-1 to 58-44A-25.

See PORTABLE CONSUMER ELECTRONIC DEVICES INSURANCE.

Photographs generally.

See PHOTOGRAPHS.

School buses.

Automated camera and video recording system.

Failure to stop for bus receiving or discharging passengers.

Use in detecting and prosecuting violation, §20-217(h).

CAMPAIGN FINANCE, §§163-278.5 to 163-278.38.

Actions.

Civil remedies other than penalties, §163-278.34(c).

District attorney, notifying and consulting with, §163-278.34(f).

Collect of penalty, §163-278.34(e).

Advertising.

Charges, §163-278.18(a).

Discrimination prohibited, §163-278.18(b).

Disclosure requirements for media advertisements, §§163-278.39 to 163-278.39C.

Indication of name of political party or political committee, §163-278.16(g).

CAMPAIGN FINANCE —Cont'd

Amounts of contributions, limitations.

Exemption from provisions, §163-278.13(e).

Generally, §163-278.13(a) to (c).

Penalties for violations, §163-278.13(f).

Reimbursement to contributing entity.

Accepting contribution for, §163-278.13(d1).

Effect of non-reimbursement, §163-278.13(d2).

Annual report.

Referendum committee, §163-278.9A(a).

Anonymous contributions or contributions made in name of another.

Acceptance prohibited, exceptions, §163-278.14(a).

Criminal penalty for violating, §163-278.27(a2).

Applicability of provisions.

General provisions as to corruption, §163-278.33.

Candidates.

Death or incapacity.

Designation of uses of funds, §163-278.16B(c).

Defined, §163-278.6.

Inactive candidates.

Procedure for, §163-278.10.

Personal estate of candidate.

Contributions not part of, §163-278.16B(c).

Cease and desist orders.

Civil remedy other than penalty, §163-278.34(c).

Certificate of election.

Filing of statements as prerequisite, §163-278.25.

Certified as true and correct.

False certification, §163-278.27(a1).

Statements and reports, §163-278.32.

Checks.

Contributions in excess of one hundred dollars, §163-278.14(b).

Expenditures by check, §163-278.8(e), (f).

Civil penalties.

Calculation and assessment, §163-278.34(e).

Civil action to collect, §163-278.34(e).

Contesting, time period, §163-278.34(e).

District attorney, notifying and consulting with, §163-278.34(f).

Illegal contributions, §163-278.34(b).

Late filing, §163-278.34(a).

Mitigation, facts, §163-278.34(d).

Voter-owned elections act, §163-278.99D.

Civil remedies other than penalties, §163-278.34(c).

District attorney, notifying and consulting with, §163-278.34(f).

Coercing state employee to support or contribute to political candidate, committee or party, §§126-14, 126-14.1.

Collection of penalty, civil action, §163-278.34(e).

Commingling of funds prohibited, §163-278.8(h).

Communications.

Process for determining whether expenditure before airing or distributions.

State board to develop, §163-278.22.

Corporations.

Acceptance of contributions, §163-278.15(a).

Defined, §163-278.6.

Political committee formed to accept contributions and make expenditures to influence elections, §163-278.19(g).

Prohibited acts, §163-278.19(a).

Exceptions, §163-278.19(b), (d), (f).

Penalties, §§163-278.19(c), 163-278.27(a2).

Council of state candidates.

Restrictions on using state funds for advertising or public service announcements, §163-278.16A.

CAMPAIGN FINANCE —Cont'd

Counties.

Use of public funds to endorse or oppose a
referendum, election or particular candidate
prohibited, §153A-456.

**Criminal penalties and prosecution of
violations.**

Certification as true and correct.

False certification, §§163-278.27(a1), 163-278.32.

Costs incurred by board to investigate.

Payment by violator as condition of probation,
§163-278.27(d).

Criminal penalty, §§163-278.19(c), 163-278.27(a).

Duty of district attorney to prosecute.

Receipt of report of violation, §163-278.27(c).

Reports by board of violations to prosecutorial
authorities, §163-278.27(b).

Statute of limitation on prosecutions,
§163-278.27(a).

Death or incapacity of candidate.

Designation of uses of funds, §163-278.16B(c).

Definitions, §163-278.6.

Disclosure requirements for media
advertisements, §163-278.38Z.

Donor.

Donation to further independent expenditure,
§163-278.12(f).

Election, §§163-278.6, 163-278.13(d).

Filer.

Donation to further independent expenditure,
§163-278.12(f).

Political party, §§163-278.6, 163-278.13(e).

Principal occupation of donor, §163-278.12(c).

Electronically filed reports, §163-278.9(j).

Evidence.

Communications are "to support or oppose the
nomination or election of one or more clearly
identified candidates,"§163-278.14A(a).

Exceptions, §163-278.14A(b).

Exemptions to reporting requirement.

Threshold amount for financial reports,
§163-278.10A.

Federal election campaign act of 1971.

Reports required to be filed under, §163-278.9(e),
(f).

Federal offices.

Candidates to file information reports,
§163-278.30.

Federal political committees.

Gifts from, §163-278.7A.

**Filing reports, statements, other required
documents.**

Late filing.

Civil late penalty, §163-278.34(a).

Manual delivery or by mail, §163-278.34(a).

Timely filing, §163-278.34(a).

Final report.

Referendum committee, §163-278.9A(a).

Forty-eight hour report, §163-278.9(a).

Referendum committee, §163-278.9A(a).

**Fundraising during legislative session,
limitation.**

Definitions, §163-278.13B(a).

Exceptions, §163-278.13B(d).

Misdemeanor for violating provisions,
§163-278.13B(e).

Prohibited contributions by limited contributor,
§163-278.13B(c).

Prohibited solicitations by limited contributor,
§163-278.13B(b).

CAMPAIGN FINANCE —Cont'd

General provisions as to corruption.

Applicability, §163-278.33.

Gifts from federal political committees,
§163-278.7A.

**Identification of donor or person or entity
making independent expenditure,**
§163-278.12(c).

Illegal contributions.

Civil penalties, §163-278.34(b).

Independent expenditures.

Communication.

Process for determining whether independent
expenditure before airing or distribution.

State board to develop, §163-278.22.

Defined, §163-278.6.

Donation to further independent expenditure,
§163-278.12(f).

Identification of person or entity making,
§163-278.12(c).

Media outlets to require written authority,
§163-278.17(d).

Persons who make, §163-278.12(a).

Reporting.

Filing, §163-278.12(g).

Required, time, §163-278.12(d).

Subsequent reporting, §163-278.12(e).

Statement of independent expenditure.

Filing required, §163-278.12(a).

Individuals.

Defined, §163-278.6.

Injunctions, §163-278.28(a).

Insurance companies.

Defined, §163-278.6.

Prohibited acts, §163-278.19(a).

Exceptions, §163-278.19(b), (d), (f).

Penalties, §§163-278.19(c), 163-278.27(a2).

Intentional violations of reporting provisions.

Costs incurred by board to investigate.

Payment by violator as condition of probation,
§163-278.27(d).

Criminal penalty, §163-278.27(a).

Duty of district attorney to prosecute.

Receipt of report of violation, §163-278.27(c).

Reports by board of violations to prosecutorial
authorities, §163-278.27(b).

Statute of limitation on prosecutions,
§163-278.27(a).

Investigations.

State board of elections.

Duties, §163-278.22.

Judicial office candidates.

Limitations on contributions, §163-278.13(e3).

Labor unions.

Prohibited acts, §163-278.19(a).

Exceptions, §163-278.19(b), (d), (f).

Penalties, §§163-278.19(c), 163-278.27(a2).

Late filing penalty, §163-278.34(a).

Legal expense funds for elected officials,
§§163-278.300 to 163-278.320.

See LEGAL EXPENSE FUNDS FOR ELECTED
OFFICIALS.

Limitation of actions.

Civil action to collect penalty, §163-278.34(e).

Limitations on contributions.

Exemptions from provisions, §163-278.13(e).

Generally, §163-278.13(a) to (c).

Penalties for violations, §163-278.13(f).

Loans.

Proceeds from financial institution,
§163-278.15(b).

Exceptions to prohibitions, §163-278.19(a2).

CAMPAIGN FINANCE —Cont'd
Loans —Cont'd
Recording separately, detailed analysis,
§163-278.8(g).
Lobbyists.
Limitation on fundraising during legislative
session, §163-278.13B.
Prohibitions, §163-278.13C.
Local boards of education.
Political endorsements or oppositions.
Public funds, restriction on use for political
activities, §115C-46.1.
Mass mailing defined, §163-278.6.
Media.
Authorizations of expenditures.
Media to require, §163-278.17(b).
Independent expenditures or electioneering
communications, §163-278.17(d).
Defined, §163-278.6.
Disclosure requirements for media
advertisements, §§163-278.39 to 163-278.39C.
Expenditures for media expenses, §163-278.8(e).
Expenditures for nonmedia expenses,
§163-278.8(f).
Misdemeanors.
Disclosure requirements for media
advertisements.
Misrepresentation of authorization,
§163-278.39(c).
Limitations on contributions.
Violations, §163-278.13(f).
Violations generally, §163-278.27(a).
Municipal campaign reporting, §§163-278.9(d),
163-278.40 to 163-278.40J.
Accounts.
Organizational report, §163-278.40A(b).
Board.
Defined, §163-278.40.
Contents, §163-278.40G.
Contributions.
Report to list, §163-278.40G.
Definitions, §163-278.40.
Filing, §163-278.40D.
Form, §163-278.40F.
Nonpartisan elections, §163-278.40C.
Nonpartisan plurality, §163-278.40E.
Primary elections, §163-278.40D.
Nonpartisan plurality method, §163-278.40E.
Notice of reports due, §163-278.40H.
Organizational report.
Contents, §163-278.40A(b).
Part 1 to apply, §163-278.40I.
Partisan elections, §163-278.40B.
Primary elections, §§163-278.40B, 163-278.40D.
Runoffs, §163-278.40C.
Schedule for committee reports, §163-278.40J.
Treasurers.
Appointment by candidate, §163-278.40A(a).
Municipalities.
Endorsement, opposition to referendum, election,
particular candidate.
Using municipal funds prohibited, §160A-499.3.
Names.
Reports to recipient, §163-278.14(c).
Oath.
Certified as true and correct.
False certification knowing information to be
untrue, criminal penalty, §163-278.27(a1).
Statements and reports required to be filed,
§163-278.32.

CAMPAIGN FINANCE —Cont'd
Organizational report, §163-278.9(a).
Referendum committee, §163-278.9A(a).
Personal estate of candidate.
Contributions not part of, §163-278.16B(c).
**Person or entity not otherwise required to
report.**
Contributions in excess of $100, reporting,
§163-278.12(b), (c), (d).
Political committees.
Acceptance and expenditure of contributions to
influence elections.
Only purpose.
Incorporation as nonprofit, §163-278.19(g).
Defined, §163-278.6.
Federal political committees, gifts from,
§163-278.7A.
Inactive committee.
Procedure for, §163-278.10.
Political parties financing fund, §§163-278.41 to
163-278.45.
Political party headquarters building funds.
Donations to, §163-278.19B.
Postprimary report, §163-278.9(a).
Pre-referendum report.
Referendum committee, §163-278.9A(a).
Prerequisites to receipts of contributions,
§163-278.16(a).
Preservation of reports, records and accounts,
§163-278.35.
County boards of election to preserve reports,
§163-278.37.
Presidential election year candidates fund,
§§163-278.41 to 163-278.45.
Presumptions.
Generally, §163-278.34A.
**Printed material identifying candidate or
potential candidate.**
Name of political party or political committee,
§163-278.16(g).
Professional associations.
Defined, §163-278.6.
Prohibited acts, §163-278.19(a).
Exceptions, §163-278.19(b), (d), (f).
Penalties, §§163-278.19(c), 163-278.27(a2).
Public campaign fund.
Generally, §§163-278.61 to 163-278.70.
See ELECTIONS.
Individual income taxpayer.
Allocation to fund by individual, §105-159.2(a).
Instructions for individual to designate
allocation, §105-159.2(c).
Returns to give individual opportunity to
designate allocation, §105-159.2(b).
Quarterly reports, §163-278.9(a).
Radio.
Disclosure requirements for media
advertisements, §§163-278.39 to 163-278.39C.
Records, §163-278.19(e).
Referenda, §163-278.19A.
Defined, §163-278.6.
Failure to comply with provisions not to invalidate
results, §163-278.38.
Referendum committees.
Defined, §163-278.6.
Inactive committees.
Procedure for, §163-278.10.
Restrictions, §163-278.13(e1).
Reimbursement to contributing entity.
Accepting contribution for, §163-278.13(d1).
Effect of non-reimbursement, §163-278.13(d2).

CAMPAIGN FINANCE —Cont'd
Remedial action.
Civil remedy other than penalty, §163-278.34(c).
Reports.
Cumulative totals reflected, §163-278.9(h).
Declaration of nomination or certificate of election.
Filing of statements as prerequisite, §163-278.25.
Electronically filed reports, §163-278.9(j).
Examination of statements within four months, §163-278.24.
Exemptions.
Threshold amount for financial reports, §163-278.10A(a).
Inapplicability of exemption, §163-278.10A(b).
Federal election campaign act of 1971, §163-278.9(e), (f).
Federal officers.
Candidates to file information reports, §163-278.30.
Filing, late filing penalty, §163-278.34(a).
Inactive candidate or committee, §163-278.10.
Independent expenditures, §163-278.12.
Information required, §163-278.9(g).
Municipal candidates and committees, §163-278.9(b).
Oath required, §163-278.9(i).
Person or entity not otherwise required to report.
Contributions in excess of $100, §163-278.12(b), (c), (d).
Preservation, §163-278.35.
County boards of elections to preserve reports, §163-278.37.
Treasurer, §163-278.9(a), (b).
Anything of value paid to be reflected, §163-278.11(b).
Best efforts used to obtain, maintain and submit information, §163-278.11(c).
Contents generally, §163-278.11(a).
Referendum committee, §163-278.9A(a), (b).
Trained treasurer, reports to be filed by, §163-278.9(k).
Violations of provisions.
Board to report to prosecuting authorities, §163-278.27(b).
Reprimand of violators.
Civil remedy other than penalty, §163-278.34(c).
Rules and regulations.
State board of elections, §163-278.21.
Sales by political party executive committees.
Exempt purchase price.
Not treated as contribution, §163-278.8A(a).
Qualification for, §163-278.8A(b).
Scope of provisions, §163-278.5.
Semiannual reports, §163-278.9(a).
Severability of provisions, §163-278.5.
State board of elections.
Administration of provisions, §163-278.21.
Appeals from board, §163-278.26.
Duties, §163-278.22.
Executive director.
Duties, §163-278.23.
Powers, §163-278.22.
Rules and regulations, §163-278.21.
Statute of limitations.
Civil action to collect penalty, §163-278.34(e).
Telephone bank.
Defined, §163-278.6.
Television.
Disclosure requirements for media advertisements, §§163-278.39 to 163-278.39C.

CAMPAIGN FINANCE —Cont'd
Transfer of funds to committee or political party account.
When deemed contribution, §163-278.19(a1).
Treasurers.
Accounts and accounting, §163-278.8(a), (b).
Appointment, §163-278.7(a).
Prerequisite to receipt of contributions, §163-278.16(a).
Defined, §163-278.6.
Prosecution of violations, §163-278.27(c).
Special prosecutors, §163-278.28(b).
Removal, §163-278.7(d).
Changes in information, §163-278.7(c).
Contents, §163-278.7(b).
Filing, §163-278.7(b).
Reports, §163-278.9(a), (b).
Anything of value paid to be reflected, §163-278.11(b).
Best efforts used to obtain, maintain and submit information, §163-278.11(c).
Contents generally, §163-278.11(a).
Referendum committee, §163-278.9A(a), (b).
Trained treasurer, reports to be filed by, §163-278.9(k).
Separate bank account for funds, §163-278.8(h).
Training for, §163-278.7(e), (f).
True and correct.
Certification.
False certification knowing information to be untrue, criminal penalty, §163-278.27(a1).
Statements and reports required to be filed, §163-278.32.
Use of contributions.
Definition of candidate campaign committee, §163-278.16B(b).
Designation in event of death or incapacity of candidate, §163-278.16B(c).
Permissible purposes, §163-278.16B(a).
Voter-owned elections act, §§163-278.95 to 163-278.99E.
Definitions, §163-278.96.
Distributions from fund.
Amount, §163-278.99(b).
Method, §163-278.99(c).
Time for, §163-278.99(a).
Fund.
Distributions from fund, §163-278.99.
Established, §163-278.97(a).
Report on evaluation and determination of fund amount, §163-278.97(c).
Sources of revenue, §163-278.97(b).
Matching funds.
Availability, §163-278.99B(a).
Electioneering communications, determinations by board, §163-278.99B(d), (e).
Limitations.
Contested general election, §163-278.99B(c).
Contested primary, §163-278.99B(b).
New-party candidates, §163-278.99C.
Participation in program.
Certification of candidate, §163-278.98(c).
Declaration of intent to participate, §163-278.98(a).
Qualifying contributions, §163-278.98(b).
Final report, §163-278.98(d).
Restrictions on contributions and expenditures, §163-278.98(e).
Revocation of decision to participate, §163-278.98(f).

CAMPAIGN FINANCE —Cont'd
Voter-owned elections act —Cont'd
Penalties for violation of provisions.
  Civil penalties, §163-278.99D.
Purpose of act, §163-278.95.
Reporting requirements.
  Certified candidates, §163-278.99A(b).
  Noncertified candidates and entities,
    §163-278.99A(a).
  Participating candidates, §163-278.99A(b).
  Public access to reports, §163-278.99A(c).
Return to fund of distributed amounts.
  Penalties for violation of provisions,
    §163-278.99D.
Unaffiliated candidates, §163-278.99C.
Voter education guide.
  Candidate information included,
    §163-278.99E(b).
  Disclaimers, §163-278.99E(c).
  List of addresses undeliverable,
    §163-278.99E(a).
  Publication with Judicial voter guide,
    §163-278.99E(d).
  Purpose, §163-278.99E(a).
Witnesses.
Self-incrimination.
  Immunity from prosecution, §163-278.29.

CAMP BUTNER RESERVATION.
Administrative procedure act.
Full exemption given department of health and
  humans services, §150B-1(c).
Butner advisory council, §§122C-413,
  122C-413.1.
Butner town manager vacancy, selection,
  §122C-413.1(b).
Chair, §122C-413(e).
Created, §122C-413(a).
Election, §122C-413(a) to (d1).
Resolutions, advising secretary of health and
  human services, §122C-413.1(a).
Vacancies, §122C-413(f).
Butner town manager vacancy, selection,
  §122C-413.1(b).
Community of Butner comprehensive
  emergency management plan, §122C-409.
County ordinances.
Application to Camp Butner reservation,
  §122C-410(b).
Enforcement of part.
Ordinances and rules for enforcement, §122C-403.
Fire protection.
Public safety authority, §122C-408.
Hospitals generally.
See HOSPITALS.
Lyons station sanitary district.
No jurisdiction over, §122C-413(g).
Municipalities.
Annexation.
  Territory extending into Camp Butner
    reservation, §122C-410(a).
Extraterritorial jurisdiction.
  Extension into Camp Butner reservation,
    §122C-410(a).
Ordinances.
Enforcement of part, §122C-403.
Police protection.
Public safety authority, §122C-408.
Special police officers, §122C-408(a5).
  Authority, §122C-408(b).

CAMP BUTNER RESERVATION —Cont'd
Public safety authority.
Created, §122C-408(a).
Dissolution, §122C-408(e).
Duties and responsibilities, §122C-408(a4).
Membership, §122C-408(a1).
Police and fire protection, providing,
  §122C-408(a5).
  Contracting for, §122C-408(c), (d).
  Funding, §122C-408(c).
Purposes, §122C-408(a).
Special police officers, §122C-408(a5).
  Authority, §122C-408(b).
Terms of membership, §122C-408(a2).
Transfer of property to, §122C-408(a3).
Rules and regulations.
Procedures applicable to rules, §122C-405.
Violations of rules, §122C-405.
Traffic laws.
Application of state highway and motor vehicle
  laws to roads, etc., at reservation, §122C-402.
Use authorized, §122C-401.
Violations made misdemeanor, §122C-406.
Water and sewer system, §122C-407(a) to (c).

CAMPERS.
Trailers generally.
See TRAILERS.

CAMPGROUNDS.
Defrauding campground owner, §14-110.
Littering, §14-399.
Membership camping, §§66-230 to 66-247.
See MEMBERSHIP CAMPING.

CAMPING TRAILERS.
Recreational vehicle, defined as, §20-4.01.

CAMPUS POLICE, §§74G-1 to 74G-13.
Arrest authority, §§74E-6(d), 74G-6(b).
Territorial jurisdiction.
  Immediate and continuous flight, §15A-402(f).
Assault with firearm upon law enforcement
  officer, §14-34.2.
Assistance to law enforcement of another
  political subdivision, §160A-288(d).
Attorney general.
Custodian of records of program, §74G-5(a).
Fees, §74G-12.
Immunity, §74G-11.
Powers, §74G-4.
Badges, §74G-7.
Certification of campus police agency.
Application for, §74G-2(c).
Expiration, §74G-10(a).
Fees, §74G-12.
Liability insurance policy or certificate of
  self-insurance, §74G-3.
Powers of attorney general, §74G-4.
Renewal, §74G-10(a).
Citation of act, §74G-1.
Civil liability for acts of, §74G-13(c).
Commission of officer.
Expiration, §74G-10(b).
Fees, §74G-12.
Renewal, §74G-10(b).
Revocation, §74G-10(b).
Compensation of officers, §74G-9.
Concealed weapons, §74G-6(d).
Firearms and other weapons, §74G-7.
Concealed weapons, §74G-6(d).
Injunction for violations, §74G-13(b).

CAMPUS POLICE —Cont'd
Liability insurance policy or certificate of self-insurance, §74G-3(a).
  Cancellation of policy, §74G-3(b).
  Suspension of agency certification for noncompliance, §74G-3(c).
Minimum standards for officers, §74G-8.
Oath of officers, §74G-6(a).
Penalties for violations, §74G-13(a).
Powers and authority of institutions, §74G-6(c), (e).
Powers and authority of officers, §74G-6(b), (d), (f).
Purpose of act, §74G-2(a), (b).
Records.
  Attorney general as custodian, §74G-5(a).
  Disclosure, §74G-5(b), (c).
Scope of act, §74G-2(c).
Standards for officers.
  Minimum standards, §74G-8.
Title of act, §74G-1.
Uniforms, §74G-7.
Vehicles, §74G-7.

CANAL COMPANIES.
No title by possession company's right-of-way, §1-44.

CANALS.
Adverse possession.
  No title by possession of right of way, §1-44.
Draining districts.
  Improvement, renovation, enlargement and extension, §§156-93.2, 156-93.3.
  Public or private ways.
    Maintenance of drainage across, §156-88.
Earth from canal removed or leveled, §156-8.
Eminent domain.
  By whom right may be exercised, §40A-3(a).
Magistrates.
  Assessment of contribution for damages or for work done on canal, §7A-292.
Maintenance for seven years presumed a necessity, §156-21.
Protection of canals, ditches and natural drains, §156-25.
Right to drain into canal, §156-10.

CANARY SEEDS.
Standard weight and measure, §81A-42.

CANCELLATION OF CONTRACTS FOR DEED.
Exercise of right, time, §47H-2(c).
Title requirements for executing contract.
  Violations, purchaser's remedies, §47G-6(c).
Violations of chapter, purchaser's remedies, §47G-8.

CANCELLATION OF COURT SESSIONS.
General court of justice.
  Adverse weather, emergency situations including catastrophic conditions, §7A-39(a).
  In chambers jurisdiction not affected, §7A-39(c).

CANCELLATION OF DISCOUNT BUYING CLUB CONTRACTS.
Customer's right, §66-133.

CANCELLATION OF INSURANCE.
Applicability of article, §58-41-10(a).
Citation of article, §58-41-1.
Commercial general liability insurance.
  Extended reporting periods, §58-40-140.
Grounds, §58-41-15(a).

CANCELLATION OF INSURANCE —Cont'd
Intent of legislature, §58-41-5(a), (b).
In-term cancellation of entire book of business, §58-41-45(b).
Legislative findings, §58-41-5(a), (b).
Loss of reinsurance, §58-41-30.
Nonpayment of premium, §58-41-15(d).
Notice.
  Copies sent to agent or broker, §58-41-15(e).
  Required, §58-41-15(b).
  Timing of notice to insured, §58-41-40(b).
Penalties, §58-41-55.
Policy in effect for less than sixty days, §58-41-15(c).
Provisions not exclusive, §58-41-10(b).
Short title, §58-41-1.
Statements or communications made in good faith.
  No liability for, §§58-41-40, 58-41-40(a).

CANCELLATION OF JUDGMENT AS TO SURETY, §26-11.

CANCELLATION OF LIS PENDENS NOTICE, §§1-119(b), 1-120.

CANCELLATION OF MEMBERSHIP CAMPING CONTRACTS.
Purchaser's right, §66-240.

CANCELLATION OF OPTION CONTRACT.
Option to purchase contract executed with residential lease agreement, §47G-2(c).
  Mortgage or lien on property securing loan.
    Seller's default, §47G-6.

CANCELLATION OF PREPAID ENTERTAINMENT CONTRACTS.
Buyer's right, §66-121.

CANCELLATION OF WILL.
Revocation of written will, §31-5.1.

CANCELLATION OF WINE DISTRIBUTION AGREEMENTS, §18B-1204.
Judicial remedies, §18B-1207.
Notice of intent, §18B-1205.

CANCELLATION, UCC.
Funds transfers.
  Payment orders, §25-4A-211.
Leases.
  Defined, §25-2A-103(1).
  Effect on rights and remedies, §25-2A-505(1), (3).
  Lessee's remedies, §25-2A-508(1).
Sale of goods, §25-2-209.
  Antecedent breach.
    Effect of cancellation on claims for, §25-2-720.
  Defined, §25-2-106(4).

CANCER, §§130A-205 to 130A-216.
Accident and health insurance.
  Breast cancer.
    Mammograms.
      Coverage, §58-51-57.
  Cervical cancer screening.
    Coverage, §58-51-57.
  Colorectal cancer examinations, laboratory tests and screening.
    Coverage, §58-3-179.
    Small employer group health plans, §58-50-155(a).
  Drugs for cancer treatment.
    Coverage of certain prescribed drugs, §58-51-59(a), (b).

CANCER —Cont'd
Accident and health insurance —Cont'd
Mammograms.
Coverage, §58-51-57.
Ovarian cancer.
Surveillance tests for women at risk, coverage, §§58-3-270, 58-50-155(a).
Administration of program.
Care and treatment of persons with cancer, §130A-205(a).
Prevention and detection of cancer, §130A-205(a).
Advisory committee on cancer coordination and control.
Administrative staff, §130A-33.50(f).
Appointment, §130A-33.50(b).
Compensation, §130A-33.50(d).
Composition, §130A-33.50(b).
Established, §130A-33.50(a).
Meetings, §130A-33.50(b).
Quorum, §130A-33.50(e).
Reports.
Annual reports, §130A-33.51(b).
Responsibilities, §130A-33.51(a).
Vacancies, §130A-33.50(c).
Breast cancer.
Cancer patient navigation program.
Breast and cervical cancer control program, §130A-216.
Mammograms.
Accident and health insurance.
Coverage, §58-51-57.
Health maintenance organizations.
Coverage, §58-67-76.
Hospital, medical and dental services corporations.
Coverage, §58-65-92.
Cancer committee of North Carolina medical society, §130A-213.
Consultation with committee, §130A-213.
Cancer patient navigation program.
Breast and cervical cancer control program, §130A-216.
Care and treatment of persons with cancer.
Establishment and administration of program, §130A-205(a).
Facilities made available, §130A-206.
Financial aid for diagnosis and treatment, §130A-206.
Central cancer registry, §130A-208.
Functions, §130A-208.
Incidence reporting of cancer, §130A-209.
Information to be received, §130A-208.
Reports.
Incidence reporting of cancer, §130A-209.
Cervical cancer screening.
Accident and health insurance.
Coverage, §58-51-57.
Hospital, medical and dental services corporations.
Coverage, §58-65-92.
Clinics, §130A-207.
Authority to establish, §130A-207.
Confidentiality of records, §130A-212.
Minimum standards, §130A-207.
Colorectal cancer examinations, laboratory tests and screening.
Health benefit plan coverage, §58-3-179.
Small employer group health plans, §58-50-155(a).
Confidentiality.
Records of cancer, §130A-212.

CANCER —Cont'd
Control program.
Administration of program, §130A-205(a).
Authority to establish clinic, §130A-207.
Committee of North Carolina medical society, §130A-213.
Financial aid for diagnosis and treatment, §130A-206.
Health and human services department.
Duties of department, §130A-214.
Incidence reporting of cancer.
Central cancer registry, §130A-208.
Medical society.
Cancer committee of the North Carolina medical society, §130A-213.
Records.
Confidentiality of records, §130A-212.
Reports.
Immunity of persons who report cancer, §130A-211.
Incidence reporting of cancer, §130A-209.
Secretary of health and human services to make report, §130A-215.
Rules and regulations, §130A-205(b).
Department of environment and natural resources.
Duties of department, §130A-214.
Secretary.
Reports by secretary, §130A-215.
Diagnosis of cancer.
Facilities made available, §130A-206.
Financial aid, §130A-206.
Establishment of program.
Care and treatment of persons with cancer, §130A-205(a).
Prevention and detection of cancer, §130A-205(a).
Financial aid.
For diagnosis and treatment, §130A-206.
To sponsored cancer clinics, §130A-207.
Food, drug and cosmetic act.
Drug or device, false advertising, §106-138(b).
Health maintenance organizations.
Colorectal cancer examinations, laboratory tests and screening.
Coverage, §58-3-179.
Drugs for cancer treatment.
Coverage of certain prescribed drugs.
Exceptions, §58-67-78(b), (c).
Generally, §58-67-78(a).
Prostate-specific antigen (PSA) tests.
Coverage, §58-67-77(a), (c).
Defined, §58-67-77(b).
Hospital, medical and dental service corporations.
Cervical cancer screening.
Coverage, §58-65-92.
Colorectal cancer examinations, laboratory tests and screening.
Coverage, §58-3-179.
Drugs for cancer treatment.
Coverage of certain prescribed drugs.
Exceptions, §58-65-94(b), (c).
Generally, §58-65-94(a).
Mammograms.
Coverage, §58-65-92.
Prostate-specific antigen (PSA) tests.
Coverage, §58-65-93(a), (c).
Defined, §58-65-93(b).
Hospitals.
Cancer clinics, §130A-207.
Confidentiality of records, §130A-212.

CANCER —Cont'd
Immunities.
Persons who report cancer, §130A-211.
Reporting of cancer, §130A-211.
Indigent persons.
Financial aid for diagnosis and treatment,
§130A-206.
Mammograms.
Accident and health insurance.
Coverage, §58-51-57.
Accreditation of facilities performing.
Medical care commission, §143B-165.
Health maintenance organizations.
Coverage, §58-67-76.
Hospital, medical and dental services
corporations.
Coverage, §58-65-92.
Small employer group health coverage,
§58-50-155(a).
Medical facilities.
Cancer clinics, §130A-207.
Confidentiality of records, §130A-212.
North Carolina medical society.
Cancer committee, §130A-213.
Ovarian cancer.
Accident and health insurance.
Surveillance tests for women at risk, coverage,
§§58-3-270, 58-50-155(a).
Pap smears.
Accreditation of facilities performing.
Medical care commission, §143B-165.
Small employer group health coverage,
§58-50-155(a).
Prevention and detection of cancer.
Establishment and administration of program,
§130A-205(a).
Prostate-specific antigen (PSA) tests.
Small employer group health coverage,
§58-50-155(a).
Records.
Central cancer registry, §130A-208.
Incidence reporting of cancer, §130A-209.
Confidentiality of records, §130A-212.
Registry.
Central cancer registry, §130A-208.
Incidence reporting of cancer, §130A-209.
Reports, §130A-215.
Central cancer registry, §130A-208.
Incidence reporting of cancer, §130A-209(a).
Control program.
Secretary of health and human services to make
report, §130A-215.
Immunity of persons who report cancer,
§130A-211.
Incidence reporting of cancer, §130A-209.
Central cancer registry, §130A-208.
Definitions, §130A-209(c).
Failure to report.
Charge for collection, §130A-209(b).
To governor and general assembly, §130A-215.
Rules and regulations.
Control program, §130A-205(b).
Establishment and administration of program,
§130A-205(b).
Small employer group health insurance.
Coverage of certain prescribed drugs for cancer
treatment, §58-50-156.
Treatment of cancer.
Financial aid for treatment, §130A-206.
University cancer research fund.
Accounting of expenditures.
Financial report, §116-29.1(g).

CANCER —Cont'd
University cancer research fund —Cont'd
Appropriations, §116-29.1(b).
Cancer research fund committee, §116-29.1(c).
Chairperson, §116-29.1(d).
Establishment, §116-29.1(a).
Financial report, §116-29.1(g).
Meetings, §116-29.1(f).
Quorum, §116-29.1(e).

C. & F.
Sale of goods, UCC, §25-2-320.
Form of bill of lading required in overseas
shipment, §25-2-323.
Net landed weight, §25-2-321.
Payment on arrival, §25-2-321.
Warranty of condition on arrival, §25-2-321.

CANDIDATES.
Campaign contributions and expenditures.
See CAMPAIGN FINANCE.
Generally.
See ELECTIONS.

CAN DOER ORGANIZATIONS.
**Community achievement network/developing
our educational resources.**
Tutoring and other services, §115C-207.

CANDY.
Sales and use tax.
Subject to tax, §105-164.13B(a).

CANNABIS.
Controlled substances generally, §§90-86 to
90-113.8.
See DRUGS AND CONTROLLED SUBSTANCES.
Food, drug and cosmetic act.
Drugs deemed misbranded, §106-134.
Marijuana.
See MARIJUANA.

CANS.
Containers generally.
See CONTAINERS.

CANTALOUPES.
Standard weight and measure, §81A-42.

**CAPACITY OF MARRIED PERSONS TO
CONTRACT,** §52-2.

CAPACITY TO MARRY, §51-2.
Want of capacity, §51-3.

CAPACITY TO SUE.
Pleading special matter, §1A-1 Rule 9(a).

CAPE CARTERET.
**Ordinances to regulate and control swimming,
personal watercraft operation, surfing and
littering in Atlantic Ocean,** §160A-176.2.

**CAPE FEAR RIVER NAVIGATION AND
PILOTAGE.**
Commission.
Appointment of members, §76A-2.
Chairman.
Designation, §76A-2.
Composition, §76A-2.
Established, §76A-1.
Expenses, §76A-24.
Jurisdiction.
Disputes as to pilotage, §76A-5(f).
Majority to constitute quorum, §76A-4.
Powers, §76A-1.
Quorum, §76A-4.

CAPE FEAR RIVER NAVIGATION AND PILOTAGE —Cont'd
Commission —Cont'd
Rules and regulations, §76A-5(a).
Terms of members, §76A-3.
Vacancies.
Filling, §76A-3.
Widows and orphans fund.
Dissolution, §76A-25.
Mutual association for pilots.
Recognition of pilotage association by commission, §76A-13.
Pilots.
Age.
Apprentices, §76A-12.
Apprentices, §76A-12.
Association.
Payments to commission for expenses, §76A-24.
Recognition by commission, §76A-13.
Bonds, surety, §76A-5(e).
Compulsory use of pilots, §76A-16.
Exceptions, §76A-18.
Disciplinary measures, §76A-5(d).
Docking masters.
Not deemed pilots, §76A-14.
Examination, §76A-5(b).
Licenses.
Apprentices, §76A-6.
Classes, §76A-6.
Full license, §76A-6.
Limited license, §76A-6.
Renewal, §76A-5(c).
Suspension or revocation, §76A-5(d).
Term, §76A-5(b).
Number of pilots, §76A-14.
Rates of pilotage, §76A-17.
Retirement, §76A-15.
Vessels not liable for pilotage, §76A-18.

CAPIAS.
Arrest in civil cases.
See ARREST IN CIVIL CASES.
Bail.
Bond of prisoner committed on capias in civil action, §162-32.
General provisions.
See BAIL.
Costs.
Arrest for nonpayment, §6-48.
Executions.
See EXECUTIONS.
Sundays.
Execution on Sundays, §103-3.

CAPITAL APPRECIATION BONDS.
Local government finance.
Authorization.
Future acts, §159-100(c).
Local government bond act, §159-100(b).
Revenue bond act, §159-100(a).
Calculating principal amount, §159-99(b).
Defined, §159-99(a).
Terms and conditions, §159-99(c).
State authority to issue, §142-15.3(b).
Provisions governing, §142-15.3(a).

CAPITAL FACILITIES FINANCE ACT, §§142-80 to 142-101.
Acquisition and construction, §142-94.
Alternative financing methods.
Purposes of act, §142-81.

CAPITAL FACILITIES FINANCE ACT —Cont'd
Certificates of participation indebtedness.
Defined, §142-82.
Documentation required, §142-87(a).
Interest, §142-87(c).
Other conditions, §142-87(e).
Procedure for delivery and sale, §142-87(b).
Sale, §142-87(c).
Trust agreement, delivered pursuant to, §142-87(d).
Debt affordability.
Annual study to establish guidelines for maintaining prudent debt levels, §142-100.
Debt affordability advisory committee.
Duties, §142-101(d).
Established, §142-101(a).
Members, §142-101(a).
Officers and staff, §142-101(b).
Per diem and allowances, §142-101(c).
Reports, §142-101(e).
Definitions, §142-82.
Financing contract indebtedness.
Bidding, §142-86(c).
Certificates of participation indebtedness, §142-87.
Credit facility, delivery to secure payment, §142-86(e).
Defined, §142-82.
Documentation required, §142-86(a).
Execution, §142-86(d).
Interest component, §142-86(b).
Terms and conditions, §142-86(f).
Findings of general assembly, §142-81.
Investments.
Special indebtedness, §142-93.
Limited obligation bonds and notes.
Authorization to issue and sell, §142-88.
Defined, §142-82.
Denominations, §142-89(b).
Expenses in preparation, sale and issuance, §142-89(c).
Form of issuance, §142-89(b).
Notes, §142-89(e).
Refunding bonds and notes, §142-89(f).
Registration, §142-89(b).
Repayment of notes, §142-89(e).
Sale, §142-89(c).
Security for payment, §142-89(g).
Signatures required, §142-89(b).
Terms and conditions, §142-89(a).
Trust agreement securing, §142-89(h).
Use of proceeds, §142-89(d).
Managing debt capacity.
Annual debt affordability study, §142-100.
Debt affordability advisory committee, §142-101.
North Carolina industrial and pollution control facilities financing act, §§159D-1 to 159D-27.
See INDUSTRIAL AND POLLUTION CONTROL FACILITIES FINANCING.
Private capital facilities finance act.
Institutions for higher education and elementary and secondary education, §§159D-35 to 159D-57.
See CAPITAL FACILITIES FINANCE AGENCY.
Procurement of capital facilities, §142-94.
Purposes of act, §142-81.
Special indebtedness.
Appropriations necessary to make payments.
Including in governor's budget, §142-85(c).
Authorization to finance costs, §142-83.

CAPITAL FACILITIES FINANCE ACT —Cont'd

Special indebtedness —Cont'd

Certificates of participation indebtedness, §142-87.

Certification that special indebtedness desirable.
State treasurer, §142-84(a).

Consultants, fiduciaries and other agents,
employment, §142-84(g).

Deficiency judgment not rendered against state,
§142-85(e).

Defined, §142-82.

Designation of facilities, §142-84(e).

Determination that indebtedness appropriate.
Notice to state treasurer, §142-84(a).

Documents for use, development, §142-84(g).

Final approval, §142-84(c).

Financing contract indebtedness, §142-86.

Financing terms, §142-84(d).

General Assembly approval, §142-83.

Investments, §142-93.

Lien or security interest.
Multiple liens, §142-85(b).
Required as security, §142-85(a).
Value, §142-85(b).

Limited obligation bonds and notes, §§142-88,
142-89.

Nonsubstitution clause prohibited, §142-85(f).

Notice to department of administration.
Appropriate to finance facilities, §142-84(a).

Notice to state treasurer.
Determination that indebtedness appropriate,
§142-84(a).

Other agreements, §142-91.

Oversight by joint legislative commission,
§142-84(h).

Preliminary approval, §142-84(b).

Protection of lender, §142-85(g).

Repayment, source, §142-85(d).

Satisfaction of payment obligations.
Net proceeds from sale or disposition of
property, §142-85(e).

State property law exemption, §142-85(h).

Tax exemption, §142-92.

Taxing power of state not pledged, §142-85(e).

Type of debt and security, determination,
§142-84(f).

Variable rate demand bonds and notes,
§142-90(a), (b).

State capital facilities finance act.

Short title, §142-80.

Tax exemption.

Special indebtedness, §142-92.

Tobacco trust fund.

Priority use.
Debt service for special indebtedness authorized
by capital facilities act of 2004, §143-719(c).

Variable rate demand bonds and notes,
§142-90(a), (b).

CAPITAL FACILITIES FINANCE AGENCY.

Board of directors, §159D-38(a).

Quorum, §159D-38(d).

**Contained within department of state
treasurer,** §159D-38(e).

Created, §159D-38(a).

General powers, §159D-39.

**North Carolina industrial and pollution
control facilities financing act,** §§159D-1 to
159D-27.

See INDUSTRIAL AND POLLUTION CONTROL
FACILITIES FINANCING.

CAPITAL FACILITIES FINANCE AGENCY
—Cont'd

Private capital facilities finance act, §§159D-35
to 159D-57.

Annual report on activities, §159D-53.

Audit of books and accounts annually, §159D-53.

Bonds or notes.
Approval by local government commission,
§159D-45(b).
Authority to issue, §159D-45(a).
Consent of other agencies not required,
§159D-45(e).
Credit of state not pledged, §159D-44.
Holders rights not limited or altered,
§159D-47(d).
Interim receipts or temporary bonds,
§159D-45(d).
Investing in, §159D-51.
Investment securities, §159D-50.
Members or officers not personally liable,
§159D-54.
Payment of principal and interest, source,
§159D-45(a).
Proceeds, use, §159D-45(c).
Public hearing, §159D-45(f).
Recovery zone facility bonds, §159D-45(g).
Refunding bonds or notes.
Authority to issue, §159D-52(a).
Purposes, §159D-52(a).
Sale or exchange, §159D-52(b).
Terms and conditions, provision governing,
§159D-52(b).
Remedies of holders, §159D-49.
Secured by trust agreement or resolution,
§159D-46.
Tax exemption, interest paid, §159D-55.
Terms and conditions, §159D-45(a).

Conflict of interest, disclosure, §159D-56.

Construction contracts, awarding by agency,
§159D-43.

Conveyance of possessory or ownership interest
acquired, §159D-42(b).

Cost of project, institution bearing, §159D-47(a).

Criteria and requirements in undertaking project,
§159D-40(a).
Factors in making determination, §159D-40(b).

Definitions, §159D-37.

Exemption from taxation, §159D-55.

Expenses incurred by agency, §159D-44.

Fees, loan repayments, purchase price payments,
rents and charges.
Fixing and collecting, §159D-47(a) to (d).
Trust funds, §159D-48.

General powers, §159D-39.

Interest directly or indirectly in contract,
disclosure, §159D-56.

Investing in bonds or notes, §159D-51.

Investment securities, bonds, notes and interest
coupons, §159D-50.

Legislative finding, §159D-36.

Lending money to institution, §159D-42(a).

Loan agreement or agreement for sale or lease,
provisions, §159D-42(a).

Procedural requirements, §159D-41.

Proposal for financing project, submittal by
institution, procedure, §159D-41.

Public hearing on proposed project and bonds,
§159D-45(f).

Refunding bonds or notes, §159D-52.

Remedies of holders of bonds and notes, §159D-49.

Report on activities, §159D-53.

CAPITAL FACILITIES FINANCE AGENCY
—Cont'd

Private capital facilities finance act —Cont'd
Sale or lease of project to institution, §159D-42(a).
Short title, §159D-35.
Supplemental and additional method for doing
things authorized, §159D-57.
Tax exemption, §159D-55.
Trust agreement or resolution securing bonds,
§159D-46.
Trust funds, money received, §159D-48.
**Revenues or assets not to inure to benefit of
private persons,** §159D-38(b).
Secretary-treasurer, §159D-38(c).

CAPITAL IMPROVEMENT PLANNING AND BUDGETING PROCESS.
State budget act, §§143C-8-1 to 143C-8-12.
See STATE BUDGET.

CAPITAL ISSUES LAW, §§78A-1 to 78A-66.
See SECURITIES.

CAPITAL PLANNING COMMISSION, §143B-374.

CAPITAL PROJECT FINANCING.
Budget of state.
Capital improvement projects, §§143C-8-1 to
143C-8-12.
See STATE BUDGET.
Development financing.
Local units of government, §158-7.3.
**Project development financing debt
instruments.**
Project development financing act, §§159-101 to
159-113.
See LOCAL GOVERNMENT FINANCE.

CAPITAL PUNISHMENT.
See DEATH PENALTY.

CAPITAL RESERVE ACTS.
Local government finance.
General provisions, §§159-1 to 159-188.
See LOCAL GOVERNMENT FINANCE.

CAPITATION TAX.
Constitution of North Carolina.
Prohibited, NC Const Art V §1.
Constitution of the United States, US Const Art
I §9.
Elections.
Denial or abridgement of right to vote for
failure to pay tax prohibited, US Const
Amd 24.

CAPITOL OF THE STATE.
Arson, §14-59.
**Carrying deadly weapons in state capitol
building.**
Prohibition, §14-269.4.
Historic properties, §121-9(h).
**"Prisoner of war/missing in action" flag
display,** §143-345.9.
State capitol police section.
Division of law enforcement.
Department of public safety, §143B-900.

CAPITOL POLICE.
Appointment of special police officers,
§143B-900(c).
Arrest power, §143B-900(d).
Chief of capitol police.
Authority to appoint special police officers,
§143B-900(b).

CAPITOL POLICE —Cont'd
Jurisdiction of special police officers,
§143B-900(d).
Oath by special police officers.
Required before exercising power to arrest,
§143B-900(c).
State buildings and grounds.
Evacuating.
Assistance of other law enforcement or
emergency agencies, §143B-900(f).
Protecting, §143B-900(f).
State capitol police section.
Established within division of law enforcement.
Department of public safety, §143B-900(a).
Special police agency of department of public
safety, §143B-900(b).
Territorial jurisdiction to exercise powers,
§143B-900(d).

CAP ON AMOUNT OF APPEAL BOND.
Staying execution of money judgment.
Noncompensatory damages of $25,000,000 or
more, §1-289(b), (c).

CAP ON COMPENSATORY OR CONSEQUENTIAL DAMAGES.
**Employee theft, larceny, shoplifting,
embezzlement or obtaining by false
pretenses.**
Civil liability, §1-538.2(a), (b).

CAP ON PUNITIVE DAMAGES, §1D-25(b).
Exemption, DWI, injury or harm arising,
§1D-26.
Not made known to trier of fact, §1D-25(c).

CAP ON TAX CREDITS.
Business and energy tax credit, §105-129.17(b).
Growing businesses tax credits, §105-129.84(b).
Mill rehabilitation tax credit, §105-129.73(b).
**Tax incentives for new and expanding
businesses,** §105-129.5(b).

CARAT.
**Standard unit for designation of weight of
diamonds,** §66-74.

CARBON MONOXIDE.
Motor vehicle emission standards, §20-128.2.

CARBON MONOXIDE DETECTORS.
Disablement or damage.
Reimbursement by tenant to landlord, §42-44(a2).
Duty of landlord to provide fit premises,
§42-42(a).
**Failure of landlord to provide, install, replace
or repair.**
Remedies, §42-44(a1).
State building code, §143-138(b2).
Tenant's duty to maintain dwelling unit,
§42-43(a).

CARBUNCLES.
Food, drug or cosmetic act.
Drug or device, false advertising, §106-138(b).

CARCASSES.
Meat inspection.
Examination and inspection of carcasses,
§106-549.18.
Application of article, §106-549.19.
Equine carcasses.
Slaughter, sale and transportation of
carcasses, §106-549.25.
Exemptions from article, §106-549.27.

CARCASSES —Cont'd
Meat inspection —Cont'd
Examination and inspection of carcasses —Cont'd
Misbranding information required,
§106-549.21(b).
Place of inspection, §106-549.19.
Marking, stamping, etc., carcass, §106-549.18.
Poultry inspections.
Condemnation of adulterated poultry,
§106-549.53(c).
Postmortem inspection of carcass, §106-549.53(b).
Rendering plants and rendering operations,
§§106-168.1 to 106-168.16.
See RENDERING PLANTS AND RENDERING
OPERATIONS.
Transportation department.
Removal of dead animals, §136-18.

CARDIAC ARREST.
Automated external defibrillator (AED),
§90-21.15.

CARDIAC REHABILITATION CERTIFICATION
PROGRAM, §§131E-165 to 131E-170.
Administrative procedure.
Applicability of provisions, §131E-168(b).
Adverse action on certificates, §131E-168(a), (b).
Applications for certification, §131E-167(a).
Definitions, §131E-166.
Denial or suspension of certificates.
Adverse action on certificates, §131E-168(a), (b).
Enforcement of provisions, §131E-169(b).
Granting of certificates, §131E-167(a).
Inspection, evaluation and certification of
programs, §131E-167(c).
Inspections, §131E-170(a), (b).
Issuance of certification, §131E-167(a).
Nontransferable or nonassignable, §131E-167(e).
Posting, §131E-167(f).
Provisional certificates, §131E-167(b).
Purpose of article, §131E-165(b).
Renewal of certificates, §131E-167(d).
Requirements for certification, §131E-167(a) to
(f).
Rules and regulations, §131E-169(a).
Title of article.
Cardiac rehabilitation certification program,
§131E-165(a).

CARDINAL.
State bird, §145-2.

CARDINAL-FLOWER.
Taking, etc., of certain wild plants from land of
another, §14-129.

CARDIOPULMONARY RESUSCITATION.
Public schools.
Health education, §115C-81(e1).

CAREER AND TECHNICAL EDUCATION.
See VOCATIONAL AND TECHNICAL
EDUCATION.

CAREER CRIMINALS.
Habitual felons, §§14-7.1 to 14-7.12.
See HABITUAL FELONS.

CARGO AIRPORT FACILITIES.
North Carolina's eastern region, §§158-30 to
158-42.
See NORTH CAROLINA'S EASTERN REGION.

CARNIVALS.
Amusement device safety generally, §§95-111.1
to 95-111.18.
See AMUSEMENT DEVICE SAFETY.

CARNIVALS —Cont'd
Counties.
Regulation of places of amusement, §153A-135.
Municipalities.
Regulation of carnivals and circuses, §160A-181.

CAROLINA BEACH.
All-terrain vehicles.
Use by employees on certain highways,
§20-171.24.
Eminent domain.
Exercise of power, purposes, modified provisions,
§40A-3(b1).
Vesting of title and right to possession,
§40A-42(a).
Ordinances to regulate and control swimming,
personal watercraft operation, surfing and
littering in Atlantic Ocean, §160A-176.2.
Room occupancy tax.
Uniform provisions.
Authorized to levy, §160A-215(g).
Generally, §160A-215.

CAROLINA LILY.
State wildflower, §145-20.

CAROLYN SONZOGNI ACT.
Accident-trauma victim identification, §§90-600
to 90-604.
See ACCIDENT-TRAUMA VICTIM
IDENTIFICATION.

CARRBORO.
Land-use development incentives.
Reduction of energy consumption, §160A-383.4.
Room occupancy tax.
Uniform provisions.
Authorized to levy, §160A-215(g).
Generally, §160A-215.

CAR RENTALS.
See RENTAL VEHICLES.

CAR REPAIRS.
Motor vehicle repairs, §§20-354 to 20-354.9.
See MOTOR VEHICLE REPAIRS.

CARRIAGES.
Bailment, lease or rental of vehicle or draft
animal.
Protection of bailor against bailee's acts, §§14-165
to 14-169.
See BAILMENTS.
Traffic laws apply to animal drawing vehicles,
§20-171.

CARRIERS.
Actions.
Carrier's right against prior carrier, §62-206.
Joinder of causes of action, §62-205.
Lost or damaged goods, §§62-203, 62-204.
Alcoholic beverages transported.
Commercial transportation permits, §18B-1115(c).
Baggage.
Careful handling required, §62-202.
Checks, §62-203(d), (e).
Sale of unclaimed baggage, §62-209.
Motor carriers of passengers.
Exemption from provisions, §62-209(d).
Notice, §62-209(a).
Record, §62-209(c).
Bills of lading.
Documents of title, §§25-7-101 to 25-7-603.
See DOCUMENTS OF TITLE.

CARRIERS —Cont'd

Bills of lading —Cont'd

Issuance on receiving property for transportation in interstate commerce, §62-203(a).

Bus companies.

See BUS COMPANIES.

Cash-on-delivery shipments.

Prompt settlement, §62-208.

Commercial code.

Documents of title, §§25-7-101 to 25-7-603.

See DOCUMENTS OF TITLE.

Common carriers.

See COMMON CARRIERS.

Confidentiality of information.

Disclosure of information as to shipments unlawful, §62-324(a).

Exceptions, §62-324(b).

Contract carriers.

Motor carriers.

Defined, §62-3.

Rates.

Conflict of laws.

Provisions controlling, §62-146(e).

Damages.

Limitation of liability.

Carrier issuing bill of lading, §25-7-309(b).

Disabled persons.

Right to use of public conveyances, §168-3.

Discrimination between connecting lines prohibited, §62-210.

Documents of title, §§25-7-101 to 25-7-603.

See DOCUMENTS OF TITLE.

Duty of carrier.

Carrier issuing bill of lading, §25-7-309(a).

Escheat.

Unclaimed baggage or freight, §62-209(c).

Franchise carriers generally.

See FRANCHISE CARRIERS.

Freight.

Bills of lading, §62-203(a).

Careful handling required, §62-202.

Charges at legal rates, §62-201.

Failure or refusal to comply, damages, §62-201.

Lost or damaged goods and property.

Additional nature of provisions, §62-203(g).

Claims.

Notice, §62-204.

Time for adjustment and payment, §62-203(b).

Penalty for failure to adjust and pay claim during time, §62-203(c).

Consolidation of actions, §62-203(f).

Failure to adjust and pay claims within required period, §62-203(c).

Liability for, §62-203(a), (c).

Limitation of actions, §62-204.

Motor carriers.

Exemptions from provisions, §62-203(h).

Reasonable time for transportation, §62-200(a), (b).

Motor carriers of passengers.

Provisions not applicable, §62-200(d).

Violations of provisions.

Forfeiture, §62-200(b).

Sale of unclaimed freight, §62-209(a).

Motor carriers of passengers.

Exemption from provisions, §62-209(d).

Notice, §62-209(a).

Record, §62-209(c).

Gasoline and oil transporters.

Invoice, bill of sale or bill of lading.

Required to be in possession of transporters, §119-42.

CARRIERS —Cont'd

Human service and volunteer transportation.

Inapplicability of laws and regulations, §62-289.5.

Intoxicated persons.

Ejection, §62-151.

Ticket refused, §62-150.

Prohibited entry, §62-150.

Joinder.

Claims between shippers and common carriers, §62-205.

Liens, §25-7-307.

Enforcement, §25-7-308(a) to (h).

Limitation of actions.

Lost or damaged goods claims, §62-204.

Lost or damaged goods and property, §§62-203, 62-204.

Motor carriers.

General provisions, §§62-259 to 62-280.1.

See MOTOR CARRIERS.

Notice.

Lost or damaged goods claims, §62-204.

Sale of unclaimed baggage or freight, §62-209(a).

Passengers refusing to pay fare or violating rules.

Ejection, §62-151.

Poultry inspections.

Violations of article, §106-549.59(b).

Prescription orders.

Rules pertaining to delivery, §90-85.32(b).

Property taxes.

Public service corporations.

Generally, §§105-333 to 105-344.

See PROPERTY TAXES.

Radioactive waste.

Safety regulations, §20-167.1(c).

Railroads.

See RAILROADS.

Rates.

Bus companies, §62-146.1.

Common carriers, §62-152.1.

Motor common carriers, §62-146.

Freight, §62-201.

Joint rates.

Common carriers, §62-152.1.

Motor common carriers, §62-146.

Mileage between points connected by more than one route, §62-145.

Motor carriers.

Allowance to shippers for transportation services, §62-272.

Collection rates and charges of carriers of property, §62-271.

Common carriers, §62-146.

Points connected by more than one route, §62-145.

Standard transportation practices, §62-152.2.

Sales of unclaimed baggage or freight, §62-209.

School buses.

See SCHOOL BUSES.

Tickets.

Intoxicated persons.

Ticket may be refused, §62-150.

Redemption, §62-149.

Utilities commission.

Free transportation for members.

Common carriers to furnish, §62-144(a).

CARROTS.

Weights and measures.

Standard weights and measures, §81A-42.

CARRYFORWARDS OF TAX CREDITS.

Business and energy tax credits.

Claimed against franchise or income tax, §105-129.17(a).

CARRYFORWARDS OF TAX CREDITS —Cont'd
Income tax credits for manufacturing cigarettes for exportation.
Increasing employment and utilizing state ports, §105-130.46(h).
Low-income housing tax credits.
Claimed against tax for which credit taken, §105-129.41(a1).
Unused portion, §105-129.41(a2).
Oysters.
Recycling oyster shells, §105-130.48(c).
Tax incentives for new and expanding businesses, §105-129.5(c).

CARRYING CONCEALED WEAPONS.
Alcoholic beverage consumption.
Carrying concealed handgun while consuming. Prohibition, §14-415.11(c2).
Alcohol or controlled substances remaining in body or blood.
Carrying concealed handgun prohibition, §14-415.11(c2).
Concealed handgun permits, §§14-415.10 to 14-415.27.
See CONCEALED HANDGUN PERMIT.
Military permittee's concealed handgun permit expired during deployment.
Carrying concealed handgun following end of deployment, §14-415.11(a).
Places authorized, §14-415.11.
Unlawful, §14-269(a).
Criminal penalties, §14-269(c).
Defense to prosecution, §14-269(b1), (b2).
Persons to which prohibition inapplicable, §14-269(b).
Pistol or gun, exceptions, §14-269(a1).
Pocket knives, inapplicability of section, §14-269(d).

CARS.
Abandoned and derelict motor vehicles, §§20-137.6 to 20-137.14.
See ABANDONED MOTOR VEHICLES.
Accidents.
See MOTOR VEHICLE ACCIDENTS.
Clubs and associations, §§58-69-2 to 58-69-60.
See MOTOR CLUBS AND ASSOCIATIONS.
Commissioner.
See MOTOR VEHICLES COMMISSIONER.
Damage appraisers.
See MOTOR VEHICLE DAMAGE APPRAISERS.
Dealers.
See MOTOR VEHICLE DEALERS.
Division.
See MOTOR VEHICLES DIVISION.
Driver's license.
Commercial drivers' licenses, §§20-37.10 to 20-37.23.
See COMMERCIAL DRIVERS' LICENSES.
Generally.
See DRIVERS' LICENSES.
Drunk driving.
See IMPAIRED DRIVING.
Equipment.
See MOTOR VEHICLE EQUIPMENT.
Financial responsibility, §§20-279.1 to 20-284.
See MOTOR VEHICLE FINANCIAL RESPONSIBILITY.
Generally.
See MOTOR VEHICLES.
Impaired driving.
See IMPAIRED DRIVING.

CARS —Cont'd
Inspections, §§20-183.2 to 20-183.8G.
See MOTOR VEHICLE INSPECTIONS.
Insurance.
See MOTOR VEHICLE INSURANCE.
Lemon law, §§20-351 to 20-351.10.
See LEMON LAW.
License plates.
See LICENSE PLATES.
Manufacturers.
See MOTOR VEHICLE MANUFACTURERS.
New motor vehicles warranty act, §§20-351 to 20-351.10.
See LEMON LAW.
Odometers, §§20-340 to 20-350.
See ODOMETERS.
Railroad grade crossing, §§20-142.1 to 20-142.5.
See RAILROAD GRADE CROSSINGS.
Reckless driving.
See RECKLESS DRIVING.
Registration.
See MOTOR VEHICLE REGISTRATION.
Rentals.
See RENTAL VEHICLES.
Service agreement companies, §§66-370, 66-372, 66-373.
See MOTOR VEHICLE SERVICE AGREEMENT COMPANIES.
Size, weight and loads.
See MOTOR VEHICLE SIZE, WEIGHT AND LOADS.
Speed.
See SPEED RESTRICTIONS AND VIOLATIONS.
Stolen vehicles.
See STOLEN PROPERTY.
Taxicabs.
See TAXICABS.
Tires.
See TIRES.
Titling.
See MOTOR VEHICLE TITLING.
Towing.
See TOWING OF VEHICLES.
Traffic lights.
See TRAFFIC LIGHTS.
Traffic regulations.
See TRAFFIC REGULATIONS.
Traffic tickets.
See TRAFFIC TICKETS.
Trailers.
See TRAILERS.

CAR SEATS, §20-137.1.
Child care facilities.
Compliance with law required, §110-91.
Seat belts generally.
See SEAT BELTS.

CARTERET COUNTY.
Acquisition of property, power, §153A-158.1(a).
Ambulances.
Obtaining ambulance services without intending to pay, §14-111.2.
Requesting ambulance falsely, §14-111.3.
Blank or master forms of mortgages, deeds of trust, etc.
Indexing and recording, inapplicability of provisions, §47-21.
Board of county commissioners.
Filling vacancies on board, §153A-27.1.
Condemnation or acquisition of land by local government unit outside county.
Consent of board of commissioners necessary, §153A-15.

CARTERET COUNTY —Cont'd
Cropper or tenant refusing to perform terms of contract.
Forfeiture of right of possession to premises, §42-27.
Eminent domain.
Exercise of power, purposes, modified provisions, §40A-3(b1).
Game laws, local acts not repealed, §113-133.1(e).
Grants in navigable waters, registration, §113-205(a).
Low-income housing tax credits.
Qualified building eligible for credit, §105-129.41(c).
North Carolina's eastern region, §§158-30 to 158-42.
Officers compensated from fees.
Statement to be rendered, §128-13.
Open fires, §106-942.
Applicability of provisions, §106-942(a).
Ground clearing activities, special permit required, §106-942(c).
Woodland fires, permit required, §106-942(b).
Registration of deeds.
Tax certification, no delinquent taxes due, §161-31(b).
Room occupancy tax levied by county, uniform provisions, §153A-155.
School property.
Acquisition and improvement, §153A-158.1.
Sheriff.
Vacancy, performance of duties until vacancy filled, §162-5.1.
Small city mixed beverage elections.
Inapplicability of provisions to, §18B-600(e1).
Special school tax, election to abolish.
Petition required, §115C-505.
Swimming, surfing and littering in Atlantic Ocean.
City ordinances effective, §160A-176.1.
Tax sales, notices by publication validated.
Inapplicability of provisions, §47-108.24.
Wild plants, taking of certain plants from land of another.
Inapplicability of provisions, §14-129.

CARTRIDGES.
Firearms generally.
See FIREARMS AND OTHER WEAPONS.
Inmates of charitable institutions.
Furnishing cartridges or ammunition for firearms, §14-258.1(a).
Teflon coated bullets.
Manufacture, sale, etc., §14-34.3.

CARTWAYS.
Abandonment or discontinuance, §§136-68, 136-70.
Application, §6-21.
Alteration, §§136-68, 136-70.
Application, §6-21.
Establishment, §§136-68, 136-69(a) to (c).
Application, §6-21.
Laying out, §136-69(a) to (c).

CAR WRECKS.
Generally.
See MOTOR VEHICLE ACCIDENTS.
Towing vehicles.
Generally.
See TOWING OF VEHICLES.

CAR WRECKS —Cont'd
Towing vehicles —Cont'd
Wreckers generally.
See WRECKERS.

CARY.
Accessory building of bona fide farm.
Building code exemption.
Zoning ordinance, §160A-360(k).
Land-use development incentives.
Reduction of energy consumption, §160A-383.4.

CASH CONVERTERS.
Generally, §§91A-1 to 91A-14.
See PAWNBROKERS AND CASH CONVERTERS.
Security agreements.
Effect of consumer protection and other laws, §25-9-201(b).

CASH FLOW CARDS.
Financial transaction card crime.
General provisions, §§14-113.8 to 14-113.17.
See FINANCIAL TRANSACTION CARDS.

CASHIER'S CHECKS.
Abandonment, presumption, time, §116B-53(c).
Defined, §25-3-104(g).
Negotiable instruments generally.
See NEGOTIABLE INSTRUMENTS.
Payment.
Obligation of issuer, §25-3-412.
Refusal to pay, §25-3-411(a) to (c).

CASH MANAGEMENT ACT, §§147-86.10 to 147-86.15.

CASH ON DELIVERY.
Common carriers to settle shipments promptly, §62-208.
Motor carriers, embezzlement of shipments, §62-273.
Sales, UCC.
Buyers not entitled to inspect goods, §25-2-513.

CASH SHORTAGES.
Deductions from employees' wages.
When withholding authorized, §95-25.8(c), (e).

CASINOS.
Houses of public entertainment, §14-293.

CASTRATION, §14-29.
Malicious castration, §14-28.

CASUALTY INSURANCE.
Actuarial opinions, §§58-10-150 to 58-10-175.
Confidentiality, §58-10-175(b), (c).
Immunity of appointed actuary, §58-10-170.
Powers of commissioner, §58-10-175(e), (f).
Privilege from testifying, §58-10-175(d).
Report and work papers, §58-10-160(a).
Failure to provide, §58-10-160(b).
Monetary penalty, §58-10-165.
Statement of, §58-10-150.
Failure to provide.
Monetary penalty, §58-10-165.
Public record, §58-10-175(a).
Summary, §58-10-155.
Failure to provide.
Monetary penalty, §58-10-165.
Community college buildings and contents, §115D-58.11(a) to (c).
Confidentiality of consumer and customer information.
Generally, §§58-39-1 to 58-39-165.
See INSURANCE CONSUMER AND CUSTOMER INFORMATION PRIVACY.

CASUALTY INSURANCE —Cont'd
Foreign or alien insurance companies.
Deposits required, §58-5-10.
Motor vehicle insurance.
Generally.
See MOTOR VEHICLE INSURANCE.
Property insurance.
Mediation of emergency or disaster claims,
§§58-44-70 to 58-44-120.
See PROPERTY INSURANCE.
Policies, §§58-44-1 to 58-44-60.
See PROPERTY INSURANCE.

CASWELL BEACH.
Eminent domain.
Vesting of title and right to possession,
§40A-42(a).
Ordinances to regulate and control swimming, personal watercraft operation, surfing and littering in Atlantic Ocean, §160A-176.2.

CASWELL COUNTY.
Ambulance services.
Attachment or garnishment and lien for,
§§44-51.4 to 44-51.8.
Obtaining ambulance services without intending
to pay, §14-111.2.
Condemnation or acquisition of land by local government unit outside county.
Consent of board of commissioners necessary,
§153A-15.
Counties generally.
See COUNTIES.
Cropper or tenant refusing to perform terms of contract.
Forfeiture of right of possession to premises,
§42-27.
Dangerous firearm use by young children, permitting.
Air rifles, air pistols and BB guns not dangerous
firearms, §14-316(b).
Dog collars.
Unlawful removal of electronic dog collars,
§14-401.17.
Foxes, open seasons for taking.
Wildlife resources commission authorized to
continue seasons from year to year,
§113-291.4(f1).
Game laws, local acts not repealed,
§113-133.1(e).
Registration of deeds.
Tax certification, no delinquent taxes due,
§161-31(b).
Room occupancy tax levied by county, uniform provision, §153A-155.
Tax elections for industrial development purposes, §§158-16 to 158-24.
Tax sales, notices by publication validated.
Inapplicability of provisions, §47-108.24.

CATALOGS.
Sale of prints.
General prohibitions applicable to art dealers,
§25C-11(a).

CATALYTIC CONVERTERS.
Person delivering to secondary metals recycler.
Receipt, fingerprint, §66-11(b).
Purchase limitations.
Secondary metals recyclers, §66-11(d).

CATASTROPHES.
State of emergency.
Government powers and proclamations generally,
§§14-288.12 to 14-288.18.
See STATE OF EMERGENCY.

CATAWBA COUNTY.
Ambulance services.
Attachment or garnishment and lien for,
§§44-51.4 to 44-51.8.
Obtaining ambulance services without intending
to pay, §14-111.2.
Condemnation or acquisition of land by local government unit outside county.
Consent of board of commissioners necessary,
§153A-15.
Counties generally.
See COUNTIES.
Game laws, local acts not repealed,
§113-133.1(e).
Oil, gas or mineral claims.
Certain ancient claims extinguished, preservation,
procedure, §1-42.2(a) to (d).
Registration of deeds.
Tax certification, no delinquent taxes due,
§161-31(b).
School property.
Acquisition and improvement, §153A-158.1.
Special school tax, election to abolish.
Petition required, §115C-505.
Wild plants, taking of certain plants from land of another.
Inapplicability of provisions, §14-129.

CATAWBA RIVER.
Mountain Island lake marine commission,
§§77-70 to 77-78.
See MOUNTAIN ISLAND LAKE.

CATAWBA, TOWN OF.
Satellite annexation.
Limitation on area of satellite corporate limits,
inapplicability, §160A-58.1(b).

CATAWBA/WATEREE RIVER BASIN ADVISORY COMMISSION.
River basins advisory commissions generally,
§§77-110 to 77-118.
See RIVER BASINS ADVISORY COMMISSIONS.

CATERING BUSINESS.
Alcoholic beverage permits.
Culinary permit.
Kind of permit that may be issued, §18B-1001.
Mixed beverages catering permit.
Kind of permit that may be issued, §18B-1001.

CATS.
Animals generally.
See ANIMALS.
Cruelty to animals.
See CRUELTY TO ANIMALS.
Euthanasia, §19A-24.
Hotel rooms, admittance of pets, §72-7.1.
Impoundment.
Leashing or restraining ordinances.
Dogs and cats in violation, §130A-192(b).
Rabies vaccination tags.
Animals not wearing, §130A-192.
Surrendered by owners, §130A-192(b).
Leashing and restraining ordinances.
Impoundment of cats in violation, §130A-192(b).
Rabies.
Defined, §130A-184.

CATS —Cont'd
Rabies —Cont'd
Generally, §§130A-184 to 130A-201.
See RABIES.
Spay/neuter program, §§19A-60 to 19A-66.
Surrender to shelter by owner, §130A-192(b).
Trust created for care of animal or animals,
§36C-4-408.

CATTLE.
Allowance to officers for keeping and
maintaining cattle taken into custody
under legal process, §1-322.
Brands generally, §§80-45 to 80-66.
See LIVESTOCK BRANDS.
Brucellosis, §§106-388 to 106-398.
See BRUCELLOSIS.
Cattle tick, §§106-351 to 106-363.
See CATTLE TICK.
Certificate of registration obtained by false
representation, §14-103.
Compensation for killing diseased animals
generally, §§106-323 to 106-335.
See LIVESTOCK DISEASES.
Control of livestock diseases generally,
§§106-400 to 106-405.
See LIVESTOCK DISEASES.
Dealer licensing generally, §§106-418.8 to
106-418.16.
See LIVESTOCK DEALER LICENSING.
Diseases generally, §§106-304 to 106-307.7.
See LIVESTOCK DISEASES.
Dogs killing cattle.
Any person may kill, §67-14.
Larceny.
Felony, §14-81(a).
Probation, conditions required, §14-81(b).
Sentencing to active sentence.
Judge's authority not limited, §14-81(b).
Livestock generally.
See LIVESTOCK.
Livestock markets, §§106-406 to 106-418.
See LIVESTOCK MARKETS.
Meat inspections generally, §§106-549.15 to
106-549.39.
See MEAT INSPECTIONS.
Promotion of use and sale of agricultural
products.
Generally, §§106-550 to 106-568.
See AGRICULTURAL PRODUCTS
PROMOTION.
Pursuing or injuring with intent to steal,
§14-85.
Quarantine of diseased animals generally.
See LIVESTOCK DISEASES.
Rendering plants and rendering operations,
§§106-168.1 to 106-168.16.
Signs for protection of cattle, §136-33.1.

CATTLE GUARDS.
Railroads, §136-194.

CATTLE RUSTLING.
Larceny of livestock, §14-81.

CATTLE TICK, §§106-351 to 106-363.
Compelling county commissioners to comply,
§106-355.
Control of livestock diseases generally,
§§106-400 to 106-405.
See LIVESTOCK DISEASES.
Counties.
Quarantine zones, §106-352.

CATTLE TICK —Cont'd
Dipping of cattle or horses, §106-351.
Counties to provide dipping vats, §106-353.
Damaging dipping vats a felony, §106-363.
Expense of owner, §106-358.
Lien on animal, §106-359.
Owners of stock to have same dipped, §106-356.
Period of dipping, §106-356.
Service of dipping notice, §106-357.
Supervision of dipping, §106-356.
Dipping vats.
Damaging dipping vats a felony, §106-363.
Enforcement of article.
Duty of sheriff, §106-360.
State veterinarian, county commissioners failing
to comply, §106-355.
Liens.
Expense of dipping as lien on animals, §106-359.
Livestock diseases generally, §§106-304 to
106-307.7.
See LIVESTOCK DISEASES.
Mandamus.
Enforcement of compliance by state veterinarian,
§106-355.
Misdemeanor, §106-362.
Notice.
Service of quarantine and dipping notice,
§106-357.
Quarantine.
Cattle placed in quarantine, §106-358.
Counties not embraced in quarantine zones,
§106-352.
Service of notice, §106-357.
Rules and regulations, §106-361.
Sheriffs.
Duty of sheriff in enforcing article, §106-360.
State veterinarian.
Enforcement of compliance with law, §106-355.
Violation of provisions, §106-362.

CAUSAL EMPLOYEES.
Workers' compensation.
Not included in definition of employee, §97-2.

CAUSEWAYS.
Special speed limitations, §20-144.

CAVEAT TO WILL.
Accountings to be filed, §31-36(a).
Alignment hearing, §31-33(b).
By whom filed, §31-32.
Commissions prohibited.
Clerk's order, §31-36(a).
Costs.
Allowance of costs to either or apportioned in
discretion of court, §6-21.
Bonds, surety, §31-33(d).
Security for costs.
Court may require, §31-33(d).
Distributions prohibited.
Clerk's order, §31-36(a).
Effect of caveat on estate administration,
§31-36.
Judgments.
Entry of judgment, §31-37.1(b).
Settlement agreements, §31-37.1(a).
Jurisdiction.
Clerks of superior court jurisdiction in estate
proceedings.
Limitation on jurisdiction, §28A-2-4(c).
Order of clerk applicable during pendency of
caveat, §31-36(a).

CAVEAT TO WILL —Cont'd
Payment of items listed in clerk's order.
Notice of intent, §31-36(b).
Pleadings, §31-33(c).
Preservation of estate, §31-36(a), (c).
Service of caveat, §31-33(a).
Settlement agreements.
Parties may enter into, §31-37.1(a).
Taxes, claims and debts of estate, §31-36(a).
Transfer of cause to superior court for trial, §31-33(a).
When filed, §31-32.

CAVE PROTECTION.
Definitions, §14-159.20.
Owners and agents liability, §14-159.23.
Speleothems.
Defined, §14-159.20.
Sale, §14-159.22.
Vandalism, §14-159.21.

CDL, §§20-37.10 to 20-37.23.
See COMMERCIAL DRIVERS' LICENSES.

CEASE AND DESIST ORDERS.
Banks.
Commissioner of banks.
Administrative orders generally, §§53-107.1, 53-107.2.
International banking, §53-232.16.
Campaign contributions and expenditures.
Civil remedy other than penalty, §163-278.34(c).
Consumer finance act, §53-187.
Continuing care retirement communities, §58-64-10(c).
Health maintenance organizations, §58-67-165(c), (d).
Injunctions.
See INJUNCTIONS.
Insurance consumer and customer information privacy, §58-39-90.
Penalty for violating, §58-39-95(b).
Insurance unfair trade practices, §58-63-35.
Issuance, modification or setting aside, §58-63-32.
Penalty for violating, §58-63-50.
Mortgages and deeds of trust.
Reverse mortgages, §53-271(a), (b).
Producer-controlled property or casualty insurers.
Lack of material compliance with section, §58-3-165(l).
Professional employer organizations, §58-89A-165(b).
Emergency orders, §58-89A-165(c).
Provider sponsored organizations.
Division of medical assistance, §131E-307(d), (e).
Savings and loan associations, §54B-59(a).
Judicial review, §54B-71.
Temporary cease and desist orders, §54B-59(b).
Savings banks.
Generally, §54C-76(a).
Judicial review, §54C-84.
Temporary cease and desist orders, §54C-76(b).
Violations of orders, §54C-79(b).
Securities regulation, §78A-47(b).
Trust companies.
Administrative enforcement, §53-369(a).
Unauthorized insurers, §§58-28-20 to 58-28-35.
Additional nature provisions, §58-28-35.
Appeal, §58-28-20(e).
Domestic companies.
Unauthorized acts by, §58-14-15.

CEASE AND DESIST ORDERS —Cont'd
Unauthorized insurers —Cont'd
Modification or setting aside, §58-28-20(b), (c).
Penalties for violations, §58-28-30.
Power of commissioner, §58-28-20(a), (d).
Viatical settlements, §58-58-290(c).
Emergency cease and desist orders, §58-58-290(d).

CEILING FANS.
Energy star qualified products.
Sales and use tax holiday, §105-164.13D(a).

CELL PHONES.
Enhanced 911 system for wireless communications.
See 911 SYSTEM.
Minors using while operating motor vehicle.
Prohibition, fine, §§20-11(c), (e), (l), 20-137.3(b), (e).
Definitions, §20-137.3(a).
Exceptions, §20-137.3(d).
Seizure or forfeiture of phone, §20-137.3(c).
Poles, ducts, conduits controlled by municipality or membership corporation.
Communications service providers.
Request to utilize, §62-350.
Portable consumer electronic devices insurance.
Claims handling, adjuster licenses, §58-33-27.
Generally, §§58-44A-1 to 58-44A-25.
See PORTABLE CONSUMER ELECTRONIC DEVICES INSURANCE.
Prepaid wireless.
911 system.
See 911 SYSTEM.
Sales and use tax on mobile telecommunications services.
Defined, §§105-164.3, 105-164.4C.
Sourcing and taxation, §105-164.4C(a), (a2).
School bus operators using while bus in motion.
Unlawful, §20-137.4(b).
Class 2 misdemeanor, fine, §20-137.4(f).
Driver's license points or insurance surcharge.
Not assessed for violation, §20-137.4(f).
Emergency situations, exception, §20-137.4(d).
Negligence per se or contributory negligence.
Violation not considered, §20-137.4(f).
Seizure or forfeiture of phone.
Prohibited unless otherwise provided by law, §20-137.4(c).
Stationary buses, inapplicability, §20-137.4(b).
Secret listening.
Electronic surveillance, §§15A-286 to 15A-298.
See ELECTRONIC SURVEILLANCE.
State correctional or local confinement facilities.
Inmates.
Giving or selling device or component to, §14-258.1(d).
Possession by inmate in local confinement facility, §14-258.1(e).
Not permitted on premises of state correctional facilities, §148-23.2.
Use by correctional employees while in vehicle, §148-23.2.
Telecommunications generally.
See TELECOMMUNICATIONS.
Text messaging or electronic mail.
Driving while using mobile phone for.
Unlawful, §20-137.4A(a).
Exceptions, §20-137.4A(b).

CELL PHONES —Cont'd
Text messaging or electronic mail —Cont'd
Driving while using mobile phone for —Cont'd
Unlawful —Cont'd
Penalty, §20-137.4A(c).
Wireless telecommunications facilities,
§§153A-349.50 to 153A-349.53.

CEMENT.
Standard weights and measures, §81A-42.
Street and highway construction contracts.
Production in United States.
Contract requirements relating to construction
materials, §136-28.7(a) to (d).

CEMETERIES, §§65-46 to 65-73.
Abandoned and neglected cemeteries.
County care of rural cemeteries, §§65-111 to
65-113.
Appropriations by county commissioners,
§65-112.
Board of trustees, §65-113.
List of public and abandoned cemeteries,
§65-111.
Powers of county commissioners, §65-113.
Definitions, §65-85.
Entering public or private property to maintain or
visit.
Consent, §65-101.
Without consent.
Order of clerk of superior court, §65-102(a).
Contents, §65-102(b).
Historic preservation program, §121-8(g).
Money for maintenance and preservation.
Clerk of superior court.
Bank or trust company substituted as trustee,
§65-95.
Bond, surety, §65-95.
Deposit with, §65-91.
Investment of funds, §65-94.
Perpetual holding of funds, §65-93.
Separate record of accounts, §65-92.
Investment, §65-94.
Tax exemption, §65-96.
Removal of graves.
Certificate to be filed, §65-106(c), (e).
Due care, §65-106(f), (g).
Eminent domain.
Authority not conferred by provisions,
§65-106(h).
Expenses, §65-106(d).
Notice, §65-106(b).
Who may disinter, move and reinter, §65-106(a).
Rural cemeteries.
County care of, §§65-111 to 65-113.
Burial.
See BURIAL.
Cemetery associations or corporations.
Change of control, §65-59.
Change of name, §65-17.
Land holdings, §65-16.
Stockholder's meetings, §65-17.1.
Cemetery brokers.
Defined, §65-48.
Licenses, §65-57.
Cemetery commission, §§65-48 to 65-54.
Cemetery management organizations.
Defined, §65-48.
Licenses, §65-57.
Cemetery sales organizations.
Defined, §65-48.
Licenses, §65-57.

CEMETERIES —Cont'd
Cities or towns.
Cemetery trustees generally, §§160A-349.1 to
160A-349.15.
See MUNICIPAL CEMETERIES.
Generally, §§160A-341 to 160A-348.
See MUNICIPAL CEMETERIES.
Columbarium.
Defined, §65-48.
Commission, §§65-48 to 65-54.
Confederate cemetery.
Labor for care of cemetery.
Division of adult correction to furnish, §65-4.
Contracts.
Individual contracts for care and maintenance,
§65-62.
Conveyances, §65-69(b), (c).
Corporate trustees.
Application for approval, §65-60.1(b).
Defined, §65-60.1(a).
Investments, §65-60.1(e).
Records, §65-60.1(c).
Removal of trustee, §65-60.1(d).
Counties.
Cemeteries for inmates of county homes.
County commissioners may establish, §65-5.
Removal and reinterment of bodies, §65-6.
Service districts, §§153A-300 to 153A-310.
Cremation.
General provisions, §§90-210.120 to 90-210.135.
See CREMATION.
Deeds.
Validation of certain deeds for cemetery lots
executed by suspended corporations, §65-73.
Defacing or desecrating grave sites.
Applicability of provisions, §14-148(b).
Archaeologists.
Applicability of provisions, §§14-148, 14-149(b).
Plowing over or covering up graves, §14-149(a).
Prohibited, §14-148(a).
Prohibited acts, §14-149(a), (a1).
Violation constitutes misdemeanor, §14-148(c).
Definitions, §65-48.
Abandoned and neglected cemeteries, §65-85.
Discrimination.
Burial without regard to race or color, §65-72(a),
(b).
Eminent domain.
Powers of local public condemnors, §40A-3(b).
Executors and administrators.
Authority provide suitable burial place for
decedent, §28A-19-9(b).
Fees.
Change of control of cemetery company.
Application.
Filing fee, §65-59.
Commission, §65-54.
Licenses, §65-54.
Cemetery companies, §65-55(c).
Sales organizations, management organizations
and brokers, §65-57(c).
Vaults.
Delivery or inspection, §65-66(n).
Fraternal orders and societies.
Exemptions from North Carolina cemetery act,
§65-47(b).
Funeral service.
General provisions, §§90-210.18A to 90-210.29B.
See FUNERAL SERVICES PROVIDERS.
Grave space.
Defined, §65-48.

CEMETERIES —Cont'd

Historic preservation program.
Abandoned cemeteries, §121-8(g).
Identification of bodies before burial or cremation, §90-210.29A.
Inscriptions on gravestone or monument.
Unlawful inscriptions.
Charging person with commission of crime, §14-401.3.
Investments.
Corporate trustees, §65-60.1(e).
Licenses.
Cemetery companies, §§65-55, 65-56.
Application, §65-55(b).
Action by commission on, §65-55(d), (e).
Filing fee, §65-55(c).
Defined, §65-48.
Denial of license, §65-55(e).
Existing companies.
Grant of license to, §65-56.
Investigation of applicant, §65-55(c).
Notice.
Granting of license, §65-55(f).
Required, §65-55(a).
Preneed funeral establishment license and preneed sales license, §90-210.67.
Renewal license.
Application, §65-67.
Assignment or transfer prohibited, §65-68.
Sale of preneed grave space, etc., §65-58.
Application, §65-58(b).
Filing fee, §65-58(c).
Fees, §65-58(c).
Judicial review of orders or decisions of commission.
Applicability of certain provisions, §65-58(f).
Notice.
Grant of license, §65-58(e).
Refusal of license, §65-58(d).
Required, §65-58(a).
Sales organizations, management organizations and brokers.
Application, §65-57(b).
Action by commission on, §65-57(e) to (g).
Filing fee, §65-57(c).
Investigation of applicant, §65-57(d).
Notice.
Denial of application, §65-57(f).
Granting of application, §65-57(g).
Required, §65-57(a).
Violations of provisions.
Misdemeanor, §65-57(h).
Local, private and special legislation prohibited, NC Const Art II §24.
Map of cemetery divided into sections based upon race.
Immediate registration by register of deeds, §161-14(e).
Mausoleums.
Defined, §65-48.
Sale of space before construction.
Time for construction, §65-70(a).
Failure to complete in time, §65-70(e).
Trust account, §65-70(b), (c).
Bond in lieu of payment to, §65-70(f).
Withdrawal of funds from, §65-70(d).
Vaults.
Fee for delivery or inspection, §65-66(n).
Requiring purchase from particular seller.
Prohibited, §65-66(n).

CEMETERIES —Cont'd

Minimum acreage, §65-69(a).
Exceptions, §65-69(d).
Minimum burial depth, §65-77.
Minor's malicious or willful destruction of property.
Recovery of damages from parents, §1-538.1.
Municipal cemeteries.
Generally, §§160A-341 to 160A-348.
See MUNICIPAL CEMETERIES.
Parent responsibility for damages.
Malicious or willful destruction of property by minors, §1-538.1.
Perpetual care funds, §§65-61 to 65-65.
Plowing over or covering up graves, §14-149.
Preneed funeral contracts and funds, §§90-210.60 to 90-210.73.
See PRENEED FUNERAL CONTRACTS AND FUNDS.
Private way to public road.
Cartway, tramway or railway.
Laying off, procedure, §136-69(a) to (c).
Property taxes.
Burial property.
Assessment, special class, §105-278.2(b).
Exemption, §105-278.2(a).
Real property defined, §105-278.2(c).
Racial minorities.
Burial without regard to race or color, §65-72(a).
Violations of provisions misdemeanors, §65-72(b).
Registration of map of cemetery divided into sections based upon race, §161-14(e).
Records, §65-60.
Corporate trustees, §65-60.1(c).
Registration of map of cemetery.
Cemetery divided into sections based upon race.
Immediate registration by register of deeds, §161-14(e).
Sale of personal property or services.
Applicability of provisions, §65-66(a).
Cancellation of contract by purchaser, §65-66(m).
Examination of business by commission, §65-66(h).
Exemptions from provisions, §65-66(k).
Interest.
Prepayments, §65-66(f).
Policy of state, §65-66(a).
Reports, §65-66(b).
Failure to make, §65-66(l).
Requirements of contracts, §65-66(b) to (e).
Trust account.
Deposit of proceeds, §65-66(b).
Bond in lieu of, §65-66(g).
Vaults, §65-66(n).
Waiver of provisions.
Prohibited, §65-66(i).
Sanitary districts.
Acceptance of gifts for nonprofit cemetery.
Corporate powers of sanitary district board, §130A-55.
Scope of act, §65-47(a).
Exceptions, §65-47(b), (c).
Taxation.
Exemption from tax, NC Const Art V §2.
Property taxes.
Exemption of burial property, §105-278.2.
Title of act.
Short title, §65-46.
Tombstones.
Defacing or desecrating grave sites, §§14-148, 14-149.

CEMETERIES —Cont'd
Transportation department.
Maintenance and repair of ingress and egress to
public or church cemeteries, §136-18.
Trespass.
Defacing or desecrating grave sites, §§14-148,
14-149.
Trust funds for care of cemeteries.
Generally.
See CEMETERY CARE TRUST FUNDS.
Perpetual care fund, §§65-61 to 65-65.
Vaults.
Fee for delivery or inspection, §65-66(n).
Requiring purchase from particular seller.
Prohibition, §65-66(n).
Veterans.
Burial.
Days for, §65-44.
Costs, §65-43.6(a) to (c).
Definitions, §65-43.
Disinterment, §65-43.4(a), (b).
Interment, §65-43.1.
Bars to eligibility, §65-43.3.
Death of family member prior to qualified
veteran, §65-43.1(c).
Eligibility, §65-43.1(a).
Number of gravesites authorized, §65-43.1(b).
Proof, §65-43.2(a), (b).
Land acquisition, §65-41.
Location of cemeteries, §65-42.
Reinterment, §65-43.5(a), (b).
Violations of North Carolina cemetery act,
§65-71(a).

CEMETERY ASSOCIATIONS OR
CORPORATIONS.
Change of control of cemetery company.
Application, §65-59.
Filing fee, §65-59.
Change of name, §65-17.
Land holdings authorized, §65-16.
Licensing of cemetery company, §§65-55, 65-56.
Meetings of certain nonprofit cemetery
corporations.
Amendment of charter.
Required vote, §65-17.1.
Calling of meeting, §65-17.1.
Notice, §65-17.1.
Quorum, §65-17.1.
Names.
Change of name, §65-17.

CEMETERY BROKERS.
Defined, §65-48.
Licenses, §65-57.

CEMETERY CARE TRUST FUNDS.
Perpetual care fund, §§65-61 to 65-65.
Advertising.
Requirements for advertising of perpetual care
fund, §65-63.
Corporate trustee.
Designation, §65-61.
Financial reports, §65-65.
Deposits, §§65-61, 65-64.
Conversion to private cemetery, §65-64(b).
Individual cemetery.
Requirements as to grave memorial markers,
§65-63.
Investment of amounts deposited, §65-64(e).
Items subject to, §65-64(d).
Special endowments, §65-64(f).

CEMETERY CARE TRUST FUNDS —Cont'd
Perpetual care fund —Cont'd
Deposits —Cont'd
Time for, §65-64(a).
Individual contracts for care and maintenance,
§65-62.
Misdemeanors.
Failure to make required contributions,
§65-71(b).
Reports.
Financial reports, §65-65.
Required trust fund, §65-61.
Withdrawal or transfer of portion of fund.
Consent of commission required, §65-61.
Preneed funeral contracts and funds,
§§90-210.60 to 90-210.73.

CEMETERY COMMISSION.
Attorneys at law.
Employment of, §65-53.
Budget.
Annual budget, §65-54.
Chairperson, §65-50(e).
Composition, §65-50.
Defined, §65-48.
Employment of staff, §65-53.
Established, §65-49.
Fees, §65-54.
Injunctions.
Power to bring action for, §65-53.
Investigations, §65-53.
Meetings.
Notice, §65-51.
Regular meetings, §65-52.
Special meetings, §65-52.
Notice.
Meetings, §65-51.
Number of members, §65-50(a).
Office.
Principal office, §65-51.
Officers.
Election, §65-50.
Powers, §65-53.
Qualifications of members, §65-50.
Quorum, §65-50(d).
Removal of members, §65-50(c).
Rules and regulations, §65-49.
Powers of commission generally, §65-53.
Selection of members, §65-50.
Term of members, §65-50(b).

CEMETERY MANAGEMENT
ORGANIZATIONS.
Defined, §65-48.
Licenses, §65-57.

CEMETERY SALES ORGANIZATIONS.
Defined, §65-48.
Licenses, §65-57.

CEMETERY TRUSTEES.
Generally, §§160A-349.1 to 160A-349.15.
See MUNICIPAL CEMETERIES.

CENSURE.
Attorney discipline.
Imposition of discipline, Bar Rule B.0123.
Issuance by grievance committee, Bar Rule
B.0113.

CENSUS.
Constitution of the United States, US Const Art
I §§2, 9.

CENSUS —Cont'd
Education of children with disabilities.
Child find.
Annual census of children with disabilities.
Conducted in each school, §115C-107.3.
Municipalities.
Electoral districts.
Reapportionment, §160A-23.
Estimates of population, §160A-486.
Special education.
Child find.
Annual census of children with disabilities.
Conducted in each school, §115C-107.3.
Traffic census.
Established, §136-18.

CENTENNIALS.
America's four hundredth anniversary committee.
Compensation of members, §143B-86.
Creation, §143B-85.
Members, §143B-86.
Powers and duties, §143B-85.
Quorum, §143B-86.
Selection of members, §143B-86.

CENTER FOR ADVANCEMENT OF TEACHING, §§115C-296.5, 115C-296.6.

CENTER FOR GEOGRAPHIC INFORMATION AND ANALYSIS.
Role, §143-725(b).

CENTER FOR HEALTH STATISTICS, §§130A-371 to 130A-374.

CENTER FOR MISSING PERSONS, §§143B-1010 to 143B-1022.
See MISSING PERSONS.

CENTER FOR NURSING, §§90-171.70 to 90-171.72.
State personnel system.
Exempt employees, §126-5(c1).

CENTER LINES.
Marking street or highway with, §136-30.1(a), (b).
Arsenic content in glass beads contained in paint used to mark highways, §136-30.2.

CENTRAL NORTH CAROLINA SCHOOL FOR THE DEAF AT GREENSBORO.
Education programs in residential schools generally, §§143B-146.1 to 143B-146.21.
See EDUCATION.
Schools for the deaf generally, §§143B-216.40 to 143B-216.44.
See DEAF AND HEARING IMPAIRED.

CENTRAL OFFICE OR AIRCRAFT FACILITY PROPERTY TAX CREDIT, §105-129.12.

CENTRAL PIEDMONT COMMUNITY COLLEGE.
Community colleges generally, §§115D-1 to 115D-81.
See COMMUNITY COLLEGES.
Financial support.
Authority to provide local financial support, §115D-60(a).
Sale, exchange or lease of property, §115D-60(b).

CENTRAL PRISON.
Delivery of prisoners to prison, §148-28.
Employees, §148-31.

CENTRAL PRISON —Cont'd
Identification bureau.
Transfer to state bureau of investigation, §114-18.
Maintenance, §148-31.
Sentencing of prisoners, §148-28.
Warden.
Powers and duties.
Generally, §148-31.
Youthful offenders, §148-28.

CENTRAL REGISTRY.
Abuse, neglect or dependency of juvenile cases or child fatalities.
Report by director of social services where maltreatment involved, §7B-307(c).

CENTRAL REGISTRY AND RESPONSIBLE INDIVIDUALS LIST.
Child abuse, neglect and dependency and child fatalities, §7B-311.
Responsible individuals list, §§7B-320 to 7B-324.

CEREBRAL PALSY.
Defined, §35A-1101.
Determination of incompetence, §§35A-1101 to 35A-1116.
See INCOMPETENCY.

CERTIFICATE OF DETERMINATION OF APPEAL.
Procedure after determination of appeal, §1-298.

CERTIFICATE OF ENVIRONMENTAL COMPATIBILITY.
Construction of transmission line by utility.
Application for certificate, §62-102.

CERTIFICATE OF PUBLIC ADVANTAGE.
Cooperative agreements among hospitals generally, §§131E-192.1 to 131E-192.13.
See HEALTH CARE FACILITIES.

CERTIFICATE OF RELIEF FROM COLLATERAL CONSEQUENCES, §§15A-173.1 to 15A-173.6.
See CRIMINAL LAW AND PROCEDURE.

CERTIFICATE OF SERVICE.
Required to accompany pleadings and papers served, §1A-1 Rule 5(b1).

CERTIFICATES OF BIRTH.
See BIRTH CERTIFICATES.

CERTIFICATES OF DEATH.
Amendment by medical examiner, §130A-385(c).
Amendment of death certificate, §130A-118(a).
Contents of death certificate, §130A-116.
Cremation.
Authorization for cremation, §130A-113(b).
Duties of local registrars, §130A-97.
Duties of medical examiners, §130A-385.
Filing of death certificate, §130A-115(a).
Information to be obtained, §130A-115(b).
Local registrar's duties, §130A-97.
Register of deeds.
Copies to be forwarded by local registrars, §130A-97.
Standard certificate of death.
Contents of death certificate, §130A-116.
Vital statistics generally.
See VITAL STATISTICS.

CERTIFICATES OF DEPOSIT.
Banks.
Unlawful issuance, §53-63.

CERTIFICATES OF MARRIAGE.
Delayed marriage certificate.
Issuance, §51-21.
Registration of marriage certificates.
Duty of registers of deeds, §130A-110(a) to (d).
Evidentiary value of copies, §130A-110(b).
Forms, §130A-110(a).
Furnishing copies, §130A-110(b), (c).

CERTIFICATES OF NEED.
Health care facilities, §§131E-175 to 130E-191.1.
See HEALTH CARE FACILITIES.

CERTIFICATES OF PUBLIC CONVENIENCE AND NECESSITY.
Coin, coinless or key-operated pay telephone service.
Special certificate issued to utility offering, §62-110(c).
Construction, acquisition or operation of utility plant or system.
Required, §62-110(a).
Construction of transmission line by utility.
Application for certificate, §62-102.
Generating facilities, certificates for construction.
Analysis for needs for expansion, §62-110.1(c).
Appeal from award order, §62-82(b).
Application.
Factors in action, §62-110.1(d).
Notice in hearing, §62-82(a).
Time period for decision on application, §62-110.1(h).
Electric membership corporations.
Inclusion in definition of public utility, §62-110.1(b).
Estimate of construction costs.
Conditions for receiving, §62-110.1(e).
Exceptions to requirements, §62-110.1(g).
Nuclear facilities.
Project development cost review, §62-110.7.
Out-of-state electric generating facilities.
Rate recovery of construction costs, §62-110.6.
Progress report by utility, §62-110.1(f).
Rate recovery of construction costs, §62-110.1(f1) to (f3).
Nuclear facilities.
Project development cost review, §62-110.7.
Out-of-state electric generating facilities, §62-110.6.
Required, §62-110.1(a).
Review by commission, §62-110.1(e1).
Local telephone exchange or exchange access services, §62-110(f1) to (f6).
Long distance service.
Issuance to utility offering, §62-110(b).
Motor carriers, certificate or permit, §62-262.
Bus companies.
Certificates of authority, §62-262.1.
Fees, §62-300.
Discontinuance or reduction in service.
Inapplicability of provision to bus companies, §62-262.2(e).
Fees, §62-300(a).
Natural gas planning, §62-36A(b1).
Nonprofit colleges or universities.
Telephone service to, §62-110(e).
Public transportation authorities.
Power to issue, §160A-579.
Public utilities, §62-110.
Alternative operator services, §62-110.4.

CERTIFICATES OF PUBLIC CONVENIENCE AND NECESSITY —Cont'd
Public utilities —Cont'd
Applications.
Fees, §62-300(a).
Definition of "certificate,"§62-3.
Long distance telephone and telegraph services, §62-110.
Natural gas planning, §62-36A(b1).
Pay telephone service, §62-110.
Telecommunication services, §62-110(f4) to (f6).
Taxicabs, §20-87.
Telephone network.
Shared use or resale of services, §62-110(b).

CERTIFICATES OF TITLE.
Boats generally, §§75A-32 to 75A-49.
See BOATS AND OTHER SMALL WATERCRAFT.
Motor vehicles generally.
See MOTOR VEHICLE TITLING.
Torrens system registration, §§43-13 to 43-25.
See TORRENS SYSTEM REGISTRATION.

CERTIFICATION BY SUPREME COURT.
Discretionary review, §7A-31, AppProc 15.

CERTIFICATION OF DEPOSITIONS, §1A-1
Rule 30(f).

CERTIFICATION OF EUTHANASIA TECHNICIANS, §19A-24.

CERTIFICATION OF LEGAL SPECIALISTS.
Bankruptcy law specialty, Bar Rules D.2201 to D.2207.
Continuing legal education, accreditation rules, Bar Rules D.1901 to D.1908.
Criminal law specialty, Bar Rules D.2501 to D.2509.
Estate planning and probate law specialty, Bar Rules D.2301 to D.2307.
Family law specialty, Bar Rules D.2401 to D.2407.
Hearing and appeal rules, Bar Rules D.1801 to D.1806.
Independent certifying organizations, rules of approval, Bar Rules D.2001 to D.2006.
Plan of legal specialization, Bar Rules D.1701 to D.1726.
Real property law specialty, Bar Rules D.2101 to D.2107.

CERTIFIED CHECKS.
Abandonment, presumption, time, §116B-53(c).
Acceptance, §25-3-409(d).
Obligation of acceptor, §25-3-413(b).
Checks generally.
See CHECKS.
Defined, §25-3-409(d).
Negotiable instruments generally.
See NEGOTIABLE INSTRUMENTS.
Refusal to pay, §25-3-411(a) to (c).

CERTIFIED MAIL.
Personal jurisdiction.
Manner of service to exercise, §1A-1 Rule 4(j).
Proof of service, §1A-1 Rule 4(j2).
Physician or surgeon licensure to practice medicine.
Service of notices required by chapter, §90-14.3.
Proof of service, §§1-75.10(a), 1A-1 Rule 4(j2).
Workers' compensation.
Notice of accident to employer, §97-23.

CERTIFIED PUBLIC ACCOUNTANTS, §§93-1 to 93-13.
See ACCOUNTANTS.

CERTIFIED SAFETY PROFESSIONALS (CSP),
§§90-671 to 90-674.

CERTIORARI.
Authorized, §1-269.
Bonds, surety, §1-269.
Undertakings to be made part of record sent up to
appellate division, §1-297.
Copies of papers, AppProc Rule 24.
Court of appeals.
Issuance of remedial writs, §7A-32(b).
Review of judgments and orders.
Scope of review, AppProc Rule 21(a).
Criminal procedure, §15A-1444.
Death penalty cases.
Petition for writ, AppProc Rule 21(f).
**Deposition of witnesses to perpetuate
testimony,** §1A-1 Rule 27(b).
Determination, AppProc Rule 21(d).
Housing appeals boards.
Review of decisions.
Proceeding in nature of certiorari, time limit,
§160A-446(e).
Issuance as substitute for appeal, §1-269.
Jurisdiction.
Stay of proceedings to permit trial in foreign
jurisdiction.
Review of rulings on motion, §1-75.12(c).
Petition for writ.
Content, AppProc Rule 21(c).
Death penalty cases, AppProc Rule 21(f).
Filing and service, AppProc Rule 21(c).
Application made by filing, AppProc Rule 21(b).
Post-conviction matters, AppProc Rule 21(e).
Death penalty cases, AppProc Rule 21(f).
Response, AppProc Rule 21(d).
Form, AppProc Appx D.
Post-conviction matters, AppProc Rule 21(e).
Death penalty cases, AppProc Rule 21(f).
Response, AppProc Rule 21(d).
Which appellate court addressed, AppProc Rule
21(b).
Scope of writ, AppProc Rule 21(a).
Supreme court.
Issuance of remedial writs, §7A-32(b).
Trial tribunal judgments and orders.
Review, scope of writ, AppProc Rule 21(a).

CERVICAL CANCER.
Accident and health insurance.
Screening for early detection.
Coverage requirements, §58-51-57(a), (e).
Defined, §58-51-57(a1).
Cancer patient navigation program.
Breast and cervical cancer control program,
§130A-216.
**Hospital, medical and dental services
corporations.**
Screening for early detection.
Coverage, §58-65-92.

CFC.
Containers manufactured with, restrictions,
§130A-309.10(b).

CHAIN GANGS, §§148-26(b), 162-58.

CHAIN LETTERS.
Pyramid and chain schemes, §14-291.2.

CHAIN OF CUSTODY.
Evidence.
Courier service or common carrier, §8-103.

CHAIN OF CUSTODY —Cont'd
Forensic analysis.
Evidence subject to, establishing, §8-58.20.
Impaired driving.
Blood or urine tests analyzed.
Procedure for establishing, §20-139.1(c3).

CHAINS.
Tire chains.
Permissible use, §20-122(b).

CHAIN SAWS.
Mechanical breakdown service agreement,
§66-374.

CHAIRLIFTS.
Passenger tramway safety, §§95-116 to 95-125.
See TRAMWAYS.

CHALLENGE OF JUROR.
Challenges for cause.
Civil cases, §§1A-1 Rule 47, 9-15(c).
Criminal cases, §9-15(c).
Appeal on grounds that challenge for cause not
allowed.
Prerequisites, §15A-1214(h).
Challenge to the panel, §15A-1211(c).
Grounds, §15A-1212.
Renewal of challenge for cause previously
denied, §15A-1214(i).
Questioning jurors without challenge, §9-15(a).
Valid cause for challenge, §9-15(b).
Criminal cases.
After juror accepted but before jury impaneled,
§15A-1214(g).
Challenge for cause, §9-15(c).
Appeal on grounds that challenge for cause not
allowed.
Prerequisites, §15A-1214(h).
Challenge to the panel, §15A-1211(c).
Grounds, §15A-1212.
Renewal of challenge for cause previously
denied, §15A-1214(i).
Judge to decide all challenges, §15A-1211(b).
Peremptory challenges, §§9-21, 15A-1214(d), (e).
Governing statutory provisions, §9-21.
Number of peremptory challenges, §15A-1217(a)
to (c).
Peremptory challenges.
Civil cases, §9-19.
Number of peremptory challenges, §9-19.
Several plaintiffs or several defendants, §9-20.
Apportionment of challenges, §9-20.
Discretion of judge, §9-20.
Criminal cases, §§9-21, 15A-1214(d), (e).
Governing statutory provisions, §9-21.
Number of peremptory challenges, §15A-1217(a)
to (c).

CHALLENGE OF VOTERS.
Absentee ballots, §163-89.
**Answer to challenge as felon not to be used on
prosecution,** §163-90.
Burden of proof, §163-90.1(b).
Challenge to absentee ballots, §163-89(c).
Day of primary or election, §163-87.
Hearing, §163-88.
Request for challenged ballot, §163-88.1.
Hearings.
Challenge on day of primary or election, §163-88.
Challenge other than on day of primary or
election, §163-86.
Challenge to absentee ballots, §163-89(e).

CHALLENGE OF VOTERS —Cont'd
Municipal elections, §163-289.
Notice.
Challenge on other than day of primary or election, §163-86(d).
Oaths.
Challenge on day of primary or election, §163-88.
Challenge other than on day of primary or election, §§163-85, 163-86(c).
False swearing, §163-90.3.
Overruled or dismissed challenge.
Action by board on, §163-90.2(c).
Appeals, §163-90.2(d).
Reasonable belief by challenger required, §163-90.1(a).
Sustained challenge.
Action by board on, §163-90.2(a), (b).
Appeals, §163-90.2(d).
Other than day of primary or election, §163-85(a) to (e).

CHAMBERS OF COMMERCE.
Franchise tax.
Exemption, §105-125(a).
Securities regulation.
Exempt securities, §78A-16.

CHANGE MACHINES.
Breaking into, §14-56.3.

CHANGE OF NAME.
Address confidentiality program participant.
Notification of attorney general, §15C-5(a).
Alcoholic beverage permittee.
New permit, issuance, fee, §18B-903(g).
Appeal of decision denying request, §101-5(f).
Application, §101-5(a).
Contents, §101-3.
Required information, §101-5(a).
Filing, §101-2(a).
Fraud or material misrepresentation, §101-5(g).
Review of information by clerk, §101-5(c).
Certificate stating change made, §101-5(d).
Confidentiality of record of proceedings, §101-2(c).
Criminal history record check.
Taking fingerprints for, §101-5(b).
Denial of request, §101-5(f).
Division of criminal information.
Updating records, §101-5(e).
Effect, §101-6.
Elections.
Registration of voters, §163-82.16.
Filing of application, §101-2(a).
Minor child, §101-2(d).
Fingerprints.
Taking for criminal history record check, §101-5(b).
Fraud or material misrepresentation, §101-5(g).
General but not private law, §101-1.
Good character, proof filed with petition, §101-4.
Hospital authorities, §131E-19(c).
Marriage licenses.
Amendment of license, §51-18.1(b).
Minors.
Filing of application, §101-2(d).
Two change limitation, §101-6(b).
Notaries, §10B-51.
Both name and county, §10B-53.
One change only, §101-6(a).
Exception from minors, §101-6(b).

CHANGE OF NAME —Cont'd
Order by clerk changing name.
Forwarded to state registrar of vital statistics, §101-5(e).
Issuance, requirements, §101-5(d).
Setting aside.
Fraud or material misrepresentation, §101-5(g).
Order denying request, §101-5(f).
Petition.
Contents of application, §101-3.
Privileges and protection under new name.
Entitlement, §101-6(a).
Procedure, §101-2.
Professional employer organizations, §58-89A-80(b).
Proof of good character, filed with petition, §101-4.
Publication of notice, §101-2(a).
When not required, §101-2(b).
Recordation, §101-7.
Secured transactions.
Financing statement.
Effect of change of name, §25-9-507(c).
Setting aside order.
Fraud or material misrepresentation, §101-5(g).
Sex offenders, §14-202.6.
Offenders registered in accordance with article 27A of chapter 14.
Prohibition, §101-6(c).
Report to sheriff in person to provide name, time, §14-208.9(f).
Special proceedings, §§101-1 to 101-8.
State registrar of vital statistics.
Duties upon receipt of order changing name, §101-5(e).
Substance abuse professionals.
Certification or registration, §90-113.41B.
Waiting period.
Unsuccessful applicant on appeal, §101-5(f).
Widow or widower.
Resumption of name, §101-8.

CHANGE OF VENUE.
See VENUE.

CHANGES AFFECTING VOTING.
Voting rights act of 1965.
Submissions to attorney general of United States, §§120-30.9A to 120-30.9I.

CHANNEL BASS.
State saltwater fish, §145-6.

CHAPEL HILL.
Land-use development incentives.
Reduction of energy consumption, §160A-383.4.
Traffic control photographic systems, §160A-300.1(d).

CHAPEL HILL TELEPHONE COMPANY.
Retirement system for teachers and state employees.
Eligibility for benefits, §135-5.2.

CHAPELS.
Generally.
See CHURCHES AND OTHER PLACES OF WORSHIP.

CHAPLAINS.
Clergymen.
See CLERGY.
Prisons and prisoners.
Employment of clinical chaplains, §148-10.1.

CHARACTER EDUCATION.
Public schools, §115C-81(h).

CHARACTER EVIDENCE.
Accused's character, §8C-1 Rule 404(a).
Credibility of witness attacked or supported,
§8C-1 Rule 608.
Hearsay exception, reputation, §8C-1 Rule 803.
Juvenile's character.
Other crimes, wrongs or acts, §8C-1 Rule 404(b).
Methods of proving character, §8C-1 Rule 405.
Not admissible to prove conduct.
Exceptions, §8C-1 Rule 404(a).
Opinion, §8C-1 Rule 405(a).
Other crimes, wrongs or acts, §8C-1 Rule 404(b).
Reputation, §8C-1 Rule 405(a).
Specific instances of conduct, §8C-1 Rule 405(b).
Victim's character, §8C-1 Rule 404(a).
Witness's character, §8C-1 Rule 404(a).

CHARCOAL.
Standard weights and measures, §81A-42.

CHARGE ACCOUNTS.
Powers of attorney.
Powers conferred by statutory short form, §32A-2.
Revolving charge account contracts.
Charges.
Annual charge, §24-11(a).
Billing date, §24-11(d).
Discount or fee, §24-11(a2).
Finance charge.
Default or deferral charges, §25A-14(c).
Insurance.
Additional charges for insurance,
§25A-17(b).
Rates, §25A-14(a).
Security interest.
Rates, §25A-14(b).
Late payment charge, §24-11(d1).
Monthly periodic rate.
Plan secured by real or personal property.
Restrictions, §24-11(c).
Revolving credit loans, §24-11(b).
Notice of proposed charge, §24-11(e).
Revolving credit loans.
Monthly periodic rate, §24-11(b).
Service charge, §24-11(a1).
Collateral.
Inapplicability of provisions, §25A-23(d).
Defined, §25A-11.
Security interests.
Finance charges, §25A-14(b).

CHARGE CARDS.
Credit cards generally.
See CREDIT CARDS.
Credit device fraud.
See CREDIT DEVICE FRAUD.
Disclosure requirements, §24-11.2.
Applicability, §24-11.2(a).
Construction and interpretation, §24-11.2(f).
Federal requirements, §24-11.2(c).
Generally, §24-11.2(b).
Penalty for violation, §24-11.2(d).
Severability of provisions, §24-11.2(e).
Fines, fees and costs owed by offenders.
Acceptance in lieu of payment by cash or check,
§7A-321(a).
Contracts with vendors to provide for.
Duty of director of administrative office of
courts, §7A-343.

CHARGE OF COURT.
Instructions.
See JURY AND JURY TRIAL.

CHARGE REDUCTIONS.
Criminal law and procedure.
Witnesses, §15A-1054.

**CHARITABLE CONTRIBUTIONS INCOME TAX
CREDIT.**
Individual income tax.
Nonitemizers, §105-151.26.

CHARITABLE GIFT ANNUITIES.
Authorized, §58-3-6(a).
Definition of education institution, §58-3-6(f).
Enforcement by insurance department,
§58-3-6(d).
Information to insurance commissioner,
§58-3-6(c).
Issuance not business of insurance, §58-3-6(e).
Notice to insurance department, §58-3-6(b).

CHARITABLE IMMUNITY, §§1-539.10, 1-539.11.
Abolition of common law defense, §1-539.9.

CHARITABLE ORGANIZATIONS.
Alcoholic beverage permits.
Special one-time permits, §18B-1002(a).
Alcoholic beverages furnished to inmates of
charitable institutions, §14-258.1(b).
Amusements.
License tax exemption, §105-40.
Auctions.
Exemptions from auction provisions, §85B-2.
Automatic dialing and recorded message
players.
Circumstances allowing, §75-104(b).
Bingo.
General provisions, §§14-309.5 to 14-309.14.
See BINGO.
Purposes of conduct of bingo games, §14-309.5.
Business corporation act.
Exemptions from, §§55-3-01(b), 55-17-01(b).
Cartridges or ammunition for firearms.
Furnishing to inmates of charitable institutions,
§14-258.1(a).
Charitable gift annuities, §58-3-6.
Charitable immunity.
Common law defense abolished, §1-539.9.
Community college employees.
Payroll deductions for charitable contributions,
§143B-426.40A(i).
Conventurers conducting sales promotion.
Accounting prepared by, §131F-18(c).
Consent from organization or sponsor.
Required prior to conducting, §131F-18(a).
Disclosures in advertising.
Adoption of rules by department, §131F-18(b).
Conveyances.
Effect as to conveyances by trustees, §59B-15(a).
Prior deeds validated, §59B-15(b).
Deadly weapons.
Furnishing to inmates of charitable institutions,
§14-258.1(a).
Deeds.
Prior deeds validated, §59B-15(b).
Definitions.
Charitable organizations, §1-539.11.
Soliciting charitable contributions by telephone,
§14-401.12(b).
Volunteers, §1-539.11.
Donated food.
Immunity for, §99B-10.

CHARITABLE ORGANIZATIONS —Cont'd
Donated food —Cont'd
Inspections, §106-141.1.
Drugs and controlled substances.
Furnishing to inmates of charitable institutions,
§14-258.1(a).
Embezzlement of funds.
Public officers and trustees, §14-92.
Treasurers, §14-93.
Establishment and operation by state, NC
Const Art XI §3.
Franchise tax exemptions, §105-125(a).
Fundraising.
Solicitation of contributions generally, §§131F-1 to
131F-24.
See CHARITABLE SOLICITATION.
Hospitals.
Property tax exemptions.
Property used for charitable hospital purposes,
§105-278.8.
Immunity.
Charitable immunity abolished, §1-539.9.
Volunteers performing services for charitable
organization, §§1-539.10, 1-539.11.
Income tax on corporations.
Contributions.
Deductions, §105-130.9.
Exemption of charitable corporations,
§105-130.1(a), (b).
Income tax on individuals.
Credit for charitable contributions by
nonitemizers, §105-151.26.
Licensing, §§131F-5 to 131F-8.
Life insurance.
Insurable interest of charitable organizations,
§58-58-86(a), (b).
Municipalities.
Regulation of solicitation campaigns, §160A-178.
Nonprofit corporations.
Certain associations deemed incorporated,
§55A-17-02.
General provisions, §§55A-1-01 to 55A-17-05.
See NONPROFIT CORPORATIONS.
**Payroll deductions for charitable
contributions.**
Public school and community college employees,
§143B-426.40A(i).
University of North Carolina system employees,
§143B-426.40A(j).
Poisons.
Furnishing poison to inmates of charitable
institution, §14-258.1(a).
**Possibility of reverter, right of entry or
executory interest.**
Time limit.
Inapplicability to charity, §41-32(b).
Property taxes.
Exemptions, §105-275.
Agencies which may obtain exemption,
§§105-278.6(a), 105-278.7(c).
Property used for charitable hospital purposes,
§105-278.8.
Property used for charitable purposes,
§§105-278.6, 105-278.7.
Prudent management of institutional funds,
§§36E-1 to 36E-11.
See PRUDENT MANAGEMENT OF
INSTITUTIONAL FUNDS.
Public schools employees.
Payroll deductions for charitable contributions,
§143B-426.40A(i).

CHARITABLE ORGANIZATIONS —Cont'd
Real property.
Conveyances.
Effect as to conveyance by trustees, §59B-15(a).
Prior deeds validated, §59B-15(b).
Sales and use tax.
Contributions deductible as charitable
contributions.
Exemption, §105-164.13.
Refunds.
Nonprofit organizations, §105-164.14(b).
Sales promotion conducted by coventurers.
Accounting prepared by, §131F-18(c).
Consent from organization or sponsor.
Required prior to conducting, §131F-18(a).
Disclosures in advertising.
Adoption of rules by department, §131F-18(b).
Securities regulation.
Exempt securities, §78A-16.
Solicitation of funds, §§131F-1 to 131F-33.
See CHARITABLE SOLICITATION.
State debt.
Educational and charitable institutions.
Interest.
Reimbursement of treasurer for interest,
§142-15.
State of North Carolina.
Establishment and operation of charitable and
correctional institutions and agencies by
state, NC Const Art XI §3.
Streets or state roadways.
Persons standing on or near to solicit
contributions.
Application authorizing, filing.
Local government authority to grant,
§20-175(e).
Tax exemption, NC Const Art V §2.
Telephone solicitation, §14-401.12.
Treasurers.
Embezzlement of funds, §14-93.
Trustees.
Conveyances by, §59B-15(a).
**University of North Carolina system
employees.**
Payroll deductions for charitable contributions,
§143B-426.40A(j).
Volunteers for charitable organizations.
Immunity, §§1-539.10, 1-539.11.

CHARITABLE SOLICITATION, §§131F-1 to
131F-33.
Actions to enforce chapter.
Attorney general bringing, §131F-24(a).
Department bringing, §131F-23(c).
Voluntary compliance.
Termination of enforcement action, §131F-24(c).
Adoption of rules.
Rule-making authority, §131F-33.
Annual report, §131F-30(c), (d).
Attorney general.
Civil action to enforce chapter, §131F-24(a).
Investigations by, §131F-24(b).
Voluntary compliance.
Termination of investigation or enforcement
action, §131F-24(c).
**Charitable contributions to governmental
agencies.**
Exemption from chapter, §131F-3.
**Clothing, household items, other items
solicited for resale.**
Collection receptacle used by person soliciting.
Collection receptacle defined, §131F-2.

CHARITABLE SOLICITATION —Cont'd
Clothing, household items, other items solicited for resale —Cont'd
Collection receptacle used by person soliciting —Cont'd
Disclosure sign or label required, §131F-9(d).
Person not charitable organization or sponsor, §131F-10.
Collection of contributions in name of charitable organization or sponsor, §131F-16(i).
Collection receptacle.
Defined, §131F-2.
Disclosure sign or label, §131F-9(d).
Persons not charitable organization or sponsor, §131F-10.
Community trust.
Exemption from chapter, §131F-3.
Continuing care retirement communities.
Exemption of nonprofit facility from provisions, §131F-3.
Conventurers conducting sales promotion.
Accounting prepared by, §131F-18(c).
Consent from organization or sponsor.
Required prior to conducting, §131F-18(a).
Conventurers defined, §131F-2.
Disclosures in advertising.
Adoption of rules by department, §131F-18(b).
Prohibited acts, §131F-20.
Deceptive or unfair trade practices.
Violation of act so designated, §131F-21.
Definitions, §131F-2.
Deposits of contributions.
Duty of solicitor, §131F-16(i).
Disclosure requirement for person not charitable organization or sponsor.
Collection receptacle disclosure, §131F-10.
Disclosures by organization or sponsor, §131F-9(b), (c).
Collection receptacle disclosure, §131F-9(d).
Disclosures by solicitors, §131F-17(a).
Distribution of contributions.
Power of attorney general to seek, §131F-24(a).
Educational institution contributions.
Exemption from chapter, §131F-3.
Exemptions from chapter.
Enumerated, §131F-3.
Expressed purpose set forth in license application.
Solicitation only for, §131F-9(a).
Fees.
Licensing, §131F-8(a) to (d).
Fundraising consultants, §131F-15(c), (f).
Fundraising consultants.
Change in information, reporting, §131F-15(g).
Contracts or agreements, requirements, §131F-15(d).
Licensing.
Application, §131F-15(b).
Partnership or corporation acting as, §131F-15(c).
Examination of application by department, §131F-15(e).
Failure to satisfy requirements, notice, hearing, §131F-15(e).
Fees, §131F-15(c).
Deposited in solicitation of contributions find, §131F-15(f).
Partnership or corporation acting as, §131F-15(c).
Required to act as, §131F-15(a).

CHARITABLE SOLICITATION —Cont'd
Fundraising consultants —Cont'd
Prohibited acts, §131F-20.
Hospital contributions.
Exemption from chapter, §131F-3.
Injunctions.
Power of attorney general to seek, §131F-24(a).
Power of department to seek, §131F-23(c).
Investigations by attorney general, §131F-24(b).
Voluntary compliance.
Termination, §131F-24(c).
Investigations by department, §131F-23(a).
Legislative intent, §131F-1.
Licensing.
Fundraising consultants, §131F-15(a) to (g).
Organizations, sponsors or individuals, §§131F-5 to 131F-8.
Solicitor's license, §131F-16(a) to (n).
Masters.
Power of attorney general to seek appointment, §131F-24(a).
Named individual trust accounts.
Required, §131F-31(a).
Use of trust funds, §131F-31(b).
Noncommercial radio or television contributions.
Exemption from chapter, §131F-3.
Notice of solicitation.
Solicitor to give, §131F-16(f).
Organizations, sponsors or individuals.
Disclosures, §131F-9(b).
Printed on solicitation or contribution, §131F-9(c).
Licensing.
Consolidated application.
Election to file, §131F-7(a).
Examination of license application, §131F-5(b).
Extension of time.
Renewal or updating information, §131F-5(d).
Fees.
Exemption from payment, §131F-8(b).
Late filing fee.
Failure to file renewal information on time, §131F-8(d).
Schedule of required fees, §131F-8(a).
Parent organization or association filing, §131F-8(c).
Financial report required, §131F-6(a).
Consolidated report, §131F-7(b).
Information required, §131F-6(a), (b).
License requirements not satisfied, notice, hearing, decision, §131F-5(b).
Renewal, §131F-5(c).
Extensions of time, §131F-5(d).
Information required, §131F-6(b).
Consolidated form, §131F-7(c).
Late filing fee, failure to file on time, §131F-8(d).
Required of organization, sponsor or person, §131F-5(a).
Press release.
Annual report released as, §131F-30(d).
Public information.
Generally, §131F-30(a).
Included information, §131F-30(b).
Purpose expressed in license application.
Solicitation only for, §131F-9(a).
Purpose of act, §131F-1.
Receivers.
Power of attorney general to seek appointment, §131F-24(a).

CHARITABLE SOLICITATION —Cont'd
Receivers —Cont'd
Power of department to seek appointment of,
§131F-23(c).
Records, §131F-32.
Religious institution charitable solicitation.
Exemption from chapter, §131F-3.
Rules and regulations, §131F-33.
Sales promotions conducted by coventurers.
Accounting prepared by, §131F-18(c).
Consent from organization or sponsor.
Required prior to conducting, §131F-18(a).
Disclosures in advertising.
Adoption of rules by department, §131F-18(b).
Sequestration of assets.
Power of attorney general to seek, §131F-24(a).
Solicitors.
Bond, §131F-16(d).
Certificate of deposit in lieu of bond, §131F-16(d1).
Change of information filed with department,
§131F-16(m).
Collection of contribution in name of charitable
organization or sponsor, §131F-16(i).
Contract or agreement with charitable
organization, §131F-16(g).
Deposit of contribution, §131F-16(i).
Disclosures, §131F-17(a).
Financial report of campaigns, §131F-16(h).
Licensing.
Applications, §131F-16(b).
Bonds, §131F-16(d).
Examination of applications by department,
§131F-16(e).
Fees, §131F-16(c).
Permanent loss of license, grounds, §131F-16(n).
Required, §131F-16(a).
Notice of solicitation, §131F-16(f).
Prohibited acts, §131F-20.
Recordkeeping requirements, §131F-16(j).
Review of records, §131F-16(l).
Tickets, §131F-16(k).
Tickets.
Donation for use by another person,
representing, §131F-17(b).
Recordkeeping, §131F-16(k).
Streets or state roadways.
Persons standing on or near to solicit
contributions.
Application authorizing, filing.
Local government authority to grant,
§20-175(e).
Subpoenas and subpoenas duces tecum.
Noncompliance with, §131F-23(c).
Power of department to issue, §131F-23(b).
**Telephone solicitation by charitable
organization.**
Definitions, §14-401.12(b).
Misdemeanor, §14-401.12(a).
Section construed, §14-401.12(c).
Tickets.
Donation for use by another person.
Solicitor representing, §131F-17(b).
Records, §131F-16(k).
Violations of act, §131F-23(d).
Criminal penalties, §131F-22.
Deceptive or unfair trade practice designation,
§131F-21.
Penalties, §§131F-23(e) to (g), 131F-24(a).
Voluntary compliance.
Termination of investigation or enforcement
action, §131F-24(c).

CHARITABLE SOLICITATION —Cont'd
Volunteer fire and rescue squad contributions.
Exemption from chapter, §131F-3.
CHARITABLE TRUSTS.
Attorney general.
Qualified beneficiaries.
Treated as, §36C-1-110.
Charitable remainder trust administration act,
§§36C-4B-1 to 36C-4B-7.
Applicability of act, §36C-4B-2.
Charitable remainder annuity trusts.
Annuity amount allocated among class of
noncharitable beneficiaries, §36C-4B-5(f).
Applicability of provisions, §36C-4B-4.
Computation of annuity amount in short or
final taxable years, §36C-4B-5(b).
Corpus paid to charity at expiration of term of
years or on death of receipt, §36C-4B-5(g).
Creation of annuity amount for period of years
or life, §36C-4B-5(a).
Deferral of annuity amount during period of
administration or settlement, §36C-4B-5(d).
Defined, §36C-4B-3.
Dollar amount annuity may be stated as
fraction or percentage, §36C-4B-5(e).
Prohibition of additional contributions,
§36C-4B-5(c).
Retention of testamentary power to revoke
noncharitable interests, §36C-4B-5(i).
Termination of annuity amount on payment
date preceding termination of noncharitable
interest, §36C-4B-5(h).
Charitable remainder unitrusts.
Additional contributions, §36C-4B-6(e).
Adjustment for incorrect valuation,
§36C-4B-6(c).
Allocation among class of noncharitable
beneficiaries, §36C-4B-6(g).
Applicability of provisions, §36C-4B-4.
Computation of unitrust amount in short and
final taxable years, §36C-4B-6(d).
Corpus paid to charity at expiration of term of
years or on death of recipient,
§36C-4B-6(h).
Creation of unitrust amount for a period of
years or life, §36C-4B-6(a).
Deferral of unitrust amount during period of
administration or settlement, §36C-4B-6(f).
Defined, §36C-4B-3.
Retention of testamentary power to revoke
noncharitable interest, §36C-4B-6(j).
Termination of unitrust amount on payment
date, §36C-4B-6(i).
Unitrust amount expressed as lesser of income
or fixed percentage, §36C-4B-6(b).
Construction of act, §36C-4B-7.
Applicability, §36C-4B-2.
Creations of remainder interests in charity,
§36C-4B-4(a).
Definitions, §36C-4B-2.
Distribution from trust used to administer an
estate, §36C-4B-4(g).
Distribution to charity during term of
noncharitable interests and distributions,
§36C-4B-4(e).
Investment restrictions on trustee, §36C-4B-4(f).
Payment of taxes on noncharitable beneficiary,
§36C-4B-4(h).
Prohibitions governing trustees, §36C-4B-4(d).
Prudent investor rule, §36C-9-906.

CHARITABLE TRUSTS —Cont'd
Charitable remainder trust administration act
   —Cont'd
  Selection of alternative charitable beneficiary.
    Remainderman not qualified under 170(b)(1)(A)
      IRS at time of distribution, §36C-4B-4(c).
    Remainderman not qualified under 170(c) IRS
      at time of distribution, §36C-4B-4(b).
  Short title, §36C-4B-1.
  Tax status of a reformed trust, §36C-4A-2.
Conveyances.
  Effect as to conveyance by trustee, §59B-15(a).
Cy pres.
  Alternative plan provided for, §36C-4-413(d).
  Application of principle, §36C-4-413(a).
  Maintenance of proceeding, §36C-4-413(b).
  Release or modification of restriction in trust
    instrument, §36C-4-413(c1).
Definitions.
  Charitable remainder trust administration act,
    §36C-4B-2.
Enforcement of trust by settlor, §36C-4-405.1(a),
  (b).
General terms, gift made in.
  Selection of charitable purposes, §36C-4-405(d).
  Validity of trust, §36C-4-405(b), (c).
Judicial proceedings under uniform trust
  code.
  Charitable trusts, notice to attorney general,
    §36C-2-205(i).
Modification.
  Cy pres, §36C-4-413.
  Settlor may maintain proceeding, §36C-4-410.
Prudent investor rule.
  Effect on charitable remainder trusts, §36C-9-906.
Prudent management of institutional funds,
  §§36E-1 to 36E-11.
  See PRUDENT MANAGEMENT OF
    INSTITUTIONAL FUNDS.
Purposes for which created, §36C-4-405(a).
Qualified beneficiaries.
  Charitable organization and attorney general
    treated as, §36C-1-110.
  Defined, §36C-1-103.
Renunciation.
  Persons who may renounce, §31B-1(a).
Selection of charitable purpose.
  Gift made in general terms, §36C-4-405(d).
Spending rules applicable to, §36C-4-405.2.
Taxation, §§36C-4A-1, 36C-4A-2.
  Prohibited transactions, §36C-4A-1.
  Reformation of charitable remainder trusts,
    §36C-4A-2.
Termination.
  Cy pres, §36C-4-413.
Uniform trust code.
  Applicability to charitable trusts, §36C-1-102.
  General provisions, §§36C-1-101 to 36C-11-1106.
    See TRUSTS AND TRUSTEES.
Vacancy in trusteeship.
  Filling, §36C-7-704(d).

CHARLES B. AYCOCK MEMORIAL
  COMMISSION.
Department of cultural resources.
  Transfer of commission to department, §143B-51.

CHARLOTTE, CITY OF.
Land-use development incentives.
  Reduction of energy consumption, §160A-383.4.
Private parking lots.
  Removal of unauthorized vehicles, §20-219.2.

CHARLOTTE, CITY OF —Cont'd
Traffic control photographic systems,
  §160A-300.1(d).

CHARLOTTE REGIONAL PARTNERSHIP, INC.
Economic development commissions.
  State board of education members as ex officio
    commission members, §158-8.4A.

CHARON COUNTY.
Acquisition of property, power, §153A-158.1(a).

CHARTER SCHOOLS, §§115C-238.29A to
  115C-238.29K.
Adequate performance.
  Criteria for, adoption, §115C-238.29G(a1).
Admission requirements, §115C-238.29F(g).
Advisory committee, §115C-238.29I(d).
Alternative timeline for submissions,
  §115C-238.29I(e).
Application, §115C-238.29B(b) to (d).
  Assistance to applicants and potential applicants,
    §115C-238.29J(c).
  Final approval, §115C-238.29D.
    Conditional approval, §115C-238.29D(c).
    Standards, §115C-238.29D(a).
  Material revision, approval required,
    §115C-238.29D(d).
  Preliminary approval, §115C-238.29C.
    Appeal process, §115C-238.29C(c).
    Standards, §115C-238.29C(b).
    Time period, §115C-238.29C(a).
  Submission for preliminary approval,
    §115C-238.29B(c).
Assets, §115C-238.29F(i).
Audits, §115C-238.29F(f).
Board of directors, §115C-238.29E(d).
Children with disabilities.
  Compliance with policies to educate,
    §115C-238.29F(d).
Contract, §115C-238.29E(c).
Conversion of existing public schools,
  §115C-238.29B(a).
Course of instruction, §115C-238.29F(d).
Criminal history checks.
  Definitions, §115C-238.29K(a).
  Determination based on results.
    Duty of state board, §115C-238.29K(d).
    Notification to board of directors of schools,
      §115C-238.29K(e).
  Findings made by state board, §115C-238.29K(d).
    Supplying board of directors of school,
      §115C-238.29K(e).
  Immunity for carrying out provisions,
    §115C-238.29K(g).
  Notification to board of directors of schools.
    Determination based on results made by state
      board, §115C-238.29K(e).
  Privileged nature of information,
    §115C-238.29K(f).
  Release or disclosure of personnel's criminal
    history.
    Prohibition, §115C-238.29K(e).
  Review of results by state board,
    §115C-238.29K(d).
  State board of education.
    Duties, §115C-238.29K(b) to (e).
Definitions.
  Criminal history checks, §115C-238.29K(a).
Department of revenue.
  Change in school status.
    Notice to department, §115C-238.29J(d).

CHARTER SCHOOLS —Cont'd
Diabetes care plans, implementation.
Information provided parents and guardians,
§115C-238.29F(a).
Driving eligibility certificates.
Designee of board of directors, duties,
§115C-238.29F(j).
Employees, §115C-238.29F(e).
Criminal history checks, §115C-238.29K.
Exemption from various statutes and rules,
§115C-238.29E(f).
Flu and meningitis and vaccine information.
Information provided parents and guardians,
§115C-238.29F(a).
Funding, §115C-238.29H(a), (a1).
Grievance procedures.
State board of education to develop,
§115C-238.29G(b).
Health and safety standards, §115C-238.29F(a).
Health insurance for employees.
State health plan for teachers and public
employees.
Election to become participating employer.
Schools operated by private nonprofit
corporations, §135-48.54.
Generally, §§135-48.1 to 135-48.61.
Late premiums, interest charged, §135-48.55.
Hours and days of instruction, §115C-238.29F(d).
Inadequate performance, §115C-238.29G(a1).
Increase in enrollment.
Material revision of charter application requiring
approval, §115C-238.29D(d).
Insurance, §115C-238.29F(c).
Liability to civil suit, §115C-238.29F(c).
Local board of education.
Accountability of charter schools to,
§115C-238.29E(a).
Location, §115C-238.29E(e).
Mediation.
Differences between charter school and state
board, §115C-238.29G(c).
Motor fuel excise tax exemption, §105-449.88.
Nonrenewal of charter, §115C-238.29G(a).
Nonsectarian requirement, §115C-238.29F(b).
North Carolina flag.
Display in classrooms, §115C-238.29F(k).
Operation.
Private nonprofit corporations, §115C-238.29E(b).
Per pupil local current expense
appropriations.
Transfer to charter school for students attending,
§115C-238.29H(b).
Pledge of allegiance.
Recitation, §115C-238.29F(k).
Private contributions, §115C-238.29J(b).
Private nonprofit corporations establishing,
§115C-238.29B(a).
Public assistance from local school
administrative units, §115C-238.29J(a).
Publicity to local community, §115C-238.29I.
Purpose, §115C-238.29A.
Renewal of charter, §115C-238.29D(d).
Nonrenewal or termination, §115C-238.29G(a).
Reporting requirements, §115C-238.29F.
Report to joint legislative education oversight
committee.
State board recommendations to modify, expand
or terminate approach, §115C-238.29I(c).

CHARTER SCHOOLS —Cont'd
Retirement system for teachers and state
employees.
Creditable service.
Credit for employment in charter school
operated by private nonprofit corporation,
§135-4(cc).
Participation by charter school operated by
nonprofit corporation.
Election by board of directors, §135-5.3(a), (b).
Effect of election or failure to elect,
§135-5.3(c), (d).
Notification to employees, §135-5.3(e).
Review and evaluation of charter school
approach.
Duty of state board, §115C-238.29I(c).
Strategic plan.
Inadequate performance, §115C-238.29G(a1).
Student assessments.
Duty to conduct, §115C-238.29F(d).
Student performance standards.
Duty to meet, §115C-238.29F(d).
Inadequate performance, §115C-238.29G(a1).
Teachers, §115C-238.29F(e).
Teacher workdays, §115C-238.29F(d).
Termination of charter, §115C-238.29G(a).
Term of initial charter, §115C-238.29D(c).
Transportation, §115C-238.29F(h).
United States flag.
Display in classrooms, §115C-238.29F(k).

CHARTERS OF CORPORATIONS, NC Const Art
VIII §1.
Counterfeiting.
Forfeiture, §14-15.
Kidnapping.
Forfeiture, §14-39.

CHARTERS OF MUNICIPAL CORPORATIONS.
Amendments.
By ordinance, §160A-102.
Charter to remain in force, §160A-110.
Referendum, §160A-103.
Copies.
Filing, §160A-111.
Effective date, §160A-109.
Filing copies, §160A-111.
Initiative petition, §160A-104.
Plan to continue for two years, §160A-107.
Officers to carry out plan, §160A-108.
Provisions dependent on form of government,
§160A-106.
Applicability of provisions, §160A-82.
Code sections and conflict repealed,
§160A-77(c).
Construction, §160A-4.
Defined, §160A-1.
Effect of provisions upon prior laws, §160A-2.
General laws.
Alternative procedure, §160A-3(a).
Superseding charter, §160A-3(c).
Supplementary charters, §160A-3(b).
Incorporation into charter.
Definition of "charter,"§160A-496(c).
Local acts.
Incorporation into charter, §160A-496(a), (b).
Name, §160A-11.
New form of government.
Charter to remain in force, §160A-110.

CHARTERS OF TRUST COMPANIES, §§53-330
to 53-365.
See TRUST COMPANIES.

CHASES BY POLICE OF VIOLATORS OF LAW.
Speed limits not applicable, §20-145.

CHATHAM COUNTY.
Ambulance services.
Attachment or garnishment and lien for,
§§44-51.4 to 44-51.8.
False pretenses and cheats.
Obtaining ambulance services without
intending to pay, §14-111.2.
Condemnation or acquisition of land by local
government unit outside county.
Consent of board of commissioners necessary,
§153A-15.
Counties generally.
See COUNTIES.
Cropper or tenant refusing to perform terms
of contract.
Forfeiture of right of possession to premises,
§42-27.
Dogs used in hunting.
Regulation by wildlife resources commission,
§113-291.5(a).
False pretenses and cheats.
Ambulance services.
Obtaining services without intending to pay,
§14-111.2.
Game laws, local acts not repealed,
§113-133.1(e).
Oil, gas or mineral interest, extinguished, title
in surface fee holder.
Failure to list interest for tax purposes for 10
years prior to January 1, 1979, §1-42.7(a) to
(d).
Protection of interest from surface fee holder,
§1-42.7(b), (d).
On-premises unfortified wine licenses.
Discretion to decline to issue, §105-113.71(b).
Room occupancy tax levied by county.
Uniform provisions, §153A-155.
Special school tax, election to abolish.
Petition required, §115C-505.

CHATTEL MORTGAGES.
Corporations.
Forms of probate for deeds and other conveyances,
§47-41.02(f).
Costs.
Attorneys' fees in addition to interest, §6-21.2.
Insurance companies.
Investments in chattel mortgages, §58-7-180(a) to
(d).
Valuation of personal property acquired,
§58-7-193(c).
Registration, §47-20.
Secured transactions, §§25-9-101 to 25-9-710.
See SECURED TRANSACTIONS.
Tobacco.
Leaf tobacco sold in auction.
Effective period for lien, §44-69.

CHATTEL PAPER.
Secured transactions.
Perfection of security interests in, §25-9-312.
Purchaser of chattel paper.
Priority, §25-9-330.

CHEATING.
Academic credit obtained by fraudulent
means, §14-118.2.
False pretenses and cheats.
See FALSE PRETENSES AND CHEATS.

CHEATING —Cont'd
Fraud generally.
See FRAUD.

CHECK-CASHING BUSINESSES, §§53-275 to
53-289.
Advancing money on security of check.
Requirements, §53-280(b).
Banks and other financial institutions.
Exemptions to provisions, §53-277(a).
Books, accounts and records, §53-282(a).
Examination by commissioner, §53-282(c).
Definitions, §53-275.
Deposit of check cashed for fee.
Time, §53-280(b).
Endorsement of instrument presented by
licensee for payment, §53-280(d).
Examination by commissioner.
Books, accounts and records, §53-282(c).
Exemptions.
Banks and other financial institutions, §53-277(a).
Money transmitters, §53-277(b).
Retailer incidentally cashing checks, §53-277(a).
Fees.
License applications, renewal, §53-278(c), (d).
Service fees, §53-280(a).
Notice of fees charged, posting, §53-280(c).
Government checks.
Fee for cashing, §53-280(a).
Hearings.
Denial of license, §53-279(b).
Incidental to retailers business.
Exemptions to provisions, §53-277(a).
Investigation for licenses, §53-278(b).
Licenses.
Application, §53-278(a).
Fee, §53-278(c).
Denial of license, §53-279(b).
Hearing, §53-279(b).
Expiration, §53-278(d).
Issuance, findings required, §53-279(b).
Liquid assets requirement, §53-279(a).
Posting at place of business, §53-280(c).
Renewal, fee, §53-278(d).
Requirement, §53-276.
Suspension or revocation.
Grounds, §53-284(a).
Notice and opportunity for hearing required,
§53-284(b).
Money orders.
Fee for cashing, §53-280(a).
Money transmitters.
Exemptions to provisions, §53-277(b).
Personal checks.
Fee for cashing, §53-280(a).
Privilege tax, §105-88.
Prohibited acts, §53-283.
Cease and desist orders, §53-285.
Civil penalty, §53-286.
Criminal penalty, §53-287.
Receipts, customer provided, §53-282(b).
Restitution.
Prohibited acts, §53-286.
Rules.
Adoption, §53-288.
Review of, §53-289.
Service fees, §53-280(a).
Notice of fees charged, posting, §53-280(c).
Taxation.
Privilege tax, §105-88.

CHECK-CASHING BUSINESSES —Cont'd
Time.
　Deposit of checked cashed for fee, §53-280(b).
CHECK GUARANTEE CARDS.
Credit cards.
　See CREDIT CARDS.
Financial transaction card crimes, §§14-113.8 to
　14-113.17.
　See FINANCIAL TRANSACTION CARDS.
CHECKING STATIONS.
Impaired driving checks, §20-16.3A.
CHECK LOAN.
Interest and service charges, §24-11(b).
CHECKOFFS.
Income tax refund contributions.
　Wildlife conservation account, §105-269.5.
CHECKS.
Accord and satisfaction.
　Use of negotiable instrument, §25-3-311.
Bad checks.
　See BAD CHECKS.
Banks.
　Exchange.
　　Payable in exchange, §53-71.
　　　Exemptions.
　　　　Checks in payment of obligations due state
　　　　　or federal government, §53-73.
　False certification of check.
　　Penalty, §53-131.
　Fees on remittances covering checks.
　　Prohibited, §53-70.
　Payable in exchange, §53-71.
　　Exemptions.
　　　Checks in payment of obligations due state
　　　　and federal government, §53-73.
　Remittances covering checks.
　　Fees not to be charged, §53-70.
Check-cashing businesses, §§53-275 to 53-289.
　See CHECK-CASHING BUSINESSES.
Collection agencies.
　Processing fee for returned checks.
　　Collection, §25-3-506.
Costs for returned checks.
　Remedies for returned check, §6-21.3(b).
Damages.
　Remedies for returned check, §6-21.3(a), (d).
Defenses.
　Returned checks.
　　Affirmative defense, §6-21.3(c).
Electronic transactions.
　Retention of electronic records, §66-322(e).
Embezzlement, §14-90.
Employment security.
　Uncertified check in payment of contribution.
　　Penalty, §96-10(h).
　　　Reduction or waiver of penalty, §96-10(j).
Fees.
　Remittances covering checks.
　　Banks and trust companies not to charge fees,
　　　§53-70.
Fiduciaries.
　Checks drawn payable to third persons, §32-6.
　Deposit in fiduciary's personal account.
　　Check drawn by fiduciary upon account, §32-10.
　Deposit in name of fiduciary.
　　Payment by bank upon check of fiduciary,
　　　§32-8.
　Deposit in name of principal.
　　Check drawn upon account of principal and
　　　bank by fiduciary, §32-9.

CHECKS —Cont'd
Fiduciaries —Cont'd
　Payable to fiduciary, §32-7.
Forgery, §14-119.
Larceny of choses in action, §14-75.
Leaf tobacco warehouses.
　Purchases to be paid for by cash or check to order,
　　§106-455.
Letters of notification and demand.
　Returned checks, §6-21.3(a1), (a2).
Loans.
　Unsolicited checks to secure loans, §75-20.
Money transmitters.
　Check-cashing businesses, §§53-275 to 53-289.
　　See CHECK-CASHING BUSINESSES.
　Generally, §§53-208.1 to 53-208.30.
　　See MONEY TRANSMITTERS.
Motor vehicles.
　Bad check in payment of fee or tax, §20-178.
Negotiable instruments generally, §§25-3-101 to
　25-3-605.
　See NEGOTIABLE INSTRUMENTS.
Payment in full.
　Accord and satisfaction.
　　Use of negotiable instrument, §25-3-311.
Powers of attorney.
　Powers conferred by statutory short form, §32A-2.
Releases.
　Accord and satisfaction.
　　Use of negotiable instrument, §25-3-311.
Remedies.
　Returned checks, §6-21.3.
Returned checks.
　Processing fee.
　　Collection, §25-3-506.
　Remedies for returned check, §6-21.3.
　Saving and loan associations.
　　Fees, §54B-147.
　Savings banks.
　　Processing fee, §54C-168.
Sale of goods, UCC.
　Payment by check, §25-2-511(3).
Savings banks.
　Returned checks.
　　Processing fee, §54C-168.
Simulation.
　Prohibited, §75-35.
Taxation.
　Bad checks in payment, §§105-236, 105-357(b).
　Property taxes.
　　Payment of taxes.
　　　Acceptance of checks, §105-357(b).
　　　Bad checks.
　　　　Penalty, §105-357(b).
Tobacco warehouses.
　Purchases of leaf tobacco to be paid for by cash or
　　check to order, §106-455.
Trusts and trustees.
　Deposit in names of two or more trustees.
　　Checks drawn upon trust account.
　　　Duty to inquire as to breach of trust, §32-11.
Unclaimed property generally, §§116B-51 to
　116B-80.
　See UNCLAIMED PROPERTY.
Unemployment compensation.
　Uncertified check in payment of contribution.
　　Penalty, §96-10(h).
　　　Reduction or waiver of penalty, §96-10(j).
Worthless checks.
　See BAD CHECKS.

CHEESE FACTORIES.
Inspections generally, §§106-246 to 106-255.
See ICE CREAM PLANTS, CREAMERIES AND CHEESE FACTORIES.

CHEMICAL ANALYSIS OF IMPAIRING SUBSTANCES IN BLOOD.
Generally.
See IMPAIRED DRIVING.

CHEMICAL DEPENDENCY.
Accident and health insurance.
Coverage for treatment, §58-51-50(a) to (e).
Group accident and health insurance.
Contracts to cover, §58-51-50(b).
Coverage not required, §58-51-55(c).
Definition of "chemical dependency,"§58-51-55(a).
Discrimination prohibited, §58-51-55(b), (c).
Plans covering both medical and surgical benefits and chemical dependency.
Paul Wellstone and Pete Domenici mental health parity and addiction equity act compliance, §58-51-50(f), (g).
Chiropractors.
Grounds for disciplinary action, §90-154(b).
Health maintenance organizations.
Contracts to cover treatment, §§58-67-70, 58-67-75.
Coverage not required, §58-67-75(c).
Defined, §58-67-75(a).
Discrimination.
Applicability of section, §58-67-75(d).
Prohibited acts, §58-67-75(b).
Sex changes.
Coverage for treatment or studies not required, §58-67-75(e).
Hospital, medical and dental service corporations.
Contracts to cover treatment, §58-65-75(a) to (g).
Incompetence, determination of, §§35A-1101 to 35A-1116.
See INCOMPETENCY.
Lawyers and judges impaired by substance abuse or addiction.
Lawyer assistance program, Bar Rules D.0601 to D.0623.
See LAWYERS ASSISTANCE PROGRAM.
Physicians and surgeons.
Grounds for denial, revocation or suspension of license, §90-14(a).
Probation.
Costs, §15A-1343(b).
Drug alcohol recovery treatment program as condition.
Screening and assessing for chemical dependency, §15A-1343(b3).
Substance abuse.
General provisions.
See MENTAL HEALTH, DEVELOPMENTAL DISABILITY, SUBSTANCE ABUSE.
Work first program recipients of assistance.
Treatment required, drug testing, §108A-29.1.

CHEMICAL DEPENDENCY TREATMENT FACILITIES.
Certificates of need, §§131E-175 to 130E-191.1.
See HEALTH CARE FACILITIES.

CHEMICAL PRESERVATIVES.
Food, drug and cosmetic act.
Foods deemed misbranded, §106-130.

CHEMICALS.
Discharges of oil or hazardous substances generally, §§143-215.83 to 143-215.94.
See OIL OR HAZARDOUS SUBSTANCES DISCHARGES.
Mass death and destruction weapons.
Nuclear, biological or chemical weapons, §§14-288.21 to 14-288.24.
See WEAPONS OF MASS DEATH AND DESTRUCTION.
Offshore oil and gas activities, §§143-215.94AA to 143-215.94JJ.
See OFFSHORE OIL AND GAS ACTIVITIES.
Oil pollution and hazardous substances control generally, §§143-215.75 to 143-215.82.
See OIL POLLUTION AND HAZARDOUS SUBSTANCES CONTROL.
Terrorist incident using nuclear, biological or chemical agents, §§130A-475 to 130A-479.
See TERRORIST INCIDENT USING NUCLEAR, BIOLOGICAL OR CHEMICAL AGENTS.
Water and air resources.
Prohibited discharges, §143-214.2(a).

CHEROKEE COUNTY.
Ambulance services.
Attachment or garnishment and lien for, §§44-51.4 to 44-51.8.
Obtaining service without intending to pay, §14-111.2.
Requesting ambulance falsely, §14-111.3.
Board of county commissioners.
Filling vacancies on board, §153A-27.1.
Condemnation or acquisition of land by local government unit outside county.
Consent of board of commissioners necessary, §153A-15.
Coroner elected as nominee of political party.
Filling vacancy in office, §152-1.
Counties generally.
See COUNTIES.
Dog collars.
Unlawful removal of electronic dog collars, §14-401.17.
Housing authority commissioners.
Tenant as commissioner, exemption from provision of law allowing, §157-5.
Oil, gas or mineral claims.
Certain ancient claims extinguished, preservation, procedure, §1-42.3(a) to (d).
Registration of deeds.
Tax certification, no delinquent taxes due, §161-31(b).
Room occupancy tax levied by county.
Uniform provisions, §153A-155.
School property.
Acquisition and improvement, §153A-158.1.
Sheriff.
Vacancy, performance of duties until vacancy filled, §162-5.1.
Western North Carolina Development Association, Inc.
Appropriation of funds to, §153A-447(a), (b).
Western North Carolina regional economic development commission, §§158-8.1 to 158-8.8.
Wild plants, taking of certain plants from land of another.
Inapplicability of provisions, §14-129.

CHEROKEE INDIANS.
Alcoholic beverages.
Tribal alcoholic beverage control, §18B-112.

CHEROKEE INDIANS —Cont'd
Amusement tax exemptions, §105-40.
Full faith and credit to judgments, decrees, and orders.
Eastern band of the Cherokee Indians.
Considered a foreign judgment, §1E-1(b).
Subject to certain provisions, §1E-1(b).
Tribal court.
Subject to full faith and credit of tribal court, §1E-1(a).
Maps of Cherokee lands.
Evidence.
Certified copies of maps, §8-14.
Motor fuel or special fuel taxes.
Refund.
Eastern band of the Cherokee Indians, §105-449.114.
National park system.
Jurisdiction over lands.
Inapplicable to lands held in trust, §104-33.
911 system.
PSAP fund distributions to.
Cherokee Indians, Eastern Band as eligible PSAP, §62A-46(f).
Robeson county.
Provision inapplicable to certain bands of Indians, §71A-2.
Rights and privileges, §71A-1.
Sales and use tax.
Exemption of sales on Cherokee Indian reservation, §105-164.13.

CHERRIES.
Standard weights and measures, §81A-42.
Unfair practices by handlers, §§106-496 to 106-501.
See FRUIT HANDLERS UNFAIR PRACTICES.

CHERRY BOMBS.
Fireworks generally, §§14-410 to 14-415.

CHERRY HOSPITAL.
Hospitals generally.
See HOSPITALS.
Joint security force, §122C-430.10.
Mental health, developmental disabilities and substance abuse.
General provisions.
See MENTAL HEALTH, DEVELOPMENTAL DISABILITY, SUBSTANCE ABUSE.

CHERRYVILLE.
All-terrain vehicles.
Use by employees on certain highways, §20-171.24.

CHESTNUTS.
Standard weight and measure, §81A-42.

CHEWING TOBACCO.
Cigarettes and tobacco products generally.
See CIGARETTES AND TOBACCO PRODUCTS.
Sale or distribution of tobacco products to minors, §14-313.

CHICK DEALERS.
Civil penalties, §106-549.01.
Defined, §106-541.
Diseases.
Compulsory testing for disease, §106-548.
False advertising, §106-545.
Fines, §106-549.01.
Grade of chicks.
Notice describing grade to be posted, §106-546.

CHICK DEALERS —Cont'd
License needed to operate, §106-542.
Misdemeanor offenses, §106-549.
Quarantine on premises, §106-548.
Records to be kept, §106-547.
Shipments from out of state, §106-544.
Violations of provisions a misdemeanor, §106-549.

CHICKENS.
Egg law, §§106-245.13 to 106-245.28.
See EGGS.
Poultry generally.
See POULTRY AND POULTRY PRODUCTS.
Poultry products inspections, §§106-549.49 to 106-549.69.
See POULTRY PRODUCTS INSPECTIONS.
Promotion of use and sale of agricultural products.
Generally, §§106-550 to 106-568.
See AGRICULTURAL PRODUCTS PROMOTION.

CHIEF INFORMATION OFFICER.
See INFORMATION TECHNOLOGY SERVICES.

CHIEF JUSTICE.
Assignment of judges, NC Const Art IV §11.
Death penalty sentencing proceedings.
Designation of judge on disability of trial judge, §15A-2003.
Election of, §7A-10(a).
Emergency justices.
Recall of justices by chief justice.
Finality of decisions regarding, §7A-39.9(a).
Termination of recall by chief justice, §7A-39.9(b).
Impeachment of governor.
Presiding judge, §123-2.
Incapacity of chief justice.
Procedure when chief justice incapacitated, §7A-39.9(c).
Salary, §7A-10(b).
Longevity pay, §7A-10(c).
Travel expense reimbursement, §7A-10(b1).
Terms of office, §7A-10(a).

CHILD ABDUCTION, §14-41(a).
Bail, §15A-534.4.
Custodial interference.
Transporting child outside state.
Intent to violate custody order, §14-320.1.
Electronic surveillance orders, §15A-290(c1).
Enticing minors out of state for purposes of employment, §14-40.
Kidnapping and abduction generally, §§14-39 to 14-41.
See KIDNAPPING.

CHILD ABUSE, NEGLECT OR DEPENDENCY, §§7B-100 to 7B-1414.
Abortion.
Consent for abortion on unemancipated minor.
Records not public record and maintained separately from juvenile records, §7B-2901(d).
Abused juvenile defined, §7B-101.
Adjudication of juvenile, §7B-807.
Court's findings on allegations in petition, §7B-807(a).
Order of adjudication.
Requirements for, §7B-807(b).
Placement on responsible individuals list, §7B-807(a1).

CHILD ABUSE, NEGLECT OR DEPENDENCY
—Cont'd
Adjudicatory hearing, §§7B-801 to 7B-808.
Clear and convincing evidence required to prove allegations, §7B-805.
Closed hearing.
Court determination, §7B-801(a).
Juvenile requesting opening hearing, §7B-801(b).
Conduct, §7B-802.
Continuance, §7B-803.
Dismissal with prejudice, court finds allegation not proven, §7B-807(a).
Due process of law, protection of juvenile's and parent's rights, §7B-802.
Finding that allegations proved, statement by court, §7B-807(a).
Held at time and place as designated by court, §7B-801(c).
Orders court permitted to enter, §7B-801(b1).
Record of hearing, §7B-806.
Record of stipulated adjudicatory facts, §7B-807(a).
Rules of evidence to apply, §7B-804.
Subsequent hearing.
Order not timely entered, §7B-807(b).
Transcript.
Reducing record to transcript upon notice of appeal, §7B-806.
Adoption.
Bringing dependents into state for placement or adoption, §§7B-3700 to 7B-3705.
See CHILD PLACEMENT.
Periodic review hearing as to placement.
Surrender of juvenile for adoption, agency plan for placement, §7B-909.
Termination of parental rights, permanent placement plan, §7B-908.
Sending dependents out of state for placement, §§7B-3702 to 7B-3705.
Aggravated circumstances.
Defined, §7B-101.
Alcohol and other drug abuse and dependence.
Drug treatment courts, §§7A-790 to 7A-801.
See DRUG TREATMENT COURTS.
Alternative dispositions, §7B-903(a).
Amendment of petition alleging abuse, neglect or dependency, §7B-800.
Appeal of final order of court.
Authority of trial court pending disposition of appeal, §7B-1003(b).
Continued exercise of jurisdiction by trial court.
Pending disposition of appeal, §7B-1003(b).
Direct appeal to court of appeals, §7B-1001(a).
Enforcement of order during appeal.
Unless stay ordered, §7B-1003(a).
Foster care placement.
Authority of court pending appeal, §7B-1003(e).
Juvenile matters which may be appealed, §7B-1001(a).
Mental health professional's opinion considered.
Before returning juvenile to custody of individual pending resolution of appeal, §7B-1003(d).
Modification of original order after affirmation by appellate court, §7B-1004.
Notice of appeal, §7B-1001(b), (c).
Permanency planning.
Notice to preserve right of appeal, §7B-507(c).
Proper parties to appeal, §7B-1002.
Right to appeal, §7B-1001.

CHILD ABUSE, NEGLECT OR DEPENDENCY
—Cont'd
Appeal of final order of court —Cont'd
Temporary order affecting custody or placement.
Authority of trial court to enter pending disposition of appeal, §7B-1003(c).
Appearance of parent, guardian, etc., personally served.
Failure to appear, contempt, §7B-407.
Appointment of counsel for parent.
Payment of court-appointed counsel, §7B-603(a) to (c).
Provisional counsel, §7B-602(a).
Summons to contain information about how to seek appointment, §7B-406(b).
Appointment of guardian, §7B-600(a).
Court's inquiry into person's qualifications to act as guardian, §7B-600(c).
Appointment of guardian ad litem, §7B-601(a).
Armed forces enlistment, authority of guardian to consent, §7B-600(a).
Assessment of report.
Abandonment alleged in report.
Immediate assessment, §7B-302(a).
Access to information, §7B-302(e).
Background check of alleged abuser.
Juvenile removed from home, §7B-302(d1).
Confidentiality, §7B-302(a).
Exceptions, §7B-302(a1).
Criminal history check of alleged abuser.
Juvenile removed from home, §7B-302(d1).
Disclosure of record, law governing, §132-1.4(l).
Duty of director of department to make, §7B-302(a).
Entry into private residence, conditions for, §7B-302(h).
Family assessment response.
Director may use, §7B-302(a).
Identity of reporter.
Confidentiality, §7B-302(a).
Immediate removal necessary, §7B-302(d).
Background check of alleged abuser.
Juvenile removed from home, §7B-302(d1).
Determination by director, §7B-302(c).
Immunity of persons cooperating in, §7B-309.
Interference or obstruction.
Contempt, order entered enforced by, §7B-303(f).
Defined, §7B-303(b).
Exparte order of respondent to cease.
Juvenile in need of immediate protection, §7B-303(d).
Hearing on petition, §7B-303(c).
Identity of person making report.
Director may be required to disclose, §7B-303(e).
Juvenile in need of immediate protection.
Exparte order of respondent to cease, §7B-303(d).
Ordering respondent to cease, §7B-303(c).
Petition ordering respondent to cease, §7B-303(a).
Service of petition, summons and notice of hearing, §7B-303(c).
Investigative assessment response.
Director may use, §7B-302(a).
Legal residence of child in another county, §7B-302(a2).
Mental health evaluation of alleged abusers.
History of violent behavior, §7B-302(d1).

CHILD ABUSE, NEGLECT OR DEPENDENCY
—Cont'd

Assessment of report —Cont'd

Missing child.

Assessment to include request to investigate. Abandonment alleged, §7B-302(a).

Notice that custody of juvenile retained by medical facility.

Director to treat as report of abuse and conduct immediate investigation, §7B-308(b).

Notice to individual determined to be responsible individual, §7B-320.

Notice to person making report.

Status of assessment, §7B-302(f), (g).

Other juveniles living at home or facility of juvenile subject of report.

Assessment, §7B-302(b).

Powers of director in performing duties, §7B-302(e).

Protective services.

Director to provide, §7B-302(c).

Protective services to include investigation and screening of complaint, §7B-300.

Report on finding evidence of abuse or neglect, §7B-307(a), (b).

Result, notice by director, §7B-307(c).

Review of director's decision not to petition the court.

Prosecutor's review, §7B-305.

Temporary custody of juvenile for juvenile's protection, §7B-302(d).

Time for initiating assessment after receipt of report, §7B-302(a).

Visit to juvenile's residence.

Assessment to include, §7B-302(a).

Attorney advocate.

Appointment when guardian ad litem nonattorney, §7B-601(a).

Standing to represent juvenile, §7B-601(a).

Attorney-client privilege, grounds for excluding evidence, §7B-310.

Baby drop off, §14-322.3.

Exceptions to child abuse, §§14-318.2, 14-318.4(c).

Background check of alleged abuser.

Assessment of report.

Juvenile removed from home, §7B-302(d1).

Best interest of juvenile.

Appointment of guardian, §7B-600(a).

Bringing dependents into state for placement or adoption, §§7B-3700 to 7B-3705.

See CHILD PLACEMENT.

Burden at adjudicatory hearing, §7B-805.

Burden at hearing on nonsecure custody, §7B-506(b).

Caretaker defined, §7B-101.

Casework.

Protective services to include, §7B-300.

Central registry and responsible individuals list.

Central registry.

Duty of department of health and human services to maintain, §7B-311(a).

Hearings or court proceedings.

Data not used at, §7B-311(a).

Source of data, §7B-311(a).

Placement on responsible individuals list following adjudication, §7B-807(a1).

Report submitted by director to, §7B-307(c).

Responsible individuals list, §§7B-320 to 7B-324.

Burden of proof in petition alleging person to be responsible individual, §7B-805.

CHILD ABUSE, NEGLECT OR DEPENDENCY
—Cont'd

Central registry and responsible individuals list —Cont'd

Responsible individuals list —Cont'd

Docket for judicial review actions.

Clerk to maintain, §7B-323(b).

Duty of department of health and human services to maintain, §7B-311(b).

Entities provided information from, §7B-311(b).

Judicial review, §§7B-320 to 7B-324.

Notice to individual determined to be responsible individual, §§7B-320, 7B-406(b).

Petition for judicial review.

Appeal of district court's decision, §7B-323(f).

Contents, §7B-323(a).

Duties of director on receipt of notice of hearing, §7B-323(b1).

Filing, §7B-323(a).

Hearing on petition, §7B-323(b), (c).

Order of district court, §7B-323(d).

Persons ineligible to petition, §7B-324(a).

Time for filing, §7B-323(a).

Stay of proceedings.

Individual named in juvenile court case resulting from same incident, §7B-324(b).

Rules regarding operation.

Social services commission to adopt, §7B-311(d).

Unlawful release of information, §7B-311(c).

Challenge to placement of name on responsible individuals list.

Judicial review, §§7B-320 to 7B-324.

Child care facilities.

See CHILD CARE FACILITIES.

Child fatality prevention system, §§7B-1400 to 7B-1414.

See CHILD FATALITY PREVENTION SYSTEM.

Children's trust fund, §7B-1302.

Civil child-custody order, §7B-911.

Clear and convincing evidence.

Adjudicatory hearing, proving allegations, §7B-805.

Clerk's office closed, magistrate issuing petition, §7B-404(a).

Authority limited to emergency situations, §7B-404(b).

Clerk to maintain complete records of juvenile cases, §7B-2901(a).

Closed hearings.

Adjudicatory hearing, §7B-801(a), (b).

Commencement of action by filing petition, §7B-405.

Community-based educational and service programs.

Program on prevention of abuse and neglect, §7B-1301.

Community-level services provided juvenile and family, §7B-900.

Conferences during prosecutor's review of director's decision, §7B-306.

Confidential information, records or reports.

Assessment of report.

Information received, §7B-302(a).

Exceptions, §7B-302(a1).

Communications between guardian ad litem and parent, §7B-602(d).

Examination of records without court order.

Persons who may examine, §7B-2901(a).

Guardian ad litem demanding, respect for confidentiality, §7B-601(c).

CHILD ABUSE, NEGLECT OR DEPENDENCY
—Cont'd
Confidential information, records or reports
—Cont'd
Permanency mediation program.
Proceedings, §7B-202(c), (d).
Records and social reports generally, §7B-2901.
Consent judgment or order, §7B-801(b1).
Consent of department of health and human services for placement of juvenile.
Sending into state or sending out of state for placement or adoption, §§7B-3700 to 7B-3705.
Consent to actions on part of juvenile.
Power of guardian, §7B-600(a).
Construction and interpretation of subchapter to implement purposes, §7B-100.
Contempt.
Failure of parent, guardian, etc., personally served to appear, §7B-407.
Failure of parent to comply with dispositional order, §7B-904(e).
Show cause orders, §7B-904(e).
Failure to comply with order generally, §7B-406(c).
Order to cease interference or obstruction with assessment of report.
Enforcement of order, §7B-303(f).
Payment of fees for court-appointed attorney or guardian ad litem.
Failure to comply with order of payment, §7B-603(c).
Show cause orders.
Failure of parent to comply with dispositional order, §7B-904(e).
Continuance of adjudicatory hearing, §7B-803.
Continuance of hearing on nonsecure custody, §7B-506(a).
Continuance of placement review hearing.
Termination of parental rights, §7B-908(b).
Continued jurisdiction of court to modify or vacate dispositional order, §7B-1000(b).
Contracts to operate community-based educational and service programs, §7B-1301(b).
Counseling services.
Protective services to include, §7B-300.
Court appointed counsel for parent.
Provisional counsel, §7B-602(a).
Criminal history check of alleged abuser.
Assessment of report.
Juvenile removed from home, §7B-302(d1).
Criminal history defined, §7B-101.
When juvenile removed from home, §7B-503(b).
Criminal investigation when evidence of abuse found, §7B-307(a).
Criminal prosecution of alleged abuse determined by district attorney, §7B-307(a).
Custodian defined, §7B-101.
Custody of juvenile.
Alternative dispositions, §7B-903(a).
Appeal of final order of court.
Temporary order affecting custody or placement.
Authority of trial court to enter pending disposition of appeal, §7B-1003(c).
Civil child-custody order.
Authorized, §7B-911(a).
Filing order in existing civil action, §7B-911(b).
Initiation of civil action.
Order treated as, §7B-911(b).
Requirements for court to issue order, §7B-911(c).

CHILD ABUSE, NEGLECT OR DEPENDENCY
—Cont'd
Custody of juvenile —Cont'd
Civil child-custody order —Cont'd
Termination of court's jurisdiction in juvenile proceeding, §7B-911(a).
Medical professionals obtaining custody in abuse cases, §7B-308.
Nonsecure custody.
Authority of court to order placement of juvenile, §7B-502.
Continued custody hearing, §7B-506.
Criteria, §7B-503.
Delegation of authority to other than district court judges, §7B-502.
Factual basis for ordering, §7B-503(a).
Hearing to determine need for continued custody, §7B-506.
Order, §7B-504.
Place of nonsecure custody, §7B-505.
Release of juvenile to parent, relative, etc.
Court's first consideration on request for nonsecure custody, §7B-503(a).
Notices, orders, authorizations and request made by telephone, §7B-508.
Placement of juvenile, periodic review hearings.
Custody removed from parent, §7B-906.
Dispositional order to direct holding of hearing, §7B-905(b).
Surrender of juvenile for adoption, agency plan, §7B-909.
Termination of parental rights, §7B-908.
Secure custody prohibited, §7B-503.
Temporary custody without court order, §7B-500(a).
Duties of person taking into temporary custody, §7B-501(a).
Time limit on holding in temporary custody, §7B-501(b).
Voluntary foster care placement, §7B-910.
Death due to maltreatment.
Assessment of report, protective services for and removal of other juveniles, §7B-302(b).
Duty to report, §7B-301.
Death of juvenile generally.
Child fatality prevention system, §§7B-1400 to 7B-1414.
See CHILD FATALITY PREVENTION SYSTEM.
Definitions, §7B-101.
Temporary custody, §7B-500(a).
Department of health and human services.
Central registry and responsible individuals list, §7B-311.
Results of assessment and report.
Department to receive, §7B-307(b), (c).
Dependent juvenile defined, §7B-101.
Director of department of social services in each county to establish protective services, §7B-300.
Director of social services to maintain record of cases, §7B-2901(b).
Disclosure of investigation records.
Law governing, §132-1.4(l).
Predisposition reports, §7B-808(c).
Discovery.
Motion, §7B-700(c).
Protective order.
Request by party served with motion for discovery, §7B-700(d).

CHILD ABUSE, NEGLECT OR DEPENDENCY
—Cont'd
Discovery —Cont'd
Redisclosure prohibited by state or federal law,
§7B-700(e).
Dismissal of petition with prejudice.
Finding by court that allegations not proved,
§7B-807(a).
Dispositional hearing, §7B-901.
Notice in summons that court will conduct,
§7B-406(b).
Dispositional order, §7B-905.
Notice in summons as types of disposition,
§7B-406(b).
Disposition of juvenile, §§7B-900 to 7B-1004.
Allowing parent or others to take appropriate
action, §7B-903(a).
Alternatives for disposition, §7B-903(a).
Appeal.
Disposition after appeal, §7B-1004.
Disposition pending appeal, §7B-1003.
Final order, §7B-1001.
Modification or alteration of original order upon
affirmation by appellate court, §7B-1004.
Proper parties to appeal final order, §7B-1002.
Authority of court to direct parents' actions,
§7B-904(d1).
Change of placement by county department of
social services.
Notice of intention given guardian ad litem or
attorney advocate, §7B-905(d).
Civil child-custody order, §7B-911.
Closed hearing unless juvenile moves to open
hearing, §7B-901.
Community-level services, providing juvenile and
family, §7B-900.
Contempt.
Failure of parent to comply with dispositional
order, §7B-904(e).
Show cause orders, §7B-904(e).
Court's inquiry into person's qualifications as to
custody, §7B-903(c).
Custody of juvenile removed from parent.
Review of order, §7B-906.
Calendaring case, timely request by director,
§7B-906(a).
Court relieved of duty to conduct review,
restoration of custody to parent,
§7B-906(d).
Court's inquiry into person's qualifications as
to custody or guardianship, §7B-906(g).
Criteria considered by court, written findings
by court, §7B-906(c).
Disposition by court after findings,
§7B-906(d).
Disposition order to set time and date of
hearing, §7B-905(b).
Foster care placement, applicability of
provisions, §7B-906(f).
Guardian, appointment by court after making
findings, §7B-906(d).
Information considered at review hearing,
§7B-906(c).
Notice of review, §7B-906(a).
Permanency-planning hearing, §7B-907(a).
Reports to court in lieu of review, §7B-906(b).
Return of juvenile to parent, hearing and
findings required, §7B-906(d).
Second or subsequent reviews, time for
conducting, §7B-906(a).

CHILD ABUSE, NEGLECT OR DEPENDENCY
—Cont'd
Disposition of juvenile —Cont'd
Custody of juvenile removed from parent —Cont'd
Review of order —Cont'd
Subsequent hearing, order not timely entered,
§7B-906(d).
Time for review, §7B-906(a).
Visitation plan, placement of juvenile with
department of social services, §7B-906(d).
Waiver of review, court authority, §7B-906(b).
Examination by physician, psychiatrist,
psychologist or other expert, §7B-903(a).
Findings or fact and conclusions of law, order to
contain, §7B-905(a).
Foster care, order directing placement of juvenile,
§7B-905(c).
Foster care placement, voluntary agreements,
review.
Addition review hearings, time for holding,
§7B-910(c).
Authority of court on making findings,
§7B-910(b).
Findings to be made by court, §7B-910(a).
Notice, §7B-910(c).
Time for conducting review, §7B-910(c).
Time limit on placement, §7B-910(c).
Hearing, §7B-901.
History of violent behavior, individual responsible
for physical abuse.
Mental health professional's opinion considered,
§7B-903(b).
Medical, psychiatric, psychological, surgical,
educational evaluations, examinations or
treatment, §7B-903(a).
Participation of parent in juvenile's treatment,
§7B-904(b).
Payment of costs, §7B-904(a), (c).
Mental health professional.
Opinion considered by court, physical abuse
suffered by juvenile, §7B-903(b).
Mentally ill or developmentally disabled juveniles,
§7B-903(a).
Missing parent, inquiry of court as to, §7B-901.
Modification or vacation of dispositional order.
Continuance of jurisdiction until terminated by
court order or emancipation, §7B-1000(b).
Original order modified after affirmation by
appellate court, §7B-1004.
Review hearing, §7B-1000(a).
Order, §7B-905.
Parents' actions.
Authority of court to direct, §7B-904(d1).
Paternity issues, inquiry of court as to, §7B-901.
Permanent placement plan.
Placement review.
Adoption placement prior to review, notice,
cancellation of review, §7B-908(e).
Considerations by court during review,
§7B-908(c).
Continuance of case, §7B-908(b).
Court authority after making findings of fact,
§7B-907(d).
Court's inquiry into person's qualifications as
to custody or guardianship, §7B-907(f).
Guardian ad litem, appointment, §7B-908(b).
Notice of review, §7B-908(b).
Purpose, §7B-908(a).
Selection of adoptive parents, §7B-1112.1.
Time for conducting, §7B-908(b).

CHILD ABUSE, NEGLECT OR DEPENDENCY
—Cont'd
Disposition of juvenile —Cont'd
Placement review, custody of juvenile removed
from parent, §7B-906.
  Calendaring case, timely request by director,
    §7B-906(a).
  Court relieved of duty to conduct review,
    restoration of custody to parent, §7B-906(d).
  Court's inquiry into person's qualifications as to
    custody or guardianship, §7B-906(g).
  Criteria considered by court, written findings by
    court, §7B-906(c).
  Disposition by court after findings, §7B-906(d).
  Disposition order to set time and date of
    hearing, §7B-905(b).
  Foster care placement, applicability of
    provisions, §7B-906(f).
  Guardian, appointment by court after making
    findings, §7B-906(d).
  Information considered at review hearing,
    §7B-906(c).
  Notice of review, §7B-906(a).
  Permanency-planning hearing, §7B-907(a).
  Reports to court in lieu of review, §7B-906(b).
  Return of juvenile to parent, hearing and
    findings required, §7B-906(d).
  Second or subsequent reviews, time for
    conducting, §7B-906(a).
  Subsequent hearing.
    Order not timely entered, §7B-906(d).
  Time for review, §7B-906(a).
  Visitation plan, placement of juvenile with
    department of social services, §7B-906(d).
  Waiver of review, court authority, §7B-906(b).
Placement review, parental rights terminated.
  Adoption placement prior to review, notice,
    cancellation of review, §7B-908(e).
  Considerations by court during review,
    §7B-908(c).
  Continuance of case, §7B-908(b).
  Court authority after making findings of fact,
    §7B-907(d).
  Court's inquiry into person's qualifications as to
    custody or guardianship, §7B-907(f).
  Guardian ad litem, appointment, §7B-908(b).
  Notice of review, §7B-908(b).
  Purpose, §7B-908(a).
  Selection of adoptive parents, §7B-1112.1.
  Time for conducting, §7B-907(b).
Placement review, surrender of juvenile for
  adoption by parent or parents.
  Notice to clerk to calendar case, §7B-909(a).
  Petition for review, notice required by,
    §7B-909(c).
  Time for conducting review, §7B-909(c).
Placement review, voluntary foster care
  placements.
  Addition review hearings, time for holding,
    §7B-910(c).
  Authority of court on making findings,
    §7B-910(b).
  Findings to be made by court, §7B-910(a).
  Notice, §7B-910(d).
  Time for conducting review, §7B-910(c).
  Time limit on placement, §7B-910(c).
Placing juvenile with department of social
  services, §7B-903(a).
  Requirements of dispositional order, §7B-905(c).
Placing juvenile with suitable person or agency,
  §7B-903(a).

CHILD ABUSE, NEGLECT OR DEPENDENCY
—Cont'd
Disposition of juvenile —Cont'd
Predisposition investigation and report,
  §7B-808(a).
  Administrative orders, §7B-808(c).
  Preparation of report, §7B-808(b).
  Rulemaking, §7B-808(c).
Purpose, §7B-900.
Show cause orders.
  Contempt.
    Failure of parent to comply with dispositional
      order, §7B-904(e).
Support of juvenile, parent ordered to pay.
  Legal custody of juvenile vested in someone
    other than parent, §7B-904(d).
Terms of disposition to be stated in order,
  §7B-905(a).
Time for entry of order, §7B-905(a).
Transfer of case to another county after
  adjudication, §7B-900.1.
Working with juvenile and family in home, initial
  approach, §7B-900.
Dispute between social services departments.
Legal residence of child.
  Referral to division of social services for
    resolution, §153A-257(d).
**District attorney notified when evidence of
  abuse found,** §7B-307(a).
District court jurisdiction.
Cases involving juvenile alleged to be abused,
  neglected or dependent, §7B-200(a).
Parent or guardian of child adjudicated abused,
  neglected or dependent, §7B-200(b).
Retention of jurisdiction until terminated by court
  or emancipation of juvenile, §7B-201(a).
Review at any time, §7B-323(e).
Termination.
  Affect, modification or enforcement of previous
    orders, prohibition, §7B-201(b).
Domestic violence generally.
See DOMESTIC VIOLENCE.
Drug treatment courts, §§7A-790 to 7A-801.
See DRUG TREATMENT COURTS.
Due process of law.
Adjudicatory hearing, §7B-802.
Duty to report abuse, neglect or dependency,
§7B-301.
Entry into private residence.
Assessment of report, §7B-302(h).
Evidence.
Dispositional hearings, §7B-901.
Excluding based on privilege, §7B-310.
Permanency planning hearings, §7B-907(b).
Placement review, parental rights terminated,
  §7B-908(a).
Review hearings, §7B-906(c).
**Evidence of abuse or neglect found by
  director, report,** §7B-307(a), (b).
Excluding evidence based on privilege,
§7B-310.
Execution of order for nonsecure custody,
§7B-504.
**Failure of parent, guardian, etc., personally
  served to appear.**
Contempt, §7B-407.
Family assessment response.
Defined, §7B-101.
Method of assessment of report, §7B-302(a).
Protective services to include, §7B-300.

CHILD ABUSE, NEGLECT OR DEPENDENCY
—Cont'd

Fatality or near fatality cases, disclosure of records.
Application for order compelling disclosure, request denied, §7B-2902(e).
Child fatality prevention team records, provisions governing access, §7B-2902(f).
Confidential records, access prohibited, §7B-2902(c).
Criminal investigative reports and criminal intelligence information, provisions governing access, §7B-2902(f).
Definition of public record not limited or narrowed, §7B-2902(h).
Definitions, §7B-2902(a).
Immunity of public agency or employee acting in good faith, §7B-2902(g).
Providing findings and information upon request, §7B-2902(d).
Request to public agency for disclosure, §7B-2902(b).
Time for providing findings and information upon request, §7B-2902(d).

Fees for court appointed attorney or guardian ad litem.
Payment, §7B-603(a) to (c).

Felony child abuse, §14-318.4(a) to (a5).
Additional offense to other civil and criminal provisions, §14-318.4(b).
Exceptions, §14-318.4(c).

Filing petition, commencement of action, §7B-405.

Final order.
Appeal, §§7B-1001 to 7B-1004.

Foster care.
Appeal of final order of court.
  Authority of court pending appeal, §7B-1003(e).
Dispositional order directing placement of juvenile, §7B-905(c).
Voluntary foster care placement agreement, review hearing, §7B-910.
  Clerk to give notice of hearings, §7B-910(d).
  Courts' authority over placements, §7B-910(b).
  Evidence considered at hearing, §7B-910(a).
  Filing of petitions of abuse, neglect or dependency.
    Time limitation in placement without filing petition, §7B-910(c).
  Timing of hearings, §7B-910(c).

Generally, 1999 provisions, §§7B-100 to 7B-1414.

Guardian.
Appointment, powers, §7B-600(a).
  Court's inquiry into person's qualifications to act as guardian, §7B-600(c).
Review of placement, custody removed from parent.
  Appointment after making findings, §7B-906(d).
  Court's inquiry into person's qualifications to act as guardian, §7B-906(g).
Termination of relationship, reintegration of juvenile into parent's home, §7B-600(b).

Guardian ad litem.
Accompanying juvenile to court in criminal matters, §7B-601(b).
Appointment by court, §7B-601(a).
Appointment for parent, §7B-602(b), (c).
Assistance to parent.
  Practices permitted, §7B-602(e).
Attorney appointed when nonattorney appointed as guardian ad litem, §7B-601(a).

CHILD ABUSE, NEGLECT OR DEPENDENCY
—Cont'd

Guardian ad litem —Cont'd
Communication between guardian, parent and parent's attorney.
  Confidentiality, privilege, §7B-602(d).
Confidentiality of information or reports demanded.
  Guardian to respect, §7B-601(c).
Demanding information or reports, authority, §7B-601(c).
Duties, §7B-601(a).
Fellow-up investigations to ensure orders executed, §7B-601(b).
Husband-wife privilege inapplicable.
  Demand for information by guardian, §7B-601(c).
Information, records, reports.
  Disclosure, sharing, §7B-700(f).
Payment, §7B-603(a) to (c).
Petition alleging abuse, neglect or dependency.
  Copy of petition to be provided to guardian ad litem office, §7B-408.
Physician-patient privilege inapplicable.
  Demand for information by guardian, §7B-601(c).
Reappointment on showing good cause, §7B-601(a).
Report to court when orders not being met, §7B-601(b).
Standing to represent juvenile in all actions under subchapter, §7B-601(a).
Termination of appointment, §7B-601(a).
Termination of parental rights, placement review, §7B-908(b).
Two years, termination of appointment, §7B-601(a).

Guardian ad litem program to provide services to juveniles, §§7B-1200 to 7B-1204.
Alternative plans, §7B-1203.
Appointment of district bar member to represent juvenile.
  Conflict of interest of local program, §7B-1202.
Attorney for local program, §7B-1200.
Conflict of interest prohibiting local program from providing representation.
  Appointment of member of district bar to represent juvenile, §7B-1202.
Coordinator of local program, paid state employee, §7B-1200.
District court operation of program.
  No local program established, §7B-1201(a).
Guardian ad litem advisory committee, §7B-1201(b).
Immunity of volunteer from civil liability, §7B-1204.
Impractical to establish local program.
  Waiver of establishment, §7B-1202.
Local program, §7B-1200.
  Conflict of interest, appointment of district bar member, §7B-1202.
  Implementation and administration, §7B-1201(a).
  Impractical to establish or alternative established, waiver of establishment, §7B-1202.
Office of guardian ad litem services.
  Established within administrative of office of the courts, §7B-1200.
Rules and regulation adopted by administrative office of the courts, §7B-1200.

CHILD ABUSE, NEGLECT OR DEPENDENCY
—Cont'd
Guardian ad litem program to provide services to juveniles —Cont'd
Volunteer guardians.
Immunity from civil liability, §7B-1204.
Part of local program, §7B-1200.
Waiver of establishment of local program, §7B-1202.
Alternative plans, §7B-1203.
Hearings.
Alleged interference or obstruction of assessment, §7B-303(c).
Determining need for continued nonsecure custody, §7B-506.
Disposition, §7B-901.
Permanency planning hearing, custody removed from parent, §7B-907(a).
Petition to review responsible individuals list, §7B-323(b), (c).
Review of placement of juvenile.
Custody removed from parent, §7B-906.
Dispositional order to direct holding of hearing, §7B-905(b).
Surrender of juvenile for adoption, agency plan, §7B-909.
Termination of parental rights, §7B-908.
Voluntary foster care placement, §7B-910.
History of violent behavior, person responsible for abuse.
Mental health professional's opinion considered, §7B-903(b).
Hospital, clinic or other medical facility administrators.
Authority in abuse cases.
Retention of physical custody of juvenile in medical facility, §7B-308(a), (f).
Husband and wife.
Privilege.
Waiver of husband-wife privilege in child abuse cases, §8-57.1.
Husband-wife privilege, inapplicability.
Demand for information by guardian ad litem, §7B-601(c).
Identity of reporter, disclosure.
Hearing on interference or obstruction of assessment, §7B-303(e).
Immunity.
Persons making reports and cooperating in assessment of report, §7B-309.
Indigent persons.
Entitlement to services of counsel, §7A-451(a).
Information sharing.
Departments of social services, §7B-700(a).
Guardian ad litem's records and reports, §7B-700(f).
Local rules.
Chief district court judge may adopt, §7B-700(b).
Redisclosure prohibited by state or federal law, §7B-700(e).
Interference with assessment of report, §7B-303.
Investigative assessment response.
Defined, §7B-101.
Method of assessment of report, §7B-302(a).
Protective services to include, §7B-300.
Issuance of summons, §7B-406.
Jurisdiction of district court.
Cases involving juvenile alleged to be abused, neglected or dependent, §7B-200(a).

CHILD ABUSE, NEGLECT OR DEPENDENCY
—Cont'd
Jurisdiction of district court —Cont'd
Parent or guardian of child adjudicated abuse, neglected or dependent, §7B-200(b).
Termination.
Affect, modification or enforcement of previous orders, prohibition, §7B-201(b).
Juvenile court counselors.
Duty to report, §7B-1700.1.
Juvenile defined, §7B-101.
Law enforcement officers.
Return and execution of order for nonsecure custody, §7B-504.
Taking juvenile into temporary custody.
Authority, §7B-500(a).
Duties upon taking juvenile into temporary custody, §7B-501(a).
Legal residence of child.
Dispute between social services departments.
Referral to division of social services for resolution, §153A-257(d).
Petition filed in county other than county of juvenile's residence.
Duty of petitioner, §7B-402(d).
Proceeding brought in district in which juvenile resides, §7B-400.
Legal services programs.
Eligible cases, §7A-474.3(b).
List of responsible individuals, §7B-311.
Judicial review, §§7B-320 to 7B-324.
Magistrate authorized to issue petition.
Clerk's office closed, §7B-404(a).
Authority limited to emergency situations, §7B-404(b).
Maltreatment of juvenile, death due to.
Duty of person or institution to report, §7B-301.
Marriage by underage parties.
District court jurisdiction, §7B-200(a).
Marriage of juvenile, authority of guardian to consent, §7B-600(a).
Mediation program.
Permanency mediation, §7B-202.
Medical professionals, authority in abuse cases.
Retention of physical custody in medical facility, §7B-308(a), (f).
Medical, psychiatric or psychological examination, treatment or care, §7B-903.
Certification by physician, nonsecure custody order, cost of treatment, §7B-308(b), (d).
Consent by guardian, §7B-600(a).
Parent ordered to undergo psychiatric or psychological examination or treatment, §7B-904(c).
Participation of parent in juvenile treatment, §7B-904(b).
Payment of cost of treatment, §7B-904(a), (c).
Mental health evaluation of alleged abusers.
Assessment of report.
History of violent behavior, §7B-302(d1).
Mental health professional.
Opinion as to disposition considered by court.
Physical abuse suffered by juvenile, §7B-903(b).
Mental health records of alleged abuser, review.
When juvenile removed from home, §7B-503(b).
Mentally ill or developmentally disabled.
Disposition on finding by court, §7B-903(a).
Misdemeanor child abuse, §14-318.2(a).
Additional offense to other civil and criminal provisions, §14-318.2(b).

CHILD ABUSE, NEGLECT OR DEPENDENCY
—Cont'd

Misdemeanor child abuse —Cont'd
Exceptions, §14-318.2(c).

Missing child.
Assessment of report, request to investigate.
Abandonment alleged, §7B-302(a).

Modification or vacation of dispositional order.
After affirmation by appellate court, §7B-1004.
Authority of court, §7B-1000(a).
Continued jurisdiction of court after finding abuse, neglect or dependency, §7B-1000(b).

Motion for discovery, §7B-700(c).

Nature of proceeding.
Summons to contain notice, §7B-406(b).

Neglected juvenile defined, §7B-101.

Nonsecure custody hearing, §7B-506.

Nonsecure custody of juvenile.
Administrative order delegating authority, §7B-502.
Authority of court to place juvenile, §7B-502.
Burden at custody hearing on state, §7B-506(b).
Continuance of hearing, §7B-506(a).
Copy of order to parent, guardian, custodian or caretaker, §7B-504.
Criteria for ordering, §7B-503.
Criteria in determining whether to continue custody, §7B-506(c).
Delegation of authority to other than district court judges, §7B-502.
Evidence and testimony at custody hearing, §7B-506(b).
Execution of order in accordance with terms, §7B-504.
Factual basis for ordering, §7B-503(a).
Findings of fact, order to contain, §7B-506(d).
Hearing to determine need for continued custody, §7B-506.
Mental health professional performing evaluation of alleged abuser.
Considered in determining need for continued custody, §7B-506(c1).
Missing parent inquiries, §7B-506(h).
Order, §7B-504.
Order continuing custody, §7B-506(d).
Findings as reasonable efforts to prevent need for placement, §7B-507(a).
Paternity inquiries, §7B-506(h).
Placing juvenile, §7B-505.
Reasonable efforts to eliminate need for placement, §7B-507.
Reasonable factual basis required to place in nonsecure custody, §7B-503.
Relatives, inquiries of.
Providing proper care and supervision in safe home, §7B-506(h).
Relative willing and able to provide care, placement with, §7B-505.
Temporary placement, §7B-506(h).
Release of juvenile first consideration when request made, §7B-503.
Release of juvenile to parent, relative, etc.
Court's first consideration on request for nonsecure custody, §7B-503(a).
Remaining juveniles in home from which juvenile removed.
Inquiry, §7B-506(h).
Return on order, §7B-504.
Rules of evidence, inapplicability at hearing, §7B-506(b).

CHILD ABUSE, NEGLECT OR DEPENDENCY
—Cont'd

Nonsecure custody of juvenile —Cont'd
Secure custody, placement in prohibited, §7B-503.
Subsequent hearing, continued custody ordered, §7B-506(e).
Waiver, §7B-506(f).
Time for hearing, §7B-506(a).
Subsequent hearing where continued custody ordered, §7B-506(e).
Waiver of subsequent hearing, §7B-506(f).

North Carolina child fatality prevention system, §§7B-1400 to 7B-1414.
See CHILD FATALITY PREVENTION SYSTEM.

Notice.
Hearing to review placement.
Custody removed from parent, §7B-906(a).
Surrender of juvenile for adoption, agency placement plan, §7B-909(a).
Termination of parental rights, §7B-908(b).
Cancellation, placement for adoption prior to review, §7B-908(e).
Voluntary foster care placement, §7B-910(c).
Intention to change placement.
County department of social services with placement responsibility to give, §7B-905(d).
Juvenile taken into temporary custody, §7B-501(a).
Permanency planning hearing, §7B-907(a).
Person determined to be responsible individual.
Contents of notice, §7B-320(c).
Mail notice.
Time for giving, §7B-320(b).
Petition for judicial review, copy to be given, §7B-320(d).
Time for giving.
Mail notice, §7B-320(b).
Written notice, §7B-320(a).
Person making report.
Assessment of report.
Status of assessment, §7B-302(f), (g).
Prosecutor's review, §7B-305.
Results of assessment.
Notification to department or state bureau of investigation, §7B-307(c).
Retention of juvenile in medical facility, §7B-308(b).
Summons, notices contained in, §7B-406(b).

Nurse privilege.
Waiver in child abuse cases, §8-53.1(a), (b).

Obstruction of assessment of report, §7B-303.

Order for nonsecure custody.
Reasonable efforts to eliminate need for placement.
Findings required, §7B-507.

Parent and child.
Protection of minors.
Contributing to delinquency and neglect by parents and others, §14-316.1.

Parents' actions.
Disposition of juvenile.
Authority of court to direct, §7B-904(d1).

Parent's right to counsel and appointed counsel, §7B-602(a).
Provisional counsel.
Appointment, dismissal, confirmation of appointment, §7B-602(a).

Parole.
Satellite-based monitoring.
Sex offenders and offenses involving abuse of minors.
Mandatory conditions, §15A-1374(b1).

CHILD ABUSE, NEGLECT OR DEPENDENCY
  —Cont'd
Parties.
  Appeal of final order of court.
    Proper parties to appeal, §7B-1002.
Payment of court-appointed attorney or guardian ad litem, §7B-603(a) to (c).
Periodic review of placement of child.
  Custody removed from parent, §7B-906.
    Dispositional order to direct holding of hearing, §7B-905(b).
    Surrender of juvenile for adoption, agency plan, §7B-909.
  Termination of parental rights, §7B-909.
  Voluntary foster care placement, §7B-910.
Permanency mediation program.
  Agreement reached by parties.
    Writing required, submitted to court, incorporated in court order, enforcement, §7B-202(e).
  Establishment by administrative office of the courts, §7B-202(a).
    Local district programs, §7B-202(b).
  Participants in mediation, §7B-202(a).
  Private and confidential proceedings, §7B-202(c), (d).
  Privilege.
    Verbal or written communication of participants, §7B-202(c), (d).
  Purpose, §7B-202(a).
Permanency planning hearing.
  Authority of judge after making findings, §7B-907(c).
  Order, requirements, time for entering, §7B-907(c).
  Removal of custody from parent, §7B-907(a).
  Subsequent hearing.
    Order not timely filed, §7B-907(c).
  Time for hearing, §7B-507(c).
Petition.
  Alleging abuse, neglect or dependency.
    Amendment, §7B-800.
    Clerk's office closed.
      Magistrate drawing, verifying and issuing.
        Chief district court judge authorizing, §7B-404(a), (b).
    Commencement of action by filing, §7B-405.
    Contents and information required, §7B-402(a), (b).
    Copies, §7B-402(c).
    Emergency situations.
      Magistrate drawing, verifying and issuing.
        Chief district court judge authorizing, §7B-404(a), (b).
    Guardian ad litem office, provision of copy to, §7B-408.
    Medical treatment needed, nonsecure custody, §7B-308(b), (e).
    More than one juvenile from same home.
      Information on, §7B-402(a).
    Pleading in action by petition, §7B-401.
    Report filed as petition, §7B-403(a).
  Alleging interference with assessment, §7B-303(a).
  Filed in county other than county of juvenile's residence.
    Duty of petitioner, §7B-402(d).
  Surrender of juvenile for adoption, agency placement plan review, §7B-909(c).
Physician-patient privilege.
  Demand for information by guardian ad litem, §7B-601(c).

CHILD ABUSE, NEGLECT OR DEPENDENCY
  —Cont'd
Physician-patient privilege —Cont'd
  Waiver in child abuse cases, §8-53.1(a), (b).
Physicians.
  Reporting certain wounds, injuries and illnesses.
    Children under age of 18, §90-21.20(c1).
  Retention of physical custody of juvenile in medical facility, §7B-308(a), (f).
Placement of juvenile.
  Alternative dispositions, §7B-903(a).
  Appeal.
    Notice to preserve right to appeal.
      Permanency planning, §7B-507(c).
    Temporary order affecting custody or placement.
      Authority of trial court to enter pending disposition of appeal, §7B-1003(c).
  Bringing dependents into state for placement or adoption, §§7B-3700 to 7B-3705.
    See CHILD PLACEMENT.
  Change of placement by county department of social services.
    Notice of intention given guardian ad litem or attorney advocate, §7B-905(d).
  Nonsecure custody, §7B-505.
  Reasonable efforts to eliminate need for placement.
    Findings required in order, §7B-507(a).
    Health and safety of juvenile as primary concern in determination of need for reasonable efforts, §7B-507(d).
    Permanency planning hearing, §7B-507(c).
    When reasonable efforts not required, §7B-507(b).
  Review hearings.
    Custody removed from parent, §7B-906.
    Surrender of juvenile for adoption, agency plan for placement, §7B-909.
    Termination of parental rights, §7B-908.
    Voluntary foster care placement, §7B-910.
  Sending juvenile out of state for placement, §§7B-3702 to 7B-3705.
  Temporary order affecting custody or placement.
    Appeal of final order of court.
      Authority of trial court to enter pending disposition of appeal, §7B-1003(c).
Pleading is by petition, §7B-401.
Post-release condition.
  Required conditions.
    Offenses involving abuse of minors, §15A-1368.4(b1).
Predisposition investigation and report, §7B-808(a).
  Administrative orders, §7B-808(c).
  Preparation of report, §7B-808(b).
  Rulemaking, §7B-808(c).
Prehearing diversion.
  Director to consider when notified that juvenile in temporary custody, §7B-501(a).
Privileged communications.
  Communications between guardian ad litem and parent, §7B-602(d).
  Not grounds for failure to report or exclude evidence, §7B-310.
Probation.
  Persons convicted of physical, mental and sexual abuse of minor.
    Special conditions, §15A-1343.
Process is summons, §7B-401.

CHILD ABUSE, NEGLECT OR DEPENDENCY
—Cont'd
Program on prevention of abuse and neglect,
§§7B-1300 to 7B-1302.
Children's trust fund.
Deposit of contributions, grants or gifts
received, §7B-1301(c).
Establishment, §7B-1302.
Contracts to operate community-based educational
and service programs, §7B-1301(b).
Contributions, grants or gifts, assistance in
implementing article, §7B-1301(c).
Definition of abuse and neglect prevention
program, §7B-1301(d).
Implementation of program, §7B-1301(a).
Intent of programs contracted for under
provisions, §7B-1301(d).
Prevention as priority of state, purposes,
§7B-1300.
Purposes of provisions, §7B-1300.
Staff and support services for implementing,
§7B-1301(a).
State-level programs to coordinate
community-based programs, limit on funding,
§7B-1301(e).
Prosecutor's review of director's decision,
§7B-305.
**Prosecutor's review of director's decision not
to file report,** §7B-403(b).
Protective order.
Request by party served with motion for
discovery, §7B-700(d).
Protective services.
Assessment of report.
Director to provide, §7B-302(c).
Protective services for juveniles, §7B-300.
Psychologist-client or patient privilege.
Exception to privilege, §8-53.3.
Publication service of summons.
Parent, guardian, custodian or caretaker not
found, §7B-407.
Public schools.
Duty to report, §115C-400.
Purposes, §7B-100.
Reasonable efforts.
Defined, §7B-101.
Elimination of need for placement, §7B-507.
Prevention of need for placement, §7B-507(a).
Reasonable factual basis.
Placing juvenile in nonsecure custody, §7B-503.
Record of adjudicatory proceedings, §7B-806.
Records and social reports in cases generally,
§§7B-2900 to 7B-2902.
Abortion of unemancipated minor, proceeding
involving complaint.
Record or proceeding not public record,
maintained separately from juvenile record,
§7B-2901(d).
Child fatality or near fatality cases, disclosure.
Application for order compelling disclosure,
request denied, §7B-2902(e).
Child fatality prevention team records,
provisions governing disclosure,
§7B-2902(f).
Confidential records not authorized to be
disclosed, §7B-2902(c).
Criminal investigative reports and criminal
intelligence information, provisions
governing disclosure, §7B-2902(f).
Definition of public record not narrowed or
limited, §7B-2902(h).

CHILD ABUSE, NEGLECT OR DEPENDENCY
—Cont'd
Records and social reports in cases generally
—Cont'd
Child fatality or near fatality cases, disclosure
—Cont'd
Definitions, §7B-2902(a).
District attorney not required to disclose
information, §7B-2902(f).
Immunity of public agency or employees for
disclosing in good faith, §7B-2902(g).
Order compelling disclosure, request denied,
§7B-2902(e).
Providing findings and information upon
request, §7B-2902(d).
Request of public agency for disclosure,
§7B-2902(b).
Time for providing findings and information
upon request, §7B-2902(d).
Clerk to maintain complete set of records of
juvenile cases, §7B-2901(a).
Definitions, §7B-2900.
Director of social services to maintain records of
cases, §7B-2901(b).
Examination of records kept by director of social
services, §7B-2901(b).
Examination of records without court order.
Persons who may examine, §7B-2901(a).
Investigative records.
Law governing disclosure, §132-1.4(l).
Sharing of information among public agencies in
case of child victim, §7B-2901(c).
Transcript, record reduced to only when notice of
appeal timely given, §7B-2901(a).
Referral of report to director for screening,
§7B-403(a).
Rehabilitative treatment.
Defendant may pay cost as condition of probation,
§15A-1343(b1).
Reintegration of juvenile into parent's home.
Termination of guardian relationship, §7B-600(b).
Relative willing and able to provide care.
Placing juvenile with, §7B-505.
**Release of juvenile taken into temporary
custody,** §7B-501(a).
Removal of custody from parents.
Periodic review hearing as to placement, §7B-906.
Removal of juvenile.
Assessment of report.
Immediate removal necessary, §7B-302(d).
Background check of alleged abuser.
Juvenile removed from home, §7B-302(d1).
Determination by director, §7B-302(c).
Nonsecure custody request.
Review of background of alleged abuser or
abusers, §7B-503(b).
Review of background of alleged abuser or
abusers, §7B-503(b).
**Report by director on finding evidence of
abuse or neglect,** §7B-307(a), (b).
Report by physician.
Children under age of 18.
Reporting certain wounds, injuries and
illnesses, §90-21.20(c1).
**Reporting abuse, neglect, dependency or death
due to maltreatment.**
Assessment of report, §7B-302.
Interference with, §7B-303.
Duty of person or institution with cause to
suspect, §7B-301.

CHILD ABUSE, NEGLECT OR DEPENDENCY
—Cont'd
Reporting abuse, neglect, dependency or death due to maltreatment —Cont'd
Identity of reporter.
Confidentiality, §7B-302(a).
Disclosure.
Hearing on interference or obstruction of assessment, §7B-303(e).
Immunity of persons making reports, §7B-309.
Information to be included in report, §7B-301.
Juvenile court counselors.
Duty to report, §7B-1700.1.
Privilege not grounds for failure to report, §7B-310.
School personnel to report child abuse, §115C-400.
Responsible individual defined, §7B-101.
Responsible individuals list, §7B-311.
Judicial review, §§7B-320 to 7B-324.
Results of assessment, notice by director, §7B-307(c).
Retention of jurisdiction by district court.
Jurisdiction to continue until terminated by court or emancipation of juvenile, §7B-201(a).
Retention of physical custody of juvenile in medical facility.
Authority of medical professionals in abuse cases, §7B-308(a), (f).
Return on order for nonsecure custody, §7B-504.
Request for review, §7B-305.
Review by district court of determination.
At any time, §7B-323(e).
Review hearings, placement of juvenile.
Custody removed from parent, §7B-906.
Dispositional order to direct holding of hearing, §7B-905(b).
Surrender of juvenile for adoption, agency plan, §7B-909.
Termination of parental rights, §7B-908.
Voluntary foster care placement, §7B-910.
Review of director's decision by prosecutor, §§7B-305, 7B-403(b).
Request by reporter, §7B-305.
Review of final order of court, §§7B-1001 to 7B-1004.
Right to counsel.
Parent's right to counsel and appointment of counsel, §7B-602(a).
Summons to contain notice, §7B-406(b).
Rules of evidence.
Applicable during adjudicatory hearing, §7B-804.
Dispositional hearings, §7B-901.
Permanency planning hearings, §7B-907(b).
Placement review, parental rights terminated, §7B-908(a).
Review hearings, §7B-906(c).
Safe haven for infants, §§14-318.2, 14-318.4.
Satellite-based monitoring.
Parole.
Sex offenders and offenses involving abuse of minors.
Mandatory conditions, §15A-1374(b1).
Post-release.
Required conditions.
Offenses involving abuse of minors, §15A-1368.4(b1).
Probation of persons convicted of abuse of minors.
Special conditions, §15A-1343(b2).
School enrollment, authority of guardian to consent, §7B-600(a).

CHILD ABUSE, NEGLECT OR DEPENDENCY
—Cont'd
Screening of report by director of social services, §7B-403(a).
Secure custody of juvenile prohibited, §7B-503.
Sending dependent out of state for placement, §§7B-3702 to 7B-3705.
Service of summons, §7B-407.
Interference or obstruction of assessment of report, §7B-303(c).
Process in action by summons, §7B-401.
Summons delivered to person authorized to serve process, §7B-406(d).
Summons directed to person summoned to appear, §7B-406(d).
Sexual abuse in child care facility.
Notice of results of assessment and report to state bureau of investigation, §7B-307(b), (c).
Notification to state bureau of investigation upon receipt of report, §7B-301.
Sharing information.
Departments of social services, §7B-700(a).
Guardian ad litem's records and reports, §7B-700(f).
Local rules.
Chief district court judge may adopt, §7B-700(b).
Redisclosure prohibited by state or federal law, §7B-700(e).
Shelter care.
Defined, §7B-101.
Show cause orders.
Contempt.
Failure of parent to comply with dispositional order, §7B-904(e).
Social services workers.
Taking juvenile into temporary custody.
Authority, §7B-500(a).
Duties upon taking juvenile into temporary custody, §7B-501(a).
State bureau of investigation.
Sexual abuse in child care facility.
Investigation, §7B-307(b), (c).
Formation of task force to investigate report, §7B-301.
Summons.
Contempt on failure to comply with order, summons to advise parent, §7B-406(c).
Delivered to person authorized to serve process, §7B-406(d).
Directed to person summoned to appear, §7B-406(d).
Form and contents, §7B-404(b).
Issuance, §7B-406(a).
Jurisdiction over parent obtained upon service, summons to advise, §7B-406(c).
Process in action by summons, §7B-401.
Service, §7B-407.
Supervision of juvenile in own home, §7B-903(a).
Support of juvenile, payment by parent.
Legal custody vested in someone other than parent, §7B-904(d).
Suspicion that juvenile abused, neglected or dependent.
Duty of person or institution to report, §7B-301.
Telephone communication authorized.
Temporary or nonsecure custody matters, §7B-508.
Temporary custody of juvenile without court order.
Authority of law enforcement officer or social services worker, §7B-500(a).

CHILD ABUSE, NEGLECT OR DEPENDENCY
—Cont'd
Temporary custody of juvenile without court order —Cont'd
Communication with director of social services, §7B-501(a).
Duties of person taking into temporary custody, §7B-501(a).
Notice to parent, guardian, custodian or caretaker, §7B-501(a).
Release to parent, guardian, custodian or caretaker.
Decision that continued custody unnecessary, §7B-501(a).
Right to be present with juvenile, parent, guardian, etc., to be advised, §7B-501(a).
Temporary custody defined, §7B-500(a).
Time limit on holding in temporary custody, §7B-501(b).
Termination of district court jurisdiction.
Affect, modification or enforcement of previous orders, prohibition, §7B-201(b).
Termination of guardian relationship, reintegration of juvenile into parent's home, §7B-600(b).
Termination of parental rights.
Generally, §§7B-1100 to 7B-1114.
See TERMINATION OF PARENTAL RIGHTS.
Grounds for terminating, §7B-1111(a).
Mediation program.
Permanency mediation, §7B-202.
Pending abuse, neglect or dependency proceeding.
Consolidation, petition filed during pending proceeding, §7B-1102(c).
Copy of motion and notice sent to attorney for parent, §7B-1102(b1).
Motion filed during, service, §7B-1102(a), (b).
Periodic review hearing as to placement, §7B-908.
Permanency mediation, §7B-202.
Time.
Hearing on nonsecure custody, §7B-506(a).
Holding juvenile in temporary custody, §7B-501(b).
Holding review hearing as to placement.
Custody removed from parent, §7B-906(a).
Surrender of juvenile for adoption, agency plan, §7B-909(a).
Termination of parental rights, §7B-908(b).
Voluntary foster care placement, §7B-909(c).
Service of summons, §7B-407.
Transcript.
Reducing record to transcript upon notice of appeal, §§7B-806, 7B-2901(a).
Transfer of juvenile to department of social services in county of residence, §7B-308(c).
Transferring case to another county.
After adjudication.
Agreement between directors of departments of social services.
Required before ordering transfer, §7B-900.1(b).
Authorized, §7B-900.1(a).
Clerk's duties upon receiving transferred case, §7B-900.1(g).
Copy of complete record of case.
Transfer to court in county to which case transferred, time, §7B-900.1(g).
Custody of juvenile transferred, §7B-900.1(c).
Factors considered before entering order, §7B-900.1(e).
Grounds, §7B-900.1(a).

CHILD ABUSE, NEGLECT OR DEPENDENCY
—Cont'd
Transferring case to another county —Cont'd
After adjudication —Cont'd
Joinder or substitution as party.
Director of social services in county to which case transferred, §7B-900.1(c).
Notice and opportunity to be heard, waiver.
Director of social services in county to which case transferred, §7B-900.1(c).
Objection by judge in district to which case transferred, §7B-900.1(d).
Order transferring, requirements, §7B-900.1(f).
Venue for proceeding, §7B-400.
Post adjudication venue.
Transferring venue to another county, §7B-900.1.
Violent behavior of person responsible for abuse, history of.
Mental health professional's opinion considered, §7B-903(b).
Visitation.
Removal of custody from parent, supervision by department of social services, §7B-906(d).
Visit to juvenile's residence.
Assessment of report.
Assessment to include, §7B-302(a).
Waiver of time for service, §7B-407.

CHILD BICYCLE SAFETY ACT, §§20-171.6 to 20-171.9.

CHILD BORN OUT OF WEDLOCK.
Adoption generally.
See ADOPTION.
Paternity.
Proceedings to establish.
See PATERNITY.
Support of illegitimate children, legitimation of illegitimate children, civil actions regarding, §§49-1 to 49-17.
See CHILDREN BORN OUT OF WEDLOCK.

CHILD CARE ADMINISTRATORS.
Qualifications, §110-91.

CHILD CARE CENTERS.
Child care facilities generally, §§110-85 to 110-107.
See CHILD CARE FACILITIES.
Defined, §110-86.
Mandatory standards for licensing, §110-91.
Sex offenders.
Residential restrictions generally, §14-208.16.
Unlawful presence on premises, §14-208.18.
Staff-child ratio, §110-91.

CHILD CARE COMMISSION, §143B-168.3(a).
Appointment of members, §143B-168.4(b).
Child abuse or neglect.
Investigation of reports and administrative action.
Commission to make rules for, §143B-168.5.
Clerical and other services, §143B-168.4(c).
Expenses, §143B-168.4(c).
Meetings, §143B-168.4(c).
Membership, §143B-168.4(a).
Officers, §143B-168.4(c).
Powers and duties, §110-88.
Religious training offered in religious-sponsored child care facilities.
Commission not to interfere with, §110-88.1.
Rules, adoption, §143B-168.3(a1), (b).
Vacancies, §143B-168.4(c).

CHILD CARE FACILITIES.
Administrative penalty, §110-102.2.
Administrative procedure.
Applicability of act, §110-94.
Administrators.
Certification of education, §110-91.
Qualifications, §110-91.
Alcohol abusers.
Persons not to be employed, §110-91.
Announced and unannounced visits,
§110-105(a).
Building standards, §110-91.
Child abuse and neglect.
Administrative action, sanctions.
Rules, adoption by commission, §110-88.
Child abuse and neglect defined, §110-105.2(a).
Child care commission.
Investigation of reports and administrative
actions, §143B-168.5.
Corrective action, §110-105.2(d).
Investigation of child sexual abuse in child care
facilities, §114-15.3.
Notice by director to department of health and
human services and state bureau of
investigation.
Finding evidence of abuse or neglect or sexual
abuse in facility, §7B-307(b).
Protective services provided juveniles alleged to be
abused, neglected or dependent.
Applicability of provisions to child care
facilities, §7B-300.
Special provisional status, §110-105.2(c).
Special unit within department of health and
human services.
Established to deal primarily with violations
involving, §143B-168.5.
Unannounced visit after issuance of written
warning, §110-105.2(b).
Use of other statutory or administrative remedies,
§110-105.2(e).
Violations, §110-105.2.
Written warning issued, §110-105.2(b).
Child abuse or neglect convictions.
Persons not to be employed, §110-91.
**Child care arrangement not meeting definition
of child care facility.**
Issuance of license to, §110-90.
Child care defined, §110-86.
Child care licensing commission.
Transfer, recodification and renaming as child
care commission, §143B-168.3.
Child care provider criminal history checks,
§114-19.5.
Civil action by child care provider on
disagreement with department decision,
§110-90.2(d).
Cost of fingerprinting and local check,
§110-90.2(g).
Definitions, §110-90.2(a).
Department of justice to provide criminal history,
§110-90.2(c).
Duties of department of health and human
services, §110-90.2(b).
Duties of division of child placement, department
of health and human services, §110-90.2(c).
Immunity from liability, §110-90.2(f).
Notice to child care provider and employer as to
qualifications to provide child care,
§110-90.2(d).
Privileged information, §110-90.2(e).

CHILD CARE FACILITIES —Cont'd
Child care provider criminal history checks
—Cont'd
Providers of treatment for or services to children,
§114-19.3.
Statement as to criminal history check,
§110-90.2(c).
Civil penalty, §110-103.1(a).
Determining amount, §110-103.1(b).
Notice of penalty, §110-103.1(c).
Remittance of proceeds, §110-103.1(d).
Communicable diseases.
Report by child care operators, §130A-136.
Compliance with provisions.
Mandatory compliance, §110-98.
**Contracts with state agencies and local boards
of education.**
Authorization to contract, §143-64.50.
Financial and legal responsibility assumed by
operators, §143-64.52.
Licensing and regulating, §143-64.51.
Procedure for approving location, §143-64.50.
Control over facilities.
Abrogation of regulations of institution, §110-46.
Authority of institution as same as parent or
guardian, §110-45.
Enticing a child from institution, §110-47.
Exception, §110-47.
Guardian.
Institution has authority of guardian, §110-45.
Institution has authority of parent or guardian,
§110-45.
Misdemeanors.
Violations a misdemeanor, §110-48.
Parent.
Institution has authority of parent, §110-45.
Rules and regulations.
Abrogation of regulations, §110-46.
Violations a misdemeanor, §110-48.
**Conviction of crime involving child neglect,
child abuse or moral turpitude.**
Persons not to be employed, §110-91.
Corporal punishment.
Banned in certain nonlicensed homes, §110-101.1.
Prohibited, §110-91.
Criminal history record checks, §§110-90.2,
114-19.3, 114-19.5. See within this heading,
"Child care provider criminal history checks."
Criminal penalties, §110-103.
Exemptions, §110-103(a).
Felonies.
Subsequent offenses, §110-103(d).
Violation causing serious injury to a child,
§110-103(c).
Willful violations, §110-103(b).
Misdemeanors, §110-103(a).
Unauthorized administration of medicine,
§110-102.1A(c), (d).
Willful violations, §110-103(b).
Death of child while in child care.
Reporting, §110-102.1(b).
Definitions, §110-86.
Department of health and human services.
Special unit.
Child abuse and neglect in child care
arrangements.
Established to deal primarily with violations
involving, §143B-168.5.
**Developmentally appropriate activities and
play materials,** §110-91.
Development of staff requirements, §110-91.

CHILD CARE FACILITIES —Cont'd
Disciplinary policy, §110-91.
Diseases.
  Communicable diseases.
    Report by operators of child care facility, §130A-136.
Drop-in or short-term child care.
  Notice to department, §110-99(b).
Drug abusers.
  Persons not to be employed, §110-91.
Drugs.
  Unauthorized administration of medicine, §110-102.1A.
Duties of local and district health departments, §110-92.
Early childhood administration credential.
  Requirement for center administrators, §110-91.
Education of children with disabilities.
  Cost of educating children in group homes, §115C-111.3.
Equipment requirements, §110-91.
Existence of child care.
  Prima facie evidence, §110-98.1.
Family child care home capacity, §110-91.
Fire prevention and safe evacuation standards, §110-91.
Fire prevention inspection, §110-92.
Food and beverage standards, §110-91.
Fraud.
  Fraudulent misrepresentation, §110-107(a), (b).
  Definitions, §110-107(c).
Furnishings requirements, §110-91.
General assembly.
  Legislative intent, §110-85.
Group sizes for infants and toddlers, §110-91.
Health assessments, §110-91.
Immunization certificate.
  Maintenance of record, §130A-155(b).
  Report to be filed, §130A-155(c).
  Submission of certificate to child care facility, §130A-155(a).
Information for parents, guardians or full-time custodians, §110-102.
Injunctive relief, §110-104.
Inspections.
  Fire departments, §110-91.
  Refusal to allow.
    Administrative warrant, §110-105(b).
  Standards and rules for, §110-105(a).
Kaitlyn's law.
  Unauthorized administration of medicine, §110-102.1A.
Lead poisoning in children.
  Generally, §§130A-131.5 to 130A-131.9H.
    See LEAD POISONING IN CHILDREN.
Legislative intent, §110-85.
Licenses.
  Applications, §110-93(a).
  Child care arrangement not meeting definition of child care facility.
    Issuance of license to, §110-90.
  Compliance history.
    Requirement, §110-90.
  Denial.
    Authority of secretary, §110-90.
  Display, §110-99(a1).
  Fees, §110-90.
  Initial licensing inspection, §110-105(a).
  Issuance, §110-93(b).
  Mandatory standards, §110-91.

CHILD CARE FACILITIES —Cont'd
Licenses —Cont'd
  Provisional licenses.
    Rules for issuance, adoption by commission, §110-88.
  Rating, §110-90.
  Required, §110-99(a).
  Revocation.
    Authority of secretary, §110-90.
  Temporary licenses.
    Issuance, rules, adoption by commission, §110-88.
Location of facility.
  Standards, §110-91.
Mandatory child care provider criminal history checks, §110-90.2.
Mandatory compliance with provisions, §110-98.
Mandatory standards for license, §110-91.
Medical care procedures, §110-91.
  Unauthorized administration of medicine, §110-102.1A.
Medicine, administration, §110-102.1A.
  Applicability, §110-102.1A(a).
  Emergency medical condition, §110-102.1A(b).
  Exceptions.
    Bona fide medical care provider, §110-102.1A(b).
  Penalty, §110-102.1A(c).
  Written authorization required, §110-102.1A(a).
Missing children.
  Reporting, §110-102.1(a).
Notice of compliance.
  Compliance history requirement maintain, §110-90.
Nutrition standards, §110-91.
Out-of-doors activities, §110-91.
Powers and duties of secretary of health, §110-90.
Powers of child care commission, §110-88.
Prima facie evidence of existence of child care facility, §110-98.1.
Public schools.
  Education of children with disabilities.
    Cost of educating children in group homes, §115C-111.3.
Purpose of article, §110-85.
Qualifications for staff, §110-91.
Rated licenses, §110-90.
Recordkeeping requirements, §110-91.
Records.
  Immunization.
    Certificate of immunization.
      Maintenance of record, §130A-155(b).
Religious sponsored child care facilities.
  Conviction of crime involving child neglect, child abuse or moral turpitude, §110-106(d).
  Corporal punishment banned in certain nonlicensed homes.
    Exemptions from provisions, §110-101.1.
  Defined, §110-106(a).
  Exemption from certain provisions, §110-106(c).
  Procedure, §110-106(b).
  Staff requirements, §110-106(e).
Reporting of missing or deceased children, §110-102.1.
Reports.
  Communicable diseases, §130A-136.
  Immunization.
    Certificate of immunization.
      Report to be filed, §130A-155(c).
Rest periods for children, §110-91.

CHILD CARE FACILITIES —Cont'd

Restraint employed by residential facility.
Collection of data on use, §131D-10.5A.

Rules.
Adoption by commission, §110-88.

Safe sleep policy, §110-91.

Sale of merchandise by governmental units.
Exception to child care facilities receiving state aid, §66-58(b).

Sanitation standards, §110-91.

Secretary of health and human services.
Powers and duties, §110-90.

Sex offenders.
Residential restrictions generally, §14-208.16.
Unlawful presence on premises, §14-208.18.

Sexual abuse in facilities.
Investigation by bureau of investigation, §114-15.3.

SIDS prevention.
Safe sleep policy, §110-91.

Smoking in public places.
No smoking except in teacher's lounge, §143-599.

Space requirements, §110-91.

Special education.
Education of children with disabilities.
Cost of educating children in group homes, §115C-111.3.

Staff-child ratio, §110-91.

Staff development standards, §110-91.

Staff qualifications, §110-91.

Standards for license, §110-91.

Summary of provisions for parents, guardian, etc., §110-102.

Supervision of children, §110-91.

Transportation, §110-91.

Visitation and inspection of child care centers, §110-92.

Visual supervision of children, §110-91.

CHILD CARE SERVICES IN STATE BUILDINGS AND PUBLIC SCHOOLS, §§143-64.50 to 143-64.52.

Authorization to contract with city, county or other political subdivision, etc., §143-64.50.

Financial and legal responsibility assumed by operators, §143-64.52.

Licensing and regulating, §143-64.51.

Location of program, procedure for approving, §143-64.50.

CHILD CUSTODY.

Abused, neglected or dependent juvenile.
Alternative dispositions, §7B-903(a).
Civil child-custody order, §7B-911.
Nonsecure custody, §§7B-502 to 7B-508.
Periodic review hearings, placement of juvenile.
Custody removed from parent, §7B-906.
Surrender of child for adoption, §7B-909.
Termination of parental rights, §7B-908.
Voluntary foster care agreement, §7B-910.
Support of juvenile paid by parent.
Custody in someone other than parent, §7B-904(d).
Suspected abused juvenile brought to medical facility.
Physician or administrator obtaining judicial authority to retain custody, §7B-308.
Temporary custody without court order, §§7B-500(a), 7B-501.
Temporary order affecting custody or placement.
Appeal of final order of court.
Authority of trial court to enter pending disposition of appeal, §7B-1003(c).

CHILD CUSTODY —Cont'd

Accident and health insurance.
Coverage of children, §58-51-120(b).

Action or proceeding for custody or visitation generally, §50-13.1.

Adoption.
Failure to consent, §50-13.2(d).
Visitation of adopted grandchild.
Action by biological grandparent, §50-13.2A.

Arbitration.
Family law arbitration generally, §§50-41 to 50-62.
See FAMILY LAW ARBITRATION.

Attorneys' fees, §50-13.6.

Attorneys specializing in family law.
Certification standards, Bar Rules D.2401 to D.2407.

Best interest and welfare of child.
Persons entitled to custody, §50-13.2(a).

Change in circumstances.
Modification of order, §50-13.7.
Family law arbitration act, §50-56.

Civil child-custody order.
Juvenile proceeding, §7B-911.

Confidentiality.
Mediation, §50-13.1(e).

Contempt.
Enforcement of orders, §50-13.3(a).

Contracts.
Mediation program.
Exemption from competitive bidding contracts, §7A-494(b).

Costs.
Allowance of costs to either party or apportioned in discretion of court, §6-21.

Delinquent and undisciplined juvenile actions.
Authority to issue orders, delegation of authority, §7B-1902.
Secure or nonsecure custody, §§7B-1903 to 7B-1906.
Telephone communications, notices, etc., §7B-1907.
Temporary custody without court order, §§7B-1900, 7B-1901.

Disabled persons.
Persons incapable of self-support upon reaching majority.
Rights same as minor child for custody purposes, §50-13.8.

Dismissal on prejudicial grounds, §50-13.1(d).

District courts.
Proper division for trial of civil actions, §7A-244.

Divorce.
Action or proceeding for custody or visitation, §50-13.1.
Enforcement of order, §50-13.3.
Grandparents' visitation, §50-13.2(b1).
Adopted grandchild.
Action by biological grandparent, §50-13.2A.
Independent actions permissible, §50-19.
Judgment provisions pertaining to custody, §50-11.2.
Change in conditions.
Jurisdiction requirements, §50-11.2.
Modification upon substantial change, §50-11.2.
Mediation program, §§7A-494, 7A-495.
Modification of orders, §50-13.7.
Persons entitled, §50-13.2(a), (b).
Persons incapable of self-support upon reaching majority, §50-13.8.

CHILD CUSTODY —Cont'd
Divorce —Cont'd
Taking child outside state, §50-13.2(c).
Domestic violence.
Award of temporary custody, §§50B-2(c1), (c2), 50B-3(a), (a1).
Emergency relief ex parte orders, §50B-2(c), (c1), (c2).
Electronic communication.
Court may set guidelines, §50-13.2(e).
Emancipation.
Persons incapable of self-support upon reaching majority.
Rights same as minor child for custody purposes, §50-13.8.
Enforcement.
Uniform child custody jurisdiction and enforcement, §§50A-101 to 50A-317.
See CHILD CUSTODY JURISDICTION AND ENFORCEMENT.
Enforcement of custody orders, §50-13.3.
Contempt, §50-13.3(a).
Injunctions, §50-13.3(b).
Pending appeals.
Enforcement by civil contempt proceedings, §50-13.3(a).
Exclusive custody, §50-13.2(b).
Family law arbitration generally, §§50-41 to 50-62.
See FAMILY LAW ARBITRATION.
General requirements for orders, §50-13.2.
Modification of order.
Change of circumstances, §50-13.7(a).
Orders entered by court of another state, §50-13.7(b).
Grandparents.
Custody and visitation rights, §50-13.5(j).
Grandparent defined, §50-13.5(j).
Visitation, §50-13.2(b1).
Adopted grandchild.
Action by biological grandparent, §50-13.2A.
Health insurance.
Coverage of children, §58-51-120(b).
Hearings by judge, §50-13.5(h).
High-conflict case.
Defined, §50-90.
Independent actions for divorce.
Maintenance of certain actions as independent actions permissible, §50-19.
Injunctions.
Enforcement of custody orders, §50-13.3(b).
Institution of action or proceeding.
Persons who may institute, §50-13.1(a).
Interlocutory orders, §50-13.5(d).
Joint custody, §50-13.2(a), (b).
Jurisdiction.
Action or proceeding for custody or visitation, §50-13.5(c).
Costs.
Allowance of costs to either party or apportioned in discretion of court, §6-21.
Uniform child custody jurisdiction and enforcement, §§50A-101 to 50A-317.
See CHILD CUSTODY JURISDICTION AND ENFORCEMENT.
Kidnapping.
Abduction of child, §14-41(a).
Bail, §15A-534.4.
Transporting child outside state.
Intent to violate custody order, §14-320.1.

CHILD CUSTODY —Cont'd
Mediation, §50-13.1(b).
Advisory committee.
Established, §7A-495(b).
Agreements.
Effect of reference as parenting agreement, §50-13.1(h).
Requirements, §50-13.1(g).
Competency to testify to communications, §50-13.1(f).
Confidentiality, §50-13.1(e).
Contracts.
Exemption from competitive bidding requirements, §7A-494(b).
Dismissal, §50-13.1(d).
Establishment of program.
Administrative office of courts to establish, §7A-494(a).
Local district programs.
Establishment, §7A-494(b).
Implementation and administration, §7A-495(a).
Orders.
Incorporation of agreements, §50-13.1(g).
Parenting agreement deemed order, §50-13.1(h).
Prejudice.
Dismissal, §50-13.1(e).
Privileged communications.
Communications with mediator, §50-13.1(e).
Purposes, §§7A-494(a), 50-13.1(b).
Qualifications to provide mediation services, §7A-494(c).
Rules for custody and visitation mediation.
Administration of program, CustodyVisit Rule 4.
Attendance at mediation session, CustodyVisit Rule 10.
Best interest of child.
Mediator to be aware of, CustodyVisit Rule 11.
Caucus with parties, CustodyVisit Rule 12.09.
Complaints about mediators or program, CustodyVisit Rule 12.11.
Confidentiality of mediation, CustodyVisit Rule 12.03.
Continuing education.
Mediators, CustodyVisit Rule 6.02.
Custody mediation advisory committee, CustodyVisit Rule 4.05.
Definitions.
Mediation, CustodyVisit Rule 3.01.
Mediator, CustodyVisit Rule 3.02.
Parenting agreement, CustodyVisit Rule 3.03.
Delinquents, placement issues.
Referral to mediation, CustodyVisit Rule 7.02.
Dismissal of mediation, CustodyVisit Rule 12.06.
Evaluation of program, CustodyVisit Rule 12.10.
Funds appropriated by general assembly.
Administration, CustodyVisit Rule 4.03.
Goals of mediation, CustodyVisit Rule 1.
Juvenile placement issues.
Referral, CustodyVisit Rule 7.02.
Length of mediation session, CustodyVisit Rule 10.
Local district programs, CustodyVisit Rule 5.
Location of mediation, CustodyVisit Rule 12.02.
Mandatory referral procedure, CustodyVisit Rule 7.01.
Mediators.
Authority, CustodyVisit Rule 12.01.
Best interest of child.
Mediator to be aware of, CustodyVisit Rule 11.

CHILD CUSTODY —Cont'd
Mediation —Cont'd
Rules for custody and visitation mediation
—Cont'd
Mediators —Cont'd
Caucus with parties, CustodyVisit Rule 12.09.
Complaints about, CustodyVisit Rule 12.11.
Continuing education, CustodyVisit Rule 6.02.
Defined, CustodyVisit Rule 3.02.
Duties in mediation process, CustodyVisit
Rule 12.
Employment, CustodyVisit Rule 4.01.
Ethics, CustodyVisit Rule 6.04.
In-house contracts for delivery of services,
CustodyVisit Rule 4.02.
Initial training period, CustodyVisit Rule
6.01.
Neutral stance, CustodyVisit Rule 11.
Performance evaluation, CustodyVisit Rule
6.03.
Qualification, CustodyVisit Rule 6.
Speaking with child, CustodyVisit Rule 12.08.
Multi-district programs, CustodyVisit Rule 4.04.
Number of mediation sessions, CustodyVisit
Rule 10.
Order to mediation, CustodyVisit Rule 7.01.
Orientation session.
Prior to mediation, CustodyVisit Rule 9.
Parenting plan, CustodyVisit Rule 12.04.
Defined, CustodyVisit Rule 3.03.
Incorporation into court order, CustodyVisit
Rule 12.05.
Performance evaluation.
Mediators, CustodyVisit Rule 6.03.
Placement of juveniles.
Referral of placement issues, CustodyVisit
Rule 7.02.
Process of mediation, CustodyVisit Rule 12.
Purpose of program, CustodyVisit Rule 2.
Referral of placement issues, CustodyVisit Rule
7.02.
Referral to mediation, CustodyVisit Rule 7.01.
Return to mediation.
Unable to resolve problems, change in
circumstances, CustodyVisit Rule 12.07.
Termination of mediation, CustodyVisit Rule
12.06.
Undisciplined juveniles, placement issues.
Referral to mediation, CustodyVisit Rule 7.02.
Waiver of mediation, CustodyVisit Rule 8.
Staff support, §7A-494(a).
Stay of action when child is subject of certain
other proceedings, §50-13.1(i).
Waiver of mandatory setting.
Good cause, §50-13.1(c).
**Mental health, developmental disabilities and
substance abuse.**
Persons incapable of self-support upon reaching
majority.
Rights same as minor child for custody
purposes, §50-13.8.
**Military personnel on temporary duty or
deployment.**
Best interest of the child prevails, §50-13.7A(g).
Definitions, §50-13.7A(b).
Electronic testimony and communication,
§50-13.7A(f).
Expedited hearings, §50-13.7A(e).
Parent with custody, §50-13.7A(c).
Parent with visitation rights, §50-13.7A(d).
Purpose of provisions, §50-13.7A(a).

CHILD CUSTODY —Cont'd
**Military personnel on temporary duty or
deployment** —Cont'd
Temporary order during parent's absence,
§50-13.7A(c).
Modification of order, §50-13.7.
Family law arbitration act, §50-56.
Motions.
Modification of orders, §50-13.7.
Notice, §50-13.5(d).
Notice.
Motions, §50-13.5(d).
Parenting coordinators, §§50-90 to 50-100.
Appointment.
Issues to be resolved, determination of scope,
§50-91(c).
Limitation of authority of coordinator, §50-91(a),
(b).
Order appointing, requirements, §50-91(c).
Selection of coordinator, §50-91(d).
When court may appoint, §50-91(a), (b).
Appointment conference.
Determined at conference, §50-90(b).
Documents required to bring, §50-90(c).
Required attendance, §50-90(a).
Authority.
Limited to certain matters, §50-92(a).
Exceptions authorized by court, §50-92(b).
Prohibited services, §50-92(c).
Review of decisions of coordinator, §50-92(b).
Definitions, §50-90.
Fees.
Disputes, request for hearing, §50-95(a).
Permissible compensation, §50-95(a).
Services contingent upon payment, §50-95(b).
Immunity, §50-100.
Meetings and communications, §50-96.
Modification or termination of appointment.
Good cause, §50-99(a).
Terms of agreement, §50-99(b).
Qualifications.
Continuing education requirements, §50-93(b).
Inclusion on list, §50-93(a).
Records.
Maintained, required, §50-98(b).
Provided to attorneys, required, §50-98(a).
Reports.
Consent orders for fundamental changes,
§50-97(c).
Notification required for certain determinations,
§50-97(a).
Hearing and review to follow, §50-97(b).
Parents' rights inter parties.
Award regardless of, §50-13.5(g).
Paternity established, §49-15.
Persons entitled to custody, §50-13.2(a).
**Preliminary injunction enjoining spouse from
interfering with, threatening or molesting
plaintiff during pendency of suit.**
Bonds not required, §1A-1 Rule 65(c).
Privileged communications.
Mediation.
Communications with mediator, §50-13.1(e).
Procedure, §50-13.5(a).
Rape.
Child born as result of commission of rape.
Child victim of rape, §14-27.2A(d).
Effect of conviction.
First degree rape, §14-27.2(c).
Second degree rape, §14-27.3(c).

CHILD CUSTODY —Cont'd
Records.
　Health, education and welfare records of child.
　　Equal access, §50-13.2(b).
Service of process.
　Action or proceeding for custody or visitation,
　　§50-13.5(d).
**Sex offender instituting proceedings for
　custody.**
　Disclosure of conviction in pleadings, §50-13.1(a).
Taking child outside of state.
　Orders providing for, §50-13.2(c).
Temporary orders pending service and notice,
　§50-13.5(d).
**Temporary restraining order enjoining spouse
　from interfering with, threatening or
　molesting plaintiff during pendency of
　suit.**
　Bond not required, §1A-1 Rule 65(c).
Termination of parental rights proceedings.
　Finding as to jurisdiction.
　　Court to make before exercising jurisdiction,
　　　§7B-1101.
Transporting child outside state.
　Intent to violate custody order, §14-320.1.
Type of actions, §50-13.5(b).
**Uniform child custody jurisdiction and
　enforcement,** §§50A-101 to 50A-317.
　See CHILD CUSTODY JURISDICTION AND
　　ENFORCEMENT.
Venue.
　Action or proceeding for custody or visitation,
　　§50-13.5(f).
Visitation.
　Abused, neglected or dependent juvenile.
　　Custody removed from parent, §7B-906(d).
　Action or proceeding for custody or visitation
　　generally, §50-13.1.
　Attorneys' fees, §50-13.6.
　Denial of parental visitation rights.
　　Written findings of fact, §50-13.5(i).
　Electronic communication.
　　Use to supplement child visitation, §50-13.2(e).
　Grandparents, §50-13.2(b1).
　　Adopted grandchild.
　　　Action by biological grandparent, §50-13.2A.
　　Custody and visitation rights, §50-13.5(j).
　Mediation.
　　Custody and visitation mediation program,
　　　§§7A-494, 7A-495.
Waiver.
　Action or proceeding for custody or visitation.
　　Mediation, §50-13.1(c).
Who may institute action or proceeding,
　§50-13.1(a).

**CHILD CUSTODY JURISDICTION AND
　ENFORCEMENT,** §§50A-101 to 50A-317.
Adoption.
　Application of provisions, §50A-103.
Appeals, §50A-314.
Appearances, §50A-210.
　Expenses, §50A-210(d).
　Limited immunity, §50A-109(a).
　　Exceptions, §50A-109(b), (c).
　Notice, §50A-210(b).
　Orders, §50A-210(a), (c).
Application of provisions, §50A-103.
　Indian tribes, §50A-104.
　International application, §50A-105.
　Notice, §50A-205(b).

**CHILD CUSTODY JURISDICTION AND
　ENFORCEMENT** —Cont'd
Communication between courts, §50A-110.
　Notice, §50A-110(c).
　Participation of parties, §50A-110(b).
　Permitted, §50A-110(a).
　Records, §50A-110(d).
　　Defined, §50A-110(e).
　Temporary emergency jurisdiction, §50A-204(d).
Confidentiality.
　Sealed information, §50A-209(e).
Cooperation between courts, §50A-112.
　Expenses, §50A-112(c).
　Permissible requests, §50A-112(a).
　　Hearings, §50A-112(b).
　Preservation of records, §50A-112(d).
Costs and fees, §50A-310(b).
　Assessed against a state, §50A-312(b).
　Awarded to prevailing party, §50A-312(a).
　Hague convention, §50A-317.
Declining jurisdiction by reason of conduct,
　§50A-208(a).
　Remedies, §50A-208(b), (c).
Definitions, §50A-102.
Duty to enforce, §50A-303.
　Available remedies, §50A-303(b).
　Out of state custody determinations, §50A-303(a).
Effect of child custody determination,
　§50A-106.
Emergency jurisdiction, §50A-204.
Emergency medical care.
　Application of provisions, §50A-103.
Enforcement, §§50A-301 to 50A-317.
　Definitions, §50A-301.
Exclusive continuing jurisdiction, §50A-202(a).
　Modification of determination, §50A-202(b).
Expedited enforcement, §50A-308.
　Petition, §50A-308(a).
　　Filing, §50A-308(c).
　　Orders, §50A-308(d).
　　Requirements, §50A-308(b).
Expenses, §50A-310(b).
　Assessed against a state, §50A-312(b).
　Awarded to prevailing party, §50A-312(a).
　Hague convention, §50A-317.
Forum non conveniens, §§50A-206(a), 50A-207.
Full faith and credit, §50A-313.
Hague convention, §50A-302.
　Costs and expenses, §50A-317.
　Prosecutor or public official, role of, §50A-315.
　　Actions by law enforcement officer, §50A-316.
Hearings.
　Enforcement, §50A-310.
Inconvenient forum, §§50A-206(a), 50A-207.
　Considerations, §50A-207(b).
　Declined to exercise jurisdiction, §50A-207(d).
　Motion, §50A-207(a).
　Stays, §50A-207(c).
Indian tribes, §50A-104.
　Applicable proceedings, §50A-104(a).
　Previous determinations, §50A-104(c).
　Tribe treated as state, §50A-104(b).
Information to be submitted to court, §50A-209.
　Additional information, §50A-209(c).
　Duty to inform, §50A-209(d).
　Not furnished, §50A-209(b).
　Required information, §50A-209(a).
　Sealed information, §50A-209(e).
Initial child custody jurisdiction, §50A-201.
　Exclusive basis, §50A-201(a), (b).

CHILD CUSTODY JURISDICTION AND ENFORCEMENT —Cont'd

Initial child custody jurisdiction —Cont'd
Physical presence or personal jurisdiction, §50A-201(c).
Injunctions.
Simultaneous proceedings, §50A-206(c).
International application, §50A-105.
Applicable proceedings, §50A-105(c).
Foreign country treated as state, §50A-105(a).
Previous determinations, §50A-105(b).
Interpretation of provisions.
Third party proceedings, §50A-205(c).
Intervention, §50A-205(c).
Jurisdiction, §§50A-201 to 50A-210.
Appearances, §50A-210.
Limited immunity, §50A-109.
Basis for determination, §50A-201.
Declined by reason of conduct, §50A-208.
Exclusive continuing jurisdiction, §50A-202.
Inconvenient forum, §50A-207.
Simultaneous proceedings, §50A-206(a).
Information to be submitted to court, §50A-209.
Modification of determination, §50A-203.
Notice, §50A-205.
Persons outside state, §50A-108.
Priority of determination, §50A-107.
Simultaneous proceedings, §50A-206.
Temporary emergency jurisdiction, §50A-204.
Law-enforcement officers.
Action by, §50A-316.
Modification of determination, §§50A-202(b), 50A-203.
Notice.
Jurisdiction, §50A-205(a).
Persons outside state, §50A-108(a), (c).
Proof of service, §50A-108(b).
Orders.
Expedited enforcement, §50A-308(d).
Full faith and credit, §50A-313.
Hearing and order, §50A-310.
Immediate physical custody, §50A-310(a).
Service of petitioner in order, §50A-309.
Petitions.
Expedited enforcement, §50A-308.
Service of petition and order, §50A-309.
Physical custody of child, warrant for, §50A-311.
Conditions, §50A-311(f).
Enforcement, §50A-311(e).
Petition, §50A-311(a).
Reasons for issuance, §50A-311(b).
Requirements, §50A-311(c).
Service, §50A-311(d).
Privilege, §50A-310(d).
Proceedings governed by other law, §50A-103.
Prosecutor or public official, role of.
Hague convention, §50A-315(a), (b).
Registration of child custody determination, §50A-305.
Confirmation, §50A-305(e), (f).
Contesting validity, §50A-305(d).
Enforcement, §50A-306(a), (b).
Notice, §50A-305(b), (c).
Procedure, §50A-305(a).
Service of process, §50A-109(b).
Short title, §50A-101.
Simultaneous proceedings, §50A-206.
Enforcement, §50A-307.
Exercise of jurisdiction, §50A-206(a).
Permissible actions, §50A-206(b), (c).

CHILD CUSTODY JURISDICTION AND ENFORCEMENT —Cont'd

Spousal privilege, §50A-310(d).
Temporary emergency jurisdiction, §50A-204.
Communication between courts, §50A-204(d).
No previous determination, §50A-204(b).
Previous determination exists, §50A-204(c).
Requirements, §50A-204(a).
Temporary visitation, §50A-304.
Orders, §50A-304(b).
Visitation schedule, §50A-304(a).
Testimony.
Failure to testify, inferences drawn, §50A-310(c).
Taking in another state, §50A-111.
Electronic means, §50A-111(b).
Evidence, §50A-111(c).
Permitted, §50A-111(a).
Title, §50A-101.
Warrants.
Physical custody of child, §50A-311.
Witnesses.
Failure to testify, inferences drawn, §50A-310(c).

CHILD FATALITY PREVENTION SYSTEM, §§7B-1400 to 7B-1414.

Access to records by state team, local teams and task force, §7B-1413(a).
Assessment of prevention system, duty of state team, §7B-1405.
Child fatality prevention team.
Chair, §7B-1407(b).
Duties, §7B-1406(b).
Establishment in county to conduct reviews, §7B-1406(b).
Local team defined, §7B-1401.
Meetings, §7B-1407(f), (g).
Membership, §7B-1407(a) to (c).
Reports to team coordinator, §7B-1406(c).
Statement of confidentiality requirement, §7B-1413(d).
Child fatality prevention team coordinator.
Duties, §7B-1408.
Ex officio member of local team, §7B-1407(d).
Closed meetings of state team and local teams, §7B-1413(b).
Community child protection team.
Chair, §7B-1407(e).
Director of county department of social services as member of team, duties, §7B-1409.
Duties, §7B-1406(a).
Establishment in counties of state, §7B-1406(a).
Geographic or governmental area larger than one county, no team to encompass, §7B-1407(a).
Local team defined, §7B-1401.
Meetings, §7B-1407(f), (g).
Membership, §7B-1407(b).
Public and nonpublic agencies in community, representation by, §7B-1407(a).
Rules in connection with reviews, adoption by social services commission, §7B-1413(f).
Statement of confidentiality requirement, §7B-1413(d).
Technical assistance provided by state team, §7B-1405.
Training of members, responsibility, §7B-1411.
Community responsibility, prevention of abuse, neglect and death, §7B-1400.
Confidentiality of information and records acquired by team, §7B-1413.
Definitions, §7B-1401.

CHILD FATALITY PREVENTION SYSTEM
—Cont'd
Director of county department of social services.
Calling first meeting of community child protection team, §7B-1407(g).
Duties as member of community child protection team, §7B-1409.
Director of local department of health.
Calling first meeting of child fatality prevention team, §7B-1407(g).
Duties as member of local team, §7B-1410.
Disclosure of records in child fatality or near child fatality cases, §7B-2902.
Provisions governing access to child fatality prevention team and fatality task force records, §7B-2902(f).
Discovery of information and records acquired by local teams, prohibition, §7B-1413(c).
Division of social services, department of health and human services.
Duty to train local team members, §7B-1411.
Entry in child's protective services records that case reviewed by local team, §7B-1413(e).
Guidelines for selecting child deaths to received detailed reviews.
Duty of state team to develop, §7B-1405.
Intent of provisions, §7B-1400.
Local team.
Composition, §7B-1407.
Creation and duties, §7B-1406.
Defined, §7B-1401.
Rules in connection with reviews, adoption by social services commission, §7B-1413(f).
Statement as to understanding of confidentiality requirements, §7B-1413(d).
Technical assistance to provided by state team, §7B-1405.
Minutes of public meetings, §7B-1413(b).
Multidisciplinary review of child deaths.
Duty of task force to develop system, §7B-1403.
Periodic public meetings held by local teams, §7B-1413(b).
Prevention of abuse, neglect and death of juveniles.
Public policy of state, §7B-1400.
Report by task force to governor and general assembly, §7B-1412.
Report to task force during existence of task force.
Duty of state team, §7B-1405.
Review of deaths attributable to abuse or neglect.
Duty of state team, §7B-1405.
Rules as to reviews conducted by community child protection team.
Social services commission to adopt, §7B-1413(f).
Statement of understanding as to confidentiality requirements.
Member of local team to sign, §7B-1413(d).
State team.
Created, §7B-1404(a).
Defined, §7B-1401.
Duties, §7B-1405.
Membership, §7B-1404(b).
Staff or consultants, hiring, §7B-1414(a).
Travel and subsistence expenses for members, staff and consultants, §7B-1414(b).
Vacancies, §7B-1404(c).

CHILD FATALITY PREVENTION SYSTEM
—Cont'd
Study of incidences and causes of child deaths and establishment of profile.
Duty of task force, §7B-1403.
Task force.
Chair, §7B-1402(c).
Created, §7B-1402(a).
Defined, §7B-1401.
Duties, §7B-1403.
Membership, §7B-1402(b).
Office space in legislative building and legislative office building, §7B-1414(c).
Report to governor and general assembly, §7B-1412.
Staff or consultants, hiring, §7B-1414(a).
Travel and subsistence expenses for members, staff and consultants, §7B-1414(b).
Vacancies, §7B-1402(c).
Testimony as to what transpired at meeting of team, prohibition, §7B-1413(c).
Training of local teams, §7B-1411.

CHILD FATALITY REVIEW TEAM.
Confidentiality requirement, members to sign statement of understanding, §143B-150.20(g).
Disclosure of information, order for.
Failure to receive information requested, §143B-150.20(d).
Established, §143B-150.20(a).
Findings and recommendations developed for each fatality review.
Division of social service to make public, not admissible, §143B-150.20(b).
Medical, hospital and other records, access to, §143B-150.20(d).
Meetings not subject to open meetings law, holding public meetings, §143B-150.20(e).
Records, confidentiality, not discoverable, not admissible, §143B-150.20(f).
Report on activities, §143B-150.20(h).
Representatives included on team, §143B-150.20(c).
Reviews of child fatalities.
Purpose, §143B-150.20(b).
Steps, §143B-150.20(a).

CHILD FATALITY TASK FORCE.
Generally, §§7B-1400 to 7B-1414.

CHILDHOOD VACCINE-RELATED INJURY COMPENSATION, §§130A-422 to 130A-434.
Actions.
Health care providers.
Right of state to bring action against, §130A-430(a).
Manufacturers.
Right of state to bring action against, §130A-430(b).
Appeals.
Decisions of commission, §130A-428(c).
Applicability of provisions, §130A-432.
Attorneys' fees, ChildhoodVaccin Rule 203.
Awards, §§130A-426(b), 130A-427(a).
Amount, §130A-427(b).
Claims.
Determination by commission, §130A-426(a).
Notice, §130A-428(b).
Entry of case upon hearing docket.
Duty of commission on receipt, §130A-425(c).

CHILDHOOD VACCINE-RELATED INJURY COMPENSATION —Cont'd

Claims —Cont'd

Filing, §130A-425(b).

  Contents of petition, §130A-425(b).

  Required, §130A-425(a).

  Time limit, §130A-429(a) to (c).

Notice of date and place of hearing.

  Duty of commission on receipt, §130A-425(c).

Requirements for filing petition, §130A-423(b1).

Rules of court.

  Applicability, §130A-425(d).

Secretary party to all proceedings, §130A-425(c).

Service of copy of petition.

  Duty of commission on receipt, §130A-425(c).

Contempt.

Industrial commission.

  Power to punish for contempt, §130A-424.

Superior court of Wake county.

  Power to punish for contempt, §130A-425(d).

Contracts.

Purchase of vaccines, §130A-433.

Covered vaccines.

Contracts for purchase, §130A-433.

Defined, §130A-422.

Distribution, §130A-433.

Fees for providing, §130A-433.

Damages.

Action by state against health care provider, §130A-430(a).

Action by state against manufacturer, §130A-430(b).

Damages awarded against vaccine manufacturers.

Authority to bring action for, §130A-423(c).

Duplicate damages, prevention, §130A-423(e).

Limitation on amount, §130A-423(d).

Definitions, §130A-422.

Diversion of vaccines, §130A-431.

Establishment of program, §130A-423(a).

Exclusive nature of remedy, §130A-423(b).

Fees.

Covered vaccines.

  Providing, §130A-433.

Forms.

Official forms of the industrial commission, ChildhoodVaccin Rule 103.

Fund.

Established, §130A-434(a).

Payments from fund, §130A-434(a).

Transfer of appropriations and receipts, §130A-434(b).

Guardian ad litem.

Filing of claims on behalf of minors or incompetent persons, §130A-429(a).

Guardian and ward.

Filing of claims on behalf of minors or incompetent persons, §130A-429(a).

Hearings.

Industrial commission.

  Power to hear and determine claims, §130A-424.

Industrial commission.

Appeals from decisions, §130A-428(c).

Attorneys' fees, ChildhoodVaccin Rule 203.

Decisions, §130A-426(b).

  Appeals from, §130A-428(c).

  Finality, §130A-428(a).

Definition of "commission,"§130A-422.

Forms.

  Official forms, ChildhoodVaccin Rule 103.

CHILDHOOD VACCINE-RELATED INJURY COMPENSATION —Cont'd

Industrial commission —Cont'd

Hearings.

  Power to hear and determine claims, §130A-424.

Hours of business, ChildhoodVaccin Rule 101.

Location of offices, ChildhoodVaccin Rule 101.

Powers, §130A-424.

Procedural rules of commission, ChildhoodVaccin Rule 202.

Rules of civil procedure.

  Applicability, ChildhoodVaccin Rule 201.

Transaction of business by commission, ChildhoodVaccin Rule 102.

Limitation of actions.

Claims, §130A-429(a) to (c).

Notice.

Decisions of commission, §130A-428(b).

Oaths.

Industrial commission.

  Power to administer oaths, §§130A-424, 130A-425(d).

Parent and child.

Filing of claims on behalf of minors or incompetent persons, §130A-429(a).

Petitions.

Information required, §130A-425(b).

Requirements for filing, §130A-423(b1).

Service, §130A-425(c).

Record of proceedings, §130A-425(d).

Rules and regulations.

Governing proceedings, commission to adopt, §130A-425(d).

Secretary of health and human services, §130A-433.

Rules of civil procedure.

Industrial commission.

  Applicability of rules of civil procedure, ChildhoodVaccin Rule 201.

Scope of provisions, §130A-432.

Service of process.

Notice of date and place of hearing, petition, §130A-425(c).

Subpoenas.

Industrial commission.

  Powers, §§130A-424, 130A-425(d).

Subrogation.

Claims under national childhood vaccine injury act.

  Filing with appropriate court, §130A-423(f).

Witnesses.

Industrial commission.

  Power to require witnesses to testify, §130A-425(d).

CHILD LABOR.

ABC permit holders.

Restrictions on employment of minors by, §95-25.5(j).

Actors or performers.

Exemption from certain provisions, §95-25.5(g).

Civil penalty, §95-25.23.

Employment certificates, §95-25.5(a).

County director of social services.

  Designation of personnel to issue, §108A-14(b).

Enforcement of youth employment laws.

Report on enforcement activities.

  Findings of legislature, §95-25.23C(a).

  Generally, §95-25.23C(c).

  Intent of legislature, §95-25.23C(b).

CHILD LABOR —Cont'd
Exemptions, §§95-25.5(g) to (k), 95-25.14(a).
Fair labor standards act.
Employment by parents.
Exemption from certain provisions, §95-25.5(i).
Newspaper distribution, §95-25.5(d).
Persons and establishments subject to.
Exemption from certain provisions, §95-25.5(k).
Fire department or rescue squad members.
Training for uncompensated members under 18
years of age, §95-25.5(n).
Hazardous occupations, §95-25.5(b).
Hours worked.
Restrictions, §95-25.5(c), (e).
Limitation of actions.
Violations of provisions.
Assessment of penalties, §95-25.23(d).
Models.
Exemption from certain provisions, §95-25.5(g).
Motor vehicles.
Eligibility to drive as part of employment,
§95-25.5(l).
Outdoor dramas.
Exemptions from certain provisions, §95-25.5(h).
Reports.
Youth employment enforcement activities,
§95-25.23C.
School term employment.
Hours of employment, §95-25.5(a1).
**University of North Carolina or North
Carolina community colleges.**
Employment of youth, §95-25.5(m).
Violations of provisions.
Civil penalty, §95-25.23(a).
Action to recover, §95-25.23(b).
Collection, §95-25.23(b).
Limitation of actions, §95-25.23(d).
Payments of sums collected into general fund,
§95-25.23(c).
**Waiver of provisions for minors over twelve
years of age.**
Power of commissioner, §95-25.5(f).

CHILD MOLESTATION.
Bail, §15A-534.4.
DNA sample.
Required upon conviction, §15A-266.4.
Rehabilitative treatment.
Defendant may pay cost as condition of probation,
§15A-1343(b1).
Statutory rape, §14-27.7(a).
Defendant at least six years older than victim,
§14-27.7A(a).
Defendant between four and six years older than
victim, §14-27.7A(b).
Taking indecent liberties with children,
§14-202.1.
Indecent liberties between children, §14-202.2.
**Testing of defendant for sexually transmitted
diseases,** §15A-615.
Venue, §15A-136.

CHILDNAPPING.
See CHILD ABDUCTION.

CHILD PASSENGER RESTRAINTS, §20-137.1.
Child care facilities.
Compliance with law required, §110-91.
Child passenger safety technicians, §20-137.5.
Placement of small children within vehicle,
§20-137.1(a1).

CHILD PASSENGER RESTRAINTS —Cont'd
Seat belts generally.
See SEAT BELTS.

CHILD PASSENGER SAFETY TECHNICIANS.
Definitions, §20-137.5(a).
Limitations of liability, §20-137.5(b).
Exceptions, §20-137.5(c).

CHILD PLACEMENT.
**Abused, neglected or dependent juvenile
actions.**
Alternative dispositions, §7B-903(a).
Disposition generally, §§7B-900 to 7B-1004.
See CHILD ABUSE, NEGLECT OR
DEPENDENCY.
Periodic review hearings, §§7B-906 to 7B-910.
**Adoption and medical assistance for adoptive
parents.**
Interstate compact on adoption and medical
assistance, §§7B-3900 to 7B-3906.
See ADOPTION.
Adoption generally, §§48-1-101 to 48-10-105.
See ADOPTION.
Agencies.
General provisions, §§131D-10.1 to 131D-10.9.
See CHILD PLACING AGENCIES.
**Bringing or sending into state child for
purposes of placement or adoption,**
§§7B-3700 to 7B-3705.
Bond required of person, agency, association, etc.,
bringing or sending child into state, §7B-3701.
Definitions, §7B-3704.
Inapplicability of provisions, §7B-3705.
Misdemeanor for violating provisions, §7B-3703.
Responsibility for child's proper care and training,
person within whom child placed,
§7B-3700(a).
Visitation and supervision, right of department of
health and human services, §7B-3700(b).
Written consent of department of health and
human services required, §7B-3700(a).
**Consent of department of health and human
services for adoption or placement of
juvenile.**
Bringing child into state or sending out of state,
§§7B-3700 to 7B-3705.
Delinquent and undisciplined juvenile actions.
Secure or nonsecure custody, §§7B-1902 to
7B-1906.
Interstate compact, §§7B-3800 to 7B-3806.
Administrator, §7B-3806.
Agreements under compact, §7B-3802.
Applicability of compact.
Adoptions, §48-3-207.
Conditions for placement, §7B-3800.
Construction and severability of provisions,
§7B-3800.
Default of performance for financial responsibility,
§7B-3801.
Definitions, §7B-3800.
Delinquent children, institutional care, §7B-3800.
Delinquent children, placement generally,
§7B-3805.
District court jurisdiction, §§7B-200(a), 7B-1603.
Enactment into law, §7B-3800.
Financial responsibility for child placed pursuant
to contract, §7B-3801.
Governor authorized to appoint compact
administrator, §7B-3806.
Limitations on compact, §7B-3800.

CHILD PLACEMENT —Cont'd
Interstate compact —Cont'd
Officers and agencies of state, agreement, §7B-3802.
Penalty for illegal placement, §7B-3800.
Placement of delinquents generally, §7B-3805.
Placements made pursuant to compact, applicability of provisions, §7B-3804.
Provisions governed between party states, §7B-3804.
Requirements for visitation, inspection or supervision, §7B-3803.
Retention of jurisdiction by sending state, §7B-3800.
Text of compact, §7B-3800.
Visitation, inspection or supervision of children, §7B-3803.
Reasonable efforts to eliminate need for placement.
Findings required in order, §7B-507(a).
Health and safety of juvenile as primary concern in determination of need for reasonable efforts, §7B-507(d).
Permanency planning hearing, §7B-507(c).
When reasonable efforts not required, §7B-507(b).
Sending child out of state for purposes of placement.
Applicability of article, §7B-3705.
Consent of department of health and human services required, §7B-3702.
Definitions, §7B-3704.
Misdemeanor, §7B-3703.
Termination of parental rights.
Generally, §§7B-1100 to 7B-1114.
See TERMINATION OF PARENTAL RIGHTS.

CHILD PLACING AGENCIES, §§131D-10.1 to 131D-10.9.
Access to premises.
Licensee or license applicant to permit department, §131D-10.3(b).
Administrative procedures act.
Applicability to notifications, hearings and appeals, §131D-10.9.
Applicability of article, §131D-10.3(d).
Criminal history records checks of foster parents.
Annual check, §131D-10.3A(b).
Confidential and privileged information, §131D-10.3A(f), (g).
Department of justice to provide information, §131D-10.3A(d).
Destruction of information, §131D-10.3A(g).
Fee for check, §131D-10.3A(i).
Hearing, request by foster parent, §131D-10.3A(f).
Immunity for action taken in carrying out provision, §131D-10.3A(h).
Mandatory checks, §131D-10.3A(a).
Notice of mandatory checks.
Placement on application, §131D-10.3A(e).
Prohibiting person from providing foster care, §131D-10.3A(c).
Review of information, right of individual, §131D-10.3A(f).
Death of resident of facility.
Civil penalty, failure to notify department, §131D-10.6B(a).
Disclosure of information, restriction, §131D-10.6B(d).
Governor's advocacy council for persons with disabilities.
Department to notify, §131D-10.6B(b).

CHILD PLACING AGENCIES —Cont'd
Death of resident of facility —Cont'd
Notice to department, §131D-10.6B(a).
Physical restraint, death occurring within 7 days of use.
Immediate investigation, §131D-10.6B(c).
Standard reporting format, secretary to establish, §131D-10.6B(e).
Declaratory rulings, commission issuing, §131D-10.5.
Definitions, §§48-1-101, 131D-10.2.
Exemptions from article, §131D-10.4.
Injunctions.
Interference with department carrying out duties, §131D-10.8(b).
Operating without license, §131D-10.8(a).
Interference with department carrying out duties.
Injunctions, §131D-10.8(b).
License to operate or provide foster care or place children.
Access to premises.
Applicant to permit department, §131D-10.3(b).
Document of compliance, §131D-10.3(g).
Duration and expiration, §131D-10.3(e).
Exemptions from article, §131D-10.4.
Injunction, operating without license, §131D-10.8(a).
Periodic review of persons licensed, §131D-10.3(c).
Powers and duties of department, §131D-10.6.
Provisional license, granting, §131D-10.3(f).
Required, §131D-10.3(a).
Unlicensed practice.
Fine, §131D-10.7.
Injunction, §131D-10.8(a).
Periodic review of persons licensed, §131D-10.3(c).
Policy of state, §131D-10.1.
Powers and duties of department, §131D-10.6.
Powers of commission, §131D-10.5.
Purpose of article, §131D-10.1.
Restraint employed by child care facility.
Collection of data on use, §131D-10.5A.
Rules, adoption by commission, §131D-10.5.
Training.
Child welfare services staff, §131D-10.6A(b).
Foster parents, §131D-10.6A(a).
Unlicensed practice.
Fine, §131D-10.7.
Injunction, §131D-10.8(a).

CHILD PORNOGRAPHY.
Electronic surveillance orders, §15A-290(c1).
Film or computer images of minor engaging in sexual activity.
Report by film and photographic processor or computer technician.
Definitions, §66-67.4(a).
Generally, §66-67.4(b), (c).
Immunity, §66-67.4(d).
Sexual exploitation of a minor, §§14-190.16, 14-190.17.

CHILD PROTECTION TEAMS.
Generally, §§7B-1400 to 7B-1414.
See CHILD FATALITY PREVENTION SYSTEM.

CHILD RAPE, §14-27.2A.
Rape generally.
See RAPE.
Sex offenses generally.
See SEX OFFENSES.

CHILD RAPE —Cont'd
Sexual offense with child, §14-27.4A.

CHILDREN AND MINORS.
Abandonment.
    Baby drop off, §§14-318.2, 14-318.4.
    Willful neglect or refusal to provide support,
        §14-322.
Abduction of children, §14-41(a).
Abortion.
    Parental or judicial consent, §§90-21.6 to 90-21.10.
    Woman's right to know act.
        Informed consent from minor and adult giving
            consent, §90-21.87.
        Real-time view of unborn child, §90-21.85(c).
Actions.
    Sales of harmful material to minors.
        Harmful material determination, injunctions,
            §§19-9 to 19-20.
Administration of estates.
    Additional costs assessed before clerk, §7A-307(d).
    Assessment of costs, §7A-307(a).
    Completeness and exclusivity of costs,
        §7A-307(c).
    Courtroom and related judicial facilities.
        Amount of facilities fee, §7A-307(b).
        Use of facilities, §7A-307(a).
    General court of justice.
        Support of court, §7A-307(a).
    Liability of parties for costs, §7A-307(e).
Adoption generally.
    See ADOPTION.
Adoptive homes.
    Regulation of agencies receiving or placing
        children, §§131D-10.1 to 131D-10.9.
        See CHILD PLACING AGENCIES.
Age of majority, §48A-2.
Air pistols or rifles.
    Permitting young children to use dangerous
        weapons, §14-316(b).
Alcoholic beverages.
    Compensation for injury caused by sales to
        underage persons, §§18B-120 to 18B-129.
        See ALCOHOLIC BEVERAGES.
    Consumption.
        Alcohol screening test.
            Authority of law enforcement to require,
                §18B-302(j).
            Evidence in court or administrative
                proceeding.
            Results, refusal to submit to, §18B-302(j).
        Exempt activities, §18B-302(k).
        Prohibition, §18B-302(b).
            Exempt activities, §18B-302(k).
            Misdemeanor, violation by 19 and 20 year
                olds, §18B-302(i).
    Conviction reports to division of motor vehicles,
        §18B-302(g).
    Driving after consuming alcohol, §20-138.3.
        Restoration of license after conviction, §20-17.6.
    Employment of youth by person holding ABC
        permits, §95-25.5(j).
    Fines and other penalties, §18B-302.1.
    Fraudulent use of identification.
        Allowing use, §18B-302(f).
    Giving to.
        Fines and other penalties, §18B-302.1(a).
        Prohibited, §18B-302(a1).
    Handling in course of employment.
        Authorized, §18B-302(h).

CHILDREN AND MINORS —Cont'd
Alcoholic beverages —Cont'd
    Purchase or possession, §18B-302(b), (i).
        Aiding and abetting, §18B-302(c).
            Fines and other penalties, §18B-302.1(b), (c).
        Allowing use of license, §18B-302(f).
        Conviction reports to division of motor vehicles,
            §18B-302(g).
        Drivers' licenses.
            Fraudulent use, §18B-302(e).
            Revocation for underage purchases, §20-17.3.
        Fraudulent use of identification.
            Allowing use, §18B-302(f).
        Nineteen or twenty year olds, §18B-302(i).
    Sales to.
        Aiding and abetting, §18B-302(c).
            Fines and other penalties, §18B-302.1(b), (c).
        Conviction reports to division of motor vehicles,
            §18B-302(g).
        Defense to violation of subsection, §18B-302(d).
        Fines and other penalties, §18B-302.1(a), (c).
        Fraudulent use of identification.
            Allowing use, §18B-302(f).
        Prohibited, §18B-302(a).
Alcoholism.
    Consent of minor to treatment sufficient,
        §90-21.5(a).
Alcohol screening test.
    Driving after consuming alcohol or drugs,
        §20-138.3(b2).
    Probable cause to believe minors consumed
        alcohol, §18B-302(j).
All-terrain vehicles.
    Age restrictions, §20-171.15.
    Helmet and eye protection required,
        §20-171.19(a1).
AMBER alert system, §143B-1021.
Anatomical gifts.
    Actions permitted by parent of minor after minor's
        death, §130A-412.10(g), (h).
    Reasonable search for parents of unemancipated
        minor, §130A-412.16(f).
    Who may make gift prior to donor's death,
        §130A-412.6.
Arrest.
    Care of child when adult supervising child
        arrested, §15A-401(g).
    Notification of parent or guardian, §15A-505(a),
        (b).
    Notification of principal of school, §15A-505(c).
    Photographs and fingerprints.
        Not authorized for juveniles, §15A-502(c).
Artificial insemination.
    Status of child, §49A-1.
Artistic and creative services contracts,
        §§48A-11 to 48A-18.
Assault and battery.
    Assault of child under certain age, §14-33.
    Inflicting serious injury or using deadly weapon in
        presence of minor, §14-33(d).
At-risk students.
    Extended service programs, §§115C-238.30 to
        115C-238.33.
Attractive nuisance doctrine.
    Child trespasser harmed by artificial condition on
        property.
        Child trespasser defined, §38B-4.
    Liability of possessor of property, §38B-3.
Authority of parent over juvenile, §§7B-3400 to
        7B-3404.
Baby drop off, §§14-318.2, 14-318.4.

CHILDREN AND MINORS —Cont'd
Baby sitting services.
Sex offender providing.
Prohibition, §14-321.1.
Banks deposits.
Operating deposit account in name of minor,
§53-43.5(a).
Bars.
Permitting minors to enter barrooms, §14-317.
Bastardy.
Illegitimate children, support, legitimation, civil
actions, §§49-1 to 49-17.
See CHILDREN BORN OUT OF WEDLOCK.
Paternity.
Proceedings to establish generally.
See PATERNITY.
BB guns.
Permitting young children to use dangerous
firearms, §14-316(b).
Betterments.
Procedure where plaintiff is under disability,
§1-349.
Bicycles, §§20-171.6 to 20-171.9.
Child bicycle safety act, §20-171.6.
Civil fine assessed parent or guardian found
responsible, §20-171.9(d).
Definitions, §20-171.8.
Helmet.
Wearing while riding roadway, bicycle path,
required, §20-171.9(a).
Infraction for violation, §20-171.9(d).
Legislative findings and declaration, §20-171.7(a).
Negligence or liability not assessed for violation,
§20-171.9(c).
Passenger on bicycle, requirements, §20-171.9(b).
Purposes of article, §20-171.7(b).
Restraining seat for small children.
Requirement to be passenger, §20-171.9(b).
Short title of act, §20-171.6.
Subsequent purchase of helmet or restraining
seat.
Waiver of fine for violation, §20-171.9(e).
Billiard rooms.
Permitting minors to enter billiard rooms,
§14-317.
Birth of child, concealing, §14-46.
Blind persons.
Personal representatives for certain recipients of
aid.
Affecting provisions for payments of minors,
§111-33.
Blood donations.
Persons under 18 years selling.
Unlawful, §130A-412.31.
Sixteen year olds donating, §130A-412.31.
Boating safety.
Personal watercraft.
Persons under 16 years of age operating,
§75A-13.3(b1).
Renting, hiring or leasing to persons under 16
years, §75A-13.3(c).
Body piercing.
Without consent of parents, §14-400(b).
Capital punishment.
Persons under 17 years of age, §14-17.
Caveat to will.
Time for filing after removal of disability, §31-32.
Cell phones.
Use while operating vehicle.
Prohibition, fine, §§20-11(c), (e), (l), 20-137.3(b),
(e).
Definitions, §20-137.3(a).

CHILDREN AND MINORS —Cont'd
Cell phones —Cont'd
Use while operating vehicle —Cont'd
Prohibition, fine —Cont'd
Exceptions, §20-137.3(d).
Seizure or forfeiture of phone, §20-137.3(c).
Center for missing persons.
General provisions, §§143B-1010 to 143B-1022.
See MISSING PERSONS.
Change of name.
Procedure, §101-2.
Two change limitation, §101-6(b).
Child abuse, neglect or dependency.
Generally, §§7B-100 to 7B-1414.
See CHILD ABUSE, NEGLECT OR
DEPENDENCY.
Child care facilities.
Adoption generally.
See ADOPTION.
Control over child care facilities, §§110-45 to
110-48.
See CHILD CARE FACILITIES.
General provisions, §§110-85 to 110-107.
See CHILD CARE FACILITIES.
Child custody generally.
See CHILD CUSTODY.
Child custody jurisdiction and enforcement,
§§50A-101 to 50A-317.
See CHILD CUSTODY JURISDICTION AND
ENFORCEMENT.
Child fatality prevention system.
Generally, §§7B-1400 to 7B-1414.
See CHILD FATALITY PREVENTION
SYSTEM.
**Childhood vaccine-related injury
compensation,** §§130A-422 to 130A-434.
See CHILDHOOD VACCINE-RELATED INJURY
COMPENSATION.
Child labor, §95-25.5.
Child placement compact, §§7B-3800 to 7B-3806.
Child placing agencies.
Regulation of agencies receiving or placing
children, §§131D-10.1 to 131D-10.9.
See CHILD PLACING AGENCIES.
Child pornography.
Sexual exploitation of minors, §§14-190.16,
14-190.17.
Child rape, §14-27.2A.
Children's trust fund, §7B-1302.
Child restraint systems, §20-137.1.
Child bicycle safety act.
Restraining seat.
Small children as passengers, §§20-171.6 to
20-171.9.
Placement of small children within vehicle,
§20-137.1(a1).
Points for violations, §§20-16(c), 20-137.1(d).
Transporting children under 12 years of age in
open bed or open cargo area of vehicle.
Exception to prohibition when child secured or
restrained by seat belt, §20-135.2B(b).
Child support generally.
See CHILD SUPPORT.
Cigarettes and tobacco products.
Sale or distribution of tobacco products to minors,
§14-313.
Use of minors by department of health and
human services to test compliance with
provisions, §14-313(d).
Use of minors by law enforcement agencies to test
compliance with provisions, §14-313(d).

CHILDREN AND MINORS —Cont'd
Cognitive impairment.
  Generally.
    See MENTAL HEALTH, DEVELOPMENTAL
        DISABILITY, SUBSTANCE ABUSE.
Common-law definition abrogated, §48A-1.
Complaints.
  Sale of harmful materials to minors.
    Civil remedy, §19-14.
Computer crimes.
  Cyber-bullying, §14-458.1.
Consent to health care for minors.
  Authorization.
    Duration, §32A-32.
    Revocation, §32A-32.
    Who may make an authorization, §32A-30.
  Custodial parents.
    Authority, §32A-30.
    Person who may make authorization, §32A-30.
  Disagreement regarding health care.
    Revocation of authorization, §32A-32(c).
  Form for authorization, §32A-34.
  Full power and authority.
    Parent authorized to grant agent, §32A-31(a).
  Incapacity or mental incompetence of authorizing
      parent.
    Authorization not effected by, §32A-32(d).
  Limitations and restrictions on authority.
    Authorization may contain, §32A-31(b).
  Protection of health care provider.
    Good faith reliance on authorization,
        §32A-33(b).
  Public policy, statement of, §32A-28(a).
  Purpose of article, §32A-28(b).
  Reliance on authorization.
    Physician, dentist or other health care provider,
        §32A-33(a), (b).
  Revocation of authorization.
    Automatic revocation, §32A-32(a).
    Disagreement regarding health care, §32A-32(c).
    Procedure for exercising right to revoke,
        §32A-32(b).
    Right to revoke, §32A-32(b).
  Treatment by physician.
    Consent of minor sufficient, §90-21.5(a).
    Consent of parent or guardian.
      When not required, §90-21.1.
  Who may make an authorization to consent,
      §32A-30.
  Withholding or discontinuing life sustaining
      procedures.
    Authorization may not contain, §32A-31(c).
Consent to intercourse and sexual offenses.
  No defense as to certain victims, §14-27.7(a).
Contempt, §§5A-31 to 5A-34.
  Age of juvenile, §5A-34(a).
  Applicability of provisions, §5A-34(a), (b).
  Delinquent and unruly children, nonapplicability
      of provisions, §7B-1707.
  Direct contempt.
    Appeal of order, §5A-32(g).
    Conditions for, §5A-31(b).
    Copy of orders placed in file by clerk, §5A-32(f).
    Oral order for custody and restraint of juvenile,
        §5A-32(e).
    Order upon finding of contempt, §5A-32(c).
    Show cause order and appointment of counsel.
      In lieu of summary imposition, §5A-32(b).
    Summary imposition of measures by presiding
        official, §5A-32(a).

CHILDREN AND MINORS —Cont'd
Contempt —Cont'd
  Direct contempt —Cont'd
    Termination or reduction of sanctions,
        §5A-32(d).
  District court jurisdiction, §7B-1603.
  Enumerated acts constituting contempt,
      §5A-31(a).
  Indirect contempt, §5A-31(c).
    Sanctions, §5A-33.
  Sale of harmful materials to minors.
    Disobedience of injunctions, §19-20.
Contracts.
  Age of majority, §48A-2.
  Artistic and creative services and talent agency
      contracts, §§48A-11 to 48A-18.
    Applicability of article, §48A-11.
    Artistic and creative services defined, §48A-11.
    Disaffirmance during minority prohibited.
      Contract approved by superior court,
          §48A-12(a).
    Documents to be provided to other party,
        §48A-13.
    Earnings set aside in trust.
      Contracts approved by court.
        Change in facts, notice, §48A-14(h).
        Continuing jurisdiction over trust
            established, §48A-14(g).
        Deposit or disbursement of funds by
            employer, §48A-14(d) to (f).
        Percentage required to be set aside,
            §48A-14(a).
        Trustee, appointment, §48A-14(b).
        Trustee's statement, providing employer,
            §48A-14(c).
      Contracts not approved by court.
        Amendment or termination, §48A-15(e).
        Change in facts, notice, §48A-15(f).
        Deposit or disbursement by employer,
            §48A-15(c), (d).
        Fiduciary relationship, parent or guardian,
            §48A-15(g).
        Gross earnings defined, §48A-15(h).
        Percentage of earning set aside, §48A-15(a).
        Trustee, appointment, §48A-15(b).
      Establishment of trust, §48A-16(a).
      Financial institutions, establishing with,
          §48A-16(d).
      Methods of handling by trustee, §48A-16(e).
      Withdrawals, restrictions, §48A-16(b).
      Written statement by trustee, §48A-16(c).
    Guardian ad litem during proceeding,
        §48A-12(d).
    Superior court approval of contracts, §48A-12(a)
        to (d).
    Talent agency contracts, §§48A-17, 48A-18.
    Talent agency contracts.
      Definitions, §48A-17(a), (b).
      Disaffirmance prohibited.
        Court approval, §48A-18.
  Deposit accounts.
    Banks operating in name of minor, §53-43.5(a).
  Disaffirmance of minors contracts.
    Determining applicable period of time, §48A-3.
  Safe deposit boxes.
    Banks leasing or renting to minors, §53-43.5(b),
        (c).
Contributing to delinquency, §14-316.1.
Controlled substances. See within this heading,
    "Drugs and controlled substances."

CHILDREN AND MINORS —Cont'd
Control over child caring facilities, §§110-45 to 110-48.
See CHILD CARE FACILITIES.
Conveyances.
Infant trustees, §39-4.
Costs.
Administration of estates, §7A-307.
Responsibility of guardian for costs against infant plaintiff, §6-30.
Credit union members.
Minimum age for holding office, §54-109.31(e).
Minimum age for voting at meetings, §54-109.31(d).
Criminal offenses, prosecution, procedure.
Alcoholic beverages. See within this heading, "Alcoholic beverages."
Arrest.
Notification, §15A-505.
Photographs and fingerprints.
Not authorized for juveniles, §15A-502(c).
Assault of child under certain age, §14-33.
Barrooms, billiard rooms.
Permitting minors to enter, §14-317.
Body piercing without consent of parents, §14-400(b).
Capital punishment.
Persons under 17 years of age, §14-17.
Child rape, §14-27.2A.
Cigarettes and tobacco products.
Sale or distribution of tobacco products to minors, §14-313.
Concealing birth of child, §14-46.
Contributing to delinquency, §14-316.1.
Criminal street gangs.
Soliciting or encouraging participation, §14-50.18.
Cyber-bullying, §14-458.1.
Drugs. See within this heading, "Drugs and controlled substances."
Evidence of other crimes, wrongs or acts.
Admissibility against juvenile, §8C-1 Rule 404(b).
Exhibition of certain children, §110-20.1.
Expungement of criminal records.
First offenders not over age twenty-one.
Drug offenses, §15A-145.2.
Toxic vapors offenses, §15A-145.3.
First offenders under age eighteen, §15A-145.
Gang offenses, §15A-145.1.
Felonious restraint, §14-43.3.
Firearms.
Generally. See within this heading, "Firearms and other weapons."
Fires.
Exposing children to fire, §14-318.
Harmful materials.
Dissemination, sales. See within this heading, "Obscenity or pornography."
Homicide.
Punishment for persons under 17 years of age, §14-17.
Inflicting serious injury or using deadly weapon in presence of minor, §14-33(d).
Molestation.
See CHILD MOLESTATION.
Murder in the first degree, §14-17.
Obscenity or pornography. See within this heading, "Obscenity or pornography."
Parent or guardian testifying, §15A-1225.

CHILDREN AND MINORS —Cont'd
Criminal offenses, prosecution, procedure —Cont'd
Prosecution of juvenile as adult.
Commission of criminal offense after superior court conviction, §7B-1604(b).
Commission of criminal offense on or after juvenile's sixteenth birthday, §7B-1604(a).
Emancipated juveniles prosecuted as adult, §7B-1604(a).
Transfer of jurisdiction of juvenile to superior court, §7B-2200.
Detention until transferred to division of adult correction, §7B-2204.
DNA samples, §7B-2201(b).
Fingerprinting juveniles, §7B-2201(a).
Pretrial release, §7B-2204.
Probable cause hearing, §7B-2202.
Transfer hearing, §7B-2203.
Prostitution. See within this heading, "Prostitution."
Rape of child, §14-27.2A.
Sex offenses.
Generally. See within this heading, "Sex offenses."
Sexual exploitation of a minor. See within this heading, "Sexual exploitation of a minor."
Shoplifting.
Notice to parent or guardian, §§14-72.1(c), 14-72(d).
State lottery.
Prize payments to minors prohibited, §18C-132(j).
Sales of tickets and shares to minors prohibited, §18C-131(d).
Defenses, §18C-131(e).
Youthful offenders.
Sentencing committed offender to central prison, §148-28.
Criminal street gangs.
Not applicable to juveniles under age of 16, §14-50.28.
Soliciting or encouraging participation, §14-50.18.
Curfews.
Cities imposing by appropriate ordinance.
Persons of age less than 18, §160A-198.
Custody generally.
See CHILD CUSTODY.
Cyber-bullying, §14-458.1.
Damages.
Malicious or willful destruction of property by minors.
Recovery of damages from parents, §1-538.1.
Negligent supervision of minor.
Right of educational entity to recover against parents, §1-538.3.
Death.
Child fatality prevention system, §§7B-1400 to 7B-1414.
See CHILD FATALITY PREVENTION SYSTEM.
Maltreatment of juvenile, report, §7B-301.
Death sentence, §14-17.
Decedents' estates.
Distribution to parent or guardian of minor, §28A-22-7.
Default judgments.
Appointment required for entry of judgment against, §1A-1 Rule 55(b).
Sale of harmful materials to minors.
Civil remedy, §19-16(b).

CHILDREN AND MINORS —Cont'd
Defenses.
  Employing or intentionally using minor to commit
    drug law violations.
    Assumption of risk or contributory negligence,
      §90-95.5.
    Mistake of age.
      Criminal prosecution, §90-95.4(c).
  Intercourse and sexual offenses with certain
    victims.
    Consent no defense, §14-27.7(a).
  Participating in a drug violation by a minor.
    Mistake of age.
      Criminal prosecution, §90-95.7(b).
  Promoting drug sales by a minor.
    Mistake of age.
      Criminal prosecution, §90-95.6(b).
  Prostitution.
    Participating in prostitution of a minor.
      Mistake of age not a defense, §14-190.19(b).
    Promoting prostitution of a minor.
      Mistake of age not a defense, §14-190.18(b).
  Sexual exploitation of a minor.
    Mistake of age not a defense, §§14-190.16(c),
      14-190.17A(c), 14-190.17(c).
Definitions.
  Age of minors, §48A-2.
  Common-law definition of minor abrogated,
    §48A-1.
  Harmful materials sales to minors, §19-12.
  Stand by guardians for minor children,
    §35A-1370.
Deformed children.
  Exhibition of certain children prohibited,
    §110-20.1.
Delinquency.
  Contributing to delinquency, §14-316.1.
  Generally, §§7B-1500 to 7B-2827.
    See DELINQUENT AND UNDISCIPLINED
      JUVENILES.
  Juvenile code.
    See JUVENILE CODE.
  Youth services.
    See YOUTH SERVICES.
Disabilities.
  Developmental disabilities generally.
    See MENTAL HEALTH, DEVELOPMENTAL
      DISABILITY, SUBSTANCE ABUSE.
  Education of children with disabilities.
    Generally, §§115C-106.1 to 115C-112.1.
      See SPECIAL EDUCATION.
  Interagency coordinating council for children from
    birth to five years of age.
    Agency cooperation, §143B-179.6.
    Compensation, §143B-179.5(e).
    Composition, §143B-179.5(b).
    Duties, §143B-179.5(d).
      Agency cooperation, §143B-179.6.
    Establishment, §143B-179.5(a).
    Organization, §143B-179.5(c).
      Clerical and staff services, §143B-179.5(f).
    Reporting, §143B-179.5(f).
  Silver alert system.
    Missing persons with cognitive impairment,
      §143B-1022.
Divorce.
  Child support.
    General provisions.
      See CHILD SUPPORT.
  Custody generally.
    See CHILD CUSTODY.

CHILDREN AND MINORS —Cont'd
Domestic violence generally, §§50B-1 to 50B-9.
  See DOMESTIC VIOLENCE.
Drainage.
  Corporations.
    Rights of infant owners protected, §156-47.
Drivers' licenses.
  Alcohol purchases by underage persons.
    Revocation of license, §20-17.3.
  Application, §20-11(i).
  Cell phones.
    Use while operating vehicle.
      Prohibition, fine, §20-11(c), (e), (l).
  Driving eligibility certificate, §20-11(n).
    Charter school's designee of board of directors,
      duties, §115C-238.29F(j).
    Principals of schools, duties, §115C-288(k).
    Private and home schools, duties, §115C-566.
    Provisional license revocation, §20-13.2(c1).
    School disciplinary actions.
      Effect on eligibility for certificate, §20-11(n1).
    State board of community colleges, adoption of
      rules, §115D-5(a3).
    State board of education, rules, duty to develop,
      §115C-12.
  Expiration, §20-11(j).
    Provisional license, §20-7(f).
  Federally issued restricted or unrestricted license
    possessed by minor on becoming resident of
    state.
    Licenses person eligible for, §20-11(h3).
  Fees, §20-11(j).
  Full provisional license, §20-11(f).
    Restrictions, §20-11(g).
  Insurance, §20-11(m).
  Limited learner's permit, §20-11(b).
    Restrictions, §20-11(c).
  Limited provisional license, §20-11(d).
    Restrictions, §20-11(e).
  Lose control, lose license, §20-11(n1).
  Mobile phones.
    Use while operating vehicle.
      Prohibition, fine, §20-11(c), (e), (l).
  Nonresidents becoming residents of state,
    §20-11(h) to (h2).
    Federally issued licenses, §20-11(h3).
  Out-of-state restricted license possessed by 16 to
    18 year old on becoming resident of state.
    Licenses person eligible for, §20-11(h1).
  Out-of-state restricted or unrestricted license
    possessed by 15 year old on becoming resident
    of state.
    Licenses person eligible for, §20-11(h2).
  Permitting unlicensed minor to drive vehicle,
    §20-32.
  Process for expanding privilege, §20-11(a).
  Provisional licensee defined, §20-4.01.
  Revocation of license or provisional license.
    Driving by provisional licensee after consuming
      alcohol or drugs, §20-13.2(a).
    Driving eligibility certificate not maintained,
      §20-13.2(c1).
    Explosives offenses, §20-13.2(c2).
      Issuance of license during revocation or
        suspension, §20-9(b1).
    Immediate civil revocation for certain criminal
      moving violations, §20-13.3.
    Impaired driving conviction, §20-13.2(b).
    Length of revocation, §20-13.2(d).
    Restoration of license, proof of financial
      responsibility, §20-13.2(e).

CHILDREN AND MINORS —Cont'd
Drivers' licenses —Cont'd
Revocation of license or provisional license
—Cont'd
Willful refusal to submit to chemical analysis,
§20-13.2(c).
Rules for issuance of driving eligibility certificates.
Duty of state board of education to develop,
§115C-12.
Supervising driver, §20-11(k).
Suspension of license of provisional licensee for
moving violation, §20-13(a).
Length of suspension, §20-13(b).
Motor vehicle moving violation defined,
§20-13(a).
Probation, placing licensee on, §20-13(b).
Restoration of license on probationary status,
hearing request, §20-13(b).
Retention of license until hearing, §20-13(a).
Suspension in addition to other remedies,
§20-13(d).
Two or more offenses committed on single
occasion, §20-13(c).
Term of license, §20-11(j).
Underage purchase of alcohol.
Revocation, §20-17.3.
Unrestricted out-of-state license possessed by 16
to 18 year old on becoming resident of state.
Licenses person eligible for, §20-11(h).
Violations, §20-11(l).
Driving after consuming alcohol or drugs.
Alcohol screening test, §20-138.3(b2).
Impaired driving offense also charged,
§20-138.3(c).
Implied consent law, subject to, §20-138.3(b).
Limited driving privilege, §20-138.3(d).
Odor insufficient, §20-138.3(b1).
Offense, §20-138.3(a).
Provisional licensee.
Restoration of license after conviction, §20-17.6.
Punishment, §20-138.3(c).
Driving motor vehicle unlicensed.
Permitting prohibited, §20-32.
Drug paraphernalia.
Delivery of drug paraphernalia to certain younger
persons, §90-113.23(c).
Drugs and controlled substances.
Delivery of drug paraphernalia to certain youths,
§90-113.23(c).
Driving after consuming drugs, §20-138.3.
Restoration of license after conviction, §20-17.6.
Employing or intentionally using minors to
commit drug law violations, §90-95.4(a), (b).
Civil liability, §90-95.5.
"Minor" defined, §90-95.4(d).
Mistake of age, §90-96(b), (d).
Expunction of records, §90-96(b), (d).
Immunity from prosecution, §90-96.1.
Participating in a drug violation by a minor,
§90-95.7(a), (c).
Mistake of age not a defense, §90-95.7(b).
Promoting drug sales by a minor, §90-95.6(a), (c).
Mistake of age not a defense, §90-95.6(b).
Treatment for drug or alcohol abuse.
Consent of minor to treatment, §90-21.5(a).
Drug treatment courts, §§7A-790 to 7A-801.
See DRUG TREATMENT COURTS.
Education.
Children with disabilities.
Generally, §§115C-106.1 to 115C-112.1.
See SPECIAL EDUCATION.

CHILDREN AND MINORS —Cont'd
Education —Cont'd
Public schools generally.
See SCHOOLS AND EDUCATION.
Emancipation, §§7B-3500 to 7B-3509.
Actions by and against juvenile after final decree,
§7B-3507.
Appeals, §7B-3508.
Burden of showing that emancipation in best
interest of petitioner, §7B-3503.
Common law provisions suspended, §7B-3509.
Considerations in determining best interest of
petitioner and need for emancipation,
§7B-3504.
Continuance of hearing and order of investigation,
§7B-3503.
Contract rights of juvenile upon emancipation,
§7B-3507.
Conveyances, right of juvenile upon final decree,
§7B-3507.
Costs of proceedings, §7B-3506.
Criminal prosecution of emancipated juveniles as
adult, §7B-1604(a).
District court jurisdiction, §§7B-200(a), 7B-1603.
Entry of final decree, §7B-3505.
Examination by psychiatrist, psychologist or
physician.
Court ordering juvenile, §7B-3503.
Hearing by court sitting without jury, §7B-3503.
Husband-wife or physician-patient privilege not
grounds for excluding evidence, §7B-3503.
Irrevocability of final decree, §7B-3507.
Juveniles sixteen years of age or older filing,
§7B-3500.
Legal effect of final decree of emancipation,
§7B-3507.
Married juvenile emancipated by provisions,
§7B-3509.
Notice of appeal, §7B-3508.
Parent relieved of legal duties and obligations
upon final decree, §7B-3507.
Petition.
Signing and verification, content requirements,
§7B-3501.
Service of summons, §7B-3502.
Summons, §7B-3502.
Taxing costs of proceedings, §7B-3506.
Temporary order pending disposition of appeal,
§7B-3508.
Transacting business as adult, effect of final
decree, §7B-3507.
**Emergency medical or surgical treatment,
judicial consent,** §7B-3600.
District court jurisdiction, §7B-1603.
Eminent domain.
Private condemnors.
Acquisition of title of infant, §40A-30.
Employment.
Child labor law generally.
See CHILD LABOR.
Employment security section.
Jurisdiction, §96-22.
Enticing out of state, §14-40.
Evidence of other crimes, wrongs or acts.
Admissibility against juvenile, §8C-1 Rule 404(b).
Execution for murder, §14-17.
Executors and administrators.
Persons disqualified to serve as personal
representative, §28A-4-2.
Settlement.
Payment into court of fund due minor,
§28A-23-2.

CHILDREN AND MINORS —Cont'd
Exemptions.
Homestead exemption.
Exemption for benefit of children, NC Const Art X §2.
Exhibition of children.
Deformed children.
Prohibited exhibition, §110-20.1(a).
Applicability of provisions, §110-20.1(d).
Penalty for violations of provisions, §110-20.1(e).
Mentally ill or retarded children.
Prohibited exhibition, §110-20.1(a).
Applicability of provisions, §110-20.1(d).
Penalty for violations of provisions, §110-20.1(e).
Participating in prohibited exhibition, §110-20.1(b), (c).
Applicability of provisions, §110-20.1(d).
Penalty for violations of provisions, §110-20.1(e).
Procuring or arranging for prohibited exhibition, §110-20.1(c).
Applicability of provisions, §110-20.1(d).
Penalty for violations of provisions, §110-20.1(e).
Expungement of criminal records.
First offenders not over age twenty-one.
Drug offenses, §15A-145.2.
Toxic vapors offenses, §15A-145.3.
First offenders under age eighteen, §15A-145.
Gang offenses, §15A-145.1.
Extradition.
Sale of harmful materials to minors.
Persons guilty of contempt, §19-20(c).
Family preservation act, §§143B-150.5, 143B-150.6.
Family purpose doctrine.
Strict liability for damage to person or property by minors, §1-538.1.
Felonious restraint, §14-43.3.
Fiduciaries.
Payments to or for minors, §32-27.
Firearms and other weapons.
Exceptions, §14-269.7(b).
Handgun sales, §14-315(a1).
Permitting young children to use dangerous firearms, §14-316(a).
Air rifles, air pistols and BB guns not deemed dangerous firearms, §14-316(b).
Possession of handgun, §14-269.7(a).
Sale or giving weapons to minors, §14-315.
Defense, §14-315(b1).
Handguns, §14-315(a1).
Weapons other than handguns, §14-315(a).
Storage of firearms to protect minors, §14-315.1.
Close proximity of weapon, §14-315.1(b).
Exemptions, §14-315.1(c).
"Minor" defined, §14-315.1(d).
Posting of warning sign, §14-315.2(b), (c).
Prohibited conduct, §14-315.1(a).
Written notice requirements, §14-315.2(a), (c).
Fires.
Exposing children to fire, §14-318.
Fishing licenses.
Salt water fishing license.
Exemption, persons 18 or younger, §113-174.2(d).
Foster care and adoption assistance.
Payments generally, §§108A-48 to 108A-50.
Foster homes.
Regulation of agencies receiving or placing children, §§131D-10.1 to 131D-10.9.
See CHILD PLACING AGENCIES.

CHILDREN AND MINORS —Cont'd
Fraternal benefit societies.
Life insurance, §58-24-75(b).
Lodge systems.
Organization and operation of lodges for children, §58-24-5(b).
Fraternal orders.
Insurance, §58-25-35.
Certificates and contributions, §58-25-40.
Continuation of certificate, §58-25-60.
Exchange of certificates, §58-25-45.
Medical examination, §58-25-40.
Reserve fund, §58-25-45.
Funds owed to minors.
Administration, delivery or distribution, §35A-1227.
Gangs.
Not applicable to juveniles under age of 16, §14-50.28.
Soliciting or encouraging participation, §14-50.18.
Gifts to minors generally, §§33A-1 to 33A-24.
See TRANSFERS TO MINORS.
Guardian ad litem, §1A-1 Rule 17.
Appointment of guardian, SuperCt Rule 7.1.
Generally.
See GUARDIAN AD LITEM.
Services to abused, neglected or dependent juveniles, §§7B-1200 to 7B-1204.
Guardians.
Generally.
See GUARDIAN AND WARD.
Standby guardians for minor children.
Authority concurrent to parental rights, §35A-1377.
Will making testamentary recommendation for appointment of guardian for minor, §§35A-1212.1, 35A-1224(d).
Incompetent minor, §35A-1225.
Handgun possession, §14-269.7.
Harmful materials.
Dissemination or sales to minors.
Criminal offenses, civil remedy. See within this heading, "Obscenity or pornography."
Health.
Childhood vaccine-related injury compensation, §§130A-422 to 130A-434.
See CHILDHOOD VACCINE-RELATED INJURY COMPENSATION.
Maternal and child health services.
County appropriations.
Local health departments not to reduce, §130A-4.1(a).
Income earned by local health departments.
Departments required to budget and expend, §130A-4.1(b).
Metabolic and other hereditary and congenital defect screening of newborns.
Establishment and administering of program, §130A-125(a).
Fees, §130A-125(c).
Rules, §130A-125(b), (b1).
Teen pregnancy prevention, §130A-131.15A.
Health benefit plan coverage.
Newborn hearing screening, §58-3-260.
Health care for minors, consent to, §§32A-28 to 32A-34.
Health insurance coverage for dependent children.
Continuation of coverage after termination.
Mentally retarded or physically handicapped children, §58-51-25(a).

CHILDREN AND MINORS —Cont'd
Health insurance coverage for dependent children —Cont'd
Continuation of coverage after termination —Cont'd
Students on medically necessary leave of absence from postsecondary educational institution, §58-51-25(b).
State health plan for teachers and state employees, §§135-48.21(g), 135-48.41(b).
Child born to covered employee.
Covered at birth without waiting period, §135-48.42(a).
Dependent younger than age 19.
Enrolled at any time without waiting period, §135-48.42(c).
Health insurance coverage for nondependent children, §58-3-290.
Coverage issued regardless of health status, §58-3-290(b).
Defined terms, §58-3-290(a).
Open enrollment, requirements, §58-3-290(b).
Premiums, adjustment, §58-3-290(d).
Rules and regulations, authority to promulgate, §58-3-290(c).
Health insurance program for children.
Act of 1998, §§108A-70.18 to 108A-70.29.
See CHILDREN'S HEALTH INSURANCE PROGRAM.
Health Choice for children.
Child health insurance fund, §108A-70.20A.
Hearing impaired.
Schools for the deaf.
See DEAF AND HEARING IMPAIRED.
Helmet law.
Bicycle safety act, §§20-171.6 to 20-171.9.
Highways, roads and streets.
Condemnation proceedings.
Appointment of guardian ad litem, §136-110.
Homestead exemption.
Exemption for benefit of children, NC Const Art X §2.
Homicide.
Punishment for persons under 17 years of age, §14-17.
Hunting and trapping licenses.
Persons under 16 years of age, license exemption, §113-276(d).
Husband and wife.
Conveyances.
Married persons under 18 competent as to certain transactions, §39-13.2(a).
Iceboxes.
Discarding or abandoning iceboxes, §14-318.1.
Identifying information.
Appeals.
Protection of identity of persons under age of 18.
Appeal information statement, AppProc Rule 41(b).
Briefs, AppProc Rule 28(a).
Form, AppProc Appx D.
Juvenile matters, AppProc Rules 3.1(b), 3(b).
Motions in appellate courts, AppProc Rule 37(c).
Oral argument, AppProc Rule 30(a).
Record on appeal.
Notice in filing involving juveniles, AppProc Rule 9(a).
Victims of sexual offenses, AppProc Rule 4(e).

CHILDREN AND MINORS —Cont'd
Identifying information —Cont'd
Local parks and recreation program records.
Limited access, §132-1.12.
Illegitimate children.
Paternity.
Proceedings to establish generally.
See PATERNITY.
Support, legitimation, civil actions regarding, §§49-1 to 49-17.
See CHILDREN BORN OUT OF WEDLOCK.
Immunity.
Motor vehicles.
Parent-child immunity, §1-539.21.
Immunization, §130A-153(d).
Childhood vaccine-related injury compensation, §§130A-422 to 130A-434.
See CHILDHOOD VACCINE-RELATED INJURY COMPENSATION.
Generally, §§130A-152 to 130A-158.
See IMMUNIZATION.
Income tax credits, §105-151.24(a), (b).
Incompetence.
Determination generally, §§35A-1101 to 35A-1116.
See INCOMPETENCY.
Indecent liberties between children, §14-202.2.
Indian child welfare.
Health and human services department.
Collaboration between division of social services and commission of Indian affairs, §143B-139.5A.
Insurance proceeds belonging to minor as beneficiary after death of insured.
Payment to and receipt by clerk of superior court or public guardian, §7A-111(a), (c).
Interstate compact for juveniles, §§7B-4000 to 7B-4002.
Interstate compact on juveniles, §§7B-2800 to 7B-2827.
See INTERSTATE COMPACT ON JUVENILES.
Interstate compact on the placement of children, §§7B-3800 to 7B-3806.
Judicial consent for emergency surgical or medical treatment, §7B-3600.
District court jurisdiction, §7B-1603.
Judicial sales.
Confirmation of public sale of real property, §1-339.28(b).
Juvenile delinquents.
Generally, §§7B-1500 to 7B-2827.
See DELINQUENT AND UNDISCIPLINED JUVENILES.
Juvenile records and social reports, §§7B-2900 to 7B-3202.
See JUVENILE RECORDS AND SOCIAL REPORTS.
Juvenile services generally.
See YOUTH SERVICES.
Kidnapping and abduction.
Abduction of children, §14-41(a).
Electronic surveillance orders, §15A-290(c1).
Employment purposes.
Enticing minors out of state for purposes of employment, §14-40.
Public officers and employees, §14-41(b).
Labor.
See CHILD LABOR.
Larceny, shoplifting, employee theft, embezzlement or false pretenses.
Civil liability for minors acts, §1-538.2(b).

CHILDREN AND MINORS —Cont'd
Larceny, shoplifting, employee theft, embezzlement or false pretenses —Cont'd
Shoplifting.
  Minors detained by merchants, agents or employees, §§14-72.1(c), 14-72(d).
Lead-based paint hazard management program, §§130A-453.01 to 130A-453.11.
See LEAD-BASED PAINT.
Lead poisoning in children.
  Generally, §§130A-131.5 to 130A-131.9H.
    See LEAD POISONING IN CHILDREN.
  Lead-based paint hazard management program, §§130A-453.01 to 130A-453.11.
    See LEAD-BASED PAINT.
Limitation of actions.
  Disabilities.
    Time for bringing action, §1-17(a).
  Malpractice, health care services.
    Time for bringing action, §1-17(c).
  Malpractice, professional services.
    Time for bringing action, §1-17(b).
  Tolled because of minority.
    Persons not yet twenty-one, §48A-3.
Local parks and recreation program participation.
  Identifying information in program records.
    Limited access, §132-1.12.
Lose control, lose license, §20-11(n1).
Lotteries.
  State lottery.
    Prize payments to minors prohibited, §18C-132(j).
    Sales of tickets and shares to minors prohibited, §18C-131(d).
      Defenses, §18C-131(e).
Malicious or willful destruction of property by minors.
  Action for recovery of damages from parents, §1-538.1.
Maltreatment of juvenile, report of death due to, §7B-301.
Marriage.
  Age to lawfully marry, §51-2(a).
  Consent to marry.
    Persons over 16 years of age and under 18 years of age.
      Required for issuance of licensee, §51-2(a1).
  District court jurisdiction.
    Marriage by underage parties, §7B-200(a).
  Emancipated minor.
    Consent to marry not required, §51-2(a1).
  Fraud or misrepresentation in procuring license, §51-2(c).
  Persons over 14 years of age and under 16 years of age, §§51-2.1, 51-2(b).
  Persons under 14 years of age.
    Unlawful to marry, §51-2(b1).
  Want of capacity, §51-3.
Maternal and child health program, §130A-124(a) to (c).
  County appropriations for services.
    Local health departments not to reduce, §130A-4.1(a).
  Income earned by local health departments.
    Departments required to budget and expend, §130A-4.1(b).
Medical treatment of minor by physician.
  Abuse of controlled substances or alcohol.
    Consent of minor sufficient, §90-21.5(a).

CHILDREN AND MINORS —Cont'd
Medical treatment of minor by physician —Cont'd
  Consent of minor.
    Sufficient for certain medical health services, §90-21.5.
  Consent of parent, guardian or person in loco parentis.
    When not required, §90-21.1.
  Consent to health care.
    Authorization.
      Duration, §32A-32.
      Revocation, §32A-32.
      Who may take on authorization, §32A-30.
    Custodial parents.
      Authority, §32A-30.
      Person who may make authorization, §32A-30.
    Definitions, §32A-29.
    Disagreement regarding health care.
      Revocation of authorization, §32A-32(c).
    Form for authorization, §32A-34.
    Full power and authority.
      Parent authorized to grant agent, §32A-31(a).
    Incapacity or mental incompetence of authorizing parent.
      Authorization not effected by, §32A-32(d).
    Limitations and restrictions on authority.
      Authorization may contain, §32A-31(b).
    Protection of health care provider.
      Good faith reliance on authorization, §32A-33(b).
    Public policy, statement of, §32A-28(b).
    Purpose of article, §32A-28(b).
    Reliance on authorization.
      Physician, dentist or other health care provider, §32A-33(a), (b).
    Revocation of authorization.
      Automatic revocation, §32A-32(a).
      Disagreement regarding health care, §32A-32(c).
      Procedure for exercising right to revoke, §32A-32(b).
      Right to revoke, §32A-32(b).
    Treatment by physician.
      Consent of minor sufficient, §90-21.5(a).
      Consent of parent or guardian.
        When not required, §90-21.1.
    Who may make an authorization to consent, §32A-30.
    Withholding or discontinuing life sustaining procedures.
      Authorization may not contain, §32A-31(c).
  Definition of "treatment," §90-21.2.
    Surgery included, §90-21.3.
  Emancipated minor.
    Consent by, §90-21.5(b).
  Emotional disturbance.
    Consent of minor sufficient, §90-21.5(a).
  Liability of physician, §90-21.4(a).
  Notification of parent, guardian or person in loco parentis.
    Physician not to notify without consent of minor, §90-21.4(b).
  Pregnancy.
    Consent of minor sufficient, §90-21.5(a).
  Surgery.
    Second opinion as to necessity, §90-21.3.
  Venereal diseases.
    Consent of minor sufficient, §90-21.5(a).

CHILDREN AND MINORS —Cont'd
Mental health, developmental disability, substance abuse.
Alcoholism or drug abuse.
Consent of minor to treatment sufficient, §90-21.5(a).
Declaring trust irrevocable and making gift of life interest.
Notice to minors, §35A-1353.
Discharge of voluntarily admitted minors.
Developmentally disabled, §122C-242.
Notice and consultation with responsible person, §122C-57(d1).
Exhibition of certain children prohibited, §110-20.1.
Rights of clients, §122C-62(c), (d).
Sexual offense.
Engaging in act with minor client constituting, §122C-65(a), (b).
Voluntary admissions.
Facilities for the mentally ill and substance abusers, §§122C-221 to 122C-224.7.
See MENTAL HEALTH, DEVELOPMENTAL DISABILITY, SUBSTANCE ABUSE.
Metabolic and other hereditary and congenital disorders.
Screening of newborns, §130A-125.
Minor defending an action.
Larceny, shoplifting, employee theft, embezzlement or false pretenses.
Civil liability for minors acts, §1-538.2(b).
Malicious or willful destruction of property by minors.
Action for recovery of damages from parents, §1-538.1.
Motor vehicles.
Abolition of parent-child immunity in motor vehicle cases, §1-539.21.
Negligent supervision of minor.
Right of educational entity to recover against parents, §1-538.3.
Missing children.
AMBER alert system, §143B-1021.
Center for missing persons.
General provisions, §§143B-1010 to 143B-1022.
See MISSING PERSONS.
Missing child defined, §143B-1011.
Silver alert system.
Missing persons with cognitive impairment, §143B-1022.
Mistake of age.
Controlled substances.
Employing or intentionally using minor to commit drug law violations, §90-95.4(c).
Participating in a drug violation by a minor, §90-95.7(b).
Promoting drug sales by a minor, §90-95.6(b).
Mobile phones.
Use while operating vehicle.
Prohibition, fine, §§20-11(c), (e), (l), 20-137.3(b), (e).
Definitions, §20-137.3(a).
Exceptions, §20-137.3(d).
Seizure and forfeiture, §20-137.3(c).
Molestation.
See CHILD MOLESTATION.
Money belonging to minor as beneficiary after death of insured.
Payment to and receipt by clerk of superior court or public guardian, §7A-111(a), (c).

CHILDREN AND MINORS —Cont'd
Mortgages and deeds of trust.
Conveyances by infant trustees, §39-4.
Motor vehicle financial responsibility, §20-279.6A.
Motor vehicles.
All-terrain vehicles.
Age restrictions, §20-171.15.
Cell phones.
Use while operating vehicle.
Prohibition, fine, §§20-11(c), (e), (l), 20-137.3(b), (e).
Definitions, §20-137.3(a).
Exceptions, §20-137.3(d).
Seizure and forfeiture, §20-137.3(c).
Child restraint systems, §20-137.1.
Placement of small children within vehicle, §20-137.1(a1).
Points for violations, §§20-16(c), 20-137.1(d).
Driving by person less than 21 years old after consuming alcohol or drugs, §20-138.3.
Driving by provisional licensee after consuming alcohol or drugs.
Restoration of license after conviction, §20-17.6.
Driving eligibility certificate, §20-11(n).
Charter school's designee, duties, §115C-238.29F(j).
Principals of schools, duties, §115C-288(k).
School disciplinary actions.
Effect on eligibility, §20-11(n1).
Revocation of provisional license, §20-13.2(c1).
State board of community colleges, rules, duty to adopt, §115D-5(a3).
State board of education, rules, duty to develop, §115C-12.
Grounds for revoking provisional license, §20-13.2.
Driving by provisional licensee after consuming alcohol or drugs, §20-13.2(a).
Driving eligibility certificate not maintained, §20-13.2(c1).
Explosives offenses, §20-13.2(c2).
Immediate civil revocation for certain criminal moving violations, §20-13.3.
Impaired driving conviction, §20-13.2(b).
Issuance of license during revocation or suspension, §20-9(b1).
Length of revocation, §20-13.2(d).
Restoration of license, proof of financial responsibility, §20-13.2(e).
Willful refusal to submit to chemical analysis, §20-13.2(c).
Mandatory usage of restraint for child passengers, §20-137.1(a).
Mobile phones.
Use while operating vehicle.
Prohibition, fine, §§20-11(c), (e), (l), 20-137.3(b), (e).
Definitions, §20-137.3(a).
Exceptions, §20-137.3(d).
Seizure and forfeiture, §20-137.3(c).
Parent-child immunity.
Abolition in motor vehicle cases, §1-539.21.
Suspension of license of provisional licensee for moving violation, §20-13(a).
Length of suspension, §20-13(b).
Motor vehicle moving violation defined, §20-13(a).
Probation, placing licensee on, §20-13(b).
Restoration of license on probationary status, hearing request, §20-13(b).
Retention of license until hearing, §20-13(a).

CHILDREN AND MINORS —Cont'd
Motor vehicles —Cont'd
Suspension of license of provisional licensee for
    moving violation —Cont'd
    Suspension in addition to other remedies,
        §20-13(d).
    Two or more offenses committed on single
        occasion, §20-13(c).
Transporting children under 12 years of age in
    open bed or open cargo area of vehicle,
    §20-135.2B(a).
    Driver's license points or insurance surcharge
        not assessed for violation, §20-135.2B(d).
    Exceptions, §20-135.2B(b).
    Infraction for violating, §20-135.2B(c).
Unlicensed driving, §20-32.
Murder in the first degree, §14-17.
Name change.
Procedure, §101-2.
Two change limitation, §101-6(b).
Negligent supervision of child.
Right of educational entity to recover against
    parent, §1-538.3.
Newborn hearing screening.
Health benefit plan coverage, §58-3-260.
Nonsupport.
Child support generally.
    See CHILD SUPPORT.
Compelling disclosure of information respecting
    nonsupporting parent, §110-131.
Support of illegitimate children, §§49-1 to 49-9.
    See CHILDREN BORN OUT OF WEDLOCK.
Willful nonsupport by supporting spouse, §14-322.
North Carolina AMBER alert system,
    §143B-1021.
North Carolina center for missing persons.
General provisions, §§143B-1010 to 143B-1022.
    See MISSING PERSONS.
**North Carolina child fatality prevention
    system,** §§7B-1400 to 7B-1414.
See CHILD FATALITY PREVENTION SYSTEM.
Obscenity or pornography.
Bureau of investigation.
    Authorized to investigate crimes, §114-15(b1).
Civil remedy for sales of harmful material to
    minors, §§19-9 to 19-20.
    Citation of act, §19-9.
    Commencement of actions, §§19-13(a), 19-14.
        Rules of civil procedure, §19-13(b).
    Complaint.
        Commencement of action, §19-14.
        Examination and reading by court, §19-15(a).
        Filing, §19-14.
        Generally, §19-14.
    Contempt.
        Defenses, §19-20(a).
        Disobedience of injunction, §19-20(a).
        Extradition, §19-20(c).
        Persons not to be guilty of contempt,
            §19-20(b).
    Default judgment, §19-16(b).
    Definitions, §19-12.
    Dismissal of action.
        No probable cause, §19-15(b).
    Extradition.
        Persons guilty of contempt, §19-20(c).
    Injunctions.
        Disobedience.
            Contempt, §19-20(a).
        Permanent injunction, §19-18(b).
        Preliminary injunction, §19-19(c), (d).

CHILDREN AND MINORS —Cont'd
Obscenity or pornography —Cont'd
Civil remedy for sales of harmful material to
    minors —Cont'd
    Injunctions —Cont'd
        Temporary restraining order, §19-19(a), (b).
    Judgments, §19-18(a), (b).
        Territorial restrictions on, §19-18(c).
    Jury.
        Right to trial by jury, §19-17(c).
    Legislative declaration, §§19-10, 19-11.
    Notice.
        Preliminary injunction, §19-19(d).
    Policy of state, §19-11.
    Purposes of provisions, §19-10.
    Respondent.
        Appearance, §19-16(a).
        Right to trial by jury, §19-17(c).
        Right to trial of issues, §19-17(b).
    Rules of civil procedure.
        Applicability to proceedings, §19-13(b).
    Summons.
        Issuance, §19-15(c).
    Title of law, §19-9.
    Trial.
        Right of respondent to trial by jury, §19-17(c).
        Right of respondent to trial of issues,
            §19-17(b).
        Setting of date, §19-17(a).
Definitions, §14-190.13.
Displaying material harmful to minors,
    §14-190.14(a).
    Penalty, §14-190.14(b).
Disseminating harmful materials to minors,
    §14-190.15(a).
    Defenses, §14-190.15(c).
    Minors under the age of 13 years, §14-190.8.
    Minors under the age of 16 years, §14-190.7.
    Penalties, §14-190.15(d).
Employing or permitting minor to assist in offense
    under article, §14-190.6.
Exhibiting harmful performance, §14-190.15(b).
    Defenses, §14-190.15(c).
    Penalties, §14-190.15(d).
Generally.
    See OBSCENITY AND PORNOGRAPHY.
Harmful to minors.
    Defined, §14-190.13.
Prostitution, §§14-190.18, 14-190.19.
    Defined, §14-190.13.
Sexual activity.
    Defined, §14-190.13.
Sexual exploitation of a minor, §§14-190.16,
    14-190.17.
Sexually explicit nudity.
    Defined, §14-190.13.
Other crimes, wrongs or acts.
Admissibility against juvenile, §8C-1 Rule 404(b).
Parental authority over juvenile, §§7B-3400 to
    7B-3404.
Parental liability for minors acts.
Larceny, shoplifting, employee theft,
    embezzlement or false pretenses.
    Civil liability for minors acts, §1-538.2(b).
Parent and child generally.
See PARENT AND CHILD.
Parks and recreation program participation.
Identifying information in local program records.
    Limited access, §132-1.12.
Parties.
Administration of estates.
    Liability for costs in administration, §7A-307(e).

CHILDREN AND MINORS —Cont'd
Parties —Cont'd
Infants to sue or defend by guardian or guardian
ad litem, §1A-1 Rule 17(b).
Partition.
Owelty.
Infant's share due at majority, §46-12.
Partition sales.
Shares to persons not sui juris secured, §46-34.
Payment for work.
Failing to pay minors for doing certain work,
§14-321.
Pederasty.
Bail, §15A-534.4.
Taking indecent liberties with children, §14-202.1.
Perinatal health care, §130A-127.
Personal watercraft.
Persons under 16 years of age operating,
§75A-13.3(b1).
Renting, hiring or leasing to persons under 16
years, §75A-13.3(c).
Pimping.
Electronic surveillance orders, §15A-290(c1).
Participating in prostitution of a minor.
Generally, §14-190.19.
Promoting prostitution of a minor.
Definitions for certain offenses concerning
minors, §14-190.13.
Generally, §14-190.18.
Placement of children.
Bringing child into state or taking child out of
state for purposes of adoption.
Consent of department of health and human
services, §§7B-3700 to 7B-3705.
Child placing agencies generally.
See CHILD PLACING AGENCIES.
Control over child placing and child care,
§§131D-10.1 to 131D-10.9.
See CHILD PLACING AGENCIES.
Foster care and adoption assistance payments,
§§108A-48 to 108A-50.
See SOCIAL SERVICES.
Interstate compact on the placement of children,
§§7B-3800 to 7B-3806.
Social services generally.
See SOCIAL SERVICES.
Precious metal dealers.
Purchasing from juvenile, §66-171.
Pregnancy.
Consent of minor to treatment sufficient,
§90-21.5(a).
Teen pregnancy prevention, §130A-131.15A.
Prior crimes, wrongs or acts.
Admissibility against juvenile, §8C-1 Rule 404(b).
Prisons and prisoners.
Disposition of child born of female prisoner,
§148-47.
**Program on prevention of abuse and neglect of
juveniles, §§7B-1300 to 7B-1302.**
Property issues.
Age of majority, §48A-2.
Condemnation proceedings.
Guardian ad litem.
Highways, roads and streets.
Appointment, §136-110.
Public condemnors.
Appointment for infants, §40A-50.
Guardians.
Private condemnors.
Appointment, §40A-30.

CHILDREN AND MINORS —Cont'd
Property issues —Cont'd
Conveyances.
Infant trustees, §39-4.
Married persons under 18 competent as to
certain transactions, §39-13.2(a).
Funds owed to minors.
Administration, delivery or distribution,
§35A-1227.
Gifts to minors generally, §§33A-1 to 33A-24.
See TRANSFERS TO MINORS.
Homestead exemption.
Exemption for benefit of children, NC Const Art
X §2.
Judicial sales.
Confirmation of public sale of real property,
§1-339.28(b).
Malicious or willful destruction.
Recovery of damages from parents, §1-538.1.
Special proceedings.
Ex parte infant petitioner.
Approval by judge, §1-402.
Talent contracts.
Earnings to be set aside in trust, §§48A-14 to
48A-16.
Prostitution.
Defined, §14-190.13.
Electronic surveillance orders, §15A-290.
Participating in prostitution of a minor.
Definitions of certain offenses concerning
minors, §14-190.13.
Elements of offense, §14-190.19(a).
Mistake of age.
Not a defense, §14-190.19(b).
Penalties, §14-190.19(c).
Sentencing, §14-190.19(c).
Promoting prostitution of a minor.
Definitions of certain offenses concerning
minors, §14-190.13.
Elements of offense, §14-190.18(a).
Mistake of age.
Not a defense, §14-190.18(b).
Penalties, §14-190.18(c).
Sentencing, §14-190.18(c).
Protection of minors, §§14-313 to 14-321.1.
Pseudoephedrine products.
Sales to minors prohibited, §90-113.52(c).
Public officers and employees.
Abduction of children, §14-41(b).
Public schools generally.
See SCHOOLS AND EDUCATION.
Rape indictments.
Essentials of bill.
Victim female child under 13 years,
§15-144.1(b).
Rape of a child, §14-27.2A.
Real property.
Conveyances by infant trustees, §39-4.
Refrigerators.
Discarding or abandoning refrigerators, §14-318.1.
Precautions required, §14-318.1.
**Remainders, reversions and executory
interests.**
Sale, lease or mortgage in case of remainders,
§41-11.
**Report of abuse, neglect, dependency or death
due to maltreatment, §7B-301.**
Representatives.
Persons representing and binding others,
§§36C-3-301 to 36C-3-305.

CHILDREN AND MINORS —Cont'd
Restraint.
Felonious restraint, §14-43.3.
Safe deposit boxes.
Banks leasing or renting to minors, §53-43.5(b), (c).
Savings and loan associations, §54B-132(b).
Savings banks, §54C-170(b).
Safe haven for infants, §§14-318.2, 14-318.4.
Safety belts.
Child restraint systems, §20-137.1.
Placement of small children within vehicle, §20-137.1(a1).
Points for violations, §§20-16(c), 20-137.1(d).
Mandatory usage of restraint for child passengers, §20-137.1(a).
Transporting children under 12 years of age in open bed or open cargo area of vehicle.
Exception to prohibition when child secured or restrained by seat belt, §20-135.2B(b).
Salt water fishing license.
Exemption, persons 18 or younger, §113-174.2(d).
Savings and loan associations.
Safe deposit boxes.
Leasing to minors, §54B-132(b).
Withdrawable accounts.
Minors as account holders, §54B-132(a).
Savings banks.
Deposit accounts.
Minors as deposit account holders, §54C-170(a).
Safe-deposit boxes.
Leased to minors, §54C-170(b).
Schools for the deaf.
See DEAF AND HEARING IMPAIRED.
Seat belts.
Child restraint systems, §20-137.1.
Effect of violations, §20-137.1(d).
Placement of small children within vehicle, §20-137.1(a1).
Points for violations, §§20-16(c), 20-137.1(d).
Mandatory usage of restraint for child passengers, §20-137.1(a).
Transporting children under 12 years of age in open bed or open cargo area of vehicle.
Exception to prohibition when child secured or restrained by seat belt, §20-135.2B(b).
Service of process on minor.
Appointment of guardian for minor.
Service of application and notices, §35A-1222.
Personal jurisdiction, §1A-1 Rule 4(j).
Manner of service on natural person under disability, §1A-1 Rule 4(j).
Sex offenses.
Bail, §15A-534.4.
Electronic surveillance orders, §15A-290(c1).
Incapacity to commit sex offense.
No presumption, §14-27.9.
Indecent liberties between children, §14-202.2.
Indictments.
Victim age 13 or less, §15-144.2(b).
Intercourse and sexual offenses with certain victims, §14-27.7(a).
Defendant at least six years older than victim, §14-27.7A(a).
Defendant between four and six years older than victim, §14-27.7A(b).
Probation for sex offenders and persons convicted of sexual abuse of minor.
Special conditions, §15A-1343.
Rape of a child, §14-27.2A.

CHILDREN AND MINORS —Cont'd
Sex offenses —Cont'd
School personnel.
Acts with victim who is student, §14-27.7(b).
Sexual offense with child, §14-27.4A.
Taking indecent liberties with children.
Elements of offense, §14-202.1.
Felony offense, §14-202.1(b).
Venue, §15A-136.
Sexual exploitation of a minor.
Definitions for certain offenses concerning minor, §14-190.13.
Electronic surveillance orders, §15A-290.
First degree.
Elements of offense, §14-190.16(a).
Inference, §14-190.16(b).
Mistake of age not a defense, §14-190.16(c).
Sentencing, §14-190.16(d).
Second degree.
Elements of offense, §14-190.17(a).
Inference, §14-190.17(b).
Mistake of age.
Not a defense, §14-190.17(c).
Penalties, §14-190.17(d).
Sentencing, §14-190.17(d).
Third degree.
Elements of offense, §14-190.17A(a).
Inferences, §14-190.17A(b).
Mistake of age.
Not defense, §14-190.17A(c).
Punishment and sentencing, §14-190.17A(d).
Shoplifting.
Notice to parent or guardian, §§14-72.1(c), 14-72(d).
Special education.
Education of children with disabilities.
Generally, §§115C-106.1 to 115C-112.1.
See SPECIAL EDUCATION.
Special proceedings.
Ex parte infant petitioner.
Approval by judge, §1-402.
Standby guardians for minor children, §§35A-1370 to 35A-1382.
See GUARDIAN AND WARD.
State child fatality review team, §143B-150.20.
State health plan for teachers and state employees.
Child born to covered employee.
Covered at birth without waiting period, §135-48.42(a).
Coverage for dependent child, §§135-48.21(g), 135-48.41(b).
Dependent younger than age 19.
Enrolled at any time without waiting period, §135-48.42(c).
State lottery.
Prize payments to minors prohibited, §18C-132(j).
Sales of tickets and shares to minors prohibited, §18C-131(d).
Defenses, §18C-131(e).
Sterilization.
Married minors.
Operation lawful upon request, §90-271.
Unmarried minors, §90-272.
Street gangs.
Not applicable to juveniles under age of 16, §14-50.28.
Soliciting or encouraging participation, §14-50.18.
Strict liability for damage to person or property by minors, §1-538.1.

CHILDREN AND MINORS —Cont'd
Supervision and control of juvenile by parents.
Armed forces members, exception to parental authority, §7B-3402.
Criminal liability not created by provisions, §7B-3403.
Definitions, §7B-3401.
Enforcement of parental authority, §7B-3404.
Juvenile leaving home and refusing to return.
Civil action to enforce parental authority, §7B-3404.
Juveniles under eighteen subject to parental control, §7B-3400.
Married juveniles, exception, §7B-3402.
Support and maintenance.
Generally.
See CHILD SUPPORT.
Illegitimate children, §§49-1 to 49-9.
See CHILDREN BORN OUT OF WEDLOCK.
Surgery.
Second opinion as to necessity, §90-21.3.
Talent agency contracts, §§48A-17, 48A-18.
Tanning equipment.
Use by persons 13 or younger.
Prescription required, §104E-9.1(a).
Tattooing.
Prohibited tattooing of persons under eighteen years of age, §14-400(a).
Tax credits, §105-151.24(a), (b).
Teen court programs, §143B-809.
Telephonic sellers.
Calls made to minors, §66-264.
Termination of parental rights.
Generally, §§7B-1100 to 7B-1114.
See TERMINATION OF PARENTAL RIGHTS.
Testamentary recommendation by parent for appointment of guardian for minor, §§35A-1224(d), 35A-1225.
Incompetent minor, §35A-1225.
Tobacco products.
Sale or distribution of tobacco products to minors, §14-313.
Torrens system registration.
Infants may sue by guardian or trustee, §43-8.
Torts.
Malicious or willful destruction of property by minors.
Recovery of damages from parents, §1-538.1.
Transfers to minors, §§33A-1 to 33A-24.
See TRANSFERS TO MINORS.
Trespass.
Harm to child trespasser caused by artificial condition.
Child trespasser defined, §38B-4.
Possessor of land subject to liability, §38B-3.
Trial.
Sale of harmful materials to minors.
Civil remedy, §19-17.
Trusts and trustees.
Conveyances by infant trustees, §39-4.
Payments to or for minors, §32-27.
Talent contracts.
Earnings to be set aside in trust, §§48A-14 to 48A-16.
Unborn infants.
Taking by deed or writing, §41-5.
Undisciplined juveniles.
Generally, §§7B-1500 to 7B-2827.
See DELINQUENT AND UNDISCIPLINED JUVENILES.

CHILDREN AND MINORS —Cont'd
Unemployment compensation.
Employment of and assistance to minors.
Jurisdiction of employment security section, §96-22.
Uniform child custody jurisdiction and enforcement, §§50A-101 to 50A-317.
See CHILD CUSTODY JURISDICTION AND ENFORCEMENT.
Uniform reciprocal enforcement of support act.
See SUPPORT AND MAINTENANCE.
Uniform transfers to minors act, §§33A-1 to 33A-24.
See TRANSFERS TO MINORS.
Vandalism.
Malicious or willful destruction of property by minors.
Recovery of damages from parents, §1-538.1.
Venereal diseases.
Consent of minor to treatment sufficient, §90-21.5(a).
Veterans.
Minor spouses of veterans, §§165-17, 165-18.
Minor veterans, §§165-12 to 165-16.
Visitation rights.
See VISITATION.
Wills.
Caveat to will.
Time for filing after removal of disability, §31-32.
Parent's will recommending appointment of guardian, §§35A-1224(d), 35A-1225.
Incompetent minors, §35A-1225.
Witnesses.
Criminal proceedings.
Parent or guardian may be present, §15A-1225.
Remote testimony by child witness, §15A-1225.1.
Work.
Failing to pay minors for certain work, §14-321.
Workers' compensation.
Agreements or receipts for payments to.
Effect, §97-48(d).
Illegally employed minors.
Compensable under provisions, §97-10.3.
Limitation of actions.
Not to run against minor, §97-50.
Trusts and trustees.
Benefits of minor employees may be paid to trustee, §97-49.
Year's allowance, when children entitled, §30-17.
Youth councils, §§143B-385 to 143B-388.
Youth employment, §95-25.5.
Youthful offenders.
Sentencing committed offender to central prison, §148-28.
Zero tolerance law.
Driving by person less than 21 years old after consuming alcohol or drugs, §20-138.3.
Driving by provisional licensee after consuming alcohol or drugs.
Restoration of license after conviction, §20-17.6.

CHILDREN BORN OUT OF WEDLOCK, §§49-1 to 49-17.
Adoption generally.
See ADOPTION.
Aid to dependent children.
Reports to district attorney of illegitimate births, §§15-155.1 to 15-155.3.

CHILDREN BORN OUT OF WEDLOCK —Cont'd
Artificial insemination.
Status of child born as a result of, §49A-1.
Bigamy.
Status of child born of voidable marriage, §50-11.1.
Birth certificates, §130A-101(f).
Affidavit acknowledging paternity.
Listing declaring father on certificate, presumption as natural father, §130A-101(f).
Illegitimate children judicially determined.
Furnishing facts as to paternity, §130A-119.
Names entered, §130A-101(f).
New certificate upon legitimation, §49-13.
Legitimation when mother married, §49-12.1(e).
Clerks of court.
Paternity of illegitimate children judicially determined.
Furnishing state registrar with facts as to paternity, §130A-119.
Confidentiality of information.
Reports to district attorneys of aid to dependent children and illegitimate births, §15-155.3.
Costs.
Allowance, apportioned, §6-21.
Custody.
Establishment of paternity, §49-15.
District attorneys.
Reports to district attorneys of aid to dependent children and illegitimate births, §§15-155.1 to 15-155.3.
Divorce.
Effects of absolute divorce.
No judgment to render children illegitimate, §50-11(b).
Voidable marriages.
Children born legitimate, §50-11.1.
General assembly.
Local, private and special legislation prohibited, NC Const Art II §24.
Intestate succession.
Descent and distribution upon intestacy, §29-20.
Legitimated children.
Succession by, through and from, §29-18.
Person's illegitimate child entitled to take by, through and from, §29-19(b).
Share of surviving spouse of illegitimate intestate, §29-21.
Shares of others than surviving spouse, §29-22.
Succession by, through and from, §29-19(a) to (d).
Jurisdiction.
Construction of section, §49-17(b).
Nonresidents, §49-17(a).
Legitimation.
Birth certificates.
New certificate upon legitimation, §49-13.
Legitimation when mother married, §49-12.1(e).
Civil action to establish paternity.
Establishment not to have effect of legitimation, §49-14(a).
Effects, §49-11.
Legitimation when mother married, §49-12.1(b).
Marriage.
By subsequent marriage, §49-12.
Legitimation when mother married, §49-12.1.
Order of court, §49-10.
Parties, §49-10.
Petition, §49-10.

CHILDREN BORN OUT OF WEDLOCK —Cont'd
Legitimation —Cont'd
Special proceedings, §49-10.
Legitimation when mother married.
Putative father may file, §49-12.1(a).
Subsequent marriage, §49-12.
When mother married, §49-12.1.
Local, private and special legislation prohibited, NC Const Art II §24.
Marriage.
Legitimacy.
By subsequent marriage, §49-12.
Legitimation when mother married, §49-12.1.
Nonresidents.
Jurisdiction over, §49-17(a).
Construction of jurisdictional basis, §49-17(b).
Nonsupport, §49-2.
Parties who may bring proceedings, §49-16.
Paternity.
Blood tests and samples.
Competency of blood test, §8-50.1.
Civil action to establish.
Action brought more than three years after birth of child.
Evidentiary requirements, §49-14(d).
Authorized, §49-14(a).
Establishment not to have effect of legitimation, §49-14(a).
Invoices for services rendered.
Admissibility, §49-14(e).
Limitations on commencement, §49-14(c).
Proof to be beyond reasonable doubt, §49-14(b).
Setting aside orders of paternity, §49-4(h).
Temporary order of child support, §49-14(d).
Trial at first session after docketing, §49-14(e).
Custody and support of illegitimate children.
When paternity established, §49-15.
Legitimation when mother married.
Special proceeding brought by putative father, §49-12.1(a).
Proceedings to establish generally.
See PATERNITY.
Witnesses.
Presumed father or mother as witnesses where paternity at issue, §8-57.2.
Support of illegitimate children.
Amount, determination, §49-7.
Bonds, future appearance, §49-9.
Child defined, §49-2.
Continuances.
Surety of person accused of being father, §49-5.
Death of mother not bar to proceedings, §49-5.
District attorneys.
Reports to district attorneys of aid to dependent children and illegitimate births, §§15-155.1 to 15-155.3.
Immunity of mother testifying, §49-6.
Issues determined by court, §49-7.
Misdemeanors.
Willful nonsupport of illegitimate child, §49-2.
Orders, §49-7.
Modification, §49-8.
Paternity.
Paternity established, §49-15.
Preliminary determination, §49-5.
Temporary order pending determination, §49-14(f).
Place of child's birth not consideration, §49-3.
Self-incrimination not excuse for mother, §49-6.
Suspension of sentence, §49-8.
Time for commencing prosecution, §49-4.

CHILDREN BORN OUT OF WEDLOCK —Cont'd
Support of illegitimate children —Cont'd
Title of article, §49-1.
Venue, §49-5.
When prosecution may be commenced, §49-4.
Willful nonsupport, §49-2.
When mother married.
Burden of proof.
Overcoming presumption of legitimacy,
§49-12.1(b).
Consent order, §49-12.1(c).
Effect of legitimation under section, §49-12.1(d).
Guardian ad litem, appointment, §49-12.1(a).
New birth certificate.
Certified copy of order of legitimation sent to
state registrar, §49-12.1(e).
Presumption of legitimacy, overcoming,
§49-12.1(b).
Special proceeding filed by putative father,
§49-12.1(a).
Wills.
Revocation by subsequent entitlement of
after-born children, §31-5.5.
Witnesses.
Paternity.
Presumed father or mother as witnesses where
paternity at issue, §8-57.2.

**CHILDREN FROM BIRTH TO FIVE WITH
DISABILITIES.**
Interagency coordinating council, §§143B-179.5,
143B-179.6.

**CHILDREN'S HEALTH INSURANCE
PROGRAM.**
Act of 1998, §§108A-70.18 to 108A-70.29.
Administration, §108A-70.20.
Application for benefits, §108A-70.26(a).
Benefits available under program, §108A-70.21(b).
Co-payment for nonemergency visits to emergency
room, §108A-70.21(b).
Cost sharing and copayments, §108A-70.21(d).
Maximum out of pocket amounts,
§108A-70.21(e).
Data collection requirements, §108A-70.27(a).
Definitions, §108A-70.18.
Dental coverage, §108A-70.21(b).
Eligibility requirements, §108A-70.21(a).
Appeal of determination, §108A-70.26(c).
Establishment, §108A-70.20.
Extended coverage, §108A-70.21(g).
Use of state funds prohibited, §108A-70.21(h).
Fee for enrollment, §108A-70.21(c).
Fraud.
Aiding and abetting in fraudulent activity,
§108A-70.28(c).
Criminal penalty, §108A-70.28(d).
Misrepresentation on application,
§108A-70.28(a).
Misrepresentation on behalf of another,
§108A-70.28(b).
Misuse of program card, §108A-70.28(c).
Person defined, §108A-70.28(e).
Health Choice program.
Rulemaking by department, §108A-70.29(f).
Hearing coverage, §108A-70.21(b).
Implementation plan, §108A-70.25.
Information dissemination and publication,
§108A-70.26(b).
Lifetime maximum.
Benefits not subject to, §108A-70.21(i).
Outreach efforts, §108A-70.26(b).

**CHILDREN'S HEALTH INSURANCE
PROGRAM** —Cont'd
Act of 1998 —Cont'd
Payments to providers, §108A-70.21(b1).
Prescription drug providers.
Payments to, §108A-70.21(b1).
Private plan coverage, §108A-70.21(f).
Purpose of provisions, §108A-70.19.
Reporting requirements, §108A-70.27(b), (c).
Review of decisions.
Coverage of services during, §108A-70.29(b).
Decisions reviewable, §108A-70.29(b).
External review, §108A-70.29(b).
Internal review, §108A-70.29(b).
Notice of decision subject to review,
§108A-70.29(d).
Program change as basis of decision,
inapplicability of review, §108A-70.29(c).
Provisions governing review process,
§108A-70.29(a).
Rulemaking by department, §108A-70.29(e), (f).
Time for completion, §108A-70.29(b).
State plan to implement program, §108A-70.25.
Title of part, §108A-70.19.
Vision coverage, §108A-70.21(b).
Health Choice for children.
Child health insurance fund, §108A-70.20A.
Provider requirements, §§108C-1 to 108C-12.

CHILDREN'S TRUST FUND, §7B-1302(a), (b).

CHILDREN'S YEAR'S ALLOWANCE.
When child entitled, §30-17.

CHILDREN WITH DISABILITIES.
Developmental disabilities generally.
See MENTAL HEALTH, DEVELOPMENTAL
DISABILITY, SUBSTANCE ABUSE.
Education expenses tax credit.
Child requiring special education and related
services, §105-151.33.
Education generally, §§115C-106.1 to 115C-112.1.
See SPECIAL EDUCATION.
Interagency coordinating council.
Children from birth to five with disabilities,
§§143B-179.5, 143B-179.6.
Silver alert system.
Missing persons with cognitive impairment,
§143B-1022.

**CHILDREN WITH SPECIAL HEALTH CARE
NEEDS COMMISSION.**
Chairperson, §143-682(c).
Compensation, §143-684.
Composition, §143-682(b).
Duties, §143-683.
Establishment, §143-682(a).
Expenses, §143-684.
Powers, §143-683.
Terms of office, §143-682(c).

CHILD RESTRAINT SYSTEMS, §20-137.1.
Bicycles, restraining seat.
Small children as passengers, §§20-171.6 to
20-171.9.
Child care facilities.
Compliance with law required, §110-91.
Child passenger safety technicians, §20-137.5.
Placement of small children within vehicle,
§20-137.1(a1).
Points for violations, §§20-16(c), 20-137.1(d).
Seat belts generally.
See SEAT BELTS.

CHILD SUPPORT.

Abandonment.

Willful neglect or refusal to provide adequate support, §14-322.

Magistrate's finding, §110-138.1.

Absent parents.

Location of parents, §110-139.

Abused, neglected or dependent juvenile action.

Parent to pay, custody of juvenile in someone other than parent, §7B-904(d).

Acknowledgment of paternity.

Agreements of support.

Filing fees, §110-134.

Force and effect of agreements, §110-132(a3).

Show cause orders, §110-132(b).

Setting aside affidavit of parentage by trial court, §110-132(a1), (a2).

Action for support of minor child generally, §50-13.4.

Administration of program, §110-128.

Adoption.

Consequences of consent by parent to adoption, §48-3-607(c).

Duty of former parent to make past-due payments.

Effect of decree of adoption, §48-1-106(c).

AEI.

High-volume, automated administrative enforcement in interstate cases, §110-139.3.

Agreements of support, §§110-132 to 110-134.

Acknowledgment of paternity.

Filing fees, §110-134.

Force and effect of agreements, §110-132(a3).

Show cause orders, §110-132(b).

Medical support, §50-13.11.

Responsible parents.

Enforceability of agreement, §110-133.

Filing fees, §110-134.

Modification of agreements, §110-133.

Voluntary support agreements, §110-133.

Acknowledgment of paternity and agreement to support, §110-132.

Filing fees, §110-134.

Filing fees, §110-134.

Amount of support, §50-13.4(c), (c1).

Employee verification form.

Amount of obligor's gross income, establishing by, §110-139(c1).

Factors considered, §50-13.4(c).

Guidelines for computation.

Uniform statewide presumptive guidelines.

Application in determining amount, §50-13.4(c).

Prescribed by conference of chief district judges, §50-13.4(c1).

Hearings on request of party, §50-13.4(c).

Modification of amount, §50-13.4(c).

Past due child support, §50-13.10.

Procedure to insure payment, §50-13.9.

Reasonable needs of child, §50-13.4(c).

Appeals.

Enforcement pending appeal.

Civil contempt, §50-13.4(f).

Expedited process.

Orders of child support hearing officer, §50-38.

Arbitration.

Family law arbitration generally, §§50-41 to 50-62.

See FAMILY LAW ARBITRATION.

CHILD SUPPORT —Cont'd

Arrearages.

At termination of support, §50-13.4(c).

Enforcement orders, §50-13.9(d).

Vesting of past due support, §50-13.10.

Arrest.

Enforcement of support.

Remedy of arrest available, §50-13.4(f).

Assignments.

Public assistance.

Acceptance of assistance constitutes assignment of support rights to state or county, §110-137.

Unemployment compensation benefits, §110-136.2.

Wages, §110-136.1.

Attachment.

Actions in which attachment may be had, §1-440.2.

Enforcement of support.

Remedy available, §50-13.4(f).

Attorneys at law.

Procedure to insure payment.

Appointment to represent party support payment owed, §50-13.9(f).

List of attorneys willing to undertake representation, §50-13.9(e).

Attorneys' fees.

Action for support of minor child, §50-13.6.

Relief from order based on nonpaternity.

Bad faith attempts to gain relief, §50-13.13(g).

Attorneys specializing in family law.

Certification standards, Bar Rules D.2401 to D.2407.

Bail.

Enforcement of support.

Remedy of arrest and bail available, §50-13.4(f).

Illegitimate children.

Continuance, surety of person accused of being father, §49-5.

Bail bondsmen and runners.

Forfeiture of licensing privilege, §50-13.12.

Licenses, suspension or revocation, §58-71-80(a).

Blood tests.

Expedited procedures to establish paternity in IV-D cases.

Subpoena to appear for blood tests to establish paternity, §110-132.2.

Bonds, surety.

Enforcement of support.

Payments secured by bond, §50-13.4(f).

Change in circumstances.

Modification of order, §50-13.7.

Family law arbitration act, §50-56.

Child support collection and disbursement unit.

Establishment, §110-139(f).

Claims against the state.

Child support obligations, assignments to meet allowed, §143B-426.40A(d).

Clerks of court.

Duty of judicial officials to assist in obtaining support, §110-138.1.

Hearing officer, §7A-183.

Past due child support.

Payments made to clerk.

When payments not past due, §50-13.10(e).

Procedure to insure payment.

Notice of delinquency.

Non-IV-D cases, §50-13.9(d).

Payments made to, §50-13.9.

Responsibilities in non-IV-D cases, §50-13.9(b2).

CHILD SUPPORT —Cont'd
Collection of spousal support, §110-130.2.
Commission of offense of failure to support child.
When offense deemed committed in state, §14-325.1.
Compromise and settlement.
District court actions.
Mediated settlement conferences or other settlement procedures, §7A-38.4A.
Computation of support, §50-13.4(c).
Guidelines.
Uniform statewide presumptive guidelines, §50-13.4(c), (c1).
Confidentiality of information.
District attorneys.
Reports to district attorneys of aid to dependent children and illegitimate births, §15-155.3.
Location of absent parents, §110-139.
Conflicting provisions.
Conformity with federal requirements, §110-140(a).
Contempt.
Compelling disclosure of information respecting nonsupporting parent.
Parent of dependent child receiving public assistance failing or refusing to cooperate, §110-131(b).
Enforcement of support, §50-13.4(f).
Failure to obey support order.
Criminal contempt, punishment, §5A-12(a).
Garnishment.
Wage garnishment order.
Garnishee violating terms of order, §110-136(e).
Procedure to insure payment.
Civil contempt.
Independent initiation of proceeding not precluded, §50-13.9(g).
Wage garnishment to enforce, garnishee violating terms, §110-136(e).
Counties.
Assignment of support rights to state or county.
Acceptance of public assistance constitutes assignment, §110-137.
Duty of county to obtain support, §110-138.
County commissioners.
Action by designated representatives, §110-130.
Responsibility for administration of program, §110-141.
Court orders.
Defined, §110-129.
Data match systems.
Agreements with financial institutions, §110-139.2.
Definitions, §§110-129, 110-142.
Abandonment and failure to support spouse and children, §14-322(a).
Expedited process, §50-31.
Garnishment for enforcement of child-support obligation.
Disposable earnings, §110-136(a).
Past due child support.
Child support payments, §50-13.10(c).
Delinquencies.
Drivers' licenses, forfeiture, §§20-17(b), 50-13.12.
Drivers' licenses, refusal to renew or issue, §20-17(b).
Enforcement order, §50-13.9(d).
Motor vehicle registration.
Refusal to register, §20-50.4(b).

CHILD SUPPORT —Cont'd
Delinquencies —Cont'd
Occupational licenses revocation when privilege forfeited for nonsupport, §93B-13(a).
Applicability of revocation period imposed by occupational licensing board, §93B-13(c).
Notice of intent, §93B-13(b).
Reinstatement upon payment of support, §93B-13(d).
Past due child support, §50-13.10.
Procedure to insure payment, §50-13.9.
Delinquent and undisciplined juvenile actions.
Parent ordered to pay, §7B-2704.
Dependent children.
Defined, §110-129.
Designated representatives.
Action by representatives of county commissioners, §110-130.
Defined, §110-129.
Responsible parents.
Duty of county to obtain support, §110-138.
Directory of new hires.
Access to information by employment security division, §110-129.2(g).
Confidentiality of information, §110-129.2(i).
Contracts with other state or private entities to perform services, §110-129.2(h).
Definitions, §110-129.2(j).
Employer reporting, §110-129.2(b).
Civil penalty for failure to report, §110-129.2(d).
Contents, §110-129.2(c).
Entry of data into directory, §110-129.2(e).
Established, §110-129.2(a).
Withholding of income notice, §110-129.2(f).
Distribution by court of marital and divisible property.
Equitable distribution without regard to child support, §50-20(f).
District attorneys.
Duty to assist in enforcing support, §110-138.1.
Reports to district attorneys of aid to dependent children and illegitimate births, §15-155.1.
Confidentiality of information, §15-155.3.
Criminal offenses.
Indictments, §15-155.2(b).
Disclosure of information by district attorney or agent, §15-155.3.
Investigations, §15-155.2(a).
District courts.
Mediated settlement conferences or other settlement procedures, §7A-38.4A.
Proper division for trial of civil actions, §7A-244.
Divorce.
Action for support of minor child, §50-13.4.
Procedure, §50-13.5.
Distribution by court of marital and divisible property.
Equitable distribution without regard to child support, §50-20(f).
Independent actions permissible, §50-19.
Judgment provisions pertaining to care, tuition and maintenance, §50-11.2.
Change of conditions.
Modification upon substantial change, §50-11.2.
Modification of orders, §50-13.7.
Past due child support, §50-13.10.
Procedure to insure payment, §50-13.9.
Domestic violence, §50B-3(a).

CHILD SUPPORT —Cont'd
Drivers' licenses.
Access to information or data storage and
retrieval system maintained by department of
transportation.
Powers of department of health and human
services, §110-129.1(a).
Forfeiture of licensing privilege for nonpayment,
§50-13.12.
Refusal to renew or issue, §20-17(b).
Driver's license suspension or revocation.
Obligors delinquent in court-ordered support or
not in compliance with orders, §§110-142,
110-142.2.
Actions authorized, §110-142.2(a).
Certification that individual no longer
delinquent or that individual in compliance
with subpoena, §110-142.2(d).
Definitions, §110-142.
Entry of order instituting sanctions,
§110-142.2(b).
Forms and procedures, development,
§110-142.2(i).
Limited driving privilege issued.
License to operate necessary to individual's
livelihood, §110-142.2(c).
Reinstatement, §110-142.2(e) to (g).
Violation of terms and conditions of stay,
§110-142.2(h).
Due process requirements met, §110-131.1.
**Duties of department of health and human
services,** §110-129.1(a).
Secretary defined, §110-129.1(b).
Effectuation of intent of article, §110-141.
Emancipation.
Termination of support, §50-13.4(c).
Exceptions, §50-13.4(c).
Employee verification form.
Amount of obligor's gross income, establishing by,
§110-139(c1).
Employer reporting of new hires to directory,
§110-129.2(b) to (e).
Employment security.
Directory of new hires.
Access to information by employment security
division, §110-129.2(g).
Voluntary assignment of unemployment
compensation benefits to child support
agency.
Assignment effective until employment security
division receives notification of revocation,
§110-136.2(d).
Payment of amount deducted and withheld by
employment security division, §110-136.2(c).
Enforcement of support.
Past due child support, §50-13.10.
Procedure to insure payment, §50-13.9.
Remedies, §50-13.4(f).
Establishment of program, §110-128.
Establishment of spousal support obligation.
Child support enforcement program not
authorized to assist, §110-130.2.
Evidence.
Employee verification form, §110-139(c1).
Executions.
Enforcement of support, §50-13.4(f).
Exemption from creditors' claims, §1C-1601(a).
Expedited process, §§50-30 to 50-39.
Appeal of order of hearing officer, §50-38(a).
Order not stayed pending appeal, §50-38(b).
Definitions, §50-31.

CHILD SUPPORT —Cont'd
Expedited process —Cont'd
Disposition of cases within 60 days, §50-32.
Extension of time, §50-32.
Establishment.
Districts required to have process, §50-34(a).
Procedure, §50-34(b).
Findings of general assembly, §50-30(a).
Hearing de novo.
Appeal of order of hearing officer, §50-38(a).
Hearing officers.
Authority, §50-35.
Contempt, §50-37.
Duties, §50-35.
Enforcement authority, §50-37.
Qualifications, §50-39(a).
Training, §50-39(b).
Hearings.
Place, §50-36(b).
Procedure, §50-36(c).
Record of proceedings, §50-36(d).
Transfer to district court judge, §50-36(e).
Public to be informed, §50-34(c).
Purpose and policy, §50-30(b).
Scheduling of cases, §50-36(a).
Waiver of requirement.
Department to seek, §50-33(a).
Districts not qualifying, §50-33(b).
Failure to obey support order.
Criminal contempt, punishment, §5A-12(a).
Failure to support child, §14-322.
Clerks of court.
Duty to assist in obtaining support, §110-138.1.
Competency of witnesses in prosecution.
Husband and wife, §8-57(b).
Enforcement order, §50-13.9(d).
Forfeiture of driver's license, §§20-17(b), 50-13.12.
Judicial officials.
Duty to assist in obtaining support, §110-138.1.
When offense deemed committed in state,
§14-325.1.
Family law arbitration generally, §§50-41 to
50-62.
See FAMILY LAW ARBITRATION.
Federal aid.
Conformity with federal requirements,
§110-140(a).
Federal parent locator service.
Access to, §110-139.1(a).
Fees.
Filing of affirmations, acknowledgments,
agreements and orders, §110-134.
Files.
Support files not to be released, §110-139.
Financial institutions data match system.
Financial institution defined, §110-139.2(c).
Immunity of financial institution for disclosure of
information, §110-139.2(b).
Lien and levy on obligor's account, §110-139.2(b1).
Mutual agreement department and financial
institutions, §110-139.2(a).
Notice to financial institution.
Lien and levy on obligor's account,
§110-139.2(b1).
**Forfeiture of licensing privilege for
nonpayment.**
Certification obligor no longer delinquent,
§50-13.12(c).
Definitions, §50-13.12(a).
Duties of licensing boards, §50-13.12(f).
Findings by court, §50-13.12(b).

CHILD SUPPORT —Cont'd
Forfeiture of licensing privilege for
nonpayment —Cont'd
Petition for reinstatement of privileges,
§50-13.12(d), (e).
Fraudulent conveyances.
Enforcement of support.
Minor child creditor within meaning of chapter,
§50-13.4(f).
Full faith and credit.
Past due child support judgment, §50-13.10(b).
Paternity determination by another state,
§110-132.1.
Garnishment.
Continuing wage garnishment proceedings.
Method for instituting, §110-136.6(b), (b1).
Time period for responding to pleadings,
§110-136(b1).
Verification of petition and statement,
§110-136(b1).
Enforcement of support.
Remedy available, §50-13.4(f).
Wage garnishment order.
Contempt.
Garnishee violating terms of order,
§110-136(e).
Definition of disposable earnings, §110-136(a).
Disposable earnings defined, §110-136(a).
Dissolution of order, §110-136(c).
Employer third-party garnishee, §110-136(b).
Modifying order, §110-136(c).
Payment of amount order to be garnished,
§110-136(d).
Percentage of disposable earnings, §110-136(c).
Review for modification and dissolution,
§110-136(c).
Time period for responding to pleadings,
§110-136(b).
Verification of motion and statement,
§110-136(b).
Genetic testing.
Expedited procedures to establish paternity in
IV-D cases.
Subpoena to appear for genetic testing,
§110-132.2.
Guidelines.
Uniform statewide presumptive guidelines.
Computation of support.
Applied in determining amount, §50-13.4(c).
Criteria for applying, §50-13.4(c1).
Generally.
See Court Rules Volume.
Modification by conference of chief district
judges, §50-13.4(c1).
Prescribed by conference of chief district
judges, §50-13.4(c1).
Purposes, §50-13.4(c1).
Review by conference of chief district judges,
§50-13.4(c1).
Health insurance.
Medical support, orders and agreements,
§50-13.11.
Hearings.
Action for support of minor child.
Heard by judge without jury, §50-13.5(h).
Amount of support payments.
Request of party, §50-13.4(c).
Expedited process.
Appeal from orders of child support hearing
officer.
De novo hearing, §50-38(a).

CHILD SUPPORT —Cont'd
Hearings —Cont'd
Procedure to insure payment.
Cases heard for enforcement.
Informing district court judge, §50-13.9(f).
Delinquency in non-IV-D cases.
Enforcement order, §50-13.9(d).
High-volume, automated administrative
enforcement in interstate cases, §110-139.3.
Hunting, fishing or trapping licenses.
Forfeiture of licensing privilege for nonpayment,
§50-13.12.
Suspension or revocation of license of delinquent
obligors, §§110-142, 110-142.2.
Actions authorized, §110-142.2(a).
Certification that individual no longer
delinquent or in compliance, §110-142.2(d).
Definitions, §110-142.
Forms and procedures, development,
§110-142.2(i).
Order instituting sanctions, §110-142.2(b).
Reinstatement, §110-142.2(e) to (g).
Stay of order, §110-142.2(b).
Violations of terms of stay, §110-142.2(h).
Husband-wife privilege.
Actions by designated representatives of county
commissioners.
Privilege not grounds for excusing mother or
father from testifying, §110-130.
Illegitimate child, §§49-1 to 49-9.
Amount.
Determination by court, §49-7.
Bond for future appearance of defendant, §49-9.
Child defined, §49-2.
Commencement of action, §49-4.
Continuances, surety of person accused of being
father, §49-5.
Death of mother not bar to proceeding, §49-5.
Immunity of mother testifying, §49-6.
Issues determined by court, §49-7.
Nonsupport of illegitimate child by parents, §49-2.
Orders, §49-7.
Power of court to modify, §49-8.
Paternity.
Custody and support when paternity
established, §49-15.
Temporary order of support.
Entry when paternity determination pending,
§49-14(f).
Place of child.
No consideration, §49-3.
Preliminary proceeding to determine, §49-5.
Reports to district attorneys of aid to dependent
children and illegitimate births, §15-155.1.
Confidentiality of information, §15-155.3.
Criminal offenses.
Indictments, §15-155.2(b).
Disclosure of information by district attorney or
agent, §15-155.3.
Investigations, §15-155.2(a).
Self-incrimination.
Mother not excused on grounds of
self-incrimination, §49-6.
Sentencing.
Power of court to extend sentence, §49-8.
Time for commencing prosecutions, §49-4.
Title of article, §49-1.
Venue, §49-5.
Income information for both parents.
Revealing to establish child support obligation,
§110-139(b).

CHILD SUPPORT —Cont'd

Income withholding, §§110-136.3 to 110-136.14.
See within this heading, "Withholding of income."

Independent actions for divorce.
Maintenance of certain actions as independent actions permissible, §50-19.

Information respecting nonsupporting responsible parent.
Compelling disclosure of information, §110-131(a).
Failure to cooperate.
Penalty for violation of provisions, §110-131(b).
Penalty for failure to cooperate, §110-131(b).
Refusal to cooperate, §110-131(a).
Declaration of ineligibility for public assistance, §110-131(a).
Needs of remaining family members, §110-131(c).

Injunctions.
Enforcement of support, §50-13.4(f).

Institution of action.
Persons who may institute, §50-13.4(a).

Insurance.
Medical insurance, §50-13.11.

Insurance settlements.
Lien on insurance settlement of child support obligor, §§58-3-135, 58-3-185(a), (b).
Receiving person charged with duty of retaining funds, §44-50.

Intent of article.
Effectuation of intent, §110-141.

Interlocutory orders, §50-13.5(d).

Interstate family support, §§52C-1-100 to 52C-9-902.
See INTERSTATE FAMILY SUPPORT.

Intervention.
Action for support of minor child, §50-13.5(e).

Job search, order of parents to perform, §50-13.4(b).

Judgments.
Lien, §50-13.4(f).
Past due child support.
Full faith and credit, §50-13.10(b).

Judicial officials.
Duty to assist in obtaining support, §110-138.1.

Jurisdiction.
Action for support of minor child, §50-13.5(c).
Transfer of IV-D cases to another jurisdiction, §50-13.4(e1).

Liability.
Primary liability, §50-13.4(b).
Secondary liability, §50-13.4(b).

License suspension or revocation.
Drivers' licenses, hunting, fishing or trapping licenses, §§110-142, 110-142.2.
Occupational, professional or business licenses, §§110-142, 110-142.1.

Licensing privileges, forfeiture for nonpayment, §50-13.12.

Liens.
Creation, §44-86(b).
Definitions, §44-86(a).
Discharge, §44-87(a).
Penalty for failure to discharge, §44-87(b).
Execution, §44-86(f).
Filing and perfection, §44-86(d).
Insurance settlements owed to obligor, §§58-3-135, 58-3-185(a), (b).
Judgment for child support, §50-13.4(f).
Liens arising out-of-state, §44-86(g).

CHILD SUPPORT —Cont'd

Liens —Cont'd
Statement of child support delinquency, §44-86(c).
Superior to subsequent liens, §44-86(e).

Limitation of actions.
Public assistance to dependent child.
Collection of debt to state created, §110-135.

Location of absent parents, §110-139.
Access to federal parent locator service, §110-139.1(a).
Banks.
Information to be provided, §110-139(d).
Confidentiality of information, §110-139.
Nonjudicial records, §110-139.1(c).
Cooperation of state, county and city agencies, officers and employees, §110-139(b).
Custody determination.
Defined, §110-139.1(b).
Employers.
Information to be provided, §110-139(c).
Financial institutions.
Information to be provided, §110-139(d).
Registry for receipt of information, §110-139(a).
Savings and loan associations.
Information to be provided, §110-139(d).
Utility companies.
Exemptions, §110-139(e).
Provision of information, §110-139(d).

Magistrates.
Child support hearing officer, §7A-178.
Duty to assist in enforcing support, §110-138.1.

Mediated settlement conferences or other settlement procedures.
District court actions, §7A-38.4A.
Rules implementing, SettlmtEquitDistrib Rules 1 to 15.
See MEDIATED SETTLEMENT CONFERENCES.

Medical support and health insurance coverage.
Agreement to provide medical support.
Authority of parties to enter into, §50-13.11(a).
Change in applicable health insurance policy.
Notice provided by party ordered to provide, §50-13.11(b).
Change in employment by obligor and health available through new employer.
Custodial obligee to notify new employer, §50-13.11(f).
Failure to maintain health insurance for benefit of child.
Liability of person ordered to maintain, §50-13.11(e).
Order to maintain health insurance for benefit of child.
Authority of court to order, §50-13.11(a1).
Order to provide medical support.
Authority of court to order, §50-13.11(a).
Payment of health related expenses.
Order or agreement may require, §50-13.11(a).
Reasonable in cost.
When health insurance considered, §50-13.11(a1).
Release of information on child's health insurance.
Ordering employer or insurer, §50-13.11(c).
Signature of each party.
Authorization for insurer to process claim, §50-13.11(d).

Modification of order, §50-13.7.
Family law arbitration act, §50-56.

CHILD SUPPORT —Cont'd

Mortgages and deeds of trust.
Enforcement of support.
Securing payment, §50-13.4(f).

Motions.
Action for support of minor child.
Notice, §50-13.5(d).
Modification of orders, §50-13.7.

Motor vehicle registration.
Access to information or data storage and
retrieval system maintained by department of
transportation.
Powers of department of health and human
services, §110-129.1(a).
Delinquent child support, refusal to register
vehicles, §20-50.4(b).
Refusal to issue to delinquent obligor or
individual not in compliance with order,
§110-142.2.

National medical support notice, §§110-136.11 to
110-136.14.

New hires, state directory, §110-129.2.

Nonrecipients of work first services.
Eligibility for collection and paternity
determination services, §110-130.1(a).
Actions brought in name of county or state
agency, §110-130.1(c).
Fees.
Annual fee in cases for which services
furnished, §110-130.1(a).
Deduction from amount collected,
§110-130.1(d).
Location of absent and deserting parent.
Use of electronic and print media authorized,
§110-130.1(c1).
Recovery of costs, §110-130.1(b1).

Nonsupporting responsible parent.
Compelling disclosure of information respecting
parent, §110-131(a).
Declaration of ineligibility for public assistance,
§110-131(a).
Needs of remaining family members,
§110-131(c).
Failure to cooperate, §110-131(a).
Penalty for violation of provisions,
§110-131(b).
Penalty for failure to cooperate, §110-131(b).
Willful nonsupport by supporting spouse, §14-322.

Notice.
Action for support of minor child.
Additional persons, §50-13.5(e).
Motions, §50-13.5(d).
Procedure to insure payment.
Delinquency in non-IV-D cases, §50-13.9(d).
Withholding of income.
Amount to be withheld.
Contents of order and notice, §110-136.6(c).
IV-D cases.
Advance notice of withholding, §110-136.4(a).
Non-IV-D cases.
Order for withholding, §110-136.5(d).
Payor, §110-136.8(a).

**Occupational, professional or business
licenses,** §93B-13(a).
Forfeiture of licensing privileges for nonpayment,
§50-13.12.
Suspension and revocation of licenses of
delinquent obligors, §§93B-13(a), 110-142,
110-142.1.
Administrative procedure act, inapplicability,
§110-142.1(n).

CHILD SUPPORT —Cont'd

Occupational, professional or business licenses
—Cont'd
Suspension and revocation of licenses of
delinquent obligors —Cont'd
Applicability of revocation period imposed by
occupational licensing board, §93B-13(c).
Definitions, §110-142.
Forms and procedures to implement provisions,
development, §110-142.1(c).
Forms for use by designated representative,
§110-142.1(l).
Furnishing licensing agency with certified list,
§110-142.1(b).
Inquiry into license status of applicant,
§110-142.1(o).
Interagency agreements, §110-142.1(m).
Motion for judicial review, §110-142.1(j).
Notice of intent to revoke or suspend license,
§§93B-13(b), 110-142.1(d), (f).
Notice of request for review, §110-142.1(h).
Notice of right to request judicial review,
judicial determination of compliance or
modification of order, §110-142.1(i).
Notice that person licensed not in compliance
with order, §110-142.1(a).
Reinstatement of license, individual no longer in
arrears, §§93B-13(d), 110-142.1(k).
Review procedures to be developed,
§110-142.1(g).
Review request, §110-142.1(h).
Severability of provisions, §110-142.1(p).
Stay of action pending review, §110-142.1(h).
Submission of certified list by designated
representative, §110-142.1(b).
Time license revoked or suspended after notice,
§110-142.1(e).

Orders.
Acknowledgment of paternity in agreement to
support.
Same force and effect as order of support,
§110-132(a3).
Agreements of support to have force and effect as
order of court, §110-133.
Attorneys' fees, §50-13.6.
Collection of spousal support, §110-130.2.
Contents, §50-13.4(h).
Definition of court order, §110-129.
Generally, §50-13.4.
Interlocutory orders, §50-13.5(d).
Medical support, §50-13.11.
Modification.
Change of circumstances, §50-13.7(a).
Orders entered by court of another state,
§50-13.7(b).
Procedure generally, §50-13.5.
Procedure to insure payment, §50-13.9.
Relief from order based on nonpaternity.
Attorney fee award for bad faith attempts to
gain relief, §50-13.13(g).
Authorized, §50-13.13(a).
Birth certificates.
Modification, §50-13.13(h).
Denial of relief.
Effect, §50-13.13(g).
Findings necessary to grant relief, §50-13.13(f).
Genetic testing, §50-13.13(d).
Guardian ad litem to protect interest of child,
§50-13.13(c).
Military service.
Tolling of time requirements, §50-13.13(i).

CHILD SUPPORT —Cont'd
Orders —Cont'd
Relief from order based on nonpaternity —Cont'd
Motions or claims for relief, §50-13.13(b).
Statute of limitations to file for relief,
    §50-13.13(b).
    Military service, tolling, §50-13.13(i).
Suspension of obligation to pay support during
    pendency of proceeding, §50-13.13(e).
Termination of support obligation upon grant of
    relief, §50-13.13(h).
Unpaid support due prior to filing for relief,
    §50-13.13(h).
Temporary orders, §50-13.5(d).
Wage garnishment order, §110-136.
Withholding of income.
Amount to be withheld, §110-136.6(c).
Expiration of order, §110-136.10.
Non-IV-D cases, §110-136.5(c).
    Notice to payor and obligor, §110-136.5(d).
Required contents of support orders,
    §110-136.3(a).
Paternity.
Acknowledgment of paternity, agreement to
    support.
Filing fees, §110-134.
Force and effect of agreement, §110-132(a3).
Setting aside affidavit of parentage by trial
    court, §110-132(a1), (a2).
Show cause orders, §110-132(b).
Determination by another state.
Full faith and credit, §110-132.1.
Established, §49-15.
Establishing paternity.
Powers of department of health and human
    services, §110-129.1(a).
Expedited procedures to establish paternity in
    IV-D cases.
Subpoena to appear for blood or genetic testing
    to establish paternity, §110-132.2(a).
Contesting subpoena, §110-132.2(b).
Preliminary proceeding, §49-5.
Temporary order of support.
Entry when paternity determination pending,
    §49-14(f).
Payment history of obligor parent, §110-139(b).
Payment of support.
Appointment of attorney to represent party
    support payment owed, §50-13.9(f).
Arrearage.
Delinquency in non-IV-D cases, §50-13.9(d).
Termination of support, §50-13.4(c).
Authority of court to order payments, §50-13.9(a).
Change of address.
Notice to court, §50-13.9(c).
Changes affecting administration.
Notice to court, §50-13.9(c).
Contempt.
Independent initiation of proceeding not
    precluded, §50-13.9(g).
Delinquency notice.
Failure to make payment, §50-13.9(d).
Disbursement of payments, §50-13.9(b).
Enforcement hearings.
Notice requirements, §50-13.9(f).
IV-D cases, §50-13.9(b1).
List of attorneys willing to undertake
    representation, §50-13.9(e).
Methods of payment, §50-13.4(e).
Non-IV-D cases.
Clerks' responsibilities, §50-13.9(b2).

CHILD SUPPORT —Cont'd
Payment of support —Cont'd
Non-IV-D cases —Cont'd
Delinquency, §50-13.9(d).
Other actions not precluded, §50-13.9(g).
Past due child support.
Child support payments defined, §50-13.10(c).
Clerks of court.
Payments made to clerk.
    When payments not past due, §50-13.10(e).
Divestment, §50-13.10(a).
Full faith and credit, §50-13.10(b).
    Judgments, §50-13.10(b).
Modification, §50-13.10(a).
Vested when it accrues, §50-13.10(a).
When support not past due, §50-13.10(d), (e).
Payments made to clerk, §50-13.9(a).
Informing clerk of change of address,
    §50-13.9(c).
Records listing amount of payment, §50-13.9(a).
Transmission payments to health and human
    services department in IV-D cases,
    §50-13.9(b).
Procedure to insure payment, §50-13.9.
To whom payments made, §50-13.4(d).
Transmission of payments to health and human
    services department, §50-13.9(b).
Withholding of income.
Immediate income withholding provisions,
    application, §50-13.9(a).
Independent initiation of proceeding not
    precluded, §50-13.9(g).
**Powers of department of health and human
    services,** §110-129.1(a).
Secretary defined, §110-129.1(b).
Premarital agreements.
Not affected, §52B-4(b).
Presumptions.
Computation of support.
Uniform statewide presumptive guidelines,
    §50-13.4(c), (c1).
Probation.
Condition of probation.
Procedure to insure payment of child support,
    §15A-1344.1.
Procedure generally, §50-13.5(a).
Production of documents and things.
Subpoena issued by department of health and
    human services, §110-129.1(a).
Professional licenses. See within this heading,
    "Occupational, professional or business
    licenses."
Public assistance.
Assignment of support rights to state or county.
Acceptance of public assistance constitutes
    assignment, §110-137.
Debt to state created, §110-135.
Nonsupporting responsible parent.
Compelling disclosure of information respecting
    parent, §110-131.
Purposes of article, §110-128.
Transfer of property.
Order transferring title, §50-13.4(f).
Receivers.
Enforcement of support, §50-13.4(f).
**Registry for receipt of information relating to
    identity or location of absent parents.**
Department of health and human services to
    serve as, §110-139(a).
Remedies.
Enforcement of support, §50-13.4(e), (f).

CHILD SUPPORT —Cont'd

Reports.

Directory of new hires.

Employer reporting, §110-129.2(b) to (e).

Responsible parents.

Agreements of support.

Enforceability of agreement, §110-133.

Filing fees, §110-134.

Modification of agreements, §110-133.

Compelling disclosure of information respecting nonsupporting parent, §110-131(a).

Declaration of ineligibility for public assistance, §110-131(a).

Needs of remaining family, §110-131(c).

Failure to cooperate, §110-131(a).

Penalty for violation of provisions, §110-131(b).

Penalty for failure to cooperate, §110-131(b).

Defined, §110-129.

Designated representatives.

Duty of county to obtain support, §110-138.

Location of absent parents, §110-139.

Salaries.

Assignment of wages, §110-136.1.

Garnishment, §110-136.

Withholding of income, §§110-136.3 to 110-136.14.

See within this heading, "Withholding of income."

Schedule of basic child support obligations.

Child support guidelines (court rules).

See Court Rules Volume.

Service of process.

Action for support of minor child, §50-13.5(d).

Services provided to nonrecipients of work first services, §110-130.1.

Setoff debt collection, §§105A-1 to 105A-16.

See SETOFF DEBT COLLECTION.

Settlement.

Mediated settlement conferences or other settlement procedures.

District court actions, §7A-38.4A.

Show cause orders.

Acknowledgment of paternity.

Agreements to support, §110-132(b).

Filing fees, §110-134.

Social security number, §50-13.4(g).

State child support collection and disbursement unit.

Establishment, §110-139(f).

State debt.

Creating debt to state, §110-135.

State directory of new hires, §110-129.2.

Subpoenas.

Actions by designated representatives of county commissioners, §110-130.

Expedited procedures to establish paternity in IV-D cases.

Appearance for blood tests or genetic tests, §110-132.2.

Powers of department of health and human services, §110-129.1(a).

Support and maintenance.

General provisions.

See SUPPORT AND MAINTENANCE.

Uniform reciprocal enforcement of support act.

See SUPPORT AND MAINTENANCE.

Temporary assistance for needy families (TANF) block grant program.

Distribution options for families receiving cash assistance under, §110-140(b).

CHILD SUPPORT —Cont'd

Temporary orders pending service and notice, §50-13.5(d).

Termination of parental rights.

Failure of noncustodial parent to pay, grounds for terminating, §7B-1111(a).

Termination of support, §50-13.4(c).

Transfers to minors.

Delivery, payment or expenditure of custodial property.

Support obligation not affected by, §33A-14(c).

Types of actions, §50-13.5(b).

Unemployment compensation.

Deductions for support obligations, §96-17(c).

Income withholding of unemployment compensation benefits.

Absence of voluntary assignment, §110-136.2(f).

Voluntary assignment of unemployment compensation benefits to child support agency, §110-136.2(a).

Assignment effective until employment security division receives notification of revocation, §110-136.2(d).

Notification to department of health and human services, §110-136.2(b).

Payment of amount deducted and withheld by employment security division, §110-136.2(c).

Proper credit ensured by department of health and human services, §110-136.2(e).

Uniform reciprocal enforcement of support act.

See SUPPORT AND MAINTENANCE.

Uniform statewide presumptive guidelines, §50-13.4(c), (c1).

Venue.

Action for support of minor child, §50-13.5(f).

Actions by designated representatives of county commissioners, §110-130.

Voluntary assignment of unemployment compensation benefits, §110-136.2.

Voluntary support agreements, §110-133.

Acknowledgment of paternity and agreement to support, §110-132.

Filing fees, §110-134.

Filing fees, §110-134.

Wages.

Assignment of wages for child support, §110-136.1.

Attachment.

Enforcement of support, §50-13.4(f).

Garnishment, §110-136.

Withholding of income, §§110-136.3 to 110-136.14.

Welfare.

Assignment of support rights to state or county.

Acceptance of public assistance constitutes assignment, §110-137.

Debt to state created, §110-135.

Nonsupporting responsible parent.

Compelling disclosure of information respecting parent, §110-131.

Who may institute action, §50-13.4(a).

Withholding of income, §§110-136.3 to 110-136.14.

Amount to be withheld.

Computation, §110-136.6(a).

Contents of order and notice, §110-136.6(c).

Limits, §110-136.6(b), (b1).

Applicability of provisions.

IV-D cases, §110-136.4(f).

Based on arrearage, §110-136.5(a).

Based on obligor's request, §110-136.5(b).

CHILD SUPPORT —Cont'd
Withholding of income —Cont'd
Disposable income.
  Defined, §110-129.
Distribution of payments received, §110-136.9.
Employer reporting to directory of new hires.
  Notice to employer to withhold income,
    §110-129.2(f).
IV-D cases.
  Applicability of provisions, §110-136.4(f).
  Contested withholding, §110-136.4(a).
  Defenses.
    Payment not a defense to withholding,
      §110-136.4(a).
  Defined, §110-129.
  Immediate income withholding, §110-136.4(b).
  Modification of withholding, §110-136.4(e).
  Multiple withholdings, §110-136.4(d).
  Notice.
    Advance notice of withholding, §110-136.4(a).
  Subsequent payors, §110-136.4(c).
  Uncontested withholding, §110-136.4(a).
Immediate income withholding, §110-136.5(c1).
  Effective date, application of provision,
    §50-13.4(d1).
  IV-D cases, §110-136.4(b).
Interstate cases, §110-136.3(d).
Interstate family support act, §§52C-5-501 to
    52C-5-507.
  See INTERSTATE FAMILY SUPPORT.
Modification of withholding.
  IV-D cases, §110-136.4(e).
  Non-IV-D cases, §110-136.5(e).
Multiple withholdings, §110-136.7.
  IV-D cases, §110-136.4(d).
National medical support notice.
  Contest of order, §110-136.13(h).
  Definition of employer, §110-136.13(a).
  Determination if qualified medical child support
    order, §110-136.14(a).
  Employer not to retaliate for withholding order,
    §110-136.13(i).
  Employer transfer of notice, §110-136.13(b).
    When notice not transferred, §110-136.13(c).
  Enrollment in plan, §110-136.14(b).
  Health insurer violations, §110-136.14(e).
  IV-D agency notice to employer, §110-136.12(a).
  IV-D notice of order expiration, §110-136.12(c).
  Liabilities of employer, §110-136.13(j).
  Newly hired employees, §110-136.12(b).
  Notice not a qualified medical child support
    order, §110-136.13(e).
  Not used, §110-136.11(b).
  Options for health care, §110-136.12(d).
  Selection of plan from options, §110-136.14(c).
  Termination of employment, notice,
    §110-136.13(g).
  Waiting period for enrollment, §§110-136.13(f),
    110-136.14(d).
  When used, §110-136.11(a).
  Withholding amount, §110-136.13(d).
Non-IV-D cases.
  Defined, §110-129.
  Modification of withholding, §110-136.5(e).
  Order for withholding.
    Notice to payor and obligor, §110-136.5(d).
  Notice.
    Amount to be withheld.
      Contents of order and notice, §110-136.6(c).
    IV-D cases.
      Advance notice of withholding, §110-136.4(a).

CHILD SUPPORT —Cont'd
Withholding of income —Cont'd
  Notice —Cont'd
    Non-IV-D cases.
      Order for withholding, §110-136.5(d).
    Payor, §110-136.8(a).
  Obligee.
    Defined, §110-129.
  Obligor.
    Change in obligor's employment, §110-136.8(c).
    Defined, §110-129.
    When obligor subject to withholding,
      §110-136.3(b).
  Orders.
    Amount to be withheld.
      Contents of order and notice, §110-136.6(c).
    Expiration of order.
      Termination of withholding, §110-136.10.
    Non-IV-D cases, §110-136.5(c).
      Notice to payor and obligor, §110-136.5(d).
    Required contents of support orders,
      §110-136.3(a).
  Payment of withheld funds, §110-136.9.
  Payment plan, §110-136.3(a).
  Payor.
    Civil penalties, §110-136.8(e), (f).
    Combining amounts withheld from obligor's
      disposable income, §110-136.8(d).
    Defined, §110-129.
    Notice to payor, §110-136.8(a).
    Prohibited conduct, §110-136.8(e).
    Responsibilities, §110-136.8(b).
  Priority.
    Multiple withholdings, §110-136.7.
  Procedure to insure payment.
    Independent initiation of proceeding not
      precluded, §50-13.9(g).
  Rules and regulations, §110-136.3(e).
  Subsequent payors.
    IV-D cases, §110-136.4(c).
  Termination of withholding, §110-136.10.
  Unemployment compensation benefits,
    §110-136.2(f).
  Work requirement for past-due support,
    §110-136.3(a1).

CHILD SUPPORT AGREEMENTS, §110-133.
**Acknowledgment of paternity in agreement to
  support,** §110-132.
Filing of affirmations, acknowledgments, etc.,
  §110-134.

**CHILD SUPPORT COLLECTION AND
  DISBURSEMENT UNIT.**
Establishment, §110-139(f).

**CHILD SUPPORT ENFORCEMENT
  PROGRAM.**
Generally, §§110-128 to 110-142.2.
  See CHILD SUPPORT.

CHILD SUPPORT GUIDELINES.
Uniform statewide presumptive guidelines.
  Computation of support.
    Applied in determining amount, §50-13.4(c).
    Criteria for applying, §50-13.4(c1).
    Generally.
      See Court Rules Volume.
    Modification by conference of chief district
      judges, §50-13.4(d).
    Prescribed by conference of chief district judges,
      §50-13.4(c1).

CHILD SUPPORT GUIDELINES —Cont'd
Uniform statewide presumptive guidelines
—Cont'd
Computation of support —Cont'd
Purposes, §50-13.4(c1).
Review by conference of chief district judges,
§50-13.4(c1).

CHILD TAX CREDIT, §105-151.24.

CHILD VISITATION.
See VISITATION.

CHIROPRACTORS, §§90-139 to 90-157.3.
Acceptable care in practice of chiropractic.
Adoption of rules to establish and define
standards, §90-154.3(b).
Enticements prohibited, §90-154.4.
Lawful scope of practice not altered, §90-154.3(d).
Unlawful to render service not conforming to
standards, §90-154.3(a).
Usual and customary method taught in majority
of recognized chiropractic colleges.
Standard of care if rule not promulgated
defining, §90-154.3(c).
Acupuncture.
Exemption from licensing, §90-452(b).
Advertising.
False or misleading advertisement, grounds for
disciplinary actions, §90-154(b).
Free or reduced rate service.
Notice to patient, §90-154.1(b).
Alcohol addiction or severe dependency.
Grounds for disciplinary action, §90-154(b).
Board of examiners.
Appointment of members, §§90-139(a), 90-140.
Certification of diagnostic imaging technicians,
§90-143.2(a), (b).
Composition, §90-139(a).
Creation, §90-139(a).
Expenditures, §90-156.
Expenses of members, §90-156.
Meetings, §90-144.
Number of members, §90-139(a).
Officers.
Election, §90-141.
Qualifications of members, §90-139(a).
Quorum, §90-141.
Records, §90-148.
Removal of members, §90-139(c).
Rules and regulations, §90-142.
Selection of members, §90-140.
Terms of members, §§90-139(b), 90-140.
Business corporations.
Limitations on ownership of practice, §90-157.3(c).
Censure of practitioner.
Powers of board of chiropractic examiners,
§90-154(a).
Certification.
Diagnostic imaging technicians, §90-143.2(a), (b).
Charge or fee violations.
Grounds for disciplinary action, §90-154(b).
Child support enforcement.
Forfeiture of licensing privilege, §50-13.12.
Control of contagious and infectious diseases.
Chiropractors subject to state and municipal
regulations as to, §90-157.
**Conviction of felony or crime involving moral
turpitude.**
Grounds for disciplinary action, §90-154(b).
Corporations.
Professional corporations generally, §§55B-1 to
55B-16.
See PROFESSIONAL CORPORATIONS.

CHIROPRACTORS —Cont'd
Costs.
Contested disciplinary hearings.
Assessment of costs upon guilty verdict,
§90-154(c).
Criminal history record checks, §114-19.22.
Confidentiality of information, §90-143.3(c).
Duties of department of justice, §90-143.3(b).
Fingerprint card, §90-143.3(a).
Immunity from liability, §90-143.3(d).
Definitions.
Chiropractic, §90-143(a).
Unethical conduct, §90-154.2.
Diagnostic imaging technicians.
Certification by board, §90-143.2(a), (b).
Discipline.
Costs of hearing upon guilty verdict, §90-154(c).
Grounds, §90-154(b).
Powers of board of examiners, §90-154(a).
Drugs.
Addiction or severe dependency.
Grounds for disciplinary action, §90-154(b).
Prescriptions.
Prohibited, §90-151.
Education requirements, §90-143(b).
Diploma, §90-143(c).
Examination scores, §90-143(d).
Enticements for treatment.
Defined, §90-154.4(a).
Marketing practices considered lawful,
§90-154.4(b).
Unlawful rebates, §90-154.4(a).
Fees.
Collection of certain fees prohibited, §90-154.1.
Diagnostic imaging technicians, §90-143.2(b).
Licenses.
Application fee, §90-149.
Renewal, §90-155.
Felony convictions.
Forfeiture of licenses, §15A-1331A.
Fines.
Unlicensed practice, §90-147.
Fraud, deception or misrepresentation.
Grounds for disciplinary action, §90-154(b).
Free choice by patient guaranteed, §90-157.1.
Free or reduced rate services.
Bills sent to patients, §90-154.1(d).
Notice to prospective patients, §90-154.1(b).
Refusal to pay certain fees.
Right of patient, §90-154.1(a).
Health benefit plans.
Right of subscriber to choose service, payment,
§58-50-30.
Identification badges required, §90-640.
Injunctions.
Unlicensed practice, §90-147.
Insurers or third-party payors.
Charging fee greater than advertised for same
service, §90-154(b).
Lewd or immoral conduct toward patient.
Ground for disciplinary action, §90-154(b).
Licenses.
Denial.
Disciplinary powers of board of examiners,
§90-154(a).
Grounds, §90-154(b).
Educational requirements, §90-143(b).
Fees.
Application fee, §90-149.
Renewal, §90-155.
Issuance, §90-145.

CHIROPRACTORS —Cont'd
Licenses —Cont'd
Privileges of licensees, §90-151.
Qualifications, §90-143(b).
Reciprocity, §§90-143.1, 90-146.
Renewal, §90-155.
Revocation or suspension.
Disciplinary powers of board of examiners,
§90-154(a).
Felony convictions, §15A-1331A.
Grounds, §90-154(b).
Unlicensed practices, §90-147.
License taxes, §105-41.
Limited partnerships.
Limitations on ownership of practice, §90-157.3(b).
**Malpractice, negligence or incompetence in
practice.**
Grounds for disciplinary actions, §90-154(b).
Malpractice actions generally, §§90-21.11 to
90-21.19B.
See MEDICAL MALPRACTICE.
Medical records, §§90-410, 90-411.
Electronic medical records, §90-412.
Misdemeanors.
Unlicensed practice, §90-147.
North Carolina chiropractic association.
Meetings, §90-144.
Nutritional supplements.
Selling to patients, §90-151.1.
Sales and use tax exemption, §105-164.13.
Ownership of practice limited, §90-157.3.
Partnerships.
Limitations on ownership of practice, §90-157.3(a).
**Physical therapy modalities, use not
restricted,** §90-270.39.
Probationary status.
Placement on, powers of board, §90-154(a).
Professional corporations generally, §§55B-1 to
55B-16.
See PROFESSIONAL CORPORATIONS.
Rebates to patients.
Grounds for disciplinary action, §90-154(b).
Reciprocity.
Licenses, §§90-143.1, 90-143(b), 90-146.
Records.
Board of examiners, §90-148.
Referral fees and solicitation payments,
§§90-400 to 90-402.
Health care provider defined, §90-400.
Prohibited, §90-401.
Sanctions, §90-402.
Reprimand.
Issuance of letter, powers of board, §90-154(a).
Rules and regulations, §90-154.3(b).
Board of examiners, §90-142.
**Rules establishing and defining standards of
acceptable care,** §90-154.3(b).
Sales.
Nutritional supplements, §90-151.1.
Self-referral, §§90-405 to 90-408.
Solicitation.
Direct solicitation prohibited, §90-401.1.
Payment prohibitions, §90-401.
Sanctions for violating prohibitions, §90-402.
**Standard of acceptable care and practice of
chiropractic.**
Enticements prohibited, §90-154.4.
Rules establishing and defining standards of
acceptable care, §90-154.3(b).
Scope or practice not altered, §90-154.3(d).

CHIROPRACTORS —Cont'd
**Standard of acceptable care and practice of
chiropractic** —Cont'd
Unlawful to render service not conforming to
standards of acceptable care, §90-154.3(a).
Usual and customary method as taught in
majority of recognized chiropractic colleges.
Standard of acceptable care if rule not defining,
§90-154.3(c).
Unethical conduct.
Defined, §90-154.2.
Unlicensed practice, §90-147.
Witnesses.
Expert witnesses, §90-157.2.

CHLAMYDIA.
**Defendants accused of offense involving
vaginal, anal or oral intercourse.**
Testing, request of victim, §15A-615.

CHLOROFLUOROCARBONS REFRIGERANTS.
Management of discarded white goods,
§§130A-309.80 to 130A-309.87.
See WHITE GOODS.

CHOICE OF LAW.
Anatomical gifts.
Law governing document, §130A-412.21(a), (b).
Commercial code.
Power to choose applicable law, §25-1-301(c).
Territorial applicability, §25-1-301(a), (b).
Conflict of laws generally.
See CONFLICT OF LAWS.
Electronic transactions.
Computer information agreement, §66-329.
Insurance policies or contracts.
Court or jurisdiction in which action or suit may
be brought.
Condition or stipulation in policy prohibited,
§58-3-35(a).

CHOLERA.
Hog cholera, §§106-310 to 106-322.3.
See HOG CHOLERA.

CHOP SHOPS.
Civil penalties, §14-72.7(c).
Definitions, §14-72.7(f).
Exceptions, §14-72.7(b).
Felonies, §14-72.7(a).
Forfeitures, §14-72.7(e).
Nuisances.
Offenses against public morals.
Abatement generally, §§19-1 to 19-8.3.
See NUISANCES.
Chop shop activity, §19-1(b2).
Private actions, §14-72.7(d).
Prohibited acts, §14-72.7(a).
Seizures, §14-72.7(e).

CHOSES IN ACTION.
Agriculture.
Delinquent fees and taxes.
Collection of delinquent fees and taxes,
§106-9.4(b).
Execution sales.
Property liable to sale under execution, §1-315(a).
Larceny, §14-75.
Obtaining property by false pretenses, §14-100.

CHOWAN COLLEGE.
Community colleges.
General provisions, §§115D-1 to 115D-81.
See COMMUNITY COLLEGES.

CHOWAN COUNTY.
Ambulance service.
Attachment or garnishment and lien for, §§44-51.4 to 44-51.8.
Blank or master forms of mortgages, deeds of trust, etc.
Indexing and recording, inapplicability of provisions, §47-21.
Dangerous firearm use by young children, permitting.
Air rifles, air pistols and BB guns not dangerous firearm, §14-316(b).
Dog collars.
Unlawful removal of electronic dog collars, §14-401.17.
Game laws, local acts not repealed, §113-133.1(e).
Grants in navigable waters, registration, §113-205(a).
Housing authority commissioners.
Tenant as commissioner, exemption from provision of law allowing, §157-5.
North Carolina's northeast commission, §§158-8.2 to 158-8.8.
Officers compensated from fees.
Statement to be rendered, §128-13.
Open fires, §106-942.
Applicability of provisions, §106-942(a).
Ground clearing activities, special permit required, §106-942(c).
Woodland fires, permit required, §106-942(b).
Registration of deeds.
Tax certification, no delinquent taxes due, §161-31(b).
School property.
Acquisition and improvement, §153A-158.1.
Special school tax, election to abolish.
Petition required, §115C-505.
Tax elections for industrial development purposes, §§158-16 to 158-24.
Wastewater systems.
Innovative septic tank systems.
Ordinance billing fee as property tax, §130A-343.1(c).
Wild plants, taking of certain plants from land of another.
Inapplicability of provisions, §14-129.

CHRISTIAN SCIENCE.
Communications between practitioner and communicant.
Competency of Christian Science practitioner as witness, §8-53.2.

CHRISTMAS DAY.
Public holiday, §103-4(a).

CHRISTMAS GREENS.
Taking, etc., of certain wild plants from land of another, §14-129.

CHRISTMAS TREES.
Official Christmas tree of state, §145-25.

CHURCH BUSES.
Motor vehicle license plates.
Permanent license plates for Sunday transportation vehicles, §20-84(b).
Speed limit for nonprofit activity buses, §20-218.2.

CHURCHES AND OTHER PLACES OF WORSHIP.
Alcoholic beverage permits.
Factors considered, establishment located within 50 feet, §18B-901(c).

CHURCHES AND OTHER PLACES OF WORSHIP —Cont'd
Billboard obstructing view at entrance, §136-102.
Breaking and entering, §14-54.1(a), (b).
Burning, §14-62.2.
Buses.
License plates.
Permanent plates for Sunday transportation vehicles, §20-84(b).
Speed limit for nonprofit activity buses, §20-218.2.
Child care facilities.
Drop-in or short-term child care not included in term child care, §110-86.
Religious training offered in.
Commission not to interfere with, §110-88.1.
Injuring churches, §14-144.
Malicious use of explosive or incendiary, §14-49(b1).
Obstructing place of worship, §14-199.
Pastoral counselors.
Certification of fee-based practicing pastoral counselors, §§90-380 to 90-395.
See PASTORAL COUNSELORS.
Professional counselors generally, §§90-329 to 90-345.
See PROFESSIONAL COUNSELORS.
Powers of attorney.
Powers conferred by statutory short form.
Continued payments incidental to membership or affiliation, §32A-2.
Religion generally.
See RELIGION.
Religious organizations and societies.
See RELIGIOUS ORGANIZATIONS AND SOCIETIES.
Roads.
Establishment, alteration or discontinuance of church road, §136-68.
Sacramental wine.
Exemptions from alcoholic beverage control regulations, §18B-103.
Sales and use tax refunds, §105-164.14(b).
Schools.
Church schools and schools of religious charter, §§115C-547 to 115C-554.
See PRIVATE AND PAROCHIAL SCHOOLS.
Swine houses, lagoons and land areas.
Siting requirements near, §106-803(a), (b).
Uniform unincorporated nonprofit association act.
Property held by association.
Effect of provisions on churches, §59B-15(a).
Volunteer immunity, §§1-539.10, 1-539.11.

CHURCH ROADS.
Establishment, alteration or discontinuance, §136-68.

CHURCH SCHOOLS AND SCHOOLS OF RELIGIOUS CHARTER, §§115C-547 to 115C-554.
See PRIVATE AND PAROCHIAL SCHOOLS.

CHURCH-SPONSORED CHILD CARE FACILITIES, §110-106.
Drop-in or short-term child care not included in term child care, §110-86.
Religious training offered in.
Commission not to interfere with, §110-88.1.

CIDER.
Exemption from alcoholic beverage provisions, §18B-103.

CIDER AND VINEGAR MANUFACTURERS.
ABC permits, §18B-1114.2.
Commercial permits for manufacturers, §18B-1100.

C.I.F.
Sale of goods, UCC, §25-2-320.
Form of bill of lading required in overseas shipment, §25-2-323.
Net landed weight, §25-2-321.
Payment on arrival, §25-2-321.
Warranty of condition on arrival, §25-2-321.

CIGAR BARS.
Defined, §130A-492.
Local government's authority to regulate smoking.
Exception, §130A-498(b1).
Smoking prohibited in restaurants and bars.
Exception, requirements, §130A-496(b).

CIGARETTES AND TOBACCO PRODUCTS.
Administration, §105-113.3(b).
Agricultural products promotion.
Exclusion of tobacco from article, §106-550.
Auctions and auctioneers.
Exemptions from auction provisions, §85B-2.
Liens.
Effective period for lien on leaf tobacco sold in auction warehouse, §44-69.
Cigarette tax, §§105-113.5 to 105-113.33.
See CIGARETTE TAX.
Citation of title.
Short title, §105-113.2.
Community colleges.
Tobacco use, §115D-20.1.
Contraband.
Cigarette packages violating certain label requirements, §14-401.18(c).
Discrimination by employers for lawful use of lawful products during nonworking hours, §95-28.2.
Distribution to minors, §14-313.
Failure of tenant to account for sales under tobacco marketing cards, §42-22.1.
Federal cigarette labeling and advertising act.
Selling cigarettes in packages differing from requirements, §14-401.18(b).
Fire-safety standard and firefighter protection act.
General provisions, §§58-92-1 to 58-92-55.
See FIRE-SAFETY STANDARD AND FIREFIGHTER PROTECTION ACT.
"For export only" selling cigarettes with label in state, §14-401.18(b).
"For use outside U. S." selling cigarettes with label in state, §14-401.18(b).
Income tax credits for manufacturing cigarettes for exportation, §105-130.45.
Amount of credit allowed, §105-130.45(b).
Cap, §105-130.45(c).
Definitions, §105-130.45(a).
Increasing employment and utilizing state ports.
Allocation, §105-130.46(f).
Allowance of credit, amount, §105-130.46(d).
Ceiling, §105-130.46(g).
Definitions, §105-130.46(b).
Documentation, §105-130.46(i).
Employment level, eligibility for full credit, §105-130.46(c).
No double credit, §105-130.46(j).
Partial credit, §105-130.46(e).

CIGARETTES AND TOBACCO PRODUCTS
—Cont'd
Income tax credits for manufacturing cigarettes for exportation —Cont'd
Increasing employment and utilizing state ports —Cont'd
Purpose, §105-130.46(a).
Reports, §105-130.46(k).
Information required by corporation attaining credit, §105-130.45(d).
Inmates in correctional or local confinement facilities.
Giving or selling to, §14-258.1(c).
Possession by inmate in local confinement facility, §14-258.1(e).
Labels.
Sale of packages of cigarettes, labeling violations, §14-401.18(b).
Tobacco seed.
Limitation on requirements, §106-277.10(c).
Landlord's lien on crops.
Failure of tenant to account for sales under tobacco marketing cards, §42-22.1.
Larceny.
Ungathered crops, §14-78.
Leaf tobacco sales, §§106-461 to 106-465.
See LEAF TOBACCO SALES.
Leaf tobacco warehouses, §§106-453 to 106-455.
Licenses.
Cancellation.
Reasons, §105-113.4B(a).
Request of license holder, §105-113.4B(a).
Summary cancellation by secretary, §105-113.4B(a), (b).
Duplicate or amended license, §105-113.4A(c).
Generally, §105-113.4A(a).
Refund of license taxes, §105-113.4A(b).
Liens.
Effective period for lien on leaf tobacco sold in auction warehouse, §44-69.
Lien on crops.
Failure of tenant to account for sales under tobacco marketing cards, §42-22.1.
Master settlement agreement.
Budget of state.
Settlement reserve fund, §143C-9-3.
Enforcement of provisions as to nonparticipating manufacturers.
Duties of attorney general and secretary of revenue, §105-113.4C.
Minors.
Sale or distribution to minors, §14-313.
Use of minors to test compliance with provisions, §14-313(d).
Motor vehicles, size and loads.
Hogsheads of tobacco.
Maximum width, §20-116(a).
Trucks hauling leaf tobacco in barrels or hogsheads.
Restrictions, §20-120.
Museums.
Establishment, §143-431.
Location of museums, §143-432.
Purposes, §143-431.
Tobacco museum board.
Transfer of board to department of cultural resources, §143B-51.
National tobacco grower settlement trust.
Board of directors of certification entity.
Appointment, §143-300.30(b).

CIGARETTES AND TOBACCO PRODUCTS
—Cont'd
National tobacco grower settlement trust
—Cont'd
Creation, proposal by tobacco companies,
§143-300.30(a).
Decedents' estates.
Phase II payments.
Property of distributees, §28A-15-9.1.
Desire of tobacco companies, §143-300.30(a).
Immunity of certification entity member,
§143-300.30(c).
**Nicotine replacement therapy program
supervision,** §90-18.6.
Oaths.
Tobacco weighers, §106-453.
Packages of cigarettes.
Sale of certain packages prohibited.
Contraband, §14-401.18(c).
Definitions, §14-401.18(a).
Offenses, §14-401.18(b).
Price fixing.
Leaf tobacco sales.
Tobacco boards of trade, §106-465.
Prisoners.
Giving or selling tobacco products to, §14-258.1(c).
Possession by inmate in local confinement facility,
§14-258.1(e).
Promotion of sale and use of tobacco,
§§106-568.18 to 106-568.37.
See TOBACCO SALES.
Public weighmasters.
Weighing tobacco, §81A-59.
Research commission, §106-568.3(b).
Sales.
Leaf tobacco sales, §§106-461 to 106-465.
See LEAF TOBACCO SALES.
Minors, §14-313.
Packages of cigarettes.
Sale of certain packages prohibited, §14-401.18.
Promotion of sale and use of tobacco, §§106-568.18
to 106-568.37.
See TOBACCO SALES.
Tobacco escrow compliance.
Sale of cigarettes on compliant nonparticipating
manufacturer's list, §66-293.
Tobacco reserve fund.
Escrow compliance, §§66-292 to 66-294.1.
Scope of tax, §105-113.3(a).
Seeds.
Label requirement for tobacco seeds,
§106-277.10(c).
Short title, §105-113.2.
Smoking generally.
See SMOKING.
State correctional institutions.
Smoking prohibited in, §148-23.1.
Taxation.
Cigarette tax, §§105-113.5 to 105-113.33.
See CIGARETTE TAX.
Tobacco products tax, §§105-113.2 to 105-113.4,
105-113.35 to 105-113.40A.
See TOBACCO PRODUCTS TAX.
Tobacco boards of trade.
Membership, §106-465.
Organization, §106-465.
Tobacco manufacturer escrow funds.
Assignment of rights to state, §143C-9-5.
Tobacco products tax, §§105-113.2 to 105-113.4,
105-113.35 to 105-113.40A.
See TOBACCO PRODUCTS TAX.

CIGARETTES AND TOBACCO PRODUCTS
—Cont'd
Tobacco reserve fund.
Tobacco product manufacturers selling cigarettes,
§§66-290, 66-291.
Escrow compliance, §§66-292 to 66-294.1.
Tobacco trust fund commission, §§143-715 to
143-723.
See TOBACCO TRUST FUND COMMISSION.
Tobacco-use cessation programs.
Nicotine replacement therapy program
supervision, §90-18.6.
Tobacco warehouses.
See TOBACCO WAREHOUSES.
**"U. S. tax exempt" selling cigarettes with label
in state,** §14-401.18(b).

CIGARETTE TAX, §§105-113.5 to 105-113.33.
Confiscation.
Non-tax-paid cigarettes, §105-113.32.
Vehicles or vessels transporting, §105-113.31(b).
Conflict of laws.
Federal constitution and statutes, §105-113.8.
Criminal penalties, §105-113.33.
Definitions, §105-113.4.
Interstate business, §105-113.9.
Place of business.
Distributors, §105-113.12(b).
Discount.
Expenses incurred in preparing records and
reports, §105-113.21(a1).
Distributors.
Licenses.
Bond, §105-113.13(b).
Investigation of applicants, §105-113.13(a).
Out-of-state distributors, §§105-113.12(c),
105-113.24(d).
Place of business.
Defined, §105-113.12(b).
Required, §105-113.12(a).
Tax, §105-113.12(a).
Out-of-state distributors, §105-113.12(c).
Manufacturers shipping to distributors.
Exemption, §105-113.10(a).
Out-of-state distributors.
Examination of books, accounts and records,
§105-113.24(b).
Licenses, §§105-113.12(c), 105-113.24(d).
Service of process.
Secretary of state as attorney for,
§105-113.24(c).
Stamps.
Sale to out-of-state distributors,
§105-113.24(a).
Refund.
Stale or unsaleable cigarettes returned to
manufacturer, §105-113.21(a).
Reports, §105-113.18.
Stale or unsaleable cigarettes.
Return to manufacturer.
Refund, §105-113.21(a).
Exemptions.
Activities tax in violation of federal constitution
and statutes, §105-113.8.
Manufacturers shipping to affiliated
manufacturers, §105-113.10(b).
Affiliated manufacturer defined, §105-113.4.
Manufacturers shipping to distributors,
§105-113.10(a).
**Identification of dispensers on vending
machines,** §105-113.17.

CIGARETTE TAX —Cont'd
Imposition of taxes, §§105-113.5, 105-113.6.
Inventories.
  Tax with respect to inventory on effective date of
      tax increase, §105-113.4D.
Levy of taxes, §§105-113.5, 105-113.6.
Licenses, §105-113.11.
  Distributors.
      Bond, §105-113.13(b).
      Investigation of applicants, §105-113.13(a).
      Out-of-state distributors, §§105-113.12(c),
          105-113.24(d).
      Place of business.
          Defined, §105-113.12(b).
          Required, §105-113.12(a).
          Tax, §105-113.12(a).
              Out-of-state distributors, §105-113.12(c).
      Required, §105-113.11.
          Distributors, §105-113.12(a).
  Unlicensed place of business.
      Prohibited, §105-113.29.
**Manufacturers shipping to affiliated
    manufacturers.**
  Exempt, §105-113.10(b).
      Affiliated manufacturer defined, §105-113.4.
Manufacturers shipping to distributors.
  Exempt, §105-113.10(a).
Non-tax-paid cigarettes.
  Confiscation, §105-113.32.
      Vehicle or vessel transporting, §105-113.31(b).
  Possession.
      Prima facie evidence, §105-113.27(c).
  Prohibited acts, §§105-113.27, 105-113.31(a).
  Sale.
      Prohibited acts, §105-113.27(a), (b).
  Transportation, §105-113.31(a).
      Requirements, §105-113.31(b).
      Seizure and confiscation of vehicle or vessel,
          §105-113.31(b).
Out-of-state shipments, §105-113.9.
Prohibited acts.
  Criminal penalties, §105-113.33.
  Non-tax-paid cigarettes, §§105-113.27,
      105-113.31(a).
  Records and reports, §105-113.30.
  Unlicensed place of business, §105-113.29.
Rate, §105-113.5.
Records.
  Required records, §105-113.26.
      Prohibited acts, §105-113.30.
Refunds, §105-113.21(b).
Reports.
  Required reports, §105-113.18.
      Prohibited acts, §105-113.30.
Stale or unsaleable cigarettes.
  Refund, §105-113.21(b).
Stamps.
  Out-of-state distributors.
      Sale to, §105-113.24(a).
Use tax.
  Levy, §105-113.6.
Vending machines.
  Identification of dispensers, §105-113.17.

CIGARETTE WRAPPING PAPERS.
Sale or distribution to minors, §14-313.

CIO.
State chief information officer.
  See INFORMATION TECHNOLOGY SERVICES.

CIRCUIT BREAKER.
Homestead circuit breaker.
  Property tax, §105-277.1B.
      Uniform provisions for payment of deferred
          taxes, §105-277.1F.

CIRCUSES.
Counties.
  Regulation of places of amusement, §153A-135.
Municipalities.
  Regulation of carnivals and circuses, §160A-181.

CISTERNS.
Cities.
  Limitations on regulating, §160A-202.
Counties.
  Limitations on regulating, §153A-145.

CITATIONS.
Contents, §15A-302(c).
**Costs of criminal process in superior or
    district courts,** §7A-304(a).
Criminal summons or warrant.
  Citation no bar to, §15A-302(f).
Defined, §15A-302(a).
**Delivery, execution and service of criminal
    process,** §15A-301.
Dismissal by prosecutor, §15A-302(e).
Forest rangers.
  Authority to issue, §106-899(b).
Form.
  Preparation, §15A-302(g).
Infractions.
  Summons and process, §15A-1113(a).
Issuance, §15A-302(b).
National guard.
  Governor's unit citation, §127A-45.1.
  Meritorious unit citation, §127A-45.2.
Occupational safety and health.
  Contest by employee of period of time fixed for
      correction violation, §95-130.
  Enforcement procedure, §95-137(b).
Service, §15A-302(d).
Summons or warrant.
  Citation no bar to, §15A-302(f).

CITIES.
Annexation.
  Extension of corporate limits generally, §§160A-29
      to 160A-58.90.
      See ANNEXATION.
Boards of education.
  Local boards of education generally, §§115C-35 to
      115C-51.
      See LOCAL BOARDS OF EDUCATION.
Cemeteries.
  Generally, §§160A-341 to 160A-348.
      See MUNICIPAL CEMETERIES.
Communications services.
  Cities providing, §§160A-340 to 160A-340.6.
      See MUNICIPAL UTILITIES.
Condemnation of unsafe buildings.
  Generally, §§160A-411 to 160A-439.
      See MUNICIPAL BUILDING INSPECTION.
Council generally.
  See CITY COUNCILS.
Council-manager cities, §§160A-147 to 160A-152.
      See COUNCIL-MANAGER CITIES.
Critical infrastructure needs.
  Special assessments, §§160A-239.1 to 160A-239.7.
Demolition of unsafe building.
  Dwellings, §160A-443.
  Nonresidential building, §160A-432(b), (b1).

CITIES —Cont'd
Demolition of unsafe building —Cont'd
Ordinance, §160A-443.
Education.
Local boards of education, §§115C-35 to 115C-51.
See LOCAL BOARDS OF EDUCATION.
Public schools generally.
See SCHOOLS AND EDUCATION.
Elections, §§163-279 to 163-306.
See MUNICIPAL ELECTIONS.
Electric service in urban areas, §§160A-331 to
160A-338.
See ELECTRIC SERVICE IN URBAN AREAS.
Extension of corporate limits generally,
§§160A-29 to 160A-58.90.
See ANNEXATION.
Generally.
See MUNICIPALITIES.
**Gross receipts tax on vehicle short-term leases
or rentals,** §160A-215.1.
Authority to levy, §160A-215.1(a).
Collection and administration, §160A-215.1(d).
Definitions, §160A-215.1(e).
Location of transaction giving rise to tax,
§160A-215.1(b).
Notation of tax in agreement, §160A-215.1(b).
Penalties and remedies, §160A-215.1(f).
Proceeds belong to city, not subject to creditor
liens, §160A-215.1(c).
Rate, §160A-215.1(a).
Heavy equipment gross receipts tax.
In lieu of property tax, §160A-215.2.
Hospitals.
Municipalities, §§131E-5 to 131E-14.2.
See MUNICIPAL HOSPITALS.
Inspection of building, §§160A-411 to 160A-439.
See MUNICIPAL BUILDING INSPECTION.
Joint municipal electric power and energy,
§§159B-1 to 159B-52.
See JOINT MUNICIPAL ELECTRIC POWER
AND ENERGY ACT.
License taxes.
Attorneys or other professions.
Levy of tax prohibited, §105-41(h).
Generally, §§105-33 to 105-109.
See MUNICIPAL LICENSE TAXES.
Local government finance, §§159-1 to 159-188.
See LOCAL GOVERNMENT FINANCE.
Local governments.
See LOCAL GOVERNMENTS.
Military property sales facilities.
Licensing, §127B-4(a) to (c).
Officers and employees generally.
See MUNICIPAL OFFICERS AND EMPLOYEES.
Outdoor advertising.
Regulation of nonconforming off-premises outdoor
advertising, §160A-199.
Planning generally, §§160A-360 to 160A-366.
See MUNICIPAL PLANNING AND
REGULATION OF DEVELOPMENT.
Property taxes.
Municipalities.
See PROPERTY TAXES.
Removal of unsafe building.
Dwellings, §160A-443.
Nonresidential building, §160A-432(b), (b1).
Ordinance, §160A-443.
Retirement, §§128-21 to 128-38.5.
See LOCAL GOVERNMENTAL EMPLOYEES'
RETIREMENT SYSTEM.

CITIES —Cont'd
Room occupancy taxes.
Uniform provisions, §160A-215.
Satellite annexation.
Annexation of noncontiguous areas, §§160A-58 to
160A-58.8.
See ANNEXATION.
Schools.
Generally.
See SCHOOLS AND EDUCATION.
Local boards of education, §§115C-35 to 115C-51.
See LOCAL BOARDS OF EDUCATION.
Smoking.
Local government regulation, §130A-498.
Solid waste disposal tax.
Distribution, use of proceeds, §105-187.63.
Special assessments.
Critical infrastructure needs, §§160A-239.1 to
160A-239.7.
Generally, §§160A-216 to 160A-238.
See SPECIAL ASSESSMENTS BY CITIES.
Subdivision regulation generally, §§160A-371 to
160A-377.
See MUNICIPAL PLANNING AND
REGULATION OF DEVELOPMENT.
Traffic control photographic systems,
§160A-300.1.
**Unsafe building, condemnation, correction of
defects,** §§160A-411 to 160A-439.
See MUNICIPAL BUILDING INSPECTION.
Zoning generally, §§160A-381 to 160A-393.
See MUNICIPAL PLANNING AND
REGULATION OF DEVELOPMENT.

CITIZENS ARREST, §§15A-404, 15A-405.
Recapture of escape prisoners, §148-40.

CITIZENS AWARENESS MONTH.
Voter registration drive, §163-82.25.

CITIZENS BAND RADIO.
Interception of communications not unlawful,
§15A-287(b).
Unauthorized use, §62-328.

CITIZENSHIP.
Concealed handgun permit qualifications,
§14-415.12(a).
Constitutional provisions, US Const Art IV §2,
Amd 14.
Convicted persons.
Restoration of citizenship, §13-1.
Filing of certificate or order of restoration,
§13-2(a).
Issuance of certificate or order of restoration,
§13-2(a).
Pardon.
Conditional pardon, §13-4.
Unconditional pardon, §13-3.
Person convicted of crime against another state
or United States.
Rights restored, provision applicable, §13-2(b).
Elections.
Presidential elections.
Residence period for presidential elections, NC
Const Art VI §2.
Registration of voters following restoration of
citizenship, §163-82.20A.
State elections.
Residence period for state elections, NC Const
Art VI §2.
Indians, §§71A-3 to 71A-7.2.

CITIZENSHIP —Cont'd
Jails.
Citizenship status of prisoners, §162-62.
Pardon.
Conditional pardon.
Endorsement of warrant, service and filing of conditional pardon, §13-4.
Unconditional pardon.
Restoration of citizenship.
Issuance, service and filing of warrant, §13-3.
Registration of voters following restoration of citizenship, §163-82.20A.
Restoration of citizenship.
Certificate or order of restoration.
Filing of certificate, §13-2(a).
Issuance, §13-2(a).
Conditions for restoration, §13-1.
Pardon.
Conditional pardon.
Endorsement of warrant, service and filing, §13-4.
Unconditional pardon.
Warrant, issuance, service, §13-3.
Person convicted of crime against another state or United States.
Rights restored, provision applicable, §13-2(b).
Rights and immunities of citizens, US Const Amd 14.

CITY CLERKS.
Deputy clerk, §160A-172.
Duties, §160A-171.
Office created, §160A-171.

CITY COUNCILS.
Abolish office, position, etc.
Power limited, §160A-146.
Applicability of part 3, §160A-82.
Charter.
Amendment, §160A-102.
City attorney.
Appointment by council, §160A-173.
Compelling production of evidence, §160A-80(a).
Compensation, §160A-64(a), (b).
Composition, §160A-66.
Deeds.
Validation of certain deeds, §160A-18.
Defined, §160A-1.
Elections, §160A-66.
Districts.
Map, §160A-23(a).
Optional form, §160A-101.
Reapportionment, §160A-23(b).
Redistricting after federal decennial census, §160A-23.1.
Optional form, §160A-101.
Hearings, §160A-81.
Investigation, §160A-80(a).
Journal.
Kept by city clerk, §160A-171.
Mayor.
Preside over council, §160A-69.
Pro tempore.
Elected by council, §160A-70.
Voting.
Right to vote, §160A-69.
Meetings.
Notice.
Given by city clerk, §160A-171.
Organizational meeting.
Date and time, §160A-68(a).
Repeal of charter and local act provisions, §160A-68(c).

CITY COUNCILS —Cont'd
Meetings —Cont'd
Organizational meeting —Cont'd
Qualifying of mayor and councilmen, §160A-68(b).
Public comment period during regular meetings, §160A-81.1.
Regular meetings.
Public comment period, §160A-81.1.
Recess and adjourn meetings, §160A-71(b1).
Time and place, §160A-71(a).
Special meetings.
Calling, §160A-71(b).
Recess and adjourn meetings, §160A-71(b1).
Minutes.
Contents, §160A-72.
Keeping, §160A-72.
Number of members, §160A-66.
Amendment of charter.
Provisions affecting charter definition of quorum, §160A-106.
Optional form, §160A-101.
Oaths.
Administration, §160A-80(a).
Organization.
City government, §160A-146.
Meetings, §160A-68.
Powers.
Exercise of corporate powers, §160A-12.
Generally, §160A-67.
Investigation, §160A-80(a).
Subpoena powers, §160A-80(a).
Procedure.
Rules of procedure, §160A-71(c).
Quorum, §160A-74.
Filling vacancies to make quorum, §160A-63.
Subpoena, §160A-80(a).
Terms of office, §160A-66.
Optional form, §160A-101.
Vacancies.
Filling, §160A-63.
Voting by members.
Ayes and noes.
Taken upon request of member, §160A-72.
Excused from voting, §160A-75.
Failure to vote.
Counted as affirmative vote, §160A-75.
Majority vote required, §160A-75.
Results of votes recorded in minutes, §160A-72.
Two thirds of membership.
Affirmative vote to adopt ordinance on date introduced, §160A-75.
Withdrawal of member from meeting without being excused.
Counted for purposes of quorum, §160A-74.
Witnesses.
Enforcement of subpoena, §160A-80(b).
Perjury, §160A-80(b).
Power to subpoena, §160A-80(a).
Use of evidence against witness prohibited, §160A-80(b).

CITY-COUNTY CONSOLIDATION ACT, §§160B-1 to 160B-21.
See CONSOLIDATED CITY-COUNTY ACT.

CITY MANAGERS.
Council-managers cities, §§160A-147 to 160A-152.
See COUNCIL-MANAGER CITIES.
Service of process.
Personal jurisdiction on city, town or village, §1A-1 Rule 4(j).

CITY SCHOOL ADMINISTRATIVE UNITS.
Administrative units generally.
See SCHOOL DISTRICTS AND
ADMINISTRATIVE UNITS.

CIVIC CENTERS.
Alcoholic beverage permits.
Convention center defined to include, §18B-1000.
Mixed beverage permit.
Kind of permit that may be issued, §18B-1001.
Recycling requirement, §18B-1006.1.
On-premises fortified wine permit.
Kind of permit that may be issued, §18B-1001.
Recycling requirement, §18B-1006.1.
On-premises malt beverage permit.
Kind of permit that may be issued, §18B-1001.
Recycling requirement, §18B-1006.1.
On-premises unfortified wine permit.
Kind of permit that may be issued, §18B-1001.
Recycling requirement, §18B-1006.1.

CIVIC LITERACY.
Basic education program, §115C-81(g).

CIVIC ORGANIZATIONS.
Alcoholic beverage permits.
Special one-time permits, §18B-1002(a).
Amusement tax exemptions, §105-40.
Solicitation of contributions, §§131F-1 to
131F-33.
See CHARITABLE SOLICITATION.

CIVIL ACTIONS.
Actions.
See ACTIONS.

CIVIL AERONAUTICS ADMINISTRATION.
Rules and regulations.
Enforcement, §63-47.

CIVIL AIR PATROL.
Benefits personnel entitled to, §143B-1031(b).
**Certificate of members in good standing
entitled to benefits.**
Deemed employees of department for purposes of
benefits, §143B-1031(b).
Duty of wing commander, §143B-1031(a).
Change in personnel.
Notification by wing commander, §143B-1031(a).
Compensation.
Service without, §143B-1032.
Contracts, debts, obligations.
State not liable, §143B-1032.
Death benefits, §§143-166.1 to 143-166.7.
See DEATH BENEFITS.
Duties of civil air patrol section, §143B-1030(b).
Establishment of civil air patrol section.
Within department of public safety,
§143B-1030(a).
Motor vehicle license plates.
Permanent license plates for patrol vehicles,
§20-84(b).
Special license plates, §20-79.4(b).
**Retirement system for teachers and state
employees.**
Not entitled to benefits, §143B-1032.
**Tort claims against state departments and
agencies.**
Provisions not applicable to, §143B-1032.
Transfer to department of public safety,
§143A-241.
Workers' compensation.
Employee defined, §97-2.
Entitlement to benefits, §143B-1031(b).

CIVIL ARREST.
See ARREST IN CIVIL CASES.

CIVIL CHILD-CUSTODY ORDER.
Juvenile proceeding, §7B-911.

CIVIL CONTEMPT, §§5A-21 to 5A-25.
See CONTEMPT.

CIVIL DEFENSE.
Civil preparedness agency.
Transfer to department of public safety,
§143A-240.
Emergency management.
General provisions, §§166A-1 to 166A-18.
See EMERGENCY MANAGEMENT.
**Interception of radio communications not
unlawful,** §15A-287(b).
Municipalities.
Property taxes.
Authorized purposes, §160A-209(c).

CIVIL DISORDERS.
Riots and civil disorders, §§14-288.1 to
14-288.20.
See RIOTS AND CIVIL DISORDERS.

CIVIL DRIVER'S LICENSE REVOCATIONS,
§20-16.5.

CIVIL INVESTIGATIVE DEMAND.
False claims act violations, §1-614.
Medicaid.
False claims by providers, §108A-70.14.

CIVIL NO-CONTACT ORDERS, §§50C-1 to
50C-11.
Additional nature of remedy, §50C-11.
Address of victim.
Omission from documents, §50C-2(d).
Commencement of action for, §50C-2(a).
Contempt.
Violations, §50C-10.
Notice that violation punishable as contempt,
§50C-5(c).
Costs not to be assessed, §50C-2(b).
Definitions, §50C-1.
Expiration of orders, §50C-8(d).
Extension of orders, §50C-8(c).
Delivery of order to sheriff, §50C-9(d).
Issuance, §50C-5(a).
Default, §50C-3(c).
Permanent order, §50C-7.
Non-exclusive nature of remedy, §50C-11.
Notice of orders, §50C-9(a).
Police department or sheriff.
Issuance to and retention by, §50C-9(c).
Service, §50C-9(b).
Notice that violation punishable as contempt,
§50C-5(c).
Permanent order, §50C-7.
Duration, §50C-8(b).
Prior sexual activity of victim inadmissible,
§50C-4.
Relief which may be granted, §50C-5(b).
Summons.
Action for order, §50C-3(a).
Service of summons and attachments,
§50C-3(b).
Temporary orders, §50C-6(a), (b).
Appearance in court for, §50C-6(c).
Court not in session, §50C-6(d).
Duration, §50C-8(a).
Venue of action for, §50C-2(c).

CIVIL NO-CONTACT ORDERS —Cont'd
Workplace violence prevention, §§95-260 to 95-271.
  See WORKPLACE VIOLENCE PREVENTION.

CIVIL PENALTY AND FORFEITURE FUND, §§115C-457.1 to 115C-457.3.
Administration, §115C-457.1(b).
Creation, §115C-457.1(a).
Deposits in, §115C-457.2.
Remittance of moneys to, §115C-457.2.
  Consolidated judicial retirement act.
    Benefits forfeited by members convicted of certain felonies, §135-75.1(d).
  Debt collectors.
    Civil penalties, §75-56(e).
  Local governmental employees' retirement system.
    Benefits forfeited by elected government officials convicted of certain felonies, §128-38.4(d).
  Motor carriers.
    Insurance verification by for-hire carriers.
      Failure to comply.
        Civil penalty, proceeds, §20-382.2(d).
  Motor vehicle or traffic violations.
    Civil penalties imposed, §20-176.1(e).
  Retirement system for teachers and state employees.
    Benefits forfeited by members convicted of certain felonies, §135-18.10(d).
State school technology fund.
  Transfer of funds to, §115C-457.3(a).
  Allocations, §115C-457.3(b).

CIVIL PREPAREDNESS.
Agency.
  Transfer to department of public safety, §143A-240.
Emergency management.
  General provisions, §§166A-1 to 166A-18.
  See EMERGENCY MANAGEMENT.
Hazardous materials emergency response, §§166A-20 to 166A-28.
  See HAZARDOUS MATERIALS EMERGENCY RESPONSE.
Municipalities.
  Property taxes.
    Authorized purposes, §160A-209(c).

CIVIL PROCEDURE.
Actions.
  Commencement of actions, §§1-105 to 1-120.2.
  See COMMENCEMENT OF ACTIONS.
  Definitions.
    Generally, §1-2.
  General provisions.
    See ACTIONS.
  Joinder.
    See JOINDER.
Adverse possession.
  See ADVERSE POSSESSION.
Advertising.
  Legal advertising, §§1-595 to 1-601.
Alimony.
  See DIVORCE.
Appeals.
  Appellate rules of procedure.
    See APPEALS.
Arbitration.
  Generally.
    See ARBITRATION.
  International commercial arbitration and conciliation, §§1-567.30 to 1-567.87.
    See INTERNATIONAL COMMERCIAL ARBITRATION AND CONCILIATION.

CIVIL PROCEDURE —Cont'd
Arbitration —Cont'd
  Revised uniform arbitration act, §§1-569.1 to 1-569.31.
    See ARBITRATION.
Arrest.
  Civil cases, §§1-409 to 1-439.
    See ARREST IN CIVIL CASES.
Attachment.
  See ATTACHMENT.
Bail.
  Civil cases.
    See BAIL.
Bankruptcy and insolvency.
  General provisions.
    See BANKRUPTCY AND INSOLVENCY.
  Receivers, §§1-501 to 1-507.11.
    See RECEIVERS.
Betterments, §§1-340 to 1-351.
  See BETTERMENTS.
Bonds, surety.
  Prosecution bonds, §§1-109 to 1-112.
Change of venue, §§1-83 to 1-87.
Claim and delivery, §§1-472 to 1-484.1.
  See CLAIM AND DELIVERY.
Class actions, §1A-1 Rule 23.
Clerks of court.
  General provisions.
    See CLERKS OF COURT.
Commencement of actions, §§1-105 to 1-120.2.
  See COMMENCEMENT OF ACTIONS.
Complaints.
  See COMPLAINTS.
Compromise and settlement, §§1-540 to 1-540.3.
  See SETTLEMENT.
Constitution of North Carolina.
  Jury trial.
    Right to jury trial in civil cases, NC Const Art I §25.
  Rules of procedure, NC Const Art IV §13.
Contempt.
  Civil contempt, §§5A-21 to 5A-25.
    See CONTEMPT.
Costs, §§6-1 to 6-62.
  See COSTS.
Counterclaims and cross-claims.
  See COUNTERCLAIMS AND CROSS-CLAIMS.
Debtors.
  Joint and several debtors, §§1-113, 1-114.
Decedents' estates.
  Rules of civil procedure.
    Applicability in estate proceedings, §28A-2-6(e).
Declaratory judgments, §§1-253 to 1-267.
  See DECLARATORY JUDGMENTS.
Defendants, §1-10.
Defenses.
  See DEFENSES.
Definitions.
  Actions.
    Civil action, §1-6.
    Criminal action, §1-5.
    Generally, §1-2.
    Kinds of actions, §1-4.
  Court.
    When court means clerk, §1-7.
  Remedies, §1-1.
  Special proceedings, §1-3.
Delivery.
  Claim and delivery, §§1-472 to 1-484.1.
    See CLAIM AND DELIVERY.

CIVIL PROCEDURE —Cont'd
Depositions.
　See DEPOSITIONS.
Deposit or delivery of money or other
　property, §§1-508 to 1-510.
Discovery.
　See DISCOVERY.
Dismissal, discontinuance and nonsuit.
　See DISMISSAL, DISCONTINUANCE AND
　　NONSUIT.
District courts.
　Applicability of civil procedure generally, §7A-193.
　Jury trials, §7A-196(a).
Divorce.
　See DIVORCE.
Electronic filing of pleadings and other
　documents, §7A-49.5.
Evidence.
　See EVIDENCE.
Executions, §§1-302 to 1-368.
　See EXECUTIONS.
Execution sales, §§1-339.41 to 1-339.71.
　See EXECUTION SALES.
Frauds, statute of.
　See STATUTE OF FRAUDS.
Garnishment.
　See GARNISHMENT.
Habeas corpus, §§17-1 to 17-46.
　See HABEAS CORPUS.
Improvements.
　Betterments, §§1-340 to 1-351.
　　See BETTERMENTS.
Injunctions.
　See INJUNCTIONS.
Interpleader and intervention.
　See INTERPLEADER AND INTERVENTION.
Interrogatories.
　See INTERROGATORIES.
Joinder.
　General provisions.
　　See JOINDER.
Joint and several debtors.
　Defenses.
　　Parties summoned after judgment, §1-114.
　Judgments, §1-113.
　　Summoning after judgment, §1-114.
　Partners, §1-113.
　Proceedings generally, §1-113.
　Summons and process, §1-113.
　　Summoning after judgment, §1-114.
Judgments.
　Declaratory judgments, §§1-253 to 1-267.
　　See DECLARATORY JUDGMENTS.
　Executions, §§1-302 to 1-368.
　　See EXECUTIONS.
Judgments and decrees.
　General provisions.
　　See JUDGMENTS AND DECREES.
Jurisdiction.
　See JURISDICTION.
Jury and jury trial.
　See JURY AND JURY TRIAL.
Legal advertising, §§1-595 to 1-601.
Limitation of actions, §§1-15 to 1-56.
　See LIMITATION OF ACTIONS.
Lis pendens, §§1-116 to 1-120.2.
　See LIS PENDENS.
Nonsuits.
　See DISMISSAL, DISCONTINUANCE AND
　　NONSUIT.

CIVIL PROCEDURE —Cont'd
Nuisances.
　See NUISANCES.
Offer of judgment, §1A-1 Rule 68(a).
　Conditional offer of judgment for damages, §1A-1
　　Rule 68(b).
Parties.
　See PARTIES.
Payment into court, §§1-508 to 1-510.
Plaintiff, §1-10.
Pleadings.
　See PLEADINGS.
Prosecution bonds, §§1-109 to 1-112.
Quo warranto.
　See QUO WARRANTO.
Receivers, §§1-501 to 1-507.11.
　See RECEIVERS.
Referees.
　See REFEREES.
Remedies.
　Civil and criminal remedies not merged, §1-8.
　Enumeration, §1-1.
　Merger.
　　Civil and criminal remedies not merged, §1-8.
Service of process.
　See SERVICE OF NOTICE, PROCESS AND
　　OTHER PAPERS.
Settlement, §§1-540 to 1-540.3.
　See SETTLEMENT.
Special proceedings.
　See SPECIAL PROCEEDINGS.
Statute of frauds.
　See STATUTE OF FRAUDS.
Statutes of limitation.
　See LIMITATION OF ACTIONS.
Stays.
　See STAYS.
Summary judgment.
　See SUMMARY JUDGMENT.
Supersedeas.
　See SUPERSEDEAS.
Supreme court.
　Rules of procedure.
　　Promulgation, NC Const Art IV §13.
Time.
　See TIME.
Trial.
　See TRIAL.
Venue.
　Change of venue, §§1-83 to 1-87.
　　See VENUE.
　General provisions, §§1-76 to 1-87.
　　See VENUE.
Verdict.
　See VERDICTS.
Waste, §§1-533 to 1-538.
Witnesses.
　See WITNESSES.

CIVIL RIGHTS.
Discrimination.
　See DISCRIMINATION.
Firearms rights.
　Restoration, §14-415.4.
Interference with.
　Civil action.
　　Compensatory and punitive damages, §99D-1(b),
　　　(b1).
　　Costs and attorney's fees, §99D-1(b), (b1).
　　Government unit or government official.
　　　Restriction on bringing against, §99D-1(c).

CIVIL RIGHTS —Cont'd
Interference with —Cont'd
Civil action —Cont'd
Human relations commission bringing, §99D-1(b1).
Personal action, §99D-1(b).
Conduct constituting, §99D-1(a).
Future acts.
Restraining and enjoining, §99D-1(b), (b1).
Mental health, developmental disabilities and substance abuse.
Rights of clients.
Retention of right to exercise all civil rights, §122C-58.
Nursing homes.
Patients' bill of rights, §§131E-115 to 131E-131.
See NURSING HOMES.
Restoration of citizenship, §§13-1 to 13-4.
Automatic restoration, §13-1.
Certificate or order of restoration.
Issuance and filing, §13-2(a), (b).
Conditional pardon.
Endorsement of warrant, service and filing, §13-4.
Unconditional pardon.
Issuance, service and filing of warrant, §13-3.
Voting rights act of 1965.
Submissions to attorney general of the United States, §§120-30.9A to 120-30.9I.

CIVIL SERVICE.
County personnel system.
Generally, §§153A-92 to 153A-99.
See COUNTY PERSONNEL SYSTEM.
Municipal personnel system, §§160A-162 to 160A-169.1.
See MUNICIPAL OFFICERS AND EMPLOYEES.
Public officers and employees generally.
See PUBLIC OFFICERS AND EMPLOYEES.
State personnel system, §§126-1 to 126-90.
See PERSONNEL SYSTEM.

CLAIM AND DELIVERY, §§1-472 to 1-484.1.
Affidavits, §1-473.
Third parties.
Property claimed by third person, §1-482.
Appeals.
Issuance or refusal to issue order to sheriff, §1-474(a).
Bonds, surety.
Defendant's undertaking for replevy, §1-478.
Qualification and justification of defendant's surety, §1-479.
Plaintiff's undertaking, §1-475.
Exceptions to undertaking, §1-477.
Sheriffs.
Liability for sufficiency of sureties, §§1-477, 1-479.
Third parties.
Property claimed by third person, §1-482.
Buildings.
Property concealed in buildings, §1-480.
Construction and interpretation.
Remedy not exclusive, §1-484.1.
Forms.
Notice of hearing, §1-474.1(c).
Waiver of hearing, §1-474.1(c).
Hearings.
Notice, §1-474.1(a).
Form, §1-474.1(c).
Waiver of rights to notice and hearing, §1-474.1(b).
Form, §1-474.1(c).

CLAIM AND DELIVERY —Cont'd
Injunctions.
Notice containing order enjoining defendant from disposing of property, §1-474.1(a).
Notice.
Bonds, surety.
Notice to sureties to justify, §§1-477, 1-479.
Hearing, §1-474.1(a).
Form of notice, §1-474.1(c).
Orders of court, §1-474(a).
Expiration of certain orders, §1-474(b).
Recovery of personal property, §1-230.
Remedy not exclusive, §1-484.1.
Requisites, §1-473.
Rights of plaintiff, §1-472.
Service of process.
Notice of hearing, §1-474.1(a).
Property claimed by third person, §1-482.
Sheriffs.
Bonds, surety.
Liability for sufficiency of sureties, §§1-477, 1-479.
Care and delivery of seized property, §1-481.
Duties, §1-476.
Care and delivery of seized property, §1-481.
Property concealed in buildings, §1-480.
Order to take and deliver property, §1-474(a).
Expiration of certain orders, §1-474(b).
Return of papers, §1-484.
Third parties.
Property claimed by third person.
Delivery of property to intervener, §1-483.
Small claims actions.
Provisional and incidental remedies, §7A-231.
Taxation.
Property taxes.
Order not to be issued, §105-379(b).
Third parties.
Property claimed by third person.
Delivery of property to intervener, §1-483.
Proceedings, §1-482.
Time, §1-472.
Waiver.
Rights to notice and hearing, §1-474.1(b).
Form of waiver, §1-474.1(c).

CLAIM OF FACTUAL INNOCENCE.
Generally, innocence inquiry commission, §§15A-1460 to 15A-1475.
See INNOCENCE CLAIM INQUIRY.

CLAIMS AGAINST BOARD OF EDUCATION MEMBER OR EMPLOYEE.
Local boards paying, §115C-43(b), (c).

CLAIMS AGAINST LOCAL UNITS OF GOVERNMENT.
Notice of claim.
Local acts not to require notice, §1-539.16.

CLAIMS AGAINST THE STATE, §§143-291 to 143-300.1A.
Adopting, amending or deleting rules.
Procedure, ICTortClaim Rule T502.
Affidavit of claimant, §143-297.
Answer, demurrer or other pleading to affidavit, §143-297.
Settlement of claims, §143-295(b).
Amateur sports, §143-299.3(b).
Appeals.
Cost, §143-291.1.
Court of appeals, §143-293.
Bond, ICTortClaim Rule T402.

CLAIMS AGAINST THE STATE —Cont'd

Appeals —Cont'd

Court of appeals —Cont'd

Motions filed, ICTortClaim Rule T403.

Rules of appellate procedure, applicability, ICTortClaim Rule T401.

Settling record, ICTortClaim Rule T404.

Supersedeas, §143-294.

Full commission, §143-292.

Assignment of error, ICTortClaim Rule T303.

Brief, ICTortClaim Rule T305.

Dismissal, failure to file assignment of error, ICTortClaim Rule T304.

Motions before full commission pending appeal, ICTortClaim Rule T307.

New evidence, prohibition, discretion to permit, ICTortClaim Rule T309.

New hearing, motion, ICTortClaim Rule T306.

Notice, ICTortClaim Rule T301.

Oral argument, waiver, ICTortClaim Rule T310.

Stays, ICTortClaim Rule T308.

Transcript, ICTortClaim Rule T302.

Transcripts.

Copies, §143-291.1.

Supersedeas.

Appeal to court of appeals to act as supersedeas, §143-294.

Assignments.

Child support obligations, §143B-426.40A(d).

Definitions, §143B-426.40A(a).

Entities exempted from prohibition, §143B-426.40A(c).

General prohibition, §143B-426.40A(b).

Payroll deductions.

Charitable contributions.

Public school and community college employees, §143B-426.40A(i).

University of North Carolina system employees, §143B-426.40A(j).

Employees' associations, payments to, §143B-426.40A(g).

Parental savings fund contributions, §143B-426.40A(f1).

State employees combined campaign, §143B-426.40A(h).

State employees' credit union accounts, §143B-426.40A(f).

Prepaid legal services, §143B-426.40A(e).

Underground storage tank cleanup funds, §143B-426.40A(l).

University of North Carolina system.

Charitable contributions, §143B-426.40A(j).

Discretionary privileges of university service, §143B-426.40A(k).

Atomic energy.

Radiation.

Tort claims against persons rendering emergency assistance, §104E-22.

Attorney general.

Duties, §§143-298, 147-17(b).

Employment of counsel in cases where state is interested, §147-17(a).

Expenses, §143-298.

Attorneys' fees, §§143-291.1, 143-291.2.

Burden of proof, §143-299.1.

Consolidation of inmate claims, ICTortClaim Rule T206.

Contested cases.

Costs, ICTortClaim Rule T207.

Hearings, ICTortClaim Rule T206.

Contributory negligence, §143-299.1.

CLAIMS AGAINST THE STATE —Cont'd

Costs, §143-291.1, ICTortClaim Rule T207.

Taxing, §143-291.2(a).

Counsel.

Employment where state is interested, §147-17.

Counterclaims by state, §143-291.3.

Court of appeals.

Appeals to, §143-293.

Supersedeas, §143-294.

Damages, §143-291(a), (a1).

Defending actions arising from activities of state employees in course of employment, §147-17.

Defenses, §143-299.1.

Contributory negligence, §143-299.1.

Department of transportation contracts.

Claims by contractors on completed contracts, §136-29(a) to (d).

Determination of claim, §143-292.

Notice, §143-292.

Docketing, §143-297.

Enlargement of time, motion for, ICTortClaim Rule T203.

Evidence.

Burden of proof, §143-299.1.

False claims act.

False or fraudulent claims generally, §§1-605 to 1-631.

See FALSE CLAIMS ACT.

Fax filing, ICTortClaim Rule T104.

Fee assessments, §143-291.2(b).

Filing.

Fees, ICTortClaim Rule T202.

Telefacsimile transmission, ICTortClaim Rule T104.

Forms.

Official forms, ICTortClaim Rule T103.

Full commission, §143-292.

Guardian ad litem.

Minors or incompetents suing, ICTortClaim Rule T204.

Hearings, ICTortClaim Rule T206.

Industrial commission, §143-291(a).

Notice, §143-297.

High school athletic association, §143-291(c).

Hours of business, ICTortClaim Rule T101.

Indigent, sue as, petition, ICTortClaim Rule T202.

Industrial commission, §143-291.1.

Costs, allocation, §143-291.1.

Court to hear and determine claims, §143-291(a).

Damages.

Determination of claims, §143-291(a).

Deputies, §143-296.

Evidence rules, §143-300.

Findings, §143-291(a).

Hearings, §143-297.

Limitation, §143-299.

Location of offices, ICTortClaim Rule T101.

Powers, §143-296.

Records.

Destruction, §143-300.

Rules and regulations, §143-300.

Rules of procedure, §143-300.

School buses, §143-300.1(a).

Claims against county or city boards of education, §143-300.1.

Settlement of claims, §143-295.

School bus accidents, §143-300.1.

Transaction of business by commission, ICTortClaim Rule T102.

CLAIMS AGAINST THE STATE —Cont'd
Industrial commission —Cont'd
Venue, §143-297.
Insurance.
Purchase by state agency, §143-291(b).
Issuance, §143-298.
Jurisdiction.
Original jurisdiction of the supreme court, §7A-25.
Limitation of actions.
Time for making claim, §143-299.
Limitations on payments by state.
Dollar amount limitation, §143-299.2.
Maximum amount of payment, §143-299.2(a), (b).
Medical malpractice cases by prison inmates.
Motion to dismiss filed by defendant, ICTortClaim Rule T201.
Medical plan, liability for noncertification.
Limitation, §143-291(d).
Minors or incompetents suing, ICTortClaim Rule T204.
Motions, ICTortClaim Rule T205.
Motor vehicle title transfers, §143-295(c).
Negligence.
Contributory negligence as defense, §143-299.1.
North Carolina High School Athletic Association, Inc.
Status under provisions, §143-291(b).
Notice.
Determination of claim, §143-292.
Hearings, §143-297.
Payment.
Limitations on payments by state, §143-299.2.
Maximum amount, §143-299.2(a).
State excess liability, §143-299.4.
Powers of industrial commission, §143-296.
Public duty doctrine, limitations on use as defense.
Law enforcement officer, defined, §143-299.1A(d).
Local government not affected, §143-299.1A(c).
When applicable, §143-299.1A(a).
When not applicable, §143-299.1A(b).
Records.
Destruction, §143-300.
Rules and regulations.
Commission, §143-300.
Rules of civil procedure.
Applicability, ICTortClaim Rule T201.
School bus accidents, §143-300.1.
Defense of claim by attorney general, §143-300.1(d).
Duties of attorney general, §143-300.1(b).
Jurisdiction, §143-300.1(a).
Payment of damages, §143-300.1(c).
Procedure, §143-300.1(a).
Settlement, §§143-295, 143-300.1.
Affidavit of claimant, §143-295(b).
Maximum amount, §143-295(a).
Smallpox vaccinations of state employees.
Claims arising from, §143-300.1A.
State employee suits against state.
Federal remedy restoration act, §143-300.35.
State excess liability.
Payment, §143-299.4.
Subpoenas.
Issuance, §143-298.
Supersedeas.
Court of appeals to act as, §143-294.
Telephonic hearings, minimal property damage, ICTortClaim Rule T206.

CLAIMS AGAINST THE STATE —Cont'd
Terrorist incident using nuclear, biological or chemical agents.
State officers, employees and agents acting pursuant to provisions.
Applicability to, §130A-478.
Time, enlargement, ICTortClaim Rule T203.
Venue, §143-297.
Waiver of rules, ICTortClaim Rule T501.

CLAIMS FOR RELIEF.
General rules of pleading, §1A-1 Rule 8(a).

CLAIMS TO PUBLIC OFFICE.
Quo warranto.
Generally, §§1-514 to 1-532.
See QUO WARRANTO.

CLAMS.
Cultivation of shellfish, §§113-201 to 113-210.
See SHELLFISH.
Sanitation of shellfish, §113-221.2.

CLAREMONT.
Satellite annexation.
Limitation on area of satellite corporate limits, inapplicability, §160A-58.1(b).

CLARK'S CALENDAR.
Proof of dates.
Use, §8-48(a).
Secretary of state.
Perpetual calendar similar to Clark's calendar. Preparation and publication, §8-48(b).

CLASS ACTIONS.
Authorized, §1A-1 Rule 23(a).
Compromise and settlement.
Approval of judge required, §1A-1 Rule 23(c).
Notice, §1A-1 Rule 23(c).
Dismissal, §1A-1 Rule 23(c).
Limited liability companies.
Derivative actions by members, §57C-8-01.
Motion picture fair competition act.
Class actions not available under provisions, §75C-5.
Secondary action by shareholders, §1A-1 Rule 23(b).
Tax refunds, §105-241.18.
Unconstitutional statute, §1A-1 Rule 23(d).
Unpaid residuals.
Distribution.
Intent and findings of legislation, §1-267.10(a).
Payment to indigent person's attorney fund and state bar for services to indigents, §1-267.10(b).

CLASSIC CARS.
Abandoned and derelict motor vehicles.
Exemption from provisions, §20-137.14.
Property taxes.
Motor vehicle taxes on antique automobiles, §105-330.9.
Special plates, §20-79.4(b).

CLASSIFIED MOTOR VEHICLES.
Property taxes, §§105-330 to 105-330.11.
See MOTOR VEHICLE TAXES.

CLASS IN ESSE.
Sale, lease or mortgage of property held by.
Membership subject to increase by persons not in esse, §41-11.1.

CLASS SIZE REDUCTION FUND, §115C-472.10.

CLAWBACKS.
Commerce department.
Economic development board, contracts, §143B-435.1.

CLAY COUNTY.
Ambulances.
Obtaining ambulance services without intending to pay, §14-111.2.
Requesting ambulance falsely, §14-111.3.
Board of county commissioners.
Filling vacancies on board, §153A-27.1.
Condemnation or acquisition of land by local government unit outside county.
Consent of board of commissioners necessary, §153A-15.
Coroner elected as nominee of political party.
Filling vacancy in office, §152-1.
Counties generally.
See COUNTIES.
Dog collars.
Unlawful removal of electronic dog collars, §14-401.17.
Foxes, open seasons for taking.
Wildlife resources commission authorized to continue seasons from year to year, §113-291.4(f1).
Housing authority commissioners.
Tenant as commissioner, exemption from provision of law allowing, §157-5.
Maps in special proceedings, recording of photographic copies, §47-32.
Violation as misdemeanor, inapplicability of provisions, §47-32.2.
Oil, gas or mineral claims.
Certain ancient claims extinguished, preservation, procedure, §1-42.3(a) to (d).
On-premises unfortified wine licenses.
Discretion to decline to issue, §105-113.71(b).
Registration of deeds.
Tax certification, no delinquent taxes due, §161-31(b).
Sheriff.
Vacancy, performance of duties until vacancy filled, §162-5.1.
Western North Carolina Development Association, Inc.
Appropriation of funds to, §153A-447(a), (b).
Western North Carolina regional economic development commission, §§158-8.1 to 158-8.8.

CLAYTON, TOWN OF.
Satellite annexation.
Limitation on area of satellite corporate limits, inapplicability, §160A-58.1(b).

CLE.
Bankruptcy law specialty, Bar Rules D.2205, D.2206.
Criminal law specialty, Bar Rules D.2505, D.2506.
Estate planning and probate law specialty, Bar Rules D.2305, D.2306.
Family law specialty, Bar Rules D.2405, D.2406.
Immigration law specialty, Bar Rules D.2601 to D.2607.
Real property law specialty, Bar Rules D.2105, D.2106.
Regulations generally, CLE Reg 1 to 10.
Rules concerning administration of program, Bar Rules D.1601 to D.1610.

CLE —Cont'd
Rules for continuing legal education.
See ATTORNEYS AT LAW.
Rules governing administration of program, Bar Rules D.1501 to D.1527.
Specialization certification, rules governing accreditation, Bar Rules D.1901 to D.1908.

CLEAN COASTAL WATER AND VESSEL ACT, §§77-125 to 77-132.
Applicability of article, §77-131.
Civil penalty for violating article, §77-130(c).
Definitions, §77-125.
Discharge of treated or untreated sewage in coastal waters.
Prevention of discharge.
Vessels with marine sanitation device, §77-129(a).
Prohibited, §77-129(a).
Violation, criminal penalty, §77-129(a).
Report of unlawful discharges.
Required of marina operators or owners or operators of vessels, §77-129(b).
Violation, civil penalty, §77-129(b).
Enforcement of articles.
Civil penalty for violating article, §77-130(c).
Officers with authority to enforce, §77-130(a).
Report of violation.
Officers enforcing article, §77-130(b).
Grants.
Installation of pumpout facilities, §77-126(b).
Large vessel marinas.
Applicability of article, §77-131.
Defined, §77-125.
Pumpout facilities.
Installation by operators in certain areas, §77-126.
Marine sanitation devices defined, §77-125.
Pumpout dates.
Record to be kept by owners or operators of vessels with marine sanitation devices, §77-127(a).
Violation, criminal penalty, §77-127(b).
Pumpout facilities.
Criteria for facilities and services.
Large vessel marinas not offering docking services.
Department to establish, §77-127(b).
Large vessel marinas offering docking services.
Department to establish, §77-127(a).
Defined, §77-125.
Installation.
Grant funds, application for, §77-126(b).
Required of large vessel marina operators in certain areas, §77-126(a).
Rules to implement, adoption, §77-132.

CLEANING AGENTS CONTAINING PHOSPHORUS.
Manufacture, storage, sale prohibited, §143-214.4(a).
Cleaning agent defined, §143-214.4(b).
Exceptions, §143-214.4(c), (d).
No adequate substitute, §143-214.4(e).
Infractions, §143-214.4(g).
Misdemeanor, fine, §143-214.4(f).

CLEANING ESTABLISHMENTS.
Cleaning agents.
Certain cleaning agents containing phosphorus prohibited, §143-214.4(a) to (g).

CLEANING ESTABLISHMENTS —Cont'd
Notice.
Unclaimed articles, §66-67(a) to (c).
Sales and use tax.
Exemption of sales to, §105-164.13.
Unclaimed articles.
Disposition, §66-67(a) to (c).

**CLEANUP OF LEAKING PETROLEUM
    UNDERGROUND STORAGE TANKS,**
    §§143-215.94A to 143-215.94Y.
See UNDERGROUND PETROLEUM STORAGE
    TANKS.

CLEAN WATER MANAGEMENT TRUST FUND,
    §§113A-251 to 113A-259.
See WATERCOURSES.

CLEAR AND CONVINCING EVIDENCE.
**Abused, neglected or dependent juvenile
    actions.**
Adjudicatory hearing, §7B-805.
Delinquent and undisciplined juvenile actions.
Petition alleging undisciplined behavior,
    §7B-2409.
Secure or nonsecure custody hearing, §7B-1906(d).
**Legitimacy presumption, when mother
    married.**
Overcome by clear and convincing evidence,
    §49-12.1(b).
Termination of parental rights proceedings.
Establishing grounds for terminating, §7B-1111(b).
Evidence standard at adjudicatory hearing,
    §7B-1109(f).

CLEAR LIGHTS.
Use on rear of vehicles, §20-130.3.

CLEATS.
Tires not to have, §20-122(b).

CLEMENCY.
Pardons.
See PARDONS.

CLERGY.
Churches generally.
See CHURCHES AND OTHER PLACES OF
    WORSHIP.
**Communications between clergymen and
    communicants, §8-53.2.**
**Employee assistance professional practice by
    members of other professional groups,**
    §90-511.
Income tax.
Withholding of income taxes from wages.
    Ordained or licensed clergyman may elect to be
        self-employed, §105-163.1A.
Marriage.
Confirmation of vows before ordained ministers,
    §51-6.
Solemnization, §51-1.
    Without license, §51-6.
Marriage and family therapists.
Exemptions from article, §90-270.48A(a).
Pastoral counselors.
Certification of fee-based practicing pastoral
    counselors, §§90-380 to 90-395.
    See PASTORAL COUNSELORS.
Professional counselors generally, §§90-329 to
    90-345.
    See PROFESSIONAL COUNSELORS.
**Property of church or religious sect, society or
    denomination.**
Authority to acquire, hold and transfer, §61-5.

CLERGY —Cont'd
Religion generally.
See RELIGION.
Religious organizations and societies.
See RELIGIOUS ORGANIZATIONS AND
    SOCIETIES.
State prison.
Employment of clinical chaplain for inmates,
    §148-10.1.

CLERICAL MISTAKES.
Relief from judgment or order, §1A-1 Rule 60(a).

CLERKS.
County clerks.
Boards of commissioners, §153A-11.
Misconduct in public office.
    Swearing falsely to official reports, §14-232.
General assembly.
Approval of bills, §120-29.1.
Journals.
    Indexing of journals by clerks, §120-28.
    Preparation and filing by clerks, §120-27.
Legislative services commission.
    Duties of enrolling clerk, §120-33.
Principal clerk.
    Bills and resolutions.
        Retention in office for certain periods,
            §120-37(f).
    Duties.
        Assignment of additional duties, §120-37(d).
        Election, §120-37(a).
        Employing temporary assistance, §120-37(e).
        Retention of books, records, etc., §120-37(f).
        Salary, §120-37(c).
    Staff employees of office.
        Additional full-time employees, §120-37(d).
    Term, §120-37(a).
Reading clerk.
    Election, §120-37(a).
    Salary, §120-37(b).
    Term, §120-37(a).
Municipalities.
Deputy clerk.
    Powers and duties.
        Generally, §160A-172.
        Provided by council, §160A-172.
Duties.
    Generally, §160A-171.
Office created, §160A-171.

CLERKS OF COURT.
Appeals.
District courts.
    Clerk to judge, §7A-251(b).
In forma pauperis.
    Fees of clerk, §1-288.
Superior courts.
    Civil actions.
        Applicability of provisions, §1-301.1(a).
        Concurrent authority of judge, §1-301.1(d).
        Duty of judge hearing appeal, §1-301.1(c).
        Filing of appeal, §1-301.1(b).
    Clerk to judge, §7A-251(a).
    Estates of decedents, minors and incompetents.
        Applicability of provisions, §1-301.3(a).
        Duty of judge, §1-301.3(d).
        Entry of judgment by clerk, §1-301.3(b).
        Filing of appeal, §1-301.3(c).
        Recording of hearings, §1-301.3(f).
        Remand to clerk, §1-301.3(e).

CLERKS OF COURT —Cont'd

Appeals —Cont'd

Superior courts —Cont'd

Special proceedings.

Appeal of clerk's decision, §1-301.2(e).

Applicability of provisions, §1-301.2(a).

Clerk's decision-authority, §1-301.2(d).

Duty of judge, §1-301.2(c).

Exceptions, §1-301.2(g), (h).

Grounds for transfer, §1-301.2(b).

Service of process, §1-301.2(f).

Arrest.

Warrant for arrest.

Clerk may issue, §15A-304(f).

Assignments for benefit of creditors.

Notice of petition.

Clerk to give, §23-14.

Attorneys at law.

Disputed monies.

Deposit with clerk of court, §93A-12.

Banks.

Superior court.

Deposit of money held by clerk, §7A-112.1.

Book of orders appointing receivers of judgment debtors.

Filing and recording appointment in book, §1-364.

Capital punishment.

Certificate of execution.

Filing, §15-192.

Duties on sentence of death, §15-189.

Child support.

Past due child support.

Payments made to clerk.

When payments not past due, §50-13.10(e).

Procedure to insure payment.

Notice of delinquency.

Non-IV-D cases, §50-13.9(d).

Payments made to, §50-13.9(a).

Informing clerk of change of address, §50-13.9(c).

Records listing amount of payment, §50-13.9(b).

Transmission to health and human services department in IV-D cases, §50-13.9(b).

Constitution of North Carolina.

Removal, NC Const Art IV §17.

Vacancies in office, NC Const Art IV §19.

Court of appeals.

Appointment of clerk, §7A-20(a).

Assistants to clerk, §7A-20(a).

Audit of financial accounts of clerk, §7A-20(b).

Bond required of clerk, §7A-20(a).

Fee bill for services of clerk, §7A-20(b).

Oath of office by clerk, §7A-20(a).

Salary of clerk, §7A-20(a).

Seal of office.

Adoption by clerk, §7A-20(a).

Crime victims compensation.

Notice.

Award made from crime victims compensation fund, §15B-15.

Deeds.

Probate and registration.

Where clerk appointed himself to sell, §47-65.

District courts.

Equipment and supplies in clerk's office, §7A-303.

Estate taxes.

Liability of clerk.

Personal representative allowed to make final settlement without presenting affirmation or certificate, §105-32.3(c).

CLERKS OF COURT —Cont'd

Executions.

Directing execution to clerk in counties which office of coroner abolished, §1-313.

Execution sales.

Procedural details.

Authority to fix, §1-339.42.

Issuance, failure to issue, requirements, §1-305(a), (b).

Returns.

Entry on judgment docket, §1-321.

Subscribed by clerk, §1-303.

Failure to discharge duties, §14-230.

Fees.

Court of appeals.

Fee bill for services, §7A-20(b).

Limitation of actions for, §1-52.

Superior courts.

Accounting for fees and other receipts, §7A-108.

Deposit of money held by clerk, §7A-308.1.

Investment of funds in clerk's hands, §7A-308.1.

Statement rendered by county officer compensated from fees, §128-13.

Foreign-money claims.

Powers and liabilities, §1C-1826(j).

Illegitimacy.

Paternity of illegitimate children judicially determined.

Furnishing state registrar with facts as to paternity, §130A-119.

In forma pauperis.

Fees upon, §1-288.

Interstate depositions and discovery.

Subpoenas.

Duties of clerk on receipt of request for, §1F-3(b).

Judgment roll.

Duty to file after entering judgment, §1-232.

Papers constituting, §1-232.

Judgments.

Entry of judgment, §1A-1 Rule 58.

Foreign judgments.

Filing in office of clerk of superior court, §1C-1703(a).

Judicial sales.

Applicability of provisions to sales ordered by clerk, §1-339.3(a).

Compensation of person holding sale.

Fixing, §1-339.11.

Judge's approval of clerk's order of public sale, §1-339.14.

Power to order public or private sale, §1-339.3A.

Procedural details.

Authority to fix, §1-339.3(c).

Report or accounting.

Authority to compel, §1-339.12.

Landlord and tenant.

Summary ejectment.

Issuance of summons by clerk, §42-28.

Limitation of actions.

Fee actions, §1-52.

Mortgages and deeds of trust.

Sales under power of sale.

Auditing and recording final account, §45-21.33(d).

Motor vehicle license plates.

Special license plates for superior court clerks, §20-79.4(b).

Notaries public.

Certification to instruct course of classroom instruction, §10B-14.

CLERKS OF COURT —Cont'd
Oaths.
Who may administer oaths of office, §11-7.1(a).
Offenses against.
Aggravating factor in sentencing, §15A-1340.16.
Pardons.
Duty of sheriff and clerk when pardon granted, §147-25.
Partition.
Docketing of owelty charges, §46-21.
Partition sales.
Clerk not to appoint self, etc., to sell, §46-31.
Paternity.
Illegitimate children judicially determined.
Furnishing state registrar with facts as to paternity, §130A-119.
Practice of law.
Private practice prohibited, §84-2.
Probate and registration.
Authorized to take probate, §47-2.
Before clerks in other states, §47-77.
Before judges of supreme or superior court or clerks before 1889, §47-58.
Certificates of clerks without seal, §47-99.
Deeds.
Where clerk appointed himself to sell, §47-65.
Defective acknowledgment on old deeds validated, §47-52.
Deputy clerks of superior court.
Validation of acknowledgments, etc., §47-108.7.
Inferior courts.
Before clerks of inferior courts, §47-59.
Interested clerk.
Order of registration by interested clerk, §47-61.
Justices of the peace.
Clerk's certificate upon probate by justice of the peace.
Validation, §47-56.
Omission of official seal by clerks of court of other states, §47-86.
Other states.
Before deputy clerks of courts of other states, §47-79.
Parties.
Order of registration by judge where clerk party, §47-60.
Probate by justice of peace or magistrate.
Clerk's certificate, form, §47-44.
State officers authorized to prove and acknowledge instruments, §47-1.
Validation of instruments in which clerk was party, §47-106.
Real estate brokers.
Disputed monies.
Deposit with clerk of court, §93A-12.
Receivers appointed in supplemental proceeding.
Recording in book of orders appointing receivers of judgment debtors, §1-364.
Renunciation of property and renunciation of fiduciary powers.
Filing renunciation with clerk, §31B-2(c).
Search warrants.
Issuance, §15A-243(b).
Service of process.
Sheriff a party.
Clerk to act in absence of office of coroner, §162-16.
Social security numbers.
Public records, restricted use.
Posting requirements, §132-1.10(g).

CLERKS OF COURT —Cont'd
Social security numbers —Cont'd
Public records, restricted use —Cont'd
Removal without request.
Documents posted on Internet web site, §132-1.10(f1).
Special proceedings.
Commissioners.
Fees.
Powers of clerk as to, §1-408.
Ex parte.
Summary action by clerks, §1-401.
Surveys.
Power to order in proceedings involving sale of land, §1-408.1.
Superior court clerks of court generally.
See SUPERIOR COURTS.
Supreme court.
Appellate division reports.
Lending prohibited, §147-51.
Responsibility of clerk, §147-51.
Appointment, §7A-11.
Assistant clerk, §7A-11.
Audit of financial accounts, §7A-11.
Bond required, §7A-11.
Duties, §7A-11.
Fees, §7A-11.
Oath of office, §7A-11.
Salaries, §7A-11.
Seal of office, §7A-11.
Torrens system registration.
Examiners.
Appointment and removal by clerk, §43-4.
Liens on registered lands.
Docketed judgments.
Duty of clerk to certify, §43-45.
Transfer of civil causes.
Retention and docketing of causes in originally designated trial division, §7A-256.
Vital statistics.
Paternity of illegitimate children judicially determined.
Furnishing state registrar with facts as to paternity, §130A-119.
When court means clerk, §1-7.
Year's allowance, §§30-19 to 30-31.2.
See SURVIVING SPOUSES.

CLEVELAND COUNTY.
All-terrain vehicles.
Use by employees on certain highways, §20-171.24.
Ambulance service.
Attachment or garnishment and lien for, §§44-51.4 to 44-51.8.
Obtaining without intending to pay, §14-111.2.
Blank or master forms of mortgages, deeds of trust, etc.
Indexing and recording, inapplicability of provisions, §47-21.
Board of county commissioners.
Filling vacancies on board, §153A-27.1.
Condemnation or acquisition of land by local government unit outside county.
Consent of board of commissioners necessary, §153A-15.
Coroner elected as nominee of political party.
Filling vacancy in office, §152-1.
Counties generally.
See COUNTIES.

CLEVELAND COUNTY —Cont'd
Cropper or tenant refusing to perform terms of contract.
Forfeiture of right of possession to premises, §42-27.
Dangerous firearm use by young children, permitting.
Air rifles, air pistols and bb guns not dangerous firearm, §14-316(b).
Game laws, local acts not repealed, §113-133.1(e).
Housing authority commissioners.
Tenant as commissioner, exemption from provision of law allowing, §157-5.
Oil, gas or mineral claims.
Certain ancient claims extinguished, preservation, procedure, §1-42.3(a) to (d).
Registration of deeds.
Tax certification, no delinquent taxes due, §161-31(b).
Sheriff.
Vacancy, performance of duties until vacancy filled, §162-5.1.
Small city mixed beverage elections.
Inapplicability of provisions to, §18B-600(e1).
Special school tax, election to abolish.
Petition required, §115C-505.
Western North Carolina regional economic development commission, §§158-8.1 to 158-8.8.

CLIENT SECURITY FUND.
Rules governing administration, Bar Rules D.1401 to D.1420.

CLINICAL LABORATORIES.
Financing health care facilities generally, §§131A-1 to 131A-25.
See HEALTH CARE FACILITY FINANCING.

CLINICAL TRIALS.
Health benefit plan coverage, §58-3-255.

CLIPPING NEWSPAPER AND MAGAZINE ARTICLES.
Work-at-home solicitations, advertising restrictions, §75-31.

CLOGGING.
Official folk dance of state, §145-24(a).

CLOSED-CIRCUIT TELEVISION.
Arraignment, §15A-941.
First appearance before district court judge, §15A-601.
Pretrial release.
Two-way audio and video transmissions authorized, §15A-532(b), (c).

CLOSED FORMULARIES.
Health insurers maintaining, §58-3-221.

CLOSED HEARINGS.
Delinquent and undisciplined juvenile actions, §7B-2402.
Mental health, developmental disability, substance abuse.
Involuntary commitment.
Substance abuser's commitment hearing, §122C-286(d).

CLOSED SHOP ACT.
Right to work law, §§95-78 to 95-84.

CLOSING ARGUMENTS, SuperCt Rule 10.
Court's control of argument, §7A-97.

CLOSING ARGUMENTS —Cont'd
Criminal proceedings.
Abusive, personal experiences, personal belief as to truth or falsity of evidence, matters outside record.
Argument prohibited, §15A-1230(a).
Length, number and order, law governing, §15A-1230(b).
Position or conclusion as to issue.
Argument permitted, §15A-1230(a).

CLOSING COURT OFFICES.
Adverse weather, other emergency situations including catastrophic conditions, §7A-39(a).

CLOSING FORESTS AND WOODLANDS TO FISHING, HUNTING AND TRAPPING.
Annulment of proclamation, §106-909.
Authority of governor, §106-908.
Publication of proclamation, §106-909.

CLOSING-OUT SALES, §§66-76 to 66-83.
Additions to stock in contemplation of sale, §66-78.
Advertising.
Advertising sale contrary to provisions, §66-81.
False advertisements, §66-82.
Applicability of provisions.
Exception of certain sales, §66-82.
Bonds, surety.
Required for license, §66-77(b).
Continuation of sale or business beyond termination date.
Prohibited, §66-80.
Definitions, §66-76.
Distress sales.
Defined, §66-76.
Inventory not required, §66-77(a).
Fees.
License fee, §66-77(b).
Injunctions, §66-83.
Inventories.
Required of applicants for licenses, §66-77(a).
Licenses.
Applications, §66-77(a).
Date of filing to be endorsed on application, §66-77(c).
False statements.
Perjury, §66-77(d).
Bonds, surety.
Required, §66-77(b).
Fees, §66-77(b).
Issuance, §66-77(b).
Required, §66-77(a).
Misdemeanor.
Advertising or conducting sale contrary to provisions, §66-81.
Perjury.
False statements in application, §66-77(d).
Prohibited acts.
Additions to stock in contemplation of sale, §66-78.
Continuation of sale or business beyond termination date, §66-80.
Replenishment of stock, §66-79.
Replenishment of stock, §66-79.
Violations of provisions.
Advertising or conducting sale contrary to provisions, §66-81.
Prohibited acts, §§66-78 to 66-80.
Restraining or enjoining, §66-83.

CLOSING THE ACHIEVEMENT GAP.
Annual performance standards, §115C-105.35(b).
Board of education model, §115C-12.

CLOTH.
Dealers of scrap, salvage or surplus, failure to keep records of purchases, §66-10(b).

CLOTHES.
Exemption from creditors' claims, §1C-1601(a).
Property taxes.
Exclusion of non-business property, §105-275.
Sales and use tax.
Defined, §105-164.3.
Tax holiday, §105-164.13C(a).
Solicitation for resale by use of collection receptacle.
Collection receptacle defined, §131F-2.
Disclosure sign or label required.
Charitable organization or sponsor soliciting, §131F-9(d).
Organization not charitable organization or sponsor soliciting, §131F-10.
Unclaimed clothing and other articles.
Disposition by laundries and dry-cleaning establishments, §66-67(a) to (c).

CLOTHES WASHERS.
Energy star qualified products.
Sales and use tax holiday, §105-164.13D(a).

CLOTHING ACCESSORIES OR EQUIPMENT.
Sales and use tax.
Defined, §105-164.3.
Tax holiday, inapplicability, §105-164.13C(b).

CLOUD ON TITLE.
Judgments by default removed.
Validated, §1-217.2.
Quieting title, §41-10.
Marketable title.
Prima facie evidence, §47B-2(d).
Torrens system registration.
Effect of decree, §43-12.
General provisions, §§43-1 to 43-64.
See TORRENS SYSTEM REGISTRATION.
Title generally.
See TITLE.

CLOVER.
Standard weights and measures, §81A-42.

CLOVER SEEDS.
Standard weights and measures, §81A-42.

CLUB FEET.
Podiatrist to surgically correct, §90-202.2(b).
Infant two years of age or less excluded from definition of podiatry, §90-202.2(a).

CLUBS.
Franchise tax.
Exemption, §105-125(a).
Hull insurance, protection and indemnity clubs, §§58-20-1 to 58-20-40.
See HULL INSURANCE, PROTECTION AND INDEMNITY CLUBS.
Powers of attorney.
Powers conferred by statutory short form.
Continued payments incidental to membership, §32A-2.
Private clubs.
Alcoholic beverage permits.
Alcoholic beverages defined, §18B-1000.
Brown-bagging permit.
Kind of permit that may be issued, §18B-1001.

CLUBS —Cont'd
Private clubs —Cont'd
Alcoholic beverage permits —Cont'd
Brown-bagging permit —Cont'd
Lockers to be provided for storing alcoholic beverages, §18B-1006(b).
Mixed beverage permit.
Kind of permit that may be issued, §18B-1001.
Recycling requirement, §18B-1006.1.
On-premises fortified wine permit.
Kind of permit that may be issued, §18B-1001.
Recycling requirement, §18B-1006.1.
On-premises malt beverage permit.
Kind of permit that may be issued, §18B-1001.
Recycling requirement, §18B-1006.1.
On-premises unfortified wine permit.
Kind of permit that may be issued, §18B-1001.
Recycling requirement, §18B-1006.1.
Permits.
Residential private clubs, §18B-1006(k).
Rules concerning retail permits, §18B-1008.
Special occasion permit.
Kind of permit that may be issued, §18B-1001.
Fair housing.
Unlawful discriminatory practices provisions.
Exemption, §41A-6(a).
Local government's authority to regulate smoking.
Exception, §130A-498(b1).
Smoking prohibited in restaurants and bars.
Exception, §130A-496(b).
Sanitation of food and lodging establishments.
Definition of private club, §130A-247.
Exemption from provisions, §130A-250.
Telephone service, shared service, §62-110(d).

COACH HOUSES.
Burning of coach houses, §14-62.

COAL.
Coke.
Weights and measures, §81A-42.
Generally.
See MINES AND MINERALS.
Mine safety and health act generally, §§74-24.1 to 74-24.20.
See MINE SAFETY AND HEALTH.
Mining act of 1971, §§74-46 to 74-68.
See MINING ACT OF 1971.
Mining permits generally.
See MINING PERMITS.
Reports.
Standard weights and measures, §81A-42.
Suppliers.
Stocks of coal, §§143-345.13, 143-345.14.

COAL-FIRED GENERATING UNITS.
Combustion products landfills.
Construction, requirements for authorization, §130A-295.4(b).
Definitions, §130A-295.4(a).
Response plan required, §130A-295.4(c).
Emissions of oxides of nitrogen and sulfur dioxide by investor-owned utilities, §143-215.107D.
Civil penalties for violations, §143-215.114A(b1).
Compliance with provisions, §143-215.107D(f), (g).

COAL-FIRED GENERATING UNITS —Cont'd
Emissions of oxides of nitrogen and sulfur
  dioxide by investor-owned utilities —Cont'd
  Criminal penalties for violations, §143-215.114B(f)
    to (h).
  Definitions, §143-215.107D(a).
  Environmental compliance costs, accelerated
    recovery, §62-133.6(b).
    Adjustments or reductions in rate base,
      §62-133.6(e), (f).
    Amortization, §62-133.6(b).
    Compliance plans, filing, §62-133.6(c).
    Defined, §62-133.6(a).
    Emissions limitations, statement by utilities
      subject to, §62-133.6(i), (j).
    Enforcement of utility compliance, §62-133.6(h).
    Final agency action not subject to review,
      §62-133.6(k).
    Hearing to review compliance costs,
      §62-133.6(d).
    Market based rates and services, authority to
      implement, §62-133.6(g).
    Rate base to remain unchanged, §62-133.6(e).
  Permits to include certain conditions,
    §143-215.107D(h).
  Prohibited acts, §143-215.107D(b) to (e).
  Statements by utility, §143-215.107D(j).
  Voluntary agreement to transfer to state certain
    emissions allowances, §143-215.107D(i).

COASTAL AREA MANAGEMENT, §§113A-100 to
  113A-134.3.
Advisory council.
  Chairman, §113A-105(e).
  Compensation, §113A-105(f).
  Creation, §113A-105(a).
  Defined, §113A-103.
  Duties, §113A-105(c).
  Functions, §113A-105(c).
  Members, §113A-105(b).
  Multiple offices, §113A-105(d).
  Vice-chairman, §113A-105(e).
Appeals.
  Denial of permits, §113A-123.
Areas of environmental concern.
  Additional grounds for designation prohibited
    unless enacted by general assembly,
    §113A-113(d).
  Designation.
    Adding new areas, §113A-115(c).
    Additional grounds for designation prohibited
      unless enacted into law by general
      assembly, §113A-113(d).
    Deleting areas, §113A-115(c).
    Generally, §113A-113.
    Geographic areas, §113A-113(a).
    Hearings, §113A-115(a).
      Notice, §113A-115(b).
    Procedural requirements, §113A-115.
    Review of designated areas, §113A-115(c).
    Rules and regulations.
      Adoption, §§113A-113, 113A-115.
  Erosion control structures, §113A-115.1.
  Generally, §113A-113.
  Hearings.
    Designation of areas, §113A-115(a).
    Notice, §113A-115(b).
  Identification, §113A-113(b), (c).
  Notice.
    Hearings, §113A-115(b).

COASTAL AREA MANAGEMENT —Cont'd
Areas of environmental concern —Cont'd
  Outstanding resource areas of environmental
    concern.
    Development in, §113A-118.2.
    Permits.
    Outstanding resource water areas of
      environmental concern.
      Development in, §113A-118.2.
Attorney general.
  Representation of commission, §113A-124(d).
Beach access program.
  Administration of program, §113A-134.2(a).
  Creation of program, §113A-134.2(a).
  Definitions, §113A-134.2(b).
  Legislative findings, §113A-134.1.
  Priorities, §113A-134.3.
  Purposes, §§113A-134.1, 113A-134.2(a).
  Standards, §113A-134.3.
Beach management plan.
  Duties of department, §113A-134.11.
  Multiyear beach management and restoration
    plan.
    Purposes, §113A-134.12(a).
    Revision, §113A-134.12(b).
Boats.
  Defined, §113A-103.
Citation of article, §113A-100.
Civil penalties.
  Permits, §113A-126(d).
Coastal habitat protection plans.
  Adoption by commission, §113A-106.1.
Coastal reserves, §§113A-129.1 to 113A-129.3.
  Acquisitions or dispositions of property,
    §113A-129.2(d).
  Administration of system, §113A-129.2(b).
  Area system established within, §113A-129.2(c).
  Creation of system, §113A-129.2(a).
  Hunting, fishing, navigation and recreation,
    §113A-129.2(e).
  Legislative findings, §113A-129.1(a).
  National estuarine reserve research system.
    Coordination with, §113A-129.3(a).
  Nature and historic preserve.
    Dedicated as components of, §113A-129.3(b).
  Purposes, §113A-129.1(b).
  Research and education.
    Lands and water within system primarily used
      for, §113A-129.2(e).
Coastal sound.
  Defined, §113A-103.
Commission.
  Appointments, §113A-104(c).
    Women and minorities, §113A-104(k).
  Attorney general.
    Representation of commission, §113A-124(d).
  Chairman, §113A-104(i).
  Compensation, §113A-104(j).
  Composition, §113A-104(b).
  Defined, §113A-103.
  Establishment, §113A-104(a).
  Meetings.
    Attendance, §113A-104(l).
  Multiple offices, §113A-104(f).
  Nominating categories, §113A-104(d).
  Office may be held concurrently with elective or
    appointive offices, §113A-104(f).
  Powers and duties, §113A-124(c).
  Residence requirements, §113A-104(e).
  Terms, §113A-104(g).

COASTAL AREA MANAGEMENT —Cont'd

Commission —Cont'd

Vacancies, §113A-104(h).

    Failure to attend meetings, §113A-104(l).

Women and minorities, §113A-104(k).

Cooperative state-local program.

Establishment, §113A-101.

Coordination with federal government, §113A-127.

Definitions, §113A-103.

Permits, §113A-118.

    Designated local officials, §113A-119(c).

Development.

Defined, §113A-103.

Discharge of oil or hazardous substances, §§143-215.83 to 143-215.94.

See OIL OR HAZARDOUS SUBSTANCES DISCHARGES.

Dredging permits, §113-229.

Eminent domain.

Commission order not applicable to certain land.

    Acquisition of fee or lesser interest in land, §113A-123(c).

Energy development, generation or transmission.

Permit for utility facility obtained from commission.

    Facility subject to regulation under article, §113A-118(e).

Erosion control structures, §113A-115.1.

Construction limitations, §113A-115.1(b).

Defined terms, §113A-115.1(a).

Permanent structures, limitations, §113A-115.1(b).

Temporary structures, limitations, §113A-115.1(b).

Terminal groins.

    Application for construction permit, §113A-115.1(e).

    Issuance of construction permit, §113A-115.1(f).

        Maximum number to be issued, §113A-115.1(g).

        Sources of funding prohibited, §113A-115.1(h).

Rules not applicable, §113A-115.1(d).

Variance permits, §113A-115.1(c).

Fees.

Permits, §113A-119.1(a), (b).

Findings, §113A-102.

Floating structures.

Defined, §113A-103.

Grants.

Planning grants, §113A-112.

Hearings.

Areas of environmental concern.

    Designation of areas, §113A-115(a).

    Notice, §113A-115(b).

Planning processes.

    Land-use plans.

        Adoption, §113A-110(e).

Injunctions.

Permits, §113A-126(a).

Judicial review.

Denial of permits, §113A-123(a), (b).

Key facilities.

Defined, §113A-103.

Landowners' rights.

Protection, §113A-128.

Land-use plans and programs.

Approval by commission, §113A-110(f).

Contents, §113A-110(a).

Copies of approval plans, §113A-110(g).

Delegation of responsibilities, §113A-110(b).

Effect, §113A-111.

COASTAL AREA MANAGEMENT —Cont'd

Land-use plans and programs —Cont'd

Hearings, §113A-110(e).

Responsibilities of bodies charged with adoption, §113A-110(c), (d).

Timetable for preparation, §113A-109.

Lead regional organizations.

Defined, §113A-103.

Legislative findings, §113A-102(a).

Legislative goals, §113A-102(b).

Letters of intent.

Planning processes, §113A-109.

Local government.

Defined, §113A-103.

Notice.

Areas of environmental concern.

    Hearings, §113A-115(b).

Permits.

    Issuance of public notice of proposed development, §113A-119(b).

    Quasi-judicial procedures.

        Giving notice by registered or certified mail, §113A-122(d).

Nursery areas.

Primary nursery areas.

    Development in, §113A-118.2.

Offshore oil and gas activities, §§143-215.94AA to 143-215.94JJ.

See OFFSHORE OIL AND GAS ACTIVITIES.

Outstanding resource water areas of environmental concern.

Development in, §113A-118.2.

Permits.

Appeals.

    Denial of permits, §113A-123(a), (b).

    Permit deemed suspended, §113A-121.1(c).

Applications, §113A-119(a).

Areas of environmental concern.

    Outstanding resource water areas of environmental concern.

    Development in, §113A-118.2.

Civil penalties, §113A-126(d).

Definitions, §113A-118(d).

Denial of permit, §§113A-120(b1), 113A-123(a), (b).

    Appeals.

        Permit deemed suspended, §113A-121.1(c).

    Hearing upon denial.

        Procedures, §113A-122.

        Request, §113A-121.1(a), (b).

    Judicial review, §113A-123(a), (b).

    Review of grant or denial of permits, §113A-121.1.

        Procedure, §113A-122.

Designated local officials.

    Defined, §113A-119(c).

    Expedited procedures, §113A-121(b).

    Fees.

        Submitted with application, §113A-119(a).

Issuance of public notice of proposed developments, §113A-119(b).

Minor developments, §113A-121(b), (c).

Notice.

    Issuance of public notice of proposed developments, §113A-119(b).

Dredging permits, §113-229.

Energy development, generation or transmission.

    Permit for utility facility obtained from commission.

        Facility subject to regulation under article, §113A-118(e).

Enforcement programs, §113A-117(c), (d).

COASTAL AREA MANAGEMENT —Cont'd
Permits —Cont'd
Erosion control structures.
  Variance permits, §113A-115.1(c).
Fees.
  Applications.
    Submitted with application, §113A-119(a).
  Credited to general fund, §113A-119.1(b).
  Graduated fee schedule.
    Establishment, §113A-119.1(a).
  Limitations, §113A-119.1(a).
  Uses, §113A-119.1(b).
General permits.
  Designation of certain classes of development,
    §113A-118.1(a).
  Issuance, §113A-118.1(b).
  Notice, §113A-118.1(c).
  Outstanding resource water areas of
    environmental concern.
    Development in, §113A-118.2.
  Primary nursery areas.
    Development in, §113A-118.2.
  Riprap, use of, §113A-118.1(e).
  Variances, appeals and enforcements,
    §113A-118.1(d).
Granting of permits, §113A-120(a), (b).
  Review of grant or denial of permits,
    §113A-121.1.
    Procedure, §113A-122.
Implementation programs, §113A-117(a), (b).
Injunctive relief, §113A-126(a).
Intent.
  Local government letter of intent, §113A-116.
Judicial review.
  Denial of permits, §113A-123(a), (b).
Local government letter of intent, §113A-116.
Minor developments.
  Applications, §113A-121(b), (c).
  Expedited procedures, §113A-121(a).
Notice.
  Issuance of public notice of proposed
    development, §113A-119(b).
  Quasi-judicial procedures.
    Giving notice by registered or certified mail,
      §113A-122(d).
Obtaining permits.
  Expedited procedure, §113A-118(b), (c).
Offshore fossil fuel facilities, review required,
  §113A-119.2.
Outstanding resource water areas of
  environmental concern.
  Development in.
    Issuance of general permit, §113A-118.2.
Primary nursery areas.
  Development in, §113A-118.2.
Publication.
  Notice of proposed development, §113A-119(b).
Quasi-judicial procedures.
  Applicability of provisions, §113A-122(b).
  Failure of commission to approve or deny
    applications, §113A-122(c).
  Notices.
    Giving by registered or certified mail,
      §113A-122(d).
Requirements, §113A-118(a).
Secretary of environment and natural resources.
  Powers and duties, §113A-124(a), (b).
Special emergency permits, §113A-118(f).
Time limit on considering record of applicant,
  §113A-120(b2).

COASTAL AREA MANAGEMENT —Cont'd
Permits —Cont'd
Transitional provisions.
  Existing regulatory permits, §113A-125(a), (c).
  Permit changeover date, §113A-125(b).
  Unified systems studies, §113A-125(d).
Variances, §113A-120.1.
Violations, §113A-126(a), (b), (c).
Petitions.
Variances, §113A-120.1(a).
Planning processes.
County letter of intent, §113A-109.
Effect of land-use plans, §113A-111.
Effect of state guidelines, §113A-108.
Grants.
  Authorization to make annual grants,
    §113A-112.
Hearings.
  Land-use plans.
    Adoption, §113A-110(e).
Land-use plans and programs.
  Approval by commission, §113A-110(f).
  Contents, §113A-110(a).
  Copies of approval plans, §113A-110(g).
  Delegation of responsibilities, §113A-110(b).
  Effect, §113A-111.
  Hearings, §113A-110(e).
  Responsibilities of bodies charged with
    adoption, §113A-110(c), (d).
  Timetable for preparation, §113A-109.
Letters of intent, §113A-109.
Scope, §113A-106.
State guidelines.
  Amendment, §113A-107(f).
  Contents, §113A-107(a).
  Effect, §113A-108.
  Preparation, adoption and amendment,
    §113A-107(b).
  Submission of proposed guidelines,
    §113A-107(c).
Timetable for preparation of land-use plans,
  §113A-109.
Policy, §113A-102.
Primary nursery areas.
Development in primary nursery areas,
  §113A-118.2.
Protection of landowners' rights, §113A-128.
Publication.
Permits.
  Public notice of proposed development,
    §113A-119(b).
**Public beach and coastal waterfront access
  program,** §§113A-134.1 to 113A-134.3.
Purposes, §113A-102.
Rules and regulations.
Areas of environmental concern, §§113A-113,
  113A-115.
Protection of landowners' rights, §113A-128.
**Secretary of environment and natural
  resources.**
Permits.
  Powers and duties, §113A-124(a), (b).
Short title, §113A-100.
Title, §113A-100.
Transitional provisions.
Permits.
  Existing regulatory permits, §113A-125(a), (c).
  Permit changeover date, §113A-125(b).
  Unified systems studies, §113A-125(d).
United States.
Coordination with federal government, §113A-127.

COASTAL AREA MANAGEMENT —Cont'd
Variances, §113A-120.1(a).
Conditions and safeguards may be imposed, §113A-120.1(b).

COASTAL CAROLINA COMMUNITY COLLEGE.
Community colleges, §§115D-1 to 115D-81.
See COMMUNITY COLLEGES.
Financial support.
Authority to provide local financial support, §115D-61.

COASTAL FISHERIES.
Commercial fishing.
See FISH AND FISHING.
Fish and fishing generally.
See FISH AND FISHING.
Promotion of coastal fisheries and seafood industry.
Generally, §§113-308 to 113-315.9.
See SEAFOOD INDUSTRY AND COASTAL FISHERIES PROMOTION.

COASTAL FISHING WATERS.
Monitoring program.
Protection of public health of swimmers and others using waters, §113-221.3(a), (b).

COASTAL HABITAT PROTECTION PLANS.
Actions to be consistent with plan adopted, §143B-279.8(c).
Adoption, §113A-106.1.
Explanation of inconsistent action by commissions, §143B-279.8(d).
Goals, §143B-279.8(a).
Preparation by department of environment and natural resources, §143B-279.8(a).
Reports, §143B-279.8(e), (f).
Review commission, §143B-279.8(b).
Revision of plan by review commission and department, §143B-279.8(b).

COASTAL RECREATIONAL FISHING LICENSES, §§113-174 to 113-174.5.
See FISH AND FISHING.

COASTAL RESERVES, §§113A-129.1 to 113A-129.3.
Acquisitions or dispositions of property, §113A-129.2(d).
Administration of system, §113A-129.2(b).
Area system established within, §113A-129.2(c).
Creation.
North Carolina coastal reserve system, §113A-129.2(a).
Hunting, fishing, navigation and recreation.
Other public uses, §113A-129.2(e).
Legislative findings, §113A-129.1(a).
National estuarine reserve research system.
Coordination with, §113A-129.3(a).
Nature and historic preserve.
Dedicated as components of, §113A-129.3(b).
Purposes, §113A-129.1(b).
Research and education.
Lands and water within system primarily used for, §113A-129.2(e).

COASTAL RESOURCES COMMISSION.
Coastal habitat protection plans, §143B-279.8.
Rulemaking.
Agencies authorized to implement and enforce environmental laws, §150B-19.3(b).
Imposing more restrictive standard, limitation, or requirement than federal law, §150B-19.3(a).

COASTAL WATERS.
Clean coastal water and vessel act, §§77-125 to 77-132.
See CLEAN COASTAL WATER AND VESSEL ACT.
Seaward boundary of private property adjoining ocean high water mark, §77-20(a) to (e).

COAST GUARD AUXILIARY.
Motor vehicle special license plates, §20-79.4(b).

COASTS AND SHORES.
Beach access program, §§113A-134.1 to 113A-134.3.
Beach area essential property insurance, §§58-45-1 to 58-45-96.
See BEACH AREA ESSENTIAL PROPERTY INSURANCE.
Beaches generally.
See BEACHES.
Clean coastal water and vessel act, §§77-125 to 77-132.
See CLEAN COASTAL WATER AND VESSEL ACT.
Coastal area management, §§113A-100 to 113A-134.3.
See COASTAL AREA MANAGEMENT.
Discharges of oil or hazardous substances, §§143-215.83 to 143-215.94.
See OIL OR HAZARDOUS SUBSTANCES DISCHARGES.
Habitat protection, §143B-279.8.
Lights.
Displaying false lights on seashore, §14-282.
Offshore oil and gas activities, §§143-215.94AA to 143-215.94JJ.
See OFFSHORE OIL AND GAS ACTIVITIES.
Reserves, §§113A-129.1 to 113A-129.3.

COCAINE.
Controlled substances generally, §§90-86 to 90-113.8.
See DRUGS AND CONTROLLED SUBSTANCES.
Food, drug and cosmetic act.
Drugs deemed misbranded, §106-134.
Schedule II controlled substances, §90-90.

COCKFIGHTING, §14-362.
Cruelty to animals generally.
See CRUELTY TO ANIMALS.

COCOA.
Food, drug and cosmetic act.
Drugs deemed misbranded, §106-134.

C.O.D.
Common carriers to settle shipments promptly, §62-208.
Motor carriers.
Embezzlement of C.O.D. shipments, §62-273.
Sale of goods, UCC.
Buyer not entitled to inspect goods, §25-2-513(3).

CODED BILL DRAFTING, §120-20.1.

CODEINE.
Controlled substances generally, §§90-86 to 90-113.8.
See DRUGS AND CONTROLLED SUBSTANCES.
Food, drug and cosmetic act.
Drugs deemed misbranded, §106-134.
Murder in second degree.
Ingestion of substance causing death of user, §14-17.

CODEINE —Cont'd
Schedule II controlled substances, §90-90.

CODE OF JUDICIAL CONDUCT.
See JUDGES.

CODE OF NORTH CAROLINA.
General statutes.
See GENERAL STATUTES.
Statutes.
See STATUTES.

CODES.
Administrative code and registry.
Publication generally, §§150B-21.17 to
150B-21.25.
See PUBLICATION OF ADMINISTRATIVE
CODE AND REGISTER.
Building codes.
General provisions, §§143-136 to 143-143.5.
See BUILDING CODES.
Juvenile code, §§7B-100 to 7B-1414.
Military justice.
Courts-martial, §§127A-47 to 127A-62.
See COURTS-MARTIAL FOR NATIONAL
GUARD.
Ordinances.
City having population of five thousand or more,
§160A-77(a) to (c).
Counties, §153A-49.

CODICILS.
Concealment, larceny or destruction of
codicils, §14-77.
Included within term will, §12-3.
Revocation of nuncupative will, §31-5.2.
Revocation of written wills, §31-5.1.
Wills generally.
See WILLS.

COERCION.
Abortion.
Woman's right to know act.
Assurance of voluntariness of informed consent,
§90-21.91.
Collection agencies.
Prohibited practices, §58-70-95.
Debt collectors.
Prohibited acts, §75-51.
Elections.
Coercing person to register or to vote, §163-275.
Farm machinery franchises.
Suppliers, §66-187.1.
Insurance.
Unfair trade practices.
Prohibited acts, §58-63-15.
Intimidation.
See INTIMIDATION.
Obscene materials.
Coercing acceptance of obscene materials by
franchises, §14-190.4.
Political activities of public employees.
Coercing employee to support or contribute to
political candidate, committee or party,
§§126-14, 126-14.1.
Private personnel services contracts,
§95-47.4(d).
Real estate appraisers.
By real estate appraisal management companies,
§93E-2-7(a).
Wine distribution agreements, §18B-1202.

COGENERATING POWER PLANTS.
Income tax credit.
Corporation or partnership constructing in state,
§105-130.25.

COGNITIVE IMPAIRMENT.
Adult care homes.
Generally.
See ADULT CARE HOMES.
Generally.
See MENTAL HEALTH, DEVELOPMENTAL
DISABILITY, SUBSTANCE ABUSE.
Incompetence, determination of, §§35A-1101 to
35A-1116.
See INCOMPETENCY.
Silver alert system.
Missing persons suffering from, §143B-1022.

COHABITATION.
Misdemeanor, §14-184.

COHARIE INDIAN TRIBE.
Indians generally.
See NATIVE AMERICANS.
Rights, privileges, immunities, obligations and
duties, §71A-6.

COIN-OPERATED MACHINES.
Blind persons.
Operation of highway vending facilities, §§111-48
to 111-52.
See BLIND AND VISUALLY IMPAIRED.
Operation of vending facilities on state property,
§§111-41 to 111-47.
See BLIND AND VISUALLY IMPAIRED.
Breaking into or forcibly opening, §14-56.1.
Damaging or destroying machine, §14-56.2.
Manufacture, sale or gift of devices for cheating
slot machines, §14-109.
Obtaining property or services from machine
by false coins or tokens, §14-108.
Slot machines.
See SLOT MACHINES.
Vending machines.
See VENDING MACHINES.
Video gaming machines, §§14-306 to 14-306.2.

COIN-OPERATED TELEPHONE SERVICE.
Certificate of convenience and necessity,
§62-110(c).

COINS.
Counterfeiting, §14-13.
Generally.
See COUNTERFEITING.
False coins or tokens.
Manufacture, sale or gift, §14-109.
Obtaining property or services by use of, §14-108.

CO-INSURANCE.
Contract or policy clauses, §58-3-15.

COKE.
Standard weights and measures, §81A-42.

COLISEUMS.
Alcoholic beverage permits.
Convention center defined to include, §18B-1000.
Mixed beverage permit.
Kind of permit that may be issued, §18B-1001.
Recycling requirement, §18B-1006.1.
On-premises fortified wine permit.
Kind of permit that may be issued, §18B-1001.
Recycling requirement, §18B-1006.1.
On-premises malt beverage permit.
Kind of permit that may be issued, §18B-1001.
Recycling requirement, §18B-1006.1.
On-premises unfortified wine permit.
Kind of permit that may be issued, §18B-1001.
Recycling requirement, §18B-1006.1.

COLISEUMS —Cont'd
Municipalities.
Power to establish and support, §160A-489.
Smoking in public places.
Applicability of article to local government, §143-601.
Nonsmoking areas in state-controlled buildings, §143-597.

COLLABORATIVE LAW PROCEEDINGS, §§50-70 to 50-79.
Agreements.
Defined, §50-71.
Judgment or order effectuating agreement, §50-75.
Notice, §50-74(a), (b).
Requirements, §50-72.
Tolling of time periods, §50-73.
Alternative dispute resolution permitted, §50-78.
Death of a party.
Survival of proceeding, §50-79.
Definitions, §50-71.
Dismissal of civil action.
Notice of agreement filed with court, restrictions, §50-74(b).
Failure to reach settlement, §50-76(a) to (c).
Filing with court.
Notice of agreement.
Civil action pending, §50-74(b).
Judgment or order effectuating agreement, §50-75.
Notice, §50-74(a), (b).
Privileged evidence, §50-77(a), (b).
Purpose, §50-70.
Tolling of time periods, §50-73.

COLLAGE.
Artwork on consignment, §§25C-1 to 25C-5.
Sale of prints, §§25C-10 to 25C-16.

COLLARD GREENS.
State collard festival, §145-27.

COLLATERAL.
Retail installment sales.
Liens.
Inapplicability of section to rights or liens granted by chapter 44-A, §25A-23(c).
Permissible collateral, §25A-23(a), (b).
Revolving charge account contracts.
Inapplicability of provisions, §25A-23(d).
Substitution of collateral, §25A-26.
Fee, §25A-26.
Transfer of equity.
Imposition of transfer fee, §25A-16.
Voidness of impermissible collateral, §25A-23(b).
Secured transactions.
See SECURED TRANSACTIONS.
Trust companies.
Multistate trust institutions.
Deposits, §53-309(d).

COLLATERAL CONTRACTS.
Sale of goods, UCC.
Remedies for breach not impaired, §25-2-701.

COLLATERAL KINSHIP.
Computation of degrees of kinship, §104A-1.

COLLATERAL SOURCE RULE.
Crime victims compensation.
Award reduction, §15B-11(d).
Claim denial, §15B-11(d).

COLLATERAL SOURCE RULE —Cont'd
Crime victims compensation —Cont'd
Definitions, §15B-2.
Subrogation, §15B-19.
Workers' compensation.
Proceedings against third parties, §97-10.2(a).

COLLATERAL WARRANTIES.
Abolished, §41-8.

COLLECTION AGENCIES, §§58-70-1 to 58-70-155.
Accounts.
Acknowledgment of accounts received.
Furnishing, §58-70-60(a).
Application of funds where there is a debtor-creditor relationship, §58-70-85.
Remittance trust account, §58-70-65(a) to (c).
Return of accounts.
Creditor may request, §58-70-75.
Termination of permit, §58-70-80.
Acknowledgment of accounts received.
Furnishing, §58-70-60(a).
Actions filed by agency plaintiffs.
Complaints by agency plaintiffs.
Allegations required, §58-70-145.
Debt buyer plaintiffs.
Attachments to complaint required, §58-70-150.
Default or summary judgment.
Prerequisites to entering against debtor, §58-70-155.
Administrative action taken against.
Report to commissioner, time, §58-70-40(e).
Alien corporations.
Applications, §58-70-5(b1).
Definitions, §58-70-5(q).
Service of process on, §58-70-40(d).
Trust accounts, §58-70-65(c).
Violations by, §58-70-5(p).
Appeals.
Denial of permit, §58-70-30.
Attorneys at law.
Practice of law by collection agencies, §58-70-120.
Shared office space, §58-70-125.
Attorneys' fees.
Services rendered to assignee or debt buyer.
Materials setting forth party's obligation to pay furnished court, §6-21.2.
Banks.
Not included in definition of "collection agency," §58-70-15(c).
Bonds, surety.
Amount, §58-70-20.
Prerequisite to issuance of permit, §58-70-20.
Building and loan associations.
Not included in definition of "collection agency," §58-70-15(c).
Business records.
Entry of default or summary judgment against debtor.
Evidence to establish amount and nature of debt, §58-70-155(b).
Checks.
Collection of processing fee for returned check, §25-3-506.
Civil penalties, §58-70-130(b), (c), (e).
Cumulative nature of provisions, §58-70-130(d).
Coercion.
Prohibited practices, §58-70-95.
Complaints in actions filed by agency plaintiffs.
Allegations required, §58-70-145.

COLLECTION AGENCIES —Cont'd
Complaints in actions filed by agency plaintiffs
—Cont'd
Debt buyer plaintiffs.
Attachments to complaint required, §58-70-150.
Conviction involving dishonesty or breach of trust.
Automatic suspension of permit, §58-70-40(b).
Commissioner notified, time, §58-70-40(b).
Correspondence.
Identification of collection agency in correspondence, §58-70-50.
Costs in criminal cases.
Collection methods, §7A-321(b).
Court process.
Simulation of court process in connection with collection of accounts, §14-118.1.
Damages.
Violations of provisions, §58-70-130(a).
Cumulative nature of provisions, §58-70-130(d).
Debt buyers.
Actions filed by buyer plaintiffs.
Complaints.
Attachments required, §58-70-150.
Defined, §58-70-15(b).
Receipt for payment received.
Requirements, §58-70-70(b).
Unfair practices, §58-70-115.
Debt collectors.
Prohibited acts by debt collectors.
Collection agencies exempted from provisions, §75-50.
Deceptive representation.
Prohibited acts, §58-70-110.
Default or summary judgment against debtor.
Evidence to establish amount and nature of debt.
Authenticated business records.
Only evidence sufficient to establish, §58-70-155(b).
Required to file prior to entry of judgment, §58-70-155(a).
Definitions, §§58-70-6, 58-70-15, 58-70-90.
Deposits.
Remittance trust account, §58-70-65(a) to (c).
Detectives.
Prohibited from acting as collection agency, §14-401.2.
Doing business without permit, §58-70-1.
Evidence to establish amount and nature of debt.
Entry of default or summary judgment against debtor, §58-70-155.
False accusations.
Prohibited practices, §58-70-95.
Fees.
Permit fees, §§58-70-35(a), 58-70-45.
Fraud.
Deceptive representation.
Prohibited acts, §58-70-110.
Simulation of court process in connection with collection, §14-118.1.
Harassment.
Prohibited practices, §58-70-100.
Hearings.
Denial of permit, §58-70-30.
Hours of business, §58-70-55.
Injunctions.
Restraining orders, §§58-2-60(a), 58-70-40(a).
Misleading representation.
Prohibited acts, §58-70-110.
Office hours, §58-70-55.

COLLECTION AGENCIES —Cont'd
Payment received in cash.
Receipt issued, §58-70-70(a).
Evidence of receipts issued, retention, §58-70-70(a).
Requirements, §58-70-70(a).
Permits.
Applications, §58-70-5.
Alien corporations, §58-70-5(b1).
Definitions, §58-70-5(q).
Violations by, §58-70-5(p).
Balance sheet, §58-70-5(k).
Subsidiary in holding company system, §58-70-5(r).
Certification of no unsatisfied judgments, §58-70-5(h).
Collection method statement, §58-70-5(g).
Contents, §58-70-5(a).
Corporations, §58-70-5(b).
Fees, §§58-70-5(j), 58-70-35(a).
Foreign corporations, §58-70-5(o).
Information to accompany, §58-70-5.
Intended business address, §58-70-5(l).
Moral turpitude statement, §58-70-5(m).
Nonresident applicants, §58-70-5(n).
Surety bond, §58-70-20(c).
Partnerships, §58-70-5(c).
Renewal of permit, §58-70-10.
Stockholder statements, §58-70-5(f).
Surety bond, §58-70-5(e).
Telephone number list, §58-70-5(i).
Trade name used, §58-70-5(d).
Assignable or transferable, §58-70-35(c).
Bond, surety, §58-70-20(a).
Application for permit, §58-70-5(e).
Cash deposit in lieu of bond, §58-70-20(b).
Nonresidents, §58-70-20(c).
Definitions, §58-70-6.
Denial, §58-70-30.
Display, §58-70-50.
Doing business without permit, §58-70-1.
Duration, §58-70-35(b).
Fees.
Application fee, §58-70-35(a).
Disposition, §58-70-45.
Guarantee of applicant's performance.
Submitted by ultimate parent of subsidiary, §58-70-5(r).
Responsibility of ultimate parent, §58-70-5(s).
Monetary penalty for violations, §58-2-70(a), (c), (d), (g).
Renewal.
Application, §58-70-10.
Required, §58-70-1.
Restitution for violations, §58-2-70(e), (f), (g).
Return of accounts and all valuable papers upon termination of permit, §58-70-80.
Revocation.
Notice and hearing, §58-2-70(b).
Violations of provisions, §58-70-40(b), (c).
Subsidiary in holding company.
Guarantee of applicant's performance.
Responsibility of ultimate parent, §58-70-5(s).
Submitted by ultimate parent, §58-70-5(r).
Ultimate parent's balance sheet filed, §58-70-5(r).
Surrender, §58-2-65.
Suspension.
Applicable provisions, §58-2-70(h).
Criminal conviction, §58-2-60(b).
Notice and hearing, §58-2-70(b).

COLLECTION AGENCIES —Cont'd
Permits —Cont'd
Suspension —Cont'd
Violations of provisions, §58-70-40(b), (c).
Practice of law.
Unauthorized practice of law, §58-70-120.
Prohibited practices, §§58-70-95, 58-70-125.
Civil liability, §58-70-130.
Publication.
Unreasonable publication as to consumer's debt.
Prohibited practices, §58-70-105.
Receipts.
Debt buyers, §58-70-70(b).
Evidence of receipts issued.
Permit holder required to keep, retention, time,
§58-70-70(a).
Required when payment received in cash,
§58-70-70(a).
Records.
Contents, §58-70-25(b).
Receipts issued, retention, §58-70-70(a).
Required, §58-70-25(a).
Remittances, §58-70-60(b).
Statements to accompany, §58-70-60(b).
Trust account, §58-70-65(a) to (c).
Restraining orders, §§58-2-60(a), 58-70-40(a).
Returned checks.
Collection of processing fee, §25-3-506.
Savings and loan associations.
Not included in definition of "collection
agency,"§58-70-15(c).
Shared office space.
Prohibited, §58-70-125.
Summary judgment against debtor.
Evidence to establish amount and nature of debt.
Prerequisites to entry of judgment, §58-70-155.
Telephones.
Harassment.
Prohibited practices, §58-70-100.
Threats.
Prohibited practices, §58-70-95.
Unfair practices, §58-70-115.
Unlawful practices, §§58-70-95, 58-70-125.
Civil liability, §58-70-130.

**COLLECTION OF WORTHLESS CHECKS
FUND,** §7A-308(c).

COLLECTORS FOR ESTATES.
Actions against collectors.
Service on or appearance of one binds all,
§28A-18-4.
Appointment, §28A-11-1.
Termination.
Duties upon termination, §28A-11-4(b).
Bond, §28A-11-2.
Commissions, §28A-23-3.
Collectors guilty of misconduct not entitled to
commission, §28A-23-3(e).
Computation, §28A-23-3(f).
Construction of section, §28A-23-3(d).
Determination of amount, §28A-23-3(b).
Entitlement, §28A-23-3(a).
Limitation on amount, §28A-23-3(c).
Statutory language, use to determine,
§28A-23-3(h).
Stipulated amount or method of payment,
§28A-23-3(g).
Compensation, §28A-11-5.
Counsel fees.
Attorneys serving as collectors, §28A-23-4.

COLLECTORS FOR ESTATES —Cont'd
**Death of person entitled to bring action before
limitation expires.**
Action by or against personal representative or
collector, §1-22.
Defined, §28A-1-1(1).
Duties, §28A-11-3(a).
Examination of accounts, §28A-11-4(c).
Letters of collection.
Issuance, §28A-11-1.
Oaths, §28A-11-2.
Personal property.
Court ordered sale or lease, §28A-16-2.
Powers, §28A-11-3(b).
When collectors' powers ceased, §28A-11-4(a).
Qualifications, §28A-11-1.
Small estates.
Subsequently appointed collectors, §28A-25-5.

**COLLECTORS OF WINE OR DECORATIVE
DECANTERS.**
Alcoholic beverage permits.
Special one-time permits, §18B-1002(a).

COLLECT TELEPHONE CALLS.
Debt collectors, harassment, §75-52.

COLLEGES AND UNIVERSITIES.
Academic common market program, §116-43.10.
Academic credit.
Fraudulent means in obtaining credit,
§14-118.2(a), (b).
**Admission status of persons charged in-state
tuition,** §116-143.4.
Alcoholic beverage permits.
Business located on campus, §18B-1006(a).
Viticulture/oenology course authorization,
§18B-1114.4.
Anatomical gifts.
Recipients of gift, §130A-412.13(a).
Armed forces members on active duty.
In-state tuition rate, §116-143.3(b).
Burden of proving entitlement, §116-143.3(d).
Definitions, §116-143.3(a).
Dependent relatives, entitlement, §116-143.3(c).
Ineligibility for certain other benefits,
§116-143.3(e).
Reassignment outside state, §116-143.3(b).
Arrest.
Campus police officers.
Territorial jurisdiction, §15A-402(f).
Arson.
Burning of buildings of educational institutions,
§14-60.
Athlete agents.
Generally, §§78C-85 to 78C-105.
See ATHLETE AGENTS.
Attorney general.
Licensing nonpublic post-secondary educational
institutions.
Enforcement, §116-15(j).
Beer and wine sales on campus.
Permit for, restrictions, §18B-1006(a).
Behavioral health problems.
Military members, veterans and families.
Collaboration on research on, §127B-20.
Board of governors.
Flexible compensation plans.
Authorized to provide, §116-17.2.
Bond.
Licensing nonpublic post-secondary educational
institutions.
Applicants, §116-15(f1).

COLLEGES AND UNIVERSITIES —Cont'd
Bond issues.
  Revenue bonds for student housing, student
    activities, physical education and recreation.
  Money received deemed trust funds, §116-192.
  State debt, §§142-1 to 142-29.7.
    See STATE DEBT.
  State education assistance authority, §§116-201 to
    116-209.40.
    See EDUCATION ASSISTANCE AUTHORITY.
  University of North Carolina.
    See UNIVERSITY OF NORTH CAROLINA.
Burning of buildings, §14-60.
Campus police officers.
  General provisions, §§74G-1 to 74G-13.
    See CAMPUS POLICE.
Capital facilities finance.
  Private capital facilities finance act.
    Institutions for higher education and
      elementary and secondary education,
      §§159D-35 to 159D-57.
      See CAPITAL FACILITIES FINANCE
        AGENCY.
Center for advancement of teaching,
  §§115C-296.5, 115C-296.6.
Civil disorders.
  State of emergency.
    Injunctions, §14-288.18(a), (b).
Community colleges.
  General provisions.
    See COMMUNITY COLLEGES.
Confidentiality.
  Emergency response plans, §132-1.6.
Constitution of North Carolina.
  Benefits extended to people of state free of
    expense, NC Const Art IX §9.
  Bond issues.
    Higher education facilities authorized, NC
      Const Art V §12.
  Maintenance of public system of higher education,
    NC Const Art IX §8.
Continuum of education programs.
  Strategic design to be developed by education
    cabinet, §116C-3.
**Contracts by minors borrowing for higher
  education,** §116-174.1.
Curfews.
  Authorized, §116-212.
  Sound-amplifying equipment.
    Defined, §116-213(a).
    Prohibited acts, §116-213(a).
  Violations.
    Punishment, §116-213(a).
      Plea of guilty or nolo contendere, §116-213(b).
Deadly weapons.
  Possessing or carrying on campus or educational
    property, §14-269.2.
Debt.
  State debt, §§142-1 to 142-29.7.
    See STATE DEBT.
Definitions.
  Defaulted student loan recovery, §105B-1(b).
  Parental loans, §116-209.24(b).
  Post-secondary educational institutions.
    Nonpublic institutions, §116-15(a2).
  State education assistance authority, §116-201(b).
  Tuition.
    Residence status for tuition purposes,
      §116-143.1(a).
  University of North Carolina.
    See UNIVERSITY OF NORTH CAROLINA.

COLLEGES AND UNIVERSITIES —Cont'd
Diplomas.
  Forgery, §14-122.1.
Disasters.
  State of emergency.
    Injunctions, §14-288.18(a), (b).
Disorderly conduct, §14-288.4.
Dormitories.
  Fire safety for residence halls, §§116-44.6 to
    116-44.8.
Driver training schools.
  License exemption, §20-326.
**Education access rewards North Carolina
  scholars fund.**
  Administration of grants, §116-209.26(e).
  Amount of grant, §116-209.26(d).
  Criteria for awarding grants, §116-209.26(c).
  Definitions, §116-209.26(a).
  Duration of grant, §116-209.26(c).
  Eligibility, §116-209.26(c).
  Escheat fund money, §116-209.26(h).
  Establishment, §116-209.26(b).
  General fund money, §116-209.26(h).
  Maximum amount, §116-209.26(d).
  Purpose, §116-209.26(b).
  Reports, §116-209.26(f).
  Unexpended funds, §116-209.26(g).
Education administration programs.
  Duties of board of governors, §116-11.2.
Education assistance authority, §§116-201 to
  116-209.40.
  See EDUCATION ASSISTANCE AUTHORITY.
Education cabinet, §116C-1.
Education commission, §§143-261 to 143-266.
  See EDUCATION COMMISSION.
Embezzlement by public officers and trustees,
  §14-92.
Emergencies.
  State of emergency.
    Injunctions, §14-288.18(a), (b).
**Energy policy and life-cycle cost analysis for
  state government.**
  Audit of state agencies or institutions of higher
    learning, §143-64.12(b1).
    Report of energy audit, §143-64.12(b2).
  Construction and renovation of facilities,
    implementation, §143-64.12(a1).
  Generally.
    See PUBLIC BUILDINGS AND GROUNDS.
  Management plans submitted by institutions of
    higher education, §143-64.12(a).
Explosives.
  Possessing or carrying on campus or educational
    property, §14-269.2.
Faculty.
  Retirement system for teachers and state
    employees.
    General provisions.
      See RETIREMENT SYSTEM FOR
        TEACHERS AND STATE EMPLOYEES.
Firearms and other weapons.
  Possessing or carrying on campus or educational
    property, §14-269.2.
Fire safety.
  Residence halls, §§116-44.6 to 116-44.8.
Fire safety loan fund.
  Supplemental fire safety protection system,
    §116-44.8.
Fire safety protection systems.
  Fraternities, sororities and residence halls,
    §§116-44.6 to 116-44.8.

COLLEGES AND UNIVERSITIES —Cont'd
First in America innovative education act,
§116C-4.
**Fluorescent lights and thermostats containing
mercury.**
Recycling program.
Establishment required, §130A-310.60(a).
Report documenting compliance required,
§130A-310.60(b).
Forgery of transcripts and diplomas, §14-122.1.
Fraternities and sororities.
Property tax exemptions, §105-275.
Supplemental fire safety protection system.
Definitions, §116-44.6.
Exemption from certain fees and charges,
§116-44.7.
Fire safety loan fund.
Administration, §116-44.8(b).
Established, §116-44.8(a).
Loans, security for, §116-44.8(d).
Operated on revolving basis, §116-44.8(c).
Fraud.
Obtaining academic credit, §14-118.2(a).
Penalty for violation of provisions, §14-118.2(b).
Funds.
Education access rewards North Carolina scholars
fund, §116-209.26.
Fire safety loan fund, §116-44.8.
Parental savings trust fund, §116-209.25.
Hazing.
Definitions, §14-35.
Kidnapping, §§14-39 to 14-41.
Self-incrimination.
No indictment founded on self-incriminating
testimony, §14-38.
Hot pursuit.
Campus police officers.
Immediate and continuous flight, §15A-402(f).
Immunization.
Certificate of immunization.
Applicability of provisions, §130A-155.1(e).
Records.
Maintenance of immunization records,
§130A-155.1(b).
Reports.
Filing of immunization report with
department, §130A-155.1(c).
Submission to college or university,
§130A-155.1(a).
Injunctions.
State of emergency.
Public or private educational institutions,
§14-288.18(a), (b).
Insurance.
University of North Carolina.
Liability insurance or self-insurance generally,
§§116-219 to 116-224.
See UNIVERSITY OF NORTH CAROLINA.
Licenses.
Post-secondary educational institutions.
Nonpublic institutions, §116-15.
Loans.
Defaulted student loan recovery.
Additional remedy, §105B-2.
Definitions, §105B-1(b).
Payor.
Prohibited conduct, §105B-4(a), (b).
Penalties.
Civil penalties, §105B-4(c).
Procedures, §105B-3.
Purpose of article, §105B-1(a).

COLLEGES AND UNIVERSITIES —Cont'd
Loans —Cont'd
Defaulted student loan recovery —Cont'd
Records.
Inspection and copying by debtor, §105B-3(c).
Remedy additional to others, §105B-2.
Schedule for repayment.
Entry, §105B-3(d).
Withholding order.
Contested withholding, §105B-3(e).
Entering, §105B-3(a).
Expiration, §105B-5.
Motion, §105B-3(b).
Termination of withholding, §105B-5.
Transmittal of payment, §105B-3(g).
Uncontested withholding, §105B-3(f).
Fund for prospective college teachers.
Amount of loans, §116-73.
Duration of fund, §116-74.
Establishment, §116-72.
Guidelines for loans, §116-73.
Interest, §116-73.
Use, §116-74.
Joint committee for administration of fund,
§116-73.
Purposes, §§116-71, 116-72.
Repaid loans and interest.
Use, §116-74.
Rules and regulations, §116-73.
Parental loans.
Assistance to parents.
Power of state education assistance authority,
§116-209.24(c).
Bond issues.
Power of authority, §116-209.24(e).
Buying and selling parental obligations.
Power of authority, §116-209.24(d).
Definitions, §116-209.24(b).
Policy of state, §116-209.24(a).
Principal fellows program, §§116-74.41 to
116-74.43.
Scholarships. See within this heading,
"Scholarships."
Social workers' education loan fund, §116-209.30.
**Meningococcal disease vaccination
information.**
Providing students, §116-260(a).
Confidential, §116-260(b).
Inapplicability, vaccine no longer recommended,
§116-260(d).
Institution not required to provide, §116-260(c).
Private right of action not created, §116-260(e).
Student health forms, information provided in,
§116-260(a).
Mercury.
Fluorescent lights and thermostats containing.
Recycling program.
Establishment required, §130A-310.60(a).
Report documenting compliance,
§130A-310.60(b).
Military personnel.
Behavioral health problems facing members,
veterans and families.
Collaboration on research on, §127B-20.
In-state tuition rate for active duty personnel,
§116-143.3.
Militia.
Commissions for commandants and officers at
qualified educational institutions, §127A-23.
Motor vehicle license plates.
Collegiate insignia plates, §§20-79.4(b),
20-81.12(a).
Application, §20-81.12(c).

COLLEGES AND UNIVERSITIES —Cont'd
National Guard tuition assistance.
Active duty personnel.
In-state rate, §116-143.3.
Generally, §§116-209.50 to 116-209.55.
See NATIONAL GUARD.
Nonpublic post-secondary educational institutions.
Licensing.
Attorney general.
Enforcement authority, §116-15(j).
Board of governors of University of North Carolina.
Regulatory authority in board, §116-15(i).
Definitions, §116-15(a2).
Denial and revocation, §116-15(h).
Enforcement authority, §116-15(j).
Exemptions, §116-15(c).
Institutions relative to religious education, §116-15(d).
Guaranty bond required of applicant, §116-15(f1).
Military posts or reservations.
Post-secondary degree activity within military, §116-15(e).
Policy of state, §§116-15, 116-15(a1).
Religious education.
Exemption of institutions, §116-15(d).
Required, §116-15(b).
Review of licensure, §116-15(g).
Severability of provisions, §116-15(k).
Standards, §116-15(f).
Nonresidents.
Tuition, §116-144.
Parental savings trust fund.
Administration, §116-209.25(d).
Contributions, §116-209.25(c).
Income tax deduction, §105-134.6(d).
Established, §116-209.25(b).
Investment manager, §116-209.25(c1).
Loan program, §116-209.25(e).
No obligation of authority or state created, §116-209.25(f).
Policy, §116-209.25(a).
Parents of students.
Loans to.
Bond issues.
Power of authority to issue, §116-209.24(e).
Buying and selling parental obligations.
Power of authority, §116-209.24(d).
Definitions, §116-209.24(b).
Policy for parental loans, §116-209.24(a).
Power of state education assistance authority, §116-209.24(c).
Piedmont Triad Research Institute, §§116-250 to 116-253.
Police officers.
Campus police officers.
See CAMPUS POLICE.
Principal fellows program, §§116-74.41 to 116-74.43.
Private capital facilities finance act.
Institutions for higher education and elementary and secondary education, §§159D-35 to 159D-57.
See CAPITAL FACILITIES FINANCE AGENCY.
Private institutions.
Licensing nonpublic post-secondary institutions, §116-15(j).

COLLEGES AND UNIVERSITIES —Cont'd
Private institutions —Cont'd
Need-based scholarships for students attending private colleges and universities, §§116-280 to 116-283.
State grants to aid eligible students attending.
Administration.
State education assistance authority, §116-43.5(c).
Definitions, §116-43.5(a).
Documentation of students receiving funs, report, §116-43.5(f1).
Eligibility, §116-43.5(b).
Incarcerated students.
Funds not used for, §116-43.5(g).
Reduction of authorized grant, §116-43.5(f).
Reversion of remaining funds, §116-43.5(e).
Shortfall in funds.
Pro rata share, §116-43.5(d).
Professional counselors.
Student intern or trainee in counseling.
Exemption from licensure, §90-332.1(a).
Protests.
Refusal to vacate building or facility.
Disorderly conduct, §14-288.4.
Refusal to vacate building or facility.
Disorderly conduct, §14-288.4.
Residence halls.
Fire safety.
Definitions, §116-44.6.
Exemption from certain fees and charges, §116-44.7.
Fire safety loan fund, §116-44.8.
Retirement system for teachers and state employees.
General provisions.
See RETIREMENT SYSTEM FOR TEACHERS AND STATE EMPLOYEES.
Optional retirement program for state institutions of higher education, §135-5.1.
Riots.
Revocation of scholarships.
Grounds, §116-174.2.
State of emergency.
Injunctions, §14-288.18(a), (b).
Roads and streets on campus.
Design, construction, etc.
Powers of department of transportation, §136-18.
Scholarships.
Generally.
See SCHOLARSHIPS.
Need-based scholarships for students attending private colleges and universities, §§116-280 to 116-283.
State education assistance authority, §§116-201 to 116-209.40.
See EDUCATION ASSISTANCE AUTHORITY.
School administrator programs.
Establishment of competitive proposal process for, §116-74.21.
Principal fellows program, §116-74.42.
Principal fellows commission, §116-74.41.
Terms of loans, §116-74.43.
Science, technology, engineering and mathematics education priorities, §116C-5.
Seizing building or facility.
Disorderly conduct, §14-288.4.
Sit-ins.
Refusal to vacate building or facility.
Disorderly conduct, §14-288.4.

COLLEGES AND UNIVERSITIES —Cont'd
Social workers' education loan fund,
§116-209.30.
Sororities.
Property tax exemptions, §105-275.
Supplemental fire safety protection program.
Definitions, §116-44.6.
Exemption from certain fees and charges,
§116-44.7.
State board of higher education.
Duties and powers, §116-158.
State debt.
Interest.
Reimbursement of treasurer for interest,
§142-15.
State education assistance authority, §§116-201
to 116-209.40.
See EDUCATION ASSISTANCE AUTHORITY.
State of emergency.
Injunctions, §14-288.18(a), (b).
Teachers.
Center for advancement of teaching,
§§115C-296.5, 115C-296.6.
Performance reports from institutions of higher
education offering teacher education,
§115C-296(b).
Teachers' retirement system.
See RETIREMENT SYSTEM FOR TEACHERS
AND STATE EMPLOYEES.
**Telephone service provided to nonprofit
college or university and affiliated medical
centers.**
Shared or resold service, §62-110(e).
Test questions.
Tampering with, §14-401.1.
Theft of property, §14-398.
Towing motor vehicles.
Private institutions, §116-229.
Trust funds.
Parental savings trust fund, §116-209.25.
Revenue bonds for student housing, student
activities, physical education and recreation.
Moneys received, §116-192.
Tuition.
See TUITION.
Tuition and fee waivers, §§115B-1 to 115B-6.
University of North Carolina.
General provisions.
See UNIVERSITY OF NORTH CAROLINA.
Veterans' children.
Scholarships for children of war veterans,
§§165-19 to 165-22.1.
Veterinary faculty certificates, §90-187.14(a), (c).
Viticulture/oenology courses.
Authorization, §18B-1114.4.
Vocational and technical education, §§115C-151
to 115C-169.
See VOCATIONAL AND TECHNICAL
EDUCATION.

COLLEGE SAVINGS PLANS.
Exemption from creditors' claims, §1C-1601(a).
Parental savings trust fund, §116-209.25.
Income tax deduction, contributions,
§105-134.6(d).

COLLISION INSURANCE.
Authorized, §58-7-15.
Mandatory or voluntary risk sharing plans.
See MANDATORY OR VOLUNTARY RISK
SHARING PLANS.

COLLISIONS.
Motor vehicles.
Generally.
See MOTOR VEHICLE ACCIDENTS.

COLLUSION.
Suit for penalty.
Reply by plaintiff that former judgment obtained
by covin, §1-59.

COLONIAL SPANISH MUSTANG.
State horse, §145-31.

COLOR ADDITIVES.
Food, drug and cosmetic act.
Additives deemed unsafe, §106-132.
Cosmetics deemed adulterated, §106-136.
Cosmetics deemed misbranded, §106-137.
Drugs deemed misbranded, §106-134.
Drugs deemed to be adulterated, §106-133.
Foods deemed misbranded, §106-130.
Foods deemed to be adulterated, §106-129.

COLORECTAL CANCER.
Health benefit plan coverage.
Examinations, tests and screening, §58-3-179.
Small employer group health plans, §58-50-155(a).

COLOR OF OFFICE.
**Limitation of action against public officer for
trespass,** §1-52.
Venue, §1-77.

COLOR OF SKIN.
Discrimination generally.
See DISCRIMINATION.
Racial minorities generally.
See RACIAL MINORITIES.

COLOR OF TITLE.
Adverse possession, §1-38.
Seven years' possession under color of title, §1-38.
Lost instruments and records.
Destroyed instrument, §98-8.

COLORS, STATE, §144-6.

COLUMBIA, TOWN OF.
Satellite annexation.
Limitation on area of satellite corporate limits,
inapplicability, §160A-58.1(b).

COLUMBINE.
**Taking, etc., of certain wild plants from land of
another,** §14-129.

COLUMBUS COUNTY.
Acquisition of property, power, §153A-158.1(a).
Agricultural tendencies in certain counties.
Terms of, §42-23.
Ambulance service.
Attachment or garnishment and lien for,
§§44-51.4 to 44-51.8.
**Blank or master forms of mortgages, deeds of
trust, etc.**
Indexing and recording, inapplicability of
provisions, §47-21.
**Condemnation or acquisition of land by local
government unit outside county.**
Consent of board of commissioners necessary,
§153A-15.
**Cropper or tenant refusing to perform terms
of contract.**
Forfeiture of right of possession to premises,
§42-27.
Dog collars.
Unlawful removal of electronic dog collars,
§14-401.17.

COLUMBUS COUNTY —Cont'd
Fair Bluff watermelon festival.
  Official Southeastern North Carolina festival,
    §145-16(b).
Game laws, local acts not repealed,
    §113-133.1(e).
Grants in navigable waters, registration,
    §113-205(a).
Low-income housing tax credits.
  Qualified building eligible for credit,
    §105-129.41(c).
School property.
  Acquisition and improvement, §153A-158.1.
**Southeastern North Carolina regional
    economic development commission,**
    §§158-8.3 to 158-8.8.

COLUMBUS DAY.
Public holiday, §103-4(a).

COLUMBUS, TOWN OF.
Satellite annexation.
  Limitation on area of satellite corporate limits,
    inapplicability, §160A-58.1(b).

COMBINATIONS IN RESTRAINT OF TRADE.
Illegality, §75-1.

COMEDIANS.
**Artistic and creative services and talent
    agency contracts.**
  Minors, §§48A-11 to 48A-18.

COMITY.
Conflict of laws generally.
  See CONFLICT OF LAWS.
Geologists.
  Licenses, §89E-11.
Soil scientist licenses, §89F-12.
Taxation.
  Reciprocal comity, §105-268.

COMMENCEMENT OF ACTIONS, §1A-1 Rule
    3(a).
**Abused, neglected or dependent juvenile
    actions,** §7B-405.
Bond for costs and damages.
  Prosecution bonds, §§1-109 to 1-112.
Civil no-contact orders.
  Workplace violence prevention.
    Filing complaint or motion, §95-262(a).
Complaints.
  Filing, §1A-1 Rule 3(a).
Death before limitation expires.
  Action by or against personal representative or
    collector, §1-22.
Defendant out of state, §1-21.
Delinquent and undisciplined juvenile actions.
  Filing of petition, §7B-1804(a).
Joint and several debtors.
  Defenses.
    Parties summoned after judgment, §1-114.
  Judgments, §1-113.
    Summoning after judgment, §1-114.
  Partners, §1-113.
  Proceedings generally, §1-113.
  Summons and process, §1-113.
    Summoning after judgment, §1-114.
Limitation of actions generally.
  See LIMITATION OF ACTIONS.
Lis pendens, §§1-116 to 1-120.2.
  See LIS PENDENS.
Medical malpractice.
  Index of actions provided senior district judge,
    §1A-1 Rule 3(a).

COMMENCEMENT OF ACTIONS —Cont'd
Prosecution bonds, §§1-109 to 1-112.
Small claims actions, §7A-213.
Special proceedings.
  Contested proceedings, §1-394.
Summons.
  Issuance, §1A-1 Rule 3(a).
Workplace violence prevention.
  Civil no-contact orders.
    Filing complaint or motion, §95-262(a).

COMMENT BY JUDGE ON VERDICT, §1-180.1.

COMMERCE.
Commercial code, §§25-1-101 to 25-11-108.
  See COMMERCIAL CODE.
Commodities, §§78D-1 to 78D-33.
  See COMMODITIES.
Constitution of North Carolina.
  Local, private and special legislation.
    Limitation, NC Const Art II §24.
Constitution of the United States, US Const Art
    I §§8, 9.
Counties.
  Inspectors of articles of commerce, §§66-1 to 66-7.
Electronic commerce in government, §§66-58.1
    to 66-58.12.
  See ELECTRONIC COMMERCE IN
    GOVERNMENT.
Limited liability companies.
  Generally, §§57C-1-01 to 57C-10-07.
  See LIMITED LIABILITY COMPANIES.
Monopolies and restraints of trade, §§75-1 to
    75-35.
  See MONOPOLIES AND RESTRAINT OF
    TRADE.
**Tax incentives for new and expanding
    businesses,** §§105-129.2 to 105-129.13.
  See TAX INCENTIVES FOR NEW AND
    EXPANDING BUSINESSES.
Unfair competitive practices.
  Regulation of method, §75-1.1.

COMMERCE DEPARTMENT.
Accounts and accounting.
  Industrial development fund.
    Utility account, §143B-437.01(b1).
Agencies.
  Organization of department, §143B-433.
Agrarian growth zones.
  Defined, §143B-437.010(a).
  Determination, §143B-437.010(b).
  Property partially within zone, §143B-437.010(c).
  Publication of list, §143B-437.010(b).
Alcoholic beverages.
  Commission.
    See ALCOHOLIC BEVERAGE CONTROL
      COMMISSION.
**Allocation of economic development
    responsibilities.**
  Economic development board, §143B-437.03.
Attorney general.
  Energy division of department.
    Employment of attorney for division, §114-4.2D.
Business license information service.
  Authorized to establish, §143B-431(e).
**Clearinghouse for business license
    information.**
  Authorized to establish, §143B-431(e).
Community development block grants,
    §143B-437.04.

COMMERCE DEPARTMENT —Cont'd

Comprehensive strategic economic development plan, §143B-434.01.
Annual report, §143B-434.01(k).
Data, plans and reports.
Availability to general assembly, §143B-434.01(l).
Economic distress defined, §143B-434.01(a).
Environmental scan, §143B-434.01(e).
Formulation of strategy, §143B-434.01(i).
Goals and objectives, §143B-434.01(h).
Implementation plan, §143B-434.01(j).
Needs assessment, §143B-434.01(f).
Plan defined, §143B-434.01(a).
Preparation of plan by board, §143B-434.01(b).
Public and private input, §143B-434.01(d).
Purpose, §143B-434.01(c).
Region defined, §143B-434.01(a).
Vision and mission statements, §143B-434.01(g).
Contested case provisions of administrative procedure.
Exemption, §150B-1(e).
Contractors.
Small business contractors, §§143B-472.100 to 143B-472.112.
Contracts.
Economic development board.
Clawbacks, §143B-435.1.
Creation, §143B-427.
Credit unions.
Commission, §143B-439.
Declaration of policy, §143B-428.
Department of natural resources and economic development.
Divisions, councils and units transferred to department of commerce, §143B-432(a) to (c).
Development tiers.
Assignment of development factor, §143B-437.08(b).
Data to be used, §143B-437.08(d).
Definition, §143B-437.08(a).
Development tier one areas.
Adjustments, §143B-437.08(f).
Exception.
Eco-industrial parks, §143B-437.08(j).
Multijurisdictional industrial parks, §143B-437.08(h).
Seafood industrial parks, §143B-437.08(i).
Two-county industrial park, §143B-437.08(g).
Ranking of counties according to development factors, §143B-437.08(c).
Small counties.
Adjustments, §143B-437.08(e).
Division of employment and training, §143B-438.13.
Division of tourism, film and sports development.
Duties and responsibilities, §143B-434.2.
Duties, §§143B-429, 143B-430(a), (b).
Federal programs, §143B-431(d).
Local planning assistance, §143B-431(c).
Economic development board.
Advertising of resources and advantages, §143B-436.
Advice and staff, §143B-434(c).
Allocation of responsibilities, §143B-437.03.
Block grants, §143B-437.04(a).
Qualifications, §143B-437.04(b).
Chairman, §143B-434(c).
Clawbacks, §143B-435.1.
Catalog, §143B-435.1(c).

COMMERCE DEPARTMENT —Cont'd

Economic development board —Cont'd
Clawbacks —Cont'd
Clawback defined, §143B-435.1(a).
Findings, §143B-435.1(b).
Purposes, §143B-435.1(b).
Reports, §143B-435.1(d).
Website to carry catalog, §143B-435.1(c).
Clerical services, §143B-434(b).
Contracts.
Clawbacks, §143B-435.1.
Creation, §143B-434(a).
Duties, §143B-434(a).
Impact studies.
Investigation of impact of proposed new and expanding industries, §143B-437.
Investigation of impact of proposed new and expanding industries, §143B-437.
Membership, §143B-434(a), (b).
Powers and duties, §143B-434(a).
Publication, §143B-435.
Reports.
Publication, §143B-435.
Review of annual report, §143B-437.05.
Economic development grants.
Economic development incentives, §143B-437.07(c).
Reporting, §143B-437.07(a).
Posting reports online, §143B-437.07(b).
Employment and training grant program, §143B-438.13.
Employment security division.
Creation, §96-3.
Unemployment compensation generally, §§96-1 to 96-29.
See UNEMPLOYMENT COMPENSATION.
Energy division.
Attorney general.
Employment of attorney for division, §114-4.2D.
Energy loan fund, §§143B-437.14 to 143B-437.16.
Established, §143B-427.
Federal funds.
Power of secretary to accept, §143B-430(b).
Federal programs.
Powers and duties with respect to, §143B-431(d).
Functions, §143B-431(a).
Funds.
Industrial development fund, §143B-437.01.
Job maintenance and capital development fund, §143B-437.012.
Main street solutions fund, §143B-472.35.
Applications, §143B-472.35(c1).
New or amended, §143B-472.35(d).
Criteria for community participation, §143B-472.35(a3).
Definitions, §143B-472.35(a2).
Disbursements, §143B-472.35(g).
Eligible projects, §143B-472.35(b).
Establishment, §143B-472.35(a).
Expenses for administration of fund, §143B-472.35(m).
Grant awards.
Amount, §143B-472.35(a1).
Use, §143B-472.35(a4).
Inspections, §143B-472.35(j).
Purpose, §143B-472.35(a3).
Reimbursable matching grants program, §143B-472.35(a1).
Reports, §143B-472.35(i), (l).
Rules, §143B-472.35(k).
Use of funds, §143B-472.35(a4), (b).

COMMERCE DEPARTMENT —Cont'd
Funds —Cont'd
NC green business fund, §§143B-437.4 to 143B-437.8.
Grants.
Main street solutions fund, §143B-472.35.
Power to apply for and accept, §143B-431(d).
Green business.
NC green business fund, §§143B-437.4 to 143B-437.8.
Housing assistance information.
Toll-free telephone number to provide information.
Established in department, §143B-431.1.
Industrial development fund.
Creation, §143B-437.01(a).
Definitions, §143B-437.01(a1).
Reports.
Annual report to general assembly, §143B-437.01(c).
Utility account, use of funds, §143B-437.01(c1).
Rules, §143B-437.01(a).
Utility account, §143B-437.01(b1).
Information resource management commission.
Administrative procedure.
Special provisions, §§150B-38 to 150B-42.
Inspections.
Main street solutions fund, §143B-472.35(j).
Job development investment grant program, §§143B-437.50 to 143B-437.63.
Job maintenance and capital development fund, §143B-437.012.
Legislative declaration, §143B-428.
Limitation on grant or loan.
Entity currently in default on loan to department, §143B-431.2.
Loans.
Main street solutions fund, §143B-472.35.
Main street solutions fund, §143B-472.35.
Major industrial projects.
Preparation of proposals.
Authority to contract for, §143B-431(b1).
Navigation and pilotage commissions transferred to department, §143B-451.
NC green business fund, §§143B-437.4 to 143B-437.8.
One North Carolina fund, §§143B-437.70 to 143B-437.74.
See ONE NORTH CAROLINA FUND.
One North Carolina small business program, §§143B-437.80 to 143B-437.83.
See ONE NORTH CAROLINA SMALL BUSINESS PROGRAM.
Organization, §143B-433.
Planning.
Local planning assistance, §143B-431(c).
Policy, §143B-428.
Port enhancement zones.
Application for designation, §143B-437.013(b).
Defined, §143B-437.013(a).
Limitation on area of county included in, §143B-437.013(b).
List of zones published annually, §143B-437.013(b).
Powers, §§143B-430(a), (b), 143B-431.
Federal programs, §143B-431(d).
Local planning assistance, §143B-431(c).
Reports.
Economic development board.
Clawbacks, §143B-435.1(d).
Publication, §143B-435.

COMMERCE DEPARTMENT —Cont'd
Reports —Cont'd
Economic development grant reporting, §143B-437.07(a).
Posting online, §143B-437.07(b).
Industrial development fund.
Annual report, §143B-437.01(c).
Utility account, use of funds, §143B-437.01(c1).
Main street solutions fund.
Reporting requirements, §143B-472.35(i).
One North Carolina fund, §143B-437.74.
Trade jobs for success initiative, §143B-438.17.
Unemployment compensation.
Duties of secretary, §96-4(c).
Retirement communities.
Certified retirement community program, §§143B-437.100, 143B-437.101.
Science and technology.
See SCIENCE AND TECHNOLOGY.
Seafood industrial park authority, §§113-315.25 to 113-315.39.
See SEAFOOD INDUSTRIAL PARK AUTHORITY.
Secretary.
Head of department, §143B-430(a).
License plate.
Special plate, number, §20-79.5.
Powers and duties, §143B-430(a), (b).
Rules, power to adopt, §143B-430(c).
Unemployment compensation.
Employment security division, duties as to.
See UNEMPLOYMENT COMPENSATION.
Site development funding, §143B-437.02.
Small business contractors, §§143B-472.100 to 143B-472.112.
See SMALL BUSINESS CONTRACTORS.
Small businesses.
Nonprofit corporations for aiding development of.
Establishment authorized, §143B-431(b).
Small business ombudsman.
Created in department, purposes, §143B-432.1.
Tax incentives for new and expanding businesses generally, §§105-129.2 to 105-129.13.
See TAX INCENTIVES FOR NEW AND EXPANDING BUSINESSES.
Trade jobs for success initiative.
Components, §143B-438.16(c).
Established within department, §143B-438.16(a).
Legislative findings, §143B-438.15(a).
Policy of state, §143B-438.15(b).
Purpose, §143B-438.15(c).
Reports, §143B-438.17.
Trade jobs for success fund, §143B-438.16(b).
Transfers to department.
Divisions and councils of department of natural resources and economic development, §143B-432(a), (c).
Navigation and pilotage commission, §143B-451.
Subunits of department of natural resources and economic development, §143B-432(b).
Travel and tourism.
Board, §143B-434.1.
Policy act, §143B-434.2.
Unemployment compensation, §§96-1 to 96-29.
See UNEMPLOYMENT COMPENSATION.
Urban progress zones.
Defined, §143B-437.09(a).
Determination of secretary, §143B-437.09(c).
Limitations on area included within, §143B-437.09(b).

COMMERCE DEPARTMENT —Cont'd
Urban progress zones —Cont'd
Property partially located within,
§143B-437.09(d).
Publication of list of zones, §143B-437.09(c).
Workforce development, §§143B-438.10 to
143B-438.13.
Workforce development commission,
§143B-438.10.

COMMERCIAL ABC PERMITS, §18B-1100.

COMMERCIAL BANKING LAW, §§53-1 to
53-208.30.
See BANKS.

COMMERCIAL BRIBERY, §14-353.

COMMERCIAL CODE.
**Amendatory act, effective date and transition
provision,** §§25-11-101 to 25-11-108.
See SECURED TRANSACTIONS.
Bank deposits and collections, §§25-4-101 to
25-4-504.
See BANK DEPOSITS AND COLLECTIONS.
Documents of title, §§25-7-101 to 25-7-603.
See DOCUMENTS OF TITLE.
Effective date, §25-10-101.
Funds transfers, §§25-4A-101 to 25-4A-507.
See FUNDS TRANSFERS.
General provisions, §§25-1-101 to 25-1-310.
Acceleration.
Option to accelerate at will, §25-1-309.
Acceptance under reservation of rights,
§25-1-308(a).
Accord and satisfaction.
Reservation of rights.
Performance or acceptance under reservation
of rights, §25-1-308(a).
Action.
Defined, §25-1-201(b)(1).
Enforceability of rights by action, §25-1-305(b).
Aggrieved party.
Defined, §25-1-201(b)(2).
Agreements.
Defined, §25-1-201(b)(3).
Applicability of act.
Territorial application, §25-1-301(a).
Bankruptcy and insolvency.
Definitions, §25-1-201(b)(22), (b)(23).
Banks and financial institutions.
Branches.
Defined, §25-1-201(b)(7).
Defined, §25-1-201(b)(4).
Bearer.
Defined, §25-1-201(b)(5).
Breach of contract.
Waiver or renunciation of claim or right after
breach, §25-1-306.
Burden of proof.
Definition of burden of establishing a fact,
§25-1-201(b)(8).
Option to accelerate at will.
Burden of establishing lack of good faith,
§25-1-309.
Buyer in ordinary course of business.
Defined, §25-1-201(b)(9).
Choice of law.
Power to choose applicable law, §25-1-301(c).
Territorial applicability, §25-1-301(a).
Citation.
Short titles, §25-1-101(a), (b).

COMMERCIAL CODE —Cont'd
General provisions —Cont'd
Common law principles.
Applicable to construction of article,
§25-1-103(b).
Conflicts of law.
Construction of chapter, §25-1-103(b).
Conspicuous.
Defined, §25-1-201(b)(10).
Construction and interpretation, §§25-1-101 to
25-1-310.
Choice of law.
Power to choose applicable law, §25-1-301(c).
Territorial applicability, §25-1-301(a).
Citation, §25-1-101(a), (b).
Common law principles applicable, §25-1-103(b).
Conflicts of law, §25-1-103(b).
Definitions, general provisions, §25-1-201(a).
Electronic signatures in global and national
commerce act.
Article modifies, limits and supersedes federal
act, §25-1-108.
Gender, reference to, §25-1-106.
Implied repeal, construction against, §25-1-104.
Liberal construction, §25-1-103(a).
Obligation of good faith, §25-1-304.
Option to accelerate at will, §25-1-309.
Presumptions, §25-1-206.
Reasonable time, §25-1-205(a).
Relations to state test, §25-1-301(a), (b).
Seasonably, §25-1-205(b).
Section captions, §25-1-107.
Severability, §25-1-105.
Singular and plural, use of, §25-1-106.
Territorial applicability, §25-1-301(a).
Variation by agreement.
Effect of chapter varied by agreement,
§25-1-302(a).
Good faith, diligence, reasonableness and
care, §25-1-302(b).
"Unless otherwise agreed" or similar words,
§25-1-302(c).
Contracts.
Defined, §25-1-201(b).
Reservation of rights.
Performance or acceptance under reservation
of rights, §25-1-308(a).
Course of dealing.
Defined, §25-1-303(b).
Express terms of an agreement, §25-1-303(e).
Vocation or trade of parties, §25-1-303(d).
Creditors.
Defined, §25-1-201(b).
Subordinated obligations, §25-1-310.
Definitions, general provisions.
Action, §25-1-201(b).
Aggrieved party, §25-1-201(b).
Agreements, §25-1-201(b).
Bank, §25-1-201(b).
Bearer, §25-1-201(b).
Bills of lading, §25-1-201(b).
Branch, §25-1-201(b).
Burden of establishing a fact, §25-1-201(b).
Buyer in ordinary course of business,
§25-1-201(b).
Conspicuous, §25-1-201(b).
Construction of words and phrases,
§25-1-201(a).
Contracts, §25-1-201(b).
Creditors, §25-1-201(b).
Defendant, §25-1-201(b).

COMMERCIAL CODE —Cont'd
General provisions —Cont'd
  Definitions, general provisions —Cont'd
    Delivery, §25-1-201(b).
    Fault, §25-1-201(b).
    Fungible, §25-1-201(b).
    Genuine, §25-1-201(b).
    Good faith, §25-1-201(b).
    Holder, §25-1-201(b).
    Honor, §25-1-201(b).
    Insolvency proceedings, §25-1-201(b).
    Insolvent, §25-1-201(b).
    Money, §25-1-201(b).
    Notice, §25-1-201(b).
    Organization, §25-1-201(b).
    Party, §25-1-201(b).
    Person, §25-1-201(b).
    Presumption, §25-1-201(b).
    Purchase, §25-1-201(b).
    Purchaser, §25-1-201(b).
    Remedy, §25-1-201(b).
    Representative, §25-1-201(b).
    Rights, §25-1-201(b).
    Security interest, §25-1-201(b).
    Send, §25-1-201(b).
    Signed, §25-1-201(b).
    Surety, §25-1-201(b).
    Telegram, §25-1-201(b).
    Term, §25-1-201(b).
    Unauthorized, §25-1-201(b).
    Value, §25-1-201(b).
    Warehouse receipt, §25-1-201(b).
    Writing, §25-1-201(b).
  Delivery.
    Defined, §25-1-201(b).
  Discover.
    Defined, §25-1-202(c).
  Due diligence.
    Notice, knowledge or a notice or notification.
      When received by an organization,
        §25-1-202(f).
  Electronic signatures in global and national
      commerce act.
    Article modifies, limits and supersedes federal
        act, §25-1-108.
  Executors and administrators.
    Representative.
      Defined, §25-1-201(b)(35).
  Fault.
    Defined, §25-1-201(b)(16).
  Fungible.
    Defined, §25-1-201(b)(17).
  Genuine.
    Defined, §25-1-201(b)(18).
  Gives.
    Defined, §25-1-202(d).
  Good faith.
    Exercising option to accelerate, §25-1-309.
    Obligation of good faith, §25-1-304.
  Holder.
    Defined, §25-1-201(b)(20).
  Honor.
    Defined, §25-1-201(b)(21).
  Indorsements.
    Unauthorized indorsements.
      Defined, §25-1-201(b).
  Knowledge.
    Defined, §25-1-202(b).
    Received by an organization.
      When effective upon, §25-1-202(f).

COMMERCIAL CODE —Cont'd
General provisions —Cont'd
  Knows.
    Defined, §25-1-202(b).
  Learn.
    Defined, §25-1-202(c).
  Leases, security interest distinguished.
    Cost of performing determination, §25-1-203(e).
    Factors for determining question of fact,
        §25-1-203(b).
    Fair market rent or fair market value
        determination, §25-1-203(e).
    Nominal additional consideration, §25-1-203(d).
    Question of fact determined by each case,
        §25-1-203(a).
    "Reasonable predictable" determination,
        §25-1-203(e).
    "Remaining economic life of the good"
        determination, §25-1-203(e).
    When security interest not created, §25-1-203(c).
  Money.
    Defined, §25-1-201(b).
  Notice.
    Defined, §25-1-201(b).
    Notifies defined, §25-1-202(d).
    Received by an organization.
      When effective upon, §25-1-202(f).
    When a person has notice of a
        "fact,"§25-1-202(a).
  Options.
    Acceleration at will, §25-1-309.
  Organization.
    Defined, §25-1-201(b).
  Parties.
    Aggrieved party.
      Defined, §25-1-201(b).
    Defendants.
      Defined, §25-1-201(b).
    Defined, §25-1-201(b).
  Performance.
    Course of performance.
      Defined, §25-1-303(a).
      Evidence relevant to show waiver or
          modification term inconsistent with,
          §25-1-303(e).
      Express terms of an agreement, §25-1-303(e).
      Vocation or trade of parties, §25-1-303(d).
  Person.
    Defined, §25-1-201(b).
  Presumptions.
    Defined, §25-1-201(b).
    Evidentiary effect, §25-1-206.
  Protests.
    Performance or acceptance under reservation of
        rights, §25-1-308(a).
  Purchasers.
    Defined, §25-1-201(b).
  Purchases.
    Defined, §25-1-201(b).
  Receives.
    Defined, §25-1-202(e).
  Remedies.
    Defined, §25-1-201(b).
    Enforceable by action, §25-1-305(b).
    Liberal administration, §25-1-305(a).
  Representatives.
    Defined, §25-1-201(b).
  Reservation of rights.
    Performance or acceptance under reservation of
        rights, §25-1-308(a).
  Scope of article, §25-1-102.

COMMERCIAL CODE —Cont'd
General provisions —Cont'd
Send.
Defined, §25-1-201(b).
Severability of provisions, §25-1-105.
Short titles, §25-1-101(a), (b).
Signed.
Defined, §25-1-201(b).
Subordinated obligations, §25-1-310.
Suretyship.
Defined, §25-1-201(b).
Telegram.
Defined, §25-1-201(b).
Third party documents.
Document in due form.
Prima facie evidence authenticity and
genuineness, §25-1-307.
Time.
Reasonable time, construed, §25-1-205(a).
Usage of trade.
Course of dealing prevails over, §25-1-303(f).
Defined, §25-1-303(c).
Evidence of relevant usage offered by a party,
§25-1-303(g).
Express terms of an agreement, §25-1-303(e).
Vocation or trade of parties, §25-1-303(d).
Value.
Defined, §25-1-201(b).
Written.
Defined, §25-1-201(b).
Global TransPark authority.
Bond issues.
Status of bonds and notes under code, §63A-17.
Investment securities, §§25-8-101 to 25-8-511.
See INVESTMENT SECURITIES.
Leases, §§25-2A-101 to 25-2A-532.
See LEASES, UCC.
Letters of credit, §§25-5-101 to 25-5-118.
See LETTERS OF CREDIT.
Local government finance.
Status of revenue bonds under code, §159-92.
Negotiable instruments, §§25-3-101 to 25-3-605.
See NEGOTIABLE INSTRUMENTS.
Prior registration statutes.
Covered transactions not subject to, §25-10-106.
Repeals.
General repealer, §25-10-103.
Specific repealer, §25-10-102(1).
Transition provision, §25-10-102(2).
Sales, §§25-2-101 to 25-2-725.
See SALE OF GOODS, UCC.
Secured transactions, §§25-9-101 to 25-9-710.
See SECURED TRANSACTIONS.

COMMERCIAL DETECTION SERVICES.
Drug detection dogs utilized, §90-102.1(h).

COMMERCIAL DRIVERS' LICENSES,
§§20-37.10 to 20-37.23.
Address.
Change of address.
Applications for duplicates, §20-37.15(b).
Age.
Minimum age for, §20-9(a).
Applications.
Contents, §20-37.15(a).
Duplicates.
Change of name or address, §20-37.15(b).
Fees, §20-37.15(a1).
Prohibition against reapplying for certain period.
Persons whose licenses canceled for failure to
give correct information or for committing
fraud, §20-15(c).

COMMERCIAL DRIVERS' LICENSES —Cont'd
Cancellation of driving privileges.
Driving commercial motor vehicle prohibited,
§20-37.12(b).
Notification required by drivers, §20-37.18(c).
Change of address.
Duplicates.
Applications for, §20-37.15(b).
Change of names.
Duplicates.
Applications for, §20-37.15(b).
**Chemical analysis of impairing substances in
blood.**
Refusal to submit to chemical test.
Disqualification.
Effect, §20-17.5(c).
Child support enforcement.
Forfeiture of licensing privilege for failure to pay,
§50-13.12.
Suspension, revocation or restriction of license,
§110-142.2.
Citation of article, §20-37.10.
Classes, §20-37.16(b).
Commissioner of motor vehicles.
Authority to enter agreements, §20-37.23.
Content of licenses, §20-37.16(a).
Controlled substances.
Disqualification from driving commercial vehicle.
Commission of felony involving drugs,
§20-17.4(c).
Testing positive in a drug or alcohol test,
§20-17.4(l).
Appeal of disqualification, §20-37.20B.
Employer's notification of division,
§20-37.19(c).
Notation on driving record, §20-37.20A.
**Convictions of violations of state law or local
ordinances relating to motor vehicle traffic
control.**
Nonresidents.
Notification of traffic convictions, §20-37.20(a).
Notification required by drivers, §20-37.18(a), (b).
Defined, §20-4.01.
Disqualification, §20-17.4(a) to (m).
Additional disqualification period.
Driving while disqualified, §20-28(d).
Article governing revocation of drivers' licenses
and disqualification of commercial drivers'
licenses, §20-24(d).
Defined, §20-4.01.
Driving while disqualified, §20-28(d).
One year disqualification, §20-17.4(a).
Drug or alcohol test.
Testing positive, §20-17.4(l).
Effect.
Conviction that requires both disqualification
and revocation, §20-17.5(b).
Conviction that requires disqualification but not
revocation, §20-17.5(a).
Disqualification for refusing to take chemical
tests, §20-17.5(c).
Restoration fee.
When disqualified person must pay,
§20-17.5(e).
Right to obtain regular class C driver's license,
§20-17.5(d).
Employers prohibited from allowing, permitting or
authorizing driver to drive commercial motor
vehicle during period of, §20-37.19(b).
Imminent hazard.
Drivers determined to constitute, §20-17.4(m).

COMMERCIAL DRIVERS' LICENSES —Cont'd
Disqualification —Cont'd
Issuance of driver's license or learner's permit
while person disqualified.
Prohibited, §20-37.13(d).
Less than year, §20-17.4(d).
Life disqualification, §20-17.4(c).
Modified life, §20-17.4(b).
Without possibility of reinstatement,
§20-17.4(c1).
Without reduction, §20-17.4(b1).
Notation on driving record, §20-37.20A.
Notification required by drivers, §20-37.18(c).
One year, §20-17.4(a).
Out-of-service order violation, §20-17.4(g).
Hazardous materials and passenger offenses,
§20-17.4(h).
Out-of-state violations, §20-17.4(i).
Person without commercial driver's license,
§20-17.4(j).
Railroad crossing offenses, §20-17.4(k).
Regular or commercial driver's license revoked,
§20-17.4(f).
Revocation or suspension of drivers' licenses
generally.
See DRIVERS' LICENSES.
Sex offenders, §20-17.4(n).
Unlawful to drive commercial passenger vehicle
or school bus while disqualified, §20-27.1.
Ten-day disqualification, §20-17.4(a1).
Three years, §20-17.4(e).
Division of motor vehicles.
Rulemaking authority, §20-37.22.
Driving after having consumed alcohol.
Disqualification from driving commercial vehicle,
§20-17.4(a1).
**Driving commercial motor vehicle without
license,** §20-37.21(a).
Driving while disqualified, §20-28(d).
One year disqualification, §20-17.4(a).
Duplicates.
Change of name or address, §20-37.15(b).
Employers.
Defined, §20-4.01.
Disqualification.
Prohibited from allowing, permitting or
authorizing driver to drive commercial
motor vehicle during period of, §20-37.19(b).
Drivers possessing more than one driver license.
Allowing, permitting or authorizing driver to
drive, §20-37.19(b).
Drug or alcohol tests.
Notification of receipt of confirmation of
employee's positive test results,
§20-37.19(c).
Information required to be supplied by drivers,
§20-37.18(d).
Employers to require, §20-37.19(a).
Out-of-service order.
Drive or vehicle subject to.
Allowing, permitting or authorizing driver to
drive, §20-37.19(b).
Endorsements.
Categories, §20-37.16(c).
Expiration of H and X endorsements,
§20-37.16(c2).
Security threat.
Person determined to constitute.
Revocation, §20-15(d).
Sex offenders.
Licenses with P or S endorsement.
Prohibited, §20-37.14A.

COMMERCIAL DRIVERS' LICENSES —Cont'd
Examinations.
Administering, §20-37.13(b).
Qualification standards, §20-37.13(a).
Waiver, §20-37.13(c), (c1).
Exemptions from provisions.
Persons taking up residence in state on
permanent basis exempt for thirty days,
§20-37.12(e).
Failure to carry license.
Production of license on date of court appearance.
No conviction, §20-37.12(f).
**Federal commercial motor vehicle safety act of
1986.**
Purpose of article to implement, §20-37.11.
**Federal license granting privilege of driving
commercial vehicle.**
Holder permitted to drive without further
examination or licensure, §20-37.12(d).
Fees.
Applications for commercial driver licenses,
§20-37.15(a1).
Issuance, §20-37.16(d).
Felonies.
Forfeiture of driving privilege after conviction,
§15A-1331A.
**Forfeiture of driving privilege after conviction
of felony,** §15A-1331A.
**Forfeiture of licensing privilege for failure to
pay child support,** §50-13.12.
Hazardous materials endorsements.
Expiration of H and X endorsements,
§20-37.16(c2).
Hit and run driving.
Disqualification from driving commercial vehicle,
§20-17.4(a).
Impaired driving.
Disqualification from driving commercial vehicle,
§20-17.4(a), (b), (b1).
Infractions.
Violation of employer responsibilities, §20-37.21(c).
Violations of notice requirements by drivers,
§20-37.21(b).
Issuance.
Fees, §20-37.16(d).
Record check and notification of license issuance,
§20-37.17.
Learners' permits, §20-37.13(e).
Sex offenders.
Permit with P or S endorsement not issued to,
§20-37.33(f).
Misdemeanors, §20-37.21(a).
Names.
Change of names.
Applications for duplicates, §20-37.15(b).
Nonresidents.
Issuance of nonresident commercial driver's
license, §20-37.14.
Notification of traffic violations, §20-37.20(a).
Requirements, §20-37.12(d).
Notice.
Drivers.
Notification required by drivers, §20-37.18.
Issuance of commercial drivers' licenses.
Notification to commercial driver license
information system, §20-37.17.
Nonresidents.
Traffic violations, §20-37.20(a).
Out-of-service order.
Defined, §20-4.01.

COMMERCIAL DRIVERS' LICENSES —Cont'd
Out-of-service order —Cont'd
Disqualification from driving.
Violation of order, §20-17.4(g), (h).
Employer allowing driver to drive vehicle.
Prohibition, §20-37.19(b).
Penalties, §20-37.21.
Points.
Schedule of point values, §20-16(c).
Possessing more than one license.
Employers prohibited from allowing, permitting or
authorizing driver to drive commercial motor
vehicle, §20-37.19(b).
Prohibited, §20-30.
Purposes of article, §20-37.11.
Qualifications, §20-37.13(a).
Railroad grade crossing offenses.
Disqualification from driving commercial vehicle,
§20-17.4(k).
Employer permitting employees to violate
requirements.
Penalties, §20-37.21(d).
Record check prior to issuance, §20-37.17.
Required, §20-37.12(a).
Waiver of requirement.
Classes of vehicles, §20-37.16(e).
Revocation or suspension.
Disqualification. See within this heading,
"Disqualification."
Driving privileges.
Driving commercial motor vehicle prohibited,
§20-37.12(b).
Driving when license revoked or suspended.
Disqualification, §20-17.4(a).
Employers prohibited from allowing, permitting or
authorizing driver to drive commercial motor
vehicle during period of, §20-37.19(b).
Issuance of commercial driver's license or
learner's permit while driver's license
suspended or revoked, §20-37.13(d).
Notification required by drivers, §20-37.18(c).
Security threat, person determined to constitute,
§20-15(d).
Sexual offense conviction requiring offender to
register as sex offender.
Revocation of license with P or S endorsement,
§20-17.9.
Rules and regulations.
Rulemaking authority of division, §20-37.22.
School bus drivers required to hold, §20-218(a).
School buses.
S endorsement, required to drive, §20-37.16(c).
School bus defined, §20-37.16(f).
Waiver of test for S endorsement, §20-37.16(c1).
Serious traffic violations.
Defined, §20-4.01.
**Sex offenders convicted of offense requiring
registration.**
Disqualification for conviction, §20-17.4(n).
Learners' permits with P or S endorsement.
Issuance prohibited, §20-37.33(f).
Licenses with P or S endorsement.
Affidavit person not on sex offender registries.
Division unable to access, §20-37.14A(b).
False affidavit, criminal penalty,
§20-37.14A(c).
Disqualification from driving during registration
period, §14-208.19A(c).
Driving without license, §14-208.19A(d).
False affidavit or swearing.
Criminal penalty, §20-37.14A(c).

COMMERCIAL DRIVERS' LICENSES —Cont'd
**Sex offenders convicted of offense requiring
registration** —Cont'd
Licenses with P or S endorsement —Cont'd
Issuance prohibited, §20-37.14A(a), (b).
Petition for hearing on denial, §20-37.14A(b).
Revocation, §20-17.9.
Search of sex offender registries.
Required prior to issuance of license,
§20-37.14A(b).
Unlawful to drive commercial passenger vehicle or
school bus without license or while
disqualified, §20-27.1.
Skills test, waiver, §20-37.13(c), (c1).
Standards.
Qualification standards, §20-37.13(a).
Suspension for child support delinquency,
§110-142.2.
Title of article, §20-37.10.
Vehicular homicide or manslaughter.
Disqualification from driving commercial vehicle,
§20-17.4(a).
Waiver of licenses.
Classes of vehicles, §20-37.16(e).
Waiver of skills test, §20-37.13(c), (c1).

COMMERCIAL FEED, §§106-284.30 to
106-284.46.
See FEED.

COMMERCIAL FERTILIZERS, §§106-655 to
106-677.
See FERTILIZERS.

COMMERCIAL FISHING.
See FISH AND FISHING.

**COMMERCIAL GENERAL LIABILITY
INSURANCE.**
Extended reporting periods, §58-40-140(a).
Health care provider professional liability
insurance, §58-40-140(b), (c).

**COMMERCIAL LOAN COMMITMENTS TO BE
IN WRITING, §22-5.**

COMMERCIAL MOTOR VEHICLES.
Defined, §20-4.01.
Generally.
See COMMERCIAL VEHICLES.

COMMERCIAL PUBLICATIONS.
Hearsay exception, §8C-1 Rule 803.

**COMMERCIAL REAL ESTATE BROKER LIEN
ACT.**
Commercial real estate defined, §44A-24.2.
Generally, §§44A-24.1 to 44A-24.14.
See REAL ESTATE BROKERS.

**COMMERCIAL SOCIAL NETWORKING WEB
SITES.**
Sex offenders banned from using, §14-202.5.

COMMERCIAL VEHICLES.
Alcoholic beverages.
Operating a commercial vehicle after consuming
alcohol, §20-138.2A.
Odor of alcohol.
Evidentiary effect, §20-138.2A(b1).
Screening test for alcohol, §20-138.2A(b2).
Operating while possessing alcoholic beverages,
§20-138.2C.
Testing positive in drug or alcohol test.
Disqualification, §20-17.4(l).
Appeal of disqualification, §20-37.20B.

COMMERCIAL VEHICLES —Cont'd
Alcoholic beverages —Cont'd
Testing positive in drug or alcohol test —Cont'd
Disqualification —Cont'd
Notation of disqualification, §20-37.20A.
Employer's notification of division, §20-37.19(c).
Alcohol screening test.
Operating a commercial vehicle after consuming
alcohol, §20-138.2A(b2).
Testing positive.
Disqualification from driving, §20-17.4(l).
Appeal of disqualification, §20-37.20B.
Notation of disqualification, §20-37.20A.
Employer's notification of division, §20-37.19(c).
Commercial motor vehicle defined, §20-4.01.
Controlled substances.
Disqualification from driving.
Commission of felony involving drugs,
§20-17.4(c).
Testing positive in a drug or alcohol test,
§20-17.4(l).
Appeal of disqualification, §20-37.20B.
Employer's notification of division,
§20-37.19(c).
Notation of disqualification, §20-37.20A.
Disqualification from driving.
Additional disqualification period.
Driving while disqualified, §20-28(d).
Article governing, §20-24(d).
Conviction requiring, §20-17.5(a), (b).
Defined, §20-4.01.
Driving while disqualified, §20-28(d).
One year disqualification, §20-17.4(a).
Employers allowing, permitting or authorizing
driver during disqualification period,
§20-37.19(b).
Imminent hazard, drivers determined to
constitute, §20-17.4(m).
Issuance of driver's license or learner's permit
while person disqualified.
Prohibited, §20-37.13(d).
Less than year, §20-17.4(d).
Life disqualification, §20-17.4(c).
Modified life, §20-17.4(b).
Without possibility of reinstatement,
§20-17.4(c1).
Without reduction, §20-17.4(b1).
Notation on driving record, §20-37.20A.
Notification required by drivers, §20-37.18(c).
One year, §20-17.4(a).
Out-of-service order violation, §20-17.4(g).
Hazardous materials and passenger offenses,
§20-17.4(h).
Out-of-state violations, §20-17.4(i).
Person without commercial driver's license,
§20-17.4(j).
Railroad crossing offenses, §20-17.4(k).
Refusing to take chemical tests, §20-17.5(c).
Regular class C driver's license.
Right to obtain, §20-17.5(d).
Regular or commercial driver's license revoked,
§20-17.4(f).
Restoration fee.
When disqualified person must pay, §20-17.5(e).
Sex offenders.
Disqualification for conviction, §20-17.4(n).
Unlawful to drive commercial passenger vehicle
or school bus while disqualified, §20-27.1.
Ten-day disqualification, §20-17.4(a1).
Testing positive in a drug or alcohol test,
§20-17.4(l).
Appeal of disqualification, §20-37.20B.

COMMERCIAL VEHICLES —Cont'd
Disqualification from driving —Cont'd
Three years, §20-17.4(e).
Double penalties for driving offenses, §20-16.01.
Drivers' licenses generally, §§20-37.10 to
20-37.23.
See COMMERCIAL DRIVERS' LICENSES.
Driving after consuming alcohol.
Disqualification from driving, §20-17.4(a1).
Driving while disqualified, §20-28(d).
One year disqualification, §20-17.4(a).
Evidence.
Operation after consuming alcohol.
Odor of alcohol, §20-138.2A(b1).
Felony using commercial motor vehicles.
Special information in judgment for conviction,
§20-24(e).
Financial responsibility, §20-309(a1).
Fines.
Out of service fines, §20-17.7.
Hit and run.
Disqualification from driving, §20-17.4(a).
Special information in judgment for conviction,
§20-24(e).
Impaired driving, §20-138.2(a).
Alcohol concentration level, §20-138.2(a).
Mandatory revocation of driver's license.
Alcohol concentration level .06 or higher, tests
conclusive, §20-17(a).
Chemical analysis of impairing substances in
blood.
Applicability, §20-138.2(g).
Rebuttal evidence as to results.
Use, §20-138.2(a1).
Defenses.
Legally entitled to use alcohol or drug.
Defense precluded, §20-138.2(b).
Preventive maintenance on testing devices not
performed.
Defense precluded, §20-138.2(b1).
Disqualification from driving, §20-17.4(a), (b), (b1).
Driving after consuming alcohol, §20-17.4(a1).
Drivers' licenses.
Mandatory revocation.
Alcohol concentration level .06 or higher, tests
conclusive, §20-17(a).
Effect when impaired driving offense also charged,
§20-138.2(e).
Gross vehicle weight rating.
Proving, §20-138.2(a2).
Implied consent offense, §20-138.2(d).
Misdemeanor, §20-138.2(e).
Offense defined, §20-138.2(a).
Operating a commercial vehicle after consuming
alcohol.
Generally, §20-138.2A(a).
Implied-consent offense, §20-138.2A(b).
Penalty, §20-138.2A(c).
Second or subsequent conviction.
Punishment, §20-138.2A(c).
What constitutes, §20-138.2A(d).
Pleading.
Sufficiency, §20-138.2(c).
Restoration of driver's license after conviction,
§20-17.6.
Special information required in judgment for
conviction, §20-24(e).
Life disqualification, §20-17.4(c).
Modified life, §20-17.4(b).
Without possibility of reinstatement, §20-17.4(c1).
Without reduction, §20-17.4(b1).

COMMERCIAL VEHICLES —Cont'd
Load protruding from rear or sides.
Federal regulation, compliance required, §20-117(b).
Markings on vehicles.
Vehicles of certain weight used in intrastate commerce, §20-101(b).
Motor carriers, §§62-259 to 62-280.1.
See MOTOR CARRIERS.
Motor vehicle financial responsibility, §20-309(a1).
Name of owner on both sides of vehicle.
Vehicles of certain weight used in intrastate commerce, §20-101(b).
Operating while possessing alcoholic beverages, §20-138.2C.
Out of service fines, §20-17.7.
Out-of-service order.
Disqualification from driving.
Violation of order, §20-17.4(g), (h).
Employer allowing driver subject to order to drive, §20-37.19(b).
Points.
Double penalties, §20-16.01.
Schedule of point values, §20-16(c).
Railroad grade crossing violations.
Disqualification from driving, §20-17.4(k).
Employer permitting employees to violate requirements.
Moving heavy equipment at crossing, §20-142.4(g).
Obedience to railroad signal, §20-142.1(e).
Penalties, §20-37.21(d).
Stopping at crossing, §20-142.3(f).
Stop sign violations, §20-142.2.
Reckless driving.
Schedule of point values, §20-16(c).
Repair of motor vehicles, §§20-354 to 20-354.9.
See MOTOR VEHICLE REPAIRS.
Sex offenders convicted of offense requiring registration.
Disqualification for conviction, §20-17.4(n).
Unlawful to drive commercial passenger vehicle or school bus without license or while disqualified, §20-27.1.
Special mobile equipment.
Towing certain vehicles, §20-140.5.
Speeding.
Schedule of point values, §20-16(c).
Tires on vehicles with GVWR of 10,001 pounds or more.
Safe tire requirement, unsafe tires, §20-122.1(a1).
Towing.
Federal regulation for vehicles used for.
Compliance required, §20-117(b).
Uninsured motorist coverage, §20-279.21(b).
Vehicular homicide.
Disqualification from driving, §20-17.4(a).
Zero tolerance law.
Disqualification from driving.
Driving after consuming alcohol, §20-17.4(a1).

COMMINGLED GOODS IN SECURED TRANSACTIONS.
Priority of security interests.
Provisions effective July 1, 2001, §25-9-336.

COMMISSIONER OF AGRICULTURE.
See AGRICULTURE COMMISSIONER.

COMMISSIONER OF BANKS, §§53-92 to 53-116.
See BANKS COMMISSIONER.

COMMISSIONER OF INSURANCE.
Generally, §§58-2-1 to 58-2-250.
See INSURANCE COMMISSIONER.

COMMISSIONER OF LABOR.
Generally.
See LABOR COMMISSIONER.

COMMISSIONER OF MOTOR VEHICLES.
Generally.
See MOTOR VEHICLES COMMISSIONER.

COMMISSIONERS.
Agriculture.
See AGRICULTURE COMMISSIONER.
Appointment.
Fees of commissioners appointed by magistrate, §7A-310.
Compensation.
Deposition taking.
Allowance of costs to either party or apportioned in discretion of court, §6-21.
Costs.
Deposition taking.
Allowance of costs to either party or apportioned in discretion of court, §6-21.
County boards of commissioners.
See COUNTY BOARDS OF COMMISSIONERS.
Fees.
Appointment by magistrate, §7A-310.
Insurance.
Generally, §§58-2-1 to 58-2-250.
See INSURANCE COMMISSIONER.
Labor.
See LABOR COMMISSIONER.
Magistrates.
Appointment of commissioner by magistrate.
Fees of commissioners, §7A-310.
Issuing notices to commissioners.
Fee of magistrate, §7A-309.
Motor vehicles.
See MOTOR VEHICLES COMMISSIONER.
Oaths.
Form of oath, §11-11.
Opening and clearing streams, §§77-1 to 77-11.
See STREAMS.
Special proceedings.
See SPECIAL PROCEEDINGS.

COMMISSIONERS OF SALE.
Special proceedings.
See SPECIAL PROCEEDINGS.

COMMISSIONS.
Boards and commissions.
See BOARDS AND COMMISSIONS.

COMMITMENT FEES.
Home loan secured by first mortgage or first deed of trust, §24-1.1A(c).

COMMITMENT FOR LOANS.
Contract rates and fees, §24-1.1.
Savings and loan association interest rates, §24-1.4.

COMMITMENT ORDERS.
Prisoners, §15A-1301.
Sentencing, §15A-1353.

COMMITMENTS AND PRELIMINARY EXAMINATIONS.
Defendants found not guilty by reason of insanity.
Civil commitment, §15A-1321(a), (b).
Generally, §15A-521(a).

COMMITMENTS AND PRELIMINARY EXAMINATIONS —Cont'd
Involuntary commitments.
  Mental health, developmental disabilities and substance abuse.
    See MENTAL HEALTH, DEVELOPMENTAL DISABILITY, SUBSTANCE ABUSE.
Orders, §15A-521(b).
  Delivery, §15A-521(c).
  Modification, §15A-521(b).
Receipt of prisoner, §15A-521(c).
Witnesses, §15A-521(d).

COMMITTEES.
Powers generally, §§32-25 to 32-27.
  See FIDUCIARIES.
Uniform fiduciaries act, §§32-1 to 32-13.
  See FIDUCIARIES.

COMMITTEES (PUBLIC BODIES).
America's four hundredth anniversary committee, §§143B-85, 143B-86.
Committee on inaugural ceremonies, §§143-532 to 143-539.
Compensation for services.
  Per diem, subsistence and travel expenses, §138-5(a) to (f).
Consumer and advocacy advisory committee for the blind, §§143B-163, 143B-164.
Economic investment committee.
  Job development investment grant program, §143B-437.54.
Ethics.
  State government ethics act, §§138A-1 to 138A-45.
Executive Mansion fine arts committee, §§143-410 to 143-415, 143B-79 to 143B-80.1.
Expiration of council created by governor or other state officials.
  Constitutional elective officers creating, §147-16.2(b).
  Executive branch officials creating, §147-16.2(c).
  Executive order of governor creating, §147-16.2(a).
Gender based appointments.
  Appointing members to statutorily created decision making or regulatory entities.
    Appointments to reflect proportion that gender represents in population of state, §143-157.1(a).
    Report by appointing authority of number of appointments of each gender, §143-157.1(b).
    Local government reporting, §143-157.1(d).
    State reporting, §143-157.1(c).
Green business fund advisory committee, §143B-437.5.
Job development investment grant program.
  Economic investment committee, §143B-437.54.
Jobs for veterans committee, §§143B-420, 143B-421.
Joint legislative committee on local government, §§120-157.1 to 120-174.
  See GENERAL ASSEMBLY.
Joint legislative economic development and global engagement oversight committee, §§120-70.130 to 120-70.132.
Joint legislative oversight committee on health and human services, §§120-208 to 120-208.4.
Joint legislative oversight committee on justice and public safety, §§120-70.93 to 120-70.95.
Joint legislative transportation oversight committee, §§120-70.50 to 120-70.52.

COMMITTEES (PUBLIC BODIES) —Cont'd
Legislative ethics committee, §§120-99 to 120-106.
NC green business fund advisory committee, §143B-437.5.
Nonpoint source pollution control program committee, §106-852.
North Carolina awards committee, §§143B-83, 143B-84.
North Carolina trails committee, §§143B-333, 143B-334.
Per diem, subsistence and travel expenses, §138-5(a) to (f).
Pesticide advisory committee, §143-439.
Professional advisory committee, §§143B-161, 143B-162.
Revenue laws study committee, §§120-70.105 to 120-70.107.
Third party administrators, §58-56-65.
Writing required to create, §147-16.2(d).

COMMODITIES, §§78D-1 to 78D-33.
Actions.
  Civil penalties.
    Enforcement of act, §78D-22(a).
  Declaratory judgments.
    Enforcement of act, §78D-22(b).
  Enforcement of chapter, §78D-22.
  Injunctive relief.
    Enforcement of act, §78D-22(b).
  Judicial review.
    Orders, §78D-31.
  Restitution of reparation.
    Enforcement of act, §78D-22(a).
Activities.
  Fraudulent conduct, §78D-6.
  Unlawful commodity activities, §78D-5.
    Board of trade.
      Failure to obtain authority of federal government, §78D-5(b).
    Licenses.
      Temporary license.
        Failure to obtain, §78D-5(a).
    Registration.
      Failure to obtain, §78D-5(a).
Administration of act, §78D-25.
  Confidentiality of information, §78D-25(c).
    Exceptions, §78D-25(c).
    Insider trading prohibited, §78D-25(b).
    Prohibited disclosures, §78D-25(b).
  Cooperation with other agencies, §78D-26.
  Powers and duties of administrator, §78D-25(a).
  Secretary of state defined as administrator, §78D-1.
Bonds, surety.
  Official action under chapter.
    Administrator not required to post, §78D-23(b).
Buys or offers to buy in state, §78D-29(b).
Cease and desist orders.
  Enforcement of act, §78D-22(a).
Civil penalties, §78D-22(a).
Confidentiality of information, §78D-25.
Conflict of laws.
  Securities and other laws unaffected, §78D-8.
Construction and interpretation.
  Comity with other agencies.
    Uniform application and interpretation of act, §78D-26(a).
  Criminal penalties.
    Violations of act, §78D-24(e).

COMMODITIES —Cont'd
Construction and interpretation —Cont'd
Liability.
Good faith compliance with agency rules, orders or forms, §78D-27(d).
Purpose of act, §78D-9.
Scope of act, §78D-29.
Cooperation with other agencies, §78D-26.
Activities for which cooperation authorized, §78D-26(b).
Uniform application and interpretation of act, §78D-26(a).
Criminal penalties, §78D-24.
Criminal procedure.
Referral for prosecution to attorney general or district attorney, §78D-24(d).
Defenses.
Affirmative defenses, §78D-33.
Definitions, §78D-1.
Qualified seller, §78D-4(b).
Enforcement of act, §78D-22.
Exempt person transactions.
Defined, §78D-3.
Exempt transactions.
Defined, §78D-4.
Enumeration, §78D-4(a).
Limitations on authority to engage in business as a qualified seller, §78D-4(d).
When limitations proper, §78D-4(d).
Revocation of exemption.
Business dissolution, §78D-4(f).
Disability warranting revocation, §78D-4(f).
Rules and regulations.
Authority of administrator to issue rules or orders, §78D-4(g).
Suspension of exemption.
Public interest or the protection of investors, §78D-4(e).
Waiver of exemption requirements.
Conditional or unconditional, §78D-4(c).
Felonies.
Violations of act, §78D-24(a).
Fines.
Violations of chapter.
When allowed, §78D-24(b), (c).
Forms.
Adoption or modification.
Approval of administrator required, §78D-27(b).
Authority of administrator to create, §78D-27(a).
Publication authority of administrator, §78D-27(c).
Fraudulent conduct, §78D-6.
Futures contracts.
Void, §16-3.
Good faith compliance with agency rules, orders or forms, §78D-27(d).
Hearings.
Commencement of administrative proceedings, §78D-30.
Investigations, §78D-21.
Injunctions, §78D-22(b).
Investigations.
Application of administrator to court to compel production of documents and attendance of witnesses, §78D-21(d).
Authority of administrator to conduct, §78D-21(a).
Discretion of administrator in appointment of law enforcement officers, §78D-21(e).
Powers and duties of administrator in investigatory proceedings, §78D-21(c).
Publication by administrator of information on violations authorized, §78D-21(b).

COMMODITIES —Cont'd
Legal or equitable remedies.
Power of court to grant, §78D-23(a) to (c).
Negligence, §78D-7(a).
Offer of sales or to buy in state.
Defined, §78D-29(d).
Parties' presence in state immaterial, §78D-29(c).
When not made in state, §78D-29(e).
Orders.
Adoption or modification.
Approval of administrator required, §78D-27(b).
Authority of administrator to issue, §78D-27(a).
Enforcement of act, §78D-22(a).
Final orders, §78D-30.
Judicial review, §78D-31.
How obtained, §78D-31(a).
Commencement of proceedings, §78D-31(b).
Procedure for entry of an order, §78D-30.
Summary orders, §78D-30.
Finality of summary orders, §78D-30.
Packages.
Information required, §81A-27.
Unit price, declaration, §81A-28.
Pleadings.
Exemptions, §78D-32.
Powers of attorney.
Powers conferred by statutory short form, §32A-2.
Principals, consulting persons and others, §78D-7.
Procedure for entry of an order.
Finality of summary orders.
When final, §78D-30(d).
Final orders.
When final, §78D-30(f).
How administrative proceedings commenced, §78D-30(a).
Notice to interested parties of hearing, §78D-30(e).
Notification to interested parties, §78D-30(b).
When matter may be set for hearing, §78D-30(c).
Prohibited commodity transactions.
Defined, §78D-2.
Purpose, §78D-9.
Qualified sellers.
Defined, §78D-4(b).
Respondeat superior, §78D-7(b).
Restitution or reparation, §78D-22(a).
Rules and regulations.
Adoption or modification.
Approval of administrator required, §78D-27(b).
Authority of administrator to adopt, §78D-27(a).
Exempt transactions.
Authority of administrator to issue rules or orders, §78D-4(g).
Sales or offer of sales in state, §78D-29(a).
Scope of act, §§78D-9, 78D-29.
Securities.
Conflict of laws, §78D-8.
Service of process.
Consent to service of process, §78D-28.
Unlawful commodity activities, §78D-5.
Board of trade.
Failure to obtain authority of federal government, §78D-5(b).
Fraudulent conduct, §78D-6.
Registration.
Failure to obtain, §78D-5(a).
Temporary license.
Failure to obtain, §78D-5(a).
Unlawful commodity transactions.
Defined, §78D-2.
Exempt person transactions, §78D-3.

COMMODITIES —Cont'd
Unlawful commodity transactions —Cont'd
Exempt transactions, §78D-4.
Fraudulent conduct, §78D-6.
Weights and measures.
Generally, §§81A-1 to 81A-88.
See WEIGHTS AND MEASURES.

COMMON CARRIERS.
Alcoholic beverages.
Commercial transportation, §18B-1115.
Commercial transportation permits, §18B-1115(a).
Wine shippers.
Direct shipments into state, §18B-1001.1(c).
Baggage.
Careful handling required, §62-202.
Checks affixed to parcels of baggage, §62-203(d),
(e).
Unclaimed baggage, sale, §62-209.
Bills of lading.
Actions by or against common carriers.
Evidence, §8-41.
Carriers generally.
See CARRIERS.
Cash-on-delivery shipments.
Prompt settlement, §62-208.
Checks affixed to parcels of baggage, §62-203(d),
(e).
Connecting lines, discrimination between,
§62-210.
Ejection of passengers.
Passengers refusing to pay fare or violating rules,
§62-151.
Free transportation.
Prohibited acts, §62-144(b).
Exceptions, §62-144(d).
Misdemeanors, §62-144(c).
Utilities commission members, §62-144(a).
Freight.
Careful handling required, §62-202.
Duty to transport within reasonable time,
§62-200(a).
Forfeiture to party aggrieved for violating
provisions, §62-200(b).
Inapplicability of section to motor carriers of
passengers, §62-200(d).
Reasonable time, determining, §62-200(c).
Freight charges settled according to rate
stipulated in bill of lading, §62-201.
Loss, damage or injury to property received for
transportation, §62-203.
Rights and remedies against prior carriers,
§62-206.
Unclaimed freight, sale, §62-209.
Human service and volunteer transportation.
Inapplicability of laws and regulations, §62-289.5.
Intoxicated persons.
Ticket may be refused, §62-150.
Joinder of causes of action.
Overcharges by carriers or undercharges by
shippers, §62-205.
Long and short hauls.
Prohibited charges, §62-141(a).
Authorization from commission, §62-141(b).
Provisions inapplicable to bus companies,
§62-141(c).
Motor carriers.
Definition of "common carrier by motor
vehicle,"§62-3.
Duties, §62-146(a).

COMMON CARRIERS —Cont'd
Motor carriers —Cont'd
Generally, §§62-259 to 62-280.1.
See MOTOR CARRIERS.
Rates, §62-146.
Additional nature of provisions, §62-146(i).
Complaints as to, §62-146(e).
Joint rates, §62-146(b), (d).
Powers of commission as to, §62-146(f).
Utilities commission.
Powers, §62-146(e) to (h).
Routes.
Deviation from regular route operations,
§62-267(a).
Overcharges.
Joinder causes of actions by shipper, §62-205.
Policy and authority of utilities commission.
Carriers of passengers, §62-2(c).
Presumption of negligence.
Injury to baggage or freight in possession or
control of carrier, §62-202.
Property taxes.
Public service corporations.
Generally, §§105-333 to 105-344.
See PROPERTY TAXES.
Railroads.
See RAILROADS.
Rates.
Definitions, §62-152.1(a).
Standard transportation practices, §62-152.2(a).
Joint rate agreements, §62-152.1(b), (c).
Antitrust law.
Exemption of parties to agreements,
§62-152.1(h).
Approval by commission, §62-152.1(d), (e), (i).
Order terminating or modifying approval,
§62-152.1(f), (g).
Investigations by commission, §62-152.1(f).
Motor common carriers, §62-146.
Standard transportation practices, §62-152.2.
Uniform rates, §62-152.1(b).
Undercharges by shippers.
Joinder of causes of actions by carrier, §62-205.
Utilities commission members.
Free transportation to, §62-144(a).
**Window tinting exception for common carrier
of passengers, §20-127(c).**

COMMON LAW.
Alcoholic beverages.
Compensation for injury caused by sales to
underage persons.
Common-law rights not abridged, §18B-128.
Attorney general.
Powers at common law, §114-1.1.
Charities.
Common law defense of charitable immunity
abolished, §1-539.9.
Commercial code.
Construction of chapter.
Applicability of common law principles,
§25-1-103(b).
Constitution of the United States.
Suits at common law, US Const Amd 7.
Contempt.
Criminal contempt.
Specified grounds for criminal contempt
exclusive, §5A-11(a).
Declared to be in force, §4-1.
Emancipation of minor.
Common law provisions superseded by article on
emancipation, §7B-3509.

COMMON LAW —Cont'd

Felony.
Defined, §14-1.

Jurisdiction.
Rule as to statutes in derogation of common law not applicable, §1-75.1.

Laws of foreign countries or states.
Proof by oral evidence, §8-3(a).

Partnerships.
Rule that statutes in derogation of common law strictly construed.
Not applicable, §59-34(a).

Phonograph records.
Restriction of or collection of royalties on commercial use.
Common law rights abrogated, §66-28.

Proof of official record.
Methods authorized by rules of evidence at common law, §1A-1 Rule 44(c).

Public lands.
Unallocated state lands.
Common law riparian or littoral rights not limited or expanded, §146-1(d).

Restraint of trade in violation of common law, §75-2.

Retaliatory employment discrimination.
Effect of article on other rights of employees under, §95-244.

Riots and civil disorders.
Provisions of article intended to supplement common law, §14-288.3.

Robbery.
Punishment for common law robbery, §14-87.1.

Rule against perpetuities.
Superseded by statutory rule, §41-22.

Securities regulation.
Crimes at common law.
Power of state to punish not restricted, §78A-57(c).

Trademarks.
Registration.
Common-law rights not adversely affected, §80-13.

Trusts and trustees.
Common law of trusts.
Supplementary to uniform code provisions, §36C-1-106.

COMMON TRUST FUNDS, §§53-163.5 to 53-163.9.

Approval of accounting, §53-163.6.

Banks.
Investment of funds held by bank, §53-163.5(d).

Court accounting, §53-163.6.

Establishment of funds, §53-163.5(a).

Short title of act, §53-163.9.

State banking commission.
Supervision by commission, §53-163.7.

Trust institutions.
Affiliation.
Criteria, §53-163.5(b).
Establishing of common trust funds, §53-163.5(a).
Investment of funds, §53-163.5(d).

Uniformity of interpretation, §53-163.8.

COMMUNICABLE DISEASES, §§130A-134 to 130A-148.

Adult care homes.
Guidelines for reporting suspected outbreaks, §131D-4.4B.
Infection prevention, §131D-4.4A.

COMMUNICABLE DISEASES —Cont'd

Adult care homes —Cont'd
Supervisors.
Infection control training, §131D-4.5C.

AIDS.
See AIDS AND HIV.

Child care operators to report, §130A-136.

Commission for public health.
Establishing lists of communicable diseases and conditions to be reported, §130A-134.
Rules of commission, §130A-147.

Confidentiality of records, §130A-143.
Access when public health concern necessitates, §130A-15.

Control measures, §130A-144(d), (e).
Compliance required, §130A-144(f).
Immunity from, §130A-144(h).
Rules to prescribe, §130A-144(g).

Death by reportable diseases.
Transportation of bodies, §130A-146.

Detention of defendant for communicable diseases.
Initial appearance before magistrate, §15A-534.3.

Diseases generally.
See DISEASES.

First responders.
Vaccination program, §130A-485(a) to (f).

Hospitals.
Reports, §130A-137.
Public health threats, emergency departments, §130A-480(a), (b).

Immunization generally, §§130A-152 to 130A-158.
See IMMUNIZATION.

Investigations by local health directors, §130A-144(a).
Access to medical records, §130A-144(b).
Immunity of persons permitting, §130A-144(c).

Isolation authority, §130A-145(a).
Entry into isolation premises, §130A-145(b).
Restrictions on applying authority, §130A-145(c), (d).

Lists of reportable diseases and conditions, §130A-134.

Local health directors.
Investigations, §130A-144(a) to (c).
Quarantine and isolation authority, §130A-145.
Reports, §130A-140.

Mass death and destruction weapons.
Nuclear, biological or chemical weapons, §§14-288.21 to 14-288.24.
See WEAPONS OF MASS DEATH AND DESTRUCTION.

Medical facilities.
Report, §130A-137.
Public health threats, emergency departments, §130A-480(a), (b).

Physicians.
Report of diseases, §130A-135.

Public health threats.
Emergency departments, reports, §130A-480(a), (b).

Quarantine authority, §130A-145(a).
Entry onto quarantine premises, §130A-145(b).
Restrictions on applying authority, §130A-145(c), (d).

Rabies, §§130A-184 to 130A-201.
See RABIES.

Records.
Confidentiality, §130A-143.
Access when public health concern necessitates, §130A-15.

COMMUNICABLE DISEASES —Cont'd
Reports.
Child care operators, §130A-136.
Form and content of reports, §130A-141.
Immunity of persons reporting, §130A-142.
Laboratories, §130A-139.
List of reportable diseases and conditions,
§130A-134.
Local health directors, §130A-140.
Medical facilities, §130A-137.
Physicians, §130A-135.
Public health threats.
Emergency departments, §130A-480(a), (b).
Restaurants and other food or drink
establishments, §130A-138.
School principals, §130A-136.
Temporary order to report health related
information, §130A-141.1.
Time limits for reporting, §130A-141.
Rules and regulations.
Control measures, §130A-144(g).
Detection, control and prevention of communicable
diseases, §130A-147.
School principals, reporting, §130A-136.
Sexually transmitted diseases.
Consent of minor for treatment sufficient,
§90-21.5(a).
Defendants accused of offense involving vaginal,
anal or oral intercourse.
Testing on request of victim, §15A-615.
Failure to obtain treatment, §130A-25(b).
Imprisonment, §130A-25(c).
Form and content of reports, §130A-141.
Laboratory reports.
Positive laboratory tests, §130A-139.
Prostitution.
Probation or parole of infected persons, §14-208.
Temporary order to report health related
information, §130A-141.1.
**Transportation of bodies of persons who have
died of reportable diseases,** §130A-146.
Venereal diseases.
Consent of minor for treatment sufficient,
§90-21.5(a).
Defendants accused of offense involving vaginal,
anal or oral intercourse.
Testing on request of victim, §15A-615(a).
Defendant in custody of division of adult
correction, §15A-615(c).
Order requiring, §15A-615(b).
Failure to obtain treatment.
Imprisonment, §130A-25(b).
Discharge, §130A-25(c).
Form and content of reports, §130A-141.
Laboratory reports.
Positive laboratory tests.
Persons in charge of laboratories to report,
§130A-139.
Prostitution.
Probation or parole of infected persons, §14-208.
Temporary order to report health related
information, §130A-141.1.
COMMUNICATIONS.
Secret listening.
Electronic surveillance, §§15A-286 to 15A-298.
See ELECTRONIC SURVEILLANCE.

COMMUNICATIONS WITH JURORS, §14-225.2.

COMMUNICATION TOWERS.
Lease of public lands, §146-29.2.

COMMUNIST PARTY.
Emergency management personnel.
Party members ineligible, §166A-13(a).

COMMUNITY ACTION PROGRAMS.
Agencies.
Activities, §108B-25.
Board of directors.
Organization, §108B-26(a).
Responsibilities, §108B-26(b).
Development zone project tax credit, §105-129.13.
Eligible agencies.
Designation, §108B-24.
Department of health and human services.
Authority, §108B-23(b).
Definition of "department,"§108B-23(a).
Municipalities.
Powers as to, §160A-492.
Purpose of article, §108B-22.
Title of article.
Short title, §108B-21.

COMMUNITY APPEARANCE COMMISSIONS,
§§160A-451 to 160A-455.
Advisory councils.
Authorized, §160A-453.
Appointment of members, §160A-451.
Authorized, §160A-451.
Composition, §160A-451.
Duties, §160A-452.
Expenses of members.
Reimbursement, §160A-451.
Funds.
Receipt and expenditure, §160A-455.
Joint commissions, §160A-451.
Number of members, §160A-451.
Powers, §160A-452.
Qualifications of members, §160A-451.
Reports.
Annual report to municipal or county governing
body, §160A-454.
Staff and technical services, §160A-453.
Terms of members, §160A-451.

**COMMUNITY BASED DEVELOPMENT
ORGANIZATION.**
Development zone project tax credit,
§105-129.13.

COMMUNITY CHILD PROTECTION TEAMS.
Generally, §§7B-1400 to 7B-1414.
See CHILD FATALITY PREVENTION SYSTEM.

COMMUNITY COLLEGES, §§115D-1 to 115D-97.
Absence of student for religious observances.
Policy to be adopted by state board, §115D-5(u).
Academic credit.
Fraudulent means in obtaining credit, §14-118.2.
Access to information, §115D-78(a).
Accounts and accounting.
Annual audits, §115D-58.5(c).
Contracts.
Approval requirements, §115D-58.5(b).
State auditor.
Responsibilities, §115D-58.5(c).
System to be maintained, §115D-58.5(a).
**Accreditation of secondary school located in
state.**
Using as factor in admissions, loans, scholarships
or other policies.
Accreditation defined, §115D-1.3(a).
Policy to prohibited, adoption required,
§115D-1.3(b).

COMMUNITY COLLEGES —Cont'd

Actions.

Tort actions against board of trustees, §115D-58.12(b), (c), (d).

Additional support for regional institutions, §115D-31(a).

Additions, improvements, renovations and repairs to property.

Acquisition of property from county, §115D-15.1(c).

Sale, lease or disposition to county in which property located, §115D-15.1(a).

Approval of state board, §115D-15.1(d).

Financing contract, county responsibility, §115D-15.1(e).

Transfer back to college after completion of project, §115D-15.1(b).

Administration of institutions.

State board of community colleges, §115D-5(a).

Administrative areas.

Board of trustees.

To be residents of administrative area, §115D-12(b).

Defined, §115D-2.

Multiple-county administrative areas, §115D-59.

Agents.

Negligence of agents.

Waiver of governmental immunity by act of obtaining liability insurance, §115D-24.

All-terrain vehicle safety training.

Authorized to provide, §20-171.20.

Annuity contracts.

Employees of institutions.

Purchase of annuity contracts for employees, §115D-25.

Appropriations.

Elections on questions of appropriations. See within this heading, "Financial support."

Architectural, engineering and surveying services.

Exemptions from article.

Capital improvement contracts, §143-64.34.

Armed forces personnel on active duty.

Tuition assistance.

Active duty members, in-state rate, §116-143.3.

Associations.

Trustee association regions.

Division into regions, §115D-62.

Athletics.

Intercollegiate athletics program.

Use of state funds, tuition or student aid to create or operate.

Prohibited, §115D-43.

Audits, §§115D-56.16(a), 147-64.6A.

EAGLE program.

Not subject to, §115D-56.16(b).

Statistical sample for program audits, §115D-5(m).

Benefits of public institutions of higher education to be extended to people of state free of charge, NC Const Art IX §9.

Board of trustees.

Access to information, §115D-78(a).

Body corporate, §115D-14.

Compensation, §115D-17.

Composition, §115D-12(a).

Conflicts of interest, §115D-26.

Cooperative innovative high school programs.

Established by local boards and community college board of trustees, §§115C-238.50 to 115C-238.55.

See COOPERATIVE INNOVATIVE HIGH SCHOOL PROGRAMS.

COMMUNITY COLLEGES —Cont'd

Board of trustees —Cont'd

Duties, §115D-20.

Elective officials serving as trustees, §115D-16.

Eminent domain, §40A-3(c).

Exchange of property, §115D-15.

Former employees.

Service on board prohibited, §115D-12(b1).

Governmental immunity.

Waiver of immunity by act of obtaining liability insurance, §115D-24.

Investment committee.

Appointment, §115D-58.6(g).

Lease of property, §115D-15.

Liability insurance, §115D-58.12(a) to (e).

Waiver of governmental immunity by act of obtaining insurance, §115D-24.

Meetings, §115D-18.

Failure to attend three consecutive meetings without a justifiable cause.

Office declared vacant, §115D-19(b).

Official meetings open to public, §115D-79.

Motor vehicle citations, fines and registration, §115D-21(c).

Negligence of agents and employees of institutions.

Waiver of governmental immunity by act of obtaining liability insurance, §115D-24.

Official title, §115D-14.

Organization of boards, §115D-18.

Powers, §§115D-14, 115D-20.

Public building contracts.

Construction contract claims.

Adjustment and resolution, §143-135.6(a) to (f).

Public/private partnerships.

Power to enter into, requirements, §115D-20.

Public records.

Availability for examination and reproduction, §115D-78(a).

Removal of trustees, §115D-19(a).

Resident of administrative area, §115D-12(b).

Sale of property, §115D-15.

Selection of trustees.

Group one, §115D-12(a).

Group two, §115D-12(a).

Group three, §115D-12(a).

Group four, §115D-12(a).

Spouses and children of employees.

Prohibited service on board, §115D-12(b1).

State government ethics act.

Official actions, participation limitations, §138A-38(d).

Terms of office, §115D-13(a).

Commencement, §115D-13(b).

Title to property, §115D-14.

Tort actions against, §115D-58.12(b) to (d).

Traffic regulations, §115D-21(b), (c).

Vacancy.

Failure to attend meetings, §115D-19(b).

Filling, §115D-12(c).

William D. Ford federal direct loan program.

Resolution to decline to participate, §115D-40.1(e).

Board reserve fund.

Use, §115D-5(j).

Bond issues.

Community colleges facilities finance, §§116D-41 to 116D-49.

See HIGHER EDUCATION BONDS.

Elections on question of issuance, §115D-36.

COMMUNITY COLLEGES —Cont'd
Bond issues —Cont'd
Local financial support of institutions.
Authority to issue bonds and notes, §115D-38.
Previously established institutions, §115D-34(b).
Bonds, surety.
Investment of idle cash, §115D-58.10.
Budgets.
Adoption, §115D-56.
Interim budget, §115D-57.
Allocation of revenue to the institution by local
tax-levying authority.
Provision of funds, §115D-58.2(a).
Purpose of funds, §115D-58.2(b).
Amendments.
Appropriations, §115D-58(b).
Rules and regulations, §115D-58(a).
Appropriations, §115D-58(b), (c).
Contracts.
Federal contracts and grants, §115D-58.1.
Disbursements.
Provision for disbursement of local money,
§115D-58.4.
Provision for disbursement of state money,
§115D-58.3.
Federal contracts and grants, §115D-58.1.
Final adoption, §115D-56.
Grants.
Federal contracts and grants, §115D-58.1.
Interim budget, §115D-57.
Management.
Approval of budget by local tax-levying
authority, §115D-55(a).
Approval of budget by state board of community
colleges, §115D-55(b).
Performance budgeting.
Publication of performance, §115D-31.3.
State board to create new accountability
measures and performance standards,
§115D-31.3(a).
Preparation and submission.
Annual submission required, §115D-54(a).
Procedures for preparation and submission,
§115D-54(b).
Provision of public funds, §115D-54(c).
Responsibility of county finance officer,
§115D-54(d).
Trust and agency fund, §115D-54(e).
Rules and regulations.
Amendments, §115D-58(a).
Vending facilities.
Disposition of revenue, §115D-58.13.
Buildings.
Construction contract claims.
Adjustment and resolution, §143-135.6(a) to (f).
Fire and casualty insurance on institutional
buildings and contents, §115D-58.11(a) to (c).
Cafeteria plans.
Flexible compensation plans, §115D-25.2.
Campus law enforcement agencies.
Board of trustees may establish and employee
police officers, §115D-21.1(a).
Joint agreement with county to extend
enforcement authority, §115D-21.1(c).
Joint agreement with municipality to extend
enforcement authority, §115D-21.1(b).
Qualifications and requirements for police officers,
powers, §115D-21.1(a).
Territorial jurisdiction of police officers,
§115D-21.1(a).

COMMUNITY COLLEGES —Cont'd
Capital improvements.
Awarding authority for contracts, §115D-9(f).
Delegation of authority, §115D-9(c).
Development of procedures, §115D-9(b).
Division of contracts to evade monetary limits,
§115D-9(e).
Expenditures requiring prior approval,
§115D-9(a).
Fee negotiations, §115D-9(b).
Minority business participation requirement.
Inapplicability, §115D-9(h).
Report to building commission, §115D-9(g).
Standard contracts for design and construction,
§115D-9(d).
Use of existing plans and specifications,
§115D-9(b).
Captive or co-opted group students.
Course of instruction, §115D-5(c).
Cash management for community colleges,
§147-86.13.
Central Piedmont community college.
Local financial support, §115D-60(a).
Sale, exchange or lease of property, §115D-60(b).
Cigarettes.
Smoking, §§115D-20.1, 143-599.
Coastal Carolina community college.
Authority to provide local financial support,
§115D-61.
College transfer program.
Addition of program to community colleges.
Approval of addition to community college,
§115D-4.1(b).
Criteria and standards to regulate addition of
program, §115D-4.1(d), (e).
Election on question of addition, §115D-36.
Reports on academic performance of transfer
students, §115D-4.1(f).
Restrictions, §115D-4.1(c).
Community colleges instructional trust fund,
§115D-42.
Community college system office.
Access to information, §115D-78(a).
Chief administrative officer, §115D-3.
Motorcycle safety instruction program.
Delivered and implemented through
department, §115D-72.
Operation of department, §115D-3.
President, §115D-3.
Compensation, §115D-3.
Professional staff members, §115D-3.
Compensation, §115D-3.
Establishing staff complement, §115D-3.
Public records.
Availability for examination and reproduction,
§115D-78(a).
Confidentiality.
Personal identifying information of applicants,
§132-1.1(f).
Conflicts of interest.
Employees of institutions, §115D-26.
Construction contract claims.
Adjustment and resolution.
Contract completed and amount claimed not
received, §143-135.6(b).
Civil action, limitation period, venue,
§143-135.6(c).
Contract not completed and amount claimed not
received, §143-135.6(a).
Definitions, §143-135.6(e).

COMMUNITY COLLEGES —Cont'd
Construction contract claims —Cont'd
Adjustment and resolution —Cont'd
Provisions applicable to community colleges
only, §143-135.6(f).
Provisions part of every contract, §143-135.6(d).
Continuation of existing law, §115D-81(a).
Rights and liabilities, §115D-81(b).
Contracts.
Annuity or retirement income contract.
Conflicts of interest, §115D-26.
Purchase of contracts for employees, §115D-25.
Local school administrative units.
Restrictions, §115D-41(a).
Public building contracts.
Construction contract claims.
Adjustment and resolution, §143-135.6(a) to
(f).
Cooperative innovative high school programs.
Established by local boards and community
college board of trustees, §§115C-238.50 to
115C-238.55.
See COOPERATIVE INNOVATIVE HIGH
SCHOOL PROGRAMS.
Correction education programs.
Reports of full-time student hours, §115D-5(c1).
Counties.
Multiple-county administrative areas, §115D-59.
Satellite campuses.
Contracts for construction, §153A-450(a) to (c).
Customized industry training program,
§115D-5.1(e) to (g).
Deadly weapons.
Possessing or carrying on campus or educational
property, §14-269.2.
Defenses.
Tort actions against board of trustees,
§115D-58.12(c).
Definitions, §115D-2.
Construction contract claims.
Adjustment and resolution, §143-135.6(c).
**Department of revenue, list of colleges
provided to,** §115D-5(n).
Dependent care assistance program.
Providing eligible employees, §115D-25.1.
Disbursements.
Provision for disbursement of local money,
§115D-58.4.
Provision for disbursement of state money,
§115D-58.3.
Discrimination.
Nondiscrimination policy, §115D-77.
**Donated property to support specific
educational purpose.**
Use of proceeds from sale or lease according to
terms of donation, §115D-15(b).
Driving eligibility certificates.
Rules established by state board, §115D-5(a3).
Dual enrollment programs.
Public school students using facilities for,
§115D-41(b).
Education cabinet, §116C-1.
Elections on questions of appropriations.
Financial support. See within this heading,
"Financial support."
Employees of institutions.
Annuity contracts.
Purchase of annuity contracts for employees,
§115D-25.
Custodial accounts in lieu of, §115D-25.

COMMUNITY COLLEGES —Cont'd
Employees of institutions —Cont'd
Confidential personnel information.
Disclosure, §115D-29(b).
Retirement system, §115D-29(c).
Who may inspect and examine, §115D-29(a).
Conflicts of interest, §115D-26.
Dependent care assistance program.
Providing eligible employees, §115D-25.1.
Flexible compensation plans, §115D-25.2.
Health insurance, §115C-340.
Negligence.
Waiver of governmental immunity by act of
obtaining liability insurance, §115D-24.
Personnel records.
Confidential information, §115D-29.
Contents, §115D-28(a).
Definition of term salary, §115D-28(b).
Employee objecting to material in file.
Remedy of employee, §115D-30.
Inspection, §§115D-27, 115D-28(c).
Maintenance, §115D-28.
Objections to material in file.
Remedy of employee, §115D-30.
Retirement income contracts.
Purchase of contracts for employees, §115D-25.
Custodial accounts in lieu of, §115D-25.
Shared leave with family member.
Family member employed by community
college, school or public agency, §115D-25.3.
State personnel system.
Exempt employees, §126-5(c2).
Voluntary shared leave.
Family member employed by community
college, school or public agency,
§§115D-25.3, 126-8.3(a).
Workers' compensation act applicable to
employees, §115D-23.
Equipment.
Allocation of funds to institutions in accordance
with equipment allocation formula,
§115D-31(d).
Lease purchase and installment purchase
contracts.
Authority of board of trustees, §115D-58.15(a).
Deficiency judgment not to be rendered for
breach of contractual obligation,
§115D-58.15(f).
Nonsubstitution clauses prohibited,
§115D-58.15(e).
Review and approval of contracts,
§115D-58.15(b).
Determining whether contract subject to
approval, §115D-58.15(d).
Local government commission approval,
§115D-58.15(c).
Taxing power of tax-levying authority and state
not to be pledged, §115D-58.15(f).
Purchases from noncertified sources,
§115D-58.14(a).
Changes of benchmarks upon review by board,
§115D-58.14(c).
Cost of purchase not to exceed bid value
benchmark, §115D-58.14(a).
Items unavailable nor substantially similar
under state contracts, §115D-58.14(a1).
Policies and procedures for monitoring
implementation, adoption, §115D-58.14(b).
Purchasing price, §115D-58.14(a).

COMMUNITY COLLEGES —Cont'd
Establishment of institutions, §115D-4.
Elections on questions of appropriations,
§115D-33(c).
Granting final approval for establishment of
institution, §115D-33(e).
State board of community colleges, §115D-5(a).
**Exchange of real or personal property no
longer desirable for purposes of
institution,** §115D-15(a).
Explosives.
Possessing or carrying on campus or educational
property, §14-269.2.
Extension courses.
Curricular courses and noncurricular courses
authorized, §115D-5(b).
Fees, §115D-5(b).
Recreation extension courses.
Financing on self-supporting basis, §115D-5(g).
Tuition charge, §115D-5(b).
Federal aid.
Budgets, §115D-58.1.
State board of community colleges.
Authority to accept, receive, use or reallocate
federal funds or aid, §115D-31(b).
**Federal law enforcement officers stationed in
state.**
Resident tuition rate, §115D-39(a1).
Fees.
Extension courses, §115D-5(b).
Fixing and regulating fees charged to students,
§115D-39(a).
Receipts state funds, deposit, §115D-39(a).
Financial assistance for students.
Administration, §115D-40.1(c).
Counselors, §115D-40.1(c).
Federal loan program participation,
§115D-40.1(d).
Resolution declining to participate,
§115D-40.1(e).
Low-enrollment programs targeted for
high-demand occupations, §115D-40.1(b).
Needs-based eligibility, §115D-40.1(a).
Targeted assistance, §115D-40.1(b).
Financial support, §§115D-31 to 115D-39.
Application for funds by board, §115D-32(c).
Capital outlay.
Responsibility for budget item, §§115D-31(a),
115D-32(a).
Central Piedmont community college.
Authority to provide local financial support,
§115D-60(a).
Coastal Carolina community college.
Authority to provide local financial support,
§115D-61.
Contracts.
Local school administrative units.
Restrictions, §115D-41(a).
Current expenses.
Responsibility for budget items, §§115D-31(a),
115D-32(a).
Supplemental current expense budget,
§115D-32(b).
Elections on questions of appropriations.
Ballot to be furnished, §115D-33(b).
Bond issues, §115D-36.
Construction of provisions, §115D-33(f).
Establishment of institution, §115D-33(c).
Granting final approval for establishment of
institution, §115D-33(e).

COMMUNITY COLLEGES —Cont'd
Financial support —Cont'd
Elections on questions of appropriations —Cont'd
Holding elections, §115D-33(d).
Power to hold elections, §115D-35(d).
Origination of formal requests for elections,
§115D-35(a).
Payment of expenses of special elections,
§115D-37.
Requests for elections to provide funds for
institutions, §115D-35.
Special elections.
Payment of expenses, §115D-37.
Special tax levies.
Maximum annual rate sort stated on formal
requests, §115D-35(c).
Submitting formal requests for elections,
§115D-35(a), (b).
Wording of ballots, §115D-33(b).
Federal aid.
Authority to accept, receive, use or reallocate
funds, §115D-31(b).
Fees.
Fixing and regulating fees charged to students,
§115D-39(a).
Institutional effectiveness plan.
Funds to be used consistent with plan,
§115D-31(b1).
Local financial support of institutions,
§115D-32(a), (b).
Appropriating nontax revenues, §115D-38.
Authority to issue bonds and notes, §115D-38.
Central Piedmont community college,
§115D-60(a).
Coastal Carolina community college, §115D-61.
Levying special taxes, §115D-38.
Previously established institutions, §115D-34(a),
(c).
Bond issues, §115D-34(b).
Satellite campuses.
Maintenance and utility costs.
Acceptance by counties, §115D-32(d).
Tax-levying authority, §§115D-32(a), 115D-33(a).
Local school administrative units.
Contracts.
Restrictions, §115D-41(a).
Regional institutions.
Responsibility for additional support,
§115D-31(a).
Satellite campuses.
Maintenance and utility costs.
Acceptance by counties, §115D-32(d).
State board of community colleges.
Budget items, §115D-31(a).
Federal aid.
Authority to accept, receive, use or reallocate,
§115D-31(b).
Reversion of funds to general fund, §115D-31(c).
State financial support of institutions, §115D-31.
Tax-levying authority.
Defined, §115D-2.
Local financial support of institutions,
§§115D-32(a), 115D-33(a).
Responsibility for budget items, §115D-32(a).
Tuition.
Fixing and regulating tuition, §115D-39(a) to
(c).
Withdrawal or withholding state support of
institutions, §115D-6.
Fines.
Traffic regulations, §115D-21(b), (c).

COMMUNITY COLLEGES —Cont'd
Fire and casualty insurance on institutional buildings and contents.
Funding, §115D-58.11(b).
Purchase authorized, §115D-58.11(c).
Purchase required, §115D-58.11(a).
Firearms and other weapons.
Possessing or carrying on campus or educational property, §14-269.2.
Fluorescent lights and thermostats containing mercury.
Recycling program.
Establishment required, §130A-310.60(a).
Report documenting compliance required, §130A-310.60(b).
Gateway to college program, §115D-5(t).
General education development (GED) test, retention of fees, §115D-5(s).
Governmental immunity.
Negligence of agents and employees of institutions.
Waiver of governmental immunity by act obtaining liability insurance, §115D-24.
Grants.
Federal contracts and grants, §115D-58.1.
Health insurance for employees, §115C-340(a), (b).
Highways, roads and streets.
Applicable provisions, §115D-21(a).
In-plant training program.
Assisting in pre-employment and in-service training of certain employees, §115D-5.1(a).
Institutional effectiveness plan.
Funds to be used consistent with plan, §115D-31(b1).
Instructional trust fund.
Allocation, §115D-42(b).
Audit, §115D-42(e).
Established, §115D-42(a).
Matching funds, §115D-42(c), (d).
Purpose, §115D-42(a).
Rules, §115D-42(b).
State funds and matching funds raised by foundation.
Use, §115D-42(c).
Intercollegiate athletics program.
Use of state funds, tuition or student aid to create or operate.
Prohibited, §115D-43.
Interest.
Deposits.
Investment of idle cash, §115D-58.6.
Investment of idle cash, §§115D-58.6 to 115D-58.10.
Bonds, surety, §115D-58.10.
Combining cash of several funds for deposit or investment, §115D-58.6(e).
Daily deposits, §115D-58.9.
Definitions, §115D-58.6(a).
Deposits, §115D-58.6(a1).
Cash balance defined, §115D-58.6(a).
Daily deposits, §115D-58.9.
Official depository defined, §115D-58.6(a).
Securing deposits, §115D-58.7(b).
Selection of depository, §115D-58.7(a).
Duties of board in managing and investing funds, §115D-58.6(h).
Facsimile signatures, §115D-58.8.
Generally, §115D-58.6(d1).
Interest earned on deposit or investment, §115D-58.6(e).

COMMUNITY COLLEGES —Cont'd
Investment of idle cash —Cont'd
Investment committee, §115D-58.6(g).
Investment securities.
Power to purchase, sell, exchange, §115D-58.6(d1).
Prudent person.
Duties of board in managing and investing funds, §115D-58.6(h).
Securities.
Power to purchase, sell, exchange, §115D-58.6(d1).
Release of registered securities, transfer, §115D-58.6(f).
Signatures.
Facsimile signatures, §115D-58.8.
Surety bonds, §115D-58.10.
Juice and bottled water.
Contracts for sale of.
Competitive bid required, §143-64.
Lateral entry program for teaching profession.
Course offerings, §115D-5(p).
Law enforcement agencies, §115D-21.1.
Law enforcement officers.
Federal law enforcement officers stationed in state.
Resident tuition rate, §115D-39(a1).
Lease of property no longer desirable for purposes of institution, §115D-15(a).
Lease purchase and installment purchase contracts.
Equipment, §115D-58.15.
State board to review, §115D-5(l).
Liability insurance.
Negligence of agents and employees of institutions.
Waiver of governmental immunity by act of obtaining insurance, §115D-24.
Professional liability insurance.
Acquisition of insurance by commission, §§58-32-15, 58-32-15(a), (b).
Declaration of public purpose, §58-32-15(d).
Sovereign immunity.
Not deemed waiver of, §58-32-15(c).
Purchase by board of trustees, §115D-58.12(a).
State funds to pay premiums, §115D-31.1.
List of colleges to department of revenue, §115D-5(n).
Low-wealth counties.
Use of funds in, §115D-31.3(j).
Maintenance of system of higher education, NC Const Art IX §8.
Meetings.
Official meetings open to public, §115D-79.
Mercury.
Fluorescent lights and thermostats containing.
Recycling program.
Establishment required, §130A-310.60(a).
Report documenting compliance, §130A-310.60(b).
Middle or early college programs.
Public school students using facilities for, §115D-41(b).
Military members.
Tuition assistance.
Adding costs of textbooks, §115D-39(d).
Armed forces personnel on active duty.
In-state rate, §116-143.3.
Motorcycle safety instruction program.
Delivered and implemented through department of community colleges, §115D-72.

COMMUNITY COLLEGES —Cont'd
Motor fuel excise tax exemption, §105-449.88.
Motor vehicles.
Citations, fines and registration.
Establishing system, §115D-21(c).
Operation of motor vehicles on campus of
institutions, §115D-21(a).
National Guard.
Tuition assistance, §§116-209.50 to 116-209.55.
Negligence.
Liability of negligence of agents and employees of
institutions.
Waiver of governmental immunity by act of
obtaining liability insurance, §115D-24.
New program.
Approval, §115D-5(f).
**North Carolina center for applied textile
technology at Gaston college,** §§115D-67.1 to
115D-67.4.
**North Carolina community colleges
instructional trust fund,** §115D-42.
Operation of institutions.
State board of community colleges, §115D-5(a).
Operation of plant.
Out-of-county head count over fifty percent of
total.
Funds provided to college, §115D-31.2.
Performance budgeting.
Low-wealth counties.
Use of funds in, §115D-31.3(j).
Mandatory performance measures, §115D-31.3(e).
Publication of performance, §115D-31.3.
Publication of performance ratings, §115D-31.3(f).
State board to create new accountability measures
and performance standards, §115D-31.3(a).
Successful performance.
Carryforward of funds for indicators achieved,
§115D-31.3(g).
Superior performance recognition,
§115D-31.3(h).
Uses of funds, §115D-31.3(i).
Personal identifying information.
Applicant records, confidentiality, §132-1.1(f).
Personal property.
Title to property, §115D-14.
Transfer to another community college,
§115D-15(a).
Personnel records and files.
Confidential information, §115D-29.
Contents, §115D-28(a).
Definition of term salary, §115D-28(b).
Disclosure, §115D-29(b).
Retirement system, §115D-29(c).
Employee objecting to material in file.
Remedy of employee, §115D-30.
Inspection, §§115D-27, 115D-28(c).
Who may inspect and examine, §115D-29(a).
Maintenance, §115D-28.
Objections to material in file.
Remedy of employee, §115D-30.
Personnel system.
Exempt employees, §126-5(c2).
Exempt from provisions of state personnel act,
§115D-5(a).
Exemption for employees, §126-5(c6).
Police, §115D-21.1.
President of system of community colleges,
§115D-3.
License plate.
Special plate, number, §20-79.5.

COMMUNITY COLLEGES —Cont'd
Private, nonprofit corporations.
Establishment to support community college
system.
State employees may assist, §115D-7.
Program audits.
Statistical sample for program audits, §115D-5(m).
Publications.
Administrative review procedures for public
documents, §143-170.2.
Procedures manuals for public documents,
§143-170.2.
Public buildings and grounds.
Fire and casualty insurance on institutional
buildings and contents, §115D-58.11(a) to (c).
Public/private partnerships.
Power of trustees to enter into, requirements,
§115D-20.
Public records.
Availability for examination and reproduction,
§115D-78(a).
Small business center network.
Documents submitted by individual seeking
counseling or assistance.
Not public records, §115D-78(b).
Public school students.
Use of facilities by.
Joint or cooperative programs, §115D-41(b).
**Public school teacher teaching college level
courses.**
Contract with local school administrative unit.
Reimbursement to community college,
§115D-41(a).
Purchasing flexibility.
Supplies, equipment and materials, §115D-58.14.
Purposes of chapter, §115D-1.
Real estate continuing education courses.
Offer on self-supporting basis, §115D-5(h).
Real property.
Acquisition, §153A-158.2(a).
Additions, improvements, renovations and repairs.
Acquisition from county, §115D-15.1(c).
Sale, lease or other disposition to county in
which property located, §115D-15.1(a), (b),
(d), (e).
Central Piedmont community college.
Sale, exchange or lease of property,
§115D-60(b).
Construction or improvement, §153A-158.2(b).
Disposition, §153A-158.2(b).
Public hearing, §153A-158.2(c).
Right-of-way easements for highway construction,
§115D-15(a).
Title to property, §115D-14.
Records.
Confidential personnel information.
Disclosures, §115D-29(b).
Retirement system, §115D-29(c).
Who may inspect and examine, §115D-29(a).
Personnel records, §§115D-27 to 115D-30.
Public records.
Available for examination and reproduction,
§115D-78(a).
Recreation extension courses.
Financing on self-supporting basis, §115D-5(g).
Regional institutions.
Defined, §115D-2.
Religious observances.
Policy to be adopted by state board regarding
absence of students, §115D-5(u).

COMMUNITY COLLEGES —Cont'd

Reports, §115D-5(o).
Capital improvements.
Report to building commission, §115D-9(g).
Customized industry training program, §115D-5.1(f).

Retirement income contracts for employees.
Purchase of contracts for employees, §115D-25.

Retirement system for teachers and state employees.
Applicability of provisions, §115D-22.
Optional retirement program.
Administration, §135-5.4(e).
Beneficiaries, §135-5.4(g).
Contracts with investment companies, §135-5.4(d).
Contributions, §135-5.4(c).
Election to participate, §135-5.4(b).
Establishment, §135-5.4(a).
Governance, §135-5.4(b).
Participation, ineligibility for other programs, §135-5.4(f).
Underwriting, §135-5.4(a).
Purchase of retirement income contracts of employees, §115D-25.

Right-of-way easements for highway construction, §115D-15(a).

Rules and regulations.
Available for examination and reproduction, §115D-78(a).

Salaries.
Community college system office.
Professional staff members, §115D-3.
Compensation of trustees, §115D-17.
State board of community colleges.
Standards, scales and salary caps, §115D-5(a).

Sale of real or personal property undesirable for purposes of institution, §115D-15(a).

Satellite campuses.
Counties.
Contracts for construction, §153A-450(a) to (c).

Saving clauses.
Continuation of existing law, §115D-81(a).
Existing rights and liabilities, §115D-81(b).

Shared leave with family member.
Family member employed by community college, public school or public agency, §115D-25.3.

Sign language instruction, §115D-5(r).

Small business center network.
Documents submitted by individual seeking counseling or assistance.
Not public records, §115D-78(b).

Smoking in public places.
Cessation and prevention resources, assistance with, §115D-20.1(e).
Definitions, §115D-20.1(a).
Policy prohibiting tobacco use, §115D-20.1(b), (c).
Adopting more restrictive policy, §115D-20.1(d).
Prohibited, §143-599.

Sports.
Intercollegiate athletics program.
Use of state funds, tuition or student aid to create or operate.
Prohibited, §115D-43.

State aid.
Financial support generally. See within this heading, "Financial support."
Withdrawal or withholding state support of institutions, §115D-6.

State board of community colleges.
Absence of student for religious observances.
Policy to be adopted by state board, §115D-5(u).

COMMUNITY COLLEGES —Cont'd

State board of community colleges —Cont'd
Access to information, §115D-78(a).
Administration of institutions, §115D-5(a).
Administrative procedure act.
Exemption, §150B-1(g).
Bookstore sales.
Adoption of rules governing expenditures of funds derived from, §115D-5(a1).
Capital improvements, §115D-9.
Chairman, §115D-2.1(e), (f).
Composition, §115D-2.1(b).
Defined, §115D-2.
Dependent care assistance program.
Providing to eligible employees of constituent institutions, §115D-25.1.
Eligibility to serve on board, §115D-2.1(d).
Established, §115D-2.1(a).
Establishment of institutions, §115D-5(a).
Exchange of information between public schools and institutions of higher education.
Planning and implementation, §115D-5(a2).
Financial support of institutions.
Authority to accept, receive, use or reallocate federal funds or aid, §115D-31(b).
Responsibility for budget items, §115D-31(a).
Reversion of funds to general fund, §115D-31(c).
Flexible compensation plans.
Authorization to provide, §115D-25.2.
Meetings, §115D-2.1(e) to (g).
Official meetings open to public, §115D-79.
Regular meetings, §115D-2.1(g).
Special meetings, §115D-2.1(g).
State board of education.
Annual meeting with, §115C-11(b1).
Officers, §115D-2.1(e), (f).
Operation of institutions, §115D-5(a).
Organization, §115D-2.1(b).
Public records.
Available for examination and reproduction, §115D-78(a).
Removal of members, §115D-2.1(b1).
Removal of trustees, §115D-19(a).
Rules to assist colleges in administration of procedures, adoption, §115D-5(a3).
Setoff debt collection.
Generally, §§105A-1 to 105A-16.
See SETOFF DEBT COLLECTION.
State board of education.
Annual meeting with, §115C-11(b1).
Terms of members, §115D-2.1(b), (c).
Vacancies, §115D-2.1(h), (i).
Withdrawal or withholding state support of institutes, §115D-6.

Statement of purpose, §115D-1.

State of emergency.
Injunctions.
Public or private educational institutions, §14-288.18(a), (b).

Statistical sample for program audits, §115D-5(m).

Student activity fees.
Receipts state funds, deposit, §115D-39(a).

Student head count from outside county of more than half of student body.
Funds provided for "operation of plant,"§115D-31.2.

Supplies.
Purchasing from noncertified sources, §115D-58.14(a).
Changes of benchmarks upon review by board, §115D-58.14(c).

COMMUNITY COLLEGES —Cont'd
Supplies —Cont'd
Purchasing from noncertified sources —Cont'd
Cost of purchase not to exceed bid value
benchmark, §115D-58.14(a).
Items unavailable nor substantially similar
under state contracts, §115D-58.14(a1).
Policies and procedures for monitoring
implementation, adoption, §115D-58.14(b).
Purchase price, §115D-58.14(a).
Tax-levying authority.
Defined, §115D-2.
Local financial support of institutions,
§§115D-32(a), 115D-33(a).
Responsibility for budget items, §115D-32(a).
Textiles.
North Carolina center for applied textile
technology at Gaston college, §§115D-67.1 to
115D-67.4.
Title to property, §115D-14.
Tobacco use, §§115D-20.1, 143-599.
Tort actions against board of trustees,
§115D-58.12(b).
Defenses, §115D-58.12(c).
Liability insurance.
Payment of premiums, §115D-58.12(e).
Reading or mentioning in presence of jury,
§115D-58.12(d).
Traffic regulations.
Applicable provisions, §115D-21(a).
Fines and penalties, §115D-21(b), (c).
Transfer of personal property to another
community college, §115D-15(a).
Trustee association regions.
Division into regions, §115D-62.
Tuition.
Armed forces personnel on active duty.
In-state rate, §116-143.3.
Textbooks purchased in college's bookstore.
Adding to tuition costs, §115D-39(d).
Eligibility for resident tuition rate.
Persons lawfully admitted to United States,
§115D-39(b), (c).
Federal law enforcement officers stationed in
state.
Resident tuition rate, §115D-39(a1).
Fixing and regulating.
State board, §115D-39(a).
Legal resident limitation, §115D-39(a).
Persons lawfully admitted to United States.
Eligibility for resident tuition rate, §115D-39(b),
(c).
Receipts state funds, deposit, §115D-39(a).
Textbooks purchased in college's bookstore.
Adding to costs billed to armed services for
enrollment of service members,
§115D-39(d).
Tuition and fees exceeding amount certified in
general fund codes.
Transfer of excess to enrollment growth fund,
§115D-31(e).
Tuition assistance, §115D-40.1.
Extension courses, §115D-5(b).
National Guard, §§116-209.50 to 116-209.55.
Tuition and fee waivers, §§115B-1 to 115B-6.
Tuition surcharge.
Authority to impose, §115D-39.1(a).
Rules promulgation, §115D-39.1(d).
Scholarship to which applicable, §115D-39.1(c).
Student exempt, §115D-39.1(b).

COMMUNITY COLLEGES —Cont'd
Use and occupancy classifications.
Business/Group B programs.
Dual enrollment programs, §115D-41(b).
Vending facilities.
Defined, §115D-2.
Disposition of revenue, §115D-58.13.
Viticulture or oenology program.
Authorization, §18B-1114.4.
Inapplicability of prohibition on governmental
units selling merchandise, §66-58(c).
Voluntary shared leave, §§115D-25.3, 126-8.3.
Withdrawal of state support.
State board of community colleges may withdraw,
§115D-6.
Workers' compensation.
Applicability of workers' compensation act to
institutional employees, §115D-23.
Youth, employment, §95-25.5(m).

COMMUNITY COLLEGES INSTRUCTIONAL
FUND, §115D-42.

COMMUNITY COLLEGE SYSTEM OFFICE,
§115D-3.

COMMUNITY CORRECTIONS, §§143B-1150 to
143B-1160.
Administrative purposes.
Percentage of funds received by service providers
used for, §143B-1156(d).
Basis of sentencing and policy advisory
commissions recommendations, §164-42.2.
Cognitive behavioral programming.
Funding eligibility, §143B-1160.
Contracts with eligible entities to operate.
Duties of division of adult corrections to enter
into, §143B-1154(a).
Contracts with service providers, §143B-1156(a).
Substance abuse treatment services,
§143B-1156(b).
Definitions, §143B-1152.
Duties of division of adult corrections,
§143B-1154(a).
Eligible population and criteria, §143B-1154(a).
Funding eligibility, §143B-1160.
Goals for programs funded under provisions,
§143B-1153.
High-risk and moderate to high need
offenders.
Focusing treatment resources on, §143B-1155(a).
Information clearinghouse.
Division of adult corrections to act as,
§143B-1155(a).
Minimum program standards, policies, rules.
Duties of division of adult corrections to develop,
§143B-1155(a).
Policy of general assembly, §143B-1151.
Primary population for programs funded,
§143B-1154(b).
Probation.
Structured sentencing provisions.
Persons sentenced to community punishment,
special rules, §15A-1343.2.
Program types eligible for funding, §143B-1160.
Purposes, §143B-1151.
Recidivism reduction plan, §143B-1155(b).
Reduction of recidivism and probation and
post-release supervision revocations.
Goals of programs, §143B-1153.
Purposes, §143B-1152.
Recidivism reduction plan, §143B-1155(b).

COMMUNITY CORRECTIONS —Cont'd
Report on recidivism rates for offenders in programs funded by provisions.
North Carolina sentencing and policy advisory commission, §143B-1159.
Report required of division of adult correction, §143B-1155(c).
Sentencing services act, §§7A-770 to 7A-777.
See SENTENCING SERVICES.
Short title.
Treatment for effective community supervision act of 2011, §143B-1150.
Standard service definitions and performance measures.
Duty to develop, §143B-1156(c).
State community corrections advisory board.
Chair and vice-chair, selection, §143B-1157(e).
Compensation, service without, §143B-1157(h).
Disclosure of contractual interest, §143B-1157(g).
Duties and responsibilities, §143B-1158.
Meetings, §143B-1157(f).
Members, §143B-1157(a).
Quorum, §143B-1157(f).
Removal of members, §143B-1157(d).
Review, evaluation, monitoring programs, §143B-1158.
Selection of members, §143B-1157(b).
Terms of members, §143B-1157(c).
Travel and subsistence expenses, §143B-1157(h).
Structured sentencing, §§15A-1340.10 to 15A-1340.23.
See SENTENCING.
Substance abuse treatment services.
Contracts, §143B-1156(b).
Contracts with service providers, §143-272.86(b).
Funding eligibility, §143B-1160.
Treatment for effective community supervision act of 2011.
Short title, §143B-1150.
Victims of crime.
Notification, responsibilities, §15A-837(a).
Time period for notifying, §15A-837(b).

COMMUNITY DEVELOPMENT BLOCK GRANTS, §143B-437.04.

COMMUNITY DEVELOPMENT CORPORATION.
Development zone project tax credit, §105-129.13.

COMMUNITY DEVELOPMENT COUNCIL.
Appointments, §143B-437.2(a).
Chairman, §143B-437.2(b).
Clerical services, §143B-437.2(g).
Compensation of members, §143B-437.2(e).
Creation, §143B-437.1.
Duties, §143B-437.1.
Meetings, §143B-437.3.
Powers and duties, §143B-437.1.
Quorum, §143B-437.2(f).
Removal of members, §143B-437.2(d).
Special meetings, §143B-437.3.
Terms of members, §143B-437.2(c).

COMMUNITY FESTIVALS.
Amusements.
License taxes.
Exemption, §105-40.

COMMUNITY HOUSING DEVELOPMENT ORGANIZATION.
Development zone project tax credit, §105-129.13.

COMMUNITY LAND TRUST PROPERTY.
Taxation, §105-277.17.

COMMUNITY MEDIATION CENTERS.
Bad checks collection program.
Assistance in establishing, fee for services, charging, §14-107.2(b1).
Determination of percentages of funding, §7A-38.6(g).
Dispute resolution fee for cases resolved in mediation, §7A-38.7(a).
Proof of payment required, §7A-38.7(b).
Evidence of statements made during negotiations not discoverable or admissible, §8-110(a).
Mediator not compelled to testify in civil or criminal proceeding, §8-110(b), (c).
Good faith effort to maintain level of non-state funding, §7A-38.6(f).
Local government entity, function as, §7A-38.6(j).
Management-related services.
State funds not to be used for such indirect costs, §7A-38.6(j).
Nonprofit organization, function as, §7A-38.6(j).
Non-state match restrictions not to apply, §7A-38.6(i).
Public interest to encourage establishment, §7A-38.5(a).
Referrals from courts, law enforcement agencies and other public agencies, §7A-38.5(b).
Reports on centers, §7A-38.6.
Annual funding and activities report, §7A-38.6(a).
Non-state funding, percentage of.
After second year, §7A-38.6(c).
Six years or more, §7A-38.6(e).
Third, fourth, and fifth years, §7A-38.6(d).
Requesting state funding for first time, §7A-38.6(b).
Waiver or special consideration for funding ratio difficulty, §7A-38.6(h).

COMMUNITY ORGANIZATIONS.
Property taxes.
Exemption of real and personal property, §105-278.7.

COMMUNITY POLICING.
Neighborhood crime watch programs.
Establishment, §153A-212.2.
Harassment of participant, §14-226.2.

COMMUNITY PROPERTY.
Disposition at death, §§31C-1 to 31C-12.
Altering interest of married persons, §31C-9.
Applicability of provisions, §31C-1.
Uniformity, §31C-11.
Citation of act, §31C-12.
Construction and interpretation, §31C-11.
Creditors' rights, §31C-8.
Elective share of spouse.
Property not subject to surviving spouses right, §31C-3.
General rule, §31C-3.
Perfection of personal representative, heir or devisee, §31C-5.
Perfection of title of surviving spouse, §31C-4.
Presumptions, §31C-2.
Purchaser for value or lender.
Inquiry as to whether lender or borrower acted properly, §31C-7(c).
Rights generally, §31C-7(a), (b).

COMMUNITY PROPERTY —Cont'd
Disposition at death —Cont'd
Purchaser for value or lender —Cont'd
Sale proceeds or creation of security interest, §31C-7(d).
Scope of provisions, §31C-1.
Severing interest of married persons, §31C-9.
Short title of act, §31C-12.
Testamentary disposition, §31C-10.
Title.
Perfection of title of personal representative, heir or devisee, §31C-5.
Perfection of title of surviving spouse, §31C-4.
Wills.
Elective share.
Property not subject to surviving spouses right, §31C-3.
Limitations on testamentary disposition, §31C-10.
Written demand, §31C-6(a).
Delivery, §31C-6(b).
Equitable distribution of marital property generally, §§50-11, 50-20 to 50-22.
Cross-actions, jurisdiction, §7A-244.
Decedents' estates.
Claim for distribution of marital or divisible property, §28A-19-19.
Mediated settlement conferences, district courts, §7A-38.4A.

COMMUNITY SCHOOLS ACT, §§115C-203 to 115C-209.1.
CAN DOER organizations.
Community achievement network/developing our educational resources.
Tutoring and other services, §115C-207.
Citation of article, §115C-203.
Community schools advisory councils, §115C-208.
Defined, §115C-205.
Community schools coordinators.
Defined, §115C-205.
Funds for employment, §115C-206.
Responsibilities, §115C-209.
Terms and conditions of employment, §115C-207.
Definitions, §115C-205.
Interagency council.
Defined, §115C-205.
Local boards of education.
Authority and responsibility, §115C-207.
Parents of students.
Membership on community schools advisory councils, §115C-208.
Public school facility.
Defined, §115C-205.
Purpose of article, §115C-204.
State board of education.
Duties and responsibilities, §115C-206.
Title of article, §115C-203.

COMMUNITY SERVICE.
Alcoholic beverages.
Minors.
Aiding and abetting sale to or purchase by underage persons, §18B-302.1(a), (c).
Fines and other penalties, §18B-302.1(b), (c).
Sales to.
Fines and other penalties, §18B-302.1(a), (c).
Bail bond remission if defendant sentenced to, §15A-547.1.
Bomb scares, §§14-69.1, 14-69.2.

COMMUNITY SERVICE —Cont'd
Delinquent juveniles, ordering to perform, §7B-2506.
Division of adult correction.
Appropriate workplace placement, §143B-708(a).
Authority to conduct community service program, §143B-708(a).
Compliance with program requirements.
Assignment of employees to assure and report, §143B-708(a).
Damages for injury or loss suffered by participant.
Liability, §143B-708(d).
Driver's license.
Revocation, willful failure to comply, §143B-708(f).
Extension of time to pay fee, §143B-708(b).
Fee to participate in program, §143B-708(b).
Hearing to determine willful failure to comply, §143B-708(f).
Notice, §143B-708(f).
Purpose of program, §143B-708(a).
Rules to conduct program, adoption, §143B-708(a).
Violation of terms of probation or deferred prosecution.
Community service staff to report, §143B-708(f).
Domestic violence.
Special probation conditions in addition to, §15A-1382.1(b).
Drivers' licenses.
Noncompliance with community service obligation.
Revocation of license, §20-17(b).
Expungement of records.
First offenders under age of eighteen.
Nonviolent felony offenses, §15A-145.4(c).
Impaired driving.
Time limits for performing, §20-179(n).
Limited driving privilege.
Driving for other than work-related purposes, §20-179.3(g2).
Willful violation.
Revocation of privilege, §20-179.3(j1).
Littering, §14-399(c), (d), (e).
Probation, §15A-1343(b1).
Person sentenced under structured sentencing provisions.
Special rules, §15A-1343.2.
Sentencing services act, §§7A-770 to 7A-777.
See SENTENCING SERVICES.
Shoplifting, §14-72.1(e).
Structured sentencing.
Community punishments generally, §§15A-1340.10 to 15A-1340.23.
See SENTENCING.
Teen court program.
Rehabilitative measures or sanctions, §143B-809(a).

COMMUNITY THEATERS.
Alcoholic beverage permits.
Brown-bagging permit.
Kind of permit that may be issued, §18B-1001.
Defined, §18B-1000.
Mixed beverage permit.
Kind of permit that may be issued, §18B-1001.
Recycling requirement, §18B-1006.1.
On-premises fortified wine permit.
Kind of permit that may be issued, §18B-1001.
Recycling requirement, §18B-1006.1.
On-premises malt beverage permit.
Kind of permit that may be issued, §18B-1001.

COMMUNITY THEATERS —Cont'd
Alcoholic beverage permits —Cont'd
On-premises malt beverage permit —Cont'd
Recycling requirement, §18B-1006.1.
On-premises unfortified wine permit.
Kind of permit that may be issued, §18B-1001.
Recycling requirement, §18B-1006.1.
Thalian association.
State community theater, §145-28.

COMMUNITY THIRD PARTY OR POOLED TRUSTS.
Benefiting persons with severe chronic disabilities, §§36D-1 to 36D-12.
Administration of trusts, §36D-4(a).
Expenditures for, §36D-4(e1).
Administrative rules, §36D-12.
Alternate services, providing, §36D-4(f).
Annual report, §36D-5(a).
Applicability of chapter, §36D-3.
Audit annually, §36D-5(b).
Beneficiaries.
Annual individual accounting statement.
Providing, §36D-5(a).
Defined, §36D-2.
Eligibility for services, §36D-4(f).
Income eligibility determination.
Interest in trust not asset for, §36D-9.
Individual services provided.
Annual statement provided trustor, §36D-5(a).
Special request on behalf of beneficiary, §36D-7.
Statement of services provided, §36D-4(i).
Board.
Administration of trusts, §36D-4(a).
Compensation for services, prohibition, §36D-4(b).
Composition, §36D-4(a).
Expenses, reimbursement, §36D-4(b).
Indemnification, §36D-4(b).
Selection, §36D-4(a).
Service providers.
Advisory capacity, §36D-4(a).
Trustee of funds.
Members not considered, §36D-4(c).
Burial expenses.
Payment for, §36D-4(e1).
Bylaws.
Adoption by board, filing, §36D-4(d).
Citation of act.
North Carolina community third party trusts, pooled trusts act, §36D-1(a).
Community third party trust defined, §36D-2.
Construction of chapter, §36D-1(c).
Contributions, devises, designations under life insurance policies.
Authority to accept, §36D-4(h).
Statement of services provided beneficiary, §36D-4(i).
Definitions, §36D-2.
Dissolution of nonprofit corporations.
Action for, §36D-11(b).
Distributions upon dissolution, merger, settlement.
Sharing in, §36D-11(c).
Final disbursement and accounting.
Trustee of medicaid pooled trust, §36D-11(a).
Fiscal accountability, §36D-5(a).
Follow-along services.
Defined, §36D-2.

COMMUNITY THIRD PARTY OR POOLED TRUSTS —Cont'd
Benefiting persons with severe chronic disabilities —Cont'd
Follow-along services —Cont'd
Paid staff to provide.
Retention by board, §36D-4(e).
Gifts.
Authority to accept, use, §36D-6(a).
Goods or services.
Expenditure of funds for, §36D-4(e1).
Guardianships.
Acceptance of appointment authorized, §36D-4(g).
Income eligibility determination.
Beneficiary's interest in trust.
Not asset for, §36D-9.
Itemized statement provided by trust, §36D-5(a).
Legal representation or professional services.
Change in trustee.
Department notified, time, §36D-4(k).
Trustee, board member, paid staff providing.
Prohibition, §36D-4(j).
Legislative findings, §36D-1(b).
Liberal construction of chapter, §36D-1(c).
Life insurance policies.
Designation of trust as beneficiary, §36D-4(h).
Statement of services provided beneficiary, §36D-4(i).
Medicaid pooled trust, pooled trust, umbrella pooled trust.
Defined, §36D-2.
Nonprofit corporations.
Applicability of chapter 55A, §36D-3.
Boards administering trusts to incorporate as, §36D-3.
Dissolution.
Action for, §36D-11(b).
Establishment of medicaid pooled trusts, §36D-2.
North Carolina community third party trusts, pooled trusts act.
Title of chapter, §36D-1(a).
Perpetuities, restraints on alienation, perpetual accumulations of trusts.
Trust not subject to laws against, §36D-10.
Pooled trusts not in conformity with chapter.
Chapter not to affect, §36D-1(d).
Recreational services.
Expenditure of funds for, §36D-4(e1).
Rules and regulations.
Adoption, §36D-12.
Scope of chapter, §36D-3.
Services provided, §36D-4(f).
Severe chronic disability defined, §36D-2.
Short title, §36D-1(a).
Sole benefit.
Defined, §36D-2.
Terms of trust not to contradict meaning, §36D-3.
Statement of services provided beneficiary, §36D-4(i).
Surplus trust funds.
Distribution.
Community third party trust funds, §36D-6(b).
Medicaid pooled trust funds, §36D-6(c), (d).
Use, retention, purposes, §36D-6(a).
Termination.
Individual pooled trust subaccount, §36D-11(a).

COMMUNITY THIRD PARTY OR POOLED
  TRUSTS —Cont'd
Benefiting persons with severe chronic
  disabilities —Cont'd
Trustee of funds.
  Corporation considered, §36D-4(c).
Uniform trust code.
  Applicability, §36D-3.

COMMUNITY WATER SYSTEMS.
Local water supply plans, §143-355.
Operating permit.
Fee, §130A-328(b).
  Disposition of fees collected, §130A-328(e).
  Failure to pay, §130A-328(d).
  Required, §130A-328(a).
Review of plans and specifications, fees,
  §130A-328(c).

COMMUTATION OF SENTENCE, NC Const Art
  II §5.
Notice of, §147-16(b).

COMPACT DISKS.
Record and tape piracy.
See RECORD AND TAPE PIRACY.

COMPACTS.
Interstate compacts.
See INTERSTATE COMPACTS.

COMPANIONS.
Wage and hour act.
Exemptions for persons employed as, §95-25.14(a).

COMPANIONSHIP.
Death by wrongful act of another.
Damages for loss of companionship, §28A-18-2(b).

COMPANY POLICE, §§74E-1 to 74E-13.
Assault and battery upon, §14-33.
Evidence of former threats upon plea of
  self-defense, §14-33.1.
Assault with deadly weapon.
Law enforcement officer assaulted with deadly
  weapon, §14-34.2.
Attorney general.
Fees, §74E-12.
Immunity, §74E-11.
Powers, §74E-4.
Records.
  Legal custodian, §74E-5.
Authority of officers, §74E-6.
Badges, §74E-7.
Certification of agency.
Expiration, renewal and termination, §74E-10.
Citation of chapter, §74E-1.
Classification, §74E-6.
Compensation, §74E-9.
Insurance.
Certificate of self-insurance, §74E-3.
Liability insurance policy required, §74E-3.
Justice department.
Transfer of powers and duties to department,
  §143A-54.
Minimum standards for officers, §74E-8.
Motor vehicles, §74E-7.
Oaths, §74E-6.
Officer commission.
Expiration, renewal and termination, §74E-10.
Payment of compensation, §74E-9.
Powers, §74E-6.
Private protective services.
Exemption from private protective services act,
  §74C-3(b).

COMPANY POLICE —Cont'd
Purpose of chapter, §74E-2.
Records.
Attorney general legal custodian, §74E-5.
Scope of chapter, §74E-2.
Short title of chapter, §74E-1.
Standards for officers.
Minimum standards, §74E-8.
Uniforms, §74E-7.
Violation of chapter.
Penalties, §74E-13(a) to (c).
Weapons, §74E-7.

COMPELLING PRODUCTION OF WILLS,
  §28A-2A-4.

COMPENSATING USE TAX, §§105-164.1 to
  105-164.44J.
See SALES AND USE TAX.

COMPENSATION FOR KILLING DISEASED
  ANIMALS, §§106-323 to 106-335.
See LIVESTOCK DISEASES.

COMPENSATION OF TRUSTEES AND OTHER
  FIDUCIARIES, §§32-53 to 32-62.
See FIDUCIARIES.

COMPENSATION TO PERSONS
  ERRONEOUSLY CONVICTED OF
  FELONIES.
Action by parole commission, §148-84.
Amount of compensation, §148-84(a).
Evidence, §148-84(a).
Forms, §148-83.
Hearings.
Nature of hearing, §148-83.
Income tax deduction, §105-134.6(b).
Innocent of charges, charges dismissed.
Provision for compensation, §148-82(b).
Job skills training, §148-84(c).
Pardon of innocence.
Provision of compensation, §148-82(a).
Petitions, §148-83.
Provision for compensation, §148-82.
Innocent of charges, charges dismissed,
  §148-82(b).
Pardon of innocence, §148-82(a).
Tuition, §148-84(c).

COMPENSATORY DAMAGES.
Civil rights, interference with, §§99D-1(b), (b1).
Damages generally.
See DAMAGES.

COMPETENCY OF WITNESSES.
Alcoholic beverage illicit sales.
Testimony enforced and immunity of witness,
  §8-55.
Child abuse cases.
Husband and wife privilege waived, §8-57.1.
Clergymen and communicants, §8-53.2.
Counselors, privileged communications,
  §8-53.8.
Dead man's statute, §8C-1 Rule 601(c).
Defendant competent but not compelled to
  testify, §8-54.
Disqualifications.
Generally, §8C-1 Rule 601(b).
Dying declarations, §8-51.1.
Wrongful death, §28A-18-2.
Exclusion by interest or crime, §8-49.
Gaming investigations.
Testimony enforced and immunity of witness,
  §8-55.

COMPETENCY OF WITNESSES —Cont'd
General rule, §8C-1 Rule 601(a).
Husband and wife privilege.
 Child abuse cases, waiver, §8-57.1.
 Civil actions, §8-56.
 Criminal actions, §8-57(a) to (c).
Interested persons disqualified, §8C-1 Rule 601(c).
Judges, §8C-1 Rule 605.
Jurors, §8C-1 Rule 606(a), (b).
Lack of personal knowledge, §8C-1 Rule 602.
Marriage and family therapists.
 Communications with clients, §§8-53.5, 8-53.6.
Optometrists, privileged communications, §8-53.9.
Parties competent as witness, §8-50(a).
Personal knowledge, §8C-1 Rule 602.
Psychologist communications with client, §§8-53.3, 8-53.6.
School counselor privilege, §§8-53.4, 115C-401.
Social worker privilege, §8-53.7.

COMPETENCY TO STAND TRIAL, §§15A-1001 to 15A-1009.
Capacity regained by defendant, §15A-1006.
Commitment.
 Civil commitment, §15A-1003(a), (b).
 Evidence admissible at proceedings, §15A-1003(c).
 Institution of proceedings, §15A-1002(b).
 Observation and treatment, §15A-1002(b).
Confidentiality of information.
 Reports to court, §15A-1002(d).
Determination of incapacity, §15A-1002(b).
Dismissal of charges, §15A-1008.
 Supplemental hearing, §15A-1007(c).
Dismissal with leave.
 Charges dismissed.
  Dismissal with leave no longer in effect, §15A-1009(e).
  Power of court not limited by section, §15A-1009(f).
 Effect, §15A-1009(b).
 Methods of entering, §15A-1009(c).
 Prosecutor authorized to enter, §15A-1009(a).
 Reinstatement of proceeding.
  Defendant becoming capable of proceeding, §15A-1009(d).
Motion, §15A-1002(a).
No proceedings when defendant mentally incapacitated, §15A-1001(a).
 Exceptions as to motions which can be handled by counsel without assistance of defendant, §15A-1001(b).
Orders for safeguarding defendant, §15A-1004(a) to (c).
 Amendment or supplementation, §15A-1004(f).
 Placement with designated individual or organization, §15A-1004(b).
 Release from custody of hospital or institution.
  Orders concerning, §15A-1004(c).
 Reports to court, §15A-1004(d).
 Return of defendant to stand trial, §15A-1004(e).
Reinstatement of proceeding.
 Dismissal with leave.
  Defendant becoming capable of proceeding, §15A-1009(d).
Reports to court, §§15A-1002(b), (b1), (d), 15A-1005.
 Hospital or institution with custody of defendant, §15A-1002(d).

COMPETENCY TO STAND TRIAL —Cont'd
Return of defendant for trial upon gaining capacity, §§15A-1004(e), 15A-1006.
Supplemental hearings, §15A-1007(a).
 Court's own determination, §15A-1007(b).
 Dismissal of charges, §15A-1007(c).
Temporary confinement of defendant, §15A-1002(c).

COMPLAINING WITNESSES.
Name, sex, age and address public record, §132-1.4(c).
 Temporarily withholding, law enforcement agencies, §132-1.4(d).

COMPLAINTS.
Account.
 Form, §1A-1 Rule 84.
Allowed pleadings, §1A-1 Rule 7(a).
Amendment changing nature of action or relief.
 Acquiring of interest in property prior to amendment not barred, §1-164.
Annulment of marriage.
 Material facts deemed denied by defendant, §50-10(a).
Attachment.
 Verified complaint used as affidavit required, §1-440.11(b).
Attorney discipline.
 Amendment, Bar Rule B.0113.
 Content requirements, Bar Rule B.0114.
 Filing, Bar Rule B.0114.
 Issuance, Bar Rule B.0113.
 Service, Bar Rule B.0114.
Child support, income withholding in non-IV-D cases, §110-136.5(a).
Civil no-contact orders.
 Workplace violence prevention.
  Filing, commencement of action, §95-262(a).
Collection agency plaintiff filing action.
 Debt buyer plaintiffs.
  Attachments to complaint required, §58-70-150.
 Requirements, §58-70-145.
Commencement of actions.
 Filing of complaint, §1A-1 Rule 3(a).
Commercial real estate broker lien act.
 Action to enforce, §44A-24.9(a).
Contractors.
 Complaints against general contractors, §87-11(a1).
Debt buyer plaintiffs filing action.
 Attachments to complaint required, §58-70-150.
Delinquent and undisciplined juvenile actions.
 Filing complaint as petition, §7B-1803(a).
 Screening of delinquency and undisciplined complaints generally, §§7B-1700 to 7B-1707.
Delivery of complaint and summons to proper person for service, §1A-1 Rule 4(a).
Divorce.
 Contents and verification, §50-8.
Expedited evictions.
 Service of complaint on defendant, §42-62(c).
Fair housing, §41A-7.
False claims act action.
 Action brought by private person, §1-608(b).
 State filing own complaint, §1-615(b).
Foreign-country money judgments.
 Recognition.
  Raising issue, §1C-1855(b).
Forms, §1A-1 Rule 84.

COMPLAINTS —Cont'd
Fraud.
Form, §1A-1 Rule 84.
General contractors, §87-11(a1).
Geologists, §89E-17(a).
Harmful material sales to minors.
Determination whether material harmful, §19-14.
Health insurance risk pool, §58-50-230.
Insanity or incompetency of party.
Supplemental complaint, §1A-1 Rule 25(b).
In the alternative.
Form, §1A-1 Rule 84.
Inverse condemnation, §40A-51(a).
Judicial standards commission.
Procedure upon receipt, JudStdsComm Rule 9.
Limited liability companies.
Derivative actions by members, §57C-8-01(b).
Lis pendens.
Failure to file within time limit.
Notice inoperative, §1-119(b).
Medical malpractice.
Requirement where complaint alleges failure to comply with applicable standard of care, §1A-1 Rule 9(j).
Money paid by mistake.
Form, §1A-1 Rule 84.
Negligence.
Forms, §1A-1 Rule 84.
Nuisances against public morals, action to abate, §19-2.2.
Pleadings generally.
See PLEADINGS.
Private personnel services, §95-47.9.
Promissory notes.
Form, §1A-1 Rule 84.
Real estate appraisal management companies.
Violation of law or unethical conduct by appraiser.
Duty of registrant to file, §93E-2-4(c).
Real estate brokers.
Commercial real estate lien.
Action to enforce, §44A-24.9(a).
Retaliatory employment discrimination, §95-242(a).
Secondary action by shareholders.
Verification by oath, §1A-1 Rule 23(b).
Sheriffs.
Delivery to for service, §1A-1 Rule 4(a).
Small claims actions, §7A-213.
Form of complaints, §7A-216.
Pleading required in assigned actions, §7A-220.
Specific performance.
Form, §1A-1 Rule 84.
Summary ejectment, §7A-223.
Supplemental complaints.
Insanity or incompetency of party, §1A-1 Rule 25(b).
Telephone services providers.
Utilities commission proceedings.
Complaints against providers, §62-73.1.
Temporary restraining order without notice.
Verified complaint, §1A-1 Rule 65(b).
Third party complaint, §1A-1 Rule 7(a).
Title of action, §1A-1 Rule 10(a).
Utilities commission proceedings.
Complaints against providers of telephone services, §62-73.1.
Action by public staff and commission, §62-73.1(b).
Notice of consumer's rights by provider, §62-73.1(a).
Complaints against public utilities, §62-73.

COMPLAINTS —Cont'd
Utilities commission proceedings —Cont'd
Complaints by public utilities, §62-74.
Workplace violence prevention.
Civil no-contact orders.
Filing, commencement of action, §95-262(a).
COMPLETENESS RULE, §8C-1 Rule 106.
COMPLEX BUSINESS CASES.
Business court judges.
Special superior court judges.
Designation to hear and decide cases, §7A-45.3.
Costs on assignment of case, §7A-305(a).
Designation, SuperCt Rule 2.1.
Mandatory complex business cases, §7A-45.4.
Judges.
Designation of special superior court judge for, SuperCt Rule 2.2.
Mandatory complex business cases.
Defined, §7A-45.4(a).
Designation, §7A-45.4.
Any party may designate, §7A-45.4(b).
Appeal to chief justice of supreme court, §7A-45.4(e).
Determination by business court judge, §7A-45.4(e).
Notice of designation.
Filing and serving, §7A-45.4(b) to (d).
Opposition to designation.
Serving and filing, §7A-45.4(e).
Proceedings, §7A-45.4(f).
Special superior court judges.
Designation to hear and decide, §7A-45.3.
COMPLIANCE BONDS.
Execution sales.
Upset bids on real property, §1-339.64(b).
Judicial sales.
Upset bid on real property at public sales, §1-339.25(b).
COMPLIMENTARY ALCOHOLIC BEVERAGES.
Air carriers serving, §18B-107(b).
COMPOSER-LAUREATE FOR STATE.
Appointment, §143-407.1(a), (b).
Governor.
Appointment, §143-407.1(a).
COMPOST.
Classification, §130A-309.11(c).
Criteria.
Establishment, §130A-309.11(a).
Investigation of potential markets, §130A-309.14(d).
Nonstandard compost.
Disposal, §130A-309.11(e).
Rules and regulations, §130A-309.11(b).
State procurement, §130A-309.14(f).
Stormwater control best management practices and process water treatment processes.
Composting operations.
Clarifications by division of water quality, §143-214.7A(b).
Compost operation stakeholder advisory group.
Department to form, §143-214.7A(e).
Establishment by department, §143-214.7A(a).
Factors considered in adopting practices and permitting procedures, §143-214.7A(f).
Federal programs, other states' procedures.
Review in adopting practices, §143-214.7A(d).
Purposes, §143-214.7A(a).

COMPOST —Cont'd
Stormwater control best management practices and process water treatment processes —Cont'd
Composting operations —Cont'd
Revised water quality permitting procedures.
Establishment for operations, §143-214.7A(c).
Use and application rates, §130A-309.11(d).

COMPOUND INTEREST.
Obligations due guardians, §24-4.

COMPROMISE AND SETTLEMENT.
See SETTLEMENT.

COMPULSORY COUNTERCLAIMS, §1A-1 Rule 13(a).

COMPULSORY REFERENCE, §1A-1 Rule 53(a).

COMPULSORY SCHOOL ATTENDANCE,
§§115C-378 to 115C-383, NC Const Art IX §3.
Age children required to attend, §115C-378(a).
Blind children, §115C-383.
Church schools and schools of religious charter, §115C-548.
Deaf children, §115C-383.
Delinquent and undisciplined juvenile.
Alternative dispositions for delinquent juveniles.
Excusing juvenile from compliance with law, §7B-2506.
Alternative dispositions for undisciplined juveniles.
Excusing from compliance with law, §7B-2503.
Encouraging absence, prohibited, §115C-378(b).
Enforcement.
Method of enforcement, §115C-379.
Excessive absences.
Notice to parent, §115C-378(e).
Parent's responsibility, §115C-378(g).
Excused absence.
Principal, superintendent or designee may excuse, §115C-378(c).
Indigency.
Investigation of indigency, §115C-382.
Investigations.
Indigency, §115C-382.
School social workers, §115C-381.
Indigency, §115C-382.
Nonpublic schools.
Required attendance, §115C-378(a).
Notice of reason for absence, §115C-378(b).
Notice to parent of excessive absences, §115C-378(e).
Parent's responsibility for absence.
Prima facie case, §115C-378(g).
Penalty for violation, §115C-380.
Private schools, §115C-556.
Records.
Nonpublic schools, §115C-378(d).
Regional schools, §115C-238.66.
Reports, §115C-381.
Nonpublic schools, §115C-378(f).
Required ages of attendance, §115C-378(a).
School social workers.
Allocation, §115C-381.
Employment, §115C-381.
General provisions, §115C-381.
Investigations, §115C-381.
Indigency, §115C-382.
Salary schedule.
State board of education to develop, §115C-381.
State board of education.
Enforcement, §115C-379.

COMPULSORY SCHOOL ATTENDANCE
—Cont'd
Teachers.
Discouragement of nonattendance.
Duty of teachers, §115C-307(f).
Violations.
Penalty for violation, §115C-380.
Regional schools, §115C-238.66.
Prima facie evidence of violations, §115C-381.

COMPUTATION OF TIME, §§1-593, 1A-1 Rule 6(a).
Act to be done falls on Saturday, Sunday or holiday, §103-5(a), (b).

COMPUTER AND TELEVISION RETAILERS.
Defined, §130A-309.131.
Label identifying manufacturer of brand.
Determination before selling, §130A-309.136(b).
Required on equipment before selling, §130A-309.136(a).
Recycled equipment.
Data or other information left on covered device.
Not liable, §130A-309.133.
Generally, §§130A-309.130 to 130A-309.141.
See RECYCLING.
Registration by manufacturer.
Required before selling, §130A-309.136(a).
Revoked or expired registration.
Retailer not responsible for unlawful sales, §130A-309.136(c).
Unlawful sales because manufacturer's registration expired or revoked.
Not responsible, §130A-309.136(c).

COMPUTER ASSISTED REMOTE HUNTING.
Prohibition, §113-291.1A.

COMPUTER BASED CLE.
Accreditation, Bar Rule D.1611.

COMPUTER CRIMES.
Accessing or causing to be accessed.
Defined, §§14-453, 14-454(c).
Felony offense, §14-454(a).
Misdemeanor offense, §14-454(b).
Applicability of provisions.
Exceptions, §14-453.1.
Authorization defined, §14-453.
Child pornography.
Report by film and photographic processor or computer technician, §66-67.4.
Computer defined, §14-453.
Computer network defined, §14-453.
Computer program defined, §14-453.
Computer software defined, §14-453.
Computer system defined, §14-453.
Computer trespass, §14-458.
Damages for.
Jurisdiction, §1-539.2A(b).
Limitations period, §1-539.2A(b).
Right to damages, §1-539.2A(a).
Cyber-bullying, §14-458.1.
Damaging computers and computer resources.
Application of provisions, §14-455(b).
Unlawful acts, §14-455(a), (a1).
Viruses.
Computer viruses, §14-454(b).
Data defined, §14-453.
Denial of computer services to authorized user, §14-456(a), (b).
Electronic mail defined, §14-453.
Exceptions, §14-453.1.

COMPUTER CRIMES —Cont'd
Extortion, §14-457.
Financial instrument defined, §14-453.
Government computers.
Accessing.
Definition, §14-454.1(d).
Prohibited acts, §14-454.1(a) to (d).
Altering, damaging or destroying, §14-455(a1).
Defined, §14-453.
Denial of services to authorized user, §14-456.1(a).
Applicability of provisions, §14-456.1(b).
Internet.
Sex offenders banned from use of social
networking sites, §14-202.5.
Solicitation of child by computer, §14-202.3.
Internet chat room.
Defined, §14-453.
Jurisdiction, §14-453.2.
Profile defined, §14-453.
Property defined, §14-453.
Resource defined, §14-453.
Services defined, §14-453.
Sex offenders.
Social networking sites.
Banned from use of, §14-202.5.
Solicitation of child by computer, §14-202.3(a).
Viruses.
Introducing computer virus, §14-455(b).
Denial of government computer services to an
authorized user, §14-456.1(b).

COMPUTER EQUIPMENT COLLECTORS.
Recycling discarded computer equipment.
Requirements, §130A-94.

COMPUTER GAMES.
Criminal offense to make unlawful payout,
§14-306(d).
Devices not considered slot machines,
§14-306(b).
Paying more than allowed by law.
Warning sticker or message as to criminal penalty
affixed to machine, §14-306(c).
Pay off in cash.
Exception to slot machine definition inapplicable,
§14-306(d).
Repurchase of prize for cash or reward in
cash.
Inapplicability of exception to slot machine
definition, §14-306(d).

COMPUTER INFORMATION TRANSACTIONS.
Electronic transactions.
Choice of law, §66-329.

COMPUTER MANUFACTURERS.
Label identifying required on equipment,
§130A-309.134(b).
Recycling computer equipment.
Computer equipment manufacturer defined,
§130A-309.131.
Generally, §§130A-309.131 to 130A-309.141.
See RECYCLING.
Plan required, §130A-309.134(c) to (h).
Registration before selling or offering for sale.
Required, §130A-309.134(a).
Fee, §130A-309.134(d).

COMPUTERS AND SOFTWARE.
Child custody jurisdiction and enforcement.
Testimony of witnesses, §50A-111.

COMPUTERS AND SOFTWARE —Cont'd
Child pornography.
Film or computer images of minor engaging in
sexual activity.
Report by film and photographic processor or
computer technician, §66-67.4.
Collectors of computer equipment for
recycling.
Requirements, §130A-94.
Computer crimes, §§14-453 to 14-458.
See COMPUTER CRIMES.
Department of revenue.
Reproduction of records.
Records stored on permanent computer-readable
media, §8-45.3(b).
Discarded computers and televisions.
Land fills.
Disposal prohibited, §130A-309.10(f).
Recycling, §§130A-309.130 to 130A-309.141.
See RECYCLING.
Driving while viewing computer located
forward of driver's seat.
Prohibited, excepted equipment, §20-136.1.
Electronic transactions, §§66-311 to 66-330.
See ELECTRONIC TRANSACTIONS.
E-mail spam.
Damage recovery, §1-539.2A.
Personal jurisdiction for actions regarding,
§1-75.4.
Employment security division.
Reproduction of records.
Records stored on permanent computer-readable
media, §8-45.3(b).
Geographical information systems databases,
§132-10.
Hunting.
Computer assisted remote hunting.
Prohibition, §113-291.1A.
Intellectual property generally.
See INTELLECTUAL PROPERTY.
Interactive digital media.
Research and development tax credit,
§105-129.56.
Internet.
See INTERNET.
Jury list.
Preparation of list.
Alternate procedure in certain counties,
§9-2.1(a).
Randomized list, §9-2.1(b).
Land fills.
Disposal of computer equipment prohibited,
§130A-309.10(f).
Manufacturers of computer equipment.
Label identifying required on equipment,
§130A-309.134(b).
Recycling computer equipment.
Computer equipment manufacturer defined,
§130A-309.131.
Generally, §§130A-309.131 to 130A-309.141.
See RECYCLING.
Plan required, §130A-309.134(c) to (h).
Registration before selling or offering for sale.
Required, §130A-309.134(a).
Fee, §130A-309.134(d).
Medical care data, §§131E-214 to 131E-214.4.
See MEDICAL CARE DATA.
Motor vehicle dealer management computer
systems, §20-305.7.
Motor vehicle equipment located forward of
driver's seat.
Driving while viewing computer prohibited,
excepted equipment, §20-136.1.

COMPUTERS AND SOFTWARE —Cont'd
Office of information technology services.
Generally, §§147-33.75 to 147-33.104A.
See INFORMATION TECHNOLOGY
SERVICES.
Portable consumer electronic devices insurance.
Claims handling, adjuster licenses, §58-33-27.
Generally, §§58-44A-1 to 58-44A-25.
See PORTABLE CONSUMER ELECTRONIC
DEVICES INSURANCE.
Privilege taxes.
Datacenter machinery and equipment,
§105-187.51C.
Software publishing companies, §105-187.51B.
Procurement of information technology,
§§147-33.95 to 147-33.104A.
Property tax exemption.
Software, §105-275.
Property tax exemptions, §105-275.
Records, §132-6.1.
Copies of databases, §132-6.2(c).
Recycling discarded computers and televisions, §§130A-309.130 to 130A-309.141.
See RECYCLING.
Registration of voters, §§163-82.11, 163-82.12.
Retailers.
Defined, §130A-309.131.
Label identifying manufacturer of brand.
Determination before selling, §130A-309.136(b).
Required on equipment before selling,
§130A-309.136(a).
Recycled equipment.
Data or other information left on covered device.
Not liable, §130A-309.133.
Generally, §§130A-309.130 to 130A-309.141.
See RECYCLING.
Registration by manufacturer.
Required before selling, §130A-309.136(a).
Revoked or expired registration.
Retailer not responsible for unlawful sales,
§130A-309.136(c).
Unlawful sales because manufacturer's
registration expired or revoked.
Not responsible, §130A-309.136(c).
Sales and use tax.
Customer computer program defined, §105-164.3.
Defined, §105-164.3.
Industrial facilities refunds, §105-164.14B(a).
Software.
Defined, §105-164.3.
Exemption, §105-164.13.
Tax holiday, §105-164.13C(a).
Schools.
Lease purchase or installment purchase contracts
by local boards.
Purchase of computers, hardware, software and
related services, §115C-528.
Solid waste management.
Land fills.
Disposal of computer equipment prohibited,
§130A-309.10(f).
Recycling discarded computers and televisions,
§§130A-309.130 to 130A-309.141.
See RECYCLING.
State departments and agencies.
Procurement of information technology,
§§147-33.95 to 147-33.104A.
COMPUTER TRESPASS.
Action by injured party, §14-458(c).
Jurisdiction, §1-539.2A(b).

COMPUTER TRESPASS —Cont'd
Action by injured party —Cont'd
Limitation period, §1-539.2A(b).
Right to damages, §1-539.2A(a).
Penalties, §14-458(b).
Prohibited acts, §14-458(a).
COMPUTER VIRUSES, §14-455(b).
Denial of government computer services to an authorized user, §14-456.1(b).
CONCEALED DEBTORS.
Arrest, §1-355.
Attachment.
Grounds for attachment, §1-440.3.
CONCEALED HANDGUN PERMIT, §§14-415.10 to 14-415.27.
Age limitation.
Qualifications of applicant, §14-415.12(a).
Alcoholic beverage consumption.
Carrying concealed handgun while.
Prohibition, §14-415.11(c), (c2).
Alcohol or controlled substances remaining in body or blood.
Carrying concealed handgun prohibition,
§14-415.11(c2).
Appeals.
Denial, revocation or nonrenewal of permit,
§14-415.15(c).
Revocation or nonrenewal of permit,
§14-415.18(a).
Application, §14-415.13(a).
Contents of form, §14-415.14(a).
Warning on form, §14-415.14(b).
Areas where concealed handgun unauthorized in spite of permit, §14-415.11(c).
Athletic facilities, athletic fields, playgrounds, swimming pools.
Municipal or county ordinance prohibiting
carrying, §14-415.23.
Bail.
Proceedings pending for disqualifying crime.
Grounds for denial of permit, §14-415.12(b).
Banks and financial institutions.
Concealed handgun prohibited, §14-415.11(c).
Bureau of investigation.
Copy of permit sent to, information available on
statewide system, §14-415.17.
Submission of fingerprints to FBI for records
check, §14-415.13(b).
Carrying a concealed handgun without permit.
Applicability of provisions, §14-415.22.
Infraction, §14-415.21(a).
Carrying of permit, §14-415.11(a).
Certificate form, §14-415.17.
Change of address.
Permittee to notify sheriff, §14-415.11(d).
Citizenship.
Qualifications of applicant, §14-415.12(a).
Conflict of laws.
Warning required on application, §14-415.14(b).
Construction of article, §14-415.22.
Controlled substance consumption.
Concealed handgun prohibited, §14-415.11(c).
Convicted felon disqualifications, §14-415.12(b).
Correctional facilities.
Concealed handgun prohibited, §14-415.11(c).
Criminal history record checks.
Fees, §14-415.19(a).
Procedure for issuance of permit, §14-415.15(a).

CONCEALED HANDGUN PERMIT —Cont'd
Criminal history record checks —Cont'd
Renewal.
Criminal history updated, §14-415.16(c).
Criminal justice education and training standards commission.
Approved courses for firearms safety, §14-415.12(a).
Certificate of completion of firearms safety course, §14-415.13(a).
Filing of course description by instructor, §14-415.12(a).
Definitions, §14-415.10.
Denial of permit, §14-415.15(a).
Appeal, §14-415.15(c).
Grounds, §14-415.12(b).
No liability of sheriff, §14-415.20.
Notice, stating grounds for denial, §14-415.15(c).
Destruction of permit.
Notification to sheriff, §14-415.11(d).
Discharge from armed forces, other than honorable.
Grounds for denial of permit, §14-415.12(b).
Display to law enforcement officer upon request, §14-415.11(a).
Failure to disclose, §14-415.21(a).
District attorneys, assistant district attorneys, investigators employed by.
Listed area prohibitions.
Not subject to unless prohibited by federal law, §14-415.27.
Domestic violence, orders issued by court.
Suspension of permit, §14-415.18(b).
Duplicate permit.
Lending or giving duplicate to another, §14-415.18(a).
Replacement of lost or destroyed permits, §14-415.11(d).
Duration of permit, §14-415.11(b).
Emergencies.
Temporary permit issuance, §14-415.15(b).
Exemptions from requirement, §14-415.25.
Failure to disclose permit to law enforcement officer.
Infraction, §14-415.21(a).
Federal office buildings.
Concealed handgun prohibited, §14-415.11(c).
Federal prosecution for possession of handgun.
Warning required on application, §14-415.14(b).
Fees, §14-415.13(a).
Criminal records checks, §14-415.19(a).
Fingerprint processing, §14-415.19(b).
Retired sworn law enforcement officer, §14-415.19(a1).
Schedule of fees, §14-415.19(a).
Fingerprints.
Fees for processing, §14-415.19(b).
Renewal.
New set, §14-415.16(b).
When not required, §14-415.16(d).
Submitted to state bureau of investigation for record check, §14-415.13(b).
Submitted with application, §14-415.13(a).
Firearms safety and training course.
Certificate of completion submitted with application, §14-415.13(a).
Exemptions.
Armed security guard licensees, §14-415.12A(b).
Law enforcement officers, §14-415.12A(a).
Qualifications of applicant, §14-415.12(a).

CONCEALED HANDGUN PERMIT —Cont'd
Firearms safety and training course —Cont'd
Renewal.
Waiver by sheriff, §14-415.16(c), (e).
Form of application, §14-415.13(a).
Contents of form, §14-415.14.
Fraud.
Revocation or suspension for fraud in obtaining, §14-415.18(a).
Fugitives from justice.
Grounds for denial of permit, §14-415.12(b).
Handgun, defined, §14-415.10.
Hunting and fishing reservations.
Openly carrying firearm or concealed carrying of handgun.
State owned reservations, §14-415.11(c3).
Identification required, §14-415.11(a).
Impaired driving.
Conviction is grounds for denial of permit, §14-415.12(b).
Indictment for felony.
Grounds for denial of permit, §14-415.12(b).
Infractions.
Surrender of permit in lieu of paying fine, §14-415.21(a).
Violations of article, §14-415.21(a).
Investigation to determine qualifications or competency.
Sheriff authorized to conduct, §14-415.15(a).
Issuance, §14-415.15(a).
Sheriffs, §14-415.11(b).
Liability, §14-415.20.
Law enforcement facilities.
Concealed handgun prohibited, §14-415.11(c).
Law enforcement officers.
Exemptions from requirement, §14-415.25.
Qualified retired law enforcement officers.
Certification.
Application for, §14-415.26(a).
Misrepresentations, §14-415.26(d).
Immunity for, §14-415.26(c).
Notice of limitations applicable, §14-415.26(b).
Private protective services.
Not exempted from requirements, §14-415.26(e).
Exemption from requirement, §14-415.25.
Multiple firearms qualifications sites throughout state, §14-415.26(b1).
Lending or giving permit to another, §14-415.18(a).
Liability of sheriff for issuance or denial, §14-415.20.
List of persons issued permits.
Sheriff to maintain, §14-415.17.
Local laws regarding concealed handgun permits prohibited, §14-415.23.
Local laws regarding posting of prohibitions.
Permissible, §14-415.23.
Lost permits.
Notification to sheriff, §14-415.11(d).
Mental health.
Disclosure of records regarding, §14-415.14(c).
Drug addict or user.
Grounds for denial of permit, §14-415.12(b).
Eligibility upon restoration of rights, §14-415.12(c).
Grounds for denial of permit, §14-415.12(b).
Release of records concerning mental health submitted with application, §14-415.13(a).
Restoration process to remove bar due to mental commitment, §122C-54.1.

CONCEALED HANDGUN PERMIT —Cont'd

Military discharge under conditions other than honorable.
Grounds for denial of permit, §14-415.12(b).

Military permittees.
Expiration of permit during deployment.
Carrying concealed handgun following end of deployment, §§14-415.11(a), 14-415.16A(b).
Validity during deployment, §14-415.16A(b).
Extension of permit.
Permit to expire during deployment, §14-415.16A(a).
Renewal after deployment, time, §14-415.16A(c).

Misdemeanors.
Grounds for denial of permit, §14-415.12(b).
Violations of article, §14-415.21(b).

Misrepresentation.
Revocation or suspension for misrepresentation in obtaining, §14-415.18(a).

Misuse of permit.
Grounds for revocation or suspension, §14-415.18(a).

Municipal or county recreational facilities.
Ordinance to prohibit carrying by posting, §14-415.23.

National rifle association.
Approved course for firearms safety, §14-415.12(a).

Notice.
Denial of permit, §14-415.15(c).

Out of state permits.
Reciprocity, §14-415.24(a).

Permit, defined, §14-415.10.

Permit information available upon request, §14-415.17.

Physical or mental infirmity preventing safe handling of handgun.
Qualifications of applicant, §14-415.12(a).

Probable cause of commission of felony.
Grounds for denial of permit, §14-415.12(b).

Property posting prohibition of concealed handguns, §14-415.11(c).

Protective order issued for protection of applicant.
Temporary permit, issuance, §14-415.15(b).

Qualifications of applicant, §14-415.12(a).

Reciprocity.
Out of state permits, §14-415.24(a).

Records.
Release of mental health records submitted with application, §14-415.13(a).

Renewal of permit.
Affidavit that permittee remains qualified, §14-415.16(b).
Application by filing renewal form, §14-415.16(b).
Continuation of permit beyond expiration date, §14-415.16(c).
Criminal history updated, §14-415.16(c).
Determination if permittee remains qualified, §14-415.16(c).
Failure to receive renewal notice.
Permittee not relieve of requirements, §14-415.16(a).
Fingerprints, §14-415.16(b).
When not required, §14-415.16(d).
Firearms safety and training course.
Sheriff may waive requirement, §14-415.16(c), (e).
Notice to permittee, §14-415.16(a).

CONCEALED HANDGUN PERMIT —Cont'd

Rest areas or rest stops along highways.
Openly carrying firearm or concealed carrying of handgun.
State owned rest areas or rest stops, §14-415.11(c3).

Revocation of permit, §14-415.18(a).
Sheriff, authority, §14-415.18(a).

State bureau of investigation.
Copy of permit sent to, information available on statewide system, §14-415.17.
Submission of fingerprints for records check, §14-415.13(b).

State office buildings.
Concealed handgun prohibited, §14-415.11(c).

State parks.
Carrying concealed handgun authorized, §14-415.11(c1).

Statewide uniformity, §14-415.23.

Surrender of permit in lieu of paying fine.
First offense infractions, §14-415.21(a).

Suspension of permit, §14-415.18(a).
Part of orders issued in domestic violence case, §14-415.18(b).

Temporary permit for emergencies, §14-415.15(b).

Transferring permit to another person.
Grounds for revocation or suspension, §14-415.18(a).

Validity period, §14-415.11(b).

Violations of article.
Punishment, §14-415.21.
Revocation or suspension of permit, §14-415.18(a).

CONCEALED PROPERTY IN BUILDINGS.
Claim for delivery of personal property, §1-480.

CONCEALED WEAPONS.
Carrying, §14-269.
Alcohol or controlled substances remaining in body or blood.
Prohibited, §14-415.11(c2).
Places authorized, §14-415.11.
While consuming alcohol.
Prohibited, §14-415.11(c2).
Concealed handgun permit generally, §§14-415.10 to 14-415.27.
See CONCEALED HANDGUN PERMIT.
Confiscation, §14-269.1.

CONCEALING BIRTH OF CHILD, §14-46.

CONCEALMENT OF DEATH, §14-401.22(a).
Aiding, abetting or counseling, §14-401.22(b).

CONCEALMENT OF MERCHANDISE.
Shoplifting, §14-72.1.
Civil liability for damages, §1-538.2.

CONCERTS.
Live concert recordings, §14-433(a) to (c).
Live music performances or productions.
Truth in music advertising act, §§75-125 to 75-128.
Scalping tickets, §§14-344, 14-344.1.
Software to interfere with operations of ticket seller, §14-344.2.

CONCESSIONS.
State parks.
Operation of public service facilities.
Authority of department of environment and natural resources, §113-35(d).

CONCILIATION.
Custody and visitation mediation program, §§7A-494, 7A-495.

CONCILIATION —Cont'd
Fair housing complaints.
Commission to seek to informally resolve
complaints, §41A-7(g).
Labor disputes, §§95-32 to 95-36.
New motor vehicles warranties act.
Utilization of informal settlement procedure.
Manufacturer requiring, §20-351.7.
Retaliatory employment discrimination.
Commissioner's attempt to eliminate violation by
informal method, §95-242(a).

CONCORD.
Land-use development incentives.
Reduction of energy consumption, §160A-383.4.
Satellite annexation.
Limitation on area of satellite corporate limits,
inapplicability, §160A-58.1(b).

CONCURRENT SENTENCES, §15A-1354.

CONCUSSIONS AND HEAD INJURIES.
Interscholastic athletic activities.
Concussion defined, §115C-12.
Information sheet.
Signing required to participate, §115C-12.
Removal of student exhibiting signs or symptoms
from activity, §115C-12.
Written clearance.
Required for student to resume activity,
§115C-12.

CONDEMNATION.
Conservation easements.
Condemnation of property encumbered by,
§§40A-80 to 40A-85.
Fertilizers.
Noncompliance with commercial fertilizer article,
§106-667.
Generally.
See EMINENT DOMAIN.
Highways generally, §§136-103 to 136-121.1.
See HIGHWAYS, ROADS AND STREETS.
Meat, adulterated or misbranded,
§106-549.52(a), (b).
Poultry, adulterated or misbranded,
§106-549.53(a) to (c).
Unsafe buildings.
Municipalities generally, §§160A-411 to 160A-439.
See MUNICIPAL BUILDING INSPECTION.

CONDITIONAL JUDGMENTS.
Garnishees.
Failure to appear, §1-440.27.

**CONDITIONAL OFFER OF JUDGMENT FOR
DAMAGES,** §1A-1 Rule 68(b).

CONDITIONAL SALES CONTRACTS.
Attorneys' fees, §6-21.2.
Claim for delivery of personal property.
Expiration of certain orders, §1-474(b).
Corporations.
Forms of probate for deeds and other conveyances,
§47-41.02(f).
Railroad property.
Sale on condition title remain in vendor until paid
for, §47-24.
Registration of contract.
Effect of registration, §47-20(a).
Place of registrations, §47-20.2(a), (b).
Instrument covering both personal and real
property, §47-20.3.
Sale under execution.
Interests of vendee, §1-315(a).

CONDITIONAL SERVICE CONTRACTS.
Sales and use tax, §105-164.12B.

CONDITION OF MIND.
Special matters, pleading, §1A-1 Rule 9(b).
**Then existing state or condition, hearsay
exception,** §8C-1 Rule 803.

CONDITIONS BROKEN, RIGHTS OF ENTRY.
Property passed by will, §31-40.

CONDITIONS PRECEDENT.
Pleading special matters, §1A-1 Rule 9(c).

CONDOMINIUMS, §§47C-1-101 to 47C-4-120.
Actions.
Breach of warranty.
Limitation of action, §47C-4-116.
Tort or contract liability.
Owners' association and declarant, §47C-3-111.
**Allocation of common element, interests, votes
and common expenses liabilities,**
§47C-2-107.
Amendment to declaration changing,
§47C-2-117(d).
Limited common elements, §47C-2-108.
Merger or consolidation of condominiums.
Reallocation of allocated interests,
§47C-2-121(c).
Alterations.
Units, §47C-2-111.
Applicability of chapter.
Generally, §47C-1-102(a).
Unit ownership act, §47C-1-102(b).
Units located outside state, §47C-1-102(c).
**Applicability of supplemental general
principles of law,** §47C-1-108.
Assessments.
Lien, §47C-3-116.
Owners' associations.
Common expenses, §47C-3-115.
Attorneys' fees.
Declarant liable to association, §47C-3-111(d).
Protection of purchasers, §47C-4-117.
Boundaries.
Relocation of boundaries between adjoining units,
§47C-2-112(a), (b).
Units, §47C-2-102.
Declaration amendment changing,
§47C-2-117(d).
Building codes.
Applicability of local building codes, §47C-1-106.
Bylaws.
Conflict with declaration, §47C-2-103(c).
Owners' association, §47C-3-106(a), (b).
Rule against perpetuities.
Not applied to defeat provisions, §47C-2-103(b).
Severability of provisions, §47C-2-103(a).
Cancellation of purchase contract.
Purchasers right, manner of canceling,
§47C-4-108(a), (b).
Citation of chapter, §47C-1-101.
Common elements.
Allocation, §47C-2-107(a), (b), (d).
Limited common elements, §47C-2-108.
Conveyance, encumbrance, subjecting to security
interest.
Access and support, unit owners not deprived
of, §47C-3-112(e).
Agreement and ratification, evidencing
agreement, §47C-3-112(b).
Contract by association, §47C-3-112(c).
Proceeds of sale or financing, §47C-3-112(a).

CONDOMINIUMS —Cont'd
Common elements —Cont'd
Conveyance, encumbrance, subjecting to security
    interest —Cont'd
    Void transactions, noncompliance with
        provisions, §47C-3-112(d).
    Votes required, §47C-3-112(a).
Damages to.
    Assessment of liability for damages by
        adjudicatory panel, §47C-3-107(d).
    Hearing by adjudicatory panel to assess
        responsibility, §47C-3-107(d).
    Repair by association when agent responsible
        for, §47C-3-107(c).
    Repair by unit owner responsible for,
        §47C-3-107(b).
Easement rights of declarants, §47C-2-116.
Insurance.
    Property insurance, §47C-3-113.
Limited common elements.
    Allocation, §47C-2-108(a).
        Element not previously allocated as limited
            element, §47C-2-108(c).
    Maintenance, repair or replacement.
        Assessment of unit owners to recover costs,
            §47C-3-115(c).
    Reallocation, §47C-2-108(b).
Maintenance, repair or replacement.
    Assessment of unit owners to recover costs,
        §47C-3-107(a).
        Limited common elements, §47C-3-115(c).
    Association responsibility, §47C-3-107(a).
Partition, not subject to, §47C-2-107(d).
Property insurance, §47C-3-113.
Security interest in common elements.
    Exercise against common elements before
        enforced against unit, §47C-3-117(b).
Transfer of undivided interest without unit to
    which interest allocated.
    Void, §47C-2-107(d).
Common expenses.
Allocation, §47C-2-107(a), (b), (d).
Assessment.
    Allocations.
        Assessment against units in accordance with,
            §47C-3-115(b).
    Annual assessment required, §47C-3-115(a).
    Benefiting fewer than all units, §47C-3-115(c).
    Insurance costs, §47C-3-115(c).
    Judgments against association, §47C-3-115(d).
    Limited common elements.
        Maintenance, repair or replacement,
            §47C-3-115(c).
    Misconduct of unit owner, §47C-3-115(e).
    Past due, interest, §47C-3-115(b).
    Payment by declarant until assessment made,
        §47C-3-115(a).
    Recalculation.
        Reallocation of expenses, §47C-3-115(f).
Consolidation, §47C-2-121.
Continuing care retirement communities.
Applicability of article, §58-64-85(b).
Contracts.
Conveyance or encumbrance of common elements,
    §47C-3-112(c).
Owners' associations.
    Tort and contract liability, §47C-3-111.
Termination of contracts and leases of declarant,
    §47C-3-105.
Conversion buildings.
Public offering statement, §47C-4-106.

CONDOMINIUMS —Cont'd
Conveyance of common elements, §47C-3-112.
Corporations.
Master associations.
    Powers exercised or delegated to corporation,
        §47C-2-120.
Cost of litigation.
Declarant liable to association, §47C-3-111(d).
Declarations.
Allocation of common element, interests, votes
    and common expenses liabilities, §47C-2-107.
Amendment.
    Action to challenge validity, time limitation,
        §47C-2-117(b).
    Affirmative vote or written agreement by unit
        owners, percentage, §47C-2-117(a).
    Exercising development rights, §47C-2-110.
    Recording and indexing, §47C-2-117(c), (e).
    Unanimous consent of unit owners.
        Required for certain matters, §47C-2-117(d).
Conflict with bylaws, §47C-2-103(c).
Development rights.
    Exercise, §47C-2-110.
Execution, §47C-2-101(a).
Leasehold condominiums.
    Every lessor must sign, §47C-2-106(a).
    Provisions required, §47C-2-106(a).
    Recording, §47C-2-106(a).
Limited common elements, §47C-2-108.
Nonmaterial errors or omissions, §47C-1-104(c).
Other provisions permitted, §47C-2-105(b).
Plats and plans, §47C-2-109.
Recordation, §47C-2-101.
Required provisions, §47C-2-105(a).
    Leasehold condominiums, §47C-2-106(a).
Rule against perpetuities.
    Not applied to defeat provisions, §47C-2-103(b).
Sales uses, §47C-2-115.
Severability of provisions, §47C-2-103(a).
Special declarant rights.
    Amendment creating or increasing, unanimous
        consent required, §47C-2-117(d).
    Transfer, §47C-3-104.
Subdividing units.
    Amending declaration, §47C-2-113(a), (b).
Substantial failure to comply.
    Marketability of title impaired, determining,
        §47C-2-103(d).
Surplus funds, §47C-3-114.
Transfer of special declarant rights, §47C-3-104.
Definitions, §47C-1-103.
Description of units, §47C-2-104.
Development rights.
Condominium subject to development right,
    §47C-4-104.
Exercise of rights.
    Amendment to declaration, §47C-2-110(a).
    Recording amendment to declaration,
        §47C-2-110(a).
Maintenance, repair and expenses.
    Responsibility of declarant, §47C-3-107(e).
Reserving rights in real estate added to
    condominium, §47C-2-110(b).
Subdividing or converting units, §47C-2-110(c).
Withdrawal, rights subject to, §47C-2-110(d).
Easements.
Declarant's right to easements through common
    elements, §47C-2-116.
Encroachments, §47C-2-114(a), (b).
Eminent domain.
Awards, §47C-1-107(a).

CONDOMINIUMS —Cont'd
Eminent domain —Cont'd
Common elements, §47C-1-107(c).
Partial taking, §47C-1-107(b).
Recordation of court decree, §47C-1-107(d).
Encroachments.
Easement for encroachment, §47C-2-114(a), (b).
Escrow of deposits.
Deposit made in connection with purchase or
reservation of unit, §47C-4-110(a), (b).
Fines.
Procedure, §47C-3-107.1.
Flags.
Display of United States or North Carolina flags,
§47C-3-121.
**Foreclosure or enforcement of lien or
encumbrance,** §47C-2-118(i), (j).
Foreclosure or sale of special declarant rights,
§47C-3-104(c), (d).
Impairment of marketability of title.
Substantial failure of declaration to comply.
Determining, §47C-2-103(d).
Implied warranty of quality.
Accrual of cause of action for breach.
Warranty of quality extending to future
performance or duration, §47C-4-116(b).
Exclusion or modification.
Agreement or expression, §47C-4-115(a).
Purchaser of unit used for residential purposes,
restrictions, §47C-4-115(b).
Improvements.
Completion of improvements labeled "must be
built,"§47C-4-119.
Declarant's obligation to complete and restore,
§47C-4-119.
Inconsistent time share provisions, §47C-1-109.
Insurance.
Assessment to pay costs, §47C-3-115(c).
Property and liability insurance, §47C-3-113.
Irrigation of landscaping, §47C-3-122.
Judgments against association.
Assessment to pay, §47C-3-115(d).
Indexing, §47C-3-117(d).
Lien in favor of judgment lienholder,
§47C-3-117(a).
Labels.
Completion of improvements labeled "must be
built,"§47C-4-119.
Promotional material, §47C-4-118.
Landscaping irrigation, §47C-3-122.
Leasehold condominiums.
Declarations.
Every lessor must sign, §47C-2-106(a).
Recording, §47C-2-106(a).
Required provisions, §47C-2-106(a).
Merger of leasehold and fee simple.
Acquisition of leasehold by owner of reversion or
remainder, §47C-2-106(c).
Reallocation of allocated interests as though units
taken by eminent domain.
Expiration or termination of leasehold reducing
units, §47C-2-106(d).
Termination after recording declaration,
restrictions, §47C-2-106(b).
Leases of declarant.
Termination, §47C-3-105.
Liens or encumbrances.
Common elements.
Subjecting common elements to encumbrance,
§47C-3-112.
Foreclosure or enforcement, §47C-2-118(i), (j).

CONDOMINIUMS —Cont'd
Liens or encumbrances —Cont'd
Judgment for money against association,
§47C-3-117(a).
Lien for assessments, §47C-3-116(a).
Claims, information required, §47C-3-116(g).
Costs and attorneys' fees, §47C-3-116(e), (e1).
Deed in lieu of foreclosure.
Authority to take, §47C-3-116(d).
Extinguished.
Failure to enforce within 3 years after
docketing, §47C-3-116(c).
Fees, charges, late charges and other charges.
Enforceable as assessments, §47C-3-116(a).
Foreclosure, §47C-3-116(a), (a1), (a2).
Holder of mortgage, deed of trust or other
purchaser.
Liability, §47C-3-116(f).
Installment payments, §47C-3-116(e2).
Limitation period on enforcement,
§47C-3-116(c).
Priority, §47C-3-116(b).
Release of liens or encumbrances.
Conveying real estate to association,
§47C-4-111(b).
Covering unit of owner paying lienholder,
§47C-3-117(c).
Sale of unit requiring public offering statement.
Purchaser not agreeing to take subject to or
assume, §47C-4-111(a).
Security interest in common elements.
Exercise against common elements before
enforced against unit, §47C-3-117(b).
Two or more units effected by lien.
Release lien attributable to owner paying,
§47C-3-117(c).
Limitation of actions.
Challenging validity of declaration amendment,
§47C-2-117(b).
Warranties, §47C-4-116.
Limited common elements, §47C-2-108.
Marketability of title impaired.
Substantial failure of declaration to comply.
Determining, §47C-2-103(d).
Master associations, §47C-2-120.
Merger or consolidation.
Agreement, §47C-2-121(b).
Authority, consequences, §47C-2-121(a).
Reallocation of allocated interests, §47C-2-121(c).
Nonprofit corporations.
Master associations.
Powers exercised or delegated to corporation,
§47C-2-120.
Ordinances.
Applicability of local ordinances, §47C-1-106.
Owners' associations.
Assessment.
Common expenses, §47C-3-115.
Budget.
Summary provided, meeting to ratify,
§47C-3-103(c).
Bylaws, §47C-3-106(a), (b).
Contract liability, §47C-3-111.
Corporate nature, §47C-3-101.
Declarant control of association.
Appointment and removal of executive board
members, termination of control,
§47C-3-103(d).
Tort or contract liability to association,
§47C-3-111(c), (d).

CONDOMINIUMS —Cont'd
Owners' associations —Cont'd
Executive board.
  Budget.
    Summary provided, meeting to ratify,
      §47C-3-103(c).
  Declarant control of association.
    Appointment and removal of executive board
      members, §47C-3-103(d).
  Election by unit owners, §47C-3-103(e), (f).
  Fiduciary relationship to association and unit
    owners, §47C-3-103(a).
  Meetings, §47C-3-108(b), (c).
  Payments to officers or members, §47C-3-118(c).
  Power to act on behalf of association,
    §47C-3-103(a).
    Restrictions, §47C-3-103(b).
  Quorum, §47C-3-109(b).
  Removal, §47C-3-103(b).
Franchise tax.
  Exemption, §105-125(a).
Judgments against.
  Assessment to pay, §47C-3-115(d).
  Indexing, §47C-3-117(d).
  Lien in favor of judgment lienholder,
    §47C-3-117(a).
Liabilities in tort in contract, §47C-3-111.
Maintenance, repair or replacement of common
  elements.
  Property covered by insurance, §47C-3-113(h).
  Responsibility, damages to, assessment,
    §47C-3-107.
Master associations.
  Corporation, nonprofit corporation or
    unincorporated association.
    Powers exercised by or delegated to,
      §47C-2-120(a).
  Delegation of powers.
    Liability of members of executive board,
      §47C-2-120(c).
  Executive board, election, §47C-2-120(e).
  Exercise of powers, restrictions, §47C-2-120(b).
  Rights and responsibilities of unit owners,
    applicability, §47C-2-120(d).
Meetings, §47C-3-108(a), (c).
  Quorum, §47C-3-109(a).
Membership, §47C-3-101.
Organization, §47C-3-101.
Powers, §47C-3-102(a).
  Restrictions on powers to deal with unit owners,
    §47C-3-102(b).
Property and liability insurance.
  Association to maintain, §47C-3-113(a).
Proxies, §47C-3-110(b).
Publication of names and addresses of officers and
  board members, §47C-3-103(g).
Records.
  Furnishing statements to unit owners,
    §47C-3-118(b).
  Maintenance, §47C-3-118(a).
Release of liens or encumbrances.
  Conveying real estate to association,
    §47C-4-111(b).
Surplus funds, §47C-3-114.
Tort and contract liability.
  Action against association, §47C-3-111(b).
    Wrongs occurring during declarant control,
      §47C-3-111(c).
  Declarant liable to association.
    Litigation expenses, §47C-3-111(d).

CONDOMINIUMS —Cont'd
Owners' associations —Cont'd
Tort and contract liability —Cont'd
  Declarant liable to association —Cont'd
    Wrong occurring during declarant control,
      §47C-3-111(c).
    Declarant's torts, §47C-3-111(a).
  Trustees, §47C-3-119.
  Voting.
    Allocation of votes, §47C-2-107(c).
    Common elements.
      Conveyance, encumbrance, subjecting to
        security interest, §47C-3-112(a).
    Lessees casting votes, §47C-3-110(c).
    Multiple owners of unit, §47C-3-110(a).
    Proxy, §47C-3-110(b).
    Subgroup voting on specified matters,
      §47C-3-110(e), (f).
    Unit allocated to association, votes not cast,
      §47C-3-110(d).
Partition.
Common elements, not subject to, §47C-2-107(d).
Plats or plans.
Altered boundaries between adjoining units.
  Preparation and recording plat or plan showing,
    §47C-2-112(b).
Certification by architect required, §47C-2-109(a).
Considered part of declaration, §47C-2-109(a).
Improvement contemplated.
  Intended location and dimensions shown,
    labeling, §47C-2-109(c).
Indexing by register of deeds, §47C-2-109(a).
New plats or plans, acquisition of development
  rights.
  Recording, §47C-2-109(d).
Recording, §47C-2-109(a).
  Fee, §47C-2-109(f).
  New plats or plans, acquisition of development
    rights, §47C-2-109(d).
  Requirements, §47C-2-109(e).
Required to show, §47C-2-109(b).
Subdividing units, §47C-2-113(a).
Political sign displays, §47C-3-121.
Powers of attorney.
Use to evade chapter, §47C-1-104(d).
Promotional material.
Labeling, §47C-4-118.
Property and liability insurance.
Assessment to pay costs, §47C-3-115(c).
Association to maintain, §47C-3-113(a).
Certificates or memoranda of insurance.
  Issuance by insurer, §47C-3-113(g).
Insurance not readily available.
  Notice to unit owners, §47C-3-113(c).
Losses covered by property insurance,
  §47C-3-113(e).
Policies, required provisions, §47C-3-113(d).
Repair or replacement of property covered by
  insurance.
  Association's duty, §47C-3-113(h).
Unit owner not prevented from obtaining,
  §47C-3-113(f).
Units having horizontal boundaries,
  §47C-3-113(b).
Varying or waiving provisions of section,
  §47C-3-113(i).
Protection of purchasers.
Applicability of article, §47C-4-101(a).
Attorneys' fees for violations, §47C-4-117.
Cancellation of contract by purchaser,
  §47C-4-108(a), (b).

CONDOMINIUMS —Cont'd
Protection of purchasers —Cont'd
Deposits made in connection with purchase or
  reservation.
  Escrow, §47C-4-110(a), (b).
Escrow of deposit.
  Deposit made in connection with purchase or
    reservation, §47C-4-110(a), (b).
Improvements.
  Declarant's obligation to complete and restore,
    §47C-4-119.
Labeling of promotional material, §47C-4-118.
Public offering statement.
  Amendment.
    Material change in information,
      §47C-4-103(b).
  Condominium registered with securities and
    exchange commission, §47C-4-107(a).
  Condominium subject to development right,
    §47C-4-104.
  Conversion buildings, §47C-4-106.
  Disclosures required, §47C-4-103(a).
  False or misleading statements, liability for,
    §47C-4-102(c).
  Investment contracts or other securities,
    condominiums deemed, §47C-4-107(b).
  Material change in information.
    Amendment, §47C-4-103(b).
  Offer of unit for own account.
    Required to prepare prior to offering,
      §47C-4-102(c).
  Required provisions, §47C-4-103(a).
  Required to prepare prior to offering,
    §47C-4-102(a).
    Exceptions, §47C-4-101(b).
    Offer of unit for own account, §47C-4-102(c).
  Single statement.
    Unit part of condominium and other real
      estate regime, §47C-4-102(d).
  Time shares, §47C-4-105(a), (b).
  Transfer of responsibility for preparing,
    §47C-4-102(b).
  False or misleading statements, responsibility
    for, §47C-4-102(c).
  When not required to prepare or deliver,
    §47C-4-101(b).
Release of liens or encumbrances.
  Conveying real estate to association,
    §47C-4-111(a).
  Sale of unit where public offering statement
    required.
    Furnishing purchaser, §47C-4-111(a).
    Surety bond, substitute collateral or
      insurance against, providing,
      §47C-4-111(a).
Resale certificate.
  When not required to prepare or deliver,
    §47C-4-101(b).
Resale of unit, §47C-4-109.
Rights of action.
  Effect of violations upon, §47C-4-117.
Statutes of limitations.
  Warranties, §47C-4-116.
Substantial completion of unit, §47C-4-120.
Warranties.
  Breach.
    Limitation of action, §47C-4-116.
  Express warranty of quality, §47C-4-113.
  Implied warranty of quality, §47C-4-114.
    Accrual of cause of action for breach.
      Warranty of quality extending to future
        performance or duration, §47C-4-116(b).

CONDOMINIUMS —Cont'd
Protection of purchasers —Cont'd
Warranties —Cont'd
  Implied warranty of quality —Cont'd
    Exclusion or modification.
      Agreement or expression, §47C-4-115(a).
      Purchaser of unit used for residential
        purposes, restrictions, §47C-4-115(b).
    Limitation of action, §47C-4-116(a).
      Warranty of quality extending to future
        performance or duration.
        Accrual of cause of action, §47C-4-116(b).
Proxies.
  Owners' associations, §47C-3-110(b).
Public offering statement, §§47C-4-102 to
  47C-4-107.
Purchase of unit.
  Protection of purchaser, §§47C-4-101 to
    47C-4-120.
Recordation.
  Amendment to declaration, §47C-2-118(c), (e).
  Declarations.
    Adding units to condominium, §47C-2-101(b).
    Creation of condominium, §47C-2-101(a).
  Plats or plans, §47C-2-109.
Records.
  Owners' association.
    Furnishing statements to unit owners,
      §47C-3-118(b).
    Maintenance, §47C-3-118(a).
Release of liens or encumbrances.
  Conveying real estate to association,
    §47C-4-111(b).
  Sale of unit requiring public offering statement.
    Purchaser not agreeing to take subject to or
      assume, §47C-4-111(a).
Resales of units.
  Protection of purchasers, §47C-4-109.
Rights of action.
  Effect of violations upon, §47C-4-117.
Rule against perpetuities.
  Not applied to defeat provisions of declarations,
    bylaws or rules and regulations,
    §47C-2-103(b).
Rules and regulations.
  Applicability of local ordinances, regulations and
    building codes, §47C-1-106.
Sales.
  Resales of units, §47C-4-109.
Sales offices, §47C-2-115.
Sales uses.
  Declaration, §47C-2-115.
Securities or investment contracts.
  Public offering statement, §47C-4-107(a), (b).
Security interest.
  Exercise against common elements before enforced
    against unit, §47C-3-117(b).
  Subjecting common elements to, §47C-3-112.
Short title, §47C-1-101.
Special declarant rights.
  Amendment creating or increasing, unanimous
    consent required, §47C-2-117(d).
  Foreclosure or sale, §47C-3-104(c), (d).
  Transfer.
    Foreclosure or sale, §47C-3-104(c), (d).
    Instrument evidencing, required, recording,
      §47C-3-104(a).
    Liability of persons who succeed to rights,
      §47C-3-104(e).
    Liability of transferor declarant, §47C-3-104(b).

CONDOMINIUMS —Cont'd
Statute of limitations.
Breach of warranty, §47C-4-116.
Challenging validity of declaration amendment, §47C-2-117(b).
Stormwater runoff rules and programs.
Transfer of stormwater management system permits to unit owners associations.
Condominiums and planned communities, §143-214.7(c2).
Subdivision of unit, §47C-2-113.
Substantial completion of unit, §47C-4-120.
Supplemental general principles of law applicable, §47C-1-108.
Surplus funds.
Owners' associations, §47C-3-114.
Suspension of condominium privileges or services, §47C-3-107.1.
Taxation.
Common elements, §47C-1-105(c).
No unit owner other than declarant, §47C-1-105(d).
Unit owners other than declarant, §47C-1-105(a), (b).
Termination.
Agreement of unit owners, §47C-2-118(a).
Condominium containing units having only horizontal boundaries, §47C-2-118(c).
Condominium containing units not having only horizontal boundaries, §47C-2-118(d).
Evidenced by execution of termination agreement, §47C-2-118(b).
Assets and proceeds from real estate sale.
Held by association as trustees, §47C-2-118(g).
Creditors liens, enforcement, §47C-2-118(g).
Interest of unit owners, §47C-2-118(h).
Sale of real estate, §47C-2-118(e).
Title to real estate.
No sale following termination, §47C-2-118(f).
Sale following termination, §47C-2-118(e).
Time shares.
Generally, §§93A-39 to 93A-59.
See TIME SHARES.
Inconsistent provisions, §47C-1-109.
Public offering statement, §47C-4-105(a), (b).
Tort and contract liability of associations, §47C-3-111.
Transfer of special declarant rights, §47C-3-104.
Trust or escrow account.
Deposits made in connection with purchase of unit, §47C-4-110(a), (b).
Trusts and trustees.
Owners' associations, §47C-3-119.
Unit boundaries, §47C-2-102.
Unit ownership, §§47A-1 to 47A-28.
See UNIT OWNERSHIP.
Units.
Access through unit.
Owner to afford association or other owners, §47C-3-107(a).
Alteration, §47C-2-111.
Boundaries, §47C-2-102.
Declaration amendment changing, §47C-2-117(d).
Relocation of boundaries between adjoining units, §47C-2-112(a), (b).
Description of unit, §47C-2-104.
Encroachments.
Easement for encroachment, §47C-2-114.
Increasing number.
Amendment to declaration, §47C-2-117(d).

CONDOMINIUMS —Cont'd
Units —Cont'd
Maintenance, repair or replacement.
Responsibility of owner of unit, §47C-3-107(a).
Purchase of unit.
Protection of purchaser, §§47C-4-101 to 47C-4-120.
Restrictions on uses.
Amendment to declaration, §47C-2-117(d).
Subdividing, §47C-2-113(a), (b).
Variations.
Agreement, §47C-1-104(b).
Declaration or bylaws, §47C-1-104(a).
Voting.
Owners' associations, §47C-3-110.
Allocation of votes, §47C-2-107(c).
Common elements.
Conveyance, encumbrance, subjecting to security interest, §47C-3-112(a).
Warranties.
Breach.
Limitation of action, §47C-4-116.
Express warranty of quality, §47C-4-113.
Implied warranty of quality, §47C-4-114.
Exclusion or modification.
Agreement or expression, §47C-4-115(a).
Purchaser of unit used for residential purposes, restrictions, §47C-4-115(b).
Limitation of action, §47C-4-116(a).
Warranty of quality extending to future performance or duration.
Accrual of cause of action, §47C-4-116(b).

CONDUCT OF WITNESS.
Credibility attacked or supported, §8C-1 Rule 608.

CONDUCT RULES GOVERNING ATTORNEYS.
See ATTORNEYS AT LAW.

CONDUITS, §136-27.

CONFEDERATE CEMETERY.
Labor for care of cemetery.
Division of adult correction to furnish, §65-4.

CONFEDERATE MEMORIAL DAY.
Public holiday, §103-4(a).

CONFERENCE OF CLERKS OF SUPERIOR COURT, §§7A-805 to 7A-809.

CONFESSION OF JUDGMENT.
Alimony.
Alimony without action, §50-16.10.
Force and effect, §1A-1 Rule 68.1(e).
Authorized, §1A-1 Rule 68.1(a).
Consumer finance act.
Licensees not to take, §53-181(c).
Costs.
Defendant's liability in criminal action, §6-47.
Entry.
Form of entry, §1A-1 Rule 68.1(d).
Where entered, §1A-1 Rule 68.1(c).
Executions.
Issuance and enforcement of executions, §1A-1 Rule 68.1(e).
Force and effect, §1A-1 Rule 68.1(e).
Insurance premium financing.
Provisions in agreements giving power of attorney to confess judgment in state.
Prohibited, §58-35-60.
Partnerships.
Power of partner to confess judgment, §59-39(c).

CONFESSION OF JUDGMENT —Cont'd
Procedure, §1A-1 Rule 68.1(b).
Retail installment sales.
Consumer credit sale.
Prohibited claims, §25A-18.
Prohibited clauses, §25A-18.
Summary ejectment, §42-30.

CONFESSIONS.
Admissions.
See ADMISSIONS.
Adultery and fornication.
Admissibility of admission or confession as
evidence, §14-184.
Delinquent and undisciplined juvenile actions.
Court acceptance of admission by juvenile.
Determination that admission product of
informed choice, §7B-2407(b).
Determination that there is factual basis for
admission, §7B-2407(c).
Duties of court before accepting, §7B-2407(a).
In-custody confession.
Admission into evidence, §7B-2101(b).

CONFIDENTIAL INTERMEDIARY.
Adoption information.
Certificate of death.
Entitlement to copy upon request, §130A-93(c2).
Child placing agencies.
Acting as for purposes of obtaining and sharing,
§48-9-104(b).
Defined, §48-9-101.
Release of identifying information, §48-9-104(b).

CONFIDENTIALITY OF INFORMATION.
Abortion.
Parental or judicial consent to abortion.
Waiver of parental consent requirement
proceedings, §90-21.8(b).
Abused, neglected or dependent juveniles.
Assessment of report.
Information received, §7B-302(a).
Exceptions, §7B-302(a1).
Authority of guardian ad litem to demand
confidential information or reports, §7B-601.
Communications between guardian ad litem and
parent, §7B-602(d).
Permanency mediation proceedings, §7B-202(c),
(d).
Records and social reports generally, §§7B-2900 to
7B-2902.
Acquired immune deficiency syndrome.
Records identifying person who has AIDS virus
infection, §130A-143.
Address confidentiality program, §§15C-1 to
15C-13.
See ADDRESS CONFIDENTIALITY PROGRAM.
Administrative hearings.
Contested tax cases, §150B-31.1(e).
Adoption.
Criminal history record check.
Prospective parent seeking adoption of child.
Privileged information, §48-3-309(f).
Records, §§48-9-101 to 48-9-109.
See ADOPTION.
Adult care homes.
Death of resident.
Reporting, §131D-34.1(d).
NC NOVA special licensure designation.
Information submitted by applicants,
§131E-154.14(c).

CONFIDENTIALITY OF INFORMATION
—Cont'd
Adult care homes —Cont'd
Quality assurance, medical, or peer review
committees, proceedings and records,
§131D-21.2(b).
Residents' bill of rights, §§131D-21, 131D-27.
Unauthorized disclosure.
Policies and procedures to ensure, §131D-2.14.
AIDS.
Records identifying person who has AIDS virus
infection, §130A-143.
Alarm system licensing.
Criminal background check, §74D-2.1(b).
Home address, telephone number of licensee,
license applicant, spouse, children, parents,
§74D-2(f).
Investigations by attorney generally, §74D-5.2.
Amusement device safety.
Trade secrets, §95-111.17.
Anatomical gifts.
Hospital and patient information, interview, etc.,
§130A-412.33(a).
Antifreeze.
Application for license.
Confidential formula information, §106-579.11.
Arbitration.
Canons of ethics for arbitrators.
Faithfulness to relationship of trust and
confidentiality inherent in office, CEA Rule
6.
Archaeological resources protection, §70-18.
**Atomic energy, radioactivity and ionizing
radiation.**
Disclosure limitations, §104E-29.
Attorney disability proceedings, Bar Rule
B.0129.
Attorney disciplinary proceedings, Bar Rule
B.0129.
Meetings of district grievance committees, Bar
Rule B.0203.
Attorneys at law, ProfCond Rule 1.6.
Confidential government information.
Lawyer acquiring as public officer or employees.
Representing client with interest adverse to
information, ProfCond Rule 1.11.
Defined, ProfCond Rule 1.0.
Disciplinary proceedings.
Documents, papers, etc, of state bar, staff,
counsel, etc, §84-32.1(a), (b).
Evidence brought forward in hearing
considered public record, §84-32.1(c).
Lawyer assistance program records not
considered public, §84-32.1(d).
Discussions with prospective clients, ProfCond
Rule 1.18.
Autopsies.
Photographs, video or audio recordings of autopsy,
§132-1.8.
Bail bondsmen and runners.
Criminal history records checks, §58-71-51(b).
Runners.
Notice of termination of appointment,
§58-71-125.
Surety bondsmen.
Notice of termination of appointment,
§58-71-115(c).
Bank compliance review documents,
§53-99.1(b).
Bank examiners.
Disclosing confidentiality information, §53-125.

CONFIDENTIALITY OF INFORMATION
    —Cont'd
Bank's regulatory rating.
    Disclosure to insurance carriers, §53-99(d).
Beach area essential property insurance.
    Information identifying policyholders, §58-45-95.
Biological agents registry, §130A-479(e).
Birth data not public record, §130A-93(b).
Birth defects monitoring program,
    §130A-131.17.
Cancer.
    Records of cancer, §130A-212.
Capital punishment.
    Witnesses to and persons carrying out execution,
        §15-190.
Carriers.
    Disclosure of information as to shipments
        unlawful, §62-324(a), (b).
Change of names.
    Confidentiality of record of proceedings, §101-2(c).
Child abuse, neglect or dependency action.
    Assessment of report.
        Information received, §7B-302(a).
            Exceptions, §7B-302(a1).
    Authority of guardian ad litem to demand
        confidential information or reports, §7B-601.
    Communications between guardian ad litem and
        parent, §7B-602(d).
    Permanency mediation proceedings, §7B-202(c),
        (d).
    Records and social reports generally, §§7B-2900 to
        7B-2902.
**Child care provider criminal history record
    check,** §110-90.2(e).
Child custody.
    Mediation, §50-13.1(e).
Child custody jurisdiction and enforcement,
    §50A-209(e).
Child fatality or near fatality case records.
    Access to confidential records prohibited,
        §7B-2902(c).
    Disclosure by public agency on request generally,
        §7B-2902.
Child fatality prevention system.
    Proceedings of state team and local teams,
        §7B-1413(c).
Child placing agencies.
    Death of resident of facility.
        Reporting, §131D-10.6B(d).
Child support enforcement.
    Directory of new hires, §110-129.2(i).
    Reports to district attorneys of aid to dependent
        children and illegitimate births, §15-155.3.
Chiropractors.
    Criminal history record checks, §90-143.3(c).
Clergymen.
    Communications between clergymen and
        communicants, §8-53.2.
**Coal and petroleum suppliers stocks and fuel
    capacity,** §143-345.14(f).
Collaborative law proceedings.
    Privileged and inadmissible evidence, §50-77(a),
        (b).
Commercial detection services.
    Utilization of drug detection dogs.
        Client records, §90-102.1(h).
Commercial feed.
    Information obtained to be confidential,
        §106-284.44(f).

CONFIDENTIALITY OF INFORMATION
    —Cont'd
Commissioner of banks.
    Records.
        Certain records not to be disclosed or be subject
            to public inspection, §§53-99(b), 53-120(c),
            (e).
        Sharing of information with state and federal
            agencies, §53-99(c).
Communicable diseases.
    Records, §130A-143.
Controlled substances.
    Practitioners.
        Treatment and rehabilitation services,
            §90-109.1(a).
    Reporting system, §90-113.74.
    Research, §90-113.3(e).
Corporations.
    Interrogatories by secretary of state, §55-1-33.
Counselors.
    Privileged communications, §8-53.8.
Credit unions.
    Agencies of state, other states or United States.
        Exchange of information permitted,
            §54-109.105(d).
    Application for new credit union.
        Public information, §54-109.105(c).
    Disclosure.
        Court of competent jurisdiction may order,
            §54-109.105(b).
    Liability for damages, §54-109.105.
    Misdemeanors for violations, §54-109.105(f).
    Penalties for violation, §54-109.105(e).
    Records of information of credit union division,
        administrator or agents, §54-109.105(a).
Criminal law and procedure.
    Address confidentiality program, §§15C-1 to
        15C-13.
        See ADDRESS CONFIDENTIALITY
            PROGRAM.
    Mental incapacity of defendant to proceed.
        Reports to court, §15A-1002(d).
    Public officers and employees.
        Misuse of confidential information, §14-234.1.
Delinquent and undisciplined juvenile actions.
    Records and social reports generally, §§7B-3000,
        7B-3001.
Dental hygienists.
    Criminal records checks for license applicants,
        §90-224(c).
Dentists.
    Criminal records checks for license applicants,
        §90-30(b).
    Peer review organizations, §§90-48.2(e), 90-48.10.
**Department of agriculture and consumer
    services.**
    Information collected and published, §106-24.1.
Department of health and human services.
    Privileged patient medical records, §143B-139.6.
DNA database and databank records,
    §15A-266.12(a).
Domestic violence.
    Programs for victims.
        Privileged communications, §8-53.12.
Drivers' licenses.
    Criminal record checks of persons manufacturing
        or producing, §114-19.24(d).
    Photographic image or signature recorded,
        §20-43(a).
Elevators.
    Trade secrets, §95-110.14.

CONFIDENTIALITY OF INFORMATION
—Cont'd

Emergency medical services.
Confidentiality of patient information, §143-518.

Emergency program to reduce home foreclosures.
Confidentiality of records, §45-106.

Emergency response plans.
Universities and hospitals, §132-1.6.

Ethics.
Misuse of public office.
Use of nonpublic information gained by official responsibilities, §138A-34.
State ethics commission.
Advisory opinions, §138A-13(e).
Inquiries, §138A-12(n).

Expunged criminal records.
Confidential agency files, §15A-151.
File of person granted expungement, §15A-146(c).
Private entities.
Dissemination of information, §15A-152(b).
Civil liability, §15A-152(c).

Fire insurance.
Information furnished by insurance companies, §58-79-40(d).

Fish and fishing.
Coastal and estuarine commercial fishing licenses.
Records, §113-170.3(c).

Freedom of information.
See FREEDOM OF INFORMATION.

Funeral service.
Criminal records checks for license applicants, §90-210.25(a).

General assembly.
Code of legislative ethics.
Disclosure of confidential information, §120-87(a), (b).
Legislative communications, §§120-129 to 120-134.
Definitions, §120-129.
Documents prepared by legislative employees, §120-131.
Drafting requests, §120-130.
Evaluation report preparation requests, §120-131.1(a1).
Fiscal note preparation requests, §120-131.1.
Information requests, §120-130.
Penalty, §§120-131.1(c), 120-134.
Redistricting communications, §120-133.
Testimony by legislative employees, §120-132.

General contractors.
Identity of complaining party, §87-15.3.

Geologists.
Examination test scores, applications, etc., §89E-14(c).
Investigations of complaints, §89E-17(c).

Grand jury proceedings, §15A-623.

Guardian ad litem.
Communications between parent, guardian ad litem and parent's counsel.
Abused, neglected or dependent juvenile actions, §7B-602(d).
Termination of parental rights proceedings, §7B-1101.1(d).

Guardians.
Status report for incompetent wards.
Restrictions on person with access to information, §35A-1242(c).

Health care facilities.
Competitive health care information, §131E-97.3.
Credentialing information, §131E-97.2.
Employee information, §131E-97.1.

CONFIDENTIALITY OF INFORMATION
—Cont'd

Health care facilities —Cont'd
Health care contracts, §131E-99.
Hospices, §131E-207(a) to (c).
Patient information, §131E-97(a), (b).

Health maintenance organizations, §58-67-180.

Hearing aid dealers and fitters.
License discipline, §93D-13(c).

Hearing impaired.
Interpreters for hearing impaired.
Criminal records checks for license applicants, §90D-7(c).
Privileged communications, §8B-5.

Home care agency employee criminal records checks, §131E-265(a).

Home care agency licensing.
NC NOVA special licensure designation.
Information submitted by applicants, §131E-154.14(c).

Home care clients' bill of rights.
Confidentiality of personal and medical, §§131E-144.3, 131E-144.7(a).

Hospices, §131E-207(a) to (c).

Hospital employee personnel files, §131E-257.2.

Hospitals.
Emergency departments, reports to state health director, §130A-480(b).
Health care contracts, §131E-99.
Privileges to practice in hospital.
Reports of disciplinary action, §90-14.13(e).

Husband and wife.
Competency as witnesses.
Child abuse cases, §8-57.1.
Civil actions, §8-56.
Criminal actions, §8-57(c).
Paternity proceedings, §8-57.2.

Illegitimacy.
District attorneys.
Reports to district attorneys of aid to dependent children and illegitimate births, §15-155.3.

Innocence claim inquiry.
Proceedings before full commission, §15A-1468(e).

Insurance.
Consumer and customer information.
Generally, §§58-39-1 to 58-39-165.
See INSURANCE CONSUMER AND CUSTOMER INFORMATION PRIVACY.
Holding companies.
Information obtained by commissioner, §58-19-40.
Interstate insurance product regulation compact.
Records, §58-91-40(b).
Market conduct analysis, financial analysis, and related documents, §58-2-240(a).
Definitions, §58-2-240(b), (c).
Medical records, §58-2-105(a).
Credentialing of medical professionals, §58-2-105(c).
Independent review organization, disclosure to, §58-2-105(b).
Misuse of borrowers' confidential information.
Prohibited, §58-63-15.
Property and casualty actuarial opinions, §58-10-175(b), (c).
Reinsurance reports, §58-10-55(b).
Asset acquisitions and dispositions, §58-10-60(a) to (d).
Risk based capital requirements.
Hearings on commissioner's determinations, §58-12-30.

CONFIDENTIALITY OF INFORMATION
   —Cont'd
Insurance —Cont'd
Risk based capital requirements —Cont'd
Information filed with commissioner,
   §58-12-35(a).
Small employer group health coverage,
   §58-50-130(g).
Supervision, rehabilitation and liquidation of
   insurers.
Hearings, §58-30-70.
Taxpayer identification numbers in public
   documents.
Redaction not required, §58-2-245.
Insurance adjusters.
Public adjusters.
Criminal history record checks of license
   applicants, §58-33A-15(e).
Proprietary information submitted to
   commissioner, §58-33A-75(c).
Interpreters for hearing impaired.
Criminal records checks for license applicants,
   §90D-7(c).
Privileged communications, §8B-5.
Interstate family support, §52C-3-311.
**Journalist's qualified privilege against
   disclosure in any legal proceeding,**
   §8-53.11(b).
Definitions, §8-53.11(a).
Eyewitness observation of criminal or tortuous
   conduct, no privilege, §8-53.11(d).
Order to compel disclosure, notice to journalist
   and hearing, §8-53.11(c).
Overcoming privilege, person seeking to compel
   disclosure, §8-53.11(c).
Judicial standards commission proceedings.
Informal advisory opinions.
Information contained in requests,
   JudStdsComm Rule 8.
Papers filed with and proceedings before
   commission, §7A-377(a1), JudStdsComm Rule
   6.
Juvenile records and social reports.
Cases of abuse, neglect and dependency generally,
   §§7B-2900 to 7B-2902.
Cases of delinquency and undiscipline, §§7B-3000,
   7B-3001.
Disclosure of information to local agencies,
   §7B-3100.
Labor dispute conciliation service, §95-36.
**Law enforcement peer support group
   counselor's privilege, §8-53.10(b).**
Child abuse or neglect.
Privilege not grounds for failure to report or
   excluding evidence, §8-53.10(d).
Definitions, §8-53.10(a).
Disabled adult in need of protective services.
Privilege not grounds for failure to report or
   excluding evidence, §8-53.10(d).
Inapplicability of privilege, §8-53.10(c).
Law firm dispute arbitration, Bar Rule E.0409.
Lawyers assistance program, Bar Rule D.0613.
Documents, papers, etc, of state bar, staff, counsel,
   etc relating to program.
Not considered public records, §84-32.1(d).
Legal expense funds for elected officials.
Limitations on donations.
Credit cards, confidentiality of credit card
   number, §163-278.316(c).
Legislative ethics committees.
Advisory opinions, §120-104(g).

CONFIDENTIALITY OF INFORMATION
   —Cont'd
Legislative ethics committees —Cont'd
Investigations of legislators, §120-103.1(l).
Libraries and librarians.
User records, §125-19(a), (b).
Limited liability companies.
Answers to interrogatories by secretary of state,
   §57C-1-33.
Trade secrets, §57C-3-04(e).
Lobbying.
Advisory opinions by state ethics commission,
   §120C-102(d), (d1).
Complaints of violations of chapter.
Records of criminal investigations,
   §§120C-600(c), 120C-601(c).
Disclosure of confidential information.
Adoption of rules to prevent, §120C-101(b).
**Local governmental employees' retirement
   system.**
List of members, §128-28(q).
Lotteries.
State lottery.
Prize winners, §18C-132(k).
Setoff debt collection.
Confidentiality of information, §18C-134(e).
Marine fisheries commission.
Personal information provided by license
   applicant, §143B-289.52(h).
Marriage and family therapists.
Communications between therapists and clients,
   §8-53.5.
Alimony and divorce actions, §8-53.6.
Mediation.
District criminal courts.
Confidentiality of work products, §7A-38.3D(i).
Standards of professional conduct for mediators,
   SPCM Rule 3.
Mediators and other neutrals.
Court ordered settlement conferences in superior
   court civil actions.
Regulation, §7A-38.2(h).
Medicaid.
Appeals by recipients, §108A-70.9A(d).
Medical board records of proceedings,
   §90-16(c).
Medical records.
Electronic medical records, §90-412(c).
Exemption from confidentiality provisions when
   public health concerns necessitate, §130A-15.
Health care facilities.
Patient information, §131E-97(a).
Insurance companies, §58-2-105(a).
Credentialing of medical professionals,
   §58-2-105(c).
Independent review organization, disclosure to,
   §58-2-105(b).
Medical care data concerning patients,
   §131E-214.3(a) to (d).
Privileged patient medical records in possession of
   department of health and human services,
   §143B-139.6.
Public health authorities, §130A-45.8(a).
Viatical life insurance settlements, §58-58-250(g).
**Medical review and quality assurance
   committees.**
Confidentiality of records and materials produced
   by committee, §90-21.22A(c).
Medical review committee.
Introduction of records into evidence.
Testimony of members of committees,
   §131E-95(b), (c).

CONFIDENTIALITY OF INFORMATION
—Cont'd
Meningococcal disease vaccination information.
Information provided students in institution of higher education, §116-260(b).
Mental health, developmental disability, substance abuse.
Area authorities.
Personnel records, privacy, §122C-158(a) to (h).
Consumer advocacy program, §122C-17.
Death of client.
Adherence to laws concerning prohibited disclosures, §122C-31(e).
Facility licenses.
Peer review and quality assurance committees' records and materials, §122C-30.
Restrictions on disclosure, §122C-25(b).
Quality assurance activities by secretary.
Review and protection of information, §122C-192(a) to (d).
Records.
Court records to be confidential, §122C-207.
Rights of clients.
See MENTAL HEALTH, DEVELOPMENTAL DISABILITY, SUBSTANCE ABUSE.
Militia.
Records of national guard, §127A-17.1.
Misuse of public office.
Use of nonpublic information gained by official responsibilities, §138A-34.
Money transmitters, §53-208.17.
Mortgage bankers, brokers and servicers.
Licensure of mortgage business specialists, §53-244.120.
Mortgages and deeds of trust.
Emergency program to reduce home foreclosures.
Confidentiality of records, §45-106.
Motor vehicle dealers.
Dealer management computer systems, §20-305.7.
Motor vehicle records, personal information, §20-43.1.
Municipal employees' personnel files, §160A-168.
Municipal tax records, §160A-208.1.
Name change.
Confidentiality of record of proceedings, §101-2(c).
National guard.
Records of national guard, §127A-17.1.
911 database, §132-1.5.
911 system.
Proprietary information, §62A-52.
Notaries public.
Statement of personal qualification.
Application for commission, §10B-7(b).
Nurse licensure compact.
Coordinated licensure information system, §90-171.88(d), (e).
Nurses.
Privileged communications, §8-53.13.
Child abuse and neglect cases.
Waiver of privilege, §8-53.13(a), (b).
Nursing home administrators.
Criminal background checks of license applicants, §90-288.01(b).
Nursing homes.
Employee criminal records checks, §131E-265(a).
NC NOVA special licensure designation.
Information submitted by applicants, §131E-154.14(c).

CONFIDENTIALITY OF INFORMATION
—Cont'd
Nursing homes —Cont'd
Nursing home medication management advisory committee.
Meetings and proceedings, confidentiality of, §131E-128.1(e).
Patients' bill of rights.
Registration of complaints, §131E-124(c).
Occupational licensing boards.
Social security numbers of applicants, §93B-14.
Occupational safety and health.
Trade secrets, §95-152.
Office of information technology services, §147-33.83(b).
Optometrists.
Disciplinary proceedings, §90-121.5.
Privileged communications, §8-53.9.
Patient health records, §130A-12.
Perfusionists committee.
Investigations, §90-685.1(a).
Personal identifying information.
Community colleges.
Applicant records, confidentiality, §132-1.1(f).
Restricted use, §132-1.10.
University of North Carolina.
Applicant records, confidentiality, §132-1.1(f).
Personnel files, §126-24.
Access to such information, §126-24.
Penalty for permitting access to unauthorized person, §126-27.
Examining, copying, etc., without authority, §126-28.
School employees, §115C-319.
Pharmacists and pharmacies.
Criminal records checks for license applicants, §90-85.15(c).
Impaired pharmacist peer review organizations, §90-85.41(e).
Pharmacy quality assurance programs, §90-85.47(d).
Records.
Availability of patient records, §90-85.35.
Pharmacy records, prescription orders.
Not public records, disclosure, restrictions, §90-85.36(a) to (c).
Physicians and surgeons.
Communications between physician and patient, §8-53.
Alimony and divorce actions, §8-53.6.
Waiver of privilege in child abuse cases, §8-53.1(a), (b).
Criminal records checks for license applicants, §90-11(b).
Information about issuance, denial, suspension or revocation, voluntary surrender, etc., of license.
Release to health care licensure board in state, §90-14(d).
Malpractice.
Reports of awards or settlements, §90-14.13(e).
Peer review agreements, §90-21.22(e).
Privileges to practice in hospital.
Reports of disciplinary action, §90-14.13(e).
Precious metal dealers.
Copies of records filed with law enforcement, §66-169(e).
Preneed funeral contracts and funds, §90-210.73.
Presentence reports, §15A-1333.

CONFIDENTIALITY OF INFORMATION
—Cont'd
Prisons and prisoners.
Administrative remedy procedure.
Records to be confidential, §148-118.5.
Capital punishment.
Witnesses to and persons carrying out
execution, §15-190.
Private personnel services.
Criminal records checks for license applicants,
§95-47.2(d).
Private protective services.
Criminal background check, §74C-8.1(b).
Home address, telephone number of licensee,
applicant for license, spouse, children,
parents, §74C-8(g).
Investigations by attorney general, §74C-7.
Privileged communications.
See PRIVILEGED COMMUNICATIONS.
Probation.
Records treated as privileged information,
§15-207.
Professional employer organization.
Health insurance plans not fully funded.
Information filed by licensee, §58-89A-106(b).
Provider sponsored organizations.
Medical information, §131E-310.
Pseudoephedrine products, sales of.
Record of disposition, §90-113.52(d).
Psychologists.
Communications between psychologists and client
or patient, §8-53.3.
Public health authorities.
Competitive health care information, §130A-45.11.
Credentialing information, §130A-45.10.
Medical review committee.
Records and materials of proceedings,
§130A-45.7(b).
Patient information, §130A-45.8.
Personnel information, §130A-45.9.
Public officers and employees.
Misuse of confidential information, §14-234.1(a),
(b).
Repayment of money owed to state.
Exemption, §143-560.
Public records, §132-1.2.
Communications by legal counsel to public board
or agency to be confidential, §132-1.1.
Economic development incentives, §132-1.8.
911 database, §132-1.5.
Tax records, §132-1.1.
Trial preparation material, §132-1.9.
Public security information, §132-1.7(a) to (c).
Public utilities.
Disclosure of information by commission
employees unlawful, §62-316.
Rape crisis centers.
Privileged communications, §8-53.12.
Real estate appraisal management companies.
Criminal history record check, §93E-2-11(b).
Real estate brokers.
Criminal records checks for license applicants,
§93A-4(b1).
Registration of voters.
Date of birth, §163-82.10B.
Information captured during registration process,
§163-82.10(a).
Retaliatory employment discrimination.
Commissioner's files and records relating to
investigation and enforcement pleadings,
§95-242(e).

CONFIDENTIALITY OF INFORMATION
—Cont'd
Retaliatory employment discrimination
—Cont'd
Informal procedures, §95-242(d).
**Retirement system for teachers and state
employees.**
Information concerning members, §135-6(p).
Savings and loan associations, §54B-63.
Compliance review documents, §54B-63.1(b).
Savings banks.
Compliance review documents, §54C-60.1(b).
Records or information of commission or
commissioner of banks, §54C-60.
Schools.
Address confidentiality program participants.
Actual address and telephone number
confidential, §115C-402(f).
Counselors.
Communications between counselors and
students, §§8-53.4, 115C-401.
Criminal records checks for employees and
applicants, §§114-19.23(c), 115C-332(f).
Employees' personnel files, §115C-319.
Penalty for disclosure of certain information,
§115C-13.
Personally identifiable student information.
Contractors prohibited from selling,
§115C-401.1.
State board of education.
Duty to maintain confidentiality of certain
information, §115C-13.
Statewide testing program.
Public records exemption, §115C-174.13.
Student records, §115C-402.
Senior citizens.
Long-term care ombudsman program,
§143B-181.22.
Setoff debt collection act, §105A-15.
Sexual assault.
Programs for victims.
Privileged communications, §8-53.12.
Social security numbers.
Occupational licensing boards, numbers for
applicants, §93B-14.
Restricted use, §132-1.10.
Social services.
Aid to families with dependent children.
Reports to district attorneys, §15-155.3.
Records, §108A-80.
Applicability of certain provisions, §108A-73.
Reports to district attorney of aid to dependent
children and illegitimate births.
Disclosure of information by district attorney or
agent, §15-155.3.
Social workers.
Disciplinary hearings, §90B-11(f).
Privileged communications, §8-53.7.
Soil scientists.
Board records, §89F-15(b).
Special identification cards.
Photographic image or signature recorded,
§20-43(a).
State center for health statistics.
Security of health data, §130A-374(a), (b).
State child fatality review team records,
§143B-150.20(f).
Members to sign statement of understanding,
§143B-150.20(g).
State ethics commission.
Advisory opinions, §138A-13(e).

CONFIDENTIALITY OF INFORMATION
—Cont'd
State ethics commission —Cont'd
Inquiries, §138A-12(n).
State health plan for teachers and state employees, §135-48.10.
State lottery.
Confidentiality of prize winners, §18C-132(k).
Setoff debt collection.
Confidentiality of information, §18C-134(e).
Student records, §115C-402.
Contractors prohibited from selling personally identifiable student information, §115C-401.1.
Subpoenas requiring disclosure of confidential information.
Protection, §1A-1 Rule 45(c).
Substance abuse professionals.
Criminal history record checks, §90-113.46A(a).
Tax cases.
Contested cases.
Administrative hearings, §150B-31.1(e).
Tax information.
Definitions, §105-259(a).
Disclosure prohibited, exceptions, §105-259(b).
Misdemeanor for violations, §105-259(c).
Municipal tax records, §160A-208.1.
Preparers of tax forms and returns.
Unauthorized disclosure of tax information prohibited, §75-28.
Tax records, §132-1.1.
Unauthorized substances taxes, §105-113.112.
Termination of parental rights proceedings.
Communications between parent, guardian ad litem and parent's counsel, §7B-1101.1(d).
Terrorist incident using nuclear, biological or chemical agents, §130A-476(e).
Biological agents registry, §130A-479(e).
Emergency departments, reports to state health director, §130A-480(b).
Toxic substances.
Identification.
Emergency information, §95-194(g).
Transportation board.
Misuse of confidential information by members, §136-14(g).
Trust companies.
Acquisition of control.
Confidential information, §53-348(c).
Private trust companies.
Application information, §53-364(b).
Unauthorized substances taxes.
Confidential tax information, §105-113.112.
Unemployment compensation.
Records and reports, §96-4(x).
University of North Carolina.
Audit of functions and programs.
Internal auditors work papers, exceptions, §116-40.7(c).
Insurance.
Confidentiality of records, §116-222.
Mediation of personnel matters, §116-3.3(a).
Uranium exploration.
Logs, surveys and reports, §74-88.
Veterans.
Records of department of administration, §165-11.1.
Viatical life insurance settlements.
Antifraud initiatives, §§58-58-268(c), 58-58-280(a).
Medical records, §58-58-250(g).
Reports to commissioner of violation of provisions, §58-58-270.

CONFIDENTIALITY OF INFORMATION
—Cont'd
Wage and hour act.
Files and other records relating to investigations and enforcement proceedings, §95-25.20.
Water and air resources, §143-215.3C.
Water and sewer authorities.
Employee personnel files, §162-6.1.
Witnesses to execution, §15-190.

CONFIDENTIAL TAX INFORMATION.
Definitions, §105-259(a).
Disclosure prohibited, exceptions, §105-259(b).
Misdemeanor for violations, §105-259(c).
Municipal tax records, §160A-208.1.
Preparers of tax forms and returns.
Unauthorized disclosure of tax information prohibited, §75-28.
Unauthorized substances taxes, §105-113.112.

CONFIRMATION OF SALE.
Execution sales.
Real property, §1-339.67.
Judicial sales.
Private sale, §1-339.37.
Public sales, §1-339.28(a) to (e).

CONFISCATION.
Controlled substances offenses.
Forfeitures of personal property used, §90-112.
Applicability of provisions, §90-113.7.
Mitigation and remission of forfeitures, §90-112.1.
Electronic surveillance devices, §15A-289.
Hunting and fishing.
Fruits and instrumentalities of offenses in question, §113-137(i).
Motor vehicles.
Reports by peace officers, §20-114(c).
Prisoners.
Unauthorized personal property in possession, §148-18.1.
Racing vehicles on streets and highways, §20-141.3(g).
Searches and seizures.
Disposition of seized, confiscated or unclaimed property, §§15-11 to 15-17.
See SEARCHES AND SEIZURES.

CONFLICT OF LAWS.
Airports.
Special airport districts.
Inconsistent laws declared inapplicable, §63-89.
Alcoholic beverages.
Tribal alcoholic beverage control, §18B-112(j).
Bail bondsmen and runners, §58-71-195.
Bank deposits and collections.
Liability of bank, §25-4-102(b).
Cigarette tax.
Federal constitution and statutes, §105-113.8.
Commercial code general provisions.
Construction of chapter, §25-1-103(b).
Commodities.
Securities and other laws unaffected, §78D-8.
Community colleges.
Construction contract claims.
Adjustment and resolution, §143-135.6.
Inconsistent contract provisions invalid, §143-135.6(d).
Concealed handgun permit.
Warning required on application, §14-415.14(b).
Contracts to improve real property.
Subject to laws of another state.
Void and against public policy, §22B-2.

CONFLICT OF LAWS —Cont'd
Contracts with forum selection provisions.
Invalid and against public policy, §22B-3.
Counties.
Planning and zoning.
Rules and regulations, §153A-346.
Custodial trusts, §33B-19(b).
Determining foreign law, §1A-1 Rule 44.1.
Documents of title.
Uniform electronic transactions act.
Conflicts between act and article, §25-7-103(d).
Electronic commerce in government,
§66-58.6(d).
Eminent domain.
Exclusive nature of provisions, §40A-1.
Federal estate tax apportionment, §28A-27-8.
Foreign-money claims.
Interest rates, §1C-1828(a).
Scope of article, §1C-1821(b).
Forum selection.
Contracts to improve real property.
Provisions making contract subject to laws of
other states.
Void and against public policy, §22B-2.
Contracts with forum selection provisions.
Invalid and against public policy, §22B-3.
Funds transfers, UCC.
Choice of law, §25-4A-507.
Exclusion of consumer transactions governed by
federal law, §25-4A-108.
Federal reserve regulations and operating
circulars supersede inconsistent provisions,
§25-4A-107.
Good Samaritan act.
Medical malpractice, §90-21.14(c).
Historic districts and landmarks, §160A-400.10.
Insurance.
Contract of insurance on property, lives or interest
in this state.
State law governs, §58-3-1.
Health care benefits providers.
Jurisdiction over, §58-49-20.
Life insurance.
Interest rates on life insurance policy loans,
§58-61-10(i).
**International commercial arbitration and
conciliation.**
Application of law as determined by conflict rules.
Failure of parties to designate applicable law,
§1-567.58(b).
Dispute decided on rules of law as chosen by
parties, §1-567.58(a).
Substantive law, designation construed to refer to,
§1-567.58(a).
Interstate family support.
Act or similar law not enacted by responding
state.
State tribunal may make findings required by
law of responding state, §52C-3-304(b).
Leases, UCC.
Leases subject to other statutes, §25-2A-104.
Limitation on power of parties to choose
applicable law and judicial forum, §25-2A-106.
Letters of credit.
Choice of law in document, §25-5-116(a).
Governing law not specified, §25-5-116(b).
Other articles of commercial code, §25-5-116(d).
Rules and custom of practice, §25-5-116(c).
Limited liability companies.
Applicability of provisions to foreign and
interstate commerce, §57C-10-02.

CONFLICT OF LAWS —Cont'd
Limited liability companies —Cont'd
Foreign limited liability companies.
Law governing, §57C-7-01.
Liability of members, managers, directors and
executives, §57C-3-30(c), (d).
Recognition of companies organized under chapter
outside boundary of state, §57C-10-07.
Limited liability partnerships.
Foreign limited liability partnerships, §59-90.
Marketing associations.
Conflicting laws not to apply, §54-138.
Medical malpractice.
Informed consent, §90-21.13(e).
Metropolitan sewerage districts.
Inconsistent laws declared inapplicable, §162A-80.
Metropolitan water districts.
Inconsistent laws declared inapplicable, §162A-58.
Motor vehicle captive finance sources.
Effect of choice of law clauses on applicability of
provisions, §20-308.22(b).
Municipalities.
General laws and charters, §160A-3.
Railroad crossings.
Local act in conflict with provisions repealed,
§160A-298.
Rail transportation liability, §160A-326(e).
Zoning, §§160A-390, 160A-391.
Negotiable instruments, §25-3-102(b).
Offshore oil and gas activities.
Duties and obligations inconsistent with federal
law, §143-215.94JJ.
Preemption of state law, §143-215.94JJ.
Oil and gas conservation, §113-415.
Open fires.
Effect on other laws, §106-949.
Overhead high-voltage line safety, §95-229.12.
Parking authorities.
Inconsistent provisions superseded, §160A-565.
Partnerships.
Liability of partners, §59-45(f).
Pollution control.
Industrial and pollution control facilities financing
act.
Inconsistent laws inapplicable, §159C-26.
Provider sponsored organizations,
§131E-308(a), (d).
Administrative procedures, §131E-305(c).
Applicability of other laws, §131E-278.
Prudent management of institutional funds,
§36E-10(a).
Public transportation authorities.
Provisions controlling, §160A-586.
**Racketeer influenced and corrupt
organization.**
Civil remedies as supplemental and cumulative,
§75D-10.
Radiation protection, §104E-21(a).
Real property improvement contracts.
Provisions making contract subject to laws of
another state.
Void and against public policy, §22B-2.
Regional public transportation authority.
Rail transportation liability, §160A-626(e).
Regional solid waste management authorities.
Compliance with other laws, §153A-430(b).
Units of local government, §153A-430(c), (d).
Retail installment sales.
Consumer credit protection act to control,
§25A-45.

CONFLICT OF LAWS —Cont'd
School budget and fiscal control act.
Conflicting laws superseded, §115C-424.
Secured transactions.
Applicability of article, §25-9-109(c).
Investment property, §25-9-305(a).
Commodity intermediary jurisdiction
determinations, §25-9-305(b).
Exceptions to general rule, §25-9-305(c).
Perfection and priority.
Agricultural liens, §25-9-302.
Certificates of title covering goods, §25-9-303.
Consignees.
When other law governs priority,
§25-9-319(b).
Debtor's location, §25-9-307.
Letter-of-credit rights, §25-9-306.
Operation of other articles of UCC, §25-9-331.
Security interests, §25-9-301.
Security agreement, §25-9-201(c).
Third party assignments.
Agreements not to assert defenses against
assignees, §25-9-403(e), (f).
Alienability of debtor's rights.
Governing law, §25-9-401(a).
Notes, general intangibles and health care
insurance receivables.
Restrictions on assignments, §25-9-408.
Notice to debtor of assignment, §25-9-406.
Social services.
Appeals, §108A-79(l).
State education assistance authority,
§§116-209.1, 116-209.23.
Transfers to minors.
Law of another state governing transfer,
§33A-2(b).
Trust companies.
Applicability of other laws, §53-366.
Trusts and trustees.
Terms of trust.
Meaning and effect.
Governing law, §36C-1-107(a).
University of North Carolina.
Bond issues.
Compliance with other laws not required,
§116-41.12.
Revenue bonds for student housing, student
activities, physical education and
recreation.
Inconsistent laws declared inapplicable,
§§116-185, 116-198.
Urban redevelopment.
Controlling effect of provisions, §160A-524.
Venue.
Person in this state injuring one in another,
§15-132.
Veterans' recreation authorities.
Provisions controlling, §165-38.
Viatical life insurance settlements.
Licenses, §58-58-210(a).
Water and sewer authorities.
Inconsistent laws declared inapplicable, §162A-19.
Weights and measures.
Repeal of conflicting laws, §81A-88.
Wells.
Construction, §87-96.

**CONFLICT RESOLUTION AND MEDIATION
MODELS.**
Basic education program, §115C-81(a4).

CONFLICTS OF INTEREST.
ABC boards, §§18B-201, 18B-700(h).
Advisory budget commission.
Purchases and contracts through department of
administration, §143-63.
Alcoholic beverage control boards, §§18B-201,
18B-700(h).
Alcoholic beverage control commission,
§18B-201.
Alcoholic beverage wholesalers.
Supplier's financial interest in wholesaler,
§18B-1119.
Animal waste management.
Review of operations, §143-215.10D(c).
Arbitration.
Arbitrators, §§1-569.11(b), 1-569.12.
Canons of ethics for arbitrators, CEA Rule 2.
Arbitrators, §§1-569.11(b), 1-569.12.
Architects.
Public works.
Employment of architects when interest in use
of materials prohibited, §133-1.
Attorney disciplinary proceedings.
Disqualification of council member or hearing
commission member due to interest, Bar Rule
B.0127.
District grievance committee members, Bar Rule
B.0207.
Attorneys at law.
Current clients, ProfCond Rule 1.7.
Specific rules, ProfCond Rule 1.8.
Former clients.
Duties to, ProfCond Rule 1.9.
Former judges, arbitrators, mediators or other
third party neutrals, ProfCond Rule 1.12.
Government officers and employees.
Special conflicts, former and current officers and
employees, ProfCond Rule 1.11.
Imputation, ProfCond Rule 1.10.
Lawyer as witness, ProfCond Rule 3.7.
Prospective clients, matters with, ProfCond Rule
1.18.
Sale or purchase of practice, notice, ProfCond
Rule 1.17.
Banking commission.
Interest in financial institution, restriction,
§53-92(b), (c).
Budget of state.
Grant funds administration, §143C-6-23(b).
Chairs of state agencies.
Duties, §138A-15(c).
Change of venue.
Judge interested as party or counsel, §1-83.
Commissioner of motor vehicles, §20-183.13.
Community colleges.
Board of trustees, §115D-26.
Employees of institutions, §115D-26.
Corporations.
Board of directors.
Business corporations, §55-8-31.
Cosmetic art.
Board of cosmetic art.
Employment of member by board for at least
one year after member's term prohibited,
§88B-3(h).
Counties.
Inspection departments.
Members of departments, §153A-355.
County planning and zoning.
Board of adjustment, §§153A-340(g),
153A-345(e1).

CONFLICTS OF INTEREST —Cont'd

Credit unions, §54-109.39.

Criminal justice information network governing board, §143-661(c).

Decedents' estates.
Clerk of superior court.
Jurisdiction where clerk subscribing witness, §28A-2-3.

Depositions.
Persons before whom depositions may be taken.
Disqualification for interest, §1A-1 Rule 28(c).

Economic interest statements, §§138A-21 to 138A-27.

Engineers.
Public works.
Employment of engineers when interest in use of materials prohibited, §133-1.

Fish and fisheries resources.
Inspectors, §113-225.

Gasoline and oil inspectors, §119-25.

General assembly.
Service by members of general assembly on certain boards and commissions, §120-123.

Global TransPark authority.
Members, officers or employees, §63A-21.

Guardian ad litem program.
Services provided to abused, neglected or dependent juveniles.
Appointment of district bar member, conflict prohibiting local program representation, §7B-1202.

Heads of state agencies.
Duties, §138A-15(c).

Health care facilities.
Finance act, §131A-22.

Hospital authorities, §131E-21.
Commissioners or employees, §157-7.

Housing finance agency, §122A-20.

Housing trust fund.
North Carolina housing partnership, §122E-4(i).

Insurance commissioner examinations, §58-2-133(a).

Job development investment grant program.
Economic investment committee, §143B-437.54(c).

Judge interested as party or counsel, §1-83.

Labor disputes.
Voluntary arbitration of labor disputes.
Disqualification of arbitrators, §95-36.4(b).

License to give trust fund commission, §20-7.5(d).

Local ABC boards, §§18B-201, 18B-700(h).

Marketing associations.
Directors, §54-146(c).

Mediation.
Standards of professional conduct for mediators, SPCM Rule 7.

Mental health facilities personnel.
Disclosure of interests when referring clients to provider agencies, §122C-26.

Mines and minerals.
Safety and health.
Commissioner of labor, director, etc., §74-24.19(c).

Misuse of public office.
Duty to inquire, §138A-35(a).

Municipal hospitals, §131E-14.2.

Nonprofit corporations.
Board of directors, §55A-8-31.

Office of information technology services.
Procurement of information technology.
Certification that information technology bids submitted without collusion, §147-33.100.

CONFLICTS OF INTEREST —Cont'd

Office of information technology services —Cont'd
Procurement of information technology —Cont'd
Financial interest of officers in sources of supply, §147-33.99.
Unauthorized use of public purchase or contract procedures for private benefit, §147-33.98.

Parking authorities.
Commissioners or employees, §160A-555.

Pollution control.
Industrial and pollution control facilities financing act.
Conflict of public officers, §159C-16.

Prisoner grievance resolution board, §148-118.7.

Property insurance.
Mediation of emergency or disaster claims.
Disqualification of mediator, §58-44-100(i).

Public contracts.
Public officers or employees benefiting from public contracts, §14-234.

Public officers or employees benefiting from public contracts, §14-234.

Public works.
Employment of architects, engineers, etc., when interest in use of materials prohibited, §133-1.

Purchases and contracts through department of administration.
Financial interest of officers in sources of supply, §143-63.

Regional sports authorities.
Members, officers and employees, §160A-479.11.

Retirement system for teachers and state employees.
Management of funds.
Personal profit or acting as surety prohibited, §135-7(e).

Savings and loan associations, §54B-104.

Savings banks.
Directors, officers and employees, §54C-104.
Savings institutions division employees, §54C-59(b) to (d).

Social services.
Medical assistance program, §108A-65.
State-county special assistance for adults.
No payments to facilities owned or operated by certain persons, §108A-47.

State auditor, §147-64.12(a), (b).

State building commission.
Interested members not to participate in contract, §143-135.28.

State ethics commission, §138A-7(d).

Statements of economic interest, §§138A-21 to 138A-27.

Tobacco trust fund commission.
Prohibited conduct, §143-717(h).

Transportation board, §136-14(b), (c), (e).
Criminal penalty, §136-14(i).

Trustees.
Administration of trust.
Conflict between trustee's fiduciary and personal interest, §36C-8-802.

Turnpike authority.
Board members, §136-89.182(h).

Urban redevelopment.
Redevelopment commissions, §160A-511.

U.S.S. North Carolina battleship commission.
Employees not to have interest, §143B-74.3.

CONFLICTS OF INTEREST —Cont'd

Veterans' recreation authorities.
Commissioners or employees, §165-29.

Vocational rehabilitation council, §143-548(d5).

Wills.
Probate of wills.
Clerk of superior court, §28A-2-3.

Workers' compensation self-insurance.
Third-party administrators and service companies, §58-47-205.

CONFORMITY ACT.

Judgments, §1-237.

CONFUSION.

Exclusion of relevant evidence, §8C-1 Rule 403.

CONGRESS.

Absent members, US Const Art I §5.

Adjournment, US Const Art I §§5, 7, Art II §3.

Admiralty, US Const Art I §8.

Age.
Representative in congress, US Const Art I §2.
Senator, US Const Art I §3.

Agriculture development act.
Funds made available by congress, §106-585.

Aliens.
Eligibility to be representative, US Const Art I §2.

Amendments to the constitution, US Const Art V.
Senate.
Equal suffrage in senate, US Const Art V.

Apportionment, US Const Art I §§2, 3, Amds 14, 17.
Action challenging state legislative or congressional plan, §§1-81.1, 1-267.1, 120-2.3 to 120-2.5.
Three-judge panel, §1-267.1.
Approval of act amending, deleting, adding to, modifying or repealing plan.
Attorney general to seek, §120-30.9B(b).
Failure to seek, §120-30.9B(b).
Severability of congressional apportionment acts, §163-201.1.

Appropriations, US Const Art I §§7, 9.

Approval by president of order, resolution or vote, US Const Art I §7.

Army and navy.
Powers of congress, US Const Art I §8.

Arrest of members, US Const Art I §6.

Bankruptcy and insolvency.
Powers of congress, US Const Art I §8.

Borrowing money, US Const Art I §8.

Changing meeting of congress, US Const Amd 20.

CLE exemption to North Carolina members, Bar Rule D.1517.

Commerce, US Const Art I §§8, 9.

Compensation of members, US Const Art I §6.
Laws varying compensation.
When to take effect, US Const Amd 27.

Consists of senate and house of representatives, US Const Art I §1.

Continuing legal education exemption to North Carolina members of congress, Bar Rule D.1517.

Copyright, US Const Art I §8.

Counterfeiting.
Powers of congress, US Const Art I §8.

Courts.
Power to constitute tribunals inferior to supreme court, US Const Art I §8.

CONGRESS —Cont'd

Debate, US Const Art I §6.

Debts.
Powers of congress, US Const Art I §8.

Declaration of war, US Const Art I §8.

Defense.
Powers of congress, US Const Art I §8.

Depositions.
Reading deposition on trial.
When depositions may be read, §8-83.

District of Columbia, US Const Art I §8.

Districts.
Congressional districts.
Number, §163-201(a).
Specified, §163-201(a).

Duties and imposts.
Powers of congress, US Const Art I §8.

Elections.
Contributions and expenditures in political campaigns.
Candidates for federal office to file information report, §163-278.30.
Date of elections, §163-1(a).
Districts.
Area not assigned to district, §163-201(d).
General assembly apportionment act.
Compliance with federal law, §163-201.2(c).
Limitation on number of divisions, §163-201.2(b).
Restriction, §163-201.2(a).
Number of districts, §163-201(a).
Specified, §163-201(a).
Voting tabulation district boundary changed.
Congressional district boundary not changed, §163-201(c).
House of representatives, US Const Art I §§2, 4.
Governor to issue commission upon certification of election, §163-182.16.
Judge of elections, returns and qualifications of members, US Const Art I §5.
Qualifications of electors, US Const Art I §2.
Reapportionment.
Election after reapportionment, §163-202.
Returns.
Judge of returns, US Const Art I §5.
Taxation.
Denial or abridgement of right to vote for failure to pay tax prohibited, US Const Amd 24.
Times, places and manner of holding, US Const Art I §4.
Payment of poll tax not required, US Const Amd 24.
Proclamation by governor of names of members of congress elected.
Judge of elections, returns and qualifications of members, US Const Art I §5.
Senate.
Electors, US Const Amds 14, 17.
Judge of elections, returns and qualifications of members, US Const Art I §5.
Qualifications of electors, US Const Amd 17.
Times, places and manner of holding, US Const Art I §4.
Vacancy in office, §§163-12, 163-115(e).
Vacancies in office.
Filling.
House of representatives, §§163-13, 163-115(b).
Senate, §§163-12, 163-115(e).

CONGRESS —Cont'd
Excises.
  Powers of congress, US Const Art I §8.
Foreign commerce, US Const Art I §8.
Freedom of speech.
  Members of congress, US Const Art I §6.
Holding other office, US Const Art I §6.
House of representatives, US Const Art I §§1, 2,
    4, 5.
  Absent members, US Const Art I §5.
  Arrest of members, US Const Art I §6.
  Compensation of members, US Const Art I §6.
    Laws varying compensation.
      When to take effect, US Const Amd 27.
  Debate, US Const Art I §6.
  Elections, US Const Art I §§2, 4.
    Governor to issue commission upon certification
      of election, §163-182.16.
    Judge of elections, returns and qualifications of
      members, US Const Art I §5.
    Qualifications of electors, US Const Art I §2.
    Reapportionment.
      Election after reapportionment, §163-202.
    Returns.
      Judge of returns, US Const Art I §5.
    Taxation.
      Denial or abridgement of right to vote for
        failure to pay tax prohibited, US Const
        Amd 24.
    Times, places and manner of holding, US Const
      Art I §4.
  Expulsion of member, US Const Art I §5.
  Freedom of speech, US Const Art I §6.
  Holding other office, US Const Art I §6.
  Impeachment, US Const Art I §2.
  Journals, US Const Art I §§5, 7.
  Libel and slander.
    Privilege of members, US Const Art I §6.
  Officers, US Const Art I §2.
  Presidential elector.
    Representative ineligible, US Const Art II §1.
  Punishment of members, US Const Art I §5.
  Qualifications.
    Electors, US Const Art I §2.
    Members, US Const Art I §2.
      Judge of qualifications, US Const Art I §5.
  Reapportionment.
    Election after reapportionment, §163-202.
    Severability of congressional apportionment
      acts, §163-201.1.
  Revenue bills, US Const Art I §7.
  Rules of procedure, US Const Art I §5.
  Speaker, US Const Art I §2.
  Term, US Const Art I §2.
  Vacancies in office, US Const Art I §2.
  Vice-president of the United States.
    Vacancy in office.
      Confirmation on nomination of president, US
        Const Amd 25 §2.
Insurrections, US Const Art I §8.
International law.
  Power to punish offenses against, US Const Art I
    §8.
Interstate commerce, US Const Art I §§8, 9.
Invasions, US Const Art I §8.
Legislative powers vested in, US Const Art I §1.
Letters of marque and reprisal, US Const Art I
    §8.
Libel and slander.
  Privilege of members of congress, US Const Art I
    §6.

CONGRESS —Cont'd
Messages to congress, US Const Art II §3.
Militia.
  Powers of congress, US Const Art I §8.
Money.
  Powers of congress, US Const Art I §8.
Motor vehicle special license plates, §20-79.4(b).
Naturalization, US Const Art I §8.
Navy.
  Powers of congress, US Const Art I §8.
Oath of office, US Const Art VI.
Patents, US Const Art I §8.
Piracy.
  Powers of congress, US Const Art I §8.
Post offices and post roads, US Const Art I §8.
Powers of congress, US Const Art I §8.
  Limitations on powers, US Const Art I §9.
President of the United States.
  Adjourning congress, US Const Art II §3.
  Convening congress, US Const Art II §3.
  Declaration of president's disability.
    Determination of issue, US Const Amd 25 §4.
  Messages to congress, US Const Art II §3.
  Special sessions of congress, US Const Art II §3.
Qualifications of members of congress, US
    Const Art I §§2, 3, 5.
Rules of procedure, US Const Art I §5.
Secretary of state.
  Distribution of acts of congress, §147-36.
Senate, US Const Amd 17.
  Absent members, US Const Art I §5.
  Adjournment, US Const Art I §§5, 7, Art II §3.
  Arrest of members, US Const Art I §6.
  Compensation of members, US Const Art I §6.
    Laws varying compensation.
      When to take effect, US Const Amd 27.
  Debate, US Const Art I §§4, 6.
  Elections.
    Electors, US Const Amds 14, 17.
    Judge of elections, returns and qualifications of
      members, US Const Art I §5.
    Qualifications of electors, US Const Amd 17.
    Times, places and manner of holding, US Const
      Art I §4.
  Equal suffrage in senate, US Const Art V.
  Expulsion of member, US Const Art I §5.
  Freedom of speech, US Const Art I §6.
  Holding other office, US Const Art I §6.
  Impeachment, US Const Art I §3.
  Journals, US Const Art I §§5, 7.
  Libel and slander.
    Privilege of members, US Const Art I §6.
  Officers, US Const Art I §3.
  President.
    Pro tempore, US Const Art I §3.
  Presidential elector.
    Senator ineligible, US Const Art II §1.
  Punishment of members, US Const Art I §5.
  Qualifications.
    Electors, US Const Amd 17.
    Members, US Const Art I §3.
      Judge of qualifications, US Const Art I §5.
  Revenue bills, US Const Art I §7.
  Rules of procedure, US Const Art I §5.
  Vice-president of the United States.
    Vacancy in office.
      Confirmation of president, US Const Amd 25
        §2.
Sessions, US Const Art I §4, Amd 20 §2.
  Special sessions, US Const Art II §3.
Suffrage, US Const Amds 15, 19, 26.

CONGRESS —Cont'd
Taxation.
Powers of congress, US Const Art I §8.
Territories, US Const Art IV §3.
Vacancies in office.
House of representatives.
Nominating procedures, §163-13(a).
Special elections, §§163-13(a), 163-115(b).
Senate.
Elections to fill, §§163-12, 163-115(e).
War.
Articles of war, US Const Art I §8.
Declaration of war, US Const Art I §8.
Weights and measures, US Const Art I §8.
Welfare.
Power of congress to provide for general welfare,
US Const Art I §8.

CONIFEROUS TREES.
Taking, etc., of certain wild plants from land of
another, §14-129.

CONNOR ACT.
Registration of conveyances, contracts to
convey, options and leases of land, §47-18.

CONOVER.
Room occupancy tax.
Uniform provisions.
Authorized to levy, §160A-215(g).
Generally, §160A-215.
Satellite annexation.
Limitation on area of satellite corporate limits,
inapplicability, §160A-58.1(b).

CONSCIENTIOUS OBJECTORS.
Exemptions from duty with the militia,
§127A-8.

CONSECUTIVE SENTENCES, §15A-1354.
Commencement date of consecutive sentence,
§15A-1355(a).

CONSENT.
Abortion.
Parental or judicial consent, §§90-21.6 to 90-21.10.
Woman's right to know act.
Informed consent required, §90-21.82.
Assurance of informed consent, §90-21.90.
Voluntariness, §90-21.91.
Minor upon whom abortion is performed,
§90-21.87.
Adoption.
Adoption of minors.
Persons whose consent is required, §48-3-601.
Agency placements, §48-3-601.
Execution of consent by agency, §48-3-605(d).
Time for execution of consent, §48-3-604(d).
Child consent, §48-3-601.
Collateral agreements, effect on consent,
§48-3-610.
Consequences, §48-3-607.
Contents, mandatory provisions, §48-3-606.
Court order dispensing with consent in certain
situations, §48-3-603(b).
Custody of minor upon revocation, §48-3-608(c).
Custody of minor upon voiding of consent,
§48-3-609(b).
Direct placement of minors for adoption,
§48-3-201(b).
Direct placements, §48-3-601.
Dismissal of adoption proceeding upon voiding of
consent, §48-3-609(c).
Effect, §48-3-607.

CONSENT —Cont'd
Adoption —Cont'd
Execution procedures.
Agencies, §48-3-605(d).
Contents, mandatory provisions, §48-3-606.
Foreign execution, §48-3-605(e).
General provisions, §48-3-605(c).
Indian children, §48-3-605(f).
Parent or guardian of minor, §48-3-605(a).
Parent under age of eighteen, §48-3-605(b).
Foreign consent, §48-3-605(e).
Fraud or duress in obtaining consent of parent or
guardian.
Statute of limitations for appeal, §48-2-607(c).
Guardian ad litem for incompetent parents,
§48-3-602.
Incompetent parents, §48-3-602.
Irrevocable consent.
Second consent to adoption by same adoptive
parents, §48-3-608(e).
Mandatory contents, §48-3-606.
Minor age twelve or older.
Consent required, §48-3-601.
Court order dispensing with consent,
§48-3-603(b).
Persons whose consent not required, §48-3-603.
Revocation of consent.
Adoption cannot proceed without another
consent, §48-3-608(d).
Attorneys' fees to person who revoked upon
failure to return minor, §48-3-608(c).
Custody of minor, §48-3-608(c).
Direct placement, §48-3-608(b).
Generally, §48-3-608(a).
Second consent by same adoptive parents.
Irrevocable, §48-3-608(e).
Stepparent's adoption of stepchild, §48-4-102.
Timing of execution, §48-3-604.
Void, §48-3-609(a).
Custody of minor, §48-3-609(b).
Dismissal of adoption proceeding, §48-3-609(c).
Alcoholic beverages.
Implied consent law, §20-16.2.
Attorney disbarment, Bar Rule B.0117.
Attorneys at law.
Informed consent.
Aggregate settlement or agreement for two or
more clients, ProfCond Rule 1.8.
Communicating with client when client's
consent required, ProfCond Rule 1.4.
Defined, ProfCond Rule 1.0.
Early childhood initiatives.
Home-centered services, §143B-168.16.
Guardian of the person.
Powers, §35A-1241(a).
Health care for minors, §§32A-28 to 32A-34.
Custodial parents.
Extent and limitations of authority, §32A-31.
Impaired driving.
Implied consent, §20-16.2.
Implied consent law, §20-16.2.
Insurance policies or contracts.
Excessive rates, §58-40-30(c).
Minors.
Cigarettes and tobacco products.
Use of minors to test compliance with
provisions.
Written parental consent required, §14-313(d).
Placement of children.
When consent of department of health and
human services required, §7B-3702.

CONSENT —Cont'd
Minors —Cont'd
Treatment of minors.
Consent of minors required, §90-21.5.
Consent of parent or guardian.
When not required, §90-21.1.
Health care consent generally, §§32A-28 to 32A-34.
Money transmitters.
Inspection, §53-208.20(d).
Motor vehicle dealers.
Computer systems.
Protection of dealership data.
Consent to access information, §20-305.7(b).
Motor vehicles.
Implied consent law, §20-16.2.
Nonprofit corporations.
Action by directors on written consent, §55A-8-21.
Action by members by written consent, §55A-7-04.
Prisons and prisoners.
Self-inflicted injuries.
Treatment of injuries upon prisoners.
Procedure when consent is refused by prisoner, §148-46.2.
Psychotherapy patient/client sexual exploitation act.
Prohibited defense, §90-21.46.
Reference by consent, §1A-1 Rule 53(a).
Jury trial, §1A-1 Rule 53(b).
Reinsurance.
Assumption reinsurance, §58-10-40.
Representation.
Persons representing and binding others, §§36C-3-301 to 36C-3-305.
Searches and seizures.
Authority pursuant to consent, §15A-221(a).
By whom given, §15A-222.
Defined, §15A-221(b).
Items seizable as result of consent search, §15A-223(b).
Person from whom effective consent may be obtained, §15A-222.
Scope of consent search.
Items seizable as result of consent search, §15A-223(b).
Limited by scope of consent, §15A-223(a).
Sexual offenses.
No defense to offense with certain victims, §14-27.7(a).
No defense to taking indecent liberties with students, §14-202.4(c).
Rape shield law, §8C-1 Rule 412.
Trial by consent.
Jury verdict having same effect as trial by jury, §1A-1 Rule 39(c).
Trusts and trustees.
Beneficiaries.
Breach of trust.
Trustee not liable, §36C-10-1009.
Noncharitable irrevocable trust.
Termination or modification, §36C-4-411.
Viatical life insurance settlements.
Viators consent to contract, §58-58-250(e).

CONSENT JUDGMENTS.
Abused, neglected or dependent juvenile actions, §7B-801(b1).
Clerks of superior courts authorized to enter, §1-209.
Money transmitters, §53-208.25(b).

CONSENT JUDGMENTS —Cont'd
State departments and agencies.
Approval by attorney general, §114-2.2(a) to (c).
Entering into, §114-2.1.

CONSENT TO HEALTH CARE FOR MINORS, §§32A-28 to 32A-34.
Authorization.
Duration, §32A-32.
Form, §32A-34.
Good faith reliance on, §32A-33.
Reliance on authorization, §32A-33.
Revocation, §32A-32.
Statutory form, §32A-34.
Who may make an authorization, §32A-30.
Custodial parents.
Authority, §32A-30.
Definitions, §32A-29.
Extent and limitations of authority, §32A-31.
Public policy, §32A-28(a).
Purpose of article, §32A-28(b).
Treatment by physician.
Consent of minor sufficient, §90-21.5(a).
Consent of parent or guardian.
When not required, §90-21.1.
Who may make an authorization to consent, §32A-30.

CONSERVATION.
Animal waste management, §§143-215.10A to 143-215.10M.
See ANIMAL WASTE MANAGEMENT.
Community conservation assistance program, §106-860.
Department of environment and natural resources.
Generally.
See ENVIRONMENT AND NATURAL RESOURCES DEPARTMENT.
Ecosystem enhancement program, §§143-214.8 to 143-214.13.
See ECOSYSTEM ENHANCEMENT PROGRAM.
Energy conservation loan authority, §122A-5.3.
Energy loan fund, §§143B-437.14 to 143B-437.16.
Environmental compact, §§113A-21 to 113A-23.
Environmental protection.
See ENVIRONMENTAL PROTECTION.
Farmland preservation, §§113A-240, 113A-241.
Floodplain regulation, §§143-215.51 to 143-215.61.
See FLOODPLAIN REGULATION.
Income tax credit.
Donations of real property for land conservation purposes, §105-151.12.
Oil and gas conservation.
See OIL AND GAS CONSERVATION.
Open space preservation, §§113A-240, 113A-241.
Parks and recreation.
Acquisition of conservation lands not included in state parks system, §113-34.1.
Plant protection and conservation, §§106-202.12 to 106-202.22.
See PLANT PROTECTION AND CONSERVATION.
Policy of state, NC Const Art XIV §5.
Soil and water conservation commission, §§106-840 to 106-844.
Southern growth policies agreement, §§143-490 to 143-506.
See SOUTHERN GROWTH POLICIES AGREEMENT.

CONSERVATION —Cont'd

Stream watch program, §§143-215.74F to
143-215.74I.

Tillage equipment.
Income tax, §§105-130.36, 105-151.13.

Water and air quality reporting, §§143-215.63 to
143-215.69.
See WATER AND AIR QUALITY REPORTING.

Water and air resources, §§143-211 to
143-215.9C.
See WATER AND AIR RESOURCES.

Water resources development projects.
Federal projects, §§143-215.38 to 143-215.43.
See WATER RESOURCES DEVELOPMENT
PROJECTS.
Generally, §§143-215.70 to 143-215.73A.
See WATER RESOURCES DEVELOPMENT
PROJECTS.

Water supply watershed protection,
§§143-214.5, 143-214.7.

CONSERVATION AGREEMENTS.

Enhanced voluntary agricultural districts.
Irrevocability, time period, automatic renewal,
time period, §106-743.2.

**CONSERVATION AND HISTORIC
PRESERVATION AGREEMENTS,** §§121-34
to 121-42.

Acquisition of agreements, §§121-37, 121-38(b).

Applicability of article, §121-36(a).

Approval of agreements, §121-37.

**Assessment of land or improvements subject to
agreement,** §121-40.

Citation of act, §§121-34, 121-42.

Construction and interpretation, §121-36(b), (c).

Definitions, §121-35.

Duration of agreements, §121-38(c).

Effectiveness of agreements, §121-38(c).

Enforceability of agreements, §121-38(a).
Right of entry, §121-39(b).
Who may enforce, §121-39(a).

Future conveyance of property.
Provision requiring payment of fee, §121-38(e).

Holders.
Defined, §121-35.
Enforceability of agreements, §121-39(a).

Public recording of agreements, §121-41.

Register of deeds.
Public recording of agreements, §121-41(a).

Releases or terminations of agreements,
§121-41(b).

Right of entry.
Enforceability of agreements, §121-39(b).

Short title, §121-34.

Taxation.
Assessment of land or improvements subject to
agreement, §121-40.

Validity of agreements, §121-38.
Imposition of continuing obligations, §121-38(d).

CONSERVATION EASEMENTS, §§113A-230 to
113A-235.

Agricultural conservation easements, §106-744.

Condemnation of property encumbered by,
§§40A-80 to 40A-85.
Appeals, §40A-85.
Applicability of provisions, §40A-80(a).
Compensation, §40A-84.
Complaint.
Additional information required, §40A-81.
Definition of conservation easement, §40A-80(b).

CONSERVATION EASEMENTS —Cont'd

Condemnation of property encumbered by
—Cont'd
No prudent and feasible alternative.
Demonstration, §40A-82(a).
Exceptions to requirement, §40A-82(c).
Judicial determination, §40A-82(b).
Petition.
Additional information required, §40A-81.
Vesting of title and right of possession, §40A-83.

Conservation grant fund.
Administration of grants from fund, §113A-234(b).
Allowable uses of grants, §113A-233(a).
Created, §113A-232(a).
Eligibility for grant, §113A-232(c), (c1).
Procedures and criteria for grants, §113A-234(a).
Prohibited uses of grants, §113A-233(b).
Sources, §113A-232(b).
Use of revenue, §113A-232(d).

Development of program to accomplish,
§113A-231.

Ecosystem enhancement program.
Recipient or grantee to grant in property acquired
under program, §143-214.12(a1).

Endowment fund.
Disbursements authorized, §113A-253.2(b).
Established, §113A-253.2(a).

Farmland preservation, §§113A-240, 113A-241.

Findings of general assembly, §113A-230.

Intent of general assembly, §113A-230.

Inventory, §113A-235(c).

Open space preservation, §§113A-240, 113A-241.

**Protection of ecological systems and
appropriate public use through
conservation easements,** §113A-235(a), (b).

Reports.
Implementation of provisions, §113A-235(c).

**CONSERVATION, FARMLAND, AND OPEN
SPACE LAND PRESERVATION.**

Generally, §113A-241(a).

Legislative intent, §113A-240(a), (b).

**Secretary of environment and natural
resources.**
Duties, §113A-241(b), (c).

CONSERVATION OF ENERGY.

Electric power rates to promote conservation,
§62-155.

CONSERVATION OFFICERS.

Special conservation officers, §113-138.

CONSERVATION TILLAGE EQUIPMENT.

Income tax.
Corporations, §105-130.36.
Individual income tax.
Credit for installation of conservation tillage
equipment, §105-151.13.

CONSERVATORS.

Banks.
Conservatorship generally, §§53-148 to 53-158.1.
See BANKS.

**Compensation of trustees and other
fiduciaries,** §§32-53 to 32-62.
See FIDUCIARIES.

Credit unions.
Conservation generally, §54-109.92.

Custodial trusts, §§33B-1 to 33B-22.
See CUSTODIAL TRUSTS.

Durable power of attorney.
Attorney-in-fact accountable to court appointed
conservator, §32A-10(a).

CONSERVATORS —Cont'd
Durable power of attorney —Cont'd
Nomination by durable power of attorney for
consideration by court, §32A-10(b).
Judicial sales.
Bond of person holding sale, §1-339.10(b), (c).
Powers of fiduciaries generally, §§32-25 to
32-27.
See FIDUCIARIES.
Representation.
Persons representing and binding others,
§§36C-3-301 to 36C-3-305.
Securities regulation.
Appointment of conservator for defendant's assets,
§78A-47(a).
Exempt transactions, §78A-17.
Trust companies, §§53-401 to 53-405.
Uniform fiduciaries act, §§32-1 to 32-13.
See FIDUCIARIES.

CONSIDERATION.
Failure as affirmative defense, pleading, §1A-1
Rule 8(c).
Leases, UCC.
Modification needs no consideration,
§25-2A-208(1).
Letters of credit, §25-5-105.
Want of consideration.
Unclaimed property act, affirmative defense,
§116B-58.

CONSIGNMENTS.
Artwork on consignment, §§25C-1 to 25C-5.
Embezzlement by consignees.
Receipt of property by virtue of office or
employment, §14-90.
Sale of goods, UCC, §25-2-326.
Sale or return, §25-2-326.
Risk of loss, §25-2-327(2).
Special incidents, §25-2-327(2).
Sale of used goods on consignment.
Records, §66-67.2(a) to (e).

CONSOLIDATED CITY-COUNTY ACT, §§160B-1
to 160B-21.
Assumption of debt, §§160B-16 to 160B-21.
Actions to set aside referendum, §160B-19(i).
Acts by localities, effect, §160B-18(c).
Applicability of article, §160B-16(a).
Approval by referendum required, §160B-18(a).
Budget preparation by governing board, §160B-17.
Canvassing of referendum, §160B-19(h).
Consolidation effective date, §160B-18(b).
Consolidation enactment publication.
Notice of assumption of debt, §160B-21(a).
Consolidations study commission.
Referendum by commission may include
referendum on assumptions of debt,
§160B-19(b).
Effective date of consolidation, §160B-18(b).
Enactment of consolidation.
Limitation on action contesting validity,
§160B-21(b).
Form of referendum on assumption of debt,
§160B-19(d).
General assembly.
Referendum of consolidation may include
referendum on assumption of debt,
§160B-19(c).
Governing board.
Budget preparation, §160B-17.
Organizational meeting, §160B-17.

CONSOLIDATED CITY-COUNTY ACT —Cont'd
Assumption of debt —Cont'd
Governing bodies of consolidating units.
Referendum on assumption of debt,
§160B-19(d).
Interim governing boards.
Referendum on assumption of debt,
§160B-19(d).
Limitation of local acts, §160B-18(c).
Limitation on action contesting validity of
consolidation enactment, §160B-21(b).
Local government commission review,
§160B-20(a).
Notice of referendum, §160B-19(g).
Organizational meeting of governing board,
§160B-17.
Outstanding debt secured by pledge of faith and
credit of consolidating city.
Approval by majority of voters, §160B-19(e).
Procedure for assumption of debt, §160B-20(b).
Referendum on assumption of debt,
§160B-19(a).
Publication of consolidation enactment.
Inclusion of assumption of debt, §160B-21(a).
Referendum approval required, §160B-18(a).
Referendum on assumption of debt.
Action to set aside, §160B-19(i).
Form, §160B-19(d).
Notice, §160B-19(g).
Time for holding, §160B-19(f).
Review by local government commission,
§160B-20(a).
Right to issue authorized debt.
Majority of approval of voters for assumption of
right, §160B-19(e).
Procedure for assumption of right, §160B-20(c).
Referendum on assumption of right,
§160B-19(a).
Scope of article, §160B-16(a).
Severability of article, §160B-16(b).
Validity of article, §160B-16(b).
Bankruptcy and insolvency.
Authority of counties, cities, towns and villages,
etc., to avail themselves of bankruptcy law,
§23-48.
Bond issues.
Authorized, §160B-13.
Debt limitations, §160B-15.
Elections on, §160B-14.
Procedure for issuance, §160B-14.
Borrowing money.
Authorized, §160B-13.
Debt limitations, §160B-15.
Citation of act.
Short title, §160B-1.
Constitution of North Carolina.
General assembly to provide for local government,
NC Const Art VII §1.
Merged or consolidated counties, NC Const Art
VII §3.
Debts.
Assumption of obligations and debts, §§160B-16 to
160B-21.
Limitation on indebtedness, §160B-15.
Definitions, §160B-2.
Dissolution.
Establishment of study commission, §160B-2.2(a).
Study commission.
Established, §160B-2.2(a).
Powers and duties generally, §160B-2.2(b).
Effective date of act, §160B-1.

CONSOLIDATED CITY-COUNTY ACT —Cont'd
Elections.
Bond issues, §160B-14.
Ethics.
Adoption of code, §160B-2.3(a).
Education requirement, §160B-2.3(b).
Local government ethics codes and education, §§160A-86, 160A-87.
General assembly.
Local government to be provided for by general assembly, NC Const Art VII §1.
Governing board.
Defined, §160B-2.
Urban service districts.
Defining districts, §§160B-3 to 160B-6.
Highways, roads and streets.
Arrangements in consolidated city-county, §136-66.6.
Limitation of actions.
Contesting validity of enactment of consolidation, §160B-21(b).
Obligations.
Assumption of debts and obligations, §§160B-16 to 160B-21.
Powers of consolidated city-county.
Generally, §160B-2.1(a).
Outside boundaries of urban service district, §160B-2.1(b).
Statute of limitations.
Contesting validity of enactment of consolidation, §160B-21(b).
Study commission for dissolution of city-county.
Establishment, §160B-2.2(a).
Powers, §160B-2.2(b).
Taxation.
Urban service districts.
Authorized, §160B-11.
Rates, §160B-11.
Title of act.
Short title, §160B-1.
Urban service districts, §§160B-3 to 160B-12.
Abolition of districts, §160B-10.
Administration, §160B-3(b).
Consolidation of district.
Effective date, §160B-8(d).
Findings required, §160B-8(a).
Hearing, §160B-8(c).
Notice of hearing, §160B-8(c).
Report.
Prerequisite to hearing, §160B-8(b).
Services, facilities and functions.
Required provision or maintenance by consolidated district, §160B-9(c).
Effective date.
Resolution defining district, §160B-6(d).
Establishment, §160B-3(a).
Defining of district prior to consolidation, §160B-4(b).
Effective date of resolution, §160B-6(c).
Findings required, §160B-6(a).
Hearing, §160B-6(c).
Notice of hearing, §160B-6(c).
Replacing municipalities abolished subsequent to consolidation, §160B-5.
Replacing municipality abolished at time of consolidation, §160B-4(a).
Report.
Prerequisite to hearing, §160B-6(b).
Services, facilities and functions.
Required provision or maintenance by new district, §160B-9(a).

CONSOLIDATED CITY-COUNTY ACT —Cont'd
Urban service districts —Cont'd
Exercise of powers, §160B-3(b).
Extension of district.
Annexation by petition, §160B-7(b).
Effective date of resolution, §160B-7(e).
Findings required, §160B-7(a).
Hearing, §160B-7(d).
Notice of hearing, §160B-7(d), (d1).
Report.
Prerequisite to hearing, §160B-7(c).
Restriction on use of provisions, §160B-7(f).
Services, facilities and functions.
Required provision or maintenance by extended district, §160B-9(b).
Governing board.
Defining districts, §§160B-3 to 160B-6.
Hearings.
Abolition of districts, §160B-10.
Consolidation of district, §160B-8(c).
Establishment of district, §160B-6(c).
Extension of district, §160B-7(d).
Notice.
Abolition of districts.
Hearings, §160B-10.
Consolidation of district.
Hearing, §160B-8(c).
Establishment of district.
Hearing, §160B-6(c).
Extension of district.
Hearing, §160B-7(d), (d1).
Purpose, §160B-3(a).
Revenues.
Allocation to urban service district by consolidated city-county, §160B-12.
Taxes.
Authorized, §160B-11.
Rates, §160B-11.

CONSOLIDATED COUNTY HUMAN SERVICES, §143B-139.7.

CONSOLIDATED HUMAN SERVICES AGENCY.
Board.
Appointing authority.
County board of commissioners, §108A-3(d).
Authority and powers generally, §§108A-15.1(a), 153A-77(d).
Chairperson, §153A-77(c).
Composition, §153A-77(c).
Creation, authority of county, §153A-77(b).
Meetings, §153A-77(c).
Number of members, §153A-77(c).
Per diem, subsistence and travel expenses, §153A-77(c).
Policy-making, rule-making and administrative board to agency, §153A-77(c).
Powers and duties of area authority, §122C-127(b).
Powers and duties of board of social services, §108A-15.1(b).
Powers and duties of local health board, §130A-43(b).
Quorum, §153A-77(c).
Removal, §153A-77(c).
Social services, power and authority, §108A-15.1(a).
Counties with population in excess of 425,000.
Applicability of section, §153A-77(f).
Creation.
Authority of county, §153A-77(b).

CONSOLIDATED HUMAN SERVICES AGENCY —Cont'd

Creation —Cont'd
County required to provide for health services, §130A-34(b).
Department of county, §122C-116(b).
Director.
Appointment, dismissal, §153A-77(e).
Duties, powers, §153A-77(e).
Director of area authority, powers and duties of, §122C-127(b).
Director of social services, powers and duties of, §108A-15.1(c).
Local health director, powers and duties of, §130A-43(c).
Report to county manager, §153A-77(e).
Duties of local health department.
Responsibility to carry out, §130A-43(a).
Human services functions.
Assignment to agency, §153A-77(b).
Local public health programs.
Authority to administer, §130A-43(a).
Mental health programs.
Authority to carry, §122C-127(a).

CONSOLIDATED JUDICIAL RETIREMENT ACT, §§135-50 to 135-75.2.
See RETIREMENT SYSTEM FOR TEACHERS AND STATE EMPLOYEES.

CONSOLIDATION.
Administrative procedure.
Hearings, §150B-26.
Arbitration.
Consolidation of separate arbitration proceedings.
Court order, §1-569.10(a), (b).
Prohibited contract provisions, §1-569.10(c).
Banks, §53-12.
Deemed one bank, §53-13.
National banks.
Consolidation, conversion or merger of state banks or trust companies with national banks, §53-16.
Wills.
Substitution as executor or trustee under will, §28A-2A-12.
Condominiums, §47C-2-121.
Counties, NC Const Art VII §3.
Commissions.
Powers, §153A-404.
Purposes, §153A-402.
Content of concurrent resolutions, §153A-403.
Establishment, §153A-401(a).
General assembly action, §153A-405(d).
Powers and duties.
Commissions, §153A-404.
Purposes of commission, §153A-402.
Referendum, §153A-405(a) to (c), (e).
Ballot propositions, §153A-405(b) to (e).
Resolutions.
Content of concurrent resolutions, §153A-403.
Support, §153A-401(b).
Decedents' estates.
Consolidation of estate proceeding and civil action, §28A-2-6(f).
Orders upon consolidation, joinder or transfer, §28A-2-6(i).
Electric membership corporations.
Articles of consolidation, §117-41(c).
Filing and recording of articles, §117-43.
Recording of articles, §117-43.
Compliance with provisions, §117-41(a).

CONSOLIDATION —Cont'd
Electric membership corporations —Cont'd
Effect of consolidation, §117-44.
Procedure, §117-41(c).
Proposition for consolidation, §117-41(b).
Validation, §117-45.
Fraternal benefit societies.
Insurance.
Reinsurance upon consolidation, §58-24-60(b).
Procedure, §58-24-65.
Hospital, medical and dental service corporations, §58-65-155.
Insurance companies, §58-7-150.
Marketing associations.
Abandonment of consolidation, §54-161(b).
Articles of consolidation, §54-162(a), (b).
Authorized, §54-160(a).
Domestic and foreign associations, §54-164.
Effect, §54-164(d), (e).
Effect, §54-163.
Objecting members, §54-166.
Plan of consolidation, §54-160(b).
Adoption, §54-161(a).
Time consolidation effected, §54-162(c).
Merger.
See MERGER.
Motor carriers, §62-111(b), (c), (e).
Municipal service districts.
Effective date, §160A-539.
Required provision or maintenance of services by consolidated district, §160A-540(c).
Mutual burial associations, §§90-210.80, 90-210.106(a) to (d), 90-210.107(a) to (f).
Public utilities, §62-111.
Retail installment sales.
Consolidation and refinancing, §§25A-27(a), 25A-31.
School districts, §115C-72(a), (b).
Administrative units in adjoining counties.
Merger of units, §115C-68.
Administrative units in same county.
Merger, §115C-67.
Administrative units merged by board of commissioners, §115C-68.1.
Administrative units merged by local boards of education, §115C-68.2.
Validation of plans, §115C-68.3.
Schools, §115C-72(a), (b).
State agencies.
Powers of governor, §147-13.1(a) to (c).
Telephone membership corporations, §117-41.
Effect of consolidation, §117-44.
Filing and recording of articles, §117-43.
Validation, §117-45.
Trusts and trustees.
Judicial proceedings involving trusts, §36C-2-205(f).

CONSOLIDATION OF ACTIONS, §1A-1 Rule 42(a).
Decedents' estates.
Consolidation of estate proceeding and civil action, §28A-2-6(f).
Orders upon consolidation, joinder or transfer, §28A-2-6(i).
Nuisances against public morals.
Action to abate and application for preliminary injunction, §19-2.4.

CONSOLIDATION OF COUNTIES, §§153A-401 to 153A-405.

CONSPIRACY.
Civil rights, interference with, §99D-1(a).
Continuing criminal enterprise, §14-7.20.
Controlled substances.
  Trafficking in certain drugs, §90-95(i).
  Violations of provisions, §90-98.
Criminal offense, §14-7.20(c).
Monopolies and restraint of trade.
  Illegal acts, §75-1.
Nuclear, biological or chemical weapons.
  Use of weapons, §14-288.22(b).
Odometer violations, §20-345.
Punishment for conspiracy to commit felony,
  §14-2.4(a).
Sentencing.
  Aggravating factors, §15A-1340.16.

CONSTITUTIONAL RIGHTS.
Enforcement or declaration of claim.
  Superior court jurisdiction, §7A-245(a).

CONSTITUTION OF NORTH CAROLINA.
Actions.
  Civil cases.
    Jury trial, NC Const Art I §25.
  Form of action, NC Const Art IV §13.
  Jury trial, NC Const Art I §25.
Acts.
  General laws.
    Defined, NC Const Art XIV §3.
Agriculture.
  Capital projects for agriculture.
    Authorization to create agency to issue bonds,
      NC Const Art V §11.
  Commissioner of agriculture.
    Acting commissioner, NC Const Art III §7.
    Compensation and allowances, NC Const Art III
      §9.
    Council of state.
      Membership, NC Const Art III §8.
    Duties, NC Const Art III §7.
    Elective officers, NC Const Art III §7.
    Incapacity.
      Determination, NC Const Art III §7.
    Interim commissioner, NC Const Art III §7.
    Vacancies.
      Filling, NC Const Art III §7.
Airports.
  Powers of general assembly as to seaport and
    airport facilities, NC Const Art V §13.
Alimony.
  Local, private and special legislation prohibited,
    NC Const Art II §24.
Allegiance to the United States, NC Const Art I
  §5.
Amendments.
  Constitutional amendments publication
    commission, §§147-54.8 to 147-54.10.
  Convention of the people.
    Revision or amendment of constitution by
      convention of the people, NC Const Art XIII
      §3.
  Legislative initiation.
    Revision or amendment by legislative initiation,
      NC Const Art XIII §4.
  Power to revise or amend constitution reserved to
    people, NC Const Art XIII §2.
  Revision or amendment by legislative initiation,
    NC Const Art XIII §4.
  Submission of acts to United States attorney
    general.
    Secretary of state, §120-30.9D.

CONSTITUTION OF NORTH CAROLINA
  —Cont'd
Appeals.
  Court of appeals.
    Decisions of the court of appeals.
      Right of appeals from certain decisions
        directly to supreme court, §7A-30.
    Jurisdiction, NC Const Art IV §12.
  Jurisdiction of the general court of justice, NC
    Const Art IV §12.
  Supreme court.
    Jurisdiction, NC Const Art IV §12.
Arson.
  Capital punishment.
    Crimes punishable by death, NC Const Art XI
      §2.
Assemblies.
  Right to assembly, NC Const Art I §12.
Attorney general.
  Acting attorney general, NC Const Art III §7.
  Compensation and allowances, NC Const Art III
    §9.
  Council of state.
    Membership, NC Const Art III §8.
  Duties, NC Const Art III §7.
  Elective officers, NC Const Art III §7.
  Incapacity.
    Determination, NC Const Art III §7.
  Interim attorney general, NC Const Art III §7.
  Qualifications, NC Const Art III §7.
Attorneys at law.
  Rights of accused to counsel, NC Const Art I §23.
Authority.
  Bond issues to finance capital projects for
    industry, NC Const Art V §9.
Bail.
  Excessive bail prohibited, NC Const Art I §27.
Bond issues.
  Capital projects for industry.
    Authorities may be created, NC Const Art V §9.
  General assembly.
    Actions on revenue bills, NC Const Art II §23.
  Health care facilities.
    Authorized, NC Const Art V §8.
  Higher education facilities.
    Authorized, NC Const Art V §12.
  Hospitals, NC Const Art V §8.
  Seaport and airport facilities.
    Authorized powers as to, NC Const Art V §13.
Boundaries.
  State boundaries, NC Const Art XIV §2.
Branches of government.
  Separation of powers, NC Const Art I §6.
Bridges.
  Local, private and special legislation prohibited,
    NC Const Art II §24.
Budget.
  Governor.
    Duties of governor, NC Const Art III §5.
Burglary.
  Capital punishment.
    Crimes punishable by death, NC Const Art XI
      §2.
Capital projects.
  Bond issues to finance.
    Counties may establish authorities to finance
      capital projects for industry, NC Const Art
      V §9.
Capital punishment.
  Enumeration of permissible punishments, NC
    Const Art XI §1.

CONSTITUTION OF NORTH CAROLINA
—Cont'd
Capital punishment —Cont'd
Offenses punishable by death, NC Const Art XI
§2.
Capitation tax.
Prohibited, NC Const Art V §1.
Cemeteries.
Local, private and special legislation prohibited,
NC Const Art II §24.
Charities.
Establishment and operation by state, NC Const
Art XI §3.
Charters.
Corporate charters, NC Const Art VIII §1.
Civil procedure.
Jury trial.
Right to jury trial in civil cases, NC Const Art I
§25.
Rules of procedure, NC Const Art IV §13.
Clerks of court.
Removal, NC Const Art IV §17.
Vacancies in office, NC Const Art IV §19.
Community colleges and technical institutes.
Benefits of public institutions of higher education
to be extended to people of state free of
charge, NC Const Art IX §9.
Maintenance of system of higher education, NC
Const Art IX §8.
Conservation.
Policy of state, NC Const Art XIV §5.
Consolidated city-county act.
General assembly to provide for local government,
NC Const Art VII §1.
Merged or consolidated counties, NC Const Art
VII §3.
Consolidation.
Counties.
Merged or consolidated counties, NC Const Art
VII §3.
**Constitutional amendments publication
commission.**
Composition, §147-54.8(b).
Duties, §147-54.10.
Established, §147-54.8(a).
Within department of secretary of state,
§147-54.8(a).
Explanation of amendment, revision or new
constitution, §147-54.10.
Meetings, §147-54.9(c).
Members, §147-54.8(b).
Officers, §147-54.9(a).
Powers, §147-54.10.
Quorum, §147-54.9(b).
Summary amendment, revision or new
constitution, §147-54.10.
Contracts.
State, political subdivisions or public corporations
may make contracts, NC Const Art V §2.
Conventions.
Amendment to the constitution.
Revision or amendment by the convention of the
people, NC Const Art XIII §3.
Composition, NC Const Art XIII §1.
Procedure for calling, NC Const Art XIII §1.
Corporations.
Charters, NC Const Art VIII §1.
Defined, NC Const Art VIII §2.
Corrections.
Establishment and operation of charitable and
correctional institutions and agencies by
state, NC Const Art XI §3.

CONSTITUTION OF NORTH CAROLINA
—Cont'd
Costs.
Revenues and expenses of the judicial
department, NC Const Art IV §20.
Council of state.
Composition, NC Const Art III §8.
Counties.
Contracts.
Authority to contract, NC Const Art V §2.
Education.
County school fund.
Composition of fund, NC Const Art IX §7.
Elections.
Sheriffs, NC Const Art VII §2.
General assembly to provide for local government,
NC Const Art VII §1.
Local treasury.
Drawing public money, NC Const Art V §7.
Merged or consolidated counties, NC Const Art
VII §3.
Sheriffs.
Election, NC Const Art VII §2.
Taxation.
Exemption from taxation, NC Const Art V §2.
Special tax areas, NC Const Art V §2.
Court of appeals.
Composition, NC Const Art IV §7.
Decisions of court of appeals.
Appeals of right from certain decisions, §7A-30.
Judges.
Election, NC Const Art IV §16.
Removal, NC Const Art IV §17.
Salaries, fees and emoluments, NC Const Art IV
§21.
Terms of office, NC Const Art IV §16.
Vacancies in office, NC Const Art IV §19.
Jurisdiction, NC Const Art IV §12.
Courts.
Administration by general assembly, NC Const
Art IV §14.
Court of appeals.
Composition, NC Const Art IV §7.
Judges.
Election, NC Const Art IV §16.
Removal, NC Const Art IV §17.
Salaries, fees and emoluments, NC Const Art
IV §21.
Terms of office, NC Const Art IV §16.
Vacancies, NC Const Art IV §19.
Jurisdiction, NC Const Art IV §12.
District courts, NC Const Art IV §10.
Judges.
Salaries, fees and emoluments, NC Const Art
IV §21.
Vacancies in office, NC Const Art IV §19.
Jurisdiction, NC Const Art IV §12.
Magistrates, NC Const Art IV §10.
General court of justice.
Appeals.
Jurisdiction, NC Const Art IV §12.
Appellate division, NC Const Art IV §5.
Court of appeals, NC Const Art IV §5.
Divisions, NC Const Art IV §2.
Judges and justices.
Retirement, NC Const Art IV §8.
Judicial power vested in general court of justice,
NC Const Art IV §1.
Jurisdiction.
Waiver, NC Const Art IV §12.

CONSTITUTION OF NORTH CAROLINA
—Cont'd
Courts —Cont'd
General court of justice —Cont'd
Retirement of justices and judges, NC Const Art IV §8.
Supreme court, NC Const Art IV §5.
Unified judicial system, NC Const Art IV §2.
Judges.
Removal by general assembly, NC Const Art IV §17.
Salaries, fees and emoluments, NC Const Art IV §21.
Open courts, NC Const Art I §18.
Superior courts.
Clerks, NC Const Art IV §9.
Removal, NC Const Art IV §17.
Districts, NC Const Art IV §9.
Judges.
Assignment, NC Const Art IV §11.
Election, NC Const Art IV §16.
Salaries, fees and emoluments, NC Const Art IV §21.
Terms of office, NC Const Art IV §16.
Vacancies in office, NC Const Art IV §19.
Jurisdiction, NC Const Art IV §12.
Open at all times, NC Const Art IV §9.
Sessions.
Trial of cases, NC Const Art IV §9.
Supreme court.
Chief justice.
Assignment of judges, NC Const Art IV §11.
Jurisdiction, NC Const Art IV §12.
Justices.
Election, NC Const Art IV §16.
Removal, NC Const Art IV §17.
Salaries, emoluments and fees, NC Const Art IV §21.
Terms of office, NC Const Art IV §16.
Vacancies in office, NC Const Art IV §19.
Membership, NC Const Art IV §6.
Procedural rules.
Authority to make, NC Const Art IV §13.
Sessions, NC Const Art IV §6.
Crime victim rights, NC Const Art I §37.
Criminal law and procedure.
Capital punishment.
Crimes punishable by death, NC Const Art XI §2.
District courts.
Prosecution in district court division, NC Const Art IV §18.
Ex post facto laws.
Prohibited, NC Const Art I §16.
Forms of actions, NC Const Art IV §13.
Jury trial.
Right to trial by jury, NC Const Art I §24.
Modes of prosecution, NC Const Art I §23.
Rights of accused, NC Const Art I §23.
Rules of procedure, NC Const Art IV §13.
Debts.
General assembly.
Actions on revenue bills, NC Const Art II §23.
Imprisonment for debt, NC Const Art I §28.
Personal property.
Exemptions from process, NC Const Art X §1.
Declaration of rights, NC Const Art I §§1 to 37.
Arms.
Right to bear arms, NC Const Art I §30.
Assembly.
Right of assembly, NC Const Art I §12.

CONSTITUTION OF NORTH CAROLINA
—Cont'd
Declaration of rights —Cont'd
Attorneys at law.
Right of accused to counsel, NC Const Art I §23.
Bail.
Excessive bail prohibited, NC Const Art I §27.
Branches of government.
Separation of powers, NC Const Art I §6.
Civil cases.
Jury trial, NC Const Art I §25.
Confrontation.
Right of accused to confrontation of witnesses against him, NC Const Art I §23.
Counsel.
Right of accused to counsel, NC Const Art I §23.
Courts.
Open courts, NC Const Art I §18.
Crime victims, NC Const Art I §37.
Criminal law and procedure.
Ex post facto laws.
Prohibited, NC Const Art I §16.
Jury trial, NC Const Art I §24.
Prosecution.
Modes of prosecution, NC Const Art I §23.
Rights of accused, NC Const Art I §23.
Cruel and unusual punishment.
Prohibited, NC Const Art I §27.
Debt.
Imprisonment for debt, NC Const Art I §28.
Discrimination.
Jury service, NC Const Art I §26.
Due process.
Law of the land, NC Const Art I §19.
Education.
State's duty to guard and maintain, NC Const Art I §15.
Elections.
Free elections, NC Const Art I §10.
Frequent elections required, NC Const Art I §9.
Property qualifications prohibited, NC Const Art I §11.
Emoluments.
Exclusive emoluments, NC Const Art I §32.
Hereditary emoluments, NC Const Art I §33.
Equality of persons, NC Const Art I §1.
Equal protection of the law, NC Const Art I §19.
Exclusive emoluments.
Prohibited, NC Const Art I §32.
Ex post facto laws.
Prohibited, NC Const Art I §16.
Fines.
Excessive fines prohibited, NC Const Art I §27.
Fraud.
Imprisonment for debt, NC Const Art I §28.
Fundamental principles.
Recurrence to fundamental principles, NC Const Art I §35.
General assembly.
Representation required, NC Const Art I §8.
Habeas corpus.
Inquiry into restraints on liberty, NC Const Art I §21.
Hereditary emoluments, NC Const Art I §33.
Honors.
Hereditary emoluments and honors prohibited, NC Const Art I §33.
Impeachment.
Modes of prosecution, NC Const Art I §22.
Incrimination.
Self-incrimination, NC Const Art I §23.

CONSTITUTION OF NORTH CAROLINA
   —Cont'd
Declaration of rights —Cont'd
Indictments.
   Modes of prosecution, NC Const Art I §22.
   Right of accused to be informed of accusation,
      NC Const Art I §23.
Information of accusation.
   Right of accused to be informed, NC Const Art I
      §23.
Inquiry into restraints on liberty, NC Const Art I
   §21.
Internal government of the state, NC Const Art I
   §3.
Involuntary servitude, NC Const Art I §17.
Jury.
   Civil cases.
      Right to jury trial in civil cases, NC Const Art
         I §25.
   Criminal cases.
      Right to jury trial in criminal cases, NC
         Const Art I §24.
   Discrimination in jury service prohibited, NC
      Const Art I §26.
Law of the land, NC Const Art I §19.
Military affairs.
   Militia, NC Const Art I §30.
   Quartering of soldiers, NC Const Art I §31.
Militia.
   Maintenance of militia, NC Const Art I §30.
Monopolies.
   Prohibited, NC Const Art I §34.
Other rights of the people.
   Enumeration does not impair or deny other
      rights retained by people, NC Const Art I
      §36.
Penalties.
   Excessive fines prohibited, NC Const Art I §27.
Perpetuities.
   Prohibited, NC Const Art I §34.
Petition.
   Right of petition, NC Const Art I §12.
Presentments.
   Modes of prosecution, NC Const Art I §22.
Press.
   Freedom of press, NC Const Art I §14.
Property qualifications.
   Political rights, privileges and offices not to be
      affected by property, NC Const Art I §11.
Prosecution.
   Modes of prosecution, NC Const Art I §22.
Public officers and employees.
   Property qualifications not to affect right to hold
      office, NC Const Art I §11.
Recurrence to fundamental principles, NC Const
   Art I §35.
Religious liberty, NC Const Art I §13.
Remedies.
   Inquiry into restraints on liberty, NC Const Art
      I §21.
Restraints of trade.
   Prohibited, NC Const Art I §34.
Retention of other rights by the people, NC Const
   Art I §36.
Retrospective laws.
   Prohibited, NC Const Art I §16.
Rights of accused, NC Const Art I §23.
Rights of persons, NC Const Art I §1.
Secession prohibited, NC Const Art I §4.
Self-incrimination, NC Const Art I §23.

CONSTITUTION OF NORTH CAROLINA
   —Cont'd
Declaration of rights —Cont'd
Sentence and punishment.
   Cruel and unusual punishment prohibited, NC
      Const Art I §27.
Separation of powers, NC Const Art I §6.
Servitude.
   Involuntary servitude.
      Prohibited, NC Const Art I §17.
Slavery, NC Const Art I §17.
Soldiers.
   Quartering of soldiers, NC Const Art I §31.
Sovereignty of the people, NC Const Art I §2.
Speech.
   Freedom of speech and press, NC Const Art I
      §14.
State of North Carolina.
   Secession prohibited, NC Const Art I §4.
   Separation of powers, NC Const Art I §6.
Suspending laws.
   Prohibited, NC Const Art I §7.
Taxation.
   Ex post facto laws.
      Prohibited, NC Const Art I §16.
   Representation required, NC Const Art I §8.
Treason.
   Conduct constituting, NC Const Art I §29.
Trial.
   Jury trial.
      Criminal cases, NC Const Art I §24.
United States.
   Allegiance to the United States, NC Const Art I
      §5.
   Secession prohibited, NC Const Art I §4.
Warrants.
   General warrants.
      Prohibited, NC Const Art I §20.
Witnesses.
   Confrontation.
      Rights of accused, NC Const Art I §23.
   Fees, costs, etc.
      Rights of accused, NC Const Art I §23.
Deeds.
Giving effect to informal deeds.
   Local, private and special legislation prohibited,
      NC Const Art II §24.
Definitions.
Corporations, NC Const Art VIII §2.
General laws, NC Const Art XIV §3.
Local government finance, NC Const Art V §4.
State debt, NC Const Art V §3.
Discrimination.
Jury service, NC Const Art I §26.
District attorneys.
Prosecutorial districts, NC Const Art IV §18.
District courts, NC Const Art IV §10.
Criminal cases.
   Prosecutions, NC Const Art IV §18.
Judges.
   Qualifications, NC Const Art IV §22.
   Salaries, fees and emoluments, NC Const Art IV
      §21.
   Vacancies in office, NC Const Art IV §19.
Jurisdiction, NC Const Art IV §12.
Districts.
General assembly.
   House of representatives, NC Const Art II §5.
   Senate districts, NC Const Art II §3.
Superior court districts, NC Const Art IV §9.

CONSTITUTION OF NORTH CAROLINA
—Cont'd

Divorce.
Local, private and special legislation prohibited, NC Const Art II §24.

Due process.
Law of the land, NC Const Art I §19.

Education.
Attendance.
School attendance, NC Const Art IX §3.
Encouragement of education, NC Const Art IX §1.
Escheats.
Disposition of escheats, NC Const Art IX §10.
Funds.
County school fund.
Composition, NC Const Art IX §7.
State fund.
Penalties, fines and forfeitures collected by state agencies (effective upon approval), NC Const Art IX §7.
State school fund.
Composition, NC Const Art IX §6.
Higher education.
Benefits of public institutions of higher education to be extended to people of state free of expense, NC Const Art IX §9.
Maintenance of public system of higher education, NC Const Art IX §8.
Public schools.
Local responsibility for public schools, NC Const Art IX §2.
Uniform system of schools to be established, NC Const Art IX §2.
State board of education.
Composition, NC Const Art IX §4.
Powers and duties, NC Const Art IX §5.
State school fund.
Composition of fund, NC Const Art IX §6.
State's duty to guard and maintain, NC Const Art I §15.
State superintendent of public instruction.
Acting superintendent, NC Const Art III §7.
Chief officer of state board of education, NC Const Art IX §4.
Compensation and allowances, NC Const Art III §9.
Council of state.
Membership, NC Const Art III §8.
Duties, NC Const Art III §7.
Elective officers, NC Const Art III §7.
Incapacity.
Determination, NC Const Art III §7.
Interim superintendent, NC Const Art III §7.
Vacancies.
Filling, NC Const Art III §7.
Students.
Escheats.
Disposition of escheats, NC Const Art IX §10.

Elections.
Ballots.
Elections by people to be by ballots, NC Const Art VI §5.
Capitation tax prohibited, NC Const Art V §1.
Continuation in office, NC Const Art VI §10.
Convention of the people.
Procedure for calling, NC Const Art XIII §1.
Counties.
Sheriffs, NC Const Art VII §2.
Court of appeals.
Judges, NC Const Art IV §16.
Disqualifications for office, NC Const Art VI §8.

CONSTITUTION OF NORTH CAROLINA
—Cont'd

Elections —Cont'd
Dual office holding, NC Const Art VI §9.
Elected officers, NC Const Art III §7.
Eligibility to elective office, NC Const Art VI §6.
Eligibility to vote, NC Const Art VI §1.
Executive branch.
Joint ballot in both houses of general assembly to decide, NC Const Art VI §5.
Felonies.
Disqualification of felon, NC Const Art VI §2.
Free elections, NC Const Art I §10.
Frequent elections required, NC Const Art I §9.
General assembly, NC Const Art II §8.
Elections by general assembly to be by viva voce, NC Const Art VI §5.
Governor, NC Const Art III §2.
Lieutenant governor, NC Const Art III §2.
Literacy requirements, NC Const Art VI §4.
Poll tax prohibited, NC Const Art V §1.
Property qualifications prohibited, NC Const Art I §11.
Qualifications of voter, NC Const Art VI §2.
Registration, NC Const Art VI §3.
Literacy requirements, NC Const Art VI §4.
Qualifications for registration, NC Const Art VI §4.
Residence.
Presidential elections, NC Const Art VI §2.
State elections, NC Const Art VI §2.
Sheriffs.
County sheriffs, NC Const Art VII §2.
Superior court.
Judges, NC Const Art IV §16.
Supreme court.
Justices, NC Const Art IV §16.
Voters.
Qualifications, NC Const Art VI §2.

Electricity.
Municipalities.
Joint ownership of generation and transmission facilities, NC Const Art V §10.

Emoluments.
Declaration of rights.
Hereditary emoluments, NC Const Art I §33.
Prohibited, NC Const Art I §33.

Equality of persons, NC Const Art I §1.

Equal protection, NC Const Art I §19.

Escheats.
Disposition of escheats, NC Const Art IX §10.

Executions.
Homestead exemption, NC Const Art X §2.
Personal property.
Exemption from process, NC Const Art X §1.
Exemptions from execution, NC Const Art X §1.

Executive branch, NC Const Art III §§1 to 11.
Elections.
Joint ballot in both houses of general assembly to decide, NC Const Art VI §5.

Exemptions.
Homestead exemption, NC Const Art X §2.
Married women.
Property of married women secured to them, NC Const Art X §4.
Personal property.
Exemption of property from execution or other process, NC Const Art X §1.

Ex post facto laws.
Prohibited, NC Const Art I §16.

CONSTITUTION OF NORTH CAROLINA
　—Cont'd
Fees.
　Judicial officers, NC Const Art IV §21.
　Revenues and expenses of the judicial
　　department, NC Const Art IV §20.
Felonies.
　Disqualifications from holding office, NC Const
　　Art VI §8.
　Elections.
　　Disqualification of felon, NC Const Art VI §2.
　Local, private and special legislation prohibited,
　　NC Const Art II §24.
Ferries.
　Local, private and special legislation prohibited,
　　NC Const Art II §24.
Finances, NC Const Art V §§1 to 14.
Fines.
　Enumeration of permissible punishments, NC
　　Const Art XI §1.
Forfeitures.
　Local, private and special legislation prohibited,
　　NC Const Art II §24.
Forms.
　Actions, NC Const Art IV §13.
Fraud.
　Imprisonment for debt, NC Const Art I §28.
Funds.
　Retirement fund.
　　Inviolability, NC Const Art V §6.
　Sinking funds.
　　Inviolability, NC Const Art V §6.
General assembly.
　Acts.
　　Style of the acts, NC Const Art II §21.
　Bills.
　　Action on bills, NC Const Art II §22.
　　Revenue bills.
　　　Requirements for passage, NC Const Art II
　　　　§23.
　　Veto by governor, NC Const Art II §22.
　Bond issues.
　　Requirements for passage, NC Const Art II §23.
　Bridges.
　　Local, private and special legislation prohibited,
　　　NC Const Art II §24.
　Cemeteries.
　　Local, private and special legislation prohibited,
　　　NC Const Art II §24.
　Cities, towns and townships.
　　Changing names not subject to local, private
　　　and special legislation, NC Const Art II §24.
　Compensation and allowances, NC Const Art II
　　§16.
　Contested elections for executive office.
　　Joint ballot of both houses to determine, NC
　　　Const Art VI §5.
　Convention of the people.
　　Procedure for calling, NC Const Art XIII §1.
　Courts.
　　Administration, NC Const Art IV §15.
　Divorce or alimony.
　　Local, private and special legislation prohibited,
　　　NC Const Art II §24.
　Elections, NC Const Art II §8.
　　Viva voce.
　　　Elections by general assembly to be by viva
　　　　voce, NC Const Art VI §5.
　Felonies.
　　Restoring citizenship rights of convicts.
　　　Local, private and special legislation
　　　　prohibited, NC Const Art II §24.

CONSTITUTION OF NORTH CAROLINA
　—Cont'd
General assembly —Cont'd
　Ferries.
　　Local, private and special legislation prohibited,
　　　NC Const Art II §24.
　Giving effect to informal deeds.
　　Local, private and special legislation prohibited,
　　　NC Const Art II §24.
　Governor.
　　Information to general assembly, NC Const Art
　　　III §5.
　　Reconvening of legislature, NC Const Art II §22,
　　　Art III §5.
　　　Request that session not be held, §120-6.1(a),
　　　　(b).
　　Sessions.
　　　Extra sessions, NC Const Art III §5.
　　Veto by governor, NC Const Art II §22.
　Health, sanitation and abatement of nuisances.
　　Local, private and special limitation prohibited,
　　　NC Const Art II §24.
　Highways, streets or alleys.
　　Local, private and special legislation prohibited,
　　　NC Const Art II §24.
　House of representatives.
　　Apportionment of representatives, NC Const Art
　　　II §5.
　　Districts, NC Const Art II §5.
　　Impeachments.
　　　Power to impeach, NC Const Art IV §4.
　　Number of representatives, NC Const Art II §4.
　　Officers of the house, NC Const Art II §15.
　　Qualifications for representatives, NC Const Art
　　　II §7.
　　Speaker, NC Const Art II §15.
　　Term of office, NC Const Art II §9.
　Indebtedness of state.
　　Requirements for passage of bills, NC Const Art
　　　II §23.
　Journals.
　　Printing of journals, NC Const Art II §17.
　　Record of votes, NC Const Art II §19.
　Judges.
　　Removal, NC Const Art IV §17.
　Jury.
　　Pay of jurors.
　　　Local, private and special legislation
　　　　prohibited, NC Const Art II §24.
　Labor.
　　Local, private and special legislation prohibited,
　　　NC Const Art II §24.
　Legislative power vested in general assembly, NC
　　Const Art II §1.
　Legitimating persons born out of wedlock.
　　Local, private and special legislation prohibited,
　　　NC Const Art II §24.
　Lieutenant governor.
　　President of the senate, NC Const Art II §13.
　Local government.
　　Provision for local government, NC Const Art
　　　VII §1.
　Local, private and special legislation.
　　Limitations, NC Const Art II §24.
　　Prohibited subjects, NC Const Art II §24.
　　Repeals.
　　　Partial repeal of general law prohibited, NC
　　　　Const Art II §24.
　　Voidness of prohibited acts, NC Const Art II
　　　§24.

CONSTITUTION OF NORTH CAROLINA
—Cont'd
General assembly —Cont'd
Magistrates.
Removal, NC Const Art IV §17.
Manufacturing.
Local, private and special legislation prohibited,
NC Const Art II §24.
Mines and minerals.
Local, private and special legislation prohibited,
NC Const Art II §24.
Municipalities.
Local, private and special legislation prohibited,
NC Const Art II §24.
Names.
Altering name of person.
Local, private and special legislation
prohibited, NC Const Art II §24.
Oaths of members, NC Const Art II §12.
Penalties.
Local, private and special legislation prohibited,
NC Const Art II §24.
Powers of general assembly, NC Const Art II §20.
President pro tempore.
Temporary succession, NC Const Art II §14.
Protests of members, NC Const Art II §18.
Quorum, NC Const Art II §11.
Reconvening of legislature, NC Const Art II §22,
Art III §5.
Request that session not be held, §120-6.1(a),
(b).
Resolutions.
Actions on resolutions, NC Const Art II §22.
School districts.
Local, private and special legislation prohibited,
NC Const Art II §24.
Senate.
Apportionment of senators, NC Const Art II §3.
Districts, NC Const Art II §3.
Impeachments.
Court for the trial of impeachments, NC
Const Art IV §4.
Number of senators, NC Const Art II §2.
Officers of the senate, NC Const Art II §14.
President of the senate.
Lieutenant governor to preside over senate,
NC Const Art II §13.
President pro tempore.
Succession to presidency, NC Const Art II
§14.
Qualifications for senator, NC Const Art II §6.
Term of office, NC Const Art II §9.
Sessions.
Extra sessions on legislative call, NC Const Art
II §11.
Regular sessions, NC Const Art II §11.
Taxation.
Classification of property, NC Const Art V §2.
Local, private and special legislation prohibited,
NC Const Art II §24.
Representation required, NC Const Art I §8.
Requirements for passage, NC Const Art II §23.
Term of office, NC Const Art II §9.
Townships.
Local, private and special legislation prohibited,
NC Const Art II §24.
Trade.
Local, private and special legislation prohibited,
NC Const Art II §24.
Vacancies, NC Const Art II §10.
Veto by governor, NC Const Art II §22.

CONSTITUTION OF NORTH CAROLINA
—Cont'd
General assembly —Cont'd
Votes.
Record votes.
Keeping in journals, NC Const Art II §19.
Waters and watercourses.
Nonnavigable streams.
Local, private and special legislation
prohibited, NC Const Art II §24.
Wills.
Giving effect to informal wills.
Local, private and special legislation
prohibited, NC Const Art II §24.
General laws.
Definition, NC Const Art XIV §3.
Governor.
Appointments, NC Const Art III §5.
Budget.
Duties of governor, NC Const Art III §5.
Clemency.
Granting reprieves, commutation and pardons,
NC Const Art III §5.
Commander-in-chief of military forces, NC Const
Art III §5, Art XII §1.
Commutation, NC Const Art III §5.
Duties, NC Const Art III §5.
Election, NC Const Art III §2.
Execution of laws, NC Const Art III §5.
Executive power of state vested in governor, NC
Const Art III §1.
General assembly.
Information to general assembly, NC Const Art
III §5.
Sessions.
Extra sessions, NC Const Art III §5.
Impeachment, NC Const Art III §3.
Mental incapacity.
Succession to office of governor, NC Const Art
III §3.
Military affairs.
Commander-in-chief, NC Const Art III §5, Art
XII §1.
Oaths, NC Const Art III §4.
Pardons, NC Const Art III §5.
Physical incapacity.
Succession to office of governor, NC Const Art
III §3.
Qualifications, NC Const Art III §2.
Reprieves, NC Const Art III §5.
Residence, NC Const Art III §5.
State departments and agencies.
Information from department heads.
Governor may require, NC Const Art III §5.
Reorganization of administration, NC Const Art
III §5.
Succession as acting governor, NC Const Art III
§3.
Succession as governor, NC Const Art III §3.
Term, NC Const Art III §2.
Habeas corpus.
Inquiry into restraints on liberty, NC Const Art I
§21.
Remedy without delay for restraint of liberty,
§17-1.
Suspension of habeas corpus, §17-2.
Health.
Local, private and special legislation prohibited,
NC Const Art II §24.
Health care facilities.
Bond issues to finance, NC Const Art V §8.

CONSTITUTION OF NORTH CAROLINA
—Cont'd

Highways.
Local, private and special legislation prohibited, NC Const Art II §24.

Homestead exemption, NC Const Art X §2.

Hospitals.
Bond issues to finance, NC Const Art V §8.

House of representatives.
Apportionment of representatives, NC Const Art II §5.
Districts, NC Const Art II §5.
Elections, NC Const Art II §8.
Impeachment.
Power to impeach, NC Const Art IV §4.
Number of representatives, NC Const Art II §4.
Officers of the house, NC Const Art II §15.
Qualifications for representative, NC Const Art II §7.
Speaker, NC Const Art II §15.
Term of office, NC Const Art II §9.

Husband and wife.
Women.
Property of married women secured to them, NC Const Art X §4.

Impeachment.
Court for the trial of impeachment.
Senate to be court, NC Const Art IV §4.
Vesting of judicial power, NC Const Art IV §1.
Governor, NC Const Art III §3.
House of representatives.
Power to impeach, NC Const Art IV §4.
Modes of prosecution, NC Const Art I §22.

Imprisonment.
Enumeration of permissible punishments, NC Const Art XI §1.

Income tax.
Limitations and restrictions, NC Const Art V §2.

Incrimination.
Self-incrimination.
Rights of accused, NC Const Art I §23.

Indictments.
Modes of prosecution, NC Const Art I §22.
Right of accused to be informed of accusation, NC Const Art I §23.

Indigent persons.
Welfare policy of state, NC Const Art XI §4.

Industry.
Capital projects for industry.
Bond issues to finance.
County may create authorities to issue bonds, NC Const Art V §9.

Insurance.
Commissioner of insurance.
Acting commissioner, NC Const Art III §7.
Compensation and allowances, NC Const Art III §9.
Council of state.
Membership, NC Const Art III §8.
Duties, NC Const Art III §7.
Elective officers, NC Const Art III §7.
Incapacity.
Determination, NC Const Art III §7.
Interim commissioner, NC Const Art III §7.
Vacancies.
Filling, NC Const Art III §7.

Involuntary servitude.
Prohibited, NC Const Art I §17.

Judges.
Assignment, NC Const Art IV §11.

CONSTITUTION OF NORTH CAROLINA
—Cont'd

Judges —Cont'd
Qualifications of judges and justices, NC Const Art IV §22.
Removal, NC Const Art IV §17.
Additional method, NC Const Art IV §17.
Retirement, NC Const Art IV §8.
Salaries.
Diminished during continuance in office prohibited, NC Const Art IV §21.
Terms of office, NC Const Art IV §16.
Vacancies in office, NC Const Art IV §19.

Judicial department, NC Const Art IV §§1 to 22.
Fees.
Revenues and expenses of the judicial department, NC Const Art IV §20.

Jurisdiction.
Courts, NC Const Art IV §12.
Waiver, NC Const Art IV §12.

Jury.
Civil cases.
Right to trial in civil cases, NC Const Art I §25, Art IV §13.
Waiver of jury trial, NC Const Art IV §14.
Criminal cases.
Right to jury trial in criminal cases, NC Const Art I §24.
Discrimination in jury service prohibited, NC Const Art I §26.
Pay of jurors.
Local, private and special legislation prohibited, NC Const Art II §24.

Labor.
Commissioner of labor.
Acting commissioner, NC Const Art III §7.
Compensation and allowances, NC Const Art III §9.
Council of state.
Membership, NC Const Art III §8.
Duties, NC Const Art III §7.
Elective officers, NC Const Art III §7.
Incapacity.
Determination, NC Const Art III §7.
Interim commissioner, NC Const Art III §7.
Vacancies.
Filling, NC Const Art III §7.
Local, private and special legislation prohibited, NC Const Art II §24.

Laborers' liens.
Exemptions from process.
Inapplicability of provisions, NC Const Art X §3.

Laws.
Continuity of laws, NC Const Art XIV §4.
General laws.
Defined, NC Const Art XIV §3.

Legitimation.
Local, private and special legislation prohibited, NC Const Art II §24.

Liens.
Mechanics' and materialmen's liens.
Inapplicability of exemption provisions, NC Const Art X §3.

Lieutenant governor.
Duties, NC Const Art III §6.
Election, NC Const Art III §2.
General assembly.
Senate.
President of the senate, NC Const Art II §13.
Qualifications, NC Const Art III §2.

CONSTITUTION OF NORTH CAROLINA
—Cont'd
Lieutenant governor —Cont'd
Succession as acting governor, NC Const Art III §3.
Succession as governor, NC Const Art III §3.
Term, NC Const Art III §2.
Life insurance.
Exemption from process, NC Const Art X §5.
Local government finance.
Authorized purposes, NC Const Art V §4.
Certain debts barred, NC Const Art V §4.
Definitions, NC Const Art V §4.
Gifts or loans of credit regulated, NC Const Art V §4.
Limitations upon increase of local government debt, NC Const Art V §4.
Outstanding debt, NC Const Art V §4.
Regulation of borrowing in debt, NC Const Art V §4.
Two-thirds limitation, NC Const Art V §4.
Local legislation.
Limitation, NC Const Art II §24.
Magistrates.
Appointment, NC Const Art IV §10.
Jurisdiction, NC Const Art IV §12.
Removal, NC Const Art IV §17.
General assembly to remove, NC Const Art IV §17.
Salaries, fees and emoluments, NC Const Art IV §21.
Vacancies in office, NC Const Art IV §19.
Manufacturing.
Local, private and special legislation prohibited, NC Const Art II §24.
Marriage.
Marriage between one man and one woman only domestic legal union, NC Const Art XIV §6 (effective upon certification).
Property of married women secured to them, NC Const Art X §4.
Merger.
Counties.
Consolidated or merged counties, NC Const Art VII §3.
Military affairs.
Governor.
Commander-in-chief, NC Const Art III §5, Art XII §1.
Militia, NC Const Art I §30.
Quartering of soldiers, NC Const Art I §31.
Mines and minerals.
Local, private and special legislation prohibited, NC Const Art II §24.
Money.
Drawing public money, NC Const Art V §7.
Monopolies.
Prohibited, NC Const Art I §34.
Municipalities.
Contracts.
Authority to contract, NC Const Art V §2.
General assembly to provide for local government, NC Const Art VII §1.
Local, private and special legislation prohibited, NC Const Art II §24.
Local treasury.
Drawing public money, NC Const Art V §7.
Public utilities.
Joint ownership of generation and transmission facilities, NC Const Art V §10.

CONSTITUTION OF NORTH CAROLINA
—Cont'd
Municipalities —Cont'd
Taxation.
Exemption from taxation, NC Const Art V §2.
Special tax areas, NC Const Art V §2.
Murder.
Capital punishment.
Crimes punishable by death, NC Const Art XI §2.
Names.
Altering name of person.
Local, private and special legislation prohibited, NC Const Art II §24.
Natural resources and community development.
Policy of state, NC Const Art XIV §5.
Newspapers.
Freedom of speech and press, NC Const Art I §14.
Nuisances.
Abatement of nuisances.
Local, private and special legislation prohibited, NC Const Art II §24.
Oaths.
General assembly, §11-7, NC Const Art II §12.
Governor, NC Const Art III §4.
Officers of state to take oath or affirmation supporting constitutions, §11-7.
Public officers and employees, NC Const Art VI §7.
Oil and gas conservation.
Policy of state, NC Const Art XIV §5.
Ordinances.
Consistent with constitution of North Carolina, §160A-174(b).
Orphans.
Welfare policy of state, NC Const Art XI §4.
Pardons.
Governor.
Duties of governor, NC Const Art III §5.
Penalties.
Excessive fines prohibited, NC Const Art I §27.
Local, private and special legislation prohibited, NC Const Art II §24.
Perpetuities.
Prohibited, NC Const Art I §34.
Personal property.
Exemptions from process, NC Const Art X §1.
Petitions.
Right to petition, NC Const Art I §12.
Plant protection and conservation.
Policy of state, NC Const Art XIV §5.
Poll tax.
Prohibited, NC Const Art V §1.
Pollution control.
Policy of state, NC Const Art XIV §5.
Ports and harbors.
Powers of general assembly as to seaport and airport facilities, NC Const Art V §13.
Power of people to amend, NC Const Art XIII §2.
Presentments.
Modes of prosecution, NC Const Art I §22.
Press.
Freedom of press, NC Const Art I §14.
Private legislation.
Limitations, NC Const Art II §24.
Project development financing, NC Const Art V §14.
Property qualifications.
Political rights, privileges and offices not to be affected by property, NC Const Art I §11.

CONSTITUTION OF NORTH CAROLINA
—Cont'd
Public officers and employees.
Continuation in office, NC Const Art VI §10.
Disqualifications for office, NC Const Art VI §8.
Dual office holding, NC Const Art VI §9.
Eligibility to hold elective office, NC Const Art VI §6.
Holding office contrary to the constitution, §128-2.
Oaths, NC Const Art VI §7.
Property qualifications not to affect right to hold office, NC Const Art I §11.
Protection of persons holding office at time of adoption of constitution, NC Const Art XIV §4.
Removal from office.
Enumeration of permissible punishments, NC Const Art XI §1.
Public schools.
Basic education program.
Knowledge and understanding required, §115C-81(g).
Public utilities.
Municipalities.
Joint ownership of generation and transmission facilities, NC Const Art V §10.
Punishment.
Cruel and unusual punishment prohibited, NC Const Art I §27.
Enumeration of permissible punishments, NC Const Art XI §1.
Quartering of soldiers, NC Const Art I §31.
Raleigh.
Seat of government to be at city of Raleigh, NC Const Art XIV §1.
Rape.
Capital punishment.
Crimes punishable by death, NC Const Art XI §2.
Reconvening of legislature, NC Const Art II §22, Art III §5.
Religion.
Liberty of religion, NC Const Art I §13.
Remedies.
Inquiry into restraints on liberty, NC Const Art I §21.
Restraints of trade.
Monopolies, NC Const Art I §34.
Retirement.
Funds.
Inviolability, NC Const Art V §6.
Judges and justices, NC Const Art IV §8.
Retrospective laws.
Prohibited, NC Const Art I §16.
Rights of crime victims, NC Const Art I §37.
Rights of persons, NC Const Art I §1.
Salaries.
General assembly, NC Const Art II §16.
Judicial officers, NC Const Art IV §21.
Sanitation.
Local, private and special legislation prohibited, NC Const Art II §24.
School districts.
Local, private and special legislation prohibited, NC Const Art II §24.
Seals.
State seal, NC Const Art III §10.
Seat of government, NC Const Art XIV §1.
Secretary of state.
Acting secretary, NC Const Art III §7.

CONSTITUTION OF NORTH CAROLINA
—Cont'd
Secretary of state —Cont'd
Compensation and allowances, NC Const Art III §9.
Council of state.
Membership, NC Const Art III §8.
Duties, NC Const Art III §7.
Elective officers, NC Const Art III §7.
Incapacity.
Determination, NC Const Art III §7.
Interim secretary, NC Const Art III §7.
Vacancies.
Filling, NC Const Art III §7.
Self-incrimination.
Rights of accused, NC Const Art I §23.
Senate.
Apportionment of senators, NC Const Art II §3.
Districts, NC Const Art II §3.
Elections, NC Const Art II §8.
Impeachment.
Court for the trial of impeachments, NC Const Art IV §4.
Lieutenant governor.
President of the senate, NC Const Art II §13.
Number of senators, NC Const Art II §2.
President of the senate.
Lieutenant governor to preside, NC Const Art II §13.
President pro tempore.
Succession to presidency, NC Const Art II §14.
Temporary succession, NC Const Art II §14.
Qualifications for senator, NC Const Art II §6.
Term of office, NC Const Art II §9.
Sentencing.
Cruel and unusual punishment prohibited, NC Const Art I §27.
Enumeration of permissible punishments, NC Const Art XI §1.
Sessions.
Extra sessions.
Governor may call, NC Const Art III §5.
Reconvening of legislature, NC Const Art II §22, Art III §5.
Sheriffs.
Election, NC Const Art VII §2.
Sinking funds.
Inviolability, NC Const Art V §6.
Slavery.
Prohibited, NC Const Art I §17.
Soldiers.
Declaration of rights.
Quartering of soldiers, NC Const Art I §31.
Sovereignty of the people, NC Const Art I §2.
Special legislation.
Limitations, NC Const Art II §24.
Speech.
Freedom of speech, NC Const Art I §14.
State auditor.
Acting auditor, NC Const Art III §7.
Compensation and allowances, NC Const Art III §9.
Council of state.
Membership, NC Const Art III §8.
Duties, NC Const Art III §7.
Elective officers, NC Const Art III §7.
Incapacity.
Determination, NC Const Art III §7.
Interim auditor, NC Const Art III §7.
Vacancies.
Filling, NC Const Art III §7.

CONSTITUTION OF NORTH CAROLINA
—Cont'd
State debt.
Authorized purposes, NC Const Art V §3.
Certain debts barred, NC Const Art V §3.
Definitions, NC Const Art V §3.
Gifts regulated, NC Const Art V §3.
Increase.
Limitations, NC Const Art V §3.
Limitations upon increase, NC Const Art V §3.
Loans regulated, NC Const Art V §3.
Standing debt, NC Const Art V §3.
Two-thirds limitation, NC Const Art V §3.
State departments and agencies.
Administrative departments.
Allocation, NC Const Art III §11.
Executive organization act of 1973.
References to constitution of North Carolina,
§143B-26.
Judicial powers of administrative agencies, NC
Const Art IV §3.
State of North Carolina.
Boundaries of state, NC Const Art XIV §2.
Contracts.
Authority to contract, NC Const Art V §2.
Declaration of rights.
Internal government of the state, NC Const Art
I §3.
Secession prohibited, NC Const Art I §4.
Drawing public money, NC Const Art V §7.
Seal of state, NC Const Art III §10.
Seat of government, NC Const Art XIV §1.
Separation of powers, NC Const Art I §6.
Taxation.
Exemption from taxation, NC Const Art V §2.
State treasurer.
Acting treasurer, NC Const Art III §7.
Compensation and allowances, NC Const Art III
§9.
Council of state.
Membership, NC Const Art III §8.
Drawing public money, NC Const Art V §7.
Duties, NC Const Art III §7.
Elective officers, NC Const Art III §7.
Incapacity.
Determination, NC Const Art III §7.
Interim treasurer, NC Const Art III §7.
Vacancies.
Filling, NC Const Art III §7.
Streets.
Local, private and special legislation prohibited,
NC Const Art II §24.
Suffrage.
Eligibility to vote, NC Const Art VI §1.
Felonies.
Disqualification of felon, NC Const Art VI §2.
Qualifications of voter, NC Const Art VI §2.
Residence.
Presidential elections, NC Const Art VI §2.
State elections, NC Const Art VI §2.
Superior courts.
Clerks of court, NC Const Art IV §9.
Removal of clerks, NC Const Art IV §17.
Salaries, fees and emoluments, NC Const Art IV
§21.
Vacancies in office, NC Const Art IV §19.
Districts, NC Const Art IV §9.
Judges.
Assignment, NC Const Art IV §11.
Election, NC Const Art IV §16.
Qualifications, NC Const Art IV §22.

CONSTITUTION OF NORTH CAROLINA
—Cont'd
Superior courts —Cont'd
Judges —Cont'd
Salaries, fees and emoluments, NC Const Art IV
§21.
Terms of office, NC Const Art IV §16.
Vacancies in office, NC Const Art IV §19.
Jurisdiction, NC Const Art IV §12.
Open at all times, NC Const Art IV §9.
Sessions.
Trial of cases, NC Const Art IV §9.
Supreme court.
Chief justice.
Assignment of judges, NC Const Art IV §11.
Court of appeals decisions.
Appeals of right from certain decisions, §7A-30.
Jurisdiction, NC Const Art IV §12.
Justices.
Election, NC Const Art IV §16.
Qualifications, NC Const Art IV §22.
Removal, NC Const Art IV §17.
Salaries, fees and emoluments, NC Const Art IV
§21.
Terms of office, NC Const Art IV §16.
Vacancies in office, NC Const Art IV §19.
Membership, NC Const Art IV §6.
Procedural rules.
Authority to make, NC Const Art IV §13.
Sessions, NC Const Art IV §6.
Suspending laws.
Prohibited, NC Const Art I §7.
Taxation.
Capitation tax prohibited, NC Const Art V §1.
Cemeteries.
Exemption from tax, NC Const Art V §2.
Charities.
Exemption from tax, NC Const Art V §2.
Classification of property, NC Const Art V §2.
Constitutional challenge of tax statute,
§105-241.17.
Exclusivity of remedy, §105-241.19.
Counties.
Exemption from taxation, NC Const Art V §2.
Special tax areas, NC Const Art V §2.
Education.
Exemption from taxation, NC Const Art V §2.
Exemptions, NC Const Art V §3.
Ex post facto laws.
Prohibited, NC Const Art I §16.
Local, private and special legislation prohibited,
NC Const Art II §24.
Municipalities.
Exemption from taxation, NC Const Art V §2.
Special tax areas, NC Const Art V §2.
Poll tax prohibited, NC Const Art V §1.
Power of taxation, NC Const Art V §2.
Property taxes.
Purposes, NC Const Art V §2.
Religion.
Exemption from tax, NC Const Art V §2.
Representation required, NC Const Art I §8.
Special tax areas, NC Const Art V §2.
Statement.
Objects, NC Const Art V §5.
Purposes to be stated, NC Const Art V §5.
State of North Carolina.
Exemption from taxation, NC Const Art V §2.
Supremacy, §105-1.1.
Towns.
General assembly to provide for local government,
NC Const Art VII §1.

CONSTITUTION OF NORTH CAROLINA
—Cont'd

Townships.
Local, private and special legislation prohibited, NC Const Art II §24.

Trade.
Local, private and special legislation prohibited, NC Const Art II §24.

Treason.
Conduct constituting, NC Const Art I §29.
Disqualifications from holding office, NC Const Art VI §8.

Trial.
Jury trial.
Civil cases, NC Const Art I §25.
Criminal cases, NC Const Art I §24.

United States.
Allegiance to the United States, NC Const Art I §5.
Declaration of rights.
Secession from Union prohibited, NC Const Art I §4.

Universities and colleges.
Benefits of public institutions of higher education to be extended to people of state free of expense, NC Const Art IX §9.
Bond issues.
Higher education facilities.
Authorized, NC Const Art V §12.
Maintenance of public system of higher education, NC Const Art IX §8.

University of North Carolina.
Benefits of public institutions of higher education to be extended to people of state free of charge, NC Const Art IX §9.
Escheats.
Disposition of escheats prior to July 1, 1971, NC Const Art IX §10.
Maintenance of system of higher education, NC Const Art IX §8.

University of North Carolina School of the Arts.
Benefits of public institutions of higher education to be extended to people of state free of charge, NC Const Art IX §9.
Maintenance of system of higher education, NC Const Art IX §8.

Warrants.
General warrants.
Prohibited, NC Const Art I §20.

Waters and watercourses.
Nonnavigable streams.
Local, private and special legislation prohibited, NC Const Art II §24.

Weapons.
Right to bear arms, NC Const Art I §30.

Welfare.
Board of public welfare.
Establishment required, NC Const Art XI §4.
Policy of state, NC Const Art XI §4.

Wills.
Giving effect to informal wills.
Local, private and special legislation prohibited, NC Const Art II §24.

Witnesses.
Confrontation.
Right of accused, NC Const Art I §23.
Fees, costs, etc.
Rights of accused, NC Const Art I §23.

Women.
Married women.
Property secured to them, NC Const Art X §4.

CONSTITUTION OF THE UNITED STATES.

Absence.
Congress.
Members of congress, US Const Art I §5.
Vice-president.
Senate to choose president pro tem, US Const Art I §3.

Accounts and accounting.
Receipts and expenditures of public money.
Publication of statement and account, US Const Art I §9.

Actions to which United States a party, US Const Art III §2.

Admiralty, US Const Art I §8.
Jurisdiction of courts, US Const Art III §2.

Age.
Congress.
Representatives, US Const Art I §2.
Senators, US Const Art I §3.
Elections.
Right to vote not to be abridged on account of age, US Const Amd 26.
Voting by persons eighteen years of age, US Const Amd 26.
President of the United States, US Const Art II §1.
Vice-president, US Const Amd 12.

Alcoholic liquors, US Const Amds 18, 21.

Aliens.
Eligibility to be representative, US Const Art I §2.
Naturalization, US Const Art I §8.
Presidency.
Ineligibility for presidency, US Const Art II §1.
Suits against state, US Const Amd 11.

Ambassadors and consuls, US Const Art II §§2, 3, Art III §2.

Amendments, US Const Art V.
Bail, US Const Amd 8.
Congress.
Compensation of members.
Laws varying compensation.
When to take effect, US Const Amd 27.
Sessions, US Const Amd 20 §2.
Terms of office, US Const Amd 20 §1.
Time of convening, US Const Amd 20 §2.
Criminal law, US Const Amds 5, 6.
Due process of law, US Const Amds 5, 14.
Effect of enumeration of rights, US Const Amd 9.
Eminent domain, US Const Amd 5.
Freedom of religion, speech and press, US Const Amd 1.
Guarantees in criminal cases, US Const Amds 5, 6.
House of representatives.
Terms of representatives, US Const Amd 20 §1.
Income tax, US Const Amd 16.
Intoxicating liquors, US Const Amds 18, 21.
Lame duck amendment, US Const Amd 20.
Manner of making amendments, US Const Art V.
Poll tax.
Denial or abridgement of right to vote upon failure to pay.
Prohibited, US Const Amd 24.
President.
Death, US Const Amd 20.
Election, US Const Amds 12, 20.
Failure to qualify, US Const Amd 20.
Succession upon death, resignation or removal of president, US Const Amd 25.
Terms of office, US Const Amds 20, 22.
Limitation on terms, US Const Amd 22.

CONSTITUTION OF THE UNITED STATES
—Cont'd

Amendments —Cont'd

Proposal and ratification of amendments, US Const Art V.

Punishments, US Const Amd 8.

Quartering soldiers in houses, US Const Amd 3.

Ratification of amendment, US Const Art V.

Repeal of the eighteenth amendment, US Const Amd 21.

Restriction of judicial power, US Const Amd 11.

Rights and immunities of citizens, US Const Amd 14.

Right to bear arms, US Const Amd 2.

Right to vote, US Const Amds 15, 26.

Searches and seizures, US Const Amd 4.

Self-incrimination, US Const Amd 5.

Senate.

   Election of senators, US Const Amd 17.

   Terms of senators, US Const Amd 20 §1.

Slavery, US Const Amd 13.

Suits against state, US Const Amd 11.

Terms of office, US Const Amd 20 §1.

   Limitation on terms of president, US Const Amd 22.

Trial by jury, US Const Amds 6, 7.

Vice-president.

   Death, US Const Amd 20.

   Election, US Const Amds 12, 20.

   Failure to qualify, US Const Amd 20.

   Terms of office, US Const Amd 20 §1.

Weapons.

   Right to bear arms, US Const Amd 2.

Women's suffrage, US Const Amd 19.

Appeals.

Decisions of the court of appeals.

   Right of appeals from certain decisions directly to supreme court, §7A-30.

Review of facts tried by jury, US Const Amd 7.

Apportionment.

Congress, US Const Amds 14, 17.

Appropriations, US Const Art I §9.

Army, US Const Art I §8.

Revenue bills, US Const Art I §7.

Approval of laws by president, US Const Art I §7.

Arms.

Right to bear, US Const Amd 2.

Army and navy, US Const Art I §8.

Commander-in-chief, US Const Art II §2.

Arrest.

Privilege from arrest, US Const Art I §6.

Assembly.

Right of, US Const Amd 1.

Attainder, US Const Art III §3.

Attorneys at law.

Right to counsel, US Const Amd 6.

Authors.

Protection of rights, US Const Art I §8.

Autrefois, acquit or convict, US Const Amd 5.

Bail.

Excessive bail, US Const Amd 8.

Bankruptcy.

Powers of congress, US Const Art I §8.

Bill of attainder, US Const Art I §§9, 10.

Bill of rights, US Const Amds 1 to 10.

Bills of credit, US Const Art I §10.

Black people, US Const Amds 14, 15.

Bribery, US Const Art II §4.

Capitation tax, US Const Art I §9.

Elections.

   Denial or abridgement of right to vote prohibited, US Const Amd 24.

CONSTITUTION OF THE UNITED STATES
—Cont'd

Census, US Const Art I §§2, 9.

Commerce, US Const Art I §§8, 9.

Common law.

Suits at, US Const Amd 7.

Compacts.

Between state and foreign power, US Const Art I §10.

Between the states, US Const Art I §10.

Congress.

Absent members, US Const Art I §5.

Adjournment, US Const Art I §§5, 7, Art II §3.

Admiralty, US Const Art I §8.

Amendments to the constitution, US Const Art V.

Appropriations, US Const Art I §9.

Approval by president of order, resolution or vote, US Const Art I §7.

Army and navy.

   Powers of congress, US Const Art I §8.

Arrest, US Const Art I §6.

Bankruptcy.

   Powers of congress, US Const Art I §8.

Borrowing money, US Const Art I §8.

Commerce, US Const Art I §§8, 9.

Compensation of members, US Const Art I §6.

   Laws varying compensation.

      When to take effect, US Const Amd 27.

Consists of senate and house of representatives, US Const Art I §1.

Copyright, US Const Art I §8.

Counterfeiting.

   Powers of congress, US Const Art I §8.

Courts.

   Power to constitute tribunals inferior to supreme court, US Const Art I §8.

Debate, US Const Art I §6.

Debt.

   Powers of congress, US Const Art I §8.

Declaration of war, US Const Art I §8.

Defense.

   Powers of congress, US Const Art I §8.

District of Columbia, US Const Art I §8.

Duties and imposts.

   Powers of congress, US Const Art I §8.

Elections.

   House of representatives, US Const Art I §§2, 4.

   Senate, US Const Art I §4, Amd 17.

Excises.

   Powers of congress, US Const Art I §8.

Foreign commerce, US Const Art I §8.

Freedom of speech.

   Members of congress, US Const Art I §6.

Holding other office, US Const Art I §6.

House of representatives, US Const Art I §§1, 2.

   Absent members, US Const Art I §5.

   Arrest of members, US Const Art I §6.

   Compensation of members, US Const Art I §6.

      Laws varying compensation.

         When to take effect, US Const Amd 27.

   Debate, US Const Art I §6.

   Elections.

      Election of representatives, US Const Art I §2.

      Times, places and manner of holding, US Const Art I §4.

   Expulsion of member, US Const Art I §5.

   Freedom of speech, US Const Art I §6.

   Holding other office, US Const Art I §6.

   Impeachment, US Const Art I §2.

   Journal, US Const Art I §§5, 7.

CONSTITUTION OF THE UNITED STATES
—Cont'd
Congress —Cont'd
House of representatives —Cont'd
Libel and slander.
Privilege of members, US Const Art I §6.
Officers, US Const Art I §2.
Presidential elector.
Representative ineligible, US Const Art II §1.
Punishment of members, US Const Art I §5.
Qualifications.
Electors, US Const Art I §2.
Members, US Const Art I §2.
Judge of qualifications, US Const Art I §5.
Revenue bills, US Const Art I §7.
Rules of procedure, US Const Art I §5.
Speaker, US Const Art I §2.
Term, US Const Art I §2.
Vacancies, US Const Art I §2.
Vice-president.
Vacancy in office.
Confirmation of nomination of president,
US Const Amd 25 §2.
Insurrections, US Const Art I §8.
International law.
Power to punish offenses against, US Const Art
I §8.
Interstate commerce, US Const Art I §§8, 9.
Journals, US Const Art I §§5, 7.
Legislative powers vested in, US Const Art I §1.
Letters of marque and reprisal, US Const Art I §8.
Messages to congress, US Const Art II §3.
Militia.
Powers of congress, US Const Art I §8.
Money.
Powers of congress, US Const Art I §8.
Naturalization, US Const Art I §8.
Navy.
Powers of congress, US Const Art I §8.
Patents, US Const Art I §8.
Piracy.
Powers of congress, US Const Art I §8.
Post office and post roads, US Const Art I §8.
Powers of congress, US Const Art I §8.
Limitations on powers, US Const Art I §9.
President of the United States.
Declaration of president's disability.
Determination of issue, US Const Amd 25 §4.
Qualifications of members of congress, US Const
Art I §§2, 3, 5.
Rules of procedure, US Const Art I §5.
Senate.
Absent members, US Const Art I §5.
Arrest of members, US Const Art I §6.
Compensation of members, US Const Art I §6.
Laws varying compensation.
When to take effect, US Const Amd 27.
Debate, US Const Art I §6.
Elections.
Election of senators, US Const Amd 17.
Times, places and manner of holding, US
Const Art I §4.
Equal suffrage in senate, US Const Art V.
Expulsion of member, US Const Art I §5.
Freedom of speech, US Const Art I §6.
Holding other office, US Const Art I §6.
Impeachment, US Const Art I §3.
Journal, US Const Art I §§5, 7.
Libel and slander.
Privilege of members, US Const Art I §6.
Officers, US Const Art I §3.

CONSTITUTION OF THE UNITED STATES
—Cont'd
Congress —Cont'd
Senate —Cont'd
President, US Const Art I §3.
Pro tempore, US Const Art I §3.
Presidential elector.
Senator ineligible, US Const Art II §1.
Punishment of members, US Const Art I §5.
Qualifications.
Electors, US Const Amd 17.
Members, US Const Art I §3.
Judge of qualifications, US Const Art I §5.
Quorum, US Const Art I §5.
Revenue bills, US Const Art I §7.
Rules of procedure, US Const Art I §5.
Vacancies, US Const Amd 17.
Vice-president of the United States.
Vacancy in office.
Confirmation of nomination of president,
US Const Amd 25 §2.
Sessions, US Const Art I §4, Amd 20 §2.
Special sessions, US Const Art II §3.
Taxation.
Powers of congress, US Const Art I §8.
Territories, US Const Art IV §3.
Vice-president.
Vacancy in office.
Nomination by president, US Const Amd 25
§2.
Confirmation by majority of both houses of
congress, US Const Amd 25 §2.
War.
Articles of war, US Const Art I §8.
Declaration of war, US Const Art I §8.
Weights and measures, US Const Art I §8.
Construction and interpretation.
Effect of enumeration of rights, US Const Amd 9.
Consuls, US Const Art II §§2, 3, Art III §2.
Contracts.
Impairment of obligations of contracts, US Const
Art I §10.
Copyright, US Const Art I §8.
Corruption of blood.
Attainder of treason not to work, US Const Art III
§3.
Counsel for defense, US Const Amd 6.
Counterfeiting, US Const Art I §8.
Court of appeals.
Decisions of court of appeals.
Appeals of right from certain decisions, §7A-30.
Courts.
Congress.
Power to constitute tribunals inferior to
supreme court, US Const Art I §8.
Inferior courts, US Const Art III §1.
Judges.
Compensation, US Const Art III §1.
Tenure, US Const Art III §1.
Restriction of judicial power, US Const Amd 11.
Criminal procedure.
Cruel and unusual punishment, US Const Amd 8.
Excessive bail, US Const Amd 8.
Extradition, US Const Art IV §2.
Fugitives from justice, US Const Art IV §2.
Guarantees in criminal cases, US Const Amds 5,
6.
Public trial, US Const Amd 6.
Self-incrimination, US Const Amd 5.
Speedy trial, US Const Amd 6.

CONSTITUTION OF THE UNITED STATES
    —Cont'd
Cruel and unusual punishment, US Const Amd
    8.
Customs.
    Congress.
        Power to lay and collect, US Const Art I §8.
        Exportations from any state.
        Duties not to be laid on, US Const Art I §9.
        Importation of persons, US Const Art I §9.
Death.
    President and vice-president of the United States.
        Duty of congress, US Const Art II §1, Amd 25.
        President elect.
            Provisions in case of, US Const Amd 20.
Debts.
    Aid of rebellion, US Const Amd 14.
    Debts and engagements contracted before
        adoption, US Const Art VI.
    Not to be questioned, US Const Amd 14.
    Powers of congress, US Const Art I §8.
Declaration of rights, US Const Amds 1 to 10.
Defense.
    Power of congress, US Const Art I §8.
Discrimination, US Const Amds 14, 15.
Double jeopardy, US Const Amd 5.
Due process of law, US Const Amds 5, 14.
Duties and imposts.
    Powers of congress, US Const Art I §8.
    States, US Const Art I §§9, 10.
Elections.
    Age.
        Right to vote not to be abridged on account of
            age, US Const Amd 26.
        Voting by persons eighteen years of age, US
            Const Amd 26.
    House of representatives, US Const Art I §§2, 4.
    President and vice-president, US Const Art II §1,
        Amds 12, 14, 23.
    Racial minorities, US Const Amd 15.
    Senate, US Const Art I §4, Amd 17.
    Suffrage, US Const Amds 15, 19.
Eminent domain, US Const Amd 5.
Emoluments, US Const Art I §9.
Equal protection of the laws, US Const Amd 14.
Equity.
    Judicial power to extend to cases in, US Const Art
        III §2.
Excessive bail, US Const Amd 8.
Excessive fines, US Const Amd 8.
Excises.
    Powers of congress, US Const Art I §8.
Execution of laws, US Const Art II §3.
Expenditures.
    Necessity for appropriations, US Const Art I §9.
    Publication of statement, US Const Art I §9.
Exports and imports, US Const Art I §§9, 10.
Ex post facto laws, US Const Art I §§9, 10.
Extradition, US Const Art IV §2.
Fines.
    Excessive fines, US Const Amd 8.
Firearms.
    Right to bear arms, US Const Amd 2.
Foreign presents, US Const Art I §9.
Former jeopardy, US Const Amd 5.
Freedom of conscience, US Const Amd 1.
Freedom of speech, US Const Amd 1.
    Members of congress, US Const Art I §6.
Freedom of the press, US Const Amd 1.
Fugitives, US Const Art IV §2.
Full faith and credit clause, US Const Art IV §1.

CONSTITUTION OF THE UNITED STATES
    —Cont'd
Gifts.
    Foreign presents to United States officials, US
        Const Art I §9.
Grand jury.
    Presentments by, US Const Amd 5.
Habeas corpus, US Const Art I §9.
Immigration, US Const Art I §9.
Immunities, US Const Art IV §2.
Impairment of obligations of contracts, US
    Const Art I §10.
Impeachment, US Const Art I §§2, 3, Art II §4, Art
    III §2.
Imports and exports, US Const Art I §§9, 10.
Income tax, US Const Amd 16.
Indictments, informations and presentments,
    US Const Amd 5.
Insurrection or rebellion, US Const Art I §8.
International law.
    Power of congress to punish offenses against, US
        Const Art I §8.
Interstate commerce, US Const Art I §§8, 9.
Intoxicating liquors.
    Prohibition, US Const Amds 18, 21.
    Repeal of the eighteenth amendment, US Const
        Amd 21.
Invasions, US Const Art I §8.
Involuntary servitude, US Const Amd 13.
Jeopardy.
    Double jeopardy, US Const Amd 5.
Journals.
    Congress, US Const Art I §§5, 7.
Judges.
    Compensation, US Const Art III §1.
    Tenure, US Const Art III §1.
Judgments.
    Full faith and credit clause, US Const Art IV §1.
    Proof, US Const Art IV §1.
Jury.
    Jury of vicinage, US Const Amd 6.
Lame duck amendment, US Const Amd 20.
Legal tender, US Const Art I §10.
Letters of marque and reprisal, US Const Art I
    §§8, 10.
Libel and slander.
    Congress.
        Privilege of members of congress, US Const Art
            I §6.
Limitations on powers of states, US Const Art I
    §10.
Liquors, US Const Amds 18, 21.
Messages to congress, US Const Art II §3.
Militia.
    Powers of congress, US Const Art I §8.
    Quartering soldiers, US Const Amd 3.
Ministers.
    Jurisdiction of cases affecting, US Const Art III
        §2.
    Receiving, US Const Art II §3.
Money, US Const Art I §§8, 10.
    Coinage, US Const Art I §§8, 10.
    Counterfeiting, US Const Art I §8.
    Powers of congress, US Const Art I §8.
Naturalization, US Const Art I §8.
Navy.
    Powers of congress, US Const Art I §8.
New states, US Const Art IV §3.
Nonresidents.
    Jurisdiction of suits against state, US Const Amd
        11.

CONSTITUTION OF THE UNITED STATES
—Cont'd
Oaths.
General assembly.
Members to take oath supporting constitutions, §11-7.
Officers to take oath or affirmation supporting constitutions, §11-7.
Ordinances.
Consistent with constitution of the United States, §160A-174(b).
Pardons, US Const Art II §2.
Patents, US Const Art I §8.
Payments.
Legal tender, US Const Art I §10.
Petitions.
Right of, US Const Amd 1.
Piracy.
Powers of congress, US Const Art I §8.
Poll tax.
Failure to pay poll or other tax.
Denial or abridgement of right to vote.
Prohibited, US Const Amd 24.
Post offices, US Const Art I §8.
Post roads, US Const Art I §8.
Powers of congress, US Const Art I §8.
Powers reserved to states and people, US Const Amd 10.
President.
Age, US Const Art II §1.
Ambassadors and consuls, US Const Art II §§2, 3.
Appointment of officers, etc., US Const Art II §2.
Approval of laws by president, US Const Art I §7.
Approval of order, resolution or vote of congress, US Const Art I §7.
Bribery, US Const Art II §4.
Commander in chief, US Const Art II §2.
Compensation, US Const Art II §1.
Congress.
Adjourning congress, US Const Art II §3.
Convening congress, US Const Art II §3.
Messages to congress, US Const Art II §3.
Special sessions of congress, US Const Art II §3.
Death, US Const Art II §1, Amd 20 §3.
Succession upon death, US Const Amd 25 §1.
Disability, US Const Art II §1.
Declaration by president.
Inability to perform duties, US Const Amd 25 §3.
Declaration by vice-president and other officers, US Const Amd 25 §4.
Determination of issue by congress, US Const Amd 25 §4.
Duties, US Const Art II §3.
Declaration by president of inability to perform duties, US Const Amd 25 §3.
Transmittal to senate and house of representatives, US Const Amd 25 §3.
Elections, US Const Art II §1, Amds 12, 14, 23.
Eligibility, US Const Art II §1.
Execution of laws, US Const Art II §3.
Executive power, US Const Art II §1.
Failure to qualify, US Const Amd 20.
Impeachment, US Const Art I §3, Art II §4.
Inability, US Const Art II §1.
Limitation on terms, US Const Amd 22.
Message to congress, US Const Art II §3.
Ministers.
Receiving, US Const Art II §3.
Opinions from principal officers in executive departments, US Const Art II §2.

CONSTITUTION OF THE UNITED STATES
—Cont'd
President —Cont'd
Pardons, US Const Art II §2.
Powers of president, US Const Art II §§2, 3.
Public officers.
Commissions, US Const Art II §3.
Qualifications, US Const Art II §1.
Removal, US Const Art II §§1, 4.
Succession upon removal, US Const Amd 25 §1.
Resignation, US Const Art II §1.
Succession upon resignation, US Const Amd 25 §1.
Signing of bills, US Const Art I §7.
Statutes.
Veto, US Const Art I §7.
Succession to office, US Const Art II §1, Amd 20.
Upon death, resignation or removal of president, US Const Amd 25 §2.
Supreme court.
Appointment of justices, US Const Art II §2.
Terms of office, US Const Art II §1, Amds 20, 22.
Limitation on terms, US Const Amd 22.
Time of taking office, US Const Amd 20.
Treason, US Const Art II §4.
Treaties, US Const Art II §2.
Vacancy in office, US Const Art II §1, Amd 20.
During senate recess, US Const Art II §2.
Veto, US Const Art I §7.
Press.
Freedom of the press, US Const Amd 1.
Privileges.
Privileged from arrest, US Const Art I §6.
Prohibition, US Const Amds 18, 21.
Protection and aid of states, US Const Art IV §4.
Public debt, US Const Art I §8.
Public officers and employees.
Appointment, US Const Art II §2.
Senate recess, US Const Art II §2.
Bribery, US Const Art II §4.
Commissions, US Const Art II §3.
Emoluments, US Const Art I §9.
Foreign office or title, US Const Art I §9.
Holding more than one office, US Const Art I §6.
Impeachment, US Const Art II §4.
Ineligibility of members of congress, US Const Art I §6.
Presents from foreign states, US Const Art I §9.
Presidential electors.
Eligibility, US Const Art II §1.
Religious tests, US Const Art VI.
Removal, US Const Art II §4.
Treason, US Const Art II §4.
Vacancies during senate recess, US Const Art II §2.
Public schools.
Basic education program.
Knowledge and understanding of constitution required, §115C-81(g).
First amendment displayed on school property, §115C-81(g3).
Public trial, US Const Amd 6.
Punishment.
Cruel and unusual punishment, US Const Amd 8.
Quartering soldiers in houses, US Const Amd 3.
Racial minorities, US Const Amds 14, 15.
Ratification, US Const Art VII.
Records.
Full faith and credit clause, US Const Art IV §1.
Proof, US Const Art IV §1.

CONSTITUTION OF THE UNITED STATES
—Cont'd
Redress of grievances.
Right to petition for, US Const Amd 1.
Religious test, US Const Art VI.
Republican form of government, US Const Art IV §4.
Reservation of rights of the people, US Const Amd 9.
Revenue bills, US Const Art I §7.
Right of assembly, US Const Amd 1.
Right of trial by jury, US Const Art III §2.
Right to bear arms, US Const Amd 2.
Right to counsel, US Const Amd 6.
Right to petition for a redress of grievances, US Const Amd 1.
Searches and seizures, US Const Amd 4.
Self-incrimination, US Const Amd 5.
Sentence and punishment, US Const Amd 8.
Capital punishment, US Const Amd 5.
Sessions of congress, US Const Art I §4.
Special sessions, US Const Art II §3.
Slavery, US Const Amds 13 to 15.
Soldiers.
Quartering prohibited, US Const Amd 3.
Speech.
Freedom of speech, US Const Amd 1.
Speedy trial, US Const Amd 6.
States.
Admission of new states, US Const Art IV §3.
Bill of attainder, US Const Art I §10.
Bills of credit, US Const Art I §10.
Commerce, US Const Art I §§8, 9.
Compacts between the states or with foreign powers, US Const Art I §10.
Contracts.
Impairing obligations of contracts, US Const Art I §10.
Controversies between citizens of different states, US Const Art III §2.
Controversies between states, US Const Art III §2.
Duties and imposts, US Const Art I §10.
Equal suffrage in senate, US Const Art V.
Exports, US Const Art I §§9, 10.
Ex post facto laws, US Const Art I §10.
Full faith and credit clause, US Const Art IV §1.
Gold and silver coin tender in payment of debts, US Const Art I §10.
Impairing obligations of contracts, US Const Art I §10.
Imports and exports, US Const Art I §10.
Invasion.
Protection against, US Const Art IV §4.
Legal tender, US Const Art I §10.
Letters of marque and reprisal, US Const Art I §10.
Limitations on powers of states, US Const Art I §10.
Money.
Coining money, US Const Art I §10.
New states, US Const Art IV §3.
Powers, US Const Art I §10.
Reserved to states, US Const Amd 10.
Protection and aid of states, US Const Art IV §4.
Republican form of government guaranteed, US Const Art IV §4.
Reservation of powers to states, US Const Amd 10.
Right to coin money, US Const Art I §10.
Suits against state, US Const Amd 11.

CONSTITUTION OF THE UNITED STATES
—Cont'd
States —Cont'd
Tender in payment of debts, US Const Art I §10.
Tonnage, US Const Art I §10.
Treaties, US Const Art I §10.
Troops or ships of war in time of peace, US Const Art I §10.
War, US Const Art I §10.
Statutes.
Approval of laws by president, US Const Art I §7.
Ex post facto laws, US Const Art I §§9, 10.
Full faith and credit clause, US Const Art IV §1.
Limitations on legislation, US Const Art I §9.
Proof, US Const Art IV §1.
Revenue bills, US Const Art I §7.
Supreme law of the land, US Const Art VI.
Veto, US Const Art I §7.
Suits against state, US Const Amd 11.
Suits against the United States, US Const Art III §2.
Supreme court.
Chief justice presides in impeachment of president, US Const Art I §3.
Court of appeals decisions.
Appeals of right from certain decisions of court of appeals, §7A-30.
Jurisdiction, US Const Art III §2.
Justices.
Appointment, US Const Art II §2.
Compensation, US Const Art III §1.
Tenure, US Const Art III §1.
Supreme law of the land, US Const Art VI.
Taxation.
Capitation tax, US Const Art I §9.
Elections.
Denial or abridgement of right to vote for failure to pay tax prohibited, US Const Amd 24.
Excises.
Powers of congress, US Const Art I §8.
Exports, US Const Art I §§9, 10.
Income tax, US Const Amd 16.
Limitations on powers of states, US Const Art I §10.
Powers of congress, US Const Art I §8.
Revenue bills, US Const Art I §7.
Tender, US Const Art I §10.
Territories, US Const Art IV §3.
Time when constitution effective, US Const Art VII.
Titles of nobility, US Const Art I §§9, 10.
Tonnage, US Const Art I §10.
Treason, US Const Art I §6, Art II §4, Art III §3.
Trial.
Public trial, US Const Amd 6.
Speedy trial, US Const Amd 6.
Venue, US Const Art III §2.
Vessels and boats.
Bound to and from one state not to be obliged to clear, etc., in another, US Const Art I §9.
Veto, US Const Art I §7.
Vice-president of the United States.
Age, US Const Amd 12.
Bribery, US Const Art II §4.
Election, US Const Art II §1, Amd 12.
Failure to qualify, US Const Amd 20.
Impeachment, US Const Art II §4.
Oaths, US Const Art VI, Amd 14.
President of senate, US Const Art I §3.
Qualifications, US Const Amd 12.

CONSTITUTION OF THE UNITED STATES —Cont'd

Vice-president of the United States —Cont'd

Removal, US Const Art II §4.

Succession to office of president, US Const Art II §1, Amds 20, 25.

Treason, US Const Art II §4.

Vacancy in office, US Const Art II §1, Amd 20.

Nomination by president, US Const Amd 25 §2.

Confirmation by congress, US Const Amd 25 §2.

War.

Articles of war, US Const Art I §8.

Declaration by congress, US Const Art I §8.

Grand jury.

Presentment as dispensable in certain cases, US Const Amd 5.

Quartering of soldiers in times of war, US Const Amd 3.

State engaging in, US Const Art I §10.

Treason.

Levying against the United States, US Const Art III §3.

Warrants.

Searches and seizures.

Conditions for issuance, US Const Amd 4.

Weights and measures, US Const Art I §8.

Welfare.

General welfare.

Powers of congress, US Const Art I §8.

Witnesses.

Confrontation with witnesses, US Const Amd 6.

Process to obtain, US Const Amd 6.

Self-incrimination, US Const Amd 5.

Treason.

Number in treason cases, US Const Art III §3.

Women's suffrage, US Const Amd 19.

CONSTRICTING SNAKES.

Regulation of reptiles generally, §§14-416 to 14-422.

See REPTILES.

CONSTRUCTION.

Building trades training.

Vocational and technical education generally.

See VOCATIONAL AND TECHNICAL EDUCATION.

Burning of building or structure in process of construction, §14-62.1.

Construction management at risk contracts.

Public contracts, §143-128.1.

Fairs.

State fair.

Board authorized to construct and finance facilities and improvements, §106-503.1.

Health care facilities.

Construction contracts, §131A-9.

Highways, roads and streets.

See HIGHWAYS, ROADS AND STREETS.

Hospitals.

Construction and enlargement of local hospitals, §131E-70.

Indemnity.

Contracts for construction indemnity agreements against public policy, §22B-1.

Interest on construction loans.

Definition, §24-10(c).

Maximum fees on loans secured by real property. Less than three hundred thousand dollars, §24-10(d).

CONSTRUCTION —Cont'd

Larceny of goods from permitted construction site, §14-72.6(b).

Criminal penalty, §14-72.6(a).

Permitted construction site defined, §14-72.6(d).

Possessing or receiving stolen goods from site, §14-72.6(c).

Payment and performance bonds generally, §§44A-25 to 44A-35.

See PAYMENT AND PERFORMANCE BONDS.

Sanitary districts.

Water supply or sewerage systems construction by corporations or individuals, §130A-58.

State fair.

Authority to construct and finance facilities and improvements, §106-503.1.

Transportation department.

State highway construction.

Powers of department, §136-18.

Vehicular surface areas.

Environmental protection.

Building permits to comply, §113A-71(b).

Water well construction, §§87-83 to 87-98.

See WATER WELL CONSTRUCTION.

CONSTRUCTION CONTRACTORS.

General contractors, §§87-1 to 87-15.4.

See GENERAL CONTRACTORS.

CONSTRUCTION EQUIPMENT.

Inside rearview mirror requirement exemption from provision, §20-126(a).

CONSTRUCTION INDEMNITY AGREEMENT.

Invalidity, §22B-1.

CONSTRUCTION LOANS.

Defined, §24-10(c).

Fees chargeable at closing, §24-1.1A(c).

Maximum fees for loans secured by real property, §24-10(a).

Prepayment fees, §24-10(b).

CONSTRUCTION OF STATUTES, §§12-2 to 12-4.

Amended statutes, §12-4.

Commercial code.

General provisions, §§25-1-101 to 25-1-310.

See COMMERCIAL CODE.

Devisee or devise, §12-3.

Fees and charges by agencies, §12-3.1(a).

Definitions, §12-3.1(b).

Inapplicability to fees or charges to state, federal or local governmental units, §12-3.1(c).

Governor, senate, solicitor, etc., §12-3.

Imprisonment for one month, §12-3.

Joint authority to three or more officers, §12-3.

Leap year, how counted, §12-3.

Masculine gender to extend and apply to females, §12-3.

Month, §12-3.

Oath to include affirmation, §12-3.

Personal property to include money, goods, etc., §12-3.

Person extended and applied to body politic and corporate, §12-3.

Preceding and following, §12-3.

Property to include all property, §12-3.

Real property.

Coextensive with land, tenements and hereditaments, §12-3.

Repeal of statute not to affect actions, §12-2.

Rules for construction generally, §12-3.

Seal, §12-3.

CONSTRUCTION OF STATUTES —Cont'd
Single and plural number, §12-3.
State, §12-3.
Sworn to include affirmed, §12-3.
United States, §12-3.
Will to construed to include codicils, §12-3.
Written and in writing construed to include printing, engraving, etc., §12-3.
Year, §12-3.

CONSTRUCTIVE NOTICE.
Eminent domain.
Filing of notice of proceedings, §40A-21.
Lis pendens, §§1-116 to 1-120.2.
See LIS PENDENS.
Mortgages and deeds of trust.
Substitution of trustees, §45-15.

CONSULS.
Constitution of the United States, US Const Art II §§2, 3, Art III §2.
Deeds probated before consular agents of the United States, §47-91.
Probate before, §47-83.
Vice-consuls and vice-consuls general, §47-84.

CONSULTANT SERVICES.
Private protective services.
Exemption of certain consultants from private protective services act, §74C-3(b).
State departments and agencies, §§143-64.20 to 143-64.24.
See STATE DEPARTMENTS AND AGENCIES.

CONSUMER AND FAMILY ADVISORY COMMITTEES.
Mental health, mental retardation, substance abuse, §§122C-170, 122C-171.

CONSUMER CREDIT.
Consumer finance act.
Loans of $10,000 or less, §§53-164 to 53-191.
See CONSUMER FINANCE ACT.
Credit cards.
See CREDIT CARDS.
Credit repair services, §§66-220 to 66-226.
Retail installment sales, §§25A-1 to 25A-45.
See RETAIL INSTALLMENT SALES.
Security freeze on consumer's credit report, §75-63.

CONSUMER CREDIT SALES.
Retail installment sales, §§25A-1 to 25A-45.
See RETAIL INSTALLMENT SALES.

CONSUMER FINANCE ACT, §§53-164 to 53-191.
Advertising.
False or misleading statements, §53-183.
Appeals.
Commission may review rules, orders or acts of commissioner, §53-188.
Assets.
Requirements for licensees, §53-168(a), (d).
Assignments.
Earnings, §53-180(b).
Attorneys' fees.
Loan agreement not to provide for payment by borrower, §53-180(e).
Borrowers.
Defined, §53-165.
Cash advances.
Applicability of provisions, §53-166(b).
Cease and desist orders.
Commissioner of banks, §53-187.

CONSUMER FINANCE ACT —Cont'd
Citation of act.
Short title, §53-164.
Commissioner of banks.
Cease and desist orders, §53-187.
Confidentiality of official records, §53-99.
Definition of "commissioner,"§53-165(e).
Fees.
Payment for expenses of supervision, §53-167.
Hearings, §53-186.
Injunctions, §53-187.
Oaths.
Power to administer, §53-186.
Powers, §§53-186, 53-187.
Publicity to investigations and findings, §53-186.
Review of rules, acts or orders by commission, §53-188.
Rules and regulations, §53-185.
State banking commission.
Commission may review rules, orders or acts of commissioner, §53-188.
Subpoenas, §53-186.
Witnesses, §53-186.
Conduct of other business in same office.
Best interest of borrowing public.
Authorizing other business found not contrary to, §53-172(b).
Revocation of authority where business contrary to, §53-172(f).
Books, records and accounts of other loans, §53-172(h).
Collections in violation of G.S. 53-190.
Section not to authorize, §53-172(g).
Purchase of goods and services sold under authorization, §53-172(d), (e).
Restriction on, §53-172(a).
Truth-in-lending act regulations.
Requirements of other business under, §53-172(c).
Confession of judgment.
Licensees not to take, §53-181(c).
Contracts.
Out-of-state loans.
When contracts unenforceable, §53-190(a).
Splitting contracts prohibited, §53-178.
Time and payment limitations, §53-180(a).
Credit life and credit accident and health insurance, §53-189(a).
Premiums, §53-189(a).
Not deemed interest or charges, §53-189(b).
Terms of agreements, §53-189(a).
Credit unions.
Exemption of cooperative credit unions, §53-191.
Deceptive trade practices.
Prohibited, §53-180(g).
Default charge.
Limitation of default provisions, §53-180(c).
Definitions, §53-165.
Discrimination.
Prohibited acts, §53-180(d).
Evasion of provisions, §53-166(b).
Exemptions.
Businesses exempted, §53-191.
False or misleading statements, §53-183.
Fees.
Commissioner of banks.
Payment for expenses of supervision, §53-167.
Operating and maintaining office of commissioner of banks, §53-122(a), (e), (f).
Processing loan.
Maximum fee, §§53-173(a1), 53-176(b).

CONSUMER FINANCE ACT —Cont'd
Fees —Cont'd
Recording fees, §53-177.
Goods and services.
Purchase under authorization to conduct other
business in same office, §53-172(d), (e).
Hearings.
Commissioner of banks, §53-186.
License applications, §53-168(b).
Home loans.
Limitation on condition to making loans,
§53-180(i).
Limitation on other loans, §53-180(h).
Injunctions, §53-187.
Installment loans.
Corporations, §53-176(f).
Due date of first payment, §53-176(e).
Election to make loan under, §53-176(d).
Loan processing fee, §53-176(b).
Interest.
Computation of charges, §53-173(b).
Credit life and credit accident and health
insurance.
Premiums not deemed interest or charges,
§53-189(b).
Judgments.
Limitation on interest after judgment,
§53-173(c).
Maturity of loan.
Limitation of interest after, §53-173(d).
Optional maturities, §53-176.
Maximum rate, §53-173(a).
Further charges prohibited, §53-178.
Optional rates, §53-176(a), (c).
Schedule of charges, §53-181(b).
Licenses.
Affiliation with other licensees.
Allocation of expense, §53-184(c).
Applications, §53-169.
Assets.
Requirements, §53-168(a), (d).
Change of location, ownership or management,
§53-170(c).
Contents, §53-168(e).
Findings required for issuance, §53-168(a).
Hearing on application, §53-168(b).
Investigation of applicants, §53-168(b).
Location of business, §53-170(a).
Additional places of business, §53-170(b).
Change of location, §53-170(c).
Multiple-office loan limitations, §53-179.
Posting, §53-168(e).
Prerequisite to issuance, §53-168(a).
Records of licensees, §53-184(a).
Reports by licensees, §53-184(b).
Required, §53-168(a).
Revocation or suspension, §53-171(a).
Preexisting contracts.
Effect, §53-171(c).
Reinstatement or issuance of new license,
§53-171(d).
Surrender of license, §53-171(a), (b).
Limitations on loans.
Conditions to making loans, §53-180(i).
Home loans and noncommercial loan over $25,000
prohibited, §53-180(h).
Negotiable check or facsimile, §53-180(k).
Misdemeanors.
Violation of provisions, §53-166(c).
Multiple-office loan limitations, §53-179.

CONSUMER FINANCE ACT —Cont'd
Noncommercial loans.
Limitation on other loans, §53-180(h).
Oaths.
Power of commissioner to administer oaths,
§53-186.
Out-of-state loans.
Licensees not to collect loan made by lender in
another state, §53-190(c).
Solicitation or other activities in state.
Subject to requirement of provisions, §53-190(b).
When contracts unenforceable, §53-190(a).
Pawnbrokers and cash converters.
Exemption, §53-191.
Payment of loans.
Payment in full.
Duties of licensees upon, §53-182(b).
Receipts, §53-182(a).
Powers of attorney.
Licensee not to permit borrower to execute,
§53-181(c).
Pretext for advance of funds.
Applicability of provisions, §53-166(b).
Processing fee.
Maximum fee, §§53-173(a1), 53-176(b).
Purchase of goods and services.
Sold under authorization to conduct other
business in same office, §53-172(d), (e).
Racial minorities.
Discrimination prohibited, §53-180(d).
Real property not security for loan, §53-180(f).
Receipts.
Payment of loans, §53-182(a).
Receivers.
Violators of provisions, §53-187.
Recording fees, §53-177.
Records.
Licensees, §53-184(a).
Religion.
Discrimination prohibited, §53-180(d).
Reports.
Licensees, §53-184(b).
Rules and regulations.
Commissioner of banks, §53-185.
State banking commission, §53-185.
Savings and loan associations.
Exemption, §53-191.
Scope of act, §53-166(a), (b).
Secured transactions.
Security agreements.
Effect of consumer protection and other laws,
§25-9-201(b), (d).
Third parties.
Assignments.
Restrictions on assignments, §§25-9-406(i),
25-9-408(f).
Solicitation of deposits.
Prohibited, §53-180(j).
State banking commission.
Commission defined, §53-165(d).
Statement to borrower, §53-181(a).
Subpoenas.
Power of commissioner, §53-186.
Title of act.
Short title, §53-164.
Unfair competition, §53-180(g).
Violation of provisions.
Penalties, §53-166(c), (d).
Void contracts, §53-166(d).
Wages.
Assignment of earnings prohibited, §53-180(b).

CONSUMER FINANCE ACT —Cont'd
Women.
Discrimination prohibited, §53-180(d).

CONSUMER GOODS.
Food, drug and cosmetic act.
Declaration of net quantity of contents,
§106-139.1.
General provisions.
See FOOD, DRUG AND COSMETIC ACT.
Regulations by board of agriculture, §106-139(c).
Exemption from certain labeling requirements,
§106-139(b).

CONSUMER HOME LOANS, §24-10.2.

CONSUMER LEASES.
Choice of judicial forum, §25-2A-106.
Defined, §25-2A-103.
Leases, UCC generally, §§25-2A-101 to 25-2A-532.
See LEASES, UCC.
Option to accelerate at will, §25-2A-109.
Unconscionability, §25-2A-108.

CONSUMER PRICE INDEX.
**Retirement system for teachers and state
employees.**
Post-retirement increases in allowances, §135-5(o).
Years 1975 and 1976 increase in allowance,
§135-5(v).

CONSUMER PROTECTION.
Advertising.
Use of term "wholesale" in advertising, §75-29.
Agriculture.
Records of sales of farm products.
Dated sales confirmation slips inapplicable to
consumers, §106-202.6(b).
Artwork on consignment, §§25C-1 to 25C-5.
**Authorized practice committee of the state
bar.**
Procedures to prevent and restrain unauthorized
practice of law, Bar Rules D.0201 to D.0207.
Automatic renewal clauses in contracts, §75-41.
Blind persons.
Consumer and advocacy advisory committee for
the blind, §§143B-163, 143B-164.
Cable television service.
State franchising of cable television service.
Standards of service, §66-356.
Check-cashing businesses, §§53-275 to 53-289.
See CHECK-CASHING BUSINESSES.
Collection agencies, §§58-70-1 to 58-70-155.
See COLLECTION AGENCIES.
Common carriers.
Unsolicited merchandise through common
carriers, §75-27.
Consumer finance act, §§53-164 to 53-191.
See CONSUMER FINANCE ACT.
Credit cards.
See CREDIT CARDS.
Credit monitoring services act, §§75-133 to
75-135.
Credit repair services, §§66-220 to 66-226.
Credit rights of women, §§25B-1 to 25B-4.
Damages.
Unfair competition and deceptive practices.
Treble damages, §75-16.
Debt collectors.
Prohibited acts, §§75-50 to 75-56.
See DEBT COLLECTORS.
Door-to-door sales, §§25A-39 to 25A-42.
Fines.
Violator subject to fine, §75-19.

CONSUMER PROTECTION —Cont'd
**Free insurance as inducement to purchase
goods or services,** §§66-380 to 66-382.
Geographical location.
Deceptive representation in telephone directory,
print advertisement or Internet, §75-42.
Gifts.
Unsolicited merchandise.
Receipt through mail, §75-27.
Home loan protection of consumers, §24-10.2.
Income tax.
Unauthorized disclosure of tax information,
§75-28.
Injunctions, §75-19.
Insurance.
Free insurance as inducement to purchase goods
or services, §§66-380 to 66-382.
Injunctions, §75-19.
Lender may not require borrower to deal with
particular insurer, §75-17.
Lender may require nondiscriminatory approval of
insurer, §75-18.
Privacy of information, §§58-39-1 to 58-39-165.
See INSURANCE CONSUMER AND
CUSTOMER INFORMATION PRIVACY.
Invoices.
Simulation of invoices, §75-35.
Leases, UCC.
Leases subject to consumer protection statute of
state, §25-2A-104(1).
Limestone, marl and landplaster.
Sale of agricultural liming materials and
landplaster, §106-92.11.
Little FTC act, §75-1.1.
Loans.
General provisions.
See LOANS.
Mail.
Unsolicited merchandise through mail, §75-27.
Manufactured homes generally.
See MANUFACTURED HOMES.
Money transmitters, §§53-208.1 to 53-208.30.
See MONEY TRANSMITTERS.
Monopolies and restraint of trade, §§75-1 to
75-35.
See MONOPOLIES AND RESTRAINT OF
TRADE.
Mortgages and deeds of trust.
Emergency program to reduce home foreclosures,
§§45-100 to 45-107.
See FORECLOSURE.
Home loan protection of consumers, §24-10.2.
Motion pictures.
Fair competition act, §§75C-1 to 75C-5.
Motor vehicle repairs, §§20-354 to 20-354.9.
See MOTOR VEHICLE REPAIRS.
Negotiable instruments.
Check-cashing businesses, §§53-275 to 53-289.
See CHECK-CASHING BUSINESSES.
Simulation of checks and invoices, §75-35.
New motor vehicles warranties act, §§20-351 to
20-351.10.
See LEMON LAW.
Prepaid entertainment contracts, §§66-118 to
66-125.
See PREPAID ENTERTAINMENT CONTRACTS.
Prizes.
Representation of eligibility to win a prize, §75-33.
Representation of winning a prize, §75-32.
Products liability, §§99B-1 to 99B-11.
Pyramid distribution plans, §14-291.2.

CONSUMER PROTECTION —Cont'd

Rebates.

Deadline for mailing consumer rebates, §75-40.

Rental referral agencies, §§66-142 to 66-146.

Representation of being specially selected, §75-34.

Retail installment sales, §§25A-1 to 25A-45.

See RETAIL INSTALLMENT SALES.

Secured transactions.

Security agreements.

Effect of consumer protection and other laws, §25-9-201(b), (d).

Taxation.

Unauthorized disclosure of tax information, §75-28.

Timber marks, §§80-15 to 80-23.

See TIMBER MARKS.

Trademarks.

Generally, §§80-1 to 80-14.

See TRADEMARKS.

Unauthorized practice of law.

Authorized practice committee of the state bar, Bar Rules D.0201 to D.0207.

Unfair trade practices generally.

See UNFAIR TRADE PRACTICES.

Unsolicited checks to secure loans, §75-20.

Unsolicited merchandise.

Receipt through mail, §75-27.

Usury.

See USURY.

Wholesale.

Unfair and deceptive trade name.

Use of term wholesale, §75-29.

Use of term in name, §75-29.

Women.

Credit rights of women, §§25B-1 to 25B-4.

Work-at-home solicitations, §75-31.

CONSUMER PROTECTION FUND OF INSURANCE DEPARTMENT.

Appropriations, §58-2-215(c).

Creation, §58-2-215(a).

Uses, §58-2-215(b).

CONSUMER REPORTS.

Credit monitoring services act, §§75-133 to 75-135.

Insurance institutions, agents or insurance-support organization.

Investigative consumer reports, §58-39-40.

Security freeze on consumer's credit report, §75-63.

CONSUMPTION AT OFF-PREMISES ESTABLISHMENTS.

Malt beverages or unfortified wine, §18B-300(b).

CONTACT LENSES.

Prescriptions, §90-236.1.

CONTAGIOUS DISEASES.

Body of person dying infected with contagious disease.

Notice to persons handling body by physician.

Proper precautions to prevent infection, §130A-395(a).

Communicable diseases.

See COMMUNICABLE DISEASES.

Diseases generally.

See DISEASES.

Food, drug and cosmetic act.

Dissemination of certain information, §106-142(b).

CONTAGIOUS DISEASES —Cont'd

Meningococcal disease vaccination information.

Universities and colleges.

Providing students information, §116-260.

Nuclear, biological or chemical agents.

Terrorist incident using, §§130A-475 to 130A-479.

See TERRORIST INCIDENT USING NUCLEAR, BIOLOGICAL OR CHEMICAL AGENTS.

Rabies.

See RABIES.

Vaccinations.

See VACCINATIONS.

CONTAINERS.

Alcoholic beverage containers.

Recycling requirements for certain permittees, §18B-1006.1.

Disposal of in landfills or by incineration.

Prohibited, §130A-309.10(f3).

Plan to collect and recycle submitted with application, §§18B-902(h), 18B-903(b2).

Aluminum cans.

Incineration, disposal by prohibited, §130A-309.10(f1).

Landfills, disposal in prohibited, §130A-309.10(f).

Commodities.

Information required, §81A-27.

Unit price, declaration, §81A-28.

Eggs.

Defined, §106-245.14.

Designation of grade and class on containers required, §106-245.15.

Labeling on containers, §106-245.18(a).

Descriptive terms, §106-245.18(b).

Food, drug and cosmetic act, §§106-120 to 106-145.

See FOOD, DRUG AND COSMETIC ACT.

Fully halogenated chlorofluorocarbons (CFC).

Containers manufactured with, restrictions, §130A-309.10(b).

Gasoline and oil inspection.

Display required on containers used in making deliveries, §119-43.

Labels generally.

See LABELS.

Matches.

Shipping containers.

Requirements, §66-15.

Metal ring or tab.

Prohibition on selling beverages in containers opened by, §130A-309.10(a).

Open container law, §18B-401(a).

Mandatory revocation of driver's license, §20-17(a).

Period of suspension or revocation, §20-19(g1).

Transporting open container of alcoholic beverage after consuming alcohol or in passenger area of vehicle, §20-138.7.

Pesticides.

Prohibited acts, §143-443(a).

Plastic containers.

Rigid containers, requirements, §130A-309.10(e).

Plastic yokes or ring type holding devices.

"Degradable" defined, §14-399.2(a).

Nondegradable devices.

Penalties for violation, §14-399.2(c).

Prohibited, §14-399.2(b).

Prosecution of violators.

Exemption, §14-399.2(d).

CONTAINERS —Cont'd
Ports authority.
Shipping in containers, §136-263.
Violations of provisions.
Penalties, §66-16.
Soil additives act.
Labeling of containers, §106-50.32.

CONTAMINATION OF SITE.
Deed or other instrument of conveyance, contaminated property statement, §143B-279.10(e).
Land use restrictions imposed by secretary of environment and natural resources.
Reduction of danger to public health, §143B-279.9(a) to (d).
Definitions, §§143B-279.9(d), 143B-279.10(d), (h).
Notice of contamination.
Cancellation after contamination eliminated, owner's request, §143B-279.10(f).
Exceptions, §143B-279.10(g).
Filing copy in register of deeds office, §143B-279.10(b).
Recording copy, §143B-279.10(c).
Secretary may prepare and file, owner's failure, §143B-279.10(d).
Survey plat submitted by owner, §143B-279.10(a).
Risk based environmental remediation of industrial sites, §§130A-310.65 to 130A-310.77.
See HAZARDOUS WASTE MANAGEMENT.

CONTEMPT.
Abused, neglected or dependent juvenile actions.
Dispositional order, parent's failure to comply, §7B-904(e).
Failure to appear, §7B-407.
Failure to comply with order, §7B-406(c).
Order to cease interference or obstruction with assessment of report.
Enforcement of order, §7B-303(f).
Alimony.
Enforcement of payment by contempt, §50-16.7(j).
Arbitration.
Grounds, §1-569.17(h).
Arrest in civil cases.
Exclusive nature of provisions.
Exception as to contempt, §1-409.
Attorneys at law.
Clerks of court.
Certification of orders, §84-36.1.
Disciplinary hearing commission of state bar.
Power to hold in contempt, §84-28.1(b1).
Suspended or disbarred attorney failing to comply with obligations, Bar Rule B.0124.
Bail.
Power of court to punish for contempt not affected, §15A-546.
Broadcasters and broadcasting.
Criminal contempt.
Basis for holding in contempt, §5A-11(b).
Child custody orders.
Enforcement, §50-13.3(a).
Childhood vaccine-related injury compensation.
Industrial commission.
Power to punish for contempt, §130A-424.
Superior court of Wake county.
Power to punish for contempt, §130A-425(d).

CONTEMPT —Cont'd
Child support enforcement, §50-13.4(f).
Compelling disclosure of information respecting nonsupporting parent.
Parent of dependent child receiving public assistance failing or refusing to cooperate, §110-131(b).
Failure to comply with support order.
Criminal contempt, punishment, §5A-12(a).
Procedure to insure payment, §50-13.9(g).
Wage garnishment to enforce, garnishee violating terms of order, §110-136(e).
Civil contempt.
Affidavit or sworn statement.
Proceeding initiated on motion of aggrieved party, §5A-23(a1).
Appeal procedures, §5A-24.
Burden of roof.
Proceeding initiated on motion of aggrieved party, §5A-23(a1).
Child support.
Imprisonment for failure to pay, §5A-21(b).
Commencement of proceedings, §5A-23(a).
Criminal contempt finding, §5A-23(g).
Dismissal of order, §5A-23(c).
Failure or refusal to purge contempt within period of imprisonment.
Recommitted to imprisonment, §5A-21(b1).
Failure to comply with order, §5A-21(a).
Findings at conclusion of hearing, §5A-23(e).
Imprisonment, §5A-21(b).
Failure to obey nontestimonial identification order, §5A-21(b1).
Maximum period, §5A-21(b2).
Recommitted for one or more successive periods, §5A-21(b2).
Imprisonment to compel compliance.
Release when civil contempt no longer continues, §5A-22(a).
Procedure for motion of contemnor, §5A-22(b).
Jurisdiction, §5A-23(b).
Motion of aggrieved party.
Initiation of proceeding by, §5A-23(a1).
Noncompliance with order, §5A-21(a).
Nontestimonial identification order.
Imprisonment for failure to obey, §5A-21(b1).
Presenting case for finding of contempt by interested persons, §5A-23(f).
Proceedings for civil contempt, §§5A-23, 5A-25.
Release when civil contempt no longer continues, §5A-22(a).
Procedure for motion of contemnor, §5A-22(b).
Same conduct.
Person held in civil contempt not found in criminal contempt, §5A-21(c).
Superior courts.
Authority of clerk to hold persons in civil contempt, §7A-103.
Authority of clerk to punish in civil contempt, §7A-103.
Trier of fact at show cause hearings, §5A-23(d).
Venue for proceedings, §5A-23(b).
Civil investigative demand.
False claims act.
Failure to comply, §1-614(g).
Civil no-contact orders.
Violations, §50C-10.
Notice that violation punishable as contempt, §50C-5(c).
Workplace violence prevention, §95-269.

CONTEMPT —Cont'd
Commissioner of labor.
Information from employers.
Power to compel giving of information, §95-7.
Statistical report from employers to commissioner.
Refusal as contempt, §95-8.
Courts-martial of national guard.
Power to punish, §127A-56.
Criminal contempt, §§5A-11 to 5A-17.
Appeal procedure, §5A-17.
Authority of court.
Impairing respect due its authority, §5A-11(a).
Child support.
Failure to comply with order.
Punishment, §5A-12(a).
Common law.
Specified grounds for criminal contempt
exclusive, §5A-11(a).
Court proceedings.
Failure to comply with schedules and practices
of court, §5A-11(a).
Interrupting proceedings, §5A-11(a).
Report of proceedings.
Court orders prohibiting publication or
broadcast of reports, §5A-11(c).
Publication of inaccurate reports of court
proceedings, §5A-11(a).
Direct criminal contempt.
Custody of person charged with criminal
contempt, §5A-16(a).
Proceedings required, §5A-13(a).
Summary proceedings for contempt, §5A-14(a).
Direct criminal contempt.
Notice of charges, §5A-14(b).
Notice of charges, §5A-14(b).
What constitutes, §5A-13(a).
Execution of court.
Interference with courts execution, §5A-11(a).
Fines.
Circumstances for fines, §5A-12(a).
Imposition of fine, §5A-12(b).
Reduction or remittance of fine, §5A-12(c).
Immunity of witnesses.
Refusal to testify or produce information,
§5A-11(a).
Imprisonment.
Circumstances for imprisonment, §5A-12(a).
Credit for imprisonment resulting from
contempt, §5A-12(e).
Imposition of imprisonment for criminal
contempt, §5A-12(b).
Reduction of sentence, §5A-12(c).
Indirect criminal contempt.
Proceedings required, §5A-13(b).
Instances enumerated, §5A-11(a).
Jury.
Improper attempt to influence deliberations,
§5A-11(a).
Nontestimonial identification order.
Failure to obey.
Punishment, §5A-12(a).
Officers of court.
Failure to perform official duties, §5A-11(a).
Order in courtroom.
Power of judge to maintain, §15A-1035.
Plenary proceedings for contempt.
Commencement of proceedings, §5A-15(a).
Custody of person charged with criminal
contempt, §5A-16(b).
Dismissal of order, §5A-15(c).

CONTEMPT —Cont'd
Criminal contempt —Cont'd
Plenary proceedings for contempt —Cont'd
Hearings.
Representation of court in hearings for
criminal contempt, §5A-15(g).
Jurisdiction of proceedings, §5A-15(b).
Representation of court in hearings for
contempt, §5A-15(g).
Self-incrimination of witnesses, §5A-15(e).
Show cause hearing.
Trier of facts at hearing, §5A-15(b).
Trier of fact at show cause hearing.
Judge, §5A-15(d).
Venue of proceedings, §5A-15(b).
Verdicts.
Establishing facts beyond reasonable doubt,
§5A-15(f).
Witnesses.
Self-incrimination, §5A-15(e).
Post-release supervision.
Willful refusal to accept or comply with,
§5A-11(a).
Proceedings for civil contempt.
Finding of criminal contempt, §5A-23(g).
Punishment, §5A-12.
Circumstances for fine or imprisonment,
§5A-12(a).
Imposition of fine or imprisonment, §5A-12(b).
Other measures, §5A-12.
Reduction of punishment, §5A-12(c).
Reports of public records banned.
Court orders prohibiting reports, §5A-11(c).
Same conduct.
Person held in criminal contempt not found in
civil contempt, §5A-12(d).
Summary proceedings for contempt.
Direct criminal contempt, §5A-14(a).
Targeted picketing of residence.
Violation of injunction, §14-277.4A(d).
Witnesses.
Immunity of witness.
Refusal to testify or produce information,
§5A-11(a).
Refusal to be sworn or to testify, §5A-11(a).
Delinquent and undisciplined juvenile actions.
Parent's noncompliance with orders, §7B-2706.
Undisciplined juveniles, failure to comply with
disposition order, §7B-2505.
Depositions.
Commissioner may punish for contempt, §8-78.
Use outside state.
Disobeyance of subpoena, §1A-1 Rule 28(d).
Direct criminal contempt, §§5A-13, 5A-14.
Discovery.
Criminal procedure.
Failure to comply with orders, §15A-910(a).
Considerations of court before granting
sanctions, §15A-910(b).
Court findings to justify sanctions,
§15A-910(d).
Presumption of good faith of prosecutors,
§15A-910(c).
Order compelling discovery.
Failure to comply, §1A-1 Rule 37(b).
District court judges.
Power to punish for contempt, §7A-291.
Divorce.
Alimony.
Enforcement of payment by contempt,
§50-16.7(j).

CONTEMPT —Cont'd
Divorce —Cont'd
Order for custody of minor child.
Enforcement, §50-13.3(a).
Domestic violence.
Enforcement of orders, §50B-4.
Evidence, rules of.
Inapplicability, §8C-1 Rule 1101(b).
Executions.
Debtor leaving state or concealing self, §1-355.
Discovery of assets of judgment debtor.
Disobedience of orders of court, §§1-352.1,
1-352.2.
Disobedience of orders, §1-368.
Expedited evictions.
Violation of injunction or preliminary relief,
§42-74.
False claims act.
Civil investigative demand.
Failure to comply, §1-614(g).
Fire investigations.
Failure to comply with summons or subpoena,
§58-79-15.
General assembly.
Committee activity.
Failure to respond to subpoena punishable as
contempt, §120-19.4.
Refusal to testify punishable as contempt,
§120-19.4.
Legislative services commission.
Subpoena and contempt powers, §120-32.4.
Grand jury.
Confidentiality of information.
Unauthorized disclosures, §15A-623(g).
Guardians.
Annual accounts.
Compelling accounting, §35A-1265(a).
Inventory or account required within three
months.
Compelling inventory or account, §35A-1262(a).
Habeas corpus.
Remand of party in custody for contempt, §17-34.
Harmful materials sales to minors.
Disobedience of injunctions, §19-20.
Industrial commission.
Holding persons, firms or corporations in
contempt, §§97-79, 97-80.
Infractions.
Enforcement of sanctions, §15A-1116(a).
**Interrogatories to discover assets of judgment
debtors.**
Disobeyance of order of court, §1-352.1.
Judgments for specific acts, §1A-1 Rule 70.
Judicial sales.
Report or accounting ordered.
Failure to comply, §1-339.12.
Judicial standards commission.
Confidentiality violations, JudStdsComm Rule 6.
Power of commission, JudStdsComm Rule 23.
Punishing for.
Authority of commission, §7A-377(a).
Power of trial court, §7A-377(c).
Juveniles, §§5A-31 to 5A-34.
Age of juvenile, §5A-34(a).
Applicability of provisions, §5A-34(a), (b).
Delinquent and unruly children, nonapplicability
of provisions, §7B-1707.
Direct contempt.
Appeal of order, §5A-32(g).
Conditions for, §5A-31(b).
Copy of orders placed in file by clerk, §5A-32(f).

CONTEMPT —Cont'd
Juveniles —Cont'd
Direct contempt —Cont'd
Oral order for custody and restraint of juvenile,
§5A-32(e).
Order upon finding of contempt, §5A-32(c).
Show cause order and appointment of counsel.
In lieu of summary imposition, §5A-32(b).
Summary imposition of measures by presiding
official, §5A-32(a).
Termination or reduction of sanctions,
§5A-32(d).
District court jurisdiction, §7B-1603.
Enumerated acts constituting contempt,
§5A-31(a).
Indirect contempt, §5A-31(c).
Sanctions, §5A-33.
Lobbying.
Subpoenas enforceable by, §§120C-600(b),
120C-601(b).
Local boards of education.
Power to punish for contempt, §115C-45(a).
Magistrates.
Power of magistrate, §7A-292.
Medical assistance provider false claims.
Failure to comply with civil investigative demand
order, §108A-70.14(j).
Monopolies and restraint of trade.
Lender requiring borrower to deal with particular
insurer.
Disregard of injunction or other court order,
§75-19.
Mortgages and deeds of trust.
Sales under power of sale.
Failure to make report, §45-21.14.
Nontestimonial identification.
Failure to obey order to appear, §15A-276.
Criminal contempt, punishment, §5A-12(a).
Resistance to compliance, §15A-279(e).
Nuisances against public morals.
Temporary order restraining removal of personal
property.
Violations generally, §19-2.3.
Occupational safety and health.
Subpoenas of commissioner of labor, §95-136(b).
Witnesses, §95-135(g).
Ordinances.
Enforcement of ordinance.
Unlawful use of real property, §160A-175(e).
Partition.
Commissioners, §46-9.
Payment into court.
Refusal to obey order, §1-509.
Plenary proceedings for contempt, §§5A-15,
5A-16.
Probation.
Willful refusal by defendant to comply with
conditions, §5A-11(a).
Willful violation of condition, §15A-1344(e1).
Receivers.
Corporations.
Refusal to answer, §1-507.5.
Referees.
Power to punish for contempt, §1A-1 Rule 53(e).
Rules of evidence.
Inapplicability, §8C-1 Rule 1101(b).
Sales and use tax.
Examination of records by secretary or agent.
Refusal to permit examination, §105-164.30.
Savings and loan associations.
Subpoenas, §54B-60(c).

CONTEMPT —Cont'd
Savings and loan associations —Cont'd
Witnesses, §54B-60(c).
Savings banks.
Subpoenas issued by administrator, §54C-57(c).
Securities regulation.
Subpoenas.
Refusal to obey, §78A-46(c).
Special proceedings.
Failure of commissioner of sale to account, §1-406.
Subpoenas.
Failure to comply, §1A-1 Rule 45(e).
Unemployment compensation, §96-4(m).
Superior court clerks' authority, §7A-103.
Supplemental proceedings.
Disobedience of orders, §1-368.
Targeted picketing of residence.
Violation of injunction, §14-277.4A(d).
Unemployment compensation.
Failure to comply with subpoena, §96-4(m).
Utilities commission.
Power to punish for contempt, §62-61.
Wills.
Probate of wills.
Failure to answer summons of clerk, §28A-2A-4.
Workplace violence prevention.
Civil no-contact orders.
Violation, §95-269.

CONTESTS.
Alcoholic beverage advertising, §18B-105(b).
Athletic contests.
See ATHLETICS.
Contested special proceedings.
Commencement, §1-394.
Complaint or petition.
Commencement of proceedings generally,
§1-394.
Filing.
Time for, §1-396.
Enlargement of time, §1-398.
Summons, §1-394.
Return, §1-395.
Elections.
Executive branch.
Joint ballot of both houses of general assembly.
General assembly to determine, NC Const Art
VI §5.
Executors and administrators.
Right to contest appointment, §28A-6-4.
Wills.
Caveat to will, §§31-32 to 31-37.1.

CONTINGENCY AND EMERGENCY FUND.
Budget of state, §143C-4-4.

**CONTINGENT FEES AND CONTINGENT FEE
AGREEMENTS.**
Attorneys, ProfCond Rule 1.5.
Lobbyists.
Prohibition, §120C-300.

**CONTINGENT INTEREST IN REAL OR
PERSONAL ESTATE.**
Property passed by will, §31-40.

CONTINGENT REMAINDERS.
Validation of transfer, §41-12.

CONTINUANCES, §1A-1 Rule 40(b).
**Abused, neglected or dependent juvenile
actions.**
Adjudicatory hearing, §7B-803.
Nonsecure custody hearings, §7B-506(a).

CONTINUANCES —Cont'd
**Abused, neglected or dependent juvenile
actions** —Cont'd
Periodic review hearings, placement of juvenile.
Termination of parental rights, §7B-908(b).
Amendments not conforming to evidence,
§1A-1 Rule 15(b).
Attorney disciplinary proceedings.
Formal hearings, Bar Rule B.0114.
Criminal law and procedure.
Entry of PJC not considered entry of judgment,
§15A-101.
Factors in superior or district court, §15A-952(g).
Delinquent and undisciplined juvenile actions.
Adjudicatory hearing, §7B-2406.
Detainers, §15-10.2(a).
District courts.
Rules of practice and procedure, SuperCt Rule 3.
Eminent domain.
Public condemnors.
Power of judge, §40A-50.
Expedited evictions.
Procedure and standards for continuances, §42-68.
Insurance.
Supervision, rehabilitation and liquidation of
insurers.
Delinquency proceedings, §58-30-50.
Judge comment on verdict, §1A-1 Rule 51(c).
Motor vehicles.
Convictions.
Third PJC filed in five-year period as conviction,
§20-4.01.
Record of PJC's, §20-26(a).
Prisons and prisoners.
Discharge of insolvent prisoner, §23-35.
Small claims actions, §7A-214.
Superior courts.
Criminal law and procedure, §15A-952(g).
Rules of practice and procedure, SuperCt Rule 3.
Support of illegitimate children.
Surety of person accused of being father, §49-5.
Termination of parental rights.
Adjudicatory hearing, §7B-1109(d).
Placement review hearing, §7B-908(b).
Unemployment compensation appeals.
Claims for benefits, §96-15(d1).

**CONTINUING CARE RETIREMENT
COMMUNITIES,** §§58-64-1 to 58-64-85.
Additional beds for facility.
Commissioner appointed as receiver, §58-64-46.
Books and papers.
Failure to exhibit or making false statements,
§58-2-200.
Cease and desist orders, §58-64-10(c).
Commissioner.
Cease and desist orders, §58-64-10(c).
Examination of books and records, §58-64-55.
Investigations.
Generally, §58-64-50.
Rehabilitation or liquidation.
Generally, §58-64-45.
Rules and regulations, §58-64-65.
Committee, §58-64-80.
Condominiums.
Applicability of article, §58-64-85(b).
Continuing care services without lodging,
§58-64-7.
Application to administer home care services,
§58-64-7(a).
Binding written service agreements, §58-64-7(b).

CONTINUING CARE RETIREMENT COMMUNITIES —Cont'd

Continuing care services without lodging —Cont'd
Financial accounting requirements, §58-64-7(c).

Contracts.
Continuing care services without lodging, §58-64-7.
Disclosure statements.
Copy of standard form of contract for continuing care.
Attachment to disclosure statement, §58-64-20(c).
Provisions of contract for continuing care, §58-64-25(a), (b).

Contracts as preferred claims on liquidation, §58-64-60.

Definitions, §58-64-1.
Applicability of certain definitions, §58-64-45(b).

Department of health and human services.
Authority, §58-64-85(a).

Disclosure statements.
Amendment for disclosure to proposed residents, §58-64-20(f).
Annual revised disclosure statement, §58-64-30(a).
Filing fee, §58-64-30(b).
Civil liability for violations, §58-64-70(a), (b).
Limitation of actions, §58-64-70(d).
Offer of refund.
Effect, §58-64-70(c).
Contents, §58-64-20(a).
Cover page, §58-64-20(b).
Continuing care services without lodging.
Financial accounting and reports, §58-64-7(c).
Contracts for continuing care.
Copy of standard form to be attached, §58-64-20(c).
Language requirements, §58-64-20(e).
Standardized format.
Commissioner may prescribe, §58-64-20(d).

Escrow account, §58-64-35(a).
Release of funds, §58-64-35(b) to (d).

Fees.
Disclosure statements.
Annual revised disclosure statement.
Filing fee, §58-64-30(b).
Entrance fee.
Defined, §58-64-1.
Return of entrance fee held in escrow, §58-64-35(d).
Licenses.
Application fee, §58-64-5(b).
Nursing beds and adult care home beds.
Licensure fees, §131E-138.1.

Financial statements, §58-64-55.

Financing health care facilities generally, §§131A-1 to 131A-25.
See HEALTH CARE FACILITY FINANCING.

Home care services.
Continuing care services without lodging.
Application to administer, §58-64-7(a).
Binding written service agreements, §58-64-7(b).
Financial accounting requirements, §58-64-7(c).

Investigations, §58-64-50(a).
Powers of commissioner, §58-64-50(b), (c).

Licenses.
Actuarial report, §58-64-5(g).
Applications, §58-64-5(b).
Correction of application, §58-64-5(d).
Notice of filing, §58-64-5(c).

CONTINUING CARE RETIREMENT COMMUNITIES —Cont'd

Licenses —Cont'd
Criminal convictions.
Suspension of license, §58-2-60(b).
Fees.
Application fee, §58-64-5(b).
Information to be provided by licensees, §58-64-5(f).
Monetary penalty for violations, §58-2-70(c), (d).
Other licensing or regulation, §58-64-85.
Required, §58-64-5(a).
Restitution for violations, §58-2-70(e) to (g).
Revocation.
Findings of fact, §58-64-10(a).
Statement of underlying facts supporting, §58-64-10(b).
Notice and hearings, §58-2-70(b).
Surrender, §58-2-65.
Suspension.
Applicable provisions, §58-2-70(h).
Criminal conviction, §58-2-60(b).
Notice and hearing, §58-2-70(b).
Transfer.
Prohibited, §58-64-15.

Limitation of actions.
Disclosure statements.
Civil liability for violations, §58-64-70(d).

Liquidation of facilities.
Application for order authorizing, §58-64-45(a), (f).
Preferred claims on.
Contracts as to, §58-64-60.
Refusal or vacation of orders, §58-64-45(g).

Marketing by unlicensed providers, §58-64-5(a).

Operating reserves, §58-64-33(a) to (c).

Orders.
Rehabilitation or liquidation, §58-64-45.

Penalties.
Criminal penalties for violations, §58-64-75.
Marketing, unlicensed providers, §58-64-5(a).

Receivership.
Additional beds for facility, §58-64-46.

Records.
Examination of books and records.
Powers of commissioner, §58-64-55.

Rehabilitation of facilities.
Application for order authorizing, §58-64-45(a), (f).
Refusal or vacation of orders, §58-64-45(g).
Termination of order, §58-64-45(c).

Reserves.
Operating reserves, §58-64-33(a) to (c).

Residents.
Defined, §58-64-1.
Meetings with residents.
Governing body to hold, §58-64-40(b).
Organization.
Right to organization, §58-64-40(a).

Rules and regulations.
Definition and description of "insolvency" and "hazardous financial condition,"§58-64-45(b).
Promulgation by commissioner, §58-64-65(a).
Time to comply with rules, §58-64-65(b).

Sale or transfer of ownership.
Approval by commissioner, §58-64-15.

Subpoenas.
Powers of commissioner, §58-64-50(c).

Supervision proceedings.
Commencement, §58-64-45(a).

CONTINUING CRIMINAL ENTERPRISE.
Defined, §14-7.20(c).

CONTINUING CRIMINAL ENTERPRISE —Cont'd
Forfeiture of profits, §14-7.20(b).
Punishment, §14-7.20(a).

CONTINUING EDUCATION.
Acupuncture, §90-457.1.
Athletic trainers.
Continuing education, §90-533(a) to (c).
Attorneys.
See CONTINUING LEGAL EDUCATION.
Auctions and auction years.
License renewal, §85B-4(e1).
Certified public accountants, §93-12.
Code enforcement officials.
Certification.
Professional development program, §143-151.13A.
Cosmetic art.
Inactive status.
Removal from list, §88B-21(h).
Teachers, §88B-21(e).
Dental hygienists, §90-225.1.
Dentists, §90-31.1.
Limited volunteer dental licenses.
Compliance required, §90-37.1(f).
Diagnostic imaging technicians, §90-143.2(a).
Election officials, §163-82.24(a).
Certification, §163-82.24(b).
Electrical contractors, §87-44.1.
Electrologists, §88A-13.
Engineers.
Sponsors of continuing professional competency activities, §89C-10(h).
Environmental health specialists, §90A-63.
Foresters.
Registration renewal, §89B-11(b).
Funeral directors, §90-210.25.
General contractors.
Designation of builders.
Equivalent education, designation according to, §87-15.4(b).
Home inspectors, §143-151.64.
Insurance adjusters, agents and brokers, §§58-33-130, 58-33-135.
Public adjusters, §58-33A-55.
Insurance instructors, §58-33-132.
Irrigation contractors, §89G-9(b).
Judges.
Accreditations.
Sponsors, CJE Rule III.
Applicability of rules, CJE Rule I.
Attendance, CJE Rule II.
Credit hours, CJE Rule II.
Delinquency.
Notice, CJE Rule IV.
Exemptions, CJE Rule V.
Expenses, CJE Rule VI.
Hours required, CJE Rule II.
Reports.
Active members.
Annual report, CJE Rule IV.
Scope of rules, CJE Rule I.
Sponsors.
Accreditation, CJE Rule III.
Laser hair practitioners, §88A-13(d).
Manufactured home manufacturers, dealers, salespersons or set-up contractors.
Licensure, §143-143.11B.
Massage and bodywork therapy, §90-632(b), (c).

CONTINUING EDUCATION —Cont'd
Mortgage bankers, brokers and servicers.
Mortgage loan originator license, §53-244.102.
Nurses, §90-171.42(a), (b).
Local health directors.
Nurse pilot program, §130A-40.1(c).
Nursing home administrators, §90-286.
Occupational therapists, §90-270.75.
Optometrists, §90-123.1.
Paralegals.
State bar, Bar Rule G.0200.
Pastoral counselors, §90-389.
Pharmacists, §90-85.18.
Podiatrists, §90-202.11.
Private protective services, §74C-22.
Real estate appraisers, §93E-1-7(b).
Fee for course sponsors, §93E-1-7(1).
Minimum standards, §93E-1-8(c).
Waiver of fee, §93E-1-7(b2).
Real estate brokers, §93A-4.1.
Recreational therapists, §90C-29.
Social workers, §90B-9.
Substance abuse professionals.
Renewal of credentials, §90-113.37A(b).
Veterinarians, §90-186.
Wastewater systems.
Certification of contractors and inspectors, §90A-79.
Well contractors, §87-98.12(a), (b).

CONTINUING LEGAL EDUCATION.
Accredited sponsors.
Application requirements, CLE Reg 3.
Agency appeals, CLE Reg 10.
Attendee's fees.
Computation, CLE Reg 6.
Authority for agency appeals, CLE Reg 10.
Bankruptcy law specialty, Bar Rules D.2205, D.2206.
Bar review/refresher course, CLE Reg 2.
Board.
Appointment of members, Bar Rule D.1506.
Chair, Bar Rule D.1510.
Committees, Bar Rule D.1601.
Defined, Bar Rule D.1601.
Duties, Bar Rule D.1516.
Executive committee, Bar Rule D.1601.
Jurisdiction, Bar Rule D.1502.
Lay participation, Bar Rule D.1505.
Meetings, Bar Rule D.1514.
Operation or responsibility, Bar Rule D.1503.
Organization, CLE Reg 9.
Powers, Bar Rule D.1516.
Quorum, Bar Rule D.1601.
Referral of matters to board by grievance committee, Bar Rule B.0112.
Removal of members, Bar Rule D.1506.
Reports, Bar Rule D.1515.
Size, Bar Rule D.1504.
Succession in office, Bar Rule D.1509.
Term of members, Bar Rule D.1507.
Staggered terms, Bar Rule D.1508.
Vice-chairperson, Bar Rule D.1511.
Compliance procedures, CLE Reg 8.
Course requirements.
Accreditation of audiovisual programs, CLE Reg 4.
Generally, CLE Reg 2.
Credit hours.
Computation, CLE Reg 5.

CONTINUING LEGAL EDUCATION —Cont'd
Criminal law specialty, Bar Rules D.2505, D.2506.
Estate planning and probate law specialty, Bar Rules D.2305, D.2306.
Family law specialty, Bar Rules D.2405, D.2406.
Fees.
Attendee's fees.
Computation, CLE Reg 6.
Reinstatement fee, CLE Reg 9.
Review of fees, CLE Reg 6.
Sponsors.
Computation, CLE Reg 6.
Uniform application, CLE Reg 6.
Immigration law specialty.
Applicability of other requirements, Bar Rule D.2607.
Applicability of provisions.
North Carolina plan of legal specialization, Bar Rule D.2604.
Definition, Bar Rule D.2602.
Establishment, Bar Rule D.2601.
Recognition as specialist, Bar Rule D.2603.
Standards for certification, Bar Rule D.2605.
Standards for continued certification, Bar Rule D.2606.
In-house continuing education.
General course approval, CLE Reg 2.
Law school courses, CLE Reg 2.
Noncompliance procedures, CLE Reg 9.
Procedures.
Compliance, CLE Reg 8.
Noncompliance, CLE Reg 9.
Review of board decision, CLE Reg 10.
Real property law specialty, Bar Rules D.2105, D.2106.
Regulations governing administration of program, Bar Rules D.1601 to D.1610.
Rules concerning administration of program, Bar Rules D.1501 to D.1527.
Scope and exemptions.
Special exemptions, CLE Reg 7.
Simultaneous broadcast, prerecorded material and computer-based CLE, Bar Rule D.1604.
Special cases, CLE Reg 7.
Specialization certification, rules governing accreditation, Bar Rules D.1901 to D.1908.
Sponsors.
Accreditation.
Application requirements, CLE Reg 3.
Video and audiovisual program accreditation, CLE Reg 4.

CONTINUOUS ALCOHOL MONITORING.
Impaired driving.
Condition of probation.
Defendants subjection to level one or two punishments, §20-179(h1), (h3).
Order to abstain from alcohol consumption.
Condition of pretrial release, §15A-534(i).
Regulations for continuous alcohol monitoring systems.
Division of adult correction, §15A-1343.3.

CONTRABAND.
Cigarettes.
Non-tax-paid cigarettes, §105-113.32.
Packages violate certain label requirements, §14-401.18(c).
Credit cards and devices.
Devices for theft, §14-113.5.

CONTRABAND —Cont'd
Credit cards and devices —Cont'd
Making, possessing or transferring device for theft, §14-113.5.
Unlawful telecommunications devices, §14-113.5(b).
Fire-safety standard and firefighter protection act.
Noncomplying cigarettes, §58-92-30(e).
Litter disposal vehicles or machines, §14-399(g).
Motion to suppress evidence.
Contraband not subject to motion, §15A-979.
Obscenity.
Dissemination of obscene materials, §14-190.1(h).
Searches and seizures, §15A-242.
Telecommunications devices, §14-113.5(b).
Trademarks.
Counterfeit trademarks, §80-11.1(d).

CONTRACEPTIVES.
Health benefit plan coverage.
Prescription contraceptive drugs and devices and outpatient contraceptive services, §58-3-178.
Small employer group health coverage.
Contraceptive drugs and devices, §58-50-155(a).

CONTRACT KILLER SENTENCING, §15A-1340.16.

CONTRACT MOTOR CARRIERS.
Defined, §62-3.

CONTRACTORS.
Architect exemption, §83A-13(b).
Child support enforcement.
Forfeiture of licensing privilege, §50-13.12.
Definitions.
Electrical contracting, §87-43.
Electrical contractors, §87-41.1.
General contractors, §87-1(a).
Exceptions, §87-1(b).
Homeowners recovery fund, §87-15.5.
Plumbing, heating and fire sprinkler contractors, §87-21(a).
Refrigeration contractors, §87-58(a), (b).
Subcontractors.
Payments to subcontractors, §22C-1.
Disabled persons.
Public building contracts.
Cooperation in promoting use of physically handicapped contractors, §143-135.5.
Disadvantaged businesses.
Transportation contracts.
Participation, §136-28.4.
Electrical contractors, §§87-39 to 87-51.
See ELECTRICAL CONTRACTORS.
Fraud.
Improvements to real property.
Furnishing false statements, §44A-24.
Furnishing false statements in connection with improvements, §44A-24.
General contractors, §§87-1 to 87-15.4.
See GENERAL CONTRACTORS.
Homeowners recovery fund, §§87-15.5 to 87-15.9.
Improvements to real property.
Provisions making contract subject to laws of another state, §22B-2.
Indemnity agreements against public policy, §22B-1.
Interest.
Subcontractors.
Payments to subcontractors.
Late payments, §22C-5.

CONTRACTORS —Cont'd
Irrigation contractors, §§89G-1 to 89G-13.
　　See IRRIGATION CONTRACTORS.
Landscape contractors, §§89D-1 to 89D-10.
　　See LANDSCAPE CONTRACTORS.
License forfeiture for felony convictions,
　　§15A-1331A.
Liens.
　　See MECHANICS' AND MATERIALMEN'S
　　　　LIENS.
Limitation of actions.
　　Real property improvements.
　　　　Recovery of damages for defective or unsafe
　　　　　　conditions.
　　　　　　Six-year limitation, §1-50(a).
　　Subcontractors.
　　　　Real property improvements.
　　　　　　Recovery of damages for defective or unsafe
　　　　　　　　conditions.
　　　　　　　　Six-year limitation, §1-50(a).
Mechanics' and materialmen's liens.
　　See MECHANICS' AND MATERIALMEN'S
　　　　LIENS.
Minorities.
　　Public building contracts.
　　　　Cooperation in promoting use of minority
　　　　　　contractors, §143-135.5.
　　Transportation contracts.
　　　　Disadvantaged businesses, participation,
　　　　　　§136-28.4.
Payment and performance bonds generally,
　　§§44A-25 to 44A-35.
　　See PAYMENT AND PERFORMANCE BONDS.
Plumbing, heating and fire sprinkler
　　contractors, §§87-16 to 87-27.1.
　　See PLUMBING, HEATING AND FIRE
　　　　SPRINKLER CONTRACTORS.
Privilege taxes.
　　Datacenter machinery and equipment.
　　　　Contractors or subcontractors,
　　　　　　§105-187.51C(a3).
Property taxes.
　　Defined, §105-273.
　　Inventories owned by contractors.
　　　　Exemptions, §105-275.
Public policy.
　　Construction indemnity agreements invalid,
　　　　§22B-1.
　　Improvements to real property contracts.
　　　　Provisions making contract subject to laws of
　　　　　　another state, §22B-2.
Public works, §§133-23 to 133-33.
　　See PUBLIC WORKS CONTRACTORS.
Refrigeration contractors, §§87-52 to 87-64.1.
　　See REFRIGERATION CONTRACTORS.
Small business contractors, §§143B-472.100 to
　　143B-472.112.
　　See SMALL BUSINESS CONTRACTORS.
Small contractors.
　　Public building contracts.
　　　　Cooperation in promoting use, §143-135.5.
Steam or gas fitters.
　　Licenses.
　　　　Revocation or suspension.
　　　　　　Felony convictions, §15A-1331A.
Subcontractors.
　　Limitation of actions.
　　　　Real property improvements.
　　　　　　Recovery of damages for defective or unsafe
　　　　　　　　conditions.
　　　　　　　　Six-year limitation, §1-50(a).

CONTRACTORS —Cont'd
Subcontractors —Cont'd
　　Payments to subcontractors.
　　　　Applicability of provisions, §22C-6.
　　　　Conditions of payment, §22C-4.
　　　　Definitions, §22C-1.
　　　　Entitlement to payment.
　　　　　　Performance by subcontractor, §22C-2.
　　　　Interest.
　　　　　　Late payments, §22C-5.
　　　　Late payments.
　　　　　　Interest, §22C-5.
　　　　Performance by subcontractor.
　　　　　　Effect, §§22C-2, 22C-3.
　　　　Scope of provisions, §22C-6.
　　　　Time for, §22C-3.
　　　　Withholding by contractor, §22C-4.
　　Prompt payment.
　　　　Public building contracts, §143-134.1(a), (b).
　　Workers' compensation.
　　　　Certificate that subcontractor has complied with
　　　　　　law, §97-19.
Transportation contracts.
　　Disadvantaged businesses, participation,
　　　　§136-28.4.
Wastewater system contractors and inspectors.
　　Certification, §§90A-70 to 90A-81.
　　See WASTEWATER SYSTEMS.
Women.
　　Public building contracts.
　　　　Cooperation in promoting use of women
　　　　　　contractors, §143-135.5.
　　Transportation contracts.
　　　　Disadvantaged businesses, participation,
　　　　　　§136-28.4.
Workers' compensation, §97-19.

CONTRACTS.
Abandoned manufactured homes.
　　Management and disposal.
　　　　County authority, §130A-309.113(b).
Abandoned property.
　　Agreement by owner to locate, deliver or recover,
　　　　§116B-78.
Accident and health insurance.
　　Group insurance.
　　　　Contracts to cover treatment, §58-51-50(b).
Accounts and accounting.
　　Itemized and verified accounts.
　　　　Evidence, §8-45.
Administrative office of the courts.
　　Assistant clerks.
　　　　Local government funding, §7A-102(g).
　　Deputy clerks.
　　　　Local government funding, §7A-102(g).
　　Judicial secretaries.
　　　　Local government funding, §7A-44.1(d).
　　Reports.
　　　　Local government services contracts,
　　　　　　§7A-346.2(a).
Adopt-a-highway participants.
　　Use of contract services to clean roadside,
　　　　§136-140.1(b).
Advisory budget commission.
　　Financial interest of officers, §143-63.
　　Purchases exempted, §§143-56, 143-57.
　　Rules covering certain purposes, §143-60.
Aeronautics.
　　Jurisdiction, §63-17.
Against public policy.
　　Construction indemnity agreements, §22B-1.

CONTRACTS —Cont'd
Against public policy —Cont'd
Forum selection provisions, §22B-3.
Improving real property.
Provisions making contract subject to laws of
another state, §22B-2.
Waiving jury trial, §22B-10.
Agricultural finance authority.
Experts and consultants.
Employment on contractual basis, §122D-5(d).
Power to contract, §122D-6.
Airport construction, repair, etc., §63-73.
Alarm system businesses.
Unlicensed or unregistered persons.
Sale, installation or service of alarm system.
Contract void, §§74D-11(f), 74D-14.
Alcoholic beverages.
Local ABC officers.
Contracts with other agencies.
Alternative to hiring local officers,
§18B-501(f).
State warehouse.
Contracting for private warehouses,
§18B-204(a).
Aliens.
Real property.
Validation of contracts to purchase or sell real
property, §64-2.
Animal waste management system operators.
Reports, §90A-47.2(b).
Annexation initiated by municipality.
Rural fire department providing fire protection,
§160A-58.57.
Solid waste collection.
Contract with private firms, §160A-58.59.
Annuities generally.
See ANNUITIES.
Antenuptial agreements, §§52B-1 to 52B-11.
See PREMARITAL AGREEMENTS.
Artistic and creative services contracts.
Minors, §§48A-11 to 48A-18.
Assignments.
Secured transactions.
Inapplicability of article 9.
Payment right assigned to one obligated to
perform under contract, §25-9-109(d).
Athlete agents.
Agency contracts generally, §§78C-85 to 78C-105.
See ATHLETE AGENTS.
Attorney general.
Review of contracts exceeding one million dollars,
§114-8.3(a).
Board for licensing of geologists.
Contracts for supplies, materials, printing,
equipment, contractual services,
§89E-5(e).
Building codes.
Contracting for examination to certify code
enforcement officials, §143-151.16(d).
Correction department.
Public contracts, §143-134(b).
Global transpark authority.
Contracts for supplies, materials, printing,
equipment, §63A-24.
Medicaid.
Contracts generally, §108A-55(b).
Purchases and contracts through department
of administration, §143-48.1(c).
North Carolina center for applied textile
technology at Gaston College, §115D-67.4.

CONTRACTS —Cont'd
Attorney general —Cont'd
Review of contracts exceeding one million dollars
—Cont'd
Purchases through department of
administration.
Generally, §143-52.2.
Medicaid, §143-48.1(c).
Soil scientists board of licensing, §89F-5(d).
State bar.
Council contracts, §84-23(d).
Transportation department.
Public contracts, §143-134(b).
Research and experimental work,
§136-28.1(h).
Trust companies.
Conservatorship, §53-401.
Foreign offices.
Agreements with bank supervisory
agencies, §53-326(d).
Out-of-state institutions.
Agreements with bank supervisory
agencies, §53-320(d).
Seizure by commissioner.
Employment of professionals, §53-391.
Turnpike authority.
Public contracting provisions, §136-89.194(g).
Attorneys at law.
Appearances.
Employment contract.
Filing or producing if requested, §84-11.
Contingent fee agreements, ProfCond Rule 1.5.
Restriction on practice, ProfCond Rule 5.6.
Attorneys' fees.
Reciprocal fees in business contracts.
Amount of fees permissible, §6-21.7(b), (f).
Consumer contracts, effect of provisions,
§6-21.7(e).
Definitions, §6-21.7(a).
Determination of reasonable fees, §6-21.7(c).
Nonapplicability of certain presumptions or
amounts awarded in other cases,
§6-21.7(d).
Insurance contracts, effect of provisions,
§6-21.7(g).
Nonapplicability of certain presumptions or
amounts awarded in other cases, §6-21.7(d).
Sales contracts, effect of provisions, §6-21.7(e).
Validity of contract provisions, §6-21.7(b).
**Automatic renewal clauses in consumer
contracts, §75-41.**
Bank reopening and closing.
Effect upon certain contracts, §53-38.
Bond for title.
Contracts for deed, §§47H-1 to 47H-8.
See CONTRACTS FOR DEED.
Book accounts.
Documentary evidence of book accounts under
$60.00, §8-42.
Boxing, requirements, §143-656.
Charitable solicitation.
Contracts between solicitor and charitable
organization or sponsor, §131F-16(g).
Fundraising consultants, §131F-15(d).
Children and minors.
Age of majority, §48A-2.
Artistic and creative services and talent agency
contracts, §§48A-11 to 48A-18.
Applicability of article, §48A-11.
Artistic or creative services defined, §48A-11.

CONTRACTS —Cont'd
Children and minors —Cont'd
Artistic and creative services and talent agency
contracts —Cont'd
Disaffirmance during minority prohibited.
Contract approved by superior court,
§48A-12(a).
Documents to be provided to other party,
§48A-13.
Earnings set aside in trust.
Contracts approved by court.
Change in facts, notice, §48A-14(h).
Continuing jurisdiction over trust
established, §48A-14(g).
Deposit or disbursement of funds by
employer, §48A-14(d) to (f).
Percentage required to be set aside,
§48A-14(a).
Trustee, appointment, §48A-14(b).
Trustee's statement, providing employer,
§48A-14(c).
Contracts not approved by court.
Amendment or termination, §48A-15(e).
Change in facts, notice, §48A-15(f).
Deposit or disbursement by employer,
§48A-15(c), (d).
Fiduciary relationship, parent or guardian,
§48A-15(g).
Gross earnings defined, §48A-15(h).
Percentage of earning set aside, §48A-15(a).
Trustee, appointment, §48A-15(b).
Establishment of trust, §48A-16(a).
Financial institutions, establishing with,
§48A-16(d).
Methods of handling by trustee, §48A-16(e).
Withdrawals, restrictions, §48A-16(b).
Written statement by trustee, §48A-16(c).
Guardian ad litem during proceeding,
§48A-12(d).
Superior court approval of contracts, §48A-12(a)
to (d).
Talent agency contracts, §48A-18.
Deposit accounts.
Banks operating in name of minor, §53-43.5(a).
Emancipation of juvenile.
Right to contract as adult, §7B-3507.
Safe deposit boxes.
Banks leasing or renting to minors, §53-43.5(b),
(c).
Commercial code.
Leases, §§25-2A-101 to 25-2A-532.
See LEASES, UCC.
Secured transactions.
General provisions, §§25-9-101 to 25-9-710.
See SECURED TRANSACTIONS.
Community-based corrections programs.
Service providers, §143B-1156(a).
Service providers.
Substance abuse treatment services,
§143B-1156(b).
Condominiums.
Conveyance or encumbrance of common elements,
§47C-3-112(c).
Constitution of North Carolina.
State, political subdivisions or public corporations
may make contracts, NC Const Art V §2.
Constitution of the United States.
Impairment of obligations of contracts, US Const
Art I §10.
Construction and interpretation.
Power of court to construe when declaratory
judgment preceding, §1-254.

CONTRACTS —Cont'd
Continuity of contracts.
European monetary union, §§53-295 to 53-300.
See EUROPEAN MONETARY UNION.
**Cooperative agreements among physicians or
between physician, hospital or others.**
Contract law to govern disputes among parties,
§90-21.36(c).
County water and sewer districts.
Validation of certain contracts, §162A-94.
**Criminal justice education and training
standards.**
Power of commission to enter into contracts,
§17C-6.
Custodial trusts.
Liability to third persons, §33B-12.
Deed.
Contracts for deed, §§47H-1 to 47H-8.
See CONTRACTS FOR DEED.
Department of administration.
Purchases and contracts through department.
Bids and bidding.
Competitive bidding procedure, §143-52.
Setting of benchmarks, §§143-53.1,
143-53.1(a).
Use of American Recovery and Reinvestment
Act funds, §143-53.1(b).
**Diversion contract with delinquent or
undisciplined juvenile and parent,
guardian or custodian, §7B-1706.**
Electronic transactions.
General provisions, §§66-311 to 66-330.
See ELECTRONIC TRANSACTIONS.
Emancipation of juvenile.
Right to contract as adult, §7B-3507.
Energy conservation finance act.
Financing contract.
See ENERGY CONSERVATION FINANCE
ACT.
Executors and administrators.
Sale of real property.
Death of vendor under contract.
Delivery of deed by executor, §28A-17-9.
Facility authorities.
Conflicts of interest.
Disclosure to authority, §160A-480.3(g).
Construction contracts, §160A-480.6.
Investment of bonds, §160A-480.8(k).
Powers of authority, §160A-480.4.
False pretenses and cheats.
Advance payments under promise to work and
pay for same, §14-104.
Nonfulfillment of contract obligation, §14-100.
Financing contract indebtedness.
State capital facilities finance act.
Special indebtedness generally, §§142-80 to
142-101.
See CAPITAL FACILITIES FINANCE ACT.
Funeral contracts.
Preneed funeral contracts and funds generally,
§§90-210.60 to 90-210.73.
See PRENEED FUNERAL CONTRACTS AND
FUNDS.
Futures contracts, §§16-3 to 16-6.
Gaming and betting contracts, §§16-1, 16-2.
**Guardian ad litem appointed for unborn
persons.**
In rem and quasi in rem actions involving
construction of contracts, §1A-1 Rule 17(b).
**Guardian's powers in administering
incompetent's estate, §35A-1251.**

CONTRACTS —Cont'd
Health and human services department.
Nursing home medication error quality initiative.
Public or private contracting entities,
§131E-128.5(a), (b).
Health benefit plans.
Contracts between plans and health care
providers, §§58-50-270 to 58-50-290.
Husband and wife.
Antenuptial agreements, §§52B-1 to 52B-11.
See PREMARITAL AGREEMENTS.
Validation of contract executed by married women
without private examination.
Contracts executed prior to Feb. 7, 1945,
§39-13.1(b).
Contracts executed since Nov. 7, 1944,
§39-13.1(a).
**Improvement to real property defective or
unsafe.**
Limitation of action for breach of contract,
§1-50(a).
**Industrial commission managed care
organizations,** ICManagedCare Rule VI.
Installment land contract.
Contracts for deed, §§47H-1 to 47H-8.
See CONTRACTS FOR DEED.
Insurance adjusters.
Public adjusters.
Between adjuster and insured, §58-33A-65.
Ministerial duties relating to licensing.
Contract with nongovernmental entities to
perform, §58-33A-40(i).
Insurance policies or contracts.
Accident and health insurance.
See HEALTH INSURANCE.
Credit insurance.
See CREDIT INSURANCE.
Fire insurance.
See FIRE INSURANCE.
Generally.
See INSURANCE POLICIES OR CONTRACTS.
Life insurance.
See LIFE INSURANCE.
Medicare, §58-54-10.
Motor vehicle insurance.
See MOTOR VEHICLE INSURANCE.
Property insurance.
See PROPERTY INSURANCE.
Interests.
Rates and fees, §24-1.1.
International commercial arbitration.
Severability of arbitration laws, §1-567.46(a).
Joint contracts of partners in trade or others.
Persons jointly liable, §1-72.
Judicial department.
Supplementation of salaries for department
employees.
Contracting with city or county for local funds,
§7A-300.1(a).
Land contract.
Contracts for deed, §§47H-1 to 47H-8.
See CONTRACTS FOR DEED.
Leases.
Option to purchase contracts executed with
residential lease agreements, §§47G-1 to
47G-7.
Residential rental agreements, §§42-38 to 42-46.
See LANDLORD AND TENANT.
Leases, UCC, §§25-2A-101 to 25-2A-532.
See LEASES, UCC.

CONTRACTS —Cont'd
Letters of credit.
Issuer not responsible for underlying contracts,
§25-5-108(f).
Rights and obligations independent of underlying
contract, §25-5-103(d).
Location and recovery of abandoned property.
Agreement by owner, §116B-78.
Lotteries.
State lottery.
Lottery game retailers, §§18C-140, 18C-141(c).
Manufactured homes.
Management and disposal of abandoned homes.
County authority, §130A-309.113(b).
Marriage settlements and other contracts.
Proof, acknowledgment, registration, §47-25.
Mechanical breakdown service agreements,
§66-374.
Medicaid.
Attorney general review of contracts exceeding
one million dollars, §108A-55(b).
Audit of contractor records, standard provision to
be included in contract, §108A-55(b).
Mid-Currituck bridge project.
Contracting for accelerated and cost-effective
completion, §136-89.183A(b).
Missing persons.
Receivers.
Operation and management of business, §28C-8.
Money transmitters.
Delegates, §53-208.19.
Motor vehicle dealers.
Captive finance sources.
Prohibited contractual requirements,
§20-308.15.
**Motor vehicle registration, registration plates
and certificates of title.**
Division contracts, §20-63(h), (h1).
Municipalities.
See MUNICIPALITIES.
Municipal service districts.
Provision of services, etc., §160A-536(d).
New or continuing contract.
Running of statute of limitations.
Writing required, §1-26.
**North Carolina center for applied textile
technology at Gaston College.**
Contracts exceeding one million dollars.
Review by attorney general, §115D-67.4.
**Option to purchase contracts executed with
residential lease agreements,** §§47G-1 to
47G-7.
Planned community act.
Tort and contract liability.
Association and lot owners, §47F-3-111.
Postal history commission.
Contracting authority, §143-676(b).
Premarital agreements generally, §§52B-1 to
52B-11.
See PREMARITAL AGREEMENTS.
Preneed funeral contracts and funds,
§§90-210.60 to 90-210.73.
See PRENEED FUNERAL CONTRACTS AND
FUNDS.
Principals of schools.
Method of employment generally, §115C-287.1.
Prisons and prisoners.
See PRISONS AND PRISONERS.
Private personnel services.
Commission-based compensation.
Anticipated earnings included in written job
order, §95-47.4(h).

CONTRACTS —Cont'd
Private personnel services —Cont'd
Defined, §95-47.1.
Filing of copy with commissioner.
　License applicant to file, §95-47.3(b).
Forms.
　Filing with commissioner, §95-47.4(c).
Opportunity for applicant to read contract,
　§95-47.4(d).
Records of executed contracts, §95-47.5.
Refund policy.
　Statements as to, §95-47.4(f), (g).
Requirements, §95-47.4(a), (b), (e) to (g).
Written contracts required, §95-47.4.
Professional employer organizations.
PEO agreement, §§58-89A-95, 58-89A-100.
　Interpretation for insurance, bonding and
　　employer's liability purposes, §58-89A-112.
Public contracts.
Generally, §§143-128 to 143-135.9.
　See PUBLIC CONTRACTS.
Public health authorities.
County Medicaid claims.
　Contracts for operation of Medicaid billing
　　system, §130A-45.13.
Punitive damages.
Breach of contract, §1D-15(d).
Railroads.
Municipalities.
　Contracts allocating financial responsibility,
　　§160A-326.
Rates and fees, §24-1.1.
Real estate brokers.
Contracts for broker services, writing and
　signature requirements, §93A-13.
Real property.
Subordination agreements, §39-6.6.
Regional public transportation authority.
Contracts allocating financial responsibility,
　§160A-626(b).
Reverse mortgages.
Contracts for shared appreciation or shared value,
　§53-270.1.
Rural fire departments.
Annexation initiated by municipality.
　Fire protection in annexed area, §160A-58.57.
Sale of merchandise by governmental units.
Actions for injunctive relief to void contract,
　§66-58(m).
Sales, §§25-2-101 to 25-2-725.
See SALE OF GOODS, UCC.
Seafood industrial park authority.
Building contracts, §113-315.36(a).
　Department of administration.
　　Services available to authority,
　　　§113-315.36(b).
Self-service storage rental contracts, §§66-305
　to 66-307.
Solid waste collection.
Annexation initiated by municipality.
　Contract with private firms, §160A-58.59.
Sports agents.
Agency contracts generally, §§78C-85 to 78C-105.
　See ATHLETE AGENTS.
State capital facilities finance act.
Special indebtedness generally, §§142-80 to
　142-101.
　See CAPITAL FACILITIES FINANCE ACT.
**State health plan for teachers and state
　employees,** §135-48.33.
To provide benefits, §135-48.32.

CONTRACTS —Cont'd
State lottery.
Lottery game retailers, §§18C-140, 18C-141(c).
Purchase of services, supplies, equipment,
　§18C-151.
State veterans home.
Operation and management of homes may be
　contracted, §165-50.
Supervisors of schools.
Method of employing administrators generally,
　§115C-287.1.
Talent agency contracts.
Minors, §§48A-17, 48A-18.
Toll bridges.
Mid-Currituck bridge project.
　Contracting for accelerated and cost-effective
　　completion, §136-89.183A(b).
Toner or inkjets.
Agreement prohibiting reusing, remanufacturing
　or refilling.
　Void and unenforceable, §75-36.
Transfers to minors.
Liability for claims based on contracts entered
　into by custodian, §33A-17.
Trusts and trustees.
Limitation on trustee's personal liability,
　§36C-10-1010.
Partnership entering into after trust's acquisition.
　Liability of trustee with interest as general
　　partner, §36C-10-1011.
Turnpike authority.
See TURNPIKE AUTHORITY.
Unborn persons.
Guardian ad litem appointed in in rem and quasi
　in rem actions involving construction, §1A-1
　Rule 17(b).
Unclaimed property act.
Agreement by owner to locate, deliver or recover,
　§116B-78.
University of North Carolina.
Review of contracts exceeding one million dollars,
　§114-8.3(b).
Viatical life insurance settlements.
Commissioner's approval, §58-58-220.
Rescission, §58-58-250(h).
Water and sewer authorities.
Services, §162A-9(b).

CONTRACTS AGAINST PUBLIC POLICY.
Construction indemnity agreements, §22B-1.
Forum selection provisions, §22B-3.
Improving real property.
Provisions making contract subject to laws of
　another state, §22B-2.
Waiving jury trial, §22B-10.

CONTRACTS FOR DEED, §§47H-1 to 47H-8.
Action by purchaser.
Title requirements for executing contract.
　Violations, purchaser's remedies, §47G-6(c).
Violations of chapter, remedies, §47G-8.
Cancellation.
Exercise of right, time, §47H-2(c).
Title requirements for executing contract.
　Violations, purchaser's remedies, §47G-6(c).
Violations of chapter, purchaser's remedies,
　§47G-8.
Content requirements, §47H-2(b).
Copy of contract.
Delivery to purchaser, §47H-2(a).
Cure the default.
Defined, §47H-1.

CONTRACTS FOR DEED —Cont'd
Cure the default —Cont'd
Right, §47H-3.
Time specified, §47H-4(a).
Default and forfeiture.
Conditions for forfeiture, §47H-3.
Effect, §47H-2(e), (f).
Notice of default and intent to forfeit.
Content requirements, §47H-4(a).
Hand delivery to purchaser, §47H-4(b).
Right to cure default, §47H-3.
Time specified, §47H-4(a).
Definitions, §47H-1.
Disclosures.
Content requirements, §47H-2(b).
Mortgage or encumbrance securing obligation
constituting lien on property, §47G-6(b).
Equitable right of redemption.
Extinguished.
Default and forfeiture, §47H-2(e), (f).
Late payment charges, §47G-7.
Memorandum of contract.
Recordation, §47H-2(d).
**Mortgage or encumbrance securing obligation
constituting lien on property.**
Execution of contract by seller, §47G-6(a).
Notice to purchaser before execution of contract,
§47G-6(b).
Violation of provisions by seller.
Purchaser's remedies, §47G-6(c).
Notice of default and intent to forfeit, §47H-4.
Notice of lien on property.
Mortgage or encumbrance securing obligation
constituting lien on property, §47G-6(b).
Past due payments.
Late payment charges, §47G-7.
Recordation, §47H-2(d).
Rescission.
Title requirements for executing contract.
Violations, purchaser's remedies, §47G-6(c).
Violations of chapter, purchaser's remedies,
§47G-8.
Right to cure default, §47H-3.
Time specified, §47H-4(a).
Signed and acknowledged, §47H-2(a).
Statements of account.
Time for providing purchaser, content
requirements, §47G-5.
Title held by seller.
Required to execute contract, §47G-6(a).
Violations, purchaser's remedies, §47G-6(c).
Unfair trade practice.
Violations of chapter, §47G-8.
Violations, remedies, §47G-8.
Writing required, §47H-2(a).

**CONTRIBUTING TO DELINQUENCY OF
MINORS,** §14-316.1.

**CONTRIBUTION AMONG JOINT
TORT-FEASORS,** §§1B-1 to 1B-7.
Actions.
Enforcement, §1B-3(a) to (c).
**Alcoholic beverage sales to underage persons,
compensation for injury.**
Joint and several liability, §18B-124.
Citation of provisions, §1B-6.
Title of act, §1B-6.
Compromise and settlement.
Right to contribution, §1B-1(d).
Construction and interpretation, §1B-5.

CONTRIBUTION AMONG JOINT
TORT-FEASORS —Cont'd
Covenant not to sue.
Effect, §1B-4.
Enforcement, §1B-3(a) to (c).
Fiduciaries.
Provisions not to apply to breaches of trust or
other fiduciary obligations, §1B-1(g).
**Improvement to real property defective or
unsafe.**
Limitation of action for contributions, §1-50(a).
Indemnification.
Right of indemnity not impaired, §1B-1(f).
Insurance.
Rights of liability insurer, §1B-1(e).
Intentional tort-feasors.
No right of contribution in favor of, §1B-1(c).
**Judgment against joint obligors or joint
tort-feasors,** §1B-7.
Preserved, §1B-7(b).
Judgment against other judgment defendants.
Motion for, enforcement by, §1B-3(b).
Liability to claimant.
Judgment of court binding, §1B-3(f).
Recovery against one tort-feasor does not
discharge others, §1B-3(e).
Liens.
Joint obligors or joint tort-feasors.
Lien of judgment preserved, §1B-7(b).
Limitation of actions.
Enforcement of right, §1B-3(c), (d).
Nonprofit corporations.
Unlawful loans or distributions by directors,
§55A-8-33(d).
Pro rata shares, §§1B-2, 1B-7(a).
Disagreement as to, §1B-7(c).
Railroads.
Applicability of provisions to employees, §1B-1(i).
Release, §1B-4.
Right to contribution, §1B-1(a).
Limitation on amount of recovery, §1B-1(b).
Separate action.
Enforcement by, §1B-3(a), (c).
Settlement with claimant.
Rights of tort-feasors who enter into, §1B-1(d).
Shares, pro rata, §§1B-2, 1B-7(a).
Disagreements as to, §1B-7(c).
State of North Carolina.
Applicability of provisions to tort claims against
state, §1B-1(h).
Suretyship.
Contribution among sureties, §26-5.
Uniformity of interpretation, §1B-5.

CONTRIBUTIONS AMONG SURETIES, §26-5.

**CONTRIBUTIONS AND EXPENDITURES IN
POLITICAL CAMPAIGNS,** §§163-278.5 to
163-278.38.
See CAMPAIGN FINANCE.

**CONTRIBUTION SOLICITATION BY
CHARITIES,** §§131F-1 to 131F-33.
See CHARITABLE SOLICITATION.

CONTRIBUTORY NEGLIGENCE.
Affirmative defense, pleading, §1A-1 Rule 8(c).
Bank deposits and collections.
Unauthorized signature or alteration,
§25-4-406(c), (d).
Burden of proof, §1-139.
**Claims against state departments and
agencies.**
Doctrine a matter of defense, §143-299.1.
Limitations on use, §143-299.1A.

CONTRIBUTORY NEGLIGENCE —Cont'd
Controlled substances.
  Employing or intentionally using minor to commit
    drug law violations, §90-95.5.
**Failure of motorist to stop vehicle within
  radius of headlights or range of vision,**
  §20-141(n).
**Failure to yield right of way at yield right of
  way signs,** §20-158.1.
Mobile phone use by school bus operator.
  Unlawful use while bus in motion.
    Violation not contributory negligence,
      §20-137.4(f).
**Motorcycle or moped overcrowded or operator
  and passengers without helmets,**
  §20-140.4(b).
**Motorcycle rearview mirror requirement
  violation not contributory negligence,**
  §20-126(c).
Negotiable instruments.
  Forged signature, altered instrument,
    §25-3-406(a) to (c).
Products liability.
  Injured parties knowledge or lack of reasonable
    care, §99B-4.
Reply to answer alleging last clear chance,
  §1A-1 Rule 7(a).

**CONTROL CORNERS IN REAL ESTATE
  DEVELOPMENTS,** §§39-32.1 to 39-32.4.
  See SUBDIVISIONS.

**CONTROLLED ACCESS
  HIGHWAYS/FACILITIES.**
  See HIGHWAYS, ROADS AND STREETS.

CONTROLLED FOREST FIRE.
Prescribed burning of forestland, §§106-966 to
  106-970.

CONTROLLED SUBSTANCE ANALOGUE.
Defined, §90-87.
Treated as schedule I substance, §90-89.1.

CONTROLLED SUBSTANCES, §§90-86 to
  90-113.8.
  See DRUGS AND CONTROLLED SUBSTANCES.

**CONTROLLED SUBSTANCES REPORTING
  SYSTEM,** §§90-113.70 to 90-113.76.
Attorney general.
  Department informed of unusual prescribing
    patterns, §90-113.74(e).
Citation of act.
  North Caroline controlled substances reporting
    system act, §90-113.70.
Confidentiality of information, §90-113.74(a).
  Exceptions, §90-113.74(g), (h).
  Penalties for violations, §90-113.75(a).
    Actions to recover damages, §90-113.75(b).
  Purging of information.
    When allowed, §90-113.74(f).
  Release of data, §90-113.74(c).
  Statistical, research, or educational uses of
    information, §90-113.74(d).
  Use of information by department, §90-113.74(b).
Damages.
  Actions to recover, §90-113.75(b).
Definitions, §90-113.72.
Establishment and maintenance, §90-113.73(a).
Immunity, §90-113.75(c).
Legislative findings, §90-113.71(a).
Penalties for violations, §90-113.75.

**CONTROLLED SUBSTANCES REPORTING
  SYSTEM** —Cont'd
Purging of information.
  When allowed, §90-113.74(f).
Purpose of act, §90-113.71(b).
Reporting requirements.
  Frequency of reports, §90-113.73(a).
  Rulemaking, §90-113.73(b).
Rulemaking, §90-113.76.
Title of act.
  North Caroline controlled substances reporting
    system act, §90-113.70.

CONTROL OF JUVENILE BY PARENTS,
  §§7B-3400 to 7B-3404.

CONTROL SHARE ACQUISITIONS.
Business combinations, §§75E-1 to 75E-9.
  See BUSINESS COMBINATIONS.
Generally, §§55-9A-01 to 55-9A-09.
  See CORPORATIONS.

**CONVENIENCE STORE ALCOHOLIC
  BEVERAGE PERMITS.**
Food business defined to include, §18B-1000.
Off-premises fortified wine permit.
  Kind of permit that may be issued, §18B-1001.
Off-premises malt beverage permit.
  Kind of permit that may be issued, §18B-1001.
On-premises malt beverage permit.
  Kind of permit that may be issued, §18B-1001.
  Recycling requirement, §18B-1006.1.

CONVENTION CENTERS.
Alcoholic beverage permits.
  Defined, §18B-1000.
  Mixed beverage permit.
    Kind of permit that may be issued, §18B-1001.
    Recycling requirement, §18B-1006.1.
  On-premises fortified wine permit.
    Kind of permit that may be issued, §18B-1001.
    Recycling requirement, §18B-1006.1.
  On-premises malt beverage permit.
    Kind of permit that may be issued, §18B-1001.
    Recycling requirement, §18B-1006.1.
  On-premises unfortified wine permit.
    Kind of permit that may be issued, §18B-1001.
    Recycling requirement, §18B-1006.1.
  Qualifications for permit, §18B-900(e).
Municipalities.
  Power to establish and support, §160A-489.

CONVENTIONS.
Centers.
  See CONVENTION CENTERS.
Winery special event authorization,
  §18B-1114.1.

CONVENTS.
Property tax exemption, §105-278.6.

**CONVERSATION BETWEEN TAXPAYER AND
  DEPARTMENT OF REVENUE.**
Advice given.
  Documentation, §105-258.2.

CONVERSION.
Arrest in civil cases, §1-410.
Bailments, §14-168.1.
District courts.
  Small claim actions.
    Form of complaint for conversion, §7A-232.
Highways, roads and streets.
  State highway fund.
    Funds and property converted to state highway
      fund, §136-16.

CONVERSION —Cont'd

Hired personal property, §14-168.1.
Prima facie evidence of intent to convert.
Property other than motor vehicle, §14-168.3.
Truck, automobile or other motor vehicle,
§14-168.5(a).
Truck, automobile or other motor vehicle.
Demand for return, §14-168.5(b).
Prima facie evidence of intent to convert,
§14-168.5(a).
**Leaf tobacco sales in auction tobacco
warehouses.**
Limitation of actions, §1-55.
Limitation of actions, §1-52.
Tobacco, §1-55.
Militia.
Care of military property.
Unlawful conversion or willful destruction of
military property, §127A-131.
Negotiable instruments, §25-3-420(a) to (c).
Preneed funeral contracts and funds,
§90-210.70(a), (c).

CONVEYANCES.
Acknowledgments.
Certification of correctness.
Failure of register of deeds to certify.
Validation of registration, §47-50.1.
Defective acknowledgment on old instruments
validated, §47-52.
Aliens.
Right to convey real property, §64-1.
Armories.
Counties and municipalities may lease, convey or
acquire property for use as armory,
§127A-165.
Prior conveyances validated, §127A-166.
Validation of prior conveyances, §127A-166.
Assignments.
Real property pledged as security, §47-17.2.
Attornment.
Unnecessary on conveyance of reversions, etc.,
§42-2.
Banks.
Validation.
Attestation by secretary or cashier, §47-42(b),
(c).
Deeds executed prior to February 14, 1939,
§47-42(b).
**Blank or master forms of instruments
conveying interest realty or personalty.**
Filing, recording, indexing, §47-21.
Boundaries.
Use of word "adjoining" instead of words "bounded
by," §39-2.
Burden of proof.
Fee presumed though word "heirs" omitted, §39-1.
Business trusts, §39-46.
Cemeteries, §65-69(b), (c).
Charities.
Effect as to conveyances by trustees, §59B-15(a).
Prior deeds validated, §59B-15(b).
Children and minors.
Emancipation of juvenile.
Right to make conveyance as adult, §7B-3507.
Condominiums.
Common elements, §47C-3-112.
Construction and interpretation.
Court to give effect to intent of parties, §39-1.1(a).
Fee presumed though word "heirs" omitted, §39-1.

CONVEYANCES —Cont'd
Construction and interpretation —Cont'd
Rule in Shelley's case.
Abolished, §41-6.3.
Section not to prevent application, §39-1.1(b).
Use of word adjoining instead of words bounded
by, §39-2.
Vagueness of description not to invalidate, §39-2.
Contaminated site.
Deed or other instrument of conveyance,
contaminated property statement,
§143B-279.10(e).
Contingent limitations.
Failure of issue.
Limitations on failure, §41-4.
Contingent remainders.
Validation of transfer, §41-12.
Contract to convey real estate.
Memorandum registering, for, §47-119.1.
Notice, §47-120.
Cooperative associations.
Effect as to conveyances by trustees, §59B-15(a).
Prior deeds validated, §59B-15(b).
Coroners.
Official selling or empowered to sell property not
in office, §39-5.
Corporations.
Corporate seal.
Required, §47-41.1.
Forms of probate for deeds and other conveyances,
§§47-41.01, 47-41.02.
Technical defects not to affect, §47-41.2.
**Court to give effect to intent of parties in
construing, §39-1.1(a).**
Covenants.
Grantees of reversion and assigns of lease have
reciprocal rights under covenants, §42-8.
Standing seized to use.
Possession transferred to use in certain
conveyances, §41-7.
Transfer fee covenants prohibited, §§39A-1 to
39A-3.
Death.
Contingent limitations depending on death of
person without heirs.
Limitations on failure of issue, §41-4.
Disclosure of death or illness of previous occupant,
§39-50.
Deeds.
See DEEDS.
Defective acknowledgment validated, §47-52.
Descriptions.
Vagueness not to invalidate, §39-2.
Disclosures.
Death or illness of previous occupant, §39-50.
Registered sex offender living in area, §39-50.
Diseases.
Disclosure of death or illness of previous occupant,
§39-50.
Draftsman.
Designation of draftsman required on instrument
in certain counties, §47-17.1.
Drainage districts, §156-114.
Electronic recording.
Uniform real property electronic recording act,
§§47-16.1 to 47-16.7.
Emancipation of juvenile.
Right to make conveyance as adult, §7B-3507.
Eminent domain.
Private condemnors.
Change of ownership pending proceedings,
§40A-33.

CONVEYANCES —Cont'd
Excise stamp tax, §§105-228.28 to 105-228.37.
  See EXCISE STAMP TAX ON CONVEYANCES.
Executors and administrators.
  Contract for sale of real property by decedent.
    Delivery of deed by personal representative,
      §28A-17-9.
  Real property conveyed to personal
    representative, §28A-17-10.
Exempt property, §1C-1604(a).
Failure of issue.
  Limitations on failure, §41-4.
Fee simple.
  Presumption of fee though word "heirs" omitted,
    §39-1.
Fraternal orders and societies.
  Effect as to conveyances by trustees, §59B-15(a).
  Prior deeds validated, §59B-15(b).
Fraudulent transfers, §§39-23.1 to 39-23.12.
  See FRAUDULENT TRANSFERS.
Future interests.
  Inter vivos and testamentary conveyances of
    future interests permitted, §39-6.3(a) to (c).
  Revocation of conveyances to persons not in esse,
    §39-6.
General services administration.
  Conveyances by United States acting by and
    through general services administration,
    §47-108.14.
Good funds settlement act, §§45A-1 to 45A-9.
  See GOOD FUNDS SETTLEMENT ACT.
Health care facility interests, §131A-8.
Hearsay exception.
  Records or documents or statements in documents
    affecting interest in property, §8C-1 Rule 803.
Heirs.
  Construed to be "children" in certain limitations,
    §41-6.
  Fee presumed though word "heirs" omitted, §39-1.
  Sale, lease or mortgage of real property,
    §28A-17-12.
Hospital authorities.
  Lease, conveyance or transfers of property to
    authority, §131E-31(a), (b).
Husband and wife.
  Acknowledgments.
    Absence of wife's acknowledgment does not
      affect deed as to husband, §39-9.
    Different times and places, §39-8.
  Acts barring property rights.
    Conveyance of property by spouse not at fault,
      §31A-1(d).
  Conveyance by spouse to both spouses.
    Tenants by the entirety, interest vested as,
      §39-13.3(b).
  Conveyance by spouse to other spouse.
    Interest vested in grantee spouse, §39-13.3(a).
    Tenants by the entirety, dissolution of interest
      held as, §39-13.3(c).
  Deed of separation.
    Conveyance by husband or wife under deed,
      §39-13.4.
  G.S. 52-10 or 52-10.1.
    Applicability of provisions to conveyances by
      spouses to spouses, §39-13.3(e).
  Instruments affecting married woman's title.
    Validation of instruments not executed by
      husband, §39-7.1.
  Joinder of spouse, §§39-7(b), (c), 39-13.3(d).
  Joint execution.
    Married persons under 18 made competent as to
      certain transactions, §39-13.2(a), (b).

CONVEYANCES —Cont'd
Husband and wife —Cont'd
  Minors.
    Married persons under 18 made competent as to
      certain transactions, §39-13.2(a).
  Notaries.
    Validation of certificates as to conveyances
      between husband and wife, §52-7.
  Party to convey without joinder, §39-7(b).
  Purchase-money mortgages.
    Spouse need not join, §39-13.
  Title.
    Validation of instruments not executed by
      husband, §39-7.1.
  Validation of conveyance executed by married
    women without private examination.
    Conveyances executed prior to Feb. 7, 1945,
      §39-13.1(b).
    Conveyances executed since Nov. 7, 1944,
      §39-13.1(a).
  Waiver of elective life estate.
    Execution of conveyance, §39-7(a), (c).
Infants.
  Conveyances by infant trustees, §39-4.
Intent.
  Court to give effect to intent of parties, §39-1.1.
  Fee presumed though word "heirs" omitted, §39-1.
Judgments.
  Directing party to execute conveyance, §1A-1 Rule
    70.
  Stay, §1-291.
  Transfer of title.
    Judgment regarded as deed of conveyance,
      §1-228.
Landlord and tenant.
  Transfer of rental property.
    Attornment by tenant unnecessary, §42-2.
Local development.
  Authority of city or county to convey interest in
    real property.
    Determinations arriving at consideration
      amount, §158-7.1(d2).
Lost instruments and records.
  Applicability of provisions, §98-18.
  Court records.
    Conveyances reciting court records.
      Prima facie evidence of destroyed court
        records, §§98-16, 98-17.
  Replacing lost official conveyances, §98-11.
Married women.
  Registration of instruments not executed by wife,
    §39-9.
  Repeal of laws requiring private examination,
    §47-14.1.
  Validation of conveyance executed by married
    women without private examination.
    Conveyances executed prior to Feb. 7, 1945,
      §39-13.1(b).
    Conveyances executed since Nov. 7, 1944,
      §39-13.1(a).
  Validation of instruments not executed by
    husband, §39-7.1.
Minors.
  Infant trustees, §39-4.
Mortgages and deeds of trust.
  See MORTGAGES AND DEEDS OF TRUST.
Next of kin, §41-6.1.
Notaries.
  Husband and wife.
    Validation of certificates of notaries as to
      conveyances between husband and wife,
      §52-7.

CONVEYANCES —Cont'd

Partnerships.

Real property, §§59-38(c), (d), 59-40.

Personal property.

Creation of interest or estate in, §39-6.2.

Planned community act.

Common elements, §47F-3-112.

Possession.

Transferred to use in certain conveyances, §41-7.

Power of sale, sales under, §§45-21.1 to 45-21.33.

See POWER OF SALE, SALES UNDER.

Presumptions and burden of proof.

Fee presumed though word "heirs" omitted, §39-1.

Probate generally.

See PROBATE.

Public lands, §§146-74 to 146-78.

Real property with manufactured home attached, §47-20.7.

Registration or recordation.

Blank or master forms of instruments conveying interest realty or personalty, §47-21.

Contract to convey real estate.

Memorandum registering, form, §47-119.1.

Notice, §47-120.

Defective acknowledgment validated, §47-52.

Generally.

See RECORDATION OR REGISTRATION OF DOCUMENTS.

Instrument conveying real estate in 2 or more counties.

Copy certified and registered, §161-15.

Necessary to pass title as against creditors or bona fide purchasers, §47-18(a), (b).

Realty conveyed with manufactured home attached, §47-20.7.

State officers authorized to prove and acknowledge, §47-1.

Religious organizations.

Effect as to conveyances by trustees, §59B-15(a).

Prior deeds validated, §59B-15(b).

Remainders, reversions and executory interests.

Attornment unnecessary, §42-2.

Conveyances of future interests, §39-6.3(a) to (c).

Grantees of reversion and assigns of lease have reciprocal rights under covenants, §42-8.

Validation of sales or mortgages, §41-12.

Renunciation of property or interest.

Bar to right to renounce property or interest, §31B-4(a).

Revenue stamps.

Excise stamp tax, §§105-228.28 to 105-228.37.

Revocation of will by subsequent conveyance.

No revocation, §31-5.6.

Right of entry.

Inter vivos and testamentary conveyances of future interests, §39-6.3(a) to (c).

Rule in Shelley's case.

Abolished, §41-6.3.

Section not to prevent application, §39-1.1(b).

School districts.

Administrative units.

Enlargement of city administrative unit.

Conveyance of school property upon, §115C-509.

Seals and sealed instruments.

Probates omitting official seals, §47-53.

Real property interests.

Seal of signatory not necessary for valid conveyance, §39-6.5.

CONVEYANCES —Cont'd

Sex offender registration.

Disclosure of registered sex offender in area not required, §39-50.

Shelley's case.

Abolished, §41-6.3.

Section not to prevent application of rule, §39-1.1(b).

Sheriffs.

Death of sheriff.

Execution by successor in office, §39-5.

Official selling or empowered to sell not in office, §39-5.

Solid waste management.

Hazardous waste landfill facility.

Land used for facility conveyed to state, §130A-292.

Stamp tax, §§105-228.28 to 105-228.37.

See EXCISE STAMP TAX ON CONVEYANCES.

State officers authorized to prove and acknowledge, §47-1.

Statute of uses, §41-7.

Stays.

Appeals.

How judgment directing conveyance stayed, §1-291.

Subordination agreements.

Interest in real property, §39-6.6(c).

Tax collectors.

Official selling or empowered to sell not in office, §39-5.

Tenants by the entirety.

Spouse conveying interest to other spouse.

Dissolution of interest held as, §39-13.3(c).

Interest created by, §39-13.3(b).

Title insurance.

Generally, §§58-26-1 to 58-27-15.

See TITLE INSURANCE.

Torrens system registration.

Method of transfer.

Conveyance of part of registered land, §43-32.

Register of deeds.

Duty of register upon part conveyance, §43-33.

Transfer fee covenants, §§39A-1 to 39A-3.

Definitions, §39A-2.

Liability of person recording, §39A-3(b).

Not to run with title, §39A-3(a).

Public policy, §39A-1.

Subsequent owner, purchaser, mortgagee.

Not binding or enforceable on, §39A-3(a).

Trusts and trustees.

Construction of provisions, §39-6.7(e).

Infant trustees, §39-4.

Property or instrument which may be conveyed, §39-6.7(d).

Sufficiency of instrument, §39-6.7(c).

Survivorship among trustees, §41-3.

Transfers by trust or trustee, §39-6.7(b).

Transfers to trust or trustee, §39-6.7(a).

Unborn infants.

Taking by deed or writing, §41-5.

United States.

General services administration.

Conveyances by United States acting by and through general services administration, §47-108.14.

Real property.

Recordation of conveyances of land acquired, §104-4.

CONVEYANCES —Cont'd
Use of word "adjoining" instead of words "bounded by,"§39-2.
Vagueness of description.
Not to invalidate, §39-2.
Water and sewer authorities.
Political subdivisions and authority, §162A-14.
Wills.
General provisions, §§31-1 to 31-47.
See WILLS.
Inter vivos and testamentary conveyances of future interests, §39-6.3(a) to (c).
No revocation by subsequent conveyance, §31-5.6.

CONVICTED FELON DISQUALIFICATIONS.
Alcoholic beverage permittees.
Certain employees prohibited, §18B-1003(b).
Concealed handgun permit, §14-415.12(b).
Executors and administrators.
Persons disqualified to serve, §28A-4-2.
Firearms possession, §14-415.1.
Physicians and surgeons.
Automatic revocation of license, §90-14(c).
Voting, §163-55(a), NC Const Art VI §2.
Concealed handgun permit, §14-415.12(b).

CONVICTION AND PJC.
Drivers' licenses.
Forwarding record to division, §20-24(b).
Entry of PJC not considered entry of judgment, §15A-101.
Motor vehicles.
Convictions.
Third PJC filed in five-year period as conviction, §20-4.01.
Records of PJC's, §20-26(a).

CONVICTION OF CRIME, IMPEACHMENT, §8C-1 Rule 609(a).
Appeal, pendency, §8C-1 Rule 609(e).
Juvenile adjudication, §8C-1 Rule 609(d).
Pardon, effect, §8C-1 Rule 609(c).
Time limit, §8C-1 Rule 609(b).

CONVICT-MADE GOODS.
Sale prohibited, §14-346(a), (b).

CONVICTS.
Discharge of insolvent prisoners.
Generally.
See DISCHARGE OF INSOLVENT PRISONERS.
Farming out convicts, §§148-66 to 148-70.
See PRISON LABOR.
Generally.
See PRISONS AND PRISONERS.
Grievance procedure generally, §§148-118.1 to 148-118.9.
See PRISONER'S GRIEVANCE PROCEDURE.
Labor of prisoners generally, §§148-26 to 148-49.
See PRISON LABOR.

COOKING SCHOOL ALCOHOLIC BEVERAGE PERMITS.
Culinary permit.
Kind of permit that may be issued, §18B-1001.
Defined, §18B-1000.
On-premises unfortified wine permit.
Kind of permit that may be issued, §18B-1001.
Recycling requirement, §18B-1006.1.
Restrictions on sales, §18B-1006(g).

COOLEEMEE.
Room occupancy tax.
Uniform provisions.
Authorized to levy, §160A-215(g).

COOLEEMEE —Cont'd
Room occupancy tax —Cont'd
Uniform provisions —Cont'd
Generally, §160A-215.

COOPERATIVE AGREEMENTS AMONG HOSPITALS.
Certificate of public advantage, §§131E-192.1 to 131E-192.13.
See HEALTH CARE FACILITIES.

COOPERATIVE AGREEMENTS AMONG PHYSICIANS OR BETWEEN PHYSICIANS, HOSPITAL OR OTHER PERSON, §§90-21.24 to 90-21.26.
Appeals.
Judicial action as to certificates of public advantage, §90-21.33.
Attorney general.
Authority, §90-21.35.
Copy of report submitted to attorney general, §90-21.32(a).
Defined, §90-21.25.
Objection to issuance of certificate of public advantage, §90-21.29.
Review after issuance of certificate of public advantage, §90-21.31.
Suit to authorize cancellation of certificate, §90-21.33(c).
Authority of department of health and human services, §90-21.35.
Certificate of need, licensure or other regulatory requirements.
Physician or other persons not exempted from compliance, §90-21.36(b).
Certificate of public advantage.
Application, §90-21.26(b).
Fee, §90-21.34(a).
Additional fee when consultants needed to complete review, §90-21.34(b).
Review of department of health and human services, §90-21.27(a).
Cancellation, suit by attorney general, §90-21.33(c).
Conditions, §90-21.28.
Consultants needed to complete review of application.
Additional fee, §90-21.34(b).
Determination of department of health and human services to issue certificate, §90-21.27(b).
Evaluating potential benefits, considerations by department of health and human services, §90-21.27(b).
Immunity from challenge or scrutiny under state antitrust laws, §90-21.36(a).
Immunity from federal or state antitrust laws, §90-21.26(a).
Issuance by department of health and human services, §90-21.28.
Judicial review of decisions.
Applicants or other person aggrieved by decision to issue or not issue, §90-21.33(a).
Attorney general suit, §90-21.33(c).
Party or other person aggrieved by decision to allow certificate to remain in effect or make changes, §90-21.33(b).
Work product of attorney general not public record, §90-21.33(b).
Objection by attorney general, §90-21.29.
Periodic reports during time certificate in effect, §90-21.32.

COOPERATIVE AGREEMENTS AMONG PHYSICIANS OR BETWEEN PHYSICIANS, HOSPITAL OR OTHER PERSON —Cont'd

Certificate of public advantage —Cont'd

Public hearing by department of health and human services, §90-21.27(a).

Recordkeeping by department of health and human services, §90-21.30.

Review after issuance of certificate, §90-21.31.

Revocation for failure to file periodic report or provide information, §90-21.32(b).

Contract law to govern disputes among parties to agreement, §90-21.36(c).

Definitions, §90-21.25.

Disputes among parties to cooperative agreement.

Governed by contract law, §90-21.36(c).

Federal or state antitrust laws.

Certificate of public advantage, immunity, §90-21.26(a).

Defined, §90-21.25.

Fees for application for certificate and periodic reports, §90-21.34.

Findings of general assembly, §90-21.24.

Judicial review of decisions as to certificate of public advantage, §90-21.33.

Notice.

Objection by attorney general to issuance of certificate of public advantage, §90-21.29.

Notice of termination, §90-21.30.

Periodic reports during time certificate of public advantage in effect, §90-21.32.

Purposes of provisions, §90-21.24.

Recordkeeping by department of health and human services, §90-21.30.

Report during time certificate of public advantage in effect.

Contents, §90-21.32(a).

Copy submitted to attorney general, §90-21.32(a).

Failure to file report or provide information, §90-21.32(b).

Fee for filings, §90-21.34(a).

Review of department of health and human services, §90-21.32(c).

Time for filing, §90-21.32(a).

Termination.

Notice, §90-21.30.

Time for filing judicial action as to certificate of public advantage.

Applicant or other person aggrieved by decision to issue or not issue, §90-21.33(a).

Party or other person aggrieved by decision to allow certificate to remain in effect or make changes, §90-21.33(b).

Venue of suit by attorney general to cancel certificate of public advantage, §90-21.33(c).

COOPERATIVE ASSOCIATIONS, §§54-111 to 54-128.

Agriculture.

Authorized purposes, §§54-111, 54-124.

Apportionment of earnings, §54-126.

Time of allocation, §54-127.

Articles of incorporation, §54-113.

Amendments, §54-125.

Fee for filing, §54-115.

Filing with secretary of state, §54-114.

Fee, §54-115.

Boards of directors, §54-123.

Businesses authorized, §§54-111, 54-124.

Bylaws, §54-116.

COOPERATIVE ASSOCIATIONS —Cont'd

Conveyances.

Effect as to conveyances by trustees, §59B-15(a).

Prior deeds validated, §59B-15(b).

Dairy products.

Authorized purposes, §§54-111, 54-124.

Deeds.

Prior deeds validated, §59B-15(b).

Dividends, §54-126.

Time for, §54-127.

Duties, §§54-124 to 54-128.

Electricity.

Authorized purposes, §§54-111, 54-124.

Fees.

Incorporation, §54-115.

Forests and forestry.

Authorized purposes, §§54-111, 54-124.

Franchise tax, §54-118.2.

Exemptions from provisions, §105-125(a).

General corporation law.

Applicability, §54-117.

General nonprofit corporation law.

Applicability, §54-117.

Housing.

Authorized purposes, §§54-111, 54-124.

Incorporation.

Admission of other corporations, §54-118.

Articles of incorporation, §54-113.

Amendments, §54-125.

Fee for filing, §54-115.

Filing with secretary of state, §54-114.

Fee, §54-115.

Authorized, §54-111.

Certificate of incorporation, §54-114.

Fees, §54-115.

Number of incorporators, §54-111.

Injunctions.

Unauthorized use of term "mutual" in name.

Violators may be enjoined from doing business, §54-112.

Irrigation.

Authorized purposes, §§54-111, 54-124.

Land and loan associations, §§54-45 to 54-73.

See LAND AND LOAN ASSOCIATIONS.

Licenses.

Taxation, §54-118.1.

Marketing associations, §§54-129 to 54-166.

See MARKETING ASSOCIATIONS.

Mines and minerals.

Authorized purposes, §§54-111, 54-124.

Names.

Bylaws to provide for, §54-116.

Use of term "mutual" restricted, §54-112.

Nonmembers, §54-117.

Officers, §54-123.

Other corporations.

Admission to provisions, §54-118.

Purchase of business.

Shares issued on, §54-121.

Powers, §§54-124 to 54-128.

Purposes, §§54-111, 54-124.

Real property.

Conveyances.

Effect as to conveyances by trustees, §59B-15(a).

Prior deeds validated, §59B-15(b).

Reports.

Annual report to secretary of state, §54-128.

Restriction on ownership of shares, §54-120.

Sewers.

Authorized purposes, §§54-111, 54-124.

COOPERATIVE ASSOCIATIONS —Cont'd
Shares and shareholders.
Amendment of articles of incorporation.
  Majority vote of shareholders, §54-125.
Bylaws.
  Matters to be provided for, §54-116.
Dividends, §§54-126, 54-127.
Election of directors, §54-123.
Increase or decrease of amount of capital, §54-125.
Information to be stated in articles of
    incorporation, §54-113.
Proxy voting, §54-122.
Purchase of business.
  Shares issued on, §54-121.
Subscriptions.
  Certificates not issued until fully paid, §54-119.
  Voting of shares by subscriber, §54-119.
Voting.
  Absent members, §54-122.
Storage.
Authorized purposes, §§54-111, 54-124.
Taxation.
Franchise taxes, §54-118.2.
Income tax.
  Corporation income tax.
    Exemptions, §105-130.11(a), (b).
License taxes, §54-118.1.
Property taxes.
  Certain farm products classified for taxation at
      reduced valuation, §105-277.01.
Telephones.
Authorized purposes, §§54-111, 54-124.
Voting.
Restriction, §54-120.
Water supply and waterworks.
Authorized purposes, §§54-111, 54-124.

**COOPERATIVE INNOVATIVE HIGH SCHOOL
    PROGRAMS,** §§115C-238.50 to 115C-238.55.
Accountable to local board of education,
    §115C-238.53(a).
Additional funds to approved programs.
Provided by appropriation only, §115C-238.51(e).
Agreement.
Operated under term of written agreement,
    §115C-238.53(b).
Application.
Information required, §115C-238.51(b).
Joint application, §115C-238.51(a).
Review, joint advisory committee, §115C-238.51(c).
Submission to state boards, §115C-238.51(c).
Appropriation of funds.
County boards of commissioners, §115C-238.54(d).
Approval, §115C-238.51(d).
Assignment of funds, §115C-238.54(a).
Definitions, §115C-238.50A.
Eligibility to attend, §115C-238.50(f).
Evaluation of student success, §115C-238.55.
Exemption from rules, §115C-238.53(f).
Facilities programs operated in,
    §115C-238.53(c).
Joint establishment.
Local boards and community college boards of
    trustee.
  Purpose of part to authorize, §115C-238.50(a).
Ninth graders, eligibility to attend,
    §115C-238.50(f).
Number of days of instruction, §115C-238.53(d).
**Other educational partner who may
    participate,** §115C-238.52(a).
Requirements, §115C-238.52(b).

**COOPERATIVE INNOVATIVE HIGH SCHOOL
    PROGRAMS** —Cont'd
Purpose of part, §115C-238.50(a).
Requirements of programs, §115C-238.50(b).
State, federal and local funds, use,
    §115C-238.53(e).
Allocation, §115C-238.54(b), (c).
Encouragement to seek other funds,
    §115C-238.54(e).
Students with disabilities.
Compliance with law and policies relating to,
    §115C-238.53(d).
Transfer of assigned funds, §115C-238.54(a).

COORDINATE SYSTEM, §§102-1 to 102-17.
See SURVEYS AND SURVEYORS.

COPIERS.
Toner or inkjets.
Agreement prohibiting reusing, remanufacturing
    or refilling.
  Void and unenforceable, §75-36.

COPIES.
Authenticated copies of public records.
Evidence, §8-35.
Certified copies.
Deeds or other instruments required to be
    registered.
  Registration, §47-31.
    Conveyance of real estate in 2 or more
        counties, §161-15.
    Copies made by alien property custodian,
        §§47-33, 47-34.
Laws of foreign countries or states.
  Admission into evidence, §8-3(b).
Ordinances.
  Prima facie evidence of existence of ordinance,
      §8-5.
Public records.
  Evidence, §8-34.
Wills.
  Evidence, §8-28.
Photographic reproductions.
Department of revenue, §8-45.3(a).
Employment security division, §8-45.3(a1).
Evidence, §8-45.1.
  Uniformity of interpretation, §8-45.2.
Public records.
Authenticated copies.
  Evidence, §8-35.
Official writings.
  Evidence, §8-34.

COPPER.
Records.
Purchase of certain metals, §66-11.
Regulation of purchase of certain metals.
Violations of provisions, §66-11.
Transportation, §66-11.1.

COPYRIGHTS.
Constitutional protection of authors' rights,
    US Const Art I §8.
Corporate income tax.
Allocation and apportionment of income,
    §105-130.4.
International commercial arbitrations.
Arbitration deemed commercial, §1-567.31(e).
Invention development.
Rights of employers and employees, §§66-57.1,
    66-57.2.
Phonograph records and tapes.
Prohibition of rights to further restrict or to
    collect royalties on commercial use, §66-28.

COPYRIGHTS —Cont'd
Real estate commission.
Publications, §93A-3(f).
Tryon's Palace.
Emblems.
Authority of commission to adopt and copyright certain emblems, §121-21.

CORAM NOBIS.
Relief now available by motion for appropriate relief, §15A-1411(c).

CORDAGE.
Dealers of scrap, salvage or surplus, failure to keep records of purchases, §66-10(b).

CORN.
Adulteration of grains generally, §§106-621 to 106-628.
See GRAIN ADULTERATION.
Grain dealers generally, §§106-601 to 106-615.
See GRAIN DEALERS.
Grain mills generally, §§73-1 to 73-28.
Granary arson, §14-62.
Larceny.
Ungathered crops, §14-78.
Liens.
Effective period, §44-69.1.
Unfair practices by handlers, §§106-498 to 106-501.
Weights and measures.
Standard weights and measures, §81A-42.

CORNELIUS.
Traffic control photographic systems, §160A-300.1(d).

CORNERS.
Control corners in real estate developments, §§39-32.1 to 39-32.4.
See SUBDIVISIONS.

CORONERS.
Appointments.
Clerk may appoint in special cases, §152-1.
Autopsies generally.
See AUTOPSIES.
Bonds, surety.
Certified copies as evidence, §152-4.
Execution, §152-3.
Official bonds of county officers generally, §§58-72-1 to 58-72-70.
See OFFICIAL BONDS OF COUNTY OFFICERS.
Registration, §152-4.
Conveyances.
Official selling or empowered to sell property not in office, §39-5.
Death.
Conveyances of real property when not in office, §39-5.
Deeds.
Official selling or empowered to sell not in office, §39-5.
Elections, §152-1.
Date of election, §163-1(a).
Escape.
Allowing prisoners to escape, §14-239.
Burden of proof, §14-239.
District attorney to prosecute officer for escape, §14-240.
Evidence.
Bonds, surety.
Certified copies as evidence, §152-4.

CORONERS —Cont'd
Executions.
Directed to coroner where sheriff is party or interested in action, §1-313.
Failure to discharge duties, §14-230.
Fees.
Generally, §152-5.
Statement rendered by county officers compensated from fees, §128-13.
Penalty for failure to file statement, §128-13.
Habeas corpus.
Hearings by coroner, §152-10.
Hearings.
Preliminary hearings.
Duties of coroners, §152-7.
Hearings by coroner in lieu of other preliminary hearing, §152-10.
Inquests.
Compensation of jurors at inquest, §152-9.
Duties of coroners, §152-7.
Medical examiners to be notified of certain deaths.
Holding of inquests by coroner, §130A-394.
Jury.
Compensation of jurors at inquest, §152-9.
Liabilities of special coroner, §152-6.
Medical examiners generally, §§130A-377 to 130A-395.
See MEDICAL EXAMINERS.
Oaths.
Taking of oath, §152-2.
Penalties.
Special coroner, §152-6.
Statement rendered by county officers compensated from fees.
Failure to file statement, §128-13.
Powers and duties, §152-7.
Special coroners, §152-6.
Preliminary hearings.
Duties, §152-7.
Salaries.
Statement rendered by county officers compensated from fees, §128-13.
Penalty for failure to file statement, §128-13.
Service of process.
Process issued by coroner, §152-11.
Sheriffs.
Acting as sheriff in certain cases, §152-8.
Service of process.
Sheriff a party.
When coroner acts, §162-16.
Vacancies in office of sheriff.
Duties performed by coroner or chief deputy, §162-5.1.
Performance of duties by coroner, §162-5.
Special coroners.
Liabilities, §152-6.
Penalties, §152-6.
Powers and duties, §152-6.
Sheriffs.
Acting as sheriff in certain cases, §152-8.
Terms of office, §163-1(a).
Vacancies in office, §152-1.

CORPORAL PUNISHMENT.
Attorneys' fees and costs in cases involving principals or teachers.
Frivolous actions, §6-21.4.
Child care facilities.
Banned in certain nonlicensed homes, §110-101.1.
Prohibited as form of discipline, §110-91.

CORPORAL PUNISHMENT —Cont'd
Mental health, developmental disabilities and substance abuse.
Rights of clients.
Use of corporal punishment prohibited, §122C-59.
Prisoners.
Prohibited, §148-20.
Public schools, §115C-390.4.
Attorneys' fees in frivolous actions, §6-21.4.
Children with disabilities, §115C-107.7(a1).
Data on each student to whom administered, §115C-276(r).
Defined, §115C-390.1(b).

CORPORATE INCOME TAX.
General provisions, §§105-130 to 105-130.41.
See INCOME TAX.
S corporations, §§105-131 to 105-131.8.
See INCOME TAX.

CORPORATE LIMITS.
Municipalities.
Annexation generally, §§160A-29 to 160A-58.90.
See ANNEXATION.

CORPORATIONS, §§55-1-01 to 55-17-05.
ABC permits.
Person to qualify for issuance, §18B-900(c).
Accountants.
Public practice of accountancy.
Prohibited, §93-8.
Use of title "certified public accountant,"§93-5.
Acknowledgments deemed sufficient.
Forms of probate for deeds and other conveyances, §47-41.01(b), (c).
Actions.
Against directors, §55-7-48.
Amendment of articles of incorporation.
Effect on actions, §55-10-09.
Derivative actions by shareholders, §§55-7-40 to 55-7-49.
Applicability of foreign corporations, §55-7-47.
Definitions, §55-7-40.1.
Demand requirement, §55-7-42.
Discontinuance or settlement, §55-7-45.
Dismissal, §55-7-44.
Jurisdiction, §55-7-40.
Payment of costs and expenses, §55-7-46.
Privileged communications, §55-7-49.
Standing, §55-7-41.
Stays, §55-7-43.
Foreign corporations.
Certificates of authority.
Consequences of failure to obtain, §55-15-02(a).
Nonprofit corporations.
Corporations already in existence, §55A-17-03(b).
Creditors action against member, §55A-6-24.
Derivative actions, §55A-7-40.
Judicial dissolution, §§55A-14-30 to 55A-14-33.
Power to sue and be sued, §55A-3-02(a).
Voluntary dissolution.
Claims against dissolved corporations, §55A-14-09(a).
Saving provisions, §55-17-03(b).
Agents.
Embezzlement.
Receipt of property by virtue of office or employment, §14-90.

CORPORATIONS —Cont'd
Agents —Cont'd
Misconduct in private office.
Malfeasance of corporation agents, §14-254(a).
Amendment of articles of incorporation, §§55-10-01 to 55-10-09.
Appraisal rights.
Corporate actions giving rise to appraisal rights, §55-13-02(a).
Articles of amendment.
Contents, §55-10-06.
Delivery to secretary of state, §55-10-06.
Issuance of classes or series of stock, filing, §55-6-02(b).
Authorized, §55-10-01(a).
Board of directors.
Amendment by board, §55-10-02.
Proposal of amendments to shareholders, §55-10-03(a) to (d).
Appraisal rights, §55-10-03(e).
Approval of proposed amendments by shareholders, §§55-10-03(b), (e), 55-10-04.
Restated articles of incorporation.
Power of board, §55-10-07(a).
Effect of amendment, §55-10-09.
Restated articles of incorporation.
Amendments may be included in, §55-10-07(b).
Articles of restatement, §55-10-07(d).
Certification by secretary of state, §55-10-07(f).
Effect, §55-10-07(e).
Power of board of directors, §55-10-07(a).
Submission to shareholders, §55-10-07(c).
Shares and shareholders.
Acquisition by corporation of own shares, §55-6-31(b).
Amendment before issuance of shares, §55-10-05.
Classes or series of stock, §55-6-02(b).
Issuance of shares.
Amendment before issuance, §55-10-05.
Restated articles of incorporation.
Submission to shareholders, §55-10-07(c).
Vested property right resulting from provisions in articles.
Stockholders not deemed to have, §55-10-01(b).
Voting groups.
Classes of shares entitled to vote as separate voting groups, §55-10-04(a).
Nonvoting shares entitled to vote as voting groups, §55-10-04(d).
Series of classes of shares entitled to vote as voting groups, §55-10-04(b), (c).
Voting on proposed amendments.
Appraisal rights, §55-10-03(e).
Required votes for adoption, §55-10-03(b), (e).
Voting groups, §55-10-04.
Amendment of bylaws.
Board of directors.
Amendment by, §55-10-20(a).
Quorum or voting requirements.
Bylaws increasing, §55-10-22.
Shareholders.
Amendment by shareholders, §55-10-20(b).
Bylaw increasing quorum or voting requirements for directors, §55-10-22.
Appeals.
Dissolution.
Administrative dissolution.
Denial of reinstatement, §55-14-23.

CORPORATIONS —Cont'd
Appeals —Cont'd
Filing of documents.
Appeal from secretary of state's refusal to file, §55D-16.
Foreign corporations.
Revocation of certificate of authority, §55-15-32.
Appearance.
Organizations generally.
Appearance by counsel or agent, §15A-773(b).
Applicability of act, §55-17-01(a).
Exceptions, §55-17-01(b).
Foreign corporations.
Qualified foreign corporations, §55-17-02.
Appraisal rights, §§55-13-01 to 55-13-40.
After-acquired shares.
Acceptance of offer of payment, §55-13-27(c).
Failure of corporation to pay.
Action against corporation, §55-13-31(d).
Sending payment for shares, §55-13-27(d).
Withholding payment, §55-13-27(a).
Notice, §55-13-27(b).
Articles of incorporation.
Limits to appraisal rights, §55-13-02(c).
Beneficial shareholders.
Asserting appraisal rights, §55-13-03(a), (b).
Defined, §55-13-01.
Corporate actions giving rise to appraisal rights, §55-13-02(a).
Remedies against proposed or completed action limited, §55-13-40(a), (b).
Definitions, §55-13-01.
Dissatisfaction with payment or offer.
Notice, §55-13-28(a).
Waiver of rights for failure to provide notice, §55-13-28(b).
Judicial appraisal of shares, §§55-13-30, 55-13-31.
Appraisers.
Appointment, §55-13-30(d).
Compensation and expenses, §55-13-31(a).
Complaint filed by corporation, §55-13-30(a).
Service of copies on parties, §55-13-30(c).
Costs, §55-13-31(a).
Fees and expenses of parties, assessment, §55-13-31(b).
When paid by others than corporation, §55-13-31(c).
Expenses of parties, assessment, §55-13-31(b).
When paid by others than corporation, §55-13-31(c).
Failure of corporation to make payments.
Action by shareholder, §55-13-31(d).
Judgment.
Amount, §55-13-30(e).
Jurisdiction of court, §55-13-30(d).
Time limitations, §55-13-30(a).
Venue, §55-13-30(b).
Notice of appraisal, §55-13-22(a).
Content of notice, §55-13-22(b).
Form of notice, §55-13-22(b).
Time to send, §55-13-22(b).
Notice of dissatisfaction with payment or offer, §55-13-28(a).
Waiver of rights for failure to provide notice, §55-13-28(b).
Notice of intent to demand payment, §55-13-21(a).
Failure to provide notice, §55-13-21(c).
Notice of rights.
Consummation of corporate change, §55-13-20(d).

CORPORATIONS —Cont'd
Appraisal rights —Cont'd
Notice of rights —Cont'd
Inclusion in notice of meeting on corporate action, §55-13-20(a).
Mergers, §55-13-20(b).
Written consent required for corporate action, §55-13-20(c).
Notice of withholding payment for after-acquired shares, §55-13-27(b).
Payment for shares.
After-acquired shares.
Acceptance of offer of payment, §55-13-27(c).
Failure of corporation to pay.
Action against corporation, §55-13-31(d).
Sending payment for shares, §55-13-27(d).
Withholding payment, §55-13-27(a).
Notice, §55-13-27(b).
Amount, §55-13-25(a).
Cash payment, §55-13-25(a).
Disclosures and other information included with payment, §55-13-25(b).
Dissatisfaction with payment or offer.
Notice, §55-13-28(a).
Waiver of rights for failure to provide notice, §55-13-28(b).
Failure to pay.
Action against corporation, §55-13-31(d).
Interest, §55-13-25(a).
Rejection of offer of payment, §55-13-28(a).
Perfection of rights, §55-13-23(a).
Failure to perfect, consequence, §55-13-23(c).
Procedure to assert, §§55-13-20 to 55-13-28.
Record shareholders.
Asserting appraisal rights, §55-13-03(a).
Reorganization.
Actions under provisions not to give rise to rights, §55-14A-01(c).
Restrictions on availability of rights, §55-13-02(b).
Withdrawal from appraisal process, §55-13-23(b).
Written consent for corporate action.
Consent, consequences on rights, §55-13-21(b), (c).
Notice of rights, §55-13-21(a).
Architects.
Licenses.
Corporate certificate, §§83A-1, 83A-8.
Practice of architecture.
Corporate practice, §§83A-1, 83A-8.
Archives and history.
Outdoor historical dramas, §143-204.8.
Articles of incorporation.
Amendments, §§55-10-01 to 55-10-09. See within this heading, "Amendment of articles of incorporation."
Appraisal rights.
Corporate actions giving rise to appraisal rights, §55-13-02(a).
Eligibility of holders of certain shares for appraisal rights, §55-13-02(d).
Limits to appraisal rights in articles, §55-13-02(c).
Contents, §55-2-02(a), (b).
Conversion of business entity to domestic corporation, §§55-2-02, 55-11A-03(a) to (c), (d).
Defined, §55-1-40.
Filing.
Commencement of corporate existence, §55-2-03(a).
Effect, §55-2-03(b).

CORPORATIONS —Cont'd
Articles of incorporation —Cont'd
Nonprofit corporations.
  See NONPROFIT CORPORATIONS.
Powers of corporation.
  Statutory powers need not be set forth,
    §§55-2-02(c), 55-3-02(b).
Suspension.
  Failure to file tax report or return or pay tax or
    fee.
    Suspension of articles of incorporation,
      §105-230(a).
    Invalidity of acts performed during
      suspension, §105-230(b).
    Receivership, liquidation, cessation of
      business, §105-232(b).
    Reinstatement of articles, §105-232(a).
Assets, disposition.
Appraisal rights.
  Corporate actions giving rise to appraisal rights,
    §55-13-02(a).
Attachment.
Grounds for attachment, §1-440.3.
Attorneys at law.
Practice of law.
  Attorney retained or employed by corporation,
    §84-5(b).
  Nonprofit corporations.
    Indigent legal services by, §84-5.1.
  Prohibition as to practice of law by corporation,
    §84-5(a).
  Regulations for professional corporations
    practicing law, Bar Rules E.0101 to E.0106.
  Violations of provisions.
    Misdemeanor, §84-8(a).
Receivers.
  Counsel fees, §1-507.9.
Attorneys' fees.
Derivative actions, §55-7-46.
Records.
  Inspection of records by shareholders.
    Court-ordered inspection, §55-16-04(c).
Auctions and auctioneers.
Licenses, §85B-4(g).
Averment of capacity, §1A-1 Rule 84.
Banks, §§53-1 to 53-272.
See BANKS.
Benefit corporations.
Appraisal rights.
  Corporate changes giving rise to appraisal
    rights, §55-13-02(a).
Board of directors.
Actions against, §55-7-48.
Amendment of articles of incorporation.
  Amendment by board, §55-10-02.
  Classes or series of stock.
    Filing articles of amendment prior to issuance
      required, §55-6-02(b).
  Proposal of amendments to shareholders,
    §§55-10-03(a) to (d).
    Appraisal rights, §55-10-03(e).
  Approval of proposed amendments by
    shareholders, §§55-10-03(b), (e), 55-10-04.
  Restated articles of incorporation.
    Power of board, §55-10-07(a).
Amendment of bylaws.
  Amendment by board of directors, §55-10-20(a).
  Quorum or voting requirements.
    Bylaws increasing, §55-10-22.
Classes or series of stock.
  Amendment of articles of incorporation.
    Filing articles of amendment prior to issuance
      required, §55-6-02(b).

CORPORATIONS —Cont'd
Board of directors —Cont'd
Classes or series of stock —Cont'd
  Preferences, limitations or rights.
    Determination by board, §55-6-02(a).
Committees.
  Approval of creation and appointment of
    members, §55-8-25(b).
  Authority, §55-8-25(d).
    Restrictions, §55-8-25(e).
  Creation, §55-8-25(a).
  Effect, §55-8-25(f).
  Meetings.
    Applicability of provisions to committees,
      §55-8-25(c).
  Number of members, §55-8-25(a).
Compensation of directors, §55-8-11.
Conflicts of interest.
  Authorization, approval, or ratification of
    transaction, §55-8-31(a), (c), (d).
  What constitutes, §55-8-31(a), (b).
Cumulative voting for, §55-7-28(b) to (e).
Dissolution.
  Voluntary dissolution, §§55-14-01 to 55-14-09.
    Adoption of proposal by shareholders,
      §55-14-02(b), (e).
    Articles of dissolution, §55-14-03(a).
    Effective date of dissolution by, §55-14-03(b).
    Notice of shareholders meeting to consider
      proposal, §55-14-02(d).
    Proposal by directors, §55-14-02(a), (c).
    Revocation of dissolution by, §55-14-04.
Election of directors, §55-8-03(d).
  Classes of shareholders, §55-8-04.
  Voting of shares, §55-7-28(a).
    Cumulative voting, §55-7-28(b) to (e).
Indemnification, §§55-8-50 to 55-8-58.
Liability of directors.
  Standards of conduct.
    Effect of provisions, §55-8-30(d), (e).
  Unlawful distributions.
    Contribution and reimbursement, §55-8-33(b).
    Generally, §55-8-33(a).
    Limitation of proceedings, §55-8-33(c).
Loans to directors.
  Indirect loan or guarantee, §55-8-32(d).
  Restrictions, §55-8-32(a), (b).
    Exceptions, §55-8-32(c).
Meetings.
  Action without meeting.
    Authorized, §55-8-21(a).
    Effect of signed consent, §55-8-21(c).
    Electronic consent, §55-8-21(a).
    When effective, §55-8-21(b).
  Assent to action taken at meeting.
    When director deemed to have assented,
      §55-8-24(d).
  Committees.
    Applicability of provisions to committees,
      §55-8-25(c).
  Communication methods, §55-8-20(b).
  Location, §55-8-20(a).
  Notice.
    Regular meetings, §55-8-22(a).
    Special meetings, §55-8-22(b).
    Waiver of notice, §55-8-23.
  Quorum, §55-8-24(a) to (c).
  Special meetings.
    Calling, §55-8-20(c).
  Telephone conference calls.
    Means of communication generally,
      §55-8-20(b).

CORPORATIONS —Cont'd
Board of directors —Cont'd
Meetings —Cont'd
Waiver of notice, §55-8-23(a).
Attendance at or participation in meeting, §55-8-23(b).
Number of directors, §55-8-03(a), (b).
Change in number, §55-8-03(b).
Effect of decrease on terms of office, §55-8-05(c).
Powers.
Dispensing with or limiting authority, §55-8-01(c).
Exercise by individual or group other than board, §55-8-01(d).
Exercise of corporate powers, §55-8-01(b).
Qualifications of directors, §55-8-02.
Quorum, §55-8-24(a) to (c).
Bylaws increasing quorum or voting requirements.
Amendment, who may amend, §55-10-22(a) to (c).
Repeal, §55-10-22(a), (b).
Removal of directors.
Entire board, §55-8-08(e).
Judicial proceeding.
Barring director from reelection, §55-8-09(b).
Corporation as party defendant, §55-8-09(c).
Generally, §55-8-09(a).
Power of superior court, §55-8-09(a).
Shareholders.
Cumulative voting, §55-8-08(c).
Notice of meeting, §55-8-08(d).
Power to remove directors, §55-8-08(a).
Removal of entire board, §55-8-08(e).
Voting groups, §55-8-08(b).
Required, §55-8-01(a).
Residence of directors.
Not required to be resident of state, §55-8-02.
Resignation of directors, §55-8-07(a).
When effective, §55-8-07(b).
Staggered terms for directors, §55-8-06.
Standards of conduct for directors.
Conflicts of interest, §55-8-31.
Generally, §55-8-30(a).
Liability.
Effect of provisions on, §55-8-30(d), (e).
Reliance on information, opinions, reports or statements, §55-8-30(b), (c).
Terms of directors, §§55-8-05, 55-8-06.
Decrease in number of directors.
Effect, §55-8-05(c).
Expiration, §55-8-05(a), (b), (d), (e).
Staggered terms, §55-8-06.
Vacancies.
Filling, §55-8-10(a), (c).
Voting groups, §55-8-10(b).
Bond issues.
Drainage, §§156-52, 156-53.
Interest.
Sale below par permitted, §24-2.
Payment of bonds enforced, §156-53.
Boxing.
Licenses for manager or promoter issued to, §143-654(b).
Brokers.
Acting as stockbroker, §14-401.7.
Burning of corporate buildings, §14-61.
Bylaws.
Adoption, §55-2-06(a).
Amendments, §§55-10-20, 55-10-22.

CORPORATIONS —Cont'd
Bylaws —Cont'd
Contents, §55-2-06(b).
Emergency bylaws.
Authorized, §55-2-07(a).
Duration of effectiveness, §55-2-07(b).
Effect, §55-2-07(c).
Nonprofit corporations, §55A-2-07.
Regular bylaws remain effective, §55-2-07(b).
When emergency exists, §55-2-07(d).
Nonprofit corporations, §§55A-2-06, 55A-2-07.
Campaign contributions and expenditures.
Acceptance of contributions by corporations.
Prohibited, §163-278.15(a).
Defined, §163-278.6.
Prohibited acts, §163-278.19(a).
Exceptions, §163-278.19(b), (d), (f).
Penalties, §§163-278.19(c), 163-278.27(a2).
Cemetery corporations.
Change of name, §65-17.
Land holdings, §65-16.
Stockholder's meetings for certain nonprofit corporations, §65-17.1.
Charities.
Exemptions from business corporation act, §55-17-01(b).
Nonprofit corporations, §§55A-1-01 to 55A-17-05.
See NONPROFIT CORPORATIONS.
Prudent management of institutional funds, §§36E-1 to 36E-11.
See PRUDENT MANAGEMENT OF INSTITUTIONAL FUNDS.
Charter, NC Const Art VIII §1.
Forfeiture.
Counterfeiting, §14-15.
Kidnapping and abduction.
Forfeiture of charter, §14-39.
Citation of act.
Short title, §55-1-01.
Class actions.
Secondary action by shareholders, §1A-1 Rule 23(b).
Collection of debts.
Simulation, §14-118.1.
Condominium owners' associations.
Master associations.
Powers exercised or delegated to corporation, §47C-2-120.
Confidentiality of information.
Interrogatories by secretary of state.
Information disclosed by, §55-1-33.
Construction and interpretation.
Control share acquisitions, §§55-9A-07, 55-9A-08.
Severability of provisions, §55-17-04.
Contractors.
Electrical contractors.
Licenses, §87-43.2.
Plumbing, heating and fire sprinkler contractors.
Licenses, §87-26(a), (d), (e).
Refrigeration contractors.
Licenses, §§87-57, 87-62.
Contracts.
Joint assumption or underwriting of risks, §58-65-5.
Control share acquisitions, §§55-9A-01 to 55-9A-09, 75E-1 to 75E-9.
Acquiring person's statement, §55-9A-02.
Applicability of provisions.
Exemptions, §55-9A-09.
Citation of act.
Short title, §55-9A-01(a).

CORPORATIONS —Cont'd
Control share acquisitions —Cont'd
Conflict of laws.
  Provisions controlling, §55-9A-08.
Construction and interpretation.
  Provisions controlling, §55-9A-08.
  Severability of provisions, §55-9A-07.
Definitions, §55-9A-01(b).
  Violation of article, §75E-1.
Exemptions from provisions, §55-9A-09.
Meeting of shareholders.
  Calling special meeting, §55-9A-03(a).
  Next special or annual meeting.
    Consideration of voting rights at,
      §55-9A-03(c).
  Notice, §55-9A-04.
  Time for, §55-9A-03(b), (d).
Nonresidents.
  Service of process.
    Designation of secretary of state, §75E-8.
Notice.
  Meeting of shareholders, §55-9A-04.
  Right of redemption by shareholders,
    §55-9A-06(b), (c).
Redemption.
  Definition of "fair value,"§55-9A-06(e).
  Notice, §55-9A-06(b), (c).
  Right of redemption by shareholders.
    Generally, §55-9A-06(a).
  Written demand by shareholder, §55-9A-06(d).
Severability of provisions, §§55-9A-07, 75E-9.
Statement by acquiring person, §55-9A-02.
Title of act.
  Short title, §55-9A-01(a).
Violation of article.
  Attorney general.
    Investigative and regulatory powers, §75E-3.
  Chapter not exclusive, §75E-7.
  Civil actions, §75E-4.
  Damages, §75E-4.
  Definitions, §75E-1.
  Penalties.
    Civil penalties, §75E-5.
  Remedies cumulative, §75E-6.
  Unlawful activities, §75E-2.
Voting rights of control shares.
  Meeting of shareholders to consider, §§55-9A-03,
    55-9A-04.
  Resolution granting, §55-9A-05(a).
    Adoption, §55-9A-05(b).
Conversion of business entity to domestic
  corporation, §§55-11A-01 to 55-11A-04.
Articles of incorporation.
  Effect, §55-11A-03(c).
  Filing by converting entity, §55-11A-03(a).
  Requirements of articles filed to effect
    conversion, §55-2-02(d).
  Withdrawal if plan of conversion abandoned,
    §55-11A-03(b).
Authorized, §55-11A-01.
Certificate of conversion.
  Registration, §55-11A-03(d).
Effect, §55-11A-04.
Plan of conversion.
  Amendment or abandonment, §55-11A-02(c).
  Approval, §55-11A-02(b).
  Contents, §55-11A-02(a).
Requirements, §55-11A-01.

CORPORATIONS —Cont'd
Conversion of domestic corporation to
  different business entity, §§55-11A-10 to
  55-11A-13.
Appraisal rights.
  Corporate changes giving rise to appraisal
    rights, §55-13-02(a).
  General provisions, §§55-13-01 to 55-13-40. See
    within this heading, "Appraisal rights."
Articles of conversion, §55-11A-12(a), (b).
  Effect, §55-11A-12(d).
  Withdrawal if plan of conversion abandoned,
    §55-11A-12(c).
Authorized, §55-11A-10.
Certificate of conversion.
  Registration, §55-11A-12(e).
Effect, §55-11A-13(a).
  Resulting entity not limited liability company or
    limited partnership, §55-11A-13(b).
Plan of conversion.
  Amendment or abandonment, §55-11A-11(g).
  Approval, §55-11A-11(b) to (f).
  Contents, §55-11A-11(a).
Requirements, §55-11A-10.
Cooperative associations, §§54-111 to 54-128.
See COOPERATIVE ASSOCIATIONS.
Costs.
Actions by state for corporation.
  Liability for costs, §6-15.
Appraisal rights.
  Judicial appraisal of shares, §55-13-31(a).
    Fees and expenses of parties, assessment,
      §55-13-31(b).
    When paid by others than corporation,
      §55-13-31(c).
Derivative actions, §55-7-46.
Records.
  Inspection of records by directors.
    Reimbursement for costs of director,
      §55-16-05(c).
  Inspection of records by shareholders.
    Court-ordered inspection, §55-16-04(c).
Counterfeiting.
Issuing substitutes for money without authority,
  §14-15.
Receiving or passing unauthorized substitutes for
  money, §14-16.
Counties.
Corporate powers of counties, §153A-11.
  Exercise of corporate powers, §153A-12.
Credit unions, §§54-109.1 to 54-110.10.
See CREDIT UNIONS.
Criminal law and procedure.
Defendants.
  Appearance by counsel or agent, §15A-773(b).
  Securing attendance of organizations,
    §15A-773(a).
    Definition of "organization,"§15A-773.
Indictments.
  Manner of alleging joint ownership of property,
    §15-148.
Securing attendance of organizations as
  defendants, §15A-773.
Cumulative voting for directors, §55-7-28(b) to
  (e).
Curative statute, §55-17-05.
Declaratory judgments.
Word "person" construed, §1-265.
Deeds and other conveyances.
Acknowledgment by corporate official.
  Form, §47-41.01(b), (c).

CORPORATIONS —Cont'd
Deeds and other conveyances —Cont'd
Corporate seal required, §47-41.1.
Error in acknowledgment of probate, §47-97.1.
Forms of probate for deeds and other conveyances.
  Acknowledgment by corporate official, §47-41.01(b), (c).
  Contracts in writing for purchase of personal property, §47-41.02(f).
  Forms deemed sufficient, §§47-41.01(a) to (c), 47-41.02(a) to (f).
    Applicability to other entities, §§47-41.01(e), 47-41.02(h).
    Definitions, §47-41.01(d).
    Other forms not excluded, §§47-41.01(a), 47-41.02(a).
    Validation of deeds and other conveyances, §47-41.02(e), (g).
  Instrument executed by president or presiding member or trustee and 2 other members of corporation, §47-41.02(b).
  Instrument executed by president or presiding member or trustee and attested by secretary or assistant secretary, §47-41.02(c), (d).
  Technical defects, errors, omissions not to affect, §47-41.2(a).
    Inapplicability of provisions, §47-41.2(b).
Mistake as to officer's name, §47-97.
Probate of deed where corporation ceased to exist, §47-16.
Validation of prior probated and recorded conveyances, §47-41.02(e), (g).
Definitions, §55-1-40.
Appraisal rights, §55-13-01.
Boards of directors, §58-65-20(a).
  Indemnification, §55-8-50(b).
  Shareholder protection act, §55-9-01(b).
    Violation of article, §75E-1.
Constitutional definition, NC Const Art VIII §2.
Control share acquisitions, §55-9A-01(b).
Foreign trade zones.
  "Public corporation,"§55C-2.
Shareholder protection act, §55-9-01(b).
  Violation of article, §75E-1.
Dental service corporations generally, §§58-65-1 to 58-66-40.
See HOSPITAL, MEDICAL AND DENTAL SERVICE CORPORATIONS.
Depositions, use in court proceedings, §1A-1 Rule 32(a).
Deposition upon oral examination, §1A-1 Rule 30(b).
Derivative actions, §§55-7-40 to 55-7-49.
Applicability of foreign corporations, §55-7-47.
Definitions, §55-7-40.1.
Demand requirement, §55-7-42.
Discontinuance or settlement, §55-7-45.
Dismissal, §55-7-44.
Jurisdiction, §55-7-40.
Nonprofit corporations.
  Members and directors, §55A-7-40.
Payment of costs and expenses, §55-7-46.
Privileged communications, §55-7-49.
Standing, §55-7-41.
Stays, §55-7-43.
Dissenting shareholders.
Appraisal rights generally, §§55-13-01 to 55-13-40.
  See within this heading, "Appraisal rights."

CORPORATIONS —Cont'd
Dissolution, §§55-14-01 to 55-14-40.
Administrative dissolution, §§55-14-20 to 55-14-24.
  Administrative procedure act.
    Inapplicability, §55-14-24.
  Appeal from denial of reinstatement, §55-14-23.
    Appeal of court's final decision, §55-14-23(d).
    Burden on corporation, §55-14-23(b).
    Notice of denial, §55-14-23(a).
    Orders of court, §55-14-23(c).
    Petition, §55-14-23(b).
    Time for, §55-14-23(b).
  Certificate of dissolution, §55-14-21(b).
  Claims against dissolved corporation.
    Applicability of certain provisions, §55-14-21(c).
  Effect of dissolution.
    Applicability of certain provisions, §55-14-21(c).
    Registered agent's authority not terminated, §55-14-21(d).
  Grounds, §55-14-20.
  Nonprofit corporations, §§55A-14-20 to 55A-14-24.
  Notice.
    Denial of reinstatement, §55-14-23(a).
    Determination that grounds exist, §55-14-21(a).
  Reinstatement, §55-14-22.
    Appeal from denial, §55-14-23.
    Application, §55-14-22(a).
    Certificate of reinstatement, §55-14-22(b).
    Effect, §55-14-22(c).
    Name, §55-14-22(a1).
Creditors.
  Unavailable shareholders and creditors.
    Disposition of amounts due to, §55-14-40.
Dissolved corporation defined, §55-14-03(c).
Forest protection and development corporations, §106-990.
Judicial dissolution, §§55-14-30 to 55-14-33.
  Claims against dissolved corporation.
    Notification of claimants, §55-14-33(b).
  Decree of dissolution, §55-14-33(a).
  Grounds, §55-14-30.
  Injunctions.
    Power of court to issue, §55-14-31(c).
  Nonprofit corporations, §§55A-14-30 to 55A-14-33.
  Parties.
    Shareholders need not be made parties, §55-14-31(b).
  Purchase of shares of complaining shareholder.
    Dissolution not ordered, §55-14-31(d).
  Receiver.
    Appointment, §§55-14-31(c), 55-14-32(a), (b).
    Compensation, §55-14-32(e).
    Powers and duties, §55-14-32(c).
  Venue of proceedings, §55-14-31(a).
  Winding up of affairs, §55-14-33(b).
Nonprofit corporations, §§55A-14-01 to 55A-14-40.
  See NONPROFIT CORPORATIONS.
Saving provisions, §55-17-03(c).
Superior court.
  Judicial dissolution generally, §§55-14-30 to 55-14-33.
Unavailable shareholders and creditors.
  Disposition of amounts due to, §55-14-40.
Voluntary dissolution, §§55-14-01 to 55-14-09.
  Articles of dissolution.
    Dissolution by board of directors and shareholders, §55-14-03(a).

CORPORATIONS —Cont'd
Dissolution —Cont'd
Voluntary dissolution —Cont'd
Articles of dissolution —Cont'd
Dissolution by incorporators or initial
directors, §55-14-01(a).
Board of directors or shareholders.
Adoption of proposal by shareholders,
§55-14-02(b), (e).
Articles of dissolution, §55-14-03(a).
Effective date of dissolution by, §55-14-03(b).
Notice of shareholders meeting to consider
proposal, §55-14-02(d).
Proposal by directors, §55-14-02(a), (c).
Revocation of dissolution by, §55-14-04.
Claims against dissolved corporation,
§§55-14-06 to 55-14-09.
Barred claims, §§55-14-06(c), 55-14-07(c).
Disposal of known claims, §55-14-06(a).
Enforcement, §55-14-08(a).
Exceptions to term "claim,"§55-14-06(d).
Limitation of actions not extended by
provisions, §55-14-08(b).
Notices, §§55-14-06(b), (c), 55-14-07.
Court proceedings.
Application for determination on claims,
§55-14-09(a).
Guardian ad litem, appointment to represent
claimants, §55-14-09(c).
Notice to claimants holding contingent claims,
§55-14-09(b).
Security to satisfy contingent claims,
§55-14-09(d).
Effective date.
Dissolution by board of directors or
shareholders, §55-14-03(b).
Dissolution by incorporators or initial
directors, §55-14-01(b).
Revocation of dissolution, §55-14-04(d).
Effect of dissolution, §55-14-05(a), (c).
Exceptions, §55-14-05(b).
Incorporators or initial directors.
Articles of dissolution, §55-14-01(a).
Effective date of dissolution by, §55-14-01(b).
Nonprofit corporations, §§55A-14-01 to
55A-14-09.
Notice of dissolution, §55-14-07(a).
Contents, §55-14-07(b).
Effect of publication, §55-14-07(c).
Known claimants, §55-14-06(b), (c).
Publication, §55-14-07(b).
Revocation of dissolution.
Articles of revocation of dissolution,
§55-14-04(c).
Authorization, §55-14-04(b).
Effective date, §55-14-04(d).
Effect of revocation, §55-14-04(e).
Time for, §55-14-04(a).
Distributions to shareholders.
Authorization, §55-6-40(a).
Restrictions, §55-6-40(c) to (g).
Compelling payment of dividends.
Shareholders rights not impair, §55-6-40(k).
Demand by shareholders, §55-6-40(h) to (j).
Payment of additional dividends, §55-6-40(i).
Parity with indebtedness to general unsecured
creditors, §55-6-40(f).
Record date for determining shareholders entitled
to distribution, §55-6-40(b).
Restrictions, §55-6-40(c), (d).
Determination of effect, §55-6-40(e) to (g).

CORPORATIONS —Cont'd
Dividends.
Distributions to shareholders generally, §55-6-40.
Income tax.
Adjustment to expenses related to, §105-130.6A.
Information filed with secretary of revenue.
Resident taxpayers receiving dividends,
§105-130.21(b).
S corporations.
Income tax.
Distributions to shareholders, §105-131.6.
Share dividends.
Generally, §55-6-23(a), (b).
Record date for shareholders entitled to share
dividend, §55-6-23(c).
Document execution.
Authority and proof generally, §47-18.3.
Officers.
Liability, §47-18.3(d).
Power of representatives to bind corporation.
Section not deemed to exclude, §47-18.3(c).
Seals and sealed instruments.
Instrument executed bearing seal.
Prima facie evidence seal duly adopted,
§47-18.3(b).
Third parties.
Validity as to innocent third parties,
§47-18.3(a).
Drainage by corporations, §§156-37 to 156-53.
See DRAINAGE BY CORPORATION.
Elected officials.
Donation of legal expense funds.
Limitations, §163-278.316(d).
Prohibited donations, §163-278.316(e).
Electric membership corporations, §§117-6 to
117-26.
See ELECTRIC MEMBERSHIP
CORPORATIONS.
Electronic transactions.
Agreement to conduct, §55-1-50.
Embezzlement.
Officers or agents of corporation.
Receipt of property by virtue of office or
employment, §14-90.
Emergency bylaws, §55-2-07.
Emergency powers, §55-3-03.
Nonprofit corporations, §55A-3-03.
Eminent domain.
By whom right may be exercised, §40A-3(a).
Engineers and land surveyors.
Practice of engineering or land surveying,
§89C-24.
Enterprise corporations, §§53A-35 to 53A-47.
See NORTH CAROLINA ENTERPRISE
CORPORATIONS.
Evidence.
Filing of documents.
Certificate of existence.
Evidentiary effect, §55-1-28(c).
Evidentiary effect of copy of filed document,
§55D-17.
Probate and registration.
Execution of corporate instruments.
Instruments executed bearing seal.
Prima facie evidence seal duly adopted,
§47-18.3(b).
Executions.
Agents of corporations.
Duties, §§1-324.2 to 1-324.4.
Penalty for violations, §1-324.5.

CORPORATIONS —Cont'd
Executions —Cont'd
Books and records.
Nonresident custodian, §§1-324.6, 1-324.7.
Debts due corporations.
Subject to execution, §1-324.4.
Information as to corporate officers and property.
Duty of agents to furnish, §1-324.2.
Information as to corporate shares.
Duty of agents to furnish, §1-324.3.
Information as to debts due corporation.
Duty of agents to furnish, §1-324.4.
Judgment against corporation.
Property subject to execution, §1-324.1.
Nonresident custodian of corporate books.
Duties, §1-324.7.
Liability, §1-324.7.
Notice to, §1-324.6.
Proceedings, §1-324.6.
Shares subject to execution, §1-324.3.
Executors and administrators.
Disqualifications for service.
Not authorized as personal representative, §28A-4-2.
Incorporation of businesses or ventures.
Power of personal representative or fiduciary, §28A-13-3(a).
Fiduciaries.
Participation in reorganizations.
Powers which may be incorporated by reference in trust instrument, §32-27.
Security transfers.
See FIDUCIARIES.
Filing of documents, §§55D-10 to 55D-18.
Advisory review of documents, §55D-12.
Appeal from secretary of state's refusal to file.
Appeal of court's final decision, §55D-16(c).
Generally, §55D-16(a).
Powers of court, §55D-16(b).
Certificate of existence.
Application for, §55-1-28(a).
Contents, §55-1-28(b).
Evidentiary effect, §55-1-28(c).
Copying, comparing or certifying documents.
Fees, §55-1-22(c).
Correcting filed document, §55D-14(a).
Articles of correction, §55D-14(b).
When effective, §55D-14(c).
Definitions, §55D-1.
Effective time and date of document, §55D-13(a).
Delayed effective time and date, §55D-13(b).
Validity or invalidity of document not affected, §55D-13(c).
Evidence.
Certificate of existence.
Evidentiary effect, §55-1-28(c).
Copy of filed document.
Evidentiary effect, §55D-17.
Expedited filings, §55D-11.
False documents.
Signing, §55D-18(a).
Misdemeanor, §55D-18(b).
Fees.
Copying, comparing or certifying documents, §55-1-22(c).
Expedited filings, §55D-11.
Nonrefundable fee for annual reports, §55-1-22(d).
Schedule of fees, §55-1-22(a).
Service of process on secretary of state, §55-1-22(b).

CORPORATIONS —Cont'd
Filing of documents —Cont'd
Forms.
Promulgation, §55-1-21(a).
Additional forms, §55-1-21(b).
Nonprofit corporations, §§55A-1-20 to 55A-1-22.
See NONPROFIT CORPORATIONS.
Professional corporations.
Applicability of provisions to, §55B-3(b).
Reorganization proceedings, §55-14A-01(b).
Requirements, §§55-1-20(a), 55D-10(b).
Execution of document, §55-1-20(b).
Satisfaction of requirements, §55D-10(a).
Rulemaking, §55D-5.
Secretary of state.
Duties, §55D-15(a), (b).
Effect of filing or refusal to file by, §55D-15(d).
Forms.
Promulgation, §55-1-21.
Refusal to file.
Appeal from, §55D-16.
Duties upon, §55D-15(c).
Effect, §55D-15(d).
Foreign corporations, §§55-15-01 to 55-15-33.
Actions.
Certificates of authority.
Consequences of failure to obtain, §55-15-02(a).
Administrative procedure act.
Revocation of certificate of authority.
Inapplicability of administrative procedure act, §55-15-33.
Appeals.
Revocation of certificate of authority, §55-15-32.
Applicability of act.
Qualified foreign corporations, §55-17-02.
Certificates of authority.
Amendment.
Procedure, §55-15-04(b).
When required, §55-15-04(a).
Applications.
Certificate of existence to accompany, §55-15-03(b).
Contents, §55-15-03(a).
Effect, §55-15-05.
Failure to obtain.
Actions may not be maintained, §55-15-02(a).
Liability to state for fees and taxes, §55-15-02(d).
Validity of corporate acts not impaired, §55-15-02(e).
Insurance companies.
Exception to requirement, §55-15-01(d).
Issuance, §55-15-03(c).
Effect, §55-15-05.
Required, §55-15-01(a).
Consequences of transacting business without authority, §55-15-02.
Exceptions, §§55-15-01(b), (d), 55-17-02.
Revocation, §§55-15-30 to 55-15-33.
Secretary of state.
Action on application for certificate, §55-15-03(c).
Dissolution.
Probate and registration.
Validation of conveyances of foreign dissolved corporations, §47-108.6.
Domestic corporations.
Certificate of authority to confer same rights and privileges, §55-15-05(b).

CORPORATIONS —Cont'd
Foreign corporations —Cont'd
Executors and administrators.
  Granting of ancillary letters, §28A-26-3(a).
Fiduciaries.
  Restrictions on foreign corporations,
    §55-15-05(a).
Franchise tax generally, §§105-114 to 105-129.
  See FRANCHISE TAX.
Insurance companies.
  See FOREIGN OR ALIEN INSURANCE
    COMPANIES.
Merger or share exchange with foreign
  corporation, §55-11-07.
  Acquisition of shares of domestic corporation.
    Power of foreign corporation not affected,
      §55-11-07(c).
  Authorized, §55-11-07(a).
  Effect, §55-11-07(b).
Names, §55D-22.
  Change of name to satisfy requirements,
    §55D-22(a).
    May not conduct business unless
      requirements satisfied, §55D-22(b).
  Registration of name.
    Generally, §§55D-24, 55D-25.
Nonprofit corporations.
  See NONPROFIT CORPORATIONS.
Probate and registration.
  Validation of certain conveyances of foreign
    dissolved corporations, §47-108.6.
Professional corporations, §55B-16.
Qualified foreign corporations.
  Exemption of previously qualified foreign
    corporation, §55-17-02.
Receivers.
  Property within state of foreign corporations,
    §1-502.
Registered agent.
  Required, §55-15-07.
  Revocation of certificate of authority.
    Authority of registered agent not terminated
      by, §55-15-31(e).
Registered office.
  Required, §55-15-07.
Revocation of certificate of authority.
  Administrative procedure act.
    Not applicable, §55-15-33.
  Appeal.
    Appeal from court's final decision,
      §55-15-32(c).
    Petition, §55-15-32(a).
    Powers of court, §55-15-32(b).
    Time for, §55-15-32(a).
  Certificate of revocation, §55-15-31(b).
  Effect, §55-15-31(c) to (e).
  Grounds, §55-15-30(a).
  New certificate of authority.
    Not granted until grounds for revocation
      corrected, §55-15-31(f).
  Notice of determination that grounds exist,
    §55-15-31(a).
  Revenue act.
    Certain provisions not repealed or modified,
      §55-15-30(b).
  Service of process.
    Effect on, §55-15-31(d).
Saving provisions, §55-17-02.
Secretary of state.
  Certificates of authority.
    Action on application for, §55-15-03(c).

CORPORATIONS —Cont'd
Foreign corporations —Cont'd
Secretary of state —Cont'd
  Certificates of authority —Cont'd
    Revocation generally, §§55-15-30 to 55-15-33.
  Power to require compliance with provisions,
    §55-15-02(f).
  Revocation of certificate of authority.
    Generally, §§55-15-30 to 55-15-33.
  Service of process.
    Merger or share exchange with foreign
      corporation, §55-11-07(b).
    Withdrawal of foreign corporation,
      §55-15-21(c).
Service of process.
  Manner of service on to exercise personal
    jurisdiction, §1A-1 Rule 4(j).
  Revocation of certificate of authority.
    Effect, §55-15-31(d).
  Secretary of state.
    Merger or share exchange with foreign
      corporation, §55-11-07(b).
    Withdrawal of foreign corporation,
      §55-15-21(c).
  Withdrawal of foreign corporation.
    Effect, §55-15-20(c).
Taxation.
  Applicability of laws, §105-250.
  Property taxes.
    Property of foreign corporations not
      exempted, §105-274(b).
Transacting business in state.
  Activities not deemed to constitute,
    §55-15-01(b).
  Previously qualified foreign corporations,
    §55-17-02.
  Requirement of certificate of authority,
    §55-15-01(a).
    Consequences of transacting business without
      authority, §55-15-02.
Venue of actions against, §1-80.
Withdrawal.
  Application for certificate, §55-15-20(b).
    Action by secretary of state on, §55-15-20(b1).
  Certificate of withdrawal.
    Application for, §55-15-20(b), (b1).
    Issuance, §55-15-20(b1).
    Required, §55-15-20(a).
    Withdrawal by reason of merger,
      consolidation, or conversion, §55-15-21.
  Effect, §55-15-20(c).
  Merger.
    Withdrawal by reason of merger,
      consolidation, or conversion, §55-15-21.
  Service of process.
    Effect on, §55-15-20(c).
  Withdrawal by reason of merger, consolidation,
    or conversion.
    Actions by secretary of state and application,
      §55-15-21(b).
    Application for certificate, §55-15-21(a).
Foreign trade zones.
Definitions.
  "Public corporation,"§55C-2.
Federal law.
  Corporations establishing foreign trade zone to
    be governed by, §55C-4.
Private corporations.
  Application for privilege for establishing foreign
    trade zone.
    Authorized, §55C-3.

CORPORATIONS —Cont'd
Foreign trade zones —Cont'd
Private corporations —Cont'd
Federal law.
Private corporation establishing foreign trade zone to be governed by, §55C-4.
Public corporations.
Application for privilege of establishing foreign trade zone.
Authorized, §55C-1.
Defined, §55C-2.
Federal law.
Public corporation establishing foreign trade zone to be governed by, §55C-4.
Foresters.
Registration.
Prohibited, §89B-9(b).
Forest protection and development corporations, §§106-980 to 106-996.
See FOREST PROTECTION AND DEVELOPMENT CORPORATIONS.
Forfeiture of charter.
Counterfeiting, §14-15.
Kidnapping and abduction, §14-39.
Forgery.
Certificates of corporate stock forged, §14-124.
Formation, §58-65-15.
Articles of incorporation.
Amendments, §§55-10-01 to 55-10-09. See within this heading, "Amendment of articles of incorporation."
Contents, §55-2-02(a), (b).
Defined, §55-1-40.
Filing.
Commencement of corporate existence, §55-2-03(a).
Effect, §55-2-03(b).
Powers of corporation.
Statutory powers need not be set forth, §§55-2-02(c), 55-3-02(b).
Bylaws, §§55-2-06, 55-2-07.
Commencement of corporate existence, §55-2-03(a).
Incorporators, §55-2-01.
Nonprofit corporations.
Incorporators, §55A-2-01.
Organizational meeting, §55A-2-05.
When corporate existence begins, §55A-2-03.
Number of incorporators, §§55-2-01, 58-65-15.
Organizational meeting, §55-2-05(a).
Location, §55-2-05(c).
Taking action without meeting, §55-2-05(b).
Purposes, §55-3-01(a).
Business subject to regulation under other statute, §55-3-01(b).
Saving provisions, §55-17-03(a).
Subscription for shares before incorporation, §55-6-20.
Forms.
Contracts in writing for purchase of personal property, §47-41.02(f).
Filing of documents, §55-1-21.
Probate of deeds and other conveyances.
Acknowledgment by corporate official, §47-41.01(b), (c).
Instrument executed by president or presiding member or trustee, §47-41.02(b).
Instrument executed by president or presiding member or trustee and attested by secretary or assistant secretary, §47-41.02(c), (d).

CORPORATIONS —Cont'd
Franchise tax.
General provisions, §§105-114 to 105-129.
See FRANCHISE TAX.
Garnishment.
Summons and process.
Delivery of garnishment process to corporate garnishee, §1-440.26.
General assembly.
Reservation of power to amend or repeal provisions, §55-1-02.
Geologists, §89E-7(a).
Guardian ad litem.
Rules of civil procedure, §1A-1 Rule 17(b), (d).
Guardians.
Accounting, procedure to compel.
Persons proceeded against, §35A-1265(a).
Administering incompetent's estate, §35A-1251.
Administering minor ward's estate, §35A-1252.
Appointment as guardian for incompetent.
Priorities for appointment, §35A-1214.
Incompetent persons.
Appointment as guardian for, §35A-1213(c).
Status reports for incompetent wards.
Procedure to compel, §35A-1244.
Health maintenance organizations, §§58-67-1 to 58-67-185.
See HEALTH MAINTENANCE ORGANIZATIONS.
Highways, roads and streets.
Defunct corporations.
Dedication of road or street.
Deemed abandoned if not used within fifteen years, §136-96.
History.
Outdoor historical dramas, §143-204.8.
Holding companies.
Insurance holding companies generally, §§58-19-1 to 58-19-70.
See INSURANCE HOLDING COMPANIES.
Hospital, medical and dental service corporations, §§58-65-1 to 58-66-40.
See HOSPITAL, MEDICAL AND DENTAL SERVICE CORPORATIONS.
Husband and wife.
Joint ownership of corporate stock and investment securities, §41-2.2(a).
Death of joint tenant, §41-2.2(c).
Inheritance laws unaffected, §41-2.2(d).
When joint tenancy and shares of corporate stock or investment securities exist, §41-2.2(b).
Immunity.
Nonprofit corporations.
Acceptance or rejection of member's vote.
Corporate action in good faith, §55A-7-27(d).
Improvements.
Internal improvements, §§124-1 to 124-7.
See INTERNAL IMPROVEMENTS.
Income tax.
General provisions, §§105-130 to 105-130.41.
See INCOME TAX.
S corporations, §§105-131 to 105-131.8.
See INCOME TAX.
Incompetent persons.
Guardian for.
Appointment, §35A-1213(c).
Indemnification, §§55-8-50 to 55-8-58.
Additional indemnification, §55-8-57(a), (b).
Agents, §55-8-56.

CORPORATIONS —Cont'd
Indemnification —Cont'd
Articles of incorporation.
Restrictions on indemnification, §55-8-58(a).
Court-ordered indemnification.
Directors, §55-8-54.
Officers, employees and agents, §55-8-56.
Definitions, §55-8-50(b).
Directors.
Advance for expenses, §55-8-53.
Authority to indemnify, §55-8-51(a) to (c).
Determinations required, §55-8-55(a), (b).
Manner of authorization, §55-8-55(c).
Conflicts of interest.
Indemnification not void or voidable on
grounds of, §55-8-51(f).
Court-ordered indemnification, §55-8-54.
Expenses in defending proceedings.
Advance for expenses, §55-8-53.
Certain powers of corporation not limited,
§55-8-58(b).
Evaluation as to reasonableness, §55-8-55(c).
Mandatory indemnification, §55-8-52.
Restrictions on indemnification, §55-8-51(d), (e).
Effective date of article.
Restriction on applicability of provisions,
§55-8-58(c).
Employees, §55-8-56.
Insurance.
Purchase and maintenance, §55-8-57(c).
Mandatory indemnification.
Directors, §55-8-52.
Officers, employees and agents, §55-8-56.
Nonprofit corporations, §§55A-8-50 to 55A-8-58.
See NONPROFIT CORPORATIONS.
Officers, §55-8-56.
Public policy of state, §55-8-50(a).
Inheritance taxes.
Joint ownership of corporate stock and investment
securities.
Inheritance tax laws unaffected, §41-2.2(d).
Injunctions.
Dissolution.
Judicial dissolution.
Powers of court, §55-14-31(c).
Franchises.
Exercise of corporate franchises not granted,
§55-3-05.
Nonprofit corporations.
Corporate power to act.
Ultra vires, §55A-3-04.
Insurance companies.
Foreign or alien insurance companies, §§58-16-1
to 58-16-55.
See FOREIGN OR ALIEN INSURANCE
COMPANIES.
Generally.
See INSURANCE COMPANIES.
Holding companies generally, §§58-19-1 to
58-19-70.
See INSURANCE HOLDING COMPANIES.
Mutual insurance companies generally, §§58-8-1
to 58-8-60.
See MUTUAL INSURANCE COMPANIES.
Interest.
Appraisal rights.
Payment for shares, §55-13-25(a).
Sale below par permitted, §24-2.
Internal improvements, §§124-1 to 124-7.
See INTERNAL IMPROVEMENTS.

CORPORATIONS —Cont'd
Interrogatories.
Secretary of state.
Answer, §55-1-31.
Sanctions for failure or refusal to answer,
§55-1-32.
Confidentiality of information disclosed by,
§55-1-33.
Failure or refusal to answer.
Misdemeanor, §55-1-32(b).
Suspension of articles or authority to do
business, §55-1-32(a).
Generally, §55-1-31.
Nonprofit corporations, §§55A-1-31 to 55A-1-33.
Interrogatories to parties, §1A-1 Rule 33(a).
Investment securities, §§25-8-101 to 25-8-511.
See INVESTMENT SECURITIES.
Joint assumption or underwriting of risks.
Contracts for, §58-65-5.
Jurisdiction.
Appraisal rights.
Judicial appraisal of shares, §55-13-30(d).
Derivative actions, §55-7-40.
Personal jurisdiction.
Grounds, §1-75.4.
Kidnapping and abduction.
Punishment for kidnapping.
Firm or corporation, §14-39(c).
Land and loan associations, §§54-45 to 54-73.
See LAND AND LOAN ASSOCIATIONS.
Landscape contractors.
Applicability of provisions, §89D-3.
Liens.
Wages for two months' lien on assets, §44-5.1.
Limitation of actions.
Appraisal rights.
Judicial appraisal of shares, §55-13-30(a).
Cash or stock dividends.
Six-year limitation, §1-50(a).
Limited liability companies, §§57C-1-01 to
57C-10-07.
See LIMITED LIABILITY COMPANIES.
Liquidation.
Voluntary dissolution proceedings.
Actions for liquidation by court after
dissolution, §§55-14-30 to 55-14-33.
Loans.
Board of directors.
Loans to directors, §55-8-32.
Malfeasance.
Officers and agents.
Misconduct in private office, §14-254.
Marketing associations, §§54-129 to 54-166.
See MARKETING ASSOCIATIONS.
Medical service corporations.
Hospital, medical and dental service corporations,
§§58-65-1 to 58-66-40.
See HOSPITAL, MEDICAL AND DENTAL
SERVICE CORPORATIONS.
Mergers, §§55-11-01 to 55-11-10.
Appraisal rights.
Corporate actions giving rise to appraisal rights,
§55-13-02(a).
General provisions, §§55-13-01 to 55-13-40. See
within this heading, "Appraisal rights."
Notice of rights, §55-13-20(b).
Articles of merger.
Contents, §55-11-05(a).
Corporation defined, §55-11-05(d).
Delivery to secretary of state, §55-11-05(a).
Authorized, §55-11-01(a).

CORPORATIONS —Cont'd

Mergers —Cont'd

Certificates of merger, §55-11-05(c).

Dissenting shareholders.

General provisions. See within this heading, "Dissenting shareholders."

Effective date, §55-11-05(b).

Effect of merger, §55-11-06(a).

Foreign corporations.

Merger with, §55-11-07.

Withdrawn by reason of merger, consolidation, or conversion, §55-15-21.

Nonprofit corporations, §55A-11-08.

Compliance with requirements, §55A-11-08(a).

Generally, §§55A-11-01 to 55A-11-10.

See NONPROFIT CORPORATIONS.

Plan of merger, §55-11-01(a).

Abandonment of plan, §55-11-03(i).

Approval, §55-11-03(b).

Notice of meeting, §55-11-03(d).

Voting groups, §55-11-03(e), (f).

Contents, §55-11-01(b), (c).

Provisions dependent upon facts ascertainable outside the plan, §55-11-01(d).

Submission to shareholders, §55-11-03(a), (c).

Subsidiary corporation, §55-11-04(b).

When action by shareholders of surviving corporation not required, §55-11-03(g), (h).

Probate and registration.

Adoption of uniform certificates of merger or consolidation, §47-18.1(b).

Certain formalities not required, §47-18.1(c).

Name of corporation formerly owning property to appear in grantor index, §47-18.1(c).

Name of corporation owning property by virtue of merger shall appear in grantee index, §47-18.1(c).

Registration of certificate, §47-18.1(a).

Share exchange.

Corporation defined, §55-11-05(d).

Shareholder protection act, §§55-9-01 to 55-9-05.

Provisions of act to control, §55-11-08.

Subsidiary corporation.

Plan of merger, §55-11-04(b).

Power of parent corporation to merge subsidiary into itself, §55-11-04(a).

Right of shareholders to dissent, §55-11-04(f).

Misdemeanors.

Filing of documents.

False document.

Signing, §55D-18(b).

Interrogatories by secretary of state.

Failure or refusal to answer, §55-1-32(b).

Money transmitters licenses.

Applications, §53-208.7(b).

Good standing required, §53-208.5(b).

Mortgages and deeds of trust.

Corporate seal.

Required, §47-41.1.

Discharge and release.

Cancellation of lost mortgages by register of deeds, §45-42.1.

Foreclosure.

Powers of receivers of corporations, §§1-507.2, 1-507.4.

Receivers.

Powers of receivers of corporations, §§1-507.2, 1-507.4.

Sales, §1-507.4.

Personal property.

Place of registration, §47-20.2(b).

CORPORATIONS —Cont'd

Mortgages and deeds of trust —Cont'd

Receivers of corporations.

Foreclosure.

Powers, §§1-507.2, 1-507.4.

Sales, §1-507.4.

Reorganization, §1-507.11.

Satisfaction of corporate mortgages by corporate officers, §45-42.

Validation of appointment of and conveyances to corporations as trustees, §45-21.

Motor vehicle certificates of title.

Change of name of corporation, §20-64(b).

Mutual insurance companies, §§58-8-1 to 58-8-60.

See MUTUAL INSURANCE COMPANIES.

Names, §§55D-20 to 55D-26.

Assumed or fictitious names, §55D-20(d).

Authorization to use.

Restrictions, §55D-20(e).

Change of name.

Certificate.

Recordation, §55D-26(a), (c).

Uniform certificates, §55D-26(b).

Definitions, §55D-1.

Dissolved entity.

Restrictions on use of name of, §55D-21(d).

Distinguishable names, §55D-21(b).

Exceptions, §55D-21(a), (c).

Foreign corporations, §55D-22.

Change of name to satisfy requirements, §55D-22(a).

May not conduct business unless requirements satisfied, §55D-22(b).

Registration of name.

Generally, §§55D-24, 55D-25.

Prohibitions, §55D-20(b), (c).

Registration of name.

Authorized, §55D-24(a).

Effect, §55D-24(e).

Filing of application, §55D-24(b).

Renewal, §55D-24(d).

Revocation, §55D-25.

When effective, §55D-24(c).

Reinstatement following administrative dissolution, §55-14-22(a1).

Requirements, §55D-20(a).

Reservation of name, §55D-23(a), (c).

Revocation, §55D-25.

Transfer of reservation.

Requirements, §55D-23(b).

Rulemaking, §55D-5.

Nonprofit corporations.

Exemptions from business corporation act, §55-17-01(b).

Generally, §§55A-1-01 to 55A-17-05.

See NONPROFIT CORPORATIONS.

Mergers with, §55A-11-08.

North Carolina enterprise corporations, §§53A-35 to 53A-47.

See NORTH CAROLINA ENTERPRISE CORPORATIONS.

Notice, §55-1-41.

Appraisal rights.

Dissatisfaction with payment or offer, §55-13-28(a).

Waiver of rights for failure to provide notice, §55-13-28(b).

Inclusion in notice of meeting on corporate action, §55-13-20(a).

CORPORATIONS —Cont'd
Notice —Cont'd
Appraisal rights —Cont'd
Intent to demand payment, §55-13-21(a).
Failure to provide notice, §55-13-21(c).
Notice of appraisal, §55-13-22(a).
Contents of notice, §55-13-22(b).
Form of notice, §55-13-22(b).
Time to send, §55-13-22(b).
Withholding payment for after-acquired shares,
§55-13-27(b).
Board of directors.
Meetings, §§55-8-22, 55-8-23.
Conflict of laws.
Requirements which govern, §55-1-41(g).
Control share acquisitions.
Meeting of shareholders, §55-9A-04.
Right of redemption by shareholders,
§55-9A-06(b), (c).
Discontinuance or settlement of derivative
proceeding, §55-7-45(a), (b).
Dissolution.
Administrative dissolution.
Denial of reinstatement, §55-14-23(a).
Determination that grounds exist,
§55-14-21(a).
Voluntary dissolution, §§55-14-06(b), (c),
55-14-07.
Foreign corporations.
Revocation of certificate of authority.
Notice of determination that grounds exist,
§55-15-31(a).
How notice given, §55-1-41(a), (b).
Meetings of shareholders.
Action without meeting, §55-7-04(d), (e).
Adjournment of meeting, §55-7-05(e).
Amendments to articles of incorporation,
§55-10-03(d).
Annual meeting.
Failure to hold, §55-7-01(c).
Location, §55-7-01(b).
Required, §55-7-01(a).
Subject matter, §55-7-01(d).
Control share acquisitions, §§55-9A-03,
55-9A-04.
Court-ordered meetings.
Powers of court as to, §55-7-03(b).
Summary order for meeting to be held,
§55-7-03(a).
Dissolution of corporation by directors and
shareholders, §55-14-02(d).
Election of directors.
Generally. See within this heading, "Board of
directors."
Merger or share exchange, §55-11-03(d).
Record date, §55-7-05(d).
Removal of directors by shareholders,
§55-8-08(d).
Requirements, §55-7-05(a) to (c).
Restated articles of incorporation, §55-10-07(c).
Transfer of assets other than in regular course
of business, §55-12-02(d).
Waiver of notice, §55-7-06.
Nonprofit corporations.
Directors' meetings, §55A-8-22.
Generally, §55A-1-41.
Waiver by directors, §55A-8-23.
Publication.
Notice by publication, §55-1-42(b).
Shareholder action without meeting, §55-7-04(d),
(e).

CORPORATIONS —Cont'd
Notice —Cont'd
Shareholders.
Inspection of records.
Exceptions, §55-16-06.
To whom addressed, §55-1-41(d).
When effective, §55-1-41(c), (e), (f).
Oaths, §11-5.
Officers, §§55-8-40 to 55-8-44.
Appointing officer.
Defined, §55-8-43(c).
Assistants.
Appointment, §55-8-40(b).
Construction of references to specific office,
§55-8-40(e).
Contract rights.
Appointment not to create, §55-8-44(a).
Removal of officer not to affect, §55-8-44(b).
Duties, §55-8-41.
Embezzlement.
Receipt of property by virtue of office or
employment, §14-90.
Generally, §55-8-40(a).
Indemnification, §§55-8-50 to 55-8-58.
Misconduct in private office.
Malfeasance of corporation officers, §14-254(a).
Mortgages and deeds of trust.
Satisfaction of corporate mortgages by corporate
officers, §45-42.
Multiple office-holding by individual, §55-8-40(d).
Nonprofit corporations.
See NONPROFIT CORPORATIONS.
Probate and registration.
Execution of corporate instruments.
Liability, §47-18.3(d).
Removal by board of directors, §55-8-43(b).
Effect on contract rights, §55-8-44(b).
Resignation, §55-8-43(a).
Secretary.
Responsibilities, §55-8-40(c).
Standards of conduct.
Generally, §55-8-42(a).
Liability of officers.
Effect of provisions on, §55-8-42(d), (e).
Reliance on information, opinions, reports, or
statements, §55-8-42(b), (c).
Tax liability.
Personal responsibility for failure to pay certain
taxes, §105-242.2.
Uniform fiduciaries act generally, §§32-1 to 32-13.
See FIDUCIARIES.
Workers' compensation.
Employee defined, §97-2.
Exclusion of executive officers by corporation,
§97-2.
Personal property.
Contracts in writing for purchase of personal
property.
Forms, §47-41.02(f).
Mortgages and deeds of trust.
Place of registration, §47-20.2(b).
Powers, §55-3-02(a).
Articles of incorporation.
Statutory powers need not be set forth,
§§55-2-02(c), 55-3-02(b).
Emergency powers, §55-3-03(a), (b).
Effect of actions taken under, §55-3-03(c).
Nonprofit corporations, §55A-3-03.
When emergency exists, §55-3-03(d).
Nonprofit corporations, §§55A-3-01 to 55A-3-07.

CORPORATIONS —Cont'd

Powers —Cont'd

Ultra vires, §55-3-04(a).

Exceptions, §55-3-04(b), (c).

Nonprofit corporations, §55A-3-04.

Practice of law by.

Regulations for professional corporations practicing law, Bar Rules E.0101 to E.0106.

Premiums or dues.

Payment, §58-65-10.

Preneed funeral contracts and funds.

Embezzling, fraudulently misapplying or converting funds.

Liability of officers, directors, agents or employees, §90-210.70(c).

Presumptions.

Annual report delinquent, §55-16-22(h).

Principal office.

Residence for purpose of venue, §1-79(a).

Private banker.

Acting as private banker, §14-401.7.

Probate and registration.

Admission to record of certain corporate deeds declared valid, §47-108.1.

By president and attested by treasurer under corporate seal, §47-70.

Error in acknowledgment or probate.

Validation of corporate deeds, §47-97.1.

Execution of corporate instruments.

Authority and proof generally, §47-18.3.

Homeowners loan corporation.

Conveyance of lands or other properties, §47-18.3(e).

Instruments executed bearing seal.

Prima facie evidence seal duly adopted corporate seal, §47-18.3(b).

Liability of corporate officers, §47-18.3(d).

Power of corporate representative to bind corporation.

Section not deemed to exclude, §47-18.3(c).

Validity with respect to innocent third parties, §47-18.3(a).

Foreign corporations.

Validation of certain conveyances of foreign dissolved corporations, §47-108.6.

Forms for probate of deeds and other conveyances, §§47-41.01, 47-41.02.

Interested corporations.

Probates before officer, §47-63.

Merger, consolidation or conversion.

Adoption of uniform certificates, §47-18.1(b).

Certain formalities not required for registration, §47-18.1(c).

Name of corporation to appear in grantor index, §47-18.1(c).

Registration of certificate, §47-18.1(a).

Mistake as to officer's name.

Validation of deeds, §47-97.

Name.

Corporate name not affixed, but signed otherwise prior to January, 1973, §47-72.

Oath of subscribing witness, §47-73.

Officers, stockholders or directors prior of January 1, 1945, §47-64.

Probate of corporate deeds where corporation ceased to exist, §47-16.

Proof of articles before officer authorized, §47-75.

Seal omitted prior to January 1, 1991, §47-71.1.

Stamps of corporate seal, §47-41.1.

Professional corporations, §§55B-1 to 55B-16.

See PROFESSIONAL CORPORATIONS.

CORPORATIONS —Cont'd

Professional counselors.

Licensed professional counselors.

Use of title by corporate entity, §90-332.

Provider sponsored organizations, §§131E-275 to 131E-314.

See PROVIDER SPONSORED ORGANIZATIONS.

Proxies, §55-7-22.

Appointment, §55-7-22(b) to (h).

Authorized, §55-7-22(a).

Death or incapacity of shareholder appointing proxy, §55-7-22(e).

Revocation of appointment, §55-7-22(d), (f), (g).

Quo warranto.

General provisions, §§1-514 to 1-532.

See QUO WARRANTO.

Railroads.

Joint construction of railroads having same location, §136-193.

Powers of railroad corporations, §136-190.

Real estate appraisers.

License or certificate not issued to, §93E-1-3(a).

Use of term licensed real estate appraiser or certified real estate appraiser, prohibited, §93E-1-3.1(c).

Real property.

Change of name or transfer of title upon merger.

Recordation of certificate, §55D-26.

Real property donations.

Credits, §105-130.34.

Receivers, §§1-507.1 to 1-507.11.

Actions.

Powers of receivers, §1-507.2.

Agents.

Appointment by receiver, §1-507.2.

Appointment of receivers, §1-507.1.

Attorneys at law.

Counsel fees, §1-507.9.

Bonds, surety, §1-507.2.

Claims.

Presentation to receiver, §1-507.6.

Proof, §1-507.6.

Report on claims to court, §1-507.7.

Exceptions, §1-507.7.

Time limit, §1-507.6.

Notice, §1-507.6.

Compensation of receivers, §1-507.9.

Contempt.

Power of receiver to examine persons and papers.

Refusal to answer, §1-507.5.

Death.

Substitution of parties, §1A-1 Rule 25(e).

Debts of corporation paid or provided for.

Discharge of receiver, §1-507.10.

Discharge of receiver, §1-507.10.

Expenses, §1-507.9.

Foreign corporations.

Property within state of foreign corporations.

Appointment of receiver, §1-502.

Inventory, §1-507.3.

Jury.

Claims.

Exceptions to report on claims, §1-507.7.

Mortgages and deeds of trust.

Foreclosure.

Powers of receivers of corporations, §§1-507.2, 1-507.4.

Notice.

Sale of property pending litigation, §1-507.8.

CORPORATIONS —Cont'd
Receivers —Cont'd
Oaths.
  Claims.
    Power of receiver to examine witnesses
      touching on claim, §1-507.6.
  Power of receivers to examine persons under
    oath, §1-507.5.
Powers of receivers, §§1-507.2 to 1-507.6.
Property.
  Inventory, §1-507.3.
  Powers of receivers generally, §1-507.2.
  Title, §1-507.3.
Removal of receivers, §1-507.1.
Reorganization, §1-507.11.
Sales.
  Mortgages and deeds of trust.
    Foreclosure.
      Powers of receivers of corporations,
        §1-507.4.
  Powers of receivers of corporations, §1-507.2.
    Foreclosure sales, §1-507.4.
  Property sold pending litigation, §1-507.8.
Superior courts.
  Proper division for actions for corporate
    receiverships, §7A-249.
Records, §§55-16-01 to 55-16-22.
Accounting records, §55-16-01(b).
Copies to be kept at principal office, §55-16-01(e).
Inspection of records by directors.
  Authorized as relates to performance of
    director's duties, §55-16-05(a).
  Costs of director, reimbursement, §55-16-05(c).
  Court-ordered inspection when director
    wrongfully refused, §55-16-05(b).
  Misuse of information, §55-16-05(c).
Inspection of records by shareholders.
  Agent of shareholder.
    Same rights as shareholder, §55-16-03(a).
  Attorney of shareholder.
    Same rights as shareholder, §55-16-03(a).
  Charges.
    Right of corporation to impose, §55-16-03(c).
  Court-ordered inspection.
    Application for, §55-16-04(b).
    Attorneys' fees, §55-16-04(c).
    Costs, §55-16-04(c).
    Generally, §55-16-04(a).
    Restrictions may be imposed, §55-16-04(d).
  Definitions, §55-16-02(f), (g).
  List of shareholders.
    Compliance by corporation with shareholder's
      demand for, §55-16-03(d).
  Notice requirements, exceptions, §55-16-06.
  Photographic copies.
    Scope of copying right, §55-16-03(b).
  Rights of shareholders, §55-16-02(a), (b), (e).
    Abolition or limitation by articles of
      incorporation or bylaws prohibited,
      §55-16-02(d).
    No common law rights, shareholders of public
      corporations, §55-16-02(i).
    Restrictions, §55-16-02(c).
    Scope of right, §55-16-03.
    Shareholder having right to elect majority of
      directors of another corporation,
      §55-16-02(h).
Minutes of meetings, §55-16-01(a).
Nonprofit corporations, §§55A-16-01 to 55A-16-05.
See NONPROFIT CORPORATIONS.

CORPORATIONS —Cont'd
Records —Cont'd
Shareholders.
  Inspection by shareholders, §§55-16-02 to
    55-16-06.
  Record of shareholders, §55-16-01(c).
Written records required, §55-16-01(d).
Registered agent, §§55D-30 to 55D-33.
Change, §55D-31(a).
  Effective date.
    Statement included in annual report,
      §55-16-22(g).
  Inclusion of information in annual report,
    §55D-31(c).
Definitions, §55D-1.
Dissolution.
  Administrative dissolution.
    Authority of registered agent not terminated,
      §55-14-21(d).
Duty, §55D-30(b).
Foreign corporations, §55-15-07.
Nonprofit corporations, §55A-5-01.
  Foreign corporations, §55A-15-07.
Required, §55D-30(a).
Resignation.
  Effect, §55D-32(c).
  Statement, §55D-32(a), (b).
Rulemaking, §55D-5.
Service of process on, §55D-33(a).
  Failure to maintain registered agent,
    §55D-33(b).
Registered office, §§55D-30, 55D-31.
Change, §55D-31(a), (b).
  Effective date.
    Statement included in annual report,
      §55-16-22(g).
  Inclusion of information in annual report,
    §55D-31(c).
Definitions, §55D-1.
Foreign corporations, §55-15-07.
Nonprofit corporations, §55A-5-01.
  Foreign corporations, §55A-15-07.
Required, §55D-30(a).
Residence for purposes of venue, §1-79(a).
Rulemaking, §55D-5.
Register of deeds.
Mortgages and deeds of trust.
  Cancellation of lost mortgages by register of
    deeds, §45-42.1.
**Registration of mortgage or deed of trust in
  personal property.**
Place of registration, §47-20.2(b).
Religious organizations and societies.
Exemption from business corporation act,
  §55-17-01(b).
Prudent management of institutional funds,
  §§36E-1 to 36E-11.
  See PRUDENT MANAGEMENT OF
    INSTITUTIONAL FUNDS.
Reorganization, §1-507.11.
Appraisal rights.
  Actions not to give rise to, §55-14A-01(c).
Filings, §55-14A-01(b).
Fundamental changes in reorganization
  proceedings, §55-14A-01.
  Execution and filing of documents,
    §55-14A-01(b).
  Final decree.
    Provisions not to apply after entry of,
      §55-14A-01(d).
  Powers of corporation, §55-14A-01(a).

CORPORATIONS —Cont'd
Reorganization —Cont'd
Generally, §55-14A-01(a).
No action to be taken after final decree,
§55-14A-01(d).
Nonprofit corporations, §55A-14-01.
Scope, §55-14A-01(a).
Reports.
Annual report, §55-16-22.
Amendment, §55-16-22(e).
Change of registered office or agent.
Statement filed in report, effective date of
change, §55-16-22(g).
Content requirements, §55-16-22(a3).
Correction of report to include required
information, §55-16-22(d).
Delinquent, presumption, §55-16-22(h).
Filing fee nonrefundable, §55-1-22(d).
Form provided, §55-16-22(a3).
Information to be included, §55-16-22(a), (b).
Correction of report which does not include
required information, §55-16-22(d).
Insurance companies, §55-16-22(a1).
Professional corporations, exemption,
§55-16-22(a2).
Required, §55-16-22(a).
Time for delivery, §55-16-22(c).
Corrected report, §55-16-22(d).
Financial statements for shareholders, §55-16-20.
Mailing.
Time for, §55-16-20(c).
Public accountant's report to accompany,
§55-16-20(b).
Required, §55-16-20(a).
Royalties.
Corporate income tax.
Payments received on use of trademarks.
Option methods of reporting, §105-130.7A.
Sanitary districts.
Construction of systems by corporations or
individuals, §130A-58.
Saving provisions, §55-17-03.
Foreign corporations, §55-17-02.
Savings and loan associations, §§54B-1 to
54B-278.
See SAVINGS AND LOAN ASSOCIATIONS.
Savings banks, §§54C-1 to 54C-212.
See SAVINGS BANKS.
Seals and sealed instruments.
Probate and registration.
By president and attested by treasurer under
corporate seal, §47-70.
Execution of corporate instruments.
Instruments executed bearing seal.
Prima facie evidence seal duly adopted,
§47-18.3(b).
Seal omitted prior to January 1, 1991, §47-71.1.
Required on certain instruments, §47-41.1.
Secretary of revenue.
Annual report, §55-16-22.
Secretary of state.
Advisory review of documents prior to submission
for filing, §55D-12.
Copying and certifying documents.
Fees, §147-37.
Dissolution.
Administrative dissolution, §§55-14-20 to
55-14-24.
Duties as to, §147-36.
Filing of documents, §§55D-10 to 55D-18.

CORPORATIONS —Cont'd
Secretary of state —Cont'd
Foreign corporations.
Certificates of authority.
Action on application for, §55-15-03(c).
Revocation generally, §§55-15-30 to 55-15-33.
Power to require compliance with provisions,
§55-15-02(f).
Revocation of certificate of authority.
Generally, §§55-15-30 to 55-15-33.
Service of process.
Merger or share exchange with foreign
corporation, §55-11-07(b).
Withdrawal of foreign corporation,
§55-15-21(c).
Service of process on secretary, §55D-33(b), (c).
Fees, §55-1-22(b).
Foreign corporations.
Merger or share exchange with foreign
corporation, §55-11-07(b).
Withdrawal of foreign corporation,
§55-15-21(c).
Securities.
Broker.
When deemed security broker, §14-401.7.
Dealing in securities on commission.
Taxed as private banker, §14-401.7.
Investment securities, §§25-8-101 to 25-8-511.
See INVESTMENT SECURITIES.
Security transfers.
See FIDUCIARIES.
Service of process.
Additional nature of provisions, §55D-33(d).
Appraisal rights.
Judicial appraisal of shares.
Complaint filed by corporation, §55-13-30(c).
Dissolution.
Administrative dissolution.
Notice of denial of reinstatement,
§55-14-23(a).
Foreign corporations.
Revocation of certificate of authority.
Effect, §55-15-31(d).
Secretary of state.
Merger or share exchange with foreign
corporation, §55-11-07(b).
Withdrawal of foreign corporation,
§55-15-21(c).
Withdrawal of foreign corporation.
Effect, §55-15-20(c).
Manner of service on to exercise personal
jurisdiction, §1A-1 Rule 4(j).
Nonprofit corporations.
See NONPROFIT CORPORATIONS.
Personal service manner of service to exercise,
§1A-1 Rule 4(j).
Registered agent, §55D-33(a).
Failure to maintain registered agent,
§55D-33(b).
Secretary of state, §55D-33(b), (c).
Fees, §55-1-22(b).
Foreign corporations.
Merger or share exchange with foreign
corporation, §55-11-07(b).
Withdrawal of foreign corporation,
§55-15-21(c).
Severability of provisions, §55-17-04.
Share exchange, §§55-11-01 to 55-11-10.
Appraisal rights.
Corporate actions giving rise to appraisal rights,
§55-13-02(a).

CORPORATIONS —Cont'd
Share exchange —Cont'd
Appraisal rights —Cont'd
Generally, §§55-13-01 to 55-13-40. See within
this heading, "Appraisal rights."
Articles of share exchange.
Contents, §55-11-05(a).
Delivery to secretary of state, §55-11-05(a).
Authorized, §55-11-02(a).
Effective date, §55-11-05(b).
Effect of share exchange, §55-11-06(b).
Foreign corporations.
Share exchange with, §55-11-07.
Merger with nonprofit corporations.
No limitation on corporate powers,
§55A-11-08(c).
Plan of exchange, §55-11-01(a).
Abandonment of plan, §55-11-03(i).
Approval, §55-11-03(b).
Notice of meeting to consider, §55-11-03(d).
Voting groups, §55-11-03(e), (f).
Contents, §55-11-02(b), (c).
Submission to shareholders, §55-11-03(a), (c).
Shareholder protection act.
Provisions of act to control, §55-11-08.
Voluntary exchanges.
Power of corporation not limited by provisions,
§55-11-02(d).
Shareholder protection act, §§55-9-01 to 55-9-05.
Applicability, §55-9-04(a), (b).
Determinations by directors, §55-9-04(c).
Business combinations.
Defined, §55-9-01(b).
Voting requirement, §55-9-02.
Exceptions, §55-9-03.
Exemptions, §55-9-05.
Citation of act.
Short title, §55-9-01(a).
Definitions, §55-9-01(b).
Fiduciary obligations.
Provisions not construed to relieve other
entities from, §55-9-04(d).
Merger or share exchange.
Applicability of act to, §55-11-08.
Nonresidents.
Service of process.
Designation of secretary of state for service,
§75E-8.
Title of act.
Short title, §55-9-01(a).
Transfer of assets.
Provisions not to modify act, §55-12-03.
Violation of article.
Attorney general.
Investigative and regulatory powers, §75E-3.
Chapter not exclusive, §75E-7.
Civil actions, §75E-4.
Damages, §75E-4.
Definitions, §75E-1.
Penalties.
Civil penalties, §75E-5.
Remedies cumulative, §75E-6.
Severability of provisions, §75E-9.
Unlawful activities, §75E-2.
Voting requirement, §55-9-02.
Exceptions, §55-9-03.
Exemptions, §55-9-05.
Shares and shareholders, §§55-6-01 to 55-7-49.
Acceptance of votes by corporation.
Good-faith acceptance.
Generally, §55-7-24(a), (b).

CORPORATIONS —Cont'd
Shares and shareholders —Cont'd
Acceptance of votes by corporation —Cont'd
Rejection of vote, §55-7-24(c), (d).
Validity of corporate action based upon,
§55-7-24(e).
Validity of corporate action based upon,
§55-7-24(e).
Action by shareholders without meeting.
All shareholders entitled to vote on certain
actions, §55-7-04(a), (a1).
Notice of proposed action, §55-7-04(d), (e).
Record date, §55-7-04(b).
Written consent, §55-7-04(a) to (c).
Agreements among shareholders.
Validity, §55-7-31(a).
Agreement among all shareholders,
§55-7-31(b), (c).
Amendment of articles of incorporation.
Acquisition by corporation of own shares,
§55-6-31(b).
Amendment before issuance of shares,
§55-10-05.
Classes or series of stock, §55-6-02(b).
Issuance of shares.
Amendment before issuance, §55-10-05.
Restated articles of incorporation.
Submission to shareholders, §55-10-07(c).
Vested property right resulting from provisions
in articles.
Stockholders not deemed to have,
§55-10-01(b).
Voting groups.
Classes of shares entitled to vote as separate
voting groups, §55-10-04(a).
Nonvoting shares entitled to vote as voting
groups, §55-10-04(d).
Series of classes of shares entitled to vote as
voting groups, §55-10-04(b), (c).
Voting on proposed amendments.
Appraisal rights, §55-10-03(e).
Required votes for adoption, §55-10-03(b), (e).
Voting groups, §55-10-04.
Amendment of bylaws, §§55-10-20, 55-10-22.
Appraisal rights, §§55-13-01 to 55-13-40. See
within this heading, "Appraisal rights."
Beneficial owner of shares registered in name of
nominee.
Recognition as shareholder by corporation.
Corporation may establish procedure,
§55-7-23(a).
What procedure may set forth, §55-7-23(b).
Certificates, §55-6-25(a).
Contents, §55-6-25(b), (c).
Shares without certificate, §55-6-26(a).
Written statement of information to be
supplied, §55-6-26(b).
Signing, §55-6-25(d), (e).
Classes of shares.
Articles of amendment.
Delivery to secretary of state before issuance,
§55-6-02(b).
Authorized classes, §55-6-01(d), (e).
Directors.
Election by certain classes of shareholders,
§55-8-04.
Generally, §55-6-01(a).
Preferences, limitations and rights.
Directors may determine, §55-6-02(a).
Required classes, §55-6-01(c).

CORPORATIONS —Cont'd
Shares and shareholders —Cont'd
Classes of shares —Cont'd
Series, §55-6-01(a).
Designation, §55-6-01(b).
Consideration for shares.
Determination before issuance, §55-6-21(c).
Effect of payment, §55-6-21(d).
Liability of purchaser to pay, §55-6-22(a).
Control share acquisitions, §§55-9A-01 to
55-9A-09.
Conversion of domestic corporation to different
business entity.
Approval of plan of conversion, §55-11A-11(b) to
(f).
Cumulative voting for directors, §55-7-28(b) to (e).
Debt securities.
Rights of holders, §55-7-21.1.
Derivative actions, §§55-7-40 to 55-7-49.
Applicability of foreign corporations, §55-7-47.
Attorney-client privilege of corporation.
Restrictions on access of shareholder to
communication within, §55-7-49.
Attorneys' fees.
Award, §55-7-46.
Authorized, §55-7-40.
Compromise and settlement.
Approval of court, §55-7-45.
Costs.
Award, §55-7-46.
Definitions, §55-7-40.1.
Demand requirement, §55-7-42.
Discontinuance or settlement, §55-7-45.
Dismissal.
Approval of court, §55-7-44.
Burden of proving proceeding not in best
interest of corporation, §55-7-44(e).
Committee appointed by independent
directors, inquiry and determination by,
§55-7-44(b), (c).
Determination that proceeding not in best
interest of corporation, §55-7-44(a).
Independent directors, inquiry and
determination by, §55-7-44(b), (c).
Panel of independent persons, inquiry and
determination by, §55-7-44(f).
Proceeding commenced after determination
rejecting shareholder's demand,
§55-7-44(d).
Jurisdiction, §55-7-40.
Payment of costs and expenses, §55-7-46.
Privileged communications, §55-7-49.
Standing, §55-7-41.
Stays, §55-7-43.
Dissenting shareholders. See within this heading,
"Dissenting shareholders."
Dissolution.
Unavailable shareholders and creditors.
Disposition of amounts due to, §55-14-40.
Voluntary dissolution, §§55-14-01 to 55-14-09.
Adoption of proposal by shareholders,
§55-14-02(b), (e).
Articles of dissolution, §55-14-03(a).
Effective date of dissolution by, §55-14-03(b).
Notice of shareholders meeting to consider
proposal, §55-14-02(d).
Proposal by directors, §55-14-02(a), (c).
Revocation of dissolution by, §55-14-04.
Distributions to shareholders.
Authorization, §55-6-40(a).
Restrictions, §55-6-40(c) to (g).

CORPORATIONS —Cont'd
Shares and shareholders —Cont'd
Distributions to shareholders —Cont'd
Compelling payment of dividends.
Shareholders rights not impair, §55-6-40(k).
Demand by shareholders, §55-6-40(h) to (j).
Demand for payment of additional dividends,
§55-6-40(i), (k).
Parity with indebtedness to general unsecured
creditors, §55-6-40(f).
Record date for determining shareholders
entitled to distribution, §55-6-40(b).
Restrictions, §55-6-40(c), (d).
Determination of effect, §55-6-40(e) to (g).
Unlawful distributions.
Liability of directors, §55-8-33.
Dividends.
Distributions to shareholders generally,
§55-6-40.
Share dividends, §55-6-23(a) to (c).
Expense of issue, §55-6-28.
Financial statements for shareholders, §55-16-20.
Fractional shares.
Authorized, §55-6-04(a).
Rights of holders, §55-6-04(c).
Script, §55-6-04(a), (b).
Conditions of issuance, §55-6-04(d).
Investment securities, §§25-8-101 to 25-8-511.
See INVESTMENT SECURITIES.
Issuance of shares.
Consideration.
Determination before issuance, §55-6-21(c).
Effect of payment, §55-6-21(d).
Escrow.
Placing certain shares in escrow, §55-6-21(e).
Expenses, §55-6-28.
Power to issue, §55-6-21(a), (b).
Liability of shareholders, §55-6-22(b).
Meetings of shareholders.
Action without meeting, §55-7-04.
Annual meeting.
Failure to hold, §55-7-01(c).
Location, §55-7-01(b).
Required, §55-7-01(a).
Subject matter, §55-7-01(d).
Control share acquisitions, §§55-9A-03,
55-9A-04.
Court-ordered meetings.
Powers of court as to, §55-7-03(b).
Summary order for meeting to be held,
§55-7-03(a).
Election of directors, §55-8-03(d).
Classes of shareholders, §55-8-04.
Voting shares, §55-7-28.
Electronic attendance, §55-7-08.
Notice.
Adjournment of meeting, §55-7-05(e).
Amendments to articles of incorporation,
§55-10-03(d).
Control share acquisitions, §55-9A-04.
Dissolution of corporation by directors and
shareholders, §55-14-02(d).
Merger or share exchange, §55-11-03(d).
Record date, §55-7-05(d).
Removal of directors by shareholders,
§55-8-08(d).
Requirements, §55-7-05(a) to (c).
Restated articles of incorporation,
§55-10-07(c).
Transfer of assets other than in regular
course of business, §55-12-02(d).

CORPORATIONS —Cont'd
Shares and shareholders —Cont'd
Meetings of shareholders —Cont'd
Notice —Cont'd
Waiver of notice, §55-7-06.
Record date.
Bylaws may fix, §55-7-07(a).
Court-ordered adjournment of meeting,
§55-7-07(d).
Notice of meeting, §55-7-05(d).
Restrictions, §55-7-07(b), (c).
Special meetings, §55-7-02(b).
Special meetings.
Location, §55-7-02(c).
Record date, §55-7-02(b).
Subject matter, §55-7-02(d).
When held, §55-7-02(a).
Voting groups.
Generally, §§55-7-25 to 55-7-27.
Voting of shares generally, §§55-7-20 to 55-7-31.
Voting trusts, §55-7-30.
Waiver of notice of meetings.
Attendance at meeting, §55-7-06(b).
Generally, §55-7-06(a).
Merger or share exchange.
Action on plan.
Generally, §55-11-03.
Nonprofit corporations.
Acquisition of shares of corporation,
§55-11-09(c).
Number of shareholders, §55-1-42(a).
More than one shareholder not required,
§55-2-03(c).
Options, §55-6-24(a).
Public corporations, §55-6-24(b).
Outstanding shares, §55-6-03(a), (c).
Reacquisition, redemption or conversion,
§55-6-03(b).
Preemptive rights of shareholders.
Definition of "shares,"§55-6-30(c).
Generally, §55-6-30(a), (d).
Statement in articles of incorporation.
Effect, §55-6-30(b).
Professional corporations.
Death of stockholder, §55B-7(b).
Disqualification of licensee stockholder,
severance of financial interest, §55B-7(a).
Distributing corporation, issuance of capital
stock to, §55B-6(b).
Issuance of capital stock, §55B-6(a).
To another professional corporation,
§55B-6(b).
Nonlicensed employee owning stock, §55B-6(a).
Percentage of stock allowed to be own by
person, §55B-6(a1).
Transfer of capital stock, §55B-6(a).
Voting trust agreements prohibited, §55B-6(a).
Proxies, §55-7-22.
Appointment, §55-7-22(b) to (h).
Authorized, §55-7-22(a).
Death or incapacity of shareholder appointing
proxy, §55-7-22(e).
Revocation of appointment, §55-7-22(d), (f), (g).
Records.
Inspection of records by shareholders,
§§55-16-02 to 55-16-06.
Record of shareholders, §55-16-01(c).
Removal of director by shareholders, §55-8-08.
Reports to shareholders, §55-16-20.
Restrictions on transfer of shares.
Authorized, §55-6-27(a).

CORPORATIONS —Cont'd
Shares and shareholders —Cont'd
Restrictions on transfer of shares —Cont'd
Definition of "shares,"§55-6-27(e).
Provisions authorized, §55-6-27(c), (d).
Validity, §55-6-27(b).
Securities generally, §§78A-1 to 78A-66.
See SECURITIES.
Series of stock.
Articles of amendment.
Delivery to secretary of state before issuance,
§55-6-02(b).
Preferences, limitations and rights.
Directors may determine, §55-6-02(a).
Share exchange, §§55-11-01 to 55-11-10.
Shareholder protection act, §§55-9-01 to 55-9-05.
Subscription for shares.
Contract.
Subscription agreement as contract,
§55-6-20(e).
Default by subscriber, §55-6-20(d).
Irrevocable, §55-6-20(a).
Payment terms, §55-6-20(b).
Effect of payment, §55-6-20(c).
Substantially similar names.
Shareholders registered in to constitute one
shareholder, §55-1-42(b).
Treasury shares.
Acquisition by corporation of own shares.
Amendment of articles of incorporation,
§55-6-31(b).
Authorized, §55-6-31(a).
Voting groups. See within this heading, "Voting
groups."
Voting of shares.
Acceptance of votes by corporation, §55-7-24.
Agreements between shareholders, §55-7-31.
Conversion of domestic corporation to different
business entity.
Approval of plan of conversion, §55-11A-11(e),
(f).
Election of directors, §55-7-28(a).
Cumulative voting, §55-7-28(b) to (e).
Electronic attendance at meetings, §55-7-08.
Entitlement to vote, §55-7-21(a).
Debt securities, §55-7-21.1.
Exceptions, §55-7-21(b) to (d).
Redeemable shares, §55-7-21(d).
List of shareholders, §55-7-20.
Availability for inspection, §55-7-20(b) to (e).
Preparation, §55-7-20(a).
Redeemable shares, §55-7-21(d).
Shareholders' agreements, §55-7-31.
Voting trusts, §55-7-30.
Voting trusts.
Authorized, §55-7-30(a).
Duration, §55-7-30(b).
Extension, §55-7-30(c).
When effective, §55-7-30(b).
Warrants for purchase of shares, §55-6-24(a).
Public corporations, §55-6-24(b).
Soil scientists.
Practice of soil science, §89F-6.
Superior courts.
Dissolution.
Administrative dissolution.
Appeal from denial of reinstatement,
§55-14-23.
Judicial dissolution generally, §§55-14-30 to
55-14-33.

CORPORATIONS —Cont'd
Superior courts —Cont'd
Proper division for actions for corporate
receiverships, §7A-249.
Surplus lines insurance.
Agents or brokers license, §58-21-65(c).
Suspended corporations, §§55-14-20 to 55-14-24.
Administrative procedure act.
Inapplicability, §55-14-24.
Authority of registered agent, §55-14-21(d).
Certificate of dissolution, §55-14-21(b).
Claims against dissolved corporations.
Applicability of certain provisions, §55-14-21(c).
Denial of reinstatement.
Appeal.
Appeal of court's final decision, §55-14-23(d).
Orders of court, §55-14-23(c).
Appeal from, §55-14-23.
Notice of denial, §55-14-23(a).
Petition, §55-14-23(b).
Grounds, §55-14-20.
Notice, §§55-14-21(a), 55-14-23(a).
Reinstatement, §55-14-22.
Application, §55-14-22(a).
Certificate, §55-14-22(b).
Denial of reinstatement.
Appeal from, §55-14-23.
Effect, §55-14-22(c).
Name, §55-14-22(a1).
Taxation.
Annual report, §105-256.1.
Failure to pay certain taxes.
Personal responsibility, §105-242.2.
Foreign corporations.
Applicability of laws, §105-250.
Property taxes.
Property of foreign corporations not
exempted, §105-274(b).
Franchise tax.
General provisions, §§105-114 to 105-129.
See FRANCHISE TAX.
Income tax.
Generally, §§105-130 to 105-130.41.
See INCOME TAX.
S corporations, §§105-131 to 105-131.8.
See INCOME TAX.
Responsible persons.
Failure to pay certain taxes.
Personal responsibility, §105-242.2.
Suspension of articles of incorporation.
Failure to file report or return or pay tax or fee,
§105-230(a).
Invalidity of acts performed during
suspension, §105-230(b).
Receivership, liquidation, cessation of
business, §105-232(b).
Reinstatement of articles, §105-232(a).
Telephone membership corporations, §§62-157,
117-28 to 117-46.
See TELEPHONE MEMBERSHIP
CORPORATIONS.
Third parties.
Probate and registration.
Execution of corporate instruments.
Validity as to innocent third parties,
§47-18.3(a).
Title of act.
Short title, §55-1-01.
Torrens system registration.
Authority to sue, §43-8.

CORPORATIONS —Cont'd
Torrens system registration —Cont'd
Certificates of title.
Dissolution of corporation.
Issuance of certificate upon dissolution,
§43-17.1.
Transfer of assets.
Mortgage of assets, §55-12-01(a).
Other than in regular course of business.
Abandonment of transaction, §55-12-02(f).
Approval by shareholders, §55-12-02(a), (b), (e).
Notice of meeting, §55-12-02(d).
Voting groups, §55-12-02(e).
Distribution to shareholders.
Not governed by provisions, §55-12-02(g).
Submission of proposed transaction to
shareholders, §55-12-02(a) to (c).
Regular course of business, §55-12-01(b).
Other than in regular course of business,
§55-12-02.
Shareholder protection act.
Provisions not to modify act, §55-12-03.
Trust companies and interstate trust business,
§§53-301 to 53-424.
See TRUST COMPANIES.
Trusts and trustees.
Criminal law and procedure.
Indictments.
Manner of alleging joint ownership of
property, §15-148.
Ultra vires, §55-3-04(a).
Exceptions, §55-3-04(b), (c).
Nonprofit corporations, §55A-3-04.
Unclaimed property generally, §§116B-51 to
116B-80.
See UNCLAIMED PROPERTY.
Usury.
Bonds may be sold below par, §24-2.
Uttering.
Forged stock certificates uttered, §14-124.
Validation of instrument.
Curative statute, §55-17-05.
Venue.
Appraisal rights.
Judicial appraisal of shares, §55-13-30(b).
Domestic corporations.
Residence, §1-79(a).
Foreign corporations, §1-80.
Verification of pleadings by corporation, §1A-1
Rule 11(d).
Veterinarians.
Practice of veterinary medicine, §90-187.11.
Voluntary dissolution, §§55-14-01 to 55-14-09. See
within this heading, "Dissolution."
Voting groups.
Amendment of articles of incorporation.
Voting on amendments by voting groups,
§55-10-04.
Directors.
Election of directors, §55-7-25(e).
Greater quorum or voting requirements.
Authorization, §55-7-27(a).
Amendment of provision for, §55-7-27(b).
Merger or share exchange.
Approval of plan, §55-11-03(e), (f).
Multiple voting groups.
Action by, §55-7-26(b).
Quorum requirements, §55-7-25(a) to (c).
Changes, §55-7-25(d).
Greater quorum or voting requirements,
§55-7-27.

CORPORATIONS —Cont'd
Voting groups —Cont'd
Removal of directors by shareholders, §55-8-08(b).
Single voting group.
Action by, §55-7-26(a).
Vacancies in board of directors.
Filling, §55-8-10(b).
When tax must be paid, §105-130.19(a).
Worthless checks, §14-107.

CORPSES.
See DEAD BODIES.

CORPUS AND INCOME OF TRUSTS,
§§37A-1-101 to 37A-6-602.
See PRINCIPAL AND INCOME ACT.

CORRECTIONAL INDUSTRIES.
Labor of prisoners, §§148-26 to 148-49.
See PRISON LABOR.

CORRECTION ENTERPRISE FUND, §148-130.
Disbursement of funds, §148-130(b).
Incentive wages and allowances, §148-130(c).
Revenue from sales, §148-130(a).

CORRECTION ENTERPRISES, §§148-128 to
148-134.
Authorization for, §148-128.
Distribution of products and services, §148-132.
Fund, §148-130.
Disbursement of funds, §148-130(b).
Incentive wages and allowances, §148-130(c).
Revenue from sales, §148-130(a).
Inmate wages and conditions of employment,
§148-133.
Incentive wages and allowances, §148-130(c).
Maximum wages, §148-133(b).
Personnel policies, adoption, §148-133(a).
Public contracts.
Preference for correction enterprise products,
§148-134.
Purposes, §148-129.
Resale of purchased products.
State and local government employees and
retirees.
Prohibition, §148-132.
Revenue from sales, §148-130(a).
Section of correction enterprises.
Established, §148-128.
Powers, §148-131.
Responsibilities, §148-131.
Self-sufficient, §148-129.
State and local government employees and
retirees.
Purchases during year, limitation on amount,
§148-132.

CORRECTIONS.
Board of correction, §143B-715.
Clerical and other services.
Supplied by secretary of public safety,
§143B-715(d).
Duties and responsibilities, §143B-715(a).
Meetings, §143B-715(c).
Members, §143B-715(b).
Per diem, travel, subsistence expenses,
§143B-715(c).
Quorum, §143B-715(c).
Secretary of public safety.
Nonvoting member, §143B-715(b).
Community-based corrections programs.
Treatment for effective community supervision act
of 2011, §§143B-1150 to 143B-1160.
See COMMUNITY CORRECTIONS.

CORRECTIONS —Cont'd
Division of adult correction, §§143B-700 to
143B-721.
See PUBLIC SAFETY DEPARTMENT.
Generally.
See PRISONS AND PRISONERS.
Jails.
See JAILS.

CORRECTIONS ADMINISTRATIVE REMEDY
PROCEDURE, §§148-118.1 to 148-118.9.
See PRISONER'S GRIEVANCE PROCEDURE.

CORRECTIONS COMPACT, §§148-119 to
148-121.
All documents public records, §148-121(b), (c).
Citation of article, §148-119.
Form of compact, §148-120.
Governor to execute, §148-120.
Proceedings to be open, §148-121(a).
Exceptions where safety of persons or property
jeopardized, §148-121(c).
Short title, §148-119.
Written documents deemed public records,
§148-121(b).

CORRESPONDENCE SCHOOLS.
General provisions, §§115D-87 to 115D-97.
See PROPRIETARY SCHOOLS.

CORROSIVE ACID OR ALKALI.
Malicious throwing, §14-30.1.

CORRUPT ELECTIONS.
Convicted officials.
Disqualification from voting, §163-276.
Removal from office, §163-276.
District attorneys.
Investigation and prosecution of violations,
§163-278.
Felonies.
Certain acts declared felonies, §163-275.
Fraud.
Felonies, §163-275.
Interference with voters.
Duties of election officers upon, §163-273(b).
Prohibited acts, §163-273(a).
Intimidation of voters by officers, §163-271.
Misdemeanors.
Generally, §§163-271 to 163-274.
Offenses of voters, §163-273(a).
Duties of election officers upon, §163-273(b).
Penalties.
Felonies, §163-275.
State board of elections.
Investigation of violations, §163-278.
Witnesses.
Self-incrimination.
Immunity from prosecution, §163-277.
Subpoenas, §§163-277, 163-278.
Powers of district attorneys, §163-278.

CORRUPTION OF BLOOD.
Attainder of treason not to work, US Const Art
III §3.

CORRUPT LAW ENFORCEMENT.
Removal of unfit officers, §128-16.

CORRUPT ORGANIZATIONS AND
RACKETEER INFLUENCE, §§75D-1 to
75D-14.
See RACKETEER INFLUENCED AND CORRUPT
ORGANIZATIONS (RICO).

CORRUPT PRACTICES ACT, §§163-271 to 163-278.
See CORRUPT ELECTIONS.

COSMETIC ART, §§88B-1 to 88B-29.
Apprentices.
Licenses.
Display of license, §88B-23(a).
Qualifications, §88B-8.
Renewal, §88B-21(c).
Failure to renew, §88B-21(f).
Practice under direct supervision of cosmetologist, §88B-22(e).
Barbers.
Exemptions from barbering provisions, §86A-14.
Board of cosmetic art.
Compensation of members, §88B-5(a).
Composition, §88B-3(a).
Disciplinary measures, §88B-24.
Costs in disciplinary proceedings, §88B-29(d).
Duties, §88B-4(a).
Employment of member by board prohibited for at least one year after member's term expires, §88B-3(h).
Established, §88B-3(a).
Executive budget act.
Applicability, §88B-6(f).
Executive director, §88B-6(b).
Collection of fees, §88B-6(e).
Inspection of shops and schools, §88B-4(b).
Meetings, §88B-5(b).
Office.
Location, §88B-6(a).
Officers, §88B-3(f).
Personnel, §88B-6(c), (d).
Powers, §88B-4(a).
Qualifications of members, §88B-3(b).
Record of proceedings, §88B-4(c).
Removal of members, §88B-3(d).
Restraining orders, §88B-28.
Rules.
Posting, §88B-26.
State personnel act.
Applicability, §88B-6(f).
Teacher's licenses not to be issued to board members, §88B-3(g).
Terms of members, §88B-3(c).
Vacancies, §88B-3(e).
Bonds, surety.
Private cosmetic art schools, §88B-17.
Citation of act, §88B-1.
Civil penalties.
Authority to assess, §88B-29(a).
Factors to be considered in assessing, §88B-29(b).
Schedule, §88B-29(c).
Conflicts of interest.
Board of cosmetic art.
Employment of member by board for at least one year after member's term prohibited, §88B-3(h).
Continuing education, §88B-21(e).
Inactive status.
Removal from list, §88B-21(h).
Cosmetic art schools.
Bond, surety.
Amount, §88B-17(b).
Required, §88B-17(a).
Waiver of requirement, §88B-17(c).
Credits.
Expired school credits, §88B-19.
Expired school credits, §88B-19.

COSMETIC ART —Cont'd
Cosmetic art schools —Cont'd
Licenses, §88B-16(a).
Bond, §88B-17.
Posting of license, §88B-23(b).
Renewal, §88B-21(g).
Required, §88B-16(b), (c).
Rules of board.
Posting, §88B-26(a), (b).
Teachers. See within this heading, "Teachers."
Cosmetic art shops.
Licenses, §88B-14(a).
Inspection for compliance.
Operation during inspection, §88B-14(c).
List of licensed cosmetologists who practice in, §88B-14(b).
Posting of license, §88B-23(b).
Renewal, §88B-21(a).
Transfer of license prohibited, §88B-14(d).
Unlicensed operation prohibited, §88B-22(c).
Practice outside shops, §§88B-15(a), 88B-22(b).
Licensed barber shop, §88B-15(b).
Rules of board.
Posting, §88B-26(a).
Cosmetologists.
Licenses.
Display of license, §88B-23(a).
Qualifications, §88B-7.
Renewal, §88B-21(b).
Failure to renew, §88B-21(f).
Costs.
Disciplinary proceedings, §88B-29(d).
Criminal law and procedure, §88B-22(f).
Definitions, §88B-2.
Disciplinary measures, §88B-24.
Costs in disciplinary proceedings, §88B-29(d).
Electrologists, §§88A-1 to 88A-23.
See ELECTROLOGISTS.
Estheticians.
Licenses.
Display of license, §88B-23(a).
Qualifications, §88B-9.
Renewal, §88B-21(c).
Failure to renew, §88B-21(f).
Restrictions on practice, §88B-22(d).
Examinations.
Licensure, §88B-18.
Fees, §88B-20(a).
Exemptions from provisions, §88B-25.
Fees.
Board of cosmetic art.
Collection by executive director, §88B-6(e).
Licensure, §88B-20.
Injunctions, §88B-28.
Inspections, §88B-27.
Board of cosmetic art.
Shops and schools, §88B-4(b).
Cosmetic art shops, §88B-4(b).
Operation while board inspects for compliance, §88B-14(c).
Licenses.
Applicants licensed in other states.
Qualifications, §88B-13(a), (b).
Teachers.
Standards for issuing license to applicant who is licensed as teacher in another state, §88B-13(c).
Apprentices. See within this heading, "Apprentices."
Cosmetic art schools. See within this heading, "Cosmetic art schools."

COSMETIC ART —Cont'd
Licenses —Cont'd
Cosmetic art shops. See within this heading,
"Cosmetic art shops."
Disciplinary measures, §88B-24.
Costs in disciplinary proceedings, §88B-29(d).
Display, §88B-23.
Estheticians. See within this heading,
"Estheticians."
Examinations.
Contents, §88B-18(b).
Fees, §88B-20(a).
Locations, §88B-18(c).
Reexamination, §88B-18(d).
Fees.
Application fees, §88B-20(b).
Examination fees, §88B-20(a).
Late fees and reinstatement fees, §88B-20(d).
License fees, §88B-20(c).
Proration of fees, §88B-20(e).
Inactive status.
Request, effect, removal, continuing education,
§88B-21(h).
Manicurists. See within this heading,
"Manicurists."
Qualifications.
Apprentices, §88B-8.
Cosmetologists, §88B-7.
Estheticians, §88B-9.
Manicurists, §88B-10.
Natural hair care specialists, §88B-10.1.
Teachers, §88B-11.
Temporary employment permit, §88B-12(a).
Renewal, §88B-21.
Refusal to renew.
Disciplinary measures generally, §88B-24.
Required, §88B-22(a).
Revocation or suspension.
Disciplinary measures generally, §88B-24.
Teachers. See within this heading, "Teachers."
Temporary employment permit, §88B-12.
Unlicensed acts prohibited, §88B-22(a) to (f).
Manicurists.
Licenses.
Display of license, §88B-23(a).
Qualifications, §88B-10.
Renewal, §88B-21(c).
Failure to renew, §88B-21(f).
Restrictions on practice, §88B-22(d).
Misdemeanors, §88B-22(f).
Natural hair care specialists.
Defined, §88B-2.
Licenses.
Qualifications, §88B-10.1.
Natural hair care teachers.
Defined, §88B-2.
Licenses.
Qualifications, §88B-11(e).
Nurses.
Exemptions from cosmetic art provisions, §88B-25.
Penalties.
Civil penalties, §88B-29.
Physicians and surgeons.
Exemptions from cosmetic art provisions, §88B-25.
Promotion of products and systems, §88B-21(e).
Reciprocity.
Licensing of applicants licensed in other states,
§88B-13.
Records.
Board proceedings, §88B-4(c).

COSMETIC ART —Cont'd
Teachers.
Continuing education.
License renewal, §88B-21(e).
Licenses.
Applicants licensed as teachers in another state.
Standards for issuing licenses to, §88B-13(c).
Display of license, §88B-23(a).
Qualifications, §88B-11(a).
Cosmetology teachers, §88B-11(b).
Esthetician teachers, §88B-11(c).
Manicurist teachers, §88B-11(d).
Natural hair care teachers, §88B-11(e).
Renewal, §88B-21(d).
Continuing education, §88B-21(e).
Failure to renew, §88B-21(f).
Required, §88B-22(d1).
Temporary employment permits.
Applicants for examination.
Applications, §88B-12(a).
Extension, §88B-12(c).
Expiration, §88B-12(b).
Limits on practice, §88B-12(c).
Qualifications, §88B-12(a).
Title of act, §88B-1.

COSMETICS.
Cosmetic art, §§88B-1 to 88B-29.
Food, drugs and cosmetics, §§106-120 to 106-145.
See FOOD, DRUG AND COSMETIC ACT.
Sales and use tax.
Clothing accessories or equipment.
Defined as including, §105-164.3.

COSMETIC SURGERY OR TREATMENT.
State health plan for teachers and state
employees.
Coverage mandate, §135-48.50.

COSMETOLOGISTS.
Cosmetic art, §§88B-1 to 88B-29.
See COSMETIC ART.

COSTS.
Abortion.
Parental or judicial consent to abortion.
Waiver of parental consent proceedings.
Cost not required of minors, §90-21.8(i).
Woman's right to know act.
Civil action, §90-21.88(c).
Absolute divorce.
Final action filed in district court, §7A-305(a2).
Administration department.
Publications.
Statement of cost, §143-170.1(a), (a1), (b).
Admissions.
Failure of party to admit, §1A-1 Rule 37(c).
Alimony.
Bond for costs unnecessary, §50-2.
Annexation.
Municipalities initiating.
Appeals, §160A-58.60(n).
Appeals, §6-33.
Discretion of appellate court in recovery of cost,
§6-33.
Federal courts.
State costs on appeals to federal courts, §6-17.
Generally, §6-33, AppProc Rule 35.
Magistrates.
Recovery of cost, §6-33.
Stay of payment, §15A-1431(f1).
Prosecution bonds.
Sureties on bonds liable for costs, §6-3.

COSTS —Cont'd

Appeals —Cont'd

Schedule of fees and costs, AppProc Appx F.

Security for costs, AppProc Rule 6.

Appraisals and appraisers.

Homestead exemption.

Laying off homestead and exemption, §6-28.

Reassessment of homestead, §6-29.

Arbitration.

Payment of fees and expenses of arbitrator and other expenses, §1-569.21(d).

Arbitration and award, §§50-51(f), (g), 50-55(d).

Judgment on award, §1-569.25(b).

Modification or correction of awards, §50-55(d).

Rules for conducting arbitration, §50-45(h).

Rules for court-ordered arbitration, Arbitration Rule 7.

Arrest.

Criminal cases in superior or district courts, §7A-304(a).

Nonpayment of fine and cost, §6-48.

Assault.

Allowance of costs to defendant, §6-19.

Allowance of costs to plaintiff, §6-18.

Assignments.

Liability of assignee for cost, §6-32.

Attorney disability proceedings, Bar Rule B.0118.

Attorneys at law.

Failure to file complaint on time.

Attorney liable for cost, §84-12.

Attorneys' fees, §§6-21.1, 6-21.2, 6-21.4, 6-21.5.

Allowance as part of costs in certain cases, §6-21.1.

Cases involving principals or teachers.

Allowance of counsel fees and costs, §6-21.4.

Chattel mortgages.

Attorneys' fees in addition to interest, §6-21.2.

Evidence of indebtedness.

Attorneys' fees in notes, etc., in addition to interest, §6-21.2.

Nonjustifiable cases, §6-21.5.

Automobile dealers.

Actions by, §20-308.1(b).

Autopsies.

Homicide investigations.

Compensation of physician, §15-7.

Bad checks.

Remedies for returned check, §6-21.3(b).

Bail.

Civil cases.

When bail to pay costs, §1-438.

Pretrial release services in district or superior courts, §7A-304(a).

Several actions on one recognizance.

Allowance of costs to defendant, §6-19.

Allowance of costs to plaintiff, §6-18.

Battery.

Allowance of costs to defendant, §6-19.

Allowance of costs to plaintiff, §6-18.

Bill of costs.

Execution for unpaid costs.

Attachment of bill of costs to execution, §6-4.

Bills of exchange.

Several actions on one instrument.

Allowance of costs to defendant, §6-19.

Allowance of costs to plaintiff, §6-18.

Blood tests and samples.

Competency of blood tests.

Taxing of expenses as cost, §8-50.1.

COSTS —Cont'd

Bond issues.

Several suits on one instrument.

Allowance of costs to defendant, §6-19.

Allowance of costs to plaintiff, §6-18.

Bonds, surety.

Defendant's liability in criminal actions.

Confession of judgment, §6-47.

Bond given to secure fine and cost, §6-47.

Mortgage in lieu of bond.

Security of costs or fine in criminal action, §58-74-5.

Cancellation of mortgage in such proceedings, §58-74-10.

Prosecution bonds, §§1-109 to 1-112.

Several suits on one instrument.

Allowance of costs to defendant, §6-19.

Allowance of costs to plaintiff, §6-18.

Cartways.

Application for establishment, alteration or discontinuance.

Allowance of costs to either party or apportioned in discretion of court, §6-21.

Case files.

Entering costs in case file, §6-7.

Chattel mortgages.

Attorneys' fees in addition to interest, §6-21.2.

Checks.

Returned check.

Remedies for returned check, §6-21.3(b).

Child care provider criminal history record check, §110-90.2(g).

Child custody.

Uniform child custody jurisdiction act.

Allowance of costs to either party or apportioned in discretion of court, §6-21.

Child support, income withholding.

Computation of amount to be withheld, §110-136.6(a).

Limitations on amount withheld, §110-136.6(b).

Chiropractors.

Contested disciplinary hearings.

Assessment of costs upon guilty verdict, §90-154(c).

Citations.

Criminal process in superior or district courts, §7A-304(a).

Civil rights, interference with, §99D-1(b), (b1).

Coastal area management.

Permit violations.

Assessment of investigative costs, §113A-126(d).

Collection assistance fee.

Criminal cases, §7A-321.

Commercial real estate broker lien act.

Action to enforce lien, §44A-24.12.

Commissioner deposition taking.

Allowance of costs to either party or apportioned in discretion of court, §6-21.

Commissioner's fees taxed as cost, §1-408.

Complex business cases.

Assignment of case, §7A-305(a).

Compromise and settlement.

Mediated settlement conferences in superior court civil actions, §7A-38.1(k).

Conditional sale contracts.

Attorneys' fees and conditional sale contract in addition to interest, §6-21.2.

Condominium assessment lien, §47C-3-116(e), (e1).

Condominium owners' associations and declarant.

Declarant liable to association, §47C-3-111(d).

COSTS —Cont'd

Construction and interpretation.

Allowance to either party or apportioned in discretion of court, §6-21.

Contracts.

Conditional sales contracts.

Attorneys' fees and contract in addition to interest, §6-21.2.

Usurious contracts.

No costs to be recovered by party seeking recovery on usurious contracts, §6-25.

Corporations.

Actions by state for corporation.

Liability for costs, §6-15.

Appraisal rights.

Judicial appraisal of shares, §55-13-31(a).

Fees and expenses of parties, assessment, §55-13-31(b).

When paid by others than corporation, §55-13-31(c).

Business corporations.

Derivative actions, §55-7-46.

Records.

Inspection of records by shareholders.

Court-ordered inspection, §55-16-04(c).

Nonprofit corporations.

Court-ordered inspections of records, §55A-16-04(c).

Cosmetic art.

Disciplinary proceedings, §88B-29(d).

Counterclaim included with pleading.

Action in superior or district court, §7A-305(a5).

Counties.

Actions by state for county.

Liability for costs, §6-15.

Prisoners.

Removal of trial from one county to another.

Liability of county, §6-40.

Public health or mental health grants from federal government.

Recovery of indirect costs on certain grants by counties, §130A-8(a).

Exception, §130A-8(b).

Special assessments.

Determination of costs, §153A-193.

Discounts authorized, §153A-193.1.

Uniform costs and fees in trial divisions.

Requirement to advance certain fees, §7A-317.

Court of appeals.

New trials.

Discretion of court in awarding cost, §6-33.

Courtroom costs in criminal actions in superior or district courts, §7A-304(a).

Credit card, charge card or debit card.

Fines, fees and costs owed by offenders.

Acceptance in lieu of cash or check, §7A-321(a).

Contracts with vendors to provide for, §7A-343.

Credit device fraud.

Telecommunication services, §14-113.6(c).

Crime laboratory services.

Costs in criminal cases, §7A-304(a).

Criminal cases, §7A-304.

Actions in superior or district courts, §7A-304.

Amendment of costs, effective date of change, §7A-304(g).

Collection assistance fee, §7A-321(b).

Retention of fee assessed by courts, §7A-321(d).

Confession of judgment.

Bond given to secure fine and cost, §6-47.

Contracts with collection agencies, §7A-321(b).

COSTS —Cont'd

Criminal cases —Cont'd

Credit card, charge card or debit card.

Fines, fees and costs owed by offenders.

Acceptance in lieu of cash or check, §7A-321(a).

Contracts with vendors to provide for, §7A-343.

Crime laboratory services, §7A-304(a).

Defendant's liability in criminal actions.

Confession of judgment.

Bond given to secure fine and cost, §6-47.

Nonpayment of costs.

Persons imprisoned for nonpayment released upon compliance with article, §23-24.

Removal of trial from one county to another.

Liability of counties for cost, §6-40.

Criminal conversation.

Allowance of costs to defendant, §6-19.

Allowance of costs to plaintiff, §6-18.

Cross-claim included with pleading.

Action in superior or district court, §7A-305(a5).

Dams.

Lowlands draining or damming.

Petitioner to pay costs, §6-22.

Debt.

Evidence of indebtedness.

Attorneys' fees in notes, etc., in addition to interest, §6-21.2.

Decedents' estates.

Actions to recover estate property, §28A-15-12(c).

Administration of estates, §7A-307.

Debts and claims.

When cost allowed against representative, §28A-19-18.

Reference of claim against deceased person.

Recovery of fees and other necessary disbursements, §6-31.

Declaratory judgments, §1-263.

Defamation.

Allowance of costs to defendant, §6-19.

Allowance of costs to plaintiff, §6-18.

Defendants.

Allowance of costs, §6-19.

Discretion of court, §§6-20, 6-21.

Attorneys' fees.

Parties appealing or defending against agency decision, §6-19.1(a).

Bonds, surety.

Confession of judgment.

Bond given to secure fine and cost, §6-47.

Confession of judgment.

Bond given to secure fine and cost, §6-47.

Notice of no personal claim.

Payment of costs by defendant unreasonably defending after notice, §6-23.

Depositions.

Compensation of referees and commissioners.

Allowance of costs to either party or apportioned in discretion of court, §6-21.

Failure of party to attend, §1A-1 Rule 37(d).

Oral examination.

Failure to attend or serve subpoena, §1A-1 Rule 30(g).

Derivative actions.

Payment, §55-7-46.

Determination of incompetence.

Fees.

Payment, §35A-1116(c).

Multidisciplinary evaluations.

Assessment of costs, §35A-1116(b).

COSTS —Cont'd
Dietitians and nutritionists.
Disciplinary actions, §90-370.
Disability of attorney proceedings, Bar Rule
B.0118.
Discovery conference.
Failure to participate, §1A-1 Rule 37(g).
Discovery, failure to comply with order, §1A-1
Rule 37(b).
Discovery, motion compelling.
Granting or denying motion, §1A-1 Rule 37(a).
Discretion of court.
Allowance of costs, §§6-20, 6-21.
Appellate court's discretion in recovery of cost,
§6-33.
**Discrimination against employees for lawful
use of lawful products during nonworking
hours.**
Court costs in civil actions for violations,
§95-28.2(e).
Dismissal of actions, §1A-1 Rule 41(d).
District courts.
Civil actions, §7A-305.
Criminal actions, §7A-304.
Divorce.
Absolute divorce.
Final action filed in district court, §7A-305(a2).
Allowance of costs to either party or apportioned
in discretion of court, §6-21.
Bond for costs unnecessary, §50-2.
DNA database and databank services.
Costs in criminal cases, §7A-304(a).
Drainage.
Allowance of costs to either party or apportioned
in discretion of court, §6-21.
Amount of contribution for repair ascertained,
§156-15.
Lowlands draining or damming.
Petitioner to pay costs, §6-22.
Repairs enforced by judgment, §156-18.
Drug treatment courts.
Payment of costs of treatment program, §7A-800.
Dry-cleaning solvent cleanup.
Reimbursement for assessment and remediation
activities generally, §143-215.104N(a) to (e).
Elective share of surviving spouse.
Expenses including attorneys' fees.
Apportionment, §30-3.4(h).
Electric, telegraph and telephone companies.
Petition for condemnation of land.
Payment of costs by petitioner, §6-22.
Electronic surveillance.
Civil action for violation of article, §15A-296(a).
Emancipation of juvenile proceedings,
§7B-3506.
Eminent domain, §40A-13.
Award of costs, §40A-8(a), (b).
Action against condemnor, §40A-8(c).
Condemnation action denied or abandoned,
§40A-8(b).
Highways, roads and streets.
Condemnation proceedings, §136-119.
Petitioner to pay costs in certain cases, §6-22.
Highways, roads and streets, §136-119.
**Employee use of lawful products during
nonworking hours.**
Actions brought pursuant to section, §95-28.2(f).
**Employer discrimination against employee for
lawful use of lawful products during
nonworking hours.**
Court costs in civil actions for violation,
§95-28.2(e).

COSTS —Cont'd
Estates.
Administration of estates, §7A-307.
Evidence.
Blood tests.
Competency of blood tests.
Taxing of expenses as cost, §8-50.1.
Executions.
Issuance of execution for unpaid costs, §6-4.
Livestock.
Cost of keeping.
Officer's account, §1-322.
Executors and administrators.
Actions for debts and claims.
When costs allowed against representative,
§28A-19-18.
Actions to recover estate property, §28A-15-12(c).
Recovery of costs when executor or administrator
a party, §6-31.
When chargeable to estate, §6-31.
Extradition.
Fugitives from this state, §15A-744.
False claims act civil actions.
Award to qui tam plaintiff, §1-610(d).
Defendant prevailing party, §1-610(g).
False imprisonment.
Allowance of costs to defendant, §6-19.
Allowance of costs to plaintiff, §6-18.
**False report of nuclear, biological or chemical
weapons,** §14-288.23(b).
Hoaxes, §14-288.24(b).
Federal courts.
Appeals.
State costs on appeals to federal courts, §6-17.
State cases.
Expenses and costs of state in connection with
state cases, §6-17.1.
Fees.
Attorneys' fees.
See ATTORNEYS' FEES.
General provisions.
See FEES.
Witnesses, §§6-51 to 6-62.
See WITNESSES.
Ferries.
Application for establishment, alteration or
discontinuance.
Allowance of costs to either party or
apportioned in discretion of court, §6-21.
Filing.
Entering costs in case file, §6-7.
Fish and fisheries resources.
Replacement costs of resources, §113-267.
Foreign-money claims.
Assessment of cost in U. S. dollars, §1C-1826(c).
Frivolous prosecutions.
Nonpayment of cost.
Imprisonment of prosecuting witness for willful
nonpayment, §6-50.
Guardian ad litem.
Responsibility of guardian for costs against infant
plaintiff, §6-30.
Guardians.
Accounts and accounting.
Annual accounts.
Compelling accounting, §35A-1265(a).
Inventory or account required within three
months.
Compelling inventory or account.
Personal liability of guardian for costs of
proceedings, §35A-1262(b).

COSTS —Cont'd
Guardians —Cont'd
Determination of incompetence.
Taxing of costs, §35A-1116(a).
Responsibility of guardian for costs against infant
plaintiff, §6-30.
Habeas corpus.
Allowance of costs to either party or apportioned
in discretion of court, §6-21.
Health.
Public health or mental health grants from
federal government.
Counties to recover indirect costs on certain
grants, §130A-8(a).
Exception, §130A-8(b).
Highways.
Application for establishment, alteration or
discontinuance.
Allowance of costs to either party or
apportioned in discretion of court, §6-21.
Highways, roads and streets.
Condemnation proceedings, §136-119.
Connection of highways with improved streets.
Pipelines and conduits, §136-27.
Public roads.
Application for establishment, etc.
Allowance of costs, §6-21.
Homestead exemption.
Appraising costs and expenses, §6-28.
Laying off homestead and exemption, §6-28.
Reallotment of homestead for increase in value.
Allowance of costs to either party or
apportioned in discretion of court, §6-21.
Reassessment of homestead, §6-29.
Husband and wife.
Judgments against married persons for costs.
Levy and collection out of separate estate,
§1-223.
Illegitimacy.
Allowance of costs to either party or apportioned
in discretion of court, §6-21.
Imprisonment for willful nonpayment.
Prosecuting witnesses.
Frivolous prosecution, §6-50.
Incompetence determinations.
Assessment in taxing, §35A-1116.
Multidisciplinary evaluation, §35A-1116.
Witness fees and fees of court-appointed counsel
or guardian ad litem, §35A-1116.
Indigent persons.
Payment of costs, §6-24.
Suits in forma pauperis.
Dismissal of actions, §1A-1 Rule 41(d).
Infant plaintiffs.
Responsibility of guardian for costs against infant
plaintiff, §6-30.
In forma pauperis.
Dismissal of actions, §1A-1 Rule 41(d).
Infractions, §15A-1118.
Inspection of land or documents.
Failure to respond to request, §1A-1 Rule 37(d).
Installment plan arrangement.
Payment of costs in criminal actions.
District courts, §7A-304(a).
Insurance.
Attorneys' fees.
Allowance of counsel fees as part of costs,
§6-21.1.
Examinations by insurance commissioner.
Reimbursement by insurer, §58-2-134.

COSTS —Cont'd
**Insurance consumer and customer information
privacy.**
Action by individual for violations, §58-39-105(c).
Interest.
Attorneys' fees in notes, conditional sale contracts,
etc., in addition to interest, §6-21.2.
Conditional sale contracts.
Attorneys' fees and conditional sale contracts in
addition to interest, §6-21.2.
Evidence of indebtedness.
Attorneys' fees in notes, conditional sale
contracts, etc., in addition to interest,
§6-21.2.
Interest from verdict to judgment added as costs,
§24-7.
Notes.
Attorneys' fees in notes in addition to interest,
§6-21.2.
**International commercial arbitration and
conciliation.**
Awarding, §1-567.61(h).
Conciliation, §1-567.85.
Interrogatories.
Failure of party to serve answers, §1A-1 Rule
37(d).
Interstate family support, §52C-3-312.
Items allowed as costs, §6-1.
Jails.
Removal of trial from one county to another.
Liability of counties for cost, §6-40.
Joinder of actions.
Plaintiff's costs.
Several suits for same cause of action, §6-18.
Judgments.
Confession of judgment.
Defendant's liability in criminal action, §6-47.
Foreign judgments.
Enforcement, §1C-1706.
Interest from verdict to judgment added as costs,
§24-7.
Judicial department.
Purposes of chapter.
Uniform costs and fees in trial divisions, §7A-2.
Revenues and expenses, NC Const Art IV §20.
Uniform costs and fees in trial divisions, §§7A-304
to 7A-318.
Juror fees.
Amount, §7A-312(a).
Waiver, §7A-312(b).
Labor.
Discrimination against lawful use of lawful
products during nonworking hours.
Court costs in civil actions for violations,
§95-28.2(e).
Retaliatory employment discrimination.
Award of costs in civil action, §95-243(c).
Landlord and tenant.
Summary ejectment.
Costs tendered by tenant, §42-33.
Light companies.
Petitions for condemnation of land.
Payment of costs by petitioners, §6-22.
**Limited liability company derivative actions
by members,** §57C-8-01(a).
Actions brought without reasonable cause,
§57C-8-01(f).
Loans.
Evidence of indebtedness.
Attorneys' fees in addition to interest, §6-21.2.

COSTS —Cont'd
Local government finance.
Bond issues.
Actions validating bonds, §159-75.
Lost instruments and records.
Proceedings under provisions, §98-14.
Magistrates.
Appeals from magistrate, §6-33.
Stay of payment, §15A-1431(f1).
Malicious prosecution.
Allowance of costs in civil cases, §§6-18, 6-19.
Marriage and family therapists.
Disciplinary actions, §90-270.60(c).
Mediated settlement conferences in superior court civil actions, §7A-38.1(k).
Mediated settlement conferences or other settlement procedures in district court.
Actions involving equitable distribution, alimony or support, §7A-38.4A(i).
Mediation.
Insurance claims, §7A-38.3A.
Ordered by superior court clerks, §7A-38.3B(f).
Medicaid.
False claims presented by providers, §108A-70.12(b).
Medical malpractice.
Arbitration of negligent health claims, §90-21.65(e).
Mental health, developmental disabilities and substance abuse.
Administration of estates, §7A-307.
Mills.
Petitions for condemnation of water millsites.
Payment of costs, §6-22.
Mines and minerals.
Trespass.
Damages.
Survey, §74-36.
Minors.
Administration of estates, §7A-307.
Responsibility of guardian for costs against infant plaintiff, §6-30.
Miscellaneous fees and expenses collected by superior court clerk, §7A-308(a).
Attorneys appointed for indigents.
Fees for copies not chargeable to, §7A-308(b1).
Not chargeable with part of regular disposition, §7A-308(b).
Worthless checks collection program.
Fee paid by person participating in, §7A-308(c1).
Misdemeanants.
Housing or confining.
Statewide misdemeanant confinement fund, §148-10.4.
Maintenance in county jails, §7A-304(a).
Missing persons' estate administration.
Additional costs assessed before clerk, §7A-307(d).
Assessment of costs, §7A-307(a).
Completeness and exclusivity of costs, §7A-307(c).
Courtroom and related judicial facilities.
Amount of facilities fee, §7A-307(b).
Use of facilities, §7A-307(a).
General court of justice.
Support of court, §7A-307(a).
Liability of parties for costs, §7A-307(e).
Mountain ridge protection.
Civil action against persons alleged in violation, §113A-211(b).
Municipalities.
Actions by state for city, town or village.
Liability for costs, §6-15.

COSTS —Cont'd
Municipalities —Cont'd
Condemnation of land.
Petitioner to pay costs in certain cases, §6-22.
Uniform costs and fees in trial divisions.
Requirement to advance certain fees, §7A-317.
Negotiable instruments.
Attorneys' fees in notes in addition to interest, §6-21.2.
Several actions on one instrument.
Allowance of costs to defendant, §6-19.
Allowance of costs to plaintiff, §6-18.
Nolle prosequi.
Prosecuting witness' liability for cost, §6-49.
Determination of prosecuting witness by court, §6-49.
Nonjustifiable cases.
Attorneys at law.
Fees, §6-21.5.
Nonpayment.
Arrest for nonpayment, §6-48.
Frivolous prosecution.
Imprisonment for willful nonpayment, §6-50.
Nonprofit corporations.
Court-ordered inspections of records, §55A-16-04(c).
Notes.
Attorneys' fees in notes in addition to interest, §6-21.2.
Notice.
Defendants with no personal claim against.
Payment of costs by defendant unreasonably defending after notice of no personal claim, §6-23.
Nuisances.
Abatement.
Offenses against public morals, §19-8.
Lien, §19-6.
Nurses.
Disciplinary action.
Assessment of costs against nurse, §90-171.27(d).
Office of information technology services.
Procurement of information technology.
Liability for violations, §147-33.102.
Oil and gas conservation.
Hearings, §113-400.
Oil pollution and hazardous substances control.
Discharges.
Removal costs and damages.
Liability of responsible party, §143-215.93A(c).
Overhead high-voltage line safety.
Precautionary safety arrangements, §95-229.10(f).
Parties.
Administration of estates, §7A-307.
Allowance of costs to either party or apportioned in discretion of court, §6-21.
Decedents' estates.
Liability for costs in administration of estates, §7A-307(e).
District courts.
Civil actions in district court.
Liability for costs, §7A-305(e).
Items allowed as costs, §6-1.
Joinder of defendants.
Several suits for same cause of action.
Allowance of costs to defendant, §6-19.
Allowance of costs to plaintiff, §6-18.

COSTS —Cont'd

Parties —Cont'd

Joinder of private party.
Civil actions by the state, §6-13.
Minors.
Administration of estates.
Liability for costs in administration,
§7A-307(e).
Superior courts.
Civil actions in superior court.
Liability for costs, §7A-305(e).
Special proceedings.
Added to costs for appeal or transfer,
§7A-306(d).
Liability of parties for costs, §7A-306(e).

Partition.

Allowance of costs to either party or apportioned
in discretion of court, §6-21.

Paupers.

Suits in forma pauperis.
Dismissal of actions, §1A-1 Rule 41(d).

Payment.

Costs in criminal actions.
District courts, §7A-304(a).
Nonpayment of fine and cost.
Arrest for nonpayment, §6-48.
Prosecuting witnesses.
Imprisonment for willful nonpayment if
prosecution frivolous, §6-50.

Personal injury.

Attorneys' fees as part of costs.
Allowance in certain cases, §6-21.1.

Personal property.

Recovery or possession.
Allowance of costs to defendant, §6-19.
Allowance of costs to plaintiff, §6-18.

Pesticides.

Condemnation, §143-447(d), (e).

Petitioners.

When petitioner to pay costs, §6-22.

Plaintiffs.

Allowance of costs, §6-18.
Infant plaintiff.
Responsibility of guardian for costs against
infant plaintiff, §6-30.

Pleadings.

Real property.
Claim of title arising on pleadings.
Allowance of costs to defendant, §6-19.
Allowance of costs to plaintiff, §6-18.

Police.

Removal of unfit officers.
Taxing of costs against unreasonable filing of
complaint, §128-20.

Pork promotion assessments.

Recovery of unpaid assessment, §106-790.

Post assessment insurance guaranty association.

Right to recover, §58-48-50(a1).

Postmortem examinations.

Homicide.
Compensation of physician, §15-7.

Powers of attorney.

Assessment of costs under powers of attorney,
§7A-307.
Gifts.
Court order authorizing, §32A-14.12.

Principals.

Actions against principals or teachers.
Allowance of counsel fees and costs, §6-21.4.

COSTS —Cont'd

Prisons and prisoners.

Removal of trial from one county to another.
Liability of counties for cost, §6-40.

Probation.

Costs of court and appointed counsel.
Payment by defendant, §15A-1343(e).
Substance abuse programs, §15A-1343(b).

Professional counselors.

Disciplinary action against licensees, §90-340(c).

Promissory notes.

Several actions on one instrument.
Allowance of costs to defendant, §6-19.
Allowance of costs to plaintiff, §6-18.

Property.

Damages.
Allowance of attorneys' fees as part of costs,
§6-21.1.
Personal property recovery or possession, §§6-18,
6-19.
Real property recovery.
Claim of title arising on pleadings, §§6-18, 6-19.

Prosecuting witnesses.

Liability for cost in certain cases, §6-49.
Determination of prosecuting witness by court,
§6-49.
Nonpayment of cost if prosecution frivolous, §6-50.
Imprisonment of prosecuting witness for willful
nonpayment, §6-50.

Prosecution bonds.

Bond for costs and damages, §§1-109 to 1-112.
Liability for costs.
Sureties on prosecution bonds liable, §6-3.

Public institutions.

Condemnation of land for water supplies.
Petitioner to pay costs in certain cases, §6-22.

Public officers and employees.

Civil actions by and against state officers, §6-14.
Improper government activities.
Reporting.
Remedies, §126-87.

Public roads.

Application for establishment, alteration or
discontinuance.
Allowance of costs to either party or
apportioned in discretion of court, §6-21.

Public utilities.

Condemnation of land.
Petitioner to pay costs in certain cases, §6-22.

Public works.

Regulation of contractors.
Estimates of cost, §133-33.

Quo warranto.

Judgments.
Recovery of costs, §1-527.

Railroads.

Petitions for condemnation of land for railroads.
Petitioner to pay costs, §6-22.

Real estate brokers.

Commercial real estate lien.
Action to enforce, §44A-24.12.

Real property.

Claim of title arising on pleadings.
Allowance of costs to defendant, §6-19.
Allowance of costs to plaintiff, §6-18.
Recovery of real property.
Allowance of costs to defendant, §6-19.
Allowance of costs to plaintiff, §6-18.

Recognizance.

Several actions on one instrument.
Allowance of costs to defendant, §6-19.

COSTS —Cont'd
Recognizance —Cont'd
Several actions on one instrument —Cont'd
Allowance of costs to plaintiff, §6-18.
Record inspections.
Nonprofit corporations.
Court-ordered, §55A-16-04(c).
Referees.
Deposition taking.
Allowance of costs to either party or
apportioned in discretion of court, §6-21.
Reference of claim against deceased person.
Recovery of fees of referees, §6-31.
Remission or revocation of fine or costs,
§§15A-1363, 15A-1364(c).
Requests for admissions, failure to admit,
§1A-1 Rule 37(c).
Rescue squad workers' relief fund.
Administration costs.
Withholding, §58-88-30.
Retaliatory employment discrimination.
Award of reasonable costs in civil action,
§95-243(c).
Sale of prints by art dealers.
Wrongful refusal to repay purchaser, §25C-15(b).
Sales representatives' commissions.
Frivolous actions by sales representatives,
§66-192(b).
Principal failing to comply with provisions,
§66-192(a).
Seduction.
Allowance of costs to defendant, §6-19.
Allowance of costs to plaintiff, §6-18.
Service of process.
Uniform civil process fees, §7A-311.
Service of process in criminal cases in
superior or district courts, §7A-304(a).
Sheriffs.
Execution for unpaid costs.
Levy of execution by sheriffs, §6-4.
Removal of unfit officers.
Taxing of costs against unreasonable filing of
complaint, §128-20.
Special proceedings, §7A-306.
Allowance in civil actions, §6-26.
Commissioner's fees taxed as cost, §1-408.
Surveyors' fees.
Taxed as costs, §1-408.1.
State departments and agencies.
Industrial commission may tax cost, §143-291.1.
Publications.
Statement of cost, §143-170.1(a), (a1), (b).
State of North Carolina, §§6-13 to 6-17.1.
Civil actions by the state.
Joinder of private party, §6-13.
Liability of state for cost, §6-13.
Officers of state in civil actions, §6-14.
Federal litigation.
Appeals, §6-17.
Expenses and costs in connection with state
cases, §6-17.1.
Liability of state for costs.
Civil actions by the state, §6-13.
Corporations.
Actions by state for corporation, §6-15.
Counties.
Actions by state for county, §6-15.
Federal court appeals, §6-17.
Joinder of private party, §6-13.
Municipalities.
Actions by state for city, town or village,
§6-15.

COSTS —Cont'd
State of North Carolina —Cont'd
Liability of state for costs —Cont'd
Officers of state.
Civil action by and against state officers,
§6-14.
Private persons.
Actions by state for private persons, §6-15.
Private persons.
Actions by state for private persons, §6-15.
State treasurer.
Banking operations of department.
Apportionment of costs, §147-68.1.
Statutes.
Persons expressly authorized by statute to
prosecute or defend actions.
Recovery of cost, §6-31.
Street railways.
Petitions for condemnation of land for street
railways.
Payment of costs, §6-22.
Subpoenas.
Criminal process in superior or district courts,
§7A-304(a).
Subrogation.
Vocational rehabilitation, §143-547(c).
Suits by indigent.
Payment of costs, §6-24.
Summary judgment.
Affidavits made in bad faith, §1A-1 Rule 56(g).
Superior courts.
Case file.
Entering costs in case file, §6-7.
Civil actions, §7A-305.
Clerks of court.
Authority of clerk to award costs and
disbursements, §7A-103.
Criminal actions, §7A-304.
Execution for unpaid costs, §6-4.
Special proceedings, §7A-306.
Support and maintenance.
Years' support for surviving spouse or children.
Allowance to either party or apportioned in
discretion of court, §6-21.
Supreme court of the United States.
Appeals to federal courts.
State costs on appeals, §6-17.
Surveyors' fees.
In actions involving sale of land.
Taxed as costs, §1-408.1.
Surviving spouses.
Allowance to either party or apportioned in
discretion of court, §6-21.
Teachers.
Actions against teachers.
Allowance of counsel fees and costs in certain
cases, §6-21.4.
Termination of parental rights proceedings.
Taxing, §7B-1110(e).
Transfer fee covenants.
Recording, liability, §39A-3(b).
Trusts and trustees.
Action or proceeding requiring construction of
trust agreement.
Allowance of costs to either party or
apportioned in discretion of court, §6-21.
Awarding in proceeding involving trust,
§36C-10-1004.
Express trusts.
Recovery of costs, §6-31.
When chargeable to fund, §6-31.

COSTS —Cont'd
Underground leaking petroleum storage tank cleanup.
Actions for fund reimbursement.
Recovery of costs, §143-215.94G(e).
Applicability of part, §143-215.94N.
Groundwater protection loan fund.
Civil action for default or violation of loan agreement, §143-215.94P(e).
Uniform civil process fees, §7A-311.
Uniform fees for jurors.
Amount, §7A-312(a).
Waiver, §7A-312(b).
Uniform fees for witnesses, §7A-314.
United States courts.
Appeals to federal courts.
State costs on appeals, §6-17.
Federal litigation arising out of state cases.
Expenses and costs of state, §6-17.1.
Usury.
Party seeking recovery on usurious contracts.
No recovery of costs, §6-25.
Vehicle mileage act violations, private civil actions, §20-348(a).
Venue changes.
Liability of counties where trial removed from one county to another, §6-40.
Vocational rehabilitation.
Subrogation, §143-547(c).
Will caveats.
Allowance of costs to either party or apportioned in discretion of court, §6-21.
Security for costs.
Court may require, §31-33(d).
Witnesses.
Fees, §§6-51 to 6-62.
See WITNESSES.
Out of state witnesses, §15A-813.
Prosecuting witness.
Liability for cost in certain cases, §6-49.
Nonpayment of cost if prosecution frivolous, §6-50.
Reference of claim against deceased person.
Recovery of fees of witness, §6-31.
Uniform fees for witnesses, §7A-314.
Worthless checks collection program.
Fee paid by person participating in, §7A-308(c1).

COST SAVINGS SUGGESTIONS OR INNOVATIONS.
State employee suggestion program (NC-Thinks), §§143-345.20 to 143-345.25.

COTENANTS.
See JOINT TENANTS AND TENANTS IN COMMON.

COTTON.
Boll weevil eradication, §§106-65.67 to 106-65.78.
See BOLL WEEVIL ERADICATION.
Commodities generally, §§78D-1 to 78D-33.
See COMMODITIES.
Definitions.
Grower's organization, §106-65.85.
Warehouses, §106-451.7.
Gins.
See COTTON GINS.
Grower's organization, §§106-65.84 to 106-65.91.
See COTTON GROWER'S ORGANIZATION.
Labels.
Requirements for cottonseed labeling, §106-277.10(c).

COTTON —Cont'd
Larceny.
Ungathered crops, §14-78.
Liens.
Effective period, §44-69.1.
Official cotton grower's organization, §§106-65.84 to 106-65.91.
Promotion of use and sale of agricultural products.
Generally, §§106-550 to 106-568.
See AGRICULTURAL PRODUCTS PROMOTION.
Referendum.
Promotion of use and sale of agricultural products.
Special provisions for cotton promotion association, §106-559.
Sales.
Promotion of use and sale of agricultural products.
Special referendum provisions for cotton promotion association, §106-559.
Seeds.
Label requirements for cottonseed, §106-277.10(c).
Weights and measures.
Standard weights and measures, §81A-42.
Warehouses, §§106-451.6 to 106-451.28, 106-451.40 to 106-451.44.
See COTTON WAREHOUSES.
Weights and measures.
Seed.
Standard weights and measures, §81A-42.

COTTON BALES.
Flat trucks loaded with.
Load to be securely fastened, §20-120.

COTTON DUST PREVENTION OR REDUCTION.
Ventilation and air conditioning systems used for.
Property tax exemption, §105-275.

COTTON GINS.
Burning of ginhouses, §14-64.
Defined, §106-451.40.
Duties, §106-451.43(a) to (d).
Injunctions.
Operation without registration, §106-451.44.
Misdemeanors.
Operation without registration, §106-451.44.
Registration.
Applications, §106-451.42(a).
Certificate.
Display, §106-451.42(c).
Denial, suspension or revocation, §106-451.43(e).
Operation without registration, §106-451.44.
Required, §106-451.41.

COTTON GROWER'S ORGANIZATION, §§106-65.74 to 106-65.91.
Agreements.
Authority to enter into, §106-65.89.
Assessments.
Basis, §106-65.88(b).
Disposition, §106-65.88(e).
Failure to pay.
Destruction of plants, §106-65.90(b).
Lien upon cotton, §106-65.90(c).
Penalties, §106-65.90(a).
Not state funds, §106-65.88(g).
Referendum, §106-65.88(a).

COTTON GROWER'S ORGANIZATION —Cont'd
Audits.
Annual audit of accounts, §106-65.88(f).
Authority to enter into agreements, §106-65.89.
Certification.
Authority of board, §106-65.86(a).
Eligibility, §106-65.86(b).
Purposes, §106-65.87(a).
Revocation, §106-65.87(b).
Definitions, §106-65.85.
Findings of fact, §106-65.84.
Purpose of article, §106-65.84.
Referendum.
Assessments, §106-65.88(a).
Votes necessary, §106-65.88(d).
Eligibility to vote, §106-65.88(c).
Votes necessary, §106-65.88(d).
Rules and regulations.
Adoption by board, §106-65.91.

COTTON MERCHANTS.
Defined, §106-451.40.
Duties, §106-451.43(a) to (d).
Injunctions.
Operation without registration, §106-451.44.
Misdemeanors.
Operation without registration, §106-451.44.
Registration.
Applications, §106-451.42(a).
Certificate.
Display, §106-451.42(c).
Denial, suspension or revocation, §106-451.43(e).
Operation without registration, §106-451.44.
Required, §106-451.41.

COTTON WAREHOUSES, §§106-451.6 to
106-451.28, 106-451.40 to 106-451.44.
Administration of article, §106-451.9.
Use of income from warehouse fund, §106-451.27.
Bonds, surety, §106-451.11(a).
Action on bond by person injured, §106-451.12.
Inspectors, §106-451.25.
Registration, §106-451.42(b).
Citation of article, §106-451.6.
**Classification, grading and weighing of cotton
stored.**
Delivery to warehouse presumed for storage,
§106-451.16.
Licenses, §106-451.14.
Suspension or revocation, §106-451.15.
Commissioner of agriculture.
Powers and duties.
Generally, §106-451.9.
**Compliance with provisions of article, rules
and regulations,** §106-451.23.
Definitions, §§106-451.7, 106-451.40.
Delivery of products stored on demand,
§106-451.21.
Conditions to delivery, §106-451.21.
Deposit of cotton deemed subject to article,
§106-451.17.
Duties, §106-451.43(a) to (d).
Enforcement of article, §106-451.9.
Examination of books, records, etc.,
§106-451.24.
Fraudulent or deceptive acts, §106-451.28.
Fund for support of system, §106-435.
Injunctions.
Operation without registration, §106-451.44.
Inspectors.
Bonds, surety, §106-451.25.
Insurance, §106-451.11(b).

COTTON WAREHOUSES —Cont'd
Liability.
Officials and employees, §106-451.26.
Licenses.
Applications.
Contents, §106-451.10(b).
Classification, grading and weighing of cotton
stored, §106-451.14.
Suspension or revocation, §106-451.15.
Issuance, §106-451.10(a).
Renewal, §106-451.10(a).
Revocation, §106-451.13.
Suspension, §106-451.13.
Term, §106-451.10(a).
Misdemeanors.
Operation without registration, §106-451.44.
Penalties.
Violation of article, §106-451.28.
Presumptions.
Delivery to warehouse, §106-451.16.
Subject to article, §106-451.17.
Receipts for cotton stored, §106-451.18.
Cancellation on delivery of cotton stored,
§106-451.22.
Contents, §106-451.19.
Delivery.
Cancellation, §106-451.22.
Issuance.
Issuance of further receipt with original
outstanding prohibited, §106-451.20.
Prohibited acts, §106-451.20.
Requirements, §106-451.19.
Records, §106-451.23.
Examination, §106-451.24.
Registration.
Applications, §106-451.42(a).
Bonds, surety, §106-451.42(b).
Certificate.
Display, §106-451.42(c).
Denial, suspension or revocation, §106-451.43(e).
Operation without registration, §106-451.44.
Required, §106-451.41.
Reports, §106-451.23.
Rules and regulations.
Board of agriculture, §106-451.8.
Short title of article, §106-451.6.
Tort actions.
Liability of officials and employees, §106-451.26.
Violation of article.
Penalties, §106-451.28.
Warehouse fund.
Use of income to administer article, §106-451.27.

COUGARS.
Captivity licenses, §113-272.5(e).

COUNCIL-MANAGER CITIES, §§160A-147 to
160A-152.
Applicability of part, §160A-152.
Council.
Ineligible to serve or act as manager, §160A-151.
Employees.
Compensation.
Manager responsible, §160A-162(a).
Manager.
Acting city manager, §160A-149.
Appointment, §160A-147(a).
Chief administrator of city, §160A-148.
County board of education, serving on,
§160A-147(b1).
Duties.
Applicability of part, §160A-152.

COUNCIL-MANAGER CITIES —Cont'd
Manager —Cont'd
Duties —Cont'd
Generally, §160A-148.
Eligibility.
Mayor and councilmen ineligible to serve or act
as manager, §160A-151.
Employees.
Compensation, §160A-162(a).
Holding elective office, §160A-147(c).
Interim city manager.
Designated by council, §160A-150.
Population figures, determining, §160A-147(d).
Powers.
Applicability of part, §160A-152.
Generally, §160A-148.
Residence in city not required, §160A-147(a).
Serving on county board of education.
Elected on non-partisan basis, §160A-147(b).
Vacancy.
Interim city manager, §160A-150.
Mayor.
Ineligible to serve or act as manager, §160A-151.
Optional form, §160A-101.
Plan of government.
Officers to carry out plan, §160A-108.
Service upon manager is service upon city,
§1A-1 Rule 4(j).

COUNCIL OF STATE.
Advertisements or public service
announcements by candidates for council.
State funds not to be used, §163-278.16A.
Capital facilities finance act.
Generally, §§142-80 to 142-101.
See CAPITAL FACILITIES FINANCE ACT.
Continuing legal education exemption, Bar
Rule D.1517.
Convening, §147-13(a).
Declared joint governmental agency, §143-186.
Internal improvements.
Control of internal improvements, §124-1.
Investigation of corporations.
Power of investigation, §124-7.
Journal, §147-13(b).
Limitation on fundraising during legislative
session, §163-278.13B.
Members-elect.
Office space and expenses, §147-31.1.
Personnel system.
Competitive service.
Determination of competitive service by council
of state, §126-12.
Quorum, §147-13(a).
Service of process, §1A-1 Rule 4(j).

COUNCIL ON EDUCATIONAL SERVICES TO
EXCEPTIONAL CHILDREN, §115C-112.1.

COUNCILS.
Apprenticeship council, §143A-71.
Brain injury advisory council, §§143B-216.65,
143B-216.66.
Building code council, §§143-136, 143-137.
Community development council, §§143B-437.1
to 143B-437.3.
Compensation for services.
Per diem, subsistence and travel expenses,
§138-5(a) to (f).
Deaf and the hard of hearing, §§143B-216.30 to
143B-216.34.

COUNCILS —Cont'd
Developmental disabilities.
Council on developmental disabilities, §§143B-177
to 143B-179.
Drought management advisory council,
§143-355.1.
Educational services to exceptional children,
§115C-112.1.
Electronic recording council, §47-16.5.
Emergency medical services.
Advisory council, §§143-507 to 143-519.
Energy policy council, §§113B-1 to 113B-12.
Expiration of council created by governor or
other state officials.
Constitutional elective officers creating,
§147-16.2(b).
Executive branch officials creating, §147-16.2(c).
Executive order of governor creating, §147-16.2(a).
Fees, §12-3.1(a), (c).
Definitions, §12-3.1(b).
Fish and fisheries resources.
Mid-Atlantic fishery management council.
North Carolina members, §113-260.
South Atlantic fishery management council.
North Carolina members, §113-259.
Gender based appointments.
Appointing members to statutorily created
decision making or regulatory entities.
Appointments to reflect proportion that gender
represents in population of state,
§143-157.1(a).
Report by appointing authority of number of
appointments of each gender, §143-157.1(b).
Local government reporting, §143-157.1(d).
State reporting, §143-157.1(c).
Governor's advisory council on aging,
§§143B-180, 143B-181.
Governor's management council, §§143B-426.22,
143B-426.23.
Housing coordination and policy council,
§§122A-5.10 to 122A-5.12.
Interagency coordinating council for children
with disabilities from birth to five years of
age, §§143B-179.5, 143B-179.6.
Internship council, §§143B-417 to 143B-419.
Juvenile crime prevention councils, §§143B-845
to 143B-851.
See JUVENILE CRIME PREVENTION
COUNCILS.
Minority health advisory council, §§130A-33.43,
130A-33.44.
Mountain resources planning act.
Technical advisory council, §153B-4.
North Carolina advisory council on the
eastern band of the Cherokee, §§143B-411.1
to 143B-411.4.
North Carolina arts council, §§143B-87, 143B-88.
North Carolina council on the Holocaust,
§143A-48.1.
North Carolina farmworker council,
§§143B-426.25, 143B-426.26.
North Carolina zoological park council,
§143B-336.1.
Per diem, subsistence and travel expenses,
§138-5(a) to (f).
Secretary of state.
Membership, NC Const Art III §8.
Sickle cell trait, §§130A-131 to 130A-131.2.
State of North Carolina.
Council of state.
See COUNCIL OF STATE.

COUNCILS —Cont'd

State youth advisory council, §§143B-385 to 143B-388.

Status of women, §§143B-393, 143B-394.

Western North Carolina public lands council, §§143B-324.1 to 143B-324.3.

Wine and grape growers' council, §143B-437.91.

Women.
Council for women, §§143B-393, 143B-394.

Writing required to create, §147-16.2(d).

Zoological park council, §§143B-335, 143B-336.

COUNSELORS.

Employee assistance professionals, §§90-500 to 90-511.
See EMPLOYEE ASSISTANCE PROFESSIONALS.

Licensed professional counselors, §§90-329 to 90-345.
See PROFESSIONAL COUNSELORS.

Marriage and family therapists.
General provisions.
See MARRIAGE AND FAMILY THERAPISTS.

Pastoral counselors.
Certification of fee-based practicing pastoral counselors, §§90-380 to 90-395.
See PASTORAL COUNSELORS.

Privileged communications, §8-53.8.

Professional counselors, §§90-329 to 90-345.
See PROFESSIONAL COUNSELORS.

School counselors.
Privileged communications, §§8-53.4, 115C-401.

COUNTERCLAIMS AND CROSS-CLAIMS, §1A-1 Rule 7(a).

Answer to crossclaim, §1A-1 Rule 7(a).

Claims for relief.
Contents, §1A-1 Rule 8(a).

Compulsory counterclaims, §1A-1 Rule 13(a).

Costs.
Action in superior or district court where counterclaim or cross-claim included in pleading, §7A-305(a5).

Counterclaim against state, §1A-1 Rule 13(d).

Counterclaim exceeding opposing claim, §1A-1 Rule 13(c).

Counterclaim maturing or acquired after pleading, §1A-1 Rule 13(e).

Crossclaim against party, §1A-1 Rule 13(g).

Default judgments.
Provisions of rule apply to parties pleading, §1A-1 Rule 55(e).

Dismissal, discontinuance and nonsuit, §1A-1 Rule 41(c).
Dismissal as to plaintiff's claim.
Effect on counterclaim, §1-183.1.

District courts.
Small claim actions.
Assigned actions, §7A-220.
Impermissible counterclaims and cross claims, §7A-219.

Divorce.
Resumption of maiden name or adoption of name of prior deceased or prior living husband.
Incorporation of petition for resumption or use of name in complaint or counterclaim for divorce, §50-12(d).

Expedited evictions.
Time for filing reply to counterclaim, §42-68.

Foreign-country money judgments.
Recognition.
Raising issue, §1C-1855(b).

COUNTERCLAIMS AND CROSS-CLAIMS —Cont'd

Foreign-money claims, §1C-1825(c).

International commercial arbitration and conciliation.
Stating counterclaims, requirements, §1-567.53(a).
Amending or supplementing, §1-567.53(b).
More than two parties to arbitration, §1-567.53(c).

Interpleader by way of crossclaim or counterclaim, §1A-1 Rule 22(a).

Joinder of claims, §1A-1 Rule 18(a).

Judgments, §1A-1 Rule 54(b).
Foreign-country money judgments.
Recognition.
Raising issue, §1C-1855(b).

Jurisdiction.
Personal jurisdiction.
Grounds for without service of summons, §1-75.7.

Mistakenly designating defense as counterclaim or crossclaim, §1A-1 Rule 8(c).

Omitted counterclaim, §1A-1 Rule 13(f).

Parties.
Additional parties brought in, §1A-1 Rule 13(h).

Permissive counterclaims, §1A-1 Rule 13(b).

Reply to counterclaim, §1A-1 Rule 7(a).

Seals and sealed instruments.
Limitation of actions, §1-47.

Separate trial, §§1A-1 Rule 13(i), 1A-1 Rule 42(b).

Service of process.
Certificate of service, §1A-1 Rule 5(b1).
Numerous defendants, §1A-1 Rule 5(c).
Pleading setting forth counterclaim or crossclaim, §1A-1 Rule 5(b).

Small claims actions.
Assigned actions, §7A-220.
Failure to file.
Claim not barred in separate action, §7A-219.
Impermissible counterclaims and crossclaims, §7A-219.

Stay of judgment as to multiple parties or multiple claims, §1A-1 Rule 62(g).

Summary judgment, §1A-1 Rule 56.

Time for serving reply to counterclaim, §1A-1 Rule 12(a).

Tort claims against state departments and agencies.
Counterclaims by state, §143-291.3.

Usurious notes or other evidences of debt, actions to recover upon.
Pleading penalty for usury as crossclaim, §24-2.

COUNTERFEIT DRUGS, §106-122.

Defined, §106-121.

COUNTERFEITING.

Bills of lading.
Felony, §21-42.

Coins, §14-109.
Counterfeiting coin and uttering coin that is counterfeit, §14-13.

Credit devices, fraudulent use, §§14-113.1 to 14-113.7A.

Forgery.
See FORGERY.

Issuing substitutes for money without authority, §14-15.

Notes, checks and other securities, §14-119.

Possessing tools for counterfeiting, §14-14.

Property obtained by, §14-108.

COUNTERFEITING —Cont'd
Receiving or passing unauthorized substitutes for money, §14-16.
Services obtained by, §14-108.
Substitutes for money.
Issuing substitutes without authority, §14-15.
Receiving or passing unauthorized substitutes for money, §14-16.
Tools.
Possessing tools for counterfeiting, §14-14.
Trademarks.
Infringement generally.
Criminal use of counterfeit trademark, §80-11.1.
Deceptive or unfair trade practices, §80-12.
Uttering.
Coin that is counterfeit, §14-13.

COUNTERINTELLIGENCE SERVICE.
Private protective services generally, §§74C-1 to 74C-30.
See PRIVATE PROTECTIVE SERVICES.

COUNTIES.
Abandoned motor vehicles, §§153A-132, 153A-132.2.
Abrogation.
Mass gatherings.
Local ordinances not abrogated, §130A-258.
Actions.
County acting outside scope of authority, successful challenge.
Attorneys' fees awarded, §6-21.6.
Damages.
Suits against counties involving governmental functions, §153A-435(a), (b).
Defense of employees and officers, §160A-167.
Inspection departments.
Failure to take corrective action, §153A-368.
Outdoor advertising.
Regulation of nonconforming off-premises outdoor advertising.
Payment of monetary compensation for removal.
Determination, §153A-143(f).
Public officers.
Retention of funds of county by delinquent official.
Citizen to recover funds, §128-10.
Riparian owners.
Venue for actions, §153A-288.
Adult care homes.
Share of costs, §143B-139.5.
Advertising.
Outdoor advertising.
Regulation of nonconforming off-premises outdoor advertising, §153A-143.
Agricultural conservation easements, §106-744.
Agricultural extension services.
Applicability of policies, §153A-439(b).
Support of activities, §153A-439(a).
Agriculture.
Agricultural extension services.
Applicability of policies, §153A-439(b).
Support of activities, §153A-439(a).
Development act.
Appropriations by counties, §§106-585, 106-587.
Utilizing facilities for installing and promoting programs, §106-582.
Nuisance liability of agricultural and forestry operations.
Local ordinances affected, §106-701(d).

COUNTIES —Cont'd
Agriculture —Cont'd
Societies.
See COUNTY AGRICULTURAL SOCIETIES.
Air pollution control programs, §143-215.112.
Airports.
Authority to operate public enterprise, §153A-275.
Establishment by counties.
Authorized, §63-3.
Financing public enterprise, §153A-276.
Powers of municipalities granted to counties, §63-57(b).
Purpose of provisions declared county purposes, §63-57(a).
Rates for public enterprise services, §153A-277.
Alcoholic beverages.
ABC boards.
Defense of employees and officers, §160A-167.
Generally, §§18B-700 to 18B-706.
See ABC BOARDS.
Confinement facilities.
Furnishing alcoholic beverages to inmates, §14-258.1.
Elections, §§18B-600 to 18B-605.
See LOCAL OPTION ELECTIONS.
Excise tax on beer, wine and liquor.
Distribution of part of taxes, §105-113.82.
Ordinances.
Consumption.
Malt beverages and unfortified wine, §18B-300(c).
Restrictions on adoption, §18B-100.
Regulation of places of amusement, §153A-135.
Alcoholic beverages tax generally.
See ALCOHOLIC BEVERAGES TAX.
All-terrain vehicles.
County and municipal employees.
Use on certain highways, §20-171.24(a) to (e).
Applicable counties and municipalities, §20-171.24(f).
Amateur radio antennas.
Zoning regulations.
Reasonable accommodation, §153A-341.2.
Ambulances.
EMS services in fire protection districts, §153A-309(a), (b).
False pretenses and cheats.
Making false ambulance request, §14-111.3.
Obtaining ambulance services without intending to pay, §§14-111.1, 14-111.2.
Health services, §153A-250.
Liens.
Attachment or garnishment.
Collection authorization, §44-51.4.
Counties to which article applicable, §44-51.8.
Discharging lien, §44-51.7.
Filing, §44-51.6.
General lien for service, §44-51.5.
Services provided by county or municipality.
Discharge of lien, §44-51.3.
Filing, §44-51.2.
Real property of recipient, §44-51.1.
Service districts, §§153A-300 to 153A-310.
Amusements.
Regulation of places of amusement, §153A-135.
Animal control officers.
Appointment authorized, §67-30.
Powers and duties of dog warden, §67-31.
Animals.
Abuse of animals, §153A-127.

COUNTIES —Cont'd

Animals —Cont'd

Dangerous animals.

Possession or harboring of dangerous animals, §153A-131.

License taxes, §153A-153.

Shelters.

Establishing, standards, §153A-442.

Spay/neuter program.

Distributions to counties, §§19A-60 to 19A-66.

Taxation, §153A-153.

Ante litem notice.

Local acts not to require notice to local unit of government claim, §1-539.16.

Applicability of chapter.

Local acts, §153A-3.

Prior laws and actions taken pursuant to prior laws, §153A-2.

Statutory references deemed amended to conform to chapter, §153A-5.

Appropriations.

Agricultural development act, §§106-585, 106-587.

Beach erosion control, §153A-438.

Cemeteries.

Abandoned and neglected cemeteries.

County care of rural cemeteries, §65-112.

Economic development commissions, §158-12.

Health services.

Counties may appropriate revenues, §153A-248(a).

Ordinances, §153A-248(b).

Hurricanes.

Flood and hurricane protection works, §153A-438.

Inspection departments.

Financial support, §153A-354.

Private entities.

Appropriation of money to private entity to carry out public purpose, §153A-449.

Public schools.

Apportionment among local school administrative units, §115C-430.

State highway fund.

Allocation of funds, §136-41.1(a) to (c).

Annual appropriation out of fund, §136-41.1(a).

Contracts for maintenance, etc., of streets, §136-41.3.

Eligible municipalities, §§136-41.1(b), 136-41.2(a) to (c).

Incorporated since January 1, 1945, §136-41.2(d).

Excess accumulation of funds, §136-41.3.

Nature of funds distributed, §136-41.1(d).

Records and annual statement, §136-41.3.

Use of funds, §136-41.3.

Western North Carolina Development Association, Inc., §153A-447(a), (b).

Arbitration.

Outdoor advertising.

Regulation of nonconforming off-premises outdoor advertising.

Relocating and reconstructing outdoor advertising, §153A-143(i).

Architectural, engineering and surveying services.

Procurement, §§143-64.31 to 143-64.34.

Armories.

Lease, conveyance or acquisition of property for use as armory, §127A-165.

Local financial support, §127A-168.

COUNTIES —Cont'd

Arson.

Burning of certain public buildings, §14-59.

Assessments.

Special assessments, §§153A-185 to 153A-210.7.

See SPECIAL ASSESSMENTS BY COUNTIES.

Assessors, §§105-294 to 105-297.

See COUNTY ASSESSORS.

Atomic energy, radioactivity and ionizing radiation.

Privileged license taxes.

Low-level radioactive and hazardous waste facilities, §153A-152.1(a) to (c).

Regulation of radioactive substances, §153A-128.

Attorneys.

See COUNTY ATTORNEYS.

Attorneys' fees.

County acting outside scope of authority.

Successful challenge, §6-21.6.

Balanced growth policy act, §§143-506.6 to 143-506.13.

See BALANCED GROWTH POLICY ACT.

Bankruptcy and insolvency.

Authority to avail themselves of bankruptcy law, §23-48.

Beach erosion control.

Appropriations, §153A-438.

Service districts, §§153A-300 to 153A-310.

Special assessments.

Authority to make, §153A-185.

Beaver damage control program.

Notification to county volunteering to participate, §113-291.10(f).

Begging regulations, §153A-126.

Bids and bidding.

Public buildings and grounds.

Architectural, engineering and surveying services, §§143-64.31 to 143-64.34.

See PUBLIC CONTRACTS.

Billboards.

Outdoor advertising.

Regulation of nonconforming off-premises outdoor advertising, §153A-143.

Billiard hall regulation, §153A-135.

Blind persons.

Aid to the blind.

Appropriations by counties, §111-17.

Boards of commissioners.

See COUNTY BOARDS OF COMMISSIONERS.

Boards of education, §§115C-35 to 115C-51.

See LOCAL BOARDS OF EDUCATION.

Boards of elections, §§163-30 to 163-37.

See COUNTY BOARDS OF ELECTIONS.

Boards of health.

See COUNTY BOARDS OF HEALTH.

Boards of social services, §§108A-1 to 108A-11.

See COUNTY BOARDS OF SOCIAL SERVICES.

Boating safety education.

State preemption.

Prohibited from enacting regulations, §75A-16.2(d).

Bond issues.

Highways, roads and streets.

Prohibition of local road bonds, §136-98(b).

Interest rate swap agreements, §§159-193 to 159-200.

See SWAP AGREEMENTS.

Local government bond act generally, §§159-43 to 159-78.

See LOCAL GOVERNMENT FINANCE.

COUNTIES —Cont'd
Bond issues —Cont'd
Local government revenue bond act generally,
§§159-80 to 159-97.
See LOCAL GOVERNMENT FINANCE.
Relocation of county seat.
Procedures if county votes to relocate, §159-67.
Savings banks.
Investment in county obligations, §54C-137.
School bonds.
Election required, §115C-501(f).
Service districts.
Authorization, §153A-308.
Solid waste management loans and bonds,
§§159I-1 to 159I-30.
See SOLID WASTE MANAGEMENT LOANS
AND SPECIAL OBLIGATION BONDS.
Watershed improvement, §139-49(a) to (g).
**Bonds of county officers generally, §§58-72-1 to
58-72-70.**
See OFFICIAL BONDS OF COUNTY OFFICERS.
Boundaries.
Disputed boundaries, §153A-18(b).
Existing boundaries, §153A-17.
Townships, §153A-19.
Uncertain boundaries, §153A-18(a), (c).
Bridges.
Authorizing bridges over navigable waters,
§153A-243.
Fishing from bridges.
Regulation or prohibition, §153A-242.
Budget.
Local government budget, §§159-7 to 159-17.
See LOCAL GOVERNMENT FINANCE.
Building codes.
See BUILDING CODES.
**Building inspections generally, §§153A-350 to
153A-375.**
See COUNTY INSPECTION DEPARTMENTS.
Buildings.
Arson.
Burning of certain public buildings, §14-59.
Bids and bidding.
Architectural, engineering and surveying
services, §§143-64.31 to 143-64.34.
See PUBLIC CONTRACTS.
Care and use of county property, §153A-169.
Contracts, §§143-128 to 143-135.9.
See PUBLIC CONTRACTS.
Damages.
Rewards for information, §153A-446.
Defined, §153A-350.
Failure of owner to comply with orders of public
authorities, §14-68.
Fire safety.
Plans for buildings to be used by counties.
Approval by commissioner of insurance,
§58-31-40(b).
Joint buildings, §153A-164.
Planning and zoning.
Applicability of provisions, §153A-347.
Statute of limitations, §§1-54, 153A-348.
Repair, closing or demolition of nonresidential
buildings, §153A-372.1.
Rewards.
Persons damaging county property, §153A-446.
Setback lines.
Authority to regulate, §153A-326.
Sites of county buildings, §153A-169.
Cable television franchises.
State franchising of cable television service,
§§66-350 to 66-360.
See CABLE TELEVISION.

COUNTIES —Cont'd
Camp Butner hospital.
Ordinances.
Application to Camp Butner reservation,
§122C-410(b).
Capital project financing.
Development financing, §158-7.3.
Project development financing debt instruments.
Project development financing act, §§159-101 to
159-113.
See LOCAL GOVERNMENT FINANCE.
Capital reserve act.
Local government finance, §§159-1 to 159-188.
See LOCAL GOVERNMENT FINANCE.
Carnivals and circuses.
Regulation of places of amusement, §153A-135.
Cattle tick.
Dipping vats provided by counties, §106-353.
Embraced in quarantine zones, §106-352.
Cemeteries.
Abandoned and neglected cemeteries.
County care of rural cemeteries, §§65-111 to
65-113.
Inmates of county homes.
County commissioners may establish, §65-5.
Removal and reinterment of bodies, §65-6.
Service districts, §§153A-300 to 153A-310.
Central Piedmont community college.
Financial support of institution.
Authority to provide local financial support,
§115D-60(a).
Child support.
Assignment of support rights to state or county.
Acceptance of public assistance constitutes
assignment, §110-137.
Duty of county to obtain support, §110-138.
Institution of civil or criminal proceedings against
responsible parent, §110-130.
**Child welfare services not provided by county
departments or boards of social services.**
Action by secretary of health and human services,
§108A-74.
Chlorofluorocarbons refrigerants.
Management of discarded white goods,
§§130A-309.80 to 130A-309.87.
See WHITE GOODS.
Cisterns.
Limitations on regulating, §153A-145.
Civil disorders.
State of emergency.
Generally, §§14-288.12 to 14-288.18.
See STATE OF EMERGENCY.
Powers of counties, §14-288.13.
Claims against local units of government.
Local acts not to require notice, §1-539.16.
Clerks.
Boards of commissioners, §153A-11.
Misconduct in public office.
Swearing falsely to official reports, §14-232.
Coastal area counties.
Service districts.
Removal of junked vehicles and street
maintenance, §153A-301(b), (c).
Coastal Carolina community college.
Financial support of institution.
Authority to provide local financial support,
§115D-61.
Commissioners.
See COUNTY BOARDS OF COMMISSIONERS.
**Community appearance commissions,
§§160A-451 to 160A-455.**

COUNTIES —Cont'd
Community colleges.
Multiple-county administrative areas, §115D-59.
Satellite campuses.
Contracts for construction, §153A-450(a) to (c).
Community development.
Acquisition and disposition of property for
redevelopment, §153A-377.
Authority of boards to engage in programs and
activities, §153A-76.
Boards of commissioners.
Advisory committees, §153A-376(c).
Exercise of powers, §153A-376(a), (b).
Loans, §153A-376(d).
Low- and moderate-income housing programs.
Authority to establish and develop, §153A-378.
Program income from economic development
grants.
Retention by economically distressed counties,
§153A-376(f).
Programs, §153A-376(a).
Property.
Acquisition and disposition of property for
redevelopment, §153A-377.
Small cities community development block grant
program.
Retention of program income by economically
distressed counties, §153A-376(f).
Taxation, §153A-376(e).
Computer equipment and televisions.
Recycling computer equipment and televisions.
Authority to manage programs, §130A-309.141.
Confinement facilities.
See JAILS.
Conflict of laws.
Planning and zoning.
Rules and regulations, §153A-346.
Conflicts of interest.
Inspection departments.
Members of departments, §153A-355.
Conservation easements.
Agricultural conservation easements, §106-744.
Consolidated case management system.
Development, §153A-77.1.
**Consolidated city-county act, §§160B-1 to
160B-21.**
See CONSOLIDATED CITY-COUNTY ACT.
**Consolidated human services agencies, boards
and directors.**
Generally.
See CONSOLIDATED HUMAN SERVICES
AGENCY.
Human services director.
Powers and duties, §108A-15.1(c).
Powers and duties, §108A-15.1(a), (b).
Consolidation.
Commissions.
Powers, §153A-404.
Purposes, §153A-402.
Content of concurrent resolutions, §153A-403.
Establishment, §153A-401(a).
General assembly action, §153A-405(d).
Merged or consolidated counties, NC Const Art
VII §3.
Powers and duties of commissions, §153A-404.
Purposes of commission, §153A-402.
Referendum, §153A-405(a).
Ballot propositions, §153A-405(b) to (e).
Resolutions.
Content of concurrent resolutions, §153A-403.
Support, §153A-401(b).

COUNTIES —Cont'd
Construction and interpretation.
Broad construction of chapter, §153A-4.
Unified government.
Construction of certain statutory references,
§153A-472.
Contracts.
Abandoned manufactured homes.
Management and disposal, authority to
contract, §130A-309.113(b).
Authority to contract, NC Const Art V §2.
Continuing contracts.
Requirements, §153A-13.
Grants from other governments, §153A-14.
Health and social services, §§153A-250, 153A-259.
Highways, roads and streets.
Appropriation to municipalities.
Contracts for maintenance, etc., of streets,
§136-41.3.
Construction of roads by local authorities.
Agreement with department of
transportation, §136-98(c).
Existing contracts, §136-98(b).
Library services, §153A-270.
Private entities.
Contracts with private entities to carry out
public purposes, §153A-449.
Public building contracts.
Architectural, engineering and surveying
services, §§143-64.31 to 143-64.34.
See PUBLIC CONTRACTS.
Rail transportation liability.
Contracts allocating financial responsibility,
§153A-279.
Controlled substances.
Confinement facilities.
Furnishing controlled substances to inmates,
§14-258.1(a).
Speedy disposition of offenses.
County appropriations for programs to protect
the public, §153A-212.1.
Corporate franchise tax.
Counties prohibited from levying, §105-122(g).
Corporate powers of counties, §153A-11.
Exercise, §153A-12.
Costs.
Actions by state for county.
Liability for costs, §6-15.
Prisoners.
Removal of trial from one county to another.
Liability of county, §6-40.
Public health or mental health grants from
federal government.
Recovery of indirect costs on certain grants by
counties, §130A-8(a).
Exception, §130A-8(b).
Special assessments.
Determination of costs, §153A-193.
Discounts authorized, §153A-193.1.
Uniform costs in fees in trial divisions.
Requirement to advance certain fees, §7A-317.
County base maps.
Program for preparation.
Secretary of state to conduct, §147-54.3(c).
County cadastral maps.
Program for preparation.
Secretary of state to conduct, §147-54.3(c1).
Countywide farmland protection plan,
§106-744(e), (f).
Criminal history record checks.
Applicants for employment, §114-19.14.

COUNTIES —Cont'd
Cruelty to animals, §153A-127.
Curfews.
Imposition of curfew on persons under 18, §153A-142.
Dance hall regulation, §153A-135.
Dangerous animals.
Possession or harboring.
Regulation, §153A-131.
Dangerous substances.
Regulation of explosives, corrosives, inflammables or radioactive substances, §153A-128.
Data processing.
Common data base.
Providing, §153A-77.1.
Debts, NC Const Art V §4.
Limitation on indebtedness, §159-55(c).
Local government finance, §§159-1 to 159-188.
See LOCAL GOVERNMENT FINANCE.
Definitions.
Buildings, §153A-350.
Inspection departments, §153A-351.
Ex officio service by county and city representatives and officials.
Official, §128-1.2.
Generally, §153A-1.
Inspection departments, §153A-351.
Library materials, §153A-262.
Local confinement facilities, §153A-217.
Managers, §153A-81.
Motor vehicles.
Junked or abandoned vehicles, §153A-132(b).
Public enterprises, §153A-274.
Roads, §153A-238(a).
Solid waste, §§153A-136(d), 153A-294.
Subdivisions, §153A-335(a).
Department of agriculture and consumer services.
Forest protection and development.
Cooperation between counties and state, §106-906.
Department of environment and natural resources.
Cooperation with counties and municipal corporations, §113-20.
Water resource surveys.
Cooperation of counties in making, §113-21.
Department of inspections, §§153A-350 to 153A-375.
See COUNTY INSPECTION DEPARTMENTS.
Departments.
Acting department heads, §153A-88.
Inspection departments, §§153A-350 to 153A-375.
See COUNTY INSPECTION DEPARTMENTS.
Interim department heads, §153A-89.
Development.
Economic development commissions, §§158-8 to 158-15.
See ECONOMIC DEVELOPMENT COMMISSIONS.
Energy consumption.
Land-use development incentives to reduce, §160A-383.4(a).
Industrial development, §§158-16 to 158-24.
See INDUSTRIAL DEVELOPMENT.
Local development generally.
See LOCAL DEVELOPMENT.
Multi-county water conservation and infrastructure district, §158-15.1.
Development agreements, §§153A-349.1 to 153A-349.13.
Acreage of developed property.
Minimum number of acres, §153A-349.4.

COUNTIES —Cont'd
Development agreements —Cont'd
Amendment.
Mutual consent of parties or successors in interest, §153A-349.9.
Applicable laws, §153A-349.7(a).
Debt approval procedures for local governments, §153A-349.12.
Exceptions, §153A-349.7(b) to (d).
Approval of governing body, §153A-349.3.
Authorized, §§153A-349.1(b), 153A-349.3.
Building code.
Relationship of agreement to, §153A-349.13.
Cancellation.
Mutual consent of parties or successors in interest, §153A-349.9.
Change of jurisdiction.
Subsequent modification or suspension, §153A-349.10(b).
Validity and duration of agreement entered into prior to, §153A-349.10(a).
Debt approval procedures for local governments.
Applicability, §153A-349.12.
Definitions, §153A-349.2.
Duration, §153A-349.4.
Agreement entered into prior to change of jurisdiction, §153A-349.10(a).
Hearing on, §153A-349.5.
Housing code.
Relationship of agreement to, §153A-349.13.
Legislative declaration, §153A-349.1(a).
Material breach by developer, §153A-349.8(b), (c).
Provisions.
Authorized provisions, §153A-349.6(b), (d).
Required provisions, §153A-349.6(a), (c).
Public hearing on, §153A-349.5.
Recordation by developer, §153A-349.11.
Successors in interest to parties.
Burdens and benefits inure to, §153A-349.11.
Supplemental nature of provisions, §153A-349.1(c).
Development financing district, §158-7.3(c).
Project development financing debt instruments, §§159-101 to 159-113.
See LOCAL GOVERNMENT FINANCE.
Development financing plan, §158-7.3(d) to (j).
Directors of social services, §§108A-12 to 108A-15.
See COUNTY DIRECTORS OF SOCIAL SERVICES.
Disasters.
State of emergency.
Generally, §§14-288.12 to 14-288.18.
See STATE OF EMERGENCY.
Powers of counties, §14-288.13.
Discrimination or retaliatory action against employees generally, §§95-240 to 95-245.
See RETALIATORY EMPLOYMENT DISCRIMINATION.
District courts.
Additional seats of court, §7A-133(c).
Appointment of judges, §7A-133(a).
Composition of split districts, §7A-133(b), (b1).
Facilities and courtrooms.
Responsibility of county for physical facilities, §7A-302.
Number of judges by districts, §7A-133(a).
Unincorporated seats of court.
Disposition of fees in counties, §7A-317.1.
Dogs.
Annual license tax.
Power to levy, §153A-153.

COUNTIES —Cont'd
Dogs —Cont'd
Dangerous dogs.
Local ordinances for control of dangerous dogs.
Article not to prevent, §67-4.5.
Potentially dangerous dogs.
Persons or board responsible for determining.
Designation, §67-4.1(c).
Provisions as to dogs applicable to all counties,
§67-18.
Supplemental nature of provisions, §67-36.
Dog wardens.
Appointment of animal control officers, §67-30.
Powers and duties, §67-31.
Rabies control officers.
Dog warden as assistant, §67-31.
Domestic violence.
County appropriations for programs to protect the
public, §153A-212.1.
Drainage districts.
See DRAINAGE DISTRICTS.
Drainage generally, §§156-139 to 156-141.
See DRAINAGE.
Drugs.
Confinement facilities.
Furnishing controlled substances to inmates,
§14-258.1(a).
Drunk in public.
Employment of officers to assist individuals
intoxicated in public, §122C-302.
Easements.
Agricultural conservation easements, §106-744.
Rights of way.
Improvement to state highways, §136-66.3(g) to
(j).
Economic development.
Interlocal agreements, §158-7.4.
Economic development and training districts,
§§153A-317.11 to 153A-317.17.
See ECONOMIC DEVELOPMENT AND
TRAINING DISTRICTS.
Economic development commissions, §158-14.
Education.
County school fund.
Composition, NC Const Art IX §7.
Generally.
See SCHOOLS AND EDUCATION.
Local boards of education, §§115C-35 to 115C-51.
See LOCAL BOARDS OF EDUCATION.
Public schools.
Responsibility, NC Const Art IX §2.
Elections.
County boards of elections generally, §§163-30 to
163-37.
See COUNTY BOARDS OF ELECTIONS.
Generally.
See COUNTY ELECTIONS.
Use of public funds to endorse or oppose a
referendum, election or particular candidate
prohibited, §153A-456.
Electrical inspections generally, §§153A-350 to
153A-375.
See COUNTY INSPECTION DEPARTMENTS.
Electronic mail subscribers.
List maintained by local government.
Public inspection.
Availability, copy, providing not required,
§132-1.13(a).
Use of list by local government, §132-1.13(b).
Electronic monitoring of offender.
Fee to cover costs of, §7A-313.1.

COUNTIES —Cont'd
Embezzlement.
Funds embezzled by public officers and trustees,
§14-92.
Emergency management, §166A-7(a).
Appropriations, §166A-7(c), (d).
Gifts and grants.
Acceptance, §166A-9.
Joint agencies between counties and
municipalities, §166A-7(b1).
Local state of emergency.
Declaration, §166A-8.
Mutual aid agreements, §166A-10(b), (c).
Powers, §166A-7(d).
State financial assistance, §166A-7(e).
State of emergency.
Generally, §§14-288.12 to 14-288.18.
See STATE OF EMERGENCY.
Powers of counties, §14-288.13.
Emergency medical services.
Fire protection districts.
EMS services in fire protection districts,
§153A-309(a), (b).
Eminent domain.
Boards of commissioners.
Local government unit outside county.
Consent of board required, §153A-15.
Federal water resources projects.
Acquisition of lands, §143-215.42(a) to (h).
Local government unit outside county.
City property within corporate limits,
inapplicability of section, §153A-15(d).
Consent of board required, §153A-15(a), (b).
Applicability of requirement, §153A-15(c).
Power to exercise, purposes, §§40A-3(b), (b1),
153A-158.
Solid waste facility.
Purchasing site by condemnation, §153A-292(c).
State psychiatric hospital.
Selection of county as site for.
Acquisition by county, conveyance to state,
§153A-178.
Water and sewer districts.
Power of district, §162A-89.1.
Watershed improvement works on projects.
Powers conferred on counties in certain cases,
§139-44(a) to (f).
Employees generally.
See COUNTY OFFICERS AND EMPLOYEES.
Employment discrimination.
Retaliatory employment discrimination, §§95-240
to 95-245.
See RETALIATORY EMPLOYMENT
DISCRIMINATION.
Energy consumption.
Land-use development incentives to reduce,
§160A-383.4(a).
Energy improvements.
Revolving loan program.
Definition of renewable energy source,
§153A-455(c).
Established, §153A-455(b).
Interest rate, §153A-455(b).
Purpose, §153A-455(a).
Enterprise tier.
Tax incentives for new and expanding businesses,
§105-129.3.
Enumeration, §153A-10.
**Environmental impact statements, major
development projects.**
Ordinance requiring statement of impact,
§113A-8(a) to (c).

COUNTIES —Cont'd

Equal employment opportunity.
Assistance in obtaining state employment, §§126-16 to 126-19.
See PERSONNEL SYSTEM.

Escape.
Confinement facilities or officers.
Prison breach and escape from facilities or officers, §14-256.

Ethics.
Local government ethics codes and education, §§160A-86, 160A-87.

E-Verify.
Defined, §153A-99.1(b).
Duty of county to register and participate, §153A-99.1(a).
Discrimination in enforcing section prohibited, §153A-99.1(c).
Work authorization verification generally, §§64-25 to 64-38.
See ALIENS.

Excise tax on beer, wine and liquor.
Distribution of part of tax, §105-113.82.

Execution sales, §153A-163.

Explosives, regulation, §153A-128.

Extortion.
Inspectors of articles of commerce.
Penalty, §66-7.

Fairs.
Application for license to commissioners, §106-517.
Penalty for violation of provisions, §106-518.
Refusal to license shows within five miles, §106-519.
County societies, §§106-505 to 106-511.
See FAIRS.
Local aid to agricultural, animal and poultry exhibits, §106-520.
Supervision of fairs, §106-520.4.

Farmland preservation generally.
Agricultural development and farmland preservation enabling act, §§106-735 to 106-744.
See FARMLAND PRESERVATION.

Farmland protection plan, §106-744(e), (f).

Federal aid.
Public health or mental health grants.
Recovery of indirect costs on certain grants by counties, §130A-8(a).
Exception, §130A-8(b).

Federal prisoners.
Contracts for confinement, §148-37(b).

Fees.
Boards of commissioners.
Commissioners to fix fees, §153A-102.
Electronic notice of new fees and increased fees, §153A-102.1.
Electronic monitoring of offender, costs of, §7A-313.1.
Inspectors of articles of commerce, §§66-3, 66-7.
New fees and increased fees.
Electronic notice, §153A-102.1.
Payment, §138-2.
Uniform fees in trial divisions.
Requirement to advance certain fees, §7A-317.

Finance.
Fiscal policy.
Commissioners to direct, §153A-101.
Fiscal year, §147-85.
Local government finance, §§159-1 to 159-188.
See LOCAL GOVERNMENT FINANCE.

COUNTIES —Cont'd

Financing public improvements, §158-7.3.

Firearms and other weapons.
Confinement facilities.
Furnishing cartridges or ammunition for firearms to inmates, §14-258.1.
Regulation, §153A-129.
Pellet guns, §153A-130.
Statewide uniformity of local regulation, §14-409.40.

Fire department.
Deceased or retiring firefighters.
Honoring, awarding helmet, §153A-236.
State volunteer fire department.
Acceptance of provisions by counties, §58-80-35.
Appropriations.
Local appropriations generally, §58-80-55.
Contracts with municipalities which have accepted provisions, §58-80-35.
No authority to render assistance to nonaccepting counties, §58-80-30.

Fires and fire protection.
Fire-fighting and prevention services, §153A-233.
Fire marshal.
Appointment, §153A-234.
Firemen's association.
Membership, §58-58-20.
Investigations.
County officers, §58-79-1.
Open fires in high hazard counties.
Enumeration of counties to which provisions applicable, §106-942(a).
Ground clearing activities, special permit, §106-942(c).
Woodland fires, permit required, §106-942(b).
Open fires in non-high hazard counties.
Applicability of provisions, §106-943(a).
Woodland fires, permit required, §106-943(b).
Plans for buildings to be used by counties.
Approval by commissioner of insurance, §58-31-40(b).
Prevention inspections generally, §§153A-350 to 153A-375.
See COUNTY INSPECTION DEPARTMENTS.
Regulation of explosive, corrosive, inflammable or radioactive substances, §153A-128.
Rural fire protection districts, §§69-25.1 to 69-25.17.
Service districts generally, §§153A-300 to 153A-310.

Fiscal control.
Finance officer, §§159-24 to 159-38.
See LOCAL GOVERNMENT FINANCE.

Fiscal impact of bills, resolutions or rules.
Local government fiscal information act, §§120-30.41 to 120-30.49.

Fiscal policy.
Commissioners to direct, §153A-101.

Fiscal year, §147-85.

Fish and fisheries resources.
Bridges.
Prohibition or regulation of fishing from bridges, §153A-242.

Flea markets.
Regulation, §153A-125.

Force account qualified labor.
Public enterprise improvements, §153A-280.

Forests and forestry.
Cooperation between counties and state in forest protection and development, §106-906.

COUNTIES —Cont'd
Forests and forestry —Cont'd
County lands acquired through tax foreclosure.
Procedure to acquire delinquent tax lands,
§106-873.
Use as demonstration forests, §106-872.
Funds paid by national forest commission,
distribution to counties, §106-880.
Restriction on certain forestry activities
prohibited.
Definitions, §153A-452(a).
Exceptions, §153A-452(c).
Generally, §153A-452(b).
Franchises.
Ambulance services, §153A-250.
Ordinances, §153A-46.
Franchise taxes on electric companies.
Additional tax imposed by county or city.
Companies not subject to, §105-116(e1).
Funded reserve.
Use against liability for damage persons or
property.
Same as purchase of liability insurance,
§153A-435(a).
Funds.
Intragovernmental service funds.
Generally, §159-13.1.
Included in budget, §159-11(d).
Local government finance, §§159-1 to 159-188.
See LOCAL GOVERNMENT FINANCE.
Garbage and trash.
Areas outside corporate limits.
Establishing and operating facilities,
§153A-292(a).
Authority to operate public enterprise, §153A-275.
Costs of providing and operating facility.
Determining for imposition of fees,
§153A-292(b).
Definitions, §§153A-136(c), (d), 153A-294.
Disposal and removal of trash and garbage.
Boards of commissioners to provide for,
§153A-132.1.
Equipment.
Agreement with department of transportation to
make available, §153A-291.
Fees.
Collection, use of facility and availability of
facility.
Authority to impose, determining amount,
§153A-292(b).
Property taxes, billing and collecting in same
manner, §153A-293.
Financing public enterprise, §153A-276.
Gate across highway leading to facility.
Erecting, §153A-292(c).
Hazardous waste facilities.
Local ordinances prohibiting facilities invalid,
§130A-293.
Privilege license taxes, §153A-152.1(a) to (c).
Highway rights-of-way, collection containers on.
Misdemeanor for placing garbage on
right-of-way, inapplicability, §136-18.3(b).
Permits, issuance by department of
transportation, §136-18.3(a).
Removal or change of location, order of
department, §136-18.3(d).
Written permission of owner of underlying fee,
required, §136-18.3(c).
Landfills.
Local government landfill liaison, §153A-136(e).
Right of entry, §153A-136(f).

COUNTIES —Cont'd
Garbage and trash —Cont'd
Landfills —Cont'd
Selection and approval of site, §153A-136(c).
Loans and bonds, §§159I-1 to 159I-30.
See SOLID WASTE MANAGEMENT LOANS
AND SPECIAL OBLIGATION BONDS.
Low-income persons, providing aid to,
§153A-292(f).
Ordinances, §153A-136(b).
Department may authorize, §130A-294(a).
Plan.
Development, §130A-309.04.
Prison and other labor.
Agreement with department of transportation to
make available, §153A-291.
Rates for public enterprise services, §153A-277.
Regional solid waste management authorities,
§§153A-421 to 153A-432.
See REGIONAL SOLID WASTE
MANAGEMENT AUTHORITIES.
Regulation of disposal facilities, nature of disposal
and method of disposal, §153A-292(a).
Regulation of solid wastes, §153A-136.
Regulation of storage, collection, transportation
and use, §153A-136(a).
Removal and disposal of trash and garbage.
Boards of commissioners to provide for,
§153A-132.1.
Service districts, §§153A-300 to 153A-310.
Site for facility.
Acquiring by purchase or condemnation,
§153A-292(c).
Use of suitable vacant land, §153A-292(c).
**Gathering, picketing or protesting on roads or
highways.**
Local ordinance regulating time, place and
manner.
Authorization, §20-174.2(a).
General assembly.
Dividing precincts in apportionment acts,
§120-2.2.
House of representatives.
Apportionment, §120-2.
Local government fiscal information, §§120-30.41
to 120-30.49.
See GENERAL ASSEMBLY.
Local government to be provided for by general
assembly, NC Const Art VII §1.
Senatorial districts, §120-1.
Severability of apportionment acts, §120-2.1.
Global TransPark authority.
Payments by county to authority, §63A-15.
Golf carts.
Regulation of use on streets, roads and highways.
Operation of golf cart, §153A-245(a).
Minors, §153A-245(b).
Registration of golf cart, §153A-245(b).
Governmental immunity waiver, §153A-435(b).
Governmental property.
Sale, exchange, lease to or lease from other
governmental unit, §160A-274(b).
Action taken by governing body, §160A-274(c).
Governmental unit defined, §160A-274(a).
Grants.
Contracts.
Acceptance of grants and loans from other
governments, §153A-14.
Public health or mental health grants from
federal government.
Recovery of indirect costs on certain grants by
counties, §130A-8(a).
Exception, §130A-8(b).

COUNTIES —Cont'd
Gross receipts tax on short-term vehicle leases or rentals, §153A-156(a).
Collection of tax, §153A-156(c), (d).
Definitions, §153A-156(e).
Penalties and remedies, §153A-156(f).
Provision noting in agreement, §153A-156(b).
Harbor master for unincorporated community situated in county.
Appointment by board of county commissioner, §76-56.
Hazardous substances.
Radioactive substances.
Low-level radioactive and hazardous waste facilities.
Privilege license taxes, §153A-152.1(a) to (c).
Regulation, §153A-128.
Health authorities.
Public health authorities generally, §§130A-45 to 130A-45.13.
See PUBLIC HEALTH AUTHORITIES.
Health boards.
See COUNTY BOARDS OF HEALTH.
Health care facilities.
Finance act.
Additional powers of public agencies, §131A-6.
Health departments generally, §§130A-34 to 130A-42.
See LOCAL HEALTH DEPARTMENTS.
Health grants by federal government.
Recovery of indirect costs on certain grants by counties, §130A-8(a).
Exception, §130A-8(b).
Health nuisances.
Abatement of public health nuisances, §153A-140.
Health services.
Ambulances.
Applicability of regulations, §153A-250(e).
Contracts for services, §153A-250(b), (d).
Franchises, §153A-250(a).
Ordinances.
Adoption, §153A-250(c).
Appropriations.
Counties may appropriate revenues, §153A-248(a).
Ordinances, §153A-248(b).
Consolidated county human services funding, §143B-139.7.
Consolidated human services agencies, boards and directors.
See CONSOLIDATED HUMAN SERVICES AGENCY.
Contracts for ambulance services, §153A-250.
Hospitals, §153A-249.
Ordinances.
Ambulances, §153A-250.
Appropriations, §153A-248(b).
Provision for public health and mental health, §153A-247.
Hearings.
Boards of commissioners.
Conduct of public hearings, §153A-52.
Inspection departments, §153A-361.
Planning and zoning.
Board of adjustment, §153A-345(b).
Research and production service districts.
Abolition of districts, §153A-316.
Establishment, §153A-312(d).
Extension, §153A-314(c).
Special assessments.
Preliminary assessment roll, §153A-195.

COUNTIES —Cont'd
Hearings —Cont'd
Special assessments —Cont'd
Preliminary resolutions, §153A-192.
Heating and air-conditioning inspectors generally, §§153A-350 to 153A-375.
See COUNTY INSPECTION DEPARTMENTS.
Heating systems.
Dwelling units leased as rental property, §160A-443.1.
Heavy equipment gross receipts tax in lieu of property tax.
Definitions, §153A-156.1(a).
Effective date, §153A-156.1(e).
Enforcement, §153A-156.1(d).
Imposition of tax, §153A-156.1(b).
Payment, §153A-156.1(c).
Repeal of tax by county, §153A-156.1(f).
Highway-rights-of way.
Garbage collection containers.
Location on rights-of-way, §136-18.3(a) to (d).
Highways.
Generally.
See COUNTY STREETS AND HIGHWAYS.
Secondary road construction programs by department of transportation.
Adoption of annual construction program for each county, §136-44.8(a) to (f).
Historical associations, assistance to.
Authorization to appropriate revenues, §153A-437(a).
Office space, §153A-437(b).
Section is supplemental, §153A-437(c).
Historic districts and landmarks.
Exercise of same powers as cities, §160A-400.2.
Historic preservation program.
Cooperation with local governments, §121-8(e).
Historic properties.
Acquisition, maintenance, etc., of property.
Procedures where assistance extended to counties, §121-11.
Hog cholera.
Purchasing and supplying serum, §106-315.
Holidays.
Public officers and employees, §153A-94(b).
Hospital authorities, §131E-30.
Hospitals.
Branch facilities, §131E-14.1.
Health services, §§153A-247 to 153A-250.
House of representatives.
Apportionment, §120-2.
Dividing precincts restricted, §120-2.2.
Severability of acts, §120-2.1.
Housing authorities and projects.
Area of operation, §157-39.1(a) to (c).
Commissioners, §157-34.
Creation of authority.
Hearings, §157-33.
Notice, §157-33.
Powers of authority, §157-34.
Regional housing authority, §§157-39.1 to 157-39.5.
Housing by local governments generally, §§160A-441 to 160A-450.
See LOCAL GOVERNMENTS.
Housing inspectors generally, §§153A-350 to 153A-375.
See COUNTY INSPECTION DEPARTMENTS.
Human service and volunteer transportation.
Local licenses and taxes prohibited, §62-289.7.

COUNTIES —Cont'd

Human services.

Consolidated human services agencies, boards and directors.

Generally.

See CONSOLIDATED HUMAN SERVICES AGENCY.

Human services director.

Powers and duties, §108A-15.1(c).

Powers and duties, §108A-15.1(a), (b).

Human services funding.

Consolidated county human services.

Allocation of funds, §143B-139.7(a).

Definitions, §143B-139.7(c).

Promulgation of rules, §143B-139.7(a), (b).

Hunting and wildlife.

Dangerous animals.

Possession or harboring, §153A-131.

Hurricanes.

Flood and hurricane protection works.

Appropriations, §153A-438.

Special assessments.

Authority to make, §153A-185.

Immunity.

Waiver of governmental immunity.

Liability insurance, §153A-435(b).

Improvements.

Development financing, §158-7.3.

Ordinances.

Submission of statement concerning improvements, §153A-325.

Project development financing debt instruments.

Project development financing act, §§159-101 to 159-113.

See LOCAL GOVERNMENT FINANCE.

Public enterprise improvements, §153A-280.

Special assessments.

Authority to make, §153A-185.

Subdivision and residential streets, §153A-205.

Income tax.

Levy prohibited, §105-247.

Industrial and pollution control facilities financing.

Industrial and pollution control facilities financing act, §§159C-1 to 159C-27.

See INDUSTRIAL AND POLLUTION CONTROL FACILITIES FINANCING.

North Carolina capital facilities financing act.

North Carolina industrial and pollution control facilities financing act, §§159D-1 to 159D-27.

See INDUSTRIAL AND POLLUTION CONTROL FACILITIES FINANCING.

Industrial development, §158-24.

Industrial or commercial parks or sites.

Interlocal agreement for development, §158-7.4.

Information technology procurement contracts.

Best value procurements, §143-135.9.

Infrastructure, §153A-349.13.

Design and construction.

Reimbursement agreements with contractors.

Authorized, §153A-451(a).

Exemption from certain provisions, §153A-451(d).

Ordinances setting forth procedures and terms, §153A-451(b).

Payment of reimbursement, §153A-451(c).

Inheritance tax.

Levy prohibited, §105-247.

COUNTIES —Cont'd

Injunctions.

Inspection departments.

Equitable enforcement of article, §153A-372.

Ordinances.

Enforcement, §153A-123(d).

Subdivisions.

Transferring lots in unapproved subdivisions, §153A-334(a).

Inspection of departments, §§153A-350 to 153A-375.

See COUNTY INSPECTION DEPARTMENTS.

Inspectors of articles of commerce, §§66-1 to 66-7.

See COUNTY INSPECTORS OF ARTICLES OF COMMERCE.

Insurance.

Defense of employees and officers.

Civil and criminal actions.

Insurer provides defense, §160A-167.

Liability insurance, §153A-435(a), (b).

Local government risk pools, §§58-23-1 to 58-23-45.

See LOCAL GOVERNMENT RISK POOLS.

Public officers and employees.

Health insurance, §153A-92.

Life insurance, §153A-92.

Rail transportation liability.

Contracts allocating financial responsibility.

Insurance required, §153A-279(c).

Interchange of governmental employees, §§126-51 to 126-58.

See PERSONNEL SYSTEM.

Interest rate swap agreements, §§159-193 to 159-200.

See SWAP AGREEMENTS.

Interlocal cooperation generally, §§160A-460 to 160A-478.

See INTERLOCAL COOPERATION.

Intoxicated in public.

Employment of officers to assist individuals intoxicated in public, §122C-302.

Intragovernmental service funds.

Generally, §159-13.1.

Included in budget, §159-11(d).

Jails.

Agreements to house misdemeanants.

Voluntary agreements with division of adult correction, §148-32.1(b1).

Generally, §§153A-216 to 153A-229.

See JAILS.

Juvenile detention facility.

Utilizing space for, §143B-819.

Statewide misdemeanant confinement program, §148-32.1(b2).

Fund, §148-10.4.

Transfer to facility operated by division of adult correction, §148-32.1(b3), (b4).

John Motley Morehead memorial commission.

Authorization for counties to assist, §143B-113.

Judicial department.

District court districts.

Additional seats of court, §7A-133(c).

Appointment of judges, §7A-133(a).

Composition of split districts, §7A-133(b), (b1).

Number of judges by districts, §7A-133(a).

Superior court division.

Organization into divisions and districts, §7A-41.

Supplementation of salaries for department employees.

Local funds of city or county, §7A-300.1.

COUNTIES —Cont'd
Judicial sales, §153A-163.
Junked or abandoned vehicles.
Coastal area counties.
Service districts to provide removal,
§153A-301(b), (c).
Regulation, restraint or prohibition.
Authority of county, §153A-132.2(a).
Junked motor vehicle defined, §153A-132.2(a).
Removal of vehicles in violation of ordinance.
Authority, request, hearing, no liability,
§153A-132.2(a1) to (a4).
Removal or disposal, §153A-132(c).
Definitions, §153A-132(b).
Exceptions, §§153A-132.2(b), 153A-132(h).
Grant of power to remove and dispose of,
§153A-132(a), (a1).
Hearing procedure, §§153A-132.2(a3),
153A-132(d).
Immunity from liability, §§153A-132.2(a4),
153A-132(g).
Indemnification of county against loss,
§153A-132.2(a2).
Jurisdiction.
Boards of commissioners.
Authority of boards in certain counties over
commissions, boards, agencies, etc.,
§153A-77.
Ordinances.
Territorial jurisdiction of county ordinances,
§153A-122.
Planning and zoning.
Territorial jurisdiction, §153A-320.
Jury commissions, §9-1.
List of deceased residents provided to,
§130A-121(a).
Juvenile crime prevention councils, §§143B-845
to 143B-851.
See JUVENILE CRIME PREVENTION
COUNCILS.
**Juvenile detention facilities operated by
county.**
Jail system space.
Utilizing as detention facility, §143B-819.
Regional detention services with surrounding
counties.
Division and county planning for, §143B-819.
Standards and rules, §7B-1905(b).
State subsidy, §143B-820.
Landfills.
Solid waste management loans and bonds,
§§159I-1 to 159I-30.
See SOLID WASTE MANAGEMENT LOANS
AND SPECIAL OBLIGATION BONDS.
Landlords.
Residential rental property registration.
Housing ordinance violations, crime or disorder
problems, §153A-364(c), (d).
**Land records improvement program, financial
assistance,** §102-15.
Land records management program.
Local governments implementing, §147-54.3.
Law enforcement.
Appropriations for programs to protect the public,
§153A-212.1.
Assistance by state law-enforcement officers,
§160A-288.1.
Assistance to state law-enforcement agencies,
§160A-288.2.
Cooperation between law-enforcement agencies,
§160A-288.

COUNTIES —Cont'd
Law enforcement —Cont'd
Cooperation in law enforcement matters,
§153A-212.
Development programs for law enforcement,
§153A-211.
Joint county and city auxiliary police, §160A-283.
Service districts, §§153A-300 to 153A-310.
Leases.
Personal property, §153A-165.
Real property, §153A-165.
Libraries.
See COUNTY LIBRARIES.
Licenses.
Animals.
Taxation, §153A-153.
Regulating and licensing businesses and trades,
§153A-134.
License taxes.
General provisions, §§105-33 to 105-109.
See LICENSE TAXES.
Privilege license taxes, §153A-152.
Attorney or other professions.
Levy of tax prohibited, §105-41(h).
Low-level radioactive and hazardous waste
facilities, §153A-152.1(a) to (c).
Liens.
Ambulances.
Attachment or garnishment.
Collection authorization, §44-51.4.
Counties to which article applicable, §44-51.8.
Discharging lien, §44-51.7.
Filing, §44-51.6.
General lien for service, §44-51.5.
Services provided by county or municipality.
Discharge of lien, §44-51.3.
Filing, §44-51.2.
Real property of recipient, §44-51.1.
Recovery for services to injured persons.
Lien created in favor of, §44-49(a).
Special assessments.
Cotenants or joint owners paying special
assessments, §153A-203.
Preliminary assessment roll, §153A-195.
Limitation of actions.
Planning and zoning, §§1-54, 153A-348.
Special assessments.
Enforcement, §153A-200(d).
Lis pendens.
Filing by counties in building inspection and
housing standards cases, §1-120.2.
Livestock.
Cattle tick.
Dipping vats provided by counties, §106-353.
Embraced in quarantine zones, §106-352.
Hog cholera.
Purchasing and supplying serum, §106-315.
**Loan agencies, check cashing businesses and
pawnbrokers.**
Privilege tax.
Levy by counties authorized, §105-88(e).
Loans.
Contracts.
Grants and loans from other governments,
§153A-14.
Local government finance, §§159-1 to 159-188.
See LOCAL GOVERNMENT FINANCE.
Solid waste management loans and bonds,
§§159I-1 to 159I-30.
See SOLID WASTE MANAGEMENT LOANS
AND SPECIAL OBLIGATION BONDS.

COUNTIES —Cont'd
Local acts.
Alternative use of procedures contained in acts or
chapter, §153A-3(b), (c).
Broad construction, §153A-4.
Not repealed or amended by chapter, §153A-3(a).
Superseded by chapter.
Act omitting or denying power, right, privilege
or immunity granted by chapter,
§153A-3(d).
Local confinement facilities.
See JAILS.
Local development.
Economic development commissions, §§158-8 to
158-15.
See ECONOMIC DEVELOPMENT
COMMISSIONS.
Generally.
See LOCAL DEVELOPMENT.
Industrial development, §§158-16 to 158-24.
See INDUSTRIAL DEVELOPMENT.
Multi-county water conservation and
infrastructure district, §158-15.1.
Local government finance generally, §§159-1 to
159-188.
See LOCAL GOVERNMENT FINANCE.
Local government fiscal information,
§§120-30.41 to 120-30.49.
See GENERAL ASSEMBLY.
Local government risk pools, §§58-23-1 to
58-23-45.
See LOCAL GOVERNMENT RISK POOLS.
Local government sales and use tax.
First one-cent local government sales and use tax,
§§105-463 to 105-474.
See SALES AND USE TAX.
Hold harmless for repealed reimbursements,
§§105-521 to 105-523.
One-quarter cent county sales and use tax,
§§105-535 to 105-538.
Second one-half cent local government sales and
use tax, §§105-495 to 105-502.
See SALES AND USE TAX.
Local governments generally.
See LOCAL GOVERNMENTS.
Local option elections, §§18B-600 to 18B-605.
See LOCAL OPTION ELECTIONS.
Low-level radioactive waste facilities.
Notice to county in which facility proposed to be
located, §104E-10.1(c).
Ordinance preventing establishment, operation or
construction of.
Invalidity, determining preemption, §104E-6.2.
Magistrates.
Number of magistrates for each county,
§§7A-133(c), 7A-171(a).
Managers, §§153A-81 to 153A-84.
Acting county manager, §153A-83.
Adoption of county-manager plan, §153A-81.
Appointment, §153A-81.
Counties not having managers, §153A-87.
Acting department heads, §153A-88.
Interim department heads, §153A-89.
Defined, §153A-81.
Designation, §153A-81.
Duties, §153A-82.
Interim county manager, §153A-84.
Officers of counties generally.
See COUNTY OFFICERS AND EMPLOYEES.
Powers, §153A-82.

COUNTIES —Cont'd
Managers —Cont'd
Service of process.
Personal jurisdiction, manner of serving on
county, §1A-1 Rule 4(j).
Manufactured homes.
Abandoned homes.
Identification, deconstruction, recycling,
disposal.
Generally, §§130A-309.111 to 130A-309.118.
See MANUFACTURED HOMES.
Zoning regulations, §153A-341.1.
Maps and plats.
County base maps.
Program for preparation.
Secretary of state to conduct, §147-54.3(c).
County cadastral maps.
Program for preparation.
Secretary of state to conduct, §147-54.3(c1).
Electoral districts, §153A-20.
Local government property mappers, §147-54.4.
Massage and bodywork therapy.
Regulation by counties, §90-636.
Mass gatherings.
Local ordinances not abrogated, §130A-258.
Medical examiners.
Appointment, §130A-382.
Cremation.
Medical examiner's permission necessary before
cremation, §130A-388(a), (b).
Duties.
Notification of medical examiners of certain
deaths, §130A-385(a).
Embalming.
When medical examiner's permission necessary
before embalming, §130A-388(a), (b).
Postmortem medicolegal examinations and
services, §§130A-377 to 130A-395.
See MEDICAL EXAMINERS.
Subpoena authority, §130A-386.
Term of office, §130A-382.
Vacancies in office, §130A-382.
Meetings of public bodies generally, §§143-318.9
to 143-318.18.
See MEETINGS.
**Mental health, developmental disabilities and
substance abuse.**
Business plan, §122C-115.2.
Consolidated county human services funding,
§143B-139.7.
Consolidated human services agency.
Generally.
See CONSOLIDATED HUMAN SERVICES
AGENCY.
Status as department of county, §122C-116(b).
Consumer and family advisory committees,
§§122C-170, 122C-171.
County programs, §122C-115.1.
Business plan, §122C-115.2.
Interlocal agreements.
Competition among public providers,
§122C-141(e).
Local management entity contracts with public
providers.
Requirements, §122C-141(d).
Mental health authorities.
Local personnel systems, §126-11(a1), (b1).
Powers and duties, §122C-115.
Provision for public health and mental health,
§153A-247.

COUNTIES —Cont'd
Mental health, developmental disabilities and
  substance abuse —Cont'd
  State psychiatric hospital.
    Selection of county as site for.
      Acquisition and conveyance of property,
        §153A-178.
Merger, NC Const Art VII §3.
Military property sales facilities.
  Licensing, §127B-4(a) to (c).
Militia.
  Support of families of soldiers, airmen and sailors
    by county.
    Privilege of organized militia, §127A-119.
Mobile homes and trailer parks.
  Registration, §153A-138.
  Zoning regulations, §153A-341.1.
Money.
  Drawing public money.
    Local treasury, NC Const Art V §7.
Monuments, memorials and parks.
  Confederate monuments.
    Contributions toward erection, §100-10.
    Fences to protect.
      Power of county commissioners to expend
        fund for, §100-9.
  Establishment, §153A-444.
  Fences to protect confederate monuments.
    Power of county commissioners to expend
      money for, §100-9.
  Local governments, §§160A-350 to 160A-356.
  World wars.
    Contributions toward erection of memorials,
      §100-10.
Mosquito control districts, §§130A-352 to
  130A-358.
Motor carriers.
  No additional local tax, §20-97(e).
Motor fuel excise tax exemption, §105-449.88.
Motor vehicle license plates.
  Marking county vehicle, private plates,
    confidential plates, §20-39.1.
  Permanent license plates for county vehicles,
    §20-84(b).
  Transporter plates.
    County receiving donated vehicles for low
      income individuals, §20-79.2(d).
Motor vehicle registration tax, §105-570.
Motor vehicle repairs.
  Inapplicability of provisions to governmental
    functions, §20-354.1.
Motor vehicles and traffic control.
  Applicability of provisions to drivers of county
    vehicles, §20-168(a).
    Exception as to highway maintenance or
      construction work, §20-168(b).
  Driveways.
    Regulation of traffic at parking areas and
      driveways, §153A-139.
  Financial responsibility.
    Exemptions, §§20-279.32, 20-318.
  Gross receipts tax on short-term vehicle leases or
    rentals, §153A-156.
  Junked and abandoned vehicles.
    Regulation, removal and disposal, §§153A-132,
      153A-132.2.
  Ordinance making power, §153A-121(b).
  Ordinances.
    Parking regulations, §153A-170.
  Parking.
    Parking on county property.
      Regulation by ordinance, §153A-170.

COUNTIES —Cont'd
Motor vehicles and traffic control —Cont'd
  Parking —Cont'd
    Regulation of traffic at parking areas and
      driveways, §153A-139.
  Powers of local authorities generally, §20-169.
  Speed limits, §20-141(b).
    Authorizing higher or lower speeds, §20-141(e),
      (e1), (f).
Motor vehicle transporter plates.
  County receiving donated vehicles for low income
    individuals, §20-79.2(d).
Mountain ridges, counties containing.
  Mountain ridge protection, §153A-448.
    Ordinances, §153A-448.
      Authority to adopt, §113A-208.
  Service districts.
    Maintenance of public roads, §153A-301(d).
Municipalities.
  Buildings.
    Joint buildings, §153A-164.
  Unified government, §§153A-471 to 153A-473.
Municipal securities.
  Local government finance, §§159-1 to 159-188.
    See LOCAL GOVERNMENT FINANCE.
Names, §153A-10.
Natural gas.
  Regional natural gas districts, §§160A-660 to
    160A-676.
    See REGIONAL NATURAL GAS DISTRICTS.
Natural gas lines located on department of
  transportation right-of-way.
  Relocation, payment of nonbetterment cost,
    §136-27.2.
Nature and historic preserves.
  Dedication of properties owned by local
    government, §143-260.8.
Noise.
  Regulation of noise by ordinance, §153A-133.
North Carolina symphony society.
  Contributions, §140-10.
Notice.
  Inspection departments.
    Condemned buildings.
      Removing prohibited, §153A-367.
  Outdoor advertising.
    Regulation of nonconforming off-premises
      outdoor advertising.
      Notice to require removal, §153A-143(c).
  Posting notices, §153A-443.
  Research and production service districts.
    Abolition of districts.
      Hearing, §153A-316.
    Establishment.
      Hearing, §153A-312(d).
    Extension.
      Hearing, §153A-314(c).
  Special assessments.
    Preliminary assessment roll.
      Notice of confirmation, §153A-196.
    Preliminary resolutions, §153A-191.
Nuisances.
  Chronic violators, notice to, §153A-140.2.
  Noise regulations, §153A-133.
  Offenses against public morals.
    Institution of action for abatement, injunction,
      §19-2.1.
  Public health nuisances.
    Abatement, §153A-140.
Number, §153A-10.

COUNTIES —Cont'd
Nutbush conservation area.
Contributions from certain counties authorized, §143-289.
Oaths.
Entry-takers.
Form of oath, §11-11.
Public officers and employees, §153A-26.
Officers generally.
See COUNTY OFFICERS AND EMPLOYEES.
Oil pollution and hazardous substances control.
Ordinances.
Effect of article, §143-215.82.
Open fires in high hazard counties.
Enumeration of counties to which provisions applicable, §106-942(a).
Ground clearing activities, special permit, §106-942(c).
Woodland fires, permit required, §106-942(b).
Open fires in non-high hazard counties.
Applicability of provisions, §106-943(a).
Woodland fires, permit required, §106-943(b).
Ordinances.
See COUNTY ORDINANCES.
Organization of county government.
Boards of commissioners to organize, §153A-76.
Outdoor advertising.
Regulation of nonconforming off-premises outdoor advertising.
Agreement in lieu of paying compensation, §153A-143(g).
Voluntary agreement for removal after set time, §153A-143(k).
Amortization.
Use to phase out nonconforming uses, §153A-143(o).
Arbitration to resolve disputes.
Relocating and reconstructing outdoor advertising, §153A-143(i).
Authority to require removal and regulate, §153A-143(b).
Eminent domain power not affected, §153A-143(n).
Notice to require removal, §153A-143(c).
Off-premises outdoor advertising defined, §153A-143(a).
Ordinances in effect on effective date of section, §153A-143(m).
Payment of monetary compensation for removal.
Action to for determination, §153A-143(f).
Determining compensation, §153A-143(e).
Monetary compensation defined, §153A-143(e).
Not required, conditions, §153A-143(d).
Relocation site not reasonably comparable to existing site, §153A-143(j).
Time period for payment, §153A-143(l).
Permit or other approval.
Relocating and reconstructing outdoor advertising, §153A-143(h).
Relocating and reconstructing outdoor advertising.
Agreement in lieu of compensation, §153A-143(g).
Arbitration to resolve disputes, §153A-143(i).
Payment of compensation by county, §153A-143(j).
Permit or other approval, §153A-143(h).
Voluntary agreement for removal after set time, §153A-143(k).

COUNTIES —Cont'd
Parking facilities.
Authority to operate public enterprise, §153A-275.
Financing public enterprise, §153A-276.
Rates for public enterprise services, §153A-277.
Parks and recreation.
Establishment, §153A-444.
Local governments generally, §§160A-350 to 160A-356.
Service districts, §§153A-300 to 153A-310.
Partition.
Land lying in more than one county.
Appointment of commissioners, §46-7.
Venue, §46-2.
Paternity of dependent child.
Institution of civil or criminal proceedings against responsible parent, §110-130.
Pawnbrokers and cash converters.
Ordinances.
Authority to adopt provisions of act by ordinance, §91A-12.
Rules and regulations.
Authority to adopt, §91A-12.
Peddlers, itinerant merchants and specialty markets.
Local regulation not affected, §66-258.
Regulation of itinerant merchants, §153A-125.
Pellet gun regulation, §153A-130.
Personal watercraft.
Local governments regulating, §75A-13.3(h).
Personnel records, §153A-98.
Personnel system, §§153A-92 to 153A-99.
See COUNTY PERSONNEL SYSTEM.
Pesticide regulation.
Preemption by state, §143-465(d).
Planning and zoning.
Generally, §§153A-320 to 153A-326, 153A-340 to 153A-349.
See COUNTY PLANNING AND ZONING.
Regional planning commissions.
Generally, §§153A-391 to 153A-398.
See REGIONAL PLANNING COMMISSIONS.
Plastic bag management.
Retailers.
Counties containing barrier islands, §§130A-309.120 to 130A-309.125.
Plumbing inspectors generally, §§153A-350 to 153A-375.
See COUNTY INSPECTION DEPARTMENTS.
Poisons.
Confinement facilities.
Furnishing poison to inmates, §14-258.1.
Police.
Assistance by state law-enforcement officers, §160A-288.1.
Assistance to state law-enforcement agencies, §160A-288.2.
Cooperation between law-enforcement agencies, §160A-288.
Joint county and city auxiliary police, §160A-283.
Unmarked vehicles, confidential plates, private plates, §20-39.1.
Pool hall regulation, §153A-135.
Port enhancement zones, §143B-437.013.
Postmortem medicolegal examinations and services, §§130A-377 to 130A-395.
See MEDICAL EXAMINERS.
Powers and duties.
Acquisition of property, §153A-158.

COUNTIES —Cont'd
Powers and duties —Cont'd
Consolidation.
Commissions, §153A-404.
Corporate powers of counties, §153A-11.
Exercise of corporate powers, §153A-12.
Eminent domain.
Power conferred, §153A-158.
Enumeration not exclusive, §153A-124.
Inspection departments, §§153A-351(a1),
153A-352.
Failure to perform duties, §153A-356.
Miscellaneous powers found in chapter 160A,
§153A-445(a).
Applicability of section, §153A-445(b).
Outdoor advertising.
Regulation of nonconforming off-premises
advertising, §153A-143.
Planning and zoning.
Grant of power, §153A-340(a) to (e).
Supplemental powers, §153A-322.
Sustainable design principles, policies to
encourage, §153A-340(i).
Regional planning commissions, §153A-395.
Taxation.
General power to impose taxes, §153A-146.
Remedies for collecting taxes other than
property taxes, §153A-147.
Prior laws.
Effect of chapter on prior laws and actions taken
pursuant to prior laws, §153A-2.
Prisons and prisoners.
Local confinement facilities.
See JAILS.
Removal of trial from one county to another.
Liability of counties for cost, §6-40.
Private personnel services.
Exemption from provisions, §95-47.11.
Privilege taxes on electric companies.
Additional tax imposed by county or city.
Companies not subject to, §105-116(e1).
Procurement.
Public contracts.
Architectural, engineering and surveying
services, §§143-64.31 to 143-64.34.
See PUBLIC CONTRACTS.
Generally, §§143-128 to 143-135.9.
See PUBLIC CONTRACTS.
**Project development financing debt
instruments.**
Project development financing act, §§159-101 to
159-113.
See LOCAL GOVERNMENT FINANCE.
Property.
Acquisition of property.
Applicability of provisions, §153A-158.1(a).
Community college property, §153A-158.2(a).
Methods of acquisition, §153A-158.1(a).
Power to acquire, §153A-158.
School property, §153A-158.1(a).
Selection of county for state psychiatric
hospital.
Conveyance to state, §153A-178.
Buildings, joint, §153A-164.
Care and use of county property, §153A-169.
Community college property.
Acquisition, §153A-158.2(a).
Construction or improvement, §153A-158.2(b).
Disposition, §153A-158.2(b).
Public hearing, §153A-158.2(c).

COUNTIES —Cont'd
Property —Cont'd
Community development.
Acquisition and disposition of property for
redevelopment, §153A-377.
Disposition of property, §153A-176.
Reconveyance of property donated to local
government, §153A-177.
Execution sales, §153A-163.
Judicial sales, §153A-163.
Leases, §153A-165.
Motor vehicle parking ordinances, §153A-170.
Open space acquisitions, §§160A-401 to 160A-407.
See LOCAL GOVERNMENTS.
Power to acquire, §153A-158.
Rewards.
Persons damaging county property, §153A-446.
School property.
Acquisition by county, §153A-158.1(a).
Construction or improvement by county,
§153A-158.1(b).
Contract for construction by board of
education, §153A-158.1(d).
Lease or sale by board of education,
§153A-158.1(c).
Scope of provisions, §153A-158.1(e).
Special assessments.
Lands exempt from, §153A-188.
Warranty deeds, power to execute and deliver,
§160A-275.
Property taxes.
See PROPERTY TAXES.
Public enterprises.
Authority to operate, §153A-275(a), (b).
Borrowing money.
Financing public enterprises, §153A-276.
Cooperation in providing enterprisory services,
§153A-278.
Debt collection.
Customer misrepresentation of identity,
§153A-277(b2).
Restrictions, §153A-277(b1).
Defined, §153A-274.
Delinquent accounts, §153A-277(b).
Financing public enterprises, §153A-276.
Improvements.
Authorized, §153A-280(a).
Property acquisition, §153A-280(b).
Joint provision of enterprisory services,
§153A-278.
Liens.
Rates, fees and charges do not constitute lien,
§153A-277(c).
Operation authorized, §153A-275(a), (b).
Penalties, §153A-277(d).
Rates.
Counties may establish, §153A-277(a), (a1).
Enforcement, §153A-277(b).
Public health authorities.
County Medicaid claims.
Contracts for operation of Medicaid billing
system, §130A-45.13.
Generally, §§130A-45 to 130A-45.13.
See PUBLIC HEALTH AUTHORITIES.
Local governmental employees' retirement system.
Membership of employees, §128-37.
**Public improvements associated with private
development projects.**
Project development financing, NC Const Art V
§14.

COUNTIES —Cont'd
Public lands.
Acquisition.
Local government unit outside county.
Consent of board required, §153A-15.
Condemnation.
Local government unit outside county.
Consent of board required, §153A-15.
Conveyances.
Admission to registration in counties, §146-77.
Grants.
Correction of grants.
Change of county line before grant issued or
registered, §146-47.
Entries in wrong county, §146-48.
Public transportation systems.
Authority to operate public enterprise,
§§136-44.20(c), 153A-275.
Financing public enterprise, §153A-276.
Local government sales and use tax, §§105-506 to
105-511.4.
See SALES AND USE TAX.
Rates for public enterprise services, §153A-277.
Quarantine inspectors, §106-354.
Tuberculosis.
Appropriations by counties for eradication of
tuberculosis, §106-343.
Amount of appropriation, §106-346.
Radioactive and hazardous waste facilities.
Privilege license taxes, §153A-152.1(a) to (c).
Radioactive substances.
Regulation, §153A-128.
Railroads.
Contracts allocating financial responsibility.
Applicability of provisions, §153A-279(f).
Authorized, §153A-279(b).
Definitions, §153A-279(a).
Effect on other laws, §153A-279(e).
Insurance required, §153A-279(c).
Limit on liability, §153A-279(d).
Corridors.
Acquisition of property for corridor preservation,
§160A-498.
Revitalization programs.
Authorization to participate in, §153A-244.
Distribution of state financial assistance,
§136-44.38.
Rain barrels.
Limitations on regulating, §153A-145.
Records.
Boards of commissioners.
Meetings.
Minutes to be kept, §153A-42.
Evidence.
Admissibility, §153A-436(e).
Inspection departments, §153A-373.
Land records management program.
Local governments implementing, §147-54.3.
Legitimacy of reproductions, §153A-436(d).
Media authorized for storage, §153A-436(f).
Original copies, §153A-436(c).
Personnel records, §153A-98.
Photographic reproduction of county records,
§153A-436(a).
Removal from depositories, §153A-436(b).
State highway fund.
Appropriation to municipalities.
Records and annual statement, §136-41.3.
Recreation.
Service districts, §§153A-300 to 153A-310.

COUNTIES —Cont'd
**Recycling computer equipment and
televisions.**
Authority to manage programs, §130A-309.141.
Referenda.
Consolidation, §153A-405(a) to (c), (e).
Regional councils of governments generally,
§§160A-470 to 160A-478.
See INTERLOCAL COOPERATION.
Regional planning commissions, §§153A-391 to
153A-398.
See REGIONAL PLANNING COMMISSIONS.
Registers of deeds, §§161-1 to 161-31.
See REGISTERS OF DEEDS.
Remedies.
Taxation.
Collection of taxes other than property taxes,
§153A-147.
Rents.
Control of rent prohibited, §42-14.1.
Death, serious illness, or certain criminal
convictions of previous occupant.
Deemed not a material fact in real property
transactions, §42-14.2.
Reports.
Boards of commissioners may require reports,
§153A-104.
Inspection departments, §153A-373.
Misconduct in public office.
Swearing falsely to official reports, §14-232.
Regional planning commissions, §153A-397.
Required by boards of commissioners, §153A-104.
Research and production service districts.
Establishment.
Required before hearing, §153A-312(c).
Extension.
Required before hearing, §153A-314(b).
Rescue.
Service districts, §§153A-300 to 153A-310.
Rescue squads.
County financial support for rescue squads,
§160A-487.
EMS services in fire protection districts,
§153A-309(a), (b).
Research and production service districts,
§§153A-311 to 153A-317.
See COUNTY RESEARCH AND PRODUCTION
SERVICE DISTRICTS.
Residential rental property registration.
Housing ordinance violations, crime or disorder
problems, §153A-364(c), (d).
Retirement.
Local governmental employees' retirement system.
General provisions, §§128-21 to 128-38.5.
See LOCAL GOVERNMENTAL
EMPLOYEES' RETIREMENT SYSTEM.
Retirement system for teachers and state
employees.
See RETIREMENT SYSTEM FOR TEACHERS
AND STATE EMPLOYEES.
Rewards.
Persons damaging county property, §153A-446.
Rights of way.
Highways, roads and streets.
Acquisition of rights of way.
County participation in improvements to state
highway system, §136-66.3(g) to (j).
Dedication of rights of way under local
ordinances, §§136-66.10, 136-66.11.
Riots and civil disorders.
State of emergency.
Generally, §§14-288.12 to 14-288.18.
See STATE OF EMERGENCY.

COUNTIES —Cont'd
Riots and civil disorders —Cont'd
State of emergency —Cont'd
Powers of counties, §14-288.13.
Riparian buffer protection program.
Delegation of responsibilities to local government,
§143-214.23.
Roads generally.
See COUNTY STREETS AND HIGHWAYS.
**Room occupancy tax, uniform provisions for
counties authorized to levy.**
Administered by taxing county, §153A-155(d).
Charge for furnishing taxable accommodation,
part of charge, §153A-155(c).
Civil and criminal penalties.
Failure to file return or pay, §153A-155(e).
Collection of tax by operator of business,
§153A-155(c).
Counties authorized to levy, applicability,
§153A-155(a), (g).
Disclosure of records, §153A-155(d).
Discount allowed operator for collecting,
§153A-155(c).
Effective date, §153A-155(b).
Levied only by resolution, §153A-155(b).
Liability for tax attaching before repeal not
affected, §153A-155(f).
Passed on to purchaser, §153A-155(c).
Public notice and public hearing on levy,
§153A-155(b).
Repeal or reduction by resolution, §153A-155(f).
Return, §153A-155(d).
Stated and charged separately, §153A-155(c).
Waiver of penalties, §153A-155(e).
When due and payable, §153A-155(d).
Rules and regulations.
Boards of commissioners, §153A-41.
Licenses.
Regulating and licensing businesses and trades,
§153A-134.
Local personnel systems, §126-11(d).
Planning and zoning.
Conflict of laws, §153A-346.
Enforcement.
Boards of commissioners to determine method
of procedure, §153A-343.
Purposes in view, §153A-341.
Public officers and employees.
Personnel rules, §153A-94(a).
Streets and highways in and around
municipalities, §136-66.4.
Transportation systems in and around
municipalities, §136-66.4.
Sales.
Disposition of property.
Governmental property generally, §153A-163.
Merchandise by governmental units.
Exception to prohibition, §66-58(b).
Real property.
Execution sales, §153A-163.
Judicial sale, §153A-163.
Sale, lease or exchange of property between
governmental units.
Action taken by governmental unit,
§160A-274(c).
Authority, §160A-274(b).
Governmental unit defined, §160A-274(a).
Sales and use tax.
First one-cent local government sales and use tax,
§§105-463 to 105-474.
See SALES AND USE TAX.

COUNTIES —Cont'd
Sales and use tax —Cont'd
First one-half cent local government sales and use
tax, §§105-480 to 105-487.
See SALES AND USE TAX.
Hold harmless for repealed reimbursements,
§§105-521 to 105-523.
Levy, §153A-151.
Limitations, §153A-151.
Modular homes, tax on.
Distribution of part of tax to counties,
§105-164.44G.
One-quarter cent county sales and use tax,
§§105-535 to 105-538.
Public transportation, §§105-506 to 105-511.4.
See SALES AND USE TAX.
Refunds, §105-164.14(c).
Second one-half cent local government sales and
use tax, §§105-495 to 105-502.
See SALES AND USE TAX.
Sanitary districts generally, §§130A-47 to
130A-85.
See SANITARY DISTRICTS.
Satellite jail/work release units, §§153A-230 to
153A-230.5.
See JAILS.
Savings and loan associations.
Investments.
County obligations, §54B-188.
Savings banks.
Investments.
County obligations, §54C-137.
School district indebtedness.
Assumption by counties, §§115C-473 to 115C-475.
Schools.
County school fund.
Composition, NC Const Art IX §7.
Generally.
See SCHOOLS AND EDUCATION.
Local boards of education.
Generally, §§115C-35 to 115C-51.
See LOCAL BOARDS OF EDUCATION.
Public schools.
Responsibility, NC Const Art IX §2.
Seats.
Relocation.
Bond issues.
Procedures if county votes to relocate county
seat, §159-67.
**Secondary road construction programs by
department of transportation.**
Adoption of annual construction program for each
county.
Board of transportation, §136-44.8(e).
Department of transportation to follow,
§136-44.8(f).
Map showing tentative road paving projects.
Posting in county courthouse, §136-44.8(a).
Notice of public meeting of board of county
commissioners.
Deviations or priority of paving projects,
§136-44.8(d).
Presentation by department of annual program
for county, §136-44.8(b).
Public meeting on annual construction program
for county, §136-44.8(c).
Notice, §136-44.8(b).
Public meeting on deviations or priority of paving
projects, §136-44.8(d).
Review of changes to which commissioners do not
consent.
Petition by board, §136-44.8(f).

COUNTIES —Cont'd
Security interest.
Entering into contracts creating, §160A-20.
Senatorial districts.
Dividing precincts into apportionment acts,
§120-2.2.
Established, §120-1.
Number of senators, §120-1.
Severability of apportionment acts, §120-2.1.
Service districts.
Economic development and training districts,
§§153A-317.11 to 153A-317.17.
See ECONOMIC DEVELOPMENT AND
TRAINING DISTRICTS.
Generally, §§153A-300 to 153A-310.
See COUNTY SERVICE DISTRICTS.
Research and production service districts,
§§153A-311 to 153A-317.
See COUNTY RESEARCH AND PRODUCTION
SERVICE DISTRICTS.
Service of process.
Personal jurisdiction.
Manner of service to exercise, §1A-1 Rule 4(j).
Setoff debt collection, §§105A-1 to 105A-16.
See SETOFF DEBT COLLECTION.
Sewage collection and disposal systems.
Service districts, §§153A-300 to 153A-310.
Sewers.
Connections.
Power to require, §153A-284.
Districts.
County water and sewer districts, §§162A-86 to
162A-94.
See COUNTY WATER AND SEWER
DISTRICTS.
Liability for failure to furnish water or sewer
services, §153A-283.
Nonliability for failure to furnish water or sewer
services, §153A-283.
Powers and duties.
Requiring connection, §153A-284.
Riparian rights.
Law not changed, §153A-286.
Venue for actions by riparian owners,
§153A-288.
Special assessments.
Authority to make, §153A-185.
Venue for actions by riparian owners, §153A-288.
Sheriffs.
Generally.
See SHERIFFS.
Training programs for law enforcement,
§153A-211.
Short-term vehicle leases or rentals.
Gross receipts tax on, §153A-156.
Signs.
Outdoor advertising.
Regulation of nonconforming off-premises
outdoor advertising, §153A-143.
Single portal of entry.
Development, §153A-77.1.
Sinking funds.
Local government finance, §§159-1 to 159-188.
See LOCAL GOVERNMENT FINANCE.
**Skateboarding, inline skating and freestyle
bicycling.**
Limitation of liability, §99E-25(b).
Duty of care not created, §99E-25(d).
Exceptions, §99E-25(c).
Independent concessionaires or other persons or
organizations.
Liability not limited by section, §99E-25(e).

COUNTIES —Cont'd
**Skateboarding, inline skating and freestyle
bicycling** —Cont'd
Limitation of liability —Cont'd
Insurance carried by entity.
Not waiver of liability limits, §99E-25(f).
Sovereign immunity not waived, §99E-25(d).
Specifically designated areas for activities.
Required to participate on property owner or
controlled by entity, §99E-25(a).
**Smallpox vaccination incident to homeland
security act.**
Adverse reaction, policy regarding sick leave,
§153A-94.1.
Smoking in public places.
Local government regulation, §130A-498.
Social services.
Appropriations.
Not to revert, §108A-91.
Authority to provide social service programs,
§153A-255.
Boards of social services, §§108A-1 to 108A-11.
See COUNTY BOARDS OF SOCIAL
SERVICES.
Child abuse, neglect or dependency cases.
Disagreement between departments as to legal
residence of child.
Resolution, referral to division of social
services, §153A-257(d).
Child welfare services not provided by county.
Action by secretary of health and human
services, §108A-74.
Consolidated county human services funding,
§143B-139.7.
Consolidated human services agencies, boards,
directors.
See CONSOLIDATED HUMAN SERVICES
AGENCY.
Contracts with other agencies, §153A-259.
County home, §153A-256.
Director of social services, §§108A-12 to 108A-15.
See COUNTY DIRECTORS OF SOCIAL
SERVICES.
Disagreement between departments as to legal
residence of child.
Child abuse, neglect or dependency cases.
Resolution, referral to division of social
services, §153A-257(d).
Failure to pay public assistance costs.
Withholding of state moneys from counties
failing to pay, §108A-93.
Programs.
Authority to provide, §153A-255.
Residence requirements.
Eligibility for financial support, §153A-257(a).
Purpose of section, §153A-257(c).
Termination, §153A-257(b).
Special county attorneys for social service
matters, §§108A-16 to 108A-18.
Taxation, §108A-90(a).
Consolidated tax, §108A-90(b).
Work first program generally, §§108A-27 to
108A-39.
See WORK FIRST PROGRAM.
Soil and water conservation districts.
Drainage projects.
Establishment and maintenance by counties,
§153A-440.1(b).
Water resources development projects.
Establishment and maintenance by counties,
§153A-440.1(b).

COUNTIES —Cont'd
Soil and water conservation districts —Cont'd
Watershed improvement works or projects.
Bond issues.
Borrowing by local units for anticipated water
supplies, §139-49(a) to (g).
Establishment and maintenance of programs by
counties, §153A-440.1(a).
Extraterritorial powers of counties, §139-45.
Participation by, §139-48(a).
Powers, §139-41(a) to (i).
Counties not authorized to levy watershed
improvement taxes, §139-41.1.
Extraterritorial powers of counties, §139-45.
Taxation.
Alternative method of financing watershed
improvement programs by special county
tax, §139-39.
Soil and water conservation promotion,
§153A-440.
Solar collectors.
Limitations on regulation, §153A-144.
Costs and attorneys' fees, courts may award,
§153A-144(c).
Prohibition or effective prohibition not allowed,
§153A-144(a).
Screening may be required, §153A-144(b).
Solicitation.
Regulation of solicitation, §153A-125.
Solid waste disposal tax.
Distribution, use of proceeds, §105-187.63.
Solid waste management.
Areas outside corporate limits.
Establishing and operating facilities,
§153A-292(a).
Authority to operate public enterprise, §153A-275.
Costs of providing and operating facility.
Determining for imposition of fees,
§153A-292(b).
Definitions, §§153A-136(c), (d), 153A-294.
Equipment.
Agreement with department of transportation to
make available, §153A-291.
Fees.
Collection, use of facility and availability of
facility.
Authority to impose, determining amount,
§153A-292(b).
Property taxes, billing and collecting in same
manner, §153A-293.
Financing public enterprise, §153A-276.
Gate across highway leading to facility.
Erecting, §153A-292(c).
Hazardous waste facilities.
Local ordinances prohibiting facilities invalid,
§130A-293.
Privilege license taxes, §153A-152.1(a) to (c).
Loans and bonds, §§159I-1 to 159I-30.
See SOLID WASTE MANAGEMENT LOANS
AND SPECIAL OBLIGATION BONDS.
Low-income persons, providing aid to,
§153A-292(f).
Ordinances.
Department may authorize, §130A-294(a).
Plan.
Development, §130A-309.04.
Prison and other labor.
Agreement with department of transportation to
make available, §153A-291.
Rates for public enterprise services, §153A-277.

COUNTIES —Cont'd
Solid waste management —Cont'd
Recycling computer equipment and televisions.
Authority to manage programs, §130A-309.141.
Regional solid waste management authorities,
§§153A-421 to 153A-432.
See REGIONAL SOLID WASTE
MANAGEMENT AUTHORITIES.
Regulation of disposal facilities, nature of disposal
and method of disposal, §153A-292(a).
Service districts, §§153A-300 to 153A-310.
Site for facility.
Acquiring by purchase or condemnation,
§153A-292(c).
Use of suitable vacant land, §153A-292(c).
Southern growth policies agreement.
Rights of state and local governments not
restricted, §143-506.
Special assessments, §§153A-185 to 153A-210.7.
See SPECIAL ASSESSMENTS BY COUNTIES.
Speed limits, §20-141(b).
Authorizing higher or lower speeds, §20-141(e),
(e1), (f).
State of emergency.
Generally, §§14-288.12 to 14-288.18.
See STATE OF EMERGENCY.
Powers of counties, §14-288.13.
State psychiatric hospital.
Selection of county as site for.
Acquisition and conveyance of property,
§153A-178.
Stormwater management programs.
Authority to operate public enterprise, §153A-275.
Financing public enterprise, §153A-276.
Ordinances to protect water quality and control
water quantity.
Authority to adopt and enforce, §153A-454(a).
Deed restrictions and protective covenants,
§153A-454(d).
Illicit discharge detection and elimination
controls, §153A-454(c).
National pollutant discharge elimination system
(NPDES) stormwater permit, §153A-454(b).
Rates for public enterprise services, §153A-277.
Stream-clearing programs.
Authorized, §153A-140.1(a).
Construction of provisions, §153A-140.1(b), (c).
Taxes.
See COUNTY TAXES.
Telecommunications.
Wireless telecommunications facilities,
§§153A-349.50 to 153A-349.53.
**Telecommunications systems for state
agencies.**
Access to, switched broadband, chief information
officer to provide, §147-33.92(a), (b).
Townships.
Boundaries and boundary changes, §153A-19(a) to
(c).
Establishing or abolishing, §153A-19(a).
Transportation department.
Local consultation on transportation projects,
§136-11.1.
Transporter plates.
County receiving donated vehicles for low income
individuals, §20-79.2(d).
**Unemployment compensation benefits
chargeable to.**
Pool account for local government unemployment
compensation, §147-86.1(a) to (d).

COUNTIES —Cont'd
Unified government, §§153A-471 to 153A-473.
Applicability of provisions, §153A-473.
Board of commissioners.
Powers and duties, §153A-471(c), (d).
Construction of certain statutory references,
§153A-472.
Generally, §153A-471(a), (b).
Property tax levy, §153A-472.1.
Used oil collection, reuse or disposal.
Grants to local governments to encourage,
§130A-309.22(a) to (d).
Vagrancy.
Regulation of begging, §153A-126.
Vesting rights.
Planning and zoning.
Land-use planning process, §153A-344.1.
Veterans.
Priority in employment assistance for United
States armed forces veterans, §§165-44.1 to
165-44.6.
Wage and hour act.
Exemption from provisions, §95-25.14(d), (e).
Waiver of governmental immunity,
§153A-435(a).
**Wastewater collection, treatment and disposal
systems.**
Authority to operate public enterprise, §153A-275.
Financing public enterprise, §153A-276.
Rates for public enterprise services, §153A-277.
Wastewater treatment, assessments.
Special assessments.
Authority to make, §153A-185.
Water and sewerage facility assessments,
§153A-185.
Water and sewer districts, §§162A-86 to 162A-94.
See COUNTY WATER AND SEWER DISTRICTS.
**Water pollution and hazardous substances
control.**
Privilege license taxes.
Low-level radioactive and hazardous waste
facilities, §153A-152.1(a) to (c).
Waters and watercourses.
Commissioners for opening and clearing streams,
§§77-1 to 77-11.
See STREAMS.
Landings.
Public landings, §77-11.
Watershed improvement projects.
Service districts, §§153A-300 to 153A-310.
Water supply and distribution systems.
Authority to operate public enterprise, §153A-275.
Financing public enterprise, §153A-276.
Rates for public enterprise services, §153A-277.
Service districts, §§153A-300 to 153A-310.
**Western North Carolina Development
Association, Inc.**
Appropriations, §153A-447(a), (b).
Wetlands.
Eminent domain.
Condemnor acquiring land for purposes of
wetlands mitigation.
Payment to county where land located,
§153A-15.1.
State agency acquiring land by purchase.
Payment to county sum equal to or in lieu of ad
valorem taxes, §§146-22.3 to 146-22.5.
White goods.
Management of discarded white goods,
§§130A-309.80 to 130A-309.87.
See WHITE GOODS.

COUNTIES —Cont'd
Wills.
Recording of wills.
Copies of wills recorded in wrong county, §8-30.
Wireless telecommunications facilities,
§§153A-349.50 to 153A-349.53.
Applications for construction or modification,
§153A-349.52(b).
Application fee, §153A-349.52(f).
Conditions on approval, §153A-349.52(g).
County review of application, §153A-349.52(c).
Written decision, time for issuance,
§153A-349.52(e).
Collocation application, §153A-349.52(d).
Streamlined process, §153A-349.53(a).
Applicability, §153A-349.53(c).
Limitations on use of process,
§153A-349.53(b).
Collocation of facilities, §153A-349.53.
Construction, §153A-349.52.
County property, may not be required,
§153A-349.52(h).
Defined terms, §153A-349.51.
Federal law, compliance with, §153A-349.50(b).
Historic districts or landmarks, §153A-349.52(i).
Purpose, §153A-349.50(a).
Support structure, siting or modification,
§153A-349.52(a).
Work first program.
Generally, §§108A-27 to 108A-39.
See WORK FIRST PROGRAM.
Zoning and planning.
Generally, §§153A-320 to 153A-326, 153A-340 to
153A-349.
See COUNTY PLANNING AND ZONING.
Regional planning commissions, §§153A-391 to
153A-398.
See REGIONAL PLANNING COMMISSIONS.
**Zoning inspectors generally, §§153A-350 to
153A-375.**
See COUNTY INSPECTION DEPARTMENTS.
Zoological authority.
Gifts, §143-177.2.

COUNTRY CLUBS.
Alcoholic beverage permits.
Residential sports club permit, §18B-1006(k).
Sports club defined to include, §18B-1000.

COUNTRY STORES.
Traditional country stores.
Defined, §130A-250.
Sanitation requirements for food and lodging
establishments.
Exemption from provisions, §130A-250.

COUNTY AGRICULTURAL SOCIETIES.
Evidence.
Records may be read in evidence, §106-511.
Exhibits exempt from state and county taxes,
§106-507.
Funds to be used in paying premiums,
§106-508.
Incorporation, §106-505.
New members, §106-506.
Officers, §106-506.
Organization, §106-506.
Powers, §106-505.
Premiums awarded by societies.
Funds to be awarded in paying premiums,
§106-508.
Publication of statements required, §106-510.

COUNTY AGRICULTURAL SOCIETIES —Cont'd
Records to be kept, §106-511.
May be read in evidence, §106-511.
Statements.
Annual statements to state treasurer, §106-509.
Publications required, §106-510.
State treasurer.
Annual statement to treasurer, §106-509.
Taxation.
Exhibits exempt from state and county taxes, §106-507.
Term of existence, §106-505.

COUNTY ASSESSORS.
Alternative to separate office of county assessor, §105-294(f).
Annual review, §105-296(j) to (m).
Exempted or excluded property, §105-296(l).
Transportation corridor official maps and amendments, §105-296(m).
Appointment, §105-294(a).
Assistant assessor, §105-297.
Bonds generally, §§58-72-1 to 58-72-70.
See OFFICIAL BONDS OF COUNTY OFFICERS.
Certification, §105-294(c).
Change in appraisal, §105-296(i).
Compensation, §105-294(e).
Duties, §105-296(a) to (c).
Instruction in appraisal or assessment of property, §105-294(d).
Inventories.
Requiring, §105-296(h).
Oath of office, §105-295.
Powers.
Generally, §105-296(g), (h).
Qualifications, §105-294(b).
Removal from office, §105-294(a).
Studies conducted by department.
Furnishing information to department, §105-296(k).
Subpoenas.
Powers, §105-296(g).
Term of office, §105-294(a).
Unknown owner.
Listing in name of, §105-302(c).
Reports on properties listed in name of, §105-302.1.
Vacancy in office, §105-294(a).

COUNTY ATTORNEYS.
Appointments, §153A-114.
Employees of counties generally.
See COUNTY OFFICERS AND EMPLOYEES.
Oaths.
Form of oaths of office, §11-11.
Police.
Removal of unfit officers.
Prosecution by county attorney, §128-17.
Powers and duties, §153A-114.
Sheriffs.
Removal of unfit officers.
Prosecution by county attorney, §128-17.
Voting rights act of 1965.
Duties as to, §§120-30.9E, 120-30.9H.

COUNTY BOARDS OF COMMISSIONERS.
Allowances, §153A-28.
Attorney.
Appointment, §153A-114.
Ayes and noes, §153A-42.
Boards, commissions and agencies.
Direct control of activities.
County with population in excess of 425,000.
Applicability of section, §153A-77(f).

COUNTY BOARDS OF COMMISSIONERS —Cont'd
Boards, commissions and agencies —Cont'd
Direct control of activities —Cont'd
County with population in excess of 425,000 —Cont'd
Assumption, §153A-77(a).
Consolidation of human services, §153A-77(b) to (e).
Public health rules, enforcement by civil penalty, §153A-77(a).
Public hearing.
Required to exercise authority, notice, publication, §153A-77(a).
Bonds, surety.
Official bonds, §58-72-60.
Liability of commissioners as surety.
Record of board conclusive as to facts stated, §58-72-65.
Vacancy declared.
Judge to file statement of proceedings with commissioners, §58-72-45.
Surety companies.
Clerk to notify county commissioners of condition of company, §58-73-10.
Brucellosis.
Cooperation of county boards, §106-394.
Buildings.
Designation of sites, §153A-169.
Chairman.
Duties, §153A-39.
Powers and duties, §153A-39.
Selection, §153A-39.
Optional methods of selection, §153A-58.
Temporary chairman, §153A-39.
Tie votes, §153A-39.
Vice-chairman, §153A-39.
Child support.
Action by designated representatives, §110-130.
Clerk.
Appointment, §153A-111.
Powers and duties, §153A-111.
Code of ordinances, §153A-49.
Community development.
Advisory committees, §153A-376(c).
Exercise of powers, §153A-376(b).
Loans, §153A-376(d).
Compensation, §§153A-28, 153A-92.
Duties, failure to discharge, §14-230.
Effective dates of alterations, §153A-62.
Elections, §§153A-60, 153A-64.
Alteration of structure of board, §153A-60.
Filing results of election, §153A-64.
Altering mode of elections, §153A-58.
Manner of election, §153A-34.
Vacancy in office, §163-115(d).
Voting systems.
Powers and duties as to, §163-165.8.
Electronic listing of personal property.
Property taxes.
Authority to provide for, §105-310.1(c).
Eminent domain.
Local government unit outside county.
Consent of board required, §153A-15.
Employees in offices of register of deeds and sheriff.
Fixing number, §153A-103.
Relatives.
Approval of board not required for employment, §153A-103.

COUNTY BOARDS OF COMMISSIONERS
—Cont'd

Ethics code.
Adoption, §153A-53(a).
Educational requirements, §153A-53(b).

Fairs.
Application for license to commissioners, §106-517.
Penalty for violation of provisions, §106-518.
Refusal to license shows within five miles, §106-519.

Fees.
Commissioners to fix fees, §153A-102.
Electronic notice of new fees and increased fees.
County web site, §153A-102.1(a1).
Inapplicability of section, §153A-102.1(c).
Method of providing notice, §153A-102.1(a).
Period of public comment, §153A-102.1(b).

Ferries.
Authority of county commissioners with regard to ferries, §136-88.

Fiscal policy of counties.
Commissioners to direct, §153A-101.
Joint meetings with local boards of education, §115C-426.2.

Franchises.
Adoption, §153A-46.

Hearings.
Conduct of public hearing, §153A-52.

Highways, roads and streets.
Responsibility of counties for upkeep, etc., terminated, §136-97(a).
Secondary roads construction programs.
Filing of annual statement, §136-44.9.
Submission of programs to county commissioners, §136-44.8(a) to (f).

Hospital districts.
Alternative procedures for creation of district, §131E-41(b).
Creation of district.
Alternative procedures, §131E-41(b).
Governing body of district, §131E-47.

Industrial development commission.
Functions and duties of commission, §158-23.

Larceny, §14-76.

Livestock.
Brucellosis.
Cooperation of county boards of commissioners, §106-394.

Meetings, §153A-42.
Adjournment, §153A-40(a).
Joint meetings with local boards of education, §115C-426.2.
Location, §153A-40(c).
Minutes to be kept, §153A-42.
Public comment period during regular meetings, §153A-52.1.
Quorum, §153A-43.
Regular meetings, §153A-40(a).
Special meetings, §153A-40(b).
Time and place, §153A-40(a).
Voting.
Ayes and noes, §153A-42.
Members excused from voting, §153A-44.

Modification in structures of boards.
Ballots.
Forms, §153A-61.
Effective date of alterations, §153A-62.
Elections.
Altering mode of elections, §153A-58.
Filing copies of resolutions, §153A-63.

COUNTY BOARDS OF COMMISSIONERS
—Cont'd

Modification in structures of boards —Cont'd
Implementation when board has members serving a combination of four and two year terms, §153A-59.
Initiation of alterations by resolution, §153A-60.
Number of commissioners.
Options, §153A-58.
Optional structures, §153A-58.
Resolutions.
Filing copies, §153A-63.
Initiation of alterations by resolution, §153A-60.
Submission of proposition to voters, §153A-61.
Filing results of election, §153A-64.
Terms of commissioners, §153A-59.

Motor vehicle license plates.
Special plates, §20-79.4(b).

Number of commissioners.
Options, §153A-58.

Oaths.
Chairman of the board of county commissioners.
Administration of oaths by chairman, §11-9.
Who may administer oaths of office, §11-7.1(a).

Optional structures, §153A-58.

Ordinances.
Adoption, §153A-45.
Book, §153A-48.
Code, §153A-49.
Pleading and proving county ordinances, §153A-50.
Technical ordinances, §153A-47.

Organization of county government.
Boards to organize, §153A-76.
Fiscal policy of county, §153A-101.

Personnel boards.
Establishment, §153A-95.

Planning and zoning.
Method of procedure, §153A-343.

Pleading and proving county ordinances, §153A-50.

Procedures, §153A-41.

Property.
Use of county property, §153A-169.

Property taxes.
Electronic listing of personal property.
Authority to provide for, §105-310.1(c).

Public comment period during regular meetings, §153A-52.1.

Public hearings.
Conduct, §153A-52.

Public schools.
Appropriations.
Allocation by purpose, function or project, discretion, §115C-429(b).
Determining amount, §115C-429(b).
Budget.
Action on, completion, time, duties, §115C-429(b).
Approval of amendment, §115C-433(b).
Transfer of funds, emergencies, §115C-433(d).
Books, records and other financial information, available to, §115C-429(c).
Deficit, not required to fund, §115C-429(d).
Dispute between board and state board of education.
Procedure for resolution, §115C-431.
Submission to commissioners, §115C-429(a).
Uniform budget format, §115C-426.
Elections.
Action of board on petition for election, §115C-506.

COUNTY BOARDS OF COMMISSIONERS
—Cont'd
Public schools —Cont'd
Money dispute between board and state board of education.
Procedure for resolution, §115C-431.
Purchase of building site.
Expenditures, approval required, §115C-426(f).
Disagreement between commissioners and board of education, §115C-426(f).
Supplementary taxes for school purposes.
Action of board on petition for election, §115C-506.
Tax levying authority, §115C-5(j).
Quorum, §153A-43.
Records, §153A-42.
Registers of deeds.
Clerk to board, §161-23.
Reports.
Commissioners may require reports, §153A-104.
Misconduct in public office.
Swearing falsely to official reports, §14-232.
Resolutions.
Filing copy of alteration resolution, §153A-63.
Initiation of alterations, §153A-60.
Rules and regulations.
Adoption, §153A-41.
Secondary roads construction programs.
Filing of annual statement, §136-44.9.
Submission of programs to county commissioners, §136-44.8(a) to (f).
Sheriffs.
Bond of sheriff.
Duties as to, §§162-9, 162-10.
Soil and water conservation districts.
Watershed improvement works or projects.
Powers, §139-41(a) to (i).
Structure, §153A-34.
Optional structures, §153A-58.
Technical ordinances, §153A-47.
Term of commissioners, §153A-59.
Implementation of optional structures.
Members serving combination of four and two year terms, §153A-59.
Toll bridges.
Authority of county commissioners with regard to toll bridges, §136-88.
Vacancies, §153A-27.
Certain enumerated counties.
Appointment to fill, §153A-27.1(a).
County executive committee of political party.
Consulting, recommendation, §153A-27.1(d), (e).
Filing, provisions repealed, §153A-27.1(f).
Eligibility for appointment, §153A-27.1(c).
Inapplicability of G.S. 53A-27, §153A-27.1(g).
List of counties which section applies, §153A-27.1(h).
Remainder of unexpired terms, §153A-27.1(b).
Term of appointee, §153A-27.1(b).
Nominations to fill.
Special provisions for obtaining nominations, §163-115(d).
Voting.
Members excused from voting, §153A-44.
Tie votes, §153A-39.

COUNTY BOARDS OF ELECTIONS.
Absentee ballots.
Certified list of executed absentee ballots.
Received on day before election, §163-232.

COUNTY BOARDS OF ELECTIONS —Cont'd
Absentee ballots —Cont'd
Certified list of executed absentee ballots —Cont'd
Received on or after election day, §163-232.1.
Counting of absentee ballots by, §163-234.
Military and overseas voters.
Electronic notice of election, §163-258.16.
Required meeting of county board, §163-230.1(c1).
Absentee voting by military.
Absentee voting at office of board of elections, §163-255.
Appointment of members, §§163-22(c), 163-30.
Appropriations.
Boards of county commissioners to make appropriations for, §163-37.
Assistants at polls.
Appointment, §163-42.
Ballots.
Duties as to, §163-33.
Preparation and production of official ballots and instructions, §163-165.3(b).
Canvassing votes, §163-182.5(b).
Certificate of nomination, election or referendum results, §163-182.15.
Chairman.
Examination of voting machines, §163-33.2.
Power to administer oaths, §163-33.1.
Compensation of members, §§163-32, 163-35(c).
Attendance at instructional meetings, §163-30.
Composition, §163-30.
Counting ballots.
Jurisdiction, §163-182.4(a).
Director of elections.
Duties, §163-35(d).
Training and certification, §163-35(e).
Vacancy in office, §163-35(a).
Disqualifications for office, §163-35(a).
Duties, §§163-33, 163-35(d).
Expenses of members, §163-32.
Full-time offices, §163-36.
Instructional meetings.
Compensation of members for attendance, §163-30.
Investigations, §163-33.
Littering notification, §163-33.3.
Maintenance of voting data by voting tabulation district, §163-132.5G.
Meetings, §163-31.
Military and overseas voters.
Electronic notice of election, §163-258.16.
Modified full-time offices, §163-36.
Municipal elections.
Administration of elections, §163-284(b).
Special district elections, §163-284.1.
Certificate of elections.
Chairman to issue, time, §163-301.
Defined, §163-298.
Special district elections.
Conducted by county board of elections, §163-284.1.
Notice.
Duties of boards, §163-33.
Military and overseas voters.
Electronic notice of election, §163-258.16.
Number of members, §163-30.
Oaths.
Oath of office of members, §163-30.
Power of chairman to administer, §163-33.1.
Official registration records for voters in all elections.
Board's registration record, §163-288.

COUNTY BOARDS OF ELECTIONS —Cont'd
Political activities by board members and employees, §§163-38 to 163-40.1.
Applicability of provisions, §163-38.
Definitions and proof of terms used, provision applicable, §163-40.1.
Limitation on activities, §163-39.
Removal, violation grounds for, §163-40.
Powers, §163-33.
Maintenance of order, §163-34.
Precinct assistants.
Appointment, §163-42.
Precincts.
Map of precinct boundaries.
Duty to prepare, §163-128(b).
Powers as to precincts, §163-128(a).
Protest of election.
Appeal of decision to superior court, §163-182.14(a), (b).
Appeal to state board after decision, §163-182.11.
Filing, §163-182.9.
Rules for conduct of hearing, §163-182.10.
Quorum, §163-31.
Recounts, §163-182.7.
Hand-to-eye recounts, §163-182.7A.
Relative of candidate not eligible to serve, §163-30.
Removal of members, §163-22(c).
Reports.
State board of elections may require reports from county boards, §163-22(c).
Rules and regulations, §163-33.
Student election assistants.
Appointment, §163-42.1.
Summary of duties.
Counting votes, canvassing, abstracts and protests, §163-182.17(c).
Termination of employment, §163-35(b).
Terms of office, §163-30.
Vacancies in office, §§163-22(c), 163-30.
Voting machines.
Examination, §163-33.2.
Voting places.
Duties as to, §§163-129, 163-166.1.
Voting systems.
Powers and duties as to, §§163-165.9, 163-165.10.

COUNTY BOARDS OF HEALTH.
Adjudicatory body, §130A-35(a).
Appointment of members, §130A-35(b).
Chairperson, §130A-35(e).
Composition, §130A-35(b).
Consolidated human services agencies, boards and directors.
See CONSOLIDATED HUMAN SERVICES AGENCY.
Expenses, §130A-35(h).
Fees.
Power to impose for services rendered by local department, §130A-39(g).
Meetings, §130A-35(i).
Per diem, §130A-35(h).
Policy-making body, §130A-35(a).
Quorum, §130A-35(f).
Removal of board members, §130A-35(g).
Rules, §130A-35(a).
Authority to adopt, §130A-39(a).
Code, standard, rule or regulation.
Adoption by reference to, §130A-39(f).
Copies, filing, §130A-39(e).
More stringent rules, power to adopt, §130A-39(b).

COUNTY BOARDS OF HEALTH —Cont'd
Rules —Cont'd
Municipalities, applicability to, §130A-39(c).
Notice prior to adoption, repeal or amendment, §130A-39(d).
Terms of office, §130A-35(c).
Vacancies in office, §130A-35(d).

COUNTY BOARDS OF SOCIAL SERVICES, §§108A-1 to 108A-11.
Appointment of members, §108A-3(a), (b).
Filling of vacancies, §108A-6.
Chairman.
Election, §108A-7.
Term of office, §108A-7.
Child welfare services not provided by boards.
Action by secretary of health and human services, §108A-74.
Compensation of members, §§108A-3(c), 108A-8.
Composition, §108A-2.
Consolidated human services boards.
Generally.
See CONSOLIDATED HUMAN SERVICES AGENCY.
Human services director.
Powers and duties, §108A-15.1(c).
Powers and duties, §108A-15.1(a), (b).
Contracts with governmental or private agencies, §108A-10.
Creation, §108A-1.
Duties, §§108A-1, 108A-9.
Fees, §108A-10.
Fraudulent public assistance program payments.
Garnishment of wages to recoup, §108A-25.3.
Meetings, §108A-7.
Number of members.
Change of number, §§108A-2, 108A-5(c).
Per diem of members, §108A-8.
Records.
Inspection of records by members, §108A-11.
Reports.
Fees received, §108A-10.
Residence requirements for membership, §108A-3(c).
Terms of members, §108A-4.
Expiration, §108A-5(a), (b).
Vacancies.
Filling, §108A-6.

COUNTY CLERKS.
Boards of commissioners, §153A-11.
Reports.
Misconduct in public office.
Swearing falsely to official reports, §14-232.

COUNTY COMMISSIONERS.
See COUNTY BOARDS OF COMMISSIONERS.

COUNTY CONSOLIDATION, §§153A-401 to 153A-405.
Cities-counties, §§160B-1 to 160B-21.
See CONSOLIDATED CITY-COUNTY ACT.

COUNTY DIRECTORS OF SOCIAL SERVICES, §§108A-12 to 108A-15.
Abuse, neglect or dependency of juveniles.
Powers and duties generally, §§7B-100 to 7B-1414.
See CHILD ABUSE, NEGLECT OR DEPENDENCY.
Adult protection.
Abuse.
Director to notify district attorney, §108A-109.

COUNTY DIRECTORS OF SOCIAL SERVICES
—Cont'd
Adult protection —Cont'd
  Contracts for provision of medical evaluations,
    §108A-103(c).
  Cooperation by certain agencies with,
    §108A-103(b).
  Definition of "director,"§108A-101(c).
  Duties of receiving reports, §§108A-14,
    108A-103(a), (d).
Appointment, §108A-12(a).
Delegation of authority, §108A-14(b).
Duties, §108A-14.
Guardians.
  Director and assistant directors as public
    guardians, §108A-15.
Investigations.
  Duties generally, §108A-14.
Joint employment by two or more boards,
  §108A-12(b).
Merit system.
  Selection or appointment of directors according to,
    §§108A-9, 108A-12(a).
Salaries, §108A-13.
Youth employment certificates.
  Designation of personnel to issue, §108A-14(b).

COUNTY ECONOMIC DEVELOPMENT AND
  TRAINING DISTRICTS.
Economic development and training districts,
  §§153A-317.11 to 153A-317.17.
  See ECONOMIC DEVELOPMENT AND
    TRAINING DISTRICTS.

COUNTY ELECTIONS.
Boards of commissioners, §153A-34.
  Altering mode of elections, §153A-58.
  Modification of structures of boards, §153A-61.
    Filing results of election, §153A-64.
Boards of elections, §§163-30 to 163-37.
  See COUNTY BOARDS OF ELECTIONS.
Consolidation.
  Plans proposed by governmental study
    commissions, §153A-405(a) to (e).
Districts.
  Applicability of provisions, §153A-22(g).
  Certified copies of resolution, §153A-22(f).
  Change in boundaries.
    Effect upon unexpired term of office of
      commissioner, §153A-22(d).
  Map of electoral districts, §153A-20.
  Redefining electoral district boundaries,
    §153A-22(b), (c).
  Resolutions adopted pursuant to provisions,
    §153A-22(e).
  Substantial inequality of population among
    districts, §153A-22(a).
Industrial development.
  Tax elections, §§158-16 to 158-24.
Sales and use tax.
  Local government sales and use tax.
    Election on adoption.
      First one-cent tax, §105-465.
Sheriffs, NC Const Art VII §2.
Structure of boards.
  Alteration.
    Effective date, §153A-62.
    Initiation of alterations by resolution.
      Filing copy, §153A-63.
    Submission of proposition to voters, §153A-61.
      Filing results of election, §153A-64.

COUNTY ELECTIONS —Cont'd
Submission of acts to United States attorney
  general.
  Alternative submission authority, §120-30.9I.
  County attorney, §120-30.9E.
Taxation.
  Property taxes, §153A-149.
Time.
  Generally, §163-1(a).
Watershed improvement programs, §§139-39,
  139-40.

COUNTY INSPECTION DEPARTMENTS,
  §§153A-350 to 153A-375.
Actions.
  Corrective action.
    Failure to take, §153A-368.
Appeals.
  General appeal to commissioner of insurance,
    §153A-374.
  Orders to take corrective action, §153A-370.
  Stop orders, §153A-361.
Appropriations.
  Financial support, §153A-354.
Buildings.
  Defined, §153A-350.
Certificates of compliance.
  Generally, §153A-363.
Composition, §153A-351(a).
Condemnation.
  Notice.
    Removing notice from condemned building,
      §153A-367.
  Unsafe buildings, §153A-366.
Conflicts of interest.
  Members of department, §153A-355.
Correction of defects in buildings, §§153A-365
  to 153A-371. See within this heading, "Defects
  in buildings."
Creation, §153A-351(a).
Defects in buildings.
  Correction, §153A-365.
    Action in event of failure to take corrective
      action, §153A-368.
    Orders to take corrective action, §153A-369.
      Appeals, §153A-370.
      Failure to comply with orders, §153A-371.
      Finality of order not appealed, §153A-370.
    Orders to take corrective action, §§153A-369 to
      153A-371.
  Removing notice from condemned building,
    §153A-367.
  Unsafe buildings condemned, §153A-366.
Enforcement of article.
  Equitable enforcement, §153A-372.
Equitable enforcement, §153A-372.
Establishment of fire limits, §153A-375.
Financial support, §153A-354.
Fire limits.
  Establishment, §153A-375.
Funds.
  Financial support, §153A-354.
Hearings.
  Stop orders, §153A-361.
Injunctions.
  Equitable enforcement of article, §153A-372.
Inspectors.
  Certification, §153A-351(b).
  Conflicts of interest, §153A-355.
  Duties, §§153A-351, 153A-352.
    Failure to perform, §153A-356.

COUNTY INSPECTION DEPARTMENTS
—Cont'd
Inspectors —Cont'd
Generally, §153A-351(a).
Powers, §§153A-351, 153A-352.
Qualifications, §§153A-351.1, 153A-351(b).
Responsibilities, §§153A-351, 153A-352.
Joint inspection departments.
Authorized, §153A-353.
Generally, §153A-353.
Other arrangements, §153A-353.
Notice.
Condemnation.
Removing prohibited, §153A-367.
Orders, failure to comply with, §14-68.
Periodic inspections.
Unsafe, unsanitary, hazardous, unlawful
conditions, §153A-364(a).
Residential rental property.
Prohibitions, registration fee, §153A-364(c),
(d).
Targeted effort within geographic area,
§153A-364(b).
Permits.
Certificates of compliance.
Generally, §153A-363.
Changes in work, §153A-359.
Delinquent property taxes owed.
Nonissuance of permit, §153A-357(c).
Erosion and sedimentation control plan required,
§153A-357(b).
Forms, §153A-357(a).
Grounds for revocation, §153A-362.
Issuance.
Requirements, §153A-357(a).
Land-disturbing activity.
Environmental compliance requirements for,
§153A-357(d).
Requirements.
Generally, §153A-357(a).
Revocation, §153A-362.
Time limitations on validity of permits,
§153A-358.
Validity.
Time limitations, §153A-358.
Work in progress.
Changes in work, §153A-359.
Generally, §153A-360.
Powers and duties, §§153A-351(a1), 153A-352.
Failure to perform duties, §153A-356.
Qualifications of inspectors, §§153A-351.1,
153A-351(b).
Records, §153A-373.
Reports, §153A-373.
Responsibilities, §§153A-351, 153A-352.
State buildings.
Inspection by counties or municipal authorities,
§143-135.1(a), (b).
Stop orders.
Appeals, §153A-361.
Hearing, §153A-361.
Tribal lands, §153A-350.1.
Unsafe buildings.
Condemnation, §153A-366.
Notice.
Removing from building, §153A-367.
Periodic inspections, §153A-364(a).
Residential rental property.
Prohibitions, registration fee, §153A-364(c),
(d).

COUNTY INSPECTION DEPARTMENTS
—Cont'd
Unsafe buildings —Cont'd
Periodic inspections —Cont'd
Targeted effort within geographic area,
§153A-364(b).
Work in progress, §§153A-359, 153A-360.

COUNTY INSPECTORS OF ARTICLES OF
COMMERCE, §§66-1 to 66-7.
Appointment.
County commissioners may appoint, §66-1.
Bonds, surety, §66-3.
Employees of counties generally.
See COUNTY OFFICERS AND EMPLOYEES.
Extortion.
Penalty, §66-7.
Falsely acting as inspector.
Penalty, §66-4.
Fees, §66-3.
Payment, §66-7.
Penalties.
Extortion, §66-7.
Falsely acting as inspector, §66-4.
Sale without inspection, §66-5.
Vessels.
Master or commander receiving articles without
inspection, §66-6.
Sale without inspection.
Penalty, §66-5.
Vessels.
Master or commander receiving articles without
inspection.
Penalty, §66-6.

COUNTY JUVENILE CRIME PREVENTION
COUNCILS, §§143B-845 to 143B-851.
See JUVENILE CRIME PREVENTION
COUNCILS.

COUNTY LAND RECORDS IMPROVEMENT
PROGRAM, §102-15.

COUNTY LIBRARIES.
Boards of trustees, §153A-265.
Powers and duties, §153A-266.
Capital outlay.
Local subdivisions to comply with laws governing
capital outlay, §125-13.
Chief librarian.
Qualifications, §153A-267(a).
Contracts for library services, §153A-270.
Declaration of state policy, §153A-261.
Definitions, §153A-262.
Employees, §153A-267(b).
Financing library systems, §153A-268.
Free library services, §153A-264.
Joint libraries, §153A-270.
Legislative declaration, §153A-261.
Local acts.
Systems operated under local acts brought under
this article, §153A-271.
Pledging of credit.
Interstate library compact, §125-13.
Powers and duties of trustees, §153A-266.
Public library systems.
Authorized, §153A-263.
Title to library property, §153A-269.

COUNTY MANAGERS, §§153A-81 to 153A-84.
Acting county manager, §153A-83.
Adoption of county-manager plan, §153A-81.
Appointment, §153A-81.

COUNTY MANAGERS —Cont'd
Counties not having, §153A-87.
Acting department heads, §153A-88.
Interim department heads, §153A-89.
Defined, §153A-81.
Designation, §153A-81.
Duties, §153A-82.
Interim county manager, §153A-84.
Officers of counties generally.
See COUNTY OFFICERS AND EMPLOYEES.
Powers, §153A-82.
Service of process.
Personal jurisdiction, manner of serving on
county, §1A-1 Rule 4(j).

COUNTY MEDICAL EXAMINERS.
Appointment, §130A-382.
Cremation.
Medical examiner's permission necessary before
cremation, §130A-388(a), (b).
Duties.
Notification of medical examiners of certain
deaths, §130A-385(a).
Embalming.
When medical examiner's permission necessary
before embalming, §130A-388(a), (b).
Employees of counties generally.
See COUNTY OFFICERS AND EMPLOYEES.
**Postmortem medicolegal examinations and
services,** §§130A-377 to 130A-395.
See MEDICAL EXAMINERS.
Subpoena authority, §130A-386.
Term of office, §130A-382.
Vacancies in office, §130A-382.

COUNTY OFFICERS AND EMPLOYEES.
Appointive offices.
Qualifications, §153A-25.
Vacancies, §153A-27.
Assessors, §§105-294 to 105-297.
See COUNTY ASSESSORS.
Attorneys.
See COUNTY ATTORNEYS.
Boards of commissioners.
See COUNTY BOARDS OF COMMISSIONERS.
Bonds, surety, §§58-72-1 to 58-72-70.
See OFFICIAL BONDS OF COUNTY OFFICERS.
Chief librarian.
Qualifications, §153A-267(a).
Clerks.
Boards of commissioners, §153A-11.
Reports, §14-232.
Compensation, §§153A-28, 153A-92.
Fixing pay schedules, §153A-92(a).
Criminal history record checks, §§114-19.14,
153A-94.2.
Defenses.
Civil or criminal actions, §160A-167.
Providing defenses for employees, §153A-97.
Dual office holding.
Ex officio service by county and city
representatives and officials, §128-1.2.
**E-Verify program to verify work authorization
of newly hired employees.**
Discrimination in enforcement prohibited,
§153A-99.1(c).
Duty of county to register and participate,
§153A-99.1(a).
E-Verify defined, §153A-99.1(b).
**Ex officio service by county and city
representatives and officials,** §128-1.2.

COUNTY OFFICERS AND EMPLOYEES
—Cont'd
Fees.
Statement rendered by county officers
compensated from fees, §128-13.
Penalty for failure to file statement, §128-13.
Fringe benefits, §153A-92(d).
Health insurance, §153A-92(d).
Holidays, §153A-94(b).
Hours and days of work, §153A-94(b).
Inspectors of articles of commerce, §§66-1 to
66-7.
See COUNTY INSPECTORS OF ARTICLES OF
COMMERCE.
Insurance.
Defense of officers and employees, §160A-167.
Health insurance, §153A-92.
Life insurance, §153A-92.
Jury commissions, §9-1.
Leaves of absence, §153A-94(a).
Sick leave.
Smallpox vaccination incident to homeland
security act.
Adverse reaction, policy regarding sick leave,
§153A-94.1.
Library employees, §153A-267(b).
Life insurance, §153A-92(d).
Managers, §§153A-81 to 153A-84.
See COUNTY MANAGERS.
Medical examiners.
See COUNTY MEDICAL EXAMINERS.
Mileage allowances.
Exempt of counties, §147-9.1.
Oath of office, §153A-26.
Official bonds of county officers generally,
§§58-72-1 to 58-72-70.
See OFFICIAL BONDS OF COUNTY OFFICERS.
Personnel records.
Allowing unauthorized access, §153A-98(e).
Confidential records, §153A-98(c), (c1).
Disclosure of certain information to retirement
organizations, §153A-98(c3).
Use for research, etc., §153A-98(c2).
Inspection and disclosure, §153A-98(a).
Maintenance and availability of information,
determination, §153A-98(b2).
Objection of employee to items in file,
§153A-98(d).
Open records, §153A-98(b).
Salary defined, §153A-98(b1).
Unauthorized access, §153A-98(f).
Personnel rules, §153A-94(a).
Employees may be made subject to rules adopted
by local governing body, §126-9(a) to (d).
Personnel system generally, §§153A-92 to
153A-99.
See PERSONNEL SYSTEM.
Political activities, §153A-99.
Coercion of employee to support or contribute to
political candidate, committee or party,
§126-14.
Qualifications for appointive offices, §153A-25.
Registers of deeds, §§161-1 to 161-31.
See REGISTERS OF DEEDS.
Reports.
Swearing falsely to official reports, §14-232.
Retaliatory employment discrimination,
§§95-240 to 95-245.
See RETALIATORY EMPLOYMENT
DISCRIMINATION.

COUNTY OFFICERS AND EMPLOYEES
—Cont'd
**Retention of funds of county by delinquent
        official.**
Citizen to recover funds, §128-10.
Retirement, §§128-21 to 128-38.5.
See LOCAL GOVERNMENTAL EMPLOYEES'
        RETIREMENT SYSTEM.
Rules and regulations.
Personnel rules, §153A-94(a).
Salaries.
Limitations of authority of boards, §153A-92(b).
Responsibilities of manager, §153A-92(c).
Schedule, §153A-92(a).
Statement rendered by county officers
        compensated from fees, §128-13.
Penalty for failure to file statement, §128-13.
Sheriffs.
See SHERIFFS.
Sick leave.
Smallpox vaccination incident to homeland
        security act.
Adverse reaction, policy regarding sick leave,
        §153A-94.1.
**Smallpox vaccination incident to homeland
        security act.**
Adverse reaction, policy regarding sick leave,
        §153A-94.1.
Social security.
Coverage of governmental employees under Title
        II of social security act, §§135-19 to 135-31.
See SOCIAL SECURITY.
Participation in social security act, §153A-96.
Social service directors, §§108A-12 to 108A-15.
See COUNTY DIRECTORS OF SOCIAL
        SERVICES.
Surveyors.
See COUNTY SURVEYORS.
Trade unions or labor unions.
Employees prohibited from becoming members of,
        §§95-98 to 95-100.
Treasurers.
See COUNTY TREASURERS.
Trust funds to be kept separate, §128-11.
Vacancies in appointive offices, §153A-27.
Veterans.
Priority in employment assistance for United
        States armed forces veterans, §§165-44.1 to
        165-44.6.
Whistleblower protection.
Retaliatory employment discrimination, §§95-240
        to 95-245.
See RETALIATORY EMPLOYMENT
        DISCRIMINATION.
Work days, §153A-94(b).

COUNTY ORDINANCES.
Adoption, §153A-45.
Alcoholic beverages.
Restriction on adoption, §18B-100.
Amusements.
Regulation of places of amusement, §153A-135.
Book, §153A-48.
Buildings.
Repair, closing or demolition of nonresidential
        buildings, §153A-372.1.
Camp Butner hospital.
Application of county ordinance to Camp Butner
        reservation, §122C-410(b).
Cisterns and rain barrels.
Limitations on regulating, §153A-145.

COUNTY ORDINANCES —Cont'd
Civil penalty, §153A-123(c).
Violation of fire prevention code, §153A-123(c1).
Code of ordinances, §153A-49.
Construction.
Board construction, §153A-4.
Dogs.
Control of dangerous dogs.
Article not to prevent, §67-4.5.
**Effect of prior laws and actions taken
        pursuant to prior laws,** §153A-2.
Enforcement, §153A-123.
Abatement, §153A-123(e).
Generally, §153A-123(a).
Injunctions, §153A-123(d).
Remedies, §153A-123(f).
**Enumeration of powers not a limit on general
        authority to adopt,** §153A-124.
Franchises, §153A-46.
Garbage and trash.
Regulation, §§153A-132.1, 153A-136.
**Gathering, picketing or protesting on roads or
        highways.**
Local ordinance regulating time, place and
        manner.
Authorization, §20-174.2(a), (b).
General ordinance-making power, §153A-121(a).
Limitations, §153A-121(b), (c).
Health services.
Ambulances, §153A-250.
Appropriations, §153A-248(b).
Improvements.
Submission of statement concerning
        improvements, §153A-325.
Jurisdiction.
Territorial jurisdiction of county ordinances,
        §153A-122.
Misdemeanors.
Violations of local ordinances, §153A-123(b).
Mobile home and trailer parks.
Registration, §153A-138.
Motor vehicles.
Parking regulations, §153A-170.
Regulation of traffic at parking areas and
        driveways, §153A-139.
Mountain ridge protection, §153A-448.
Noise regulation, §153A-133.
Parking, §153A-170.
Planning and zoning.
Adoption.
Procedure, §153A-323.
Agency establishment, §153A-321.
Amendment.
Procedure, §153A-323.
Enforcement, §153A-324.
Additional enforcement provisions,
        §153A-324(a).
Illegally collected fee, tax or contribution,
        return with interest, §153A-324(b).
Repeal.
Procedure, §153A-323.
Unified ordinance, §153A-322(d).
Zoning ordinance.
Amendments, §153A-344(a).
Consent of landowner in certain cases,
        §153A-344(b).
Board of adjustment, §153A-345(c).
Certificate to boards of commissioners,
        §153A-344(a).
Preparation, §153A-344(a).

COUNTY ORDINANCES —Cont'd
Pleading and proving county ordinances,
   §153A-50.
   See COUNTY ORDINANCES.
Solar collectors.
   Limitations on regulation, §153A-144.
     Costs and attorneys' fees, courts may award,
       §153A-144(c).
     Prohibition or effective prohibition not allowed,
       §153A-144(a).
     Screening may be required, §153A-144(b).
Subdivisions.
   Contents, §153A-331.
     Procedure for plat approval, §153A-332.
   Plat approval, §153A-332.
Technical ordinances.
   Adoption, §153A-47.
Violations.
   Injunctions, §153A-123(d).
   Misdemeanors, §153A-123.
   Separate and distinct offenses, §153A-123(g).

COUNTY PERSONNEL SYSTEM, §§153A-92 to
   153A-99.
Application to local employees, §126-1.
Boards, §153A-95.
Compensation.
   Governing body to set, §153A-92(a).
   County manager system, §153A-92(c).
   Insurance coverage as part of compensation,
     §153A-92(d).
   Limitations, §153A-92(b).
Defense of employees, §§153A-97, 160A-167.
Deferred compensation plan, §153A-93(e).
Hours and days of work, §153A-94(b).
Interchange of governmental employees,
   §§126-51 to 126-58.
Local personnel system.
   Approval, §126-11(a).
   Establishment, §126-11(a).
   Maintenance, §126-11(a).
   Mental health authorities.
     Determination of whether system meets
       requirements, §126-11(b1).
     Establishment and maintenance, §126-11(a1).
   Monitoring, §126-11(c).
   Petitions regarding meeting of requirements,
     §126-11(b).
   Rules and regulations, §126-11(d).
Office of state personnel.
   Services and facilities available to local
     subdivisions of state, §126-10.
Personnel records.
   Allowing unauthorized access, §153A-98(e).
   Confidential records, §153A-98(c), (c1).
     Disclosure of certain information to retirement
       organizations, §153A-98(c3).
     Use for research, etc., §153A-98(c2).
   Inspection and disclosure, §153A-98(a).
   Maintenance and availability of information,
     determination, §153A-98(b2).
   Objection of employee to items in file,
     §153A-98(d).
   Open records, §153A-98(b).
   Salary defined, §153A-98(b1).
   Unauthorized access, §153A-98(f).
Political activity.
   Conflicts with local regulations or ordinances,
     §153A-99(f).
   Definitions, §153A-99(b).
   Prohibitions, §153A-99(c) to (e).

COUNTY PERSONNEL SYSTEM —Cont'd
Political activity —Cont'd
   Purpose, §153A-99(a).
Retirement benefits.
   Certification by actuary, §153A-93(b).
     Definition of certified actuary, §153A-93(c).
   Deferred compensation plan, §153A-93(e).
   Governing body may provide for, §153A-93(a).
   Health insurance, §153A-93(d) to (d2).
Rules.
   Governing body may provide for, §153A-94(a).
   Hours and days of work, §153A-94(b).
Rules adopted by local governing body.
   Employees of county may be made subject to
     rules, §126-9(a) to (d).
Social security act.
   Participation, §153A-96.

COUNTY PLANNING AND ZONING, §§153A-320
   to 153A-326, 153A-340 to 153A-349.
Agency, §153A-344(a).
   Established, §153A-321.
Amateur radio antennas.
   Reasonable accommodation, §153A-341.2.
Appeals.
   Board of adjustment, §153A-345(b).
   Certiorari, appeals to superior court.
     Entities, definitions, §153A-349(b).
     Governing provisions, §153A-349(a).
     Impermissible conflict, §153A-349(c).
   Defense of invalidity of ordinance, raising,
     §153A-348(c).
Applicability of provisions, §153A-347.
Appropriations.
   Supplemental powers, §153A-322(c).
Board of adjustment.
   Appeals, §153A-345(b).
   Appointment, §153A-345(a).
   Chairman, §153A-345(f).
   Compensation, §153A-345(a).
   Conflicts of interest, §§153A-340(g), 153A-345(e1).
   Hearings, §153A-345(b).
   Modification of regulations, §153A-345(d).
   Planning agency.
     Designation to perform duties of board of
       adjustment, §153A-345(a).
   Review of decisions, §153A-345(e2).
   Subpoena power, §153A-345(g2).
   Votes, §153A-345(e).
   Zoning ordinance, §153A-345(c).
Boards of commissioners.
   Method of procedure, §153A-343.
   Voting on matter having financial impact on
     member, §153A-340(g).
Buildings.
   Applicability of provisions, §153A-347.
   Setback lines, §153A-326.
Certiorari to superior court.
   Entities, definitions, §153A-349(b).
   Governing provisions, §153A-349(a).
   Impermissible conflict, §153A-349(c).
Challenging validity of ordinance.
   Statute of limitation, §153A-348(b).
Changes caused by adoption or amendment of
   ordinance.
   Notice, §153A-323(b).
Conditional use.
   Validity, statute of limitation, §153A-348(a).
Conflict of laws, §153A-346.
Contracts.
   Supplemental powers, §153A-322(b).

COUNTY PLANNING AND ZONING —Cont'd
Defense of invalidity of ordinance.
Raising, §153A-348(c).
Districts.
Designation, §153A-342(a) to (d).
Energy consumption.
Land-use development incentives to reduce,
§160A-383.4(a).
Enforcement.
Ordinances, §153A-324.
Additional enforcement provisions,
§153A-324(a).
Illegally collected fee, tax or contribution,
return with interest, §153A-324(b).
Enforcement of ordinance.
Defense of invalidity, raising, §153A-348(c).
Farm purposes.
Regulations affecting property used for,
§153A-340(b), (j).
Federal aid.
Power to accept, receive and disburse,
§153A-322(a).
Hearings.
Board of adjustment, §153A-345(b).
Jurisdiction.
Territorial jurisdiction, §153A-320.
Zoning less than entire jurisdiction, §153A-342(d).
Limitation of actions, §§1-54, 153A-348.
Validity of ordinance or amendment contested,
§1-54.1.
Lot sizes.
Ordinances prohibiting, restrictions, §153A-340(j).
Manufactured homes.
Zoning regulations for, §153A-341.1.
Method of procedure, §153A-343(a).
Exceptions, §153A-343(b), (d).
Military bases.
Change of permitted uses near.
Adoption or modification of ordinance resulting
in.
Notice, §153A-323(b).
Moratoria on development, §153A-340(h).
Notice.
Actual notice of proposed amendment and public
hearing, §153A-343(b1).
Changes.
Adoption or amendment of ordinance resulting
in, §153A-323(b).
Mail notice of public hearing, §153A-343(a).
Exceptions to requirement, §153A-343(b).
Public hearing.
Adoption, amendment or repeal of ordinance,
§153A-323(a).
Ordinances.
Adoption.
Procedure, §153A-323(a), (b).
Agency establishment, §153A-321.
Amendment.
Procedure, §153A-323(a), (b).
Challenging validity.
Statute of limitation, §153A-348(b).
Enforcement, §153A-324.
Additional enforcement provisions,
§153A-324(a).
Defense of invalidity, raising, §153A-348(c).
Illegally collected fee, tax or contribution,
return with interest, §153A-324(b).
Repeal.
Procedure, §153A-323(a), (b).
Unified ordinance, §153A-322(d).

COUNTY PLANNING AND ZONING —Cont'd
Ordinances —Cont'd
Zoning ordinance.
Amendments, §153A-344(a).
Consent of landowner in certain cases,
§153A-344(b).
Board of adjustment, §153A-345(c).
Certification to boards of commissioners,
§153A-344(a).
Preparation, §153A-344(a).
Powers and duties.
Grant of power, §153A-340(a) to (e).
Supplemental powers, §153A-322.
Publication.
Notice of public hearing.
Adoption, amendment or repeal of ordinance,
§153A-323(a).
Public hearing.
Adoption, amendment or repeal of ordinance,
§153A-323(a).
Purposes in view, §153A-341.
Regional planning commissions, §§153A-391 to
153A-398.
See REGIONAL PLANNING COMMISSIONS.
Rezoning request.
Validity, statute of limitation, §153A-348(a).
Rules and regulations.
Conflict of laws, §153A-346.
Enforcement.
Boards of commissioners to determine method
of procedure, §153A-343(a).
Purposes in view, §153A-341.
Single-family detached residential uses.
Ordinances prohibiting, restrictions, §153A-340(j).
Special use permits, §153A-340(c1).
Validity, statute of limitation, §153A-348(a).
Statute of limitations, §§1-54, 153A-348.
Subdivisions, §§153A-330 to 153A-336.
Supplemental powers, §153A-322.
**Sustainable design principles, policies to
encourage,** §153A-340(i).
**Swine farms served by animal waste
management systems.**
Regulations affecting, §153A-340(b).
Temporary moratoria on development,
§153A-340(h).
Validity of ordinance.
Challenging, statute of limitation, §153A-348(b).
Defense of invalidity, raising, §153A-348(c).
Varying application of regulation, §153A-340(c).
Vesting rights, §153A-344.1.
Declaration of legislature, §153A-344.1(a).
Definitions, §153A-344.1(b).
Duration of vested right, §153A-344.1(d).
Establishment of vested right, §153A-344.1(c).
County's failure to adopt ordinance.
How established, §153A-344.1(f).
Judicial determination, §153A-344.1(f).
Subsequent changes.
When permitted, §153A-344.1(e).
Vested right not a personal right,
§153A-344.1(f).
Subsequent changes.
When permitted, §153A-344.1(e).
Termination of vested right, §153A-344.1(d).
Water and sewer authorities.
Rates, fees, charges relating to construction of
development.
Imposition or increase, notice, §162A-9(a1) to
(a4).

COUNTY PLANNING AND ZONING —Cont'd
Zoning map changes.
Adoption or modification of ordinance resulting in.
Notice, §153A-323(b).
Validity, statute of limitation, §153A-348(a).

**COUNTY RESEARCH AND PRODUCTION
SERVICE DISTRICTS,** §§153A-311 to
153A-317.
Abolition, §153A-316.
Advisory committee.
Board of directors for industrial park corporate
owner serving as, §153A-313(b).
General provisions, §153A-313(a).
Establishment.
Effective date of resolution, §153A-312(e).
Hearing, §153A-312(d).
Multi-county districts, §153A-312(b).
Purposes, §153A-311.
Report, §153A-312(c).
Standards, §153A-312(a).
Multi-county districts, §153A-312(b).
Extension.
Effective date of resolution, §153A-314(d).
Hearing, §153A-314(c).
Notice.
Hearing, §153A-314(c).
Provision or maintenance of services.
Requirements for extended district,
§153A-315(b).
Report.
Required prior to hearing, §153A-314(b).
Standards, §153A-314(a).
Hearings.
Abolition of districts, §153A-316.
Establishment, §153A-312(d).
Extension, §153A-314(c).
Removal of territory.
Public hearing, §153A-314.1(c).
Multi-county districts.
Abolition, §153A-316.
Establishment, §153A-312(b).
Notice.
Abolition of districts.
Hearing, §153A-316.
Establishment.
Hearing, §153A-312(d).
Extension.
Hearing, §153A-314(c).
Removal of territory.
Public hearing, §153A-314.1(c).
Provision or maintenance of services.
Extended district, §153A-315(b).
New district, §153A-315(a).
Purposes, §153A-311.
Removal of territory.
Annexation, general law.
Applicability to removed territory,
§153A-314.1(d).
Effective date of resolution removing territory,
§153A-314.1(e).
Findings required, §153A-314.1(a).
Notice of public hearing, §153A-314.1(c).
Public hearing before adopting resolution,
§153A-314.1(c).
Report prior to public hearing, §153A-314.1(b).
Resolution of board of commissioners,
§153A-314.1(a).
Reports.
Establishment.
Required before public hearing, §153A-312(c).

**COUNTY RESEARCH AND PRODUCTION
SERVICE DISTRICTS** —Cont'd
Reports —Cont'd
Extension.
Required before hearing, §153A-314(b).
Standards, §153A-312(a).
Extension, §153A-314(a).
Multi-county districts, §153A-312(b).
Taxation.
Authorized taxes, §153A-317(a).
Public transportation funding, levy for,
§153A-317(c).
Rate limitation, §153A-317(b).

COUNTY SCHOOL ADMINISTRATIVE UNITS.
Administrative units generally.
See SCHOOL DISTRICTS AND
ADMINISTRATIVE UNITS.

COUNTY SERVICE DISTRICTS, §§153A-300 to
153A-310.
Abolition, §153A-306.
Research and production service districts,
§153A-316.
Ambulance and rescue.
Establishing district to provide, §153A-301(a).
Property tax reduction in district, §153A-310(a),
(b).
Annexation.
Authority, findings required, §153A-303(a).
By petition of owners, §153A-303(b).
Effective date of resolution, §153A-303(f).
Fire protection district.
Chapter 69 district annexing, §153A-304.2(a),
(b).
Municipality annexing all or part of district,
§153A-304.1(a) to (d).
Hearing on resolution, §153A-303(e).
Law enforcement district.
Tax reduction and refund.
Annexation of portion of district by
municipality, §153A-304.4.
Notice of hearing, §153A-303(e).
Report, §153A-303(d).
Required provision or maintenance of services,
§153A-305(b).
Sanitary districts within city limits, §153A-303(c).
Aquatic weed control, §153A-301(e).
Beach erosion control.
Establishing district to provide, §153A-301(a).
Bonds authorized, §153A-308.
Boundaries.
Extending by annexation, §153A-303.
Boundary changes between adjoining districts.
Effective date of resolution, §153A-304.3(d).
Generally, §153A-304.3(a).
Notice and hearing, §153A-304.3(c).
Report, §153A-304.3(b).
Cemeteries.
Establishing district to provide, §153A-301(a).
Coastal area counties.
Junk automobile removal and street maintenance.
Establishing districts for removal, §153A-301(b),
(c).
Considerations in establishing, §153A-302(a).
Consolidation.
Authority, findings required, §153A-304(a).
Effective date, §153A-304(d).
Hearing on resolution, §153A-304(c).
Notice of hearing on resolution, §153A-304(c).
Report, §153A-304(b).

COUNTY SERVICE DISTRICTS —Cont'd
Consolidation —Cont'd
Required provision or maintenance of services,
§153A-305(c).
County containing protected mountain ridge.
Maintenance of public roads, §153A-301(d).
County service district act of 1973.
Article cited as, §153A-300.
Economic development and training districts,
§§153A-317.11 to 153A-317.17.
See ECONOMIC DEVELOPMENT AND
TRAINING DISTRICTS.
Effective date of resolution establishing,
§153A-302(d).
EMS in fire protection districts, §153A-309(a),
(b).
Establishment.
Research and production service districts,
§§153A-311, 153A-312.
Extending boundaries.
Annexation, §153A-303.
Extension.
Research and production service districts,
§153A-314.
Findings for establishing, §153A-302(a1).
Exceptions, §153A-302(f).
Fire protection.
Annexation by chapter 69 district, §153A-304.2(a),
(b).
Annexation of all or part of district by
municipality, §153A-304.1(a).
Fire protection tax, levy by commissioners,
§153A-304.1(a) to (d).
EMS in fire protection districts, §153A-309(a), (b).
Establishing district to provide, §153A-301(a).
Industrial property.
Removal from district and creation of new
district for, §153A-309.3(a).
Abolition of district, §153A-309.3(d).
Effective date of resolution, §153A-309.3(e).
Notice and hearing, §153A-309.3(b).
Rate limitation on property taxes,
§153A-309.3(c).
Property tax rate reduction, §153A-309.2(a), (b).
Hearings.
Abolition, §153A-306.
Annexation of territory, §153A-303(e).
Before adopting resolution, §153A-302(c).
Consolidation, §153A-304(c).
Junked automobile removal.
Coastal area counties.
Establishing districts for, §153A-301(b), (c).
Law enforcement.
Annexation of portion of district by municipality.
Tax reduction and refund, §153A-304.4.
Establishing district to provide, requirement,
§153A-301(a).
Requirements not applicable to countywide
district, §153A-302(e).
Notice.
Abolition.
Public hearing, §153A-306.
Annexation of territory.
Public hearing, §153A-303(e).
Boundary changes between adjoining districts.
Hearing on, §153A-304.3(c).
Consolidation.
Hearing on resolution, §153A-304(c).
Fire protection.
Industrial property.
Removal from district and creation of new
district for, hearing on, §153A-309.3(b).

COUNTY SERVICE DISTRICTS —Cont'd
Notice —Cont'd
Public hearing before adopting resolution,
§153A-302(c).
Exceptions, §153A-302(f).
Property taxes.
Authorized, rate, §153A-307.
Ambulance and rescue district, rate reduction,
§153A-310(a), (b).
Fire protection districts, rate reduction,
§153A-309.2(a), (b).
Fire protection district.
Annexation by chapter 69 district.
Fire protection tax, commissioners levying
and collecting, §153A-304.2(a), (b).
Annexation of all or part of district by
municipality.
Fire protection tax, levy by commissioners,
§153A-304.1(a) to (d).
Publication.
Annexation of territory.
Notice of public hearing, §153A-303(e).
Consolidation.
Notice of public hearing, §153A-304(c).
Notice of public hearing before adopting
resolution, §153A-302(c).
Exceptions, §153A-302(f).
Purposes, §153A-301.
Research and production service districts,
§153A-311.
Recreation.
Establishing district to provide, §153A-301(a).
Removal of territory.
Research and production districts, §153A-314.1.
**Report of boundary changes between
adjoining districts,** §153A-304.3(b).
Report on establishing, §153A-302(b).
**Required provision or maintenance of
services.**
Consolidated district, §153A-305(c).
Extended district, §153A-305(b).
New districts, §153A-305(a).
Research and production districts, §§153A-311
to 153A-317.
Sanitary districts within city limits.
Annexation, §153A-303(c).
Sewage collection and disposal.
Establishing district to provide, §153A-301(a).
Solid waste collection.
Establishing district to provide, §153A-301(a).
Standards.
Considerations in establishing, §153A-302(a).
Street maintenance.
Coastal area counties.
Establishing districts for, §153A-301(b), (c).
Taxation.
Fire protection district.
Annexation by chapter 69 district.
Fire protection tax, commissioners levying
and collecting, §153A-304.2(a), (b).
Annexation of all or part of district by
municipality.
Fire protection tax, levy by commissioners,
§153A-304.1(a) to (d).
Law enforcement districts.
Annexation of portion of district by
municipality.
Tax reduction and refund, §153A-304.4.
Property taxes authorized, rate, §153A-307.
Ambulance and rescue district, rate reduction,
§153A-310(a), (b).

COUNTY SERVICE DISTRICTS —Cont'd
Taxation —Cont'd
  Property taxes authorized, rate —Cont'd
    Fire protection districts, rate reduction,
      §153A-309.2(a), (b).
  Research and production service districts,
    §153A-317.
Water supply and water distribution.
  Establishing district to provide, §153A-301(a).

COUNTY STREETS AND HIGHWAYS.
Abandonment or change in secondary road.
  Request by board of county commissioners,
    §136-63(a).
Adopt-a-highway program, §136-140.1.
Appropriation to municipalities, §136-41.1(a).
  Allocation of funds, §136-41.1(a) to (c).
  Contracts for maintenance, etc., of streets,
    §136-41.3.
  Eligible municipalities, §§136-41.1(b), 136-41.2(a)
    to (c).
    Incorporated before January 1, 1945,
      §136-41.2A(a), (b).
    Incorporated since January 1, 1945,
      §136-41.2(d).
  Excess accumulation of funds, §136-41.3.
  Nature of funds distributed, §136-41.1(d).
  Records and annual statement, §136-41.3.
  Use of funds, §136-41.3.
Assigning street numbers in unincorporated
  areas, §153A-239.1(a).
Bond issues.
  Prohibition of local road bonds, §136-98(b).
Closing public roads or easements, §153A-241.
Coastal area counties.
  Service districts.
    Street maintenance provided, §153A-301(b), (c).
Construction of roads by local authorities,
  §136-98(b).
  Under agreement with department of
    transportation, §136-98(c).
Controlled-access facilities.
  Authority of local units to consent, §136-89.54.
Coordinated street system.
  Development of system, §136-66.2.
County containing protected mountain ridge.
  Service districts.
    Maintenance of public roads, §153A-301(d).
Filing complaints with department of
  transportation, §136-64.
Fishing from bridges.
  Regulation or prohibition, §153A-242.
Golf carts.
  Regulation of use on streets, roads and highways,
    §153A-245.
Improvements to state highway system.
  County participation, §136-66.3.
Incorporation of county roads into state
  highway system, §§136-51 to 136-64.1.
  See HIGHWAYS, ROADS AND STREETS.
Municipal street system.
  Responsibility for streets inside municipalities,
    §136-66.1.
Naming roads and assigning street numbers in
  unincorporated areas, §153A-239.1(a).
Public road.
  Defined, §153A-238(a).
Responsibility for streets inside
  municipalities, §136-66.1.
Responsibility of counties for upkeep, etc.,
  terminated, §136-97(a).

COUNTY STREETS AND HIGHWAYS —Cont'd
Rights of way.
  Dedication of rights of way under local
    ordinances, §§136-66.10, 136-66.11.
Road equipment.
  Department of transportation.
    Authority to furnish, §136-34.
Rules and regulations.
  Authority of municipalities, §136-66.4.
Secondary road construction programs by
  department of transportation.
  Adoption of annual construction program for each
    county.
    Board of transportation, §136-44.8(e).
    Department of transportation to follow,
      §136-44.8(f).
  Map showing tentative road paving projects.
    Posting in county courthouse, §136-44.8(a).
  Notice of public meeting of board of county
    commissioners.
    Deviations or priority of paving projects,
      §136-44.8(d).
    Presentation by department of annual program
      for county, §136-44.8(b).
  Public meeting on annual construction program
    for county, §136-44.8(c).
    Notice, §136-44.8(b).
  Public meeting on deviations or priority of paving
    projects, §136-44.8(d).
  Review of changes to which commissioners do not
    consent.
    Petition by board, §136-44.8(f).
Service districts for road maintenance.
  Section not to prohibit, §136-98(b).
Special assessments, §§153A-185 to 153A-210.7.
  See SPECIAL ASSESSMENTS BY COUNTIES.
State highway system.
  Maintenance of system by municipalities,
    §136-66.1.
  Responsibility for streets inside municipalities,
    §136-66.1.
Taxation.
  Prohibition of local road taxes, §136-98(b).

COUNTY SUBDIVISIONS, §§153A-330 to
  153A-336.
Appeal of decisions regarding plats.
  Administrative or ministerial decisions,
    §153A-336(b).
  Quasi-judicial decisions, §153A-336(a), (c).
Classes of subdivisions.
  Expedited review for, §153A-335(b).
Definitions, §153A-335(a).
Funds to be provided by developer.
  Ordinance provisions authorized, §153A-331(c).
Injunctions.
  Penalties for transferring lots in unapproved
    subdivisions, §153A-334(a).
Ordinances.
  Contents, §153A-331.
    Procedure for plat approval, §153A-332.
  Plat approval, §153A-332.
Plats.
  Appeal of decisions regarding, §153A-336.
  Ordinance provisions authorized, §153A-331(b).
Public utilities.
  Ordinance may provide for, §153A-331(a).
Regulations, §153A-330.
  Plats.
    Approval, §153A-332.
      Effect on dedication, §153A-333.

COUNTY SUBDIVISIONS —Cont'd
Regulations —Cont'd
Plats —Cont'd
Effect of plat approval on dedications, §153A-333.
Ordinance to contain procedure for plat approval, §153A-332.
Recommendations by certain agencies, §153A-332.
Recordation, §153A-332.
Statement by owner, §153A-332.
Transfer of lots in unapproved subdivisions.
Penalties, §153A-334(a).
Exceptions, §153A-334(b), (c).

COUNTY SURVEYORS.
Appointment of county surveyor, §153A-441.
Bonds, surety generally, §§58-72-1 to 58-72-70.
See OFFICIAL BONDS OF COUNTY OFFICERS.
Coordinate system.
Assistance.
Board of county commissioners to apply for assistance, §102-16.
County projects eligible for assistance, §102-17.
Duties, failure to discharge, §14-230.
Employees of counties generally.
See COUNTY OFFICERS AND EMPLOYEES.
Fees.
Statement rendered by county officers compensated from fees, §128-13.
Penalty for failure to file statement, §128-13.
Oaths.
Administration of oaths.
When county surveyors may administer, §11-10.
Form of oath, §11-11.
Penalties.
Statement rendered by county officers compensated from fees.
Failure to file statement, §128-13.
Salaries.
Statement rendered by county officers compensated from fees, §128-13.
Penalty for failure to file statement, §128-13.

COUNTY TAXES.
Agricultural societies and fairs.
Exhibits exempt, §106-507.
Alcoholic beverages.
Excise tax on beer, wine and liquor.
Distribution of part of taxes, §105-113.82.
License tax.
Beer and wine retail licenses, §105-113.78.
Appraisals.
Reserve for octennial reappraisal, §153A-150.
Board of equalization and review, §105-322.
Collection of taxes.
Remedies for collecting taxes other than property taxes, §153A-147.
Community development, §153A-376(e).
Continuing taxes, §153A-148.
Disclosure of certain information prohibited, §153A-148.1(a).
Penalties, §153A-148.1(b).
Economic development and training districts.
Property taxes.
County may levy within district, rate limitation, §153A-317.17.
Exemptions from tax, NC Const Art V §2.
Food tax.
Local tax administered by secretary, §105-164.13B(d).

COUNTY TAXES —Cont'd
Gross receipts tax on short-term vehicle leases or rentals, §153A-156(a).
Collection of tax, §153A-156(c), (d).
Definitions, §153A-156(e).
Penalties and remedies, §153A-156(f).
Provision noting in agreement, §153A-156(b).
Heavy equipment gross receipts tax in lieu of property tax.
Definitions, §153A-156.1(a).
Effective date, §153A-156.1(e).
Enforcement, §153A-156.1(d).
Imposition of tax, §153A-156.1(b).
Payment, §153A-156.1(c).
Repeal of tax by county, §153A-156.1(f).
Highways, roads and streets.
Prohibition of local road taxes, §136-98(b).
Income tax.
Levy prohibited, §105-247.
Inheritance tax.
Levy prohibited, §105-247.
Liability upon governing bodies of local units for failure to levy taxes.
Repeal of laws imposing, §105-270.
Licenses.
Privilege license taxes, §153A-152.
Low-level radioactive and hazardous waste facilities, §153A-152.1(a) to (c).
Loan agencies, check cashing businesses and pawnbrokers.
Privilege tax.
Levy by counties authorized, §105-88(e).
Low-level radioactive and hazardous waste facilities.
Privilege license taxes, §153A-152.1(a) to (c).
Meals taxes.
Penalties, §153A-154.1(a).
Scope of uniformity requirement, §153A-154.1(b).
Motor vehicles.
Gross receipts tax on short-term vehicle leases or rentals, §153A-156.
Powers and duties.
Continuing taxes, §153A-48.
General power to impose taxes, §153A-146.
Remedies for collecting taxes other than property taxes, §153A-147.
Privilege license taxes, §153A-152(a).
Animal taxes, §153A-153.
Low-level radioactive and hazardous waste facilities, §153A-152.1(a) to (c).
Telecommunications restriction, §153A-152(b).
Property taxes.
Generally.
See PROPERTY TAXES.
Rates.
Property taxes.
Increase, §153A-149(e).
Reappraisals.
Reserve for octennial reappraisals, §153A-150.
Remedies.
Collection of taxes other than property taxes, §153A-147.
Research and production service districts.
Authorized taxes, §153A-317(a).
Public transportation funding, levy for, §153A-317(c).
Rate limitation, §153A-317(b).
Room occupancy tax, uniform provisions for counties authorized to levy.
Administered by taxing county, §153A-155(d).

COUNTY TAXES —Cont'd
Room occupancy tax, uniform provisions for counties authorized to levy —Cont'd
Charge for furnishing taxable accommodation, part of charge, §153A-155(c).
Civil and criminal penalties.
  Failure to file return or pay, §153A-155(e).
Collection of tax by operator of business, §153A-155(c).
Counties authorized to levy, applicability, §153A-155(a), (g).
Disclosure of records, §153A-155(d).
Discount allowed operator for collecting, §153A-155(c).
Effective date, §153A-155(b).
Levied only by resolution, §153A-155(b).
Liability for tax attaching before repeal not affected, §153A-155(f).
Passed on to purchaser, §153A-155(c).
Public notice and public hearing on levy, §153A-155(b).
Repeal or reduction by resolution, §153A-155(f).
Return, §153A-155(d).
Stated and charged separately, §153A-155(c).
Waiver of penalties, §153A-155(e).
When due and payable, §153A-155(d).
Sales and use tax, §153A-151.
Local food tax.
  Administered by secretary, §105-164.13B(d).
Service districts.
Research and production service districts, §153A-317.
Short-term vehicle leases or rentals.
Gross receipts tax on, §153A-156.
Special assessments, §§153A-185 to 153A-210.7.
  See SPECIAL ASSESSMENTS BY COUNTIES.
Special tax areas, NC Const Art V §2.
Vehicle registration tax, §105-570.

COUNTY TREASURERS.
Bonds, surety generally, §§58-72-1 to 58-72-70.
  See OFFICIAL BONDS OF COUNTY OFFICERS.
Finance officer.
Fiscal control, §§159-24 to 159-38.
  See LOCAL GOVERNMENT FINANCE.
Local government finance.
General provisions, §§159-1 to 159-188.
  See LOCAL GOVERNMENT FINANCE.
Oaths.
Form of oath, §11-11.
Officers of counties generally.
See COUNTY OFFICERS AND EMPLOYEES.
Reports.
Misconduct in public office.
  Swearing falsely to official reports, §14-232.

COUNTY VEHICLE REGISTRATION TAX.
Distribution and retention of proceeds, §105-570(c).
Interlocal agreements, §105-570(f).
Operation of transit system as requirement, §105-570(b), (e).
Regional transit authority, status of county, §105-570(a).
Supplemental nature of article, §105-570(g).
Use of proceeds, §105-570(d).

COUNTY WATER AND SEWER DISTRICTS, §§162A-86 to 162A-94.
Abolition, §162A-87.2.
Contracts for conveyance of land to city, §162A-87.2(b).

COUNTY WATER AND SEWER DISTRICTS —Cont'd
Abolition —Cont'd
Conveyance of land to a private person, §162A-87.2(c).
Effective date of resolution, §162A-87.2(d).
Public hearing, §162A-87.2(a).
Assessments.
Special assessments authorized, §162A-92.
Assumption of indebtedness of district, §162A-101.
Board of county commissioners.
Creation of district, §§162A-86, 162A-87.
Defined, §162A-86(a1).
Governing body of district, §162A-89(a).
Bond issues.
Authorized, §162A-90.
Boundaries, initial.
Exclusion of areas, §162A-87.1A(a).
Interpretation and construction, §162A-87.1A(c).
Noncontiguous portions, §162A-87.1A(b).
Consolidated city-county governing board.
Governing body of district, §162A-89(b).
Contracts.
Contracts with private entities, §162A-88.1.
Validation of certain contracts, §162A-94.
Creation.
Authorized, §162A-86(a).
Hearings, §162A-86(b), (c).
  Notice, §162A-86(b).
  Public hearing, §162A-86(b1).
Resolution.
  Findings required, §162A-87(a).
  Publication, §162A-87(b).
Defined, §162A-86(a1).
Eminent domain.
Power of district, §162A-89.1.
Extension.
Annexation by petition, §162A-87.1(b).
Annexation of property within city or sanitary district, §162A-87.1(c).
Effective date of resolution, §162A-87.1(f).
Hearing, §162A-87.1(e).
Notice.
  Hearing, §162A-87.1(e).
  Report, §162A-87.1(d).
Standards, §162A-87.1(a).
Hearings.
Creation of district, §162A-86(b), (c).
  Notice, §162A-86(b).
  Public hearings, §162A-86(b1).
Extension of districts, §162A-87.1(e).
Limitation of actions.
Creation of district.
  Action to set aside resolution, §162A-87(b).
Municipalities.
Area annexed by city, §162A-93(c), (d).
Duplicating water or sewer services provided by district, §162A-93(a), (b).
Notice.
Creation of district.
  Hearing, §162A-86(b).
  Resolution, §162A-87(b).
Extension of district.
  Hearing, §162A-87.1(e).
Petitions.
Extension of districts.
  Annexation by petition, §162A-87.1(b).
Public hearings.
Creation of district, §162A-86(b1).

COUNTY WATER AND SEWER DISTRICTS
—Cont'd
Reports.
Extension of districts, §162A-87.1(d).
Services outside district.
Authorized, §162A-87.3(a).
Corporate limits of city or sanitary district.
Limitations, §162A-87.3(c).
Customers lying within another county.
Limitations, §162A-87.3(d).
Rates and charges.
Different schedule, §162A-87.3(b).
State-owned property.
Transfer from one district to another,
§162A-87.1B.
Status, §162A-88.
Taxation.
Powers of district, §162A-91.
Tax anticipation notes.
Authorized, §162A-90.
Validation of certain contracts, §162A-94.

COUNTYWIDE BASE MAPS.
Financial assistance, §102-17.
Improvement of county land records program,
§102-15.

COUNTYWIDE FARMLAND PROTECTION
PLAN, §106-744(e), (f).

COURIERS.
Private protective services generally, §§74C-1
to 74C-30.
See PRIVATE PROTECTIVE SERVICES.

COURSE OF DEALING.
Commercial code general provisions.
Defined, §25-1-303(b).
Express terms of an agreement, §25-1-303(e).
Vocation or trade of parties, §25-1-303(d).
Leases, UCC.
Explaining or supplementing terms,
§25-2A-202(a).
Implied warranties may arise from, §25-2A-212(3).
Sale of goods, UCC.
Implied warranties, §25-2-314(3).
Exclusion or modification, §25-2-316(3).
Used to explain terms of contracts, §25-2-202.

COURSE OF PERFORMANCE.
Commercial code general provisions.
Defined, §25-1-303(a).
Evidence relevant to show waiver or modification
term inconsistent with, §25-1-303(e).
Express terms of an agreement, §25-1-303(e).
Vocation or trade of parties, §25-1-303(d).
Leases, UCC.
Explaining or supplementing terms,
§25-2A-202(a).
Sale of goods, UCC.
Used to explain terms of contract, §25-2-202.

COURT-APPOINTED COUNSEL.
Abused, neglected or dependent juvenile
actions, §§7B-602, 7B-603.
Delinquent and undisciplined juvenile actions,
§§7B-1906(c), 7B-2000, 7B-2002.
Fees for preparation of copies.
Not chargeable to attorney appointed to represent
indigent at state expense, §7A-308(b1).
Indigent defense services.
General provisions, §§7A-450 to 7A-458.
Indigent defense services act, §§7A-498 to
7A-498.8.
See INDIGENT DEFENSE SERVICES.

COURT-APPOINTED COUNSEL —Cont'd
Indigent defense services —Cont'd
Indigent services rules, IDS Rules 1.1 to 3.7.
See INDIGENT DEFENSE SERVICES.
Interstate compact on juvenile.
Return of escapees or absconders, §7B-2805(c).
Mental health, developmental disability,
substance abuse.
Involuntary commitment.
Substance abuser's commitment hearing,
§122C-286(d).
Termination of parental rights proceeding,
§7B-1109(b).
Parent's right to counsel and appointment of
counsel, §7B-1101.1(a).

COURT COSTS.
See COSTS.

COURTHOUSES.
Acquisition of land by US to be added to
military bases, §104-7.

COURT INFORMATION TECHNOLOGY FUND.
Establishment, §7A-343.2(a).
Reports, §7A-343.2(c).
Revenues, §7A-343.2(a).
Use of funds, §7A-343.2(b).

COURT OF APPEALS, §§7A-16 to 7A-21.
Administration department.
Providing adequate quarters for court, §7A-19(b).
Administrative agency decisions.
Appeal of right from certain administrative
agencies, §7A-29(a).
Appeals of right from superior courts.
Final judgments of superior court upon review
of decision, §7A-27(b).
Appeal of right from court of appeals, §7A-30.
Appeals generally.
See APPEALS.
Arrest.
Warrant for arrest.
Judges may issue, §15A-304(f).
Audits.
Clerk of court.
Financial accounts of clerk audited, §7A-20(b).
Bonds, surety.
Clerk of court, §7A-20(a).
Certification of cause for discretionary review
by supreme court, §7A-31, AppProc 15.
Certiorari.
Issuance of remedial writs.
Power of court of appeals to issue, §7A-32(b).
Review of court judgments and orders.
Scope of review, AppProc Rule 21(a).
Chief judge.
Compensation of judges, §7A-18(a).
Longevity pay, §7A-18(b).
Designation, §7A-16.
Disability of chief judge, §7A-16.
Expenses.
Reimbursement for travel and subsistence
expenses, §7A-18(a), (a1).
Oath of office, §7A-16.
Panels.
Assignment of members to panels, §7A-16.
Sessions.
Scheduling sessions, §7A-19(c).
Clerk of court.
Appointment of clerk, §7A-20(a).
Assistants to clerk, §7A-20(a).
Audit of financial accounts, §7A-20(b).

COURT OF APPEALS —Cont'd
Clerk of court —Cont'd
Bond required, §7A-20(a).
Fee bill for services, §7A-20(b).
Oath of office, §7A-20(a).
Salary of clerk, §7A-20(a).
Seal of office, §7A-20(a).
Composition, organization, etc., §7A-16, NC
    Const Art IV §7.
Cost.
New trials.
    Discretion of court in awarding cost, §6-33.
Courts-martial review.
Certification for review from superior court,
    §7A-31.1(a).
Finality of decisions, §7A-28(c).
Grounds for discretionary review, §7A-31.1(b).
Rules of practice and procedure applicable,
    §7A-31.1(c).
Creation, §7A-16.
Delinquent and undisciplined juvenile actions.
Appeal of decision transferring jurisdiction of
    juvenile to superior court, §7B-2603(d).
    Waiver of right to raise transfer issue in court
        of appeals.
        Failure to appeal transfer order to superior
            court, §7B-2603(a).
Appeal of final order of court in review matter
    before court of appeals, §7B-2602.
Department of administration.
Providing adequate quarters for court, §7A-19(b).
**Department of environment and natural
    resources.**
Final orders and decisions of secretary.
    Right of appeal to court, §7A-29(a).
Department of health and human services.
Final orders and decisions.
    Right of appeal to court, §7A-29(a).
Depositions.
Reading deposition on the trial.
    When witness is judge of court of appeals,
        §8-83.
**Discretionary review on certification by
    supreme court,** §7A-31, AppProc 15.
District attorneys, removal from office.
Appeal to court of appeals, §7A-66.
District courts.
Appeals of right from district court.
    Final judgments of district courts in civil
        actions, §7A-27(c).
    Interlocutory orders or judgments of district court.
    Appeals of right from district court to court of
        appeals, §7A-27(d).
Elections.
Judges of court elected by qualified voters, §7A-16,
    NC Const Art IV §16.
Judicial voter guide.
    Candidate information, §163-278.69(b).
    Disclaimer statement, §163-278.69(c).
    Publication by board, §163-278.69(a).
State board of elections.
    Appeal of right to court, §7A-29(a).
Emergency judges, recall to active service.
Applicability of provisions.
    Generally, §7A-39.12.
Article applicable to previously retired justices,
    §7A-39.10.
Commission, application to governor, §7A-39.6.
Compensation, §7A-39.3.
Emergency judge.
    Defined, §7A-39.1.

COURT OF APPEALS —Cont'd
Emergency judges, recall to active service
    —Cont'd
Emergency recall judges, §7A-39.15.
Jurisdiction and authority, §7A-39.7.
Recall of judges reaching mandatory retirement
    age, §7A-39.13.
Retired judges recalled to active service, §7A-39.3.
Supreme court authorized to adopt rules,
    §7A-39.7.
Temporary incapacity of judge, §7A-39.5.
Temporary vacancies, §7A-39.14.
Termination of recall, §7A-39.9.
Evidence.
Review of errors, §8C-1 Rule 103(d).
Fees.
Clerk of court.
    Fee bill for services, §7A-20(b).
Judges, NC Const Art IV §21.
Habeas corpus.
Issuance of remedial writs.
    Power of court of appeals to issue, §7A-32(a).
Health and human services department.
Appeals of right from department, §7A-29(a).
Incompetence, determination of.
Appeal from order adjudicating incompetence,
    §35A-1115.
Industrial commission.
Appeals of right from industrial commission,
    §7A-29(a).
Jurisdiction of court of appeals.
    Power of court of appeals to issue remedial
        writs, §7A-32(c).
Review of final orders, §7A-250(b).
Insurance.
Commissioner of insurance.
    Appeals of right from commissioner to court of
        appeals, §7A-29(a).
Interlocutory orders.
Appeals of right from the courts of the trial
    divisions, §7A-27(d).
Discretionary review on certification by supreme
    court, AppProc Rule 15(h).
Judges.
Age limit for service as justice or judge for general
    court of justice, §7A-4.20.
Appointments.
    Temporary appointments, §7A-16.
Assignment of judges, NC Const Art IV §11.
Consolidated judicial retirement act, §§135-50 to
    135-75.2.
    See RETIREMENT SYSTEM FOR TEACHERS
        AND STATE EMPLOYEES.
Depositions.
    Reading deposition on the trial.
        When witness is judge of court of appeals,
            §8-83.
Disbarment or suspension.
    Salary suspension pending appeal, §7A-410.1.
    Vacancy in office declared upon, §7A-410.
Election, §7A-16, NC Const Art IV §16.
Emergency judges, recall to active service,
    §§7A-39.1 to 7A-39.15.
Expenses.
    Reimbursement for travel and subsistence
        expenses, §7A-18(a), (a1).
Habeas corpus, application for writ, §17-6.
Habeas corpus, issuance of writ, §17-8.
Increase in number of judges, §7A-16.
Judicial standards commission.
    Chair of commission to be court of appeals
        judge, §7A-375(a).

COURT OF APPEALS —Cont'd
Judges —Cont'd
  Jurisdiction.
    Emergency judges, §7A-39.7.
  Oaths.
    Who may administer oaths of office, §11-7.1(b).
  Panels of judges, §7A-16.
  Qualifications, NC Const Art IV §22.
  Quorum constituted, §7A-16.
  Recall of retired judges to active service,
    §§7A-39.1 to 7A-39.15.
  Removal, NC Const Art IV §17.
  Retirement, NC Const Art IV §§8, 21.
    Age limit for service as justice or judge of
      general court of justice, §7A-4.20.
    Consolidated judicial retirement act, §§135-50
      to 135-75.2.
    See RETIREMENT SYSTEM FOR
      TEACHERS AND STATE EMPLOYEES.
  Salaries, fees and emoluments, §7A-18(a), NC
    Const Art IV §21.
    Longevity pay, §7A-18(b).
  Search warrants.
    Issuance of warrant valid throughout state,
      §15A-243(a).
  Terms of office, §7A-16, NC Const Art IV §16.
  Vacancies in office, NC Const Art IV §19.
    Appointment by governor to fill, §163-9(a), (c).
    Term of appointee, §163-9(a).
Judicial standards commission.
  Chair of commission to be court of appeals judge,
    §7A-375(a).
Jurisdiction, NC Const Art IV §12.
  Administrative agencies.
    Appeals of right from certain administrative
      agencies, §7A-29(a).
  Appellate jurisdiction, §7A-26.
  Certiorari.
    Power of court of appeals to issue remedial
      writs, §7A-32(b).
  Habeas corpus.
    Power of court of appeals to issue remedial
      writs, §7A-32(a).
  Industrial commission.
    Power of court of appeals to issue remedial
      writs, §7A-32(c).
  Judges.
    Emergency judges, §7A-39.7.
  Mandamus.
    Power of court of appeals to issue remedial
      writs, §7A-32(b).
  Prohibition.
    Power of court of appeals to issue remedial
      writs, §7A-32(b).
  Remedial writs.
    Power of court of appeals to issue remedial
      writs, §7A-32.
  Supersedeas.
    Power of court of appeals to issue remedial
      writs, §7A-32(b).
  Utilities commission.
    Power of court of appeals to issue remedial
      writs, §7A-32(c).
Locations.
  Seats and sessions of court, §7A-19(a).
Mandamus.
  Issuance of remedial writs.
    Power of court of appeals to issue, §7A-32(b).
Marshal, §7A-21.
Motions.
  Decisions on post trial motions for appropriate
    relief.
    Finality, §7A-28(a).

COURT OF APPEALS —Cont'd
Motions —Cont'd
  Decisions upon review of valuation of exempt
    property.
    Finality, §7A-28(b).
New trials.
  Cost.
    Discretion of appellate court, §6-33.
Oaths.
  Clerk of court, §7A-20(a).
  Judges of court to take oath of office, §7A-16.
Opinions.
  Unpublished opinions, AppProc Rule 30(e).
Organization, §7A-16.
  Appellate division of general court of justice,
    §7A-5.
Powers.
  Remedial writs.
    Issuance of remedial writs by court of appeals,
      §7A-32.
Prohibition.
  Issuance of remedial writs.
    Power of court of appeals to issue, §7A-32(b).
**Property tax commission orders and decisions,
  appeal of.**
  Appeal from court of appeals to supreme court,
    §105-345.4.
  Appeal to lie to, §105-345(d).
  Panels, assignment of hearing to, §105-345(e).
  Right of appeal from commission to court of
    appeals, §7A-29(a).
Public utilities.
  Jurisdiction of court of appeals.
    Power to issue remedial writs in utilities
      commission proceedings, §7A-32(c).
Quorum, §7A-16.
Recall, §§7A-39.1 to 7A-39.15.
Removal.
  Certification of cause for discretionary review by
    supreme court, §7A-31, AppProc Rule 15.
Reporters.
  Appointment by supreme court for appellate
    division, §7A-6(a).
Scope of review of decisions by supreme court,
  AppProc Rule 16.
Seal of office adoption, §7A-20(a).
Search warrants.
  Judges of court of appeals.
    Issuance of search warrant valid throughout
      state, §15A-243(a).
**Secretary of environment and natural
  resources.**
  Final orders and decisions.
    Right of appeal to court, §7A-29(a).
Sessions and sittings, AppProc Rule 29(a).
  Scheduling of sessions by chief judge, §7A-19(c).
  Seats and sessions of court, §7A-19.
State auditor.
  Clerk of the court.
    Financial accounts of the clerk audited,
      §7A-20(b).
State bar.
  Appeals of right from North Carolina state bar to
    court of appeals, §7A-29(a).
State departments and agencies.
  Decisions of agency.
    Appeals of right from superior courts.
      Final judgments upon review of decision,
        §7A-27(b).
Superior courts.
  Administrative agency decisions.
    Final judgment of superior court upon review of
      decision, §7A-27(b).

COURT OF APPEALS —Cont'd
Superior courts —Cont'd
Appeals of right from superior courts, §7A-27.
　Final judgments of superior court, §7A-27(b).
Interlocutory orders or judgments of superior
　　court.
　Appeals of right from superior court to court of
　　　appeals, §7A-27(d).
Statutory authorized appeals.
　Direct appeal to court of appeals, §7A-27(e).
Supersedeas.
Issuance of remedial writs.
　Power of court of appeals to issue, §7A-32(b).
Transfer of case to supreme court.
Certification of cause for discretionary review by
　　supreme court, §7A-31, AppProc Rule 15.
Trial divisions.
Appeals of right from courts of the trial divisions,
　　§7A-27.
Unpublished opinions, AppProc Rule 30(e).
Utilities commission.
Appeals of right from utilities commission to court
　　of appeals, §7A-29(a).
Jurisdiction of court of appeals.
　Power of court of appeals to issue remedial
　　　writs, §7A-32(c).
Review of final orders, §7A-250(b).
Workers' compensation.
Appeals of right from industrial commission,
　　§7A-29(a).
Jurisdiction of court of appeals.
　Issuing remedial writs, §7A-32(c).
Writs.
Remedial writs.
　Power of court of appeals to issue, §7A-32.

COURT REPORTERS.
Appellate division of general court of justice,
　§7A-6(a).
Blind lawyers.
Lending North Carolina reports to blind lawyers,
　　§111-29.
Copies of appellate division reports.
Administrative office of courts.
　Distribution of copies, §7A-343.1.
Depositions.
Independent contractors.
　Persons before whom deposition may be taken,
　　　§1A-1 Rule 28(c).
District courts.
Appointment of reporter, §7A-198(f).
Compensation and allowances, §7A-198(f).
　Civil trials, §7A-198.
Electronic or mechanical devices.
　Inaccurate record produced, §7A-198(g).
　Operation of device while in progress,
　　　§7A-198(c).
　State of the art and techniques of recording
　　　testimony, §7A-198(b).
Magistrates.
　No provisions for reporting of trials before
　　　magistrates, §7A-198(e).
Utilization of personnel for reporting civil trials,
　　§7A-198(a).
Waiver of reporting of trial by consent of parties,
　　§7A-198(d).
Perpetuation of testimony.
Certified transcript of court reporter, §8-85.
Superior courts.
Appointment of reporters, §7A-95(e).
Availability of personnel, §7A-95(a).

COURT REPORTERS —Cont'd
Superior courts —Cont'd
Compensation and allowances of reporters,
　　§7A-95(e).
Electronic or mechanical devices.
　Operation of device while trial in progress,
　　　§7A-95(c).
　Use of in recording testimony, §7A-95(b).
Sick leave.
　Transfer of sick leave of court reporters earned
　　　as county or municipal employees,
　　　§7A-102.1(a) to (c).
Testimony.
　Investigating state of the art and techniques of
　　　recording testimony, §7A-95(b).
Waiver of reporting by consent of party, §7A-95(d).

COURTROOM COSTS.
Administration of estates, §7A-307(a).
Civil actions in district or superior courts,
　§7A-305(a).
Criminal actions in superior or district courts,
　§7A-304(a).
Special proceedings in superior court,
　§7A-306(a).

COURTROOM DECORUM.
**Power of judge in maintaining order in
　courtroom,** §§15A-1031 to 15A-1035.

COURTS.
Administration by general assembly, NC Const
　Art IV §14.
Administrative office of the courts, §§7A-340 to
　7A-346.
See ADMINISTRATIVE OFFICE OF THE
　　COURTS.
Appeals.
Cost on appeal, §6-33.
Court of appeals, §§7A-16 to 7A-21.
　See COURT OF APPEALS.
General court of justice.
　Appellate division, NC Const Art IV §5.
General provisions.
　See APPEALS.
Supreme court, §§7A-5 to 7A-13.
　See SUPREME COURT OF NORTH
　　　CAROLINA.
Appellate division reports.
Distribution of copies, §7A-343.1.
Child custody jurisdiction and enforcement.
Cooperation between courts, §50A-112.
Civil contempt, §§5A-21 to 5A-25.
See CONTEMPT.
Clerks of court.
See CLERKS OF COURT.
Closed.
Adverse weather, other emergency situations
　　including catastrophic conditions, §7A-39(a).
Day for doing act falls on, §103-5(a), (b).
Commission, §§7A-506 to 7A-510.
See COURTS COMMISSION.
Congress.
Power to constitute tribunals inferior to supreme
　　court, US Const Art I §8.
Contempt.
Civil contempt, §§5A-21 to 5A-25.
　See CONTEMPT.
Criminal contempt, §§5A-11 to 5A-17.
　See CONTEMPT.
Costs.
Courtrooms, §§7A-304 to 7A-307.
　See COURTROOM COSTS.

COURTS —Cont'd
Costs —Cont'd
General provisions, §§6-1 to 6-62.
See COSTS.
Discipline of judges or justices.
Judicial standards commission, §§7A-374.1 to
7A-378, JudStdsComm Rules 1 to 26.
See JUDICIAL STANDARDS COMMISSION.
District courts.
See DISTRICT COURTS.
Drug treatment courts, §§7A-790 to 7A-801.
See DRUG TREATMENT COURTS.
General assembly.
Administration, NC Const Art IV §15.
General court of justice.
See GENERAL COURT OF JUSTICE.
Judges.
See JUDGES.
Judicial standards commission, §§7A-374.1 to
7A-378, JudStdsComm Rules 1 to 26.
See JUDICIAL STANDARDS COMMISSION.
Jurisdiction generally, NC Const Art IV §12.
Juvenile court.
Delinquent and undisciplined juveniles.
Delinquent juveniles.
Jurisdiction over, §7B-1601.
Extended jurisdiction, §7B-1602.
District court exercising jurisdiction pursuant to
chapter, §7B-1501.
Generally, §§7B-1500 to 7B-2827.
See DELINQUENT AND UNDISCIPLINED
JUVENILES.
Limitations on jurisdiction, §7B-1604.
Undisciplined juvenile.
Jurisdiction over, §7B-1600.
Missing persons.
Release of information to by center, §143B-1018.
Open courts, NC Const Art I §18.
Orders.
See ORDERS.
Payment into court, §§1-508 to 1-510.
Qualifications or conduct of judges.
Investigation and resolution of inquiries
concerning.
Judicial standards commission, §§7A-374.1 to
7A-378, JudStdsComm Rules 1 to 26.
See JUDICIAL STANDARDS COMMISSION.
Records mutilation, larceny or destruction,
§14-76.
Reporters.
See COURT REPORTERS.
Reports.
Administrative officer of the courts, §7A-6(b).
Appellate division reports.
Distribution of copies, §7A-343.1.
Blind lawyers.
Lending North Carolina reports to blind
lawyers, §111-29.
Designation of commercial reports as official
reports, §7A-6(b1).
Restriction of judicial power, US Const Amd 11.
Seals.
Governor to procure, §147-28.
New seals when necessary, §147-30.
Superior courts.
See SUPERIOR COURTS.
Supreme court, §§7A-5 to 7A-13.
See SUPREME COURT OF NORTH CAROLINA.
Therapeutic court.
Activities.
Participation as condition of probation or
deferred prosecution, §7A-272(f).

COURTS —Cont'd
United States courts.
See UNITED STATES COURTS.
Weapons possession in courthouses, §14-269.4.

COURTS COMMISSION, §§7A-506 to 7A-510.
Administrative officer of the courts.
Ex officio members, §7A-507.
Appointment, §7A-506(a).
Bar association.
Representative of association to be ex officio
member, §7A-507.
Chairman, §7A-509.
Compensation of members, §7A-509.
Composition, §7A-506(b) to (e).
Creation, §7A-506(a).
Duties, §7A-508.
Supporting services, §7A-510.
Ex officio members, §7A-507.
Meetings.
Designation of times and places of meetings by
chairman, §7A-509.
Number of members, §7A-506(a).
State bar council.
Representative of council to be ex officio member,
§7A-507.
Supporting services, §7A-510.
Terms, §7A-506(f).
Vacancies, §7A-506(g).

COURTS-MARTIAL FOR NATIONAL GUARD,
§§127A-47 to 127A-62.
Administrative procedure act.
Full exemption, §150B-1(c).
Appeals.
Applicable law, §127A-62(e).
Appointment of judge advocate.
Representation of defendant and state,
§127A-62(h).
Appointment of judge to hear, §127A-62(d).
Attorney-client privilege waived.
Ineffectiveness of prior counsel ground for relief,
§127A-62(h).
Court of appeals.
Certification for review from superior court,
§7A-31.1(a).
Finality of decisions, §7A-28(c).
Grounds for discretionary review, §7A-31.1(b).
Rules of practice and procedure applicable,
§7A-31.1(c).
Errors asserted or waived, §127A-62(c).
Filing, time, filing fee, §127A-62(b).
Ineffectiveness of prior counsel ground for relief.
Attorney-client privilege waived, §127A-62(h).
Jurisdiction, §127A-62(a).
Modifying or setting aside finding or sentence.
Grounds, §127A-62(f).
Rehearing ordered, §127A-62(g).
Rehearing ordered.
Findings or sentence set aside, §127A-62(g).
Remand for evidentiary hearings, other
proceedings, §127A-62(g).
Representation of defendant.
Appointment of judge advocate, §127A-62(h).
Representation of state.
Appointment of judge advocate, §127A-62(h).
Review of decisions of Wake county superior court,
§127A-62(i).
Right to appeal, §127A-62(a).
Rules for practice and procedure for review.
Requirements, §127A-62(j).
Venue, §127A-62(a).

COURTS-MARTIAL FOR NATIONAL GUARD
—Cont'd

Appeals —Cont'd
Wake county superior court.
Jurisdiction, §127A-62(a).
Review of decisions, §127A-62(i).
Rules of practice and procedure, §127A-62(j).

Arrest warrants.
Power to issue, §127A-56.

Bail.
Pretrial confinement.
Provisions applicable, §127A-54(b).

Confinement.
Appeals, §127A-62.
General courts-martial.
Imposition, restrictions, §127A-48.
Local confinement facility.
Transfer of physical custody to, §127A-54(c).
Placed into custody of division of adult correction, §127A-54(c).
Pretrial confinement, §127A-54(a), (b).
Special courts-martial.
Imposition, restrictions, §127A-49.
Summary courts-martial.
Imposition, prohibition, §127A-50.

Contempt.
Power to punish, §127A-56.

Criminal history records.
Pertinent information included, §127A-59.

Disqualification from holding commission.
Officer dismissed from service, §127A-60.

Execution of processes and sentences, §127A-57.

Fines.
Disposition of fines, §127A-61.

Forms for courts-martial procedure, §127A-55.

General courts-martial, §127A-47.
Confinement, imposition, restrictions, §127A-48.
Convening, §127A-48.
Powers, §127A-48.

Habeas corpus.
Pretrial confinement.
Right not abridged, §127A-54(b).

Jurisdiction, §127A-52.

Local confinement facility.
Transfer of physical custody to, §127A-54(c).

Manual for courts-martial, §127A-53.
Sentences.
Execution, §127A-57.

Military judges.
Appointment, §127A-50.1.
Qualifications, §127A-50.1.

Nonjudicial punishment, §127A-51.
No right to demand trial by special courts-martial, §127A-51.

Officer dismissed from service.
Disqualification from holding commission, §127A-60.

Powers, §§127A-47, 127A-56.
General courts-martial, §127A-48.
Special courts-martial, §127A-49.
Summary courts-martial, §127A-50.

Pretrial confinement, §127A-54(a), (b).

Procedure, §127A-47.
Forms for courts-martial procedure, §127A-55.

Processes.
Execution, §127A-57.

Sentences, §127A-59.
Appeals, §127A-62.
Approval of governor required, §127A-60.
Certificate, §127A-59.

COURTS-MARTIAL FOR NATIONAL GUARD
—Cont'd

Sentences —Cont'd
Confinement.
General courts-martial.
Imposition, restrictions, §127A-48.
Local confinement facility.
Transfer of physical custody to, §127A-54(c).
Placed into custody of division of adult correction, §127A-54(c).
Pretrial confinement, §127A-54(a), (b).
Special courts-martial.
Imposition, restrictions, §127A-49.
Summary courts-martial.
Imposition, prohibition, §127A-50.
Execution of processes and sentences, §127A-57.
Nonjudicial punishment, §127A-51.
No right to demand trial by special courts-martial, §127A-51.

Special courts-martial, §127A-47.
Appointment, §127A-49.
Authority, §127A-49.
Confinement, imposition, restrictions, §127A-49.
No rights to demand trial by special courts-martial.
Nonjudicial punishment, §127A-51.
Summary courts-martial, §127A-50.
Power and authority, §127A-49.
Punishments, imposition, power, §127A-49.

Subpoenas and subpoenas duces tecum.
Power to issue, §127A-56.

Summary courts-martial, §127A-47.
Appointment, §127A-50.
Composition, §127A-50.
Confinement, imposition, prohibition, §127A-50.
No right to demand trial by special courts-martial, §127A-50.
Powers, §127A-50.
Punishments, imposition, power, §127A-50.

Trials and proceedings.
Manual for courts-martial, §127A-53.

Warrants for arrest.
Power to issue, §127A-56.

Witnesses.
Attendance.
Enforcement by attachment, power, §127A-56.

COURTS OF THE UNITED STATES.
See UNITED STATES COURTS.

COVENANTS.
Contribution among joint tortfeasors.
Effect of release or covenant not to sue, §1B-4.

Conveyances generally.
See CONVEYANCES.

Covenant to stand seized to use.
Possession transferred to use in certain conveyances, §41-7.

Interest.
Default judgments.
Clerk to ascertain interest upon default judgment on covenant to pay money, §24-6.

Joint tortfeasor contributions.
Effect of release or covenant not to sue, §1B-4.

Life estates.
Warranties by life tenants deemed covenants, §41-8.

Remainders, reversions and executory interests.
Grantees of reversion and assigns of lease have reciprocal rights under covenants, §42-8.

COVENANTS —Cont'd
Solar collectors.
Deed restrictions, covenants or other agreements prohibiting installation.
Void and unenforceable, exception, §22B-20(a) to (e).
State officers authorized to prove or acknowledge, §47-1.
Transfer fee covenants, §§39A-1 to 39A-3.
Definitions, §39A-2.
Liability of person recording, §39A-3(b).
Not to run with title, §39A-3(a).
Public policy, §39A-1.
Subsequent owner, purchaser, mortgagee.
Not binding or enforceable on, §39A-3(a).
Unit ownership compliance with, §47A-10.

COVENTRY ACT.
Maiming, §§14-30, 14-30.1.
Malicious maiming, §14-30.

COVER.
Leases, UCC.
Cover by lessor, §25-2A-518.
Sale of goods, UCC.
Buyer's inability to effect cover.
Right to specific performance, §25-2-716.
Buyer's remedies, §§25-2-711, 25-2-712.
Merchant buyer's duties as to rightfully rejected goods, §25-2-603.

COVERED CLINICAL TRIALS.
Health benefit plan coverage, §58-3-255.

COVIN.
Suit for penalty.
Plaintiff's reply that former judgment obtained by, §1-59.

COWS.
Brands generally, §§80-45 to 80-66.
See LIVESTOCK BRANDS.
Brucellosis, §§106-388 to 106-398.
See BRUCELLOSIS.
Cattle tick, §§106-351 to 106-363.
See CATTLE TICK.
Compensation for killing diseased animals generally, §§106-323 to 106-335.
See LIVESTOCK DISEASES.
Control of livestock diseases generally, §§106-400 to 106-405.
See LIVESTOCK DISEASES.
Diseases generally, §§106-304 to 106-307.7.
See LIVESTOCK DISEASES.
Larceny, §14-81.
Livestock dealer licensing generally, §§106-418.8 to 106-418.16.
See LIVESTOCK DEALER LICENSING.
Livestock generally.
See LIVESTOCK.
Markets for livestock, §§106-406 to 106-418.
See LIVESTOCK MARKETS.
Meat inspections, §§106-549.15 to 106-549.39.
See MEAT INSPECTIONS.
Running at large generally, §§68-17 to 68-24.
See LIVESTOCK RUNNING AT LARGE.
Signs for protection of cattle, §136-33.1.

COYOTES.
Hunting preserves.
Controlled hunting preserve operator license, §113-273(g).
Trapping.
Traps or snares used, §113-291.6(h).

COYOTES —Cont'd
Unlawfully transporting or breeding, §113-294(o).

CPA'S, §§93-1 to 93-13.
See ACCOUNTANTS.

CPR EDUCATION.
Public schools.
Health education, §115C-81(e1).

CRAFTS.
Artwork on consignment, §§25C-1 to 25C-5.
Promotion of arts, §§143-403 to 143-407.1.
Sale of prints, §§25C-10 to 25C-16.

CRAMERTON.
All-terrain vehicles.
Use by employees on certain highways, §20-171.24.
Room occupancy tax.
Uniform provisions.
Authorized to levy, §160A-215(g).
Generally, §160A-215.
Satellite annexation.
Limitation on area of satellite corporate limits, inapplicability, §160A-58.1(b).

CRAPS.
Video craps.
Ban on new machines, regulation of existing machines, §§14-306.1A, 14-306.4.

CRASHES.
Motor vehicle accidents generally.
See MOTOR VEHICLE ACCIDENTS.

CRASH PARTS.
Nonoriginal crash repair parts.
Definitions, §58-36-95(a).
Disclosure to claimant by insurer.
Estimate of repair based on use, §58-36-95(b).
Repair facility submitting invoice for original repair part, §58-36-90(b).
Reporting fraud, §58-36-90(c).
Original equipment manufactured crash parts, coverage specifying.
Development of policy endorsement permitting policyholders election, §58-36-41.

CRAVEN COUNTY.
Agricultural tenancies in certain counties.
Terms of, §42-23.
Ambulance service.
Attachment or garnishment and lien for, §§44-51.4 to 44-51.8.
Condemnation or acquisition of land by local government unit outside county.
Consent of board of commissioners necessary, §153A-15.
Cropper or tenant refusing to perform terms of contract.
Forfeiture of right of possession to premises, §42-27.
Dog collars.
Unlawful removal of electronic dog collars, §14-401.17.
Game laws, local acts not repealed, §113-133.1(e).
Grants in navigable waters, registration, §113-205(a).
Low-income housing tax credits.
Qualified building eligible for credit, §105-129.41(c).

CRAVEN COUNTY —Cont'd
North Carolina's eastern region, §§158-30 to
    158-42.
    See NORTH CAROLINA'S EASTERN REGION.
Open fires, high hazard counties.
    Applicability of provisions, §106-942(a).
    Ground clearing activities, special permit,
        §106-942(c).
    Woodland fires, permit required, §106-942(b).
Private parking lots.
    Removal of unauthorized vehicles, §20-219.2.
**Room occupancy tax levied by county, uniform
    provision,** §153A-155.
School property.
    Acquisition and improvement, §153A-158.1.
Special school tax, election to abolish.
    Petition required, §115C-505.

CREAM.
Regulation of milk and cream.
    Generally.
        See MILK AND MILK PRODUCTS.

CREAMERY INSPECTIONS.
Generally, §§106-246 to 106-255.
    See ICE CREAM PLANTS, CREAMERIES AND
        CHEESE FACTORIES.

CREATIVE WRITING.
Promotion of arts, §§143-403 to 143-407.1.

CREDIBILITY OF WITNESSES.
Impeachment generally.
    See IMPEACHMENT OF WITNESSES.

CREDIT, US Const Art I §10.
Cards.
    See CREDIT CARDS.
Crime victims credit protection, §15B-26.
Device fraud.
    See CREDIT DEVICE FRAUD.
Equity lines of credit, §§45-81 to 45-84.
    See EQUITY LINES OF CREDIT.
Interest and service charges, §24-11(b).
Letters of credit, §§25-5-101 to 25-5-118.
    See LETTERS OF CREDIT.
Libraries.
    Pledging of credit.
        Political subdivisions to comply with pledging of
            credit, §125-13.
Married women.
    Equal availability of credit for women, §25B-1(a).
Repair services, §§66-220 to 66-226.
    See CREDIT REPAIR SERVICES.
Retail installment sales, §§25A-1 to 25A-45.
    See RETAIL INSTALLMENT SALES.
Secured transactions, §§25-9-101 to 25-9-710.
    See SECURED TRANSACTIONS.
Women.
    Actions.
        Enforcement of article, §25B-3(a).
    Equal availability of credit for women.
        Construction of term "credit,"§25B-1(c).
        Married women, §25B-1(a).
        Unmarried women, §25B-1(b).
    Granting of credit not otherwise affected, §25B-4.
    Injunctions.
        Enforcement of article, §25B-3(b).
    Reporting agencies.
        Separate credit histories to be maintained,
            §25B-2.
    Unmarried women.
        Equal availability of credit for women,
            §25B-1(b).

CREDIT CARDS.
Account numbers or expiration date.
    Printing more than 5 digits upon receipt provided
        cardholder at point of sale.
        Prohibited, §14-113.24(b).
            Penalty, §14-113.24(c).
            Person defined, §14-113.24(a).
Charges, §24-11.
    Revolving charge account contracts.
        Annual charge, §24-11(a).
        Billing date, §24-11(d).
        Discount or fee, §24-11(a2).
    Finance charge.
        Default or deferral charges, §25A-14(c).
        Insurance.
            Additional charges for insurance,
                §25A-17(b).
        Rates, §25A-14(a).
        Security interest.
            Rates, §25A-14(b).
    Late payment charge, §24-11(d1).
    Monthly periodic rate.
        Plan secured by real or personal property.
            Restrictions, §24-11(c).
        Revolving credit loans, §24-11(b).
    Notice of proposed charge, §24-11(e).
    Revolving credit loans.
        Monthly periodic rate, §24-11(b).
    Service charge, §24-11(a1).
Credit insurance on credit card balances,
    §58-57-105.
    Premium rate allowed, §58-57-105(b).
    Solicitation or negotiation by credit card facilities,
        §58-57-105(a).
    Unsolicited telephone calls or facsimile
        transmissions.
        Prohibited solicitation, §58-57-105(a).
Disclosure requirements.
    Applicability, §24-11.1(a).
    Charge cards, §24-11.2.
    Construction and interpretation, §24-11.1(f).
    Federal requirements, §24-11.1(c).
    Generally, §24-11.1(b).
    Penalty for violation, §24-11.1(d).
    Severability of provisions, §24-11.1(e).
Financial transaction cards, §§14-113.8 to
    14-113.17.
    See FINANCIAL TRANSACTION CARDS.
Fines, fees and costs owed by offenders.
    Acceptance in lieu of payment by cash or check,
        §7A-321(a).
        Contracts with vendors to provide for, §7A-343.
Fraud by generally.
    See CREDIT DEVICE FRAUD.
Identity fraud.
    Generally, §§14-113.20 to 14-113.25.
Insurance.
    Credit card guaranty or collateral.
        Prohibited, §58-3-147.
    Solicitation, negotiation or payment of premiums
        through credit card or debit card services,
        §58-3-145.
**Insurance institution, agent or support
    organization.**
    Sharing consumer's account number.
        General prohibition, §58-39-76.
Interest.
    Disclosure requirements.
        Generally, §24-11.1.
    Loans exempt from interest rate and fee
        limitations, §24-9(d).

CREDIT CARDS —Cont'd
Legal expense funds for elected officials.
Limitations on donations.
Credit cards, confidentiality of credit card
number, §163-278.316(c).
**Loans exempt from interest rate and fee
limitations,** §24-9(d).
**Possession or manufacture of false or
fraudulent identification cards,** §14-100.1.
Retail installment sales.
General provisions, §§25A-1 to 25A-45.
See RETAIL INSTALLMENT SALES.
Savings and loan associations power to issue,
§54B-77.
Savings banks.
Stock savings banks.
Powers as to, §54C-146(a).
Statewide accounts receivable program.
Payment by, §147-86.22(b).
Unemployment compensation.
Taxes, payment by credit card, §96-9(a).

CREDIT DEVICE FRAUD.
Actions.
Civil action for damages, §14-113.6(c).
Applicability of article, §14-113.7A.
Construction of article.
Article not construed as repealing section 14-100,
§14-113.7.
Electric companies, §§14-113.4, 14-113.5.
Financial transaction cards, §§14-113.8 to
14-113.17.
Knowledge.
Use of credit devices as prima facie evidence of
knowledge, §14-113.3.
Multiple violations made felony, §14-113.6(a).
Notice of revocation.
Definition of "notice,"§14-113.2.
Prima facie evidence of receipt of notice,
§14-113.2.
Use after notice, §14-113.1.
Repealing provision.
Article not construed as repealing section 14-100,
§14-113.7.
Restitution or reparation.
Violation of provisions, §14-113.6(b).
Revocation.
Use after notice of revocation, §14-113.1.
Telecommunication services.
Avoiding or attempting to avoid payment,
§14-113.4.
Civil actions, §14-113.6(c).
Concealment of existence, origin or destination of
any telecommunication, §14-113.5.
Definitions, §14-113.5(c).
Destination of telecommunication.
Concealment of destination, §14-113.5.
Existence of telecommunication.
Concealment of existence, §14-113.5.
Making, possessing or transferring device for theft
of service, §14-113.5.
Origin of telecommunication.
Concealment of origin, §14-113.5.
Publication of information regarding schemes,
devices, means or methods for theft,
§14-113.5.
Venue of offenses, §14-113.6A(b).
Theft of service.
Making, possessing or transferring device for
theft, §14-113.5.

CREDIT DEVICE FRAUD —Cont'd
Telecommunication services —Cont'd
Theft of service —Cont'd
Publication of information regarding schemes,
devices, means or methods for theft,
§14-113.5.
Venue of offenses, §14-113.6A(a).
Unauthorized use of another's credit device,
§14-113.1.
Use of false or counterfeit credit device,
§14-113.1.
Venue of offenses, §14-113.6A(a), (b).
Violations made misdemeanor, §14-113.6(a).

CREDIT INSURANCE, §§58-57-1 to 58-57-115.
Amount of insurance authorized.
Credit accident and health insurance,
§58-57-15(b).
Credit life insurance, §58-57-15(a).
Credit unemployment insurance, §58-57-15(b).
Appeals.
Orders of commissioner, §58-57-75.
Applicability of provisions, §58-57-1.
Authorized, §58-7-15.
Automobile physical damage insurance.
Authorized, §58-57-100(a).
Conditions, §58-57-100(a).
Filing of documents with commissioner,
§58-57-100(b).
Choice of insurer, §58-57-65.
Claims.
Acknowledgment, §58-57-60(d).
Adjustment, §58-57-60(c).
Payment, §58-57-60(b).
Report to insurer, §58-57-60(a).
Settlement, §58-57-60(a).
Commissioner.
Credit unemployment insurance.
Rulemaking to implement, §58-57-110(b).
Enforcement authority, §58-57-71(a).
Orders.
Judicial review, §58-57-75.
Confidentiality of information.
Consumer and customer information.
Generally, §§58-39-1 to 58-39-165.
See INSURANCE CONSUMER AND
CUSTOMER INFORMATION PRIVACY.
Credit card balances, §58-57-105.
Premium rate allowed, §58-57-105(b).
Solicitation or negotiation by credit card facilities,
§58-57-105(a).
Unsolicited telephone calls or facsimile
transmissions.
Prohibited solicitation, §58-57-105(a).
Credit property insurance, §58-57-90.
Definitions.
Dual credit property, §58-57-90(a).
Personal household property, §58-57-90(a).
Single interest credit property, §58-57-90(a).
Dual credit property.
Defined, §58-57-90(a).
Premium, §58-57-90(b).
Credit unemployment insurance.
Policy provisions, §58-57-110(a) to (c).
Rate standards, §58-57-110(a).
Joint coverage rates, §58-57-110(c).
Rulemaking to implement, §58-57-110(b).
Definitions, §58-57-5.
Enforcement.
Civil penalties, §58-57-71(a), (c).
Grounds, §58-57-71(a).

CREDIT INSURANCE —Cont'd

Enforcement —Cont'd

Licenses, suspension, revocation or restriction, §58-57-71(a), (b), (d), (e).

Existing insurance.

Option of furnishing required insurance through, §58-57-65.

Family leave credit insurance, §58-57-115.

Coverage, §58-57-115(b).

Definitions, §§58-57-5, 58-57-115(a).

Eligibility for coverage, §58-57-115(c).

Evidence of employer approval of qualified leave, §58-57-115(h).

Exclusions from coverage, §58-57-115(e).

Lump-sum payments, §58-57-115(h).

Minimum monthly benefit amount, §58-57-115(g).

Notice that benefits paid, §58-57-115(f).

Premium rates, §58-57-115(i).

Qualifying events for payment of benefits, §58-57-115(d).

Refund of unearned premium, §58-57-115(h).

Reports by insurers offering, §58-57-115(j).

Waiting period for benefits, §58-57-115(h).

Forms.

Disapproval by commissioner, §58-57-30(b).

Notice, §58-57-30(c).

Filing with commissioner, §58-57-30(a).

Action by commissioner on, §58-57-30(b).

Withdrawal of approval by commissioner, §58-57-30(d), (e).

Licenses.

Revocation or suspension, §58-57-71(a), (b), (d), (e).

Mortgages and deeds of trust.

Consumer home loans.

Financing credit insurance by lender, §24-10.2(b).

Policies.

Amounts authorized, §58-57-15.

Contents, §58-57-25(b).

Credit unemployment insurance.

Provisions, §58-57-110(a) to (c).

Generally.

See INSURANCE POLICIES OR CONTRACTS.

Insurance to be evidenced by individual policy, §58-57-25(a).

Issuance, §58-57-55.

Kinds of policies authorized, §58-57-10.

Notification when policy not delivered to debtor, §58-57-25(e).

Prohibited provisions, §58-57-25(d).

Required provisions, §58-57-25(c).

Premiums.

Credit property insurance, §58-57-25(b).

Credits, §58-57-50(e).

Rate standards.

Adjustment during critical period, §58-57-35(d).

Credit accident and health insurance.

Applicability of rate standards, §58-57-45(a).

Gainful employment debtor may be required, §58-57-45(c).

Generally, §58-57-45(d) to (g).

Joint accident and health coverage, §58-57-45(h).

Restrictiveness of definition of "disability,"§58-57-45(b).

Credit life insurance.

Applicability of provisions, §58-57-40(a).

Generally, §58-57-40(c) to (h).

Joint life insurance coverage, §58-57-40(d).

Level term life insurance, §58-57-40(e).

CREDIT INSURANCE —Cont'd

Premiums —Cont'd

Rate standards —Cont'd

Credit life insurance —Cont'd

More restrictive forms, §58-57-40(b).

Credit unemployment insurance, §58-57-110(a).

Joint coverage, §58-57-110(c).

Generally, §58-57-35(a), (b).

Determination according to age, §58-57-35(c).

Refunds.

Calculations, §58-57-50(b), (c).

Generally, §58-57-50(a) to (e).

Minimum amount, §58-57-50(d).

Rates.

Credit property insurance.

Premium rates, §58-57-90(b).

Scope of provisions, §58-57-1.

Single interest credit property.

Defined, §58-57-90(a).

Premium, §58-57-90(b).

Termination prior to scheduled maturity, §58-57-20.

Term of insurance, §58-57-20.

CREDIT MONITORING SERVICES ACT, §§75-133 to 75-135.

Consumer's right to one free credit report per year.

Disclosure required, §75-135(a).

Attorney general to enforce, §75-135(c).

Services offered in telephone call, §75-135(b).

Violation, §75-135(c).

Credit monitoring services defined, §75-134.

Definitions, §75-134.

Short title, §75-133.

CREDITORS.

See DEBTORS AND CREDITORS.

CREDITORS' BILLS.

Supplemental proceedings, §§1-352 to 1-368.

See SUPPLEMENTAL PROCEEDINGS.

CREDIT REPAIR SERVICES, §§66-220 to 66-226.

Acts prohibited, §66-223.

Applicability of chapter, §66-226.

Bonds, surety.

Required, §66-222.

Citation of article, §66-220.

Contracts.

Cancellation, §66-224.

Contents, §66-224.

Voiding.

Use of untrue or misleading statements, §66-225.

Definitions, §66-221.

Felonies.

Violation of provisions, §66-225.

Injunctions.

Violation of provisions, §66-225.

Prohibited acts, §66-223.

Purposes of article, §66-220.

Scope of article, §66-226.

Short title of article, §66-220.

Trust account.

Required, §66-222.

Violation of provisions, §66-225.

Waiver of provisions.

Void and unenforceable, §66-225.

CREDIT REPORTING AGENCIES.

Credit monitoring services act, §§75-133 to 75-135.

CREDIT REPORTING AGENCIES —Cont'd
Security freeze placed on consumer's credit report, §75-63.
Separate credit histories for married persons, responsibility to maintain, §25B-2.

CREDIT REPORTS.
Credit monitoring services act, §§75-133 to 75-135.
Security freeze on consumer's credit report, §75-63.

CREDIT SALES, §§25A-1 to 25A-45.
See RETAIL INSTALLMENT SALES.

CREDIT SCORING.
Motor vehicle or property insurance, §58-36-90.

CREDITS UPON JUDGMENTS, §1-242.

CREDIT SUSPENSION DIRECTIVE, §45-36.7A.

CREDIT UNIONS, §§54-109.1 to 54-110.10.
Actions.
Power to sue and be sued, §54-109.21.
Administrator of credit unions.
Assistants, §54-109.10.
Confidential information, §54-109.105(a).
Duties, §§54-109.11, 54-109.12.
Liquidation of credit unions, §54-109.13.
Removal of officers, §54-109.19.
Revocation of certificate of approval, §54-109.13.
Rules and regulations, §54-109.12.
Supervision of credit unions, §54-109.12.
Supervision of division, §54-109.10.
Suspension and conservation, §54-109.92.
Agents.
Personal agency accounts.
Generally, §54-109.63.
Age of members.
Minimum age to hold office, §54-109.31(e).
Minimum age to vote at meetings, §54-109.31(d).
Appeals.
Suspension and conservation.
Decisions of administrator, §54-109.92(k).
Appraisal fees.
Loans secured by real property, §24-10(h).
Articles of incorporation, §54-109.2(b).
Amendment, §54-109.4(a).
When effective, §54-109.4(b).
Form, §54-109.3.
Assets.
Liquidation.
Voluntary liquidation.
Use of assets, §54-109.93(g).
Associations.
Membership, §54-109.27.
Representation and voting at meetings, §54-109.31(c).
Attorneys at law.
Selection of attorneys to handle loan-closing proceedings, §54-109.18.
Audits.
Supervisory committee, §54-109.49.
Bankruptcy and insolvency.
Suspension and conservation, §54-109.92.
Board of directors.
Conflicts of interest, §54-109.39.
Dividends.
Declaring, §54-109.54.
Duties, §54-109.44.
Election of directors, §54-109.35(a).
Executive committee, §54-109.42.
Meetings, §54-109.43.

CREDIT UNIONS —Cont'd
Board of directors —Cont'd
Executive committee —Cont'd
Number of members, §54-109.42.
Executive officers.
Election or employment, §54-109.40(a), (d).
Expenses of directors, §54-109.38.
General direction of credit union, §54-109.41.
Immunity of director or officer of nonprofit corporation, §55A-8-60(c).
Loans.
Duties of directors as to, §54-109.44.
Meetings, §54-109.43.
Number of directors, §§54-109.2(d), 54-109.35.
Organization.
Selection, §54-109.2(d).
Powers, §54-109.41.
Record of members, §54-109.36.
Removal of directors.
Grounds, §54-109.19(a).
Hearing, §54-109.19(b).
Notice, §54-109.19(b).
Order of removal, §54-109.19(b).
Power of administrator of credit unions, §54-109.19(a).
Procedure, §54-109.19(b).
Vacancies, §54-109.37.
Bonds, surety.
Blanket fidelity bond.
Purchase by board of directors, §54-109.44.
Generally, §54-109.11.
Borrowing money.
Powers of credit unions generally, §54-109.21.
Bylaws.
Amendment, §54-109.4(a).
When effective, §54-109.4(b).
Form, §54-109.3.
Preparation and adoption, §54-109.2(c).
Capital.
Composition, §54-109.53(a).
Carolina credit union foundation.
Special license plates, §20-81.12(b82).
Changes in corporate status, §§54-109.92 to 54-109.95.
Child support enforcement.
Location of absent parents.
Information to be provided, §110-139(d).
Commercial loan commitments to be in writing, §22-5.
Commission.
Created, §143B-439(a).
Meetings, §143B-439(a).
Members, §143B-439(a).
Powers and duties, §143B-439(c).
Quorum, §143B-439(a).
Relationship between secretary of economic and community development and credit union commission, §143B-439(b).
Terms, §143B-439(a).
Confidentiality, §54-109.105.
Agencies of state, other states or United States.
Exchange of information permitted, §54-109.105(d).
Application for new credit union.
Public information, §54-109.105(c).
Disclosure.
Court of competent jurisdiction may order, §54-109.105(b).
Liability for damages, §54-109.105.
Misdemeanors for violations, §54-109.105(f).
Penalties for violation, §54-109.105(e).

CREDIT UNIONS —Cont'd
Confidentiality —Cont'd
  Records of information of credit union division,
    administrator or agents, §54-109.105(a).
Conflicts of interest, §54-109.39.
Conservation.
  Appeals from decisions of administrator,
    §54-109.92(k).
  Appointment of conservator, §54-109.92(b), (e).
  Costs, §54-109.92(g).
  Duration, §54-109.92(i).
  Duties of conservator, §54-109.92(f).
  Grounds, §54-109.92(a).
  Jurisdiction.
    Suits during conservation, §54-109.92(h).
  Liquidating agent.
    Appointment, §54-109.92(j).
  Liquidation.
    Order of liquidation, §54-109.92(j).
  Merger.
    Order of merger, §54-109.92(j).
  Order, §54-109.92(b), (e).
    Appeal from order, §54-109.92(k).
    Effect, §54-109.92(c).
    Reply to order, §54-109.92(c).
      Effect of failure to file, §54-109.92(l).
      Hearing, §54-109.92(d).
      Service, §54-109.92(b).
  Reports by conservator, §54-109.92(f).
Consumer finance act.
  Exemption of cooperative credit unions, §53-191.
Contracts.
  Power to make contracts, §54-109.21.
Conversion of charter, §54-109.95.
Cooperative marketing arrangements.
  Authorized, §54-109.77.
Corporate credit unions, §§54-110.1 to 54-110.10.
  Applicability of article, §54-110.10.
  Application form, §54-110.4(a).
  Articles of incorporation, §54-110.4(b).
  Bylaws, §54-110.4(c).
  Central financial system.
    Participation in, §54-110.6.
  Charter exclusive, §54-110.3.
  Defined, §54-110.1(a).
  Directors.
    Meetings, §54-110.5(d).
  Fees.
    Operating fees, §54-110.8.
  Liens.
    Shares and deposit accounts, §54-110.7(b).
  Membership, §54-110.2(a).
  Name exclusive, §54-110.3.
  Operating fees, §54-110.8.
  Participation in central system, §54-110.6.
  Powers, §54-110.5(a), (b), (e).
  Purposes, §54-110.1(b).
  Reserves, §54-110.9.
  Security.
    Loans, §54-110.7(c).
  Setoff.
    Right of setoff, §54-110.7(a).
  Taxation.
    Exemption, §54-110.5(c).
  Voting representatives.
    Designation, §54-110.2(b).
Credit committee.
  Appointment, §54-109.35(c).
  Authority, §54-109.45.
  Conflicts of interest, §54-109.39.
  Dispensing with, §54-109.48.

CREDIT UNIONS —Cont'd
Credit committee —Cont'd
  Expenses of members, §54-109.38.
  Loan officers in lieu of, §§54-109.35(c), 54-109.48.
  Loans.
    Majority of committee must approve,
      §54-109.46.
  Meetings, §54-109.46.
  Number of members, §54-109.35(c).
  Powers, §54-109.45.
  Record of members, §54-109.36.
  Vacancies, §54-109.37.
Definitions, §54-109.1.
  Corporate credit unions, §54-110.1(a).
  Interest, §54-109.65.
  "Membership,"§54-109.26(a).
  Risk assets, §54-109.88.
Deposits.
  Insurance.
    Share and deposit insurance, §54-109.78(a).
      Prerequisite to granting of charter,
        §54-109.78(b).
  Lien on deposit, §54-109.59.
  Savings accounts, §54-109.55.
Direction of affairs, §§54-109.35 to 54-109.49.
Dividends, §54-109.54.
  Lien on accumulated dividends, §54-109.59.
  Power to declare dividends, §54-109.21.
Division.
  Administrator of credit unions. See within this
    heading, "Administrator of credit unions."
  Creation, §54-109.10.
  Supervision, §54-109.10.
Equity line of credit.
  Future advances.
    Notice regarding, form, §45-82.3(f).
  Request to terminate made by.
    Notice to borrower, form, §45-82.2(d).
Evidence.
  Records.
    Photostatic or photographic reproductions,
      §54-109.17(c).
Examinations.
  Administrator of credit unions.
    Duties, §54-109.11.
  Annual examinations required, §54-109.16.
  Costs.
    Payment, §54-109.16.
  Fees, §54-109.14(a).
Federal credit unions.
  Conversion into state credit union, §54-109.95(b).
  Conversion of state credit union into,
    §54-109.95(a).
Fees.
  Disposition of moneys collected, §54-109.14(b), (c).
  Examination fees, §54-109.14(a).
  Organization, §54-109.2(e).
  Supervision fees, §54-109.14(a).
Fiduciaries.
  Power of credit unions generally, §54-109.21.
Financial records privacy generally, §§53B-1 to
  53B-10.
  See FINANCIAL RECORDS PRIVACY.
**Foreign credit unions conducting business in
  state.**
  Approval.
    Denial or revocation, §54-109.106(c).
    Prerequisites, §54-109.106(a).
    Required, §54-109.106(a).
    Requirements, §54-109.106(a), (b).

CREDIT UNIONS —Cont'd
Group purchasing.
Cooperative marketing arrangements authorized, §54-109.77.
Hearings.
Removal of officers, §54-109.19(b).
Suspension and conservation.
Reply to order, §54-109.92(d).
Immunity.
Director or officer of nonprofit corporation, §55A-8-60(c).
Installment loans, §54-109.69.
Insurance.
Members.
Cooperative marketing arrangements to facilitate members' purchase of, §54-109.75(b).
Purchase of insurance for, §54-109.75(a).
Source of insurance, §54-109.75(c).
Officers.
Liability insurance for, §54-109.76.
Share and deposit insurance, §54-109.78(a).
Prerequisite to granting of charter, §54-109.78(b).
Insurance premium financing.
Exception to license requirement, §58-35-10(a).
Interest, §54-109.65.
Investments, §54-109.82.
Authorized investments, §54-109.82.
Joint accounts.
Additions.
Effect, §54-109.58(c).
Establishment, §54-109.58(a).
Estate tax provisions not repealed, §54-109.58(b).
Form of statement establishing, §54-109.58(a).
Incidents of account, §54-109.58(a).
Section deemed not exclusive, §54-109.58(a1).
Withdrawals.
Effect, §54-109.58(c).
Liens, §54-109.59.
Line of credit, §54-109.70.
Liquidation, voluntary.
Assets.
Use, §54-109.93(g).
Authorized, §54-109.93(a).
Certificate of dissolution, §54-109.93(h).
Continuation of existence for certain purposes, §54-109.93(f).
Notice.
Board of directors to notify administrator, §54-109.93(c).
Meeting of members to consider question, §54-109.93(e).
Records.
Retention, §54-109.93(h).
Resolution, §54-109.93(b).
Submission of question to members, §54-109.93(b), (d), (e).
Loan officers.
Appointment, §54-109.47(a).
Delegation of powers by credit committee, §54-109.47(a).
In lieu of credit committee, §§54-109.35(c), 54-109.48.
Review by credit committee of loan applications not approved by, §54-109.47(b).
Loans, §§54-109.65 to 54-109.71.
Applications, §54-109.66.
Authorized investments generally, §54-109.82.
Boards of directors.
Duties of directors as to, §54-109.44.

CREDIT UNIONS —Cont'd
Loans —Cont'd
Commercial loan commitments to be in writing, §22-5.
Conditional sales contracts of members.
Purchase, §54-109.71(c).
Credit committee.
Majority of committee must approve, §54-109.46.
Guaranteed loan programs of federal and state governments.
Participation in, §54-109.71(b).
Installments, §54-109.69.
Interest, §54-109.65.
Joint loans.
Participation in, §54-109.71(a).
Limitations, §54-109.67.
Line of credit, §54-109.70.
Other credit unions.
Loans to as authorized investments, §54-109.82.
Powers of credit unions generally, §54-109.21.
Purposes, §54-109.65.
Restrictions, §54-109.67.
Security, §54-109.68.
Terms, §54-109.65.
Written documents.
Loans to be evidenced by, §54-109.66.
Members, §§54-109.26 to 54-109.31.
Age.
Minimum age to hold office, §54-109.31(e).
Minimum age to vote at meetings, §54-109.31(d).
Associations, §54-109.27.
Representation and voting at meetings, §54-109.31(c).
Expulsion.
Power of credit unions, §54-109.21.
Generally, §54-109.26.
Groups, §§54-109.26(b), 54-109.27.
Representation and voting at meetings, §54-109.31(c).
Insurance.
Cooperative marketing arrangements to facilitate members' purchase of, §54-109.75(b).
Purchase of insurance for, §54-109.75(a).
Source of insurance, §54-109.75(c).
Leaving field of membership.
Retention of membership, §54-109.29.
Liquidation, voluntary.
Submission of question to members, §54-109.93(b), (d), (e).
Meetings.
Election of directors, §54-109.35(a).
Generally, §54-109.31(a).
Voting, §54-109.31(b).
Age.
Minimum age, §54-109.31(d).
Societies, associations, copartnerships or corporations having membership, §54-109.31(c).
Other credit unions, §54-109.28.
Proxy voting.
Prohibited, §54-109.31(b).
Retention of membership on leaving field, §54-109.29.
Societies, §54-109.27.
Representation and voting at meetings, §54-109.31(c).
Voting at meetings, §54-109.31(b) to (d).
Withdrawal from membership, §54-109.21.

CREDIT UNIONS —Cont'd
Merger, §54-109.94.
Minors as members.
Minimum age for holding office, §54-109.31(e).
Minimum age for voting at meetings,
§54-109.31(d).
Mortgage bankers, brokers and servicers.
Persons engaged in the mortgage business.
State or federally chartered credit union claim
and confirm exemption, §53-244.050(h).
Names.
Articles of incorporation to state, §§54-109.2(a),
54-109.3.
Exclusive use of name, §54-109.5.
Notice.
Liquidation.
Voluntary liquidation.
Board of directors to notify administrator,
§54-109.93(c).
Meeting of members to consider question,
§54-109.93(e).
Removal of officers, §54-109.19(b).
Suspension of operations.
Notification to members of credit union
commission, §54-109.92(n).
Office facilities.
Change of place of business, §54-109.6(b).
Facilities at location other than main office,
§54-109.6(a).
Sharing office space with other credit unions,
§54-109.6(c).
Officers.
Age.
Minimum age to hold office, §54-109.31(e).
Board of directors. See within this heading,
"Board of directors."
Compensation, §54-109.38.
Conflicts of interest, §54-109.39.
Duties, §54-109.40(c).
Enumerated, §54-109.40(a), (d).
Executive officers.
Election by board, §54-109.40(a).
Immunity of director or officer of nonprofit
corporation, §55A-8-60(c).
Insurance.
Liability insurance for, §54-109.76.
Record of names and addresses, §54-109.36.
Removal.
Grounds, §54-109.19(a).
Hearing, §54-109.19(b).
Notice, §54-109.19(b).
Order of removal, §54-109.19(b).
Power of administrator of credit unions,
§54-109.19(a).
Procedure, §54-109.19(b).
Terms of office, §54-109.40(b).
Operating fees.
Corporate credit unions, §54-110.8.
Orders.
Confidential information.
Disclosure orders, §54-109.105(b).
Conservation, §54-109.92.
Organization.
Applications for new credit unions.
Information contained in application to be
public information, §54-109.105(c).
Articles of incorporation, §54-109.2(b).
Amendment, §54-109.4(a).
When effective, §54-109.4(b).
Form, §54-109.3.

CREDIT UNIONS —Cont'd
Organization —Cont'd
Board of directors.
Selection, §54-109.2(d).
Bylaws.
Preparation and adoption, §54-109.2(c).
Certificate of approval, §54-109.2(e).
Revocation, §54-109.13.
Charter members.
Number, §54-109.2(a).
Fees, §54-109.2(e).
Procedure, §54-109.2.
Supervisory committee.
Selection, §54-109.2(d).
Other credit unions.
Joint loans with.
Participation in, §54-109.71(a).
Loans to.
Authorized investments, §54-109.82.
Membership, §54-109.28.
Merger with, §54-109.94.
Out-of-state business, §54-109.7.
Payable on death (POD) accounts.
Additions, withdrawal, payment or change of
beneficiary, effect, §54-109.57A(c).
Establishment, §54-109.57A(a).
Estate taxes, provisions not repealed or modified,
§54-109.57A(d).
Form of statement creating, §54-109.57A(a).
Incidents of accounts, §54-109.57A(a).
Penalties.
Confidential information, §54-109.105.
Reports.
Neglect to make report, §54-109.15(b).
Unlawful use of name containing words "credit
union,"§54-109.5.
Personal agency accounts.
Creation, §54-109.63(a), (c).
Effect, §54-109.63(d), (e).
Survivorship, §54-109.63(b).
Place of business.
Change of place of business, §54-109.6(b).
Facilities at locations other than main office,
§54-109.6(a).
Powers, §§54-109.21, 54-109.22.
Conducting business outside state, §54-109.7.
Generally, §54-109.21.
Incidental powers, §54-109.22.
Privacy of financial records generally, §§53B-1
to 53B-10.
See FINANCIAL RECORDS PRIVACY.
Purposes, §54-109.1.
Incidental powers for, §54-109.22.
Raffles.
Savings promotion raffles, §§14-309.15(h),
54-109.64.
Records.
Board and committee members, §54-109.36.
Confidential information, §54-109.105(a).
Destruction of records after expiration of retention
time, §54-109.17(b).
Generally, §54-109.17(a).
Liquidation.
Voluntary liquidation.
Retention of records, §54-109.93(h).
Photostatic or photographic reproductions.
Admissibility as evidence, §54-109.17(c).
Privacy of financial records generally, §§53B-1 to
53B-10.
Reduction in shares, §54-109.61.
Regular reserve, §§54-109.86, 54-109.87.

CREDIT UNIONS —Cont'd
Reports.
Conservation.
Reports by conservator, §54-109.92(f).
Neglect to make report.
Penalty, §54-109.15(b).
Revocation of certificate of approval, §54-109.13.
Required, §54-109.15(a).
Reserves, §§54-109.86 to 54-109.88.
Corporate credit unions, §54-110.9.
Regular reserve.
Transfers to, §54-109.86(a).
Increase or decrease of requirement,
§54-109.86(b).
Use, §54-109.87.
Requirements not to be construed as limiting,
§54-109.86(d).
Risk assets.
Defined, §54-109.88.
Special reserves, §54-109.86(c).
Rules and regulations.
Administrator of credit unions, §54-109.12.
Savings accounts, §§54-109.53 to 54-109.64.
Deposits, §54-109.55.
Joint accounts, §54-109.58.
Savings promotion raffles, §§14-309.15(h),
54-109.64.
Seals and sealed instruments.
Power to adopt and use seal, §54-109.21.
Securities regulation.
Exempt securities, §78A-16.
Security for loans, §54-109.68.
Service of process.
Foreign credit unions.
Agent for service of process.
Required, §54-109.106(b).
Suspension and conservation.
Order, §54-109.92(b).
Shareholder liability, §54-109.30.
Shares and shareholders.
Articles of incorporation.
Information to be included, §§54-109.2(b),
54-109.3.
Certificates.
Not required, §54-109.53(c).
Insurance.
Share and deposit insurance, §54-109.78(a).
Prerequisite to granting of charter,
§54-109.78(b).
Liability of shareholders, §54-109.30.
Lien on shares, §54-109.59.
Reduction in shares.
Conditions for, §54-109.61(a).
Excess divided among members, §54-109.61(b).
Majority vote of members at special meeting,
§54-109.61(a).
Subscriptions, §54-109.53(b).
Transfer of shares, §54-109.53(b).
Small estates.
Collection of property by affidavit.
Transfer of rights by representation of affidavit,
§28A-25-1(c).
Social security.
Coverage under title II of social security act.
State employees' credit union.
Elections relating to membership,
contributions and service, §135-27(e).
State departments and agencies.
Information exchangers, §54-109.105(d).
Supervisory committee.
Appointment, §54-109.35(b).

CREDIT UNIONS —Cont'd
Supervisory committee —Cont'd
Audits, §54-109.49.
Clerical and auditing assistants in lieu of,
§54-109.35(b).
Conflicts of interest, §54-109.39.
Duties, §54-109.49.
Expenses of members, §54-109.38.
Number of members, §§54-109.2(d), 54-109.35(b).
Organization.
Selection, §54-109.2(d).
Record of members, §54-109.36.
Removal or suspension of members, §54-109.35(b).
Vacancies, §54-109.37.
Survivorship.
Personal agency accounts, §54-109.63(b).
Trust accounts.
Governing provisions, §54-109.57A.
Suspension of operations.
Appeals from decisions of administrator,
§54-109.92(k).
Extension of period of suspension, §54-109.92(m).
Grounds, §54-109.92(a).
Notification of members of credit union committee,
§54-109.92(n).
Order, §54-109.92(b).
Appeals, §54-109.92(k).
Effect, §54-109.92(c).
Reply to order, §54-109.92(c).
Effect of failure to file, §54-109.92(l).
Hearing on, §54-109.92(d).
Taxation.
Exemptions, §54-109.99.
Restriction, §54-109.99.
Thrift accounts, §54-109.56.
Trust accounts.
Shares and deposits in trust, §54-109.59.
United States.
Exchange of information permitted,
§54-109.105(d).

CREEK OBSTRUCTIONS.
Free passage of boats, §77-12.
Natural drainage, §77-14.
Natural flow, §77-13.

CREMATION, §§90-210.120 to 90-210.135.
Access to crematory area.
Persons authorized, §90-210.129(f).
Amputated body parts, §90-210.129(q).
Authorizing agent.
Anatomical gifts.
Inapplicability of provisions, §90-210.124(d).
Cancellation of cremation, instructions.
Revocation of authorization to cremate,
§90-210.125(d).
Cremation authorization form, §90-210.125.
Defined, §90-210.121.
Disposition of remains.
Responsibility, §90-210.130(b).
Persons authorized to serve as, §90-210.124(a).
Reimbursing licensee.
Responsibility, §90-210.130(b).
Waiver of right to authorize disposition,
§90-210.124(b).
Authorizing cremation and disposition.
Persons eligible, §90-210.124(c).
**Burial-transit permit/cremation authorization
form.**
Required prior to cremation.
Deaths investigated by medical examiner,
§90-210.128(c).

CREMATION —Cont'd
Cancellation of cremation, instructions.
Revocation of authorization to cremate,
§90-210.125(d).
Caskets.
Rules requiring remains be placed in or cremated
in.
Prohibition, §90-210.128(a).
Cemeteries.
Constructing adjacent to, §90-210.123(b).
Construction of crematory.
Local zoning and environmental regulations.
Consistency with required, §90-210.123(b).
Cremating within 24 hours after death.
Restriction, §90-210.129(e).
Cremation authorization form.
Disclosure, §90-210.126(b).
Information required, §90-210.125(a).
Instructions contained in authorization.
Duty to cremate and dispose of remains in
accordance with, §90-210.126(d).
Legal right to cremate upon receipt,
§90-210.125(c).
Liability of authorizing agent signing,
§90-210.125(b).
No liability for cremation pursuant to,
§90-210.131(b).
Persons in possession of executed form.
Duty to ensure remains cremated,
§90-210.126(c).
Receipt by crematory before cremation.
Required, §§90-210.128(b), 90-210.131(b).
Required to cremate, §90-210.125(a).
Revocation by authorizing agent, cancellation of
cremation, §90-210.125(d).
Standard form and procedures.
Board may adopt, §90-210.134(a).
Vital statistics, §130A-113(b).
Warranty of truthfulness of facts.
Authorizing agent signing, §§90-210.125(b),
90-210.131(a).
Cremation containers.
Defined, §90-210.121.
Initial containers or urns.
Placement of remains in, §90-210.129(l), (m).
Shipping remains, packaging requirements,
§90-210.129(n).
Remains cremated in enclosed containers,
§90-210.129(g).
Rules by crematory licensees.
Restrictions, §90-210.128(a), (b).
Cremation only in licensed facility,
§90-210.123(f).
Cremation procedures, §90-210.129(a) to (n).
Cremation societies.
Registration required, §90-210.135(a).
Crematory authority.
Chairman, vice chairman, secretary,
§90-210.122(e).
Established, §90-210.122(a).
Meetings, quorum, §90-210.122(f).
Number of members, §90-210.122(b).
Per diem and travel and subsistence expenses,
§90-210.122(d).
Terms of members, §90-210.122(c).
Crematory manager.
Application for licensure to identify,
§90-210.123(d).
Defined, §90-210.121.
Names and address, informing board,
§90-210.123(d).

CREMATION —Cont'd
Crematory manager —Cont'd
Permit fee, §90-210.132(a).
Crematory technicians.
Application for licensure to identify,
§90-210.123(d).
Defined, §90-210.121.
Educational certificates included on license
application, §90-210.123(d).
Employment by crematory required,
§90-210.123(d).
Names and address, informing board,
§90-210.123(d).
Replacing at time of license renewal.
Continued operation, time, §90-210.123(d).
Crime of violence in connection with death.
Requesting or authorizing cremation,
§90-210.134(d).
Criminal penalty for violations of article,
§90-210.134(c).
Death certificate.
Required before cremating, information required,
§90-210.128(a).
Definitions, §90-210.121.
Discipline, §90-210.123(g) to (i).
**Disposition of remains of terminated
pregnancies,** §130A-131.10.
Dispute concerning cremation.
Refusal to accept body or perform cremation,
§90-210.131(d).
Refusal to release or dispose of remains,
§90-210.131(e).
Environmental regulations.
Construction consistent with, §90-210.123(b).
Fees.
Disposition, §90-210.132(b).
Schedule of fees, §90-210.132(a).
Felony convictions.
Forfeiture of license, §15A-1331A.
Fetal remains.
Acknowledgment of delivery, §90-210.129(o).
Fetal report of death, §90-210.129(p).
Final dispositions.
Authorizing agent, responsibility, §90-210.130(b).
Licensee disposing of, §90-210.130(b).
Manner of disposing of, §90-210.130(c), (d), (f).
Release of cremated remains by licensee,
§90-210.130(e).
Statement specifying ultimate disposition.
Authorizing agent to provide, §90-210.130(a).
Storing or retaining remains.
At direction of authorizing agent, records,
§90-210.130(a).
Funeral Establishments.
Constructing adjacent to, §90-210.123(b).
Hearings, §90-210.123(i).
Holding and processing facility requirements,
§90-210.129(i).
Identification of bodies before, §90-210.29A.
Impossible or impractical cremations.
Not required, §90-210.129(k).
Initial containers or urns.
Placement of remains in, §90-210.129(l), (m).
Shipping remains, packaging requirements,
§90-210.129(n).
License as crematory licensee.
Application, §90-210.123(c).
Crematory manager and crematory technician.
Application to identify, §90-210.123(d).
Expiration, §90-210.123(e).
Fees, §90-210.132(a).

CREMATION —Cont'd
License as crematory licensee —Cont'd
Issuance, requirements for, §90-210.123(c).
Renewal, §90-210.123(e).
Required to operate crematory, §90-210.123(a).
Suspension or revocation.
Felony convictions, §15A-1331A.
Suspension, revocation or refusal to issue or renew.
Grounds, §90-210.123(g).
Manner of disposing of cremated remains, §90-210.130(c), (d), (f).
Medical examiners.
Postmortem medicolegal examinations and services.
When medical examiner's permission necessary before cremation, §130A-388(a), (b).
Medical waste.
Inapplicability of article to cremation, §90-210.134(b).
North Carolina crematory act.
Short title, §90-210.120.
North Carolina crematory authority, §90-210.122.
Operation of crematory in state.
License required, §90-210.123(a).
Persons or entities who may operate, §90-210.123(a).
Pacemakers, defibrillators or other implants.
Cremating body containing prohibited, §90-210.129(d).
Per cremation fee, §90-210.132(a).
Placement of cremated remains in container, §90-210.129(l).
Preneed cremation arrangements.
Action in accordance with required, §90-210.126(d).
Authorizations prior to effective date of act.
Inapplicability of provisions, §90-210.126(f).
Authorizing cremation and final disposition by, §90-210.126(a).
Best efforts to ensure cremation and final disposition.
Persons in possession of authorization, §90-210.126(c).
Cancellation of authorization, §90-210.126(a).
Copy of form.
Retention, sent to funeral establishment, §90-210.126(a).
Discharge from legal obligation.
Compliance with terms, §90-210.126(e).
Disclosure required in authorization form, §90-210.126(b).
Final disposition specified, §90-210.126(e).
Transfer of authorization, right, §90-210.126(a).
Probation.
Placing licensee on, §90-210.123(h).
Procedures for cremation, §90-210.128(a) to (n).
Processing and pulverizing remains, standards, compliance, §90-210.129(j).
Receipt.
Furnished person delivering remains, §90-210.127(a).
Furnished to person receiving remains, §90-210.127(b).
Record keeping requirements, §90-210.127(a), (b).
Retention and disposition records, §90-210.130(a).
Registration of cremation societies, §90-210.135(a).

CREMATION —Cont'd
Reimbursing licensee.
Authorizing agent, responsibility, §90-210.130(b).
Release of cremated remains by licensee, §90-210.130(e).
Residue.
Removal from chamber, separation from foreign residue, §90-210.129(g).
Rights of licensees, §90-210.133(a) to (c).
Rules for carrying out and enforcement of provisions.
Adoption by board, §90-210.134(a).
Rules for management and operation of crematory.
Right of licensee to adopt, §90-210.133(a).
Scattering remains over uninhabited lands, public water ways or sea, §90-210.130(c), (d), (f).
Shipping remains, packaging requirements, §90-210.129(n).
Short title.
North Carolina crematory act, §90-210.120.
Simultaneous cremation.
Prohibited, §90-210.129(h).
Societies.
Registration required, §90-210.135(a).
Storing or retaining remains.
At direction of authorizing agent, records, §90-210.130(a).
Unauthorized persons viewing cremation chamber.
Prohibition, §90-210.129(f).
Urn or receptacle.
Initial containers or urns.
Placement of remains in, §90-210.129(l), (m).
Shipping remains, packaging requirements, §90-210.129(n).
Rules requiring remains be placed in or cremated in.
Prohibition, §90-210.128(b).
Valuables delivered to licensee.
Licensee not liable for, §90-210.131(c).
Vital statistics.
Authorization for cremation, §130A-113(b).
Waiver of right to authorize disposition, §90-210.124(b).
Zoning regulations.
Construction consistent with, §90-210.123(b).

CRESWELL, TOWN OF.
Satellite annexation.
Limitation on area of satellite corporate limits, inapplicability, §160A-58.1(b).

CRIME AGAINST NATURE, §14-177.

CRIME COMMISSION.
Governor's crime commission, §§143B-1100 to 143B-1102.
Transfer to department of public safety, §143A-244.

CRIME LABORATORIES.
Costs of services in criminal case, §7A-304(a).
State crime laboratory ombudsman, §114-16.2.

CRIME VICTIMS.
Compensation, §§15B-1 to 15B-37.
See CRIME VICTIMS COMPENSATION.
DNA analysis, §§15A-266 to 15A-270.
See DNA.
Financial recovery assistance act, §§15B-30 to 15B-37.
See CRIME VICTIMS FINANCIAL RECOVERY ASSISTANCE ACT.

CRIME VICTIMS —Cont'd
Generally.
See VICTIMS OF CRIME.
Rights.
See VICTIMS OF CRIME.
Sex offense victims assistance program,
§143B-1200.

CRIME VICTIMS COMPENSATION, §§15B-1 to
15B-37.
Action by claimant for damages.
Attorney general's duties after notice from
commission, §15B-16(c).
Notice to commission prerequisite for bringing,
§15B-16(c).
Special verdict to indicate separate award for
noneconomic detriment, punitive damages
and economic loss, §15B-16(d).
Application for award.
Contents, §15B-7(a).
False or fraudulent application, §15B-7(b).
Filing, §15B-7(a).
Procedure, §15B-8(a).
Procedure.
Filing, §15B-8(a).
Appropriations.
Compensation payable.
Available to extent that general assembly
appropriates funds, §15B-25.
Attorney general.
Action by claimant for damages.
Duty after notice from commission, §15B-16(c).
Representation of state, §15B-5.
Availability of award.
Providing information to victim, §15B-20.
Award.
Claims exceeding $5,000 or involving future
economic loss, §15B-10(b).
Claims not exceeding $5,000 and not including
future economic loss, §15B-10(a).
Clerks of court.
Notice to, §15B-15.
Contested cases.
Claimants dissatisfied with decision,
§15B-10(d).
Economic loss.
Documentation establishing submitted to
commission, §15B-10(c).
Specific statements of loss.
Included in trial courts judgment.
Considered in making award, §15B-14(c).
When compensation awarded, §15B-4.
Written statement of decision, §15B-10(d).
Citation of chapter, §15B-1.
Civil tort law.
Rules of liability applicable to.
Commission to follow, §15B-4(a).
Clerks of court.
Notice.
Award made from crime victims compensation
fund, §15B-15.
Commission.
Action by claimant for damages.
Notice to attorney general of action, §15B-16(c).
Attorney general authorized to assert rights,
§15B-16(f).
Chairman, §15B-3(d).
Compensation, §15B-3(f).
Composition, §15B-3(a).
Director, §15B-3(g).
Established, §15B-3.

CRIME VICTIMS COMPENSATION —Cont'd
Commission —Cont'd
Powers, §15B-6(a).
Quorum, §15B-3(e).
Records.
Confidentiality, §15B-8.1(b).
Reports.
Annual report, §15B-21.
Terms of office, §15B-3(b).
Vacancies in office, §15B-3(c).
Compensation payable.
Available to extent that general assembly
appropriates funds, §15B-25.
Injury to or death of victim.
Maximum compensation payable, §15B-11(g).
Construction and interpretation.
Right to receive compensation.
Act not construed to create, §15B-25.
Contested cases.
Commenced by claimants dissatisfied with
decision, §15B-10(d).
Evidence.
Exclusion of persons from hearings, §15B-12(h).
Juvenile proceedings records, §15B-12(g).
Law enforcement officers providing copies of
information gathered in investigation,
§15B-12(d).
Medical or psychological reports, §15B-12(e).
Mental or physical examination of claimants,
§15B-12(c).
Method of taking evidence, §15B-12(a).
Official record open to public inspection,
§15B-12(i).
Privileges, §15B-12(b).
Requesting evidence not admissible prohibited,
§15B-12(f).
Conviction of claimant.
Felony conviction within three years of claimed
injury.
Denial of claim, §15B-11(c1).
Conviction of offender.
Effect, §15B-14(a).
Credit protection, §15B-26.
Crime victims financial recovery assistance
act, §§15B-30 to 15B-37.
Criminal injurious conduct.
Basis for award, §15B-4(b).
Definitions, §15B-2.
Denial of claim.
Claimant convicted of felony within three years of
claimed injury, §15B-11(c1).
Contributory misconduct, §15B-11(b).
Discretion of commission or director, §15B-11(b1).
Failure to cooperate with law enforcement
agencies, §15B-11(c).
Grounds, §15B-11(a).
Reconsideration or reopening claim, §15B-11(h).
Reimbursement from collateral sources,
§15B-11(d).
Director.
Claims of fund or commission.
Authority to pursue, §15B-18(f).
Powers, §15B-6(b).
Disbursements, §15B-22.
Economic loss.
Future economic loss.
Payment of claim for, §15B-16(c).
Paid for only, §15B-4(a).
Evidence.
Contested cases, §15B-12.

CRIME VICTIMS COMPENSATION —Cont'd
Evidence —Cont'd
Establishing requirements for award met,
§15B-4(a).
Execution.
Award not subject to, §15B-17(b).
**Failure to cooperate with law enforcement
agencies.**
Denial of claim, reduction of award,
reconsideration of award, §15B-11(c).
Fees.
Application for award.
Filing fee, §15B-7(a).
Financial recovery assistance act.
See CRIME VICTIMS FINANCIAL RECOVERY
ASSISTANCE ACT.
Fund.
Attorney general authorized to assert rights,
§15B-16(f).
Clerks of court.
Notified of awards made from, §15B-15.
Deposited with state treasurer, §15B-23.
Established, §15B-23.
Information provided to victims and dependents
concerning existence, §15B-20.
Insufficient funds.
Payment delayed until sufficient funds
available, §15B-22.
Investments by state treasurer, §15B-23.
Oversight of state auditor, §15B-23.
Restitution, eligible recipient for, §15B-16(b).
Subrogation to claimant's rights to recover for
economic loss, §15B-16(a).
Disposition of funds recovered, §15B-16(e).
Surplus, §15B-23.
Future economic loss.
Payment of claim for, §15B-16(c).
Hearings.
Contested cases.
Evidence, §15B-12.
Suspension.
Disposition of criminal prosecution, §15B-14(b).
Investments.
Crime victims compensation fund.
Investments by state treasurer, §15B-23.
Noneconomic loss.
Not paid for, §15B-4(a).
Notice.
Award made from crime victims compensation
fund.
Clerks of court to be notified, §15B-15.
Payment.
Future economic loss, §15B-16(c).
Installments, §15B-16(b).
Insufficient funds.
Delay until sufficient funds available, §15B-22.
Lump sum, §15B-16(b).
Manner of payment, §15B-16(a).
Negotiations with service providers.
Reduction of amount claimed by provider,
§15B-16(e).
Refunds, §15B-16(d).
Privileges.
Applicability, §15B-8.1(a).
Prosecution or conviction of offender.
Effect, §15B-14(a).
Providing information to victims, §15B-20.
Publicity.
Information provided to victims and dependents of
existence of crime victims compensation fund,
§15B-20.

CRIME VICTIMS COMPENSATION —Cont'd
Reports.
Commission.
Annual report, §15B-21.
Restitution.
Crime victims compensation fund, §15B-18(a).
Eligible recipient, §15B-16(b).
Requiring defendant to pay encouraged, §15B-24.
Right to receive compensation.
Act construed not to create, §15B-25.
Secured transactions.
Third parties.
Assignments.
Restrictions on assignments, §§25-9-406(i),
25-9-408(f).
Short title of chapter, §15B-1.
State auditor.
Crime victims compensation fund.
Oversight.
Responsibilities, §15B-23.
State treasurer.
Crime victims compensation fund.
Deposited with, §15B-23.
Investments by, §15B-23.
Subrogation.
Collateral sources, §15B-19.
Crime victims compensation fund, §15B-18(a).
Disposition of funds recovered, §15B-16(e).
State, §15B-18.
Taxation.
Exemption, §15B-17(a).

**CRIME VICTIMS FINANCIAL RECOVERY
ASSISTANCE ACT, §§15B-30 to 15B-37.**
Action to recover profits or funds, §15B-34(a).
Commission, responsibilities of, §15B-34(c).
Notice by eligible persons, §15B-34(b).
Standing, §15B-34(d).
**Contract or agreement to pay an offender
profit from crime or other funds.**
Notice to commission, §15B-32(a).
Notice to eligible persons, §15B-32(b).
**Conviction overturned or pardon issued,
§15B-37.**
Definitions, §15B-31.
Evasive action void, §15B-37.
Legislative intent, §15B-30.
Penalties.
Escrow account.
Establishment and notice, §15B-33(d).
Satisfaction of judgment from, §15B-33(e).
Unclaimed funds, return of, §15B-33(f).
Failure to give notice, §15B-33(a).
Failure to pay, §15B-33(c).
Notice and opportunity to be heard required,
§15B-33(b).
Public policy, §15B-30.
Evasive action void, §15B-37.
Subrogation, §15B-35.

CRIMINAL CASE DOCKETING.
Superior courts, §7A-49.4.

CRIMINAL CONTEMPT, §§5A-11 to 5A-17.
See CONTEMPT.

CRIMINAL CONVERSATION, §52-13.
Costs.
Allowance of costs to defendant, §6-19.
Allowance of costs to plaintiff, §6-18.
Limitation of actions, §§1-52, 52-13(b).
Natural person as party, §52-13(c).
Parties as witnesses, §8-50(a).

CRIMINAL CONVERSATION —Cont'd
Permanent physical separation of spouse,
§52-13(a).

CRIMINAL FORFEITURES.
Generally.
See FORFEITURES.

CRIMINAL HISTORY RECORD CHECKS,
§§114-19.01 to 114-19.50.
Adoption.
Adoptive parents seeking to adopt minor in
custody of county department of social
services, §§48-3-309, 114-19.7.
Agency placements, §48-3-203(d1).
Definition of "criminal history,"§48-1-101.
Preplacement assessments, §48-3-303(d).
Minor in custody or placement responsibility of
county department of social services,
§48-3-309.
Adult care home providers and employees,
§§114-19.3, 114-19.10, 131D-40.
Alarm system licensing.
Applicants for license or registration, §74D-2.1.
Archaeological investigations.
Permit applicants, §70-13.1.
**Area mental health, developmental disabilities,
and substance abuse services authorities,**
§114-19.10.
Attorneys at law.
Applicants for admission to practice, §84-24.
**Auctioneer, apprentice auctioneer or auction
firm license.**
Applicants, §§85B-3.2, 114-19.8.
Bail bondsmen and runners.
Applicants for license, §§58-71-50(a), 58-71-51.
Renewal in even numbered years, §58-71-75(c).
Change of name.
Taking fingerprints for, §101-5(b).
Charter schools, §115C-238.29K.
Child abuse, neglect or dependency reports.
Assessment of report.
History of violent behavior by abuser,
§7B-302(d1).
When juvenile removed from home.
Check of alleged abuser or abusers, §7B-503(b).
Child care providers, §§110-90.2, 114-19.5.
Chiropractors, §§90-143.3, 114-19.22.
Concealed handgun permit.
Fees, §14-415.19(a).
Procedure for issuance of permit, §14-415.15(a).
Renewal.
Criminal history updated, §14-415.16(c).
Counselors.
Applicants for licensure as professional
counselors, §§90-345, 114-19.26.
County employees, §§114-19.14, 153A-94.2.
Dental hygienist license applicants, §90-224(c).
Dental license applicants, §90-30(b).
Department of health and human services.
Employees and applicants for employment,
§114-19.6.
Department of public instruction.
Employees and applicants, §114-19.23(f).
Division of criminal statistics, §§114-10 to
114-10.02.
Division of juvenile justice.
Employees and applicants for employment,
§114-19.6.
Domestic violence.
Bail and pretrial release.
Criminal history report for defendant.
Condition of pretrial release, §15A-534.1.

CRIMINAL HISTORY RECORD CHECKS
—Cont'd
Drivers' licenses.
Persons manufacturing or producing, §114-19.24.
Petitioner for restoration of revoked license,
§114-19.31.
Drug detection dog handlers, §90-102.1(d).
Emergency medical services, §§114-19.21,
131E-159(g).
Euthanasia technicians, §§19A-24(d), 114-19.29.
**Exploration, recovery or salvage operations
and archaeological investigations.**
Applicants for permits or licenses, §114-19.17.
Expunction of criminal records.
First offenders not over age twenty-one.
Drug offenses.
Application for check, §15A-145.2(a).
Toxic vapors offenses.
Application for check, §15A-145.3(a).
First offenders under age 18.
Application for check filed with petition,
§15A-145(a).
Gang offenses, §15A-145.1(a).
Nonviolent felony offenses, §15A-145.4(c).
Misdemeanor larceny conviction.
Application for check filed with petition,
§15A-145(d1).
Fees.
Conducted for purposes other than administration
of criminal justice, §114-19.1(a).
Firearms.
Concealed handgun permit.
Fees, §14-415.19(a).
Procedure for issuance of permit, §14-415.15(a).
Renewal.
Criminal history updated, §14-415.16(c).
Out of state purchases by citizens of state,
§14-409.10.
Petitioner for restoration of rights.
Conduct of check by bureau, §114-19.28(b).
Department of justice instant background check
system check, §14-415.4(h).
Fee to offset cost, §114-19.28(d).
Information to superior court clerk,
§114-19.28(c).
Submission of fingerprints, forms and
information, §114-19.28(a).
Fire departments, applicants, §114-19.12.
Foster parents, §§114-19.4, 131D-10.3A(a) to (i).
Funeral service license applicants,
§90-210.25(a).
General assembly appointees, §§114-15(a),
120-19.4(a).
Home care agencies, §114-19.10.
Applicants for employment, §131E-265.
Identification cards.
Persons manufacturing or producing, §114-19.24.
Information technology services office,
§114-19.20.
Insurance adjusters.
Public adjusters.
Confidentiality of information, §58-33A-15(e).
National criminal history record check,
§58-33A-15(c).
Business entity, §58-33A-15(d).
**Insurance company incorporators and key
persons,** §58-7-37.
Insurance producer license applicants,
§58-33-48.
**Interpreter and transliterator license
applicants,** §90D-7(c).

CRIMINAL HISTORY RECORD CHECKS
—Cont'd
Judicial department.
Refusal by employee, contractor or volunteer to consent to.
Denial or termination of employment, contract or volunteer opportunity, §7A-349.
Justice department employees, volunteers and contractors, §114-19.19.
Locksmith licensing, §§74F-18, 114-19.15.
Requesting department of justice to conduct on applicants.
Power of board, §74F-6.
Manufactured home manufacturers, dealers, salespersons or set-up contractors.
Applicants for licensure, §143-143.10A.
Marriage and family therapists.
Applicants for licensure, §§90-270.63, 114-19.27.
Marriage and family therapy associates.
Applicants for licensure, §§90-270.63, 114-19.27.
Massage and bodywork therapy, §114-19.11B.
Generally, §90-629.1.
Submission of fingerprint card, §90-629.
McGruff house program volunteers, §114-19.9.
Criminal record checks, §114-19.9.
Medicaid.
Provider requirements, §108C-4.
Mental health, developmental disability, substance abuse.
Area authorities and providers, §§114-19.3, 114-19.10, 122C-80.
Providers, §§114-19.3, 114-19.10, 122C-80.
Mortgage bankers, brokers and servicers.
Criminal history records check and fingerprints.
Grounds for denial of renewal, §53-244.101(e).
Municipal officers and employees, §160A-164.2.
Contents of application, §114-19.14.
Names.
Change of name.
Taking fingerprints for, §101-5(b).
National crime prevention and privacy compact, §114-19.50.
Nurses.
Registered or licensed practical nurse, §114-19.11.
Nursing home administrators, §§90-288.01, 114-19.25.
Nursing home employees and applicants for employment, §§114-19.10, 131E-265.
Pharmacists and pharmacies.
License applicants, §90-85.15(c).
Physicians and surgeons.
License applicants, §90-11(b).
Police information network, §114-10.1.
Positions that must be confirmed by general assembly, §§114-15, 120-19.4A.
Precious metals dealers.
Applicants for permits, §66-165(a), (c).
Employees, §66-165(b).
Priority in processing, §114-19.1(c).
Private personnel services.
License applicants, §95-47.2(d).
Private protective services, §74C-8.1.
Applicants for license.
Requirement, §74C-8(d).
Professional counselors.
Applicants for licensure, §§90-345, 114-19.26.
Professional employer organizations.
License applicant furnished department upon request, §58-89A-60(d).

CRIMINAL HISTORY RECORD CHECKS
—Cont'd
Providers of treatment for or services to children, the elderly, mental health patients, the sick and the disabled, §114-19.3.
Adoption.
Prospective adoptive parent, §114-19.3(d).
Consent, §114-19.3(b).
Fees, §114-19.3(e).
Foster care.
Prospective foster care parent, §114-19.3(d).
Generally, §114-19.3(a).
Psychologists, §§90-270.22, 114-19.18.
Public utility employees, screening employment applications, §62-333.
Real estate appraisal management companies.
Applicants for registration or registrants, §§93E-2-11, 114-19.30.
Real estate appraisers and registered trainees, §93E-1-6(c), (d).
Real estate brokers.
License applicants, §93A-4(b1).
Regional schools, §115C-238.73.
Residential school personnel, §143B-146.16.
Respiratory care practitioners.
Applicants for license, §90-652(a).
Rights to receive records of bureau.
Not enlarged, §114-19.1(d).
Salvage.
Abandoned shipwrecks and other underwater sites.
Applicants for permit or license, §121-25.1.
School employees, §§114-19.2, 115C-332.
Charter schools, §115C-238.29K.
Concealed handgun permit, §14-415.15(a).
Contractors.
Sex offender registry checks, §115C-332.1.
Department of public instruction employees and applicants, §114-19.23(f).
Regional schools, §115C-238.73.
Residential schools, §143B-146.16.
State lottery.
Contracts for purchase of services, supplies, equipment.
Background investigations, §18C-151(c).
State lottery employees, retailers, contractors and vendors, §114-19.16.
Structural pest control.
Licenses, §106-65.26(d), (e).
Substance abuse professionals, §90-113.46A.
Applicants for registration, certification or licensure, §114-19.11A.
Volunteer fire departments, §114-19.12.

CRIMINAL INDEX RECORDS IN SUPERIOR COURTS.
Certified copies, admissibility, §8-35.2.

CRIMINAL INTELLIGENCE INFORMATION.
Withholding from public disclosure, §132-1.4(d).
Defined, §132-1.4(b).

CRIMINAL INVESTIGATION RECORDS.
Child abuse investigation records.
Law governing, §132-1.4(l).
Complaining witness.
Temporarily withholding name or address by law enforcement, §132-1.4(d).
Court records considered public record, §132-1.4(k).
Definitions, §132-1.4(b).

CRIMINAL INVESTIGATION RECORDS
—Cont'd

Deletion of information not public record.
Law enforcement to make clear deletion made,
§132-1.4(j).

Disclosure of records transmitted to prosecuting attorney.
Law governing, §132-1.4(g).

Information considered public records,
§132-1.4(c).

Information not required to be disclosed,
§132-1.4(h).

Innocence claim inquiry, §§15A-1460 to
15A-1475.
See INNOCENCE CLAIM INQUIRY.

911 or other communications.
Time required to maintain tape recordings,
§132-1.4(i).

Not public record, §132-1.4(a).

Order of court preventing disclosure of information.
Law enforcement agency seeking, §132-1.4(e).

Release by order of court, §132-1.4(a).

Use of public record in custody of another public agency, §132-1.4(f).

CRIMINAL JUSTICE EDUCATION AND TRAINING STANDARDS COMMISSION,
§§17C-1 to 17C-13.

Ad hoc members.
Appointment, §17C-4(b).

Age requirement for holding certification.
Authority of commission to establish, §93B-9.

Appeals.
Denial, suspension or revocation of certification,
§17C-11(b).

Attorney general.
Chairman.
Designation, §17C-5(a).
Custody of books, papers and other property,
§17C-7(b).
Staff assistance.
Attorney general to provide, §17C-7(a).

Certification denied, suspended or revoked.
Appeal, §17C-11(b).

Certification procedure.
Officers, §17C-10.
Powers of commission, §17C-6(a).

Chairman.
Appointment, §17C-5(a).

Compensation of members, §17C-4(a).

Composition, §17C-3(a).

Concealed handgun permit.
Approved courses for firearms safety,
§14-415.12(a).
Certificate of completion of firearms safety course,
§14-415.13(a).
Filing of course description by instructor,
§14-415.12(a).

Contracts.
Power to enter into contracts, §17C-6(a).

Criminal justice agencies.
Defined, §17C-2.

Criminal justice officers.
Defined, §17C-2.
Standards for, §17C-10(b), (c).
Certificates evidencing satisfaction of
requirements, §17C-10(d).

Definitions, §17C-2.

Effect of standards, §17C-10(a).

CRIMINAL JUSTICE EDUCATION AND TRAINING STANDARDS COMMISSION
—Cont'd

Electronic speed measuring device.
Minimum standards, §17C-6(a).

Entry level.
Defined, §17C-2.
Standards for appointment at entry level,
§17C-10(b).

Established, §17C-3(a).

Expenses of members, §17C-4(a).

Felony conviction.
Denial, suspension or revocation of certification,
§17C-13(b).

Grants.
Acceptance, §17C-12(a).
Reimbursement by commission of political
subdivisions, §17C-12(b), (d).

Injunctions to prevent violations, §17C-11(c).

Law enforcement officers.
Certification, §17C-10.

Legislative findings, §17C-1.

Meetings, §17C-5(c).

Noncompliance by criminal justice officer.
Exercise of powers prohibited, enforcement,
§17C-11(a).
Injunctions against performing functions,
§17C-11(c).

Noncompliance by instructor or school director, §17C-11(a1).

Noncompliance by training school, program or course of instruction, §17C-11(a1).

Number of members, §17C-3(a).

Officers.
Certification, §17C-10.

Pardons.
Denial, suspension or revocation of certification.
Persons granted an unconditional pardon.
Prohibited, §17C-13(a).

Policy of state, §17C-1.

Political subdivisions.
Reimbursement of funds, §17C-12.

Powers.
Advisory powers, §17C-6(b).
Enforceable powers, §17C-6(a).
Generally, §17C-6(a).

Qualifications of members, §17C-3(a).

Radar.
Establishing minimum standards, §17C-6(a).

Recommendations.
Advisory powers, §17C-6(b).

Records.
Personnel files.
Disclosure requirements, §17C-7(c).

Reports, §17C-5(d).
Advisory powers, §17C-6(b).
Grant, §17C-12(a).

Research.
Advisory powers, §17C-6(b).

Rules and regulations, §17C-6(a).
Duration, §17C-6(c).
Grant program, §17C-12(c).
Powers enforceable through rules and regulations,
§17C-6(a).
Relation to federal standards, §17C-6(d).

Speed-measuring instruments, §17C-6(a).

Staff assistance.
Attorney general to provide, §17C-7(a).

System.
Establishment of system, §17C-8.

Terms of members, §17C-3(b).

CRIMINAL JUSTICE EDUCATION AND TRAINING STANDARDS COMMISSION —Cont'd

Vice-chairman.
Selection, §17C-5(b).

CRIMINAL JUSTICE INFORMATION NETWORK GOVERNING BOARD, §§143-660 to 143-664.

Appropriations, use, §143-663(b).
Conflicts of interest, §143-661(c).
Creation, §143-661(a).
Definitions, §143-660.
Duties, §143-663(a).
Expenses of members, §143-662.
Grants, use, §143-663(b).
Meetings, §143-664(a).
Members, §143-661(b).
Officers, §143-664(a).
Powers, §143-663(a).
Staff, §143-664(b).

CRIMINAL JUSTICE STANDARDS DIVISION, §17C-9.

Administrative duties and responsibilities, §17C-9(c).
Created, §17C-9(a).
Director.
Appointment by attorney general, §17C-9(b).

CRIMINAL LAW AND PROCEDURE.
ABC board members and employees.
Embezzlement, malfeasance, §18B-702(w).
Abduction, §§14-39 to 14-41.
Abortion.
General provisions, §§14-44 to 14-46.
See ABORTION.
Obstructing abortion clinics, §14-277.4(c).
Parental consent to abortion violation, §90-21.10.
Abuse of children, §§14-318.2, 14-318.4.
Abuse of disabled or elder adults, §14-32.3(a).
Abuse of patients.
Physical abuse, §14-32.2.
Accessories.
See ACCOMPLICES AND ACCESSORIES.
Accomplices.
See ACCOMPLICES AND ACCESSORIES.
Acid or alkali.
Malicious throwing, §14-30.1.
Acting as officer before qualifying, §14-229.
Actions arising out of a criminal act.
Civil actions seeking to recover damages.
Statutes of limitation and repose, §1-15.1.
Address confidentiality program, §§15C-1 to 15C-13.
See ADDRESS CONFIDENTIALITY PROGRAM.
Adoption.
Prohibited placement activities, §48-10-101.
Unauthorized disclosure of identifying information, §48-10-105.
Unlawful payments related to adoption, §48-10-102.
Adult care homes.
Criminal history record checks of employees.
Furnishing false information, §131D-40(e).
Operation without license, §131D-2.6(b).
Adult day care programs.
Harming or willfully neglecting person under care, §131D-6(c1).
Adulterated or misbranded food, drugs or cosmetics.
Intent to cause serious injury or death, §14-34.4(a).

CRIMINAL LAW AND PROCEDURE —Cont'd
Adulterated or misbranded food, drugs or cosmetics —Cont'd
Intent to extort, §14-34.4(b).
Adultery, §14-184.
Adult establishments, §§14-202.10 to 14-202.12.
Adult protection.
Abuse of disabled or elder adults, §14-32.3(a).
Neglect of disabled or elder adult, §14-32.3(b).
Advertising.
Defacing, destroying, injuring, §§14-384, 14-385.
Affidavits.
Motion for appropriate relief.
Supporting affidavits, §15A-1420(b).
Pretrial motion to suppress evidence.
Affidavit supporting motion, §15A-977(a).
Affrays.
Aggravated affrays.
Habitual misdemeanor assault, §14-33.2.
Punishment for misdemeanor affrays, §14-33(b), (c).
Self-defense.
Evidence of former threats upon plea of self-defense, §14-33.1.
Simple affray.
Punishment for misdemeanor affrays, §14-33(a).
Aggravating factors.
Admissions, acceptance, §15A-1022.1(a) to (e).
Air bags.
Unlawful installation or reinstallation, §20-136.2.
Alarm systems licensing.
Confidentiality of certain information concerning applicants and licensees.
Disclosure, §74D-2(f).
Albemarle Sound.
Lumbermen failing to remove obstructions, §76-42.
Alcoholic beverages.
Criminal offenses, criminal procedure.
See ALCOHOLIC BEVERAGES.
Aliens.
Verification of work authorization.
Complaints.
False and frivolous complaints, §64-28(b).
Alligator propagation and production.
Untagged or undocumented alligator possessed by operator of facility, §106-763.1(c).
Alternative fuel, §105-449.139(b).
Ambulance, false request, §14-286.1.
Ambulatory surgical facility licensure.
Unlicensed operation, §131E-151.
American Legion emblem, §14-395.
Amusement device safety.
Death resulting from violation, §95-111.13(i).
Anatomical gifts.
Falsification of document, §130A-412.19.
Sale or purchase of parts, §130A-412.18(a).
Animal auctions.
Unlicensed operation, §19A-33.
Animal baiting, §14-362.1.
Dog baiting, §14-362.2.
Animal cruelty investigators.
Interference in performance of official duties, §19A-48.
Animal dealers.
Acting without license, §19A-34.
Cruelty to animals, §19A-35.
Animal fighting, §14-362.1.
Cockfighting, §14-362.
Dog fighting, §14-362.2.

CRIMINAL LAW AND PROCEDURE —Cont'd
Animal shelters.
Cruelty to animals, §19A-35.
Antifreeze solutions compounded with organic salts or petroleum distillates.
Manufacture or sale, §66-66.
Appeals.
See APPEALS.
Appearance.
See APPEARANCES.
Apples.
Selling immature apples, §106-189.2(b).
Appointment of counsel for indigent persons.
Generally, §§7A-450 to 7A-458.
See INDIGENT DEFENSE SERVICES.
Indigent defense services act, §§7A-498 to 7A-498.8.
See INDIGENT DEFENSE SERVICES.
Indigent services rules, IDS Rules 1.1 to 3.7.
See INDIGENT DEFENSE SERVICES.
Aquatic weed control.
Violations as misdemeanors, §113A-226(a).
Armed robbery, §14-87(a).
Arraignment, §§15A-941 to 15A-945.
Arrest.
Civil cases.
See ARREST IN CIVIL CASES.
General provisions.
See ARREST.
Arson, §§14-58 to 14-69.3.
See ARSON.
Assault and battery.
See ASSAULT AND BATTERY.
Assignments for benefit of creditors.
False swearing as to verified claims filed with clerk, §23-9.
Trustees violating duty, §23-12.
Assistance animal.
Assaulting, §14-163.1.
Assisted living administrators.
Practicing without certificate, §90-288.20.
Athlete agents, §78C-99.
Athletics.
Alcoholic beverages.
Publicly displaying at athletic contests, §18B-301(f).
Bonuses.
Not forbidden, §14-379.
Bribery.
Acceptance of bribes by players, managers, etc., §14-374.
Completion of offenses, §14-375.
Completion of offenses, §14-375.
Definition of bribe, §14-376.
Elements of offense of bribery of players, managers, etc., §14-373.
Intentionally losing contests, §14-377.
Limiting margin of victory or defeat, §14-377.
Throwing, dropping, etc., objects at sporting events.
Offenses against the public safety, §14-281.1.
Venue.
Protection of athletic contests.
Proper venue of prosecutions under article, §14-378.
Atomic energy, radioactivity and ionizing radiation.
Disclosure of confidential information, §104E-29(c).
Radiation protection violations, §104E-23(a).

CRIMINAL LAW AND PROCEDURE —Cont'd
Attempts to commit crime.
See ATTEMPTS TO COMMIT CRIME.
Attorneys at law.
See ATTORNEYS AT LAW.
Audiovisual recording devices.
Unlawful operation in motion picture theater, §14-440.1.
Autopsies.
Photographs, video or audio recordings of autopsy.
Unlawful disclosure, §130A-389.1(c).
Willful violations, §130A-389.1(g).
Bad checks.
See BAD CHECKS.
Bail.
See BAIL.
Bailments.
See BAILMENTS.
Ballistic knives.
Possession and sale, §14-269.6(a), (b).
Bankruptcy and insolvency.
Solicitation of claims of creditors in proceedings, §23-47.
Barrooms and billiard rooms.
Permitting minor to enter, §14-317.
Battery.
See ASSAULT AND BATTERY.
Battleship commission.
Employees with interest, §143B-74.3.
Bawdy houses, §14-188.
Beacons.
Displaying false lights on seashore, §14-282.
Bicycles.
Child bicycle safety act violations, §20-171.9(d).
Bigamy, §14-183.
Billboards.
Highways, roads and streets.
Obstructing view at entrance to building on public highway, §136-102.
Bill of particulars, §15A-925.
Bills of lading.
False bills.
Issuing false bills made felony, §21-42.
Violations of chapter made felony, §21-42.
Birth of child, concealing, §14-46.
Black bears.
Placing food products as bait in area with open season for black bears, §113-294(r).
Violation of protection provisions, §19A-13.
Blacklisting employees, §14-355.
Blood banks.
Supervision by licensed physician.
Violation of requirements, §90-220.12.
Blue Ridge Parkway.
Control of outdoor advertising.
Violations as misdemeanors, §113A-170.
Boating safety.
Flashing blue light, use of, §75A-17(c).
Fraudulent safety certification card, §75A-16.1(f).
Medical waste.
Depositing or discharging, §75A-10(e).
Navigation rules violations, §75A-6.1(c).
Skin and scuba divers, §75A-13.1(d).
Slowing in no-wake zone, §75A-17(f).
Stopping when directed by law enforcement, §75A-17(e).
Vessel agents, §75A-5.2(h).
Violations generally, §75A-18(a).
Boat sanitation devices.
Discharge of sewage in coastal waters, §77-129(a).

CRIMINAL LAW AND PROCEDURE —Cont'd

Boat sanitation devices —Cont'd
Pumpout of marine sanitation devices.
Record to be kept by vessel owner or operator.
Violation, §77-128(b).
Body piercing.
Minors, without consent of parents, §14-400(b).
Boilers.
Violations, §95-69.20.
Boll weevil eradication.
Violations of provisions, §106-65.78(a), (b).
Bonds, surety.
Forfeitures.
When execution to issue, §1-305(a).
Model payment and performance bonds.
Failure of official to require bond as
misdemeanor, §44A-32.
Mortgage in lieu of bond.
Recognizance for appearance in criminal
proceeding, §58-74-5.
Cancellation of mortgage in such proceedings,
§58-74-10.
Security of costs or fine in criminal action,
§58-74-5.
Cancellation of mortgage in such proceedings,
§58-74-10.
Bottles and bottling.
Polluting bottles used for beverages.
Unlawful to pollute, §14-288.
Boxing, §143-658(b).
Brake system.
Violations of sales restriction, §20-124(h).
Breaking and entering.
See BREAKING AND ENTERING.
Bribery.
See BRIBERY.
Bridges.
Fastening vessels to bridges, §136-80.
Load limits for safe capacity.
Capacity violations, §136-72.
Budget of state.
Criminal penalties for violations, §143C-10-1.
Building code of state.
Representation of self as qualified
code-enforcement official, §143-151.18.
Building permits.
Violation of requirements for issuance, §87-14(b).
Buoys, beacons and day marks.
Interfering with, §76-58.
Burden of proof.
Generally.
See BURDEN OF PROOF.
Bureau of investigation, §§114-12 to 114-20.1.
See BUREAU OF INVESTIGATION.
Burglary.
See BURGLARY.
Buying and selling offices, §14-228.
Calendar for criminal trial sessions.
Superior court, criminal case docketing, §7A-49.4.
Calendaring of actions for trial.
Calendaring by district attorney for
administrative purposes, §15A-941(e).
Campus police, §74G-13(a).
Capital punishment.
Generally.
See DEATH PENALTY.
Carrying concealed weapons.
Concealed handgun permit, §§14-415.10 to
14-415.27.
See CONCEALED HANDGUN PERMIT.
Castration, §§14-28, 14-29.

CRIMINAL LAW AND PROCEDURE —Cont'd

Cattle rustling, §14-81.
Cattle tick, §106-362.
Cave protection, §§14-159.20 to 14-159.23.
Cell phones.
School bus operators.
Unlawful use while bus in motion, §20-137.4.
Text messaging or electronic mail.
Driving while using mobile phone for,
§20-137.4A.
**Certificate of relief from collateral
consequences,** §§15A-173.1 to 15A-173.6.
Appearance by district attorney, §15A-173.4(c).
Collateral sanctions not within scope of relief,
§15A-173.3.
Conditions for issuance, §15A-173.2(b).
Definitions, §15A-173.1.
Denial, §15A-173.2(g).
Disqualification.
Consideration for, §15A-173.2(d).
Eligibility to petition for, §15A-173.2(a).
Evidence of due care.
Reliance on certificate as, §15A-173.5.
Expunction.
Certificate not constituting, §15A-173.2(e).
Investigation or verification of person's conduct.
Probation officers, §15A-173.4(d).
Issuance, §15A-173.4(a).
Judge to hear petition, §15A-173.2(a).
Just cause for revocation or modification,
§15A-173.4(b).
Material disputed issues or fact or law,
§15A-173.4(d).
Modification of certificate, §15A-173.4(b).
Motion to modify or revoke, §15A-173.4(b).
Negligence actions.
Evidence of due care, reliance on certificate as,
§15A-173.5.
Notice to district attorney of motion to modify or
revoke, §15A-173.4(b).
Notice to district attorney of petition,
§15A-173.4(a).
Notice to victim, §15A-173.6.
Pardon.
Certificate not constituting, §15A-173.2(e).
Public record, status as, §15A-173.4(e).
Reapplication of petition.
Conditions for, §15A-173.4(a).
Restrictions and collateral sanctions or
disqualifications excluded, §15A-173.2(c).
Revocation, §15A-173.2(f).
Certificate, §15A-173.4(b).
Scope of relief, §15A-173.2(d).
Collateral sanctions not within scope of relief,
§15A-173.3.
Subsequent petition following denial,
§15A-173.2(g).
Victims of crime, rights, §15A-173.6.
Certified public accountants.
Violations of provision, §93-13.
Certiorari.
Petition for writ in post conviction matters,
AppProc 21(e), (f).
Change machines, burglary, §14-56.3.
Change of venue.
Motion, §15A-957.
Charitable solicitations by telephone,
§14-401.12.
Check-cashing businesses, §53-287.
Child abduction, §14-41(a).
Child abuse, §§14-318.2, 14-318.4.

CRIMINAL LAW AND PROCEDURE —Cont'd
Child care facilities, §110-103.
　Unauthorized administration of medicine,
　　§110-102.1A(c), (d).
Child custody orders.
　Enforcement.
　　Criminal contempt, §50-13.3(a).
**Childhood vaccine-related injury
　compensation.**
　Diversion of certain vaccines, §130A-431.
Child placing agencies.
　Unlicensed operation, §131D-10.7.
Child rape, §14-27.2A.
Children and minors.
　See CHILDREN AND MINORS.
Children's health insurance program.
　Fraud and misrepresentation, §108A-70.28.
Child support.
　Enforcement of support.
　　Criminal contempt, §50-13.4(f).
　Failure to support, §14-322.
Chlamydia.
　Defendant accused of offense involving sexual
　　intercourse.
　　Testing on victim's request, §15A-615.
Chop shops, §14-72.7.
Cigarettes and tobacco products.
　Sale of certain packages of cigarettes, §14-401.18.
　Sale or distribution to minors, §14-313.
Cigarette tax.
　Violations as misdemeanors, §105-113.33.
Citations, §§15A-301, 15A-302.
Civil rights restored to convicted persons,
　　§§13-1 to 13-4.
　Automatic restoration, §13-1.
　Certificate or order of restoration.
　　Issuance and filing, §13-2.
　Conditional pardon.
　　Endorsement of warrant, service and filing,
　　　§13-4.
　Unconditional pardon.
　　Issuance, service and filing of warrant, §13-3.
Claim of factual innocence.
　Generally, innocence inquiry commission,
　　§§15A-1460 to 15A-1475.
　　See INNOCENCE CLAIM INQUIRY.
　Post-trial motions, §15A-1401.
Classified motor vehicles.
　Motor vehicle taxes.
　　Criminal penalty for evasion of taxes,
　　　§105-330.3(d).
Clean coastal water and vessel act.
　Discharge of sewage in coastal waters, §77-129(a).
　Pumpout of marine sanitation devices.
　　Record to be kept by vessel owner or operator.
　　　Violation, §77-128(b).
Cleaning agents containing phosphorus.
　Water and air resources.
　　Manufacturing, selling or distributing,
　　　§143-214.4(f).
Clerks of court.
　Superior court clerks.
　　Misapplying money received by virtue of office,
　　　§7A-112(d).
Coal and petroleum suppliers.
　Stocks of coals and petroleum fuel capacity.
　　Refusal to provide administration department,
　　　§143-345.14(d).
Coastal area management.
　Permits.
　　Violations as misdemeanors, §113A-126(c).

CRIMINAL LAW AND PROCEDURE —Cont'd
Coast and shore lights.
　Displaying false lights on seashore, §14-282.
Cockfighting, §14-362.
Coin-operated machines generally.
　Breaking into or forcibly opening, §14-56.1.
　Damaging or destroying machine, §14-56.2.
　Devices for cheating slot machines.
　　Manufacture, sale or gift, §14-109.
　False tokens or coins.
　　Obtaining property or services from machine by,
　　　§14-108.
College curfews.
　Violations, §116-213(a).
Combinations and restraint of trade, §75-1.
Commercial bribery, §14-353.
Commercial drivers' licenses.
　Sex offenders prohibited from obtaining license
　　with P or S endorsement.
　　False affidavit or swearing, §20-37.14A(c).
Commercial vehicles.
　Driving while disqualified, §20-28(d).
　Operating after consuming alcohol, §20-138.2A(c).
Commitments and preliminary examinations.
　Generally, §15A-521(a).
　Orders, §15A-521(b).
　　Delivery, §15A-521(c).
　　Modification, §15A-521(b).
　Receipt of prisoner, §15A-521(c).
　Witnesses, §15A-521(d).
Commodities.
　Violations of act, §78D-24(a).
　　Referral for prosecution to attorney general or
　　　district attorney, §78D-24(d).
Communications.
　Magazines or periodicals.
　　Libelous matter communicated, §14-47.
　Newspapers.
　　Libelous matter communicated to newspapers,
　　　§14-47.
Community corrections programs.
　Sentencing services, §§7A-770 to 7A-777.
　　See SENTENCING SERVICES.
Community service.
　See COMMUNITY SERVICE.
Company police.
　Violation of chapter, §74E-13.
Compensation to victims of crimes.
　Financial recovery assistance act, §§15B-30 to
　　15B-37.
　　See CRIME VICTIMS FINANCIAL RECOVERY
　　　ASSISTANCE ACT.
　Generally, §§15B-1 to 15B-37.
　　See CRIME VICTIMS COMPENSATION.
Competency to stand trial, §§15A-1001 to
　15A-1009.
　See COMPETENCY TO STAND TRIAL.
Computer crimes, §§14-453 to 14-458.
Concealed handgun permit, §§14-415.10 to
　14-415.27.
　See CONCEALED HANDGUN PERMIT.
Concealment of death, §14-401.22.
Confidentiality.
　Address confidentiality program, §§15C-1 to
　　15C-13.
　　See ADDRESS CONFIDENTIALITY
　　　PROGRAM.
　Mental incapacity of defendant to proceed.
　　Reports to court, §15A-1002(d).
　Public officers and employees.
　　Misuse of confidential information, §14-234.1.

CRIMINAL LAW AND PROCEDURE —Cont'd
Consent searches, §§15A-222, 15A-223.
  Defined, §15A-221(b).
Conspiracy.
  See CONSPIRACY.
**Contaminating food or drink to render one
    mentally incapacitated or physically
    helpless,** §14-401.16.
Contempt.
  Criminal contempt, §§5A-11 to 5A-17.
    See CONTEMPT.
Continuances.
  Superior or district court, §15A-952(g).
Continuing care retirement communities.
  Marketing by unlicensed providers, §58-64-5(a).
Contributing to delinquency of minor,
    §14-316.1.
Controlled substances offenses.
  Generally.
    See DRUGS AND CONTROLLED
      SUBSTANCES.
Conversation.
  Criminal conversation.
    Allowance of costs, §§6-18, 6-19.
Convict made goods.
  Sale prohibited, §14-346(a), (b).
Coram nobis.
  Relief formerly available now available by motion
    for appropriate relief, §15A-1411(c).
Corporations.
  Defendants.
    Appearance by counsel or agent, §15A-773(b).
    Securing attendance of organizations,
      §15A-773(a).
    Definition of "organization,"§15A-773.
  Nonprofit corporations.
    Failure to answer interrogatories propounded
      by secretary.
        Officers and directors, §55A-1-32(b).
Cosmetic art, §88B-22(f).
Costs.
  See COSTS.
Counterfeiting.
  See COUNTERFEITING.
Counties.
  Defense of employees and officers in criminal
    actions, §160A-167.
  Inspection departments.
    Certificates of compliance.
      Violations as misdemeanor, §153A-363.
    Defects in buildings.
      Orders to take corrective action.
        Failure to comply as misdemeanor,
          §153A-371.
    Failure to perform duties as misdemeanor,
      §153A-356.
    Notices.
      Removing as misdemeanor, §153A-367.
    Permits.
      Violations as misdemeanors, §153A-357(a).
    Stop orders.
      Violations as misdemeanor, §153A-361.
  Public officers and employees.
    Privacy of employee personnel records.
      Violations, §153A-98(f).
  Subdivisions.
    Transferring lots in unapproved subdivisions,
      §153A-334(a).
  Taxation.
    Disclosure of certain information,
      §153A-148.1(b).

CRIMINAL LAW AND PROCEDURE —Cont'd
Credit card, charge card or debit card.
  Fines, fees and costs.
    Acceptance in lieu of payment by cash or check,
      §7A-321(a).
      Contracts with vendors to provide for,
        §7A-343.
Credit device fraud, §§14-113.1 to 14-113.7A.
  See CREDIT DEVICE FRAUD.
Credit repair service violations, §66-225(f).
Credits on sentence, §§15-196.1 to 15-196.4.
Creeks, obstructing, §§77-12 to 77-14.
Cremation, §90-210.134(c).
Crime against nature, §14-177.
Crime victims.
  Compensation.
    Financial recovery assistance act, §§15B-30 to
      15B-37.
      See CRIME VICTIMS FINANCIAL
        RECOVERY ASSISTANCE ACT.
    Generally, §§15B-1 to 15B-37.
      See CRIME VICTIMS COMPENSATION.
  Generally.
    See VICTIMS OF CRIME.
Criminal case docketing.
  Superior courts, §7A-49.4.
Criminal contempt, §§5A-11 to 5A-17.
  See CONTEMPT.
**Criminal justice education and training
    standards.**
  See CRIMINAL JUSTICE EDUCATION AND
    TRAINING STANDARDS COMMISSION.
Criminal street gangs, §§14-50.15 to 14-50.30.
  See GANGS.
Criminologists.
  State bureau of investigation.
    Employment of criminologists, §114-16.
Crossbows.
  Sale.
    Dealer record violation, §14-408.
Cruel and unusual punishment, US Const Amd
    8.
Cruelty to animals.
  See CRUELTY TO ANIMALS.
Currituck Sound, obstructing, §76-41.
Custodial interference.
  Bail, §15A-534.4.
  Transporting child outside state intending to
    violate custody order, §14-320.1.
Cyber-bullying, §14-458.1.
Cyberstalking, §14-196.3.
Dairy milk case or crate larceny, §14-72.4.
Damages.
  Civil actions seeking to recover damages arising
    out of criminal act.
    Statutes of limitation and repose, §1-15.1.
  Dam safety, §143-215.36(a).
Data processing, §§14-453 to 14-458.
Death by vehicles.
  Double prosecution for manslaughter.
    Prohibition, §20-141.4(c).
  Felony death by vehicle, §20-141.4(a1).
    Aggravated felony death by vehicle,
      §20-141.4(a5).
    Repeat offenders.
      Second degree murder, §20-141.4(a6).
  Misdemeanor death by vehicle, §20-141.4(a2).
  Punishments, §20-141.4(b).
Death penalty.
  General provisions.
    See DEATH PENALTY.

CRIMINAL LAW AND PROCEDURE —Cont'd
Debt adjusters.
Appointment of receiver for money and property
employed, §14-425.
Definitions, §14-423.
Engaging, etc., in business of debt adjusting a
misdemeanor, §14-424.
Persons not deemed debt adjusters, §14-426.
Practice of debt adjusting enjoined, §14-425.
Transactions not deemed debt adjustment,
§14-426.
Defamation, §14-47.
Defendants.
Attendance.
Securing attendance of criminal defendants
confined in institutions within state,
§15A-711(a) to (c).
Detainers, §15A-711(d).
Civil commitment of defendants found not guilty
by reason of insanity, §15A-1321(a), (b).
Depositions, §8-74.
First appearance before district court judge,
§§15A-601 to 15A-606.
Indigent persons, §15A-603.
Information to be given defendant, §15A-605.
Right to counsel, §15A-603.
Warning against self-incrimination, §15A-602.
Incapacity of defendant to proceed, §§15A-1001 to
15A-1009.
Insanity defense, §15A-959.
Joinder, §15A-926(b).
Objection to joinder, §15A-927(c).
Failure to prove grounds for joinder,
§15A-927(d).
Physical restraint of defendant.
Maintenance of order in courtroom, §15A-1031.
Temporary restraint of mentally ill, §15A-1322.
Pleadings.
Each defendant to be charged with separate
pleading, §15A-926(b).
Pleas generally.
See PLEAS.
Prisons and prisoners.
Securing attendance of criminal defendants
confined in institutions within state,
§15A-711(a) to (c).
Detainers, §15A-711(d).
Probable cause hearings.
See PROBABLE CAUSE.
Removal of disruptive defendant.
Maintenance of order in courtroom,
§15A-1032(a), (b).
Representation of self at trial, §15A-1242.
Standby counsel, §15A-1243.
Restraint of defendant.
Maintenance of order in courtroom, §15A-1031.
Securing attendance.
Defendants confined in federal prisons,
§15A-771(a).
Certificate by superior court, §15A-771(b).
Defendants who are outside United States.
Application by governor to secretary of state
of United States, §15A-772(b).
Application to governor, §15A-772(a).
Extradition.
Applicability of provisions to, §15A-772(c).
Organizations, §15A-773(a).
Appearance by counsel or agent, §15A-773(b).
Defined, §15A-773(c).
Temporary restraint.
Mentally ill defendants, §15A-1322.

CRIMINAL LAW AND PROCEDURE —Cont'd
Defense of insanity.
Notice.
Intent to introduce expert testimony,
§15A-959(b).
Pretrial determination of insanity, §15A-959(c).
Pretrial hearing, §15A-959(a).
Defenses generally.
See DEFENSES.
Defensive force.
Defense of person, §14-51.3.
Justification not available, §14-51.4.
Protection of home, workplace, motor vehicle,
§14-51.2.
Deferred prosecution, §15A-1341(a1), (a2).
Dismissal with leave pursuant to deferred
prosecution agreement, §15A-932(a1).
Method of delivery to court by prosecutor,
§15A-932(c).
Reinstitution of proceedings if defendant fails to
comply, §15A-932(e).
Removal of case from docket, all processes
retain validity, §15A-932(b).
Definitions, §15A-101.
Appeals.
Prejudicial error, §15A-1443(a).
Bail, §15A-531.
Citation, §15A-302(a).
Criminal summons, §15A-303(a).
Disposition of cases, §15A-1381.
Electronic technology in criminal process and
procedure, §15A-101.1.
Grand jury, §15A-621.
Indictments, §15A-641(a).
Informations, §15A-641(b).
Motion to suppress evidence, §15A-971.
Order for arrest, §15A-305(a).
Presentments, §15A-641(c).
Unborn child, §14-23.1.
Warrant for arrest, §15A-304(a).
Witnesses.
Securing attendance.
Witnesses from without state, §15A-811.
Delinquent or undisciplined juvenile actions.
Willful violation of nontestimonial identification
procedures, §7B-2109.
Demurrer to the evidence, §15-173.
Dental hygienists.
Violations of provision, §90-233.1.
Dentists.
Extraoral services performed for dentist,
§90-29.2(d), (e).
Limited volunteer dental licenses.
Unauthorized practice, §90-37.1(g).
Practicing dentistry without license, §90-40.
Subpoenas of board of dental examiner.
Neglect or refusal to obey, §90-27.
Unauthorized practices, §90-40.
Violations of rules and regulations of board,
§90-48.
Department of health and human services.
Buildings and grounds.
Rules governing deportment of persons in and
suppression of nuisances and disorders,
§143-116.6(b).
Department of justice.
See JUSTICE DEPARTMENT.
Desertion and nonsupport.
Abandonment and failure to support spouse and
children, §14-322.

CRIMINAL LAW AND PROCEDURE —Cont'd
Detainers.
Interstate agreement on detainers, §§15A-761 to 15A-767.
See DETAINERS.
Mandatory disposition of detainers, §§15-10.1 to 15-10.4.
See DETAINERS.
Detectives collecting claims, accounts, etc., §14-401.2.
Discharge of firearm or barreled weapons.
Into occupied property or conveyance while in operation, §14-34.1.
Discovery, §§15A-901 to 15A-910.
See DISCOVERY.
Discrimination against military personnel, §127B-15.
Dismissal, discontinuance and nonsuit generally.
See DISMISSAL, DISCONTINUANCE AND NONSUIT.
Dismissal with leave for nonappearance.
Methods for delivery by prosecutor, §15A-932(c).
Reinstitution upon apprehension, notice, §15A-932(d).
Removal of case from docket, all processes retain validity, §15A-932(b).
Waiver of trial or hearing and payment of fines and costs by defendant.
Acceptance without need for reinstitution by prosecutor, §15A-932(d1).
When prosecutor may enter, §15A-932(a).
Dismissal with leave pursuant to deferred prosecution agreement.
Methods for delivery by prosecutor, §15A-932(c).
Reinstitution upon violation of agreement, §15A-932(e).
Removal of case from docket, all processes retain validity, §15A-932(b).
When prosecutor may enter, §15A-932(a1).
Disorderly conduct, §14-275.1.
Militia.
Commander may prevent trespass and disorder, §127A-148.
Public buildings and grounds, §143-345.2.
Trespasses to land and fixtures, §14-132.
Disorderly houses, §14-188.
Disposition of cases.
Defined, §15A-1381.
Fingerprints.
Report of disposition of charges, §15A-1382(a).
Plans for implementation of article, §15A-1383(a).
Modification, §15A-1383(c).
Not considered rules, §15A-1383(d).
Punishment for failure to comply, §15A-1383(b).
Reports, §15A-1382(a).
Domestic violence to be indicated in report, §15A-1382.1(a).
Felonies, §15A-1382(b).
Disruptive defendant.
Removal from courtroom.
Authority of judge, §15A-1032(a).
Instruction to jury, §15A-1032(b).
Opportunity given defendant to learn of proceedings while absent, §15A-1032(b).
Reason, entry into record, §15A-1032(b).
Warning, required, issued out of presence of jury, §15A-1032(a).
District attorneys.
General provisions.
See DISTRICT ATTORNEYS.

CRIMINAL LAW AND PROCEDURE —Cont'd
District attorneys —Cont'd
Prosecution of actions, NC Const Art IV §18.
District courts.
Appeal by defendant, §15A-1431.
Appeal by state, §15A-1432.
Costs in criminal actions, §7A-304.
General provisions.
See DISTRICT COURTS.
Prosecution in district court division, NC Const Art IV §18.
Seat of court in municipality with corporate limits extending into two or more contiguous counties.
Venue in criminal case, authority of judge, §7A-199(c).
Division of criminal statistics, §§114-10 to 114-10.02.
Division of motor vehicles.
Witness failure to obey summons, §20-47(b).
Divorce.
Alimony.
Willful disobedience of order for payment.
Enforcement of payment by criminal contempt, §50-16.7(j).
DNA.
Evidence, preservation, §15A-268.
Expungement of records.
Charges dismissed, finding of not guilty or not responsible, §15A-146(b1), (b2).
Charges dismissed on appeal or pardon of innocence granted, §15A-148.
General provisions, §§15A-266 to 15A-270.
See DNA.
Samples from crime scene.
Defendant's access before trial, §15A-267.
Testing after conviction.
Motion by defendant, §§15A-269 to 15A-270.1.
Dockets.
Superior courts.
Criminal case docketing, §7A-49.4.
Dogs.
See DOGS.
Dog wardens.
Animal welfare act violations, §19A-36.
Cruelty to animals, §19A-35.
Domestic criminal trespass, §14-134.3.
Domestic violence.
See DOMESTIC VIOLENCE.
Double jeopardy.
See DOUBLE JEOPARDY.
Drainage.
Jurisdiction of county commissioners.
Refusal to comply with requirements, §156-33.
Refusal to serve on board, §156-32.
Obstructions, §§156-19, 156-24, 156-25.
Drainage districts.
Assessments.
Failure of sheriff to make settlements, §156-111.
Failure of treasurer to make payments, §156-112.
Conveyance of land.
Failure of chairman or board to act, §156-114(e).
Injuring or damaging bridges, fences, ditches, etc., §156-92.
Reports.
Failure of commissioners to make reports, §156-132.
Drivers' licenses generally.
See DRIVERS' LICENSES.

CRIMINAL LAW AND PROCEDURE —Cont'd
Driver training schools.
  Violations of licensing provisions, §20-327.
Driving after notification or failure to appear.
  Impaired driver's license revocation, §20-28(a2).
Driving by person less than 21 years old after consuming alcohol or drugs, §20-138.3(a), (c).
Driving under the influence.
  See IMPAIRED DRIVING.
Droughts.
  Violation of water conservation measures, §143-355.6(d).
Drug and alcohol screening tests.
  Defrauding test, §14-401.20.
Drug offenses generally.
  See DRUGS AND CONTROLLED SUBSTANCES.
Drug paraphernalia.
  Control of potential drug paraphernalia products.
    Sale of glass tubes or splitters, §90-113.83.
Drunk driving.
  See IMPAIRED DRIVING.
Drunk in public, §§14-443 to 14-447, 122C-301 to 122C-303.
  See INTOXICATION.
Dry-cleaning solvent cleanup, §143-215.104Q(a) to (i).
Dune buggies used in violation of municipal ordinance, §160A-308.
Easements.
  Highways, roads and streets.
    Regulation of scenic easements, §136-125.
Eavesdropping, §§14-227.1 to 14-227.3.
Economic interests statements.
  State government ethics act.
    Concealing or failing to disclose information, §138A-26.
    False information, §138A-27.
Egg promotion tax.
  Handlers, §106-245.38.
Eggs.
  Warnings in lieu of criminal prosecutions, §106-245.25.
Election offenses generally.
  See ELECTIONS.
Electrologists.
  Violations of chapter, §88A-4(b).
Electronic commerce in government, §66-58.8.
Electronic communications.
  Cyberstalking, §14-196.3.
Electronic dog collars.
  Unlawful removal, §14-401.17.
Electronic mail.
  Driving while using mobile phone for, §20-137.4A.
Electronic monitoring devices.
  Interference with, §14-226.3.
Electronic repository for criminal process.
  Definitions, §15A-101.1.
  Generally, §15A-301.1(a) to (d).
  Printing of process in paper form, §15A-301.1(e), (f).
  Service of process in, §15A-301.1(g), (j) to (n).
  Tracking information, §15A-301.1(h), (i), (m).
Electronic surveillance generally, §§15A-286 to 15A-298.
  See ELECTRONIC SURVEILLANCE.
Electronic technology in criminal process and procedure.
  Definitions, §15A-101.1.
  Electronic repository for criminal process, §15A-301.1.

CRIMINAL LAW AND PROCEDURE —Cont'd
Elementary and secondary education.
  See SCHOOLS AND EDUCATION.
Elevator violations, §95-110.11.
E-mail.
  Cyberstalking, §14-196.3.
Emancipated juvenile prosecuted as adult, §7B-1604(a).
Embezzlement.
  See EMBEZZLEMENT.
Emergency communication, interfering with, §14-286.2.
Emergency medical services.
  Regulation of emergency medical services.
    Violations of article, §131E-161.
Employment relations.
  Blacklisting employees, §14-355.
  Earnings of employees in interstate commerce.
    Collection out of state to avoid exemption, §95-75.
  Influencing employees to violate duties owed employers, §§14-353, 14-354.
  Labor union violations by public employee, §95-99.
  Medical examination as condition of employment, §14-357.1.
  Payments to or for benefit of labor organization.
    Violations, §95-104.
Employment security.
  False statements or representation, §96-18(a), (b).
  Violations of chapter or rules or regulation, §96-18(c).
  Witness intimidation, §96-15.2.
Endangered plant species.
  Unlawful acts, §106-202.19(a), (a1).
Energy.
  Crisis administration.
    Violations as misdemeanors, §113B-24(b).
Environmental health specialists.
  Violations, §90A-66.
Errors at trial.
  Appropriate relief, §15A-1401.
  Motion for appropriate relief, §§15A-1411 to 15A-1422, MOTION FOR APPROPRIATE RELIEF.
Escape.
  See ESCAPE.
Ethen's law.
  Unborn victims of violence act, §§14-23.1 to 14-23.8.
Ethics.
  State government ethics act.
    Misuse of public office.
      Failure to resign, §138A-39(b).
      Gifts, violations of section, §138A-32(i).
    Remedies available, §138A-45(f).
    Statements of economic interest.
      Concealing or failing to disclose information, §138A-26.
      False information, §138A-27.
Ethnic intimidation, §14-401.14(a), (b).
Evasion of tax, §105-236.
Evidence.
  DNA samples and testing, §§15A-266 to 15A-270.
    See DNA.
  Generally.
    See EVIDENCE.
  Motion to suppress evidence.
    See EVIDENCE.
Examination question, tampering with, §14-401.1.
Excessive bail, US Const Amd 8.

CRIMINAL LAW AND PROCEDURE —Cont'd

Exclusionary rule.
Motion to suppress evidence. See within this heading, "Evidence."

Execution on forfeiture of bonds.
Issuance, §1-305(a).

Executions.
Capital punishment.
See DEATH PENALTY.
Corporate agents, §1-324.5.
Supplemental proceedings.
Examination of parties and witnesses.
Incriminating answers not to be used in criminal proceedings, §1-357.

Exploitation of elder adult or disabled adult, §14-112.2.

Explosives.
See EXPLOSIVES.

Ex post facto laws.
Prohibited, NC Const Art I §16.

Expungement of records.
See EXPUNGEMENT OF RECORDS.

Extension of session of court by trial judge, §15-167.

Extortion.
See EXTORTION.

Extradition.
Uniform criminal extradition act, §§15A-721 to 15A-750.
See EXTRADITION.

Eyewitness identification reform, §§15A-284.50 to 15A-284.53.

Failure to appear, §15A-543.
Dismissal with leave when defendant fails to appear and cannot be found readily, §15A-932.

Failure to pay minor for certain work, §14-321.

False fire alarms.
Giving false fire alarms, §14-286.
Molesting fire alarm, §14-286.

False pretenses and cheats.
See FALSE PRETENSES AND CHEATS.

False reports concerning mass violence on educational property, §14-277.5.

False reports to law enforcement officers, §14-225.

False swearing.
Perjury generally.
See PERJURY.

Federal law enforcement officers.
Assistance in enforcing criminal laws in state.
Authority to assist, §15A-406(b).
Federal tort claims act, applicability, §15A-406(e).
Independent investigation into state law violations not authorized, §15A-406(f).
List of federal law enforcement officers, §15A-406(a).
Not considered officer, employee of state or local agency, §15A-406(d).
Powers when assisting, §15A-406(c).

Felonies.
See FELONIES.

Felonious restraint, §14-43.3.

Felony death by vehicle, §20-141.4(a1).

Felony death or serious injury by vehicle, §20-141.4(a3).
Aggravated felony death by vehicle, §20-141.4(a5).
Aggravated felony serious injury by vehicle, §20-141.4(a4).
Punishment, §20-141.4(b).

CRIMINAL LAW AND PROCEDURE —Cont'd

Felony death or serious injury by vehicle —Cont'd
Repeat offenders.
Second degree murder, §20-141.4(a6).

Felony sentencing, §§15A-1340.13 to 15A-1340.17.

Feral swine.
Live feral swine caught in traps.
Unlawful to remove and to transport after removal, §113-294(s).

Ferries.
Chain guards or gates.
Safety violations, §136-89.

Financial transaction cards.
Credit cards and devices.
Fraud, §§14-113.1 to 14-113.7A.
See CREDIT DEVICE FRAUD.
Generally, §§14-113.8 to 14-113.17.
See FINANCIAL TRANSACTION CARDS.

Fire alarms.
False alarms, tampering with, §14-286.

Firearms.
See FIREARMS AND OTHER WEAPONS.

Fire department.
Volunteer fire department.
Defense of employees and officers in civil or criminal actions, §160A-167.

Fire-detection or fire-extinguishing system.
Molesting, §14-286.

Fire insurance.
Unauthorized insurer violations, §58-28-45(h).

Fires.
Arson, §§14-58 to 14-69.3.
See ARSON.
Exposing minor to fire, §14-318.

Fireworks, §§14-410 to 14-415.

Fish and fisheries resources.
See FISH AND FISHING.

Flag desecration, §14-381.

Flat trucks.
Violation of operation restriction, §20-120.

Floodplain regulation.
Violations, §143-215.58(a), (b).

Fluorescent lights containing mercury.
Disposal in unlined landfills, §§130A-25(d), 130A-309.10(m).

Food and nutrition services.
Fraud, §108A-53.
Illegal possession or use, §108A-53.1.

Food, drug and cosmetic act.
Advertising violations, §106-124.
Prosecution of violations, §106-126.

Forensic analysis.
Admissible in evidence without testimony of analyst who prepared report, §8-58.20(a).
Affidavit by analyst, §8-58.20(c).
Chain of custody of evidence subject to forensic analysis.
Establishing without calling unnecessary witnesses, §8-58.20(g).
Copy of laboratory report and affidavit.
Service on attorney for defendant, §8-58.20(d).
Determination of admissibility.
Objection to report and affidavit timely filed, §8-58.20(f).
Impaired driving prosecutions.
Laboratory results of chemical analysis of blood or urine, §20-139.1(c1) to (c3).
Indication whether laboratory report and affidavit offered for evidence, §8-58.20(d).

CRIMINAL LAW AND PROCEDURE —Cont'd
Forensic analysis —Cont'd
Admissible in evidence without testimony of
analyst who prepared report —Cont'd
Objection to use of laboratory report.
Defendant or defendant's attorney to file,
time, §8-58.20(e).
Failure to timely file, §8-58.20(f).
Performed in accordance with adopted rules and
procedures, §8-58.20(b).
Chain of custody of evidence subject to forensic
analysis.
Establishing without calling unnecessary
witnesses, §8-58.20(g).
Determination of admissibility of statement.
Objection timely filed, §8-58.20(g).
Impaired driving prosecutions.
Lab results of chemical analysis of blood or
urine, §20-139.1(c3).
Objection to introduction of statement filed by
persons in chain of custody, §8-58.20(g).
Failure to file, §8-58.20(g).
Statement signed by each successive person
in chain of custody, §8-58.20(g).
Forest fires.
Summons to assist in extinguishing.
Failure to comply as misdemeanor, §106-899(a).
Forestry notices.
Destruction, §106-905.
Forfeitures.
See FORFEITURES.
Forgery.
See FORGERY.
Forms of action, NC Const Art IV §13.
Fornication, §14-184.
Fowl.
Permitting domestic fowl to run at large after
notice, §68-25(a).
Commercial poultry operations.
Permitting by operation of fowl running on
adjoining property, §68-25(c).
Permitting fowl on lands of operations,
§68-25(b).
Franchise tax.
Limited liability companies.
Controlled companies.
Underpayment, fraud to evade, penalty,
§105-114.1(h).
Fraud.
See FRAUD.
Fugitives from justice, US Const Art IV §2.
Fundraising during legislative session,
§163-278.13B(e).
Funeral contracts and funds.
Violations generally, §90-210.70(a), (b).
Funeral service.
Unlawful practices, §90-210.25(f).
Futures.
Entering into or aiding, §16-4.
Opening office for sales, §16-5.
Gambling, gaming.
General provisions, §§14-289 to 14-300.
See GAMBLING.
Gangs.
Criminal street gangs, §§14-50.15 to 14-50.30.
See GANGS.
Gasoline.
Adulteration, §119-35.
Inspection violations, §119-39.
Inspectors.
Conflicts of interest, §119-25.

CRIMINAL LAW AND PROCEDURE —Cont'd
Gasoline —Cont'd
Inspectors —Cont'd
Failure or refusal to exhibit records to, §119-32.
Pumps.
Devices calculated to falsify measure, §119-33.
Display of grade rating, §119-27.
Tax.
Acts that are misdemeanors, §105-449.120.
Use of non-tax-paid fuel on highway,
§105-449.117(a).
General assembly.
Fundraising during legislative session,
§163-278.13B(e).
General contractors.
Building permits.
Violation of requirements for issuance,
§87-14(b).
Glue sniffing, §90-113.13.
Gonorrhea.
Defendant accused of offense involving sexual
intercourse.
Testing on victim's request, §15A-615.
Governor.
Emergency war powers.
Violations of orders, rules or regulations,
§147-33.3.
Grand jury.
See GRAND JURY.
Gravestones, inscribing charging of crime,
§14-401.3.
Greyhound racing, §14-309.20(c).
Guarantees in criminal cases, US Const Amds 5,
6.
Guilty pleas.
Generally.
See GUILTY PLEAS.
Pleas generally.
See PLEAS.
Habeas corpus, §§17-1 to 17-46.
See HABEAS CORPUS.
Habitual breaking and entering status offense,
§§14-7.25 to 14-7.31.
See BREAKING AND ENTERING.
Habitual felons, §§14-7.1 to 14-7.12.
See HABITUAL FELONS.
Habitual misdemeanor assault, §14-33.2.
Halloween food, distributing certain food,
§14-401.11.
Hazardous waste management.
Class I felonies, §130A-26.1(f).
Class J felonies, §130A-26.1(g).
False reporting, §130A-26.2.
Hazing, §§14-35, 14-38.
Definitions, §14-35.
Indictments.
Self-incriminating testimony.
No indictment to be founded on
self-incriminating testimony, §14-38.
Punishment for hazing, §14-35.
Witnesses in hazing trials, §14-38.
Health.
Violations of chapter or rules, §130A-25(a).
Health care facility, obstruction, §14-277.4.
Hearings.
Interpreters generally.
See INTERPRETERS.
Mental incapacity of defendant to proceed.
Determination of incapacity, §15A-1002(b).
Supplemental hearings, §15A-1007(a).
Court's own determination, §15A-1007(b).

CRIMINAL LAW AND PROCEDURE —Cont'd
Hearings —Cont'd
Mental incapacity of defendant to proceed
—Cont'd
Supplemental hearings —Cont'd
Dismissal of charges, §15A-1007(c).
Motion for appropriate relief, §15A-1420(c).
Motion to suppress evidence.
Motion made during trial.
Hearing out of presence of jury, §15A-977(e).
Pretrial motion, §§15A-976(c), 15A-977(d).
Pretrial motions.
Date for hearing, §15A-952(f).
Motion to suppress evidence, §§15A-976(c),
15A-977(d).
Probable cause hearings.
See PROBABLE CAUSE.
Hepatitis B.
Defendant accused of offense involving sexual
intercourse.
Testing on victim's request, §15A-615.
Highway inspection reports or test reports.
Falsification, §136-13.2.
Highway signs.
Commercial signs prohibited, §136-32(a).
Political signs in right-of-way.
Unlawful removal, §136-32(e).
Hired property.
See HIRED PROPERTY.
Historical and cultural resources.
Violations of regulations, §121-4.
HIV.
Defendant accused of offense involving sexual
intercourse.
Testing on victim's request, §15A-615.
Home care agency licensure.
Unlicensed operation, §131E-141.1.
Home inspectors.
Violations as misdemeanors, §143-151.59.
Homicide.
Generally.
See HOMICIDE.
Manslaughter.
See MANSLAUGHTER.
Murder.
See MURDER.
Horse show officials or judges, bribery,
§14-380.1.
Attempts at bribery to be reported, §14-380.2.
Definitions of "bribe,"§14-380.3.
Printing provisions of article in horse show
schedules, §14-380.4.
Hospice licensure.
Unauthorized disclosure of inspection information,
§131E-207(b).
Hospital discharged patient.
Failure or refusal to leave hospital, §131E-90.
Hospital employee personnel files.
Unlawful disclosure, §131E-257.2(g).
Unlawful examination or use, §131E-257.2(h).
Hospital inspections by department.
Disclosure of confidential or privileged
information, §131E-80(d).
Hospital licensure.
Disclosure of information, §131E-80(d).
Unlicensed operation, §131E-81(a).
Willful violations, §131E-81(b).
Hotel admittance of pets, §72-7.1.
Hotel, false registration as husband and wife,
§14-186.

CRIMINAL LAW AND PROCEDURE —Cont'd
Hotel room occupied by opposite sexes for
immoral purposes, §14-186.
Household goods carriers.
Lack of certificate to operate as.
Prohibited activities, criminal enforcement,
§62-280.1(b).
Marking or identification of vehicles, §20-398(d).
Housemovers.
Article or rules violations, §20-371(a).
Houses of ill repute, §14-188.
Housing authorities and projects.
Fraudulent misrepresentation in obtaining
housing assistance, §157-29.1(a), (b).
Human remains.
Concealing evidence of death.
Dismembering, destroying.
Criminal penalty, §14-401.22(d).
Death not of natural causes, §14-401.22(e).
Defined, §14-401.22(f).
Disturbing, vandalizing, desecrating.
Criminal penalty, exceptions, §14-401.22(c).
Human trafficking, §§14-43.10 to 14-43.13.
See HUMAN TRAFFICKING.
Hunting and wildlife.
Generally.
See HUNTING AND WILDLIFE.
Husband and wife.
Competency as witnesses in criminal action,
§8-57(a) to (c).
Postnuptial crimes, §52-12.
Icebox abandonment, §14-318.1.
Identification.
DNA analysis, §§15A-266 to 15A-270.
See DNA.
Nontestimonial identification, §§15A-271 to
15A-282, IDENTIFICATION.
Identification cards.
Nonoperators of motor vehicles.
Fraud or misrepresentation in application,
§20-37.7(e).
Wrongful issuance, §20-34.1.
Identifying marks on machines or apparatus.
Removing, defacing, etc., §14-401.4.
Identity theft, §§14-113.20 to 14-113.25.
Ignition interlock system.
Tampering with system, §20-17.8A.
Illegitimacy.
Nonsupport of illegitimate child by parents, §49-2.
Immunity of witnesses.
Evidence of grant of immunity may be fully
developed, §15A-1055(a).
Jury.
Argument to jury as to impact of immunity,
§15A-1055(b).
Order to testify or produce other information,
§15A-1051(a).
Application for.
Court proceedings, §15A-1052(a), (b).
Grand jury proceedings, §15A-1053(a), (b).
Court proceedings, §15A-1052(a).
Definition of "other information,"§15A-1051(c).
Grand jury proceedings, §15A-1053(a).
Application, §15A-1053(a), (b).
Jury trial.
Judge to inform jury of grant of immunity,
§15A-1052(c).
When effective, §15A-1051(b).
Self-incrimination, §15A-1051(a).
Sentence concessions, §15A-1054(a).
Evidence of testimonial arrangement may be
fully developed, §15A-1055(a).

CRIMINAL LAW AND PROCEDURE —Cont'd
Immunity of witnesses —Cont'd
Sentence concessions —Cont'd
Jury.
Argument to jury as to impact of agreement, §15A-1055(b).
Notice of agreement, §15A-1054(c).
Recommendations, §15A-1054(b).
Impaired driving, §§20-38.1 to 20-38.7.
See IMPAIRED DRIVING.
Impersonation.
Emergency medical services personnel, §14-276.1.
Firemen, §14-276.1.
Law enforcement officers, §14-277(a) to (e).
Public officer or employee, §14-277(e).
Implied consent offenses.
Impaired driving, §§20-38.1 to 20-38.7.
See IMPAIRED DRIVING.
Imprisonment.
Prison terms.
See PRISON TERMS.
Sentencing generally.
See SENTENCING.
Incapacity of defendant to proceed, §§15A-1001 to 15A-1009.
See INCAPACITY OF DEFENDANT TO PROCEED.
Incest, §14-178.
Inciting riot, §14-288.2.
Indecent exposure, §14-190.9.
Indecent liberties between children, §14-202.2.
Indecent liberties with minor, §14-202.1.
Indictments.
See INDICTMENTS.
Indigent persons.
False material statements as to indigency.
Defendant seeking appointment of counsel, §7A-456(a).
Guilty pleas.
Waiver of right to counsel, §7A-457(b).
Representation of indigent persons.
Generally, §§7A-450 to 7A-458.
See INDIGENT DEFENSE SERVICES.
Indigent defense services act, §§7A-498 to 7A-498.8.
See INDIGENT DEFENSE SERVICES.
Indigent services rules, IDS Rules 1.1 to 3.7.
See INDIGENT DEFENSE SERVICES.
Motion for appropriate relief.
Appointment of counsel for indigent defendant, §15A-1421.
Informations, §§15A-641 to 15A-646.
Information technology procurement.
Office of information technology services.
Bribery, §147-33.99.
False certification that bid submitted without collusion, §147-33.100.
Financial interest of officers in sources of supply, §147-33.99.
Unauthorized use of procedures for private gain, §147-33.98(c).
Injuring vehicle with intent to steal, §20-107(b).
Innocence claim inquiry.
Generally, innocence inquiry commission, §§15A-1460 to 15A-1475.
See INNOCENCE CLAIM INQUIRY.
Post-trial motions, §15A-1401.
Insanity defense.
Notice.
Discovery generally, §15A-905(c), (d).

CRIMINAL LAW AND PROCEDURE —Cont'd
Insanity defense —Cont'd
Notice —Cont'd
Intent to introduce expert testimony, §15A-959(b).
Pretrial hearing, §15A-959(a).
Pretrial determination of insanity, §15A-959(c).
Insolvent or imprisoned debtor.
False swearing, §23-43.
Inspections.
Alcoholic beverages.
Interference with inspections, §18B-502(b).
Instructions to jury.
See JURY AND JURY TRIAL.
Insufficiency of evidence to prove crime charged.
Preserving issue for appeal at trial, AppProc Rule 10(a).
Insurance adjusters.
Acting for unauthorized company, §58-33-115.
Acting without license or violating insurance law generally, §§58-3-130, 58-33-120.
Insurance agents, brokers, administrators.
Brokers.
Acting without license or violating insurance law generally, §58-3-130.
Unauthorized insurers.
Soliciting, negotiating or selling insurance for, §58-33-95(a).
Embezzlement, §§58-2-162, 58-2-163.
False statement to procure or deny benefit of policy or certificate, §58-2-161(b).
Insurance commissioner.
False statements to, §58-2-180.
Insurance companies.
Alien governments.
Companies owned or controlled by violations, §58-16-20(c).
Books and papers.
Failure to exhibit or making false statements, §58-2-200.
Insurance consumer and customer information privacy.
False pretenses.
Obtaining information under, criminal penalty, §58-39-115.
Insurance policies.
Violations, §58-50-70.
Interfering with emergency communications, §14-286.2.
Internal improvements.
Report of railroad, canal, etc.
Failure to report, §124-3.
Interstate agreement on detainers, §§15A-761 to 15A-767.
See DETAINERS.
Interstate earnings of employee.
Collection out of state to avoid exemption, §95-75.
Intoxication, §§14-443 to 14-447, 122C-301 to 122C-303.
See INTOXICATION.
Investment advisers.
Criminal penalties, §78C-39.
Jail keepers causing injuries to prisoners, §162-55.
Jails.
See JAILS.
Joinder.
Defendants, §15A-926(b).
Objection to joinder, §15A-927(c).
Failure to prove grounds for joinder, §15A-927(d).

CRIMINAL LAW AND PROCEDURE —Cont'd

Joinder —Cont'd

Offenses, §15A-926(a).

Failure to join related offenses, §15A-926(c).

Venue.

Concurrent venue, §15A-132.

Journalist's qualified privilege against disclosure in any legal proceeding, §8-53.11.

Judges.

Admonitions to jurors, §15A-1236(a).

Death, §15A-1224(b).

Disability, §15A-1224(a), (b).

Disqualification.

Motion of state or defendant, §15A-1223(b), (c).

Time for filing, §15A-1223(d).

Own motion, §15A-1223(a).

Witness in case, §15A-1223(e).

Opinion.

Expression of opinion in presence of jury prohibited, §15A-1222.

Verdict.

Comment on verdict.

Prohibited, §1-180.1.

Judicial comment on verdict, §15A-1239.

Judgments, entry of unauthorized judgment, §14-221.2.

Junk dealers.

Restrictions as to location of junkyards, §136-145.

Jurisdiction for appeals.

Correction of errors by appellate division, §15A-1448(a).

Lack of jurisdiction on part of trial court.

Errors which may be reviewed even though no objection, exception or motion made, §15A-1446(d).

Grounds for correction, §15A-1442.

Jury and jury trial.

See JURY AND JURY TRIAL.

Justice academy, §§17D-1 to 17D-4.

Justice department.

See JUSTICE DEPARTMENT.

Justifiable use of defensive force.

Defense of person, §14-51.3.

Justification not available, §14-51.4.

Protection of home, workplace, motor vehicle, §14-51.2.

Juvenile prosecuted as adult.

Commission of criminal offense after superior court conviction, §7B-1604(b).

Commission of criminal offense on or after sixteenth birthday, §7B-1604(a).

Emancipated juvenile prosecuted as adult, §7B-1604(a).

Transfer of jurisdiction of juvenile to superior court, §7B-2200.

Court not transferring case to superior court, §7B-2203(d).

Detention pending release, §7B-2204.

Detention pending transfer to division of adult correction, §7B-2204.

DNA sample of juvenile transferred, §7B-2201(b).

Fingerprinting juvenile transferred, §7B-2201(b).

Jurisdiction of superior court on transfer, §7B-2203(c).

Pretrial release, §7B-2204.

Probable cause hearing.

Burden of state, §7B-2202(c).

Conducted in felony cases, §7B-2202(a).

Continuing for good cause, §7B-2202(a).

CRIMINAL LAW AND PROCEDURE —Cont'd

Juvenile prosecuted as adult —Cont'd

Transfer of jurisdiction of juvenile to superior court —Cont'd

Probable cause hearing —Cont'd

Probable cause found and transferred to superior court not required, proceeding to transfer hearing, §7B-2202(e).

Probable cause not found, §7B-2202(f).

Prosecutor representing state, §7B-2202(b).

Representation of juvenile by counsel, §7B-2202(b).

Testimony and cross-examination, §7B-2202(b).

Time for conducting, §7B-2202(a).

Waiver of right and stipulating to finding of probable cause, §7B-2202(d).

Transfer hearing, §7B-2203(a).

Factors considered, §7B-2203(b).

Transfer order, §7B-2203(c).

Kaitlyn's law.

Child care facilities.

Unauthorized administration of medicine, §110-102.1A.

Kennels.

Cruelty to animals, §19A-35.

Unlicensed operation, §19A-33.

Kerosene.

Sale location prohibitions, §119-16.3.

Kerosene distributors, suppliers and terminal operators.

Bond or letter of credit.

Required for license, failure to comply, §119-15.3(c).

Kidnapping and abduction.

See KIDNAPPING.

Lake lure marine commission.

Regulations applicable to lake and shoreline area.

Violations, §77-87(b).

Landlord and tenant.

Lien on crops.

Tobacco marketing cards.

Failure of tenant to account for sales as misdemeanor, §42-22.1.

Unlawful seizure by landlord or removal by tenant, §42-22.

Sexual harassment in rental of residential property, §14-395.1(a).

Willful destruction by tenant, §42-11.

Wrongful surrender to other landlord, §42-13.

Landscape architects.

Practice without registration or license, §89A-8(a).

Larceny, §§14-70 to 14-86.1.

See LARCENY.

Laser devices.

Unlawful to intentionally point, §14-34.8.

Aircraft, §14-280.2.

Law enforcement agency animal.

Assaulting, §14-163.1.

Law enforcement association publications.

Soliciting advertising, §14-401.10.

Law enforcement vehicles.

Operating vehicles resembling, §20-137.2(b).

Lease of motor vehicles.

Sublease and loan assumption arranging, §20-106.2(d), (e).

Legal expense funds for elected officials, §163-278.301(f).

Statements filed with board.

False certification as true and correct, §163-278.308(e).

CRIMINAL LAW AND PROCEDURE —Cont'd
Legal services programs.
Limitations on eligible cases, §7A-474.3(c).
Legislative retirement system.
Improper receipt of decedent's retirement
allowance, §120-4.34.
Legislators.
Bribery, §120-86(a).
Extortion, §120-86(b) to (e).
Letters.
Anonymous or threatening letters, §14-394.
Opening of sealed letters.
Unauthorized opening, §14-372.
Publishing of sealed letters.
Unauthorized publishing, §14-372.
Reading of sealed letters.
Unauthorized reading, §14-372.
Library books.
Failure to return, §125-11.
**Library, museum, gallery, etc., theft or
destruction of property,** §14-398.
**License agents for wildlife resources
commission.**
Prohibited acts, criminal penalty, §113-270.1(d).
License plates.
Alteration, disguise or concealment of numbers,
§20-63(g).
Borrowing or lending, §20-111.
Failure to surrender, §20-45(b).
Manufacturer's and dealer's special plates.
Registration violations, §20-79(e).
Neglect or refusal to clean plates, §20-63(e).
Operating with false numbers, §20-63(f).
Refusal to surrender illegible plates, §20-63(a).
Transporter, dealer-transporter plates,
§20-79.2(b2).
Liens.
Docketing in violation of restrictions, §44A-12.1(c).
Lighthouses.
Anchorage in range of, §76-43.
Displaying false lights on seashore, §14-282.
Lights.
Red or blue lights.
Operating vehicles resembling law enforcement
vehicle, §20-137.2(b).
Violations of prohibition, §20-130.1(e).
Limitation of actions.
Civil actions seeking to recover damages arising
out of criminal act, §1-15.1.
Dismissal of criminal charges.
Motion to dismiss.
Grounds, §15A-954(a).
Voluntary dismissal by state.
Statute of limitations not tolled, §15A-931(b).
Misdemeanors, §15-1.
Limited insurance representatives.
Unauthorized insurers.
Soliciting, negotiating or selling insurance for,
§58-33-95(a).
Limited liability companies.
Franchise tax.
Controlled companies.
Underpayment, fraud to evade, penalty,
§105-114.1(h).
Interrogatories by secretary of state.
Manager's refusal or failure to answer,
§57C-1-32(b).
Liquefied petroleum gas dealers.
Violations, §119-59(a).
Liquid fuels, lubricating oils, greases, etc.
Violations of article, §119-13.

CRIMINAL LAW AND PROCEDURE —Cont'd
Littering, §14-399.
Livestock.
Larceny, §14-81.
Livestock diseases.
Failure to destroy animal with glanders or farcy,
§106-404.
Livestock running at large.
Domestic fowl.
Permitting domestic fowl to run at large after
notice, §68-25(a).
Commercial poultry operations.
Lands of operations, §68-25(b).
Running on adjoining property, §68-25(c).
Loans, usurious.
Household and kitchen furniture, §14-391.
Lobbying.
Criminal penalty for violations, §120C-602(a).
Local ABC board members and employees.
Embezzlement, malfeasance, §18B-702(w).
Local boards of education.
Defense of members in criminal action,
§115C-43(a) to (c).
**Local governmental employees' retirement
system.**
Improper receipt of decedent's retirement
allowance, §128-38.5.
Local government finance.
Fiscal control.
Annual independent audit.
Violations of requirements as misdemeanors,
§159-34(a).
Local governments.
Buildings unfit of human habitation.
Occupancy of buildings so posted, §160A-443.
Local officers government and employees.
Defense of criminal proceedings, §160A-167.
Locksmith licensing.
Unlicensed operation, §74F-3.
Long-term care ombudsman.
Unlawful disclosures, §143B-181.20(a).
Willful interference, §143B-181.25.
Looting, §14-288.6(b).
Lotteries, §§14-289 to 14-291.2.
Lubricating oils.
Violations of article, §§119-4, 119-13.
Machine guns.
Sale, use or possession, §14-409.
Magazines.
Communicating libelous matter to magazines,
§14-47.
Magistrates.
Appeals, §15A-1431.
Implied consent offenses.
Initial appearance before magistrate, §20-38.4.
Powers of magistrates, §7A-273.
Arrest warrants.
Issuance of warrant, §7A-273.
Bail.
Granting of bail for noncapital offense,
§7A-273.
Infraction cases, §7A-273.
Initial appearances.
Conduct of, §7A-273.
Judgments and decrees.
Entering judgments of chief district judge,
§7A-273.
Misdemeanor cases, §7A-273.
Search warrants.
Issuance of warrant, §7A-273.

CRIMINAL LAW AND PROCEDURE —Cont'd
Magistrates —Cont'd
Powers of magistrates —Cont'd
Written appearances.
Acceptance of, §7A-273.
Maiming.
Malicious maiming, §14-30.
Malfeasance.
Corporation officers and agents.
Misconduct in private office, §14-254.
Local ABC board members and employees,
§18B-702(w).
Malicious conduct by prisoners, §14-258.4(a).
Manslaughter.
See MANSLAUGHTER.
**Manufactured home manufacturers, dealers,
salespersons or set-up contractors.**
Engaging in business without license,
§143-143.24.
Manufactured homes.
Uniform standards.
Health and safety of purchaser threatened,
§143-151(b).
Marine fisheries commission rules violations,
§113-135(a) to (c).
Marine fisheries inspectors.
Refusal of person to stop in obedience to
directions of, §113-136(j).
Marine sanitation devices.
Discharge of sewage in coastal waters, §77-129(a).
Pumpout.
Record to be kept by vessel owner or operator.
Violation, §77-128(b).
Marriage.
Licenses.
Obtaining by false representation as
misdemeanor, §51-15.
Solemnizing without license as misdemeanor,
§51-7.
Massage and bodywork therapy.
Approval of schools, violations, §90-634(b2).
Unlicensed acts, §90-634(b).
Mass death and destruction weapons.
Manufacture, assembly, possession, etc.,
§14-288.8.
Nuclear, biological or chemical weapons.
False report or hoax, §§14-288.23, 14-288.24.
Manufacture, assembly, possession, etc.,
§14-288.21.
Use and delivery of weapons, §14-288.22.
Mass violence on educational property.
False reports concerning, §14-277.5.
Meat of diseased animal, selling, §14-342.
Mechanic's or storage liens.
Failure to report unclaimed vehicles, §20-77(d).
Medicaid.
Conflicts of interest, §108A-65(b).
Fraud.
Providers, §108A-63(c), (e), (f).
Recipients, §108A-64(c).
Kickbacks, bribes or rebates.
Activities inapplicable, §108A-63(i).
Construction of provisions in relation to federal
statute, §108A-63(j).
Offering or paying, §108A-63(h).
Soliciting or receiving, §108A-63(g).
Property of patients' violations, §108A-60(b).
Withholding of information, §108A-57(b), (c).
Medical waste.
Depositing in navigable waters, §76-40(a1).

CRIMINAL LAW AND PROCEDURE —Cont'd
Medical waste —Cont'd
Water and air resources.
Prohibited disposal, §143-214.2A(a), (c).
Meetings of public bodies.
Disrupting, §143-318.17.
**Mental health, developmental disabilities,
substance abuse.**
Advance instruction for mental health treatment.
Alteration, forgery, concealment or destruction
of instrument, §122C-76.
Area authorities.
Unlawful access or disclosure of personnel
records, §122C-158(g), (h).
Camp Butner and community of Butner.
Violations of ordinances or rules, §122C-406.
Consumer advocacy program.
Confidentiality violations, §122C-17(b).
Willful interference with consumer advocate,
§122C-20.
Death penalty for mentally retarded defendants,
§15A-2005.
Defendant regains capacity for trial, §15A-1006.
Defendants incapable of proceeding, §15A-1005.
Defense of insanity.
Notice, §§15A-905(c), (d), 15A-959(a).
Intent to introduce expert testimony,
§15A-959(b).
Pretrial determination of insanity, §15A-959(c).
Escape and commission of crime after escape or
while resident of facility, §122C-254.
Furnishing false information, §122C-80(f).
Incapacity of defendant to proceed, §§15A-1001 to
15A-1009.
See INCAPACITY OF DEFENDANT TO
PROCEED.
Not guilty by reason of insanity.
Temporary restraint of defendant, §15A-1322.
Verdict to state, §15A-1237(c).
Operating a licensable facility without a license,
§122C-28.
Quality assurance activities.
Unlawful disclosure of confidential information
by secretary or his agent, §122C-192(b).
Unlawful disclosure of confidential information
generally, §122C-52(e).
Unlawful disclosure of information gathered
during inspections, §122C-25.
Violations of clients' rights, §§122C-62,
122C-65(a), (b), 122C-66.
Witnesses with developmental disabilities or
mental retardation.
Remote testimony, §15A-1225.2.
Methamphetamine watch program.
Immunity from civil and criminal liability.
Good faith actions, §114-43.
Migrant farm workers.
Motor carriers.
Violations of regulations, §20-215.4.
Military personnel.
Discrimination against, §127B-15.
Military property sales facilities.
Perjury.
Application for permit, §127B-5.
Violations of provisions by dealers, §127B-7.
Militia.
Composition of unauthorized militia.
Convicted felons excepted, §127A-7.
Conversion or destruction of military property,
§127A-131.

CRIMINAL LAW AND PROCEDURE —Cont'd
Militia —Cont'd
Muster role.
Placing name wrongfully, §127A-152.
Organizing company without authority,
§127A-151.
Milk case or crate larceny, §14-72.4.
Mines and minerals.
Notice of beginning business of manufacturing
products from mineral resources of state.
Violations as misdemeanors, §113-25.
Minors.
See CHILDREN AND MINORS.
Miscarriage.
Injury to pregnant woman resulting in
miscarriage or stillbirth.
Use of instruments or drugs, §14-45.
Misconduct in private office.
Corporation officers and agents.
Malfeasance of officers and agents, §14-254(a).
Definition of "person,"§14-254.
Railroad officers.
Failure of certain officers to account with
successors, §14-253.
Misconduct in public office, §§14-228 to 14-252.
Misdemeanor death by vehicle, §20-141.4(a2).
Punishment, §20-141.4(b).
Misdemeanors.
See MISDEMEANORS.
Missing persons.
Improper release of information, §143B-1020.
Mistrial.
Deadlocked jury, §15A-1235(d).
Disability of trial judge, §15A-1224(a).
Finding of facts required, §15A-1064.
Grounds.
Hung jury, §15A-1063.
Impossibility of proceeding, §15A-1063.
Prejudice to defendant, §15A-1061.
Prejudice to state, §15A-1062.
Hung jury, §15A-1063.
Impossibility of proceeding, §15A-1063.
Prejudice to defendant, §15A-1061.
Prejudice to state, §15A-1062.
Procedure following mistrial, §15A-1065.
Misuse of public office.
State government ethics act.
Failure to resign, §138A-39(b).
Gifts, violations of section, §138A-32(i).
Mobile phones.
School bus operators.
Unlawful use while bus in motion, §20-137.4.
Text messaging, electronic mail.
Driving while using mobile phone for,
§20-137.4A.
Modes of prosecution, NC Const Art I §23.
Money transmitters, §53-208.26.
Mortgage bankers, brokers and services.
Unlicensed activity, §53-244.112.
Mortgages and deeds of trust.
Residential mortgage fraud.
General provisions, §§14-118.10 to 14-118.17.
Secondary or junior mortgages.
Willful or knowing violations, §24-17.
Motion for appropriate relief, §§15A-1411 to
15A-1422.
See MOTION FOR APPROPRIATE RELIEF.
Motions.
See MOTIONS.
Motor carriers.
Embezzlement of COD shipments, §62-273.

CRIMINAL LAW AND PROCEDURE —Cont'd
Motor carriers —Cont'd
False information to department, §20-397.
Household goods carriers.
Lack of certificate to operate as.
Prohibited activities, criminal enforcement,
§62-280.1(b).
Marking or identification of vehicles, §20-398(d).
Migrant farm workers.
Violations of regulations, §20-215.4.
Refusal to allow inspections, §20-390.
Registration fees.
Carrying charge, §20-94.
Taxation.
Road tax on carriers using fuel purchased
outside state.
Violations of provisions as misdemeanors,
§105-449.51.
Unlawful motor carrier operations, §20-396.
Willful evasion of department of public safety
regulations, §§20-396, 20-397.
Willful injury to property of motor carrier,
§20-395.
Motor vehicle accidents.
Failure to stop and give name, §20-166(c), (c1).
Passengers, §20-166.2(b).
Leaving scene of accident, §20-166(a), (b).
Injury occurring in accident, §20-166(a1).
Passengers, §20-166.2(a).
Reports, §20-166.1(k).
False information, §20-279.31(b).
Motor vehicle certificates of title.
Altering or forging, §20-71(a).
Borrowing or lending, §20-111.
Failure to surrender ownership documents,
§20-45(b).
Registration of security interest.
False filing, §20-58(b).
Reproducing or possessing blank title, §20-71(b).
Satisfaction of liens.
Lienor refusal to surrender certificate, §20-59.
Secondary metals recyclers and salvage yards.
Purchase of vehicles without certificate for scrap
and parts only.
Violations, §20-62.1(c).
Transfer of title or interest.
Assignment of blank title.
Dealer or insurance company, §20-75.
Assignment with blank signature, §20-72(b).
Failure of new owner to apply for new
certificate, §20-73(c).
False statement in making an application,
§20-74.
Motor vehicle dealers.
License applications.
Violations of license provisions, §20-308.
Motor vehicle financial responsibility,
§20-279.31(b) to (d).
Failure of owner to deliver certificate of
registration and plates, §20-312.
False certification, §20-313.1(a).
False information concerning another's
responsibility, §20-313.1(b).
Unlawful operation of motor vehicle, §20-313(a).
Motor vehicle inspections, §20-183.8(c).
Motor vehicle insurance.
Total loss claim vehicle.
Removal of permanent marker affixed to
vehicles doorjam, §20-71.4(c).
Motor vehicle manufacturers.
Certificate of origin.
Assignment with blank signature, §20-52.1(c).

CRIMINAL LAW AND PROCEDURE —Cont'd
Motor vehicle manufacturers —Cont'd
Certificate of origin —Cont'd
False sworn certification, §20-52.1(d).
License applications.
Violations of license provisions, §20-308.
Motor vehicle parts.
Felony larceny, §14-72.8.
Motor vehicle registration.
Application.
False or fictitious statement, §20-111.
Motor vehicle safety or emissions inspections.
Performing without license, §20-183.8(b1).
Motor vehicle sales.
Damage to vehicle.
Failure to disclose when transferring, §20-71.4(d).
Motor vehicle serial or engine numbers.
Altering or changing numbers, §20-109(a), (b).
Prohibitions as to vehicles without numbers, §20-108(a).
Motor vehicle taxes.
Classified motor vehicles.
Criminal penalty for evasion of taxes, §105-330.3(d).
Mountain ridge protection.
Violations subject to criminal sanctions, §113A-211(a).
Municipalities.
Building inspection certificates of compliance.
Violations of provisions, §160A-423.
Building inspection department members.
Failure to perform duties, §160A-416.
Building inspector stop orders.
Violations, §160A-421(b).
Building permit violations, §160A-417(a).
Defense of employees and officers in criminal actions, §160A-167.
Notice of unsafe building.
Removal, §160A-427.
Personnel records.
Knowingly, willfully and with malice permitting access to, §160A-168(e).
Removing or copying confidential personnel files, §160A-168(f).
Subdivisions.
Transferring lots in unapproved subdivisions, §160A-375(a).
Swearing falsely at investigation by council, §160A-80(b).
Taxation.
Disclosure of information, §160A-208.1(b).
Vehicle used on foreshore, beach strand and barrier dune systems.
Violation of ordinance regulating, §160A-308.
Zoning boards of adjustment.
Swearing falsely before, §160A-388(g).
Murder.
See MURDER.
Mutual burial associations.
Accepting application without collecting membership fee or assessment, §90-210.91.
False entries on books of association, §90-210.90.
False or fraudulent statement or representation, §90-210.97.
Free services, failure to assess, §90-210.93.
Operating without authority of board, §90-210.84.
Operation in noncompliance with bylaws, §90-210.88.
Wrongfully inducing change in membership, §90-210.89.

CRIMINAL LAW AND PROCEDURE —Cont'd
Narcotics.
Drugs and controlled substances generally.
See DRUGS AND CONTROLLED SUBSTANCES.
National crime prevention and privacy compact, §114-19.50.
Navigable waters.
Medical waste, depositing, §76-40(a1).
Structures erected on floor of navigable waters, §76-40(b).
Failure to remove abandoned structures, §76-40(c).
Necessity.
Peace officers.
Non-law-enforcement actions when urgently necessary, §15A-285.
Neglect of disabled or elder adult, §14-32.3(b).
Neighborhood crime watch programs.
Establishment, §153A-212.2.
Harassment of participant, §14-226.2.
Newspapers.
Libel and slander.
Communicating libelous matter to newspapers, §14-47.
New trial.
Appeals.
Correction of errors by appellate division.
Duties of clerk of superior court upon order of new trial, §15A-1452(c).
Relief available upon appeal, §15A-1447(a).
Motion for appropriate relief.
Motion for new trial.
Relief formerly available now available by motion for appropriate relief, §15A-1411(c).
Relief available, §15A-1417(a).
911 system.
Misuse of system, §14-111.4.
No contest pleas.
Generally.
See NO CONTEST PLEAS.
Pleas generally.
See PLEAS.
Nolo contendere.
Generally.
See NO CONTEST PLEAS.
Nonprofit corporations.
Failure to answer interrogatories propounded by secretary.
Officers and directors, §55A-1-32(b).
Nontestimonial identification, §§15A-271 to 15A-282.
See IDENTIFICATION.
North Carolina state flag.
Desecration, §14-381.
Notaries public.
Electronic notary public act.
Electronic signature.
Wrongfully obtaining coding, file or program enabling affixation, §10B-146(b).
Software or hardware.
Wrongful manufacture, distribution or possession, §10B-146(a).
Felonies, §10B-60(e), (f).
Misdemeanors, §10B-60(b), (c).
Not guilty by reason of insanity.
Civil commitment of defendant, §15A-1321(a), (b).
Not guilty pleas, §15A-1011.
Notice.
Appeals.
Correction of errors by appellate division.
Notice of appeal, §15A-1448(b).

CRIMINAL LAW AND PROCEDURE —Cont'd
Notice —Cont'd
  DNA evidence disposal.
    Prior to expiration of time period for preserving, §15A-268(b), (c).
  Insanity defense.
    Discovery generally, §15A-905(c), (d).
    Intent to introduce expert testimony, §15A-959(b).
    Pretrial hearing, §15A-959(a).
Nuclear fuel.
  Transportation of spent nuclear fuel, §20-167.1(d).
Nursing home administrators.
  Violations of provision, §90-288.
Nursing home licensure.
  Inspection violations, §131E-109(b).
  Prohibited acts, §131E-109(d).
  Unlicensed operation, §131E-109(a).
Nursing pools.
  Unauthorized disclosure of inspection information, §131E-154.8(b).
Obscenity, §§14-190.1 to 14-190.20.
  See OBSCENITY AND PORNOGRAPHY.
Obstructing health care facilities, §14-277.4(c).
Obstructing justice, §§14-221 to 14-227.
  See OBSTRUCTING JUSTICE.
Occupational safety and health.
  Criminal penalties, §95-139.
Occupational therapists.
  Violations of provision, §90-270.79.
Odometers.
  Prohibited acts, §20-350.
  Unlawful change of mileage, §20-350.
Offering bribe, §14-218.
Office of information technology services.
  Procurement of information technology.
    Bribery, §147-33.99.
    False certification that information technology bid submitted without collusion, §147-33.100.
    Financial interest of officers in sources of supply, §147-33.99.
    Unauthorized use of public purchase or contract procedures for private benefit, §147-33.98(c).
Off-premises sales, failure to give right to cancel, §14-401.13.
Oil and gas conservation.
  Violations as misdemeanors, §§113-380, 113-409.
Oil dispensing devices.
  Falsification of measures, §119-33.
Oil inspection violations.
  Generally, §119-39.
Oil inspectors.
  Conflicts of interest, §119-25.
  Failure or refusal to exhibit records to, §119-32.
Oil or hazardous substances discharges, §143-215.88B.
Oil refining facility permit violations, §143-215.102(b).
Oils.
  Lubricating oils.
    Violations of article, §§119-4, 119-13.
  Rerefined or reprocessed oil.
    Violations of article, §119-13.3.
Oil terminal facilities.
  Violations of provisions, §143-215.98.
Open container law, §20-138.7(e).
  Pleading and prosecutions, §20-138.7(g).
Open fires violations, §106-948.

CRIMINAL LAW AND PROCEDURE —Cont'd
Opticians.
  Allowing unlicensed person to use certificate or license, §90-251.
  Sale of flammable frame, §90-255.1.
  Unlicensed practice, §90-252.
Options to purchase rented property.
  Failing to return.
    Misdemeanor, §14-168.4(a).
    Presumptions from evidence.
      Intent to commit crime, §14-168.4(b).
    Prosecution, §14-168.4(c).
Optometrists.
  Rules and regulations violation, §90-124.
  Unauthorized practices, §90-118.11.
Orders.
  Commitment order, §15A-1301.
  Imprisonment.
    Order of commitment, §15A-1301.
  Suppression of evidence, §15A-979(a).
Orders of court, violating, §14-226.1.
Ordinance violation, misdemeanor, §14-4(a).
Organized crime.
  RICO generally, §§75D-1 to 75D-14.
    See RACKETEER INFLUENCED AND CORRUPT ORGANIZATIONS (RICO).
Organized retail theft, §§14-86.5, 14-86.6.
Outdoor advertising.
  Control act violations, §136-135.
Overloaded vehicles.
  Weighing or removing.
    Refusal to permit law enforcement officer, §20-118.1.
Overtaking and passing.
  Driver of overtaken vehicle not giving way to right in favor of overtaking vehicle, §20-149(b).
Paper currency machine burglary, §14-56.3.
Parent and child.
  Exclusion of witnesses.
    Exception to provisions, §15A-1225.
  Failure to support parent, §14-326.1.
Parking.
  Ports authority regulations, §136-269(c).
  Private lots.
    Unauthorized vehicles, §20-219.2(b).
  Private parking space, §14-401.9.
  Public grounds, §143-340.
Parks and recreation.
  State parks.
    Violation of department rules for use by public, §113-35(a).
Parole.
  See PAROLE.
Partnerships.
  Appearance by counsel or agent, §15A-773(b).
  Securing attendance of organizations, §15A-773(a).
    Definition of "organization,"§15A-773(c).
Party lines, refusal to relinquish, §14-401.8.
Patient abuse.
  Unlawful to physically abuse patient, §14-32.2.
Pawnbrokers and cash converters.
  Receiving stolen goods.
    Criminal penalties, §91A-11(b).
  Violations, §91A-11(a).
Peace officers.
  Motor vehicles.
    Rights of misdemeanor arrestee, §20-114(a).
Peddlers, itinerant merchants and specialty markets, §66-257.
  Prohibited sales, §66-254.1.

CRIMINAL LAW AND PROCEDURE —Cont'd
Peeping into room occupied by another person, §14-202.
Pen registers and trap and trace devices, §§15A-260 to 15A-264.
Periodicals.
Communicating libelous matter to periodicals, §14-47.
Perjury, §§14-209 to 14-211.
See PERJURY.
Personnel system.
Political activities of employees.
Coercing employee to support or contribute to political candidate, committee or party, §§126-14, 126-14.1.
Restrictions, §126-13(b).
Pesticide applicators and consultants.
Applying or combining prohibited substances, §143-458(c) to (e).
Reporting of shipments and volumes of pesticides, §143-459.
Pesticide violations, §143-469(a).
Applying or combining prohibited substances, §143-458(c) to (e).
Petitions.
Review of criminal trials.
Generally, §15A-1420(b1).
Pet shops.
Cruelty to animals, §19A-35.
Unlicensed shops, §19A-33.
Pharmacists and pharmacies.
Violations of article, §90-85.40.
Phonograph records and tapes, §§14-432 to 14-437.
Civil action for damages by owner of recorded device, §14-436.
Definitions, §14-432.
Live concert recordings.
Unlawful in certain circumstances, §14-433(a) to (c).
Retailers.
Unlawful retailing of certain recorded devices, §14-434.
Violation of article, §14-437(a).
Physical therapists.
Unlicensed practice, §90-270.35.
Physician assistants.
Limited volunteer license to practice.
Violation of practice restriction, §90-12.4A(e).
Physician assistant retired limited volunteer license, §90-12.4B(e).
Physicians and surgeons.
Limited volunteer license to practice.
Violation of practice restriction, §90-12.1A(f).
Retired limited volunteer license, §90-12.1B(e).
Medical school faculty.
Unauthorized practice, §90-12.3(b).
Practicing without license, §90-18(a).
Special purpose license.
Unauthorized practice, §90-12.2A(b).
Picketing or parading within certain distance of general court of justice, §14-225.1.
Plastic yoke and ring type holding devices, §14-399.2.
Plea bargaining.
See PLEAS.
Pleadings in criminal cases.
See PLEADINGS.
Pleas.
See PLEAS.

CRIMINAL LAW AND PROCEDURE —Cont'd
Poisons generally.
See POISONS.
Pollution control.
Sedimentation pollution control act of 1973.
Violations as misdemeanors, §113A-64(b).
Water pollution on lands used for dairy purposes, §14-382.
Polysomnography.
Prohibited acts, §90-723(b).
Portable smelters, §66-173.
Portable toilets or pumper trucks.
Larceny, destruction, defacement, vandalism, §14-86.2.
Post conviction DNA testing.
Motion by defendant, §§15A-269 to 15A-270.1.
Post-trial motions, §15A-1401.
Prayer for judgment continued.
Entry of PJC not considered entry of judgment, §15A-101.
Precious metal dealers, §66-172.
Copies of records filed with law enforcement.
Unauthorized disclosure by public official or law enforcement employee, §66-169(e).
Pregnant women.
Abortion, §§14-44 to 14-46.
Injury to pregnant woman resulting in miscarriage or stillbirth.
Use of instruments or drugs, §14-45.
Prejudicial error.
Appeals.
Burden of proof, §15A-1443(a).
Definition of prejudicial error, §15A-1443(a).
Preneed funeral contracts and funds.
Failure of person to obey subpoena, §90-210.69(b).
Presentments.
Contents, §15A-644(c).
Defined, §15A-641(c).
Modes of prosecution, NC Const Art I §22.
Signatures.
Foreman of grand jury.
Signature attesting concurrence of twelve or more grand jurors, §15A-644(c).
Venue.
Grand jury's venue.
To present or indict, §15A-631.
Pretrial conference in capital cases, SuperCt Rule 24.
Previous convictions.
Alleging, pleading and proving, §§15A-924, 15A-928.
Price tags, transfer, §14-72.1(d).
Principals and accessories, §§14-5.2, 14-7.
Prisons and prisoners.
General provisions.
See PRISONS AND PRISONERS.
Private office.
Misconduct in private office.
Corporation officers and agents.
Malfeasance of officers and agents, §14-254(a).
Definition of "person," §14-254(b).
Railroad officers.
Failure of certain officers to account to successors, §14-253.
Private personnel services.
Operation without license, §95-47.9(e).
Unlicensed operation, §95-47.9(e).
Probable cause hearings.
See PROBABLE CAUSE.
Probate and registration.
Maps and plats.
Violations of certain provisions as misdemeanors, §47-32.2.

CRIMINAL LAW AND PROCEDURE —Cont'd

Probate and registration —Cont'd

Registration of military discharges.

Forgery or alteration of discharge certificate as misdemeanor, §47-112.

Probation.

See PROBATION.

Process.

Electronic repository for criminal process, §15A-301.1.

Definitions, §15A-101.1.

Failure to return or false return, §14-242.

Professional counselors.

Conviction of a crime.

Disciplinary action against licensee.

Grounds, §90-340(a).

Violation punishable as crime, §90-341.

Property tax offenses generally.

See PROPERTY TAXES.

Proprietary schools.

Operating without license or bond, §115D-96.

Prosecution of juvenile as adult, §17B-1604.

Transfer of jurisdiction of juvenile to superior court, §§17B-2200 to 17B-2204.

Prostitution.

See PROSTITUTION.

Protection of home, workplace, motor vehicle.

Defensive force, §14-51.2.

Psychologists.

Prohibited acts, §90-270.17.

Public buildings and grounds.

Disorderly conduct in and injury to, §143-345.2.

Motor vehicle regulations and parking, §143-340.

Violations of regulations, §143-345.1.

Public intoxication.

Generally, §§14-443 to 14-447, 122C-301 to 122C-303.

See INTOXICATION.

Public lands.

Piers.

Erection on state lakes.

Violations of permits, §146-13.

Trees and timber.

Cutting before obtaining grant, §146-43.

Public morality and decency.

Offenses against public morality and decency, §§14-177 to 14-202.6.

Public officers and employees.

Bribery of officials, §14-217.

Insurance committee, §58-31-60(d).

Misconduct in public office, §§14-228 to 14-252.

See MISCONDUCT IN PUBLIC OFFICE.

Political activities of employees.

Coercing employee to support or contribute to political candidate, committee or party, §§126-14, 126-14.1.

Restrictions, §126-13(b).

Receiving compensation of subordinates for appointment or retention, §128-4.

Violations of law, §143-115.

Public peace.

Offenses against the public peace, §§14-269 to 14-277.5.

Public records.

Cultural resources department.

Disposition of records at end of official's term, §132-4.

Destruction, §121-5.

Unauthorized removal or destruction, §132-3.

Unlawful possession, §132-5.

CRIMINAL LAW AND PROCEDURE —Cont'd

Public safety.

Offenses against the public safety, §§14-278 to 14-288.

Public schools.

Contractors selling personally identifiable student information.

Criminal penalty, §115C-401.1(c).

Criminal act on school property.

Policies of board regarding.

Report by principal, §115C-288(g).

Public trial, US Const Amd 6.

Public utilities.

Allowing or accepting rebates, §62-318.

Property, willful damaging, §62-323.

Refusal to permit commission to inspect records, §62-313.

Public works.

Chapter violations, §133-4.

Contractor affidavits.

Perjury in affidavit, §133-31.

Contractor gifts and favors.

Public officers and employees, §133-32(b).

Quo warranto.

Official papers.

Refusal to surrender by person against whom judgment rendered, §1-531.

Racing on streets and highways, §20-141.3(a) to (c).

Railroad grade crossing.

Vehicles required to stop, §20-142.3(c).

Railroads.

Cattle guards and crossings.

Failure to erect and maintain, §136-194.

Intoxicated person boarding train after being forbidden by conductor, §136-197.

Obstructing highways.

Failure to repair after notice, §136-192(c).

Riding on train unlawfully, §§14-460, 62-319.

Switch-lock keys.

Unauthorized manufacture or sale, §§14-461, 62-322.

Rape.

See RAPE.

Rape shield law, §8C-1 Rule 412.

Real estate appraisal management companies.

Violations, §93E-2-10(a).

Real estate appraisers.

Practicing without license or certificate, §93E-1-13(a).

Real property.

Furnishing false statements in connection with improvements as misdemeanor, §44A-24.

Rebellion, §14-10.

Punishment for rebellion, §14-8.

Rebirthing technique.

Practicing unlawful, §14-401.21.

Reckless driving, §20-140(d).

Commercial motor vehicle carrying a load, §20-140(f).

Refrigerator abandonment, §14-318.1.

Registers of deeds.

Failure to discharge duties, §161-27.

Registration of voters.

Application forms.

Misdemeanor violations regarding, §163-82.6(a1).

Removal of disruptive defendant from courtroom.

Authority of judge, §15A-1032(a).

Instruction to jury, §15A-1032(b).

CRIMINAL LAW AND PROCEDURE —Cont'd
Removal of disruptive defendant from courtroom —Cont'd
Opportunity given defendant to learn of proceedings while absent, §15A-1032(b).
Reason, entry into record, §15A-1032(b).
Warning, required, issued out of presence of jury, §15A-1032(a).
Rental vehicles.
Fraud, §20-106.1.
Options to purchase.
Failing to return rented property on which there is purchase option, §14-168.4.
Sublease and loan assumption arranging, §20-106.2(e).
Violations of insurance provisions, §20-284.
Reports.
Disposition of cases, §15A-1382(a), (b).
Representation of indigent persons.
Generally, §§7A-450 to 7A-458.
See INDIGENT DEFENSE SERVICES.
Reptiles.
Regulation of certain reptiles generally, §§14-416 to 14-422.
See REPTILES.
Residential mortgage fraud.
General provisions, §§14-118.10 to 14-118.17.
Resisting officers, §14-223.
Respiratory care practitioners.
Regulatory violations, §90-662.
Restitution or reparation.
See RESTITUTION.
Restoration of citizenship rights to convicted persons, §§13-1 to 13-4.
Automatic restoration, §13-1.
Certificate or order of restoration.
Issuance and filing, §13-2.
Conditional pardon.
Endorsement of warrant, service and filing, §13-4.
Unconditional pardon.
Issuance, service and filing of warrant, §13-3.
Restraint.
Felonious restraint, §14-43.3.
Retirement system for counties, cities and towns, §§128-28, 128-32.
Confidentiality of information, §128-28(q).
Retirement system for teachers and state employees.
Consolidated judicial retirement act.
Improper receipt of decedent's retirement allowance, §135-75.2.
Disclosure of confidential information concerning members, §135-6(p).
False statements or falsified records, §135-10.
Improper receipt of decedent's retirement allowance, §135-18.11.
Review of criminal trials.
Petitions, §15A-1420(b1).
Riding on train unlawfully, §§14-460, 62-319.
Rights of accused, NC Const Art I §23.
Rights of victims. See within this heading, "Victims of crime."
Right to counsel, §15-4, NC Const Art I §23, US Const Amd 6.
Riots and civil disorders, §§14-288.1 to 14-288.20.
See RIOTS AND CIVIL DISORDERS.
Rivers.
Obstructing natural drainage, §77-14.
Obstructing natural flow, §77-13.

CRIMINAL LAW AND PROCEDURE —Cont'd
Rivers —Cont'd
Obstructing passage, §77-12.
Robbery.
See ROBBERY.
Rules of procedure, NC Const Art IV §13.
Rustling cattle, §14-81.
Safety belt.
Violations of mandatory use provision, §20-135.2A(e).
Sales.
Convict made goods, §14-346(a), (b).
Diseased animal meat, §14-342.
Railroad tickets, §14-343.
Scalping tickets, §§14-344, 14-344.1.
Software to interfere with operations of ticket seller, §14-344.2.
Sales and use tax.
Absorption of tax.
Advertisement to absorb tax as misdemeanor, §105-164.9.
Salvage of abandoned shipwrecks and other underwater archaeological sites.
Violations of article, §121-28.
Salvage vehicle certificate of title violations, §20-109.1(f).
Salvage vehicles.
Certificate of title violations, §20-109.1(f).
Salvia divinorum.
Manufacture, sale, delivery, possession.
Unlawful, §14-401.23.
Sanitary districts.
Noncompliance with board promulgated rules, §130A-55.
Sewer line or disposal plant.
Connection or reconnection without permit, §130A-65.
Scalping tickets, §§14-344, 14-344.1.
Software to interfere with operations of ticket seller, §14-344.2.
School buses.
Mobile phones.
Unlawful use by operator while bus in motion, §20-137.4.
Operating after consuming alcohol, §20-138.2B(c).
Passing stopped school bus, §20-217.
Trespassing upon, damaging or impeding progress, §14-132.2.
School employees.
Defense of board of education members and employees, §115C-43(a) to (c).
Personnel files.
Inspection.
Confidential information in personnel file, §115C-321(c), (d).
School of science and mathematics.
Nonattendance, §116-235(b).
Traffic violations, §116-235(e).
Searches and seizures.
See SEARCHES AND SEIZURES.
Secondary metals recyclers and salvage yards.
Motor vehicles purchased without title certificate.
Purchases for scrap and parts recovery only, violations, §20-62.1(c).
Secret listening, §§14-227.1 to 14-227.3.
Secretly peeping into room occupied by another person, §14-202.
Secret societies, §§14-12.1 to 14-12.15.
See SECRET SOCIETIES.
Securities, §78A-57.
Dealing in securities on commission.
Taxed as private banker, §14-401.7.

CRIMINAL LAW AND PROCEDURE —Cont'd

Securities —Cont'd

Exemptions from securities regulation.

Burden of proof, §78A-18(b).

Securities regulation.

Obstruction of investigation, §78A-58.

Security agreements.

Filing false security agreements, §14-401.19.

Seized property.

Disposition of unclaimed property, §§15-11 to 15-17.

See SEARCHES AND SEIZURES.

General provisions.

See SEARCHES AND SEIZURES.

Self-defense.

Affrays.

Evidence of former threats upon plea of self-defense, §14-33.1.

Assaulting law enforcement, assistance or search and rescue animals, §14-163.1(f).

Justifiable use of defensive force.

Defense of person, §14-51.3.

Justification not available, §14-51.4.

Protection of home, workplace, motor vehicle, §14-51.2.

Self-incrimination.

Generally.

See SELF-INCRIMINATION.

Sentencing.

Community corrections programs.

Sentencing services, §§7A-770 to 7A-777.

See SENTENCING SERVICES.

Death sentence.

See DEATH PENALTY.

Felony sentencing, §§15A-1340.13 to 15A-1340.17.

See SENTENCING.

General provisions.

See SENTENCING.

Sentencing services act, §§7A-770 to 7A-777.

See SENTENCING SERVICES.

Service animals.

Prohibited acts, §168-4.5.

Service of process.

Citation, §15A-302(d).

Criminal process generally, §15A-301(c).

Electronic repository for criminal process.

Process in, §15A-301.1(g), (j) to (n).

Motion for appropriate relief, §15A-1420(a).

Motions, §15A-951(b).

Proof of service, §15A-951(c).

Recall of process, §15A-301(g).

Severance of offenses.

Generally, §15A-927(b).

Motion.

Motion of court, §15A-927(e).

Renewal, §15A-927(a).

Time for, §15A-927(a).

Waiver, §15A-927(a).

Sex offender and public protection registration.

General provisions, §§14-208.5 to 14-208.32.

See SEX OFFENDER AND PUBLIC PROTECTION REGISTRATION.

Sex offender monitoring, §§14-208.40 to 14-208.45.

See SEX OFFENDER MONITORING.

Sex offenses.

Generally.

See SEX OFFENSES.

Rape.

See RAPE.

CRIMINAL LAW AND PROCEDURE —Cont'd

Sexual exploitation of minor, §§14-190.16 to 14-190.17A.

Sexually transmitted infections.

Testing defendant accused of offense involving sexual intercourse.

Request of victim, §15A-615(a).

Defendant in custody of division of adult correction, §15A-615(c).

Order requiring, §15A-615(b).

Sharecroppers.

Landlord failing to make advance, §§14-358, 14-359.

Receiving advance with intent to defraud, §§14-358, 14-359.

Shellfish cultivation.

Leases.

Forms for determining amount of shellfish.

False statements as misdemeanors, §113-202(o).

Polluted shellfish.

Taking or selling at night or with prior convictions as felony, §113-209(d).

Ships and shipping.

Lights.

Displaying false lights on seashore, §14-282.

Shopping carts.

Removal from shopping premises, §14-72.3.

Slander.

Magazines or periodicals.

Libelous matter communicated, §14-47.

Newspapers.

Communicating libelous matter to newspapers, §14-47.

Slot machines, §§14-301 to 14-309.1.

See SLOT MACHINES.

Smoke screen.

Violations of prohibition, §20-136(b).

Social services.

Local confinement facilities.

Refusal to provide information, §131D-13.

Social workers.

Violations, §90B-12.

Soil and water conservation commission.

Refusing entry, resisting, delaying or obstructing employee or agent of commission, §106-840(c).

Soil scientists, §89F-22.

Solicitation of contributions.

Willful violations of chapter, §131F-22.

Solid waste management.

Disclosure of information received pursuant to article, §130A-304(b).

Used oil.

Disposal at landfills, §130A-309.15(a).

Registration violations, §130A-309.17(h).

Special prosecution division.

Duties, §114-11.6.

Established, §114-11.6.

Speech and language pathologists and audiologists.

Violations of provision, §90-306.

Speeding.

Commercial motor vehicle carrying a load, §20-141(j3).

Speeding to elude arrest, §20-141.5.

Speedy trial, US Const Amd 6.

Denial.

Grounds for motion to dismiss, §15A-954(a).

Felonies, §15-10.

Quo warranto, §1-521.

Treason, §15-10.

CRIMINAL LAW AND PROCEDURE —Cont'd

Sporting events, throwing, dropping, etc., objects at, §14-281.1.

Spring loaded projectile knives.
Possession and sale, §14-269.6(a), (b).

Stalking, §14-277.3A.
Cyberstalking, §14-196.3.

State auditor.
Obstruction of audit, §147-64.7A.

State bureau of investigation, §§114-12 to 114-20.1.
See BUREAU OF INVESTIGATION.

State flag.
Desecration, §14-381.

State forests.
Concessions for operation of public service facilities.
Violation of rules regarding, §106-877(c).

State legislative building.
Removal of state-owned furniture, fixtures or equipment, §120-32.
Use and maintenance.
Violations of regulations, §120-32.1.

State of emergency.
County ordinance or proclamation dealing with, violation, §14-288.13(d).
Extension of municipal restrictions into county, violation, §14-288.14(e).
Governor's proclamation, violation, §14-288.15(e).
Municipal ordinance and proclamation, violation, §14-288.12(e).

State parks.
Violation of rules for use of facilities, §113-35(a).

State personnel records.
Unlawful disclosure, §§126-27, 126-28.

State personnel system.
Compensation for assisting person in obtaining state employment, §126-18.
Political activity of employees, §§126-14, 126-14.1.

State treasurer.
Deposits.
Unauthorized depositories, §147-80.
Violations of provisions, §147-79(c).
False entries in books, §147-76.

Status offenders.
Habitual breaking and entering status offense.
Generally, §§14-7.25 to 14-7.31.
See BREAKING AND ENTERING.
Status offender defined, §14-7.25.
Habitual felons.
Charging as, §14-7.1.
Generally, §§14-7.1 to 14-7.12.
See HABITUAL FELONS.

Statute of limitations.
Civil actions seeking to recover damages arising out of criminal act, §1-15.1.
Dismissal of criminal charges.
Motion to dismiss.
Grounds, §15A-954(a).
Voluntary dismissal by state.
Statute of limitations not tolled, §15A-931(b).
Misdemeanors, §15-1.

Stays.
Appeals.
Correction of errors by appellate division, §15A-1451(a).
No stay when state appeals, §15A-1451(b).

Stillbirth.
Injury to pregnant woman resulting in miscarriage or stillbirth.
Use of instruments or drugs, §14-45.

CRIMINAL LAW AND PROCEDURE —Cont'd

Stolen vehicles.
False report of theft or conversion, §20-102.1.

Street gangs, §§14-50.15 to 14-50.30.
See GANGS.

Subdivisions.
Highways, roads and streets.
Developer noncompliance with standards, §136-102.6.

Submachine guns.
Sale, use or possession, §14-409.

Subornation of perjury, §14-210.

Subpoenas.
Documentary evidence, §15A-802.
General provisions.
See SUBPOENAS.
Witnesses, §15A-801.
Material witnesses.
Securing attendance, §15A-803(g).

Subversion.
Activities aimed at overthrow of government, §14-11.
Certain subversive activities made unlawful, §14-12.1.
Punishment for violations, §14-12.

Summons and criminal process, §§15A-301, 15A-303.

Superior court costs, §7A-304.

Superior court procedure applicability, §15A-1101.

Support and maintenance.
Abandonment and failure to support spouse and children, §14-322.
Failure to support parent, §14-326.1.

Suppression of evidence.
Motion to suppress evidence, §§15A-971 to 15A-980. See within this heading, "Evidence."

Surveys and surveyors.
Coordinate system.
Damaging, defacing or destroying monuments, §102-4.

Sweepstakes.
Electronic machines and devices prohibited, §14-306.4(f).

Swine kept near state institutions, §143-153.

Switch-lock keys used by railroads.
Unauthorized manufacture or sale, §§14-461, 62-322.

Syphilis.
Defendant accused of offense involving sexual intercourse.
Testing on victim's request, §15A-615.

Taking indecent liberties with minor, §14-202.1.

Tampering with ignition interlock system, §20-17.8A.

Tampering with vehicle, §20-107(a).

Tandem trailers and semitrailer.
Load limitation violations, §20-115.1(i).

Targeted picketing of residence, §14-277.4A.

Tattooing, §14-400(a).

Taxation.
Attempt to evade or defeat tax as felony, §105-236.
Fraud.
Aid or assistance as felony, §105-236.
Tax information confidentiality, §105-259(c).
Willful failure to collect, withhold or pay over tax as misdemeanor, §105-236.
Willful failure to file return, supply information or pay tax as misdemeanor, §105-236.

CRIMINAL LAW AND PROCEDURE —Cont'd

Tax preparers' unauthorized disclosure of tax information, §75-28.

Tear gas, unlawful possession, use, etc., §14-401.6.

Teflon-coated bullets.
Manufacture sale, purchase or possession unlawful, §14-34.3(a).
Inapplicability of provisions, §14-34.3(b).
Misdemeanor, §14-34.3(c).

Telecommunications services, theft, §14-113.5.

Telegraphic and telephonic messages.
Delivery of message.
Failure to deliver promptly, §14-371.
Opening of sealed telegram.
Unauthorized opening, §14-372.
Publishing of sealed telegram.
Unauthorized publishing, §14-372.
Reading of sealed telegram.
Unauthorized reading, §14-372.
Transmission of message.
Failure to transmit promptly, §14-371.
Violating privacy of messages, §14-371.
Wrongfully obtaining or divulging knowledge of messages, §14-370.

Telephone party lines, refusal to relinquish, §14-401.8.

Telephone records privacy protection.
General provisions, §§14-113.30 to 14-113.33.

Telephone sales recovery services, §14-401.15.

Telephone threats, harassment, obscenity, etc., §14-196.

Text messaging.
Driving while using mobile phone for, §20-137.4A.

Theft.
See THEFT.

Thermostats containing mercury.
Disposal in unlined landfills, §§130A-25(d), 130A-309.10(m).

Threats.
Communicating, §14-277.1.
Telephones, §14-196.
Transmitting anonymous letters, §14-394.

Ticket scalping, §§14-344, 14-344.1.
Software to interfere with operations of ticket seller, §14-344.2.

Timber marks.
Altering timber trademark, §80-22.
Fraudulent use of mark, §80-20.
Possession of branded logs without consent, §80-23.

Time shares.
Registration of violations, §93A-40(b).
Time share registrar violation, §93A-58.
Violations of provision, §93A-56.

Tobacco products.
Sale or distribution to minors, §14-313.

Toxic substances.
Disclosure of hazardous substance trade secret, §95-197.
Distribution or disclosure of emergency information, §95-194.
Dumping, §14-284.2.

Toxic vapors.
Violations of provision, §90-113.13.

Train surfing.
Riding on train unlawfully, §§14-460, 62-319.

Tramways.
Juvenile to be prosecuted as adult, §§7B-2200 to 7B-2204.

CRIMINAL LAW AND PROCEDURE —Cont'd

Tramways —Cont'd
Operation of passenger route tramway without registration, §95-124.

Transportation board.
Malfeasance, §136-13(c).
Profiting from proposed project, §136-14(f).

Transportation department.
Airport landing area construction and alteration, §136-18.
Highway inspection reports.
Falsifying reports, §136-13.2(a), (b).
Highway vending machines in rest areas, §136-18.
Ordinance violations, §136-18.
Utility lines and services, §136-18.

Tree cutting on town watershed.
Disposal violations, §14-383.

Trespass, §§14-127 to 14-165.
See TRESPASS.

Trial.
Generally.
See TRIAL.
Jury trial.
See JURY AND JURY TRIAL.

Truck routes.
Designation violation, §20-116(h).

Trust companies.
Records violations, §53-355.
Reporting offenses or shortages, §53-358(c).

Trust funds held by public officers.
Failure to keep separate, §128-12.

Tuition and fee waivers.
Misrepresentation of eligiblity, §115B-6.

Unauthorized insurers.
Soliciting, negotiating or selling insurance for, §58-33-95(a).

Unauthorized substances taxes.
Information obtained by department, testimony of officer, employee or agent of department.
Prohibition on use or testimony, misdemeanor for providing, §105-113.112.

Unborn victims of violence act/Ethen's law, §§14-23.1 to 14-23.8.
Abortion.
Prosecution not permitted for lawful acts, §14-23.7.
Assault inflicting serious bodily injury on unborn child, §14-23.5(a).
Class F felony, §14-23.5(c).
Serious bodily harm defined, §14-23.5(b).
Battery on unborn child, §14-23.6(a).
Class A1 misdemeanor, §14-23.6(b).
Exceptions, §14-23.7.
Intent of defendant to cause death or injury to unborn child.
Proof not required, §14-23.8.
Involuntary manslaughter of unborn child, §14-23.4(a).
Class F felony, §14-23.4(b).
Knowledge that victim of underlying offense pregnant.
Proof not required, §14-23.8.
Miscarriage or stillbirth.
Act committed by pregnant woman resulting in not prosecuted, §14-23.7.
Murder of unborn child, §14-23.2(a).
Class A felony, punishment, §14-23.2(b).
Unborn child defined, §14-23.1.
Usual and customary standards of medical practice.
Acts committed pursuant to not prosecuted, §14-23.7.

CRIMINAL LAW AND PROCEDURE —Cont'd
Unborn victims of violence act/Ethen's law
    —Cont'd
   Voluntary manslaughter of unborn child,
     §14-23.3(a).
   Class D felony, §14-23.3(b).
**Underground petroleum storage tank leak
    cleanup.**
   Circumstantial evidence to prove actual
     knowledge, §143-215.94X(e).
   Defenses, affirmative defenses and bars to
     prosecution, applicability, §143-215.94X(g).
   Federal violations, conviction of, §143-215.94X(d).
   Knowingly and willfully committing offenses,
     §143-215.94X(b), (c), (f).
   Negligently committing offenses, §143-215.94X(a).
Unemployment compensation.
   False statements or representation, §96-18(a), (b).
   Violations of chapter or rules or regulation,
     §96-18(c).
   Witness intimidation, §96-15.2.
**Uniform criminal extradition act, §§15A-721 to
    15A-750.**
   See EXTRADITION.
United States courts.
   Solicitors.
     Prosecution of cases removed to federal courts,
       §147-89.
United States flag.
   Desecration, §14-381.
Used goods sold on consignment.
   Recordkeeping violations, §66-67.2(c).
Used oil.
   Registration violations, §130A-309.17(h).
Usurious loans.
   Household and kitchen furniture, §14-391.
Vagrancy.
   Counties.
     Regulation of begging, §153A-126.
   Municipalities.
     Regulation of begging, §160A-179.
Vandalism.
   Generally.
     See VANDALISM.
Venue in criminal cases.
   See VENUE.
Verdict.
   General provisions.
     See VERDICTS.
Veterans guardianship act.
   Securities.
     Investment by guardians in certain securities.
       Violations as misdemeanors, §34-13.
Veterinarians.
   Directing or permitting technician, intern or
     preceptee to commit practice violations,
     §90-187.6(g).
   Unauthorized practices, §90-187.12.
**Veterinary technicians, student interns or
    student preceptees.**
   Practice violations, §90-187.6(f).
Victims of crime.
   Compensation.
     See CRIME VICTIMS COMPENSATION.
   Generally.
     See VICTIMS OF CRIME.
   Restitution or reparation.
     Sentencing, §§15A-1340.34 to 15A-1340.38.
       See SENTENCING.
   Rights.
     See VICTIMS OF CRIME.

CRIMINAL LAW AND PROCEDURE —Cont'd
Violent habitual felons, §§14-7.7 to 14-7.12.
Vital statistics.
   Birth certificates.
     Registration outside.
       Time period for filing, §130A-103.
   Misdemeanors and felonies, §130A-26A(a), (b).
Vocational rehabilitation services.
   Withholding of information, §143-547(f).
Voter registration.
   Application forms.
     Misdemeanor violations regarding,
       §163-82.6(a1).
Wage and hour act.
   Violations, §95-25.21(c).
Waiver.
   Appeals.
     Correction of errors by appellate division.
       Waiver of right to assert error upon appeal.
         Failure to make appropriate and timely
           motion or objection, §15A-1446(b).
   Appearance.
     Defendant may execute written waiver and
       plead not guilty, §15A-1011(d), (e).
   Arraignment, §15A-945.
   Indictment, §15A-642(b), (c).
   Probable cause hearings, §15A-606(a).
     Evidence of waiver not to be admitted at trial,
       §15A-606(b).
     Proceedings upon waiver, §15A-606(c).
   Venue, §15A-133(a).
Warrants.
   Arrest.
     See ARREST.
   Searches and seizures.
     See SEARCHES AND SEIZURES.
Wastewater systems.
   Certification of contractors and inspectors,
     §90A-81(d).
Water and air resources.
   Air pollution control violations, §143-215.114B(a)
     to (i).
   Classifications, standards or limitations.
     Violations, §143-215.6B(f) to (i).
   Cleaning agents containing phosphorus.
     Manufacturing, selling or distributing,
       §143-214.4(f).
   Conservation and use of diverted waters within
     emergency areas.
     Violations of regulations, §143-354.
   Enforcement procedures.
     Criminal penalties, §143-215.6B.
   Local air pollution control programs.
     Violations, §143-215.112(d).
   Medical waste.
     Prohibited disposal, §143-214.2A(a), (c).
   Reporting of quality.
     Violations of part, §143-215.69(a).
   Violations of part regulating water usage,
     §143-215.17(a).
Water and sewer authorities.
   Personnel records.
     Disclosure of confidential information,
       §162A-6.1(g), (h).
Waters and watercourses.
   Lake Wylie marine commission.
     Jurisdiction.
       Trial.
         Criminal violations of regulations,
           §77-38(c).

CRIMINAL LAW AND PROCEDURE —Cont'd
Waters and watercourses —Cont'd
Natural and scenic rivers system.
Violations as misdemeanors, §113A-42(b).
Water supply of public institutions.
Injuring, §143-152.
Weapons.
See FIREARMS AND OTHER WEAPONS.
Weight of vehicles and load.
Excessive size or weight.
Violations of special permit terms and condition,
§20-119(d).
Weights and measures offenses, §81A-29.
Well drilling, construction, etc., §143-355(i).
Wells.
Leaving unused well open and exposed, §14-287.
Wildlife protectors.
Refusal of person to stop in obedience to
directions of, §113-136(j).
Wildlife resources commission rules violations,
§§113-135.1(a), (b), 113-135(a) to (c).
Witnesses.
See WITNESSES.
Workers' compensation.
Coercing or attempting to coerce employee into
agreeing to compensation.
Threatening employee with criminal
prosecution, §97-88.2(c).
False statements or representations, §97-88.2(a).
Insurance carrier violation, §97-100(g).
Insurance or proof of financial ability to pay
benefit.
Refusal or neglect to secure compensation,
§97-94(c).
Receiving fee, other consideration or gratuity on
account of services rendered, §97-90(b).
Unlawful deduction by employers, §97-21.
Work first program fraud, §108A-39.
Worship places, obstructing way, §14-199.

CRIMINAL LAW SPECIALTY.
Certification standards, Bar Rules D.2501 to
D.2509.

CRIMINAL PENALTIES.
Crimes and offenses generally.
See CRIMINAL LAW AND PROCEDURE.
Felonies.
See FELONIES.
Fines.
See FINES.
Infractions.
See INFRACTIONS.
Misdemeanors.
See MISDEMEANORS.
Prison terms.
See PRISON TERMS.
Sentencing procedure for imposing
punishment.
See SENTENCING.

CRIMINAL PROCESS.
Arrest warrants and orders for arrest.
Time for serving, §15A-301(d).
To whom directed, §15A-301(b).
Copy delivered to person arrested or served,
§15A-301(c).
Copy made and original transmitted to
appropriate county.
Wrong venue, §15A-301(e).
Copy of charges filed against defendant.
Furnishing defendant, §15A-301(e).

CRIMINAL PROCESS —Cont'd
Copy when original lost, §15A-301(e).
Corporations.
Serving criminal summons on, §15A-301(c).
Criminal summons.
Corporations, serving, §15A-301(c).
Time for serving, §15A-301(d).
To whom directed, delivery, service, §15A-301(b).
Execution or service, §15A-301(c).
Redelivery for further attempts at service,
§15A-301(d).
Time for serving, §15A-301(d).
Failure to return.
Process not invalidated, §15A-301(d).
Formal requirements, §15A-301(a).
Immunity of server for due service, §15A-301(f).
Lost original.
Copy when original lost, §15A-301(e).
Protection of process server, §15A-301(f).
Record of process issued maintained,
§15A-301(a).
Redelivery for further attempts at service,
§15A-301(d).
Return, §15A-301(d).
Service or execution, §15A-301(c).
Redelivery for further attempts at service,
§15A-301(d).
Time for serving, §15A-301(d).
Signed and dated, requirement, §15A-301(a).
Time for serving, §15A-301(d).
To whom directed, §15A-301(b).
Wrong venue.
Copy made and original transmitted to
appropriate county, §15A-301(e).

CRIMINAL RECORD CHECKS.
See CRIMINAL HISTORY RECORD CHECKS.

CRIMINAL STREET GANGS, §§14-50.15 to
14-50.30.
See GANGS.

CRISIS INTERVENTION PROGRAM,
§108A-25.4.

CROATAN INDIANS.
Indians of Robeson county.
Rights and privileges, §71A-1.

CROCODILIANS.
Regulation of reptiles generally, §§14-416 to
14-422.
See REPTILES.

CROPS.
Burning crops in the field.
Criminal trespass, §14-141.
Commodities.
General provisions, §§78D-1 to 78D-33.
See COMMODITIES.
Corn.
See CORN.
Damage to agricultural commodities or
production systems.
Definitions, §1-539.2B(c).
Double damage liability, §1-539.2B(a).
Valuation, §1-539.2B(b).
Decedents' estates.
Ungathered crops at death of decedent,
§28A-15-1(d).
Destroying crops in the field.
Criminal trespass, §14-141.
Execution not to be levied on growing crops
until matured, §1-315(c).

CROPS —Cont'd
Exemption from creditors' claims, §1C-1601(a).
Gleaned crops.
Income tax.
Individual income tax.
Credits, §105-151.14.
Grain adulteration, §§106-621 to 106-628.
See GRAIN ADULTERATION.
Grain dealers, §§106-601 to 106-615.
See GRAIN DEALERS.
Income tax credit for gleaned crops.
Corporation donating harvested crop to nonprofit
organization, §105-130.37.
Landlord and tenant.
In lieu of emblements, farm lessee holds out year,
with rents apportioned, §42-7.
Lien on crops, §§42-15 to 42-25.
Neglecting crops by tenant, §14-359.
Larceny.
Ungathered crops, §14-78.
Liens on crops, §§42-15 to 42-25.
Action to settle disputes between parties, §42-17.
Tenant's undertaking upon continuance or
appeal, §42-18.
Advances, §42-15.
Appeals.
Tenant's undertaking on continuance or appeal,
§42-18.
Assigns, §42-15.
Claim for delivery of personal property, §42-16.
Compliance with prices provided by agricultural
liens, §42-15.
Delivery of crops to landlord on his undertaking,
§42-19.
Enforcement, §§42-15, 42-15.1.
Executions.
Tenant's crop not subject to execution against
landlord, §42-21.
Failure to make fair decision, §42-16.
Insurance.
Landlord's lien on crop insurance for rents,
advances, etc., §42-15.1.
Priority, §42-15.
Removal of crops, §42-15.
Unlawful removal by tenant, §42-22.
Rents, §42-15.
Rights of tenant, §42-16.
Sale of crops if neither party gives undertaking,
§42-20.
Seizures.
Unlawful seizure by landlord or removal by
tenant misdemeanor, §42-22.
Terms of agricultural tenancies in certain
counties, §42-23.
Tobacco.
Failure of tenant to account for sales under
tobacco marketing cards, §42-22.1.
Wages.
Persons entitled to part of crop as wages.
Tenant's crop not subject to execution against
landlord, §42-21.
**Promotion of use and sale of agricultural
products.**
Generally, §§106-550 to 106-568.
See AGRICULTURAL PRODUCTS
PROMOTION.
Sale of goods, UCC, §25-2-107(2).
Definition of goods, §25-2-105(1).
Identification of goods, §25-2-501(1).
Secured transactions.
Priority of security interests in, §25-9-334(i).

CROPS —Cont'd
Secured transactions —Cont'd
Production-money crops.
Defined, §25-9-102(a).
Status of security interest in, §25-9-103.1(a).
Production-money obligation.
Application of payments, §25-9-103.1(b).
Defined, §25-9-102(a).
Production-money security interests.
Priority, §25-9-324.1.
Status, §25-9-103.1(a).
Burden of establishing, §25-9-103.1(d).
Continuation of status, §25-9-103.1(c).
Production of crops.
Defined, §25-9-102(a).
Surety on crops.
Appeals, §§42-18 to 42-20.
Trespass.
Burning or otherwise destroying crops in the field.
Criminal trespass, §14-141.
Criminal trespass.
Injury to crops of another, §14-128.
Warehouse receipts.
Storage under government bond, §25-7-201(b).

CROP SEED IMPROVEMENT BOARD,
§§106-269 to 106-276.
See SEEDS.

CROSSBOWS.
Sale, §§14-402 to 14-408.
Collection.
Issuance of permit to nonresident, §14-404(a).
Dealer records, requirements, §14-406(a).
Misdemeanor for violating, §14-408.
License or permit required, §14-402(a).
Collection, issuance to nonresident, §14-404(a).
Expiration date, §14-403.
Fee for sheriffs services, §14-404(e).
Form, §14-403.
Inapplicability, §§14-402(b), 14-404(d).
Informing applicant as to action on issuance,
§14-404(f).
Issuance by sheriff, §14-403.
Mental health denial, eligibility upon
restoration of rights, §14-404(g).
Records kept by sheriffs, §14-405.
Refusal to issue, grounds, appeal, §14-404(b).
Mail or other parcel delivery.
Display of permit or license, §14-402(a).

CROSS-CLAIMS.
Generally.
See COUNTERCLAIMS AND CROSS-CLAIMS.

CROSSES.
Burning or flaming crosses.
Placing on property of another or public street or
highway, §14-12.12.
Placing with intent of intimidating, §§14-12.13,
14-12.14.

CROSS-EXAMINATION, US Const Amd 5.
Criminal defendants competency, §8-54.
Depositions.
Oral examinations, §1A-1 Rule 30(c).
Leading questions, §8C-1 Rule 611(c).
Scope, §8C-1 Rule 611(b).

CROSS-INDEX OF JUDGMENTS, §1-233.

CROSS-INDEX OF LIS PENDENS, §1-117.
Effect on subsequent purchasers, §1-118.

**CROSSING OF UTILITY LINES AND RIGHTS
OF WAY BY OTHER UTILITIES,** §62-39.

CROSSINGS.
Controlled-access facilities.
　Elimination of crossings, §§136-20, 136-89.53.
Public utilities.
　Crossing of lines and rights of way, §62-39.
Railroad grade crossings, §§20-142.1 to 20-142.5.
　See RAILROAD GRADE CROSSINGS.

CROSSWALKS.
Pedestrians.
　Right of way, §§20-155(c), 20-173(a), (b).
　　Blind persons, §20-175.2.
　When required to cross at crosswalk, §20-174(c).
Stopping when traffic obstructed, §20-142.5.

CROWDERS MOUNTAIN STATE PARK.
Removal of land from state nature and historic
　preserve, §143-260.10G(a).
　Exchange of property by state, permitted
　　purposes, §143-260.10G(c).
　Property deleted from state parks system,
　　§143-260.10G(b).

CRUELTY TO ANIMALS.
Abandonment, §14-361.1.
Baby chicks.
　Living baby chicks or other fowl under eight
　　weeks of age.
　　Disposing of as pets or novelties forbidden,
　　　§14-363.1.
Baiting, §14-362.1.
　Dog baiting, §14-362.2.
Care for animal pending hearing, §19A-3.
Care of animals subjected to illegal treatment.
　Defendant ordered to provide necessary care,
　　§19A-70(f).
　Deposit by defendant for reasonable expenses.
　　Acquittal.
　　　Refund of deposit, §19A-70(e).
　　Disposing of animal prior to 30 day period,
　　　§19A-70(e).
　　Forfeiture of animal.
　　　Failure to deposit funds, §19A-70(d).
　　Funds necessary for 30 days care.
　　　Court to set amount for, §19A-70(c).
　　　Posting of amount ordered, §19A-70(d).
　　Hearing on petition to determine need for care,
　　　notice, §19A-70(b).
　　Order for funds to be deposited, §19A-70(c).
　　Petition by animal shelter taking custody of
　　　animal, §19A-70(a).
　　Posting of amount ordered, §19A-70(d).
　　Refund of deposit, §19A-70(e).
Civil remedies for the protection of animals,
　§§19A-1 to 19A-4.
　Appeals.
　　Custody and care pending, §19A-4(d).
　Care for animals pending hearing on merits.
　　Employment of veterinarian to provide medical
　　　care, §19A-3(b).
　　Foster care provider.
　　　Placement of animal with, §19A-3(c).
　　Preliminary injunction giving plaintiff right to
　　　provide.
　　　Request by plaintiff, §19A-3(a).
　Costs of food, water, shelter and care.
　　Included as part of costs allowed, §19A-4(b).
　Custody and care pending appeals, §19A-4(d).
　Definitions, §19A-1.
　Exemptions from article, §19A-1.1.
　Foster care provider.
　　Placement of animal with pending hearing,
　　　§19A-3(c).

CRUELTY TO ANIMALS —Cont'd
Civil remedies for the protection of animals
　—Cont'd
　Injunction.
　　New animals.
　　　Enjoining defendant from acquiring,
　　　　§19A-4(b).
　　Permanent injunction.
　　　Authority of court to enter, §19A-4(a).
　　Preliminary injunction, §19A-3(a).
　Medical care.
　　Employment of veterinarian to provide,
　　　§19A-3(b).
　Merits determined without jury, §19A-4(a).
　New animals.
　　Enjoining defendant from acquiring, §19A-4(b).
　Orders of court deemed appropriate.
　　Authority of court to enter, §19A-4(a).
　Preliminary injunction, §19A-3(a).
　Purpose of article, §19A-2.
　Real party in interest as defendant, §19A-2.
　Real party in interest as plaintiff, §19A-2.
　Removal from owner or other person possessing.
　　Plaintiff taking possession as custodian.
　　　Preliminary injunction allowing for,
　　　　§19A-3(a).
　Return of animal to defendant, §19A-4(c).
　Termination of defendant's ownership, §19A-4(b).
　Transfer of ownership to plaintiff or successor
　　owner, §19A-4(b).
　Veterinarian.
　　Employment to provide medical care, §19A-3(b).
Cockfighting, §14-362.
Confiscation of cruelly treated animals,
　§14-363.2.
Construction and interpretation, §14-360.
Conveying animals in cruel manner, §14-363.
Counties.
　Regulation by local ordinance, §153A-127.
Custody of confiscated animals, §14-363.2.
Definitions, §§14-360(c), 19A-1.
Dogs.
　Dog fighting, §14-362.2.
　Restraining dogs in cruel manner, §14-362.3.
Exclusions, §14-360(c).
Fights, §14-362.1.
　Dog fighting, §14-362.2.
Foster care provider.
　Placement of animal by plaintiff with, §19A-3(c).
Fowl.
　Living baby chicks or other fowl under eight
　　weeks of age.
　　Disposing of as pets or novelties forbidden,
　　　§14-363.1.
Injunction.
　New animals.
　　Enjoining defendant from acquiring, §19A-4(b).
　Permanent injunction.
　　Authority of court to enter order, §19A-4(a).
　Preliminary injunction, §19A-3(a).
Instigating cruelty, §14-361.
Intentional cruelty, §14-360(a).
Intentional deprivation of necessary
　substances, §14-360(a1).
Investigators, §§19A-45 to 19A-49.
Malicious cruelty, §14-360(b).
Municipalities.
　Abuse of animals.
　　City may define and prohibit abuse of animals,
　　　§160A-182.

CRUELTY TO ANIMALS —Cont'd
Permanent injunction.
Authority of court to enter order, §19A-4(a).
Preliminary injunction, §19A-3(a).
Promoting cruelty, §14-361.
Rabbits.
Eight weeks of age or under.
Disposing of as pets or novelties forbidden, §14-363.1.
Societies for the prevention of cruelty to animals.
Property used for charitable purposes, §105-278.6.
Veterinarians.
Employment by plaintiffs to provide care, §19A-3(b).
Immunity for reporting, §14-360.1.

CRUELTY TO SPOUSE.
Divorce from bed and board, §50-7.

CRUISE VESSELS.
Alcoholic beverages for use on oceangoing ships, §18B-106.

CRUSTACEA.
Adulterated or misbranded crustacea.
Embargoes, §113-221.4.
Sanitation of shellfish and crustacea, §113-221.2.
Shellfish.
General provisions.
See SHELLFISH.

CRUTCHES.
Sales and use tax exemptions, §105-164.13.

CRYPTS.
Hearsay exception, engravings on, §8C-1 Rule 803.

CUCUMBERS.
Weights and measures, §81A-42.

CULTURAL ACTIVITIES.
Agritourism activity liability, §§99E-30 to 99E-32.

CULTURAL RESOURCES DEPARTMENT.
Admission fees.
Museums owned by department, §121-7.3.
African-American heritage commission.
Creation, §143B-135(a).
Appropriations.
Promotion of arts, §143-407.
Archival and historical agency of state, §121-3.
Artifacts owned by state and in custody of office of archives and history.
Selling, trading or placing on permanent loan, §121-7(a).
Budget requests, procedure for preparing, §121-12.2.
Defined, §121-2.
Grants-in-aid.
Expending appropriation, §121-12.2.
Responsibility for administering appropriations, §121-12.1.
Museum of history, maintenance and administration by department, §121-7(a).
Transfer of commission to department, §143B-51.
Tryon's Palace, §§121-14 to 121-21.1.
Bentonville Battlefield fund, §121-7.5.
Commissions and divisions.
Organization of department, §143B-53.
Creation, §143B-49.

CULTURAL RESOURCES DEPARTMENT —Cont'd
Definitions.
Arts, §143-403.
Employees.
Salaries, promotions and leave.
Exemptions from state personnel classification rules, §143B-53.2(c).
Executive Mansion.
Authority of department of administration not affected, §143-415.
Powers of department, §143-411.
Purpose of provisions, §143-410.
Functions of department, §143B-51(a).
Transfer, §143B-51(b).
Funds.
Promotion of arts, §143-407.
General assembly.
Retention of books, records, etc., by department, §120-37(f).
Gifts.
Promotion of arts.
Acceptance of gifts by department, §143-407.
Graveyard of the Atlantic Museum.
Administration by department, §121-7.4.
Head of department, §143B-52.
Historical markers.
Cooperation of department of transportation, §136-42.2.
Lake Mattamuskeet Lodge Preservation.
Plans for repair and renovation subject to commission review, §121-9.1(b).
Repair and renovation by department, §121-9.1(a).
Libraries.
State library agency, §§125-1 to 125-11.
See LIBRARIES.
Museums owned by department.
Admission fees, §121-7.3.
North Carolina register of historic places.
Power to establish, expand and maintain, §121-4.1(a).
North Carolina transportation museum special fund.
Audit, §121-7.6(d).
Created in department, §121-7.6(a).
Emergency reserve fund, §121-7.6(c).
Money credited to fund, §121-7.6(b).
Organization of department, §143B-53.
Personnel.
Salaries, promotions and leave.
Exemption from state personnel classification rules, §143B-53.2(c).
Powers and duties, §§121-4, 143B-49, 143B-50.
Executive Mansion, §143-411.
Transfer, §143B-51(b).
Promotion of arts.
Appropriations, §143-407.
Definitions, §143-403.
Duties of department, §143-406.
Funds, §143-407.
Gifts.
Acceptance, §143-407.
Reports.
Submission of biennial report to governor, §143-406.
Public records.
Administration of records management program by department, §132-8.1.
Assistance by and to department, §132-8.
Disposition of records at end of official's term, §132-4.

CULTURAL RESOURCES DEPARTMENT
 —Cont'd
Register of historic places.
  Power to establish, expand and maintain,
    §121-4.1(a).
Reports.
  Biennial report to governor.
    Submission, §143-406.
Roanoke Island commission, §§143B-131.1 to
    143B-131.10.
Secretary.
  Head of department, §143B-52.
  License plate.
    Special plate, number, §20-79.5.
State historic sites special fund.
  Applicability, §121-7.7(b).
  Created in division of historic sites, §121-7.7(a).
  Money in fund, §121-7.7(a).
  Reports, §121-7.7(c).
Transportation department.
  Historical markers on highway.
    Cooperation with department of cultural
      resources, §136-42.2.
Veterans' memorial commission.
  See VETERANS' MEMORIAL COMMISSION.

CUMBERLAND COUNTY.
Agricultural tenancies in certain counties.
  Terms of, §42-23.
Ambulance service.
  Attachment or garnishment and lien for,
    §§44-51.4 to 44-51.8.
  Obtained without intending to pay, §14-111.2.
Board of county commissioners.
  Filling vacancies on board, §153A-27.1.
Condemnation or acquisition of land by local
    government unit outside county.
  Consent of board of commissioners necessary,
    §153A-15.
Counties generally.
  See COUNTIES.
Cropper or tenant refusing to perform terms
    of contract.
  Forfeiture of right of possession to premises,
    §42-27.
Dangerous firearm use by young children,
    permitting.
  Air rifles, air pistols and BB guns not dangerous
    firearm, §14-316(b).
Dog collars.
  Unlawful removal of electronic dog collars,
    §14-401.17.
Game laws, local acts not repealed,
    §113-133.1(e).
Probates and registration orders before clerks
    of inferior courts validated, §47-59.
Room occupancy tax levied by county, uniform
    provisions, §153A-155.
School property.
  Acquisition and improvement, §153A-158.1.
Southeastern North Carolina regional
    economic development commission,
    §§158-8.3 to 158-8.8.
Wild plants, taking of certain plants from land
    of another.
  Inapplicability of provisions, §14-129.

CURATIVE ACTS AND STATUTES.
Acknowledgments.
  Banks.
    Stockholders, officers or directors, §47-93.

CURATIVE ACTS AND STATUTES —Cont'd
Acknowledgments —Cont'd
  Building and loan associations.
    Officer or stockholder, §47-94.
  Deeds.
    Proof of execution, §47-100.
  Failure of register of deeds to certify correctness
      of acknowledgment.
    Registrations validated, §47-50.1.
  Handwriting.
    Probates on proof of handwriting of maker
        refusing to acknowledge, §47-57.
  Married women.
    Taken by officer who has grantor, §47-105.
  Notary public.
    Holding another office, §§47-104, 47-108.2.
    Interested as trustee or holding other office,
      §47-95.
  Officer in wrong capacity, §47-55.
  Resident taking out-of-state, §47-78.
  Savings and loan associations, §47-94.
  Seals.
    Omission of seal of acknowledging officer,
      §47-101.
  Taking out-of-state by resident, §47-78.
Banks.
  Acknowledgments taken by stockholders, officers,
      or directors, §47-93.
  Nonresident banks.
    Validation of certain deeds, §47-108.16.
  Probate before stockholders and directors of
      banks, §47-92.
Building and loan associations.
  Acknowledgment and registration by officer or
      stockholder, §47-94.
Certificate alleging examination of grantor
    instead of witness, §47-74.
Clerks of court.
  Before clerks before year 1889, §47-58.
  Before justices of the peace where clerk's
      certificate or order of registration defective,
      §47-56.
  Deeds where clerk appointed himself to sell,
      §47-65.
  Defective certification or adjudication of clerk,
      etc., admitting to registration, §47-49.
  Deputy clerks of superior court, §47-108.6.
  Inferior courts, §47-59.
  Interested clerks.
    Instruments in which clerk of court was party,
      §47-106.
    Order of registration by interested clerk, §47-61.
  Order of registration by judge where clerk party,
      §47-60.
  Other states, §47-77.
  Prior certificates.
    Certificate failing to pass on all prior
        certificates, §47-48.
  Seals.
    Certificates of clerks without seal, §47-99.
    Probate omitting seals, etc., §47-53.
Commissioners.
  Validation of instruments acknowledged before
      United States commissioners, §47-108.12.
Commissioners of deeds.
  Before commissioners, §47-81.
Commissioners of oaths, §47-81.1.
Consuls.
  Probate of deeds before consular agents of the
      United States, §47-91.
  Consuls general, §47-83.

CURATIVE ACTS AND STATUTES —Cont'd
Consuls —Cont'd
Probate of deeds before consular agents of the
    United States —Cont'd
Vice-consuls and vice-consuls general, §47-84.
Corporations.
By president and attested by treasurer under
    corporate seal, §47-70.
By president and attested by witness before
    January 1, 1900, §47-71.
Deeds.
Error in acknowledgment or probate, §47-97.1.
Foreign corporations.
Validation of certain conveyances of foreign
    dissolved corporations, §47-108.6.
Mistake as to officer's name.
Validation of corporate deed, §47-97.
Name.
Corporate name not affixed, but signed
    otherwise prior to January, 1973, §47-72.
Oath of subscribing witness, §47-73.
Probates before officer of interested corporation,
    §47-63.
Proof of corporate articles before officer authorized
    to probate, §47-75.
Registration.
Validation of registration of certain corporate
    deeds, etc., §47-108.1.
Seal.
Corporate seal omitted prior to January 1, 1991,
    §47-71.1.
Validation of registration of certain corporate
    deeds, etc., §47-108.1.
Deeds.
Clerk's deeds where clerk appointed himself to
    sell, §47-65.
Corporate deeds.
Validation of certain deeds where admitted to
    record, §47-108.1.
Guardians.
Deeds by guardians omitting seal, prior to
    January 1, 1944, validated, §35A-1360.
Nonresident banks.
Validation of certain deeds, §47-108.16.
Official capacity not designated, §47-108.17.
Examinations.
Notaries holding other office, §47-108.2.
Foreign probates.
Commission of seal, §47-82.
Governor.
Sister state probates without governor's
    authentication, §47-80.
Guardians.
Deeds.
Guardians omitting seal, prior to January 1,
    1944, validated, §35A-1360.
Validation of certain private sales, §35A-1361.
Handwriting.
Proof of handwriting of maker refusing to
    acknowledge, §47-57.
Husband and wife.
Before different officers, §47-68.
Different officers of deeds by husband and wife,
    §47-87.
Probates in wrong order, §47-67.
Instruments that were not acknowledged.
Validation of certain recorded instruments,
    §47-108.20.
Judges.
Before judges of supreme or superior courts or
    clerks before 1889, §47-58.

CURATIVE ACTS AND STATUTES —Cont'd
Jurisdiction.
Officer acting in wrong capacity or out of
    jurisdiction, §47-55.
Magistrates.
Clerk's certificate or order of registration
    defective, §47-56.
Maps and plats.
Register of deeds.
Acts in recording validated, §47-108.8.
Validation of certain maps and plats that cannot
    be copies, §47-108.19.
Validation of registration of plats upon probate in
    accordance with section 47-30, §47-108.10.
Married women.
Acknowledgment and private examination by
    officer who was grantor, §47-105.
Acknowledgments of instruments of married
    women made since February 7, 1945,
    §47-108.4.
Certificate of wife's "previous" examination,
    §47-66.
Wife free trader.
No examination or husband's assent, §47-69.
Masters in chancery.
Probate before masters in chancery, §§47-85,
    47-85.1.
Military officers.
Instruments proved before officers of certain
    ranks, §47-81.2.
Name of grantor omitted from record, §47-107.
Notaries public.
Acknowledgments and examinations before
    notaries holding other office, §47-108.2.
Acknowledgments before notaries under age,
    §47-108.
Acknowledgments taken by notaries holding other
    office.
Validation, §47-90.
Acts prior to November 26, 1921, §47-108.3.
Interested parties.
Probates before interested notaries, §47-95.
Notary holding another office.
Acknowledgments, §47-104.
Other states, §47-77.
Probates before interested notaries, §47-62.
Seals.
Absence of notarial seal, §47-102.
Trustees.
Taking acknowledgments when interested as
    trustee, §47-95.
Validation of certain instruments containing
    notarial jurat, §47-108.18.
Oaths.
Before commissioner of oaths, §47-81.1.
**Officer acting in wrong capacity or out of
jurisdiction,** §47-55.
**Officers, stockholders or directors prior to
January 1, 1945,** §47-64.
Officials of wrong state, §47-76.
Order of registration.
Omitted, §47-50.
Registration without formal order validated,
    §§47-88, 47-89, 47-108.15.
Other states.
Certain deeds executed in other states where seal
    omitted, §47-108.5.
Defective probates beyond state, §47-98.
Notaries and clerks in other states, §47-77.
Officials of other states, §47-108.15.
Seal omitted, §§47-86, 47-108.5.

CURATIVE ACTS AND STATUTES —Cont'd

Other states —Cont'd

Sister state probates without governor's
authentication, §47-80.

Public lands.

Conveyances of state-owned lands, §146-78.

Grants signed by deputy secretary of state.
Validation, §146-54.

Validation of irregular entries, §146-53.

Register of deeds.

Acts of register in recording plats and maps,
§47-108.8.

Clerks or deputies.

Registration by register's deputies, assistants or
clerks, §§47-54, 47-54.1.

Prior certificates.

Certificate failing to pass on all prior
certificates, §47-48.

Registration.

Defective probates beyond state, §47-98.

Instruments registered prior to January 1, 1934.
Validation, §47-108.13.

Validation of instruments registered without
probate, §47-96.

Sales.

Guardians.

Certain private sales validated, §35A-1361.

Savings and loan associations, §47-94.

Seals.

Clerks of court.

Certificates of clerks without seal, §47-99.

Foreign probate omitting seals, §47-82.

Notarial seal.

Absence, §47-102.

Omitted, §§47-51, 47-53.1, 47-101, 47-108.5.

Validation where seal omitted, §47-108.11.

Subscribing witnesses, §47-108.9.

Superior courts.

Before judges of superior court, §47-58.

Supreme court.

Before judges of supreme court, §47-58.

United States.

Conveyance acting by and through general
services administration, §47-108.14.

**Validation of certain recorded instruments
that were not acknowledged,** §47-108.20.

Veterans' guardianship act.

Validation of prior acts, §34-2.1.

CURATORS.

Powers of fiduciaries generally, §§32-25 to
32-27.

See FIDUCIARIES.

Uniform fiduciaries act, §§32-1 to 32-13.

See FIDUCIARIES.

CURBS.

Disabled persons.

Curb ramps or curb cuts, §136-44.14.

Special assessments by counties, §§153A-185 to
153A-210.7.

See SPECIAL ASSESSMENTS BY COUNTIES.

CURFEW.

Frisk of curfew violators, §14-288.10.

Persons under 18 years.

Cities imposing, §160A-198.

Counties imposing, §153A-142.

Delinquent juveniles, §7B-2506.

Teen court program.

Rehabilitative measures or sanctions,
§143B-809(a).

CURFEW —Cont'd

Universities and colleges, §§116-212, 116-213.

CURRENCY.

Commodities.

General provisions, §§78D-1 to 78D-33.

See COMMODITIES.

Counterfeiting, §§14-13 to 14-16.

See COUNTERFEITING.

European monetary union.

Continuity of contracts, §§53-295 to 53-300.

See EUROPEAN MONETARY UNION.

Foreign-money claims, §§1C-1820 to 1C-1834.

See FOREIGN-MONEY CLAIMS.

Money.

See MONEY.

Money transmitters, §§53-208.1 to 53-208.30.

See MONEY TRANSMITTERS.

CURRENT ACCOUNT ACTIONS.

**Accrual of cause of action to recover balance
due,** §1-31.

CURRITUCK COUNTY.

All-terrain vehicles.

Use by employees on certain highways,
§20-171.24.

Bridges.

Mid-Currituck toll bridge project, §136-89.183A.

**Condemnation or acquisition of land by local
government unit outside county.**

Consent of board of commissioners necessary,
§153A-15.

**Cropper or tenant refusing to perform terms
of contract.**

Forfeiture of right of possession to premises,
§42-27.

Game commission.

Regulatory authority not appealed or abridged,
§113-133.1(b).

Game laws, local acts not repealed,
§113-133.1(e).

Grants in navigable waters, registration,
§113-205(a).

Housing.

Tenant as commissioner, exemption from provision
of law allowing, §157-5.

North Carolina's northeast commission,
§§158-8.2 to 158-8.8.

Officers compensated from fees.

Statement to be rendered, §128-13.

Open fires, high hazard counties.

Applicability of provisions, §106-942(a).

Ground clearing activities, special permit,
§106-942(c).

Woodland fires, permit required, §106-942(b).

Registration of deeds.

Tax certification, no delinquent taxes due,
§161-31(b).

**Room occupancy tax levied by county, uniform
provision,** §153A-155.

School property.

Acquisition and improvement, §153A-158.1.

Special school tax, election to abolish.

Petition required, §115C-505.

**Swimming, surfing and littering in Atlantic
Ocean.**

City ordinances effective, §160A-176.1.

Tax sales, notices by publication validated.

Inapplicability of provisions, §47-108.24.

Wastewater systems.

Innovative septic tank systems.

Ordinance billing fee as property tax,
§130A-343.1(c).

CURRITUCK COUNTY —Cont'd
Wild plants, taking of certain plants from land of another.
Inapplicability of provisions, §14-129.

CURRITUCK SOUND.
Mid-Currituck bridge project.
Environmental protection provisions, §136-89.183A(d).
Obstructing waters, §76-41.

CURSING.
See PROFANITY.

CURTESY.
Abolished, §§29-4, 41-4.
Renunciation by married person under age of 21, §39-13.2(c).

CURVES.
Provisions marking of "pull off" areas, §136-18.4.

CUSTODIAL INTERFERENCE.
Abduction of child, §14-41(a).
Bail, §15A-534.4.
Transporting child outside state.
Intent to violate custody order, §14-320.1.

CUSTODIAL INTERROGATION OF JUVENILES.
Delinquent or undisciplined juveniles, §7B-2101.

CUSTODIAL TRUSTS, §§33B-1 to 33B-22.
Acceptance of custodial trust property.
Custodial trustee, §33B-4.
Accounting by trustee, §33B-15.
Applicability of provisions, §33B-19(a).
Uniformity of application, §33B-20.
Beneficiaries.
Defined, §33B-1.
Directions of beneficiary.
Duty of trustee to follow, §33B-7(b).
Incapacitated beneficiaries.
Administration of trust for incapacitated beneficiary.
Determination of incapacity by trustee, §33B-10(c).
Requirements for, §33B-10(a).
Determination by trustee, §33B-10(b).
Administration of trust for incapacitated beneficiary, §33B-10(c).
Trustee not liable for good faith determination, §33B-10(f).
Effect of determination, §33B-10(e).
Payment or expenditure for use and benefit of beneficiary, §33B-9(b).
Petition for determination, §33B-10(d).
Liability to third persons, §33B-12(c), (d).
Payment or expenditure for use and benefit of beneficiary, §33B-9(a).
Incapacitated beneficiaries, §33B-9(b).
Separate custodial trust, §33B-6(b).
Single beneficiary, §33B-6(a).
Checking, savings or other accounts.
Establishment, withdrawal of funds, §33B-9(c).
Citation of act.
Short title, §33B-21.
Conflict of laws, §33B-19(b).
Construction and interpretation.
Other means of creating trusts not displaced or restricted, §33B-2(h).
Uniformity of construction, §33B-20.

CUSTODIAL TRUSTS —Cont'd
Contracts enter into by trustee during administration.
Asserting claim against trustee, §33B-12(a).
Personal liability of beneficiary, §33B-12(c).
Personal liability of trustee, §33B-12(b).
Protection as insured by liability insurance, §33B-12(d).
Creation of custodial trust, §33B-2(a), (b).
Custodial trust to begin in the future, §33B-3(a).
Customary methods of transferring or evidencing ownership of property, §33B-18(b).
Forms, §33B-18(a).
Custodial trustee.
Acceptance of custodial trust property.
Form of acceptance and receipt, §33B-4(b).
Obligations arise upon, §33B-4(a).
Statement provided by trustee, §33B-15(a).
Subject to person jurisdiction of state upon, §33B-4(c).
Accounting by trustee.
Instructions issued or review of actions.
Authority of court, §33B-15(f).
Legal representative, account by, §33B-15(d).
Petition, §33B-15(b), (c).
Removal, §33B-15(e).
Statements provided as to administration, §33B-15(a).
Actions against.
Limitation of actions, §33B-16(a).
Fraud, misrepresentation or concealment, §33B-16(b).
When claims for relief not barred, §33B-16(c).
Bond, §33B-14.
Checking, savings or other accounts.
Establishment, withdrawal of funds, §33B-9(c).
Collect, manage, invest and reinvest trust property.
Duty, §33B-7(c).
Control of trust property.
Duty to take, §33B-7(c).
Custodial trust property.
Powers as to, §33B-8(a).
Custodial trust to begin in the future, §33B-3(b).
Dealing with trust property.
Prudent person standard of care, §33B-7(b).
Declining to serve.
Notice, substitute, designation, §33B-13(a).
Defined, §33B-1.
Directions of beneficiary.
Duty to follow, §33B-7(b).
Duties, §33B-7.
Liability for violation, §33B-8(b).
Expenses, §33B-14.
Incapacity of beneficiary.
Determination, §33B-10.
Ineligibility, death or incapacity.
Successor, §33B-13(c).
Liability for violation of duties, §33B-8(b).
Liability to third person, §33B-12(b), (d).
Obligations.
Arise on acceptance of trust property, §33B-4(a).
General duties, §33B-7.
Payment or expenditure for use and benefit of beneficiary, §33B-9(a).
Incapacitated beneficiary, §33B-9(b).
Personal jurisdiction of state.
Subject to, §33B-4(c).
Powers, §33B-8.
Prudent person standard of care.
Dealing with trust property, §33B-7(b).

CUSTODIAL TRUSTS —Cont'd
Custodial trustee —Cont'd
Recordation or registration of instrument vesting title.
　Duty of trustee if appropriate, §33B-7(a).
Records of transactions.
　Duty to keep, §33B-7(e).
Removal.
　Accounting by trustee, §33B-15(e).
　Petition for, §33B-13(f).
Resignation.
　Notice, successor, designation, §33B-13(b).
Separate from other property.
　Duty to keep, §33B-7(d).
Special skill or expertise.
　Standard of care, §33B-7(b).
Standard of care.
　Dealing with trust property, §33B-7(b).
Statements provided by trustee, §33B-15(a).
Substitute trustee.
　Designating.
　　Person originally designated declines to serve, §33B-13(a).
Successor custodial trustee.
　Designation, §33B-2(g).
Successor trustee.
　Accounting by predecessor.
　　Petition, §33B-15(c).
　Designating, §33B-13(b) to (d).
　Property and records, possession and control, §33B-13(e).
Transfers to by fiduciary or obligor, §33B-5(a), (b).
　Exceptions, §33B-5(c).
Custodial trust property.
Acceptance by trustee, §33B-4.
Augmentation of existing custodial trust property, §33B-2(f).
Custodial trustee.
　Powers as to property, §33B-8(a).
Defined, §33B-1.
Limitation on value, §33B-22.
Recordation.
　Adequate identification of property for record, §33B-7(d).
Registration.
　Adequate identification of property for record, §33B-7(d).
Title, §33B-2(c).
Custodial trust to begin in the future, §33B-3.
Definitions, §33B-1.
Durable power of attorney for incapacitated person.
Effective to terminate or direct administration or distribution of property.
　Specific provision required, §33B-7(f).
Forms.
Custodial trustee's receipt and acceptance, §33B-4(b).
Declaration of trust under act, §33B-18(a).
Transfer under act, §33B-18(a).
Fraud.
Limitation of actions against custodial trustee, §33B-16(b).
Incapacity of beneficiary.
Determination, §33B-10.
Limitation of actions against custodial trustee, §33B-16.
Notice.
Trustee declining to serve or resigning, §33B-13(a), (b).

CUSTODIAL TRUSTS —Cont'd
Obligations arising from ownership or control of property.
Asserting claim against trustee, §33B-12(a).
Personal liability of beneficiary, §33B-12(c).
Personal liability of trustee, §33B-12(b).
Protection as insured by liability insurance, §33B-12(d).
Payment or expenditure for use and benefit of beneficiary, §33B-9(a), (b).
Petitions.
Accounting by trustee, §33B-15(b), (c).
Incapacity of beneficiary, determination, §33B-10(d).
Removal of trustee, §33B-13(f).
Successor trustee, designation, §33B-13(d).
Prudent person rule.
Trustee dealing with property.
　Standard of care, §33B-7(b).
Recordation.
Adequate identification of property for record, §33B-7(d).
Duty of trustee to record instrument if appropriate, §33B-7(a).
Records.
Transaction records, duty to keep, §33B-7(d), (e).
Registration.
Adequate identification of trust property for registration, §33B-7(d).
Termination of custodial trust, §33B-2(d), (e).
Distribution on, §33B-17(a), (d).
Death of beneficiary.
　Effect, §33B-17(c).
Incapacitated distributee, §33B-17(b).
Third parties.
Liability to third person, §33B-12.
Third-party transactions, §33B-11.
Title of act.
Short title, §33B-21.
Title to custodial trust property, §33B-2(c).
Tort committed in course of administering trust.
Asserting claim against trustee, §33B-12(a).
Value of custodial trust property.
Limitation on, §33B-22.

CUSTODIANS.
Custodial trusts and trustees, §§33B-1 to 33B-22.
See CUSTODIAL TRUSTS.
Powers of fiduciaries generally, §§32-25 to 32-27.
See FIDUCIARIES.
Transfers to minors, §§33A-1 to 33A-24.
See TRANSFERS TO MINORS.
Uniform fiduciaries act, §§32-1 to 32-13.
See FIDUCIARIES.

CUSTODY.
Child custody generally.
See CHILD CUSTODY.

CUSTODY AND VISITATION MEDIATION PROGRAM, §§7A-494, 7A-495.

CUSTOM-BUILT VEHICLES.
Title, registration, §20-53.1.

CUSTOMHOUSES.
Acquisition of land by US to be added to military bases, §104-7.

CUSTOMS OF THE ALCOHOLIC BEVERAGE TRADE, §18B-1116(b).

CUSTOMS SERVICE OFFICERS' AUTHORITY, §15A-406.

CUTOUT MUFFLERS, §20-128(b).
Motorboats, use of, §75A-9(a).

CUTTING TREES FOR TIMBER.
Damages for unlawful cutting, removal or burning, §1-539.1(a).
Injunctions.
  Insolvency of defendant need not be alleged, §1-486.
  Trial of title to, §1-487.
  When timber may be cut, §1-488.
Timber of another, §14-135.

CYBER-BULLYING.
Computer or computer network used with intent to intimidate or torment minor.
  Unlawful acts, §14-458.1(a).
Deferral of proceeding, placement on probation, §14-458.1(c).
Fake profile or web site.
  Building, unlawful, §14-458.1(a).
Follow minor online or into Internet chat room.
  Unlawful, §14-458.1(a).
Planting statement.
  Unlawful, §14-458.1(a).
Pornographic Internet site.
  Signing up minor, unlawful, §14-458.1(a).
Pose as a minor.
  Unlawful, §14-458.1(a).
Private, personal or sexual information regarding minor.
  Posting on Internet, unlawful, §14-458.1(a).
Punishment, §14-458.1(b).
Real or doctored image of minor.
  Posting on Internet, unlawful, §14-458.1(a).

CYBERSTALKING, §14-196.3(b).
Class 2 misdemeanor, §14-196.3(d).
Constitutionally protected rights of speech, protest or assembly.
  Section not to impair, §14-196.3(e).
Definitions, §14-196.3(a).
DNA sample for DNA analysis.
  Obtaining upon arrest for certain offenses, §15A-266.3A.
Peaceable, nonviolent or nonthreatening activity.
  Inapplicability to, §14-196.3(e).
Venue.
  Offense committed by email or electronic communication, §14-196.3(c).

CY PRES.
Charitable trusts.
  Alternative plan provided for, §36C-4-413(d).
  Application of principle, §36C-4-413(a).
  Maintenance of proceeding, §36C-4-413(b).
  Release or modification of restriction in trust instrument, §36C-4-413(c1).

D

DAGGERS.
Carrying concealed weapons, §§14-269, 14-269.2.
Historic edged weapons defined, §14-409.12.
Weapons generally.
  See FIREARMS AND OTHER WEAPONS.

DAIRIES AND DAIRY PRODUCTS.
Cooperative associations.
  Authorized purposes, §§54-111, 54-124.

DAIRIES AND DAIRY PRODUCTS —Cont'd
Ice cream plants, creameries and cheese factories.
  Inspections generally, §§106-246 to 106-255.
    See ICE CREAM PLANTS, CREAMERIES AND CHEESE FACTORIES.
Marketing associations, §§54-129 to 54-166.
  See MARKETING ASSOCIATIONS.
Milk cases or crates.
  Unauthorized taking or sale, §14-72.4.
North Carolina dairy stabilization and growth program, §§106-812 to 106-815.
Pollution control.
  Water pollution on lands used for dairy purposes, §14-382.
Production, distribution, inspection, grading and testing generally, §§106-267 to 106-268.1.
  See MILK AND MILK PRODUCTS.
Southern dairy compact, §§106-810, 106-811.

DAIRY STABILIZATION AND GROWTH PROGRAM, §§106-812 to 106-815.

DALE EARNHARDT HIGHWAY, §136-18.5B.

DALLAS.
All-terrain vehicles.
  Use by employees on certain highways, §20-171.24.
Room occupancy tax.
  Uniform provisions.
    Authorized to levy, §160A-215(g).
    Generally, §160A-215.
Satellite annexation.
  Limitation on area of satellite corporate limits, inapplicability, §160A-58.1(b).

DAMAGES.
Ad damnum clause, §1A-1 Rule 8(a).
Adoption.
  Failure to disclose nonidentifying information.
    Civil action for monetary relief, §48-10-104.
  Unauthorized disclosure of information.
    Civil action for monetary relief, §48-10-105.
Aeronautics.
  Forced landing, §63-13.
Agricultural commodities or production systems, injury to.
  Definitions, §1-539.2B(c).
  Double damage liability, §1-539.2B(a).
  Valuation, §1-539.2B(b).
Alcoholic beverages.
  Beer franchises.
    Transfer of wholesaler's business.
      Disapproval or prevention of transfer, §18B-1307(c).
    Wrongful termination of agreement, §18B-1306(b).
  Sales to underage persons.
    Compensation for injury caused by, limitation, §18B-123.
Appeal bond to stay execution on money judgment, §1-289(a).
  Cap in amount, noncompensatory damages of $25,000,000 or more, §1-289(b), (c).
Appeals.
  Frivolous appeals, AppProc Rule 34(b).
Arbitration.
  Additional remedies, §1-569.21(c).
  Grounds for awarding, §1-569.21(b).
  Payment of arbitrator's expenses, §1-569.21.
  Punitive damages, §1-569.21(a), (e).

DAMAGES —Cont'd

Athlete agents.
Action by education institution against agent or student-athlete, §78C-100(b).

Attorneys at law.
Fraudulent practice.
Liability of attorney in double damages, §84-13.
Unauthorized practice of law.
Actions by private persons damaged by unauthorized practice, §84-10.1.

Automobile dealers.
Punitive damages, §20-308.1(b).

Bad checks.
Remedies for returned check, §6-21.3(a), (d).

Baggage lost, damaged or destroyed by innkeeper's negligence, §72-2.

Bank deposits and collections, §25-4-103.

Banks.
Directors' liability, §53-82.

Betterments.
Assessment of damages.
Annual value of land and waste charged against defendant, §1-341.
Execution suspended for, §1-340.
Value of improvements estimated, §1-342.
Value of premises without improvements.
Estimate, §1-346.

Bills of lading.
Limitations of liability in bill of lading, §25-7-309.

Bonds, surety.
Actions on bonds.
Officer unlawfully detaining money liable for damages, §58-76-20.

Breach of trust, §36C-10-1002.

Budget of state.
Civil liability for violations, §143C-10-2.

Buildings.
Dismantling.
Joint owner dismantling portion of building, §1-539.2.

Business combinations unlawful.
Treble damages, §75E-4.

Business opportunity sales.
Remedy of purchaser, §66-100(b).

Cable television franchises.
Civil penalties for theft of service, §14-118.5.

Campaign contributions and expenditures.
Disclosure requirements for media advertisements.
Television and radio advertisements supporting or opposing the nomination or election of one or more clearly identified candidates.
Legal remedy, §163-278.39A(f).

Cap on amount of appeal bond.
Staying execution on money judgment.
Noncompensatory damages of $25,000,000 or more, §1-289(b), (c).

Cap on compensatory or consequential damages.
Employee theft, larceny, shoplifting, embezzlement or obtaining by false pretenses.
Civil liability, §1-538.2(a), (b).

Cap on punitive damages, §1D-25(b).
Exemption, DWI, injury or harm arising, §1D-26.
Not made known to trier of fact, §1D-25(c).

Carriers.
Limitation of liability.
Carrier issuing bill of lading, §25-7-309(b).

Checks.
Remedies for returned check, §6-21.3(a), (d).

DAMAGES —Cont'd

Childhood vaccine-related injury compensation.
Action by state against manufacturer, §130A-430(b).
Actions by state against health care provider, §130A-430(a).
Amount awarded against vaccine manufacturers.
Duplicate damages, prevention, §130A-423(c).
Limitation on amount, §130A-423(d).

Civil rights, interference with, §99D-1(b), (b1).

Claims against state departments and agencies, §143-291(a).
False or fraudulent claims against state.
False claims act, §1-607.
Retaliation for lawful acts done to prevent violations.
Private right of action, §1-613.
Retention of portion of damages recovered, §1-608(c).

Collection agencies, §58-70-130(a), (d).

Compromise and settlement.
Motor vehicles.
Property damage claims from collisions or accidents, §1-540.2.

Computer trespass.
Action by injured party, §14-458(c).
Jurisdiction, §1-539.2A(b).
Limitations period, §1-539.2A(b).
Right to damages, §1-539.2A(a).

Conditional offer of judgment, §1A-1 Rule 68(b).

Contracts for deed.
Title requirements for executing contract.
Violations, purchaser's remedies, §47G-6(c).
Violations of chapter, purchaser's remedies, §47G-8.

Contribution among joint tort-feasors, §§1B-1 to 1B-7.

Control share acquisitions unlawful.
Treble damages, §75E-4.

Credit rights for married women.
Actions to enforce articles, §25B-3(a).

Crime victims compensation.
Claimant's action for damages.
Notice to commission, attorney general's duties, §15B-16(c).
Special verdict to indicate separate award for noneconomic detriment, punitive damages and economic loss, §15B-16(d).

Crime victims' rights.
No claim for damages created, §15A-839.

Criminal law and procedure.
Civil actions seeking to recover damages arising out of criminal act.
Statutes of limitation and repose, §1-15.1.

Criminal trespass.
Gas companies.
Injuring fixtures and property of gas companies, §14-152.

Dam safety law.
Actions brought by state.
Liability for damages, §143-215.35.

Debt collectors.
Liability in private actions, §75-56(b).

Discharge of employee called to jury duty, §9-32(b).

Discount buying clubs.
Breach of contract.
Action against bond, §66-135(c).
Action for damages, §66-136(a).

DAMAGES —Cont'd

Discrimination against employees for lawful use of lawful products during nonworking hours.

Civil actions for violations, §95-28.2(e).

Discrimination in business.

Actions by persons injured by violations, §75B-4.

Documents of title.

Limitation of liability in bill of lading, §25-7-309(b).

Limitation of warehouse's liability, §25-7-204(a), (b).

Dogs.

Dangerous dogs.

Damages for injuries or property damage inflicted by dog.

Strict liability, §67-4.4.

Killing or injuring livestock.

Liability of owner, §67-1.

Mad dogs.

Failure to kill, §67-4.

Permitting dogs to run at large at night.

Liability of owner, §67-12.

Double damages.

Attorneys, fraudulent practice, §84-13.

Unlawful cutting, removal or burning of timber, §1-539.1(a).

Drainage.

Assessments, §156-70.

Compensation for damage to lands.

Corporations, §156-48.

Petitions.

Agreement for construction.

Payment of damages, §156-27.

Railroads, §156-89.

Electronic surveillance.

Civil action for violation of article.

Actual damages, §15A-296(a).

Embezzlement, civil liability.

Compensatory and punitive damages, §1-538.2(a) to (d).

Eminent domain.

Compensation.

Generally.

See EMINENT DOMAIN.

Public condemnors.

Action in tort for damage to property.

Common law right not affected, §40A-51(c).

Right of entry prior to condemnation.

Reimbursement to owner for damages resulting, §40A-11.

Employee theft, civil liability.

Compensatory and punitive damages, §1-538.2(a) to (d).

Employer discrimination for lawful use of lawful products during nonworking hours.

Civil actions for violations, §95-28.2(e).

Employment security.

Claims for benefits.

Discharge, demotion or intimidation of witnesses, §96-15.1(a) to (d).

Excessive damages.

New trial, grounds for motion, §1A-1 Rule 59(a).

Executors and administrators.

Wrongful death actions, §28A-18-2(b).

Exemplary damages.

Civil rights, interference with, §99D-1(b), (b1).

Motor fuel marketing violations, private actions, §75-86.

Trade secrets, willful and malicious misappropriations, §66-154(c).

DAMAGES —Cont'd

Exemption from creditors' claims.

Compensation from personal injury, §1C-1601(a).

False claims act.

False or fraudulent claims against state, §1-607.

Retaliation for lawful acts done to prevent violations.

Private right of action, §1-613.

Retention of portion of damages recovered, §1-608(c).

False pretenses and cheats, civil liability.

Compensatory and punitive damages, §1-538.2(a) to (d).

False report of nuclear, biological or chemical weapons, §14-288.23(b).

Hoaxes, §14-288.24(b).

Financial records privacy.

Disclosures in violation of article, §53B-10(a).

Frivolous appeals, AppProc Rule 34(b).

Funds transfers.

Improper execution or failure to execute payment order, §25-4A-305(c).

Obligation of beneficiary's bank to pay and give notice to beneficiary.

Refusal to pay after demand and receipt of notice, §25-4A-404(a).

Good funds settlement act.

Violation of chapter, §45A-7.

Habeas corpus.

Order of discharge.

Failure to comply, §17-23.

Health benefit plans.

Liability for negligent decision, §§90-21.50 to 90-21.56.

See HEALTH CARE LIABILITY.

Home foreclosure rescue scams.

Action for, §75-122.

Husband and wife.

Judgments against married persons for damages.

Levy and collection out of separate estate, §1-223.

Recovery by person suing alone, §52-4.

Tort actions arising out of acts occurring outside state, §52-5.1.

Torts between husband and wife, §52-5.

Identity theft, §1-539.2C.

Civil liability, §14-113.22(b).

Publication of personal information, §75-66(e).

Inadequate damages.

New trial, grounds for motion, §1A-1 Rule 59(a).

Injunctions.

Dissolution, §1A-1 Rule 65(e).

Insurance.

Accident and health insurance.

Pharmacy of choice, §58-51-37(h).

Insurance consumer and customer information privacy.

Action by individual for violations, §58-39-105(b).

Jail keepers causing injuries to prisoners, §162-55.

Labor.

Discrimination for lawful use of lawful products during nonworking hours.

Civil actions for violations of section, §95-28.2(e).

Retaliatory employment discrimination.

Relief in civil actions, §95-243(c).

Right to work law.

Recovery of damages by persons denied employment, §95-83.

DAMAGES —Cont'd
Landlord and tenant.
Accidental damages.
Liability of tenant, §42-10.
Military personnel.
Early termination of rental agreement.
Liquidated damages, liability for, §42-45(b).
Summary ejectment.
Assessment to trial, §42-32.
Claims for damages, §42-28.
Disposition of tenant.
Damages to tenant for dispossession if proceedings quashed, §42-36.
Surrender by lessee where building destroyed or damaged, §42-12.
Wrongful surrender to other landlord misdemeanor, §42-13.
Willful destruction by tenant misdemeanor, §42-11.
Leases, UCC.
Consequential damages.
Limiting, altering or excluding, §25-2A-503(3).
Cover by lessor, §25-2A-518.
Lessee's incidental and consequential damages, §25-2A-520.
Lessee's remedies for default by lessor, §25-2A-508(1), (4).
Lessor's damages, §25-2A-523.
Incidental damages, §25-2A-530.
Liquidation, §25-2A-504.
Market rent, §25-2A-507.
Nonacceptance of goods.
Lessor's damages, §25-2A-528.
Nondelivery, repudiation, default and breach of warranty, §25-2A-519.
Lemon law, §§20-351.3(a), 20-351.8.
Liens.
Enforcement of lien by sale.
Noncompliance, §44A-4(g).
Recoveries for personal injuries.
Accounting for disbursements, §44-50.1(a) to (c).
Limitation on damages.
Alcoholic beverage sales to underage persons, compensation for injury, §18B-123.
Liquefied petroleum gas dealers.
Liability limitations, §119-62.
Littering.
Felony violations, §14-399(e), (h).
Livestock impoundment.
Demand upon owner, §68-18.
Determination by selected landowners or by referee, §68-19.
Right of impounder to recover, §68-17.
Magistrates.
Dam, canal or ditch work.
Power of magistrate to assess contributions for damages or for work done, §7A-292.
Marketing associations.
Merger, consolidation or other fundamental changes.
Rights of objecting members.
Failure of association to mention provisions of section in notices, §54-166(d).
Medicaid.
False claims submitted by providers, §108A-70.12(b).
Medical malpractice.
Arbitration of negligent health claims.
Damage limitations, §90-21.65(b).
Noneconomic damages.
Cap on liability, §90-21.19(a).

DAMAGES —Cont'd
Medical malpractice —Cont'd
Noneconomic damages —Cont'd
Conditions in which no limit imposed, §90-21.19(b).
Definitions, §90-21.19(c).
Verdict, statement of award, §§90-21.19B, 90-21.19(d).
Membership camping, §66-247.
Mill construction.
Action for damages in superior court, §73-25.
Abatement of mill as nuisance when damages cannot be collected, §73-26.
Annual sum as damages, §73-27.
Cost, §73-28.
Execution, §73-28.
Judgment.
Annual sum as damages, §73-27.
Final judgment, §73-28.
Mines and minerals.
Trespass, §74-32.
Persons entitled to bring suit, §74-33.
Survey, §§74-34 to 74-36.
Application for, §74-34.
Costs, §74-36.
Free access to mine for, §74-35.
Order for, §74-34.
Water and drainage rights, §74-28.
Minors.
Malicious or willful destruction of property by minors.
Recovery of damages from parents, §1-538.1.
Negligent supervision of minor.
Right of educational entity to recover against parents, §1-538.3.
Monopolies and restraint of trade.
Treble damages, §75-16.
Mortgage debt collection and servicing.
Remedies of borrower, §45-94.
Mortgages and deeds of trust.
Reverse mortgages.
Actions by borrowers, §53-271(d).
Motion pictures.
Fair competition.
Enforcement of provisions, §75C-5.
Motor fuel marketing violations, private actions, §75-86.
Motor vehicle insurance.
Rate evasion fraud, §58-2-164(h).
Motor vehicle repairs.
Remedies for violation of article, §20-354.9.
Motor vehicles.
First aid or emergency assistance at scene of accident, §20-166(d).
Lemon law, §§20-351.3(a), 20-351.8.
New motor vehicles warranties act, §§20-351.3(a), 20-351.8.
Odometer violations, §20-348(a), (b).
Repairs, remedies for violating article, §20-354.9.
Settlement of accident not to constitute admission of liability, §1-540.2.
Sublease and loan assumption arranging, §20-106.2(f).
Mountain ridge protection.
Civil action against persons alleged in violation, §113A-211(b).
Municipalities.
Rail transportation liability.
Liability limits, §160A-326(d).
New motor vehicles warranties act, §20-351.8.

DAMAGES —Cont'd

Nuisances.
Remedies, §1-539.

Offer of judgment.
Conditional offer of judgment for damages, §1A-1 Rule 68(b).

Oil pollution and hazardous substances control.
Damage to public resources, §§143-215.90 to 143-215.94.
Contesting assessment of damages.
Time for filing petition, §143-215.90(b).
Failure to pay, §143-215.90(b).
Joint and several liability, §143-215.94.
Liability for damages caused, §143-215.94.
Offshore oil and gas activities.
Actions for damages, §143-215.94DD(b).
Defined, §143-215.94BB.
Liability, §143-215.94CC(a).
Exceptions, §143-215.94CC(b).
Create no defense, §143-215.94DD(b).
Personal injury.
Exclusions from liability, §143-215.94DD(b).
Violations of part, §143-215.94FF(a).
Removal of oil discharges.
Liability of responsible party for removal costs and damages, §143-215.93A(c).
Limitation on liability of persons engaged in, §143-215.93A(a).
Exceptions, §143-215.93A(b).

Option to purchase contracts executed with residential lease agreements.
Violations.
Option purchaser's remedies, §47G-7.

Pain and suffering.
See PAIN AND SUFFERING.

Parent and child.
Malicious or willful destruction of property by minors.
Recovery of damages from parents, §1-538.1.
Negligent supervision of minor.
Right of educational entity to recover against parents, §1-538.3.

Party walls.
Dismantling portion of building, §1-539.2.

Personal property.
Interference with property rights, §99A-1.
Judgments in action for recovery of personal property, §1-230.

Pesticides.
Rules and regulations.
Prevention of damages, §143-458(a), (b).

Pleadings.
Ad damnum clause, §1A-1 Rule 8.
Punitive damages, §1A-1 Rule 9(k).
Special damage, §1A-1 Rule 9(g).

Prepaid entertainment contracts.
Remedies of buyer, §66-125(a).
Additional nature of remedies, §66-125(b).

Property damage suits.
Attorneys' fees.
Allowance of counsel fees as part of costs, §6-21.1.

Psychotherapy patient/client sexual exploitation act, §90-21.43.

Public officers and employees.
Unconstitutional taxes.
Employee collecting or administering tax, §143-300.9.

Public schools.
Liability of students and their parents or guardians for damages to buildings, furnishings or textbooks, §115C-398.

DAMAGES —Cont'd

Public schools —Cont'd
Negligent supervision of minor.
Right of educational entity to recover against parents, §1-538.3.
School buses, §115C-399.

Public works.
Regulation of contractors.
Civil damages, §133-28(a), (b).
Relocation assistance.
Administrative payments, §133-17.

Punitive damages.
Aggravating factors, §1D-15(a).
Burden of proof, §1D-15(b).
Amount.
Considerations by trier of fact, §1D-35.
Trier of fact to determine amount, §1D-25(a).
Appeal bond, staying execution on money judgment, §1-289(c).
Cap on amount, noncompensatory damages of $25,000,000 or more, §1-289(b).
Automobile dealers, §20-308.1(b).
Bifurcated trial, §1D-30.
Breach of contract, §1D-15(d).
Cap on amount awarded, §1D-25(b).
Exemption, DWI, injury or harm arising, §1D-26.
Not made know to trier of fact, §1D-25(c).
Cap on amount of appeal bond.
Staying execution on money judgment.
Noncompensatory damages of $25,000,000, §1-289(b), (c).
Civil rights, interference with, §99D-1(b), (b1).
Criminal actions, §99A-1.
Definitions, §1D-5.
Election of extracompensatory remedies, §1D-20.
Exemption from cap, §1D-26.
Family law arbitration, §50-51(e).
Frivolous claims, §1D-45.
Judicial review of award, §1D-50.
Jury instructions, §1D-40.
Larceny, shoplifting, employee theft, embezzlement and obtaining by false pretenses.
Civil liability, §1-538.2(a) to (d).
Limitation on amount of recovery, §1D-25(b), (c).
Driving while impaired exemption, §1D-26.
Malicious claims, §1D-45.
Motor fuel marketing violations, private actions, §75-86.
Pleadings, stating demand for monetary relief, §1A-1 Rule 8(a).
Special matters, §1A-1 Rule 9(k).
Psychotherapy patient/client sexual exploitation act, §90-21.43.
Purpose of punitive damages, §1D-1.
Reptiles.
Regulated reptiles.
Violations, §14-422(d).
Scope of chapter, §1D-10.
Separate determination, §§1D-25(a), 1D-30.
Staying execution on money judgment.
Appeal bond, §1-289(c).
Cap on amount, noncompensatory damages of $25,000,000 or more, §1-289(b), (c).
Trade secrets, willful and malicious misappropriations, §66-154(c).
Trier of fact to determine amount, §1D-25(a).
Vicarious liability, §1D-15(c).

Railroads.
Limitation of actions, §1-51.

DAMAGES —Cont'd
Records and tapes.
Civil action for damages by owner of recorded device, §14-436.
Regional public transportation authority.
Rail transportation liability.
Liability limits, §160A-626(d).
Registers of deeds.
Liability for damages.
Liability insurance coverage.
County decision not to provide insurance coverage, §161-4.2.
Rental referral agencies.
Action on bond, §66-145(c).
Actions for damages, §66-146(a).
Reptiles.
Regulated reptiles.
Violations, §14-422(d).
Restitution or reparation.
Civil actions seeking to recover damages arising out of criminal act.
Crediting of restitution against judgment, §1-15.1(b).
Retail installment sales.
Action by buyer injured by violation, §25A-44.
Retaliatory employment discrimination, §95-243(c).
RICO civil remedies.
Treble damages, §75D-8(c).
Sale of goods, UCC.
Antecedent breach.
Effect of cancellation or rescission on claim, §25-2-720.
Buyer's damages, §§25-2-713 to 25-2-718.
Liquidation or limitation of damages, §§25-2-718, 25-2-719.
Proof of market price, §25-2-723.
Market price.
Admissibility of market quotations, §25-2-724.
Proof, §25-2-723.
Time and place, §25-2-723.
Seller's damages for repudiation, §25-2-708.
Seller's incidental damages, §25-2-710.
Third parties.
Who can sue third parties for injuries to goods, §25-2-722.
Sales.
Commissions.
Actions for damages, §66-192(a).
Savings and loan associations.
Civil penalties.
Separate action for damages not precluded, §§54B-64(d), 54B-65(d).
Confidentiality of information, §54B-63(e).
Savings banks.
Civil penalties.
Actions for damages not precluded, §§54C-77(d), 54C-78(d).
Confidentiality of information, §54C-60(e).
School buses.
Public schools, §115C-399.
Secured transactions.
Remedies for noncompliance with article, §25-9-625(b).
Consumer goods transactions.
Statutory damages, §25-9-625(c).
Limitation of liability, §25-9-628.
Statutory damages.
Consumer goods transactions, §25-9-625(c).
Generally, §25-9-625(e).

DAMAGES —Cont'd
Secured transactions —Cont'd
Remedies for noncompliance with article —Cont'd
Statutory damages —Cont'd
Requests for accounting, collateral, etc., §25-9-625(f).
Surplus or deficiency an issue.
Applicable rules, §25-9-626(a).
Deficiency eliminated or reduced, §25-9-625(d).
Nonconsumer transactions, §25-9-626(b).
Securities regulation.
Civil liabilities generally, §78A-56.
Manipulation of market, §78A-56(b1).
Seed law, claim of defective seeds.
Damages recoverable, §106-277.34(b).
Shellfish.
Cultivation of oysters and clams.
Taking of property, §113-206(e).
Shoplifting, civil liability.
Compensatory and punitive damages, §1-538.2(a) to (d).
Social networking sites.
Sex offenders banned from using.
Liability of web site, §14-202.5A(a).
Special damage, pleading, §1A-1 Rule 9(g).
State institutions, damage of personal property.
Appeals, §143-127.6.
Negligence.
No reimbursement, §143-127.3.
Other remedies.
Good faith effort as prerequisite to reimbursement, §143-127.4.
Reimbursement.
Amount.
Restriction, §143-127.5.
Negligence.
No reimbursement, §143-127.3.
Other remedies.
Good faith effort required, §143-127.4.
Restriction on amount, §143-127.5.
Staying execution on money judgment.
Appeal bond, §1-289(a).
Cap on amount of appeal bond.
Noncompensatory damages of $25,000,000 or more, §1-289(b), (c).
Street and highway condemnation proceedings.
Determination of issues of damages, §136-109(d).
Interest as part of just compensation, §136-113.
Measure of damages, §136-112.
Structured settlement agreements.
Violation of provisions, §1-543.15(b).
Telephone records privacy protection, §14-113.33(b).
Telephone solicitations.
Action by subscriber for violation, §75-105(b).
Torrens system registration.
Assurance fund.
Action for indemnity, §43-50.
Fund not liable for breach of trust, §43-54.
Trademarks.
Infringement, §§80-11, 80-12.
Trade secrets.
Misappropriation, §66-154(b), (c).
Transfer fee covenants.
Recording, liability, §39A-3(b).
Treble damages.
Business combinations or control share acquisitions unlawful, §75E-4.

DAMAGES —Cont'd
Treble damages —Cont'd
Cable television systems theft, §14-118.5.
False claims act.
  False or fraudulent claims against the state,
    §1-607.
Littering, §14-399(e), (h).
Monopolies and restraints of trade, private civil
  actions, §75-16.
New motor vehicles warranties act.
  Manufacturer unreasonably refusing to comply,
    §20-351.8.
Retaliatory employment discrimination,
    §95-243(c).
Returned checks, §6-21.3.
RICO civil remedies, §75D-8(c).
Trespass to public lands, §14-130.
Vehicle mileage act violations, §20-348(a).
Waste, §1-538.
Trees and timber.
Unlawful burning of timber, §1-539.1(b).
Unlawful cutting or removal of timber,
    §1-539.1(a).
  Misrepresentation of property lines, §1-539.1(c).
Trespass.
Mines and minerals. See within this heading,
    "Mines and minerals."
Personal property.
  Interference with property rights, §99A-1.
Public lands.
  Treble damages, §14-130.
Trusts and trustees.
Breach of trust, §36C-10-1002.
Unauthorized practice of law.
Actions by private persons damaged by
  unauthorized practice, §84-10.1.
Unemployment compensation.
Claims for benefits.
  Discharge, demotion or intimidation of
    witnesses, §96-15.1(a) to (d).
Uniform contribution among tort-feasors,
  §§1B-1 to 1B-6.
Unit ownership.
Failure to comply with regulations and covenants,
    §47A-10.
Partition sale on resolution not to restore,
    §47A-25.
Vandalism by minors.
Recovery of damages from parents, §1-538.1.
Victims' rights.
No claim for damages created by provisions,
    §15A-839.
Waste, §1-533.
Treble damages and possession, §1-538.
Water and air resources.
Floodplain regulation.
  Liability for damages in actions, §143-215.60.
Wrongful death, §28A-18-2.

DAM SAFETY, §§143-215.23 to 143-215.37.
See DAMS AND RESERVOIRS.

DAMS AND RESERVOIRS, §§143-215.23 to
  143-215.37.
Alteration of dams, §143-215.27(a), (b).
Appeals, §143-215.33.
Attorney general.
Civil penalties, action to recover, §143-215.36(b).
Injunctive relief, §143-215.36(c).
Citation of part, §143-215.23.
Civil penalties, §143-215.36(b).
Action to recover, §143-215.36(b).

DAMS AND RESERVOIRS —Cont'd
Civil penalties —Cont'd
Remission, §143-215.36(b).
Construction of dams.
Application, §143-215.28(a) to (d).
  Action by environmental management
    commission.
    Approval or disapproval, §143-215.28(a).
    Commencement of construction,
      §143-215.28(d).
    Defective applications, §143-215.28(b).
    Return of disapproved applications with
      statement of objections, §143-215.28(c).
  Appeals, §143-215.33.
  Fees, §143-215.28A(a).
    Dam safety account, §143-215.28A(b).
  Generally, §§143-215.26, 143-215.27.
Certification of final approval, §143-215.30(c), (d).
Commencement, §143-215.28(d).
Modification during work, §143-215.29(c).
Notice of completion, §143-215.30(a).
Repair, alteration or removal, §143-215.27(a), (b).
Reports, §143-215.29(b).
Requirements, §143-215.26(a).
  Applications, §143-215.26(b).
Supervision by qualified engineers,
    §143-215.29(a).
Contested cases.
Civil penalties.
  Filing petitions, §143-215.36(b).
Criminal penalties.
Violations of article, §143-215.36(a).
Damages.
Liability, §143-215.35.
Declaration of purpose, §143-215.24.
Definitions, §143-215.25.
Employment of consultants, §143-215.34.
Enforcement procedures.
Generally, §143-215.36.
Enlargement.
Supplementary drawings and descriptive matter.
  Applicability to new work only, §143-215.30(b).
Exempt dams, §143-215.25A(a).
Limited applicability, §143-215.25A(b).
Fees.
Applications for construction, §143-215.28A.
Fish and fisheries resources.
Inspecting plans and specifications of dams,
    §113-263.
Keeping open fishways in dams, §113-293(c).
Obstructing rivers or creeks, §113-293.
Hearings.
Administrative hearing, §143-215.33.
Impounded water.
Right of withdrawal, §§143-215.44 to 143-215.50.
  Applicability of provisions, §143-215.50.
  Assignment of right of withdrawal, §143-215.45.
  Community water supplies.
    Right of withdrawal for use, §143-215.49.
  Definitions, §143-215.44(b) to (d).
  Determining streamflows.
    Authority to make determinations,
      §143-215.48(b).
    Minimum average flow, §143-215.48(a).
  Discharges of water.
    Effect of right of withdrawal, §143-215.47.
  Exercise of right of withdrawal, §143-215.46.
  Generally, §143-215.44(a).
  Interpretation with other statutes, §143-215.50.
  Transfer of right of withdrawal, §143-215.45.
  Use in community water supplies, §143-215.49.

DAMS AND RESERVOIRS —Cont'd
Injunctions, §143-215.36(c).
Inspections.
Authorization, §143-215.32(a).
Dangerous or unsafe dams, §143-215.32(c).
Orders to repair dams, §143-215.32(b).
Service on owner, §143-215.32(d).
Plans and specifications of dams, §113-263.
Right of entry, §143-215.37.
Investigations, §143-215.34.
Right of entry, §143-215.37.
Judicial review, §143-215.33.
Legislative declaration, §143-215.24.
Liability for damages, §143-215.35.
Lowlands draining or damming.
Petitioner to pay costs, §6-22.
Magistrates.
Assessment of contribution for damages or for
work done.
Power of magistrate, §7A-292.
Minimum streamflow, §143-215.31(c) to (e).
Misdemeanors, §143-215.36(a).
Natural and scenic rivers system.
Restriction on project works, §113A-44.
Navigable waters.
Reservoirs not included definition, §76-40(d).
Notice.
Civil penalties.
Assessment, §143-215.36(b).
Construction of dams.
Notice of completion, §143-215.30.
Petitions.
Civil penalties.
Contested cases, §143-215.36(b).
Purpose, §143-215.24.
Repair of dams.
Applications, §143-215.27(a).
Immediate work in emergency cases,
§143-215.27(b).
Reports.
Construction of dams, §143-215.29(b).
Right of entry, §143-215.37.
Rules and regulations, §143-215.34.
Short title, §143-215.23.
Supervision by qualified engineers, §143-215.29.
**Supervision over maintenance and operation
of dams.**
Commission jurisdiction and supervision,
§143-215.31(a).
Conditions or requirements in orders and written
approvals, §143-215.31(b).
Minimum streamflow, §143-215.31(c) to (e).
Trespass.
Criminal trespass.
Injuries to dams of mills and factories, §14-142.
Violations of part.
Civil penalties, §143-215.36(b).
Water supply watershed protection,
§§143-214.5, 143-214.7.

DANCE.
Obscene exhibitions, §14-190.1.
Promotion of arts, §§143-403 to 143-407.1.

DANCE HALLS.
Counties.
Regulation of places of amusement, §153A-135.
Municipalities.
Regulation of dance halls, §160A-181.

DANCING LESSONS.
Prepaid entertainment contracts generally,
§§66-118 to 66-125.
See PREPAID ENTERTAINMENT CONTRACTS.

DANGEROUS DOGS, §§67-4.1 to 67-4.5.
Applicability of provisions, §67-4.1(b).
Attacks by dangerous dogs, §67-4.3.
Precautions against, §67-4.2.
Definitions, §67-4.1(a).
**Determination that dog is potentially
dangerous,** §67-4.1(c).
Leaving dangerous dogs unattended, §67-4.2(a).
Local programs for control of dangerous dogs,
§67-4.5.
**Permitting dangerous dogs to go beyond
owner's real property,** §67-4.2(a).
Potentially dangerous dogs.
Defined, §67-4.1(a).
Determination, §67-4.1(c).
**Precautions against attacks by dangerous
dogs,** §67-4.2.
Strict liability.
Damages for injuries or property damage inflicted
by dangerous dog, §67-4.4.
**Transfer of ownership or possession of
dangerous dog.**
Notice by owner, §67-4.2(b).

DANGEROUS DRUGS.
Drugs and controlled substances generally.
See DRUGS AND CONTROLLED SUBSTANCES.

DANGEROUS WEAPONS.
Generally.
See FIREARMS AND OTHER WEAPONS.

DANIEL BOONE MEMORIAL COMMISSION,
§143B-51.

DARE COUNTY.
Ambulance service.
Attachment or garnishment and lien for,
§§44-51.4 to 44-51.8.
**Blank or master forms of mortgages, deeds of
trust, etc.**
Indexing and recording, inapplicability of
provisions, §47-21.
Board of county commissioners.
Filling vacancies on board, §153A-27.1.
Eminent domain.
Exercise of power, purposes, modified provisions,
§40A-3(b1).
**Game and wildlife commission, regulatory
authority not appealed or abridged,**
§113-133.1(b).
Game laws, local acts not repealed,
§113-133.1(e).
Grants in navigable waters, registration,
§113-205(a).
Housing authority commissioners.
Tenant as commissioner, exemption from
provisions of law allowing, §157-5.
Low-income housing tax credits.
Qualified building eligible for credit,
§105-129.41(c).
North Carolina's northeast commission,
§§158-8.2 to 158-8.8.
Open fires, high hazard counties.
Applicability of provisions, §106-942(a).
Woodland fires and ground clearing activities,
permits, §106-942.
Private parking lots.
Removal of unauthorized vehicles, §20-219.2.
Registration of deeds.
Tax certification, no delinquent taxes due,
§161-31(b).

DARE COUNTY —Cont'd

Room occupancy tax levied by county, uniform provisions, §153A-155.

School property.
Acquisition and improvement, §153A-158.1.

Swimming, surfing and littering in Atlantic Ocean.
City ordinances effective, §160A-176.1.

Wild plants, taking of certain plants from land of another.
Inapplicability of provisions, §14-129.

DARFUR.

Sudan (Darfur) divestment act, §§147-86.41 to 147-86.49.

DARKENING WINDSHIELDS ON MOTOR VEHICLES, §20-127(b) to (f).

DATA MATCH SYSTEMS.

Child support enforcement.
Agreements with financial institutions, §110-139.2.

DATA PROCESSING.

Child custody jurisdiction and enforcement.
Testimony of witnesses, §50A-111.

Computer crimes, §§14-453 to 14-458.

Computers and software generally.
See COMPUTERS AND SOFTWARE.

Electronic data-processing records, §132-6.1.

Jury lists.
Preparation of jury list.
Alternate procedure in certain counties, §9-2.1(a).
Randomized list, §9-2.1(b).

Medical care data, §§131E-214 to 131E-214.4.
See MEDICAL CARE DATA.

Office of information technology services.
Generally, §§147-33.75 to 147-33.104A.
See INFORMATION TECHNOLOGY SERVICES.

Privilege taxes.
Datacenter machinery and equipment, §105-187.51C.

Records.
Electronic data-processing records, §132-6.1.
Public records.
Copies of databases, §132-6.2(c).
Geographical information systems databases, §132-10.

Sales and use tax.
Definitions, §105-164.3.

Software property tax exemption, §105-275.

Voter registration, §§163-82.11, 163-82.12.

DATA TRANSMISSION LINE ENVIRONMENTAL DOCUMENT, §113A-12.

DATE RAPE DRUG.

Gamma hydroxybutyric acid (GHB), §90-89.

DATING SERVICES.

Prepaid entertainment contracts generally, §§66-118 to 66-125.
See PREPAID ENTERTAINMENT CONTRACTS.

DAVIDSON, CITY OF.

Communication services provided by joint agency.
Service area, §160A-340.2(c).

DAVIDSON COUNTY.

Ambulance service.
Attachment or garnishment and lien for, §§44-51.4 to 44-51.8.

DAVIDSON COUNTY —Cont'd

Board of county commissioners.
Filling vacancies on board, §153A-27.1.

Condemnation or acquisition of land by local government unit outside county.
Consent of board of commissioners necessary, §153A-15.

Coroner elected as nominee of political party.
Filling vacancy in office, §152-1.

Counties generally.
See COUNTIES.

Cropper or tenant refusing to perform terms of contract.
Forfeiture of right of possession to premises, §42-27.

Dog collars.
Unlawful removal of electronic dog collars, §14-401.17.

Oil, gas or mineral claims.
Certain ancient claims extinguished, preservation, procedure, §1-42.2(a) to (d).

Registration of deeds.
Tax certification, no delinquent taxes due, §161-31(b).

School property.
Acquisition and improvement, §153A-158.1.

Sheriff.
Vacancy, performance of duties until vacancy filled, §162-5.1.

Special school tax, election to abolish.
Petition required, §115C-505.

Uwharrie regional resources act, §§153C-1 to 153C-4.

DAVIDSON, TOWN OF.

All-terrain vehicles.
Use by employees on certain highways, §20-171.24.

DAVIE COUNTY.

Ambulance service.
Attachment or garnishment and lien for, §§44-51.4 to 44-51.8.
Obtaining services without intending to pay, §14-111.2.
Requesting ambulance falsely, §14-111.3.

Board of county commissioners.
Filling vacancies on board, §153A-27.1.

Condemnation or acquisition of land by local government unit outside county.
Consent of board of commissioners necessary, §153A-15.

Coroner elected as nominee of political party.
Filling vacancy in office, §152-1.

Counties generally.
See COUNTIES.

Game laws, local acts not repealed, §113-133.1(e).

Registration of deeds.
Tax certification, no delinquent taxes due, §161-31(b).

Room occupancy tax levied by county, uniform provision, §153A-155.

School property.
Acquisition and improvement, §153A-158.1.

Sheriff.
Vacancy, performance of duties until vacancy filled, §162-5.1.

Uwharrie regional resources act, §§153C-1 to 153C-4.

DAY-CARE FACILITIES.

Generally, §§110-85 to 110-107.
See CHILD CARE FACILITIES.

DAY MARKS.
Interfering with, §76-58.
Rafts to exercise care in passing, §76-57.

DEA AUTHORITY.
U.S. department of justice, §15A-406.

DEAD ANIMALS.
See CARCASSES.

DEAD BODIES.
AIDS.
Handling and transportation of bodies,
§130A-395(a), (c).
Anatomical gifts, §§130A-412.3 to 130A-412.33.
See ANATOMICAL GIFTS.
Autopsies.
General provisions, §§130A-398 to 130A-401.
See AUTOPSIES.
Unclaimed bodies.
Consent of commission of anatomy,
§130A-415(d).
Burial.
General provisions.
See BURIAL.
Cemeteries.
General provisions, §§65-4 to 65-113.
See CEMETERIES.
Commission of anatomy, §§130A-33.30 to
130A-33.32.
Unclaimed bodies.
Adoption of rules, §130A-416.
Autopsies.
Consent of commission, §130A-415(d).
Notification to commission, §130A-415(a), (g),
(i).
Cremation.
General provisions, §§90-210.120 to 90-210.135.
See CREMATION.
Disinterment.
Exhumations, §130A-390(a) to (c).
Disposition of body or body parts.
Delegation of right to dispose of own body,
§130A-420(a1).
Disposition of bodies as anatomical gifts.
Inapplicability of provisions, §130A-420(d).
Persons authorized to determine method of
disposition.
Decedent leaving no written authorization,
§130A-420(b).
Written authorization by decedent, §130A-420(a),
(c).
Disposition of unclaimed bodies, §130A-415.
Exhumations, §130A-390(a) to (c).
Funeral service.
General provisions, §§90-210.18A to 90-210.29B.
See FUNERAL SERVICES PROVIDERS.
Handling.
Contagious diseases, §130A-395(a) to (c).
Hepatitis.
Handling and transportation of bodies,
§130A-395(a), (c).
Identification before burial or cremation,
§90-210.29A.
Medical examiners.
Unclaimed bodies.
Provisions inapplicable to bodies within
jurisdiction of medical examiner,
§130A-415(h).
Orders.
Exhumation, §130A-390(b).

DEAD BODIES —Cont'd
Remains of terminated pregnancies.
Manner of disposition, §130A-131.10.
Rulemaking authority.
Unclaimed bodies.
Commission of anatomy, §130A-416.
Shielding from public view.
Unclaimed bodies, §130A-415(e).
Smallpox.
Handling and transportation of bodies,
§130A-395(a), (b).
Transportation.
Contagious diseases, §130A-395(a) to (c).
Unclaimed bodies.
Anatomical gift.
Inapplicability of provision to, §130A-415(f).
Autopsy performed on.
Consent of commission of anatomy required,
§130A-415(d).
Bodies of minors in custody of county at time of
death.
Inapplicability of provisions, §130A-415(g).
Claiming for final disposition.
Ten day period, §130A-415(a), (b), (b1).
Commission of anatomy.
Adoption of rules, §130A-416.
Delivery to commission, §130A-415(a), (b).
Notification, time, §130A-415(a).
Director of social services for county.
Duty to arrange for prompt final disposition.
Commission of anatomy declining body,
§130A-415(c).
Lifeguardianship Council of the Association of
Retarded Citizens.
Release of body claimed by council,
§130A-415(i).
Medical examiner.
Inapplicability of provisions to bodies under
jurisdiction, §130A-415(h).
Migrant farm workers and their dependents.
Delivery of bodies to commission of anatomy,
§130A-418(b).
Reasonable efforts to contact relative,
§130A-415(a).
Rules and regulations.
Adoption by commission of anatomy, §130A-416.
Shielding from public view.
Due caution taken, §130A-415(e).
Ten day period for claiming for final disposition,
§130A-415(a), (b), (b1).
Waters and watercourses.
Burial at sea, §§130A-113(b), 130A-388(b).

DEADLY FORCE.
Arrest by law enforcement officers, §15A-401.
Investigations of use of deadly force by law
enforcement officers, §147-90.
Statistics on use of deadly force by law
enforcement officers.
Collection by division of criminal statistics,
§114-10.02.

DEADLY WEAPONS.
Weapons generally.
See FIREARMS AND OTHER WEAPONS.

DEAD MAN'S STATUTE, §8C-1 Rule 601(c).

DEAF AND HEARING IMPAIRED.
American sign language.
High school modern foreign language,
§115C-81.3(a).

DEAF AND HEARING IMPAIRED —Cont'd
Assault and battery.
Assault upon handicapped persons, §14-32.1.
DNA sample.
Required upon conviction for assaulting, §15A-266.4.
Commission to study the care of the aged and handicapped, §§143-279 to 143-283.
Council for the deaf and hard of hearing.
Appointment of members, §143B-216.32(a).
Chairman, §143B-216.32(c).
Clerical assistance, §143B-216.32(f).
Composition, §143B-216.32(a).
Creation, §143B-216.31.
Definitions, §143B-216.30.
Duties, §143B-216.31.
Expenses of members.
Reimbursement, §143B-216.32(e).
Meetings, §143B-216.32(d).
Quorum, §143B-216.32(d).
Terms of members, §143B-216.32(b).
Definitions.
Council for the deaf and hard of hearing, §143B-216.30.
Division of services for the deaf and hard of hearing, §143B-216.30.
Interpreters for hearing impaired, §§8B-1, 90D-3.
Division of services for the deaf and hard of hearing.
Communication services program.
Established, §143B-216.34(a).
Creation, §143B-216.33(a).
Definitions, §143B-216.30.
Division under authority of department of health and human services, §143B-216.33(b).
Duties, §143B-216.33(a), (b).
Funding, §143B-216.33(c).
Powers, §143B-216.33(a).
Rules, §§143B-216.33(d), 143B-216.34(b).
Sheriffs.
Central communications office of county sheriff's department, §143B-216.34(c).
TDD equipment, §143B-216.34(c), (d).
Evidence.
Statement taken under custody without interpreter present.
Admissibility, §8B-2.
False representation as to physical disability.
Obtaining money by, §14-113.
Fees.
Interpreters for hearing impaired.
Licenses, §90D-10(b).
Service fee, §8B-10.
Training and licensing preparation program fee, §8B-10.
Governor's council on employment of the handicapped, §§143-283.1 to 143-283.8.
Hearing aids.
Health insurance.
Deductibles, coinsurance and other limitations, §58-3-285(b).
Medical necessity determination, utilization review, §58-3-285(c).
Required coverage, §58-3-285(a).
High schools.
American sign language.
High school modern foreign language, §115C-81.3(a).
Insurance on motor vehicles.
Discriminatory practices prohibited, §58-3-25(b).

DEAF AND HEARING IMPAIRED —Cont'd
Interpreters.
Administrative office of the courts.
Policies and procedures for appointment and payment, §7A-343.
Administrative proceedings.
Appointment if deaf person party or witness before, §8B-2(c).
Appointment, §§8B-1, 8B-2(a) to (g).
Compensation, §8B-8.
Waiver of appointed interpreter, §8B-3(a), (b).
Arrest of deaf person.
Arresting officer to procure, §8B-2(d).
Civil, criminal or juvenile proceedings.
Appointment if deaf person party or witness, §8B-2(a).
Compensation, fees and expenses.
Administrative agencies.
Payment for services before, §8B-8(e).
City or county administrative proceedings.
Payment for services, §8B-8(f).
Civil cases and special proceedings.
Payment for services, §8B-8(c).
Criminal and juvenile proceedings.
Payment for services, §8B-8(b).
Fixed by appointing authority, §8B-8(a).
Legislative bodies.
Payment for services before, §8B-8(d).
Reasonable fee for services, entitlement, included in, §8B-8(a).
Travel and subsistence expenses, §8B-8(a).
Competence.
Determination, §8B-1.
Confidentiality.
Privileged communications, §8B-5.
Coordination of interpreter services, §8B-6.
Definitions, §8B-1.
Determination of competence, §8B-1.
Fees.
Licenses, §90D-10(b).
Training and licensing preparation program fee, §8B-10.
Funds.
Responsibility for payment to implement chapter, §8B-9.
Legislative committees.
Appointment if deaf person witness before, §8B-2(b).
Licenses, §§90D-1 to 90D-14.
See INTERPRETERS.
Lists of interpreters, §8B-6.
Notice.
Need for interpreter, §8B-4.
Oath, §8B-7.
Parent of juvenile brought before court deaf.
Appointment for parent, §8B-2(e).
Preliminary determination for appointment, §8B-2(f).
Privileged communications, §8B-5.
Proof of deafness, §8B-4.
Removal, §8B-2(g).
Responsibility for payment of funds to implement chapter, §8B-9.
Right to interpreter, §8B-1.
Training and licensing preparation program fee, §8B-10.
Waiver of appointed interpreter, §8B-3(a), (b).
Motor vehicle insurance.
Discriminatory practices prohibited, §58-3-25(b).
Parent and child.
Failure to enroll deaf child in school, §115C-383(b).

DEAF AND HEARING IMPAIRED —Cont'd

Schools for the deaf, §§143B-216.40 to 143B-216.44.

ABC's program.
Annual performance goals, §143B-146.3.
Defined, §143B-146.1(b).
Participation, §143B-146.2.
Age limits, §115C-383(a).
Age of students, §115C-383(a).
Agreements with local governing authorities, §143B-216.43.
Athletic fees, §143B-216.44.
Calendars, §143B-146.11.
Classroom equipment, §143B-216.41(c).
Compulsory attendance of children, §115C-383(a).
Courses of study, §143B-216.41(c).
Criminal history checks of personnel, §143B-146.16.
Criteria for admission, §143B-216.41(a).
Dispute resolution, §143B-146.15.
Education programs in residential schools generally, §§143B-146.1 to 143B-146.21.
See EDUCATION.
Establishment of schools, §143B-216.40.
Failure of parent, guardian or custodian to enroll child in school, §115C-383(b).
Failure of parent, guardian or custodian to send child to school, §115C-383(c).
Free textbooks, §143B-216.42.
Institutions of higher education.
Collaborative relationship with, maintaining, §143B-216.41(d).
Low-performing residential schools, §§143B-146.5 to 143B-146.9.
Dismissal of administrators and teachers in schools identified as low-performing, §115C-325(p1).
Minimum attendance, §115C-383(a).
Mission, §143B-146.1.
Nonresidents.
Admission to schools, §143B-216.41(b).
Operation and maintenance of schools.
Department of health and human services responsible for, §143B-216.40.
Parents.
Failure to enroll child in school, §115C-383(b).
Purchase and rental system operated by state, §143B-216.42.
Report of deaf children in school.
Local superintendent, §115C-383(d).
Sale of merchandise by governmental units.
Exception to prohibition, §66-58(b).
School technology plans, §143B-146.13.

Service animals, §§168-4.2 to 168-4.6.
Donation for training, §168-4.6.
Prohibited acts, §168-4.5.
Registration and training, §168-4.3.
Responsibility for, §168-4.4.
Right to be accompanied by, §168-4.2.
Penalty for depriving of right, §168-4.5.
Tags, §168-4.2(a).

Telecommunications relay service, §62-157.

Vocational rehabilitation, §168-14.

Witnesses.
Interpreters for deaf parties or witnesses, §8B-2(a) to (g).

Workers' compensation.
Loss of hearing.
Rates of compensation, §97-31.
Occupational diseases.
Loss of hearing caused by harmful noise in employment, §97-53.

DEALERS.

Animal dealers.
Defined, §19A-23.
Licenses.
Change in ownership, management or operation of business, §19A-31.
Fees, §19A-29.
Penalty for acting as dealer without license, §19A-34.
Refusal, suspension or revocation, §19A-30.
Appeals, §19A-32.
Required, §19A-29.
Transfer prohibited, §19A-31.

Art dealers.
Sale of fine prints, §§25C-10 to 25C-16.

Chick dealers.
Civil penalties, §106-549.01.
Compulsory testing for disease, §106-548.
Defined, §106-541.
False advertising, §106-545.
Fines, §106-549.01.
Misdemeanor offenses, §106-549.
Notice describing grade to be posted, §106-546.
Quarantine on premises, §106-548.
Records to be kept, §106-547.
Shipments from out of state, §106-544.
Violations of provisions a misdemeanor, §106-549.

Crossbows.
Sale, §§14-402 to 14-408.
See CROSSBOWS.

Grain dealers, §§106-601 to 106-615.
See GRAIN DEALERS.

Liquefied petroleum gas, §119-56.

Livestock dealer licensing, §§106-418.8 to 106-418.16.
Application for license, §106-418.11(a).
Information required, §106-418.11(a).
Citation of act, §106-418.15.
Civil penalties, §106-418.16.
Definitions, §106-418.8.
Exemptions from provisions, §106-418.9.
Fines, §106-418.16.
Hearings required, §106-418.12.
Maintenance of records, §106-418.13.
Penalties, §§106-418.14, 106-418.16.
Prohibited conduct, §106-418.10.
Refusal to issue license, §106-418.11(c), (d).
Renewal of licenses, §106-418.11(a).
Revocation of license, §106-418.11(b), (d).
Short title, §106-418.15.
Suspension of license, §106-418.11(b), (d).
Unlawful acts, §106-418.10.

Manufactured homes.
Licensure, §§143-143.8 to 143-143.54.
See MANUFACTURED HOMES.

Motor vehicles.
See MOTOR VEHICLE DEALERS.

Pesticide dealers.
Dealer responsible for actions of employees, §143-450(b).
Defined, §143-460.
Employer to list on license application, §143-450(a).
Licenses, §§143-448 to 143-451.
Supervision of employees, agents, etc., to prevent making deceptive or misleading statements about pesticides, §143-442(j).

Precious metal dealers, §§66-163 to 66-173.
See PRECIOUS METAL DEALERS.

Securities.
Bonds, surety, §78A-37(d).

DEALERS —Cont'd
Securities —Cont'd
Defined, §78A-2.
Records.
 Registered dealers, §78A-38(a), (d).
Registration, §§78A-36 to 78A-40.
Reports.
 Financial reports by registered dealers,
  §78A-38(b).
Seeds.
Complaints by buyers, §106-277.30(a).
 Damages recoverable, §106-277.34(b).
 Evidence introduced in action, §106-277.34(a).
 Notice of procedure, §106-277.31.
Licensing of dealers, §106-277.18.
 Revocation or refusal of license for cause,
  §106-277.19.
Referral of investigation to seed board,
 §106-277.30(c).
Registration, §106-277.18.
Requesting investigation, §106-277.30(b).

DEAL-MAKING BY PROSECUTION
 WITNESSES.
Immunity, charge reduction or sentence
 concessions, §§15A-1051 to 15A-1055.

DEATH.
Adoption.
Death of joint petitioner pending final decree,
 §48-2-204.
Adult care homes.
Reporting death of resident, §131D-34.1.
Advancements.
Death of advancee before intestate donor, §29-27.
Anatomical gifts, §§130A-412.3 to 130A-412.33.
See ANATOMICAL GIFTS.
Attachment.
Defendant.
 Death after levy.
  Effect, §1-440.34.
Attorneys at law.
Appointment to protect clients' interests, Bar Rule
 B.0122.
Bail bondsman, §58-71-121.
Bank deposits and collections.
Death of customer.
 Authority of payor or collecting bank,
  §25-4-405(a), (b).
  Controlling provisions, §25-4-405(c).
Benefits act, §§143-166.1 to 143-166.7.
Blind persons.
Aid to the blind.
 Award and assistance check payable to
  decedents, §111-18.1(a), (b).
Boating safety.
Death, injury or disappearance resulting from
 occurrence.
 Filing of report, §75A-11(b).
 Notice to law enforcement agency, §75A-11(c).
Brain death, §90-323.
Burial at sea.
Certification and duties of medical examiners,
 §§130A-113(b), 130A-388(b).
Child care facilities.
Report of death of child while in child care,
 §110-102.1(b).
Child fatality or near fatality cases.
Disclosure of records, §7B-2902.
Child fatality prevention system, §§7B-1400 to
 7B-1414.
See CHILD FATALITY PREVENTION SYSTEM.

DEATH —Cont'd
Child fatality review team, §143B-150.20.
Child placing agencies.
Reporting death of resident, §131D-10.6B.
Community property rights.
Disposition at death, §§31C-1 to 31C-12.
 See COMMUNITY PROPERTY.
Competency of witnesses.
Dying declarations, §8-51.1.
Concealing evidence of death.
Dismembering or destroying human remains,
 §14-401.22(d).
 Death not of natural causes, §14-401.22(e).
 Human remains defined, §14-401.22(f).
Concealment, §14-401.22(a).
Aiding, abetting or counseling, §14-401.22(b).
Conveyances.
Contingent limitations depending on death of
 person without heirs.
 Limitations on failure of issue, §41-4.
Disclosure of death or illness of previous occupant,
 §39-50.
Coroners.
Conveyances of real property when not in office,
 §39-5.
Death benefits, §§143-166.1 to 143-166.7.
See DEATH BENEFITS.
Death with dignity, §§90-320 to 90-323.
Declarations.
Right to natural death.
 Advance directive, §90-321.
 Procedures in absence of declaration, §90-322.
Deeds.
Contingent limitations on death of person without
 heirs.
 Limitations on failure of issue, §41-4.
Definitions.
Brain death, §90-323.
Right to natural death, §90-321(a).
Depositions.
Reading deposition on trial.
 When deposition may be read on trial, §8-83.
Determination that death has occurred,
 §90-323.
Dismembering or destroying human remains.
Concealing evidence of death, §14-401.22(d).
 Death not of natural causes, §14-401.22(e).
 Human remains defined, §14-401.22(f).
Disposition of body or body parts of decedent.
Decedent authorizing disposition in will, written
 statement, etc., §130A-420(a).
Delegation of right to dispose of own body,
 §130A-420(a1).
Inapplicability of provisions to disposition of
 bodies as anatomical gifts, §130A-420(d).
Persons authorized to determine method of
 disposition of decedent's body.
 Decedent leaving no written authorization,
  §130A-420(b).
Written authorization for disposition of body
 parts, §130A-420(c).
Disturbing human remains, §14-401.22(c).
Human remains defined, §14-401.22(f).
Dying declarations, §8C-1 Rule 804(b).
Competency of witnesses, §8-51.1.
Executors and administrators.
Appointment of successor, §28A-6-3.
Letters testamentary or of administration.
 Evidence of death, §28A-6-1(c).
Powers and duties of successor, §28A-13-7.

DEATH —Cont'd
Executors and administrators —Cont'd
Surviving personal representative.
Powers, §28A-13-9.
Extraordinary means of postponing.
Right to natural death, §§90-320 to 90-323.
Federal officers and employees.
Finding of presumed death, §8-37.1(a), (b).
Authority to certify evidence, §8-37.3.
Deemed signed and issued pursuant to law,
§8-37.3.
Report or record that person died, §8-37.2.
Certified copies deemed signed and issued
pursuant to law, §8-37.3.
Authority to certify evidence, §8-37.3.
Felony death by vehicle, §20-141.4.
Fetal death registration.
Report of death, §130A-114(a).
Preparation and filing of report, §130A-114(c).
Required medical information, §130A-114(b).
Guardians.
Appointment of successor guardian, §35A-1293.
Mortgages.
Powers passed to succeeding guardian, §45-19.
Health.
Communicable diseases.
Transportation of bodies of persons who have
died of reportable diseases, §130A-146.
Health care powers of attorney, §§32A-15 to
32A-26.
See HEALTH CARE POWERS OF ATTORNEY.
Hearsay exception.
Family history, §8C-1 Rule 803.
Records of religious organizations, §8C-1 Rule
803.
Statements under belief of impending death,
§§8-51.1, 8C-1 Rule 804(b).
Highway patrol.
Badges and service sidearms of deceased
members, §20-187.2(a).
Joint tenants and tenants in common.
Ownership of corporate stock and investment
securities, §41-2.2(c).
Landlord and tenant.
Apportionment of rent.
Leases terminated by death, §42-5.
Right to payment terminated by death, §42-6.
Death, serious illness, or certain criminal
convictions of previous occupant.
Deemed not a material fact in real property
transactions, §42-14.2.
Leases.
Apportionment of rent where lease terminated by
death, §42-5.
Death, serious illness, or certain criminal
convictions of previous occupant.
Deemed not a material fact in real property
transactions, §42-14.2.
Legislative retirement system.
Death benefits, §120-4.27.
Distributions, §120-4.26A.
Survivor's alternative benefit, §120-4.28.
Limitation of actions.
Personal representative or collector.
Action by or against in event of death before
limitation expires, §1-22.
Limited liability company member.
Cessation of membership, §57C-3-02.
Limited partnerships, revised act.
Exercise of partnership rights by legal
representative, §59-705.

DEATH —Cont'd
Living will.
Right to natural death, §§90-320 to 90-323.
**Local governmental employees' retirement
system.**
Benefits.
Death benefit plan, §128-27(l).
Maltreatment of juvenile.
Disclosure of records in child fatality or near
fatality cases, §7B-2902.
Report of death due to maltreatment, §7B-301.
Medical certification as to cause, §130A-115(c).
Nurse practitioners.
Medical certification deemed authorized by
supervisor, §90-18.2(e1).
Physician assistants.
Medical certification deemed authorized by
supervisor, §90-18.1(e1).
Medical examiners.
Notification of certain deaths, §130A-383(a).
Duties of medical examiners upon receipt of
notice, §130A-385(a).
Out of state bodies, §130A-384.
Postmortem medicolegal examinations and
services, §§130A-377 to 130A-395.
See MEDICAL EXAMINERS.
Military affairs.
Absentees in military service.
Termination of receivership, §28B-8(b).
Evidence.
Finding of presumed death, §8-37.1(a), (b).
Honor and Remember Flag.
Armed forces members who have died in the
line of duty, §145-32.
Powers of attorney.
Death of principal.
Affidavit of agent as to possessing no
knowledge of death of principal, §165-40.
Provisions for revocation not affected,
§165-42.
Report of "missing" not to constitute
revocation, §165-41.
Validity of acts of agent, §165-39.
Militia.
Third party injuring or killing guard personnel.
Proceedings against third party, §127A-110.
Minors.
Child fatality or new fatality cases, disclosure of
records, §7B-2902.
Child fatality prevention system, §§7B-1400 to
7B-1414.
See CHILD FATALITY PREVENTION
SYSTEM.
Report of death due to maltreatment, §7B-301.
Misdemeanor death by vehicle, §20-141.4.
Missing persons.
Final finding and decree of absentee's death,
§28C-11(a).
Termination of receivership, §28C-12.
Monuments and memorials.
Not to be erected within 25 years of death of
person, §100-8.
Mortgages and deeds of trust.
Guardians.
Powers passed to succeeding guardian, §45-19.
Representative succeeds on death of mortgagee or
trustee in deeds of trust, §45-4.
Survivorship among donees of power of sale,
§45-8.

DEATH —Cont'd
Motor vehicle accidents.
Death as result of accident within twelve months after accident.
Supplemental report by investigating law enforcement officer, §20-166.1(e).
Hospitals to notify medical examiner of death resulting from accidents, §20-166.1(f).
Medical examiner to report death resulting from accident, §20-166.1(f).
Vehicular homicide, §20-141.4.
Motor vehicle registration.
Death of owner of registered vehicle.
Continuation of registration, §20-64(e).
National guard.
Mutual assistance compact.
Death benefits, §127A-177(h).
Injury or death while going to or returning from duty, §127A-183.
Pensions for members of national guard.
Cessation of payments upon death of individual, §127A-40(b).
Natural death.
Right to natural death, §§90-320 to 90-323.
Notary.
Electronic notary public act.
Delivery of electronic records to secretary, §10B-126(g).
Disposition of coding, file or program enabling affixation of electronic signature, §10B-128(a), (b).
Notice to secretary, delivery of seal by estate, §10B-55(c).
Parties.
Substitution of parties, §1A-1 Rule 25(a), (e), (f).
Partnerships.
Claims against partnership when one partner has died.
Failure to present claims in six months, §59-80.
Payment pro rata, §59-79.
Dissolution and winding up.
Continuation of business.
Rights of estate of deceased partner when business continued, §59-72.
Death of partner as cause of dissolution, §59-61.
Liability of individual property of deceased partner for obligations of partnership, §59-66(d).
Fiduciary obligations of partner.
Applicability to representatives of deceased partner, §59-51(b).
Surviving partners, §§59-74 to 59-84.1.
Physicians and surgeons.
Determination that person is dead, §90-323.
Police.
Badges and service side arms of deceased members, §20-187.2(a).
Postmortem medicolegal examinations and services, §§130A-377 to 130A-395.
See MEDICAL EXAMINERS.
President of the United States.
Duty of congress, US Const Art II §1.
President-elect.
Provision in case of, US Const Amd 20.
Succession upon death, US Const Amd 25 §1.
Presumption, §28C-1.
Prisons and prisoners.
Investigation of inmate's death.
Death other than natural causes, §148-25.
Public schools.
School employees.
Payment of wages after death, §115C-324.

DEATH —Cont'd
Real property.
Death, serious illness, or certain criminal convictions of previous occupant.
Deemed not a material fact in real property transactions, §42-14.2.
Rents.
Apportionment.
Lease terminated by death, §42-5.
Right to payment terminated by death, §42-6.
Retirement system for teachers and state employees, §135-5.
Consolidated judicial retirement act.
Benefits on death after retirement, §135-64(a) to (i).
Benefits on death before retirement, §135-63(a) to (d).
Death benefit plan, §135-5(l).
Survivor's alternate benefit, §135-5(m), (m3).
Right to natural death, §§90-320 to 90-323.
See RIGHT TO NATURAL DEATH.
Sheriffs.
Deeds.
Official selling or empowered to sell property not in office, §39-5.
Pensions.
Sheriffs' supplemental pension fund act of 1985.
Cessation of benefits on death of pensioner, §143-166.85(c).
Simultaneous death, revised act, §§28A-24-1 to 28A-24-8.
See SIMULTANEOUS DEATH.
Social services.
Checks payable to decedents, §108A-72.
State child fatality review team, §143B-150.20.
Substitution of parties, §1A-1 Rule 25(a), (e), (f).
Suicide.
Crime of suicide abolished, §14-17.1.
Health care powers of attorney.
Actions under not considered suicide, §32A-24(c).
Homicide.
Crime of suicide abolished, §14-17.1.
Medical examiners.
Postmortem medicolegal examinations and services.
Notification of medical examiners of certain deaths, §130A-383(a).
Workers' compensation.
No compensation payable, §97-12.
Superintendents of schools.
Vacancies in office, §115C-275.
Tax collectors.
Official selling real property not in office.
Execution by successor, §39-5.
Trusts and trustees.
Contingent limitations on death of person without heirs.
Limitations on failure of issue, §41-4.
Representative succeeds on death of trustee in deeds of trust, §45-4.
Unclaimed bodies, §§130A-415, 130A-416.
Uniform transfer on death security registration act, §§41-40 to 41-51.
See UNIFORM TRANSFER ON DEATH SECURITY REGISTRATION ACT.
Vice-president, US Const Art II §1.
Vital statistics generally, §§130A-90 to 130A-121.
See VITAL STATISTICS.
Wills.
Testator's death.
Construction of will, §31-41.

DEATH —Cont'd
Witnesses.
  Competency of witnesses.
    Dying declarations, §8-51.1.
Workers' compensation.
  See WORKERS' COMPENSATION.
Wrongful death.
  See WRONGFUL DEATH.

DEATH BENEFITS, §§143-166.1 to 143-166.7.
Applicability of article, §143-166.7.
Awards.
  Conclusiveness, §143-166.4.
Definitions.
  Dependent child, §143-166.2(a).
  Dependent parent, §143-166.2(b).
  Generally, §143-166.2.
  Killed in the line of duty, §143-166.2(c).
    Official duties, §143-166.2(f).
  Spouse, §143-166.2(e).
Effect of payments on other benefits,
  §143-166.5.
Industrial commission rules.
  Abandonment of grounds for appeal.
    Failure to include ground in statement,
      ICDeathBenefits Rule IV.
  Amendment of rules, ICDeathBenefits Rule V.
  Appeal to full commission, ICDeathBenefits Rule
    IV.
  Briefs on appeal, ICDeathBenefits Rule IV.
  Determination of claim, ICDeathBenefits Rule III.
  Grounds for appeal.
    Statement, requirements, time for filing,
      ICDeathBenefits Rule IV.
  Guardian ad litem.
    Appointment for infants and incompetents,
      ICDeathBenefits Rule III.
  Hearing on award.
    Insufficient evidence or information,
      ICDeathBenefits Rule III.
  Insufficient evidence or information.
    Hearing on award, ICDeathBenefits Rule III.
  Location of commission office, ICDeathBenefits
    Rule I.
  New evidence on appeal, prohibition,
    ICDeathBenefits Rule IV.
  New hearing to take additional evidence.
    Motion, ICDeathBenefits Rule IV.
  Notice of appeal, ICDeathBenefits Rule IV.
  Oral argument on appeal, waiver,
    ICDeathBenefits Rule IV.
  Rehearing, ordering, ICDeathBenefits Rule III.
  Settlement for less than maximum amount.
    Commission ordering or approving,
      ICDeathBenefits Rule III.
  Statement of facts and circumstances furnished by
    claimant.
    Copy furnished opposing party, ICDeathBenefits
      Rule III.
  Statement of grounds for appeal.
    Time for filing, ICDeathBenefits Rule IV.
  Sufficient evidence or information.
    Award without hearing, ICDeathBenefits Rule
      III.
  Transacting business, continuous session,
    ICDeathBenefits Rule II.
Legislative findings, §143-166.1.
Payments.
  Amounts, §143-166.3(b).
  Awards exempt from taxes, §143-166.6.
  Determination, §143-166.3(a).

DEATH BENEFITS —Cont'd
Payments —Cont'd
  Other benefits not affected, §143-166.5.
  Remainder of payments, §143-166.3(c).
  Service or merchandise payments.
    Insurance company contracts, §58-3-55.
  Subsequent ineligibility, §143-166.3(c), (d).
Purpose, §143-166.1.
Renunciation of succession, §31B-1.
Source of funds, §143-166.4.
Taxation.
  Awards exempt from taxes, §143-166.6.

DEATH BY VEHICLE.
Felony death by vehicle, §20-141.4(a1).
  Aggravated felony death by vehicle, §20-141.4(a5).
  Repeat offender.
    Second degree murder, §20-141.4(a6).
Mandatory revocation of driver's license,
  §20-17(a).
  Permanent revocation, §20-19(i).
Misdemeanor death by vehicle, §20-141.4(a2).
No double prosecution for manslaughter,
  §20-141.4(c).
Punishments, §20-141.4(b).

DEATH BY WRONGFUL ACT.
See WRONGFUL DEATH.

DEATH CERTIFICATES.
Amendment, §130A-118(a).
  By medical examiner, §130A-385(c).
  Fee, §130A-118(d).
Contents of death certificate, §130A-116.
Cremation.
  Authorization for cremation, §130A-113(b).
  Required before cremating, information required,
    §90-210.128(a).
Duties of local registrars, §130A-97.
Duties of medical examiners, §130A-385.
Fee for registering or amending, copies,
  §161-10(a).
Felonies and misdemeanors.
  Generally, §130A-26A(a), (b).
Filing of death certificate, §130A-115(a).
  Information to be obtained, §130A-115(b).
Local registrar's duties, §130A-97.
Medical certification of cause of death,
  §130A-115(c).
  Nurse practitioners.
    Medical certification deemed authorized by
      supervisor, §90-18.2(e1).
  Physician assistants.
    Medical certification deemed authorized by
      supervisor, §90-18.1(e1).
Register of deeds.
  Copies to be forwarded by local registrars,
    §130A-97.
Simultaneous death.
  Evidence of death, §28A-24-7.
Standard certificate of death.
  Contents of death certificate, §130A-116.

DEATH OF A PARTY.
Substitution of party upon death, §1A-1 Rule
  25(a).

DEATH OF JUVENILE.
Child fatality prevention system, §§7B-1400 to
  7B-1414.
  See also CHILD FATALITY PREVENTION SYSTEM.
**Disclosure of records in child fatality or near
  fatality cases,** §7B-2902.

DEATH OF JUVENILE —Cont'd
Maltreatment, report, §7B-301.

DEATH PENALTY.
Age of defendant.
Mitigating circumstances, §15A-2000(f).
Aggravating circumstances.
Consideration by jury, §15A-2000(b), (c).
Enumerated, §15A-2000(e).
Agreement to accept life imprisonment.
Plea of guilty to first degree murder,
§15A-2001(b).
State may agree at any point in prosecution,
§15A-2004(a).
Upon remand from Supreme Court.
State may agree, §15A-2001(d).
Appeals.
Automatic review of judgment and sentence,
§15A-2000(d).
Briefs.
Filing and serving, time, AppProc Rule 13(a).
Direct appeal to supreme court.
Death sentences included in superior court
judgments, §7A-27(a).
Indigent persons, representation of, §7A-451(b) to
(e), IndigCounsel Model Plan Art VIII §8.2.
New trial.
Notice of new trial, §15-193.
Prisoner taken to place of trial when new trial
granted, §15-195.
Notice of appeals, §15-189.
Notice of reprieve or new trial, §15-193.
Arson.
Aggravating circumstances.
Capital punishment in commission of arson,
§15A-2000(e).
Bail.
Discretion of judge as to pretrial release,
§15A-533(c).
Burglary.
Aggravating circumstances.
Capital felony in commission of burglary,
§15A-2000(e).
Certiorari.
Petition for writ in post conviction matters,
AppProc 21(e), (f).
Clerks of court.
Certificate of execution.
Filing, §15-192.
Duties on sentence of death, §15-189.
Confidentiality.
Witnesses to and persons carrying out execution,
§15-190.
Contact with victims' family members.
Death row inmates, §148-10.2(a).
Crimes punishable by death, NC Const Art XI
§2.
Discretion of prosecutor to seek death penalty,
§15A-2004(a).
Discrimination.
Race as basis of judgment, §§15A-2010 to
15A-2012.
District attorneys.
Argument for death penalty, §15-176.1.
Duties on sentence of death, §15-189.
Drugs.
Manner of execution, §15-187.
Duress.
Mitigating circumstances, §15A-2000(f).
Electrocution.
Abolished, §15-187.

DEATH PENALTY —Cont'd
Electrocution, death by.
Abolished, §15-187.
Enumeration of permissible punishments, NC
Const Art XI §1.
Escape.
Aggravating circumstances.
Capital felony committed for purpose of
effecting escape, §15A-2000(e).
Execution, §§15-187 to 15-195.
Certificate of execution, §15-192.
Confidentiality of witnesses and executioner,
§15-190.
Designation of person or persons to execute
sentence, §15-190.
Electrocution.
Abolished, §15-187.
Fee, §15-190.
Manner of execution, §§15-187, 15-188.
Pending sentences unaffected, §15-191.
Pending sentences unaffected, §15-191.
Place of execution, §15-188.
Race as basis of judgment.
Execution prohibited, §15A-2010.
Supervision of execution, §15-190.
Time for execution, §15-194.
Who shall be present, §15-190.
Findings in support of sentence of death,
§15A-2000.
Guilty plea entered to capital offense.
Entry of plea at any time after indictment,
§15A-2001(a).
Jury impanel for limited purpose of sentence
recommendation.
Notice given of intent to seek death penalty,
§15A-2001(c).
Life imprisonment.
Agreement by state or defendant to accept life
imprisonment, §15A-2001(b).
Notice of intent to seek death penalty not given,
§15A-2001(b).
Notice of intent to seek death penalty given by
state, §15A-2001(c).
Habeas corpus.
Procedure when considering application, SuperCt
Rule 25.
Indictment may not be waived in capital case,
§15A-642(b).
Indigent persons, representation of.
Appointment of counsel in capital cases,
IndigCounsel Model Plan Art VII.
Appellate appointments, §7A-451(b) to (e),
IndigCounsel Model Plan Art VIII §8.2.
Indigent defense services.
Generally, §§7A-450 to 7A-458.
See INDIGENT DEFENSE SERVICES.
Indigent defense services act, §§7A-498 to
7A-498.8.
See INDIGENT DEFENSE SERVICES.
Indigent services rules, IDS Rules 1.1 to 3.7.
See INDIGENT DEFENSE SERVICES.
Judges.
Duties on sentence of death, §15-189.
Judgments, §15-189.
Jury.
Alternate jurors in capital cases, §15A-1215(b).
Arguments of counsel to jury.
Consequences of guilty verdict, §15-176.5.
District attorney may argue for death penalty,
§15-176.1.
No limit as to number, §7A-97.

DEATH PENALTY —Cont'd
Jury —Cont'd
Informing potential jurors on consequences of
guilty verdict, §15-176.3.
Instructions to jury on consequences of guilty
verdict, §15-176.4.
Peremptory challenges.
Number in capital cases, §15A-1217(a).
Questioning potential jurors on consequences of
guilty verdict, §15-176.3.
Selection of jurors in capital cases, §15A-1214(j).
Sentencing proceedings.
Generally, §15A-2000(a).
Recommendation by jury as to sentence,
§15A-2000(b).
Findings in support of sentence of death,
§15A-2000(c).
Sentencing upon, §15A-2002.
Kidnapping.
Aggravating circumstances.
Capital felony in commission of kidnapping,
§15A-2000(e).
Lethal injection.
Manner of carrying out, obtaining drugs, §15-187.
Manner of execution, §15-187.
Mentally ill.
Mitigating circumstances, §15A-2000(f).
Mentally retarded defendants.
Death sentence prohibited, §15A-2005(b).
Burden of proof on defendant, §15A-2005(a), (c),
(f).
Definitions, §15A-2005(a).
Jury determination of aggravating or mitigating
circumstance.
Consideration of evidence of retardation,
§15A-2005(g).
Legal defenses not precluded by pretrial
determination, §15A-2005(d).
Noncapital case, court declaration,
§15A-2005(c).
Other sentence not precluded, §15A-2005(h).
Pretrial hearing to determine retardation,
§15A-2005(c).
Special issue submitted to jury.
Pretrial determination of retardation not
found, §15A-2005(e).
Minors who commit murder, §14-17.
Mitigating circumstances.
Consideration by jury, §15A-2000(b), (c).
Enumerated, §15A-2000(f).
Motions.
Superior courts.
Motions for appropriate relief in capital cases,
SuperCt Rule 25.
New trial.
Notice of reprieve or new trial, §15-193.
Prisoner taken to place of trial when new trial
granted, §15-195.
Noncapital proceeding.
Notice of intent to seek death penalty not given,
§15A-2001(c).
North Carolina racial justice act, §§15A-2010 to
15A-2012.
Notice of intent to seek death penalty.
Required to impose sentence, §15A-2001(b).
Offenses punishable by death, NC Const Art XI
§2.
Peace officers.
Aggravating circumstances.
Capital felony committed against peace officer,
§15A-2000(e).

DEATH PENALTY —Cont'd
Place of execution, §15-188.
Plea of guilty to first degree murder.
Entry of plea at any time after indictment,
§15A-2001(a).
Jury impanel for limited purpose for sentence
recommendation.
Notice given of intent to seek death penalty,
§15A-2001(c).
Life imprisonment.
Agreement by state or defendant to accept life
imprisonment, §15A-2001(b).
Notice of intent to seek death penalty not given,
§15A-2001(b).
Notice of intent to seek death penalty given by
state, §15A-2001(c).
Pretrial conference in capital cases, SuperCt
Rule 24.
Prisoner taken to penitentiary, §15-189.
Prosecutorial discretion to seek death penalty,
§15A-2004(a).
Race as basis of judgment, §§15A-2010 to
15A-2012.
Burden of proof, §15A-2011(c).
Finding of, §15A-2011(a).
Evidence relevant to establishing, §15A-2011(b).
Hearing on claim of, §15A-2012(a).
Motion seeking relief, §15A-2012(b), (c).
Sentence of death or execution prohibited,
§15A-2010.
Rape.
Aggravating circumstances.
Capital punishment in commission of rape,
§15A-2000(e).
Remand of case from Supreme court.
Agreement to accept life imprisonment,
§15A-2001(d).
Reprieve.
Notice, §15-193.
Review of judgment and sentence, §15A-2000(d).
Sentencing, §15A-2002.
Aggravating circumstances.
Consideration by jury, §15A-2000(b), (c).
Enumerated, §15A-2000(e).
Enumeration of permissible punishments, NC
Const Art XI §1.
Mitigating circumstances.
Consideration by jury, §15A-2000(b), (c).
Enumerated, §15A-2000(f).
Offenses punishable by death, NC Const Art XI
§2.
Review of sentence.
Automatic review, §15A-2000(d).
Separate sentencing proceeding.
Disability of trial judge.
Chief justice to designate judge to conduct
proceedings, §15A-2003.
Generally, §15A-2000(a).
Recommendation by jury as to sentence,
§15A-2000(b).
Findings in support of sentence of death,
§15A-2000(c).
Sentencing upon, §15A-2002.
Superior courts.
Motions for appropriate relief in capital cases,
SuperCt Rule 25.
Time.
Execution, §15-194.
**Time for filing notice of intent to seek death
penalty,** §15A-2001(b).

DEATH PENALTY —Cont'd
Verdict.
Consequences of guilty verdict.
Argument to jury, §15-176.5.
Informing and questioning potential jurors,
§15-176.3.
Instruction to jury, §15-176.4.
Warden.
Presence at execution, §15-190.
Supervision of execution, §15-190.
Witnesses.
Aggravating circumstances.
Capital felony committed against witness,
§15A-2000(e).

DEATH PRESUMPTION.
Not presumed from mere absence, §28C-1(a).
Specific peril exposure considered, §28C-1(b).

DEATH TAX.
Estate tax generally, §§105-32.1 to 105-32.8.
See ESTATE TAXES.

DEATH WITH DIGNITY, §§90-320 to 90-323.
Advance directive, §90-321.
Absence of declaration.
Procedure for natural death, §90-322(a), (b).
Health care power of attorney form.
Combination with or incorporation into,
§§32A-26, 90-321(j).
Advance health care directive registry,
§§130A-465 to 130A-471.
Affirmative or deliberate ending of life not
authorized, §90-320(b).
Brain death.
Defined, §90-323.
Use as sole basis for determination of death,
§90-323.
Cause of death.
Withholding or discontinuance of extraordinary
means not to constitute, §§90-321(h),
90-322(d).
Comatose persons.
Procedures for natural death in absence of
declaration, §90-322(a), (b).
Definitions, §90-321(a).
Determination of death, §90-323.
Form.
Advance directive, §90-321(d).
Health care powers of attorney.
General provisions, §§32A-15 to 32A-26.
See HEALTH CARE POWERS OF ATTORNEY.
Insurance.
Signing of declaration not to be required as
condition for becoming insured, §90-321(g).
Legislative declaration, §90-320(a).
Suicide.
Execution and consummation of declaration not to
constitute, §90-321(f).

DEBIT CARDS.
Account numbers or expiration date.
Printing more than 5 digits upon receipt provided
cardholder at point of sale.
Prohibited, §14-113.24(b).
Penalty, §14-113.24(c).
Person defined, §14-113.24(a).
Financial transaction card crimes, §§14-113.8 to
14-113.17.
See FINANCIAL TRANSACTION CARDS.
Fines, fees and costs owed by offenders.
Acceptance in lieu of payment by cash or check,
§7A-321(a).
Contracts with vendors to provide, §7A-343.

DEBIT CARDS —Cont'd
Identity theft.
Generally, §§14-113.20 to 14-113.25.
See IDENTITY THEFT.
Insurance.
Solicitation, negotiation or payment of premiums
through credit card or debit card services,
§58-3-145.
Statewide accounts receivable program.
Payments by, authorized, §147-86.22(b).

DEBT ADJUSTERS.
Definitions, §14-423.
Engaging, etc., in business of debt adjusting a
misdemeanor, §14-424.
Injunctions.
Appointment of receiver for money and property
employed, §14-425.
Practice of debt adjusting enjoined, §14-425.
Persons not deemed debt adjusters, §14-426.
Receivers.
Appointment of receiver for money and property
employed, §14-425.
Transactions not deemed debt adjustment,
§14-426.

DEBT BUYERS.
Actions filed by buyer plaintiffs.
Complaints.
Attachments required, §58-70-150.
Collection agencies generally, §§58-70-1 to
58-70-130.
See COLLECTION AGENCIES.
Defined, §58-70-15(b).
Receipt for payment received.
Requirements, §58-70-70(b).
Unfair practices, §58-70-115.

DEBT COLLECTORS.
Actions.
Liability in private action, §75-56(b).
Arrests.
Representing that nonpayment may result in
arrest, §75-51.
Civil penalties, §75-56(d).
Civil penalty and forfeiture fund.
Remitted to, §75-56(e).
Coercion, §75-51.
Collection agencies.
General provisions, §§58-70-1 to 58-70-155.
See COLLECTION AGENCIES.
Prohibited acts by debt collectors.
Collection agencies exempted from provisions,
§75-50.
County public enterprise services.
Customer misrepresentation of identity,
§153A-277(b2).
Restrictions on debt collection practices,
§153A-277(b1).
Damages.
Liability in private actions, §75-56(b).
Deceptive representations, §75-54.
Definitions, §75-50.
Harassment, §75-52.
Municipal utilities.
Customer misrepresentation of identity,
§160A-314(b2).
Restricted practices, §160A-314(b1).
Obscenity.
Profane or obscene language, §75-52.
Private actions.
Liability, §75-56(b).

DEBT COLLECTORS —Cont'd
Publication.
  Unreasonable publication, §75-53.
**Remedies cumulative and in addition to other
  remedies,** §75-56(c).
Telephone harassment, §75-52.
Threats, §75-51.
Unconscionability, §75-55.
Unfair or deceptive acts or practices.
  Provisions of article to constitute, §75-56(a).

DEBT COUNSELING.
Credit repair services, §§66-220 to 66-226.
  See CREDIT REPAIR SERVICES.

DEBT OF ANOTHER, PROMISE TO ANSWER.
Contract required to be in writing, §22-1.

DEBTOR LEAVING STATE.
Arrest, §1-355.

DEBTORS AND CREDITORS.
Assignments for benefit of creditors.
  See ASSIGNMENTS FOR BENEFIT OF
    CREDITORS.
Commercial code generally.
  Defined, §25-1-201(b)(12).
  Subordinated obligations, §25-1-310.
Community property rights at death, §31C-8.
Conveyances.
  Intent to defraud, §§39-23.1 to 39-23.12.
    See FRAUDULENT TRANSFERS.
Debts generally.
  See DEBTS.
Decedents' estates.
  Community property rights at death, §31C-8.
  Limitation of actions.
    Action against decedent's personal or real
      representative, §1-49.
  Notice for claims, §§28A-14-1 to 28A-14-3.
    Notice to creditors without administration of
      estate, §§28A-29-1 to 28A-29-5.
  Sale, lease or mortgage of real property by heirs,
    §28A-17-12.
Executors and administrators.
  When creditors may sue on claim, §28A-18-5.
Funds transfers.
  Creditor process served on receiving bank,
    §25-4A-502.
Leases, UCC.
  Creditors' special rights, §25-2A-308.
Lien creditors.
  Lis pendens.
    Notice of filing, §1-116(d).
Limited liability companies.
  Judgment creditors rights in members interest,
    §57C-5-03.
Nonprofit corporations.
  Distribution of amounts due to unavailable
    creditors upon dissolution, §55A-14-40.
Powers of appointment.
  Limitation against creditors and purchasers for
    value, §39-35.
Sale of goods, UCC.
  Creditor's rights.
    Consignment sales, §25-2-326.
    Rights of seller's creditors against sold goods,
      §25-2-402.
    Sale on approval, §25-2-326.
    Sale or return, §25-2-326.
Settlor of trust.
  Creditor's claims against settlor.
    Trust containing spendthrift provisions.
      Power of withdrawal, §36C-5-505(b).

DEBTORS AND CREDITORS —Cont'd
Settlor of trust —Cont'd
  Creditor's claims against settlor —Cont'd
    Trust containing spendthrift provisions —Cont'd
      Rules, §36C-5-505(a).
Supplemental proceedings to recover assets,
    §§1-352 to 1-368.
  See SUPPLEMENTAL PROCEEDINGS.
Transfers.
  Intent to defraud, §§39-23.1 to 39-23.12.
    See FRAUDULENT TRANSFERS.
Trust beneficiary's creditors.
  Attachment of distributions for beneficiary's
    benefit, §36C-5-501(a).
  Discretionary trusts, §36C-5-504.
  Exceptions, §36C-5-501(b).
  Mandatory distribution overdue, §36C-5-506.
  Spendthrift provisions, §§36C-5-502, 36C-5-503.
Trustee's personal obligations.
  Trust property not subject to, §36C-5-507.

DEBTS.
Absentees in military service.
  Receivers.
    Collection and payment of debts, §28B-6.
Accounts and accounting.
  Prisons and prisoners.
    Trustee for estate of debtor, §23-20.
Adjusters, §§14-423 to 14-426.
  See DEBT ADJUSTERS.
Adoption.
  Debts and engagements contracted before, US
    Const Art VI.
Aid of rebellion, US Const Amd 14.
Alimony.
  Dependent spouse deemed creditor, §50-16.7(h).
Arrest in civil cases.
  Removal or disposition of property with intent to
    defraud creditors.
    Cases in which arrest allowed, §1-410.
Art dealers.
  Creditors of art dealer may not reach works of
    fine art on consignment with art dealer,
    §25C-4.
Assignments for benefit of creditors.
  See ASSIGNMENTS FOR BENEFIT OF
    CREDITORS.
Attachment.
  Intent to defraud creditors.
    Grounds for attachment, §1-440.3.
Attorneys at law.
  Appearance for creditor in insolvency and certain
    other proceedings.
    Unlawful for anyone except attorney, §84-9.
Bonds, surety.
  Actions on bonds.
    Officer liable for negligence in collecting debt,
      §58-76-30.
  Official bonds.
    Justification of sureties.
      Official bonds considered debts and liabilities,
        §58-72-40.
Collection agencies.
  Debt collectors, §§75-50 to 75-56.
    See DEBT COLLECTORS.
  General provisions, §§58-70-1 to 58-70-155.
    See COLLECTION AGENCIES.
Congress.
  Powers of congress, US Const Art I §8.
Consolidated city-county act.
  Assumption of debt, §§160B-16 to 160B-21.
    See CONSOLIDATED CITY-COUNTY ACT.

DEBTS —Cont'd

Consolidated city-county act —Cont'd

Limitation on indebtedness, §160B-15.

Contracts.

Promise to answer for debt of another.

Statute of frauds provisions, §22-1.

Costs.

Evidence of indebtedness.

Attorneys' fees in notes, etc., in addition to interest, §6-21.2.

Court process.

Collection of debt.

Simulation of court process in connection with collection, §14-118.1.

Credit repair services, §§66-220 to 66-226.

See CREDIT REPAIR SERVICES.

Debt collectors.

Collection agencies, §§58-70-1 to 58-70-155.

See COLLECTION AGENCIES.

General provisions, §§75-50 to 75-56.

See DEBT COLLECTORS.

Decedents' estates.

Debts and claims generally.

See DECEDENTS' ESTATES.

Notice to creditors, §§28A-14-1 to 28A-14-3.

Definitions.

Setoff debt collection act, §105A-2.

Electric membership corporations.

Contracting debt.

Specific grant of power, §117-18.

Executors and administrators.

Appointment of executor.

No discharge of debt due to decedent's estate, §28A-15-11.

Notice to creditors, §§28A-14-1 to 28A-14-3.

Satisfying debts or claims against decedent's estate, §28A-13-3(a).

False swearing by imprisoned debtor, §23-43.

Fiduciaries.

Transfer of negotiable instruments.

Security for personal debt.

Liability of creditor or transferee, §32-5.

Fraud.

Court process in connection with collection of claim.

Simulation of court process, §14-118.1.

Garnishment.

Payment to defendant by garnishee, §1-440.31.

General assembly.

Indebtedness of state.

Requirements for passage of revenue bills, NC Const Art II §23.

Imprisonment for debt, NC Const Art I §28.

Joint and several debtors, §§1-113, 1-114.

Life insurance.

Exemption of benefits from claims of creditors except in case of fraud, §58-58-115.

Local government finance.

Authorized purposes, NC Const Art V §4.

Certain debts barred, NC Const Art V §4.

General provisions, §§159-1 to 159-188.

See LOCAL GOVERNMENT FINANCE.

Outstanding debt, NC Const Art V §4.

Regulation, NC Const Art V §4.

Two-thirds limitation in increase, NC Const Art V §4.

Missing persons.

Receivers.

Power to collect or pay, §28C-8.

Not to be questioned, US Const Amd 14.

DEBTS —Cont'd

Oaths.

Prisons and prisoners.

Trustee for estate of debtor, §23-20.

Partition.

Petition by judgment creditor of cotenant, §46-5.

Personal property.

Exemptions from process, NC Const Art X §1.

Powers of appointment.

Limitation against creditors and purchasers for value.

Requisites, §39-35.

Powers of congress, US Const Art I §8.

Prisons and prisoners.

Bankruptcy and insolvency, §§23-18 to 23-45.

See DISCHARGE OF INSOLVENT PRISONERS.

Bounds of jail.

Imprisoned debtor may take benefit of bounds, §23-45.

False swearing.

Perjury, §23-43.

Fees.

Creditor liable for jail fee, §23-42.

Fraud.

Superior or district court tries issue, §23-39.

Jail bounds.

Imprisoned debtor may take benefit of prison bounds, §23-45.

Perjury.

False swearing, §23-43.

Trustee for estate of debtor.

Accounting, §23-20.

Appointments.

Successor, §23-22.

Superior court appoints, §23-19.

Bonds, surety.

Release of insolvent upon giving bond, §23-40.

Surrender of principal.

Surety authorized to surrender, §23-41.

Copy of sentence to be produced, §23-19.

Court may appoint several trustees, §23-21.

Creditor liable for jail fees, §23-42.

Duties, §23-20.

False swearing.

Penalized as perjury, §23-43.

Fraud.

Superior or district court tries issue, §23-39.

Multiple trustees may be appointed, §23-21.

Oath, §23-20.

Persons who may apply for trustee, §23-18.

Powers, §23-44.

Removal, §23-22.

Superior court appoints, §23-19.

Probate and registration.

Conveyances.

Registration necessary to pass title as against creditors, §47-18.

Proprietary schools.

Evidence of indebtedness with unlicensed schools null and void, §115D-97.

Retail installment sales generally, §§25A-1 to 25A-45.

See RETAIL INSTALLMENT SALES.

Secured transactions.

General provisions governing secured debt, §§25-9-101 to 25-9-710.

See SECURED TRANSACTIONS.

Small estates.

Debts of decedent, §§28A-25-1 to 28A-25-6.

See SMALL ESTATES.

DEBTS —Cont'd
State debt.
See STATE DEBT.
Statewide accounts receivable program,
§§147-86.20 to 147-86.27.
See STATEWIDE ACCOUNTS RECEIVABLE PROGRAM.
Statute of frauds.
Promise to answer for debt of another.
Writing required, §22-1.
Revival of debt of bankrupt, §22-4.
Suretyship.
Joinder of debtor by surety, §26-12.
Notice to creditor to take action.
Effect of failure of creditor to take action.
Discharge, §26-9(a).
Separate notice of co-sureties, co-indorsers or co-guarantors, §26-9(c).
Waiver of defense provisions, §26-9(b).
Evidence of notice, §26-8(c).
Method of giving notice, §26-8(a).
Service of notice returned, §26-8(b).
Surety, indorser or guarantor may notify creditor to take action, §26-7(a).
Applicability of section, §26-7(d).
Extent of notice, §26-7(b).
Holder or owner of obligation to disclose other sureties, indorsers or guarantors, §26-7(c).
Tax debts.
Collection of tax debts.
Collection assistance fee, §105-243.1(d).
Use of fee by department, §105-243.1(e).
Contracting for collection, §105-243.1(b).
Definitions, §105-243.1(a).
Notice that debt submitted to contractor for collection, §105-243.1(b).
Outsourcing collection, §105-243.1(b).
Report by department, §105-243.1(f).
Secrecy of collection.
Contract for collection conditioned on, §105-243.1(c).
Termination of contract for collection.
Violation of secrecy requirement, §105-243.1(c).
Status of tax as debt, §105-238.
Torrens system registration.
Method of transfer.
Land conveyed as security, §43-36.
Transfers to minors.
Obligor of debt owed to minor.
Transfer for benefit of minor, §33A-7.
Trusts and trustees.
Trustee for estate of debtor.
Prisons and prisoners. See within this heading, "Prisons and prisoners."
Venue.
Deficiency debtor, §1-76.1.
Workers' compensation.
Claims exempt from debt, §97-21.

DECEDENTS' ESTATES.
Absentees in military service, §§28B-1 to 28B-10.
See ABSENTEES IN MILITARY SERVICE.
Accounts and accounting.
Collectors.
Settlement of accounts, §28A-11-4(b).
Executors and administrators, §§28A-21-1 to 28A-21-6.
See EXECUTORS AND ADMINISTRATORS.

DECEDENTS' ESTATES —Cont'd
Actions.
Powers of personal representatives or fiduciaries, §28A-13-3(a).
Recovery of estate property, §28A-15-12(a1) to (d).
Survival of actions, §28A-18-1(a).
Actions in favor of decedent which do not survive, §28A-18-1(b).
Transfers or conveyances by decedent to defraud creditors.
Actions by personal representative to recover, §28A-15-10.
Administration of estates.
Costs of administration, §7A-307.
Additional costs assessable on appeal or upon transfer or cause, §7A-307(d).
Amount of facilities fee, §7A-307(b).
Assessment of costs, §7A-307(a).
Completeness and exclusivity of costs, §7A-307(c).
Courtroom and related judicial facilities.
Amount of facilities fee, §7A-307(b).
Use of facilities, §7A-307(a).
General court of justice.
Support of court, §7A-307(a).
Liability of parties for costs, §7A-307(e).
Miscellaneous fees, §7A-307(b1).
Summary administration, §§28A-28-1 to 28A-28-7.
See within this heading, "Summary administration."
Administrators generally.
See EXECUTORS AND ADMINISTRATORS.
Adoption.
Inheritance rights of child subject to adoption.
Consequences of consent by parent to adoption, §48-3-607(c).
Intestate succession, §29-17.
Share of after-adopted children, §28A-22-2.
Advancements, §§29-23 to 29-29.
Death of advancee before intestate donor, §29-27.
Effect, §29-25.
Generally, §29-23.
Gift inter vivos.
Presumption of gift, §29-24.
Inventory.
Failure to give inventory, §29-28.
Release by advancee, §29-29.
Taking into account and computation of estate, §29-23.
Valuation.
Determination, §29-26.
After-born children.
Shares, §28A-22-2.
Agriculture.
Continuation of farming operations, §§28A-13-3, 28A-13-4.
Crops of deceased persons, §28A-15-1.
Ancillary administration, §§28A-26-1 to 28A-26-9.
See EXECUTORS AND ADMINISTRATORS.
Annexation of wills.
Powers and duties of administrator with will annexed, §28A-13-8.
Annuities.
Killing decedents.
Additional liability for annuity company, §31A-11(c).
Proceeds payable to slayer, §31A-11(a).
Appeals.
Estate proceedings.
Applicable provisions, §28A-2-9(a), (c).

DECEDENTS' ESTATES —Cont'd

Appeals —Cont'd

Special proceedings.

Applicable provisions, §28A-2-9(b), (c).

Appointment.

Annexation of will.

Powers and duties of administrator with will annexed, §28A-13-8.

Powers and duties of successor personal representative, §28A-13-7.

Appraisers.

Employment, §28A-20-4.

Arbitration and award.

Disputed claims, §28A-19-15.

Assets.

Abatement, §28A-15-5(a).

Availability for discharge of debts and claims, §28A-15-1(a).

Encumbered assets.

Payment of encumbrance by personal representative, §28A-15-4.

Joint deposit accounts.

Sources of assets to satisfy claims against estate, §28A-15-10(a).

Order in which assets appropriated, §28A-15-5(a).

Powers of personal representative, §28A-13-3.

Special proceedings to obtain possession, custody, etc.

Jurisdiction.

Clerk of superior court, §28A-2-5.

Attachment.

Defendant's death after levy, §1-440.34.

Attorneys specializing in estate planning and probate law.

Certification standards, Bar Rules D.2301 to D.2307.

Auctions and auctioneers.

Sales in settlement in decedents' estates.

Exemptions from auction provisions, §85B-2.

Bonds, surety.

Collectors, §28A-11-2.

Debts and claims.

Distribution of estate despite contingent or unliquidated claim.

Bond of heirs and devisees, §28A-19-5.

Executors and administrators, §§28A-8-1 to 28A-8-6.

See EXECUTORS AND ADMINISTRATORS.

Burial places and gravestones.

Authority to provide suitable burial place, §28A-19-9(b).

Authority to provide suitable gravestone, §28A-19-9(a).

Costs associated with.

Claims against estate.

Third class claims, §28A-19-6(a).

Caveat.

Effect on estate administration, §31-36.

Jurisdiction.

Clerks of superior court jurisdiction in estate proceedings.

Limitation on jurisdiction, §28A-2-4(c).

Cemeteries.

Perpetual care of cemetery lot, §28A-19-10.

Children born out of wedlock, intestate succession.

Descent and distribution upon intestacy, §29-20.

Legitimated children.

Succession, by, through and from, §29-18.

Person's illegitimate child entitled to take by, through and from, §29-19(b).

DECEDENTS' ESTATES —Cont'd

Children born out of wedlock, intestate succession —Cont'd

Shares of others than surviving spouse, §29-22.

Succession by, through and from, §29-19(a) to (d).

Surviving spouse.

Share of surviving spouse of illegitimate intestate, §29-21.

Shares of others than surviving spouse, §29-22.

Claims against estate. See within this heading, "Debts and claims."

Collectors.

Actions against collectors.

Service on or appearance of one binds all, §28A-18-4.

Appointment, §28A-11-1.

Termination.

Duties upon termination, §28A-11-4(b).

Bond, §28A-11-2.

Commissions, §28A-23-3.

Collectors guilty of misconduct not entitled to commission, §28A-23-3(e).

Computation, §28A-23-3(f).

Construction of section, §28A-23-3(d).

Determination of amount, §28A-23-3(b).

Entitlement, §28A-23-3(a).

Limitation on amount, §28A-23-3(c).

Statutory language, use to determine, §28A-23-3(h).

Stipulated amount or method of payment, §28A-23-3(g).

Compensation, §28A-11-5.

Counsel fees.

Attorneys serving as collectors, §28A-23-4.

Defined, §28A-1-1(1).

Duties, §28A-11-3(a).

Estate proceedings.

Examination of persons believed to have possession of estate property, §28A-15-12(b1).

Costs of proceedings, responsibility, §28A-15-12(c).

Cumulative nature of remedy, §28A-15-12(d).

Examination of accounts, §28A-11-4(c).

Letters of collection, §28A-11-1.

Oaths, §28A-11-2.

Personal property.

Court ordered sale or lease, §28A-16-2(a) to (d).

Powers, §28A-11-3(b).

When collectors' powers ceased, §28A-11-4(a).

Qualifications, §28A-11-1.

Small estates.

Subsequently appointed collectors, §28A-25-5.

Commissions.

Personal representatives, §28A-23-3.

Community property rights.

Disposition at death, §§31C-1 to 31C-12.

See COMMUNITY PROPERTY.

Compensation.

Personal representatives.

Commissions generally, §28A-23-3.

Compromise and settlement.

Family settlements.

Approval of settlement agreements, §28A-2-10.

Jurisdiction.

Clerks of superior court jurisdiction in estate proceedings, §28A-2-4(a).

Powers of personal representatives, §28A-13-3(a).

Settlement of estate proceedings, §28A-2-4(a).

Contracts.

Debts and claims.

Limitation on claims based on contract, §28A-19-3(b).

DECEDENTS' ESTATES —Cont'd
Contracts —Cont'd
Powers of personal representative, §28A-13-3(a).
Costs.
Actions to recover estate property, §28A-15-12(c).
Administration of estates, §7A-307.
Additional costs assessable on appeal or upon
transfer of cause, §7A-307(d).
Amount of facilities fee, §7A-307(b).
Assessment of costs, §7A-307(a).
Completeness and exclusivity of costs,
§7A-307(c).
Courtroom and related judicial facilities.
Amount of facilities fee, §7A-307(b).
Use of facilities, §7A-306(a).
General court of justice.
Support of court, §7A-307(a).
Liability of parties for costs, §7A-307(e).
Miscellaneous fees, §7A-307(b1).
Reference of claim against deceased person.
Recovery of fees and other necessary
disbursements, §6-31.
Creditors.
Jurisdiction.
Clerks of superior court jurisdiction in estate
proceedings.
Limitation on jurisdiction, §28A-2-4(c).
Priorities among creditors, §28A-2-4(a).
Notice to creditors, §§28A-14-1 to 28A-14-3.
Without administration of estate, §§28A-29-1 to
28A-29-5.
Transfers to hinder, delay or defraud.
Clerks of superior court jurisdiction in estate
proceedings.
Limitation on jurisdiction, §28A-2-4(c).
Crops.
Ungathered crops at death of decedent,
§28A-15-1(d).
Damages.
Jurisdiction.
Clerks of superior court jurisdiction in estate
proceedings.
Limitation on jurisdiction, §28A-2-4(c).
Death presumption, §28C-1.
Debts and claims.
Arbitration and award.
Referral of disputed claim, §28A-19-15.
Assets available for discharge of debts and claims,
§28A-15-1.
Claims due representative not preferred,
§28A-19-12.
Claims not due, §28A-19-14.
Classes of claims, §28A-19-6(a).
Preferences within class prohibited, §28A-19-13.
Commission of personal representative,
§28A-19-6(b).
Contingent claims.
Payment of contingent or unliquidated claims,
§28A-19-5.
Contracts.
Limitation on claims based on contract,
§28A-19-3(b).
Costs.
When costs against representative allowed,
§28A-19-18.
Determination of property for discharge of debt,
§28A-15-1(b).
Disputed claims.
Claims not referred barred in three months,
§28A-19-16.
Referral, §28A-19-15.

DECEDENTS' ESTATES —Cont'd
Debts and claims —Cont'd
Equitable distribution.
Action for distribution.
Claimant may file, §28A-19-19(c).
Claims against estate, provisions inapplicable,
§28A-19-19(a).
Distribution, agreement by representative
providing for, §28A-19-19(b).
Fraudulent transfers or conveyances.
Actions by personal representative to recover,
§28A-15-10(b).
Limitation of actions.
Disputed claims not referred barred in three
months, §28A-19-16.
Pleading statute of limitations, §28A-19-11.
Presentation of claims, §28A-19-3(a) to (j).
Marital or divisible property.
Action for distribution.
Claimant may file, §28A-19-19(c).
Claims against estate, provisions inapplicable,
§28A-19-19(a).
Distribution, agreement by representative
providing for, §28A-19-19(b).
Mortgages.
Limitations on presentation of claims.
Exception as to enforcement of mortgage,
§28A-19-3(g).
Notice to creditors, §§28A-14-1 to 28A-14-3.
See EXECUTORS AND ADMINISTRATORS.
Notice to creditors without administration of
estate, §§28A-29-1 to 28A-29-5.
See EXECUTORS AND ADMINISTRATORS.
Order of payment.
Classification of claims, §28A-19-6(a).
Commission of personal representative,
§28A-19-6(b).
Payment of claims and charges, §28A-19-4.
Preferences within class prohibited, §28A-19-13.
Presentation of claims.
Affidavit of claimant.
Right of personal representative or collector
to require, §28A-19-2(b).
Contents, §28A-19-1(a).
Further information required by personal
representative or collector, §28A-19-2(a).
Limitations on presentation, §28A-19-3(a) to (j).
Exceptions, §28A-19-3(g) to (i).
Notice of claims.
Effect, §28A-19-3(d) to (f).
State of North Carolina, subdivisions and
agencies.
Applicability of limitations, §28A-19-3(j).
Manner of presentation, §28A-19-1.
Method of presentation, §28A-19-1(a).
Substitution of personal representatives,
§28A-19-1(c).
When commencement of action deemed
presentation, §28A-19-1(b).
Writing required, §28A-19-1(a).
Rebate of interest on claims not due, §28A-19-14.
Reopening administration.
Assertion of claims already barred in opened
administration, §28A-23-5.
Retaining property in satisfaction of
representative claim, §28A-19-12.
Satisfaction of claims other than by payment,
§28A-19-7.
Small estates.
Debts owed decedent, §§28A-25-1 to 28A-25-6.
See SMALL ESTATES.

DECEDENTS' ESTATES —Cont'd
Debts and claims —Cont'd
Tentative trusts.
Sources of assets to satisfy claims,
§28A-15-10(a).
When charges and claims paid, §28A-19-4.
Wrongful death.
Application of recovery to payment of debts and
claims against estate, §28A-15-10(c).
Declaratory judgments.
Jurisdiction.
Clerks of superior court jurisdiction in estate
proceedings.
Preservation of right to file for declaratory
judgment, §28A-2-4(b).
Definitions, §28A-1-1.
Federal estate tax.
Apportionment, §28A-27-1.
Killing decedents, §31A-3.
Deposits.
Powers of personal representative or fiduciary,
§28A-13-3(a).
Devise.
Construction of term appearing in statute, §12-3.
Devisees.
Ascertainment of heirs or devisees.
Jurisdiction.
Clerks of superior court jurisdiction in estate
proceedings, §28A-2-4(a).
Construction of term appearing in statute, §12-3.
Defined, §28A-1-1(1a).
Service of process, §28A-13-3.
Disbursement.
Scheme of distribution, §28A-22-1.
**Discretion of executor or trustee over
distributions,** §28A-22-8.
Distribution.
After-born and after-adopted children.
Shares, §28A-22-2.
Discretion of executor or trustee, §28A-22-8.
Federal marital deduction.
Agreements with taxing authorities, §28A-22-6.
Guardians, §28A-22-7.
Inoperative trust, assets of, §28A-22-10.
Known but unlocated devisees or heirs,
§28A-22-9(a) to (e).
Minors.
Guardian or parent of minor, §28A-22-7(a) to
(d).
Nonresident trustees.
Appointment of process agent required,
§28A-22-4(a), (b).
Parents, §28A-22-7.
Satisfaction of devises and transfers.
Distribution of assets in kind, §28A-22-5(a).
Requirements, §28A-22-5(b).
Special proceeding against unknown heirs,
§28A-22-3.
Unlocated devisees or heirs, §28A-22-9(a) to (e).
Elective life estate.
Marital interest in real property, §29-30(a) to (h).
Elective share of surviving spouse, §§30-3.1 to
30-3.6, 31-5.3.
Equitable distribution.
Action against surviving spouse.
Collaborative law proceedings, §50-79.
Limitation of actions, §50-20(l).
Action for distribution.
Claimant may file, §28A-19-19(c).
Claims against estate, provisions inapplicable,
§28A-19-19(a).
Eighth class claim, §28A-19-6(a).

DECEDENTS' ESTATES —Cont'd
Equitable distribution —Cont'd
Distribution, agreement by representative
providing for, §28A-19-19(b).
Escheats.
Unclaimed personalty on settlements of decedents'
estates to the escheat fund, §116B-3.
Estate proceedings.
Appeals.
Applicable provisions, §28A-2-9(a), (c).
Consolidation of estate proceeding and civil action,
§28A-2-6(f).
Orders upon consolidation, joinder or transfer,
§28A-2-6(i).
Contested estate proceedings.
Commencement, §28A-2-6(a).
Pleadings, §28A-2-6(c).
Defined, §28A-1-1(1b).
Elective share of surviving spouse.
Procedure for elective share proceedings,
§30-3.4(e1).
Examination of persons believed to have
possession of estate property, §28A-15-12(b1).
Costs of proceedings, responsibility,
§28A-15-12(c).
Cumulative nature of remedy, §28A-15-12(d).
Extension of time, §28A-2-6(d).
Intestate succession.
Controversies concerning intestate succession.
Determination as estate proceeding, §29-12.1.
Joinder of claims, §28A-2-6(g).
Orders upon consolidation, joinder or transfer,
§28A-2-6(i).
Jurisdiction.
Clerk of superior court, §28A-2-1.
Declaratory judgment.
Preservation of right to file for declaratory
judgment, §28A-2-4(b).
Limitation on jurisdiction, §28A-2-4(c).
Subject matter jurisdiction, §28A-2-4(a).
Parties.
Representation of parties, §28A-2-7(a).
Service on representative, §28A-2-7(b).
Waiver of notice, §28A-2-8.
Personal representative's powers as to,
§28A-13-3(d).
Probate of wills.
Solemn form, §28A-2A-7(a).
Rules of civil procedure.
Applicability, §28A-2-6(e).
Settlements, §28A-2-10.
Transfer of estate proceeding.
Notice of transfer, §§28A-2-4(a), 28A-2-6(h).
Orders upon consolidation, joinder or transfer,
§28A-2-6(i).
Uncontested estate proceedings.
Commencement, §28A-2-6(b).
Estate taxes, §§105-32.1 to 105-32.8.
See ESTATE TAXES.
Evidence.
Killing decedent.
Record determining slayer admissible, §31A-13.
Examinations.
Persons or corporations believed to have
possession of property of decedent,
§28A-15-12(a1) to (d).
Executions.
Defendant dying in execution.
Rights against property of defendant, §1-312.
Executors generally.
See EXECUTORS AND ADMINISTRATORS.

DECEDENTS' ESTATES —Cont'd
False imprisonment.
Rights of action not surviving decedent,
§28A-18-1.
Family settlements.
Approval of settlement agreements, §28A-2-10.
Jurisdiction.
Clerks of superior court jurisdiction in estate
proceedings, §28A-2-4(a).
Farming.
Continuation of farming operations, §28A-13-4.
**Federal estate tax and generation-skipping tax
referenced in will or trust.**
Construction of formula provisions in trusts.
Applicability, §36C-1-113(b).
Construction generally, §36C-1-113(c).
Proceeding to determine settlor's intention.
Authorized, statute of limitations,
§36C-1-113(d).
Purpose, §36C-1-113(a).
Construction of formula provisions in wills.
Applicability, §31-46.1(b).
Construction generally, §31-46.1(c).
Proceeding to determine settlor's intention.
Authorized, statute of limitations, §31-46.1(d).
Purpose, §31-46.1(a).
Federal estate tax apportionment.
Collection of uncollected taxes, §28A-27-4.
Definitions, §28A-27-1.
Determination.
Personal representative, §28A-27-3(a).
Differences with federal estate tax law, §28A-27-8.
Distribution of property prior to final
apportionment, §28A-27-7(b).
Effective date of article, §28A-27-9.
Expenses, §28A-27-3(c).
Generally, §28A-27-2(a).
Inequitable apportionment, §28A-27-3(b).
Method described in will, §28A-27-2(b).
Personal representative.
Withholding amount of tax apportioned,
§28A-27-7(a).
Temporary and remainder interests.
No apportionment between, §28A-27-6.
Uncollected taxes.
Proceedings to recover, §28A-27-4.
Federal marital deduction.
Agreements with taxing authorities, §28A-22-6.
Fees.
Clerks of court.
Miscellaneous fees in administration of estates,
§7A-307(b1).
Personal representatives.
Commissions generally, §28A-23-3.
Fiduciaries.
Breach of fiduciary duty.
Jurisdiction.
Clerks of superior court jurisdiction in estate
proceedings.
Limitation on jurisdiction, §28A-2-4(c).
Collection of rent, income, etc., §32-27.
Distribution in cash or kind.
Powers which may be incorporated by reference
in trust instrument, §32-27.
General duties of representatives, §28A-13-2.
Incorporation by reference of certain powers.
Restriction on exercise of such powers,
§32-26(b), (c).
Foreign personal representatives.
Defined, §28A-1-1(2).

DECEDENTS' ESTATES —Cont'd
Fraud.
Jurisdiction.
Clerks of superior court jurisdiction in estate
proceedings.
Limitation on jurisdiction, §28A-2-4(c).
Funeral expenses.
Claims against estate.
Second class claims, preferential limitation,
§28A-19-6.
Deemed obligation of estate, §28A-19-8(a), (b).
Generation-skipping transfers.
Taxation, §105-32.1.
Gifts causa mortis.
Sources of assets to satisfy claims, §28A-15-10(a).
Guardian ad litem.
Unknown heirs.
Appointment of guardian ad litem, §28A-22-3.
Guardians.
Distribution to guardian of minor, §28A-22-7.
Heirs.
Agreements with heirs to recover share of
decedents' estates.
Provisions governing, §28A-22-11.
Ascertainment of heirs or devisees.
Jurisdiction.
Clerks of superior court jurisdiction in estate
proceedings, §28A-2-4(a).
Construed to be "children" in certain limitations,
§41-6.
Declaratory judgments.
Who may apply for declaration, §1-255.
Defined, §§28A-1-1(3), 29-2.
Guardian ad litem.
Appointment for unknown heir, §28A-22-3.
Limitations on failure of issue, §41-4.
Renunciation of succession, right to renounce,
§31B-1.
Sale, lease or mortgage of real property,
§28A-17-12.
Service of process, §28A-13-3.
Unknown heirs.
Special proceedings prior to distribution,
§28A-22-3.
Jurisdiction.
Clerk of superior court, §28A-2-5.
Waste.
Action by heirs, §1-537.
Wills.
See WILLS.
Homicide.
Killing decedent, §§31A-3 to 31A-15.
See SLAYER ACT.
Household effects.
Election of appropriate effects to be excluded from
carry over basis, §28A-13-3(a1).
Sales, §28A-16-3.
Husband and wife.
Spouse sole beneficiary.
Summary administration, §§28A-28-1 to
28A-28-7. See within this heading,
"Summary administration."
Surviving spouses.
See SURVIVING SPOUSES.
Identity theft.
Damages.
Recovery by estate, §1-539.2C(b).
Illegitimate children, intestate succession.
Descent and distribution upon intestacy, §29-20.
Legitimated children.
Succession, by, through and from, §29-18.

DECEDENTS' ESTATES —Cont'd
Illegitimate children, intestate succession
—Cont'd
Person's illegitimate child entitled to take by,
through and from, §29-19(b).
Succession by, through and from, §29-19(a) to (d).
Surviving spouses.
Share of surviving spouse of illegitimate
intestate, §29-21.
Shares of others than surviving spouse, §29-22.
Income.
Allocation of income.
Powers of personal representatives, §28A-13-3.
Inoperative trust.
Distribution of assets of, §28A-22-10.
Intestate succession.
General provisions, §§29-1 to 29-30.
See INTESTATE SUCCESSION.
Small estates, §§28A-25-1 to 28A-25-6.
See SMALL ESTATES.
Inventory.
Compelling inventory, §28A-20-2(a).
Failure to file.
Liability for costs, §28A-20-2(b).
Removal of representative, §28A-20-2(a).
Required within three months, §28A-20-1.
Supplemental inventory.
Enforcement, §28A-20-3(b).
Erroneous or misleading inventory,
§28A-20-3(a).
Investments.
Powers of personal representative or fiduciary,
§28A-13-3(a).
Joint tenants and tenants in common.
Survivorship in joint tenancy, §41-2.
Judgments.
Claims against estates.
Sixth class claim, §28A-19-6(a).
Jurisdiction.
Assistant clerk of superior court, §28A-2-2.
Clerk of superior court, §28A-2-1.
Estate proceedings.
Declaratory judgment.
Preservation of right to file for declaratory
judgment, §28A-2-4(b).
Limitation on jurisdiction, §28A-2-4(c).
Special proceedings, §28A-2-5.
Jurisdiction where clerk interested, §28A-2-3.
Killing decedent, §§31A-3 to 31A-15.
See SLAYER ACT.
Kinship.
Degree computation, §§29-5, 104A-1.
Interpretation rule, §41-6.2.
Listing of personal property, §105-306.
Partnership rights, §59-55.
Renunciation of property interest, §31B-1.
Wills, §41-6.1.
Probate of nuncupative, §28A-2A-10.
Workers' compensation, §97-10.1.
Order of compensation, §97-37.
Out-of-state accidents, §97-36.
Payments, §§97-38, 97-40.
Leases.
Abatement, §28A-15-5(b).
Personal property.
Sale or lease, §§28A-16-1 to 28A-16-3.
Real property.
Personal representative leasing, §28A-17-11.
Void leases, §28A-17-12(a).
Legitimation, effect, §49-11.
Mother married, legitimation when, §49-12.1.

DECEDENTS' ESTATES —Cont'd
Legitimation, effect —Cont'd
Subsequent marriage, legitimation by, §49-12.
Letters testamentary.
Certified copy of record.
Admissibility as evidence, §8-36.
Libel and slander.
Rights of action not surviving defendant,
§28A-18-1.
Liens.
Actions against personal representatives.
No lien created by suit, §28A-19-17.
Claims against decedent's estate.
First class claims, §28A-19-6.
Nonexoneration of encumbered property,
§28A-15-3.
Payment of encumbered assets, §28A-15-4.
Limitation of actions.
Claims against the state.
Pleading statute of limitations, §28A-19-11.
Creditor of decedent against representative.
Seven-year limitation, §1-49.
Equitable distribution claim against surviving
spouse, §50-20(l).
Injury to incorporeal hereditament.
Six-year limitation, §1-50(a).
Presentation of claims, §28A-19-3(a) to (j).
Limited personal representatives.
Notice to creditors without administration of
estate, §§28A-29-1 to 28A-29-5.
See EXECUTORS AND ADMINISTRATORS.
Loans.
Borrowing money.
Powers of personal representatives or
fiduciaries, §28A-13-3(a).
Lottery winners.
Payment of state lottery prizes.
Estate of deceased winner, §18C-132(h).
Marital or divisible property.
Action for distribution.
Claimant may file, §28A-19-19(c).
Claims against estate, provisions inapplicable,
§28A-19-19(a).
Distribution, agreement by representative
providing for, §28A-19-19(b).
Medicaid.
Medicaid estate recovery plan, §108A-70.5.
Military affairs.
Absentees in military service, §§28B-1 to 28B-10.
See ABSENTEES IN MILITARY SERVICE.
Minors.
Distribution to parent or guardian of minor,
§28A-22-7.
Missing persons, §§28C-1 to 28C-22.
See MISSING PERSONS.
Mortgages and deeds of trust.
Abatement, §28A-15-5(b).
Debts and claims.
Limitations on presentation of claims.
Exception as to enforcement of mortgage,
§28A-19-3(g).
Mortgaging property for payment of debts,
§28A-15-1(c).
Defined, §28A-1-1(4).
Encumbered assets.
Payment, §28A-15-4.
Nonexoneration of encumbered property,
§28A-15-3.
Murder.
Killing decedent, §§31A-3 to 31A-15.
See SLAYER ACT.

DECEDENTS' ESTATES —Cont'd
Negligence.
Jurisdiction.
Clerks of superior court jurisdiction in estate
proceedings.
Limitation on jurisdiction, §28A-2-4(c).
Newly discovered property.
Reopening administration, §28A-23-5.
Notary.
Death.
Notice to secretary, delivery of seal by estate,
§10B-55(c).
Oaths.
Collectors, §28A-11-2.
Parent and child.
Distribution to parent, §28A-22-7.
Parties.
Costs in administration of estates.
Liability for costs, §7A-307(e).
Defined, §28A-1-1(4a).
Estate proceedings.
Representation of parties, §28A-2-7(a).
Service on representative, §28A-2-7(b).
Waiver of notice, §28A-2-8.
Personal property.
Actions by personal representative to recover
property, §28A-15-12(a1).
Costs of proceedings, responsibility,
§28A-15-12(c).
Cumulative nature of remedy, §28A-15-12(d).
Assets available for discharge of debts and claims,
§28A-15-1.
Examination of persons believed to have
possession of estate property, §28A-15-12(b1).
Costs of proceedings, responsibility,
§28A-15-12(c).
Cumulative nature of remedy, §28A-15-12(d).
Nonexoneration of encumbered property,
§28A-15-3.
Powers of personal representative, §28A-13-3.
Sale or lease.
Court ordered sale or lease, §28A-16-2(a) to (d).
Household furnishings, §28A-16-3.
Power of personal representative to sell or
lease, §§28A-13-3, 28A-16-1(a).
Special report not required, §28A-16-1(b).
Title and right of possession, §28A-15-2(a).
Personal representatives.
Defined, §28A-1-1(5).
General provisions.
See EXECUTORS AND ADMINISTRATORS.
Person defined, §28A-1-1(4b).
Persons interested in estate.
Relation to persons, §28A-13-2.
Phase II payments.
Tobacco growers and quota owner.
Property of distributees, §28A-15-9.1.
Powers of attorney.
Powers conferred by statutory short form, §32A-2.
Presumption of death, §28C-1.
Pretermitted children.
Shares, §28A-22-2.
Principal and income act.
Apportionment of receipts and disbursements
when decedent dies, §37A-3-302(a) to (c).
Determination of net income, §37A-2-201.
Distribution from estate during administration of
trust, §37A-4-402.
Distribution of net income, §§37A-2-201,
37A-2-202.

DECEDENTS' ESTATES —Cont'd
Principal and income act —Cont'd
General provisions, §§37A-1-101 to 37A-6-602.
See PRINCIPAL AND INCOME ACT.
Probate of wills, §§28A-2A-1 to 28A-2A-23.
See WILLS.
Public administrators, §§28A-12-1 to 28A-12-8.
See EXECUTORS AND ADMINISTRATORS.
Real property.
Abandoning or relinquishing rights in property.
Powers of personal representatives or
fiduciaries, §28A-13-3(a).
Actions by personal representative to recover
property, §28A-15-12(a1).
Costs of proceedings, responsibility,
§28A-15-12(c).
Cumulative nature of remedy, §28A-15-12(d).
Assets available for discharge of debts and claims,
§28A-15-1.
Examination of persons believed to have
possession of estate property, §28A-15-12(b1).
Costs of proceedings, responsibility,
§28A-15-12(c).
Cumulative nature of remedy, §28A-15-12(d).
Executors and administrators.
See EXECUTORS AND ADMINISTRATORS.
Nonexoneration of encumbered property,
§28A-15-3.
Sale, lease or mortgage, §§28A-17-1 to 28A-17-13.
See EXECUTORS AND ADMINISTRATORS.
Summary administration.
Spouses as to real property.
Effect of clerks order, §28A-28-4(b).
Title and possession, §28A-15-2(b).
Record of administration.
Authenticated copy of record.
Admissibility as evidence, §8-36.
Reference of claim against deceased person.
Cost.
Recovery of fees and other necessary
disbursements, §6-31.
Renunciation.
Power of personal representative, §28A-13-3.
Reopening administration, §28A-23-5.
Safe deposit boxes, §28A-15-3.
Clerk of court.
Presence not required, §28A-15-13(c).
Presence required, §28A-15-13(b).
Opening and inventorying, §28A-15-3.
Definitions, §28A-15-13(a).
Release of contents by financial institution,
§28A-15-13(e).
Tax waiver, not required, §28A-15-13(f).
Will or testamentary instrument in box,
§28A-15-13(d).
Secured transactions.
Financing statements.
Name of debtor and secured party, §25-9-503(a).
Service of process.
Devisees and heirs made parties, §28A-13-3.
Distribution to nonresident trustees.
Appointment of process agent required,
§28A-22-4(a), (b).
Estate proceedings.
Contested estate proceedings.
Commencement, §28A-2-6(a).
Representation of parties.
Service on representative, §28A-2-7(b).
Simultaneous death, revised act, §§28A-24-1 to
28A-24-8.
See SIMULTANEOUS DEATH.

DECEDENTS' ESTATES —Cont'd
Slayer act, §31A-6.
  Killing decedent generally, §§31A-3 to 31A-15.
    See SLAYER ACT.
Small estates, §§28A-25-1 to 28A-25-6.
  See SMALL ESTATES.
Special proceedings.
  Appeals.
    Applicable provisions, §28A-2-9(b), (c).
  Jurisdiction.
    Clerk of superior court, §28A-2-5.
State lottery winners.
  Payment of state lottery prizes.
    Estate of deceased winner, §18C-132(h).
Stock and stockholders.
  Powers of personal representative or fiduciary,
    §28A-13-3.
  Selling or exercising stock subscription or
    conversion rights.
    Powers of personal representatives or
      fiduciaries, §28A-13-3.
Summary administration, §§28A-28-1 to
    28A-28-7.
  Appointment of personal representative or
    collector.
    Discharge of spouses liability, §28A-28-7(b).
  Clerks order, §§28A-28-3, 28A-28-4.
    Spouses assumption of liabilities, §28A-28-6.
  Order by clerk, §§28A-28-3, 28A-28-4.
    Spouses assumption of liabilities, §28A-28-6.
  Personal representative.
    Discharge of spouses liability on appointment,
      §28A-28-7(b).
    Petition for appointment, §28A-28-7.
  Petition by surviving spouse, §28A-28-1.
    Contents, §28A-28-2(a).
    Filing, §28A-28-2(b).
    Signature, §28A-28-2(a).
  Real property.
    Spouses as to real property.
      Effect of clerks order, §28A-28-4(b).
  Spousal assumption of debt, §28A-28-6.
  Transfer of property to surviving spouse.
    Action to compel, §28A-28-5.
    Effect, §28A-28-5.
    Effect of clerks order, §28A-28-4(a).
  When authorized, §28A-28-1.
Superior courts.
  Administration of decedents' estates.
    Original jurisdiction in probate and
      administration of decedents' estates,
      §7A-241.
    Transfer of civil causes, §7A-257.
  Clerks, appeals of estate matters, §1-301.3.
Surviving spouses.
  Elective share, §31-5.3.
  Spouse as sole beneficiary.
    Summary administration, §§28A-28-1 to
      28A-28-7. See within this heading,
      "Summary administration."
  Year's allowance, §§30-15 to 30-31.2.
    See SURVIVING SPOUSES.
Taxation.
  Carry over provisions.
    Election of appropriate household effects,
      §28A-13-3(a1).
  Claims against estate.
    Fourth and fifth class claims, §28A-19-6.
  Domicile of decedent.
    Agreements with respect to, §105-240.1.

DECEDENTS' ESTATES —Cont'd
Taxation —Cont'd
  Estate taxes, §§105-32.1 to 105-32.8.
    See ESTATE TAXES.
  Excess funds, §28A-15-9.
  Federal estate tax.
    Apportionment, §§28A-27-1 to 28A-27-9.
    Formula provisions in trusts referencing.
      Construction applicable to estates of
        decedents dying in 2010, §36C-1-113.
    Formula provisions in wills referencing.
      Construction applicable to estates of
        decedents dying in 2010, §31-46.1.
  Federal income tax refunds, §28A-15-6.
    Separate returns, §28A-15-7.
  Federal marital deduction.
    Agreements with taxing authorities, §28A-22-6.
  Generation-skipping transfers, §105-32.1.
  Income tax.
    Estates and trusts, §§105-160 to 105-160.8.
      See INCOME TAX.
  Joint returns.
    Federal income tax refunds, §28A-15-6.
  Powers of personal representatives or fiduciaries,
    §28A-13-3(a).
  Property taxes.
    Preference accorded taxes in liquidation of
      debtors' estates, §105-365.
  Separate returns.
    Federal income tax refunds, §28A-15-7.
  State income tax returns, §28A-15-8.
Title.
  Personal property, §28A-15-2(a).
  Real property, §28A-15-2(b).
Tobacco growers and quota owners.
  Phase II payments.
    Property of distributees, §28A-15-9.1.
Transfers to minors.
  Authorized by will or trust, §33A-5.
  Irrevocable transfer for benefit of minor.
    Authority of personal representative or trustee
      to make as custodian, §33A-6(a), (c).
Trusts and trustees.
  Distribution to nonresident trustees.
    Appointment of process agent required,
      §28A-22-4(a), (b).
  General provisions, §§36C-1-101 to 36C-11-1106.
    See TRUSTS AND TRUSTEES.
  Tentative trusts.
    Sources of assets to satisfy claims against
      estate, §28A-15-10(a).
**Uniform transfer on death security
    registration act,** §§41-40 to 41-51.
  See UNIFORM TRANSFER ON DEATH
    SECURITY REGISTRATION ACT.
Unknown heirs.
  Special proceeding prior to distribution,
    §28A-22-3.
Venue.
  Jurisdiction.
    Clerks of superior court jurisdiction in estate
      proceedings.
      Limitation on jurisdiction, §28A-2-4(c).
Wages due decedent's employees.
  Claims against estates.
    Seventh class claim, §28A-19-6(a).
Wills.
  General provisions, §§31-1 to 31-47.
    See WILLS.
Witnesses.
  Clerk of superior court.
    Jurisdiction where clerk subscribing witness,
      §28A-2-3.

DECEDENTS' ESTATES —Cont'd
Wrongful death.
Application of recovery to payment of debts and claims, §28A-15-10(c).
Killing decedent.
Acts barring property rights, §§31A-3 to 31A-15.
See SLAYER ACT.
Year's allowance, §§30-15 to 30-31.2.
See SURVIVING SPOUSES.

DECEIT.
See FRAUD.

DECEPTIVE TRADE PRACTICES, §75-1.1.
Fruit handlers, §§106-496 to 106-501.
See FRUIT HANDLERS UNFAIR PRACTICES.
Insurance unfair trade practices, §§58-63-1 to 58-63-75.
See INSURANCE UNFAIR TRADE PRACTICES.
Monopolies and restraint of trade.
See MONOPOLIES AND RESTRAINT OF TRADE.
Mortgage bankers, brokers and servicers.
Prohibited acts, §53-244.111.
Motor vehicle rentals.
Advertising and sales practices, §66-206.
Price gouging during states of disaster, §75-38.
Solicitation of contributions, §131F-21.
Vegetable handlers, §§106-496 to 106-501.
See VEGETABLE HANDLERS' UNFAIR PRACTICES.

DECLARATION OF INDEPENDENCE.
Basic education program, §115C-81(g).

DECLARATION OF WAR.
Powers of congress, US Const Art I §8.

DECLARATIONS.
Admissions.
See ADMISSIONS.
Confessions, §14-184.
Hearsay evidence.
See EVIDENCE.
Right to natural death.
Advance directive, §90-321.
Procedures in absence of declaration, §90-322.

DECLARATORY JUDGMENTS, §§1-253 to 1-267, 1A-1 Rule 57.
Administration of article.
Liberal administration, §1-264.
Administrative procedure.
Rulemaking procedure.
Temporary rules.
Rule returned to agency, §150B-21.1(b2), (c1).
Affirmative or negative in form and effect, §1-253.
Appeals.
Review, §1-258.
Attorney general.
Party to proceedings involving constitutionality, §1-260.
Authorized, §1-253.
Automobile dealers associations, §20-308.1(d).
Citation of act.
Short title, §1-267.
Construction and interpretation.
Liberal construction of provisions, §1-264.
"Person" defined, §1-265.
Uniformity of interpretation, §1-266.
Contracts.
Power of courts to construe, §1-254.
Costs, §1-263.

DECLARATORY JUDGMENTS —Cont'd
Decedents' estates.
Jurisdiction.
Clerks of superior court jurisdiction in estate proceedings.
Preservation of right to file for declaratory judgment, §28A-2-4(b).
Deeds.
Power of courts to construe, §1-254.
Discretion of court, §1-257.
Effect, §1-253.
Establishment or disestablishment of statute, ordinance or regulation.
Superior court jurisdiction, §7A-245(a).
Fiduciaries.
Renunciation compatible with fiduciary duties, §31B-1.2(b).
Who may apply for declaration, §1-255.
Forms.
Complaint for interpleader and declaratory relief, §1A-1 Rule 84.
Franchises.
Attorney general as party to proceedings involving constitutionality, §1-260.
Municipality as party to proceedings involving validity, §1-260.
Power of courts to construe, §1-254.
Guardian and ward.
Who may apply for declaration, §1-255.
Hearings.
Judge.
Hearing before judge where no issues of fact raised or jury trial waived, §1-262.
Heirs.
Who may apply for declaration, §1-255.
Hospital, medical and dental service corporations.
Protection or enforcement of rights of public, §58-65-132(d).
Instruments.
Power of courts to construe, §1-254.
Jury.
Hearing before judge where no issues of fact raised or jury trial waived, §1-262.
Trial by jury, §1-261.
Waiver of jury trial.
Hearing before judge, §1-262.
Meetings violation.
Public bodies, §§143-318.16A to 143-318.16C.
Motor fuel marketing violations, §75-86.
Notice.
Hearing before judge, §1-262.
Ordinances.
Municipality as party to proceedings affecting validity, §1-260.
Power of courts to construe, §1-254.
Parties, §1-260.
Who may apply for declaration, §1-255.
Personal representatives.
Who may apply for declaration, §1-255.
Petitions.
Supplemental relief, §1-259.
Power of courts, §§1-253, 1-254.
Purpose of article, §1-264.
Refusal to render or enter.
Discretion of court, §1-257.
Removal of uncertainty by judgment or decree.
Enumeration of declarations not exclusive, §1-256.
Renunciation.
Right of fiduciary to institute, §31B-1.2(b).

DECLARATORY JUDGMENTS —Cont'd
Review, §1-258.
Rule adopted by administrative agency.
Emergency rules.
Standing to seek, §150B-21.1A(c).
Temporary rules.
Standing to seek, §150B-21.1(c).
Rulemaking procedure.
Temporary rules.
Rule returned to agency, §150B-21.1(b2), (c1).
Scope.
Enumeration not exclusive, §1-256.
Power of courts to construe instruments, §1-254.
Who may apply for declaration, §1-255.
Statutes.
Attorney general as party to proceedings involving
constitutionality, §1-260.
Power of courts to construe, §1-254.
Summary judgment, §1A-1 Rule 56.
Supplemental relief, §1-259.
Termination of controversy by judgment or
decree.
Enumeration of declarations not exclusive, §1-256.
Title of act.
Short title, §1-267.
Trusts and trustees.
Declaratory relief, right to seek, §36C-2-203(c).
Who may apply for declaration, §1-255.
Wills.
Power of courts to construe, §1-254.

DECLARATORY RULINGS.
Administrative procedure, §150B-4.

DECODERS.
Cable television service theft, §14-118.5.

DECREES.
See JUDGMENTS AND DECREES.

DEDICATION.
Highways, roads and streets.
Abandonment of road or street for fifteen years,
§136-96.
Partition, §46-17.1.
Special proceeding to declare right of way for
public use, §136-96.1.
Withdrawal of public use dedication by property
owners association, §136-96.2.
Judicial sales.
Property subdivided for sale.
Dedicated to public, §1-339.9(b).
State preserves, §§143-260.6 to 143-260.10F.

DEEDS.
Acknowledgments, §47-17.
Corporate deeds and other conveyances.
Forms for probate, §47-41.01(b), (c).
Defective acknowledgment on old deeds validated,
§47-52.
Failure of register of deeds to certify correctness.
Validation of registration, §47-50.1.
Agents.
Execution of deed.
Dated before 1835.
Evidence of due execution, §8-13.
Torrens system registration.
Instruments describing party as agent not to
operate as notice, §§43-63, 43-64.
Alien property custodian.
Certified copies of deeds made by.
Evidence, §47-34.
Registration, §47-33.

DEEDS —Cont'd
Anson county.
Evidence.
Records of deeds in Anson, §8-26.
Assignment for benefit of creditors.
Generally, §§23-1 to 23-12.
See ASSIGNMENTS FOR BENEFIT OF
CREDITORS.
Attornment.
Unnecessary on conveyance of reversions, etc.,
§42-2.
Banks.
Validation of deeds and conveyances.
Attestation by secretary or cashier, §47-42(b),
(c).
Executed by nonresident bank, §47-108.16.
Bargain and sale.
Possession transferred to use in certain
conveyances, §41-7.
Blank or master forms.
Filing, recording, indexing, §47-21.
Register of deeds to fill in blank forms with line,
§47-35.
Business trusts.
Prior deeds validated, §39-47.
Cemeteries.
Validation of certain deeds for cemetery lots
executed by suspended corporations, §65-73.
Charities.
Prior deeds validated, §59B-15(b).
Clerks of court.
Probate and registration.
Where clerk appointed himself to sell, §47-65.
Contaminated site transferred.
Contaminated property statement,
§143B-279.10(e).
Contingent limitations.
Failure of issue.
Limitations on failure, §41-4.
Contingent remainders.
Validation of transfer, §41-12.
Contracts for deed, §§47H-1 to 47H-8.
See CONTRACTS FOR DEED.
Conveyances generally.
See CONVEYANCES.
Cooperative associations.
Prior deeds validated, §59B-15(b).
Copies.
Registration of certified copies, §47-31(a).
Deeds made by United States alien property
custodian, §47-33.
Evidence, §47-31(a).
Deeds made by alien property custodian,
§47-34.
Validation of instruments registered prior to
July 6, 1993, §47-31(b).
Coroners.
Official selling or empowered to sell not in office,
§39-5.
Corporations.
Corporate seal.
Imprinting required, §47-41.1.
Error in acknowledgment of probate, §47-97.1.
Forms of probate for deeds and other conveyances,
§§47-41.01, 47-41.02.
Technical defects not to affect, §47-41.2.
Mistake as to officer's name, §47-97.
Probate of corporate deeds where corporation has
ceased to exist, §47-16.
Corrective affidavit and notice.
Errors in recorded deeds, §47-36.1.

DEEDS —Cont'd
Covenants to stand seized to use.
Possession transferred to use in certain conveyances, §41-7.
Curative acts.
Before commissioners of deeds, §47-81.
Clerk's deeds where clerk appointed himself to sell, §47-65.
Corporate deeds.
Validation of certain deeds where admitted to record, §47-108.1.
Defective acknowledgment on old deeds, §47-52.
Guardians.
Deeds by guardians omitting seal, prior to January 1, 1944, validated, §35A-1360.
Nonresident banks.
Validation of certain deeds, §47-108.16.
Official capacity not designated, §47-108.17.
Death.
Contingent limitations on death of person without heirs.
Limitations on failure of issue, §41-4.
Declaratory judgments.
Power of court to construe declaratory judgment preceding, §1-254.
Defective acknowledgment on old deeds validated, §47-52.
Definitions.
Next of kin, §41-6.1.
Descriptions of land.
Vagueness not to invalidate, §39-2.
Drafters' errors in registered instruments, §47-36.1.
Draftsman required to be designated on instrument required in certain counties, §47-17.1.
Drainage districts, §156-115.
Warranty in deed runs to purchaser who pays assessment, §156-115.
Dry-cleaning solvent cleanup.
Notice of dry-cleaning solvent remediation.
Notice of restrictions in deed of sale, lease or conveyance, §143-215.104M(d).
Easements.
Registration necessary, §47-27.
Electronic recording, §§47-16.1 to 47-16.7.
See REAL PROPERTY ELECTRONIC RECORDING.
Errors in recorded deeds.
Corrective affidavit and notice, §47-36.1.
Petition to correct to clerk of superior court.
Filing, hearing, notice, appeal, §47-36.
Evidence.
Anson county.
Records of deeds in Anson, §8-26.
Certified copies.
From other states, §8-32.
1835 or before.
Date on deed.
Execution of deed, §8-13.
Lost or destroyed deeds.
Presumed to be in due form, §8-21.
Registered instruments as evidence.
Certified copies of registered instruments, §§8-18, 47-31(a), (b).
Copies made by alien property custodian, §47-34.
Lost or destroyed records.
Presumed to be in due form, §8-21.
Tax deeds.
Recitals in tax deeds in Haywood and Henderson counties, §8-22.

DEEDS —Cont'd
Evidence —Cont'd
Tax deeds —Cont'd
Richmond county, §8-22.1.
Tracts of land.
Common survey of contiguous tracts as evidence, §8-19.
Excise stamp tax on conveyances, §§105-228.28 to 105-228.37.
See EXCISE STAMP TAX ON CONVEYANCES.
Execution sales.
Real property sold, §1-339.68(a).
Executors and administrators.
Contract for sale of real property by decedent.
Delivery of deed by personal representative, §28A-17-9.
Omitting seals, §47-51.
Failure of issue.
Limitations on failure, §41-4.
Forgery, §14-122.
Fraternal orders.
Prior deeds validated, §59B-15(b).
Fraudulent transfers, §§39-23.1 to 39-23.12.
See FRAUDULENT TRANSFERS.
Future interests.
Revocation of conveyances to persons not in esse, §39-6.
Validation of deeds, §39-6.1.
General assembly.
Giving effect to informal deeds.
Local, private and special legislation prohibited, NC Const Art II §24.
Gifts.
Registration required, §47-26.
Guardians.
Validation of deeds by guardians omitting seal, prior to January 1, 1944, §35A-1360.
Hearsay exception.
Records or documents or statements in documents affecting interest in property, §8C-1 Rule 803.
Heirs.
Construed to be "children" in certain limitations, §41-6.
Sale, lease or mortgage of real property, §28A-17-12.
Husband and wife.
Acknowledgments.
Absence of wife's acknowledgment not to affect deed as to husband, §39-9.
Different times and places, §39-8.
Conveyances under deed of separation, §39-13.4.
Fraud.
Certain conveyances not affected by fraud if acknowledgment or privy examination regular, §39-11.
Joint execution.
Married persons under 18 made competent as to certain transactions, §39-13.2(a), (c).
Power to convey property without joinder, §39-7(b).
Probates.
Different officers of deeds, §47-87.
Validation of deed executed by married women without private examination.
Deeds executed prior to Feb. 7, 1945, §39-13.1(b).
Deeds executed since Nov. 7, 1944, §39-13.1(a).
Validation of instruments not executed by husband, §39-7.1.
Index.
Consolidated index maintained in register's office, §161-21.

DEEDS —Cont'd
Index —Cont'd
Immediate prior owners of land, §161-22.1.
Parcel identifier number indexes, §161-22.2.
Registered instruments generally, §161-22.
Informal deeds.
Giving effect to informal deeds.
Local, private and special legislation prohibited,
NC Const Art II §24.
Judgments in which transfer of title declared
regarded as deed of conveyance, §1-228.
Judicial sales.
Private sale of real property, §1-339.38(a).
Public sale of real property, §1-339.29(a), (b).
Lease and release.
Possession transferred to use in certain
conveyances, §41-7.
Livery of seizin.
Probate and registration sufficient, §47-17.
Maps attached to deeds submitted for
recording.
Electronic documents meeting requirements,
§47-30(o).
Size requirements, §47-30(m), (n).
Married women.
Private examination.
Repeal of laws requiring, §47-14.1.
Registration of instruments not executed by wife,
§39-9.
Validation of deed executed by married women
without private examination.
Deeds executed prior to Feb. 7, 1945,
§39-13.1(b).
Deeds executed since Nov. 7, 1944, §39-13.1(a).
Validation of instruments not executed by
husband, §39-7.1.
Mistake or error.
Corrective affidavit and notice, §47-36.1.
Petition to clerk of superior court to correct.
Filing, hearing, notice, appeal, §47-36.
Mortgages and deeds of trust.
Generally.
See MORTGAGES AND DEEDS OF TRUST.
Municipalities.
Conveying property by, §160A-275.
Validation of certain deeds, §160A-18.
Next of kin.
Defined, §41-6.1.
Notary public.
Seal of notary not affixed.
Validation of deed, §47-103.
Partition sales.
Deed to purchaser, §46-30.
Effect of deed, §46-30.
Personal property.
Creation of interest or estate in, §39-6.2.
Presumptions.
Unborn infants.
When child presumed in esse, §41-5.
Probate and registration.
Banks.
Validation of deeds and conveyances.
Attestation by secretary or cashier, §47-42(b),
(c).
Before commissioners of deeds, §47-81.
Blank or master forms.
Filing, recording, indexing, §47-21.
Register of deeds to fill in blank forms with
line, §47-35.
Certified copies, §47-31(a), (b).
Deeds made by United States alien property
custodian, §§47-33, 47-34.

DEEDS —Cont'd
Probate and registration —Cont'd
Consolidated index maintained in register's office,
§161-21.
Conveyance of real estate in 2 or more counties.
Copy certified and registered, §161-15.
Conveyance of realty with manufactured home
attached.
Recording deed, §47-20.7.
Corporations.
Corporate seal required, §47-41.1.
Forms of probate for deeds and other
conveyances, §§47-41.01, 47-41.02.
Technical defects not to affect, §47-41.2.
Probate of corporate deeds where corporation
has ceased to exist, §47-16.
Deeds of gift.
Registration required, §47-26.
Defective acknowledgment on old deeds validated,
§47-52.
Easements.
Registration necessary, §47-27.
Electronic recording.
Uniform real property electronic recording act,
§§47-16.1 to 47-16.7.
Errors in registration.
Corrective affidavit and notice, §47-36.1.
Petition to clerk of superior court to correct.
Filing, hearing, notice, appeal, §47-36.
Evidence.
Certified copies, §47-31(a).
Copies made by alien property custodian,
§47-34.
Failure to register instrument.
Liability of register of deeds, §161-16.
Index of registered instrument, §161-22.
Immediate prior owners of land, §161-22.1.
Parcel identifier number indexes, §161-22.2.
Judgment in which transfer of title declared,
§1-228.
Certified registered copy evidence, §1-229.
Livery of seizin.
Probate and registration sufficient without
livery, §47-17.
Maps attached to deeds submitted for recording.
Size requirements, §47-30(m), (n).
Passing property interest as against lien creditors
and purchasers for value.
Registration of conveyance required, §47-18(a),
(b).
Recordation or registration generally.
See RECORDATION OR REGISTRATION OF
DOCUMENTS.
State officers authorized to prove or acknowledge,
§47-1.
Tax certification.
No delinquent taxes due.
Required to register, specified counties,
§161-31.
Unregistered deeds prior to January, 1920.
Registration on affidavit, §47-19.
Public lands.
Execution, §146-75.
Failure to register.
Forfeiture of grants, §146-20.
Governor.
Signing of deeds, §146-75.
Swamplands.
Forfeiture for failure to register deeds, §146-20.
Public schools.
Custody of deeds to property, §115C-519.

DEEDS —Cont'd

Real property with manufactured home attached, §47-20.7.

Receivers.
Seals.
Omitting seals, §47-51.

Recordation or registration.
Generally. See within this heading, "Probate and registration."

Register of deeds, §§161-1 to 161-31.
See REGISTERS OF DEEDS.

Religious organizations.
Prior deeds validated, §59B-15(b).

Remainders, reversions and executory interests.
Attornment unnecessary, §42-2.
Validation of sale or mortgage of contingent remainder, §41-12.

Seals and sealed instruments.
Guardians.
Deeds by guardians omitting seal, prior to January 1, 1944, validated, §35A-1360.
Official deeds omitting seals, §47-51.
Probates omitting official seals, §47-53.

Sheriffs.
Official selling or empowered to sell property not in office, §39-5.
Omitting seal, §47-51.

Solar collectors.
Deed restrictions, covenants or other agreements prohibiting installation.
Void and unenforceable, exception, §22B-20(a) to (e).

Stamp tax on conveyances, §§105-228.28 to 105-228.37.
See EXCISE STAMP TAX ON CONVEYANCES.

States.
Certified copies of deeds of other states, §8-32.

Statute of uses, §41-7.

Substitute for incompetent trustee appointed in special proceedings, §23-4.

Tax certification.
No delinquent taxes due.
Required to register, specified counties, §161-31.

Tax collectors.
Official selling or empowered to sell not in office, §39-5.

Tax deeds.
Hayward county, §8-22.
Henderson county, §8-22.
Richmond county, §8-22.1.

Trusts and trustees.
Torrens system registration.
Instruments describing party as trustee not to operate as notice, §§43-63, 43-64.

Tryon's Palace.
Execution of deeds, §121-14.

Unborn infants.
Taking by deed or writing, §41-5.

Unit ownership.
Conveying units, §47A-14.1(a).
Validation of conveyances, §47A-14.1(b).

Vagueness of description not to invalidate, §39-2.

DEEDS OF GIFT.
Proved, registration, required, time, §47-26.

DEEDS OF TRUST.
Assignments for benefit of creditors, §§23-1 to 23-12.
See ASSIGNMENTS FOR BENEFIT OF CREDITORS.

DEEDS OF TRUST —Cont'd

General provisions, §§45-4 to 45-84.
See MORTGAGES AND DEEDS OF TRUST.

Notary named as trustee only.
Validation, §10B-65(c).

DEEMER PROVISIONS.

Insurance policies or contracts.
Filing or contract deemed approved, §58-3-151.

DEER.

Black-tailed deer.
Unlawfully transporting or possessing, §113-294(p).

Captivity licenses.
Issuance, §113-272.6(d).
Regulations, §113-272.6(a).
Violations, forfeitures, §113-272.6(e).

Captivity permits.
Issuance, §113-272.6(d).
Regulations, §113-272.6(a).
Violations, forfeitures, §113-272.6(e).

Dogs.
Injuring or killing deer on wildlife management area, killing, §67-14.1(a).

Farmed deer.
Captivity licenses.
Issuance, §113-272.6(d).
Regulations, §113-272.6(a).
Violations, forfeitures, §113-272.6(e).
Captivity permits.
Issuance, §113-272.6(d).
Regulations, §113-272.6(a).
Violations, forfeitures, §113-272.6(e).
Possession and transportation of cervids.
Regulations, §113-272.6(a).
Production and sale for commercial purposes, §§106-549.97, 106-549.98.
Regulation of farmed cervids, §106-549.97(a).

Hunting.
Antlerless deer tags, §113-291.2(e).
Dogs chasing deer.
Muzzle loading firearms season.
Dogs not used for hunting, §113-291.2(a).
Regulation of use in hunting, limitation on regulations, §113-291.5(a) to (f).
Muzzle loading firearms season.
Dogs not used for hunting, §113-291.2(a).
Taking one antlerless deer, §113-291.2(a).
Special antlerless deer tags, §113-291.2(e).
Spotlighting.
Prima facie evidence, §113-302(b).
Sweeping area with lights at night, §113-291.1(e1), (e2).
Unlawfully selling, possessing for sale or buying, §113-294(b).
Unlawfully taking, possessing or transporting, §113-294(d).
Night hunting with artificial lights, §113-294(e).
Penalty, §113-294(d).

Mule deer.
Unlawfully transporting or possessing, §113-294(p).

Possession and transportation of cervids, §106-549.97(b).
Captivity licenses.
Issuance, §113-272.6(d).
Regulations, §113-272.6(a).
Violations, forfeitures, §113-272.6(e).
Captivity permits.
Issuance, §113-272.6(d).
Regulations, §113-272.6(a).

DEER —Cont'd
Possession and transportation of cervids
—Cont'd
Captivity permits —Cont'd
Violations, forfeitures, §113-272.6(e).
Regulations, §113-272.6(a).
Transportation permits.
Issuance, §113-272.6(d).
Notice, compliance requirements, §113-272.6(b).
Regulations, §113-272.6(a).
Production and sale for commercial purposes,
§§106-549.97, 106-549.98.
Defined terms, §106-549.97(c).
Inspection fees, §106-549.98.
Possession and transportation of cervids,
§106-549.97(b).
Notice, compliance requirements, §113-272.6(b).
Regulations, §113-272.6(a).
Regulation of farmed cervids, §106-549.97(a).
Regulations, §113-272.6(c).
Transportation of cervids, §113-272.6.
Transportation permits.
Issuance, §113-272.6(d).
Notice, compliance requirements, §113-272.6(b).

DEFAMATION.
Allowance of costs, §§6-18, 6-19.
Answer alleging truth or mitigating
circumstances, §1A-1 Rule 9(i).
Banks.
Willfully and maliciously making derogatory
reports, §53-128.
Congress.
Privilege of members of congress, US Const Art I
§6.
Decedents' estates.
Rights of action not surviving defendant,
§28A-18-1.
Defenses.
Justification or truth as defense to libel, §15-168.
Elections.
False and derogatory reports as to candidates,
§163-274(a).
Executors and administrators.
Actions in favor of decedent which do not survive,
§28A-18-1.
Insurance.
Unfair trade practices, §58-63-15.
Insurance consumer and customer information
privacy.
Immunity from suit.
Disclosure in accordance with article,
§58-39-110.
Justification.
Defense to libel, §15-168.
Larceny, shoplifting, employee theft,
embezzlement or false pretense.
Civil liability, demand letter for payment prior to
action.
Qualified privilege of sender, §1-538.2(c3).
Limitation of actions, §1-54.
Magazines.
Communicating libelous matter to magazines,
§14-47.
Negligence.
Radio and television.
Negligence in permitting defamatory
statements, §99-5.
Newspapers.
Anonymous publication, §99-3.

DEFAMATION —Cont'd
Newspapers —Cont'd
Communicating libelous matter to newspapers,
§14-47.
Notice before action against newspaper, §99-1(a).
Publication in good faith and retraction, §99-2(a).
Notice.
Action against newspaper, §99-1(a).
Action against radio or television station, §99-1(b).
Periodicals.
Communicating libelous matter to periodicals,
§14-47.
Pleading, §1A-1 Rule 9(i).
Radio and television.
Anonymous communications, §99-3.
Broadcast in good faith and retraction, §99-2(b).
Negligence in permitting defamatory statements,
§99-5.
Notice before action against radio or television
station, §99-1(b).
Retraction.
Newspapers.
Publication in good faith and retraction,
§99-2(a).
Radio and television.
Broadcast in good faith and retraction, §99-2(b).
Savings banks, §54C-64.
Truth as defense, §15-168.
Pleading affirmative defense, §1A-1 Rule 8(c).

DEFAULTED STUDENT LOANS.
Withholding earnings, §§105B-1 to 105B-5.
Contested withholding, §105B-3(e).
Definitions, §105B-1(b).
Disposable earnings, §105B-3(a).
Discharge from employment by payor, §105B-4(b).
Election remedy in addition to and not
substitution for other remedies, §105B-2.
Entering withholding order, §105B-3(a).
Immunity of payor for withholding sum provided
in notice or order, §105B-4(c).
Inspection and copying of records by debtors,
§105B-3(c).
Motion for withholding order, §105B-3(b).
Payor willfully refusing to comply with provisions,
§105B-4(a).
Purposes, §105B-1(a).
Schedule for repayment.
Written agreement with state education
assistance authority, §105B-3(d).
Termination of withholding, §105B-5.
Transmittal of amount ordered to be withheld to
clerk of superior court, §105B-3(g).
Uncontested withholding, §105B-3(f).
Verified motion for withholding order, §105B-3(b).

DEFAULT JUDGMENTS, §1A-1 Rule 55(b).
Adult publications.
Adjudication on potentially harmful materials,
§19-16.
Applicability of provisions of civil rule, §1A-1
Rule 55(e).
Attorney disciplinary proceedings, Bar Rule
B.0114.
Bonds, surety.
Plaintiff, §1A-1 Rule 55(c).
Civil no-contact orders.
Workplace violence prevention.
Failure of respondent to answer, §95-263(c).
Clerk.
Entry of judgment by, §1A-1 Rule 55(b).

DEFAULT JUDGMENTS —Cont'd
Clerk —Cont'd
Superior court.
Authorized to enter, §§1-209, 7A-103.
Collection agencies.
Entry of judgment against debtor.
Evidence to establish amount and nature of
debt.
Prerequisites to entry of judgment,
§58-70-155.
Counterclaims.
Provisions of rule apply to parties pleading, §1A-1
Rule 55(e).
Cross-claims.
Provisions of rule apply to party pleading, §1A-1
Rule 55(e).
Demand for judgment, §1A-1 Rule 54(c).
Divorce, §50-10(e).
Entry of default, §1A-1 Rule 55(a).
By clerk, §1A-1 Rule 55(b).
By judge, §1A-1 Rule 55(b).
State of North Carolina or officers and officials.
No judgment by default entered against, §1A-1
Rule 55(f).
Expedited evictions.
Failure to plead in accordance with time periods,
§42-68.
Harmful materials sales to minors, §19-16(b).
Hearings.
Taking account, determining damages,
establishing truth of averment, §1A-1 Rule
55(b).
Infants or incompetents.
Guardian ad litem.
Appointment required for entry of judgment
against, §1A-1 Rule 55(b).
Interest.
Clerk to ascertain, §24-6.
Judge.
Entry of judgment by, §1A-1 Rule 55(b).
Motions.
Decided without hearing, §1A-1 Rule 55(b).
Plaintiffs.
Provisions of rule applied to, §1A-1 Rule 55(e).
Publication, service by.
Bond of plaintiff prior to entering, §1A-1 Rule
55(c).
Quo warranto.
Judgment by default and inquiry on failure of
defendant to give bond, §1-525.
Service by publication.
Bond of plaintiff prior to entering, §1A-1 Rule
55(c).
Service of process.
Process or judgment by default not to be attacked
on certain grounds, §1A-1 Rule 4(j4).
Registered or certified mail, signature
confirmation or designated delivery service.
Proof of service, §1A-1 Rule 4(j2).
Setting aside entry of default, §1A-1 Rule 55(d).
Superior courts.
Authority of clerk to enter default judgment,
§§1-209, 7A-103.
Third-party plaintiffs.
Provisions of rule applied to, §1A-1 Rule 55(e).
Torrens system registration.
Prohibited, §43-11(d).
Validation, §§1-217, 1-217.2.
Judgments by default to remove cloud from title
to real estate, §1-217.2.

DEFAULT JUDGMENTS —Cont'd
Workplace violence prevention.
Civil no-contact orders.
Failure of respondent to answer, §95-263(c).

DEFAULT ON CRIMINAL FINES, §15A-1364.

**DEFECTIVE IMPROVEMENT TO REAL
PROPERTY.**
Limitation of actions, §1-50(a).

DEFENDANTS.
Arrest in civil cases.
See ARREST IN CIVIL CASES.
Attendance.
Securing attendance of criminal defendants
confined in institutions within state,
§15A-711(a) to (c).
Detainers, §15A-711(d).
Civil procedure, §1-10.
Costs.
Allowance of costs, §6-19.
Discretion of court, §§6-20, 6-21.
Attorneys' fees.
Parties appealing or defending against agency
decision, §6-19.1(a).
Bonds, surety.
Confession of judgment.
Bond given to secure fine and cost, §6-47.
Confession of judgment.
Bond given to secure fine and cost, §6-47.
Judgment confessed.
Bond given to secure fine and cost, §6-47.
Notice of no personal claim.
Payment of costs by defendant unreasonably
defending after notice, §6-23.
Defined, §1-75.2.
Depositions.
Criminal actions, §8-74.
Discovery in criminal cases generally.
See DISCOVERY.
First appearance before district court judge.
See APPEARANCES.
Hearing impaired.
Interpreters, §8B-2.
Incapacity to proceed, §§15A-1001 to 15A-1009.
See INCAPACITY OF DEFENDANT TO
PROCEED.
Interpreters.
Deaf or hearing impaired persons, §8B-2.
Joinder, §15A-926(b).
Objections to joinder, §15A-927(c).
Failure to prove grounds for joinder,
§15A-927(d).
Jurisdiction.
Defined, §1-75.2.
Limitation of actions.
Out of state defendants.
When action begun or judgment enforced, §1-21.
Mentally ill.
Civil commitment of defendants found not guilty
by reason of insanity, §15A-1321(a), (b).
Incapacity of defendant to proceed, §§15A-1001 to
15A-1009.
See INCAPACITY OF DEFENDANT TO
PROCEED.
Temporary restraint, §15A-1322.
Parties generally, §§1-57 to 1-72.
See PARTIES.
Physical restraint of defendant.
Maintenance of order in courtroom, §15A-1031.

DEFENDANTS —Cont'd
Pleadings.
Each defendant to be charged with separate
pleading, §15A-926(b).
Pleas.
See PLEAS.
Prisons and prisoners.
Securing attendance of criminal defendants
confined in institutions within state,
§15A-711(a) to (c).
Detainer, §15A-711(d).
Probable cause hearings.
See PROBABLE CAUSE.
Removal of disruptive defendant.
Maintenance of order in courtroom, §15A-1032(a),
(b).
Representation of self at trial, §15A-1242.
Standby counsel, §15A-1243.
Restraint of defendant.
Maintenance of order in courtroom, §15A-1031.
Securing attendance.
Defendants confined in federal prisons,
§15A-771(a).
Certificate by superior court, §15A-771(b).
Defendants who are outside United States.
Application by governor to secretary of state of
United States, §15A-772(b).
Application to governor, §15A-772(a).
Extradition.
Applicability of provisions to, §15A-772(c).
Organizations, §15A-773(a).
Appearance by counsel or agent, §15A-773(b).
Defined, §15A-773(c).
Small claim actions.
Answer of defendant, §7A-218.
Methods of subjecting persons of defendant to
jurisdiction, §7A-217.
Temporary restraint.
Mentally ill defendants, §15A-1322.
Witnesses.
Criminal actions.
Defendant in criminal action competent but not
compellable to testify, §8-54.

DEFENSE OF MARRIAGE.
Same sex marriage ban, §51-1.2.

DEFENSE OF PUBLIC SCHOOL EMPLOYEES,
§§143-300.13 to 143-300.18.

DEFENSE OF STATE EMPLOYEES, §§143-300.2
to 143-300.18.
See PUBLIC OFFICERS AND EMPLOYEES.

DEFENSES.
Affirmative defenses.
Accord and satisfaction.
Pleading, §1A-1 Rule 8(c).
Arbitration and award.
Pleading, §1A-1 Rule 8(c).
Assumption of risk.
Pleading, §1A-1 Rule 8(c).
Bad checks, §6-21.3(c).
Bankruptcy and insolvency.
Discharge, pleading, §1A-1 Rule 8(c).
Commodities.
Failure to make physical delivery, §78D-33.
Commodities trading, §78D-33.
Consideration, failure.
Pleading, §1A-1 Rule 8(c).
Contributory negligence.
Pleading, §1A-1 Rule 8(c).

DEFENSES —Cont'd
Affirmative defenses —Cont'd
Defamation.
Truth, pleading, §1A-1 Rule 8(c).
Disabled persons.
Protection act.
Affirmative defenses of employers, §168A-9.
Duress.
Pleading, §1A-1 Rule 8(c).
Estoppel.
Pleading, §1A-1 Rule 8(c).
Eviction.
Retaliatory eviction, §42-37.1.
Expedited evictions.
Evidence of isolated or nonrecurring incidents.
Admissible only to support affirmative
defense, §42-67.
Fellow servant doctrine.
Pleading, §1A-1 Rule 8(c).
Foreign-country money judgments.
Recognition.
Raising issue, §1C-1855(b).
Fraud.
Pleading, §1A-1 Rule 8(c).
Laches.
Pleading, §1A-1 Rule 8(c).
Limitation of actions.
Pleading, §1A-1 Rule 8(c).
Motor vehicles.
Lemon law, §20-351.4.
New motor vehicles warranties act, §20-351.4.
Obscenity.
Disseminating or exhibiting harmful materials
to minors, §14-190.15(c).
Pleading, §1A-1 Rule 8(c).
Release.
Pleading, §1A-1 Rule 8(c).
Res judicata.
Pleading, §1A-1 Rule 8(c).
Statute of frauds.
Pleading, §1A-1 Rule 8(c).
Statute of limitations.
Pleading, §1A-1 Rule 8(c).
Unclaimed property act.
Payment, satisfaction, discharge and want of
consideration, §116B-58.
Usury.
Pleading, §1A-1 Rule 8(c).
Waiver.
Pleading, §1A-1 Rule 8(c).
Affrays.
Plea of self-defense.
Evidence of former threats upon plea, §14-33.1.
Aircraft.
Operation while impaired.
Infliction of serious bodily injury.
Preclusion of defense, §63-28(b).
Preclusion of defense, §63-27(b).
Alcoholic beverages.
Minors.
Sales to.
Defense to violation of subsection,
§18B-302(d).
Assault and battery.
Self-defense.
Assaulting law enforcement, assistance or
search and rescue animals, §14-163.1(f).
Evidence of former threats upon plea, §14-33.1.
Assignment of thing in action.
Action by assignee without prejudice to, §1-57.

DEFENSES —Cont'd
Assumption of risk.
Controlled substances.
Employing or intentionally using minor to commit drug law violations, §90-95.5.
Roller skaters and spectators, §§99E-13, 99E-14.
Bad checks.
Affirmative defense, §6-21.3(c).
Bigamy.
Prosecutions for bigamy, §14-183.
Breach of trust.
Consent, release or ratification by beneficiaries.
Trustee not liable, §36C-10-1009.
Reliance on trust instrument, §36C-10-1006.
Business necessity.
Fair housing violation, §41A-5(a).
Carrying concealed weapon, §14-269(b1), (b2).
Charitable immunity.
Defense abolished, §1-539.9.
Checks.
Returned checks.
Affirmative defense, §6-21.3(c).
Child prostitution.
Participating in prostitution of a minor.
Mistake of age not a defense, §14-190.19(b).
Promoting prostitution of a minor.
Mistake of age not a defense, §14-190.18(b).
Cigarettes and tobacco products.
Sale or distribution to minors.
Reliance upon proof of age, §14-313(b).
Commodities trading.
Affirmative defenses, §78D-33.
Community colleges.
Tort actions against board of trustees, §115D-58.12(c).
Consent to intercourse and sexual offense.
No defenses as to certain victims, §14-27.7(a).
Consolidation of defenses in motion, §1A-1 Rule 12(g).
Contributory negligence.
Bank deposits and collections.
Unauthorized signature or alteration, §25-4-406(c), (d).
Burden of proof, §1-139.
Claims against state departments and agencies.
Doctrine a matter of defense, §143-299.1.
Limitations on use, §143-299.1A.
Controlled substances.
Employing or intentionally using minor to commit drug law violations.
Doctrine no defense to civil liability, §90-95.5.
Controlled substances.
Employing or intentionally using minor to commit drug law violations.
Assumption of risk, §90-95.5.
Contributory negligence, §90-95.5.
Mistake of age, §90-95.4(c).
Participating in a drug violation by a minor.
Mistake of age not a defense, §90-95.7(b).
Promoting drug sales by a minor.
Mistake of age, §90-95.6(b).
Counties.
Public officers and employees.
Providing defenses for employees, §153A-97.
Criminal law and procedure.
Insanity defense.
Notice, §§15A-905(c), (d), 15A-959(a).
Intent to introduce expert testimony, §15A-959(b).
Pretrial determination of insanity, §15A-959(c).

DEFENSES —Cont'd
Criminal law and procedure —Cont'd
Mistake of age.
Controlled substances.
Employing or intentionally using minor to commit drug law violations, §90-95.4(c).
Participating in a drug violation by a minor, §90-95.7(b).
Promoting drug sales by a minor, §90-95.6(b).
Disabled persons.
Protection act.
Employers.
Affirmative defenses, §168A-9.
Discovery.
Criminal law and procedure.
Notice to state of defenses and witnesses, §15A-905(c), (d).
Drivers' licenses.
Failure to carry license, §20-35(c).
Drugs.
Controlled substances.
Employing or intentionally using minor to commit drug law violations, §§90-95.4(c), 90-95.5.
Participating in a drug violation by a minor.
Mistake of age not a defense, §90-95.7(b).
Promoting drug sales by a minor.
Mistake of age, §90-95.6(b).
Electronic surveillance.
Actions for violation of article.
Good faith reliance, §15A-296(b).
Expedited evictions.
Evidence of isolated or nonrecurring criminal activity.
Impermissible as defense, admissible as support of affirmative defenses, §42-67.
Fair housing.
Business necessity, §41A-5(a).
Unlawful discriminatory housing practices.
Acting for another person no defense, §41A-5(b).
Flour, corn meal and grain.
Adulteration of grains.
Nonposting of sign not a defense, §106-626.
Foreign-money claims, §1C-1825(b), (c).
Fraudulent transfers, §39-23.8.
Gaming.
Slot machines.
Possession of slot machine, §14-309.1(a).
Return of slot machine to defendant, §14-309.1(b).
Hazardous waste management.
Felonies, §130A-26.1(e), (i).
Health care liability.
Actions for damages, §90-21.51(c), (e).
How presented, §1A-1 Rule 12(b).
Impaired driving.
Commercial vehicles.
Legal entitlement to use alcohol or drug, §20-138.2(b).
Preventive maintenance on testing devices not performed, §20-138.2(b1).
Preventive maintenance on testing devices not performed, §§20-138.1(b1), 20-138.2(b1).
Incest.
Child under age of sixteen, when other person at least four years older, §14-178(c).
Insanity defense.
Notice, §15A-959(a).
Discovery generally, §15A-905(c), (d).
Intent to introduce expert testimony, §15A-959(b).

DEFENSES —Cont'd
Insanity defense —Cont'd
Pretrial determination of insanity, §15A-959(c).
Intercourse and sexual offenses with certain victims.
Consent no defense, §14-27.7(a).
International commercial arbitration and conciliation.
Stating, requirements, §1-567.53(a).
Amending or supplementing, §1-567.53(b).
More than two parties to arbitration, §1-567.53(c).
Intoxicated and disruptive in public.
Alcoholism as defense, §14-445.
Investment securities, §§25-8-202, 25-8-203.
Joint and several debtors.
Parties summoned after judgment, §1-114.
Judgments.
Foreign judgments.
Notice of defense.
Filing by judgment debtors, §1C-1705(a).
Leases, UCC.
Unconscionability, §25-2A-108(3).
Lemon law.
Affirmative defenses, §20-351.4.
Libel and slander.
Justification as defense to libel, §15-168.
Lotteries.
State lottery.
Sales of tickets or shares to minors, §18C-131(e).
Manufactured homes.
Conversion to another use.
Failure to give statutory notices, §42-14.3(a).
Mental health, developmental disabilities and substance abuse.
Area authorities.
Defense of agents, employees and board members, §122C-153.
Minors.
Employing or intentionally using minor to commit drug law violations.
Assumption of risk, §90-95.5.
Contributory negligence, §90-95.5.
Mistake of age, §90-95.4(c).
Intercourse and sexual offenses with certain victims.
Consent no defense, §14-27.7(a).
Lotteries.
State lottery.
Sale of ticket or share to minors, §18C-131(e).
Participating in a drug violation by a minor.
Mistake of age, §90-95.7(b).
Promoting drug sales by a minor.
Mistake of age, §90-95.6(b).
Prostitution.
Participating in prostitution of a minor.
Mistake of age not a defense, §14-190.19(b).
Promoting prostitution of a minor.
Mistake of age not a defense, §14-190.18(b).
Sexual exploitation of a minor.
Mistake of age not a defense, §§14-190.16(c), 14-190.17A(c), 14-190.17(c).
Sexual offenses.
Intercourse and sexual offenses with certain victims.
Consent no defense, §14-27.7(a).
State lottery.
Sale of ticket or share to minors, §18C-131(e).
Motions, defenses presented by, §1A-1 Rule 12(b).

DEFENSES —Cont'd
Motor vehicle equipment.
Window tinting, §20-127(e).
Motor vehicle inspections.
Infractions, §20-183.8(b).
Municipal planning and zoning.
Invalidity of ordinance, §160A-364.1(c).
Negotiable instruments.
Burden of establishing effectiveness of signature and holder in due course, §25-3-308(a).
Defenses generally, §25-3-305.
New motor vehicles warranties act.
Affirmative defenses, §20-351.4.
Obscenity.
Disseminating harmful material to minors, §14-190.15(c).
Exhibiting harmful performances to minors, §14-190.15(c).
Sexual exploitation of a minor.
Mistake of age not a defense, §§14-190.16(c), 14-190.17A(c), 14-190.17(c).
Oil pollution and hazardous substances control.
Offshore oil and gas activities.
Liability exceptions.
Exceptions constitute no defense, §143-215.94DD(b).
Patient abuse and neglect, §14-32.2(f).
Peddlers, itinerant merchants and specialty markets.
Misdemeanor violations, §66-257(d).
Pleading, §1A-1 Rule 8(b).
Affirmative defenses, §1A-1 Rule 8(c).
How presented, §1A-1 Rule 12(d).
Preliminary hearings, §1A-1 Rule 12(d).
Products liability.
Breach of warranty, §99B-1.2.
Property insurance.
Failure to render timely proof of loss, §58-44-50.
Retail installment sales.
Preservation of consumers' claims and defenses, §25A-25(a).
Compliance with federal trade commission requirements, §25A-25(c).
Notice to be included in instrument, §25A-25(b).
Roller skating rink safety and liability.
Assumption of risk of skaters and spectators, §§99E-13, 99E-14.
Seeds.
Use of disclaimers, nonwarranties and limited warranties, §106-277.11.
Sexual offenses.
Intercourse and sexual offenses with certain victims.
Consent no defense, §14-27.7(a).
Minors.
Intercourse and sexual offenses with certain victims.
Consent no defense, §14-27.7(a).
Spouse of person as victim.
Defense that victim is spouse of person committing act, §14-27.8.
Taking indecent liberties with a student.
Consent no defense, §14-202.4(c).
Solid waste management.
Hazardous waste.
Felonies, §130A-26.1(e), (i).
Spouse of person as victim.
Defense that victim is spouse of person committing act, §14-27.8.

DEFENSES —Cont'd

State lottery.

Sales of tickets or shares to minors, §18C-131(e).

Taking indecent liberties with a student.

Consent not a defense, §14-202.4(c).

Trusts and trustees.

Breach of trust.

Consent, release or ratification by beneficiaries. Trustee not liable, §36C-10-1009.

Reliance on trust instrument, §36C-10-1006.

Ultra vires.

Business corporations, §55-3-04.

Nonprofit corporations, §55A-3-04.

Surety companies not to plead, §58-73-20.

Unclaimed property act.

Payment, satisfaction, discharge and want of consideration, §116B-58.

Underage drinking.

Sale to or purchase of alcoholic beverages by underage persons, §18B-302(d).

Waiver or preservation of certain defenses, §1A-1 Rule 12(h).

Warranties.

Products liability, §99B-1.2.

Water and air resources.

Criminal penalties.

Applicability of general defenses, affirmative defenses and other bars to prosecution, §143-215.6B(e).

Window tinting of motor vehicles, §20-127(e).

Zoning.

Municipal planning and zoning.

Invalidity of ordinance, §160A-364.1(c).

DEFENSIVE FORCE.

Defense of person.

Justified in using force.

Deadly force, §14-51.3(a).

Except deadly force, §14-51.3(a).

Immunity, exceptions, §14-51.3(b).

Home, workplace, motor vehicle protection.

Defenses under common law.

No repealed or limited, §14-51.2(g).

Definitions, §14-51.2(a).

Exceptions to justification and immunity in using force, §14-51.2(e).

Fear of imminent death or personal bodily harm to occupant or another when using defensive force.

Presumption, §14-51.2(b).

Rebuttable, inapplicable, §14-51.2(c).

Home defined, §14-51.2(a).

Intent to commit unlawful act with force or violence.

Presumption.

Unlawful and forceful entry, §14-51.2(d).

Justified in using force, immunity, exceptions, §14-51.2(e).

Motor vehicle defined, §14-51.2(a).

No duty to retreat from intruder, §14-51.2(f).

Workplace defined, §14-51.2(a).

Justification not available, §14-51.4.

DEFERRED COMPENSATION PLANS.

Divorce.

Distribution of pension, retirement and deferred compensation benefits, §50-20.1.

Principal and income act.

Deferred compensation, annuities, similar payments.

Allocation, §37A-4-409.

Public employees, §143B-426.24.

DEFERRED COMPENSATION PLANS —Cont'd

Renunciation to succession, §31B-1.

DEFERRED INTEREST.

Home loan secured by first mortgages or first deeds of trust, §24-1.1A(g).

DEFERRED PROSECUTION.

Dismissal with leave pursuant to agreement, §15A-932.

Drug offenses.

First offenders.

Conditional discharge, §90-96(a), (a1), (e).

Generally, §15A-1341(a1), (a2).

Prayer for judgment continued.

Entry of PJC not considered entry of judgment, §15A-101.

Motor vehicles.

Convictions.

Third PJC filed in five-year period as conviction, §20-4.01.

Records of PJC's, §20-26(a).

Speeding in excess of 25 mph of posted speed. Ineligibility, §20-141(p).

Therapeutic court activities.

Participation, §7A-272(f).

Toxic vapors offenses.

Conditional discharge.

First offenses, §90-113.14(a), (a1).

DEFERRED TAX PROGRAMS.

Agricultural, horticultural and forestland.

Present use value.

Property taxes, §105-277.4.

Historic properties.

Property taxes, §105-278(b).

Inventory property tax deferral.

Builder constructed and owned property, §105-277.1D.

Property tax homestead circuit breaker program, §105-277.1B.

Uniform provision for payment, §105-277.1F.

Wildlife conservation land.

Property taxes, §105-277.15.

Working waterfront property.

Property taxes, §105-277.14.

DEFIBRILLATORS, §90-21.15.

DEFICIENCY JUDGMENTS, MORTGAGES AND DEEDS OF TRUST.

Abolished.

Mortgage represents part of purchase price, §45-21.38.

Mortgage secured by primary residence, §45-21.38A.

Certain sections not applicable to tax suits, §45-21.37.

Severability of provisions, §45-21.38C.

Tax foreclosures, §45-21.37.

Value of property.

Right of mortgagor to prove by way of defense, §45-21.36.

DEFINED TERMS.

Abandoned.

Animals, §90-187.7(c).

Cemeteries, §65-85.

Child custody jurisdiction and enforcement, §50A-102.

Abandoned dry-cleaning facility site.

Dry-cleaning solvent cleanup act, §143-215.104B(b).

Abandoned manufactured home, §130A-309.112.

DEFINED TERMS —Cont'd

Abandoned motor vehicle.
Defined, §20-137.7.
Removal and disposal, §§153A-132(b), 160A-303(b1).

Abandoned vessel.
Boating safety, §75A-2.

Abandoned well.
Well construction, §87-85.

Abatement.
Asbestos hazard management, §130A-444.
Lead poisoning in children, §130A-131.7.

ABC commission.
Alcohol taxation, §105-113.68.

ABC law.
Alcoholic beverages, §18B-101.

ABC permit.
Alcoholic beverages, §18B-101.
Alcohol taxation, §105-113.68.

ABC's program.
Education programs in residential schools, §143B-146.1(b).

ABC system.
Alcoholic beverages, §18B-101.

Abnormal market disruption.
Price gouging during state of disaster, §75-38(e).

Abode.
Tuition of active duty personnel in armed forces, §116-143.3(a).

Abortion.
Parental or judicial consent to abortion, §90-21.6.
Woman's right to know act, §90-21.81.

Absentee in military service.
Estates, §28B-1.

Absolute auction, §85B-1.

Abstract.
Elections, §163-182.
Property taxes, §105-273.

Abuse.
Adult care homes, §131D-2.1.
Civil no-contact orders, §50C-1.
Patient abuse, §14-32.2(e1).
Protection of disabled adults, §108A-101.

Abused juveniles.
Abused, neglected or dependent juveniles, §7B-101.

Abused or neglected.
Assignment of student to particular school, §115C-366(h).

Academic year.
Education access rewards North Carolina scholars fund, §116-209.26(a).
National Guard tuition assistance, §116-209.52(a).
Need-based scholarships for students attending private colleges and universities, §116-280.
Scholarships, §115C-499.1.

Academy.
Justice academy, §17D-1.

Academy property.
Justice academy, §17D-1.

Accept.
Educational personnel qualifications, §115C-350.
Letters of credit, §25-5-102(b).
Private personnel services, §95-47.1.

Acceptance.
Letters of credit, §25-5-102(b).
Negotiable instruments, §25-3-409(a).

Acceptance of a power of attorney.
Powers of attorney, §32A-41(b).

Accepted.
Limitation on fundraising during legislative session, §163-278.13B(a).

DEFINED TERMS —Cont'd

Acceptor.
Criminal law, §14-107.1.
Negotiable instruments, §25-3-103.

Access.
Social networking sites.
Sex offenders banned from using, §14-202.5A(b).

Accessing or causing to be accessed.
Computer related crime, §14-454(c).

Accession.
Secured transactions, §25-9-102(a).

Access or cause to be accessed.
Computer crimes, §14-453.
Government computers, §14-454.1(d).

Accident.
Insurance, §58-3-30.
Medical service corporations, §58-65-80(b).
Mines, §74-24.2.
Workers' compensation, §97-52.

Accidental injury.
Insurance, §58-3-30.
Medical service corporations, §58-65-80(b).

Accidental means.
Insurance, §58-3-30.
Medical service corporations, §58-65-80(b).

Accident and health insurance, §58-51-95(j).
Insurance companies, closure of a block of business, §58-3-275(c).

Accommodation bondsman.
Bail, §15A-531.
Bail bondsmen and runners, §58-71-1.

Account.
Banking, §25-4-104(a).
Insurance guaranty association, §58-48-20.
Secured transactions, §25-9-102(a).
Trust companies, §53-301(a).

Accountant, §93-1.
Annual audited financial reports.
Insurance companies, §58-10-190.

Account debtor.
Secured transactions, §25-9-102(a).

Accounting.
Incompetency, §35A-1202.
Secured transactions, §25-9-102(a).

Accounting period.
Principal and income act, §37A-1-102.

Accounting system.
Administrative office of the court.
Internal audit division, §7A-343.5.
State auditor, §147-64.4.
State controller, §143B-426.35.

Account number.
Insurance information privacy, §58-39-76.

Accounts receivable.
Statewide accounts receivable program, §147-86.20.

Accreditation.
Massage and bodywork therapy, §90-622.

Accreditation board.
Public health, §130A-2.

Accredited college or university.
Speech and language pathologists and audiologists licensure, §90-293.

Accredited educational institution.
Pastoral counselors, §90-382.

Accredited school of veterinary medicine, §90-181.

Accredited sponsor.
Continuing legal education, rules governing administration, Bar Rule D.1501.

DEFINED TERMS —Cont'd

Accredited state.
Producer-controlled property or casualty insurers,
§58-3-165(a).

Accrediting body.
Occupational therapists, §90-270.67.

Accumulated contributions.
Judicial retirement, §135-53.
Legislative retirement system, §120-4.8.
Retirement, §128-21.
State retirement system, §135-1.

Accused.
Crime victims' rights, §15A-830(a).

Accused delinquent.
Interstate compact for juveniles, §7B-4001.

Accused status offender.
Interstate compact for juveniles, §7B-4001.

Acknowledgment.
Impaired driving, §20-28.2(a1).
Notaries public act, §10B-3.

Acquire.
Banking, §53-210.
Electric membership corporations, §117-7.
Regional reciprocal savings and loan acquisition
act, §54B-48.2.

Acquired lands.
State lands, §146-64.

Acquiring persons statement.
Corporations, §75E-1.

Acquisition of a branch.
Interstate branch banking, §53-224.9.

Act as a fiduciary.
Trust companies, §53-301(a).

Act as a mortgage servicer.
Emergency program to reduce home foreclosures,
§45-101.

Action.
Civil procedure, §1-2.
Foreign-money claims, §1C-1820.
Residential rental agreements, §42-40.
UCC, §25-1-201(b).
Uniform trust code, §36C-1-103.

Active business operations.
Sudan (Darfur) divestment act, §147-86.42.

Active duty.
Life insurance.
Dishonest and predatory sales to military
personnel, §58-58-335.

Active federal service.
Children of war veterans scholarships, §165-20.

Active ingredient.
Pesticide board, §143-460.

Actively engaged.
Athletic trainers, §90-530(b).

Active member.
Continuing legal education, rules governing
administration, Bar Rule D.1501.

Active North Carolina main street community.
Main street solutions fund, §143B-472.35(a2).

Active period or periods.
Unemployment compensation.
Seasonal pursuits, §96-16(j).

Active punishment.
Structured sentencing, §15A-1340.11.

Actual address.
Address confidentiality program, §15C-2.

Actuarial certification.
Small employer group health coverage,
§58-50-110.

Actuarial equivalent.
Judicial retirement, §135-53.

DEFINED TERMS —Cont'd

Actuarial equivalent —Cont'd
Legislative retirement system, §120-4.8.
Retirement, §128-21.
State retirement system, §135-1.

Acupuncture, §90-451.

Additional child fatality.
Child fatality prevention system, §7B-1401.

Additional technology.
Unlawful use of mobile phone by minors,
§20-137.3(a).

Additive.
Gasoline tax, §105-449.60.

Address.
Address confidentiality program, §15C-2.

Address confidentiality program, §15C-2.

Address for giving a notification.
Satisfaction of deeds of trust and mortgages,
§45-36.4.

Address of record.
Bail, §15A-531.

Adequate feed.
Protection of animals, §19A-23.

Adequate water.
Protection of animals, §19A-23.

Adjudicated delinquent.
Interstate compact for juveniles, §7B-4001.

Adjudicated status offender.
Interstate compact for juveniles, §7B-4001.

Adjusted for inflation.
Tobacco reserve fund, §66-290.

Adjusted gross income.
Taxation, §105-134.1.

Adjusted risk-based capital report.
Insurance companies, §58-12-2.

Adjuster.
Licensing, §58-33-10.

Adjustment.
Weights and measures, §81A-9.

Administer.
Controlled substance, §90-87.
Pharmacy, §90-85.3(a).

Administration.
National defense housing projects, §157-53.

Administration of criminal justice.
Background investigations, §114-19.1(b).

Administrative area.
Community colleges, §115D-2.

Administrative committee.
Continuing legal education, Bar Rule D.1501.

Administrative district.
Organization of schools, §115C-69.

Administrative law judge, §150B-2.

Administrator.
Commodities act, §78D-1.
Drinking water, §130A-313.
Health insurance risk pool, §58-50-175.
Mediation of emergency or disaster property
insurance claims, §58-44-75.
Nursing homes, §131E-116.
Securities, §78A-2.

Administrator-in-training.
Assisted living administrators, §90-288.13.
Nursing home administrators, §90-276.

Admitted insurer.
Surplus lines, §58-21-10.
Unauthorized insurers, §58-28-12.

Admonition.
Discipline and disability rules of state bar, Bar
Rule B.0103.

DEFINED TERMS —Cont'd

Adopt.

Administrative procedure, §150B-2.

Adoptee, §48-1-101.

Adoption, §§48-1-101, 131D-10.2.

Workers' compensation, §97-2.

Adoption assistance state.

Interstate compact on adoption and medical
assistance, §7B-3901.

Adoption facilitator, §48-1-101.

Adoptive home.

Child placing and care, §131D-10.2.

Adult.

Adoption, §48-1-101.

Anatomical gifts, §130A-412.4.

Custodial trusts, §33B-1.

Transfers to minors, §33A-1.

Adult bookstore, §14-202.10.

Adult care facility.

State health plan for teachers and state
employees.

Long-term care benefits, §135-48.61(a).

Adult care home, §131D-2.1.

Bill of rights, §131D-20.

Certificates of need, §131E-176.

Facility licensure act, §131E-101.

Long-term care insurance, §58-55-35(a).

State-county special assistance, §108A-41(a).

Adult care home resident discharge team.

Adult care homes, §131D-2.1.

Adult care home staff.

Infection prevention requirements, §131D-4.4A(a).

Adult day care program.

Long-term care insurance, §58-55-35(a).

Adulterated.

Meat inspection, §106-549.15.

Pesticide board, §143-460.

Poultry products inspection, §106-549.51.

Soil additives act, §106-50.30.

Adulterated grain, §106-621.

Adulteration.

Milk regulation, §106-268(b).

Adult establishment, §14-202.10.

Adult live entertainment, §14-202.10.

Adult live entertainment business, §14-202.10.

Adult mini motion picture theater, §14-202.10.

Adult motion picture theater, §14-202.10.

Advance.

Mortgages and deeds of trust, §45-67.

Advance instruction.

Mental health treatment, §122C-72.

**Advance instruction for mental health
treatment.**

Power of attorney, §32A-16.

Advancement.

Decedents' estates, §29-2.

Adverse action.

Credit scoring to rate motor vehicle and property
insurance, §58-36-90(a).

Nurse licensure compact, §90-171.82.

Adverse claim.

Investment securities, §25-8-102.

Adverse determination.

Medicaid appeals by recipients, §108A-70.9A(a).

Provider requirements for Medicaid or Health
Choice, §108C-2.

Adverse underwriting decision.

Insurance information and privacy protection act,
§58-39-15.

Advertisement.

Antifreeze law, §106-579.3.

DEFINED TERMS —Cont'd

Advertisement —Cont'd

Campaign contributions and expenditures.

Disclosure requirements for media
advertisements, §163-278.38Z.

Food, drugs and cosmetics, §106-121.

Funeral services, §90-210.20(a).

Interstate insurance product regulation compact,
§58-91-10.

Seed law, §106-277.2.

Advertising.

Viatical life insurance settlements, §58-58-205.

Advisers.

Letters of credit, §25-5-102(a).

Advisory committee.

Nursing home medication management advisory
committee, §131E-128.1(a).

Aeronautical facilities, §63-79.

Aeronautics, §63-1.

Aeronautics instructor, §63-1.

Affected land.

Mining, §74-49.

Affiliate.

Annual audited financial reports.

Insurance companies, §58-10-190.

Appraisal rights, §55-13-01.

Banking, §53-104.1.

Brownfields property reuse act, §130A-310.31(b).

Collection agencies, §58-70-6.

Corporate franchise tax, §105-122(b).

Dry-cleaning solvent cleanup act,
§143-215.104B(b).

Fraudulent transfers, §39-23.1.

Insurance guaranty association, §58-48-20.

Insurance holding companies, §58-19-5.

Insurance information and privacy protection act,
§58-39-15.

Mining, §74-49.

Mortgage bankers, brokers and servicers,
§53-244.030.

Mortgages, high cost home loans, §24-1.1E(a).

Motor fuel, §75-81.

Savings and loan associations, §54B-4.

Savings banks, §54C-4(b).

Shareholder protection act, §55-9-01(b).

Tax credit for qualified business investments,
§105-163.010.

Telephone solicitations, §75-101.

Third party administrators, §58-56-2.

Tobacco reserve fund, §66-290.

Tobacco taxation, §105-113.4.

Trust companies, §53-301(a).

Underground storage tank cleanup, §143-215.94A.

Workers' compensation self-insurance, §97-165.

Employer groups, §58-47-60.

Affiliated.

Annual audited financial reports.

Insurance companies, §58-10-190.

Insurance holding companies, §58-19-5.

Insurance information and privacy protection act,
§58-39-15.

Affiliated group.

Corporate income tax.

Adjustment for expenses related to dividends,
§105-130.6A(a).

Intercompany transaction lacking economic
substance and not at fair market value,
§105-130.5A(i).

Franchise tax, §105-114.1(a).

Affiliated manufacturer.

Tobacco taxation, §105-113.4.

DEFINED TERMS —Cont'd

Affiliated provider.
Provider sponsored organizations, §131E-276.
Affiliate of a declarant.
Condominiums, §47C-1-103.
Affiliate transfer.
Trust companies, §53-301(a).
Affiliation period.
Health insurance portability and accountability.
Preexisting condition exclusions, §58-68-30(g).
Affirmation.
Notaries public act, §10B-3.
Affordable housing unit.
Housing trust, §122E-2.
African bee.
Bee and honey act, §106-635.
After-acquired property.
Probate and registration, §47-20.5(b).
After-acquired property clause.
Probate and registration, §47-20.5(a).
After-adopted.
Wills, §31-5.5(c).
After-born.
Wills, §31-5.5(c).
Aftercare.
Interstate compact on mental health, §122C-361.
Afternoon.
Banking, §25-4-104(a).
AFV.
Energy credit and banking program, §143-58.1(a).
Agencies authorized to implement and enforce state and federal environmental laws.
Rulemaking, §150B-19.3(b).
Agencies of the United States.
Soil and water conservation districts, §139-3.
Agency.
Administrative procedure, §150B-2.
Adoption, §48-1-101.
Archives and history, §121-2.
Coastal fisheries, §113-308.
Consultant service contracts, §143-64.20(a).
Department of administration, §143-336.
Executive organization, §143B-3.
Fees and charges by state agencies, §12-3.1(b).
Housing finance agency, §122A-3.
Housing trust, §122E-2.
Pollution control, §§159C-3, 159D-3.
Publications, §143-169.2(b).
Public telecommunications, §143B-426.8.
Relocation assistance, §133-7.
Seaward boundary of coastal lands, §77-20(c).
State government reorganization, §143A-3.
Surplus state property, §143-64.02.
Agency contract.
Athlete agents, §78C-86.
Agency head.
Internal auditing requirements for state agencies, §143-745(a).
Agency identified adoption, §48-1-101.
Agency of North Carolina.
Address confidentiality program, §15C-2.
Agency of the state.
Service of process, §1A-1 Rule 4(j).
Soil and water conservation districts, §139-3.
Agent.
Anatomical gifts, §130A-412.4.
Consent to health care of minor, §32A-29.
Controlled substances, §90-87.
Fire-safety standard and firefighter protection act, §58-92-10.

DEFINED TERMS —Cont'd

Agent —Cont'd
Insurance information and privacy protection act, §58-39-15.
Licensing, §58-33-10.
Mines, §74-24.2.
Nature of policies, §58-51-80(d).
Privileged communications, rape crisis centers and domestic violence programs, §8-53.12.
Aggravated circumstances.
Abused, neglected or dependent juveniles, §7B-101.
Aggravated offense.
Sex offender and public protection registration, §14-208.6.
Aggregate data.
Local health departments billing Medicaid, §130A-34.2(f).
Aggregate withdrawal value of withdrawable accounts.
Savings and loan associations, §54B-4.
Aggrieved party.
Alcoholic beverages, §18B-120.
UCC, §25-1-201(b).
Aggrieved person.
Electronic surveillance, §15A-286.
Agrarian growth zone.
Commerce department, §143B-437.010(a).
Tax incentives for new and expanding businesses, §105-129.3B(a).
Agreement.
Alcoholic beverages, §18B-1201.
City and town annexation agreements, §160A-58.22.
Electronic transactions, §66-312.
Farm machinery franchises, §66-180.
Job development investment grant program, §143B-437.51.
Membership camping, §66-232.
Sales, §25-2-106.
UCC, §25-1-201(b).
Uniform sales and use tax administration act, §105-164.42B.
Agreement for electronic presentment.
Banking, §25-4-110(a).
Agreement materials.
Radiation protection, §104E-5.
Agreement state.
Radiation protection, §104E-5.
Agricultural.
Development, §106-581.1.
Agricultural commodities.
Double damage liability, §1-539.2B(c).
Agricultural conservation easement, §106-744(b).
Agricultural employment.
Migrant housing, §95-223.
Agricultural land.
Taxation, §105-277.2.
Agricultural lien.
Secured transactions, §25-9-102(a).
Agricultural loan, §122D-3.
Agricultural operation.
Nuisance liability of agriculture and forest operations, §106-701(b).
Agricultural products.
Marketing associations, §54-130.
Water and air resources, §143-215.1(a5).
Agricultural seeds.
Seed law, §106-277.2.

DEFINED TERMS —Cont'd

Agricultural spreader vehicle.
Exemption from motor vehicle registration and certificate of title requirements, §20-51.

Agriculture, §122D-3.
Development, §106-581.1.
Wage and hour act, §95-25.2.

Agritourism activity.
Agritourism activity liability, §99E-30.

Agritourism professional.
Agritourism activity liability, §99E-30.

AHERA.
Asbestos hazard management, §130A-444.

Air ambulance.
Certificate of need, §131E-176.

Air cleaning device.
Water and air resources, §143-213.

Air contaminant, §143-213.

Air contamination, §143-213.

Air contamination source, §143-213.

Air courier services.
Growing businesses tax credits, §105-129.81.
Industrial facilities sales tax refunds, §105-164.14B(a).
Tax incentives for new and expanding businesses, §105-129.2.

Aircraft.
Aeronautics, §63-1.
Aircraft labor and storage liens, §44A-50.
Global TransPark authority, §63A-2.
Littering, §14-399(i).
Pointing laser devices at, §14-280.2(b).

Aircraft maintenance and repair.
Growing businesses tax credits, §105-129.81.

Aircraft manufacturing.
Industrial facilities sales tax refunds, §105-164.14B(a).

Air instruction, §63-1.

Airline company.
Public service taxation, §105-333.

Airman, §63-1.

Air navigation, §63-1.

Air navigation facility, §63-1.

Air pollution, §143-213.

Air pollution control, §143-215.105.

Air pollution control facility, §159C-3.
North Carolina industrial and pollution control facilities financing act, §159D-3.

Airport, §§63-1, 63-65.

Airport hazard, §63-1.

Airport protection privileges, §63-1.

Air school, §63-1.

Alarm system business, §74D-2(a).

Alarm systems business, §74D-2.

Alcohol.
Motor vehicles, §20-4.01.

Alcohol concentration.
Motor vehicles, §20-4.01.

Alcoholic beverages, §18B-101.
Alcohol taxation, §105-113.68.
Open container law, §20-138.7(f).

Alcoholism.
Public intoxication, §14-443.

ALE section.
Alcoholic beverages, §18B-101.

Alien company.
Insurance, §58-1-5.

Alien corporation.
Collection agencies, §58-70-5(q).

Alien country.
Insurers supervision, §58-30-10.

DEFINED TERMS —Cont'd

Alien or foreign government.
Foreign insurers, §58-16-20(a).

Alimony, §50-16.1A.

Allocable share.
Tobacco reserve fund, §66-290.

Allocated interests.
Condominiums, §47C-1-103.
Planned community act, §47F-1-103.

Allowable expenses.
State health plan for teachers and state employees, §135-48.1.
Victims compensation, §15B-2.

Allowed amount.
State health plan for teachers and state employees, §135-48.1.

All-terrain vehicle, §20-4.01.

Alteration.
Negotiable instruments, §25-3-407(a).

Alternate standby guardian, §35A-1370.

Alternative education services.
Discipline of students, §115C-390.1(b).

Alternative fuel, §105-449.130.
Energy credit and banking program, §143-58.1(a).
Gasoline and oil inspection, §119-15.

Alternative programs.
Nurse licensure compact, §90-171.82.

Amateur.
Boxing commission, §143-651.

Ambient temperature.
Protection of animals, §19A-23.

Ambulance.
Emergency medical services, §131E-155.
Motor vehicles, §20-4.01.

Ambulatory surgical facility, §131E-146.
Certificate of need, §131E-176.

Ambulatory surgical program, §131E-146.
Certificate of need, §131E-176.

Amendment.
Contracts between health benefit plans and health care providers, §58-50-270.

Amenities.
Adult care homes, §131D-2.1.

American vessel.
Unemployment compensation, §96-8.

Ammunition.
Soliciting unlawful purchase of firearm, §14-408.1(a).

Amount financed.
Installment sales, §25A-9.

Amount of the loan.
Banking, §53-165(a).

Amusement device safety, §95-111.3(a).

Amusement park.
Safety, §95-111.3(b).

Anaerobic lagoon.
Animal waste management, §143-215.10I(a).

Anaerobic process.
Animal waste management, §143-215.10I(a).

Analytical services.
Sales and use tax, §105-164.3.

Anatomical gift, §130A-412.4.

Anatomic pathology services, §90-701(e).

Ancillary security instrument.
Automatic release of ancillary security instruments, §45-42.3(a).

Ancillary service.
Sales and use tax, §105-164.3.

Ancillary state.
Insurers supervision, §58-30-10.

DEFINED TERMS —Cont'd
And official seal.
  Corporate conveyance forms, §47-41.01(d).
Animal clinic.
  Veterinarians, §90-181.1(b).
Animal control officer.
  Rabies, §§130A-134, 130A-184.
Animal dentistry, §90-181.
Animal exhibition.
  Regulation, §106-520.3A(b).
Animal feed.
  Biological residues, §106-549.81.
Animal food manufacturer.
  Meat inspection, §106-549.15.
  Poultry products inspection, §106-549.51.
Animal health center.
  Veterinarians, §90-181.1(b).
Animal hospital, §90-181.1(b).
Animal operation.
  Animal waste management, §143-215.10B.
Animal produce.
  Biological residues, §106-549.81.
Animals.
  Biological residues, §106-549.81.
  Biologics law, §106-708.
  Conservation, §113-129.
  Cruelty to animals, §14-360(c).
  Protection of animals, §§19A-1, 19A-23.
  Regulation of animal exhibitions, §106-520.3A(b).
  Structural pest control act, §106-65.24.
  Veterinarians, §90-181.
Animal shelter.
  Protection of animals, §19A-23.
  Sodium pentobarbital and other drugs for
    euthanasia of animals.
    Registration for purpose of obtaining and using,
      §90-101(a2).
Animal technician.
  Veterinarians, §90-181.
Animal waste, §143-215.10B.
  Animal waste management system operators,
    §90A-47.1.
Animal waste management system,
  §143-215.10B.
Annexation.
  City and town agreements, §160A-58.22.
Announcer.
  Boxing commission, §143-651.
Annual audited financial report.
  Insurance companies, §58-10-190.
Annual federal poverty guidelines.
  Student loan collection, §105B-1.
Annual license continuation fee.
  Insurance companies, §58-6-15.
Annual percentage rate.
  High cost home loans, §24-1.1E(a).
  Rate spread home loans, §24-1.1F(a).
Annual statement filing.
  Workers' compensation self-insurance.
    Employer groups, §58-47-60.
Annuitant.
  Group annuity contracts, §58-58-145(a).
Annuity.
  Legislative retirement system, §120-4.8.
  Retirement, §128-21.
  State retirement system, §135-1.
  Suitability in annuity transactions, §58-60-165.
Annuity buyer's guide.
  Annuity disclosure, §58-60-130.
Annuity issuer.
  Structured settlement protection, §1-543.11.

DEFINED TERMS —Cont'd
Annuity reserve.
  Legislative retirement system, §120-4.8.
  Retirement, §128-21.
  State retirement system, §135-1.
An offense involving assault.
  Domestic violence in disposition report,
    §15A-1382.1(c).
Anomalous endorsement.
  Negotiable instruments, §25-3-205(d).
Antenna.
  Wireless telecommunications facilities,
    §§153A-349.51, 160A-400.51.
Antifreeze and summer coolant, §106-579.3.
Antimicrobial.
  Pesticide board, §143-460.
Antique airplanes.
  Property taxes, §105-277.12(a).
Antique automobiles.
  Property taxes, §105-330.9(a).
Antique firearm, §14-409.11(a).
  Exclusions from definition, §14-409.11(b).
  Sale of pistols and crossbows, §14-402(c).
A period of war.
  Employment preference for veterans, §128-15(b).
  Veteran's preference, §126-81.
Apiary.
  Bee and honey act, §106-635.
Apparent owner.
  Unclaimed property act, §116B-52.
Appeal.
  Criminal procedure, §15A-101.
Appeals panel.
  Mental health, developmental disability,
    substance abuse, §122C-151.4(a).
Appearance in person before notary.
  Notaries public act, §10B-3.
Appellant.
  Discretionary review on certification by supreme
    court, AppProc Rule 15(i).
  Scope of review of decisions of court of appeals,
    AppProc Rule 16(c).
Appellate division.
  Discipline and disability rules of state bar, Bar
    Rule B.0103.
  Procedures for the authorized practice committee
    of the state bars, Bar Rule D.0204.
Appellee.
  Discretionary review on certification by supreme
    court, AppProc Rule 15(i).
  Scope of review of decisions of court of appeals,
    AppProc Rule 16(c).
Applicable percentage rate.
  Sales and use tax, §105-164.4(a).
Applicable state entity.
  Drivers' licenses, lose control, lose license,
    §20-11(n1).
Applicant.
  Accredited sponsor.
    Continuing legal education, Bar Rule D.1902.
  Archaeological investigations.
    Criminal record checks of permit applicants,
      §70-13.1(a).
  Auctions and auctioneers.
    Criminal history record checks of applicants for
      license, §85B-3.2(a).
  Child support, §110-142.
  CLE.
    Specialization certification, Bar Rule D.1902.
  Client security fund of North Carolina state bar,
    rules governing, Bar Rule D.1401.

DEFINED TERMS —Cont'd
Applicant —Cont'd

Continuing legal education, Bar Rule D.1902.
Energy assistance for low-income persons,
§143B-472.122.
Fire departments, criminal history record checks,
§114-19.12(a).
Health insurance risk pool.
Notice regarding by insurers to applicants,
§58-3-276(d).
Homeowner's recovery fund, §87-15.5.
Insurance information and privacy protection act,
§58-39-15.
Insurance rate evasion fraud, §58-2-164(a).
Letters of credit, §25-5-102(a).
Licensure of manufactured home manufacturers,
dealers, salespersons or set-up contractors.
Criminal history record checks, §143-143.10A.
Locksmith licensing, §74F-18(a).
Long-term care insurance, §58-55-20.
Marriage and family therapists.
Criminal history record checks of license
applicants, §90-270.63(a).
Medicare supplement insurance, §58-54-1.
Money transmitters, §53-208.2(a).
Nurses, §90-171.48(a).
Nursing home administrators, §90-288.01(a).
Private personnel services, §95-47.1.
Professional counselors.
Criminal history record checks of license
applicants, §90-345(a).
Professional employer organizations, §58-89A-5.
Provider requirements for Medicaid or Health
Choice, §108C-2.
Public assistance program, §108A-24.
Real estate appraisal management companies.
Criminal history record checks, §93E-2-11(a).
Recovery from insurers providing additional
coverage to Medicaid-eligible persons,
§108A-55.4(a).
Refund anticipation loan act, §53-246.
Salvage.
Abandoned shipwrecks and other underwater
sites.
Criminal record checks of applicants for
permit or license, §121-25.1(a).
Solid waste management, environmental
compliance requirements, §130A-295.3(a).
Specialty field.
Continuing legal education, specialization
certification, Bar Rule D.1902.
Sponsor.
Continuing legal education, Bar Rule D.1902.
Substance abuse professionals, §90-113.31A.
**Applicant for a certified applicator's
identification card.**
Structural pest control act, §106-65.24.
Applicant for a license.
Structural pest control act, §106-65.24.
Applicant for employment.
Employer and employee, §14-357.1.
Applicant supervisor.
Substance abuse professionals, §90-113.31A.
Application.
Animal waste management system operators,
§90A-47.1.
Savings and loan associations, §54B-4.
Wireless telecommunications facilities,
§§153A-349.51, 160A-400.51.
Application assistant.
Address confidentiality program, §15C-2.

DEFINED TERMS —Cont'd
Appointing authority.

Interpreters for hearing impaired, §8B-1.
Notice of public office appointments, §143-47.6.
Repayment of money owed to state, §143-555.
Appointing officer.
Corporations, §55-8-43(c).
Apportionable income.
Corporate income tax, §105-130.4(a).
Appraisal.
Property taxes, §105-273.
Real estate appraisers, §93E-1-4.
Relocation assistance, §133-7.
Appraisal assignment.
Real estate appraisers, §93E-1-4.
Appraisal foundation.
Real estate appraisals, §93E-1-4.
Appraisal management company.
Real estate appraisal management companies,
§93E-2-2(a).
Appraisal management services.
Real estate appraisal management companies,
§93E-2-2(a).
Appraisal panel or fee panel.
Real estate appraisal management companies,
§93E-2-2(a).
Appraisal report.
Real estate appraisers, §93E-1-4.
Appraisal review.
Real estate appraisal management companies,
§93E-2-2(a).
Appraised value.
Recreation and natural heritage, §113-77.6.
Apprentice, §94-6.
Cosmetic art, §88B-2.
Locksmiths, §74F-4.
Appropriate court.
Interstate agreement on detainers, §15A-762.
**Appropriate evidence of appointment or
incumbency.**
Investment securities, §25-8-402(c).
Appropriate state agency.
Certificates of public convenience and necessity,
§62-110(f6).
Appropriation.
Budget of state, §143C-1-1(d).
Approved activity.
Continuing legal education, rules governing
administration, Bar Rule D.1501.
Approved forest management plan.
Forest development act, §106-1012.
Approved laboratory.
Controlled substance examination regulation,
§95-231.
Approved practices.
Forest development act, §106-1012.
Approving a site.
Counties.
Solid waste collection and disposal,
§153A-136(c).
Public enterprises, §160A-325(a).
Aquaculture, §106-758.
Aquaculture facility, §106-758.
A qualified voter.
Soil and water conservation districts, §139-3.
Aquatic species.
Aquaculture development, §106-758.
Aquifer.
Well construction, §87-85.
Arbitral award.
Civil procedure, §1-567.32.

DEFINED TERMS —Cont'd

Arbitral tribunal.
Civil procedure, §1-567.32.
Arbitration.
Civil procedure, §1-567.32.
Arbitration agreement.
Civil procedure, §1-567.37.
Arbitration institution.
Family law arbitration, §50-45(g).
Arbitration organization, §1-569.1.
Arbitrator, §1-569.1.
Archaeological investigation, §70-12.
Indian antiquities, §70-48.
Archaeological resource, §70-12.
Indian antiquities, §70-48.
Architect, §83A-1.
Area authority.
Mental health, §122C-3.
Area board.
Mental health, §122C-3.
Area director.
Mental health, §122C-3.
Area facility.
Mental health, §122C-3.
Area of operation.
Urban redevelopment, §160A-503.
Area of the state.
Water and air resources, §143-212.
Areas of environmental concern.
Land policy act, §113A-152.
Armed forces.
Children of war veterans scholarships, §165-20.
Life insurance.
Dishonest and predatory sales to military
personnel, §58-58-335.
Armed private investigator, §74C-13(a1).
Armed security guard, §74C-13(a1).
Armed services.
Tuition of active duty personnel in armed forces,
§116-143.3(a).
Armory, §127A-161.
Armory car profession, §74C-3.
Armory site, §127A-161.
Arrestee.
DNA database and databanks, §15A-266.2.
Arresting law enforcement agency.
Crime victims' rights, §15A-830(a).
Arrest order.
Criminal process, §15A-305.
Arrest warrant.
Criminal process, §15A-304.
Arson.
Criminal law, §14-58.
Art dealer.
Sales, §25C-10.
Article.
Records, tapes and other recorded devices,
§14-432.
State education assistance authority, §116-201.
Article 65 corporation.
Insurance company taxation, §105-228.3.
Articles of dedication.
Nature preserves act, §113A-164.3.
Articles of incorporation.
Business corporations, §55-1-40.
Nonprofit corporations, §55A-1-40.
Articles of organization.
Limited liability companies, §57C-1-03.
Artificial construction.
Floodplain regulations, §143-215.52(a), (b).

DEFINED TERMS —Cont'd

Artisan bakery.
Sales and use tax, §105-164.13B(a).
Artist.
Minors, talent contracts, §48A-17.
Sales, §25C-10.
Artistic or creative services.
Minors, talent contracts, §48A-11.
Arts, §143-403.
Asbestos, §130A-444.
Asbestos containing material, §130A-444.
Asbestosis.
Workers' compensation, §97-62.
As-extracted collateral.
Secured transactions, §25-9-102(a).
ASHRAE.
Performance standards for sustainable,
energy-efficient public buildings, §143-135.36.
Assessment.
Property taxes, §105-273.
Assessment agreement.
Dry-cleaning solvent cleanup act,
§143-215.104B(b).
Asset-backed security.
Principal and income act, §37A-4-415(a).
Asset management plan.
Water infrastructure, §159G-20.
Assets, §58-13-15.
Fraudulent transfers, §39-23.1.
Long-term care partnerships, §58-55-55.
Medicaid, §108A-70.4(a).
Medicaid, transfer of assets for less than market
value to qualify, §108A-58.1(e).
Assigned area.
Urban electrical service, §160A-331.
Assigned employee.
Interchange of governmental employees, §126-52.
Professional employer organizations, §58-89A-5.
Assigned supplier.
Urban electrical service, §160A-331.
Assignment.
Claims against the state, §143B-426.40A(a).
Assignment of leases, rents, issues or profits.
Probate and registration, §47-20.
Assistance animal.
Assaulting law enforcement or assistance animals,
§14-163.1(a).
Assistance eligible individual.
Group accident and health insurance.
Continuation of coverage, §58-53-41(a).
Assistant display operator.
Pyrotechnics licenses, §58-82A-1.1.
Assisted living administrators, §90-288.13.
Assisted living facility.
State health plan for teachers and state
employees.
Long-term care benefits, §135-48.61(a).
Assisted living residence.
Adult care homes, §131D-2.1.
Adult care home's bill of rights, §131D-20.
Assisted living administrators, §90-288.13.
Assistive technology device.
Discipline of students.
Seclusion and restraint, §115C-391.1(b).
Associate.
Savings and loan associations, §54B-4.
Savings banks, §54C-4(b).
Shareholder protection act, §55-9-01(b).
Associate home inspector, §143-151.45.
Association.
Beach property insurance, §58-45-5.

DEFINED TERMS —Cont'd
Association —Cont'd
  Planned community act, §47F-1-103.
  Savings and loan interstate branches, §54B-266.
  Self-insurance security association, §97-130.
  Solicitation of contributions, §131F-2.
Association aggregate security system.
  Self-insurance security association, §97-130.
  Workers' compensation self insurance, §97-165.
Association of unit owners, §47A-3.
Assorted chicks, §106-541.
Assuming insurer.
  Reinsurance, §58-10-25(a).
Assumption reinsurance agreement,
  §58-10-25(a).
Athlete.
  Athletic trainers, §90-523.
Athlete agent, §78C-86.
Athletic director.
  Athlete agents, §78C-86.
Athletic trainer, §90-523.
At no cost other than periodic user fees.
  Annexation initiated by municipality.
    Water and sewer service, §160A-58.56(h).
Atomic energy.
  Radiation protection, §104E-5.
Attack.
  Local government during emergencies, §162B-7.
Attempted robbery.
  Criminal law, §14-87.1.
Attempted telephone solicitation, §66-260.
Attempt to perform an abortion.
  Woman's right to know act, §90-21.81.
Attending physician.
  Advance instruction for mental health treatment,
    §122C-72.
  Standby guardianship, §35A-1370.
Attending practitioner.
  Adoption, §48-3-401.
Attending providers.
  Drive-thru deliveries, §58-3-169(a).
Attest.
  Notaries public act, §10B-3.
Attestation.
  Notaries public act, §10B-3.
Attorney.
  Client security fund, rules governing
    administration, Bar Rule D.1401.
  Procedures, Bar Rule D.0101.
  Reciprocal insurance, §58-15-5.
Attorney general.
  Address confidentiality program, §15C-2.
  Cooperative agreements.
    Health care facilities, §131E-192.2.
  Cooperative agreements among physicians or
    between physician, hospital or others,
    §90-21.25.
  Electronic surveillance, §15A-286.
  False claims act, §1-606.
  Medical assistance provider false claims act,
    §108A-70.11.
  National crime prevention and privacy compact,
    §114-19.50.
  RICO act, §75D-3.
Attorney of record.
  Criminal procedure, §15A-101.
ATV.
  Motor vehicles, §20-4.01.
At will.
  Leases, UCC, §25-2A-109(1).
Auction, §85B-1.

DEFINED TERMS —Cont'd
Auctioneer, §85B-1.
Auctioneering, §85B-1.
Auction firm, §85B-1.
Audiologist.
  Licensure, §90-293.
Audio-visual master.
  Sales and use tax exemption, §105-164.13.
Audiovisual recording device.
  Unlawful use of audiovisual recording device in
    motion picture theater, §14-440.1(c).
Audiovisual work.
  Sales and use tax, §105-164.3.
Audio work.
  Sales and use tax, §105-164.3.
Audit.
  State auditor, §147-64.4.
Audit committee.
  Annual audited financial reports.
    Insurance companies, §58-10-190.
Audited financial report.
  Workers' compensation self-insurance.
    Employer groups, §58-47-75(a).
Audited GAAP financial statement.
  Professional employer organizations, §58-89A-5.
Audited statement of financial condition.
  Mortgage bankers, brokers and servicers,
    §53-244.030.
Aural transfer.
  Electronic surveillance, §15A-286.
Authenticate.
  Secured transactions, §25-9-102(a).
Authentication.
  Document authentication, §66-271.
  Electronic medical records, §90-412(b).
Authority.
  Facility authorities, §160A-480.2.
  Need-based scholarships for students attending
    private colleges and universities, §116-280.
  Regional transit authority registration tax,
    §105-560.
  Regional transit authority vehicle rental tax,
    §105-550.
  Regional transportation authorities, §160A-631.
  Water and sewer, §162A-2.
Authority service area.
  Public health authorities, §130A-45.01.
Authorization.
  Computer crimes, §14-453.
Authorization to consent to health care for
  minor, §32A-29.
Authorized account.
  Funds transfers, UCC, §25-4A-105(a).
Authorized agent.
  Weights and measures, §81A-9.
Authorized control event.
  Risk based capital requirements, insurance
    companies, §58-12-21(a).
Authorized control level risk-based capital.
  Insurance companies, §58-12-2.
Authorized delegate.
  Money transmitters, §53-208.2(a).
Authorized insurer.
  Motor vehicle service agreement companies,
    §66-370(b).
Authorized investments.
  State debt, §142-29.2.
Authorized lender.
  Reverse mortgages, §53-257.
Authorized officer.
  Public obligations, §159E-2.

DEFINED TERMS —Cont'd

Authorized person.
Instruments to secure equity lines of credit, §45-81.

Authorized representative.
Egg law, §106-245.14.
Meat inspection, §106-549.15.

Authorized shares.
Business corporations, §55-1-40.

Authorized trust institution.
Trust companies, §53-301(a).

Authorizing agent.
Cremation, §90-210.121.

Autism.
Competency, §35A-1101.

Auto insurance.
Rate evasion fraud, §58-2-164(a).

Automated banking device.
Criminal law, §14-113.8.

Automated claims adjudication system.
Portable consumer electronic devices insurance, §58-33-27(a).

Automated external defibrillator, §90-21.15(b).

Automated ordering system.
Motor vehicle warranties, §20-305.1(h).

Automated transaction.
Electronic transactions, §66-312.

Automatic dialing and recorded message player.
Telephone solicitations, §75-101.

Automatic vending.
Aid to the blind, §111-49(a).

Automobile graveyard.
Junkyard control, §136-143.

Average final compensation.
Judicial retirement, §135-53.
Retirement, §128-21.
State retirement system, §135-1.

Average installation of a connection for a residential lot.
Annexation initiated by municipality.
Water and sewer service, §160A-58.56(h).

Average prime offer rate.
Rate spread home loans, §24-1.1F(a).

Average weekly insured wage.
Unemployment compensation, §96-8.

Average weekly wages.
Workers' compensation, §97-2.

Aversive procedure.
Discipline of students.
Seclusion and restraint, §115C-391.1(b).

Aviation gasoline.
Gasoline and oil inspection, §119-15.
Gasoline tax, §105-449.60.

Axle group.
Motor vehicles, §20-118.

B-20.
Energy credit and banking program, §143-58.1(a).

Baby sitting service.
Sex offender providing, §14-321.1(a).

Background standard.
Risk based environmental remediation of industrial sites, §130A-310.65.

Bail agent, §15A-531.

Bail bond, §§15A-531, 58-71-1.

Bail bondsman, §58-71-1.

Bailee.
Oil and hazardous substance control, §143-215.77.
UCC, §25-7-102(a).

Bailment surcharge.
Alcoholic beverages, §18B-101.

DEFINED TERMS —Cont'd

Bakery items.
Sales and use tax, §105-164.13B(a).

Ballot.
Elections, §163-165.

Ballot item.
Elections, §163-165.

Ballot style.
Elections, §163-165.

Bank, §§32-2, 53-1.
Bank holding company act, §53-226.
Funds transfers, UCC, §25-4A-105(a).
Good funds settlement act, §45A-3.
Interstate branch banking, §53-224.9.
Loans exempt from rate and fee limitations, §24-9(a).
Manufactured housing, §143-143.9.
Reciprocal banking act, §53-210.
Secured transactions, §25-9-102(a).
Trust companies, §53-301(a).
UCC, §25-1-201(b).
Uniform fiduciaries act, §32-2(a).

Bank acceptances, §53-56.

Bank holding company.
Bank holding company act, §53-226.
Corporate income tax.
Adjustment for expenses related to dividends, §105-130.6A(a).
Interstate branch banking, §53-224.9.
Reciprocal banking act, §53-210.

Banking, §53-127(a).

Banking business day.
Livestock prompt pay law, §106-418.3.

Banking commission.
Mortgage bankers, brokers and servicers, §53-244.030.

Banking day, §25-4-104(a).

Banking entity, §53-127(a).

Banking institution.
Rate of survivorship and joint deposits, §41-2.1(e).

Banking office.
Reciprocal banking act, §53-210.

Bank of below ground crypts.
Cemeteries, §65-48.

Bank-offered spot rate.
Foreign-money claims, §1C-1820.

Bankrupt.
Limited liability companies, §57C-1-03.
Partnerships, §59-32.

Bankruptcy law specialty, Bar Rule D.2202.

Bank supervisory agency.
Interstate branch banking, §53-224.9.
Trust companies, §53-301(a).

Bar.
Procedures for ruling on questions of legal ethics, Bar Rule D.0101.
Smoking in restaurants and bars, §130A-492.

Barrel.
Oil and hazardous substance control, §143-215.77.
Weights and measures, §81A-9.

Base flood.
Floodplain regulations, §143-215.52(a).

Base floodplain.
Floodplain regulations, §143-215.52(a).

Baseline reversion.
State employee suggestion program (NC-Thinks), §143-345.20.

Base period.
Unemployment compensation, §96-8.

Base premium rate.
Small employer group health coverage, §58-50-110.

DEFINED TERMS —Cont'd
Base rate of compensation.
Disability income plan, §135-101.
Base year exportation volume.
Tax credit for manufacturing cigarettes for
exportation, §105-130.45(a).
Base years.
Job development investment grant program,
§143B-437.51.
Basic health care plan.
Small employer group health coverage,
§58-50-110.
Basin.
Cooperative state-local coalition water quality
protection plans, §143-214.14(a).
Beach area.
Beach property insurance, §58-45-5.
Beach bingo games.
Lotteries and gaming, §14-309.6.
Bearer.
UCC, §25-1-201(b).
Bearer form.
Investment securities, §25-8-102.
Bed and breakfast inn.
Sanitation, §130A-247.
Bed capacity.
Certificate of need, §131E-176.
Bedding, §106-65.95.
Bees, §106-635.
Bee yard.
Bee and honey act, §106-635.
Begin to construct.
Public utilities, §62-100.
Behavioral intervention.
Discipline of students.
Seclusion and restraint, §115C-391.1(b).
Below ground crypts.
Cemeteries, §65-48.
Beneficial interest.
Asset-backed securities facilitation, §53-425.
RICO act, §75D-3.
Beneficial owner.
Appraisal rights, §55-13-01.
Beneficial ownership.
Control share acquisitions, §55-9A-01(b).
Beneficial shareholder.
Appraisal rights, §55-13-01.
Beneficiary.
Community third party trusts, pooled trusts act,
§36D-2.
Custodial trusts, §33B-1.
Disability income plan, §135-101.
Funds transfers, UCC, §25-4A-103(a).
Judicial retirement, §135-53.
Letters of credit, §25-5-102(a).
Local government law-enforcement retirement,
§143-166.50(a).
Principal and income act, §37A-1-102.
Provider sponsored organizations, §131E-276.
Retirement, §128-21.
State law-enforcement retirement, §143-166.30(a).
State retirement system, §135-1.
Uniform trust code, §36C-1-103.
Beneficiary designation.
Renunciation, §31B-2.1(a).
Beneficiary form.
Uniform transfer on death security registration
act, §41-40.
Beneficiary of the remainder interest.
Principal and income act, §37A-1-102.

DEFINED TERMS —Cont'd
Beneficiary's bank.
Funds transfers, UCC, §25-4A-103(a).
Benefit booklet.
Readable insurance policies, §58-38-15.
Readable medical insurance, §58-66-15.
Benefit contract.
Fraternal benefit societies, §58-24-15(a).
Benefit member.
Fraternal benefit societies, §58-24-15(b).
Benefit period.
State health plan for teachers and state
employees, §135-48.1.
Benefit plan.
Health insurance risk pool, §58-50-175.
Transfers to minors, §33A-1.
Benefits.
Direct access to obstetrician-gynecologist,
§58-51-38(a).
Disability income plan, §135-101.
Health benefit plan external review, §58-50-75(c).
State health plan for teachers and state
employees, §135-48.1.
Unemployment compensation, §96-8.
Veterans, §34-2.
Benefit year.
Unemployment compensation, §96-8.
Unemployment insurance, §96-8.
Best value procurements.
Public contracts, §143-135.9(a).
Between merchants.
Sales, §25-2-104.
Bicycle, §136-71.7.
Child bicycle safety act, §20-171.8.
Motor vehicles, §20-171.1.
Bid.
Motion pictures, §75C-2.
Biennium.
Budget of state, §143C-1-1(d).
Big game.
Conservation, §113-129.
Bikeway, §136-71.7.
Billing date.
Revolving credit charges, §24-11(d).
Billing information.
Taxation, §132-1.1(c).
Bill of lading.
UCC, §25-1-201(b).
Bingo game.
Lotteries and gaming, §14-309.6.
Biodiesel.
Gasoline tax, §105-449.60.
Biodiesel provider.
Gasoline tax, §105-449.60.
Biological agent.
Biological agents registry, §130A-479(b).
Biological evidence, §15A-268(a).
Biological organism, §106-65.44.
Biological residue.
Animals, §106-549.81.
Biologics, §106-708.
Bioprocessing.
Industrial facilities sales tax refunds,
§105-164.14B(a).
Bioterrorism.
First responders vaccination program,
§130A-485(f).
Birds.
Conservation, §113-129.
Birth defect.
Monitoring program, §130A-131.16(b).

DEFINED TERMS —Cont'd

Blanket accident and health insurance.
Nature of policies, §58-51-75.

Blanket encumbrance.
Membership camping, §66-232.

Blend.
Seed law, §106-277.2.

Blended fuel.
Gasoline tax, §105-449.60.

Blender.
Gasoline tax, §105-449.60.

Blighted area.
Urban redevelopment, §160A-503.

Blighted parcel.
Urban redevelopment, §160A-503.

Blind bidding.
Motion pictures, §75C-2.

Blind person, §111-11.
License tax for privilege to practice profession.
Exemption, §105-41(b).

Blind trust.
State government ethics act, §138A-3.

Blind vendor.
Aid, §111-49(b).

Block of business.
Insurance companies, closure of a block of
business, §58-3-275(c).

Blood.
Wholesale prescription drug distributors,
§106-145.2.

Blood component.
Wholesale prescription drug distributors,
§106-145.2.

Blue light.
Use of red or blue lights on vehicle, §20-130.1(c).

Board.
Education, §115C-5.
Interpreters and transliterators licensure act,
§90D-3.
University of North Carolina, §116-2.

Board-approved school.
Massage and bodywork therapy, §90-622.

Boarding kennel.
Protection of animals, §19A-23.

Board of county commissioners.
County water and sewer districts, §162A-86(a1).
Mental health, §122C-3.
Public hospitals, §131E-16.

Board of directors.
Falls Lake watershed association, §77-140.
Trust companies, §53-301(a).

Board of trade.
Commodities act, §78D-1.

Board of trustees.
Disability income plan, §135-101.
Judicial retirement, §135-53.
Local government sales and use tax for public
transportation, §105-506.1.
Regional natural gas districts, §160A-661(b).
Regional public transportation, §160A-601.
Regional transit authority registration tax,
§105-560.
Regional transportation authorities, §160A-631.
State retirement system, §135-1.

Boat.
Coastal area management, §113A-103.

Boating and fishing access area.
Conservation, §113-129.

Body parts.
Anatomical gifts, §130A-412.4.
Cremation, §90-210.121.

DEFINED TERMS —Cont'd

Boiler.
Uniform act, §95-69.9(b).

Boll weevil, §106-65.69.

Bona fide association.
Health insurance portability and accountability,
§58-68-25(a).

Bona fide farm purposes.
Accessory building of bona fide farm.
Building code exemption, §160A-360(k).
Municipalities initiating annexation,
§160A-58.54(c).

Bona fide loan discount points.
Mortgages, high cost home loans, §24-1.1E(a).

Bona fide medical care provider.
Child care facilities, administration of medicine,
§110-102.1A(b).

Bona fide title insurance agency, §58-27-5(c).

Bona fide title insurance agent, §58-27-5(c).

Bona fide title insurance company, §58-27-5(c).

Bond documentation.
State debt, §142-29.2.

Bonded importer.
Gasoline tax, §105-449.60.

Bonded indebtedness.
Capital facilities finance act, §142-82.

Bond resolution.
State education assistance authority, §116-201.

Bonds.
Agricultural finance act, §122D-3.
City and town parking authorities, §160A-551.
Electric power, §159B-3.
Financing capital facilities, §116D-7.
Health facilities finance, §131A-3.
Higher education bonds, §116D-26(f).
Housing authorities, §157-3.
Housing finance agency, §122A-3.
Pollution control, §§159C-3, 159D-3.
Private capital facilities finance act, §159D-37.
Public hospitals, §131E-16.
Solid waste, §159I-3(a).
State debt, §142-29.2.
State education assistance authority, §116-201.
University of North Carolina, §116-41.1.
Urban redevelopment, §160A-503.

Bonds or notes.
Capital facilities finance act, §142-82.

Bone marrow transplantation services.
Certificate of need, §131E-176.

Books and records.
Workers' compensation.
Self-insurance.
Third-party administrators and service
companies, §58-47-150.
Workers' compensation self-insurance.
Employer groups, §58-47-60.

Booth.
Cosmetic art, §88B-2.

Booth renter.
Cosmetic art, §88B-2.

Borrower.
Banking, §53-165(b).
Good funds settlement act, §45A-3.
Instruments to secure equity lines of credit,
§45-81.
Reverse mortgages, §53-257.
Satisfaction of deeds of trust and mortgages,
§45-36.4.
Savings and loan associations, §54B-4.

Boxer, §143-651.

Boxing match, §143-651.

DEFINED TERMS —Cont'd
Brain death.
  Natural death right, §90-323.
Branch.
  Banking, §53-1.
  Interstate branch banking, §53-224.9.
  Savings and loan interstate branches, §54B-266.
  Savings interstate branch banks, §54C-200.
  Trust companies, §53-301(a).
  UCC, §25-1-201(b).
Branch manager.
  Mortgage bankers, brokers and servicers,
    §53-244.030.
Branch of an employer.
  Unemployment compensation.
    Seasonal pursuits, §96-16(j).
Branch office.
  Mortgage bankers, brokers and servicers,
    §53-244.030.
  Regional reciprocal savings and loan acquisition
    act, §54B-48.2.
  Savings and loan associations, §54B-4.
  Savings banks, §54C-4(b).
  Structural pest control act, §106-65.24.
Branch or district office.
  Motor clubs and associations, §58-69-2.
Brand.
  Livestock brands, §80-58.
  Seed law, §106-277.2.
Brand family.
  Tobacco escrow compliance, §66-292.
Brand name.
  Commercial feed law, §106-284.33.
  Commercial fertilizer, §106-657.
Brand style.
  Fire-safety standard and firefighter protection act,
    §58-92-10.
Brazilian bee.
  Bee and honey act, §106-635.
Breach of the peace.
  Public morals, §19-1.1.
Breaking and entering.
  Habitual breaking and entering status offense,
    §14-7.25.
Bribe.
  Athletic contests, §§14-376, 14-380.3.
Bribery of officials, §14-217.
Broadband service.
  Public utilities, §62-3.
Broadcasting station.
  Political campaigns, §163-278.6.
Broker.
  Commercial real estate broker lien act, §44A-24.2.
  Investment securities, §25-8-102.
  Licensing, §58-33-10.
  Public utilities, §62-3.
  Reinsurance intermediaries, §58-9-2(a).
  Transfers to minors, §33A-1.
Broker services.
  Commercial real estate broker lien act, §44A-24.2.
Brokers-in-charge.
  Real estate brokers, §93A-2(a1).
Brother.
  Adoptee's new birth certificate, §48-9-107(c).
  Workers' compensation, §97-2.
Brownfields agreement, §130A-310.31(b).
Brownfields property, §130A-310.31(a).
Brownfields site, §130A-310.31(b).
Brucellosis, §106-389.
Budget.
  Budget of state, §143C-1-1(d).

DEFINED TERMS —Cont'd
Budget —Cont'd
  Local government finance, §159-7.
  School budgets, §115C-423.
Budget ordinance.
  Local government finance, §159-7.
Budget resolution.
  School budgets, §115C-423.
Budget year.
  Budget of state, §143C-1-1(d).
  Local government finance, §159-7.
  School budgets, §115C-423.
Building, §47A-3.
  Counties, §153A-350.
  Criminal law, §§14-58.1, 14-159.11.
  Criminal trespass, §14-132.
Building and loan association, §54B-4.
Building inspection official.
  Volunteer architect during an emergency or
    disaster, §83A-13.1(d).
  Volunteer engineer during emergency or disaster,
    §89C-19.1(d).
Building permit.
  Wireless telecommunications facilities,
    §§153A-349.51, 160A-400.51.
Building that is a place of religious worship.
  Breaking and entering, §14-54.1(b).
Building trades training.
  Vocational and technical education, §115C-160.
Bulk.
  Soil additives act, §106-50.30.
Bulk end-user.
  Alternative fuel, §105-449.130.
  Gasoline tax, §105-449.60.
Bulk fertilizer.
  Commercial fertilizer, §106-657.
Bulk plant.
  Gasoline tax, §105-449.60.
Bulk sale.
  Weights and measures, §81A-9.
Bullying and harassing behavior.
  School violence prevention, §115C-407.15(a).
Bundled transaction.
  Sales and use tax, §105-164.3.
Burden of establishing a fact.
  UCC, §25-1-201(b).
Bureau.
  Controlled substances, §90-87.
  Veterans, §34-2.
Burglary.
  Criminal law, §14-51.
Burial, §90-210.20(c).
Burn intensive care services.
  Certificate of need, §131E-176.
Bus company.
  Public utilities, §62-3.
Bushel.
  Conservation, §113-129.
  Weights and measures, §81A-9.
Business.
  Business discrimination, §75B-1.
  Enterprise corporations, §53A-37.
  Growing businesses tax credits, §105-129.83(j).
  Identity theft, §75-61.
  Job development investment grant program,
    §143B-437.51.
  Limited liability companies, §57C-1-03.
  Partnerships, §§59-32, 59-102.
  Relocation assistance, §133-7.
  Sales and use tax, §105-164.3.
  State government ethics act, §138A-3.

DEFINED TERMS —Cont'd

Business —Cont'd
Tax credit for qualified business investments, §105-163.010.
Business agreement.
Tangible personal property, §105-304.
Business associate.
Health information exchange, §90-413.3.
Business associate contract.
Health information exchange, §90-413.3.
Business association.
Transportation board, §136-14(h).
Unclaimed property act, §116B-52.
Business bankruptcy law, Bar Rule D.2202.
Business combination.
Corporations, §75E-1.
Shareholder protection act, §55-9-01(b).
Business contract.
Reciprocal attorneys' fees in business contracts, §6-21.7(a).
Business day.
Invention development services, §66-209.
Legislative services commission enrolling clerk, §120-33(d2).
Membership camping, §66-232.
Sales, §14-401.13.
State directory of new hires, §110-129.2(j).
Business district.
Motor vehicles, §20-4.01.
Business entity.
Building codes, §143-143.4(g).
Business corporations, §55-1-40.
Derivative transactions, insurance companies, §58-7-205(a).
Discarded computer equipment and television management, §130A-309.131.
Insurance producers, §58-33-10.
Limited liability companies, §57C-1-03.
Partnerships, §59-102.
Conversion and merger, §59-73.1.
Political campaigns, §163-278.6.
Public adjusters, §58-33A-5.
Solid waste management, §130A-290(a).
Taxation, §105-277.2.
Personal liability when taxes not paid, §105-242.2(a).
Wildlife conservation land.
Special class of property for property tax purposes, §105-277.15(a).
Business firm.
Engineering, §89C-3.
Business of viatical settlements.
Viatical life insurance settlements, §58-58-205.
Business operations.
Sudan (Darfur) divestment act, §147-86.42.
Business opportunity.
Sales, §66-94.
Business or trade school.
National Guard tuition assistance, §116-209.52(a1).
Business paper.
Banking, §53-55.
Business premises.
Tangible personal property, §105-304(b).
Business property.
Business and energy tax credit, §105-129.15.
Growing businesses tax credits, §105-129.81.
Business trust, §39-44.
Business with which associated.
Legislative ethics, §120-85.1.
Local ABC boards, §18B-201(g).

DEFINED TERMS —Cont'd

Business with which associated —Cont'd
State government ethics act, §138A-3.
Bus line company.
Public service taxation, §105-333.
Butterfly ballot, §163-165.4B.
Buyer.
Manufactured housing, §143-143.9.
Pork promotion assessment, §106-792.
Sales, §25-2-103.
Seed law, §106-277.2.
Sublease of motor vehicle and loan assumption arranging, §20-106.2(a).
Buyer in ordinary course of business.
Leases, UCC, §25-2A-103(1).
UCC, §25-1-201(b).
Buyer's guide.
Annuity disclosure, §58-60-130.
Life insurance solicitation, §58-60-10.
Bylaws.
Interstate compact for juveniles, §7B-4001.
Interstate insurance product regulation compact, §58-91-10.
Nonprofit corporations, §55A-1-40.
By-product material.
Radiation protection, §104E-5.
Cable service.
Sales and use tax, §105-164.3.
State franchising of cable television service, §66-350.
Cable system.
State franchising of cable television service, §66-350.
Calendar quarter.
Unemployment compensation, §96-8.
Call-by-call basis.
Sales and use tax on telecommunications, §105-164.4C(h).
Call center.
Sales and use tax on telecommunications, §105-164.4C(h).
Caller identification record.
Telephone records privacy protection, §14-113.30.
Call taking.
911 system, §62A-40.
Campaign-related expenditure.
Voter-owned elections act, §163-278.96.
Camp Butner reservation.
Mental health, §122C-3.
Campgrounds.
Membership camping, §66-232.
Camping site.
Membership camping, §66-232.
Camping trailer.
Motor vehicles, §20-4.01.
Campus.
Certificate of need, §131E-176.
University of North Carolina, §116-44.3.
Cancellation.
Leases, UCC, §25-2A-103(1).
Sales, §25-2-106.
Cancelled.
Motor vehicles, §20-4.01.
Candidate.
Campaign contributions and expenditures.
Disclosure requirements for media advertisements, §163-278.38Z.
Elections, candidacy challenge, §163-127.1.
Political campaigns, §163-278.6.
Public campaign fund, §163-278.62.
Voter-owned elections act, §163-278.96.

DEFINED TERMS —Cont'd

Candidate campaign committee.
Campaign contributions and expenditures.
Disclosure requirements for media advertisements, §163-278.38Z.

Candidate-specific communication.
Electioneering communications, §163-278.100.
Mass mailings and telephone banks, §163-278.110.

Candling and grading.
Egg law, §106-245.14.

Candy.
Sales and use tax, §105-164.3.

Canned pet food.
Commercial feed law, §106-284.33.

Canvass.
Elections, §163-182.5(a).

Capable of use as human food.
Meat inspection, §106-549.15.
Poultry products inspection, §106-549.51.

Capital.
Banking, §53-62(a).
Surplus lines, §58-21-10.

Capital costs.
Project development financing debt instruments, §159-103(a).

Capital expenditure.
Certificate of need, §131E-176.

Capital expenditure project.
Certificate of need, §131E-176.

Capital facility.
Capital facilities finance act, §142-82.
Higher education bonds, §116D-1.

Capital improvement.
Budget of state, §143C-1-1(d).

Capital improvements appropriations act.
Budget of state, §143C-1-1(d).

Capital interest.
Franchise tax, §105-114.1(a).

Capital project.
Local government finance, §159-13.2.

Capital stock.
Savings and loan associations, §54B-4.
Savings banks, §54C-4(b).

Capitation arrangement.
Purchases and contracts through department of administration.
Medicaid program exemption, §143-48.1(b).

Captive insurer.
Producer-controlled property or casualty insurers, §58-3-165(a).

Captive REIT.
Real estate investment trusts, §105-130.12(a).

Card holder.
Criminal law, §14-113.8.

Cardiac angioplasty equipment.
Certificate of need, §131E-176.

Cardiac catheterization equipment.
Certificate of need, §131E-176.

Cardiac catheterization services.
Certificate of need, §131E-176.

Cardiac rehabilitation program, §131E-166.

Care.
Costs paid by persons admitted to institutions of department of health and human services, §143-117.1.

Career development; introductory.
Vocational and technical education, §115C-152.

Career employee.
Educational personnel, §115C-325(a).

Career growth recognition award.
Personnel system.
Comprehensive compensation system, §126-7(a2).

DEFINED TERMS —Cont'd

Career school administrator, §115C-325(a).

Career state employee.
State personnel system, §126-1.1.

Career teacher.
Education personnel, §115C-325(a).

Care for a term of years.
Health facilities finance, §131A-3.

Care for life.
Health facilities finance, §131A-3.

Caregiver adult.
Assignment of student to particular school, §115C-366(h).

Caretaker.
Abused, neglected and dependent juveniles, §7B-101.
Abuse, neglect or exploitation of disabled or elder adults.
Criminal offense, §14-32.3(d).
Protection of disabled adults, §108A-101.

Carnival area.
Safety, §95-111.3(b1).

Carrier.
Health maintenance organizations, §58-67-5(n).
Oil and hazardous substance control, §143-215.77.
Small employer group health coverage, §58-50-110.

Carry a concealed handgun.
Concealed handgun permits, §14-415.10.

Case characteristics.
Small employer group health coverage, §58-50-110.

Cash.
Banking, §53-51(b).
Money transmitters, §53-208.2(a).
Pawnbrokers and cash converters, §91A-3.

Cash advance.
Banking, §53-165(c).

Cash balance.
Community colleges.
Deposits, §115D-58.6(a).

Cash buyer.
Grain dealers, §106-601.

Cash converter.
Pawnbrokers and cash converters, §91A-3.

Cash dividend.
Life insurance solicitation, §58-60-10.

Cashier's check.
Good funds settlement act, §45A-3.

Cashing.
Check-cashing businesses, §53-275.

Cash price.
Installment sales, §25A-7.

Cash proceeds.
Secured transactions, §25-9-102(a).

Casket.
Cremation, §90-210.121.

Casual sale of property.
Corporate income tax, §105-130.4(a).

Cat, §130A-134.
Rabies vaccination, §130A-184.

Catastrophe recovery charge.
Beach property insurance, §58-45-5.

Catastrophic conditions.
Cancellation of court sessions, closing court offices, §7A-39(a).

Catastrophic incident.
Public adjusters, §58-33A-5.

Catastrophic loss amount.
Student protection fund, proprietary schools, §115D-95.1(a).

DEFINED TERMS —Cont'd

Catchment area.
Mental health, §122C-3.

Cave.
Criminal law and procedure, §14-159.20.

C corporation.
Taxation, §§105-130.2, 105-131.

CDL.
Commercial driver's license, §20-4.01.

Cede.
Vehicle reinsurance, §58-37-1.

Cemetery, §65-48.
Abandoned and neglected cemeteries, §65-85.

Cemetery broker, §65-48.

Cemetery company, §65-48.

Cemetery management organization, §65-48.

Cemetery sales organization, §65-48.

Censure.
Discipline and disability rules of state bar, Bar
Rule B.0103.
Judicial standards commission, §7A-374.2.

Centennial campus, §116-198.33.

Center.
Privileged communications, rape crisis centers
and domestic violence programs, §8-53.12.

Central office or aircraft facility.
Tax incentives for new and expanding businesses,
§105-129.2.

CERCLA/SARA.
Solid waste management, §§130A-290(a),
130A-310.
Superfund program, §130A-310.20.

Cerebral palsy.
Competency, §35A-1101.

Certificate.
Boll weevil eradication, §106-65.69.
Drivers' licenses, lose control, lose license,
§20-11(n1).
Fraternal benefit societies, §58-24-15(c).
Long-term care insurance, §58-55-20.
Medicare supplement insurance, §58-54-1.
Notaries public act, §10B-3.
Public utilities, §62-3.

Certificated registered public obligation,
§159E-2.

Certificated security.
Investment securities, §25-8-102.

Certificate holder.
Hospital, medical and dental service corporations.
Conversion, §58-65-131(b).

Certificate of approval.
Savings and loan associations, §54B-4.

Certificate of conviction.
Discipline and disability rules of state bar, Bar
Rule B.0103.

Certificate of coverage.
Accident and health insurance.
Utilization review, §58-50-61(a).

Certificate of cremation, §90-210.121.

Certificate of deposit.
Negotiable instruments, §25-3-104.

Certificate of election.
Elections, §163-182.

Certificate of incorporation or charter.
Savings and loan associations, §54B-4.
Savings banks, §54C-4(b).

Certificate of limited partnership, §59-102.

Certificate of need, §131E-176.

Certificate of number.
Boating safety, §75A-2.

DEFINED TERMS —Cont'd

Certificate of registration.
Environmental health specialists, §90A-51.

Certificate of title.
Secured transactions, §25-9-102(a).

Certificates of insurance.
Insurance policies or contracts, §58-3-150(d).

Certificates of participation.
Capital facilities finance act, §142-82.
Energy conservation finance act, §142-61.
Lease or purchase of prison facilities constructed
by private firm, §148-37.2(b).

Certificates of participation indebtedness.
Capital facilities finance act, §142-82.

Certification.
Cardiac rehabilitation program, §131E-166.

Certification authority.
Electronic commerce in government, §66-58.2.

Certification of crop seeds.
Crop seed improvement board, §106-274.

Certified applicator.
Structural pest control act, §106-65.24.

Certified audit.
Workers' compensation self insurance, §97-165.

Certified automated system.
Uniform sales and use tax administration act,
§105-164.42B.

Certified budget.
Budget of state, §143C-1-1(d).

Certified candidate.
Public campaign fund, §163-278.62.
Voter-owned elections act, §163-278.96.

Certified check.
Good funds settlement act, §45A-3.
Negotiable instruments, §25-3-409(d).

Certified child passenger safety technician,
§20-137.5(a).

Certified clinical perfusionist, §90-682.

Certified clinical supervisor.
Substance abuse professionals, §90-113.31A.

Certified copy.
Savings and loan associations, §54B-4.

**Certified criminal justice addictions
professional.**
Substance abuse professionals, §90-113.31A.

Certified disaster service volunteer, §166A-31.

Certified dust sampling.
Lead-based paint renovation activities,
§130A-453.22(b).

Certified employee assistance professionals,
§90-500.

Certified general real estate appraiser,
§93E-1-4.

Certified historic structure.
Historic rehabilitation tax credit, §105-129.35(c).
Mill rehabilitation tax credit, §105-129.70.

Certified industrial hygienist, §90-515.

Certified laboratory.
Drinking water, §130A-313.

Certified list.
Child support, §110-142.

Certified mail.
Public utilities, §62-3.

Certified master social worker, §90B-3.

Certified prescribed burner.
Prescribed burning of forestlands, §106-966.

Certified public accountant, §93-1.
Workers' compensation self insurance, §97-165.

Certified rabies vaccinator, §130A-134.
Rabies vaccination, §130A-184.

DEFINED TERMS —Cont'd

Certified rehabilitation.
Historic rehabilitation tax credit, §105-129.36(b).
Mill rehabilitation tax credit, §§105-129.36, 105-129.70.

Certified renovation firm.
Lead-based paint renovation activities, §130A-453.22(b).

Certified renovator.
Lead-based paint renovation activities, §130A-453.22(b).

Certified residential real estate appraiser, §93E-1-4.

Certified seeds.
Seed law, §106-277.2.

Certified service provider.
Uniform sales and use tax administration act, §105-164.42B.

Certified social worker, §90B-3.

Certified social work manager, §90B-3.

Certified statement of financial condition.
Mortgage bankers, brokers and servicers, §53-244.030.

Certified substance abuse counselor.
Substance abuse professionals, §90-113.31A.

Certified substance abuse prevention consultant.
Substance abuse professionals, §90-113.31A.

Certified substance abuse residential facility director.
Substance abuse professionals, §90-113.31A.

Certified vegetable plants for transplanting.
Vegetable plant law, §106-284.16.

Cervid or cervidae.
Conservation, §113-129.
Deer, production and sale for commercial purposes, §106-549.97(c).

Cession.
Vehicle reinsurance, §58-37-1.

CFS.
Job training, education and placement information management, §96-31.

CFTC rule.
Commodities act, §78D-1.

Chairlift.
Passenger tramway safety, §95-117.

Chairman.
Local government finance, §159-1.

Chairman of the board of county commissioners.
Civil disorders, §14-288.1.

Chairperson of the grievance committee.
Discipline and disability rules of state bar, Bar Rule B.0103.

Challenge.
Challenge to a candidacy, §163-127.1.

Chancellor.
University of North Carolina, §116-2.

Change in bed capacity.
Certificate of need, §131E-176.

Change in ownership or control.
Licensure of manufacturers, dealers, salespersons or set-up contractors, §143-143.11A(c).

Channel.
State franchising of cable television service, §66-350.

Chapter 119 of the United States code.
Electronic surveillance, §15A-286.

Charge.
Liability of landowners associated with watershed improvement projects, §139-41.3.

DEFINED TERMS —Cont'd

Charge —Cont'd
Recreational trespass, §38A-2.
Exclusions from definition, §38A-3.

Charged.
Implied consent to chemical analysis, §20-16.2(a1).

Charging officer.
Motor vehicles, §20-16.5(a).

Charitable.
Solicitation of contributions, §131F-2.

Charitable gift annuity.
Annuity disclosure, §58-60-130.

Charitable organization.
Solicitation of contributions, §131F-2.
Volunteer immunity, §1-539.11.

Charitable or religious corporations.
Nonprofit corporations, §55A-1-40.

Charitable purpose.
Property tax exemption, §§105-278.6(b), 105-278.7(f).
Prudent management of institutional funds, §36E-2.
Solicitation, §14-401.12.
Taxation, §105-278.3(d).

Charitable remainder annuity trust.
Charitable remainder trust administration act, §36C-4B-3.

Charitable remainder trust.
Charitable remainder trust administration act, §36C-4B-3.

Charitable remainder unitrust.
Charitable remainder trust administration act, §36C-4B-3.

Charitable sales promotion.
Solicitation of contributions, §131F-2.

Charitable trust.
Uniform trust code, §36C-1-103.

Charter.
Cities and towns, §160A-1.
Marketing associations, §54-130.
Regional sports authorities, §160A-479.
Trust companies, §53-301(a).

Charter operations.
Public utilities, §62-3.

Charter party.
Public utilities, §62-260.

Charter school.
Taxation, §105-228.90(b).

Chattel paper.
Secured transactions, §25-9-102(a).

Check.
Negotiable instruments, §§25-3-104, 25-3-312(a).

Check-cashing service, §53-275.

Check passer.
Bad checks, §14-107.2(a).
Criminal law, §14-107.1.

Check taker, §14-107.2(a).
Criminal law, §14-107.1.

Chemical analysis.
Motor vehicles, §20-4.01.

Chemical analyst.
Motor vehicles, §20-4.01.

Chemical dependency.
Accident and health insurance, §58-51-50(a).
Health maintenance organizations, §58-67-70(a).
Hospital, medical and dental service corporations, §58-65-75(a).
State health plan for teachers and state employees, §135-48.1.

DEFINED TERMS —Cont'd
Chemical dependency treatment beds.
  Certificate of need, §131E-176.
Chemical dependency treatment facility.
  Certificate of need, §131E-176.
Chemical manufacturer.
  Toxic or hazardous substance identification,
    §95-174(a).
Chemical name.
  Toxic or hazardous substance identification,
    §95-174(b).
Chemical or portable toilet.
  Solid waste management, §130A-290(a).
Chick dealer, §106-541.
Chief court counselor.
  Delinquent and undisciplined juveniles, §7B-1501.
  Division of juvenile justice, §143B-805.
Chief district court judge, §7A-200(a).
Chief executive officer.
  Annuities, §147-9.2.
  Insurers supervision, §58-30-12.
Chief inspector.
  Boiler and pressure vessel regulation,
    §95-69.9(b1).
Child.
  Adoption, §48-1-101.
  Child custody jurisdiction and enforcement,
    §50A-102.
  Child placing and care, §131D-10.2.
  Children of war veterans scholarships, §165-20.
  Remote testimony by child witness,
    §15A-1225.1(a).
  Support of illegitimate children, §49-2.
  Workers' compensation, §97-2.
Child care, §110-86.
  Mandatory child care provider criminal history
    checks, §110-90.2(a).
Child care administrator, §110-86.
Child care center, §110-86.
Child care facility, §110-86.
Child care provider.
  Mandatory criminal history checks, §110-90.2(a).
Child care subsidy.
  Fraudulent misrepresentation, §110-107(c).
Child care vehicles.
  Motor vehicles, §20-4.01.
Child-custody determination.
  Child custody jurisdiction and enforcement,
    §50A-102.
Child-custody proceeding.
  Child custody jurisdiction and enforcement,
    §50A-102.
Child fatality.
  Disclosure of records in child fatality or near
    fatality cases, §7B-2902(a).
Child interstate family support, §52C-1-101.
Child-occupied facility.
  Lead-based paint renovation activities,
    §130A-453.22(b).
  Lead poisoning in children, §130A-131.7.
Child placing agency, §131D-10.2.
Children's camp.
  Child placing and care, §131D-10.2.
Child support case, §50-31.
Child support hearing officer, §50-31.
Child support obligation.
  Unemployment insurance, §96-17(d).
Child support order.
  Interstate family support, §52C-1-101.
Child support payment.
  Vesting of past due support, §50-13.10(c).

DEFINED TERMS —Cont'd
Child trespasser.
  Trespasser responsibility act, §38B-4.
Child with disability.
  Education of children with disabilities,
    §115C-106.3.
Chiropractic, §90-143(a).
Chlorofluorocarbon refrigerant.
  Solid waste management, §130A-290.
Chore.
  Long-term care insurance, §58-55-35(a).
Chronically ill.
  Viatical life insurance settlements, §58-58-205.
Chunking.
  Motor vehicles, §20-122.1.
Church plan.
  Health insurance portability and accountability.
    Guaranteed availability of individual coverage
      to certain individuals with prior group
      coverage, §58-68-60(h).
Cigar.
  Taxation, §105-113.4.
Cigar bar.
  Smoking in restaurants and bars, §130A-492.
Cigarette.
  Fire-safety standard and firefighter protection act,
    §58-92-10.
  Taxation, §105-113.4.
  Tobacco reserve fund, §66-290.
Cistern.
  Building codes, §143-138(b12).
Citation.
  Criminal process, §15A-302.
  Interstate wildlife violator compact, §113-300.6.
  Motor vehicles, §20-4.18.
Citizens band radio equipment, §62-328.
City, §160A-1.
  Annexation of noncontiguous areas, §160A-58.
  Counties, §153A-1.
  Housing authorities, §§157-3, 157-41.
  Housing standards, §160A-442.
  Insurance, §58-84-5.
  Local government finance, §159-1.
  Mental health, §122C-3.
  Municipal campaign reporting, §163-278.40.
  Parking authorities, §160A-551.
  Public hospitals, §§131E-6, 131E-16.
  Room occupancy taxes, §160A-215(a).
  Taxation, §105-228.90(b).
  Urban redevelopment, §160A-503.
  Veterans' recreation, §165-25.
  Water and sewer authorities, §162A-5.1(a).
  Zoning, §160A-385.1(b).
City board of education, §115C-5.
City clerk.
  City and town parking authorities, §160A-551.
  Housing authorities, §157-3.
  Public hospitals, §131E-16.
  Veterans' recreation, §165-25.
City council.
  City and town parking authorities, §160A-551.
  Metropolitan water districts, §162A-32(a).
  Public hospitals, §131E-16.
City employee, §160A-169.
City hold harmless threshold.
  Third one-half cent tax.
    County hold harmless for repealed taxes,
      §105-523(b).
City-owned communications service provider.
  Cities providing communications services,
    §160A-340.

DEFINED TERMS —Cont'd

Civil action.
Civil procedure, §1-6.
Civil aircraft.
Aeronautics, §63-1.
Civil air patrol members.
Death benefits, §143-166.2(d).
Civil investigative demand.
False claims act, §1-614(a).
Civil no-contact order, §50C-1.
Workplace violence prevention, §95-260.
Civil or criminal action or proceeding.
Legal defense of state employees, §143-300.2.
Civil proceeding.
RICO act, §75D-3.
Claim.
Claims against the state, §143B-426.40A(a).
Counties.
Contracts with railroads to allocate financial
responsibility, §153A-279(a).
Elective share of surviving spouse, §30-3.2.
False claims act, §1-606.
Fraudulent transfers, §39-23.1.
Medical assistance provider false claims act,
§108A-70.11.
Rail transportation liability, §160A-326(a).
Claimant agency.
Debt collection, §105A-2.
Claimants.
Asset protection, §58-13-15.
Bonds, §44A-25.
Insurance guaranty association, §58-48-20.
Negotiable instruments, §25-3-312(a).
Products liability, §99B-1.
Prompt claim payments under health benefit
plans, §58-3-225(a).
Punitive damages, §1D-5.
Vaccine-related injury, §130A-422.
Victims compensation, §15B-2.
Claim of factual innocence.
Innocence inquiry commission, §15A-1460.
Claims processor.
State health plan for teachers and state
employees, §135-48.1.
Claim submission policy.
Health plans, disclosure to providers,
§58-3-227(a).
Class A motor vehicle, §20-4.01.
Class B motor vehicle, §20-4.01.
Class C motor vehicle, §20-4.01.
Classified motor vehicle.
Taxation, §105-330.
Classified service.
Occupational safety and health, §95-127.
Class of business.
Small employer group health coverage,
§58-50-110.
Clawbacks.
Commerce department, economic development
board, §143B-435.1(a).
CLE, Bar Rule D.1501.
Clean risk.
Vehicle reinsurance, §§58-37-35, 58-37-35(l).
Clearing corporation.
Investment securities, §25-8-102.
Clearinghouse.
Banking, §25-4-104(a).
Clerk.
Abused, neglected and dependent juveniles,
§7B-101.
Counties, §153A-1.

DEFINED TERMS —Cont'd

Clerk —Cont'd
Criminal procedure, §15A-101.
Delinquent and undisciplined juveniles, §7B-1501.
General assembly.
Contesting a seat, §120-10.2.
Incompetency, §§35A-1101, 35A-1202.
Insurance, §58-84-5.
Local government finance, §159-1.
Military or naval leaves of absence for county or
municipal employees, §128-42(f).
Motor vehicles, §20-16.5(a).
Provisional license revocation, §20-13.3(a).
Clerk of superior court.
Judicial retirement, §135-53.
Client.
Domestic violence shelters.
Limited civil liability, §1-620.
Mental health, §122C-3.
Mental health, developmental disability,
substance abuse.
Appeals panel, §122C-151.4(a).
Psychotherapy patient/client sexual exploitation
act, §90-21.41.
Trust companies, §53-301(a).
Client advocate.
Mental health, §122C-3.
Client company.
Professional employer organizations, §58-89A-5.
Client law enforcement client.
Peer support group counselor's privilege,
§8-53.10(a).
Clinical experience.
Marriage and family therapists, §90-270.47.
Clinical peer.
Accident and health insurance.
Utilization review, §58-50-61(a).
Clinical pharmacist practitioners.
Pharmacy practice, §90-85.3(b1).
Clinical review criteria.
Accident and health insurance.
Utilization review, §58-50-61(a).
Clinical social work practice, §90B-3.
Clinical supervisor intern.
Substance abuse professionals, §90-113.31A.
Clinical trials.
State health plan for teachers and state
employees, §135-48.1.
Clone.
Seed law, §106-277.2.
Closed block.
Insurance companies, conversion, §58-10-12(a).
Closed block of business.
Insurance companies, §58-3-275(c).
Closed formulary.
Health insurers maintaining, §58-3-221(c).
Closing.
Good funds settlement act, §45A-3.
Closing funds.
Good funds settlement act, §45A-3.
Closing-out sale, §66-76.
Closure.
Solid waste management, §130A-290(a).
Closure date.
Insurance companies, closure of a block of
business, §58-3-275(c).
Clothing.
Sales and use tax, §105-164.3.
Clothing accessories or equipment.
Sales and use tax, §105-164.3.

DEFINED TERMS —Cont'd
Club.
  Commercial fisherman's hull insurance, §58-20-5.
CMRS.
  Telecommunications relay service, §62-157(a1).
CMRS connection.
  911 system, §62A-40.
  Telecommunications relay service, §62-157(a1).
CMRS provider.
  911 system, §62A-40.
  Telecommunications relay service, §62-157(a1).
CMS.
  Hospital provider assessments, §108A-121.
Coal-fired generating unit.
  Air pollution control, §143-215.107D(a).
  Environmental compliance costs, §62-133.6(a).
  Solid waste management, §130A-290(a).
Coalition plan.
  Cooperative state-local coalition water quality
      protection plans, §143-214.14(a).
Coastal area.
  Beach property insurance, §58-45-5.
  Coastal area management, §113A-103.
Coastal fisheries.
  Conservation, §113-129.
Coastal fishing.
  Conservation, §113-129.
Coastal fishing waters, §113-129.
  Offshore oil and gas activities, §143-215.94BB.
  Review of offshore fossil fuel facilities for potential
      of unauthorized discharge, §113A-119.2(a).
  Working waterfront property taxation,
      §105-277.14(a).
Coastal property insurance pool.
  Beach property insurance, §58-45-5.
Coastal sound, §113A-103.
Coastal wetlands.
  Conservation, §113-230.
COBRA continuation provision.
  Health insurance portability and accountability,
      §58-68-25(a).
Code.
  Elective share of surviving spouse, §30-3.2.
  Express total return unitrust, §37A-1-104.21(b).
  Gasoline tax, §105-449.60.
  Manufactured housing, §143-143.9.
  Officials qualification board, §143-151.8(a).
  Pollution control, §§159C-3, 159D-3.
  Principal and income act, §37A-1-104.1.
  Property taxes, §105-273.
  Public obligations, §159E-2.
  Taxation, §§105-33.1, 105-114, 105-130.2,
      105-134.1, 105-228.90(b).
Code book.
  Locksmith licensing, §74F-4.
Code designation.
  Seed law, §106-277.2.
Code enforcement.
  Officials qualification board, §143-151.8(a).
Codifier of rules.
  Administrative procedure, §150B-2.
CODIS.
  DNA database and databanks, §15A-266.2.
Coercion.
  Human trafficking, §14-43.10(a).
Coin or currency operated machine.
  Criminal law, §14-56.1.
Collaborative law.
  Divorce, §50-71.
Collaborative law agreement.
  Divorce, §50-71.

DEFINED TERMS —Cont'd
Collaborative law procedures.
  Divorce, §50-71.
Collaborative law settlement agreement.
  Divorce, §50-71.
Collateral.
  Interstate wildlife violator compact, §113-300.6.
  Secured transactions, §25-9-102(a).
Collateral assignment.
  Probate and registration, §47-20.
Collateral consequence.
  Criminal procedure, certificate of relief from
      collateral consequences, §15A-173.1.
Collateral or bond.
  Motor vehicles, §20-4.18.
Collateral sanction.
  Criminal procedure, certificate of relief from
      collateral consequences, §15A-173.1.
Collateral source.
  Victims compensation, §15B-2.
Collected funds.
  Good funds settlement act, §45A-3.
Collecting authority.
  Taxation, §105-330.
Collecting bank, §25-4-105.1(c).
  Banking, §25-4-105.
Collection agency, §58-70-15(a), (b).
  Prohibited collection practices, §58-70-90.
Collection receptacle.
  Solicitation of contributions, §131F-2.
Collection site.
  Scrap tire disposal, §130A-309.53.
Collector.
  Decedents' estates, §28A-1-1.
  Property taxes, §105-273.
  Rendering plants, §106-168.1.
Collision damage waiver.
  Rental cars, §66-201.
Collocation.
  Wireless telecommunications facilities,
      §§153A-349.51, 160A-400.51.
Colony.
  Bee and honey act, §106-635.
Color.
  Food, drugs and cosmetics, §106-121.
Color additive.
  Food, drugs and cosmetics, §106-121.
  Meat inspection, §106-549.15.
  Poultry products inspection, §106-549.51.
Columbarium.
  Cemeteries, §65-48.
Comb.
  Bee and honey act, §106-635.
Combination home.
  Facility licensure act, §131E-101.
  Long-term care insurance, §58-55-35(a).
Combined general rate.
  Sales and use tax, §105-164.3.
Combined heat and power system.
  Renewable energy and energy efficiency portfolio
      standard (REPS), §62-133.8(a).
Combustion products.
  Solid waste management, §130A-290(a).
Combustion products landfill.
  Solid waste management, §130A-290(a).
Commencement.
  Child custody jurisdiction and enforcement,
      §50A-102.
Commercial.
  Solid waste management, §130A-290(a).

DEFINED TERMS —Cont'd
Commercial aircraft.
Insurance, §58-1-5.
Commercial beekeeper.
Bee and honey act, §106-635.
Commercial cave.
Criminal law and procedure, §14-159.20.
Commercial detection service.
Controlled substances, §90-102.1(a).
Commercial domicile.
Corporate income tax, §105-130.4(a).
Commercial driver's license, §20-4.01.
Commercial driver training school, §20-320.
Commercial electronic mail.
Computer crimes, §14-453.
Commercial feed, §106-284.33.
Commercial fertilizer, §106-657.
Commercial fisherman, §58-20-5.
Commercial fishing boats, §75A-5.1.
Commercial fishing operation.
Coastal and estuarine commercial fishing licenses, §113-168.
Working waterfront property taxation, §105-277.14(a).
Commercial fund.
Petroleum cleanup, §143-215.94A.
Commercial hazardous waste treatment facility, §130A-295.01(a).
Commercial loan commitment.
Contracts to be in writing, §22-5.
Commercial mortgages.
Insurance policies or contracts, §58-3-150(d).
Commercial motor vehicle, §20-4.01.
Commercial paper.
Banking, §53-55.
Commercial poultry operations.
Fowl running at large, permitting at commercial operations, §68-25(b).
Commercial production.
Strawberry assessment, §106-783.
Commercial purposes.
Littering, §14-399(i).
Commercial real estate.
Commercial real estate broker lien act, §44A-24.2.
Commercial social networking web site, §14-202.5(b).
Commercial tort claim.
Secured transactions, §25-9-102(a).
Commercial underground storage tank.
Petroleum cleanup, §143-215.94A.
Commercial unit.
Leases, UCC, §25-2A-103(1).
Sales, §25-2-105.
Commercial vehicle.
Motor vehicles, §20-4.2.
Commercial water pollution control system operating firm, §90A-46.
Commingled goods.
Secured transactions priority of security interests, §25-9-336(a).
Commission.
Commercial real estate broker lien act, §44A-24.2.
Notaries public act, §10B-3.
Commission chairperson.
Discipline and disability rules of state bar, Bar Rule B.0103.
Commissioner of banks.
Regional reciprocal savings and loan acquisition act, §54B-48.2.
Commissioner's designee.
Insurance licensees or applicants for licenses. Electronic filing, §58-2-250(a).

DEFINED TERMS —Cont'd
Committee.
General assembly.
Contesting a seat, §120-10.2.
Job development investment grant program, §143B-437.51.
Commodity, §78D-1.
Commodity account.
Secured transactions, §25-9-102(a).
Commodity contract, §78D-1.
Secured transactions, §25-9-102(a).
Commodity customer.
Secured transactions, §25-9-102(a).
Commodity exchange act, §78D-1.
Commodity futures trading commission, §78D-1.
Commodity intermediary.
Secured transactions, §25-9-102(a).
Commodity merchant, §78D-1.
Commodity option, §78D-1.
Common areas and facilities, §47A-3.
Common carrier.
Public utilities, §62-3.
Common carrier by motor vehicle.
Public utilities, §62-3.
Common carriers of passengers.
Motor vehicles, §20-4.01.
Common control.
Wholesale prescription drug distributors, §106-145.2.
Common elements.
Condominiums, §47C-1-103.
Planned community act, §47F-1-103.
Common expense liability.
Condominiums, §47C-1-103.
Planned community act, §47F-1-103.
Common expenses.
Condominiums, §47C-1-103.
Planned community act, §47F-1-103.
Unit ownership, §47A-3.
Common name.
Toxic or hazardous substance identification, §95-174(c).
Common profits.
Unit ownership, §47A-3.
Common stock.
Shareholder protection act, §55-9-01(b).
Communicable condition.
Public health, §130A-2.
Communicable disease.
Public health, §130A-2.
Communicate.
Investment securities, §25-8-102.
Secured transactions, §25-9-102(a).
Communications common carrier.
Electronic surveillance, §15A-286.
Communications equipment.
Purchases through department of administration.
Multiple award schedule contracts, §143-52.3.
Communications media.
Political campaigns, §163-278.6.
Communications service.
Certificates of public convenience and necessity, §62-110(f6).
Cities providing communications services, §160A-340.
Communications service providers.
Utilization of poles controlled by municipalities or membership corporations, §62-350.
Community advisory committee.
Facility licensure act, §131E-101.

DEFINED TERMS —Cont'd

Community-based development organization.
Development zone project tax credit,
§105-129.13(b).

Community-based program.
Abused, neglected and dependent juveniles,
§7B-101.
Delinquent and undisciplined juveniles, §7B-1501.
Division of juvenile justice, §143B-805.

Community college, §115D-2.
Construction contract claims, §143-135.6(e).

Community college buildings.
Department of administration, §143-336.

Community development corporation.
Development zone project tax credit,
§105-129.13(b).

Community development purpose.
Development zone project tax credit,
§105-129.13(b).

Community facilities.
Housing authorities, §157-3.

Community general hospital, §131E-6.
Public hospitals, §131E-16.

Community land trust developer.
Community land trust property, taxation,
§105-277.17(b).

Community land trust property, §105-277.17(b).

Community punishment.
Structured sentencing, §15A-1340.11.

Community schools advisory council.
Community schools act, §115C-205.

Community schools coordinator, §115C-205.

Community service.
Public assistance program, §108A-24.

Community theatre.
Alcoholic beverages, §18B-1000.

Community third party trust.
Community third party trusts, pooled trusts act,
§36D-2.

Community water system, §143-355.
Drinking water, §130A-313.

Compact administrator.
Interstate compact for juveniles, §7B-4001.
Interstate compact on mental health, §122C-361.

Compacting state.
Interstate compact for juveniles, §7B-4001.
Interstate insurance product regulation compact,
§58-91-10.

Compact officer.
National crime prevention and privacy compact,
§114-19.50.

Company.
Bank holding company act, §53-226.
Insurance, §58-1-5.
Insurance taxation, §105-228.8(b).
Regional reciprocal savings and loan acquisition
act, §54B-48.2.
Sudan (Darfur) divestment act, §147-86.42.
Trust companies, §53-301(a).
Vehicle reinsurance, §58-37-1.

Company action level event.
Risk based capital requirements, insurance
companies, §58-12-11(a).

Company action level risk-based capital.
Insurance companies, §58-12-2.

Company headquarters.
Growing businesses tax credits, §105-129.81.

Comparable replacement dwelling.
Relocation assistance, §133-7.

Comparative market analysis.
Real estate appraisers, §93E-1-4.

DEFINED TERMS —Cont'd

Compensation.
Corporate income tax, §105-130.4(a).
Disability income plan, §135-101.
Home inspectors, §143-151.45.
Judicial retirement, §135-53.
Legislative retirement system, §120-4.8.
Lotteries, §14-291.2(b).
Retirement, §128-21.
State government ethics act, §138A-3.
State retirement system, §135-1.
Tax withholding, §105-163.1.
Workers' compensation, §97-2.

Compensatory agent.
Adult care homes, §131D-2.1.

Compensatory damages.
Punitive damages, §1D-5.

Compensatory mitigation.
Ecosystem enhancement program, §143-214.11(a).

Compensatory mitigation bank.
Ecosystem enhancement program, §143-214.11(a).

Compensatory programs.
Tobacco trust fund commission, §143-716.

Compensatory time.
Municipal firefighters, §160A-295.

Competent evidence.
Municipal zoning appeals, §160A-393(k).

Competent local attorneys.
Banking, §53-20(w).

Competing local provider.
Public utilities, §62-3.

Competitor.
Winter sports safety, §99C-1.

Complainant or complaining witness.
Discipline and disability rules of state bar, Bar
Rule B.0103.
Procedures for the authorized practice committee
of the state bars, Bar Rule D.0203.
Public records, §132-1.4.

Complaint.
Discipline and disability rules of state bar, Bar
Rule B.0103.
Private personnel services, §95-47.1.
Procedures for the authorized practice committee
of the state bars, Bar Rule D.0203.

Completed operations liability.
Liability risk retention, §58-22-10.

Complete eviction.
Expedited evictions, §42-59.

Complex sources.
Water and air resources, §143-213.

Compliance.
Interstate wildlife violator compact, §113-300.6.

Compliance review documents.
Savings and loan associations, §54B-63.1(a).
Savings banks, §54C-60.1(a).

Compliance with an order for support.
Child support, §110-142.

Complicit.
Sudan (Darfur) divestment act, §147-86.42.

Component parts manufacturers.
Automobile dealer warranty obligations,
§20-305.1(f1).

Composite abstract.
Elections, §163-182.

Compounding.
Pharmacy practice, §90-85.3(c).

Comprehensive health benefit plan.
State health plan for teachers and state
employees, §135-48.1.

DEFINED TERMS —Cont'd
Comprehensive health coverage.
Children's health insurance program,
§108A-70.18.
Comprehensive plan.
Development agreements, §160A-400.21.
Counties, §153A-349.2.
Comprehensive planning.
Regional sewage disposal, §162A-27.
Comprehensive vocational and technical
education, §115C-152.
Computer.
Computer crimes, §14-453.
Sales and use tax, §105-164.3.
Computer-assisted remote hunting,
§113-291.1A(b).
Computer database.
Electronic data-processing records, §132-6.1(d).
Computer equipment.
Discarded computer equipment and television
management, §130A-309.131.
Computer equipment manufacturer.
Discarded computer equipment and television
management, §130A-309.131.
Computer hardware.
Electronic data-processing records, §132-6.1(d).
Computer network.
Computer crimes, §14-453.
Computer program.
Computer crimes, §14-453.
Electronic data-processing records, §132-6.1(d).
Electronic transactions, §66-312.
Computer services.
Computer crimes, §14-453.
Computer software.
Computer crimes, §14-453.
Electronic data-processing records, §132-6.1(d).
Sales and use tax, §105-164.3.
Computer supply.
Sales and use tax, §105-164.3.
Computer system.
Computer crimes, §14-453.
Tax incentives for new and expanding businesses,
§105-129.2.
Computer system design and related services.
Tax incentives for new and expanding businesses,
§105-129.2.
Computer technician.
Film or computer images of minor engaging in
sexual activity.
Report by film and photographic processor or
computer technician, §66-67.4(a).
Concert or public exhibition.
Fireworks, §14-410(c).
Concurrently maintainable.
Sales and use tax, §105-164.3.
Condemnation.
Eminent domain, §40A-2.
Condemned equipment.
Weights and measures, §81A-9.
Condemnor.
Eminent domain, §40A-2.
Conditional service contract.
Sales and use tax, §105-164.12B(a).
Conditioning.
Seed law, §106-277.2.
Condominium, §§47A-3, 47C-1-103.
Planned community act, §47F-1-103.
Condominium unit, §47A-3.
Conduct.
Domestic violence shelters.
Limited civil liability, §1-620.

DEFINED TERMS —Cont'd
Confidential information.
Legislative ethics, §120-85.1.
Mental health, §122C-3.
State government ethics act, §138A-3.
Confidential intermediary.
Adoption, §48-1-101.
Confidential license plate.
Publicly owned vehicles, §20-39.1(d).
Confirmed lead poisoning, §130A-131.7.
Confirmers.
Letters of credit, §25-5-102(a).
Conflict of interest.
Savings and loan associations, §54B-4.
Savings banks, §54C-4(b).
Conflict of interest transaction.
Nonprofit corporations, §55A-3-01(a).
Conformed copy.
Partnerships, §59-102.
Savings and loan associations, §54B-4.
Conforming.
Leases, UCC, §25-2A-103(1).
Conforming to contract.
Sales, §25-2-106.
Conformity.
Planning regionally significant transportation
projects, §136-200.
Congressionally chartered veterans'
organizations.
Alcoholic beverages, §18B-1000.
Consent.
Criminal procedure, §15A-221.
Conservation.
Endangered wildlife, §113-331.
Plant protection and conservation, §106-202.12.
Conservation agreement.
Historic preservation agreements, §121-35.
Conservation easement.
Condemnation of property encumbered by,
§40A-80(b).
Soil and water conservation districts, §139-3.
Conservator.
Uniform trust code, §36C-1-103.
Conserve.
Endangered wildlife, §113-331.
Plant protection and conservation, §106-202.12.
Consideration.
Bail bondsman and runners, §58-71-1.
Negotiable instruments, §25-3-303(b).
Consignee.
Secured transactions, §25-9-102(a).
UCC, §25-7-102(a).
Consignment.
Auctions and auctioneers, §85B-1.
Secured transactions, §25-9-102(a).
Consignor.
Secured transactions, §25-9-102(a).
UCC, §25-7-102(a).
Consolidated city-county, §160B-2.
Consolidated county human services agency,
§143B-139.7(c).
Consolidated housing authorities, §157-39.5.
Consolidated human services board,
§143B-139.7(c).
Consolidated judicial retirement system,
§135-53.
Consolidated metropolitan planning
organization.
Planning regionally significant transportation
projects, §136-200.

DEFINED TERMS —Cont'd

Consolidation of cases.
Discipline and disability rules of state bar, Bar Rule B.0103.

Conspicuous.
Business corporation, §55-1-40.
Nonprofit corporations, §55A-1-40.
UCC, §25-1-201(b).

Conspiracy to commit bribery.
Public officers and employees, §14-217(a).

Constituent institution.
Cooperative innovative high school programs, §115C-238.50A.
University of North Carolina, §116-2.

Constitutional officers of the state.
State government ethics act, §138A-3.

Construction.
Mountain ridge protection, §113A-206.
Sewage systems, §130A-334.
Solid waste management, §130A-290(a).
University of North Carolina, §116-41.1.

Construction contract.
Bonds, §44A-25.

Construction contract agreement.
Lease of purchase of prison facilities constructed by private firm, §148-37.2(b).

Construction contractor.
Property taxes, §105-273.

Construction costs.
Water infrastructure, §159G-20.

Construction equipment.
Purchases through department of administration. Multiple award schedule contracts, §143-52.3.

Construction loans.
Maximum fees on loans secured by real property, §24-10(c).

Construction management at risk services, §143-128.1(a).

Construction management services, §143-128.1(a).

Construction manager at risk, §143-128.1(a).

Construction of wells, §87-85.

Consulting forester, §89B-2.

Consult or consultation.
Employee assistance professionals, §90-500.

Consumer.
Credit monitoring services act, §75-134.
Credit repair business, §66-221.
Debt collectors, §75-50.
Discarded computer equipment and television management, §130A-309.131.
Egg law, §106-245.14.
Identity theft, §75-61.
MH/DD/SA consumer advocacy program, §122C-11.
Prohibited collection practices, §58-70-90.
Rebates.
Deadline for mailing consumer rebates, §75-40(a).
Sales and use tax, §105-164.3.
Tanning equipment operators, §104E-9.1(c).

Consumer advocate.
MH/DD/SA consumer advocacy program, §122C-15(a).

Consumer bankruptcy law, Bar Rule D.2202.

Consumer commodity.
Food, drugs and cosmetics, §106-121.

Consumer contract.
Reciprocal attorneys' fees in business contracts, §6-21.7(a).

DEFINED TERMS —Cont'd

Consumer credit installment sale contract.
Installment sales, §25A-12.

Consumer credit protection act.
Installment sales, §25A-13.

Consumer credit sale.
Installment sales, §§25A-2, 25A-24.

Consumer debtor.
Secured transactions, §25-9-102(a).

Consumer goods or services.
Free insurance as inducement to purchase goods or services, §66-380.
Sales, §14-401.13.
Secured transactions, §25-9-102(a).

Consumer-goods transaction.
Secured transactions, §25-9-102(a).

Consumer home loans.
Interest, consumer protection in home loans, §24-10.2(a).

Consumer lease.
Leases, UCC, §25-2A-103(1).

Consumer obligor.
Secured transactions, §25-9-102(a).

Consumer price index.
Medical malpractice, §90-21.19(c).

Consumer report.
Credit monitoring services act, §75-134.
Identity theft, §75-61.
Insurance information and privacy protection act, §58-39-15.

Consumer reporting agency.
Identity theft, §75-61.
Insurance information and privacy protection act, §58-39-15.

Consumer service center.
Tax incentives for new and expanding businesses, §105-129.2.

Consumer testing.
Fire-safety standard and firefighter protection act, §58-92-10.

Consumer transaction.
Electronic transactions, §66-312.
Secured transactions, §25-9-102(a).

Consumptive use.
Water and air resources, §143-215.21.

Contact.
Inmates prohibited from contacting victims' family members, §148-10.2(a), (b).

Container.
Egg law, §106-245.14.
Poultry products inspection, §106-549.51.

Contaminant.
Brownfields property reuse act, §130A-310.31(b).
Drinking water, §130A-313.
Dry-cleaning solvent cleanup act, §143-215.104B(b).
Risk based environmental remediation of industrial sites, §130A-310.65.

Contaminated industrial site.
Risk based environmental remediation of industrial sites, §130A-310.65.

Contaminated with filth.
Food, drugs and cosmetics, §106-121.

Contaminating a public water system.
Criminal law, §14-159.1.

Contamination.
Risk based environmental remediation of industrial sites, §130A-310.65.

Contents.
Electronic surveillance, §15A-286.

DEFINED TERMS —Cont'd

Contest.
Boxing commission, §143-651.
Elections.
Executive branch, §163-182.13A(l).
General assembly.
Contesting a seat, §120-10.2.

Contestant.
Boxing commission, §143-651.
General assembly.
Contesting a seat, §120-10.2.

Contested case.
Administrative procedure, §150B-2.

Contested primary and contested general election.
Public campaign fund, §163-278.62.
Voter-owned elections act, §163-278.96.

Contestee.
General assembly.
Contesting a seat, §120-10.2.

Contiguous area.
Annexation initiated by municipality, §160A-58.51.

Continually low-performing schools, §115C-105.37A(a).

Continuation statement.
Secured transactions, §25-9-102(a).

Continuing care, §58-64-1.
Health facilities finance, §131A-3.

Continuing director.
Shareholder protection act, §55-9-01(b).

Continuing legal education, Bar Rule D.1501.

Continuity of control.
Unemployment compensation, §96-9(c).

Continuous alcohol monitoring system, §15A-1343.3.

Contract.
Athlete agents, §78C-86.
Contracts between health benefit plans and health care providers, §58-50-270.
Contracts for deed, §47H-1.
Electronic transactions, §66-312.
Housing authorities, §157-3.
Invention development services, §66-209.
Membership camping, §66-232.
Mental health, developmental disability, substance abuse.
Appeals panel, §122C-151.4(a).
Option to purchase contracts executed with residential lease agreements, §47G-1.
Private personnel services, §95-47.1.
Public hospitals, §131E-16.
Sales, §25-2-106.
State government ethics act, §138A-3.
UCC, §25-1-201(b).

Contract carrier of property vehicles.
Motor vehicles, §20-4.01.

Contract costs.
Membership camping, §66-232.

Contract feeder.
Commercial feed law, §106-284.33.

Contract for construction or repair work.
Community colleges, §143-135.6(e).

Contract for deed, §47H-1.

Contract for sale.
Sales, §25-2-106.
UCC, §25-7-102(b).

Contracting body.
Bonds, §44A-25.

Contractor, §87-21(a).
Bonds, §44A-25.

DEFINED TERMS —Cont'd

Contractor —Cont'd
Certification of wastewater contractors and inspectors, §90A-71.
Commercial fertilizer, §106-657.
Community college construction claims, §143-135.6(e).
Liens, §44A-17.
Mental health, developmental disability, substance abuse.
Appeals panel, §122C-151.4(a).
Public contracts.
Resolution and adjustment of state construction contract claim, §143-135.3(a).
Subcontractors, §22C-1.
Tax withholding, §105-163.1.

Contract owner.
Annuity disclosure, §58-60-130.

Contract provider.
Accident and health insurance, §58-51-37(b).
Pharmacy of choice, §58-51-37(b).

Contract security company, §74C-13(a1).

Contract term.
Small business contractors, §143B-472.101.

Contractual obligation.
Insurance guaranty associations, §58-62-16.

Contractual personnel.
Schools, sex offender registry checks of contractors, §115C-332.1(a).

Contribute.
Political campaigns, §163-278.6.

Contribution.
Legal expense funds for elected officials, §163-278.300.
Partnerships, §59-102.
Public campaign fund, §163-278.62.
Solicitation, §§14-401.12, 131F-2.
Unemployment compensation, §96-8.
Voter-owned elections act, §163-278.96.

Contributions tax preparer.
Unemployment compensation, §96-18(b1).

Control.
Bank holding company act, §53-226.
Banks, §53-42.1(a).
Collection agencies, §58-70-6.
Condominiums, §47C-1-103.
Development zone project tax credit, §105-129.13(b).
Insurance guaranty association, §58-48-20.
Insurance holding companies, §58-19-5.
Insurance information and privacy protection act, §58-39-15.
Interstate branch banking, §53-224.9.
Managing general agents, §58-34-2(a).
Money transmitters, §53-208.2(a).
Mortgage bankers, brokers and servicers, §53-244.030.
Producer-controlled property or casualty insurers, §58-3-165(a).
Professional employer organizations, §58-89A-5.
Reciprocal banking act, §53-210.
Regional reciprocal savings and loan acquisition act, §54B-48.2.
Savings and loan associations, §54B-4.
Savings banks, §54C-4(b).
Substances, §90-87.
Tax credit for qualified business investments, §105-163.010.
Trust companies, §53-301(a).
Workers' compensation self-insurance, §97-165.

Controlled-access facility, §136-89.49.

DEFINED TERMS —Cont'd

Controlled insurer.
Producer-controlled property or casualty insurers, §58-3-165(a).

Controlled substance, §90-87.
Controlled substances reporting system, §90-113.72.
Examination regulation, §95-231.
Unauthorized substances taxes, §105-113.106.

Controlled substance analogue, §90-87.

Controller.
Budget of state, §143C-1-1(d).

Controlling.
Collection agencies, §58-70-6.
Insurance holding companies, §58-19-5.
Workers' compensation self-insurance, §97-165.

Controlling capital stock.
Insurance holding companies, §58-19-17(a).

Controlling person.
Annual audited financial reports.
Insurance companies, §58-10-190.
Money transmitters, §53-208.2(a).
Reinsurance intermediaries, §58-9-2(a).

Controlling producer.
Producer-controlled property or casualty insurers, §58-3-165(a).

Control of the business enterprise.
Unemployment compensation, §96-9(c).

Control share acquisition, §55-9A-01(b).
Corporations, §75E-1.

Control shares, §55-9A-01(b).

Control zone.
Protection of forest, §106-922.

Conventional water system.
Certification of wastewater contractors and inspectors, §90A-71.

Convention center.
Alcoholic beverages, §18B-1000.

Conversion.
Hospital, medical and dental service corporations, §58-65-131(b).

Conversion building, §47A-34.
Condominiums, §47C-1-103.

Conversion date.
Foreign-money claims, §1C-1820.

Converted policy.
Group health insurance, §58-53-1.

Converting mutual.
Insurance companies, conversion, §58-10-12(a).

Conveyance.
Partnerships, §59-32.

Conveyor.
Passenger tramway safety, §95-117.

Convicted.
Crime victims financial recovery assistance act, §15B-31.
Habitual breaking and entering status offense, §14-7.25.

Conviction.
Alcoholic beverages, §18B-900(b).
DNA database and databanks, §15A-266.2.
Firearms, §14-415.1.
Interstate wildlife violator compact, §113-300.6.
Licenses and permits, §113-277.
Motor vehicles, §20-4.01.
North Carolina rate bureau, §58-36-65(i).
Safe driver incentive program, §58-36-75(g).
Unlawful for felon to possess firearm, §14-415.1(b).

Cooking school.
Alcoholic beverages, §18B-1000.

DEFINED TERMS —Cont'd

Cooperative.
Planned community act, §47F-1-103.

Cooperative agreements.
Health care facilities, §131E-192.2.

Cooperative agreements among physicians or between physician, hospital or others, §90-21.25.

Cooperative innovative high school, §115C-238.50A.

Coordinated licensure information system.
Nurse licensure compact, §90-171.82.

Co-owners with rights of survivorship.
Simultaneous death, §28A-24-1.

Copayment.
Accident and health insurance, §58-51-37(b).
Pharmacy of choice, §58-51-37(b).

Copy.
Criminal process and procedure.
Electronic technology, §15A-101.1.

Cord.
Motor vehicles, §20-122.1.
Weights and measures, §81A-9.

Core services.
Mental health, §122C-3.

Corporal punishment.
Discipline of students, §115C-390.1(b).

Corporate certificate.
Architects, §83A-1.

Corporate credit unions, §54-110.1(b).

Corporate practice of architecture.
Architects, §83A-1.

Corporate surety.
Workers' compensation self insurance, §97-165.

Corporation, NC Const Art VIII §2.
Appraisal rights, §55-13-01.
Articles of merger or share exchange, §55-11-05(d).
Business corporations, §§55-1-40, 55-8-50(b).
Corporate conveyance forms, §47-41.01(d).
Electric membership corporations, §117-7.
Estimated income tax, §105-163.38.
Hospital, medical and dental service corporations.
Conversion, §58-65-131(b).
Limited liability companies, §57C-1-03.
Medical service corporations, §58-65-166(b).
Nonprofit corporations, §55A-1-40.
Political campaigns, §163-278.6.
Property taxes, §105-273.
Taxation, §§105-114, 105-130.2.

Corporation, foreign or domestic, authorized to do business in North Carolina.
Public hospitals, §§131E-6, 131E-16.

Correct.
Weights and measures, §81A-9.

Corrective order.
Insurance companies, §58-12-2.

Cosmetic.
Food, drugs and cosmetics, §106-121.

Cosmetic art, §88B-2.

Cosmetic art school, §88B-2.

Cosmetic art shop, §88B-2.

Cosmetologist, §88B-2.

Cosmetology, §88B-2.

Cosmetology teacher, §88B-2.

Cost.
Bonds for student housing, §116-175.
Business and energy tax credit, §105-129.15.
Capital facilities finance act, §142-82.
Centennial campus and Horace William campus financing act, §116-198.33.

DEFINED TERMS —Cont'd

Cost —Cont'd

Electric power, §159B-3.

Energy conservation finance act, §142-61.

Growing businesses tax credits, §105-129.81.

Health facilities finance, §131A-3.

Higher education bonds, §116D-1.

Higher education student housing, §116-189.

Metropolitan sewerage districts, §162A-65(a).

Metropolitan water districts, §162A-32(a).

Motor fuel, §75-81.

Pollution control, §§159C-3, 159D-3.

Private capital facilities finance act, §159D-37.

Solid waste, §159I-3(a).

Tax incentives for new and expanding businesses, §105-129.2.

University of North Carolina, §116-41.1.

Water and sewer, §162A-2.

Cost certification.

Mill rehabilitation tax credit, §105-129.70.

Cost-effective cleanup.

Petroleum cleanup, §143-215.94A.

Cost-of-living adjustment.

Personnel system.

Comprehensive compensation system, §126-7(a2).

Cost of operation.

Education food service, §115C-264(c).

Cost of repairing a motor vehicle.

Felony larceny of motor vehicle parts, §14-72.8.

Cost plus percentage of cost contract.

State lottery, §18C-150.

Cost price.

Tobacco taxation, §105-113.4.

Costs of collection.

Political campaign, §163-278.6.

Costs of construction.

Tax incentives for railroad intermodal facilities, §105-129.95.

Cotton.

Boll weevil eradication, §106-65.69.

Cotton gin, §106-451.40.

Cotton grower, §106-65.85.

Cotton merchant, §106-451.40.

Cotton warehouse, §106-451.40.

Council.

Mountain resources planning act, §153B-2.

Counsel.

Discipline and disability rules of state bar, Bar Rule B.0103.

Counseling.

Substance abuse professionals, §90-113.31A.

Counseling agency.

Housing finance agency, §122A-3.

Counselor.

Discipline and disability rules of state bar, Bar Rule B.0103.

Reverse mortgages, §53-257.

Counterfeit.

Instruments, §14-119(c).

Counterfeit controlled substance, §90-87.

Counterfeit drug.

Food, drugs and cosmetics, §106-121.

Counterfeit mark.

Trademarks, §80-11.1(a).

Counterintelligence service profession, §74C-3.

Counterparty exposure.

Derivative transactions, insurance companies, §58-7-205(a).

County, §153A-1.

Public health authorities, §130A-45.01.

DEFINED TERMS —Cont'd

County —Cont'd

Public hospitals, §131E-16.

Public utilities, §62-100.

Taxation, §105-228.90(b).

Tribal lands, §153A-350.1.

County block grant.

Public assistance program, §108A-24.

County board of commissioners.

Public health authorities, §130A-45.01.

County board of education, §115C-5.

County board of elections.

Municipal elections, §163-298.

County clerk.

Public hospitals, §131E-16.

County councils.

Division of juvenile justice, §143B-805.

County department of social services.

Public assistance program, §108A-24.

County employee.

Counties, §153A-99(b).

County of residence.

Mental health, §122C-3.

County plan.

Public assistance program, §108A-24.

County program.

Mental health, §122C-3.

County registry.

Sex offender and public protection registration, §14-208.6.

County water and sewer district, §162A-86(a1).

Countywide farmland protection plan, §106-744(e), (f).

Courier service profession, §74C-3.

Course of conduct.

Stalking, §14-277.3A(b).

Course of dealing.

UCC, §25-1-303(b).

Course of performance.

UCC, §25-1-303(a).

Court.

Abused, neglected and dependent juveniles, §7B-101.

Arbitration, §1-569.1.

Child custody jurisdiction and enforcement, §50A-102.

Civil procedure, §1-7.

Custodial trusts, §33B-1.

Delinquent and undisciplined juveniles, §7B-1501.

Division of juvenile justice, §143B-805.

Family law arbitration, §50-59(a).

Insurers supervision, §58-30-10.

Interstate compact for juveniles, §7B-4001.

Interstate compact on juveniles, §7B-2803.

Interstate wildlife violator compact, §113-300.6.

Limited liability companies, §57C-1-03.

Mediated settlement conferences or other settlement procedures, §7A-38.3D(n).

Partnerships, §59-32.

Transfers to minors, §33A-1.

Court competent jurisdiction.

Savings and loan associations, §54B-4.

Court of competent jurisdiction.

Abused, neglected and dependent juveniles, §7B-101.

Court officer.

Endangering officers, §14-16.10.

Court or courts of the state.

Discipline and disability rules of state bar, Bar Rule B.0103.

DEFINED TERMS —Cont'd
Court or courts of the state —Cont'd
Procedures for the authorized practice committee
of the state bars, Bar Rule D.0203.
Court order.
Child support, §110-129.
Coventurer.
Solicitation of contributions, §131F-2.
Coverage.
Health insurance portability and accountability,
§58-68-25(a).
Covered benefits.
Health benefit plan external review, §58-50-75(c).
Covered claim.
Insurance guaranty association, §58-48-20.
Self-insurance security association, §97-130.
Covered clinical trials.
Health benefit plan coverage, §58-3-255(a).
Covered corporation.
Control share acquisitions, §55-9A-01(b).
Covered device.
Discarded computer equipment and television
management, §130A-309.131.
Covered entity.
Health information exchange, §90-413.3.
Covered equipment.
Overhead high-voltage line safety, §95-229.6.
Covered governmental entity.
Persons with disabilities protection, §168A-3.
Covered items.
Overhead high-voltage line safety, §95-229.6.
Covered lease agreement.
Option to purchase contracts executed with
residential lease agreements, §47G-1.
Covered multifamily dwellings, §41A-3.
Covered person.
Accident and health insurance.
Utilization review, §58-50-61(a).
Criminal history record checks.
Department of public instruction, §114-19.23(a).
Employees of department of health and human
services and division of juvenile justice,
§114-19.6(a).
Health benefit plan external review, §58-50-75(c).
Health insurance risk pool, §58-50-175.
State government ethics act, §138A-3.
Covered policy.
Insurance guaranty associations, §58-62-16.
Covered service.
Contracts between health benefit plans and dental
service providers, §58-50-290(b).
State health plan for teachers and state
employees, §135-48.1.
Covered vaccine.
Vaccine-related injury, §130A-422.
Covered visit services.
Health insurance, locum tenens contracts,
§58-3-231(a).
Covered voter.
Uniform military and overseas voters act,
§163-258.2.
Coworker.
Voluntary shared leave program, §§115C-12.2(a),
126-8.3(a).
CPA.
Workers' compensation self insurance, §97-165.
Crash.
Motor vehicles, §20-4.01.
Creation of a security interest.
Leases, UCC, §25-2A-303(1).

DEFINED TERMS —Cont'd
Credential.
Substance abuse professionals, §90-113.31A.
Credentialing body.
Substance abuse professionals, §90-113.31A.
Credible witness.
Notaries public act, §10B-3.
Credit.
Equal availability of credit for women, §25B-1(c).
Worthless checks, §14-107(c).
Creditable coverage.
Health insurance portability and accountability,
§§58-51-17(a), 58-68-30(c).
Creditable service, §128-21.
Judicial retirement, §135-53.
Law enforcement officers, §143-166.42(b).
Law-enforcement separation allowances,
§143-166.41(b).
Legislative retirement system, §120-4.12(a).
State law-enforcement retirement, §143-166.30(a).
State retirement system, §135-1.
Credit accident and health insurance, §58-57-5.
Credit card.
Identity theft, §75-61.
Credit card business.
Insurance, solicitation, negotiation or payment of
premiums through, §58-3-155.
Credit facility.
Capital facilities finance act, §142-82.
Energy conservation finance act, §142-61.
Facility authorities, §160A-480.2.
Global TransPark authority, §63A-2.
Higher education bonds, §116D-1.
Local government bonds, §159-79(c).
Solid waste, §159I-7.
Solid waste management loan program.
Special obligation bonds and notes of local
governments, §159I-30(g).
State debt, §142-29.2.
Credit hour.
Continuing legal education, Bar Rule D.1501.
Credit insurance agent, §58-57-5.
Credit life insurance, §§58-57-5, 58-58-10.
Credit monitoring services, §75-134.
Creditor.
Credit insurance, §58-57-5.
Fraudulent transfers, §39-23.1.
Insurers supervision, §58-30-10.
Refund anticipation loan act, §53-246.
UCC, §25-1-201(b).
Creditor process.
Funds transfers, UCC, §25-4A-502(a).
Credit repair business, §66-221.
Credit report.
Credit scoring to rate motor vehicle and property
insurance, §58-36-90(a).
Identity theft, §75-61.
Credit score.
Credit scoring to rate motor vehicle and property
insurance, §58-36-90(a).
Credit suspension directive.
Satisfaction of deeds of trust and mortgages,
§45-36.4.
Credit transaction.
Credit insurance, §58-57-5.
Credit unemployment insurance, §58-57-5.
Credit union, §54-109.1.
Cremated remains, §90-210.121.
Cremation, §90-210.121.
Cremation chamber, §90-210.121.
Cremation container, §90-210.121.

DEFINED TERMS —Cont'd

Cremation interment container, §90-210.121.
Cremation society, §90-210.121.
Crematorium, §90-210.121.
Crematory, §90-210.121.
Crematory licensee, §90-210.121.
Crematory manager, §90-210.121.
Crematory technician, §90-210.121.
Crest.
Mountain ridge protection, §113A-206.
CRFL.
Coastal recreational fishing licenses, §113-174.
Crime.
Victims and witnesses, §15A-824.
Crime insurance.
Beach property, §58-45-5.
Fair access to insurance requirements,
§58-46-1(c).
Crime memorabilia.
Crime victims financial recovery assistance act,
§15B-31.
Criminal action.
Civil procedure, §1-5.
Criminal activity.
Expedited evictions, §42-59.
Criminal appellate practice.
Certification standards for criminal law specialty,
Bar Rule D.2502.
Criminal history.
Abused, neglected and dependent juveniles,
§7B-101.
Adoption, §48-1-101.
Archaeological investigations.
Criminal record checks of permit applicants,
§70-13.1(a).
Auctions and auctioneers.
Criminal history record checks of applicants for
license, §85B-3.2(a).
Charter schools, §115C-238.29K(a).
Department of public instruction, §114-19.23(a).
Employees of department of health and human
services and division of juvenile justice,
§114-19.6(a).
Fire departments, criminal history record checks,
§114-19.12(a).
Licensure of manufactured home manufacturers,
dealers, salespersons or set-up contractors.
Criminal history record checks, §143-143.10A.
Locksmith licensing, §74F-18(a).
Mandatory child care provider criminal history
checks, §110-90.2(a).
Marriage and family therapists.
Criminal history record checks of license
applicants, §90-270.63(a).
Nurses, §90-171.48(a).
Nursing home administrators, §90-288.01(a).
Professional counselors.
Criminal history record checks of license
applicants, §90-345(a).
Real estate appraisal management companies.
Criminal history record checks, §93E-2-11(a).
Residential school personnel criminal history
checks, §143B-146.16(a).
Salvage.
Abandoned shipwrecks and other underwater
sites.
Criminal record checks of applicants for
permit or license, §121-25.1(a).
School personnel, §115C-332(a).
Substance abuse professionals, §90-113.31A.

DEFINED TERMS —Cont'd

Criminal history record check.
Massage and bodywork therapy, §90-622.
Criminal history record repository.
National crime prevention and privacy compact,
§114-19.50.
Criminal history records.
National crime prevention and privacy compact,
§114-19.50.
Criminal justice.
National crime prevention and privacy compact,
§114-19.50.
Criminal justice agencies.
Criminal justice education, §17C-2.
DNA database and databanks, §15A-266.2.
Justice academy, §17D-1.
National crime prevention and privacy compact,
§114-19.50.
Criminal justice officers.
Criminal justice education, §17C-2.
Criminal justice personnel.
Justice academy, §17D-1.
Criminal justice services.
National crime prevention and privacy compact,
§114-19.50.
Criminal law specialty, Bar Rule D.2502.
Criminally injurious conduct.
Victims compensation, §15B-2.
Criminal moving violation.
Provisional license revocation, §20-13.3(a).
**Criminal offense showing professional
unfitness.**
Discipline and disability rules of state bar, Bar
Rule B.0103.
Criminal proceeding.
Remote testimony by child witness,
§15A-1225.1(a).
RICO act, §75D-3.
Criminal street gang, §14-50.16(b).
Aggravating factors in sentencing,
§15A-1340.16(d).
Criminal street gang activity, §14-50.16(c).
Criminal summons.
Criminal process, §15A-303.
Critical access hospital.
Hospital licensure, §131E-76.
Hospital provider assessments, §108A-121.
Critical period conversion ratio.
Credit insurance, §58-57-5.
Critical period coverage.
Credit insurance, §58-57-5.
Critical tire information.
Purchase of tires for school buses, §115C-249.1(a).
State vehicles, tire purchase, repair or
refurbishment, §143-63.2(a).
Cruel treatment.
Protection of animals, §19A-1.
Cruelty.
Cruelty to animals, §14-360(c).
Protection of animals, §19A-1.
Cruelty to animals.
Veterinarians, §90-181.
Crustaceans.
Conservation, §113-129.
Cued speech.
Interpreters and transliterators licensure act,
§90D-3.
Culpably negligent.
Patient abuse, §14-32.2(e).
Cultural purpose.
Taxation, §105-278.3(d).

DEFINED TERMS —Cont'd

Cure the default.
Contracts for deed, §47H-1.
Option to purchase contracts executed with residential lease agreements, §47G-1.

Curfew.
Emergency management.
Availability of emergency supplies and utility services, §166A-6.03(f).

Curfew area.
Emergency management.
Availability of emergency supplies and utility services, §166A-6.03(f).

Current assets.
Provider sponsored organizations, §131E-276.

Current beneficiary.
Second trust, §36C-8-816.1(a).

Current liabilities.
Provider sponsored organizations, §131E-276.

Current model.
Farm machinery franchises, §66-180.

Current net price.
Farm machinery, §66-180.

Current operations appropriations act.
Budget of state, §143C-1-1(d).

Current ratio.
Provider sponsored organizations, §131E-276.

Current significant investigative information.
Nurse licensure compact, §90-171.82.

Current standards.
Dry-cleaning solvent cleanup act, §143-215.104B(b).

Custodial accounts.
Livestock prompt pay law, §106-418.3.

Custodial agency.
Crime victims' rights, §15A-830(a).
DNA database and databanks, §15A-266.2.

Custodial agent.
Managing general insurance agents, §58-34-2(a).

Custodial parents.
Consent to health care for minor, §32A-29.

Custodial property.
Transfers to minors, §33A-1.

Custodial trustee, §33B-1.

Custodial trust property, §33B-1.

Custodian.
Abused, neglected and dependent juveniles, §7B-101.
Delinquent and undisciplined juveniles, §7B-1501.
Division of juvenile justice, §143B-805.
Transfers to minors, §33A-1.

Custom built vehicle.
Motor vehicles, §20-4.01.

Customer.
Banking, §25-4-104(a).
Disposal of dyes, molds, forms and patterns, §66-67.3(a).
Financial privacy, §53B-2.
Funds transfers, UCC, §25-4A-105(a).
Insurance customer information safeguards, §58-39-140.
Invention development services, §66-209.
Motor vehicle repairs, §20-354.2.
Portable consumer electronic devices insurance, §58-44A-1.
Telephone records privacy protection, §14-113.30.

Customer computer software.
Sales and use tax, §105-164.3.

Customer-formula feed.
Commercial feed law, §106-284.33.

DEFINED TERMS —Cont'd

Customer information.
Insurance customer information safeguards, §58-39-140.

Customer information systems.
Insurance customer information safeguards, §58-39-140.

Customer service call center.
Growing businesses tax credits, §105-129.81.

CWSRF.
Water infrastructure, §159G-20.

Dairy case.
Criminal law, §14-72.4.

Dam.
Safety, §143-215.25.

Damage.
Contractors, §87-101.
Medical assistance provider false claims act, §108A-70.11.
Offshore oil and gas activities, §143-215.94BB.
Rental cars, §66-201.

Dangerous dog, §67-4.1.

Dangerous to himself or others.
Mental health, §122C-3.

Dangerous weapon or substance.
Civil disorders, §14-288.1.

Data.
Computer crimes, §14-453.

Datacenter.
Sales and use tax, §105-164.3.

Data entry and preparation.
Tax incentives for new and expanding businesses, §105-129.2.

Data processing.
Tax incentives for new and expanding businesses, §105-129.2.

Date of test.
Seed law, §106-277.2.

Day.
Education personnel, §115C-325(a).
Local government finance, §159-2.
Migrant housing, §95-223.
Occupational safety and health, §95-127.
Political campaign, §163-278.6.
Satisfaction of deeds of trust and mortgages, §45-36.4.

Day of adjournment.
Rulemaking procedure, §150B-21.3(d).

Dead human bodies, §90-210.20(c1).

Deaf.
Health and human services division, §143B-216.30.

Deaf person.
Interpreters for hearing impaired, §8B-1.

Dealer.
Farm machinery, §66-180.
Firearms, §14-409.39.
Liquefied petroleum gases, §119-54(a).
Motor vehicles, §20-4.01.
Precious metals, §66-164.
Protection of animals, §19A-23.
Securities, §78A-2.
Seed law, §106-277.2.
Unauthorized substances taxes, §105-113.106.
Wildlife dealer licenses, §113-273(a).

Dealer management computer system.
Motor vehicle dealers, §20-305.7(f).

Dealer management computer system vendor.
Motor vehicle dealers, §20-305.7(f).

Dealership facilities.
Motor vehicles, §20-286.

DEFINED TERMS —Cont'd
Dealing in furs.
Fur-dealer licenses, §113-273(f).
Death.
Workers' compensation, §97-2.
Death taxes.
Elective share of surviving spouse, §30-3.2.
Debilitation.
Standby guardianship, §35A-1370.
Debit card.
Identity theft, §75-61.
Debris.
Solid waste management, §130A-290(a).
Debt, NC Const Art V §§3, 4.
Debt collection, §105A-2.
Debt collectors, §75-50.
Fraudulent transfers, §39-23.1.
Prohibited collection practices, §58-70-90.
Debt adjuster, §14-423.
Debt adjusting, §14-423.
Debt buyer.
Collection agencies, §58-70-15(b).
Debt collector, §75-50.
Debt instrument.
Solid waste, §159I-7.
Debtor.
Credit insurance, §58-57-5.
Debt adjusting, §14-423.
Debt collection, §105A-2.
Fraudulent transfers, §39-23.1.
Refund anticipation loan act, §53-246.
Secured transactions, §25-9-102(a).
Statewide accounts receivable program,
§147-86.20.
Student loan collections, §105B-1.
Debtor's correct name.
Secured transactions financing statements,
§25-9-506(d).
Debt security.
Trust companies, §53-301(a).
Debt service.
Local government finance, §159-7.
Debt service reserve supplement requirement.
Revenue bonds, §159-97.
Decedent.
Anatomical gifts, §130A-412.4.
Decedents' estates, §31A-3.
Deceit.
Securities, §78A-2.
Deception.
Human trafficking, §14-43.10(a).
Deceptive acts or practices.
Unfair trade practices, §58-63-15.
Decision-making board.
Municipal planning and regulation of
development, appeals, §160A-393(b).
Declarant.
Condominiums, §47C-1-103.
Conversion building rental, §47A-34.
Evidence, §8C-1 Rule 801(b).
Natural death right, §90-321(a).
Planned community act, §47F-1-103.
Declaration.
Condominiums, §47C-1-103.
Planned community act, §47F-1-103.
Unit ownership, §47A-3.
Declaration of loss.
Negotiable instruments, §25-3-312(a).
Declared state of emergency.
Civil disorders, §14-288.1.

DEFINED TERMS —Cont'd
Declination of insurance coverage.
Insurance information and privacy protection act,
§58-39-15.
Dedicate.
Nature preserves act, §113A-164.3.
Dedicated natural gas vehicle.
Motor vehicles, §20-4.01.
Deductible.
State health plan for teachers and state
employees, §135-48.1.
Deed of trust.
Sales under power of sale, §45-21.1(b).
Deemed status.
Substance abuse professionals, §90-113.31A.
Deep water.
State lands, §146-64.
Deer.
Conservation, §113-129.
Default.
Home foreclosure rescue scams, §75-120.
Defendant, §1-10.
Bail, §15A-531.
Civil procedure, §1-75.2.
Discipline and disability rules of state bar, Bar
Rule B.0103.
Procedures for the authorized practice committee
of the state bars, Bar Rule D.0203.
Punitive damages, §1D-5.
UCC, §25-1-201(b).
Definite beneficiary.
Uniform trust code, §36C-4-402.
Defoliant.
Pesticide board, §143-460.
Defraud.
Securities, §78A-2.
Delegates.
Nonprofit corporations, §55A-1-40.
Delinquency proceeding.
Insurers supervision, §58-30-10.
Delinquent income tax debt.
Electrical contractors, §87-44.2(a).
Engineers.
Licensing of nonresidents, §89C-18.1(a).
General contractors.
Licensing of nonresidents, §87-10.1(a).
Plumbing, heating and fire sprinkler contractors,
§87-22.2(a).
Delinquent insurer.
Insurance guaranty associations, §58-62-16.
Delinquent juvenile.
Delinquent and undisciplined juveniles, §7B-1501.
Division of juvenile justice, §143B-805.
Interstate compact on juveniles, §7B-2803.
Deliver.
Business corporations, §55-1-40.
Controlled substances, §90-87.
Nonprofit corporations, §55A-1-40.
Pharmacy practice, §90-85.3(d).
Renunciation, §31B-2.1(a).
Salvia divinorum.
Manufacture, sale, delivery, possession,
§14-401.23(d).
Delivered electronically.
Sales and use tax, §105-164.3.
Delivery.
UCC, §25-1-201(b).
Delivery charges.
Sales and use tax, §105-164.3.
Delivery damages.
Motor vehicles, §20-305.1.

DEFINED TERMS —Cont'd

Delivery order.
UCC, §25-7-102(a).

Delivery receipt.
Personal jurisdiction, manner of serving, §1A-1
Rule 4(j).
Proof of service of process, §1-75.10(b).

Demand deposits.
Banking, §53-1.

Demand-side management.
Renewable energy and energy efficiency portfolio
standard (REPS), §62-133.8(a).

Demolisher.
Motor vehicles, §20-137.7.

Demolition.
Solid waste management, §130A-290(a).

Demote.
Educational personnel, §115C-325(a).

De novo branch.
Interstate branch banking, §53-224.9.

Dental hygiene, §90-221(a).

Dental hygienist, §90-221(b).

Dental service plan, §58-65-1(a).

Dentistry, §90-29.

Departmental receipt.
Budget of state, §143C-1-1(d).

Department of defense personnel.
Life insurance.
Dishonest and predatory sales to military
personnel, §58-58-335.

Dependent.
Deceased migrant agricultural workers,
§130A-417.
Health insurance risk pool, §58-50-175.
Small employer group health coverage,
§58-50-110.
State health plan for teachers and state
employees, §135-48.1.
Tax withholding, §105-163.1.
Uniform military and overseas voters act,
§163-258.2.
Victims compensation, §15B-2.

Dependent child.
Child support, §110-129.
Death benefits, §143-166.2(a).
Public assistance program, §108A-24.
State health plan for teachers and state
employees, §135-48.1.

Dependent juvenile.
Abused, neglected or dependent juveniles,
§7B-101.

Dependent parent.
Death benefits, §143-166.2(b).

Dependent's economic loss.
Victims compensation, §15B-2.

Dependent spouse.
Alimony, §50-16.1A.
Support and maintenance, §14-322(a).

Dependent's replacement service loss.
Victims compensation, §15B-2.

Deployment.
Military personnel on temporary duty or
deployment, child custody or visitation,
§50-13.7A(b).

Deposit.
Manufactured housing, §143-143.9.
Regional reciprocal savings and loan acquisition
act, §54B-48.2.

Deposit account.
Right of survivorship in bank deposits, §41-2.1(e).
Secured transactions, §25-9-102(a).

DEFINED TERMS —Cont'd

Depositary bank.
Banking, §25-4-105.

Depository institution.
Mortgage bankers, brokers and servicers,
§53-244.030.
Savings banks, §54C-4(b).
Trust companies, §53-301(a).
Trust institutions acting in fiduciary capacity,
§53-158.10.

Depository library, §125-11.6.

Depreciation.
Principal and income act, §37A-5-503(a).

Deputy.
Opening and inventory of decedent's safe-deposit
box, §28A-15-13(a).

Deputy commissioner.
Banking, §53-165(f).
Occupational safety and health, §95-127.

Deputy compact administrator.
Interstate compact for juveniles, §7B-4001.

Deputy inspector.
Boiler and pressure vessel regulation,
§95-69.9(d1).

Derelict vehicle.
Motor vehicles, §20-137.7.

Derivative.
Principal and income act, §37A-4-414(a).

Derivative instrument.
Derivative transactions, insurance companies,
§58-7-205(a).

Derivative proceedings, §55-7-40.1.

Derivative transaction.
Insurance companies, §58-7-205(a).

DES.
Job training, education and placement
information management, §96-31.

Desiccant.
Pesticide board, §143-460.

Designated agency.
Incompetency, §§35A-1101, 35A-1202.

Designated downtown area.
Main street solutions fund, §143B-472.35(a2).

Designated family member.
Motor vehicles, §20-286.

Designated health care services.
Self-referrals by health care providers, §90-405.

Designated individual.
Lobbying, §120C-100(a).

Designated micropolitan.
Main street solutions fund, §143B-472.35(a2).

Designated person.
Auctions and auctioneers, §85B-1.

Designated relative.
Private trust companies, §53-363(a).

Designated representative.
Child support, §110-129.

Designated state official.
Educational personnel qualifications, §115C-350.

Designation.
Standby guardianship, §35A-1370.

Designator.
Standby guardianship, §35A-1370.

Desktop computer.
Discarded computer equipment and television
management, §130A-309.131.

Destination state.
Gasoline tax, §105-449.60.

Destructive device.
Discipline of students, §115C-390.1(b).

DEFINED TERMS —Cont'd

Detailed accounts.
Legal expense funds for elected officials,
§163-278.307(c).

Detection of deception examiner.
Private protective services, §74C-3.

Detention.
Delinquent and undisciplined juveniles, §7B-1501.
Division of juvenile justice, §143B-805.

Detention facility.
Delinquent and undisciplined juveniles, §7B-1501.
Division of juvenile justice, §143B-805.

Determinable elements.
Annuity disclosure, §58-60-130.

Determination date.
Urban electrical service, §160A-331.

Determination of debilitation.
Standby guardianship, §35A-1370.

Determination of incapacity.
Standby guardianship, §35A-1370.

Develop.
Certificate, §131E-176.

Developed losses.
Insurance rates, §58-36-100(b).

Developer.
Development agreements, §160A-400.21.
Counties, §153A-349.2.
Time shares, §93A-41.

Development.
Coastal area management, §113A-103.
Counties.
Forestry activities, §153A-452(a).
Development agreements, §160A-400.21.
Counties, §153A-349.2.
Municipal planning and regulation of
development.
Forestry activities, §160A-458.5(a).
National defense housing projects, §157-53.

Developmental disability.
Council, §143B-178.
Mental health, §122C-3.

Development permit.
Development agreements, §160A-400.21.
Counties, §153A-349.2.

Development project.
Local development, development financing,
§158-7.3(a).

Development rights.
Condominiums, §47C-1-103.

Development tier.
Commerce department, §143B-437.08(a).
Sales and use tax, §105-164.3.

Development tier area.
Mill rehabilitation tax credit, §105-129.70.

Development tier one area.
Research and development expenses tax credit,
§105-129.50.

Development zone.
Tax incentives for new and expanding businesses,
§105-129.2.

Development zone agency.
Development zone project tax credit,
§105-129.13(b).

Deviation.
Structural pest control act, §106-65.24.

Device.
Food, drugs and cosmetics, §106-121.
Pesticide board, §143-460.
Pharmacy practice, §90-85.3(e).

Devise.
Testamentary additions to trusts, §31-47(e).

DEFINED TERMS —Cont'd

Devisee.
Decedents' estates, §28A-1-1.
Uniform transfer on death security registration
act, §41-40.
Wills, antilapse statute, §31-42(d).

Diagnostic center.
Certificate of need, §131E-176.

Diamond.
Unfair trade practices, §§66-73, 66-74.

Diamond industry.
Unfair trade practices, §§66-73, 66-74.

Diamond Shamrock Litigation Funds.
Housing trust, §122E-2.

Diesel fuel.
Gasoline tax, §105-449.60.

Dietary supplement.
Sales and use tax, §105-164.3.

Dietetics/nutrition, §90-352.

**Differs substantially from text of proposed
rule.**
Administrative rulemaking, §150B-21.2(g).

Digital code.
Sales and use tax, §105-164.3.

Direct access.
National crime prevention and privacy compact,
§114-19.50.

Direct holdings.
Sudan (Darfur) divestment act, §147-86.42.

Direct mail.
Sales and use tax, §105-164.3.

Director.
Limited liability companies, §57C-1-03.
State lottery, §18C-103.
Trust companies, §53-301(a).

Director of indigent defense services.
Consolidated judicial retirement act, §135-53.

Direct supervision.
Polysomnography practice act, §90-721.
Respiratory care practices act, §90-648.

Direct-to-home satellite services.
Sales and use tax, §105-164.3.

Disability.
Education of children with disabilities,
§115C-106.3.

Disability income insurance policy,
§58-51-130(a).

Disabled adult.
Abuse, neglect or exploitation of disabled or elder
adults.
Criminal offense, §14-32.3(d).
Exploitation, §14-112.2(a).
Protection, §108A-101.

Disabled business enterprise.
Global TransPark authority, §63A-19.
Procurement, §143-48(b).

Disabled or disability.
Discipline and disability rules of state bar, Bar
Rule B.0103.
Income plan, §135-101.
Workers' compensation, §§97-2, 97-55.

Disabled veteran.
Disabled veteran property tax homestead
exclusion, §105-277.1C(b).

Disablement.
Workers' compensation, §97-54.

Disabling condition, §168A-3.

Disadvantaged business.
Transportation contracts, §136-28.4(c).

Disaster.
Emergency management, §166A-4.

DEFINED TERMS —Cont'd

Disaster —Cont'd
Volunteer leave, §166A-31.

Disaster area.
Emergency management, §166A-4.

Disaster location.
First responders vaccination program, §130A-485(f).

Discarded computer equipment.
Discarded computer equipment and television management, §130A-309.131.

Discarded computer equipment or television collector.
Discarded computer equipment and television management, §130A-309.131.

Discarded television.
Discarded computer equipment and television management, §130A-309.131.

Discharge.
Liability for hazardous materials abatement, §143-215.103.
Oil and hazardous substance control, §143-215.77.
Review of offshore fossil fuel facilities for potential of unauthorized discharge, §113A-119.2(a).

Discharge for misconduct with work.
Unemployment insurance, §96-14.

Discharge of waste, §143-213.

Disciplinary action.
Drivers' licenses, lose control, lose license, §20-11(n1).

Disciplinary suspension.
Educational personnel, §115C-325(a).

Disclose.
Health information exchange, §90-413.3.

Disclosure.
Health information exchange, §90-413.3.

Disclosure date.
Electioneering communications.
Candidate-specific communication, §§163-278.100, 163-278.110.

Disclosure document.
Annuity disclosure, §58-60-130.

Discontinuance.
Health maintenance organizations, §58-67-5(o).

Discount buying club, §66-131.

Discounted present value.
Structured settlement protection, §1-543.11.

Discover.
UCC, §25-1-202(c).

Discovered property.
Property taxes, §105-273.

Discriminatory practice.
Persons with disabilities protection, §168A-3.

Disease.
Bee and honey act, §106-635.

Dishonest conduct.
Client security fund, rules governing administration, Bar Rule D.1401.
Homeowner's recovery fund, §87-15.5.

Dishonor.
Letters of credit, §25-5-102(a).

Disinterested directors.
Savings and loan associations, §54B-4.
Savings banks, §54C-4(b).

Disinterested person.
Principal and income act, §37A-1-104.1.

Disinterested public agent.
Incompetency, §35A-1202.

Disinterested witness.
Anatomical gifts, §130A-412.4.

DEFINED TERMS —Cont'd

Disorder.
Bee and honey act, §106-635.

Disorderly conduct.
Civil disorders, §14-288.1.

Dispatch.
Hunting and wildlife, §113-291.1(k).

Dispense.
Controlled substances, §90-87.
Pharmacy practice, §90-85.3(f).

Dispenser.
Controlled substances, §90-87.
Controlled substances reporting system, §90-113.72.

Dispensing optician, §90-235.

Dispersement of settlement proceeds.
Good funds settlement act, §45A-3.

Displaced homemaker, §143B-394.4.

Displaced person.
Relocation assistance, §133-7.

Display a real-time view of the unborn child.
Woman's right to know act, §90-21.81.

Display operator.
Fireworks, §14-410(c).

Disposable earnings.
Child support, §110-136.
Debt collection, §105B-3.
Debts owed public hospitals, §131E-48.
Garnishment for enforcement of child-support obligations, §110-136(a).

Disposable income.
Child support, §110-129.
Garnishment of wages to recoup fraudulent public assistance program payments, §108A-25.3(a).

Disposal.
Dry-cleaning solvent cleanup act, §143-215.104B(b).
Identity theft, §75-61.
Solid waste management, §130A-290(a).

Disposal fee.
Scrap tire disposal, §130A-309.53.

Disposal system.
Water and air resources, §143-213.

Dispose.
Child support, §50-31.
Condominiums, §47C-1-103.
Conversion building rental, §47A-34.

Disposed of.
Growing businesses tax credits, §105-129.88(d).

Disposition.
Child support, §50-31.
Condominiums, §47C-1-103.
Conversion building rental, §47A-34.
Criminal procedure, §15A-1381.

Disposition of remains.
Power of attorney, §32A-16.

Dispute.
Education of children with disabilities, §115C-106.3.

Disputed claim.
Mediation of emergency or disaster property insurance claims, §58-44-75.

Disqualification.
Criminal procedure, certificate of relief from collateral consequences, §15A-173.1.
Motor vehicles, §20-4.01.

Disqualified person.
Professional corporations, §55B-2.

Disqualifying conflict of interest.
Ethics, misuse of public office, §138A-39(d).

DEFINED TERMS —Cont'd
Dissolution.
Partnerships, §59-59.
Dissolved corporation.
Articles of dissolution, §55-14-03(c).
Distinguishing license plate.
Handicapped parking privileges, §20-37.5.
Distressed area.
Annexation by petition of property owners,
§160A-31(j).
Distress sale, §66-76.
Distributable system property.
Public service taxation, §105-333.
Distribute.
Antifreeze law, §106-579.3.
Commercial feed law, §106-284.33.
Controlled substances, §90-87.
Seed law, §106-277.2.
Soil additives act, §106-50.30.
Youth access to tobacco products, §14-313(a).
Distributed information technology assets.
Office of information technology services,
§147-33.81.
Distribution.
Business corporations, §55-1-40.
Limited liability companies, §57C-1-03.
Nonprofit corporations, §55A-1-40.
Distribution proceeding.
Foreign-money claims, §1C-1820.
Distributive award.
Divorce, §50-20(b).
Distributor.
Commercial feed law, §106-284.33.
Commercial fertilizer, §106-657.
Controlled substances, §90-87.
Egg law, §106-245.14.
Fire-safety standard and firefighter protection act,
§58-92-10.
Gasoline tax, §105-449.60.
Motion pictures, §75C-2.
Motor vehicles, §20-286.
Soil additives act, §106-50.30.
Tobacco taxation, §105-113.4.
Toxic or hazardous substance identification,
§95-174(d).
Distributor branch.
Motor vehicles, §20-286.
Distributor representative.
Motor vehicles, §20-286.
District.
Abused, neglected and dependent juveniles,
§7B-101.
Aeronautics, §63-79.
Delinquent and undisciplined juveniles, §7B-1501.
Division of juvenile justice, §143B-805.
Metropolitan sewerage, §162A-65(a).
Metropolitan water, §162A-32(a).
Organization of schools, §115C-69.
Pollution control act, §113A-52.
Regional natural gas district, §160A-661(b).
Soil and water conservation, §139-3.
District attorney.
Consolidate judicial retirement act, §135-53.
Criminal procedure, §15A-101.
Certificate of relief from collateral consequences,
§15A-173.1.
Judicial retirement, §135-53.
District bar.
Attorneys at law, §84-19.
District court.
Criminal procedure, §15A-101.

DEFINED TERMS —Cont'd
District court —Cont'd
Protection of disabled adults, §108A-101.
Diversion.
Gasoline tax, §105-449.60.
Dividend credit.
Business corporations, §55-1-40.
Dividends.
Corporate income tax, §105-130.4(f).
Adjustment for expenses related to dividends,
§105-130.6A(a).
Dividends on stock.
Savings and loan associations, §54B-4.
Savings banks, §54C-4(b).
Dividends on withdrawable accounts.
Savings and loan associations, §54B-4.
Division of entomology.
Biological organism act, §106-65.44.
Division of water quality.
Water infrastructure, §159G-20.
DNA, §15A-266.2.
DNA record, §15A-266.2.
DNA sample, §15A-266.2.
Docket book.
Civil procedure, §1-208.1.
Doctor of veterinary medicine, §90-181.
Document.
Confidential legislative communications, §120-129.
Criminal process and procedure.
Electronic technology, §15A-101.1.
Letters of credit, §25-5-102(a).
Property taxes, §105-273.
Real property electronic recording, §47-16.2.
Satisfaction of deeds of trust and mortgages,
§45-36.4.
Secured transactions, §25-9-102(a).
State depository library system, §125-11.6.
UCC, §25-7-102(a).
Documentary draft.
Banking, §25-4-104(a).
Documentary material.
RICO act, §75D-3.
Document of gift.
Anatomical gifts, §130A-412.4.
Document of rescission.
Satisfaction of deeds of trust, §45-36.6(a).
Document of title.
UCC, §25-1-201(b).
Dog, §130A-134.
Rabies vaccination, §130A-184.
Dog handler.
Controlled substances, §90-102.1(a).
Doing business.
Insurers supervision, §58-30-10.
Taxation, §105-114.
Doing business in this state.
Telephone solicitations, §75-101.
Domestic.
Venue, §1-79(b).
Domestic company.
Insurance, §58-1-5.
Domestic corporation.
Business corporations, §55-1-40.
Limited partnerships, §59-102.
Nonprofit corporations, §55A-1-40.
Partnerships, §59-32.
Taxation, §105-130.2.
Domestic guaranty association.
Insurers supervision, §58-30-10.
Domestic insurer.
Insurance companies, §58-12-2.

DEFINED TERMS —Cont'd
Domestic insurer —Cont'd
Protected cell companies, §58-10-80.
Domestic limited liability company.
Limited partnerships, §59-102.
Partnerships, §59-32.
Domestic limited partnership.
Partnerships, §59-32.
Domestic nonprofit corporation.
Limited partnerships, §59-102.
Partnerships, §59-32.
Domestic partnership.
Conversion and merger, §59-73.1.
Domestic setting.
Abuse, neglect or exploitation of disabled or elder
adults, §14-32.3(d).
Domestic violence, §50B-1(a).
Domestic violence victim.
Domestic violence victim assistance act,
§7A-474.17.
Privileged communications, rape crisis centers
and domestic violence programs, §8-53.12.
Domicile.
Liability risk retention, §58-22-10.
Unclaimed property act, §116B-52.
Domiciliary state.
Insurers supervision, §58-30-10.
Interstate insurance product regulation compact,
§58-91-10.
Donor.
Anatomical gifts, §130A-412.4.
Campaign finance.
Donation to further independent expenditure,
§163-278.12(f).
Electioneering communications.
Reporting costs incurred for producing or airing,
§163-278.12C(c).
Donor registry.
Anatomical gifts, §130A-412.4.
Do not call registry.
Telephone solicitations, §75-101.
Door to door.
Life insurance.
Dishonest and predatory sales to military
personnel, §58-58-335.
Down payment.
Contracts for deed, §47H-1.
Downtown development project.
City and town planning, §160A-458.3.
**Downtown economic development
organization.**
Main street solutions fund, §143B-472.35(a2).
Downtown organization.
Main street solutions fund, §143B-472.35(a2).
Downtown revitalization project, §160A-536(b).
Drawee.
Negotiable instruments, §25-3-103.
Drawer.
Negotiable instruments, §25-3-103.
Drilling wastes.
Offshore oil and gas activities, §143-215.94BB.
Drinking water reserve.
Water infrastructure, §159G-20.
Drinking water rules, §130A-313.
Driver.
Motor vehicles, §20-4.01.
Driver's license.
Anatomical gifts, §130A-412.4.
Drug.
Commercial feed law, §106-284.33.
Controlled substances, §90-87.

DEFINED TERMS —Cont'd
Drug —Cont'd
Food, drugs and cosmetics, §106-121.
Pharmacy practice, §90-85.3(g).
Sales and use tax, §105-164.3.
Drug dependent person.
Controlled substances, §90-87.
Drug detection dog.
Controlled substances, §90-102.1(a).
Drug sample.
Wholesale prescription drug distributors,
§106-145.2.
Dry-cleaning facility.
Dry-cleaning solvent cleanup act,
§143-215.104B(b).
Dry-cleaning solvent tax, §105-187.30.
Dry-cleaning operation.
Dry-cleaning solvent cleanup act,
§143-215.104B(b).
Dry-cleaning solvent.
Dry-cleaning solvent cleanup act,
§143-215.104B(b).
Dry-cleaning solvent tax, §105-187.30.
Dry-cleaning solvent assessment agreement.
Dry-cleaning solvent cleanup act,
§143-215.104B(b).
Dry-cleaning solvent contamination.
Dry-cleaning solvent cleanup act,
§143-215.104B(b).
Dry-cleaning solvent remediation agreement.
Dry-cleaning solvent cleanup act,
§143-215.104B(b).
Dual credit property.
Credit property insurance, §58-57-90(a).
Dual relationship.
Substance abuse professionals, §90-113.31A.
Due notice.
Soil and water conservation districts, §139-3.
Due on sale clause.
Maximum fees on loans secured by real property,
§24-10(d).
Duly authorized representative of the state.
Home schools, §115C-563(b).
**Duly certified fee-based practicing pastoral
counselor.**
Health benefit plans, choosing services,
§58-50-30(c1).
Duly certified substance abuse professional.
Health benefit plans, choosing services,
§58-50-30(c2).
Duly licensed clinical social worker.
Health benefit plans, choosing services,
§58-50-30(c).
Duly licensed professional counselor.
Health benefit plans, choosing services,
§58-50-30(c3).
Duly licensed psychologist.
Health benefit plans, choosing services,
§58-50-30(b).
Dumbwaiter.
Elevator safety, §95-110.3(c).
Duplicate.
Evidence, §8C-1 Rule 1001.
Duplicate record.
Workers' compensation self-insurance.
Employer groups, §58-47-75(a).
Durable equipment.
Insurance companies, investments in chattel
mortgages, §58-7-180(b).
Insurance companies, investments in mortgage
loans, §58-7-179(b).

DEFINED TERMS —Cont'd

Durable medical equipment.
Sales and use tax, §105-164.3.
Durable medical supplies.
Sales and use tax, §105-164.3.
Durable power of attorney, §32A-8.
Duties.
Assault on school employees or volunteers, §14-33(c).
Duty of support.
Interstate family support, §52C-1-101.
D. V. M., §90-181.
Dwelling.
Housing standards, §160A-442.
Mortgage bankers, brokers and servicers, §53-244.030.
DWSRF.
Water infrastructure, §159G-20.
Dyed diesel fuel.
Gasoline tax, §105-449.60.
Dyed diesel fuel distributor, §119-15.
Early childhood, §143B-168.11.
Earnable compensation.
Retirement, §128-21.
State retirement system, §135-1.
Earned income.
Crime victims financial recovery assistance act, §15B-31.
Earnings.
Disability income plan, §135-101.
Eating establishment.
Alcoholic beverages, §18B-1000.
E-blend fuel.
Dispensing equipment standards for ethanol blends, §143-143.6(a).
Ecological flow.
Basinwide hydrologic models, §143-355(o).
Ecological integrity.
Basinwide hydrologic models, §143-355(o).
Economically distressed county.
Industrial development fund, §143B-437.01(a), (a1).
Economically distressed units of local government.
Clean water management trust fund, §113A-252.
Economic development.
Fisherman, §113-315.17.
Economic development incentives.
Economic development grants, §143B-437.07(c).
Economic distress.
Comprehensive strategic economic development, §143B-434.01(a).
Economic interest.
Legislative ethics, §120-85.1.
State government ethics act, §138A-3.
Economic life.
Energy in state buildings, §143-64.11.
Economic loss.
Annexation initiated by municipality.
Private firm providing solid waste collection services, §160A-58.59(i).
Victims compensation, §15B-2.
Economic substance.
Corporate income tax.
Intercompany transactions lacking, §105-130.5A(f).
Educational decision.
Assignment of student to particular school, §115C-366(h).
Educational institution, §105-134.1.
Charitable gift annuities, §58-3-6.

DEFINED TERMS —Cont'd

Educational institution —Cont'd
Taxation, §105-278.4.
Educational interpreter or transliterator.
Interpreters and transliterators licensure act, §90D-3.
Educational personnel, §115C-350.
Educational property.
Discipline of students, §115C-390.1(b).
False reports concerning mass violence on educational property, §14-277.5(a).
Negligent supervision of minor, §1-538.3.
Weapons on educational property, §14-269.2(a).
Educational purpose.
Liability of landowners associated with watershed improvement projects, §139-41.3.
Property tax exemption.
Exemption of real and personal property used for, §105-278.7(f).
Recreational trespass, §38A-2.
Taxation, §§105-278.3(d), 105-278.4.
Educational services.
Education of children with disabilities, §115C-106.3.
Education partner.
Cooperative innovative high school programs, §115C-238.50A.
E-85.
Energy credit and banking program, §143-58.1(a).
Effective county tax rate.
Public school building capital fund, §115C-546.2(d).
Effective date of notice.
Business corporations, §55-1-40.
Effluent standards or limitations, §143-213.
Eggs, §106-245.14.
EIS.
Unemployment compensation, §96-8.
Unemployment insurance, §96-8.
Elder adult.
Abuse, neglect or exploitation of disabled or elder adults, §14-32.3(d).
Exploitation, §14-112.2(a).
Elderly person.
Adult care homes, §131D-2.1.
Roads and highways, §136-44.27(b).
Elected officer.
Legal expense funds for elected officials, §163-278.300.
Election, §163-165.
Challenge to a candidacy.
Single or multicounty panel, §163-127.6(a).
Statewide panel, §163-127.6(b).
Political campaigns, §163-278.6.
Electioneering communication.
Public campaign fund, §163-278.62.
Voter-owned elections act, §163-278.96.
Elective supplier.
Gasoline tax, §105-449.60.
Electrical contracting, §87-43.
Electrical system.
Electric power, §159B-3.
Electric generating facility.
Boating safety, §75A-2.
Electricity demand reduction.
Renewable energy and energy efficiency portfolio standard (REPS), §62-133.8(a).
Electric membership corporation.
Public service taxation, §105-333.
Electric personal assistive mobility device, §§20-4.01, 20-175.6(a).

DEFINED TERMS —Cont'd

Electric power company.
Public service taxation, §105-333.

Electric power holding companies.
Corporate income tax.
Adjustment for expenses related to dividends, §105-130.6A(a).

Electric power supplier.
Renewable energy and energy efficiency portfolio standard (REPS), §62-133.8(a).

Electric supplier.
Public utilities, §62-110.2.

Electrologist, §88A-3.

Electrology, §88A-3.

Electrolysis, §88A-3.

Electronic.
Criminal process and procedure, §15A-101.1.
Electronic notary public act, §10B-101.
Electronic transactions, §66-312.
Property taxes.
Electronic listing of personal property, §105-310.1(d).
Real property electronic recording, §47-16.2.
Sales and use tax, §105-164.3.
Satisfaction of deeds of trust and mortgages, §45-36.4.

Electronic agent.
Electronic transactions, §66-312.

Electronically monitor.
Criminal process and procedure, §15A-101.1.

Electronically stored information.
Discovery, scope of discovery, §1A-1 Rule 26(b).

Electronic bidding.
Procurement of information technology, §147-33.95(c).

Electronic chattel paper.
Secured transactions, §25-9-102(a).

Electronic communication.
Child custody and visitation, §50-13.2(e).
Cyberstalking, §14-196.3(a).
Electronic surveillance, §15A-286.
Wiretaps, §15A-260.

Electronic communication service.
Electronic surveillance, §15A-286.

Electronic communication system.
Electronic surveillance, §15A-286.

Electronic data-processing system, §132-6.1(d).

Electronic document.
Electronic notary public act, §10B-101.
Real property electronic recording, §47-16.2.

Electronic funds transfer.
Local government.
Payment of bills, claims or invoices, §159-28(d).
Taxation, §105-228.90(b).

Electronic inspection authorization.
Motor vehicle inspections, §20-183.2(c).

Electronic instrument.
Money transmitters, §53-208.2(a).

Electronic listing.
Property taxes, §105-310.1(d).

Electronic machine or device.
Sweepstakes, §14-306.4(a).

Electronic mail.
Computer related crime, §14-453.
Cyberstalking, §14-196.3(a).
Sex offender and public protection registration, §14-208.6.

Electronic mail order house.
Tax incentives for new and expanding businesses, §105-129.2.

DEFINED TERMS —Cont'd

Electronic mail service provider.
Computer crimes, §14-453.

Electronic means.
Military personnel on temporary duty or deployment, custody and visitation, §50-13.7A(f).
Transportation contracts, §136-28.1(k).

Electronic, mechanical or other device, §15A-286.

Electronic monitoring.
Criminal process and procedure, §15A-101.1.

Electronic notarial act.
Electronic notary public act, §10B-101.

Electronic notarization.
Electronic notary public act, §10B-101.

Electronic notary.
Electronic notary public act, §10B-101.

Electronic notary public.
Electronic notary public act, §10B-101.

Electronic notary seal.
Electronic notary public act, §10B-101.

Electronic payment.
Local government.
Payment of bills, claims or invoices, §159-28(d).
Statewide accounts receivable program, §147-86.20.

Electronic record.
Electronic transactions, §66-312.

Electronic recording.
Electronic recording of custodial interrogations, §15A-211(c).

Electronic repository.
Criminal process and procedure, §15A-101.1.

Electronic seal.
Electronic notary public act, §10B-101.

Electronic shopping and mail order houses.
Growing businesses tax credits, §105-129.81.

Electronic signature.
Criminal process and procedure, §15A-101.1.
Electronic commerce in government, §66-58.2.
Electronic notary public act, §10B-101.
Electronic transactions, §66-312.
Real property electronic recording, §47-16.2.

Electronic storage.
Electronic surveillance, §15A-286.

Electronic surveillance, §15A-286.

Elementary school, §115C-75(a).

Elevated blood lead level, §130A-131.7.

Elevator.
Safety, §95-110.3(d).

Eligibility certification.
Mill rehabilitation tax credit, §105-129.70.

Eligibility period.
Unemployment insurance, §96-12.01(a1).

Eligibility site.
Mill rehabilitation tax credit, §105-129.70.

Eligible applicant.
Insurance rate evasion fraud, §58-2-164(a).

Eligible assaultive and violent children.
Mental health, §122C-3.

Eligible client.
Judicial department, §7A-474.2.

Eligible dependent.
Education expenses credit, §105-151.33(a).

Eligible donor.
Drug, supplies, and medical device repository program, §90-85.44(a).

Eligible employee.
Small employer group health coverage, §58-50-110.

DEFINED TERMS —Cont'd
Eligible entity.
Emergency management, §166A-4.
Treatment for effective community supervision act
of 2011, §143B-1152.
Eligible firefighter.
Income tax deduction, §105-134.6(d).
Eligible fireman.
Pension fund, §58-86-25.
Eligible individual.
Health insurance portability and accountability.
Guaranteed individual coverage for certain
individuals with prior group coverage,
§58-68-60(b).
Eligible industry.
Industrial development fund, §143B-437.01(a1).
Eligible infants and toddlers.
Mental health, §122C-3.
Eligible institution.
Forgivable education for service program,
§116-209.45(b).
State education assistance authority, §116-201.
Eligible Internet data center.
Sales and use tax, §105-164.3.
Eligible landowner.
Forest development act, §106-1012.
Eligible lands.
Forest development act, §106-1012.
Eligible local government.
Main street solutions fund, §143B-472.35(a2).
Eligible major industry.
Tax incentives for new and expanding business,
§105-129.2.
Eligible member.
Insurance companies, conversion, §58-10-12(a).
Eligible municipality.
Third one-half cent tax.
City hold harmless for repealed taxes,
§105-522(a).
Eligible patient.
Drug, supplies, and medical device repository
program, §90-85.44(a).
Eligible person.
Crime victims financial recovery assistance act,
§15B-31.
Eligible position.
Job development investment grant program,
§143B-437.51.
Eligible postsecondary institution.
Education access rewards North Carolina scholars
fund, §116-209.26(a).
Scholarships, §115C-499.1.
Eligible private postsecondary institution.
Need-based scholarships for students attending
private colleges and universities, §116-280.
Eligible projects.
Housing trust, §122E-6(b).
Eligible property owner.
Annexation initiated by municipality,
§160A-58.51.
Eligible psychologists.
Mental health, §122C-3.
Eligible railroad intermodal facility.
Sales and use tax, §105-164.3.
Tax incentives for railroad intermodal facilities,
§105-129.95.
Eligible rescue squad worker.
Income tax deduction, §105-134.6(d).
Pension fund, §58-86-30.
Eligible risk.
Vehicle reinsurance, §58-37-1.

DEFINED TERMS —Cont'd
Eligible student.
Education access rewards North Carolina scholars
fund, §116-209.26(c).
Eligible surplus lines insurer, §58-21-10.
Eligible unit.
Workers' compensation fund for the benefit of
volunteer safety workers, §58-87-10(a).
Eligible veteran, §126-81.
Employment preference for veterans, §128-15(b).
Emancipated minor.
Pharmacy practice, §90-85.3(h).
Embalmer.
Funeral services, §90-210.20(d).
Embalming.
Funeral services, §90-210.20(e).
Emergency.
National Guard compact, §127A-177.
Protection of disabled adults, §108A-101.
Radiation protection, §104E-5.
Telephones, §14-401.8.
Emergency circumstances.
Drinking water, §130A-323.
Emergency communication.
Offenses against public safety, §14-286.2(b1).
Emergency facility.
Veterinarians, §90-181.1(b).
Emergency interim successor.
Local government during emergencies, §162B-7.
Emergency judge.
Judicial department, §§7A-39.1(b), 7A-50.
Emergency justice.
Judicial department, §7A-39.1(b).
Emergency management, §166A-4.
Emergency management agency, §166A-4.
Waiver of commission rules for hospitals during
disasters, §131E-84(b).
Emergency medical condition.
Accident and health insurance.
Utilization review, §58-50-61(a).
Child care facilities, administration of medicine,
§110-102.1A(b).
Health information exchange, §90-413.3.
Insurance coverage for emergency care,
§58-3-190(g).
Emergency medical dispatcher.
Emergency medical services, §131E-155.
Emergency medical services, §131E-155.
**Emergency medical services-nurse
practitioner,** §131E-155.
**Emergency medical services peer review
committee,** §131E-155.
Emergency medical services personnel,
§131E-155.
**Emergency medical services-physician
assistant,** §131E-155.
Emergency medical technician, §131E-155.
Emergency medical technician-intermediate,
§131E-155.
Emergency medical technician-paramedic,
§131E-155.
Emergency meeting.
Open meetings act, §143-318.12(f).
Emergency need.
Financial assistance for nursing students and
inactive nurses, §90-171.51.
Emergency personnel.
Civil disorders, §14-288.9.
Emergency recall judge.
Judicial department, §7A-39.1(b).

DEFINED TERMS —Cont'd

Emergency response operator.
Underground petroleum storage tank operator training, §143-215.94OO.

Emergency service employees.
Solicitation of contributions, §131F-2.

Emergency services.
Accident and health insurance.
Utilization review, §58-50-61(a).
Insurance coverage for emergency care, §58-3-190(g).
Protection of disabled adults, §108A-101.
Volunteer immunity, §1-539.11.

Eminent domain, §40A-2.

Emission, §143-213.

Emissions county.
Motor vehicle inspections, §20-183.2(c).

Employ.
Aliens, verification of work authorization, §64-25.
Wage and hour act, §95-25.2.

Employed.
Sex offender and public protection registration, §14-208.6.

Employee.
Adult care homes, immunization, §131D-9(g).
Annuities, §147-9.2.
Assault on school employees or volunteers, §14-33(c).
Confidentiality of legislative communications, §120-131.1(b).
Disability income plan, §135-101.
Group health insurance, §58-53-1.
Health insurance portability and accountability, §58-68-25(a).
Health maintenance organizations, §58-67-85(d), (d1).
Home care agencies, smoking prohibited, §131E-143(a).
Legal defense by state, §143-300.2.
Medical services corporations, §58-65-60(e1), (e3).
Mortgage bankers, brokers and servicers, §53-244.030.
Motor vehicle repairs, §20-354.2.
Nature of policies, §58-51-80(c).
Negotiable instruments, §25-3-405(a).
Nursing homes, immunization, §131E-113(g).
Occupational safety and health, §95-127.
Private personnel services, §95-47.1.
Public school employees.
Employment benefits, §115C-338(a).
Real estate appraisal management companies, §93E-2-2(a).
Repayment of money owed to state, §143-552.
Retirement, §128-21.
Safety and health, §95-250.
Smoking in public buildings and places of employment, §130A-492.
Social security eligibility, §135-20.
State directory of new hires, §110-129.2(j).
State personnel files, privacy, §126-22(b).
State retirement system, §135-1.
Structural pest control act, §106-65.24.
Tax withholding, §105-163.1.
Toxic or hazardous substance identification, §95-174(e).
Verification of work authorization, §64-25.
Wage and hour act, §95-25.2.
Water and sewer authorities, §162A-6.1(a).
Weapons on educational property, §14-269.2(a).
Workers' compensation, §97-2.
Access to relevant medical information, §97-25.6(k).

DEFINED TERMS —Cont'd

Employee assistance certification commission, §90-500.

Employee assistance professionals, §90-500.

Employee life insurance, §58-58-150.

Employee on leave.
Governmental employees, §126-52.

Employee or officer.
Confidentiality of tax information, §105-259(a).

Employee or state employee.
State health plan for teachers and state employees, §135-48.1.

Employer.
Annuities, §147-9.2.
Disability income plan, §135-101.
Employer and employee, §14-357.1.
Health insurance portability and accountability, §58-68-25(a).
Industrial commission managed care organizations, ICManagedCare Rule II.
Local government law-enforcement retirement, §143-166.50(a).
Motor vehicles, §20-4.01.
Nature of policies, §58-51-80(c).
Occupational safety and health, §95-127.
Persons with disabilities protection, §168A-3.
Private personnel services, §95-47.1.
Retirement, §128-21.
Smoking in public buildings and places of employment, §130A-492.
State directory of new hires, §110-129.2(j).
State law-enforcement retirement, §143-166.30(a).
State personnel files, privacy, §126-22(b).
State retirement system, §135-1.
Tax withholding, §105-163.1.
Toxic or hazardous substance identification, §95-174(f).
Tuition and fee waivers, §115B-1.
Unemployment compensation, §96-8.
Verification of work authorization, §64-25.
Wage and hour act, §95-25.2.
Workers' compensation, §97-2.
Access to relevant medical information, §97-25.6(k).
Workplace violence prevention, §95-260.

Employer network.
Industrial commission managed care organizations, ICManagedCare Rule II.

Employing entity.
Repayment of money owed to state, §§143-552, 143-555, 143-558.
State government ethics act, §138A-3.

Employing unit.
State health plan for teachers and state employees, §135-48.1.
Unemployment compensation, §96-8.

Employment.
Legal defense of state employees, §143-300.2.
Private personnel services, §95-47.1.
Public assistance program, §108A-24.
Social security eligibility, §135-20.
Unemployment compensation, §96-8.
Workers' compensation, §97-2.

Employment agency.
Persons with disabilities protection, §168A-3.

Employment contract.
Reciprocal attorneys' fees in business contracts, §6-21.7(a).

Employment level.
Tax credit for manufacturing cigarettes for exportation, §105-130.46(b).

DEFINED TERMS —Cont'd

Employment office.
Unemployment compensation, §96-8.

Employment security administration fund.
Unemployment compensation, §96-8.

Employment security law.
Unemployment compensation, §96-8.

EMS.
Rescue squad workers' relief fund, §58-88-1.

EMS provider.
Emergency medical services, §131E-155.

Enclosed area.
Smoking in restaurants and bars, §130A-492.

Encoded or scrambled signal.
Cable television theft, §14-118.5.

Encounter-level data.
Local health departments billing Medicaid, §130A-34.2(f).

Encryption.
Identity theft, §75-61.

Encumbrance.
Budget of state, §143C-1-1(d).
Secured transactions, §25-9-102(a).

Endangered species, §113-331.
Plant protection and conservation, §106-202.12.

Endangered species act, §113-331.
Plant protection and conservation, §106-202.12.

End-of-life-vehicle.
Mercury switch removal, motor vehicles, §130A-310.50.

End of state of disaster.
Price gouging during states of disaster, §75-38(c).

Endorsement.
Investment securities, §25-8-102.

Endorsement contract.
Athlete agents, §78C-86.

Endowment fund.
Marine resources endowment fund, §113-175.
Prudent management of institutional funds, §36E-2.

Endowment investment income.
Marine resources endowment fund, §113-175.

Endowment license revenue.
Marine resources endowment fund, §113-175.

Energy conservation loan.
Housing finance agency, §122A-3.

Energy conservation measure.
Energy conservation finance act, §142-61.
Guaranteed energy savings contracts, §143-64.17.

Energy conservation property.
Energy conservation finance act, §142-61.

Energy-consuming system.
Energy policy and life-cycle cost analysis for state government, §143-64.11.

Energy-consumption analysis.
State buildings, §143-64.11.

Energy crisis, §113B-20(a).

Energy efficiency measure.
Renewable energy and energy efficiency portfolio standard (REPS), §62-133.8(a).

Energy policy act.
Energy credit and banking program, §143-58.1(a).

Energy savings.
Guaranteed energy savings contracts, §143-64.17.

Energy star qualified product.
Sales and use tax, §105-164.3.

Enforcement agency.
Structural pest control act, §106-65.24.

Enforcement costs.
Political campaign, §163-278.6.

DEFINED TERMS —Cont'd

Engaged in business.
Sales and use tax, §105-164.3.

Engage in an equine activity.
Equine activity liability, §99E-1.

Engaging in the mortgage business.
Mortgage bankers, brokers and servicers, §53-244.030.

Engineer, §89C-3.

Engineered barrier.
Radiation protection, §104E-5.

Engineering intern, §89C-3.

Enhanced 911 service.
911 system, §62A-40.

Enrolled.
Time shares, §93A-41.

Enrolled customer.
Portable consumer electronic devices insurance, §58-44A-1.

Enrollee.
Health maintenance organizations, §58-67-5(b).

Enrollment date.
Health insurance portability and accountability, §58-68-30(b).

Enter.
Sweepstakes, §14-306.4(a).

Entered.
Criminal process and procedure.
Electronic technology, §15A-101.1.

Enterprise.
RICO act, §75D-3.
Wage and hour act, §95-25.2.

Enterprise tier.
Job development investment grant program, §143B-437.51.
Tax incentives for new and expanding businesses, §105-129.2.

Entertaining display.
Sweepstakes, §14-306.4(a).

Entire premises.
Expedited evictions, §42-59.

Entitled after-born.
Wills, §31-5.5(c).

Entitled person.
Satisfaction of deeds of trust and mortgages, §45-36.4.

Entitlement holder.
Investment securities, §25-8-102.

Entitlement order.
Investment securities, §25-8-102.

Entity.
Business corporations, §55-1-40.
Franchise tax, §105-114.1(a).
Nonprofit corporations, §55A-1-40.
Principal and income act, §37A-4-401(a).
Securities regulation, §78A-2.
Self-referrals by health care providers, §90-405.
Sex offender and public protection registration, §14-208.6.

Entrance fee.
Continuing care retirement communities, §58-64-1.

Entrance fee per withdrawable account.
Savings and loan associations, §54B-4.

Entry.
Sweepstakes, §14-306.4(a).

Entry level.
Criminal justice education, §17C-2.

Entry of judgment.
Criminal procedure, §15A-101.

DEFINED TERMS —Cont'd
Entry permit.
Hunting and fishing on registered property of
another, §113-281.
Enumerated student conduct.
Drivers' licenses, lose control, lose license,
§20-11(n1).
Environmental assessment, §113A-9.
Environmental compliance costs, §62-133.6(a).
Environmental contamination.
Brownfields property reuse act, §130A-310.31(b).
Environmental disqualifying event.
Growing businesses tax credits, §105-129.81.
Environmental document, §113A-9.
Environmental health practice, §90A-51.
Environmental health specialist, §90A-51.
Environmental impact statement, §113A-9.
Environmental law.
Fiduciaries, §32-27.
Uniform trust code, §36C-1-103.
Environmental management commission.
Soil and water conservation districts, §139-3.
Well construction, §87-85.
EPAct credit.
Energy credit and banking program, §143-58.1(a).
Epilepsy.
Incompetency, §35A-1101.
Equine.
Equine activity liability, §99E-1.
Equine activity.
Equine activity liability, §99E-1.
Equine activity sponsor.
Equine activity liability, §99E-1.
Equine infectious anemia.
Animal diseases, §106-405.15.
Equine professional.
Equine activity liability, §99E-1.
Equipment.
Pesticide board, §143-460.
Secured transactions, §25-9-102(a).
Equipment enclosure.
Wireless telecommunications facilities,
§§153A-349.51, 160A-400.51.
Equity assessment.
Hospital provider assessments, §108A-121.
Equity capital.
Trust companies, §53-301(a).
Equity line of credit, §45-81.
Loans exempt from rate and fee limitations,
§24-9(a).
Equity line securing instrument.
Instruments to secure equity lines of credit,
§45-81.
Equity security.
Domestic companies, §58-7-145(f).
Enterprise corporations, §53A-37.
Tax credit for qualified business investments,
§105-163.010.
Trust companies, §53-301(a).
Equivalent drug product.
Pharmacy practice, §90-85.27.
Equivalent level annual dividend.
Life insurance solicitation, §58-60-10.
Equivalent level death benefit.
Life insurance solicitation, §58-60-10.
Erect.
Outdoor advertising control, §136-128.
Erosion.
Pollution control act, §113A-52.
Erosion control structures.
Coastal area management, erosion control
structures, §113A-115.1(a).

DEFINED TERMS —Cont'd
Escalator.
Elevator safety, §95-110.3(e).
Escheated lands.
State lands, §146-64.
Escrow agreement.
Tobacco escrow compliance, §66-292.
Escrow or trust account.
Manufactured housing, §143-143.9.
Escrow or trust account funds.
Manufactured housing, §143-143.9.
ESS.
Unemployment compensation, §96-8.
Unemployment insurance, §96-8.
Essential parts.
Motor vehicles, §20-4.01.
Essential property insurance.
Beach property insurance, §58-45-5.
Essential public health services, §130A-1.1(b).
Essentials.
Emergency management.
Availability of emergency supplies and utility
services, §166A-6.03(f).
Essential services.
Protection of disabled adults, §108A-101.
Essential water use.
Water resources, §143-350.
Established business relationship.
Telephone solicitations, §75-101.
Unsolicited facsimiles, §75-115.
Established federal standard.
Migrant housing, §95-223.
Occupational safety and health, §95-127.
Established legal services program.
Domestic violence victim assistance act,
§7A-474.17.
Judicial department, §7A-474.2.
Established name.
Pharmacy practice, §90-85.27.
Established office.
Motor vehicles, §20-286.
Established place of business.
Motor vehicles, §20-4.01.
Established salesroom.
Motor vehicles, §20-286.
Establishment.
Growing businesses tax credits, §105-129.81.
Sanitation, §130A-247.
Tax incentives for new and expanding businesses,
§105-129.2.
Wage and hour act, §95-25.2.
Establishment that prepares or serves drink.
Sanitation, §130A-247.
Establishment that prepares or serves food.
Sanitation, §130A-247.
Estate.
Decedents' estates, §29-2.
Federal estate tax, §28A-27-1.
Incompetency, §35A-1202.
Medicaid estate recovery plan, §108A-70.5(b).
Veterans, §34-2.
Estate planning and probate law specialty, Bar
Rule D.2302.
Estate proceedings.
Decedents' estates, §28A-1-1(1b).
Estate recovery.
Long-term care partnerships, §58-55-55.
Medicaid, §108A-70.4(a).
Estate sale.
Auction and auctioneers, §85B-1.
Esthetician, §88B-2.

DEFINED TERMS —Cont'd
Esthetician teacher, §88B-2.
Esthetics, §88B-2.
Estimated tax, §105-163.38.
Estuarine shoreline.
Coastal area management, erosion control
structures, §113A-115.1(a).
E-10 fuel.
Dispensing equipment standards for ethanol
blends, §143-143.6(a).
Ethics advisory.
Procedures for ruling on questions of legal ethics,
Bar Rule D.0101.
Ethics decision.
Procedures for ruling on questions of legal ethics,
Bar Rule D.0101.
Euro.
European monetary union, §53-295.
European currency unit (ECU).
European monetary union, §53-295.
Euthanasia.
Protection of animals, §19A-23.
Event employee.
Pyrotechnics licenses, §58-82A-1.1.
Event of withdrawal of a general partner.
Limited partnerships, §59-102.
Partnerships, §59-102.
E-Verify.
Duty of county to register and participate,
§153A-99.1(b).
Duty of municipality to register and participate,
§160A-169.1(b).
Verification of work authorization, §64-25.
Evidence.
Criminal procedure, §15A-971.
Obstruction of justice, §14-221.1.
Evidence of coverage.
Health maintenance organizations, §58-67-5(c).
Examination and investigation.
Insurance commissioner, §58-2-131(b).
Psychology practice act, §90-270.2.
Savings and loan associations, §54B-4.
Savings banks, §54C-4(b).
**Examinations and laboratory tests for the
screening for the early detection of
cervical cancer.**
Accident and health insurance, §58-51-57(a1).
Health maintenance organizations, §58-67-76(a1).
Hospital, medical and dental services
corporations, §58-65-92(a1).
Examinee.
Controlled substance examination regulation,
§95-231.
Examiner.
Controlled substance examination regulation,
§95-231.
Insurance commissioner, §58-2-131(b).
Examining body.
Occupational therapists, §90-270.67.
Excavation.
Contractors, §87-101.
Excepted benefits.
Health insurance portability and accountability,
§58-68-25(b).
Excess value of water.
Impounded water, §143-215.44(c).
Exchange access facility.
911 system, §62A-40.
Telecommunications relay service, §62-157(a1).
Exchange act.
Shareholder protection act, §55-9-01(b).

DEFINED TERMS —Cont'd
Exchange company.
Time shares, §93A-41.
Exchange program.
Time shares, §93A-41.
Exchange teacher, §115C-325(a).
Excluded corporation.
Corporate income tax, §105-130.4(a).
Excluded shares.
Appraisal rights, §55-13-01.
Exclusive economic zone.
Offshore oil and gas activities, §143-215.94BB.
Exclusive mortgage broker.
Mortgage bankers, brokers and servicers,
§53-244.030.
Excursion passenger vehicles.
Motor vehicles, §20-4.01.
Executed.
Funds transfers, UCC, §25-4A-301(a).
Execution date.
Funds transfers, UCC, §25-4A-301(b).
Execution sale, §1-339.41(a).
Executive.
Limited liability companies, §57C-1-03.
Executive action.
Lobbying, §120C-100(a).
Executive authority.
Criminal extradition, §15A-721.
Executive board.
Condominiums, §47C-1-103.
Planned community act, §47F-1-103.
Executive committee.
Pest control, §106-65.55.
Executive director.
Health insurance risk pool, §58-50-175.
Executive head.
Motor vehicles, §20-183.21.
Executive officer.
Endangering officers, §14-16.10.
Money transmitters, §53-208.2(a).
Trust companies, §53-301(a).
Executive order.
National crime prevention and privacy compact,
§114-19.50.
Exempt commercial purchaser.
Surplus lines insurance, streamlined application
for commercial purchasers, §58-21-16(b).
Exempt for-hire vehicles.
Motor vehicles, §20-4.01.
Exempt loan.
Loans exempt from rate and fee limitations,
§24-9(a).
Exempt managerial position.
Personnel system, §126-5(b).
Exempt organization.
Lotteries and gaming, §14-309.6.
Exempt policymaking position.
Personnel system, §126-5(b).
Exempt position.
Personnel system, §126-5(b).
Exempt transaction.
Home foreclosure rescue scams, §75-120.
Exhaustee.
Unemployment insurance, §96-12.01(a1).
Exhibit.
Motion pictures, §75C-2.
Placing exhibit while wearing mask or hood,
§14-12.14.
Placing exhibit with intention of intimidating,
§14-12.13.

DEFINED TERMS —Cont'd

Exhibition.
Boxing commission, §143-651.

Exhibitor.
Motion pictures, §75C-2.

Existing agreement.
Distribution of sales and use taxes.
Supplemental PEG channel support, §105-164.44J(a).
State franchising of cable television service, §66-350.

Existing facilities.
Centennial campus and Horace Williams campus financing act, §116-198.33.
Higher education bonds, §116D-22.
Higher education student housing, §116-189.

Existing local compensatory mitigation bank.
Ecosystem enhancement program, §143-214.11(a).

Existing sanitary landfill.
County solid waste disposal, §153A-136(c).
Public enterprises, §160A-325(a).

Existing trees.
Outdoor advertising, §136-133.5(d).

Exotic species.
Plant protection and conservation, §106-202.12.

Expedited process.
Child support, §50-31.

Expedited review.
Certificate of need, §131E-176.

Expenditure.
Legal expense funds for elected officials, §163-278.300.
Political campaigns, §163-278.6.
Public campaign fund, §163-278.62.
Voter-owned elections act, §163-278.96.

Expense adjustment.
Corporate income tax.
Adjustment for expenses related to dividends, §105-130.6A(a).

Expenses.
Appraisal rights, §55-13-01.
Business corporations, §55-8-50(b).
Insurance rates, §58-36-100(b).
Medical service corporations, §58-65-166(b).
Workers' compensation self-insurance.
Employer groups.
Premium rates, §58-47-110(a).

Experience.
Contractors, §87-21(a).

Experience rate modifier.
Safety and health, §95-250.

Experimental/investigational.
State health plan for teachers and state employees, §135-48.1.

Expiration date.
Prescription labels, §90-85.29.

Expired financial transaction card.
Criminal law, §14-113.8.

Explanation.
Secured transactions, disposition of collateral after default, §25-9-616(a).

Exploitation.
Adult care homes, §131D-2.1.
Adult care home's bill of rights, §131D-20.
Protection of disabled adults, §108A-101.

Exploration.
Offshore oil and gas activities, §143-215.94BB.

Exploration activity.
Mining, §74-76.

Explosive or incendiary device or substance.
Criminal law, §§14-50.1, 14-72.

DEFINED TERMS —Cont'd

Explosives.
Motor vehicles, §20-4.01.
Offenses against safety, §14-284.1.

Export.
Gasoline tax, §105-449.60.
Surplus lines, §58-21-10.

Exportation.
Tax credit for manufacturing cigarettes for exportation, §105-130.45(a).
Increasing employment and utilizing state ports, §105-130.46(b).

Exposed.
Bee and honey act, §106-635.

Express invitation or permission.
Telephone solicitations, §75-101.

Express total return unitrust.
Principal and income act, §37A-1-104.21(a).

Expulsion.
Discipline of students, §115C-390.1(b).

Extended benefit period.
Unemployment insurance, §96-12.01(a1).

Extended benefits.
Unemployment insurance, §96-12.01(a1).

Extended family.
State government ethics act, §138A-3.

Extracorporeal circulation.
Perfusionists, §90-682.

Extraordinary medical expenses.
State prisons, §148-32.1.

Eye bank.
Anatomical gifts, §130A-412.4.

Eyewitness.
Eyewitness identification reform, §15A-284.52(a).

Facilitator.
Refund anticipation loan act, §53-246.

Facilities.
Armories, §127A-161.
Continuing care, §58-64-1.
Dry-cleaning solvent cleanup act, §143-215.104B(b).
Egg law, §106-245.14.
Energy in state buildings, §143-64.11.
Industrial facilities sales tax refunds, §105-164.14B(a).
Membership camping, §66-232.
Mental health, §122C-3.
Nursing homes, §131E-116.
Toxic or hazardous substance identification, §95-174(g).
Underground storage tank cleanup, §143-215.94A.
Vehicle reinsurance, §58-37-1.

Facility.
Assignment of student to particular school, §115C-366(h).

Facsimile seal.
Public obligations, §159E-2.

Facsimile signature.
Public obligations, §159E-2.

Fact expert witness.
Medicolegal guidelines for attorney-physician relationship, MLG Rule 3.

Factory branch.
Motor vehicles, §20-286.

Factory representative.
Motor vehicles, §20-286.

Failure to list property.
Property taxes, §105-273.

Fair.
Supervision, §106-520.1.

DEFINED TERMS —Cont'd

Fair consideration.
Insurers supervision, §58-30-10.

Fair Labor Standards Act, §95-25.2.

Fair market value.
Impaired driving, §20-28.2(a1).
Medicaid, transfer of assets for less than market value to qualify, §108A-58.1(f).
Self-referrals by health care providers, §90-405.

Fair value.
Appraisal rights, §55-13-01.
Protected cell companies, §58-10-80.

Falconry.
Public activities, §113-130.

Falls Lake watershed.
Falls Lake watershed association, §77-140.

Fall zone.
Wireless telecommunications facilities, §§153A-349.51, 160A-400.51.

Familial status.
Fair housing act, §41A-3.

Family.
Debts owed public hospitals, §131E-48.
Fair housing act, §41A-3.
Public assistance program, §108A-24.
Student loan collections, §105B-1.

Family assessment response.
Abused neglected or dependent juveniles, §7B-101.

Family business entity.
Wildlife conservation land.
Special class of property for property tax purposes, §105-277.15(a).

Family care home.
Adult care homes, §131D-2.1.
Adult care home's bill of rights, §131D-20.
Handicapped person, §168-21.
Long-term care insurance, §58-55-35(a).

Family child care home, §110-86.

Family foster home.
Child placing and care, §131D-10.2.

Family income.
Children's health insurance program, §108A-70.18.
Student loan collections, §105B-1.

Family income of debtor.
Debts owed public hospitals, §131E-48.

Family law specialty, Bar Rule D.2402.

Family leave credit insurance, §58-57-5.

Family member.
Adoption.
Release of identifying information, §48-9-104(c).
Community third party trusts, pooled trusts act, §36D-2.
Farm machinery franchises, §66-180.
Private trust companies, §53-363(a).
Victims and witnesses, §15A-824.

Family trust.
Wildlife conservation land.
Special class of property for property tax purposes, §105-277.15(a).

Family unit.
Mental health, developmental disabilities and substance abuse, voluntary admissions, §122C-211(g).

Farm building.
Building codes, §143-138(b4).

Farmed cervid.
Conservation, §113-129.
Deer, production and sale for commercial purposes, §106-549.97(c).

DEFINED TERMS —Cont'd

Farmer.
Property-hauling vehicle registration fees, §20-88(b).

Farmers of low income.
Housing authorities, §157-3.

Farming.
Agricultural development act, §106-581.1.

Farming activity.
Mediation of farm nuisance disputes, §7A-38.3(a).

Farming operation.
Secured transactions, §25-9-102(a).

Farm machinery.
Taxation, §105-151.21.

Farm nuisance dispute.
Prelitigation mediation, §7A-38.3(a).

Farm operation.
Relocation assistance, §133-7.

Farm products.
Property-hauling vehicle registration fees, §20-88(b).
Secured transactions, §25-9-102(a).

Farm resident.
Mediation of farm nuisance disputes, §7A-38.3(a).

Farm tractor.
Motor vehicles, §20-4.01.

Father.
Marriage proceedings, §51-2.2.

Fault.
Leases, UCC, §25-2A-103(1).
UCC, §25-1-201(b).

FBI.
DNA database and databanks, §15A-266.2.
National crime prevention and privacy compact, §114-19.50.

FCC order.
911 system, §62A-40.

Feasibility study.
Liability risk retention, §58-22-10.

Federal act.
Drinking water, §130A-313.
Food, drugs and cosmetics, §106-121.
Occupational safety and health, §95-127.

Federal agency.
Drinking water, §130A-313.
Electric membership corporations, §117-7.
State auditor, §147-64.4.

Federal association.
Regional reciprocal savings and loan acquisition act, §54B-48.2.
Savings and loan associations, §54B-4.

Federal banking agencies.
Mortgage bankers, brokers and servicers, §53-244.030.

Federal clean air act, §143-213.

Federal determination.
Limitation on tax refunds and assessments, §105-241.10.

Federal expedited process requirement.
Child support, §50-31.

Federal food, drug and cosmetic act.
Meat inspection, §106-549.15.
Poultry products inspection, §106-549.51.

Federal government.
Agricultural finance act, §122D-3.
Housing authorities, §157-3.
Interstate environmental compact, §113A-23.
National defense housing projects, §157-53.
Public health authorities, §130A-45.01.
Public hospitals, §131E-16.
Veterans' recreation, §165-25.

DEFINED TERMS —Cont'd
Federal installation.
Motor vehicle inspections, §20-183.2(c).
Federal insurance contributions act.
Governmental employees and social security, §135-20.
Federal international banking institution.
International banking act, §53-232.2(a).
Federally chartered savings institution.
Trust companies, §53-301(a).
Federally guaranteed security.
Health facilities finance, §131A-3.
Federally insured mortgage note.
Health facilities finance, §131A-3.
Federally insured securities.
Housing finance agency, §122A-3.
Federal meat inspection act, §106-549.15.
Federal or state antitrust laws.
Cooperative agreements among physicians or between physician, hospital or others, §90-21.25.
Health care facilities.
Cooperative agreements, §131E-192.2.
Federal poultry products inspection act, §106-549.51.
Federal poverty level.
Children's health insurance program, §108A-70.18.
Federal reserve act, §53-61(a).
Federal reserve banks, §53-61(a).
Federal reserve board, §53-61(a).
Federal retirement benefits.
Individual income tax, §105-151.20(a).
Federal safety and hazardous material regulations.
Motor carriers, §20-376.
Federal TANF funds, §108A-24.
Federated fundraising organization.
Solicitation of contributions, §131F-2.
Fee.
Mortgages, high cost home loans, §24-1.1E(a).
Private personnel services, §95-47.1.
Fee-based pastoral counseling associate, §90-382.
Fee-based pastoral counselor, §90-382.
Fee-based practice of pastoral counseling, §90-382.
Fee-based professional pastoral counseling services, §90-382.
Feed ingredient.
Commercial feed law, §106-284.33.
Feedlot.
Animal waste management, §143-215.10B.
Felony.
Crime victims financial recovery assistance act, §15B-31.
Criminal law, §14-1.
Expedited evictions, §42-59.
Felony offense.
Habitual felons, §14-7.1.
Feral.
Rabies vaccination, §130A-184.
Feral swine.
Conservation, §113-129.
Ferret.
Rabies vaccination, §130A-184.
Fertilizer coated seed.
Commercial fertilizer, §106-657.
Fertilizer material.
Commercial fertilizer, §106-657.

DEFINED TERMS —Cont'd
FICA.
Public assistance program, §108A-24.
Fiduciary, §32-25.
Federal estate tax, §28A-27-1.
Negotiable instruments, §25-3-307(a).
Principal and income act, §37A-1-102.
Trusts and trustees, §32-70.
Uniform fiduciaries act, §32-2(a).
Fiduciary record.
Trust companies, §53-301(a).
Field.
Oil and gas conservation, §113-389.
Field of operation.
Urban redevelopment, §160A-503.
Fifth wheel trailer.
Motor vehicles, §20-4.01.
File number.
Secured transactions, §25-9-102(a).
Filer.
Campaign finance.
Donation to further independent expenditure, §163-278.12(f).
Electioneering communications.
Reporting costs incurred for producing or airing, §163-278.12C(c).
Filing.
Child support, §50-31.
Criminal process and procedure.
Electronic technology, §15A-101.1.
Judicial retirement, §135-53.
Legislative retirement system, §120-4.8.
Retirement, §128-21.
State retirement system, §135-1.
Filing office.
Secured transactions, §25-9-102(a).
Filing-office rule.
Secured transactions, §25-9-102(a).
Filing person.
State government ethics act, §138A-3.
Filing with the court.
Civil procedure, §1A-1 Rule 5.
Filler.
Eyewitness identification reform, §15A-284.52(a).
Final compensation.
Judicial retirement, §135-53.
Final disposition.
Cremation, §90-210.121.
Final overpayment, assessment or fine.
Provider requirements for Medicaid or Health Choice, §108C-2.
Finance charge.
Installment sales, §25A-8.
Finance lease.
Leases, UCC, §25-2A-103(1).
Finance officer.
Alcoholic beverages, §18B-101.
Local government bonds, §159-44.
Financial asset.
Asset-backed securities facilitation, §53-425.
Investment securities, §25-8-102.
Financial assurance.
Solid waste management facilities, §130A-295.2(a).
Financial institution.
Collection of taxes by attachment or garnishment, §105-242.1(d).
Commodities act, §78D-1.
Data match systems.
Child support enforcement, §110-139.2.
Fair housing act, §41A-3.

DEFINED TERMS —Cont'd
Financial institution —Cont'd
Financial privacy, §53B-2.
Forgery, §14-119(c).
Funeral and burial trust funds, §90-210.60.
Savings and loan associations, §54B-4.
Tax credit for qualified business investments,
§105-163.010.
Transfers to minors, §33A-1.
Financial instrument.
Computer crimes, §14-453.
Financial intermediary.
Public obligations, §159E-2.
Financial organization.
Unclaimed property act, §116B-52.
Financial qualification.
Solid waste management facilities,
§130A-295.2(a).
Financial record.
Financial privacy, §53B-2.
Financial report.
Incompetency, §35A-1202.
Financial responsibility.
Professional employer organizations, §58-89A-5.
Solid waste management facilities,
§130A-295.2(a).
**Financial services, securities operations and
related systems development.**
Industrial facilities sales tax refunds,
§105-164.14B(a).
Financial statement analysis.
Insurance commissioner, confidentiality of
information, §58-2-240(b).
Financial statement analysis work papers.
Insurance commissioner, confidentiality of
information, §58-2-240(b).
Financial transaction card.
Criminal law, §14-113.8.
Financing agency.
Sales, §25-2-104.
Financing agreement.
Global TransPark authority, §63A-2.
Pollution control, §§159C-3, 159D-3.
Financing contract.
Capital facilities finance act, §142-82.
Energy conservation finance act, §142-61.
Financing contract indebtedness.
Capital facilities finance act, §142-82.
Financing entity.
Viatical life insurance settlements, §58-58-205.
Financing statement.
Secured transactions, §25-9-102(a).
Finding of no significant impact.
Environmental policy act, §113A-9.
Findings and information.
Disclosure of records in child fatality or near
fatality cases, §7B-2902(a).
Fine print.
Sales, §25C-10.
Fingerprints.
Public adjusters, §58-33A-5.
FINRA.
Insurance producers, §58-33-10.
Firearm, §14-409.39.
Criminal law, §14-72.
Discipline of students, §115C-390.1(b).
Unlawful for felons to purchase, own, possess,
care or control, §14-415.1(a).
Firearms rights.
Restoration of firearms rights, §14-415.4(a).

DEFINED TERMS —Cont'd
Fire chief.
Toxic or hazardous substance identification,
§95-174(h).
Fire department.
Toxic or hazardous substance identification,
§95-174(j).
Fire district.
Insurance, §58-84-5.
Firefighter, §106-955.
Municipal firefighters, §160A-295.
Retirement, §128-21.
State health plan for teachers and state
employees, §135-48.1.
Tuition and fee waivers, §115B-1.
Fireman.
Death benefits, §143-166.2(e).
Fire protection.
Rural fire protection districts, §69-25.4(b).
Fire sprinkler.
Contractors, §87-21(a).
Fire suppression duties, §106-955.
Firm.
Annexation initiated by municipality.
Private firm providing solid waste collection
services, §160A-58.59(i).
Meat inspection, §106-549.15.
Rules of professional conduct, ProfCond Rule 1.0.
First-degree murder.
Criminal law, §14-17.
First-degree rape.
Criminal law, §14-27.2.
First-degree sexual offense.
Criminal law, §14-27.4.
First generation student.
Regional schools, §115C-238.61.
First responders.
Vaccination program, §130A-485(f).
First-tier subcontractor, §143-128.1(a).
Liens, §44A-17.
First-year licensee.
Bail bondsman and runners, §58-71-1.
Fiscal note.
Local government, §120-30.44.
Fiscal period.
Budget of state, §143C-1-1(d).
Capital facilities finance act, §142-82.
Higher education bonds, §116D-1.
Fiscal year.
Budget of state, §143C-1-1(d).
Capital facilities finance act, §142-82.
Estimated income tax, §105-163.38.
Higher education bonds, §116D-1.
Local government finance, §159-7.
School budgets, §115C-423.
Taxation, §§105-130.2, 105-134.1.
Fish.
Conservation, §113-129.
Sales and use tax exemptions, §105-164.13.
Fisheries director.
Conservation, §113-128.
Marine fisheries compact, §113-251.
Fisheries resources, §113-129.
Fisherman.
Fishermen's economic development, §113-315.17.
Fishing related industry.
Fishery resource grant program, §113-200(b).
Fish processing.
Working waterfront property taxation,
§105-277.14(a).

DEFINED TERMS —Cont'd
Fitting and selling hearing aids.
Dealers and board, §93D-1.
Five model years.
Failure to disclose damage to vehicle, §20-71.4(a1).
Fixed.
Records, tapes and other recorded devices, §14-432.
Fixed location.
Dealing in regulated metals property, §66-11(a).
Fixed route.
Public utilities, §62-3.
Fixture filing.
Secured transactions, §25-9-102(a).
Fixtures.
Secured transactions, §25-9-102(a).
Flesch scale analysis readability score.
Readable insurance policies, §58-38-15.
Readable medical insurance, §58-66-15.
Flight equipment.
Public service taxation, §105-333.
Flipping.
Interest, consumer protection in home loans, §24-10.2(a).
Floating structure.
Coastal area management, §113A-103.
Flood hazard.
Floodplain regulations, §143-215.52(a).
Flood vehicle.
Motor vehicles, §20-4.01.
Florist wire sale.
Sales and use tax, §105-164.4B(d).
Flour.
Weights and measures, §81A-9.
Fluid fertilizer.
Commercial fertilizer, §106-657.
Flying club.
Aeronautics, §63-1.
Focused growth institution.
Distinguished professors endowment trust fund, §116-41.13A.
Food.
Food, drugs and cosmetics, §106-121.
Sales and use tax, §105-164.3.
Food additive.
Food, drugs and cosmetics, §106-121.
Meat inspection, §106-549.15.
Poultry products inspection, §106-549.51.
Food business.
Alcoholic beverages, §18B-1000.
Food sold through vending machines.
Sales and use tax, §105-164.3.
Foreclosure rescue transaction.
Home foreclosure rescue scams, §75-120.
Foreign bank.
Trust companies, §53-301(a).
Foreign commerce.
Motor carriers, §20-376.
Public utilities, §62-3.
Foreign company.
Insurance, §58-1-5.
Foreign corporation.
Business corporations, §55-1-40.
Collection agencies, §58-70-5(q).
Limited liability companies, §57C-1-03.
Limited partnerships, §59-102.
Nonprofit corporations, §55A-1-40.
Partnerships, §59-32.
Taxation, §105-130.2.

DEFINED TERMS —Cont'd
Foreign country.
Foreign legal consultants, §84A-1(c).
International banking act, §53-232.2(a).
Recognition of foreign-country money judgments, §1C-1851.
Sales and use tax exemptions, §105-164.13.
Foreign-country judgment.
Recognition of foreign-country money judgments, §1C-1851.
Foreign entity.
Electrical contractors, §87-44.2(a).
Engineers.
Licensing of nonresidents, §89C-18.1(a).
General contractors, §87-10.1(a).
Plumbing, heating and fire sprinkler contractors, §87-22.2(a).
Foreign government.
Business discrimination, §75B-1.
Filing of agreements between North Carolina and foreign governments, §66-280(c).
Foreign guaranty association.
Insurers supervision, §58-30-10.
Foreign insurer.
Insurance companies, §58-12-2.
Foreign judgment.
Judgments, §1C-1702.
Foreign jurisdiction.
Document authentication, §66-271.
Interstate depositions and discovery, §1F-2.
Foreign limited liability company, §57C-1-03.
Partnerships, §§59-32, 59-102.
Foreign limited liability partnership, §59-32.
Limited partnerships, §59-102.
Foreign limited partnership.
Limited liability companies, §57C-1-03.
Partnerships, §§59-32, 59-102.
Foreign money.
Foreign-money claims, §1C-1820.
Foreign nonprofit corporation.
Limited partnerships, §59-102.
Partnerships, §59-32.
Foreign official.
Document authentication, §66-271.
Foreign partnership.
Electrical contractors, §87-44.2(a).
Engineers.
Licensing of nonresidents, §89C-18.1(a).
General contractors, §87-10.1(a).
Plumbing, heating and fire sprinkler contractors, §87-22.2(a).
Foreign person.
Business discrimination, §75B-1.
Corporate income tax, §105-130.5(b).
Foreign personal representative.
Decedents' estates, §28A-1-1.
Foreign registered public accounting firm.
Workers' compensation self-insurance, §97-165.
Foreign subpoena.
Interstate depositions and discovery, §1F-2.
Foreign trade relationships.
Business discrimination, §75B-1.
Foreign trust institution.
Trust companies, §53-301(a).
Foreign vehicle.
Motor vehicles, §20-4.01.
Forensic medical examination.
Assistance program for victims of rape and sex offenses, §143B-1200(i).
Forest development assessment.
Forest development act, §106-1012.

DEFINED TERMS —Cont'd
Forest development cost sharing payment.
  Forest development act, §106-1012.
Forest development fund, §§106-1012, 106-1027.
Forester, §89B-2.
Forestland.
  Counties, §153A-452(a).
  Municipal planning and regulation of
    development, §160A-458.5(a).
  Protection of forest, §106-922.
  Taxation, §105-277.2.
Forest laws, §106-897.
Forest management plan.
  Municipal planning and regulation of
    development, §160A-458.5(a).
Forest operation.
  Nuisance liability of agriculture and forest
    operations, §106-701(b1).
Forest ranger.
  Regulation of open fires, §106-941.
Forestry, §89B-2.
  Counties, §153A-452(a).
  Municipal planning and regulation of
    development, §160A-458.5(a).
Forestry activity.
  Counties, §153A-452(a).
  Municipal planning and regulation of
    development, §160A-458.5(a).
Forestry equipment.
  Purchases through department of administration.
    Multiple award schedule contracts, §143-52.3.
Forestry management plan.
  Counties, §153A-452(a).
Forest trees, §106-922.
Forfeiture.
  Contracts for deed, §47H-1.
  Option to purchase contracts executed with
    residential lease agreements, §47G-1.
For hire boat.
  Coastal recreational fishing licenses, §113-174.
For-hire motor carrier, §20-4.01.
For hire passenger vehicles.
  Motor vehicles, §20-4.01.
Formal delinquency proceeding.
  Insurers supervision, §58-30-10.
Formal ethics opinion.
  Procedures for ruling on questions of legal ethics,
    Bar Rule D.0101.
Former Article 9 record.
  Secured transactions filing office transition,
    §25-9-710(a).
Former contractor.
  Mental health, developmental disability,
    substance abuse.
    Appeals panel, §122C-151.4(a).
Former franchisee.
  Motor vehicle manufacturers.
    Unfair methods of competition, §20-305.2(c).
Former insurer.
  Appointment of bondsmen, §58-71-141(c).
Former mutual.
  Insurance companies, conversion, §58-10-12(a).
Form of identification, §14-100.1(d).
Fortified mulch.
  Commercial fertilizer, §106-657.
Fortified wine.
  Alcoholic beverages, §18B-101.
  Alcohol taxation, §105-113.68.
Foster care.
  Children, §131D-10.2.

DEFINED TERMS —Cont'd
Foster child.
  Family leave credit insurance, §58-57-115(a).
  Insurance, §58-51-30(a).
Foster parent.
  Child placing and care, §131D-10.2.
Foundation.
  Hospital, medical and dental service corporations.
    Conversion, §58-65-131(b).
Foundation seeds.
  Seed law, §106-277.2.
FPG.
  Health coverage for workers with disabilities act,
    §108A-54.1(b).
FPL.
  Children's health insurance program,
    §108A-70.18.
Franchise.
  Motor vehicles, §20-286.
  Public utilities, §62-3.
Franchise accident and health insurance,
  §58-51-90.
Franchise motor vehicle dealer, §20-286.
Franchise-related form agreements.
  Motor vehicle dealers, §20-297.1(a).
Fraternal orders, §58-25-5.
Fraud alert.
  Credit monitoring services act, §75-134.
Fraud or fraudulent.
  Punitive damages, §1D-5.
  Rules of professional conduct, ProfCond Rule 1.0.
  Securities, §78A-2.
Fraudulent endorsement.
  Negotiable instruments, §25-3-405(a).
Fraudulent payment.
  Garnishment of wages to recoup fraudulent public
    assistance program payments, §108A-25.3(a).
Fraudulent viatical settlement act.
  Viatical life insurance settlements, §58-58-205.
Free appropriate public education.
  Education of children with disabilities,
    §115C-106.3.
Free clinic.
  Drug, supplies, and medical device repository
    program, §90-85.44(a).
  Volunteer health care providers, §90-21.16(c).
Free-flowing.
  Natural and scenic rivers, §113A-33.
Freeholders in petition for special taxes.
  Estates, §41-13.
Free insurance.
  Free insurance as inducement to purchase goods
    or services, §66-380.
Freestanding ambulatory surgical facility.
  Medical care data, §131E-214.1.
Freestyle terrain.
  Winter sports safety, §99C-1.
Freight car line companies.
  Taxation, §105-228.2.
Friable.
  Asbestos hazard management, §130A-444.
Frontage road.
  Controlled-access facilities, §136-89.49.
Fuel alcohol.
  Gasoline tax, §105-449.60.
Fuel alcohol provider.
  Gasoline tax, §105-449.60.
Fuel cell electric vehicle.
  Motor vehicles, §20-4.01.
Full cost.
  Tuition.
    Full scholarship students attending constituent
      institutions, §116-143.6(b).

DEFINED TERMS —Cont'd
Full scholarship.
Tuition, §116-143.6(b).
Full-screen.
Campaign contributions and expenditures.
Disclosure requirements for media
advertisements, §163-278.38Z.
Full service corporation.
Medical service plan or hospital service plan,
§58-65-1(a).
Full-time employee.
Job development investment grant program,
§143B-437.51.
Full-time employment.
Public assistance program, §108A-24.
Full-time job.
Growing businesses tax credits, §105-129.81.
Tax credit for manufacturing cigarettes for
exportation.
Increasing employment and utilizing state
ports, §105-130.46(b).
Tax incentives for new and expanding businesses,
§105-129.2.
Fully funded.
Protected cell companies, §58-10-80.
Fumigants.
Structural pest control act, §106-65.24.
Fund.
Armories, §127A-161.
Auction and auctioneers, §85B-1.
Budget of state, §143C-1-1(d).
Client security fund, rules governing
administration, Bar Rule D.1401.
Dry-cleaning solvent cleanup act,
§143-215.104B(b).
Forgivable education for service program,
§116-209.45(b).
Homeowner's recovery fund, §87-15.5.
Housing trust, §122E-2.
Local government finance, §159-7.
Manufactured housing, §143-143.9.
Recreation and natural heritage, §113-77.6.
Rescue squad workers' relief fund, §58-88-1.
Risk based environmental remediation of
industrial sites, §130A-310.65.
School budgets, §115C-423.
Self-insurance security association, §97-130.
Unemployment compensation, §96-8.
University of North Carolina hospital at Chapel
Hill, §116-37.2(a).
Voter-owned elections act, §163-278.96.
Fund cap amount.
Student protection fund, proprietary schools,
§115D-95.1(a).
Funding agreements.
Annuity disclosure, §58-60-130.
Insurance, §58-7-16(a).
Fundraising consultant.
Solicitation of contributions, §131F-2.
Fundraising cost.
Solicitation of contributions, §131F-2.
Funds of an offender.
Crime victims financial recovery assistance act,
§15B-31.
Funds-transfer business day, §25-4A-105(a).
Funds-transfers, §25-4A-104(a).
Funds-transfer system, §25-4A-105(a).
Funds-transfer system rule, §25-4A-501(b).
Funeral chapel, §90-210.20(e1).
Funeral directing, §90-210.20(f).
Funeral director, §90-210.20(g).

DEFINED TERMS —Cont'd
Funeral establishment, §90-210.20(h).
Funeral expenses.
Sales and use tax exemptions, §105-164.13.
Funeral processions, §20-157.1(a).
Funeral service licensee, §90-210.20(i).
Funeral service profession, §90-210.20(j).
Fungi.
Structural pest control act, §106-65.24.
Fungible.
UCC, §25-1-201(b).
Fungicide.
Pesticide board, §143-460.
Fungus.
Pesticide board, §143-460.
Fur-bearing animals.
Conservation, §113-129.
Furniture requirements contracts, §143-57.1(b).
Future goods.
Sales, §25-2-105.
GAAP financial statement.
Workers' compensation self insurance, §97-165.
Employer groups, §58-47-60.
Gallon.
Weights and measures, §81A-9.
Game.
Conservation, §113-129.
State lottery, §18C-103.
Game animals.
Conservation, §113-129.
Game birds.
Conservation, §113-129.
Game fish.
Conservation, §113-129.
Game lands.
Conservation, §113-129.
Gamma knife.
Certificate of need, §131E-176.
Garbage, §130A-290(a).
Animal diseases, §106-405.1.
Garnishee, §1-440.21(b).
Debts owed public hospitals, §131E-48.
Garnishment of wages to recoup fraudulent public
assistance program payment, §108A-25.3(a).
Gas.
Oil and gas conservation, §113-389.
Gas city.
Piped natural gas tax, §105-187.40.
Gas company.
Public service taxation, §105-333.
Gasohol.
Gasoline tax, §105-449.60.
Gasoline.
Gasoline and oil inspection, §119-15.
Taxation, §105-449.60.
Gas operators.
Public utilities, §62-50.
Gastrointestinal endoscopy room.
Hospital licensure, §131E-76.
Gate.
Cave protection, §14-159.20.
General account.
Protected cell companies, §58-10-80.
General advertisement.
Life insurance.
Dishonest and predatory sales to military
personnel, §58-58-335.
General assets.
Insurers supervision, §58-30-10.
General contractor, §87-1(a).
Homeowner's recovery fund, §87-15.5.

DEFINED TERMS —Cont'd
General election.
  Municipal elections, §163-298.
General fund operating budget.
  Budget of state, §143C-1-1(d).
General guardian.
  Custodial trusts, §33B-1.
  Incompetency, §35A-1202.
General intangible.
  Secured transactions, §25-9-102(a).
General laws, NC Const Art XIV §3.
  Cities and towns, §160A-1.
  Counties, §153A-1.
General license.
  Radiation protection, §104E-5.
General manager.
  Alcoholic beverages, §18B-101.
General obligation bonds.
  Metropolitan sewerage districts, §162A-65(a).
  Metropolitan water districts, §162A-32(a).
General partner.
  Partnerships, §59-102.
General power of appointment.
  Elective share of surviving spouse, §30-3.2.
General reserve.
  Savings and loan associations, §54B-4.
General supervision.
  Polysomnography practice act, §90-721.
General verdict, §1A-1 Rule 49(a).
Generic name.
  Annuity disclosure, §58-60-130.
  Life insurance solicitation, §58-60-10.
Genetic characteristic.
  Discrimination in employment based on genetic
    information, §95-28.1A(b).
Genetic information.
  Discrimination in employment based on genetic
    information, §95-28.1A(b).
  Health insurance, §58-3-215(a).
Genetic test.
  Discrimination in employment based on genetic
    information, §95-28.1A(b).
Genuine.
  UCC, §25-1-201(b).
Geologist, §89E-3.
Geologist-in-training, §89E-3.
Geology, §89E-3.
Geriatric.
  Medical release of inmates, §15A-1369.
Germination.
  Seed law, §106-277.2.
Gift.
  State government ethics act, §138A-3.
Gift card.
  Maintenance fees, §66-67.5(c).
Gift instrument.
  Prudent management of institutional funds,
    §36E-2.
Gift or prize.
  Telephonic sellers, §66-260.
GIS mapping.
  911 system, §62A-40.
Gives.
  UCC, §25-1-202(d).
Glass tube.
  Drug paraphernalia control act, §90-113.81.
Gleaning.
  Tax credit for gleaned crop, §105-130.37(b).
Global TransPark complex, §158-32.
Gold.
  Precious metals, §66-164.

DEFINED TERMS —Cont'd
Gold Star parents.
  State veterans home, §165-53.
Golf cart, §20-4.01.
Good cause.
  Farm machinery franchises, §66-180.
  Motor vehicles, §20-305.
Good faith.
  Funds transfers, UCC, §25-4A-105(a).
  Investment securities, §25-8-102.
  Letters of credit, §25-5-102(a).
  Motor vehicles, §20-286.
  Negotiable instruments, §25-3-103.
  Sales, §25-2-103.
  Satisfaction of deeds of trust and mortgages,
    §45-36.4.
  UCC, §25-1-201(b).
Good manufacturing practice.
  Pharmacy practice, §90-85.27.
Good moral character.
  Architects, §83A-1.
  Geologist, §89E-3.
  Professional employer organizations, §58-89A-5.
Goods.
  Installment sales, §25A-4.
  Leases, UCC, §25-2A-103(1).
  Sales, §25-2-105.
  Secured transactions, §25-9-102(a).
  UCC, §25-7-102(a).
Governing board.
  Consolidated city-county, §160B-2.
  Cooperative innovative high school programs,
    §115C-238.50A.
  Electric power, §159B-3.
  Local government bonds, §159-44.
  Pest control, §106-65.55.
Governing body, §162A-2.
  Aeronautics, §63-79.
  Bond sales, §159-120.
  City and town transportation authorities,
    §160A-576.
  Counties, §153A-217.
  Development agreements, §160A-400.21.
    Counties, §153A-349.2.
  Hospital licensure, §131E-76.
  Housing standards, §160A-442.
  Metropolitan sewerage districts, §162A-65(a).
  Metropolitan water districts, §162A-32(a).
  Pollution control, §§159C-3, 159D-3.
  Urban redevelopment, §160A-503.
Governing instrument.
  Simultaneous death, §28A-24-1.
Governing law.
  Franchise tax, §105-114.1(a).
Government.
  Housing authorities, §157-3.
  Interstate environmental compact, §113A-23.
  Public health authorities, §130A-45.01.
  Public hospitals, §131E-16.
  Soil and water conservation districts, §139-3.
  Urban redevelopment, §160A-503.
  Veterans' recreation, §165-25.
Government agency.
  Small business contractors, §143B-472.101.
Governmental agency.
  Contractors for public works, §133-23.
  Electronic transactions, §66-312.
  Housing finance agency, §122A-3.
Governmental entities.
  Hazardous recreation activities, §99E-22.
  Sales tax, §105-164.14.

DEFINED TERMS —Cont'd

Governmental plan.
Health insurance portability and accountability.
Guaranteed of availability of individual
coverage to certain individuals with prior
group coverage, §58-68-60(h).

Governmental subdivision.
Business corporations, §55-1-40.
Nonprofit corporations, §55A-1-40.

Governmental unit.
Forgery, §14-119(c).
Guaranteed energy savings contracts, §143-64.17.
Sale, lease, exchange and joint use of
governmental property, §160A-274(a).
Secured transactions, §25-9-102(a).
Swap agreements, §159-193.

Government authority.
Financial privacy, §53B-2.

Government computer.
Computer crimes, §14-453.

Government computer service.
Computer crimes, §14-456.1(a).

Government entity.
Ecosystem enhancement program, §143-214.11(a).

Government inquiry.
Financial privacy, §53B-2.

Government of Sudan.
Sudan (Darfur) divestment act, §147-86.42.

Government-vendor partnership.
Best value procurements, §143-135.9(a).

Governor.
Criminal extradition, §15A-721.
Interstate family support, §52C-8-801(a).

Grade "A" milk, 106-266.30.

Grades.
Commercial fertilizer, §106-657.
Egg law, §106-245.14.

Gradient compression garments.
Lymphedema.
Health benefit plan coverage, §58-3-280(c).

Grain.
Adulteration, §106-621.
Dealers, §106-601.

Grain dealer, §106-601.
Adulteration of grain, §106-621.

Grandchild.
Workers' compensation, §97-2.

Grand jury.
Grand jury proceedings, §15A-621.

Grandparent.
Visitation rights, §50-13.2(b1).

Grant.
Budget of state, §143C-6-23(a).
Water infrastructure, §159G-20.

Grantee.
Budget of state, §143C-6-23(a).

Grant funds.
Budget of state, §143C-6-23(a).

Granting entity.
Tax credit for qualified business investments,
§105-163.010.

Grant project.
Local government finance, §159-13.2.

Grave.
Abandoned and neglected cemeteries, §65-85.

Grave space.
Cemeteries, §65-48.

Gray water.
Water resources, §143-350.

Gray water system.
Water resources, §143-350.

DEFINED TERMS —Cont'd

Greenhouse.
Building codes, §143-138(b4).

Grievance.
Accident and health insurance.
Utilization review, §58-50-61(a).
Discipline and disability rules of state bar, Bar
Rule B.0103.

Grievance committee.
Discipline and disability rules of state bar, Bar
Rule B.0103.
Procedures for ruling on questions of legal ethics,
Bar Rule D.0101.

Gross combination weight rating.
Motor vehicles, §20-4.01.

Gross combined weight.
Motor vehicles, §20-4.01.

Gross earnings.
Freight line taxation, §105-228.2.
Minors, talent contracts, §48A-15(h).

Gross gallons.
Gasoline tax, §105-449.60.

Gross income.
Taxation, §§105-130.2, 105-134.1.

Gross sales.
Sales and use tax, §105-164.3.

Gross tonnage of newsprint consumed.
Taxation, §105-102.6.

Gross vehicle weight.
Motor vehicles, §20-4.01.

Gross vehicle weight rating.
Motor vehicles, §20-4.01.

Gross weight.
Motor vehicles, §20-118.

Ground lease.
Community land trust property taxation,
§105-277.17(b).

Ground maintenance equipment.
Purchases through department of administration.
Multiple award schedule contracts, §143-52.3.

Grounds.
Smoking in public places, §143-596.
Smoking in state buildings and state vehicles,
§130A-492.

Groundwater resource.
Basinwide hydrologic models, §143-355(o).

Group.
Self-insurance security association, §97-130.
Workers' compensation self-insurance.
Employer groups, §58-47-60.

Group accident and health insurance.
Nature of policies, §58-51-80(a).

Group annuity contracts, §58-58-145(a).

Group health insurance.
Providers of health benefits, §58-50-40(a).

Group health insurance coverage.
Health insurance portability and accountability,
§58-68-25(a).

Group Health plan.
Health insurance portability and accountability,
§58-68-25(a).

Group health plan.
Providers of health benefits, §58-50-40(a).

Group life insurance, §58-58-135.

Group long-term care insurance, §58-55-20.

Group market.
Health insurance portability and accountability,
§58-68-25(a).

Group of insurers.
Annual audited financial reports.
Insurance companies, §58-10-190.

DEFINED TERMS —Cont'd
Group policy, §58-53-1.
Group practice.
Self-referrals by health care providers, §90-405.
Group self-insurance.
Self-insurance security association, §97-130.
Grower.
Seed law, §106-277.2.
Swine integrator registration, §143-215.10H(a).
Guaranteed.
Securities, §78A-2.
Guaranteed elements.
Annuity disclosure, §58-60-130.
Guaranteed energy savings contract,
§143-64.17.
Guarantee of the signature.
Investment securities, §25-8-402(c).
Guarantor.
Workers' compensation self insurance, §97-165.
Guaranty association.
Savings and loan associations, §54B-4.
Guard-dog service profession, §74C-3.
Guardian.
Adoption, §48-1-101.
Anatomical gifts, §130A-412.4.
Interstate compact on mental health, §122C-361.
Mental health, §122C-3.
Transfers to minors, §33A-1.
Uniform trust code, §36C-1-103.
Veterans, §34-2.
Guardian ad litem.
Incompetency, §§35A-1101, 35A-1202.
Guardian of the estate.
Custodial trusts, §33B-1.
Incompetency, §35A-1202.
Guardian of the person.
Custodial trusts, §33B-1.
Incompetency, §35A-1202.
Guest.
Expedited evictions, §42-59.
Habilitation.
Mental health, §122C-3.
Habitual felons.
Criminal law, §14-7.1.
Halogenated hydrocarbon.
Dry-cleaning solvent cleanup act,
§143-215.104B(b).
Handgun, §14-409.39.
Concealed handgun permits, §14-415.10.
Prohibitions on handguns for minors, §14-269.7(c).
Soliciting unlawful purchase of firearm,
§14-408.1(a).
Handicapped.
Motor vehicles, §20-37.5.
Handicapped person.
Assault on, §14-32.1.
Handicapping condition, §41A-3.
Handler.
Egg promotion tax, §106-245.33(b).
Handling.
Ports authority income tax, §105-130.41(c).
Ports authority individual income tax,
§105-151.22(c).
Harasses or harassment.
Stalking, §14-277.3A(b).
Harassment of jurors.
Obstructing justice, §14-225.2.
Harass on the basis of sex.
Criminal law, §14-395.1.
Hard of hearing.
Health and human services division,
§143B-216.30.

DEFINED TERMS —Cont'd
Hard seeds.
Seed law, §106-277.2.
Harm.
Assaulting law enforcement or assistance animals,
§14-163.1(a).
Domestic violence shelters.
Limited civil liability, §1-620.
Harmful material.
Public morals, §19-12.
Harmful noise.
Workers' compensation, §97-53.
Harmful to minors.
Offenses against morality, §14-190.13.
Public morals, §19-12.
Has a record of such an impairment.
Persons with disabilities protection, §168A-3.
Hatchery, §106-541.
Hatching egg dealer, §106-541.
**Having control over oil or other hazardous
substances,** §143-215.77.
Hazardous chemical.
Toxic or hazardous substance identification,
§95-174(k).
Hazardous condition.
Trust companies, §53-301(a).
Trust institutions acting in fiduciary capacity,
§53-158.10.
Hazardous financial condition.
Continuing care retirement communities,
§58-64-1.
Liability risk retention, §58-22-10.
Professional employer organizations, §58-89A-5.
Workers' compensation self insurance, §97-165.
Employer groups, §58-47-60.
Hazardous materials.
Emergency responses, §166A-21.
Liability for abatement, §143-215.103.
Motor vehicles, §20-4.01.
**Hazardous materials emergency response
team,** §166A-21.
Hazardous materials incident.
Emergency responses, §166A-21.
Hazardous recreation activity, §99E-22.
Hazardous solvent.
Dry-cleaning equipment tax credit,
§105-129.16C(c).
Hazardous substance, §130A-310.
Control, §143-215.77.
Fiduciaries, §32-27.
Hazardous substance list.
Toxic or hazardous substance identification,
§95-174(l).
Hazardous substance trade secret.
Toxic or hazardous substance identification,
§95-174(m).
Hazardous waste, §130A-290(a).
Dry-cleaning solvent cleanup act,
§143-215.104B(b).
Hazardous waste constituent, §130A-290(a).
Hazardous waste disposal facility, §130A-290(a).
Hazardous waste facility, §130A-290(a).
Hazardous waste generation.
Solid waste management, §130A-290(a).
Hazardous waste management, §130A-290(a).
Hazardous waste management program,
§130A-290(a).
Hazardous waste transfer facility.
Solid waste management, §130A-290(a).
Hazard risk management.
Emergency management, §166A-4.

DEFINED TERMS —Cont'd

Hazing.
Criminal law, §14-35.

Hazmat team.
Hazardous materials emergency response, §166A-21.

HCWD.
Health coverage for workers with disabilities act, §108A-54.1(b).

HE.
Property taxes, §105-273.

Head.
Assistance by out-of-state law enforcement officers, §160A-288.3(b).

Head of department.
Executive organization, §143B-3.
State government reorganization, §143A-2.

Head of household.
Taxation, §105-134.1.

Health benefit plan, §58-3-200(a).
Applicability of acts of general assembly to health benefit plans, §58-3-167(a).
Claims, §§58-3-171(c), 58-3-172.
Closed formulary, health insurers maintaining, §58-3-221(c).
Contracts between health benefit plans and health care providers, §58-50-270.
Coordination of benefits with Medicaid, §58-51-115(a).
Covered clinical trials, §58-3-255(a).
Dental procedures performed in hospital or ambulatory surgical facility, §58-3-122(b).
Diagnosis and evaluation of osteoporosis and low bone mass, §58-3-174.
Direct access to obstetrician-gynecologist, §58-51-38(a).
Direct payment to government, §58-3-175(a).
Drive-thru deliveries, §58-3-169(a).
Emergency care coverage, §58-3-190(g).
Employer obligations, §108A-69(a).
Genetic information, §58-3-215(a).
Health care liability, §90-21.50.
Insurance discrimination, §58-3-121(a) to (c).
Lien on insurance settlement of child support obligor, §58-3-185(b).
Managed care access to specialists, §58-3-223(b).
Maternity coverage, §58-3-170(b).
Nondependent child coverage, §58-3-290(a).
Pharmacy of choice, §58-51-37(b).
Postmastectomy inpatient care coverage, §58-3-168(b).
Prescription contraceptive drugs, devices and services covered by health benefit plan, §58-3-178(c).
Prompt claim payments under health benefit plans, §58-3-225(a).
Reporting and disclosure requirements, §58-3-191(c).
Small employer group health coverage, §58-50-110.
Treatment discussions, §58-3-176.
Uniform prescription drug identification cards issued by health benefit plan, §58-3-177(e).
Uniform provider credentialing, §58-3-230(c).
Utilization review, §58-50-61(a).

Health benefits representative.
State health plan for teachers and state employees, §135-48.1.

Health care.
Consent to health care for minor, §32A-29.
Power of attorney, §32A-16.

DEFINED TERMS —Cont'd

Health care agent.
Power of attorney, §32A-16.

Health care decision.
Anatomical gifts, §130A-412.4.
Health care liability, §90-21.50.

Health care delivery assets.
Provider sponsored organizations, §131E-276.

Health care facilities, §131A-3.
Adoption, §48-3-401.
Cancer reporting, §130A-209(c).
Health plans, disclosure to providers, §58-3-227(a).
Nursing pools, §131E-154.2.
Obstruction of health care facilities, §14-277.4(f).
Patient abuse, §14-32.2(c).
Prompt claim payments under health benefit plans, §58-3-225(a).
Terrorist incident using nuclear, biological or chemical agents, §130A-476(g).
Verification of nurse licensure status, §90-171.43A(b).

Health-care-insurance receivable.
Secured transactions, §25-9-102(a).

Health care operations.
Patient medical records, confidentiality of, §130A-12.

Health care plan.
Health maintenance organizations, §58-67-5(d).

Health care power of attorney, §32A-16.

Health care practitioners.
Identification, §90-640(a).

Health care professional.
Umbilical cord stem cells and umbilical cord blood banking.
Providing women with information, §130A-128.1(a).

Health care provider.
Accident and health insurance.
Utilization review, §58-50-61(a).
Cancer reporting, §130A-209(c).
Contracts between health benefit plans and health care providers, §58-50-270.
Health care liability, §90-21.50.
Health plans, disclosure to providers, §58-3-227(a).
Industrial commission managed care organizations, ICManagedCare Rule II.
Medical malpractice, §90-21.11.
Medical records, §90-410.
Nursing, §90-171.20.
Pharmacy practice, §90-85.3(i).
Prompt claim payments under health benefit plans, §58-3-225(a).
Provider sponsored organizations, §131E-276.
Referral fees and solicitation payments, §90-400.
Self-referrals, §90-405.
Temporary order by state health director to report health related information, §130A-141.1.
Terrorist incident using nuclear, biological or chemical agents, §130A-476(g).
Workers' compensation, §97-2.

Health care services.
Accident and health insurance.
Utilization review, §58-50-61(a).
Direct access to obstetrician-gynecologist, §58-51-38(a).
Health care liability, §90-21.50.
Health maintenance organizations, §58-67-5(e).
Obstruction of health care facilities, §14-277.4(g).

DEFINED TERMS —Cont'd
Health certificate.
Bee and honey act, §106-635.
Health Choice.
Provider requirements for Medicaid or Health
Choice, §108C-2.
Health data.
Health statistics, §130A-372.
Health information.
Managed care patient assistance program,
§143-730.
Health information system or HIS.
Local health departments billing Medicaid,
§130A-34.2(f).
Health insurance.
Insurance guaranty associations, §58-62-16.
Health insurance coverage.
Health insurance portability and accountability,
§58-68-25(a).
Health insurance risk pool, §58-50-175.
Notice regarding by insurers to applicants,
§58-3-276(d).
Health insurance for the aged act, §58-54-1.
Health insurance plan.
Health insurance portability and accountability,
§58-68-25(a).
Health insurer, §58-12-2.
Coordination of benefits with Medicaid,
§58-51-115(a).
Employer obligations, §108A-69(a).
Health insurance portability and accountability,
§58-68-25(a).
Recovery from insurers providing additional
coverage to Medicaid-eligible persons,
§108A-55.4(a).
Health maintenance organization, §58-67-5(f).
Certificate of need, §131E-176.
Health organization.
Risk based capital requirements, §58-12-2.
Health or life would be endangered.
Medicaid, transfer of assets for less than market
value to qualify, §108A-58.2(e).
Health plan contract.
Provider sponsored organizations, §131E-276.
Health related services.
Continuing care retirement communities,
§58-64-1.
Health service.
Certificate of need, §131E-176.
Psychology practice act, §90-270.2.
Health service facility.
Certificate of need, §131E-176.
Health service facility bed.
Certificate of need, §131E-176.
Health status-related factor.
Health insurance portability and accountability,
§58-68-25(a).
Hearing aid.
Dealers and board, §93D-1.
Hearing aid specialist, §93D-1.
Hearing committee.
Discipline and disability rules of state bar, Bar
Rule B.0103.
Hearing officer.
Administrative procedure, §150B-2.
Child support, §50-31.
Educational personnel, §115C-325(a).
Education of children with disabilities,
§115C-106.3.
Physicians and surgeons, §90-1.1.

DEFINED TERMS —Cont'd
Hearing unit.
Adult care homes, §131D-2.1.
Hearsay.
Evidence, §8C-1 Rule 801(c).
Heart-lung bypass machine.
Certificate of need, §131E-176.
Heating.
Contractors, §87-21(a).
Heating, group 1.
Contractors, §87-21(a).
Heating, group 2.
Contractors, §87-21(a).
Heating, group 3.
Contractors, §87-21(a).
Heating oil.
Petroleum cleanup, §143-215.94A.
Heavy equipment.
Heavy equipment gross receipts tax in lieu of
property tax, §153A-156.1(a).
Municipal heavy equipment gross receipts tax,
§160A-215.2(a).
Heir.
Decedents' estates, §§28A-1-1, 29-2.
Uniform transfer on death security registration
act, §41-40.
Help America Vote act, §163-82.27.
Hemoglobin C trait, §58-58-25.
Labor discrimination, §95-28.1.
Herbicide.
Pesticide board, §143-460.
Hernia.
Workers' compensation, §97-2.
HIE network.
Health information exchange, §90-413.3.
High-calcium foods and beverages.
School boards to give preference to,
§115C-264.1(a).
High-conflict case.
Child custody, §50-90.
High cost home loans.
Mortgages, high cost home loans, §24-1.1E(a).
Higher education.
Executive organization, §143B-3.
Highest annual salary.
Legislative retirement system, §120-4.8.
Highly compensated individual.
Tax credit for qualifying expenses of production
company, §§105-130.47(a), 105-151.29(a).
High Rock lake.
High Rock lake marine commission, §77-50.
High school, §115C-75(a).
High unemployment period.
Unemployment insurance, §96-12.01(a1).
High-unit-cost project.
Water infrastructure, §159G-20.
High-unit-cost threshold.
Water infrastructure, §159G-20.
High-voltage lines.
Overhead high-voltage line safety, §95-229.6.
Highway.
Alternative fuel, §105-449.130.
Contractors, §87-101.
Gasoline tax, §105-449.60.
Motor vehicles, §20-4.01.
Public utilities, §62-3.
Roads and highways, §136-91.
Highway vehicle.
Alternative fuel, §105-449.130.
Gasoline tax, §105-449.60.
Underinsured motorist coverage, §20-279.21(b).

DEFINED TERMS —Cont'd
Highway vending facilities.
  Aid to the blind, §111-49(c).
Highway work zone.
  Speed limits, §20-141(j2).
HIPAA.
  Health information exchange, §90-413.3.
Hire.
  Criminal law, §14-168.2.
Historic ABC establishment.
  Alcoholic beverages, §18B-101.
Historically underutilized business.
  Higher education bonds, §116D-1.
  Public contracts, §143-128.4.
Historic district.
  City and towns, §160A-400.3.
Historic edged weapon.
  Sale of pistols and crossbows, §§14-402(c),
    14-409.12.
Historic preservation.
  Archives and history, §121-2.
Historic properties, §121-2.
  Main street solutions fund, §143B-472.35(a2).
Hive.
  Bee and honey act, §106-635.
HMO, §58-67-5(f).
Holder.
  Historic preservation agreements, §121-35.
  UCC, §25-1-201(b).
  Unclaimed property act, §116B-52.
Holder in due course.
  Negotiable instruments, §25-3-302(a).
Hold harmless amount.
  Third one-half cent tax.
    City hold harmless for repealed taxes,
      §105-522(a).
Hold harmless threshold.
  Third one-half cent tax.
    County hold harmless for repealed taxes,
      §105-523(b).
Holding and processing facility.
  Cremation, §90-210.121.
Holding company.
  Corporate income tax.
    Adjustment for expenses related to dividends,
      §105-130.6A(a).
  Taxation, §105-120.2.
Holding company system.
  Collection agencies, §58-70-6.
  Workers' compensation self insurance, §97-165.
Holdover facility.
  Delinquent and undisciplined juveniles, §7B-1501.
Home.
  Defensive force to protect, §14-51.2(a).
  Medicaid estate recovery plan, §108A-70.5(b).
Home appliance.
  Service agreement companies, §66-371(b).
Home appliance service agreement.
  Service agreement companies, §66-371(b).
Home appliance service agreement company,
    §66-371(b).
Home care agency, §131E-136.
  State health plan for teachers and state
    employees.
    Long-term care benefits, §135-48.61(a).
Home care agency director.
  Home care agencies licensing, §131E-136.
Home care client.
  Home care agencies licensing, §131E-136.
Home care services, §131E-136.
  Continuing care retirement communities,
    §58-64-1.

DEFINED TERMS —Cont'd
Home consumer-sized package.
  Antifreeze law, §106-579.3.
Home country.
  Trust companies, §53-301(a).
Home country regulator.
  Trust companies, §53-301(a).
Home health agency, §131E-136.
  Certificate of need, §131E-176.
Home health services.
  Certificate of need, §131E-176.
  Long-term care insurance, §58-55-35(a).
Home inspection, §143-151.45.
Home inspector, §143-151.45.
Homeless.
  Assignment of student to particular school,
    §115C-366(h).
Home loan.
  Contract rates on home loan secured by first
    mortgage or first deed of trust, §24-1.1A(e).
  Emergency program to reduce home foreclosures,
    §45-101.
  Mortgage debt collection and servicing, §45-90.
Homemaker services.
  Long-term care insurance, §58-55-35(a).
Home office.
  Structural pest control act, §106-65.24.
Home school, §115C-563(a).
Home service business, §58-10-25(a).
Home-solicitation sale.
  Installment sales, §25A-38.
Home state.
  Child custody jurisdiction and enforcement,
    §50A-102.
  Insurance producers, §58-33-10.
  Interstate branch banking, §53-224.9.
  Interstate family support, §52C-1-101.
  Interstate wildlife violator compact, §113-300.6.
  Nurse licensure compact, §90-171.82.
  Public adjusters, §58-33A-5.
  Savings and loan interstate branches, §54B-266.
  Savings interstate branch banks, §54C-200.
  Surplus lines insurance, §58-21-11(b).
  Trust companies, §53-301(a).
Home state action.
  Nurse licensure compact, §90-171.82.
Home state regulator.
  Trust companies, §53-301(a).
Honey, §106-635.
Honeybees, §106-635.
Honeyflow, §106-635.
Honey plants, §106-635.
Honor.
  Letters of credit, §25-5-102(a).
  UCC, §25-1-201(b).
Honorable military service.
  Veterans cemeteries, §65-43.
Honorarium.
  State government ethics act, §138A-3.
Horace Williams campus, §116-198.33.
Horticultural land.
  Taxation, §105-277.2.
Hospice, §131E-201.
  Certificate of need, §131E-176.
  Long-term care insurance, §58-55-35(a).
Hospice inpatient facility.
  Certificate of need, §131E-176.
  Hospice licensure, §131E-201.
Hospice patient, §131E-201.
Hospice patient's family, §131E-201.

DEFINED TERMS —Cont'd
Hospice residential care facility.
　Certificate of need, §131E-176.
　Hospice licensure, §131E-201.
Hospice services.
　Hospice licensure, §131E-201.
Hospice team, §131E-201.
Hospital.
　Anatomical gifts, §130A-412.4.
　Certificate of need, §131E-176.
　Cooperative agreements.
　　Certificate of public advantage, §131E-192.2.
　Cooperative agreements among physicians or
　　between physician, hospital or others,
　　§90-21.25.
　Licensure, §131E-76.
　Medical care data, §131E-214.1.
　Terrorist incident or communicable diseases,
　　detection of, §130A-480(d).
Hospital authority.
　Public hospitals, §131E-16.
Hospital facilities, §131E-6.
　Public hospitals, §131E-16.
Hospitalization.
　Insurance, §58-51-105.
Hospital land, §131E-6.
　Public hospitals, §131E-16.
Hospital medical records.
　Evidence, §8-44.1.
Hospital service corporation, §58-65-1(a).
Hospital service plan, §58-65-1(a).
Hospital services.
　Debts owed public hospitals, §131E-48.
Host.
　Boll weevil eradication, §106-65.69.
Host state.
　Interstate branch banking, §53-224.9.
　Trust companies, §53-301(a).
Hotel.
　Alcoholic beverages, §18B-1000.
Hours worked.
　Wage and hour act, §95-25.2.
House.
　Criminal law, §14-58.1.
　Motor vehicles, §20-356.
House arrest.
　Delinquent and undisciplined juveniles, §7B-1501.
House arrest with electronic monitoring.
　Bail, §15A-531.
　Structured sentencing, §15A-1340.11.
House car.
　Motor vehicles, §20-4.01.
Household support loss.
　Victim's compensation, §15B-2.
Housemover.
　Motor vehicles, §20-356.
House trailer.
　Motor vehicles, §20-4.01.
Housing accommodation, §41A-3.
Housing authority, §157-41.
　National defense housing projects, §157-53.
Housing facility.
　Protection of animals, §19A-23.
Housing finance agency.
　Emergency program to reduce home foreclosures,
　　§45-101.
　Low-income housing tax credits, §105-129.40(b).
Housing for older persons.
　Fair housing, §41A-6(e).
Housing project, §157-41.
　Housing authorities, §157-3.

DEFINED TERMS —Cont'd
Hub.
　Sales and use tax, §105-164.3.
　Tax incentives for new and expanding businesses,
　　§105-129.2.
HUD.
　Uniform standards for manufactured homes act,
　　§143-145.
Hull insurance and protection and indemnity,
　§58-20-5.
Human remains.
　Cemeteries, §65-48.
　Cremation, §90-210.121.
　Disturbing, dismembering, §14-401.22(f).
Human service agency.
　Public utilities, §62-289.3.
Human services field.
　Substance abuse professionals, §90-113.31A.
Human service transportation.
　Public utilities, §62-289.3.
Human skeletal remains.
　Burial sites, §70-28.
Hybrid.
　Seed law, §106-277.2.
Hydrocarbon.
　Dry-cleaning solvent cleanup act,
　　§143-215.104B(b).
Hydroelectric generator.
　Business and energy tax credits, §105-129.15.
Hydrologic area.
　Ecosystem enhancement program, §143-214.11(a).
Hypothecation lender.
　Membership camping, §66-246(a).
IDEA.
　Administrative procedure, §150B-22.1(c).
　Education of children with disabilities,
　　§115C-106.3.
Identifiable hospice administration.
　Hospice licensure, §131E-201.
Identification card.
　Anatomical gifts, §130A-412.4.
Identifying information.
　Identity theft, §14-113.20(b).
　Long-term care partnerships.
　　Information sharing, §58-55-80(d).
　Public records, restricted use, §132-1.10(b).
Identifying number.
　Condominiums, §47C-1-103.
IEP.
　Discipline of students.
　　Seclusion and restraint, §115C-391.1(b).
IEP team.
　Education of children with disabilities,
　　§115C-106.3.
III system.
　National crime prevention and privacy compact,
　　§114-19.50.
Illegal gas.
　Oil and gas conservation, §113-389.
Illegal oil.
　Oil and gas conservation, §113-389.
Illegal product.
　Oil and gas conservation, §113-389.
Illegal signs.
　Outdoor advertising control, §136-128.
Illegal slot machines.
　Lotteries and gaming, §14-296.
Illicit drug.
　Discipline and disability rules of state bar, Bar
　　Rule B.0103.

DEFINED TERMS —Cont'd

Illicit mixed beverage.
Unauthorized substances taxes, §105-113.106.
Illicit sexual behavior.
Alimony, §50-16.1A.
Illicit spirituous liquor.
Unauthorized substances taxes, §105-113.106.
Immediate container.
Food, drugs and cosmetics, §106-121.
Poultry products inspection, §106-549.51.
Immediate family.
Coastal and estuarine commercial fishing licenses, §113-168.
Custodial institutions, §14-259.
Legislative ethics, §120-85.1.
Local ABC boards, §18B-700(k).
Peer support group counselor's privilege, §8-53.10(a).
Savings and loan associations, §54B-4.
Savings banks, §54C-4(b).
State government ethics act, §138A-3.
Transportation board, §136-14(h).
Unemployment compensation, §96-8.
Unemployment insurance, §96-8.
Immediate family member.
Family leave credit insurance, §58-57-115(a).
Mortgage bankers, brokers and servicers, §53-244.030.
Self-referrals by health care providers, §90-405.
Voluntary shared leave program, §§115C-12.2(a), 126-8.3(a).
Immediate precursor.
Controlled substances, §90-87.
Imminent danger.
Mines, §74-24.2.
Occupational safety and health, §95-127.
Imminent hazard.
Dry-cleaning solvent cleanup act, §143-215.104B(b).
Public health generally, §130A-2.
Impaired.
Insurers supervision, §58-30-12.
Impaired driving.
Motor vehicles, §20-138.1.
Impaired driving license revocation, §20-28.2(a).
Impaired insurer.
Insurance guaranty associations, §58-62-16.
Small employer group health coverage, §58-50-110.
Impairing substance.
Motor vehicles, §20-4.01.
Impervious surface.
Vehicle surface areas, §113A-70(b).
Implement of husbandry.
Motor vehicles, §20-4.01.
Implied-consent offense, §20-16.2(a1).
Import.
Gasoline tax, §105-449.60.
Important mountain resources, §153B-2.
Important regional resources.
Uwharrie regional resources act, §153C-2.
Importer.
Alcohol taxation, §105-113.68.
Impound.
Impounded water, §143-215.44(d).
Improve.
Statutory liens on real property, §44A-7.
Subcontractors, §22C-1.
Improvement project.
Development zone project tax credit, §105-129.13(b).

DEFINED TERMS —Cont'd

Improvements.
Statutory liens on real property, §44A-7.
Subcontractors, §22C-1.
Water and sewer, §162A-2.
Inaccessible.
Mercury switch removal, motor vehicles, §130A-310.50.
Inactive business operations.
Sudan (Darfur) divestment act, §147-86.42.
Inactive hazardous substance or waste disposal site, §130A-310.
Inactive licensee.
Engineering, §89C-3.
Inactive member.
Continuing legal education, Bar Rule D.1501.
Inactive period or periods.
Unemployment compensation.
Seasonal pursuits, §96-16(j).
Inaugural period.
Ceremonies committee, §143-532.
Inaugural planning period.
Ceremonies committee, §143-532.
Inbred line.
Seed law, §106-277.2.
In bulk.
Seed law, §106-277.2.
Incapable.
Advance instruction for mental health treatment, §122C-72.
Incapacity or incapacitated.
Custodial trusts, §33B-1.
Discipline and disability rules of state bar, Bar Rule B.0103.
Judicial standards commission, §7A-374.2.
Standby guardianship, §35A-1370.
Incapacity to proceed.
Criminal law and procedure, §15A-1001.
Inclined or vertical wheelchair lift.
Elevator safety, §95-110.3(g).
Inclined stairway chair lift.
Elevator safety, §95-110.3(f).
Includes.
Business corporations, §55-1-40.
Nonprofit corporations, §55A-1-40.
Income.
Community land trust property taxation, §105-277.17(b).
Interstate family support, §52C-1-101.
Medicaid, transfer of assets for less than market value to qualify, §108A-58.2(e).
Principal and income act, §37A-1-102.
Property tax homestead exclusion, §105-277.1(b).
Veterans, §34-2.
Income attributable to the state.
Taxation, §105-131.
Income beneficiary.
Principal and income act, §37A-1-102.
Income interest.
Principal and income act, §37A-1-102.
Income not attributable to the state.
Taxation, §105-131.
Income tax return preparer.
Taxation, §105-228.90(b).
Income trust.
Principal and income act, §37A-1-104.1.
Income-withholding order.
Interstate family support, §52C-1-101.
Income year.
Taxation, §§105-114, 105-130.2.

DEFINED TERMS —Cont'd
Incompetent adult.
Incompetency, §35A-1101.
Mental health, §122C-3.
Incompetent child.
Incompetency, §35A-1101.
Incompetent person.
Incompetency, §35A-1202.
Incomplete instrument.
Negotiable instruments, §25-3-115(a).
In-county scrap tire, §130A-309.53.
Increase the scope.
Budget of state, §143C-1-1(d).
Incremental fuel cost.
Energy credit and banking program, §143-58.1(a).
Incremental vehicle cost.
Energy credit and banking program, §143-58.1(a).
Indebtedness.
Corporate franchise tax, §105-122(b).
Credit insurance, §58-57-5.
Indemnification.
Annual audited financial reports.
Insurance companies, §58-10-190.
Indemnity trigger.
Protected cell companies, §58-10-80.
Independent administrator.
Eyewitness identification reform, §15A-284.52(a).
Independent certified public accountant.
Annual audited financial reports.
Insurance companies, §58-10-190.
Independent escrow agent.
Time shares, §93A-41.
Independent expenditure.
Political campaigns, §163-278.6.
Public campaign fund, §163-278.62.
Voter-owned elections act, §163-278.96.
Independent expert witness.
Medicolegal guidelines for attorney-physician
relationship, MLG Rule 3.
Independent medical examination.
Medicolegal guidelines for attorney-physician
relationship, MLG Rule 3.
Independent motor vehicle dealer, §20-286.
Independent professional advice.
Structured settlement protection, §1-543.11.
Independent review organization.
Health benefit plan external review, §58-50-75(c).
NC NOVA special licensure designation,
§131E-154.13.
Independent study.
Substance abuse professionals, §90-113.31A.
Index rate.
Small employer group health coverage,
§58-50-110.
Indictment, §15A-641.
Indigent.
Incompetency, §35A-1101.
Protection of disabled adults, §108A-101.
Indigent persons.
Judicial department, §7A-450.
Rules governing legal services provided by
students, Bar Rule C.0202.
Rules governing practical training of law
students, Bar Rule C.0202.
Indirect holdings.
Sudan (Darfur) divestment act, §147-86.42.
Indirect interest in transaction.
Nonprofit corporations, §55A-3-01(b).
Individual.
Business corporations, §55-1-40.
Conservation, §113-130.

DEFINED TERMS —Cont'd
Individual —Cont'd
Health information exchange, §90-413.3.
Insurance information and privacy protection act,
§58-39-15.
Limited liability companies, §57C-1-03.
Medicaid, transfer of assets for less than market
value to qualify, §108A-58.1(g).
Mortgage bankers, brokers and servicers,
§53-244.030.
Nonprofit corporations, §55A-1-40.
Political campaigns, §163-278.6.
Public adjusters, §58-33A-5.
Respiratory care practices act, §90-648.
Taxation, §105-134.1.
Tax withholding, §105-163.1.
Individual education program.
Education of children with disabilities,
§115C-106.3.
Individual health insurance coverage.
Health insurance portability and accountability,
§58-68-25(a).
Individually identifiable energy information.
Stocks of coal and petroleum fuels, §143-345.14(f).
Individually owned.
Taxation, §105-277.2.
Individual market.
Health insurance, nondependent child coverage,
§58-3-290(a).
Health insurance portability and accountability,
§58-68-25(a).
Individual policy.
Group health insurance, §58-53-1.
Individual rental unit.
Expedited evictions, §42-59.
Individual self-insurer.
Self-insurance security association, §97-130.
Indorsement.
Negotiable instruments, §25-3-204(a).
Indorser.
Negotiable instruments, §25-3-204(b).
Industrial bank, §53-136.
Industrial hygiene, §90-515.
Industrial hygienist, §90-515.
Industrial hygienist in training, §90-515.
Industrial life insurance, §58-58-5.
Industrial machinery.
Building codes, §143-138(b9).
Industrial plant.
Public utilities, §62-3.
Industrial project.
Pollution control, §159C-3.
Industrial-quality eye protective devices.
Vocational education, §115C-168.
Industrial sick benefit insurance.
Nature of policies, §58-51-65.
Industrial solid waste, §130A-290.
Industrial waste, §143-213.
Industry.
Passenger tramway safety, §95-117.
Small employer group health coverage,
§58-50-110.
Inebriety.
Incompetency, §35A-1101.
Inert debris.
Solid waste management, §130A-290(a).
Inert ingredient.
Pesticide board, §143-460.
Inert matter.
Seed law, §106-277.2.

DEFINED TERMS —Cont'd

Infant or toddler with a disability.
Education of children with disabilities,
§115C-106.3.

Infected.
Bee and honey act, §106-635.

Infection.
Protection of forest, §106-922.

Infestation.
Protection of forest, §106-922.

Infested.
Bee and honey act, §106-635.
Boll weevil eradication, §106-65.69.

Infirmary.
Hospital licensure, §131E-76.

Informal bids.
Roads and highways, §136-28.1(b).

Informal ethics advisory.
Procedures for ruling on questions of legal ethics,
Bar Rule D.0101.

Information, §15A-641.
Electronic transactions, §66-312.

Information center.
Outdoor advertising control, §136-128.

Information processing system.
Electronic transactions, §66-312.

Information service.
Sales and use tax, §105-164.3.

Information technology.
Best value procurements, §143-135.9(a).
Budget of state, §143C-1-1(d).
Office of information technology services,
§147-33.81.
Persons with disabilities protection, §168A-3.

Information technology and service.
Growing businesses tax credits, §105-129.81.

**Information technology enterprise
management.**
Office of information technology services,
§147-33.81.

Information technology portfolio management.
Office of information technology services,
§147-33.81.

Infraction.
Criminal law, §14-3.1.

In good faith.
Uniform fiduciaries act, §32-2(b).

Ingredient statement.
Pesticide board, §143-460.

Inherent risk.
Hazardous recreation activities, §99E-22.

Inherent risks of agritourism activity.
Agritourism activity liability, §99E-30.

Inherent risks of equine activities.
Equine activity liability, §99E-1.

In-house continuing legal education, Bar Rule
D.1501.

Initial capital.
Trust companies, §53-301(a).

Initial container.
Cremation, §90-210.121.

Initial cost.
Energy policy for state government, §143-64.11.

Initial determination.
Child custody jurisdiction and enforcement,
§50A-102.

Initial investment basis.
Community land trust property taxation,
§105-277.17(b).

Initial pledges for withdrawable accounts.
Savings and loan associations, §54B-4.

DEFINED TERMS —Cont'd

Initiating party.
Child support, §§50-31, 110-129.

Initiating state.
Interstate family support, §52C-1-101.

Initiating tribunal.
Interstate family support, §52C-1-101.

In its entirety.
Electronic recording of custodial interrogations,
§15A-211(c).

Injured party.
Offshore oil and gas activities, §143-215.94BB.

Injury.
Alcoholic beverages, §18B-120.
Workers' compensation, §97-2.

Inland fishing waters, §113-129.

Inland game fish.
Conservation, §113-129.

Inland marine insurance.
Insurance rates, §58-40-5.

Inmate.
Medical release of inmates, §15A-1369.
State prisons, §148-120.

In need of protective services.
Protection of disabled adults, §108A-101.

Innocent owner.
Impaired driving, §20-28.2(a1).

Inoperable blue light.
Use of red or blue lights on vehicle, §20-130.1(c1).

Inoperable vehicle, §20-4.01.

Inquiry.
Domestic violence in disposition report,
§15A-1382.1(c).

Insect.
Pesticide board, §143-460.
Structural pest control act, §106-65.24.

Insecticides.
Pesticide board, §143-460.
Structural pest control act, §106-65.24.

Inside.
Long-term care facilities, smoking prohibited
within, §§131D-4.4(b), 131E-114.3(a).
Smoking in mental health facilities, §122C-6(a).

Insider.
Fraudulent transfers, §39-23.1.

Insolvency.
Banking, §53-1.
Health maintenance organizations, §58-67-5(m).
Insurers supervision, §58-30-10.

Insolvency proceedings.
UCC, §25-1-201(b).

Insolvent.
Health maintenance organizations, §58-67-5(m).
Insurers supervision, §§58-30-10, 58-30-12.
Trust companies, §53-301(a).
UCC, §25-1-201(b).

Insolvent insurer.
Insurance guaranty association, §§58-48-20,
58-62-16.

Inspection.
Certification of wastewater contractors and
inspectors, §90A-71.

Inspection certificate.
Boiler and pressure vessel regulation, §95-69.9(e).

Inspection department.
Uniform standards for manufactured homes act,
§143-145.

Inspection service.
Poultry products inspection, §106-549.51.

Inspector.
Certification of wastewater contractors and
inspectors, §90A-71.

DEFINED TERMS —Cont'd
Inspector —Cont'd
Conservation, §113-128.
Poultry products inspection, §106-549.51.
Inspector's commission.
Boiler and pressure vessel regulation, §95-69.9(f).
Installation.
Weights and measures, §81A-9.
Installation of pumps and pumping equipment.
Well construction, §87-85.
Installment lease contract.
Leases, UCC, §25-2A-103(1).
Instant message.
Sex offender and public protection registration, §14-208.6.
In-state-only supplier.
Gasoline tax, §105-449.60.
Institution.
Bonds for student housing, §116-175.
Centennial campus and Horace Williams campus financing act, §116-198.33.
Community colleges, §115D-2.
Decedents' estates, safe deposit boxes, §28A-15-13(a).
Higher education bonds, §116D-22.
Higher education student housing, §116-189.
Interstate compact on mental health, §122C-361.
Mutual deposit guaranty associations, §54B-236.
Private educational institutions, §116-22.
Prudent management of institutional funds, §36E-2.
State grants to students attending private universities or colleges, §116-43.5(a).
State prisons, §148-120.
University of North Carolina, §§116-2, 116-15.
Institutional consumer.
Egg law, §106-245.14.
Institutional controls.
Risk based environmental remediation of industrial sites, §130A-310.65.
Institutional fund.
Prudent management of institutional funds, §36E-2.
Institutionalized individual.
Medicaid, transfer of assets for less than market value to qualify, §108A-58.1(h).
Institutional source.
Insurance information and privacy protection act, §58-39-15.
Institution for elementary and secondary education.
Private capital facilities finance act, §159D-37.
Institution of higher education.
Higher education tuition and fees, §116-143.1.
Performance standards for sustainable, energy-efficient public buildings, §143-135.36.
Private capital facilities finance act, §159D-37.
Psychology practice act, §90-270.2.
Sex offender and public protection registration, §14-208.6.
Unemployment compensation, §96-8.
Unemployment insurance, §96-8.
Instruction.
Investment securities, §25-8-102.
Instructional personnel.
Education programs in residential schools, §143B-146.1(b).
Instructor.
Motor vehicles, §20-320.
Instrument.
Forgery, §14-119(c).

DEFINED TERMS —Cont'd
Instrument —Cont'd
Negotiable instruments, §25-3-104.
Registration by register of deeds, §161-14(d).
Secured transactions, §25-9-102(a).
Instrumentality.
Chop shops, §14-72.7(f).
Insurable interest.
Beach property insurance, §§58-45-35, 58-45-35(a).
Insurable property.
Beach property insurance, §58-45-5.
Insurance.
Group health insurance, §58-53-1.
Insurance producers, §58-33-10.
Liability risk retention, §58-22-10.
Third party administrators, §58-56-2.
Insurance arrangement.
Health insurance risk pool, §58-50-175.
Insurance company, §58-1-5.
Bail, §15A-531.
Funeral and burial trust funds, §90-210.60.
Impaired driving, §20-28.2(a1).
Political campaigns, §163-278.6.
Regulatory charge, §58-6-25(e).
State of disaster, §58-2-46.
Unclaimed property act, §116B-52.
Insurance fiduciary.
Providers of health benefits, §58-50-40(a).
Insurance fund.
Pest control, §106-65.55.
Insurance holding company system, §58-19-5.
Insurance institution.
Insurance information and privacy protection act, §58-39-15.
Insurance of deposit accounts.
Savings banks, §54C-4(b).
Insurance of withdrawable accounts.
Savings and loan associations, §54B-4.
Insurance policy or contract.
Readable insurance policies, §58-38-15.
Insurance premium finance agreement, §58-35-1.
Insurance premium finance company, §58-35-1.
Insurance proceeds.
Impaired driving, §20-28.2(a1).
Insurance producer, §58-33-10.
Interagency consultation by insurance commissioner, §58-2-128(d).
Life insurance.
Dishonest and predatory sales to military personnel, §58-58-335.
Insurance product.
Public officers and employees, §58-31-60(a).
Insurance regulator, §58-2-131(b).
Insurance guaranty associations, §58-62-16.
Insurance-support organization.
Insurance information and privacy protection act, §58-39-15.
Insurance transaction.
Insurance information and privacy protection act, §58-39-15.
Insured.
Health insurance risk pool, §58-50-175.
Insured or enrollee.
Group health insurance, §58-53-1.
Health care liability, §90-21.50.
Insurer.
Accident and health insurance.
Pharmacy of choice, §58-51-37(b).
Annual audited financial reports, §58-10-190.

DEFINED TERMS —Cont'd
Insurer —Cont'd
Applicability of acts of general assembly to health
    benefit plans, §58-3-167(a).
Bail bondsman and runners, §58-71-1.
Closed formulary, health insurers maintaining,
    §58-3-221(c).
Closure of a block of business, §58-3-275(c).
Dental procedures performed in hospital or
    ambulatory surgical facility, §58-3-122(b).
Diagnosis and evaluation of osteoporosis and low
    bone mass, §58-3-174.
Drive-thru deliveries, §58-3-169(a).
Elderly insurance, §58-52-1.
Emergency care coverage, §58-3-190(g).
False statement to procure or deny benefit of
    policy or certificate, §58-2-161(a).
Genetic information in health insurance,
    §58-3-215(a).
Group health insurance, §58-53-1.
Health benefit plans, §58-3-200(a).
Health care liability, §90-21.50.
Health insurance, locum tenens contracts,
    §58-3-231(a).
Health insurance risk pool, §58-50-175.
    Notice regarding by insurers to applicants,
        §58-3-276(d).
Health plans, disclosure to providers,
    §58-3-227(a).
Insurance, §58-1-5.
Insurance commissioner, confidentiality of
    information, §58-2-240(c).
Insurance company taxation, §105-228.3.
Insurance holding companies, §58-19-5.
Insurers supervision, §58-30-10.
Interstate insurance product regulation compact,
    §58-91-10.
Life insurance.
    Dishonest and predatory sales to military
        personnel, §58-58-335.
Managed care access to specialists, §58-3-223(b).
Managing general agents, §58-34-2(a).
Medicare supplement insurance, §58-54-1.
Pharmacy of choice, §58-51-37(b).
Preferred providers, §58-50-56(a).
Prescription contraceptive drugs, devices and
    services covered by health benefit plan,
    §58-3-178(c).
Producer-controlled property or casualty insurers,
    §58-3-165(a).
Prompt claim payments under health benefit
    plans, §58-3-225(a).
Property insurance policies, §58-44-60(b).
Rate evasion fraud, §58-2-164(a).
Rates, §58-36-100(b).
Readable insurance policies, §58-38-15.
Regulatory charge, §58-6-25(e).
Third party administrators, §58-56-2.
Treatment discussions, §58-3-176.
Uniform provider credentialing, §58-3-230(c).
Use of nonoriginal crash parts, §58-36-95(a).
Utilization review, §58-50-61(a).
Workers' compensation, §97-2.
Intact.
Management of abandoned manufactured homes,
    §130A-309.112.
Intake.
Delinquent and undisciplined juveniles, §7B-1501.
Intangible personal property.
Property taxes, §105-273.

DEFINED TERMS —Cont'd
Integrated wholesale dealer.
Tobacco taxation, §105-113.4.
Integrative medicine.
Physicians and surgeons, §90-1.1.
Intentional interference.
Interference with emergency communications,
    §14-286.2(b1).
Interactive digital media.
Research and development tax credit,
    §105-129.56(a).
Interagency council.
Community schools act, §115C-205.
Intercept.
Electronic surveillance, §15A-286.
Intercollegiate sport.
Athlete agents, §78C-86.
Interconceptional care.
Midwifery practice, §90-178.2.
Interconnected VoIP service.
911 system, §62A-40.
Interdisciplinary team, §131E-201.
Interest.
Appraisal rights, §55-13-01.
State community corrections advisory board,
    §143B-1157(h).
Interested distributee.
Principal and income act, §37A-1-104.1.
Interested parties.
Structured settlement protection, §1-543.11.
Unemployment compensation.
    Seasonal pursuits, §96-16(j).
Interested persons.
Appraisal rights, §55-13-01.
Nonjudicial settlement agreements, §36C-1-111.
Interested shares.
Control share acquisitions, §55-9A-01(b).
Interested transactions.
Appraisal rights, §55-13-01.
Interested trustee.
Principal and income act, §37A-1-104.1.
Interest in real property.
Subordination agreements, §39-6.6(f).
Interests of the beneficiaries.
Uniform trust code, §36C-1-103.
Interface.
Planning regionally significant transportation
    projects, §136-200.
Interim association.
Savings and loan associations, §54B-4.
Interim guardian.
Incompetency, §35A-1101.
Interlocal agreement.
Cities providing communications services,
    §160A-340.
**Interlocal small business economic
    development project.**
Main street solutions fund, §143B-472.35(a2).
Intermediary.
Reinsurance intermediaries, §58-9-2(a).
Intermediary bank.
Banking, §25-4-105.
Funds transfers, UCC, §25-4A-104(b).
Intermediate accident.
Safe driver incentive program, §58-36-75(a).
Intermediate care facility.
Long-term care insurance, §58-55-35(a).
**Intermediate care facility for the mentally
    retarded.**
Certificate of need, §131E-176.

DEFINED TERMS —Cont'd
Intermediate punishment.
Structured sentencing, §15A-1340.11.
Intermodal facility.
Tax incentives for railroad intermodal facilities, §105-129.95.
Internal auditing.
Administrative office of the court.
Internal audit division, §7A-343.5.
Internal control.
State governmental accountability and internal control act, §143D-3.
Internal control over financial reporting.
Annual audited financial reports.
Insurance companies, §58-10-190.
Internal Revenue Code.
Exemptions from creditors' claims, §1C-1601(b).
Securities, §78A-2.
Small business contractors, §143B-472.101.
International bank agency.
International banking act, §53-232.2(a).
International bank branch.
International banking act, §53-232.2(a).
International banking corporation.
International banking act, §53-232.2(a).
International banking facility.
Corporate income tax, §105-130.5(b).
International fuel tax agreement.
Fuel taxes, §105-449.37(a).
International organization.
Business discrimination, §75B-1.
International representative office.
International banking act, §53-232.2(a).
International symbol of access.
Handicapped parking privileges, §20-37.5.
Internet.
Sex offender and public protection registration, §14-208.6.
Internet access service, §105-164.3.
Internet chat room.
Computer crimes, §14-453.
Interpreter.
Interpreters and transliterators licensure act, §90D-3.
Interpreting.
Interpreters and transliterators licensure act, §90D-3.
Intersection.
Motor vehicles, §20-4.01.
Intersection of highway.
Motor vehicles, §20-150.
Interstate air business.
Sales and use tax, §105-164.3.
Interstate air courier.
Sales and use tax, §105-164.3.
Tax incentives for new and expanding businesses, §105-129.2.
Interstate cases.
Child support income withholding procedures, §110-136.3(b).
Interstate commerce.
Motor carriers, §20-376.
Public utilities, §62-3.
Interstate commission.
Interstate compact for juveniles, §7B-4001.
Interstate compact on juveniles, §7B-1501.
Interstate environment pollution.
Interstate environmental compact, §113A-23.
Interstate freight air carrier.
Sales and use tax, §105-164.3.

DEFINED TERMS —Cont'd
Interstate merger transaction.
Branch banking, §53-224.9.
Interstate motor carrier.
Motor carrier safety regulation unit, §20-376.
Interstate passenger air carrier.
Sales and use tax, §105-164.3.
Tax incentives for new and expanding businesses, §105-129.2.
Interstate system.
Junkyard control, §136-143.
Outdoor advertising control, §136-128.
Interview.
Private personnel services, §95-47.1.
In the presence of a minor.
Assault, §14-33(d).
In this (the) state.
Sales and use tax, §105-164.3.
Intoxicated.
Mental health, §122C-3.
Public intoxication, §14-443.
Intoxication.
Toxic vapors act, §90-113.9.
Workers' compensation, §97-12.
Intrapartum care.
Midwifery practice, §90-178.2.
Intrastate commerce.
Meat inspection, §106-549.15.
Motor carriers, §20-376.
Poultry products inspection, §106-549.51.
Public utilities, §62-3.
Intrastate motor carrier.
Motor carrier safety regulation unit, §20-376.
Intrastate operations.
Public utilities, §62-3.
Intrastate system.
Highway trust fund, §136-175.
Introduction of the Euro.
European monetary union, §53-295.
Invention.
Invention development services, §66-209.
Invention developer, §66-209.
Invention development services, §66-209.
Inventory.
Farm machinery, §66-180.
Property taxes, §105-273.
Secured transactions, §25-9-102(a).
Investigating law enforcement agency.
Crime victims' rights, §15A-830(a).
Investigation.
Discipline and disability rules of state bar, Bar Rule B.0103.
Judicial standards commission, §7A-374.2.
Procedures for the authorized practice committee of the state bars, Bar Rule D.0203.
Investigative assessment response.
Abused neglected or dependent juveniles, §7B-101.
Investigative consumer report.
Insurance information and privacy protection act, §58-39-15.
Investigative information.
Optometrists, §90-121.5(b).
Investigative or law enforcement officer.
Electronic surveillance, §15A-286.
Investigator.
Discipline and disability rules of state bar, Bar Rule B.0103.
Procedures for the authorized practice committee of the state bars, Bar Rule D.0203.
Investment adviser, §78C-2.

DEFINED TERMS —Cont'd

Investment adviser covered under federal law, §78C-2.

Investment adviser representative, §78C-2.

Investment advisers act of 1940, §78C-2.

Investment company act of 1940.
Securities, §78A-2.

Investment company security, §25-8-103.

Investment interest.
Self-referrals by health care providers, §90-405.

Investment property.
Secured transactions, §25-9-102(a).

Investor.
Self-referrals by health care providers, §90-405.

Investor-owned drinking water corporation.
Water infrastructure, §159G-20.

Investor-owned public utility.
Air pollution control, §143-215.107D(a).
Environmental compliance costs, §62-133.6(a).

Invitation to bid.
Motion pictures, §75C-2.

Invited.
State government ethics act, §138A-32(e).

Involuntary servitude.
Human trafficking, §14-43.10(a).

Ionizing radiation.
Radiation protection, §104E-5.

Irrigation construction or contracting, §89G-1.

Irrigation contractor, §89G-1.

Irrigation system, §89G-1.

Isolation.
Discipline of students.
Seclusion and restraint, §115C-391.1(b).

Isolation authority.
Public health, §130A-2.

Isomer.
Controlled substances, §90-87.

Is regarded as having an impairment.
Persons with disabilities protection, §168A-3.

Issue.
Negotiable instruments, §25-3-105.
Occupational safety and health, §95-127.

Issued.
Criminal process and procedure.
Electronic technology, §15A-101.1.

Issuer.
Criminal law, §14-113.8.
Letters of credit, §25-5-102(a).
Negotiable instruments, §25-3-105.
Public obligations, §159E-2.
Securities, §78A-2.
UCC, §25-7-102(a).

Issuer's jurisdiction.
Investment securities, §25-8-110.

Issuing court.
Child custody jurisdiction and enforcement, §50A-102.

Issuing state.
Child custody jurisdiction and enforcement, §50A-102.
Interstate family support, §52C-1-101.
Interstate wildlife violator compact, §113-300.6.

Issuing tribunals.
Interstate family support, §52C-1-101.

Issuing unit.
Local government finance, §159-160.

Item.
Banking, §25-4-104(a).
Telephonic sellers, §66-260.

ITIN contractor.
Tax withholding, §105-163.1.

DEFINED TERMS —Cont'd

Itinerant merchant, §66-250.

Itinerant vendor.
Bedding, §106-65.95.

ITIN holder.
Tax withholding, §105-163.1.

IV-D case child support, §110-129.

J bar, T bar or platter pull.
Passenger tramway safety, §95-117.

Jeopardized.
Trust companies, §53-301(a).

Jet fuel.
Gasoline and oil inspection, §119-15.
Gasoline tax, §105-449.60.

Jobber, §106-541.

Job listing service, §95-47.19.

Job order.
Private personnel services, §95-47.1.

Job performance.
Employer disclosing information, §1-539.12(b).

Joint accident and health coverage.
Credit insurance, §58-57-5.

Joint agency.
Cities providing communications services, §160A-340.
Electric power, §159B-3.

Joint fishing waters.
Conservation, §113-129.

Joint life coverage.
Credit insurance, §58-57-5.

Joint municipal assistance agency.
Electric power, §159B-3.

Joint ordinance.
High Rock lake marine commission, §77-50.
Lake Wylie marine commission, §77-30.

Joint resolution.
Mountain Island lake marine commission, §77-70.

Journalist.
Journalist's qualified privilege, §8-53.11(a).

Judge.
Abused, neglected and dependent juveniles, §7B-101.
Boxing commission, §143-651.
Civil procedure, §1A-1 Rule 30.
Condemnation, §136-115.
Delinquent and undisciplined juveniles, §7B-1501.
Depositions upon oral examinations, §1A-1 Rule 30(h).
Division of juvenile justice, §143B-805.
Electronic surveillance, §15A-286.
Eminent domain, §40A-2.
Judicial standards commission, §7A-374.2.
Retirement, §135-53.

Judge of the court of appeals.
Judicial department, §7A-39.1(a).

Judgment.
Civil procedure, §1A-1 Rule 54.
Motor vehicles, §20-279.1.

Judgment book.
Civil procedure, §1-208.1.

Judgment creditor.
Judgments, §1C-1702.

Judgment debtor.
Judgments, §1C-1702.

Judgment docket.
Civil procedure, §1-208.1.

Judicial district.
Abused, neglected and dependent juveniles, §7B-101.
Attorneys at law, §84-19.
Delinquent and undisciplined juveniles, §7B-1501.

DEFINED TERMS —Cont'd
Judicial district —Cont'd
Division of juvenile justice, §143B-805.
Judicial employee.
State government ethics act, §138A-3.
Judicial officer.
State government ethics act, §138A-3.
Judicial official.
Criminal procedure, §15A-101.
Motor vehicles, §20-16.5(a).
Provisional license revocation, §20-13.3(a).
Judicial review panel.
Electronic surveillance, §15A-286.
Judicial sale.
Civil procedure, §1-339.1(a).
Judiciary.
False claims act, §1-606.
Junior high school, §115C-75(a).
Junk.
Yard control, §136-143.
Junked motor vehicle, §153A-132(b).
Removal and disposal, §160A-303(b2).
Junk vehicle, §20-4.01.
Junkyard, §136-143.
Jurat.
Notaries public act, §10B-3.
Jurisdiction.
Motor vehicles, §20-4.2.
Psychology practice act, §90-270.2.
Uniform trust code, §36C-1-103.
Jurisdictional waters.
Ecosystem enhancement program, §143-214.11(a).
Jurisdiction of organization.
Secured transactions, §25-9-102(a).
Juror.
Obstructing justice, §14-225.2.
Justice officer.
Sheriffs' education, §17E-2.
Justice of the supreme court.
Judicial department, §7A-39.1(a).
Juvenile.
Abused, neglected and dependent juveniles,
§7B-101.
Delinquent and undisciplined juveniles, §7B-1501.
Division of juvenile justice, §143B-805.
Interstate compact for juveniles, §7B-4001.
Juvenile court.
Delinquent and undisciplined juveniles, §7B-1501.
Division of juvenile justice, §143B-805.
Juvenile court counselor.
Delinquent and undisciplined juveniles, §7B-1501.
Division of juvenile justice, §143B-805.
Keeper.
Disorderly houses, §14-188.
Keg.
Alcoholic beverages, §18B-101.
Kerosene.
Gasoline and oil inspection, §119-15.
Gasoline tax, §105-449.60.
Kerosene distributor.
Gasoline and oil inspection, §119-15.
Kerosene supplier.
Gasoline and oil inspection, §119-15.
Key facilities.
Coastal area management, §113A-103.
Land policy act, §113A-152.
Key shareholder.
Money transmitters, §53-208.2(a).
Kickboxer, §143-651.
Kickboxing match, §143-651.

DEFINED TERMS —Cont'd
Kidnapping.
Criminal law, §14-39.
Kidney disease treatment centers.
Certificate of need, §131E-176.
Killed in the line of duty.
Death benefits, §143-166.2(c).
Kind.
Seed law, §106-277.2.
Kind of insurance.
Unauthorized insurers, §58-28-12.
Kinds of actions.
Civil procedure, §1-4.
Know.
Anatomical gifts, §130A-412.4.
Knowing.
False claims act, §1-606.
Knowingly.
False claims act, §1-606.
Life insurance.
Dishonest and predatory sales to military
personnel, §58-58-335.
Medical assistance provider false claims act,
§108A-70.11.
Rules of professional conduct, ProfCond Rule 1.0.
Unemployment compensation, §96-8.
Knowingly and willfully.
Public health generally, §130A-26.1(d).
Underground petroleum storage tank leak
cleanup, §143-215.94X(b).
Knowledge.
Arbitration, §1-569.1.
Public morals, §19-1.1.
UCC, §25-1-202(b).
Knowledge of the minor's age.
Public morals, §19-12.
Knowledge of the nature of the material.
Public morals, §19-12.
Knows.
UCC, §25-1-202(b).
Label.
Antifreeze law, §106-579.3.
Commercial feed law, §106-284.33.
Food, drugs and cosmetics, §106-121.
Meat inspection, §106-549.15.
Pesticide board, §143-460.
Pharmacy practice, §90-85.3(j).
Poultry products inspection, §106-549.51.
Soil additives act, §106-50.30.
Structural pest control act, §106-65.24.
Toxic or hazardous substance identification,
§95-174(n).
Uniform standards for manufactured homes act,
§143-145.
Labeling.
Antifreeze law, §106-579.3.
Commercial feed law, §106-284.33.
Food, drugs and cosmetics, §106-121.
Meat inspection, §106-549.15.
Pesticide board, §143-460.
Pharmacy practice, §90-85.3(k).
Poultry products inspection, §106-549.51.
Seed law, §106-277.2.
Soil additives act, §106-50.30.
Structural pest control act, §106-65.24.
Labor organization.
Payment or benefits, §95-101.
Persons with disabilities protection, §168A-3.
Labor or materials.
Bonds, §44A-25.

DEFINED TERMS —Cont'd

Labor union.
Political campaigns, §163-278.6.

Lacks the capacity to consent.
Protection of disabled adults, §108A-101.

Lagoon.
Animal waste management, §143-215.10I(a).
Swine farms, §106-802.

Lake Lure.
Lake lure marine commission, §77-80.

Lake Wylie.
Lake Wylie marine commission, §77-30.

Land.
Clean water management trust fund, §113A-252.
Liability of landowners associated with watershed
improvement projects, §139-41.3.
Mining, §§74-49, 74-76.
Pesticide board, §143-460.
Property taxes, §105-273.
Public utilities, §62-100.
Recreational trespass, §38A-2.
Recreation and natural heritage, §113-77.6.
State lands, §146-64.

Land adjoining.
Mining permits, §74-50(b).

Land and loan associations, §54-45.

Land-clearing debris.
Solid waste management, §130A-290(a).

Land development regulations.
Development agreements, §160A-400.21.
Counties, §153A-349.2.
Wireless telecommunications facilities,
§§153A-349.51, 160A-400.51.

Land-disturbing activity.
Pollution control act, §113A-52.
Vehicle surface areas, §113A-70(b).

Landfill.
Solid waste management, §130A-290(a).

Landholder.
Conservation, §113-130.

Landlord, §42-40.
Expedited evictions, §42-59.

Land occupier.
Soil and water conservation districts, §139-3.

Landowner.
City and town zoning, §160A-385.1(b).
Counties, §153A-344.1.
Satisfaction of deeds of trust and mortgages,
§45-36.4.
Soil and water conservation districts, §139-3.

Landscape architect, §89A-1.

Landscape architecture, §89A-1.

Landscape contractor, §89D-2.

Landscaping.
Condominiums, §47C-3-122.
Planned community act, §47F-3-122.

Land surveyor intern, §89C-3.

Large community water system.
Water resources, §143-350.

Large constricting snakes, §14-417.1.

Large employer.
Health insurance portability and accountability,
§58-68-25(a).

Large group market.
Health insurance portability and accountability,
§58-68-25(a).

Large investment.
Tax incentives for new and expanding businesses,
§105-129.2.

Larger systems.
Marriage and family therapists, §90-270.47.

DEFINED TERMS —Cont'd

Large-scale.
Certification of property mappers, §147-54.4.

Large vessel marina.
Clean coastal water and vessel act, §77-125.

Laser.
Criminal use of laser device, §14-34.8(a).
Pointing laser devices at aircraft, §14-280.2(b).

Laser hair practitioner, §88A-3.

Laser, light source or pulsed-light devices.
Electrologists, §88A-3.

Laser, light source or pulsed-light treatments.
Electrologists, §88A-3.

Last known address.
Storage facilities, §44A-40.

Late enrollee.
Health insurance portability and accountability,
§58-68-30(b).
Small employer group health coverage,
§58-50-110.

Law.
Egg law, §106-245.14.
Electric membership corporations, §117-7.
Interstate family support, §52C-1-101.

Law enforcement agency.
Assistance by out-of-state law enforcement
officers, §160A-288.3(b).
Crime victims' rights, §15A-830(a).

Law enforcement agency animal.
Assaulting law enforcement or assistance animals,
§14-163.1(a).

Law enforcement officers.
Civil disorders, §14-288.1.
Claims against the state, §143-299.1A(d).
Collection of statistics on use of deadly force,
§114-10.02(b).
Collection of traffic law enforcement statistics,
§114-10.01(b).
Dealing in regulated metals property, §66-11(a).
Death benefits, §143-166.2(d).
Defensive force to protect home, workplace, motor
vehicle, §14-51.2(a).
Discipline of students.
Seclusion and restraint, §115C-391.1(b).
Littering, §14-399(i).
Local government retirement, §143-166.50(a).
Mental health, §122C-3.
Retirement, §128-21.
Solicitation of contributions, §131F-2.
State retirement, §143-166.30(a).
State retirement system, §135-1.
Tuition and fee waivers, §115B-1.

Law-enforcement officers' retirement system,
§143-166.30(a).
Local government, §143-166.50(a).

Law enforcement official.
Volunteer architect during an emergency or
disaster, §83A-13.1(d).
Volunteer engineer during emergency or disaster,
§89C-19.1(d).

Law practice assistance program.
Continuing legal education, Bar Rule D.1501.

Law-related services.
Rules of professional conduct, ProfCond Rule 5.7.

Laws.
Development agreements, §160A-400.21.
Counties, §153A-349.2.
Fraternal benefit societies, §58-24-15(e).

Layaway contract.
Sales, §25-2-106.

DEFINED TERMS —Cont'd
Lead agency.
Relocation assistance, §133-7.
Lead-based paint hazard, §130A-131.7.
Lead poisoning hazard, §130A-131.7.
Lead regional organizations.
Coastal area management, §113A-103.
Lead-safe housing, §130A-131.7.
Lead teacher.
Child care facility, §110-86.
Learn.
UCC, §25-1-202(c).
Lease.
Credit insurance, §58-57-5.
Criminal law, §14-168.2.
Leases, UCC, §25-2A-103(1).
Sales and use tax, §105-164.3.
Sublease of motor vehicle and loan assumption
arranging, §20-106.2(a).
Lease agreement.
Leases, UCC, §25-2A-103(1).
Option to purchase contracts executed with
residential lease agreements, §47G-1.
Lease contract.
Leases, UCC, §25-2A-103(1).
Leased residential premises.
Expedited evictions, §42-59.
Leasehold condominium, §47C-1-103.
Leasehold interest.
Leases, UCC, §25-2A-103(1).
Leasehold planned community, §47F-1-103.
Lease-purchase agreement.
Lease or purchase of prison facilities constructed
by private firm, §148-37.2(b).
Least restrictive environment.
Education of children with disabilities,
§115C-106.3.
Legal action.
Legal expense funds for elected officials,
§163-278.300.
Legal aid clinic.
Rules governing practical training of law
students, Bar Rule C.0202.
Legal assistance.
Domestic violence victim assistance act,
§7A-474.17.
Judicial department, §7A-474.2.
Legal custodian.
Assignment of student to particular school,
§115C-366(h).
Legal custody.
Adoption, §48-1-101.
Legal disability.
Compensation of trustees and other fiduciaries,
§32-53.
Principal and income act, §37A-1-104.1.
Legal entity.
Liability of landowners associated with watershed
improvement projects, §139-41.3.
Legal expense donation.
Legal expense funds for elected officials,
§163-278.300.
Legal expense fund.
Legal expense funds for elected officials,
§163-278.300.
Legal intern.
Rules governing legal services provided by
students, Bar Rule C.0202.
Legally responsible person.
Mental health, §122C-3.

DEFINED TERMS —Cont'd
Legal possessor.
Liens on personal property, §44A-1.
Legal proceeding.
Journalist's qualified privilege, §8-53.11(a).
Trial preparation materials, access to, §132-1.9(h).
Legal representation.
Funeral and burial trust funds, §90-210.60.
Legal representative.
Custodial trusts, §33B-1.
Transfers to minors, §33A-1.
Legal residence.
Higher education tuition and fees, §116-143.1.
Legal resident.
Veterans cemeteries, §65-43.
Legal services corporation.
Rules governing legal services provided by
students, Bar Rule C.0202.
Legislative action.
Lobbying, §120C-100(a).
State government ethics act, §138A-3.
Legislative commission.
Confidential communications, §120-129.
Legislative day.
Rulemaking procedure, §150B-21.3(d).
Legislative employee.
Confidential legislative communications, §120-129.
Lobbying, §120C-100(a).
State government ethics act, §138A-3.
Legislative officer.
Endangering officers, §14-16.10.
Legislator.
Confidential communications, §120-129.
Legislative ethics, §120-85.1.
Lobbying, §120C-100(a).
State government ethics act, §138A-3.
Lender.
Good funds settlement act, §45A-3.
Reverse mortgages, §53-257.
Lender is obligated, §45-81.
Lending institution.
Agricultural finance act, §122D-3.
Lessee.
Condominiums, §47C-1-103.
Criminal law, §14-395.1.
Leases, UCC, §25-2A-103(1).
Motor vehicles, §20-341.
Planned community act, §47F-1-103.
Sublease of motor vehicle and loan assumption
arranging, §20-106.2(a).
Lessee in ordinary course of business.
Leases, UCC, §25-2A-103(1).
Lessee in the ordinary course of business.
UCC, §25-7-102(b).
Lessor.
Leases, UCC, §25-2A-103(1).
Motor vehicles, §20-341.
Sublease of motor vehicle and loan assumption
arranging, §20-106.2(a).
Lessor's residual interest.
Leases, UCC, §25-2A-103(1).
Letter of authority.
Decedents' estates, safe deposit boxes,
§28A-15-13(a).
Letter of caution.
Discipline and disability rules of state bar, Bar
Rule B.0103.
Judicial standards commission, §7A-374.2.
Procedures for the authorized practice committee
of the state bars, Bar Rule D.0203.

DEFINED TERMS —Cont'd
Letter-of-credit right.
Secured transactions, §25-9-102(a).
Letter of notice.
Discipline and disability rules of state bar, Bar
Rule B.0103.
Procedures for the authorized practice committee
of the state bars, Bar Rule D.0203.
Letter of warning.
Discipline and disability rules of state bar, Bar
Rule B.0103.
Letters of credit, §25-5-102(a).
Lever machine voting system, §163-165.4A(a1).
Lewd matter.
Public morals, §19-1.1.
Lewdness.
Public morals, §19-1.1.
Liabilities, debts and obligations.
Limited liability companies, §57C-1-03.
Liability.
Business corporations, §55-8-50(b).
Insurers supervision, §58-30-10.
Medical service corporations, §58-65-166(b).
Risk retention, §58-22-10.
Liaison personnel.
Lobbying, §120C-100(a).
Library.
Records, §125-18.
Library agreement.
Interstate library compact, §125-12.
Library materials.
Counties, §153A-262.
Library record, §125-18.
Licensable facility.
Mental health, §122C-3.
License.
Administrative procedure, §150B-2.
Alcohol taxation, §105-113.68.
Architects, §83A-1.
Athletic trainers, §90-523.
Banking, §53-165(g).
Child care facility, §110-86.
Child support, §110-142.
Dental hygiene, §90-221(c).
Electronic filing.
Insurance licensees or applicants for licenses,
§58-2-250(a).
Geologist, §89E-3.
Insurance companies.
Notifications to insurance commissioner,
§58-2-69(a).
Insurance customer information safeguards,
§58-39-140.
Insurance producer, §58-33-10.
Interpreters and transliterators licensure act,
§90D-3.
Interstate wildlife violator compact, §113-300.6.
Locksmith licensing, §74F-4.
Manufactured housing, §143-143.9.
Motor vehicles, §20-4.01.
Nursing, §90-171.20.
Occupational boards, §93B-1.
Pharmacy practice, §90-85.3(l).
Physicians and surgeons, §90-1.1.
Real estate appraisers, §93E-1-4.
Reciprocal insurance, §58-15-5.
Respiratory care practices act, §90-648.
Soil scientists, §89F-3.
Speech and language pathologists and
audiologists, §90-293.
Trust companies, §53-301(a).

DEFINED TERMS —Cont'd
License agreement.
Motion pictures, §75C-2.
Licensed clinical addictions specialist.
Substance abuse professionals, §90-113.31A.
Licensed clinical social workers, §90B-3.
Licensed dealer.
Soliciting unlawful purchase of firearm,
§14-408.1(a).
Licensed dietitian/nutritionist, §90-352.
Licensed distributor.
Tobacco taxation, §105-113.4.
Licensed facility.
Assignment of student to particular school,
§115C-366(h).
Licensed geologist, §89E-3.
Licensed insurer.
Motor vehicle service agreement companies,
§66-370(b).
Licensed marriage and family therapist,
§90-270.47.
Licensed physician.
Polysomnography practice act, §90-721.
Licensed professional counselor, §90-330(a).
Licensed professional counselor associate,
§90-330(a).
Licensed professional counselor supervisor,
§90-330(a).
Licensed psychological associate, §90-270.2.
Licensed psychologist, §90-270.2.
Licensed recreational therapist, §90C-22.
Licensed recreational therapy assistant,
§90C-22.
Licensed residential real estate appraiser,
§93E-1-4.
Licensed soil scientist, §89F-3.
Licensed veterinarian, §90-181.
Licensee.
Banking, §53-165(h).
Boxing commission, §143-651.
Check-cashing service, §53-275.
Child support, §110-142.
Electronic filing.
Insurance licensees or applicants for licenses,
§58-2-250(a).
Insurance companies.
Notifications to insurance commissioner,
§58-2-69(a).
Manufactured housing, §143-143.9.
Money transmitters, §53-208.2(a).
Mortgage bankers, brokers and servicers,
§53-244.030.
Motor clubs and associations, §58-69-2.
Nurse licensure compact, §90-171.82.
Perfusionists, §90-682.
Private personnel services, §95-47.1.
Professional corporation, §55B-2.
Professional employer organizations, §58-89A-5.
Real estate appraisers, §93E-1-4.
Regulations for professional corporations and
professional limited liability companies
practicing law, Bar Rule E.0101.
Respiratory care practices act, §90-648.
Structural pest control act, §106-65.24.
Licensee in ordinary course of business.
Secured transactions priority of security interests,
§25-9-321(a).
License exempt organization.
Lotteries and gaming, §14-309.6.
License year.
Coastal and estuarine commercial fishing licenses,
§113-168.

DEFINED TERMS —Cont'd
Licensing.
Administrative procedure, §150B-2.
Licensing agency.
Forfeiture of licensing privilege after conviction of felony, §15A-1331A.
Licensing authority.
Interstate wildlife violator compact, §113-300.6.
Licensing board.
Forfeiture of licensing privilege for non-payment of child support, §50-13.12(a).
Nurse licensure compact, §90-171.82.
Professional corporations, §55B-2.
Licensing privilege.
Forfeiture after conviction of felony, §15A-1331A.
Forfeiture of licensing privilege for non-payment of child support, §50-13.12(a).
Licensure student.
Scholarship funds provided private colleges and universities, §116-22.
Lien.
Fraudulent transfers, §39-23.1.
Leases, UCC, §25-2A-103(1).
Motor vehicle titling, §20-58.8(c).
Lien claimant.
Commercial real estate broker lien act, §44A-24.2.
Lien creditor.
Secured transactions, §25-9-102(a).
Lienholder.
Impaired driving, §20-28.2(a1).
Lienor.
Personal property, §44A-1.
Storage facilities, §44A-40.
Life care.
Health facilities finance, §131A-3.
Life-cycle cost analysis.
Energy policy and life-cycle cost analysis for state government, §143-64.11.
Life insurance.
Dishonest and predatory sales to military personnel, §58-58-335.
Insurance information and privacy protection act, §58-39-15.
Life insurance cost indexes.
Life insurance solicitation, §58-60-10.
Life insurance surrender cost index.
Life insurance solicitation, §58-60-10.
Life insurer, §58-12-2.
Life-prolonging measures.
Power of attorney, §32A-16.
Life-sustaining procedures.
Consent to health care for minor, §32A-29.
Light-traffic roads.
Motor vehicles, §20-118.
Limited common areas and facilities.
Unit ownership, §47A-3.
Limited common element.
Condominiums, §47C-1-103.
Planned community act, §47F-1-103.
Limited contributee.
Limitation on fundraising during legislative session, §163-278.13B(a).
Limited contributor.
Limitation on fundraising during legislative session, §163-278.13B(a).
Limited driving privilege, §20-179.3(a).
Driving with revoked license, §20-20.1(a).
Limited food services establishment.
Sanitation, §130A-247.
Limited liability company, §57C-1-03.
Corporate income taxation, §105-130.2.

DEFINED TERMS —Cont'd
Limited liability company —Cont'd
Individual income taxation, §105-134.1.
Limited liability limited partnership.
Limited partnerships, §59-102.
Limited license.
Rental car companies selling insurance, §58-33-17(a).
Limited licensee.
Self service storage renter's insurance, §58-33-18(a).
Limited line credit insurance.
Insurance producer, §58-33-10.
Limited line credit insurance producer, §58-33-10.
Limited lines insurance.
Insurance producers, §58-33-10.
Limited lines producer.
Insurance producers, §58-33-10.
Limited obligation bond.
Capital facilities finance act, §142-82.
Limited partnership.
Limited liability company, §57C-1-03.
Limited representative.
Licensing, §58-33-10.
Limited service facility.
Banking, §53-1.
Limited veterinary license, §90-181.
Line.
Public utilities, §§62-100, 62-110.2.
Urban electrical service, §160A-331.
Lineal decedents.
Decedents' estates, §29-2.
Elective share of surviving spouse, §30-3.2.
Lineal descendant of a deceased adoptee.
Adoption, §48-1-101.
Linear accelerator.
Certificate of need, §131E-176.
Lineor.
Aircraft labor and storage liens, §44A-50.
Lineup.
Eyewitness identification reform, §15A-284.52(a).
Lineup administrator.
Eyewitness identification reform, §15A-284.52(a).
Liquefied petroleum gas, §119-54(a).
Liquidating asset.
Principal and income act, §37A-4-410(a).
Liquidity fund.
Savings and loan associations, §54B-4.
Liquor.
Alcoholic beverages, §18B-101.
List.
Property taxes, §105-273.
Listed.
Dispensing equipment standards for ethanol blends, §143-143.6(a).
Listed qualified individual.
Electrical contractors, §87-41.1.
Listing.
Property taxes, §105-273.
Literary purpose.
Property tax exemption, §105-278.7(f).
Taxation, §105-278.3(d).
Lithotriptor.
Certificate of need, §131E-176.
Litter, §14-399(i).
Live lineup.
Eyewitness identification reform, §15A-284.52(a).
Live poultry or ratite dealer, §106-541.
Live sporting event.
Tax credit for qualifying expenses of production company, §§105-130.47(a), 105-151.29(a).

DEFINED TERMS —Cont'd
Livestock, §68-15.
  Dealer licensing, §106-418.8.
  Livestock brands, §80-58.
Livestock dealer.
  Licensing, §106-418.8.
Living unit.
  Continuing care retirement communities,
    §58-64-1.
Llama.
  Classification as livestock, §106-22.4.
Loan, §66-106.
  Loans exempt from rate and fee limitations,
    §24-9(a).
  Reverse mortgages, §53-257.
  Solid waste, §159I-3(a).
  Water infrastructure, §159G-20.
Loanable assets.
  Banking, §53-165(i).
Loan agreement.
  Solid waste, §159I-3(a).
Loan amount.
  Loans exempt from rate and fee limitations,
    §24-9(a).
Loan broker, §66-106.
Loan closing.
  Good funds settlement act, §45A-3.
Loan documents.
  Good funds settlement act, §45A-3.
Loan funds.
  Good funds settlement act, §45A-3.
  Petroleum cleanup, §143-215.94A.
Loan of credit.
  State debt, NC Const Art V §§3, 4.
Loan processor or underwriter.
  Mortgage bankers, brokers and servicers,
    §53-244.030.
Loan production office.
  Savings banks, §54C-4(b).
Loan-related goods, products and services.
  Interest rates, §24-8(d).
Lobbying, §120C-100(a).
  State government ethics act, §138A-3.
Lobbyist, §120C-100(a).
Lobbyist's principal.
  Lobbying, §120C-100(a).
Local act.
  Cities and towns, §160A-1.
  Counties, §153A-1.
Local agency.
  Debt collection, §105A-2.
Local authorities.
  Motor vehicles, §20-4.01.
Local board, §115C-5.
  Alcoholic beverages, §18B-101.
Local board of education.
  Cooperative innovative high school programs,
    §115C-238.50A.
Local board of health.
  Public health generally, §130A-2.
Local board of trustees.
  Cooperative innovative high school programs,
    §115C-238.50A.
Local confinement facility.
  Counties, §153A-217.
Local consumer advocacy program.
  MH/DD/SA consumer advocacy program,
    §122C-11.
Local consumer advocate.
  MH/DD/SA consumer advocacy program,
    §122C-11.

DEFINED TERMS —Cont'd
Local distribution company.
  Piped natural gas tax, §105-187.40.
Local educational agency.
  Education of children with disabilities,
    §115C-106.3.
Local exchange carrier.
  911 system, §62A-40.
Local exchange company.
  Alternative regulation, tariffing and deregulation
    of telecommunications utilities, §62-133.5(h).
  Certificates of public convenience and necessity,
    §62-110(f6).
  Public utilities, §62-3.
Local fire chief.
  Fire departments, criminal history record checks,
    §114-19.12(g).
Local food.
  Sustainable local food advisory council,
    §106-830(b).
Local funds.
  Mental health, §122C-3.
Local governing body.
  Dedication of property to nature and historic
    preserve, §143-260.8(a).
Local government.
  Brownfields property reuse act, §130A-310.31(b).
  Certification of property mappers, §147-54.4.
  Coastal area management, §113A-103.
  Cooperative state-local coalition water quality
    protection plans, §143-214.14(a).
  Dedication of property to nature and historic
    preserves, §143-260.8(a).
  Development agreements, §160A-400.21.
    Counties, §153A-349.2.
  Dry-cleaning solvent cleanup act,
    §143-215.104B(b).
  Falls Lake watershed association, §77-140.
  Floodplain regulations, §143-215.52(a).
  Land policy act, §113A-152.
  Local sales and use tax, §105-521(a).
  Pollution control act, §113A-52.
  Risk pools, §58-23-1.
  Smoking in public buildings, §130A-492.
  Smoking in public places, §143-596.
**Local governmental employees' retirement
  system.**
  Law enforcement, §143-166.50(a).
Local governmental entities.
  Office of information technology services,
    §147-33.82(b).
Local governmental unit.
  Energy loan fund, §143B-437.16(f).
  Guaranteed energy savings contracts, §143-64.17.
Local government building.
  Smoking in public buildings, §130A-492.
Local government commission.
  Global TransPark authority, §63A-2.
  Solid waste, §159I-3(a).
Local government unit.
  Clean water management trust fund, §113A-252.
  Water infrastructure, §159G-20.
Local government user.
  Criminal justice information network governing
    board, §143-660.
Local health department.
  Public health generally, §130A-2.
Local health director.
  Public health generally, §130A-2.
Local inspection department.
  Code officials qualification board, §143-151.8(a).

DEFINED TERMS —Cont'd
Local law enforcement agency.
  Lotteries and gaming, §14-309.6.
  Precious metals, §66-164.
  Unauthorized substances tax, §105-113.106.
Locally assigned rolling stock.
  Public service taxation, §105-333.
Local management entity or LME.
  Mental health, §122C-3.
Local partnership.
  Early childhood initiatives, §143B-168.11.
Local planning board.
  Development agreements.
    Counties, §153A-349.2.
Local sales tax share.
  Local sales and use tax, §105-521(a).
Local school administrative unit.
  Education, §115C-5.
Local service provider.
  Telecommunications relay service, §62-157(a1).
Local tax district.
  Organization of schools, §115C-69.
Local tax official.
  Property taxes, §105-273.
Local team.
  Child fatality prevention system, §7B-1401.
Local vehicle.
  Smoking in state owned buildings and state
    vehicles, §130A-492.
Location.
  Portable consumer electronic devices insurance,
    §58-44A-1.
  Sewage systems, §130A-334.
Location of underground utilities.
  Contractors, §87-101.
Locksmith.
  Locksmith licensing, §74F-4.
Locksmith services.
  Locksmith licensing, §74F-4.
Locksmith tools.
  Locksmith licensing, §74F-4.
Locum tenens agencies.
  Health insurance, locum tenens contracts,
    §58-3-231(a).
Locum tenens physicians.
  Health insurance, locum tenens contracts,
    §58-3-231(a).
Lodge.
  Fraternal benefit societies, §58-24-15(h).
Lodging.
  Continuing care retirement communities,
    §58-64-1.
Lodging establishment.
  Smoking in restaurants or bars, §130A-492.
Long term care facility.
  Ombudsman program, §143B-181.16.
  Smoking prohibited within, §§131D-4.4(b),
    131E-114.3(a).
  Temporary management, §131E-231.
Long-term care hospital.
  Certificate of need, §131E-176.
Long-term care insurance, §58-55-20.
Long-term lease or rental.
  Highway use tax, §105-187.1.
  Regional transit authority vehicle rental tax,
    §105-550.
Long-term suspension.
  Discipline of students, §115C-390.1(b).
Long-term unemployed worker.
  Growing businesses tax credits, §105-129.81.

DEFINED TERMS —Cont'd
Loss mitigation specialist.
  Mortgage bankers, brokers and servicers,
    §53-244.030.
Loss trending.
  Insurance rates, §58-36-100(b).
Lot owner.
  Planned community act, §47F-1-103.
Lots.
  Egg law, §106-245.14.
  Leases, UCC, §25-2A-103(1).
  Planned community act, §47F-1-103.
  Sales, §25-2-105.
  Seed law, §106-277.2.
Lottery.
  State lottery, §18C-103.
Lottery contractor.
  State lottery, §18C-103.
Lottery game.
  State lottery, §18C-103.
Lottery game retailer.
  State lottery, §18C-103.
Lottery law.
  Alcoholic beverages, §18B-101.
Lottery potential contractor.
  State lottery, §18C-103.
Lottery retailer.
  State lottery, §18C-103.
Lottery supplier.
  State lottery, §18C-103.
Low dose screening mammography.
  Accident and health insurance, §58-51-57(a1).
  Health maintenance organizations, §58-67-76(b).
  Hospital, medical and dental services
    corporations, §58-65-92(b).
Lowest floor.
  Floodplain regulations, §143-215.52(a).
Low-income person.
  Spay/neuter account, §19A-63(b).
Low-income residents.
  Water infrastructure, §159G-23.
Low-level radioactive waste.
  Radiation protection, §104E-5.
Low-speed vehicle, §20-4.01.
Low-street value drug.
  Unauthorized substances taxes, §105-113.106.
Lubricating oil.
  Regulation of rerefined or reprocessed oil,
    §119-13.1.
Machine guns, §14-409(a).
Machinery and equipment.
  Tax incentives for new and expanding businesses,
    §105-129.2.
  Tax incentives for recycling facilities, §105-129.25.
Made.
  Limitation on fundraising during legislative
    session, §163-278.13B(a).
Magnetic resonance imaging scanner.
  Certificate of need, §131E-176.
Mailed.
  Business corporations, §55-1-40.
Mail order sale.
  Sales and use tax, §105-164.3.
Main permanent campus.
  Need-based scholarships for students attending
    private colleges and universities, §116-280.
  Scholarship funds provided private colleges and
    universities, §116-22.
  State grants to students attending private
    universities or colleges, §116-43.5(a).

DEFINED TERMS —Cont'd

Main street center.
Main street solutions fund, §143B-472.35(a2).

Main street organization.
Main street solutions fund, §143B-472.35(a2).

Main street program.
Main street solutions fund, §143B-472.35(a2).

Maintain.
Forest development act, §106-1012.

Maintenance.
Sewage systems, §130A-334.
Solicitation of contributions, §131F-2.
Weights and measures, §81A-9.

Maintenance fee.
Gift cards, §66-67.5(c).

Maintenance standard.
Lead poisoning in children, §130A-131.7.

Major accident.
Safe driver incentive program, §58-36-75(a).

Major development project.
Environmental policy act, §113A-9.

Major economic dislocation.
Industrial development fund, §143B-437.01(a),
   (a1).

Major facility construction project.
Performance standards for sustainable,
   energy-efficient public buildings, §143-135.36.

Major facility renovation project.
Performance standards for sustainable,
   energy-efficient public buildings, §143-135.36.

Major hypothecation loan.
Membership camping, §66-246(a).

Majority.
Unit ownership, §47A-3.

Majority of unit owners, §47A-3.

Major life activities.
Persons with disabilities protection, §168A-3.

Major medical equipment.
Certificate of need, §131E-176.

Major recycling facility.
Sales and use tax, §105-164.3.
Tax incentives for recycling facilities, §105-129.25.

Make a residential mortgage loan.
Mortgage bankers, brokers and servicers,
   §53-244.030.

Maker.
Negotiable instruments, §25-3-103.

Malice.
Punitive damages, §1D-5.

Maliciously.
Cruelty to animals, §§14-360(c), 14-362.3.

Malt beverage.
Alcoholic beverages, §18B-101.
Alcohol taxation, §105-113.68.

Managed care entity.
Health care liability, §90-21.50.

Managed care organization.
Industrial commission, ICManagedCare Rule II.
Workers' compensation, §97-2.

Managed care plan.
Utilization review, §58-50-61(a).

Managed services.
Professional employer organizations, §58-89A-5.

Management.
Asbestos hazards, §130A-444.
Workers' compensation self insurance, §97-165.

Management contract.
Managing general insurance agents, §58-34-2(a).

Management functions.
Executive reorganization act of 1971, §143A-6(c).

DEFINED TERMS —Cont'd

Management of the affairs.
Limited liability companies, §57C-1-03.

Manager.
Boxing commission, §143-651.
County managers, §153A-81.
Limited liability companies, §57C-1-03.
Private personnel services, §95-47.1.
Reinsurance intermediaries, §58-9-2(a).

Managing agent.
Lead poisoning in children, §130A-131.7.
Time shares, §93A-41.

Managing general agent, §58-34-2(a).

Mandatory business case, §7A-45.4.

Mandatory control level event.
Risk based capital requirements, insurance
   companies, §58-12-25(a).

Mandatory control level risk-based capital.
Insurance companies, §58-12-2.

Mandatory income.
Principal and income act, §37A-1-102.

Manicuring, §88B-2.

Manicurist, §88B-2.

Manicurist teacher, §88B-2.

Manifest.
Solid waste management, §130A-290(a).

Manipulated manures.
Commercial fertilizer, §106-657.

Manipulative key.
Preparation to commit breaking or entering into
   motor vehicle, §14-56.4(a).

Manlift.
Elevator safety, §95-110.3(h).

Manufacture.
Bedding, §106-65.95.
Commercial feed law, §106-284.33.
Controlled substances, §90-87.
Salvia divinorum.
   Manufacture, sale, delivery, possession,
      §14-401.23(d).

Manufactured home.
Housing standards, §160A-442.
Management of abandoned manufactured homes,
   §130A-309.112.
Manufactured housing, §143-143.9.
Sales and use tax, §105-164.3.
Secured transactions, §25-9-102(a).
Uniform standards for manufactured homes act,
   §143-145.

Manufactured home dealer.
Manufactured housing, §143-143.9.

Manufactured home manufacturer.
Manufactured housing, §143-143.9.

Manufactured home salesperson.
Manufactured housing, §143-143.9.

Manufactured home transaction.
Secured transactions, §25-9-102(a).

**Manufacture of an unlawful
   telecommunication device, §14-113.5.**

Manufacturer.
Commercial fertilizer, §106-657.
Discarded computer equipment management,
   §130A-309.91.
Fire-safety standard and firefighter protection act,
   §58-92-10.
Motor vehicles, §§20-4.01, 20-286.
Pesticide board, §143-460.
Pharmacy practice, §90-85.27.
Products liability, §99B-1.
Property taxes, §105-273.

DEFINED TERMS —Cont'd
Manufacturer —Cont'd
Registration of prescription drug manufacturer, §106-140.1(j).
Tobacco taxation, §105-113.4.
Wholesale prescription drug distributors, §106-145.2.
Manufacturer's certificate.
Motor vehicles, §20-4.01.
Manufacturing.
Growing businesses tax credits, §105-129.81.
Industrial development fund, §143B-437.01(a1).
Tax incentives for new and expanding businesses, §105-129.2.
Manufacturing facility.
Toxic or hazardous substance identification, §95-174(o).
Marginalized populations of Sudan.
Sudan (Darfur) divestment act, §147-86.42.
Marijuana.
Controlled substances, §90-87.
Unauthorized substances taxes, §105-113.106.
Marine and estuarine resources.
Conservation, §113-129.
Offshore oil and gas activities, §143-215.94B(b).
Marine fisheries commission.
Conservation, §113-128.
Marine fisheries inspector.
Conservation, §113-128.
Marine resources fund, §113-175.
Marine resources investment income.
Marine resources fund, §113-175.
Marine resources license revenue.
Marine resources fund, §113-175.
Marine sanitation device.
Clean coastal water and vessel act, §77-125.
Marine vessel.
Gasoline tax, §105-449.60.
Marital misconduct.
Alimony, §50-16.1A.
Marital property.
Divorce, §50-20(b).
Market.
Egg law, §106-245.14.
Pork promotion assessment, §106-792.
Market analysis.
Insurance commissioner, confidentiality of information, §58-2-240(b).
Market conduct action.
Insurance commissioner, confidentiality of information, §58-2-240(b).
Marketing of eggs.
Egg law, §106-245.14.
Market price.
Tax credit for gleaned crop, §105-130.37(b).
Market share.
Discarded computer equipment and television management, §130A-309.131.
Marriage and family therapy, §90-270.47.
Married individual.
Taxation, §105-134.1.
Mash.
Unauthorized substances taxes, §105-113.106.
Massage.
Adult establishments, §14-202.10.
Massage and bodywork therapist, §90-622.
Massage and bodywork therapy, §90-622.
Massage and bodywork therapy school, §90-622.
Massage business.
Adult establishments, §14-202.10.

DEFINED TERMS —Cont'd
Mass gathering, §130A-252(a).
Mass mailing.
Political campaigns, §163-278.6.
Mastectomy.
Accident and health insurance, §58-51-62(b).
Health maintenance organizations, §58-67-79(b).
Hospital, medical and dental service corporations, §58-65-96(b).
Postmastectomy inpatient care coverage, §58-3-168(c).
Master association.
Condominiums, §47C-1-103.
Planned community act, §47F-1-103.
Master key.
Preparation to commit breaking or entering into motor vehicle, §14-56.4(a).
Master settlement agreement.
Tobacco reserve fund, §66-290.
Tobacco trust fund commission, §143-716.
Match.
Boxing commission, §143-651.
Matchmaker.
Boxing commission, §143-651.
Material.
False claims act, §1-606.
Offenses against morality, §14-190.13.
Material litigation.
Money transmitters, §53-208.2(a).
Materially false information.
Soliciting unlawful purchase of firearm, §14-408.1(a).
Material safety data sheet.
Pesticide board, §143-460.
Toxic or hazardous substance identification, §95-174(p).
Matriculated status.
Education access rewards North Carolina scholars fund, §116-209.26(a).
Need-based scholarships for students attending private colleges and universities, §116-280.
Scholarships, §115C-499.1.
Matter.
Public morals, §19-1.1.
Mausoleum.
Cemeteries, §65-48.
Mausoleum section.
Cemeteries, §65-48.
Maximum contaminant level.
Drinking water, §130A-313.
Maximum imposed term.
Post-release supervision, §15A-1368(a).
Maximum qualifying contribution.
Public campaign fund, §163-278.62.
Voter-owned elections act, §163-278.96.
Mayor.
Cities and towns, §160A-1.
Civil disorders, §14-288.1.
Housing authorities, §157-3.
Public hospitals, §131E-16.
Veterans' recreation, §165-25.
McKinney-Vento homeless Education Assistance Improvements Act of 2001.
Assignment of student to particular school, §115C-366(h).
MCO.
Industrial commission managed care organizations, ICManagedCare Rule II.
Meal.
Weights and measures, §81A-9.

DEFINED TERMS —Cont'd

Meals tax.
Uniform penalties, §153A-154.1(b).

Means.
Business corporations, §55-1-40.
Nonprofit corporations, §55A-1-40.

Meat broker.
Meat inspection, §106-549.15.

Meat food product.
Meat inspection, §106-549.15.

Meat inspection, §106-549.15.

Mechanical restraint.
Discipline of students.
Seclusion and restraint, §115C-391.1(b).

Mediated settlement conference.
Administrative procedure, §150B-23.1(b).
Superior court civil actions, §7A-38.1(b).

Mediation.
Education of children with disabilities,
§115C-106.3.
Mediated settlement conferences, §7A-38.1(b).

Mediator.
Administrative procedure, §150B-23.1(b).
Education of children with disabilities,
§115C-106.3.
Farm nuisance dispute mediation, §7A-38.3(a).
Mediated settlement conferences, §7A-38.1(b).
Mediation of emergency or disaster property
insurance claims, §58-44-75.

Medicaid.
Long-term care partnerships, §§58-55-55,
108A-70.4(a).
Provider requirements for Medicaid or Health
Choice, §108C-2.

Medicaid equity payment.
Hospital provider assessments, §108A-121.

**Medicaid pooled trust, pooled trust or
umbrella pooled trust.**
Community third party trusts, pooled trusts act,
§36D-2.

Medical assistance.
Medicaid estate recovery plan, §108A-70.5(b).
Recovery from insurers providing additional
coverage to Medicaid-eligible persons,
§108A-55.4(a).

Medical assistance program.
Children's health insurance program,
§108A-70.18.
Medical assistance provider false claims act,
§108A-70.11.

Medical board.
Disability income plan, §135-101.
Judicial retirement, §135-53.
Legislative retirement system, §120-4.8.
Perfusionists, §90-682.
Retirement, §128-21.
State retirement system, §135-1.

Medical care.
Health insurance portability and accountability,
§58-68-25(a).
Health insurance risk pool, §58-50-175.

Medical-care institution.
Insurance information and privacy protection act,
§58-39-15.

Medical compensation.
Workers' compensation, §97-2.

Medical director.
Respiratory care practices act, §90-648.

Medical emergency.
Woman's right to know act, §90-21.81.

DEFINED TERMS —Cont'd

Medical equipment.
Pharmacy practice, §90-85.3(11).

Medical examiner.
Anatomical gifts, §130A-412.23(d).

Medical expense policy.
Narcotics and intoxicants, accident and health
insurance, §58-51-16(c).

Medically necessary services or supplies.
Accident and health insurance.
Utilization review, §58-50-61(a).

Medical malpractice action, §90-21.11.

Medical necessity or medically necessary.
State health plan for teachers and state
employees, §135-48.1.

Medical professional.
Insurance information and privacy protection act,
§58-39-15.

Medical-record information.
Insurance information and privacy protection act,
§58-39-15.

Medical records, §90-410.
Health statistics, §130A-372.
Medicolegal guidelines for attorney-physician
relationship, MLG Rule 3.

Medical rehabilitation.
Industrial commission utilization of rehabilitation
professionals, ICRehabProf Rule III.

Medical release.
Medical release of inmates, §15A-1369.

Medical release plan.
Medical release of inmates, §15A-1369.

Medical report.
Medicolegal guidelines for attorney-physician
relationship, MLG Rule 3.

Medical responder.
Emergency medical services, §131E-155.

Medical review committee, §90-21.22A(a).
Facility licensure act, §131E-101.
Hospital licensure, §131E-76.

Medical service plan, §58-65-1(a).

Medical waste.
Solid waste management, §130A-290(a).

Medical witness.
Medicolegal guidelines for attorney-physician
relationship, MLG Rule 3.

Medicare, §58-54-1.
Group health insurance, §58-53-1.
Health benefit plans.
Continuing care retirement community
residents, §58-3-200(f).

Medicare contract.
Provider sponsored organizations, §131E-276.

Medication-related error.
Nursing home medication management advisory
committee, §131E-128.1(a).

Medium to lower quality obligations.
Investment diversification, insurance companies,
§58-7-170(e).

Member.
Disability income plan, §135-101.
Discipline and disability rules of state bar, Bar
Rule B.0103.
Facility authorities, §160A-480.2.
Group health insurance, §58-53-1.
Insurance companies, conversion, §58-10-12(a).
Insurance rates, §58-40-5.
Interstate insurance product regulation compact,
§58-91-10.
Judicial retirement, §135-53.
Limited liability companies, §57C-1-03.

DEFINED TERMS —Cont'd
Member —Cont'd
Local government law-enforcement retirement, §143-166.50(a).
Marketing associations, §54-130.
Nonprofit corporations, §55A-1-40.
Retirement, §128-21.
Savings and loan associations, §54B-4.
Savings banks, §54C-4(b).
Self-insurance security association, §97-130.
State law-enforcement retirement, §143-166.30(a).
State retirement system, §135-1.
Taxation, §105-277.2.
Uniform unincorporated nonprofit association act, §59B-2.
Wildlife conservation land.
Special class of property for property tax purposes, §105-277.15(a).
Workers' compensation self-insurance.
Employer groups, §58-47-60.
Member bank, §53-61(a).
Member in service.
Legislative retirement system, §120-4.8.
Member insurer.
Insurance guaranty association, §§58-48-20, 58-62-16.
Member of his or her own family.
Barbers, §86A-26.
Member of minor's family.
Transfers to minors, §33A-1.
Member of the beneficiary's family.
Custodial trusts, §33B-1.
Member of the diamond industry.
Unfair trade practices, §66-73.
Member self-insurer.
Self-insurance security association, §97-130.
Membership.
Credit unions, §54-109.26(a).
Solicitation of contributions, §131F-2.
Membership camping agreements, §66-232.
Membership camping contracts, §66-232.
Membership camping operators, §66-232.
Membership interest.
Insurance companies, conversion, §58-10-12(a).
Limited liability companies, §57C-1-03.
Membership service.
Disability income plan, §135-101.
Judicial retirement, §135-53.
Legislative retirement system, §120-4.12(b).
Retirement, §§128-21, 135-1.
Member state.
Uniform sales and use tax administration act, §105-164.42B.
Mental abnormality.
Sex offender and public protection registration, §14-208.6.
Mental deficiency, §122C-361.
Mental health treatment.
Advance instruction, §122C-72.
Power of attorney, §32A-16.
Mental illness, §§122C-3, 122C-361.
Group health benefit plans, §58-3-220(h).
Incompetency, §35A-1101.
Mentally defective.
Criminal law, §14-27.1.
Mentally incapacitated.
Criminal law, §14-27.1.
Mentally retarded.
Death sentence prohibited, mentally retarded defendants, §15A-2005(a).

DEFINED TERMS —Cont'd
Mentally retarded with accompanying behavior disorder, §122C-3.
Mental retardation, §122C-3.
Incompetency, §35A-1101.
Merchant.
Sales, §25-2-104.
Merchant lessee.
Leases, UCC, §25-2A-103(1).
Mercury recovery performance ratio.
Mercury switch removal, motor vehicles, §130A-310.50.
Mercury switch.
Motor vehicles, §130A-310.50.
Merger.
Business corporations, §55-1-40.
Metal tire.
Motor vehicles, §20-4.01.
Metropolitan planning organization.
Planning regionally significant transportation projects, §136-200.
Metro region of the state.
Sustainable communities task force.
Reports, §143B-344.38(c).
MEWA.
Providers of health benefits, §58-49-30.
Mezzanine finance.
Enterprise corporations, §53A-37.
MGA, §58-34-2(a).
MH/DD/SA.
Consumer advocacy program, §122C-11.
Middle school, §115C-75(a).
Midnight deadline.
Banking, §25-4-104(a).
Midwifery, §90-178.2.
Migrant, §95-223.
Migrant agricultural worker, §130A-417.
Migrant housing, §95-223.
Migratory birds.
Conservation, §113-129.
Migratory farm worker.
Motor vehicles, §20-215.1.
Migratory game birds, §113-129.
Migratory waterfowl, §113-129.
Mileage.
Motor vehicles, §20-341.
Military equipment.
Sudan (Darfur) divestment act, §147-86.42.
Military installation.
Life insurance.
Dishonest and predatory sales to military personnel, §58-58-335.
Military-overseas ballot.
Uniform military and overseas voters act, §163-258.2.
Military property, §127B-2.
Military property sales facility, §127B-1.
Military service.
Power of sale barred during, §45-21.12A(d).
Military service medal.
Law enforcement officers wearing military service medals, §165-44.01(d).
Millennial campus, §116-198.33.
Mine, §74-24.2.
Miner, §74-24.2.
Mineral extraction activities.
Sudan (Darfur) divestment act, §147-86.42.
Mineral feed.
Commercial feed law, §106-284.33.
Mineral oil.
Oil or hazardous substances discharges, §§143-215.84(a2), 143-215.85(c).

DEFINED TERMS —Cont'd

Mineral proceeds.
Unclaimed property act, §116B-52.

Minerals.
Mining, §74-49.
Unclaimed property act, §116B-52.

Minimal cost.
Public records, §132-1(b).

Minimally adequate services.
Mental health, §122C-3.

Minimum amount of consideration.
Savings and loan associations, §54B-4.

Minimum amount on deposit in withdrawable accounts.
Savings and loan associations, §54B-4.

Minimum criteria.
Environmental policy act, §113A-9.

Minimum flows.
Dam safety, §143-215.25.

Minimum imposed term.
Post-release supervision, §15A-1368(a).

Minimum stream flows.
Dam safety, §143-215.25.

Mining, §§74-37, 74-49.

Minister.
Pastoral counselors, §90-382.

Ministerial functions.
Lobbying, §120C-100(a).

Minor.
Adoption, §48-1-101.
Anatomical gifts, §130A-412.4.
Assault, §14-33(d).
Consent to health care for minor, §32A-29.
Drug law violations, §90-95.4(d).
Human trafficking, §14-43.10(a).
Incompetency, §35A-1202.
Offenses against morality, §14-190.13.
Parental or judicial consent to abortion, §90-21.6.
Prohibition on handguns for minors, §14-269.7(c).
Public morals, §19-12.
Storage of firearms to protect minors, §14-315.1(d).
Transfers to minors, §33A-1.

Minor accident.
Safe driver incentive program, §58-36-75(a).

Minor child.
Child custody, §50-90.
Standby guardianship, §35A-1370.

Minority.
Transportation contracts, §136-28.4(c).

Minority business.
Public contracts, §§143-128.2(g), 143-128.4.

Minority business enterprise.
Global TransPark authority, §63A-19.

Minority person.
Global TransPark authority, §63A-19.
Public contracts, §143-128.2(g).

Misappropriation.
Trade secrets, §66-152.

Misbranded.
Meat inspection, §106-549.15.
Milk regulation, §106-268(c).
Pesticide board, §143-460.
Poultry products inspection, §106-549.51.

Miscarriage.
Unborn victims of violence act/Ethen's law, §14-23.7.

Miscellaneous payroll period.
Tax withholding, §105-163.1.

Misconduct connected with work.
Unemployment insurance, §96-14.

DEFINED TERMS —Cont'd

Misdemeanors.
Criminal law, §14-1.

Missing child.
Center for missing persons, §143B-1011.

Missing person.
Center for missing persons, §143B-1011.

Missing person report.
Center for missing persons, §143B-1011.

Mistake of fact.
Child support, §110-129.
Student loan collections, §105B-1.

Mitigation banking instrument.
Ecosystem enhancement program, §143-214.11(a).

Mixed beverage.
Alcoholic beverages, §18B-101.
Sales and use tax exemptions, §105-164.13.

Mixed chicks, §106-541.

Mixed fertilizers.
Commercial fertilizer, §106-657.

Mixed martial artist.
Boxing commission, §143-651.

Mixed martial arts.
Boxing commission, §143-651.

Mixed-use centers.
Main street solutions fund, §143B-472.35(a2).

Mixture.
Seed law, §106-277.2.

Mobile facility.
Veterinarians, §90-181.1(b).

Mobile home.
Housing standards, §160A-442.
Taxation, §105-316.7.
Tenancy by the entirety, §41-2.5(c).

Mobile intensive care nurse.
Emergency medical services, §131E-155.

Mobile pharmacy, §90-85.3(12).

Mobile phone.
Unlawful use of mobile phone by minors, §20-137.3(a).

Mobile telecommunication center.
Sales and use tax on telecommunications, §105-164.4C(h).

Mobile telecommunications service.
Sales and use tax, §105-164.3.

Mobility enhancing equipment.
Sales and use tax, §105-164.3.

Mobilization.
Military personnel on temporary duty or deployment, child custody or visitation, §50-13.7A(b).

Modality.
Physicians and surgeons, §90-1.1.

Modification.
Child custody jurisdiction and enforcement, §50A-102.

Modified permit.
Solid waste management, §130A-295.01(a).

Modular home.
Sales and use tax, §105-164.3.

Modular homebuilder.
Sales and use tax, §105-164.3.

Molders.
Disposal of dyes, molds, forms and patterns, §66-67.3(a).

Monetary compensation.
Regulation of nonconforming off-premises outdoor advertising, §§153A-143(e), 160A-199(e).

Monetary transmission.
Money transmitters, §53-208.2(a).

DEFINED TERMS —Cont'd
Monetary value.
  Money transmitters, §53-208.2(a).
Money.
  Foreign-money claims, §1C-1820.
  UCC, §25-1-201(b).
Money of the claim.
  Foreign-money claims, §1C-1820.
Month.
  Local government finance, §159-2.
Moody's corporate bond yield average.
  Insurance guaranty associations, §58-62-16.
Moped.
  Motor vehicles, §20-4.01.
  Sales and use tax, §105-164.3.
Moral turpitude.
  Notaries public act, §10B-3.
Morehead city tariff, terminal tariff.
  Ports authority income tax, §105-130.41(c).
  Ports authority individual income tax,
    §105-151.22(c).
Mortgage.
  Decedents' estates, §28A-1-1.
  Housing authorities, §157-3.
  Housing finance agency, §122A-3.
  Sales under power of sale, §45-21.1(b).
  Secured transactions, §25-9-102(a).
Mortgage broker.
  High cost home loans, §24-1.1E(a).
  Mortgage bankers, brokers and servicers,
    §53-244.030.
  Rate spread home loans, §24-1.1F(a).
Mortgagee.
  Sales under power of sale, §45-21.1(b).
**Mortgage guaranty insurers' report of
  policyholder's position, §58-10-120.**
Mortgage lender.
  Emergency program to reduce home foreclosures,
    §45-101.
  Housing finance agency, §122A-3.
  Mortgage bankers, brokers and servicers,
    §53-244.030.
Mortgage lending process.
  Residential mortgage fraud, §14-118.11.
Mortgage loan.
  Housing finance agency, §122A-3.
  Residential mortgage fraud, §14-118.11.
Mortgage loan originator.
  Mortgage bankers, brokers and servicers,
    §53-244.030.
Mortgage servicer.
  Emergency program to reduce home foreclosures,
    §45-101.
  Mortgage bankers, brokers and servicers,
    §53-244.030.
Most qualified persons.
  Personnel system, §126-14.2(b).
Mother.
  Marriage proceedings, §51-2.2.
Motion picture film.
  Public morals, §19-1.1.
Motion picture theater.
  Unlawful use of audiovisual recording device in
    motion picture theater, §14-440.1(c).
Motions.
  Criminal procedure, §15A-951.
Motorboat.
  Boating safety, §75A-2.
Motor carrier, §20-4.01.
  Fuel taxes, §105-449.37(a).
  Public utilities, §62-3.

DEFINED TERMS —Cont'd
Motor carrier of migratory farm workers.
  Motor vehicles, §20-215.1.
Motor carrier transportation contract.
  Indemnity agreements in motor carrier
    transportation contracts, §62-212(b).
Motor club, §58-69-2.
Motorcycle.
  Motor vehicles, §20-4.01.
  Regional transit authority vehicle rental tax,
    §105-550.
Motor freight carrier company.
  Public service taxation, §105-333.
Motor fuel, §75-81.
  Alternative fuel, §105-449.130.
  Gasoline and oil inspection, §119-15.
  Gasoline tax, §105-449.60.
  Larceny, §14-72.5(b).
Motor fuel merchant, §75-81.
Motor fuel outlet, §75-81.
Motor fuel rate.
  Alternative fuel, §105-449.130.
  Gasoline tax, §105-449.60.
Motor fuel transporter.
  Gasoline tax, §105-449.60.
Motor home.
  Motor vehicles, §20-4.01.
Motorists services directional signs.
  Exemption from removal, §136-140.7.
Motorized all terrain vehicle.
  Trespass to land, §14-159.3(b).
Motorsports facility.
  Growing businesses tax credits, §105-129.81.
Motorsports racing team.
  Growing businesses tax credits, §105-129.81.
Motor vehicle, §§20-4.01, 20-286.
  Counties, §153A-132(b).
  Defensive force to protect, §14-51.2(a).
  Fuel taxes, §105-449.37(a).
  Liens on personal property, §44A-1.
  Motor vehicle repairs, §20-354.2.
  Open container law, §20-138.7(a3).
  Public utilities, §62-3.
  Removal or disposal of junked or abandoned
    motor vehicles, §160A-303(b).
  Sales and use tax, §105-164.3.
  Taxation, §105-330.
  Vehicle reinsurance, §58-37-1.
Motor vehicle damage appraiser.
  Licensing, §58-33-10.
Motor vehicle dealer.
  Motor vehicles, §20-286.
Motor vehicle insurance.
  Vehicle reinsurance, §58-37-1.
Motor vehicle liability policy.
  Motor vehicles, §20-279.21.
Motor vehicle manufacturing.
  Industrial facilities sales tax refunds,
    §105-164.14B(a).
Motor vehicle oil filter.
  Solid waste management, §130A-290(a).
Motor vehicle owner.
  Impaired driving, §20-28.2(a1).
Motor vehicle repair, §20-354.2.
Motor vehicle repair shop, §20-354.2.
Motor vehicle salesman.
  Motor vehicles, §20-286.
Motor vehicle service agreement.
  Service agreement companies, §66-370(b).
Motor vehicle service agreement company,
  §66-370(b).

DEFINED TERMS —Cont'd

Mountain Island lake.
Marine commission, §77-70.

Mountain region of Western North Carolina.
Mountain resources planning act, §153B-2.

Movable frame hive.
Bee and honey act, §106-635.

Moving walk.
Elevator safety, §95-110.3(i).

MSDS.
Pesticide board, §143-460.
Toxic or hazardous substance identification,
§95-174(p).

MTBE, §119-26.3(a).

Mulch.
Commercial fertilizer, §106-657.

Multicar aerial passenger tramway.
Passenger tramway safety, §95-117.

Multidisciplinary evaluation.
Competency, §35A-1202.
Incompetency, §35A-1101.

Multiple award schedule contract.
Purchases through department of administration,
§143-52.3.

Multiple birth siblings.
Classroom placement, §115C-366.3(a).

Multiple distribution paths.
Sales and use tax, §105-164.3.

Multiple employer welfare arrangement.
Providers of health benefits, §58-49-30.

Multiplier.
Insurance rates, §58-36-100(b).
Workers' compensation self-insurance.
Employer groups.
Premium rates, §58-47-110(a).

Multispecialty ambulatory surgical program.
Certificate of need, §131E-176.

Multistate licensure privilege.
Nurse licensure compact, §90-171.82.

Multiunit assisted housing with services.
Adult care homes, §131D-2.1.

Municipal corporation.
Property taxes, §105-273.
Taxation, §105-330.

Municipality.
Aeronautics, §63-1.
Armories, §127A-161.
Civil disorders, §14-288.1.
Electric power, §159B-3.
Housing authorities, §§157-3, 157-41.
Local government finance, §159-160.
Property taxes, §105-273.
Public hospitals, §§131E-6, 131E-16.
Public utilities, §§62-3, 62-100.
Revenue bonds, §159-81.
Transportation authorities, §160A-576.
Urban redevelopment, §160A-503.
Well construction, §87-85.

Municipality's chief administrative official.
Parking authorities, §160A-576.

Municipal solid waste, §130A-290(a).

Municipal solid waste management facility,
§130A-290(a).

Mutual association.
Savings and loan associations, §54B-4.

Mutual responsibility agreement (MRA).
Public assistance program, §108A-24.

Mutual savings bank, §54C-4(b).

My commission expires.
Corporate conveyance forms, §47-41.01(d).

DEFINED TERMS —Cont'd

MyPay.
Life insurance.
Dishonest and predatory sales to military
personnel, §58-58-335.

NAICS.
Growing businesses tax credits, §105-129.81.
Insurance, §58-1-5.
Sales and use tax, §105-164.3.
Taxation, §105-228.90(b).
Tax incentives for new and expanding businesses,
§105-129.2.

Named storm.
Beach property insurance, §58-45-5.

Narcotic drug.
Controlled substances, §90-87.

Narrow channel.
Personal watercraft, §75A-13.3(f1).

Narrow therapeutic index drugs.
Pharmacy practice, §90-85.27.

National bank.
Trust companies, §53-301(a).

National board.
Boiler and pressure vessel regulation, §95-69.9(f1).

National fingerprint file.
National crime prevention and privacy compact,
§114-19.50.

National Guard members.
State health plan for teachers and state
employees, §135-48.1.

National identification index.
National crime prevention and privacy compact,
§114-19.50.

National indices.
National crime prevention and privacy compact,
§114-19.50.

National mercury recovery performance ratio.
Mercury switch removal, motor vehicles,
§130A-310.50.

National primary drinking water regulations,
§130A-313.

National tobacco grower settlement trust.
Tobacco trust fund commission, §143-716.

**Nationwide mortgage licensing system and
registry.**
Mortgage bankers, brokers and servicers,
§53-244.030.

Natural area.
Nature preserves act, §113A-164.3.

Natural gas.
Offshore activities, §143-215.94B(b).
Offshore oil and gas activities, §143-215.94BB.

Natural gas system.
Regional natural gas district, §160A-661(b).

Natural hair care, §88B-2.

Natural hair care specialist, §88B-2.

Natural hair care teacher, §88B-2.

Natural obstruction.
Floodplain regulations, §143-215.52(a).

Natural organic fertilizer.
Commercial fertilizer, §106-657.

Natural person.
Boxing commission, §143-651.

Natural resources, §130A-290(a).
Offshore oil and gas activities, §143-215.94BB.

Natural shellfish bed.
Cultivation of shellfish, §113-201.1.

Nature preserve.
Nature preserves act, §113A-164.3.

Navigable air space.
Aeronautics, §63-1.

DEFINED TERMS —Cont'd
Navigable waters.
State lands, §146-64.
NC HIE.
Health information exchange, §90-413.3.
NC NOVA partner team, §131E-154.13.
NC NOVA provider information manual,
§131E-154.13.
NC-Thinks.
State employee suggestion program, §143-345.20.
NDIS.
DNA database and databanks, §15A-266.2.
Near fatality.
Disclosure of records in child fatality or near
fatality cases, §7B-2902(a).
Near relative.
Absentee ballots, §163-230.1(f).
Necessary information.
Accident and health insurance.
Utilization review, §58-50-61(f), (g).
Necessary land connection.
Annexation initiated by municipality,
§160A-58.51.
Needy North Carolina students.
Need-based scholarships for students attending
private colleges and universities, §116-281.
Scholarships, §115C-499.2.
Negative.
Sales, §25C-10.
Negative trend.
Insurance companies, §58-12-2.
Neglect.
Adult care homes, §131D-2.1.
Adult care home's bill of rights, §131D-20.
Protection of disabled adults, §108A-101.
Neglected.
Cemeteries, §65-85.
Neglected juvenile.
Abused, neglected or dependent juveniles,
§7B-101.
Negotiate.
Insurance producers, §58-33-10.
Negotiation.
Negotiable instruments, §25-3-201(a).
Neighboring.
Mining, §74-49.
Nematicide.
Pesticide board, §143-460.
Nematode.
Pesticide board, §143-460.
Neonatal intensive care services.
Certificate of need, §131E-176.
Nesting tobacco.
Leaf tobacco sales, §106-461.
Net cost.
Farm machinery, §66-180.
Net direct premiums.
Beach property insurance, §58-45-5.
Net direct written premiums.
Insurance guaranty association, §58-48-20.
Net disposable earnings.
Repayment of money owed to state, §143-552.
Net dividends.
Corporate income tax, §105-130.4(f).
Net earnings.
Banking, §53-1.
Net economic loss.
Taxation, §105-130.8.
Net estate.
Decedents' estates, §29-2.

DEFINED TERMS —Cont'd
Net gallons.
Gasoline tax, §105-449.60.
Net income.
Principal and income act, §37A-1-102.
Net pension tax.
Individual income tax, §105-151.20(a).
Net proceeds.
Land sales, §146-15.
Local government sales and use tax for public
transportation, §105-506.1.
Net proceeds collected.
Debt collection, §105A-2.
Net property passing to surviving spouse.
Elective share of surviving spouse, §30-3.2.
Net taxable sales.
Sales and use tax, §105-164.3.
Net withdrawal value of withdrawable
accounts.
Savings and loan associations, §54B-4.
Network.
Criminal justice information network, §143-660.
Network plan.
Health insurance portability and accountability,
§58-68-25(a).
Network user.
Criminal justice information network, §143-660.
Net worth.
Health maintenance organizations, §58-67-5(i).
Savings and loan associations, §54B-4.
Savings banks, §54C-4(b).
Neuropsychological.
Psychology practice, §90-270.2.
Neutral observer.
Mediated settlement conferences in district court,
§7A-38.3D(n).
Mediated settlement conferences in superior court,
§7A-38.1(l).
Mediation order by superior court clerks,
§7A-38.3B(g).
New applicant.
Private protective services, §74C-30.
New article.
Sales and use tax exemptions, §105-164.13.
New article 9.
1975 amendatory act, §25-11-101.1.
Newborn care.
Midwifery practice, §90-178.2.
New business premium rate.
Small employer group health coverage,
§58-50-110.
New communities and large-scale
developments.
Land policy act, §113A-152.
New debtor.
Secured transactions, §25-9-102(a).
New drug.
Food, drugs and cosmetics, §106-121.
New employee.
Job development investment grant program,
§143B-437.51.
New facility.
Solid waste management, §130A-295.01(a).
New institutional health services.
Certificate of need, §131E-176.
New job.
Growing businesses tax credits, §105-129.81.
New location.
Sewage systems, §130A-334.
Newly admitted active member.
Continuing legal education, Bar Rule D.1501.

DEFINED TERMS —Cont'd

New material.
Bedding, §106-65.95.

New motor vehicle, §20-286.

New permit.
Solid waste management, fees for permits, §130A-295.8(b).

New renewable energy facility.
Renewable energy and energy efficiency portfolio standard (REPS), §62-133.8(a).

New retail outlet.
Motor fuel, §75-81.

New sanitary landfill.
County solid waste disposal, §153A-136(c).
Public enterprises, §160A-325(a).

News medium.
Journalist's qualified privilege, §8-53.11(a).

Newsprint.
Taxation, §105-102.6.

New swine farm.
Swine farm siting, §106-806(a).

New value.
Secured transactions, §25-9-102(a).

Next of kin.
Crime victims' rights, §15A-830(a).
Mental health, §122C-3.
Workers' compensation, §97-40.

Niche.
Cremation, §90-210.121.

Nickname.
Notaries public act, §10B-3.

911 board, §62A-40.

911 fund, §62A-40.

911 state plan, §62A-40.

911 system, §62A-40.

No longer authorized to practice law.
Vacancy in office declared upon disbarment, §7A-410.

Nominal consideration.
Debt adjusters, §14-423.

Nominated person.
Letters of credit, §25-5-102(a).

Nominating petition.
Soil and water conservation districts, §139-3.

Nonadmitted insurer.
Surplus lines, §58-21-10.
Unauthorized insurers, §58-28-12.

Nonadverse trustee.
Elective share of surviving spouse, §30-3.2.

Nonapportionable income.
Corporate income tax, §105-130.4(a).

Nonattainment area, §143-213.

Nonbanking entity, §53-127(a).

Non-business property.
Property taxes, §105-275.

Noncash proceeds.
Secured transactions, §25-9-102(a).

Noncertification.
Accident and health insurance.
Utilization review, §58-50-61(a).

Noncharitable irrevocable trust.
Uniform trust code, §36C-4-411.

Noncommercial fund.
Petroleum cleanup, §143-215.94A.

Noncommercial private passenger motor vehicle.
Credit scoring to rate motor vehicle and property insurance, §58-36-90(a).

Noncommercial underground storage tank.
Petroleum cleanup, §143-215.94A.

DEFINED TERMS —Cont'd

Noncommunity water system.
Drinking water, §130A-313.

Noncompacting state.
Interstate compact for juveniles, §7B-4001.
Interstate insurance product regulation compact, §58-91-10.

Noncompensatory damages.
Stay of execution on money judgment, §1-289(b).

Nonconforming sign.
Outdoor advertising control, §136-128.

Nonconsensual.
Civil no-contact orders, §50C-1.

Nonconsumptive use.
Water and air resources, §143-215.21.

Noncorporate limited liability company.
Franchise tax, §105-114.1(a).

Noncriminal justice purposes.
National crime prevention and privacy compact, §114-19.50.

Nondependent child policy.
Health insurance, nondependent child coverage, §58-3-290(a).

Nondistributable system property.
Public service taxation, §105-333.

Nondisturbance agreement.
Membership camping, §66-246(a).

Noneconomic damages.
Medical malpractice, §90-21.19(c).

Noneconomic detriment.
Victims compensation, §15B-2.

Nonfleet.
Insurance rates, §58-40-10.

Nonfleet private passenger motor vehicle.
Limited driving privilege, §20-179.3(l).
Motor vehicles, §§20-13.2, 20-16.1.

Nongame animals.
Conservation, §113-129.

Nongame fish.
Conservation, §113-129.

Nonguaranteed elements.
Annuity disclosure, §58-60-130.

Nonindemnity trigger.
Protected cell companies, §58-10-80.

Non-institutionalized individual.
Medicaid, transfer of assets for less than market value to qualify, §108A-58.1(h).

Nonionizing radiation.
Radiation protection, §104E-5.

Nonissuer.
Securities, §78A-2.

Non-IV-D case.
Child support, §110-129.

Nonmanufacturing facility.
Toxic or hazardous substance identification, §95-174(q).

Nonoffender.
Interstate compact for juveniles, §7B-4001.

Nonoriginal crash repair part, §58-36-95(a).

Nonparticipating candidate.
Public campaign fund, §163-278.62.
Voter-owned elections act, §163-278.96.

Nonparticipating manufacturer.
Tobacco escrow compliance, §66-292.

Nonparty state.
National crime prevention and privacy compact, §114-19.50.

Nonpotable mineralized water.
Well construction, §87-85.

Nonprofit.
Public utilities, §62-289.3.

DEFINED TERMS —Cont'd

Nonprofit agency.
Health facilities finance, §131A-3.

Nonprofit association.
Public hospitals, §131E-6.
Uniform unincorporated nonprofit association act, §59B-2.

Nonprofit community health referral service.
Volunteer health care providers, §90-21.16(e).

Nonprofit corporation, §55A-1-40.
Falls Lake watershed association, §77-140.

Nonprofit corporation or organization with which associated.
Legislative ethics, §120-85.1.
State government ethics act, §138A-3.

Nonprofit organization.
Alcoholic beverage permits, §18B-1002(a).
Energy loan fund, §143B-437.16(f).
Tax credit for gleaned crop, §105-130.37(b).

Nonprofit tax exempt organizations.
Surplus state property agency, §143-64.02.

Nonprofit water corporation.
Water infrastructure, §159G-20.

Nonprofit work center for the blind and the severely disabled, §143-48(b).

Nonrecoupable assessment.
Beach property insurance, §58-45-5.

Nonresident.
Higher education tuition and fees, §116-143.1.
Motor vehicles, §§20-4.01, 20-4.18.
Taxation, §105-134.5.

Nonresident bidders.
Preferences to state products and citizens, §143-59(c).

Nonresident contractor.
Tax withholding, §105-163.1.

Nonresident entity.
Tax withholding, §105-163.1.

Nonresidential redevelopment area, §160A-503.

Nonresident individual.
Taxation, §105-134.1.

Nonresident retail or wholesale merchant.
Sales and use tax, §105-164.3.

Nonresident's operating privilege.
Motor vehicles, §20-279.1.

Nonresident student.
Sex offender and public protection registration, §14-208.6.

Nonresident worker.
Sex offender and public protection registration, §14-208.6.

Nonseasonal wages.
Unemployment compensation.
Seasonal pursuits, §96-16(j).

Nonsmoking area, §143-596.

Nonspousal assets.
Elective share of surviving spouse, §30-3.2.

Nonstandard working hours.
Limited driving privilege.
Driving with revoked license, §20-20.1(a).

Non-state entity.
Budget of state, §143C-1-1(d).

Nonsystem property.
Public service taxation, §105-333.

Nontax district.
Organization of schools, §115C-69.

Nontaxpaid alcoholic beverage.
Alcoholic beverages, §18B-101.

Nontax revenue.
Budget of state, §143C-1-1(d).

DEFINED TERMS —Cont'd

Nontestimonial identification.
Criminal law and procedure, §15A-271.
Delinquent or undisciplined juvenile actions, §7B-2103.

Nontraditional mortgage loan, §45-21.38A(a).

Nontraditional mortgage product.
Mortgage bankers, brokers and servicers, §53-244.030.

Non-U.S.A. vehicle.
Motor vehicles, §20-4.01.

Nonvested easement in gross, §41-28.

Nonviolent felony.
Expungement of records, §15A-145.4(a).
Restoration of firearms rights, §14-415.4(a).

Nonvirgin newsprint.
Taxation, §105-102.6.

North Carolina association.
Regional reciprocal savings and loan acquisition act, §54B-48.2.

North Carolina bank.
Interstate branch banking, §53-224.9.
Reciprocal banking act, §53-210.

North Carolina bank holding company.
Reciprocal banking act, §53-210.

North Carolina coordinate system, §102-1.

North Carolina enterprise corporation.
Tax credit for qualified business investments, §105-163.010.

North Carolina Global TransPark, §158-32.

North Carolina health information exchange, §90-413.3.

North Carolina museum of history, §121-2.

North Carolina new organizational vision award (NC NOVA), §131E-154.13.

North Carolina public livestock market advisory board.
Livestock prompt pay law, §106-418.3.

North Carolina public school.
NBPTS certification, §115C-296.2(b).

North Carolina resident.
Coastal and estuarine commercial fishing licenses, §113-168.
Coastal recreational fishing licenses, §113-174.
Salt water fishing license, §113-174.

North Carolina savings and loan holding company.
Regional reciprocal savings and loan acquisition act, §54B-48.2.

North Carolina seed analysis tag.
Seed law, §106-277.2.

North Carolina state archives, §121-2.

North Carolina state bank.
Interstate branch banking, §53-224.9.

North Carolina state health coordinating council, §131E-176.

North Carolina taxable income, §§105-134.1, 105-134.5.

North Carolina university research expenses.
Research and development expenses tax credit, §105-129.50.

Notarial act.
Notaries public act, §10B-3.

Notarial certificate.
Notaries public act, §10B-3.

Notary.
Notaries public act, §10B-3.

Notary act.
Notaries public act, §10B-3.

Notary public.
Document authentication, §66-271.

DEFINED TERMS —Cont'd
Notary public —Cont'd
  Notaries public act, §10B-3.
Notary's electronic signature.
  Electronic notary public act, §10B-101.
Notebook computer.
  Discarded computer equipment and television
    management, §130A-309.131.
Notes.
  Agricultural finance act, §122D-3.
  Financing capital facilities, §116D-7.
  Health facilities finance, §131A-3.
  Housing finance agency, §122A-3.
  Private capital facilities finance act, §159D-37.
  Solid waste, §159I-3(a).
  State debt, §142-29.2.
Notice.
  Business corporations, §55-1-40.
  Conservation, §113-128.
  Criminal law, §14-113.2.
  UCC, §25-1-201(b).
Notice of intent.
  General assembly.
    Contesting a seat, §120-10.2.
Notice regarding future advances.
  Instruments to secure equity lines of credit,
    §45-81.
Notification.
  Satisfaction of deeds of trust and mortgages,
    §45-36.4.
Notification date.
  Secured transactions disposition of collateral after
    default, §25-9-611(a).
Notifies.
  UCC, §25-1-202(d).
Novelty lighter.
  Retail sale prohibited, §66-16.1(a).
No-wake speed.
  Boating safety, §75A-2.
Noxious aquatic weed.
  Aquatic weed control, §113A-221.
  County service districts, §153A-301(e).
Noxious-weed seeds.
  Seed law, §106-277.2.
Nuclear, biological or chemical weapon of
    mass destruction.
  Weapons of mass death and destruction,
    §14-288.21(c).
Nudity.
  Public morals, §19-12.
Nuisance.
  Mediation of farm nuisance disputes, §7A-38.3(a).
  Nuisance tire collection sites, §130A-309.60(f).
  Public morals, §19-1.
Nurses.
  Nurse licensure compact, §90-171.82.
Nursing, §90-171.20.
Nursing care.
  Certificate of need, §131E-176.
Nursing home.
  Administrators, §90-276.
  Facility licensure act, §131E-101.
  Long-term care insurance, §58-55-35(a).
  Nursing home medication management advisory
    committee, §131E-128.1(a).
  State health plan for teachers and state
    employees.
    Long-term care benefits, §135-48.61(a).
Nursing home administrator, §90-276.
Nursing home facility.
  Certificates of need, §131E-176.

DEFINED TERMS —Cont'd
Nursing pool, §131E-154.2.
Nursing program, §90-171.20.
Nutrition care services, §90-352.
NVMSRP.
  Mercury switch removal, motor vehicles,
    §130A-310.50.
OAH.
  Medicaid appeals by recipients, §108A-70.9A(a).
Oath or affirmation.
  Notaries public act, §10B-3.
Object or line item.
  Budget of state, §143C-1-1(d).
Obligated bank.
  Negotiable instruments, §§25-3-312(a),
    25-3-411(a).
Obligated resources.
  Higher education bonds, §116D-22.
Obligations.
  False claims act, §1-606.
  Housing finance agency, §122A-3.
  Public obligations, §159E-2.
  Swap agreements, §159-193.
Obligee.
  Child support, §110-129.
  Failure to pay child support, §50-13.12(a).
  Interstate family support, §52C-1-101.
  Urban redevelopment, §160A-503.
Obligee of the authority.
  Housing authorities, §157-3.
Obligee of the commission.
  Urban redevelopment, §160A-503.
Obligor.
  Bail, §15A-531.
  Bail bondsman and runners, §58-71-1.
  Child support, §§110-129, 110-142.
  Failure to pay child support, §50-13.12(a).
  Global TransPark authority, §63A-2.
  Interstate family support, §52C-1-101.
  Liens, §44A-17.
  Pollution control, §§159C-3, 159D-3.
  Secured transactions, §25-9-102(a).
Obscene matter.
  Public morals, §19-1.1.
Obstruction or interference with assessment.
  Abused, neglected or dependent children,
    §7B-303(b).
Occasional importer.
  Gasoline tax, §105-449.60.
Occupant.
  Self service storage renter's insurance,
    §58-33-18(a).
  Storage facilities, §44A-40.
Occupant or occupants of the office from
    which.
  Retirement system for superior court judges,
    §7A-51(d).
Occupational diseases.
  Workers' compensation, §97-53.
Occupational license.
  Administrative procedure, §150B-2.
  Failure to pay child support, §50-13.12(a).
  Forfeiture of licensing privilege after conviction of
    felony, §15A-1331A.
Occupational licensing agency.
  Administrative procedure, §150B-2.
Occupational licensing board, §93B-1.
Occupational loss of hearing.
  Workers' compensation, §97-53.
Occupational safety and health standards,
    §95-127.

DEFINED TERMS —Cont'd
Occupational skill development.
Vocational and technical education, §115C-152.
Occupational therapist, §90-270.67.
Occupational therapy, §90-270.67.
Occupational therapy assistant, §90-270.67.
Occupied residence.
Swine farms, §106-802.
Occupier of land.
Soil and water conservation districts, §139-3.
Occurrence.
Boating safety, §75A-11(a).
Ocean beach area.
All-terrain vehicles, §20-171.22(c).
Ocean beaches.
Seaward boundary of coastal lands, §77-20(e).
Oceangoing vessel.
Alcoholic beverages, §18B-106.
Ocean marine insurance.
Insurance guaranty association, §58-48-20.
Ocean shoreline.
Coastal area management, erosion control
structures, §113A-115.1(a).
Odometer.
Motor vehicles, §20-341.
Off-campus program.
Contracts with private institutions to aid North
Carolina students, §116-19(b).
Offender.
Crime victims financial recovery assistance act,
§15B-31.
Offense.
Revocation of driver's license, §20-24.1(e).
Offense against a minor.
Sex offender and public protection registration,
§14-208.6.
Offense involving impaired driving.
Motor vehicles, §20-4.01.
Offer.
Certificate of need, §131E-176.
Commodities act, §78D-1.
Membership camping, §66-232.
Securities, §78A-2.
Offering.
Condominiums, §47C-1-103.
Conversion building rental, §47A-34.
Membership camping, §66-232.
Offer to sell.
Securities, §78A-2.
Office.
Counties, §153A-230.1.
Delinquent or undisciplined juveniles, §7B-1501.
Elections, candidacy challenge, §163-127.1.
Local government during emergencies, §162B-7.
Public campaign fund, §163-278.62.
Sheriffs' education, §17E-2.
State controller, §143B-426.35.
Trust companies, §53-301(a).
Veterinarians, §90-181.1(b).
Voter-owned elections act, §163-278.96.
Office of the counsel.
Discipline and disability rules of state bar, Bar
Rule B.0103.
Procedures for the authorized practice committee
of the state bars, Bar Rule D.0203.
Office of the secretary.
Discipline and disability rules of state bar, Bar
Rule B.0103.
Procedures for the authorized practice committee
of the state bars, Bar Rule D.0203.

DEFINED TERMS —Cont'd
Officer.
Criminal procedure, §15A-101.
Death benefits, §143-166.2(d).
Local government law-enforcement retirement,
§143-166.50(a).
Motor vehicles, §20-137.7.
State law-enforcement retirement, §143-166.30(a).
Official.
Document authentication, §66-271.
Public obligations, §159E-2.
Official action.
Public obligations, §159E-2.
State government ethics act, §138A-3.
Transportation board, §136-14(h).
Official ballot.
Elections, §163-165.
Official capacity.
Business corporations, §55-8-50(b).
Legal expense funds for elected officials,
§163-278.300.
Medical service corporations, §58-65-166(b).
Official certificate.
Meat inspection, §106-549.15.
Poultry products inspection, §106-549.51.
Official certifying agency.
Seed law, §106-277.2.
Official compendium.
Food, drugs and cosmetics, §106-121.
Official depository.
Community colleges.
Deposits, §115D-58.6(a).
Official device.
Meat inspection, §106-549.15.
Poultry products inspection, §106-549.51.
Official duties.
Death benefits, §143-166.2(f).
Official establishment.
Poultry products inspection, §106-549.51.
Official governmental flag, §144-7(c).
Official inspection legend.
Meat inspection, §106-549.15.
Poultry products inspection, §106-549.51.
**Official in the executive branch of state
government.**
State officers, §147-16.2(c).
Official mark.
Meat inspection, §106-549.15.
Poultry products inspection, §106-549.51.
Official meeting.
Public bodies, §143-318.10(d).
Official misconduct.
Notary public act, §10B-3.
Official record.
Administrative procedure, §150B-42.
Official sales.
Installment sales, §25A-10.
Official sample.
Commercial feed law, §106-284.33.
Commercial fertilizer, §106-657.
Off indicator.
Unemployment insurance, §96-12.01(a1).
Off-premises outdoor advertising.
Regulation of nonconforming off-premises outdoor
advertising, §§153A-143(a), 160A-199(a).
Off-premises sale.
Sales, §14-401.13.
Offshore fossil fuel facility.
Review of offshore fossil fuel facilities for potential
of unauthorized discharge, §113A-119.2(a).

DEFINED TERMS —Cont'd
Offshore waters.
 Offshore oil and gas activities, §143-215.94BB.
 Oil and gas activities, §143-215.94B(b).
Oil.
 Offshore activities, §§143-215.94B(b),
   143-215.94BB.
 Oil and gas conservation, §113-389.
 Pollution control, §143-215.77.
 Review of offshore fossil fuel facilities for potential
   of unauthorized discharge, §113A-119.2(a).
Oil and gas developer operations.
 Oil and gas conservation, §113-389.
Oil and gas developer or operator.
 Oil and gas conservation, §113-389.
Oil-related activities.
 Sudan (Darfur) divestment act, §147-86.42.
Oil terminal facility.
 Oil and hazardous substance control, §143-215.77.
Old article 9.
 1975 amendatory act, §25-11-101.1.
On-call emergency service.
 Veterinarians, §90-181.1(b).
Oncology treatment center.
 Certificate of need, §131E-176.
On duty.
 City and town personnel, §160A-169.
 Counties, §153A-99(b).
One bedding unit, §106-65.103(f).
100-year floodplain.
 Floodplain regulations, §143-215.52(a).
Ongoing special condition.
 Health maintenance organizations, §58-67-88.
On indicator.
 Unemployment insurance, §96-12.01(a1).
Online identifier.
 Sex offender and public protection registration,
   §14-208.6.
On-site wastewater system.
 Certification of wastewater contractors and
   inspectors, §90A-71.
Open area.
 Cities and towns, §160A-407(a).
Open container.
 Alcoholic beverages.
   Ordinance regulating malt beverages and
     unfortified wine, §18B-300(c).
   Open container law, §20-138.7(f).
Open dump, §130A-290(a).
Open-end credit.
 Credit insurance, §58-57-5.
Open enrollment.
 Health insurance, nondependent child coverage,
   §58-3-290(a).
Open-heart surgery services.
 Certificate of need, §131E-176.
Open road toll.
 Toll collection on turnpike projects, §136-89.210.
Open road tolling system.
 Toll collection on turnpike projects, §136-89.210.
Open space.
 Cities and towns, §160A-407(b).
Open space land.
 Cities and towns, §160A-407(b).
Open space uses.
 Cities and towns, §160A-407(b).
**Open to competition from competing local
   providers.**
 Alternative regulation, tariffing and deregulation
   of telecommunications utilities, §62-133.5(h).

DEFINED TERMS —Cont'd
Operate.
 Boating safety, §75A-2.
Operating agreement.
 Limited liability companies, §57C-1-03.
Operating costs.
 Mental health, §122C-3.
Operating procedures.
 Interstate insurance product regulation compact,
   §58-91-10.
Operating rights railroad.
 Counties.
   Contracts with railroads to allocate financial
     responsibility, §153A-279(a).
   Rail transportation liability, §§160A-326(a),
     160A-626(a).
Operating room.
 Certificate of need, §131E-176.
 Hospital licensure, §131E-76.
Operation of aircraft.
 Aeronautics, §63-1.
Operation of wells.
 Well construction, §87-85.
Operations.
 Fuel taxes, §105-449.37(a).
Operator.
 Amusement device safety, §95-111.3(e).
 Child bicycle safety act, §20-171.8.
 Child care facility, §110-86.
 Dry-cleaning solvent cleanup act,
   §143-215.104B(b).
 Elevator safety, §95-110.3(j).
 Global TransPark authority, §63A-2.
 Migrant housing, §95-223.
 Mining, §74-49.
 Motor vehicles, §20-4.01.
 Oil and hazardous substance control, §143-215.77.
 Passenger tramway safety, §95-117.
 Petroleum cleanup, §143-215.94A.
 Pollution control, §§159C-3, 159D-3.
 Roller skating rink safety and liability, §99E-10.
 Solid waste management, §§130A-290(a),
   130A-310.
 Water pollution control system, §90A-46.
 Water treatment facilities, §90A-20.1.
Operator in charge.
 Animal waste management system operators,
   §90A-47.1.
Operator in responsible charge.
 Water pollution control system, §90A-46.
 Water treatment facilities, §90A-20.1.
Opiate.
 Controlled substances, §90-87.
Opium poppy.
 Controlled substances, §90-87.
**Optional alternative comprehensive benefit
   plans.**
 State health plan for teachers and state
   employees, §135-48.1.
Option contract.
 Option to purchase contracts executed with
   residential lease agreements, §47G-1.
Option fee.
 Option to purchase contracts executed with
   residential lease agreements, §47G-1.
**Option in gross with respect to an interest in
   land,** §41-28.
Option purchaser.
 Option to purchase contracts executed with
   residential lease agreements, §47G-1.

DEFINED TERMS —Cont'd

Option seller.
Option to purchase contracts executed with
residential lease agreements, §47G-1.

Optometry, §90-114.

Opt out.
Health information exchange, §90-413.3.
Interstate insurance product regulation compact,
§58-91-35(c).

Oral communication.
Electronic surveillance, §15A-286.

Order.
Negotiable instruments, §25-3-103.

Order for arrest.
Criminal process, §15A-305.

Order of forfeiture.
Impaired driving, §20-28.2(a1).

Ordinary care.
Health care liability, §90-21.50.
Negotiable instruments, §25-3-103.

Ordinary pocketknife.
Carrying concealed weapons, §14-269(d).

Organic fertilizer.
Commercial fertilizer, §106-657.

Organization.
Securing attendance of organizations for criminal
actions, §15A-773.
UCC, §25-1-201(b).

Organizer.
Limited liability companies, §57C-1-03.

Organ procurement organization.
Anatomical gifts, §130A-412.4.

Origin.
Seed law, §106-277.2.

Original.
Criminal process and procedure.
Electronic technology, §15A-101.1.
Evidence, §8C-1 Rule 1001.

Original debtor.
Secured transactions, §25-9-102(a).

Original incorporators.
Savings and loan associations, §54B-4.
Savings banks, §54C-4(b).

Original instrument.
Registers of deeds, §161-14.1(a).

Original parties.
Satisfaction of deeds of trust and mortgages,
§45-36.4.

Original record.
Workers' compensation self-insurance.
Employer groups, §58-47-75(a).

Original trust.
Second trust, §36C-8-816.1(a).

Originating state.
Educational personnel qualifications, §115C-350.

Originator.
Funds transfers, UCC, §25-4A-104(c).

Originator's bank.
Funds transfers, UCC, §25-4A-104(d).

Orphan discarded computer equipment.
Discarded computer equipment management,
§130A-309.91.

OSHNC standard.
Toxic or hazardous substance identification,
§95-174(r).

Other consideration to be received.
Shareholder protection act, §55-9-01(b).

Other crop seeds.
Seed law, §106-277.2.

Other entity.
Shareholder protection act, §55-9-01(b).

DEFINED TERMS —Cont'd

Other necessities of life.
Medicaid, transfer of assets for less than market
value to qualify, §108A-58.2(e).

Other public right-of-way.
Child bicycle safety act, §20-171.8.

Other recipient.
Mental health, §122C-3.

Other valid coverage.
Nature of policies, §58-51-15(b).

Other waste.
Water and air resources, §143-213.

Outbreak.
Public health, §130A-2.

Outdoor advertising.
Control, §136-128.

Outdoor pyrotechnics display.
Pyrotechnics licenses, §58-82A-1.1.

Outdoor recreational facility.
Swine farm, §106-802.

Outer banks of this state, §68-46.

Outlet.
Water and air resources, §143-213.

Out-of-counties scrap tire.
Scrap tire disposal, §130A-309.53.

Out-of-network services.
Provider sponsored organizations, §131E-276.

Out of service order.
Motor vehicles, §20-4.01.

Out-of-state.
Motor vehicles, §20-4.01.
Savings interstate branch banks, §54C-200.

Out-of-state association.
Savings and loan interstate branches, §54B-266.

Out-of-state bank.
Interstate branch banking, §53-224.9.

Out-of-state law enforcement agency.
Assistance by out-of-state law enforcement
officers, §160A-288.3(b).

Out-of-state law enforcement officer.
Assistance by out-of-state law enforcement
officers, §160A-288.3(b).

Out-of-state state bank.
Interstate branch banking, §53-224.9.

Out-of-state trust institution.
Trust companies, §53-301(a).

Outpatient contraceptive services.
Prescription contraceptive drugs, devices and
services covered by health benefit plan,
§58-3-178(c).

Outpatient treatment.
Mental health, §122C-3.

Outstanding balance.
Contempt, §6-21.2.
Reverse mortgages, §53-257.

Outstanding obligations.
State debt, §142-29.2.

Outstanding payment instrument.
Money transmitters, §53-208.2(a).

Overburden.
Mining, §74-49.

Overdue tax debt.
Business tax incentives, §105-129.2.
Collection, §105-243.1(a).
Job development investment grant program,
§143B-437.51.

Overfished, §113-129.

Overfishing, §113-129.

Overhanging tobacco.
Leaf tobacco sales, §106-461.

DEFINED TERMS —Cont'd
Overseas voter.
Uniform military and overseas voters act,
§163-258.2.
Over-the-counter drug.
Sales and use tax, §105-164.3.
Owner.
Aircraft labor and storage liens, §44A-50.
Amusement device safety, §95-111.3(f).
Auctions and auctioneers, §85B-1.
Boating safety, §75A-2.
Cave protection, §14-159.20.
Commercial real estate broker lien act, §44A-24.2.
Condemnation, §136-115.
Conservation, §113-130.
Dangerous dogs, §67-4.1.
Elevator safety, §95-110.3(k).
Eminent domain, §40A-2.
Housing standards, §160A-442.
Industrial facilities sales tax refunds,
§105-164.14B(a).
Instruments to secure equity lines of credit,
§45-81.
Joyriding, §14-72.2.
Liability of landowners associated with watershed
improvement projects, §139-41.3.
Liens on personal property, §44A-1.
Motor vehicles, §20-4.01.
Nature preserves act, §113A-164.3.
Oil and gas conservation, §113-389.
Petroleum cleanup, §143-215.94A.
Private personnel services, §95-47.1.
Property tax homestead exclusion, §105-277.1(b).
Records, tapes and other recorded devices,
§14-432.
Recreational trespass, §38A-2.
Residential property disclosure act, §47E-3.
Solicitation of contributions, §131F-2.
Solid waste management, §130A-310.
Statutory liens on real property, §44A-7.
Storage facilities, §44A-40.
Subcontractors, §22C-1.
Tax incentives for recycling facilities, §105-129.25.
Telephonic sellers, §66-260.
Unclaimed property act, §116B-52.
Owner and/or operator.
Provider requirements for Medicaid or Health
Choice, §108C-2.
Owner-controlled or wrap-up insurance.
Public works projects, §58-31-65(b).
Owner of land.
Soil and water conservation districts, §139-3.
Owners association.
Planned community act, §47F-1-103.
Owner's real property.
Dangerous dogs, §67-4.1.
Own or control.
Real estate investment trusts, §105-130.12(a).
Package.
Antifreeze law, §106-579.3.
Food, drugs and cosmetics, §106-121.
Poultry products inspection, §106-549.51.
Tobacco taxation, §105-113.4.
Weights and measures, §81A-9.
Packaged, labeled and released for shipment.
Pesticide board, §143-460.
Packer.
Egg law, §106-245.14.
Palladium.
Precious metals, §66-164.

DEFINED TERMS —Cont'd
Palliative care.
Hospice licensure, §131E-201.
PALS committee.
Discipline and disability rules of state bar, Bar
Rule B.0103.
Panel.
Public utilities, §62-3.
Paper from pulp manufacturing.
Industrial facilities sales tax refunds,
§105-164.14B(a).
Parent.
Adoptee's new birth certificate, §48-9-107(c).
Adoption, §48-1-102.
Anatomical gifts, §130A-412.4.
Brownfields property reuse act, §130A-310.31(b).
Corporate franchise tax, §105-122(b).
Discipline of students, §115C-390.1(b).
Dry-cleaning solvent cleanup act,
§143-215.104B(b).
Education assistance authority, §116-209.24.
Education of children with disabilities,
§115C-106.3.
Marriage proceedings, §51-2.2.
Mining, §74-49.
Public assistance program, §108A-24.
Solid waste management, §130A-290(a).
Suspension or expulsion of student,
§115C-391(d5).
Underground storage tank cleanup, §143-215.94A.
Vision screening for children entering
kindergarten, §130A-440.1(h).
Workers' compensation, §97-2.
Parental loans.
Education assistance authority, §116-209.24.
Parental obligations.
Education assistance authority, §116-209.24.
Parent company.
Insurance companies, conversion, §58-10-12(a).
Parenting coordinator.
Child custody, §50-90.
Parent of a sponsoring provider.
Provider sponsored organizations, §131E-276.
Parent organization.
Solicitation of contributions, §131F-2.
Par formula.
Capital facilities finance act, §142-82.
Facility authorities, §160A-480.2.
Global TransPark authority, §63A-2.
Higher education bonds, §116D-1.
Local government bonds, §159-79(c).
Solid waste management loan program.
Special obligation bonds and notes of local
governments, §159I-30(g).
State debt, §142-29.2.
Park.
State parks act, §113-44.9.
Parking project.
Parking authorities, §160A-551.
Parole.
Interstate compact for juveniles, §7B-4001.
Interstate compact on juveniles, §7B-2803.
Part.
Water and air resources, §143-215.6B(a1).
Partial eviction.
Expedited evictions, §42-59.
Participant.
Agritourism activity liability, §99E-30.
Boxing commission, §143-651.
Disability income plan, §135-101.
Equine activity liability, §99E-1.

DEFINED TERMS —Cont'd

Participant —Cont'd

Health insurance portability and accountability, §58-68-25(a).

State law-enforcement retirement, §143-166.30(a).

Participate.

State government ethics act, §138A-3.

Participating agency.

State employee suggestion program (NC-Thinks), §143-345.20.

Participating candidate.

Public campaign fund, §163-278.62.

Voter-owned elections act, §163-278.96.

Participating city.

City and town annexation agreements, §160A-58.22.

Participating community college.

Research and development expenses tax credit, §105-129.50.

Participating institution.

Private capital facilities finance act, §159D-37.

Participating manufacturer.

Tobacco escrow compliance, §66-292.

Participating provider.

Accident and health insurance.

Utilization review, §58-50-61(a).

Health maintenance organizations, §58-67-5(l).

Participating school.

Education programs in residential schools, §143B-146.1(b).

Participating units.

Regional schools, §115C-238.61.

Participatory CLE.

Continuing legal education, Bar Rule D.1501.

Parties in interests.

Housing standards, §160A-442.

Minimum standards for nonresidential structures, §160A-439(p).

Partner.

Partnerships, §59-102.

Rules of professional conduct, ProfCond Rule 1.0.

Partnership, §59-36.

Conversion and merger, §59-73.1.

Housing trust, §122E-2.

Individual income taxation, §105-134.1.

Partnership interest, §59-102.

Part-year residents.

Taxation, §105-134.5.

Party line.

Telephones, §14-401.8.

Party or parties.

Administrative procedure, §150B-2.

Adoption, §48-1-101.

Business corporations, §55-8-50(b).

Civil procedure, §1-567.32.

Condemnation, §136-115.

Decedents' estates, §28A-1-1(4a).

Discipline and disability rules of state bar, Bar Rule B.0103.

Education of children with disabilities, §115C-106.3.

Good funds settlement act, §45A-3.

Industrial commission utilization of rehabilitation professionals, ICRehabProf Rule III.

Mediation of emergency or disaster property insurance claims, §58-44-75.

Mediation of farm nuisance disputes, §7A-38.3(a).

Medical service corporations, §58-65-166(b).

Negotiable instruments, §25-3-103.

Procedures for the authorized practice committee of the state bars, Bar Rule D.0203.

DEFINED TERMS —Cont'd

Party or parties —Cont'd

UCC, §25-1-201(b).

Party state.

Interstate wildlife violator compact, §113-300.6.

National crime prevention and privacy compact, §114-19.50.

Nurse licensure compact, §90-171.82.

Pass a household.

State franchising of cable television service, §66-350.

Passenger.

Child bicycle safety act, §20-171.8.

Winter sports safety, §99C-1.

Passenger area of a motor vehicle.

Alcoholic beverages, §18B-401(c).

Open container law, §20-138.7(f).

Passenger rail services.

Counties.

Contracts with railroads to allocate financial responsibility, §153A-279(a).

Rail transportation liability, §§160A-326(a), 160A-626(a).

Passenger tramway.

Safety, §95-117.

Winter sports safety, §99C-1.

Passenger vehicles.

Motor vehicles, §20-4.01.

Pass-through entity.

Historic rehabilitation tax credit, §105-129.35(c).

Low-income housing tax credits, §105-129.40(b).

Mill rehabilitation tax credit, §§105-129.70, 105-228.90.

Taxation, §105-228.90(b).

Tax credit for qualified business investments, §105-163.010.

Tax withholding, §105-163.1.

Past corrected Type A1 or type A2 violation.

Nursing homes, §131E-129(a).

Past due.

Statewide accounts receivable program, §147-86.20.

Pastoral counseling, §90-382.

Pastoral psychotherapy.

Counseling, §90-382.

Patient.

Emergency medical services, §131E-155.

Interstate compact on mental health, §122C-361.

Nursing homes, §131E-116.

Patient counseling.

Hospital licensure, §131E-79.1(b).

Patient data.

Medical care data, §131E-214.1.

Patient identifying information.

Medical care data, §131E-214.1.

Patient safety organization.

Medical review committee, §131E-95(c).

Patient's representative.

Portable do not resuscitate orders, §90-21.17(c).

Pattern of criminal street gang activity, §14-50.16(d).

Pattern of residential mortgage fraud, §14-118.11.

Patterns of racketeering activity.

RICO act, §75D-3.

Pawn, §91A-3.

Pawnbroker, §91A-3.

Pawnshop, §91A-3.

Pawn transaction, §91A-3.

Payable at a definite time.

Negotiable instruments, §25-3-108.

DEFINED TERMS —Cont'd

Payable at bank, §25-4-105.1(b).

Payable in installments.
　Installment sales, §25A-3.

Payable on demand.
　Negotiable instruments, §25-3-108.

Payable through bank, §25-4-105.1(a).

Payday.
　Wage and hour act, §95-25.2.

Payee.
　Structured settlement protection, §1-543.11.

Payment.
　Patient medical records, confidentiality of,
　　§130A-12.

Payment date.
　Funds transfers, UCC, §25-4A-401.

Payment for services.
　Lobbying, §120C-100(a).

Payment instrument.
　Money transmitters, §53-208.2(a).

Payment intangible.
　Secured transactions, §25-9-102(a).

Payment order.
　Funds transfers, UCC, §25-4A-103(a).

Payoff amount.
　Satisfaction of deeds of trust and mortgages,
　　§45-36.4.

Payoff statement.
　Satisfaction of deeds of trust and mortgages,
　　§45-36.4.

Payor.
　Alimony, §50-16.1A.
　Child support, §110-129.
　Simultaneous death, §28A-24-1.
　Student loan collections, §105B-1.
　Tax withholding, §105-163.1.

Payor bank.
　Banking, §25-4-105.

Pay periods.
　Wage and hour act, §95-25.2.

Payroll period.
　Tax withholding, §105-163.1.

Peak.
　Mining, §74-49.

Peddler, §66-250.

Peer counselor.
　Peer support group counselor's privilege,
　　§8-53.10(a).

Peer review committee.
　Facility licensure act, §131E-101.

PEG channel.
　Distribution of sales and use taxes.
　　Supplemental PEG channel support,
　　　§105-164.44J(a).
　State franchising of cable television service,
　　§66-350.

PEG channel operator.
　Distribution of sales and use taxes.
　　Supplemental PEG channel support,
　　　§105-164.44J(a).

Penal institution.
　Sex offender and public protection registration,
　　§14-208.6.

Pen register.
　Wiretaps, §15A-260.

Pension.
　Legislative retirement system, §120-4.8.
　Retirement, §128-21.
　State retirement system, §135-1.

Pension payer.
　Tax withholding, §105-163.1.

DEFINED TERMS —Cont'd

Pension payment.
　Tax withholding, §105-163.1.

Pension reserve.
　Legislative retirement system, §120-4.8.
　Retirement, §128-21.
　State retirement, §135-1.

PEO agreement.
　Professional employer organizations, §58-89A-5.

Percent.
　Commercial feed law, §106-284.33.
　Commercial fertilizer, §106-657.
　Soil additives act, §106-50.30.

Percentage.
　Commercial feed law, §106-284.33.
　Soil additives act, §106-50.30.

Performance bonus.
　Personnel system, §126-7(a2).

Performance information.
　Budget of state, §143C-1-1(d).

Performing group.
　Truth in music advertising act, §75-125(b).

Perfusion protocols.
　Perfusionists, §90-682.

Period of measurement.
　Research and development expenses tax credit,
　　§105-129.50.

Period of military service.
　Power of sale barred during, §45-21.12A(d).

Period of war.
　Children of war veterans scholarships, §165-20.

Permanent designee.
　State government ethics act, §138A-3.

Permanent house guests.
　Sanitation, §130A-247.

Permanently and totally disabled.
　Medical release of inmates, §15A-1369.

**Permanently and totally disabled as a direct
　result of a traumatic injury sustained in
　the line of duty.**
　Tuition and fee waivers, §115B-1.

Permanent no contact order.
　Order prohibiting future contact by convicted sex
　　offender with victim, §15A-1340.50(a).

Permanent residence.
　Disabled veteran property tax homestead
　　exclusion, §105-277.1C(b).
　Property tax homestead exclusion, §105-277.1(b).

Permissible investments.
　Money transmitters, §53-208.2(a).

Permissive supplier.
　Gasoline tax, §105-449.60.

Permit.
　Bee and honey act, §106-635.
　Boll weevil eradication, §106-65.69.
　Concealed handgun permits, §14-415.10.
　Pharmacy practice, §90-85.3(m).
　Wildlife permit, §113-274(a).

Permit amendment.
　Solid waste management, fees for permits,
　　§130A-295.8(b).

Permit boundaries.
　Mining permits, §74-50(b).

Permit modification.
　Solid waste management, fees for permits,
　　§130A-295.8(b).

Permitted analytical variation.
　Commercial feed law, §106-284.33.

Permitted area.
　Mining permits, §74-50(b).

DEFINED TERMS —Cont'd
Permitted construction site.
Larceny of goods from, §14-72.6(d).
Perpetrator.
Domestic violence shelters, limited civil liability,
§1-620.
Person.
Address confidentiality program, §15C-2.
Administrative procedure, §150B-2.
Aeronautics, §63-1.
Agricultural finance act, §122D-3.
Agritourism activity liability, §99E-30.
Aircraft labor and storage liens, §44A-50.
Alcoholic beverages, §18B-101.
Amusement device safety, §95-111.3(g).
Anatomical gifts, §130A-412.4.
Animal diseases, §106-405.1.
Antifreeze law, §106-579.3.
Arbitration, §1-569.1.
Athlete agents, §78C-86.
Automated external defibrillator (AED),
§90-21.15(b).
Banking, §§53-42.1(a), 53-99.1(a), 53-165(j).
Banks.
Total loans and extension of credit to one
person, §53-48(d).
Beach property insurance, §58-45-6.
Biological agents registry, §130A-479(b).
Biological residues, §106-549.81.
Boating safety, §75A-2.
Boiler and pressure vessel regulation, §95-69.9(f2).
Boll weevil eradication, §106-65.69.
Boxing commission, §143-651.
Business corporations, §55-1-40.
Business discrimination, §75B-1.
Capital facilities finance act, §142-82.
Cave protection, §14-159.20.
Cemeteries, §65-48.
Certificate of need, §131E-176.
Certification of wastewater contractors and
inspectors, §90A-71.
Check-cashing service, §53-275.
Child care facilities.
Fraudulent misrepresentation, §110-107(c).
Child custody jurisdiction and enforcement,
§50A-102.
Child placing and care, §131D-10.2.
Children's health insurance program,
§108A-70.28(e).
Civil procedure, §1-75.2.
Coastal area management, §113A-103.
Collection agencies, §58-70-6.
Commercial feed law, §106-284.33.
Commercial fertilizer, §106-657.
Commodities act, §78D-1.
Community service program.
Division of adult correction, §143B-708(d).
Condemnation, §136-115.
Condominiums, §47C-1-103.
Conservation, §113-130.
Contractors, §87-101.
Contractors for public works, §133-23.
Controlled substances, §90-87.
Cooperative agreements among physicians or
between physician, hospital or others,
§90-21.25.
Corporations, §75E-1.
Cotton warehousing, §106-451.7.
Credit monitoring services act, §75-134.
Custodial trusts, §33B-1.
Debt adjusting, §14-423.

DEFINED TERMS —Cont'd
Person —Cont'd
Decedents' estates, §§28A-1-1(4b), 28A-19-7.
Development agreements, §160A-400.21.
Counties, §153A-349.2.
Drinking water, §130A-313.
Dry-cleaning solvent cleanup.
Criminal penalties, §143-215.104Q(i).
Egg law, §106-245.14.
Electric membership corporations, §117-7.
Electronic commerce in government, §66-58.2.
Electronic surveillance, §15A-286.
Electronic transactions, §66-312.
Elevator safety, §95-110.3(l).
Eminent domain, §40A-2.
Energy conservation finance act, §142-61.
Engineering, §89C-3.
Fair access to insurance requirements, §58-46-2.
Fair housing act, §41A-3.
Family law arbitration, §50-59(b).
Federal estate tax, §28A-27-1.
Food, drugs and cosmetics, §106-121.
Foreign-money claims, §1C-1820.
Fraudulent transfers, §39-23.1.
Fuel taxes, §105-449.37(a).
Gasoline and oil inspection, §119-15.
Gasoline tax, §105-449.60.
Global TransPark authority, §63A-2.
Grain adulteration, §106-621.
Grain dealers, §106-601.
Health care facilities, §131E-1.
Certificate of public advantage, §131E-192.2.
Health maintenance organizations, §58-67-5(g).
Identity theft, §§14-113.24(a), 75-61.
Publication of personal information, §75-66(b).
Instruments to secure equity lines of credit,
§45-81.
Insurance, §58-1-5.
Insurance commissioner examinations,
§58-2-131(b).
Insurance guaranty associations, §58-62-16.
Insurance holding companies, §58-19-5.
Insurance producers, §58-33-10.
Insurer supervision, rehabilitation and
liquidation, §58-30-22(a).
Interstate depositions and discovery, §1F-2.
Investment advisers, §78C-2.
Irrigation contractors, §89G-1.
Liability for hazardous materials abatement,
§143-215.103.
Limited liability companies, §57C-1-03.
Livestock brands, §80-58.
Livestock dealer licensing, §106-418.8.
Manufactured housing, §143-143.9.
Marketable title, §47B-8.
Marketing associations, §54-130.
Mediation of farm nuisance disputes, §7A-38.3(a).
Membership camping, §66-232.
Mental health, §122C-3.
Metropolitan sewerage districts, §162A-65(a).
Metropolitan water districts, §162A-32(a).
Migrant housing, §95-223.
Money transmitters, §53-208.2(a).
Mortgage bankers, brokers and servicers,
§53-244.030.
Motion pictures, §75C-2.
Motor fuel, §75-81.
Motor vehicles, §§20-4.01, 20-286, 20-356.
Mountain ridge protection, §113A-206.
Municipal planning and regulation of
development, appeals, §160A-393(b).

DEFINED TERMS —Cont'd
Person —Cont'd

Nonprofit corporations, §55A-1-40.
Nursing program, §90-171.20.
Occupational safety and health, §95-127.
Occupational therapy, §90-270.67.
Oil and gas conservation, §113-389.
Oil and hazardous substance control, §143-215.77.
Overhead high-voltage line safety, §95-229.6.
Partnerships, §§59-32, 59-102.
Patient abuse, §14-32.2(d).
Pawnbrokers and cash converters, §91A-3.
Peddlers, itinerant merchants and specialty markets, §66-250.
Persons with disabilities protection, §168A-3.
Pesticide board, §143-460.
Pharmacy practice, §90-85.3(n).
Planned community act, §47F-1-103.
Political campaigns, §163-278.6.
Pollution control act, §113A-52.
Pork promotion assessment, §106-792.
Poultry products inspection, §106-549.51.
Principal and income act, §37A-1-102.
Private personnel services, §95-47.1.
Professional employer organizations, §58-89A-5.
Property taxes, §105-273.
Protection of animals, §§19A-1, 19A-23.
Prudent management of institutional funds, §36E-2.
Public adjusters, §58-33A-5.
Public health generally, §§130A-2, 130A-26.1(a).
Public morals, §§19-1.1, 19-12.
Public utilities, §§62-3, 62-289.3.
Radiation protection, §104E-5.
Readable insurance policies, §58-38-15.
Real property electronic recording, §47-16.2.
Reciprocal insurance, §58-15-5.
Recreational therapists, §90C-22.
Refund anticipation loan act, §53-246.
Regulation of open fires, §106-941.
Relocation assistance, §133-7.
Rendering plants, §106-168.1.
Rental cars, §66-201.
Residential mortgage fraud, §14-118.11.
Respiratory care practices act, §90-648.
Retaliatory work discrimination, §95-240.
Sales, §§25C-10, 66-76.
Sales and use tax, §105-164.3.
Sales representatives, §66-190.
Satisfaction of deeds of trust and mortgages, §45-36.4.
Savings and loan associations, §54B-63.1(a).
Savings banks, §54C-60.1(a).
Securities, §78A-2.
Seed law, §106-277.2.
Soil additives act, §106-50.30.
Solid waste management, §130A-290(a).
Speech and language pathologists and audiologists licensure, §90-293.
Sport shooting range protection, §14-409.45.
State government ethics act, §138A-3.
State lottery, §18C-103.
State psychiatric hospital finance act, §142-101.
Statewide accounts receivable program, §147-86.20.
Structural pest control act, §106-65.24.
Sublease of motor vehicle and loan assumption arranging, §20-106.2(a).
Taxation, §§105-33.1, 105-134.1, 105-228.90(b).
Telephone records privacy protection, §14-113.30.
Telephone solicitations, §75-101.

DEFINED TERMS —Cont'd
Person —Cont'd

Telephonic sellers, §66-260.
Time shares, §93A-41.
Tobacco taxation, §105-113.4.
Trade secrets, §66-152.
Transfers to minors, §33A-1.
Trust companies, §53-301(a).
Trusts and trustees, §§32-70, 32-72.
UCC, §25-1-201(b).
Unauthorized substances taxes, §105-113.106.
Unclaimed property act, §116B-52.
Unfair trade practices, §58-63-5.
Uniform fiduciaries act, §32-2(a).
Uniform sales and use tax administration act, §105-164.42B.
Uniform transfer on death security registration act, §41-40.
Uniform trust code, §36C-1-103.
Uniform unincorporated nonprofit association act, §59B-2.
Unit ownership, §47A-3.
Vehicle reinsurance, §58-37-1.
Veterans, §34-2.
Veterinarians, §90-181.
Wage and hour act, §95-25.2.
Water and air resources, §§143-212, 143-215.6B(a).
Water and sewer, §162A-2.
Weights and measures, §81A-9.
Well construction, §87-85.
Well contractor certification, §87-98.2.
Wholesale prescription drug distributors, §106-145.2.
Workers' compensation self-insurance, §97-165.
Work first program fraud, §108A-39(c).
Person acting as a parent.
Child custody jurisdiction and enforcement, §50A-102.
Person affiliated with.
Workers' compensation self-insurance, §97-165.
Person aggrieved.
Administrative procedure, §150B-2.
Personal advantage.
Bribery of officials, §14-217(d).
Personal appearance.
Notaries public act, §10B-3.
Personal care services.
Adult care homes, §131D-2.1.
Personal household property.
Credit property insurance, §58-57-90(a).
Personal identification code.
Criminal law, §14-113.8.
Personal information.
Identity theft, §75-61.
Publication of personal information, §75-66(c).
Insurance information and privacy protection act, §58-39-15.
Personality disorder.
Sex offender and public protection registration, §14-208.6.
Personal knowledge or personally know.
Notaries public act, §10B-3.
Personal property.
Storage facilities, §44A-40.
Personal recognizance.
Interstate wildlife violator compact, §113-300.6.
Motor vehicles, §20-4.18.
Personal relationship.
Domestic violence, §50B-1(b).

DEFINED TERMS —Cont'd
Personal relationship —Cont'd
Domestic violence in disposition report,
§15A-1382.1(c).
Personal representative.
Custodial trusts, §33B-1.
Decedents' estates, §28A-1-1.
Estate taxes, §105-32.1.
Transfers to minors, §33A-1.
Uniform transfer on death security registration
act, §41-40.
Personal risk liability, §58-22-10.
Personal watercraft, §75A-13.3(a).
Person associated with the shelter.
Domestic violence shelters.
Limited civil liability, §1-620.
Person financially responsible.
Contractors, §87-101.
Person having custody of prisoner.
Approval of education and other training
programs, §162-59.1.
Person in loco parentis.
Pharmacy practice, §90-85.3(o).
Person interested in the estate.
Federal estate tax, §28A-27-1.
Person in the position of a seller.
Sales, §25-2-707.
Personnel.
School-based management and accountability
program, §115C-105.36(a).
Personnel file.
State personnel files, privacy, §126-22(b).
Personnel hoist.
Elevator safety, §95-110.3(m).
Personnel placement services.
Professional employer organizations, §58-89A-5.
Personnel professional.
Personnel system, §126-5(b).
Person related to, individual.
Secured transactions, §25-9-102(a).
Person related to, organization.
Secured transactions, §25-9-102(a).
Person responsible for the work to be done.
Overhead high-voltage line safety, §95-229.6.
Persons admitted.
Costs paid by persons admitted to institutions of
department of health and human services,
§143-117.1.
Persons and families of lower income.
Housing finance agency, §122A-3.
Persons and families of moderate income.
Housing finance agency, §122A-5.4.
Persons engaged in national defense activities.
National defense housing projects, §157-53.
Persons insured.
Uninsured motorist coverage, §20-279.21(b).
Persons of low income.
Housing authorities, §157-3.
National defense housing projects, §157-53.
Persons of moderate income.
Housing authorities, §157-3.
Persons who rent to transients.
Sales and use tax, §105-164.4(a).
Person with a disability, §168A-3.
Person with disabilities.
Family care home, §168-21.
Pest.
Pest control, §106-65.55.
Pesticide board, §143-460.
Structural pest control act, §106-65.24.

DEFINED TERMS —Cont'd
Pest control consultant.
Pesticide board, §143-460.
Pesticide.
Board, §143-460.
Structural pest control act, §106-65.24.
Pesticide applicator, §143-460.
Pesticide board, §143-460.
Pesticide chemical.
Food, drugs and cosmetics, §106-121.
Meat inspection, §106-549.15.
Poultry products inspection, §106-549.51.
Pesticide classified for restricted use, §143-460.
Pesticide dealer.
Board, §143-460.
Pet.
Commercial feed law, §106-284.33.
Pet food.
Commercial feed law, §106-284.33.
Petition.
Education of children with disabilities,
§115C-106.3.
Soil and water conservation districts, §139-3.
Petitioner.
Abused, neglected or dependent juveniles,
§7B-101.
Child custody jurisdiction and enforcement,
§50A-301.
Delinquent and undisciplined juveniles, §7B-1501.
Standby guardianship, §35A-1370.
Petroleum.
Oil or hazardous substances discharge,
§143-215.85(b).
Underground storage tank cleanup, §143-215.94A.
Petroleum product.
Underground storage tank cleanup, §143-215.94A.
Pet shop.
Protection of animals, §19A-23.
**Pharmaceutical and medicine manufacture
and distribution.**
Industrial facilities sales tax refunds,
§105-164.14B(a).
Pharmacist, §90-85.3(p).
Pharmacy, §90-85.3(q).
Pharmacy audit rights, §90-85.50(a).
Pharmacy of choice, §58-51-37(b).
Pharmacy personnel, §90-85.3(q1).
Pharmacy quality assurance programs,
§90-85.46.
Pharmacy technician, §90-85.3(q2).
Phased development plan.
Counties, §153A-344.1.
Phased development planning.
City and town zoning, §160A-385.1(b).
Photograph.
Evidence, §8C-1 Rule 1001.
Sales, §25C-10.
Photographic image.
Secretly peeping into room occupied by another
person, §14-202(b).
Photo lineup.
Eyewitness identification reform, §15A-284.52(a).
**Photovoltaic materials or modules use in
producing electricity.**
Industrial facilities sales tax refunds,
§105-164.14B(a).
Physical custody.
Adoption, §48-1-101.
Child custody jurisdiction and enforcement,
§50A-102.

DEFINED TERMS —Cont'd
Physical injury.
Assault on law enforcement, detention, probation, parole officer, §14-34.7(c).
Physically helpless.
Criminal law, §14-27.1.
Physical or mental impairment.
Persons with disabilities protection, §168A-3.
Physical restraint.
Discipline of students.
Seclusion and restraint, §115C-391.1(b).
Physical therapist, §90-270.24.
Physical therapist assistant, §90-270.24.
Physical therapy, §90-270.24.
Physical therapy aide, §90-270.24.
Physician.
Accident and health insurance.
Diabetes treatment coverage, §58-51-61(b).
Anatomical gifts, §130A-412.4.
Boxing commission, §143-651.
Cooperative agreements among physicians or between physician, hospital or others, §90-21.25.
Health care liability, §90-21.50.
Health maintenance organizations.
Diabetes treatment coverage, §58-67-74(b).
Hospital, medical and dental service corporations.
Diabetes treatment coverage, §58-65-91(b).
Industrial commission utilization of rehabilitation professionals, ICRehabProf Rule III.
Medicolegal guidelines for attorney-physician relationship, MLG Rule 3.
Mental health, §122C-3.
Natural death right, §90-321(a).
Respiratory care practices act, §90-648.
Woman's right to know act, §90-21.81.
Pipeline.
Gasoline tax, §105-449.60.
Oil and hazardous substance control, §143-215.77.
Pipeline company.
Public service taxation, §105-333.
Place.
Public morals, §19-1.1.
Placed for adoption.
Health insurance portability and accountability, §58-68-25(a).
Placement.
Adoption, §48-1-101.
Placement for adoption.
Insurance, §58-51-30(a).
Placement in the foster home.
Family leave credit insurance, §58-57-115(a).
Insurance, §58-51-30(a).
Place of business.
Sales, §14-401.13.
Secured transactions debtor's location, §25-9-307(a).
Sewage systems, §130A-334.
Place of detention.
Electronic recording of custodial interrogations, §15A-211(c).
Place of primary use.
Sales and use tax, §§105-163.3, 105-164.3.
Telecommunications, §105-164.4C(h).
Place of public accommodations.
Persons with disabilities protection, §168A-3.
Place of public assembly.
Sewage systems, §130A-334.
Plaintiff, §1-10.
Civil procedure, §1-75.2.

DEFINED TERMS —Cont'd
Plaintiff —Cont'd
Discipline and disability rules of state bar, Bar Rule B.0103.
Procedures for the authorized practice committee of the state bar, Bar Rule D.0203.
Plan.
Annuities, §147-9.2.
Disability income, §135-101.
Health insurance portability and accountability, §58-68-25(a).
Self-insurance security association, §97-130.
Separate insurance benefits for law enforcement, §143-166.60(a).
State parks act, §113-44.9.
Plan member.
State health plan for teachers and state employees, §135-48.1.
Planned community, §47F-1-103.
Planning commission.
Urban redevelopment, §160A-503.
Plan of conversion.
Insurance companies, conversion, §58-10-12(a).
Savings and loan associations, §54B-4.
Savings banks, §54C-4(b).
Plan of operation.
Beach area essential property insurance, §58-45-30(f).
Beach property insurance, §58-45-5.
Health insurance risk pool, §58-50-175.
Liability risk retention, §58-22-10.
Small employer group health coverage, §58-50-150(d).
Vehicle reinsurance, §58-37-1.
Plan or state health plan.
State health plan for teachers and state employees, §135-48.1.
Plant.
Plant protection and conservation, §106-202.12.
Plant pest, §106-419.
Plant regulator.
Pesticide board, §143-460.
Plan year.
State health plan for teachers and state employees, §135-48.1.
Plastic bag.
Plastic bag management, §130A-309.121.
Plate.
Sales, §25C-10.
Platinum.
Precious metals, §66-164.
Pledged goods.
Pawnbrokers and cash converters, §91A-3.
Plug-in electric vehicle.
Motor vehicles, §20-4.01.
Plumbing.
Contractors, §87-21(a).
Pneumatic tire.
Motor vehicles, §20-4.01.
Podiatry, §90-202.2(a).
Points and fees.
Mortgages, high cost home loans, §24-1.1E(a).
Point source, §143-213.
Policy.
Insurance guaranty associations, §58-62-16.
Long-term care insurance, §58-55-20.
Medicare supplement insurance, §58-54-1.
Readable insurance policies, §58-38-15.
Viatical life insurance settlements, §58-58-205.
Policyholder.
Assumption reinsurance, §58-10-25(a).

DEFINED TERMS —Cont'd
Policyholder —Cont'd
Insurance companies, closure of a block of
    business, §58-3-275(c).
Insurance guaranty association, §58-48-20.
Insurance information and privacy protection act,
    §58-39-15.
Policyholder-related liabilities.
Asset protection, §58-13-15.
Policyholders position.
Mortgage guaranty insurers, §58-10-120.
Policyholders surplus.
Mortgage guaranty insurers, §58-10-120.
Policy summary.
Life insurance solicitation, §58-60-10.
Political action committee.
Campaign contributions and expenditures.
    Disclosure requirements for media
        advertisements, §163-278.38Z.
Political committee.
Campaigns, §163-278.6.
Candidates' financing fund, §163-278.45.
Public campaign fund, §163-278.62.
Voter-owned elections act, §163-278.96.
Political organization.
Alcoholic beverage permits, §18B-1002(a).
Political party, §163-96(a).
Campaigns, §163-278.6.
State government ethics act, §138A-3.
Political party organization.
Campaign contributions and expenditures.
    Disclosure requirements for media
        advertisements, §163-278.38Z.
Political sign.
Highway signs, §136-32(c).
Political subdivision.
Emergency management, §166A-4.
Governmental employees and social security,
    §135-20.
Local government during emergencies, §162B-7.
Metropolitan sewerage districts, §162A-65(a).
Metropolitan water districts, §162A-32(a).
North Carolina trail system, §113A-85.
Pollution control, §§159C-3, 159D-3.
Water and sewer, §162A-2.
Pollutants.
Pollution control, §159C-3.
Polluted water.
Well construction, §87-85.
Pollution.
Pollution control, §§159C-3, 159D-3.
Pollution control project, §159C-3.
Polysomnography, §90-721.
Pool.
Health insurance risk pool, §58-50-175.
Oil and gas conservation, §113-389.
Small employer group health coverage,
    §58-50-110.
Poppy straw.
Controlled substances, §90-87.
Population.
Regional public transportation, §160A-601.
Regional transportation authorities, §160A-631.
Porcine animal.
Pork promotion assessment, §106-792.
Pork producer.
Promotion assessment for pork, §106-792.
Portability.
Group life insurance, §58-58-141(a).
Portable consumer electronic devices.
Portable consumer electronic devices insurance,
    §58-33-27(a).

DEFINED TERMS —Cont'd
Portable electronics.
Portable consumer electronic devices insurance,
    §58-44A-1.
Portable electronics insurance.
Portable consumer electronic devices insurance,
    §58-44A-1.
Portable electronics transaction.
Portable consumer electronic devices insurance,
    §58-44A-1.
Portable toilet.
Clean coastal water and vessel act, §77-125.
Position holder.
Gasoline tax, §105-449.60.
Positive identification.
National crime prevention and privacy compact,
    §114-19.50.
Positron emission tomography scanner.
Certificate of need, §131E-176.
Possessor.
Trespasser responsibility act, §38B-4.
Possessory liens.
Secured transactions priority of security interests,
    §25-9-333(a).
Postconsumer recovered paper.
Newspaper taxation, §105-102.6.
Postconsumer waste material.
Tax incentives for recycling facilities, §105-129.25.
Posted property, §113-281.
Postpaid calling service.
Sales and use tax on telecommunications,
    §105-164.4C(h).
Postpartum care.
Midwifery practice, §90-178.2.
Post-release supervision, §15A-1368(a).
Delinquent and undisciplined juveniles, §7B-1501.
Division of juvenile justice, §143B-805.
Post-secondary degree.
University of North Carolina, §116-15.
Post-secondary degree activity.
University of North Carolina, §116-15.
Post-termination transition period.
Taxation, §105-131.
Potential contractor.
State lottery, §18C-103.
Potentially dangerous dog, §67-4.1.
Potentially responsible party.
Brownfields property reuse act, §130A-310.31(b).
Dry-cleaning solvent cleanup act,
    §143-215.104B(b).
Potential medication-related error.
Nursing home medication management advisory
    committee, §131E-128.1(a).
Potential testimony.
Criminal procedure, §15A-971.
Poultry.
Product inspection, §106-549.51.
Regulation, §106-541.
Poultry composting facility.
Poultry products inspection, §106-549.51.
Poultry product.
Inspection, §106-549.51.
Poultry products broker.
Poultry products inspection, §106-549.51.
Pound.
Weights and measures, §81A-9.
Power of withdrawal.
Uniform trust code, §36C-1-103.
Power production activities.
Sudan (Darfur) divestment act, §147-86.42.
Practical banker, §53-1.

DEFINED TERMS —Cont'd

Practical examination.
Emergency medical services, §131E-155.

Practice law.
Attorneys at law, §84-2.1.

Practice of acupuncture, §90-451.

Practice of architecture, §83A-1.

Practice of audiology.
Licensure, §90-293.

Practice of counseling.
Licensed professional counselors, §90-330(a).

Practice of engineering, §89C-3.

Practice of forestry, §89B-2.

Practice of funeral service, §90-210.20(k).

Practice of land surveying, §89C-3.

Practice of marriage and family therapy,
§90-270.47.

Practice of massage and bodywork therapy,
§90-622.

Practice of medicine or surgery.
Physicians and surgeons, §90-1.1.

Practice of nursing by a licensed practical
nurse, §90-171.20.

Practice of nursing by a registered nurse,
§90-171.20.

Practice of perfusion, §90-682.

Practice of pharmacy, §90-85.3(r).

Practice of polysomnography, §90-722(a).

Practice of psychology, §90-270.2.

Practice of respiratory care.
Respiratory care practices act, §90-648.

Practice of social work, §90B-3.

Practice of soil science, §89F-3.

Practice of veterinary medicine, §90-181.

Practice supervisor.
Substance abuse professionals, §90-113.31A.

Practitioner.
Controlled substances, §90-87.
Drug, supplies, and medical device repository
program, §90-85.44(a).
Food, drugs and cosmetics, §106-121.

Prearrangement insurance policy.
Funeral and burial trust funds, §90-210.60.

Preceptor.
Assisted living administrators, §90-288.13.
Nursing home administrators, §90-276.

Precious metal, §66-164.
Commodities act, §78D-1.

Predecessor plan.
Children's health insurance program,
§108A-70.18.
State health plan for teachers and state
employees, §135-48.1.

Preeffective-date financing statement.
Secured transactions transitional provisions
regarding financing statements, §25-9-707(a).

Preemptive right in the nature of a right to
first refusal in gross with respect to an
interest in land, §41-28.

Preexisting condition.
Long-term care insurance, §58-55-30(c).
Nature of policies, §58-51-80(b).

Preexisting condition exclusion.
Health insurance portability and accountability,
§58-68-30(b).

Preexisting-conditions provision.
Small employer group health coverage,
§58-50-110.

Preexisting swine farm.
Swine farm siting, §106-806(a).

DEFINED TERMS —Cont'd

Preferred claim.
Insurers supervision, §58-30-10.

Preferred provider, §§58-50-56(a), 58-65-1(a).

Preferred provider benefit plan, §58-50-56(a).

Preferred provider organization, §58-50-56(a).

Preferred shares.
Appraisal rights, §55-13-01.

Preliminary damage assessment.
Emergency management, §166A-4.

Preliminary hearing.
Discipline and disability rules of state bar, Bar
Rule B.0103.
Procedures for the authorized practice committee
of the state bars, Bar Rule D.0203.

Premarital agreement, §52B-2.

Premises, §42-40.
Alcoholic beverages, §18B-101.
Larceny of shopping carts, §14-72.3.
Piped natural gas tax, §105-187.40.
Public utilities, §62-110.2.
Urban electrical service, §160A-331.

Premium.
Fraternal benefit societies, §58-24-15(d).
Group health insurance, §58-53-1.
Insurance guaranty associations, §58-62-16.
Providers of health benefits, §58-50-40(a).
Small employer group health coverage,
§58-50-110.

Prenatal care.
Midwifery practice, §90-178.2.

Preneed funeral contract, §90-210.60.

Preneed funeral contract beneficiary,
§90-210.60.

Preneed funeral funds, §90-210.60.

Preneed funeral planning, §90-210.60.

Preneed licensee.
Funeral and burial trust funds, §90-210.60.

Pre-1983 landfill.
Solid waste management, §130A-290(a).

Prepaid calling service.
Sales and use tax, §105-164.3.

Prepaid entertainment contract, §66-118.

Prepaid health services.
Medicaid program exemption, §143-48.1(b).

Prepaid legal services plan or group services
plan.
Rules of professional conduct, ProfCond Rule 7.3.

Prepaid telephone calling arrangement.
Sales and use tax, §105-164.3.

Prepaid telephone calling service.
Sales and use tax on telecommunications,
§105-164.4C(h).

Prepaid wireless calling service.
Sales and use tax, §105-164.3.

Prepaid wireless telephone service.
911 system, §62A-40.

Preparation for advanced education.
Vocational and technical education, §115C-152.

Prepared.
Meat inspection, §106-549.15.

Prepared food.
Sales and use tax, §105-164.3.

Prepared foods retailer.
Plastic bag management, §130A-309.121.

Preplacement assessment.
Adoption, §48-1-101.

Preschool child with a disability.
Education of children with disabilities,
§115C-106.3.

Prescribed burning, §106-966.

DEFINED TERMS —Cont'd
Prescriber.
  Pharmacy practice, §90-85.27.
Prescription.
  Controlled substances, §90-87.
  Prescribed burning of forestlands, §106-966.
  Sales and use tax, §105-164.3.
Prescription contraceptive drugs and devices.
  Prescription contraceptive drugs, devices and
    services covered by health benefit plan,
    §58-3-178(c).
Prescription drug.
  Pharmacy practice, §90-85.3(s).
  Registration of prescription drug wholesalers,
    manufacturers or repackagers, §106-140.1(j).
  Wholesale prescription drug distributors,
    §106-145.2.
Prescription order.
  Pharmacy practice, §90-85.3(t).
Presentation.
  Letters of credit, §25-5-102(a).
Presenters.
  Letters of credit, §25-5-102(a).
Presenting.
  Criminal law, §14-113.8.
Presenting bank.
  Banking, §25-4-105.
**Presently exercisable general power of
  appointment.**
  Elective share of surviving spouse, §30-3.2.
Present member of the general assembly.
  Legislative retirement system, §120-4.8.
Presentment, §15A-641.
  Negotiable instruments, §25-3-501(a).
Present sale.
  Sales, §25-2-106.
Present-use value.
  Taxation, §105-277.2.
Present value.
  Leases, UCC, §25-2A-103(1).
  UCC, §25-1-201(b).
Preservation agreement, §121-35.
Preserving the status quo.
  Public morals, §19-1.1.
President.
  University of North Carolina, §116-2.
Pressure vessel.
  Uniform act, §95-69.9(g).
Presumption.
  UCC, §25-1-201(b).
Pretext interview.
  Insurance information and privacy protection act,
    §58-39-15.
Pretreatment.
  Sewage systems, §130A-334.
Pretreatment facility, §143-213.
Pretreatment standards, §143-213.
Prevailing ecological conditions.
  Basinwide hydrologic models, §143-355(o).
Prevention.
  Substance abuse professionals, §90-113.31A.
Prevention of significant deterioration.
  Water and air resources, §143-213.
Previously used material.
  Bedding, §106-65.95.
Previous system.
  Judicial retirement, §135-53.
Prewritten computer software.
  Sales and use tax, §105-164.3.
Primarily educational institution.
  Child placing and care, §131D-10.2.

DEFINED TERMS —Cont'd
Primary corporate limits.
  City and town annexation of noncontiguous areas,
    §160A-58.
Primary enclosure.
  Protection of animals, §19A-23.
Primary forest product, §106-1027.
Primary operator.
  Underground petroleum storage tank operator
    training, §143-215.94OO.
Primary PSAP.
  911 system, §62A-40.
Primary standards.
  Weights and measures, §81A-9.
Primary system.
  Junkyard control, §136-143.
  Outdoor advertising control, §136-128.
Prime suppliers.
  Stocks of coal and petroleum fuels, §143-345.14(b).
  Urban electrical service, §160A-331.
Principal.
  Advance instruction for mental health treatment,
    §122C-72.
  Bail, §15A-531.
  Bail bondsman and runners, §58-71-1.
  Discipline of students, §115C-390.1(b).
  Education, §115C-5.
  Notaries public act, §10B-3.
  Power of attorney, §32A-16.
  Principal and income act, §37A-1-102.
  Regional schools, §115C-238.61.
  Sales representatives, §66-190.
  Telephonic sellers, §66-260.
  Uniform fiduciaries act, §32-2(a).
Principal amount.
  Interest, §24-13.
Principal executive officer.
  State governmental accountability and internal
    control act, §143D-3.
Principally engaged.
  Vehicle reinsurance, §58-37-1.
Principal occupation of donor.
  Campaign finance, §163-278.12(c).
  Electioneering communications.
    Reporting costs incurred for producing or airing,
      §163-278.12C(c).
Principal office.
  Business corporations, §55-1-40.
  Limited liability companies, §57C-1-03.
  Limited partnerships, §59-102.
  Mortgage bankers, brokers and servicers,
    §53-244.030.
  Nonprofit corporations, §55A-1-40.
  Savings and loan associations, §54B-4.
  Savings banks, §54C-4(b).
  Trust companies, §53-301(a).
Principal officer.
  Land policy act, §113A-152.
Principal place of administration.
  Uniform trust code, §36C-1-103.
Principal place of business.
  Preferences to state products and citizens,
    §143-59(c).
  Reciprocal banking act, §53-210.
  Regional reciprocal savings and loan acquisition
    act, §54B-48.2.
Principal shareholder.
  Trust companies, §53-301(a).
Principal state department.
  Executive organization, §143B-3.

DEFINED TERMS —Cont'd

Principle display panel.
Food, drugs and cosmetics, §106-121.

Print.
Sales, §25C-10.

Print media.
Campaign contributions and expenditures.
Disclosure requirements for media
advertisements, §163-278.38Z.

Prior conviction.
Structured sentencing, §15A-1340.11.

Priority.
Priority in employment assistance for United
States armed forces veteran, §165-44.3.

Prior rehabilitation.
Disability income plan, §135-101.

Prior service.
Judicial retirement, §135-53.
Legislative retirement system, §120-4.12(c).
Retirement, §128-21.
State retirement system, §135-1.

Prisoner.
Counties, §153A-217.
State prisons, §148-118.4.

Private act.
Cities and towns, §160A-1.

Private carrier.
Public utilities, §62-3.

Private club.
Alcoholic beverages, §§18B-1000, 18B-1006.
Sanitation, §130A-247.
Smoking in restaurants or bars, §130A-492.

Private compensatory mitigation bank.
Ecosystem enhancement program, §143-214.11(a).

Private detectives and investigators, §74C-3.

Private drinking water well.
Well construction, §87-85.

Private educational institution.
Children of war veterans scholarships, §165-20.
National Guard tuition assistance, §116-209.52(b).

Private entity.
Adult care homes, criminal history record checks
for providers and employees, §131D-40(h).
Nursing homes and home care agencies, criminal
history record checks, §131E-265(h).

Private facility.
Mental health, §122C-3.

Private hauler vehicles.
Motor vehicles, §20-4.01.

Private institution.
State education assistance authority, §116-201.

Private investment.
Main street solutions fund, §143B-472.35(a2).

Private library agency.
Interstate library compact, §125-12.

Private license plate.
Publicly owned vehicles, §20-39.1(d).

Private motor carrier, §20-4.01.

Private nonprofit utilities.
Emergency management, §166A-4.

Private passenger automobile, §20-135.4.

Private passenger motor vehicle.
Credit scoring to rate motor vehicle and property
insurance, §58-36-90(a).
Insurance rates, §58-40-10.

Private passenger vehicles.
Motor vehicles, §20-4.01.
Vehicle surface areas, §113A-70(b).

Private personnel service, §§95-47.1, 95-47.19.

Private pond, §113-129.

Private protective services, §74C-3.

DEFINED TERMS —Cont'd

Private real estate school, §93A-32.

Private residence.
Smoking in public buildings or places of
employment, §130A-492.

Private road or driveway.
Motor vehicles, §20-4.01.

Private seller.
Soliciting unlawful purchase of firearm,
§14-408.1(a).

Private telecommunication service.
Sales and use tax on telecommunications,
§105-164.4C(h).

Private trust company.
Trust companies, §53-301(a).

Private vehicle.
Smoking in public buildings or places of
employment, §130A-492.

Privilege communication.
Peer support group counselor's privilege,
§8-53.10(a).

Privileged information.
Insurance information and privacy protection act,
§58-39-15.

Prize.
Sweepstakes, §14-306.4(a).

Probable cause.
Discipline and disability rules of state bar, Bar
Rule B.0103.
Procedures for the authorized practice committee
of the state bars, Bar Rule D.0203.

Probable gestational age.
Woman's right to know act, §90-21.81.

Probation.
Delinquent and undisciplined juveniles, §7B-1501.
Division of juvenile justice, §143B-805.
Interstate compact for juveniles, §7B-4001.
Interstate compact on juveniles, §7B-2803.

Probationary state employee.
State personnel system, §126-15.1.

Probationary teacher.
Education personnel, §115C-325(a).

Proceeding.
Business corporations, §§55-1-40, 55-8-50(b).
Medical service corporations, §58-65-166(b).
Nonprofit corporations, §55A-1-40.

Proceeds.
Secured transactions, §25-9-102(a).

Processed.
Poultry products inspection, §106-549.51.

Processing.
Cremation, §90-210.121.
Solid waste management, §130A-290(a).

Processing site.
Scrap tire disposal, §130A-309.53.

Processor.
Forest product assessment act, §106-1027.

Processor of photographic images.
Film or computer images of minor engaging in
sexual activity.
Report by film and photographic processor or
computer technician, §66-67.4(a).

Procurement organization.
Anatomical gifts, §130A-412.4.

Producer.
Cotton warehousing, §106-451.7.
Grain dealers, §106-601.
Oil and gas conservation, §113-389.
Producer-controlled property or casualty insurers,
§58-3-165(a).
Reinsurance intermediaries, §58-9-2(a).

DEFINED TERMS —Cont'd
Producer —Cont'd
Sweet potato assessment, §106-564.4(d).
Producing broker.
Surplus lines, §58-21-10.
Product.
Interstate insurance product regulation compact, §58-91-10.
Oil and gas conservation, §113-389.
Weights and measures, §81A-51.
Production.
Controlled substances, §90-87.
Oil and gas conservation, §113-423.
Salvia divinorum.
Manufacture, sale, delivery, possession, §14-401.23(d).
Production company.
Sales and use tax, §105-164.3.
Exemption of audio-visual master, §105-164.13.
Tax credit for qualifying expenses of production company, §§105-130.47(a), 105-151.29(a).
Production-money crops.
Secured transactions, §25-9-102(a).
Production-money obligation.
Secured transactions, §25-9-102(a).
Production of crops.
Secured transactions, §25-9-102(a).
Production operations.
Unemployment compensation.
Seasonal pursuits, §96-16(j).
Production systems.
Double damage liability for damage to agricultural systems, §1-539.2B(c).
Production work.
Vocational and technical education, §115C-160.
Product liability.
Liability risk retention, §58-22-10.
Product liability action, §99B-1.
Product name.
Commercial feed law, §106-284.33.
Soil additives act, §106-50.30.
Professional.
Boxing commission, §143-651.
Professional archaeologists.
Burial sites, §70-28.
Professional association.
Political campaigns, §163-278.6.
Professional bondsman.
Bail, §15A-531.
Bail bondsman and runners, §58-71-1.
Professional corporations, §55B-2.
Regulations for practicing law, Bar Rule E.0101.
Professional discipline.
Substance abuse professionals, §90-113.31A.
Professional employer organization, §58-89A-5.
Professional employer organization group, §58-89A-5.
Professional employer services, §58-89A-5.
Professional engineer, §89C-3.
Professional engineer, retired, §89C-3.
Professional fundraising counsel.
Solicitation, §14-401.12.
Professionalism.
Continuing legal education, Bar Rule D.1501.
Professional land surveyor, §89C-3.
Professional limited liability company or companies.
Regulations for practicing law, Bar Rule E.0101.
Professional motorsports racing team.
Sales and use tax, §105-164.3.

DEFINED TERMS —Cont'd
Professional responsibility.
Continuing legal education, Bar Rule D.1501.
Professional service.
Professional corporations, §55B-2.
Professional solicitor.
Solicitation, §14-401.12.
Professional-sports-services contract.
Athlete agents, §78C-86.
Profile.
Computer crimes, §14-453.
Profit.
Transportation board, §136-14(h).
Profit from crime.
Crime victims financial recovery assistance act, §15B-31.
Program.
Bicycle and bikeway act, §136-71.7.
Birth defects monitoring program, §130A-131.16(b).
Child support, §110-129.
Forgivable education for service program, §116-209.45(b).
Indian antiquities, §70-48.
Relocation assistance, §133-7.
Program director.
Mental health, §122C-3.
Program evaluation.
Commission on governmental operations, §120-72.
Program participant.
Address confidentiality program, §15C-2.
Assignment of student to particular school, §115C-366(h).
Program-related asset.
Prudent management of institutional funds, §36E-2.
Prohibited noxious-weed seeds.
Seed law, §106-277.2.
Project.
Bonds for student housing, §116-175.
Centennial campus and Horace Williams campus financing act, §116-198.33.
Certificate of need, §131E-176.
Electric power, §159B-3.
Global TransPark authority, §63A-2.
Higher education student housing, §116-189.
Lease or purchase of prison facilities constructed by private firm, §148-37.2(b).
Pollution control, §§159C-3, 159D-3.
Private capital facilities finance act, §159D-37.
Relocation assistance, §133-7.
Solid waste, §159I-3(a).
University of North Carolina, §116-41.1.
Project broker.
Time shares, §93A-41.
Project of regional impact.
Land policy act, §113A-152.
Promise.
Negotiable instruments, §25-3-103.
Promisee.
Indemnity agreements in motor carrier transportation contracts, §62-212(b).
Promissory note.
Secured transactions, §25-9-102(a).
Promoter.
Boxing commission, §143-651.
Prompt payment discounts.
Motor fuel, §75-81.
Proof of age.
Youth access to tobacco products, §14-313(a).

DEFINED TERMS —Cont'd
Proof of financial responsibility.
  Motor vehicles, §§20-279.1, 20-280.
Proper identification.
  Identity theft, §75-61.
Properly payable.
  Banking, §25-4-104(a).
Property, §47A-3.
  City and town zoning, §160A-385.1(b).
  Computer crimes, §14-453.
  Contracts for deed, §47H-1.
  Counties, §153A-344.1.
  Decedents' estates, §31A-3.
  Dedication of property to nature and historic
    preserves, §143-260.8(a).
  Development agreements, §160A-400.21.
    Counties, §153A-349.2.
  Eminent domain, §40A-2.
  Fraudulent transfers, §39-23.1.
  Home foreclosure rescue scams, §75-120.
  Municipalities initiating annexation,
    §160A-58.54(c).
  Option to purchase contracts executed with
    residential lease agreements, §47G-1.
  Premarital agreements, §52B-2.
  Sales under power of sale, §45-21.1(b).
  Unclaimed property act, §116B-52.
  Uniform transfer on death security registration
    act, §41-40.
  Uniform trust code, §36C-1-103.
Property-hauling vehicles.
  Motor vehicles, §20-4.01.
Property mappers.
  Certification of local government property
    mappers, §147-54.4.
Property or casualty insurer, §58-12-2.
Property owner.
  Annexation initiated by municipality,
    §160A-58.51.
Property passing to surviving spouse.
  Elective share of surviving spouse, §30-3.2.
Property registered.
  Motor vehicles, §20-4.2.
Property subsequently acquired.
  Probate and registration, §47-20.5(b).
Property taxes, §§105-151.21, 105-163.2.
Property tax relief.
  Disabled veteran property tax homestead
    exclusion, §105-277.1C(b).
Proposal.
  Secured transactions, §25-9-102(a).
Proposed association.
  Savings and loan associations, §54B-4.
Proposed savings bank, §54C-4(b).
Proprietary information.
  911 system, §62A-40.
Proprietary school, §115D-87.
Proprietary security organization, §74C-13(a1).
Pro rata share.
  Taxation, §105-131.
Prosecutor.
  Abused, neglected or dependent juveniles,
    §7B-101.
  Criminal procedure, §15A-101.
  Delinquent and undisciplined juveniles, §7B-1501.
Prosecutorial districts.
  Judicial department, §7A-60.
Prospective client.
  Rules of professional conduct, ProfCond Rule 1.18.
Prospective developer.
  Brownfields property reuse act, §130A-310.31(b).

DEFINED TERMS —Cont'd
Prospective donor.
  Anatomical gifts, §130A-412.4.
Prospective lessee.
  Criminal law, §14-395.1.
Prospective loss costs.
  Insurance rates, §58-36-100(b).
  Workers' compensation self-insurance.
    Employer groups.
      Premium rates, §58-47-110(a).
Prospective purchaser.
  Telephonic sellers, §66-260.
**Prostate-specific antigen (PSA) tests or
  equivalent test for the presence of prostate
  cancer, §58-51-58.**
  Health maintenance organizations, §58-67-77(b).
  Hospital, medical and dental service corporations,
    §58-65-93(b).
Prosthetic device.
  Sales and use tax, §105-164.3.
Prostitution.
  Criminal law, §14-203.
  Offenses against morality, §14-190.13.
  Public morals, §19-1.1.
Protected animal.
  Endangered wildlife, §113-331.
Protected animal list, §113-331.
Protected cell.
  Protected cell companies, §58-10-80.
Protected cell account.
  Protected cell companies, §58-10-80.
Protected cell assets.
  Protected cell companies, §58-10-80.
Protected cell company, §58-10-80.
Protected cell company insurance, §58-10-80.
Protected cell liabilities.
  Protected cell companies, §58-10-80.
Protected health information.
  Health information exchange, §90-413.3.
Protected mountain ridges, §113A-206.
Protected plant.
  Plant protection and conservation, §106-202.12.
Protected tenant.
  Residential rental agreements, §42-40.
Protective bicycle helmet.
  Child bicycle safety act, §20-171.8.
Protective equipment.
  Sales and use tax, §105-164.3.
Protective order.
  Domestic violence, §50B-1(c).
Protective services.
  Protection of disabled adults, §108A-101.
Protective supervision.
  Delinquent and undisciplined juveniles, §7B-1501.
  Division of juvenile justice, §143B-805.
Protective trusts.
  Trusts and trustees, §36C-5-508.
Protector.
  Conservation, §113-128.
Protest.
  Elections, §163-182.
Prove.
  Funds transfers, UCC, §25-4A-105(a).
  Negotiable instruments, §25-3-103.
Provider.
  Accident and health insurance.
    Utilization review, §58-50-61(a).
  Continuing care retirement communities,
    §58-64-1.
  Health insurance risk pool, §58-50-175.
  Health maintenance organizations, §58-67-5(h).

DEFINED TERMS —Cont'd

Provider —Cont'd

Industrial commission managed care
organizations, ICManagedCare Rule II.

Mental health, developmental disabilities and
substance abuse, §122C-80(e).

Provider requirements for Medicaid or Health
Choice, §108C-2.

Provider sponsored organizations, §131E-276.

Provider of alternative fuel, §105-449.130.

Provider of support services.

Mental health, §122C-3.

Provider sponsored organization, §131E-276.

Provisional license.

Child placing and care, §131D-10.2.

Interpreters and transliterators licensure act,
§90D-3.

**Provisional licensed clinical addictions
specialist.**

Substance abuse professionals, §90-113.31A.

Provisional licensed clinical social workers,
§90B-3.

Provisional licensee.

Motor vehicles, §20-4.01.

Provisional license revocation, §20-13.3(a).

**Provisionally approved septic tank or
innovative septic tank system,**
§130A-343.1(a).

Provisional official ballot.

Elections, §163-165.

Proximate audience display.

Pyrotechnics licenses, §58-82A-1.1.

Proximate audience display operator.

Pyrotechnics licenses, §58-82A-1.1.

Pseudoephedrine product.

Methamphetamine lab prevention, §90-113.51(a).

Psychiatric facility, §131E-176.

Psychologist, §§90-270.2, 122C-3.

Psychotherapist.

Psychotherapy patient/client sexual exploitation
act, §90-21.41.

Public adjuster, §58-33A-5.

Public agency.

Disclosure of records in child fatality or near
fatality cases, §7B-2902(a).

Electronic commerce in government, §66-58.2.

Health facilities finance, §131A-3.

Performance standards for sustainable,
energy-efficient public buildings, §143-135.36.

Public aircraft.

Aeronautics, §63-1.

Public area.

Asbestos hazard management, §130A-444.

Public assistance program.

Garnishment of wages to recoup fraudulent public
assistance program payment, §108A-25.3(a).

Publication.

Counties, §153A-1.

Local government finance, §159-1.

Public morals, §19-1.1.

Public auction.

Protection of animals, §19A-23.

Public authority.

Budget of state, §143C-1-1(d).

Housing standards, §160A-442.

Local government finance, §159-7.

Public bicycle path.

Child bicycle safety act, §20-171.8.

Public body.

Meetings, §143-318.10(b), (c).

DEFINED TERMS —Cont'd

Public building or facility.

Criminal trespass, §14-132.

Public buildings.

Department of administration, §143-336.

Public buildings and grounds.

Department of administration, §143-336.

Public cemetery.

Abandoned and neglected cemeteries, §65-85.

Public corporation.

Business corporations, §55-1-40.

Foreign trade zones, §55C-2.

Public defender.

Judicial retirement, §135-53.

Public disturbance.

Civil disorders, §14-288.1.

Public document.

Publications, §143-169.2(a).

Public employee.

False claims act, §1-606.

Public employment.

False claims act, §1-606.

Public enterprise, §160A-311.

Counties, §153A-274.

Public entity.

Public obligations, §159E-2.

Public event.

State government ethics act, §138A-3.

Public facilities.

Development agreements, §160A-400.21.

Counties, §153A-349.2.

Public-finance transaction.

Secured transactions, §25-9-102(a).

Public fishing waters, §113-129.

Public fund.

Sudan (Darfur) divestment act, §147-86.42.

Public grounds.

Department of administration, §143-336.

Public health.

Dry-cleaning solvent cleanup act,
§143-215.104B(b).

Public health authority, §130A-45.01.

Public health facility.

Public health authorities, §130A-45.01.

Public health program services.

Local health departments billing Medicaid,
§130A-34.2(f).

Public health purposes.

Health information exchange, §90-413.3.

Public health threat.

Terrorist incident using nuclear, biological or
chemical agents, §130A-475(d).

Public hospital.

Debts owed public hospitals, §131E-48.

Donation of surplus equipment, §131E-250(a).

Hospital provider assessments, §108A-121.

Public hospital personnel act, §131E-257(e).

Public hunting grounds.

Conservation, §113-129.

Public improvements.

Main street solutions fund, §143B-472.35(a2).

Public infrastructure.

Main street solutions fund, §143B-472.35(a2).

Public land.

Environmental policy act, §113A-9.

Public law enforcement agencies.

Public records, §132-1.4.

Public library agency.

Interstate library compact, §125-12.

Public livestock market.

Livestock prompt pay law, §106-418.3.

DEFINED TERMS —Cont'd
Public-local act.
  Cities and towns, §160A-1.
Publicly registered name.
  University of North Carolina, §116-15.
Public meetings.
  Smoking in public places, §143-596.
Public mills, §73-1.
Public mountain trout waters.
  Special license for fishing mountain trout waters,
    §113-272(c).
Public office.
  Legal expense funds for elected officials,
    §163-278.300.
  Notice of appointments, §143-47.6.
  Political campaigns, §163-278.6.
  Repayment of money owed to state, §143-555.
Public officer.
  Housing standards, §160A-442.
  Public contracts, §14-234(a1).
Public official.
  False claims act, §1-606.
  Repayment of money owed to state, §143-555.
  Volunteer architect during an emergency or
    disaster, §83A-13.1(d).
  Volunteer engineer during emergency or disaster,
    §89C-19.1(d).
Public operator.
  Pesticide board, §143-460.
Public or community sewage systems,
  §130A-334.
Public place.
  Public intoxication, §14-443.
  Smoking in public buildings or places of
    employment, §130A-492.
Public practice of accountancy, §93-1.
Public practice of geology.
  Geologist, §89E-3.
Public record, §132-1(a).
  Address confidentiality program, §15C-2.
  Archives and history, §121-2.
Public reprimand.
  Judicial standards commission, §7A-374.2.
Public road.
  Counties, §153A-238(a).
Public roadway.
  Child bicycle safety act, §20-171.8.
Public safety answering point (PSAP).
  911 system, §62A-40.
Public safety officer.
  Law enforcement officers wearing military service
    medals, §165-44.01(d).
Public safety official.
  Volunteer architect during an emergency or
    disaster, §83A-13.1(d).
  Volunteer engineer during emergency or disaster,
    §89C-19.1.
Public school.
  Child care facilities, §110-86.
  State retirement system, §135-1.
Public school buildings.
  Public school building capital fund, §115C-546.2.
Public school employee, §143-300.13.
Public school facility.
  Community schools act, §115C-205.
Public servants.
  State government ethics act, §138A-3.
Public service company.
  Public service taxation, §105-333.
  Taxation, §105-330.

DEFINED TERMS —Cont'd
Public services.
  Mental health, §122C-3.
Public service vehicle.
  Parked or standing on roadside giving warning
    signal, §20-157(f).
Public spaces.
  Contractors, §87-101.
Public transportation.
  Cities and towns, §160A-576.
  Regional authority, §160A-601.
  Regional transportation authorities, §160A-631.
Public transportation system.
  Cities and towns, §160A-576.
  Local government sales and use tax for public
    transportation, §105-506.1.
  Regional authority, §160A-601.
  Regional transit authority registration tax,
    §105-560.
  Regional transit authority vehicle rental tax,
    §105-550.
  Regional transportation authorities, §160A-631.
Public trust resources.
  Beach access program, §113A-134.2(b).
  Jurisdiction of conservation agencies, §113-131(e).
Public trust rights.
  Beach access program, §113A-134.2(b).
  No adverse possession of property subject to,
    §1-45.1.
Public use and enjoyment.
  City and town open space, §160A-407(b).
Public used oil collection center.
  Solid waste management, §130A-290(b).
Public utility, §§62-3, 62-100.
  Corporate income tax, §105-130.4(a).
Public utility holding company act of 1935.
  Securities, §78A-2.
Public vehicular area.
  Motor vehicles, §20-4.01.
  Roads and highways, §136-91.
Public water or sewer system.
  Annexation initiated by municipality,
    §160A-58.56(a).
Public waters.
  Conservation, §113-129.
Public water system.
  Drinking water, §130A-313.
  Water infrastructure, §159G-20.
  Water treatment facility operators, §90A-20.1.
Public weighmaster.
  Weights and measures, §81A-51.
Publish.
  Cities and towns, §160A-1.
  Local development, development financing,
    §158-7.3(a).
  Unlawful telecommunications devices, §14-113.5.
Published.
  Procedures for ruling on questions of legal ethics,
    Bar Rule D.0101.
Published monthly average.
  Life insurance loan interest rates, §58-61-5.
Publisher.
  Newspaper taxation, §105-102.6.
Pulverization.
  Cremation, §90-210.121.
Pumpout facility.
  Clean coastal water and vessel act, §77-125.
Pumps, §87-85.
Punchboards.
  Lotteries and gaming, §14-296.
Punitive damages, §1D-5.

DEFINED TERMS —Cont'd

Purchase.

Business and energy tax credit, §105-129.15.

Leases, UCC, §25-2A-103(1).

Pawnbrokers and cash converters, §91A-3.

Sales and use tax, §105-164.3.

Tax incentives for new and expanding businesses, §105-129.2.

Tax incentives for recycling facilities, §105-129.25.

UCC, §25-1-201(b).

Purchase agreement.

Lease or purchase of prison facilities constructed by private firm, §148-37.2(b).

Purchase money.

Membership camping, §66-232.

Purchase-money collateral.

Secured transactions, §25-9-103(a).

Purchase-money obligation.

Secured transactions, §25-9-103(a).

Purchase price.

Sales, §14-401.13.

Sales and use tax, §105-164.3.

Purchaser.

Condominiums, §47C-1-103.

Contracts for deed, §47H-1.

Membership camping, §66-232.

Option to purchase contracts executed with residential lease agreements, §47G-1.

Planned community act, §47F-1-103.

Residential property disclosure act, §47E-3.

Telephonic sellers, §66-260.

Time shares, §93A-41.

UCC, §25-1-201(b).

Purchasing group.

Liability risk retention, §58-22-10.

Pure seed.

Seed law, §106-277.2.

Purity.

Seed law, §106-277.2.

Purpose or program.

Budget of state, §143C-1-1(d).

Pursuant to commitment.

Secured transactions, §25-9-102(a).

Pursuit.

Unemployment compensation.

Seasonal pursuits, §96-16(j).

Pyramid distribution plan.

Lotteries, §14-291.2(b).

Pyrotechnics.

Licenses, §58-82A-1.1.

Sale of pyrotechnics, §14-414.

Pyrotechnics display operator.

Pyrotechnics licenses, §58-82A-1.1.

Qualifications.

Personnel system, §126-7.1(d).

Priority given employee separated due to reduction in force, §126-7.1(d).

Qualified actuary.

Counties, §153A-93.

Managing general agents, §58-34-2(a).

Workers' compensation self insurance, §97-165.

Employer groups, §58-47-60.

Qualified agricultural programs.

Tobacco trust fund commission, §143-716.

Qualified allocation plan.

Low-income housing tax credits.

Federal credit allocation on or after January 1, 2003, §105-129.42(a).

Qualified assignment agreement.

Structured settlement protection, §1-543.11.

DEFINED TERMS —Cont'd

Qualified beneficiary.

Compensation of trustees and other fiduciaries, §32-53.

Principal and income act, §37A-1-104.1.

Uniform trust code, §36C-1-103.

Qualified business.

Tax credit for qualified business investments, §105-163.010.

Qualified business venture.

Tax credit for qualified business investments, §105-163.010.

Qualified charitable organization.

Claims against the state, §143B-426.40A(a).

Qualified clearinghouse.

Derivative transaction, insurance companies, §58-7-205(a).

Qualified code-enforcement official.

Board, §143-151.8(a).

Qualified contingency.

Charitable remainder trust administration act, §36C-4B-3.

Qualified dry-cleaning equipment.

Dry-cleaning equipment tax credit, §105-129.16C(c).

Qualified escrow fund.

Tobacco reserve fund, §66-290.

Qualified exchange.

Derivative transaction, insurance companies, §58-7-205(a).

Qualified foreign exchange.

Derivative transaction, insurance companies, §58-7-205(a).

Qualified former sworn law enforcement officer.

Concealed handgun permits, §14-415.10.

Qualified geologist, §89E-3.

Qualified grantee business.

Tax credit for qualified business investments, §105-163.010.

Qualified individual.

Diagnosis and evaluation of osteoporosis and low bone mass, §58-3-174.

Electrical contractors, §87-41.1.

Qualified interpreter.

Interpreters for hearing impaired, §8B-1.

Qualified licensee business.

Tax credit for qualified business investments, §105-163.010.

Qualified lien holder.

Instruments to secure equity lines of credit, §45-81.

Satisfaction of deeds of trust and mortgages, §45-36.4.

Qualified long-term care partnership policy.

Long-term care partnerships, §58-55-55.

Qualified motor vehicle.

Fuel taxes, §105-449.37(a).

Qualified North Carolina business.

Enterprise corporations, §53A-37.

Qualified North Carolina low-income building.

Low-income housing tax credits, §105-129.41(c).

Federal credit allocation on or after January 1, 2003, §105-129.42(a).

Qualified North Carolina research expenses.

Research and development expenses tax credit, §105-129.50.

Qualified observer.

Annual evaluation of teachers, §115C-333.1(c).

Qualified organization.

Health information exchange, §90-413.3.

DEFINED TERMS —Cont'd

Qualified person.
Decedents' estates, safe deposit boxes, §28A-15-13(a).

Qualified person with a disability, §168A-3.

Qualified policy.
Long-term care partnerships, §58-55-55.

Qualified professional.
Mental health, §122C-3.
Woman's right to know act, §90-21.81.

Qualified provider.
Guaranteed energy savings contracts, §143-64.17.

Qualified rehabilitation expenditures.
Historic rehabilitation tax credit, §105-129.35(c).
Mill rehabilitation tax credit, §105-129.70.

Qualified residential unit.
Low-income housing tax credits.
Federal credit allocation on or after January 1, 2003, §105-129.42(a).

Qualified retired law enforcement officer.
Concealed handgun permits, §14-415.10.

Qualified risk manager.
Surplus lines insurance, streamlined application for commercial purchasers, §58-21-16(b).

Qualified sworn law enforcement officer.
Concealed handgun permits, §14-415.10.

Qualified technician.
Woman's right to know act, §90-21.81.

Qualified United States financial institution.
Asset protection, insurance companies, §58-13-20(c).
Domestic companies, §58-7-26(b).
Reinsurance intermediaries, §58-9-2(a).

Qualified veteran.
Veterans cemeteries, §65-43.

Qualified witness.
Advance instruction for mental health treatment, §122C-72.
Power of attorney, §32A-16.

Qualifying agent.
Alarm system business, §74D-2(c).

Qualifying contribution.
Public campaign fund, §163-278.62.
Voter-owned elections act, §163-278.96.

Qualifying expenses.
Tax credit for qualifying expenses of production company, §§105-130.47(a), 105-151.29(a).

Qualifying improvements.
Property taxes on Brownfields properties, §105-277.13(b).

Qualifying individual.
Mortgage bankers, brokers and servicers, §53-244.030.

Qualifying owner.
Community land trust property taxation, §105-277.17(b).
Disabled veteran property tax homestead exclusion, §105-277.1C(b).

Qualifying PEG channel.
Distribution of sales and use taxes.
Supplemental PEG channel support, §105-164.44J(a).

Qualifying period.
Public campaign fund, §163-278.62.
Voter-owned elections act, §163-278.96.

Quality assurance committee, §90-21.22A(a).
Facility licensure act, §131E-101.
Nursing home medication management advisory committee, §131E-128.1(a).

Quality control and quality assurance program.
Fire-safety standard and firefighter protection act, §58-92-10.

DEFINED TERMS —Cont'd

Quarantine authority.
Public health, §130A-2.

Quasi-judicial decision.
Municipal planning and regulation of development, appeals, §160A-393(b).

Rabies vaccine, §130A-184.

Rack.
Gasoline tax, §105-449.60.

Racketeering activity.
RICO act, §75D-3.

Radiation, §104E-5.

Radiation machine, §104E-5.

Radio.
Campaign contributions and expenditures.
Disclosure requirements for media advertisements, §163-278.38Z.

Radioactive material.
Radiation protection, §104E-5.

Radiology.
Practice of medicine, §90-18(c).

Railroad.
Counties.
Contracts with railroads to allocate financial responsibility, §153A-279(a).
Rail transportation liability, §§160A-326(a), 160A-626(a).

Railroad company.
Public service taxation, §105-333.

Railroad intermodal facility.
Tax incentives for railroad intermodal facilities, §105-129.95.

Railroad operating revenue.
Corporate income tax, §105-130.4(m).

Rape crisis center.
Privileged communications, rape crisis centers and domestic violence programs, §8-53.12.

Raptor.
Conservation, §113-129.

Rate.
Insurance, §58-36-100(b).
Public utilities, §62-3.
Workers' compensation self-insurance.
Employer groups, §58-47-60.

Ratemaking.
Lobbying, §120C-100(a).

Rate of exchange.
Foreign-money claims, §1C-1820.

Rate of insured unemployment.
Unemployment insurance, §96-12.01(a1).

Rate spread home loan, §24-1.1F(a).

Rating period.
Small employer group health coverage, §58-50-110.

Ratite.
Meat inspection, §106-549.15.
Regulation of dealers, §106-541.

Raw agricultural commodity.
Food, drugs and cosmetics, §106-121.
Meat inspection, §106-549.15.
Poultry products inspection, §106-549.51.

Raw material.
Rendering plants, §106-168.1.

RCGL.
Coastal and estuarine commercial fishing licenses, §113-168.

RCRA.
Solid waste management, §130A-290(a).

Readily accessible lead-bearing substance, §130A-131.7.

DEFINED TERMS —Cont'd

Readily accessible to the general public.
Electronic surveillance, §15A-286.

Real estate.
Appraisers, §93E-1-4.
Condominiums, §47C-1-103.
Planned community act, §47F-1-103.
Property taxes, §105-273.

Real estate appraisal, §93E-1-4.

Real estate appraiser, §93E-1-4.

Real estate appraising, §93E-1-4.

Real estate brokerage activity.
Mortgage bankers, brokers and servicers, §53-244.030.

Real estate broker or salesperson, §93A-2(a), (b).
Fair housing act, §41A-3.

Real estate contract.
Residential property disclosure act, §47E-3.

Real-estate related business.
Tax credit for qualified business investments, §105-163.010.

Real estate transaction, §41A-3.

Real property, §41A-3.
Appraisers, §93E-1-4.
Automatic release of ancillary security instruments, §45-42.3(a).
City and town parking authorities, §160A-551.
Housing authorities, §157-3.
Mortgages and deeds of trust.
Sales under power of sale, §45-21.1(b).
Partnerships, §59-32.
Property taxes, §105-273.
Public health authorities, §130A-45.01.
Public hospitals, §131E-16.
Residential property disclosure act, §47E-3.
RICO act, §75D-3.
Statutory liens, §44A-7.
Subcontractors, §22C-1.
Urban redevelopment, §160A-503.
Veterans' recreation, §165-25.

Real property law-business, commercial and industrial transactions, Bar Rule D.2102.

Real property law-residential transactions, Bar Rule D.2102.

Real property law specialty, Bar Rule D.2102.

Reasonable.
Rules of professional conduct, ProfCond Rule 1.0.

Reasonable accommodations.
Persons with disabilities protection, §168A-3.

Reasonable and customary.
Group health insurance, §58-53-1.

Reasonable attorneys' fees.
Planned community act, §47F-1-103.

Reasonable belief.
Rules of professional conduct, ProfCond Rule 1.0.

Reasonable cause.
Municipal building inspection.
Periodic inspections, §160A-424(a).

Reasonable efforts.
Abused, neglected or dependent juveniles, §7B-101.

Reasonable person.
Stalking, §14-277.3A(b).

Reasonably available.
Anatomical gifts, §130A-412.4.

Reasonably should know.
Rules of professional conduct, ProfCond Rule 1.0.

Rebate.
Deadline for mailing consumer rebates, §75-40(a).

Receipt.
Cotton warehousing, §106-451.7.

DEFINED TERMS —Cont'd

Receipt —Cont'd
Research and development expenses tax credit, §105-129.50.
Sales, §25-2-103.
UCC, §25-7-102(b).

Receiver.
Insurers supervision, §58-30-10.

Receives.
Criminal law, §14-113.8.
UCC, §25-1-202(e).

Receiving agency.
Interchange of governmental employees, §126-52.

Receiving bank.
Funds transfers, UCC, §25-4A-103(a).

Receiving state.
Educational personnel qualifications, §115C-350.
Interstate agreement on detainers, §15A-761.
Interstate compact on mental health, §122C-361.
State prisons, §148-120.

Recidivist.
Sex offender and public protection registration, §14-208.6.

Recipient.
Anatomical gifts, §130A-412.4.
Medicaid appeals by recipients, §108A-70.9A(a).
Public assistance program, §108A-24.
Recovery from insurers providing additional coverage to Medicaid-eligible persons, §108A-55.4(a).

Reciprocal.
Reciprocal insurance, §58-15-5.

Reciprocal attorneys' fees provisions, §6-21.7(a).

Reciprocal insurance, §58-15-5.

Reciprocal program.
Membership camping, §66-232.

Reciprocal state.
Insurers supervision, §58-30-10.

Reciprocating state.
Motor vehicles, §20-4.18.

Reckless driving.
Motor vehicles, §20-140.

Reclaiming.
Solid waste management, §130A-290(b).

Reclamation.
Mining, §74-49.

Reclamation plan.
Mining, §74-49.

Recognized educational institution.
Marriage and family therapists, §90-270.47.

Recognized hybrid designation.
Seed law, §106-277.2.

Recognized variety name.
Seed law, §106-277.2.

Recommendation.
Suitability in annuity transactions, §58-60-165.

Reconstructed vehicle.
Motor vehicles, §20-4.01.

Reconstructive breast surgery.
Accident and health insurance, §58-51-62(b).
Health maintenance organizations, §58-67-79(b).
Hospital, medical and dental service corporations, §58-65-96(b).

Record.
Adoption, §48-9-101(a).
Anatomical gifts, §130A-412.4.
Arbitration, §1-569.1.
Athlete agents, §78C-86.
Child custody jurisdiction and enforcement, §50A-110.

DEFINED TERMS —Cont'd

Record —Cont'd

Electronic transactions, §66-312.

Indian antiquities, §70-48.

Letters of credit, §25-5-102(a).

Notaries public act, §10B-3.

Prudent management of institutional funds, §36E-2.

Secured transactions, §25-9-102(a).

State personnel files, privacy, §126-22(b).

Unclaimed property act, §116B-52.

Recordation.

Unit ownership, §47A-3.

Record center.

Archives and history, §121-2.

Record date.

Business corporations, §55-1-40.

Nonprofit corporations, §55A-1-40.

Recording data.

Registers of deeds, §161-14.1(a).

Satisfaction of deeds of trust and mortgages, §45-36.4.

Recording group.

Truth in music advertising act, §75-125(b).

Recordings.

Evidence, §8C-1 Rule 1001.

Records.

Identity theft, §75-61.

Record shareholder.

Appraisal rights, §55-13-01.

Records of criminal intelligence information.

Public records, §132-1.4.

Records of criminal investigations.

Public records, §132-1.4.

Recover.

Discarded computer equipment and television management, §130A-309.131.

Recovered materials.

Solid waste management, §130A-290(a).

Recreation.

Cities and towns, §160A-352.

Local affairs, §143-320.

Recreational fishing.

Coastal recreational fishing licenses, §113-174.

Salt water fishing license, §113-174.

Recreational purpose.

Liability of landowners associated with watershed improvement projects, §139-41.3.

Recreational trespass, §38A-2.

Recreational therapy, §90C-22.

Recreational therapy aide, §90C-22.

Recreational vehicle, §20-4.01.

Highway use tax, §105-187.1.

Recreation authority.

Veterans, §165-25.

Recreation district.

Alcoholic beverage permits, §18B-1006(j).

Recyclable material, §130A-290(a).

Surplus state property, §143-64.02.

Recycle.

Discarded computer equipment and television management, §130A-309.131.

Recycled content.

Plastic bag management, §130A-309.121.

Recycled content percentage.

Taxation, §105-102.6.

Recycled content tonnage.

Taxation, §105-102.6.

Recycled oil, §119-13.1.

Recycled paper bag.

Plastic bag management, §130A-309.121.

DEFINED TERMS —Cont'd

Recycler.

Discarded computer equipment and television management, §130A-309.131.

Recycling, §130A-290(a), (b).

Newspaper taxation, §105-102.6.

Recycling tonnage.

Newspaper taxation, §105-102.6.

Redaction.

Identity theft, §75-61.

Redeveloper.

Urban redevelopment, §160A-503.

Redevelopment, §160A-503.

Redevelopment area, §160A-503.

Redevelopment commission, §160A-503.

Redevelopment contract, §160A-503.

Redevelopment plan, §160A-503.

Redevelopment project, §160A-503.

Redevelopment proposal, §160A-503.

Red light.

Use of red light or blue lights on motor vehicles, §20-130.1(a).

Redundant capacity components.

Sales and use tax, §105-164.3.

Reemployment services.

Unemployment compensation, §96-8.

Refer.

Private personnel services, §95-47.1.

Referee.

Boxing commission, §143-651.

Referendum.

Elections, §163-165.

Political campaigns, §163-278.6.

Referendum committee.

Political campaigns, §163-278.6.

Public campaign fund, §163-278.62.

Referral.

Self-referrals by health care providers, §90-405.

Refiner.

Gasoline tax, §105-449.60.

Motor fuel, §75-81.

Refinery.

Gasoline tax, §105-449.60.

Refrigeration contractor, §87-58(a).

Refrigeration trade or business.

Refrigeration contractors, §87-58(b).

Refund.

Debt collection, §105A-2.

Refund anticipation loan.

Refund anticipation loan act, §53-246.

Refund anticipation loan fee.

Refund anticipation loan act, §53-246.

Refunding obligations.

State debt, §142-29.2.

Refusal.

Anatomical gifts, §130A-412.4.

Refuse.

Mining, §74-49.

Solid waste management, §130A-290(a).

Refuse-derived fuel.

Solid waste management, §130A-290(a).

Region.

Land policy act, §113A-152.

Reciprocal banking act, §53-210.

Regional bank.

Reciprocal banking act, §53-210.

Regional bank holding company.

Reciprocal banking act, §53-210.

Regional facility.

Facility authorities, §160A-480.2.

DEFINED TERMS —Cont'd

Regional institution.
Community colleges, §115D-2.

Regionally significant project.
Planning regionally significant transportation projects, §136-200.

Regional natural gas district, §160A-661(b).

Regional ombudsman.
Long-term care program, §143B-181.16.

Regional public transportation authority,
§160A-601.
Territorial jurisdiction, §160A-602.

Regional response team.
Hazardous materials emergency response, §166A-21.

Regional school, §115C-238.61.

Regional school board of directors or board of directors.
Regional school, §115C-238.61.

Regional sewage disposal system, §162A-27.

Regional transportation authority, §160A-631.

Regional travel demand model.
Planning regionally significant transportation projects, §136-200.

Regional water system, §162A-22.

Register.
Interstate family support, §52C-1-101.
Uniform transfer on death security registration act, §41-40.

Registered agent.
Savings and loan associations, §54B-4.
Savings banks, §54C-4(b).

Registered classified motor vehicle.
Taxation, §105-330.

Registered environmental consultant.
Risk based environmental remediation of industrial sites, §130A-310.65.

Registered environmental health specialist,
§90A-51.

Registered environmental health specialist intern, §90A-51.

Registered forester, §89B-2.

Registered form.
Investment securities, §25-8-102.

Registered handler.
Egg promotion tax, §106-245.33(b).

Registered limited liability partnerships.
Partnerships, §59-32.

Registered mortgage loan originator.
Mortgage bankers, brokers and servicers, §53-244.030.

Registered organization.
Secured transactions, §25-9-102(a).

Registered owner.
Impaired driving, §20-28.2(a1).

Registered pesticide.
Structural pest control act, §106-65.24.

Registered polysomnographic technologist,
§90-721.

Registered property.
Hunting and fishing on registered property of another, §113-281.

Registered public obligation, §159E-2.

Registered seeds.
Seed law, §106-277.2.

Registered sponsor.
Hearing aids, §93D-1.

Registered technician.
Structural pest control act, §106-65.24.

Registered trainee.
Real estate appraisers, §93E-1-4.

DEFINED TERMS —Cont'd

Registering entity.
Uniform transfer on death security registration act, §41-40.

Registering tribunal.
Interstate family support, §52C-1-101.

Register of deeds.
Satisfaction of deeds of trust and mortgages, §45-36.4.

Registrant.
Controlled substances, §90-87.
Hunting and fishing on registered property of another, §113-281.
Pesticide board, §143-460.
Real estate appraisal management companies, §93E-2-2(a).
Refund anticipation loan act, §53-246.
Soil additives act, §106-50.30.
Substance abuse professionals, §90-113.31A.

Registration.
Adult care homes, §131D-2.1.
Athlete agents, §78C-86.
Nature preserves act, §113A-164.3.

Registration as a trainee.
Real estate appraisers, §93E-1-4.

Registration fees.
Taxation, §105-330.

Regular accumulated contributions.
State law-enforcement retirement, §143-166.30(a).

Regular benefits.
Unemployment insurance, §96-12.01(a1).

Regular boarder.
Sanitation, §130A-247.

Regular driver's license.
Motor vehicles, §20-4.01.

Regular interest, §128-21.
Legislative retirement system, §120-4.8.
State retirement system, §135-1.

Regularly visits.
Lead poisoning in children, §130A-131.7.

Regular physicians.
Health insurance, locum tenens contracts, §58-3-231(a).

Regular place of work or business.
Notaries public act, §10B-3.

Regular remuneration.
Contingency fees collected by lobbyists, §120C-300(b).

Regular resident superior court judge of the district or set of districts.
Judicial department, §7A-41.1(a).

Regular session.
Limitation on fundraising during legislative session, §163-278.13B(a).

Regular vending facility.
Aid to the blind, §111-42(a).

Regulated article.
Bee and honey act, §106-635.
Boll weevil eradication, §106-65.69.

Regulated metals property.
Dealing in, §66-11(a).

Regulated substance.
Brownfields property reuse act, §130A-310.31(b).
Dry-cleaning solvent cleanup act, §143-215.104B(b).

Regulatory action level event.
Risk based capital requirements, insurance companies, §58-12-11(a).

Regulatory action level risk-based capital.
Insurance companies, §58-12-2.

DEFINED TERMS —Cont'd

Rehabilitation.
Housing finance agency, §122A-3.

Rehabilitation, conservation and reconditioning area.
Urban redevelopment, §160A-503.

Rehabilitation expenses.
Historic rehabilitation tax credit, §105-129.36(b).
Mill rehabilitation tax credit, §§105-129.36, 105-129.70.

Rehabilitation facility, §131E-176.

Reimbursable loss.
Client security fund, rules governing administration, Bar Rule D.1401.
Homeowner's recovery fund, §87-15.5.

Reimbursement policy.
Health plans, disclosure to providers, §58-3-227(a).

Reinsurance intermediaries, §58-9-2(a).

Reinsurer.
Reinsurance intermediaries, §58-9-2(a).

Reinsuring carrier.
Small employer group health coverage, §58-50-110.

REIT.
Real estate investment trusts, §105-130.12(a).

Rejected equipment.
Weights and measures, §81A-9.

Related degree.
Marriage and family therapists, §90-270.47.

Related entity.
Industrial facilities sales tax refunds, §105-164.14B(a).

Related member.
Job development investment grant program, §143B-437.51.
Sales and use tax, §105-164.3.
Tax credit for qualifying expenses of production company, §§105-130.47(a), 105-151.29(a).

Related or subordinate party.
Principal and income act, §37A-1-104.1.

Related party.
Small business contractors, §143B-472.101.

Related person.
Research and development expenses tax credit, §105-129.50.

Related provider trust.
Viatical life insurance settlements, §58-58-205.

Related services.
Education expenses credit, §105-151.33(i).
Education of children with disabilities, §115C-106.3.

Relative.
Fraudulent transfers, §39-23.1.
Taxation, §105-277.2.
Wildlife conservation land.
Special class of property for property tax purposes, §105-277.15(a).

Release.
Decedents' estates, §28A-19-7.
Dry-cleaning solvent cleanup act, §143-215.104B(b).
Mortgages and deeds of trust, §45-36.6(a).
Sex offender and public protection registration, §14-208.6.
Solid waste management, §130A-310.

Released claims.
Tobacco reserve fund, §66-290.

Releasing parties.
Tobacco reserve fund, §66-290.

DEFINED TERMS —Cont'd

Relevant evidence.
Evidence, §8C-1 Rule 401.

Relevant market area.
Motor vehicle manufacturers.
Unfair methods of competition, §20-305.2(c).

Relevant market area or trade area.
Motor vehicles, §20-286.

Relevant medical information.
Workers' compensation, §97-25.6(b).

Relevant offense.
Mental health, developmental disabilities and substance abuse, §122C-80(e).

Relevant time after driving.
Motor vehicles, §20-4.01.

Religious assembly.
Governing body of assembly authorized to adopt regulations, §61-7(f).
Religious societies, §61-7.

Religious institution.
Solicitation of contributions, §131F-2.

Religious purpose.
Property taxes, §105-278.3(d).
Taxation, §105-278.3.

Religious sponsored child care facilities, §110-106.

Relinquishment.
Adoption, §48-1-101.

Relocation officer, §133-7.

Remainder beneficiary.
Principal and income act, §37A-1-102.

Remedial action.
Solid waste management, §130A-310.

Remedial action plan.
Risk based environmental remediation of industrial sites, §130A-310.65.

Remedial program.
Brownfields property reuse act, §130A-310.31(b).
Dry-cleaning solvent cleanup act, §143-215.104B(b).

Remediation.
Brownfields property reuse act, §130A-310.31(b).
Dry-cleaning solvent cleanup act, §143-215.104B(b).
Lead poisoning in children, §130A-131.7.
Risk based environmental remediation of industrial sites, §130A-310.65.

Remedy.
Civil procedure, §1-1.
Solid waste management, §130A-310.
UCC, §25-1-201(b).

Remit.
Money transmitters, §53-208.2(a).

Remitter.
Negotiable instruments, §25-3-103.

Remitting bank.
Banking, §25-4-105.

Remote sale.
Sales and use tax, §105-164.3.

Remote state action.
Nurse licensure compact, §90-171.82.

Remote states.
Nurse licensure compact, §90-171.82.

Remote testimony.
Child witness, §15A-1225.1(a).
Developmentally disabled or mentally retarded, §§8C-1 Rule 616, 15A-1225.2(a).

Removable windshield placard.
Handicapped parking privileges, §20-37.5.

Removal.
Asbestos hazard management, §130A-444.

DEFINED TERMS —Cont'd

Removal —Cont'd

Gasoline tax, §105-449.60.

Judicial standards commission, §7A-374.2.

Remove.

Judicial standards commission, §7A-374.2.

Solid waste management, §130A-310.

Renderer.

Meat inspection, §106-549.15.

Poultry products inspection, §106-549.51.

Rendering operation, §106-168.1.

Rendering plant, §106-168.1.

Renewable biomass resources.

Business and energy tax credits, §105-129.15.

Renewable energy certificate.

Renewable energy and energy efficiency portfolio standard (REPS), §62-133.8(a).

Renewable energy facility.

Renewable energy and energy efficiency portfolio standard (REPS), §62-133.8(a).

Renewable energy property.

Business and energy tax credits, §105-129.15.

Renewable energy resource.

Renewable energy and energy efficiency portfolio standard (REPS), §62-133.8(a).

Renewable energy source.

Energy improvements revolving loan program.

Cities, §160A-459.1(c).

Counties, §153A-455(c).

Renewable fuel.

Business and energy tax credits, §105-129.15.

Renewal certificate, §90-221(d).

Renovate.

Bedding, §106-65.95.

Renovation activities.

Lead-based paint renovation activities, §130A-453.22(b).

Renovation or construction.

Swine farm siting, §106-806(a).

Rent.

Corporate income tax, §105-130.4.

Rental agreement.

Rental car companies selling insurance, §58-33-17(a).

Rental cars, §66-201.

Self service storage renter's insurance, §58-33-18(a).

Storage facilities, §44A-40.

Rental car company, §66-201.

Rental car companies selling insurance, §58-33-17(a).

Rental referral agency, §66-142.

Rental vehicle.

Motor vehicles, §20-84.2.

Renter.

Rental car companies selling insurance, §58-33-17(a).

Rental cars, §66-201.

Self service storage renter's insurance, §58-33-18(a).

Rents, issues or profits.

Criminal law, §14-168.2.

Probate and registration, §47-20.

Repackager.

Registration of prescription drug repackager, §106-140.1(j).

Repair.

Motor vehicles, §20-341.

Sewage systems, §130A-334.

Weights and measures, §81A-9.

Well construction, §87-85.

DEFINED TERMS —Cont'd

Repealed reimbursement amount.

Local sales and use tax, §105-521(a).

Repealed sales tax amount.

Third one-half cent tax.

County hold harmless for repealed taxes, §105-523(b).

Repeatability.

Fire-safety standard and firefighter protection act, §58-92-10.

Repeated violation.

Mines, §74-24.2.

Repellents.

Structural pest control act, §106-65.24.

Replacement equipment.

Certificate of need, §131E-176.

Replacement revenue.

Local sales and use tax, §105-521(a).

Replacement services loss.

Victims compensation, §15B-2.

Replication transaction.

Derivative transaction, insurance companies, §58-7-205(a).

Replica vehicle.

Motor vehicles, §20-4.01.

Report.

False reports concerning destructive devices, §14-69.1(e).

Weapons of mass death and destruction, §14-288.23(c).

Reportable conviction.

Sex offender and public protection registration, §14-208.6.

Reportable crash.

Motor vehicles, §20-4.01.

Reportable expenditure.

Lobbying, §120C-100(a).

Report to the court.

Adoption, §48-1-101.

Representative.

Compensation of trustees and other fiduciaries, §32-53.

Principal and income act, §37A-1-104.1.

UCC, §25-1-201(b).

Representative payee.

Nursing homes, §131E-116.

Representative trust office.

Trust companies, §53-301(a).

Represented person.

Negotiable instruments, §25-3-307(a).

Reprimand.

Discipline and disability rules of state bar, Bar Rule B.0103.

Reproduction.

Sales, §25C-10.

Request.

Recovery from insurers providing additional coverage to Medicaid-eligible persons, §108A-55.4(a).

Request for an accounting.

Secured transactions, §25-9-210(a).

Requesting state.

National Guard compact, §127A-177.

Pest control, §106-65.55.

Request regarding a list of collateral.

Secured transactions, §25-9-210(a).

Request regarding a statement of account.

Secured transactions, §25-9-210(a).

Requests.

Secured transactions, information as to collateral, §25-9-210(a).

DEFINED TERMS —Cont'd
Requests for proposals.
Guaranteed energy savings contracts, §143-64.17.
Request to terminate an equity line of credit.
Instruments to secure equity lines of credit,
§45-81.
Requisites of contract, §58-58-1.
Rerefined oil, §119-13.1.
Rerefining, §130A-290(b).
Resale.
Mortgages and deeds of trust.
Sales under power of sale, §45-21.1(a).
Resale restrictions.
Community land trust property taxation,
§105-277.17(b).
Rescue, §58-87-5(c).
Rescue squad.
Highway use tax, §105-187.1.
Insurance, volunteer rescue/EMS fund and safety
workers assistance, §58-87-5(c).
Rescue squad worker.
Death benefits, §143-166.2(d).
Retirement, §128-21.
State health plan for teachers and state
employees, §135-48.1.
Tuition and fee waivers, §115B-1.
Rescue unit, §58-87-5(c).
Research and development.
Growing businesses tax credits, §105-129.81.
Research and production service district.
Counties, §153A-312.
Research facility.
Protection of animals, §19A-23.
Research purposes.
Health information exchange, §90-413.3.
Research university.
Research and development expenses tax credit,
§105-129.50.
Reservation deposit, §116B-54(b).
Reserve.
Banking, §§53-51(a), 53-84.
Reserve assets.
Asset protection, §58-13-15.
**Reserve components of the armed forces of the
United States.**
Motor vehicles, §20-4.01.
Reserve trust fund.
State education assistance authority, §116-201.
Reside.
Education of children with disabilities,
§115C-106.3.
Residence.
Administrative procedure, §150B-2.
Asbestos hazard management, §130A-444.
Continuing care retirement communities,
§58-64-1.
Education of children with disabilities,
§115C-106.3.
False advertising, §58-29-5.
Insurance guaranty associations, §58-62-16.
Interstate compact on juveniles, §7B-2803.
Inventory property tax deferral on builder
constructed and owned residence,
§105-277.1D(a).
Sewage systems, §130A-334.
Targeted picketing, §14-277.4A(a).
Voting, §163-57.
Residence state.
Interstate compact on adoption and medical
assistance, §7B-3901.

DEFINED TERMS —Cont'd
Residency.
Municipal voting, §163-282.
Resident.
Adult care homes, §131D-2.1.
Adult care home's bill of rights, §131D-20.
Bail bondsman and runners, §58-71-1.
Conservation, §113-130.
Expedited evictions, §42-59.
Health insurance risk pool, §58-50-175.
Higher education tuition and fees, §116-143.1.
Insurance guaranty association, §58-48-20.
Long-term care ombudsman program,
§143B-181.16.
Motor vehicles, §20-4.01.
Public assistance program, §108A-24.
Taxation, §105-134.1.
Temporary management of long-term care
facilities, §131E-231.
Resident bidders.
Preferences to state products and citizens,
§143-59(c).
Resident for tuition purposes.
Higher education tuition and fees, §116-143.1.
Residential building.
Home inspectors, §143-151.45.
Residential care facility.
Patient abuse, §14-32.2(c1).
Residential child-care facility, §131D-10.2.
Residential district.
Motor vehicles, §20-4.01.
Residential facility.
Mental health, §122C-3.
Residential housing.
Housing finance agency, §122A-3.
Residential manufactured home.
Installment sales, §25A-15.
Residential mortgage loan or mortgage loan.
Mortgage bankers, brokers and servicers,
§53-244.030.
Residential private club.
Alcoholic beverages, §18B-1000.
Residential property.
Credit scoring to rate motor vehicle and property
insurance, §58-36-90(a).
Solar collectors.
County limitations on regulation, §153A-144(a).
Municipal limitations on regulation,
§160A-201(a).
Vacation rentals, §42A-4.
Residential purposes.
Condominiums, §47C-1-103.
Conversion building rental, §47A-34.
Residential real estate.
Mortgage bankers, brokers and servicers,
§53-244.030.
Real estate appraisers, §93E-1-4.
Residential real property.
Residential mortgage fraud, §14-118.11.
Residential school personnel.
Criminal history checks, §143B-146.16(a).
Residential treatment facility.
Mental health, developmental disabilities and
substance abuse, §122C-23.1.
Resident plant or resident species.
Plant protection and conservation, §106-202.12.
Resident trainee.
Funeral services, §90-210.20(l).
Residual market mechanism.
Insurance information and privacy protection act,
§58-39-15.

DEFINED TERMS —Cont'd

Resolution.
State education assistance authority, §116-201.

Resource disregard.
Long-term care partnerships, §58-55-55.
Medicaid, §108A-70.4(a).

Resource protection.
Long-term care partnerships, §58-55-55.
Medicaid, §108A-70.4(a).

Resource recovery.
Solid waste management, §130A-290(a).

Resources.
Computer crimes, §14-453.
Long-term care partnerships, §58-55-55.
Medicaid, §108A-70.4(a).
Medicaid, transfer of assets for less than market value to qualify, §108A-58.2(e).

Respiratory care.
Respiratory care practices act, §90-648.

Respiratory care practitioner, §90-648.

Respite care, institutional.
Long-term care insurance, §58-55-35(a).

Respite care, noninstitutional.
Long-term care insurance, §58-55-35(a).

Respondent.
Child custody jurisdiction and enforcement, §50A-301.
Discipline and disability rules of state bar, Bar Rule B.0103.
Incompetency, §35A-1101.
Temporary management of long-term care facilities, §131E-231.
Vaccine-related injury, §130A-422.

Responding state, §127A-177.
Interstate family support, §52C-1-101.
Pest control, §106-65.55.

Responding tribunal.
Interstate family support, §52C-1-101.

Response costs.
Dry-cleaning solvent cleanup act, §143-215.104B(b).

Responsibility.
Negotiable instruments, §25-3-405(a).

Responsibility for streets.
Municipal streets and highways, §136-66.1.

Responsible administrative authority.
Structured settlement protection, §1-543.11.

Responsible charge.
Engineering, §89C-3.

Responsible charge of work.
Geologist, §89E-3.
Soil scientists, §89F-3.

Responsible individual.
Abused, neglected and dependent juveniles, §7B-101.

Responsible parent.
Child support, §110-129.

Responsible party.
Management of abandoned manufactured homes, §130A-309.112.
Manufactured housing, §143-143.9.
Pharmacy audit rights, §90-85.50(a).
Solid waste management, §130A-310.

Responsible person.
Elective share of surviving spouse, §30-3.2.
Offshore oil and gas activities, §143-215.94BB.
Taxation.
Personal liability when taxes not paid, §105-242.2(a).

Responsible person's nonspousal assets.
Elective share of surviving spouse, §30-3.2.

DEFINED TERMS —Cont'd

Responsible professional.
Mental health, §122C-3.

Restaurant.
Alcoholic beverages, §18B-1000.
Smoking in public places, §143-596.
Smoking in restaurants and bars, §130A-492.

Restoration.
Oil and hazardous substance control, §143-215.77.

Restraining seat.
Child bicycle safety act, §20-171.8.

Restricted access drug and device.
Health insurers maintaining, §58-3-221(c).

Restricted area.
Aeronautics, §63-1.

Restricted noxious-weed seeds.
Seed law, §106-277.2.

Restricted use pesticide.
Pesticide board, §143-460.
Structural pest control act, §106-65.24.

Restriction.
Notaries public act, §10B-3.

Resulting bank.
Interstate branch banking, §53-224.9.

Resumption of marital relation, §52-10.2.

Retail business.
Alcoholic beverages, §18B-1000.

Retail dealer.
Fire-safety standard and firefighter protection act, §58-92-10.
Tobacco taxation, §105-113.4.

Retailer.
Alternative fuel, §105-449.130.
Commercial fertilizer, §106-657.
Discarded computer equipment and television management, §130A-309.131.
Drug paraphernalia control act, §90-113.81.
Egg law, §106-245.14.
Gasoline tax, §105-449.60.
Highway use tax, §105-187.1.
Methamphetamine lab prevention, §90-113.51(b).
Plastic bag management, §130A-309.121.
Sales and use tax, §105-164.3.
State lottery, §18C-103.

Retail installment sale.
Motor vehicles, §20-286.

Retail merchant.
Property taxes, §105-273.

Retail property.
Organized retail theft, §14-86.5.

Retail property fence.
Organized retail theft, §14-86.5.

Retail sale or sale at retail.
Sales and use tax, §105-164.3.

Retail sales value.
Counterfeit trademarks, §80-11.1(a).

Retail transactions.
911 system, §62A-40.

Retained expert witness.
Medicolegal guidelines for attorney-physician relationship, MLG Rule 3.

Retaliatory action.
Employment discrimination, §95-240.

Retired employee.
State health plan for teachers and state employees, §135-48.1.

Retiree.
State health plan for teachers and state employees, §135-48.1.

Retirement, §128-21.
Disability income plan, §135-101.

DEFINED TERMS —Cont'd
Retirement —Cont'd
Judiciary, §135-53.
Legislature, §120-4.8.
State retirement, §135-1.
Retirement allowance, §128-21.
Judiciary, §135-53.
State law-enforcement, §143-166.30(a).
State retirement, §135-1.
Retirement benefits.
Taxation, §105-134.1.
Retirement system, §128-21.
Disability income plan, §135-101.
Judiciary, §135-53.
State retirement, §135-1.
Retrospective compensation agreements.
General insurance agents, §58-34-5(b).
Return to work.
Industrial commission utilization of rehabilitation professionals, ICRehabProf Rule III.
Reusable bag.
Plastic bag management, §130A-309.121.
Reuse, §130A-290(a).
Revalidation.
Provider requirements for Medicaid or Health Choice, §108C-2.
Revenue bond project, §§159-81, 159-97.
Special assessments by counties for critical infrastructure needs, §153A-210.6(b).
Revenue bonds, §159-81.
Metropolitan sewerage districts, §162A-65(a).
Metropolitan water districts, §162A-32(a).
State education assistance authority, §116-201.
University of North Carolina, §116-41.1.
Revenue-neutral property tax rate.
Local budgets, §159-11(e).
Revenues.
Centennial campus and Horace Williams campus financing act, §116-198.33.
Global TransPark authority, §63A-2.
Higher education student housing, §116-189.
Metropolitan sewerage districts, §162A-65(a).
Metropolitan water districts, §162A-32(a).
Pollution control, §§159C-3, 159D-3.
Revenue bonds, §159-81.
Solid waste, §159I-3(a).
Special assessments by counties for critical infrastructure needs, §153A-210.6(b).
University of North Carolina, §116-41.1.
Water and sewer, §162A-2.
Reverse auction.
Procurement of information technology, §147-33.95(c).
Public contracts, §143-129.9(a).
Reverse mortgage loan, §53-257.
Revised rules of professional conduct.
Discipline and disability rules of state bar, Bar Rule B.0103.
Procedures for ruling on questions of legal ethics, Bar Rule D.0101.
Revocable.
Uniform trust code, §36C-1-103.
Revocation or suspension.
Motor vehicles, §20-4.01.
Notaries public act, §10B-3.
Revocation report.
Motor vehicles, §20-16.5(a).
Provisional license revocation, §20-13.3(a).
Revoked financial transaction card.
Criminal law, §14-113.8.

DEFINED TERMS —Cont'd
Revolving charge account contract.
Installment sales, §25A-11.
Revolving loan programs for private investment.
Main street solutions fund, §143B-472.35(a2).
Ridge.
Mining, §74-49.
Mountain ridge protection, §113A-206.
Right of withdrawal.
Impounded water, §143-215.44(b).
Rights.
UCC, §25-1-201(b).
Ring official.
Boxing commission, §143-651.
Ring signaling device.
Deaf and the hard of hearing, §143B-216.30.
Ringtone.
Sales and use tax, §105-164.3.
Riot, §14-288.2(a).
Civil disorders, §14-288.1.
Riparian owner.
Cultivation of shellfish, §113-201.1.
Risk assets.
Cooperative organizations' reserve allocations, §54-109.88.
Risk-assuming carrier.
Small employer group health coverage, §58-50-110.
Risk-based.
Contamination of site, §143B-279.9(d).
Risk-based capital level.
Insurance companies, §58-12-2.
Risk retention group, §58-22-10.
River.
Natural and scenic rivers, §113A-33.
River basin, §77-110.
Water withdrawals and transfers, §143-215.22G.
Road.
Natural and scenic rivers, §113A-33.
Road construction.
Contractors, §87-101.
Road maintenance.
Contractors, §87-101.
Road tractors.
Motor vehicles, §20-4.01.
Roadway.
Motor vehicles, §20-4.01.
Roanoke river basin.
Roanoke river basin commission, §77-90.
Robbery.
Criminal law, §14-87.1.
Rodenticides.
Pesticide board, §143-460.
Structural pest control act, §106-65.24.
Roller skater.
Roller skating rink safety and liability, §99E-10.
Roller skating rink.
Roller skating rink safety and liability, §99E-10.
Rolling stock.
Public service taxation, §105-333.
Room.
Secretly peeping into room occupied by another person, §14-202(b).
Room operator.
Telephonic sellers, §66-260.
Rope tow.
Passenger tramway safety, §95-117.
Route.
Public utilities, §62-3.

DEFINED TERMS —Cont'd
Royalties.
Corporate income tax, §105-130.4.
RSCFL.
Coastal and estuarine commercial fishing licenses, §113-168.
Rules.
Education of children with disabilities, §115C-106.3.
Fraternal benefit societies, §58-24-15(f).
Interstate compact for juveniles, §7B-4001.
Interstate insurance product regulation compact, §58-91-10.
Rules and regulations.
Administrative procedure, §150B-2.
Continuing legal education, Bar Rule D.1501.
Fees and charges by state agencies, §12-3.1(b).
Savings and loan associations, §54B-4.
Rules of professional conduct.
Discipline and disability rules of state bar, Bar Rule B.0103.
Run.
Motion pictures, §75C-2.
Runner.
Bail bondsman and runners, §58-71-1.
Rural areas.
Enterprise corporations, §53A-37.
Rural fire department.
Cities and towns, §160A-1.
Rural hospital network.
Hospital licensure, §131E-76.
Rural transportation planning organizations.
Transportation department, §136-210.
Sadomasochistic abuse.
Public morals, §19-12.
Safe home.
Abused, neglected or dependent juveniles, §7B-101.
Safekeeping property.
Rules of professional conduct, ProfCond Rule 1.15-1.
Safety glass.
Motor vehicles, §20-135(b).
Safety rest area.
Outdoor advertising control, §136-128.
Safety zone.
Motor vehicles, §20-4.01.
Salary.
Community college employee records, §115D-28(b).
County personnel system, records, §153A-98(b1).
Mental health, developmental disability, substance abuse.
Area authorities, personnel file of employees, §122C-158(b1).
School employees, §115C-320(b).
State employee's personnel records, §126-23(b).
Water and sewer authorities, §162A-6.1(b).
Sale.
Alcoholic beverages, §18B-101.
Alcohol taxation, §105-113.68.
Bedding, §106-65.95.
Civil procedure, §1-339.41(b).
Commercial fertilizer, §106-657.
Corporate income tax, §105-130.4(a).
Fire-safety standard and firefighter protection act, §58-92-10.
Judicial sales, §1-339.1(b).
Motor fuel, §75-81.
Public morals, §19-1.1.
Sales, §25-2-106.
Sales and use tax, §105-164.3.

DEFINED TERMS —Cont'd
Sale —Cont'd
Sales under power of sale, §45-21.1(a).
Securities, §78A-2.
Soil additives act, §106-50.30.
Tobacco taxation, §105-113.4.
Weights and measures, §81A-9.
Sale of obscene or lewd matter.
Public morals, §19-1.1.
Sales assessment ratio studies.
Public school building capital fund, §115C-546.2(d).
Sales customer.
Piped natural gas tax, §105-187.40.
Salesman.
Securities, §78A-2.
Salespersons.
Membership camping, §66-232.
Telephonic sellers, §66-260.
Sales price.
Sales and use tax, §105-164.3.
Sales representative, §66-190.
Sales tax.
Uniform sales and use tax administration act, §105-164.42B.
Sales territory.
Alcoholic beverages, §18B-1201.
Salvage motor vehicle, §20-4.01.
Salvage rebuilt vehicle.
Motor vehicles, §20-4.01.
Salvage yard.
Motor vehicles, §20-137.7.
Same professional services.
Medical malpractice, §90-21.19(c).
Sample.
Youth access to tobacco products, §14-313(a).
Sanctioned amateur.
Boxing commission, §143-651.
Sanctioned amateur match.
Boxing commission, §143-651.
SANE nurse.
Assistance program for victims of rape and sex offenses, §143B-1200(i).
Sanitary landfill, §130A-290(a).
Sanitary sewage systems, §130A-334.
Sanitize.
Bedding, §106-65.95.
Protection of animals, §19A-23.
Satellite corporate limits.
City and town annexation of noncontiguous areas, §160A-58.
Satellite digital audio radio service.
Sales and use tax, §105-164.3.
Satellite jail/work release unit.
Counties, §153A-230.1.
Satisfactory evidence.
Notaries public act, §10B-3.
Satisfy.
Satisfaction of deeds of trust and mortgages, §45-36.4.
Savings and loan association, §§54B-4, 54C-4(a).
Savings and loan holding company.
Regional reciprocal savings and loan acquisition act, §54B-48.2.
Savings association.
Trust companies, §53-301(a).
Savings bank, §54C-4(b).
Savings interstate branch banks, §54C-200.
Savings institution, §54C-4(b).
SBI.
DNA database and databanks, §15A-266.2.

DEFINED TERMS —Cont'd

Scale technician.
Weights and measures, §81A-9.

Scan line.
Campaign contributions and expenditures.
Disclosure requirements for media
advertisements, §163-278.38Z.

Scanning device.
Financial transaction cards, §14-113.8.

Scattering area.
Cremation, §90-210.121.

Scenic easement.
Natural and scenic rivers, §113A-33.
North Carolina trail system, §113A-85.

SCFL.
Coastal and estuarine commercial fishing licenses,
§113-168.

Schedule of fees.
Health plans, disclosure to providers,
§58-3-227(a).

Scholarship, §115C-499.1.
Lobbying, §120C-800(g).
Need-based scholarships for students attending
private colleges and universities, §116-280.

School.
Attendance, §115C-378.
Dissemination of criminal intelligence
information, §14-50.27A.
Drivers' licenses, lose control, lose license,
§20-11(n1).
Leave for parent involvement in schools,
§95-28.3(a).
Taking indecent liberties with a student,
§14-202.4(d).
Weapons on educational property, §14-269.2(a).

School activity bus, §20-4.01.

School administrator, §115C-325(a).
Drivers' licenses, lose control, lose license,
§20-11(n1).

School bus, §20-4.01.
Tire purchases, §115C-249.1(a).

School district.
Funding bonds, §115C-481.

School instructional material.
Sales and use tax, §105-164.3.

School official.
Discipline of students, §115C-390.1(b).

School personnel.
Charter schools.
Criminal history checks, §115C-238.29K(a).
Criminal history records checks, §115C-332(a).
Discipline of students, §115C-390.1(b).
Seclusion and restraint, §115C-391.1(b).
Taking indecent liberties with a student,
§14-202.4(d).

School property.
Drivers' licenses, lose control, lose license,
§20-11(n1).
Education programs at residential schools.
Duty to report certain acts to law enforcement,
§143B-146.15.
Principals to report certain acts to law
enforcement, §115C-288(g).

School safety officer.
Taking indecent liberties with a student,
§14-202.4(d).

School supply.
Sales and use tax, §105-164.3.

School system.
Organization of schools, §115C-74.

DEFINED TERMS —Cont'd

Scientific committee.
Plant protection and conservation, §106-202.12.

Scientific council.
Endangered wildlife, §113-331.

Scientific purposes.
Property tax exemption, §105-278.7(f).
Taxation, §105-278.3(d).

Scope of recreational therapy.
Recreational therapists, §90C-22.

S corporations and partnerships.
Taxation, §§105-130.2, 105-131, 105-134.1,
105-134.5.

Scrap fishing, §113-185(b).

Scrap-metal recycling facility.
Mercury switch removal, motor vehicles,
§130A-310.50.

Scrap tire, §130A-309.53.
Tire disposal tax, §105-187.15.

Screened.
Rules of professional conduct, ProfCond Rule 1.0.

Screening.
Controlled substance examination regulation,
§95-231.

Scrutinized business operations.
Sudan (Darfur) divestment act, §147-86.42.

Scrutinized company.
Sudan (Darfur) divestment act, §147-86.42.

Sealed record information.
National crime prevention and privacy compact,
§114-19.50.

Sealed with its corporate seal.
Corporate conveyance forms, §47-41.01(d).

Seals.
Notaries public act, §10B-3.

Search and rescue animal.
Assaulting, §14-163.1(a).

Search ring.
Wireless telecommunications facilities,
§§153A-349.51, 160A-400.51.

Search warrant, §15A-241.

Seasonal food service establishment.
Wage and hour act, §95-25.2.

**Seasonal or religious nonprofit educational
conference center or a seasonal
amusement or recreational establishment.**
Wage and hour act, §95-25.2.

Seasonal pursuit.
Unemployment compensation, §96-16(a).

Seasonal wages.
Unemployment compensation.
Seasonal pursuits, §96-16(j).

Seasonal worker.
Unemployment compensation.
Seasonal pursuits, §96-16(j).

SEC.
Audited financial reports.
Insurance companies, §58-10-190.

Seclusion.
Discipline of students, §115C-391.1(b).

Second.
Boxing commission, §143-651.

Secondary metals recycler.
Dealing in regulated metals property, §66-11(a).

Secondary obligor.
Secured transactions, §25-9-102(a).

Secondary standards.
Weights and measures, §81A-9.

Secondary supplier.
Urban electrical service, §160A-331.

DEFINED TERMS —Cont'd
Second-degree murder.
Criminal law, §14-17.
Second-degree rape.
Criminal law, §14-27.3.
Second-degree sexual offense.
Criminal law, §14-27.5.
Secondhand bedding, §106-65.95.
Second tier subcontractor.
Liens, §44A-17.
Second trust, §36C-8-816.1(a).
Secretary.
Business corporations, §55-1-40.
Nonprofit corporations, §55A-1-40.
Sanitary districts, creation by commission,
§130A-47(b).
Solid waste management, §130A-290(a).
Secretary of health, education and welfare.
Governmental employees and social security,
§135-20.
Secretary-treasurer.
Rescue squad workers' relief fund, §58-88-1.
Secret military society.
Criminal law, §14-12.2.
Secret political society.
Criminal law, §14-12.2.
Secret society.
Criminal law, §14-12.2.
Section.
Boxing commission, §143-651.
Section 404.
Annual audited financial reports.
Insurance companies, §58-10-190.
Section 404 report.
Annual audited financial reports.
Insurance companies, §58-10-190.
Secured claim.
Insurers supervision, §58-30-10.
Secured creditor.
Satisfaction of deeds of trust and mortgages,
§45-36.4.
Trustee in deed of trust, §45-45.3(a).
Secured obligation.
Satisfaction of deeds of trust and mortgages,
§45-36.4.
Secured party, §44A-1.
Secured transactions, §25-9-102(a).
Sublease of motor vehicle and loan assumption
arranging, §20-106.2(a).
Securities act of 1933.
Securities, §78A-2.
Securities exchange act of 1934.
Securities, §78A-2.
Securities intermediary.
Investment securities, §25-8-102.
Securitization.
Asset-backed securities facilitation, §53-425.
Security, §78A-2.
Enterprise corporations, §53A-37.
Investment securities, §25-8-102.
Joint ownership of securities, §41-2.2.
Public utilities, §62-3.
Tax credit for qualified business investments,
§105-163.010.
Uniform transfer on death security registration
act, §41-40.
Security account.
Uniform transfer on death security registration
act, §41-40.
Security agreement.
Motor vehicles, §20-4.01.

DEFINED TERMS —Cont'd
Security agreement —Cont'd
Secured transactions, §25-9-102(a).
Security breach.
Identity theft, §75-61.
Motor vehicle dealers, §20-305.7(f).
Security certificate.
Investment securities, §25-8-102.
Security covered under federal law.
Securities, §78A-2.
Security document.
Global TransPark authority, §63A-2.
Pollution control, §§159C-3, 159D-3.
Security entitlement.
Investment securities, §25-8-102.
Security freeze.
Identity theft, §75-61.
Security guard and patrol profession, §74C-3.
Security holder.
Insurance holding companies, §58-19-5.
Security instrument, §45-67.
Satisfaction of deeds of trust and mortgages,
§45-36.4.
Security interest, §44A-1.
Motor vehicles, §20-4.01.
Satisfaction of deeds of trust and mortgages,
§45-36.4.
Sublease of motor vehicle and loan assumption
arranging, §20-106.2(a).
UCC, §25-1-201(b).
Security procedure.
Electronic transactions, §66-312.
Funds transfers, UCC, §25-4A-201.
Sediment.
Pollution control act, §113A-52.
Seed offered for sale, §106-277.2.
Seeking only part-time work.
Unemployment compensation, §96-8.
Seizure.
Seed law, §106-277.2.
Selected contractors.
Lease or purchase of prison facilities constructed
by private firm, §148-37.2(b).
Self-insurer.
Insurance company taxation, §105-228.3.
Workers' compensation.
Third-party administrators and service
companies, §58-47-150.
Workers' compensation self insurance, §97-165.
Self-propelled pole carrier, §20-116(f).
Self-service storage company.
Self service storage renter's insurance,
§58-33-18(a).
Self-service storage facility, §44A-40.
Self-supporting agencies.
State-owned office space.
Fees for use by, §143-342.1.
Sell.
Commercial fertilizer, §106-657.
Fire-safety standard and firefighter protection act,
§58-92-10.
Insurance producers, §58-33-10.
Securities, §78A-2.
Soil additives act, §106-50.30.
Seller.
Contracts for deed, §47H-1.
Installment sales, §25A-6.
Option to purchase contracts executed with
residential lease agreements, §47G-1.
Products liability, §99B-1.
Sales, §§14-401.13, 25-2-103.

DEFINED TERMS —Cont'd
Selling.
Sales and use tax, §105-164.3.
Selling or leasing at retail.
Tax credit for qualified business investments, §105-163.010.
Semiconductor manufacturing.
Industrial facilities sales tax refunds, §105-164.14B(a).
Semitrailers.
Motor vehicles, §20-4.01.
Send.
Secured transactions, §25-9-102(a).
UCC, §25-1-201(b).
Sender.
Funds transfers, UCC, §§25-4A-103(a), 25-4A-202(d).
Sending agency.
Interchange of governmental employees, §126-52.
Sending state.
Interstate agreement on detainers, §15A-761.
Interstate compact on mental health, §122C-361.
State prisons, §148-120.
Senior executive branch official.
False claims act, §1-606.
Senior executives.
Appraisal rights, §55-13-01.
Senior high school, §115C-75(a).
Sensitive land use.
Commercial hazardous waste treatment facilities, §130A-295.01(f).
Sentencing plan.
Sentencing services act, §7A-771.
Sentencing services program, §7A-771.
Separate property.
Divorce, §50-20(b).
Septage.
Solid waste management, §130A-290(a).
Septage management firm.
Solid waste management, §130A-290(a).
Septic tank system.
Sewage systems, §130A-334.
Serious bodily harm.
Assault inflicting serious bodily injury to unborn child, §14-23.5(b).
Serious bodily injury.
Assault, §14-32.4(a).
Child abuse, §14-318.4(d).
Failure to yield right of way, §20-160.1(b).
Serious harm.
Assaulting law enforcement or assistance animals, §14-163.1(a).
Serious neglect.
Abused, neglected or dependent juveniles, §7B-101.
Serious or chronic degenerative, disabling or life-threatening disease or condition.
Managed care access to specialists, §58-3-223(b).
Serious physical injury.
Child abuse, §14-318.4(d).
Serious traffic violation.
Motor vehicles, §20-4.01.
Serious violation.
Occupational safety and health, §95-127.
Server-based electronic game promotion, §14-306.3(c).
Service.
Computer crimes, §14-453.
Disability income plan, §135-101.
District attorneys, §7A-65(c), (d).
Installment sales, §25A-5.

DEFINED TERMS —Cont'd
Service —Cont'd
Privileged communications, rape crisis centers and domestic violence programs, §8-53.12.
Public utilities, §62-3.
Retirement, §128-21.
State retirement, §135-1.
Weights and measures, §81A-9.
Service agreement, §66-372(b).
Service agreement company, §66-372(b).
Service area.
Certificate of need, §131E-176.
Costs for solid waste management, determining, §130A-309.08(c).
Service certificate.
Weights and measures, §81A-73.
Service charges.
University of North Carolina, §116-41.1.
Service company.
Workers' compensation.
Self-insurance, §58-47-150.
Employer groups, §58-47-60.
Service corporation.
Regional reciprocal savings and loan acquisition act, §54B-48.2.
Savings and loan associations, §54B-4.
Savings banks, §54C-4(b).
Service member.
Life insurance.
Dishonest and predatory sales to military personnel, §58-58-335.
Servicemember.
Power of sale barred during military service, §45-21.12A(d).
Service provider.
Insurance customer information safeguards, §58-39-140.
Servicer.
Mortgage debt collection and servicing, §45-90.
Service-related industry.
Tax credit for qualified business investments, §105-163.010.
Services rendered.
Sales and use tax exemptions, §105-164.13.
Service supplier.
911 system, §62A-40.
Servicing facility.
Self-insurance security association, §97-130.
Set of districts.
District court districts, §7A-200(a).
Judicial department, §7A-41.1(a).
Settle.
Banking, §25-4-104(a).
Settled claim.
Structured settlement protection, §1-543.11.
Settlement.
Good funds settlement act, §45A-3.
Medical malpractice.
Reports to medical board of judgments, awards, payments and settlements, §§90-5.3(e), 90-121.6(d).
Settlement agent.
Good funds settlement act, §45A-3.
Settlor.
Principal and income act, §37A-1-104.1.
Uniform trust code, §36C-1-103.
Setup.
Manufactured housing, §143-143.9.
Set-up contractor.
Manufactured housing, §143-143.9.

DEFINED TERMS —Cont'd
7Q10 conditions.
  Solid waste management, §130A-295.01(a).
Severe and persistent mental illness, §122C-3.
Severe chronic disability.
  Community third party trusts, pooled trusts act,
    §36D-2.
Severe injury.
  Dangerous dogs, §67-4.1.
Severely disabled veteran.
  Unemployment compensation, §96-8.
Sewage, §§130A-334, 143-213, 162A-2.
  Clean coastal water and vessel act, §77-125.
  Metropolitan districts, §162A-65(a).
Sewage disposal system, §162A-2.
  Metropolitan districts, §162A-65(a).
Sewerage system.
  Metropolitan districts, §162A-65(a).
  Metropolitan water districts, §162A-32(a).
Sewers, §162A-2.
  Metropolitan districts, §162A-65(a).
  Metropolitan water districts, §162A-32(a).
Sewer system, §§143-213, 162A-2.
Sex offense.
  Permanent no contact order prohibiting future
    contact by convicted sex offender with victim,
    §15A-1340.50(a).
Sexual act.
  Criminal law, §14-27.1.
Sexual activity.
  Offenses against morality, §14-190.13.
Sexual assault.
  Assistance program for victims of rape and sex
    offenses, §143B-1200(i).
  Privileged communications, rape crisis centers
    and domestic violence programs, §8-53.12.
Sexual assault evidence collection kit.
  Assistance program for victims of rape and sex
    offenses, §143B-1200(i).
Sexual assault victim.
  Privileged communications, rape crisis centers
    and domestic violence programs, §8-53.12.
Sexual behavior.
  Rape shield law, §8C-1 Rule 412.
Sexual conduct.
  Civil no-contact orders, §50C-1.
  Obscene literature, §14-190.1.
  Public morals, §19-12.
Sexual contact.
  Sex offenses, §14-27.1.
Sexual excitement.
  Public morals, §19-12.
Sexual exploitation.
  Psychotherapy patient/client sexual exploitation
    act, §90-21.41.
Sexual history.
  Psychotherapy patient/client sexual exploitation
    act, §90-21.41.
Sexually explicit nudity.
  Offenses against morality, §14-190.13.
Sexually oriented devices.
  Adult establishments, §14-202.10.
Sexually violent offense.
  Sex offender and public protection registration,
    §14-208.6.
Sexually violent predator.
  Sex offender and public protection registration,
    §14-208.6.
Sexual penetration.
  Civil no-contact orders, §50C-1.

DEFINED TERMS —Cont'd
Sexual relations with clients.
  Rules of professional conduct, ProfCond Rule 1.19.
Sexual servitude.
  Human trafficking, §14-43.10(a).
SFL.
  Salt water fishing license, §113-174.
SGLI.
  Life insurance.
    Dishonest and predatory sales to military
      personnel, §58-58-335.
Shallow land burial.
  Radiation protection, §104E-5.
Shampooing, §88B-2.
Shared appreciation.
  Reverse mortgages, §53-257.
Shared value.
  Reverse mortgages, §53-257.
Shareholder.
  Appraisal rights, §55-13-01.
  Business corporations, §55-1-40.
  Derivative actions, §55-7-40.1.
Shares.
  Business corporations, §55-1-40.
  Decedents' estates, §29-2.
  State lottery, §18C-103.
Shellfish, §113-201.1.
  Conservation, §113-129.
Shellfish lease.
  Conservation, §113-269.
Shelter.
  Domestic violence shelters.
    Limited civil liability, §1-620.
Shelter care.
  Abused, neglected or dependent juveniles,
    §7B-101.
Sheriff.
  Civil procedure, §1-339.41(b).
  Sex offender and public protection registration,
    §14-208.6.
Sheriffs' association.
  Statewide misdemeanant confinement fund,
    §148-10.4(a).
Shingling tobacco.
  Leaf tobacco sales, §106-461.
Shipping container.
  Poultry products inspection, §106-549.51.
Shopping cart.
  Larceny, §14-72.3.
Shoreline area.
  High Rock lake marine commission, §77-50.
  Lake lure marine commission, §77-80.
  Lake Wylie marine commission, §77-30.
Short-pay amount.
  Satisfaction of deeds of trust and mortgages,
    §45-36.4.
Short-pay statement.
  Satisfaction of deeds of trust and mortgages,
    §45-36.4.
Short-term lease or rental.
  Heavy equipment gross receipts tax in lieu of
    property tax, §§105-187.1, 153A-156.1(a).
  Highway use tax, §105-187.1.
  Municipal heavy equipment gross receipts tax,
    §160A-215.2(a).
  Regional transit authority vehicle rental tax,
    §105-550.
Short-term suspension.
  Discipline of students, §115C-390.1(b).
Sickle cell trait.
  Labor discrimination, §95-28.1.

DEFINED TERMS —Cont'd
Side fund.
  Life insurance.
    Dishonest and predatory sales to military
      personnel, §58-58-335.
Sign.
  Anatomical gifts, §130A-412.4.
  Satisfaction of deeds of trust and mortgages,
    §45-36.4.
Signator.
  Interstate environmental compact, §113A-23.
Signature.
  Criminal process and procedure.
    Electronic technology, §15A-101.1.
Signed.
  UCC, §25-1-201(b).
Signed print.
  Sales, §25C-10.
Significant limitations in adaptive functioning.
  Death sentence prohibited, mentally retarded
    defendants, §15A-2005(a).
**Significantly subaverage general intellectual
    functioning.**
  Death sentence prohibited, mentally retarded
    defendants, §15A-2005(a).
Silent mortgage amount.
  Community land trust property taxation,
    §105-277.17(b).
Silicosis.
  Workers' compensation, §97-62.
Silver.
  Precious metals, §66-164.
Simulator.
  Certificate of need, §131E-176.
Simultaneous conversion/merger.
  Mutual and stock associations, §54B-37.1(a).
Single-axle weight.
  Motor vehicles, §20-118.
Single-family residential dwelling unit.
  Homeowner's recovery fund, §87-15.5.
Single family unit.
  Cultivation of shellfish, §113-201.1.
Single interest credit property.
  Credit property insurance, §58-57-90(a).
Single-line basic residential service.
  Alternative regulation, tariffing and deregulation
    of telecommunications utilities, §62-133.5(h).
Single service corporation.
  Dental service plan, §58-65-1(a).
Singular.
  Workers' compensation, §97-2.
Sinking fund.
  Local government bonds, §159-44.
  Local government finance, §159-7.
Sister.
  Adoptee's new birth certificate, §48-9-107(c).
  Workers' compensation, §97-2.
Site.
  Solid waste management, §130A-310.
  Specific development plan.
    Counties, §153A-344.1.
Site development, §143B-437.02(c).
Site evaluation.
  Swine farms, §106-802.
Site plan.
  Sewage systems, §130A-334.
Site specific development plan.
  City and town zoning, §160A-385.1(b).
Situated.
  Tangible personal property, §105-304(b).

DEFINED TERMS —Cont'd
Size or weight class.
  Egg law, §106-245.14.
Skeletal analyst.
  Burial sites, §70-28.
Ski area, §99C-1.
Ski area operator, §99C-1.
Skier, §99C-1.
Skilled nursing facility.
  Long-term care insurance, §58-55-35(a).
Skimobile.
  Passenger tramway safety, §95-117.
Slayer.
  Decedents' estates, §31A-3.
Slot device.
  Lotteries and gaming, §14-306(a).
Slot machine.
  Lotteries and gaming, §14-306(a).
Sludge.
  Solid waste management, §130A-290(a).
Sludge management facility.
  Construction, design and operation, §143-129.2(a).
Small business.
  Business and energy tax credits, §105-129.16E(c).
  Main street solutions fund, §143B-472.35(a2).
  Research and development expenses tax credit,
    §105-129.50.
Small claim action.
  Judicial department, §7A-210.
Small employer.
  Health insurance portability and accountability,
    §58-68-25(a).
  Small employer group health coverage,
    §58-50-110.
Small employer carrier.
  Small employer group health coverage,
    §58-50-110.
Small group market.
  Health insurance portability and accountability,
    §58-68-25(a).
Small power producer.
  Public utilities, §62-3.
Small town main street program.
  Main street solutions fund, §143B-472.35(a2).
Smoking, §143-596.
  Home care agencies, smoking prohibited,
    §131E-143(a).
  Long-term care facilities, prohibited within,
    §131E-114.3(a).
  Mental health facilities, §122C-6(a).
  Safety, minimum requirements, §131D-4.4(b).
  Smoking in state government buildings,
    §130A-492.
Social development company.
  Sudan (Darfur) divestment act, §147-86.42.
**Socially and economically disadvantaged
    individual.**
  Public contracts, §143-128.2(g).
Social security act.
  Governmental employees, §135-20.
Social security breakpoint.
  State retirement system, §135-1.
Social worker.
  Certification, §90B-3.
Society.
  Fraternal benefit societies, §58-24-15(g).
Socioeconomic and demographic data.
  County solid waste disposal, §153A-136(c).
  Public enterprises, §160A-325(a).
Soft drink.
  Sales and use tax, §105-164.3.

DEFINED TERMS —Cont'd
Software.
Secured transactions, §25-9-102(a).
Soil.
Soil scientists, §89F-3.
Soil additive, §106-50.30.
Soil and water conservation commission,
    §139-3.
Soil and water conservation district, §139-3.
Soil science, §89F-3.
Soil scientist, §89F-3.
Soil scientist-in-training, §89F-3.
Solar electricity generating material
    manufacturing.
Industrial facilities sales tax refunds,
    §105-164.14B(a).
Sold.
Bedding, §106-65.95.
Sole benefit.
Community third party trusts, pooled trusts act,
    §36D-2.
Solicit.
Insurance producers, §58-33-10.
Solicitation, §14-401.12.
Solicitation.
Civil procedure, §1-75.2.
Life insurance, dishonest and predatory sales to
    military personnel, §58-58-330(c).
Solicitation of contributions, §131F-2.
Solicitation of others.
Lobbying, §120C-100(a).
Solicitor.
Solicitation of contributions, §131F-2.
Solid organ transplantation service.
Certificate of need, §131E-176.
Solid tire.
Motor vehicles, §20-4.01.
Solid waste, §130A-290(a).
Counties, §§153A-136(d), 153A-294, 153A-421(a).
Pollution control, §§159C-3, 159D-3.
Public enterprises, §160A-325(b).
Solid waste disposal facility, §159C-3.
Pollution control, §159D-3.
Solid waste disposal site, §130A-290(a).
Solid waste generation, §130A-290(a).
Solid waste management, §130A-290(a).
Solid waste management facility, §130A-290(a).
Solution-based solicitation.
Best value procurements, §143-135.9(a).
Sound-amplifying equipment.
Disruption of state-owned campuses, §116-213.
Sound management program.
Taxation, §105-277.2.
Sound recording.
Truth in music advertising act, §75-125(b).
Source material.
Radiation protection, §104E-5.
Southern region association.
Regional reciprocal savings and loan acquisition
    act, §54B-48.2.
Southern region savings and loan holding
    company.
Regional reciprocal savings and loan acquisition
    act, §54B-48.2.
Southern region states.
Regional reciprocal savings and loan acquisition
    act, §54B-48.2.
SOX-complaint entity.
Annual audited financial reports.
    Insurance companies, §58-10-190.

DEFINED TERMS —Cont'd
Special ABC area.
Alcoholic beverages, §18B-101.
Special act.
Cities and towns, §160A-1.
Special annuity account accumulated
    contributions.
State law-enforcement retirement, §143-166.30(a).
Special annuity accounts.
State law-enforcement retirement, §143-166.30(a).
Special care service.
Adult day care programs.
    Alzheimer's disease, §131D-6(b4).
Special care unit.
Adult care homes, §131D-4.6(a).
Nursing homes, §131E-114(e).
Special concern species.
Endangered wildlife, §113-331.
Plant protection and conservation, §106-202.12.
Special corporation.
Capital facilities finance act, §142-82.
Energy conservation finance act, §142-61.
Special declarant rights.
Condominiums, §47C-1-103.
Planned community act, §47F-1-103.
Special deposit claim.
Insurers supervision, §58-30-10.
Special deputy.
Sheriffs' education, §17E-2.
Special district.
Local government finance, §159-7.
Special education.
Education expenses credit, §105-151.33(i).
Education of children with disabilities,
    §115C-106.3.
Special equipment.
Elevator safety, §95-110.3(n).
Special fund for individual schools,
    §115C-448(c).
Special funds for individual institutions.
University of North Carolina constituent
    institutions, §116-36.2(b).
Special indebtedness.
Capital facilities finance act, §142-82.
Special limited guard and patrol profession,
    §74C-3.
Specially constructed vehicles.
Motor vehicles, §20-4.01.
Special mobile equipment.
Motor vehicles, §20-4.01.
Sales and use tax, §105-164.3.
Special needs institution.
Distinguished professors endowment trust fund,
    §116-41.13A.
Special nonprofit corporation.
Lease or purchase of prison facilities constructed
    by private firm, §148-37.2(b).
Special nuclear material.
Radiation protection, §104E-5.
Special obligation bond project.
Higher education bonds, §116D-22.
Special proceedings.
Civil procedure, §1-3.
Special purpose entity.
Asset-backed securities facilitation, §53-425.
Viatical life insurance settlements, §58-58-205.
Special purpose institution.
Private capital facilities finance act, §159D-37.
Special purpose project.
Pollution control, §159C-3.

DEFINED TERMS —Cont'd

Special-purpose unit of government.
Environmental policy act, §113A-9.
Specialty ambulatory surgical program.
Certificate of need, §131E-176.
Specialty fertilizer.
Commercial fertilizer, §106-657.
Specialty market, §66-250.
Specialty market operator, §66-250.
Specialty market vendor, §66-250.
Specialty pet.
Commercial feed law, §106-284.33.
Specialty pet food.
Commercial feed law, §106-284.33.
Specialty services.
Mental health, §122C-3.
Specialty vehicles, §20-4.01.
Special user project.
Global TransPark authority, §63A-2.
Special verdict, §1A-1 Rule 49(a).
Special wastes.
Solid waste management, §130A-290(a).
Specific appointment.
Life insurance.
Dishonest and predatory sales to military
personnel, §58-58-335.
Specifications.
Rerefined or reprocessed oil, §119-13.1.
Specific contracted work site.
Owner-controlled or wrap-up insurance,
§58-31-65(b).
Specific license.
Radiation protection, §104E-5.
Specific reserve account.
Savings and loan associations, §54B-4.
Specified anatomical areas.
Adult establishments, §14-202.10.
Specified sexual activities.
Adult establishments, §14-202.10.
Specimen.
Document authentication, §66-271.
Spectator.
Roller skating rink safety and liability, §99E-10.
Speech and language pathologist.
Licensure, §90-293.
Speech impaired.
Health and human services division,
§143B-216.30.
Speleothem.
Cave protection act, §14-159.20.
Spendthrift provision.
Uniform trust code, §36C-1-103.
Spirituous liquor.
Alcoholic beverages, §18B-101.
Alcohol taxation, §105-113.68.
Sales and use tax exemptions, §105-164.13.
Splitter.
Drug paraphernalia control act, §90-113.81.
Spoil bank.
Mining, §74-49.
Sponsor.
Campaign contributions and expenditures.
Disclosure requirements for media
advertisements, §163-278.38Z.
Continuing legal education, Bar Rule D.1501.
Solicitation of contributions, §131F-2.
Sponsoring organization.
Child passenger safety technicians, §20-137.5(a).
Sponsoring providers.
Provider sponsored organizations, §131E-276.

DEFINED TERMS —Cont'd

Sponsor purpose.
Solicitation of contributions, §131F-2.
Sponsor sales promotion.
Solicitation of contributions, §131F-2.
Sport or recreational equipment.
Sales and use tax, §105-164.3.
Sports club.
Alcoholic beverages, §18B-1000.
Sports events.
Assault and battery, §14-33.
Sport shooting range, §14-409.45.
Sports officials.
Assault and battery, §14-33.
Spot rate.
Foreign-money claims, §1C-1820.
Spotter plane.
Coastal and estuarine commercial fishing licenses,
§113-171.1(a).
Spousal-support order.
Interstate family support, §52C-1-101.
Spouse.
Death benefits, §143-166.2(e).
Taxation, §105-277.2.
SSI.
Health coverage for workers with disabilities act,
§108A-54.1(b).
Stabilize.
Accident and health insurance.
Utilization review, §58-50-61(a).
Stable Internet web site.
Woman's right to know act, §90-21.81.
Stafford act.
Emergency management, §166A-4.
Stalking.
Civil no-contact orders, §50C-1.
Stamp.
Notaries public act, §10B-3.
Stand-alone basic residential line.
Alternative regulation, tariffing and deregulation
of telecommunications utilities, §62-133.5(h).
Standard health care plan.
Small employer group health coverage,
§58-50-110.
Standard program county.
Public assistance program, §108A-24.
Standards.
Vegetable plant law, §106-284.16.
Water and air resources, §143-213.
Standards for quality.
Egg law, §106-245.14.
Standard transportation practices.
Joint rate agreements, §62-152.2(a).
Standard work first program.
Public assistance program, §108A-24.
Standard working hours.
Limited driving privilege, §20-179.3(f1).
Standby guardian, §35A-1370.
State.
Aeronautics, §63-1.
Agricultural finance act, §122D-3.
Anatomical gifts, §130A-412.4.
Biological residues, §106-549.81.
Business corporations, §55-1-40.
Capital facilities finance act, §142-82.
Child custody jurisdiction and enforcement,
§50A-102.
Claims against the state, §143B-426.40A(a).
Controlled substances, §90-87.
Criminal extradition, §15A-721.
Criminal procedure, §15A-101.

DEFINED TERMS —Cont'd

State —Cont'd

Custodial trusts, §33B-1.

Disability income plan, §135-101.

Educational personnel qualifications, §115C-350.

Electric power, §159B-3.

Electronic transactions, §66-312.

Foreign-money claims, §1C-1820.

Health facilities finance, §131A-3.

Housing authorities, §157-3.

Housing finance agency, §122A-3.

Insurance taxation, §105-228.8(b).

Interstate agreement on detainers, §15A-761.

Interstate branch banking, §53-224.9.

Interstate compact for juveniles, §7B-4001.

Interstate compact on adoption and medical assistance, §7B-3901.

Interstate compact on education, §115C-104.

Interstate compact on juveniles, §7B-2803.

Interstate compact on mental health, §122C-361.

Interstate depositions and discovery, §1F-2.

Interstate environmental compact, §113A-23.

Interstate family support, §52C-1-101.

Interstate insurance product regulation compact, §58-91-10.

Interstate wildlife violator compact, §113-300.6.

Law-enforcement retirement, §143-166.30(a).

Legal defense of employees, §143-300.2.

Limited liability companies, §57C-1-03.

Local government law-enforcement retirement, §143-166.50(a).

Mines, §§74-24.2, 74-37.

Motor vehicles, §20-4.01.

National crime prevention and privacy compact, §114-19.50.

Nonprofit corporations, §55A-1-40.

Nurse licensure compact, §90-171.82.

Occupational safety and health, §95-127.

Partnerships, §59-102.

Pest control, §106-65.55.

Private capital facilities finance act, §159D-37.

Public health authorities, §130A-45.01.

Public hospitals, §131E-16.

Public utilities, §62-3.

Reciprocal banking act, §53-210.

Regional reciprocal savings and loan acquisition act, §54B-48.2.

Satisfaction of deeds of trust and mortgages, §45-36.4.

Secured transactions, §25-9-102(a).

Securities, §78A-2.

Soil and water conservation districts, §139-3.

State prisons, §148-120.

Transfers to minors, §33A-1.

Unclaimed property act, §116B-52.

Unemployment compensation, §96-8.

Uniform military and overseas voters act, §163-258.2.

Uniform sales and use tax administration act, §105-164.42B.

Uniform transfer on death security registration act, §41-40.

Uniform trust code, §36C-1-103.

Uniform unincorporated nonprofit association act, §59B-2.

Veterans' recreation, §165-25.

Water infrastructure, §159G-20.

Witnesses, §15A-811.

State acquisition and relocation fund.

Emergency management, §166A-4.

DEFINED TERMS —Cont'd

State action.

Dentist peer review organizations, §90-48.2(f).

State agency.

Aid to the blind, §111-42(b).

Budget of state, §143C-1-1(d).

Capital facilities finance act, §142-82.

Criminal justice information network, §143-660.

Debt collection, §105A-2.

Depository library system, §125-11.6.

Disaster service volunteer leave, §166A-31.

Employees and social security, §135-20.

Energy in state buildings, §143-64.11.

Environmental policy act, §113A-9.

Internal auditing requirements for state agencies, §143-745(a).

Office of information technology services, §147-33.81.

Office of the controller, §143B-426.35.

Sales and use tax, §105-164.3.

State auditor, §147-64.4.

State governmental accountability and internal control act, §143D-3.

State government ethics act, §138A-3.

State lands, §146-64.

State officers, §147-86.11.

Statewide accounts receivable program, §147-86.20.

State airway.

Aeronautics, §63-1.

State archaeologist.

Burial sites, §70-28.

Indian antiquities, §70-48.

State-assisted state facility.

Energy in state buildings, §143-64.11.

State association.

Regional reciprocal savings and loan acquisition act, §54B-48.2.

Savings and loan associations, §54B-4.

Savings and loan interstate branches, §54B-266.

State average effective tax rate.

Public school building capital fund, §115C-546.2(d).

State bank.

Trust companies, §53-301(a).

State bar.

Client security fund, rules governing administration, Bar Rule D.1401.

State board.

Community colleges, §115D-2.

Education, §115C-5.

State building.

Aid to the blind, §111-42(c).

Department of administration, §143-336.

Sales and use tax exemptions, §105-164.13.

State capital improvement project.

State building commission, §143-135.27.

State-certified historic structure.

Historic rehabilitation tax credit, §105-129.36(b).

Mill rehabilitation tax credit, §§105-129.36, 105-129.70.

State consumer advocacy program.

MH/DD/SA consumer advocacy program, §122C-11.

State consumer advocate.

MH/DD/SA consumer advocacy program, §122C-11.

State corporate income tax, §105-130.4(a).

State correctional facility.

Smoking prohibition, §148-23.1(d).

DEFINED TERMS —Cont'd
State criminal law.
  Certification standards for criminal law specialty,
    Bar Rule D.2502.
State DNA databank, §15A-266.2.
State DNA database, §15A-266.2.
State educational institution.
  Children of war veterans scholarships, §165-20.
  National Guard tuition assistance, §116-209.52(d).
**State education assistance authority loan
    fund,** §116-201.
State employee.
  State employee suggestion program (NC-Thinks),
    §143-345.20.
State employee credit union.
  Claims against the state, §143B-426.40A(a).
State environmental management commission.
  Soil and water conservation districts, §139-3.
State facility.
  Energy in state buildings, §143-64.11.
  Mental health, §122C-3.
State fire marshal.
  Fireworks, §14-410(c).
  State volunteer fire department, §58-80-1.
State-funded program.
  Job training, education and placement
    information management, §96-31.
State funds.
  Budget of state, §143C-1-1(d).
  Office of the controller, §143B-426.35.
State government.
  Smoking in public places, §143-596.
  Smoking in state government buildings,
    §130A-492.
State governmental unit.
  Guaranteed energy savings contract, §143-64.17B.
State government building.
  Smoking in state government buildings,
    §130A-492.
State historic preservation officer.
  Historic rehabilitation tax credit, §105-129.36(b).
  Historic structure rehabilitation tax credit,
    §105-129.35(c).
  Mill rehabilitation tax credit, §§105-129.36,
    105-129.70.
State historic site, §121-2.
State hospital.
  Unemployment compensation, §96-8.
  Unemployment insurance, §96-8.
State institution of higher learning.
  Energy in state buildings, §143-64.11.
**State job training, education and placement
    program,** §96-31.
State lands, §146-64.
  Archaeology, §70-12.
State law.
  Outdoor advertising control, §136-128.
  Unemployment insurance, §96-12.01(a1).
State law enforcement agency.
  Unauthorized substances tax, §105-113.106.
State legislative buildings and grounds,
    §120-32.1(d).
State library agency.
  Interstate library compact, §125-14.
State medical facilities plan.
  Certificate of need, §131E-176.
Statement.
  Evidence, §8C-1 Rule 801(a).
  False statement to procure or deny benefit of
    policy or certificate, §58-2-161(a).

DEFINED TERMS —Cont'd
State net income.
  Taxation, §105-130.2.
State of emergency.
  Alcoholic beverages, §18B-110.
  Civil disorders, §14-288.1.
State official.
  Environmental policy act, §113A-9.
State ombudsman.
  Long-term care program, §143B-181.16.
**State or local child support enforcement
    agency.**
  Unemployment insurance, §96-17(d).
State or local consumer advocate.
  Mental health, §122C-3.
State-owned passenger motor vehicle.
  Assignment of vehicles by department of
    administration, §143-341.
State parks and forest road system.
  Motor vehicle laws applicable to, §143-116.8.
State parks system, §113-44.9.
State plan.
  Children's health insurance program,
    §108A-70.18.
  Mental health, §122C-3.
  Public assistance program, §108A-24.
State practice laws.
  Nurse licensure compact, §90-171.82.
State property.
  Aid to the blind, §111-42(c).
State publication.
  Depository library system, §125-11.6.
State public body.
  National defense housing projects, §157-53.
State public health veterinarian.
  Rabies, §130A-184.
State public work project.
  State prisons, §148-26.1.
State recreational forest.
  State forest acquisition and control, §106-870(b).
State recreation trails.
  North Carolina trail system, §113A-86.
State resources.
  Budget of state, §143C-1-1(d).
  Mental health, §122C-3.
State retirement system.
  Law-enforcement, §143-166.30(a).
State revenue.
  Budget of state, §143C-1-1(d).
State's annual medicaid payment.
  Hospital provider assessments, §108A-121.
State savings association.
  Trust companies, §53-301(a).
State savings bank, §54C-4(b).
  Savings interstate branch banks, §54C-200.
State scenic trails.
  North Carolina trail system, §113A-86.
State team.
  Child fatality prevention system, §7B-1401.
State trails system.
  North Carolina trail system, §113A-85.
State trust company.
  Trust companies, §53-301(a).
State trust company facility, §53-340(b).
  Trust companies, §53-301(a).
State trust institution.
  Trust companies, §53-301(a).
State vehicle.
  Smoking in state controlled passenger carrying
    vehicle, §130A-492.

DEFINED TERMS —Cont'd

State vehicle —Cont'd

Tire purchase, repair or refurbishment,
§143-63.2(a).

Statewide data processor.

Medical care data, §131E-214.1.

Statewide registry.

Sex offender and public protection registration,
§14-208.6.

Statistical organization.

Insurance rates, §58-40-5.

Rate bureau, §58-36-4(a).

Statistical plan.

Insurance rates, §58-40-5.

Rate bureau, §58-36-4(a).

Status offender.

Habitual breaking and entering status offense,
§14-7.25.

Status report.

Incompetency, §35A-1202.

Statutory appropriation.

Budget of state, §143C-1-1(d).

Stepparent.

Adoption, §48-1-101.

Stillbirth.

Unborn victims of violence act/Ethen's law,
§14-23.7.

Stock association.

Savings and loan associations, §54B-4.

Stock savings bank, §54C-4(b).

Stop-sale.

Seed law, §106-277.2.

Storage.

Sales and use tax, §105-164.3.

Storage and container.

Solid waste management, §130A-290(a).

Toxic or hazardous substance identification,
§95-174(s).

Storage media.

Sales and use tax, §105-164.3.

Storage unit.

Self service storage renter's insurance,
§58-33-18(a).

Stored value.

Money transmitters, §53-208.2(a).

Stormwater, §143-213.

Stormwater quality project.

Clean water management trust fund, §113A-252.

Water infrastructure, §159G-20.

Strawberry plant seller, §106-783.

Stray.

Rabies vaccination, §130A-184.

Stream.

Floodplain regulations, §143-215.52(a).

Streamlined agreement.

Sales and use tax, §105-164.3.

Street.

Contractors, §87-101.

Motor vehicles, §20-4.01.

Roads and highways, §136-41.1.

Street address.

Telephonic sellers, §66-262(b).

Street gang, §14-50.16(b).

Street rod vehicle.

Motor vehicles, §20-4.01.

Strike.

Public employees and unions, §95-98.2.

Stripper Well Litigation Funds.

Housing trust, §122E-2.

Structural pest control, §106-65.24.

Structural pest control act, §106-65.24.

DEFINED TERMS —Cont'd

Structure.

Floodplain regulations, §143-215.52(a), (b).

Structured settlement, §1-543.11.

Structured settlement agreement, §1-543.11.

Structured settlement annuity.

Annuity disclosure, §58-60-130.

Insurance guaranty associations, §58-62-16.

Structured settlement obligor, §1-543.11.

Structured settlement payment rights,
§1-543.11.

Student.

Conservation, §113-130.

Drivers' licenses, lose control, lose license,
§20-11(n1).

Polysomnography practice act, §90-721.

Private educational institutions, §116-22.

Sex offender and public protection registration,
§14-208.6.

State education assistance authority, §116-201.

State grants to students attending private
universities or colleges, §116-43.5(a).

Taking indecent liberties with a student,
§14-202.4(d).

Weapons on educational property, §14-269.2(a).

Student-athlete.

Athlete agents, §78C-86.

Student loans.

Education assistance authority, §§116-201,
116-209.24.

National Guard tuition assistance, §116-209.52(f).

Student loan collections, §105B-1.

Student obligations.

State education assistance authority, §116-201.

Student teacher, §115C-309(a).

Student teaching, §115C-309(a).

Subcontractor, §22C-1.

Bonds, §44A-25.

Subdivision.

City and town planning, §160A-376(a).

Counties, §153A-335(a).

Subgrantee.

Budget of state, §143C-6-23(a).

Energy assistance for low-income persons,
§143B-472.122.

Sublease.

Leases, UCC, §25-2A-103(1).

Motor vehicle and loan assumption arranging,
§20-106.2(a).

Sublease arranger.

Motor vehicle and loan assumption arranging,
§20-106.2(a).

Submachine gun, §14-409(a).

Submerged lands.

State lands, §146-64.

Submit for recording.

Satisfaction of deeds of trust and mortgages,
§45-36.4.

Subordinate.

Geologist, §89E-3.

Soil scientists, §89F-3.

Subordinated debt.

Enterprise corporations, §53A-37.

Tax credit for qualified business investments,
§105-163.010.

Subordination agreements.

Real property, §39-6.6(f).

Subpoena.

Interstate depositions and discovery, §1F-2.

Subscriber.

Business corporations, §55-1-40.

DEFINED TERMS —Cont'd

Subscriber —Cont'd

Health maintenance organizations, §58-67-5(k).

Insurance rates, §58-40-5.

911 system, §62A-40.

Reciprocal insurance, §58-15-5.

Recovery from insurers providing additional coverage to Medicaid-eligible persons, §108A-55.4(a).

State health plan for teachers and state employees, §135-48.1.

Subscribing witness.

Notaries public act, §10B-3.

Subscriptions.

Savings and loan associations, §54B-4.

Subsequent instrument.

Registers of deeds, §161-14.1(a).

Subsidiary.

Bank holding company act, §53-226.

Brownfields property reuse act, §130A-310.31(b).

Corporate franchise tax, §105-122(b).

Dry-cleaning solvent cleanup act, §143-215.104B(b).

Insurance holding companies, §58-19-5.

Mining, §74-49.

Reciprocal banking act, §53-210.

Regional reciprocal savings and loan acquisition act, §54B-48.2.

Solid waste management, §130A-290(a).

Trust companies, §53-301(a).

Underground storage tank cleanup, §143-215.94A.

Workers' compensation self-insurance, §97-165.

Subsidiary of a specified person.

Collection agencies, §58-70-6.

Substance abuse.

Mental health, §122C-3.

Substance abuse counseling.

Substance abuse professionals, §90-113.31A.

Substance abuse counselor intern.

Substance abuse professionals, §90-113.31A.

Substance abuse professional, §90-113.31A.

Substance abuser, §122C-3.

Substandard unit.

Housing trust, §122E-2.

Substantial.

Rules of professional conduct, ProfCond Rule 1.0.

Substantial action.

Sudan (Darfur) divestment act, §147-86.42.

Substantial change in use.

Sport shooting range protection, §14-409.45.

Substantial completion.

Civil procedure, §1-50(a).

Substantial defect.

Manufactured housing, §143-143.9.

Substantial economic impact.

Rulemaking procedure, §150B-21.4(b1).

Substantial emotional distress.

Stalking, §14-277.3A(b).

Targeted picketing, §14-277.4A(b).

Substantial evidence.

Abused, neglected and dependent juveniles, §7B-101.

Administrative procedure, §150B-2.

Discipline of students, §115C-390.1(b).

Victims compensation, §15B-2.

Substantial fault.

Unemployment insurance, §96-14.

Substantially equivalent.

State personnel system, §126-11.

Substantial plurality.

Primary elections, §163-111(a).

DEFINED TERMS —Cont'd

Substantial proportion of the services.

Provider sponsored organizations, §131E-276.

Substantial understatement.

Property tax, §105-273.

Substantive violation.

Migrant housing, §95-223.

Substitute address.

Address confidentiality program, §15C-2.

Successor external review process.

Health care liability, §90-21.50.

Successor in business.

Tax credit for manufacturing cigarettes for exportation, §105-130.45(a).

Increasing employment and utilizing state ports, §105-130.46(b).

Successor manufacturer.

Motor vehicle manufacturers.

Unfair methods of competition, §20-305.2(c).

Successors in interest.

Uniform trust code, §36C-1-103.

Successors of a beneficiary.

Letters of credit, §25-5-102(a).

Suitable employment.

Industrial commission utilization of rehabilitation professionals, ICRehabProf Rule III.

Unemployment insurance, §96-14.

Workers' compensation, §97-2.

Suitable transportation.

Assignment of suitable transportation to state employee or agency by department of administration, §143-341.

Suitable work.

Unemployment insurance, §96-12.

Summons.

Witnesses, §15A-811.

Superintendent.

Discipline of students, §115C-390.1(b).

Education, §115C-5.

Superior court.

Civil procedure, §1-567.32.

Criminal procedure, §15A-101.

Superior court district.

Sentencing services act, §7A-771.

Superior court judge.

Criminal procedure, §15A-101.

Superseded part.

Farm machinery franchises, §66-180.

Supervised living facility of developmentally disabled adults.

Long-term care insurance, §58-55-35(a).

Supervisee.

Post-release supervision, §15A-1368(a).

Supervising attorney.

Rules governing legal services provided by students, Bar Rule C.0202.

Supervising bail bondsman, §58-71-1.

Supervising entity.

Portable consumer electronic devices insurance, §58-44A-1.

Supervision.

Dental hygiene, §90-221(f).

Pyrotechnics licenses, §58-82A-1.1.

Supervisor.

Education, §115C-5.

Licensed professional counselors, §90-330(a).

Savings and loan interstate branches, §54B-266.

Savings interstate branch banks, §54C-200.

Soil and water conservation districts, §139-3.

Supervisory agency.

Financial privacy, §53B-2.

DEFINED TERMS —Cont'd
Supervisory personnel.
Municipal firefighters, §160A-295.
Supplemental address.
Lead poisoning in children, §130A-131.7.
Supplemental PEG channel support funds.
Distribution of sales and use taxes.
Supplemental PEG channel support,
§105-164.44J(a).
Supplemental retirement income plan.
State law-enforcement, §143-166.30(a).
Supplementary rating information.
Insurance, §58-36-100(b).
Workers' compensation self-insurance.
Employer groups.
Premium rates, §58-47-110(a).
Supplier.
Beer franchises, §18B-1301.
Farm machinery, §66-180.
Gasoline tax, §105-449.60.
Leases, UCC, §25-2A-103(1).
Manufactured housing, §143-143.9.
Supplier of water.
Drinking water, §130A-313.
Supplies.
Drug, supplies, and medical device repository
program, §90-85.44(a).
Supply contract.
Leases, UCC, §25-2A-103(1).
Support activities.
Respiratory care practices act, §90-648.
Support enforcement agency.
Interstate family support, §52C-1-101.
Supporting obligation.
Secured transactions, §25-9-102(a).
Supporting spouse.
Alimony, §50-16.1A.
Support and maintenance, §14-322(a).
Support order.
Interstate family support, §52C-1-101.
Supreme court.
Client security fund, rules governing
administration, Bar Rule D.1401.
Discipline and disability rules of state bar, Bar
Rule B.0103.
Procedures for the authorized practice committee
of the state bars, Bar Rule D.0203.
Supreme court orders.
Client security fund, rules governing
administration, Bar Rule D.1401.
Surety.
Bail, §15A-531.
Bail bondmen and runners, §58-71-1.
UCC, §25-1-201(b).
Surety bondsman.
Bail bondsman and runners, §58-71-1.
Surface owner.
Oil and gas conservation, §113-389.
Surface water.
Water withdrawals and transfers, §143-215.22G.
Surface water resource.
Basinwide hydrologic models, §143-355(o).
Surplus.
Banking, §53-1.
Surplus lines, §58-21-10.
Surplus funds.
Drainage, §156-82.1(c).
Surplus lines insurance, §58-21-10.
Surplus lines licensee, §58-21-15.
Surplus trust funds.
Community third party trusts, pooled trusts act,
§36D-2.

DEFINED TERMS —Cont'd
Surrender of a driver's license.
Motor vehicles, §20-16.5(a).
Surveying and platting.
Limitations of actions, §1-47.
Surviving spouse.
State health plan for teachers and state
employees, §135-48.1.
Suspend.
Judicial standards commission, §7A-374.2.
Suspends payments.
Banking, §25-4-104(a).
Suspension.
Interstate wildlife violator compact, §113-300.6.
Judicial standards commission, §7A-374.2.
Motor vehicles, §20-4.01.
Notaries public act, §10B-3.
Sustainable food, §106-830(b).
Sustainable harvests.
Conservation, §113-129.
Swamplands.
State lands, §146-64.
Swap agreement, §159-193.
Sweepstakes.
Gambling, §14-306.4(a).
Swine farm, §106-802.
Animal waste management, §143-215.10I(a).
Swine integrator registration, §143-215.10H(a).
Swine house, §106-802.
Swine operation integrator, §143-215.10H(a).
Switchblade knife.
Weapons on educational property, §14-269.2(a).
Symptomless carrier.
Bee and honey act, §106-635.
System.
State parks act, §113-44.9.
Systemic toxicant.
Risk based environmental remediation of
industrial sites, §130A-310.65.
System of registration.
Public obligations, §159E-2.
System property.
Public service taxation, §105-333.
System transfer.
Gasoline tax, §105-449.60.
Table-funded transaction.
Mortgages, high cost home loans, §24-1.1E(a).
Tablefunding.
Mortgage bankers, brokers and servicers,
§53-244.030.
Tag.
Motor vehicles, §20-137.7.
Talent agency.
Minors, talent contracts, §48A-17.
Tall buildings or structures.
Mountain ridge protection, §113A-206.
Tandem-axle weight.
Motor vehicles, §20-118.
Tangible chattel paper.
Secured transactions, §25-9-102(a).
Tangible personal property.
Property taxes, §105-273.
Sales and use tax, §105-164.3.
Tank system.
Underground petroleum storage tank operator
training, §143-215.94OO.
Tank wagon.
Gasoline tax, §105-449.60.
Tank wagon importer.
Gasoline tax, §105-449.60.
Tanning equipment, §104E-9.1(c).

DEFINED TERMS —Cont'd

Tanning facility, §104E-9.1(c).

Targeted interest rate project.
Water infrastructure, §159G-20.

Targeted picketing, §14-277.4A(a).

Targeted population.
Mental health, §122C-3.

Targeted to the relevant electorate.
Electioneering communication.
Candidate-specific communication,
§§163-278.100, 163-278.110.

Target housing.
Lead-based paint renovation activities,
§130A-453.22(b).

Task force.
Child fatality prevention system, §7B-1401.

Tattooing, §130A-283(a).

Tax, §105-228.90(b).
Federal estate tax, §28A-27-1.
Fiduciaries, §32-26.
Gasoline tax, §105-449.60.
Local government finance, §159-7.
Property taxes, §105-273.
Real estate investment trusts, §105-130.12(a).

Taxable income, §105-134.1.

Taxable period.
Taxation, §105-131.

Taxable year, §§105-130.2, 105-134.1, 105-163.2.
Estimated income tax, §105-163.38.
Tax withholding, §105-163.1.

Tax collector.
Property taxes, §105-273.

Tax debt.
Collection, §105-243.1(a).

Taxicab.
Motor vehicles, §20-87.

Tax information.
Confidentiality, §105-259(a).

Taxing unit, §§105-151.21, 105-163.2.
Property taxes, §105-273.

Tax-levying authority.
Community colleges, §115D-2.
Education, §115C-5.

Taxpayer, §§105-130.2, 105-134.1, 105-163.2,
105-228.90(b).
Property taxes, §105-273.
Sales and use tax, §105-164.3.

Tax year.
Individual income tax, §105-151.20(a).

TDD.
Deaf and the hard of hearing, §143B-216.30.

Teacher.
Disability income plan, §135-101.
Education personnel, §115C-325(a).
Leaves of absence, §115C-302.1(d).
NBPTS certification, §115C-296.2(b).
State retirement system, §135-1.

Team coordinator.
Child fatality prevention system, §7B-1401.

Technical specialist.
Animal waste management, §143-215.10B.

Technician.
Anatomical gifts, §130A-412.4.

Technician-level entry capability.
Hazardous materials emergency response,
§166A-21.

Teen court program.
Delinquent and undisciplined juveniles, §7B-1501.

Telecommunications.
Public agency, §143B-426.8.

DEFINED TERMS —Cont'd

Telecommunications device.
Deaf and the hard of hearing, §143B-216.30.
Electronic surveillance, §14-113.5.

Telecommunication service.
Sales and use tax on telecommunications,
§§105-164.3, 105-164.4C(h).
Unlawful telecommunications devices, §14-113.5.

Telecommunication service provider.
Unlawful telecommunications devices, §14-113.5.

Telecommunications service provider.
Certificates of public convenience and necessity,
§62-110(f6).

Telegram.
UCC, §25-1-201(b).

Telegraph company.
Public service taxation, §105-333.

Telemarketing sales rule.
Telephone solicitations, §75-101.

Telemedicine.
Mental health, developmental disability,
substance abuse, §122C-263(c).

Telephone bank.
Electioneering communications.
Candidate-specific communications,
§163-278.110.
Political campaigns, §163-278.6.

Telephone company.
Public service taxation, §105-333.

Telephone facsimile machine.
Unsolicited facsimiles, §75-115.

Telephone record.
Telephone records privacy protection, §14-113.30.

Telephone room.
Securities regulation, §78A-11.

Telephone service.
Telephone records privacy protection, §14-113.30.

Telephone service provider.
Telephone records privacy protection, §14-113.30.

Telephone solicitation, §75-101.

Telephone solicitor, §75-101.

Telephone subscriber.
Telephone solicitations, §75-101.

Telephonic communications.
Criminal law and procedure, §14-196.

Telephonic seller, §66-260.

Television.
Campaign contributions and expenditures.
Disclosure requirements for media
advertisements, §163-278.38Z.
Discarded computer equipment and television
management, §130A-309.131.

Television manufacturer.
Discarded computer equipment and television
management, §130A-309.131.

Teller's check.
Good funds settlement act, §45A-3.
Negotiable instruments, §25-3-104.

Temporarily.
Hospitals, §131E-83.

Temporary.
Public assistance program, §108A-24.

Temporary appraiser licensure or certification.
Real estate appraisers, §93E-1-4.

Temporary duty.
Military personnel on temporary duty or
deployment, child custody or visitation,
§50-13.7A(b).

Temporary employees.
Professional employer organizations, §58-89A-5.

DEFINED TERMS —Cont'd

Temporary intergovernmental law enforcement agreement.
Assistance by out-of-state law enforcement officers, §160A-288.3(b).

Tenant.
Expedited evictions, §42-59.

Tenant year.
Agricultural leases, §42-23.

Tender.
Oil and gas conservation, §113-389.

Term.
UCC, §25-1-201(b).

Terminal.
Gasoline and oil inspection, §119-15.
Gasoline tax, §105-449.60.
Public service taxation, §105-333.

Terminal groin.
Coastal area management, erosion control structures, §113A-115.1(a).

Terminally ill.
Medical release of inmates, §15A-1369.
Viatical life insurance settlements, §58-58-205.

Terminal operator.
Gasoline and oil inspection, §119-15.
Gasoline tax, §105-449.60.

Terminal supplier.
Motor fuel, §75-81.

Terminal transfer system.
Gasoline tax, §105-449.60.

Terminate.
Insurance producers, §58-33-10.
Sales representative commissions, §66-190.

Termination.
Farm machinery, §66-180.
Health maintenance organizations, §58-67-88.
Leases, UCC, §25-2A-103(1).
Sales, §25-2-106.

Termination of employment.
State health plan for teachers and state employees, §135-48.44(d).

Termination of insurance coverage.
Insurance information and privacy protection act, §58-39-15.

Termination of mining, §74-49.

Termination request.
Instruments to secure equity lines of credit, §45-81.

Termination statement.
Secured transactions, §25-9-102(a).

Term of a trust.
Principal and income act, §37A-1-102.

Term of court.
Expungement of records, §15A-146(a1).

Terms of a trust.
Uniform trust code, §36C-1-103.

Terms of the citation.
Interstate wildlife violator compact, §113-300.6.

Terms of the structured settlement, §1-543.11.

Territory.
Alcoholic beverages, §18B-1201.

Territory of the United States.
Trust companies, §53-301(a).

Testimony of witness unavailable.
Probate of attested written will, §28A-2A-8(c).

Theatre.
Motion pictures, §75C-2.

Theft.
Organized retail theft, §14-86.5.

Therapeutic court, §7A-272(f).

DEFINED TERMS —Cont'd

Therapeutic deception.
Psychotherapy patient/client sexual exploitation act, §90-21.41.

Therapeutic foster home, §131D-10.2.

Therapeutic recreation.
Recreational therapists, §90C-22.

Thing of value.
Bribery of officials, §14-217(d).

Third party.
Sublease of motor vehicle and loan assumption arranging, §20-106.2(a).

Third party administrator, §58-56-2.
Unauthorized insurers, §58-33-95(d).
Workers' compensation.
Self-insurance, §58-47-150.
Workers' compensation self-insurance.
Employer groups, §58-47-60.

Third-party expert.
Divorce, §50-71.

Third-party filer.
Interstate insurance product regulation compact, §58-91-10.

Third tier subcontractor.
Liens, §44A-17.

36D trust.
Community third party trusts, pooled trusts act, §36D-2.

This state.
Savings and loan associations, §54B-4.
Taxation, §105-134.1.

Threatened species.
Endangered wildlife, §113-331.
Plant protection and conservation, §106-202.12.

Three counties.
Lake Wylie marine commission, §77-30.

Thresholds.
Mortgages, high cost home loans, §24-1.1E(a).

Throughput.
Ports authority income tax, §105-130.41(c).
Ports authority individual income tax, §105-151.22(c).

Ticket.
State lottery, §18C-103.

Ticket seller.
Software to interfere with operation of ticket seller, §14-344.2(a).

Ticket to work.
Health coverage for workers with disabilities act, §108A-54.1(b).

Tier 1, 2 or 3 counties.
Main street solutions fund, §143B-472.35(a2).

Time deposits, §53-1.

Timekeeper.
Boxing commission, §143-651.

Timely postdelivery care.
Drive-thru deliveries, §58-3-169(e).

Time-out.
Discipline of students, §115C-391.1(b).

Time share, §93A-41.
Condominiums, §47C-1-103.

Time share instrument, §93A-41.
Time share program, §93A-41.
Time share project, §93A-41.
Time share registrar, §93A-41.
Time share salesmen, §93A-41.
Time share unit, §93A-41.

Tip.
Wage and hour act, §95-25.2.

Tipped employee.
Wage and hour act, §95-25.2.

DEFINED TERMS —Cont'd
Tire.
  Scrap tire disposal, §130A-309.53.
  Tire disposal tax, §105-187.15.
Tire collector.
  Scrap tire disposal, §130A-309.53.
Tire-derived fuel.
  Solid waste management, §130A-290(a).
Tire hauler.
  Scrap tire disposal, §130A-309.53.
Tire processor.
  Scrap tire disposal, §130A-309.53.
Tire retailer.
  Scrap tire disposal, §130A-309.53.
Tissue.
  Anatomical gifts, §130A-412.4.
Tissue banks.
  Anatomical gifts, §130A-412.4.
Title II.
  Water and air resources, §143-213.
Title III.
  Water and air resources, §143-213.
Title IV.
  Scholarships, §115C-499.1.
    Need-based scholarships for students attending
        private colleges and universities, §116-280.
  Water and air resources, §143-213.
Title IV-A.
  Public assistance program, §108A-24.
Title transaction.
  Marketable title, §47B-8.
Title V.
  Water and air resources, §143-213.
Title V account.
  Water and air resources, §143-213.
Title XXI.
  Children's health insurance program,
      §108A-70.18.
Tobacco product.
  Smoking in community colleges, §115D-20.1(a).
  State correctional facilities, §148-23.1(d).
  Taxation, §105-113.4.
  Youth access to tobacco products, §14-313(a).
Tobacco product component business.
  Tobacco trust fund commission, §143-716.
Tobacco product manufacturer.
  Tobacco reserve fund, §66-290.
Tobacco-related business.
  Tobacco trust fund commission, §143-716.
Tobacco-related employment.
  Tobacco trust fund commission, §143-716.
Tobacco shop.
  Smoking in public buildings or places of
      employment, §130A-492.
Tobacco use.
  Smoking in community colleges, §115D-20.1(a).
To buy.
  Public activities, §113-130.
To discover property.
  Property taxes, §105-273.
TODS.
  Tourist-oriented directional sign program,
      §136-140.15(b).
To fish.
  Public activities, §113-130.
To hunt.
  Public activities, §113-130.
Ton.
  Commercial feed law, §106-284.33.
  Commercial fertilizer, §106-657.
  Weights and measures, §81A-9.

DEFINED TERMS —Cont'd
Torment.
  Cruelty to animals, §14-360(c).
Torture.
  Cruelty to animals, §14-360(c).
To sell.
  Public activities, §113-130.
To stabilize.
  Emergency care coverage, §58-3-190(g).
To take.
  Public activities, §113-130.
Total actual investment in tangible property.
  Corporate franchise tax, §105-122(d).
Total assets.
  Elective share of surviving spouse, §30-3.2.
  Savings and loan associations, §54B-4.
Total extended benefit amount.
  Unemployment insurance, §96-12.01(a1).
Total hospital costs.
  Hospital provider assessments, §108A-121.
Total loan amount.
  Mortgages, high cost home loans, §24-1.1E(a).
Totally and permanently disabled.
  Property tax homestead exclusion, §105-277.1(b).
Total net assets.
  Elective share of surviving spouse, §30-3.2.
Total operating revenues.
  Hospital authorities, §131E-32(e).
Total return intrust.
  Principal and income act, §37A-1-104.1.
Total taxable payroll.
  Unemployment compensation, §96-9(h).
To trap.
  Public activities, §113-130.
Touching.
  Sex offenses, §14-27.1.
Tough man contestant, §143-651.
Tough man event, §143-651.
Tourism ABC establishment, §18B-101.
Tourism resort.
  Alcoholic beverages, §18B-101.
Tourist-oriented business.
  Tourist-oriented directional sign program,
      §136-140.15(b).
Tourist-oriented facility.
  Tourist-oriented directional sign program,
      §136-140.15(b).
**To use any pesticide in a manner inconsistent
    with its labeling.**
  Pesticide board, §143-460.
Tow.
  Motor vehicles, §20-219.9.
Tower.
  Motor vehicles, §20-219.9.
Towing fee.
  Motor vehicles, §20-219.9.
Town.
  Insurance, §58-84-5.
  Public hospitals, §131E-6.
  Public utilities, §62-3.
Toxic waste, §143-213.
TPA.
  Third party administrators, §58-56-2.
  Workers' compensation self-insurance, §58-47-150.
      Employer groups, §58-47-60.
Tract.
  Pollution control act, §113A-52.
Trade acceptance.
  Banks, §53-55.
Trade adjustment assistance program.
  Health insurance risk pool, §58-50-175.

DEFINED TERMS —Cont'd
Trade screening.
Motion pictures, §75C-2.
Trade secret, §66-152.
Trade time.
Municipal firefighters, §160A-295.
Traditional country stores.
Sanitation of food and lodging establishments.
Exemption from provisions, §130A-250.
Traditional financial institutions.
Enterprise corporations, §53A-37.
Trail.
North Carolina trail system, §113A-85.
Trailers.
Motor vehicles, §20-4.01.
Trained renovation worker.
Lead-based paint renovation activities,
§130A-453.22(b).
Trainee.
Real estate appraisers, §93E-1-4.
Trainee registration.
Real estate appraisers, §93E-1-4.
Training.
Automated external defibrillator (AED),
§90-21.15(b).
Transact business with the general public.
Private trust companies, §53-363(a).
Transacting insurance business.
Unauthorized insurers, §58-28-12.
Transaction.
Electronic commerce in government, §66-58.2.
Electronic transactions, §66-312.
Transaction account.
Insurance information privacy, §58-39-76.
Transfer.
Community land trust property taxation,
§105-277.17(b).
Fraudulent transfers, §39-23.1.
Insurers supervision, §58-30-10.
Motor vehicles, §20-341.
Oil and hazardous substance control, §143-215.77.
Structured settlement protection, §1-543.11.
Sublease of motor vehicle and loan assumption
arranging, §20-106.2(a).
Transfer fee covenants, §39A-2.
Transfers to minors, §33A-1.
Water, §143-215.22G.
Transferability.
Sales, §25-2-105.
Transferable record.
Electronic transactions, §66-326(a).
Transfer agreement.
Structured settlement protection, §1-543.11.
Transferee.
Motor vehicles, §20-341.
Transferee trust institution.
Trust companies, §53-301(a).
Transfer fee.
Transfer fee covenants, §39A-2.
Transfer fee covenant, §39A-2.
Transferor.
Asset-backed securities facilitation, §53-425.
Custodial trusts, §33B-1.
Motor vehicles, §20-341.
Transfers to minors, §33A-1.
Transferred.
Solid waste, §153A-421(d).
Transferring insurer.
Assumption reinsurance, §58-10-25(a).
Transferring trust institution.
Trust companies, §53-301(a).

DEFINED TERMS —Cont'd
Transfer statement.
Secured transactions title transfers upon default,
§25-9-619(a).
Transit oriented development.
Municipal service districts, §160A-536(c1).
Transliterating.
Interpreters and transliterators licensure act,
§90D-3.
Transliterator.
Interpreters and transliterators licensure act,
§90D-3.
Transmission line.
Public utilities, §62-100.
Transmitting utility.
Secured transactions, §25-9-102(a).
Transmix.
Gasoline tax, §105-449.60.
Transplant hospital.
Anatomical gifts, §130A-412.4.
Transportation authority.
Local government sales and use tax for public
transportation, §105-506.1.
Transportation customer.
Piped natural gas tax, §105-187.40.
Transportation equipment.
Sales and use tax, §105-164.4B(c).
Transportation improvement program.
Highway trust fund, §136-175.
Transportation system.
Department of transportation, §136-5.1.
Transport refrigeration contractor, §87-58(b1).
Transport truck.
Gasoline tax, §105-449.60.
Trap and trace device.
Wiretaps, §15A-260.
Trash fishing, §113-185(b).
Trauma.
Nursing pools, §131E-154.2.
Traveler's check.
Negotiable instruments, §25-3-104.
Travel trailer.
Motor vehicles, §20-4.01.
Tread.
Motor vehicles, §20-122.1.
Tread depth.
Motor vehicles, §20-122.1.
Treasurer.
Housing trust, §122E-2.
Legal expense funds for elected officials,
§163-278.300.
Political campaigns, §163-278.6.
Unclaimed property act, §116B-52.
Treasury regulations.
Express total return unitrust, §37A-1-104.21(c).
Principal and income act, §37A-1-104.1.
Treated.
Seed law, §106-277.2.
Treatment.
Dry-cleaning solvent cleanup act,
§143-215.104B(b).
Medical care of minors, §§90-21.2, 90-21.3.
Patient medical records, confidentiality of,
§130A-12.
Solid waste management, §130A-290(a).
Treatment facility.
Incompetency, §35A-1101.
Treatment technique requirement.
Drinking water, §130A-313.
Treatment works, §143-213.

DEFINED TERMS —Cont'd

Trespasser.
Trespasser responsibility act, §38B-4.

Trial division.
Involuntary commitment, §122C-268.1(g).
Mental health, §122C-268.1.

Trial preparation material.
Public records, §132-1.9(h).

Trial tribunal, AppProc Rule 1(d).

Tribal lands.
Inapplicability of hunting, trapping and fishing license provisions, §113-276(l).

Tribe.
Child custody jurisdiction and enforcement, §50A-102.

Tribunal.
Interstate family support, §52C-1-101.
Rules of professional conduct, ProfCond Rule 1.0.

Tricycle.
Child bicycle safety act, §20-171.8.

Trigger for matching funds.
Voter-owned elections act, §163-278.96.

Triggering event.
Price gouging during state of disaster, §75-38(d).
Standby guardianship, §35A-1370.

Trigger or rescue funds.
Public campaign fund, §163-278.62.

Truck camper.
Motor vehicles, §20-4.01.

Truck tractors.
Motor vehicles, §20-4.01.

True lease.
Global TransPark authority, §63A-2.

True mileage, §20-342.

Truncated coverage.
Credit insurance, §58-57-5.

Trust.
Compensation of trustees and other fiduciaries, §32-53.

Trust business.
Trust companies, §53-301(a).

Trust company, §53-301(a).
Custodial trusts, §33B-1.
Transfers to minors, §33A-1.

Trustee.
Community third party trusts, pooled trusts act, §36D-2.
Gasoline tax, §105-449.60.
Medical service corporations, §58-65-166(b).
Mortgages and deeds of trust.
Sales under power of sale, §45-21.1(b).
Principal and income act, §§37A-1-102, 37A-1-104.1.
Recreation and natural heritage, §113-77.6.
RICO act, §75D-3.
Satisfaction of deeds of trust and mortgages, §45-36.4.
Trustee in deed of trust, §45-45.3(a).
Uniform trust code, §36C-1-103.

Trust fund.
Highways, §136-175.

Trust indenture.
Housing authorities, §157-3.

Trust institution.
Fiduciary capacity, trust institutions acting, §53-158.10.
Trust companies, §53-301(a).

Trust instrument.
Uniform trust code, §36C-1-103.

Trust marketing.
Trust companies, §53-301(a).

DEFINED TERMS —Cont'd

Trust office.
Trust companies, §53-301(a).

Tuition.
Tuition and fee waivers, §115B-1.

Tuition assistance.
Tuition of active duty personnel in armed forces, §116-143.3(a).

Turbine manufacturing.
Industrial facilities sales tax refunds, §105-164.14B(a).

Turnpike authority, §136-89.181.

Turnpike project, §136-89.181.

Turnpike system, §136-89.181.

24-hour facility.
Mental health, §122C-3.

Two-car aerial passenger tramway.
Safety, §95-117.

Two-cent sales taxes.
Local sales and use tax, §105-521(a).

Two counties.
High Rock lake marine commission, §77-50.

Two-party exchange.
Gasoline tax, §105-449.60.

Type A1 violation.
Adult care home resident's bill of rights violation, §131D-34(a).
Nursing homes, §131E-129(a).

Type A2 violation.
Adult care home resident's bill of rights violation, §131D-34(a).
Nursing homes, §131E-129(a).

Type B violation.
Adult care home resident's bill of rights violation, §131D-34(a).
Nursing homes, §131E-129(a).

U-drive-it passenger vehicle, §20-4.01.
Regional transit authority vehicle rental tax, §105-551.

U-drive-it vehicles, §20-4.01.

Ultimate user.
Controlled substances, §90-87.
Controlled substances reporting system, §90-113.72.

Umbilical cord blood.
Umbilical cord stem cells and umbilical cord blood banking.
Providing women with information, §130A-128.1(a).

Unaccompanied youth.
Assignment of student to particular school, §115C-366(h).

Unallocated annuity contract.
Insurance guaranty associations, §58-62-16.

Unarmed combat, §143-651.

Unassigned surplus.
Insurance dividends, §58-7-130(b).

Unauthorized.
UCC, §25-1-201(b).

Unauthorized aliens.
Aliens, verification of work authorization, §64-25.

Unauthorized insurer.
Insurance information and privacy protection act, §58-39-15.

Unauthorized substance.
Unauthorized substances taxes, §105-113.106.

Unauthorized trust activity.
Trust companies, §53-301(a).

Unavailability as a witness.
Evidence, §8C-1 Rule 804(a).

DEFINED TERMS —Cont'd
Unavailable.
Local government during emergencies, §162B-7.
Unavoidably unsafe.
Products liability for prescription drugs, §99B-6.
Unborn child.
Unborn victims of violence act/Ethen's law, §14-23.1.
Uncertificated registered public obligation, §159E-2.
Uncertificated security.
Investment securities, §25-8-102.
Unclaimed firearm.
Criminal procedure, disposition of articles, §15-11.2(a).
Uncompensated value.
Medicaid, transfer of assets for less than market value to qualify, §108A-58.1(f).
Uncovered expenditures.
Health maintenance organizations, §58-67-5(p).
Underage person.
Alcoholic beverages, §18B-120.
Underground storage tank.
Underground petroleum storage tank operator training, §143-215.94OO.
Underground storage tank system.
Underground petroleum storage tank operator training, §143-215.94OO.
Underground utility.
Contractors, §87-101.
Underinsured motor vehicle, §20-279.21(b).
Underlying offense.
Limited driving privilege.
Driving with revoked license, §20-20.1(a).
Undertaking.
City and town cooperation, §160A-460.
Under the direct supervision of a certified applicator.
Structural pest control act, §106-65.24.
Under the influence.
Workers' compensation, §97-12.
Under the influence of an impairing substance.
Motor vehicles, §20-4.01.
Underway.
Boating safety, §75A-2.
Underwrite.
Managing general agents, §58-34-2(a).
Underwriting.
Third party administrators, §58-56-2.
Workers' compensation.
Self-insurance.
Employer groups, §58-47-60.
Third-party administrator and service companies, §58-47-150.
Undisciplined juvenile.
Delinquent or undisciplined juveniles, §7B-1501.
Division of juvenile justice, §143B-805.
Undistributed income.
Principal and income act, §37A-3-303(a).
Undivided profits.
Banking, §53-1.
Undue family hardship.
Unemployment compensation, §96-8.
Unemancipated minor.
Parental or judicial consent to abortion, §90-21.6.
Unemployment compensation, §96-17(d).
Unethical acts.
Speech and language pathologists and audiologists licensure, §90-301A.
Unethical conduct.
Chiropractic, §90-154.2.

DEFINED TERMS —Cont'd
Unethical practices.
Speech and language pathologists and audiologists licensure, §90-301A.
Unfair methods of competition.
Unfair trade practices, §58-63-15.
Unfair trade practice act.
False advertising, §58-29-5.
Unfair trade practices, §66-73.
Unfortified wine.
Alcoholic beverages, §18B-101.
Alcohol taxation, §105-113.68.
Uniform application.
Insurance producers, §58-33-10.
Uniform business entity application.
Insurance producers, §58-33-10.
Public adjuster, §58-33A-5.
Uniformed service.
Uniform military and overseas voters act, §163-258.2.
Uniformed-service voter.
Uniform military and overseas voters act, §163-258.2.
Uniform manual.
Roads and highways, §136-30(d).
Uniform portal process.
Mental health, §122C-3.
Uniform standard.
Interstate insurance product regulation compact, §58-91-10.
Unimpaired capital fund.
Banking, §53-1.
Unincorporated entity.
Business corporations, §55-1-40.
Nonprofit corporations, §55A-1-40.
Uninsured.
Children's health insurance program, §108A-70.18.
Uninsured motor vehicle, §20-279.21(b).
Union school, §115C-75(a).
Unique identifier.
Mortgage bankers, brokers and servicers, §53-244.030.
Unit, §47A-3.
Aeronautics, §63-79.
Armories, §127A-161.
City and town cooperation, §160A-460.
Condominiums, §47C-1-103.
Counties, §153A-217.
Local government bonds, §159-44.
Local government finance, §§159-7, 159-160.
Property taxes, §105-277.2.
Time shares, §93A-41.
Unit designation, §47A-3.
Unit dose medication system.
Pharmacy practice, §90-85.3(u).
United States.
Business corporations, §55-1-40.
Nonprofit corporations, §55A-1-40.
Soil and water conservation districts, §139-3.
Uniform military and overseas voters act, §163-258.2.
Unit of local government.
Budget of state, §143C-1-1(d).
City and town cooperation, §160A-460.
Counties, §153A-421(a).
Ecosystem enhancement program, §143-214.11(a).
Local government finance, §159-160.
Local government fiscal information, §120-30.42.
North Carolina's eastern region act, §158-32.

DEFINED TERMS —Cont'd
Unit of local government —Cont'd
Project development financing debt instruments,
    §159-102.
Public health generally, §130A-2.
Regional councils, §160A-470.
Regional natural gas district, §160A-661(b).
Regional public transportation, §160A-601.
Regional sports authorities, §160A-479.
Regional transportation authorities, §160A-631.
Septic tank systems, §130A-343.1(b).
Solid waste, §159I-3(a).
Solid waste management, §130A-290(a).
Water resources, §143-350.
Water treatment facility operators, §90A-20.1.
Unit of local government's chief administrative
    official.
Regional natural gas district, §160A-661(b).
Regional public transportation, §160A-601.
Regional transportation authorities, §160A-631.
Unit owner, §47A-3.
Condominiums, §47C-1-103.
Unit owners' associations.
Condominiums, §47C-1-103.
Unitrust amount.
Principal and income act, §37A-1-104.1.
Units sold.
Tobacco reserve fund, §66-290.
University.
Higher education bonds, §116D-1.
University of North Carolina, §116-41.1.
University enterprises.
University of North Carolina, §116-41.1.
University of North Carolina School of the
    Arts, §116-64.
University property.
University of North Carolina, §116-44.3.
Unlawful conduct.
Civil no-contact orders, §50C-1.
Workplace violence prevention, §95-260.
Unlawful telecommunications device, §14-113.5.
Unmanipulated manures.
Commercial fertilizer, §106-657.
Unmarked human burial.
Burial sites, §70-28.
Unobscured.
Campaign contributions and expenditures.
    Disclosure requirements for media
        advertisements, §163-278.38Z.
Unregistered classified motor vehicle.
Taxation, §105-330.
Unreserved fund balance.
Budget of state, §143C-1-1(d).
Unrestricted use standards.
Brownfields property reuse tax, §130A-310.31(b).
Contamination of site, §143B-279.9(d).
Risk based environmental remediation of
    industrial sites, §130A-310.65.
Unsafe practices.
Motor vehicles, §20-356.
Unsolicited.
Computer crimes, §14-453.
Unsolicited advertisement.
Unsolicited facsimiles, §75-115.
Unsolicited telephone call.
Telephone solicitations, §75-101.
Unsuccessful candidate.
General assembly.
    Contesting a seat, §120-10.2.
Unwithdrawn deposit.
Right of survivorship in bank deposits, §41-2.1(e).

DEFINED TERMS —Cont'd
Unzoned area.
Junkyard control, §136-143.
Outdoor advertising control, §136-128.
Upgrading supplement requirement.
Revenue bonds, §159-97.
UPL.
Hospital provider assessments, §108A-121.
Upland game birds.
Conservation, §113-129.
UPL assessment.
Hospital provider assessments, §108A-121.
UPL gap.
Hospital provider assessments, §108A-121.
UPL payment.
Hospital provider assessments, §108A-121.
Upper pay limit (UPL).
Hospital provider assessments, §108A-121.
Urban area.
Outdoor advertising control, §136-128.
Urban area revitalization project, §160A-536(c).
Urban forester, §89B-2.
Urban progress zone.
Commerce department, §143B-437.09(a).
Growing businesses tax credits, §105-129.81.
Urban service districts.
Consolidated city-county, §§160B-3 to 160B-6.
Usage of trade.
UCC, §25-1-303(c).
U.S. drought monitor.
Water resources, §143-350.
Use.
Sales and use tax, §105-164.3.
Tobacco taxation, §105-113.4.
Used for profit.
Public morals, §19-1.1.
Used for residential purposes.
Annexation initiated by municipality,
    §160A-58.51.
Used motor vehicle dealer.
Motor vehicles, §20-286.
Used oil.
Regulation of rerefined or reprocessed oil,
    §119-13.1.
Solid waste management, §130A-290(b).
Used oil recycling facility.
Solid waste management, §130A-290(b).
Use of public land.
Environmental policy act, §113A-9.
User.
Criminal justice information network, §143-660.
Electronic surveillance, §15A-286.
Gasoline tax, §105-449.60.
Use tax.
Sales and use tax, §105-164.3.
Uniform sales and use tax administration act,
    §105-164.42B.
Utility.
Road construction, §136-102.6(e).
Unclaimed property act, §116B-52.
Utility or public service enterprise.
Local government bonds, §159-44.
Utility owner.
Contractors, §87-101.
Utility pole.
Wireless telecommunications facilities,
    §§153A-349.51, 160A-400.51.
Utility vehicles, §20-4.01.
Utilization review, §58-50-61(a).
Utilization review organization, §58-50-61(a).

DEFINED TERMS —Cont'd
Uwharrie region of North Carolina.
Uwharrie regional resources act, §153C-2.
Vacant and unappropriated lands.
State lands, §146-64.
Vacant industrial warehouse.
Minimum standards for nonresidential structures, §160A-439(p).
Vacant manufacturing facility.
Minimum standards for nonresidential structures, §160A-439(p).
Vacation rental, §42A-4.
Vacation rental agreement, §42A-4.
Vaccination.
Rabies, §130A-184.
Vaccine-related injury, §130A-422.
Valid lien.
Fraudulent transfers, §39-23.1.
Valid protective order.
Domestic violence, §§50B-4.1(f), 50B-4(f).
Valuation.
Property taxes, §105-273.
Value.
Exemptions from creditors' claims, §1C-1601(b).
Letters of credit, §25-5-102(b).
Organized retail theft, §14-86.5.
Secured transactions third party assignees, §25-9-403(a).
UCC, §§25-1-201(b), 25-1-204.
Variety.
Seed law, §106-277.2.
Vault.
Cemeteries, §65-48.
Vegetable plants, §106-284.16.
Vegetable seeds, §106-277.2.
Vehicle, §§14-399(i), 20-4.01(49).
Alcoholic beverages, §18B-120.
Criminal procedure, §15A-101.
Gross receipts tax on short-term leases or rentals, §153A-156(e).
Mercury switch removal, motor vehicles, §130A-310.50.
Motor vehicles, §§20-4.01, 20-137.7, 20-138.1.
Rental car companies selling insurance, §58-33-17(a).
Rental cars, §66-201.
Vehicle crusher.
Mercury switch removal, motor vehicles, §130A-310.50.
Vehicle dismantler.
Mercury switch removal, motor vehicles, §130A-310.50.
Vehicle identification number.
Chop shops, §14-72.7(f).
Vehicle license and registration fees.
Rental cars, §66-201.
Vehicle manufacturer.
Mercury switch removal, motor vehicles, §130A-310.50.
Vehicle part identification number.
Chop shops, §14-72.7(f).
Vehicle recycler.
Mercury switch removal, motor vehicles, §130A-310.50.
Vehicle recycling.
Motor vehicles, §20-137.7.
Vehicle surface area, §113A-70(b).
Vending facilities.
Aid to the blind, §111-42(d).
Community colleges, §115D-2.
Local government finance, §159-7.

DEFINED TERMS —Cont'd
Vending facilities —Cont'd
School budgets, §115C-423.
University of North Carolina, §116-2.
Vendor.
Portable consumer electronic devices insurance, §58-44A-1.
Seed law, §106-277.2.
Verification or proof.
Notaries public act, §10B-3.
Vessel.
Boating safety, §75A-2.
Clean coastal water and vessel act, §77-125.
Conservation, §113-130.
Liens on personal property, §44A-1.
Oil and hazardous substance control, §143-215.77.
Vested right.
City and town zoning, §160A-385.1(b).
Counties, §153A-344.1.
Vested trust.
Legislative ethics, §120-85.1.
State government ethics act, §138A-3.
Veteran, §§126-81, 165-3.
Children of war veterans scholarships, §165-20.
Employment preference for veterans, §128-15(b).
Minor spouses of veterans, §165-17.
Minor veterans, §165-13.
Priority in employment assistance for United States armed forces veterans, §165-44.2.
Recreation, §165-25.
Veterans' organization, §165-3.
Veterans' recreation project, §165-25.
Veterinarian, §90-181.
Veterinary clinic, §90-181.1(b).
Veterinary hospital, §90-181.1(b).
Veterinary license, §90-181.
Veterinary medicine, §90-181.
Veterinary student intern, §90-181.
Veterinary student preceptee, §90-181.
Veterinary technician, §90-181.
VGLI.
Life insurance.
Dishonest and predatory sales to military personnel, §58-58-335.
Viatical settlement broker.
Viatical life insurance settlements, §58-58-205.
Viatical settlement contract.
Securities, §78A-2.
Viatical life insurance settlements, §58-58-205.
Viatical settlement provider.
Viatical life insurance settlements, §58-58-205.
Viatical settlement purchase agreement.
Viatical life insurance settlements, §58-58-205.
Viatical settlement purchaser.
Viatical life insurance settlements, §58-58-205.
Viaticated policy.
Viatical life insurance settlements, §58-58-205.
Viator.
Viatical life insurance settlements, §58-58-205.
Victim.
Crime victims, §§15A-824, 15A-830(a).
Crime victims financial recovery assistance act, §15B-31.
Innocence inquiry commission, §15A-1460.
Permanent no contact order prohibiting future contact by convicted sex offender with victim, §15A-1340.50(a).
Restitution, §15A-1340.34.
Victims compensation, §15B-2.
Victim advocate.
Domestic violence shelters.
Limited civil liability, §1-620.

DEFINED TERMS —Cont'd
Victim of a sexual offense.
Address confidentiality program, §15C-2.
Victim of domestic violence.
Address confidentiality program, §15C-2.
Victim of human trafficking.
Address confidentiality program, §15C-2.
Victim of stalking.
Address confidentiality program, §15C-2.
Video gaming machine, §14-306.1A(b).
Video programming.
Sales and use tax, §105-164.3.
State franchising of cable television service,
§66-350.
Viewing zone.
Outdoor advertising, §136-133.5(d).
Village.
Public hospitals, §131E-6.
Violations of the law.
Public records, §132-1.4.
Virgin newsprint.
Newspaper taxation, §105-102.6.
Virulent hog-cholera virus, §106-316.2.
Visible.
Junkyard control, §136-143.
Outdoor advertising control, §136-128.
Visually impaired person, §111-11.
Vital records.
Public health generally, §130A-2.
Vocational rehabilitation.
Industrial commission utilization of rehabilitation
professionals, ICRehabProf Rule III.
Voice communications service.
911 system, §62A-40.
Voice communications service connection.
911 system, §62A-40.
Voice communications service provider.
911 system, §62A-40.
VoIP provider.
911 system, §62A-40.
**Volatile substances capable of producing toxic
effect.**
Household cleaners, §66-85.
Volume control handset.
Deaf and the hard of hearing, §143B-216.30.
Voluntary dissolution.
Savings and loan associations, §54B-4.
Savings banks, §54C-4(b).
Voluntary market.
Beach property insurance, §58-45-5.
Voluntary market area.
Beach property insurance, §58-45-5.
Volunteer.
Assault on school employees or volunteers,
§14-33(c).
Domestic violence shelters.
Limited civil liability, §1-620.
Volunteer immunity, §1-539.11.
Volunteer firefighter.
Tuition and fee waivers, §115B-1.
Volunteer transportation.
Public utilities, §62-289.3.
Vote.
Nonprofit corporations, §55A-1-40.
Voting booth.
Elections, §163-165.
Voting enclosure.
Elections, §163-165.
Voting group.
Business corporations, §55-1-40.

DEFINED TERMS —Cont'd
Voting place.
Elections, §163-165.
Voting security.
Collection agencies, §58-70-6.
Insurance holding companies, §58-19-5.
Voting shares.
Shareholder protection act, §55-9-01(b).
Voting system.
Elections, §163-165.
Wage.
Child support, §110-129.
Governmental employees and social security,
§135-20.
Tax withholding, §105-163.1.
Unemployment compensation, §96-8.
Seasonal pursuits, §96-16(j).
Wage and hour act, §95-25.2.
Waiting period.
Health insurance portability and accountability,
§58-68-30(b).
Guaranteed individual coverage for certain
individuals with prior group coverage,
§58-68-60(b).
Ward.
Incompetency, §§35A-1101, 35A-1202.
Veterans, §34-2.
Warehouse.
Cotton warehousing, §106-451.7.
Warehouseman.
Cotton warehousing, §106-451.7.
UCC, §25-7-102(a).
Warehouse receipt.
UCC, §25-1-201(b).
Warehousing.
Growing businesses tax credits, §105-129.81.
Warehousing and distribution.
Tax incentives for new and expanding businesses,
§105-129.2.
Warning sign.
Overhead high-voltage line safety, §95-229.6.
Warrant.
Child custody jurisdiction and enforcement,
§50A-102.
Warrant for arrest.
Criminal process, §15A-304.
Wartime.
Children of war veterans scholarships, §165-20.
Waste.
Oil and gas conservation, §113-389.
Solid waste management, §130A-290(a).
Water and air resources, §143-213.
Water pollution control system operators, §90A-46.
Waste treatment management practice,
§143-213.
Wastewater collection system.
Clean water management trust fund, §113A-252.
Water infrastructure, §159G-20.
Wastewater reserve.
Water infrastructure, §159G-20.
Wastewater system.
Water infrastructure, §159G-20.
Wastewater treatment facility.
Certification of wastewater contractors and
inspectors, §90A-71.
Wastewater treatment works.
Clean water management trust fund, §113A-252.
Water infrastructure, §159G-20.
Water column.
Cultivation of shellfish, §113-201.1.

DEFINED TERMS —Cont'd
Watercraft.
Littering, §14-399(i).
Water distribution system.
Metropolitan water districts, §162A-32(a).
Water infrastructure fund.
Water infrastructure, §159G-20.
Water pollution, §143-213.
Water pollution control facility.
Pollution control, §§159C-3, 159D-3.
Water pollution control system.
Operators, §90A-46.
Water quality protection.
Cooperative state-local coalition water quality
protection plans, §143-214.14(a).
Waters.
Dry-cleaning solvent cleanup act,
§143-215.104B(b).
Oil and hazardous substance control, §143-215.77.
Water and air resources, §143-212.
Watershed, §143-213.
Watershed improvement project.
Soil and water conservation, §139-3.
Watershed improvement work.
Soil and water conservation, §139-3.
Water shortage emergency, §143-350.
Waterslide.
Safety, §95-111.3(h).
Waters of this state.
Aquatic weed control, §113A-221.
Boating safety, §75A-2.
Water supply well.
Well construction, §§87-85, 87-88(k).
Water system, §162A-2.
Metropolitan water districts, §162A-32(a).
Water treatment facility.
Operators, §90A-20.1.
Water treatment or purification plant.
Metropolitan water districts, §162A-32(a).
Weapon of like kind.
Deadly weapons, §14-269.1.
Weapon of mass death and destruction.
Civil disorders, §14-288.8.
Weapons.
Educational property, §14-269.2(a).
Weather-based irrigation controller.
Performance standards for sustainable,
energy-efficient public buildings, §143-135.36.
Weatherization.
Energy assistance for low-income persons,
§143B-472.122.
Weed.
Pesticide board, §143-460.
Weed seeds.
Seed law, §106-277.2.
Week.
Unemployment compensation, §96-8.
Unemployment insurance, §96-8.
Weekly benefit amount.
Unemployment compensation, §96-8.
Weigh.
Weights and measures, §81A-51.
Weight.
Weights and measures, §§81A-9, 81A-51.
Well.
Well construction, §87-85.
Well contractor.
Certification, §87-98.2.
Well contractor activity.
Well contractor certification, §87-98.2.

DEFINED TERMS —Cont'd
Well driller.
Well construction, §87-85.
Well seal.
Well construction, §87-85.
Wet marine and transportation insurance.
Surplus lines, §58-21-10.
Wharfage.
Ports authority income tax, §105-130.41(c).
Ports authority individual income tax,
§105-151.22(c).
When he deems himself insecure.
Leases, UCC.
Option to accelerate at will, §25-2A-109(1).
White goods.
Solid waste management, §130A-290(a).
White goods disposal tax, §105-187.20.
White-tailed deer.
Deer, production and sale for commercial
purposes, §106-549.97(c).
Wholesale dealer.
Tobacco taxation, §105-113.4.
Wholesale distribution.
Wholesale prescription drug distributors,
§106-145.2.
Wholesale distribution facility.
Dry-cleaning solvent cleanup act,
§143-215.104B(b).
Wholesale distributor, §106-145.2.
Dry-cleaning solvent cleanup act,
§143-215.104B(b).
Wholesale merchant.
Property taxes, §105-273.
Sales and use tax, §105-164.3.
Wholesaler.
Alcohol taxation, §105-113.68.
Beer franchises, §18B-1301.
Commercial fertilizer, §106-657.
Motor vehicles, §20-286.
Registration of prescription drug wholesalers,
§106-140.1(j).
Seed law, §106-277.2.
Wholesale sale.
Sales and use tax, §105-164.3.
Wholesale trade.
Growing businesses tax credits, §105-129.81.
Tax incentives for new and expanding businesses,
§105-129.2.
Widow.
Workers' compensation, §97-2.
Widower.
Workers' compensation, §97-2.
Wild animals.
Conservation, §113-129.
Endangered wildlife, §113-331.
Wild birds.
Conservation, §113-129.
Wilderness program.
Delinquent and undisciplined juveniles, §7B-1501.
Wildlife.
Conservation, §113-129.
Interstate wildlife violator compact, §113-300.6.
Pesticide board, §143-460.
Resources commission, §143-238.
Wildlife commission.
High Rock lake marine commission, §77-50.
Lake lure marine commission, §77-80.
Lake Wylie marine commission, §77-30.
Wildlife law.
Interstate wildlife violator compact, §113-300.6.

DEFINED TERMS —Cont'd

Wildlife officer.
Interstate wildlife violator compact, §113-300.6.
Wildlife protector.
Conservation, §113-128.
Wildlife refuge.
Conservation, §113-129.
Wildlife resources.
Commission, §143-238.
Conservation, §113-129.
Offshore oil and gas activities, §143-215.94B(b).
Wildlife resources commission, §113-128.
Will.
Discipline and disability rules of state bar, Bar
    Rule B.0103.
Willful.
Insurance rates, §58-40-5.
Willfully.
Unemployment compensation, §96-8.
Willful or wanton conduct.
Punitive damages, §1D-5.
Wilmington tariff, terminal tariff.
Ports authority income tax, §105-130.41(c).
Ports authority individual income tax,
    §105-151.22(c).
Wine.
Alcohol taxation, §105-113.68.
Wine producer, §18B-1000.
Winery.
Alcoholic beverages, §18B-1201.
Wine shipper permittee.
Alcoholic beverages tax, §105-113.68.
Wine wholesaler.
Alcoholic beverages, §18B-1201.
Winter sports, §99C-1.
Wire communication.
Electronic surveillance, §15A-286.
Wireless facility.
Wireless telecommunications facilities,
    §§153A-349.51, 160A-400.51.
Wireless support structure.
Wireless telecommunications facilities,
    §§153A-349.51, 160A-400.51.
Wireless telephone service.
Unlawful use of mobile phone by minors,
    §20-137.3(a).
Withdrawable accounts.
Savings and loan associations, §54B-4.
Withholding agent.
Tax withholding, §105-163.1.
Withholdings.
Job development investment grant program,
    §143B-437.51.
Without authority.
Computer trespass, §14-458(a).
Witness.
Victims and witnesses, §15A-824.
Witnesses, §15A-811.
Woman.
Woman's right to know act, §90-21.81.
Women.
Transportation contracts, §136-28.4(c).
Women's business enterprise.
Global TransPark authority, §63A-19.
Wooden pallet.
Solid waste management, §130A-290(a).
Woodland.
Regulation of open fires, §106-941.
Setting fire to woodlands, §14-138.1.
Work.
Public assistance program, §108A-24.

DEFINED TERMS —Cont'd

Work day.
Contractors, §87-101.
Workers' compensation, §97-2.
Disability income plan, §135-101.
Workers' compensation act.
Industrial commission managed care
    organizations, ICManagedCare Rule II.
Work first diversion assistance.
Public assistance program, §108A-24.
Work first family assistance.
Public assistance program, §108A-24.
Work first program.
Public assistance program, §108A-24.
Work first program assistance.
Public assistance program, §108A-24.
Work first services.
Public assistance program, §108A-24.
Working capital, §58-67-5(j).
Local ABC boards, §18B-702(g).
Working day.
Abused, neglected and dependent juveniles,
    §7B-101.
Pollution control act, §113A-52.
Working waterfront property, §105-277.14(a).
Work loss.
Victims compensation, §15B-2.
Work of art.
Sales, §25C-10.
Sales and use tax exemptions, §105-164.13.
State monuments, §100-2.
Workplace.
City and town personnel, §160A-169.
Counties, §153A-99(b).
Defensive force to protect, §14-51.2(a).
Worksite.
Safety and health, §95-250.
Work week.
Wage and hour act, §95-25.2.
Wreckers.
Motor vehicles, §20-4.01.
Property-hauling vehicle registration fees,
    §20-88(b).
Write-off.
Statewide accounts receivable program,
    §147-86.20.
Writings.
Evidence, §8C-1 Rule 1001.
UCC, §25-1-201(b).
Written.
UCC, §25-1-201(b).
Yard trash.
Solid waste management, §130A-290(a).
Year.
Continuing legal education, Bar Rule D.1501.
Educational personnel, §115C-325(a).
Judicial retirement, §135-53.
Legislative retirement system, §120-4.8.
Local government finance, §159-2.
Retirement, §128-21.
State retirement system, §135-1.
Youth development center.
Delinquent and undisciplined juveniles, §7B-1501.
Division of juvenile justice, §143B-805.

DEFORMED CHILDREN.
Prohibited exhibition, §110-20.1.

DEGREES OF KINSHIP.
Computation, §§29-5, 104A-1.
Intestate succession, §29-7.

DEHUMIDIFIERS.
Energy star qualified products.
Sales and use tax holiday, §105-164.13D(a).

DELINQUENCY HISTORY LEVELS, §§7B-2507,
7B-2508(b).
Disposition chart, §7B-2508(f).
Level one to level three dispositions,
§7B-2508(b) to (e).

DELINQUENCY PROCEEDINGS, INSURERS.
Generally, §§58-30-1 to 58-30-310.
See INSURER SUPERVISION,
REHABILITATION AND LIQUIDATION.

DELINQUENT AND UNDISCIPLINED
JUVENILES, §§7B-1500 to 7B-2827.
Absconding juveniles.
Returning from one state to another.
Interstate compact on juveniles generally,
§§7B-2800 to 7B-2827.
See INTERSTATE COMPACT ON
JUVENILES.
Taking juvenile into temporary custody, §7B-1900.
Transporting to nearest secure facility,
§7B-1901(c).
Adjudication of juvenile, §7B-2411.
Delinquent adjudication not considered conviction
of criminal offense nor cause for forfeiture of
citizenship rights, §7B-2412.
Written order, requirements, §7B-2411.
Adjudicatory hearing.
Admissibility of statement made by juvenile to
juvenile court counselor during preliminary
inquiry, §7B-2408.
Admissions by juvenile, when accepted by court,
§7B-2407.
Clear and convincing evidence, petition alleging
undisciplined behavior, §7B-2409.
Conduct of hearing, §7B-2405.
Continuance, §7B-2406.
Due process rights protected, §7B-2405.
Jeopardy attaches, §7B-2414.
Rights of juvenile and parent, guardian or
custodian protected to assure due process,
§7B-2405.
Rules of evidence, §7B-2408.
Time and place for holding, §7B-2403.
Admissions by juvenile, when accepted by
court.
Duties of court before accepting, §7B-2407(a).
Factual basis for admission determination,
§7B-2407(c).
Product of informed choice determination by
court, §7B-2407(b).
Statement made to juvenile court counselor
during preliminary inquiry, §7B-2408.
Adoption.
Bringing juvenile delinquents into state for
placement or adoption, §§7B-3700 to 7B-3705.
See CHILD PLACEMENT.
Sending child out of state for purposes of
placement, §§7B-3702 to 7B-3705.
Adult, prosecution of juvenile as.
Commission of offense after superior court
conviction, §7B-1604(b).
Emancipated juvenile prosecuted as adult for
commission of criminal offense, §7B-1604(a).
Juvenile committing criminal offense on or after
sixteenth birthday, §7B-1604(a).
Transfer of jurisdiction to superior court,
§§7B-2200 to 7B-2204.
Appeal, §7B-2603.

DELINQUENT AND UNDISCIPLINED
JUVENILES —Cont'd
Age governs for purposes of determining
jurisdiction.
Jurisdiction over delinquent juveniles,
§7B-1601(a).
Jurisdiction over undisciplined juvenile,
§7B-1600(a).
Alcohol rehabilitation center.
Taking absconding juvenile into temporary
custody, §7B-1900.
Duties of persons taking juvenile into
temporary custody, §7B-1901(a).
Transporting to approved secure custody
facility, §7B-1901(c).
Allowing family opportunity to meet needs of
juvenile, §7B-2501(d).
Alternative dispositions for delinquent
juveniles, §7B-2506.
Alternative dispositions for undisciplined
juvenile, §7B-2503.
Amendment of petition, §7B-2400.
Appeal of final order of court.
County appeals, limitations, §7B-2604(c).
Modification or alteration of original order upon
affirmation of order by appellate court,
§7B-2606.
Notice of appeal, §7B-2602.
Parties, §7B-2604(a).
Release of juvenile pending disposition of appeal,
§7B-2605.
Review of final order before court of appeals,
§7B-2602.
Right to appeal, §7B-2602.
Transfer decision, §7B-2603.
State appeal, limitations, §7B-2604(b).
Temporary order affecting custody or placement
pending disposition, §7B-2605.
Time for filing notice, §7B-2602.
Transfer of jurisdiction of juvenile to superior
court for prosecution as adult.
Abuse of discretion, review by superior court,
§7B-2603(a).
Appeal to court of appeals, §7B-2603(d).
Appeal to superior court for hearing on record,
§7B-2603(a).
Interlocutory order, order of superior court
considered, §7B-2603(d).
Notice of appeal, §7B-2603(a).
Pretrial release of juvenile, §7B-2603(b).
Probable cause or underlying offense findings,
superior court not to review, §7B-2603(a).
Remanding case to juvenile court, §7B-2603(c).
Transfer of case to superior court docket,
§7B-2603(a).
Waiver of right to raise issue of transfer before
court of appeals, §7B-2603(a).
Who may take appeal, §7B-2604.
Appearance of parent, guardian or custodian.
Contempt, failure to appear, §§7B-1805(c),
7B-1806.
Excusing appearance, §7B-2700.
Requirement as to attending hearings, §7B-2700.
Appointment of counsel for indigent parent,
guardian or custodian.
Summons to notify of right, §7B-1805(b).
Appointment of counsel for juvenile,
§7B-2000(a).
Conclusive presumption of indigence, §7B-2000(b).
Payment, §§7B-2002, 7B-2704.
Secure or nonsecure custody hearing, §7B-1906(c).

**DELINQUENT AND UNDISCIPLINED
    JUVENILES** —Cont'd
Attorneys.
Juvenile delinquency law specialist.
    Recognition as specialist, Bar Rule D.2503.
    Standards for certification, Bar Rule D.2508.
        Continuing certification, Bar Rule D.2509.
    Subspecialty, criminal law specialist, Bar Rule
        D.2502.
**Audio and video transmission, continued
    custody hearing conducted by,** §7B-1906(h).
**Authority over parents of juveniles
    adjudicated delinquent or undisciplined.**
Appearance at hearings required, §7B-2700.
Compliance with orders, §7B-2703(a).
Contempt for failure to comply with provisions,
    §7B-2706.
Cooperation with and assisting juvenile in
    complying with terms and conditions of
    probation or orders, §7B-2703(b).
Court-appointed attorneys' fees, ordering
    payment, §7B-2704.
Employment discrimination unlawful for
    compliance with provisions of articles,
    §7B-2705.
Excusing appearance of parent, §7B-2700.
Insurance coverage to cover medical costs while
    juvenile in out-of-home custody, ordering,
    §7B-2704.
Medical, surgical, psychiatric, psychological or
    other evaluation or treatment ordered,
    §7B-2702.
Parental responsibility classes, ordering parent to
    attend, §7B-2701.
Probation supervision fees or residential facility
    costs, ordering payment, §7B-2704.
Support of juvenile, payment ordered, §7B-2704.
Transportation for juvenile to keep appointment
    with juvenile court counselor, court ordering,
    §7B-2703(a).
Beyond reasonable doubt quantum of proof.
Petition alleging juvenile delinquent, §7B-2409.
Black Mountain center.
Juvenile absconders, taking into temporary
    custody, §7B-1900.
    Duties of persons taking juvenile into
        temporary custody, §7B-1901(a).
Blood specimens.
Grounds for obtaining, §7B-2105(b).
Nontestimonial identification order procedures,
    §§7B-2103 to 7B-2109.
Books, papers, documents, etc.
Disclosure by juvenile, §7B-2301(b).
Disclosure by petitioner, §7B-2300(c).
**Bringing juvenile delinquents into state for
    placement or adoption,** §§7B-3700 to
    7B-3705.
    See CHILD PLACEMENT.
Burden at adjudicatory hearing, §7B-2409.
**Burden at secure or nonsecure custody
    hearing,** §7B-1906(d).
Chart of dispositions of delinquent juveniles.
Class of offense in delinquency history level,
    §7B-2508(f).
Chief court counselor.
Appointment for each district, §143B-806(b).
Defined, §7B-1501.
Delegation of court's authority to issue secure and
    nonsecure custody orders to, §7B-1902.
Establishment of intake services, §7B-1700.

**DELINQUENT AND UNDISCIPLINED
    JUVENILES** —Cont'd
Chief court counselor —Cont'd
Maintenance or records, confidentiality,
    §7B-3001(a).
Powers and duties, §143B-830.
Citizenship rights, forfeiture.
Delinquent adjudication not cause for, §7B-2412.
Classification of offenses, §7B-2508(a).
Consolidation of offenses, §7B-2508(h).
Delinquency history levels, §§7B-2507, 7B-2508(b).
Disposition chart, §7B-2508(f).
Levels one to three dispositions, §7B-2508(c) to
    (e).
Clear and convincing evidence.
Petition alleging undisciplined behavior,
    §7B-2409.
Secure or nonsecure custody hearing, §7B-1906(d).
Clerk to maintain complete records,
    §7B-3001(a).
Closure of hearing, §7B-2402.
Commencement of action by filing petition,
    §7B-1804(a).
**Commencement of proceeding in district other
    than that of juvenile's residence,**
    §7B-1800(a).
**Commitment of delinquent juvenile to division
    of juvenile justice.**
Commitment services in a program not located in
    a youth development center or detention
    facility, §7B-2513(e).
Placement in youth development center,
    §7B-2513.
    Extended commitment, §7B-2515.
    Post-release supervision, §§7B-2514, 7B-2516(c).
**Community service, juveniles ordered to
    perform,** §7B-2506.
Complaint filed as petition, §7B-1803.
Juvenile court counselor determination, §7B-1702.
Juvenile court counselor's findings as to
    commission of certain nondivertible offenses,
    §7B-1702.
Notice to complainant on determination that
    petition should not be filed, §7B-1703(c).
Time for filing after juvenile court counselor
    determination, §7B-1703(b).
**Comprehensive juvenile delinquency and
    substance abuse prevention plan,**
    §143B-840.
**Compulsory school attendance law, excusing
    juvenile.**
Delinquent juveniles, §7B-2506.
Undisciplined juveniles, §7B-2503.
Conditions of protective supervision.
Undisciplined juvenile placed under, §7B-2504.
Confidentiality of records and social reports,
    §7B-3000(b).
Chief court counselor's records, §7B-3001(a).
Division of juvenile justice records and files,
    §7B-3001(c).
Law enforcement records and files, §7B-3001(b).
Sealing of records, §7B-3000(c).
Sharing of information between designated local
    agencies, §7B-3100.
Confinement in detention facility.
Alternative disposition for delinquent juvenile,
    §7B-2506.
Contempt of court for undisciplined juvenile,
    §7B-2505.

DELINQUENT AND UNDISCIPLINED JUVENILES —Cont'd

Consent of department of health and human services for purposes of placement of juvenile.

Bringing or sending juvenile into state or sending juvenile out of state, §§7B-3700 to 7B-3705.

Contempt.

Failure of parent, guardian or custodian to appear.

Show cause order for contempt, §7B-1806.

Summons to notify parent, guardian or custodian, §7B-1805(c).

Nonapplicability of provisions to direct contempt proceedings, §7B-1707.

Undisciplined juveniles, failure to comply with disposition order, §7B-2505.

Continuance of adjudicatory hearing, §7B-2406.

Continued jurisdiction of court to modify or vacate order, §7B-2600(c).

Continued jurisdiction until terminated by court order or emancipation of juvenile.

Jurisdiction over delinquent juveniles, §7B-1601(a).

Jurisdiction over undisciplined juveniles, §7B-1600(b).

Juvenile placed in youth development center for committing certain offenses, §7B-1602.

Continued secure or nonsecure custody hearing, §7B-1906.

Contributing to delinquency, §14-316.1.

Conviction of criminal offense, delinquent adjudication not considered, §7B-2412.

County appeals, limitations, §7B-2604(c).

County or unit of government operating juvenile detention facility.

Required standards and rules, §7B-1905(b).

Criminal process, provisions applicable to juvenile process, §7B-1806.

Criminal prosecution of juvenile as adult.

Commission of offense after superior court conviction, §7B-1604(b).

Commission of offense by juvenile on or after sixteenth birthday, §7B-1604(a).

Emancipated juvenile prosecuted as, §7B-1604(a).

Transfer of jurisdiction of juvenile to superior court, §7B-2200.

Appeal of transfer order, §7B-2603(a).

Appeal of superior court decision to court of appeals, §7B-2603(d).

Appeal to superior court for hearing on record, §7B-2603(a).

Authority of superior court on review, §7B-2603(a).

Interlocutory order, superior court order considered, §7B-2603(d).

Notice of appeal, §7B-2603(a).

Pretrial release of juvenile, §7B-2603(b).

Remanding case to juvenile court for adjudication or upholding transfer order, §7B-2603(c).

Waiver of right to raise issue of transfer before court of appeal.

Failing to appeal transfer order to superior court, §7B-2603(a).

Case not transferred, §7B-2203(d).

Detention pending pretrial release, §7B-2204.

Detention pending transfer to division of adult correction, §7B-2204.

DNA sample of juvenile transferred, §7B-2201(b).

DELINQUENT AND UNDISCIPLINED JUVENILES —Cont'd

Criminal prosecution of juvenile as adult —Cont'd

Transfer of jurisdiction of juvenile to superior court —Cont'd

Fingerprinting juvenile transferred, §7B-2201(a).

Pretrial release, right once order entered, §7B-2204.

Probable cause found and transfer to superior court not required, §7B-2202(e).

Probable cause hearing.

Burden of state, §7B-2202(c).

Conducting, §7B-2202(a).

Representation of state, juvenile, testimony and cross-examination of witnesses, §7B-2202(b).

Time for conducting, §7B-2202(a).

Waiver of right and stipulating to finding, §7B-2202(d).

Probable cause not found, §7B-2202(f).

Transfer hearing, §7B-2203(a).

Factors considered for transfer, §7B-2203(b).

Transfer order, §7B-2203(c).

Curfew, imposition on delinquent juvenile, §7B-2506.

Custodial interrogation procedures.

Admissibility of in-custody admission or confession, §7B-2101(b).

Admission into evidence of statement resulting from interrogation, court findings required, §7B-2101(d).

Advising juvenile of rights, §7B-2101(a).

Ceasing questioning when juvenile indicates a wish not to be questioned, §7B-2101(c).

Custody of juvenile.

Administrative order, delegation of court's authority, §7B-1902.

Authority of court to issue custody orders, §7B-1902.

Delegation of court's authority to chief court counselor or chief court counselor's counseling staff, §7B-1902.

Law enforcement procedures after juvenile taken into custody, §§7B-2100 to 7B-2109.

Secure or nonsecure custody, §§7B-1903 to 7B-1906.

Taking into temporary custody, §§7B-1900, 7B-1901.

Law enforcement, roles and permitted actions, §7B-2100.

Telephone communications, notices, orders, authorizations and requests, §7B-1907.

Day programs, disposition of delinquent juvenile, §7B-2506.

Definitions, §7B-1501.

Delinquent juvenile, §143B-805.

Nontestimonial identification, §7B-2103.

Undisciplined juvenile, §143B-805.

Delinquency history levels.

Calculating, §7B-2507(a).

Classification of offenses, §7B-2508.

Classification of prior adjudication from other jurisdictions, §7B-2507(e).

Classification of prior offense, §7B-2507(c).

Consolidation of offenses for disposition.

Adjudication of more than one offense during session, §7B-2508(h).

Determination, §7B-2508(b).

Dispositional chart, §7B-2508(f).

DELINQUENT AND UNDISCIPLINED
   JUVENILES —Cont'd
Delinquency history levels —Cont'd
Juvenile adjudicated delinquent for more than one
   offense in single session of district court,
   §7B-2507(d).
Level one, community disposition, §7B-2508(c).
Level two, intermediate disposition, §7B-2508(d).
Level three, commitment, §7B-2508(e).
Low, medium, high, §7B-2507(c).
Minor offense, committed to level three
   disposition, §7B-2508(g).
Points, assignments, §7B-2507(b).
Prior adjudications.
   Classification when from other jurisdiction,
      §7B-2507(e).
   Methods for proving, §7B-2507(f).
   Multiple adjudications obtained in one court
      session, §7B-2507(d).
Delinquent juvenile defined, §§7B-1501,
   143B-805.
Delivery of notification to school, §7B-3101(a).
Detention.
Generally, §§143B-815 to 143B-821.
See JUVENILE DETENTION.
Determination of incapacity to proceed.
Cases in which juvenile alleged to be delinquent,
   §7B-2401.
**Disclosure of evidence by petitioner or
   juvenile,** §§7B-2300 to 7B-2303.
Disclosure of information by local agencies,
   §7B-3100.
Discovery and disclosure of evidence.
Continuing duty to disclose, §7B-2303.
Denying, restricting or deferring discovery or
   inspection, §7B-2302(a).
   Supporting affidavits or statements for in
      camera inspection, §7B-2302(b).
Disclosure by juvenile.
   Books, papers, documents, etc., inspection and
      copying by petitioner, §7B-2301(b).
   Names of persons to be called as witnesses,
      §7B-2301(a).
   Physical or mental examinations or tests,
      inspecting and copying, §7B-2301(c).
   Tests, measurements or experiments, inspection
      and copying, §7B-2301(c).
Disclosure by petitioner.
   Books, papers, documents, etc., inspection and
      copying by juvenile, §7B-2300(c).
   Furnishing names of persons to be called as
      witnesses, §7B-2300(b).
   Internal documents, records or memoranda not
      subject to disclosure, §7B-2300(e).
   Oral statements, divulging in written or
      recorded form, §7B-2300(a).
   Physical evidence, inspecting, examining and
      testing by juvenile, §7B-2300(d).
   Physical or mental examinations, juvenile to
      inspect and copy, §7B-2300(d).
   Record of witnesses under age of sixteen, copy
      furnished juvenile, §7B-2300(b).
   Tests, measurements or experiments, inspection
      and copying by juvenile, §7B-2300(d).
   Voluntary disclosures not prohibited,
      §7B-2300(f).
   Work product not subject to disclosure,
      §7B-2300(e).
   Written or recorded statements by juvenile,
      §7B-2300(a).

DELINQUENT AND UNDISCIPLINED
   JUVENILES —Cont'd
Dismissal of petition with prejudice.
Allegations not proved, §7B-2411.
Dispositional hearing, §7B-2501(a).
Court to proceed to hearing upon receipt of
   predisposition report, §7B-2413.
Opportunity to present evidence and advise court
   as to disposition in best interest of juvenile,
   §7B-2501(b).
Dispositional order, §7B-2512.
Disposition chart, delinquent juveniles,
   §7B-2508(f).
Dispositions in juvenile actions.
Allowing family opportunity to meet needs of
   juvenile, §7B-2501(d).
Alternatives for delinquent juvenile, §7B-2506.
Alternatives for undisciplined juveniles, §7B-2503.
Appeals, §§7B-2603 to 7B-2606.
Commitment of delinquent to office of juvenile
   justice, §7B-2513.
   Notification of extended commitment, plan of
      treatment, §7B-2515.
Consideration by court in developing, §7B-2500.
Considerations of court in selecting disposition,
   §7B-2501(c).
Contempt of court for undisciplined juveniles,
   §7B-2505.
Delinquency history levels, §7B-2507.
   Limitations, §7B-2508.
Evaluation and treatment of juveniles, §7B-2502.
Hearing, §7B-2501(a).
   Opportunity to present evidence and advise
      court as to disposition in best interest of
      juvenile, §7B-2501(b).
Limits for each class of offense and delinquency
   history level, §7B-2508.
Modification or vacation of disposition, §7B-2600.
   Request of modification for lack of suitable
      services, §7B-2601.
Most appropriate disposition, court to select,
   §7B-2501(c).
Order, §7B-2512.
Post-release supervision, §7B-2514.
   Revocation, §7B-2516(a) to (c).
Probation, §7B-2510.
Probation termination, §7B-2511.
Protective supervision for undisciplined juveniles,
   conditions, §7B-2504.
Purposes, §7B-2500.
Transfer of juvenile by governor from jail or penal
   facility to residential facility, §7B-2517.
District court jurisdiction, §§7B-1600 to 7B-1604.
**Diversion contract with juvenile and parent,
   guardian or custodian,** §7B-1706(b).
Compliance determination by juvenile court
   counselor, §7B-1706(e).
Destruction of contract when juvenile reaches age
   of eighteen years or no longer under
   jurisdiction of court, §7B-1706(d).
Maintenance of contract to determine whether
   complaint previously diverted, §7B-1706(d).
Not public records, §7B-1706(d).
**Diversion of juvenile pursuant to diversion
   plan,** §7B-1706(a).
Compliance determination by juvenile court
   counselor, §7B-1706(e).
Destruction of plans when juvenile reaches age of
   eighteen years or no longer under jurisdiction
   of court, §7B-1706(d).

DELINQUENT AND UNDISCIPLINED JUVENILES —Cont'd

Diversion of juvenile pursuant to diversion plan —Cont'd

Maintenance of plans to determine whether complaint previously diverted, §7B-1706(d).

Plans not public records, §7B-1706(d).

Teen court programs.

Operated as community resource for, §143B-809(a).

Emancipated juvenile prosecuted as adult, §7B-1604(a).

Escaped delinquent juveniles.

Disclosure of information, §7B-3102(a).

Effort to notify parents prior to disclosure, §7B-3102(e).

Felony offense committed, §7B-3102(b).

Maintaining photograph of juveniles in custody, §7B-3102(d).

Return to custody prior to disclosures, §7B-3102(c).

Returning from one state to another.

Interstate compact on juveniles, §§7B-2800 to 7B-2827.

See INTERSTATE COMPACT ON JUVENILES.

Evaluation of complaint, §7B-1702.

Notice to complainant on determination that petition should not be filed, §7B-1703(c).

Time for completing by juvenile court counselor, §7B-1703(a).

Time for filing complaint as petition after juvenile court counselor determination, §7B-1703(b).

Evaluation of progress of juvenile.

Periodic evaluation by office of juvenile justice, §7B-2514(a).

Evidence, §§7B-2300 to 7B-2303.

Adjudicatory hearings, §7B-2408.

Dispositional hearings, §7B-2501(a).

Rebutting predisposition report, opportunity to juvenile, §7B-2413.

Examination and copying of evidence.

Discovery and disclosure of evidence generally, §§7B-2300 to 7B-2303.

Exclusive original jurisdiction over delinquent juveniles, §7B-1601(a).

Exclusive original jurisdiction over undisciplined juvenile, §7B-1600(a).

Expunction of juvenile records.

Effect of expunction, §7B-3101.

Failure to recite or acknowledge record or response after expunction.

Person not guilty of perjury or giving false statements, §7B-3201(a).

Notice of expunction, §7B-3202.

Person adjudicated, undisciplined or delinquent.

Ordering and directing expungement, §7B-3200(d), (e).

Petition filed by person adjudicated delinquent, §7B-3200(b), (c).

Petition filed by person adjudicated undisciplined, §7B-3200(a), (c).

Retention or disposal of records maintained by juvenile court counselor or intake officer, §7B-3200(f).

Retention or disposition of records maintained by residential facility, §7B-3200(g).

Service of petition, §7B-3200(c).

Person alleged to be delinquent or undisciplined.

Hearing on objection to petition, §7B-3200(h).

Petition, §7B-3200(h).

DELINQUENT AND UNDISCIPLINED JUVENILES —Cont'd

Expunction of juvenile records —Cont'd

Person alleged to be delinquent or undisciplined —Cont'd

Service of petition, §7B-3200(h).

Report clerk of superior court of names persons granted expunction, §7B-3200(i).

Testimony with respect of whether juvenile adjudicated delinquent.

Juvenile defendant in choosing to testify or juvenile called as witness, §7B-3201(b).

Extended jurisdiction of juvenile court, §§7B-1601(f), 7B-1602.

Failure of parent, guardian or custodian to appear.

Show cause order for contempt, §7B-1806.

Summons to notify parent, guardian or custodian, §7B-1805(c).

Filing of petition.

Time for filing after determination that complaint should be filed as petition, §7B-1703(b).

Fines, delinquent juveniles, §7B-2506.

Fingerprinting and photographing juveniles.

County juvenile detention facilities, §7B-2102(a1).

Destruction of records, §7B-2102(e).

Escape of juvenile from facility or law enforcement.

Release of photograph to public, §7B-3102.

Juvenile adjudicated delinquent, §7B-2102(b).

Maintaining photograph of juveniles in custody, §7B-3102(d).

Nondivertible offense, juvenile in custody for, §7B-2102(a).

Nontestimonial identification order procedures, §§7B-2103 to 7B-2109.

Not public records, §7B-2102(d).

Proper format for transfer to state bureau of investigation and federal bureau of investigation, §7B-2102(c).

First appearance for felony cases.

Continuance to time certain for good cause, §7B-1808(a).

Duty of court to inform juveniles, §7B-1808(b).

Place of hearing when juvenile in secure or nonsecure custody, §7B-1808.

Time for juvenile's appearance, §7B-1808(a).

Footprinting juvenile.

Nontestimonial identification order procedures, §§7B-2103 to 7B-2109.

Forfeiture of citizenship rights.

Delinquent adjudication not cause for, §7B-2412.

Governor.

Transferring juvenile from jail or penal facility to residential facility, §7B-2517.

Guardian appointed for juvenile, §7B-2001.

Hair samples.

Nontestimonial identification order procedures, §§7B-2103 to 7B-2109.

Handling of notice by principal, §7B-3101(c).

Handwriting exemplars.

Nontestimonial identification order procedures, §§7B-2103 to 7B-2109.

Hearings to be open to public unless court closes hearing, §7B-2402.

Holdover facilities.

Defined, §7B-1501.

Retaining juvenile allegedly committing Class A, B1, B2, C, D or E felony, §7B-1905(c).

House arrest of delinquent juvenile, §7B-2506.

**DELINQUENT AND UNDISCIPLINED
   JUVENILES** —Cont'd
Identification procedures, nontestimonial,
   §§7B-2103 to 7B-2109.
**Identifying information not to be disclosed or
   shared,** §7B-3100(b).
Incapacity to proceed, determination.
   Cases in which juvenile alleged to be delinquent,
      §7B-2401.
Inspection and copying of evidence.
   Discovery and disclosure of evidence generally,
      §§7B-2300 to 7B-2303.
**Inspection of predisposition report by
   juvenile,** §7B-2413.
Intake counselor.
   Defined, §7B-1501.
   Referral of juvenile to teen court program,
      §7B-1706(c).
Intake process, steps included, §7B-1702.
Intake services.
   Establishment by chief court counselor, §7B-1700.
   Juvenile court counselors.
      Field investigations, prohibition from engaging
         in, §7B-1700.
      Purposes, §7B-1700.
**Interpretation and construction of subchapter
   to implement purposes and policies,**
      §7B-1500.
**Interrogation procedures when juvenile in
   custody.**
   Admission into evidence of statement resulting
      from interrogation, court findings required,
      §7B-2101(d).
   Admission or confession resulting from
      interrogation, admissibility into evidence,
      §7B-2101(b).
   Advising juvenile of rights, §7B-2101(a).
   Ceasing questioning when juvenile indicates a
      wish not to be questioned further,
      §7B-2101(c).
Interstate compact on juveniles, §§7B-2800 to
   7B-2827.
   See INTERSTATE COMPACT ON JUVENILES.
**Interstate compact on the placement of
   children,** §§7B-3800 to 7B-3806.
**Interviews with complainant, victim, juvenile,
   etc.**
   Intake process to include, §7B-1702.
Jeopardy attaches in adjudicatory hearing,
   §7B-2414.
Jurisdiction of court to modify order.
   Continued jurisdiction, §7B-2600(b).
Jurisdiction over delinquent juveniles.
   Age governs for determining jurisdiction,
      §7B-1601(a).
   Continued jurisdiction of juvenile court.
      Juvenile committed to youth development
         center.
         Class B1, B2, C, D OR E felony, §7B-1602(b).
         First-degree murder, first-degree rape or
            first-degree sexual offense, §7B-1602(a).
   Continued jurisdiction until terminated by court
      order or emancipation of juvenile,
      §7B-1601(b).
   Exclusive original jurisdiction of district court,
      §7B-1601(a).
   Extended jurisdiction of juvenile court,
      §7B-1601(f).
   Parent, guardian or custodian, jurisdiction over,
      §7B-1601(g).

**DELINQUENT AND UNDISCIPLINED
   JUVENILES** —Cont'd
Jurisdiction over delinquent juveniles —Cont'd
   Preliminary inquiry.
      Personal jurisdiction, §7B-1701.
   Probable cause hearing and transfer hearing,
      §7B-1601(c), (d).
   Retention of jurisdiction for purposes of probable
      cause hearing and transfer hearing.
      Delinquent proceedings not concluded before
         juvenile reaches age of 18 years,
         §7B-1601(c).
   Violation of terms of juvenile's post-release
      supervision, §7B-1601(e).
**Jurisdiction over parent, guardian or
   custodian.**
   Authority of court generally, §§7B-2700 to
      7B-2706.
   Court having jurisdiction over delinquent juvenile,
      §7B-1601(g).
   Court having jurisdiction over undisciplined
      juvenile, §7B-1600(c).
   Summons to advise, §7B-1805(c).
Jurisdiction over undisciplined juveniles.
   Age governs for determining jurisdiction,
      §7B-1600(a).
   Continued jurisdiction until terminated by court
      order or emancipation of juvenile,
      §7B-1600(b).
   Exclusive original jurisdiction of district court,
      §7B-1600(a).
   Parent, guardian or custodian, jurisdiction over,
      §7B-1600(c).
Juvenile court counselors.
   Abuse, neglect, dependency.
      Duty to report, §7B-1700.1.
   Assumption of custody of juveniles.
      Powers and duties, §143B-831.
   Chief court counselor.
      Appointment for each district, §143B-806(b).
      Defined, §7B-1501.
      Delegation of court's authority to issue secure
         and nonsecure custody orders to, §7B-1902.
      Establishment of intake services, §7B-1700.
      Maintenance of records, confidentiality,
         §7B-3001(a).
      Powers and duties, §143B-830.
   Complaint alleging juvenile delinquent or
      undisciplined.
      Duty to screen and evaluate, §143B-831.
   Court counselor training and development
      program.
      Duty to develop, §143B-806(b).
   Defined, §§7B-1706(b), 143B-805.
   Diversion contract with juvenile and parent,
      guardian or custodian, §7B-1706(b).
      Compliance determination by juvenile court
         counselor, §7B-1706(e).
   Diversion of juvenile pursuant to diversion plan,
      §7B-1706(a).
      Compliance determination by juvenile court
         counselor, §7B-1706(e).
   Evaluation of complaint, §7B-1702.
      Notice to complainant on determination that
         petition should not be filed, §7B-1703(c).
      Time for completing, §7B-1703(a).
      Time for filing complaint as petition after
         determination, §7B-1703(b).
   Intake services.
      Field investigations, prohibition from engaging
         in, §7B-1700.

DELINQUENT AND UNDISCIPLINED JUVENILES —Cont'd

Juvenile court counselors —Cont'd
Petition drawn by counselor, §7B-1803(a).
Powers and duties, §143B-831.
Preliminary determination upon receipt of complaint, §7B-1702.
Referral of juvenile to teen court program, §7B-1706(c).
Taking juvenile into temporary custody without court order, §7B-1900.
Duties, §7B-1901(a).
Training and professional development program. Division of juvenile justice.
Duty to develop, §143B-806(b).

Juvenile court jurisdiction, §§7B-1600 to 7B-1604.
Juvenile court defined as district court exercising jurisdiction, §7B-1501.

Juvenile crime prevention councils, §§143B-845 to 143B-851.
See JUVENILE CRIME PREVENTION COUNCILS.

Juvenile detention facility operated by county or unit of government.
Standards and rules required, §7B-1905(b).

Lack of suitable services, request for modification, §7B-2601.

Law enforcement officers taking juvenile into temporary custody, §7B-1900.
Duties, §7B-1901(a).
Selecting appropriate course of action, permitted action, §7B-2100.

Law enforcement records and files.
Kept separate from records and files of adults, confidentiality, §7B-3001(b).

Level one disposition, delinquent juveniles, §7B-2508(c).

Level two disposition, delinquent juveniles, §7B-2508(d).

Level three disposition, delinquent juveniles, §7B-2508(e).

Liberty restrictions on release from secure custody, §7B-1906(f).

Lineups.
Nontestimonial identification order procedures, §§7B-2103 to 7B-2109.

Local agencies.
Designated to share information, §7B-3100.

Magistrates drawing and verifying petition, §7B-1804(b).

Mail service of summons.
Parent, guardian or custodian not found, §7B-1806.

Malicious conduct by prisoners, §14-258.4(a).

Measurements taken from juvenile.
Nontestimonial identification order procedures, §§7B-2103 to 7B-2109.

Medical, surgical, psychiatric or psychological evaluation, examination or treatment.
Court ordering examination, §7B-2502(a).
Direct involvement of parent in evaluation or treatment, court ordering, §7B-2702(b).
Disclosure of examination results by juvenile, §7B-2301(c).
Disclosure of examination results by petitioner, §7B-2300(d).
Hearing to determine whether juvenile in need of evaluation or treatment, §7B-2502(b).
Ordering parent to undergo evaluation or treatment, §7B-2702(c), (d).

DELINQUENT AND UNDISCIPLINED JUVENILES —Cont'd

Medical, surgical, psychiatric or psychological evaluation, examination or treatment —Cont'd
Payment of costs of treatment or care by parent or other responsible party, court ordering, §7B-2702(a).

Mental illness or developmental disability, court presented with evidence to effect.
Institutionalization of juvenile, requirements, §7B-2502(c).
Referral of juvenile to area mental health, developmental disabilities and substance abuse services director, §7B-2502(c).

Minor offenses.
Commission to level three disposition, §7B-2508(g).
Delinquency history levels, §§7B-2507, 7B-2508(b).
Disposition chart, §7B-2508(f).
Levels one to three disposition, §7B-2508(c) to (e).
Offense classification, §7B-2508(a).

Modification or vacation of order.
Authority of court to modify or alter order after affirmation by appellate court, §7B-2606.
Changes in circumstances or needs of juvenile, §7B-2600(a).
Continued jurisdiction of court to modify order, §7B-2600(c).
Duration of disposition of delinquent, reduction, §7B-2600(b).
Lack of suitable services, request for modification, §7B-2601.
Nature of disposition of delinquent, reduction, §7B-2600(b).
Reduction of delinquent's nature or duration of disposition, §7B-2600(b).
Review hearing to determine, §7B-2600(a).

Multipurpose group homes, residential placement of delinquent juvenile, §7B-2506.

Nontestimonial identification orders where juvenile alleged to be delinquent, §§7B-2103 to 7B-2109.
Affidavit required for issuance of order, §7B-2105.
Authority to issue order, §7B-2103.
Blood specimen to be obtained, grounds, §7B-2105(b).
Destruction of records, §7B-2108.
Grounds, §7B-2105(a).
Blood specimen to be obtained, §7B-2105(b).
Juvenile requesting order, §7B-2107.
Misdemeanor for willful violation of procedures, §7B-2109.
Nontestimonial identification defined, §7B-2103.
Procedure for issuance of order upon showing grounds, §7B-2106.
Request for order by juvenile, §7B-2107.
Request for order made prior to taking juvenile into custody or after custody and prior to adjudicatory hearing, §7B-2104.
Retention of records in court file, §7B-2108.

North Carolina sentencing and policy advisory commission.
Juvenile crime prevention council grants, programs receiving.
Biennial report on effectiveness, §164-49.
Juvenile recidivism.
Biennial report on, §164-48.

Notice of date and time of scheduled hearings to parent and juvenile, §7B-1807.

DELINQUENT AND UNDISCIPLINED JUVENILES —Cont'd

Notice requirements of summons, §7B-1805(b), (c).

Notice that petition should not be filed.

Juvenile court counselor determination, §7B-1703(c).

Notice to juvenile's parent, guardian or custodian.

Person taking juvenile into temporary custody without court order, §7B-1901(a).

Notification of principals of schools when juvenile alleged or found to be delinquent, §7B-3101.

Offense classification, §7B-2508(a).

Consolidation of offenses, §7B-2508(h).

Dispositional chart, §7B-2508(f).

Level one disposition, community disposition, §7B-2508(c).

Level two disposition, intermediate disposition, §7B-2508(d).

Level three disposition, commitment, §7B-2508(e).

Minor offense, commission to level three disposition, §7B-2508(g).

Open hearings, §7B-2402.

Order of adjudication.

Written order, requirements, §7B-2411.

Palm printing juvenile.

Nontestimonial identification order procedures, §§7B-2103 to 7B-2109.

Parties to appeal, §7B-2604(a).

Payment of support or other expenses, parent ordered to pay, §7B-2704.

Contempt.

Parent's failure to comply with orders, §7B-2706.

Discrimination in employment for complying with provisions, §7B-2705.

Employer discharging, demoting or denying promotion to employee complying with provisions of article.

Prohibition, §7B-2705.

Insurance coverage to cover medical costs of juvenile while in detention.

Parent ordered to assign private insurance coverage, §7B-2704.

Probation.

Parent ordered to pay fee for supervision, §7B-2704.

Support of juvenile, parent ordered to pay, §7B-2704.

Personal service of summons, §7B-1806.

Petition alleging delinquency or undiscipline, §7B-1802.

Amendment, §7B-2400.

Commencement of action by filing, §7B-1804(a).

Complaint filed as petition, §7B-1803.

Time for filing, §7B-1703(b).

Copy attached to summons, §7B-1805.

Law enforcement officer seeking upon taking custody of juvenile, §7B-2100.

Magistrate drawing and verifying petition, §7B-1804(b).

Person taking juvenile into temporary custody requesting, §7B-1901(a).

Pleading in juvenile action by petition, §7B-1801.

Petition should not be filed.

Notice to complainant, juvenile court counselor determination, §7B-1703(c).

Review by prosecutor of juvenile court counselor's decision, §7B-1705.

Request, §7B-1704.

DELINQUENT AND UNDISCIPLINED JUVENILES —Cont'd

Photographing and fingerprinting juveniles.

At time juvenile adjudicated delinquent, §7B-2102(b).

County juvenile detention facilities, §7B-2102(a1).

Destruction of records, §7B-2102(e).

Escape of juvenile from facility or law enforcement.

Release of photograph to public, §7B-3102.

Maintaining photograph of juveniles in custody, §7B-3102(d).

Nondivertible offense, juvenile in custody for, §7B-2102(a).

Nontestimonial identification order procedures, §§7B-2103 to 7B-2109.

Not public records, §7B-2102(d).

Proper format for transfer to state bureau of investigation and federal bureau of investigation, §7B-2102(c).

Placement of juvenile.

Alternative disposition for delinquent juvenile, §7B-2506.

Alternative disposition for undisciplined juveniles, §7B-2503.

Bringing delinquents into state for placement or adoption, §§7B-3700 to 7B-3705.

See CHILD PLACEMENT.

Interstate compact on the placement of children, §§7B-3800 to 7B-3806.

Secure or nonsecure custody orders, §§7B-1902 to 7B-1906.

Sending child out of state for purposes of placement, §§7B-3702 to 7B-3705.

Pleading in juvenile action by petition, §7B-1801.

Points, assignment.

Delinquency history levels, §7B-2507(b).

Post-release supervision.

Credit for definite term for time juvenile spends on supervision, §7B-2514(f).

Defined, §§7B-1501, 143B-805.

Hearing on violation of terms.

Rights of juvenile, §7B-2516(a).

Hearing to review progress, §7B-2516(a).

Indefinite commitment, period to be served before release, §7B-2514(e).

Initiation of planning process, §7B-2514.

Jurisdiction of district court for determining whether juvenile violated terms, §7B-1601(e).

Length of supervision, §7B-2514(b).

Notification before releasing juvenile, §7B-2514(d).

Planning process, what included, §7B-2514(a).

Revocation, §7B-2516(b), (c).

Secure custody for juvenile violating conditions, §7B-1903(d).

Supervision by juvenile court counselor, §7B-2514(g).

Termination of supervision order, §7B-2514(g).

Time for releasing juvenile, §7B-2514(c).

Violation of terms, revocation, §7B-2516(a), (b).

Predisposition investigation and report, §7B-2413.

Preliminary determination as to whether court has jurisdiction.

Juvenile court counselor to make determination upon receipt of complaint, §7B-1702.

Pretrial release of juvenile.

Appeal of order transferring jurisdiction to superior court, §7B-2603(b).

DELINQUENT AND UNDISCIPLINED JUVENILES —Cont'd

Pretrial release of juvenile —Cont'd
Release of juvenile once transfer order entered, §7B-2204.

Principals of schools notified when juvenile alleged or found to be delinquent, §7B-3101.
Use of information, §115C-404.

Prior adjudication of delinquent juvenile.
Delinquency history levels.
Adjudications from other jurisdiction, §7B-2507(e).
Methods of proving, §7B-2507(f).
Multiple adjudications obtained in one court session, §7B-2507(d).

Probable cause hearing.
Transfer of jurisdiction of juvenile to superior court, §7B-2202.

Probation.
Alternative disposition for delinquent juvenile, §7B-2506.
Conditions, §7B-2510(a).
Additional conditions, §7B-2510(b).
Extension of order for additional period, §7B-2510(c).
Length order to remain in force, §7B-2510(c).
Level three disposition for violation of conditions not to be ordered by court.
Juvenile adjudicated delinquent for minor offense, §7B-2510(f).
Modification of conditions or duration, §7B-2510(d).
Review of progress of juvenile, §7B-2510(d).
Secure custody for juvenile violating conditions, §7B-1903(d).
Termination by written order, §7B-2511.
Violation of conditions, authority of court on finding, §7B-2510(e).
Visitation by juvenile court counselor of juvenile in home, §7B-2510(a).

Production of books, records, documents, etc., for inspection and copying.
Disclosure by juvenile, §7B-2301(b).
Disclosure by petitioner, §7B-2300(d).

Prosecution review of intake counselor's decision not approving filing of petition, §§7B-1705, 7B-1803(b).

Prosecution review of juvenile court counselor's decision not to approve filing of petition, §§7B-1705, 7B-1803(b).
Request for review, §7B-1704.

Prosecutor to represent state, §7B-2404.

Protective orders.
Regulation of discovery, §7B-2302.

Protective supervision by juvenile court counselor.
Placing undisciplined juveniles under, §7B-2503.
Conditions, §7B-2504.

Public access to hearings, §7B-2402.

Publication service of summons.
Parent, guardian or custodian not found, §7B-1806.

Purposes of subchapter, §7B-1500.

Recidivism, report.
North Carolina sentencing and policy advisory commission.
Biennial report on juvenile recidivism, §164-48.

Recording adjudicatory and dispositional hearings and hearings on probable cause and transfer, §7B-2410.

DELINQUENT AND UNDISCIPLINED JUVENILES —Cont'd

Records and social reports in juvenile cases.
Chief court counselor to maintain records of cases, §7B-3001(a).
Clerk to maintain complete set of records, §7B-3000(a).
Confidentiality generally, §7B-3000(b).
Confidentiality of chief court counselor's records, §7B-3001(a).
Confidentiality of information shared among local agencies, §7B-3100(a).
Confidentiality of law enforcement records and files, §7B-3001(b).
Confidentiality of records and files maintained by office of juvenile justice, §7B-3001(c).
Designation of local agencies to share information, §7B-3100(a).
Destruction of juvenile records, §7B-3000(g).
Expunction of juvenile records, §§7B-3200 to 7B-3202.
Family background information to be contained in chief court counselor's records, §7B-3001(a).
Identifying information not be disclosed by local agency, §7B-3100(b).
Law enforcement records and files kept separate from records and files of adults, §7B-3001(b).
Local agencies authorized to share information, §7B-3100(a).
Person who may exam juvenile records, §7B-3000(b).
Probation officers for persons subject to probation supervision, §7B-3000(e1).
Notification of existence of juvenile record, §7B-3001(d).
Probation officers for persons subject to probation supervision.
Examination of juvenile records, §7B-3000(e1).
Notification of existence of juvenile record, §7B-3001(d).
Prosecutor sharing information with law enforcement officers, §7B-3000(b).
School notified when juvenile alleged or found to be delinquent.
Actions requiring notification, §7B-3101(a).
Delivery of notifications, §7B-3101(a).
Handling of notification by principals, §7B-3101(c).
Juvenile transferring to another school, §7B-3101(b).
School defined, §7B-3101(d).
Time for delivering notice, §7B-3101(a).
Use of information by schools.
Burning, shredding or destroying documents to protect confidentiality, §115C-404(a).
Confidentiality of records, §115C-404(a).
Dismissal of employee for failure to maintain confidentiality, §115C-404(b).
Maintaining documents in safe, locked storage, §115C-404(a).
Return of documents to juvenile court counselor, §115C-404(c).
Suspension or expelling student on basis of documents, prohibition, §115C-404(b).
Sealing juveniles' record, §7B-3000(c).
Transcribing electronic or mechanical recording of hearing upon filing notice of appeal, §7B-3000(d).
Use of record of adjudication of delinquency for offense that would be felony if committed by adult, §7B-3000(e), (f).

DELINQUENT AND UNDISCIPLINED
   JUVENILES —Cont'd
Reduction of nature or duration of
   delinquent's disposition, §7B-2600(b).
Referral to teen court program, §7B-1706(c).
Regimented training program.
   Delinquent juvenile ordered to participate in,
      §7B-2506.
Registration of juvenile for certain sexual
   offenses, §7B-2509.
Relative willing and able to provide care and
   supervision.
   Placing juvenile in nonsecure custody,
      §7B-1905(a).
Release from secure or nonsecure custody.
   Allegations in petition not proved, §7B-2411.
   Restrictions on liberty, §7B-1906(f).
Release of juvenile pending disposition of
   appeal, §7B-2605.
Release of juvenile to juvenile's parent,
   guardian or custodian.
   Action by law enforcement officer after taking
      juvenile into custody, §7B-2100.
   Person taking juvenile into temporary custody
      without court order, §7B-1901(a).
Restitution, delinquent juveniles, §7B-2506.
Restraint in courtroom at hearing, §7B-2402.1.
Returning from one state to another of
   delinquent juveniles escaping or
   absconding.
   Interstate compact on juveniles generally,
      §§7B-2800 to 7B-2827.
   See INTERSTATE COMPACT ON JUVENILES.
Review by prosecutor of juvenile court
   counselor's decision not to approve filing
   of petition, §§7B-1704, 7B-1705, 7B-1803(b).
Review hearing as to modification or vacation
   of order, §7B-2600(a).
Right to counsel, §7B-2000(a).
   Summons to contain notice of parent's guardian's
      or custodian's right, §7B-1805(b).
Risk and needs assessment.
   Included in predisposition report, §7B-2413.
Rules of evidence.
   Adjudicatory hearings, §7B-2408.
   Dispositional hearings, §7B-2501(a).
Saliva samples.
   Nontestimonial identification order procedures,
      §§7B-2103 to 7B-2109.
School defined, §7B-3101(b).
School notification when juvenile alleged or
   found to be delinquent, §7B-3101.
   Actions requiring notification, §7B-3101(a).
   Delivery of notification, §7B-3101(a).
   Handling of notification by principal, §7B-3101(c).
   Juvenile transferring to another school,
      §7B-3101(b).
   Use of juvenile court information by school.
      Burning, shredding or destroying documents to
         protect confidentiality, §115C-404(a).
      Confidential records, §115C-404(a).
      Dismissal of employee for failure to maintain
         confidentiality, §115C-404(b).
      Maintaining documents in safe, locked storage,
         §115C-404(a).
      Returning documents to juvenile court
         counselor, §115C-404(c).
      Suspending or expelling student solely on basis
         of information, prohibition, §115C-404(b).
Sealing of juvenile's records, §7B-3000(c).

DELINQUENT AND UNDISCIPLINED
   JUVENILES —Cont'd
Secure or nonsecure custody.
   Administrative order issued by chief court
      counselor, §7B-1902.
   Appointment of counsel for juvenile, §7B-1906(c).
   Assignment of counsel, court to determine,
      §7B-1906(c).
   Audio and video transmission, continued custody
      hearings, §7B-1906(h).
   Authority of court to issue custody order,
      §7B-1902.
   Burden at custody hearing, §7B-1906(d).
   Circumstances required to exist for ordering
      secure custody, §7B-1903(b).
   Clear and convincing evidence standard at
      custody hearing, §7B-1906(d).
   Confidential communications with attorney during
      hearing, §7B-1906(h).
   Continuance or waiver of custody hearing
      prohibited, §7B-1906(a).
   Continued custody hearings, §7B-1906(b).
      Audio and video transmission, hearing
         conducted by, §7B-1906(h).
      Criteria in determining whether continued
         custody warranted, §7B-1906(e).
      Order for continued custody, issuance,
         §7B-1906(g).
      Testimony and opportunity to introduce
         evidence, §7B-1906(d).
   County or unit of government operating juvenile
      detention facility, standards, §7B-1905(b).
   Delegation of court's authority to issue orders,
      §7B-1902.
   Department of social services, placing juvenile in
      nonsecure custody, §7B-1905(a).
   Execution of order for custody, §7B-1904.
   Hearings, §7B-1906.
   Holdover facility, placing juvenile in secure
      custody.
      Juvenile committing offense classified as Class
         A, B1, B2, C, D or E felony, §7B-1905(c).
   Law enforcement procedure after taking juvenile
      into custody, §§7B-2100 to 7B-2109.
   Order directing officer or authorized person to
      assume custody, secure custody, §7B-1903(e).
   Pending dispositional hearing or placement,
      ordering secure custody, §7B-1903(c).
   Placing juvenile in nonsecure custody,
      §7B-1905(a).
   Reasonable factual basis to believe juvenile
      committed offense alleged.
      Required for order for nonsecure custody,
         §7B-1903(b).
   Reasonable factual basis to believe matters
      alleged true.
      Required for order for nonsecure custody,
         §7B-1903(a).
   Relative of juvenile willing and able to provide
      care and supervision, nonsecure custody,
      §7B-1905(a).
   Release of juvenile to juvenile's parent, guardian,
      custodian or other responsible adult.
      First consideration of court on request for
         nonsecure custody, §7B-1903(a).
   Request made for nonsecure custody, §7B-1903(a).
   Request made for secure custody, §7B-1903(b).
   Requirements for order for secure or nonsecure
      custody, §7B-1904.
   Restrictions on liberty of juvenile released from
      secured custody, §7B-1906(f).

DELINQUENT AND UNDISCIPLINED JUVENILES —Cont'd

Secure or nonsecure custody —Cont'd

Retention of counsel, court to determine, §7B-1906(c).

Telephone communications, notices, orders, etc., §7B-1907.

Temporary detention in approved detention facility, §7B-1905(b).

Temporary residential placement, nonsecure custody, §7B-1905(a).

Time for holding custody hearing, §7B-1906(a).
Continued custody hearing, §7B-1906(b).

Violation of conditions of probation or post-release supervision, ordering secure custody, §7B-1903(d).

Secure or nonsecure custody hearings, §7B-1906.

Selecting most appropriate disposition.
Considerations by court, §7B-2501(c).

Sending delinquent juvenile out of state for purposes of placement, §§7B-3702 to 7B-3705.

Serious offenses.
Delinquency history levels, §§7B-2507, 7B-2508(b).
Disposition chart, §7B-2508(f).
Levels one to three disposition, §7B-2508(c) to (e).
Offense classification, §7B-2508(a).

Service of summons, §7B-1806.
Criminal contempt for failure to appear, notice, §7B-1805(c).
Criminal process applicable to juvenile process, §7B-1806.
Delivered to person authorized to serve process, §7B-1805(d).
Directed to person summoned to appear, §7B-1805(d).
Form and notice requirements, §7B-1805(b).
Issuance of summons after petition filed, §7B-1805(a).
Jurisdiction over parent, guardian or custodian, notice, §7B-1805(c).
Mail or publication, parent, guardian or custodian not found, §7B-1806.
Personal service, §7B-1806.
Process is summons, §7B-1801.
Show cause order for contempt.
Failure of parent, guardian or custodian to appear, §7B-1806.
Time for service, §7B-1806.

Sex offender registration.
Juveniles adjudicated delinquent for committing certain offenses generally, §§14-208.26 to 14-208.32.
See SEX OFFENDER AND PUBLIC PROTECTION REGISTRATION.
Requirement generally, §7B-2509.

Sharing of information by local agencies, §7B-3100.

State appeals, limitations, §7B-2604(b).

Statements made by juvenile.
Disclosure by petitioner, §7B-2300(a).

State represented by prosecutor, §7B-2404.

Substance abuse prevention.
Comprehensive juvenile delinquency and substance abuse prevention plan, §143B-840.

Substance abuse testing for juvenile adjudicated delinquent.
Procedures, establishment.
Division of juvenile justice, §143B-806(b).

DELINQUENT AND UNDISCIPLINED JUVENILES —Cont'd

Summons.
Copy of petition attached to summons, §7B-1805(a).
Criminal contempt for failure of parent, guardian or custodian to appear.
Notice in summons, §7B-1805(c).
Delivered to person authorized to serve process, §7B-1805(d).
Directed to person summoned to appear, §7B-1805(d).
Form and content requirements, §7B-1805(b).
Issuance after petition filed, §7B-1805(a).
Jurisdiction over parent, guardian or custodian upon service, §7B-1805(c).
Process in juvenile action by, §7B-1801.
Service, §7B-1806.

Superior court, transfer of jurisdiction of juvenile, §§7B-2200 to 7B-2204.
Appeal of transfer decision, §7B-2603.

Suspension of imposition of disposition.
Delinquent juvenile, §7B-2506.

Taking juvenile into temporary custody, §§7B-1900, 7B-1901.
Law enforcement officers role, permitted actions, §7B-2100.

Teen court program.
Administered by division of juvenile justice, §143B-809(a).
Community resource for diversion of juveniles, §143B-809(a).
Defined, §7B-1501.
Referral of juvenile to, §7B-1706(c).
Rehabilitative measures or sanctions, §143B-809(a).
Rules and reporting requirements of division.
Compliance with, §143B-809(b).
School problems.
Resource to handle, §143B-809(a).
Trial by other juveniles, §143B-809(a).

Temporary custody of juvenile without court order.
Authority of court to issue orders, §7B-1902.
Circumstances allowing, §7B-1900.
Delegation of court's authority to issue orders, §7B-1902.
Duties of persons taking juvenile into custody, §7B-1901(a).
Law enforcement officers role, permitted actions, §7B-2100.
Law enforcement procedures after taking juvenile into custody, §§7B-2100 to 7B-2109.
Notice to juvenile's parent, guardian or custodian.
Duty of persons taking juvenile into custody, §7B-1901(a).
Release of juvenile to juvenile's parent, guardian or custodian, §7B-1901(a).
Requesting that petition be drawn if juvenile not released, §7B-1901(a).
Telephone communications, notices, orders, etc., §7B-1907.
Temporary custody defined, §7B-1900.
Time limitation on holding juvenile, §7B-1901(b).
Transporting absconders to nearest facility providing secure custody, §7B-1901(c).

Temporary detention in approved detention facility, §7B-1905(b).

Tests, measurements or experiments made in connection with case.
Disclosure by juvenile, §7B-2301(c).

DELINQUENT AND UNDISCIPLINED JUVENILES —Cont'd

Tests, measurements or experiments made in connection with case —Cont'd
Disclosure by petitioner, §7B-2300(d).

Time for completing evaluation of complaint, §7B-1703(a).

Time for holding secure or nonsecure custody hearing, §7B-1906(a).
Continued custody hearing, §7B-1906(b).

Time for notice of date and time of scheduled hearings, §7B-1807.

Time for service of summons, §7B-1806.

Time limit on holding juvenile in temporary custody, §7B-1901(a).

Transcripts.
Reducing recording of proceeding when notice of appeal filed, §7B-3000(d).

Transfer hearing.
Transfer of jurisdiction of juvenile to superior court, §7B-2203.

Transfer of jurisdiction of juvenile to superior court, §7B-2200.
Appeal of transfer decision to superior court for hearing on record, §7B-2603.
Appealing transfer issue to court of appeals, §7B-2603(d).
Waiver of right for failure to appeal order to superior court, §7B-2603(a).
Authority of superior court on review, §7B-2603(a).
Interlocutory order, superior court order considered, §7B-2603(d).
Notice of appeal, §7B-2603(a).
Pretrial release of juvenile, §7B-2603(b).
Remanding case to juvenile court for adjudication or upholding transfer order, §7B-2603(c).
Waiver of right to raise issue on appeal to court of appeals.
Failure to appeal transfer order to superior court, §7B-2603(a).
Commission of offense by juvenile after superior court conviction.
Prosecution as adult, §7B-1604(a).
Court not transferring case, §7B-2203(d).
Detention pending pretrial release, §7B-2204.
Detention pending transfer to division of adult correction, §7B-2204.
DNA sample of juvenile transferred, §7B-2201(b).
Fingerprinting juvenile, §7B-2201(a).
Pretrial release, right once order of transfer entered, §7B-2204.
Probable cause found and transfer not required, §7B-2202(e).
Probable cause hearing.
Burden of state, §7B-2202(c).
Conducting, §7B-2202(a).
Jurisdiction of district court for purposes of conducting, §7B-1601(c), (d).
Representation of state and juvenile, testimony and cross-examination, §7B-2202(b).
Time for conducting, §7B-2202(a).
Waiver and stipulation to finding, §7B-2202(d).
Probable cause not found, §7B-2202(f).
Transfer hearing, §7B-2203(a).
Factors considered for transfer, §7B-2203(b).
Jurisdiction of district court for purposes of conducting, §7B-1601(c), (d).
Transfer order, §7B-2203(c).

DELINQUENT AND UNDISCIPLINED JUVENILES —Cont'd

Transfer of juvenile from jail or penal facility to residential facility.
Governor's authority to order, §7B-2517.

Transfer of proceeding to court in district where juvenile resides, §7B-1800(b).

Undisciplined juvenile defined, §§7B-1501, 143B-805.

Urine specimens.
Nontestimonial identification order procedures, §§7B-2103 to 7B-2109.

Venue of proceedings, §7B-1800.

Victim-offender reconciliation program, delinquent juvenile participation, §7B-2506.

Violent offenses.
Delinquency history levels, §§7B-2507, 7B-2508(b).
Disposition chart, §7B-2508(f).
Levels one to three disposition, §7B-2508(c) to (e).
Offense classifications, §7B-2508(a).

Voice samples.
Nontestimonial identification order procedures, §§7B-2103 to 7B-2109.

Wilderness program.
Defined, §7B-1501.
Delinquent juvenile ordered to cooperate with placement in, §7B-2506.

Witnesses, names of persons to be called.
Disclosure by juvenile, §7B-2301(a).
Disclosure by petitioner, §7B-2300(b).

Work product.
Disclosure of reports, memoranda or other internal documents made in connection with investigation or prosecution.
Disclosure by petitioner not required, §7B-2300(e).

Youth development center.
Commitment of delinquent juvenile to division of juvenile justice for placement, §7B-2513(a).
Age limit, §7B-2513(a).
Commitment order to be forwarded to division, §7B-2513(e).
Continued commitment beyond maximum commitment period.
Notice, §7B-2515(a).
Review by court, §7B-2515(c).
Continuing jurisdiction over juvenile and parent not terminated by placement, §7B-2513(g).
Controlled substance or alcohol testing of juvenile, §7B-2513(i).
Extended commitment, notification, review, §7B-2515.
Housing delinquent juvenile in holdover facility pending placement, §7B-2513(h).
Indefinite term of at least six months, §7B-2513(a).
Modification of plan of care or treatment, §7B-2515(b).
Notice of intention to continue commitment beyond maximum commitment period, §7B-2515(a).
Plan for care or treatment, §7B-2513(f).
Post-release supervision planning process, §7B-2514(a).
Credit for definite term for time juvenile spends, §7B-2514(f).
Notification prior to release of juvenile, §7B-2514(d).
Release of juvenile under indefinite commitment, §7B-2514(e).
Release of juvenile under plan, §7B-2514(c).

DELINQUENT AND UNDISCIPLINED JUVENILES —Cont'd

Youth development center —Cont'd

Commitment of delinquent juvenile to division of juvenile justice for placement —Cont'd

Post-release supervision planning process —Cont'd

Revocation of post-release supervision, §7B-2516(c).

Supervision by juvenile court counselor, §7B-2514(g).

Termination of release by court order, §7B-2514(g).

Time for completing, §7B-2514(b).

Previous adjudication for two or more felony offenses and previous commitment to youth development center.

Length of term, §7B-2513(b).

Progress evaluation, §7B-2514(a).

Records requested to accompany juvenile, §7B-2513(d).

Review by court of decision to extend commitment, §7B-2515(c).

Term time limitation, §7B-2513(a).

Transporting juvenile to, §7B-2513(c).

Victim and members of victim's immediate family notified of placement, §7B-2513(j).

Continued jurisdiction of court, §7B-1602.

Defined, §143B-805.

Phasing out.

Division of juvenile justice.

Duty of secretary of public safety as head of division, §143B-806(b).

Placement of delinquent juveniles in, §7B-2506.

DELINQUENT TAXES.

Property taxes.

Collection, §105-365.1(b).

Date deemed delinquent, §105-365.1(a).

DELIVERY.

Claim and delivery, §§1-472 to 1-484.1.

See CLAIM AND DELIVERY.

Commercial code generally.

Defined, §25-1-201(b).

Documents of title.

See DOCUMENTS OF TITLE.

Sale of goods, UCC.

See SALE OF GOODS, UCC.

DEMAND DEPOSITS, BANKS, §53-65.

DEMAND FOR JUDGMENT, §1A-1 Rule 54(c).

DEMAND FOR JURY TRIAL, §1A-1 Rule 38(b).

Small claims actions.

Appeals, §7A-230.

Specification of issues, §1A-1 Rule 38(c).

DEMAND LETTER.

Bad checks.

Form, §6-21.3(a2).

Civil liability for larceny, shoplifting, employee theft, embezzlement or false pretense.

Seeking damages prior to action, §1-538.2(c2) to (c4).

DEMANDS FOR SERVICE, §1A-1 Rule 5(a).

DEMENTIA.

Silver alert system.

Missing persons suffering from, §143B-1022.

DEMOLISHER STATEMENTS.

Purchase or acquisition of abandoned or derelict vehicles.

Statement under oath that vehicle shredded or recycled, §20-137.11.

DEMOLITION.

Buildings with fluorescent lights or thermostats containing mercury.

Removal and recycling, §130A-310.61.

Construction indemnity agreements invalid, §22B-1.

Local historic districts.

Demolition of buildings and landmarks within district.

Delay, §160A-400.14.

Municipalities.

Contributing structures outside local historic districts.

Demolition by neglect ordinance, applicability, §160A-40.15.

Dwellings, ordinance, lien, §160A-443.

Nonresidential building, §160A-432(b).

Lien for costs of removal, §160A-432(b).

Additional lien on other property of owner, §160A-432(b1).

Ordinance, §160A-443.

DEMONSTRATIONS.

Firearms and other weapons.

Possession, §14-277.2.

Private health care facilities.

Possession of weapon, §14-277.2.

Riots and civil disorders, §§14-288.1 to 14-288.20.

See RIOTS AND CIVIL DISORDERS.

Secret societies.

Masks, hoods or disguises.

Holding demonstrations while wearing masks, hoods, etc., §14-12.10.

Permitting, etc., demonstrations of prohibited secret societies, §14-12.5.

DEMURRER.

Abolished, §1A-1 Rule 7(c).

Evidence.

Criminal law and procedure, §15-173.

DENATURED ALCOHOL.

Exemption from alcoholic beverage provisions, §18B-103.

DE NOVO TRIALS.

Abortion.

Parental or judicial consent to abortion.

Waiver of parental consent requirement, appeal by minor, §90-21.8(h).

Appeals.

District courts, §15A-1431.

Magistrates, §15A-1431.

Small claims actions, §§7A-228, 7A-229.

Criminal contempt appeals, §5A-17.

District courts.

Appeals, §15A-1431.

Superior court, §7A-196(b).

Incompetence, determination of.

Appeal from order adjudicating incompetence, §35A-1115.

Incompetence, restoration.

Appeal from clerk's order denying petition, §35A-1130(f).

DE NOVO TRIALS —Cont'd
Judgment of magistrate in civil action improperly assigned or not assigned.
Appeal to district court judge, §7A-212.
Magistrates.
Appeals, §15A-1431.
Small claim action appeals, §§7A-228, 7A-229.
Jury trial, §7A-230.
Special proceedings.
Clerk ordering survey, appeal, §1-408.1.

DENTAL HEALTH PROGRAM.
Children's health insurance program.
Dental coverage, §108A-70.21(b).
Establishment, §130A-366(a).
Problem access areas.
Dental providers for, §130A-367.
Rules and regulations, §130A-366(b).

DENTAL HYGIENISTS, §§90-221 to 90-233.1.
Administration of provisions.
Board of dental examiners, §90-222.
Board of dental examiners.
Administration of provisions, §90-222.
Clinical examinations, contracts for, §90-223(a).
Definition of "board,"§90-221(e).
Duties, §90-223(c), (d).
Impaired dental hygienist programs, authority to provide, §90-223(e).
Powers, §90-223(a), (b).
Disciplinary measures, §90-229(a).
Records, §90-223(c).
Rules and regulations, §90-223(b).
Examinations, §90-224(b).
Renewal certificates, §90-227(b).
Subpoenas.
Power to issue, §90-231(c).
Child support enforcement.
Forfeiture of licensing privilege, §50-13.12.
Continuing education, §90-225.1.
Criminal law and procedure.
Violations of provision, §90-233.1.
Definitions, §90-221.
Disciplinary proceedings.
Definition of "licensee,"§90-229(b).
Grounds, §90-229(a).
Hearings.
Conduct of hearings, §90-231(c).
Consent order in lieu of, §90-231(b).
Right to hearing, §90-231(a).
Powers of board, §90-229(a).
Provisional licensees subject to, §90-226(e).
Drugs.
Chronic or persistent use as grounds for disciplinary measures, §90-229(a).
Employment of two dental hygienists by dentists, §90-233(b).
Fees.
Generally, §90-232.
Felony convictions.
Forfeiture of license, §15A-1331A.
Grounds for disciplinary measures, §90-229(a).
Fraud.
Grounds for disciplinary measures, §90-229(a).
Hearings.
Disciplinary proceedings, §90-231.
Impaired dental hygienist programs.
Annual renewal fee to finance, §90-232(c).
Board's authority to provide, §90-223(e).
Peer review organizations for impaired dentists.
Inclusion of dental hygienists in programs, §90-48.3.

DENTAL HYGIENISTS —Cont'd
Intoxication.
Grounds for disciplinary measures, §90-229(a).
Licenses.
Certificate upon transfer to another state, §90-230.
Credentials, license by, §90-224.1(a) to (e).
Fees, §90-232.
Criminal records checks for license applicants, §90-224(c).
Defined, §90-221(c).
Display.
Place for display to be determined by board, §90-225(b).
Examinations.
Credentials, license by, §90-224.1(a), (c), (d).
Fee, §90-232(b).
Notification of successful candidates.
Board to determine method and time, §90-225(b).
Power of board to conduct examinations, §90-223(a).
Rules and regulations of board as to, §90-224(b).
Fees, §90-232(a).
Issuance, §90-225(a).
Practice of dental hygiene.
Required, §90-233(c).
Provisional license, §90-226.
Applications, §90-226(d).
Disciplinary proceedings.
Provisional licensee subject to, §90-226(e).
Eligibility for, §90-226(a), (c).
Fee, §90-232.
Issuance, §90-226(a).
Term, §90-226(b).
Qualifications of applicants, §90-224(a).
Credentials, license by, §90-224.1(a) to (e).
Renewal certificates.
Defined, §90-221(d).
Fee, §90-232.
Issuance, §90-227(a).
Power of board, §90-223(a).
Renewal of license of dental hygienists who fails to obtain renewal certificate, §90-228.
Rules and regulations as to, §90-227(b).
Revocation or suspension.
Felony convictions, §15A-1331A.
Misdemeanors.
Violations, §90-233.1.
Peer review organizations for impaired dentists.
Inclusion of dental hygienists in programs, §90-48.3.
Practice of dental hygiene.
Acts and practices which do not constitute, §90-233(c).
Definition of "dental hygiene,"§90-221(a).
Disciplined hygienist, §90-233(a3).
Licenses.
Required, §90-233(c).
Report by dentist, §90-233(a4).
Separate facility for, prohibited, §90-233(a2).
Standards for infection control and patient treatment, §90-233(a5).
Supervision by dentists required, §90-233(a).
Definition of "supervision,"§90-221(f).
Exception, §90-233(a1).
Records.
Board of dental examiners, §90-223(c).
Criminal records checks for license applicants, §90-224(c).

DENTAL HYGIENISTS —Cont'd
Referral fees and solicitation payments,
§§90-400 to 90-402.
Health care provider defined, §90-400.
Prohibited, §90-401.
Sanctions, §90-402.
Removal from state.
Certificate upon transfer to another state,
§90-230.
Rules and regulations.
Board of dental examiners, §90-223(b).
Examinations, §90-224(b).
Renewal certificates, §90-227(b).
Separate facility for dental hygiene services,
prohibited, §90-233(a2).
Subpoenas.
Hearings.
Power of board to issue, §90-231(c).
Supervision by licensed dentist, §90-233(a).
Definition of "supervision,"§90-221.
Exception, §90-233(a1).
Violations of provisions.
Misdemeanors, §90-233.1.

DENTISTS AND DENTISTRY, §§90-22 to 90-48.2.
Actions.
Injunctions.
Unauthorized practice.
Action for injunction, §90-40.1.
Alcoholic beverages.
Exemption from chapter, §18B-103.
Anatomic pathology services.
Billing for services, §90-701.
Anesthesia and parenteral sedation.
Practice of dentistry, §90-29(b).
Standards for general anesthesia and parenteral
sedation.
Board of dental examiners to establish by
regulation, §90-30.1.
Board of dental examiners.
Agreements with special peer review
organizations for impaired dentist, §90-48.2.
Anesthesia and parenteral sedation.
Standards for general anesthesia and
parenteral sedation.
Board to establish by regulation, §90-30.1.
Bylaws, §90-28(a).
Compensation of members, §§90-22(d), 90-43.
Composition, §90-22(b).
Disciplinary action, §90-41.
Hearings, §90-41.1.
Election of members, §90-22(c).
Expenses of members, §§90-22(d), 90-43.
Hearings.
Disciplinary proceedings, §90-41.1.
Meetings.
Adjourned meetings.
Effect, §90-24.
Annual meetings, §90-26.
Notice, §90-26.
Special meetings, §90-26.
Nominations of members, §90-22(c).
Number of members, §90-22(b).
Oaths.
Power to administer, §90-27.
Officers, §90-23.
Qualifications of members, §90-22(b).
Quorum, §90-24.
Records, §90-25.
Reports.
Annual report, §90-44.

DENTISTS AND DENTISTRY —Cont'd
Board of dental examiners —Cont'd
Rules and regulations, §§90-28(a), 90-48.
Seal, §90-23.
Secretary, §90-22(e).
Subpoenas.
Powers, §90-27.
Terms of members, §90-22(b).
Vacancies, §90-22(b).
Charges at issue.
Injured party as witness.
Competency to give evidence regarding amount
of charges, §8-58.1(a).
Reasonableness, presumption, §8-58.1(c).
Testimony of person establishing, §8-58.1(b).
Services reasonable and necessary, permissive
presumption, §8-58.1(c).
Child support enforcement.
Forfeiture of licensing privilege, §50-13.12.
Confidentiality of information.
Criminal records checks for license applicants,
§90-30(b).
Peer review committees.
Proceedings and records, §90-48.10.
Consent to health care for minors.
Reliance on agent's authorization, §32A-33.
Construction and interpretation.
Liberal construction of provisions, §90-22(a).
Continuing education, §90-31.1.
Limited volunteer dental licenses.
Compliance required, §90-37.1(f).
Corporations.
Dental service corporations generally, §§58-65-1 to
58-66-40.
See HOSPITAL, MEDICAL AND DENTAL
SERVICE CORPORATIONS.
Professional corporations generally, §§55B-1 to
55B-16.
See PROFESSIONAL CORPORATIONS.
Criminal law and procedure.
Extraoral services performed for dentist,
§90-29.2(d), (e).
Practicing dentistry without license, §90-40.
Subpoenas of board of dental examiner.
Neglect or refusal to obey, §90-27.
Unauthorized practice, §90-40.
Violations of rules and regulations of board,
§90-48.
Dental health program.
Problem access areas.
Dental providers for, §130A-367.
Dental hygienists.
See DENTAL HYGIENISTS.
Dental service corporations generally,
§§58-65-1 to 58-66-40.
See HOSPITAL, MEDICAL AND DENTAL
SERVICE CORPORATIONS.
Disciplinary action, §90-41.
Attorneys at law.
Employment of legal counsel by board,
§90-41(e).
Definition of "licensee,"§90-41(f).
Grounds, §90-41(a).
Hearings.
Consent orders, §90-41.1(b).
Rights of parties, §90-41.1(c).
Right to hearing, §90-41.1(a).
Initiation of proceedings by board, §90-41(c).
Intern permit.
Holder subject to, §90-29.4.

DENTISTS AND DENTISTRY —Cont'd
Disciplinary action —Cont'd
Investigators.
  Appointment by board, §90-41(d).
Powers of board, §90-41(a).
Provisional licensee subject to, §90-29.3(e).
Records.
  Confidentiality of information, §90-41(g).
  Public records.
    Access to records, §90-41(g).
Revocation or suspension of license, §90-41(a).
  Practice while license suspended, §90-41(b).
  Restoration of revoked license, §90-42.
Drugs.
Chronic or persistent use.
  Grounds for disciplinary action, §90-41(a).
Prescriptions, §90-46.
Elections.
Board of dental examiners.
  Nominations and elections of members,
    §90-22(c).
Evidence.
Medical charges at issue.
  Injured party as witness.
    Competency to give evidence regarding
      amount of charges, §8-58.1(a).
  Reasonableness, presumption, §8-58.1(c).
    Testimony of person establishing, §8-58.1(b).
  Services reasonable and necessary, permissive
    presumption, §8-58.1(c).
Examinations.
Licenses, §90-30(a).
Extraoral services performed for dentists,
  §90-29.1.
Prohibited acts, §90-29.2(d), (e).
Work orders.
  Copies.
    Retention, §90-29.2(b).
  Subwork orders, §90-29.2(c).
  Written work orders required, §90-29.2(a).
Fees.
Anesthesia and parenteral sedation.
  Standards for general anesthesia and
    parenteral sedation.
    Board of dental examiners to establish by
      regulation, §90-30.1.
Examination and inspection.
  Dental offices, §90-30.1.
Intern permits, §90-39.
Licenses, §90-39.
  Duplicate licenses, §90-35.
  Renewal, §§90-31, 90-39.
Felony convictions.
Forfeiture of license, §15A-1331A.
Grounds for disciplinary action, §90-41(a).
Fines.
Subpoenas of board of medical examiner.
  Neglect or refusal to obey, §90-27.
Unauthorized practice, §90-40.
Violations of rules and regulations of board,
  §90-48.
Fraud.
Grounds for disciplinary action, §90-41(a).
Licenses.
  Obtained through fraud void, §90-30(a).
Free choice by patient, §90-48.1.
Health benefit plans.
Contracts between health benefit plans and health
  care providers.
  Dental services, §58-50-290.
    Covered services defined, §58-50-290(b).

DENTISTS AND DENTISTRY —Cont'd
Health benefit plans —Cont'd
Contracts between health benefit plans and health
  care providers —Cont'd
  Dental services —Cont'd
    No limitation on fees for noncovered services,
      §58-50-290(a).
Right of subscriber to choose service, payment,
  §58-50-30.
Hearings.
Disciplinary proceedings, §90-41.1.
Identification badges required, §90-640.
Immunity.
Peer review committees.
  Members, §90-48.8.
  Witnesses, §90-48.9.
Injunctions.
Unauthorized practice, §90-40.1.
  Action for injunction, §90-40.1(a).
    Plaintiff entitled to examination of adverse
      party and witnesses, §90-40.1(d).
    Venue, §90-40.1(c).
  Judgment.
    Effect, §90-40.1(b).
  Venue for actions, §90-40.1(c).
Instructors.
Licenses, §90-29.5.
Fee, §90-39.
Intern permits, §90-29.4.
Fee, §90-39.
Legislative declaration, §90-22(a).
Licenses.
Certificate issued to dentist moving out of state,
  §90-37.
  Fee, §90-39.
Contents of original license, §90-32.
Credentials, license by.
  Application, §90-36(d).
  Authority to issue, §90-36(a).
  Conditions, §90-36(c).
  Eligibility, §90-36(a), (b).
  Establishment of practice location in and
    actively practice in state.
    Required, time, failure, license void, §90-36(e).
  Fees, §90-39.
Criminal records checks for license applicants,
  §90-30(b).
Denial.
  Grounds, §90-30(a).
Display, §90-33.
Duplicate licenses, §90-35.
  Fee, §90-35.
Examinations, §90-30(a).
Fees, §90-39.
  Duplicate licenses, §90-35.
  Renewal, §§90-31, 90-39.
Former dentists who have moved back into state
  or resumed practice, §90-38.
Fraud or false representation.
  License obtained through.
    Void, §90-30(a).
Instructors, §90-29(c).
  Application, §90-29.5(c).
  Authority of holder, §90-29.5(b).
  Authority to issue, §90-29.5(a).
  Eligibility, §90-29.5(a).
  Fee, §90-39.
Intern permits, §90-29.4.
  Fee, §90-39.
Limited volunteer dental licenses.
  Application, §90-37.1(e).

DENTISTS AND DENTISTRY —Cont'd
Licenses —Cont'd
  Limited volunteer dental licenses —Cont'd
    Authority to issue, §90-37.1(a).
    Conditions, §90-37.1(d).
    Continuing education requirements.
      Compliance, §90-37.1(f).
    Eligibility, §90-37.1(a) to (c).
    Fees, §90-39.
    List of nonprofit facilities serving low-income
      population, §90-37.1(h).
    Rules, adoption, §90-37.1(i).
    Unauthorized practice.
      Criminal penalty, §90-37.1(g).
  Provisional licenses.
    Applications, §90-29.3(d).
    Authorized, §90-29.3(a).
    Disciplinary action.
      Provisional licensee subject to, §90-29.3(e).
    Eligibility, §90-29.3(a), (c).
    Fee, §90-39.
    Term, §90-29.3(b).
  Qualifications, §90-30(a).
  Reciprocity, §90-36.
    Fees, §90-39.
  Renewal, §90-31.
    Certificate of renewal, §90-31.
      Display, §90-33.
    Fees, §90-39.
      Additional late fee, §90-31.
    Refusal to grant, §90-34.
  Required, §90-29(a).
  Revocation or suspension, §90-41(a).
    Anatomic pathology services billing violations,
      §90-701(j).
    Felony convictions, §15A-1331A.
    Practicing while license suspended, §90-41(b).
    Restoration of revoked license, §90-42.
  Statewide license for privilege of practicing.
    Firm or corporation.
      Not issued in name of, §105-41(e).
    License not authorization to practice, §105-41(i).
    Not transferable, §105-41(a).
    Personal privilege licenses, §105-41(e).
    Required, §105-41(a).
    Tax for each license, §105-41(a).
      Counties and cities levying, prohibition,
        §105-41(h).
      Exemptions, §105-41(b).
  Temporary permits for volunteer dentists.
    Issuance, §90-37.2(a).
    Rules of board, §90-37.2(b).
License taxes.
  Statewide license for privilege of practicing,
    §105-41.
Liens, recoveries for personal injuries, §44-49.
  Attorneys' fees, §44-50.
  Charges, §44-50.
  Disputed claims to be settled before payment,
    §44-51.
  Evidence, §44-50.
  Limit on recovery, §44-50.
  Receiving person charged with duty of retaining
    funds, §44-50.
Limited volunteer dental licenses, §90-37.1.
  Fees, §90-39.
Malpractice.
  Actions generally, §§90-21.11 to 90-21.19B.
    See MEDICAL MALPRACTICE.
  Grounds for disciplinary action, §90-41(a).
  Pleading special matters, §1A-1 Rule 9(j).

DENTISTS AND DENTISTRY —Cont'd
Medical records, §§90-410, 90-411.
  Electronic medical records, §90-412.
Misdemeanors.
  Extraoral services performed for dentists.
    Prohibited acts, §90-29.2(d), (e).
  Rules and regulations.
    Violations, §90-48.
  Subpoenas of board of dental examiners.
    Neglect or refusal to obey, §90-27.
  Unauthorized practice, §90-40.
Negligence.
  Grounds for disciplinary action, §90-41(a).
Notice.
  Board of dental examiners.
    Meetings, §90-26.
Oaths.
  Board of dental examiners.
    Power to administer oaths, §90-24.
Peer review committees.
  Citation of act.
    Short title, §90-48.7.
  Confidentiality of proceedings and records,
    §90-48.10.
  Immunity of members, §90-48.8.
  Immunity of witnesses, §90-48.9.
  Previous privileges and immunities not limited,
    §90-48.11.
  Savings clause.
    No limitation on previous privileges and
      immunities, §90-48.11.
  Title of act.
    Short title, §90-48.7.
  Witnesses.
    Immunity, §90-48.9.
Peer review organizations for impaired
  dentists.
  Board agreements, §90-48.2.
  Composition and activities, §90-48.2(a).
  Confidentiality, §90-48.2(e).
  Dental hygienists, inclusion, §90-48.3.
  Immunity from liability, §90-48.2(f).
  Powers, §90-48.2(b).
  Programs, §90-48.2(c).
  Reporting requirements, §90-48.2(d).
Penalties.
  Rules and regulations.
    Violations, §90-48.
Practice of dentistry.
  License required, §90-29(a).
  Unauthorized practice.
    Injunction, §90-40.1.
    Misdemeanor, §90-40.
  What constitutes, §90-29(b).
  What does not constitute, §90-29(c).
    Extraoral services performed for dentists,
      §90-29.1.
Prescriptions, §90-46.
Presumptions.
  Medical charges at issue.
    Reasonableness of charges, rebuttable
      presumption.
      Testimony of person establishing, §8-58.1(b).
    Services reasonable and necessary.
      Permissive presumption, §8-58.1(c).
Prison terms.
  Subpoenas of board of medical examiner.
    Neglect or refusal to obey, §90-27.
  Unauthorized practice, §90-40.
  Violations of rules and regulations of board,
    §90-48.

DENTISTS AND DENTISTRY —Cont'd
Privileges to practice in hospitals, §131E-85.
Professional corporations generally, §§55B-1 to
 55B-16.
  See PROFESSIONAL CORPORATIONS.
Reciprocity.
 Licenses, §90-36.
  Fees, §90-39.
Records.
 Board of dental examiners, §90-25.
 Disciplinary action.
  Confidentiality of information, §90-41(g).
  Public records.
   Access to records, §90-41(g).
 Peer review committees.
  Confidentiality of records, §90-48.10.
Referral fees and solicitation payments,
 §§90-400 to 90-402.
 Health care provider defined, §90-400.
 Prohibited, §90-401.
 Sanctions, §90-402.
Removal from state.
 Certificate of license issued to dentist moving out
  of state, §90-37.
  Fee, §90-39.
 Licensing former dentists who have moved back
  into state, §90-38.
Reports.
 Board of dental examiners.
  Annual report, §90-44.
Residency programs.
 Establishment of public health programs,
  §130A-11.
**Residency programs established in public
 health,** §130A-11.
Rules and regulations.
 Anesthesia and parenteral sedation.
  Standards for general anesthesia and
   parenteral sedation.
   Board of dental examiners to establish by
    regulation, §90-30.1.
 Board of dental examiners, §§90-28(a), 90-48.
Seals and sealed instruments.
 Board of dental examiners, §90-23.
Sedation standards, §90-30.1.
Self-referrals, §§90-405 to 90-408.
Solicitation.
 Direct solicitation prohibited, §90-401.1.
 Grounds for disciplinary action, §90-41(a).
 Payment prohibitions, §90-401.
 Sanctions for violating prohibitions, §90-402.
Subpoenas.
 Board of dental examiners.
  Powers, §90-27.
Unauthorized practice.
 Limited volunteer dental licenses.
  Criminal penalty, §90-37.1(g).
Unlicensed practice.
 Injunction, §90-40.1.
 Misdemeanor, §90-40.
Venue.
 Injunctions.
  Unauthorized practice.
   Actions for injunctions, §90-40.1(c).
Volunteers.
 Limited volunteer dental licenses, §90-37.1.
 Temporary permits, §90-37.2.
Witnesses.
 Medical charges at issue.
  Injured party as witness.
   Competency to give evidence regarding
    amount, §8-58.1(a).

DENTISTS AND DENTISTRY —Cont'd
Witnesses —Cont'd
 Medical charges at issue —Cont'd
  Reasonableness of charges, rebuttable
   presumption.
   Testimony of person establishing, §8-58.1(b).
  Services reasonable and necessary, permissive
   presumption, §8-58.1(c).
 Peer review committees.
  Immunity of witnesses, §90-48.9.

DEPARTMENT OF ADMINISTRATION.
Generally.
 See ADMINISTRATION DEPARTMENT.

**DEPARTMENT OF AGRICULTURE AND
 CONSUMER SERVICES,** §§143A-56 to
 143A-65.
See AGRICULTURE AND CONSUMER SERVICES
 DEPARTMENT.

DEPARTMENT OF CULTURAL RESOURCES,
 §§143B-49 to 143B-133.1.
See CULTURAL RESOURCES DEPARTMENT.

**DEPARTMENT OF ENVIRONMENT AND
 NATURAL RESOURCES.**
See ENVIRONMENT AND NATURAL
 RESOURCES DEPARTMENT.

**DEPARTMENT OF HEALTH AND HUMAN
 SERVICES.**
Generally, §§143B-136.1 to 143B-216.70.
 See HEALTH AND HUMAN SERVICES
  DEPARTMENT.

DEPARTMENT OF INSURANCE.
See INSURANCE DEPARTMENT.

DEPARTMENT OF JUSTICE, §§143A-49 to
 143A-55.2.
See JUSTICE DEPARTMENT.

DEPARTMENT OF LABOR, §§143A-67 to
 143A-72.
See LABOR DEPARTMENT.

DEPARTMENT OF PUBLIC INSTRUCTION.
See EDUCATION.

DEPARTMENT OF PUBLIC SAFETY,
 §§143A-239 to 143A-245, 143B-600 to
 143B-1201.
See PUBLIC SAFETY DEPARTMENT.

DEPARTMENT OF REVENUE, §§143B-217 to
 143B-220.
See REVENUE DEPARTMENT.

DEPARTMENT OF SECRETARY OF STATE,
 §§143A-19 to 143A-23.
See SECRETARY OF STATE.

DEPARTMENT OF STATE AUDITOR, §§143A-24
 to 143A-29.
See STATE AUDITOR.

DEPARTMENT OF STATE TREASURER,
 §§143A-30 to 143A-38.1.
See STATE TREASURER.

DEPARTMENT OF TRANSPORTATION,
 §§143B-345 to 143B-360.
See TRANSPORTATION DEPARTMENT.

DEPENDENT CHILDREN.
Abused, neglected or dependent juveniles.
 Generally, §§7B-100 to 7B-1414.
  See CHILD ABUSE, NEGLECT OR
   DEPENDENCY.

DEPENDENT CHILDREN —Cont'd
Defined, §7B-101.
Domestic violence generally.
　See DOMESTIC VIOLENCE.

DEPOSIT IN LIEU OF BAIL.
Arrest in civil cases, §1-426.
　Application of deposit to plaintiff's judgment,
　　§1-429.
　Bail substituted for deposit, §1-428.

DEPOSIT IN LIEU OF PROSECUTION BOND.
Plaintiffs, for cost, §1-109.

DEPOSIT INSURANCE.
Banks, §53-9.1.

DEPOSITIONS.
Administrative procedure.
　Hearings, §§150B-28(a), 150B-39(a).
　Subpoenas.
　　Witnesses.
　　　Fees, §150B-39(c).
Appeals.
　Pending appeal, §1A-1 Rule 27(b).
Arbitration.
　Discovery permitted, §1-569.17(b).
Before action, §1A-1 Rule 27(a).
Change of venue.
　Removal for fair trial.
　　Taking after cause directed to be removed,
　　　§1-87(b).
Commissioners.
　Allowance of costs to either party or apportioned
　　in discretion of court, §6-21.
　Witnesses.
　　Attendance before commissioner enforced, §8-79.
　　Defaulting witness before commissioner.
　　　Remedies against defaulting witness, §8-80.
　　Enforcement of attendance before commissioner,
　　　§8-79.
　　Power to subpoena witnesses, §8-78.
　　Punishment for contempt, §8-78.
Conflicts of interest.
　Persons before whom depositions may be taken.
　　Disqualification for interest, §1A-1 Rule 28(c).
Congress.
　Reading deposition on trial, §8-83.
Contempt.
　Commissioner may punish for contempt, §8-78.
Costs.
　Compensation of referees and commissioners.
　　Allowance of costs to either party or
　　　apportioned in discretion of court, §6-21.
Court of appeals.
　Reading deposition on trial.
　　When witness is judge of court of appeals,
　　　§8-83.
Court reporters.
　Perpetuation of testimony.
　　Certified transcription of court reporter, §8-85.
Criminal actions.
　Defendant's deposition in criminal actions, §8-74.
Death.
　Reading deposition on trial.
　　When deposition may be read, §8-83.
Defendants.
　Criminal actions, §8-74.
Discovery generally.
　See DISCOVERY.
District attorneys.
　Reading deposition on trial.
　　When deposition may be read, §8-83.

DEPOSITIONS —Cont'd
Errors or irregularities in depositions.
　Effect, §1A-1 Rule 32(d).
Failure of party to attend at own deposition,
　§1A-1 Rule 37(d).
Fee of magistrate, §7A-309.
Foreign countries.
　Reading deposition on trial.
　　When deposition may be read, §8-83.
General assembly.
　Contesting a seat, §120-10.6(a).
Governor.
　Reading deposition on trial.
　　When deposition may be read, §8-83.
Interrogatories.
　See INTERROGATORIES.
Interstate depositions and discovery, §§1F-1 to
　1F-7.
　Application and construction of statutory
　　provisions, §1F-7.
　Applications to court for relief, §1F-6.
　Definitions, §1F-2.
　Disputes, appropriate court to resolve, §1F-6.
　Rules of civil procedure applicable, §1F-5.
　Short title of act, §1F-1.
　Subpoenas.
　　Contents required, §1F-3(c).
　　Duties of clerk on receipt of request, §1F-3(b).
　　Request for issuance, §1F-3(a).
　　Service, §1F-4.
Judges.
　Reading deposition on trial.
　　When deposition may be read, §8-83.
Larceny.
　Mutilation, larceny or destruction of public
　　records and papers, §14-76.
Leaving county or country.
　Deposition upon oral examination, leave of court
　　not required, §1A-1 Rule 30(b).
Magistrates.
　Authority to take depositions.
　　Power of magistrates, §7A-292.
　Fee for taking deposition, §7A-309.
　Reading deposition on trial.
　　When deposition may be read, §8-83.
Medical malpractice.
　Arbitration of negligent health claims,
　　§90-21.63(d).
Mentally ill.
　Reading deposition on trial.
　　When deposition may be read, §8-83.
Municipalities.
　Taking deposition before municipal authorities,
　　§8-76.
Nonresidents.
　Reading deposition on trial.
　　When deposition may be read, §8-83.
Notice, §1A-1 Rule 27(a), (b).
　Oral examination, §1A-1 Rule 30(b).
　Written questions, §1A-1 Rule 31(a).
Objections to admissibility, §1A-1 Rule 32(b).
Occupational safety and health.
　Commission, §95-135(d).
Oral examination.
　Certification of deposition by officer, §1A-1 Rule
　　30(f).
　Cross-examination, §1A-1 Rule 30(c).
　Failure to attend or serve subpoenas.
　　Expenses, §1A-1 Rule 30(g).
　Filing of deposition by officer, §1A-1 Rule 30(f).
　General requirements, §1A-1 Rule 30(b).

DEPOSITIONS —Cont'd
Oral examination —Cont'd
"Judge" defined, §1A-1 Rule 30(h).
Leave of court not required.
　Circumstances, §1A-1 Rule 30(b).
Leaving county or country.
　Leave of court not required, §1A-1 Rule 30(b).
Limitation of examination.
　Motion, §1A-1 Rule 30(d).
Notice, §1A-1 Rule 30(b).
Oath, §1A-1 Rule 30(c).
Objections, §1A-1 Rule 30(c).
Organizations, §1A-1 Rule 30(b).
Record of examination, §1A-1 Rule 30(c).
Signing of deposition by deponent, §1A-1 Rule
　30(e).
Submission of deposition to deponent, §1A-1 Rule
　30(e).
Termination of examination.
　Motion, §1A-1 Rule 30(d).
Voyage to sea.
　Leave of court not required, §1A-1 Rule 30(b).
When depositions may be taken, §1A-1 Rule 30(a).
Orders, §1A-1 Rule 27(a), (b).
Pending appeal, §1A-1 Rule 27(b).
Perjury.
Punishment for perjury, §14-209.
Perpetuation of testimony, §1A-1 Rule 27(a).
Pending appeal, §1A-1 Rule 27(b).
Perpetuation by action, §1A-1 Rule 27(c).
**Persons before whom depositions may be
　taken.**
Conflicts of interest.
　Disqualification for interest, §1A-1 Rule 28(c).
Depositions to be used outside state, §1A-1 Rule
　28(d).
In foreign countries, §1A-1 Rule 28(b).
In United States, §1A-1 Rule 28(a).
Petitions, §1A-1 Rule 27(a), (b).
Physicians and surgeons.
Hearings before board, §90-14.5(b).
Reading deposition on trial.
　When deposition may be read, §8-83.
President of the United States.
Reading deposition on trial.
　When deposition may be read, §8-83.
Prisons and prisoners.
Reading deposition on trial.
　When deposition may be read, §8-83.
Production of documents and things.
Oral examination.
　Service of subpoena duces tecum, §1A-1 Rule
　　30(b).
Public officers and employees.
Reading deposition on trial.
　When deposition may be read, §8-83.
Public utilities.
Utilities commission, §62-66.
Quashing deposition.
Trial.
　Deposition not quashed after trial begun, §8-82.
Referees.
Compensation of referees.
　Allowance of costs to either party or
　　apportioned in discretion of court, §6-21.
Remedies.
Witnesses before commissioner.
　Remedies against defaulting witness, §8-80.
Removal for fair trial, §1-87(b).
Sealing.
Protective orders, §1A-1 Rule 26(c).

DEPOSITIONS —Cont'd
Service of process, §1A-1 Rule 27(a), (b).
Oral examination notice, §1A-1 Rule 30(b).
Written questions, §1A-1 Rule 31(a).
State auditor.
Authority to take depositions, §147-64.7(c).
State departments and agencies.
Reading deposition on trial.
　When deposition may be read, §8-83.
Stipulations regarding discovery procedure,
　§1A-1 Rule 29.
Subpoena duces tecum.
Oral examination.
　Service of subpoena, §1A-1 Rule 30(b).
Subpoenas.
Commissioner may subpoena witnesses, §8-78.
Summary judgment.
Affidavit supplemented or opposed by, §1A-1 Rule
　56(e).
Supreme court.
Reading deposition on trial.
　When witness is justice of supreme court, §8-83.
Trial.
Objection to deposition before trial, §8-81.
Quashing deposition after trial begun, §8-82.
Reading deposition on trial.
　When deposition may be read, §8-83.
When deposition may be read on trial, §8-83.
Uniform interstate depositions and discovery,
　§§1F-1 to 1F-7. See within this heading,
　"Interstate depositions and discovery."
University of North Carolina, president.
Reading deposition on trial, §8-83.
Use of depositions, §1A-1 Rule 27(a), (b).
Court proceedings, §1A-1 Rule 32(a).
Effect of taking or using depositions, §1A-1 Rule
　32(c).
Objections to admissibility, §1A-1 Rule 32(b).
Voyages to sea.
Deposition upon oral examination, leave of court
　not required, §1A-1 Rule 30(b).
Wage and hour act.
Power of commissioner of labor to take
　depositions, §95-25.16(b).
Witnesses.
Commissioner to take depositions.
　Attendance before commissioner enforced, §8-79.
　Punishment for contempt, §8-78.
　Remedies against defaulting witness before
　　commissioner, §8-80.
Reading deposition on trial.
　When deposition may be read, §8-83.
Workers' compensation.
Contested cases, ICWorkComp Rule 612.
Industrial commission, §97-80(d).
Written questions.
Cross questions, service, §1A-1 Rule 31(a).
Notice, §1A-1 Rule 31(a).
Person to take responses and prepare record,
　§1A-1 Rule 31(b).
Service of questions, §1A-1 Rule 31(a).

DEPOSIT MADE TO SECURE JUDGMENT.
Supersedeas to suspend execution.
Filing for judgment sought to be vacated, §1-269.

DEPOSITS.
ABC boards, §18B-702(t).
Bail.
Deposit in lieu of bail.
　Civil cases, §§1-426 to 1-429.

DEPOSITS —Cont'd
Bail bondsmen and runners.
Deposit of securities, §§58-71-135 to 58-71-160.
Bank deposits.
See BANKS.
Bank deposits and collections, §§25-4-101 to
25-4-504.
See BANK DEPOSITS AND COLLECTIONS.
Bonds, surety.
State funds, §147-79.
Certificate of deposit.
Negotiable instruments.
General provisions, §§25-3-101 to 25-3-605.
See NEGOTIABLE INSTRUMENTS.
Clerks of court.
Superior court.
Money held by clerk of superior court,
§7A-112.1.
Fees, §7A-308.1.
Collection agencies.
Remittance trust account, §58-70-65(a) to (c).
Community college investments.
Daily deposits, §115D-58.9.
Securing deposits, §115D-58.7(b).
Selection of depository, §115D-58.7(a).
Community colleges, §115D-58.6(a1).
Credit unions.
Insurance.
Share and deposit insurance, §54-109.78(a).
Prerequisite to granting of charter,
§54-109.78(b).
Lien on deposit, §54-109.59.
Savings accounts, §54-109.55.
Decedents' estates.
Powers of personal representative or fiduciary,
§28A-13-3(a).
Drainage districts.
Bond issues.
Receipt of bonds as deposits, §156-102.
Economic development commissions, §158-12.1.
Electrologists.
Fees payable to board of electrologist examiners,
§88A-7.
Estates.
Survivorship in bank deposit created by written
agreement, §41-2.1.
Fiduciaries.
Banking deposits in name of fiduciary, §32-8.
Personal account of fiduciary, §32-10.
Principal.
Deposit in name of principal, §32-9.
Trustees.
Deposits in name of two or more trustees,
§32-11.
Foreign or alien insurance companies.
Generally, §§58-5-5 to 58-5-40.
See FOREIGN OR ALIEN INSURANCE
COMPANIES.
Highways, roads and streets.
Condemnation proceedings.
Disbursement of deposit, §136-105.
Serving copy of disbursing order, §136-105.
Refund of deposit, §136-121.
Home inspector licensure board.
Moneys received by, §143-151.63(b).
Housing authorities and projects.
National defense housing projects.
Security for public deposits, §157-57.
Security for funds deposited, §157-24.
Insurance.
Banks.
Requirements as to deposit insurance, §53-9.1.

DEPOSITS —Cont'd
Insurance —Cont'd
Foreign or alien insurance companies, §§58-5-5 to
58-5-40.
See FOREIGN OR ALIEN INSURANCE
COMPANIES.
Liens.
Discharge of liens, §44-48.
Local ABC boards, §18B-702(t).
Local government finance.
Fiscal control.
Daily deposits.
Required, §159-32.
Selection of depository, §159-31.
Mortgages and deeds of trust.
Sales under power of sale.
Failure of bidder to cash deposit, §45-21.30(a).
Requirement of cash deposit at sale, §45-21.10.
Nurses.
Board of nursing.
Funds, §90-171.25.
Parking authorities.
Moneys of authority, §160A-559.
Payment into court, §§1-508 to 1-510.
Powers of attorney.
Powers conferred by statutory short form, §32A-2.
Prisons and prisoners.
Canteens.
Revenue from prison canteens, §148-2(c).
Provider sponsored organizations.
See PROVIDER SPONSORED ORGANIZATIONS.
Public officers and employees.
Daily deposit of funds to credit of state treasurer,
§147-77.
Report of daily deposits to state treasurer,
§147-84.
Rental referral agencies, §66-143(b).
Savings banks.
Deposit accounts.
See SAVINGS BANKS.
Security deposits of tenants, §§42-50 to 42-56.
Application of article, §42-56.
Deposit in trust accounts, §42-50.
Deposits from tenant, §42-50.
Landlord may furnish bond from insurance
company, §42-50.
Landlord to notify tenant of bank holding deposit,
§42-50.
Obligations of landlord, §42-52.
Permitted uses of deposit, §42-51.
Pet deposits, §42-53.
Recovery of deposit, §42-55.
Remedies, §42-55.
Rent.
Use for deposit, §42-51.
Transfer of dwelling units, §42-54.
Withholding of deposit.
Normal wear and tear, §42-52.
State departments and agencies.
Daily deposit of funds to credit of state treasurer,
§147-77.
Report of daily deposits to state treasurer,
§147-84.
State treasurer.
Contracts, §147-81.
Daily deposit of funds to credit of treasurer,
§147-77.
Good faith deposits.
Master trust, §147-78.1.
Interest.
Contracts as to interest, §147-81.

DEPOSITS —Cont'd
State treasurer —Cont'd
Number of depositories, §147-81.
Office declared office of deposit and disbursement, §147-74.
Receipts from federal government and gifts not affected, §147-83.
Reports of depositories, §147-79.
Security for deposits, §147-79.
Selection.
Treasurer to select depositories, §147-78.
State funds.
Deposits of state funds in banks and savings and loans regulated, §147-69.
Superior courts.
Clerks of court.
Money held by clerk, §7A-112.1.
Fees, §7A-308.1.
Taxation.
Collection of taxes.
Bank deposits subject to attachment or garnishment, §105-242(b).
Tenant security deposits, §§42-50 to 42-56.
Trust companies.
Financial holding companies.
Trust funds, §53-366(f).
Multistate trust institutions, §53-309.
Seizure by commissioner.
Deposit of funds collected, §53-390.
Trusts and trustees.
Deposit in name of two or more trustees, §32-11.
Unclaimed property generally, §§116B-51 to 116B-80.
See UNCLAIMED PROPERTY.
University of North Carolina.
Trust funds, §116-36.1(h).
Official depositories, §116-36.1(h).

DEPOSITS INTO COURT.
Arrest in civil cases.
Application of deposit to plaintiff's judgment, §1-429.
Bail substituted for deposit, §1-428.
Deposit in lieu of bail.
Paid into court, §1-427.
Discharge of defendants, §1-419.
Interpleader.
Funds to competing claims by parties, §1A-1 Rule 22(b).
Order paid into court, §1-508.
Orders seized by sheriff, §1-509.
Staying execution on money judgment, §1-289(a).

DEPOTS.
No title by possession of real estate condemned by railroad, plank road, etc., for, §1-44.

DEPRECIATION.
Corporate income tax.
Recapture of depreciation required under internal revenue code.
Inclusion in state net income, §105-130.5(e).
Individual income tax.
Accelerated depreciation.
Deductions to taxable income, §105-134.6(b).
Public utilities.
Depreciation charges, §62-35(c).

DEPRESSANTS.
Schedule I controlled substances, §90-89.
Schedule II controlled substances, §90-90.

DEPRESSANTS —Cont'd
Schedule IV controlled substances, §90-92(a).
Exemption of compounds, mixtures or preparations, §90-92(b).
Unauthorized substances taxes, §§105-113.105 to 105-113.113.
See UNAUTHORIZED SUBSTANCES TAXES.

DEPUTY SHERIFFS.
Allowing prisoners to escape, §14-239.
District attorney to prosecute officer for escape, §14-240.
Compensation, §153A-103.
Vacancy in office of sheriff.
Performance of duties, §162-5.
Workers' compensation benefits, §160A-282(c).

DERELICT MOTOR VEHICLES.
Generally, §§20-137.6 to 20-137.14.
See ABANDONED MOTOR VEHICLES.

DERIVATIVE ACTIONS, §1A-1 Rule 23(b).
Attorneys' fees.
Payment, §55-7-46.
Costs and expenses.
Payment, §55-7-46.
Definitions, §55-7-40.1.
Demand requirement, §55-7-42.
Discontinuance or settlement, §55-7-45.
Dismissal, §55-7-44.
Foreign corporations.
Applicability, §55-7-47.
Jurisdiction, §55-7-40.
Limited liability companies, §57C-8-01.
Limited partners, §§59-1001 to 59-1006.
Nonprofit corporations.
Members and directors, §55A-7-40.
Privileged communications, §55-7-49.
Standing, §55-7-41.
Stays, §55-7-43.

DESCENT AND DISTRIBUTION.
Decedents' estates.
Distribution, §§28A-22-1 to 28A-22-11.
See DECEDENTS' ESTATES.
Degrees of kinship.
How computed, §104A-1.
Executors and administrators.
See EXECUTORS AND ADMINISTRATORS.
Intestate succession, §§29-1 to 29-30.
See INTESTATE SUCCESSION.

DESCRAMBLERS.
Cable television service theft, §14-118.5.

DESECRATION OF FLAG, §14-381.

DESERTION AND NONSUPPORT.
Child support enforcement program generally, §§110-128 to 110-142.2.
See CHILD SUPPORT.
Compelling disclosure of information respecting parent, §110-131.
Illegitimate children, §49-2.
Support and maintenance.
General provisions.
See SUPPORT AND MAINTENANCE.
Willful abandonment and failure to support spouse and children, §14-322(b), (c).
Child support, payment order, determining, §14-322(e).
Definitions, §14-322(a).
Dependent spouse defined, §14-322(a).
First offense, penalty, §14-322(f).

DESERTION AND NONSUPPORT —Cont'd
Willful abandonment and failure to support spouse and children —Cont'd
Parents, §14-322(d).
Second or subsequent offense, §14-322(f).
Supporting spouse defined, §14-322(a).
Supporting spouse living with dependent spouse, §14-322(c).

DESIGNATED DELIVERY SERVICE.
Service of process.
Definition of delivery receipt, §1-75.10(b).
Personal jurisdiction, manner of serving, §1A-1 Rule 4(j).
Proof of service by, §§1-75.10(a), 1A-1 Rule 4(j2).

DESTRUCTION OF INSTRUMENTS AND RECORDS.
Deeds.
Evidence.
Presumed to be in due form, §8-21.
Grants.
Burke county, §8-10.
Public records, destruction regulated, §132-3.
Wills, §31-5.1.
Evidence.
Proved and lost before recorded, §8-31.

DESTRUCTION OF WILL, §31-5.1.
Evidence.
Proved and lost before recorded, §8-31.

DETAINERS.
Continuance, §15-10.2(a).
Information to be furnished prisoner, §15-10.2(b).
Interstate agreement on detainers, §§15A-761 to 15A-767.
Administrator, §15A-766.
Designation of central administrator, §15A-766.
Appropriate court.
Defined, §15A-762.
Cooperation in enforcement, §15A-763.
Copies of provisions.
Distribution, §15A-767.
Courts.
Cooperation in enforcement, §15A-763.
Definitions, §15A-761.
"Appropriate court,"§15A-762.
Designation of enforcement officer, §15A-766.
Distribution of copies of provisions, §15A-767.
Enactment, §15A-761.
Escape from temporary custody, §15A-764.
General provisions, §15A-761.
Information agent, §15A-761.
Designation, §15A-766.
Penal or correctional institutions.
Officials in charge.
Authority and duty, §15A-765.
Public officers and employees.
Cooperation in enforcement, §15A-763.
Set forth, §15A-761.
State departments and agencies.
Cooperation in enforcement, §15A-763.
Temporary custody, §15A-761.
Escape from temporary custody, §15A-764.
Text of agreement, §15A-761.
Warden's, etc., duties, §15A-765.
Mandatory disposition of detainers, §§15-10.1 to 15-10.4.
Continuance, §15-10.2.
Information to be furnished prisoner, §15-10.2.

DETAINERS —Cont'd
Mandatory disposition of detainers —Cont'd
Mentally ill.
Exception as to prisoners who are mentally ill, §15-10.4.
Procedure, §15-10.3.
Request for final disposition of charges, §15-10.2.
Return of prisoner after trial, §15-10.3.
Manner of use, §15-10.1.
Mentally ill persons.
Mandatory disposition of detainer.
Exceptions as to mentally ill prisoners, §15-10.4.
Purpose, §15-10.1.
Request for final disposition of charges, §15-10.2(a).
Securing attendance of criminal defendants confined in institutions within state, §15A-711(d).

DETECTIVES.
Misdemeanor for detective to collect claims, accounts, etc., §14-401.2.
Private protective services generally, §§74C-1 to 74C-30.
See PRIVATE PROTECTIVE SERVICES.
State departments and agencies.
Use of private investigators limited, §114-15.2.

DETENTION OF JUVENILES.
Generally, §§143B-815 to 143B-821.
See JUVENILE DETENTION.

DETINUE.
Claim and delivery, §§1-472 to 1-480.

DETOURS.
Road repair, §136-25.

DEVELOPMENT.
Armories.
Fostering development of armories and facilities.
Authority to foster, §127A-162.
Authorities, borrowing, §159-188.
Balanced growth policy act, §§143-506.6 to 143-506.13.
See BALANCED GROWTH POLICY ACT.
Economic development commissions, §§158-8 to 158-15.
See ECONOMIC DEVELOPMENT COMMISSIONS.
Environmental impact statements.
Ordinances requiring statements for major development projects, §113A-8(a) to (c).
Industrial development, §§158-16 to 158-24.
See INDUSTRIAL DEVELOPMENT.
Local development generally.
See LOCAL DEVELOPMENT.
Multi-county water conservation and infrastructure district, §158-15.1.
Subdivisions.
Control corners in real estate developments, §§39-32.1 to 39-32.4.
Highways, roads and streets.
Minimum standards of board of transportation.
Compliance with standards required of developers, §136-102.6.

DEVELOPMENT AGREEMENTS.
Cities and towns, §§160A-400.20 to 160A-400.32.
Acreage of developed property.
Minimum number of acres, §160A-400.23.
Amendment.
Mutual consent of parties or successors in interest, §160A-400.28.

DEVELOPMENT AGREEMENTS —Cont'd

Cities and towns —Cont'd

Applicable laws, §160A-400.26(a).

Debt approval.

Applicability of constitutional and statutory procedures for, §160A-400.31.

Exceptions, §160A-400.26(b) to (d).

Approval by governing body, §160A-400.22.

Authorized, §§160A-400.20(b), 160A-400.22.

Building code.

Relationship to, §160A-400.32.

Cancellation.

Mutual consent of parties or successors in interest, §160A-400.28.

Change of jurisdiction.

Subsequent modification or suspension, §160A-400.29(b).

Validity and duration of agreement entered into before, §160A-400.29(a).

Contents.

Authorized contents, §160A-400.25(b), (d).

Required contents, §160A-400.25(a), (c).

Debt approval.

Applicability of constitutional and statutory procedures for, §160A-400.31.

Definitions, §160A-400.21.

Duration, §160A-400.23.

Agreement entered into prior to change of jurisdiction, §160A-400.29(a).

Hearings.

Public hearing on proposed agreement, §160A-400.24.

Housing code.

Relationship to, §160A-400.32.

Legislative findings, §160A-400.20(a).

Material breach by developer, §160A-400.27(b), (c).

Periodic review to assess compliance with, §160A-400.27(a).

Public hearing on proposed agreement, §160A-400.24.

Recordation by developer, §160A-400.30.

Successors in interest to parties.

Benefits and burdens inure to, §160A-400.30.

Supplemental nature of provisions, §160A-400.20(c).

Counties, §§153A-349.1 to 153A-349.13.

Acreage of developed property.

Minimum number of acres, §153A-349.4.

Amendment.

Mutual consent of parties or successors in interest, §153A-349.9.

Applicable laws, §153A-349.7(a).

Debt approval procedures for local governments, §153A-349.12.

Exceptions, §153A-349.7(b) to (d).

Approval of governing body, §153A-349.3.

Authorized, §§153A-349.1(b), 153A-349.3.

Building code.

Relationship of agreement to, §153A-349.13.

Cancellation.

Mutual consent of parties or successors in interest, §153A-349.9.

Change of jurisdiction.

Subsequent modification or suspension, §153A-349.10(b).

Validity and duration of agreement entered into prior to, §153A-349.10(a).

Debt approval procedures for local governments.

Applicability, §153A-349.12.

Definitions, §153A-349.2.

DEVELOPMENT AGREEMENTS —Cont'd

Counties —Cont'd

Duration, §153A-349.4.

Agreement entered into prior to change of jurisdiction, §153A-349.10(a).

Hearing on, §153A-349.5.

Housing code.

Relationship of agreement to, §153A-349.13.

Legislative declaration, §153A-349.1(a).

Material breach by developer, §153A-349.8(b), (c).

Provisions.

Authorized provisions, §153A-349.6(b), (d).

Required provisions, §153A-349.6(a), (c).

Public hearing on, §153A-349.5.

Recordation by developer, §153A-349.11.

Successors in interest to parties.

Burdens and benefits inure to, §153A-349.11.

Supplemental nature of provisions, §153A-349.1(c).

DEVELOPMENTAL DISABILITIES.

Adult care homes.

Generally.

See ADULT CARE HOMES.

Generally.

See MENTAL HEALTH, DEVELOPMENTAL DISABILITY, SUBSTANCE ABUSE.

Incompetence, determination of, §§35A-1101 to 35A-1116.

See INCOMPETENCY.

Missing persons with cognitive impairment.

Silver alert system, §143B-1022.

DEVELOPMENT FINANCING DISTRICTS.

Annexation of district established by county, §159-107(e).

Base valuation in development finance district.

Adjustments during lifetime of district, §159-107(b).

Determination by tax assessor, §159-107(a).

Duration, §159-107(g).

Project development financing debt instruments, §§159-101 to 159-113.

See LOCAL GOVERNMENT FINANCE.

Property taxes.

Assessment of property.

District subject to agreement, §§105-277.11, 105-284(d).

Levy within development financing district, §159-107(d).

Revenue increment fund, §159-107(c).

Use of money, §159-107(f).

DEVELOPMENT ZONES.

Tax credit, §105-129.13.

Business tax incentives.

Sunset provision for taxpayers located in zones, §105-129.2A(a3).

Zone designation, §105-129.3A.

Zone project credit, §105-129.13.

DEVISAVIT VEL NON, §31-35.

DEVISEES' RIGHT TO RENOUNCE, §31B-1.

DEVISES.

Agriculture.

Hall of fame.

Acceptance, §106-568.17.

Construction of term appearing in statute, §12-3.

Wills generally.

See WILLS.

DIABETES.
Accident and health insurance.
Coverage for certain treatment, §58-51-61(a).
Definition of "physician,"§58-51-61(b).
Charter schools.
Diabetes care plans, implementation.
Information provided parents and guardians, §115C-238.29F(a).
Food, drug or cosmetic act.
Drug or device, false advertising, §106-138(b).
Health maintenance organizations.
Coverage for certain treatment, §58-67-74(a).
Definition of "physician,"§58-67-74.
Hospital, medical and dental service corporations.
Coverage for certain treatment, §58-65-91(a).
Definition of "physician,"§58-65-91(b).
Jail prisoner unconscious or semiconscious.
Duty of custodial personnel.
Reasonable effort to determine if prisoner wearing emergency alert symbol, §153A-225.1(a) to (c).
Police assistance to persons arrested while unconscious or semiconscious, §15A-503.
Program establishment, §130A-221(a), (b).
Public schools.
Guidelines to support and assist students with, §115C-375.3.

DIAGNOSTIC CENTERS.
Certificates of need, §§131E-175 to 130E-191.1.
See HEALTH CARE FACILITIES.

DIAMOND INDUSTRY TRADE PRACTICES.
Definitions, §66-73.
Violations of provisions.
Penalty, §66-75.
What constitutes unfair trade practice, §66-74.

DIESEL EMISSIONS.
Diesel powered motor vehicles, §20-128.1(a).
Reduction of school student's exposure.
Duty of local boards, §115C-47.
Duty of state board of education, §115C-12.

DIESEL FUEL TAX.
Gasoline tax generally, §§105-449.60 to 105-449.126.
See GASOLINE TAX.

DIESEL POWERED VEHICLES.
Manufacturer's warranty.
Vehicles purchased by state, §20-351.11.

DIETARY SUPPLEMENTS.
Sales and use tax.
Defined, §105-164.3.
Subject to tax, §105-164.13B(a).

DIETITIANS AND NUTRITIONISTS, §§90-350 to 90-370.
Applicability of provisions.
Persons and practices not affected, §90-368.
Board of dietetics/nutrition.
Appointment of members, §90-354(a).
Compensation, §90-354(f).
Composition, §90-353(a).
Professional members, §90-353(b).
Public at large members.
Professions excluded from appointment, §90-353(c).
Creation, §90-353(a).
Defined as "board,"§90-352.
Meetings, §90-355(b).

DIETITIANS AND NUTRITIONISTS —Cont'd
Board of dietetics/nutrition —Cont'd
Officers.
Election of, §90-355(a).
Powers and duties, §90-356.
Quorum, §90-355(b).
Removal of members, §90-354(d).
Responsibilities, §90-356.
Terms of members, §90-354(b).
Limitation, §90-354(c).
Vacancies, §90-354(e).
Child support enforcement.
Forfeiture of licensing privilege, §50-13.12.
Citation of title.
Dietetics/nutrition practice act, §90-350.
Criminal law and procedure.
Violations of provision, §90-366.
Definitions, §90-352.
Disciplinary actions, §90-363.
Costs, §90-370.
Grounds.
Prohibited conduct, §90-363(a).
Hearing required, §90-363(b).
Prohibited conduct.
Grounds for disciplinary action, §90-363(a).
Education.
License requirements, §90-357.
Examinations.
Fee for examination or reexamination, §90-364.
Fees.
Schedule of fees, §90-364.
Felony convictions.
Forfeiture of license, §15A-1331A.
Fines.
Violations of provision, §90-366.
Inapplicability of provisions, §90-368.
Injunctions.
Violation of provisions, §90-367.
Legislative declaration.
Purpose of provisions, §90-351.
Letters.
"LD," "LN" or "LDN."
Use of letters or any facsimile or combination.
License required, §90-365.
Licensed dietitian/nutritionist.
Defined, §90-352.
Use of words.
License required, §90-365.
Licenses.
Application, §90-357.
Evaluation.
Notification of applicant, §90-358.
Initial application fee, §90-364.
Display requirement, §90-362(b).
Evaluation of application.
Notification of applicant, §90-358.
Examinations, §90-359.
Administration, §90-359.
Granting license without examination, §90-360.
Fees, §90-357.
Granting license without examination, §90-360.
Inactive status.
Application for active status, §90-362(g).
Request by licensee, §90-362(g).
Issuance.
Fee, §90-364.
Late renewal.
Fee, §90-364.
Notification requirements, §90-362(c).
Practice of dietetics/nutrition.
Requirement of license, §90-365.

DIETITIANS AND NUTRITIONISTS —Cont'd
Licenses —Cont'd
Property of board.
  License as constituting, §90-362(a).
Provisional licenses, §90-361.
  Fee, §90-364.
Renewal, §90-362(d).
  Board notification, §90-362(e).
  Fee, §90-364.
  Late renewal, §90-362(f).
Requirements, §90-357.
Revocation or suspension.
  Felony convictions, §15A-1331A.
  Reinstatement, §90-363(b).
Misdemeanors.
Violation of provisions, §90-366.
Nutrition care services.
Defined, §90-352.
"Nutritionist" or "licensed nutritionist."
Use of words.
  License required, §90-365.
Prison terms.
Violations of provision, §90-366.
Purpose of provisions, §90-351.
Referral fees and solicitation payments,
  §§90-400 to 90-402.
Health care provider defined, §90-400.
Prohibited, §90-401.
Sanctions, §90-402.
Rules and licensure standards.
Copy fees, §90-364.
Rules and regulations.
Board of dietetics/nutrition.
  Licensure standards and rules.
    Copy fees, §90-364.
  Rulemaking authority, §90-356.
Short title.
Dietetics/nutrition practice act, §90-350.
Third-party reimbursement, §90-369.
Limitation on modifications, §90-369.
Title.
Use of title "dietitian/nutritionist."
  License required, §90-365.
Title of act.
Dietetics/nutrition practice act, §90-350.
Unlawful use of title, words or letters, §90-365.
Words.
"Dietitian" or "licensed dietitian.."
  Use of words.
    License required, §90-365.

DIGGING.
Underground damage prevention, §§87-100 to
  87-114.
  See UNDERGROUND DAMAGE PREVENTION.

DIGITAL CAMERAS.
**Portable consumer electronic devices
  insurance.**
Claims handling, adjuster licenses, §58-33-27.
Generally, §§58-44A-1 to 58-44A-25.
  See PORTABLE CONSUMER ELECTRONIC
    DEVICES INSURANCE.

DIGITAL SIGNATURES.
Electronic commerce in government, §§66-58.1
  to 66-58.12.
  See ELECTRONIC COMMERCE IN
    GOVERNMENT.
Electronic medical records, authorization,
  §90-412(b).

DIGITAL SIGNATURES —Cont'd
Electronic transactions generally, §§66-311 to
  66-330.
  See ELECTRONIC TRANSACTIONS.
Identity theft.
Generally, §§14-113.20 to 14-113.25.

DILATORY PLEADINGS, §1A-1 Rule 11(a).

DIMMING HEADLIGHTS, §20-131(a).
Failure to dim, §20-181.

DIPHTHERIA.
Childhood vaccine-related compensation,
  §§130A-422 to 130A-434.
Drug or device, false advertising, §106-138(b).
Immunization, §§130A-152 to 130A-158.

DIPLOMAS.
Forgery, §14-122.1.
Obtaining by fraudulent means, §14-118.2.
World War II veterans.
Special high school diplomas.
  Powers of board of education, §115C-12.

DIPLOMATS.
Foreign diplomat.
Holder of driver's license issued by United States
  department of state.
  Notice to department of state.
    Violation of state or local traffic law,
      revocation order, §20-37.20.

DIRECT CRIMINAL CONTEMPT, §5A-13.
Summary proceedings, §5A-14.

DIRECTED VERDICT MOTIONS, §1A-1 Rule
  50(a).
Judgment notwithstanding verdict, §1A-1 Rule
  50(b) to (d).

**DIRECTING, CONTROLLING OR
  REGULATING TRAFFIC.**
**Willful failure to obey law-enforcement or
  traffic-control officer,** §20-114.1.

DIRECTIONAL FLOW PEAK TRAFFIC LANES,
  §20-146.2(c).

**DIRECTIONAL SIGNALS ON MOTOR
  VEHICLES.**
Motorcycles.
Provisions not applicable, §20-125.1(d).
Requirements generally, §20-125.1(a), (b).
Safety inspections, scope, §20-183.3(a).
Trailers.
When not required, §20-125.1(c).

DIRECT MAIL MARKETING.
**Insurance consumer's or customer's account
  number.**
Insurance institution, agent or support
  organization sharing.
  General prohibition, §58-39-76.

DIRECT MAIL SALES.
Sales and use tax.
Direct mail defined, §105-164.3.
Direct pay permit, §105-164.27A(a1).
Sourcing sale of product.
  Inapplicability of principles, §105-164.3(d).

DIRECTOR OF THE BUDGET.
See BUDGETS.

DIRECTORY OF NEW HIRES, §110-129.2.

DIRECT-TO-HOME SATELLITE SERVICES.
Sales and use tax.
Defined, §105-164.3.

DIRKS.
Carrying concealed weapons, §14-269.
Carrying or possessing on educational
  property, §14-269.2.
Sale to minors, §14-315.
Weapons generally.
  See FIREARMS AND OTHER WEAPONS.

DIRT ROADS.
Driving farm tractors on dirt roads from farm
  to farm, §20-122(d).
Natural and scenic rivers system.
  Road defined, §113A-33.

DISABILITY HISTORY AND AWARENESS
  MONTH, §103-11.

DISABILITY INCOME INSURANCE.
Interstate insurance product regulation
  compact, §§58-91-1 to 58-91-80.
  See INTERSTATE INSURANCE PRODUCT
    REGULATION COMPACT.
Policy standards, §58-51-130.
  Applicability of provisions, §58-51-130(b).
  Definitions, §58-51-130(a).
  Disclosure standards, §58-51-130(c).
  Exceptions, §58-51-130(e).
  Other income sources, §58-51-130(h).
  Other provisions applicable, §58-51-130(g).
  Preexisting conditions, when denial of claim
    prohibited, §58-51-130(d).
  Required provisions, §58-51-130(f).

DISABILITY INCOME PLAN, §§135-100 to
  135-114.
Amendment of provisions.
  Reservation of power, §135-113.
Benefits.
  Adjustments.
    Post disability benefit adjustments, §135-108.
  Defined, §135-101.
  Long-term disability benefits.
    Amount, §135-106(b), (c).
    Forfeiture of rights to benefits, receipt of early
      retirement allowance, return of
      accumulated contribution.
    Irrevocable election by participant or
      beneficiary, §135-106(d).
    Generally, §135-106(a).
    Medical review.
      Annual medical review, §135-106(a).
      Trial rehabilitation, return to service for,
        §135-106(c1).
  Post disability benefit adjustments, §135-108.
  Short-term disability benefits.
    Administration of provisions, §135-105(d).
    Amount, §135-105(c).
    Commencement, §135-105(b).
    Determination of eligibility, §135-105(f).
    Extension, §135-105(g).
    Generally, §135-105(a).
    Return to service for trial rehabilitation,
      §135-105(e).
  Status.
    Not part of an employment contract, §135-113.
  Waiting period, §135-104(a).
    Return to service for trial rehabilitation,
      §135-104(b).
    Salary continuation, §135-104(a).
Board of trustees.
  Administration of provisions, §135-102(a).
  Defined, §135-101.
  Powers, §135-102(c), (e).

DISABILITY INCOME PLAN —Cont'd
Board of trustees —Cont'd
  Rules and regulations, §135-102(c).
  Trust fund.
    Board as trustee of fund, §135-110(a).
Citation of article.
  Short title, §135-100(a).
Compensation.
  Base rate of compensation.
    Defined, §135-101.
  Defined, §135-101.
Consolidated judicial retirement system.
  Reciprocity of membership service, §135-114.
Contributions.
  Employers, §135-110(b), (c).
Definitions, §135-101.
Disability salary continuation plan.
  Transition provisions.
    Benefit recipients under former disability salary
      continuation plan, §135-112(b), (c).
Earnings.
  Defined, §135-101.
  Reports of earnings, §135-109.
Employers.
  Contributions, §135-110(b), (c).
  Defined, §135-101.
Exemptions.
  Applicability of provisions to plan, §135-111.
Investigations.
  Medical board, §135-102(d).
Investments.
  Trust fund.
    Assets of fund, §135-110(d).
Legislative retirement system.
  Reciprocity of membership service, §135-114.
Medical board, §135-102(d).
  Composition, §135-102(d).
  Defined, §135-101.
  Duties, §135-102(d).
Modification of provisions.
  Reservation of power, §135-113.
Optional retirement program, §135-107.
Other pension laws.
  Applicability, §135-111.
Participants.
  Cessation of participation, §135-103(b).
  Defined, §135-101.
  Eligible participants, §135-103(a).
Powers of plan, §135-102(b).
Purpose of article, §135-100(b).
Repeal of provisions.
  Reservation of power, §135-113.
Reports.
  Earnings, §135-109.
Retirement.
  Defined, §135-101.
  Optional retirement program, §135-107.
  Retirement system for teachers and state
    employees.
    Member being paid under plan, §135-5(a).
Rules and regulations, §135-102(c).
Short title of article, §135-100(a).
State treasurer.
  Administration of provisions, §135-102(a).
  Powers, §135-102(c), (e).
  Rules and regulations, §135-102(c).
  Trust fund.
    Custodian of fund, §135-110(d).
Teachers.
  Defined, §135-101.
  Eligible participants, §135-103(a).

DISABILITY INCOME PLAN —Cont'd
Title of article.
Short title, §135-100(a).
Transition provisions.
Disability salary continuation plan.
Benefit recipients under former disability salary
continuation plan, §135-112(b), (c).
Generally, §135-112(a).
Trust fund, §135-110(a).
Board of trustees.
Board as trustee of fund, §135-110(a).
Investment of assets, §135-110(d).
State treasurer.
Custodian of fund, §135-110(d).

DISABILITY OF ATTORNEYS.
Disability proceedings generally, Bar Rules
B.0101 to B.0217.
See ATTORNEYS AT LAW.

DISABILITY OF JUDGE, §1A-1 Rule 63.

DISABILITY OF MARRIAGE.
Adverse possession, §1-18.

DISABLED ADULT PROTECTION ACT,
§§108A-99 to 108A-111.
See ABUSED, NEGLECTED OR EXPLOITED
DISABLED ADULTS.

DISABLED AMERICAN VETERANS.
Property tax exclusion, §105-275.

DISABLED IN LINE OF DUTY.
**Law enforcement officers, firefighters, rescur
squad workers.**
Tuition and fee waivers to spouse or child,
§§115B-1 to 115B-6.

DISABLED PERSONS.
Access to and use of public places, §168-2.
Actions.
Protection act.
Civil actions for discriminatory practices,
§§168A-11, 168A-12.
Adult care homes.
Generally, §§131D-2.1 to 131D-2.18.
See ADULT CARE HOMES.
Adult protection.
Protection of abused, neglected or exploited
adults, §§108A-99 to 108A-111.
See ABUSED, NEGLECTED OR EXPLOITED
DISABLED ADULTS.
**Aids or adaptations for persons with
disabilities.**
Enjoyment of public services provided by state or
political subdivisions.
Required, §168A-7(a), (b).
Alcoholic beverages.
Refusal to sell not to be discriminatory,
§18B-305(c).
All-terrain vehicles.
Disabled sportsman program.
Use by persons qualified under program,
§20-171.26.
Amusements.
Right to use of places of public amusement,
§168-3.
Animals.
Service animals, §§168-4.2 to 168-4.6.
Assault and battery.
Aggravated assault, §14-32.1(e).
Assaults upon handicapped persons, §14-32.1.
Punishments, §14-32.1.

DISABLED PERSONS —Cont'd
Assault and battery —Cont'd
Definition of handicapped person, §14-32.1(a).
DNA sample.
Required upon conviction, §15A-266.4.
Simple assault, §14-32.1(f).
Assistance dogs.
See ASSISTANCE ANIMALS.
**Assistance granted to persons in adult care
homes.**
State-county special assistance, §§108A-40 to
108A-47.1.
See SOCIAL SERVICES.
Assisted living facilities.
Adult care homes generally, §§131D-2.1 to
131D-2.18.
See ADULT CARE HOMES.
Attorney general.
Designation of attorney specializing in law of the
handicapped, §114-4.2F.
Attorneys, CLE substitute program, Bar Rule
D.1607.
Aviation.
Right to use of public conveyances, §168-3.
Betterments.
Procedure where plaintiff is under disability,
§1-349.
Blind persons.
General provisions, §§111-4 to 111-47.
See BLIND AND VISUALLY IMPAIRED.
Boats.
Right to use of public conveyances, §168-3.
Buses.
Right to use of public conveyances, §168-3.
Carriers.
Right to use of public conveyances, §168-3.
Charities.
Governor's council on employment of the
handicapped.
Council to be nonpartisan and nonprofit,
§143-283.8.
Child custody.
Persons incapable of self-support upon reaching
majority.
Rights same as minor child for custody
purposes, §50-13.8.
Children with disabilities.
Education of children with disabilities.
Generally, §§115C-106.1 to 115C-112.1.
See SPECIAL EDUCATION.
Interagency coordinating council for children from
birth to five years of age.
Agency cooperation, §143B-179.6.
Compensation, §143B-179.5(e).
Composition, §143B-179.5(b).
Duties, §143B-179.5(d).
Agency cooperation, §143B-179.6.
Establishment, §143B-179.5(a).
Organization, §143B-179.5(c).
Clerical and support services, §143B-179.5(f).
Reporting, §143B-179.5(f).
Commission for the blind.
Consumer and advocacy advisory committee for
the blind, §§143B-163, 143B-164.
General provisions, §§143B-157 to 143B-160.
See BLIND AND VISUALLY IMPAIRED.
Professional advisory committee, §§143B-161,
143B-162.
**Commission to study the care of the aged and
handicapped,** §§143-279 to 143-283.
See SENIOR CITIZENS.

DISABLED PERSONS —Cont'd

Community third party or pooled trusts.
Persons with severe chronic disabilities, §§36D-1 to 36D-12.
See COMMUNITY THIRD PARTY OR POOLED TRUSTS.

Contractors.
Public building contracts.
Small, minority, physically handicapped and women contractors.
Cooperation in promoting use, §143-135.5.

Council on developmental disabilities, §§143B-177 to 143B-179.
See MENTAL HEALTH, DEVELOPMENTAL DISABILITY, SUBSTANCE ABUSE.

Curb ramps or curb cuts.
Minimum requirements, §136-44.14.

Custody.
Persons incapable of self-support upon reaching majority.
Rights same as minor child for custody purposes, §50-13.8.

Deaf and hearing impaired.
See DEAF AND HEARING IMPAIRED.

Defenses.
Protection act.
Employers.
Affirmative defenses, §168A-9.

Definitions.
Council on developmental disabilities, §143B-178.
Protection act, §168A-3.

Developmental disabilities.
General provisions.
See MENTAL HEALTH, DEVELOPMENTAL DISABILITY, SUBSTANCE ABUSE.
Protection act.
General provisions, §§168A-1 to 168A-12. See within this heading, "Protection act."

Disability history and awareness month, §103-11.

Discrimination.
Protection act, §§168A-1 to 168A-12. See within this heading, "Protection act."

Divorce.
Custody.
Persons incapable of self-support upon reaching majority, §50-13.8.

Dogs.
Assistance dogs.
See ASSISTANCE ANIMALS.

Drivers' licenses.
Persons not to be licensed, §20-9(e).
When persons may be licensed, §20-9(g).

Education.
Right to habilitation and rehabilitation services, §168-8.

Education of children with disabilities.
Generally, §§115C-106.1 to 115C-112.1.
See SPECIAL EDUCATION.

Elections.
Accessible polling places, §163-131.
Assistance to voters, §163-166.8.
Curbside voting, §163-166.9.
Satellite voting places for disabled voters, §163-130.

Employment.
Governor's council on employment of the handicapped, §§143-283.1 to 143-283.8. See within this heading, "Governor's council on employment of the handicapped."

DISABLED PERSONS —Cont'd

Employment security.
Disability benefits.
Eligibility conditions, §96-14.

Exploitation of disabled adult.
Disabled adult defined, §14-112.2(a).
Obtaining or using funds, assets or property with intent to deprive.
Person knowing that adult lacks capacity to consent, §14-112.2(c).
Criminal penalties, §14-112.2(e).
Persons standing in position of trust and confidence or business relationship, §14-112.2(b).
Criminal penalties, §14-112.2(d).

Facsimile signatures.
Use by person with disability, §22A-1.

Fair housing.
Generally, §§41A-1 to 41A-10.
See FAIR HOUSING.
Unlawful discriminatory housing practices, §41A-4(f).

False representation as to physical disability.
Obtaining money by, §14-113.

Family care homes.
Charges and assessments for services, utilities and improvements.
Deemed residential use property for determining, §168-22(b).
Definitions, §168-21.
Private agreements.
Certain agreements void, §168-23.
Public policy, §168-20.
Zoning.
Deemed residential use of property, §168-22(a).
Permits not required, §168-22(a).

Firemen's pension fund.
Monthly pensions upon retirement.
Totally and permanently disabled members, §58-86-55.

Global TransPark authority.
Goals for participation by, §63A-19.

Governor's council on employment of the handicapped, §§143-283.1 to 143-283.8.
Celebration of National Employ the Physically Handicapped Week, §143-283.3.
Charitable organization, §143-283.8.
Citation of article, §143-283.1.
Cooperation with president's committee, §143-283.2.
National Employ the Physically Handicapped Week.
Celebration, §143-283.3.
Nature of council, §143-283.8.
Nonpartisan organization, §143-283.8.
Nonprofit organization, §143-283.8.
Purpose of article, §143-283.2.
Short title, §143-283.1.
Title of article, §143-283.1.

Health coverage for workers with disabilities act.
Medicaid buy-in for workers with disabilities, §108A-54.1.

Health insurance for physically handicapped children.
Continuation of coverage, §58-51-25(a).

Hearing impaired.
See DEAF AND HEARING IMPAIRED.

Highways.
Right of access to and use of public places, §168-2.

DISABLED PERSONS —Cont'd
Highways, roads and streets.
Condemnation proceedings.
Appointment of guardian ad litem for person with disability, §136-110.
Curb ramps or curb cuts for handicapped, §136-44.14.
Right of access to and use of public places, §168-2.
Holidays.
National Employ the Physically Handicapped Week.
Celebration, §143-283.3.
Homestead exclusion.
Property taxes, §105-277.1.
Disabled veterans, §105-277.1C.
Notice on abstract, §105-309(f).
Hotels, inns and other transient lodging places.
Right to use of public accommodations, §168-3.
Housing.
Fair housing, §§41A-1 to 41A-10.
See FAIR HOUSING.
Right to housing, §168-9.
Human service and volunteer transportation, §§62-289.1 to 62-289.7.
See HUMAN SERVICE AND VOLUNTEER TRANSPORTATION.
Hunting and fishing.
Disabled sportsman program, §113-296.
Motorized all-terrain vehicles.
Use by persons qualified under program, §20-171.26.
Income tax credits, §105-151.18.
Construction of dwelling units for, §105-151.1.
Definitions, §105-151.18(c).
Disabled dependent, §105-151.18(b).
Disabled taxpayer, §105-151.18(a).
Limitations, §105-151.18(d).
Injunctions.
Protection act.
Relief available, §168A-11(b).
Insurance.
Discrimination.
Prohibited, §168-10.
Proceeds belonging to incapacitated adults.
Payment to and receipt by clerks of superior courts or public guardians, §7A-111(b), (d).
Jurisdiction.
Protection act.
Civil actions, §168A-11(c).
Jury duty.
Excused, deferred or exempted.
Request, §9-6.1.
Legislative declaration, §168-1.
Legislative retirement system.
Disability retirement benefits, §120-4.22.
Reexamination for disability retirement allowance, §120-4.23.
Limitation of actions.
Protection act.
Civil actions for discriminatory practices, §168A-12.
Local governmental employees' retirement system.
Benefits.
Allowance on disability retirement, §128-27(d).
Disability retirement benefits, §128-27(c).
Restriction of benefits, municipal officers and employees, §160A-163(g).
Increase in benefits.
Those persons on disability retirement who were retired prior to July 1, 1971, §128-27(p), (t).

DISABLED PERSONS —Cont'd
Local governmental employees' retirement system —Cont'd
Reexamination of beneficiaries retired on account of disability, §128-27(e).
Low-income energy assistance program, §108A-25.4.
Mattresses and bedding.
Exemptions for bedding manufactured, sanitized or renovated by nonprofit agency for the blind or severely handicapped, §106-65.106(a).
Medicaid buy-in for workers with disabilities.
Health coverage for workers with disabilities act, §108A-54.1.
Mentally ill.
General provisions.
See MENTAL HEALTH, DEVELOPMENTAL DISABILITY, SUBSTANCE ABUSE.
Money belonging to incapacitated adults.
Payment to and receipt by clerks of superior courts or public guardians, §7A-111(b), (d).
Motor carriers.
Right to use of public conveyances, §168-3.
Motorized wheelchairs.
Registration and certificate of title.
Exemption from requirements, §20-51.
Nonprofit work centers for the blind and severely disabled.
Public contracts.
Purchases from, §143-129.5.
Purchases through department of administration.
Agency procurement of goods directly from center, §143-48.2(a).
Agency procurement of services directly from center, §143-48.2(b).
Bids and making offers by center, §143-48.2(c).
Parking.
Designation of parking places, §20-37.6(d).
Enforcement of handicapped parking privileges, §20-37.6(e).
License plates.
Distinguishing license plates, §20-37.6(b), (c1).
Out-of-state plates, §20-37.6A.
Penalties for violations, §20-37.6(f).
Placards.
Out-of-state placards, §20-37.6A.
Windshield placards, §20-37.6(c) to (c2).
Privileges generally, §20-37.6(a).
Definitions, §20-37.5.
Public vehicular areas.
Signs differing from uniform signs, §136-30(c).
Violations of provisions.
Penalties, §20-37.6(f).
Prohibited acts, §20-37.6(e).
Personnel system.
Discrimination against handicapped prohibited, §128-15.3.
Recruitment, etc., of handicapped persons, §128-15.3.
Prisons and prisoners.
Medical release, §§15A-1369 to 15A-1369.5.
Property taxes.
Homestead exclusion, §105-277.1.
Disabled veterans, §105-277.1C.
Notice on abstract, §105-309(f).
Reduced valuation of permanent residence.
Abstract notice, §105-309(f).
Protection act.
Actions.
Attorneys' fees.
Award, §168A-11(d).

DISABLED PERSONS —Cont'd
Protection act —Cont'd
Actions —Cont'd
Jurisdiction, §168A-11(c).
Limitation of actions, §168A-12.
Relief, §168A-11(b).
Right of action, §168A-11(a).
Citation.
Short title, §168A-1.
Defenses.
Employers.
Affirmative defenses, §168A-9.
Definitions, §168A-3.
Discriminatory practices.
Defined, §168A-3.
Employment, §168A-5(a).
Exemptions, §168A-5(b).
Public accommodations, §168A-6.
Public service, §168A-7(a), (b).
Public transportation, §168A-8.
Transportation.
Public transportation, §168A-8.
Employers.
Defenses.
Affirmative defenses, §168A-9.
Defined, §168A-3.
Discriminatory practices, §168A-5.
Retaliation.
Prohibited, §168A-10(a), (b).
Employment agencies.
Defined, §168A-3.
Discriminatory practices, §168A-5.
Retaliation.
Prohibited, §168A-10(a).
Injunctions.
Relief available, §168A-11(b).
Jurisdiction.
Civil actions, §168A-11(c).
Legislative findings, §168A-2(b).
Limitation of actions, §168A-12.
Public accommodations.
Definition of "place of public
accommodations,"§168A-3.
Discriminatory practices, §168A-6.
Public service.
Discriminatory practices, §168A-7(a), (b).
Public transportation.
Discriminatory practices, §168A-8.
Purpose of act, §168A-2(a).
Qualified person with a disability.
Defined, §168A-3.
Reasonable accommodations.
Defined, §168A-3.
Duties as to, §168A-4.
Investigation of whether there are reasonable
accommodations that can be made,
§168A-4(b).
Request for.
Duties of qualified handicapped person,
§168A-4(a).
Retaliation.
Prohibited, §168A-10(a), (b).
Short title, §168A-1.
Title.
Short title, §168A-1.
Transportation.
Discrimination in public transportation,
§168A-8.
**Protection of abused, neglected or exploited
adult,** §§108A-99 to 108A-111.
See ABUSED, NEGLECTED OR EXPLOITED
DISABLED ADULTS.

DISABLED PERSONS —Cont'd
Public buildings.
Right of access to and use of public places, §168-2.
Public contracts.
Nonprofit work centers for the blind and severely
disabled.
Purchases from, §143-129.5.
**Public services provided by state or political
subdivisions.**
Aids or adaptations for persons with disabilities to
enjoy.
Required, §168A-7(a), (b).
Public transportation.
Elderly and disabled transportation assistance
program.
General provisions, §136-44.27.
**Purchases through department of
administration.**
Cooperation in promoting use of small contractors,
minority contractors, physically disabled
contractors and women contractors, §143-48.
Purposes of provisions, §168-1.
Railroads.
Right to use of public conveyances, §168-3.
Ramps.
Curb ramps or curb cuts.
Minimum requirements, §136-44.14.
Rape.
Indictments.
Essentials of bill.
Victim physically helpless, §15-144.1(c).
Retirement system for superior court judges.
Total and permanent disability, §§7A-55, 7A-56.
**Retirement system for teachers and state
employees.**
Disability retirement, §135-5.
Consolidated judicial retirement act, §§135-59,
135-60.
Rights.
Generally, §§168-1 to 168-10.
School buses.
Authority to expend funds for transportation of
students with disabilities, §115C-250.
Schools.
Employment of handicapped, §115C-330.
Medicaid for students with disabilities.
Collaboration of agencies to ensure maximum
funding, §108A-55.2.
Special education.
Education of children with disabilities.
Generally, §§115C-106.1 to 115C-112.1.
See SPECIAL EDUCATION.
Service animals, §§168-4.2 to 168-4.6.
Service of process.
Personal jurisdiction.
Manner of service to exercise, §1A-1 Rule 4(j).
Sexual offenses.
Indictments.
Essentials of bill.
Victim physically helpless, §15-144.2(c).
Signature facsimile.
Use by person with disability, §22A-1.
Special education.
Education of children with disabilities.
Generally, §§115C-106.1 to 115C-112.1.
See SPECIAL EDUCATION.
Sundays, holidays and special days.
National Employ the Physically Handicapped
Week.
Celebration, §143-283.3.

DISABLED PERSONS —Cont'd
Taxation on property.
Abstracts.
Information on tax relief for, §105-309(f).
Failure to give required information,
§105-309(g).
Unemployment compensation.
Disability benefits.
Eligibility conditions, §96-14.
Visually handicapped, §§111-4 to 111-47.
See BLIND AND VISUALLY IMPAIRED.
Voting.
Accessible voting places, §163-131.
Assistance to voters, §163-166.8.
Curbside voting, §163-166.9.
Satellite voting places for disabled voters,
§163-130.
Wage and hour act.
Minimum wage established by commissioner,
§95-25.3(c).

DISABLED SPORTSMAN PROGRAM, §113-296.
Motorized all-terrain vehicles.
Use by persons qualified under program,
§20-171.26.

DISABLED VEHICLES.
Abandoned and derelict motor vehicles
generally, §§20-137.6 to 20-137.14.
See ABANDONED MOTOR VEHICLES.
Unattended motor vehicles standing on public
highway or public vehicular area.
Stopping engine, setting brake, etc., §20-163.

DISABLED VETERAN PROPERTY TAX
HOMESTEAD EXCLUSION, §105-277.1C.

DISAFFIRMANCE OF MINOR'S CONTRACT.
Artistic and creative services contracts,
§48A-12(a) to (d).
Talent agency contracts, §48A-18.
Determining applicable period of time, §48A-3.

DISASTER RELIEF.
Client assistance debit card issued for disaster
assistance.
Sales and use tax exemption.
Purchases with, §105-164.13.
Disaster service volunteer leave, §§166A-30 to
166A-32.
Emergency management.
Assistance compact, §§166A-40 to 166A-53.
General provisions, §§166A-1 to 166A-18.
See EMERGENCY MANAGEMENT.
Hazardous materials emergency response,
§§166A-20 to 166A-28.
See HAZARDOUS MATERIALS EMERGENCY
RESPONSE.
Individual income tax.
Deductions to taxable income.
Amounts paid from disaster relief reserve fund,
§105-134.6(b).
Low-income housing tax credits.
Hurricane damage or hurricane disaster.
Qualified North Carolina low-income building,
§105-129.41(c).
Nuclear, biological or chemical agents.
Terrorist incident using, §§130A-475 to 130A-479.
See TERRORIST INCIDENT USING
NUCLEAR, BIOLOGICAL OR CHEMICAL
AGENTS.
Sales and use tax exemption.
Client assistance debit card issued for disaster
assistance.
Purchases with, §105-164.13.

DISASTER RELIEF —Cont'd
State of emergency.
Government powers and proclamations generally,
§§14-288.12 to 14-288.18.
See STATE OF EMERGENCY.

DISASTER RELIEF VEHICLES.
Motor vehicle license plates.
Permanent license plates for privately owned
vehicles dedicated to support of disaster
relief, §20-84(b).

DISASTER RESPONSE PLAN OF THE STATE
BAR, Bar Rules D.0301 to D.0303.

DISASTERS.
Accident and health insurance.
Prescription drugs.
Extra prescriptions during state of emergency
or disaster, §58-3-228.
Alcoholic beverage tax.
Exemptions, §105-113.81(a).
Architects.
Qualified immunity for volunteers during
emergency or disaster, §83A-13.1.
Department of public safety.
Powers and duties of secretary, §143B-602.
Emergencies.
See EMERGENCIES.
Emergency management.
See EMERGENCY MANAGEMENT.
Engineers.
Qualified immunity for volunteers during
emergency or disaster, §89C-19.1.
First responders vaccination program,
§130A-485(a) to (f).
Immunity of volunteers performing emergency
services, §§1-539.10, 1-539.11.
Insurance.
Incident affecting operations of department.
Stay of deadlines, §58-2-47.
Stay of proof of loss requirements, §58-2-46.
Militia.
Unorganized militia.
Ordered out for service, §127A-87.
Physicians and surgeons.
Waiver of provisions, §90-12.5.
Presidentially declared disaster.
Tax penalties not assessed, §105-249.2(b).
Price gouging during states of disaster.
Abnormal market disruption, §75-38(e), (f).
Deceptive trade practice, §75-38(a).
Determining whether price unreasonably
excessive.
Considerations, §75-38(a).
End of state of disaster, §75-38(c).
Public policy, §75-37.
Statement that seller not in violation.
Issuance by attorney general, §75-38(b).
Triggering event, defined, §75-38(d).
Property insurance.
Mediation of emergency or disaster claims,
§§58-44-70 to 58-44-120.
See PROPERTY INSURANCE.
Riots and civil disorders, §§14-288.1 to
14-288.20.
See RIOTS AND CIVIL DISORDERS.
Secretary of public safety.
Powers and duties of secretary, §143B-602.
State of disaster.
Declaration by governor or general assembly,
powers, §166A-6.

DISASTERS —Cont'd
State of disaster —Cont'd
Insurance.
Stay of proof of loss requirements, §58-2-46.
Price gouging during state of disaster, §§75-37, 75-38.
State of disaster assistance funds, §166A-6.01.
State of emergency.
Government powers and proclamations generally, §§14-288.12 to 14-288.18.
See STATE OF EMERGENCY.
Tax penalties during presidentially declared disaster.
Not assessed, §105-249.2(b).
Trespass during emergencies, §14-288.6.
Unemployment compensation.
Waiting period credit not required or waived, §96-13(c).
Waiting period for benefit year not required, §96-13(c1).
Volunteers, qualified immunity.
Architects, §83A-13.1.
Engineers, §89C-19.1.
Warnings regarding personal safety issued during disaster.
Civil liability for cost of rescue when willfully ignoring, §166A-15.1.

DISASTER SERVICE VOLUNTEER LEAVE, §§166A-30 to 166A-32.
Certified disaster service volunteer.
Defined, §166A-31.
Citation of provisions, §166A-30.
Disaster.
Defined, §166A-31.
Personnel called into service, §166A-17.
Persons eligible for leave, §166A-32.
Requests for leave, §166A-32.
Short title, §166A-30.
State agency.
Defined, §166A-31.
Workers' compensation, §166A-32.

DISBARMENT OF ATTORNEYS, §84-28(c).
Consent to disbarment, Bar Rule B.0117.
Disciplinary and disability rules of state bar generally, Bar Rules B.0101 to B.0217.
See ATTORNEYS AT LAW.
Employing as legal clerk or assistant, ProfCond Rule 5.5.
Forfeiture of license for felony conviction, §15A-1331(a).
Imposition of discipline, Bar Rule B.0123.
Obligations of disbarred or suspended attorneys, Bar Rule B.0124.
Reinstatement, Bar Rule B.0125.
Resignation while under investigation, order disbarring member, Bar Rule B.0117.

DISCARDED COMPUTER EQUIPMENT AND TELEVISION MANAGEMENT.
Recycling computers and televisions, §§130A-309.130 to 130A-309.141.
See RECYCLING.

DISCHARGE AND RELEASE.
Generally.
See RELEASES.
Mortgages and deeds of trust, §§45-36.2 to 45-42.1.
See MORTGAGES AND DEEDS OF TRUST.
Unclaimed property act, affirmative defense, §116B-58.

DISCHARGE FROM CIVIL ARREST, §1-419.
DISCHARGE OF ATTACHMENT.
Giving bond, §1-440.39.
DISCHARGE OF CLAIMS OR MONEY DEMANDS.
Advance payments to person claiming bodily injury, §1-540.3.
By agreement receipt of less sum is discharged, §1-540.
Motor vehicle accident settlements, §1-540.2.

DISCHARGE OF FIREARM FROM WITHIN ENCLOSURE, §14-34.9.

DISCHARGE OF INSOLVENT PRISONERS, §§23-18 to 23-45.
Arrests, §23-29.
Bail, §23-29.
Bonds, surety.
Release of insolvent upon giving bond, §23-40.
Surrender of principal, §23-41.
Continuance granted for cause, §§23-35, 23-45.
Creditor liable for jail fees, §23-42.
Executions, §23-29.
False swearing punished as perjury, §23-43.
Fraud.
Absent suggestion of fraud, discharge granted, §23-34.
Imprisonment for fraud, §23-37.
Suggestion of fraud, §23-28.
Superior or district court tries issue of fraud, §§23-29, 23-39.
Trial required before discharge, §23-36.
Who may suggest, §23-33.
Nonpayment of costs in criminal cases, §23-24.
Notice, §23-32.
Petition, §23-25.
Oath, §23-23.
Order of discharge, §23-38.
Persons taken in arrest and bail proceedings or in execution, §23-29.
Petition.
Before whom made, §23-25.
Contents, §23-31.
Notice, §23-25.
Proceeding on application, §23-27.
Verification, §23-31.
When filed, §23-30.
Proceeding on application, §23-27.
Provisional release, §23-30.1.
Release, §23-30.1.
Service of notice, §23-25.
Warrant issued for prisoner, §23-26.

DISCHARGE OF RECEIVERS.
Corporate receivers, debts provided for, §1-507.10.

DISCHARGES FROM MILITARY.
Concealed handgun permit eligibility.
Discharged other than honorably, §14-415.12(b).
Registration, §§47-109 to 47-114.
Book for record of discharges in office of register of deeds, §47-109.
Certified copies of registration, §47-113.
Expenses.
Payment of expenses incurred, §47-114.
Fees.
Lost certificates.
Certificate of lost discharge, §47-110.
Oath of applicant, §47-111.
Recordation without charge, §47-110.

DISCHARGES FROM MILITARY —Cont'd
Registration —Cont'd
Forgery, §47-112.
Operation, §47-112.
Register of deeds.
Inquiry by register, §47-111.
Specifications, §47-109.
Removal or review of discharge paper.
Restricting access to military discharge
documents, §47-113.2.
Restricting access to military discharge
documents.
Construction of terms, §47-113.2(l).
Copies, availability of, §47-113.2(d), (h).
Cost of compliance with provision, §47-113.2(j).
Filing office responsibility, §47-113.2(o).
Documents on file for over 50 years, §47-113.2(m).
Fees, charging, restriction, §47-113.2(n).
Filing fees authorized, §47-113.2(i).
Filing requirements, §47-113.2(c).
Good faith immunity, §47-113.2(k).
Immunity of recording officials.
Good faith compliance with provisions,
§47-113.2(p).
Indexing and document images, §47-113.2(f).
Parties authorized access, §47-113.2(b).
Preservation of prior records, §47-113.2(g).
Public records with restricted access, §47-113.2(a).
Refusal of filing officer to accept, §47-113.2(d).
Register of deeds defined, §47-113.2(q).
Rulemaking authority, §47-113.2(e).

DISCHARGES OF OIL OR HAZARDOUS
SUBSTANCES.
Dry-cleaning solvent cleanup, §§143-215.104A to
143-215.104U.
See DRY-CLEANING SOLVENT CLEANUP.
Generally, §§143-215.83 to 143-215.94.
See OIL OR HAZARDOUS SUBSTANCES
DISCHARGES.
Offshore oil and gas activities, §§143-215.94AA
to 143-215.94JJ.
See OFFSHORE OIL AND GAS ACTIVITIES.
Underground petroleum storage tanks.
Leak cleanup, §§143-215.94A to 143-215.94Y.
See UNDERGROUND PETROLEUM
STORAGE TANKS.
Operator training, §§143-215.94NN to
143-215.94UU.
See UNDERGROUND PETROLEUM
STORAGE TANKS.

DISCHARGING WEAPON INTO OCCUPIED
PROPERTY OR CONVEYANCE WHILE IN
OPERATION, §14-34.1.

DISCIPLINE OF ATTORNEYS.
Disciplinary rules of state bar generally, Bar
Rules B.0101 to B.0217.
See ATTORNEYS AT LAW.

DISCIPLINE OF JUDGES OR JUSTICES.
Judicial standards commission, §§7A-374.1 to
7A-378, JudStdsComm Rules 1 to 26.
See JUDICIAL STANDARDS COMMISSION.

DISCIPLINE OF STUDENTS.
Generally, §§115C-390.1 to 115C-392.
See SCHOOLS AND EDUCATION.

DISCLAIMER.
Intestate succession renunciation, §§31B-1 to
31B-7.
See INTESTATE SUCCESSION.

DISCLAIMER —Cont'd
Seeds.
Use of disclaimer as defense in prosecution or
proceedings, §106-277.11.
Torrens system registration.
Deemed admission of allegations, §43-9.
Will renunciation, §§31B-1 to 31B-7.
See WILLS.

DISCLOSURES.
Art dealers.
Sale of prints, §25C-14.
Confidential information.
See CONFIDENTIALITY OF INFORMATION.
Credit cards sales, requirements, §§24-11.1,
24-11.2.
Loan brokers, §66-107.
Membership camping operator, §66-238.
Motor vehicle records.
Personal information, §20-43.1.
Motor vehicle transfers.
Mileage, §20-347.
Notice generally.
See NOTICE.
Residential real property sales, §§47E-1 to
47E-10.
See RESIDENTIAL PROPERTY DISCLOSURE
ACT.

DISCONTINUANCE.
Generally.
See DISMISSAL, DISCONTINUANCE AND
NONSUIT.

DISCOUNT BUYING CLUBS.
Bonds, surety, §66-135(a).
Actions on bond, §66-135(c).
Violation of requirement.
Felony, §66-135(d).
Contracts.
Breach.
Action against bond, §66-135(c).
Cancellation.
Business days.
Defined, §66-133(e).
Customer's right to cancel, §66-133(a).
Statement of right to be included in contract,
§66-132(a).
Notice, §66-133(b) to (d).
When cancellation occurs, §66-133(b).
Contents, §66-132(a).
Waiver of certain formalities.
Requirements for waiver, §66-132(b).
Formalities.
Waiver of certain formalities.
Requirements for waiver, §66-132(b).
Written contracts required, §66-132(a).
Damages.
Breach of contract.
Action against bond, §66-135(c).
Violations of provisions.
Action against bond, §66-135(c).
Action for damages, §66-136(a).
Defined, §66-131.
Felonies.
Bond and trust account requirements.
Violations, §66-135(d).
Mail.
Cancellation of contract by customer.
Notice of cancellation, §66-133(c).
Notice.
Cancellation of contract by customer, §66-133(b)
to (d).

DISCOUNT BUYING CLUBS —Cont'd
Prohibited acts, §66-134.
Sales and use tax, §66-137.
Taxation, §66-137.
Trust account.
Required, §66-135(b).
Exceptions, §66-135(b).
Violation of requirement.
Felony, §66-135(d).
Violations of provisions.
Bond and trust account requirements.
Felonies, §66-135(d).
Damages.
Action against bond, §66-135(c).
Action for damages, §66-136(a).
Prohibited acts, §66-134.
Remedies, §66-136(a), (b).
Additional nature of remedies, §66-136(c).
Unfair acts and practices.
Violations to constitute, §66-136(b).

DISCOUNT FEES.
Loans secured by real property, §24-10(a).
Revolving credit charges, §24-11(a2).
Structured settlement transfers, §1-543.12.

DISCOUNT POINTS.
**Home loan secured by first mortgage or first
deed of trust,** §24-1.1A(c).

DISCOUNTS.
Gasoline tax.
Suppliers filing return, §105-449.97.
Property taxes.
Payment prior to due date, §105-360(c).

DISCOVERED PROPERTY.
Property taxes, listing assessing and taxing,
§105-312.

**DISCOVERING ASSETS OF JUDGMENT
DEBTOR.**
Supplemental proceedings, §§1-352 to 1-368.
See EXECUTIONS.

DISCOVERY.
Administrative procedure.
Hearings, §150B-39(b).
Subpoenas.
Witnesses.
Fees, §150B-39(c).
Admissions.
See ADMISSIONS.
Adult care homes.
Quality assurance, medical, or peer review
committee information, immunity from
discovery, §131D-21.2(b).
Amendment of responses, §1A-1 Rule 26(e).
Arbitration.
Grounds for permitting, §1-569.17(c).
Issuance of process, §1-569.17(d).
Attorney disciplinary proceedings, Bar Rule
B.0114.
Attorneys at law.
Frivolous discovery, ProfCond Rule 3.4.
Bank compliance review documents.
Undiscoverable matter, §53-99.1(b).
Bills of lading.
Actions by or against common or connecting
carriers.
Bills of lading as evidence, §8-41.
**Child abuse, neglect or dependency
proceedings,** §7B-700.

DISCOVERY —Cont'd
Child fatality prevention system.
Confidential information and records created by
local teams, prohibition, §7B-1413(c).
Civil investigative demand.
False claims act.
Express demand for product of discovery,
§1-614(d).
Conference, §1A-1 Rule 26(f).
Failure to participate in framing of discovery
plan, §1A-1 Rule 37(g).
Medical malpractice, §1A-1 Rule 26(f1).
Contempt.
Criminal procedure.
Failure to comply with orders, §15A-910(a).
Considerations of court before granting
sanctions, §15A-910(b).
Court findings to justify sanctions,
§15A-910(d).
Presumption of good faith of prosecutors,
§15A-910(c).
Order compelling discovery.
Failure to comply, §1A-1 Rule 37(b).
Criminal procedure.
Applicability of provisions, §15A-901.
Contempt.
Failure to comply with orders, §15A-910(a).
Considerations of court before granting
sanctions, §15A-910(b).
Court findings to justify sanctions,
§15A-910(d).
Presumption of good faith of prosecutors,
§15A-910(c).
Continuing duty to disclose, §15A-907.
Defendant.
Case files and expert witness information.
Disclosure by state, §15A-903(a).
Disclosure of information by defendant.
Documents, §15A-905(a).
Exemptions, §15A-906.
Reports of examinations and tests,
§15A-905(b).
Tangible objects, §15A-905(a).
Law enforcement agency disclosures to state,
§15A-903(c).
Notice to state of defenses and witnesses,
§15A-905(c), (d).
Omission or misrepresentation of evidence,
criminal offense, §15A-903(d).
Statements of co-defendants.
Disclosure by state, §15A-903(b).
DNA records.
Requests to access, §15A-266.12(d).
Documents.
Disclosure by defendant, §15A-905(a).
Disclosure by state.
Certain information not subject to disclosure,
§15A-904(a).
Duty to disclose.
Continuing duty, §15A-907.
Failure to comply with orders.
Sanctions, §15A-910(a).
Considerations of court before granting,
§15A-910(b).
Court findings to justify sanctions,
§15A-910(d).
Presumption of good faith of prosecutors,
§15A-910(c).
Manner of discovery.
Orders must specify, §15A-909.

DISCOVERY —Cont'd
Criminal procedure —Cont'd
Motion for discovery, §15A-902(a), (f).
Hearing before superior court judge,
§15A-902(c).
Physical and mental examinations.
Disclosure of results by defendant, §15A-905.
Place of discovery.
Orders must specify, §15A-909.
Procedure, §15A-902.
Protective orders, §15A-908(a).
Supporting affidavits or statements.
Submission to court for in camera inspection,
§15A-908(b).
Reports of examinations and tests.
Disclosure by defendant, §15A-905(b).
State of North Carolina.
Defendant's defenses and witnesses,
§15A-905(c), (d).
Disclosure of evidence by state.
Case files and expert witness information,
§15A-903(a).
Confidential informant's identity,
§15A-904(a1).
Crime Stoppers, persons providing
information to, §15A-904(a3).
Defendant's defenses and witnesses,
§15A-905(c), (d).
Exemptions, §15A-904(a), (b), (c).
Omission or misrepresentation of evidence,
criminal offense, §15A-903(d).
Personal identifying information of witness,
§15A-904(a2).
Statement of co-defendant, §15A-903(b).
Victim impact statements, §15A-904(a4).
Law enforcement agency disclosures to state,
§15A-903(c).
Voluntary discovery.
Exemptions from required disclosure of
evidence not to preclude voluntary
disclosures or waiver of protections,
§15A-904(b).
Request by defendant for voluntary discovery
from state, §15A-902(d).
Request by state for voluntary discovery from
defendant, §15A-902(e).
Tangible objects.
Disclosure by defendant, §15A-905(a).
Time of discovery.
Orders must specify, §15A-909.
Voluntary compliance with discovery request.
Effect, §15A-902(b).
Request for or written agreement required,
§15A-902(a).
Scope of disclosure, §15A-903(b).
State of North Carolina.
Request for voluntary discovery from
defendant, §15A-902(e).
Request for voluntary discovery from state,
§15A-902(d).
Delinquent and undisciplined juvenile actions.
Continuing duty to disclose, §7B-2303.
Denying, restricting or deferring discovery,
§7B-2302(a).
Submission of supporting affidavits or
statements for court in camera inspection,
§7B-2302(b).
Disclosure of evidence by juvenile.
Inspection and copying of books, papers,
documents, etc., §7B-2301(b).

DISCOVERY —Cont'd
Delinquent and undisciplined juvenile actions
—Cont'd
Disclosure of evidence by juvenile —Cont'd
Names of persons to be called as witnesses,
§7B-2301(a).
Physical or mental examination or test results,
§7B-2301(c).
Tests, measurements or experiments made in
connection with case, §7B-2301(c).
Disclosure of evidence by petitioner.
Books, papers, documents, etc., §7B-2300(c).
Names of persons to be called as witness,
§7B-2300(b).
Oral statements of juvenile, §7B-2300(a).
Physical or mental examination or test results,
§7B-2300(d).
Tests, measurements or experiments made in
connection with case, §7B-2300(d).
Voluntary disclosures permitted, §7B-2300(f).
Work product of petitioner, law enforcement
officers or other persons.
Production of reports, memoranda or other
internal documents in connection with
investigation not required to be disclosed,
§7B-2300(e).
Written or recorded statements of juvenile,
§7B-2300(b).
Protective orders, §7B-2302.
Depositions.
See DEPOSITIONS.
Discipline of attorneys, Bar Rule B.0114.
District courts, SuperCt Rule 8.
Civil actions.
Fee on filing verified petition, §7A-305.1.
Divorce.
Distribution by court of marital and divisible
property.
Equitable distribution.
Discovery and scheduling conference,
§50-21(d).
Procedures in actions, §50-21(a).
Sanctions for delay, §50-21(e).
DNA records.
Requests to access in criminal proceeding,
§15A-266.12(d).
Electronically stored information.
Admissions, failure to admit, expenses, §1A-1
Rule 37(c).
Defined, scope of discovery, §1A-1 Rule 26(b).
Failure to make, §1A-1 Rule 37.
Lost information, §1A-1 Rule 37(b1).
Order compelling discovery.
Failure to comply with order, §1A-1 Rule 37(b).
Motion for, §1A-1 Rule 37(a).
Production, §1A-1 Rule 34.
Scope of discovery, §1A-1 Rule 26(b).
**Entry on land for inspection and other
purposes,** §§1A-1 Rule 26(a), 1A-1 Rule 34.
Executions.
Assets of judgment debtor.
Generally, §1-352.2.
Interrogatories, §1-352.1.
Expedited evictions.
Authority to conduct discovery generally,
§42-70(a).
Injunction against illegal activity pending
completion of discovery, §42-70(e).
Interrogatories.
Time for response, §42-70(d).

DISCOVERY —Cont'd
Expedited evictions —Cont'd
Request for admissions.
Time for response, §42-70(d).
Request for production of documents.
Time for response, §42-70(d).
Time for initiation by defendant, §42-70(b).
Time for initiation by plaintiff, §42-70(c).
Experts.
Trial preparation, scope of discovery, §1A-1 Rule 26(b).
False claims act.
Civil investigative demand.
Express demand for product of discovery, §1-614(d).
Frequency or extent of use of discovery methods.
Limitation by court, §1A-1 Rule 26(b).
Frivolous discovery.
Attorneys at law, ProfCond Rule 3.4.
General assembly.
Contesting a seat, §120-10.6.
Committee.
Compelling discovery, §120-10.8(c).
Health care liability.
Separate discovery on claims, §90-21.53.
Insurance agreements.
Scope of discovery, §1A-1 Rule 26(b).
International commercial arbitration and conciliation.
Assistance of superior court in obtaining, request, §1-567.57(a).
Tribunal conducting proceeding, §1-567.49(b).
Interrogatories.
See INTERROGATORIES.
Interstate depositions and discovery, §§1F-1 to 1F-7.
Application and construction of statutory provisions, §1F-7.
Applications to court for relief, §1F-6.
Definitions, §1F-2.
Disputes, appropriate court to resolve, §1F-6.
Rules of civil procedure applicable, §1F-5.
Short title of act, §1F-1.
Subpoenas.
Contents required, §1F-3(c).
Duties of clerk on receipt of request, §1F-3(b).
Request for issuance, §1F-3(a).
Service, §1F-4.
Interstate family support.
Tribunal requesting assistance with, §52C-3-317.
Judicial standards commission.
Disclosure prior to disciplinary hearing, JudStdsComm Rule 15.
Managed care entities, claims involving.
Separate discovery and trial, §1A-1 Rule 42(b).
Mediated settlement conferences in superior court civil actions.
Statements made and conduct occurring.
Not subject to discovery, exceptions, §7A-38.1(l).
Mediated settlement conferences or other settlement procedures in district court.
Actions involving equitable distribution, alimony or support.
Statements made or conduct during mediation.
Prohibition, exceptions, §7A-38.4A(j).
Mediation ordered by superior court clerks.
Statements and conduct during mediation.
Prohibition, exceptions, §7A-38.3B(g).
Medical board proceedings.
Provision of information to subject of proceedings, §90-16(e).

DISCOVERY —Cont'd
Medical malpractice.
Arbitration of negligent health claims, §90-21.63(c), (d).
Discovery conference, §1A-1 Rule 26(f1).
Meeting, §1A-1 Rule 26(f).
Methods of discovery, §1A-1 Rule 26(a).
Motions.
Child abuse, neglect or dependency proceedings, §7B-700(c).
Order compelling discovery.
Motion for, §1A-1 Rule 37(a).
Nonresidents.
Subpoenas.
Discovery from persons residing outside state, §1A-1 Rule 45(f).
Notice.
Discovery conference, service, §1A-1 Rule 26(f).
Objections.
Production of documents, electronically stored information and things, §1A-1 Rule 34(b1).
Request for entry on land for inspection, §1A-1 Rule 34(b1).
Order compelling discovery.
Failure to comply with order.
Sanctions, §1A-1 Rule 37(b).
Motion for, §1A-1 Rule 37(a).
Physical and mental examination of persons, §§1A-1 Rule 26(a), 1A-1 Rule 35.
Plan, §1A-1 Rule 26(f).
Failure to participate in framing of discovery plan, §1A-1 Rule 37(g).
Production of documents, electronically stored information and things, §§1A-1 Rule 26(a), 1A-1 Rule 34.
Protective orders, §1A-1 Rule 26(c).
Child abuse, neglect or dependency proceedings, §7B-700(d).
Criminal procedure, §15A-908.
Delinquent and undisciplined juvenile actions, §7B-2302.
Trade secrets, actions for misappropriation, §66-156.
Psychotherapy patient/client sexual exploitation act.
Clients conduct.
Specific information or examples, §90-21.44(b).
Sexual history of client, §90-21.44(a).
Response.
Production of documents, electronically stored information and things, §1A-1 Rule 34(b1).
Request for entry on land for inspection, §1A-1 Rule 34(b1).
Savings and loan associations.
Compliance review documents, §54B-63.1(b).
Scope of discovery, §1A-1 Rule 26(b).
Sealing deposition.
Protective orders, §1A-1 Rule 26(c).
Sequence and timing of discovery, §1A-1 Rule 26(d).
Service of process.
Notice of motion for discovery conference, §1A-1 Rule 26(f).
Papers relating to discovery, §1A-1 Rule 5(a).
Subpoenas for production of documentary evidence, §8-61.
Signing of discovery requests, responses and objections, §1A-1 Rule 26(g).
Stipulations regarding discovery procedure, §1A-1 Rule 29.

DISCOVERY —Cont'd
Superior courts, SuperCt Rule 8.
Civil actions.
Fee on filing verified petition, §7A-305.1.
Criminal procedure, §§15A-901 to 15A-910. See
within this heading, "Criminal procedure."
Supplementation of responses, §1A-1 Rule 26(e).
Trade secrets.
Protective orders, §1A-1 Rule 26(c).
Trial preparation.
Scope of discovery, §1A-1 Rule 26(b).
University of North Carolina.
Mediation of personnel matters.
Not subject to discovery, §116-3.3(a).
Wage and hour act.
Files and other records relating to investigations
and enforcement proceedings, §95-25.20.
Workers' compensation.
Contested cases, ICWorkComp Rules 605, 606.
Industrial commission.
Power to limit discovery, §97-80(f).
Work product.
Health care facility certificate of public advantage.
Actions on issuing or remaining in effect.
Department's or attorney general's work
product, §131E-192.10(d).
Trial preparation, scope of discovery, §1A-1 Rule
26(b).

DISCOVERY CONFERENCE, §1A-1 Rule 26(f).
Failure to participate, §1A-1 Rule 37(g).
Medical malpractice, §1A-1 Rule 26(f1).

DISCOVERY MEETING, §1A-1 Rule 26(f).

**DISCOVERY OF INJURY, LOSS, DEFECT OR
DAMAGE.**
Malpractice action.
Time limitation for commencing action, §1-15(c).

**DISCOVERY OF JUDGMENT DEBTOR
ASSETS.**
Supplemental proceedings generally, §§1-352 to
1-368.
See SUPPLEMENTAL PROCEEDINGS.

DISCOVERY PLAN, §1A-1 Rule 26(f).
**Failure to participate in framing of discovery
plan,** §1A-1 Rule 37(g).

**DISCRETIONARY REVIEW ON
CERTIFICATION BY SUPREME COURT,**
§7A-15, AppProc 15.

DISCRIMINATION.
Actions.
Discrimination in business.
Enforcement of provisions, §75B-4.
Agricultural marketing authority.
Prohibition on discrimination, §106-531.
Alcoholic beverages.
Refusal to sell not to be discriminatory,
§18B-305(c).
Tribal alcoholic beverage control.
Discrimination against non-Indians, prohibition,
§18B-112(g).
Alternative dispute resolution.
Persons with disabilities.
Public service discrimination cases, §168A-10.1.
Attorney general.
Discrimination in business.
Enforcement of provisions.
Actions, §75B-4.

DISCRIMINATION —Cont'd
Burial without regard to race or color,
§65-72(a).
Violations of provisions.
Misdemeanors, §65-72(b).
Business.
Actions.
Enforcement of provisions, §75B-4.
Attorney general.
Enforcement of provisions.
Actions, §75B-4.
Construction and interpretation.
Provisions not exclusive, §75B-7.
Contracts.
Prohibited contracts, §75B-2.
Void contracts, §75B-6.
Cumulative nature of remedies, §75B-5.
Damages.
Actions for.
Persons injured by violations, §75B-4.
Definitions, §75B-1.
Enforcement of provisions, §75B-4.
Cumulative nature of remedies, §75B-5.
Injunctions.
Enforcement of provisions, §75B-4.
Prohibited acts, §75B-2.
Actions not prohibited, §75B-3.
Cable television.
State franchising of cable television service.
Discrimination against service area residents,
§66-356(a).
Capital punishment.
Race as basis of judgment, §§15A-2010 to
15A-2012.
Carriers.
Connecting lines.
Discrimination between connecting lines
prohibited, §62-210.
Cemeteries.
Burial without regard to race or color, §65-72(a).
Violations of provisions.
Misdemeanors, §65-72(b).
Community colleges.
Nondiscrimination policy, §115D-77.
Constitution of North Carolina.
Jury service, NC Const Art I §26.
Constitution of the United States, US Const
Amds 14, 15.
Consumer finance act.
Prohibited acts, §53-180(d).
Contracts.
Discrimination in business.
Prohibited contracts, §75B-2.
Void contracts, §75B-6.
Damages.
Discrimination in business.
Actions by persons injured by violations,
§75B-4.
Death penalty.
Race as basis of judgment, §§15A-2010 to
15A-2012.
Definitions.
Discrimination in business, §75B-1.
Disabled persons.
Protection act.
General provisions, §§168A-1 to 168A-12.
See DISABLED PERSONS.
Elections.
Voting rights act of 1965.
Submission of charges to United States attorney
general, §§120-30.9A to 120-30.9I.
See ELECTIONS.

DISCRIMINATION —Cont'd
Electric membership corporations.
Prohibition on discrimination, §117-16.1.
Emergency management.
Prohibited, §166A-12.
Employment.
Equal employment practices, §§143-422.1 to
143-422.3.
Citation of article, §143-422.1.
Human relations council.
Charges of discrimination.
Receipt, §143-422.3.
Conciliations, §143-422.3.
Investigations, §143-422.3.
Legislative declaration, §143-422.2.
Purpose of article, §143-422.2.
Short title, §143-422.1.
Lawful use of lawful products during nonworking
hours, §95-28.2.
Personnel system.
Assistance in obtaining state employment,
§§126-16 to 126-19.
Retaliatory employment discrimination, §§95-240
to 95-245.
Civil action by employees, §95-243(a).
Civil action filed by commissioner or employee,
§95-242(b).
Complaint, §95-242(a).
Conciliation, §95-242(a), (b).
Confidential information, §95-242(d), (e).
Informal procedures, §95-242(b).
Definitions, §95-240.
Discrimination prohibited, §95-241(a).
Effect of article on other rights, §95-244.
Exception to violation of article, §95-241(b).
Investigation, §95-242(a).
Reopening of investigation, §95-242(b1).
Jury trial in civil actions, §95-243(d).
Other rights afforded employee.
Effect of article on, §95-244.
Relief in civil actions, §95-243(c).
Reopening of investigation, §95-242(b1).
Required for employee to bring actions,
§95-243(e).
Right-to-sue letter, §95-242(a) to (c).
Subpoenas, §95-242(f).
Time for commencing civil actions, §95-243(b).
Use of leave for parent involvement in schools,
§95-28.3(b), (c).
Venue of civil action by employees, §95-243(a).
Sickle cell trait or hemoglobin C trait.
Discrimination against persons possessing,
§95-28.1.
Equal employment practices, §§143-422.1 to
143-422.3.
Ethnic intimidation.
Assaulting person or damaging or defacing
property, §14-401.14(a).
Teaching techniques, §14-401.14(b).
Fair housing, §§41A-1 to 41A-10.
See FAIR HOUSING.
Felonies.
Offenses committed because of victim's race, etc.,
§14-3(c).
Firefighters' relief fund.
No discrimination on account of race, §58-84-55.
Genetic testing, information or counseling.
Employment discrimination.
Based on person's genetic information,
§95-28.1A(a).
Genetic characteristic defined, §95-28.1A(b).

DISCRIMINATION —Cont'd
Genetic testing, information or counseling
—Cont'd
Employment discrimination —Cont'd
Genetic information defined, §95-28.1A(b).
Genetic test defined, §95-28.1A(b).
Person requesting genetic test or counseling,
§95-28.1A(a).
Health maintenance organizations.
Mentally ill and chemically dependent.
Applicability of section, §58-67-75(d).
Coverage, §58-67-75(b1), (c).
Prohibited acts, §58-67-75(b).
Sex changes.
Coverage for treatment or studies not
required, §58-67-75(e).
Prohibited acts, §58-67-65(f).
**Hospital, medical and dental service
corporations.**
Mentally ill and chemically dependent.
Applicability of section, §58-65-90(d).
Coverage, §58-65-90(b1), (c).
Definitions, §58-65-90(a).
Prohibited acts, §58-65-90(b).
Exceptions, §58-65-90(c).
Sex change.
Coverage for treatment or studies not
required, §58-65-90(e).
Prohibited practices, §58-65-85.
Housing.
Disabled persons.
Right to housing, §168-9.
Fair housing, §§41A-1 to 41A-10.
See FAIR HOUSING.
Human relations council, §§143-422.1 to
143-422.3.
Injunctions.
Discrimination in business.
Enforcement of provisions, §75B-4.
Insurance.
Accident and health insurance.
Coverage of bones and joints, §58-3-121(a) to (c).
Group accident and health insurance.
Mentally ill and chemically dependent.
Applicability, §58-51-55(d).
Coverage, §58-51-55(b1), (c).
Definitions, §58-51-55(a).
Prohibited acts, §58-51-55(b), (c).
Sex changes, coverage of treatment or
studies not required, §58-51-55(e).
Bones, coverage of, §58-3-121(a) to (c).
Disabled persons.
Prohibited, §168-10.
Employer discrimination against lawful use of
lawful products during nonworking hours.
Health, disability or life insurance policies
distinguishing between employees,
§95-28.2(b).
Joints, coverage of, §58-3-121(a) to (c).
Life insurance.
Prohibited acts, §58-58-35.
Motor vehicles.
Prohibited practices, §58-3-25.
Race, color or national or ethnic origin.
Prohibited acts, §58-3-25(c).
Rates not to be unfairly discriminatory,
§58-40-20(a), (e).
Method of rate making, §58-36-10.
Unfair trade practices.
Prohibited acts, §58-63-15.

DISCRIMINATION —Cont'd

Insurance companies.

Between individuals of same class, prohibition, §58-3-120(b).

In favor of any person, prohibition, §58-3-120(a).

Lawful use of lawful products by employees during nonworking hours, §95-28.2.

Military personnel, discrimination against.

Employer discrimination prohibited, §127B-14.

Misdemeanors, §127B-15.

Penalties.

Violations of article, §127B-15.

Private discrimination prohibited, §127B-11.

Public discrimination prohibited, §127B-12.

Purpose of article, §127B-10.

Refusing entrance prohibited, §127B-13.

Violation of article.

Penalties, §127B-15.

Misdemeanors.

Offenses committed because of victim's race, etc., §14-3(c).

Motor carriers.

Penalty, §62-325(a).

Motor vehicle manufacturers.

Discriminating among dealers, §20-305.6.

Notaries.

Fees charged, §10B-30(b).

Nursing home administrators.

Grounds for revocation or suspension of license, §90-285.1.

Occupational safety and health.

Prohibited, §95-151.

Personnel system.

Disabled persons.

Prohibited discrimination against, §128-15.3.

Equal employment opportunity.

Assistance in obtaining state employment, §§126-16 to 126-19.

Compensation for assisting person barred, §126-18.

Equal employment opportunity institute.

Training, §126-16.1.

Local political subdivisions, §126-16.

Retaliation against protecting employees, §126-17.

Newly appointed managers and supervisors.

Training, §126-16.1.

State departments and agencies, §126-16.

Retaliation against protecting employees, §126-17.

Training, §126-16.1.

Grounds for filing contested case, §126-34.1(a).

Denial of equal opportunity, §126-34.1(b).

Persons with disabilities.

Alternative dispute resolutions.

Public service discrimination cases, §168A-10.1.

Pregnant or parenting students.

Policies prohibiting discrimination against, §115C-375.5(b).

Provider sponsored organizations.

Prohibited acts, §131E-290(c).

Public schools.

Assignment on certain basis prohibited, §115C-367.

Pregnant or parenting students.

Policies prohibiting discrimination against, §115C-375.5(b).

Public utilities.

Prohibited, §62-140(a), (c).

Rules and regulations to prevent, §62-140(b).

DISCRIMINATION —Cont'd

Retaliatory employment discrimination, §§95-240 to 95-245.

Whistleblower protection.

Retaliatory employment discrimination, §§95-240 to 95-245.

Wine distribution agreements.

Inducement, coercion or discrimination prohibited, §18B-1202.

Intent of article to prohibit unlawful discrimination, §18B-1215.

Notice of intent to terminate, §18B-1205(a).

Wholesalers, §§18B-1203(b), 18B-1211.

DISCS.

Compact discs.

Record and tape piracy generally.

See RECORD AND TAPE PIRACY.

DISEASES.

Adult care homes.

Guidelines for reporting suspected communicable disease outbreaks, §131D-4.4B.

Infection prevention, §131D-4.4A.

Medication aides.

Infection control, in-service training, §131D-4.5B.

Supervisors.

Infection control training, §131D-4.5C.

AIDS.

See AIDS AND HIV.

Bee and honey industry.

Authority of commissioner to protect industry from diseases, §106-640.

Giving false information to commissioner, §106-641.

Defined, §106-635.

Minimum standards for disease tolerance levels, §106-638.

Moveable frame hives, §106-641.

Regulations for control and prevention, §106-639.

Bioterrorism.

Nuclear, biological or chemical agents.

Terrorist incident using, §§130A-475 to 130A-479.

See TERRORIST INCIDENT USING NUCLEAR, BIOLOGICAL OR CHEMICAL AGENTS.

Blood banks.

Selection of donors.

Risk of diseased transmission to be minimized, §90-220.13.

Cancer.

See CANCER.

Child care operators.

Communicable diseases.

Reports, §130A-136.

Chiropractors.

Control of contagious and infectious diseases.

Chiropractors subject to state and municipal regulations as to, §90-157.

Communicable diseases generally, §§130A-134 to 130A-148.

See COMMUNICABLE DISEASES.

Community third party or pooled trusts.

Persons with severe chronic disabilities, §§36D-1 to 36D-12.

See COMMUNITY THIRD PARTY OR POOLED TRUSTS.

Conveyances.

Disclosure of death or illness of previous occupant, §39-50.

DISEASES —Cont'd
Dead bodies.
Contagious diseases.
Handling and transportation of bodies,
§130A-395(a) to (c).
Health emergency.
Nuclear, biological or chemical agents.
Terrorist incident using, §§130A-475 to
130A-479.
See TERRORIST INCIDENT USING
NUCLEAR, BIOLOGICAL OR
CHEMICAL AGENTS.
Hearing aid dealers and fitters.
Freedom from contagious or infectious diseases.
Prerequisite to issuance of license, §93D-5(a).
Heart disease and stroke.
Justus-Warren heart disease and stroke
prevention task force, §143B-216.60.
HIV.
See AIDS AND HIV.
Immunization.
Childhood vaccine-related injury compensation,
§§130A-422 to 130A-434.
See CHILDHOOD VACCINE-RELATED
INJURY COMPENSATION.
Generally, §§130A-152 to 130A-158.
See IMMUNIZATION.
Kidneys.
Chronic renal disease program, §130A-220(a), (b).
Livestock.
Bang's disease, §§106-388 to 106-398.
See BRUCELLOSIS.
Brucellosis, §§106-388 to 106-398.
See BRUCELLOSIS.
Cattle tick, §§106-351 to 106-363.
See CATTLE TICK.
Compensation for killing diseased animals,
§§106-323 to 106-335.
See LIVESTOCK DISEASES.
Control of livestock diseases generally, §§106-400
to 106-405.
See LIVESTOCK DISEASES.
Equine infectious anemia, §§106-405.15 to
106-405.20.
Generally, §§106-304 to 106-307.7.
See LIVESTOCK DISEASES.
Hog cholera, §§106-310 to 106-322.3.
See HOG CHOLERA.
Tuberculosis, §§106-336 to 106-350.
See TUBERCULOSIS IN LIVESTOCK.
Meat and meat products.
Regulation, §14-342.
Rendering operations.
Disposal of diseased animals, §106-168.10.
**Meningococcal disease vaccination
information.**
Universities and colleges.
Providing students information, §116-260.
Occupational diseases generally.
Workers' compensation.
See WORKERS' COMPENSATION.
Occupational diseases, reportable.
Avoidance of duplication of reports, §130A-455.
Department of labor.
Reports to, §130A-460.
Immunity of persons who report, §130A-459.
Laboratories, §130A-458.
Medical facilities, §130A-457.
Physicians and surgeons, §130A-456.
Rules and regulations, §130A-455.

DISEASES —Cont'd
Physicians and surgeons.
Reports of diseases, §130A-135.
Quarantine.
Livestock and poultry.
See QUARANTINE.
Rabies, §§130A-184 to 130A-201.
See RABIES.
Schools.
Communicable diseases.
Report by school principals, §130A-136.
Sexually transmitted diseases.
AIDS.
See AIDS AND HIV.
General provisions.
See VENEREAL DISEASES.
Schools.
Prevention, instruction, health education,
§115C-81(e1).
Testing defendant accused of offense involving
sexual intercourse.
Victim's request, §15A-615(a).
Defendant in custody of division of adult
correction, §15A-615(c).
Order requiring, §15A-615(b).
Sickle cell trait.
Accident and health insurance.
Policies to be issued to persons possessing sickle
cell trait or hemoglobin C trait, §58-51-45.
Council, §§130A-131 to 130A-131.2.
Employers.
Discrimination against persons possessing
sickle cell trait, §95-28.1.
Hospital, medical and dental service corporations.
Contracts to cover persons possessing sickle cell
trait, §58-65-70.
Life insurance.
Policies not to be denied to person possessing
sickle cell trait or hemoglobin C trait,
§58-58-25.
Local health departments.
Duties, §130A-130.
Sickle cell program, §130A-129.
Terrorism.
Nuclear, biological or chemical agents.
Terrorist incident using, §§130A-475 to
130A-479.
See TERRORIST INCIDENT USING
NUCLEAR, BIOLOGICAL OR
CHEMICAL AGENTS.
Tuberculosis.
See TUBERCULOSIS.
Venereal diseases.
See VENEREAL DISEASES.
Wildlife resources commission.
Emergency powers regarding wildlife diseases.
Rules governing, §113-306(f).

DISGUISES.
**Entry, etc., upon premises of another while
wearing disguises,** §14-12.9.
Exemptions from provisions of article,
§14-12.11.
**Exhibit with intention of intimidating, etc.,
another.**
Placing exhibit while wearing disguise, §14-12.14.
Holding meetings while wearing disguise,
§14-12.10.
Use of disguises for illegal purposes, §14-12.4.
Wearing of masks, hoods, etc., on public ways,
§14-12.7.

DISHWASHING DETERGENT.
Containing phosphorus.
Manufacture, storage or sale.
Prohibition, exceptions, penalties, §143-214.4(a) to (g).

DISINTERMENT, §130A-390(a) to (c).
Permits.
Disinterment and reinterment, §130A-113(c).
Veterans.
Disinterment of, §65-43.4(a), (b).

DISMEMBERING HUMAN REMAINS.
Concealing evidence of death, §14-401.22(d).
Death not of natural causes, §14-401.22(e).

DISMISSAL, DISCONTINUANCE AND NONSUIT.
Abused, neglected or dependent juvenile actions.
Court finding allegations not proven, §7B-807(a).
Adoption.
Petition to adopt minor, §48-2-604(a), (b).
Appeals.
Brief.
Failure to file, AppProc Rule 13(c).
Appeal of right from court of appeals to supreme court, AppProc Rule 14(d).
Discretionary review on certification by supreme court, AppProc Rule 15(g).
Costs.
Taxing, AppProc Rule 35(a).
Failure of appellant to take timely action, AppProc Rule 25(a).
Frivolous appeals, AppProc Rule 34(b).
Security for costs.
Failure to file, defect in security, AppProc Rule 6(d).
Brief in support or opposition to motion to dismiss.
Service, §1A-1 Rule 5(a1).
Business corporations.
Derivative proceedings, §55-7-45.
Dismissal of proceedings, §55-7-44.
Child custody.
Action or proceeding for custody or visitation.
Dismissal on prejudicial grounds, §50-13.1(d).
Class actions, §1A-1 Rule 23(c).
Cost, §1A-1 Rule 41(d).
Counterclaims and cross-claims, §1A-1 Rule 41(c).
Dismissal as to plaintiff's claim.
Effect on counterclaim, §1-183.1.
Criminal procedure.
Deferred prosecution agreement.
Dismissal with leave, §15A-932(a1).
Effect, §15A-932(b).
Entry of dismissal, §15A-932(c).
Reinstitution of proceedings for failure to comply, §15A-932(e).
Demurrer to the evidence, §15-173.
Dismissal with leave pursuant to deferred prosecution agreement, §15A-932(a1).
Effect, §15A-932(b).
Entry of dismissal, §15A-932(c).
Reinstitution of proceedings for failure to comply, §15A-932(e).
Dismissal with leave when defendant fails to appear and cannot be readily found, §15A-932(a).
Effect, §15A-932(b).
Entry of dismissal, §15A-932(c).

DISMISSAL, DISCONTINUANCE AND NONSUIT —Cont'd
Criminal procedure —Cont'd
Dismissal with leave when defendant fails to appear and cannot be readily found —Cont'd
Later appearance by defendant and payment tendered, §15A-932(d1).
Reinstitution of proceedings, §15A-932(d).
Mental incapacity of defendant to proceed.
Dismissal of charges, §15A-1008.
Supplemental hearings, §15A-1007(c).
Dismissal with leave, §15A-1009(a) to (f).
Motion for appropriate relief.
Relief available.
Dismissal of charges, §15A-1417(a).
Motion for dismissal.
Death of defendant.
Dismissal required, §15A-954(b).
Deferral of ruling on motion to dismiss when charge to be reinstituted, §15A-956.
Grounds, §15A-954(a).
Motion to dismiss indictment, §15A-955.
Insanity of defendant, §15A-959.
Insufficiency of evidence.
Reviewable on appeal regardless of whether motion made during trial, §15A-1227(d).
Ruling by judge on motion before trial may proceed, §15A-1227(c).
Time for motion, §15A-1227(a), (b).
Time for, §15A-954(c).
Probable cause hearings.
Dispositional alternatives, §15A-612(a).
Voluntary dismissal of criminal charges by state, §15A-931(a), (a1).
Statute of limitations not tolled by charges dismissed, §15A-931(b).
Deferred prosecution agreement.
Dismissal with leave pursuant to, §15A-932.
Derivative proceedings.
Business corporations, §55-7-45.
Dismissal of proceedings, §55-7-44.
Dismissal with leave for nonappearance, §15A-932.
Dismissal with leave pursuant to deferred prosecution agreement, §15A-932.
Dismissal without prejudice.
Involuntary dismissal, §1A-1 Rule 41(b).
Voluntary dismissal, §1A-1 Rule 41(a).
Double jeopardy.
Motion to dismiss.
Grounds, §15A-954(a).
Eminent domain.
Abandonment of condemnation proceedings by petitioner.
Petitioner taxed with fee for respondent's attorney, §1-209.1.
Voluntary nonsuit authorized, §1-209.2.
Voluntary nonsuit by petitioner in condemnation proceedings, §1-209.2.
Petitioner taxed with fee for respondent's attorney, §1-209.1.
False claims act actions.
Action brought by private person, §1-608(b).
State proceeding with action, §1-609(b).
Frivolous complaints by prisoners, §1-110(b).
Impaired driving, implied consent offenses.
Explanation by prosecutor.
Dismissal of impaired driving charge, §20-138.4.
Motions to dismiss or suppress evidence, §20-38.6.
Incompetence, determination of.
Finding that respondent not incompetent, §35A-1112(c).

DISMISSAL, DISCONTINUANCE AND NONSUIT —Cont'd
Incompetence, determination of —Cont'd
Voluntary dismissal, §35A-1112(g).
Appointment of interim guardian, §35A-1114(f).
Indictments.
Grounds for motion to dismiss, §15A-955.
Involuntary dismissal, §1A-1 Rule 41(b).
Effect, §1A-1 Rule 41(b).
Limitation of actions.
Motion to dismiss.
Grounds, §15A-954(a).
Limited liability companies.
Derivative actions by members, §57C-8-01(b).
New action after voluntary dismissal.
Time for commencing, §1A-1 Rule 41(a).
Quo warranto.
Failure to bring action within requisite time, §1-522.
Small claims actions.
Dismissal of appeal for failure to pay costs, §7A-228(b).
Summons and process.
No endorsement of summons nor issuance of alias or pluries.
Summons within time specified.
Action discontinued, §1A-1 Rule 4(e).
Superior courts.
Judgments of voluntary nonsuit.
Clerk of court may enter, §1-209.
Termination of parental rights proceedings.
Best interest of child require rights not be terminated, §7B-1110(b).
Circumstances authorizing do not exist, §7B-1110(c).
Third-party practice, §1A-1 Rule 41(c).
Voluntary dismissal, §1A-1 Rule 41(a).
Effect, §1A-1 Rule 41(a).
Voluntary nonsuit.
Clerks of superior courts.
Authorized to enter judgment, §1-209.
Petitioner in condemnation proceeding, §1-209.2.
Workers' compensation.
Contested cases, ICWorkComp Rule 613.

DISMISSAL WITH LEAVE FOR NONAPPEARANCE, §15A-932.

DISMISSAL WITH LEAVE PURSUANT TO DEFERRED PROSECUTION AGREEMENT, §15A-932.

DISMISSAL WITHOUT PREJUDICE.
Involuntary dismissal, §1A-1 Rule 41(b).
Voluntary dismissal, §1A-1 Rule 41(a).

DISORDERLY CONDUCT, §14-288.4.
Administrative department.
Public buildings and grounds.
Disorderly conduct in and injury to, §143-345.2.
Airports, §14-275.1.
Alcoholic beverage permittees.
Unlawful conduct on premises, §18B-1005(a).
Buildings.
Public buildings and facilities.
Trespasses to land and fixtures, §14-132.
Bus stations, §14-275.1.
Conduct constituting, §14-288.4(a).
Court orders abating disorderly conduct.
Violation of court orders, §14-226.1.
Failure to disperse when commanded, §14-288.5.

DISORDERLY CONDUCT —Cont'd
Militia.
Commander may prevent trespass and disorder, §127A-148.
Public intoxication, §§14-443 to 14-447.
Punishment, §14-288.4(b), (c).
Railroad stations, §14-275.1.
Riots and civil disorders generally, §§14-288.1 to 14-288.20.
See RIOTS AND CIVIL DISORDERS.

DISORDERLY HOUSES, §14-188.
Evidence of reputation or character of house admissible, §14-188(a).
Prostitution generally, §§14-203 to 14-208.
See PROSTITUTION.

DISPATCHERS OF EMERGENCY COMMUNICATIONS.
Interfering with, §14-286.2.

DISPENSING CONTROLLED SUBSTANCES.
Controlled substances generally.
See DRUGS AND CONTROLLED SUBSTANCES.
Date of dispensing.
Entry on face of prescription, §90-106(h).
Defined, §90-87.
Prescriptions.
Generally.
See PRESCRIPTION DRUGS.
Prohibited acts, §90-108(a).
Registration of manufacturers, distributors and dispensers, §§90-101 to 90-104.
Schedule V, §90-106(d).
Schedule VI, §90-106(e).

DISPENSING OPTICIANS.
See OPTICIANS.

DISPLACED HOMEMAKERS.
Center.
Establishment, §143B-394.5.
Evaluation of programs, §143B-394.9(b).
Funding, §143B-394.7.
Grants to.
Criteria, §143B-394.5A(b).
Location, §143B-394.5A(a).
Services to be provided, §143B-394.8(a), (b).
Staff, §143B-394.6.
Definitions, §143B-394.4.
Establishment of center, §143B-394.5.
Evaluation of program, §143B-394.9(b).
Funding, §143B-394.7.
Location of center, §143B-394.5A(a).
North Carolina fund for displaced homemakers, §143B-394.10(a).
Rules to implement, §143B-394.10(b).
Rules and regulations.
Promulgation by department, §143B-394.9(a).
Staff for center, §143B-394.6.

DISPLACED PERSONS.
Public works relocation assistance, §§133-5 to 133-18.
See RELOCATION ASSISTANCE.

DISPOSAL OF PROPERTY WITH INTENT TO DEFRAUD CREDITORS.
Arrest in civil cases, §1-410.

DISPOSITION OF DECEDENT'S BODY OR BODY PARTS, §130A-420.
Delegation of right to dispose of own body, §130A-420(a1).

DISPOSITION OF DECEDENT'S BODY OR BODY PARTS —Cont'd

Disposition of bodies as anatomical gifts.
Inapplicability of provisions, §130A-420(d).

Persons authorized to determine method of disposition.
Decedent leaving no written authorization, §130A-420(b).

Unclaimed bodies, §130A-415.

Written authorization by decedent, §130A-420(a), (c).

DISPOSITION OF JUVENILE.

Abused, neglected or dependent juvenile actions, §§7B-900 to 7B-1004.
See CHILD ABUSE, NEGLECT OR DEPENDENCY.

Delinquent or undisciplined juveniles, §§7B-2500 to 7B-2606.
See DELINQUENT AND UNDISCIPLINED JUVENILES.

DISPOSITION OF SEIZED, CONFISCATED OR UNCLAIMED PROPERTY, §§15-11 to 15-17.
See SEARCHES AND SEIZURES.

DISPOSITION OF UNCLAIMED PROPERTY.
Generally, §§116B-51 to 116B-80.
See UNCLAIMED PROPERTY.

DISPUTE RESOLUTION.
Arbitration.
Generally.
See ARBITRATION.
Revised uniform arbitration act, §§1-569.1 to 1-569.31.
See ARBITRATION.

Community mediation centers, §7A-38.5.
Negotiation not discoverable or admissible in evidence, §8-110.

Custody and visitation mediation program, §§7A-494, 7A-495.

Education of children with disabilities.
Mediation of disputes, §115C-109.4.

Interstate insurance product regulation compact, §58-91-45.

Labor disputes.
Conciliation service and mediation of disputes generally, §§95-32 to 95-36.
See LABOR DISPUTES.
Voluntary arbitration, §§95-36.1 to 95-36.9.
See LABOR DISPUTES.

Mediated settlement conferences in superior court civil actions, §7A-38.1.

Mediation generally.
See MEDIATION.

Medical malpractice.
Arbitration of negligent health claims, §§90-21.60 to 90-21.69.
See MEDICAL MALPRACTICE.

New motor vehicles warranties act.
Utilization of informal settlement procedure.
Manufacturer requiring, §20-351.7.

Nurse licensure compact, §90-171.92.

Office of information technology services.
Services, fees and charges.
Dispute resolution panel, §147-33.93.

Public contracts, §143-128(g).

Public schools.
Education of children with disabilities.
Mediation of disputes, §115C-109.4.

Special education.
Education of children with disabilities.
Mediation of disputes, §115C-109.4.

DISPUTE RESOLUTION —Cont'd
Superior courts.
Mediated settlement conferences in superior court civil actions, §7A-38.1.
Mediators and other neutrals.
Regulation, §7A-38.2.
Rules implementing, SuperCtMediatedSettlemt Rules 1 to 15.
See MEDIATED SETTLEMENT CONFERENCES.

DISPUTE RESOLUTION CENTERS, §7A-38.1.
Negotiation not discoverable or admissible in evidence, §8-110.

DISPUTE RESOLUTION COMMISSION.
Court ordered mediated settlement conferences in superior court civil actions.
Regulation of mediators and other neutrals, §7A-38.2(b) to (k).

DISSECTION PRIVILEGES.
Schools for teaching mortuary science, §90-210.23(g).

DISSENTING FROM A WILL.
Acts bearing rights of spouse, §31A-1(b).

DISSENTING SHAREHOLDERS.
Appraisal rights generally, §§55-13-01 to 55-13-40.
See CORPORATIONS.
Trust companies.
Merger or share exchange.
Appraisal rights, §53-362.

DISSOLUTION.
Attachment orders.
Jury trial, §1-440.36(c).
Motion for, §1-440.36(a).
Hearing of motion, §1-440.36(b), (c).
Remedies of third person claiming attached property or interest therein, §1-440.43.
Service of process.
Noncompliance with time limit, §1-440.7(b).
Stay of order dissolving order of attachment, §1-440.38.

Banks.
See BANKS.

Corporations.
Generally, §§55-14-01 to 55-14-40.
See CORPORATIONS.
Nonprofit corporations, §§55A-14-01 to 55A-14-40.
See NONPROFIT CORPORATIONS.

District health department, §130A-38.

Facility authorities.
Dissolution of authority by general assembly, §160A-480.5.

Forest protection and development corporations, §106-990.

Interstate insurance product regulation compact, §58-91-70(c).

Limited liability companies, §§57C-6-01 to 57C-6-09.
See LIMITED LIABILITY COMPANIES.

Marriage.
Annulment of marriage.
See ANNULMENT OF MARRIAGE.
Divorce.
See DIVORCE.

Mosquito control districts.
Procedure for dissolution of certain mosquito control districts, §130A-358.

DISSOLUTION —Cont'd
Mutual burial associations.
  Request for voluntary dissolution, §90-210.107(h)
    to (k).
Partnerships, §§59-59 to 59-73.
  See PARTNERSHIPS.
Public health authorities, §130A-45.2.
Sanitary districts.
  See SANITARY DISTRICTS.
Trust companies.
  Foreign offices.
    Change in control, transactions causing,
      §53-328.
  Out-of-state institutions.
    Notice of change in control, §53-322.
  Voluntary dissolution, §§53-372 to 53-376.

DISTILLERY PERMITS, §18B-1105(a), (b).

**DISTINGUISHED PROFESSORS
  ENDOWMENT TRUST FUND,** §§116-41.13 to
  116-41.19.
See UNIVERSITY OF NORTH CAROLINA.

DISTRAINT, §42-25.7.

DISTRESS, REMEDY, §42-25.7.

DISTRESS SALES.
Closing-out sales, §§66-76 to 66-83.
  See CLOSING-OUT SALES.

DISTRESS SIGNALS.
**Interception of radio communications not
  unlawful,** §15A-287(b).

DISTRIBUTION AGREEMENTS, WINE,
  §§18B-1200 to 18B-1216.
See WINE DISTRIBUTION AGREEMENTS.

DISTRIBUTION BUSINESSES.
**Tax incentives for new and expanding
  businesses generally,** §§105-129.2 to
  105-129.13.
  See TAX INCENTIVES FOR NEW AND
    EXPANDING BUSINESSES.

DISTRIBUTION OF APPELLATE REPORTS,
  §7A-343.1.

**DISTRIBUTION OF CONTROLLED
  SUBSTANCES.**
Controlled substances generally.
  See DRUGS AND CONTROLLED SUBSTANCES.
Definition of "distribute,"§90-87.
Order forms, §90-105.
  Inspection, §90-107.
Prohibited acts, §90-108(a).
**Registration of manufacturers, distributors
  and dispensers,** §§90-101 to 90-104.
Samples, §90-106(i).

DISTRIBUTION OF DECEDENTS' ESTATES.
Executors and administrators.
  See EXECUTORS AND ADMINISTRATORS.
General provisions, §§28A-22-1 to 28A-22-11.
  See DECEDENTS' ESTATES.
Intestate succession, §§29-1 to 29-30.
  See INTESTATE SUCCESSION.

**DISTRIBUTION OF MARITAL AND DIVISIBLE
  PROPERTY,** §50-20.
Absolute divorce, effects, §50-11(e), (f).
Procedures, §50-21.

**DISTRIBUTORS, DISTRIBUTOR BRANCHES,
  DISTRIBUTOR REPRESENTATIVES.**
Motor vehicles.
  Automobile dealers licensing act.
    Generally, §§20-285 to 20-308.22.
      See MOTOR VEHICLE DEALERS.

**DISTRIBUTORS OF MILK AND MILK
  PRODUCTS.**
Generally.
  See MILK AND MILK PRODUCTS.

DISTRICT ATTORNEYS.
Abuse, neglect or dependency of juveniles.
  Report by director on finding evidence of abuse,
    §7B-307(a).
  Review of director's decision that petition not be
    filed, §§7B-306, 7B-403(b).
  Request for review, §7B-305.
Acting district attorneys, §7A-62.
**Administrative and victim and witness
  services assistants.**
  Allocation to offices, §7A-347.
Administrative assistants.
  Appointment, §7A-68(a).
  Duties, §7A-68(b).
  Expenses.
    Entitled to reimbursement, §7A-68(c).
Advance sheets.
  Furnishing advance sheets without charge,
    §7A-6(c).
Aid to families with dependent children.
  Reports to district attorneys, §§15-155.1 to
    15-155.3.
Allowances, §7A-65(a).
  Service.
    What constitutes, §7A-65(c).
Antifreeze.
  Violations of article.
    Institution and prosecution of proceedings,
      §106-579.12(c).
Assistant district attorneys.
  Allowances, §7A-65(a).
  Appointment, §7A-63.
  Carrying concealed weapons.
    Inapplicability of prohibition, exceptions,
      §14-269(b).
    Valid permit to carry concealed handgun.
      Listed prohibited areas inapplicable,
        §14-415.27.
  Compensation, §7A-65(a).
  Duties, §7A-63.
  Number of full-time assistants in prosecutorial
    districts, §7A-60(a1), (a2).
  Oath of office, §7A-63.
  Travel and subsistence expenses, §7A-65(a).
  Vacancies in office, §7A-63.
Attorney general.
  Consulting and advising prosecutors.
    Duties of attorney general, §114-2.
Bad checks cases.
  Establishment of collection program, §14-107.2(b).
Biologics.
  Prosecution of violations.
    Concurrent jurisdiction with attorney general,
      §106-714(a).
**Calendaring of criminal cases in superior
  court.**
  Criminal case docketing plan, §7A-49.4(a).

DISTRICT ATTORNEYS —Cont'd
**Calendaring of criminal cases in superior
  court** —Cont'd
  Order in which case called for trial, announcing,
    §7A-49.4(f).
  Publication of trial calendar, §7A-49.4(e).
Capital punishment.
  Argument for death penalty, §15-176.1.
  Duties on sentence of death, §15-189.
Carrying concealed weapons.
  Inapplicability of prohibition, exceptions,
    §14-269(b).
  Valid permit to carry concealed handgun.
    Listed prohibited areas inapplicable, §14-415.27.
**Certificate of relief from collateral
  consequences.**
  Appearance by district attorney, §15A-173.4(c).
  Notice to district attorney of motion to modify or
    revoke, §15A-173.4(b).
  Notice to district attorney of petition,
    §15A-173.4(a).
Child support.
  Duty to assist in enforcing support, §110-138.1.
  Reports to district attorneys of aid to dependent
    children and illegitimate births, §§15-155.1 to
    15-155.3.
Commercial feed.
  Prosecution of violations of article, §106-284.44(c).
Compensation, §7A-65(a).
  Longevity pay, §7A-65(c), (d).
  Service.
    What constitutes, §7A-65(c).
Conference of district attorneys.
  Bylaws, §7A-412(d).
  Clerical support, §7A-414.
  Establishment, §7A-411.
  Executive committee, §7A-412(c).
  Executive secretary, §7A-414.
  Meetings.
    Annual meetings, §7A-412(a).
    Attendance.
      Duty to attend, §7A-412(e).
    Calling of meetings, §7A-412(e).
  Officers.
    Election, §7A-412(b).
  Organization, §7A-412(d).
  Powers.
    Adoption of rules, §7A-413(b).
    Generally, §7A-413(a).
  Purposes, §7A-411.
Confidentiality of information.
  Child support.
    Reports to district attorneys of aid to dependent
      children and illegitimate births, §15-155.3.
Corruption.
  Elections.
    Investigation and prosecution of violations,
      §163-278.
**Criminal case records to identify attorney
  representing state,** §7A-109.2(a).
**Criminal investigation and intelligence
  information.**
  Disclosure of records transmitted to district
    attorneys, §132-1.4(g).
Criminal law and procedure.
  Prosecution of actions, NC Const Art IV §18.
Deadly force.
  Investigations of use of deadly force by law
    enforcement officers, §147-90.
Defined, §15A-101.

DISTRICT ATTORNEYS —Cont'd
Delinquent and undisciplined juvenile actions.
  Representation of state, §7B-2404.
  Review of juvenile court counselor's decision not to
    approve filing of petition, §§7B-1705,
    7B-1803(b).
  Request for review, §7B-1704.
Depositions.
  Reading deposition on the trial.
    When deposition may be read, §8-83.
Disbarment or suspension.
  Salary suspension pending appeal, §7A-410.1.
  Vacancy in office declared upon, §7A-410.
District court division, §7A-132.
District court prosecutors.
  Advance sheets.
    Furnishing advance sheets without charge,
      §7A-6(c).
Dockets.
  Preparation of trial dockets, §7A-61.
Duties.
  Dockets.
    Preparation of trial dockets, §7A-61.
  Generally, §147-89.
  Juvenile cases.
    Representation of state in cases in which
      juvenile represented by attorney, §7A-61.
Elections, §7A-60(b).
  Corruption.
    Investigation and prosecution of violations,
      §163-278.
  Prosecutorial districts, §7A-60(b).
  Vacancies in office.
    Election to fill, §163-10.
Employment security.
  Prosecution of violations, §96-7(b).
Escape.
  Allowing prisoners to escape.
    Prosecution of sheriffs or other officers for
      escape, §14-240.
Expunction of criminal records.
  First offenders under age 18.
    Petition.
      Service on, objection, filing, time, §15A-195(a).
        Gang offenses, §15A-145.1(a).
        Nonviolent felony offenses, §15A-145.4(c).
  Misdemeanor larceny conviction.
    Petition.
      Service on, objection, filing, time,
        §15A-145(d1).
Federal courts.
  Prosecution of cases removed to federal courts,
    §147-89.
Firearms.
  Carrying concealed weapons.
    Inapplicability of prohibition, exceptions,
      §14-269(b).
    Valid permit to carry concealed handgun.
      Listed prohibited areas inapplicable,
        §14-415.27.
Food, drugs and cosmetics.
  Prosecution of violations of article, §106-126.
General assembly.
  Appointment of district attorneys, NC Const Art
    IV §18.
Habeas corpus.
  Notice, §17-30.
Harmful material sales to minors.
  Civil remedy.
    Harmful material determination, injunction,
      §§19-9 to 19-20.

DISTRICT ATTORNEYS —Cont'd

Illegitimacy.
Child support.
Reports to district attorneys of aid to dependent children and illegitimate births, §§15-155.1 to 15-155.3.

Implied consent offense procedures.
Access to chemical analysis room.
Written policies, establishment, §20-38.5(a).

Infractions.
Hearing procedure.
Duties, §15A-1114(e).
Preparation of trial dockets, §7A-61.

Innocence claim inquiry.
Special prosecutor.
Prosecutorial misconduct allegations, §7A-64(a1).

Interchangeable use of terms "solicitor" and "district attorney," §7A-66.1(a).
Authorized in proceedings, documents and quotations, §7A-66.1(c).

Investigations.
Deadly force.
Investigations of use of deadly force by law enforcement officers, §147-90.

Investigatorial assistants, §7A-69.

Juvenile courts.
Duties of district attorney.
Representation of state and juvenile cases in which juvenile represented by attorney, §7A-61.

License plates, §20-79.4(b).

Lobbying.
Prosecution of violations.
District attorney of district including Wake County, §120C-603.

Milk and milk products.
Ice cream plants, creameries and cheese factories.
Closure of plants for violation of article.
Certificate to district attorney, §106-252.

Missing persons.
Release of information to by center, §143B-1018.

Monopolies and restraint of trade.
Prosecution of violations.
Assistants to attorney general, §75-13.

Motion for appropriate relief.
Signature indicating opportunity to consent or object.
Required, granting motion without, §15A-1420(a).

Motor vehicles.
Antifreeze.
Violations of article.
Institution and prosecution of proceedings, §106-579.12(c).

Nuisances against public morals, action to abate, §19-2.1.

Oaths.
Acting district attorneys, §7A-62.
Assistant district attorneys, §7A-63.
Form of oaths of office, §11-11.

Obscenity or pornography.
Harmful material sales to minors.
Civil remedy.
Harmful material determination, injunction, §§19-9 to 19-20.
Search warrant or criminal process.
Issuance, §14-190.20.

Offenses against.
Aggravating factor in sentencing, §15A-1340.16.

DISTRICT ATTORNEYS —Cont'd

Patient abuse.
Issuance of criminal process only upon request of, §14-32.2(g).

Powers.
Generally, §147-89.

Practice of law.
Prohibition on private practice of law, §§7A-61, 84-2.

Prosecutorial districts, NC Const Art IV §18.
Allocation of office and term of district attorney from prosecutorial district 12, §7A-60(c).
Division of state into districts, §7A-60(a), (a1).
Election of district attorney, §7A-60(b).
Full-time assistant district attorneys.
Number, §7A-60(a1), (a2).

Public lands.
Trees and timber.
Cutting before obtaining grant.
Prosecution, §146-43.

Removal from office, §7A-66.

Removal of causes.
United States courts.
Prosecution of cases removed to federal courts, §147-89.

Residential mortgage fraud.
Authority to investigate and prosecute, §14-118.14.

Salary.
Suspension pending appeal of disbarment or suspension from practice, §7A-410.1.

Search warrants for obscenity offenses.
Issuance upon request of prosecutors, §14-190.20.

Secretaries.
Sick leave.
Transfer of earned leave as county or municipal employees, §7A-102.1(a) to (c).

Solicitors.
Denomination of office of solicitor as office of district attorney, §7A-66.1(a).

Special prosecutor.
Innocence claim inquiry.
Prosecutorial misconduct allegations, §7A-64(a1).

Special responsibilities, ProfCond Rule 3.8.

Subpoenas.
Witnesses proving single material fact.
No more than two witnesses may be subpoenaed, §6-60.

Suspension, §7A-66.

Temporary assistance to district attorneys.
Application to director of administrative office of the courts, §7A-64(a).
Innocence claim inquiry.
Special prosecutor in case of prosecutorial misconduct allegations, §7A-64(a1).
Length of service and compensation to temporary appointee, §7A-64(c).
Required showing in order to provide assistance, §7A-64(b).

Term of office, §7A-60(b).

Travel and subsistence expenses, §7A-65(a).

Unemployment compensation.
Prosecution of violations, §96-7(b).

United States courts.
Prosecution of cases removed to federal courts, §147-89.

Vacancies in office.
Filling, §§7A-60(a), 163-10.

Witnesses.
Discharge of state's witnesses.
Announcement of discharge by district attorney, §6-62.

DISTRICT ATTORNEYS —Cont'd
Witnesses —Cont'd
Subpoenaing witnesses to prove single material
fact.
No more than two witnesses may be
subpoenaed, §6-60.

DISTRICT BOARDS OF HEALTH.
Adjudicatory bodies, §130A-37(a).
Appointment of members, §130A-37(b), (c).
Attorney at law.
Contracting for services, §130A-37(k).
Chairperson, §130A-37(f).
Compensation of board members, §130A-37(i).
Composition, §130A-37(a), (b).
Dissolution of board, §130A-37(d).
Expenses, §130A-37(i).
Fees.
Power to impose for services rendered by local
department, §130A-39(g).
Liability insurance contracts, §130A-37(k).
Meetings, §130A-37(j).
Policy-making body, §130A-37(a).
Quorum, §130A-37(g).
Removal of board members, §130A-37(h).
Rules, §130A-37(a).
Authority to adopt, §130A-39(a).
Code, standard, rule or regulation.
Adoption by reference to, §130A-39(f).
Copies, filing, §130A-39(e).
More stringent rules, power to adopt, §130A-39(b).
Municipalities, applicability to, §130A-39(c).
Notice prior to adoption, repeal or amendment,
§130A-39(d).
Secretary, §130A-37(f).
Terms of office, §130A-37(c).
Vacancies, §130A-37(e).

**DISTRICT COURT DIVISION OF GENERAL
COURT OF JUSTICE.**
Age.
Official actions of twenty-fifth judicial district
judges.
Validation of actions after mandatory
retirement age, §7A-4.21.
Composition, §7A-130.
Creation, §7A-130.
Districts.
Composition of split districts, §7A-133(b), (b1).
Number of judges by districts, §7A-133(a).
Organization into territorial districts, §7A-130.
Establishment of district courts, §7A-131.
Transfer of pending cases when present inferior
court replaced by district courts, §7A-135.
Inferior courts replaced by district courts.
Transfer of pending cases, §7A-135.
Judges, §7A-132.
Mandatory retirement age.
Official actions of twenty-fifth judicial district
judges.
Validation of actions performed after
mandatory retirement age, §7A-4.21.
Number of judges by districts, §7A-133(a).
Judicial districts.
Trial court administrators, §7A-355.
Duties, §7A-356.
Magistrates, §7A-132.
Number of magistrates for each county,
§7A-133(c).
Number of judges by districts, §7A-133(a).
Organization into territorial districts, §7A-130.

**DISTRICT COURT DIVISION OF GENERAL
COURT OF JUSTICE** —Cont'd
Schedule of establishment of district courts,
§7A-131.
Seats of court, §7A-130.
Additional seats, §7A-133(c).
Appointment of judges, §7A-133(a).
Solicitors, §7A-132.
Transfer of pending cases.
When present inferior courts replaced by district
courts, §7A-135.
Trial court administrators.
Duties, §7A-356.
Judicial districts having administrator, §7A-355.

DISTRICT COURT JUDGES.
Age.
Limit for service as judge, §7A-4.20.
Official actions of judges of twenty-fifth judicial
district.
Validation of actions after mandatory
retirement age, §7A-4.21.
Appeals.
Entry of orders by trial judges under rules of
appellate procedure.
Authorization, AppProc Rule 36.
Assignment of judges, NC Const Art IV §11.
Assignment of judge to another district or
specialized duty, §7A-141.
Chambers.
Hearings and orders in chambers, §7A-191.
Interlocutory orders in chambers, §7A-192.
Chief judge.
Administrative authority, §7A-146.
Annual conference of chief district judges.
Purposes of conference, §7A-148(a).
Designation of chief judge, §7A-141, NC Const Art
IV §10.
Duties, §7A-146.
Implied consent offense procedures.
Access to chemical analysis room.
Written policies, establishment, §20-38.5(a).
Multicopy uniform traffic ticket and complaint,
§7A-148(b).
Powers, §7A-146.
Compensation, §7A-144(a), NC Const Art IV §21.
Longevity pay, §7A-144(b).
Concealed handgun.
Carrying or possessing in court building,
§14-269.4.
Depositions.
Judge defined, §1A-1 Rule 30(h).
Disability of judge.
Performance of duties, §1A-1 Rule 63.
Disbarment or suspension.
Salary suspension pending appeal, §7A-410.1.
Vacancy in office declared upon, §7A-410.
Election, §§7A-140, 163-321, 163-335.
Applicability of provisions, §163-321.
Ballots.
Counting, §163-334.
Furnished by county boards, §163-332(b).
Official ballots, printing, names of candidates,
§163-332(a).
Certificate that candidate registered voter.
Filing with notice of candidacy, §163-323(d).
Certification of candidate.
Acknowledgment of receipt, §163-326(c).
To local boards of elections, §163-326(b).
To secretary of state, §163-326(a).
Date of election, §163-1(a).

DISTRICT COURT JUDGES —Cont'd
Election —Cont'd
Death, disqualification or resignation of candidate.
  After the election, §163-328(e).
  Before election, §163-328(b), (c).
Districts 13, 22A, 22B, §7-133(b2) to (b4).
Fees.
  Petition in lieu of payment of fees, §163-325.
  Refund, §163-324(b).
  Schedule, §163-324(a).
Insufficient number of candidates, §163-328(a).
Nonpartisan primary election.
  Date, §163-331.
  Determination of election winners, §163-322(c).
  Determination of nominees, §163-322(b).
  Generally, §163-322(a).
  Voting, §163-330.
Notice of candidacy.
  Certification, §163-326.
  Form, §163-323(a).
  For more than one office, prohibition, §163-323(e).
  Indicating vacancy, §163-323(f).
  Specialized judgeship, §163-323(f).
  Time for filing, §163-323(b).
  Withdrawal, §163-323(c).
Other rules, §163-335.
Petition in lieu of payment of fees, §163-325(a).
  Requirements, deadline for filing, §163-325(b).
Withdrawal after close of filing, §163-328(d).
Emergency judges, recall to active service.
Commission, application to governor, §7A-53.
Compensation for emergency judges on recall, §7A-52(b).
Jurisdiction of emergency district court judges, §7A-53.1.
Recall of judges who have reached mandatory retirement age, §7A-57.
Retired judge may become emergency judge subject to recall, §7A-52(a).
Firearms.
Concealed handgun.
  Carrying or possessing in court building, §14-269.4.
Interlocutory orders.
By whom power to enter orders exercised, §7A-192.
Judicial sales, §§1-339.1 to 1-339.40.
See JUDICIAL SALES.
Jurisdiction, §7A-149(a).
License plates, §20-79.6(c).
Marriage.
Solemnization, §51-1.
Number of judges, §7A-140.
Oaths.
Administration of oaths, §7A-291.
Oath of office, §7A-140.
Orders in chambers, §7A-191.
Powers, §7A-291.
Practice of law.
Prohibition on practice of law, §7A-140.
Qualifications, §7A-140, NC Const Art IV §22.
Residence in district for which elected.
Requirement, NC Const Art IV §10.
Retirement.
Age limit for service as judge, §7A-4.20.
Consolidated judicial retirement, §§135-50 to 135-75.2.
  See RETIREMENT SYSTEM FOR TEACHERS AND STATE EMPLOYEES.

DISTRICT COURT JUDGES —Cont'd
Retirement —Cont'd
Recall to active service, §7A-52(a).
  Compensation for emergency judges on recall, §7A-52(b).
  Limitation upon compensation, §7A-52(b).
Validation of actions performed after mandatory retirement age, §7A-4.21.
Salary, §7A-144(a), NC Const Art IV §21.
Longevity pay, §7A-144(b).
Suspension pending appeal of disbarment or suspension from practice, §7A-410.1.
Selection of nominees, Bar Rule A.1013.
Specialized judgeships.
Designation of specialty, §7A-147(a).
Filling of positions, §7A-147(a).
Juvenile cases, §7A-147(c).
Powers of specialized judge, §7A-147(b).
Sessions for trial of specialized cases, §7A-147(b).
Temporary or specialized duty.
Assignment of judge to another district, §7A-141.
Term of office, §§7A-140, 163-1(a), NC Const Art IV §10.
Travel and subsistence expenses, §7A-144(a).
Vacancies in office, NC Const Art IV §§10, 19.
Appointment by governor to fill.
  Nominations submitted by district bar, §7A-142.
Filling, §§7A-142, 163-9(d).

DISTRICT COURTS, NC Const Art IV §10.
Abortion.
Parental or judicial consent to abortion.
  Jurisdiction over proceedings, §7B-200(a).
Absence of party or counsel during trial.
Civil actions, SuperCt Rule 13.
Accounts and accounting.
Small claim actions.
  Form of complaint on account, §7A-232.
Additional seats of court authorized.
Clerical functions furnished by clerk of superior court, §7A-182(a), (b).
Administrative office of the courts, §§7A-340 to 7A-346.
See ADMINISTRATIVE OFFICE OF THE COURTS.
Advance sheets.
Furnishing advance sheets without charge, §7A-6(c).
Age.
Twenty-fifth judicial district judges.
  Validation of official acts performed after mandatory retirement age, §7A-4.21.
Alimony.
Mediated settlement conferences or other settlement procedures in actions involving, §7A-38.4A.
Amount in controversy.
Determination of proper division for trial of civil actions, §7A-243.
Annulment of marriage.
Proper division for trial of civil actions, §7A-244.
Appeals.
Appeal from judge, §1-277(a).
Clerk to judge, §7A-251(b).
Costs in civil actions.
  Collection of advance court costs, §7A-305(c).
  Cumulative nature of costs, §7A-305(b).
Costs in criminal actions, §7A-304(b).
Criminal law and procedure.
  Appeals by defendant, §15A-1431.
  Appeals by state, §15A-1432.

DISTRICT COURTS —Cont'd

Appeals —Cont'd

Entry of orders by trial judges under rules of appellate procedure.

Authorization, AppProc Rule 36.

Final judgment of district court in civil actions.

Direct appeal to court of appeals, §7A-27(c).

Game commission rulings.

Heard in district court division, §7A-250(c).

Interlocutory orders.

Direct appeal to court of appeals, §7A-27(d).

Liens.

Possessory liens on personal property.

Action to regain possession of motor vehicle or vessel.

Appeal to district court for trial de novo, §44A-6.1(b).

Procedure after determination of appeal, §1-298.

Settling record on appeal.

Power of trial judge, §1-283.

Small claim actions.

Indigent persons, §7A-228(b1).

Jury trial on appeal, §7A-230.

Priority of judgment when appeal taken, §7A-226.

Stay of execution on appeal, §7A-227.

Trial de novo, §7A-228(a).

Dismissal of appeal, §7A-228(c).

Oral notice of appeal, §7A-228(a).

Perfection of appeal, §7A-228(b).

Procedure generally, §7A-229.

Appearances.

Attorneys at law.

Withdrawal of appearance, SuperCt Rule 16.

First appearance before district court judge, §§15A-601 to 15A-606.

See APPEARANCES.

Applicability of rules of practice and procedure, SuperCt Rule 1.

Arguments.

Opening and concluding arguments, SuperCt Rule 10.

Arrest.

Costs in criminal actions, §7A-304(a).

Warrant for arrest.

Judges may issue, §15A-304(f).

Attorneys at law.

Courtroom decorum, SuperCt Rule 12.

Scheduling conflicts.

Guidelines for resolving, SuperCt Rule 3.1.

Withdrawal of appearance, SuperCt Rule 16.

Bail.

Criminal actions.

Status of bail bond, §7A-290.

Judges of district court.

Power to set bail, §7A-291.

Boats.

Possessory liens on personal property.

Action to regain possession of vessel.

Involuntary relinquishment of possession by lienor.

Appeal to district court for trial de novo, §44A-6.1(b).

Calendars.

Civil cases, SuperCt Rule 2.

Certificate of readiness.

Form, SuperCt Rule 24.

Chambers of judge.

Hearings and orders in chambers, §7A-191.

Interlocutory orders in chambers, §7A-192.

DISTRICT COURTS —Cont'd

Chief court counselors.

Duties and powers, §143B-830.

Chief judge.

Administrative authority, §7A-146.

Annual conference of chief district judges.

Purposes of conference, §7A-148(a).

Designation of, §7A-141.

Duties, §§7A-146, 7A-200(b).

Multicopy uniform traffic ticket and complaint, §7A-148(b).

Powers, §7A-146.

Child abuse, neglect or dependency.

Generally, §§7B-100 to 7B-1414.

See CHILD ABUSE, NEGLECT OR DEPENDENCY.

Child custody.

Action or proceeding for custody or visitation.

Denial of parental visitation rights.

Written findings of fact, §50-13.5(i).

Proper division for trial of civil actions, §7A-244.

Child support.

Proper division for trial of civil actions, §7A-244.

Civil actions.

Absence of party or counsel during trial, SuperCt Rule 13.

Applicability of civil procedure generally, §7A-193.

Calendaring of civil cases, SuperCt Rule 2.

Costs in civil actions.

Appeal costs.

Collection of advance court costs, §7A-305(c).

Cumulative nature of costs, §7A-305(b).

Assessment of costs, §7A-305(a).

Completeness and exclusivity of costs, §7A-305(d).

Courtroom and related judicial facilities.

Use of facilities, §7A-305(a).

Cross-claim or counterclaim included in pleadings, §7A-305(a5).

General court of justice.

Support of court, §7A-305(a).

Filings containing certain motions, §7A-305(f).

Liability of parties for costs, §7A-305(e).

Designation of case or group of cases as exceptional, SuperCt Rule 2.1.

Discovery procedures.

Fee on filing verified petition, §7A-305.1.

Efiling pilot project, SuperCt Supp Rules 1 to 9.

Fees.

Uniform civil process fees, §7A-311.

Amount, §7A-311(a).

Collection of fees in advance, §7A-311(b).

Completeness and exclusivity of fees and commissions, §7A-311(c).

Jury trials, §7A-196(a).

Motions, SuperCt Rule 6.

Reporting of civil trials.

Appointment of reporters, §7A-198(f).

Compensation and allowances of reporters, §7A-198(f).

Electronic or mechanical devices.

Inaccurate record produced, §7A-198(g).

Operation of device while trial in progress, §7A-198(c).

State of the art and techniques of recording testimony, §7A-198(b).

Magistrates.

No provisions for reporting of trial before magistrates, §7A-198(e).

DISTRICT COURTS —Cont'd
Civil actions —Cont'd
  Reporting of civil trials —Cont'd
    Utilization of court-reporting personnel,
      §7A-198(a).
    Waiver of reporting of trial by consent of party,
      §7A-198(d).
Clerks of court.
  Additional seats of court authorized.
    Clerical functions furnished by clerk of superior
      court, §7A-182(a), (b).
  Appeal of clerk to judge, §7A-251(b).
  Equipment and supplies in clerk's office, §7A-303.
  Jurisdiction, §7A-149(c).
Complex business cases.
  Designation, SuperCt Rule 2.1.
  Superior court judges.
    Designation of special superior court judge for,
      SuperCt Rule 2.2.
Construction and interpretation, SuperCt Rule
  1.
Contempt.
  Civil contempt.
    Proceedings for civil contempt, §5A-23.
  Judges of district courts.
    Power to punish for contempt, §7A-291.
Continuances, SuperCt Rule 3.
Conversion.
  Small claim actions.
    Form of complaint for conversion, §7A-232.
Costs.
  Civil actions, §7A-305.
  Criminal actions, §7A-304.
  Determination and disbursement after date court
    established.
    Administration of estates, §7A-318(b).
    Assessment of matter pending in general court
      of justice, §7A-318(a).
    Disbursement according to prior law,
      §7A-318(d), (e).
    General court of justice fee and facilities fee
      remission to state, §7A-318(c).
  Fees are exclusive, §7A-320.
  Uniform costs and fees in trial divisions, §§7A-304
    to 7A-318.
Counterclaims and cross-claims.
  Small claim actions.
    Impermissible counterclaims and cross-claims,
      §7A-219.
Counties.
  Facilities and courtrooms.
    Responsibility of county for physical facilities,
      §7A-302.
  Unincorporated seats of court.
    Disposition of fees in counties, §7A-317.1.
Court of appeals.
  Appeals of right from district court.
    Final judgments of district courts in civil
      actions, §7A-27(c).
  Interlocutory orders or judgments of district court.
    Appeals of right from district court, §7A-27(d).
Court reporters.
  Appointment of reporter, §7A-198(f).
  Compensation and allowances, §7A-198(f).
    Civil trials, §7A-198.
  Electronic or mechanical devices.
    Inaccurate record produced, §7A-198(g).
    Operation of device while in progress,
      §7A-198(c).
    State of the art and techniques of recording
      testimony, §7A-198(b).

DISTRICT COURTS —Cont'd
Court reporters —Cont'd
  Magistrates.
    No provisions for reporting of trials before
      magistrates, §7A-198(e).
  Utilization of personnel for reporting civil trials,
    §7A-198(a).
  Waiver of reporting of trial by consent of parties,
    §7A-198(d).
Courtroom decorum, SuperCt Rule 12.
Criminal law and procedure.
  Appeals.
    Appeals by defendant, §15A-1431.
    Appeals by state, §15A-1432.
  Costs in criminal actions, §7A-304.
    Amendment of costs, effective date of change,
      §7A-304(g).
    Appeal costs, §7A-304(b).
    Arrest or personal service of criminal process,
      §7A-304(a).
    Assessment of costs, §7A-304(a).
    Collection of costs, §7A-304(a).
    Completeness and exclusivity of costs,
      §7A-304(c).
    Courtroom and related judicial facilities.
      Use of facilities, §7A-304(a).
    Determination, §7A-304(d).
    DNA database and databank services,
      §7A-304(a).
    General court of justice.
      Support of general court of justice,
        §7A-304(a).
    Installment plan arrangement.
      Payment, §7A-304(f).
    Law-enforcement officers' benefit and retirement
      fund.
      Assessment and collection of costs,
        §7A-304(a).
    Misdemeanor maintenance in county jails,
      §7A-304(a).
    Payment, §7A-304(f).
    Personal service of criminal process, §7A-304(a).
  Felony guilty or no contest pleas.
    Transfer of case from superior court to district
      court, §15A-1029.1(a).
  Infractions.
    Procedure for hearing and disposition,
      §§15A-1111 to 15A-1118.
    See INFRACTIONS.
  Judge.
    Finder of fact, §15A-1201.
  Jurisdiction of district court, §7A-270.
    Accepting guilty plea or no contest plea to
      certain felonies, §7A-272(c), (d).
    Petty offenses triable by court, §7A-272(a).
    Preliminary examinations.
      Conduct of examinations, §7A-272(b).
  Prosecution in district court division, NC Const
    Art IV §18.
  Record of proceeding,
    Guilty or no contest plea to certain felonies,
      §7A-191.1.
  Seat of court in municipality with corporate limits
    extending into two or more contiguous
    counties.
    Venue in criminal case, authority of judge,
      §7A-199(c).
  Trial procedure.
    Applicability of superior court procedure,
      §15A-1101.

DISTRICT COURTS —Cont'd
Definitions.
Chief district court judge, §7A-200(a).
Set of districts, §7A-200(a).
Small claim actions, §7A-210.
Delinquent and undisciplined juveniles.
Generally, §§7B-1500 to 7B-2827.
See DELINQUENT AND UNDISCIPLINED
JUVENILES.
Jurisdiction over delinquent juveniles.
Age governs for purposes of determining
jurisdiction, §7B-1601(a).
Continued jurisdiction of juvenile court.
Placement in youth development center for
offense classified as class B1, B2, C, D
OR E felony, §7B-1602(b).
Placement in youth development center for
offense of first-degree murder, first-degree
rape or first-degree sexual offense,
§7B-1602(a).
Until terminated by court order or
emancipation of juvenile, §7B-1601(b).
Exclusive original jurisdiction, §7B-1601(a).
Extended jurisdiction of juvenile court.
Persons 18 years of age or older.
Under extended jurisdiction, §7B-1601(f).
Parent, guardian or custodian of juvenile,
jurisdiction over, §7B-1601(g).
Retention of jurisdiction when proceedings not
concluded before juvenile reaches age of 18
years, §7B-1601(c).
Violation of terms of post-release supervision,
§7B-1601(e).
When court has not obtained jurisdiction over
juvenile before juvenile reaches age of 18.
Jurisdiction over felony and related
misdemeanors committed by juvenile
after thirteenth and prior to sixteenth
birthday, §7B-1601(d).
Jurisdiction over undisciplined juveniles.
Age governs for purposes of determining
jurisdiction, §7B-1600(a).
Continued jurisdiction until terminated by court
order or emancipation of juvenile,
§7B-1600(b).
Exclusive original jurisdiction, §7B-1600(a).
Parent, guardian or custodian of juvenile,
jurisdiction over, §7B-1600(c).
Limitations on juvenile court jurisdiction.
Emancipated juveniles prosecuted as adult,
§7B-1604(a).
Juvenile committing criminal offense after
superior court conviction as adult,
§7B-1604(b).
Juvenile committing criminal offense on or after
sixteenth birthday subject to prosecution as
adult, §7B-1604(a).
**Designation of case or group of cases as
exceptional.**
Civil actions, SuperCt Rule 2.1.
Discovery, SuperCt Rule 8.
Civil actions.
Fee on filing verified petition, §7A-305.1.
Districts.
Composition of split districts, §7A-133(b), (b1).
Divorce and alimony.
Cost of final action for absolute divorce,
§7A-305(a2).
Mediated settlement conference or other
settlement procedures.
Actions involving equitable distribution,
alimony and support.
Administrative fee, §7A-38.4A(l).

DISTRICT COURTS —Cont'd
Divorce and alimony —Cont'd
Mediated settlement conference or other
settlement procedures —Cont'd
Actions involving equitable distribution,
alimony and support —Cont'd
Appointment of mediator by district court
judge.
Failure of parties to designate mediator,
§7A-38.4A(f).
Attendance at settlement conference, parties
required to attend, §7A-38.4A(d).
Authority of chief district court judge to order,
§7A-38.4A(c).
Compelling mediator or neutral to testify or
produce evidence.
Prohibition, §7A-38.4A(j).
Costs, born by parties, §7A-38.4A(i).
Definitions applicable to section,
§7A-38.4A(b).
Designation of mediators, §7A-38.4A(f).
Design, implementation and evaluation of
pilot program, purpose of section,
§7A-38.4A(a).
Evidence of statements in conduct not subject
to discovery and inadmissible in action or
other actions, §7A-38.4A(j).
Failure of persons required to attend,
monetary sanctions, §7A-38.4A(e).
Fees of mediators, payment, §7A-38.4A(i).
Immunity of mediators and neutrals acting
pursuant to section, §7A-38.4A(h).
Jury trial, right not restricted, §7A-38.4A(n).
Mediator or neutral not to be compelled to
testify or produce evidence, §7A-38.4A(j).
Monetary sanctions.
On person failing to attend, §7A-38.4A(e).
Neutrals, selection and compensation.
Other settlement procedures authorized,
§7A-38.4A(g).
Order to attend and participate in other
settlement procedure, §7A-38.4A(f).
Purpose of section, §7A-38.4A(a).
Report of statistical data about settlement
procedures by judges, §7A-38.4A(m).
Rules to implement section, supreme court
may adopt, §7A-38.4A(o).
Standards for certification and conduct of
mediators and neutrals, supreme court
may adopt, §7A-38.4A(k).
Statements made or conduct during
mediation.
Inadmissibility, discovery restrictions,
exceptions, §7A-38.4A(j).
Proper division for trial of civil actions, §7A-244.
Domestic relations.
Proper division for trial of civil actions, §7A-244.
Drug treatment court probation.
Revocation, jurisdiction, §7A-271(f).
Supervision, jurisdiction, §7A-272(e).
Efiling pilot project, SuperCt Supp Rules 1 to 9.
Emancipation of juvenile.
Jurisdiction over proceedings to determine,
§§7B-200(a), 7B-1603.
**Emergency medical treatment of juveniles,
authorization,** §7B-3600.
Jurisdiction over proceedings involving judicial
consent, §§7B-200(a), 7B-1603.
Entries on records, SuperCt Rule 17.
Equitable distribution.
Mediated settlement conferences or other
settlement procedures in actions involving,
§7A-38.4A.

DISTRICT COURTS —Cont'd
Evidence.
Custody and disposition, SuperCt Rule 14.
Judges of district court.
Power to compel production of evidence, §7A-291.
Exceptional civil case.
Designation, SuperCt Rule 2.1.
Facilities.
Costs in civil actions.
Use of courtroom and related judicial facilities, §7A-305(a).
Costs in criminal actions.
Use of courtroom and related judicial facilities, §7A-304(a).
Responsibility for physical facilities.
Counties and municipalities responsible, §7A-302.
Fees.
Civil process.
Uniform civil process fees, §7A-311.
Amount, §7A-311(a).
Collection of fees in advance, §7A-311(b).
Completeness and exclusivity of fees and commissions, §7A-311(c).
Costs are exclusive, §7A-320.
Discovery procedures.
Filing of verified petition, §7A-305.1.
Judges, NC Const Art IV §21.
Uniform costs and fees in trial divisions, §§7A-304 to 7A-318.
Unincorporated seats of court.
Disposition of fees in counties, §7A-317.1.
Felony offenses, guilty or no contest pleas.
Appeals, §15A-1029.1(b).
Record of proceedings, §7A-191.1.
Transfer of case from superior court to district court, §15A-1029.1(a).
Foster care placement of juvenile.
Jurisdiction over proceedings to review, §7B-200(a).
Game commission rulings.
Appeals heard in district court division, §7A-250(c).
General assembly.
Organization and establishment of district courts, NC Const Art IV §10.
Guardian ad litem.
Appointment for minors, SuperCt Rule 7.1.
Guardian ad litem program.
Providing services to abused, neglected or dependent juveniles, §§7B-1200 to 7B-1204.
Hearings.
Chambers.
Hearings and orders in chambers, §7A-191.
Interlocutory orders in chambers, §7A-192.
Conduct of hearings, §7A-191.
Infractions.
Cost in criminal actions.
Applicability of section to infractions disposed of in district courts, §7A-304(e).
Hearings conducted in open court, §7A-191.
Jurisdiction for adjudication and disposition, §7A-253.
No right to trial by jury in adjudicatory hearings, §7A-196(c).
Procedure for hearing and disposition, §§15A-1111 to 15A-1118.
See INFRACTIONS.
Reporting not provided in hearings to adjudicate, §7A-198(e).

DISTRICT COURTS —Cont'd
Injunctions.
Extension, modification or vacation.
Applications.
Before whom heard, §1-498.
Jurisdiction of judge, §1-493.
Return, §1-494.
Statutes.
Enforcement or invalidation of statutes.
Grounds for transfer, §7A-245(b).
Interlocutory orders.
Appeals of right from district courts to court of appeals, §7A-27(d).
Exercise of power to enter interlocutory orders, §7A-192.
Interstate compact on the placement of children.
Jurisdiction of court, §§7B-200(a), 7B-1603.
Judges.
See DISTRICT COURT JUDGES.
Judgments.
Appeals of right from district courts to court of appeals.
Direct appeal to court of appeals, §7A-27(d).
Final judgments of district courts in civil action, §7A-27(c).
Small claim actions.
Lien and execution of judgment, §7A-225.
Priority of judgment when appeal taken, §7A-226.
Rendition and entry of judgment, §7A-224.
Judicial districts.
Trial court administrators, §7A-355.
Jurisdiction, NC Const Art IV §12.
Abused, neglected or dependent juveniles, §7B-200.
Retention of jurisdiction until terminated by court or emancipation, §7B-201(a).
Termination of district court jurisdiction.
Affect, modification or enforcement of previous orders, prohibition, §7B-201(b).
Accepting guilty plea or no contest plea to certain felonies, §7A-272(c), (d).
Clerks, §7A-149(c).
Concurrently held original jurisdiction.
Allocation between trial divisions, §7A-242.
Contempt of juvenile, §7B-1603.
Criminal actions.
General jurisdiction for trial of criminal actions, §7A-270.
Petty misdemeanors triable by court, §7A-272(a).
Preliminary examinations.
Conduct of examinations, §7A-272(b).
Delinquent and undisciplined juveniles.
Extended jurisdiction over delinquent juvenile, §7B-1602.
Jurisdiction over delinquent juveniles, §7B-1601.
Jurisdiction over undisciplined juveniles, §7B-1600.
Limitations on juvenile court jurisdiction, §7B-1604.
Drug treatment court probation.
Revocation, §7A-271(f).
Supervision, §7A-272(e).
Emancipation of juvenile, proceeding to determine, §§7B-200(a), 7B-1603.
Emergency medical or surgical treatment for juvenile, judicial consent proceedings, §§7B-200(a), 7B-1603.

DISTRICT COURTS —Cont'd
Jurisdiction —Cont'd
Foster care placement, proceedings to review,
§7B-200(a).
Infractions, §7A-253.
Interstate compact on the placement of children,
proceedings under, §§7B-200(a), 7B-1603.
Judges, §7A-149(a).
Marriage by underage parties, §7B-200(a).
Original civil jurisdiction.
Alimony proceedings, §7A-244.
Amount in controversy.
Proper division for trial of civil actions
generally determined by amount in
controversy, §7A-243.
Annulment of marriage proceedings, §7A-244.
Child custody proceedings, §7A-244.
Child support proceedings, §7A-244.
Concurrently held original jurisdiction allocated
between trial divisions, §7A-242.
Divorce proceedings, §7A-244.
Domestic relations, §7A-244.
Generally, §7A-240.
Parental or judicial consent to abortion
proceedings, §7B-200(a).
Parent, guardian or custodian of juvenile,
§7B-200(b).
Parent or guardian of juvenile adjudicated abused,
neglected or dependent, §7B-200(b).
Small claim actions.
Defendants.
Methods of subjecting person of defendant to
jurisdiction, §7A-217.
Objections to jurisdiction over person, §7A-221.
Termination or reinstatement of parental rights
proceedings, §7B-200(a).
Jury.
Jury instruction conference, SuperCt Rule 21.
Petit jurors.
Applicability of provisions, §7A-197.
Seat of court in municipality with corporate limits
extending into two or more contiguous
counties.
Summoning jury, challenges, §7A-199(b).
Summary jury trial, SuperCt Rule 23.
Trial by jury.
No right to jury trial in criminal cases,
§7A-196(b).
Right to trial by jury in conformity with rules of
civil procedure, §7A-196(a).
Juvenile code.
Specialized judgeships, §7A-147(c).
Juvenile court.
Defined, §143B-805.
Juvenile court counselors.
Chief court counselors.
Duties and powers, §143B-830.
Defined, §143B-805.
Duties and powers, §143B-831.
Landlord and tenant.
Summary ejectment.
Appeals to district court, §42-32.
Liens.
Possessory liens on personal property.
Action to regain possession of motor vehicle or
vessel.
Involuntary relinquishment of possession by
lienor.
Appeal to district court for trial de novo,
§44A-6.1.

DISTRICT COURTS —Cont'd
Liens —Cont'd
Small claim actions.
Enforcement of motor vehicle mechanic and
storage liens, §7A-211.1.
Execution and lien of judgment, §7A-225.
Local court rules, SuperCt Rule 22.
Magistrates.
Assignment of small claim actions to magistrates,
§7A-211.
Judgment of magistrate in civil action
improperly assigned or not assigned,
§7A-212.
Number of magistrates for each county,
§7A-133(c).
Reporting of civil trials.
No provision for reporting before magistrates,
§7A-198(e).
Small claim actions.
Assignment of small claim actions to
magistrates.
Request for and notice of assignment,
§7A-213.
Form of magistrate summons, §7A-232.
New trial before magistrate, §7A-228(a).
Stay of execution on appeal, §7A-227.
**Mediated settlement conferences or other
settlement procedures.**
Actions involving equitable distribution, alimony
and support, §7A-38.4A.
Administrative fees, §7A-38.4A(l).
Appointment of mediator by judge, parties
failure to designate, §7A-38.4A(f).
Attendance at mediated settlement conference.
Failure to attend, monetary sanctions,
§7A-38.4A(e).
Parties required to attend, §7A-38.4A(d).
Attendance at settlement procedure in lieu of
attending mediated settlement conference,
§7A-38.4A(g).
Compelling mediator or neutral to testify,
prohibition, §7A-38.4A(j).
Costs of mediated settlement conference,
§7A-38.4A(i).
Definitions applying to section, §7A-38.4A(b).
Designation of mediator by parties,
§7A-38.4A(f).
Design, implementation and evaluation of pilot
program, purposes of section, §7A-38.4A(a).
Discovery.
Statements made and conduct during
mediation, §7A-38.4A(j).
Evidence.
Statements made or conduct during
mediation, §7A-38.4A(j).
Fees of mediators, payment, §7A-38.4A(i).
Immunity of mediators and neutrals,
§7A-38.4A(h).
Neutrals acting at settlement procedure,
selection and compensation, §7A-38.4A(g).
Report as to statistical data, §7A-38.4A(m).
Right to jury trial not limited, §7A-38.4A(n).
Rules to implement section, supreme court may
adopt, §7A-38.4A(o).
Sanctions for failure to attend conference,
§7A-38.4A(e).
Standards for certification and conduct of
mediators and neutrals, adoption by
supreme court, §7A-38.4A(k).
Agreements reached to be in writing,
§7A-38.3D(l).

DISTRICT COURTS —Cont'd
Mediated settlement conferences or other
		settlement procedures —Cont'd
	Authority of mediator, §7A-38.3D(e).
	Civil district court action, judge to encourage,
		§7A-38.5(d).
	Community mediation center, §7A-38.3D(c).
	Confidentiality of work products, §7A-38.3D(i).
	Criminal district court action, judge to encourage,
		§7A-38.5(c).
	Definitions, §7A-38.3D(n).
	Delay of prosecution pending mediation,
		§7A-38.3D(b).
	Dismissal of case, fee, §7A-38.3D(m).
	Divorce and alimony.
		Actions involving equitable distribution,
			alimony and support.
			Authority of chief district court judge to order,
				§7A-38.4A(c).
	Enabling authority, §7A-38.3D(b).
	Immunity of mediator, §7A-38.3D(h).
	Inadmissibility of negotiations, §7A-38.3D(j).
	Oversight, §7A-38.3D(g).
	Purpose of provisions, §7A-38.3D(a).
	Qualification of mediator, §7A-38.3D(f).
	Rules of procedure, §7A-38.3D(d).
	Testimony of mediator or neutral witness,
		§7A-38.3D(k).
Motions.
	Civil actions, SuperCt Rule 6.
Motor vehicle mechanic and storage liens.
	Small claim actions.
		Enforcement of liens, §7A-211.1.
Motor vehicles.
	Chief district judges.
		Multicopy uniform traffic ticket and complaint.
			Judges to prescribe, §7A-148(b).
	Possessory liens on personal property.
		Action to regain possession.
			Involuntary relinquishment of possession by
				lienor.
				Appeal to district court for trial de novo,
					§44A-6.1(b).
Motor vehicle special registration plates.
	Judges, §20-79.6(c).
Municipalities.
	Facilities and courtrooms.
		Responsibility of municipalities for physical
			facilities, §7A-302.
	Seat of court in municipality with corporate limits
		extending into two or more contiguous
		counties.
		Venue, special rules, place for recording
			judgments, §7A-199(a) to (d).
No contest plea to felony.
	Record of proceeding, §7A-191.1.
Notice.
	Criminal actions.
		Notice of appeal, §7A-290.
	Small claim actions.
		Appeal for trial de novo.
			Oral notice of appeal, §7A-228(a).
		Assignment of actions.
			Form of notice, §7A-232.
Number of judges by districts, §7A-133(a).
Oaths.
	Judges of district court.
		Administration of oaths, §7A-291.
		Oath of office, §7A-140.
Open.
	Court always open, §7A-190.

DISTRICT COURTS —Cont'd
Opening statements, SuperCt Rule 9.
Orders in chambers, §7A-191.
	Interlocutory orders, §7A-192.
Parental or judicial consent to abortion.
	Jurisdiction over proceedings, §7B-200(a).
Personal injury.
	Small claim actions.
		Form of complaint for injury to person, §7A-232.
Photographs or reproduction of court
		proceedings, SuperCt Rule 15.
Place court to sit, NC Const Art IV §10.
Pleadings.
	Form, SuperCt Rule 5.
	Small claim actions.
		No required pleadings other than complaint,
			§7A-220.
Presence of counsel during jury deliberations.
	Criminal actions, SuperCt Rule 13.
Pre-trial procedure, SuperCt Rule 7.
	Conferences in capital cases, SuperCt Rule 24.
	Order on final pre-trial conference.
		Form, SuperCt Forms.
Promissory notes.
	Small claim actions.
		Form of complaint on promissory note, §7A-232.
Property.
	Small claim actions.
		Form of complaint for injury to property,
			§7A-232.
Receivers.
	Appointment of receivers.
		Jurisdiction of judges, §1-501.
Remedies.
	Small claim actions.
		Provisional and incidental remedies, §7A-231.
Removal for fair trial, §1-84.
	Affidavits on hearing, §1-85.
	Depositions, §1-87(b).
	Subsequent proceedings, §1-87(a).
	Transcripts, §1-87(a).
Reporting of civil trials.
	Appointment of reporters, §7A-198(f).
	Compensation and allowances of reporters,
		§7A-198(f).
	Electronic or mechanical devices.
		Inaccurate record produced, §7A-198(g).
		Operation of device while trial in progress,
			§7A-198(c).
		State of art and techniques of recording
			testimony, §7A-198(b).
	Infractions.
		No reporting of hearings to adjudicate and
			dispose of, §7A-198(e).
	Magistrates.
		No provisions for reporting trials before
			magistrate, §7A-198(e).
	Utilization of court-reporting personnel,
		§7A-198(a).
	Waiver of reporting of trial by consent of party,
		§7A-198(d).
Retirement system for teachers and state
		employees.
	Consolidated judicial retirement act, §§135-50 to
		135-75.
		See RETIREMENT SYSTEM FOR TEACHERS
			AND STATE EMPLOYEES.
Rules of civil procedure govern procedure,
	§1A-1 Rule 1.
Scheduling conflicts.
	Guidelines for resolving, SuperCt Rule 3.1.

DISTRICT COURTS —Cont'd
Search warrants.
  Judges of district courts.
    Issuance of search warrant, §15A-243(b).
Seat of court.
  Additional seat, §7A-133(c).
    Appointment of judges, §7A-133(a).
    Clerical functions furnished by clerk of superior
      court, §7A-182(a), (b).
    Unincorporated seats of court.
      Disposition of fees in counties, §7A-317.1.
    Unincorporated seats of court.
      Disposition of fees in counties, §7A-317.1.
    Venue.
      Special venue rule when court sits without jury
        and seat of court lies in more than one
        county, §7A-199(a) to (d).
Sessions, §7A-149(b).
Settlement procedures and mediated
  settlement conferences.
  Actions involving equitable distribution, alimony
    and support, §7A-38.4A.
Small claims actions, §§7A-210 to 7A-232.
  See SMALL CLAIMS.
Statutes.
  Injunctive and declaratory relief.
    Enforcement or invalidation of statutes.
      Grounds for transfer, §7A-245(b).
Stays.
  Small claim actions.
    Execution on appeal, §7A-227.
Summary jury trial, SuperCt Rule 23.
Summons and process.
  Fees.
    Uniform civil process fees, §7A-311.
  Judges of district court.
    Power to issue process and orders, §7A-291.
Superior court clerks.
  Additional seats of district court.
    Clerical functions at additional seats, §7A-182.
  Assistant clerks.
    Functions of assistant clerks in district court
      matters, §7A-181.
  Deputy clerks.
    Functions of deputy clerks in district court
      matters, §7A-181.
  Functions of clerk in district court matters,
    §7A-180.
Support and maintenance.
  Mediated settlement conferences or other
    settlement procedures in actions involving
    support, §7A-38.4A.
Supreme court.
  Rules of practice and procedure in trial courts.
    Power of supreme court to prescribe, §7A-34.
Sureties, SuperCt Rule 20.
Termination of parental rights.
  Generally, §§7B-1100 to 7B-1114.
    See TERMINATION OF PARENTAL RIGHTS.
  Jurisdiction over proceedings, §7B-200(a).
Third party practice.
  Small claim actions.
    Impermissible third party claims, §7A-219.
Time.
  Enlargement of time, SuperCt Rule 4.
Traffic ticket and complaint.
  Chief judge.
    Prescribing multicopy uniform traffic ticket and
      complaint, §7A-148(b).
Transfer of cases.
  Felony guilty or no contest pleas, §15A-1029.1(a).

DISTRICT COURTS —Cont'd
Transfer of cases —Cont'd
  Judge's own motion, §7A-259(b).
  Review of matters, §7A-260.
Trial court administrators.
  Duties, §7A-356.
Trials.
  Chambers.
    Hearings and orders in chambers, §7A-191.
      Interlocutory orders in chambers, §7A-192.
  Conducted in open court, §7A-191.
  Jury trials.
    No right to jury trial on criminal cases,
      §7A-196(b).
    Right to trial by jury in conformity with the
      rules of civil procedure. §7A-196(a).
  On merits conducted at regularly scheduled trial
    sessions, §7A-190.
Undisciplined juveniles.
  Generally, §§7B-1500 to 7B-2827.
    See DELINQUENT AND UNDISCIPLINED
      JUVENILES.
  Jurisdiction over, §7B-1600.
Venue.
  Seat of court in municipality with corporate limits
    extending into two or more contiguous
    counties.
    Civil jury actions, summoning jurors,
      challenges, §7A-199(b).
    Criminal cases, §7A-199(c).
    Nonjury civil or juvenile matters, §7A-199(a).
    Recording judgment, place for, §7A-199(d).
  Small claim actions.
    Objections to venue, §7A-221.
Vessels.
  Possessory liens on personal property.
    Action to regain possession.
      Involuntary relinquishment of possession by
      lienor.
        Appeal to district court for trial de novo,
          §44A-6.1(b).
Warrants.
  Judges of district court.
    Power to issue arrest and search warrants,
      §7A-291.
Witnesses.
  Examination, SuperCt Rule 11.
  Judges of district court.
    Power to compel attendance of witnesses,
      §7A-291.

DISTRICT OF COLUMBIA, US Const Art I §8.

DISTRICTS.
Agricultural districts.
  Voluntary agricultural districts.
    Agricultural development and farmland
      preservation enabling act generally,
      §§106-735 to 106-744.
    See FARMLAND PRESERVATION.
Airports.
  Special airport districts, §§63-78 to 63-89.
    See AIRPORTS.
Congress.
  Area not assigned to district, §163-201(d).
  General assembly apportionment act.
    Compliance with federal law, §163-201.2(c).
    Limitation on number of divisions,
      §163-201.2(b).
    Restriction, §163-201.2(a).
  Number of districts, §163-201(a).

DISTRICTS —Cont'd
Congress —Cont'd
  Severability of congressional apportionment acts,
    §163-201.1.
  Specified, §163-201(a).
  Voting tabulation district boundary changed.
    Congressional district boundary not changed,
      §163-201(c).
Consolidated city-county act.
  Urban service districts.
    See CONSOLIDATED CITY-COUNTY ACT.
Constitution of North Carolina.
  General assembly.
    House of representatives, NC Const Art II §5.
    Senate, NC Const Art II §3.
    Superior court districts, NC Const Art IV §9.
Counties.
  Economic development and training districts,
    §§153A-317.11 to 153A-317.17.
    See ECONOMIC DEVELOPMENT AND
      TRAINING DISTRICTS.
  Mosquito control districts, §§130A-352 to
    130A-358.
  Research and production service districts,
    §§153A-311 to 153A-317.
    See COUNTY RESEARCH AND PRODUCTION
      SERVICE DISTRICTS.
  Water and sewer districts, §§162A-86 to 162A-94.
    See COUNTY WATER AND SEWER
      DISTRICTS.
County service districts.
  Economic development and training districts,
    §§153A-317.11 to 153A-317.17.
    See ECONOMIC DEVELOPMENT AND
      TRAINING DISTRICTS.
  Generally, §§153A-300 to 153A-310.
    See COUNTY SERVICE DISTRICTS.
  Research and production service districts,
    §§153A-311 to 153A-317.
    See COUNTY RESEARCH AND PRODUCTION
      SERVICE DISTRICTS.
Drainage districts, §§156-54 to 156-138.4.
  See DRAINAGE DISTRICTS.
Eminent domain power, §40A-3(c).
Fire protection districts.
  Rural fire protection districts, §§69-25.1 to
    69-25.17.
    See RURAL FIRE PROTECTION DISTRICTS.
General assembly.
  Dividing precincts in apportionment acts,
    §120-2.2.
  Representative districts, §120-2(a) to (d), NC
    Const Art II §5.
  Senatorial districts, §120-1(a) to (d), NC Const Art
    II §3.
  Severability of apportionment acts, §120-2.1.
Historic districts generally, §§160A-400.1 to
    160A-400.14.
  See HISTORIC DISTRICTS AND LANDMARKS.
Hospital districts.
  See HOSPITAL DISTRICTS.
Judicial department.
  District court division.
    Composition of split districts, §7A-133(b), (b1).
    Number of judges by districts, §7A-133(a).
    Organization into territorial district, §7A-130.
Libraries.
  Interstate library districts, §125-12 Art III.
    Governing board, §125-12 Art IV.
  State and federal aid to districts, §125-15.

DISTRICTS —Cont'd
Local government finance.
  General provisions, §§159-1 to 159-188.
    See LOCAL GOVERNMENT FINANCE.
Metropolitan sewerage districts, §§162A-64 to
    162A-81.
  See METROPOLITAN SEWERAGE DISTRICTS.
Metropolitan water districts, §§162A-31 to
    162A-58.
  See METROPOLITAN WATER DISTRICTS.
Mosquito control districts, §§130A-352 to
    130A-358.
Municipal service districts, §§160A-535 to
    160A-544.
  See MUNICIPAL SERVICE DISTRICTS.
Public school districts.
  Generally.
    See SCHOOL DISTRICTS AND
      ADMINISTRATIVE UNITS.
Regional natural gas districts, §§160A-660 to
    160A-676.
  See REGIONAL NATURAL GAS DISTRICTS.
**Sale, lease or exchange of property between
    governmental units.**
  Action taken by governmental unit, §160A-274(c).
  Authority, §160A-274(b).
  Governmental unit defined, §160A-274(a).
Sanitary districts, §§130A-47 to 130A-85.
  See SANITARY DISTRICTS.
School districts.
  See SCHOOL DISTRICTS AND
    ADMINISTRATIVE UNITS.
Soil and water conservation districts, §§139-1
    to 139-57.
  See SOIL AND WATER CONSERVATION
    DISTRICTS.
Superior courts, NC Const Art IV §9.
Transportation department.
  Administrative districts.
    Establishment, §136-15.
Water supply and waterworks.
  County water and sewer districts, §§162A-86 to
    162A-94.
    See COUNTY WATER AND SEWER
      DISTRICTS.
  Metropolitan water districts, §§162A-31 to
    162A-58.
    See METROPOLITAN WATER DISTRICTS.

DISTURBING HUMAN REMAINS, §14-401.22(c).

DISTURBING OFFICIAL MEETINGS,
    §143-318.17.

DISTURBING THE PEACE.
Disorderly conduct.
  See DISORDERLY CONDUCT.
Public intoxication, §§14-443 to 14-447.
Riots and civil disorders, §§14-288.1 to
    14-288.20.
  See RIOTS AND CIVIL DISORDERS.

DITCHES.
**Assessment or contribution for damages or for
    work done on ditch.**
  Power of magistrate to assess, §7A-292.
Diverting water from public road, §136-95.
Open drains within thirty feet of ditch, §156-9.

DIVER'S FLAGS.
Skin and scuba divers, §75A-13.1.

**DIVERSION OF DELINQUENT OR
    UNDISCIPLINED JUVENILES,** §7B-1706.

DIVIDENDS.
Bank holding companies.
Income tax.
Adjustment to expenses related to,
§105-130.6A(c), (e), (f), (h).
Banks, §§53-87, 53-87.1.
Dissolution and liquidation, §§53-18, 53-20(m).
Preferred stock, §53-155.
Issuance to the United States Treasury,
§53-87.1(a), (b).
Use of surplus, §53-88.
Cooperative associations, §54-126.
Time for, §54-127.
Corporations.
Distributions to shareholders generally, §55-6-40.
Income tax.
Adjustment to for expenses related to,
§105-130.6A.
Information filed with secretary of revenue.
Persons receiving dividends, §105-130.21(b).
S corporations.
Distributions to shareholders, §105-131.6.
Information filed with secretary of revenue.
Resident taxpayers receiving dividends,
§105-130.21(b).
Nonprofit corporations.
Unlawful distributions by directors, §55A-8-33.
Credit unions, §54-109.54.
Lien on accumulated dividends, §54-109.59.
Power to declare dividends, §54-109.21.
Electric power holding companies.
Income tax.
Adjustment for expenses related to,
§105-130.6A(d), (g), (h).
Income tax.
Bank holding companies.
Adjustment to for expenses related to,
§105-130.6A(c), (e), (f), (h).
Corporations.
Adjustment to for expenses related to,
§105-130.6A.
Information filed with secretary of revenue.
Persons receiving dividends, §105-130.21(b).
S corporations.
Distributions to shareholders, §105-131.6.
Electric power holding companies.
Adjustment for expenses related to,
§105-130.6A(d), (g), (h).
Insurance companies.
Conversion of stock corporations into mutual
corporations.
Repayment of dividends to corporation for
beneficiaries, §58-10-5.
Impairment of capital.
Dividends not payable when capital impaired,
§58-7-125.
Liability of stockholders for unlawful
stockholders, §58-7-125.
Rate bureau.
Payment of dividends not prohibited or
regulated by rate bureau division,
§58-36-60.
Restrictions, requirements for declaring,
§58-7-130.
Insurance holding companies.
Extraordinary dividends, §58-19-30(c).
Reporting of dividends by registered insurers,
§58-19-25(d).
Limitation of actions.
Actions on account of, §1-50(a).

DIVIDENDS —Cont'd
Mutual insurance companies.
Dividends to policyholders, §58-8-25(a), (b).
Nonprofit corporations.
Unlawful distributions by directors, §55A-8-33.
Partition, §§46-10, 46-11.
Principal and income act.
Interest, dividends, payments made in lieu of.
Allocation, §37A-4-409.
Savings and loan associations.
Approval by commissioner required, §54B-43.
Withdrawable accounts, §§54B-122, 54B-123.
Forced retirement.
Effect, §54B-126(b), (c).
Savings banks.
Stock dividends, §54C-44.
Share dividends.
Generally, §55-6-23(a), (b).
Record date for shareholders entitled to share
dividend, §55-6-23(c).
Trust companies.
Seizure by commissioner.
Dividends to shareholders and claimants,
§53-389.
Unclaimed dividends, §53-392.
Unclaimed property generally, §§116B-51 to
116B-80.
See UNCLAIMED PROPERTY.

DIVINER'S SAGE.
Salvia divinorum.
Manufacture, sale, delivery, possession.
Unlawful, §14-401.23.

DIVISION OF ADULT CORRECTION.
Department of public safety, §§143B-700 to
143B-721.
See PUBLIC SAFETY DEPARTMENT.

DIVISION OF EMPLOYMENT SECURITY.
Creation, §96-3.
**Job training, education and placement
information management,** §§96-30 to 96-35.
See JOB TRAINING, EDUCATION AND
PLACEMENT INFORMATION
MANAGEMENT.
Unemployment compensation, §§96-1 to 96-29.
See UNEMPLOYMENT COMPENSATION.

DIVISION OF JUVENILE JUSTICE.
Department of public safety, §§143B-800 to
143B-851.
See PUBLIC SAFETY DEPARTMENT.

DIVISION OF MOTOR VEHICLES.
See MOTOR VEHICLES DIVISION.

DIVORCE, §§50-2 to 50-22.
Abandonment.
Grounds for divorce, §50-7.
Absolute divorce.
Acts barring rights, §31A-1(a).
Answer of summons by defendant, §50-9.
Certificate failing to comply with former section
52-6.
Effect of decree on, §52-9.
Cost of final action, §7A-305(a2).
Effects, §50-11.
Equitable distribution judgment not entered prior
to decree, §50-21(a).
Incompetent spouses, §50-22.
Incurable insanity, §50-5.1.
Judgments entered prior to January 1, 1981
validated, §50-11.3.

DIVORCE —Cont'd
Absolute divorce —Cont'd
Maiden or premarriage surname.
Resumption by woman or man, §50-12.
Separation of one year, §50-6.
Summary judgment, §50-10(d).
Accident and health insurance.
Coverage of children, §58-51-120(c).
Actions.
Competency of witnesses.
Communications between marital counselor and
parties, §8-53.6.
Acts barring rights of spouse, §31A-1(a).
Adoption.
Visitation of adopted grandchild.
Action by biological grandparent, §50-13.2A.
Adultery.
Grounds for divorce, §50-7.
Alcohol abuse.
Grounds for divorce, §50-7.
Alimony.
Absolute divorce.
Effects, §50-11(c).
Divorce obtained outside state in which
jurisdiction over dependent spouse not
obtained.
Right to alimony not impaired or destroyed,
§50-11(d).
Actions.
Independent actions.
Maintenance of certain actions as
independent actions permissible,
§50-19(a).
Separate action prosecuted during
pendency, §50-19(b).
Maintenance of certain actions as independent
actions permissible, §50-19(a).
Without action, §50-16.10.
Amount, §50-16.3A(b).
Determination of amount, §50-16.3A.
Arrest.
Remedy available, §50-16.7(d).
Attachments.
Remedy available, §50-16.7(e).
Attorney at law.
Fees.
Action for alimony, §50-16.4.
Attorneys' fees, §50-16.4.
Bail.
Remedy available, §50-16.7(d).
Barred by separation agreement or premarital
agreement provisions, §50-16.6(b).
Bonds, surety.
Bond for costs unnecessary, §50-2.
Change in circumstances.
Modification.
Family law arbitration act, §50-56.
Cohabitation of dependent spouse.
Termination of alimony, §50-16.9(b).
Confession of judgment, §1A-1 Rule 68.1(e).
Costs.
Bond for costs unnecessary, §50-2.
Debtors and creditors.
Dependent spouse deemed creditor, §50-16.7(h).
Decree.
Enforcement, §50-16.7.
Definitions, §50-16.1A.
Dependent spouse.
Deemed creditor, §50-16.7(h).
Defined, §50-16.1A.

DIVORCE —Cont'd
Alimony —Cont'd
Distribution by court of marital and divisible
property.
Equitable distribution.
Without regard to alimony, §50-20(f).
Duration, §50-16.3A(b).
Effects of absolute divorce, §50-11(c).
Divorce obtained outside state in which
jurisdiction over dependent spouse not
obtained.
Right to alimony not impaired or destroyed,
§50-11(d).
Entitlement, §50-16.3A(a).
Equitable distribution.
Hearing claim for alimony prior to, effect,
§50-16.3A(a).
Execution, execution sales and supplemental
proceedings.
Remedies available, §50-16.7(k).
Execution of judgment.
Time limitation as to execution not to apply,
§1-306.
Exemption from creditors' claims, §1C-1601(a).
Findings of fact, §50-16.3A(c).
Garnishment.
Remedy available, §50-16.7(e).
Grounds for alimony, §50-16.3A.
Illicit sexual behavior.
Defined, §50-16.1A.
Dependent or supporting spouse participating
in, §50-16.3A(a).
Income withholding.
Application to court by dependent spouse,
§50-16.7(l1).
Limitation on amount withheld, §110-136.6(b1).
Incompetent spouse.
Actions on behalf of, §50-22.
Independent actions.
Maintenance of certain actions as independent
actions permissible, §50-19(a).
Separate action prosecuted during pendency,
§50-19(b).
Injunctions.
Remedy available, §50-16.7(f).
Judgments.
Not lien against real property, §50-16.7(i).
Jury trial, §50-16.3A(c).
Liens.
Judgment not lien, §50-16.7(i).
Local, private and special legislation prohibited,
NC Const Art II §24.
Lump sum payments, §50-16.7(a).
Marital misconduct.
Defined, §50-16.1A.
Mediated settlement conferences or other
settlement procedures.
District court actions, §7A-38.4A.
Military affairs.
Residence of military personnel, §50-18.
Modification.
Change in circumstances.
Family law arbitration act, §50-56.
Mortgages and deeds of trust.
Securing payments, §50-16.7(b).
Orders.
Modification, §50-16.9(a).
Payment.
How paid, §50-16.7.
Willful disobedience of order for payment,
§50-16.7(j).
Contempt to enforce payment, §50-16.7(j).

DIVORCE —Cont'd
Alimony —Cont'd
  Personal property.
    Transfer as part of order, §50-16.7(c).
  Postseparation support. See within this heading, "Postseparation support."
  Preliminary injunction enjoining spouse from interfering with threatening or molesting plaintiff during pendency of suit.
    Bond not required, §1A-1 Rule 65(c).
  Real property.
    Transfer as part of order, §50-16.7(c).
    Writ of possession issued, §50-17.
  Receivers.
    Appointment, §50-16.7(g).
  Reference by consent, §1A-1 Rule 53(a).
  Remarriage of dependent spouse.
    Termination of alimony, §50-16.9(b).
  Remedies supplemental, §50-16.7(l).
  Removal of action, §50-3.
  Supporting spouse.
    Defined, §50-16.1A.
  Temporary restraining order enjoining spouse from interfering with threatening or molesting plaintiff during pendency of suit.
    Bond not required, §1A-1 Rule 65(c).
  Termination, §50-16.9(b).
  Travel expenses of defendant.
    Payment, §50-18.
  Without action, §50-16.10.
A mensa et thoro.
  Bed and board.
    Grounds for divorce, §50-7.
Annulment of marriage.
  General provisions.
    See ANNULMENT OF MARRIAGE.
Appearances.
  Failure of defendant to appear in action.
    Notice of trial not required, §50-10(b).
Arbitration.
  Family law arbitration generally, §§50-41 to 50-62.
    See FAMILY LAW ARBITRATION.
Arrest.
  Remedy available, §50-16.7(d).
Attorneys' fees.
  Action for alimony, §50-16.4.
  Barred by separation agreement or premarital agreement provisions, §50-16.6(b).
  Custody and support of minor children.
    Counsel fees in actions for, §50-13.6.
Attorneys specializing in family law, Bar Rules D.2401 to D.2407.
A vinculo.
  Effects of absolute divorce, §50-11.
  Grounds for absolute divorce.
    Separation of one year, §50-6.
  Incompetent spouses, §50-22.
  Summary judgment.
    Applicability of provisions, §50-10(d).
Bed and board divorce grounds, §50-7.
Bonds, surety.
  Bond for costs unnecessary, §50-2.
Change of venue, §1-83.
Child custody.
  Action or proceeding for child custody or visitation, §50-13.1.
    Procedure, §50-13.5.
  Electronic communications.
    Court may set guidelines, §50-13.2(e).
  Enforcement of order, §50-13.3.

DIVORCE —Cont'd
Child custody —Cont'd
  General provisions.
    See CHILD CUSTODY.
  Grandparents' visitation, §50-13.2(b1).
    Adopted grandchild.
      Action by biological grandparent, §50-13.2A.
  Independent actions permissible, §50-19.
  Judgment provisions pertaining to custody, §50-11.2.
    Change in conditions.
      Jurisdiction requirements, §50-11.2.
      Modification upon substantial change, §50-11.2.
  Mediation program, §§7A-494, 7A-495.
  Modification of orders, §50-13.7.
  Persons entitled, §50-13.2(a), (b).
  Persons incapable of self-support upon reaching majority, §50-13.8.
  Taking child outside state, §50-13.2(c).
Child support.
  Action for support of minor child, §50-13.4.
    Procedure, §50-13.5.
  Distribution by court of marital and divisible property.
    Equitable distribution without regard to child support, §50-20(f).
  General provisions.
    See CHILD SUPPORT.
  Independent actions permissible, §50-19.
  Judgment provisions pertaining to care, tuition and maintenance, §50-11.2.
    Change of conditions.
      Modification upon substantial change, §50-11.2.
  Modification of orders, §50-13.7.
  Past due child support, §50-13.10.
  Procedure to insure payment, §50-13.9.
Collaborative law proceedings, §§50-70 to 50-79.
  See COLLABORATIVE LAW PROCEEDINGS.
Community property.
  Equitable distribution of marital property generally, §§50-11, 50-20 to 50-22.
  Cross-actions, jurisdiction, §7A-244.
  Decedents' estates.
    Claim for distribution of marital or divisible property, §28A-19-19.
  Mediated settlement conferences, district courts, §7A-38.4A.
Complaint.
  Contents of complaint, §50-8.
  Material facts deemed denied by defendant, §50-10(a).
  Resumption of maiden name or adoption of name of prior deceased or living husband.
    Incorporation for petition of resumption or use in complaint for divorce, §50-12(d).
  Verification, §50-8.
Confession of judgment.
  Alimony.
    Alimony without action, §50-16.10.
Contempt.
  Alimony.
    Payment.
      Willful disobedience of order for payment.
        Enforcement of payment by contempt, §50-16.7(j).
  Order for custody of minor child.
    Enforcement, §50-13.3(a).
Costs.
  Allowance of costs to either party or apportioned in discretion of court, §6-21.

DIVORCE —Cont'd
Costs —Cont'd
Bond for costs unnecessary, §50-2.
Counterclaims and cross-claims.
Resumption of maiden name or adoption of name
of prior deceased or prior living husband.
Incorporation of petition for resumption or use
of name in complaint or counterclaim for
divorce, §50-12(d).
**Cruel or barbarous treatment endangering life
of the other.**
Grounds for divorce, §50-7.
Decrees.
Alimony.
Enforcement, §50-16.7.
Default judgments, §50-10(e).
Deferred compensation plans.
Distribution of pension, retirement and deferred
compensation benefits, §50-20.1.
Definitions, §50-16.1A.
Distribution by court of marital and divisible
property.
Equitable distribution, §50-20(b).
Disabled persons.
Custody.
Persons incapable of self-support upon reaching
majority.
Physically incapable of self-support, §50-13.8.
Discovery.
Distribution by court of marital and divisible
property.
Equitable distribution.
Discovery and scheduling conference,
§50-21(d).
Procedures in actions, §50-21(a).
Prejudicial delays.
Sanctions for, §50-21(e).
**Distribution by court of marital and divisible
property.**
Absolute divorce.
Equitable distribution.
Effects of absolute divorce, §50-11(e), (f).
Cross action for equitable distribution.
Jurisdiction.
District court division, §7A-244.
Decedents' estates.
Claim for distribution of marital or divisible
property, §28A-19-19.
Equitable distribution, §50-20.
Absolute divorce.
Effects of absolute divorce, §50-11(e), (f).
Agreements providing for equitable distribution,
§50-20(d).
Alimony.
Equitable distribution without regard to,
§50-20(f).
Hearing claim prior to distribution,
§50-16.3A(a).
Child support.
Equitable distribution without regard to,
§50-20(f).
Death of party, §50-20(c), (l).
Definitions, §50-20(b).
Discovery, §50-20(a).
Discovery and scheduling conference,
§50-21(d).
Prejudicial delay sanctions, §50-21(e).
Distributive award.
Defined, §50-20(b).
Duties of court, §50-20(a).

DIVORCE —Cont'd
**Distribution by court of marital and divisible
property** —Cont'd
Equitable distribution —Cont'd
Equal division.
By using net value of marital property,
§50-20(b), (c).
Equity between parties.
Distributive award in order to achieve,
§50-20(e).
Filing of claims, §50-21(a).
Incompetent spouse.
Ordering equitable distribution on behalf of,
§50-22.
Injunctive relief, §50-20(i).
Interim distribution.
Partial distribution, §50-20(i1).
Judgments.
Entry, §50-21(a).
Jury trial.
Section not to restrict or extend right,
§50-21(c).
Lis pendens, §50-20(h).
Marital property.
Defined, §50-20(b).
Mediated settlement conference or other
settlement procedures.
District court actions, §7A-38.4A.
Rules implementing procedures,
SettlmtEquitDistrib Rules 1 to 15.
See MEDIATED SETTLEMENT
CONFERENCES.
Net value of marital property.
Equal division, §50-20(c).
Partial distribution, §50-20(i1).
Pensions, retirement and deferred compensation
benefits, §50-20.1.
Distributive award, §50-20(b).
Personal property.
Located outside of state.
Subject to equitable distribution, §50-21(a).
Order transferring title, §50-20(g).
Pretrial conference, §50-21(d).
Procedures, §50-21.
Qualified domestic relations order.
Distributive award, §50-20(b).
Real property.
Located outside of state.
Subject to equitable distribution, §50-21(a).
Order transferring title, §50-20(g).
Rights of parties.
Species of common ownership, §50-20(k).
Second or subsequent spouse.
Interest in marital or divisible property,
§50-20(c1).
Separate property.
Defined, §50-20(b).
Transfer of title, §50-20(g).
Valuation of marital property.
Date, §50-21(b).
Vesting of rights, §50-20(k).
Waste or destruction of marital or separate
property.
Temporary orders preventing, §50-21(a).
Written findings of fact.
Requirement, §50-20(j).
Pension or retirement benefits.
Actual receipt of benefits.
Payment upon, §50-20.1(c).
Applicability of provisions, §50-20.1(h).
Basis of award, §50-20.1(d).

DIVORCE —Cont'd
Distribution by court of marital and divisible property —Cont'd
Pension or retirement benefits —Cont'd
Death of person receiving award.
Passing of unpaid balance, §50-20.1(f).
Determination of award, §50-20.1(d).
Maximum percentage of benefits received, §50-20.1(e).
Nonvested benefits, §50-20.1(b).
Qualified domestic relations order.
Distribution by, §50-20.1(g).
Vested benefits, §50-20.1(a).
Presumption of marital property, §50-20(b).
Second or subsequent spouse.
Interest in marital or divisible property, §50-20(c1).
District courts.
Proper division for trial of civil actions, §7A-244.
Drugs.
Grounds for divorce, §50-7.
Equitable distribution, §§50-20 to 50-22.
Alimony claim.
Hearing claim prior to distribution, §50-16.3A(a).
Mediated settlement conferences or other settlement procedures.
District court actions, §7A-38.4A.
Rules implementing procedures, SettlmtEquitDistrib Rules 1 to 15.
See MEDIATED SETTLEMENT CONFERENCES.
Family law arbitration generally, §§50-41 to 50-62.
See FAMILY LAW ARBITRATION.
General assembly.
Local, private and special legislation prohibited, NC Const Art II §24.
Grandparent visitation, §§50-13.2(b1), 50-13.5(j).
Adopted grandchild.
Action by biological grandparent, §50-13.2A.
Grounds.
Abandonment.
Bed and board, §50-7.
Adultery.
Bed and board, §50-7.
Alcohol or drugs.
Excessive use.
Bed and board, §50-7.
Bed and board, §50-7.
Bonds of matrimony.
Insanity of spouse, §50-5.1.
Separation of one year, §50-6.
Cruelty.
Bed and board, §50-7.
Insanity of spouse.
Bonds of matrimony, §50-5.1.
Maliciously turning other out of doors.
Bed and board, §50-7.
Separation of one year.
Bonds of matrimony, §50-6.
Health care power of attorney.
Revocation of health care agent's authority.
Health care agent spouse of principal, §32A-20(c).
Health insurance.
Coverage of children, §58-51-120(c).
Hearsay exception.
Statement of personal or family history, §§8C-1 Rule 803, 8C-1 Rule 804.

DIVORCE —Cont'd
Illegitimacy.
Effects of absolute divorce.
No judgment to render children illegitimate, §50-11(b).
Voidable marriages.
Children born legitimate, §50-11.1.
Incompetent spouses.
Actions on behalf of, §50-22.
Independent actions.
Maintenance of certain actions as independent actions permissible, §50-19(a).
Separate action prosecuted during pendency of independent action, §50-19(b).
Injunctions.
Distribution by court of marital and divisible property.
Equitable distribution, §50-20(i).
Order for custody of minor child.
Enforcement, §50-13.3(b).
Judges.
Jury trial or trial before judge without jury.
Determination, §50-10(c).
Material facts found by judge or jury.
Judgment not given in favor of plaintiff until, §50-10(a).
Judgments.
Collaborative law agreement.
Entry of judgment to effectuate, §50-75.
Default judgments, §50-10(e).
Distribution by court of marital and divisible property.
Equitable distribution.
Entry of judgment, §50-21(a).
Material facts found by judge or jury.
Judgment in favor of plaintiff not given until, §50-10(a).
Provisions pertaining to care, custody, tuition and maintenance of minor children, §50-11.2.
Validation of certain judgments entered prior to January 1, 1981, §50-11.3.
Validation of certain judgments entered prior to October 1, 1983, §50-11.4.
Jurisdiction.
Child custody or child support actions, §50-13.5(c).
In rem or quasi in rem jurisdiction.
Grounds, §1-75.8.
Personal jurisdiction based on marital relationship, §1-75.4.
Jury.
Distribution by court of marital and divisible property.
Equitable distribution.
Jury trial.
Nothing in section to restrict or extend right, §50-21(c).
Jury trial or trial before judge without jury.
Determination, §50-10(c).
Material facts found by judge or jury.
Judgment not given in favor of plaintiff until, §50-10(a).
Lis pendens.
Distribution by court of marital and divisible property.
Equitable distributions, §50-20(h).
Local, private and special legislation prohibited, NC Const Art II §24.
Maiden or premarriage surname.
Resumption, §50-12(a).
Application, §50-12(b).
Man applying to change surname to premarriage surname, §50-12(a1).

DIVORCE —Cont'd
Maiden or premarriage surname —Cont'd
Resumption —Cont'd
Fee, §50-12(e).
Incorporation of petition for resumption in complaint or counterclaim for divorce, §50-12(d).
Man applying to change surname to premarriage surname, §50-12(a1).
Validation of previous resumptions, §50-12(c).
Maliciously turning out of doors.
Grounds for divorce, §50-7.
Marital property.
Decedents' estates.
Claim for distribution of marital or divisible property, §28A-19-19.
Defined, §50-20(b).
Equitable distribution, §§50-20 to 50-22.
Presumptions, §50-20(b).
Marriage generally.
See MARRIAGE.
Material facts found by judge or jury.
Genuine issue of material fact.
Determination, §50-10(d).
Judgment not given in favor of plaintiff until, §50-10(a).
Material facts in complaint deemed denied by defendant, §50-10(a).
Mediated settlement conference and other settlement procedures.
District court actions involving equitable distribution, alimony or support, §7A-38.4A.
Equitable distribution and other family financial cases.
Rules implementing, SettlmtEquitDistrib Rules 1 to 15.
See MEDIATED SETTLEMENT CONFERENCES.
Rules.
Agreement of parties.
Finalizing settlement, SettlmtEquitDistrib Rule 4(B).
Selection of mediator, SettlmtEquitDistrib Rule 2(A).
Selection of neutrals, SettlmtEquitDistrib Rule 10(C)(10).
Appointment of mediator by court, SettlmtEquitDistrib Rule 2(B).
Attendance at settlement conference, SettlmtEquitDistrib Rule 4(A).
Other settlement procedures, SettlmtEquitDistrib Rule 10(C)(8).
Sanction for failure to attend, SettlmtEquitDistrib Rule 10(C)(9).
Sanction for failure to attend, SettlmtEquitDistrib Rule 5.
Authority of mediators, SettlmtEquitDistrib Rule 6.
Authorizing procedures other than mediated settlement conference, SettlmtEquitDistrib Rule 1(C)(3).
Bias.
Disclosure by mediator, SettlmtEquitDistrib Rule 6(B)(2).
Disclosure by neutral, SettlmtEquitDistrib Rule 10(C)(13).
Certification of mediators, SettlmtEquitDistrib Rule 8.
Certification of mediator training programs, SettlmtEquitDistrib Rule 9.

DIVORCE —Cont'd
Mediated settlement conference and other settlement procedures —Cont'd
Rules —Cont'd
Certified family financial mediator.
Selection, SettlmtEquitDistrib Rule 2.
Child custody and visitation.
Including in settlement proceedings, SettlmtEquitDistrib Rule 1(C)(2).
Compelling mediator or neutral to testify.
Prohibition, SettlmtEquitDistrib Rule 10(C)(5).
Compensation of mediator.
Generally, SettlmtEquitDistrib Rule 7.
Paid by parties, SettlmtEquitDistrib Rules 4(C), 7(C).
Compensation of neutral, SettlmtEquitDistrib Rule 10(C)(8), (C)(12).
Computation of time limits, SettlmtEquitDistrib Rule 15.
Confidentiality.
Judicial settlement conference, SettlmtEquitDistrib Rule 12(C).
Counsel consultations with clients and opposing counsel.
Duty, SettlmtEquitDistrib Rule 1(B).
Court appointment of mediator, SettlmtEquitDistrib Rule 2(B).
Decertification of mediators, SettlmtEquitDistrib Rule 8.
Definitions.
AOC forms, SettlmtEquitDistrib Rule 14(B).
Court, SettlmtEquitDistrib Rule 14(A).
Family financial case, SettlmtEquitDistrib Rule 14(C).
Delay of other proceedings.
Mediated settlement conference.
Not cause for, SettlmtEquitDistrib Rule 3(E).
Other settlement procedures.
Not cause for delay, SettlmtEquitDistrib Rule 10(C)(4).
Designation of mediator by agreement.
Filing with court, SettlmtEquitDistrib Rule 2(A).
Dispensing with settlement.
Motion, SettlmtEquitDistrib Rule 1(C)(6).
Disqualification of mediator, SettlmtEquitDistrib Rule 2(D).
Disqualification of neutral, SettlmtEquitDistrib Rule 10(C)(11).
Duties of mediators, SettlmtEquitDistrib Rule 6(B).
Equitable distribution actions.
Requirement for settlement procedures.
Scheduling order to include, SettlmtEquitDistrib Rule 1(C)(1).
Evidence of statements and conduct at settlement proceeding.
Inadmissibility, SettlmtEquitDistrib Rule 10(C)(5).
Executing final agreement.
Time, SettlmtEquitDistrib Rule 4(B).
Ex parte communication.
By mediators, SettlmtEquitDistrib Rule 6(A)(2).
Fee of mediator.
Generally, SettlmtEquitDistrib Rule 7.
Paid by parties, SettlmtEquitDistrib Rules 4(C), 7(C).

DIVORCE —Cont'd
Mediated settlement conference and other settlement procedures —Cont'd
Rules —Cont'd
Fee of neutral, SettlmtEquitDistrib Rule 10(C)(8), (C)(12).
Finalizing settlement agreement, SettlmtEquitDistrib Rule 4(B).
Impasse.
Mediator declaring, SettlmtEquitDistrib Rule 6(A)(3).
Inability to pay.
Failure to move court promptly for determination.
Sanctions, SettlmtEquitDistrib Rule 7(F).
Indigent status.
Failure to move court promptly for indigency determination.
Sanctions, SettlmtEquitDistrib Rule 7(F).
Judicial settlement conference.
Authorized settlement procedures, SettlmtEquitDistrib Rule 10(B)(2).
Conduct of conference.
By district court judge, SettlmtEquitDistrib Rule 12(A).
Discretion of judge, SettlmtEquitDistrib Rule 12(B).
Confidentiality, SettlmtEquitDistrib Rule 12(C).
Disqualification of settlement judge to hear action, SettlmtEquitDistrib Rule 12(A).
Imposition of settlement prohibited, SettlmtEquitDistrib Rule 12(B).
Report by judge, SettlmtEquitDistrib Rule 12(C).
Selection of settlement judge, SettlmtEquitDistrib Rule 12(A).
Local rule making, SettlmtEquitDistrib Rule 13.
Mediated settlement conference.
Attendance.
Excused or modified attendance, SettlmtEquitDistrib Rule 4(A)(2).
Persons required to attend, SettlmtEquitDistrib Rule 4(A)(1).
Phone, attendance by, SettlmtEquitDistrib Rule 4(A)(2).
Sanction for failure to attend, SettlmtEquitDistrib Rule 5.
Authority of mediators, SettlmtEquitDistrib Rule 6.
Deadline for completion, SettlmtEquitDistrib Rule 3(B).
Request to extend, SettlmtEquitDistrib Rule 3(C).
Delay of other proceedings prohibited, SettlmtEquitDistrib Rule 3(E).
Duties of mediators, SettlmtEquitDistrib Rule 6(B).
Postponement of conference, SettlmtEquitDistrib Rule 7(E).
Recesses, SettlmtEquitDistrib Rule 3(D).
When held, SettlmtEquitDistrib Rule 3(B).
Where held, SettlmtEquitDistrib Rule 3(A).
Mediator directory, SettlmtEquitDistrib Rule 2(C).
Mediators.
Authority, SettlmtEquitDistrib Rule 6(A).
Brochure.
Distributing before conference, SettlmtEquitDistrib Rule 6(B)(6).
Certification, SettlmtEquitDistrib Rule 8.

DIVORCE —Cont'd
Mediated settlement conference and other settlement procedures —Cont'd
Rules —Cont'd
Mediators —Cont'd
Compelling mediator or neutral to testify.
Prohibition, SettlmtEquitDistrib Rule 10(C)(5).
Compensation, SettlmtEquitDistrib Rule 7(B).
Agreement of parties to compensation, SettlmtEquitDistrib Rule 7(A).
Court order, SettlmtEquitDistrib Rule 7(B).
Duty of parties to pay, SettlmtEquitDistrib Rule 4(C).
Inability of party to pay full share, SettlmtEquitDistrib Rule 7(D).
Payment by parties, SettlmtEquitDistrib Rule 7(C).
Postponement fee, SettlmtEquitDistrib Rule 7(E).
Sanctions for failure to pay mediator's fee, SettlmtEquitDistrib Rule 7(F).
Control of conference, SettlmtEquitDistrib Rule 6(A)(1).
Disclosures, SettlmtEquitDistrib Rule 6(A)(1).
Bias, prejudice or partiality, SettlmtEquitDistrib Rule 6(A)(2).
Disqualification, SettlmtEquitDistrib Rule 2(D).
Duties, SettlmtEquitDistrib Rule 6(B).
Evaluation forms.
Distributing at conference, SettlmtEquitDistrib Rule 6(B)(7).
Fee.
Compensation generally, SettlmtEquitDistrib Rule 7.
Payment, SettlmtEquitDistrib Rules 4(C), 7(C).
Impasse, declaring, SettlmtEquitDistrib Rule 6(A)(3).
Other settlement procedures.
General rules, SettlmtEquitDistrib Rule 10(C).
Postponement fee, SettlmtEquitDistrib Rule 7(E).
Private communications with participant during conference, SettlmtEquitDistrib Rule 6(A)(2).
Report of results of conference, SettlmtEquitDistrib Rule 6(B)(4).
Revocation of mediator certification, SettlmtEquitDistrib Rule 8.
Scheduling and holding conference, SettlmtEquitDistrib Rule 6(B)(5).
Selection.
Agreement of parties, SettlmtEquitDistrib Rule 2(A).
Certified family financial mediator, SettlmtEquitDistrib Rule 2(A), (B).
Designation of mediator by agreement, SettlmtEquitDistrib Rule 2(A).
Nomination of non-certified family financial mediator, SettlmtEquitDistrib Rule 2(A).
Training and experience.
Certification, SettlmtEquitDistrib Rule 8.
Certification of mediator training programs, SettlmtEquitDistrib Rule 9.
Mediators' fee.
Compensation generally, SettlmtEquitDistrib Rule 7.

DIVORCE —Cont'd
Mediated settlement conference and other settlement procedures —Cont'd
Rules —Cont'd
Mediators' fee —Cont'd
Payment, SettlmtEquitDistrib Rule 4(C).
Mediator training programs.
Certification.
Administrators' fees, payment to complete certification, SettlmtEquitDistrib Rule 9(D).
Before attendance at program, SettlmtEquitDistrib Rule 9(C).
Curriculum, SettlmtEquitDistrib Rule 9(A), (B).
Minimum hours of instruction, SettlmtEquitDistrib Rule 9(A), (B).
Programs attended prior to rules, SettlmtEquitDistrib Rule 9(C).
Motions.
Court appointment of mediator, SettlmtEquitDistrib Rule 2(B).
Dispensing with settlement, SettlmtEquitDistrib Rule 1(C)(6).
Disqualification of mediator, SettlmtEquitDistrib Rule 2(D).
Extension of time to complete settlement conference, SettlmtEquitDistrib Rule 3(C).
Inability to pay share of mediator's fee, SettlmtEquitDistrib Rule 7(D).
Sanction for failure to attend conference, SettlmtEquitDistrib Rule 5.
Settlement procedures in other family financial cases, SettlmtEquitDistrib Rule 1(C)(5).
Use of settlement procedures other than mediated settlement conference, SettlmtEquitDistrib Rule 1(C)(3).
Neutral evaluation.
Abbreviated presentation of facts and issues, SettlmtEquitDistrib Rule 11(A).
Authorized settlement procedures, SettlmtEquitDistrib Rule 10(B)(1).
Conference procedure, SettlmtEquitDistrib Rule 11(E).
Modification, SettlmtEquitDistrib Rule 11(F).
Neutral evaluator.
Assistance to parties in settlement discussions, SettlmtEquitDistrib Rule 11(H).
Duties, SettlmtEquitDistrib Rule 11(G).
Opening statements, SettlmtEquitDistrib Rule 11(G)(1).
Report to court, SettlmtEquitDistrib Rule 11(G)(3).
Report to parties, SettlmtEquitDistrib Rule 11(G)(2).
Responsibilities, SettlmtEquitDistrib Rule 11(A).
Pre-conference submissions, SettlmtEquitDistrib Rule 11(C).
Replies, SettlmtEquitDistrib Rule 11(D).
Time.
Pre-conference submissions, SettlmtEquitDistrib Rule 11(C).
When conference held, SettlmtEquitDistrib Rule 11(B).
Neutrals.
Agreement of parties.
Selection of neutrals, SettlmtEquitDistrib Rule 10(C)(10).

DIVORCE —Cont'd
Mediated settlement conference and other settlement procedures —Cont'd
Rules —Cont'd
Neutrals —Cont'd
Authority and duties, SettlmtEquitDistrib Rule 10(C)(13).
Bias, prejudice or partiality, disclosure, SettlmtEquitDistrib Rule 10(C)(13).
Compensation, SettlmtEquitDistrib Rule 10(C)(8), (C)(12).
Control of proceeding, SettlmtEquitDistrib Rule 10(C)(13).
Disclosures, SettlmtEquitDistrib Rule 10(C)(13).
Disqualification, SettlmtEquitDistrib Rule 10(C)(11).
Fee, SettlmtEquitDistrib Rule 10(C)(8), (C)(12).
Holding proceeding, SettlmtEquitDistrib Rule 10(C)(13).
Reporting results, SettlmtEquitDistrib Rule 10(C)(13).
Scheduling proceeding, SettlmtEquitDistrib Rule 10(C)(13).
Selection of neutrals, SettlmtEquitDistrib Rule 10(C)(10).
Nomination of non-certified family mediator.
Selecting mediator by agreement.
Filing with court, SettlmtEquitDistrib Rule 2(A).
Notarized agreement.
Finalizing settlement agreement, SettlmtEquitDistrib Rule 4(B).
Ordering settlement procedures, SettlmtEquitDistrib Rule 1(C).
Contents of order, SettlmtEquitDistrib Rule 1(C)(4).
Other family financial cases, SettlmtEquitDistrib Rule 1(C)(5).
Other settlement procedures, SettlmtEquitDistrib Rule 10(A).
Other settlement procedures.
Attendance, SettlmtEquitDistrib Rule 10(C)(8).
Sanctions for failure to attend, SettlmtEquitDistrib Rule 10(C)(9).
Delay of other proceedings.
Prohibited, SettlmtEquitDistrib Rule 10(C)(4).
Duties of parties, SettlmtEquitDistrib Rule 10(C)(8).
Finalizing agreement, SettlmtEquitDistrib Rule 10(C)(8).
General rules, SettlmtEquitDistrib Rule 10(C).
Inadmissibility of proceedings, SettlmtEquitDistrib Rule 10(C)(5).
Neutrals.
Selection, disqualification, compensation, authority, duties, SettlmtEquitDistrib Rule 10(C).
Neutral's fee.
Payment, SettlmtEquitDistrib Rule 10(C)(8).
Order authorizing, SettlmtEquitDistrib Rule 10(A).
Procedures authorized by rules, SettlmtEquitDistrib Rule 10(B).
Record not made, SettlmtEquitDistrib Rule 10(C)(6).

DIVORCE —Cont'd
**Mediated settlement conference and other
    settlement procedures** —Cont'd
Rules —Cont'd
  Other settlement procedures —Cont'd
    Time for conducting, SettlmtEquitDistrib
        Rule 10(C)(1).
      Extension, SettlmtEquitDistrib Rule
          10(C)(2).
    When proceeding conducted,
        SettlmtEquitDistrib Rule 10(C)(1).
    Where conducted, SettlmtEquitDistrib Rule
        10(C)(3).
  Partiality.
    Disclosure by mediator, SettlmtEquitDistrib
        Rule 6(B)(2).
    Disclosure by neutral, SettlmtEquitDistrib
        Rule 10(C)(13).
  Phone.
    Attendance at settlement conference by,
        SettlmtEquitDistrib Rule 4(A)(2).
  Postponement fee.
    Mediators, SettlmtEquitDistrib Rule 7(E).
  Postponement of conference,
      SettlmtEquitDistrib Rule 7(E).
  Prejudice.
    Disclosure by mediator, SettlmtEquitDistrib
        Rule 6(B)(2).
    Disclosure by neutral, SettlmtEquitDistrib
        Rule 10(C)(13).
  Private communication.
    By mediators, SettlmtEquitDistrib Rule
        6(A)(2).
  Purpose of mandatory settlement procedures,
      SettlmtEquitDistrib Rule 1(A).
  Recesses.
    Mediated settlement conference,
        SettlmtEquitDistrib Rule 3(D).
  Report by mediator.
    Results of conference, SettlmtEquitDistrib
        Rule 6(B)(4).
  Report by neutral, SettlmtEquitDistrib Rule
      10(C)(13).
  Report by neutral evaluator.
    To court, SettlmtEquitDistrib Rule 11(G)(3).
    To parties, SettlmtEquitDistrib Rule 11(G)(2).
  Report by settlement judge, SettlmtEquitDistrib
      Rule 12(C).
  Revocation of mediator certification,
      SettlmtEquitDistrib Rule 8.
  Sanctions.
    Failure to attend settlement conference,
        SettlmtEquitDistrib Rule 5.
    Failure to attend settlement proceeding,
        SettlmtEquitDistrib Rule 10(C)(9).
    Failure to pay mediator's fee,
        SettlmtEquitDistrib Rule 7(F).
  Scheduling conference.
    Equitable distribution action.
      Scheduling order requiring settlement
          procedure, SettlmtEquitDistrib Rule
          1(C)(1).
    Selection of mediator, SettlmtEquitDistrib
        Rule 2.
  Scheduling order.
    Order requiring settlement procedures,
        SettlmtEquitDistrib Rule 1(C).
    Contents of order, SettlmtEquitDistrib Rule
        1(C)(4).
    Other family financial cases,
        SettlmtEquitDistrib Rule 1(C)(5).

DIVORCE —Cont'd
**Mediated settlement conference and other
    settlement procedures** —Cont'd
Rules —Cont'd
  Scope of settlement proceedings,
      SettlmtEquitDistrib Rule 1(C)(2).
  Selection of certified family financial mediator.
    Appointment by court, SettlmtEquitDistrib
        Rule 2(B).
    By agreement of parties, SettlmtEquitDistrib
        Rule 2(A).
    Mediator directory, SettlmtEquitDistrib Rule
        2(C).
  Selection of non-certified family financial
      mediator.
    By agreement.
      Filing nomination of non-certified family
          financial mediator, SettlmtEquitDistrib
          Rule 2(A).
  Settlement conference.
    Authority of mediators, SettlmtEquitDistrib
        Rule 6.
    Duties of mediators, SettlmtEquitDistrib Rule
        6(B).
    Duties of parties attorneys and participants,
        SettlmtEquitDistrib Rule 4.
    Generally, SettlmtEquitDistrib Rule 3.
    Judicial settlement conference.
      Authorized settlement procedures,
          SettlmtEquitDistrib Rule 10(B)(2).
    Other settlement procedures,
        SettlmtEquitDistrib Rule 10.
    Postponement of conference,
        SettlmtEquitDistrib Rule 7(E).
    Sanctions for failure to attend,
        SettlmtEquitDistrib Rule 5.
  Summary memorandum.
    Essential terms of settlement agreement
        reduced to, SettlmtEquitDistrib Rule
        4(B).
  Telephone.
    Attendance at settlement conference by,
        SettlmtEquitDistrib Rule 4(A)(2).
  Time.
    Completion of settlement conference,
        SettlmtEquitDistrib Rule 3(B).
      Extension of time, SettlmtEquitDistrib Rule
          3(C).
    Computation of limits, SettlmtEquitDistrib
        Rule 15.
    Executed final agreement,
        SettlmtEquitDistrib Rule 4(B).
    Neutral evaluation pre-conference submission,
        SettlmtEquitDistrib Rule 11(C).
      Replies, SettlmtEquitDistrib Rule 11(D).
    Neutral evaluator's report to court,
        SettlmtEquitDistrib Rule 11(G)(3).
    Other settlement procedures,
        SettlmtEquitDistrib Rule 10(C)(1).
      Extension, SettlmtEquitDistrib Rule
          10(C)(2).
    Report by mediator on results of conference,
        SettlmtEquitDistrib Rule 6(B)(4).
    Waiver or extension of limits allowed,
        SettlmtEquitDistrib Rule 15.
  Training and experience.
    Certification of mediators,
        SettlmtEquitDistrib Rule 8.
  Training programs for mediators.
    Certification, SettlmtEquitDistrib Rule 9.

DIVORCE —Cont'd
Mediation.
Child custody and visitation.
Action or proceeding for custody or visitation, §50-13.1.
Custody and visitation mediation program, §§7A-494, 7A-495.
Mental health, developmental disabilities and substance abuse.
Custody.
Persons incapable of self-support upon reaching majority.
Mentally incapable of self-support, §50-13.8.
Incurable insanity.
Grounds for absolute divorce, §50-5.1.
Names.
Adoption of prior deceased husband's name, §50-12(a).
Application, §50-12(b).
Fee, §50-12(e).
Incorporation of petition for adoption in complaint or counterclaim for divorce, §50-12(d).
Validation of use, §50-12(c).
Resumption of maiden or premarriage surname, §50-12(a).
Application, §50-12(b).
Man applying to change surname to premarriage surname, §50-12(a1).
Fee, §50-12(e).
Incorporation of petition for resumption in complaint or counterclaim for divorce, §50-12(d).
Man applying to change surname to premarriage surname, §50-12(a1).
Validation of use of name, §50-12(c).
Use of surname of prior living husband, §50-12(a).
Application, §50-12(b).
Fee, §50-12(e).
Incorporation of petition for use of name in complaint or counterclaim for divorce, §50-12(d).
Validation of use, §50-12(c).
No-fault divorce.
Separation of one year, §50-6.
Nonresidents.
Venue and service on, §50-8.
Notice.
Child custody or child support actions, §50-13.5(d), (e).
Failure of defendant to appear in action.
Notice of trial not required, §50-10(b).
Offering indignities causing intolerable and burdensome conditions.
Grounds for divorce, §50-7.
Pensions and retirement benefits.
Distribution, §§50-20.1, 50-20(b).
Personal jurisdiction based on marital relationship, §1-75.4.
Personal property distribution by court.
Equitable distribution.
Generally, §§50-20, 50-21.
Orders transferring title, §50-20(g).
Personal property located outside of state, §50-21(a).
Pleadings.
Verification.
When verification required, §50-8.
Postseparation support.
Attorneys' fees, §50-16.4.

DIVORCE —Cont'd
Postseparation support —Cont'd
Barred by separation agreement or premarital agreement provisions, §50-16.6(b).
Basis of award, §50-16.2A(b).
Change in circumstances.
Modification.
Family law arbitration act, §50-56.
Considerations in awarding support, §50-16.2A(b).
Marital misconduct of dependent spouse, §50-16.2A(d), (e).
Court's duty, §50-16.8.
Defined, §50-16.1A.
Either party may move for, §50-16.2A(a).
Enforcement of decree, §50-16.7.
Entitlement of dependent spouse to award, §50-16.2A(c).
How paid, §50-16.7.
Income withholding.
Limitation on amount withheld, §110-136.6(b1).
Maintenance of certain actions as independent actions permissible, §50-19.
Marital misconduct of dependent spouse.
Considering, §50-16.2A(d), (e).
Modification, §50-16.9.
Change in circumstances.
Family law arbitration act, §50-56.
Procedure, §50-16.8.
Verified pleading, motion or affidavit.
Requirements, §50-16.2A(a).
Preliminary injunction enjoining spouse from interfering with, threatening or molesting plaintiff during pendency of suit.
Bond not required, §1A-1 Rule 65(c).
Premarital agreements generally, §§52B-1 to 52B-11.
See PREMARITAL AGREEMENTS.
Presumptions.
Marital property, §50-20(b).
Qualified domestic relations orders.
Distribution by court of marital and divisible property, §§50-20.1(g), 50-20(b).
Real property distribution by court.
Equitable distribution.
Generally, §§50-20, 50-21.
Lis pendens, §50-20(h).
Orders transferring title, §50-20(g).
Real property located outside of state, §50-21(a).
Reference by consent, §1A-1 Rule 53(a).
Removal of action, §50-3.
Retirement property distribution by court, §50-20(b).
Rights arising out of marriage.
Effects of absolute divorce, §50-11(a).
Separate property.
Defined, §50-20(b).
Separation.
One year separation on application of either party, §50-6.
Separation agreements, §52-10.1.
Service of process.
Absolute divorce for incurable insanity, §50-5.1.
Child custody or child support actions, §50-13.5(d).
Nonresidents, §50-8.
Validation where summons answered, §50-9.
State health plan for teachers and state employees.
Continuation of coverage.
Legally divorced or separated spouses and eligible dependent children, §135-48.44(e), (f).

DIVORCE —Cont'd
Summary judgment.
When summary judgment provisions applicable, §50-10(d).
Support and maintenance.
Child support.
General provisions.
See CHILD SUPPORT.
General provisions.
See SUPPORT AND MAINTENANCE.
Mediated settlement conferences or other settlement procedures.
District court actions, §7A-38.4A.
Postseparation support, §50-16.2A.
Attorneys' fees, §50-16.4.
Barred by separation agreement or premarital agreement provisions, §50-16.6(b).
Basis of award, §50-16.2A(b).
Change in circumstances.
Modification.
Family law arbitration act, §50-56.
Considerations in awarding support, §50-16.2A(b).
Marital misconduct of dependent spouse, §50-16.2A(d), (e).
Court's duty, §50-16.8.
Defined, §50-16.1A.
Either party may move for, §50-16.2A(a).
Enforcement of decree, §50-16.7.
Entitlement of dependent spouse to award, §50-16.2A(c).
How paid, §50-16.7.
Maintenance of certain actions as independent actions permissible, §50-19.
Marital misconduct of dependent spouse.
Considering, §50-16.2A(d), (e).
Modification, §50-16.9.
Change in circumstances.
Family law arbitration act, §50-56.
Procedure, §50-16.8.
Verified pleading, motion or affidavit.
Requirements, §50-16.2A(a).
Temporary restraining order enjoining spouse from interfering with, threatening or molesting plaintiff.
Bond not required, §1A-1 Rule 65(c).
Title.
Distribution by court of marital and divisible property.
Personal or real property.
Orders transferring title, §50-20(g).
Trial.
Jury trial or trial before judge without jury.
Determination, §50-10(c).
Notice of trial.
Failure of defendant to appear in action.
Notice not required, §50-10(b).
Trusts and trustees.
Loss resulting from trustee's lack of knowledge.
Trustee not liable, reasonable care exercised, §36C-10-1007.
Revocable trusts.
Divorce or annulment of marriage of settlor.
Provisions of trust revoked, §36C-6-606.
Validation.
Judgments entered prior to January 1, 1981, §50-11.3.
Judgments entered prior to October 1, 1983, §50-11.4.
Prior judgments or decrees, §§50-8, 50-9.

DIVORCE —Cont'd
Venue, §50-3.
Change of venue, §1-83.
Child custody or child support actions, §50-13.5(f).
Nonresidents, §50-8.
Verification.
Complaint verified, §50-8.
Pleadings.
When verifications required, §50-8.
Visitation.
Action or proceeding for child custody or visitation, §50-13.1.
Denial of parental visitation rights.
Written findings of fact, §50-13.5(i).
Electronic communication.
Use to supplement child visitation, §50-13.2(e).
Grandparents, §§50-13.2(b1), 50-13.5(j).
Adopted grandchild.
Action by biological grandparent, §50-13.2A.
Mediation, §§7A-494, 7A-495.
Vital statistics.
Registration of divorce, §130A-111.
Void ab initio.
What marriages may be declared void upon application of either party, §50-4.
Voidable marriage.
Children born legitimate, §50-11.1.
Waste.
Temporary orders preventing, §50-21(a).
Will revocation and revival, §31-5.4.

DIVORCE FROM BED AND BOARD.
Acts barring rights of spouse, §31A-1(a).
Divorce generally.
See DIVORCE.
Grounds, §50-7.
Reference by consent, §1A-1 Rule 53(a).

DIVORCE FROM BONDS OF MATRIMONY.
Acts barring rights of spouse, §31A-1(a).
Divorce generally.
See DIVORCE.
Effect of answer of summons by defendant, §50-9.
Effects of absolute divorce, §50-11.
Equitable distribution judgment not entered prior to decree, §50-21(a).
Former section 52-6, effect of decree or certificate not complying with, §52-9.
Incurable insanity, §50-5.1.
Judgments entered prior to January 1, 1981 validated, §50-11.3.
Maiden or premarriage surname.
Resumption by woman or man, §50-12.
Separation for one year, §50-6.
Summary judgment.
Applicability of provisions, §50-10(d).

DNA, §§15A-266 to 15A-270.
Arrest for certain offenses.
Obtaining DNA sample for DNA analysis, §15A-266.3A(a).
Acquittal.
Removal of record and destruction of samples, §15A-266.3A(f).
Arresting law enforcement officer to obtain, §15A-266.3A(b).
Dismissal of charges.
Removal of record and destruction of samples, §15A-266.3A(f).
Expunction of DNA sample.
Circumstances requiring removal and destruction of records, §15A-266.3A(g) to (i).

DNA —Cont'd
Arrest for certain offenses —Cont'd
Obtaining DNA sample for DNA analysis —Cont'd
Expunction of DNA sample —Cont'd
Notice of procedures for seeking provided,
§15A-266.3A(b2).
List of offenses requiring sample,
§15A-266.3A(d).
Attempts, solicitation, conspiracy to commit
offenses, §15A-266.3A(e).
Method of obtaining, §15A-266.3A(b).
Procedures to comply with section.
Adoption, §15A-266.3A.
Record regarding sample taken.
Person obtaining to make, §15A-266.3A(b1).
Removal of record and destruction of samples.
Circumstances requiring, §15A-266.3A(f).
Expunction, §15A-266.3A(g) to (i).
Required, §15A-502.1.
Storage of record of identification
characteristics, §15A-266.3A(c).
Time for obtaining, §15A-266.3A(b).
When obtained, §15A-266.3A(b).
Availability of results to local, state and
federal law enforcement, §15A-266.8(a).
Blood sample taken instead of cheek swab.
Persons authorized to draw blood, immunity,
§15A-266.6(b).
Cancellation of authority to exchange records,
§15A-266.9.
Capacity of DNA database, §15A-266.3.
Citation of provisions, §15A-266.
CODIS.
Defined, §15A-266.2.
Collection and storage of samples and records,
§15A-266.12.
Confidentiality.
Computer software and database structures,
§15A-266.12(f).
Records, §15A-266.12(a).
Contracting out typing analysis to laboratory.
Authority of SBI, §15A-266.8(a).
Convictions requiring samples, §15A-266.4(a).
Listed crimes, §15A-266.4(b).
Costs in criminal actions in superior or
district courts, §7A-304(a).
Crime scene samples.
Access by defendant before trial, §15A-267.
Crimes requiring samples.
Upon conviction or finding of not guilty by reason
of insanity, §15A-266.4(a).
Listed crimes, §15A-266.4(b).
Database and databank, §§15A-266 to
15A-266.12.
Database exchange, §15A-266.8.
Definitions, §15A-266.2.
Disclosing individually identifiable
information, §15A-266.11(a).
Discovery.
Requests to access DNA records in criminal
proceeding, §15A-266.12(d).
DNA defined, §15A-266.2.
DNA record defined, §15A-266.2.
Establishment of state database and databank,
§15A-266.3.
Evidence, preservation.
Court instructions, §15A-268(a3), (a4).
Disposal before expiration of time period.
Conditions to be met, §15A-268(b).
Notification to dispose of evidence, §15A-268(b),
(c).

DNA —Cont'd
Evidence, preservation —Cont'd
Disposal before expiration of time period —Cont'd
Order to dispose of evidence, §15A-268(d).
Appeal of order, §15A-268(f).
Reasonable measures to preserve portions of
evidence, §15A-268(e).
Guidelines, §15A-268(a2).
Inability to produce evidence required to be
preserved, §15A-268(g).
Prohibited acts, §15A-268(i).
Records documenting.
Retention, §15A-268(h).
Required.
Government agency collecting evidence,
§15A-268(a1).
Time period, §15A-268(a6).
Waiver of duty to preserve by defendant,
§15A-268(a5).
Exchange of information, §15A-266.8.
Cancellation of authority, §15A-266.9.
Expungement of DNA records.
Arrest for certain offenses.
Obtaining DNA sample for DNA analysis.
Circumstances requiring removal of record
and destruction of samples,
§15A-266.3A(g) to (i).
Notice of procedures for seeking provided,
§15A-266.3A(b2).
Automated procedure to facilitate.
Study, report, §15A-266.5(d).
Dismissal of charges or person found not guilty or
not responsible, §15A-146(b1), (b2).
Failure to appear to provide sample.
Persons not sentenced to term of incarceration,
§15A-266.6(a).
FBI.
Defined, §15A-266.2.
Records provided by SBI, §15A-266.3.
Forensic analysis.
Admissibility in evidence in criminal prosecutions
without testimony of analyst, §8-58.20.
Identification of persons.
Policy of state, §15A-266.1.
Immunity.
Persons authorized to draw blood, §15A-266.6(b).
Individually identifiable information.
Disclosure, §15A-266.11(a).
Obtaining, §15A-266.11(b).
Juvenile actions.
Transfer of jurisdiction to superior court for
prosecution as adult, §7B-2201(b).
Listed crimes.
Samples required on conviction, §15A-266.4(b).
Not guilty by reason of insanity and
committed to mental health facility.
Crimes requiring samples, §15A-266.4(a).
Listed crimes, §15A-266.4(b).
Obtaining samples for analysis.
Arrest for certain offenses, §15A-266.3A.
Blood sample provided instead of cheek swab.
Persons authorized to draw blood, immunity,
§15A-266.6(b).
Court order to provide sample.
Persons not sentenced to incarceration,
§15A-266.6(a).
Failure to appear to provide sample.
Persons not sentenced to incarceration,
§15A-266.6(a).
Materials, supplies, envelopes supplied by SBI,
§15A-266.6(c).

DNA —Cont'd
Obtaining samples for analysis —Cont'd
Persons not sentenced to incarceration.
Immediately following sentencing,
§15A-266.6(a).
Persons sentenced to incarceration.
At place of incarceration, §15A-266.6(a).
Procedures for collection, security, submission,
identification, storage.
SBI to adopt, §15A-266.7(a).
Quality assurance guidelines.
SBI to adopt, §15A-266.7(a).
Storage, §15A-266.7(b).
Order of court.
Obtaining samples.
Persons not sentenced to term of incarceration,
§15A-266.6(a).
Paternity.
Genetic testing.
Competency of tests as evidence, §8-50.1.
Expedited procedures to establish paternity in
IV-D cases, §110-132.2.
Setting aside orders of paternity, §49-4(h).
Penalties, §15A-266.11.
**Persons not sentenced to term of
incarceration.**
Obtaining samples from, §15A-266.6(a).
Policy, §15A-266.1.
Population database.
Creation of separate database, sharing,
§15A-266.8(c).
Post conviction DNA testing.
Motion by defendant.
Agreement of parties, §15A-269(h).
Appeal of denial, §15A-270.1.
Appointment of counsel for indigent defendant,
§15A-269(c).
Conditions to be met, §15A-269(a).
Costs of testing, defendant to bear, §15A-269(d).
Delay of proceedings or execution of sentence
pending testing.
Miscarriage of justice, §15A-269(e).
Discharge of defendant, ordering on favorable
results, §15A-270(c).
Facility to conduct testing, §15A-269(b1).
Favorable results, order entered serving interest
of justice, §15A-270(c).
Granting motion, determinations required,
§15A-269(b).
Hearing to evaluate results, §15A-270(a).
Inventory of evidence by custodial agency,
§15A-269(f).
New trial, ordering on favorable results,
§15A-270(c).
Resentencing, ordering on favorable results,
§15A-270(c).
Time for testing order pursuant to motion,
§15A-269(e).
Unfavorable results, dismissal of motion,
§15A-270(b).
Vacating and setting aside judgment, ordering
on favorable results, §15A-270(c).
Victim services.
Reactivation, §15A-269(g).
Preservation of DNA evidence, §15A-268.
Pretrial access to crime scene samples.
Defendants, §15A-267(a).
Costs of further testing, defendant to bear,
§15A-267(d).
Statutes governing access, §15A-267(b).

DNA —Cont'd
Pretrial release.
Collection of sample as condition of pretrial
release, §15A-534.
**Procedures for collection, security, submission,
identification, storage.**
SBI to adopt, §15A-266.7(a).
Public records.
Records and samples not public records,
§15A-266.12(c).
Quality assurance guidelines.
SBI to adopt, §15A-266.7(a).
Records.
Arrest for certain offenses.
Obtaining DNA sample for DNA analysis,
§15A-266.3A(b1).
Cancellation of authority to exchange, §15A-266.9.
Collection and storage, §15A-266.12(b).
Confidentiality, §15A-266.12(a).
Not public records, §15A-266.12(c).
Testing records, §15A-266.7(c).
Release of DNA records and DNA samples.
Authorized purposes, §15A-266.12(e).
Release to appropriate parties.
Court orders directing, §15A-266.8(a).
Report by SBI.
Annual report, §15A-266.5(c).
Repository for samples obtained.
State DNA databank to serve as, §15A-266.3.
Rules for obtaining information.
SBI to adopt, §15A-266.8(b).
Sample defined, §15A-266.2.
**Samples taken upon conviction or finding of
not guilty by reason of insanity,** §15A-266.4.
SBI.
Administration of state database and databank,
§15A-266.3.
Annual report, §15A-266.5(c).
Defined, §15A-266.2.
Materials, supplies, envelopes for obtaining
sample.
Duty to provide, §15A-266.6(c).
Procedures, adoption, §15A-266.7.
Short title, §15A-266.
State DNA databank defined, §15A-266.2.
State DNA database defined, §15A-266.2.
**Storage of record of identification
characteristics in database,** §15A-266.5(b).
Arrest for certain offenses.
Obtaining DNA sample for DNA analysis,
§15A-266.3A(c).
Storage of samples in databank, §§15A-266.5(b),
15A-266.7(b).
Storage of typing results in database,
§15A-266.7(b).
Testing records, §15A-266.7(c).
Tests to be performed.
Purposes, §15A-266.5(a).
Storage of record of identification characteristics
in database, §15A-266.5(b).
Storage of sample in databank, §15A-266.5(b).
Unauthorized use of databank, §15A-266.11.

DNA ANALYSIS, §§15A-266 to 15A-270.
See DNA.

**DNA DATABASE AND DATABANK ACT OF
1993,** §§15A-266 to 15A-270.
See DNA.

DNR.
Do not resuscitate orders, §90-21.17.

DOBSON.
Room occupancy tax.
Uniform provisions.
Authorized to levy, §160A-215(g).
Generally, §160A-215.
Satellite annexation.
Limitation on area of satellite corporate limits, inapplicability, §160A-58.1(b).

DOCKET BOOK.
Defined, §1-208.1.
Judgments.
Cancellation, assignment, etc., of judgments, §1-239.1.

DOCKETS.
Appeals.
Docketing appeal, AppProc Rule 12(b).
Appeal of right from court of appeals to supreme court, AppProc Rule 14(c).
Discretionary review on certification by supreme court, AppProc Rule 15(e).
Stays.
Docket entry of stay, §1-293.
Attachment.
Levy on real property, §1-440.17.
Child abuse, neglect and dependency.
Judicial review of responsible individuals lists.
Separate docket for review actions, §7B-323(b).
Criminal case docketing.
Superior courts, §7A-49.4.
District attorneys.
Preparation of trial dockets, §7A-61.
Docket book.
See DOCKET BOOK.
Executions.
County to which execution to be issued.
Docketing in as prerequisite to issuance, §1-308.
Returns.
Entry on judgment docket, §1-321.
Judgment docket and judgment in docket book.
Defined, §1-208.1.
Judgments, §§1-233, 1-234.
Assignment of judgment.
Entry on judgment docket, §1-246.
Deemed rendered and docketed on first day of session, §1-233.
Federal court judgments, §1-237.
Foreign judgments, §1C-1703(b).
Judgment of appellate division docketed in superior court, §1-235.
Modification of judgment on appeal, §1-242.
Payment to clerk.
Docket credited, §1-239(a).
Entry of payment on docket, §1-239(c).
Liens.
Restrictions on docketing, §44A-12.1.
Magistrates to keep, §7A-175.
Stays.
Appeals.
Docket entry of stay, §1-293.
Summons, §1A-1 Rule 4(g).
Superior courts.
Clerks, record-keeping procedures, §7A-109(a) to (e).
Criminal case docketing, §7A-49.4.
Torrens system registration.
Liens on registered lands.
Docketed judgments, §43-45.

DOCTOR-PATIENT PRIVILEGE.
Communications between doctor and patient, §8-53.
Alimony and divorce actions, §8-53.6.
Waiver of privilege in child abuse cases, §8-53.1(a), (b).
Medical review committee.
Testimony of members of committees, §131E-95(b), (c).
Workers' compensation.
Medical examinations, facts not privileges, §97-27(a).
Policy of state to protect, §97-25.6(a).

DOCTORS.
Chiropractors, §§90-139 to 90-157.3.
See CHIROPRACTORS.
Dentists, §§90-22 to 90-48.11.
See DENTISTS AND DENTISTRY.
Generally.
See PHYSICIANS AND SURGEONS.
Optometrists, §§90-114 to 90-127.3.
See OPTOMETRISTS.
Osteopaths.
See OSTEOPATHS.
Podiatrists, §§90-202.2 to 90-202.14.
See PODIATRISTS.
Psychologists, §§90-270.1 to 90-270.22.
See PSYCHOLOGISTS.
Veterinarians, §§90-179 to 90-187.15.
See VETERINARIANS.

DOCTRINE OF WORTHIER TITLE.
Abolished, §41-6.2(a).
Applicable to revocable trusts, §41-6.2.

DOCUMENTARY DRAFTS.
Negotiable instruments generally.
See NEGOTIABLE INSTRUMENTS.

DOCUMENTARY EVIDENCE.
Accounts and accounting.
Itemized and verified accounts, §8-45.
Bills of lading in evidence, §8-41.
Book accounts.
Copies of accounts in evidence, §8-44.
Executors and administrators.
Approving book accounts by personal representative, §8-43.
Under $60, §8-42.
Carriers.
Actions by or against common or connecting carriers.
Bills of lading in evidence, §8-41.
Contract actions.
Book accounts under $60, §8-42.
Copies of book accounts in evidence, §8-44.
Executors and administrators.
Book accounts approved by personal representative, §8-43.
Hospital records.
Copies of medical records, §8-44.1.
Itemized and verified accounts, §8-45.
Meat inspection.
Production of documentary evidence, §106-549.36(b), (c).
Medical records.
Copies of medical records, §8-44.1.
Parol evidence.
Identifying land described, §8-39.
Real property.
Parol evidence to identify land described, §8-39.

DOCUMENTARY EVIDENCE —Cont'd
Remainder of or related writings or recorded statements, §8C-1 Rule 106.
Subpoena for production, §8-61.

DOCUMENT AUTHENTICATION.
Certificates of authentication.
Authority of secretary of state, §66-270.
Definitions, §66-271.
Issuance of certificate, §66-272.
Limitation on authority of secretary, §66-274(c).
Non-certifiable documents, §66-274(b).
Other methods of authentication, §66-275.
Prerequisites to authentication, §66-273.
Purpose of certificate precluding issuance, §66-274(a).

DOCUMENT OF RESCISSION.
Release or satisfaction of security instrument.
Erroneous recorded release or erroneous satisfaction, §45-36.6.

DOCUMENTS OF TITLE, §§25-7-101 to 25-7-603.
Alteration of instruments.
Bills of lading, §25-7-306.
Warehouse receipts, §25-7-208.
Applicability of chapter, §25-7-103(a).
Attachment of goods covered by a negotiable document, §25-7-602.
Bailee.
Defined, §25-7-102(a).
Bills of lading.
Altered bills, §25-7-306.
Attachment of goods covered by a negotiable document, §25-7-602.
Care.
Contractual limitation of carrier's liability, §25-7-309(b).
Duty of care, §25-7-309(a).
Change of instructions, §25-7-303(a).
Claims.
Time and manner of presentation, §25-7-309(c).
Damages.
Limitation of liability, §25-7-309(b).
Defined, §25-1-201(b).
Destination bills, §25-7-305(a).
Substitute bills, §25-7-305(b).
Diversion, §25-7-303(a).
Duty of carrier, §25-7-309(a).
Evidence.
Actions by or against common or connecting carriers, §8-41.
Handling.
Proper handling, §25-7-301(a).
Improper load.
Liability for damages, §25-7-301(d).
Instructions.
Change of instructions, §25-7-303(a).
Liability for non-receipt or misdescription.
"Said to contain,"§25-7-301(a).
"Shipper's weight, load and count,"§25-7-301(a), (b).
Liability of carrier.
Contractual limitation of liability of carrier, §25-7-309(b).
Duty of carrier, §25-7-309(a).
Lien of carrier, §25-7-307(a), (b).
Enforcement, §25-7-308(a) to (h).
Limitation of actions.
Limitations in bill of lading or tariff, §25-7-309(a).

DOCUMENTS OF TITLE —Cont'd
Bills of lading —Cont'd
Misdescription.
Liability for misdescription, §25-7-301(e).
Negotiability, §25-7-104(a).
Negotiation. See within this heading, "Negotiation."
Non-negotiable bills of lading, §25-7-104(b), (c).
Non-receipt.
Liability for non-receipt, §25-7-301(a), (e).
Original terms.
Holding to original terms, §25-7-303(b).
Overseas shipment.
Form of bill, §25-2-323.
Reconsignment, §25-7-303(a).
"Said to contain,"§25-7-301(a).
Sets.
Tangible bill of lading in a set, §25-7-304(a) to (e).
"Shipper's weight, load and count,"§25-7-301(a), (c).
Substitute bills, §25-7-305(b).
Tangible bill of lading in a set, §25-7-304(a) to (e).
Through bills of lading and similar documents, §25-7-302(a), (b).
Issuers, §25-7-302(c).
Citation of chapter.
Short title, §25-7-101.
Claims.
Conflicting claims, §25-7-603.
Commercial code general provisions, §§25-1-101 to 25-1-310.
See COMMERCIAL CODE.
Consignee.
Defined, §25-7-102(a).
Consignor.
Defined, §25-7-102(a).
Construction and interpretation.
Applicability of chapter, §25-7-103(a).
Modification or repeal of existing laws, §25-7-103(b).
Relation of chapter to treaties, statutes, tariffs, etc., §25-7-103(a).
Contract for sale.
Defined, §25-7-102(b).
Damages.
Limitation of liability in bill of lading, §25-7-309(b).
Limitation of warehouseman's liability, §25-7-204(a), (b).
Defeated.
Document of title to goods defeated in certain cases, §25-7-503(a) to (d).
Definitions, §§25-1-201(b), 25-7-102(a), (b).
Bailees, §25-7-102(a).
Bills of lading, §25-1-201(b).
Consignee, §25-7-102(a).
Consignor, §25-7-102(a).
Delivery order, §25-7-102(a).
Documents, §25-7-102(a).
Goods, §25-7-102(a).
Index of definitions, §25-7-102(a).
Issuer, §25-7-102(a).
Warehouseman, §25-7-102(a).
Warehouse receipts, §25-1-201(b).
Delivery.
Excuse, §25-7-403(a), (c).
Good faith delivery.
No liability for good faith delivery pursuant to receipt or bill, §25-7-404.

DOCUMENTS OF TITLE —Cont'd
Delivery —Cont'd
Liens.
Satisfaction before delivery, §25-7-403(b).
No liability for good faith delivery pursuant to receipt or bill, §25-7-404.
Obligation of warehouseman or carrier to deliver, §25-7-403(a), (c).
Seller's stoppage of delivery, §25-7-504(4).
Without indorsement, §25-7-506.
Delivery order.
Defined, §25-7-102(a).
Destroyed documents, §25-7-601(a).
Delivery by bailee, §25-7-601(b).
Due negotiation.
Absence of due negotiation.
Rights acquired in absence, §25-7-504(1), (2).
Duplicates, §25-7-402.
Electronic document of title.
Evidentiary effect, §25-7-105(b).
Issuance of electronic substitute, §25-7-105(c).
Issuance of tangible document of title, §25-7-105(a).
Substitution for a tangible document of title, §25-7-105(d).
Electronic signatures in global and national commerce act.
Article modifies, limits and supersedes federal act, §25-7-103(c).
Executions.
Lien on goods covered by a negotiable document, §25-7-602.
Fungible goods.
Buyer in the ordinary course of business.
Delivery by warehouseman, §25-7-205.
Goods.
Defined, §25-7-102(a).
Guaranty.
Indorser not guarantor for other parties, §25-7-505.
Indorsement, §25-7-501(a).
Compelling indorsement.
Right to compel, §25-7-506.
Delivery to compel indorsement, §25-7-506.
Indorser not guarantor for other parties, §25-7-505.
Power to compel indorsement, §25-7-506.
Requirements of due negotiation, §25-7-501.
Injunctions.
Enjoining negotiations of document, §25-7-602.
Interpleader and intervention, §25-7-603.
Irregularities in issue or conduct of issuer, §25-7-401.
Issuance.
Irregularities in issue, §25-7-401.
Overissue, §25-7-402.
Issuer.
Conduct.
Irregularities in conduct of issuer, §25-7-401.
Defined, §25-7-102(a).
Irregularities in conduct of issuer, §25-7-401.
Lessee in the ordinary course of business.
Defined, §25-7-102(b).
Liability.
No liability for good faith delivery pursuant to receipt or bill, §25-7-404.
Liens.
Carrier, §25-7-307(a), (b).
Enforcement, §25-7-308(a) to (h).
Satisfaction before delivery, §25-7-403(b).

DOCUMENTS OF TITLE —Cont'd
Liens —Cont'd
Warehouseman, §25-7-209(a)(1).
Enforcement of lien, §25-7-210(a) to (i).
Good faith purchaser, §25-7-209(c).
Loss of lien, conduct constituting, §25-7-209(e).
Limitation of actions.
Bill of lading or tariff, §25-7-309(c).
Warehouse receipt or tariff, §25-7-204(c).
Lost instruments and records, §25-7-601(a).
Delivery by bailee, §25-7-601(b).
Missing documents, §25-7-601(a).
Delivery by bailee, §25-7-601(b).
Negotiation.
Absence of due negotiation.
Rights acquired in the absence of due negotiation, §25-7-504(1), (2).
Attachment of goods covered by a negotiable document, §25-7-602.
Contract.
When adequate compliance with commercial contract, §25-7-509.
Defeated.
Document of title to goods defeated in certain cases, §25-7-503(a) to (d).
Delivery.
Seller's stoppage of delivery, §25-7-504(1).
Without indorsement, §25-7-506.
Diversion.
Change of shipping instructions, §25-7-504(3).
Effect of diversion, §25-7-504(3).
Due negotiation.
Rights acquired by due negotiation, §25-7-502(a), (b).
Rights acquired in the absence of due negotiation, §25-7-504(1), (2).
Electronic document of title, §25-7-501(b).
Enjoining negotiation of document, §25-7-602.
Form of negotiation, §25-7-501.
Indorsement.
Compelling indorsement, §25-7-506.
Delivery without indorsement, §25-7-506.
Due negotiation, §25-7-501(a).
Form of negotiation, §25-7-501.
Indorser not guarantor for other parties, §25-7-505.
Non-negotiable document, §25-7-501(a), (c).
Power to compel, §25-7-506.
Right to compel, §25-7-506.
Naming of a person for notice upon arrival of goods, §25-7-501(d).
Negotiability, §25-7-104(a).
Warranties, §25-7-507.
Collecting bank.
Warranties of collecting bank as to documents, §25-7-508.
Non-negotiable documents, §25-7-104(b), (c).
Indorsement, §25-7-501(a), (c).
Rights acquired by due negotiation, §25-7-502(a), (b).
Warranties.
Collecting bank, §25-7-508.
Negotiation or transfer of receipt or bill, §25-7-507.
When adequate compliance with commercial contract, §25-7-509.
Obligation of warehouseman or carrier to deliver, §25-7-403(a), (c).
Overissue, §25-7-402.
Receipt.
Defined, §25-7-102(b).

DOCUMENTS OF TITLE —Cont'd
Relation of chapter to treaties, statutes, tariffs, etc., §25-7-103(a).
Retail installment sales.
 Payment.
  Return of title documents upon full payment, §25A-22(b).
Sale of goods, UCC.
 Bill of lading required in overseas shipment, §25-2-323.
 When deliverable on acceptance and when on payment, §25-2-514.
Secured transactions.
 Priority of security interests, §25-9-331.
Short title of chapter, §25-7-101.
Stolen documents, §25-7-601(a).
 Delivery by bailee, §25-7-601(b).
Storage.
 Termination of storage at warehouseman's option, §25-7-206.
  Delivery upon due demand, §25-7-206(d).
  Hazardous property due to quality or condition, §25-7-206(c).
  Lien on proceeds of sale or disposition, §25-7-206(e).
  Payment of charge, notice of, §25-7-206(a).
  Public sale to prevent decline in value, §25-7-206(b).
  Removal of goods, notice of, §25-7-206(a).
Suretyship.
 Indorser not guarantor for other parties, §25-7-505.
Tariffs.
 Relation of chapter to tariffs, §25-7-103(a).
Transfer.
 Warranties, §25-7-507.
Treaties.
 Relation of chapter to treaty, §25-7-103(a).
Uniform electronic transactions act.
 Conflicts between act and article, §25-7-103(d).
United States statutes.
 Relation of chapter to statute, §25-7-103(a).
Warehouseman.
 Defined, §25-7-102(a).
Warehouse receipts.
 Agricultural commodities stored under government bond, §25-7-201(b).
 Alcoholic beverages.
  Distilled spirits stored under government bond, §25-7-201(b).
 Altered warehouse receipts, §25-7-208.
 Contents, §25-7-202(b).
 Contractual limitation of warehouseman's liability, §25-7-204(d).
 Crops.
  Storage under government bond, §25-7-201(b).
 Defined, §§25-1-201(b), 25-7-201.
 Distilled spirits.
  Storage under government bond, §25-7-201(b).
 Duty of care, §25-7-204(a).
 Forms, §25-7-202(a).
 Fungible goods, §25-7-207(b).
  Title of buyer in ordinary course of business, §25-7-205.
 Goods must be kept separate, §§25-7-204, 25-7-207.
 Insertion of contrary provisions, §25-7-202(c).
 Issuance.
  Who may issue, §25-7-201(a).
  Liability for damages, §25-7-202(b).

DOCUMENTS OF TITLE —Cont'd
Warehouse receipts —Cont'd
 Liability for non-receipt or misdescription, §25-7-203.
  Contractual limitation of warehouseman's liability, §25-7-204(d).
 Lien of warehouseman, §25-7-209(a), (b).
  Damages, liability for, §25-7-210(i).
  Enforcement, §25-7-210(a) to (i).
  Good faith purchaser, §25-7-209(c), (e).
  Goods other than stored goods, §25-7-210(b).
  Household goods, §25-7-209(d).
  Loss of lien, conduct constituting, §25-7-209(e).
  Merchant in course of business, §25-7-210(h).
  Purchase at public sale, §25-7-210(d).
  Retention of goods under claim of right, §25-7-210(c).
  Right in addition to other rights, §25-7-210(g).
  Satisfaction of lien from sale proceeds, §25-7-210(f).
 Limitation of actions.
  Contractual limitation of warehouseman's liability, §25-7-204(c), (d).
 Misdescription.
  Liability for, §25-7-203.
 Non-negotiable warehouse receipts, §25-7-104(b), (c).
 Non-receipt.
  Liability for, §25-7-203.
 Storage.
  Under government bond, §25-7-201(b).
 Termination of storage at warehouseman's option, §25-7-206.
  Delivery upon due demand, §25-7-206(d).
  Hazardous property due to quality or condition, §25-7-206(c).
  Lien on proceeds of sale or disposition, §25-7-206(e).
  Payment of charge, notice of, §25-7-206(a).
  Public sale to prevent decline in value, §25-7-206(b).
  Removal of goods, notice of, §25-7-206(a).
 Title under warehouse receipt defeated in certain cases, §25-7-205.
 Who may issue, §25-7-201(a).
Warranties.
 Collecting banks.
  Warranties of collecting bank as to documents, §25-7-508.
 Negotiation, §25-7-507.

DOG BAITING, §14-362.2.

DOG FIGHTING, §14-362.2.
Care of animals subjected to illegal treatment, §19A-70.
Cruelty to animals generally.
 See CRUELTY TO ANIMALS.

DOGS.
Animals generally.
 See ANIMALS.
Applicability of provisions, §67-18.
Assistance dogs.
 Service animals generally. See within this heading, "Service animals."
Beagles.
 Field trials.
  Hunting license exemption, §113-276(k).
Biting dogs.
 Rabies.
  General provisions, §§130A-184 to 130A-201.
  See RABIES.

DOGS —Cont'd
Care of animals subjected to illegal treatment,
§19A-70.
Cruelty to animals.
Generally.
See CRUELTY TO ANIMALS.
Restraining dogs in cruel manner, §14-362.3.
Damages.
Dangerous dogs.
Damages for injuries or property damage
inflicted by dog.
Strict liability, §67-4.4.
Killing or injuring livestock.
Liability of owner, §67-1.
Mad dogs.
Failure to kill, §67-4.
Permitting dogs to run at large at night.
Liability of owner, §67-12.
Dangerous dogs, §§67-4.1 to 67-4.5.
Appeals.
Dog potentially dangerous, §67-4.1(c).
Applicability of provisions, §67-4.1(b).
Assault, torment or abuse of dog.
Injury inflicted by dog.
Inapplicability of provisions, §67-4.1(b).
Attacks by dangerous dogs, §67-4.3.
Precautions against, §67-4.2.
Violations by owners, §67-4.2(c).
Definitions, §67-4.1(a).
Determination that dog is potentially dangerous,
§67-4.1(c).
Herding dogs.
Inapplicability of provisions, §67-4.1(b).
Hunting dogs.
Inapplicability of provisions, §67-4.1(b).
Injuries or property damage inflicted by
dangerous dog.
Strict liability, §67-4.4.
Injury inflicted on person committing tort.
Inapplicability of provisions, §67-4.1(b).
Law enforcement dogs.
Inapplicability of provisions, §67-4.1(b).
Leaving dangerous dogs unattended, §67-4.2(a).
Local ordinances for control, §67-4.5.
Ordinances.
Local programs for control, §67-4.5.
Owner defined, §67-4.1(a).
Owner's real property defined, §67-4.1(a).
Permitting dangerous dog to go beyond owner's
real property unless leashed and muzzled,
§67-4.2(a).
Potentially dangerous dog.
Appeal from final decisions, §67-4.1(c).
Defined, §67-4.1(a).
Determination, §67-4.1(c).
Hearing, §67-4.1(c).
Notice of determination, §67-4.1(c).
Persons or board responsible for determining.
Designation, §67-4.1(c).
Precautions against attacks by dangerous dogs,
§67-4.2.
Predator control dogs.
Inapplicability of provisions, §67-4.1(b).
Strict liability.
Damages for injuries or property damage
inflicted by dangerous dog, §67-4.4.
Transfer of ownership or possession.
Notice, §67-4.2(b).
Trespass.
Injury inflicted by dog on person committing
willful trespass.
Inapplicability of provisions, §67-4.1(b).

DOGS —Cont'd
Dog wardens.
Appointment of animal control officers, §67-30.
Duties, §67-31.
Powers, §67-31.
Rabies control officers.
Dog warden as assistant, §67-31.
Drug detection dogs.
Handlers, commercial detection services,
§90-102.1.
Earthdog trials.
Dog fighting and baiting.
Exception to, §14-362.2(e).
Electronic dog collars.
Enforcement, §14-401.17(c).
Jurisdiction, §14-401.17(c).
Penalties, §14-401.17(b).
Unlawful removal, §14-401.17(a).
Euthanasia, §19A-24.
Female dogs in heat.
Running at large, §67-2.
Field trials for beagles.
Hunting license exemption, §113-276(k).
Foxes.
Taking with dogs at night or day or year-round
basis, §113-291.4(b).
Greyhound racing, §14-309.20.
Guide dogs.
Service animals generally. See within this
heading, "Service animals."
Herding dogs.
Dog fighting and baiting.
Exception to, §14-362.2(f).
Hotel rooms, admittance of pets, §72-7.1.
Hunting and wildlife.
Dangerous dogs.
Dogs used in lawful hunt.
Inapplicability of provisions of article to,
§67-4.1(b).
Dog fighting and baiting.
Exception as lawful taking of animals,
§14-362.2(d).
Field trials with dogs, §113-291.1(d).
Foxes, §113-291.4(b).
Muzzle loading firearm deer season.
Using dogs to hunt deer prohibited,
§113-291.2(a).
Raccoon and opossum hunting at night,
§113-291.1(e).
Regulation of use, §113-291.5.
Limitations on authority, §113-291.5.
Training during closed season, §113-291.1(d1).
Use in taking wildlife, §113-291.1(a).
Use to retrieve wounded or dead big game
animals, §113-291.1(k).
Impoundment.
Leashing or restraining ordinances.
Dogs and cats in violation, §130A-192(b).
Rabies vaccination tags.
Animals not wearing, §130A-192.
Surrendered by owners, §130A-192(b).
Wildlife management areas.
Unmuzzled dogs running at large, §67-14.1(b) to
(e).
Larceny.
Felony, §14-81(a1).
Probation, conditions required, §14-81(b).
Sentencing to active sentence.
Judge's authority not limited, §14-81(b).
Taking dogs for temporary purpose, §14-82.

DOGS —Cont'd
Law enforcement dogs.
Assaulting, §14-163.1.
Dangerous dogs.
Inapplicability of article to dogs used by, §67-4.1(b).
Leashing or restraining ordinances.
Impoundment of dogs in violation, §130A-192(b).
Liability of owners.
Dangerous dogs.
Attacks by dangerous dogs, §67-4.3.
Precautions against.
Violations of section by owners, §67-4.2(c).
Strict liability in civil damages for injuries, §67-4.4.
Killing or injuring livestock or fowl, §67-1.
Liability to discharge duties imposed under provision.
Penalty, §67-16.
Mad dogs.
Failure of owner to kill, §67-4.
Permitting dogs to run at large at night.
Liability for damages, §67-12.
License tax.
Power of county to levy, §153A-153.
Livestock.
Dangerous dogs.
Herding dogs.
Inapplicability of provisions of article to, §67-4.1(b).
Killing or injuring livestock.
Liability of owner, §67-1.
Sheep-killing dogs.
Any person may kill, §67-14.
Refusal to kill, penalty, §67-3.
Mad dogs.
Killing.
Any person may kill, §67-14.
Failure to kill.
Liability of owner, §67-4.
Municipal regulation of domestic animals, §160A-186.
Nighttime.
Permitting dogs to run at large, §67-12.
Plott hound.
State dog, §145-13.
Police dogs.
Assaulting, §14-163.1.
Dangerous dogs.
Inapplicability of article to dogs used by, §67-4.1(b).
Property tax exemption, §105-275.
Provisions as to dogs applicable to all counties, §67-18.
Rabies, §§130A-184 to 130A-201.
See RABIES.
Racing, greyhounds, §14-309.20.
Restraining dogs in cruel manner, §14-362.3.
Running at large.
Female dogs in heat, §67-2.
Nighttime, permitting to run, §67-12.
Sheep-killing dogs, §67-3.
Wildlife management areas.
Unmuzzled dogs running at large.
Impoundment, §67-14.1(b) to (e).
Search and rescue dogs.
Assaulting, killing, §14-163.1.
Service animals.
Assaulting, §14-163.1.
Blind pedestrians rights and privileges without guide dog, §20-175.3.

DOGS —Cont'd
Service animals —Cont'd
Common carrier fares for blind person accompanied by, §62-144(b).
Prohibited acts as to, §168-4.5.
Registration, §168-4.3.
Responsibility for, §168-4.4.
Right of way.
Guide dog to serve as signal for the blind, §20-175.2.
Right to be accompanied by, §168-4.2.
Penalty for depriving of right, §168-4.5.
Tags, §168-4.2.
Training, §168-4.3.
Donation for training, §168-4.6.
Spay/neuter program, §§19A-60 to 19A-66.
State dog.
Plott hound, §145-13.
Superior courts.
Dangerous dogs.
Determination that dog is potentially dangerous dog.
Appeals to superior court of final decisions, §67-4.1(c).
Supplemental nature of provisions, §67-36.
Surrender of dog to shelter by owner, §130A-192(b).
Trust created for care of animal or animals, §36C-4-408.
Vicious animals.
Confinement or leashing of vicious animals, §130A-200.
Dangerous dogs. See within this heading, "Dangerous dogs."
Wildlife management areas.
Killing or injuring deer or bear.
Dog may be killed without liability, §67-14.1(a).
Running at large.
Unmuzzled dogs running at large.
Impoundment, §67-14.1(b) to (e).

DOG WARDENS.
Appointment of animal control officer by county, §67-30.
Powers and duties, §67-31.

DOGWOOD.
State flower, §145-1.
Trespass.
Taking, etc., of flowering dogwood from land of another, §14-129.

DOLPHIN PROTECTION, §113-189(b).

DOMESTICATED ANIMALS.
Animals generally.
See ANIMALS.
Animal welfare act generally, §§19A-20 to 19A-41.
See ANIMAL WELFARE.
Cats.
See CATS.
Dead animals.
Disposition of, §106-403.
Dogs generally.
See DOGS.

DOMESTIC CRIMINAL TRESPASS, §14-134.3.
Arrest without warrant, §15A-401.
Deadly weapons.
Trespass on property of safe house, §14-134.3(b).
Defined, §14-134.3(a).
Evidence that couple living apart, §14-134.3(a).

DOMESTIC CRIMINAL TRESPASS —Cont'd
Safe houses.
Trespass with a deadly weapon, §14-134.3(b).

DOMESTIC RECIPROCALS.
Generally, §§58-15-100 to 58-15-150.
See RECIPROCAL INSURANCE.

DOMESTIC RELATIONS.
Alimony.
See DIVORCE.
Annulment of marriage.
See ANNULMENT OF MARRIAGE.
Antenuptial agreements, §§52B-1 to 52B-11.
See PREMARITAL AGREEMENTS.
Attorneys specializing in family law.
Certification standards, Bar Rules D.2401 to
D.2407.
Child custody.
See CHILD CUSTODY.
Child support.
See CHILD SUPPORT.
District courts.
Proper division for trial of civil actions, §7A-244.
Divorce.
See DIVORCE.
Domestic violence, §§50B-1 to 50B-9.
See DOMESTIC VIOLENCE.
Husband and wife.
See HUSBAND AND WIFE.
Marriage.
See MARRIAGE.
Married women.
See MARRIED WOMEN.
Minors.
See MINORS.
Parent and child.
See PARENT AND CHILD.
Premarital agreements, §§52B-1 to 52B-11.
See PREMARITAL AGREEMENTS.
Trespass.
Criminal trespass, §14-134.3.
Arrest without warrant, §15A-401.
Violence, §§50B-1 to 50B-9.
See DOMESTIC VIOLENCE.

DOMESTIC SERVANTS.
Workers' compensation.
Exceptions to provisions, §97-13(b).

DOMESTIC VIOLENCE.
Actions.
Institution of civil action, §50B-2(a).
Who may institute, §50B-2(a).
Shelters, limited civil liability, §§1-620, 1-621.
Adultery.
Effect upon prosecution for violation of section
14-184 or other offense against public morals,
§50B-8.
Agreements.
Contents, §50B-3(a).
Arrest.
Violation of order, §50B-4(b).
Attorney General.
Domestic violence-related homicides.
Reporting and database system, §114-2.7.
Attorneys' fees, §50B-3(a).
Attorneys specializing in family law.
Certification standards, Bar Rules D.2401 to
D.2407.
Bail, §15A-534.1(a).
Criminal history report for defendant.
Condition of pretrial release, §15A-534.1(a).

DOMESTIC VIOLENCE —Cont'd
Bail —Cont'd
Retention of defendant in custody without action,
time limitation, §15A-534.1(b).
Centers for victims of domestic violence.
Domestic violence center fund.
Fees collected for issuance of marriage licenses,
§161-11.2.
Purposes, §50B-9.
Child abuse generally, §§7B-100 to 7B-1414.
See CHILD ABUSE, NEGLECT OR
DEPENDENCY.
Child custody.
Award of temporary custody, §§50B-2(c1), (c2),
50B-3(a), (a1).
Emergency relief ex parte orders, §50B-2(c) to
(c2).
Child support, §50B-3(a).
Commission, §§143B-394.15, 143B-394.16.
See DOMESTIC VIOLENCE COMMISSION.
Community punishment.
Special probation conditions in addition to,
§15A-1382.1(b).
Concealed handgun permit.
Suspension as part of orders issued by court,
§14-415.18(b).
Temporary permit.
Issuance to holder of protective order,
§14-415.15(b).
Construction and interpretation.
Construction of chapter, §50B-6.
Contempt.
Enforcement of orders, §50B-4.
Copies.
Issuance of copy of order to parties, §50B-3(c).
Counties.
Appropriations. for programs to protect the public,
§153A-212.1.
Criminal history report for defendant.
Bail and pretrial release.
Condition of pretrial release, §15A-534.1(a).
Defined, §50B-1.
Disposition report, indication on,
§15A-1382.1(a).
Division of adult corrections.
Treatment program for inmates committing.
Establishment, §143B-704(e).
Domestic violence commission, §§143B-394.15,
143B-394.16.
Domestic violence-related homicides.
Reporting and database system, §114-2.7.
Emergency assistance, §50B-5(a).
Who may request, §50B-5(a).
Emergency relief.
Custody ex parte orders, §50B-2(c) to (c2).
Enforcement of orders.
Generally, §50B-4.
Ex parte orders, §50B-2(c).
Authorized magistrates, §50B-2(c1), (c2).
Firearms.
Surrender required, §50B-3.1(a), (d).
Disposal, §50B-3.1(h).
Retrieval, §50B-3.1(e).
Motion, §50B-2(b).
Pro se forms, §50B-2(d).
Relief authorized.
Generally, §50B-3.
Employment discrimination.
Persons seeking relief under provisions.
Prohibited acts by employers, §50B-5.5(a).
Enforcement, §50B-5.5(b).

DOMESTIC VIOLENCE —Cont'd
Eviction.
Orders for relief, §50B-3(a).
Firearms.
Emergency or ex parte orders.
Surrender of firearms required, §50B-3.1(a), (d).
Additional relief, §50B-3.1(l).
Disposal, §50B-3.1(h).
Exemptions for official use, §50B-3.1(k).
Hearings, §50B-3.1(b), (c).
Motions for return of firearms, §50B-3.1(f), (g).
Retrieval of firearms, §50B-3.1(e).
Violations, §50B-3.1(i), (j).
Purchase or possession by person subject to order prohibited, §14-269.8.
Forms.
Pro se forms, §50B-2(d).
Fornication.
Effect upon prosecution for violation of section 14-184 or other offense against public morals, §50B-8.
Funds.
Domestic violence center fund, §50B-9.
Fees collected for issuance of marriage licenses, §161-11.2.
Grants.
Domestic violence center fund, §50B-9.
Harassment.
Orders for relief, §50B-3(a).
Hearings.
Emergency relief, §50B-2(b).
Firearms.
Inquiry as to defendants' access to firearms, §50B-3.1(b), (c).
Homicide.
Attorney General.
Domestic violence-related homicides.
Reporting and database system, §114-2.7.
Housing.
Orders for relief, §50B-3(a).
Trespass on property of safe house with a deadly weapon, §14-134.3(b).
Jurisdiction.
District court to have original jurisdiction, §50B-2(a).
Landlord and tenant.
Victim protection.
Changing of locks, §42-42.3.
Early termination of rental agreement by victim, §42-45.1.
Unlawful termination or other modification of rental agreement by landlord, §42-42.2.
Law enforcement officers.
Emergency assistance, §50B-5(a).
Who may request, §50B-5(a).
Liability, §50B-5(b).
Legal services programs.
Eligible cases for legal assistance, §7A-474.3(b).
Magistrates.
Emergency relief ex parte orders, §50B-2(c1), (c2).
Motions.
Contempt, §50B-4(a).
Emergency relief, §50B-2(b).
Who may move, §50B-2(b).
Firearms, return of, §50B-3.1(f), (g).
North Carolina Coalition Against Domestic Violence, Inc.
Domestic violence center fund.
Purposes, §50B-9.

DOMESTIC VIOLENCE —Cont'd
Notice.
Emergency relief hearings, §50B-2(b).
Prisoners found to have committed acts of domestic violence.
Treatment program.
Completion of program prior to completion of incarceration, §143B-704(e).
Establishment, §143B-704(e).
Programs for victims.
Privileged communications.
Definitions, §8-53.12(a).
Duty in cases of abuse or neglect, §8-53.12(c).
Generally, §8-53.12(b).
Pro se forms, §50B-2(d).
Protective orders, §50B-3(a).
Arrest for violation, §50B-4(b).
Copies.
Issuance to parties, §50B-3(c).
Defined, §50B-1(c).
Enforcement, §§50B-4, 50B-4(a), (b).
Full faith and credit, §50B-4(d).
Out-of-state orders, §50B-4(e).
Who may seek enforcement, §50B-4(b).
Without further order, §50B-4(c).
Entry into information registry, §50B-3(d).
Ex parte orders, §50B-2(c).
Firearms.
Surrender required, §50B-3.1(a), (d).
Disposal, §50B-3.1(h).
Retrieval, §50B-3.1(e).
False statement regarding, §50B-4.2.
Firearms.
Purchase or possession by person subject to order prohibited, §14-269.8.
Surrender and disposal.
Emergency or ex parte orders, §50B-3.1.
Period of time, §50B-3(b).
Temporary orders.
Ex parte orders, §50B-2(c).
Valid protective order defined, §§50B-4.1(f), 50B-4(f).
Violation of valid protective order as felony, §50B-4.1(d), (f).
Entry into safe house or haven where protected person is residing, §50B-4.1(g1).
Possession of deadly weapon, §50B-4.1(g).
Violation of valid protective order as misdemeanor, §50B-4.1(a).
Warrantless arrest by law enforcement officer, §50B-4.1(b), (c).
Relief.
Generally, §50B-3(a).
Remedies not exclusive, §50B-7.
Reporting and database system.
Domestic violence-related homicides, §114-2.7.
Safe houses.
Trespass with a deadly weapon, §14-134.3(b).
Shelters.
Entry into safe house or haven where person protected under order is residing.
Felony violation, §50B-4.1(g1).
Limited civil liability.
Definitions, §1-620.
Excepted conduct, §1-621(b).
Scope of immunity, §1-621(a).
Spousal assault.
Competency of spouse as witness, §8-57(b).
Superior courts.
Secure area for victims waiting for hearing, §7A-114.

DOMESTIC VIOLENCE —Cont'd
Victim assistance act, §§7A-474.16 to 7A-474.20.
Victims programs.
Privileged communications.
Definitions, §8-53.12(a).
Duty in cases of abuse or neglect, §8-53.12(c).
Generally, §8-53.12(b).

DOMESTIC VIOLENCE CENTERS.
Domestic violence center fund, §50B-9.
Fees collected for issuance of marriage licenses, §161-11.2.
Entry into safe house or haven where person protected under order is residing.
Felony violation, §50B-4.1(g1).
Limited civil liability.
Domestic violence shelters, §1-620.

DOMESTIC VIOLENCE COMMISSION,
§§143B-394.15, 143B-394.16.
Chair, §143B-394.15(e).
Established, §143B-394.15(a).
Located within department of administration, §143B-394.15(a).
Meetings, §143B-394.15(i).
Membership, §143B-394.15(c).
Office space provided by department of administration, §143B-394.15(k).
Per diem, subsistence and travel allowances, §143B-394.15(g).
Powers and duties, §143B-394.16(a).
Purpose, §143B-394.15(b).
Quorum, §143B-394.15(j).
Removal, §143B-394.15(h).
Report on findings and recommendations, §143B-394.16(b).
Staffing, §143B-394.15(l).
Terms, §143B-394.15(d).
Vacancies, §143B-394.15(f).

DOMESTIC VIOLENCE VICTIM ASSISTANCE ACT, §§7A-474.16 to 7A-474.20.
Definitions, §7A-474.17.
Eligible activities, §7A-474.18(a).
Eligible cases, §7A-474.18(b).
Funding, §7A-474.19.
Legislative declaration, §7A-474.16.
Prohibited purposes for funds, §7A-474.18(c).
Records, §7A-474.20.
Reports, §7A-474.20.

DOMESTIC WORKERS.
Wage and hour act exemptions, §95-25.14(a).

DOMICILE.
Residency.
See RESIDENCY.

DOMICILIARY HOMES.
Adult care homes.
Generally.
See ADULT CARE HOMES.
Sales and use tax refunds for nonprofits, §105-164.14(b).

DONATIONS.
Bees and honey.
Authority of board to accept, §106-637.
Food.
Food bank information and referral service.
Maintenance of information by department of agriculture and consumer services, §106-21.2.
Immunity for, §99B-10.

DONATIONS —Cont'd
Food —Cont'd
Inspections by department of agriculture and consumer services, §106-141.1.
Gifts generally.
See GIFTS.
Hospitals.
Surplus medical equipment, §131E-250(a), (b).
Housing authorities and projects.
Municipal cooperation and aid.
Advances and donations by city and municipality, §157-43.
Justice department.
Justice academy, §17D-3.
Nonprofit corporations.
Acceptance after mergers, §55A-11-07.
Organ donations.
See ANATOMICAL GIFTS.
Public schools.
Powers of local boards of education, §115C-47.
Secretary of state.
International relations, authority to accept, §147-54.6(b).
Sheriffs' education and training standards commission, §17E-10(a).

DONKEYS.
Equine activity liability, §§99E-1 to 99E-3.
Equine infectious anemia, §§106-405.15 to 106-405.20.
See EQUINE INFECTIOUS ANEMIA.

DO NOT CALL LAW, §§75-100 to 75-103.
Notification to telephone subscribers.
Opportunity to object to telephone solicitation, §62-54.

DO NOT RESUSCITATE ORDERS, §90-21.17.
Immunity from liability, §90-21.17(d).
Issuance, §90-21.17(b).
Official form, §90-21.17(c).
Forms in existence prior to effective date.
Not affected, §90-21.17(f).
Public policy, §90-21.17(a).
Reciprocal acceptance, §90-21.17(e).

DO NOT SEND LAW.
Unsolicited facsimiles, §§75-115 to 75-118.

DONUTS.
Sales and use tax exemption.
Bakery items sold by artisan bakeries, §105-164.13B(a).

DOOR CLOSING ACT.
Deficiency judgments, §45-21.38.

DOOR LOCK EXEMPTION PERMITS, §143-143.4.

DOOR-TO-DOOR SALES.
Buyer's right.
Limitation on buyer's right, §25A-39(e).
Notice, §25A-39(b) to (d).
Restoration of down payment, §25A-41(a).
Goods as down payment, §25A-41(b).
Retention of goods, §25A-41(d).
Return and care of goods, §25A-42(a).
Cancellation.
Buyer's right, §25A-39(a).
Delay of seller, §25A-39(f).
No compensation for services of seller prior to cancellation, §25A-42(c).
Care of goods by buyer, §25A-42(b).
Defined, §25A-38.

DOOR-TO-DOOR SALES —Cont'd
Failure to give right to cancel in off premises sales, §14-401.13.
Form of agreement or offer, §25A-40(b).
Negotiation or transfer of note, contract or other evidence of indebtedness.
Compensation, §25A-42(b).
Time limitation, §25A-42(d).
Statement of buyer's rights, §25A-40(a).

DORMITORY FIRE SAFETY, §§116-44.6 to 116-44.8.

DORMITORY TELEPHONE SERVICE, §62-110(d).

DOROTHEA DIX HOSPITAL JOINT SECURITY FORCE, §122C-430.20.

DOUBLE BOTTOM TRAILERS.
Department of transportation not authorized to permit to operate over state highways, §20-119(a).

DOUBLE DAMAGES.
Attorneys, fraudulent practice, §84-13.
Unlawful cutting, removal or burning of timber, §1-539.1(a).

DOUBLE JEOPARDY, US Const Amd 5.
Appeals.
Correction of errors by appellate division.
When charges must be dismissed with prejudice, §15A-1447(g).
Death by vehicle.
Manslaughter.
Subsequent prosecutions prohibited, §20-141.4(c).
Dismissal motions, §15A-954(a).
Manslaughter.
Death by vehicle.
Subsequent prosecutions prohibited, §20-141.4(c).
Probable cause hearings.
Findings by judge not to preclude subsequent prosecution for same offense, §15A-612(b).
Subsequent prosecution for same offense not barred, §15A-612.

DOVES.
Hunting and wildlife generally.
See HUNTING AND WILDLIFE.

DOWER.
Abolished, §29-4.
Renunciation by married person under age of 21, §39-13.2(c).

DOWNTOWN REVITALIZATION.
Defined, §160A-536(b).
Municipal service districts.
Authorized purpose of district, §160A-536(a).
Generally, §§160A-535 to 160A-544.
See MUNICIPAL SERVICE DISTRICTS.

DRAFT ANIMALS.
Passing horses or other draft animals, §20-216.

DRAFTS.
Checks.
See CHECKS.
False pretenses and cheats.
Worthless checks, draft or order.
Obtaining property in return for worthless check, etc., §14-106.
Negotiable instruments generally, §§25-3-101 to 25-3-605.
See NEGOTIABLE INSTRUMENTS.

DRAFTS —Cont'd
Powers of attorney.
Powers conferred by statutory short form, §32A-2.
Unclaimed property generally, §§116B-51 to 116B-80.
See UNCLAIMED PROPERTY.

DRAG RACING.
Racing on streets and highways generally, §20-141.3.

DRAINAGE, §§156-1 to 156-53.
Appeals.
Canals.
Right to drain into canal, §156-10.
Petitions.
Agreement for construction, §156-29.
Apportionment.
Expenses for repairs, §156-11.
Assessments.
Deficiencies.
Supplemental assessments to make up deficiencies, §156-22.
Jurors.
Vacancy appointments of assessment jurors, §156-22.
Liens.
Drainage assessments declared liens, §156-21.
Petitions.
Agreement for construction.
Viewers, §156-28.
Subsequent owners bound, §156-14.
Supplemental assessment to make up deficiencies, §156-22.
Vacancy appointments of assessment jurors, §156-22.
Bond issues.
Payment of bonds authorized, §156-53.
Bonds, surety.
Petitions.
Agreement for construction, §156-26(d).
Canals.
Earth from canal removed or leveled, §156-8.
Maintenance for seven years presumed a necessity, §156-21.
Necessity that canals be maintained for seven years, §156-21.
Protection of canals, ditches and natural drains, §156-25.
Right to drain into canal, §156-10.
Commissioners.
Appointments, §156-2.
Corporations, §§156-38, 156-40, 156-43.
Duties.
Generally, §156-3.
Examination of lands and making reports, §156-17.
Jurisdiction in county commissioners. See within this heading, "Jurisdiction in county commissioners."
Liens, §156-21.
Powers, §156-3.
Reports, §156-4.
Confirmation, §156-4.
Examination of lands and making reports, §156-17.
Vacancy appointments, §156-22.
Contributions.
Amount of contribution for repair ascertained, §156-15.
Subsequent owners bound, §156-14.

DRAINAGE —Cont'd

Corporations, §§156-37 to 156-53.
See DRAINAGE BY CORPORATION.

Costs.
Allowance of costs to either party or apportioned
in discretion of court, §6-21.
Amount of contribution for repair ascertained,
§156-15.
Lowlands draining or damming.
Petitioner to pay costs, §6-22.
Repairs enforced by judgment, §156-18.

Damages.
Compensation for damage to lands.
Corporations, §156-48.
Petitions.
Agreement for construction.
Payment of damages, §156-27.

Dams.
Earth for construction of, §156-7.

Default.
Judgment against owner in default, §156-13.

Districts, §§156-54 to 156-138.4.
See DRAINAGE DISTRICTS.

Ditches.
Open drains within thirty feet of, §156-9.

Easements.
Acquisition, §156-4.
Petition by servient owner against dominant
owner, §156-16.
Repairs.
Right of dominant owner to repair, §156-20.
Surrender of drainage easements, §156-23.
Width of right of way for repairs, §156-5.

Eminent domain.
Powers of local public condemnors, §40A-3(b).
Supplemental proceeding, §156-1.

Fences.
Right of owner, §156-6.

Hearings.
Petitions.
Agreement for construction, §156-26(c).

Highways, roads and streets.
Application to court, §136-21.
Appointment of commissioners, §136-21.
Judgment of commissioners, §136-22.
Right to appeal, §136-23.
Obstructing highway drains misdemeanor,
§136-92.
Special proceedings.
Rights of parties, §136-24.
Summons and process, §136-21.
View by commissioners, §136-22.
Report, §136-22.
Water must be diverted from public road by ditch
or drain, §136-95.

Judgments.
Corporations, §156-42.
Cost of repairs enforced by judgment, §156-18.
Default.
Judgment against owner in default, §156-13.
Expenses of repairs, §156-11.
Owners in default, §156-13.
Repairs.
Cost of repairs enforced by judgment, §156-18.
Subsequent owners bound, §156-14.

Jurisdiction in county commissioners.
Board.
Appointment, §156-32.
Chairman, §156-32.
Compensation, §156-36.
Compliance with requirements, §156-33.

DRAINAGE —Cont'd

Jurisdiction in county commissioners —Cont'd
Board —Cont'd
Composition, §156-32.
Duties, §156-33.
Meetings, §156-33.
Notice to landowners, §156-32.
Penalties.
Refusal to comply with requirements,
§156-33.
Refusal to serve, §156-32.
Powers, §156-33.
Qualifications of members, §156-32.
Refusal to serve, §156-32.
Reports.
Filing, §156-34.
Ditches.
Owners to keep open, §156-35.
Obstructions.
Keeping ditch open, §156-35.
Penalties.
Board.
Refusal to comply with requirements,
§156-33.

Jury.
Assessment jurors.
Vacancy appointments, §156-22.
Petitions.
Agreement for construction.
Trial by jury, §156-29.

Liens.
Default judgments, §156-13.
Drainage assessment declared liens, §156-21.
Judgments against owners in default, §156-13.
Laborer's lien for work on canal, §156-50.
Subsequent owners bound, §156-14.

Magistrates.
Contributions for repairs.
Amount ascertained, §156-15.

Mechanic liens.
Laborer's lien for work on canal, §156-50.

Misdemeanors.
Obstructions in drainage ditches, §77-14.

Municipal service districts.
Authorized purposes of districts, §160A-536(a).

Notice.
Easements.
Surrender of drainage easements, §156-23.
Petitions.
Agreement for construction, §156-26.
Landowners, §156-28.
Repairs, §156-12.

Obstructions.
Canals, ditches and natural drains, §156-25.
Canals or ditches dug under agreement, §156-19.
Drainage districts.
Penalty, §77-14.
Drains cut by consent, §156-24.
Keeping ditches open, §156-35.
Protection of canals, ditches and natural drains,
§156-25.

Open drains.
No open drains within thirty feet, §156-9.

Owners.
Right of dominant owner to repair, §156-20.
Subsequent owners bound, §156-14.

Petitions.
Agreement for construction.
Appeals, §156-29.
Assessments made by viewers, §156-28.

DRAINAGE —Cont'd
Petitions —Cont'd
  Agreement for construction —Cont'd
    Benefits.
      Recovery, §156-27.
    Bonds, surety, §156-26(d).
    Confirmation of reports, §156-30.
    Construction authorized, §156-26(e).
    Damages.
      Payment, §156-27.
    Hearings, §156-26(c).
    Installment payments, §156-31.
    Jury trials, §156-29.
    Names filed, §156-26(a).
    Notice, §156-26(b).
      Landowners, §156-28.
    Payment in installments, §156-31.
    Payment of damages, §156-27.
    Procedure upon agreement, §156-26.
    Recovery for benefits, §156-27.
    Reports, §156-26(d).
      Confirmation, §156-30.
      Filing, §156-29.
    Viewers, §156-26(c).
      Assessments, §156-28.
  Contents, §156-2.
  Corporations.
    Filing in superior court, §156-37.
  Filing, §156-2.
Repairs.
  Amount of contribution for repair ascertained,
    §156-15.
  Cost of repairs enforced by judgment, §156-18.
  Entry for repairs, §156-6.
  Judgments against owners in default, §156-13.
  Notice, §156-12.
  Right of dominant owner to repair, §156-20.
  Right of way for repairs, §156-5.
  Subsequent owners bound, §156-14.
  Width of right of way, §156-5.
Reports.
  Canals already constructed, §156-43.
  Commissioners, §156-4.
    Examination of land, §156-17.
  Confirmation, §156-4.
  Corporations.
    Commissioners, §156-38.
      Confirmation, §156-40.
  Jurisdiction in county commissioners.
    Board appointed by county commissioners,
      §156-34.
  Petitions.
    Agreement for construction, §156-26(d).
      Confirmation of report, §156-30.
      Filing of reports, §156-29.
Right of entry.
  Repairs, §156-6.
Rights of way.
  Widths, §156-5.
Special proceedings.
  Dissolution of corporations, §156-49.
Summons and process.
  Petition by servient owner against dominant
    owner, §156-16.
Surveys and surveyors.
  Corporations.
    Employment of surveyors, §156-39.
  County surveyor as chairman of board, §156-32.

DRAINAGE BY CORPORATION.
Actions.
  Payment of bonds enforced, §156-53.

DRAINAGE BY CORPORATION —Cont'd
Assessments, §156-42.
  Canal already constructed, §156-43.
  Payment of dues entitles to use of canal, §156-46.
  Penalty for nonpayment of assessments, §156-51.
  Shareholders to pay assessments, §156-45.
Board of directors, §156-42.
Bond issues, §§156-52, 156-53.
  Actions to enforce payment, §156-53.
  Payment of bonds enforced, §156-53.
Canals.
  Payment of dues entitles to use, §156-46.
Capital stock.
  Amount, §156-41.
Commissioners.
  Appointment, §156-38.
  Canals already constructed, §156-43.
  Duties.
    Generally, §156-38.
  Reports, §156-38.
    Confirmation, §156-40.
Corporate name, §156-42.
Damages.
  Compensation for damage to lands, §156-48.
Dissolution of corporations, §156-49.
Eminent domain, §156-48.
Infants.
  Rights of infant owners protected, §156-47.
Judgments.
  Assessments, §156-42.
Liens.
  Assessments, §156-42.
  Bond issues constitute liens, §156-52.
  Laborer's lien for work on canal, §156-50.
Minors.
  Rights of infant owners protected, §156-47.
Name, §156-42.
Officers, §156-42.
Organization, §156-42.
Payment.
  Entitles to use of canal, §156-46.
Petitions.
  Filing in superior court, §156-37.
Powers.
  Generally, §156-42.
Proprietors become a corporation, §156-41.
Reports.
  Canals already constructed, §156-43.
  Confirmation, §156-40.
  Contents, §156-38.
Shares of stock annexed to land, §156-44.
Stock.
  Amount of capital stock, §156-41.
  Shareholders to pay assessments, §156-45.
  Shares of stock annexed to land, §156-44.
Surveyors' employees, §156-39.

DRAINAGE DISTRICTS.
Accounts and accounting.
  Expenses.
    Filing account of expenses, §156-77.
Actions.
  Bond issues.
    Holder's remedy, §156-99.
Amendments, §156-104.
Anticipation notes, issuing, §156-93.1(g).
Appeals.
  Acquiring title for purpose of easements or
    rights-of-way, §156-70.1.
  Bonds, surety, §156-66.
  Construction of drainage law, §156-135.

DRAINAGE DISTRICTS —Cont'd

Appeals —Cont'd

Easements, §156-70.1.

Hearings.

Final hearings, §156-75.

Improvement, renovation, enlargement and extension of canals, structures and boundaries, §§156-93.2, 156-93.3.

Notice, §156-70.1.

Publication in case of unknown owners, §156-58.

Public or private ways.

Maintenance of drainage across, §156-88.

Railroads.

Drainage across railroads, §156-90.

Right of appeal, §156-66.

Rights of way, §156-70.1.

Applicability of provisions.

Local drainage laws not affected, §156-137.

Appointments.

Commissioners.

Amended act, §156-81.

Method of appointment, §156-81(a).

Failure to appoint, §156-81(e).

Original act, §156-79.

Statutory appointment of elected commissioners, §156-82.2.

Validation of election of members of drainage commission, §156-82.

Statutory appointment of elected drainage commissioners, §156-82.2.

Curative statutes.

Validation of election of members of drainage commission, §156-82.

Statutory appointment of elected drainage commissioners, §156-82.2.

Validation of prior actions of members of drainage commission, §156-82.3(a), (b).

Assessments.

Adjustment of delinquent assessments.

Amount of assessments limited, §156-129.

Approval of adjustment by local government commission, §156-128.

Authorized, §156-125.

Distribution of collections, §156-127.

Extension, §156-126.

Fund.

Distribution of collections, §156-127.

Special fund set up, §156-127.

Limitation on amount of assessments, §156-129.

Local government commission.

Approval of adjustments, §156-128.

Reassessments regulated, §156-129.

Advancement of funds and repayment from assessments, §156-61.

Amendment or reformation of proceedings, §156-104.

Application of amendatory provisions of certain sections, §156-104.

Arrears.

Authority to collect arrears, §156-110.

Benefits.

Classification, §156-71.

Collection.

Authority to collect arrears, §156-110.

Fees, §156-113.

Installments, §156-95.

Not collectible out of other property of delinquent, §156-106.

Procedure generally, §§156-105, 156-106.

Construction of drainage law, §156-135.

DRAINAGE DISTRICTS —Cont'd

Assessments —Cont'd

Conveyance of land.

Change in assessment rolls, §156-114.

Costs.

Total cost of improvement.

Ascertained for three years, §156-94.

Rate per acre, §156-95.

Damages, §156-70.

Default.

Authority to collect arrears, §156-110.

Delinquent assessments, §156-105.

Adjustment, §§156-125 to 156-129.

Authority to collect arrears, §156-110.

Eminent domain.

Damages, §156-70.

Estimates, §156-61.

Excess assessments, §156-98.

Extension of adjusted installments, §156-126.

Fees.

Collection fees, §156-113.

Improvements.

Renovation, enlargement and extension of canals, structures and boundaries, §156-93.5.

Judgments, §156-103.

Levy.

No assessments to be levied on property when once paid in full, §156-124.

Liens, §§156-61, 156-105.

Payment of assessments which become liens after original bond issue, §156-100.2.

Maintenance, §§156-92, 156-93.1(a), (e).

Modification of assessments.

Additional bonds issued, §156-116(e).

Insufficient funds, §156-116(d).

Manner of issue, §156-116(f).

Relevy, §156-116(a).

Surplus funds, §156-116(c).

Upon sale of land for assessments, §156-116(b).

Not collectible out of other property of delinquent, §156-106.

Notice, §156-95.

Requirements generally, §156-138.3.

Payment, §156-61.

Assessments may not be levied on property when once paid in full, §156-124.

Assessments which become liens after original bond issue, §156-100.2.

Time of payment, §156-95.

Warranty in deed runs to purchaser who pays assessment, §156-115.

Power to assess, §156-54.

Public or private ways.

Maintenance of drainage across, §156-88.

Railroads.

Drainage across railroads, §156-89.

Receipt book.

Land in two or more counties, §156-109.

Preparation, §156-108.

Rolls.

Change in assessment rolls.

Effect, §156-114.

Procedure, §156-114.

Contents, §156-103.

Copies, §156-103.

Preparation, §156-103.

Recording, §156-103.

Sale of land.

Delinquent assessments, §156-105.

DRAINAGE DISTRICTS —Cont'd

Assessments —Cont'd

Sale of land —Cont'd

Sheriff in good faith selling property for assessment not liable for irregularity, §156-107.

Sheriffs.

Authority to collect arrears, §156-110.

Collection, §156-105.

Fees, §156-113.

Liability for good faith selling of property, §156-107.

Monthly settlements to be made, §156-111.

Penalty for failure to make, §156-111.

Subdistricts.

Formation of subdistricts, §156-117.

Surplus assessments, §156-98.

Treasurer.

Duty of treasurer to make payments, §156-112.

Waiver.

Defense to assessment waived, §156-96.

Warranty in deed runs to purchaser who pays assessment, §156-115.

Attorneys at law.

Petitions, §156-60.

Payment of petitioners attorney, §156-61.

Auditor.

Appointment, §156-133.

Compensation, §156-133.

Duties, §§156-133, 156-134.

Removal, §156-136.

Reports.

Duties of auditor, §§156-133, 156-134.

Benefits.

Assessments.

Classification, §156-71.

Railroads.

Assessment benefits, §156-89.

Bids and bidding.

Construction of improvements.

Regulations, §156-84.

Bond issues.

Actions.

Holder's remedy, §156-99.

Amendment or reformation of proceedings, §156-104.

Amount, §156-97.

Anticipation notes, §156-97.

Force and effect of bonds, §156-97.1.

Form, §156-98.

Interest rate, §156-97.1.

Issuance, §156-97.1.

Sale, §156-100.1.

Sinking fund, §156-100.3.

Application of amendatory provisions of certain sections, §156-104.

Application of funds, §156-99.

Collection.

Holder's remedy, §156-99.

Commissioners.

Powers and duties of board, §156-82.1(a).

Consent to issuance.

Failure to pay deemed consent to bond issue, §156-96.

Construction of drainage law, §156-135.

Construction of improvements.

Destruction of work.

Assessments, §156-116.

Conveyance of land.

Assessments.

Modification of assessments, §156-116.

DRAINAGE DISTRICTS —Cont'd

Bond issues —Cont'd

Cost.

Total cost for three years ascertained, §156-94.

Default.

Holder's remedy, §156-99.

Deposits.

Drainage bonds received as deposits, §156-102.

Excess assessments, §156-98.

Extinguishing debt, §156-122.

Form, §156-98.

Improvements and maintenance.

Increase to extinguish debt, §156-122.

Proceedings as for original bond issue, §156-123.

Redress to dissatisfied landowners, §156-121.

Renovation, enlargement and extension of canals, structures and boundaries, §156-93.5.

Increase to extinguish debt, §156-122.

Installments, §156-97.

Interest, §§156-95, 156-97.

Collection, §156-97.

Payment.

Duty of treasurer, §156-112.

Rate, §156-97.

Issuance.

Additional bonds, §156-116.

Modification of assessments, §156-116.

Failure to pay deemed consent to bond issue, §156-96.

Generally, §156-97.

Maintenance anticipation notes, §156-93.1(g).

Modification of assessments, §156-116.

Notice, §156-95.

Sale of bonds, §156-100.

Payments.

Enforcement, §156-99.

Installments, §156-97.

Time, §156-97.

Procedure.

Generally, §156-97.

Recreational facilities, §156-82.1(g).

Redress to dissatisfied landowners, §156-121.

Refunding bonds.

General provisions, §156-101.

Increase to extinguish debt, §156-122.

Proceedings as for original bond issue, §156-123.

Requirements.

Generally, §156-97.

Sale of bonds, §§156-99, 156-100.

Sinking fund, §156-100.3.

Bonds, surety.

Amount of penalty, §156-57.

Appeals, §156-66.

Construction of improvements.

Contractors, §156-84.

Penalties.

Amount of penalty, §156-57.

Petitions.

Filing with petition, §156-57.

Treasurer, §156-81.1.

Boundaries.

Establishment, §156-65.

Existing districts may act together to extend boundaries, §156-93.7.

Extension, §156-93.3.

Existing districts may act together, §156-93.7.

Bridges.

Control and repairs by commissioners, §156-92.

DRAINAGE DISTRICTS —Cont'd

Bridges —Cont'd

Public or private ways.

Maintenance of drainage across, §156-88.

Canals.

Improvement, renovation, enlargement and
extension.

Procedures generally, §§156-93.2, 156-93.3.

Public or private ways.

Maintenance of drainage across, §156-88.

Channelization.

Procedures to be followed, §156-138.4.

Rules and regulations, §156-138.4.

Classification.

Lands and benefits, §156-71.

Redress to dissatisfied landowners, §156-121.

Commissioners.

Amendment or reformation of proceedings,
§156-104.

Application of amendatory provisions of certain
sections, §156-104.

Application of section, §156-81(h).

Appointments.

Amended act, §156-81.

Failure to appoint, §156-81(e).

Method of appointment, §156-81(a).

Original act, §156-79.

Statutory appointment of elected
commissioners, §156-82.2.

Validation of election of members of drainage
commission, §156-82.

Statutory appointment of elected drainage
commissioners, §156-82.2.

Chairman, §§156-79, 156-81(b).

Compensation, §156-81(g).

Construction of improvements.

Control and repairs by commissioners, §156-92.

Control and repairs by commissioners, §156-92.

Duties, §156-82.1(a) to (i).

Elected commissioners.

Statutory appointment, §156-82.2.

Meetings, §156-81(f).

Names of districts, §156-80.

Organization, §156-81(b).

Original act, §156-79.

Powers, §§156-79, 156-82.1(a) to (i).

Prior actions.

Validation of prior actions of members of
drainage commission, §156-82.3(a), (b).

Removal, §156-136.

Repairs, §156-92.

Reports.

Annual reports, §156-131.

Penalty for failure to make, §156-132.

Statements to be made, §156-130.

Subdistricts.

Powers and authority, §156-117.

Superintendent of construction.

Appointment, §156-83.

Term of office, §156-81(c).

Treasurer.

Appointment, §156-81.1.

Elected treasurer.

Statutory appointment, §156-82.2.

Statutory appointment of elected treasurer,
§156-82.2.

Vacancies, §§156-79, 156-81(d).

Compensation of viewers, §156-76.

Condemnation of land, §156-67.

Consolidation of services and equipment.

Board, setting up, §156-93.1(d).

DRAINAGE DISTRICTS —Cont'd

Construction and interpretation.

Construction of drainage law, §156-135.

Local drainage laws not affected, §156-137.

Construction of improvements.

Bids and bidding.

Regulations, §156-84.

Bonds, surety.

Contractors, §156-84.

Commissioners.

Control and repairs by commissioners, §156-92.

Contracts.

Bids and bidding, §156-84.

Failure of contractors, §156-86.

Letting contracts, §156-84.

Monthly estimates for work and payments
thereon, §156-85.

Payment, §156-85.

Reletting contract, §156-86.

Improvement, renovation, enlargement and
extension of canals, structures and
boundaries.

Assessments, §156-93.5.

Bond issues, §156-93.5.

Coordination of proceedings, §156-93.4.

Easements, §156-93.6.

Existing districts may act together, §156-93.7.

Extension of boundaries, §156-93.3.

Procedures.

Coordination of proceedings, §156-93.4.

Generally, §§156-93.2, 156-93.3.

Rights of way, §156-93.6.

Lateral drains, §156-93.

Notice.

Letting contracts, §156-84.

Payments.

Final payments, §156-85.

Monthly estimates for work and payments
thereon, §156-85.

Publication.

Letting contracts, §156-84.

Public or private ways.

Maintenance of drainage across, §156-88.

Railroads.

Appeals, §156-90.

Construction across railroads, §156-91(a) to (d).

Drainage across railroads, §156-89.

Reports.

Contracts, §156-84.

Right of entry, §156-87.

Superintendent of construction.

Appointment, §156-83.

Duties, §156-83.

Estimates.

Monthly estimates for work and payments
thereon, §156-85.

Powers, §156-83.

Removal, §156-136.

Trees and timber.

Removal of timber, §156-87.

Contracts.

Construction of improvements.

Bids and bidding, §156-84.

Failure of contractors, §156-86.

Letting contracts, §156-84.

Monthly estimates for work and payments
thereon, §156-85.

Payment, §156-85.

Reletting contract, §156-86.

Conveyance of land.

Application of section, §156-114(l).

DRAINAGE DISTRICTS —Cont'd
Conveyance of land —Cont'd
Assessments.
  Change in assessment rolls, §156-114.
  Rolls.
    Costs.
      Determined, §156-114(j).
    Effect in change of assessment roll,
      §156-114(g).
    Number of copies, §156-114(i).
    Preparation of new rolls by clerk, §156-114(h).
Chairman.
  Represents board, §156-114(k).
Costs.
  Determination of costs, §156-114(j).
Deeds.
  Warranty in deed runs to purchaser who pays
    assessment, §156-115.
Delinquent assessments.
  Collection, §156-105.
Duty of chairman of commissioners, §156-114(d).
Establishment of districts.
  Conveyance afterwards, §156-114(c).
Failure of chairman or board to act, §156-114(e).
Lease to or from federal or state government or
  agency thereof, §156-138.1.
Petition, §156-114(f).
Reports.
  Before final report, §156-114(b).
  Conveyance before final report, §156-114(b).
Sale of land.
  Delinquent assessments, §156-105.
Status of land fixed, §156-114(a).
When owner may file petition with clerk,
  §156-114(f).
Costs.
Assessments.
  Total cost of improvements.
    Ascertained for three years, §156-94.
    Rate per acre, §156-95.
Bond issues.
  Total cost for three years ascertained, §156-94.
Conveyance of land.
  Determination of costs, §156-114(j).
Payment by petitioners, §156-74.
Counties.
Article applicable to certain counties only,
  §156-141.
Cleaning and draining of streams under
  supervision of governmental agencies,
  §156-139.
Drainage by certain counties.
  Article applicable to certain counties only,
    §156-141.
  Cleaning and draining of streams, §156-139.
  Tax levy, §156-140.
Taxation.
  Levy of tax, §156-140.
Curative statutes.
Appointments.
  Validation of election of members of drainage
    commission, §156-82.
  Statutory appointment of elected drainage
    commissioners, §156-82.2.
Prior actions.
  Validation of prior actions of members of
    drainage commission, §156-82.3(a), (b).
Damages.
Assessments, §156-70.
Railroads.
  Drainage across railroads, §156-89.

DRAINAGE DISTRICTS —Cont'd
Deeds.
Conveyance of land.
  Warranty in deed runs to purchaser who pays
    assessment, §156-115.
Definitions.
Majority of resident landowners, §156-138.2.
Owners of three fifths of land area, §156-138.2.
Deposits.
Bond issues.
  Drainage bonds received as deposits, §156-102.
Disposing of equipment, §156-93.1(c).
Disposition of lands, §156-138.1.
Ditches.
Control and repairs by commissioners, §156-92.
Easements, §156-70.1.
Improvements.
  Renovation, enlargement and extension of
    canals, structures and boundaries,
    §156-93.6.
Elections.
Commissioners.
  Elected commissioners.
    Statutory appointment, §156-82.2.
Eminent domain.
Acquisition and disposition of lands.
  Generally, §156-138.1.
Assessments.
  Damages, §156-70.
Compensation of landowners.
  When title deemed acquired for purpose of
    easements or rights of way, §156-70.1.
Condemnation of land, §156-67.
**Employing engineering assistance, equipment,
  superintendents and equipment operators,**
  §156-93.1(a), (b).
Equipment.
Consolidation of services and equipment.
  Board, setting up, §156-93.1(d).
Disposing of equipment, §156-93.1(c).
Duty of commissioners to maintain, §156-82.1(b).
Employing engineering assistance, equipment,
  superintendents and equipment operators,
  §156-93.1(a), (b).
Establishment.
Adjudication upon final report, §156-74.
Conveyance of land after district established,
  §156-114(c).
Jurisdiction, §156-54.
Special proceedings, §156-55.
Survey, plan and specifications, §§156-68, 156-69.
Venue, §156-55.
Expenses.
Account of expenses filed, §156-77.
Advancement of funds and repayment from
  assessments, §156-61.
Estimate of expense and manner of payment,
  §156-61.
Fees, §156-113.
Fish and fisheries resources.
Conservation and replacement of fish and wildlife
  habitat, §156-69.
Forms.
Receipt books, §§156-108, 156-109.
Funds.
Advancement of funds.
  Repayment from assessments, §156-61.
Investment of surplus funds, §156-135.1.
Sinking fund, §156-100.3.
Surplus funds.
  Investment, §156-135.1.

DRAINAGE DISTRICTS —Cont'd
Good faith.
Sheriffs.
Liability for good faith selling of property, §156-107.
Governmental agencies, contracting with, §156-82.1(d).
Hearings.
Appeals.
Final hearings, §156-75.
Final hearings.
Adjudication upon final report, §156-74.
Appeals, §156-75.
Notice, §156-73.
First hearing of preliminary report, §156-63.
Further hearings.
District established, §156-65.
Generally, §156-65.
Improvement, renovation, enlargement and extension of canals, structures and boundaries, §§156-93.2, 156-93.3.
Notice.
Final hearings, §156-73.
Further hearing, §§156-64, 156-73.
Reports.
First hearing of preliminary report, §156-63.
Highways.
Public or private ways.
Maintenance of drainage across, §156-88.
Highways, roads and streets.
Public or private ways.
Drainage across public or private ways, §156-88.
Hunting and wildlife.
Conservation and replacement, §156-69.
Improvements.
Assessments.
Renovation, enlargement and extension of canals, structures and boundaries, §156-93.5.
Canals, structures and boundaries.
Renovation, enlargement and extension.
Procedures generally, §§156-93.2, 156-93.3.
Construction of improvements. See within this heading, "Construction of improvements."
Easements.
Renovation, enlargement and extension of canals, structures and boundaries, §156-93.6.
Interest.
Bond issues, §§156-95, 156-97.
Anticipation notes, §156-97.1.
Payment.
Duty of treasurer, §156-112.
Investments.
Surplus funds, §156-135.1.
Joint use of facility for impoundment or storage of water.
Contracts for, §156-82.1(h).
Judgments.
Adjudication upon final report, §156-74.
Assessments, §156-103.
Establishment of district, §156-65.
Jurisdiction.
Establishment of districts, §156-54.
Lateral drains.
Construction, §156-93.
Leases.
Acquisition and disposition of lands, §156-138.1.
Liens.
Assessment liens, §§156-61, 156-105.
Payment of assessments which become liens after original bond issue, §156-100.2.

DRAINAGE DISTRICTS —Cont'd
Local government finance generally, §§159-1 to 159-188.
See LOCAL GOVERNMENT FINANCE.
Maintenance assessments, §§156-92, 156-93.1(a), (e).
Majority of resident landowners.
Defined, §156-138.2.
Maps and plats.
Contents, §156-69.
Copies kept by clerk, §156-78.
Municipalities.
Classification of lands and benefits, §156-71.
Contribution of funds, §156-78.1(b).
Necessary expenses, §156-78.1(c).
Participation in works or projects, §156-78.1(a).
Permissive nature of applicable section, §156-78.1(d).
Names, §156-80.
Notice.
Acquisition of title for purpose of easements or rights of way, §156-70.1.
Appeals, §156-70.1.
Assessments, §156-95.
Bond issues, §156-95.
Sale of bonds, §156-100.
Construction of improvements.
Letting contracts, §156-84.
Hearings.
Final hearings, §156-73.
Further hearings, §§156-64, 156-73.
Improvement, renovation, enlargement and extension of canals, structures and boundaries, §§156-93.2, 156-93.3.
Maintenance assessment, meeting to determine levy, §156-93.1(a).
Publication in case of unknown owners, §§156-57, 156-58.
Railroads.
Drainage across railroads, §§156-89, 156-90.
Requirements generally, §156-138.3.
Obstructions.
Penalty, §77-14.
Officers.
Removal, §156-136.
Owners of three fifths of land area.
Defined, §156-138.2.
Parties.
Unknown owners.
Publication in case of unknown owners, §156-58.
Petitions.
Adjudication upon final report, §156-74.
Amendments, §156-65.
Attorneys for petitioners, §156-60.
Payment, §156-61.
Bonds, surety.
Filing with petition, §156-57.
Contents, §156-56.
Conveyance of land, §156-114(f).
Costs.
Payment by petitioners, §156-74.
Filing, §156-56.
Hearings.
First hearing of preliminary report, §156-63.
Improvement, renovation, enlargement and extension of canals, structures and boundaries, §§156-93.2, 156-93.3.
Prosecution bonds.
Institution of actions without being required to give, §1-109.

DRAINAGE DISTRICTS —Cont'd
Public or private ways, §156-88.
Purchasing, selling or leasing equipment,
§156-93.1(c).
Railroads.
Appeals.
Drainage across railroads, §156-90.
Assessments.
Drainage across railroads, §156-89.
Benefits.
Assessment benefits, §156-89.
Construction across.
Agreement as to exact time work to be done,
§156-91(a).
Utilities commission to settle disagreements,
§156-91(b).
Duty of railroad, §156-91(a).
Expenses for railroad opening tracks.
Bill for, payment, §156-91(d).
Penalty for delay of construction, §156-91(c).
Removal of rails, ties and other obstructions.
Duty of railroad, §156-91(b).
Penalty for delay, §156-91(c).
Construction of improvements.
Appeals, §156-90.
Drainage across railroads, §156-89.
Damages.
Drainage across railroads, §156-89.
Notice.
Drainage across railroads, §§156-89, 156-90.
Receipt books.
Land in two or more counties, §156-109.
Preparation, §156-108.
Records.
Assessments.
Rolls, §156-103.
Bond issue recorded, §156-99.
Drainage record.
Certificate of assessment recorded, §156-95.
Clerk to keep book, §156-78.
Recreational facilities.
Contracts for operating, authority, §156-82.1(g).
Issuance of revenue bonds or notes, §156-82.1(g).
Recreational purpose.
Use of stored or impounded water for, authorizing,
§156-82.1(g).
Redress to dissatisfied landowners, §156-121.
Refunding bonds, §§156-101, 156-122, 156-123.
Release of areas taken for rights-of-way,
§156-82.1(e).
Reports.
Auditor.
Duties of auditor, §§156-133, 156-134.
Commissioners.
Annual reports, §156-131.
Penalty for failure to make, §156-132.
Statements to be made, §156-130.
Construction of improvements.
Contracts, §156-84.
Conveyance of land.
After final report, §156-114(c).
Before final report, §156-114(b).
Extension of time for reports, §156-72.
Final reports.
Adjudication upon final report, §156-74.
Filing, §156-73.
Hearings.
First hearing of preliminary report, §156-63.
Improvement, renovation, enlargement and
extension of canals, structures and
boundaries, §§156-93.2, 156-93.3.

DRAINAGE DISTRICTS —Cont'd
Reports —Cont'd
Penalties.
Failure of commissioners to make reports,
§156-132.
Preliminary report of viewers, §156-62.
First hearing of preliminary report, §156-63.
Right of entry.
Construction of improvements.
Entry upon lands, §156-87.
Rights of way.
Appeals, §156-70.1.
Improvement, renovation, enlargement and
extension of canals, structures and
boundaries, §156-93.6.
When title deemed acquired for purpose of
easements or rights of way.
Claim for compensation, §156-70.1.
Notice to landowner, §156-70.1.
Rules and regulations.
Channelization, §156-138.4.
Sales.
Assessments.
Delinquent assessments.
Sale of land, §156-105.
Bond issues, §§156-99, 156-100.
Anticipation notes, §156-100.1.
Sheriffs.
Assessments.
Authority to collect arrears, §156-110.
Collection of assessments, §156-105.
Fees, §156-113.
Good faith.
Liability for good faith selling of property,
§156-107.
Monthly settlements to be made, §156-111.
Penalty for failure to make, §156-111.
Sale of land.
Delinquent assessments, §156-105.
Liability for good faith selling of property,
§156-107.
Sinking fund.
Bond issues, §156-100.3.
Special proceedings.
Establishment of districts, §156-55.
Storage of water, §156-69.
Subdistricts, §156-117.
Summons and process.
Issuance, §156-57.
Unknown owners, §156-58.
Surplus funds, use, §156-82.1(c).
Surveys and surveyors.
Classification of lands and benefits, §156-71.
Complete survey ordered, §156-68.
Expenses.
Account of expenses filed, §156-77.
Nature of survey, §156-69.
Taxation.
Power to levy taxes, §156-54.
Treasurer.
Appointment, §156-81.1.
Assessments.
Duty of treasurer to make payments, §156-112.
Penalty for failure to make, §156-112.
Bonds, surety, §156-81.1.
Elected treasurer.
Statutory appointment, §156-82.2.
Fees.
Collection and disbursement of funds, §156-113.
Jurisdiction where lands in two or more counties,
§156-109.

DRAINAGE DISTRICTS —Cont'd
Treasurer —Cont'd
Qualifications, §156-81.1.
Removal, §156-136.
Statutory appointment of elected treasurer, §156-82.2.
Term of office, §156-81.1.
Trees and timber.
Construction of improvements.
Removal of timber, §156-87.
Venue.
Establishment of districts, §156-55.
Viewers.
Appointment, §156-59.
Classification of lands and benefits, §156-71.
Compensation, §156-76.
Duties.
Generally, §156-59.
Examination of lands, §156-62.
Expenses.
Account of expenses filed, §156-77.
Qualifications, §156-59.
Removal, §156-136.
Reports.
Adjudication upon final report, §156-74.
Correction and modification by commissioners, §156-84.
Extension of time for reports, §156-72.
Final reports.
Filing, §156-73.
Hearings.
First hearing of preliminary report, §156-63.
Preliminary reports, §156-62.
Violations.
Penalties generally, §156-138.
Waiver.
Assessments.
Defense to assessment waived, §156-96.
Warranties.
Deed runs to purchaser who pays assessment, §156-115.
Water-retardant structures.
Maintaining and operating, §156-93.1(f).
Waters and watercourses.
Control of water, §156-69.
Injuring or damaging, §156-92.
Storage of water, §156-69.

DRAINAGE DITCH OBSTRUCTIONS, §77-14.

DRAINAGE PROJECTS.
Special assessments by counties, §§153A-185 to 153A-210.7.
See SPECIAL ASSESSMENTS BY COUNTIES.

DRAMA.
Promotion of arts, §§143-403 to 143-407.1.

DRAM SHOP LIABILITY.
Compensation for injury caused by sales to underage persons, §§18B-120 to 18B-129.
Intoxicated persons.
Sales to prohibited, §18B-305(a).
Refusal to sell.
Discretion for seller, §18B-305(b).
Discriminatory refusals prohibited, §18B-305(c).

DRAWINGS.
Artwork on consignment, §§25C-1 to 25C-5.

DREDGING.
Coastal wetlands, §113-230.
Permits.
Appeals, §113-229(f), (g).

DREDGING —Cont'd
Permits —Cont'd
Applicability of section, §113-229(m).
Applications, §113-229(b).
Beach-quality sand, §113-229(h1), (h2), (i).
Civil actions, §113-229(l).
Coastal wetlands.
Orders to control activities.
Powers and duties of department as to permits not repealed by section, §113-230(h).
Conditions, §113-229(e).
Construction of terms, §113-229(n).
Coordination, §113-229(e).
Definitions, §113-229(n).
Denial of applications, §113-229(e).
Emergency dredging, §113-229(d), (e1).
Federal laws, compliance with requirements, §113-229(j).
Issuance, §113-229(c).
Major or minor development.
General or blanket permits issued, §113-229(c1).
Objections.
Circulating among agencies for opportunity to raise objections, §113-229(e).
Required, §113-229(a).
Rules.
General permits issued as, §113-229(c2).
Time for action on application, §113-229(e).
Violations, §113-229(k).

DRESSING ROOMS.
Secretly peeping into room occupied by another person, §14-202.

DRIED APPLES.
Standard weights and measures, §81A-42.

DRILLING FOR OIL AND GAS.
Applications.
Punishment for making false entries, §113-409.
Residence address of applicant to be included, §113-408.
Bond, surety.
Required, §113-378.
Development of lands.
Cooperative development not in restraint of trade, §113-393(c).
Variation from vertical, §113-393(d).
When each owner may drill, §113-393(b).
Filing log of drilling and development of each well, §113-379.
Keeping under control.
Required, §113-396.
Location of wells, §113-392(c).
Notice and payment of fee to department, §113-395.
Offshore oil and gas activities, §§143-215.94AA to 143-215.94JJ.
See OFFSHORE OIL AND GAS ACTIVITIES.
Pools.
Units in pools, §113-392(b).
Test drilling or boring.
Filing record of results, §136-102.3.
Penalty for violations of provisions, §136-102.4.
Right of way.
Authorization required, §136-102.2.
Filing record of results, §136-102.2.
Variation from vertical, §113-393(d).
When each owner may drill, §113-393(b).

DRINKING WATER.
Community water systems.
Local water supply plans, §143-355.

DRINKING WATER —Cont'd
Community water systems —Cont'd
Permits.
Fees, §130A-328(b).
Disposition of fees collected, §130A-328(e).
Failure to pay, §130A-328(d).
Required, §130A-328(a).
Review of plans and specifications, fees,
§130A-328(c).
Enforcement of provisions, §130A-327.
Interpretation of article.
Construction of provisions, §130A-327.
Penalties.
Prohibited acts, §130A-22(b).
Prohibited acts.
Administrative penalties, §130A-22(b).
**Regulation of public water systems supplying
drinking water,** §§130A-311 to 130A-329.
See WATER SUPPLY AND WATERWORKS.
Violations of provisions.
Administrative penalties, §130A-22(b).
Water infrastructure loans and grants.
Generally, §§159G-20 to 159G-67.
See WATER INFRASTRUCTURE.
Wells.
Construction of private wells.
Bernard Allen memorial emergency drinking
water fund, §87-98.
Chlorination of well, §87-97(f).
Construction of provisions, §87-97(l).
Emergency drinking water fund, §87-98.
Maintenance or pump repair, §87-97(c).
Permits, inspections and testing.
Certificate of completion, §87-97(g).
Chlorination of well, §87-97(f).
Expiration of permit, §87-97(f).
Issuance of permit, §87-97(e).
Maintenance or pump repair, §87-97(c).
Mandatory local programs, §87-97(a).
Registry of permits and test results,
§87-97(k).
Requirement for permit, §87-97(b).
Results of tests, §87-97(j).
Revocation of permit, §87-97(f).
Rules for testing, §87-97(i).
Site evaluation, §87-97(d).
Testing procedures, §87-97(h).
Standards, §87-88(a).

DRIVE-BY SHOOTINGS.
**Discharge of firearm into occupied property or
conveyance while in operation,** §14-34.1.

DRIVER EDUCATION AND TRAINING.
Driver license handbook, §20-88.1(d).
Expenses.
Payment out of highway fund, §20-88.1(c).
Public schools, §§115C-215, 115C-216.
School-based management and accountability
program, §115C-105.25(b).
Training schools.
Licensing, §§20-320 to 20-328.
See DRIVER TRAINING SCHOOLS.

DRIVER IMPROVEMENT CLINICS.
Fee, §20-16(e).
Points deducted for attending, §20-16(c).

DRIVER LICENSE HANDBOOK.
Division to prepare, §20-88.1(d).

DRIVER'S LICENSE COMPACT, §§20-4.21 to
20-4.30.
Administration of information, §20-4.28.

DRIVER'S LICENSE COMPACT —Cont'd
Commissioner.
Authority to make reciprocity agreements,
arrangements or declarations, §20-4.22.
Construction and severability, §20-4.30.
Conviction reports, §20-4.24.
Convictions to be reported, §20-4.24(a).
Effect, §20-4.24(b).
Effect on laws or agreements, §20-4.26.
Effect on other state driver's license laws,
§20-4.27.
Exchange of information, §20-4.28.
Findings and policy, §20-4.23(a), (b).
Findings of legislature, §20-4.23.
License status in other states.
Review upon application for license in member
state, §20-4.25.
Policy of state, §20-4.23.
Title of article, §20-4.21.
Withdrawal from compact, §20-4.29.

DRIVERS' LICENSES, §§20-5 to 20-37.
Accidents.
Failure to report reportable accident.
Suspension of license, §20-279.31(a).
Failure to stop and render assistance.
Revocation or suspension, §20-166(e).
Mandatory revocation, §20-17(a).
Active duty military designation.
Issuance, renewal, §20-7(q).
Affidavits.
False affidavits.
Perjury, §20-31.
Age, §20-9(a).
**Alcohol and drug education traffic (ADED)
school.**
Impaired driving.
Condition of probation, §20-179(g) to (k).
Restoration of license after impaired driving
conviction or conviction for driving while less
than 21 years old after consuming alcohol or
drugs.
Obtaining certificate of completion, §20-17.6(c).
Alcoholic beverages.
Issuance of drivers' licenses to habitual
drunkards.
Prohibited, §20-9(c).
Minors.
Sale to or purchase by underage persons.
Allowing use of identification, §18B-302(f).
Defense, §18B-302.
Fraudulent use of identification, §18B-302(e).
Use of fraudulent license, §18B-302.
Revocation or suspension.
Mental incompetents, alcoholics and habitual
users of narcotic drugs, §20-17.1.
Aliens.
Cancellation.
Legal presence of licensee in country no longer
authorized, §20-15(a).
Limited duration license.
Expiration, §20-7(f).
Issuance to applicant in country under valid
visa, §20-7(s).
Issuance to applicant presenting documentation
demonstrating legal presence, §20-7(s).
Anatomical gifts.
Access to records by procurement organizations,
§130A-412.16(b).
Invalidation of driver's license upon which gift is
made, effect, §130A-412.7(c).

DRIVERS' LICENSES —Cont'd
Anatomical gifts —Cont'd
Method of making gift prior to donor's death,
§130A-412.7(a).
Appeals.
Denial, cancellation, suspension or revocation,
§20-25.
Applications, §20-7(b).
Contents, disclosures and other information,
§20-7(b1).
False statements or information.
Prohibited, §20-30.
Fraud or incorrect information.
Grounds for cancellation of license, §20-15(a).
Prohibition against reapplying for commercial
driver's license, §20-15(c).
Minors.
Signatures, §20-11(i).
Armed forces members.
Eye exam exemption.
Renewing by mail, §20-7(r).
Military designation.
Active duty military designation, §20-7(q).
Veteran military designation, §20-7(q1).
Nonresident military spouses licensed in home
state.
Exemption, §20-8.
Persons operating vehicles owned by and in
service of military.
Exemption, §20-8.
Renewal, §20-7(f).
Authorization of license, §20-7(a).
Bomb scares.
Revocation or suspension of license.
Minors, §20-13.2(c2).
Issuance of license during revocation or
suspension, §20-9(b1).
Cancellation, §20-15(a).
Appeals, §20-25.
Commercial drivers' licenses.
Driving during cancellation.
Prohibited, §20-37.12(b).
Notice of cancellation, §20-37.18(c).
Surrender of license, §20-15(b).
Carrying license while driving.
Required, §20-7(a).
Change of address.
Application for duplicate license, §20-7.1(a).
Change of name.
Application for duplicate license, §20-7.1(b).
Child support.
Access to information or data storage and
retrieval system maintained by department of
transportation.
Powers of department of health and human
services, §110-129.1(a).
Forfeiture of licensing privilege for failure to pay,
§50-13.12.
Suspension or revocation.
Delinquent obligors or individuals not in
compliance with orders, §§110-142,
110-142.2.
Mandatory revocation, §20-17(b).
Classes of motor vehicles allowed to be driven,
§20-7(a).
Classes of regular drivers' licenses, §20-7(a).
Color photocopies or color reproductions.
Prohibition, §20-30.
Color photograph, §20-7(n).
Commercial drivers' licenses, §§20-37.10 to
20-37.23.
See COMMERCIAL DRIVERS' LICENSES.

DRIVERS' LICENSES —Cont'd
Community service.
Mandatory revocation.
Noncompliance with obligations, §20-17(b).
Division of adult correction program,
§143B-708(f).
Compact, §§20-4.21 to 20-4.30.
See DRIVER'S LICENSE COMPACT.
**Confidentiality of photographic image or
signature recorded in format,** §20-43(a).
Convictions.
Forwarding record of conviction to division,
§20-24(b).
Substituting period of probation for revocation
or disqualification, failure to receive record,
§20-24(b1).
Special information required, §20-24(e).
Counterfeiting.
Prohibited, §20-30.
**Criminal record checks of persons
manufacturing or producing.**
Confidentiality, §114-19.24(d).
Department of justice, §114-19.24(a).
Fee to offset costs, §114-19.24(e).
Fingerprints, §114-19.24(c).
Information provided to department,
§114-19.24(b).
**Defect or disease affecting operation of
vehicle.**
Certificate of applicant's condition.
Requirement, §20-7(e).
Defenses.
Failure to carry license, §20-35(c).
Defined, §20-4.01.
Denial.
Appeals, §20-25.
Disclosure of impairments, §20-9.1.
Driver license handbook.
Division to prepare, §20-88.1(d).
Drivers license technology fund, §20-37.01.
Driving eligibility certificate.
Minors, §20-11(n).
Charter school's designee, duties,
§115C-238.29F(j).
Duty of state board of education to develop
rules for issuance, §115C-12.
Principals of schools, duties, §115C-288(k).
Private and home schools, duties, §115C-566.
School disciplinary actions.
Effect on eligibility for certificate, §20-11(n1).
Provisional license revocation, §20-13.2(c1).
State board of community colleges, adoption of
rules, §115D-5(a3).
Driving while intoxicated. See within this
heading, "Impaired driving."
Driving while license suspended or revoked.
Application for new license after license revoked,
§20-28(c).
Conditional restoration.
Impaired driving revocation, §20-28(c3) to (c5).
Imprisonment for misdemeanor violation.
Restriction, §20-176(c1).
Issuance of new license.
Proof required, §20-28(c1).
Limited driving privilege.
Application, §20-20.1.
Moving offense during.
Additional period of revocation, §20-28.1(a), (b).
New license, §20-28.1(c).
Prohibited, §20-28(a).

DRIVERS' LICENSES —Cont'd

Driving while license suspended or revoked
—Cont'd
Restrictions or conditions on new license.
Imposing, §20-28(c2).
When treated as driving without a license,
§20-28(a1).

Drugs.
Issuance of driver's license to habitual user.
Prohibited, §20-9(c).
Revocation or suspension.
Mental incompetents, alcoholics and habitual
users of narcotic drugs, §20-17.1.

Drunk driving. See within this heading, "Impaired
driving."

Duplicate licenses, §20-14.
Change of address.
Application for duplicate license, §20-7.1(a).
Change of name.
Application for duplicate license, §20-7.1(b).
Commercial drivers' licenses, §20-37.15(b).
Fees, §20-7.1(c).

Duration, §20-7(f).

Electronic system to verify information.
Collection or retention of information prohibited,
§20-37.02(c).
Costs of equipment and communications lines.
Retailers responsibility, §20-37.02(d).
Division to establish and operate, §20-37.02(a).
Fictitious identification.
System used to prevent, §20-37.02(a).
Funding, §20-37.02(e).
Verification of information.
Retailers and ABC permit holders, §20-37.02(b).

Endorsement required to drive vehicle,
§20-7(a).
Motorcycle endorsement, §20-7(a1).
Fee, §20-7(i).
Requirements for obtaining, §20-7(b).

Examinations, §20-7(c).
Exclusive nature of provisions, §20-37.
Reexamination.
Commissioner may require, §20-29.1.

Exclusive nature of provisions, §20-37.

Exemptions, §20-8.
Mopeds, §20-8.

Expiration, §20-7(f).

Explosives.
Revocation or suspension of license.
Minors, §20-13.2(c2).
Issuance of license during revocation or
suspension, §20-9(b1).

Expunction of criminal records.
First offenders under age 18.
Civil revocation of driver's license expunged,
§15A-145.

Eye exam.
Exemption when renewing by mail.
Armed forces members, national guard
members and reservists, §20-7(r).

Fake IDs.
Electronic system to verify information, §20-37.02.
Presenting license with fake name in commission
of felony, §20-30.
Violations of license or learner's permit provisions,
§20-30.
Wrongful issuance of drivers' licenses, §20-34.1.

Farm tractors.
Exemption from driver's license requirement,
§20-8.

DRIVERS' LICENSES —Cont'd

Fees, §20-7(i).
Duplicate licenses, §20-14.
Highway fund, placing in, §20-7(j).
Learners' permits, §20-7(l).
Limited driving privileges.
Processing fee, §20-20.2.
Minors, expanding privileges, §20-11(j).
Records.
Copies.
Furnishing, §20-26(c).
Not subject to provisions of chapter 132,
§20-26(d).
Refund in event of mistake on part of person
ordering, §20-26(e).
Restoration fee.
Person whose license has been revoked,
§20-7(i1).

Fictitious names.
Electronic system to verify information, §20-37.02.
Presenting license with fake name in commission
of felony, §20-30.

Financial responsibility.
Proof required for issuance, forms of proof,
§20-7(c1).
Revocation.
Appeals, §20-279.2.
Surrender of license, §20-279.30.
Misdemeanor for failure to surrender,
§20-279.31(c).
Suspension, §20-279.5(b).
Duration, §20-279.7.
Licenses in other states, §20-279.8(c).
Nonpayment of judgments, §20-279.13(a).
Continuation of suspension until judgment
satisfied, §20-279.14.
Default on installment payment,
§20-279.16(c).
Exceptions, §20-279.13(b), (c).
Surrender of license, §20-279.30.

Foreign licenses.
No operation under during suspension or
revocation in state, §20-21.

Forfeited privileges.
Revocation when privileges forfeited, §20-15.1.

**Forfeiture of licensing privilege after
conviction of felony, §15A-1331A.**
Limited driving privilege.
Eligibility of persons whose license revoked,
§20-179.3(b).

**Forfeiture of licensing privilege for failure to
pay child support, §50-13.12.**

Format, §20-7(n).

Full provisional license, §20-11(f), (g).

Habitual drunkards.
Issuance of license to prohibited, §20-9(c).
Revocation or suspension, §20-17.1.

Handbook.
Copies given to clerks of superior courts, §20-7(p).

Highway fund.
Placing fees in, §20-7(j).

Hospitals for mentally disordered.
Persons not to be licensed, §20-9(d), (e).

Identity theft.
Generally, §§14-113.20 to 14-113.25.

Ignition interlock system.
Impaired driving conviction.
Restoration of license conditioned on use.
Duration of condition, §20-17.8(c).
Habitual impaired driving.
Applicability of provisions, §20-17.8(a1).

DRIVERS' LICENSES —Cont'd
Ignition interlock system —Cont'd
Impaired driving conviction —Cont'd
Restoration of license conditioned on use
—Cont'd
Limited driving privilege, effect, §20-17.8(d).
Medical exception to requirement.
Requesting, requirements for issuing,
§20-17.8(l).
Notice of requirement, §20-17.8(e).
Scope, §20-17.8(a).
Vehicles subject to requirement, §20-17.8(c1).
Violation as driving while license revoked,
§20-17.8(f), (g).
Commencement of revocation, §20-17.8(h).
Hearings, §20-17.8(j).
Notification of revocation, §20-17.8(i).
Restoration after revocation for violating
this section, §20-17.8(k).
When required, §20-17.8(b).
Limited driving privileges.
When allowed, §20-179.3(g3).
When required as condition, §20-179.3(g5).
Tampering with system, §20-17.8A.
Immediate civil license revocation.
Implied consent violations.
Civil actions, §20-16.5(o).
Costs, §20-16.5(j).
Definitions, §20-16.5(a).
Effect of revocation, §20-16.5(i).
Exceptions, §20-16.5(n).
Hearing, contesting validity, §20-16.5(g).
Limited driving privilege, §20-16.5(p).
Modification of order, §20-16.5(m).
Persons charged with violations, §20-16.5(b).
Precharge test results basis for revocation,
§20-16.5(b1).
Refusal to submit to chemical analysis,
§20-16.5(b).
Report to division, §20-16.5(k).
Report to judicial officials.
Duty of charging officers, §20-16.5(c).
Judicial officer with whom report filed,
§20-16.5(d).
Person not present, procedure for filing,
§20-16.5(f).
Person present, procedure for filing,
§20-16.5(e).
Restoration fee, person with no license,
§20-16.5(l).
Return of license, §20-16.5(h).
Fee as cost for action, §20-16.5(j).
Impaired driving.
Driving after notification or failure to appear.
License revoked, §20-28(a2).
Conditional restoration, §20-28(c3) to (c5).
Habitual impaired driving.
Permanent revocation, §20-138.5(d).
Limited driving privilege.
License revoked for refusal to submit to test,
§20-16.2(e1).
Provisional license.
Revocation or suspension, §20-13.2(b), (c).
Refusal to submit to chemical test, §20-16.5(b).
Revocation, §20-16.2(d).
Death or critical injury involved, §20-16.2(d1).
Limited driving privilege, §20-16.2(e1).
Restoration after conviction, §20-17.6.
Driving after notification or failure to appear.
Conditional restoration, §20-28(c3) to (c5).

DRIVERS' LICENSES —Cont'd
Impaired driving —Cont'd
Restoration after conviction —Cont'd
Ignition interlock as condition.
Duration of condition, §20-17.8(c).
Habitual impaired driving.
Applicability of section, §20-17.8(a1).
Limited driving privilege, effect, §20-17.8(d).
Medical exception to requirement.
Requesting, requirements for issuing,
§20-17.8(l).
Notice of requirement, §20-17.8(e).
Scope, §20-17.8(a).
Tampering with system, §20-17.8A.
Vehicles subject to requirement, §20-17.8(c1).
Violation as driving while license revoked,
§20-17.8(f), (g).
Commencement of revocation, §20-17.8(h).
Hearings, §20-17.8(j).
Notification of revocation, §20-17.8(i).
Restoration after revocation for violating
this section, §20-17.8(k).
When required, §20-17.8(b).
Probation, conditions, §20-170(g) to (k).
Revocation.
Conditional restoration, §20-28(c3).
After ten years, §20-19(e4).
After three years, §20-19(e1).
After two years, §20-19(e2).
Cancellation, imposition of remaining
revocation period, §20-28(c5).
Conditions or restrictions, §20-19(e3).
Substance abuse assessment, §20-28(c4).
Driving after notification or failure to appear,
§20-28(a2).
Immediate civil license revocation, §20-16.5.
Mandatory revocation, §20-17(a).
Period of suspension or revocation, §20-19(c1)
to (e).
Permanent revocation, §20-19(e).
Permanent revocation, §20-19(e).
Habitual impaired driving, §20-138.5(d).
Refusal to submit to chemical test, §20-16.2(d).
Death or critical injury involved, §20-16.2(d1).
Limited driving privilege, §20-16.2(e1).
Implements of husbandry.
Exemption from driver's license requirement,
§20-8.
Incendiaries.
Revocation or suspension of license.
Minors, §20-13.2(c2).
Issuance of license during revocation or
suspension, §20-9(b1).
Information, §20-7(n).
Instruction.
Supervising driver or approved instructor.
Giving instructions while under influence of
impairing substances or after consumption
of alcohol, §20-12.1(a), (b).
Instruction permit, §20-7(m).
Learner's permit generally, §20-7.
Insurance points.
Offenses for which points charged, §58-36-75.
Issuance, §20-7(c1).
Disabled persons.
Persons not to be licensed, §20-9(e).
When license may be issued, §20-9(g).
During period of revocation or suspension,
§20-9(b), (f).
Explosives offenses by minors, §20-9(b1).
Habitual user of drugs or alcohol, §20-9(c).

DRIVERS' LICENSES —Cont'd
Issuance —Cont'd
Mentally ill.
Persons not to be licensed, §20-9(d), (e).
When license may be issued, §20-9(g).
What persons should not be licensed, §20-9.
Wrongful issuance, §20-34.1(a).
Jury commissions.
Current list of licensed drivers.
Providing to commission, §20-43.4.
Larceny of motor fuel.
Second or subsequent conviction.
Limited driving privilege.
Allowed person whose license revoked,
§20-16(e2).
Mandatory revocation of driver's license,
§20-17(a).
Period of revocation of driver's license,
§20-19(g2).
Learners' permits, §20-7(l).
Age for obtaining, §20-7(l).
Applications, §20-7(b).
Color photocopies or color reproductions.
Prohibition, §20-30.
Expiration, §20-7(l).
Fees, §20-7(l).
Motorcycle learner's permit, §20-7(a2).
Prohibited acts as to, §20-30.
Renewal, §20-7(l).
Resident of state.
Proof required for issuance, documents
evidencing, §20-7(b2), (b3), (b4).
Social security number or tax payer identification
number.
Providing required for issuance of license,
§20-7(b1).
**Legal presence of licensee in country no
longer authorized.**
Cancellation, §20-15(a).
**Limited driving privileges, §§20-16.1(b1),
20-16(e1).**
Application for, §20-179.3(d).
Driving with revoked license underlying offense
resulting in license revocation.
Petition, §20-20.1(d).
Community service violations.
Willful violation.
Revocation of privilege, §20-179.3(j1).
Conviction for excessive speeding.
Limited driving permits for first offenders.
Proof of financial responsibility, §20-16.1(g).
Conviction of motor fuel larceny.
Allowed person whose license revoked on second
conviction, §20-16(e2).
Copy of privilege to division, §20-179.3(k).
Court-ordered revocation, privilege not effective
until after compliance, §20-179.3(c).
Definition of limited driving privilege,
§20-179.3(a).
Driving with revoked license underlying offense
resulting in license revocation, §20-20.1(a).
Driving by person less than 21 years old after
consuming alcohol or drugs, §20-138.3(d).
Driving for other than work-related purposes,
§20-179.3(g2).
Driving for work-related purposes.
Nonstandard hours, §20-179.3(g1).
Driving with revoked license underlying
offense resulting in license revocation,
§20-20.1(g).

DRIVERS' LICENSES —Cont'd
Limited driving privileges —Cont'd
Driving for work-related purposes —Cont'd
Standard working hours, §20-179.3(g).
Driving with revoked license underlying
offense resulting in license revocation,
§20-20.1(f).
Driving with revoked license underlying offense
resulting in license revocation.
Alcohol restrictions, §20-20.1(i).
Conditions, §20-20.1(i).
New license issued after expiration of term,
§20-20.1(j).
Costs, §20-20.1(d).
Definitions, §20-20.1(a).
Eligibility to apply for, §20-20.1(b).
Revocation compliance period, §20-20.1(c).
Employment related driving.
Nonstandard working hours, §20-20.1(g).
Standard working hours, §20-20.1(f).
Essential driving purposes.
Scope of privilege, §20-20.1(e).
Expiration of term.
Reinstatement of driving privilege,
§20-20.1(j).
Financial responsibility.
Providing proof required, §20-20.1(i).
Household maintenance driving, §20-20.1(h).
Invalid privilege, §20-20.1(i).
Issuance to eligible person, §20-20.1(d).
Modification or revocation of privilege,
§20-20.1(k).
Offense of driving while license revoked.
Violation of privilege, effect, §20-20.1(l).
Petition.
Filing, application for, §20-20.1(d).
Reinstatement of driving privilege.
Expiration of term, §20-20.1(j).
Revocation of compliance period to be eligible,
§20-20.1(c).
Scope of privilege, §20-20.1(e).
Employment related driving.
Nonstandard working hours, §20-20.1(g).
Standard working hours, §20-20.1(f).
Household maintenance, §20-20.1(h).
Term, §20-20.1(j).
Violation of privilege, effect, §20-20.1(l).
Eligibility of persons whose license revoked for
privilege, §20-179.3(b).
Driving with revoked license underlying offense
resulting in license revocation, §20-20.1(b).
Exception to restriction set forth, §20-179.3(g4).
Hearings.
Scheduling of subsequent hearings,
§20-179.3(d).
Ignition interlock system.
When allowed, §20-179.3(g3).
When required as condition, §20-179.3(g5).
Impaired driving.
Privilege restrictions, high-risk drivers,
§20-179.3(c1).
Refusal to submit to chemical test.
License revoked for refusal to submit to test,
§§20-16.2(e1), 20-16.5(p).
Insurance verification, §20-179.3(l).
Invalidity of privilege, action taken, §20-179.3(k).
Limited basis for and effect of privilege,
§20-179.3(e).
Modification or revocation of privilege,
§20-179.3(i).
Driving with revoked license underlying offense
resulting in license revocation, §20-20.1(k).

DRIVERS' LICENSES —Cont'd
Limited driving privileges —Cont'd
Nonfleet private passenger motor vehicle.
Defined, §20-179.3(l).
Open container law violations, §20-138.7(g).
Other mandatory and permissive conditions or
restrictions, §20-179.3(h).
Processing fee, §20-20.2.
Proof of financial responsibility, §20-179.3(l).
Driving with revoked license underlying offense
resulting in license revocation, §20-20.1(i).
Restoration of license after impaired driving
conviction or conviction for driving while less
than 21 years old after consuming alcohol or
drugs.
Persons subject to section not eligible for,
§20-17.6(e).
Revocation.
Community service violations.
Willful violation, §20-179.3(j1).
Standard working hours.
Defined, §20-179.3(f1).
Use of privilege, overall provisions, §20-179.3(f).
Violations of restrictions, effect, §20-179.3(j).
Driving with revoked license underlying offense
resulting in license revocation, §20-20.1(l).
Limited duration license.
Applicant presenting documentation
demonstrating legal presence in country.
Expiration, §20-7(f).
Issuance, §20-7(s).
Limited learner's permit, §20-11(b), (c).
Limited licenses.
Issuance, §20-29.1.
Limited provisional license, §20-11(d), (e).
Lose control, lose license, §20-11(n1).
Mail.
License sent by, §20-7(f).
Renewal, §20-7(f).
Active duty military designation, §20-7(q).
**Mental health, developmental disabilities and
substance abuse.**
Persons not to be licensed, §20-9(d), (e).
Retention of motor vehicle driver's license by
clients, §122C-62(b).
Military.
Active duty military designation, §20-7(q).
Eye exam exemption.
Renewal by mail, §20-7(r).
Nonresident military spouses licensed in home
state.
Exemption, §20-8.
Persons operating vehicles owned by and in
service of military.
Exemption, §20-8.
Renewal.
Members of armed forces and reserved
components on active duty and stationed
outside state, §20-7(f).
Selective service system registration
requirements, §20-9.2.
Veteran military designation, §20-7(q1).
Minors.
Cell phones.
Use while operating vehicle.
Prohibition, fine, §20-11(c), (e), (l).
Driving eligibility certificate, §20-11(n).
Charter school's designee, duties,
§115C-238.29F(j).
Principals of schools, duties, §115C-288(k).
Private and home schools, duties, §115C-566.

DRIVERS' LICENSES —Cont'd
Minors —Cont'd
Driving eligibility certificate —Cont'd
Rules for issuance.
Duty of state board of education to develop,
§115C-12.
School disciplinary actions.
Effect on eligibility for certificate, §20-11(n1).
Provisional license revocation, §20-13.2(c1).
State board of community colleges.
Adoption of rules, §115D-5(a3).
Expiration, §20-11(j).
Provisional license, §20-7(f).
Fees, §20-11(j).
Full provisional license, §20-11(f).
Restrictions, §20-11(g).
Insurance, §20-11(m).
Length of suspension, §20-13(b).
Limited learner's permit, §20-11(b).
Restrictions, §20-11(c).
Limited provisional license.
Restrictions, §20-11(e).
Lose control, lose license, §20-11(n1).
Mobile phones.
Use while operating vehicle.
Prohibition, fine, §20-11(c), (e), (l).
Motor vehicle moving violation defined, §20-13(a).
Nonresidents becoming residents, §20-11(h) to
(h2).
Federally issued licenses, §20-11(h3).
Permitting unlicensed minor to drive motor
vehicle.
Prohibited, §20-32.
Probation, placing licensee on, §20-13(b).
Process for expanding privileges, §20-11(a).
Provisional licensee defined, §20-4.01.
Restoration of license on probationary status,
hearing request, §20-13(b).
Retention of license until hearing held, §20-13(a).
Revocation of provisional license.
Driving after consuming alcohol or drugs,
§20-13.2(a).
Driving eligibility certificate not maintained,
§20-13.2(c1).
Explosives offenses, §20-13.2(c2).
Immediate civil revocation for certain criminal
moving violations, §20-13.3.
Impaired driving conviction, §20-13.2(b).
Issuance of license during revocation or
suspension, §20-9(b1).
Length of revocation, §20-13.2(d).
Restoration of license, proof of financial
responsibility, §20-13.2(e).
Willful refusal to submit to chemical analysis,
§20-13.2(c).
Supervising driver for minor, §20-11(k).
Suspension.
In addition to other remedies, §20-13(d).
License of provisional licensee, §20-13(a).
Two or more offenses committed on single
occasion, §20-13(c).
Underage purchase of alcohol.
Revocation, §20-17.3.
Violations, §20-11(l).
Mopeds.
Driver's license not required, §§20-7(a1), 20-8.
Nor motorcycle endorsement, §20-7(a1).
Motorcycles, §20-7(a1).
Learner's permit, §20-7(a2).
Motor vehicle accidents.
Suspension of license for failure to report
reportable accident, §20-279.31(a).

DRIVERS' LICENSES —Cont'd
National guard.
Eye exam exemption.
Renewing by mail, §20-7(r).
National sex offender public registry.
Search by division.
Applicant residing in state less than 12 months, §20-9(i).
New residents of state.
Time for obtaining license after becoming resident, §20-7(a).
Nonresidents.
Exemption.
In possession of valid license issued in home state or country, §20-8.
Minors, §20-11(h) to (h2).
Federally issued licenses, §20-11(h3).
Surrender of license issued by other jurisdiction.
Prerequisite to issuance of driver's license, §20-9(h).
Open container law violations.
Limited driving privileges, §20-138.7(h).
Operating privileges of persons not holding licenses.
Suspending or revoking, §20-23.1.
Oral test, §20-7(c).
Organ, eye and tissue donor cards.
Availability at division offices issuing drivers' licenses, §20-7.3.
Perjury.
False affidavits, §20-31.
Permanent revocation.
Habitual impaired driving, §20-138.5(d).
Photographic image or signature recorded in format.
Confidentiality, §20-43(a).
Photostating or otherwise reproducing.
Prohibited, §20-30.
Physicians and psychologists disclosing impairments.
Authority to disclose, §20-9.1(a).
Immunity of disclosing person, §20-9.1(c).
Use of information, §20-9.1(b).
Points.
Suspension, §20-16(c).
Probation.
Substituted for revocation or disqualification.
Failure of division to receive record of conviction, §20-24(b1).
Surrender of drivers' license, §15A-1343(b1).
Prohibited acts, §20-30.
False affidavits, §20-31.
Permitting unlicensed minor to drive motor vehicle, §20-32.
Permitting violations of provisions, §20-34.
Proof of financial responsibility.
Required for issuance, forms of proof, §20-7(c1).
Provisional licensees.
Defined, §20-4.01.
Driving by licensee after consuming alcohol or drugs.
Restoration after conviction, §20-17.6.
Revocation of operator's license, §20-13.2.
Suspension of operator's license, §20-13.
Provisional license revocation.
Driving after consuming alcohol or drugs, §20-13.2(a).
Driving eligibility certificate not maintained, §20-13.2(c1).
Grounds for revoking provisional license.
Explosives offenses, §20-13.2(c2).

DRIVERS' LICENSES —Cont'd
Provisional license revocation —Cont'd
Grounds for revoking provisional license —Cont'd
Issuance of license during revocation or suspension, §20-9(b1).
Immediate civil revocation for certain criminal moving violations.
Captions in civil actions, §20-13.3(g).
Definitions, §20-13.3(a).
Duties of official receiving report, §20-13.3(d).
Effect of revocation, §20-13.3(f).
Initial appearance of licensee, §20-13.3(c).
License subject to revocation, §20-13.3(b).
Limited driving privilege not applicable, §20-13.3(f).
Notice to division of issuance of revocation order, §20-13.3(e).
Period of revocation, §20-13.3(d).
Points or insurance surcharge not assessed, §20-13.3(h).
Probable cause determination, §20-13.3(d).
Report by law enforcement officer to judicial official, §20-13.3(c).
Impaired driving conviction, §20-13.2(b).
Length of revocation, §20-13.2(d).
Restoration of license, proof of financial responsibility, §20-13.2(e).
Willful refusing to submit to chemical analysis, §20-13.2(c).
Provisional license suspension, §20-13(a).
Length of suspension, §20-13(b).
Motor vehicle moving violation defined, §20-13(a).
Probation, placing licensee on, §20-13(b).
Restoration of license on probationary status, request for hearing, §20-13(b).
Retention of license until hearing held, §20-13(a).
Suspension in addition to other remedies, §20-13(d).
Two or more motor vehicle moving offenses committed on single occasion, §20-13(c).
Pump and run.
Second or subsequent conviction.
Limited driving privilege.
Allowed person whose license revoked, §20-16(e2).
Mandatory revocation of driver's license, §20-17(a).
Period of revocation, §20-19(g2).
Racing vehicles on streets and highways.
Revocation or suspension, §20-141.3(d) to (f).
Records.
Availability, §20-27(a).
Issuance.
Prior record check requirement, §20-37.17.
Convictions.
Forwarding of record of conviction to division, §20-24(b).
Substituting period of probation for revocation, failure to receive record, §20-24(b1).
Copies, §20-26(b).
Furnishing, §20-26(c).
Charges not subject to provisions of chapter 132, §20-26(d).
Division to furnish to insurance agents, insurance companies and to insurance support organizations, §20-26(f).
Fees, §20-26(c).
Refund of fee in event of mistake on part of person ordering, §20-26(e).
Generally, §20-26(a).

DRIVERS' LICENSES —Cont'd
Records —Cont'd
  Inspection, §20-27(a).
  Weight of vehicles.
    Evidentiary effect of records, §20-26(b1).
Renewal, §20-7(f).
  Armed forces members, members of reserve
    components, §20-7(f).
  Expiration of renewed license, §20-7(f).
  Learners' permits, §20-7(l).
  Mail, §20-7(f).
  Military designation, active duty, §20-7(q).
  Proof of financial responsibility.
    Furnishing not required, §20-7(c1).
  Road test, when required, §20-7(c).
  Temporary license.
    License renewed by mail, §20-7(f).
  Time period prior to expiration.
    Application for renewal allowed, §20-7(f).
Rental vehicles.
  Insurance sales or solicitation.
    Rental car company representatives.
      Agent license required, §66-205.
Required, §20-17.6.
  Certificate of completion.
    Required for restoration, §20-17.6(b).
    Requirements for obtaining, §20-17.6(c).
  Limited driving privileges.
    Person subject to section not eligible for,
      §20-17.6(e).
  Notice of requirements of section, §20-17.6(d).
  Requirements for restoring license, §20-17.6(b).
  Scope of sections, §20-17.6(a).
Required to drive, §20-7(a).
Resident of state.
  Proof required for issuance, documents
    evidencing, §20-7(b2), (b3), (b4), (b5).
Residents residing outside state.
  Renewal by mail, §20-7(f).
Restoration fee.
  Person whose license has been revoked, §20-7(i1).
Restricted instruction permit, §20-7(m).
Restricted licenses, §20-7(e).
  Issuance, §20-29.1.
  Operating vehicle without complying with
    restriction.
    Deemed operating vehicle without license,
      §20-7(e).
Restrictions, imposing, §20-7(e).
Revocation or suspension, §20-16(d).
  Accidents.
    Failure to stop and render assistance,
      §20-166(e).
      Mandatory revocation, §20-17(a).
    Suspension of license until reported,
      §20-279.31(a).
  Alcoholic beverages.
    Underage purchasers of alcohol, §20-17.3.
  Appeals, §20-25.
    No suspension pending appeal of conviction,
      §20-16(b).
  Article governs revocation and disqualification,
    §20-24(b).
  Assault with motor vehicle.
    Mandatory revocation, §20-17(a).
  Authority of division to suspend license, §20-16(e).
  Child support scofflaws.
    Mandatory revocation, §§20-17(b), 110-142,
      110-142.2.
  Community service noncompliance, §20-17(b).
    Division of adult correction program,
      §143B-708(f).

DRIVERS' LICENSES —Cont'd
Revocation or suspension —Cont'd
  Conditional restoration.
    Impaired driving, §20-28(c3).
      Cancellation, imposition of remaining
        revocation period, §20-28(c5).
      Conditions or restrictions on restoration,
        §20-19(e3).
      Restoration after ten years, §20-19(e4).
      Restoration after three years, §20-19(e1).
      Restoration after two years, §20-19(e2).
      Substance abuse assessment, §20-28(c4).
  Convictions.
    Criminal convictions.
      Limited driving privilege.
        Eligibility of persons whose driver's license
          revoked, §20-179.3(b).
    Forwarding record of conviction to division,
      §20-24(b).
    Substituting probation for revocation, failure
      to receive record, §20-24(b1).
    Impaired driving in federal court, §20-23.2.
    In another state.
      Suspending resident's license upon, §20-23.
    Special information required, §20-24(e).
    Ten-year-old convictions not considered, §20-36.
  Criminal history records check.
    Petitioner for restoration of revoked license,
      §114-19.31.
  Death by vehicle.
    Mandatory revocation, §20-17(a).
    Period of suspension, §20-19(a).
  Defined, §20-4.01.
  Driving by person less than 21 years old after
    consuming alcohol or drugs.
    Limited driving privilege, §20-138.3(d).
  Driving while license suspended or revoked.
    Application for new license after license
      revoked, §20-28(c).
    Conditional restoration.
      Impaired driving revocation, §20-28(c3) to
        (c5).
    Imprisonment for misdemeanor violation.
      Restriction, §20-176(c1).
    Issuance of new license.
      Proof required, §20-28(c1).
    Limited driving privilege.
      Application, §20-20.1.
    Moving offense during.
      Additional period of revocation, §20-28.1(a),
        (b).
      New license, §20-28.1(c).
    Prohibited, §20-28(a).
    Restrictions or conditions on new license.
      Imposing, §20-28(c2).
    When treated as driving without a license,
      §20-28(a1).
  Explosives offenses by minors, §20-13.2(c2).
  Issuance of license during revocation or
    suspension, §20-9(b1).
  Expunction of criminal records.
    First offenders under age 18.
      Civil revocation of driver's license expunged,
        §15A-145.
  Failure to appear or pay fines, penalties or costs,
    §20-24.1(a).
    Duration of revocation, §20-24.1(b).
    "Offense" defined, §20-24.1(e).
    Reports to DMV, §20-24.2(a).
      Section not applicable to offenses in which
        order of forfeiture of cash bond entered
        and reported to division, §20-24.2(b).

DRIVERS' LICENSES —Cont'd
Revocation or suspension —Cont'd
Failure to appear or pay fines, penalties or costs
    —Cont'd
    Restoration of license, §20-24.1(c).
    Copy of notice of compliance given person,
        §20-24.1(d).
    Trial or hearing afforded within reasonable time
        of defendant's appearance, §20-24.1(b1).
Failure to stop and render aid, §20-17(a).
False or fictitious name or address in application.
    Mandatory revocation, §20-17(a).
Federal traffic conviction, §20-23.2.
Fee upon restoration of license.
    Person whose license has been revoked,
        §20-7(i1).
Felony convictions, §15A-1331A.
Felony in commission of which motor vehicle used.
    Mandatory revocation, §20-17(a).
Financial responsibility.
    Misdemeanor for refusal to surrender,
        §20-279.31(c).
Foreign license.
    No operation under during suspension or
        revocation in state, §20-21.
Forfeiture of licensing privileges.
    Revocation when privilege forfeited, §20-15.1.
Grounds.
    Suspension, §20-16(a).
Headlamps.
    Failure to dim or low beam headlamps not
        grounds for revocation or suspension,
        §20-18.
Hearings, §20-16(d).
Immediate civil license revocation, §20-16.5.
Impaired driving, §20-19(c1) to (e).
    Amended revocation orders, §20-19(j).
    Conditional restoration, §20-28(c3).
        After ten years, §20-19(e4).
        After three years, §20-19(e1).
        After two years, §20-19(e2).
        Cancellation, imposition of remaining
            revocation period, §20-28(c5).
        Conditions or restrictions, §20-19(e3).
        Substance abuse assessment, §20-28(c4).
    Conviction in federal court, §20-23.2.
    Habitual impaired driving.
        Permanent revocation, §20-138.5(d).
    Implied consent, §20-16.2.
    Mandatory revocation, §20-17(a).
    Mental incompetents, alcoholics and habitual
        users of narcotic drugs, §20-17.1.
    Period of suspension or revocation, §20-19(c1) to
        (e2).
        Permanent revocation, §§20-19(e), (i),
            20-138.5(d).
    Refusal to submit to chemical test.
        Revocation, §20-16.2(d).
        Death or critical injury involved,
            §20-16.2(d1).
    Restoration after conviction, §20-17.6.
        Conditional restoration, §20-28(c3).
            After ten years, §20-19(e4).
            After three years, §20-19(e1).
            After two years, §20-19(e2).
            Cancellation, imposition of remaining
                revocation period, §20-28(c5).
            Conditions or restrictions, §20-19(e3).
            Substance abuse assessment, §20-28(c4).
        Ignition interlock as condition, §20-17.8(a),
            (b).
        Duration of condition, §20-17.8(c).

DRIVERS' LICENSES —Cont'd
Revocation or suspension —Cont'd
Impaired driving —Cont'd
    Restoration after conviction —Cont'd
        Ignition interlock as condition —Cont'd
            Habitual impaired driving, applicability,
                §20-17.8(a1).
            Limited driving privilege, effect,
                §20-17.8(d).
            Medical exception to requirement,
                §20-17.8(l).
            Notice of requirement, §20-17.8(e).
            Restoration after revocation for violating
                this section, §20-17.8(k).
            Tampering with system, §20-17.8A.
            Vehicles subject to requirement,
                §20-17.8(c1).
            Violation results in revocation, §20-17.8(f)
                to (j).
Implied consent offenses, §20-16.2.
    Immediate civil license revocation, §20-16.5.
Issuance of license during period of revocation or
    suspension.
    Prohibited, §20-9(b), (f).
Larceny of motor fuel, §14-72.5(c).
Larceny of motor vehicle, second or subsequent
    conviction.
    Limited driving privilege may be allowed by
        judge, §20-16(e2).
    Mandatory revocation of driver's license,
        §20-17(a).
    Period of revocation, §20-19(g2).
Limitation of actions.
    Ten-year-old convictions not considered, §20-36.
Limited driving privilege, §§20-16(e1), 20-179.3.
    Community service violations.
        Willful violation, revocation, §20-179.3(j1).
    Driving by person less than 21 years old after
        consuming alcohol or drugs, §20-138.3(d).
    Open container law violations, §20-138.7(h).
    Violations of restrictions, effect, §20-179.3(j).
Mandatory revocation.
    Grounds, §20-17(a).
Manslaughter or negligent homicide.
    Mandatory revocation, §20-17(a).
Mental incompetents, alcoholics and habitual
    users of narcotic drugs.
    Adjudication.
        Copy of abstract to commissioner, §20-17.1(b).
    Generally, §20-17.1(a).
    Institutions.
        Agreements for care and treatment,
            §20-17.1(d).
        Information to be furnished, §20-17.1(e).
    Legislative intent, §20-17.1(d).
    Review of revocation, §20-17.1(f).
Motor fuel larceny conviction.
    Limited driving privilege may be allowed by
        judge, §20-16(e2).
    Mandatory revocation of driver's license.
        Second or subsequent conviction, §20-17(a).
    Period of revocation, §20-19(g2).
Nonresidents.
    Suspending privileges of nonresidents,
        §20-22(a).
Notice, §20-16(d).
Open container law violations.
    Limited driving privilege, §20-138.7(h).
    Second or subsequent conviction, mandatory
        revocation, §20-17(a).

DRIVERS' LICENSES —Cont'd
Revocation or suspension —Cont'd
Operating privilege of person not holding license, §20-23.1.
Period of suspension or revocation.
Death by vehicle, §20-19(a).
Driving under the influence, §20-19(c1) to (e).
Conditional restoration after 2 years, §20-19(e2).
Conditional restoration after 3 years, §20-19(e1).
Conditional restoration after 10 years, §20-19(e4).
Conditions or restrictions on restoration, §20-19(e3).
Financial responsibility.
Proof required on seeking to have license restored, §20-19(k).
Generally, §20-19(c), (f), (g).
Permanent revocation, §20-19(e).
Provisional license revoked, §20-13.2(b).
Restoration.
Proof of financial responsibility required, §20-19(k).
Speeding, §20-19(a), (b).
Perjury or false affidavit or statement under oath to division.
Mandatory revocation, §20-17(a).
Permanent revocation, §20-19(e).
Habitual impaired driving, §20-138.5(d).
Points.
Child restraint systems, failure to use, §20-137.1(d).
Generally, §20-16(c).
Schedule of point values, §20-16(c).
Probation.
Condition, §15A-1343(b1).
Substituted for revocation.
Failure to receive record of conviction, §20-24(b1).
Provisional licensees.
Financial responsibility.
Proof required prior to restoration, §20-13.2(e).
Immediate civil revocation for certain criminal moving violations, §20-13.3.
Impaired driving, §20-13.2(b).
Period of revocation, §20-13.2(d).
Receipt of record of conviction, §20-13.2(a).
Refusal to submit to chemical analysis, §20-13.2(c).
Suspension upon moving violation conviction, §20-13(a).
Length of suspension, §20-13(b).
Motor vehicle moving violation defined, §20-13(a).
Probation, placing licensee on, §20-13(b).
Restoration of license on probationary status, hearing request, §20-13(b).
Retention of license until hearing, §20-13(a).
Suspension in addition to other remedies, §20-13(d).
Two or more offenses committed on single occasion, §20-13(c).
Provisional licenses.
Driving after consuming alcohol or drugs, §20-13.2(a).
Driving eligibility certificate not maintained, §20-13.2(c1).
Immediate civil revocation for certain criminal moving violations, §20-13.3.

DRIVERS' LICENSES —Cont'd
Revocation or suspension —Cont'd
Provisional licenses —Cont'd
Impaired driving conviction, §20-13.2(b).
Length of revocation, §20-13.2(d).
Restoration, proof of financial responsibility, §20-13.2(e).
Willful refusing to submit chemical analysis, §20-13.2(c).
Racing vehicles on streets and highways, §20-141.3(d) to (f).
Reckless driving.
Two charges within 12 month period or transportation of illegal intoxicants.
Mandatory revocation, §20-17(a).
Record of conviction, forwarding to division, §20-24(b).
Probation substituted for revocation, failure to receive record, §20-24(b1).
Restoration, conditions upon, §20-19(c3).
Impaired driving, §20-17.6.
Conditional restoration, §20-28(c3).
After ten years, §20-19(e4).
After three years, §20-19(e1).
After two years, §20-19(e2).
Cancellation, imposition of remaining revocation period, §20-28(c5).
Conditions or restrictions, §20-19(e3).
Substance abuse assessment, §20-28(c4).
Violation of conditions.
Hearing, §20-19(c5).
Procedure, §20-19(c4).
Review of division's decision, §20-19(c6).
Restoration fee.
Person whose license has been revoked, §20-7(i1).
Speeding.
Mandatory revocation for excessive speeding, §20-17(a).
Mandatory suspension for excessive speeding, §20-16.1(a).
Limited driving permits for first offenders, §20-16.1(b1).
Longer period of suspension authorized, §20-16.1(e).
Reckless driving on same occasion as speeding offense, §20-16.1(d).
Second or subsequent offense, §20-16.1(c).
Period of suspension, §20-19(a), (b).
Speeding to elude arrest convictions, §20-141.5(d).
Surrender of license to court or child support enforcement agency, §20-24(a).
Road test, §20-7(c).
Safe driver incentive plan.
Offenses for which insurance points charged, §58-36-75.
Sale.
Reproduction or facsimile or simulation of driver's license.
Prohibited, §20-30.
School bus drivers.
Requirements, §20-218(a).
Seizure.
By division, §20-45(a).
By law enforcement officers, §20-45(c).
Selective service system registration requirements, §20-9.2(a).
Forwarding of information to selective service system, §20-9.2(b).
Sex offenders.
Commercial drivers' licenses.
Disqualification from driving for conviction requiring registration, §20-17.4(n).

DRIVERS' LICENSES —Cont'd
Sex offenders —Cont'd
Commercial drivers' licenses —Cont'd
Driving commercial passenger vehicle or school
bus without license or while disqualified,
§20-27.1.
Learners permit with P or S endorsement.
Issuance prohibited to persons convicted
offenses requiring registration,
§20-37.13(f).
Licenses with P or S endorsement.
Disqualification from driving during
registration period, §14-208.19A(c).
Driving without license because person
convicted of offense requiring
registration, §14-208.19A(d).
Issuance prohibited, §20-37.14A.
Issuance restrictions, §14-208.19A.
Revocation.
Conviction of offense requiring person to
register as sex offender, §20-17.9.
Denial of license to registered offenders, §20-9(i).
Notification of registration requirements, §20-9.3.
Search of national sex offender public registry.
Applicant residing in state less than 12 months,
§20-9(i).
Social security number or tax payer
identification number.
Providing, required for issuance, disclosure,
§20-7(b1), (b2).
Special identification cards for nonoperators,
§§20-37.7, 20-37.8.
Application, §20-7(b).
Confidentiality of photographic image or signature
recorded, §20-43(a).
Resident of state.
Proof required for issuance, documents
evidencing, §20-7(b2), (b3), (b4).
Social security number or tax payer identification
number.
Providing required for issuance of license,
§20-7(b1).
Speeding.
Revocation or suspension, §20-17(a).
Period of suspension, §20-19(a), (b).
Substance abuse assessment.
Impaired driving.
Condition of probation, §20-179(g) to (k).
Restoration of license after conviction.
Obtaining certificate of completion,
§20-17.6(c).
Supervising driver for minor, §20-11(k).
Impaired supervision or instruction, §20-12.1(a),
(b).
Surrender of license.
Conviction of offense requiring revocation,
§20-24(a).
Financial responsibility.
Misdemeanor for failure to surrender,
§20-279.31(c).
Generally, §20-29.
Notice, failure to surrender, §20-45(b).
Tamperproof, §20-7(n).
Taxicabs.
Cities and towns.
Power to regulate, §20-37.
Temporary driving certificate, §20-7(f).
Temporary license.
License renewed by mail, §20-7(f).
Tests of physical and mental ability, §20-7(c).

DRIVERS' LICENSES —Cont'd
Time for obtaining license after becoming
resident, §20-7(a).
Title of act, §20-5.
Uniform driver's license act.
Citation of provisions, §20-5.
Veteran military designation.
Issuance, renewal, §20-7(q1).
Violations of provisions.
Failure to carry license.
When person may not be convicted of, §20-35(c).
False affidavits, §20-31.
General penalty provision, §20-35(a).
Permitting unlicensed minor to drive motor
vehicle, §20-32.
Permitting violations of provisions, §20-34.
Prohibited acts, §20-30.
Vision test, §20-7(c).
Exemption when renewing by mail.
Armed forces members, national guard
members and reservists, §20-7(r).
Written test for literate applicants, §20-7(c).
Wrongful issuance, §§20-34.1, 20-34.1(a).
Defenses precluded, §20-34.1(b).

DRIVER'S LICENSE TECHNOLOGY FUND,
§20-37.01.

DRIVER'S PRIVACY PROTECTION ACT.
Disclosure of personal information in motor
vehicle records, §20-43.1.

DRIVER TRAINING SCHOOLS.
Licensing, §§20-320 to 20-328.
Cancellation of licenses, §20-325.
Commissioner of motor vehicles.
Administration and enforcement of provisions,
§20-321(b).
Powers, §20-321(a).
Regulations as to requirements, §§20-322(b),
20-323(b).
Definitions, §20-320.
Denial of licenses, §20-325.
Division of motor vehicles.
Administration of provisions, §20-328.
Employers and employees.
Exemptions from provisions, §20-326.
Examining of applications.
Duty of commissioner or authorized
representative, §20-321(a).
Exemptions from provisions, §20-326.
Expiration of licenses, §20-324(a).
Fees, §20-324(b).
Inspecting school facilities, records and
equipment.
Duty of commissioner or authorized
representative, §20-321(a).
Instructors.
Defined, §20-320.
Licenses required, §20-323(a).
Renewal of licenses, §20-324(a).
Refusal to renew, §20-325.
Requirements.
Licenses for instructors, §20-323(a).
Licenses for schools, §20-322(a).
Regulations as to requirements, §§20-322(b),
20-323(b).
Rules and regulations.
Commissioner of motor vehicles, §§20-321(a),
20-322(b), 20-323(b).
Penalty for violation, §20-327.
Suspension or revocation of licenses, §20-325.

DRIVER TRAINING SCHOOLS —Cont'd
Licensing —Cont'd
Violations of provisions or regulations, §20-327.

DRIVE-THRU DELIVERIES, §58-3-169.

DRIVEWAYS.
Driver emerging from or entering to yield right of way to pedestrian, §20-173(c).
Environmental document not required for construction of driveway connecting public roadway, §113A-12.
Parking in front of private driveway, §20-162(a).
Right of way of vehicle about to enter or cross, §20-156(a).
Subcontractors, payments to, §§22C-1 to 22C-6.

DRIVING AFTER CONSUMING ALCOHOL.
Commercial vehicle drivers.
Disqualification from driving, §20-17.4(a1).
Persons less than 21 years old.
Alcohol screening test, §20-138.3(b2).
Impaired driving offense also charged, §20-138.3(c).
Implied consent law, subject to, §20-138.3(b).
Limited driving privilege, §20-138.3(d).
Odor insufficient, §20-138.3(b1).
Offense, §20-138.3(a).
Punishment, §20-138.3(c).

DRIVING AFTER NOTIFICATION OR FAILURE TO APPEAR.
Impaired driver's license revocation, §20-28(a2).

DRIVING BY PROVISIONAL LICENSEE AFTER CONSUMING ALCOHOL OR DRUGS.
Restoration of license after conviction, §20-17.6.

DRIVING ELIGIBILITY CERTIFICATE, §20-11(n).
Charter school's designee, duties, §115C-238.29F(j).
Principals of schools, duties, §115C-288(k).
School disciplinary actions.
Effect on eligibility, §20-11(n1).
Revocation of provisional license, §20-13.2(c1).
State board of community colleges, rules, duty to adopt, §115D-5(a3).
State board of education, rules, duty to develop, §115C-12.

DRIVING ON RIGHT SIDE OF HIGHWAY, §20-146.

DRIVING UNDER THE INFLUENCE.
Generally.
See IMPAIRED DRIVING.

DRIVING WHILE DISQUALIFIED, §20-28(d).
One year disqualification, §20-17.4(a).

DRIVING WHILE IMPAIRED TREATMENT COURT PROGRAMS.
Drug treatment courts generally, §§7A-790 to 7A-801.
See DRUG TREATMENT COURTS.

DRIVING WHILE INTOXICATED.
Generally.
See IMPAIRED DRIVING.

DRIVING WHILE LICENSE REVOKED, §20-28(a).
Impaired driving.
Conditional restoration.
Impaired driving license revocation, §20-28(c3) to (c5).
Driving after notification or failure to appear, §20-28(a2).
Seizure and forfeiture of vehicle, §20-28.3.
Imprisonment for misdemeanor violation.
Restrictions, §20-176(c1).
Limited driving privilege.
Application for after expiration of revocation period for underlying offense, §20-20.1.
Moving offense during.
Additional period of revocation, §20-28.1(a), (b).
New license, §20-28.1(c).
Restoration of license or new license.
Conditional restoration.
Impaired driving license revocation, §20-28(c3) to (c5).
Issuance, proof required, §20-28(c1).
Restrictions or conditions, imposing, §20-28(c2).
When person may apply, §20-28(c).
When treated as driving without a license, §20-28(a1).

DRIVING WITHOUT LICENSE.
Commercial driver's license.
Criminal penalty, §20-37.21(a).
Defenses, §20-35(c).
License revoked as result of prior impaired driving offenses.
Seizure and forfeiture of vehicle, §20-28.3.
Restricted licenses.
Operating vehicle without complying with restriction.
Deemed operating vehicle without license, §20-7(e).

DROPOUT PREVENTION.
Committee on.
Administrative costs, §115C-64.6(a).
Duties, §115C-64.6(b).
Established within department of public instruction, §115C-64.6(a).
Members, §115C-64.6(b).
Terms, §115C-64.6(b).
Grants.
Criteria, §115C-64.7.
Evaluation of impact, §115C-64.9.
Nonprofit organizations receiving.
Contract requiring fidelity bonding, §115C-64.8.
Report by recipients, §115C-64.9.

DROPOUT RATES.
Reporting, reducing.
Powers and duties of state board of education, §115C-12.

DROPSY.
Drug or device, false advertising, §106-138(b).

DROUGHT ADVISORIES.
Issuance by drought management advisory council, §143-355.1(e).
Considerations before issuing, §143-355.1(f).
Variation from U.S. drought monitor, §143-355.1(f1).

DROUGHT MANAGEMENT ADVISORY COUNCIL.
Chair.
Employee of department designated as, §143-355.1(d).
Drought advisory, issuance, §143-355.1(e).
Considerations before issuing, §143-355.1(f).
Established by department of environment and natural resources, §143-355.1(a).
Meetings, §143-355.1(d).
Purpose, §143-355.1(a).
Report, §143-355.1(g).
Representatives to serve on council.
Expertise, §143-355.1(b1).
Organizations to designate, §143-355.1(b), (c).

DROUGHTS.
Closing of forests and woodlands to hunting, fishing and trapping, §§106-908, 106-909.
Fire patrols designated during season of drought, §106-899(a).
Graywater.
Policies on reuse of water, §143-355.5.
Open burning prohibited statewide during periods of hazardous forest fire conditions, §106-944.
Water conservation measures.
Area drought designation, §143-355.2(e).
Car washes, trade association representing.
Voluntary conservation and efficiency measures, §143-355.2(h1).
Default measures for locality without plan, §143-355.2(f).
Time for implementation, §143-355.2(g).
Enforcement provisions.
Civil penalty for violations, §143-355.6(a).
Notification, §143-355.6(e).
Local government failure to implement conservation measures, §143-355.6(c).
Action to recover unpaid penalties, §143-355.6(c3).
Amount of penalty imposed, §143-355.6(c1).
Request for remission of civil penalty, §143-355.6(c2).
Separate violations each day, §143-355.6(b).
Violation of conservation measures, criminal offense, §143-355.6(d).
Implementation of more stringent measures, §143-355.2(b).
Considerations, §143-355.2(c).
Limitations on applicability, §143-355.2(j).
Public water service or large community water system, §143-355.2(h).
Implementation of plan or next tier of plan, §143-355.2(d).
Public water service or large community water system.
Implementation of more stringent measures, §143-355.2(h).
Time for report, §143-355.2(i).
Violation of conservation measures, criminal offense, §143-355.6(d).
Water shortage response plan contents, §143-355.2(a).
Water reuse provisions, §143-355.5.
Water shortage emergency powers.
Compensation for water allocated or diverted, §143-355.3(d).
Construction of provisions, §143-355.3(e).
Declaration of emergency, §143-355.3(a).
Powers and duties of secretary, §143-355.3(b).

DROUGHTS —Cont'd
Water shortage emergency powers —Cont'd
Right of way for temporary water lines, §143-355.3(c).
Water system efficiency, §143-355.4.

DRUG ABUSE OR ADDICTION.
Chemical dependency.
See CHEMICAL DEPENDENCY.
Chiropractors.
Grounds for disciplinary action, §90-154(b).
Drug treatment courts, §§7A-790 to 7A-801.
See DRUG TREATMENT COURTS.
Generally.
See MENTAL HEALTH, DEVELOPMENTAL DISABILITY, SUBSTANCE ABUSE.
Incompetence, determination of, §§35A-1101 to 35A-1116.
See INCOMPETENCY.
Lawyers and judges impaired by substance abuse or addiction.
Lawyer assistance program, Bar Rules D.0601 to D.0623.
See LAWYERS ASSISTANCE PROGRAM.
Physicians and surgeons.
Ground for denial, revocation or suspension of license, §90-14(a).
Referral of physician to state medical society physician health and effectiveness committee, §90-14(b).
Prisons and prisoners.
Substance abuse program.
See PRISONS AND PRISONERS.
Work first program recipients of assistance.
Treatment required, drug testing, §108A-29.1.

DRUG ALCOHOL RECOVERY TREATMENT PROGRAM.
Probation.
Special condition.
Costs, §15A-1343(b).
Screening and assessing for chemical dependency, §15A-1343(b3).

DRUG DETECTION DOGS.
Commercial detection services utilizing.
Certification of dogs, §90-102.1(h).
Confidentiality of client records, exception, §90-102.1(h).
Defined, §90-102.1(a).
Disclosure of dog alert or discovery, §90-102.1(h).
Defined, §90-102.1(a).
Handlers.
Acquisition of controlled substances for training, §90-102.1(e).
Record keeping, inventory maintenance, §90-102.1(f).
Complaints against handlers.
Investigation, §90-102.1(j).
Defined, §90-102.1(a).
Dog alert or discovery of controlled substances.
Notifying and informing law enforcement, §90-102.1(g).
Commercial detection services, §90-102.1(h).
Disclosure of requirement in contracts, §90-102.1(i).
Inapplicability to law enforcement agencies, §90-102.1(k).
Registration if controlled substances used in training, §90-102.1(b).
Criminal record check, §90-102.1(d).
Denial, revocation or suspension, §90-102.1(j).

DRUG DETECTION DOGS —Cont'd
Handlers —Cont'd
Registration if controlled substances used in training —Cont'd
Prerequisites, §90-102.1(c).

DRUG ENFORCEMENT ADMINISTRATION AGENTS' AUTHORITY, §15A-406.

DRUG EXAMINATION AND SCREENING OF EMPLOYEES, §§95-230 to 95-235.
Action to recover amount of civil penalty, §95-234(b).
Chain of custody, §95-232(e).
Civil penalty for violation, §95-234.
Collection of samples, §95-232(b).
Compliance with procedural requirements, §95-232(a).
Confirmation of samples, §95-232(c1).
Current employees, screening of, §95-232(c).
Definitions, §95-231.
Defrauding drug and alcohol screening tests.
Penalties, §14-401.20(c).
Unlawful acts, §14-401.20(a), (b).
Determination of whether violation occurred, §95-234(a).
Disposition of civil penalties collected, §95-234(c).
Duty of examiners to conduct examinations.
No duty to examine, §95-233.
Exemption.
Certain federal agencies, §95-235.
Federal agencies.
Certain ones exempted, §95-235.
Intent of general assembly, §95-230.
No duty to examine, §95-233.
Procedural requirements, §95-232.
Prospective employees, screening of, §95-232(c).
Purposes, §95-230.
Requirements, §95-232.
Retention of samples, §95-232(d).
Retesting of positive samples, §95-232(f).
Rules, adoption, §95-234(e).
Statute of limitations on assessment of penalties, §95-234(d).
Violations, §95-234.

DRUGGISTS, §§90-85.2 to 90-85.44.
See PHARMACISTS AND PHARMACIES.

DRUG PARAPHERNALIA.
Advertising.
Penalties, §90-113.24(b).
Prohibited acts, §90-113.24(a).
Citation of act.
Short title, §90-113.20.
Control of potential drug paraphernalia products —§§90-113.80 to 90-113.84.
Citation of act, §90-113.80.
Criminal penalties, §90-113.83.
Definitions, §90-113.81.
Sale of glass tubes or splitters.
Immunity.
Retailers and employees, §90-113.84.
Record, §90-113.82(b).
Availability for inspection, §90-113.82(d).
False statements as misdemeanors, §90-113.83(b).
Maintenance, §90-113.82(c).
Restrictions, §90-113.82(a).
Training of agents or employees by retailers, §90-113.82(e).

DRUG PARAPHERNALIA —Cont'd
Control of potential drug paraphernalia products —Cont'd
Sale of glass tubes or splitters —Cont'd
Violations by retailers as misdemeanors, §90-113.83(a).
Title of act, §90-113.80.
Defined, §90-113.21(a).
Delivery, §90-113.23.
To minors, §90-113.23(c).
Enumerated, §90-113.21(a).
Evidence.
Determination where object is drug paraphernalia.
What may be considered, §90-113.21(b).
Manufacture.
Penalty, §90-113.23(c).
Prohibited acts, §90-113.23(a), (b).
Minors.
Delivery of drug paraphernalia to certain younger persons.
Felony, §90-113.23(c).
Possession.
Penalty, §90-113.22(b).
Prohibited, §90-113.22(a).
Prohibited acts as to, §§90-113.22 to 90-113.24.
Short title of act, §90-113.20.

DRUG PARAPHERNALIA CONTROL ACT OF 2009, §§90-113.80 to 90-113.84.

DRUG PRODUCT SELECTION.
Definitions, §90-85.27.
Equivalent drug product.
Defined, §90-85.27.
Price.
Limitation on selected drugs, §90-85.28(c).
Selection by pharmacist, §90-85.28(a).
Liability of prescriber and pharmacist not extended, §90-85.31.
Prescriber may permit or prohibit, §90-85.28(b).
Liability of prescriber and pharmacist not extended, §90-85.31.
Prescriptions.
Label, §90-85.29.
Record, §90-85.30.

DRUG RECOGNITION EXPERTS.
Testimony as to under the influence of impairing substances and category of substances, §8C-1 Rule 702(a1).

DRUGS AND CONTROLLED SUBSTANCES, §§90-86 to 90-113.8.
Abortion.
Destroying unborn child.
Using drugs or instruments to destroy, §14-44.
Injuring pregnant woman.
Using drugs to injure, §14-45.
Miscarriages.
Using drugs to produce miscarriage, §14-45.
Actions.
Employing or intentionally using minor to commit drug law violations, §90-95.5.
Additional nature of penalties, §90-97.
Administrative proceedings.
Pending proceedings, §90-113.7(c).
Aircraft.
Forfeiture of conveyances used in controlled substances violations, §§90-112, 90-112.1.
Operation of aircraft while impaired, §63-27.
Infliction of serious bodily injury, §63-28.

DRUGS AND CONTROLLED SUBSTANCES
—Cont'd
Alcoholic beverage permittees.
Certain conduct unlawful on premises,
§18B-1005(a).
Factors considered when issuing permits.
Illegal drug activity on or about licensed
premises, §18B-901(c).
Amphetamines, trafficking, §90-95(h).
Amusement device operators.
Operating device equipment under the influence,
§95-111.11(b).
Anabolic steroids, §90-91(k).
Animal shelters.
Sodium pentobarbital and other drugs for
euthanasia of animals.
Registration for purpose of obtaining and using,
§90-101(a2).
Appeals.
Judicial review of drug commission, §90-113.2.
Attempts to commit crime, §90-98.
**Attorney disciplinary amnesty in elicit drug
use cases,** Bar Rule B.0130.
Bail.
Conditions of pretrial release.
Presumptions concerning conditions in
controlled substance cases, §15A-533(d).
Methamphetamine manufacturing, §15A-534.6.
Bail bondsmen and runners.
Misdemeanor drug violations.
Denial of license, §58-71-80(b2).
Revocation or refusal to renew license,
§58-71-80(b1).
Board of pharmacy.
Enforcement of provisions, §90-113.5.
Boating safety.
Operation of boat or manipulation of water skis
while under influence of drugs, §75A-10(b),
(b1).
**Buprenorphine for treatment of opiate
dependence.**
Physicians prescribing or dispensing, §90-101(a1).
Burden of proof.
Exemptions or exceptions, §90-113.1(a).
Registration or order form, §90-113.1(b).
Capital punishment.
Manner of execution, §15-187.
Charitable institutions.
Furnishing substances to inmates, §14-258.1(a).
**Chemical analysis of impairing substances in
blood generally.**
See IMPAIRED DRIVING.
Child care facilities.
Unauthorized administration of medicine,
§110-102.1A.
Chiropractors.
Addiction or severe dependency.
Grounds for disciplinary action, §90-154(b).
Prescriptions.
Prohibited, §90-151.
Citation of act.
Short title, §90-86.
Commercial detection services.
Drug detection dogs utilized by service, §90-102.1.
Commercial vehicles.
Disqualification from driving.
Commission of felony involving drugs,
§20-17.4(c).
Commission.
Defined, §90-87.
Judicial review, §90-113.2.

DRUGS AND CONTROLLED SUBSTANCES
—Cont'd
Commission —Cont'd
Power to add, delete or reschedule substances,
§90-88(a) to (d).
Rules and regulations, §90-100.
Conditional discharge.
First offenders, §90-96(a), (a1), (e).
**Conditions of prescribed punishments and
degree of offenses,** §90-95(e).
Confidentiality of information.
Research, §90-113.3(e).
Conspiracy.
Trafficking in certain drugs, §90-95(i).
Violations of provisions, §90-98.
Continuing criminal enterprise.
Electronic surveillance orders, §15A-290(a1).
Felony, §90-95.1(a).
Forfeitures, §90-95.1(b).
Grand juries.
Examination of witnesses by prosecutor,
§15A-623(h).
Petition for convening, §15A-622(h).
What constitutes, §90-95.1(c).
Controlled substance analogue.
Defined, §90-87.
Treated as schedule I substance, §90-89.1.
Counterfeit substances.
Defined, §90-87.
Prohibited acts, §90-95(a).
Penalties, §90-95(c).
County confinement facilities.
Furnishing controlled substances to inmates,
§14-258.1(a).
Death from use.
Distributor liability, §14-17.
Defenses.
Employing or intentionally using minor to commit
drug law violations, §§90-95.4(c), 90-95.5.
Mistake of age not a defense.
Participating in a drug violation by a minor,
§90-95.7(b).
Promoting drug sales by a minor, §90-95.6(b).
Deferred prosecution.
Conditional discharge.
First offenders, §90-96(a), (a1), (e).
Definitions, §90-87.
Law enforcement agencies, §90-95.2(b).
Dental hygienists.
Grounds for disciplinary measures, §90-229(a).
Dentists.
Grounds for disciplinary action, §90-41(a).
Prescriptions, §90-46.
Depressants.
Schedule I, §90-89.
Schedule II, §90-90.
Exemption of compounds, mixtures or
preparations, §90-92(b).
Schedule IV, §90-92(a).
**Discrimination by employer for lawful use of
lawful products during nonworking hours,**
§95-28.2.
Dispensing.
Date of dispensing.
Entry on face of prescription, §90-106(h).
Defined, §90-87.
Prescriptions.
Generally.
See PRESCRIPTION DRUGS.
Prohibited acts, §90-108(a).

DRUGS AND CONTROLLED SUBSTANCES
  —Cont'd
Dispensing —Cont'd
  Registration of manufacturers, distributors and
    dispensers, §§90-101 to 90-104.
  Schedule V, §90-106(d).
  Schedule VI, §90-106(e).
Distribution.
  Definition of "distribute,"§90-87.
  Order forms, §90-105.
    Inspection, §90-107.
  Prohibited acts, §90-108(a).
  Registration of manufacturers, distributors and
    dispensers, §§90-101 to 90-104.
  Samples, §90-106(i).
Divorce grounds, §50-7.
Drivers' licenses.
  Habitual users.
    Prohibited, §20-9(c).
    Revocation or suspension, §20-17.1.
  Instruction by supervising driver or approved
    instructor.
    Giving instructions while under the influence,
      §20-12.1(a), (b).
**Driving by person less than 21 years old after
    consuming,** §20-138.3.
**Driving by provisional licensee after
    consuming.**
  Restoration of license after conviction, §20-17.6.
Driving under the influence generally.
  See IMPAIRED DRIVING.
Drug detection dogs.
  Certification.
    Dogs utilized by commercial detection services,
      §90-102.1(h).
  Commercial detection services.
    Utilization, §90-102.1.
  Handlers, §90-102.1.
Drug education schools, §90-96.01(a).
  Fees, §90-96.01(a).
    Failure to pay, §90-96.01(b).
Drug testing employees.
  Employee examination and screening for
    controlled substances, §§95-230 to 95-235.
Drug treatment courts, §§7A-790 to 7A-801.
  See DRUG TREATMENT COURTS.
Drug use review program.
  Rules implementing, §108A-68.
Effective date of provisions, §90-113.7(d).
Embezzlement, §90-108(a).
**Employee examination and screening for
    controlled substances,** §§95-230 to 95-235.
**Employer discrimination for lawful use of
    lawful products during nonworking hours,**
    §95-28.2.
**Employing or intentionally using minor to
    commit drug law violations,** §90-95.4(a), (b).
Enforcement of provisions, §90-113.5.
  Advance of funds by state treasurer for,
    §90-113.6(c).
  Cooperative arrangements, §90-111.
  Information concerning violations.
    Payments to persons providing, §90-113.6(a).
  No liability on authorized officers, §90-113.1(c).
**Eviction of drug traffickers and other
    criminals,** §§42-59 to 42-76.
  See EXPEDITED EVICTIONS.
Evidence.
  Chain of custody, §90-95(g1).
  Reports of analysis, §90-95(g).

DRUGS AND CONTROLLED SUBSTANCES
  —Cont'd
Exemptions and exclusions from provisions,
    §90-88(e) to (g).
  List, §90-88(i).
  Schedule III, §90-91(i).
  Schedule IV, §90-92.
**Expungement of records of certain drug
    offenders.**
  First offenders not over twenty-one years of age,
    §15A-145.2.
Fees.
  Expunction of records, §90-96(f).
  Wholesale prescription drug distributors.
    License application fees, §106-145.4(b).
Firearms and other weapons.
  Controlled substance in body or blood.
    Carrying concealed handgun prohibited,
      §14-415.11(c2).
First offenders.
  Conditional discharge, §90-96(a), (a1), (e).
    Superior courts to file names of persons granted
      conditional discharge, §90-96(c).
  Expunction of records, §90-96(b), (d), (f).
Fish or wildlife taken by use of, §113-262(a), (b).
  Permit authorizing, §113-261(b).
Food and nutrition services program.
  Eligibility of individual convicted of felony offense
    to participate in, §108A-25.2.
Food, drug and cosmetic act, §§106-120 to
    106-145.
  See FOOD, DRUG AND COSMETIC ACT.
Forfeiture.
  Applicability of article, §90-113.7.
  Contraband, §90-112(e).
  Conveyances subject to forfeiture, §90-112(f).
  Custody, §90-112(c).
  Disposition of property, §90-112(c), (d).
  Manner of forfeitures, §90-112(f).
  Money, §90-112(a), (d1).
  Pending proceedings not affected, §90-113.7(b).
  Process, §90-112(b).
    When seizure without process authorized,
      §90-112(b).
  Property subject to forfeiture, §90-112(a).
  Release, §90-112(c).
  Remission or mitigation of forfeitures, §90-112.1.
    Joint claims, §90-112.1(c).
    Jurisdiction of courts, §90-112.1(a).
    Proof required, §90-112.1(b).
    Vehicles held for purpose of evidence,
      §90-112.1(d).
Forgery.
  Acquiring or obtaining possession by, §90-108(a).
Fraud.
  Prohibited acts, §90-108(a).
**Free samples of prescription drugs given
    physicians and other medical
    practitioners.**
  Property tax exemption or exclusion, §105-275.
Grand juries.
  Examination of witnesses by prosecutor,
    §15A-623(h).
  Petition for convening, §15A-622(h).
Hallucinogenic substances.
  Schedule I, §90-89.
  Schedule II, §90-90.
Heroin trafficking, §90-95(h).
  Conspiracy, §90-95(i).
  Penalties, §90-95(h).

DRUGS AND CONTROLLED SUBSTANCES
  —Cont'd
Hospitals.
  Licensed chiropractors may practice in public
     hospitals, §90-153.
Hypodermic syringes and needles generally.
  See DRUG PARAPHERNALIA.
Immediate precursor.
  Defined, §90-87.
Impaired driving generally.
  See IMPAIRED DRIVING.
Information concerning violations.
  Payments to persons providing, §90-113.6(a).
Injunctions.
  Jurisdiction of superior court, §90-110(a).
  Violations of injunctions.
    Trial, §90-110(b).
Inmates of mental institutions.
  Furnishing substances to inmates of mental
     institutions, §14-258.1(a).
Inspections, §90-107.
Intentionally committed prohibited acts,
  §90-108(b).
Isomer.
  Defined, §90-87.
Justice department.
  Enforcement of provisions, §90-113.5.
  Purchase of controlled substances.
    Reimbursement, §90-113.6(b).
Ketamine.
  Schedule III controlled substances, §90-91(m).
Lab cleanup costs.
  Restitution to law enforcement agencies,
    §90-95.3(c).
Labels.
  Requirements, §90-106(f).
Law enforcement agencies.
  Cooperation between, §90-95.2(a).
    Jurisdiction or authority not reduced,
      §90-95.2(c).
  Definitions, §90-95.2(b).
  Restitution for illegal lab cleanup costs,
    §90-95.3(c).
  Undercover purchases.
    Restitution to law enforcement agencies,
      §90-95.3(a).
Law enforcement officers.
  Enforcement of provisions, §90-113.5.
Licenses.
  Nonprofessional treatment.
    Required, §90-109.
  Wholesale prescription drug distributors,
    §§106-145.3 to 106-145.6.
Liens.
  Medical attention to injured persons, §44-49.
    Charges, §44-50.
    Evidence, §44-50.
    Funds for purpose.
      Duty of receiving person, §44-50.
    Limit on recovery, §44-50.
    Settlement.
      Disputed claims to be settled before payment,
        §44-51.
Lists.
  Schedule I, §90-89.
  Schedule II, §90-90.
  Schedule III, §90-91(b) to (n).
  Schedule IV, §90-92.
  Schedule V, §90-93.
  Schedule VI, §90-94.

DRUGS AND CONTROLLED SUBSTANCES
  —Cont'd
Manufacture.
  Defined, §90-87.
  Enhanced sentencing in certain cases,
    §15A-1340.16D.
  Penalties, §90-95(b).
  Prohibited acts, §§90-95(a), 90-108(a).
  Registration of manufacturers, distributors and
    dispensers, §§90-101 to 90-104.
Marijuana.
  Conspiracy, §90-95(i).
  Defined, §90-87.
  Schedule VI, §90-94.
  Trafficking in, §90-95(h).
MDA/MDMA, trafficking, §90-95(h).
MDPV, trafficking, §90-95(h).
Medicaid.
  Prior authorization requirement.
    Exemptions, §108A-68.1.
Mental health, developmental disabilities and
  substance abuse.
  General provisions.
    See MENTAL HEALTH, DEVELOPMENTAL
      DISABILITY, SUBSTANCE ABUSE.
Mephedrone.
  Trafficking, §90-95(h).
Methamphetamine.
  Manufacture.
    Bail, §15A-534.6.
    Committed in area where minors live, are
      present or are otherwise endangered.
    Aggravating factors in sentencing,
      §15A-1340.16(d).
    Decontamination of property used for
      manufacture of drug, §130A-284.
    Serious injury inflicted upon law enforcement or
      emergency personnel.
      Enhanced sentencing, §15A-1340.16D.
  Precursor chemicals.
    Methamphetamine lab prevention act,
      §§90-113.50 to 90-113.61.
      See METHAMPHETAMINE LAB
        PREVENTION.
    Possession or distribution with intent to
      manufacture, §90-95(d1).
    List of chemicals to which subsection applies,
      §90-95(d2).
  Trafficking, §90-95(h).
  Watch program.
    Immunity from civil and criminal liability.
      Good faith actions, §114-43.
Minors.
  Driving after consuming drugs.
    Restoration of license after conviction, §20-17.6.
  Driving by person less than 21 years old after
    consuming alcohol or drugs, §20-138.3.
  Employing or intentionally using minor to commit
    drug law violations, §90-95.4(a), (b).
    Civil liability, §90-95.5.
    Definition of "minor,"§90-95.4(d).
    Mistake of age, §90-95.4(c).
  Expunction of records, §90-96(b), (d).
  Immunity from prosecutions, §90-96.1.
  Methamphetamine, manufacture.
    Committed in area where minors live, are
      present or are otherwise endangered.
    Aggravating factors in sentencing,
      §15A-1340.16(d).
  Participating in a drug violation by a minor,
    §90-95.7(a), (c).
    Mistake of age not a defense, §90-95.7(b).

DRUGS AND CONTROLLED SUBSTANCES
—Cont'd
Minors —Cont'd
Promoting drug sales by a minor, §90-95.6(a), (c).
Mistake of age not a defense, §90-95.6(b).
Treatment for abuse of controlled substances or
alcohol.
Abuse of controlled substances.
Consent of minor to treatment sufficient,
§90-21.5(a).
Misrepresentation.
Acquiring or obtaining possession by, §90-108(a).
Motor vehicles.
Forfeiture of conveyances used in violations of
provisions.
Generally, §§90-112, 90-112.1.
Municipalities.
Confinement facilities.
Furnishing controlled substances to inmates,
§14-258.1.
Drug abuse programs, §160A-494.
Murder in the second degree, §14-17.
Narcotic drugs.
Defined, §90-87.
Schedule III, §90-91.
Schedule IV, §90-92(a).
Schedule V, §90-93.
New drugs.
Regulations for sale of, §106-135.
Nonprofessional treatment.
Licenses.
Required, §90-109.
Non-use as probation condition, §15A-1343(b1).
Nuisances.
Abatement of offenses against public morals,
§§19-1 to 19-8.3.
See NUISANCES.
Nurses.
Grounds for revocation, suspension or denial of
license, §90-171.37.
Opiates.
Defined, §90-87.
Schedule I, §90-89.
Schedule II, §90-90.
Opium.
Schedule II, §90-90.
Opium derivatives.
Schedule I, §90-89.
Opium trafficking, §90-95(h).
Conspiracy, §90-95(i).
Penalties, §90-95(h).
Optometrists.
Prescriptions, §90-118(e).
Copy of prescription.
Furnished on request, §90-127.3.
Filling, §90-127.2.
Order forms, §90-105.
Inspection, §90-107.
Outdated prescription drugs.
Wholesale prescription drug distributors.
Duties, §106-145.7(e).
Over-the-counter drugs.
Sales and use tax.
Defined, §105-164.3.
Paraphernalia, §§90-113.20 to 90-113.24.
See DRUG PARAPHERNALIA.
Paregoric, U.S.P..
Sales, §90-91(e) to (h).
Participating in a drug violation by a minor,
§90-95.7(a), (c).
Mistake of age not a defense, §90-95.7(b).

DRUGS AND CONTROLLED SUBSTANCES
—Cont'd
Peace officers.
Enforcement of provisions, §90-113.5.
Pending prosecutions and other proceedings.
Not affected by repealers or amendments,
§90-113.7(a) to (d).
Pharmacists and pharmacies generally,
§§90-85.2 to 90-85.44.
See PHARMACISTS AND PHARMACIES.
Physicians and surgeons.
Optometry provisions not to apply, §90-127.
Possession.
Penalties, §90-95(d).
Prohibited, §90-95(a).
Practitioners.
Defined, §90-87.
Treatment and rehabilitation services.
Confidentiality of information, §90-109.1(a).
Examination and evaluation by practitioner,
§90-109.1(b).
Reports, §90-109.1(c).
Precursor chemicals.
Designation, §90-95(d2).
Methamphetamine lab prevention act, §§90-113.50
to 90-113.61.
See METHAMPHETAMINE LAB
PREVENTION.
Possession or distribution with intent to
manufacture controlled substance or
methamphetamine.
Penalties, §90-95(d1), (d1a).
Prescriptions.
See PRESCRIPTION DRUGS.
Prisons and prisoners.
Employees of state prison system.
Use of intoxicants, narcotic drugs or profanity.
Prohibited, §148-23.
Furnishing substances to inmates, §14-258.1(a).
Probation.
Conditional discharge on first offense, §90-96(a),
(a1), (e).
Drug alcohol recovery treatment program as
condition.
Screening and assessing for chemical
dependency, §15A-1343(b3).
Non-use as condition, §15A-1343(b1).
Prohibited acts generally, §90-108.
Pseudoephedrine.
Products marketed for children, §90-113.61.
Records.
Prescription drugs.
Wholesale distributors.
Duties, §106-145.8.
Registration of manufacturers, distributors and
dispensers.
Records of registrants, §90-104.
**Registration of manufacturers, distributors
and dispensers.**
Animal shelters.
Sodium pentobarbital and other drugs for
euthanasia of animals.
Registration for purpose of obtaining and
using, §90-101(a2).
Buprenorphine for treatment of opiate
dependence.
Physicians prescribing or dispensing,
§90-101(a1).
Drug detection dog handlers, §90-102.1(b) to (d).
Persons initially permitted to register, §90-102(e).

DRUGS AND CONTROLLED SUBSTANCES
—Cont'd
Registration of manufacturers, distributors and dispensers —Cont'd
Places of business.
Inspection, §90-101(f).
Separate registration required at each principal place of business, §90-101(e).
Privileges of registrants, §90-101(b), (g).
Restrictions, §90-102(b).
Public interest.
Determination.
Factors considered, §90-102(a).
Records of registrants, §90-104.
Required, §90-101(a).
Exceptions, §90-101(c), (i).
Waiver of requirement by commission, §90-101(d).
Research, §90-102(c), (d).
Revocation or suspension.
Disposition of controlled substances possessed by registrant, §90-103(e).
Grounds, §90-103(a).
Imminent danger to public health or safety, §90-103(d).
Notice of orders to bureau, §90-103(f).
Order to show cause why registration should not be revoked or suspended, §90-103(c).
Powers of commission, §90-103(a), (b).
Sodium pentobarbital and other drugs for euthanasia of animals.
Animal shelters, §90-101(a2).
Reporting system, §§90-113.70 to 90-113.76.
See CONTROLLED SUBSTANCES REPORTING SYSTEM.
Research.
Authorization for possession and distribution of controlled substances, §90-113.3(f).
Confidentiality of information, §90-113.3(e).
Contracts for research activities, §90-113.3(d).
Powers of department of health and human services, §90-113.3(c).
Registration, §90-102(c), (d).
Returned prescription drugs.
Wholesale prescription drug distributors.
Duties, §106-145.7(e).
Rules and regulations, §90-100.
Continuation of regulations, §90-113.8.
Sales.
Paregoric, U.S.P., §90-91(e) to (h).
Penalties, §90-95(b).
Prohibited, §90-95(a).
Sales and use tax.
Defined, §105-164.3.
Exemptions, §105-164.13.
Over-the-counter drugs.
Defined, §105-164.3.
Exemption, §105-164.13.
Prescription drugs.
Defined, §105-164.3.
Exemption, §105-164.13.
Samples.
Distribution, §90-106(i).
Schedule I, §90-89.
Controlled substance analogue treated as, §90-89.1.
Schedule II, §90-90.
Prescriptions, §90-106(a), (b).
Photo identification to be provided to pharmacy, §90-106.1(a).
Delivery to health care facilities, exception, §90-106.1(c).

DRUGS AND CONTROLLED SUBSTANCES
—Cont'd
Schedule II —Cont'd
Prescriptions —Cont'd
Photo identification to be provided to pharmacy —Cont'd
Identifying information available in controlled substances reporting system, §90-106.1(b).
Person seeking dispensation and person to whom prescription issued not same person, §90-106.1(c).
Schedule III, §90-91(b) to (n).
Dispensing or distributing, §90-106(c).
Schedule IV, §90-92.
Dispensing or distributing, §90-106(c).
Schedules, §90-94.
Dispensing or distributing, §90-106(e).
Republishing, §90-99.
Schedule V, §90-93.
Dispensing or distributing, §90-106(d).
Schools.
Activities contracts, §90-113.3(b).
Basic education program.
Alcohol and drug education program, §115C-81(a3).
Instruction in dangers of harmful or illegal drugs, §115C-81(c).
Driving eligibility certificate.
Effect of disciplinary action for enumerated student conduct, §20-11(n1).
Drug addicted children.
Appropriate education provided for.
Policy of state to insure, §115C-149.
Children with special needs.
Drug addicted children excluded from article, §115C-149.
Policy of state, §115C-149.
State board of education to adopt rules, §115C-150.
Programs to prevent and deter misuse and abuse, §90-113.3(a).
Special education.
Children with chemical dependency.
Drug addicted children excluded from provisions of article, §115C-149.
Sentencing.
Conditions governing prescribed punishments and degree of offenses, §90-95(e).
Trafficking in certain drugs, §90-95(h).
Sodium pentobarbital and other drugs for euthanasia of animals.
Animal shelters.
Registration for purpose of obtaining and using, §90-101(a2).
Special education.
Children with chemical dependency.
Drug addicted children excluded from provisions of article, §115C-149.
Speedy disposition of offenders.
County appropriations for programs to protect the public, §153A-212.1.
State departments and agencies.
Cooperative arrangements, §90-111.
Statements obtained from person under the influence of drugs.
Presumption of fraud, §8-45.5.
Steroids.
Anabolic steroids.
Schedule III, §90-91(k).

DRUGS AND CONTROLLED SUBSTANCES
—Cont'd

Stimulants.
Schedule I, §90-89.
Schedule II, §90-90.
Schedule IV, §90-92(b).
Exempt compounds, mixtures or preparations, §90-92(b).

Storage.
Prescription drugs.
Wholesale distributors, §106-145.7.

Structures or vehicles.
Knowingly keeping or maintaining places resorted to by persons using, §90-108(a).

Substance abuse generally.
See MENTAL HEALTH, DEVELOPMENTAL DISABILITY, SUBSTANCE ABUSE.

Substance abuse professionals, §§90-113.30 to 90-113.46A.
See SUBSTANCE ABUSE PROFESSIONALS.

Synthetic cannabinoids.
Schedule VI, §90-94.

Tax, §§105-113.105 to 105-113.113.
See UNAUTHORIZED SUBSTANCES TAXES.

Title of act.
Short title, §90-86.

Trademarks, trade names or identification marks.
Making, distributing, etc., thing designed to print, imprint or reproduce, §90-108(a).

Trafficking in certain drugs, §90-95(h).
Conspiracy, §90-95(i).
Electronic surveillance orders, §15A-290(a1).

Unauthorized substances taxes, §§105-113.105 to 105-113.113.
See UNAUTHORIZED SUBSTANCES TAXES.

Undercover purchases.
Restitution to law enforcement agencies, §90-95.3(a).

Wholesale prescription drug distributors generally, §§106-145.1 to 106-145.13.
See WHOLESALE PRESCRIPTION DRUG DISTRIBUTORS.

Workers' compensation.
Impairment by use of controlled substances.
Rebuttable presumption, §97-12.
Injury or death caused by employee being under influence.
No compensation payable, §97-12.

Work first program.
Eligibility of individual convicted of felony offense to participate in, §108A-25.2.

Zero tolerance law.
Driving by person less than 21 years old after consuming alcohol or drugs, §20-138.3.

DRUGSTORES.

Alcoholic beverage permits.
Food business defined to include, §18B-1000.
Off-premises fortified wine permit.
Kind of permit that may be issued, §18B-1001.
Off-premises malt beverage permit.
Kind of permit that may be issued, §18B-1001.
On-premises malt beverage permit.
Kind of permit that may be issued, §18B-1001.
Recycling requirement, §18B-1006.1.
On-premises unfortified wine permit.
Kind of permit that may be issued, §18B-1001.
Recycling requirement, §18B-1006.1.
Special occasion permit.
Kind of permit that may be issued, §18B-1001.

DRUGSTORES —Cont'd

Generally.
See PHARMACISTS AND PHARMACIES.

DRUG TESTING EMPLOYEES.
Examination and screening of employees, §§95-230 to 95-235.

DRUG THERAPY MANAGEMENT.
Clinical pharmacist practitioners generally.
See PHARMACISTS AND PHARMACIES.
Practicing medicine without a license.
Exception, §90-18(c).

DRUG TRAFFICKING, §90-95(h).
Children or minors.
Delivery of drug paraphernalia to certain youths, §90-113.23.
Employing or intentionally using minors to commit drug law violations, §90-95.4(a), (b).
Civil liability, §90-95.5.
"Minor" defined, §90-95.4(d).
Mistake of age, §90-96(b), (d).

Conspiracy, §90-95(i).

Electronic surveillance.
Issuance of orders for surveillance, §15A-290(a1).

Landlord and tenant.
Eviction of drug traffickers and other criminals, §§42-59 to 42-76.
See EXPEDITED EVICTIONS.

DRUG TREATMENT COURTS, §§7A-790 to 7A-801.
Advisory committee, §7A-795.
Citation of act, §7A-790.
Costs of treatment program, §7A-800.
Eligibility guidelines, §7A-797.
Establishment of programs, §7A-793.
Fund administration, §7A-794.
Goals of programs, §7A-792.
Guidelines for court operation, §7A-797.
Local drug treatment court management committees, §7A-796.
Monitoring and reports, §7A-801.
Probation revocation.
Authority, §15A-1344(a1).
Jurisdiction, appeal, §7A-271(f).
Probation supervision.
Authority, §15A-1344(a1).
Jurisdiction, §7A-272(e).
Purpose of act, §7A-791.
Reports, §7A-801.
Right to treatment not conferred, §7A-799.
Short title, §7A-790.
State drug treatment court advisory committee, §7A-795.
Treatment not guaranteed, §7A-799.

DRUNK DRIVING.
Generally.
See IMPAIRED DRIVING.

DRUNK IN PUBLIC.
Generally.
See INTOXICATION.

DRY CLEANERS.
Generally.
See LAUNDRIES AND DRY CLEANING ESTABLISHMENTS.

DRY-CLEANING EQUIPMENT TAX CREDIT.
Equipment not using hazardous substances, §105-129.16C(a) to (d).

DRY-CLEANING SOLVENT CLEANUP,
§§143-215.104A to 143-215.104U.
Action for reimbursement cost.
Remediation of uncertified site, §143-215.104O(a), (b).
Administrative functions of commission,
§143-215.104D(a).
Appeals, §143-215.104S.
Assessment agreements.
Costs for reimbursement equals or exceeds money in fund.
Notice, further agreement prohibited, §143-215.104N(d).
Determination no remediation or further action required, §143-215.104H(f).
Determination of risk to public health acceptable. §143-215.104H(e).
Generally, §143-215.104H(a).
Liability protection of potentially responsible persons, §143-215.104K.
Obligation to reimburse response cost.
Expressed in agreement, §143-215.104N(d).
Petition generally, §143-215.104H(a).
Refusal of commission to enter into, §143-215.104H(c), (d).
Renegotiation or termination generally, §143-215.104J.
Requirements for petitioning for, §143-215.104F.
Terms and conditions, §143-215.104H(b).
Brownfields notice.
Notice of dry-cleaning solvent remediation in lieu of notice, §143-215.104M(g).
Certification of facilities and abandoned sites,
§143-215.104(a).
Assessment or remediation of contamination by person with access to property, §143-215.104G(d).
Changing initial priority ranking, §143-215.104G(a).
Costs not reimbursed from fund, §143-215.104F(c1).
Decertification generally, §143-215.104J.
Information provided by potentially responsible party, §143-215.104G(c).
Requirements for petitioning, §143-215.104F.
Citation of act, §143-215.104A.
Civil penalties.
Amounts, §143-215.104P(a), (b).
Assessment by secretary, §143-215.104P(a).
Civil action for unpaid penalty, §143-215.104P(f).
Considerations in determining, §143-215.104P(c).
Notice of assessment, §143-215.104P(d).
Remission, request for, §143-215.104P(e).
Construction of provisions, §143-215.104T(a).
Cost of assessment and remediation activities.
Reimbursement generally, §143-215.104N.
Criminal penalties and prosecutions.
Applicability of general defenses, affirmative defenses and bars to prosecution, §143-215.104Q(g), (h).
Circumstantial evidence, §143-215.104Q(e).
Knowingly and willfully committing offense, §143-215.104Q(b).
Person in imminent danger of death or serious bodily injury, §143-215.104Q(c).
Knowingly and willfully or knowingly, proving state of mind, §143-215.104Q(f).
Negligently committing offense, §143-215.104Q(a).
Person defined, §143-215.104Q(i).
Previous conviction of federal violation based upon same facts, §143-215.104Q(d).

DRY-CLEANING SOLVENT CLEANUP —Cont'd
Decertification of facility, renegotiation or termination of assessment agreement or remediation agreement, §143-215.104J(a).
Notice of opportunity for hearing, §143-215.104J(b).
Rights of other petitioners not affected, §143-215.104J(c).
Definitions, §143-215.104B(b).
Applicability, §143-215.104B(a).
Delegation of functions of commission to contractors, §143-215.104D(a).
Delegation of rights, duties and responsibilities to department,
§143-215.104D(d).
Disbursement of assessment and remediation costs, §143-215.104N.
Dry-cleaning solvent cleanup fund.
Established, §143-215.104C(a).
Investigation of inactive hazardous substance disposal sites contaminated by dry-cleaning solvent.
Use of fund for, §143-215.104C(d).
Payment of claims filed from money in fund, §143-215.104C(c).
Sources of revenue, §143-215.104C(b).
Transfer of sales and use taxes to fund, §105-164.44E.
Financial responsibility for certification of facility, assessment agreement or remediation agreement, §143-215.104F(f).
Immunity of state, agencies, officers, etc.,
§143-215.104T.
Injunctions, §143-215.104R.
Intention of provisions, §143-215.104T.
Land-use restrictions.
Notice of dry-cleaning solvent remediation, §143-215.104M.
Liability protection when entering into assessment or remediation agreement.
Persons conducting environmental assessment or transaction screen, §143-215.104K(b).
Potentially responsible parties, §143-215.104K(a).
Violations of land-use restrictions, §143-215.104K(c).
Notice of dry-cleaning solvent remediation,
§143-215.104M(a).
Cancellation, §143-215.104M(e).
Enforcement of restrictions on current or future use of property, §143-215.104M(f).
Notice in lieu.
Brownfields notice, §143-215.104M(g).
Recordation, §§47-29.1(e), 143-215.104M(c).
Restrictions contained in notice, §143-215.104M(b).
Sale, lease, conveyance or transfer of property.
Notice in deed, §143-215.104M(d).
Notice of intent to remediate, §143-215.104L(a), (b).
Petition for certification of facility, assessment agreement or remediation agreement.
Assessment agreements generally, §143-215.104H.
Certification of facilities generally, §143-215.104G.
Fee, §143-215.104F(a1).
Financial responsibility requirement, §143-215.104F(f).
Grounds for rejecting petition, §143-215.104F(d), (e).
Potentially responsible persons, requirements generally, §143-215.104F(b).
Property owners, requirements, §143-215.104F(c).

DRY-CLEANING SOLVENT CLEANUP —Cont'd

Petition for certification of facility, assessment agreement or remediation agreement —Cont'd

Public meetings on proposed agreement, §143-215.104L(c).

Refusal to enter into, §143-215.104I(d) to (f).

Rejection of petition not to effect rights of other petitioners, §143-215.104G(e).

Remediation agreements generally, §143-215.104I.

Renegotiation or termination generally, §143-215.104J.

Requirements for petitioning for, §143-215.104F.

Requirements generally, §143-215.104F(a).

Terms and conditions, §143-215.104I(g).

Publication of notice of intent to remediate, §143-215.104L(b).

Public meeting on proposed remediation agreement, §143-215.104L(c).

Reimbursement for assessment and remediation agreements, §§143-215.104M(a), 143-215.104N(a).

Cost equaling or exceeding money in fund. Notice of determination, §143-215.104N(d).

Exhaustion of financial resources by petitioner required, §143-215.104N(c).

Express statement as to reimbursement obligation in agreements.

Contingent on money in fund, §143-215.104N(d).

Limitations, §§143-215.104M(b), 143-215.104N(b).

Reimbursable response cost, §143-215.104N(e).

Remediation agreements.

Costs for reimbursement equals or exceeds money in fund.

Notice, further agreement prohibited, §143-215.104N(d).

Description of site and statement required, §143-215.104I(c).

Failure to comply, violation of provisions, §143-215.104I(h).

Future uses, refusal to accept limitations on, §143-215.104I(e).

Generally, §143-215.104I(a).

Land-use restrictions, reliance on when negotiating, §143-215.104I(b).

Liability protection of potentially responsible persons, §143-215.104K.

Notice of intent to remediate, §143-215.104L(a), (b).

Obligation to reimburse response cost.

Expressed in agreement, §143-215.104N(d).

Petition for certification of facility. See within this heading, "Petition for certification of facility, assessment agreement or remediation agreement."

Remediation of uncertified site.

Civil action to secure reimbursement of cost, §143-215.104O(b), (c).

Renegotiating assessment agreement or remediation agreement.

Generally, §143-215.104J.

Report by secretary, §143-215.104U(a).

Time for reporting, §143-215.104U(b).

Response cost.

Reimbursement generally, §143-215.104N.

Rulemaking, §143-215.104D(b).

Applicability to dry-cleaning facilities, wholesale distribution facilities and abandoned dry-cleaning facilities, §143-215.104D(c).

DRY-CLEANING SOLVENT CLEANUP —Cont'd

Termination of assessment agreement or remediation agreement.

Generally, §143-215.104J.

Uncertified site, remediation, §143-215.104O.

DRY-CLEANING SOLVENT TAX, §§105-187.30 to 105-187.35.

Collected and administered in same manner as sales and use tax, §105-187.32.

Credit of taxes to dry-cleaning solvent cleanup funds, §105-187.34.

Definitions, §105-187.30.

Excise tax imposed on dry-cleaning solvent purchased outside state, §105-187.31.

Exemptions not to apply, §105-187.33.

Privilege tax imposed on dry-cleaning solvent retailers, §105-187.31.

Rate of privilege tax and excise tax, §105-187.31.

Refunds to apply, §105-187.33.

Sunset of provisions, §105-187.35.

DUAL OFFICEHOLDING, NC Const Art VI §9.

Elections.

Notification regarding dual-office holding requirements.

Electors for presidential election, §163-209(b).

Political parties, §163-209.1.

Running for 2 separate offices at same time.

Prohibition, exception, §163-124.

"Elective office" defined, §128-1.1(d).

Ex officio service by county and city representatives and officials, §128-1.2.

Mountain resources planning act.

Technical advisory council, §153B-4(d).

No person shall hold more than one office, §128-1.

When allowed, §128-1.1(a) to (c).

DUCK BLINDS.

Hunting, fishing or trapping on posted property, §§14-159.6 to 14-159.10.

DUCKS.

Baby ducklings.

Disposing of as pets or novelties.

Cruelty to animals, §14-363.1.

Hunting and wildlife generally.

See HUNTING AND WILDLIFE.

DUCK, TOWN OF.

All-terrain vehicles.

Use by employees on certain highways, §20-171.24.

DUDE RANCHES.

Agritourism activity liability, §§99E-30 to 99E-32.

DUE ON SALE CLAUSE FEES.

Mortgages or deeds of trust, §24-10(d).

DUE PROCESS, NC Const Art I §19, US Const Amds 5, 14.

Abused, neglected or dependent juvenile actions.

Adjudicatory hearing, §7B-802.

Banking.

Administrative orders of commissioner.

Hearings, §53-107.1.

Basic education program in public schools.

Civil literacy, §115C-81(g).

Delinquent and undisciplined juvenile actions.

Adjudicatory hearing.

Protection of due process rights, §7B-2405.

DUE PROCESS —Cont'd
Interstate family support.
Issuance of support orders, §52C-4-401.
Teachers.
Probationary teachers, dismissal, §115C-325(m).
Trust companies.
Administrative enforcement, §53-370.
Foreign offices.
Emergency enforcement, waiver of due process,
§53-327(c).
Out-of-state institutions, offices.
Violation of provisions.
Waiver of due process in emergency,
§53-321(c).

DUI.
Generally.
See IMPAIRED DRIVING.

DUKE MEDICAL SCHOOL.
Grants to students.
Administration, §116-21.6(c).
Eligibility, §116-21.6(b).
Funding, §116-21.6(a).
Reversion of remaining funds, §116-21.6(f).
Transfer when appropriation insufficient,
§116-21.6(e).
Statistical information and reporting,
§116-21.6(g).
Termination of enrollment, refund of grant,
§116-21.6(d).

DUMBWAITERS.
**Elevator safety act generally, §§95-110.1 to
95-110.15.**
See ELEVATORS.
Inspection fees.
Assessment and collection, §95-107.
Disposition, §95-108.

DUMPING LITTER, §14-399.

**DUMPING OF RADIOACTIVE MATERIALS OR
TOXIC SUBSTANCES, §14-284.2.**

DUNE BUGGIES.
Municipalities.
Regulation, §160A-308.
Utility easements.
Operating vehicle upon after being forbidden to do
so, §14-134.2.

DUNKERS.
Affirmations in lieu of oaths, §11-4.

DUPLIN COUNTY.
Acquisition of property, power, §153A-158.1(a).
Agricultural tendencies in certain counties.
Terms of, §42-23.
**Ambulance service, attachment or
garnishment and lien for, §§44-51.4 to
44-51.8.**
Ambulances requested falsely, §14-111.3.
**Condemnation or acquisition of land by local
government unit outside county.**
Consent of board of commissioners necessary,
§153A-15.
Counties generally.
See COUNTIES.
**Cropper or tenant refusing to perform terms
of contract.**
Forfeiture of right of possession to premises,
§42-27.
Evidence.
Partition of real estate in Duplin.
Records of partition, §8-24.

DUPLIN COUNTY —Cont'd
Evidence —Cont'd
Wills in Duplin.
Records of wills, §8-25.
Game laws, local acts not repealed,
§113-133.1(e).
Housing authority commissioners.
Tenant as commissioner, exemption from provision
of law allowing, §157-5.
Low-income housing tax credits.
Qualified building eligible for credit,
§105-129.41(c).
**North Carolina's eastern region, §§158-30 to
158-42.**
Officers compensated from fees.
Statement to be rendered, §128-13.
On-premises unfortified wine licenses.
Discretion to decline to issue, §105-113.71(b).
Open fires, §106-942.
Applicability of provisions, §106-942(a).
Ground clearing activities, special permit,
§106-942(c).
Woodland fires, permit required, §106-942(b).
Partition.
Evidence.
Records of partition in Duplin, §8-24.
**Probates and registration orders before clerks
of inferior courts validated, §47-59.**
Records.
Partition of real estate in Duplin.
Evidence of records of partition, §8-24.
Wills in Duplin.
Evidence, §8-25.
Registration of deeds.
Tax certification, no delinquent taxes due,
§161-31(b).
School property.
Acquisition and improvement, §153A-158.1.
Special school tax, election to abolish.
Petition required, §115C-505.
**Wild plants, taking of certain plants from land
of another.**
Inapplicability of provisions, §14-129.
Wills.
Evidence.
Records of wills in Duplin, §8-25.

**DURABLE POWER OF ATTORNEY, §§32A-8 to
32A-14.**
Accounts.
Filing.
Incapacity or incompetence of principal,
§32A-11(b).
Acknowledgment of substitution, §32A-12(b).
Appointment, §32A-12(a).
Attorney-in-fact.
Relations to court-appointed fiduciary, §32A-10.
Compensation of attorney-in-fact.
Incapacity or incompetence of principal,
§32A-11(c).
Trustees and other fiduciaries generally, §§32-53
to 32-62.
See FIDUCIARIES.
Copy of power.
Filing.
Incapacity or incompetence of principal,
§32A-11(a).
Custodial trusts.
Effective to terminate or direct administration or
distribution of property.
Specific provision required in power, §33B-7(f).

DURABLE POWER OF ATTORNEY —Cont'd

Death of attorney-in-fact.

Substitution, §32A-12(b).

Definition, §32A-8.

Execution of power prior to October 1, 1988 pursuant to G.S. 47-115.1.

Deemed durable power, §32A-14(a).

Fiduciaries.

Relation of attorney-in-fact to court-appointed fiduciary, §32A-10.

Generally.

See POWER OF ATTORNEY.

Good faith dealing with attorney-in-fact.

Incapacity or incompetence of principal, §32A-9(c).

Health care powers of attorney, §§32A-15 to 32A-26.

See HEALTH CARE POWERS OF ATTORNEY.

Incapacity of attorney-in-fact to act.

Substitution, §32A-12(b).

Incapacity or mental incompetence of principal.

Commissions attorney-in-fact to receive, §32A-11(c).

Custodial trust, terminating or directing distribution.

Specific provision required in power, §33B-7(f).

Filing copy of power with clerk, §32A-11(a).

Inventories and accounts, filing, §32A-11(b).

Records of transactions, attorney-in-fact to keep, §32A-11(a).

Substitution of attorney-in-fact.

Recordation, §32A-12(b).

Validity of acts done by attorney-in-fact, §32A-9(a).

Protection of person dealing in good faith with attorney-in-fact, §32A-9(c).

Registration of power required, §32A-9(b).

Inventories.

Filing.

Incapacity or incompetence of principal, §32A-11(b).

Notice of substitution, §32A-12(b).

Reference to chapter 32B.

Authority to refer to chapter 32B, §32A-14(b).

Registration.

Incapacity or incompetence of principal, §32A-9(b).

Removal, §32A-12(a).

Resignation, §32A-12(a).

Revocation, §32A-13(a), (b).

Affidavit of attorney-in-fact, §32A-13(c).

Rights, powers, duties and responsibilities, §32A-12(a).

Substitution, §32A-12(a), (b).

DURESS.

Adoption proceedings.

Waiver of notice, §48-2-406(c).

Affirmative defense, pleading, §1A-1 Rule 8(c).

Capital punishment.

Mitigating circumstances, §15A-2000(f).

Child support.

Relief from order based on nonpaternity.

Finding that initial order of support based on fraud, duress, etc, §50-13.13(h).

Criminal procedure.

Notice to state of defenses, §15A-905(c), (d).

Evidence.

Statements, releases, etc., obtained from persons in shock or under the influence of drugs.

Presumption of fraud, §8-45.5.

DURESS —Cont'd

Husband and wife.

Conveyances.

Certain conveyances not affected by fraud or duress, §39-11.

Insurance.

Statements, releases, etc., obtained from persons in shock or under the influence of drugs.

Presumption of fraud, §8-45.5.

Paternity.

Setting aside orders of paternity, §49-4(h).

Private personnel services contracts, §95-47.4(d).

Special matters, pleading, §1A-1 Rule 9(b).

Trusts.

Creation induced by duress, §36C-4-406.

DURHAM, CITY OF.

Land-use development incentives.

Reduction of energy consumption, §160A-383.4.

Private parking lots, removal of unauthorized vehicles, §20-219.2.

Satellite annexation.

Limitation on area of satellite corporate limits, inapplicability, §160A-58.1(b).

Traffic control photographic systems, §160A-300.1(d).

DURHAM COUNTY.

Ambulance service.

Attachment or garnishment and lien for, §§44-51.4 to 44-51.8.

Condemnation or acquisition of land by local government unit outside county.

Consent of board of commissioners necessary, §153A-15.

Counties generally.

See COUNTIES.

Dangerous firearm use by young children, permitting.

Air rifles, air pistols and BB guns not dangerous firearm, §14-316(b).

Durham-Orange historical commission.

Transfer of commission to department, §143B-51.

Local government sales and use tax for public transportation.

Regional transportation authority (Triangle), §§105-509, 105-509.1.

Motor vehicle emission inspections.

Counties inspections required to be performed in, §143-215.107A(c).

Oil, gas or mineral claims.

Certain ancient claims extinguished, preservation, procedure, §1-42.1(a) to (d).

Registration of deeds.

Tax certification, no delinquent taxes due, §161-31(b).

School property.

Acquisition and improvement, §153A-158.1.

Water and sewer systems within Camp Butner reservation, §122C-407(b).

DUTCHMAN'S BREECHES.

Taking, etc., of certain wild plants from land of another, §14-129.

DUTY FREE INSTRUCTIONAL PLANNING TIME.

Teachers, §115C-301.1.

DWI.

Generally.

See IMPAIRED DRIVING.

DYED DIESEL FUEL.
Gasoline tax.
  Accidental mix with tax paid motor fuel.
    Refund, §105-449.105(c).
  Backup tax, liability, §105-449.87.
  Defined, §105-449.60.
  Listed on shipping document.
    Joint and several liability where fuel not dyed
      diesel fuel, §105-449.82(c).
  Motor fuel excise tax, §105-449.86.
    Liability, §105-449.86(b).
    Rate, §105-449.86(a).
  Unlawful for highway use, §105-449.117(a) to (c).

DYES, MOLDS, FORMS AND PATTERNS,
  §66-67.3.
Definitions, §66-67.3(a).
Ownership and transfer, §66-67.3(b).
  Procedure for transfer, §66-67.3(c).
  Use upon transfer, §66-67.3(d).
Rights under state and federal laws, §66-67.3(e).

DYING DECLARATIONS, §8C-1 Rule 804(b).
Admissibility, §8-51.1.
  Wrongful death, §28A-18-2.

DYNAMITE.
Burglary using explosives, §14-57.
Exploding cartridges, §14-283.
Explosives generally.
  See EXPLOSIVES.
Keeping for sale or selling without license,
  §14-284.

E

EAGLES.
Unlawfully taking, possessing, transporting,
  etc., §113-294(l).

EARLY CHILDHOOD ADMINISTRATION
  CREDENTIAL.
Child center administrators.
  Requirements, §110-91.

EARLY CHILDHOOD INITIATIVES.
Consent.
  Home-centered services, §143B-168.16.
Definitions, §143B-168.11(b).
Findings of legislature, §143B-168.10.
Home-centered services, §143B-168.16.
Legislative findings, §143B-168.10.
Local partnerships.
  Audit and review by state auditor,
    §143B-168.14(b).
  Capital projects, funding guidelines,
    §143B-168.12(e).
  Conditions for receiving state funds,
    §143B-168.14(a).
  Contractors.
    Requirements as to, §143B-168.12(c).
  Defined, §143B-168.11(b).
  Long-term plans, §143B-168.15(c).
  Needs improvement rating.
    Annual audit, §143B-168.14(b).
  Qualifying expenses.
    Monitoring, §143B-168.12(f).
  State funds.
    Conditions for receiving, §143B-168.14(a).
    County expenditures.
      State funds not to supplant, §143B-168.15(e).
    Expansion of child care subsidies,
      §143B-168.15(g).

EARLY CHILDHOOD INITIATIVES —Cont'd
Local partnerships —Cont'd
  State funds —Cont'd
    Start-up and related activities, §143B-168.15(d).
    Unexpended funds, §143B-168.15(h).
    Use, §143B-168.15(a).
      Direct services, §143B-168.15(b).
  Superior or satisfactory rating.
    Biennial audit, §143B-168.14(b).
  Technical and administrative assistance,
    §143B-168.13(a).
North Carolina Partnership for Children, Inc.
  Audit and review by state auditor,
    §143B-168.12(b).
  Board of directors, §143B-168.12(a).
  Defined, §143B-168.11(b).
  Conditions for receiving state funds,
    §143B-168.12(a).
  Definition of "North Carolina
    partnership,"§143B-168.11(b).
  Local partnerships.
    Capital projects, funding guidelines,
      §143B-168.12(e).
  Qualifying expenses.
    Uniform guidelines and reporting format,
      establishment.
      Documentation of qualifying expenses,
        §143B-168.12(f).
  Reports, §143B-168.12(a), (d).
  Uniform guidelines and reporting format,
    establishment.
    Documentation of qualifying expenses,
      §143B-168.12(f).
Purpose of provisions, §143B-168.11(a).
Records.
  Home-centered services.
    Parents to have access to records, §143B-168.16.
Rules to implement part, adoption,
  §143B-168.13(a).
Statewide needs and resource assessment,
  §143B-168.13.

EARLY PERIODIC SCREENING, DIAGNOSIS
  AND TREATMENT PROGRAM.
Child care facilities.
  Health assessments, §110-91.

EARLY RETIREMENT.
Retirement system for teachers and state
  employees, §135-5(a1).
  Law enforcement officers, §135-5(a2).

EARNED INCOME TAX CREDIT.
Amount, §105-151.31(a).
Nonresident or part-time resident.
  Reduction, §105-151.31(a).
Refund of excess, §105-151.31(b).
Sunset, §105-151.31(c).

EARNED TIME CREDIT.
Felonies, structured sentencing.
  Authorization, §15A-1340.13(d).
Good behavior, §15A-1355(c).
Impaired drivers, §15A-1355(c).
Mentally and physically unfit inmates,
  §15A-1355(d).
Misdemeanors, §15A-1340.20(d).

EARNINGS.
Garnishment.
  See GARNISHMENT.
Salaries.
  See SALARIES.

EARNINGS —Cont'd
Wages.
See WAGES.

EARTHQUAKES.
Property insurance.
Notice of non-coverage for flood, earthquake, mudslide or landslide, §58-44-60(a).

EASEMENTS.
Abandonment of railroad easement.
Presumptive ownership, §1-44.2(a), (b).
Airports.
Municipal airports.
Acquisition of easements, §63-49(c).
Cartways, etc.
Abandonment or discontinuance, §§136-68, 136-70.
Alteration, §§136-68, 136-70.
Establishment, §§136-68, 136-69(a) to (c).
Procedure for laying out, §136-69(a) to (c).
Condominiums.
Encroachments, §47C-2-114(a), (b).
Conservation easements, §§113A-230 to 113A-235.
Agricultural conservation easements, §106-744.
Condemnation of property encumbered by, §§40A-80 to 40A-85.
North Carolina conservation easement endowment fund, §113A-253.2.
Creation, §39-6.4(a).
Deeds of easement.
Registration required, §47-27.
Doctrine of merger, §39-6.4(b).
Drainage.
Acquisition, §156-4.
Petition by servient owner against dominant owner, §156-16.
Repairs.
Right of dominant owner to repair, §156-20.
Surrender of drainage easements, §156-23.
Width of right of way for repairs, §156-5.
Drainage districts, §156-70.1.
Improvements.
Renovation, enlargement and extension of canals, structures and boundaries, §156-93.6.
Highways, roads and streets.
Metropolitan sewerage districts, §162A-74.
Metropolitan water districts, §162A-54.
Neighborhood roads, cartways, church roads, etc.
General provisions, §§136-67 to 136-71.
Public utility lines laid out on petition.
Procedure, §136-71.
Scenic beauty of areas along highways.
Regulation of scenic easements, §136-125.
Metropolitan sewerage districts.
Highways, roads and streets, §162A-74.
Metropolitan water districts.
Highways, roads and streets, §162A-54.
Mosquito control districts.
Acquisition and holding of easements, §130A-355.
Municipalities.
Grant of easements, §160A-273.
Natural resources easement fund, §146-14.1.
Navigation.
Filling navigable water.
Application for easement, §146-6(c).
Nonvested easement in gross.
Defined, §41-28.
Time limit, §41-31.

EASEMENTS —Cont'd
Presumptive ownership of abandoned railroad easement, §1-44.2(a), (b).
Public lands.
Allocated state lands.
Exemptions, §146-32.
Filling navigable water.
Application for easements, §146-6(c).
Granting, §146-11.
Lands covered by water, §146-12(a) to (n).
Natural resources easement fund, §146-14.1.
Public schools.
Granting, §115C-518(b).
Public utilities.
Lines laid out on petition.
Procedure, §136-71.
Trespass.
Motor vehicles.
Operating vehicle upon easements after being forbidden to do so, §14-134.2.
Utility easement at William B. Umstead State Park, §143-260.10E(a) to (c).
Railroads.
Presumptive ownership of abandoned easement, §1-44.2(a), (b).
Registration of deed of easement, §47-27.
Right of way.
See RIGHT OF WAY.
Sanitary districts.
Acquisition and holding of easements.
Corporate powers of sanitary district board, §130A-55.
Power to purchase and condemn property, §130A-57.
Trails.
North Carolina trails system.
Scenic easements within right of way, §113A-90.
Trespass.
Motor vehicles.
Operating vehicle upon utility easements after being forbidden to do so, §14-134.2.
Unit ownership.
Unit owners not to impair easements, §47A-11.
Waters and watercourses.
Natural and scenic rivers system.
Charitable deductions.
Claim and allowance for contribution or gift of easement, §113A-39.
New river.
Acquisition of land and easement, §113A-35.1(a).

EAST CAROLINA UNIVERSITY.
Brody School of Medicine.
Accrediting agencies.
Meeting requirements of, §116-40.4.
Medical faculty practice plan, §116-40.6.
Clinical programs and facilities, operating, §116-40.6(a).
Construction and renovation of buildings, facilities and other property, §116-40.6(e).
Division of school of medicine, §116-40.6(a).
Open-end design agreements, using, §116-40.6(e).
Personnel, §116-40.6(b).
Property, acquiring or disposing of, §116-40.6(d).
Purchases, §116-40.6(c).
Medicare reimbursements.
Request for, use of funds, §116-36.6.
Smoking in public places, §143-599.

EAST CAROLINA UNIVERSITY —Cont'd
Constituent institution of University of North Carolina, §116-4.
Military members, veterans and families.
Behavioral health problems facing.
Collaboration on research on, §127B-20.

EASTERN NORTH CAROLINA AGRICULTURAL CENTER FUND, §106-6.2(a).

EASTERN NORTH CAROLINA HOSPITAL.
Department of environment and natural resources.
Control of certain hospitals transferred to department, §131E-67.
Power of secretary to regulate, §131E-67.

EASTERN NORTH CAROLINA SCHOOL FOR THE DEAF AT WILSON.
Education programs in residential schools generally, §§143B-146.1 to 143B-146.21.
See EDUCATION.
Schools for the deaf generally, §§143B-216.40 to 143B-216.44.
See DEAF AND HEARING IMPAIRED.

EATING PLACES.
See RESTAURANTS.

EAVESDROPPING.
Conference between prisoner and his attorney, §14-227.1(a).
Admissibility as evidence, §14-227.1(b).
Violations made misdemeanors, §14-227.3.
Deliberations of grand or petit jury, §14-227.2.
Violations made misdemeanors, §14-227.3.
Electronic surveillance generally, §§15A-286 to 15A-298.
See ELECTRONIC SURVEILLANCE.
Telephones.
Unauthorized connections, §14-155.

E-BOOK READERS.
Portable consumer electronic devices insurance.
Claims handling, adjuster licenses, §58-33-27.
Generally, §§58-44A-1 to 58-44A-25.
See PORTABLE CONSUMER ELECTRONIC DEVICES INSURANCE.

ECCLESIASTICAL OFFICERS.
Property of church or religious sect, society or denomination.
Power to acquire, hold and transfer, §61-5.

ECOLOGICAL PROTECTION.
Air pollution control.
See AIR POLLUTION.
Balanced growth policy act generally, §§143-506.6 to 143-506.13.
See BALANCED GROWTH POLICY ACT.
Biological organism act generally, §§106-65.42 to 106-65.49.
See BIOLOGICAL ORGANISM ACT.
Community conservation assistance program, §106-860.
Department of environment and natural resources.
See ENVIRONMENT AND NATURAL RESOURCES DEPARTMENT.
Discharges of oil or hazardous substances.
Generally, §§143-215.83 to 143-215.94.
See OIL OR HAZARDOUS SUBSTANCES DISCHARGES.

ECOLOGICAL PROTECTION —Cont'd
Discharges of oil or hazardous substances —Cont'd
Offshore oil and gas activities, §§143-215.94AA to 143-215.94JJ.
See OFFSHORE OIL AND GAS ACTIVITIES.
Dry-cleaning solvent cleanup, §§143-215.104A to 143-215.104U.
See DRY-CLEANING SOLVENT CLEANUP.
Ecosystem enhancement program, §§143-214.8 to 143-214.13.
See ECOSYSTEM ENHANCEMENT PROGRAM.
Environmental compact, §§113A-21 to 113A-23.
Environmental impact statements, §§113A-8 to 113A-13.
See ENVIRONMENTAL IMPACT STATEMENTS.
Environmental management commission, §§143B-282 to 143B-285.
See ENVIRONMENTAL MANAGEMENT COMMISSION.
Environmental policy act, §§113A-1 to 113A-13.
See ENVIRONMENTAL POLICY ACT.
Environmental review commission, §§120-70.41 to 120-70.47.
See ENVIRONMENTAL REVIEW COMMISSION.
Floodplain regulation, §§143-215.51 to 143-215.61.
See FLOODPLAIN REGULATION.
Industrial and pollution control facilities financing.
Industrial and pollution control facilities financing act, §§159C-1 to 159C-27.
See INDUSTRIAL AND POLLUTION CONTROL FACILITIES FINANCING.
North Carolina capital facilities financing act.
North Carolina industrial and pollution control facilities financing act, §§159D-1 to 159D-27.
See INDUSTRIAL AND POLLUTION CONTROL FACILITIES FINANCING.
Office of environmental education and public affairs, §§143B-285.20 to 143B-285.25.
Pesticides generally.
See PESTICIDES.
Pollution control generally.
See POLLUTION.
Sedimentation control commission, §§113A-50 to 113A-67.
See SEDIMENTATION CONTROL COMMISSION.
Stream watch program, §§143-215.74F to 143-215.74I.
Underground petroleum storage tanks.
Leak cleanup, §§143-215.94A to 143-215.94Y.
See UNDERGROUND PETROLEUM STORAGE TANKS.
Operator training, §§143-215.94NN to 143-215.94UU.
See UNDERGROUND PETROLEUM STORAGE TANKS.
Water and air quality reporting, §§143-215.63 to 143-215.69.
See WATER AND AIR QUALITY REPORTING.
Water and air resources.
See WATER AND AIR RESOURCES.
Water resources development projects.
Federal projects, §§143-215.38 to 143-215.43.
See WATER RESOURCES DEVELOPMENT PROJECTS.
Generally, §§143-215.70 to 143-215.73A.
See WATER RESOURCES DEVELOPMENT PROJECTS.

ECOLOGICAL PROTECTION —Cont'd
Water supply watershed protection,
§§143-214.5, 143-214.7.

ECONOMICALLY DISADVANTAGED.
Indigent persons.
See INDIGENT PERSONS.
Minimum wage, subminimum wage, §95-25.3(d).

**ECONOMIC AND COMMUNITY
DEVELOPMENT.**
Commerce department generally.
See COMMERCE DEPARTMENT.
**Joint legislative economic development and
global engagement oversight committee,**
§§120-70.130 to 120-70.132.
Urban redevelopment, §§160A-500 to 160A-526.
See URBAN REDEVELOPMENT.

**ECONOMIC DEVELOPMENT AND TRAINING
DISTRICTS,** §§153A-317.11 to 153A-317.17.
Abolition, §153A-317.16.
Advisory committee for district.
Creation in resolution establishing district,
§153A-317.13(a).
Membership, §153A-317.13(b).
Recommendations.
Prior to establishing budget and levying tax,
§153A-317.13(c).
Annexation of territory to district.
Effective date of resolution, §153A-317.14(d).
Findings required, §153A-317.14(a).
Notice of public hearing, §153A-317.14(c).
Public hearing, §153A-317.14(c).
Report by board prior to public hearing,
§153A-317.14(b).
Resolution of board of commissioners,
§153A-317.14(a).
Establishment.
Effective date of resolution creating,
§153A-317.12(e).
Findings required to establish, §153A-317.12(b).
Notice of public hearing, §153A-317.12(d).
Public hearing, §153A-317.12(d).
Report by board of commissioners.
Prior to public hearing on establishing,
§153A-317.12(c).
Resolution of board of commissioners,
§153A-317.12(a).
Standards for area or areas of county where
established, §153A-317.12(a).
Petition requesting abolition, §153A-317.16.
Property taxes.
County may levy within district, rate limitation,
§153A-317.17.
Purposes for which created, §153A-317.11.
Skills training center.
Additions to.
Required when district extended,
§153A-317.15(b).
Providing for and maintaining.
Required when creating new district,
§153A-317.15(a).
Purposes for creating district, §153A-317.11.

ECONOMIC DEVELOPMENT COMMISSIONS,
§§158-8 to 158-15.
Appropriations.
Localities, §158-12.
Charlotte Regional Partnership, Inc.
State board of education members as ex officio
commission members, §158-8.4A.

ECONOMIC DEVELOPMENT COMMISSIONS
—Cont'd
Committees.
Appointment, §158-9.
Composition, §158-8.
Contracts.
Service contracts, §158-10.
Counties.
Regional planning and economic development
commissions.
Authorized, §158-14.
Creation.
Authorized, §158-8.
Deposits, §158-12.1.
Duties.
General provisions, §158-13.
Equipment.
Lease or purchase, §158-11.
Federal aid.
Acceptance, §158-12.
Meetings, §158-9.
North Carolina's northeast commission.
Annual reporting, §158-8.5.
Counties served, §158-8.2(a).
Created, §158-8.2(a).
Director of economic development, §158-8.2(g).
Director of tourism, §158-8.2(g).
Economic development advisory board,
§158-8.2(e).
Meetings.
Initial meeting, §158-8.2(d1).
Members, §158-8.2(b).
Nonvoting ex officio members, §158-8.2(b1).
Office space, §158-8.2(g).
Orientation for board members, §158-8.8.
Per diem and travel expenses, §158-8.2(h).
Personnel, §158-8.2(g).
Powers and duties, §158-8.2(f).
Removal of members, §158-8.4.
Reports to general assembly, §158-8.2(f).
Terms of members, §158-8.2(c).
Uniform standards, §158-8.6.
Use of state funds, §158-8.7.
Vacancies, §158-8.2(d).
Offices.
Lease or rent of space, §158-11.
Organization, §158-9.
Piedmont triad regional partnership.
State board of education members as ex officio
commission members, §158-8.4A.
Powers.
General provisions, §158-13.
Supplementary, §158-15.
Regional commissions.
Authorized, §158-14.
Joining, §158-8.
Withdrawal from commission, §158-8.
Research triangle regional partnership.
State board of education members as ex officio
commission members, §158-8.4A.
Rules and regulations.
Adoption, §158-9.
Sales and use tax.
Refunds, §105-164.14(c).
**Southeastern North Carolina regional
economic development commission.**
Annual reporting, §158-8.5.
Contracts, §158-8.3(f).
Counties served, §158-8.3(a).
Created, §158-8.3(a).

ECONOMIC DEVELOPMENT COMMISSIONS
—Cont'd
Southeastern North Carolina regional
economic development commission
—Cont'd
Meetings.
Initial meeting, §158-8.3(c1).
Members, §158-8.3(b).
Nonvoting ex officio members, §158-8.3(b1).
Orientation for board members, §158-8.8.
Per diem and travel expenses, §158-8.3(d).
Personnel, §158-8.3(f).
Powers and duties, §158-8.3(e).
Removal of members, §158-8.4.
Report to general assembly, §158-8.3(e).
Terms, §158-8.3(c).
Uniform standards, §158-8.6.
Use of state funds, §158-8.7.
Vacancies, §158-8.3(c).
Staff, §158-10.
State board of education.
Members as ex officio commission members,
§158-8.4A.
Western North Carolina regional economic
development commission.
Annual reporting, §158-8.5.
Counties served, §158-8.1(a).
Created, §158-8.1(a).
Meetings.
Initial meeting, §158-8.1(c1).
Members, §158-8.1(b).
Nonvoting ex officio members, §158-8.1(b1).
Orientation for board members, §158-8.8.
Per diem and travel expenses, §158-8.1(d).
Powers and duties, §158-8.1(e).
Removal of members, §158-8.4.
Terms of members, §158-8.1(c).
Uniform standards, §158-8.6.
Use of state funds, §158-8.7.
Vacancies, §158-8.1(c).

ECONOMIC INTEREST STATEMENTS.
State government ethics act.
Statements of economic interest, §§138A-21 to
138A-27.
See STATE GOVERNMENT ETHICS ACT.

ECONOMIC OR MONETARY LOSS.
Action to recover damages for defective or
unsafe condition of improvement to real
property.
Limitation of actions, §1-50(a).
Retaliatory employment discrimination civil
actions.
Award to employee, §95-243(c).
Trade secrets, action for misappropriation.
Actual damages recovered measured by,
§66-154(b).

ECONOMIC PROGRESS.
Balanced growth policy act, §§143-506.6 to
143-506.13.

ECOSYSTEM ENHANCEMENT PROGRAM,
§§143-214.8 to 143-214.13.
Basinwide restoration plans.
Development, §143-214.10.
Compensatory mitigation.
Coordination with basinwide restoration plans,
§143-214.11(b).
Defined, §143-214.11(a).
Existing local compensatory mitigation bank.
Sale of mitigation credits, §143-214.11(h).

ECOSYSTEM ENHANCEMENT PROGRAM
—Cont'd
Compensatory mitigation —Cont'd
Mitigation banks, §143-214.11(f).
Nutrient offset credits.
Purchase to offset nutrient loadings to surface
waters, §143-214.26.
Payment schedule, §143-214.11(e).
Replacement function, §143-214.11(c).
Satisfaction of requirements by applicant.
Applicants other than department of
transportation, §143-214.11(d1).
Department of transportation, §143-214.11(d).
Taxes lost by county.
Payment of sum in lieu of, §143-214.11(g).
Composting operations.
Stormwater control best management practices
and process water treatment processes,
§143-214.7A.
Conservation easement granted by recipient
or grantee in property acquired,
§143-214.12(a1).
Conveyance of property acquired under
program, §143-214.12(a1).
Established, §143-214.8.
Fund.
Accounting for payments, §143-214.12(c).
Distribution directly to recipient, §143-214.12(a1).
Established, §143-214.12(a).
Methods of payment, §143-214.12(b).
Inventory of property, §143-214.13(b).
Nutrient offset credits.
Purchase to offset nutrient loadings to surface
waters, §143-214.26.
Purposes, §143-214.9.
Reports, §143-214.13(a).
Riparian buffer protection program,
§143-214.25A.
Surface water identification training and
certification.
Riparian buffer protection, §143-214.25A.

EDDIE BRIDGES FUND, §143-250.1(a) to (h).

EDEN.
Room occupancy tax.
Uniform provisions.
Authorized to levy, §160A-215(g).
Generally, §160A-215.

EDENTON HISTORICAL COMMISSION.
Appointments, §143B-98.
Compensation of members, §143B-98.
Creation, §143B-95.
Department of cultural resources.
Transfer of commission to department, §143B-51.
Duties, §143B-95.
Exemption from provisions, §143B-96.
Members, §143B-98.
Powers and duties, §143B-95.
Quorum, §143B-98.
Reports, §143B-97.
Selection of members, §143B-98.
Status, §143B-96.

EDGECOMBE COUNTY.
Agricultural tendencies in certain counties.
Terms of, §42-23.
Ambulance service.
Attachment or garnishment and lien for,
§§44-51.4 to 44-51.8.
Condemnation or acquisition of land by local
government unit outside county.
Consent of board of commissioners necessary,
§153A-15.

EDGECOMBE COUNTY —Cont'd

Cropper or tenant refusing to perform terms of contract.
Forfeiture of right of possession to premises, §42-27.

Game laws, local acts not repealed, §113-133.1(e).

Housing authority commissioners.
Tenant as commissioner, exemption from provision of law allowing, §157-5.

Industrial development.
Tax elections, §§158-16 to 158-24.
See INDUSTRIAL DEVELOPMENT.

Low-income housing tax credits.
Qualified building eligible for credit, §105-129.41(c).

North Carolina's eastern region, §§158-30 to 158-42.
See NORTH CAROLINA'S EASTERN REGION.

Probate and registration orders before clerks of inferior courts validated, §47-59.

Registration of deeds.
Tax certification, no delinquent taxes due, §161-31(b).

School property.
Acquisition and improvement, §153A-158.1.

Sheriff.
Vacancy, performance of duties until vacancy filled, §162-5.1.

Tax elections for industrial development purposes, §§158-16 to 158-24.

Taxicabs.
Certificates of necessity and convenience, §20-87.

Wild plants, taking of certain plants from land of another.
Inapplicability of provisions, §14-129.

EDUCATION.

Academic credit.
Fraudulent means in obtaining credit, §14-118.2(b).

Accountants, §93-12.

Administrative procedure, §115C-2.

Adult education.
Entitlement to attend, §115C-231(c).
Free tuition.
Persons 18 years of age or older not having completed high school, §115C-231(b).
No adult left behind initiative, §143B-438.14.
Organization and administration of program, §115C-231(a).
Removal or prohibiting enrollment.
Persons having attained age of 21 years, §115C-231(c).

Arts.
University of North Carolina School of the Arts, §§116-63 to 116-69.1.
See UNIVERSITY OF NORTH CAROLINA SCHOOL OF THE ARTS.

At-risk students.
Extended service programs, §§115C-238.30 to 115C-238.33.
See AT-RISK STUDENTS.

Attorneys at law.
Continuing legal education.
See CONTINUING LEGAL EDUCATION.

Bail bondsmen and runners, §58-71-71.
Instructor's qualifications, §§58-71-72, 58-71-72(b).

Barber schools.
See BARBERS.

EDUCATION —Cont'd

Black Mountain Advancement Center for Women.
Educational and vocational training for inmates, §143B-269(f).

Blind children.
Governor Morehead school, §§143B-164.10 to 143B-164.18.
See GOVERNOR MOREHEAD SCHOOL.

Boards of education.
Local boards, §§115C-35 to 115C-51.
See LOCAL BOARDS OF EDUCATION.
State board of education.
See STATE BOARD OF EDUCATION.

Boating safety education.
Required to operate motorboats, §75A-16.2.

Bond issues.
State debt, §§142-1 to 142-29.7.
See STATE DEBT.

Budgets.
Public schools generally, §§115C-425 to 115C-434.
See SCHOOL DISTRICTS AND ADMINISTRATIVE UNITS.

Buildings.
Generally, §§115C-517 to 115C-530.
See SCHOOL BUILDINGS AND PROPERTY.

Buses.
School buses.
See SCHOOL BUSES.

Cabinet, §116C-1.

Capital facilities finance.
Private capital facilities finance act.
Institutions for higher education and elementary and secondary education, §§159D-35 to 159D-57.
See CAPITAL FACILITIES FINANCE AGENCY.

Center for the advancement of teaching, §§115C-296.5, 115C-296.6.

Charitable gift annuities.
Generally, §58-3-6.

Charter schools, §§115C-238.29A to 115C-238.29K.
See CHARTER SCHOOLS.

Cheating.
Academic credit obtained by fraudulent means, §14-118.2.

Children with chemical dependency, §§115C-149, 115C-150.

Children with disabilities.
Generally, §§115C-106.1 to 115C-112.1.
See SPECIAL EDUCATION.

Chiropractors.
Requirements for licensure, §90-143(b).

Church schools and schools of religious charter, §§115C-547 to 115C-554.
See PRIVATE AND PAROCHIAL SCHOOLS.

Colleges.
See COLLEGES AND UNIVERSITIES.

Community colleges, §§115D-1 to 115D-97.
See COMMUNITY COLLEGES.

Community schools act, §§115C-203 to 115C-209.1.
See COMMUNITY SCHOOLS ACT.

Compulsory attendance law, §§115C-378 to 115C-383.
See COMPULSORY SCHOOL ATTENDANCE.

Consolidation of administrative units and school districts, §§115C-68 to 115C-72.

Continuum of education programs.
Strategic design to be developed by education cabinet, §116C-3.

EDUCATION —Cont'd
Criminal justice education and training standards, §§17C-1 to 17C-13.
  See CRIMINAL JUSTICE EDUCATION AND TRAINING STANDARDS COMMISSION.
Department of public instruction.
  Confidentiality of certain records.
    Disclosure by member, officer or employee, §115C-13.
  Created, §143A-44.1.
  Criminal history records checks for employees and applicants.
    Conditional offer of employment pending check, §114-19.23(f).
    Confidentiality of information, §114-19.23(c).
    Convictions, effect of finding, §114-19.23(d).
    Definitions, §114-19.23(a).
    Provision for generally, §114-19.23(b).
    Refusal to consent, §114-19.23(e).
  Head of department.
    State board of education, §143A-44.1.
  Impaired driving.
    Forfeiture of motor vehicles.
      Contracts for services to tow, store, process, maintain, and sell seized vehicles.
        Authorized, §20-28.9(a).
        Fees, §20-28.9(b), (c).
  Interstate compact for education.
    Rights, duties and privileges, §143A-45.
  Office of environmental education and public affairs.
    Liaison between office and department, §143B-285.25.
  Office of superintendent of public instruction.
    Transferred to department of public instruction, §143A-44.3.
  Records.
    Duty to maintain confidentiality of certain records, §115C-13.
  Salaries for employees injured during an episode of violence, §115C-338.
  State board of education.
    Head of department, §143A-44.1.
    Transfer of powers and duties to state board, §143A-44.2.
  Superintendent of public instruction to be secretary and chief administrative officer of state board of education, §143A-44.3.
  Textbook commission.
    Transfer to department of public instruction, §143A-48.
  Transfer of powers and duties to state board of education, §143A-44.2.
  Transferred to department of public instruction, §143A-44.3.
Dietitians and nutritionists.
  License requirements, §90-357.
Disabled persons.
  Right to habilitation and rehabilitation services, §168-8.
Discipline of students, §§115C-390.1 to 115C-392.
  See SCHOOLS AND EDUCATION.
Districts.
  Local government finance generally, §§159-1 to 159-188.
    See LOCAL GOVERNMENT FINANCE.
  School districts.
    See SCHOOL DISTRICTS AND ADMINISTRATIVE UNITS.
Driver education, §§20-88.1, 115C-215, 115C-216.

EDUCATION —Cont'd
Driver training schools.
  Licensing, §§20-320 to 20-328.
    See DRIVER TRAINING SCHOOLS.
Drug addicted children, §§115C-149, 115C-150.
Early childhood initiatives, §§143B-168.10 to 143B-168.16.
  See EARLY CHILDHOOD INITIATIVES.
Education assistance authority, §§116-201 to 116-209.40.
  See EDUCATION ASSISTANCE AUTHORITY.
Education commission, §§143-261 to 143-266.
  See EDUCATION COMMISSION.
Education expenses tax credit.
  Child with disability requiring special education and related services, §105-151.33.
Electrologists.
  Continuing education.
    License renewal.
      Requirements, §88A-13.
Elementary and secondary education.
  Generally.
    See SCHOOLS AND EDUCATION.
Embezzlement.
  Funds embezzled by public officers and trustees, §14-92.
Emergency paramedical program.
  Duty of state board of education to provide for, §115C-12.
Encouragement of education, NC Const Art IX §1.
Engineers and land surveyors.
  Requirements for licensure generally, §89C-13.
Environmental education and public affairs, office of, §§143B-285.20 to 143B-285.25.
Environmental health specialists.
  Continuing education, §90A-63(c).
Exemption from taxation, NC Const Art V §2.
  Endowment funds, §115C-494.
  Real and personal property, §105-278.4.
  Vehicles owned by boards of education, §115C-520.
Eye protection devices, §§115C-166 to 115C-169.
  See VOCATIONAL AND TECHNICAL EDUCATION.
First in America innovative education act.
  Annual report, §116C-4(c).
  Cooperative efforts.
    Secondary schools and institutions of higher education, §116C-4(a).
  Funding, §116C-4(b).
Fiscal control of public schools, §§115C-435 to 115C-452.
  See SCHOOL DISTRICTS AND ADMINISTRATIVE UNITS.
Forgery.
  Diplomas, §14-122.1.
  Transcripts, §14-122.1.
Fraud.
  Academic credit by fraudulent means.
    Assisting, etc., in obtaining credit, §14-118.2(a), (b).
Funds.
  Generally.
    See SCHOOLS AND EDUCATION.
  Scholarship loan fund for prospective teachers, §§116-209.33, 116-209.34.
    See TEACHERS.
  State literary fund, §§115C-458, 115C-459.
General assembly.
  Joint legislative education oversight committee, §§120-70.80 to 120-70.83.

EDUCATION —Cont'd
General assembly —Cont'd
Local government fiscal information act,
§§120-30.41 to 120-30.49.
Geologists.
Licenses.
Minimum qualifications, §89E-9.
Gifts.
Charitable gift annuities, §58-3-6.
State board of education.
Power to accept gifts, §115C-410.
Governor Morehead School.
Education programs in residential schools
generally, §§143B-146.1 to 143B-146.21. See
within this heading, "Residential schools."
State school for sight impaired children,
§§143B-164.10 to 143B-164.18.
See GOVERNOR MOREHEAD SCHOOL.
Hearing aid dealers and fitters.
Occupational instruction courses.
Board may require as prerequisite to license
renewal, §93D-11.
Qualifications for licenses, §93D-5(a).
Hearing-impaired children.
Schools for the deaf generally, §§143B-216.40 to
143B-216.44.
See DEAF AND HEARING IMPAIRED.
Higher education.
Benefits of public institutions to the people of
state free of expense, NC Const Art IX §9.
Community colleges, §§115D-1 to 115D-97.
See COMMUNITY COLLEGES.
Generally.
See COLLEGES AND UNIVERSITIES.
Maintenance of public system of higher education,
NC Const Art IX §8.
Students.
Escheats.
Disposition of escheats after June 30, 1971,
NC Const Art IX §10.
University of North Carolina, §§116-1 to 116-44.5.
See UNIVERSITY OF NORTH CAROLINA.
University of North Carolina School of the Arts,
§§116-63 to 116-69.1.
See UNIVERSITY OF NORTH CAROLINA
SCHOOL OF THE ARTS.
Home schools, §§115C-563 to 115C-565.
Hospitals.
Health education facilities.
Sale or lease, §131E-8.1.
Income tax credit.
Education expenses.
Child with disability requiring special education
and related services, §105-151.33.
Indians.
State advisory council on Indian education,
§§115C-210 to 115C-210.4.
See NATIVE AMERICANS.
Insurance.
Continuing education program for licensees,
§§58-33-130, 58-33-135.
Local boards of education.
Liability insurance, §115C-42.
State insurance of public school property,
§§115C-533 to 115C-543.
See SCHOOL BUILDINGS AND PROPERTY.
**Interstate agreement on qualifications of
educational personnel,** §§115C-349 to
115C-358.
See SCHOOL EMPLOYEES.

EDUCATION —Cont'd
Interstate compact for education.
Department of public education.
Rights, duties and privileges, §143A-45.
Enactment of compact, §115C-104.
State superintendent of public instruction.
Rights, duties and privileges, §143A-45.
Text of compact, §115C-104.
**Joint legislative education oversight
committee,** §§120-70.80 to 120-70.83.
Justice academy, §§17D-1 to 17D-4.
Juvenile facilities.
Salary supplement for teachers and instructional
personnel, §143B-806(b).
Kindergarten children.
Comprehensive eye examination required,
§130A-440.1.
Health assessments, §130A-440.
Lobbying education program, §120C-103.
Local boards of education, §§115C-35 to 115C-51.
See LOCAL BOARDS OF EDUCATION.
Local government finance.
Budget and fiscal control.
Application of article to school administrative
units, §159-7(d).
Local government fiscal information act,
§§120-30.41 to 120-30.49.
See GENERAL ASSEMBLY.
Marriage and family therapists.
Continuing education requirements, §90-270.58C.
Licensing requirements, §90-270.54(a).
Marriage and family therapy associates,
§90-270.54A(a).
Recognized educational institution.
Defined, §90-270.47.
Massage and bodywork therapy.
Approval of schools, §90-631.
Continuing education.
License renewal, §90-632(b), (c).
Qualifications for licensure, §90-629.
Meetings.
Open meetings law, §115C-4.
**Merger of administrative units and school
districts,** §§115C-68 to 115C-72.
Military children.
Interstate compact on educational opportunity for
military children, §§115C-407.5 to 115C-407.8.
Militia.
Commissions for commandants and officers at
qualified educational institutions, §127A-23.
Nonprofit corporations.
Certain associations deemed incorporated,
§55A-17-02.
**North Carolina center for the advancement of
teaching,** §§115C-296.5, 115C-296.6.
Notaries.
Commission.
Course of classroom instruction, §10B-8.
Instructor certification, §10B-14.
Electronic notary registration.
Course of instruction and examination,
§10B-107.
Nurses.
Baccalaureate in nursing candidate credits,
§90-171.41.
Continuing education.
Approval of programs by board, §90-171.42(a).
Advanced skills, §90-171.42(b).
Emergency financial assistance fund.
Established, §90-171.51.
Licensing exam follow-up assistance, §90-171.52.

EDUCATION —Cont'd
Nurses —Cont'd
Local health directors.
Nurse pilot program, §130A-40.1(a) to (c).
Publicity program.
Salary levels, job opportunities, refresher
courses and license renewal requirements.
Developing publicity on, §90-171.53.
Scholarship and loan information.
Consolidation, §90-171.50.
Nursing home administrators.
Continuing education.
Powers of board as to, §90-286.
Qualifications for licenses, §90-278.
Occupational safety and health.
Commissioner of labor.
Powers and duties, §95-147(a), (b).
Open meetings law, §115C-4.
Opticians.
Qualifications, §90-237.
Optometrists.
Continuing education courses required, §90-123.1.
Parochial schools generally, §§115C-547 to
115C-554.
See PRIVATE AND PAROCHIAL SCHOOLS.
**Personnel evaluation of certified school
employees,** §§115C-333 to 115C-335.
Podiatrists.
Continuing education courses required,
§90-202.11.
Qualifications for examination, §90-202.5.
Principals, §§115C-284 to 115C-289.
See PRINCIPALS OF SCHOOLS.
Prisons and prisoners.
Facilities and programs for selected inmates,
§148-22.1(a), (b).
Salary supplement paid teachers, other
instructional personnel, §148-22.1(c).
Private and parochial schools.
See PRIVATE AND PAROCHIAL SCHOOLS.
Private capital facilities finance act.
Institutions for higher education and elementary
and secondary education, §§159D-35 to
159D-57.
See CAPITAL FACILITIES FINANCE
AGENCY.
Property taxes.
Supplementary taxes for school purposes,
§§115C-500 to 115C-513.
See SCHOOL DISTRICTS AND
ADMINISTRATIVE UNITS.
Proprietary schools, §§115D-87 to 115D-97.
See PROPRIETARY SCHOOLS.
Prudent management of institutional funds,
§§36E-1 to 36E-11.
See PRUDENT MANAGEMENT OF
INSTITUTIONAL FUNDS.
**Public school buildings and property
generally,** §§115C-517 to 115C-530.
See SCHOOL BUILDINGS AND PROPERTY.
Public school employees.
Evaluation of certified employees, §§115C-333 to
115C-335.
Generally.
See SCHOOL EMPLOYEES.
Principals, §§115C-284 to 115C-289.
See PRINCIPALS OF SCHOOLS.
Superintendents of schools, §§115C-271 to
115C-278.
See SUPERINTENDENTS OF SCHOOLS.

EDUCATION —Cont'd
Public school employees —Cont'd
Supervisors, §§115C-284 to 115C-289.
See SUPERVISORS OF SCHOOLS.
Teachers, §§115C-295 to 115C-310.
See TEACHERS.
Public schools generally.
See SCHOOLS AND EDUCATION.
Recreational trespass.
Definition of "educational purpose,"§38A-2.
Generally, §§38A-1 to 38A-4.
Regional organization of schools, §115C-65.
Regional schools, §§115C-238.60 to 115C-238.73.
See REGIONAL SCHOOLS.
Residential schools.
ABC's program.
Annual performance goals, §143B-146.3.
Decision making and parental involvement,
§143B-146.2(c).
Defined, §143B-146.1(b).
Participation in program, §143B-146.2(a).
Flexibility in use of funds, §143B-146.2(d).
Guidelines, §143B-146.2(b).
Appeals from decisions of school personnel to
secretary, §143B-146.14.
Calendars, §143B-146.11.
Criminal acts.
Duty to report to law enforcement,
§143B-146.15.
Criminal history checks of school personnel.
Definitions, §143B-146.16(a).
Department of justice.
Duties, §143B-146.16(c).
Fingerprints.
Applicant not to be required to pay for being
fingerprinted, §143B-146.16(c).
Negligence.
Immunity from liability, §143B-146.16(g).
Privileged information, §143B-146.16(f).
Review by state board of education,
§143B-146.16(e).
Review of criminal history by secretary,
§143B-146.16(d).
Secretary to require, §143B-146.16(b).
Definitions, §143B-146.1(b).
Criminal history checks of school personnel,
§143B-146.16(a).
School property, §143B-146.15.
Dispute resolution, §143B-146.14.
Duties of secretary of health and human services,
§143B-146.21(a), (b).
Independent living facilities.
Policies to ensure that students are given
priority to residing in, §143B-146.21(d).
Low-performing schools.
Annual review of progress, §143B-146.6(d).
Assessment teams, §143B-146.9.
Duties, §143B-146.9.
Assistance teams, §143B-146.6(a), (b).
Recommendations, §143B-146.6(c).
Certificated personnel.
Action plans, §143B-146.8(b).
Annual evaluations, §143B-146.8(a).
Reevaluation, §143B-146.8(c).
Standards and criteria for, §143B-146.10.
Assessment teams, §143B-146.9.
Consequences of identification as
low-performing school for, §143B-146.7(b)
to (d).
Dismissal.
State board notification, §143B-146.8(d).

EDUCATION —Cont'd
Residential schools —Cont'd
Low-performing schools —Cont'd
Certificated personnel —Cont'd
Negligence in action taken under provisions.
Civil immunity, §143B-146.8(e).
Performance standards and criteria for,
§143B-146.10.
Contracts of school administrators.
Termination if dismissed, §143B-146.7(e).
Identification, §143B-146.5(a), (b).
Written notification to parents,
§143B-146.5(c).
Principals.
Consequences of identification as
low-performing school for principal,
§143B-146.7(a).
Evaluation, §143B-146.8(f).
Mission of schools, §143B-146.1(a).
Performance recognition, §143B-146.4(a).
Allocation of funds for awards, §143B-146.4(b).
Professional development opportunities.
Availability to be offered and communicated,
§143B-146.21(c).
Salary supplements.
Setting, §143B-146.21(e).
School calendar, §143B-146.11.
School technology plan, §143B-146.13(a).
Use of funds, §143B-146.13(b).
Safe and orderly schools.
Local plans for maintaining, §§115C-105.45,
115C-105.46.
School administrative units.
Generally.
See SCHOOL DISTRICTS AND
ADMINISTRATIVE UNITS.
**School-based management and accountability
program.**
Generally, §§115C-105.20 to 115C-105.40.
See SCHOOLS AND EDUCATION.
Residential schools.
ABC's program, §§143B-146.1 to 143B-146.21.
See within this heading, "Residential
schools."
School boards.
Local boards of education, §§115C-35 to 115C-51.
See LOCAL BOARDS OF EDUCATION.
State board of education.
See STATE BOARD OF EDUCATION.
School budget and fiscal control act.
Generally, §§115C-422 to 115C-452.
See SCHOOL DISTRICTS AND
ADMINISTRATIVE UNITS.
School buildings and property, §§115C-517 to
115C-530.
See SCHOOL BUILDINGS AND PROPERTY.
School buses.
See SCHOOL BUSES.
School districts.
See SCHOOL DISTRICTS AND
ADMINISTRATIVE UNITS.
School employees.
See SCHOOL EMPLOYEES.
School for sight impaired children.
Governor Morehead school, §§143B-164.10 to
143B-164.18.
See GOVERNOR MOREHEAD SCHOOL.
Schools for the deaf.
Education programs in residential schools
generally, §§143B-146.1 to 143B-146.21. See
within this heading, "Residential schools."

EDUCATION —Cont'd
Schools for the deaf —Cont'd
Generally, §§143B-216.40 to 143B-216.44.
See DEAF AND HEARING IMPAIRED.
Schools generally.
See SCHOOLS AND EDUCATION.
**Science and mathematics school of the
University of North Carolina,** §§116-230.1 to
116-238.5.
See UNIVERSITY OF NORTH CAROLINA.
**Science, technology, engineering and
mathematics education priorities,** §116C-5.
Seized, confiscated or unclaimed property.
Sale proceeds to county boards of education,
§15-15.
**Sheriffs' education and training standards
commission,** §§17E-1 to 17E-12.
See SHERIFFS' EDUCATION AND TRAINING
STANDARDS COMMISSION.
Special education.
Children with disabilities.
Generally, §§115C-106.1 to 115C-112.1.
See SPECIAL EDUCATION.
**Speech and language pathologists and
audiologists.**
Qualifications of applicants for licensure, §90-295.
Sports medicine.
State board of education.
Duty to provide for, §115C-12.
State board of education.
See STATE BOARD OF EDUCATION.
State education assistance authority, §§116-201
to 116-209.40.
See EDUCATION ASSISTANCE AUTHORITY.
State education commission, §§143-261 to
143-266.
See EDUCATION COMMISSION.
State literary fund, §§115C-458, 115C-459.
State school for sight impaired children.
Governor Morehead school, §§143B-164.10 to
143B-164.18.
See GOVERNOR MOREHEAD SCHOOL.
State schools for hearing-impaired children.
Schools for the deaf generally, §§143B-216.40 to
143B-216.44.
See DEAF AND HEARING IMPAIRED.
State superintendent of public instruction.
See SUPERINTENDENT OF PUBLIC
INSTRUCTION.
Statewide testing program, §§115C-174.10 to
115C-174.14.
See SCHOOLS AND EDUCATION.
Superintendent of public instruction.
See SUPERINTENDENT OF PUBLIC
INSTRUCTION.
Superintendents of schools, §§115C-271 to
115C-278.
See SUPERINTENDENTS OF SCHOOLS.
Supervisors of schools, §§115C-284 to 115C-289.
See SUPERVISORS OF SCHOOLS.
Supplementary taxes for school purposes,
§§115C-500 to 115C-513.
See SCHOOL DISTRICTS AND
ADMINISTRATIVE UNITS.
Taking indecent liberties with a student,
§14-202.4.
Taxation.
Supplementary taxes for school purposes,
§§115C-500 to 115C-513.
See SCHOOL DISTRICTS AND
ADMINISTRATIVE UNITS.

EDUCATION —Cont'd
Teacher enhancement program.
  Teaching fellows commission, §§115C-363.22, 115C-363.23.
  Teaching fellows program, §115C-363.23A.
Teachers.
  Generally, §§115C-295 to 115C-310.
    See TEACHERS.
  Retirement system for teachers and state employees.
    See RETIREMENT SYSTEM FOR TEACHERS AND STATE EMPLOYEES.
Technical education generally.
  See VOCATIONAL AND TECHNICAL EDUCATION.
Technology.
  School technology commission, §§115C-102.5 to 115C-102.7.
  School technology plan, §§115C-102.6A to 115C-102.6D.
  Statewide testing program, §§115C-174.10 to 115C-174.14.
    See SCHOOLS AND EDUCATION.
Textbooks generally, §§115C-85 to 115C-102.
  See TEXTBOOKS.
Trespass.
  Recreational trespass.
    Definition of "educational purpose,"§38A-2.
    Generally, §§38A-1 to 38A-4.
      See RECREATIONAL TRESPASS.
Trusts and trustees.
  Performance of educational requirements.
    Loss resulting from trustee's lack of knowledge.
      Trustee not liable, reasonable care exercised, §36C-10-1007.
Uniform system of schools, §115C-1, NC Const Art IX §2.
Universities.
  See COLLEGES AND UNIVERSITIES.
University of North Carolina, §§116-1 to 116-44.5.
  See UNIVERSITY OF NORTH CAROLINA.
University of North Carolina School of the Arts, §§116-63 to 116-69.1.
  See UNIVERSITY OF NORTH CAROLINA SCHOOL OF THE ARTS.
Veterinarians.
  Continuing education.
    Powers of board as to, §90-186.
Vocational education generally.
  See VOCATIONAL AND TECHNICAL EDUCATION.
Voted tax supplements for school purposes, §§115C-500 to 115C-513.
  See SCHOOL DISTRICTS AND ADMINISTRATIVE UNITS.
Wastewater treatment.
  Certification of water pollution control system operators.
    Powers of certification commission, §90A-43.
Water treatment facility operators.
  Powers of board as to, §90A-28.
  Qualifications for certificates.
    Establishment, §90A-24.

EDUCATION ACCESS REWARDS NORTH CAROLINA SCHOLARS FUND, §116-209.26.

EDUCATIONAL ASSOCIATIONS.
Sales and use tax refunds.
  Educational institutions not operated for profit, §105-164.14(b).

EDUCATIONAL ASSOCIATIONS —Cont'd
Solicitation of contributions, §§131F-1 to 131F-33.
  See CHARITABLE SOLICITATION.

EDUCATIONAL DISTRICTS ENUMERATED, §115C-65.

EDUCATIONAL PERSONNEL QUALIFICATIONS.
Interstate agreement, §§115C-349 to 115C-358.
  See SCHOOL EMPLOYEES.
Personnel evaluation of certified employees, §§115C-333 to 115C-335.

EDUCATIONAL TELEVISION.
Agency for public telecommunications, §§143B-426.8 to 143B-426.20.
  See PUBLIC TELECOMMUNICATIONS, AGENCY FOR.

EDUCATION ASSISTANCE AUTHORITY, §§116-201 to 116-209.40.
Acquisition of obligations, §§116-206, 116-207.
Acts or undertakings.
  Defined, §116-201(b).
  Fees.
    Powers as to, §116-204.
  Limited to revenues, §116-202.
Board of directors.
  Members, §116-203(b).
  Officers, §116-203(f).
  Per diem and expenses, §116-203(h).
  Quorum for transaction of business, §116-203(g).
  Removal of member, §116-203(e).
  Terms of office, §116-203(c).
  Vacancies in office, §116-203(d).
Board of governors of University of North Carolina.
  Cooperation, §116-209.21.
Bond issues.
  Authorized, §116-209.4.
  Bond holder remedies, §116-209.8.
  Credit of state not pledged, §116-209.12.
  Definitions, §116-201(b).
  Investments.
    Eligibility for investment, §116-209.10.
  Issuance of bonds, §116-209.4.
  Maturity of bonds, §116-209.4.
  Negotiability of bonds, §116-209.9.
  Parental loans.
    Power of authority to issue bonds, §116-209.24(e).
  Refunding bonds, §116-209.4.
  Remedies of bondholders, §116-209.8.
  Reserves, §116-209.2.
  Resolution, §116-209.5.
  Revenues.
    Sufficiency to pay bonds, §116-209.6.
  Security of bonds.
    Additional pledge, §116-209.11.
    Credit of state not pledged, §116-209.12.
    Reserve trust fund.
      Pledge of security interest for payment of bonds, §116-209.
    Trust agreement, §116-209.5.
      Remedies of bond holders, §116-209.8.
  Tax exemption, §116-209.13.
  Terms and conditions of bonds, §116-209.4.
  Trust agreement, §116-209.5.
    Remedies of bond holders, §116-209.8.
  Trust funds, §116-209.7.
    Merger, §116-209.15.

EDUCATION ASSISTANCE AUTHORITY
—Cont'd
Bond issues —Cont'd
United States funds.
Pledge for security of bonds, §116-209.11.
Collection of loan repayments.
Scholarship loan fund for prospective teachers,
§116-204.
Teaching fellows program, §115C-363.23A(g).
Conflict of laws.
Inconsistent laws inapplicable, §116-209.23.
Repeal of certain provisions to extent of conflict,
§116-209.1.
Construction and interpretation.
Liberal construction of provisions, §116-208.
Severability of provisions, §116-209.22.
Creation, §116-203(a).
Definitions, §116-201(b).
**Education access rewards North Carolina
scholars fund.**
Administration of grants, §116-209.26(e).
Expenditures.
Public purpose, §116-209.20.
**Forgivable education loans for service
program.**
Administration, §116-209.45(c).
Advisory group, §116-209.45(g).
Amount of loans.
Authority to establish, §116-209.45(f).
Criteria for eligibility for loans.
Authority to establish, §116-209.45(e).
Criteria for forgiveness.
Authority to establish, §116-209.45(f).
Death or disability.
Impossible for recipient to repay, §116-209.45(f).
Definitions, §116-209.45(b).
Eligible institution.
Defined, §116-209.45(b).
Established, §116-209.45(c).
Finding of general assembly, §116-209.45(a).
Fund.
Established, administration, purpose,
§116-209.45(d).
Money placed in, use, §116-209.45(h).
Future teachers, nurses, allied health
professional.
Initial target of program, §116-209.45(c).
Hardship, §116-209.45(f).
Promissory notes.
Loans evidenced by, §116-209.45(f).
Purpose, §116-209.45(c).
Repayment of loans, §116-209.45(f).
Report to general assembly, §116-209.45(j).
Residents of state.
Eligibility for loans, §116-209.45(e).
Rules, §116-209.45(i).
Standards.
Authority to develop, §116-209.45(e).
Terms and conditions of loans, §116-209.45(f).
**Future teachers of North Carolina scholarship
loan fund.**
Criteria for awarding loans, §116-209.38(b).
Established, §116-209.38(a).
Information regarding availability of and criteria
for loans, §116-209.38(d).
Purpose, §116-209.38(a).
Repayment of loans on noncompliance,
§116-209.38(c).
Reports, §116-209.38(f).
Rulemaking, §116-209.38(e).
Grants to students, §116-209.19.

EDUCATION ASSISTANCE AUTHORITY
—Cont'd
Legislative declaration, §116-201(a).
Loan fund, §116-209.3.
**Need-based scholarships for students
attending private colleges and universities,**
§§116-280 to 116-283.
Obligations.
Acquisition, §116-206.
Terms of acquisitions, §116-207.
Defined, §116-201(b).
Power to buy and sell students obligations,
§116-202.
Offices, §116-205(c).
Parental loans.
Assistance to parents.
Powers of authority, §116-209.24(c).
Bond issues.
Power of authority to issue, §116-209.24(e).
Buying and selling parental obligations.
Power of authority, §116-209.24(d).
Definitions, §116-209.24(b).
Purpose, §116-209.24(a).
Powers.
Generally, §§116-204, 116-209.3, 116-209.16.
Student assistance program, §§116-209.16 to
116-209.18.
Property.
Powers as to, §116-204.
State property.
Consent to use, §116-205(b).
Title to property in name of authority,
§116-205(a).
Purposes, §116-201(a).
Expenditures to be for public purpose,
§116-209.20.
Reports.
Annual report, §116-209.14.
Reserves, §116-209.2.
Revenues, §116-209.6.
Undertakings of authority limited to revenues,
§116-202.
Scholarship loans.
Future teachers of North Carolina scholarship
loan fund, §116-209.38.
Need-based scholarships for students attending
private colleges and universities, §§116-280 to
116-283.
Severability of provisions, §116-209.22.
Status, §116-203(a).
Student assistance program.
Powers as to, §116-209.16.
Administration of program, §116-209.18.
Establishment of program, §116-209.17.
Students.
Defined, §116-201(b).
Grants to students, §116-209.19.
Obligations.
Acquisition, §§116-206, 116-207.
Defined, §116-201(b).
Power to buy and sell, §116-202.
Taxation.
Exemptions, §116-209.13.
Teacher assistant scholarship fund, §116-209.35.
Trust funds.
Generally, §116-209.7.
Merger, §116-209.15.
Reserve trust fund.
Creation, §116-209.
Escheat fund.
Transfer, §116-209.

EDUCATION CABINET.
Created, §116C-1(a).
Duties, §116C-1(c).
First in America innovative education act.
Annual report, §116C-4(c).
Funding, §116C-4(b).
Members, §116C-1(b).
Science, technology, engineering and
mathematics education priorities, §116C-5.
Staff, §116C-1(d).
Strategic design for continuum of education
programs, §116C-3.

EDUCATION COMMISSION, §§116C-2, 143-261
to 143-266.
Appointments, §143-261.
Compensation, §143-264.
Duties, §§116C-2, 143-261.
Elections.
Officers, §143-262.
Executive secretary.
Powers, §143-266.
Salary, §143-265.
Expenses, §143-264.
Members, §116C-2.
Status, §143-262.
Membership, §143-261.
Officers.
Election, §143-262.
Organization meeting, §143-262.
Per diem expenses, §143-264.
Powers of executive secretary, §143-266.
Purpose, §143-261.
Comprehensive study of education problems,
§143-263.
Salaries.
Executive secretary, §143-265.
Status of members, §143-262.
Studies.
Commission to make comprehensive studies of
educational problems, §143-263.
Travel allowances, §143-264.

EDUCATION EXPENSES TAX CREDIT.
Child with disability requiring special
education and related services, §105-151.33.

EDUCATION OF CHILDREN WITH
DISABILITIES, §§115C-106.1 to 115C-112.1.
See SPECIAL EDUCATION.

EFFECTIVE DATES OF STATUTES AND ACTS,
§§120-20, 164-8.

EFFLUENT STANDARDS AND LIMITATIONS.
Contents of standards and limitations,
§143-215(b).
Powers of commission, §143-215(a).

E-FILING, §1A-1 Rule 5(e).
Contract with vendor to provide.
Administrative office of the courts, §7A-49.5(c).
Deposit of funds received from vendor.
Court information technology fund, §7A-49.5(d).
Establishment and operation of systems and
services.
Duty of director of administrative office of the
courts, §7A-343.
Legislative findings, §7A-49.5(a).
Rules.
Supreme court may adopt, §7A-49.5(b).
Waiver of fees for indigents.
Rules to address, §7A-49.5(b).

EGG PROMOTION TAX, §§106-245.30 to
106-245.39.
Amount, §106-245.32.
Collection.
Delinquent taxes, §106-245.36.
Definitions, §106-245.31.
Effect on Article 50 of Chapter 106, §106-245.39.
Exemptions, §106-245.34.
Eggs assessed under agricultural marketing
agreement act of 1937, §106-245.34A.
Funds.
North Carolina egg fund, §106-245.37.
Handlers.
Defined, §106-245.33(b).
Exemptions, §106-245.34.
False reports or records, failure to record.
Criminal penalty, §106-245.38(a).
Functions, §106-245.33(b).
Payment by handler, §106-245.33(a).
Records, §106-245.35.
Registration, §106-245.33(b).
Failure, criminal penalty, §106-245.38(b).
Report of tax, §106-245.33(a).
Interest.
Delinquent taxes, §106-245.36.
Legislative findings, §106-245.30.
Levy of tax, §106-245.32.
Purpose of article, §106-245.30.
Records, §106-245.35.
Return of tax.
Taxes paid on exempt eggs or processed eggs,
§106-245.34.
Rules and regulations.
Promulgation, §106-245.32.

EGGS, §§106-245.13 to 106-245.28.
Advertising.
Designation in block letters, §106-245.20.
Agents.
Act of agent as that of principal, §106-245.28.
Aiding and abetting.
Violations of egg act.
Persons punishable as principals,
§106-245.27(a), (b).
Citation of act, §106-245.13.
Commissioner of agriculture.
Defined, §106-245.14.
Power of commissioner, §106-245.23.
Sanitary conditions.
Approval of methods by commissioner,
§106-245.22(a).
Construction and interpretation.
Rule of construction, §106-245.13.
Containers.
Defined, §106-245.14.
Grades.
Designation of grade and class on containers
required, §106-245.15.
Conformity with designation, §106-245.15.
Exemption, §106-245.15.
Labeling on containers, §106-245.18(a).
Descriptive terms, §106-245.18(b).
Size or weight class.
Designation of grade and class on containers
required, §106-245.15.
Conformity with designation, §106-245.15.
Exemption, §106-245.15.
Criminal law and procedure.
Warnings in lieu of criminal prosecutions,
§106-245.25.
Definitions, §106-245.14.

EGGS —Cont'd

Grades.

Containers, designation of grade and class on, §106-245.15.

Defined, §106-245.14.

Establishment and promulgation of grades, §106-245.16.

Injunctions.

Granting temporary or permanent injunction, §106-245.24(b).

Invoices.

Copy of invoice to be filed, §106-245.19(b).

Furnishing to purchaser at time of delivery, §106-245.19(a).

Labels.

Container labeling, §106-245.18(a).

Descriptive terms, §106-245.18(b).

Misdemeanors.

Violations of egg law, §106-245.24.

Orders.

Stop-sale orders, §106-245.17.

Penalties.

Violations of the egg law, §106-245.24.

Principal and agent.

Act of agent as that of principal, §106-245.28.

Promotion of use and sale of agricultural products.

Generally, §§106-550 to 106-568.

See AGRICULTURAL PRODUCTS PROMOTION.

Promotion tax, §§106-245.30 to 106-245.39.

See EGG PROMOTION TAX.

Publications.

Rules and regulations to be published, §106-245.21.

Remedies.

Cumulative nature of remedies, §106-245.26.

Rules and regulations.

Publication and copies, §106-245.21.

Rules of construction, §106-245.13.

Sanitation.

Approval of methods by commissioner of agriculture, §106-245.22(a).

Scope of article, §106-245.13.

Short title, §106-245.13.

Size or weight classes.

Containers, designation of grade and class, §106-245.15.

Defined, §106-245.14.

Establishment and promulgation of classes, §106-245.16.

Standards for quality.

Defined, §106-245.14.

Establishment and promulgation of standards, §106-245.16.

Stop-sale orders.

Violations of article, §106-245.17.

Taxation.

Promotion tax, §§106-245.30 to 106-245.39.

See EGG PROMOTION TAX.

Title of article, §106-245.13.

Venue.

Proceedings for violations of article, §106-245.24(c).

Violations of article.

Penalties, §106-245.24(a).

Persons punishable as principals, §106-245.27(a), (b).

Stop-sale orders, §106-245.17.

Venue of proceedings, §106-245.24(c).

EIGHT LINER.

Video gaming machines.

Ban on new machines, regulation of existing machines, §§14-306.1A, 14-306.4.

EJECTMENT.

Expedited evictions of drug traffickers and other criminals, §§42-59 to 42-76.

See EXPEDITED EVICTIONS.

Landlord and tenant.

Residential tenants, §§42-25.6 to 42-25.9.

See LANDLORD AND TENANT.

Retaliatory eviction, §§42-37.1 to 42-37.3.

Summary ejectment, §§42-26 to 42-36.2.

See LANDLORD AND TENANT.

Small claim actions.

Form of complaint, §7A-232.

Practice and procedure in actions for summary ejectment, §7A-223.

Summary ejectment.

Defendant's bond for costs and damages in land actions.

Not required in summary ejectment action, §1-112(b).

Generally, §§42-26 to 42-36.2.

See LANDLORD AND TENANT.

Practice and procedure in actions for, §7A-223.

ELBOW PADS.

Skateboard parks.

Wearing required, §99E-23.

ELDERLY OR DISABLED PROPERTY TAX HOMESTEAD EXCLUSION, §105-277.1.

ELDERLY PERSONS.

See SENIOR CITIZENS.

ELECTIONEERING COMMUNICATIONS.

Automatic dialing and recorded message players.

Circumstances allowing, §75-104(b).

Candidate-specific communications, §§163-278.100 to 163-278.103.

Mass mailings and telephone banks, §§163-278.110 to 163-278.113.

Costs incurred for producing or airing.

Donation to further electioneering communication, §163-278.12C(c).

Reports to be filed, §163-278.12C(a).

Manner of filing, §163-278.12C(d).

Subsequent reports, §163-278.12C(b).

Time for, §163-278.12C(b).

Determination by state board as to status of communication.

Appeal of determination.

Candidate-specific communications, §§163-278.103(b), 163-278.113(b).

Mass mailings and telephone banks, §163-278.113(b).

Process for determining.

Candidate-specific communications, §§163-278.103(b), 163-278.113(b).

Mass mailings and telephone banks, §163-278.113(b).

Request for determination.

Candidate-specific communications, §§163-278.103(a), 163-278.113(a).

Mass mailings and telephone banks, §163-278.113(b).

Determining whether communication electioneering communication.

State board to develop process, §163-278.22.

ELECTIONEERING COMMUNICATIONS
—Cont'd
Disclosures, prohibited sources.
Mass mailings and telephone banks.
Candidate-specific communications,
§§163-278.110 to 163-278.113.
Election observers, prohibitions, §163-45.
Media outlets to require written authority,
§163-278.17(d).
Public campaign fund.
Determination of eligibility for matching funds,
§163-278.67(d), (e).
Reporting.
Costs incurred for producing or airing,
§163-278.12C.
Voter-owned elections act.
Determination of eligibility for matching funds,
§163-278.99B(d), (e).

ELECTION OFFENSES.
Generally.
See ELECTIONS.

ELECTION OFFICERS.
Accepting bribes, §163-275.
County boards of elections generally.
See COUNTY BOARDS OF ELECTIONS.
Precinct election officials, §§163-41 to 163-48.
See PRECINCT ELECTION OFFICIALS.
State board of elections generally.
See STATE BOARD OF ELECTIONS.

ELECTION OF RIGHTS AND REMEDIES.
Betterments.
Election by plaintiff that defendant take premises,
§1-347.
Bonds, surety.
Actions on bonds.
Suing officer individually, §58-76-10.
Judges.
Consolidated judicial retirement act.
Transfer of members to another system,
§135-70.
**Retirement system for teachers and state
employees.**
Consolidated judicial retirement act.
Optional allowance election, §135-61.
Transfer of members to another system,
§135-70.
State institutions of higher education.
Optional retirement program, §135-5.1(b).
Social security.
Coverage of governmental employees under title II
of social security act.
Local governmental employees' retirement
system.
Transfer of members to employment covered
by retirement system, §135-28.
Transfers from state to certain association
service, §135-27.
Uniform judicial retirement system.
Transfer of members to employment covered
by retirement system, §135-28.1.

**ELECTION OF TAX AGAINST WHICH CREDIT
CLAIMED.**
Business tax credit, §105-129.17(a).
**Tax incentives for new and expanding
businesses,** §105-129.5(a).

ELECTIONS.
Absentee ballots.
Generally, §§163-226 to 163-239.
See ABSENTEE BALLOTS.

ELECTIONS —Cont'd
Absentee ballots —Cont'd
Military and overseas voters.
Uniform military and overseas voters act,
§§163-258.1 to 163-258.31.
See ABSENTEE BALLOTS.
Voting in person on day of election, §163-258.28.
Abstracts.
Composite abstracts, §163-182.6(b).
Forms, §163-182.6(d).
Preparation by county board, §163-182.6(a).
Secretary of state, duties, §163-182.6(c).
Actions.
State board of elections.
Authority to assist in litigation, §163-25.
Address confidentiality program.
Substitute address.
Use by boards of elections, §15C-8(e).
Administrative procedure.
Precinct boundaries.
Exemption of state board of elections,
§163-132.5B.
Advertising.
Charges by media, §163-278.18(a), (b).
Disclosure requirements for media
advertisements, §§163-278.39 to 163-278.39C.
Definitions, §163-278.38Z.
Misrepresentation of authorization,
§163-278.39(c).
Requirements, §163-278.39(a), (b).
Scope, §163-278.39C.
Television and radio advertisements
supporting or opposing the nomination or
election of one or more clearly identified
candidates, §163-278.39A.
Scope of requirements, §163-278.39C.
Television and radio advertisements supporting
or opposing the nomination or election of
one or more clearly identified candidates.
Choice of supporting or opposing a candidate,
§163-278.39A(e).
Communications act of 1934.
Relation to, §163-278.39A(g).
Criminal liability not created,
§163-278.39A(i).
Expanded disclosure requirements,
§163-278.39A(a).
Radio, §163-278.39A(c).
Television, §163-278.39A(b).
Immunity of television or radio outlets,
§163-278.39A(h).
Join sponsors, §163-278.39A(e1).
Legal remedy, §163-278.39A(f).
Placement of disclosure statement in
advertisements, §163-278.39A(d).
Age.
Persons eighteen years of age, US Const Amd 26.
Qualifications of voters.
Minimum age, §163-55(a).
Right to vote not to be abridged on account of age,
US Const Amd 26.
Agriculture.
Commissioner of agriculture, §106-10.
Airports.
Special airport districts.
Bond elections, §63-87.
Creation, §63-80(c).
Alcoholic beverages.
See LOCAL OPTION ELECTIONS.

ELECTIONS —Cont'd
Appeals.
Contributions and expenditures in political
  campaigns.
  State board of elections.
    Appeals from board, §163-278.26.
Protest of election.
  Appeal of decision to state board, §163-182.11.
  Appeal of decision to superior court,
    §163-182.14(a), (b).
  Appeal to general assembly or house thereof,
    §163-182.14(c).
  Attorneys' fees not to be awarded against state
    board of elections, §163-182.14(d).
Arrest.
County boards of elections.
  Power to maintain order, §163-34.
Interference with voters.
  Election officers to cause violators to be
    arrested, §163-273(b).
Offenses by voters.
  Election officers to cause violators to be
    arrested, §163-273(b).
Precinct election officials.
  Power to maintain order, §163-48.
State board of elections.
  Power to maintain order, §163-24.
Assistance to voters.
Admission of person rendering assistance to
  voting booth, §163-166.8(c).
Generally, §163-166.8(a).
Request for, §163-166.8(b).
Assistants at polls.
Appointment.
  County boards of election, §163-42(a).
    Names recommended by political parties,
      §163-42(b).
  Emergency election day assistants, §163-42(c).
  Registered voters in other precincts, §163-42(b).
Compensation, §163-46.
Emergency election day assistants, §163-42(c).
Number appointed, §163-42(a).
Qualified voters in precinct appointed, §163-42(a).
Recommendation for appointment.
  Chairman of each political party, §163-42(b).
Student election assistants, §163-42.1.
Attorney general.
Date of election, §163-1(a).
Elective officers, NC Const Art III §7.
Vacancy in office.
  Election to fill, §163-8.
Ballot boxes.
State board of elections.
  Access to ballot boxes, §163-22(j).
Ballot counters, §163-43.
Ballots.
Absentee ballots generally, §§163-226 to 163-239.
  See ABSENTEE BALLOTS.
Arrangement of official ballots, §163-165.6.
Butterfly ballots.
  Use prohibited, §163-165.4B.
Candidate ballot items.
  Order of precedence, §163-165.6(a) to (d).
Changes.
  Late changes in ballots, §163-165.3(c).
Characteristics for official ballots, §163-165.4.
Coding of ballots.
  Duties of state board, §163-165.3(a).
Combining ballot items on single ballot,
  §163-165.5B.
Confidentiality of voted ballots, §163-165.1(e).

ELECTIONS —Cont'd
Ballots —Cont'd
Contents of official ballots, §163-165.5.
Counting ballots. See within this heading,
  "Counting ballots."
Counting of votes, §§163-182 to 163-182.5.
County boards of elections.
  Preparation and production of official ballots
    and instructions, §163-165.3(b).
Documents resembling official ballot.
  Disclaimer, §163-165.2(b).
Headings of official ballots, §163-165.5.
Instructions to voters.
  English and Spanish, §163-165.5A.
  Posting of voter information, §163-166.7A.
  Preparation and production by county boards,
    §163-165.3(b).
Lever machines, use of, §163-165.4A(a1).
  Effective date of provision, §163-165.4A(b).
New elections.
  Candidates on ballot, §163-182.13(e).
Other uses prohibited, §163-165.1(d).
Persons previously registered by mail who have
  not voted for federal office.
  Exemptions, §163-166.12(d).
  Identification proof submitted by voter.
    County board to note, §163-166.12(b1).
    Voting when identification numbers not
      matched, §163-166.12(b2).
  In-person voting, §163-166.12(a).
  Mail-in absentee voting, §163-166.12(b).
  Provisional voting, §163-166.12(c).
Primary elections.
  Order of candidates, §163-165.6(c).
Provisional ballots.
  Persons previously registered by mail,
    §163-166.12(c).
  Posting of voter information, §163-166.7A(a).
  Procedures generally, §163-166.11.
  Voting after hours, §163-166.01.
Punch-card ballots.
  Use prohibited, §163-165.4A(a).
    Effective date, §163-165.4A(b).
Referendum questions.
  Order of precedence, §163-165.6(g).
Requirements, §163-165.1(b).
  Compliance with provisions, §163-165.1(c).
Return and accounting of ballots.
  Procedures after close of voting, §163-166.10.
Sample ballots, §163-165.2(a).
  Posting of voter information, §163-166.7A(a).
Scope of provisions, §163-165.1(a).
Special ballots, §163-165.3(d).
Standards for official ballots, §163-165.4.
State board of elections.
  Responsibilities in connection with official
    ballots, §163-165.3(a), (c), (d).
Straight-party voting, §163-165.6(e).
Voted ballots.
  Confidentiality and disclosure, §163-165.1(e).
Voting procedures.
  Distribution of official ballots, §163-166.7(b).
Write-in voting, §163-165.6(f).
Blind persons.
Assistance to voters, §163-166.8.
Boards of elections.
County boards of elections, §§163-30 to 163-37.
  See COUNTY BOARDS OF ELECTIONS.
Political activities by board members and
  employees, §§163-38 to 163-40.1.
  Applicability of provisions, §163-38.

ELECTIONS —Cont'd
Boards of elections —Cont'd
Political activities by board members and
    employees —Cont'd
    Definitions and proof of terms used, provision
        applicable, §163-40.1.
    Limitation on activities, §163-39.
    Removal, violation grounds for, §163-40.
State board of elections, §§163-19 to 163-28.
    See STATE BOARD OF ELECTIONS.
Boundaries.
Precincts, §§163-132.3 to 163-132.5F.
Bribery.
Officers of elections.
    Accepting bribes.
        Felony, §163-275.
Butner advisory council, §122C-413(a) to (d1).
Butterfly ballot.
Use prohibited, §163-165.4B.
Campaign contributions and expenditures.
Coercing state employees to contribute, §§126-14,
    126-14.1.
Counties.
    Use of public funds to endorse or oppose a
        referendum, election or particular candidate
        prohibited, §153A-456.
Generally, §§163-278.5 to 163-278.38.
    See CAMPAIGN FINANCE.
Local boards of education.
    Political endorsements or oppositions.
        Public funds, restriction on use for political
            activities, §115C-46.1.
Municipal campaign reporting, §§163-278.40 to
    163-278.40J.
    See CAMPAIGN FINANCE.
Municipalities.
    Endorsement, opposition to referendum,
        election, particular candidate.
        Using municipal funds prohibited,
            §160A-499.3.
Public campaign fund, §§163-278.61 to 163-278.70.
Candidates.
Automatic dialing and recorded message players.
    Circumstances allowing, §75-104(b).
Challenge to a candidacy, §§163-127.1 to
    163-127.6.
    Appeals, §163-127.6.
    Board rulemaking authority, §163-127.4(e).
    Burden of proof, §163-127.5(a), (b).
    Compelling attendance of witnesses,
        §163-127.4(a).
    Conduct of hearing by panel, §§163-127.3,
        163-127.4.
    Defect discovered after deadline, §163-127.2(c).
    Definitions, §163-127.1.
    Depositions, §163-127.4(a).
    Evidence, presentation of, §163-127.4(c).
    Findings of fact and conclusions of law,
        §163-127.4(d).
    Grounds for protest, §163-127.2(c).
    How made, §163-127.2(b).
    Multicounty.
        Appeal from, §163-127.6(a).
        Hearing on challenge, §163-127.3(a)(2).
    Notice of hearing, §163-127.4(b).
    Production of documents and things,
        §163-127.4(a).
    Question of residency, §163-127.5(b).
    Recordation of proceedings, §163-127.4(c).
    Single county, §163-127.3(a)(3).
        Hearing on challenge, §163-127.3(a)(1).

ELECTIONS —Cont'd
Candidates —Cont'd
Challenge to a candidacy —Cont'd
    Single or multicounty panel, §163-127.6(a).
    Statewide panel, §163-127.6(b).
    Time and place, §163-127.4(a).
    When made, §163-127.2(a).
Contributions not part of personal estate,
    §163-278.16B(c).
Death or incapacity.
    Designation of uses of contributions made,
        §163-278.16B(c).
Economic interest statements, §138A-22(d), (d1).
    Notice by state board of elections, §138A-22(e).
Municipal elections generally.
    See MUNICIPAL ELECTIONS.
No run for 2 separate offices at same time,
    §163-124(a).
    Applicability, §163-124(b).
    Exception, §163-124(a).
Political parties.
    Certificate of party affiliation, §163-106(f).
Primary elections.
    Certificate of registration, §163-106(f).
    Death of candidate before primary.
        Filling vacancy, §163-112.
    Felony convictions, disclosure of, §163-106(a1).
    Nomination determined by substantial
        plurality, §163-111(a).
    Nominee's right to withdraw as candidate,
        §163-113.
    Notice of candidacy, §163-106(a).
        Certification, §163-108(a) to (d).
        Acknowledgment, §163-108(d).
        Eligibility to file, §163-106(b).
        Felony convictions, disclosure of,
            §163-106(a1).
        Filing fees, §163-107(a).
        Petition in lieu of payment of fee,
            §163-107.1.
        Refund, §163-107(b).
        Filing for more than one office, §163-106(h).
        Inspection of registration records upon receipt
            of notice, §163-106(g).
        Petition in lieu of payment of filing fee.
            County, municipal and district primaries,
                §163-107.1(c).
            Generally, §163-107.1(a), (b).
            Nonpartisan primaries and elections,
                §163-107.1(d).
        Time for filing, §163-106(c).
        Vacancies in office.
            Notice of candidacy for certain offices to
                indicate vacancy, §163-106(d).
        Withdrawal, §163-106(e).
    Presidential preference primary.
        Names to appear on ballot or voting machine,
            §163-213.7.
        Nomination by petition, §§163-213.5,
            163-213.6.
        Nomination by state board of elections,
            §§163-213.4, 163-213.6.
        Notification of nomination, §163-213.6.
    Sole candidate declared nominee, §163-110.
    Unaffiliated voters, §163-119.
    Withdrawal.
        Nominee's right to withdraw as candidate,
            §163-113.
State board of elections.
    Certifying names of candidates to county board,
        §163-22(h).

ELECTIONS —Cont'd
Candidates —Cont'd
Two sperate offices.
  Candidate not to run for, §163-124(a).
    Applicability, §163-124(b).
    Exception, §163-124(a).
Unaffiliated candidate.
  Nomination by petition, §163-122(a).
    Cancellation of petition.
      Failure to meet qualifications for office,
        §163-122(d).
    Filing fee, §163-122(e).
    Form, §163-122(b).
    Inapplicability of provisions, §163-122(c).
Write-in candidates.
  Counting and recording of votes, §163-123(f).
  Declaration of intent, §163-123(b).
  Defeated primary candidate, §163-123(e).
  Municipal and nonpartisan elections excluded,
    §163-123(g).
  Petitions, §163-123(c).
    Forms, §163-123(d).
  Procedure for qualifying as, §163-123(a).
Canvassing votes.
County board, §163-182.5(b).
Definitions of canvass, §163-182.5(a).
State board, §163-182.5(c).
Capitation tax prohibited, NC Const Art V §1.
Census data by precinct, §163-132.5F.
Certain acts declared misdemeanors.
Class 1 misdemeanors, §163-274(b).
Class 2 misdemeanors, §163-274(a).
Certificate of election.
Appeal of decision to superior court.
  Stay of certificate, §163-182.14(a), (b).
Contributions and expenditures in political
  campaigns.
  Filing of statements as prerequisite,
    §163-278.25.
Copy to secretary of state, §163-182.15(c).
Governor to issue commission upon certification of
  election.
  Certain offices, §163-182.16.
Municipal elections.
  Chairman of election to furnish certificate,
    §163-301.
When county board to issue, §163-182.15(a).
When state board to issue, §163-182.15(b).
Certificate of nomination.
Copy to secretary of state, §163-182.15(c).
When county board to issue, §163-182.15(a).
When state board to issue, §163-182.15(b).
Challenge of voters.
Absentee ballots.
  Burden of proof, §163-89(c).
  Hearing, §163-89(e).
  Separate challenge to each ballot, §163-89(c).
  Signing of challenge, §163-89(c).
  Time for challenge, §163-89(a).
  To whom challenge addressed, §163-89(d).
  Who may challenge, §163-89(b).
Burden of proof, §163-90.1(b).
  Challenge to absentee ballots, §163-89(c).
Day of primary or election.
  Authorized, §163-87.
  Grounds, §163-87.
  Hearing, §163-88.
  Oath of challenged registrant, §163-88.
  Request for challenged ballot, §163-88.1(a), (b).
    Preservation of such ballots, §163-88.1(c).

ELECTIONS —Cont'd
Challenge of voters —Cont'd
Felonies.
  Answer to challenge as felon not to be used on
    prosecution, §163-90.
Hearings.
  Challenge on day of primary or election,
    §163-88.
  Challenge other than on day of primary or
    election, §163-86.
  Challenge to absentee ballots, §163-89(e).
Municipal elections, §163-289.
Notice.
  Challenge on other than day of primary or
    election, §163-86(d).
Oaths.
  Challenge on day of primary or election.
    Challenged registrant, §163-88.
  Challenge other than on day of primary or
    election.
    Challenged registrant, §163-86(c).
  False swearing.
    Felony, §163-90.3.
Other than on day of primary or election.
  Action by county board of elections on
    challenge, §163-85(b).
  Grounds, §163-85(c).
    Challenge to specify, §163-85(b).
  Hearing, §163-86(a).
    Appearance by challenged registrant,
      §163-86(d).
    Notice, §163-86(b).
    Scheduling, §163-85(d).
  Notice of challenge, §163-86(b).
  Oath of challenged registrant, §163-86(c).
  Time for challenge, §163-84.
  Voter no longer residing in precinct, prima facie
    evidence, §163-85(e).
  Who may challenge, §163-85(a).
Overruled or dismissed challenge.
  Action by board on, §163-90.2(c).
  Appeals, §163-90.2(d).
Reasonable belief by challenger required,
  §163-90.1(a).
Sustained challenge.
  Action by board on, §163-90.2(a), (b).
  Appeals, §163-90.2(d).
Challenge to a candidacy, §§163-127.1 to
163-127.6.
Changes affecting voting.
Voting rights act of 1965.
  Submissions to attorney general of United
    States, §§120-30.9A to 120-30.9I.
Citizenship.
Presidential elections.
  Residence period for presidential elections, NC
    Const Art VI §2.
State elections.
  Residence period for state elections, NC Const
    Art VI §2.
Closing voting places.
Hours for voting, §163-166.01.
Coercing person to register or to vote,
§163-275.
Community colleges.
Financial support.
  Elections on questions of appropriations.
    See COMMUNITY COLLEGES.
Composite abstracts, §163-182.6(b).
Confidentiality.
Address confidentiality program.
  Substitute address.
    Use by boards of elections, §15C-8(e).

ELECTIONS —Cont'd
Confidentiality —Cont'd
Voted ballots, §163-165.1(e).
Congress.
Contributions and expenditures in political
  campaigns.
  Candidates for federal office to file information
    report, §163-278.30.
Date of elections, §163-1(a).
Districts.
  General assembly apportionment act.
    Compliance with federal law, §163-201.2(c).
    Limitation on number of divisions,
      §163-201.2(b).
    Restriction, §163-201.2(a).
  Names and boundaries.
    Area not assigned to district, §163-201(d).
  Number of districts, §163-201(a).
  Severability of congressional apportionment
    acts, §163-201.1.
  Specified, §163-201(a).
  Voting tabulation district boundary changed.
    Congressional district boundary not changed,
      §163-201(c).
House of representatives.
  Reapportionment.
    Election after reapportionment, §163-202.
Senate.
  Vacancy in office, §§163-12, 163-115(e).
Severability of congressional apportionment acts,
  §163-201.1.
Vacancies in office.
  Filling.
    House of representatives, §§163-13,
      163-115(b).
    Senate, §§163-12, 163-115(e).
Consolidated city-county act.
Bond issues, §160B-14.
Contests.
Executive branch.
  Applicability of procedures, §163-182.13A(a), (i).
  Basis for decision, §163-182.13A(f).
  Copies of filings, §163-182.13A(h).
  Definition of contest, §163-182.13A(l).
  Final determination, §163-182.13A(e), (g).
    Not reviewable, §163-182.13A(k).
  Joint ballot of both houses of general assembly,
    §163-182.13A(e).
  General assembly to determine, NC Const Art
    VI §5.
  Judicial proceedings abated, §163-182.13A(j).
  Jurisdiction of general assembly,
    §163-182.13A(c).
  Notice of intent to contest, §163-182.13A(b).
  Select committee of general assembly,
    §163-182.13A(d).
General assembly members, §§120-10.1 to
  120-10.14.
  See GENERAL ASSEMBLY.
Legal expense funds for elected officials,
  §§163-278.300 to 163-278.320.
  See LEGAL EXPENSE FUNDS FOR ELECTED
    OFFICIALS.
Continuation in office, NC Const Art VI §10.
**Contributions and expenditures in political
  campaigns.**
Generally, §§163-278.5 to 163-278.38.
  See CAMPAIGN FINANCE.
Municipal campaign reporting, §§163-278.40 to
  163-278.40J.
  See CAMPAIGN FINANCE.

ELECTIONS —Cont'd
Convention of the people.
Procedure for calling, NC Const Art XIII §1.
Coroners, §152-1.
Date of election, §163-1(a).
Corruption.
Convicted officials.
  Disqualification from voting, §163-276.
  Removal from office, §163-276.
District attorneys.
  Investigation and prosecution of violations,
    §163-278.
Felonies.
  Certain acts declared felonies, §163-275.
Fraud.
  Felonies, §163-275.
Interference with voters.
  Duties of election officers upon, §163-273(b).
  Prohibited acts, §163-273(a).
Intimidation of voters by officers, §163-271.
Misdemeanors.
  Generally, §§163-271 to 163-274.
  Offenses of voters, §163-273(a).
  Duties of election officers upon, §163-273(b).
Penalties.
  Felonies, §163-275.
State board of elections.
  Investigation of violations, §163-278.
Witnesses.
  Self-incrimination.
    Immunity from prosecution, §163-277.
  Subpoenas, §§163-277, 163-278.
  Powers of district attorneys, §163-278.
Counties.
Alcoholic beverages.
  See LOCAL OPTION ELECTIONS.
Boards of commissioners, §153A-34.
  Altering mode of elections, §153A-58.
  Modification of structures of boards, §§153A-61
    to 153A-64.
Voting systems.
  Powers and duties as to, §163-165.8.
Consolidation.
  Plans proposed by governmental study
    commissions, §153A-405(a) to (e).
Electoral districts, §153A-22.
  Map of districts, §153A-20.
Endorsement, opposition to referendum, election,
  political candidate.
  Use of public funds prohibited, §153A-456.
Industrial development.
  Tax elections, §§158-16 to 158-24.
Sales and use tax.
  Local government sales and use tax.
    Election on adoption.
      First one-cent tax, §105-465.
Sheriffs, NC Const Art VII §2.
Structure of boards of commissioners.
  Alteration.
    Effective date, §153A-62.
    Initiation of alterations by resolution.
      Filing copy, §153A-63.
    Submission of proposition to voters, §153A-61.
      Filing results of election, §153A-64.
Taxation.
  Property taxes, §153A-149.
Time generally, §163-1(a).
Watershed improvement programs, §§139-39,
  139-40.
Counting ballots.
Chief judge of precinct, duties, §163-182.3.

ELECTIONS —Cont'd
Counting ballots —Cont'd
County boards of elections.
Duties as to, §163-33.
Definitions, §163-182.
Elections by people to be by ballot, NC Const Art
VI §5.
General principles, §163-182.1(a).
Initial ballot count.
General principles, §163-182.2(a).
Rules promulgation, §163-182.2(b).
Jurisdiction.
County board, §163-182.4(a).
Duties of those having jurisdiction,
§163-182.4(c).
State board, §163-182.4(b).
Military voting absentee.
See ABSENTEE BALLOTS.
Official ballots only, §163-182.1(a).
Political parties.
New political party, §163-98.
Presidential elections.
Electors.
Names not printed on ballots, §163-209.
Presidential preference primaries, §163-213.7.
Presidential preference primaries, §163-213.7.
Promulgation of rules, §163-182.1(b).
Protest filed with county board, §163-182.9.
Standards and procedures, adoption,
§163-182.1(b).
State board of elections.
Duties as to, §163-22(e), (f).
Write-in votes, §163-182.1(a).
County boards of elections, §§163-30 to 163-37.
See COUNTY BOARDS OF ELECTIONS.
Court of appeals.
Judges of court elected by qualified voters, §7A-16,
NC Const Art IV §16.
Judicial voter guide.
Candidate information, §163-278.69(b).
Disclaimer statement, §163-278.69(c).
Publication by board, §163-278.69(a).
Public campaign fund, §§163-278.61 to 163-278.70.
Criminal offenses.
Absentee ballot violations, §§163-226.3(a),
163-237.
County boards of elections, §163-236.
Appropriations from North Carolina political
parties financing fund.
Violations of provisions, §163-278.44.
Certain acts declared felonies, §163-275.
Certain acts declared misdemeanors, §163-274.
Challenge of voters.
False swearing, §163-90.3.
Contributions and expenditures in political
campaigns.
Disclosure requirements for media
advertisements.
Misrepresentation of authorization,
§163-278.39(c).
False certification knowing information to be
untrue, criminal penalty, §§163-278.27(a1),
163-278.32.
Fundraising from lobbyists, §163-278.13(a), (d).
Limitation on contribution violations,
§163-278.13(f).
Violations by business organizations and labor
unions, §§163-278.19(a), 163-278.27(a2).
Violations generally, §163-278.27(a).
Interference with voters, §163-273.
Intimidation of voters by officers, §163-271.

ELECTIONS —Cont'd
Criminal offenses —Cont'd
Misdemeanor punishments, §163-272.1.
Offenses by voters, §163-273.
Signing name of another on petition, §163-221(c).
Voting systems.
Vendors.
Willful violation of duties, §163-165.9A(b).
Curbside voting, §163-166.9.
Death of candidate before primary.
Filling vacancy, §163-112.
Definitions, §163-165.
Butterfly ballot, §163-165.4B.
Challenge to a candidacy, §163-127.1.
Contributions and expenditures in political
campaigns, §163-278.6.
Election, §§163-278.6, 163-278.13(d).
Political party, §§163-278.6, 163-278.13(e).
Counting ballots, canvassing votes, etc., §163-182.
Election.
Residence requirement, §163-55(c).
Funds.
Appropriations from North Carolina political
parties financing fund, §163-278.45.
Political parties, §§163-96(a), 163-278.6,
163-278.13(e).
Residence, §163-57.
Uniform military and overseas voters act,
§163-258.2.
Dental examiners board, §90-22(c).
Disabled persons.
Accessible polling places, §163-131.
Satellite voting places for disabled voters,
§163-130.
Disabled voters.
Assistance to voters, §163-166.8.
Curbside voting, §163-166.9.
Discrimination.
Voting rights act of 1965.
Submission of charges to United States attorney
general, §§120-30.9A to 120-30.9I. See
within this heading, "Voting rights act of
1965."
Disqualifications for office, NC Const Art VI §8.
District attorneys.
Corruption.
Investigation and prosecution of violations,
§163-278.
Prosecutorial districts, §7A-60(a).
Vacancies in office.
Election to fill, §163-10.
District courts.
Judges of district courts, §7A-140.
Generally, §§163-321 to 163-335.
See DISTRICT COURT JUDGES.
Dual office holding, NC Const Art VI §9.
Running for 2 separate offices at same time.
Prohibition, exception, §163-124.
Economic interest statements.
Candidates for public office, §138A-22(d), (d1).
Notice by state board of elections, §138A-22(e).
Education.
Commission.
Officers, §143-262.
Local boards of education, §§115C-35(a), 115C-37.
Elected officers, NC Const Art III §7.
Electioneering communications.
Candidate-specific communications, §§163-278.100
to 163-278.103.
Contents of disclosure, §163-278.101(b).
Mass mailings and telephone banks,
§163-278.111(b).

ELECTIONS —Cont'd
Electioneering communications —Cont'd
  Candidate-specific communications —Cont'd
    Definitions, §163-278.100.
    Determination if communication is
      candidate-specific, §163-278.103.
      Mass mailings and telephone banks,
        §163-278.113.
    Disclosure statement required, §163-278.101(a).
      Mass mailings and telephone banks,
        §163-278.111(a).
    Mass mailings and telephone banks.
      Definitions, §163-278.110.
    Organization of multiple organizations to avoid
      compliance, §163-278.101(c).
      Mass mailings and telephone banks,
        §163-278.111(c).
    Penalties, §163-278.102.
      Mass mailings and telephone banks,
        §163-278.112.
  Costs incurred for producing or airing.
    Donation to further electioneering
      communication, §163-278.12C(c).
    Reports to be filed, §163-278.12C(a).
      Manner of filing, §163-278.12C(d).
      Subsequent reports, §163-278.12C(b).
      Time for, §163-278.12C(b).
  Determination by state board as to status of
    communication.
    Appeal of determination.
      Candidate-specific communications,
        §§163-278.103(b), 163-278.113(b).
      Mass mailings and telephone banks,
        §163-278.113(b).
    Process for determining.
      Candidate-specific communications,
        §§163-278.103(b), 163-278.113(b).
      Mass mailings and telephone banks,
        §163-278.113(b).
    Process for determining, board to develop,
      §163-278.22.
    Request for determination.
      Candidate-specific communications,
        §§163-278.103(a), 163-278.113(a).
      Mass mailings and telephone banks,
        §163-278.113(b).
  Media outlets to require written authority,
    §163-278.17(d).
  Reporting.
    Costs incurred for producing or airing,
      §163-278.12C.
Eligibility to elective office, NC Const Art VI §6.
Eligibility to vote, NC Const Art VI §1.
Executive branch.
  Contested elections.
    Applicability of procedures, §163-182.13A(a), (i).
    Basis for decision, §163-182.13A(f).
    Copies of filings, §163-182.13A(h).
    Definition of contest, §163-182.13A(l).
    Final determination, §163-182.13A(e), (g).
      Not reviewable, §163-182.13A(k).
    Joint ballot of both houses of general assembly,
      §163-182.13A(e).
    General assembly to determine, NC Const Art
      VI §5.
    Judicial proceedings abated, §163-182.13A(j).
    Jurisdiction of general assembly,
      §163-182.13A(c).
    Notice of intent to contest, §163-182.13A(b).
    Select committee of general assembly,
      §163-182.13A(d).

ELECTIONS —Cont'd
Expenses.
  Primary elections.
    Payment, §163-105.
Faithless elector statute.
  Failure of presidential elector to attend and vote,
    §163-212.
Felonies.
  Absentee ballots.
    Prohibited act, §163-226.3(a).
  Challenge of voters.
    Answer to challenge as felon not to be used on
      prosecution, §163-90.
    False swearing, §163-90.3.
  Corruption.
    Certain acts declared felonies, §163-275.
  Disqualification from office, NC Const Art VI §8.
  Disqualification from voting, §163-55(a), NC Const
    Art VI §2.
Fines.
  Penalties for misdemeanors, §163-272.1.
Fire district elections.
  Absentee voting not permitted, §163-226(b).
Fish and fisheries.
  Coastal fisheries and seafood industry promotion
    referenda, §§113-312 to 113-315.7.
Forgery.
  Absentee ballots, §163-237(c).
Fraud.
  Absentee ballots.
    Misdemeanors, §163-237(c).
  Felonies, §163-275.
  Registration of voters.
    Felonies, §163-275.
  State bureau of investigation.
    Authority to make investigations, §114-15(a).
Free elections, NC Const Art I §10.
Frequent elections required, NC Const Art I §9.
Full-time election offices.
  County boards of elections.
    Modified full-time offices, §163-36.
Funds.
  Political parties financing fund, §§163-278.41 to
    163-278.45.
Gambling.
  Bet or wager on election.
    Misdemeanor, §163-274(a).
General assembly, NC Const Art II §8.
  Apportionment act.
    Congressional districts, §§163-201 to 163-201.2.
  Contests, §§120-10.1 to 120-10.14.
    See GENERAL ASSEMBLY.
  Corrupt practices in election.
    Expulsion for corrupt practices, §120-8.
  Date of election, §163-1(a).
  Elections by general assembly to be by viva voce,
    NC Const Art VI §5.
  House of representatives.
    Nomination of candidates, §163-108.1.
  Joint legislative elections oversight committee,
    §§120-70.140 to 120-70.143.
  Primaries moved from date provided.
    Holding on same day, §163-1(d).
Governor, NC Const Art III §2.
  Commission of certain offices issued upon
    certification of election, §163-182.16.
  Date of election, §163-1(a).
  Governor-elect and lieutenant governor-elect.
    Office space and expenses, §147-31.1.
  Summary of duties.
    Counting votes, canvassing, abstracts and
      protests, §163-182.17(f).

ELECTIONS —Cont'd
Governor —Cont'd
Vacancy in office.
Election to fill, §163-8.
Hand counting of ballots, §163-182.1(a).
Hearings.
Challenge of voters.
Challenge on day of primary or election,
§163-88.
Challenge other than on day of primary or
election, §163-86.
Challenge to absentee ballots, §163-89(e).
Help America Vote act compliance.
Complaint procedure.
Administrative procedure act exemptions,
§163-91(b), (c).
Establishment, §163-91(a).
Proposed plan, §163-91(b).
Computerized voter registration, §163-82.11(c).
Drivers' license offices, duties, §163-82.19(b).
Election fund established, §163-82.28.
Generally, §163-82.27.
Posting of voter information, §163-166.7A(b).
Holidays.
Election day as public holiday, §103-4(a).
Hospital districts.
Referendum on repeal of tax levy, §131E-46(a) to
(d).
Hours for voting, §163-166.01.
Husband and wife.
Precinct election officials.
Certain relatives prohibited from serving
together, §163-41.1.
Residence.
Eligibility to establish separate domicile,
§163-57.
Inaugural ceremonies committee, §§143-532 to
143-539.
Industrial development.
Tax elections for industrial development purposes,
§§158-16 to 158-24.
Injunctions.
Contributions and expenditures in political
campaigns.
Violations of provisions, §163-278.28(a).
Insurance commissioner, §58-2-5.
Interference with voters, §163-273.
Intimidation.
Officers of election.
Felony, §163-275.
Voters.
Intimidation by officers, §163-271.
Misdemeanor, §163-274(a).
Investigations.
County boards of elections, §163-33.
State board of elections, §163-22(d).
Judges of election.
Appointment, §163-41(a).
Chief judge, §163-47.
Compensation, §163-46.
Counting ballots.
Chief judge of precinct, duties, §163-182.3.
Duties, §163-47.
Jurisdiction.
Counting ballots, §163-182.4.
Labor.
Commissioner of labor, §95-2.
Date of election, §163-1.
Lawyer candidate for judicial office.
Compliance with Code of Judicial Conduct,
ProfCond Rule 8.2.

ELECTIONS —Cont'd
Legal expense funds for elected officials,
§§163-278.300 to 163-278.320.
See LEGAL EXPENSE FUNDS FOR ELECTED
OFFICIALS.
Libel and slander.
False and derogatory reports as to candidates.
Misdemeanors, §163-274(a).
Libraries and librarians.
Registration of voters.
Designation of library employees to register
voters, §153A-272.
Lieutenant governor, NC Const Art III §2.
Date of election, §163-1(a).
Vacancy in office.
Election to fill, §163-8.
Literacy.
Qualifications of voters, NC Const Art VI §4.
Littering.
County boards of elections.
Littering notification, §163-33.3.
State board of elections.
Littering notification, §163-22.3.
Livestock.
Tuberculosis.
Appropriations by counties for eradication of
tuberculosis, §§106-343, 106-344.
Lobbyists.
Influencing, prohibition, §120C-301.
Local boards of education.
Election of members, §§115C-35(a), 115C-37.
Public funds, restriction on use for political
activities, §115C-46.1.
Local development.
Industrial development taxation, §§158-16 to
158-24.
Married women.
Residence.
Eligibility to establish separate domicile,
§163-57.
Media advertising.
Disclosure requirements for media
advertisements, §§163-278.39 to 163-278.39C.
Metropolitan sewerage districts.
Assumption of sewerage system indebtedness of
political subdivision by district, §162A-77.
Inclusion of additional political subdivision or
unincorporated areas, §162A-68(d).
Merger of metropolitan sewerage districts into
cities or towns, §162A-77.1.
Metropolitan water districts.
Inclusion of unincorporated area, §162A-35.
Military and overseas voters.
Registration of voters.
Change of status of covered voter registering
under article.
Validity of registration, §163-258.27.
Declaration accompanying federal write-in
absentee ballot.
Method used to register, §163-258.6(b).
Electronic transmission system.
Capability to accept registration method,
§163-258.6(c).
Federal postcard application.
Method used to register, §163-258.6(a).
Receipt of registration prior to election.
Time, §163-258.6(d).
Registration in person including day of election
or primary, §163-258.28.
Uniform military and overseas voters act,
§§163-258.1 to 163-258.31.
See ABSENTEE BALLOTS.

ELECTIONS —Cont'd
Military and overseas voters —Cont'd
Voting in person on day of election, §163-258.28.
Mosquito control districts.
Formation of districts.
Procedure for forming, §130A-353(b) to (g).
Mountain ridge protection.
Exemption from coverage, binding referendum, §113A-214(a).
Municipalities.
Electoral districts.
Census 2010 redistricting data program.
Purpose, §163-132.1B(a).
Reporting of unchanged voting tabulation districts, §163-132.1B(a2).
Reporting of voting tabulation districts, §163-132.1B(a1).
Rules and regulations, §163-132.1B(b).
Endorsement, opposition to referendum, election, particular candidate.
Using municipal funds prohibited, §160A-499.3.
Generally, §§163-279 to 163-306.
See MUNICIPAL ELECTIONS.
Municipal campaign reporting, §§163-278.40 to 163-278.40J.
See CAMPAIGN FINANCE.
Nepotism.
Precinct election officials.
Certain relatives prohibited from serving together, §163-41.1.
New elections.
Candidates on ballot, §163-182.13(e).
Jurisdiction, §163-182.13(d).
Procedures set by state board, §163-182.13(b).
Tie votes, §163-182.13(f).
Voter eligibility, §163-182.13(c).
When ordered, §163-182.13(a).
Nonpartisan elections.
County board of elections.
Notice of candidacy, §163-106(a).
Local boards of education, §115C-37(a), (h).
Municipal elections generally.
See MUNICIPAL ELECTIONS.
Sanitary districts, board members, §139-6.
Write-in candidates.
Municipal and nonpartisan elections excluded, §163-123(g).
Notice.
Challenge of voters.
Challenge on other than day of primary or election, §163-86(d).
County boards of elections.
Duties of boards, §163-33.
Military and overseas voters.
Electronic notice, §163-258.16.
Municipal campaign reporting.
Notice of reports due, §163-278.40H.
Precinct boundaries.
Alterations to approved precinct boundaries.
Disapproval, §163-132.3(c).
Presidential preference primaries.
National committees of political parties to be notified of provisions, §163-213.9.
Nomination.
Notification to candidates, §163-213.6.
Primary elections.
Candidacy, §163-106(a).
Certification of notice of candidacy, §163-108(a) to (d).
Acknowledgment, §163-108(d).

ELECTIONS —Cont'd
Notice —Cont'd
Primary elections —Cont'd
Candidacy —Cont'd
Filing fees, §163-107(a).
Petition in lieu of payment of fee, §163-107.1.
Refund, §163-107(b).
Petition in lieu of payment of filing fee, §163-107.1(a), (b).
County, municipal and district primaries, §163-107.1(c).
Nonpartisan primaries and elections, §163-107.1(d).
Time for filing, §163-106(c).
Vacancies in office.
Notice of candidacy for certain offices to indicate vacancy, §163-106(d).
Withdrawal of notice of candidacy, §163-106(e).
Protest filed with county board.
Appeal of decision to state board, §163-182.11(a).
Notice of hearing, §163-182.10(b).
Special elections.
Municipality holding, §163-287.
Oaths.
Challenge of voters.
Challenge on day of primary or election.
Challenged registrant, §163-88.
Challenge other than on day of primary or election.
Challenged registrant, §163-86(c).
False swearing, §163-90.3.
County boards of elections.
Oath of office of members, §163-30.
Power of chairman to administer, §163-33.1.
False swearing.
Felony, §163-275.
Precinct assistants, §163-42(d).
Precinct election officials.
Oaths of office.
Ballot counters, §163-43.
Judges of election and registrars, §163-41(a).
State board of elections.
Oath of office of members, §163-19.
Offenses by voters, §163-273.
Officers of elections.
Bribery.
Accepting bribes, §163-275.
County boards of elections generally.
See COUNTY BOARDS OF ELECTIONS.
Delegation of tasks among, §163-166.6.
Intimidation of officers.
Felony, §163-275.
Precinct election officials, §§163-41 to 163-48.
See PRECINCT ELECTION OFFICIALS.
State board of elections generally.
See STATE BOARD OF ELECTIONS.
One stop voting.
Buffer zones, §163-166.4(d).
Procedure, §163-227.2.
Opening voting places.
Hours for voting, §163-166.01.
Ordinances.
Ballots.
Submission of proposition to voters, §160A-105.
Out-out-precinct voting places, §163-130.1.
Overvotes.
Counting ballots, §163-182.1(a).

ELECTIONS —Cont'd
Parent and child.
Precinct election officials.
Certain relatives prohibited from serving
together, §163-41.1.
Perjury.
Corruptly taking oath prescribed for voters,
§163-275.
Personnel system.
Interchange of governmental employees.
Authority to interchange employees.
Participation of elected officials in program,
§126-53(d).
Petitions.
Limitation on petitions, §163-219.
Petition circulated prior to July 1, 1957,
§163-220.
Notice of circulation of petition.
Registration, §163-218.
Petition void after one year from registration,
§163-219.
Political parties.
New political party.
Petition for formation, §163-96(b).
Presidential preference primaries.
Nomination by petition, §§163-213.5, 163-213.6.
Notification to candidates, §163-213.6.
Primary elections.
Notice of candidacy.
Petition in lieu of payment of filing fee,
§163-107.1.
Signing name of another.
Penalty, §163-221(c).
Prohibited, §163-221(a), (b).
Unaffiliated candidate.
Nomination by petition, §163-122.
Political activities of government employees,
§§126-13 to 126-15.1.
See POLITICAL ACTIVITIES.
Political advertising.
Candidate-specific communications, §§163-278.110
to 163-278.113.
Charges, §163-278.18(a), (b).
Disclosure requirements for media
advertisements, §§163-278.39 to 163-278.39C.
Mass mailings and telephone banks.
Candidate-specific communications,
§§163-278.110 to 163-278.113.
Political campaign contributions and
expenditures.
Coercing state employees to contribute, §§126-14,
126-14.1.
Counties.
Endorsement, opposition to referendum,
election, political candidate.
Use of public funds prohibited, §153A-456.
Generally, §§163-278.5 to 163-278.38.
See CAMPAIGN FINANCE.
Local boards of education.
Political endorsements or oppositions.
Public funds, restriction on use for political
activities, §115C-46.1.
Municipal campaign reporting, §§163-278.40 to
163-278.40J.
See CAMPAIGN FINANCE.
Municipalities.
Endorsement, opposition to referendum,
election, particular candidate.
Using municipal funds prohibited,
§160A-499.3.

ELECTIONS —Cont'd
Political parties.
Ballots.
New political party, §163-98.
Defined, §§163-96(a), 163-278.6, 163-278.13(e).
New political party.
General election participation by, §163-98.
Petition for formation, §163-96(b).
Notification regarding dual-office holding
requirements, §163-209.1.
Observers, §163-45.
Placement of available funds in fund,
§163-278.41(c).
Political parties financing fund, §§163-278.41 to
163-278.45.
Public buildings.
Use for political meetings, §163-99.
Registration of voters.
Change of party affiliation, §163-82.17.
Voters affiliated with expired political party,
§163-97.1.
Schools.
Use for political meetings, §163-99.
Termination of status as political party, §163-97.
Voters affiliated with expired political party,
§163-97.1.
Political parties financing fund, §§163-278.41 to
163-278.45.
Administration and enforcement ,rules, adoption,
§163-278.43(c1).
Contributions, receipts reported as,
§163-278.43(c2).
Criminal penalty for violations, §163-278.44.
Definitions, §163-278.45.
Disbursement of deposited funds.
Application for, §163-278.41(a) to (c).
Disbursement of funds by state chairman,
§163-278.42(a) to (f).
Eligibility to receive funds.
Review and certification of applications,
§163-278.43(c1).
Expenditures, disbursement reported as,
§163-278.43(c2).
Payment of funds held by state treasurer,
§163-278.41(b), (c).
Placement of available funds in fund,
§163-278.41(c).
Records of parties receipts, expenditures and
disbursements, §163-278.43(a).
Report on parties receipts, expenditures and
disbursements, §163-278.43(b).
Unlawful use of fund, §163-278.42(g).
Poll tax.
Failure to pay poll or other tax.
Denial or abridgement of right to vote by reason
of failure prohibited, US Const Amd 24.
Prohibited, NC Const Art V §1.
Precinct assistants.
Appointment.
County boards of election, §163-42(a).
Names recommended by political parties,
§163-42(b).
Emergency election day assistants, §163-42(c).
Registered voters in other precincts, §163-42(b).
Compensation, §163-46.
Emergency election day assistants, §163-42(c).
Number appointed, §163-42(a).
Oath required, §163-42(d).
Qualified voters in precinct appointed, §163-42(a).
Recommendation for appointment.
Chairman of each political party, §163-42(b).

ELECTIONS —Cont'd
Precinct assistants —Cont'd
Student election assistants, §163-42.1.
Precinct election officials, §§163-41 to 163-48.
Assistants at polls.
Student election assistants, §163-42.1.
Ballot counters, §163-43.
Compensation, §163-46.
Initial ballot count.
General principles, §163-182.2(a).
Judges of election.
Appointment, §163-41(a).
Chief judge, §163-47.
Duties, §163-47.
Oath of office, §163-41(a).
Observers, §163-45.
Power to maintain order of place of registration
voting, §163-48.
Publication of names, §163-41(c).
Relatives prohibited from serving together,
§163-41.1.
Special registration commissioners, §163-41(b).
Student election assistants, §163-42.1.
Summary of duties.
Counting votes, canvassing, abstracts and
protests, §163-182.17(b).
Precincts.
Alteration to precinct name, §163-132.3A.
Boundaries.
Administrative procedure act.
State board exempt from act, §163-132.5B.
Alterations to approved precinct boundaries.
Approval of maps and written descriptions,
§163-132.3(b).
Disapproval of precinct boundaries,
§163-132.3(c).
Examination of maps of proposed new or
altered precincts, §163-132.3(b).
Notice of disapproval, §163-132.3(c).
Reporting election returns by voting
tabulation districts, §163-132.3(a).
Report of boundary changes, §163-132.3(a).
Submission of certain alterations to United
States attorney general.
State board of elections, §120-30.9B(a).
Uniform standards for boundaries,
§163-132.3(a).
Census data by precinct, §163-132.5F.
Cooperation of state and local agencies,
§163-132.5.
Crossing township lines, §163-132.5C(b).
Directives, §163-132.4.
Local act, §163-132.5C(a).
Maps.
Retention of precinct maps, §163-132.5D.
Retention of precinct maps, §163-132.5D.
Census data by precinct.
State to request, §163-132.5F.
Census redistricting data program.
Census 2010.
Purpose, §163-132.1B(a).
Reporting of unchanged voting tabulation
districts, §163-132.1B(a2).
Reporting of voting tabulation districts,
§163-132.1B(a1).
Rules and regulations, §163-132.1B(b).
Purpose, §163-132.1(a).
Rules and regulations, §163-132.1(f).
Cooperation of state and local agencies.
Establishment of boundaries, §163-132.5.

ELECTIONS —Cont'd
Precincts —Cont'd
County boards of elections.
Map of precinct boundaries.
Duty to prepare, §163-128(b).
Powers as to precincts, §163-128(a).
Directives.
Boundaries, §163-132.4.
Division of counties into precincts, §163-128(a).
Maps.
Maps of counties showing precinct boundaries.
County boards of elections to prepare,
§163-128(b).
Retention, §163-132.5D.
Name.
Alteration, §163-132.3A.
Overseas voters.
Precinct of address of last place of residence.
Assigning overseas voters, §163-258.5.
Prima facie evidence.
Voter no longer living in precinct, §163-85(e).
Two voting places for certain precincts.
Temporary designation, §163-130.2.
Preclearance pursuant to voting rights act.
Submissions to attorney general of United States,
§§120-30.9A to 120-30.9I. See within this
heading, "Voting rights act of 1965."
Presidential elections.
Generally.
See PRESIDENTIAL ELECTIONS.
Preference primary, §§163-213.1 to 163-213.9.
See PRESIDENTIAL PREFERENCE PRIMARY.
Presidential election year candidates fund,
§§163-278.41 to 163-278.45.
Administration and enforcement ,rules, adoption,
§163-278.43(c1).
Contributions, receipts reported as,
§163-278.43(c2).
Criminal penalty for violations, §163-278.44.
Definitions, §163-278.45.
Eligibility to receive funds.
Review and certification of applications,
§163-278.43(c1).
Expenditures, disbursement reported as,
§163-278.43(c2).
Payment of funds held by state treasurer,
§163-278.41(b).
Placement of available funds in fund,
§163-278.41(c).
Records of parties receipts, expenditures and
disbursements, §163-278.43(a).
Report on parties receipts, expenditures and
disbursements, §163-278.43(b).
Unlawful use of fund, §163-278.42(g).
Primary elections.
Generally, §§163-1, 163-104 to 163-119.
See PRIMARY ELECTIONS.
Municipal elections generally.
See MUNICIPAL ELECTIONS.
Presidential preference primary, §§163-213.1 to
163-213.9.
See PRESIDENTIAL PREFERENCE PRIMARY.
Prison terms.
Penalties for misdemeanors, §163-272.1.
Property qualifications prohibited, NC Const
Art I §11.
Protest filed with county board.
Appeal of decision to state board.
Consideration of appeal, §163-182.11(b).
Decision, §163-182.11(b).
Filing, §163-182.11(a).

ELECTIONS —Cont'd
Protest filed with county board —Cont'd
Appeal of decision to state board —Cont'd
Notice, §163-182.11(a).
Who may appeal, §163-182.11(a).
Appeal of decision to superior court,
§163-182.14(a), (b).
Appeal to general assembly or house thereof,
§163-182.14(c).
Attorneys' fees not to be awarded against board,
§163-182.14(d).
Conduct of hearing, §163-182.10(c).
Contents, §163-182.9(b).
Effect on canvass, §163-182.10(a).
Findings of fact and conclusions of law,
§163-182.10(d).
Forms, §163-182.9(c).
Initial consideration, §163-182.10(a).
Notice of hearing, §163-182.10(b).
Order, §163-182.10(c), (d).
Promulgation of rules, §163-182.10(e).
Time for filing, §163-182.9(b).
Who may file, §163-182.9(a).
Protest initiated by state board, §163-182.12.
Appeal of decision to superior court,
§163-182.14(a), (b).
Appeal to general assembly or house thereof,
§163-182.14(c).
Attorneys' fees not to be awarded against board,
§163-182.14(d).
Provisional ballots.
Persons previously registered by mail,
§163-166.12(c).
Posting of voter information, §163-166.7A(a).
Procedures generally, §163-166.11.
Voting after hours, §163-166.01.
Provisional official ballots.
Initial count, §163-182.2(a).
Public campaign fund, §§163-278.61 to
163-278.70.
Administration of article, §163-278.67.
Amount of fund distributions, §163-278.65(b).
Availability of matching funds, §163-278.67(a).
Certification of candidates, §163-278.64(c).
Civil penalty, §163-278.70.
Declaration on intent to participate,
§163-278.64(a).
Definitions, §163-278.62.
Demonstration of support of candidacy,
§163-278.64(b).
Determination of fund amount, §163-278.63(c).
Distributions from the fund, §163-278.65.
Electioneering communications.
Communications affecting all candidates
equally, no matching funds, §163-278.67(f).
Determination of eligibility for matching funds,
§163-278.67(d), (e).
Enforcement of article, §163-278.67.
Establishment, §163-278.63(a).
Expedited distribution of matching funds,
§163-278.67(c1).
Individual income taxpayer.
Allocation to fund by individual, §105-159.2(a).
Instructions for individual to designate
allocation, §105-159.2(c).
Returns to give individual opportunity to
designate allocation, §105-159.2(b).
Judicial voter guide, §163-278.69.
Legislative intent, §163-278.61.
Limit on matching funds.
Contested general election, §163-278.67(c).

ELECTIONS —Cont'd
Public campaign fund —Cont'd
Limit on matching funds —Cont'd
Contested primary, §163-278.67(b).
Matching funds, §163-278.67.
Method of fund distributions, §163-278.65(c).
Noncertified candidates and independent
expenditure entities.
Reporting requirements, §163-278.66(a).
Participating and certified candidates.
Reporting requirements, §163-278.66(b).
Restrictions on contributions and expenditures,
§163-278.64(d).
Public policy, §163-278.61.
Reporting requirements, §163-278.66.
Revocation of decision to participate,
§163-278.64(e).
Source of funding, §163-278.63(b).
Timing of fund distributions, §163-278.65(a).
Vacancy elections, candidates in.
Allocations, §163-278.64A(c).
Participation, §163-278.64A(a).
Qualifying period, §163-278.64A(b).
Public officers and employees.
Continuation in office, NC Const Art VI §10.
Disqualifications for office, NC Const Art VI §8.
Dual office holding, NC Const Art VI §9.
Eligibility to elective office, NC Const Art VI §6.
Felonies.
Disqualifications from holding office, NC Const
Art VI §8.
Oaths, NC Const Art VI §7.
Officers of state institutions.
Generally, §§143-108 to 143-116.
See STATE DEPARTMENTS AND
AGENCIES.
Public schools, supplementary taxes for.
Districts created from portions of contiguous
counties, §115C-510.
Effective date of action after election,
§115C-508(b).
Frequency of elections, §115C-502(b).
Petitions.
Action of counties or municipalities, §115C-506.
Boards of education must consider, §115C-505.
Necessary information, §115C-504.
Who may petition for election, §115C-503.
Purposes for which elections may be called,
§115C-501.
Rules governing, §115C-507.
Public witness of ballot count, §163-182.2(a).
Qualifications of voters.
Absentee ballots.
Who may vote absentee ballot.
Primary elections, §163-226.1.
Convicted persons.
Restoration of citizenship rights, §§13-1 to 13-4.
Municipal elections, §§163-282, 163-283.
Presidential preference primaries, §163-213.2.
Independent voters not to participate,
§163-213.7.
Primary elections, §163-59.
Municipal elections, §163-283.
Person who will not be qualified until general
election following primary, §163-283.1.
Registration a prerequisite to voting, §163-54.
Primary elections, §163-59.
Residence requirements, §163-55(a).
Precincts and election districts, §163-55(b).
Racial minorities, US Const Amd 15.

ELECTIONS —Cont'd
Radio.
Disclosure requirements for media
  advertisements, §§163-278.39 to 163-278.39C.
Recounts.
Demand, §163-182.7(b), (c).
Discretionary recounts, §163-182.7(a).
Hand-to-eye recounts.
  Applicable rules, §163-182.7A(b).
  Generally, §163-182.7A(a).
  Restrictions on conducting, §163-182.7A(c).
Mandatory recounts.
  County board jurisdiction, §163-182.7(b).
  State board jurisdiction, §163-182.7(c).
Rules of conducting, §163-182.7(d).
  Hand-to-eye recounts, §163-182.7A.
Referenda.
See REFERENDUM.
Registers of deeds, §§161-1, 161-2.
Registration of voters, §§163-82.1 to 163-91.
See VOTER REGISTRATION.
Reports.
Contributions and expenditures in political
  campaigns.
  Declaration of nomination or certificate of
    election.
    Filing of statements as prerequisite,
      §163-278.25.
  Examination of statements within four months,
    §163-278.24.
  Federal officers.
    Candidates to file information reports,
      §163-278.30.
  Inactive candidate or committee, §163-278.10.
  Preservation, §163-278.35.
    County boards of elections to preserve
      reports, §163-278.37.
  Violations of provisions.
    Board to report to prosecuting authorities,
      §163-278.27(b).
County boards of elections.
  State board of elections may require reports
    from county boards, §163-22(c).
Electioneering communications, §163-278.12C.
Residence.
Challenge to a candidacy.
  Burden of proof, §163-127.5(b).
Married women.
  Establishment of separate domicile, §163-57.
Presidential elections.
  Period for presidential elections, NC Const Art
    VI §2.
Qualifications to vote, §163-55(a).
  Definition of residence, §163-57.
  Election defined for purposes of residence
    requirements, §163-55(c).
  Precincts and election districts, §163-55(b).
State election.
  Period for state elections, NC Const Art VI §2.
Returns.
Abstract of returns.
  Municipal elections.
    Disposition of duplicate abstracts, §163-300.
Abstracts, §163-182.6.
Canvassing votes, §163-182.5.
Counting ballots, §§163-182 to 163-182.5.
False or fraudulent returns.
  Felony, §163-275.
New election ordered, §163-182.13.
Presidential elections, §163-208.
Presidential preference primaries, §163-213.3.

ELECTIONS —Cont'd
Returns —Cont'd
Primary elections.
  Presidential preference primaries, §163-213.3.
Protest of election, §163-182.9.
Recounts, §163-182.7.
  Hand-to-eye recounts, §163-182.7A.
Tie votes, §163-182.8.
Right to vote, US Const Amds 14, 19, 26.
Rules and regulations.
Absentee ballots.
  Military absentee voting.
    State board of elections, §163-256(a).
Contributions and expenditures in political
  campaigns.
  State board of elections, §163-278.21.
County boards of elections, §163-33.
State board of elections, §163-22(a).
  Power to promulgate temporary rules and
    regulations, §163-22.2.
  Publication, §163-22(b).
  Temporary rules and regulations, §163-22.2.
Rural fire protection districts.
Abolition, §69-25.10.
Tax question, §§69-25.1 to 69-25.4.
Sales and use tax.
Local government sales and use tax.
  Election on adoption of tax.
    First one-cent tax, §105-465.
    One-quarter cent county tax, §105-537(b).
      Ballot question, §105-537(c).
    Second one-half cent tax, ballot question,
      form, §105-499(a).
  Election on repeal of levy.
    First one-cent tax, §105-473(a), (b).
    Second one-half cent tax, ballot question,
      form, §105-499(b).
Sanitary districts, §§130A-52.1, 130A-53.
Board members, §130A-50(b), (c).
County with no incorporated city, §130A-50(b2).
Meetings for purpose of election, §130A-50(a).
Multi-county districts, §130A-50(b1).
Results of election certified, §130A-50(d).
Validation of election of members of district
  boards, §130A-79(a), (b).
Extension of district.
  Procedure for extension, §130A-69.
Removal of member of board, §130A-66.
Returns of elections, §130A-68.
Special election if election not held in November
  of 1981, §130A-52(a) to (d).
Two contiguous sanitary districts merger,
  §130A-83.
Satellite voting places, §163-130.
School elections.
Merger of administrative units.
  Units in adjoining counties, §115C-68(c).
Supplementary taxes for school purposes,
  §§115C-500 to 115C-511.
See SCHOOL DISTRICTS AND
  ADMINISTRATIVE UNITS.
Secretary of state.
Abstracts, duties, §163-182.6(c).
Date of election, §163-1(a).
Elective officers, NC Const Art III §7.
Summary of duties.
  Counting votes, canvassing, abstracts and
    protests, §163-182.17(e).
Vacancy in office.
  Election to fill, §163-8.

ELECTIONS —Cont'd
Senior citizens.
  Accessible polling places, §163-131.
  Curbside voting, §163-166.9.
  Satellite voting places, §163-130.
Sex offenders.
  Unlawful presence on premises for use, care or
    supervision of children.
    Voting exception, §14-208.18(e).
Sheriffs, §162-1.
  County sheriffs, NC Const Art VII §2.
  Date of election, §163-1(a).
Signs.
  Political signs, §136-32.
Soil and water conservation districts.
  Watershed improvement works or projects.
    Alternative method of financing watershed
      improvement programs by special county
      tax, §139-39.
      Conduct of election, §139-40(a).
    Appointment of judges and election officials,
      §139-40(c).
    Conduct of elections, §139-40(a).
    Form of question, §139-40(b).
    Majority vote, §139-40(d).
Special elections.
  Municipality holding, §163-287.
Split-ticket votes.
  Counting ballots, §163-182.1(a).
State auditor.
  Date of election, §163-1(a).
  Elective officers, NC Const Art III §7.
  Vacancy in office.
    Election to fill, §163-8.
State board of elections, §§163-19 to 163-28.
  See STATE BOARD OF ELECTIONS.
State departments and agencies.
  Influencing election or political activities.
    Removal by governor, §143B-16.
Statements of economic interest.
  Candidates for public office, §138A-22(d), (d1), (e).
State superintendent of public instruction,
  §115C-18.
State treasurer.
  Date of election, §163-1(a).
  Elective officers, NC Const Art III §7.
  Vacancy in office.
    Election to fill, §163-8.
Stay of certificate.
  Appeal of decision to superior court,
    §163-182.14(a), (b).
Straight-party tickets.
  Ballots, §163-165.6(e).
  Counting, §163-182.1(a).
Student election assistants, §163-42.1.
Subpoenas.
  Corruption.
    Witnesses, §§163-277, 163-278.
  State board of elections.
    Powers of chairman, §163-23.
Suffrage, US Const Amds 15, 19.
Summary of officials' duties, §163-182.17(a).
Superintendent of public instruction, §115C-18.
Superior courts.
  Clerks of court, §7A-100(a).
    Date of election, §163-1(a).
    Vacancy or people failing to elect, §163-115(a).
  Judges, §7A-41.2, NC Const Art IV §16.
    Date of election, §163-1(a).
    Generally, §§163-321 to 163-335.
    See SUPERIOR COURT JUDGES.

ELECTIONS —Cont'd
Supreme court justices, NC Const Art IV §16.
  Judicial voter guide.
    Candidate information, §163-278.69(b).
    Disclaimer statement, §163-278.69(c).
    Publication by board, §163-278.69(a).
  Qualified electors of state to elect justices,
    §7A-10(a).
Taxation.
  Denial or abridgment of right to vote.
    Failure to pay poll or other tax, US Const Amd
      24.
  Poll tax.
    Prohibited, NC Const Art V §1.
Television.
  Campaign contributions and expenditures.
    Disclosure requirements for media
      advertisements, §§163-278.39 to
      163-278.39C.
Tie vote.
  New elections, §163-182.13(f).
  Resolution, §163-182.8.
Time.
  Generally, §163-1(a).
  Municipal elections, §163-279.
    Special elections, §163-287.
  Presidential elections, §163-1(c).
  Primary elections, §163-1(b), (d).
    Modification of time schedule.
      Power of state board of elections, §163-104.
      Presidential preference primaries, §163-213.2.
Training for election officials, §163-82.24(a).
  Certification, §163-82.24(b).
Transportation board.
  Use of position to influence elections or political
    action, §136-13.1.
Transportation department.
  Use of position to influence elections or political
    action, §136-13.1.
Treason.
  Disqualifications from office, NC Const Art VI §8.
Two separate offices.
  Running for at same time prohibited, §163-124(a).
    Applicability, §163-124(b).
    Exception, §163-124(a).
Unaffiliated candidate.
  Nomination by petition, §163-122(a).
    Cancellation of petition.
      Failure to meet qualifications for office,
        §163-122(d).
    Filing fee, §163-122(e).
    Form, §163-122(b).
    Inapplicability of provisions, §163-122(c).
Uniform military and overseas voters act,
  §§163-258.1 to 163-258.31.
  See ABSENTEE BALLOTS.
Vacancies in office.
  County boards of elections.
    Filling, §163-30.
  Elections to fill.
    Congress.
      House of representatives.
        Nominating procedures, §163-13(b).
        Special election, §§163-13(a), 163-115(b).
      Senate, §163-12.
    District attorneys, §163-10.
    State executive offices, §163-8.
  Primary elections.
    Death of candidate before primary.
      Filling vacancy, §163-112.

ELECTIONS —Cont'd
Vacancies in office —Cont'd
  Primary elections —Cont'd
    Nominees.
      Filling vacancies among party nominees
        occurring after nomination and before
        election, §163-114.
      Notice of candidacy for certain offices to indicate
        vacancy, §163-106(d).
      Special provisions for obtaining nominations
        when vacancies occur in certain offices,
        §163-115(a) to (e).
    State board of elections.
      Filling, §163-19.
    State or district office other than U.S. house of
      representatives, §163-115(c).
Vote-buying, §163-275.
Voter-owned elections act, §§163-278.95 to
  163-278.99E.
  See CAMPAIGN FINANCE.
Voter registration, §§163-82.1 to 163-91.
  See VOTER REGISTRATION.
Voters.
  Age.
    Minimum age, §163-55(a).
    Persons eighteen years of age, US Const Amd
      26.
    Right to vote not to be abridged on account of
      age, US Const Amd 26.
  Aged voters.
    Curbside voting, §163-166.9.
    Assistance to voters, §163-166.8.
  Blind voters.
    Assistance to voters, §163-166.8.
  Challenge of voters.
    Absentee ballots, §163-89.
    Answer to challenge as felon not to be used on
      prosecution, §163-90.
    Burden of proof, §163-90.1(b).
      Challenge to absentee ballots, §163-89(c).
    Day of primary or election, §§163-87 to
      163-88.1.
    False swearing.
      Felony, §163-90.3.
    Municipal elections, §163-289.
    Other than on day of primary or election,
      §§163-85, 163-86.
    Overruled or dismissed challenge.
      Action by board on, §163-90.2(c).
      Appeals, §163-90.2(d).
    Reasonable belief by challenger required,
      §163-90.1(a).
    Sustained challenge.
      Action by board on, §163-90.2(a), (b).
      Appeals, §163-90.2(d).
  Disabled voters.
    Assistance to voters, §163-166.8.
    Curbside voting, §163-166.9.
  Eligibility to vote, NC Const Art VI §1.
  Felons, restoration of citizenship after conviction.
    Persons who become qualified to register and
      vote, §163-82.6(e).
  Intimidation of voters.
    Misdemeanors, §163-274(a).
    Officers, §163-271.
  Naturalized citizens.
    Persons who become qualified to register and
      vote, §163-82.6(e).
  No longer living in precinct.
    Prima facie evidence, §163-85(e).

ELECTIONS —Cont'd
Voters —Cont'd
  Party primaries.
    Right to participate or vote in, §163-59.
      Municipal elections, §163-283.
        Person who will not be qualified until
          general election following primary,
          §163-283.1.
  Persons eighteen years of age, US Const Amd 26.
  Persons who become qualified to register and vote,
    §163-82.6(e).
  Preventing from voting or other irregularities.
    New elections, §163-182.13(a).
      Voter eligibility, §163-182.13(c).
  Prima facie evidence.
    Voter no longer living in precinct, §163-85(e).
  Qualifications of voters.
    Absentee ballots.
      Who may vote absentee ballot.
        Primary elections, §163-226.1.
    Convicted persons.
      Restoration of citizenship rights, §§13-1 to
        13-4.
    Municipal elections, §§163-282, 163-283.
    Presidential preference primaries, §163-213.2.
      Independent voters not to participate,
        §163-213.7.
    Primary elections, §163-59.
      Municipal elections, §163-283.
        Person who will not be qualified until
          general election following primary,
          §163-283.1.
    Registration a prerequisite to voting, §163-54.
      Primary elections, §163-59.
    Residence requirements, §163-55(a).
      Precincts and election districts, §163-55(b).
  Registration of voters, §§163-82.1 to 163-91.
  See VOTER REGISTRATION.
Voting data maintenance.
  Voting tabulation districts, §163-132.5G.
Voting places.
  Accessible polling places, §163-131(a).
    Definitions, §163-131(b).
  Access to voting enclosure.
    Limiting, §163-166.3.
  Activity in voting place and buffer zone around it.
    Limitations on, §163-166.4.
  Agreements for election-related activity,
    §163-166.4(b).
  Area provided for election-related activity,
    §163-166.4(a1).
  Arrangement of voting enclosure, §163-166.2.
  Assistance to voters, §163-166.8.
  Buffer zones and adjacent areas, §163-166.4(a).
    Agreements for election-related activity,
      §163-166.4(b).
    Areas for election-related activity,
      §163-166.4(a1).
    Notice to public, §163-166.4(c).
    One-stop sites, §163-166.4(d).
  Closing voting places.
    Hours for voting, §163-166.01.
    Procedures after close of voting, §163-166.10.
  Contents of voting enclosure, §163-166.2.
  County boards of elections.
    Duties, §163-166.1.
    Duties as to, §163-129.
  Curbside voting, §163-166.9.
  Electioneering.
    Limitations on activity in voting place and
      buffer zone around it, §163-166.4.

ELECTIONS —Cont'd
Voting places —Cont'd
Hours for voting, §163-166.01.
Limiting access to voting enclosure, §163-166.3.
Marking off limits, §163-129.
Opening voting places.
Hours for voting, §163-166.01.
Out-of-precinct voting places, §163-130.1.
Photographing of voted ballot prohibited, §163-166.3(c).
Photographing of voters prohibited, §163-166.3(b).
Political activity.
Limitations on activity in voting place and buffer zone around it, §163-166.4.
Posting of voter information, §163-166.7A(a).
Intent, §163-166.7A(b).
Procedure for voting, §163-166.7.
Procedures after close of voting, §163-166.10.
Procedures before voting begins, §163-166.5.
Satellite voting places, §163-130.
Setting up voting place.
Procedures before voting begins, §163-166.5.
Structures at, §163-129.
Two voting places for certain precincts.
Temporary designation, §163-130.2.
Who may enter enclosure, §163-166.3(a).
Voting rights act of 1965.
Submission of acts to United States attorney general, §§120-30.9A to 120-30.9I.
Constitutional amendments.
Secretary of state, §120-30.9D.
Counties.
Alternate submission authority, §120-30.9I.
County attorney, §120-30.9E.
Judicial system.
Administrative office of the court, §120-30.9C.
Municipalities.
Municipality attorney, §120-30.9F.
North Carolina register.
Decision letters of U. S. attorney general.
Published in North Carolina register, §120-30.9H.
Publication of decision letters of U. S. attorney general in North Carolina register, §120-30.9H.
Purpose of article, §120-30.9A.
School administrative units.
Alternate submission authority, §120-30.9I.
Boards of education attorney, §120-30.9G(b).
State board of education, §120-30.9G(a).
Statewide statutes.
State board of elections, §120-30.9B(a), (b).
Voting systems.
Boards of county commissioners.
Powers and duties, §163-165.8.
Certification by state board of elections.
Decertification of types, makes and models, §163-165.7(b).
Required, §163-165.7(a).
Review prior to, §163-165.7(c).
County boards of elections.
Powers and duties, §§163-165.9, 163-165.10.
Examination by county board of elections, §163-33.2.
Federal assistance.
State board may use, §163-165.7(a1).
Lever machines or punch cards, use of, §163-165.4A(a1).
Effective date of provision, §163-165.4A(b).
Rules for adoption, handling, operation and honest use, §163-165.7(d).

ELECTIONS —Cont'd
Voting systems —Cont'd
State board of elections.
Access to voting machines, §163-22(j).
Powers and duties, §163-165.7.
Testing.
Duties of county board of elections, §163-165.9(a).
Training and support to be facilitated, §163-165.7(e).
Vendors.
Duties, §163-165.9A(a).
Penalties for violations, §163-165.9A(b).
Warranty maintenance, §163-165.9(b).
Voting tabulation districts.
County to maintain voting data, §163-132.5G.
Watershed improvement programs.
Generally, §§139-39, 139-40.
Wildlife resource commission offices, §143-243.
Witnesses.
Contributions and expenditures in political campaigns.
Self-incrimination.
Immunity from prosecution, §163-278.29.
Corruption.
Self-incrimination.
Immunity from prosecution, §163-277.
Subpoenas, §§163-277, 163-278.
Power of district attorneys, §163-278.
State board of elections.
Powers of chairman as to witnesses, §163-23.
Woman suffrage, US Const Amd 19.
Write-in votes.
Ballots, §163-165.6(f).
Counting ballots, §163-182.1(a).

ELECTIVE LIFE ESTATE.
Marital interest in real property, §29-30(a) to (h).
Waiver, §39-7(a), (c).

ELECTIVE SHARE OF SURVIVING SPOUSE, §§30-3.1 to 30-3.6, 31-5.3.
Apportionment of liability to surviving spouse, §30-3.5(a1).
Beneficial interest of spouse.
Valuation of property, §30-3.3A(e).
Bond or other security by responsible person, §30-3.5(e).
Claim.
Defined, §30-3.2.
Petition prior to marriage, §31-5.3.
Time limits on making, §30-3.4(b).
Date of death.
Valuation of property, §30-3.3A(a).
Death before claim settled.
Succession to surviving spouse's right.
Personal representative, §30-3.4(a).
Definitions, §30-3.2.
Determining, procedure, §30-3.4.
Disposal of total net assets.
Prohibition.
Standstill order, §30-3.5(b).
Estate proceedings.
Procedure for elective share proceedings, §30-3.4(e1).
Examination regarding total net assets, §30-3.4(e2).
Exercise of right only during lifetime, §30-3.4(a).
Expenses including attorneys' fees.
Apportionment, §30-3.4(h).

ELECTIVE SHARE OF SURVIVING SPOUSE
—Cont'd
Fair market value.
Valuation of property, §30-3.3A(a).
**Findings and conclusions after notice and
hearing,** §30-3.4(f).
Generally, §30-3.1(a).
General power of appointment.
Defined, §30-3.2.
Presently exercisable general power of
appointment.
Defined, §30-3.2.
Valuation of property, §30-3.3A(c).
Gift property.
Valuation of property, §30-3.3A(a).
Inability or refusal to pay, §30-3.5(a3).
Incapacity of surviving spouse.
Time limit for making claim not tolled, §30-3.4(b).
**Jointly owned property with right of
survivorship.**
Valuation of property, §30-3.3A(b).
Liability to surviving spouse.
Apportionment, §30-3.5(a1).
Inability or refusal to pay, §30-3.5(a3).
Recovery from responsible person, §30-3.5(a2).
**Life estate or income interest terminating
upon death or remarriage of surviving
spouse.**
Valuation of property, §30-3.3A(e).
Life expectancy of surviving spouse.
Contingent interest dependent upon.
Valuation of property, §30-3.3A(e).
Lifetime of surviving spouse.
Exercise of right during.
Required, §30-3.4(a).
Mediation of disputes, §30-3.4(d).
Net property passing to surviving spouse.
Defined, §30-3.2.
Nonspousal assets.
Apportionment of liability to surviving spouse,
§30-3.5(a1).
Defined, §30-3.2.
Responsible person's nonspousal assets.
Defined, §30-3.2.
Persons who may exercise right, §30-3.4(a).
Petition.
Filing, §30-3.4(b).
Procedure for determining, §30-3.4.
Property passing to surviving spouse.
Defined, §30-3.2.
Net property passing to surviving spouse.
Defined, §30-3.2.
Recovery from responsible person, §30-3.5(a2).
Inability or refusal to pay, §30-3.5(a3).
Reduction of applicable share, §30-3.1(b).
Responsible person defined, §30-3.2.
Standstill order.
Prohibiting disposal of total net assets, §30-3.5(b).
Succession to surviving spouse's right.
Death before claim settled.
Personal representative, §30-3.4(a).
Time limits on making claim, §30-3.4(b).
Total assets.
Defined, §30-3.2.
Total net assets.
Defined, §30-3.2.
Examination regarding, §30-3.4(e2).
Information submitted to clerk, §30-3.4(e2).
Standstill order.
Prohibiting disposal of total net assets,
§30-3.5(b).

ELECTIVE SHARE OF SURVIVING SPOUSE
—Cont'd
Trusts.
Beneficial interest of spouse.
Valuation of property, §30-3.3A(e).
Valuation of property.
Basic principles, §30-3.3A(a).
Beneficial interest of spouse, §30-3.3A(e).
Determined as of date of death, §30-3.3A(a).
Evidence regarding value.
Determining value, §30-3.3A(f).
Fair market value, §30-3.3A(a).
Gift property, §30-3.3A(a).
Good faith agreement.
Determining value, §30-3.3A(f).
Jointly owned property with right of survivorship.
Partial interest, §30-3.3A(b).
Life estate or income interest terminating upon
death or remarriage of surviving spouse,
§30-3.3A(e).
Life expectancy of surviving spouse.
Contingent interest dependent upon,
§30-3.3A(e).
Method for determining, §30-3.3A(f).
Partial or contingent interest property,
§30-3.3A(e).
Presently exercisable general power of
appointment, §30-3.3A(c).
Transfers with retained interest, §30-3.3A(d).
Trusts.
Beneficial interest of spouse, §30-3.3A(e).
Waiver of right to claim, §30-3.6(a).
Effective waiver, §30-3.6(c).
Unenforceable waiver, §30-3.6(b).

**ELECTRICAL APPLIANCE AND EQUIPMENT
SALES,** §§66-23 to 66-27.01.
Actions.
Enforcement of provisions, §66-27.01.
Compliance with provisions required, §66-23.
Evidence.
Acceptable listings as to safety of goods, §66-25.
Identification marks, §66-24.
Installation.
Legal responsibility for proper installation
unaffected, §66-26.
Liability.
Effect of provisions, §66-26.
Merchantability.
Acceptable listings as to safety of goods, §66-25.
Misdemeanors.
Violations of provisions, §66-27.
Safety.
Acceptable listings as to safety of goods, §66-25.
Testing.
Acceptable listings as to safety of goods, §66-25.

ELECTRICAL CONTRACTORS, §§87-39 to 87-51.
Applicability of provisions.
Exceptions, §87-43.1.
Board of examiners.
Appointment of members, §87-39.
Classification of licenses.
Standards for, §87-43.3.
Composition, §87-39.
Disciplinary proceedings.
Generally, §87-47.
Duties, §87-42.
Meetings, §87-39.
Oath of office of members, §87-39.
Office.
Principal office, §87-39.

ELECTRICAL CONTRACTORS —Cont'd
Board of examiners —Cont'd
Officers, §87-39.
Powers, §87-42.
Public awareness program, §87-50.1.
Quorum, §87-39.
Seal, §87-41.
Secretary-treasurer, §87-40.
Terms of members, §87-39.
Vacancies, §87-39.
Child support enforcement.
Forfeiture of licensing privilege, §50-13.12.
Complaints against licensees.
Records, §87-47(c).
Continuing education requirements, §87-44.1.
Corporations.
Licenses, §87-43.2.
Definitions, §87-41.1.
Electrical contracting, §87-43.
Discipline.
Authority of board and staff to prefer charges,
§87-47(a4).
Final decision, entry, imposition of penalty,
§87-47(a5).
Hearing on receipt of notice of violation.
Request, time, conduct, §87-47(a4).
Notice of violation, issuance, §87-47(a4).
Penalties, §87-47(a2).
Civil penalties, §87-47(a3).
Compromise, amount, §87-47(e).
Prohibited activities, §87-47(a1).
Records regarding charges and notice.
Duty to keep, §87-47(c).
Reinstatement of certificate or license, §87-47(d).
Rules, adoption, §87-47(b).
Education.
Continuing education requirements, §87-44.1.
Examinations.
No examination required of licensed contractors,
§87-49.
Exceptions to provisions, §87-43.1.
Fees.
Licenses, §87-44.
Use of funds collected, §87-45.
Injunctions.
Violations of provisions, §87-48(b).
Licenses.
Cancellation.
No listed qualified individual employed by
applicant, §87-43.2(b).
Classification of licenses, §87-43.3.
Corporations, §87-43.2.
Disciplinary actions, §87-47(a1) to (a3).
Display, §87-43.
Eligibility for license or renewal, §87-43.2(a).
Examinations.
No examination required of licensed contractors,
§87-49.
Fees, §87-44.
Use of funds collected, §87-45.
Issuance, §87-43.2.
Listed qualified individuals employed by
applicant.
Names and classifications indicated on license,
§87-43.2(b).
Nonresidents.
Definitions, §87-44.2(a).
Delinquents, §87-44.2(d).
Information, §87-44.2(c).
Prerequisites to issuance of license, §87-44.2(b).
Partnerships, §87-43.2.

ELECTRICAL CONTRACTORS —Cont'd
Licenses —Cont'd
Reciprocity, §87-50.
Registry of licenses, §87-43.
Renewal, §87-44.
Residential dwelling license, §87-43.4.
Responsibilities of licensees, §87-46.
Revocation or suspension.
Felony convictions, §15A-1331(a).
Reissuance, §87-47(d).
Rules governing, §87-47(b).
Signing, §87-43.
Term, §87-44.
Negligence.
Immunity of board for negligent acts of license
holders, §87-46.
Nonresidents.
Licensing of nonresidents, §87-44.2.
Partnerships.
Licenses, §87-43.2.
Prohibited activities, §87-47(a1).
Authority of board and staff to prefer charges,
§87-47(a4).
Final decision, entry, imposition of penalty,
§87-47(a5).
Hearing on receipt of notice of violation.
Request, time, conduct, §87-47(a4).
Notice of violation, issuance, §87-47(a4).
Penalties, §87-47(a2).
Civil penalties, §87-47(a3).
Compromise, amount, §87-47(e).
Records regarding charges and notice.
Duty to keep, §87-47(c).
Reinstatement of certificate or license, §87-47(d).
Rules, adoption, §87-47(b).
Public awareness program, §87-50.1.
Residential dwelling license, §87-43.4.
Severability of provisions, §87-51.
Violations of provisions.
Injunctions, §87-48(b).
Penalty, §87-48(a).

ELECTRICAL INSPECTORS.
County inspection departments generally,
§§153A-350 to 153A-375.
See COUNTY INSPECTION DEPARTMENTS.

ELECTRIC CHAIR, DEATH BY.
Abolished, §15-187.

ELECTRIC COMPANIES.
All terrain vehicles operated by electric
service employees.
Head and eye protection equipment.
Required while engaged in power line
inspection, §20-171.19(a2).
Bills to show reading or meter, §66-9.
Child support enforcement.
Location of absent parents.
Information to be provided, §110-139(d).
Coal-fired generating units.
Emissions of oxides of nitrogen and sulfur dioxide
by investor-owned utilities, §143-215.107D.
Environmental compliance costs recovery,
§62-133.6.
Cogenerating power plants.
Income tax credit.
Corporation or partnership constructing in
state, §105-130.25(a).
Application for credit, §105-130.25(d).
Ceiling on credit, §105-130.25(e).

ELECTRIC COMPANIES —Cont'd
Cogenerating power plants —Cont'd
Income tax credit —Cont'd
Corporation or partnership constructing in state
—Cont'd
Cogenerating power plant defined,
§105-130.25(b).
Cost paid during earlier year, alternative
method, §105-130.25(c).
**Cost recovery for demand-side management
and energy efficiency measures,** §62-133.9.
Costs of petitions for condemnation of land,
§6-22.
Eminent domain.
By whom right may be exercised, §40A-3(a).
Dwelling house, yard, kitchen, etc., of owner
taken under certain cases, §62-184.
Exercise of right, parties interest only taken,
§62-185.
Grant, §62-183.
Petition costs, §6-22.
Powers granted corporations exercisable by
persons, firms or copartnerships, §62-189.
Proceedings as under eminent domain, §62-187.
Use or occupancy of public highway, §62-181.
Environmental compliance costs recovery.
Coal-fired generating units, §62-133.6.
Franchise or privilege tax.
Additional tax imposed by county or city.
Companies not subject to, §105-116(e1).
Annual tax imposed, §105-116(a).
City not to impose or collect greater tax,
§105-116(e).
County or city imposing additional tax.
Companies not subject to, §105-116(e1).
Distribution to cities, §105-116(d).
City's share, §105-116.1(b).
Definitions, §105-116.1(a).
Hold-back amount for 1995-96 fiscal year,
§105-116.1(c) to (d).
Municipality incorporated on or after January 1,
2000, §105-116.1(e).
Payment, return, report, §105-116(b).
Rate of tax, §105-116(a).
Generating facilities, §§62-82, 62-110.1.
Joint municipal electric power and energy,
§§159B-1 to 159B-52.
See JOINT MUNICIPAL ELECTRIC POWER
AND ENERGY ACT.
Membership corporations, §§117-6 to 117-26.
See ELECTRIC MEMBERSHIP
CORPORATIONS.
Meters.
Electric light bills to show reading of meter, §66-9.
Master electrical meters.
Prohibition, §143-151.42(a).
Exception, §143-151.42(b).
Municipalities.
Electric service in urban areas, §§160A-331 to
160A-338.
See ELECTRIC SERVICE IN URBAN AREAS.
Electric service outside of municipalities,
§62-110.2.
Joint municipal electric power and energy,
§§159B-1 to 159B-52.
See JOINT MUNICIPAL ELECTRIC POWER
AND ENERGY ACT.
Joint ownership of generation and transmission
facilities, NC Const Art V §10.
Public enterprises generally, §§160A-311 to
160A-328.
See MUNICIPAL UTILITIES.

ELECTRIC COMPANIES —Cont'd
Nuclear facilities producing electricity, fees,
§166A-6.1.
Overhead high-voltage line safety, §§95-229.5 to
95-229.13.
See OVERHEAD HIGH-VOLTAGE LINE
SAFETY.
Property taxes.
Public service corporations.
Generally, §§105-333 to 105-344.
See PROPERTY TAXES.
Public service vehicles used to restore service.
Parked or standing on roadside giving warning
signal.
Motorist's duties when approaching, §20-157(f).
Public utilities generally, §§62-1 to 62-350.
See PUBLIC UTILITIES.
Rates for electric power.
Conservation of energy.
Change of rates.
Application to be accompanied by report of
probable effect, §62-155(e).
Generally, §62-155(b) to (d).
Policy of state, §62-155.
Exemption of certain electric utilities, §62-134(d).
Fuel and fuel-related charge adjustment,
§62-133.2.
Hearing, §62-134(b), (c).
Increase notices, §62-81(b).
Small power producers.
Power sales to public utilities, §62-156(a).
Determinations by commission, §62-156(b).
Surplus power rates, §62-154.
Rates for public utilities generally, §§62-130 to
62-159.
See PUBLIC UTILITY RATES.
**Renewable energy and energy efficiency
portfolio standard (REPS),** §62-133.8.
Right-of-way.
Acquisition by contract, §62-182.
Grant of eminent domain, §62-183.
Rural electrification authority, §§117-1 to 117-5.
See RURAL ELECTRIFICATION AUTHORITY.
Transmission line construction, §§62-180,
113A-12.
Transmission line siting, §§62-100 to 62-107.
See ELECTRIC TRANSMISSION LINE SITING.
Trespass.
Criminal trespass.
Damaging wires and other fixtures, §§14-154,
14-156.
Felling trees onto electric-power wires, §14-157.
Interfering with electric appliances, §14-151.
Underground damage prevention, §§87-100 to
87-114.
See UNDERGROUND DAMAGE PREVENTION.
Wastewater systems.
Limitation on electrical service, §130A-339.
Temporary electrical service, §130A-339.

ELECTRIC FENCES.
Electronic dog collars, unlawful removal,
§14-401.17.

ELECTRICITY.
Actions.
Sale of electrical materials, devices, appliances
and equipment.
Enforcement of provisions, §66-27.01.
Building codes.
Certificates for occupancy, §143-139.2(b).
Applicability of provisions, §143-139.2(c).

ELECTRICITY —Cont'd

Building codes —Cont'd

Insulation requirements, §143-139.2(a), (b).
Applicability of provisions, §143-139.2(c).
Wiring of houses, buildings and structures.
Requirements, §143-143.2.

Coal-fired generating units.

Emissions of oxides of nitrogen and sulfur dioxide by investor-owned utilities, §143-215.107D.
Environmental compliance costs recovery, §62-133.6.

Cogenerating power plants.

Income tax credit.
Corporation or partnership constructing in state, §105-130.25.

Companies.

See ELECTRIC COMPANIES.

Contractors, §§87-39 to 87-51.

See ELECTRICAL CONTRACTORS.

Cooperative associations.

Authorized purposes, §§54-111, 54-124.

Electric membership corporations, §§117-6 to 117-26.

See ELECTRIC MEMBERSHIP CORPORATIONS.

Environmental compliance costs recovery.

Coal-fired generating units, §62-133.6.

Landlord and tenant.

Charging tenants in same contiguous premises for costs of electric service, §42-42.1(a).
Disconnection or termination of service for nonpayment.
Prohibited, §42-42.1(b).
Security deposits, permitted uses.
Costs of, §42-51.
Separate leases for each bedroom of units.
Charging by lessor for costs of providing electricity.
Procedures to allow, utilities commission authority, §62-110(h).

Public service vehicles used to restore service.

Parked or standing on roadside giving warning signals.
Duties of motorist when approaching, §20-157(f).

Public utilities generally.

See PUBLIC UTILITIES.

Sales and use tax.

Rate of tax, §105-164.4(a).
Sale reported on accrual basis, §105-164.20.

ELECTRIC MEMBERSHIP CORPORATIONS,
§§117-6 to 117-26.

Amendments.

Certificate of incorporation, §117-25.

Assessments, §117-19.

Board of directors.

Bylaws.
Power of board to adopt and amend, §117-14.
Compensation, §117-13.
Election, §117-13.
Indemnification of directors, §117-46.
Powers.
Adoption and amendment of bylaws, §117-14.
Delegation of powers, §117-14.
Enumerated, §117-14.
President, §117-13.
Rules and regulations.
Powers of board, §117-14.
Secretary, §117-13.

ELECTRIC MEMBERSHIP CORPORATIONS
—Cont'd

Bond issues, §117-21.

Agreements for security of bonds, §117-22.
Cancellation of bonds, §117-23.
Covenants or agreements for security of bonds, §117-22.
Purchase and cancellation of bonds, §117-23.
Specific grant of power, §117-18.

Borrowing money.

Specific grant of power, §117-18.

Bylaws.

Power of board of directors to adopt and amend, §117-14.

Certificate of dissolution, §117-24.

Certificate of incorporation.

Amendment of certificate, §117-25.
Authorized formation, §117-10.
Contents, §117-11.
Execution of certificate by residents of territory served, §117-12.
Filing of certificate by residents of territory served, §117-12.
Formation authorized, §117-10.
Permissible provisions, §117-11(b).
Required provisions, §117-11(a).

Certificates of membership, §117-15.

Citation of act, §117-6.

Communications service providers.

Utilization of poles controlled by corporation, §62-350.

Conditions of membership, §117-16.

Consolidation.

Articles of consolidation, §117-41(c).
Filing and recording of articles, §117-43.
Recording of articles, §117-43.
Compliance with provisions, §117-41(a).
Effect of consolidation, §117-44.
Procedure, §117-41(c).
Proposition for consolidation, §117-41(b).
Validation, §117-45.

Construction of lines between June 1, 2005 and May 31, 2007, §117-10.3.

Contracts.

Specific grant of power, §117-18.

Corporate purpose, §117-16.

General grant of powers, §117-17.

Cost recovery for demand-side management and energy efficiency measures, §62-133.9.

Debts.

Contracting debt.
Specific grant of power, §117-18.

Definitions, §117-7.

Discrimination prohibited, §117-16.1.

Dissolution.

Certificate of dissolution, §117-24.

Federal aid.

Acceptance of gifts or grants, §117-18.
Application for grant or loan from governmental agency, §117-26.

Fees.

Applicability, §62-300(e).
Regulatory fee, §117-3.1.
Rate, §62-302(b1).

Foreign corporations, §117-28.

Domestication, §117-28.
Privileges, §117-28.
Rights and privileges, §117-28.

Formation in unserved communities, §117-8.

Application.
Filed with rural electrification authority, §117-8.

ELECTRIC MEMBERSHIP CORPORATIONS
—Cont'd
Formation in unserved communities —Cont'd
Application —Cont'd
Issuance of privilege for formation of such
corporation, §117-9.
Authorized, §117-10.
Privilege for formation of such corporation.
Issuance of privilege, §117-9.
Franchises.
Eligibility to receive franchise, §117-10.1.
Restriction on municipal service, §117-10.2.
Grants.
Application for grant or loan from governmental
agency, §117-26.
Indemnification.
Directors, officers, employees and agents, §117-46.
Lines.
Construction between June 1, 2005 and May 31,
2007, §117-10.3.
Loans.
Application for grant or loan from governmental
agency, §117-26.
Membership.
Certificates of membership, §117-15.
Conditions of membership, §117-16.
Terms of membership, §117-16.
Merger.
Articles of merger, §117-42(c).
Filing and recording of articles, §117-43.
Recording of articles, §117-43.
Compliance with provisions, §117-42(a).
Effect of merger, §117-44.
Procedure, §117-42(c).
Proposition for merger, §117-42(b).
Validation, §117-45.
Municipal franchises.
Eligibility to receive franchise, §117-10.1.
Restriction on municipal service, §117-10.2.
Political subdivision.
No corporation to be or have rights of political
subdivision of state, §117-19(a).
Powers.
General grant of powers, §117-17.
Specific grant of powers, §117-18.
Property.
Acquiring, holding and disposing of property.
Specific grant of power, §117-18.
Disposal of property, §117-20.
Encumbrance of property, §117-20.
Property taxes.
Public service corporations.
Generally, §§105-333 to 105-344.
See PROPERTY TAXES.
Public agency.
No corporation to be public agency, §117-19(a).
Purpose.
Corporate purpose, §§117-16, 117-17.
General grant of powers, §117-17.
Rates.
Discrimination prohibited, §117-16.1.
Regulatory fee.
Due date, §117-3.1(c).
Imposition, purpose, use, §117-3.1(a).
North Carolina rural electrification authority
fund.
Creation, proceeds deposited in, §117-3.1(d).
Rate, §117-3.1(b).
**Renewable energy and energy efficiency
portfolio standard (REPS) for,** §62-133.8(c).

ELECTRIC MEMBERSHIP CORPORATIONS
—Cont'd
Rural electric membership corporations.
Sale of merchandise by governmental units.
Exception to prohibition, §66-58(b).
Sale of merchandise by governmental units.
Exception to provisions, §66-58(b).
Seal.
Specific grant of powers, §117-18.
Subsidiary business activities, §117-18.1(a).
Employment of director or spouse, §117-18.1(c).
Prohibited activities, §117-18.1(b).
Taxes and assessments.
Subject to certain taxes, §117-19(b).
Telephone corporations.
Applicability of provisions, §117-30(a).
Terms and conditions of membership, §117-16.
Title of article, §117-6.
Utilities commission.
Regulation by commission, §62-53.

**ELECTRIC PERSONAL ASSISTIVE MOBILITY
DEVICES.**
Defined, §§20-4.01, 20-175.6(a).
Municipal regulation, §20-175.6(d).
Registration and certificate of title.
Exemption, §§20-51, 20-175.6(b).
Use, §20-175.6(c).

ELECTRIC POWER AND ENERGY ACT,
§§159B-1 to 159B-52.
See JOINT MUNICIPAL ELECTRIC POWER AND
ENERGY ACT.

ELECTRIC POWER HOLDING COMPANIES.
Dividends.
Income tax.
Adjustment for expenses related to,
§105-130.6A(d), (g), (h).

ELECTRIC POWER RATES.
Conservation of energy.
Change of rates.
Application to be accompanied by report of
probable effect, §62-155(e).
Generally, §62-155(b) to (d).
Policy of state, §62-155.
**Cost recovery for demand-side management
and energy efficiency measures.**
Assessment to be submitted, §62-133.9(c).
Definitions applicable, §62-133.9(a).
Generally, §62-133.9(d) to (g).
Implementation of measures, §62-133.9(b).
Rulemaking, §62-133.9(h).
Summary of proceedings, §62-133.9(i).
**Electric public utility purchase or
construction of carbon offset facility.**
Retention of fuel and fuel-related cost savings,
§62-133.10.
Exemption of certain electric utilities,
§62-134(d).
Fuel and fuel-related charge adjustment,
§62-133.2.
Hearing, §62-134(b), (c).
Notice of rate increase, §62-81(b).
Small power procedures.
Power sales to public utilities, §62-156(a).
Determinations by commission, §62-156(b).
Surplus power rates, §62-154.

ELECTRIC SERVICE IN URBAN AREAS,
§§160A-331 to 160A-338.
Agreements of electric suppliers.
Legislative findings, §160A-331.2(a).

ELECTRIC SERVICE IN URBAN AREAS
—Cont'd
Agreements of electric suppliers —Cont'd
Utilities commission.
Assignments or reassignments, §160A-331.2(e).
Jurisdiction to resolve issues related to
negotiations, §160A-331.2(c).
Orders to furnish service, §160A-331.2(d).
City facilities, §160A-336.
Contracts, §160A-322.
Definitions, §160A-331.
Electric membership corporations.
Agreements of electric suppliers generally,
§160A-331.2.
Load management, §160A-323.
Peak load pricing, §160A-323.
Police powers, §160A-338.
Rates, §160A-323.
Suppliers.
Assigned supplier.
Defined, §160A-331.
Police power, §160A-338.
Primary supplier.
Defined, §160A-331.
Effect of provisions, §160A-337.
Furnishing electric service for city facilities,
§160A-336.
Rights and restrictions, §160A-332(a).
Cities incorporated after April 20, 1965,
§160A-332(b).
Prohibited acts, §160A-332(c).
Secondary supplier.
Defined, §160A-331.
Discontinuance of service and transfer of
facilities by, §160A-335.
Temporary electric service, §160A-333.
Temporary electric service, §160A-333.
Utilities commission.
Agreements of electric suppliers.
Assignments or reassignments, §160A-331.2(e).
Jurisdiction to resolve issues related to
negotiations, §160A-331.2(c).
Orders to furnish service, §160A-331.2(d).
Authority and jurisdiction, §160A-334.
Discontinuance of service and transfer of facilities
by secondary supplier, §160A-335.
Orders, §§160A-331.2(d), 160A-334.

**ELECTRIC TRANSMISSION LINE
CONSTRUCTION.**
Environmental document.
Not required when constructing, maintaining or
removing lines across right of way of street or
highway, §113A-12.
**Rights of persons operating to construct and
maintain along highways and railroads,**
§62-180.

ELECTRIC TRANSMISSION LINE SITING.
Construction certificate.
Application.
Amendment of certificate, §62-102(e).
Contents, §62-102(a).
Inadvertent failure of service on or notice to,
§62-102(d).
Notice, §62-102(c).
Service of copies, §62-102(b).
Burden of proof, §62-105.
Compliance with certificate, §62-101(b).
Conditions, §62-105.
Effect of local ordinances, §62-106.
Exemptions, §62-101(c).

ELECTRIC TRANSMISSION LINE SITING
—Cont'd
Construction certificate —Cont'd
Hearing or making complaint, §§62-101(f), 62-104.
Initial construction without certificate, §62-101(e).
Intervention in proceedings, §62-103(b).
Parties to proceedings, §62-103(a).
Required, §62-101(a).
Rules and regulations, §62-107.
Waiver of notice and hearing requirement,
§62-101(d).
Definition, §62-100.
Underground damage prevention, §§87-100 to
87-114.
See UNDERGROUND DAMAGE PREVENTION.

ELECTRIC UTILITIES.
Generally.
See ELECTRIC COMPANIES.
Municipal utilities.
See MUNICIPAL UTILITIES.
Public utilities generally.
See PUBLIC UTILITIES.

ELECTRIC VEHICLES.
Energy credit and banking act.
Participation by state departments, institutions
and agencies.
Purchase, §143-58.4.
High occupancy vehicle lanes.
Lane restrictions inapplicable, §20-146.2(a).
Low speed vehicle defined, §20-4.01.
**Operation on certain roadways, restrictions,
equipment, registration, insurance,**
§20-121.1.
Registration fees, §20-87.

ELECTROCUTION, CAPITAL PUNISHMENT.
Abolished, §15-187.

ELECTROLOGISTS, §§88A-1 to 88A-23.
Actions.
Reports of violations of chapter.
Immunity from suit, §88A-23.
Venue for actions brought under chapter,
§88A-22(b).
Advertisement.
Board of electrologist examiners.
Powers to regulate, §88A-6.
Disseminating false, deceptive or misleading
advertising.
Grounds for disciplinary action, §88A-21(a).
Applicability of chapter.
Persons not affected, §88A-15.1.
Board of electrologist examiners.
Appointment of members, §88A-5(a), (b).
"Board" defined, §88A-3.
Compensation, §88A-5(f).
Composition, §88A-5(a).
Created, §88A-5(a).
Custody and use of funds, §88A-7.
Disciplinary authority, §88A-21.
Duties.
Generally, §88A-6.
Expenses.
Reimbursement, §88A-5(f).
Grants, contributions, devises, etc.
Accepted, §88A-8.
Meetings, §88A-5(h).
Number of members, §88A-5(a).
Officers.
Elections, §88A-5(g).

ELECTROLOGISTS —Cont'd
Board of electrologist examiners —Cont'd
Powers.
Generally, §88A-6.
Quorum, §88A-5(h).
Removal of members, §88A-5(e).
Terms of members, §88A-5(c).
Vacancies.
Filling, §88A-5(d).
Bribery.
Grounds for disciplinary actions, §88A-21(a).
Calls outside office, §88A-16(d).
Change of address, §88A-16(b).
Citation of chapter.
Short title, §88A-1.
Continuing education.
License renewal requirement, §88A-13.
Conviction of crime.
Grounds for disciplinary actions, §88A-21(a).
Criminal law and procedure.
Violations of chapter, §88A-4(b).
Definitions, §88A-3.
Deposits.
Fees payable to board of electrologist examiners,
§88A-7.
Disciplinary actions.
Certification, §88A-21(b).
Grounds, §88A-21(a).
Licenses.
Reinstatement of revoked license or removal of
restrictions, §88A-21(c).
Restrictions, revocation or suspension,
§88A-21(b), (c).
Remedial education.
Requiring, §88A-21(b).
Reprimands.
Letters of reprimand, §88A-21(b).
Education.
Continuing education.
License renewal.
Requirements, §88A-13.
Electrology.
Defined, §88A-3.
Electrology instructors.
Certification.
Examinations, §88A-17(b).
Failure to renew, §88A-18.
Issuance of certificate, §88A-17(c).
Renewal.
Annual renewal, §88A-18.
Failure to renew.
Examination, §88A-18.
Requirements, §88A-17(a).
Electrolysis.
Defined, §88A-3.
Examinations.
Certification of electrology instructors, §88A-17(b).
Failure to renew certificate, §88A-18.
Licenses, §88A-10(b).
Without examination, §88A-11.
Expenses, §88A-9(a).
Fees.
Board of electrologist examiners.
Duties to collect, §88A-6.
Deposits, §88A-7.
Salaries, compensation and expenses incurred
paid from, §88A-9(a).
Schedule, §88A-9(b).
Felonies.
Violations of chapter, §88A-4(b).

ELECTROLOGISTS —Cont'd
Felony convictions.
Forfeiture of license, §15A-1331A.
Financial obligations binding upon state.
Prohibited, §88A-9(a).
Forfeitures.
Schools of electrology.
Failure to renew certification, §88A-20.
Fraud.
Grounds for disciplinary actions, §88A-21(a).
Gifts.
Acceptance by board of electrologist examiners,
§88A-8.
Grants.
Acceptance by board of electrologist examiners,
§88A-8.
Hearings.
Reports of violations of chapter.
Notice of administrative hearing, §88A-23.
Immunity.
Reports of violations of chapter, §88A-23.
Injunctions, §88A-22(a).
Intent of chapter, §88A-2.
Investigations.
Board of electrologist examiners.
Powers, §88A-6.
Laser hair practitioners.
Ablative procedures, §88A-11.1(f).
Continuing education, §88A-13(d).
Instructors.
Issuance of license, §88A-17.1(b).
Requirements for license, §88A-17.1(a).
Issuance of license, §88A-11.1(b).
Medication, prohibited from dispensing,
§88A-11.1(d).
Physician supervision, §88A-11.1(c).
Requirements for license, §88A-11.1(a).
School of laser, light-source or pulse-light
treatments.
Application for certificate, §88A-19.1(a).
Change in ownership or management,
§88A-19.1(d).
Change of location, §88A-19.1(c).
Display of certification, §88A-19.1(e).
Issuance of certificate, §88A-19.1(b).
Use of approved devices, §88A-19.1(f).
Use of approved devices, §88A-11.1(e).
Licenses.
Board of electrologist examiners.
Powers, §88A-6.
Continuing education.
License renewal requirements, §88A-13.
Display in conspicuous place, §88A-16(c).
Education.
Continuing education requirements, §88A-13.
Examinations, §88A-10(b).
Licensure without examination, §88A-11.
Exemptions from licensure, §88A-15.
Fees.
Schedule, §88A-9(b).
Inactive status, §88A-14.
Issuance, §88A-10(c).
Laser hair practitioners, §88A-11.1.
Nonresidents.
Licensure without examination, §88A-11.
Statement of intent to practice, §88A-10(d).
Practice of electrolysis without license.
Unlawful practice, §88A-4(a).
Proof to be furnished board, §88A-10(a1).
Records.
Continuing education.
Records of educational course work,
§88A-13(c).

ELECTROLOGISTS —Cont'd
Licenses —Cont'd
Renewal.
Annual renewal, §88A-12(a).
Continuing education.
Approval of program, §88A-13(b).
Hours and subject matter, §88A-13(a).
Maintenance and distribution of appropriate
records of educational course work,
§88A-13(c).
Failure to renew.
Reinstatement, §88A-12(b).
Inactive status.
Removal from inactive status, §88A-14.
Late renewal, §88A-12(a).
Requirements, §88A-10(a).
Restrictions, revocation or suspension.
Disciplinary actions, §88A-21(b).
Reinstatement of revoked license or removal
of restrictions, §88A-21(c).
Felony convictions, §15A-1331A.
Temporary license.
Issuance, §88A-10.1.
Malpractice.
Grounds for disciplinary actions, §88A-21(a).
**Mental health, developmental disabilities and
substance abuse.**
Judicial determination of mental incompetency.
Grounds for disciplinary actions, §88A-21(a).
Nonresidents.
Licensure without examination, §88A-11.
Statement of intent to practice, §88A-10(d).
Notice.
Change of address or opening of new office,
§88A-16(b).
Reports of violations of chapter.
Notice of administrative hearing, §88A-23.
Opening of new offices.
Notice, §88A-16(b).
Permanent establishments.
Required, §88A-16(a).
Persons not affected by chapter, §88A-15.1.
Physicians and surgeons.
Exemptions from licensure, §88A-15.
Persons not affected by chapter, §88A-15.1.
Place of business.
Calls outside office, §88A-16(d).
Change of address or opening of new office.
Notice, §88A-16(b).
Permanent establishment.
Required, §88A-16(a).
Practice of electrolysis.
Unlawful practice, §88A-4(a).
Purposes of chapter, §88A-2.
Records.
Board of electrologist examiners.
Duty to maintain records of proceedings,
§88A-6.
Continuing education requirements.
Records of educational course work, §88A-13(c).
Reports.
Violations of chapter, §88A-23.
Immunity from suit, §88A-23.
Reprimands.
Disciplinary actions.
Letters of reprimand, §88A-21(b).
Rules and regulations.
Board of electrologist examiners.
Powers to adopt, §88A-6.
Salaries, §88A-9(a).

ELECTROLOGISTS —Cont'd
Schools of electrology.
Certification.
Display, §88A-19(e).
Forfeiture.
Failure to renew, §88A-20.
Issuance of certificate, §88A-19(b).
Renewal.
Annual renewal, §88A-20.
Failure to renew.
Forfeiture, §88A-20.
Requirements, §88A-19(a).
Transferability of certificates, §88A-19(d).
Valid for location named in application only,
§88A-19(c).
Epilators.
Used in school.
Approval by food and drug administration of
United States government, §88A-19(f).
Renewal.
Failure to renew.
Examination, §88A-18.
Seals and sealed instruments.
Board of electrologist examiners.
Powers to adopt, §88A-6.
Short title, §88A-1.
Superior courts.
Venue for actions brought under chapter,
§88A-22(b).
Temporary license.
Issuance, §88A-10.1.
Title of chapter.
Short title, §88A-1.
Unprofessional conduct.
Grounds for disciplinary actions, §88A-21(a).
Venue.
Actions brought under chapter, §88A-22(b).
Violations of chapter.
Criminal penalty, §88A-4(b).
Injunctions, §88A-22.
Reports, §88A-23.
Immunity from suit, §88A-23.

ELECTROMAGNETIC RADIATION.
Radiation protection act generally, §§104E-1 to
104E-29.
See RADIATION PROTECTION.

ELECTRONIC ACCESS TO STATE SERVICES.
Electronic and digital transactions.
Access to services through.
Agencies encouraged to maximize, §66-58.12(a).
Fees, §66-58.12(b), (c).
Judicial department exempt from provisions,
§66-58.12(d).
Webportal system.
Agency links, §66-58.20(b).
Development and implementation, §66-58.20(a).

ELECTRONICALLY STORED INFORMATION.
Discovery, production, §1A-1 Rule 34.
Admissions, failure to admit, expenses, §1A-1
Rule 37(c).
Defined, §1A-1 Rule 26(b).
Failure to make, §1A-1 Rule 37.
Lost information, §1A-1 Rule 37(b1).
Objections, §1A-1 Rule 34(b1).
Order compelling discovery.
Failure to comply with order, §1A-1 Rule 37(b).
Motion for, §1A-1 Rule 37(a).
Persons not parties, §1A-1 Rule 34(c).
Procedure, §1A-1 Rule 34(b).

ELECTRONICALLY STORED INFORMATION
—Cont'd
Discovery, production —Cont'd
Response, §1A-1 Rule 34(b1).
Scope of discovery, §1A-1 Rule 26(b).
Scope of request, §1A-1 Rule 34(a).
Subpoenas.
Confidentiality of information.
Subpoenas requiring disclosure of confidential
information, protection, §1A-1 Rule 45(c).
Issuance, §1A-1 Rule 45(a).
Service, §1A-1 Rule 45(b).

ELECTRONIC AUCTION SERVICE.
**Disposition of seized, confiscated or unclaimed
property,** §15-14.1.
State surplus property.
Sale or disposal using, §143-64.03(d).

ELECTRONIC CHATTEL PAPER.
Secured transactions.
Control, §25-9-105.
Perfection by control, §25-9-314(a).

**ELECTRONIC COMMERCE IN
GOVERNMENT,** §§66-58.1 to 66-58.12.
**Access to services through electronic and
digital transactions.**
Agencies encouraged to maximize, §66-58.12(a).
Fees, §66-58.12(b), (c).
Judicial department exempt from provisions,
§66-58.12(d).
Certification authorities.
Licensing, §66-58.3.
Civil penalties for violations, §66-58.7.
Conflict of other rights, §66-58.6(d).
Criminal penalties for violations, §66-58.8(a).
Definitions, §66-58.2.
Deposit of fees, §66-58.10(c).
Electronic signatures.
Acceptance and use by public agencies, §66-58.4.
Enforceability of transactions, §66-58.5(b).
Presumptions and burden of proof not effected,
§66-58.5(c).
Validity, §66-58.5(a).
Enforcement of provisions, §66-58.6(a).
Evidence of criminal violations, §66-58.8(b).
Exemptions from article, §66-58.9.
Jurisdiction over transactions, §66-58.6(b).
Legislative purpose, §66-58.1.
**Limitation of authority for criminal
punishment,** §66-58.8(c).
Non-applicability of article, §66-58.9.
Purpose of article, §66-58.1.
Reciprocal agreements, §66-58.11.
Representation by Attorney General,
§66-58.6(c).
Rulemaking.
Procedures, §66-58.10(a).
Temporary rules, §66-58.10(b).

ELECTRONIC DOG COLLARS.
Enforcement, §14-401.17(c).
Jurisdiction, §14-401.17(c).
Penalties, §14-401.17(b).
Unlawful removal, §14-401.17(a).

**ELECTRONIC FILING BY INSURANCE
LICENSEES OR APPLICANTS FOR
LICENSES,** §58-2-250.

**ELECTRONIC FILING OF PLEADINGS AND
OTHER DOCUMENTS,** §1A-1 Rule 5(e).
Appeals, AppProc Rule 26(a).
Service of process by electronic means, AppProc
Rule 26(c).

**ELECTRONIC FILING OF PLEADINGS AND
OTHER DOCUMENTS** —Cont'd
Contract with vendor to provide.
Administrative office of the courts, §7A-49.5(c).
Deposit of funds received from vendor.
Court information technology fund, §7A-49.5(d).
District courts and superior courts.
Efiling pilot project, SuperCt Supp Rules 1 to
Super Ct Supp Rule 9.
**Establishment and operation of systems and
services.**
Duty of director of administrative office of the
courts, §7A-343.
Legislative findings, §7A-49.5(a).
Rules.
Supreme court may adopt, §7A-49.5(b).
Waiver of fees for indigents.
Rules to address, §7A-49.5(b).

ELECTRONIC FUNDS TRANSFERS.
Funds transfers generally, §§25-4A-101 to
25-4A-507.
See FUNDS TRANSFERS.
Local government finance.
Acceptance of electronic payments, §159-32.1.
Public hospitals, §159-39(i), (i1).
Statewide accounts receivable program.
Payments by, authorized, §147-86.22(b).
Taxes.
Payment by, §105-241(b).
Penalty for bad transfer, §105-236(a).

ELECTRONIC MAIL.
**Driving while using mobile phone to send
electronic mail.**
Unlawful, §20-137.4A(a).
Driver's license points or insurance surcharge
not assessed, §20-137.4A(c).
Exceptions, §20-137.4A(b).
Penalty, §20-137.4A(c).
While operating school bus.
Penalty, §20-137.4A(c).
E-filing, §§1A-1 Rule 5(e), 7A-49.5.
Electronic records and signatures.
Uniform electronic transactions act, §§66-311 to
66-330.
See ELECTRONIC TRANSACTIONS.
**List of electronic mail subscribers maintained
by local government.**
Public inspection.
Availability, copy, providing not required,
§132-1.13(a).
Use of list by local government, §132-1.13(b).
Military and overseas voters.
Confirmation of receipt of application and voted
ballot.
Electronic free access system, §163-258.14.
Electronic mail address provided by covered voter,
§163-258.15.
Transmission of ballots and ballot materials to
covered voters.
Electronic transmission system, §163-258.9(b).
**Municipal subdivision construction or
development.**
Imposition or increase in fees or charges.
Communicating notice of meeting, §160A-4.1(a).
Sanitary districts.
New or increased services charges or rates.
Notice of meeting, §130A-64.1.
Service by electronic mail not authorized,
§1A-1 Rule 4(j6).

ELECTRONIC MAIL —Cont'd

Spam.

Damage recovery, §1-539.2A.

Personal jurisdiction for actions regarding, §1-75.4.

Stalking, §14-277.3A.

Cyberstalking, §14-196.3.

ELECTRONIC MEDICAL RECORDS, §90-412.

Health information exchange, §§90-413.1 to 90-413.8.

ELECTRONIC MONITORING.

Costs of monitoring pretrial and sentenced offenders.

Reimbursement to division of adult correction, §148-10.3.

Counties.

Fee to cover costs of monitoring, §7A-313.1.

Parole.

Conditions, §15A-1374(b).

Impaired driving, §15A-1374(a1).

Removal, destruction or circumventing operation of electronic monitoring devices.

Unlawful, §14-226.3(b).

Electronic monitoring device defined, §14-226.3(a).

Persons for which section applies, §14-226.3(b).

Punishment, §14-226.3(e).

Request or solicitation, §14-226.3(c).

Sex offender monitoring, inapplicability, §14-226.3(d).

Satellite-based monitoring.

Probation, post-release supervision, parole.

See SATELLITE-BASED MONITORING.

Sex offenders, §§14-208.40 to 14-208.45.

See SEX OFFENDER MONITORING.

ELECTRONIC MONITORING DEVICES, §15A-1343(b1).

County fee to cover costs of monitoring, §7A-313.1.

Fees, §15A-1343(c2).

House arrest with electronic monitoring, defined, §15A-1340.11.

Removal, destruction or circumventing operation of electronic monitoring devices.

Unlawful, §14-226.3(b).

Electronic monitoring device defined, §14-226.3(a).

Persons for which section applies, §14-226.3(b).

Punishment, §14-226.3(e).

Request or solicitation, §14-226.3(c).

Sex offender monitoring, inapplicability, §14-226.3(d).

ELECTRONIC NOTARY PUBLIC ACT, §§10B-100 to 10B-146.

See NOTARIES PUBLIC.

ELECTRONIC OR DIGITAL RECORDS AND SIGNATURES.

Electronic commerce in government, §§66-58.1 to 66-58.12.

See ELECTRONIC COMMERCE IN GOVERNMENT.

Electronic medical records, authorization, §90-412(b).

Generally, §§66-311 to 66-330.

See ELECTRONIC TRANSACTIONS.

Identity theft.

Generally, §§14-113.20 to 14-113.25.

ELECTRONIC OR DIGITAL RECORDS AND SIGNATURES —Cont'd

Public agency transactions, §§66-58.1 to 66-58.12.

See ELECTRONIC COMMERCE IN GOVERNMENT.

Uniform electronic transactions act, §§66-311 to 66-330.

See ELECTRONIC TRANSACTIONS.

ELECTRONIC SURVEILLANCE.

Actions.

Civil cause of action for violation of article.

Damages authorized, §15A-296.

Administrative subpoena to compel production of business records, §15A-298.

Advertisement for surveillance devices.

Felony, §15A-288(a2).

Aggrieved person.

Defined, §15A-286.

Appeals.

Order granting motion to suppress, §15A-294(h).

Attorneys' fees.

Civil action for violation of article, §15A-296(a).

Aural transfers.

Defined, §15A-286.

Bugging devices.

Advertisements for, §15A-288(a2).

Confiscation of, §15A-289.

Manufacture, §15A-288.

Citizens band radio communications.

Interception not unlawful, §15A-287(b2).

Civil action for violation of article.

Damages authorized, §15A-296.

Civil defense signals.

Interception not unlawful, §15A-287(b2).

Communications common carriers.

Defined, §15A-286.

Permissible manufacture, assembly, possession, purchase or sale of surveillance devices, §15A-288(b1).

Confiscation of electronic surveillance devices, §15A-289.

Conformity to federal law, §15A-297.

Conspiracy to commit certain crimes.

Issuance of orders for surveillance, §15A-290(a2).

Continuing criminal enterprise.

Issuance of orders for electronic surveillance, §15A-290(a1).

Costs.

Civil action for violation of article, §15A-296(a).

Damages.

Civil action for violation of article.

Actual damages, §15A-296(a).

Defenses.

Actions for violation of article.

Good faith reliance, complete defense, §15A-296(b).

Definitions.

Generally, §15A-286.

Disclosure of communications.

Discretion of judicial review panel to disclose to party or counsel, §15A-294(e).

Evidence.

Copy of order and application must be furnished to parties, §15A-294(f).

Law enforcement officers in performance of duty, §15A-294(a), (b).

Orders, specification of facilities or place of interception.

Exceptions, §15A-294(i), (j).

ELECTRONIC SURVEILLANCE —Cont'd
Disclosure of communications —Cont'd
Testifying under oath, §15A-294(c).
Distress or public use signals.
Interception not unlawful, §15A-287(b2).
Drug-trafficking violations.
Issuance of orders for surveillance, §15A-290(a1).
Electronic communications.
Authorized interception by law enforcement
personnel, §15A-290(d).
Defined, §15A-286.
Disclosure by law enforcement officer in
performance of duty, §15A-294(a).
Use of contents by law enforcement officer in
performance of duty, §15A-294(b).
Willful disclosure, felony, §15A-287(a3).
Willful interception, felony, §15A-287(a1).
Electronic communication services.
Administrative subpoena to compel production of
business records, §15A-298.
Defined, §15A-286.
Interception by agent of providers.
Not unlawful if necessary to services,
§15A-287(c).
Electronic communication systems.
Defined, §15A-286.
Electronic storage.
Defined, §15A-286.
Evidence.
Admissibility of contents of communications.
Copy of order and application must be furnished
to parties, §15A-294(f).
Disclosure of communications.
Copy of order and application must be furnished
to parties, §15A-294(f).
Motion to suppress contents of communications,
§15A-294(g).
Appeal of order granting motion, §15A-294(h).
Extortion.
Electronic surveillance orders, §15A-290(b).
Federal communications commission officers.
Interception in discharge of monitoring
responsibilities.
Not unlawful, §15A-287(d).
Federal law, legislative intent of conformity,
§15A-297.
Felony offenses, surveillance orders to be
issued.
Adulteration of food, drugs or cosmetics,
§15A-290(c5).
Assault or threats against executive or legislative
officers, §15A-290(c4).
Assault with deadly weapon of government
officers, §15A-290(c4).
Intimidation or harassment of jurors or witnesses,
§15A-290(c3).
Mass death or destruction weapons.
Manufacture, assembly, etc., §15A-290(c5).
Murder, kidnapping, robbery, etc., §15A-290(b).
Obstructing criminal investigations, §15A-290(c2).
Offenses against minors, §15A-290(c1).
Forfeiture of electronic surveillance devices,
§15A-289.
Good faith reliance.
Complete defense to actions for violation of article,
§15A-296(b).
Ham radio communications.
Interception not unlawful, §15A-287(b2).
Judicial review panels.
Applications for electronic surveillance orders,
§§15A-291(a), 15A-292(a).
Contents, §15A-291(d).

ELECTRONIC SURVEILLANCE —Cont'd
Judicial review panels —Cont'd
Compliance with federal statute, §15A-291(b).
Composition, §15A-291(a).
Contents of application for surveillance order,
§15A-291(d).
Defined, §15A-286.
Determination of probable cause for orders,
§15A-291(e).
Disclosure of recorded material.
Discretion to disclose to party or counsel,
§15A-294(e).
Emergency applications for surveillance orders.
Compliance with federal statute, §15A-291(b).
Examination of applicant under oath, §15A-291(e).
Interception of communications by law
enforcement personnel.
Felonies other than those specified, §15A-290(d).
Judge may preside over trial resulting from
surveillance order, §15A-291(c).
Orders for surveillance.
Application and granting, §15A-292(a).
Applications sealed by panel, §15A-293(d2).
Contents of order, §15A-293(b).
Custody of applications for orders,
§15A-293(d2).
Denial, §15A-294(h).
Destruction of orders, §15A-293(d2).
Determinations necessary for issuance,
§15A-293(a).
Inventory of parties upon issuance of order,
§15A-294(d).
Notice to parties upon issuance of order,
§15A-294(d), (d1).
Reports, §15A-293(d).
Probable cause for surveillance orders,
determination of, §15A-291(e).
Recorded material.
Custody of recordings, §15A-293(d).
Discretion to disclose portion of material to
party or counsel, §15A-294(e).
Report to supreme court regarding surveillance
orders, §15A-292(c).
Trials resulting from electronic surveillance order.
Member of panel may not preside, §15A-291(c).
Law enforcement communications available to
general public.
Interception not unlawful, §15A-287(b2).
Manufacture of surveillance devices.
Felony, §15A-288(a1).
Law enforcement use, permissible manufacture,
§15A-288(c).
Mobile radio communications.
Interception not unlawful, §15A-287(b2).
Notice.
Orders for surveillance.
Application and granting of order, §15A-292(a).
Oral communications.
Defined, §15A-286.
Disclosure by law enforcement officer in
performance of duty, §15A-294(a).
Lawful interception by law enforcement
personnel, §15A-290(d).
Use of contents by law enforcement officer in
performance of duty, §15A-294(b).
Willful disclosure, felony, §15A-287(a3).
Willful interception, felony, §15A-287(a1).
Order denying application for surveillance
order, §15A-294(h).
Orders for surveillance.
Appeal of order denying application, §15A-294(h).

ELECTRONIC SURVEILLANCE —Cont'd
Orders for surveillance —Cont'd
Application, §15A-292(a).
Application by attorney general independent of
    law enforcement agencies, §15A-292(b).
Authorized duration of order, §15A-293(c).
Contents required, §15A-293(b).
    Specification of facilities or place of interception,
        exceptions, §15A-294(i), (j).
Custody of applications and orders, §15A-293(d2).
Destruction of applications or orders,
    §15A-293(d2).
Determinations by judicial review panel,
    §15A-293(a).
Duration of order, §15A-293(c).
Implementation generally, §15A-293.
Notice of application and granting, §15A-292(a).
Notice to parties of issuance, §15A-294.
Obstruction of investigation or prosecution of
    surveillance subject matter.
    Grossly negligent disclosure, misdemeanor,
        §15A-287(f).
    Willful disclosure, felony, §15A-287(e).
Offenses for which orders may be granted,
    §15A-290.
Persons authorized to conduct interceptions,
    §15A-293(c).
Progress reports to judicial review panel required
    in order, §15A-293(d).
Reports to supreme court, §15A-292(c).
Request of attorney general for applications,
    §15A-292(a).
Sealed by judicial review panel, §15A-293(d2).
Time period authorized, §15A-293(c).
Possession of surveillance devices.
Felony, §15A-288(a1).
Law enforcement use, §15A-288(c).
Privileged character of communications,
    §15A-290(e).
Public officers and employees.
Obstruction of investigation or prosecution of
    subject matter of surveillance.
    Removal from office, §15A-287(g).
Permissible manufacture, possession, purchase or
    sale of devices for surveillance, §15A-288(b2).
Punitive damages.
Civil action for violation of article, §15A-296(a).
Purchase of surveillance devices.
Felony, §15A-288(a1).
Law enforcement use, §15A-288(c).
Radio communications.
Interception not unlawful, §15A-287(b2).
Readily accessible to the general public.
Defined, §15A-286.
Interception of or access to electronic
    communications.
    Not unlawful, §15A-287(b1).
Recorded material.
Custody of recordings, §15A-293(d).
Destruction of recordings, §15A-293(d).
Disclosure by law enforcement officers in
    performance of duties, §15A-294(a).
Disclosure of contents in testimony under oath,
    §15A-294(c).
Duplicate recordings, §15A-293(d).
Judicial review panels.
    Discretion to disclose portion of material to
        party or counsel, §15A-294(e).
Use of contents by law enforcement officer in
    performance of duty, §15A-294(b).

ELECTRONIC SURVEILLANCE —Cont'd
Recording equipment.
Procedures for use established by attorney
    general, §15A-293(f).
State bureau of investigation to own and operate
    equipment, §15A-293(e).
Recording of communications, procedure,
    §15A-293(d).
Records of business.
Subpoena duces tecum, §15A-298.
Reports.
Attorney general report to administrative office of
    United States court, §15A-295.
Copy of attorney general's report filed with
    administrative office of courts of North
    Carolina, §15A-295.
Orders for surveillance, report to supreme court,
    §15A-292(c).
Progress reports on orders for surveillance,
    §15A-293(d).
Sale of surveillance devices.
Felony, §15A-288(a1).
Law enforcement use, §15A-288(c).
Service of process.
Issuance of surveillance order.
    Inventory served on parties, §15A-294(d).
State bureau of investigation.
Operation of recording equipment, §15A-293(e).
Subpoenas.
Issuance to communications carriers or services
    for production of business records, §15A-298.
Suppression of evidence.
Appeal of order granting motion, §15A-294(h).
Motion to suppress contents of communications,
    §15A-294(g).
Switchboard operators.
Interception or disclosure of communications in
    normal course of employment.
    Not unlawful, §15A-287(c).
**Training of law enforcement officers for
    surveillance.**
Attorney general, §15A-293(f).
Users.
Defined, §15A-286.
Willful use of contents of wire or oral
    communications, felony, §15A-287(a4).
Willful use of devices to intercept oral
    communications, felony, §15A-287(a2).
Wire communications.
Defined, §15A-286.
Disclosure by law enforcement officer in
    performance of duty, §15A-294(a).
Lawful interception by law enforcement
    personnel, §15A-290(d).
Use of contents by law enforcement officer in
    performance of duty, §15A-294(b).
Willful disclosure, felony, §15A-287(a3).
Willful interception, felony, §15A-287(a1).

ELECTRONIC SURVEILLANCE ORDERS,
    §15A-290(b).

ELECTRONIC TRANSACTIONS, §§66-311 to
    66-330.
Agreements.
Defined, §66-312.
Effect, §66-315(b), (c).
Waiver of provisions by agreement, §66-315(d).
Applicability of act, §§66-313(a), (c), 66-315(b),
    66-316.
Exceptions, §66-313(b), (e).
Prospective application, §66-314.

ELECTRONIC TRANSACTIONS —Cont'd
Athlete agents and agency contracts.
Law governing electronic records and signatures,
§78C-103.
Automated transactions, §66-324.
Citation of act, §66-311.
Computer information agreement.
Choice of law, §66-329.
Construction of provisions, §66-316.
Severability, §66-330.
Consumer transactions.
Consent to electronic records, §66-327(c).
Entered into in state, §66-327(f).
Federal law compliance, §66-328.
Written copy of contract, §66-327(d).
Contracts.
Automated transactions, §66-324.
Consumer transactions.
Written copy of contract, §66-327(d).
Defined, §66-312.
Corporations.
Agreement to conduct, §55-1-50.
Criminal process and procedure.
Definitions relating to electronic technology,
§15A-101.1.
Electronic repository for criminal process,
§15A-301.1.
Definitions, §66-312.
Transferable record, §66-326(a).
Electronic records.
Acknowledgment, §66-321.
Attribution, §66-319(a).
Change.
Effect, §66-320.
Consumer transactions.
Consent to electronic records, §66-327(c).
Defined, §66-312.
Effect, §66-319(b).
Error.
Effect, §66-320.
Evidence.
Admissibility, §66-323.
Inhibiting of ability of recipient to store or print
by sender.
Record not enforceable against recipient,
§66-318(c), (d).
Legal consequences.
Determination, §66-315(e).
Legal effect, §66-317(a) to (d).
Notarization, §66-321.
Posting or display, §66-318(b), (d).
Receipt.
Effect, §66-325(f), (g).
What constitutes, §66-325(b) to (e).
Retention, §66-322(a) to (g), (f).
Additional requirements by governmental
agencies, §66-322(g).
Checks, §66-322(e).
Sending.
What constitutes, §66-325(a), (d).
Transferable records.
Control, §66-326(b) to (d), (f).
Defined, §66-326(a).
Obligor's rights and defenses, §66-326(e).
Proof of control, §66-326(f).
Trusts and trustees.
Uniform trust code, §36C-11-1102.
Use not required by provisions, §66-315(a).
Electronic signatures.
Acknowledgment, §66-321.

ELECTRONIC TRANSACTIONS —Cont'd
Electronic signatures —Cont'd
Athlete agents and agency contracts.
Law governing, §78C-103.
Attribution, §66-319(a).
Commercial code.
Electronic signatures in global and national
commerce act.
Article modifies, limits and supersedes federal
act, §25-1-108.
Criminal process and procedure.
Definitions relating to electronic technology,
§15A-101.1.
Defined, §66-312.
Effect, §66-319(b).
Evidence.
Admissibility, §66-323.
Legal consequences.
Determination, §66-315(e).
Legal effect, §66-317(a), (d).
Notarization, §66-321.
Prudent management of institutional funds.
Electronic signatures in global and national
commerce act.
Relation to, §36E-9.
Public agencies.
Acceptance and use, §66-58.4.
Validity.
Transactions between person and agency,
§66-58.5.
Trusts and trustees.
Uniform trust code, §36C-11-1102.
Use not required by provisions, §66-315(a).
Evidence.
Admissibility of electronic signatures and records,
§66-323.
Filing of pleadings and papers electronically,
§1A-1 Rule 5(e).
E-filing, §7A-49.5.
Funds transfers.
Generally, §§25-4A-101 to 25-4A-507.
See FUNDS TRANSFERS.
Money transmitters, §§53-208.1 to 53-208.30.
See MONEY TRANSMITTERS.
Insurance licensees or applicants for licenses.
Electronic filing, §58-2-250.
Nonprofit corporations.
Action by members by written consent, §55A-7-04.
Action by written ballot, §55A-7-08.
Action without meeting, consent, §55A-8-21(a).
Agreement to conduct, §55A-1-70.
Notice communicated by corporation, §55A-1-41(c).
Signature of proxy, §55A-7-24(a).
Notaries public.
Electronic notary public act, §§10B-100 to
10B-146.
See NOTARIES PUBLIC.
Oral communications, §66-327(e).
Other applicable laws, §66-313(d).
Determination of legal consequences of electronic
record or signature, §66-315(e).
Prospective application of act, §66-314.
Prudent management of institutional funds.
Electronic signatures in global and national
commerce act.
Relation to, §36E-9.
Public agencies.
Electronic signatures.
Acceptance and use, §66-58.4.
Validity.
Transactions between person and agency,
§66-58.5.

ELECTRONIC TRANSACTIONS —Cont'd
Real property electronic recording, §§47-16.1 to 47-16.7.
See REAL PROPERTY ELECTRONIC RECORDING.
Retention of electronic records, §66-322(a) to (g), (f).
Additional requirements by governmental agencies, §66-322(g).
Checks, §66-322(e).
Severability of provisions, §66-330.
Title of act, §66-311.
Trusts and trustees.
Electronic records and signatures, §36C-11-1102.
Writing.
Consumer transactions.
Written copy of contract, §66-327(d).
Provision of information in writing, §66-318(a), (d).

ELECTRONS.
Radiation protection act generally, §§104E-1 to 104E-29.
See RADIATION PROTECTION.

ELEMENTARY AND SECONDARY EDUCATION.
Generally.
See SCHOOLS AND EDUCATION.

ELEVATING HEIGHT OF PASSENGER MOTOR VEHICLE, §20-135.4(d).

ELEVATOR INSURANCE, §58-7-15.
Mandatory or voluntary risk sharing plans.
See MANDATORY OR VOLUNTARY RISK SHARING PLANS.

ELEVATORS, §§95-110.1 to 95-110.15.
Accidents.
Investigations, §95-110.9(b).
Operating after accident, §95-110.9(c).
Removal of damaged equipment, §95-110.9(d).
Reports.
Required, §95-110.9(a).
Appeals.
Violations of article, §95-110.10.
Applicability of article, §95-110.2.
Attorney general.
Representing department of labor, §95-110.12.
Building codes.
Enforcement, §143-139(d).
Special safety to life requirements applicable to existing high-rise buildings.
Class I buildings, §143-138(i).
Class II buildings, §143-138(i).
Class III buildings, §143-138(i).
Certificate of operation.
Required, §95-110.7(a).
Suspension, revocation or refusal to issue or renew.
Operation after commissioner has refused to issue or has revoked, §95-110.7(c).
Violations of article, §95-110.6(b).
Commissioner of labor.
Powers and duties.
Generally, §95-110.5.
Compliance with article, §95-110.7(b).
Confidentiality.
Trade secrets, §95-110.14.
Construction of article, §95-110.15.
Criminal law and procedure, §95-110.11.

ELEVATORS —Cont'd
Definitions, §95-110.3.
Elevator and amusement device division, §95-110.4.
Exemptions from article, §95-110.2.
Federal law.
Agreements for enforcement, §95-110.13.
Fines, §95-110.11.
Inspection fees.
Assessment and collection, §95-107.
Disposition, §95-108.
Misdemeanors.
Violations, §95-110.11.
Noncomplying devices and equipment.
Appeals, §95-110.6(c).
Stopping or limiting use, §95-110.6(a).
Penalties, §95-110.10.
Prison terms, §95-110.11.
Purpose of general assembly, §95-110.1.
Rules and regulations.
Adoption, §95-110.5.
Construction, §95-110.15.
Scope of article, §95-110.2.
Severability of article, §95-110.15.
Short title of article, §95-110.1.
Smoking in, §143-599.
Trade secrets.
Confidentiality, §95-110.14.
Unsafe device or equipment.
Operation, §95-110.8.
Violation of article.
Appeals, §95-110.10.
Certificate of operation.
Suspension, revocation or refusal to issue or renew, §95-110.6(b).
Civil penalties, §95-110.10.
Criminal penalties, §95-110.11.

ELIZABETH CITY.
Room occupancy tax.
Uniform provisions.
Authorized to levy, §160A-215(g).
Generally, §160A-215.
Satellite annexation.
Limitation on area of satellite corporate limits, inapplicability, §160A-58.1(b).

ELIZABETH CITY STATE UNIVERSITY.
Constituent institution of University of North Carolina, §116-4.
Generally.
See UNIVERSITY OF NORTH CAROLINA.
Distinguished professors endowment trust fund.
Focused growth institutions.
Allocation, §116-41.15(b).
Contributions, matching, §116-41.16(b).
Defined, §116-41.13A.

ELKIN.
Room occupancy tax.
Uniform provisions.
Authorized to levy, §160A-215(g).
Generally, §160A-215.

ELUDING ARREST OR APPREHENSION.
Police chases, speed limits not applicable, §20-145.
State parks and forest road system, §143-116.8(b).

E-MAIL.

Driving while using mobile phone to send electronic mail.

Unlawful, §20-137.4A(a).

Driver's license points or insurance surcharge not assessed, §20-137.4A(c).

Exceptions, §20-137.4A(b).

Penalty, §20-137.4A(c).

While operating school bus.

Penalty, §20-137.4A(c).

E-filing, §§1A-1 Rule 5(e), 7A-49.5.

Electronic records and signatures.

Uniform electronic transactions act, §§66-311 to 66-330.

See ELECTRONIC TRANSACTIONS.

General assembly commissions, committees or subcommittees meeting.

Notice, §143-318.14A(b).

Improper government activities.

Reports.

State auditor to provide e-mail address for receipt of reports, §147-64.6B(a).

Insurance companies.

Licensees and license applicants.

Information provided commission, §58-2-69(b).

List of electronic mail subscribers maintained by local government.

Public inspection.

Availability, copy, providing not required, §132-1.13(a).

Use of list by local government, §132-1.13(b).

Military and overseas voters.

Confirmation of receipt of application and voted ballot.

Electronic free access system, §163-258.14.

Electronic mail address provided by covered voter, §163-258.15.

Transmission of ballots and ballot materials to covered voters.

Electronic transmission system, §163-258.9(b).

Municipal subdivision construction or development.

Imposition or increase in fees or charges.

Communicating notice of meeting, §160A-4.1(a).

Notaries public.

Electronic notary public act, §§10B-100 to 10B-146.

See NOTARIES PUBLIC.

Sanitary districts.

New or increased services charges or rates.

Notice of meeting, §130A-64.1.

Spam.

Damage recovery, §1-539.2A.

Personal jurisdiction for actions regarding, §1-75.4.

Stalking, §14-277.3A.

Cyberstalking, §14-196.3.

Trusts and trustees.

Electronic message.

Permissible method of notice or sending documents, §36C-1-109(a).

EMANCIPATION, §§7B-3500 to 7B-3509.

Age of minor, §48A-2.

Answer, time for filing, §7B-3502.

Appeals, §7B-3508.

Burden of showing emancipation in petitioner's best interest, §7B-3503.

Child support.

Termination of support, §50-13.4(c).

EMANCIPATION —Cont'd

Common law.

Provisions superseded by provisions of chapter, §7B-3509.

Considerations in determining best interest of petitioner, §7B-3504.

Continuing hearing and ordering investigation by juvenile court counselor, §7B-3503.

Contracting as adult, right of emancipated juvenile, §7B-3507.

Conveyances as adult, legal effect of final decree, §7B-3507.

Costs of proceeding, taxing, §7B-3506.

Criminal prosecution of emancipated juvenile as adult, §7B-1604(a).

Custody.

Persons incapable of self-support upon reaching majority, §50-13.8.

District court jurisdiction, §§7B-200(a), 7B-1603.

Entry of final decree of emancipation, §7B-3505.

Examination of juvenile by psychiatrist, psychologist or physician.

Court ordering, §7B-3503.

Final decree of emancipation, §7B-3505.

Hearing by court without jury, §7B-3503.

Husband-wife privilege, inapplicability, §7B-3503.

Irrevocability of decree, §7B-3507.

Legal effect of final decree, §7B-3507.

Married juvenile emancipated by provisions of article, §7B-3509.

Married persons, §52-2.

Notice of appeal, §7B-3508.

Parent relieved of legal duties and obligations, §7B-3507.

Petition.

Juveniles sixteen years or older filing, §7B-3500.

Signing and verifying, content requirements, §7B-3501.

Physician-patient privilege, inapplicability, §7B-3503.

Service of summons, §7B-3502.

Summons, §7B-3502.

Temporary order pending disposition of appeal, §7B-3508.

Transacting business as adult, legal effect of final decree, §7B-3507.

EMBALMERS.

Defined, §90-210.20(d).

Embalming defined, §90-210.20(e).

Funeral services providers generally.

See FUNERAL SERVICES PROVIDERS.

License qualifications, §90-210.25(a).

Medical examiner's permission necessary before embalming, §130A-388(a), (b).

EMBARGOES.

Authority of department of agriculture and consumer services.

Not limited, §130A-21(d).

Construing adulterated and misbranded, §130A-21(e).

Detention of product or article suspected of being misbranded or adulterated, §106-125.

Exercise of authority, §130A-21(a).

Milk and milk products, §106-266.36.

Scallops, shellfish or crustacea, §113-221.4.

Secretary or local health director.

Exercise of authority, §130A-21(a).

EMBEZZLEMENT.
ABC board members and employees,
§18B-702(w).
Arrest in civil cases.
Cases in which arrest allowed, §1-410.
Banks.
Conservators.
Applicability of provisions, §53-157.
Prohibited acts, §53-129.
Charities.
Funds embezzled by public officers and trustees,
§14-92.
Treasurers of charitable organizations, §14-93.
Civil liability for damages, §1-538.2(a).
Action brought regardless of criminal action,
§1-538.2(c).
Consequential and punitive damages and
attorneys' fees.
Additional recovery allowed, §1-538.2(a).
Amount of damages, cap, §1-538.2(a).
Parent or legal guardian liable for acts of
minor, §1-538.2(b).
Consequential damages, included in,
§1-538.2(c1).
Demand letter, seeking damages prior to action,
§1-538.2(c2).
Payment of money demanded, no further
action, §1-538.2(c4).
Demand letter, seeking damages prior to action,
§1-538.2(c2).
Payment of money demanded, no further action,
§1-538.2(c4).
Qualified privilege of sender, §1-538.2(c3).
Libel and slander.
Demand letter, seeking damages prior to action.
Qualified privilege of sender, §1-538.2(c3).
Other theories of law, recovery under, §1-538.2(d).
Parent or legal guardian liable for acts of minor,
§1-538.2(b).
Recovery of value of goods and merchandise,
§1-538.2(a).
Counties.
Funds embezzled by public officers and trustees,
§14-92.
Drugs.
Controlled substances, §90-108(a).
Education.
Funds embezzled by public officers and trustees,
§14-92.
Executors and administrators.
Liability, §28A-13-10.
Fiduciaries.
Property received by virtue of office or
employment, §14-90.
Fraternal benefit societies.
Treasurers of benevolent organizations, §14-93.
Good funds settlement act.
Settlement agents.
Closing funds received by, §45A-8(c).
Indictments.
Description in bill for embezzlement of money,
§15-150.
Insurance agents, brokers or administrators,
§§58-2-162, 58-2-163.
Larceny by servant or employee, §14-74.
Limited partnerships.
Appropriation of partnership funds by partner to
personal use, §14-97.
Surviving partner embezzling property, money or
effects of partnership, §14-98.

EMBEZZLEMENT —Cont'd
Local government finance.
Penalty, §159-181(b).
Motor carriers.
C.O.D. shipments, §62-273.
Municipalities.
Funds embezzled by public officers and trustees,
§14-92.
Partnerships.
Appropriation of partnership funds by partner to
personal use, §14-97.
Surviving partner embezzling property, money or
effects of partnership, §14-98.
Preneed funeral contracts and funds,
§90-210.70(a), (c).
Prisons and prisoners.
Funds embezzled by public officers and trustees,
§14-92.
**Property received by virtue of office or
employment.**
Agent, consignee, clerk, bailee, servant.
Applicability of section, §14-90(a).
Applicability of section, §14-90(a).
Corporate officers and agents.
Applicability of section, §14-90(a).
Felony, §14-90(b).
Fiduciaries.
Applicability of section, §14-90(a).
Person exercising public trust.
Applicability of section, §14-90(a).
Person holding public office.
Applicability of section, §14-90(a).
Value of property.
Punishment, §14-90(c).
Public officers and employees.
Property of state embezzled by officers and
employees, §14-91.
Property received by virtue of office or
employment, §14-90.
Taxes embezzled by officers, §14-99.
Railroads.
Officers of railroad companies, §14-94.
Religious societies.
Funds embezzled by public officers and trustees,
§14-92.
Treasurers of religious organizations, §14-93.
Seized items under warrant, §15A-242.
Social services.
Medical assistance program.
Property of patients.
Prohibited acts, §108A-60(a).
State bureau of investigation.
Misuse of state property, §114-15.1.
State of North Carolina.
Property of state.
Public officers and employees of embezzling
state property, §14-91.
Taxation.
Officers embezzling taxes, §14-99.
Trusts and trustees.
Funds embezzled by public officers and trustees,
§14-92.
Property received by virtue of office or
employment, §14-90.
Universities and colleges.
Funds embezzled by public officers and trustees,
§14-92.

EMBLEMENTS.
Crops.
See CROPS.

EMBLEMS.
Insurance companies, §58-3-50.
Motor clubs and associations.
Approval by commissioner of insurance, §58-69-20.
Tryon's Palace, §121-21.

EMERALD.
State stone, §145-8.

EMERALD ISLE.
All-terrain vehicles.
Use by employees on certain highways, §20-171.24.
Eminent domain.
Exercise of power, purposes, modified provisions, §40A-3(b1).
Vesting of title and right to possession, §40A-42(a).
Ordinances to regulate and control swimming, personal watercraft operation, surfing and littering in Atlantic Ocean, §160A-176.2.

EMERGENCIES.
Abortion.
Parental consent requirement waiver, §90-21.9.
Woman's right to know act.
Abortion compelled by medical emergency, §90-21.86.
Accident and health insurance.
Prescription drugs.
Extra prescriptions during state of emergency or disaster, §58-3-228.
Adult care homes.
Waiver of rules for certain homes providing shelter or service during disaster or emergency, §131D-7(a).
Alcoholic beverages.
State of emergency.
Powers of governor, §18B-110.
Ambulances.
See AMBULANCES.
Archives and history.
Historic properties.
Acquisition where funds not immediately available, §121-9(f).
Banks.
Suspension of business.
Authorization, §53-77.3(b).
Construction and interpretation, §53-77.3(d).
Definitions, §53-77.3(a).
Legal holiday for certain purposes, §53-77.3(c).
Bees and honey.
Action by commissioner, §106-642.
Bioterrorism.
Nuclear, biological or chemical agents.
Terrorist incident using, §§130A-475 to 130A-479.
See TERRORIST INCIDENT USING NUCLEAR, BIOLOGICAL OR CHEMICAL AGENTS.
Civil preparedness, §§166A-1 to 166A-18.
See EMERGENCY MANAGEMENT.
Concealed handgun permit.
Temporary permit issuance, §14-415.15(b).
Contracts.
Purchases and contracts through department of administration.
Purchase of articles in certain emergencies, §143-57.
Corporations.
Business corporations.
Emergency bylaws, §55-2-07.

EMERGENCIES —Cont'd
Corporations —Cont'd
Business corporations —Cont'd
Emergency powers, §55-3-03.
Court offices, closing.
Response to emergency situations, §7A-39(a).
In chambers jurisdiction not affected, §7A-39(c).
Court sessions, cancellation.
Response to emergency situations, §7A-39(a).
In chambers jurisdiction not affected, §7A-39(c).
Definitions.
Emergency communication, §14-286.2(b1).
Department of public safety.
Powers and duties of secretary, §143B-602.
Disasters.
See DISASTERS.
Drinking water, public water system supplying.
Definition of emergency circumstances, §130A-323(b).
Plan for provision of drinking water under emergency circumstances, §130A-323(a).
Emergency management, §§166A-1 to 166A-18.
See EMERGENCY MANAGEMENT.
Emergency management assistance compact, §§166A-40 to 166A-53.
Emergency management certification program, §§166A-60 to 166A-63.
Emergency medical services, §§143-507 to 143-519.
See EMERGENCY MEDICAL SERVICES.
Emergency war powers act, §§147-33.1 to 147-33.6.
See GOVERNOR.
Energy crisis administration, §§113B-20 to 113B-24.
Energy program, §113B-9.
Engineers.
Qualified immunity for volunteers during emergency or disaster, §89C-19.1.
Evacuation of public building.
Power of governor to order evacuation.
Willful refusal to leave building, §14-288.19(b).
Extension of time or period of limitation.
Catastrophic conditions existing in one or more counties.
Authority of chief justice, entry of order, §7A-39(b).
Firearms and other weapons.
Temporary concealed handgun permit, §14-415.15(b).
Governor.
Emergency management.
Mutual aid agreements.
Power to establish, §166A-10(a), (a1).
Emergency war powers, §§147-33.1 to 147-33.6.
See GOVERNOR.
Evacuation of public buildings.
Power of governor to order evacuation, §14-288.19(a).
Penalty for willful refusal to leave building, §14-288.19(b).
Succession to office of governor, §147-11.1(a) to (f).
Guns.
Concealed handgun permit, §14-415.15(b).
Hazardous materials emergency response, §§166A-20 to 166A-28.
See HAZARDOUS MATERIALS EMERGENCY RESPONSE.

EMERGENCIES —Cont'd
Health care facilities.
Temporary shelter or temporary services during disaster or emergency.
Waiver of rules for facilities that provide, §131E-112(a).
Hospitals.
Temporary waiver of rules of commission, §131E-84(a).
Ignoring warning regarding personal safety during disaster.
Civil liability for cost of rescue effort, §166A-15.1.
Immunity of volunteers performing emergency services, §§1-539.10, 1-539.11.
Interfering with emergency communication.
Definitions, §14-286.2(b1).
Penalties, §14-286.2(a).
Prohibited, §14-286.2(a).
Livestock diseases.
Threat imminent.
Warrantless inspection, §106-399.5.
Loans.
State debt, §§142-16 to 142-19.
State treasurer.
Short-term notes in emergencies, §147-70.
Management, §§166A-1 to 166A-18.
See EMERGENCY MANAGEMENT.
Medical emergencies.
Parental consent requirement for abortion, waiver, §90-21.9.
Mental health, developmental disabilities and substance abuse.
Involuntary commitment.
Special emergency procedure for individuals needing immediate hospitalization, §122C-262.
Substance abusers, §122C-282.
Militia.
Arrest power in certain emergencies, §127A-149.
Unorganized militia.
Ordered out for service, §127A-87.
Misdemeanors.
Interfering with emergency communication, §14-286.2(a).
Motor carriers.
Grant of emergency operating authority, §62-265.
Municipalities.
Vehicles in riot areas or approaching municipalities during emergencies.
Warrants to inspect vehicles, §14-288.11.
National guard.
Mutual assistance compact, §§127A-175 to 127A-184.
See NATIONAL GUARD.
911 system.
Enhanced 911 system for wireless communications.
See 911 SYSTEM.
General provisions.
See 911 SYSTEM.
Nurses.
Assistance by person in case of emergency.
Not prohibited, §90-171.43.
Parking on highway, §20-161(a).
Peace officers.
Urgent necessity.
Non-law-enforcement actions authorized, §15A-285.
Permits for concealed handguns, §14-415.15(b).
Personnel.
Assault on emergency personnel, §14-288.9.

EMERGENCIES —Cont'd
Pesticides.
Registration.
Emergency suspension, §143-447(a).
Pharmacists and pharmacies.
Declaration of disaster or state of emergency by governor.
Waiver of certain requirements, §90-85.25(a).
Price gouging during states of disaster.
Abnormal market disruption, §75-38(e), (f).
Deceptive trade practice, §75-38(a).
Determining whether price unreasonably excessive.
Considerations, §75-38(a).
End of state of disaster, §75-38(c).
Public policy, §75-37.
Statement that seller not in violation.
Issuance by attorney general, §75-38(b).
Triggering event, defined, §75-38(d).
Property insurance.
Mediation of emergency or disaster claims, §§58-44-70 to 58-44-120.
See PROPERTY INSURANCE.
Rabies emergencies, §130A-201.
Radiation protection.
See ATOMIC ENERGY, RADIOACTIVITY AND IONIZING RADIATION.
Retirement system for teachers and state employees.
Provision for emergency expenses of integration of system, §135-18.5.
Riots and civil disorders.
Assault on emergency personnel, §14-288.9(a).
Definition of term "emergency personnel,"§14-288.9(b).
Penalties for violations of provisions, §14-288.9(c).
Dangerous weapon or substance.
Transporting weapon or substance during emergency, §14-288.7.
Exceptions, §14-288.7(b).
Penalty for violation of provisions, §14-288.7(c).
Declared state of emergency defined, §14-288.1.
Definitions.
Declared state of emergency, §14-288.1.
Savings and loan associations.
Withdrawable accounts.
Limitations on amounts withdrawable or payable, §54B-125.
Savings banks.
Powers of commissioner of banks.
Imposition of limitation, §54C-87.
Secretary of public safety.
Powers and duties of secretary, §143B-602.
Sex offenders.
Unlawful presence on premises for use, care or supervision of children.
Emergency medical care exception, §14-208.18(b).
State bar disaster response plan, Bar Rules D.0301 to D.0303.
State board of elections.
Executive director.
Emergency powers, §163-27.1.
State debt.
Borrowing in emergencies, §§142-16 to 142-19.
State of emergency.
Government powers and proclamations generally, §§14-288.12 to 14-288.18.
See STATE OF EMERGENCY.

EMERGENCIES —Cont'd
State treasurer.
  Short-term notes in emergencies.
    Authorization to make, §147-70.
Telephones.
  False statement of emergencies.
    Securing use of party telephone line by false
      statement, §14-401.8.
  Refusing to relinquish party telephone line in
    emergency, §14-401.8.
  Securing use of party telephone line.
    False statement of emergency, §14-401.8.
Terrorism.
  Nuclear, biological or chemical agents.
    Terrorist incident using, §§130A-475 to
      130A-479.
      See TERRORIST INCIDENT USING
        NUCLEAR, BIOLOGICAL OR
        CHEMICAL AGENTS.
Trespass during, §14-288.6(a).
Vehicle size, weight and load restrictions.
  Vehicles responding to emergency event.
    Single trip emergency permit, §20-119(a1).
Volunteers performing emergency services.
  Immunity, §§1-539.10, 1-539.11.
**Warnings regarding personal safety during
    disaster.**
  Civil liability for cost of rescue when willfully
    ignoring, §166A-15.1.
War powers act, §§147-33.1 to 147-33.6.
  See GOVERNOR.
Water and air resources.
  Water emergencies, §143-354.
Waters and watercourses.
  Withdrawing, diverting or obtaining water.
    Surface water transfers.
      Emergency transfers, §143-215.22L(q).
Wildlife resources commission.
  Emergency powers regarding wildlife diseases.
    Rules governing, §113-306(f).

EMERGENCY CARE INSURANCE COVERAGE.
Definitions, §58-3-190(g).
Information to covered persons, §58-3-190(f).
Requirements, §58-3-190(a) to (e).

**EMERGENCY COMMUNICATION
    INTERFERENCE,** §14-286.2.

EMERGENCY ENERGY PROGRAM.
Contents, §113B-9(f).
Contingency plans, §113B-9(d).
Cooperative and joint plans, §113B-9(c).
Emergency curtailment plan.
  Electric and gas utilities to submit proposed plan,
    §113B-9(b).
Governor.
  Authority to accept and enforce federal programs,
    §113B-9(k).
  Duties, §113B-9(i).
Hearings.
  Council to hold public hearing, §113B-9(e).
Investigations.
  Council to carry out investigations and studies,
    §113B-9(g).
National supply curtailment.
  Oil producers to submit, §113B-9(b).
Preparation, §113B-9(a).
Recommendations, §113B-9(h).
State departments and agencies.
  Council to collect contingency plans, §113B-9(d).
Updating program, §113B-9(j).

EMERGENCY JUSTICE OR JUDGE.
Applicability of provisions, §7A-39.12.
Commission as, application to governor,
  §7A-39.6.
Court of appeals emergency recall judges,
  §7A-39.15.
Decisions regarding recall.
  Final, §7A-39.9(a).
Defined, §7A-39.1(b).
District courts.
  Commission, application to governor, §7A-53.
  Compensation, §7A-52(b).
  Jurisdiction, §7A-53.1.
  Recall of judges reaching mandatory retirement
    age, §7A-57.
  Retired judges may become emergency judges,
    §7A-52(a).
**Emergency recall judges of the court of
    appeals,** §7A-39.15.
Emergency special judges of superior court.
  Jurisdiction, §7A-48.
Jurisdiction and authority, §7A-39.7.
Recall for temporary vacancy, §7A-39.14.
**Recall of judges reaching mandatory
    retirement age,** §7A-39.13.
  Superior court, §7A-57.
**Recall upon temporary incapacity of justice or
    judge,** §7A-39.5.
Retired justices and judges may become,
  §7A-39.3.
  Superior court, §7A-52(a).
Special judges of superior court, §7A-45.2.
Superior court.
  Commission, application to governor, §7A-53.
  Compensation, §7A-52(b).
  Emergency judge.
    Defined, §7A-50.
  Recall of active and emergency trial judges
    reaching mandatory retirement age, §7A-57.
  Retired judge may become emergency judge,
    §7A-52(a).
Supreme court authorized to adopt rules,
  §7A-39.8.
**Termination of recall by chief justice or chief
    judge,** §7A-39.9(b).

EMERGENCY MANAGEMENT, §§166A-1 to
  166A-18.
All-terrain vehicles.
  Use on certain highways, §20-171.23(a) to (f).
**Availability of emergency supplies and utility
    services.**
  Abnormal market disruption, waivers due to,
    §166A-6.03(e).
  Certification of persons transporting essentials,
    §166A-6.03(c).
  Definitions, §166A-6.03(f).
  Executive order of governor, §166A-6.03.
  Maximum hours of service, waiver, §166A-6.03(b).
  Persons transporting essentials, allowing to enter
    or remain, §166A-6.03(a).
    Certification of persons, §166A-6.03(c).
    Scope of authority, §166A-6.03(d).
Bioterrorism.
  Nuclear, biological or chemical agents.
    Terrorist incident using, §§130A-475 to
      130A-479.
      See TERRORIST INCIDENT USING
        NUCLEAR, BIOLOGICAL OR
        CHEMICAL AGENTS.

EMERGENCY MANAGEMENT —Cont'd
State emergency management vehicles.
Red or blue lights on vehicles, §20-130.1(b).
State emergency response account.
Establishment, §166A-6.02(a).
Reporting requirement, §166A-6.02(c).
Use of funds, §166A-6.02(b).
State of disaster.
Governor or general assembly declaring,
    §166A-6(a).
Governor's powers, §166A-6(b).
Concurrence of council of state, §166A-6(c).
National guard training.
Use of funds in preparation for, §166A-6(d).
Preliminary damage assessment.
Providing governor and general assembly,
    §166A-6(a1).
Price gouging during state of disaster, §§75-37,
    75-38.
State of disaster assistance funds.
Governor to make available, §166A-6.01(a).
Type I disaster, §166A-6.01(b).
Type II disaster, §166A-6.01(c).
Type III disaster, §166A-6.01(d).
Termination.
Proclamation or governor or resolution of
    general assembly, §166A-6(a2).
Type I disaster.
Declaring, expiration, §166A-6(a1).
State of disaster assistance funds,
    §166A-6.01(b).
Type II disaster.
Declaring, expiration, §166A-6(a1).
State of disaster assistance funds,
    §166A-6.01(c).
Type III disaster.
Declaring, expiration, §166A-6(a1).
State of disaster assistance funds,
    §166A-6.01(d).
State of emergency, §§14-288.12 to 14-288.18.
Alcoholic beverages, governor's powers, §18B-110.
County powers.
Authority to determine and declare.
Delegation of authority to chairman of board
    of county commissioners, §14-288.13(b).
Authority to enact ordinance, §14-288.13(a).
Class 3 misdemeanor, violation of ordinance or
    proclamation, §14-288.13(d).
Extension of municipal restrictions into county.
Class 3 misdemeanor, violation of restrictions,
    §14-288.14(e).
County imposition of restrictions not
    precluded, §14-288.14(d).
Deemed state of emergency validly found and
    declared, §14-288.14(b).
Exercise of authority not dependent on county
    ordinance, §14-288.14(d).
Notice of terms to those likely affected,
    §14-288.14(c).
Power of chairman of board of county
    commissioners.
Request of municipality, §14-288.14(a).
Request of municipality.
Power of chairman of board of county
    commissioners, §14-288.14(a).
Termination of prohibitions or restriction
    proclaimed, §14-288.14(c).
Municipal jurisdiction, inapplicability of county
    ordinance, §14-288.13(c).
Ordinance effective immediately.
State of emergency exists or imminent,
    §14-288.17(a), (b).

EMERGENCY MANAGEMENT —Cont'd
State of emergency —Cont'd
County powers —Cont'd
Prohibitions and restrictions permitted,
    §14-288.13(b).
Extension of municipal restrictions into
    county, §14-288.14.
Declared state of emergency.
Defined, §14-288.1.
Defined, §14-288.1.
Emergency war powers act, §§147-33.1 to
    147-33.6.
See GOVERNOR.
Governor's authority.
Local control deemed insufficient, §14-288.15(a).
Class 2 misdemeanor, violation of
    proclamation, §14-288.15(e).
Finding local control insufficient,
    requirements, §14-288.15(b).
Giving directions to local and state agencies
    and officers, power, §14-288.15(c).
Prohibitions and restrictions permitted,
    §14-288.15(c), (d).
Insurance deadlines and proof of loss
    requirements.
Stay during state of disaster, §§58-2-46,
    58-2-47.
Municipal powers.
Authority to enact ordinance, §14-288.12(a).
Class 3 misdemeanor.
Violation of ordinance or proclamation,
    §14-288.12(e).
Continuation of ordinance in force without
    reenactment, §14-288.12(d).
Extension of prohibitions and restriction into
    county.
Power of chairman of board of county
    commissioners, §14-288.14.
Mayor, authority to determine and proclaim.
Ordinance may delegate authority to,
    §14-288.12(b).
Ordinance effective immediately.
State of emergency exists or imminent,
    §14-288.17(a), (b).
Prohibitions and restrictions permitted,
    §14-288.12(b).
Extension into county, power of chairman of
    board of county commissioners,
    §14-288.14.
Supplemental authority and power,
    §14-288.12(c).
Ordinance effective immediately.
State of emergency exists or imminent,
    §14-288.17(a), (b).
Price gouging during state of disaster, §§75-37,
    75-38.
Proclamations imposing prohibitions and
    restrictions.
Amending or rescinding, §14-288.16(c).
Duration, expiration, §14-288.16(c).
Effective upon publication, §14-288.16(a), (b).
Extension as to time or area, §14-288.16(c).
Publication requiring compliance, §14-288.16(b).
Property insurance.
Mediation of emergency or disaster claims,
    §§58-44-70 to 58-44-120.
See PROPERTY INSURANCE.
Public or private educational institutions.
Injunction to cope with emergencies,
    §14-288.18(a), (b).

EMERGENCY MANAGEMENT —Cont'd
Terrorism.
Nuclear, biological or chemical agents.
Terrorist incident using, §§130A-475 to 130A-479.
See TERRORIST INCIDENT USING NUCLEAR, BIOLOGICAL OR CHEMICAL AGENTS.
Title of act.
Short title, §166A-1.
Vehicle size, weight and load restrictions.
Vehicles responding to emergency event.
Single trip emergency permit, §20-119(a1).
Volunteer leave, §§166A-30 to 166A-32.
Personnel called into service, §166A-17.
Volunteers performing emergency services.
Immunity, §§1-539.10, 1-539.11.
Warnings regarding personal safety during disaster.
Civil liability for cost of rescue on willfully ignoring warning, §166A-15.1.
Workers' compensation.
Right to receive benefits not affected by performance of functions, §166A-14(b).

EMERGENCY MANAGEMENT ASSISTANCE COMPACT, §§166A-40 to 166A-53.
Action by party state requested to render mutual aid, §166A-44(a).
Additional provisions, §166A-53.
Compensation and death benefits to injured members of emergency forces, §166A-48.
Consultation between state officials, §166A-43(c).
Deposit of authenticated copies with party state, §166A-51.
Effective date, §166A-51(a).
Entering into compact, §166A-40(b).
Evacuation and interstate recession of portions of civilian population, §166A-50.
Formulation of appropriate interstate mutual aid plans and procedures.
Official responsible, §166A-42(c).
Liability of officers or employees of party state rendering aid, §166A-46.
Mutual cooperation, §166A-41(b).
Powers, duties, rights and privileges of forces of party state.
Rendering mutual aid, §166A-44(b).
Principle of articles of compact, §166A-42(b).
Purposes, §166A-41(a).
Recognition by party state, §166A-42(a).
Recognition of licenses and permits issued by party state, §166A-45.
Reimbursement of party state rendering aid in another state, §166A-49.
Requesting assistance of other party states, §166A-43(b).
Responsibility of party states, §166A-43(a).
Supplementary agreement, §166A-47.
Title of provisions, §166A-40(a).
Validity, §166A-52.
Withdrawal from compact, §166A-51(b).

EMERGENCY MANAGEMENT CERTIFICATION PROGRAM, §§166A-60 to 166A-63.
Advanced certification.
Renewal, §166A-63(d).
Establishment, §166A-60.
Expiration of certification, §166A-63(e).
Reinstatement time limit, §166A-63(f).

EMERGENCY MANAGEMENT CERTIFICATION PROGRAM —Cont'd
Issuance of certification, §166A-63(a).
Reciprocity, §166A-63(b).
Purpose, §166A-60.
Renewal of certification, §166A-63(c).
Advanced certification, §166A-63(d).
Standards and guidelines.
Consultation and cooperation with other entities, §166A-61(b).
Contents, §166A-61(a).
Reports and recommendations, §166A-61(c).
Training and standards advisory board, §166A-62.
Training and standards advisory board.
Duties, §166A-62(c).
Established, §166A-62(a).
Meetings, §166A-62(d).
Members, §166A-62(b).
Voluntary program, §166A-60.

EMERGENCY MEDICAL OR SURGICAL TREATMENT OF JUVENILE.
Judicial consent, §7B-3600.
District court jurisdiction over proceedings, §7B-1603.

EMERGENCY MEDICAL SERVICES, §§143-507 to 143-519.
Advisory council.
Appointments of members, §143-510(a).
Chairperson and vice-chairperson.
Election annually, §143-510(f).
Composition, §143-510(a).
Created, §143-510(a).
Duties.
Generally, §143-511.
Expenses, §143-510(d).
Members, §143-510(a).
Per diem and travel expenses, §143-510(d).
Powers.
Generally, §143-511.
Quorum to transact business, §143-510(e).
Terms of office, §143-510(b).
Vacancies, §143-510(c).
Ambulance permit.
Application, §131E-156(b).
Equipment, failure to meet standards on inspection.
Revocation of permit, §131E-157(c).
Inspection of records, §131E-156(d).
Required, §131E-156(a).
Temporary permits, §131E-156(c).
Ambulance support for citizens, §143-517.
Arson.
Burning of rescue-squad building, §14-61.
Assault or affray while discharging official duties, §14-34.6(a).
Infliction of bodily injury, §14-34.6(b).
Use of deadly weapon other than firearms, §14-34.6(b).
Use of firearms, §14-34.6(c).
Assault with deadly weapon, §14-34.6(b).
Electronic surveillance orders, §15A-290(c4).
Personnel assaulted with deadly weapon, §14-34.2.
Automated external defibrillator (AED), §90-21.15.
Background checks, §114-19.21.
Credentialing requirements.
Criminal background checks, §131E-159(g).

EMERGENCY MEDICAL SERVICES —Cont'd
Terrorist incident using nuclear, biological or chemical agents.
Emergency departments, surveillance by state health director, reporting requirements, §130A-480(a), (b).
Traffic lights.
Preempting.
Local authority to permit, §20-169.
Trauma system, establishment, §143-509.
Vaccinations.
First responder vaccination program.
First responders exposed to infectious diseases when deployed to disaster locations, §130A-485.
Vehicles exempt, §131E-160.
Violations of article, §131E-161.
Wage and hour act.
Exemptions, §95-25.14(b1).

EMERGENCY MEDICAL TECHNICIANS.
Arson or other unlawful burning.
Serious injury to emergency medical technician, §14-69.3.
Automated external defibrillator (AED), §90-21.15.
Bioterrorism.
First responder vaccination program.
First responders exposed to infectious diseases when deployed to disaster locations, §130A-485.
Disasters.
First responder vaccination program.
First responders exposed to infectious diseases when deployed to disaster locations, §130A-485.
Immunization.
First responder vaccination program.
First responders exposed to infectious diseases when deployed to disaster locations, §130A-485.
License plates, §20-79.4(b).
Offenses against.
Aggravating factor in sentencing, §15A-1340.16.
Regulation of emergency medical services, §§131E-155 to 131E-161.
See EMERGENCY MEDICAL SERVICES.
Vaccination.
First responder vaccination program.
First responders exposed to infectious diseases when deployed to disaster locations, §130A-485.

EMERGENCY PROGRAM TO REDUCE HOME FORECLOSURES ACT.
Mortgages and deeds of trust, §§45-100 to 45-107.
See FORECLOSURE.

EMERGENCY ROAD SERVICE.
Motor clubs and associations, §58-69-2.

EMERGENCY TELEPHONE SYSTEM.
Enhanced 911 system for wireless communications.
See 911 SYSTEM.
General provisions.
See 911 SYSTEM.

EMERGENCY VEHICLES.
Ambulances.
See AMBULANCES.
Fire trucks and vehicles generally.
See FIRE TRUCKS AND VEHICLES.

EMERGENCY VEHICLES —Cont'd
Law enforcement officers.
Motor vehicles.
See LAW ENFORCEMENT OFFICERS.

EMERGENCY WAR POWERS ACT, §§147-33.1 to 147-33.6.
See GOVERNOR.

EMINENT DOMAIN.
Abandonment of condemnation proceeding.
Petitioner abandoning taxed with fee for respondent's attorney, §1-209.1.
Agricultural development and farmland preservation enabling act.
Voluntary agricultural districts.
Public hearing on condemning land within district.
Required, §106-740.
Airports.
Municipal airports, §§63-5, 63-6, 63-49(b).
Joint operation of airports, §63-56(h).
Special airport districts.
Powers of districts, §63-83.
Zoning.
Acquisition of air rights, §63-36.
Answers.
Private condemnors.
Petitions.
Answer to petition, §40A-25.
Public condemnors, §40A-45(a).
Determination of issues raised, §40A-42(d).
Failure to answer, §40A-46.
Reply to answer, §40A-45(b).
Service of answer, §40A-45(b).
Time for filing answer, §40A-46.
Appeals, §40A-13.
Conservation easements.
Condemnation of property encumbered by, §40A-85.
Private condemnors, §40A-28(c).
Jury trial, §40A-29.
Appraisals, right of entry to make, §40A-11.
Archives and history.
Historic properties.
Power to acquire property by condemnation, §121-9(g).
Attorneys at law.
Abandonment of condemnation proceedings by petitioner.
Petitioner taxed with fee for respondent's attorney, §1-209.1.
Attorneys' fees.
Petitioner abandoning proceeding taxed with fee for respondent's attorney, §1-209.1.
Right of entry prior to condemnation.
Recovery for damages resulting, §40A-11.
Authorities.
Power of eminent domain, §40A-3(c).
Blue Ridge parkway.
Control of outdoor advertising.
Condemnation procedure, §113A-169.
Borings, right of entry to make, §40A-11.
Bridges.
By whom right may be exercised, §40A-3(a).
Buildings.
Removal of structures on condemned land, §40A-9.
Bus stations.
By whom right may be exercised, §40A-3(a).
Canals.
By whom right may be exercised, §40A-3(a).

EMINENT DOMAIN —Cont'd
Cemeteries.
Abandoned and neglected cemeteries.
  Removal of graves.
    Authority not conferred by provisions,
      §65-106(h).
  Powers of local public condemnors, §40A-3(b).
Children and minors.
Guardian ad litem.
  Public condemnors.
    Appointment for infants, §40A-50.
Guardians.
  Private condemnors.
    Acquisition of title of infants.
      Power of court to appoint guardian,
        §40A-30.
Coastal area management.
Commission order not applicable to certain land.
  Acquisition of fee or lessor interest in land,
    §113A-123(c).
Commercial feed.
Detained commercial feeds, §106-284.43(b).
Commissioners.
Private condemnors.
  Appointment, §40A-25.
  Meetings.
    Notice, §40A-26.
  New commissioners.
    Appointment, §40A-32(b).
  Oath of office, §40A-26.
  Powers, §40A-26.
  Qualifications, §40A-25.
  Report of assessed compensation, §40A-26.
    Exceptions to, §40A-28(a).
    Form, §40A-27.
  Subpoenas.
    Power to issue, §40A-26.
Public condemnors.
  Appointment, §40A-48(a).
Community colleges.
Board of trustees, §40A-3(c).
Compensation.
Applicability of principles, §40A-62.
Conservation easements.
  Condemnation of property encumbered by,
    §40A-84.
Date of valuation.
  Day of filing of petition or complaint, §40A-63.
Determination of amount, §40A-63.
  Conservation easements.
    Condemnation of property encumbered by,
      §40A-84.
  Effect of condemnation procedure on value,
    §40A-65(a), (c).
  Project expanded or changed to require taking
    of additional property, §40A-65(b).
Entire tract, §40A-67.
Fair market value, §40A-64(a).
Project as planned.
  Compensation to reflect, §40A-66.
Removal of timber, buildings or other
    permanent improvements or fixtures.
  Value not included, §40A-64(c).
Taking of less than entire tract.
  Measure of compensation, §40A-64(b).
Entire tract.
  Determination of amount, §40A-67.
Fair market value.
  Measure of amount, §40A-64(a).
Lien.
  Acquisition of property subject to lien, §40A-68.

EMINENT DOMAIN —Cont'd
Compensation —Cont'd
Life tenancy.
  Taking of property subject to, §40A-69.
Measure of compensation, §40A-64(a), (b).
Principles governing, §40A-62.
Private condemnors.
  Ascertainment and determination by
    commissioners, §40A-26.
  Deposit by condemnor with clerk of superior
    court, §40A-28(d).
  Failure to pay.
    Effect, §40A-28(f).
  Rights of claimants of fund.
    Determination, §40A-31.
Project as planned.
  Compensation to reflect, §40A-66.
Public condemnors.
  Deposit of estimated compensation to
    accompany complaint, §40A-41.
    Disbursement of deposit, §40A-44.
    Refund of deposit, §40A-56.
  Interest as part of just compensation, §40A-53.
  Measure of compensation, §40A-52.
  Payment of compensation, §40A-55.
  Refund of deposit, §40A-56.
  Remedy where no declaration of taking filed,
    §40A-51(a).
Remainder, value of.
  Tacking of less than entire track, §40A-66(a),
    (b).
Tacking of less than entire track.
  Value of remainder, §40A-66(a), (b).
Value of remainder.
  Tacking of less than entire track, §40A-66(a),
    (b).
Complaints of public condemnors.
Conservation easements.
  Condemnation of property encumbered by.
    Additional information required, §40A-81.
Contents, §40A-41.
Deposit of estimated compensation to accompany
    complaint, §40A-41.
    Disbursement of deposits, §40A-44.
    Refund of deposit, §40A-56.
Filing, §40A-41.
Memorandum of action, §40A-43.
Recordation, §40A-51(b).
Condemnors.
Defined, §40A-2.
Private condemnors. See within this heading,
    "Private condemnors."
Public condemnors. See within this heading,
    "Public condemnors."
Condominiums.
Awards, §47C-1-107(a).
Common elements, §47C-1-107(c).
Partial taking, §47C-1-107(d).
Recording of court decree, §47C-1-107(d).
Conflict of laws.
Exclusive nature of provisions, §40A-1.
Conservation easements.
Condemnation of property encumbered by,
    §§40A-80 to 40A-85.
Constitution of the United States, US Const
    Amd 5.
Constructive notice.
Filing of notice of proceedings, §40A-21.
Continuances.
Public condemnors.
  Power of judge, §40A-50.

EMINENT DOMAIN —Cont'd

Conveyances.
Private condemnors.
Change of ownership pending proceedings, §40A-33.

Corporations.
By whom right may be exercised, §40A-3(a).

Costs, §40A-13.
Award of costs, §40A-8(a), (b).
Action against condemnor, §40A-8(c).
Condemnation action denied or abandoned, §40A-8(b).
Highways, roads and streets.
Condemnation proceedings, §136-119.
Petitioner to pay costs in certain cases, §6-22.
Highways, roads and streets, §136-119.

Counties.
Federal water resources projects.
Acquisition of lands, §143-215.42(a) to (h).
Local government unit outside county.
City property within corporate limits, inapplicability of section, §153A-15(d).
Consent of board required, §153A-15(a), (b).
Applicability of requirement, §153A-15(c).
Power to exercise, purposes, §§40A-3(b), (b1), 153A-158.
Public condemnors generally. See within this heading, "Public condemnors."
Public lands.
Acquisition or condemnation.
Local government unit outside county.
Consent of board required, §153A-15.
Solid waste facility.
Purchasing site by condemnation, §153A-292(c).
State psychiatric hospital.
Selection of county as site for.
Acquisition by county, conveyance to state, §153A-178.
Water and sewer districts.
Power of district, §162A-89.1.

Damages.
Compensation.
Generally. See within this heading, "Compensation."
Public condemnors.
Action in tort for damage to property.
Common law right not affected, §40A-51(c).

Deed of trust covering property to be condemned.
Trustee neither necessary or proper party, §45-45.3(c).

Definitions, §40A-2.
Conservation easement.
Condemnation of property encumbered by, §40A-80(b).

Deposit of estimated compensation to accompany complaint, §40A-41.
Disbursement, §40A-44.
Refund, §40A-56.

Dismissal, discontinuance and nonsuit.
Abandonment of condemnation proceedings by petitioner.
Petitioner taxed with fee for respondent's attorney, §1-209.1.
Voluntary nonsuit authorized, §1-209.2.
Voluntary nonsuit by petitioner in condemnation proceedings, §1-209.2.
Petitioner taxed with fee for respondent's attorney, §1-209.1.

Disposition of land condemned, §40A-10.

EMINENT DOMAIN —Cont'd

Districts.
Power of eminent domain, §40A-3(c).

Drainage.
Corporations, §156-48.
Powers of local public condemnors, §40A-3(b).
Supplemental proceeding, §156-1.

Drainage districts.
Acquisition and disposition of lands.
Generally, §156-138.1.
Assessments.
Damages, §156-70.
Compensation of landowners.
When title deemed acquired for purpose of easements or rights of way, §156-70.1.
Condemnation of land, §156-67.

Easements.
Conservation easements.
Condemnation of property encumbered by, §§40A-80 to 40A-85.

Electric companies.
By whom right may be exercised, §40A-3(a).
Costs of petitions for condemnation of land.
Petitioner to pay costs in certain cases, §6-22.
Dwelling house of owner taken under certain cases, §62-184.
Exercise of right, parties interest only taken, §62-185.
Grant of eminent domain, §62-183.
Powers granted corporations exercisable by persons, firms or copartnerships, §62-189.
Proceedings as under eminent domain, §62-187.
Use or occupancy of public highway, §62-181.

Emergency management.
Compensation for taking of property, §166A-11.

Entry.
Right to enter prior to condemnation, §40A-11.

Environment and natural resources department.
Marine and estuarine resources.
Powers as to, §113-226(a).

Examinations, right of entry to make, §40A-11.

Exclusive nature of provisions, §40A-1.

Farmland preservation.
Voluntary agricultural districts.
Public hearing on condemning land within district.
Required, §106-740.

Fire stations.
Powers of local public condemnors, §40A-3(b).

Fish and fisheries resources.
Coastal wetlands, orders to control activities.
Taking fee of land order inapplicable to, §113-230(g).
Seafood industrial park authority, §113-315.32.

Fixtures.
Removal of fixtures on condemned land, §40A-9.

Flumes.
Flume companies exercising right to become common carriers, §62-191.

Forms.
Private condemnors.
Commissioners.
Report of assessed compensation, §40A-27.
Public condemnors.
Commissioners.
Report of assessed compensation, §40A-48(c).

Global TransPark authority.
Powers, §63A-6(b).

EMINENT DOMAIN —Cont'd

Guardians.

Private condemnors.

Acquisition of title of infants, incompetents, inebriates or trustees without power of sale.

Power of court to appoint guardian, §40A-30.

Highways, roads and streets.

Cartways, church roads or mill roads.

Special proceeding for establishment, alteration or discontinuance, §136-68.

Condemnation, §§136-103 to 136-121.1.

See HIGHWAYS, ROADS AND STREETS.

Powers of local public condemnors, §40A-3(b).

Historic districts and landmarks.

Powers of local public condemnors, §40A-3(b).

Hospital authorities. §131E-10.

Power of eminent domain, §§40A-3(c), 131E-24(a).

Certificate of public convenience and necessity.

Prerequisite to exercise of power, §131E-24(c).

Restrictions, §131E-24(b).

Hospitals.

Municipal hospitals, §131E-10.

Powers of local public condemnors, §40A-3(b).

Housing authorities and projects.

Certificate of convenience and necessity.

Required, §157-28.

Declaration of necessity, §157-48.

Exercise of right, §157-50.

Finding and declaration of necessity, §157-48.

Housing project.

Defined, §157-49.

Municipal cooperation and aid.

Restrictions on exercise of right, §157-45.

Power of eminent domain, §§40A-3(c), 157-11, 157-50.

Restrictions on right, §157-28.

Hydraulic power corporations.

Use or occupancy of public highway, §62-181.

Injunctions.

Private condemnors.

Provisions not to preclude injunctive relief, §40A-28(g).

Public condemnors.

Remedy not precluded by provisions, §40A-42(f).

Interest.

Public condemnors.

Compensation.

Interest as part of just compensation, §40A-53.

Inverse condemnation, §40A-51.

Judges.

Power to make additional orders and rules of procedure, §40A-12.

Judgments.

Private condemnors, §40A-28(b).

Powers of judge to carry into effect, §40A-28(e).

Public condemnors.

Final judgments, §40A-54.

Junkyard control, §136-150.

Jury.

Private condemnors.

Appeals.

Provision for jury trial, §40A-29.

Right to trial by jury granted to parties in condemnation proceedings, §1A-1 Rule 38(e).

View by jury, §1-181.1.

Land policy act.

Taking of property without compensation.

Protection of rights, §113A-158.

Legislative declaration, §40A-1.

EMINENT DOMAIN —Cont'd

Libraries.

Powers of local public condemnors, §40A-3(b).

Liens.

Compensation.

Acquisition of property subject to lien, §40A-68.

Removal of structures on condemned land, §40A-9.

Life estates.

Taking of property subject to life tenancy.

Compensation, §40A-69.

Limitation of actions.

Inverse condemnation, §40A-51(a).

Lis pendens.

Filing of notice of proceedings, §40A-21.

Local governments.

Federal water resources projects.

Acquisition of lands, §143-215.42(a) to (h).

Powers, §40A-3(b), (b1).

Public condemnors generally. See within this heading, "Public condemnors."

Maps and plats.

Public condemnors.

Filing of plat, §40A-45(c).

Metropolitan sewerage districts.

Powers of districts, §162A-69.

Metropolitan water districts.

Powers of districts, §162A-36(a).

Mining, water and drainage rights.

Appraisers.

Appointment, §74-27.

Duties, §74-27.

Number, §74-27.

Report, §74-27.

Confirmation, §74-28.

Registration, §74-29.

Fee, §74-29.

Damages.

Payment, §74-28.

Obstructing mining drains.

Misdemeanor, §74-30.

Petition for, §74-25.

Contents, §74-26.

Waste.

Disposition, §74-31.

Mosquito control districts.

Powers of boards of commissioners, §§40A-3(c), 130A-355.

Motor carriers.

By whom right may be exercised, §40A-3(a).

Municipalities.

Cemeteries.

Authority to condemn cemeteries, §160A-345.

Authority to condemn easements for perpetual care, §160A-346.

Trustees, §160A-349.10.

Costs.

Petitions for condemnation of land.

Petitioner to pay costs in certain cases, §6-22.

Federal water resources projects.

Acquisition of lands, §143-215.42(a) to (h).

Joint municipal electric power and energy act, §159B-33.

Powers, §§40A-3(b), (b1), 160A-240.1.

Procedures for exercise of power, §160A-240.1.

Public condemnors generally. See within this heading, "Public condemnors."

Streets and alleys.

Acquiring land, §160A-296(a).

Extraterritorial planning jurisdiction, exercising power in, §160A-296(a1).

EMINENT DOMAIN —Cont'd
Notice.
Private condemnors.
Meeting of commissioners, §40A-26.
Proceedings by, §40A-21.
Public condemnors.
Determination of issues other than damages,
§40A-47.
Intent to institute action to condemn property,
§40A-40.
Right of entry.
Notice to owner of entry prior to condemnation,
§40A-11.
Orders.
Power of judges to effectuate provisions, §40A-12.
Public condemnors.
Power of judge to enter orders, §40A-42(e).
Outdoor advertising, §136-132.
Parking authorities.
Acquisition of real property, §§160A-556,
160A-557(d).
Parks and recreation.
Condemnation of land for state parks, §113-34(a).
Powers of local public condemnors, §40A-3(b).
Perfection of title.
Private condemnation proceedings, §40A-34.
Persons under legal disabilities.
Private condemnation proceedings.
Procedure, §40A-30.
Petitions.
Conservation easements.
Condemnation of property encumbered by.
Additional information required, §40A-81.
Private condemnors, §§40A-20, 40A-25.
Answer to petition, §40A-25.
Contents, §40A-20.
Filing, §40A-20.
Pipelines.
By whom right may be exercised, §40A-3(a).
Right conferred on pipeline companies, §62-190.
Planned community act.
Common elements, §47F-1-107(d).
Compensation of lot owner, §47F-1-107(a), (b).
Decree.
Recordation, §47F-1-107(e).
Reallocation of interests, §47F-1-107(a), (b).
Amendment to declaration reflecting,
§47F-1-107(c).
Pollution control.
Industrial and pollution control facilities financing
act.
No power of eminent domain, §159C-20.
Ports authority.
Power of eminent domain, §136-267.
Poultry and poultry products.
Inspections.
Seizure or condemnation proceedings,
§106-549.66.
Principal and income act.
Allocation of receipts not normally apportioned
during administration of trust, §37A-4-404.
Prior purchase offer.
Not necessary, §40A-4.
Private condemnors.
Amendments of proceedings.
Power of clerk or judge, §40A-32(b).
Appeals, §40A-28(c).
Jury trial, §40A-29.
Commissioners.
Appointment, §40A-25.

EMINENT DOMAIN —Cont'd
Private condemnors —Cont'd
Commissioners —Cont'd
Meetings.
Notice, §40A-26.
New commissioners.
Appointment, §40A-32(b).
Oath of office, §40A-26.
Powers, §40A-26.
Qualifications, §40A-25.
Report of assessed compensation, §40A-26.
Exceptions to report, §40A-28(a).
Form, §40A-27.
Subpoenas.
Power to issue, §40A-26.
Compensation.
Ascertainment and determination by
commissioners, §40A-26.
Deposit by condemnor with clerk of superior
court, §40A-28(d).
Failure to pay.
Effect, §40A-28(f).
Rights of claimants of fund.
Determination, §40A-31.
Condemnation proceedings by, §§40A-19 to
40A-34.
Conveyances.
Change of ownership pending proceeding,
§40A-33.
Defective title.
How cured, §40A-34.
Guardians.
Acquisition of title of infants, incompetents,
inebriates or trustees without power of sale.
Power of court to appoint guardian, §40A-30.
Incompetent persons.
Acquisition of title of.
Powers of court upon, §40A-30.
Infants.
Acquisition of title of.
Powers of court upon, §40A-30.
Injunctions.
Provisions not to preclude, §40A-28(g).
Judgments, §40A-28(b).
Powers of judge to carry into effect, §40A-28(e).
Jury.
Appeals.
Provision for jury trial on appeal, §40A-29.
Notice.
Meeting of commissioners, §40A-26.
Proceedings by, §40A-21.
Petitions.
Answer to petition, §40A-25.
Contents, §40A-20.
Filing, §40A-20.
Proceedings for condemnation by, §§40A-19 to
40A-34.
Right of eminent domain, §§40A-3(a), 40A-19.
Service of process, §40A-22.
Special proceedings.
Service as in special proceedings in absence of
other provisions, §40A-24.
Unknown parties, §40A-23.
Title.
Defective title.
How cured, §40A-34.
Transfer of property pending proceedings,
§40A-33.
Trustees.
Acquisition of title of trustees without power of
sale.
Powers of court upon, §40A-30.

EMINENT DOMAIN —Cont'd
Private condemnors —Cont'd
Unknown parties.
  Attorney for unknown parties.
    Appointment, §40A-32(a).
  Service where parties unknown, §40A-23.
Property tax reimbursement, §40A-6(a).
Deferred taxes paid by owner, §40A-6(b).
Public condemnors.
Answers, §40A-45(a).
  Determination of issues raised, §40A-42(d).
  Failure to answer, §40A-46.
  Reply, §40A-45(b).
  Service, §40A-45(b).
  Time for filing, §40A-46.
Commissioners.
  Appointment, §40A-48(a).
Compensation.
  Deposit of estimated compensation to
    accompany complaint, §40A-41.
    Disbursement of deposit, §40A-44.
    Refund of deposit, §40A-56.
  Interest as part of just compensation, §40A-53.
  Measure of compensation, §40A-52.
  Payment of compensation, §40A-55.
  Refund of deposit, §40A-56.
  Remedy where no declaration of taking filed,
    §40A-51(a).
  Transfer of case to civil docket, §40A-49.
Complaints.
  Contents, §40A-41.
  Deposit of estimated compensation to
    accompany complaint, §40A-41.
    Disbursement of deposit, §40A-44.
    Refund of deposit, §40A-56.
  Filing, §40A-41.
  Memorandum of action, §40A-43.
    Recordation, §40A-51(b).
Condemnation proceedings by, §§40A-40 to
  40A-56.
Continuances.
  Power of judge, §40A-50.
Damages.
  Action in tort for damaged property.
    Common law right not affected, §40A-51(c).
Guardian ad litem.
  Appointment for infants or incompetents,
    §40A-50.
Injunctions.
  Remedy not precluded, §40A-42(f).
Interest.
  Compensation.
    Part of just compensation, §40A-53.
Issues other than damages.
  Determination, §40A-47.
Judgments.
  Final judgments, §40A-54.
Local public condemnors.
  Power to exercise, purposes.
    Modified provision for certain localities,
      §40A-3(b1).
    Standard provision, §40A-3(b).
Memorandum of action, §40A-43.
  Recordation, §40A-51(b).
Notice.
  Determination of issues other than damages,
    §40A-47.
  Intent to institute action to condemn property,
    §40A-40(a).
  Vesting of title and right of possession,
    §40A-40(b).

EMINENT DOMAIN —Cont'd
Public condemnors —Cont'd
Notice —Cont'd
  Time for filing, manner of serving owners,
    §40A-40(a).
Number, §40A-48(a).
Orders.
  Power of judge to enter orders, §40A-42(e).
Plat.
  Filing, §40A-45(c).
Powers, §40A-48(b).
Proceedings for condemnation by, §§40A-40 to
  40A-56.
Qualifications, §40A-48(a).
Report of assessed compensation, §40A-48(b).
  Exceptions to, §40A-48(d).
  Form, §40A-48(c).
  Service on parties, §40A-48(d).
Request for appointment, §40A-48(a).
  Procedure when no request, §40A-49.
Return of condemned property, §40A-70.
Right of eminent domain, §40A-3(b), (c).
Service of process.
  Answer, §40A-45(b).
  Report of commissioners.
    Service of copies on parties, §40A-48(d).
Title.
  Vesting of title, §40A-42(a) to (c).
Torts.
  Action in tort for damages to property.
    Common law right not affected, §40A-51(c).
Unknown parties.
  Appointment of attorney for, §40A-50.
Public institutions.
Costs of petitions for condemnation of land.
  Petitioner to pay costs in certain cases, §6-22.
Public lands.
Consent of state to taking, §40A-5(a).
Public schools.
Acquisition of school sites, §115C-517.
Powers of local boards of education, §40A-3(b).
Public utilities.
Burial grounds, §62-184.
By whom right may be exercised.
  Private condemnors, §40A-3(a).
Costs of petitions for condemnation of land.
  Petitioner to pay costs in certain cases, §6-22.
Dwelling houses, §62-184.
Exercise of power by persons, firms or
  copartnerships, §62-189.
Exercise of right under general eminent domain
  provisions, §62-185.
Flume companies exercising right become common
  carriers, §62-191.
Grant of eminent domain, §62-183.
  Dwelling houses, etc., §62-184.
  Exceptions, §62-183.
  Powers granted to be exercisable by persons,
    firms or copartnerships, §62-189.
Highways.
  Use of highways generally, §§62-180, 62-181.
Pipeline companies.
  Right of eminent domain conferred upon,
    §62-190.
Proceedings as under eminent domain, §62-187.
Surveys.
  No survey required, §62-185.
Public water systems, §130A-319.
Public works relocation assistance, §§133-5 to
  133-18.
See RELOCATION ASSISTANCE.

EMINENT DOMAIN —Cont'd
Purposes.
Local public condemnors.
Modified provisions for certain localities,
§40A-3(b1).
Standard provisions, §40A-3(b).
Other public condemnors, §40A-3(c).
Railroads.
By whom right may be exercised, §40A-3(a).
Costs.
Petitions for condemnation of land.
Petitioner to pay costs in certain cases, §6-22.
Fee simple condemnations, §40A-3(a).
Intersection with highways, §136-191.
Limitation of actions.
Damages or compensation for railroad right of
way, §1-51.
Powers of railroad corporations, §136-190.
Right of eminent domain.
Consent of state required, §40A-5(a).
Regional natural gas districts.
Continuing power, §160A-674(a).
Procedure when exercising power, §160A-674(b).
Regional transportation authorities.
Continuing power, §160A-649(a).
Procedures when exercising powers, §160A-649(b).
Right of eminent domain, §40A-3(c).
Relocation assistance, §§133-5 to 133-18.
See RELOCATION ASSISTANCE.
Remainder of track.
Less than entire tract taken.
Value of, §40A-66(a), (b).
Removal of structures on condemned land,
§40A-9.
Reports of assessed compensation.
Private condemnors.
Commissioners, §40A-26.
Exceptions to report, §40A-28(a).
Form of report, §40A-27.
Public condemnors.
Commissioners, §40A-48(b) to (d).
Residential property disclosure act.
Applicability of act, §47E-2.
Return of condemned property.
Public condemnors, §40A-70.
Right of eminent domain.
No prior purchase offer necessary, §40A-4.
Private condemnors, §§40A-3(a), 40A-19.
Property owned by other condemnors, §40A-5(b).
Public condemnors, §40A-3(b), (c).
Railroads, state owned.
Consent of state requires, §40A-5(a).
State property.
Consent of state required, §40A-5(a).
Who may exercise right, §40A-3.
Right of entry prior to condemnation, §40A-11.
Sales.
Disposition of land condemned, §40A-10.
Sanitary districts.
Power of boards, §§40A-3(c), 130A-57.
Schools.
Acquisition of school sites, §115C-517.
By whom right may be exercised.
Private condemnor, §40A-3(a).
Powers of local boards of education, §40A-3(b).
Seafood industry park authorities, §113-315.32.
Service of process.
Private condemnors, §40A-22.
Special proceedings.
Service as in special proceedings in absence of
other provisions, §40A-24.

EMINENT DOMAIN —Cont'd
Service of process —Cont'd
Private condemnors —Cont'd
Unknown parties, §40A-23.
Public condemnors.
Answer, §40A-45(b).
Report of commissioners.
Service of copies on parties, §40A-48(d).
Sewers.
Powers of local public condemnors, §40A-3(b).
Public sewerage systems.
Private condemnors, §40A-3(a).
Soil and water conservation districts.
Watershed improvement districts.
Power of eminent domain, §40A-3(c).
State lands.
Acquiring allocated lands.
Administration department.
Powers generally, §146-24.1.
Procedure to obtain, §146-24(c).
State of North Carolina.
Taking of state lands.
Consent of state required, §40A-5(a).
State parks.
Condemnation of land for, §113-34(a).
Statute of limitations.
Inverse condemnation, §40A-51(a).
Street railways.
Costs of petitions for condemnation of land.
Petitioner to pay costs in certain cases, §6-22.
Subpoenas.
Private condemnors.
Commissioners.
Power to issue, §40A-26.
Summons and process.
Private condemnors, §40A-22.
Unknown parties, §40A-23.
Superior courts.
Proper division for trial of actions and
proceedings, §7A-248.
Surveys, right of entry to make, §40A-11.
Taxation.
Reimbursement of owner for taxes paid on
condemned property, §40A-6(a).
Deferred taxes paid, §40A-6(b).
Telephone and telegraph companies, §§62-183
to 62-189.
By whom may be exercised, §40A-3(a).
Petition costs, §6-22.
Title.
Conservation easements.
Condemnation of property encumbered by.
Vesting of title and right of possession,
§40A-83.
Private condemnation proceedings.
Curing of defective title, §40A-34.
Vesting of title and right to possession, §40A-42.
Conservation easements.
Condemnation of property encumbered by,
§40A-83.
Torts.
Public condemnors.
Action in tort for damage to property.
Common law right not affected, §40A-51(c).
Tramways.
By whom right may be exercised, §40A-3(a).
Transportation department.
Powers of department, §§136-18, 136-19.
Trespass.
Right of entry prior to condemnation not deemed,
§40A-11.

EMINENT DOMAIN —Cont'd
Trusts and trustees.
Private condemnors.
Acquisition of title of trustee without power of sale.
Powers of court upon, §40A-30.
Tryon's Palace restoration, §121-16.
Turnpike authority.
Power, §136-89.184(a).
Procedure, §136-89.184(b).
Urban redevelopment, §160A-515.
Powers of redevelopment commissions generally, §160A-512.
Vesting of title and right to possession, §40A-42(b).
Conservation easements.
Condemnation of property encumbered by, §40A-83.
Modified provision for certain localities, §40A-42(a).
Property owned by private condemnor, §40A-42(c).
Standard provision, §40A-42(a).
Voluntary agricultural districts.
Public hearing on condemning land within district.
Required, §106-740.
Voluntary nonsuit, §1-209.2.
Petitioner taxed with fee for respondent's attorney, §1-209.1.
Water and air resources.
Federal water resources development projects, §143-215.42(a) to (h).
Water and sewer authorities.
Power of authority, §162A-6(a), (c).
Waters and watercourses.
Natural and scenic rivers system.
Acquisition of land by administration department, §113A-38(b).
Watershed improvement works or projects.
Certification of copies of findings to applicant district, §139-44(b).
Interest in land acquired pursuant to section, §139-44(e).
Power conferred on county, §139-44(a).
Procedure, §139-44(d).
Repeal of inconsistent provisions, §139-44(f).
Words construed, §139-44(c).
Water supply and waterworks.
By whom right may be exercised, §40A-3(a).
Public water systems supplying drinking water, §130A-319.
Wetlands mitigation.
Condemnor seeking to acquire land for purposes of.
Payment to county where land located by condemnor, §153A-15.1(a), (b).
Applicability of provisions, §153A-15.1(e).
Estimated amount of ad valorem taxes that would have accrued for next 20 years defined, §153A-15.1(c).
Exception, §153A-15.1(d).
Wharves.
Powers of local public condemnors, §40A-3(b).
Whole parcel or building.
Acquisition.
Generally, §40A-7(a), (c).
Sale or disposal of residues required under provisions, §40A-7(b).

EMISSIONS FROM MOTOR VEHICLES, §§20-128.1, 20-128.2.
Commissioner of motor vehicles.
Rules and regulations, §20-39.

EMISSIONS FROM MOTOR VEHICLES
—Cont'd
Control devices, §20-128(c).
Exception for pollution reduction modifications, §20-128(d).
Safety inspections, scope, §20-183.3(a).
Enforcement of provisions, §20-128.1(c).
Inspections.
Counties, inspections performed in, §143-215.107A(c).
Additional counties, requiring tests in, §143-215.107A(c).
Decentralized network of test and repair stations.
Performing inspections, §143-215.107A(a).
Emission mechanic license.
Required of persons performing, §§20-183.4A, 143-215.107A(a).
Exemptions.
Vehicle principally garaged in state but primarily operated outside county subject to inspections.
Temporary exemption, §20-183.4C(c).
General provisions, §143-215.107A(a).
Inspection in jurisdiction where vehicle located, §20-183.4C(a).
License to perform emissions inspection.
Mechanic qualifications, §20-183.4A(c).
Performing without license, criminal penalty, §20-183.8(b1).
Required, §§20-183.4A, 143-215.107A(a).
Self-inspector qualifications, §20-183.4A(d).
Station qualifications, §20-183.4A(b).
Scope, §20-183.3(b), (b1).
Temporary exemption.
Vehicle principally garaged in state but primarily operated outside county subject to inspections, §20-183.4C(c).
Vehicle subject to, §20-183.2(b).
Waiver after failing inspection.
Electronic inspection authorization, expiration, §20-183.5(d).
Missing emission control devices.
Electronic inspection authorization, expiration, §20-183.5A(d).
Procedure for obtaining, §20-183.5A(b).
Repairs equaling or exceeding waiver amount.
Repairs and costs not considered in determining, §20-183.5A(c).
Requirements for waiver, §20-183.5A(a).
Procedure, §20-183.5(b).
Repairs, §20-183.5(c).
Requirements, §20-183.5(a).
When vehicle must be inspected, §20-183.4C(a).
Municipal regulations, §160A-185.
Requirements generally, §§20-128.1(a), 20-128(a).
Standards.
Rules and regulations, §20-128.2(a).
State plans to reduce emissions from job-related travel.
Alternative-fueled or low emission vehicles, purchase by state, §143-215.107C(a) to (c).
Plan for private sector employees, §143-215.107C(e).
Plan for state employees, §143-215.107C(d).
Violations of provisions.
Penalty, §20-128.1(d).
Time for bringing vehicle into conformity with standards, §20-128.1(b).

EMOTIONAL CONDITION, HEARSAY EXCEPTION, §8C-1 Rule 803.

EMOTIONAL DISTRESS.
Childhood vaccine injury compensation.
Commission awards, §130A-427(a).
Ejectment of residential tenants.
Damages in action by tenant not to include, §42-25.9(a).
Stalking, §14-277.3A.

EMPLOYEE ASSISTANCE PROFESSIONALS, §§90-500 to 90-511.
Advertising.
Representation as licensed professional, §90-508.
Board.
Chair, §90-501(j).
Compensation, §90-501(i).
Composition, §90-501(b).
Creation, §90-501(a).
Diversity, §90-501(h).
Duties, §90-502.
Independence, §90-501(l).
List of nominees, §90-501(e).
Meetings, §90-501(k).
Powers, §90-502.
Prerequisites, §90-501(d).
Qualifications, §90-501(c).
Removal of members, §90-501(f).
Secretary, §90-501(j).
Vacancies, §90-501(g).
Definitions, §90-500.
Enforcement of article, §90-506.
Considerations, §90-506(b).
Enforcement options, §90-506(a).
Hearings, §90-507.
Fees.
License application fee, §90-503.
Hearings.
Enforcement or disciplinary actions, §90-507.
Identification badges required, §90-640.
Immunities.
Good faith report of violations, §90-510.
Investigations.
Violations of provisions, §90-510.
Licenses.
Denial, suspension or revocation, §90-509.
Duration, §90-503.
Qualifications, §90-503.
Renewals, §90-504.
Misrepresentation.
Prohibited, §90-509.
Representation as licensed professional, §90-508.
Nonresidents.
Requirements for persons licensed out-of-state, §90-505.
Practice by members of other professional groups, §90-511.
Prohibited activities, §90-509.
Reciprocity, §90-505.
Representation as licensed professional, §90-508.
Violations of article, §90-506.

EMPLOYEE BENEFIT PLAN SUCCESSION RENUNCIATION, §31B-1.

EMPLOYEE SAFETY AND HEALTH PROGRAMS, §§95-250 to 95-256.
Additional rights, §95-253.
Amount of civil penalties, §95-256(a).
Appeals of civil penalty, §95-256(c).

EMPLOYEE SAFETY AND HEALTH PROGRAMS —Cont'd
Certification that employer meets requirement, §95-255(b).
Civil penalties, §95-256.
Committees.
Composition, §95-252(d).
Establishment, §95-252(a).
Requirements, §95-252(c).
Selection, §95-252(d).
Temporary help services not counted as employee, §95-252(b).
Definitions, §95-250.
Determination of amount of civil penalties, §95-256(b).
Employee assistance professionals, §§90-500 to 90-511.
See EMPLOYEE ASSISTANCE PROFESSIONALS.
Establishment of program, §95-251(a).
Experience rate modifiers.
Defined, §95-250.
Goals of program, §95-254(a).
Notice that employer to comply with provision, §95-255(a), (c).
Technical assistance, §95-255.1.
Pay during time employees participating.
No loss of pay, §95-251(c).
Payment of civil penalties into general fund, §95-256(d).
Reports, §95-255.
Requirements of program, §95-251(b).
Rights additional to other rights, §95-253.
Rules, §95-254(b).
Worksite.
Defined, §95-250.

EMPLOYEE THEFT.
Civil liability for damages, §1-538.2(a).
Action brought regardless of criminal action, §1-538.2(c).
Consequential and punitive damages and attorneys' fees.
Additional recovery allowed, §1-538.2(a).
Amount of damages, cap, §1-538.2(a).
Parent or legal guardian liable for acts of minor, §1-538.2(b).
Consequential damages, included in, §1-538.2(c1).
Demand letter, seeking damages prior to action, §1-538.2(c2).
Payment of money demanded, no further action, §1-538.2(c4).
Demand letter, seeking damages prior to action, §1-538.2(c2).
Payment of money demanded, no further action, §1-538.2(c4).
Qualified privilege of sender, §1-538.2(c3).
Libel and slander.
Demand letter, seeking damages prior to action. Qualified privilege of sender, §1-538.2(c3).
Other theories of law, recovery under, §1-538.2(d).
Parent or legal guardian liable for acts of minor, §1-538.2(b).
Recovery of value of goods and merchandise, §1-538.2(a).
Embezzlement.
See EMBEZZLEMENT.

EMPLOYER REPORTS TO DIRECTORY OF NEW HIRES, §110-129.2(b) to (e).

EMPLOYMENT AGENCIES.
Immunity of employer for disclosure of information.
Employee's job performance or job history.
Employer includes job placement service, §1-539.12(c).
Job listing services, §§95-47.19 to 95-47.32.
See JOB LISTING SERVICES.
Private personnel services, §§95-47.1 to 95-47.15.
See PRIVATE PERSONNEL SERVICES.
Professional employer organization act, §§58-89A-1 to 58-89A-180.
See PROFESSIONAL EMPLOYER ORGANIZATIONS.

EMPLOYMENT AND TRAINING GRANT PROGRAM.
Workforce development, §143B-438.13.

EMPLOYMENT DISCRIMINATION.
Domestic violence.
Persons seeking relief under provisions.
Prohibited acts by employers, §50B-5.5(a).
Enforcement, §50B-5.5(b).
Equal employment practices, §§143-422.1 to 143-422.3.
Citation of article, §143-422.1.
Human relations council.
Charges of discrimination.
Receipt, §143-422.3.
Conciliations, §143-422.3.
Investigations, §143-422.3.
Legislative declaration, §143-422.2.
Purpose of article, §143-422.2.
Short title, §143-422.1.
Genetic information, testing or counseling services.
Basis of genetic information, §95-28.1A(a).
Genetic characteristic defined, §95-28.1A(b).
Genetic information defined, §95-28.1A(b).
Genetic test defined, §95-28.1A(b).
Person having requested genetic tests or counseling, §95-28.1A(a).
Lawful use of lawful products during nonworking hours, §95-28.2.
Personnel system.
Assistance in obtaining state employment, §§126-16 to 126-19.
Persons possessing sickle cell trait or hemoglobin C trait, §95-28.1.
Retaliatory employment discrimination, §§95-240 to 95-245.
Civil action by employees, §95-243(a).
Civil action filed by commissioner or employee, §95-242(b).
Complaint, §95-242(a).
Conciliation, §95-242(a), (b).
Confidential information, §95-242(d), (e).
Informal procedures, §95-242(b).
Definitions, §95-240.
Discrimination prohibited, §95-241(a).
Effect of article on other rights, §95-244.
Exception to violation of article, §95-241(b).
Investigation, §95-242(a).
Reopening of investigation, §95-242(b1).
Jury trial in civil actions, §95-243(d).
Other rights afforded employee.
Effect of article on, §95-244.
Relief in civil actions, §95-243(c).

EMPLOYMENT DISCRIMINATION —Cont'd
Retaliatory employment discrimination —Cont'd
Reopening of investigation, §95-242(b1).
Required for employee to bring actions, §95-243(e).
Right-to-sue letter, §95-242(a) to (c).
Subpoenas, §95-242(f).
Time for commencing civil actions, §95-243(b).
Use of leave for parent involvement in schools, §95-28.3(b), (c).
Venue of civil action by employees, §95-243(a).
Sickle cell trait or hemoglobin C trait.
Discrimination against persons possessing, §95-28.1.
Whistleblower protection.
Retaliatory employment discrimination, §§95-240 to 95-245.
See RETALIATORY EMPLOYMENT DISCRIMINATION.

EMPLOYMENT PREFERENCE ACT, VETERANS, §128-15(a) to (d).
Preferences generally.
See PERSONNEL SYSTEM.
Priority in employment assistance for United States armed forces veterans, §§165-44.1 to 165-44.6.

EMPLOYMENT RELATIONS.
Actions.
Discrimination against lawful use of lawful products during nonworking hours.
Civil actions for violation of section, §95-28.2(e).
Examination and screening of employees for controlled substances.
Recovery of civil penalty imposed, §95-234(b).
Advance obtained under promise to work and pay for, §14-104.
Agents.
Violating duties owed employers, §14-353.
Witness required to give self-incriminating evidence, §14-354.
Agriculture.
Housing standards for migrant farm workers, §§95-222 to 95-229.1.
See MIGRANT FARM WORKERS.
Alarm systems licensees' employees.
Registration, §74D-8.
Alcoholic beverages.
Discharge of employees.
Violations of chapter, §18B-202.
Lawful use of lawful products by employees during nonworking hours.
Discrimination prohibited, §95-28.2.
Aliens.
Verification of work authorization, §§64-25 to 64-38.
Anonymous complaints, §64-28(a).
Appeal of orders, §64-36.
Complaints.
Anonymous complaints, §64-28(a).
False and frivolous complaints.
Criminal offense, §64-28(b).
Filing, §64-28(a).
Forms.
Contents, §64-27(b).
Design and promulgation, §64-27(a).
Hearings, §64-30.
Investigation of complaints, §64-29(a).
Certain categories of complaints not investigated, §64-29(b).

EMPLOYMENT RELATIONS —Cont'd
Aliens —Cont'd
Verification of work authorization —Cont'd
Complaints —Cont'd
Investigation of complaints —Cont'd
Federal government verification exclusive
method of determining authorization,
§64-35.
State bureau of investigation assistance in
investigating, §64-29(c).
Subpoenas for production of documents in
aid of investigation, §64-29(d).
Process following complaint, §64-30.
Counties.
E-Verify.
Duty to register and participate,
§153A-99.1.
Definitions, §64-25.
Employ.
Defined, §64-25.
Employees.
Defined, §64-25.
Employers.
Defined, §64-25.
E-Verify.
Counties.
Duty to register and participate,
§153A-99.1.
Defined, §64-25.
Employers to use, §64-26(a).
Seasonal temporary employee exception to
requirement, §64-26(c).
Violations, consequences, §§64-31 to 64-33.
Municipalities.
Duty to register and participate,
§160A-169.1.
Records.
Preservation of E-Verify forms, §64-26(b).
Seasonal temporary employees.
Exception to requirement, §64-26(c).
State departments, agencies, etc.
Verification of legal status after hiring new
employees, §126-7.1(f).
Labor commissioner.
Appeal of orders, §64-36.
Complaint forms, §64-27.
Definition of commissioner, §64-25.
Filing complaints with commissioner,
§64-28(a).
Independent determination of authorization.
Prohibited, §64-35.
Investigation of complaints, §64-29(a), (b).
Federal government verification exclusive
method of determining authorization,
§64-35.
Law enforcement assistance, §64-29(c).
Subpoenas for production of documents,
§64-29(d).
Rulemaking to implement provisions, §64-37.
Violations, consequences.
Duties of commissioner, §§64-31 to 64-33.
Municipalities.
E-Verify.
Duty to register and participate,
§160A-169.1.
Notice of presence of unauthorized alien,
§64-30.
Rulemaking to implement provisions, §64-37.
State departments, agencies, etc.
Verification of legal status after hiring new
employees, §126-7.1(f).

EMPLOYMENT RELATIONS —Cont'd
Aliens —Cont'd
Verification of work authorization —Cont'd
Statutory construction.
Employers not to be required to violate
federal or state law, §64-38.
Unauthorized aliens.
Defined, §64-25.
Notice of presence of unauthorized alien,
§64-30.
Violations, consequences.
Copies of orders.
Retention, §64-34.
First violation.
Affidavit, §64-31(a).
Second violation, §64-32.
Third and subsequent violations, §64-33.
Apprenticeship, §§94-1 to 94-12.
See APPRENTICESHIP.
Arbitration of labor disputes.
Conciliation service and mediation, §§95-32 to
95-36.
See LABOR DISPUTES.
Voluntary arbitration, §§95-36.1 to 95-36.9.
See LABOR DISPUTES.
Attorney general.
Enforcement of rules and regulations, §95-13.
Attorneys' fees.
Discrimination against lawful use of lawful
products during nonworking hours.
Civil actions for violations, §95-28.2(e).
Blacklisting.
Employees blacklisted, §14-355.
Blind persons.
Promoting employment of blind persons, §111-27.
Bribery.
Employees violating duties owed employers,
§14-353.
Career education.
Vocational and technical education, §§115C-151 to
115C-169.
See VOCATIONAL AND TECHNICAL
EDUCATION.
Child labor, §95-25.5.
Child support.
Directory of new hires.
Employer reporting, §110-129.2(b) to (e).
Employee verification form.
Establishing obligor's gross income,
§110-139(c1).
Garnishment for enforcement of child-support
obligation.
Employer third-party garnishee, §110-136(b).
Location of parent, employer information,
providing, §110-139(c).
Withholding of income.
Generally, §§110-136.3 to 110-136.14.
See CHILD SUPPORT.
Interstate family support act, §§52C-5-501 to
52C-5-507.
See INTERSTATE FAMILY SUPPORT.
Cigarettes and tobacco products.
Distribution to minor employee in performance of
duties, §14-313(b).
Lawful use of lawful products during nonworking
hours by employees.
Discrimination against prohibited, §95-28.2.
Civil no-contact orders.
Workplace violence prevention, §§95-260 to
95-271.
See WORKPLACE VIOLENCE PREVENTION.

EMPLOYMENT RELATIONS —Cont'd
Commercial bribery, §14-353.
Commissioner of labor.
See LABOR COMMISSIONER.
Conciliation service and mediation of labor disputes, §§95-32 to 95-36.
See LABOR DISPUTES.
Constitution of North Carolina.
Local, private and special legislation prohibited, NC Const Art II §24.
Contempt.
Information from employers.
Refusal as contempt, §95-7.
Statistical report from employers to commissioner.
Refusal as contempt, §95-8.
Controlled substances.
Examination and screening of employees for, §§95-230 to 95-235.
Costs.
Discrimination against lawful use of lawful products during nonworking hours.
Court costs in civil actions for violations, §95-28.2(e).
Criminal law and procedure.
Earnings of employees in interstate commerce.
Collection out of state to avoid exemption, §95-75.
Labor union violations by public employee, §95-99.
Payments to or for benefit of labor organization.
Violations, §95-104.
Victims or witnesses.
Employer intercession services, §15A-825.
Damages.
Discrimination for lawful use of lawful products during nonworking hours.
Civil actions for violations of section, §95-28.2(e).
Right to work law.
Recovery of damages by persons denied employment, §95-83.
Definitions.
Lawful use of lawful products during nonworking hours.
Discrimination against employees prohibited, §95-28.2(a).
Medical examination as condition of employment.
Requiring payment for examination, §14-357.1(b), (c).
Occupational safety and health, §95-127.
Retaliatory employment discrimination, §95-240.
Safety and health program, §95-250.
Unions.
Payments to or for benefit of labor organizations.
Definition of "labor organization,"§95-101.
Wage and hour act, §95-25.2.
Department of labor generally.
See LABOR DEPARTMENT.
Disabled persons.
Governor's council on employment of the handicapped, §§143-283.1 to 143-283.8.
See DISABLED PERSONS.
Discharge of employee.
Employee called to jury duty.
Prohibition, §9-32(a).
Action for damages, §9-32(b), (c).
Retaliatory employment discrimination, §§95-240 to 95-245.
Disclosure of information by employer.
Employee's job performance or job history.
Immunity, §1-539.12(a) to (d).

EMPLOYMENT RELATIONS —Cont'd
Discrimination.
Equal employment practices, §§143-422.1 to 143-422.3.
Generally.
See EMPLOYMENT DISCRIMINATION.
Genetic testing, information or counseling, §95-28.1A.
Lawful use of lawful products during nonworking hours by employees, §95-28.2.
Leave for parent involvement in schools, §95-28.3(b), (c).
Retaliatory employment discrimination, §§95-240 to 95-245.
See EMPLOYMENT DISCRIMINATION.
Sickle cell trait or hemoglobin C trait.
Discrimination against persons possessing, §95-28.1.
Driver's license.
Limited driving privilege, driving for work-related purposes.
Nonstandard hours, §20-179.3(g1).
Driving with revoked license underlying offense resulting in license revocation, §20-20.1(g).
Standard working hours, §20-179.3(g).
Driving with revoked license underlying offense resulting in license revocation, §20-20.1(f).
Drugs.
Examination and screening of employees for controlled substances, §§95-230 to 95-235.
Lawful use of lawful products during nonworking hours by employees.
Discrimination against prohibited, §95-28.2.
Duties owed employer.
Influencing employees to violate duties, §§14-353, 14-354.
Earnings of employees in interstate commerce, §§95-73 to 95-77.
Embezzlement.
By servant or employee, §14-74.
Generally.
See EMBEZZLEMENT.
Receipt of property by virtue of office or employment, §14-90.
Employee assistance professionals, §§90-500 to 90-511.
See EMPLOYEE ASSISTANCE PROFESSIONALS.
Employee examination and screening for controlled substances, §§95-230 to 95-235.
Employee's job history or performance.
Immunity, employer disclosing information, §1-539.12(a) to (d).
Employment agencies.
Job listing services, §§95-47.19 to 95-47.32.
See JOB LISTING SERVICES.
Private personnel services, §§95-47.1 to 95-47.15.
See PRIVATE PERSONNEL SERVICES.
Professional employer organization act, §§58-89A-1 to 58-89A-180.
See PROFESSIONAL EMPLOYER ORGANIZATIONS.
Employment security.
General provisions, §§96-1 to 96-29.
See UNEMPLOYMENT COMPENSATION.
Equal employment practices, §§143-422.1 to 143-422.3.
Citation of article, §143-422.1.

EMPLOYMENT RELATIONS —Cont'd
Equal employment practices —Cont'd
Human relations council.
Charges of discrimination, §143-422.3.
Legislative declaration, §143-422.2.
Purpose of article, §143-422.2.
Short title, §143-422.1.
E-Verify program.
Counties.
Duty to register and participate, §153A-99.1.
Definition of E-Verify, §64-25.
Employers to use, §64-26(a).
Seasonal temporary employee exception to
requirement, §64-26(c).
Violations, consequences, §§64-31 to 64-33.
Municipalities.
Duty to register and participate, §160A-169.1.
State departments, agencies, etc.
Verification of legal status after hiring new
employees, §126-7.1(f).
Work authorization verification generally, §§64-25
to 64-38.
Evidence.
Earnings of employees in interstate commerce.
Collections out of state to avoid exemptions,
§95-76.
Family leave credit insurance, §58-57-115.
Garnishment.
See GARNISHMENT.
General assembly.
Local, private and special legislation prohibited,
NC Const Art II §24.
Genetic testing, information or counseling.
Discrimination against persons based on,
§95-28.1A.
Harassment.
Workplace violence prevention.
Civil no-contact orders, §§95-260 to 95-271.
See WORKPLACE VIOLENCE
PREVENTION.
Health of employees.
Occupational safety and health, §§95-126 to
95-155.
See OCCUPATIONAL SAFETY AND HEALTH.
Safety and health programs generally, §§95-250 to
95-256.
See EMPLOYEE SAFETY AND HEALTH
PROGRAMS.
Hemoglobin C trait.
Discrimination against persons possessing
hemoglobin C trait, §95-28.1.
Hospital authorities.
Conflicts of interest of employees, §131E-21.
Hospital employees.
Garnishment for debts owed public hospitals.
Discharge or disciplinary action because
employee subject to garnishment, §131E-50.
Public hospital personnel act, §§131E-257 to
131E-257.2.
Hours of labor.
Wage and hour act.
General provisions, §§95-25.1 to 95-25.25.
See WAGE AND HOUR ACT.
Housing standards.
Migrant farm workers, §§95-222 to 95-229.1.
See MIGRANT FARM WORKERS.
Immigration.
Verification of work authorization.
E-Verify program.
Counties.
Duty to register and participate,
§153A-99.1.

EMPLOYMENT RELATIONS —Cont'd
Immigration —Cont'd
Verification of work authorization —Cont'd
E-Verify program —Cont'd
Definition of E-Verify, §64-25.
Municipalities.
Duty to register and participate,
§160A-169.1.
State departments, agencies, etc.
Verification of legal status after hiring new
employees, §126-7.1(f).
Generally, §§64-25 to 64-38.
Immunity of employer.
Disclosure of information.
Employee's job history or performance,
§1-539.12(a) to (d).
Income withholding.
Child support.
Generally, §§110-136.3 to 110-136.14.
See CHILD SUPPORT.
Interstate family support act, §§52C-5-501 to
52C-5-507.
See INTERSTATE FAMILY SUPPORT.
**Influencing employees in violating duties owed
employers,** §§14-353, 14-354.
Witness required to give self-incriminating
evidence, §14-354.
No suit or prosecution to be founded thereon,
§14-354.
Inspection service fees, §§95-107, 95-108.
Insurance.
Discrimination against lawful use of lawful
products during nonworking hours prohibited.
Health, disability or life insurance policies
distinguishing between employees,
§95-28.2(b).
Interstate commerce.
Earnings of employees in interstate commerce.
Collections out of state to avoid exemptions,
§§95-73 to 95-77.
Construction and interpretation, §95-77.
Evidence of intent to violate provisions,
§95-76.
Institution of foreign suit as evidence of
intent to violate, §95-76.
Penalty, §95-75.
Remedies for violation, §95-75.
Resident not to abet collection out of state,
§95-74.
Inventions developed by employees.
Certain employment agreements void, §66-57.1.
Reporting inventions to employer.
Employer may require, §66-57.2.
Right of employees to certain inventions, §66-57.1.
Rights of employers, §66-57.2.
Involuntary servitude.
Constitution of the United States, US Const Amds
13, 15.
Job listing services, §§95-47.19 to 95-47.32.
See JOB LISTING SERVICES.
Job performance or job history.
Disclosure of information by employer.
Immunity, §1-539.12(a) to (d).
**Job training, education and placement
information management,** §§96-30 to 96-35.
See JOB TRAINING, EDUCATION AND
PLACEMENT INFORMATION
MANAGEMENT.
Jury duty.
Discharge of employee called to jury duty.
Damages suffered by employee, employer liable
for, §9-32(b).
Burden of proof on employee, §9-32(b).

EMPLOYMENT RELATIONS —Cont'd
Jury duty —Cont'd
Discharge of employee called to jury duty —Cont'd
Damages suffered by employee, employer liable
for —Cont'd
Statute of limitation, §9-32(c).
Prohibition, §9-32(a).
Jury trial.
Retaliatory employment discrimination,
§95-243(d).
Kidnapping and abduction.
Enticing minors out of state for employment
purposes, §14-40.
Labor disputes.
See LABOR DISPUTES.
Labor organizations generally.
See LABOR UNIONS.
Larceny by servant or employee, §14-74.
**Lawful use of lawful products during
nonworking hours by employees.**
Discrimination against.
Action for violation of section, §95-28.2(e).
Court costs and attorneys' fees in actions for
violations of section, §95-28.2(d).
Employer defined, §95-28.2(a).
Exceptions to section, §95-28.2(c).
Health, disability or life insurance policies
distinguishing between employees,
§95-28.2(d).
Unlawful employment practice, §95-28.2(a).
Leave for parent involvement in schools,
§95-28.3.
Liens.
Wages for two months' lien on assets, §44-5.1.
Limitation of actions.
Discrimination for lawful use of lawful products
during nonworking hours.
Civil actions for violations, §95-28.2(e).
Examination and screening of employees for
controlled substances.
Assessment of penalties, §95-234(b).
Limited driving privilege.
Driving for work-related purposes.
Nonstandard hours, §20-179.3(g1).
Driving with revoked license underlying
offense resulting in license revocation,
§20-20.1(g).
Standard working hours, §20-179.3(g).
Driving with revoked license underlying
offense resulting in license revocation,
§20-20.1(f).
**Local, private and special legislation
prohibited,** NC Const Art II §24.
Managed care organizations, ICManagedCare
Rules I to X.
See INDUSTRIAL COMMISSION.
Medical examinations.
Conditions of employment.
Requiring payment for examination as condition
of employment, §14-357.1(a).
Definitions, §14-357.1(b), (c).
Penalty for violation of provisions,
§14-357.1(d).
Migrant farm workers.
Housing standards, §§95-222 to 95-229.1.
See MIGRANT FARM WORKERS.
Minimum wage.
Wage and hour act, §§95-25.1 to 95-25.25.
See WAGE AND HOUR ACT.
Minors.
Child labor, §95-25.5.

EMPLOYMENT RELATIONS —Cont'd
Minors —Cont'd
Failure to pay for certain work, §14-321.
Kidnapping and abduction.
Enticing minors out of state for purposes of
employment, §14-40.
National guard.
Reemployment rights, §§127A-201 to 127A-203.
No-contact orders.
Workplace violence prevention.
Civil no-contact orders, §§95-260 to 95-271.
See WORKPLACE VIOLENCE
PREVENTION.
Notice of laws.
Employers to post, §95-9.
Occupational safety and health.
General provisions, §§95-126 to 95-155.
See OCCUPATIONAL SAFETY AND HEALTH.
Safety and health programs, §§95-250 to 95-256.
See EMPLOYEE SAFETY AND HEALTH
PROGRAMS.
Overhead high-voltage line safety act,
§§95-229.5 to 95-229.13.
See OVERHEAD HIGH-VOLTAGE LINE
SAFETY.
Personnel system.
See PERSONNEL SYSTEM.
Precinct election officials.
Discharge or demotion of employee because of
appointment as, §163-41.2.
**Priority in employment assistance for United
States armed forces veterans,** §§165-44.1 to
165-44.6.
Prisoner labor.
Farming out prisoners, §§148-66 to 148-70.
See PRISON LABOR.
Generally, §§148-26 to 148-49.
See PRISON LABOR.
Private personnel services, §§95-47.1 to 95-47.15.
See PRIVATE PERSONNEL SERVICES.
Private protective services, §§74C-1 to 74C-30.
See PRIVATE PROTECTIVE SERVICES.
Professional employer organization act,
§§58-89A-1 to 58-89A-180.
See PROFESSIONAL EMPLOYER
ORGANIZATIONS.
Proprietary schools.
Schools maintained or classes conducted by
employers for employees.
Exemptions from article, §115D-88.
Public hospital personnel act, §§131E-257 to
131E-257.2.
Public officers and employees.
General provisions.
See PUBLIC OFFICERS AND EMPLOYEES.
Unions, §§95-98 to 95-100.
Public utilities.
Screening employment applications.
Criminal history record from state bureau of
investigation, §62-333.
Willful acts of employees deemed those of public
utility, §62-311.
Rehabilitation.
See VOCATIONAL REHABILITATION.
Reports.
Directory of new hires.
Employer reporting, §110-129.2(b) to (e).
Employers required to make statistical report to
commissioner, §95-8.
Safety and health programs and committees,
§95-255.

EMPLOYMENT RELATIONS —Cont'd
Reports —Cont'd
Workplace fatal injuries.
Medical examiners.
Death investigation report, §130A-385(e).
Retaliatory employment discrimination,
§§95-240 to 95-245.
See EMPLOYMENT DISCRIMINATION.
**Retirement system for teachers and state
employees.**
See RETIREMENT SYSTEM FOR TEACHERS
AND STATE EMPLOYEES.
Right to work law, §§95-78 to 95-84.
Agreements between employers and unions.
Certain agreements declared illegal, §§95-79,
95-102.
Applicability of provisions, §95-84.
Exception as to governmental units and their
employees, §95-100.
Damages.
Recovery of damages by persons denied
employment, §95-83.
Legislative declaration, §95-78.
Membership in labor organization as condition of
employment, §95-80.
Nonmembership in labor organization as condition
of employment, §95-81.
Union dues.
Payment of dues as condition of employment,
§95-82.
Rules and regulations, §95-4.
Division of standards and inspection, §95-11(f).
Enforcement, §95-13.
Organization with divisions, §95-3.
Retaliatory employment discrimination, §95-245.
Safety and health programs and committees,
§95-254.
Voluntary arbitration of labor disputes.
Commissioner of labor, §95-36.3(c).
Safety and health programs, §§95-250 to 95-256.
See EMPLOYEE SAFETY AND HEALTH
PROGRAMS.
Salaries.
See SALARIES.
**Screening employees for controlled
substances,** §§95-230 to 95-235.
Seasonal temporary employees.
Verification of work authorization.
E-Verify.
Exception to requirement, §64-26(c).
Self-incrimination.
Influencing agents and employees in violating
duties owed employers.
Witness required to give self-incriminating
evidence, §14-354.
Sickle cell trait.
Discrimination against persons possessing sickle
cell trait, §95-28.1.
Smoking.
Lawful use of lawful products during nonworking
hours by employees.
Discrimination against prohibited, §95-28.2.
State employees.
General provisions.
See PUBLIC OFFICERS AND EMPLOYEES.
Retirement system for teachers and state
employees.
General provisions.
See RETIREMENT SYSTEM FOR
TEACHERS AND STATE EMPLOYEES.

EMPLOYMENT RELATIONS —Cont'd
State employees —Cont'd
State personnel system.
See PERSONNEL SYSTEM.
State institutions.
Wage and hour act.
Exemption of persons confined, §95-25.14(a).
Statutes of limitation.
Discrimination for lawful use of lawful products
during nonworking hours.
Civil actions for violations, §95-28.2(e).
Examination and screening of employees for
controlled substances.
Assessment of penalties, §95-234(b).
Strikes.
Employment security.
Disqualification for benefits, §96-14.
Generally.
See LABOR DISPUTES.
Public employees.
Definition of "strike,"§95-98.2.
Prohibited, §95-98.1.
Voluntary arbitration of labor disputes, §§95-36.1
to 95-36.9.
Subpoenas.
Retaliatory employment discrimination.
Investigations, §95-242(f).
Tests of employees for controlled substances,
§§95-230 to 95-235.
Theft by employees.
Civil liability, §1-538.2(a) to (d).
Threats.
Workplace violence prevention.
Civil no-contact orders, §§95-260 to 95-271.
See WORKPLACE VIOLENCE
PREVENTION.
Tobacco products.
Distribution to minor employee, §14-313(b).
Unemployment compensation.
General provisions, §§96-1 to 96-29.
See UNEMPLOYMENT COMPENSATION.
Unions generally.
See LABOR UNIONS.
United States.
Fair labor standards act.
Agreement with certain federal agencies for
enforcement of act, §95-14.
Verification of work authorization.
E-Verify program.
Counties.
Duty to register and participate, §153A-99.1.
Definition of E-Verify, §64-25.
Municipalities.
Duty to register and participate, §160A-169.1.
State departments, agencies, etc.
Verification of legal status after hiring new
employees, §126-7.1(f).
Generally, §§64-25 to 64-38.
Veterans priority in employment assistance,
§§165-44.1 to 165-44.6.
Violence in the workplace.
Prevention.
Civil no-contact orders, §§95-260 to 95-271.
See WORKPLACE VIOLENCE
PREVENTION.
Vocational and technical education.
See VOCATIONAL AND TECHNICAL
EDUCATION.
Wage and hour act, §§95-25.1 to 95-25.25.
See WAGE AND HOUR ACT.

EMPLOYMENT RELATIONS —Cont'd
Wages generally.
See WAGES.
Whistleblower protection.
Retaliatory employment discrimination, §§95-240 to 95-245.
See EMPLOYMENT DISCRIMINATION.
Withholding of income.
Child support.
Generally, §§110-136.3 to 110-136.14.
See CHILD SUPPORT.
Interstate family support act, §§52C-5-501 to 52C-5-507.
See INTERSTATE FAMILY SUPPORT.
Witnesses.
Adverse parties.
Examination of employee of adverse party, §1A-1 Rule 43(b).
Commissioner of labor.
Powers as to, §95-4.
Workforce development, §§143B-438.10 to 143B-438.13.
Workplace fatal injuries.
Medical examiner's report.
Copy forwarded to commissioner, §130A-385(e).
Workplace violence prevention.
Civil no-contact orders, §§95-260 to 95-271.
See WORKPLACE VIOLENCE PREVENTION.
Youth employment.
Child labor, §95-25.5.

EMPLOYMENT SECURITY DIVISION.
Creation, §96-3.
Job training, education and placement information management, §§96-30 to 96-35.
See JOB TRAINING, EDUCATION AND PLACEMENT INFORMATION MANAGEMENT.
Unemployment compensation generally, §§96-1 to 96-29.
See UNEMPLOYMENT COMPENSATION.

ENCROACHMENT UPON PUBLIC WAY.
No title by possession, §1-45.

ENDANGERED SPECIES.
Plants.
Board, §§106-202.14, 106-202.15.
Criteria and procedures for placing on list, §106-202.16.
Declaration of policy, §106-202.13.
Definitions, §106-202.12.
Enforcement of article, §106-202.19(b).
Ginseng dealers.
Permits, §106-202.21.
Illegally possessed plants.
Forfeiture and disposition, §106-202.20.
Injunctive relief.
Violations of article, §106-202.19(c).
Legislative findings, §106-202.13.
Permits.
Denial, suspension or revocation, §106-202.22.
Ginseng dealers, §106-202.21.
Policy of state, NC Const Art XIV §5.
Declaration, §106-202.13.
Right of entry.
Enforcement of article, §106-202.19(b).
Scientific committee, §§106-202.17, 106-202.18.
Unlawful acts, §106-202.19(a).
Civil penalties, §106-202.19(a2).
Criminal penalties, §106-202.19(a1).

ENDANGERED SPECIES —Cont'd
Wildlife.
Declaration of policy, §113-332.
Definitions, §113-331.
Federal list species.
Same status on state list, §113-334(a).
Nongame wildlife advisory committee, §§113-335, 113-336.
Placing on protected lists.
Examination of relevant scientific and economic data.
Commission finding probable merit in proposal, §113-334(c).
Federal list species.
Same status on state list, §113-334(a).
Notice of proposed rulemaking, publication, §113-334(d).
Resolution proposing adding or removing species.
Advisory committee proposing to commission, §113-334(b).
Tentative determine on regulatory action, §113-334(d).
Policy of state, §113-332.
Unlawful acts, §113-337(a).
Misdemeanors, §113-337(b).
Wildlife resources commission.
Bat exclusion and eviction curriculum, §113-333(d).
Conservation plan, §113-333(b), (c).
Powers and duties, §113-333(a).

ENDANGERING EXECUTIVE, LEGISLATIVE OR COURT OFFICERS, §§14-16.6 to 14-16.10.
Electronic surveillance orders, §15A-290(c4).

ENDORSEMENTS.
Check-cashing business.
Instrument presented by licensee for payment, §53-280(d).
Commercial code general provisions.
Unauthorized indorsements defined, §25-1-201(b)(43).
Commercial paper.
See NEGOTIABLE INSTRUMENTS.
Documents of title, §25-7-501(a).
Compelling endorsement.
Right to compel, §25-7-506.
Delivery to compel endorsement, §25-7-506.
Endorser not guarantor for other parties, §25-7-505.
Power to compel endorsement, §25-7-506.
Requirements of due negotiation, §25-7-501.
Investment securities, §25-8-107.
Assurance that indorsements are effective, §25-8-402.
Warranties in direct holding, §25-8-108.
Negotiable instruments generally.
See NEGOTIABLE INSTRUMENTS.
Uttering instrument containing forged endorsement, §14-120.

ENDOWMENT FUNDS.
Conservation easement endowment fund, §113A-253.2.
Prudent management of institutional funds, §§36E-1 to 36E-11.
See PRUDENT MANAGEMENT OF INSTITUTIONAL FUNDS.
Public schools, §§115C-490 to 115C-494.

ENERGY.
Coal and petroleum suppliers.
Reporting petroleum fuel capacity, §§143-345.13, 143-345.14.
Conservation loan authority, §§122A-5.3, 122A-6.1.
County energy improvements revolving loan program, §153A-455.
Crisis administration, §§113B-20 to 113B-24.
See ENERGY CRISIS ADMINISTRATION.
Emergency energy program, §113B-9.
Energy assistance to low-income persons, §§143B-472.121 to 143B-472.123.
Definitions, §143B-472.122.
Legislative findings, §143B-472.121(a).
Methods to be utilized to increase energy efficiency, §143B-472.121(b).
Office of economic opportunity.
Administration of program, §143B-472.123(a).
Final decision-making authority, §143B-472.123(b).
Powers and duties, §143B-472.123(a).
Energy conservation.
Energy conservation finance act, §§142-60 to 142-70.
Public buildings.
Performance standards for sustainable, energy-efficient buildings, §§143-135.35 to 143-135.40.
See PUBLIC BUILDINGS AND GROUNDS.
University of North Carolina.
Budget effect of energy conservation savings, §116-30.3B.
Energy efficiency incentives.
Municipalities, §160A-383.4(a).
Energy efficiency program, §113B-7.
Energy loan fund, §§143B-437.14 to 143B-437.16.
Energy savings contracts.
Guaranteed energy savings contracts, §§143-64.17 to 143-64.17M, 143-129.4.
Guaranteed energy savings contracts, §§143-64.17 to 143-64.17M, 143-129.4.
Local governmental units.
Installment and lease purchase contracts, §143-64.17I.
Reports, §143-64.17G.
State governmental units.
Financing by, §143-64.17J.
Inspection and compliance certification for, §143-64.17K.
Reports, §143-64.17H.
Use of contracts when feasible, rules, recommendation, §143-64.17F.
University of North Carolina constituent institutions, §143-64.17L.
Energy savings analyses required, §143-64.17M.
Low-income energy assistance program, §108A-25.4.
Management plan, §113B-8.
Municipal energy efficiency incentives, §160A-383.4(a).
Municipal program to finance energy improvements, §160A-459.1.
Nuclear facility fees.
Carried forward amount of fees, §166A-6.1(c).
Oil and gas conservation, §§113-378 to 113-424.
See OIL AND GAS CONSERVATION.
Policy council, §§113B-1 to 113B-12.
See ENERGY POLICY COUNCIL.

ENERGY —Cont'd
Public buildings and grounds.
Energy conservation.
Performance standards for sustainable, energy-efficient buildings, §§143-135.35 to 143-135.40.
See PUBLIC BUILDINGS AND GROUNDS.
Energy policy and life-cycle cost analysis for state government, §§143-64.10 to 143-64.16.
Guaranteed energy savings contracts, §§143-64.17 to 143-64.17M, 143-129.4.
Renewable energy and energy efficiency portfolio standard (REPS), §62-133.8.
Southern states energy compact, §§104D-1 to 104D-5.
State energy conservation finance act, §§142-60 to 142-70.
See ENERGY CONSERVATION FINANCE ACT.
University of North Carolina.
Budget effect of energy conservation savings, §116-30.3B.

ENERGY ASSISTANCE TO LOW-INCOME PERSONS, §§143B-472.121 to 143B-472.123.
Definitions, §143B-472.122.
Legislative findings, §143B-472.121(a).
Methods to be utilized to increase energy efficiency, §143B-472.121(b).
Office of economic opportunity.
Administration of program, §143B-472.123(a).
Final decision-making authority, §143B-472.123(b).
Powers and duties, §143B-472.123(a).

ENERGY CONSERVATION FINANCE ACT, §§142-60 to 142-70.
Certificates of participation.
Defined, §142-61.
Interest, §142-67(b).
Investment eligibility, §142-70.
Other agreements authorized, §142-69.
Powers of state treasurer, §142-67(a).
Sale, §142-67(b).
Tax exemption, §142-68.
Trust agreement, §142-67(c).
Citation of act, §142-60.
Credit facility.
Defined, §142-61.
Security for payments under financing contract, §142-65(g).
Definitions, §142-61.
Financing contract.
Aggregate principal amount payable by the state, §142-63.
Authorization, §142-63.
Breach.
Deficiency judgment not to be rendered against state in action for, §142-65(b).
Defined, §142-61.
Entry into.
Certification of availability of funds to make payments due under, §142-64(d).
Conditions, §142-64(b).
Factors in determining whether to approve, §142-64(c).
Request for approval, §142-64(a).
Faith and credit of state not pledged, §142-66.
Interest component of installment payments under.
Calculation, §142-65(f).
Investment eligibility, §142-70.
Nonsubstitution clauses prohibited, §142-65(c).

ENERGY CONSERVATION FINANCE ACT
  —Cont'd
Financing contract —Cont'd
  Other agreements authorized, §142-69.
  Payments under, §142-66.
  Provisions authorized, §142-65(d), (e).
  Security for performance of state's obligations
    under.
    Credit facility, §142-65(g).
    Lien on conservation property, §142-65(a).
  Tax exemption, §142-68.
Liens.
  Security for performance of state's obligations
    under financing contract.
    Lien on conservation property, §142-65(a).
Title of act, §142-60.

ENERGY CREDIT AND BANKING PROGRAM.
Alternative fuel revolving fund.
  Definitions, §143-58.5(a).
  Established, distribution, §143-58.5(b).
  Report on expenditures, §143-58.5(e).
  Rules, §143-58.5(d).
  Use, §143-58.5(c).
Definitions, §143-58.4(a).
Department of transportation.
  Participation, §136-28.13.
Establishment, §143-58.4(b).
Purposes, §143-58.4(b).
Rules, adoption, §143-58.4(c).

ENERGY CRISIS ADMINISTRATION, §§113B-20
    to 113B-24.
Attorney general enforcement, §113B-24(a).
Declaration of crisis.
  Energy policy council.
    Emergency energy coordinating body.
      Council to become upon declaration of energy
        crisis, §113B-23(a).
  Implementation and enforcement of emergency
    energy program, §113B-23(b).
  Power of governor, §§113B-20(b), 113B-23(c).
Definitions, §113B-20(a).
Emergency energy coordinating body.
  Declaration of energy crisis.
    Energy policy council, §113B-23(a).
Emergency proposals.
  Consultation by governor with committee,
    §113B-22(b).
  Contents, §113B-22(d).
  Duration, §113B-22(c).
  Effective date, §113B-22(b).
  Procedure for adoption, §113B-22(a).
Energy policy council.
  Declaration of energy crisis.
    Emergency energy coordinating body,
      §113B-23(a).
    Duties, §113B-23(a).
Enforcement.
  Powers and duties of attorney general,
    §113B-24(a).
Governor.
  Declaration of crisis, §113B-20(b).
  Powers, §113B-23(c).
Implementation and enforcement of
    emergency energy programs.
  Declaration of energy crisis, §113B-23(b).
Injunctions.
  Enforcement of article, §113B-24(c).
Legislative committee.
  Composition, §113B-21(a).
  Created, §113B-21(a).

ENERGY CRISIS ADMINISTRATION —Cont'd
Legislative committee —Cont'd
  Governor to consult with, §113B-22(b).
  Meetings, §113B-21(b).
  Reimbursement of members, §113B-21(c).
Penalties, §113B-24(b).
Violations.
  Injunctions, §113B-24(c).
  Penalty, §113B-24(b).

ENERGY EFFICIENCY PROGRAM.
Attorney general.
  Assignment of attorney for program, §114-4.2D.
Contents, §113B-7(c).
Initial plan.
  Completion, §113B-7(a).
Municipal energy efficiency incentives,
    §160A-383.4(a).
Municipal program to finance energy
    improvements, §160A-459.1.
Preparation by council, §113B-7(a).
Purpose of plan, §113B-7(b).
Recommendations of council, §113B-7(c), (d).
Review of plan, §113B-7(g).
Transmission to governor, §113B-7(e).
Transmission to legislature, §113B-7(f).

ENERGY LOAN FUND, §§143B-437.14 to
    143B-437.16.
Administrative expenses.
  Applicability of stripper well settlement,
    §143B-437.16(e).
Definitions, §143B-437.16(f).
Interest rates, §143B-437.16(d).
Lead agency, §143B-437.16(a).
Powers and duties, §143B-437.16(b).
Purpose, §143B-437.15.
Revolving fund.
  Annual interest rate charged for use,
    §143B-437.16(c).
  Establishment, §143B-437.16(b).
Short title, §143B-437.14.

ENERGY MANAGEMENT PLAN.
Components of plan, §113B-8(b).
Contents, §113B-8(c).
Governor.
  Authority, §113B-8(g), (h).
Preparation, §113B-8(a).
Purpose of plan, §113B-8(b).
Recommendations, §113B-8(d).
Transmission to governor and legislature,
    §113B-8(e).
Updating plan by council, §113B-8(f).

ENERGY POLICY COUNCIL, §§113B-1 to
    113B-12.
Advisory committees.
  Authority to create, §113B-5(c).
Appointments, §113B-3(b).
Attorney general.
  Assignment of attorney for council, §114-4.2D.
Chair, §113B-4(a).
Composition, §113B-3(a).
Creation, §113B-2(a).
Declaration of energy crisis.
  Emergency energy coordinating body, §113B-23(a).
  Duties, §113B-23(a).
Duties, §§113B-2(b), 113B-6.
Emergency energy program.
  Preparation, §113B-9(a).
Energy efficiency program.
  Administrative responsibility.
    Assignment by governor, §113B-7(e).

ENERGY POLICY COUNCIL —Cont'd
Energy efficiency program —Cont'd
Attorney general.
Assignment of attorney for program, §114-4.2D.
Distribution, §113B-7(d).
Governor.
Transmission to senate, §113B-7(f).
Preparation, §113B-7(a).
Purpose of plan, §113B-7(b).
Recommendations of council, §113B-7(c), (d).
Review by council, §113B-7(g).
Transmission to governor for approval or
disapproval, §113B-7(e).
Funds.
Authority to allocate and dispense, §113B-11(d).
Grants.
Authority of council to apply and utilize,
§113B-11(c).
Information.
Authority of council to secure, §113B-11(a).
Legislative findings, §113B-1.
Management plan.
Governor.
Authority, §113B-8(g), (h).
Procedures, §113B-8(e).
Preparation, §113B-8(a).
Purpose of plan, §113B-8(b).
Recommendations, §113B-8(d).
Updating by council, §113B-8(f).
Organization, §113B-5(a).
Powers, duties and functions, §§113B-2(b),
113B-6.
Purpose of article, §113B-1.
Purpose of council, §113B-2(c).
Qualifications, §113B-3(c).
Reimbursement of members, §113B-4(c).
Reports, §113B-12(a), (b).
Annual report, §113B-11(a).
Council may require filing, §113B-11(b).
Rules of procedure.
Adoption, §113B-5(b).
Staff, §113B-11(e).
Vacancies, §113B-4(b).

ENERGY SAVINGS CONTRACTS.
Guaranteed energy savings contracts,
§§143-64.17 to 143-64.17M, 143-129.4.
Local governmental units.
Installment and lease purchase contracts,
§143-64.17I.
Reports, §143-64.17G.
State governmental units.
Financing by, §143-64.17J.
Inspection and compliance certification for,
§143-64.17K.
Reports, §143-64.17H.
University of North Carolina constituent
institutions, §143-64.17L.
Energy savings analyses required,
§143-64.17M.
Use of contracts when feasible, rules,
recommendations, §143-64.17F.

ENERGY STAR QUALIFIED PRODUCT.
Sales and use tax.
Defined, §105-164.3.
Tax holiday, §105-164.13D(a).
Qualified products, §105-164.13D(a).
Unqualified products, §105-164.13D(b).

**ENFORCEMENT OF CHILD SUPPORT
PROGRAM.**
Generally, §§110-128 to 110-142.2.
See CHILD SUPPORT.

ENFORCEMENT OF FOREIGN JUDGMENTS,
§§1C-1701 to 1C-1708.
See FOREIGN JUDGMENTS.

ENGINEERS.
Air pollution control.
Expedited review of applications certified by
professional engineer, §143-215.108(h).
Appeals.
Disciplinary action.
Judicial review, §89C-22(d).
Applicability of provisions.
Limitations, §89C-25.
Architects.
Exemption of architectural work incidental to
engineering project, §83A-13(a).
Attorney general.
Legal adviser to board, §89C-23.
Board of examiners.
Appointment of members, §89C-4.
Compensation of members, §89C-6.
Composition, §89C-4.
Continuing professional competency activities.
Licensing of sponsors, §89C-10(h).
Creation, §89C-4.
Executive director, §89C-9.
Bond, surety, §89C-9.
Expenses of members, §89C-6.
Funds, §89C-11.
Injunctions.
Power to seek, §89C-10(c).
Instructional programs.
Powers as to, §89C-10(g).
Licensure by discipline.
Submission of program, §89C-25.2.
Meetings, §89C-8.
Number of members, §89C-4.
Officers, §89C-8.
Powers.
Generally, §89C-10.
Qualifications of members, §§89C-4, 89C-5.
Quorum, §89C-8.
Real property, powers, §89C-10(i).
Records, §89C-12.
Removal of members, §89C-7.
Reports.
Annual report to governor, §89C-12.
Residence requirements for membership, §89C-5.
Rules and regulations, §89C-10(a).
Rules of professional conduct.
Promulgation, §89C-20.
Seal, §89C-10(b).
Secretary.
Duties, §89C-11.
Election, §89C-8.
Terms of members, §89C-4.
Vacancies, §§89C-4, 89C-7.
Bonds, surety.
Board of examiners.
Executive director, §89C-9.
Child support enforcement.
Forfeiture of licensing privilege, §50-13.12.
Citation of act.
Short title, §89C-1.
Conflicts of interest.
Public works.
Employment of engineers when interest in use
of materials prohibited, §133-1.
Construction of act.
Citation of title, §89C-1.
Exemptions from act's provisions, §89C-25.

ENGINEERS —Cont'd
Construction of act —Cont'd
Limitations on act's applicability, §89C-25.
Public policy, §89C-2.
Severability of provisions, §89C-27.
Continuing education.
Sponsors of continuing professional competency
    activities.
Licensing, §89C-10(h).
Corporations.
Practice of engineering or land surveying,
    §89C-24.
Definitions, §89C-3.
Disciplinary action, §89C-22.
Appeals.
Judicial review, §89C-22(d).
Certificate of authorization of corporation.
Revocation or suspension, §89C-21(b).
Reissuance, §89C-22(e).
Charges, §89C-22(a).
Hearing, §89C-22(b).
Grounds, §89C-21(a).
Penalties.
Civil penalties, §89C-21(c), (d).
Penalties authorized, §89C-22(c).
Revocation or suspension of certificate,
    §89C-21(a).
Reissuance, §89C-22(e).
Education.
Continuing education.
Licensing of sponsors of professional
    competency activities, §89C-10(h).
Requirements for licensure generally, §89C-13.
Emergency or disaster.
Qualified immunity for volunteers, §89C-19.1(a) to
    (d).
Engineering interns.
Licenses.
Qualifications, §89C-13(a).
Evidence.
Licenses.
Certificates of licensure.
Evidentiary effect, §89C-16(b).
Examinations, §89C-15.
Power of board, §89C-10(d).
Reexamination, §89C-14(e).
Requirements for licensure generally, §89C-13.
Scope, §89C-15(b).
Time and place, §89C-15(a).
Exemptions from provisions, §89C-25.
Fees.
Continuing professional competency activities.
Sponsors' licenses, §89C-10(h).
Felony convictions.
Forfeiture of license, §15A-1331A.
Highways, roads and streets.
Right-of-way acquisitions.
Preliminary engineering annual report,
    §136-44.11(a).
Immunity.
Emergency or disaster.
Qualified immunity for volunteers, §89C-19.1(a)
    to (d).
Injunctions, §89C-10(c).
Instructional programs.
Board of examiners.
Powers as to, §89C-10(g).
Investigations.
Duties of board, §89C-10(f).
Land surveyor interns.
Licenses.
Qualifications, §89C-13(b).

ENGINEERS —Cont'd
Land surveyors.
Soil scientists.
Unlawful acts as to land surveying, §89F-19(e).
Legislative declaration, §89C-2.
Licenses.
Applications, §89C-14(a).
Certificates of licensure.
Evidentiary effect, §89C-16(b).
Expiration, §89C-17.
Issuance, §89C-16(a).
Power of board, §89C-10(e).
Lost or destroyed certificates.
Duplicate certificate, §89C-18.
Renewal, §89C-17.
Comity or indorsement.
Requirements for licensure by.
Professional engineer, §89C-13(a).
Professional land surveyor, §89C-13(b).
Corporations and business firms, §89C-24.
Engineering interns.
Qualifications, §89C-13(a).
Examinations, §89C-15.
Reexamination, §89C-14(e).
Requirements for licensure generally, §89C-13.
Scope, §89C-15(b).
Time and place, §89C-15(a).
Existing licensure not affected, §89C-28.
Expiration of certificates, §89C-17.
Fees, §89C-14(b), (c).
Corporations and business firms, §89C-24.
Duplicate certificates, §89C-18.
Renewal of certificate, §89C-17.
Return on denial of certificate, §89C-14(d).
Issuance of certificate of licensure.
Power of board, §89C-10(e).
Land surveyor interns.
Qualifications, §89C-13(b).
Nonresidents.
Definitions, §89C-18.1(a).
Delinquents, §89C-18.1(d).
Generally, §89C-18.1(b).
Information, §89C-18.1(c).
Photogrammetrists.
Qualifications, §89C-13(b).
Professional engineers.
Qualifications, §89C-13(a).
Professional land surveyors.
Qualifications, §89C-13(b).
Qualifications, §89C-13.
Renewal of certificate, §89C-17.
Required, §89C-2.
Revocation or suspension.
Disciplinary action generally, §§89C-21, 89C-22.
Felony convictions, §15A-1331A.
Saving clause, §89C-28.
Statewide license for privilege of practicing.
Firm or corporation.
Not issued in name of, §105-41(e).
License not authorization to practice, §105-41(i).
Not transferable, §105-41(a).
Personal privilege licenses, §105-41(e).
Required, §105-41(a).
Tax for each license, §105-41(a).
Counties and cities levying, prohibition,
    §105-41(h).
Exemptions, §105-41(b).
Supervision of unlicensed individuals by licensed
    person, §89C-25.1.
License tax.
Statewide license for privilege of practicing,
    §105-41.

ENGINEERS —Cont'd
Licensure by discipline.
Board to submit program, §89C-25.2.
Limitation of actions.
Real property improvements.
Recovery of damages for defective or unsafe conditions.
Six-year limitation, §1-50(a).
Nonresidents.
Licensing of nonresidents, §89C-18.1.
Penalties.
Violations of provisions, §89C-23.
Practice of engineering.
Corporations and business firms, §89C-24.
Practice of land surveying.
Corporations and business firms, §89C-24.
Professional corporations, §55B-14(b).
Professional engineers.
Licenses.
Qualifications, §89C-13(a).
Professional land surveyors.
Licenses.
Qualifications, §89C-13(b).
Public buildings and grounds.
Bids and bidding.
Architectural, engineering and surveying services, §§143-64.31 to 143-64.34.
See PUBLIC CONTRACTS.
Certain buildings involving public funds to be designed, etc., by engineer, §133-1.1.
Public works.
Bids and bidding.
Architectural, engineering and surveying services, §§143-64.31 to 143-64.34.
See PUBLIC CONTRACTS.
Buildings involving expenditure of public funds.
Certain buildings involving public funds to be designed, etc., by engineer, §133-1.1.
Employment of engineers when interest in use of materials prohibited, §133-1.
Requirements, §89C-19.
Records.
Board of examiners, §89C-12.
Reports.
Board of examiners.
Annual report to governor, §89C-12.
Rules and regulations of board of examiners, §89C-10(a).
Rules of professional conduct, §89C-20.
Safety professionals, §§90-671 to 90-674.
Sanitary districts.
Employment of engineers.
Corporate powers of sanitary district board, §130A-55.
Plan for accomplishment of objects of district.
Engineers to provide plans and supervise work, §130A-63(a), (c).
Report on problems of sanitary district, §130A-59.
Consideration of reports and adoption of plan, §130A-60(a), (b).
Seals and sealed instruments, §89C-16(c).
Board of examiners, §89C-10(b).
Confidential information.
Records submitted for project approval revealing, §132-1.2.
Severability of provisions, §89C-27.
Soil scientists.
Unlawful acts by soil scientists as to engineering, §89F-19(f).
Subcontractors, payments to for improvements upon real property, §§22C-1 to 22C-6.

ENGINEERS —Cont'd
Supervision of unlicensed individuals by licensed person, §89C-25.1.
Title of act.
Short title, §89C-1.
Transportation department.
Division engineer to manage personnel department, §136-14.2.
Unit ownership.
Plans of buildings.
Certificate of engineer, §47A-15(a).
Violations of provisions.
Injunctions, §89C-10(c).
Penalties, §89C-23.
Prohibited act, §89C-23.
Volunteering services at disaster or emergency.
Qualified immunity for volunteers, §89C-19.1(a) to (d).

ENGINE NUMBERS.
Altering or changing.
Prohibited acts, §20-109(a).
Intent to conceal or misrepresent true identity of vehicle, §20-109(b).
New.
Division to be notified on installation, §20-70(a).
When required, §20-70(c).
Surrender of certificate of title and registration card on installation, §20-70(b).
Removal or obliteration.
New engine number, §20-69.
Surrender of registration card and certificate of title, §20-70(b).
Vehicles without manufacturer's numbers.
Prohibitions as to, §20-108(a) to (j).

ENGINE TAMPERING, §14-153.

ENGLISH LANGUAGE.
Public schools.
Basic education program.
Classes to be conducted in English, §115C-81(c).
State language, §145-12.

ENGRAVINGS.
Sale of prints, §§25C-10 to 25C-16.

ENLARGEMENT OF TIME, §§1-593, 1A-1 Rule 6(b).

ENTERPRISE CORPORATIONS, §§53A-35 to 53A-47.
See NORTH CAROLINA ENTERPRISE CORPORATIONS.

ENTERPRISE TIER.
Tax incentives for new and expanding businesses.
Agrarian growth zone designation.
Relationship with enterprise tiers, §105-129.3B(d).
Defined, assignment and rankings of counties, §105-129.3.
Development zone designation.
Relationship with enterprise tiers, §105-129.3A(c).
Eligibility for credits, forfeiture, §105-129.4.

ENTERTAINMENT CONTRACTS.
See PREPAID ENTERTAINMENT CONTRACTS.

ENTERTAINMENT TAX.
License tax by city but not county, §105-37.1(d).
Privilege tax on gross receipts, admission fee charged, §105-37.1(a).
Rate and payment, §105-37.1(b).

ENTICING MINOR OUT OF STATE FOR EMPLOYMENT PURPOSES, §14-40.

ENTRAPMENT.
Criminal law and procedure.
Notice to state of defenses, §15A-905(c), (d).

ENTRY OF JUDGMENT, §1A-1 Rule 58.
Confession of judgment, §1A-1 Rule 68.1(d).
Default, §1A-1 Rule 55(a), (b).
Setting aside, §1A-1 Rule 55(d).
Judgment by confession, §1A-1 Rule 68.1.
Multiple claims or parties, §1A-1 Rule 54(b).
Small claims actions, §7A-224.

ENTRY, RIGHT OF.
See RIGHT OF ENTRY.

ENVIRONMENTAL COMPACT, §§113A-21 to
113A-23.
Citation of article, §113A-21.
Compact provisions, §113A-23.
Legislative findings, §113A-22.
Provisions generally, §113A-23.
Purposes, §113A-22.
Short title, §113A-21.

ENVIRONMENTAL COMPLIANCE COSTS.
Accelerated costs recovery.
Coal-fired investor-owned generating units,
§62-133.6(b).
Adjustments or reductions in rate base,
§62-133.6(e), (f).
Amortization, §62-133.6(b).
Compliance plans, filing, §62-133.6(c).
Defined, §62-133.6(a).
Emissions limitations, statement by utilities
subject to, §62-133.6(i), (j).
Enforcement of utility compliance, §62-133.6(h).
Final agency action not subject to review,
§62-133.6(k).
Hearing to review compliance costs,
§62-133.6(d).
Market based rates and services, authority to
implement, §62-133.6(g).
Rate base to remain unchanged, §62-133.6(e).
Electric public utility purchase or
construction of carbon offset facility.
Retention of fuel and fuel-related cost savings,
§62-133.10.
Adjustment of fuel and fuel-related costs,
§62-133.10(a), (f).
Carbon offset facility, defined, §62-133.10(b).
Conduct of investigation, §62-133.10(d).
Filing petition with commission, §62-133.10(c),
(d).
Other permits and certificates not affected,
§62-133.10(e).

ENVIRONMENTAL CONTAMINATION.
Brownfields property reuse act of 1997,
§§130A-310.30 to 130A-310.40.
See BROWNFIELDS PROPERTY REUSE.
Risk based environmental remediation of
industrial sites, §§130A-310.65 to
130A-310.77.
See HAZARDOUS WASTE MANAGEMENT.

**ENVIRONMENTAL EDUCATION AND PUBLIC
AFFAIRS, OFFICE OF,** §§143B-285.20 to
143B-285.25.
Awards.
Objectives, §143B-285.24.
Citation of act.
Short title, §143B-285.20.

**ENVIRONMENTAL EDUCATION AND PUBLIC
AFFAIRS, OFFICE OF** —Cont'd
Creation, §143B-285.22.
Department of public instruction.
Liaison with, §143B-285.25.
Grants.
Objectives, §143B-285.24.
Legislative declaration, §143B-285.21.
Powers and duties, §143B-285.23.
Purpose of act, §143B-285.21.
Secretary.
Powers and duties, §143B-285.23.
Title of act.
Short title, §143B-285.20.

**ENVIRONMENTAL ENFORCEMENT
OFFICERS.**
Municipalities.
Enforcing restrictions on illegal disposal of solid
waste, §160A-185.

ENVIRONMENTAL HEALTH SPECIALISTS,
§§90A-50 to 90A-67.
Applicability of chapter, §90A-58.
Board of environmental health specialist
examiners.
Applicability of chapter, §90A-58.
Compensation of members, §90A-56.
Created, §90A-50(a).
Current registry of all environmental health
specialists and interns, §90A-59(c).
Disciplinary action.
Generally, §90A-64.
Election of officers, §90A-57(a).
Ethics.
Adoption of code of ethics, §90A-67.
Expenses, §90A-56.
List of candidates to governor, §90A-55(c).
Membership, §90A-55(a).
Oaths.
Administration, §90A-57(b).
Officers.
Terms, §90A-57(a).
Purpose, §90A-50(b).
Record of proceedings, §90A-59(a).
Availability to public, §90A-59(d).
Register of applications for registration,
§90A-59(b).
Removal of members, §90A-55(d).
Seal.
Official seal of board, §90A-57(b).
Terms of office, §90A-55(b).
Officers, §90A-57(a).
Certificates of registration. See within this
heading, "Registration."
Criminal law and procedure.
Violations, §90A-66.
Defense of state employees.
Local environmental health specialists,
§143-300.8.
Definitions, §90A-51.
Disciplinary action.
Grounds, §90A-64(a), (a1).
Immunity of board, §90A-64(d).
Investigations, §90A-64(c).
Procedure, §90A-64(b).
Education.
Continuing education.
Renewal of certificates, §90A-63(c).
Ethics.
Code of ethics, §90A-67.

ENVIRONMENTAL HEALTH SPECIALISTS
—Cont'd
Fraudulent representation as a registered environmental health specialist, §90A-65.
Injunctions, §90A-66.
Interns.
Practice allowed, §90A-52(b).
Qualifications, §90A-53(a).
Representing oneself as a registered environmental health specialist intern, §90A-65.
Temporary certificates, §90A-53(b).
Misdemeanors.
Violations, §90A-66.
Oaths.
Board of environmental health specialist examiners, §90A-57(b).
Penalties, §90A-66.
Reciprocity.
Environmental health specialists certified or registered in other states, §90A-62.
Records.
Board of environmental health specialist examiners, §90A-59.
Registration.
Examinations, §§90A-53, 90A-53(a).
Failure to renew certificate, §90A-63(b).
Fraudulent representation as a registered environmental health specialist, §90A-65.
Practice without certificate unlawful, §90A-52.
Qualifications, §§90A-53, 90A-53(a).
Interns, §90A-53(a).
Reciprocity, §90A-62.
Refusal to grant.
Disciplinary action generally, §90A-64.
Renewal of certificates, §90A-63(a).
Representing oneself as a registered environmental health specialist, §90A-65.
Revocation or suspension.
Disciplinary action generally, §90A-64.
Temporary certificates.
Interns, §90A-53(b).
Violations, §90A-66.
Seals and sealed instruments.
Board of environmental health specialist examiners, §90A-57(b).
Venue.
Injunctions, §90A-66.

ENVIRONMENTAL IMPACT STATEMENTS, §§113A-8 to 113A-13.
Environmental documents.
Defined, §113A-9.
Review, §113A-13.
Where not required, §§113A-12, 113A-13.
Major development projects in counties, cities or towns.
Ordinance requiring statement of impact, §113A-8(a) to (c).
Provisions supplemental, §113A-10.
Rules adoption, §113A-11.

ENVIRONMENTAL MANAGEMENT COMMISSION, §§143B-282 to 143B-285.
Air pollution control, §§143B-215.105 to 143-215.114C.
See AIR POLLUTION.
Appointments, §143B-283(a).
Conflicts of interest, §143B-283(c).
General assembly appointments, §143B-283(d).
Officers, §143B-284.

ENVIRONMENTAL MANAGEMENT COMMISSION —Cont'd
Chairman, §143B-284.
Committee on civil penalty remissions.
Appointment of members, §143B-282.1(c).
Civil actions.
Institution for civil penalty remissions, §143B-282.1(e).
Clerical and other services, §143B-283(b4).
Coastal fishing waters.
Monitoring water quality, §113-221.3(b).
Coastal habitat protection plans, §143B-279.8.
Committee on civil penalty remissions.
Appointment by chairman, §143B-282.1(c).
Conditions for remission, §143B-282.1(d).
Institution of civil action.
When allowed, §143B-282.1(e).
Conflicts of interest, §143B-283(c).
Contested cases.
Final agency decision.
Procedures, §143B-282.1(b).
Creation, §143B-282(a).
Within department of natural resources and community development, §143B-282(a).
Discharges of oil or hazardous substances, §§143-215.83 to 143-215.94.
See OIL OR HAZARDOUS SUBSTANCES DISCHARGES.
Dry-cleaning solvent cleanup act, §§143-215.104A to 143-215.104U.
See DRY-CLEANING SOLVENT CLEANUP.
Duties, §143B-282(a).
Geographic representation on, §143B-282(e).
Impaired waters.
Identifying and prioritizing, §143B-282(c).
Meetings, §143B-285.
Members, §143B-283(a).
Conflicts of interest, §143B-283(c).
General assembly appointments, §143B-283(d).
Officers, §143B-284.
Oil or hazardous substances discharges, §§143-215.83 to 143-215.94.
See OIL OR HAZARDOUS SUBSTANCES DISCHARGES.
Per diem and travel and subsistence expenses, §143B-283(b2).
Powers and duties, §143B-282(a).
Procedures.
Contested cases, §143B-282.1(b).
Quasi-judicial powers, §143B-282.1(a).
Quorum, §143B-283(b), (b3).
Removal of members, §143B-283(b1).
Reports, §143B-282(b).
Rulemaking.
Agencies authorized to implement and enforce environmental laws, §150B-19.3(b).
Imposing more restrictive standard, limitation, or requirement than federal law, §150B-19.3(a).
Secretary.
Defined, §143B-282.1(f).
Special meetings, §143B-285.
Terms, §143B-283(b).
Use of water resource regulation, §§143-215.11 to 143-215.22B.
See WATER RESOURCE USE REGULATION.
Vice-chairman, §143B-284.
Water and air resources.
See WATER AND AIR RESOURCES.
Water quality standards.
Adopting rules setting out strategies necessary for assuring, §143B-282(d).

ENVIRONMENTAL NOTICES.
Recording, §47-29.1.

ENVIRONMENTAL ORGANIZATIONS.
Solicitation of contributions, §§131F-1 to
     131F-33.
     See CHARITABLE SOLICITATION.

ENVIRONMENTAL PERMITS.
Department of environment and natural
     resources.
     One-stop permit application assistance and
          tracking system.
          Duties of department upon submission of
               application, §143B-279.12(a).
          Establishment, §143B-279.12(a).
     Timely processing by department.
          Automatic granting of permit.
               Failure of department to act in timely
                    manner, §143B-279.12(c).
          Date of final decision on application.
               Estimate provided by department,
                    §143B-279.12(b).
          Report on application taking longer than ninety
               days to process, §143B-279.15.
          Rules to implement provision, adoption,
               §143B-279.12(f).
     Time required to process applications.
          Department to track and compare,
               §143B-279.12(d).

**ENVIRONMENTAL POLICY ACT, §§113A-1 to
     113A-13.**
Actions.
     Review of agency actions involving major adverse
          changes or conflicts, §113A-5.
Administrative procedures.
     Conformity to state environmental policy,
          §113A-6.
Agencies.
     Cooperation, §113A-4.
     Statutory obligations of agencies, §113A-7.
Appeals.
     Review of agency actions involving major adverse
          changes or conflicts, §113A-5.
Availability of information, §113A-4.
Bridges.
     Replacement program for bridges.
          Applicability of act to replacement program,
               §136-76.1(b).
Citation, §113A-1.
Conformity of administrative procedures to
     state environmental policy, §113A-6.
     Other statutory obligations of agencies, §113A-7.
Cooperation of agencies, §113A-4.
Declaration of state environmental policy,
     §113A-3.
Definitions, §113A-9.
Driveway connections to public roadways.
     Environmental document not required, §113A-12.
Environmental documents.
     Defined, §113A-9.
     Review.
          Administrative and judicial review, §113A-13.
     When not required, §§113A-12, 113A-13.
Information.
     Availability, §113A-4.
Legislative declaration, §§113A-2, 113A-3.
Major development projects, §113A-8(a) to (c).
Policy.
     Declaration of state environmental policy,
          §113A-3.

ENVIRONMENTAL POLICY ACT —Cont'd
Projects.
     Major development projects, §113A-8(a) to (c).
Provisions supplemental, §113A-10.
Public money expended for payment of
     incentives.
     Environmental documents.
          When not required, §113A-12.
Purposes, §113A-2.
Release or permit granted by state agency.
     Environmental document not required, §113A-12.
Reports.
     Submission, §113A-4.
Review of actions.
     Agency actions involving major adverse changes
          or conflicts, §113A-5.
Rules and regulations.
     Adoption by department of administration,
          §113A-11(a).
     Adoption by state agencies to establish minimum
          criteria, §113A-11(b).
     State agencies.
          Establishment of minimum criteria,
               §113A-11(b).
Short title, §113A-1.
Statutes.
     Other statutory obligations of agencies, §113A-7.
Supplemental provisions, §113A-10.
Surface water transfers.
     Environmental assessment, §113A-8.1.
Title, §113A-1.
Utility line construction, etc.
     Environmental document not required, §113A-12.

ENVIRONMENTAL PROTECTION.
Air pollution control.
     See AIR POLLUTION.
Balanced growth policy act, §§143-506.6 to
     143-506.13.
     See BALANCED GROWTH POLICY ACT.
Biological organism act.
     General provisions, §§106-65.42 to 106-65.49.
     See BIOLOGICAL ORGANISM ACT.
Clean coastal water and vessel act, §§77-125 to
     77-132.
     See CLEAN COASTAL WATER AND VESSEL
          ACT.
Community conservation assistance program,
     §106-860.
Composting operations.
     Stormwater control best management practices
          and process water treatment processes,
          §143-214.7A.
Corporate franchise tax.
     Deducted reserves, §105-122(d).
     Deductible liabilities, §105-122(b).
Discharges of oil or hazardous substances.
     Generally, §§143-215.83 to 143-215.94.
          See OIL OR HAZARDOUS SUBSTANCES
               DISCHARGES.
     Offshore oil and gas activities, §§143-215.94AA to
          143-215.94JJ.
          See OFFSHORE OIL AND GAS ACTIVITIES.
Dry-cleaning equipment not using hazardous
     substances.
     Business and energy tax credits, §105-129.16C(a)
          to (d).
Dry-cleaning solvent cleanup, §§143-215.104A to
     143-215.104U.
     See DRY-CLEANING SOLVENT CLEANUP.

ENVIRONMENTAL PROTECTION —Cont'd

Ecosystem enhancement program, §§143-214.8 to 143-214.13.
　See ECOSYSTEM ENHANCEMENT PROGRAM.

Environmental policy act, §§113A-1 to 113A-13.
　See ENVIRONMENTAL POLICY ACT.

Floodplain regulation, §§143-215.51 to 143-215.61.
　See FLOODPLAIN REGULATION.

Hazardous substances.
　Discharges generally, §§143-215.83 to 143-215.94.
　　See OIL OR HAZARDOUS SUBSTANCES DISCHARGES.
　Oil pollution and hazardous substances control generally, §§143-215.75 to 143-215.82.
　　See OIL POLLUTION AND HAZARDOUS SUBSTANCES CONTROL.

Industrial and pollution control facilities financing.
　Industrial and pollution control facilities financing act, §§159C-1 to 159C-27.
　　See INDUSTRIAL AND POLLUTION CONTROL FACILITIES FINANCING.
　North Carolina capital facilities financing act.
　North Carolina industrial and pollution control facilities financing act, §§159D-1 to 159D-27.
　　See INDUSTRIAL AND POLLUTION CONTROL FACILITIES FINANCING.

Lead-based paint.
　Hazard management program, §§130A-453.01 to 130A-453.11.
　　See LEAD-BASED PAINT.
　Renovation activities.
　　Certification and accreditation, §§130A-453.22 to 130A-453.31.
　　　See LEAD-BASED PAINT.

Mid-Currituck bridge project, §136-89.183A(d).

Motor vehicles.
　Vehicular surface areas, §§113A-70, 113A-71.

Nutrient offset credits.
　Purchase to offset nutrient loadings to surface waters, §143-214.26.

Offshore oil and gas activities, §§143-215.94AA to 143-215.94JJ.
　See OFFSHORE OIL AND GAS ACTIVITIES.

Oil or hazardous substances discharges, §§143-215.83 to 143-215.94.
　See OIL OR HAZARDOUS SUBSTANCES DISCHARGES.

Oil pollution and hazardous substances control generally, §§143-215.75 to 143-215.82.
　See OIL POLLUTION AND HAZARDOUS SUBSTANCES CONTROL.

Parking.
　Vehicular surface areas, §§113A-70, 113A-71.

Pesticide applicators, §§143-452 to 143-459.
　See PESTICIDE APPLICATORS.

Pesticide board.
　See PESTICIDE BOARD.

Pesticide consultants, §§143-455, 143-456.

Pesticide dealers and manufacturers licenses, §§143-448 to 143-451.

Pesticide registration.
　See PESTICIDE REGISTRATION.

Pesticides generally.
　See PESTICIDES.

Plastic bag management.
　Retailers.
　　Counties containing barrier islands, §§130A-309.120 to 130A-309.125.

ENVIRONMENTAL PROTECTION —Cont'd

Pollution control.
　Air pollution control.
　　See AIR POLLUTION.
　Generally.
　　See POLLUTION.
　Water and air resources.
　　See WATER AND AIR RESOURCES.

Powers of fiduciaries to comply with, §32-27.

Riparian buffer protection program, §143-214.25A.

Risk based environmental remediation of industrial sites, §§130A-310.65 to 130A-310.77.
　See HAZARDOUS WASTE MANAGEMENT.

Sedimentation control commission, §§113A-50 to 113A-67.
　See SEDIMENTATION CONTROL COMMISSION.

Solid waste management.
　Environmental compliance requirements for applicants and permit holders, §130A-295.3.

Stream watch program, §§143-215.74F to 143-215.74I.

Surface water identification training and certification.
　Riparian buffer protection, §143-214.25A.

Sustainable communities task force, §§143B-344.34 to 143B-344.38.

Underground petroleum storage tanks.
　Leak cleanup, §§143-215.94A to 143-215.94Y.
　　See UNDERGROUND PETROLEUM STORAGE TANKS.
　Operator training, §§143-215.94NN to 143-215.94UU.
　　See UNDERGROUND PETROLEUM STORAGE TANKS.

Vehicular surface areas, §§113A-70, 113A-71.

Water and air quality reporting, §§143-215.63 to 143-215.69.
　See WATER AND AIR QUALITY REPORTING.

Water and air resources.
　See WATER AND AIR RESOURCES.

Water resources development projects.
　Federal projects, §§143-215.38 to 143-215.43.
　　See WATER RESOURCES DEVELOPMENT PROJECTS.
　Generally, §§143-215.70 to 143-215.73A.
　　See WATER RESOURCES DEVELOPMENT PROJECTS.

Water supply watershed protection, §§143-214.5, 143-214.7.

ENVIRONMENTAL REVIEW COMMISSION, §§120-70.41 to 120-70.47.

Allocation of money to fund commission, §120-70.47.

Clerical staff, §120-70.46.

Co-chairs, §120-70.42(b).

Compensation, §120-70.45.

Consolidation and reorganization of environmental agency.
　Study, §120-70.43(b).

Consultants and employees.
　Authority to contract for and hire, §120-70.44(c).

Created, §120-70.41.

Department of environment and natural resources.
　Report to commission on well drilling activities, §143-355(n).

Duties, §120-70.43(a) to (c).

ENVIRONMENTAL REVIEW COMMISSION
—Cont'd
Established, §120-70.41.
Expenses, §120-70.45.
Clerical staff, §120-70.46.
Funding, §120-70.47.
Hazardous waste management.
Powers and duties, §120-70.43(c).
Inactive hazardous sites.
Annual report to, §130A-310.10(a).
Meetings, §120-70.44(a).
Membership, §120-70.42(a).
Powers, §120-70.43(a) to (c).
Additional powers, §120-70.44(a).
Quorum, §120-70.42(d).
Recommendations as to studies or reports.
Proposed legislation.
Introduction and consideration, §120-70.44(b).
Staffing, §120-70.46.
Term, vacancy, §120-70.42(c).

ENVIRONMENTAL SAFETY.
Safety professionals, §§90-671 to 90-674.

ENVIRONMENT AND NATURAL RESOURCES DEPARTMENT.
Abandoned manufactured homes.
Identification, deconstruction, recycling, disposal.
Report activities in state related to, §130A-309.06(c).
Administrative penalties, §130A-22.
Advertising.
Blue Ridge parkway.
Control of outdoor advertising, §§113A-165 to 113A-170.
Agreements with federal agencies, §113-17.
Air pollution control program administration, §143-215.106.
Appalachian trail system, §§113A-72 to 113A-77.
Appeals from final order or decision of secretary.
Right of appeal to court of appeals, §7A-29(a).
Applicability of certain provisions, §143B-279.1(b).
Arrest.
Special peace officers.
Arrest powers, §113-28.2.
Balanced growth policy act, §§143-506.6 to 143-506.13.
See BALANCED GROWTH POLICY ACT.
Biennial state of environment report.
Cooperation in preparing report, §143B-279.5(b).
Included in report, §143B-279.5(a).
Time secretary to report, §143B-279.5(a).
Blue Ridge parkway.
Control of outdoor advertising, §§113A-165 to 113A-170.
Brownfields property reuse act of 1997, §§130A-310.30 to 130A-310.40.
See BROWNFIELDS PROPERTY REUSE.
Bureau of mines.
Establishment, §113-26.1.
Civil penalties.
Extension of time between notice of violation and assessment, §143B-279.18(a), (b).
Clean coastal water and vessel act.
Pumpout facilities at large vessel marinas.
Criteria, §77-127.
Rules, adoption, §77-132.
Coastal area management.
General provisions, §§113A-100 to 113A-128.
See COASTAL AREA MANAGEMENT.

ENVIRONMENT AND NATURAL RESOURCES DEPARTMENT —Cont'd
Coastal habitat protection plans.
Actions of commission to be consistent with protection plan, §143B-279.8(c).
Explanation of inconsistent actions by commission, §143B-279.8(d).
Preparation and goal of plans, §143B-279.8(a).
Reports, §143B-279.8(e), (f).
Review commission, §143B-279.8(b).
Coastal wetlands.
Orders controlling activities in, §113-230.
Community development council, §§143B-437.1 to 143B-437.3.
See COMMUNITY DEVELOPMENT COUNCIL.
Compacts.
Marine fisheries compact, §§113-251 to 113-258.
Southeastern interstate forest fire protection compact, §§106-930 to 106-933.
Composting operations.
Stormwater control best management practices and process water treatment processes, §143-214.7A.
Conferences with federal agencies, §113-17.
Conservation as policy of state, NC Const Art XIV §5.
Conservation easements, §§113A-230 to 113A-235.
Contamination at site.
Deed or other instrument of conveyance, contaminated property statement, §143B-279.10(e).
Land-use restrictions to reduce danger to public health, §143B-279.9.
Authority to impose, §143B-279.9(a).
Definitions, §§143B-279.9(d), 143B-279.10(d), (h).
Obligations and liabilities imposed by other laws, §143B-279.9(c).
Remedial action plan, §143B-279.9(b).
Notice of contamination.
Cancellation after contamination eliminated, owner's request, §143B-279.10(f).
Exceptions, §143B-279.10(g).
Filing copy in register of deeds office, §143B-279.10(b).
Recording copy, §143B-279.10(c).
Secretary may prepare and file, owner's failure, §143B-279.10(d).
Survey plat submitted by owner, §143B-279.10(a).
Cooperation with agencies of federal government, §113-16.
Cooperation with counties and municipal corporations, §113-20.
Water resource surveys, §113-21.
Cooperation with other state departments, §113-19.
Corporations for protection and development of forest.
See FOREST PROTECTION AND DEVELOPMENT CORPORATIONS.
Corrective action.
Extension of time between notice of violation and assessment of penalty, §143B-279.18(a), (b).
Counties.
Cooperation with counties and municipal corporations, §113-20.
Soil and water conservation work.
Promotion, §153A-440.

ENVIRONMENT AND NATURAL RESOURCES DEPARTMENT —Cont'd

Counties —Cont'd

Water resource surveys.

Cooperation of counties with state in making, §113-21.

Creation, §143B-279.1(a).

Crime control division.

Transfer to department of public safety, §143A-245.

Dam safety law, §§143-215.23 to 143-215.37.

See DAMS AND RESERVOIRS.

Definitions.

Meaning of terms, §113-1.

Discharges of oil or hazardous substances.

Generally, §§143-215.83 to 143-215.94.

See OIL OR HAZARDOUS SUBSTANCES DISCHARGES.

Offshore oil and gas activities, §§143-215.94AA to 143-215.94JJ.

See OFFSHORE OIL AND GAS ACTIVITIES.

Underground petroleum storage tanks.

Leak cleanup, §§143-215.94A to 143-215.94Y.

See UNDERGROUND PETROLEUM STORAGE TANKS.

Operator training, §§143-215.94NN to 143-215.94UU.

See UNDERGROUND PETROLEUM STORAGE TANKS.

Division of North Carolina aquariums, §§143B-289.40, 143B-289.41.

Division of parks and recreation.

Litter enforcement, prevention, removal efforts.

Detailed information delivered to governor, time, §147-12(b).

Divisions created within department, §143B-279.3(c).

Drainage districts, §§156-54 to 156-138.4.

See DRAINAGE DISTRICTS.

Drinking water.

Regulation of public water systems supplying, §§130A-311 to 130A-328.

See WATER SUPPLY AND WATERWORKS.

Drought management advisory council, §143-355.1.

Dry-cleaning solvent cleanup, §§143-215.104A to 143-215.104U.

See DRY-CLEANING SOLVENT CLEANUP.

Eminent domain.

Marine and estuarine resources.

Powers as to, §113-226(a).

Environmental management commission, §§143B-282 to 143B-285.

Environmental permits.

One-stop permit application assistance and tracking system.

Duties of department upon submission of application, §143B-279.12(a).

Establishment, §143B-279.12(a).

Timely processing by department.

Automatic granting of permit.

Failure of department to act in timely manner, §143B-279.12(c).

Date of final decision on application.

Estimate provided by department, §143B-279.12(b).

Report on application taking longer than ninety days to process, §143B-279.15.

Rules to implement provision, adoption, §143B-279.12(f).

ENVIRONMENT AND NATURAL RESOURCES DEPARTMENT —Cont'd

Environmental permits —Cont'd

Timely processing by department —Cont'd

Time required to process applications.

Department to track and compare, §143B-279.12(d).

Environmental policy act generally, §§113A-1 to 113A-13.

See ENVIRONMENTAL POLICY ACT.

Express permit and certification reviews.

Development of program, §143B-279.13(a).

Express review fund, §143B-279.14.

Fees may be determined by department, §143B-279.13(b).

Report of findings on success of program, §143B-279.15.

Falls Lake watershed association.

Memoranda of understanding with association, §77-142.

Federal agencies.

Agreements, negotiations and conferences with, §113-17.

Cooperation with agencies, §113-16.

Federal power commission.

Department authorized to receive funds from, §113-18.

Fish and fisheries resources.

Administrative authority, §113-226.

Cooperative agreements.

Authority to enter into, §113-224.

License fees.

Government owned property unaffected, §113-39.

Fish kill response protocols.

Development by department, §143B-279.7(a).

Necessary and appropriate steps to carry out purposes, §143B-279.7(b).

Report, §143B-279.7(c).

Floodplain regulation, §§143-215.51 to 143-215.61.

See FLOODPLAIN REGULATION.

Food defense.

Protection from intentional contamination, §130A-481.

Funds.

Express review fund, §143B-279.14.

Federal power commission.

Department authorized to receive funds, §113-18.

Health.

Powers of secretary generally.

See HEALTH.

Highway construction projects.

Permits issued by department for.

Modification and cancellation, restrictions, §136-44.7B.

Highways, roads and streets.

Test drilling or boring upon public land.

Filing record of results with secretary, §136-102.3.

Hotels or tourist inns in parks over which department has jurisdiction.

Department not to construct, maintain, operate or lease, §66-58(b).

Hunting and wildlife.

General provisions.

See HUNTING AND WILDLIFE.

License fees.

Government owned property unaffected, §113-39.

ENVIRONMENT AND NATURAL RESOURCES DEPARTMENT —Cont'd

Informal resolution of matters.
Extension of time between notice of violation and assessment of penalty, §143B-279.18(a), (b).

Interstate compacts.
Marine fisheries compacts, §§113-251 to 113-258.
Southeastern interstate forest fire protection compact, §§106-930 to 106-933.

Land policy act, §§113A-150 to 113A-159.
See LAND POLICY ACT.

Leaking petroleum underground storage tank cleanup, §§143-215.94A to 143-215.94Y.
See UNDERGROUND PETROLEUM STORAGE TANKS.

Local affairs, §§143-320 to 143-326.
See LOCAL AFFAIRS.

Marine fisheries commission, §§143B-289.50 to 143B-289.61.
See MARINE FISHERIES COMMISSION.

Marine fisheries compact, §§113-251 to 113-258.

Maritime museum.
Selling or exchanging objects from collections, §143B-344.22.

Mattresses and bedding.
Enforcement of part, §106-65.105(a).

Meaning of terms, §113-1.

Mineral museum.
Establishment, §113-26.1.

Mines and minerals.
Beginning business of manufacturing products from mineral resources.
Notice to department, §113-25.
Bureau of mines.
Established as part of department, §113-26.1.
Mineral museum.
Established as part of department, §113-26.1.

Mining commission, §§143B-290 to 143B-293.

Monuments, memorials and parks.
Control of Mount Mitchell park and other state parks.
Department to have control, §113-23.

Motor vehicle laws applicable to state parks and forest road system, §143-116.8.

Mount Mitchell park.
Control of park, §§100-11, 113-23.
Fees.
Powers as to, §100-13.
Powers, §§100-11 to 100-13.
Protection of property, §100-12.
Rules and regulations, §100-13.

Municipalities.
Cooperation with counties and municipal corporations, §113-20.

Museum of natural sciences.
Selling or exchanging objects from collection, §143B-344.22.

Natural and scenic rivers system.
Administrative agency, §113A-36(a).

Nature preserves, §§113A-164.1 to 113A-164.11.
See NATURAL HERITAGE AREAS REGISTRY.

North Carolina aquarium division.
Created in department, §143B-289.40.
Organization, §143B-289.41(a).
Powers and duties, §143B-289.41(a).
Rules and procedures, §143B-289.41(b).

North Carolina sustainable communities task force, §§143B-344.34 to 143B-344.38.

Notice.
Mines and mining.
Beginning business of manufacturing products from mineral resources of state, §113-25.

ENVIRONMENT AND NATURAL RESOURCES DEPARTMENT —Cont'd

Notice —Cont'd
Violation of environmental statute.
Extension of time period between notice and assessment of civil penalty, §143B-279.18(a), (b).

Nutbush conservation area, §§143-286.1, 143-289.

Oaths.
Special peace officers.
Required, §113-28.4.

Office of environmental education and public affairs, §§143B-285.20 to 143B-285.25.

Offshore oil and gas activities, §§143-215.94AA to 143-215.94JJ.
See OFFSHORE OIL AND GAS ACTIVITIES.

Oil and gas conservation, §§113-397, 113-398.
Actions by department, §113-399.
Appeals, §113-401.
Effect of pendency of judicial review, §113-406.
Bonds, surety.
Stay of proceedings, §113-407.
Drilling wells.
Applications to include residence address, §113-408.
False entries.
Penalties, §113-409.
Hearings.
Contested cases, §113-402.
Costs, §113-400.
Parties, §113-401.
Stay of proceedings, §113-406.
Bond, §113-407.
Injunctions, §113-408.
Jurisdiction and authority, §113-391.
Misrepresentation.
Punishment, §113-409.
Orders, §113-391.
Parties to hearings, §113-401.
Penalties.
Violations, §§113-409, 113-410.
Rules and regulations, §113-391.
Service of process, §113-408.
Stay of proceedings, §113-406.
Bond, §113-407.
Suits by department, §113-399.
Violations.
Penalties, §§113-409, 113-410.

Oil or hazardous substances discharges, §§143-215.83 to 143-215.94.
See OIL OR HAZARDOUS SUBSTANCES DISCHARGES.

Oil pollution and hazardous substance control generally, §§143-215.75 to 143-215.82.
See OIL POLLUTION AND HAZARDOUS SUBSTANCES CONTROL.

Outer continental shelf task force.
Administration, §143B-279.2.

Parks.
Acquisition and control of state parks, §§113-29 to 113-44.
Control of Mount Mitchell park and other state parks, §113-23.
Power to acquire lands, §113-34.

Parks and recreation authority.
Administered by department, §143B-313.1.

Peace officers.
Special peace officers, §§113-28.1 to 113-28.4.

Penalties.
Administrative penalties, §130A-22.

**ENVIRONMENT AND NATURAL RESOURCES
    DEPARTMENT** —Cont'd
Penalties —Cont'd
Assessment of civil penalties.
    Extension of time between notice of violation
        and assessment, §143B-279.18(a), (b).
Pollution control.
Generally.
    See POLLUTION.
Offshore oil and gas activities generally,
    §§143-215.94AA to 143-215.94JJ.
    See OFFSHORE OIL AND GAS ACTIVITIES.
Pollution prevention pays programs.
    Established within department, §113-8.01.
Pollution prevention pays programs, §113-8.01.
Powers and duties, §§113-3(a), 113-8,
    143B-279.1(a), 143B-279.2.
Additional powers and duties.
    Solid waste management, §130A-309.06(a).
Generally, §§113-8, 143B-279.3(d).
Promotion of seashore industry and recreation,
    §113-14.1(b).
Transferred to and vested in department,
    §§143-355, 143B-279.3(a), (b).
Prisons and prisoners.
Supervision of sanitary and health conditions of
    prisoners, §148-10.
Property of department.
Regulatory power over property, §113-264.
Removal, damage or destruction, §113-264(b).
**Protection and development of forest
    corporations.**
See FOREST PROTECTION AND
    DEVELOPMENT CORPORATIONS.
Publications.
Resources material, §113-14.3.
Public lands.
Disposition of mineral deposits in state lands
    under water, §146-8.
Recreation and natural heritage trusts,
    §§113-77.6 to 113-77.9.
See NATURAL HERITAGE TRUST FUND.
Reports.
Biennial state of environment report,
    §143B-279.5.
Coastal habitat protection plan, §143B-279.8(f).
Environmental permits taking longer than ninety
    days to process, §143B-279.15.
Express permit and certification reviews.
    Report of findings on success of program,
        §143B-279.15.
Fish kill response protocols, §143B-279.7(c).
Publication, §113-14.3.
Sedimentation pollution control act.
    Annual report by department, §113A-67.
Rulemaking.
Agencies authorized to implement and enforce
    environmental laws, §150B-19.3(b).
Imposing more restrictive standard, limitation,
    or requirement than federal law,
    §150B-19.3(a).
Sale of merchandise by governmental units.
Exception to prohibition, §66-58(b).
Seashore industry and recreation.
Promotion, §113-14.1(b).
Secretary.
Appeal of final order or decision.
    Right of appeal to court of appeals, §7A-29(a).
Biennial state of the environment report,
    §143B-279.5.
Deputy secretaries, §143B-279.4(b).

**ENVIRONMENT AND NATURAL RESOURCES
    DEPARTMENT** —Cont'd
Secretary —Cont'd
Head of department, §143B-279.4(a).
Health.
    Powers of secretary generally.
        See HEALTH.
Highways, roads and streets.
    Test drilling or boring upon public land.
        Filing record of results with secretary,
            §136-102.3.
License plate.
    Special plate, number, §20-79.5.
Natural history museum.
    Advisory commission.
        Member of commission, §143B-344.18.
Office of environmental education and public
    affairs.
    Powers and duties of secretary, §143B-285.23.
Recreation and natural heritage trusts, §§113-77.6
    to 113-77.9.
    See NATURAL HERITAGE TRUST FUND.
Sedimentation control commission, §§143B-298,
    143B-299.
Sedimentation pollution control act of 1973,
    §§113A-50 to 113A-67.
See SEDIMENTATION CONTROL
    COMMISSION.
Shellfish generally.
See SHELLFISH.
Solid waste management.
Authority in establishing program, §130A-294(a).
Division of waste management.
    Legislative declaration, §130A-291(a), (b).
Powers and duties.
    Additional powers and duties, §130A-309.06.
Reports.
    Annual report, §130A-309.06(c).
Septage.
    Duties and septage management program,
        §130A-291.1.
Single agency designation, §130A-299.
**Southeastern interstate forest fire protection
    compact,** §§106-930 to 106-933.
Special peace officers, §§113-28.1 to 113-28.4.
Arrest powers, §113-28.2.
Commissioned as special peace officers.
    Designated employees commissioned special
        peace officers by governor, §113-28.1.
Cooperation between law enforcement agencies,
    §113-28.2A.
Designated employees commissioned special
    officers by governor, §113-28.1.
Governor.
    Designated employees commissioned special
        officers by, §113-28.1.
Oaths.
    Required, §113-28.4.
Powers.
    Arrest, §113-28.2.
State departments and agencies.
Cooperation with other state departments,
    §113-19.
State parks system.
Acquisition and control of state parks, §§113-29 to
    113-44.
Control of Mount Mitchell park and other parks
    in, §113-23.
State prison.
Supervision of sanitary and health conditions of
    prisoners, §148-10.

ENVIRONMENT AND NATURAL RESOURCES DEPARTMENT —Cont'd

Statutes.

Repeal of certain public, public-local, special and private acts, §113-377.8.

Surveys and surveyors.

Cooperation of counties with state in making water resources surveys, §113-21.

Sustainable communities task force, §§143B-344.34 to 143B-344.38.

Terms.

Meaning, §113-1.

Traffic laws applicable to state parks and forest road system, §143-116.8.

Trails.

See TRAILS.

Trails committee, §§143B-333, 143B-334.

Transfer of functions, powers, duties and obligations to department, §§143-355, 143B-279.3(a), (b).

Trespass.

Land under option by federal government, §14-131.

Underground petroleum storage tanks.

Leak cleanup, §§143-215.94A to 143-215.94Y.

See UNDERGROUND PETROLEUM STORAGE TANKS.

Operator training, §§143-215.94NN to 143-215.94UU.

See UNDERGROUND PETROLEUM STORAGE TANKS.

Violations of environmental statutes.

Notice of violation and assessment of civil penalty.

Extension of time period between, §143B-279.18(a), (b).

Waste management division, §130A-291(a), (b).

Created within department, §143B-279.3(c).

Water and air quality reporting, §§143-215.63 to 143-215.69.

See WATER AND AIR QUALITY REPORTING.

Water and air resources.

Research functions, §143-215.3(b).

Water pollution control system operators.

Certification commission, §§143B-300, 143B-301.

Water resources development projects.

Federal projects, §§143-215.38 to 143-215.43.

See WATER RESOURCES DEVELOPMENT PROJECTS.

Generally, §§143-215.70 to 143-215.73A.

See WATER RESOURCES DEVELOPMENT PROJECTS.

Well contractor certification, §§87-98.1 to 87-98.13.

See WELL CONTRACTORS.

Well contractor certification commission, §§143B-301.10 to 143B-301.12.

Western North Carolina public lands council, §§143B-324.1 to 143B-324.3.

Wetlands.

Coastal wetlands.

Orders controlling activities in, §113-230.

Wildlife generally.

See HUNTING AND WILDLIFE.

Wildlife resources commission.

Transfer to department, §143B-281.1.

Zoological park council, §§143B-335, 143B-336.

EPIDEMICS.

Immunization.

See IMMUNIZATION.

EPIDEMICS —Cont'd

Infectious and communicable diseases generally.

See DISEASES.

EPILEPSY.

Arrest.

Police assistance to persons arrested while unconscious or semiconscious, §15A-503.

Defined, §35A-1101.

Determination of incompetence, §§35A-1101 to 35A-1116.

See INCOMPETENCY.

Jail prisoner unconscious or semiconscious.

Duty of custodial personnel.

Reasonable effort to determine if prisoner wearing emergency alert symbol, §153A-225.1(a) to (c).

E-PROCUREMENT SERVICE.

Purchases through department of administration.

Electronic procurement, §143-48.3.

EQUAL AVAILABILITY OF CREDIT FOR WOMEN, §25B-1.

EQUAL EMPLOYMENT OPPORTUNITY.

Citation of article, §143-422.1.

Conciliations.

Human relations council to use good offices, §143-422.3.

Human relations council.

Charges of discrimination.

Receipt, §143-422.3.

Conciliations, §143-422.3.

Investigations, §143-422.3.

Legislative declaration, §143-422.2.

Personnel system.

Assistance in obtaining state employment.

Compensation for assisting person barred, §126-18.

Exception, §126-18.

Equal employment opportunity institute.

Training, §126-16.1.

Local political subdivisions, §126-16.

Retaliation against protesting employees, §126-17.

Managers.

Newly appointed managers.

Training, §126-16.1.

State departments and agencies, §126-16.

Retaliation against protesting employees, §126-17.

Supervisors.

Newly appointed supervisor.

Training, §126-16.1.

Training, §126-16.1.

Plans.

Development and submission by certain agencies, §126-19(a).

Reports, §126-19(b).

State personnel director.

Maintenance of services by, §126-19(c).

Purpose of article, §143-422.2.

Short title, §143-422.1.

EQUAL JUSTICE UNDER THE LAW.

Basic education program in public schools.

Civic literacy, §115C-81(g).

EQUAL PROTECTION, NC Const Art I §19, US Const Amd 14.

EQUINE ACTIVITY LIABILITY, §§99E-1 to 99E-3.
Acts not preventing or limiting liability, §99E-2(b).
Definitions, §99E-1.
Immunity of liability generally for injury or death of participant, §99E-2(a).
Products liability law.
Liability not prevented or limited for violation, §99E-2(c).
Warning notice.
Contents, §99E-3(b).
Failure to comply, §99E-3(c).
Posting requirement, §99E-3(a).

EQUINE BOARDING, TRAINING, TEACHING FACILITIES.
Alcoholic beverages.
Sports clubs.
ABC permit, §18B-1006(k).
Defined, §18B-1001.

EQUINE INFECTIOUS ANEMIA, §§106-405.15 to 106-405.20.
Control and eradication program.
Implementation of program, §106-405.18.
Defined, §106-405.15.
Fine, §106-405.20.
Implementation of control and eradication program, §106-405.18.
Penalties, §106-405.20.
Quarantine of infected or exposed animals, §106-405.16.
Rules and regulations.
Authority to promulgate and enforce, §106-405.17.
Violation made misdemeanor, §106-405.19.

EQUIPMENT IDENTIFICATION OR MARKS, §14-401.4.

EQUITABLE DISTRIBUTION OF MARITAL PROPERTY, §50-20.
Absolute divorce, effects, §50-11(e), (f).
Collaborative law proceedings, §§50-70 to 50-79.
See COLLABORATIVE LAW PROCEEDINGS.
Decedents' estates.
Claim against estate.
Distribution of marital or divisible property, §28A-19-19.
Eighth class claim, §28A-19-6(a).
Mediated settlement conferences or other settlement procedures.
District court actions, §7A-38.4A.
Rules implementing procedures,
SettlmtEquitDistrib Rules 1 to 15.
See MEDIATED SETTLEMENT CONFERENCES.
Pensions, retirement and deferred compensation benefits, §50-20.1.
Procedures, §50-21.

EQUITY.
Commercial code.
Construction of chapter.
Principles of law and equity, §25-1-103(b).
Divorce.
Distribution by court of marital and divisible property, §50-20.
Absolute divorce, effect, §50-11.
Mediated settlement conference, §7A-38.4A.
Procedure, §50-21.
Mortgages and deeds of trust.
Injunctions.
Enjoining sales on equitable grounds, §45-21.34.

EQUITY —Cont'd
Nuisances.
See NUISANCES.
Ordinances.
Enforcement of ordinance by appropriate equitable remedies, §160A-175(d).

EQUITY LINES OF CREDIT.
Applicability of provisions.
Article not exclusive, §45-84.
Future advances statute not to apply, §45-83.
Article not exclusive, §45-84.
Definitions, §45-81.
Equity line of credit.
Defined, §45-81(a).
Equity line security instrument.
Defined, §45-81.
Priority, §45-82.
Extension of period for advances.
Priority of extension, §45-82.1(b).
Term of extension, §45-82.1(a).
Future advances statute not to apply, §45-83.
Interest rates.
Adjustable or variable interest, §24-1.2A(a).
Contract in writing, §24-1.2A(a).
Fees for modification, renewal, extension, §24-1.2A(b).
Loans exempt from interest rate and fee limitations, §24-9(c).
Lender is obligated.
Defined, §45-81(b).
Loans exempt from interest rate and fee limitations, §24-9(c).
Notice regarding future advances, §45-82.3(a).
Advances secured by equity security instrument, §45-82.3(c).
Form, §45-82.3(e).
Attorney, bank, other financial institution, title insurance company giving, §45-82.3(f).
Receipt of notice action adversely affecting lender's security, §45-82.3(d).
Termination of borrowers right to obtain additional advances.
Lender's authority, §45-82.3(d).
Time for lender to act on notice, §45-82.3(b).
Payment and satisfaction of interest.
Lender to make written entry upon security instrument to that effect, §45-81(c).
Prepayment penalty, §45-83.4.
Priority of equity line security instrument, §45-82.
Extension, §45-82.1(b).
Termination of equity line of credit.
Attorney, bank, other financial instruction making request.
Notice to borrower, form, §45-82.2(d).
Duty of lender upon receipt of request, §45-82.2(a).
Form of request to terminate, §45-82.2(b).
Title insurance company making request.
Notice to borrower, form, §45-82.2(c).

EQUITY OF REDEMPTION.
Execution sales.
Sheriff's deed on sale of equity of redemption, §1-317.

EQUIVALENT DRUG PRODUCT.
Defined, §90-85.27.
Liability of prescriber and pharmacist not extended, §90-85.31.

EQUIVALENT DRUG PRODUCT —Cont'd
Prescriptions.
Label, §90-85.29.
Record, §90-85.30.
Price.
Limitation on selected drugs, §90-85.28(c).
Selection by pharmacist, §90-85.28(a).
Liability of prescriber and pharmacist not
extended, §90-85.31.
Prescriber may permit or prohibit, §90-85.28(b).

EROSION.
County equipment.
Authority to provide farmers with erosion
equipment, §106-532.
Municipalities.
Control of erosion and sedimentation, §160A-458.
Sedimentation control commission, §§113A-50
to 113A-67.
See SEDIMENTATION CONTROL
COMMISSION.
Transportation department.
Control of erosion.
Powers of department, §136-18.

ERRONEOUS CONVICTION OR
IMPRISONMENT.
Compensation to individual, §§148-82 to 148-84.

ERROR.
Generally.
See MISTAKE OR ERROR.
Harmless error, §1A-1 Rule 61.

ESCALATORS.
Inspection fees.
Assessment and collection, §95-107.
Disposition, §95-108.
Safety, §§95-110.1 to 95-110.15.

ESCAPE.
Aiding or assisting.
Penalty, §148-45(d).
Allowing prisoners to escape.
Burden of proof on officers to show escape not by
consent, §14-239.
Arrest.
Peace officers.
Prevention of escape.
Use of force in arrest, §15A-401(d).
Persons escaped from penal institutions, §162-35.
Burden of proof.
Allowing prisoners to escape.
Burden of proof upon sheriff or other officer,
§14-239.
Capital punishment.
Aggravating circumstances.
Capital felony committed for purpose of
effecting escape, §15A-2000(e).
Convicted felon.
Classifying person convicted of escape, §148-45(f).
Coroners allowing prisoners to escape, §14-239.
District attorney to prosecute officer for escape,
§14-240.
Counties.
Confinement facilities or officers.
Prison breach and escape from facilities or
officers, §14-256.
Delinquent and undisciplined juveniles.
Absconding juveniles, taking into temporary
custody, §7B-1900.
Transporting to nearest secure custody facility,
§7B-1901(c).

ESCAPE —Cont'd
Detainers.
Escape from temporary custody, §15A-764.
District attorney.
Prosecution of officers for allowing prisoners to
escape, §14-240.
Extended limits of confinement.
Failure of prisoner to remain within, §148-4.
Firearms and other weapons.
Conveying to convicts and other prisoners,
§14-258.
Use in assisting prisoner to escape, §14-258.2(b).
Guards.
Degree of protection against allowed, §148-46(a),
(b).
Harboring or aiding escaped prisoners,
§14-259.
Interstate compact on juveniles, §§7B-2800 to
7B-2827.
See INTERSTATE COMPACT ON JUVENILES.
Jails.
Allowing prisoners to escape.
Burden of proof upon jailer to show that escape
was not by consent or negligence, §14-239.
District attorney to prosecute jailer for escape,
§14-240.
Reduction of sentence for work, education or
training programs.
Forfeiture of reduction, §162-60(c).
Juvenile escapees.
Delinquent and undisciplined juveniles,
§§7B-1900, 7B-1901.
Disclosure of information, §7B-3102.
Limitation of actions.
Public officers.
Actions against for escape of prisoner arrested
or imprisoned on civil process, §1-54.
Mental health, developmental disabilities and
substance abuse.
Assisting client to leave facility without authority,
§122C-65(a), (b).
Discharge of clients who escape or breach
conditions of release, §122C-205.1(a), (b), (d).
Notice, §122C-205.1(c).
Involuntary commitment.
Commission of criminal offense, §122C-254(a) to
(d).
Denial of pretrial release, §122C-254(a).
Notice of discharge of clients who escape or breach
conditions of release, §122C-205.1(c).
Notice of escape or breach of conditional release,
§122C-205(d).
Return of clients to 24-hour facilities,
§122C-205(a) to (c).
Messages.
Conveying messages to convicts and other
prisoners, §14-258.
Municipalities.
Confinement facilities or officers.
Prison breach and escape from facilities or
officers, §14-256.
Peace officers.
Prevention of escape.
Force.
Use of force in arrest, §15A-401(d).
Penalty.
Class 1 misdemeanor, §148-45(a).
Aiding or assisting, §148-45(d).
Class H felony, §148-45(b).
Classifying person as convicted felon, §148-45(f).
Private correction facilities, §14-256.1.

ESCAPE —Cont'd

Recapture of escaped prisoners, §§148-40, 148-41.

Rewards.
Governor may offer rewards, §15-53.

Sentencing.
Aggravating factor, §15A-1340.16.

Sheriffs allowing prisoners to escape, §14-239.
District attorney to prosecute officer for escape, §14-240.

Solicitor.
Allowing prisoners to escape.
Prosecution of sheriffs or other officers for escape, §14-240.

State institutions.
Persuading inmates to escape, §§14-266, 14-268.

Temporary custody.
Interstate agreement on detainers, §15A-764.
Juvenile escapees.
Delinquent and undisciplined juveniles, §§7B-1900, 7B-1901.

Working prisoners escaping from custody, §14-255.

Work-release program, §148-45(g).

ESCHEAT FUND, §§116B-5 to 116B-7.

ESCHEATS, §§116B-1 to 116B-4.

Attorney to perform title search, employment, §116B-8.

Claim for, §116B-4.

Consultants, real estate managers and others with specialized skills.
Employment, §116B-8.

Disposition of, NC Const Art IX §10.

Escheat fund, §§116B-5 to 116B-7.
Distribution, §116B-7(a), (b).
Escheat account.
Excess funds, §116B-6(e).
Investments, §116B-6(b).
Limitation on amount of secured obligation, §116B-6(d).
Placement of funds, §116B-6(a).
Security interest, §116B-6(c).
Expenditures from fund, §116B-6(h).
Payments into, §116B-1.
Property paid into fund, §116B-5.
Records, §116B-6(i).
Refund reserve, §116B-6(f).
Refunds, additional funds, §116B-6(g).
Report by secretary of revenue, §105-256(d).

Locating owners of unclaimed property.
Information furnished treasurer.
Duty of certain governmental agencies, §116B-6(j).

Personal property, §116B-2.
Decedents' estates, §116B-3.

Real property, §116B-2.

Unclaimed property generally, §§116B-51 to 116B-80.
See UNCLAIMED PROPERTY.

ESCORT VEHICLES.

Oversize or overweight loads.
Escort driver training and certification program, §20-119(f).
Highway patrol.
Escort fee.
Oversized and hazardous shipment, §20-196.4.

ESCROW ACCOUNTS.

Insurance adjusters.
Public adjusters.
Deposit of funds held on behalf of insured, §58-33A-70.

Mortgage bankers, brokers and servicers, §53-244.105(d).

ESCROW ACCOUNTS IN PREPAID ENTERTAINMENT CONTRACTS, §66-124.

ESCROW OF FUNDS BY TOBACCO MANUFACTURERS.
Tobacco reserve fund, §§66-290, 66-291.
Escrow compliance, §§66-292 to 66-294.1.

ESPIONAGE, INDUSTRIAL.
Larceny of secret technical processes, §14-75.1.

ESTABLISHED LEGAL SERVICES PROGRAMS, §§7A-474.1 to 7A-474.5.
See LEGAL SERVICES PROGRAMS.

ESTATE PLANNING AND PROBATE LAW SPECIALTY.
Certification standards, Bar Rules D.2301 to D.2307.

ESTATES.

Absentees in military service, §§28B-1 to 28B-10.
See ABSENTEES IN MILITARY SERVICE.

Contingent limitations.
Death of person without heirs.
Limitations on failure, §41-4.

Conversion of fee tail into fee simple, §41-1.

Conveyances.
General provisions.
See CONVEYANCES.

Decedents' estates.
See DECEDENTS' ESTATES.

Deeds.
General provisions.
See DEEDS.

Definitions.
Freeholders in petition for special taxes, §41-13.
Time limits on options in gross and certain other interests in land, §41-28.

Deposits.
Survivorship in bank deposit created by written agreement, §41-2.1.

Devise presumed to be in fee, §31-38.

Doctrine of worthier title.
Abolished, §41-6.2(a).

Executions.
Execution sales.
Leasehold estates.
Liability to sale under execution, §1-315(a).
Trust estates.
Title of purchaser, §1-316.

Executors and administrators.
See EXECUTORS AND ADMINISTRATORS.

Failure of issue.
Limitations on failure, §41-4.

Freeholders.
Taxation.
Freeholders in petition for special taxes.
Defined, §41-13.

Income tax on estates and trusts.
Amount, §105-160.2.
Changes, §105-160.8.
Corrections, §105-160.8.
Credits, §105-160.3(a).
Credits not allowed, §105-160.3(b).
Income taxes paid to other states, §105-160.4.

ESTATES —Cont'd
Income tax on estates and trusts —Cont'd
Definitions, §105-160.1.
Imposition of tax, §105-160.2.
Payment.
Place of payment, §105-160.7(a).
Returns, §105-160.5.
Place of filing, §105-160.6.
Time of filing, §105-160.6.
Taxable income, §105-160.2.
Inheritance tax generally.
See INHERITANCE TAX.
Issue.
Limitations on failure of issue, §41-4.
Joint tenants and tenants in common.
See JOINT TENANTS AND TENANTS IN
COMMON.
Landlord and tenant.
See LANDLORD AND TENANT.
Life estates.
See LIFE ESTATES.
Military service.
Absentees in military service, §§28B-1 to 28B-10.
See ABSENTEES IN MILITARY SERVICE.
Missing persons, §§28C-1 to 28C-22.
See MISSING PERSONS.
Next of kin.
Defined, §41-6.1.
Possession.
Transferred to use in certain conveyances, §41-7.
Possibility of reverter.
Time limits, §41-32.
Powers of attorney.
Powers conferred by statutory short form, §32A-2.
Presumptions and burden of proof.
Fee presumed though word heirs omitted, §39-1.
Unborn infants.
Presumed in esse, §41-5.
Probate of wills.
General provisions, §§28A-2A-1 to 28A-2A-23.
See WILLS.
Quieting title.
Actions, §41-10.
Real property generally.
See REAL PROPERTY.
Rule in Shelley's case.
Abolished, §41-6.3.
Small estates, §§28A-25-1 to 28A-25-6.
See SMALL ESTATES.
State.
Trying title to land where state claims interest,
§41-10.1.
Time limits on certain interests in land, §§41-28
to 41-33.
Applicability of provisions.
Prospective application, §41-33.
Definitions, §41-28.
Leases to commence in the future, §41-30.
Nonvested easement in gross, §41-31.
Defined, §41-28.
Option in gross with respect to an interest in
land, §41-29.
Defined, §41-28.
Possibility of reverter, §41-32.
Preemptive right, §41-29.
Defined, §41-28.
Prospective application to divisions, §41-33.
Title.
See TITLE.
Trusts and trustees.
General provisions, §§36C-1-101 to 36C-11-1106.
See TRUSTS AND TRUSTEES.

ESTATES —Cont'd
Unborn infants.
Taking by deed or writing, §41-5.
**Uniform transfer on death security
registration act,** §§41-40 to 41-51.
See UNIFORM TRANSFER ON DEATH
SECURITY REGISTRATION ACT.
Waste, §§1-533 to 1-538.
See WASTE.
Wills.
General provisions, §§31-1 to 31-47.
See WILLS.

ESTATE TAXES, §§105-32.1 to 105-32.8.
Administration, §105-32.4(e).
Amount, §105-32.2(b).
Federal determination which changes, §105-32.8.
Assets of estates.
Payable from, §105-32.3(a).
Sale to obtain money due, §105-32.4(d).
Clerk of court.
Liability for tax.
Allowing personal representative to make final
settlement without presenting affirmation
or certificate, §105-32.3(c).
**Correct amount of tax payable, return
reflecting.**
Federal determination changing amount payable,
§105-32.8.
Deficiencies, penalty, §105-236(a).
Definitions, §105-32.1.
Due date, §105-32.4(a).
Generation-skipping transfer, §105-32.7(c).
**Estate property located in state other than
North Carolina.**
Amount of tax, §105-32.2(b).
**Federal determination changing amount of
tax,** §105-32.8.
Federal estate tax.
Apportionment, §§28A-27-1 to 28A-27-9.
Credits, §28A-27-5(b) to (d).
Deductions, §28A-27-5(a).
Definitions, §28A-27-1.
Determining apportionment.
Personal representative to determine,
§28A-27-3(a).
Basis for determining, §28A-27-3(b).
Expenses for apportionment to be
apportioned, §28A-27-3(c).
Distribution before final apportionment.
Personal representative may require bond for
tax liability, §28A-27-7(b).
Effective date of provisions, §28A-27-9.
Exemptions, §28A-27-5(a).
Computations, §28A-27-5(d).
Federal tax law to determine liabilities imposed,
§28A-27-8.
Method of apportionment, §28A-27-2(a).
Choosing method, §28A-27-2(b).
Rights and duties of personal representative,
§28A-27-7(a).
Temporary and remainder interests need not be
apportioned, §28A-27-6.
Uncollected taxes, §28A-27-4.
Trusts referencing.
Construction of formula provisions.
Estates of decedents dying in 2010,
§36C-1-113.
Wills referencing.
Construction of formula provisions.
Estates of decedents dying in 2010, §31-46.1.

ESTATE TAXES —Cont'd
Generation-skipping transfer.
Amount, §105-32.7(b).
Correct amount of tax payable, return reflecting.
Federal determination changing amount
payable, §105-32.8.
Due date, §105-32.7(c).
Imposition of tax, §105-32.7(a).
Net value of property located in state,
§105-32.7(b).
Payment, §105-32.7(c).
Return, §105-32.7(c).
State percentage of tax, §105-32.7(b).
Trusts referencing federal tax.
Construction of formula provisions.
Estates of decedents dying in 2010,
§36C-1-113.
Wills referencing federal tax.
Construction of formula provisions.
Estates of decedents dying in 2010, §31-46.1.
Imposition on estate of decedent, §105-32.2(a).
Individual income tax.
Adjustments to taxable income, §105-134.6(d).
Inheritance tax.
See INHERITANCE TAX.
Installment payments, §105-32.5.
Intestate succession.
Descent and distribution, §29-13(a).
Determination of 120-hour survivorship
requirement, §29-13(b).
Liability for tax.
Clerk of court.
Allowing personal representative to make final
settlement without presenting affirmation
or certificate, §105-32.3(c).
Generation-skipping transfer, §105-32.7(c).
Personal representative.
Tax not paid within 2 years after tax due,
§105-32.3(b).
Person who receives property, §105-32.3(a).
Liens, §105-32.6.
Payable on death (POD) accounts.
Savings banks.
Statutory construction.
Estate tax provisions not affected by
provisions, §54C-166.1(d).
Payment of tax.
Due date, §105-32.4(a).
Filing return, §105-32.4(b), (c).
Generation-skipping transfer, §105-32.7(c).
Installment payments, §105-32.5.
Selling assets to obtain money due, §105-32.4(d).
Personal representative.
Liability for tax.
Tax not paid within 2 years after tax due,
§105-32.3(b).
**Renunciation of property and fiduciary
powers,** §31B-1(b).
Return.
Due date, §105-32.4(a).
Filing, §105-32.4(b).
Extension of time, §105-32.4(c).
Generation-skipping transfer, §105-32.7(c).
Sale of assets of estates.
Obtaining money due, §105-32.4(d).
Savings banks.
Payable on death (POD) accounts.
Statutory construction.
Estate tax provisions not affected by
provisions, §54C-166.1(d).

ESTATE TAXES —Cont'd
Wills.
Federal estate tax apportionment.
Method described in will, §28A-27-2(b).

ESTHETICIANS.
Cosmetic art generally, §§88B-1 to 88B-29.
See COSMETIC ART.

ESTOPPEL.
Affirmative defense, pleading, §1A-1 Rule 8(c).
False claims act.
False or fraudulent claims against the state.
Final judgment rendered in favor of state in
criminal proceeding, §1-615(d).
Limited liability companies.
Applicability of law under chapter, §57C-10-03(b).
Medicaid.
False claims by providers.
Final judgment rendered in favor of state in
criminal proceeding, §108A-70.13(d).
Partnerships.
Applicability of law of estoppel, §59-34(b).
Partner by estoppel.
Agent of persons consenting to representation,
§59-46(b).
Liability, §59-46(a).
RICO criminal convictions, §75D-8(e).
Small claims actions, §7A-219.

ESTRAYS.
Dogs running at large.
Dangerous dogs.
Permitting dangerous dog to go beyond owner's
real property unless leashed and muzzled.
Unlawful, §67-4.2(a).
Female dogs in heat.
Penalty, §67-2.
Nighttime.
Permitting to run at large at night.
Penalty, §67-12.
Sheep-killing dogs.
Penalty for permitting such dog to run at large,
§67-3.
Wildlife management areas.
Unmuzzled dogs running at large.
Impoundment, §67-14.1(b) to (e).
Livestock running at large.
Allowing livestock to run at large prohibited,
§68-16.
Diseased livestock, §106-307.7.
Outer Banks.
Impoundment.
Applicability of general provisions, §68-45.
Penalty, §68-44.
Prohibited, §68-42.
Protection of livestock running at large, §14-366.
Molesting, §14-366.

ESTUARINE WATER BEACHES.
Coastal area management generally, §§113A-100
to 113A-128.
See COASTAL AREA MANAGEMENT.

ETCHINGS.
Artwork on consignment, §§25C-1 to 25C-5.
Sale of fine prints, §§25C-10 to 25C-16.

ETHANOL.
**Dispensing equipment standards for E-blend
fuel.**
Definitions, §143-143.6(a).
Labels on pumps or other dispensing devices,
§119-27.2(a), (b).

ETHANOL —Cont'd
Dispensing equipment standards for E-blend fuel —Cont'd
Requirements, §143-143.6(b).
Gasoline tax.
Excise tax on motor fuel.
Liability for tax on fuel grade ethanol, §105-449.83A.
Renewable fuel facility construction tax credit, §105-129.16D.

ETHEN'S LAW.
Unborn victims of violence act/Ethen's law, §§14-23.1 to 14-23.8.
See CRIMINAL LAW AND PROCEDURE.

ETHICS.
ABC boards.
Requirements, §18B-706.
Arbitration.
Canons of ethics for arbitrators.
Integrity of arbitration process.
Upholding, CEA Rule 1.
Consolidated city-county act.
Ethics code adoption, §160B-2.3.
County boards of commissioners.
Ethics code adoption, §153A-53.
Environmental health specialists.
Code of ethics, §90A-67.
Facility authorities.
Authority created under this provision to be treated as board for purposes of state government ethics act, §160A-480.3(h).
Judicial standards commission, §§7A-374.1 to 7A-378, JudStdsComm Rules 1 to 26.
See JUDICIAL STANDARDS COMMISSION.
Legal ethics, procedures for ruling on questions of, Bar Rules D.0101 to D.0104.
Definitions, Bar Rule D.0101.
Ethics advisories, Bar Rule D.0103.
Requests for, Bar Rule D.0102.
Ethics decisions, Bar Rule D.0104.
Formal ethics opinion, Bar Rule D.0104.
General provisions, Bar Rule D.0102.
Informal ethics advisories, Bar Rule D.0103.
Requests for, Bar Rule D.0102.
Legislative ethics, §§120-85.1 to 120-106.
See LEGISLATIVE ETHICS.
Local ABC boards.
Requirements, §18B-706.
Local government ethics codes and education, §§160A-86, 160A-87.
Privileged communications.
See PRIVILEGED COMMUNICATIONS.
Rules of professional conduct.
Attorneys.
See ATTORNEYS AT LAW.
Sanitary districts.
Governing boards.
Code of ethics for members, §130A-49.5.
Soil scientists.
Code of professional conduct, §89F-17.
Speech and language pathologists and audiologists.
Unethical acts and practices, §90-301A.
Transportation board.
Disclosures, §143B-350(i) to (l).
Education program on ethics, §143B-350(m).
Ethics policy, §143B-350(k).

ETHICS COMMISSION.
State government ethics act.
State ethics commission, §§138A-6 to 138A-15.
See STATE GOVERNMENT ETHICS ACT.

ETHNIC ANIMOSITY.
Punishment of offenses committed with, §14-3(c).

ETHNIC DISCRIMINATION.
Discrimination generally.
See DISCRIMINATION.

ETHNIC INTIMIDATION.
Assaulting person or damaging or defacing property, §14-401.14(a).
Teaching techniques, §14-401.14(b).

ETHYL ALCOHOL.
Exemption from alcoholic beverage provisions, §18B-103.

EUGENICS BOARD PROGRAM.
Records.
Not public records as to persons impacted by program, §132-1.23(a).
Person impacted may obtain person's individual records, §132-1.23(b).

EUROPEAN MONETARY UNION.
Application of provisions, §53-299.
Other currency alterations, §53-300.
Continuity of contracts, §§53-295 to 53-300.
Currency alterations generally.
Application of provisions, §53-300.
Currency substitutions.
Commercially reasonable substitutes, §53-296(a), (b).
Designated by contract, §53-296(c).
Effect, §53-297.
Definitions, §53-295.
References to ECU in contracts, §53-298(a), (b).

EUTHANASIA OF ANIMALS.
Defined, §19A-23.
Gas method approved.
Rules, requirements, §19A-24(a).
Methods allowed, §19A-24(a).
Procedures for euthanasia, §19A-24(a).
Rules, adoption, §19A-24(a).
Sodium pentobarbital and other drugs for euthanasia of animals.
Animal shelters.
Registration for purpose of obtaining and using, §90-101(a2).
Technicians performing euthanasia.
Certification, rules, §19A-24(b).
Denial, revocation, suspension, §19A-24(c).
Fingerprints, providing, criminal background check, §§19A-24(d), 114-19.29.
Training for person participating in process.
Mandatory training, §19A-24(a).

EVACUATION OF PUBLIC BUILDINGS.
Power of governor to order, §14-288.19.
State legislative building, §120-32.1A.

EVALUATION OF CERTIFIED SCHOOL EMPLOYEES, §§115C-333 to 115C-335.

EVASION OF TAX, §105-236.

E-VERIFY PROGRAM.
Counties.
Duty to register and participate, §153A-99.1.
Definition of E-Verify, §64-25.
Employers to use, §64-26(a).
Seasonal temporary employee exception to requirement, §64-26(c).
Violations, consequences, §§64-31 to 64-33.

E-VERIFY PROGRAM —Cont'd
Municipalities.
Duty to register and participate, §160A-169.1.
State departments, agencies, etc.
Verification of legal status after hiring new employees, §126-7.1(f).
Work authorization verification generally, §§64-25 to 64-38.
See ALIENS.

EVICTION.
Betterments.
Defendant evicted may recover from plaintiff, §1-350.
Criminals, expedited evictions, §§42-59 to 42-76.
See EXPEDITED EVICTIONS.
Domestic violence.
Orders for relief, §50B-3(a).
Ejectment of residential tenants, §§42-25.6 to 42-25.9.
Abandoned personal property of tenant.
Determination of abandonment, §42-25.9(e).
Disposition, §42-25.9(d).
Liability of recipient, §42-25.9(f).
Contrary lease provisions.
Void, §42-25.8.
Damages.
Remedies, §42-25.9(a), (b).
Distraint.
Prohibited, §42-25.7.
Distress.
Prohibited, §42-25.7.
Execution of writ of possession.
Personal property valued at less than $100. Disposition, §42-25.9(h).
Notice to tenant of sale of personal property left on premises, §42-25.9(g).
Seizure of personal property of tenant prohibited, §42-25.7.
Exclusive nature of provisions, §42-25.6.
Lease provisions.
Contrary lease provisions void, §42-25.8.
Manner of ejectment, §42-25.6.
Personal property of tenant abandoned.
Delivery of property into custody of nonprofit organization, §42-25.9(d).
No liability to owner of property for disposition of such property, §42-25.9(f).
Determination of abandonment, §42-25.9(e).
Policy of state, §42-25.6.
Remedies, §42-25.9(a), (b).
Supplementary nature, §42-25.9(c).
Expedited eviction of drug traffickers and other criminals, §§42-59 to 42-76.
See EXPEDITED EVICTIONS.
Retaliatory eviction, §§42-37.1 to 42-37.3.
Actions for summary ejectment.
Tenant may raise affirmative defense of retaliatory evictions, §42-37.1(b).
Activities protected by law, §42-37.1(a).
Complaints.
Good faith complaints.
Activities protected by law, §42-37.1(a).
Health or safety laws.
Good faith complaints to government agencies. Activities protected by law, §42-37.1(a).
Public policy estate, §42-37.1(a).
Remedies.
Court may deny request for judgment, §42-37.2(a).
Generally, §42-37.2(a), (b).

EVICTION —Cont'd
Retaliatory eviction —Cont'd
Remedies —Cont'd
Supplementary to existing common law and statutory rights and remedies, §42-37.2(b).
Repairs.
Good faith or request to repairs.
Activities protected by law, §42-37.1(a).
Summary ejectment.
When landlord may prevail in action, §42-37.1(c).
Tenant unions.
Activities protected by law, §42-37.1(a).
Waiver of rights, §42-37.3.
Sale of abandoned personal property, §42-25.9.
Summary ejectment, §§42-26 to 42-36.2.
See LANDLORD AND TENANT.
Vacation rentals.
Expedited eviction proceedings, §§42A-23 to 42A-27.

EVIDENCE, §8C-1 Rule 412.
Absentees in military service.
Transfer of property.
Court order authorizing transfer, §§28B-9(c), 28B-10(f).
Absolute divorce for incurable insanity, §50-5.1.
Abstracts of grants, certified copies, §§8-6, 8-7.
Recording of certified copies, §8-8.
Validation, §8-9.
Abused, neglected or dependent juvenile actions.
Adjudicatory hearing, applicability of rules of evidence, §7B-804.
Dispositional hearings, §7B-901.
No privilege except attorney-client grounds for failing to report or excluding evidence, §7B-310.
Permanency planning hearings, §7B-907(b).
Placement review, parental rights terminated, §7B-908(a).
Review hearings, §7B-906(c).
Accident reports by motor carriers.
Inadmissibility, §62-274.
Accident reports involving public utilities not admissible, §62-41.
Accounts and accounting.
Book accounts.
Copies of book accounts in documentary evidence, §8-44.
Documentary evidence of book accounts under $60, §8-42.
Executors and administrators to approve book accounts, §8-43.
Documentary evidence.
Itemized and verified accounts, §8-45.
Accused's character.
Admissibility of evidence of pertinent trait, §8C-1 Rule 404(a).
Acts of the general assembly.
Certified copies as evidence, §8-1.
Administrative procedure.
Appeals.
New evidence, §150B-49.
Dying declarations, §8-51.1.
Hearings, §150B-41(a), (b).
Opportunity to present evidence, §§150B-25(c), 150B-40(a).
Rules of evidence, §150B-29(a), (b).
Subpoenas, §§150B-27, 150B-39(c).

EVIDENCE —Cont'd

Admissibility.

Character evidence.

Not admissible to prove conduct, §8C-1 Rule 404(a).

Collaborative law proceedings.

Privileged and inadmissible evidence, §50-77(a), (b).

Compromises and offers to compromise, §8C-1 Rule 408.

Dying declarations, §8-51.1.

Evidence of other crimes, wrongs or acts, §8C-1 Rule 404.

Irrelevant evidence.

Inadmissible, §8C-1 Rule 402.

Limited admissibility, §8C-1 Rule 105.

Medical, hospital or other expenses.

Evidence of furnishing or offering or promising to pay.

Inadmissible to prove liability for injury, §8C-1 Rule 409.

Pleas, plea discussions and related statements.

Inadmissibility, §8C-1 Rule 410.

Questions of admissibility generally, §8C-1 Rule 104(a).

Relevant evidence, §8C-1 Rule 402.

Exclusions.

Prejudice, confusion or waste of time, §8C-1 Rule 403.

Rulings on, §1A-1 Rule 46(a).

Subsequent remedial measures, §8C-1 Rule 407.

Adult care homes.

Temporary management.

Hearing on petition for appointment of temporary manager, §131E-233(b).

Adverse possession.

Seven years possession under color of title, §1-38(b).

Affrays.

Plea of self-defense.

Evidence of former threats upon plea, §14-33.1.

Age of child registering for school.

Birth certificates prima facie evidence, §130A-103.

Secondary proof, §130A-103.

Agriculture.

Marketing and branding farm products.

Certificate of grade or classifications of farm product prima facie evidence, §106-192.

Seed law, claim of defective seeds, §106-277.34(a).

Alcoholic beverages.

Alcohol screening test.

Minor suspected of consuming alcohol.

Results, refusal to submit, §18B-302(j).

Compensation for injury caused by sales to underage persons.

Admissibility, §18B-122.

Open container law.

Alcohol screening test, §20-138.7(d).

Odor, sufficiency to determine whether alcohol remains in driver's body, §20-138.7(c).

Possession for purpose of sale.

Prima facie evidence.

Possession by person not permitted to possess, §18B-304(b).

Alcohol screening test.

Impaired driving.

Positive or negative results, §20-16.3(d).

Minor suspected of consuming alcohol.

Results, refusal to submit, §18B-302(j).

EVIDENCE —Cont'd

Aliens.

Real property.

Certified copies of deeds made by alien property custodians.

Admissible in evidence, §47-34.

Altering, destroying, etc., evidence of criminal conduct, §14-221.1.

Amendment of pleading to conform to evidence, §1A-1 Rule 15(b).

Annuities.

Mortality tables.

Worth of annuities.

Establishing present worth, §8-47.

Antifreeze.

Enforcement of article.

Copy of analysis administered as evidence, §106-579.10(c).

Appeals.

Exceptions, §1-186(b).

Applicability of rules, §8C-1 Rule 1101(a).

Arbitration.

Compelling attendance of witnesses, §1-569.17(a).

Depositions permitted, §1-569.17(b).

Discovery.

Grounds for permitting, §1-569.17(c).

Issuance of process, §1-569.17(d).

Presentation of case, §1-569.7(c).

Rules for court-ordered arbitration.

Exhibits.

Copies admissible, Arbitration Rule 3.

Law of evidence used as guide, Arbitration Rule 3.

Trial de novo.

No evidence of arbitration admissible, Arbitration Rule 5.

Rules of evidence.

Applicability to proceedings, §1-569.7(f).

Inapplicability, exception, §1-569.15(e).

Assault and battery.

Plea of self-defense.

Evidence of former threats upon plea, §14-33.1.

Assumed names.

Business under assumed name.

Copy of certificate prima facie evidence, §66-69.1.

Attorneys at law.

Altering, destroying or concealing, ProfCond Rule 3.4.

Appearances.

Attorney-client relationship.

Filing or producing if requested, §84-11.

Disciplinary proceedings.

Confidentiality of documents, papers, etc, of state bar, staff, counsel, etc.

Considering evidence brought forward in hearing as public record, §84-32.1(c).

Formal hearings, Bar Rule B.0114.

Preservation of evidence, Bar Rule B.0118.

False evidence offered, ProfCond Rule 3.3.

Obstructing party's access to, ProfCond Rule 3.4.

Prohibited acts as to opposing party and counsel, ProfCond Rule 3.4.

Attorneys' fees in nonjustifiable cases, §6-21.5.

Authentication and identification.

General provisions, §8C-1 Rule 901(a).

Illustration of examples, §8C-1 Rule 901(b).

Self-authentication, §8C-1 Rule 902.

Subscribing witness.

Testimony not necessary to authenticate, §8C-1 Rule 903.

EVIDENCE —Cont'd

Bad checks.
Prima facie evidence in worthless check cases, §14-107.1.

Bail bondsmen and runners.
Commissioners' actions, §58-71-5(b).

Bailments.
Conversion.
Prima facie evidence of intent to convert.
Property other than motor vehicle, §14-168.3.
Truck, automobile or other motor vehicle, §14-168.5(a).
Options to purchase.
Failing to return rented property on which there is purchase option.
Intent to commit crime.
Presumptions from evidence, §14-168.4(b).

Banks.
Records.
Certified copies, §53-113.

Bawdy houses, keeping, §14-188(a).

Best evidence.
Contents of writings, recordings and photographs, §§8C-1 Rule 1001 to 8C-1 Rule 1008.

Bills of lading.
Actions by or against common or connecting carriers, §8-41.

Birth certificate as evidence, §130A-109.

Bladen county.
Records in Bladen.
Copies of lost records, §8-33.

Blind persons.
Aid to the blind.
Personal representatives for certain recipients of aid.
Findings not competent as evidence in other proceedings, §111-32.

Blood tests and samples.
Competency of blood tests.
Civil actions, §8-50.1(b1).
Jury charge, §8-50.1(b1).
Taxing of expenses as cost, §8-50.1(b1).
Cost.
Taxing of expenses as cost, §8-50.1.
Criminal actions, §8-50.1(a).
Jury charge, §8-50.1(a).
Taxing of expenses as cost, §8-50.1(a).
Jury charge, §8-50.1.

Boating safety.
Proof of ownership of vessel, §75A-10.2.

Boats.
Certificate of title.
Prima facie evidence of ownership, §75A-37(a).

Bonds, surety.
Actions on bonds.
Evidence against principal admissible against sureties, §58-76-25.
Model payment and performance bond.
Certified copies of bonds.
Prima facie evidence, §44A-31(b).

Breaking and entering.
Habitual breaking and entering status offense.
Prior convictions, §14-7.29.

Brunswick county.
Wills in Brunswick.
Records of wills, §8-27.

Burden of proof.
See BURDEN OF PROOF.

Bureau of investigation.
Availability to district attorneys, §114-15(c).

EVIDENCE —Cont'd

Burke county.
Grants.
Copies of grants in Burke.
Admission into evidence, §8-10.

Business corporation document filing.
Certificate of existence.
Evidentiary effect, §55-1-28(c).
Evidentiary, §55D-17.

Calendar.
Proof of dates.
Clark's calendar may be used, §8-48(a).

Campaign contributions and expenditures.
Communications are "to support or oppose the nomination or election of one or more clearly identified candidates,"§163-278.14A(a).

Carriers.
Actions by or against common or connecting carriers.
Bills of lading in evidence, §8-41.

Chain of custody.
Courier service and contract carriers, §8-103.

Character evidence.
Accused's character, §8C-1 Rule 404(a).
Credibility of witness, §8C-1 Rule 608.
Juvenile's character.
Other crimes, wrongs or acts, §8C-1 Rule 404(b).
Methods of proving character, §8C-1 Rule 405.
Not admissible to prove conduct.
Exceptions, §8C-1 Rule 404(a).
Opinion, §8C-1 Rule 405(a).
Other crimes, wrongs or acts, §8C-1 Rule 404(b).
Juveniles, §8C-1 Rule 404(b).
Reputation, §8C-1 Rule 405(a).
Specific instances of conduct, §8C-1 Rule 405(b).
Victim's character, §8C-1 Rule 404(a).
Witness's character, §8C-1 Rule 404(a).

Cherokee Indians.
Maps of Cherokee lands.
Certified copies of maps, §8-14.

Child care facilities.
Prima facie evidence of existence, §110-98.1.

Child custody jurisdiction and enforcement.
Testimony, §50A-111.

Child support.
Agency payment records as admissible evidence, §50-13.9(b).
Employee verification form, §110-139(c1).

Child witnesses.
Remote testimony.
Criminal cases, §15A-1225.1.

Citation of rules of evidence, §8C-1 Rule 1102.

Clergymen.
Communications between clergymen and communicants, §8-53.2.

Code, §§8C-1 Rule 101 to 8C-1 Rule 1102.

Collaborative law proceedings.
Privileged and inadmissible evidence, §50-77(a), (b).

Collection agencies.
Entry of default or summary judgment against debtor.
Evidence to establish amount and nature of debt, §58-70-155.

Commercial code.
Breach of contract.
Waiver or renunciation of claim or right after breach, §25-1-306.
Course of performance.
Evidence relevant to show waiver or modification term inconsistent with, §25-1-303(e).

EVIDENCE —Cont'd
Commercial code —Cont'd
Option to accelerate at will.
Burden of establishing lack of good faith, §25-1-309.
Presumption of fact.
Evidentiary effect, §25-1-206.
Third party documents.
Document in due form.
Prima facie evidence authenticity and genuineness, §25-1-307.
Usage of trade.
Evidence of relevant usage offered by a party, §25-1-303(g).
Commercial vehicles.
Operation after consuming alcohol.
Odor of alcohol, §20-138.2A(b1).
Common carriers.
Actions by or against common carriers.
Bills of lading, §8-41.
Common law.
Laws of foreign countries or states.
Proof by oral evidence, §8-3(a).
Competency of witnesses.
See COMPETENCY OF WITNESSES.
Completeness rule, §8C-1 Rule 106.
Compromise and settlement.
Offering or accepting.
Admissibility, §8C-1 Rule 408.
Conduct of witness.
Credibility, §8C-1 Rule 608.
Construction and interpretation.
Photographing and photostating public records.
Uniformity of interpretation, §8-45.2.
Rules of evidence, §8C-1 Rule 102(a).
Contractors.
General contractors license certificate, §87-12.
Controlled substances.
Chain of custody, §90-95(g1).
Conviction of crime.
Impeachment, §8C-1 Rule 609.
Copies.
Use of registered copies as evidence, §47-31(a), (b).
Coroners.
Bonds, surety.
Certified copies evidence, §152-4.
Corporations.
Business corporation documents filing.
Certificate of existence.
Evidentiary effect, §55-1-28(c).
Evidentiary effect of copy of filed document, §55D-17.
Probate and registration.
Execution of corporate instruments.
Instruments executed bearing seal.
Prima facie evidence seal duly adopted, §47-18.3(b).
Cost.
Blood tests.
Competency of blood tests.
Taxing of expenses as cost, §8-50.1.
Counselors.
Privileged communications, §8-53.8.
Court reporters.
Perpetuation of testimony.
Certified transcription of court reporter, §8-85.
Credit cards and devices fraud, §14-113.3.
Credit unions.
Records.
Photostatic or photographic reproductions, §54-109.17(c).

EVIDENCE —Cont'd
Crime victims compensation.
Contested cases, §15B-12.
Criminal law and procedure.
Additional evidence.
Introduction at any time prior to verdict.
Discretion of judge, §15A-1226(b).
Altering, destroying or stealing evidence of conduct.
Obstructing justice, §14-221.1.
Appeals.
Insufficiency of evidence to prove crime charged.
Preserving issue for appeal at trial, AppProc Rule 10(a).
Bawdy houses, keeping.
Reputation or character of house admissible, §14-188(a).
Breaking and entering.
Habitual breaking and entering status offense.
Prior convictions, §14-7.29.
Demurrer to the evidence, §15-173.
DNA samples and testing, §§15A-266 to 15A-270.
See DNA.
Errors in admission or exclusion of evidence.
Correction of errors by appellate division, §15A-1442.
Forensic analysis.
Admissible in evidence without testimony of analyst who prepared report, §8-58.20.
Impaired driving prosecutions.
Lab results of chemical analysis of blood or urine, §20-139.1(c1) to (c3).
Fruit of the poisonous tree doctrine, §15A-974.
Habitual breaking and entering status offense.
Prior convictions, §14-7.29.
Hearsay.
Probable cause hearings, §15A-611(b).
Impaired driving, implied consent offenses.
Motion to suppress evidence, §20-38.6.
Insufficiency of evidence.
Grounds for correction of errors by appellate division, §15A-1442.
Insufficiency of evidence to prove crime charged.
Preserving issue for appeal at trial, AppProc Rule 10(a).
Jury.
Review of testimony, §15A-1233(a).
Motion to suppress evidence.
Appeals.
Order denying motion, §15A-979(b).
Order granting motion, §15A-979(c).
State may appeal, §15A-1445(b).
Definitions, §15A-971.
During trial.
District court, §15A-973.
Hearing on motion.
Outside presence of jury, §15A-977(e).
Superior court, §15A-975(b).
Written or oral motion, §15A-977(e).
Exclusive method of provisions, §15A-979(d).
Findings of fact and conclusions of law, §15A-974(b).
Judgment set forth, §15A-977(f).
Good faith belief that actions were lawful, §15A-974(a).
Grounds for exclusion or suppression of unlawfully obtained evidence, §15A-974(a).
Hearing of jury, §8C-1 Rule 104(c).
Impaired driving, implied consent offenses, §20-38.6.
Order of suppression, §15A-979(a).

EVIDENCE —Cont'd
Criminal law and procedure —Cont'd
Motion to suppress evidence —Cont'd
Prior to trial.
Affidavit supporting motion, §15A-977(a).
Answer by state, §15A-977(a).
District court, §15A-973.
Hearing on motion, §§15A-976(c), 15A-977(d).
Service of copies of motion, §15A-977(a).
Superior court, §§15A-972, 15A-975(a).
Time for motion, §15A-976(a), (b).
Written motion required, §15A-977(a).
Procedure, §15A-977.
Renewal of motion, §15A-975(c).
Searches and seizures.
Challenge to probable cause supporting
search warrant on grounds of
truthfulness, §15A-978(a).
Identity of informant to be disclosed,
§15A-978(b).
Challenge to truthfulness of testimony offered
in support of search without warrant,
§15A-978(c).
Summary grant or denial of motion.
Grounds, §15A-977(b), (c).
Pleadings used in criminal prosecution as proof of
fact admitted or alleged, §1-49.
Plea discussion and arrangement.
Inadmissible, §15A-1025.
Prior convictions.
Breaking and entering.
Habitual breaking and entering status
offense, §14-7.29.
Probable cause hearings, §15A-611(b).
Prostitution prosecution.
Reputation and prior convictions, admissibility,
§14-206.
Rebuttal evidence, §15A-1226(a).
Records.
Superior courts.
Criminal index maintained by clerk of court.
Records admissible in certain cases,
§8-35.2.
Subpoena duces tecum, §15A-802.
Superior courts.
Clerks of court.
Criminal index.
Records admissible in certain cases,
§8-35.2.
Suppression of evidence.
Motion to suppress evidence, §§15A-971 to
15A-980.
Impaired driving, implied consent offenses,
§20-38.6.
Testimony by accused, §8C-1 Rule 104(d).
Victims, impact of crime, §15A-833.
Custody.
Chain of custody.
Courier service and contract carriers, §8-103.
Dead man's statute, §8C-1 Rule 601(c).
Death.
Competency of witnesses.
Dying declarations, §8-51.1.
Federal officers and employees.
Finding of presumed death, §8-37.1(a), (b).
Authority to certify evidence, §8-37.3.
Deemed signed and issued pursuant to law,
§8-37.3.
Report or record that person died, §8-37.2.
Certified copies deemed signed and issued
pursuant to law, §8-37.3.
Authority to certify evidence, §8-37.3.

EVIDENCE —Cont'd
Death presumption.
Federal officers and employees, §§8-37.1, 8-37.3.
Specific peril exposure, §28C-1(b).
Decedents' estates.
Killing decedent.
Record determining slayer admissible, §31A-13.
Deeds.
Anson county.
Records of deeds in Anson, §8-26.
Certified copies.
From other states, §8-32.
Registered instruments, §§8-18, 47-31.
Copies made by alien property custodian,
§47-34.
Lost or destroyed records.
Presumed to be in due form, §8-21.
1835 or before.
Date on deed.
Execution of deed, §8-13.
Execution of deed.
Dated before 1835.
Evidence of due execution, §8-13.
Lost or destroyed deeds.
Presumed to be in due form, §8-21.
Tax deeds.
Recitals in tax deeds in Haywood and
Henderson counties, §8-22.
Richmond county, §8-22.1.
Tracts of land.
Common survey of contiguous tracts as
evidence, §8-19.
Deer hunting.
Spotlighting.
Prima facie evidence, §113-302(b).
Definitions.
Hearsay, §8C-1 Rule 801(a) to (c).
Relevant evidence, §8C-1 Rule 401.
Writings, recordings and photographs, §8C-1 Rule
1001.
Delinquent and undisciplined juvenile actions.
Court acceptance of admission by juvenile,
§7B-2407.
Custodial interrogation of juvenile.
In-custody admission, confession or other
statement, §7B-2101(b), (c).
Dispositional hearings, §7B-2501(a).
Rules of evidence at hearing, §7B-2408.
Dentists.
Medical charges at issue.
Competency of injured party to give evidence
regarding amount of charges, §8-58.1(a).
Reasonableness of charges, rebuttable
presumption.
Testimony of person establishing, §8-58.1(b).
Services reasonable and necessary.
Permissive presumption, §8-58.1(c).
**Department of health and human services
actions to recover costs of care.**
Prima facie evidence, §143-121(c).
Depositions, §§8-74 to 8-83.
Use in court proceedings, §1A-1 Rule 32.
Developmentally disabled.
Remote testimony.
Civil cases and special proceedings, §8C-1 Rule
616.
Disability of attorney proceedings.
Preservation, Bar Rule B.0118.
Discipline of attorneys.
Formal hearings, Bar Rule B.0114.

EVIDENCE —Cont'd
Disorderly conduct.
Remaining at scene after command to disperse, §14-288.5(c).
Disorderly houses, keeping, §14-188(a).
District courts.
Custody and disposition, SuperCt Rule 14.
Judges of district court.
Power to compel production of evidence, §7A-291.
Divorce.
Absolute divorce for incurable insanity, §50-5.1.
DNA samples and testing, §§15A-266 to 15A-270.
See DNA.
Doctor-patient privilege, §8-53.
Waiver of privilege in child abuse cases, §8-53.1(a), (b).
Documentary evidence.
Accounts and accounting.
Itemized and verified accounts, §8-45.
Bills of lading in evidence, §8-41.
Book accounts.
Copies of accounts in evidence, §8-44.
Executors and administrators.
Approving book accounts by personal representative, §8-43.
Under $60, §8-42.
Carriers.
Actions by or against common or connecting carriers.
Bills of lading in evidence, §8-41.
Contract actions.
Book accounts under $60, §8-42.
Copies of book accounts in evidence, §8-44.
Executors and administrators.
Book accounts approved by personal representative, §8-43.
Hospital records.
Copies of medical records, §8-44.1.
Itemized and verified accounts, §8-45.
Meat inspection.
Production of documentary evidence, §106-549.36(b), (c).
Medical records.
Copies of medical records, §8-44.1.
Parol evidence.
Identifying land described, §8-39.
Real property.
Parol evidence to identify land described, §8-39.
Remainder of or related writings or recorded statements, §8C-1 Rule 106.
Subpoena for production, §8-61.
Drug paraphernalia.
Determination where object is drug paraphernalia.
What may be considered, §90-113.21(b).
Drug recognition expert.
Under the influence of impairing substances and category of substances, §8C-1 Rule 702(a1).
Drugs.
Controlled substances.
Reports of analysis, §90-95(g).
Duplin county.
Partition of real estate in Duplin.
Records of partition, §8-24.
Wills in Duplin.
Records of wills, §8-25.
Duress.
Statements, releases, etc., obtained from persons in shock or under the influence of drugs.
Presumption of fraud, §8-45.5.

EVIDENCE —Cont'd
Dying declarations.
Admissibility, §8-51.1.
Wrongful death actions.
Admissibility, §28A-18-2(d).
Elections.
Challenge to a candidacy.
Compelling attendance of witnesses, §163-127.4(a).
Conduct of hearing, §163-127.4(c).
Production of documents and things, §163-127.4(a).
Challenge to voter.
Voter no longer living in precinct, prima facie evidence, §163-85(e).
Protest filed with county board.
Conduct of hearing, §163-182.10(c).
Electronic recording of custodial interrogations.
Admissibility as evidence, §15A-211(e).
Electronic surveillance.
Admissibility of contents of communications.
Copy of order and application must be furnished to parties, §15A-294(f).
Motion to suppress contents of communications, §15A-294(g).
Appeal of order granting motion, §15A-294(h).
Electronic transactions.
Admissibility of electronic signatures and records, §66-323.
Employment security division.
Reproduction of records stored on permanent computer-readable media, §8-45.3(b).
Engineer licensure certificates, §89C-16(b).
Exceptions, §1A-1 Rule 46(a), (b).
Exceptions to decisions of court, §1-186.
Excluded evidence.
Judicial standards commission.
Failure to disclose, JudStdsComm Rule 15.
Penalty for failure to comply with discovery order, §15A-910(a).
Considerations of court before granting, §15A-910(b).
Record, §1A-1 Rule 43(c).
Executors and administrators.
Book accounts proved by personal representative, §8-43.
Letters testamentary or of administration.
Death, evidence of, §28A-6-1(c).
Medical, hospital or other charges at issue.
Competency to give evidence regarding amount, §8-58.1(a).
Rebuttable presumption of reasonableness.
Testimony establishing, §8-58.1(b).
Services reasonable and necessary.
Permissive presumption, §8-58.1(c).
Vouchers.
Presumptive evidence of disbursement, §28A-21-5.
Wrongful death actions.
Evidence establishing elements of damages, §28A-18-2(c).
Expert witnesses.
See EXPERT WITNESSES.
Fair housing.
Intent to discriminate, establishing, §41A-5(a).
Fairs.
County societies.
Records may be read in evidence, §106-511.
False pretenses and cheats.
Worthless check cases.
Prima facie evidence in cases, §14-107.1.

EVIDENCE —Cont'd
Family law arbitration, §50-49.
Financial transaction cards.
Forgery of transaction card.
Prima facie evidence of forgery, §14-113.12(a),
(b).
Theft of financial transaction card.
Prima facie evidence of theft, §14-113.10.
Firearm possessed by felon.
Records of prior conviction proving violation,
§14-415.1(b).
Fireworks.
Possession prima facie evidence of violation,
§14-412.
Fish and fisheries resources.
Possession of illegally killed fish as evidence,
§113-262(b).
Replacement costs of resources, §113-267.
Unlawful possession of game fish, §113-302(a).
Warning tickets not to constitute evidence of
commission of offense, §113-140(g).
Foreign country laws.
Admission into evidence, §8-3(a).
Exhibiting copy of law from printed volume,
§8-3(b).
Judicial notice of laws, §8-4.
Forensic analysis.
Criminal prosecutions.
Admissible in evidence without testimony of
analyst who prepared report, §8-58.20.
Impaired driving prosecutions.
Lab reports of chemical analysis of blood or
urine, §20-139.1(c1) to (c3).
Form, §1A-1 Rule 43(a).
Francis X. Martin.
Collection of Martin's private acts, §8-2.
Fraud.
Statements, releases, etc., obtained from persons
in shock or under the influence of drugs.
Presumption of fraud, §8-45.5.
Frivolous actions.
Attorneys' fees in nonjustifiable cases, §6-21.5.
Funeral charges at issue.
Competency to give evidence regarding amount,
§8-58.1(a).
Rebuttable presumption of reasonableness.
Testimony establishing, §8-58.1(b).
Services reasonable and necessary.
Permissive presumption, §8-58.1(c).
Futures contracts.
Prosecutions under provisions, §16-6.
Gasoline and oil inspection.
Certified copies of official tests admissible in
evidence, §119-36.
General statutes.
Printed statutes and certified copies as evidence,
§8-1.
Supplements.
Prima facie evidence of laws, §164-11(a).
Cumulative supplements, §164-11.1.
Grants.
Abstracts of grants.
Certified copies, §8-7.
Recording of certified copies, §8-8.
Secretary of state or state archivist to certify,
§8-6.
Burke county.
Copies of grants in Burke.
Admission into evidence, §8-10.
Certified copies, §8-7.
Recording of certified copies, §8-8.

EVIDENCE —Cont'd
Grants —Cont'd
Certified copies —Cont'd
Validation by clerk of secretary of state, §8-9.
H.E. McCulloch grants.
Evidence of title under grants, §8-16.
Conveyances, §8-17.
Moore county.
Copies of grants in Moore, §8-11.
Onslow county.
Copies of grants in Onslow.
Admission into evidence, §8-12.
Secretary of state.
Validation of copies of grants certified by clerk
of secretary, §8-9.
Guardians.
Ancillary guardian appointed for nonresident
ward with property in state.
Certified or exemplified copy of appointment,
§35A-1280(c).
Medical, hospital or other charges at issue.
Competency to give evidence regarding amount,
§8-58.1(a).
Rebuttable presumption of reasonableness.
Testimony establishing, §8-58.1(b).
Services reasonable and necessary.
Permissive presumption, §8-58.1(c).
Habeas corpus ad testificandum, §§17-41 to
17-46.
See HABEAS CORPUS AD TESTIFICANDUM.
Habits of person.
Relevant to prove conduct of person, §8C-1 Rule
406.
Habitual breaking and entering status offense.
Prior convictions, §14-7.29.
Habitual felons.
Prior convictions, §14-7.4.
Violent habitual felons, §14-7.10.
Violent habitual felons, §14-7.10.
Harmless error, §1A-1 Rule 61.
Haywood county.
Tax deeds in Haywood.
Recitals in tax deeds, §8-22.
Hazardous waste management.
Felonies.
Circumstantial evidence of defendant's
possession of actual knowledge,
§130A-26.1(c).
Health care liability.
Admissibility of evidence, §90-21.55(b).
Hearing impaired.
Statement taken under custody without
interpreter present.
Admissibility, §8B-2.
Hearing of jury, §8C-1 Rule 104(c).
Hearsay.
Attacking credibility of declarant, §8C-1 Rule 806.
Credibility of declarant.
Attacking and supporting, §8C-1 Rule 806.
Definitions, §8C-1 Rule 801(a) to (c).
Exceptions.
Admissions by party-opponent, §8C-1 Rule
801(d).
Availability of declarant immaterial, §8C-1 Rule
803.
Declarant unavailable, §8C-1 Rule 804.
Enumeration, §8C-1 Rule 803.
Hearsay within hearsay, §8C-1 Rule 805.
Probable cause hearings, §15A-611(b).
Rule generally, §8C-1 Rule 802.

EVIDENCE —Cont'd
Hearsay —Cont'd
Supporting credibility of declarant, §8C-1 Rule 806.
H.E. McCulloch grants.
Title under grants, §8-16.
Conveyances, §8-17.
Henderson county.
Tax deeds in Henderson.
Recitals in tax deeds, §8-22.
Homicide.
Killing decedents.
Record determining slayer admissible in evidence, §31A-13.
Hospital authorities.
Certificate of incorporation.
Copy of certificate admissible in evidence, §131E-19.
Hospitals.
Medical records.
Copies of medical records as documentary evidence, §8-44.1.
Medical review committee.
Introduction of records into evidence, §131E-95(b), (c).
Testimony of members of committees, §131E-95(b), (c).
Hunting and wildlife.
Possession of illegally killed wildlife as evidence, §113-262(b).
Spotlighting deer.
Prima facie evidence, §113-302(b).
Warning tickets not to constitute evidence of commission of offense, §113-140(g).
Husband and wife.
Competency of witnesses.
Paternity proceedings, §8-57.2.
Privilege.
Child abuse cases, §8-57.1.
Civil actions, §8-56.
Criminal actions, §8-57(a) to (c).
Illustrative evidence.
Photographs as substantive or illustrative evidence, §8-97.
Impaired driving.
Alcohol screening test.
Positive or negative results, §20-16.3(d).
Chemical analysis of impairing substances in blood.
Admissibility, §20-139.1(a).
Blood and urine tests, §20-139.1(c1) to (c4).
Breath analysis, §20-139.1(b3).
Refusal to submit to analysis, §20-139.1(f).
Requirements to be admissible, §20-139.1(b).
Affidavit of chemical analyst.
Admissibility without further authentication or testimony of analyst, §20-139.1(e1).
Requirements, §20-139.1(e2).
Alcohol screening test.
Positive or negative results, §20-16.3(d).
Blood and urine test.
Admissibility.
Lab results, requirements for admissibility, §20-139.1(c1) to (c4).
Inadmissibility.
Preventive maintenance on breath testing devices not performed, §§20-138.1(b1), 20-139.1(b2).
Impaired driving in commercial vehicle, §20-138.2(b1).

EVIDENCE —Cont'd
Impaired driving —Cont'd
Chemical analysis of impairing substances in blood —Cont'd
Laboratory results on blood and urine tests.
Admissibility.
Without further authentication or testimony of analyst, §20-139.1(c1) to (c3).
Rebuttal evidence as to alcohol concentration level.
Use of results, §20-138.1(a1).
Impaired driving in commercial vehicle, §20-138.2(a1).
Refusal to submit to analysis.
Admissibility, §20-139.1(f).
Breath analysis.
Second or subsequent sample, §20-139.1(b3).
Expert testimony.
Impairment, alcohol concentration level, impairing substances, §8C-1 Rule 702(a1).
Gross vehicle weight rating.
Impaired driving in commercial vehicle, §20-138.2(a2).
Motion to suppress, §20-38.6.
Sentencing hearing.
Aggravating or mitigating factors, existence.
Evidentiary standards, §20-179(o).
Impoundment.
Property impounded for evidence, §15-11.1.
Inapplicability of rules, §8C-1 Rule 1101(b).
Insufficiency of evidence.
New trial.
Grounds, §1A-1 Rule 59(a).
Insurance.
Documents executed by commissioner.
Certificate as evidence of authority to do business, §58-2-115.
Originals and certified copies, §58-2-110.
Liability insurance.
Evidence of existence of insurance inadmissible, §8C-1 Rule 411.
Existence inadmissible.
Mental health area authorities, §122C-152(f).
Tort action against community college trustees, §115D-58.12(d).
Motor vehicle accident reports, §20-279.11.
International commercial arbitration and conciliation.
Admissions and documents, §1-567.81.
Documentary evidence, translation, tribunal ordering, §1-567.52(b).
Tribunal conducting proceeding.
Not limited to rules of evidence, §1-567.49(b).
Interstate commerce.
Earnings of employees in interstate commerce.
Collections out of state to avoid exemptions.
Evidence of intent to violate provisions, §95-76.
Investment securities.
Certificated securities, §25-8-114.
Journalist's qualified privilege against disclosure in any legal proceeding, §8-53.11(b).
Definitions, §8-53.11(a).
Eyewitness observation of criminal or tortuous conduct, no privilege, §8-53.11(d).
Order to compel disclosure, notice to journalist and hearing, §8-53.11(c).
Overcoming privilege, person seeking to compel disclosure, §8-53.11(c).

EVIDENCE —Cont'd
Judgments, §1-229.
Judicial notice.
  Adjudicative facts.
    Instructing jury, §8C-1 Rule 201(g).
    Kinds of facts, §8C-1 Rule 201(b).
    Opportunity to be heard, §8C-1 Rule 201(e).
    Scope of rule, §8C-1 Rule 201(a).
    Time of taking notice, §8C-1 Rule 201(f).
    When discretionary, §8C-1 Rule 201(c).
    When mandatory, §8C-1 Rule 201(d).
  Laws of United States, other states and foreign
    countries, §8-4.
Judicial standards commission.
  Disclosure prior to disciplinary hearing,
    JudStdsComm Rule 15.
  Exclusion.
    Failure to disclose, JudStdsComm Rule 15.
  Rules of evidence.
    Public proceedings under rules, applicability,
      JudStdsComm Rule 20.
  Subpoenas.
    Issuance, request, service, JudStdsComm Rule
      19.
    Right of respondent to issue, JudStdsComm
      Rule 18.
Jurisdiction.
  Proof of jurisdiction.
    Judgment against nonappearing defendant,
      §1-75.11.
Jury.
  Blood tests.
    Competency of blood tests.
      Charge to jury, §8-50.1.
  Use of evidence by jury during deliberation,
    §1-181.2.
Juvenile code.
  Character.
    Other crimes, wrongs or acts, §8C-1 Rule
      404(b).
  Conviction of crime.
    Impeachment in juvenile adjudication, §8C-1
      Rule 609(d).
Labor.
  Interstate commerce.
    Earnings of employees in interstate commerce.
      Collections out of state to avoid exemptions.
        Evidence of intent to violate, §95-76.
Land surveyors' licensure certificate,
  §89C-16(b).
Land tracts.
  Contiguous tracts as evidence.
    Common survey of contiguous tracts, §8-19.
Larceny.
  Concealment of merchandise in mercantile
    establishments.
    Prima facie evidence of willful concealment,
      §14-72.1(a).
Leases, UCC.
  Extrinsic evidence, §25-2A-202.
  Proof of market rent, §25-2A-507.
  Unconscionability.
    Parties afforded reasonable opportunity to
      present, §25-2A-108(3).
Legal notices.
  Newspapers.
    Proof of publication of notice in newspaper.
      Prima facie evidence, §1-600(b).
    Qualification.
      Sworn statement prima facie evidence of
        qualification, §1-598.

EVIDENCE —Cont'd
Letters testamentary.
  Certified copies, §8-36.
Liability insurance.
  Evidence of existence of insurance inadmissible,
    §8C-1 Rule 411.
  Existence inadmissible, §8C-1 Rule 411.
    Mental health area authorities, §122C-152(f).
    Tort action against community college trustees,
      §115D-58.12(d).
Liens.
  Physicians and surgeons.
    Recoveries for personal injuries, §44-50.
Life tables.
  Annuities.
    Present worth of annuities, §8-47.
  Establishing expectancy of continued life of
    person, §8-46.
Limited liability companies.
  Certificate of existence or authorization,
    §57C-1-28(c).
  Filing of articles of organization, §57C-2-20(b).
Limiting instruction on admissibility, §8C-1
  Rule 105.
Lost instruments and records.
  Bladen county.
    Copies of lost records in Bladen, §8-33.
  Copies, §98-1.
    Wills, §98-5.
  Court records.
    Conveyances reciting court records.
      Prima facie evidence thereof, §§98-16, 98-17.
    Proof of destroyed instruments set out therein,
      §98-12.
  Deeds and records thereof lost.
    Presumed to be in due form, §8-21.
  Wills.
    Copy of lost will, §98-5.
Lotteries.
  "Numbers" tickets.
    Possession prima facie evidence of violation,
      §14-291.1.
  Possession, §14-290.
Malpractice.
  Medical malpractice.
    Standard of health care, §90-21.12(a).
      Emergency medical condition, treatment of,
        §90-21.12(b).
    Statements by health care provider to
      ameliorate or mitigate adverse outcomes,
      §8C-1 Rule 413.
Maps and plats.
  Certified copies of maps, §8-14.
  Copies of plats.
    Certification, §8-6.
  Tennessee.
    Certified copies of certain surveys and maps
      obtained from state of Tennessee, §8-15.
Market value.
  Sale of goods, UCC, §§25-2-723, 25-2-724.
Marriage and family therapists privilege.
  Alimony and divorce actions, §8-53.6.
  Communications between therapists and clients,
    generally, §8-53.5.
Marriage certificate registration, §130A-110(b).
Marriage proceedings.
  Underage pregnant females.
    Action for judicial authorization to marry,
      §51-2.1(f).
Material facts.
  Proof of single material fact.
    No more than two witnesses may be
      subpoenaed to prove, §6-60.

EVIDENCE —Cont'd
Meat and meat product inspections,
§106-549.36(c).
Mediated settlement conferences in district court.
Equitable distribution, alimony or support actions.
Statements made and conduct occurring in settlement proceeding, §7A-38.4A(j).
Mediated settlement conferences in superior court civil actions.
Statements and conduct during mediation.
Inadmissibility, exceptions, §7A-38.1(l).
Mediation ordered by superior court clerks.
Statements and conduct during mediation.
Inadmissibility, exceptions, §7A-38.3B(g).
Medicaid.
Contested case procedures.
New evidence, submission, §108A-70.9B(e).
Medical board.
Closed sessions.
Evidence regarding treatment of patient, §90-16(b).
Entries in record books, §90-16(a).
Medical examiners.
Postmortem medicolegal examinations and services.
Reports and records received as evidence, §130A-392.
Medical, hospital or other expenses.
Evidence of furnishing or offering or promising to pay.
Inadmissible to prove liability for injury, §8C-1 Rule 409.
Injured as witness when medical charges an issue.
Competency to give evidence regarding amount, §8-58.1(a).
Past medical expenses, §8C-1 Rule 414.
Rebuttable presumption of reasonableness.
Testimony establishing, §8-58.1(b).
Services reasonable and necessary.
Permissive presumption, §8-58.1(c).
Mental health, developmental disabilities and substance abuse.
Involuntary commitment.
District court hearing.
Admissible evidence, §122C-268(f).
Hearing following automatic commitment, §122C-268.1(f), (h), (i).
Substance abuser's commitment hearing, §122C-286(c).
Mentally retarded.
Remote testimony.
Civil cases and special proceedings, §8C-1 Rule 616.
Microfilm.
Admissible photographic reproductions, §8-45.1.
Citation of act, §8-45.4.
Uniformity of interpretation, §8-45.2.
Department of revenue.
Reproductions of records, §8-45.3(a).
Employment security division.
Reproduction of records, §8-45.3(a1).
Military affairs.
Death.
Finding of presumed death, §8-37.1(a), (b).
Missing in action.
Report or record that person is missing in action.
Prima facie evidence, §8-37.2.
Missing persons records and reports.
Certified copies deemed signed and issued pursuant to law, §8-37.3.

EVIDENCE —Cont'd
Missing persons records and reports —Cont'd
Prima facie evidence, §8-37.2.
Mode and order of presenting evidence.
Control of court, §8C-1 Rule 611(a).
Moore county.
Grants.
Copies of grants in Moore, §8-11.
Mortality tables.
Annuities.
Present worth of annuities, §8-47.
Establishing expectancy of continued life of person, §8-46.
Mortgages and deeds of trust.
Registered instruments as evidence.
Certified copies of registered instruments, §8-18.
Sales under power of sale.
Requests for copies of notice, §45-21.17A(e).
Motions.
Evidence on motions, §1A-1 Rule 43(e).
Suppression of evidence, §§15A-971 to 15A-980.
Impaired driving, implied consent offenses, §20-38.6.
Motor carrier accident reports, §62-274.
Motor vehicle accidents.
Reports, §20-166.1(i).
Information on financial responsibility contained in accident report, §20-279.11.
Settlements, §1-540.2.
Motor vehicle financial responsibility.
Matters not to be evidence in civil suit, §20-279.11.
Operation of vehicle without, §20-313(b).
Motor vehicle license plates.
Ownership, §8-37.
Motor vehicle registration.
Ownership evidence, §20-71.1(b).
Motor vehicles.
Altering to increase potential speed.
Prima facie rule of evidence as to operation, §20-141.2.
Antifreeze.
Enforcement of article.
Copy of analysis administered as evidence, §106-579.10(c).
Impaired driving.
Records of division of motor vehicles.
Admissibility of records as prima facie evidence of convictions, §8-35.1.
Open container law.
Alcohol screening test, §20-138.7(d).
Odor, sufficiency to determine whether alcohol remains in driver's body, §20-138.7(c).
Ownership.
Certificate of commissioner as to ownership, §8-37.
Evidence of defendant's responsibility for conduct of operation, §20-71.1(a).
Motor vehicles commissioner.
Certified copies of documents issued by, §20-42(b).
Proceedings before, §20-279.2.
Motor vehicles division.
Certified copies of records, §20-42(b).
Sent by police information network, facsimile or other electronic means, §20-48(a).
Motor vehicle size, weight and loads.
Registered or declared weight.
Prima facie evidence, §20-26(b1).
Municipalities.
Compelling the production of evidence.
Powers of council, §160A-80(a).

EVIDENCE —Cont'd
Municipalities —Cont'd
Ordinances, §160A-79.
Negligence.
Liability insurance.
Admissibility, §8C-1 Rule 411.
Subsequent remedial measures.
Admissibility, §8C-1 Rule 407.
Negotiable instruments.
Dishonor, §25-3-505(a).
Newly discovered evidence.
New trial.
Grounds, §1A-1 Rule 59(a).
Relief from judgment or order, §1A-1 Rule 60(b).
Nonprofit corporations.
Articles of incorporation, §55A-2-03(b).
Certificates of existence or authorization.
Conclusive evidence of existence or authority,
§55A-1-28(c).
North Carolina's eastern region.
Certificate of incorporation as conclusive evidence
on region creation and establishment,
§158-33(d).
Nuisances.
Abatement.
Offenses against public morals, §19-3(b), (c).
Nurses.
Privileged communications, §8-53.13.
Child abuse or neglect cases.
Waiver of privilege, §8-53.1(a), (b).
Nursing homes.
Temporary management.
Hearing on petition for appointment of
temporary manager, §131E-233(b).
Objections, §§1A-1 Rule 46(a), (b), 8C-1 Rule
103(a).
Admissibility of evidence, §1A-1 Rule 46(a).
Matters other than admissibility of evidence,
§1A-1 Rule 46(b).
Obscenity.
Literature and exhibitions.
Dissemination of obscene material, §14-190.1(d).
Obstructing justice.
Altering, destroying or stealing evidence of
criminal conduct, §14-221.1.
Offer of judgment.
Withdrawn offer, §1A-1 Rule 68(a).
Offer of proof, §8C-1 Rule 103(a), (b).
Offer to compromise, §8C-1 Rule 408.
**Oil pollution and hazardous substances
control.**
Offshore oil and gas activities.
Removal of prohibited discharges.
Actions taken not to be construed as
admission of liability for discharge,
§143-215.94EE(d).
Onslow county grants, copies of, §8-12.
Open container law.
Alcohol screening test, §20-138.7(d).
Odor on driver's breath as determining whether
alcohol remains in driver's body, §20-138.7(c).
Options.
Failing to return rented property on which there
is purchase option.
Intent to commit crime.
Presumptions from evidence, §14-168.4(b).
Optometrists.
Privileged communications, §8-53.9.
Rules and regulations.
Certified copies, §90-124.

EVIDENCE —Cont'd
Ordinances.
Certified under seal by city clerk, §160A-79(b).
Code of ordinances, §160A-79(b).
Map book.
Copies, §160A-79(b).
Proving city ordinances, §160A-79(c).
Uniform law, §160A-79(e).
Town ordinances certified.
Prima facie evidence of existence of ordinance,
§8-5.
Other crimes, wrongs or acts, §8C-1 Rule 404(b).
Parking violations.
Prima facie rule of evidence, §20-162.1.
Parol evidence.
Documentary evidence.
Identifying land described by parol evidence,
§8-39.
Leases.
Recovery for use and occupation, §42-4.
Leases, UCC, §25-2A-202.
Sale of goods, UCC.
Contracts, §25-2-202.
Statute of frauds, §§22-1 to 22-4.
See STATUTE OF FRAUDS.
Partition.
Duplin county.
Records of partition in Duplin, §8-24.
Partition sales.
Order confirming sale.
Evidence required of purchasers, §46-28.1(c).
Revocation of confirmation order.
Proof required of purchaser, §46-28.1(c).
Partnerships.
Admission of partner, §59-41.
Continuation of partnership beyond fixed term.
Continuation of business as prima facie
evidence, §59-53(b).
Past medical expenses, §8C-1 Rule 414.
Paternity actions.
Action brought more than three years after birth
of child.
Required evidence, §49-14(d).
Blood or genetic marker tests, §49-14(d).
Invoices for services rendered, §49-14(g).
Proof of paternity beyond reasonable doubt,
§49-14(b).
Temporary order of child support.
Clear, cogent and convincing evidence, §49-14(f).
Perpetuation of testimony.
Deposition before action, §1A-1 Rule 27(a).
Deposition pending appeal, §1A-1 Rule 27(b).
Perpetuation by action, §1A-1 Rule 27(c).
Personal knowledge, §8C-1 Rule 602.
Personal property.
Impoundment, §15-11.1.
Return to victim as soon as possible, §15A-825.
Photographs and reproductions.
Admissibility of other evidence of contents, §8C-1
Rule 1004.
Admissible photographic reproductions, §8-45.1(a).
Destruction of originals, §8-45.1(a).
Records stored on permanent,
computer-readable media, §8-45.1(b).
Citation of act, §8-45.4.
Construction and interpretation.
Uniformity of interpretation, §8-45.2.
Definitions, §8C-1 Rule 1001.
Department of revenue.
Reproductions of records, §8-45.3(a).
Records stored on computer readable media,
§8-45.3(b).

EVIDENCE —Cont'd
Photographs and reproductions —Cont'd
Destruction of originals, §8-45.1(a).
Duplicates.
Admissibility, §8C-1 Rule 1003.
Employment security division.
Reproduction of records, §8-45.3(a1).
Records stored on computer readable media, §8-45.3(b).
Functions of court and jury, §8C-1 Rule 1008.
Original.
Requirement, §8C-1 Rule 1002.
Revenue department.
Reproduction of records, §8-45.3(a).
Records stored on computer readable media, §8-45.3(b).
Substantive or illustrative evidence, §8-97.
Summaries, §8C-1 Rule 1006.
Testimony or written admission of party, §8C-1 Rule 1007.
Title of article, §8-45.4.
Physicians and surgeons.
Charges.
Competency of injured party to give evidence regarding amount, §8-58.1(a).
Evidence of furnishing or offering or promising to pay.
Inadmissible to prove liability for injuring, §8C-1 Rule 409.
Reasonableness of charges.
Rebuttable presumption, §8-58.1(b).
Services reasonable and necessary.
Permissive presumption, §8-58.1(c).
Communications between physician and patient.
Confidentiality of information, §8-53.
Alimony and divorce actions, §8-53.6.
Waiver of privilege in child abuse cases, §8-53.1(a), (b).
Hearings before board, §90-14.6(a) to (d).
Medical board record books, entries in, §90-16(a).
Plats.
Copies of plats.
Certification by secretary of state or state archivist, §8-6.
Pleas.
Inadmissibility of pleas, plea discussions and related statements, §8C-1 Rule 410.
Poultry and poultry products.
Inspections.
Receiving evidence, §106-549.68(b).
Powers of attorney.
Registered instruments as evidence.
Certified copies of registered instruments, §8-18.
Preliminary questions, §8C-1 Rule 104.
Accused testimony upon preliminary matter.
Not subject to cross-examination on other matters, §8C-1 Rule 104(d).
Admissibility, §8C-1 Rule 104(a).
Hearings, §8C-1 Rule 104(c).
Relevancy.
Conditions on fact, §8C-1 Rule 104(b).
Weight or credibility, §8C-1 Rule 104(e).
Presumption of death.
Specific peril exposure, §28C-1(b).
Presumptions.
See PRESUMPTIONS.
Prima facie evidence.
Alarm system business.
Good moral character and temperate habits.
License applicant does not possess, §74D-2(d).
Bad checks, §14-107.1.

EVIDENCE —Cont'd
Prima facie evidence —Cont'd
Baggage or property lost, damaged or destroyed by innkeeper's negligence.
Proof of loss, §72-2.
Child care facility existence, §110-98.1.
Conveyances reciting destroyed court records.
Prima facie evidence of records, §98-17.
Devisavit vel non.
Affidavit of witness to will, §31-35.
Elections.
Challenge to voter.
Voter no longer living in precinct, §163-85(e).
Fraternal benefit society license.
Copy or duplicate, §58-24-130.
Motor carriers embezzlement of COD shipments, §62-273.
Motor vehicle operated so as to increase potential speed, §20-141.2.
Parking violations, §20-162.1.
Privation protective services.
Good moral character and temperate habits.
Applicant for license does not possess, §74C-8(d).
Surety, indorser or guarantor notifying creditor to take action, §26-8(c).
Unclaimed property act.
Record of issuance of check, draft or similar instrument, §116B-58.
Watercraft titling, ownership, §75A-49.
Printed statutes.
Admission into evidence, §8-1.
Prior convictions.
Breaking and entering.
Habitual breaking and entering status offense, §14-7.29.
Prior crimes, wrongs or acts, §8C-1 Rule 404(b).
Prior statements of witness, §8C-1 Rule 613.
Prisoners of war.
Report or record that person is beleaguered, besieged or captured by enemy.
Prima facie evidence, §8-37.2.
Prisons and prisoners.
Compensation to persons erroneously convicted of felonies, §148-84(a).
Habeas corpus ad testificandum, §§17-41 to 17-46.
See HABEAS CORPUS AD TESTIFICANDUM.
Private protective services.
License suspension or revocation.
Prima facie evidence, §74C-12(a).
Privileges.
General rule, §8C-1 Rule 501.
Proof of official records.
Copies, authentication, §1A-1 Rule 44(a).
Lack of record, §1A-1 Rule 44(b).
Other proof, §1A-1 Rule 44(c).
Prostitution.
Reputation and prior conviction admissible as evidence, §14-206.
Psychologist-patient privilege.
Disclosure of information, §8-53.3.
Alimony and divorce actions, §8-53.6.
Psychotherapy patient/client sexual exploitation act.
Sexual history.
Admissibility of evidence, §90-21.45(a), (b).
Reputation or opinion evidence, §90-21.45(c).
Public lands.
Record of surveys, §146-42.
Public utility accident reports.
Not admissible in evidence, §62-41.

EVIDENCE —Cont'd
Public utility rate schedules, §62-143.
Punitive damages.
Bifurcated trial, §1D-30.
Rape shield law, §8C-1 Rule 412.
Real property.
Identifying land described.
Parol evidence to identify, §8-39.
Record chain of title, §1-42.
Rebuttal.
Deposition evidence, §1A-1 Rule 32(c).
Records.
Administration of decedents' estates.
Record of administration.
Authenticated copy of record, §8-36.
Admissibility of other evidence of contents, §8C-1
Rule 1004.
Admission of remainder of or related writings or
recorded instruments, §8C-1 Rule 106.
Anson county.
Deeds and wills in Anson, §8-26.
Bladen county.
Records in Bladen.
Copies of lost records, §8-33.
Brunswick county.
Wills in Brunswick, §8-27.
Criminal index of clerk of superior court.
Records admissible in certain cases, §8-35.2.
Death of federal officers and employees.
Certified record deemed signed and issued
pursuant to law, §8-37.3.
Authority to certify evidence, §8-37.3.
Prima facie evidence that person is dead,
§8-37.2.
Deeds and records thereof lost.
Presumed to be in due form, §8-21.
Definitions, §8C-1 Rule 1001.
Duplicates.
Admissibility, §8C-1 Rule 1003.
Duplin county.
Partition of real estate in Duplin, §8-24.
Wills in Duplin, §8-25.
Functions of court and jury, §8C-1 Rule 1008.
Grants and abstracts.
Certified copies of grants and abstracts to be
recorded, §8-8.
Internment in neutral country.
Certified record deemed signed and issued
pursuant to law, §8-37.3.
Authority to certify evidence, §8-37.3.
Prima facie evidence that person is interned,
§8-37.2.
Lost instruments and records.
See LOST INSTRUMENTS AND RECORDS.
Medical records.
Copies of medical records as documentary
evidence, §8-44.1.
Missing in action.
Prima facie evidence that person is missing in
action, §8-37.2.
Missing persons.
Certified record deemed signed and issued
pursuant to law, §8-37.3.
Authority to certify evidence, §8-37.3.
Prima facie evidence that person is missing,
§8-37.2.
Motor vehicles.
Driving under the influence.
Convictions.
Admissibility of records of division as prima
facie evidence, §8-35.1.

EVIDENCE —Cont'd
Records —Cont'd
Motor vehicles —Cont'd
Ownership.
Certificate of commissioner as to ownership,
§8-37.
Original.
Requirement of original, §8C-1 Rule 1002.
Prisoners of war.
Certified record deemed signed and issued
pursuant to law, §8-37.3.
Authority to certify evidence, §8-37.3.
Prima facie evidence that person is beleaguered,
besieged or captured by enemy, §8-37.2.
Proof of official record.
Authentication of copy, §1A-1 Rule 44(a).
Generally, §1A-1 Rule 44(c).
Proof of lack of record, §1A-1 Rule 44(b).
Public records, §8C-1 Rule 1005.
Reproduction of county records.
Admissibility in evidence, §153A-436(e).
Summaries, §8C-1 Rule 1006.
Superior courts.
Clerks of court.
Criminal index.
Records admissible in certain cases,
§8-35.2.
Testimony or written admission of party, §8C-1
Rule 1007.
Tyrrell county.
Copies of records from Tyrrell, §8-23.
Refreshing memory.
Writing or object used, §8C-1 Rule 612.
Registered instruments.
Certified copies, §47-31(a), (b).
Copies made by alien property custodian,
§47-34.
Relevancy.
Conditions on fact, §8C-1 Rule 104(b).
Habits of a person, §8C-1 Rule 406.
Irrelevant evidence.
Inadmissible, §8C-1 Rule 402.
Relevant evidence.
Admissibility, §8C-1 Rule 402.
Defined, §8C-1 Rule 401.
Exclusion.
Prejudice, confusion or waste of time, §8C-1
Rule 403.
Routine practice.
Organizations, §8C-1 Rule 406.
Sexual behavior, §8C-1 Rule 412.
Subsequent remedial measures, §8C-1 Rule 407.
Religious beliefs or opinions, §8C-1 Rule 610.
Remote testimony.
Child witnesses.
Criminal cases, §15A-1225.1.
Developmentally disabled, mentally retarded.
Civil cases and special proceedings, §8C-1 Rule
616.
Reports.
Death of federal officers and employees.
Certified report deemed signed and issued
pursuant to law, §8-37.3.
Authority to certify evidence, §8-37.3.
Finding of presumed death, §8-37.1(a), (b).
Authority to certify evidence, §8-37.3.
Deemed signed and issued pursuant to law,
§8-37.3.
Prima facie evidence that person is dead,
§8-37.2.

EVIDENCE —Cont'd
Reports —Cont'd
Internment in neutral country.
Certified report deemed signed and issued
pursuant to law, §8-37.3.
Authority to certify evidence, §8-37.3.
Prima facie evidence that person is interned,
§8-37.2.
Missing in action.
Prima facie evidence that person is missing in
action, §8-37.2.
Missing persons.
Certified report deemed signed and issued
pursuant to law, §8-37.3.
Prima facie evidence that person is missing,
§8-37.2.
Prisoners of war.
Certified report deemed signed and issued
pursuant to law, §8-37.3.
Authority to certify evidence, §8-37.3.
Prima facie evidence that person is beleaguered,
besieged or captured by enemy, §8-37.2.
**Required evidence in prosecutions under
article,** §14-27.10.
Retail installment sales.
Unconscionability, §25A-43(b).
Richmond county tax deeds, §8-22.1.
Riots and civil disorders.
Command to disperse.
Failure to disperse when commanded.
Prima facie evidence, §14-288.5(c).
Remaining at scene after command to disperse,
§14-288.2(c).
Routine practice of organization.
Relevant to prove conformity with routine
practice, §8C-1 Rule 406.
Rule of completeness, §8C-1 Rule 106.
Rules review commission.
Failure of commission to object to rule,
§143B-30.4.
Rulings on evidence, §1A-1 Rule 46(a), (b).
Erroneous rulings.
Effect, §8C-1 Rule 103(a).
Review where justice requires, §8C-1 Rule
103(d).
Hearing of jury, §8C-1 Rule 103(c).
Objections, §8C-1 Rule 103(a).
Offer of proof, §8C-1 Rule 103(a).
Record, §8C-1 Rule 103(b).
Record, §8C-1 Rule 103(b).
Safety belts.
Failure to wear, §20-135.2A(d).
Sale of evidence.
Proceeds.
Use for public school fund, §15-15.
Sale of goods, UCC.
Extrinsic evidence, §25-2-202.
Parol evidence, §25-2-202.
Preserving evidence of goods in dispute,
§25-2-515.
Remedies.
Market quotations.
Admissibility, §25-2-724.
Price.
Proof of market price, §25-2-723.
Savings and loan associations.
Certificate of incorporation, §54B-14(d).
Compliance review documents, §54B-63.1(b).
Records.
Reproductions, §54B-55(e).

EVIDENCE —Cont'd
School buses.
Failure to stop for bus receiving or discharging
passengers.
Photograph or video recording from automated
camera or video recording system,
§20-217(h).
Operating a school bus, school activity bus, or
child care vehicle after consuming alcohol.
Odor of alcohol, §20-138.2B(b1).
School counselor-student privilege, §§8-53.4,
115C-401.
Scope of evidence rules, §8C-1 Rule 101.
Searches and seizures.
Item subject to seizure under search warrant,
§15A-242.
Seat belts.
Failure to wear, §20-135.2A(d).
Secret listening.
Conference between prisoner and his attorney.
Admissibility as evidence, §14-227.1(b).
Seized property, §15-11.1.
Self-incrimination.
See SELF-INCRIMINATION.
Sentencing hearings.
Rules of evidence, inapplicability, §§8C-1 Rule
1101(b), 15A-1334(b).
Seven years possession under color of title,
§1-38(b).
Sexual offenses.
Rape shield law, §8C-1 Rule 412.
Records of in camera hearings.
Inspection, §8C-1 Rule 412(e).
Required evidence and prosecutions of article,
§14-27.10.
Sexual behavior.
Defined, §8C-1 Rule 412(a).
Introduction of evidence, §8C-1 Rule 412(d).
Not proved by reputation or opinion, §8C-1 Rule
412(c).
Relevancy, §8C-1 Rule 412(b).
Shop-book rule, §§8-42 to 8-44.
Shoplifting, §14-72.1(a).
Short title.
Rules of evidence, §8C-1 Rule 1102.
Simultaneous death.
Evidence of death, §28A-24-7.
Small claims actions.
Rules of evidence generally observed, §7A-222.
Social workers.
Privileged communications, §8-53.7.
Solid waste management.
Hazardous waste.
Felonies.
Circumstantial evidence concerning
defendant's possession actual knowledge,
§130A-26.1(c).
Speed-measuring instruments.
Results of use.
Admissibility, §8-50.2(a), (b), (d).
**State child fatality review team findings and
records.**
Inadmissible, §143B-150.20(b), (f).
State departments and agencies.
Rules review commission.
Failure of commission to object to rules,
§143B-30.4.
States.
Deeds from other states.
Certified copies of deeds, §8-32.

EVIDENCE —Cont'd

States —Cont'd

Laws of other states.

Admission into evidence, §8-3(a).

Exhibition of copy of law from printed volume, §8-3(b).

Judicial notice of laws, §8-4.

Wills from other states.

Certified copies of wills, §8-32.

Statutes.

Foreign countries.

Laws of foreign countries, §8-3.

Printed statutes.

Admission into evidence, §8-1.

States.

Laws of other states, §§8-3, 8-4.

Stolen property.

Return to victim as soon as possible, §15A-825.

Subdivisions.

Control corners.

Use of corners to fix distances and boundaries, prima facie evidence of correct method, §39-32.4.

Subdivisions of rules of evidence, §8C-1 Rule 102(b).

Subpoenas.

Documentary evidence.

Production of documentary evidence, §8-61.

Subsequent remedial measures, §8C-1 Rule 407.

Substantive evidence.

Photographs as substantive or illustrative evidence, §8-97.

Summons.

Issuance.

Date.

Prima facie evidence, §1A-1 Rule 4(a).

Superior courts.

Custody and disposition, SuperCt Rule 14.

Suppression of evidence.

Motion to suppress evidence, §§15A-971 to 15A-980.

Impaired driving, implied consent offenses, §20-38.6.

Surveys and surveyors.

Certificates of survey.

Copies of certificates.

Certification by secretary of state or state archivist, §8-6.

Contiguous tracts of land.

Common survey of contiguous tracts as evidence, §8-19.

Tennessee.

Certified copies of certain surveys and maps obtained from state of Tennessee, §8-15.

Tax deeds.

Haywood county.

Recitals in tax deeds in Haywood, §8-22.

Henderson county.

Recitals in tax deeds in Henderson, §8-22.

Richmond county, §8-22.1.

Tennessee.

Surveys and maps obtained from state of Tennessee.

Certified copies of certain surveys and maps, §8-15.

Testimony.

By accused, §8C-1 Rule 104(d).

Expert witnesses.

See EXPERT WITNESSES.

Time.

Proof of dates.

Clark's calendar may be used, §8-48(a).

EVIDENCE —Cont'd

Torrens system registration.

Decree.

Conclusive evidence that person or corporation is owner of land, §43-12.

Powers of examiner to take and call for evidence, §43-11(d).

Town ordinances.

Certification of ordinances.

Prima facie evidence of existence of ordinance, §8-5.

Trademarks.

Registration.

Certificate of registration, §80-4.

Timber marks.

Evidence of ownership, §80-19.

Trees and timber.

Trademark on timber evidence of ownership, §80-19.

Trespass.

Marketable title.

Actions for recovery of real property.

Quieting title, etc.

Prima facie evidence of title ownership, §47B-2(d).

Prima facie evidence of title ownership, §47B-2(d).

Trusts and trustees.

Oral trusts.

Clear and convincing evidence to establish, §36C-4-407.

Tyrrell county.

Records from Tyrrell.

Copies of records, §8-23.

Undue influence.

Statements, releases, etc., obtained from persons in shock or under the influence of drugs.

Presumption of fraud, §8-45.5.

Unemployment compensation.

Disputed claims.

Compelling witnesses and evidence, administration of oaths, §96-4(k).

Employment security division.

Admissibility of findings, determinations, conclusions or judgments, §96-4(x).

Reproduction of records stored on permanent computer-readable media, §8-45.3(b).

United States.

Laws of United States.

Judicial notice of laws, §8-4.

University of North Carolina.

Mediation of personnel matters.

Inadmissible, §116-3.3(a).

Utilities commission hearings.

Affidavits, §62-68.

Depositions, §62-66.

Rules of evidence, §62-65(a).

Vacation rentals.

Expedited evictions, §42A-24(c).

Veterans' guardianship act.

Certificate as evidence in regard to guardianship of mentally incompetent wards, §34-7.

Certificate of director.

Prima facie evidence of necessity for appointment of guardian, §34-6.

Victim's character.

Evidence of pertinent trait, §8C-1 Rule 404(a).

Victims, impact of crime, §15A-833.

Victims of crime.

Return of stolen or personal property, §15A-825.

EVIDENCE —Cont'd
Videotape.
Substantive or illustrative evidence, §8-97.
Violent habitual felons.
Prior convictions, §14-7.10.
Vital statistics.
Certified copies of records.
Evidentiary effect, §130A-93(h).
Marriage certificates.
Copies as evidence, §130A-110(b).
Water and air resources.
Criminal penalties.
Enforcement procedures.
Use of circumstantial evidence,
§143-215.6B(c).
Judicial notice.
Commission.
Judicial notice of official studies, reports and
statistical data.
Authority as to, §143-215.4(d).
Weights and measures.
Regular use of devices.
Presumptive evidence, §81A-31.
Wills.
Affidavit of witnesses as evidence, §31-35.
Anson county.
Records of wills in Anson, §8-26.
Brunswick county.
Records of wills in Brunswick, §8-27.
Copies of wills, §8-28.
From other states, §8-32.
Lost wills, §98-5.
Proved and lost before recorded, §8-31.
Recording of wills.
Proved and lost before recorded, §8-31.
Wrong county, §8-30.
Secretary of state's office to contain copies,
§8-29.
Counties.
Copies of wills recorded in wrong county, §8-30.
Duplin county.
Records, §8-25.
Lost wills.
Copy of lost will, §98-5.
Recording of wills.
Lost before recorded.
Copy of will proved and lost before recorded,
§8-31.
Wrong county.
Copies of wills recorded in wrong county,
§8-30.
Witnesses.
Character and conduct of witnesses, §§8C-1 Rule
404(a), 8C-1 Rule 608.
Competency of witnesses.
See WITNESSES.
Expert witnesses.
See EXPERT WITNESSES.
General provisions, §§8-49 to 8-64.
See WITNESSES.
Proof of single material fact.
No more than two witnesses may be
subpoenaed, §6-60.
Wills.
Affidavit of witness as evidence, §31-35.
Workers' compensation.
Electronically transmitted or recorded documents,
§97-92(f).
Work first program.
Mismanagement of assistance, appointment of
personal representative.
Use of evidence in other proceedings prohibited,
§108A-37(d).

EVIDENCE —Cont'd
Writings.
Admissibility of other evidence of contents, §8C-1
Rule 1004.
Definitions, §8C-1 Rule 1001.
Documentary evidence. See within this heading,
"Documentary evidence."
Duplicates.
Admissibility, §8C-1 Rule 1003.
Functions of court and jury, §8C-1 Rule 1008.
Original.
Requirement of original, §8C-1 Rule 1002.
Probate of wills.
Proof and examination in writing, §28A-2A-6.
Summaries, §8C-1 Rule 1006.
Testimony or written admission of party, §8C-1
Rule 1007.
Wrongful death.
Dying declarations.
Admissibility, §28A-18-2(c).
X rays.
Photographs as substantive or illustrative
evidence, §8-97.

EXAMINATION QUESTION TAMPERING,
§14-401.1.

EXAMINATIONS.
Accountants.
Powers and duties of board as to, §93-12.
Qualifications of applicants, §93-12.
New requirements.
Effect, §93-12.1.
Alarm systems licensing.
Board may require, §74D-2(e).
Animal waste management system operators,
§90A-47.3(b).
Architects.
Licensing by examination, §83A-7(a).
Qualification requirements, §83A-7(a).
Bail bondsmen and runners.
Commissioner of insurance, §58-71-170.
Educational requirements for taking, §58-71-71(a).
Licenses, §58-71-70.
Fees, §58-71-70.
Bank examiners, §§53-117 to 53-123.
See BANK EXAMINERS.
Barbers.
Applications, §86A-8.
Apprenticeship, §86A-24(a).
Retaking.
Requirement, §86A-24(c).
Fees, §86A-25.
Payment required, §86A-8.
Frequency, §86A-9.
Instructors, §86A-23(a).
Applications for, §86A-23(b).
Qualifications for certificate of registration,
§86A-3.
Times and places, §86A-9.
Blind persons.
Eye examinations.
Aid to the blind.
Application for aid, §111-14.
Arranging for examination of eyes, §111-8.
Medical and surgical treatment, §111-8.
Bonds, surety.
Annual examination of official bonds, §58-72-20.
Cosmetic art.
Licensure, §88B-18.
Fees, §88B-20(a).

EXAMINATIONS —Cont'd

Credit unions.
Administrator of credit unions.
Duties, §54-109.11.
Annual examinations required, §54-109.16.
Costs.
Payment, §54-109.16.
Fees, §54-109.14(a).

Decedents' estates.
Persons or corporations believed to have
possession of property of decedent,
§28A-15-12.

Dental hygienists.
Credentials, license by, §90-224.1(a), (c), (d).
Fee, §90-232(b).
Notification of successful candidates.
Board to determine method and time,
§90-225(b).
Power of board to conduct examinations,
§90-223(a).
Rules and regulations of board as to, §90-224(b).

Dentists.
Licenses, §90-30(a).

Discovery methods, §1A-1 Rule 26(a).

Electrologists.
Certification of electrology instructors, §88A-17(b).
Failure to renew certificate, §88A-18.
Licenses, §88A-10(b).
Without examination, §88A-11.

Emergency medical services.
Credentialing requirements, §131E-159(a).
Waiver of examination, §131E-159(c), (d).

Engineers, §89C-15.
Power of board, §89C-10(d).
Reexamination, §89C-14(e).
Requirements for licensure generally, §89C-13.
Scope, §89C-15(b).
Time and place, §89C-15(a).

Food, drugs and cosmetics.
Conduct of examinations, §106-141(b).

Foresters.
Fees, §89B-12.
Registration, §89B-12.

Fraternal benefit societies, §58-24-135(a).
Agents, §58-24-160(a).

Geologists, §89E-10.
Confidentiality of results, §89E-14(c).
Qualifications for license, §89E-9.

Health maintenance organizations.
Powers of commissioner, §58-67-100(a).
Report in lieu of, §58-67-100(d).

Hearing aid dealers and fitters, §93D-8(a).
Scope, §93D-8(a).
Successfully passing examination required,
§93D-5(b).

Home inspectors.
Failure of examination.
Subsequent application.
Additional application fee not required,
§143-151.57(b).
Knowledge gained through experience to be
emphasized, §143-151.49(b).

Husband and wife.
Conveyances.
Certain conveyances not affected by fraud if
acknowledgment or privy examination
regular, §39-11.

Insurance commissioner generally.
See INSURANCE COMMISSIONER.

Irrigation contractors, §89G-6(b).

EXAMINATIONS —Cont'd

Laboratories.
State laboratory of public health, §130A-88(a).

Landscape contractors.
Certificates of registration, §89D-5(b).
Exemptions, §§89D-8, 89D-9.

Marriage and family therapists, §90-270.55.
Licensing requirement, §90-270.54(a).
Marriage and family therapy associates,
§90-270.54A(a).

Married women.
Certificate of wife's "previous" examination,
§47-66.
Repeal of laws requiring private examination,
§47-14.1.

Massage and bodywork therapy.
Licensure, §90-629.

Medical examiners.
Postmortem medicolegal examinations and
services, §§130A-377 to 130A-395.
See MEDICAL EXAMINERS.

Medical malpractice.
Arbitration of negligent health claims,
§90-21.63(c).

**Mental health, developmental disabilities and
substance abuse.**
Involuntary commitment, §122C-263.

Notaries.
Requirement for commission, §10B-8.

Nurses.
Follow-up assistance.
Nursing licensing exam follow-up assistance,
§90-171.52.
Frequency, §90-171.30.
Generally, §90-171.30.
Licensure by examination, §90-171.30.
Notice, §90-171.30.
Qualifications of applicant, §90-171.29.
Reexamination, §90-171.31.

Occupational licensing board.
Disclosure of questions or answers.
Restrictions, §93B-8(d).
Failure to pass.
Review of examination, §93B-8(c).
Identification of applicants by number only,
§93B-8(b).
Written examinations, §93B-8(a).

Opticians.
Fee, §90-246.
Frequency, §90-240(c).
National examinations.
Board may include, §90-240(e).
Notice, §90-240(c).
Qualifications for taking examination, §90-240(a).
Scope, §90-240(b).
Scores.
Applicant may receive upon request, §90-240(d).
Waiver of examination requirements, §90-241(a),
(b).
Application, §90-241(c).

Physical and mental examination of persons,
§1A-1 Rule 26(a).
Order for examination, §1A-1 Rule 35(a).
Report of examining physician, §1A-1 Rule 35(b).

Physician and surgeon licenses.
Accepted examinations for licensure, §90-10.1.
Rules and regulations governing, §90-8.1.

Podiatrists.
Clinical residency requirements, §90-202.5(a).
Failure to pass.
Reexamination, §90-202.6(c).

EXAMINATIONS —Cont'd
Podiatrists —Cont'd
Fee, §§90-202.5(a), 90-202.9.
   Reexamination, §90-202.6(c).
Frequency, §90-202.6(a).
Postgraduate clinical program requirements,
   §90-202.5(a).
Qualifications of applicants, §90-202.5(a).
Reexamination, §90-202.6(c).
Scope, §90-202.6(a).
Waiver of examination, §90-202.6(b).
Postmortem medicolegal examinations and
   services, §§130A-377 to 130A-395.
   See MEDICAL EXAMINERS.
Provider sponsored organizations, §131E-296.
Racketeer influenced and corrupt
   organizations.
False testimony, §75D-7.
Power to compel examination, §75D-6.
Real estate brokers.
Licenses, §93A-4(b).
Records.
Public records, §132-6.
Refrigeration contractors, §87-58(d).
Fees, §87-64.
Licenses granted without examination, §87-58(f).
Retirement system for teachers and state
   employees.
Consolidated judicial retirement act.
   Disability retirement benefits.
      Medical examination required, §135-60(b).
Sales and use tax.
Examination of records, §105-164.30.
Savings and loan associations.
See SAVINGS AND LOAN ASSOCIATIONS.
Savings banks.
Administrator of savings institution division,
   §54C-54(a).
Confidentiality of information, §54C-60.
Costs.
   Extended audit, examination or reevaluation,
      §54C-56(b).
   Payment when person not employed by
      administrator's office appointed to make,
      §54C-55(c).
Extended audit, examination or reevaluation,
   §54C-56(a).
   Payment of expenses, §54C-56(b).
Fees, §54C-55(a), (b).
Powers in connection with examinations.
   Misdemeanors, §54C-54(c), (d).
   Report, §54C-54(a), (b).
Service corporations, §54C-144(c).
Soil scientists.
Licenses, §89F-11.
   Passing examination as qualification,
      §89F-10(a).
Speech and language pathologists and
   audiologists, §§90-295, 90-296.
American Speech and Hearing Association.
   Certificate of clinical competence.
      Examination not required of person who holds
         certificate, §90-296(c).
Fee, §90-305.
Frequency, §90-296(b).
Required, §90-296(a).
   Exceptions, §90-296(c).
State departments and agencies.
Special investigations, §143-158.
   Conduct, §143-160.
   Stenographic record of proceedings, §143-161.

EXAMINATIONS —Cont'd
State departments and agencies —Cont'd
Special investigations —Cont'd
   Subjects, §143-159.
Statewide testing program, §§115C-174.10 to
   115C-174.14.
   See SCHOOLS AND EDUCATION.
Structural pest control.
Applicants for certified applicator's identification
   card, §106-65.27.
Substance abuse professionals, §90-113.41.
Applications, §90-113.41(a).
Criteria for examinations, §90-113.41(b).
Obtaining and reviewing scores, §90-113.41(d).
Time and place, §90-113.41(c).
Tampering with examination questions a
   misdemeanor, §14-401.1.
Teachers.
Licensure requirements, §115C-296(a), (a1).
Torrens system registration.
Title, §43-11(d).
Trust companies.
Conservatorship.
   Oversight by commissioner, §53-402.
Foreign offices, §53-326(a).
Out-of-state institutions, offices, §53-320(a).
Voluntary dissolution, §53-375.
Unit ownership.
Availability of records for examinations, §47A-20.
Veterinarians.
Applications.
   Time for, §90-187.1.
Frequency, §90-187.1.
Licensure without examination, §§90-187.3(a), (b),
   90-187(d).
   Oral or practical examination of person
      qualifying, §90-187.3(c).
Notification of results, §90-187.1.
Viatical life insurance settlements.
Conducted in accordance with examination law,
   §58-58-230(b).
Examiners and costs of examiners, §58-58-230(d).
Foreign or alien persons, §58-58-230(c).
Frequency of examination by commissioner,
   §58-58-230(a).
Wastewater treatment plant operators, §90A-39.

EXAMINERS OF BANKS, §§53-117 to 53-123.
See BANK EXAMINERS.

EXCAVATION.
Construction indemnity agreements invalid,
   §22B-1.
Subcontractors, payments to, §§22C-1 to 22C-6.
Underground damage prevention, §§87-100 to
   87-114.
   See UNDERGROUND DAMAGE PREVENTION.

EXCEPTIONS FOR INSUFFICIENCY, §1A-1
   Rule 7(c).

EXCEPTIONS TO DECISIONS OF COURT,
   §1-186.

EXCEPTIONS TO RULINGS ON EVIDENCE,
   §1A-1 Rule 46(a), (b).

EXCISE STAMP TAX ON CONVEYANCES,
   §§105-228.28 to 105-228.37.
Actions.
Taxes recoverable by action, §105-228.33.
Administrative provisions.
Applicability, §105-228.35.

EXCISE STAMP TAX ON CONVEYANCES
—Cont'd
Applicability of provisions, §§105-228.28, 105-228.35.
Collection of tax before instrument recorded, §105-228.32.
Consideration not due or paid, exempted transfer, §105-228.29.
County registers of deeds.
Remittance of net proceeds to county finance officer, §105-228.30(b).
Exempted transfers, §105-228.29.
Failure to pay tax.
Recovery of tax by action, §105-228.33.
Gift, transfer by exempted, §105-228.29.
Imposition of tax, §105-228.30(a).
Intestacy, transfer by exempted, §105-228.29.
Lease for term of years, exempted transfer, §105-228.29.
Marking instrument indicating tax paid.
Before recording of instrument, §105-228.32.
Merger, conversion, consolidation, exempted transfer, §105-228.29.
Operation of law, transfers by, exemption, §105-228.29.
Overpayment.
Refund, §105-228.37.
Payment of tax.
County finance officer.
Who to pay, §105-228.30(b).
Recovery of tax by action, §105-228.33.
Who to pay, §105-228.30(b).
Rate of tax, §105-228.30(a).
Recovery of unpaid taxes by action, §105-228.33.
Refund of overpayment.
Assessment of taxpayer for amount, §105-228.37(c).
Correct deed recorded before tax refunded, §105-228.37(e).
Denial of request.
Departmental review, §105-228.37(d).
Filing request, time, §105-228.37(a).
Hearing on request by county commissioners.
Notice, time for holding, decision, §105-228.37(b).
Interest on overpayment, §105-228.37(f).
Refund with interest, §105-228.37(c).
Remittance of net proceeds, §105-228.30(b).
Report of amount of tax due.
Presentation for registration, §105-228.32.
Securing indebtedness, instrument exempted, §105-228.29.
Wills, transfers by, exempted, §105-228.29.

EXCISE TAXES.
Dry-cleaning solvent tax, §§105-187.30 to 105-187.35.
Piped natural gas tax, §§105-187.40 to 105-187.46.
See PIPED NATURAL GAS TAX.
Solid waste disposal tax, §§105-187.60 to 105-187.63.
Use of proceeds, §130A-295.9.

EXCITED UTTERANCE, §8C-1 Rule 803.

EXCLUDED EVIDENCE OR TESTIMONY RECORD, §1A-1 Rule 43(c).

EXCLUSIONARY RULE.
Judicial standards commission.
Failure to disclose, JudStdsComm Rule 15.

EXCLUSIONARY RULE —Cont'd
Motion to suppress evidence, §§15A-971 to 15A-980.

EXCLUSION OF WITNESSES, §8C-1 Rule 615.

EXCLUSIVE OUTLETS.
Alcoholic beverage manufacturers, bottlers or wholesalers.
Acquiring prohibited, §18B-1116.

EXCUSABLE NEGLECT.
Enlargement of time, §§1-593, 1A-1 Rule 6(b).
Paternity.
Setting aside orders of paternity, §49-4(h).
Relief from judgment or order, §1A-1 Rule 60(b).
Small claims actions.
Setting aside order or judgment, §7A-228(a).

EXECUTION OF POWER OF APPOINTMENT BY WILL, §31-4.

EXECUTION OF WILLS.
Attestation, §31-3.3.
Compliance required, §31-3.1.
Establishment of due execution, §28A-2A-8(b).
Holographic will, §31-3.4(a), (b).
Nuncupative, §31-3.5.
Power of appointment, §31-4.
Revival of revoked will, §31-5.8.
Seal not required, §31-3.6.
Self-proved will, §31-11.6.
Signature of testator, §31-3.3(b), (c).
Who may make, §31-1.

EXECUTIONS, §§1-302 to 1-368.
Absconders.
Debtor leaving state or concealing self.
Arrest, §1-355.
Against property, §1-303.
Forms, §1-313.
Against the person, §§1-303, 1-311.
Findings of fact required, §1-311.
Form, §1-313.
Indigent defendants.
Appointment of counsel, §1-311.
Contents of execution, §1-313.
Alimony.
Time limitation for enforcing execution not to apply, §1-306.
Alimony, remedies available, §50-16.7(k).
Appeals.
Procedure after determination, §1-298.
Arrest.
Debtor leaving state or concealing self, §1-355.
Assets of judgment debtor.
Discovery.
Generally, §1-352.2.
Interrogatories, §1-352.1.
Unsatisfied execution.
Debtor ordered to answer concerning his property, §1-352.
Withholding of property from execution.
Proceedings for application of property, §1-353.
Attachment.
See ATTACHMENT.
Attorney general.
Execution sales.
Notification of attorney general, §1-339.55.
Attorneys at law.
Execution against the person.
Indigent defendants.
Appointment of counsel, §1-311.

EXECUTIONS —Cont'd

Bail bond forfeiture.
Final judgment, §15A-544.7(c), (d).

Bank deposits and collections.
When item subject to legal process, §25-4-303(a).

Betterments.
Suspension of execution for assessment, §1-340.

Bills of lading.
Lien on goods covered by a negotiable document, §25-7-602.

Blind persons.
Aid to the blind.
Payment of awards.
Exemption from execution, §111-18.

Bona fide purchasers.
Execution against property of judgment debtor not lien on personal property as against, §1-313.

Bonds, surety.
Amount of bond, determination, §1-289(a2).
Debtor leaving state or concealing self, §1-355.
Execution sales.
Special proceedings to determine ownership of surplus.
Transfer of proceedings to civil issue docket of superior court, §1-339.71(c).
Upset bid on real property.
Compliance bond, §1-339.64(b).
Forthcoming bond for personal property.
Generally, §1-318.
Procedure on giving bond, §1-319.
Subsequent levies, §1-319.
Summary remedy on bond, §1-320.
Staying personal property, §1-290.
Stay in judgment for real property, §1-292.
Stay of execution on money judgment, §1-289(a).
Cap on amount, noncompensatory damages of $25,000,000 or more awarded, §1-289(b), (c).

Breaking and entering.
When executing officer may break and enter premises or vehicle, §15A-251.

Child support.
Enforcement of support, §50-13.4(f).

Choses in action.
Execution sales.
Property liable to sale under execution, §1-315(a).

Clerks of court.
Directing execution to clerk in counties which office of coroner abolished, §1-313.
Execution sales.
Procedural details.
Authority to fix, §1-339.42.
Issuance.
Duties, §1-305(a).
Time for, §1-305(a).
Violations of provisions.
Penalty, §1-305(a).
When clerk may not issue, §1-305(b).
Returns.
Entry on judgment docket, §1-321.
Violations of provisions.
Penalty, §1-321.
Subscribed by clerk, §1-303.

Commercial code.
Bank deposits and collections.
When items subject to legal process, §25-4-303(a).
Documents of title.
Lien on goods covered by a negotiable document, §25-7-602.

EXECUTIONS —Cont'd

Confession of judgment.
Issuance and enforcement, §1A-1 Rule 68.1(e).

Contempt.
Debtor leaving state or concealing self, §1-355.
Discovery of assets of judgment debtor.
Disobedience of orders of court, §§1-352.1, 1-352.2.
Interrogatories to discover assets.
Disobedience of order of court, §1-352.1.
Orders of court.
Disobedience, §1-368.

Contents, §1-313.

Conveyance directed by judgment.
Stay, §1-291.

Coroners.
Directed to coroner where sheriff is party or interested in action, §1-313.

Corporations.
Agents of corporations.
Duties, §§1-324.2 to 1-324.4.
Penalty for violations, §1-324.5.
Books and records.
Nonresident custodian, §§1-324.6, 1-324.7.
Debts due corporations.
Subject to execution, §1-324.4.
Information as to corporate officers and property.
Duty of agents to furnish, §1-324.2.
Information as to corporate shares.
Duty of agents to furnish, §1-324.3.
Information as to debts due corporation.
Duty of agents to furnish, §1-324.4.
Judgment against corporation.
Property subject to execution, §1-324.1.
Nonresident custodian of corporate books.
Duties, §1-324.7.
Liability, §1-324.7.
Notice to, §1-324.6.
Proceedings, §1-324.6.
Shares subject to execution, §1-324.3.

Costs.
Issuance of execution for unpaid costs, §6-4.
Livestock.
Cost of keeping.
Officer's account, §1-322.

Crime victims compensation.
Award not subject to, §15B-17(b).

Criminal law and procedure.
Supplemental proceedings.
Examination of parties and witnesses.
Incriminating answers not to be used in criminal proceedings, §1-357.

Crops.
Execution not to be levied on growing crops until matured, §1-315(c).

Dating.
When dated, §1-310.

Death of defendant in execution.
Rights against property of defendant, §1-312.

Debtors and creditors.
Debtor leaving state or concealing self.
Bonds, surety, §1-355.
Debtors of judgment debtor.
Execution on property of debtors, §1-360.1.
Receivers.
Actions by receiver against, §1-366.
Satisfaction of execution, §1-359.
Summoning, §1-360.
Rights against property of defendant dying in execution, §1-312.

EXECUTIONS —Cont'd
Decedents' estates.
Defendant dying in execution.
Rights against property of defendant, §1-312.
Defective title.
Remedy of purchaser against defendant, §1-323.
Definitions.
Execution sales, §1-339.41(a).
Delivery of possession of real or personal property, §1-303.
Form of execution, §1-313.
Discovery.
Assets of judgment debtor.
Generally, §1-352.2.
Interrogatories, §1-352.1.
Docket entry of stay, §1-293.
Dockets.
County to which execution to be issued.
Docketing in as prerequisite to issuance, §1-308.
Returns.
Entry on judgment docket, §1-321.
Documents of title.
Lien on goods covered by a negotiable document, §25-7-602.
Enforcement as of course, §1-306.
Enforcement of judgments by execution, §1-302.
Secreting property to hinder enforcement of lien after judgment, §14-115.
Equity of redemption.
Execution sales.
Sheriff's deed on sale of equity of redemption, §1-317.
Estates.
Execution sales.
Trust estates.
Title of purchaser, §1-316.
Execution sales, §§1-339.41 to 1-339.71.
See EXECUTION SALES.
Executors and administrators.
Action by creditors.
When execution to issue, §28A-18-5.
Defendant dying in execution.
Rights against property of defendant, §1-312.
Form of execution against property in hands of personal representative, §1-313.
Successors in office, §28A-18-7.
Exemptions.
Limitation of wage garnishment, §1-362.
Mechanics' and materialmen's liens.
Inapplicability of exemption, NC Const Art X §3.
Property from creditors' claims.
See EXEMPTION OF PROPERTY FROM CREDITOR CLAIMS.
Fee of magistrate for proof of execution, §7A-309.
Fines.
Docketed judgments for fines, §15A-1365.
Payment as authorized condition of parole, §15A-1374(b).
Forfeiture of bonds in criminal cases.
When execution to issue, §1-305(a).
Forms, §1-313.
Garnishment.
Generally.
See GARNISHMENT.
Issuance of execution against garnishee, §1-440.32(a).
Bonds, surety.
Garnishee retaining possession, §1-440.32(b).

EXECUTIONS —Cont'd
Governor.
Execution sales.
Notification of governor, §1-339.55.
Habeas corpus.
Party held in execution not to be discharged, §17-36.
Homestead exemptions.
Generally.
See HOMESTEAD EXEMPTIONS.
Time limitation not to apply to enforcing lien of judgment upon, §1-306.
Housing authorities and projects.
Exemptions of property from execution, §157-21.
Husband and wife.
Married women.
Levy and collection from separate property, §1-304.
Indigent persons.
Execution against the person.
Appointment of counsel, §1-311.
Entitlement to services of counsel, §7A-451(a).
Contents of execution, §1-313.
Injunctions.
Execution sales.
Dissolution of order restraining or enjoining sale.
Procedure upon, §1-339.59(a), (b).
Insurance.
Life insurance.
Group insurance.
Exemptions from execution, §58-58-165.
Supervision, rehabilitation and liquidation of insurers.
Levy of execution prohibited during pendency of liquidation proceeding, §58-30-295.
Interrogatories.
Discovery of assets of judgment debtor, §1-352.1.
Issuance.
Clerks of court.
Duties, failure to issue, when not to issue, §1-305(a), (b).
Court of rendition.
Issuance from, §1-307.
Time limits, §1-306.
To what counties issued, §1-308.
Joint debtors.
Supplemental proceedings against, §1-354.
Judgment directing payment of money.
Appeal bond, stay, §1-289(a).
Amount of bond, determination, §1-289(a2).
Cap on amount, noncompensatory damages of $25,000,000 or more, §1-289(b), (c).
Judicial sales.
See JUDICIAL SALES.
Kinds of executions, §1-303.
Laborers' liens.
Exemptions from process.
Inapplicability, NC Const Art X §3.
Landlord and tenant.
Lien on crops.
Tenant's crop not subject to execution against landlord, §42-21.
Leasehold estates.
Liability to sale under execution, §1-315(a).
Liens.
Execution sales.
Real property.
Property remains subject to liens, §1-339.68(b).

EXECUTIONS —Cont'd

Liens —Cont'd

Mechanics, laborers and materialmen dealing with owner.

Sale of property in satisfaction of judgment. Execution sale, §44A-14(a).

Secreting property to hinder enforcement after judgment, §14-115.

Limitation of actions.

Issuance of executions requiring payment of money or recovery of personal property, §1-306.

Livestock.

Cost of keeping.

Officer's account, §1-322.

Local governmental employees' retirement system.

Exemptions from execution, §128-31.

Married women.

Execution against, §1-304.

Money.

Execution sales.

Sale to be made for cash, §1-339.47.

Judgment for payment of money.

Enforcement by execution, §1-302.

Time limit on issuance of execution, §1-306.

Nonresidents.

Corporations.

Nonresident custodian of corporate books, §§1-324.6, 1-324.7.

Orders of court.

Contempt.

Disobedience of orders, §1-368.

Debtors of judgment debtor.

Summoning, §1-360.

Discovery of assets, §§1-352.1, 1-352.2.

Disposition of property.

Order forbidden, §1-358.

Property withheld from execution.

Application of property, §1-353.

Receivers.

Appointment, §§1-363 to 1-365.

Sale of debtor's property, §1-362.

Unsatisfied execution.

Order for debtor to answer, §1-352.

Where proceedings instituted and defendant examined, §1-361.

Parties.

Supplemental proceedings.

Contempt.

Disobedience of orders, §1-368.

Examination of parties and witnesses, §1-356.

Incriminating answers not privileged, §1-357.

Partition.

Right of judgment creditor to sue execution on judgment, §46-5.

Penalties.

Clerks of court.

Issuance.

Violations of provisions, §1-305(a).

Corporations.

Agents.

Violations of duties, §1-324.5.

Execution sales.

Sheriffs.

Return of no sale for want of bidders.

Failure to make required statement, §1-339.50.

Selling contrary to law, §1-339.49.

Returns.

Entry on judgment docket.

Violations of provisions by clerk, §1-321.

EXECUTIONS —Cont'd

Person.

Execution against person, §1-303.

Personal property.

Bonds, surety.

Forthcoming bond for personal property, §§1-318 to 1-320.

Execution for delivery of possession of personal property, §1-303.

Execution sales.

Bids.

Defaulting bidder, §1-339.69(a).

Bill of sale, §1-339.62.

Defective title.

Remedy of purchaser against defendant, §1-323.

Delivery of property, §1-339.62.

Description of property.

Notice of sale to contain, §1-339.51.

Report of sale to contain, §1-339.63(b).

Exemptions from process, NC Const Art X §1.

Notice of sale.

Posting, §1-339.53.

Place of sale, §1-339.44(c).

Posting of notice, §1-339.53.

Presence of property at sale required, §1-339.45.

Property liable to sale under execution, §1-315(a).

Judgment for delivery of personal property.

Enforcement by execution, §1-302.

Time limit on issuance of execution, §1-306.

Stay of judgment, §1-290.

Prisons and prisoners.

Debtor and creditor.

Discharge of insolvent prisoners.

Persons taken in execution, §23-29.

Property of debtor of judgment debtor, §1-360.1.

Property of judgment debtor, §1-303.

Purchase money of land.

Form of execution, §1-313.

Real property.

Execution for delivery of possession of real property, §1-303.

Execution sales, §1-309.

Bids.

Defaulting bidder, §1-339.69(b).

Confirmation of sale, §1-339.67.

Deed, §1-339.68(a).

Defective title.

Remedy of purchaser against defendant, §1-323.

Description of property.

Notice of sale to contain, §1-339.51.

Report of sale to contain, §1-339.63(b).

Liens.

Property remains subject to, §1-339.68(b).

Notice of sale.

Judgment debtor, §1-339.54.

Posting, §1-339.52(a), (c).

Publication, §1-339.52(a) to (c).

Orders for possession, §1-339.68(c), (d).

Place of sale, §1-339.44(a), (b).

Posting of notice, §1-339.52(a), (c).

Property liable to sale under execution, §1-315(a).

Sale as a whole or in parts, §1-339.46.

Judgment for delivery of real property.

Enforcement by execution, §1-302.

Stays, §1-292.

EXECUTIONS —Cont'd
Receivers.
Actions.
Receiver to sue debtors of judgment debtor, §1-366.
Appointment, §1-363.
Filing, §1-364.
Record, §1-364.
Where order of appointment recorded, §1-365.
Debtors of judgment debtor.
Actions by receiver against, §1-366.
Title.
Vesting of property in receiver, §1-364.
Reports.
Execution sales.
Contents, §1-339.63(b).
Required, §1-339.63(a).
Retirement system for teachers and state employees.
Exemption from execution, §135-9.
Return.
Clerks of superior court.
Return to clerk, §1-210.
Court of rendition.
Return to, §1-307.
Judgment docket.
Entry of returns on, §1-321.
No sale for want of bidders, §1-339.50.
Unsatisfied execution.
Order for debtor to answer, §1-352.
Proceedings against joint debtors, §1-354.
When returnable, §1-310.
Sales.
Execution sales, §§1-339.41 to 1-339.71.
See EXECUTION SALES.
Judicial sales, §§1-339.1 to 1-339.40.
See JUDICIAL SALES.
Seals and sealed instruments.
Executions running out of county.
Seal of court required, §1-303.
Self-incrimination.
Supplemental proceedings.
Examination of parties and witnesses.
Incriminating answers not privileged, §1-357.
Service of process.
Discovery of assets of judgment debtor.
Interrogatories, §1-352.1.
Notice of motion, §1-352.2.
Interrogatories to discover assets, §1-352.1.
Shares of stock.
Corporate shares subject to execution, §1-324.3.
Sheriffs.
Conflicts of interest.
Directed to coroner where sheriff interested in action, §1-313.
Costs.
Levy of execution for unpaid costs, §6-4.
County where judgment docketed.
Issuance to sheriff of such county, §1-308.
Directed to sheriff, §1-313.
Execution sales.
See EXECUTION SALES.
Forthcoming bond for personal property, §§1-318 to 1-320.
Livestock.
Cost of keeping.
Officer's account, §1-322.
Payment of money collected on execution, §162-18.
Return of execution.
Clerk of superior court, §1-210.
Small claims actions, §7A-225.

EXECUTIONS —Cont'd
Stays, §1A-1 Rule 62.
Docket entry, §1-293.
Execution on money judgment.
Amount of bond, determination, §1-289(a2).
Appeal bond, §1-289(a).
Cap on amount, noncompensatory damages of $25,000,000 or more awarded, §1-289(b), (c).
Judgment directing conveyance, §1-291.
Judgment for real property, §1-292.
Personal property judgment, §1-290.
Sundays.
Execution sales.
Holding on Sunday prohibited, §1-339.43.
Superior court clerks, §1-210.
Supplemental proceedings.
Contempt.
Disobedience of orders, §1-368.
Debtor leaving state or concealing self, §1-355.
Debtors of judgment debtor.
Satisfaction of execution, §1-359.
Summoning, §1-360.
Discovery of assets.
Generally, §1-352.2.
Interrogatories, §1-352.1.
Disposition of property.
Order forbidden, §1-358.
Examination of parties and witnesses, §1-356.
Incriminating answers not privileged, §1-357.
Inspection and copying of designated documents, papers, books, etc., of judgment debtor, §1-352.2.
Joint debtors.
Proceedings against, §1-354.
Parties.
Contempt.
Disobedience of orders, §1-368.
Examination, §1-356.
Incriminating answers not privileged, §1-357.
Receivers, §§1-363 to 1-366.
Referees.
Appointment, §1-367.
Examination of parties and witnesses, §1-356.
Reference to, §1-367.
Sale of debtor's property, §1-362.
Statute of limitations.
Additional method of discovering assets, §1-352.2.
Unsatisfied execution.
Debtor ordered to answer, §1-352.
Proceedings against joint debtors, §1-354.
Where proceedings instituted and defendant examined, §1-361.
Witnesses.
Contempt.
Disobedience of orders, §1-368.
Examination, §1-356.
Incriminating answers not privileged, §1-357.
Suretyship.
Principal and surety distinguished in judgment and execution, §26-1.
Principal liable on execution before surety, §26-2.
Stay of execution.
Dissenting surety not liable to surety on stay of execution, §26-6.
Surviving spouses.
Exemption from execution, §30-15.
Taxation.
Collection of taxes, §105-242(a).

EXECUTIONS —Cont'd
Torrens system registration.
Conveyance as security for debts.
Sale under lien, §43-36(f).
Trust estate sales, §1-316.
Unincorporated associations, organizations or societies, §1-69.1(b).
Findings of fact, §1-69.1(a).
Variance between judgment and execution.
Effect, §1-314.
Venue.
Against the person, §1-311.
Sale of land under execution, §1-309.
To what counties issued, §1-308.
Where proceedings instituted and defendant examined, §1-361.
Warehouse receipts.
Lien on goods covered by a negotiable document, §25-7-602.
Witnesses.
Supplemental proceedings.
Contempt.
Disobedience of orders, §1-368.
Examination of parties and witnesses, §1-356.
Incriminating answers not privileged, §1-357.
Year's allowance.
Assignment in superior court.
Judgment and order for commissioners.
Execution to enforce judgment, §30-31.2.

EXECUTIONS AGAINST THE PERSON,
§§1-303, 1-311.
Form, §1-313.

EXECUTION SALES, §§1-339.41 to 1-339.71.
Alimony, remedies available, §50-16.7(k).
Attorneys' fees.
Special proceeding to determine ownership of surplus, §1-339.71(d).
Bill of sale, §1-315(b).
Bonds, surety.
Special proceedings to determine ownership of surplus.
Transfer of proceedings to civil issue docket of superior court, §1-339.71(c).
Upset bid on real property.
Compliance bond, §1-339.64(b).
Cash.
Sale to be made for cash, §1-339.47.
Clerks of court.
Procedural details.
Authority to fix, §1-339.42.
Commencement.
Time for, §1-339.60(a), (b).
When sale commenced, §1-339.48.
Confirmation.
Sale of real property, §1-339.67.
Validation.
Certain sales confirmed prior to time prescribed by law, §1-339.77.
Continuance of sale, §1-339.60(c).
Uncompleted sale, §1-339.61.
Validation of certain sales continued beyond time prescribed by law, §1-339.75.
Days on which sale may be held, §1-339.43.
Validation of sales held on other days, §§1-339.73, 1-339.74.
Defaulting bidder.
Liability on bid, §1-339.69(c).
Other remedies against defaulting bidders unimpaired, §1-339.69(d).
Personal property, §1-339.69(a).

EXECUTION SALES —Cont'd
Defaulting bidder —Cont'd
Real property, §1-339.69(b).
Defective title.
Remedy of purchaser against defendant, §1-323.
Deferred payments.
More than two years.
Validation of sale, §1-339.76.
Definitions, §1-339.41(a), (b).
Equity of redemption.
Sheriff's deed on sale, §1-317.
Exemptions.
Mechanics' and materialmen's liens, NC Const Art X §3.
Fees.
Uniform civil process fees, §7A-311(a).
Homestead exemption, NC Const Art X §§2, 3.
Injunctions.
Dissolution of order restraining or enjoining sale.
Procedure upon, §1-339.59(a), (b).
Leasehold estates.
Liability to sale under execution, §1-315(a).
Liens.
Real property remains subject to liens, §1-339.68(b).
Motor vehicles, §20-77.
Notice.
Attorney general, §1-339.55.
Contents of notice of sale, §1-339.51.
Exception as to perishable property, §1-339.56.
Governor.
Notice to, §1-339.55.
Judgment debtor of sale of real property, §1-339.54.
Posting and publishing sale of real property, §1-339.52(a) to (c).
Posting sale of personal property, §1-339.53.
Postponement of sale, §1-339.58(b), (c).
Real property.
Judgment debtor.
Notice to, §1-339.54.
Validation of certain sales as to publication of notice, §1-339.72.
Payment deferred more than two years.
Validation of sale, §1-339.76.
Payment of judgment.
Application of proceeds to, §1-339.70(b).
Penalties.
Sheriffs.
Return of no sale for want of bidders.
Failure to make required statement, §1-339.50.
Selling contrary to law, §1-339.49.
Perishable property, §1-339.56.
Personal property.
Bids.
Defaulting bidder, §1-339.69(a).
Bill of sale, §1-339.62.
Defective title.
Remedy of purchaser against defendant, §1-323.
Delivery of property, §1-339.62.
Description of property.
Notice of sale to contain, §1-339.51.
Report of sale to contain, §1-339.63(b).
Exemptions from process, NC Const Art X §1.
Notice of sale.
Posting, §1-339.53.
Place of sale, §1-339.44(c).
Posting of notice, §1-339.53.
Presence of property at sale required, §1-339.45.
Property liable to sale under execution, §1-315(a).

EXECUTION SALES —Cont'd

Place of sale, §1-339.44.

Posting and publishing notice.

Exception as to perishable property, §1-339.56.

Sale of personal property, §1-339.53.

Sale of real property, §1-339.52(a) to (c).

Posting in area designated by clerk, §1-339.32(a).

Property situated in more than one county, §1-339.32(c).

Publishing in newspaper, §1-339.32(a), (b).

Postponement.

Grounds, §1-339.58(a).

Notice, §1-339.58(b), (c).

Proceeds.

Disposition, §1-339.70(a) to (c).

Surplus.

Disposition, §1-339.70(c).

Special proceedings to determine ownership of surplus, §1-339.71(a) to (d).

Property liable to sale under execution, §1-315(a).

Real property.

Confirmation, §1-339.67.

Deed, §1-339.68(a).

Defaulting bidder, §1-339.69.

Failure of bidder to comply with bid, §1-339.69.

Liens effective prior to lien of judgment property sold remains subject to, §1-339.68(b).

Notice of sale.

Notice to judgment debtor, §1-339.54.

Posting and publishing, §1-339.52(a) to (c).

Order for possession, §1-339.68(c).

Resale.

Failure of bidder to comply with bid, §1-339.69.

Upset bid on real property, §1-339.64(a).

Binding terms of original notice, §1-339.64(h).

Compliance bonds, §1-339.64(b).

Notice, §1-339.64(e), (f).

Orders of clerk of court, §1-339.64(i).

Release of last bidder, §1-339.64(g).

Resale order, §1-339.66A.

Separate upset bids when real property sold in parts, §1-339.65.

Receipt for proceeds.

Clerk to furnish sheriff, §1-339.70(a).

Reports.

Contents, §1-339.63(b).

Required, §1-339.63(a).

Residential property disclosure act.

Applicability of act, §47E-2.

Return of no sale for want of bidders, §1-339.50.

Satisfaction of judgment before sale completed, §1-339.57.

Secured transactions.

Default.

Effect, §25-9-601(e).

Sheriffs.

Defined, §1-339.41(b).

Equity of redemption.

Sheriff's deed on sale, §1-317.

Fees.

Uniform civil process fees, §7A-311(a).

Penalties.

Return of no sale for want of bidders.

Failure to make required statement, §1-339.50.

Selling contrary to law, §1-339.49.

Real property, §1-309.

EXECUTION SALES —Cont'd

Special proceeding to determine ownership of surplus.

Attorneys' fees, §1-339.71(d).

Defendants in proceeding, §1-339.71(b).

Instituted by person claiming money, §1-339.71(a).

Transfer of proceeding to civil case docket.

Issues of fact as to ownership, §1-339.71(c).

Sundays.

Sale may not be held on Sunday, §1-339.43.

Supplemental proceedings.

Debtor's property ordered sold, §1-362.

Time for sale, §1-339.60.

Commencement of sale, §1-339.60(a), (b).

Continuance of sale, §§1-339.60(c), 1-339.61.

Failure to hold sale by time fixed, §1-339.58(d).

Trust estates.

Title of purchaser, §1-316.

Upset bid.

Binding terms of original notice, §1-339.64(h).

Bonds, surety.

Compliance bond, §1-339.64(b).

Generally, §1-339.64(a).

Notice, §1-339.64(e), (f).

Orders of clerk of court, §1-339.64(i).

Release of last prior bidder, §1-339.64(g).

Resale order, §1-339.66A.

Separate upset bids when real property sold in parts, §1-339.65.

Validation.

Confirmation of sales prior to time prescribed by law, §1-339.77.

Continuation of sale for longer period than prescribed by law, §1-339.75.

Notice.

Validation of certain sales as to publication of notice, §1-339.72.

Payment deferred more than two years, §1-339.76.

Payment deferred over two years, §1-339.76.

Sales held on days other than day required by statute, §§1-339.73, 1-339.74.

Variance between judgment and execution.

Title of purchaser not invalidated, §1-314.

Venue.

Place of sale, §1-339.44.

When sale may be held, §1-339.43.

EXECUTIVE BUDGET ACT.

See BUDGETS.

EXECUTIVE MANSION.

Carrying deadly weapons in.

Prohibition, §14-269.4.

Department of cultural resources.

Authority of administration department not affected, §143-415.

Powers of department, §143-411.

Purposes, §143-410.

Secretary.

Executive mansion fine arts committee.

Committee to give aid and advice, §143B-79.

Fine arts committee, §§143B-79, 143B-80.

See EXECUTIVE MANSION FINE ARTS COMMITTEE.

EXECUTIVE MANSION FINE ARTS COMMITTEE.

Appointments, §143B-80.

Compensation of members, §143B-80.

Creation, §143B-79.

Department of cultural resources.

Transfer of commission to department, §143B-51.

EXECUTIVE MANSION FINE ARTS COMMITTEE —Cont'd

Duties, §143B-79.
Members, §143B-80.
Powers and duties, §143B-79.
Quorum, §143B-80.
Selection of members, §143B-80.

EXECUTIVE ORGANIZATION ACT OF 1971.
State departments and agencies.
See STATE DEPARTMENTS AND AGENCIES.

EXECUTIVE ORGANIZATION ACT OF 1973.
State departments and agencies.
See STATE DEPARTMENTS AND AGENCIES.

EXECUTORS AND ADMINISTRATORS.
Abatement, revival and survival of actions.
Death before limitation expires.
Action by or against personal representative or collector, §1-22.
Presentation of claims.
Substitution of personal representative to constitute, §28A-19-1(c).
Rights of action not surviving decedent, §28A-18-1.
Wrongful death, §28A-18-2.
Absence.
Service by publication on executor without bond, §28A-18-6.
Absentees in military service, §§28B-1 to 28B-10.
See ABSENTEES IN MILITARY SERVICE.
Accounts and accounting.
Annual accounts.
Filing required, §28A-21-1.
Book accounts.
Proved by personal representative, §8-43.
Certification of final account, §28A-21-2(a).
Clerk may order account, §28A-21-4.
Contents of accounts, §28A-21-3.
Evidence.
Vouchers presumptive evidence, §28A-21-5.
Examination by clerk, §28A-21-1.
Failure to make account, §28A-21-4.
Final accounts, §28A-21-2(b).
Limited personal representative, §28A-21-2.2.
Notice.
Permissive notice of final account, §28A-21-6.
Time for filing, §28A-21-2(a).
Grounds for summary revocation of letters testamentary, §28A-9-2.
Improper appointment.
Filing accounting with clerk of superior court, §28A-3-3.
Limited personal representative.
Final accounting.
Affidavit or report filed, §28A-21-2.2(a).
Review and recordation by clerk, §28A-21-2.2(b).
Clerk of superior court.
Actions by, §28A-21-2.2(b).
Filing requirement, §28A-21-2.2(a).
Permissive notice of final account, §28A-21-6.
Presumptions.
Vouchers presumptive evidence, §28A-21-5.
Public administrator.
Procedure after removal from office, §28A-12-7.
Resignation.
Statement of account, §28A-10-3.
Revocation of letters.
Filing accounting, §28A-9-3.

EXECUTORS AND ADMINISTRATORS —Cont'd
Accounts and accounting —Cont'd
Vouchers.
Lost vouchers, §28A-21-5.
Presumptive evidence of disbursement, §28A-21-5.
What accounts must contain, §28A-21-3.
Actions.
Actions brought by or against in representative capacity, §28A-18-3.
Bonds, surety.
Action against obligors on bond, §28A-8-6.
Costs.
When costs against representative allowed, §28A-19-18.
Creditors.
When creditors may sue on claim, §28A-18-5.
False imprisonment.
Rights of action not surviving decedent, §28A-18-1.
Libel and slander.
Rights of actions which do not survive, §28A-18-1.
Liens.
Commencement of actions against personal representatives not lien, §28A-19-17.
Recovery of estate property, §28A-15-12(a1) to (d).
Representative capacity.
To sue or defend in representative capacity, §28A-18-3.
Revocation of letters.
Actions to continue, §28A-18-8.
Service on or appearance of one binds all, §28A-18-4.
Survival of actions, §28A-18-1(a).
Actions which do not survive, §28A-18-1(b).
Venue of actions against executors and administrators, §1-78.
Wrongful death.
Power to maintain actions, §28A-13-3(a).
Age.
Persons disqualified to serve, §28A-4-2.
Agriculture.
Continuation of farming operations, §28A-13-4.
Powers of personal representative, §28A-13-3(a).
Crops.
Ungathered at death of deceased person, §28A-15-1(d).
Ancillary administration, §§28A-26-1 to 28A-26-9.
Assets.
Assets in jurisdiction outside state subject to ancillary administration, §28A-26-1.
Nonresident decedents.
Assets subject to claims, allowances, etc., §28A-26-8(a).
Remission of surplus assets, §28A-26-9.
Authority of domiciliary.
Personal representative for nonresident decedent, §28A-26-5.
Bonds, surety.
Personal representatives granted ancillary letters, §28A-26-4(a).
Claims.
Certain claims binding, §28A-26-8(b).
Limitation on presentation, §28A-26-8(c).
Payment, §28A-26-8(d).
Duties of personal representatives in ancillary administration, §28A-26-8.
Foreign corporations.
Authority to act as ancillary personal representative, §28A-26-3(a).

EXECUTORS AND ADMINISTRATORS —Cont'd
Ancillary administration —Cont'd
General provisions, §28A-26-1.
Granting ancillary letters, §28A-26-3(a).
  Bond for personal representative, §28A-26-4.
  Nonexistence of domiciliary personal
    representative, §28A-26-3(b).
Jurisdiction.
  Domiciliary personal representative of
    nonresident decedent.
    Invoking or submission to jurisdiction of state
      courts, §28A-26-6.
  Nonresident decedents.
    Personal jurisdiction by service of process,
      §28A-26-7.
No ancillary administrator within ninety days.
  Payment of debt and delivery of property to
    nonresident domiciliary, §28A-26-2(c).
Nonresident decedents.
  Assets subject to claims, etc., §28A-26-8(a).
Payment of debt and delivery of property without
  ancillary administration in state, §28A-26-2.
Appeals.
Resignation, §28A-10-6.
Revocation of letters, §28A-9-4.
Stay of further proceedings in court below.
  Security limited for fiduciaries, §1-294.
Appearances.
Actions against personal representatives or
  collectors.
  Service on or appearance of one binds all,
    §28A-18-4.
Appointment.
Carrying out powers and duties prior to
  appointment, §28A-13-1.
Delay in appointment, §28A-6-1(b).
Discharge of debt due, §28A-15-11.
Improper appointment.
  Liability of personal representative appointed in
    improper county, §28A-3-4.
  Procedure after determination, §28A-3-3.
Powers and duties accrue upon appointment,
  §28A-13-1.
Reopening administration, §28A-23-5.
Resignation.
  Rights and duties devolve on successor,
    §28A-10-7.
  When appointment of successor not required,
    §28A-10-8.
Revocation of letters, §28A-9-6.
  Rights and duties devolve on successor,
    §28A-9-7.
Right to contest appointment, §28A-6-4.
Successors, §28A-6-3.
Appraisers.
Employment, §28A-20-4.
Arbitration and award.
Referral of disputed claim, §28A-19-15.
Assets.
Ancillary administration.
  Jurisdiction outside of state, §28A-26-1.
  Nonresident decedents, §28A-26-8(a).
  Remission of surplus assets, §28A-26-9.
Encumbered assets.
  Payment by personal representative, §28A-15-4.
Improper appointment.
  Surrender of assets, §28A-3-3.
Nonresident decedents.
  Assets subject to claims, allowances, etc.,
    §28A-26-8(a).

EXECUTORS AND ADMINISTRATORS —Cont'd
Assets —Cont'd
Retaining in satisfaction of representative claim,
  §28A-19-12.
Revocation of letters.
  Surrender of assets, §28A-9-3.
Sources of assets to satisfy claims against estate.
  Tentative trusts, §28A-15-10(a).
Surplus assets.
  Remission by ancillary representatives,
    §28A-26-9.
Attachment.
Death of defendant after levy.
  Judgment against real property enforced
    through defendant's personal
    representative, §1-440.34(b).
  Service on personal representative for levy to
    remain in force, §1-440.34(a).
Attorneys at law.
Counsel fees allowable to attorneys serving as
  representatives, §28A-23-4.
Employing attorneys.
  Powers of personal representatives and
    fiduciaries, §28A-13-3(a).
Audits and auditors.
Employment of auditors.
  Powers of personal representatives,
    §28A-13-3(a).
Banks.
Fiduciaries generally.
  See BANKS.
Stockholders.
  Executors and administrators not personally
    liable as, §53-40.
Blind persons.
Aid to the blind.
  Personal representatives for certain recipients
    of aid, §§111-30 to 111-33.
Bonds, surety.
Actions.
  Right of action against obligor on bond of
    personal representative, §28A-8-6.
Amount, §28A-8-2.
Ancillary administration.
  Personal representatives granted ancillary
    letters, §28A-26-4.
Appeal perfected staying further proceedings in
  court below.
  Security limited for fiduciaries, §1-294.
Breach of bond.
  Action against obligors, §28A-8-6.
Deposited money.
  Exclusion from computation of bond, §28A-8-1.1.
Failure to give additional bond, §28A-8-4.
Increase of bond or security in case of inadequacy
  or insufficiency, §28A-8-3(a).
Increase of bond upon sale of real estate,
  §28A-8-3(b).
Judicial sales.
  Person holding sale, §1-339.10(b), (c).
Limitation of action against surety, §1-52.
Manner of security, §28A-8-2.
Modification of bond, §28A-8-3.
  Increase.
    Inadequacy or insufficiency, §28A-8-3(a).
    Real estate sale, §28A-8-3(b).
  Reduction, §28A-8-3(c).
  Substitution of security, §28A-8-3(d).
Mortgages and deeds of trust.
  Bonds secured by mortgage or deed of trust,
    §28A-8-3.

EXECUTORS AND ADMINISTRATORS —Cont'd

Bonds, surety —Cont'd

Provisions of bond, §28A-8-2.

Public administrator, §28A-12-3.

Reduction, §28A-8-3(c).

Required prior to issuance of letters, §28A-8-1(a).

Rights of surety in danger of loss, §28A-8-5.

Service of process on executor without bond, §28A-18-6.

Substitution of security, §28A-8-3(d).

When bond not required, §28A-8-1(b).

Book accounts proved by personal representative.

Evidence, §8-43.

Breach of duty, §28A-13-10(c).

Burial arrangements.

Carrying out prior to appointment, §28A-13-1.

Burial place.

Authority to provide, §28A-19-9(b).

Caveat.

Effect on estate administration, §31-36.

Cemeteries.

Perpetual care of cemetery lot.

Authorized, §28A-19-10.

Claims against estate.

General provisions.

See DECEDENTS' ESTATES.

Notice for claims, §28A-14-1.

Delivery or mailing, §28A-14-1(b), (c).

Personal notice to creditors, §28A-14-3.

Proof of notice, §28A-14-2.

Publication, §28A-14-1(a).

Validation of certain notices, §28A-14-1.1(a), (b).

Notice to creditors without administration of estate, §§28A-29-1 to 28A-29-5. See within this heading, "Creditors."

Collateral attack.

Letters not subject to attack, §28A-6-5.

Collectors, §§28A-11-1 to 28A-11-5.

See DECEDENTS' ESTATES.

Commercial code.

Representative defined, §25-1-201(b)(35).

Commingling of estates.

Liability, §28A-13-10(c).

Commissions, §28A-23-3(a).

Computation, §28A-23-3(f).

Construction of section, §28A-23-3(d).

Determination of amount, §28A-23-3(b).

Entitlement, §28A-23-3(a).

Limitation on amount, §28A-23-3(c).

Personal representatives guilty of misconduct not entitled to commission, §28A-23-3(e).

Statutory language, use to determine, §28A-23-3(h).

Stipulated amount or method of payment, §28A-23-3(g).

Compensation.

Commissions generally, §28A-23-3.

Compensation of trustees and other fiduciaries, §§32-53 to 32-62.

See FIDUCIARIES.

Compromise and settlement.

Wrongful death actions, §28A-13-3(a).

Contests.

Right to contest appointment, §28A-6-4.

Continuation of businesses or ventures.

Powers of personal representative and fiduciary, §28A-13-3(a).

Contracts.

Exoneration from personal liability.

Powers of personal representative, §28A-13-3(a).

EXECUTORS AND ADMINISTRATORS —Cont'd

Contracts —Cont'd

Sale of real property.

Death of vendor under contract.

Delivery of deed by executor, §28A-17-9.

Conveyances.

Contract for sale of real property by decedent.

Delivery of deed by personal representative, §28A-17-9.

Real property conveyed to personal representative, §28A-17-10.

Convicted felons.

Persons disqualified to serve, §28A-4-2.

Corporations.

Disqualifications for service.

Not authorized as personal representative, §28A-4-2.

Incorporation of businesses or ventures.

Power of personal representative or fiduciary, §28A-13-3(a).

Costs.

Actions to recover estate property, §28A-15-12(c).

Administration of estates, §7A-307.

Recovery of costs when executor or administrator a party, §6-31.

When chargeable to estate, §6-31.

Creditors.

Notice to creditors. See within this heading, "Notice."

Notice to creditors without administration of estate, §§28A-29-1 to 28A-29-5.

Administration of claims presented, §28A-29-4.

Applicability of procedure.

Decedent dies leaving no property subject to probate, §28A-29-1.

Failure to file claims.

Claims barred, §28A-29-4.

Limited personal representative to provide notice.

Administration of claims presented, §28A-29-4.

Application for appointment, §28A-29-2(a).

Filing upon payment of fee, indexing, §28A-29-2(c).

Duty to provide notice, §28A-29-3.

Issuance of letters of administration, §28A-29-2(b).

Persons eligible to be appointed, §28A-29-1.

Proof of notice provided, §28A-29-3.

Personal representative to administer estate.

Appointment after claims presented, §28A-29-4.

Right to petition for appointment, §28A-29-5.

Presentation of claims by creditors, §28A-29-4.

When creditors may sue on claim, §28A-18-5.

Damages.

Wrongful death actions, §28A-18-2(b).

Death.

Appointment of successor, §28A-6-3.

Letters testamentary and of administration.

Evidence of death, §28A-6-1(c).

Powers and duties of successor, §28A-13-7.

Surviving personal representative.

Powers, §28A-13-9.

Debts and claims.

Discharge of debt by appointment, §28A-15-11.

Notice to creditors, §§28A-14-1 to 28A-14-3.

Satisfying debts or claims against decedent's estate, §28A-13-3(a).

Declaratory judgments.

Who may apply for declaration, §1-255.

EXECUTORS AND ADMINISTRATORS —Cont'd

Deeds.
Contract for sale of real property by decedent.
Delivery of deed by personal representative, §28A-17-9.
Omitting seals, §47-51.

Definitions, §28A-1-1.

Deposits.
Estate funds deposited in bank, §28A-13-3(a).

Designation.
Successors.
When appointment of successor not required, §28A-10-8.

Devisees.
Defined, §28A-1-1(1a).
Service of process, §28A-13-3.

Disqualifications, §28A-4-2.

Distribution, §§28A-22-1 to 28A-22-11.
See DECEDENTS' ESTATES.

Domiciliary administration.
Foreign corporations.
Authority to act as ancillary personal representative, §28A-26-3(a).
Jurisdiction, §28A-26-1.
Nonresident decedents.
Invoking jurisdiction, §28A-26-6(a).
Personal jurisdiction by service of process, §28A-26-7.
No ancillary administrator qualifying within ninety days.
Payment of debt or delivery of property, §28A-26-2(c).
Nonexistence of domiciliary personal representative.
Issuance of ancillary letters, §28A-26-3(b).
Nonresidents.
Authority of domiciliary personal representative, §28A-26-5.
Jurisdiction.
Invoking jurisdiction of state, §28A-26-6(a).
Personal jurisdiction by service of process, §28A-26-7.
Submission to jurisdiction of state courts, §28A-26-6(b).
Payment of debt and delivery of property without ancillary administration, §28A-26-2(a).
Release of debt, §28A-26-2(b).
Remission of surplus assets, §28A-26-9.
Taxation.
Right and duty to pay off federal and state taxes, §28A-26-1.

Duties.
Annexation of will.
Powers and duties of administrator with will annexed, §28A-13-8.
General duties, §28A-13-2.
Settlement of estate, §28A-13-2.
Successors, §28A-13-7.
Time of accrual of duties, §28A-13-1.

Embezzlement.
Liability, §28A-13-10.
Property.
Receipt of property by virtue of office or employment, §14-90.

Employment of persons to assist in performance of duties.
Powers of personal representatives, §28A-13-3(a).

Estate taxes.
Liability of personal representative.
Tax not paid within 2 years after due, §105-32.3(b).

EXECUTORS AND ADMINISTRATORS —Cont'd

Evidence.
Book accounts proved by personal representative, §8-43.
Letters testamentary and of administration.
Death, evidence of, §28A-6-1(c).
Medical, hospital or other charges at issue.
Competency to give evidence regarding amount, §8-58.1(a).
Rebuttable presumption of reasonableness.
Testimony establishing, §8-58.1(b).
Services reasonable and necessary.
Permissive presumption, §8-58.1(c).
Vouchers.
Presumptive evidence of disbursement, §28A-21-5.
Wrongful death actions.
Evidence establishing elements of damages, §28A-18-2(c).

Examination of persons believed to have possession of estate property, §28A-15-12(b1).
Costs of proceedings, responsibility, §28A-15-12(c).
Cumulative nature of remedy, §28A-15-12(d).

Executions.
Action by creditors.
When execution to issue, §28A-18-5.
Defendant dying in capital offense execution.
Rights against property of defendant, §1-312.
Form of execution against property in hands of personal representative, §1-313.
Successors in office, §28A-18-7.

False imprisonment.
Rights of action which do not survive, §28A-18-1.

Farming.
Continuation of farming operations, §28A-13-3(a).

Federal estate tax apportionment.
Personal representative to determine apportionment, §28A-27-3.

Fees.
Commissions generally, §28A-23-3.

Fiduciaries generally, §§32-1 to 32-13.
See FIDUCIARIES.

Foreclosures.
Validation, §45-5.

Foreign personal representatives.
Ancillary administration, §§28A-26-1 to 28A-26-9.
Defined, §28A-1-1(2).

Fraud.
Sales of real property.
Conveyance by deceased in fraud of creditors.
Property subject to sale, §28A-17-5.
Transfers or conveyances by decedent to defraud creditors.
Action by personal representative to recover, §28A-15-10.

Funerals.
Carrying out funeral arrangements prior to appointment, §28A-13-1.

Gravestones.
Authority to provide, §28A-19-9(a).

Hearings.
Contesting appointments, §28A-6-4.
Letters testamentary and of administration.
Revocation, §28A-9-1.
Resignation.
Hearing on petition, §28A-10-4.

Heirs.
Defined, §28A-1-1(3).
Parties to proceeding, §28A-13-3.
Service of process, §28A-13-3.

EXECUTORS AND ADMINISTRATORS —Cont'd

Household furnishings.
Sales, §28A-16-3.

Illiterates.
Persons disqualified to serve, §28A-4-2.

Improper appointment.
Liability of personal representative appointed in improper county, §28A-3-4.
Procedure after determination, §28A-3-3.

Income.
Allocation of state income.
Powers of personal representatives, §28A-13-3.

Incorporation of businesses or ventures.
Powers of personal representative or fiduciary, §28A-13-3.

Inheritance tax.
See INHERITANCE TAX.

Interested person.
Disqualified to testify against, exception, §8C-1 Rule 601(c).

Inventory, §§28A-20-1 to 28A-20-4.
See DECEDENTS' ESTATES.

Joint personal representatives.
Exercise of powers by one or more than one, §28A-13-6.
Fiduciary powers, §28A-13-6(c).
Shares in corporate stock or other securities, ownership of, §28A-13-6(d).
Will provisions, governance by, §28A-13-6(b).
Written agreement, §28A-13-6(c1), (f).

Joint tenants and tenants in common.
Personal representatives to hold in joint tenancy, §28A-13-5.

Judgments and decrees.
Execution by successor in office, §28A-18-7.

Judicial sales.
Authority to hold sale, §1-339.4.
Bond of person holding sale, §1-339.10(b), (c).

Jurisdiction.
Clerk of superior court.
Jurisdiction for administration of estates, §28A-2-1.
Nonresident decedents.
Invoking jurisdiction by domiciliary personal representative, §28A-26-6.
Personal jurisdiction by service of process, §28A-26-7.
Personal jurisdiction.
Grounds, §1-75.4.

Leases.
Authority to lease real property, §28A-17-11.
Certain leases void as to creditors and personal representatives, §28A-17-12(a), (b).
Leasing property for payment of debts, §28A-15-1.
Personal property.
Sale or lease, §§28A-16-1 to 28A-16-3.
Real property, §28A-17-11.

Letters of collection, §28A-11-1.

Letters testamentary and of administration.
Actions.
Continuation though letters revoked, §28A-18-4.
Ancillary administration.
Granting ancillary letters, §28A-26-3(a).
Application.
Form, §28A-6-1(a).
Recording, §28A-6-1(a).
Clerks of superior courts.
Authority of clerk to grant and revoke letters, §7A-103.
Jurisdiction.
Subject matter jurisdiction in estate proceedings, §28A-2-4(a).

EXECUTORS AND ADMINISTRATORS —Cont'd

Letters testamentary and of administration —Cont'd
Collateral attack.
Validity of letters not subject to, §28A-6-5.
Contesting appointment, §28A-6-4.
Death.
Evidence of death, §28A-6-1(c).
Delaying of appointment, §28A-6-1(b).
Equally entitled applicants, §28A-4-1.
Issuance, §28A-6-1(b).
Oath required prior to issuance, §28A-7-1.
Without notice, §28A-6-2.
Jurisdiction.
Assistant clerk of superior court, §28A-2-2.
Clerk of superior court.
Subject matter jurisdiction in estate proceedings, §28A-2-4(a).
Limitation of actions.
Time during controversy on granting letters, §1-24.
Notice.
Issuance without notice, §28A-6-2.
Oaths.
Required prior to issuance, §28A-7-1.
Order of persons qualified to serve, §28A-4-1.
Public administrator.
Revocation for false representation, §28A-12-6.
When administrator to apply for letters, §28A-12-4.
Renunciation.
Express renunciation, §28A-5-2(a).
Implied renunciation, §28A-5-2(b).
Nomination by person renouncing, §28A-5-2(c).
Revocation.
Accounting.
Required, §28A-9-3.
Actions.
Continuation of actions though letters revoked, §28A-18-8.
Appeals, §28A-9-4.
Appointment of successor, §§28A-6-3, 28A-9-6.
Effect, §28A-9-3.
Failure to give additional bond, §28A-8-4.
Grounds, §28A-9-1(a).
Summary revocation, §28A-9-2(a).
Hearing, §28A-9-1.
Interlocutory orders, §28A-9-5.
Procedure, §28A-9-1(b).
Summary revocation, §28A-9-2(b).
Rights and duties devolve on successor, §28A-9-7.
Stays, §28A-9-4.
Summary revocation.
Grounds, §28A-9-2(a).
Procedure, §28A-9-2(b).
Surrender of assets upon revocation, §28A-9-3.
Time pleaded as bar to action.
Controversy on granting letters, §1-24.
Validity.
Collateral attack on validity, §28A-6-5.

Liability.
Property not part of estate, §28A-13-10(b).
Property of estate, §28A-13-10(a).

Libel and slander.
Actions in favor of decedent which do not survive, §28A-18-1.

Liens.
Actions against personal representatives.
No lien by suit, §28A-19-17.
Payment of encumbered assets, §28A-15-4.

EXECUTORS AND ADMINISTRATORS —Cont'd
Limitation of actions.
Ancillary administration.
Presentation of claims, §28A-26-8(c).
Bonds, surety, §1-50(a).
Action against surety, §1-52.
Claims against the estate, §28A-19-3(a).
Creditor against personal representative, §1-49.
Death before limitation expires.
Action by or against personal representative or collector, §1-22.
Time during controversy on granting of letters, §1-24.
Limited personal representatives.
Final accounting.
Affidavit or report filed, §28A-21-2.2(a).
Action by clerk after review and recording, §28A-21-2.2(b).
Review and recording by clerk, §28A-21-2.2(b).
Notice to creditors without administration of estate, §§28A-29-1 to 28A-29-5.
Applicability of procedure.
Decedent leaving no property to probate, §28A-29-1.
Appointment of limited representative to give notice.
Application for appointment, §28A-29-2(a).
Filing on payment of fee, indexing, §28A-29-2(a).
Issuance of letters of limited administration, §28A-29-2(b).
Persons eligible, §28A-29-1.
Duty to provide notice, §28A-29-3.
Personal representative.
Appointment after claim presented, §28A-29-4.
Right to petition for appointment, §28A-29-5.
Presentment of claims after notice provided, §28A-29-4.
Failure, claim barred, §28A-29-4.
Proof of notice provided, §28A-29-3.
Qualification.
Cost assessed, §7A-307(a).
Mentally ill.
Persons disqualified to serve, §28A-4-2.
Military affairs.
Estates of absentees in military service, §§28B-1 to 28B-10.
See ABSENTEES IN MILITARY SERVICE.
Minors.
Persons disqualified to serve as personal representative, §28A-4-2.
Settlement.
Payment into court of fund due minor, §28A-23-2.
Missing persons.
Estates of missing persons, §§28C-1 to 28C-22.
See MISSING PERSONS.
Mortgages and deeds of trust.
Authority to mortgage real property, §28A-17-11.
Bonds secured by mortgage, §28A-8-3(d).
Certain mortgages void as to creditors and personal representatives, §28A-17-12(a), (b).
Debts and claims.
Mortgaging property for payment of debts, §28A-15-1.
Definition of "mortgage,"§28A-1-1(4).
Foreclosures.
Validation, §45-5.

EXECUTORS AND ADMINISTRATORS —Cont'd
Mortgages and deeds of trust —Cont'd
Jurisdiction.
Clerk of superior court, §28A-2-5.
Payment of encumbered assets, §28A-15-4.
Renunciation by representative, §45-6.
Newly discovered property.
Reopening administration, §28A-23-5.
Nonresidents.
Domiciliary administration.
Authority of domiciliary personal representative for nonresident decedent, §28A-26-5.
Personal jurisdiction by service of process, §28A-26-7.
Submission to jurisdiction of court, §28A-26-6(b).
Persons disqualified to serve, §28A-4-2.
Service of process.
Service on personal representative, §28A-26-7.
Notice.
Final account, permissive notice, §28A-21-6.
Letters testamentary and of administration.
Issuance without notice, §28A-6-2.
Notice to creditors, §28A-14-1.
Delivery or mailing, §28A-14-1(b), (c).
Personal notice to creditors, §28A-14-3.
Proof of notice, §28A-14-2.
Publication, §28A-14-1(a).
Real property.
Sale, lease or mortgage by heirs or devisees.
Certain transactions void as to creditors and personal representatives, §28A-17-12(a), (b).
Validation of certain notices, §28A-14-1.1(a), (b).
Without administration of estate, §§28A-29-1 to 28A-29-5. See within this heading, "Limited personal representatives."
Resignation.
Petition, §28A-10-2.
Oaths.
Form of oaths of office, §11-11.
Letters testamentary and of administration.
Oath required before issuance, §28A-7-1.
Public administrator, §28A-12-2.
Order of persons qualified to serve.
Letters of administration, §28A-4-1(b).
Disqualification of persons listed, petition alleging, §28A-4-1(c).
Letters testamentary, §28A-4-1(a).
Parent and child.
Acts barring rights of parents, §31A-2.
Parties, §1A-1 Rule 17(a).
Sales of real property.
Adverse claimant to be heard, §28A-17-6.
Heirs and devisees necessary parties, §28A-17-4.
Partition.
Petitions by personal representative of cotenant, §46-3.
Partnerships.
Continuing partnerships.
Powers of personal representatives, §28A-13-3(a).
Fiduciary obligations of partners.
Applicability to representatives of deceased partner, §59-51(b).
Personal property.
Action to recover, §28A-15-12(a1).
Costs of proceedings, responsibility, §28A-15-12(c).
Cumulative nature of remedy, §28A-15-12(d).

EXECUTORS AND ADMINISTRATORS —Cont'd
Personal property —Cont'd
Examination of persons believed to have
    possession of estate property, §28A-15-12(b1).
  Costs of proceedings, responsibility,
    §28A-15-12(c).
  Cumulative nature of remedy, §28A-15-12(d).
Sale or lease, §§28A-16-1 to 28A-16-3.
Personal representatives defined, §28A-1-1(5).
Petitions.
Resignation of office, §28A-10-2.
Powers, §28A-13-3(a) to (d).
Annexation of will.
  Powers and duties of administrator with will
    annexed, §28A-13-8.
Carrying out powers and duties prior to
    appointment, §28A-13-1.
Initiating estate proceeding to enforce,
    §28A-13-3(d).
Powers of fiduciaries generally, §§32-25 to 32-27.
Successors, §28A-13-7.
Surviving personal representative, §28A-13-9.
Time of accrual of powers, §28A-13-1.
Presumptions.
Medical, hospital or other charges at issue.
  Reasonableness, rebuttable presumption,
    testimony establishing, §8-58.1(b).
  Services reasonable and necessary, permissive
    presumption, §8-58.1(c).
Principal and income act.
General provisions, §§37A-1-101 to 37A-6-602.
See PRINCIPAL AND INCOME ACT.
Probate of wills.
Application for probate, §28A-2A-1.
Substitution of consolidated bank as executor or
    trustee, §28A-2A-12.
Prudent person rule.
Liability for loss to the estate, §28A-13-10(c).
Public administrators.
Accounts and accounting.
  Procedure after removal from office, §28A-12-7.
Appointment, §28A-12-1.
Bonds, surety, §28A-12-3(a).
Commissions, §28A-23-3(a).
  Computation, §28A-23-3(f).
  Construction of section, §28A-23-3(d).
  Determination of amount, §28A-23-3(b).
  Entitlement, §28A-23-3(a).
  Limitation on amount, §28A-23-3(c).
  Public administrator guilty of misconduct not
    entitled to commission, §28A-23-3(e).
  Statutory language, use to determine,
    §28A-23-3(h).
  Stipulated amount or method of payment,
    §28A-23-3(g).
Compensation, §28A-12-8.
Counsel fees.
  Attorney serving as representatives, §28A-23-4.
Duties, §28A-12-5(a).
Letters testamentary and of administration.
  Revocation, §28A-12-6.
  When administrator to apply for letters,
    §28A-12-4.
Missing persons.
  Appointment of public administrator as
    receiver, §28C-17.
Nonresidents.
  Removal from office upon becoming nonresident,
    §28A-12-6.
Oath of office, §28A-12-2.
Permanent bond, §28A-12-3(b).

EXECUTORS AND ADMINISTRATORS —Cont'd
Public administrators —Cont'd
Powers, §28A-12-5(a).
Removal from office, §28A-12-6.
  Procedure after removal, §28A-12-7.
Term, §28A-12-1.
  Expiration.
    Administering estates upon expiration,
      §28A-12-5(b).
Qualifications.
Age, §28A-4-2.
Convicted felons, §28A-4-2.
Equally entitled applicants, §28A-4-1.
Illiterates, §28A-4-2.
Incompetents, §28A-4-2.
Mentally ill, §28A-4-2.
Nonresidents, §28A-4-2.
Order of persons qualified to serve.
  Letters of administration, §28A-4-1(b).
    Petition alleging disqualification of persons
      listed, §28A-4-1(c).
  Letters testamentary, §28A-4-1(a).
Persons disqualified to serve, §28A-4-2.
Real estate brokers.
Exemptions from provisions, §93A-2(c).
Real property.
Action to recover, §28A-15-12(a1).
  Costs of proceedings, responsibility,
    §28A-15-12(c).
  Cumulative nature of remedy, §28A-15-12(d).
Assets available for discharge of debts and claims,
    §28A-15-1.
Conveyance to personal representative.
  Title in personal representative for estate,
    §28A-17-10.
Damages to property.
  Actions to recover damages, §28A-13-3(a).
Death of vendor under contract.
  Delivery of deed by personal representative,
    §28A-17-9.
Deeds.
  Death of vendor under contract.
    Delivery of deed by personal representative,
      §28A-17-9.
  Warranties.
    Death of vendor under contract, §28A-17-9.
Examination of persons believed to have
    possession of estate property, §28A-15-12(b1).
  Costs of proceedings, responsibility,
    §28A-15-12(c).
  Cumulative nature of remedy, §28A-15-12(d).
Fraud.
  Property subject to sale.
    Conveyance by deceased in fraud of creditors,
      §28A-17-5.
Leases.
  Certain leases void as to creditors and personal
    representatives, §28A-17-12(a), (b).
  Jurisdiction.
    Clerk of superior court, §28A-2-5.
  Personal representative may lease, §28A-17-11.
Mortgages and deeds of trust. See within this
    heading, "Mortgages and deeds of trust."
Order authorizing possession, custody or control.
  Petition to clerk of court, §28A-13-3(c).
Partition.
  Petition for partition, §28A-17-3.
Power to sell or lease, §28A-13-3(a).
Prior validating acts, §28A-17-13.
Purchase of property belonging to decedent's
    estate.
  Powers of personal representative, §28A-13-3(a).

EXECUTORS AND ADMINISTRATORS —Cont'd

Real property —Cont'd

Sales, §§28A-17-1 to 28A-17-13.

Adverse claimants.

Making party to proceeding, §28A-17-6.

Application to clerk, §28A-17-1.

Certain sales void as to creditors and personal representatives, §28A-17-12(a), (b).

Conveyance by deceased in fraud of creditors.

Property subject to sale, §28A-17-5.

Guardian ad litem.

Appointment for heirs and devisees, §28A-17-4.

Heirs or devisees.

Necessary parties, §28A-17-4.

Void sales, etc., §28A-17-12(a), (b).

Increase of bond, §28A-8-3(b).

Joinder of issues of law or fact, §28A-17-6.

Jurisdiction.

Clerk of superior court, §28A-2-5.

Partition.

Petition for partition, §28A-17-3.

Petitions, §28A-17-1.

Contents of petition for sale, §28A-17-2.

Partition, §28A-17-3.

Private sales, §28A-17-7.

Property recovered from fraudulent alienee subject to sale, §28A-17-5.

Property subject to sale, §28A-17-5.

Summary orders, §28A-17-7.

Wills.

Public or private sales, §28A-17-8.

Title.

Actions to determine title.

Powers of personal representative, §28A-13-3(a).

Renunciation.

Declaratory judgment proceeding.

Compatible with fiduciary duties, §31B-1.2(b).

Express renunciation by executor, §28A-5-1(a).

Implied renunciation by executor, §28A-5-1(b).

Letters of administration.

Express renunciation, §28A-5-2(a).

Implied renunciation, §28A-5-2(b).

Nomination by person renouncing, §28A-5-2(c).

Persons disqualified to serve, §28A-4-2.

Power of personal representative, §28A-13-3.

Procedure upon renunciation, §28A-5-1(c).

Review.

Declaratory judgment proceeding, §31B-1.2(b).

Institution of proceeding by fiduciary, notice, §31B-1.2(a).

Requirements of proceedings instituted, §31B-1.2(c).

Right to renounce succession, §31B-1(a).

Reopening administration, §28A-23-5.

Representation.

Persons representing and binding others, §§36C-3-301 to 36C-3-305.

Resignation.

Accounting to successor.

When resignation becomes effective, §28A-10-5.

Appeals, §28A-10-6.

Appointment of successor, §28A-6-3.

Clerk's power to accept, §28A-10-1.

Petition.

Contents, §28A-10-2(a).

Hearing on petition, §28A-10-4.

Notice of petition, §28A-10-2(b).

Powers and duties of successor, §28A-13-7.

Statement of account, §28A-10-3.

EXECUTORS AND ADMINISTRATORS —Cont'd

Resignation —Cont'd

Stays, §28A-10-6.

Successors.

Rights and duties devolve on successor, §28A-10-7.

When appointment of successor not required, §28A-10-8.

When resignation becomes effective, §28A-10-5.

Revocation of letters, §§28A-9-1 to 28A-9-7.

Sales.

Personal property.

Sale or lease, §§28A-16-1 to 28A-16-3.

Seals and sealed instruments.

Deeds.

Official deeds omitting seals, §47-51.

Securities regulation.

Exempt transactions, §78A-17.

Self-dealing.

Losses to estate through self-dealing.

Liability of personal representative, §28A-13-10(c).

Service of process.

Actions against personal representatives or collectors.

Service on or appearance of one binds all, §28A-18-4.

Devisees and heirs made parties by service, §28A-13-3.

Executors without bond, §28A-18-6.

Nonresident decedents.

Nonresident drivers.

Personal representatives of deceased nonresident drivers, §1-105.

Service on personal representative, §28A-26-7.

Settlement, §28A-13-2.

After final account filed, §28A-23-1.

Discharge of personal representative from liability, §28A-23-1.

Investments.

Funds due minor, §28A-23-2.

Minor.

Payment into court of fund due minor, §28A-23-2.

Small estates.

Subsequently appointed personal representative or collector, §28A-25-5.

Statute of frauds.

Contracts charging representative personally, §22-1.

Stays.

Resignation, §28A-10-6.

Revocation of letters, §28A-9-4.

Security limited for fiduciaries, §1-294.

Stock and stockholders.

Powers of personal representatives, §28A-13-3.

Summary administration of estates.

Appointment of personal representative.

Discharge of spouses liability, §28A-28-7(b).

Petition, §28A-28-7(a).

Surviving spouses.

Right to administer estate of other spouse.

Acts barring rights of spouse, §31A-1(b).

Taxation.

Carry-over basis provision.

Election of excluded items, §28A-13-3(a1).

Domiciliary representative to pay off federal and state taxes, §28A-26-1.

Marital deduction.

Power of personal representative to secure benefit of marital deduction, §28A-13-3(a).

EXECUTORS AND ADMINISTRATORS —Cont'd
Taxation —Cont'd
Power to enter agreements with taxing
  authorities, §28A-13-3(a).
Property taxes.
  Payment of taxes by fiduciaries, §105-383.
Title.
Actions to determine title.
  Powers of personal representative, §28A-13-3.
Transfers to minors.
Authority to make transfer, §33A-5(a).
Designation of custodians by personal
  representative, §33A-5(c).
Irrevocable transfer for benefit of minor.
  Authority to make as custodian, §33A-6(a), (c).
Trust companies.
Acting as executor or administrator authorized,
  §53-159.
Trusts and trustees.
General provisions, §§36C-1-101 to 36C-11-1106.
  See TRUSTS AND TRUSTEES.
Uniform fiduciaries act, §§32-1 to 32-13.
  See FIDUCIARIES.
Validation.
Notice to creditors, §28A-14-1.1(a), (b).
Venue.
Actions against executors and administrators,
  §1-78.
Improper appointment.
  Liability of personal representative appointed in
    improper county, §28A-3-4.
  Procedure after determination, §28A-3-3.
Priority of venue, §28A-3-5.
Proceedings commenced in more than one county,
  §28A-3-2(a).
Proceedings to determine venue, §28A-3-2.
  Interested persons may file, §28A-3-2(a1).
  Referral to judge to determine, §28A-3-2(a1).
Proper county, §28A-3-1.
Waiver, §28A-3-5.
When proceeding deemed commenced,
  §28A-3-2(b).
Waiver.
Venue, §28A-3-5.
Wills.
Appointment of successor to personal
  representative required by will, §28A-6-3.
Bonds, surety.
  Execution without giving bond, §28A-26-4(b).
Executor competent witness, §31-9.
Probate of wills generally.
  See WILLS.
Witnesses.
Interested person.
  Disqualified to testify against, exception, §8C-1
    Rule 601.
Medical, hospital or other charges at issue.
  Competency to give evidence regarding amount,
    §8-58.1(a).
  Rebuttable presumption of reasonableness.
    Testimony establishing, §8-58.1(b).
  Services reasonable and necessary.
    Permissive presumption, §8-58.1(c).
Wills.
  Executor competent witness, §31-9.
Wrongful death.
Damages recoverable by personal representative,
  §28A-18-2(b).
Distribution of sums recovered from wrongful
  death.
  Powers of personal representative, §28A-13-3(a).

EXECUTORS AND ADMINISTRATORS —Cont'd
Wrongful death —Cont'd
Dying declarations.
  Admissibility, §28A-18-2(d).
Evidence establishing elements of damages,
  §28A-18-2(c).
Maintaining action for wrongful death.
  Powers of personal representative and fiduciary,
    §28A-13-3(a).
Survival of actions, §28A-18-2(a).
  Authority of personal representative or collector
    to pay reasonable and necessary expenses
    from assets of estate, §28A-18-2(a).

EXECUTORY INTERESTS.
General provisions.
See REMAINDERS, REVERSIONS AND
  EXECUTORY INTERESTS.

EXEMPLARY DAMAGES.
Civil rights, interference with, §99D-1(b), (b1).
**Motor fuel marketing violations, private
  actions,** §75-86.
**Trade secrets, willful and malicious
  misappropriations,** §66-154(c).

**EXEMPTION OF PROPERTY FROM
  CREDITOR CLAIMS.**
Alternative exemptions, §1C-1602.
Amount of personal or real property,
  §1C-1601(a).
Bankruptcy code exemptions.
Inapplicable to residents of state, §1C-1601(f).
Conveyances.
Effect of exemption of property.
  Conveyance of exempt property, §1C-1604(a).
Homestead, NC Const Art X §2.
Definitions, §1C-1601(b).
Disability income plan.
Applicability of provisions to plan, §135-111.
Effect of exemption of property, §1C-1604(a).
Exceptions, §1C-1601(e).
Executions.
Limitation of wage garnishment, §1-362.
Mechanics' and materialmen's liens.
  Inapplicability of exemption, NC Const Art X
    §3.
Forms.
Setting aside exempt property.
  Statement by debtor, §1C-1603(c).
Gifts.
Continuation of exemption of property,
  §1C-1604(b).
Homestead.
See HOMESTEAD EXEMPTIONS.
Husband and wife.
Property of married women secured to them, NC
  Const Art X §4.
Property passing by devise, intestate succession or
  gift to dependent spouse.
  Continuation of exemption, §1C-1604(b).
Intestate succession.
Continuation of exemption of property,
  §1C-1604(b).
Laborers' liens, NC Const Art X §3.
Life insurance.
Proceeds of life policy exempt from process of
  predators, NC Const Art X §5.
Limitation of actions.
Effect of exemption of property, §1C-1604(a1).
Married women.
Property of married women secured to them, NC
  Const Art X §4.

EXEMPTION OF PROPERTY FROM CREDITOR CLAIMS —Cont'd

Mechanics' and materialmen's liens, NC Const Art X §3.

Minors.

Homestead exemption.

Exemption for benefit of children, NC Const Art X §2.

Motions.

Setting aside exempt property, §1C-1603(a), (b).

Notice.

Setting aside exempt property.

Notice to persons affected, §1C-1603(d).

Partition.

Assignment of homestead, §46-5.

Personal property, §1C-1601.

Exemption of personal property from execution or other process, NC Const Art X §1.

Laborers' liens.

Inapplicability of exemption provisions, NC Const Art X §3.

Mechanics' and materialmen's liens.

Inapplicability of exemption from process, NC Const Art X §3.

Personnel system, §126-5.

Petitions.

Setting aside exempt property, §1C-1603(a), (b).

Physical therapists, §§90-270.34, 90-270.39.

Private protective services, §74C-3(b).

Real property, §1C-1601.

Recent purchases not exempt, exception, §1C-1601(d).

Securities regulation, §§78A-16 to 78A-18.

Setting aside exempt property.

Modification, §1C-1603(g).

Motion, §1C-1603(a).

Contents, §1C-1603(b).

Notation of order on motion docket, §1C-1603(f).

Notice to persons affected, §1C-1603(d).

Petition, §1C-1603(a).

Contents, §1C-1603(b).

Procedure, §1C-1603(e).

Statement by debtor, §1C-1603(c).

Surviving spouse.

Homestead exemption.

Exemption for benefit of surviving spouse, NC Const Art X §2.

Wage and hour act, §95-25.14.

Wages.

Limitation on wage garnishment, §1-362.

Waiver, §1C-1601(c).

Women.

Married women.

Property of married women secured to them, NC Const Art X §4.

EXEMPTIONS FROM TAXATION.

See TAXATION.

EXHAUST SYSTEMS.

Motor vehicle inspections generally, §§20-183.2 to 20-183.8G.

See MOTOR VEHICLE INSPECTIONS.

EXHIBITION OF CHILDREN.

Prohibited exhibition, §110-20.1.

EXHIBITIONS.

Fireworks.

Use at public exhibitions requires permit, §14-413.

Obscenity, §§14-190.1 to 14-190.20.

See OBSCENITY AND PORNOGRAPHY.

EXHIBITIONS —Cont'd

Secret societies.

Placing exhibit with intention of intimidating, §14-12.13.

Wearing of disguise, §14-12.14.

Theft.

Destruction or theft of property of exhibition, §14-398.

EXHIBITS.

Part of pleading, §1A-1 Rule 10(c).

Record on appeal, AppProc 9(d).

Use of evidence by jury during deliberation, §1-181.2.

EXHUMATIONS, §130A-390(a) to (c).

EX MERO MOTU.

Findings of fact and conclusions of law necessary, §1A-1 Rule 52(a).

Removal for fair trial, §1-84.

EXONERATION.

Contribution among joint tort-feasors, §§1B-1 to 1B-7.

Decedents' estates.

Nonexoneration of encumbered property, §28A-15-3.

EXONERATION OF BAIL.

Arrest in civil cases, §1-433.

Surrender of defendant, §1-434.

EXPANDING BUSINESSES.

Tax incentives for new and expanding businesses generally, §§105-129.2 to 105-129.13.

See TAX INCENTIVES FOR NEW AND EXPANDING BUSINESSES.

EX PARTE PROCEEDINGS.

Discovery.

Protective orders, §15A-908(a).

Guardians.

Motions in the cause, §35A-1207(d).

Referees meetings.

Failure of party to appear, §1A-1 Rule 53(f).

Special proceedings, §§1-400 to 1-402.

EXPEDITED EVICTIONS, §§42-59 to 42-76.

Actions.

Nature of cause of action of landlord, §42-60.

Parties.

Defendants to action, §42-62(b).

Who may bring action, §42-62(a).

Standard of proof, §42-61.

Adjudication of delinquency.

Conclusive proof in civil action, §42-69(b).

Effect in civil action, §42-69(a).

Admissions.

Request for, §42-70(d).

Affirmative defenses.

Complete evictions, §42-64(a).

Evidence of isolated or nonrecurring incidents.

May be offered only to support affirmative defense, §42-67.

Subsequent actions, availability of affirmative defense, §42-64(b).

Answers.

Time for filing, §42-68.

Applicability of provisions, §42-59.1.

Applicability of rules of civil procedure, §42-68.

Availability of law enforcement resources to plaintiffs, §42-72.

EXPEDITED EVICTIONS —Cont'd

Burden of proof.
Affirmative defense to subsequent action for complete eviction, §42-64(b).
Civil causes of action, §42-61.
Exemption from complete eviction where grounds established, §42-64(c).

Civil immunity from liability, §42-76.

Civil procedure rules.
Applicability, §42-68.

Collection of rent by landlord not waiver of default, §42-73.

Complaints.
Service of complaint on defendant, §42-62(c).

Complete evictions.
Affirmative defenses, §42-64(a).
Subsequent action, availability of defense, §42-64(b).
Defined, §42-59.
Exemption, §42-64(c).
Grounds, §42-63(a).

Conditional evictions.
Order against tenant.
Removal order issued against person other than tenant, §42-63(b), (c).

Contempt.
Violation of injunction or preliminary relief, §42-74.

Continuances.
Procedure in standards for continuances, §42-68.

Conviction of criminal activity.
Conclusive proof in civil action, §42-69(b).
Effect in civil action, §42-69(a).

Counterclaims.
Time for filing reply to counterclaim, §42-68.

Criminal activity.
Conviction as proof in civil action, §42-69(b).
Defined, §42-59.

Criminal proceedings.
Adjudication of delinquency.
Conclusive proof in civil action, §42-69(b).
Pendency of proceedings not to preclude civil action, §42-69(a).
Admissibility of sealed records in civil action, §42-69(d).
Admissibility of trial recordings or transcripts in civil action, §42-69(c).
Conviction of criminal activity.
Conclusive proof in civil action, §42-69(b).
Pendency of criminal proceedings not to preclude civil action, §42-69(a).

Cumulative remedies, §42-75.

Default judgments.
Failure to plead in accordance with time periods, §42-68.

Defenses.
Affirmative defenses. See within this heading, "Affirmative defenses."
Evidence of isolated or nonrecurring criminal activity.
Impermissible as defense, admissible as support of affirmative defenses, §42-67.

Definitions, §42-59.

Discovery.
Authority to conduct discovery generally, §42-70(a).
Injunction against illegal activity pending complete of discovery, §42-70(e).
Interrogatories.
Time for response, §42-70(d).

EXPEDITED EVICTIONS —Cont'd

Discovery —Cont'd
Request for admissions.
Time for response, §42-70(d).
Request for production of documents.
Time for response, §42-70(d).
Time for initiation by defendant, §42-70(b).
Time for initiation by plaintiff, §42-70(c).

Entire premises.
Defined, §42-59.

Evidence.
Criminal proceeding sealed records.
Admissibility in civil actions, §42-69.
Isolated or nonrecurring criminal activities, §42-67.

Exemption from complete eviction where grounds established, §42-64(c).

Felonies.
Defined, §42-59.

Grounds for complete eviction, §42-63(a).

Grounds for partial eviction and issuance of removal order, §42-63(b).

Guests.
Defined, §42-59.

Hearings.
Procedure for expedited hearing, §42-68.

Immunities.
Civil liability, §42-76.

Individual rental units.
Defined, §42-59.

Injunctions.
Preliminary injunction against illegal activity pending completion of discovery, §42-70(e).
Preliminary injunction in emergency situation, §42-74.

Intent of provisions, §42-59.1.

Interrogatories.
Time for response, §42-70(d).

Landlords.
Defined, §42-59.

Law enforcement resources.
Availability of police or lab reports to plaintiffs, §42-72.

Leased residential premises.
Defined, §42-59.

Mandatory evictions, §42-66(b).

Motions.
Enforcement of eviction and removal orders.
Expedited hearings, §42-66(a).

Notice.
Service of complaint, §42-62(c).

Obstructing execution or enforcement of removal or eviction order, §42-65.

Orders for eviction.
Mandatory eviction, §42-66(b).
Motion to enforce, §42-66(a).
Obstruction of execution or enforcement, §42-65.

Partial evictions.
Defined, §42-59.
Grounds, §42-63(b).

Parties.
Defendants, §42-62(b).
Who may bring action, §42-62(a).

Preliminary or emergency relief, §42-74.

Protection of threatened witnesses or affiants, §42-71.

Public policy statement, §42-59.1.

Records.
Admissibility of sealed criminal proceeding records in civil action, §42-69(d).

Remedies, cumulative nature, §42-75.

EXPEDITED EVICTIONS —Cont'd
Removal orders.
Grounds to remove from premises person other
than tenant, §42-63(b).
Conditional eviction order against tenant,
§42-63(c).
Motion to enforce, §42-66(a).
Obstruction of execution or enforcement, §42-65.
Rents.
Collection of rent by landlord does not constitute
waiver, §42-73.
Reports.
Availability of police or lab reports to plaintiffs,
§42-72.
Residents.
Defined, §42-59.
Rules of civil procedure, applicability, §42-68.
Service of process.
Complaint, §42-62(c).
Small claim actions.
Applicability of expedited process for summary
ejectment, §42-68.
Nature of actions, §42-60.
Standard of proof, §42-61.
Subpoena duces tecum, §42-70(d).
Temporary restraining orders.
Preliminary or emergency relief, §42-74.
Tenants.
Defined, §42-59.
Threats against witnesses.
Protection by court, §42-71.
Time for filing.
Extensions of time, §42-68.
Transcripts.
Admissibility of criminal trial recordings or
transcripts in civil action, §42-69(c).
Vacation rentals, §§42A-23 to 42A-27.
Violation of injunctions or preliminary relief.
Civil or criminal contempt, §42-74.
Violations of orders.
Mandatory eviction, §42-66(b).
Witnesses.
Protection of threatened witnesses, §42-71.

**EXPEDITED PROCESS FOR CHILD
SUPPORT,** §§50-30 to 50-39.
See CHILD SUPPORT.

EXPEDITED REFEREES PROCEEDINGS,
§1A-1 Rule 53(f).

EXPENSES OF LITIGATION.
See COSTS.

**EXPERIENCE AND CAREER EXPLORATION
PROGRAMS.**
Hours of work per week of enrollees,
§95-25.5(c).

EXPERTS IN CAPITAL CASES.
Indigent defense services.
Appointment and compensation, other expenses,
IDS Rules 2D.1 to 2D.5.

EXPERT WITNESSES.
Accident reconstruction experts.
Opinion on speed of vehicle, §8C-1 Rule 702(i).
Alcohol concentration level.
Testimony on specific level prohibited, §8C-1 Rule
702(a1).
Basis of opinion testimony, §8C-1 Rule 703.
Court appointed experts, §8C-1 Rule 706.
**Disclosure of facts and data underlying
opinion,** §8C-1 Rule 705.

EXPERT WITNESSES —Cont'd
Drug recognition expert.
Whether person under influence of impairing
substances and category of substances, §8C-1
Rule 702(a1).
Fees.
Uniform fees for witnesses, §7A-314(d).
Horizontal gaze nystagmus test (HGN).
Testimony as to results, §8C-1 Rule 702(a1).
Impairing substances.
Whether person under influence of and category
of, §8C-1 Rule 702(a1).
Impairment.
Testimony solely on issue of, §8C-1 Rule 702(a1).
Indigent defense services.
Fees paid by state, §7A-454.
Insanity defense.
Notice required, §15A-959.
**International commercial arbitration and
conciliation,** §1-567.56.
Limitation of number, pre-trial conference,
§1A-1 Rule 16(a).
Medical malpractice actions.
Arbitration of negligent health claims, §90-21.63.
Contingency fee testimony prohibited, §8C-1 Rule
702(f).
Discovery conference, §1A-1 Rule 26(f1).
Qualifications of expert.
General provisions, §8C-1 Rule 702(b).
Testimony against general practitioner, §8C-1
Rule 702(c).
Testimony regarding administrative or other
nonclinical issues, §8C-1 Rule 702(h).
Testimony regarding medical support staff,
§8C-1 Rule 702(d).
Waiver of requirements by resident judge, §8C-1
Rule 702(e).
Review of records by person reasonably expected
to qualify as expert witness.
Complaint to specifically assert, §1A-1 Rule 9(j).
Trial court disqualification of expert.
Power not limited by section, §8C-1 Rule 702(g).
**Medicolegal guidelines for attorney-physician
relationship,** MLG Rules 1 to 6.
Notice to defense of intent to call, §15A-903(a).
Notice to state of intent to call, §15A-905(c), (d).
Physicians and surgeons.
Hearing before medical board.
Right of licensee to call, §90-14.6(b).
Specialized knowledge, §8C-1 Rule 702(a).
Testimony generally, §8C-1 Rule 702(a).
Ultimate issue to be decided by trier of fact,
§8C-1 Rule 704.

**EXPLOITATION OF ELDER ADULT OR
DISABLED ADULT.**
Definitions, §14-112.2(a).
**Obtaining or using funds, assets or property
with intent to deprive.**
Person knowing that adult lacks capacity to
consent, §14-112.2(c).
Criminal penalties, §14-112.2(e).
Persons standing in position of trust and
confidence or business relationship,
§14-112.2(b).
Criminal penalties, §14-112.2(d).

**EXPLOITED, ABUSED OR NEGLECTED
DISABLED ADULTS,** §§108A-99 to 108A-111.
See ABUSED, NEGLECTED OR EXPLOITED
DISABLED ADULTS.

EXPLORATION FOR OIL AND GAS OFFSHORE, §§143-215.94AA to 143-215.94JJ. See OFFSHORE OIL AND GAS ACTIVITIES.

EXPLOSIVES.
Attempts to commit crime.
Malicious use of explosive or incendiary.
Property occupied by persons, §14-49.1.
Punishment, §14-49.1.
Bombs.
Exploding bombs, §14-283.
License.
Keeping for sale or selling explosives without license, §14-284.
Burglary.
Use of explosives in burglary, §14-57.
Campus or other education property, possessing or carrying unlawful.
Class 1 felony, §14-269.2(b1).
Class 1 misdemeanors, §14-269.2(f).
Definitions, §14-269.2(a).
Exceptions, §14-269.2(g), (h).
Minors, aiding to possess or carry.
Class 1 felony, §14-269.2(c1).
Civil disorders, §14-288.20.
Construction and interpretation.
Regulation of sale of explosives, §14-284.1(g).
Counties.
Regulation, §153A-128.
Definitions.
Incendiary device or explosive or material, §14-50.1.
Drivers' licenses.
Revocation or suspension of license.
Minors, §20-13.2(c2).
Dynamite.
Exploding dynamite cartridges, §14-283.
License.
Keeping for sale or selling explosives without license, §14-284.
Failure of town or city officer to inspect incendiary fires, §14-69.
False reports concerning destructive device.
Destructive device located in any building or vehicle, §14-69.1(a).
Destructive device located in public building, §14-69.1(c).
Report defined, §14-69.1(d).
Restitution, costs and consequential damages, ordering, §14-69.1(d).
Fireworks, §§14-410 to 14-415.
Fish or wildlife taken by use of.
Permit authorizing, §113-261(b).
Hoax by use of false bomb or other device, §14-69.2(a).
Public buildings, §14-69.2(c).
Restitution, costs and consequential damages, ordering, §14-69.2(d).
Larceny.
Felony larceny.
When value of property in question irrelevant, §14-72.
Licenses.
Sale or selling explosives without license, §14-284.
Malicious use of explosive or incendiary, §14-49(a), (b).
Churches and other buildings of worship, §14-49(b1).
Government buildings, §14-49(b2).
Punishment, §14-49.1.

EXPLOSIVES —Cont'd
Mass death and destruction weapons.
Manufacture, assembly, etc., §14-288.8.
Minors detonating in schools.
Parental liability for damages, §1-538.3.
Motor vehicles transporting, §20-167.
Municipalities.
Regulation of explosive substances, §160A-183.
Penalties.
Regulation of sale of explosives, §14-284.1(f).
Possessing or carrying on campus or other educational property, §14-269.2.
Powerful explosives.
Defined, §14-284.1(d).
Property occupied by persons.
Malicious damage by use of explosive or incendiary, §14-49.1.
Attempt to commit crime, §14-49.1.
Punishment for malicious use of explosive or incendiary.
Attempt to commit crime.
Property occupied by persons, §14-49.1.
Occupied property damaged.
Punishment, §14-49.1.
Records.
Regulation of sale of explosives, §14-284.1(b).
Safecracking, §14-89.1.
Sales.
License.
Keeping for sale or selling explosives without license, §14-284.
Regulation of sale of explosives, §14-284.1.
Applicability of provisions, §14-284.1(f).
Application of person or agent of person purchasing or receiving explosive, §14-284.1(a).
Construing provisions, §14-284.1(g).
Definition of term "powerful explosives,"§14-284.1(d).
Exceptions, §14-284.1(f).
Identifying purchaser, §14-284.1(a).
Penalties for violation of provisions, §14-284.1(e).
Powerful explosives.
Defined, §14-284.1(d).
Record of sales or deliveries, §14-284.1(b).
Storage of explosives, §14-284.1(c).
School, community college, college or university.
Possessing or carrying on campus or educational property, §14-269.2.
Storage.
Regulation of sale of explosives, §14-284.1(c).
Transporting, §20-167.
Weapons generally.
See FIREARMS AND OTHER WEAPONS.

EXPORTS AND IMPORTS.
Alcoholic beverages.
Denatured alcohol.
Exemption from provisions, §18B-103.
Liquor importer/bottler permit, §18B-1105.1.
Malt beverages.
Importer.
Authorization of permit, §18B-1108.
Unauthorized imports and exports prohibited, §18B-102(a).
Violation a misdemeanor, §18B-102(b).
Wine importer.
Authorization of permit, §18B-1106(a).
Distribution agreements, §18B-1106(b).

EXPORTS AND IMPORTS —Cont'd
Alcoholic beverages —Cont'd
Wine importer —Cont'd
Primary American source of supply of wine,
§18B-203(a).
Ammunition.
Teflon-coated bullets, §14-34.3.
Constitution of the United States, US Const Art
I §§9, 10.
Fertilizers.
Commercial fertilizers.
Sales or exchanges between imports, §106-676.
Livestock.
Tubercular animals.
Importation of cattle, §106-345.
Pesticides.
Foreign exports.
Exceptions, §143-445(b).
Sales and use tax.
Exemptions, §105-164.13.
Wildlife exportation or importation permits,
§113-274(c).

EX POST FACTO LAWS, NC Const Art I §16, US
Const Art I §§9, 10.

EXPRESS TOTAL RETURN UNITRUSTS.
Distribution, §§37A-1-104.21 to 37A-1-104.26.
See PRINCIPAL AND INCOME ACT.

EXPRESS TRUSTS.
Uniform trust code.
General provisions, §§36C-1-101 to 36C-11-1106.
See TRUSTS AND TRUSTEES.

EXPRESS WARRANTIES.
Leases, UCC, §25-2A-210.
Displacement of inconsistent implied warranties,
§25-2A-215(c).
Third-party beneficiaries, §25-2A-216.
New motor vehicles warranties act, §§20-351 to
20-351.10.
See LEMON LAW.
Sale of goods, UCC, §25-2-313.
Cumulation and conflict, §25-2-317.
Third party beneficiaries, §25-2-318.

EXPULSION OF STUDENTS, §115C-390.11.
Assault on teacher resulting in expulsion.
Return to teacher's classroom on readmission
prohibited, §115C-390.12(c).
Data on each student disciplined, §115C-276(r).
Denial or restriction on admission,
§115C-366(a5).
Discipline generally, §§115C-390.1 to 115C-392.
See SCHOOLS AND EDUCATION.
Expulsion defined, §115C-390.1(b).
Policies to minimize use, §115C-390.2(f).
Readmission, request for, §115C-390.12.
Serious violations of code of student conduct.
Examples, §115C-390.2(f).
Limited to, §115C-390.2(f).
Transfers.
Statement by parent relating to, §115C-366(a4).
Violations provided in state and federal laws,
§115C-390.2(e).

EXPUNGEMENT OF RECORDS.
Certificate of verification, §15A-152(d).
Confidential agency files.
Administrative office of courts.
Disclosure, §15A-151(a).
Duty to maintain, §15A-151(a).

EXPUNGEMENT OF RECORDS —Cont'd
Confidential agency files —Cont'd
Agencies required to expunge records providing
information to private entities, §15A-151(b).
Criminal street gangs.
First offenders under age of 18.
Discharge on completion of probation,
§14-50.29(d).
Petition, §15A-145.1.
Procedure, §§14-50.30, 15A-145.1.
**Dismissal of charges, finding of not guilty or
not responsible.**
Application to court, §15A-146(a).
As result of identity theft, §15A-147.
Confidential file containing names of persons
granted expungement.
Administrative office of the courts to maintain,
§15A-146(c).
Costs taxed against petitioner, §15A-146(b).
DNA records, application to expunge,
§15A-146(b1), (b2).
Failure to recite or acknowledge expunged
records.
Not perjury or false statement, §15A-146(a).
Hearing on application, §15A-146(a).
Law enforcement agencies order to expunge
records, §15A-146(b).
Multiple offenses, §15A-146(a1).
Names of persons granted expungement.
Filed with administrative office of the courts,
§15A-146(c).
Order of court, §15A-146(a), (b).
Division of motor vehicles.
Expungement specifically prohibited by certain
federal acts.
Division not required to expunge, §15A-151(c).
DNA records.
Arrest for certain offenses.
Obtaining DNA sample for DNA analysis.
Circumstances requiring removal of record
and destruction of samples,
§15A-266.3A(g) to (i).
Notice of procedures for seeking provided,
§15A-266.3A(b2).
Automated procedure to facilitate.
Study, report, §15A-266.5(d).
Charges dismissed, finding of not guilty or not
responsible, §15A-146(b1), (b2).
Charges dismissed on appeal or pardon of
innocence granted, §15A-148(a), (b).
Drug offenses, §90-96.
First offenders not over age twenty-one,
§15A-145.2.
Application to court, §15A-145.2(a).
Content requirements, §15A-145.2(a).
Criminal record check.
Application filed by applicant,
§15A-145.2(a).
Fee, §15A-145.2(d).
Good behavior affidavit.
Applicant to file, §15A-145.2(a).
Good character and reputation affidavit.
Persons not related to applicant to file,
§15A-145.2(a).
Notification requirements, §15A-150.
Order of court, §15A-145.2(a), (c).
Possession of controlled substance,
§15A-145.2(b), (c).
Possession of drug paraphernalia, §15A-145.2(c).
Restoration to status prior to arrest, indictment
or information, §15A-145.2(a).

EXPUNGEMENT OF RECORDS —Cont'd
Firearms rights, restoration.
Expunction not restoration, §14-415.4(i).
First offenders not over age twenty-one.
Drug offenses, §15A-145.2.
Toxic vapors offenses, §15A-145.3.
First offenders under age of eighteen.
Gang offenses, §15A-145.1.
  Discharge on completion of probation,
    §14-50.29(d).
  Notification requirements, §15A-150.
  Order, §15A-145.1(b).
  Petition, §15A-145.1(a).
  Procedure, §14-50.30.
  Restoration to status prior to arrest, indictment
    or information, §15A-145.1(b).
  Supplemental nature of provisions,
    §15A-145.1(c).
Misdemeanor or civil revocation of driver's license.
Expunged, §15A-145(c).
Nonviolent felony offenses.
Affidavit of petitioner, §15A-145.4(c).
Community service requirement, §15A-145.4(c).
Conditions for granting petition, §15A-145.4(e).
Court records, expunction from, §15A-145.4(g).
Court, steps taken on receipt of petition,
  §15A-145.4(d).
Criminal record check, application for,
  §15A-145.4(c).
Definition of nonviolent felony, §15A-145.4(a).
Duties of district attorney, §15A-145.4(c).
Failure to acknowledge arrest after expunction,
  effect, §15A-145.4(f).
Filing petition for expungement, §15A-145.4(c).
Law enforcement records, expunction from,
  §15A-145.4(g).
Multiple nonviolent felonies committed at same
  time, §15A-145.4(b).
Notice to offender of eligibility for expunction,
  §15A-145.4(i).
Order of court for expunction and restoration of
  status, §15A-145.4(e).
Service of petition on district attorney,
  §15A-145.4(c).
State or local government agency records,
  expunction from, §15A-145.4(h).
Notification requirements, §15A-150.
Orders of court, §15A-145(b), (c).
  Gang offenses, §15A-145.1(b).
  Notification to state and local agencies.
    Duty of clerk, §15A-145(d).
Petition, §15A-145(a).
  Content requirements, §15A-145(a).
  Criminal record check.
    Application for, §15A-145(a).
  Fee for filing, §15A-145(e).
  Gang offenses, §15A-145.1(a).
  Good behavior affidavit by petitioner,
    §15A-145(a).
  Good character and reputation affidavits.
    Persons not related to petitioner, §15A-145(a).
  No restitution or civil judgments outstanding.
    Affidavit by petitioner, §15A-145(a).
  Objection by district attorney.
    Time for filing, §15A-145(a).
  Service upon district attorney, §15A-145(a).
  Time for filing, §15A-145(a).
Restoration to status before arrest, indictment or
  information, §15A-145(b).
Gang offenses.
First offenders under age of eighteen.
  Discharge on completion of probation,
    §14-50.29(d).

EXPUNGEMENT OF RECORDS —Cont'd
Gang offenses —Cont'd
First offenders under age of eighteen —Cont'd
  Notification requirements, §15A-150.
  Order, §15A-145.1(b).
  Petition, §15A-145.1(a).
    Content requirements, §15A-145.1(a).
    Criminal record check.
      Application filed with petition,
        §15A-145.1(a).
    Good behavior affidavit.
      Filed by petitioner, §15A-145.1(a).
    Good character and reputation affidavit.
      Filed by persons not related to petitioner,
        §15A-145.1(a).
    No restitution or civil judgments outstanding.
      Affidavit filed with petition, §15A-145.1(a).
    Objection by district attorney, filing, time,
      §15A-145.1(a).
    Service on district attorney, §15A-145.1(a).
    Time for filing, §15A-145.1(a).
  Procedure, §14-50.30.
  Restoration to status prior to arrest, indictment
    or information, §15A-145.1(b).
  Supplemental nature of provisions,
    §15A-145.1(c).
Identity theft.
Dismissal of charges, finding of not guilty, another
  using identifying information.
  Division of motor vehicles to expunge records,
    §15A-147(c), (d).
  Failure to acknowledge records not perjury,
    §15A-147(b).
  Hearing on petition or motion, court to hold,
    §15A-147(a).
  Insurance companies charging additional
    insurance points premium, refund,
    §15A-147(f).
  Law enforcement agencies and other agencies
    ordered to expunge, §15A-147(c).
  Order to expunge, §15A-147(a).
  Petition or motion, §15A-147(a).
  State or local agencies ordered to expunge,
    §15A-147(c), (e).
Juveniles alleged or adjudicated delinquent.
Effect of expunction, §7B-3201.
Notice of expunction, §7B-3202.
Ordering and directing expungement,
  §7B-3200(d), (e).
Petition filed by person adjudicated delinquent or
  undisciplined, §7B-3200(a), (c).
Petition filed by person alleged delinquent or
  undisciplined, §7B-3200(h).
Report by clerk of superior court of names of
  persons granted expunction, §7B-3200(i).
Retention or disposition of records.
  Juvenile court counselor, §7B-3200(f).
  Residential facility, §7B-3200(g).
Minors.
Drug offenses, §90-96.
First offense, §15A-145.
  Drug offenses.
    First offenders not over age twenty-one,
      §15A-145.2.
  Gang offenses, §15A-145.1.
  Toxic vapors offenses.
    First offenders not over age twenty-one,
      §15A-145.3.
Juveniles alleged or adjudicated delinquent,
  §§7B-3200 to 7B-3202.

EXPUNGEMENT OF RECORDS —Cont'd
Misdemeanor larceny conviction 15 years prior to filing petition.
Notification requirements, §15A-150.
Order of court, §15A-145(d1).
Petition, §15A-145(d1).
Content requirements, §15A-145(d1).
Criminal record check.
Application for, §15A-145(d1).
Fee, §15A-145(e).
Good behavior affidavit.
Petitioner to file, §15A-145(d1).
Good character and reputation affidavit.
Persons not related to petitioner to file, §15A-145(d1).
No restitution orders or civil judgments outstanding.
Affidavit filed by petitioner, §15A-145(d1).
Objection by district attorney.
Filing, time, §15A-145(d1).
Service on district attorney, §15A-145(d1).
Restoration to status before arrest, indictment or information, §15A-145(d1).
Notice.
Administrative office of the courts, §15A-150(a).
Confidential agency files, §15A-151.
FBI, §15A-150(c).
Private entities, §15A-150(d).
Record removal.
Request by person subject of expunged record, §15A-152(e).
SBI, §15A-150(c).
State and local agencies generally, §15A-150(b).
Nurse licensure compact.
Coordinated licensure information system, §90-171.88(f).
Pardon of innocence granted.
Application, §15A-149(a).
Order, §15A-149(b).
Perjury not charged for denial or failure to acknowledge record, §15A-149(c).
Presentence reports, §15A-1333.
Private entities.
Deletion of records.
Duty to delete, §15A-152(a).
Dissemination of information, §15A-152(b).
Civil liability, §15A-152(c).
Notice of record removal.
Request by person subject of expunged record.
Notification to private entity, §15A-152(e).
Public schools.
Special education.
Education of children with disabilities.
Incorrect, outdated, misleading or irrelevant entries in child's records, §115C-109.3(c).
Student records, §115C-402(b).
Special education.
Education of children with disabilities.
Incorrect, outdated, misleading or irrelevant entries in child's records, §115C-109.3(c).
Student records, §115C-402(b).
Education of children with disabilities.
Incorrect, outdated, misleading or irrelevant entries in child's records, §115C-109.3(c).
Toxic vapors offenses.
First offenders not over age twenty-one, §15A-145.3.
Application to court, §15A-145.3(a) to (c).
Content requirements, §15A-145.3(a).
Criminal record check.
Application for, §15A-145.3(a).

EXPUNGEMENT OF RECORDS —Cont'd
Toxic vapors offenses —Cont'd
First offenders not over age twenty-one —Cont'd
Application to court —Cont'd
Good behavior affidavit.
Filed by applicant, §15A-145.3(a).
Good character and reputation affidavit.
Filed by persons not related to applicant, §15A-145.3(a).
Notification requirements, §15A-150.
Order of court, §15A-145.3(a) to (c).
Restoration to status prior to arrest, indictment or information, §15A-145.3(a).

EXTENSION OF MUNICIPAL CORPORATION LIMITS, §§160A-29 to 160A-58.90.
See ANNEXATION.

EXTENSION OF TIME FOR FILING AND OTHER ACTS.
Catastrophic conditions existing in one or more counties.
Authority of chief justice, entry of order, §7A-39(b).
Tax reports or returns, §105-263(b).

EXTENSION SERVICE.
Agricultural development generally, §§106-580 to 106-587.
See AGRICULTURAL DEVELOPMENT.

EXTORTION.
Adulterated or misbranded food, drugs or cosmetics.
Intent to extort, §14-34.4(b).
Computer-related crime, §14-457.
County inspectors of articles of commerce, §66-7.
Electronic surveillance orders, §15A-290(b).
Elements of offense, §14-118.4.
General assembly.
Legislative ethics act, §120-86(b) to (e).
Police.
Removal of unfit officers, §128-16.
Sheriffs.
Removal of unfit officers, §128-16.

EXTRADITION, §§15A-721 to 15A-750, US Const Art II §2, Art IV §2.
Assisting arresting officer.
Refusing assistance, §15A-729.
Asylum.
No right of asylum, §15A-748.
Citation of act.
Short title, §15A-750.
Construction and interpretation, §15A-749.
Definitions, §15A-721.
Evidence, rules of, §8C-1 Rule 1101(b).
Fugitives from other states, §§15A-728, 15A-729.
Arrest by officers from other states, §15A-403.
Arrest prior to requisition, §15A-733.
Bail.
Conditions of bond, §15A-736.
Forfeiture of bail, §15A-738.
Generally, §§15A-735, 15A-736.
Methamphetamine manufacture, §15A-534.6.
Recovery on bond, §15A-738.
Commitment to await requisition, §15A-735.
Extension of time of commitment, §15A-737.
Confinement in jail when necessary, §15A-732.
Criminal charges pending in this state, §15A-739.
Demand for extradition.
Contents, §15A-723.

EXTRADITION —Cont'd
Fugitives from other states —Cont'd
Demand for extradition —Cont'd
Form, §15A-723.
Investigation.
Governor may cause investigation to be made, §15A-724.
Governor.
Duty as to, §15A-722.
Investigation.
Governor may cause investigation to be made, §15A-724.
Warrant of arrest, §§15A-727 to 15A-729.
Guilt or innocence of accused.
When inquired into, §15A-740.
Habeas corpus.
Application for, §15A-730.
Imprisoned or awaiting trial in another state, §15A-725.
Intent of fugitive irrelevant, §15A-725.
Jail.
Commitment to await requisition, §15A-735.
Extension of time of commitment, §15A-737.
Confinement in jail when necessary, §15A-732.
Commitment to await requisition, §15A-735.
Officers or agents passing through state.
Confinement of prisoner in local jails, §15A-732.
Persons imprisoned or awaiting trial in another state or who have left the demanding state under compulsion, §15A-725.
Persons not present in demanding state at time of commission of crime, §15A-726.
Persons under criminal prosecution in this state at time of requisition, §15A-739.
Persons who left state under compulsion, §15A-725.
Presence in demanding state not required, §15A-726.
Rights of accused person, §§15A-730, 15A-731.
Violation, §15A-731.
Warrantless arrest, §15A-734.
Warrant of arrest.
Alias.
Issuance, §15A-741.
Execution of warrant.
Commanding aid, §§15A-728, 15A-729.
Time and place, §15A-728.
Issuance, §15A-727.
Recall of warrant, §15A-741.
Recitals, §15A-727.
Fugitives from this state.
Costs, §15A-744.
Demand, §15A-742.
Expenses, §15A-744.
Governor.
Duty, §15A-742.
Immunity from civil process, §15A-745.
Requisition.
Application for issuance, §15A-743(a), (b).
Contents, §15A-743(c).
Service of process.
Immunity from service of process in certain civil actions, §15A-745.
Fugitives in other countries.
Securing attendance, §15A-772.
Guilt or innocence of accused.
Fugitives from other states, §15A-740.
Harmful materials sales to minors.
Contempt.
Persons guilty of contempt, §19-20(c).

EXTRADITION —Cont'd
Immunities.
No immunity from other criminal prosecution while in this state, §15A-748.
Indigent persons.
Entitlement to services of counsel, §7A-451(a).
International fugitives.
Procedure for extraditing fugitives in other countries, §15A-772.
Interstate compact on juveniles, §§7B-2800 to 7B-2827.
See INTERSTATE COMPACT ON JUVENILES.
Interstate family support.
Interstate rendition, §§52C-8-801, 52C-8-802.
Multiple jurisdiction.
Fugitives from other states awaiting prosecution in this state, §15A-739.
Rules of evidence.
Inapplicability, §8C-1 Rule 1101(b).
Title of act.
Short title, §15A-750.
Waiver.
Nonwaiver by this state, §15A-747.
Written waiver of extradition proceedings, §15A-746.

EXTRAJUDICIAL STATEMENTS.
Attorneys at law, ProfCond Rule 3.6.

EXTRAORDINARY REMEDIES.
Habeas corpus, §§17-1 to 17-46.
See HABEAS CORPUS.
Mandamus.
See MANDAMUS.
Prohibition, §7A-32(b).
Quo warranto, §§1-514 to 1-532.
See QUO WARRANTO.
Receivers.
General provisions.
See RECEIVERS.
Waste, §§1-533 to 1-538.
See WASTE.

EYE DONOR CARDS.
Availability at division of motor vehicles offices, §20-7.3.

EYEGLASSES.
Contact lenses.
Prescriptions.
Requirements for filling, §90-236.1.
Opticians.
General provisions, §§90-234 to 90-255.1.
See OPTICIANS.
Optometrists.
General provisions, §§90-114 to 90-127.3.
See OPTOMETRISTS.
Sales.
Flammable frames.
Prohibited, §90-255.1.
Opticians.
Requirements, §90-250.
Sales and use tax.
Exemption, §105-164.13.

EYE PROTECTION.
Operating ATV.
Requirement, §20-171.19(a).
Electric service employee engaged in power line inspection, §20-171.19(a2).
Minors, §20-171.19(a1).
Schools, §§115C-166 to 115C-169.
Corrective protective devices, §115C-169.

EYE PROTECTION —Cont'd
Schools —Cont'd
Industrial quality eye protective devices.
Defined, §115C-168.
Required in certain courses, §115C-166.
Visitors to wear, §115C-167.

EYES.
Armed forces members.
Eye exam exemption.
Renewal of driver's license by mail, §20-7(r).
Blind persons.
Eye examinations.
Arranging for examination of eyes, §111-8.
Medical and surgical treatment, §111-8.
Children's health insurance program.
Vision benefits, §108A-70.21(b).
Glaucoma.
Department of environment and natural
resources.
Establishment of program, §130A-221(a), (b).
Kindergarten children.
Comprehensive eye examination required,
§130A-440.1.
Opticians generally, §§90-234 to 90-255.1.
See OPTICIANS.
Optometrists generally, §§90-114 to 90-127.3.
See OPTOMETRISTS.
**Vision screening for children entering
kindergarten,** §130A-440.1.
Workers' compensation.
Loss of eyes.
Permanent total disability.
Qualification for, lifetime compensation,
§97-29(d).

EYEWITNESS IDENTIFICATION REFORM,
§§15A-284.50 to 15A-284.53.
**Alternative methods in lieu of independent
lineup,** §15A-284.52(c).
Definitions, §15A-284.52(a).
Live lineups, independent administration,
§15A-284.52(b).
Photo lineups, §15A-284.52(c).
Purpose of provisions, §15A-284.51.
Remedies for noncompliance, §15A-284.52(d).
Title of act, §15A-284.50.
Training of law enforcement officers,
§15A-284.53.

EYEWITNESS OBSERVATIONS.
Journalist's qualified privilege.
Eyewitness observation of criminal or tortuous
conduct, no privilege, §8-53.11(d).

F

FACE BONES AND JOINTS.
Insurance discrimination, §58-3-121(a) to (c).

FACILITY AUTHORITIES, §§160A-480.1 to
160A-480.15.
Accounts and accounting.
Fiscal accountability, §160A-480.3(f).
Actions.
Powers of authority, §160A-480.4.
Arenas.
Seating at regional facility arena, §160A-480.7.
Bids and bidding.
Construction contracts, §160A-480.6.
Bond issues.
Approval, §160A-480.8(g).

FACILITY AUTHORITIES —Cont'd
Bond issues —Cont'd
Basis of investment, §160A-480.8(k).
Certification of approval, §160A-480.8(g).
Details of bonds or notes, §160A-480.8(j).
Faith and credit of state not pledged,
§160A-480.11.
Investment basis, §160A-480.8(k).
Investment securities, §160A-480.8(i).
Issuance generally, §160A-480.8(f).
Liability, §160A-480.15.
Pledge of state, §160A-480.8(h).
Powers of authority, §160A-480.4.
Proceeds from bonds deemed trust funds,
§160A-480.10.
Proceeds, use, §160A-480.8(b).
Refunding bonds, §160A-480.12.
Revenue, §160A-480.8(d).
Securities eligible for investment, §160A-480.13.
Security interest, §160A-480.8(e).
Security of bonds, §160A-480.8(c).
State pledge, §160A-480.8(h).
Tax exemption, §160A-480.14.
Terms of bonds, §160A-480.8(a).
Trust agreements securing bonds, §160A-480.9.
Use of proceeds, §160A-480.8(b).
Bylaws, §160A-480.3(d).
Powers of authority to adopt, §160A-480.4.
Charter, §160A-480.3(d).
Citation of act.
Short title, §160A-480.1.
Conflicts of interest.
Members, officers or employees.
Disclosure to authority, §160A-480.3(g).
Construction contracts, §160A-480.6.
Consultants, employment.
Powers of authority, §160A-480.4.
Contracts.
Conflicts of interest.
Disclosure to authority, §160A-480.3(g).
Construction contracts, §160A-480.6.
Investment of bonds, §160A-480.8(k).
Powers of authority, §160A-480.4.
Creation of authority, §160A-480.3(a).
Credit facilities.
Defined, §160A-480.2.
Definitions, §160A-480.2.
Dissolution.
Dissolution of authority by general assembly,
§160A-480.5.
Ethics.
Authority created under this to be treated as
board for purposes of state government ethics
act, §160A-480.3(h).
Fees.
Powers of authority, §160A-480.4.
Fiscal accountability, §160A-480.3(f).
Grants.
Powers of authority, §160A-480.4.
Investment securities.
Bond issues, §160A-480.8(i).
Bond issues made securities eligible for
investment, §160A-480.13.
Jurisdiction.
Territorial jurisdiction of authority,
§160A-480.3(a).
Liability of members or officers, §160A-480.15.
Loans.
Powers of authority, §160A-480.4.
Meetings, §160A-480.3(e).

FACILITY AUTHORITIES —Cont'd
Members.
Appointment, §160A-480.3(b).
Defined, §160A-480.2.
Disclosure of conflicts of interest to authority,
§160A-480.3(g).
Liability for bond issues, §160A-480.15.
Terms, §160A-480.3(b).
Par formulas.
Defined, §160A-480.2.
Personal property.
Powers of authority, §160A-480.4.
Powers generally, §160A-480.4.
Purpose of authority, §160A-480.3(c).
Real property.
Powers of authority, §160A-480.4.
Refunding bonds, §160A-480.12.
Regional facilities.
Construction and operation, powers of authority,
§160A-480.4.
Defined, §160A-480.2.
Seating at arenas, §160A-480.7.
Sales and use tax refunds, §105-164.14(c).
Seals and sealed instruments.
Power of authority to adopt official seal,
§160A-480.4.
Security interest.
Bond issues, §160A-480.8(e).
Short title, §160A-480.1.
State debt not created by bond issues,
§160A-480.11.
Surveys and surveyors.
Powers of authority, §160A-480.4.
Taxation.
Bond issues exempt from taxation, §160A-480.14.
Trusts and trustees.
Receipt of proceeds from sale of bonds deemed
trust funds, §160A-480.10.
Trust agreement or resolution securing bond
issues, §160A-480.9.
University of North Carolina.
Athletic events at regional facility arena.
Student seating, §160A-480.7.

FACSIMILE TRANSACTIONS.
Generally.
See FAX.
Uniform electronic transactions act, §§66-311 to
66-330.
See ELECTRONIC TRANSACTIONS.

FACTORS.
Agents generally.
See AGENTS.
Brokers generally.
See BROKERS.
Disclosure of real parties.
Person trading as "factor" to disclose, §66-72.
Sale of goods, UCC.
Consignment sales, §25-2-326.
Power to transfer title, §25-2-403.
Sale on approval or return, §25-2-326.
Trader or merchant transacting business with
addition of words factor.
Disclosure of name of principal or partner by sign
placed conspicuously in place of business,
§66-72.

FACTORY BRANCHES AND FACTORY
REPRESENTATIVES.
Motor vehicles.
Automobile manufacturers licensing act.
Generally.
See MOTOR VEHICLE MANUFACTURERS.

FACTORY BRANCHES AND FACTORY
REPRESENTATIVES —Cont'd
Motor vehicles —Cont'd
Automobile manufacturers' licensing act.
Generally, §§20-285 to 20-308.22.

FACTUAL INNOCENCE.
Claim generally, innocence inquiry
commission, §§15A-1460 to 15A-1475.
See INNOCENCE CLAIM INQUIRY.

FAILURE OF CONSIDERATION.
Affirmative defense, pleading, §1A-1 Rule 8(c).

FAILURE TO APPEAR.
Abused, neglected or dependent juvenile
actions, §7B-407.
Delinquent and undisciplined juvenile actions.
Contempt for parent's guardian's or custodian's
failure to appear, §§7B-1805(b), (c), 7B-1806.
Dismissal with leave when defendant fails to
appear and cannot readily be found,
§15A-932.
Divorce or annulment.
Notice of trial not required, §50-10(b).
Garnishees, §1-440.27.
Motor vehicle offenses.
Court to report failure to appear, §20-24.2.
Revocation of driver's license, §20-24.1.
Pretrial release, conditions imposed.
Prior failure to appear and answer charges,
§15A-534(d1).
Property insurance.
Mediation of emergency or disaster claims.
Failure of insurer to appear, §58-44-100(f).
Referees meetings, §1A-1 Rule 53(f).
Service of pleadings and other papers on party
in default not required, §1A-1 Rule 5(a).
Small claims actions.
Appeals, §7A-228(c).

FAILURE TO DIM HEADLIGHTS, §20-181.

FAILURE TO DISPERSE WHEN
COMMANDED, §14-288.5.

FAILURE TO JOIN PARTY.
Defense by pretrial motion, §1A-1 Rule 12(b).

FAILURE TO SHOW RIGHT TO RELIEF.
Involuntary dismissal, §1A-1 Rule 41(b).

FAILURE TO STATE CLAIM.
Defense by pretrial motion, §1A-1 Rule 12(b).
Involuntary dismissal, plaintiff failed to show
right to relief, §1A-1 Rule 41(b).

FAILURE TO YIELD RIGHT-OF-WAY.
Interstate or defense highways or
controlled-access highways, §20-140.3.
Point schedule, §20-16(c).
Stop signs or signals, §20-158(b).

FAIR ACCESS TO INSURANCE, §§58-46-1 to
58-46-60.
See PROPERTY INSURANCE.

FAIR HOUSING, §§41A-1 to 41A-10.
Actions.
Commission may bring to obtain relief, §41A-7(h).
Complaints.
Judicial review.
Final agency decision, §41A-7(m).
Jury trial, §41A-7(k).
Right-to-sue letter.
Issuance, §41A-7(h).
Time for issuing, §41A-7(i).

FAIR HOUSING —Cont'd
Actions —Cont'd
Superior courts.
Filing of certified copy of commission's final
order.
Clerk of court to enter order enforcing
council's final order, §41A-7(n).
Venue, §41A-10.
Appeals.
Final agency decisions, §41A-7(m).
**Building code provisions applicable to
handicapped.**
Exemption from chapter, §41A-6(d).
Business necessity.
Not violation, §41A-5(a).
Certification.
Commission certification by federal department
prerequisite to acceptance of complaints,
§41A-7(a).
Citation of chapter, §41A-1.
Coercion, intimidation, threats or interference,
§41A-4(e).
Commercial real estate.
Exemption from chapter, §41A-6(a).
Complaints.
Actions.
Commission issuance of notice of conciliation
failure.
Actions of council when civil action not
elected, §41A-7(l).
Issuance of right-to-sue letter, §41A-7.
Judicial review.
Final agency decision, §41A-7(m).
Right-to-sue letter.
Time for issuance, §41A-7(i).
Answers.
Filing, §41A-7(b).
Appeals.
Final agency decisions, §41A-7(m).
Assignment of administrative law judges,
§41A-7(l).
Certification.
Commission certification by federal department
prerequisite to acceptance of complaints,
§41A-7(a).
Conciliation.
Agreements.
Commission to approve, §41A-7(g).
Public disclosure, §41A-7(g).
Commission to seek to informally resolve
complaint, §41A-7(g).
Failure of conciliation.
Actions of commission, §41A-7(h).
Notice of conciliation failure, §41A-7(k).
Resolution by conciliation, §41A-7(d).
Conference.
Commission to seek to bring about informal
resolution through conference, §41A-7.
Resolution by informal conference, §41A-7(d).
Dismissal, §41A-7(f).
Filing, §41A-7(a), (b).
Final decision.
Commission's panel composition, §41A-7(l).
Final administrative disposition.
Time in which commission shall make,
§41A-7(b).
Judicial review, §41A-7(m).
Penalties of commission, §41A-7(l).
Remedies of commission, §41A-7(l).
Form, §41A-7(a).

FAIR HOUSING —Cont'd
Complaints —Cont'd
Grounds for belief of occurrences.
Unlawful discriminatory housing practices.
Steps council to take, §41A-7(g).
Injunction, §41A-7(j).
Investigations, §41A-7(e).
Jurisdiction, §41A-7(c).
Notice, §41A-7(a).
Persuasion.
Commission to seek informal resolution through
persuasion, §41A-7(g).
Resolution of complaint by persuasion,
§41A-7(d).
Relief.
Commission may grant appropriate relief,
§41A-7(j).
Resolution.
Failure to resolve.
Actions of commission, §41A-7(h).
Informal resolution, §41A-7(d).
Commission to attempt to bring about,
§41A-7(g).
Respondent.
Notice of procedural rights and obligations,
§41A-7(a).
Serving of complaint, §41A-7(a).
Right-to-sue letter.
Council issuance of notice of conciliation failure.
Actions of commission when letter not
requested, §41A-7(l).
Time for determination, §41A-7(e).
Damages.
Actual and punitive damages, §41A-7(j).
Defenses.
Business necessity, §41A-5(a).
Unlawful discriminatory housing practices.
Acting for another no defense, §41A-5(b).
Definitions, §41A-3.
Residential real estate related transactions,
§41A-4(b1).
Disclosures.
Conciliation agreements, §41A-7(g).
Evidence.
Intent to discriminate, establishing, §41A-5(a).
Exemptions.
Building code provisions, §41A-6(d).
Familial status.
Inapplicability to housing for older persons,
§41A-6(e).
Generally, §41A-6(a).
Maximum number of occupants.
Local or state restrictions, §41A-6(c).
Threat to health or safety.
Tenancy constituting, §41A-6(b).
**Familial status provisions contained in
chapter.**
Inapplicability to housing for older persons,
§41A-6(e).
Financial institutions.
Unlawful discriminatory housing practices,
§41A-4(b).
Four families or less, accommodations for.
Exemption from chapter, §41A-6(a).
Handicapped persons.
Unlawful discriminatory housing practices,
§41A-4(f).
Housing for older persons.
Inapplicability of familial status provisions,
§41A-6(e).

FAIR HOUSING —Cont'd
Injunctions.
  Appropriateness of relief, §41A-7(j).
Intent of chapter, §41A-2.
Intent to discriminate.
  Establishing, §41A-5(a).
Investigations, §41A-8(a).
  Complaints, §41A-7(e).
Land-use decisions.
  Unlawful discriminatory housing practices,
    §41A-4(g).
Maximum number of occupants.
  Local or state restrictions.
    Exemption from chapter, §41A-6(c).
Municipalities.
  Fair housing ordinance.
    Amendment, §160A-499.2(b).
    Authority to adopt, §160A-499.2(a).
    Complaints and results of inspections not
      subject to inspection, §160A-499.2(e).
    Creation of committee to enforce ordinance,
      §160A-499.2(d).
    Exemption from coverage, §160A-499.2(c).
    Meetings of committee, §160A-499.2(f).
Notice.
  Complaints, §41A-7(a).
    Respondent.
      Notice of procedural rights and obligations,
        §41A-7(a).
  Conciliation.
    Notice of conciliation failure, §41A-7(k).
Orders, §41A-7.
  Commission.
    Final decision orders, §41A-7(l).
  Superior courts.
    Clerk of court to enter order enforcing
      commission's final orders, §41A-7(n).
Penalties.
  Complaints.
    Commission's final decisions, §41A-7(l).
Private clubs.
  Exemption from chapter, §41A-6(a).
Private house, rental of room or rooms.
  Exemption from chapter, §41A-6(a).
Purpose of chapter, §41A-2.
Real estate brokers.
  Unlawful discriminatory housing practices,
    §41A-4(d).
Real estate transactions.
  Unlawful discriminatory housing practices,
    §41A-4(c).
Religious institutions.
  Exemption from chapter, §41A-6(a).
Remedies.
  Complaints.
    Commission's final decisions, §41A-7(l).
Residential real estate related transactions.
  Defined, §41A-4(b1).
Single sex dormitory.
  Exemption from chapter, §41A-6(a).
Subpoenas.
  Issuance, §41A-8(b).
  Refusal to obey, §41A-8(d).
  Respondent, entitlement to issuance, §41A-8(c).
Superior courts.
  Filing of certified copy of council's final order.
    Clerk of court to enter order enforcing
      commission's final order, §41A-7(n).
Threat to health or safety.
  Exemption from chapter, §41A-6(b).
Title of chapter, §41A-1.

FAIR HOUSING —Cont'd
Unlawful discriminatory housing practices.
  Acting for another no defense, §41A-5(b).
  Enumeration, §41A-4.
  Generally, §41A-4(a).
  Proof of violation, §41A-5(a).
  Steps commission to take, §41A-7(g).
  Violations.
    Proof of violation, §41A-5(a).
Venue.
  Civil actions, §41A-10.

FAIR LABOR STANDARDS ACT OF 1938.
Enforcement, §95-14.
Limitation of actions, §1-52.

FAIR MARKET VALUE.
Eminent domain.
  Compensation for taking, §40A-64.

FAIR PLAN.
Fair access to property insurance, §§58-46-1 to
  58-46-60.
  See PROPERTY INSURANCE.

FAIRS.
Agricultural exhibits.
  Local aid, §106-520.
Animal exhibitions.
  Regulation, §106-520.3A.
Animal exhibits.
  Local aid, §106-520.
Commissioner of agriculture.
  Supervision of fairs, §106-520.3.
County commissioners.
  Application for license to commissioners,
    §106-517.
    Penalty for violation of provisions, §106-518.
    Refusal to license shows within five miles,
      §106-519.
County societies.
  Evidence.
    Records may be read in evidence, §106-511.
  Exhibits exempt from state and county taxes,
    §106-507.
  Funds to be used in paying premiums, §106-508.
  Incorporation, §106-505.
  New members, §106-506.
  Officers, §106-506.
  Organization, §106-506.
  Powers, §106-505.
  Premiums awarded by societies.
    Funds to be used in paying premiums,
      §106-508.
  Publication of statements required, §106-510.
  Records to be kept, §106-511.
    May be read in evidence, §106-511.
  Statements.
    Annual statements to state treasurer, §106-509.
    Publication required, §106-510.
  State treasurer.
    Annual statement to treasurer, §106-509.
  Taxation.
    Exhibits exempt from state and county taxes,
      §106-507.
  Term of existence, §106-505.
Definitions.
  Supervision of fairs, §106-520.1.
Exhibitors' license to be paid if near fairs,
  §106-516.
  Unlicensed exhibiting a misdemeanor, §106-518.
General assembly.
  Land set apart for state fair.
    Repossession of land at will of general
      assembly, §106-504.

FAIRS —Cont'd
Licenses.
Application for license to county commissioners, §106-517.
Penalty for violation of provisions, §106-518.
Refusal to license shows within five miles, §106-519.
Exhibitors near fairs to pay license, §106-516.
Protection and regulation of fairs.
Lien against licensees' property to secure charge, §106-512.
Notice of sale to owner, §106-513.
Refusal to license shows within five miles, §106-519.
Vendors near fairs to pay license, §106-516.
Liens.
Protection and regulation of fairs.
Lien against licensees' property to secure charge, §106-512.
Notice of sale to owner, §106-513.
Local aid to agricultural, animal and poultry exhibits, §106-520.
Supervision of fairs, §106-520.4.
Permits.
Carnivals and similar amusements not to operate without permit, §106-516.1.
Poultry exhibits.
Local aid, §106-520.
Property.
Theft or destruction of property of fairs, §14-398.
State fair.
Admission to fair grounds.
Fees or charges.
Establishment by regulations, §106-503.
Board of agriculture.
Constructing and financing facilities and improvements for fair, §106-503.1.
Operation of fair, §106-503(a).
Bond issues, §106-503.1(a).
Borrowing money, §106-503.1(a).
Constructing facilities and improvements of fair, §106-503.1.
Contracts and leases, §106-503.1(b).
Dedication of land, §106-502.
Repossession of land at will of general assembly, §106-504.
Endowments, §106-503.1(c).
Fees or charges.
Admission to fair grounds.
Establishment by regulations, §106-503(b).
Financing facilities and improvements for fair, §106-503.1.
Gate receipts.
Pledge of receipts, §106-503.1(b).
General assembly.
Land dedicated by state may be repossessed at will, §106-504.
Gifts and endowments, §106-503.1(c).
Land set apart, §106-502.
Leases, §106-503.1(b).
Operation of fair, §106-503(a).
Pledge of gate receipts, etc., §106-503.1(b).
Recycling bins.
Providing and maintaining, §106-503(d).
Rental rates.
Establishment of schedule, §106-503(c).
Rules and regulations.
Fees for admission to fair grounds, §106-503(b).
Sale of merchandise by governmental units.
Exception to prohibition, §66-58(b).

FAIRS —Cont'd
State fair —Cont'd
State lands.
Land set aside for state fair, §106-502.
Repossession of land at will of general assembly, §106-504.
State lands.
Land set apart for state fair, §106-502.
Repossession of land at will of general assembly, §106-504.
Supervision of fairs and animal exhibitions.
Animal exhibitions.
Aedin's law.
Cites as, §106-520.3A(a).
Attorney general.
Representation of department in actions and proceedings.
Duty, §106-520.3A(g).
Civil penalty for violation, §106-520.3A(f).
Definitions, §106-520.3A(b).
Health risks.
Education outreach, §106-520.3A(e).
Operation permit.
Required, inspection required, suspension or revocation, §106-520.3A(c).
Purpose of section, §106-520.3A(a).
Rules concerning operation.
Adoption by commissioner, requirements, §106-520.3A(d).
Commissioner of agricultural to regulate, §106-520.3.
Definition of fair, §106-520.1.
Local supervision of fairs, §106-520.4.
Misdemeanors, §106-520.7.
Name of exhibition.
Use of "fair" in name, §106-520.2.
Premiums and premium lists supplemented, §106-520.6.
Reports, §106-520.5.
Supplementing premiums and premium lists, §106-520.6.
Use of "fair" in name of exhibition, §106-520.2.
Violations made misdemeanor, §106-520.7.
Theft.
Destruction or theft of property of fair, §14-398.
Unlawful entry on grounds.
Assisting unlawful entry a misdemeanor, §106-515.
Misdemeanor offenses, §§106-514, 106-515.
Vendors' licenses to be paid if near fairs, §106-516.
Unlicensed vending a misdemeanor, §106-518.

FAIR TRADE.
Monopolies and restraint of trade.
See MONOPOLIES AND RESTRAINT OF TRADE.

FAITHLESS ELECTOR STATUTE.
Failure of presidential elector to attend and vote, §163-212.

FAKE ID'S.
Alcoholic beverage sales to or purchases by underage persons.
Fraudulent use of identification, §18B-302(e).
Conviction report to division, §18B-302(g).
Driver's license information verification system, §20-37.02.
Possession or manufacture, §14-100.1.
Violations of driver's license or learner's permit provisions, §20-30.

FAKE ID'S —Cont'd
Wrongful issuance of drivers' licenses or special identification cards, §20-34.1.

FALCONRY.
Licenses, §113-270.3(b).
Method of taking wild animals or wild birds, §113-291.1(a).

FALLOW DEER.
Meat inspections.
Generally, §§106-549.15 to 106-549.39.
See MEAT INSPECTIONS.

FALLS LAKE WATERSHED ASSOCIATION, §§77-140 to 77-143.
Authority granted in addition to other authority, §77-143.
Board of directors, §77-141(b).
Definitions, §77-140.
Falls Lake watershed.
Defined, §77-140.
Local government.
Authority granted in addition to other authority granted, §77-143.
Defined, §77-140.
Meetings of public bodies.
Subject to requirements, §77-141(d).
Memoranda of understanding with association.
Department of environment and natural resources, §77-142.
Nonprofit corporation.
Defined, §77-140.
Election to incorporate or establish using existing corporation, §77-141(a).
Public records.
Subject to requirements, §77-141(e).
Purposes, §77-141(c).

FALSE ADVERTISING.
Generally.
See ADVERTISING.
Live music performance or production.
Truth in music advertising act, §§75-125 to 75-128.
Unauthorized insurers false advertising process act, §§58-29-1 to 58-29-25.
See UNAUTHORIZED INSURERS.

FALSE AMBULANCE REQUESTS, §14-286.1.

FALSE BILLS OF LADING.
Issuing, §21-42.

FALSE CLAIMS ACT, §§1-605 to 1-631.
Acts for which liability attaches, §1-607(a).
Attorney general.
Civil action for violations, §1-608(a).
Civil investigative demand.
Administrative subpoena, §1-614.
Investigation of violations, §1-608(a).
Report, §1-617(b).
Retention of portion of damages recovered, §1-608(c).
Rules, adoption, §1-618.
Civil actions.
Action brought in name of state.
Private persons bringing action, §1-608(b).
Attorney general.
Responsibilities, §1-608(a).
Burden of proof, §1-615(c).
Certain actions barred, §1-611.
Complaint filed by state, §1-615(b).
Complaint filed in camera under seal.
Action brought by private person, §1-608(b).

FALSE CLAIMS ACT —Cont'd
Civil actions —Cont'd
Dismissal of action brought by private person, §1-608(b).
State proceeding with action brought by private person.
Dismissal of action for cause, §1-609(b).
Domestic violence shelters.
Limited civil liability, §§1-620, 1-621.
Estoppel.
Final judgment rendered in favor of state in criminal proceeding, §1-615(d).
Expenses incurred by persons bringing action.
State not liable, §1-612.
Extensions of time in action brought by private person.
Motion by state, §1-608(b).
Federal, state, local authorities named as co-plaintiffs.
Service on, §1-615(f).
General assembly members, judiciary, senior executive branch officials.
No jurisdiction over actions against, §1-611(a).
Information obtained from news media.
Actions based on, restrictions, §1-611(d).
Law governing procedure, §1-615(g).
Private persons bringing actions for violations, §1-608(b).
Award to qui tam plaintiff, §1-610.
Certain actions barred, §1-611.
Expenses incurred by persons bringing action.
State not liable, §1-612.
Rights of parties to qui tam actions, §1-609.
Public employees or officials bringing actions.
Restrictions, §1-611(c).
Qui tam plaintiff.
Award to.
Amount of proceeds award, §1-610(a), (b).
Reduction, plaintiff planned and initiated violation, §1-610(f).
State not proceeding with action, §1-610(e).
Expenses, attorneys' fees and costs, §1-610(d).
Defendant prevailing party, §1-610(g).
Payments, §1-610(c).
Reduction of award.
Plaintiff planned and initiated violation, §1-610(f).
Discovery stayed, §1-609(g).
Imposition of restrictions on participation, §1-609(d), (e).
Right to conduct action.
State not electing not to proceed, §1-609(f).
Right to continue as party, §1-609(a).
State not bound by acts, §1-609(a).
Response by defendant to complaint.
Actions brought by private persons, §1-608(b).
Retaliation for lawful acts done to prevent violations.
Private right of action, §1-613.
Settlement of action.
State proceeding with action brought by private person, §1-609(c).
State already party to proceeding.
No action may be based on, §1-611(b).
State proceeding with action brought by private person.
Alternate remedies.
Pursuing claim through, §1-609(h).
Dismissal of action for cause, §1-609(b).
Qui tam plaintiff.
Award to, §1-610.

FALSE CLAIMS ACT —Cont'd
Civil actions —Cont'd
State proceeding with action brought by private
person —Cont'd
Qui tam plaintiff —Cont'd
Discovery stayed, §1-609(g).
Imposition of restrictions on participation,
§1-609(d), (e).
Right to conduct action.
State not electing not to proceed, §1-609(f).
Right to continue as party, §1-609(a).
State not bound by acts, §1-609(a).
Responsibility for prosecuting action, §1-609(a).
Settlement of action, §1-609(c).
Statute of limitations, §1-615(a).
Venue, §1-615(e).
Civil investigative demand.
Administrative subpoena, §1-614(a).
Custodian of documents and objects produced.
Designation by attorney general, §1-614(j).
Enforcement.
Action for order to enforce, §1-614(f).
Examination of documents and objects produced.
Availability while in possession of custodian,
§1-614(k), (l).
Failure to comply, sanctions, §1-614(g).
Issuance by attorney general, §1-614(a).
Petition for order to modify or set aside, §1-614(h).
Product of discovery.
Express demand for, §1-614(d).
Requirements, §1-614(b).
Return of documents and objects produced,
§1-614(m).
Rules of civil procedure, applicability, §1-614(n).
Sworn certification.
Production made under, §1-614(e).
Time for production of document or object,
§1-614(c).
Use of documents and objects produced, §1-614(i).
Civil penalty.
Liability, §1-607(a).
Claim defined, §1-606.
**Cost of civil action brought to recover
penalties.**
Liability, §1-607(a).
Damages, §1-607(a).
Limitation of damages assessed, §1-607(b).
Retention of portion by attorney general,
§1-608(c).
Definitions, §1-606.
Domestic violence shelters.
Limited liability.
Definitions, §1-620.
Excepted conduct, §1-621(b).
Scope of immunity, §1-621(a).
Estoppel.
Final judgment rendered in favor of state in
criminal proceeding, §1-615(d).
Exclusion from chapter, §1-607(c).
Federal false claims act.
Consistency in interpretation and construction,
§1-616(c).
Liability, §1-607(a).
Limitation of damages assessed, §1-607(b).
**Private persons bringing actions for
violations,** §1-608(b).
Rights of parties to qui tam actions, §1-609.
Procedure generally, §1-615.
Prohibited acts.
Liability, §1-607(a).
Purpose, §1-605(b).

FALSE CLAIMS ACT —Cont'd
Remedies under other laws, §1-616(a).
Reports, §1-617.
**Retaliation for lawful acts done to prevent
violations.**
Private right of action, §1-613.
Rules, adoption, §1-618.
Severability of provisions, §1-616(b).
Short title, §1-605(a).
Statute of limitations.
Civil actions, §1-615(a).
Tax claims.
Inapplicability of chapter, §1-607(c).
**Terms and disbursements under settlement,
final order or judgment.**
Report, §1-617(a).
Three times amount of damages state sustains.
Liability, §1-607(a).
Whistleblower protection.
Retaliation for lawful acts done to prevent
violations.
Private right of action, §1-613.

**FALSE CLAIMS BY MEDICAL ASSISTANCE
PROVIDERS,** §§108A-70.10 to 108A-70.16.
See MEDICAID.

FALSE COINS OR TOKENS.
Counterfeiting and uttering, §14-13.
Manufacture, sale or gift, §14-109.
Obtaining property or services by use of,
§14-108.

FALSE FIRE ALARMS.
Giving false fire alarms, §14-286.
Molesting fire-alarm, §14-286.

FALSE IMPERSONATION.
See IMPERSONATION.

FALSE IMPRISONMENT.
Allowance of costs to defendant, §6-19.
Allowance of costs to plaintiff, §6-18.
Limitation of actions, §1-52.
Rights of action not surviving decedent,
§28A-18-1.
Shoplifting.
Detention or arrest of suspects.
Liability for false imprisonment, §§14-72.1(c),
14-72(d).

FALSE NAMES.
Boxing under fictitious or assumed name,
§143-654(b).
Business names, §§66-68 to 66-71.
See ASSUMED NAMES.
Drivers' licenses.
Presenting license with fake name in commission
of felony, §20-30.
Identification cards.
Presenting identification card with fake name in
commission of felony, §20-37.8(b).
Professional employer organizations.
Conducting business under, §58-89A-80(a).

FALSE PRETENSES AND CHEATS, §§14-100 to
14-113.
Absentees in military service.
Receiver appointment obtained by false
representation, §28B-7.
**Advances under promise to work and pay for
same.**
Obtaining advances, §14-104.
Property.
Written promise to pay therefor out of
designated property, §14-105.

FALSE PRETENSES AND CHEATS —Cont'd
Ambulances.
Obtaining ambulance services without intending
    to pay, §§14-111.1, 14-111.2.
Animal pedigree.
Obtaining property by false representation of
    pedigree, §14-102.
Animal registration.
Obtaining certificate of registration by false
    representation, §14-103.
Bad checks, §14-107.
Obtaining property in return for worthless check,
    draft or order, §14-106.
Prima facie evidence in worthless check cases,
    §14-107.1.
Bed and breakfast establishments.
Defrauding innkeeper, §14-110.
Bounced checks.
Obtaining property in return for worthless check,
    draft or order, §14-106.
Worthless check, draft or order, §14-107.
    Prima facie evidence in worthless check cases,
        §14-107.1.
Campgrounds.
Defrauding campground owner, §14-110.
Checks.
Worthless check, draft or order, §14-107.
    Obtaining property in return for worthless
        check, etc., §14-106.
    Prima facie evidence in worthless check cases,
        §14-107.1.
Choses in action.
Obtaining property by false pretenses, §14-100.
Civil liability for damages, §1-538.2(a).
Action brought regardless of criminal action,
    §1-538.2(c).
Consequential and punitive damages and
    attorneys' fees.
    Additional recovery allowed, §1-538.2(a).
    Amount of damages, cap, §1-538.2(a).
        Parent or legal guardian liable for acts of
            minor, §1-538.2(b).
    Consequential damages, included in,
        §1-538.2(c1).
    Demand letter, seeking damages prior to action,
        §1-538.2(c2).
        Payment of money demanded, no further
            action, §1-538.2(c4).
    Demand letter, seeking damages prior to action,
        §1-538.2(c2).
    Payment of money demanded, no further action,
        §1-538.2(c4).
    Qualified privilege of sender, §1-538.2(c3).
    Libel and slander.
        Demand letter, seeking damages prior to action.
            Qualified privilege of sender, §1-538.2(c3).
    Other theories of law, recovery under, §1-538.2(d).
    Parent or legal guardian liable for acts of minor,
        §1-538.2(b).
    Recovery of value of goods and merchandise,
        §1-538.2(a).
Coin-operated machines.
Manufacture, sale, or gift of devices for cheating
    slot machines, §14-109.
Obtaining property or services from machine by
    false coins or tokens, §14-108.
Contracts.
Advance payments under promise to work and
    pay for same, §14-104.
Nonfulfillment of contract obligation, §14-100.

FALSE PRETENSES AND CHEATS —Cont'd
Credit cards, §§14-113.1 to 14-113.7A.
See CREDIT CARDS.
Definitions.
Person, §14-100(c).
Disabled persons.
Obtaining money by false representation of
    physical disability, §14-113.
Drafts.
Worthless check, draft or order, §14-107.
    Obtaining property in return for worthless
        check, etc., §14-106.
    Prima facie evidence in worthless check cases,
        §14-107.1.
Forgery.
Generally.
    See FORGERY.
Obtaining signatures by false pretenses, §14-101.
Fraud.
See FRAUD.
Hotels.
Defrauding innkeeper, §14-110.
Identification, false or fraudulent, §14-100.1.
Insurance consumer and customer information
    privacy.
Obtaining information under false pretenses,
    §58-39-115.
Kennel clubs.
Animal registration certificate obtained by false
    representation, §14-103.
Letters testamentary and of administration.
Grounds for revocation, §28A-9-1.
Marriage license obtained by false pretenses,
    §51-15.
Merchants.
Obtaining merchandise on approval, §14-112.
Money.
Counterfeiting generally, §§14-13 to 14-16.
    See COUNTERFEITING.
911 system.
Misuse of system, §14-111.4.
Nuclear, biological or chemical weapons.
Hoax or false report, §§14-288.23, 14-288.24.
Obtaining money by false representation of
    physical disability, §14-113.
Person.
Defined, §14-100(c).
Physically disabled persons.
Obtaining money by false representation of,
    §14-113.
Promises to work and pay for same.
Obtaining advances under promise to work,
    §14-104.
    Written promise to pay therefor out of
        designated property, §14-105.
Property.
Advances under promise to work and pay for
    same.
    Obtaining advances under written promise
        therefor out of designated property,
        §14-105.
Definition of "person,"§14-100(c).
Obtaining property by false pretenses, §14-100.
    Elements of offense, §14-100(a).
        Establishing element of intent to defraud,
            §14-100(b).
Restaurants.
Failure to pay for services, §14-110.
Security agreements.
Filing false security agreements, §14-401.19.

FALSE PRETENSES AND CHEATS —Cont'd
Signatures.
Obtaining signatures by false pretenses, §14-101.
Slot machines.
Manufacture, sale, or gift of devices for cheating machines, §14-109.
Obtaining property or services from machines by false coins or tokens, §14-108.
Telecommunications.
Concealment of destination of telecommunications, §14-113.5.
Payment for telecommunication services.
Avoiding or attempting to avoid payment, §14-113.4.
Telephones.
Obtaining property or services by false or fraudulent use, §14-113.6A.
Wastewater system contractors and inspectors.
Certification, §90A-81(d).

FALSE REPORTS.
Destructive devices, §14-69.1.
Mass violence on educational property, §14-277.5.
To law enforcement, §14-225.

FALSE RETURN OF PROCESS, §14-242.

FALSE STATEMENT TO PROCURE OR DENY INSURANCE BENEFIT, §58-2-161.

FALSE SWEARING.
Perjury generally.
See PERJURY.

FALSE TEETH.
Sales and use tax.
Exemptions, §105-164.13.

FAMILY AND MARRIAGE THERAPY LICENSURE ACT, §§90-270.45 to 90-270.63.
See MARRIAGE AND FAMILY THERAPISTS.

FAMILY CARE HOMES, §§168-20 to 168-23.
Charges and assessments for services, utilities and improvements.
Deemed residential use property for determining, §168-22(b).
Definitions, §168-21.
Family child care homes.
Capacity, §110-91.
Child care facilities generally, §§110-85 to 110-107.
See CHILD CARE FACILITIES.
Defined, §110-86.
Private agreements.
Certain agreements void, §168-23.
Public policy, §168-20.
Zoning.
Deemed residential use of property, §168-22(a).
Permits not required, §168-22(a).

FAMILY FOSTER HOMES.
Regulation of agencies receiving or placing children, §§131D-10.1 to 131D-10.9.
See CHILD PLACING AGENCIES.

FAMILY HISTORY.
Hearsay exceptions, §§8C-1 Rule 803, 8C-1 Rule 804.

FAMILY LAW.
Alimony.
See DIVORCE.
Annulment of marriage.
See ANNULMENT OF MARRIAGE.

FAMILY LAW —Cont'd
Attorneys specializing in.
Certification standards, Bar Rules D.2401 to D.2407.
Child custody.
General provisions.
See CHILD CUSTODY.
Jurisdiction and enforcement, §§50A-101 to 50A-317.
See CHILD CUSTODY JURISDICTION AND ENFORCEMENT.
Child support.
See CHILD SUPPORT.
Divorce.
See DIVORCE.
Domestic violence, §§50B-1 to 50B-9.
See DOMESTIC VIOLENCE.
Husband and wife.
See HUSBAND AND WIFE.
Marriage, §§51-1 to 51-21.
See MARRIAGE.
Minors.
See MINORS.
Parent and child.
See PARENT AND CHILD.

FAMILY LAW ARBITRATION, §§50-41 to 50-62.
Appeals, §50-60.
Application of law by arbitrator, §50-60(b).
Generally, §50-60(a).
Manner of appeals, §50-60(c).
Application of provisions.
Enforcement, §50-42(b).
Applications, §50-43(c).
Motions, §50-58.
Appointment of arbitrators, §50-45.
Court appointment, §50-45(d).
Method, §50-45(b).
Arbitrators.
Appointment, §50-45.
Change award, §50-52.
Application for change, requirements, §50-52(b).
Permissible reasons for modification, §50-52(a).
Disclosure of impartiality, §50-45.1.
Before accepting appointment, required, §50-45.1(a).
Continuing obligation, §50-45.1(b).
Ground for vacating award.
Compliance with agreed upon procedures as condition precedent, §50-45.1(f).
Failure to disclose, §50-45.1(d).
Objection to fact disclosed, §50-45.1(c).
Presumption of partiality, §50-45.1(e).
Hearings, §50-47.
Liability, §50-45(f).
Majority action, §50-46.
Number of arbitrators, §50-45(a).
Powers, §§50-45(c), 50-49(a), (b).
Majority action, §50-46.
Awards, §50-51.
Change award, §50-52.
Application for change, requirements, §50-52(b).
Permissible reasons for modification, §50-52(a).
Confirmation, §50-53.
Application for, §50-53(a).
Costs, §50-53(b).
Correction, §50-55.
Interest, §50-51(c).
Modification, §§50-55, 50-56.
Orders or judgments on award, §50-57.
Costs, award, §50-57(a).

FAMILY LAW ARBITRATION —Cont'd
Awards —Cont'd
Orders or judgments on award —Cont'd
Enforcement, entry and docketing of order or
judgment, §50-57(a).
Sealing of order or judgment, §50-57(b).
Punitive damages, §50-51(e).
Reasons upon which based, §50-51(b).
Requirements, §50-51(a).
Specific performance, §50-51(d).
Vacating, §50-54.
Child abuse or neglect, §50-44(h).
Collaborative law proceedings.
Alternative dispute resolution permitted, §50-78.
Consolidation.
Some claims and not others may be consolidated,
§50-50.1(b).
Terms of agreement given force, §50-50.1(c).
When court may allow, §50-50.1(a).
Construction of provisions, §50-62(a).
Electronic records or signatures, provisions
governing, §50-62(b).
Costs.
Awards, §50-51(f), (g).
Modification or correction of awards, §50-55(d).
Rules for conducting arbitration, §50-45(h).
Definitions.
Appointment of arbitrators, §50-45(g).
Court, §50-59(a).
Person, §50-59(b).
Enforcement, §50-42(a).
Evidence, §50-49(d).
Hearings, §50-47.
Attorneys at law, §50-48.
Interest.
Awards, §50-51(c).
Interim relief, §50-44.
Applicable law, §50-44(a).
Findings of fact, §50-44(e).
Jurisdiction, §50-44(f).
Prior written agreement limiting, §50-44(g).
Remedies, §50-44(c).
Request for, §50-44(i).
Right to seek, §50-44(b).
Waiver of right to arbitrate, not considered,
§50-44(j).
Interpretation of provisions, §50-61.
Electronic records or signatures, provisions
governing, §50-62(b).
Uniformity of interpretation, §50-62(a).
Jurisdiction, §50-59(a).
Modification or correction of award, §§50-55,
50-56.
Alimony, postseparation support, child custody or
child support.
Change in circumstances, §50-56.
Application, §50-55(a).
Vacating award, §50-55(c).
Change in circumstances.
Applicability of G.S. 50-55, §50-56(f).
Authority of court or arbitrators to modify,
§50-56(a).
Child support or child custody, §50-56(c).
Post separation support or alimony, §50-56(b).
Confirmation of award.
Matters submitted to arbitrators, §50-56(d),
(e).
Confirmation, §50-55(b).
Costs, §50-55(d).
Notice of initiation of proceedings, §50-42.2.
Action which constitutes notice.
Giving notice, §50-42.2(c).

FAMILY LAW ARBITRATION —Cont'd
Notice of initiation of proceedings —Cont'd
Action which constitutes notice —Cont'd
Having notice, §50-42.2(d).
Receiving notice, §50-42.2(e).
Manner of notice, §50-42.2(a).
Sufficiency of notice, objections to, §50-42.2(b).
Orders, §50-43(d).
Interim relief, §50-44(d).
Refusal to grant, §50-43(e).
Proceedings to compel, §50-43(a).
Punitive damages, §50-51(e).
Purpose, §50-41(a).
Refusal to grant order or stay, §50-43(e).
Retroactive application, §50-61.
Rules for arbitration, §50-45(e).
Short title, §50-41(b).
Specific performance, §50-51(d).
Stays, §50-43(b).
Orders, §50-43(d).
Refusal to grant, §50-43(e).
Subpoenas.
Powers of arbitrators, §50-49(a), (c), (e).
Vacating awards.
Application to vacate, §50-54(a), (b).
Denial, §50-54(d).
Grounds, §50-54(c).
Modification or correction of awards, §50-55(c).
Validity of arbitration agreements, §50-42(a).
Waiver of provisions, §50-42.1.
Effect of unlawful waivers, §50-42.1(d).
Interim relief, not a waiver of right to arbitrate,
§50-44(j).
In writing requirement, §50-42.1(a).
Prohibitions, §50-42.1(b), (c).
Scope of right to waive, §50-42.1(a).
Unreasonable restrictions, §50-42.1(b).

FAMILY LAW SPECIALTY.
Certification standards, Bar Rules D.2401 to
D.2407.

FAMILY LEAVE.
Credit insurance.
Defined, §58-57-5.
Policy standards and provisions, §58-57-115.
Coverage, §58-57-115(b).
Definitions, §58-57-115(a).
Eligibility for coverage, §58-57-115(c).
Evidence of employer approval of qualified
leave, §58-57-115(h).
Exclusions from coverage, §58-57-115(e).
Lump-sum payments, §58-57-115(h).
Minimum monthly benefit amount,
§58-57-115(g).
Notice that benefits paid, §58-57-115(f).
Premium rates, §58-57-115(i).
Qualifying events for payment of benefits,
§58-57-115(d).
Refund of unearned premium, §58-57-115(h).
Reports by insurers offering, §58-57-115(j).
Waiting period for benefits, §58-57-115(h).
School employees.
Parental leave, §115C-336.1.
Teachers.
Parental leave, §115C-302.1(j).

FAMILY LIFE EDUCATION.
Public schools.
Basic education program.
Health education, §115C-81(e1).

FAMILY MEDICINE.
Primary care physicians, medical education, §143-613.

FAMILY PRESERVATION, §§143B-150.5, 143B-150.6.
Cooperation of state agencies, §143B-150.5(d).
Development and implementation of family preservation services program, §143B-150.5(a).
Eligible families for services, §143B-150.6(b).
Services delivered to, §143B-150.6(c).
Establishment of family preservation services program, §143B-150.5(a).
Financing family preservation services.
Grants, §143B-150.5(c).
Grants.
Awarding to local agencies, §143B-150.6(d).
Financing family preservation services, §143B-150.5(c).
Purposes of family preservation services program, §143B-150.5(b).
Services delivered to eligible families, §143B-150.6(c).
Services provided under family preservation services program, §143B-150.6(a).
Use of funds available to divisions to support program, §143B-150.6(e).

FAMILY PURPOSE DOCTRINE.
Boating safety.
Applicability of doctrine, §75A-10.1.
Strict liability for damage to person or property by minors, §1-538.1.

FAMILY RECORDS.
Hearsay exception, §8C-1 Rule 803.

FAMILY RESOURCE CENTER GRANT PROGRAM, §§143B-152.10 to 143B-152.15.
Administration of programs, §143B-152.11.
Agency cooperation.
State and local agencies, §143B-152.14.
Applications.
Grants, §143B-152.12(b), (c).
Grant review, §143B-152.13(a), (b).
Considerations for determining amount of funds received, §143B-152.13(c).
Cooperation of state and local agencies, §143B-152.14.
Creation, §143B-152.10(a).
Eligible applicants, §143B-152.12(a).
Evaluation of program, §143B-152.15(a).
Grants.
Applications, §143B-152.12(b), (c).
Review of applications, §143B-152.13(a), (b).
Considerations for determining amount of funds received, §143B-152.13(c).
Secretary to award, §143B-152.13(d).
Intent of general assembly, §143B-152.10(b), (c).
Program administration, §143B-152.11.
Reports, §143B-152.15(b), (c).

FAMILY SUPPORT.
Interstate family support, §§52C-1-100 to 52C-9-902.
See INTERSTATE FAMILY SUPPORT.

FAMILY THERAPY, §§90-270.45 to 90-270.63.
See MARRIAGE AND FAMILY THERAPISTS.

FAMILY VIOLENCE.
See DOMESTIC VIOLENCE.

FARM AND HOME DEVELOPMENT PROGRAM.
Agricultural development generally, §§106-580 to 106-587.
See AGRICULTURAL DEVELOPMENT.

FARM CREDIT ADMINISTRATION.
Banks.
Investment in farm loan bonds, §53-60.
Obligations of agencies supervised by.
Investments in, §53-44.1.
Securities for deposit of public funds, §53-43.1.

FARM EQUIPMENT AND MACHINERY.
See FARM MACHINERY, VEHICLES AND IMPLEMENTS OF HUSBANDRY.

FARMERS MARKETS.
Sale of merchandise by governmental units.
Department of agriculture and consumer services operated markets, exception in provisions, §66-58(b).

FARM FORECLOSURES.
Legal services programs.
Eligible cases, §7A-474.3(b).

FARMING OUT CONVICTS, §§148-66 to 148-70.
See PRISON LABOR.

FARMLAND PRESERVATION, §§106-735 to 106-744.
Administration of provisions of act, §106-735(c).
Agricultural advisory board, §106-739.
Ordinance adopting agricultural district, §106-739.
Agricultural conservation easements, §106-744.
Agricultural development and farmland preservation enabling act.
Short title, §106-735(a).
Agricultural development and farmland preservation trust fund committee, §106-744(g) to (i).
Condemnation of land within district.
Public hearing required, §106-740.
Conservation agreements.
Enhanced voluntary agricultural districts.
Irrevocability, time period, automatic renewal, time period, §106-743.2.
Conservation easements.
Agricultural conservation easements, §106-744.
Consultation with commissioner of agriculture.
Prior to adopting ordinance, §106-743.
Countywide farmland protection plan, §106-744(e), (f).
Easements.
Agricultural conservation easements, §106-744.
Establishment of programs by ordinances, §106-736(a).
North Carolina agricultural development and farmland preservation trust fund, §106-744(c) to (c3).
Notice.
Record notice of proximity to farmlands, §106-741(a).
Immunities from liability in connection with, §106-741(b), (c).
Ordinances.
Adopting voluntary agricultural district, §106-738(a).
Agricultural advisory board.
Ordinance to provide for, §106-739.

FARMLAND PRESERVATION —Cont'd
Ordinances —Cont'd
Commissioner of agriculture.
Consultation with before adopting ordinance, §106-743.
Enhanced districts voluntary agricultural districts, §106-743.1.
Establishment of programs by, §106-736(a).
Recording in office of commissioner of agriculture, §106-743.
Waiver of water and sewer assessment.
Farms inside or outside agricultural district, §106-742.
Programs to promote growth, development and sustainability of farming.
Authority of counties and cities to develop, §106-736(b).
Purpose of article, §106-735(b).
Qualifying farmland.
Inclusion in voluntary agricultural district, §106-737.
Reports.
Counties to report to commissioner of agriculture, §106-743.
Report to commissioner of agriculture, §106-743.
Short title.
Agricultural development and farmland preservation enabling act, §106-735(a).
Voluntary agricultural districts.
Agricultural advisory board.
Ordinance to provide for, authority, §106-739.
Condemnation of land within.
Public hearing required, §106-740.
Enhanced districts.
Abeyance of utility assessments until farm connected to system.
Assessment procedures, §106-743.5(d).
Authority of localities not diminished, §106-743.5(e).
Authority to provide for in ordinance, §106-743.5(a).
Payment of assessment at end of abeyance, §106-743.5(b).
Statutes of limitations suspended, §106-743.5(c).
Additional benefits, §106-743.4.
Areas ordinance effective in, §106-743.1(c).
Benefits of voluntary districts.
Entitlement to, §106-743.3.
Conservation agreements.
Irrevocability, time period, automatic renewal, §106-743.2.
Entitlement to benefits of voluntary districts, §106-743.3.
Grants, priority consideration, §106-743.4(c).
Nonfarm products, additional benefits, §106-743.4(a).
Ordinance establishing, §106-743.1(a).
Adopted simultaneously with ordinance creating district, §106-743.1(d).
Purpose of establishing, §106-743.1(b).
Ordinances adopting, requirements, §106-738(a).
Enhanced districts, §106-743.1.
Purposes, §106-738(b).
Qualifications of land for inclusion in, §106-737.
Waiver of water and sewer assessment.
Ordinances providing for, §106-742.
Water and sewer assessments.
Holding in abeyance for farms until connected to system.
Assessment procedures, §106-742(d).

FARMLAND PRESERVATION —Cont'd
Water and sewer assessments —Cont'd
Holding in abeyance for farms until connected to system —Cont'd
Authority of locality to hold assessments in abeyance.
Not diminished by section, §106-742(e).
Ordinance may provide for, §106-742(a).
Payment of assessment when abeyance ends, §106-742(b).
Statutes of limitations suspended during abeyance, §106-742(c).

FARM MACHINERY, VEHICLES AND IMPLEMENTS OF HUSBANDRY.
Age for operation, §20-10.
Brakes.
Trailers used by farmers, §20-124(g).
Certificate of title exemptions, §20-51.
Defined, §20-4.01.
Driver's license requirement exemptions, §20-8.
Farm machinery franchises.
Commercial practices.
Uniformity, §66-186.
Definitions, §66-180.
Usage of trade, §66-181.
Notice.
Termination by dealer.
Contents requirements, §66-182(c).
Required, §66-182(b).
Termination by supplier.
Contents requirements, §66-182(c).
Required, time limit, §66-182(a).
Prohibited acts, §66-187.1.
Repurchase.
Cost of shipping and handling, §66-184(d).
Death of dealer or majority stockholder.
Exercise of heir's options, §66-184(g).
Supplier's duty, §66-183(b).
Exceptions to repurchase requirements, §66-185.
Full payment, time for, §66-184(e).
New agreement to operate dealership, §66-184(h).
Payments to dealer, §66-184(b).
Succession agreement, §66-184(i).
Supplier's duty to repurchase, §66-183.
Failure to repurchase, §66-188(a) to (c).
Termination by death or incompetence of dealer, §66-183(b).
Termination by either party, §66-183(a).
Terms, §66-184.
Time for, §66-184(a).
Transfer of title, §66-184(f).
Termination.
Supplier's duty to repurchase, §66-183.
Exceptions, §66-185.
Failure to repurchase, §66-188(a) to (c).
Repurchase terms, §66-184.
Termination by dealer.
Notice.
Contents requirements, §66-182(c).
Required, §66-182(b).
Termination by supplier.
Cure of deficiency.
Notice void, §66-182(a).
Good cause.
Notice not required, §66-182(a1).
Notice.
Contents requirements, §66-182(c).
Required, time limit, §66-182(a).

FARM MACHINERY, VEHICLES AND IMPLEMENTS OF HUSBANDRY —Cont'd

Farm machinery franchises —Cont'd

Termination by supplier —Cont'd

Right-to-cure deficiency.

Required to provide dealer, §66-182(a).

Uniform commercial practice, §66-186.

Effect on security interests, §66-186(a).

Representatives to inspect parts, §66-186(c).

Warranties.

Claim for work prior to termination, §66-187(c).

Errors, adjustment for, §66-187(h).

Expenses excluded under warranty, §66-187(f).

Indemnification, §66-187(a), (b).

Interest on unpaid claims, §66-187(d).

Obligations, §66-187.

Payment for parts, §66-187(g).

Reasonable and customary rates, §66-187(e).

Reimbursement in lieu of warranty provisions, §66-187(i).

Farm tractors.

Age for operation, §20-10.

Certificates of title exemptions, §20-51.

Defined, §20-4.01.

Driver's license exemptions, §20-8.

Identification marks.

Removing.

Defacing, etc., §14-401.4.

Motor vehicle repairs.

Applicability of provisions to farm vehicles, §20-354.1.

Registration exemptions, §20-51.

Tires.

Driving on dirt roads from farm to farm, §20-122(d).

Movable tracks.

Special permits, §20-122(c).

Identification marks, removing, defacing, etc., §14-401.4.

Inside rearview mirror requirement exempt from provisions, §20-126(a).

Mechanical breakdown service agreement, §66-374.

Motor vehicle repairs.

Applicability of provisions to farm vehicles, §20-354.1.

Registration exemptions, §20-51.

Tax credit.

Property taxes paid on farm machinery, §105-151.21.

Trailers used by farmers.

Brakes, §20-124(g).

FARM NAME REGISTRATION, §§80-33 to 80-39.

Application for registry, §80-36.

Hearing on, §80-36.

Publication, §80-36.

Authorized, §80-33.

Cancellation of registry, §80-39.

Fee, §80-39.

Continuation of name.

When transfer of farm carries name, §80-38.

Distinctive name required, §80-35.

Effect, §80-34.

Fees, §80-37.

Cancellation of registry, §80-39.

Hearing on application, §80-36.

Non-confusing name required, §80-35.

Similar names not to be registered after registry, §80-34.

FARM NAME REGISTRATION —Cont'd

Transfer of farm.

When transfer carries name, §80-38.

FARM NUISANCE DISPUTES.

Prelitigation mediation, §7A-38.3.

Certification that mediation concluded, FarmMediation Rule 8.

Compensation of mediator, FarmMediation Rule 6.

Completion, FarmMediation Rule 4.

Conclusion.

Certification, FarmMediation Rule 8.

Certification training programs, FarmMediation Rule 10.

Compensation, FarmMediation Rule 8.

Selection, FarmMediation Rule 3.

Submission of dispute, FarmMediation Rule 1.

Waiver, FarmMediation Rule 7.

FARM OPERATIONS COMMISSION.

Exception to prohibition of merchandise sales by state agencies, §66-58(b).

FARM PRODUCTS MARKETING AND BRANDING, §§106-185 to 106-196.

Agents.

Power to employ, §106-186.

Aggregate state service credit for graders, §106-190.1.

Appeal from classification of farm products, §106-191.

Apple grade standards.

Requirements for maturity, adoption, §106-189.2(a).

Criminal penalty for violating, §106-189.2(b).

Assistants.

Power to employ assistants, §106-186.

Board of agriculture.

Investigating marketing of farm products, §106-187.

Classification of farm products.

Appeal from classification, §106-191.

Prima facie evidence, §106-192.

Unwholesome products not classified, §106-193.

Conformity to requirements of article.

Sale and receptacles of standardized products must conform, §106-189.

Construction of term "farm products," §106-185(a).

Employment of agents and assistants, §106-186.

Evidence.

Certificate of grade or classification of farm product prima facie evidence, §106-192.

Federal-state cooperation, §106-185(b).

Grades.

Aggregate state service credit for graders, §106-190.1.

Authorized graders, §106-190.

Certificate of grade.

Prima facie evidence, §106-192.

Establishment and maintenance of standard grades, §§106-185(a), 106-188.

Health officer.

Notification in cases of unwholesome products, §106-193.

Immature apples.

Apple grade standards including requirements for maturity, adoption, §106-189.2(a).

Criminal penalty for violating, §106-189.2(b).

Inspections.

Authorized farm products, §106-194.

**FARM PRODUCTS MARKETING AND
  BRANDING** —Cont'd
Inspections —Cont'd
Farm product inspection account, §106-194.1.
Inspectors.
Authorized, §106-190.
Investigations.
Board of agriculture to investigate marketing of
  farm products, §106-187.
Licenses.
Revocation of license, §106-190.
Misdemeanors.
Violation of article or regulations a misdemeanor,
  §106-196.
Packages.
Establishment and maintenance of standard
  packages, §106-185(a).
Prescribing rules and regulations, §106-195.
**Promotion of use and sale of agricultural
  products.**
Generally, §§106-550 to 106-568.
  See AGRICULTURAL PRODUCTS
    PROMOTION.
Purpose of article, §106-185(a).
Receptacles of standardized products.
Conforming as to requirements, §106-189.
Establishment and promulgation of standards for
  opened and closed receptacles, §106-188.
Marks, brands and labels, §106-188.
Requirements of article.
Sale and receptacles of standardized products
  must conform, §106-189.
Rules and regulations.
How prescribed, §106-195.
Misdemeanor offenses, §106-196.
Sampling of farm products.
Authorized, §106-194.
Standardized products.
Conforming to requirements, §106-189.
State service credit.
Aggregate credit for graders, §106-190.1.
Unwholesome products.
Classification of farm products, §106-193.
Notification of health officer, §106-193.
Violations of article.
Misdemeanor offenses, §106-196.

FARMS AND FARMERS.
Adulteration of grain, §§106-621 to 106-628.
See GRAIN ADULTERATION.
**Agricultural water resources assistance
  program, §139-60.**
Agriculture generally.
See AGRICULTURE.
**Agritourism activity liability, §§99E-30 to
  99E-32.**
All-terrain vehicles, §20-171.22(a).
Animals generally.
See ANIMALS.
**Animal waste management, §§143-215.10A to
  143-215.10M.**
See ANIMAL WASTE MANAGEMENT.
Aquaculture development, §§106-756 to 106-764.
Auction of livestock.
Livestock markets.
  Generally, §§106-406 to 106-418.
  See LIVESTOCK MARKETS.
Bees and honey.
See BEES AND HONEY.
**Biological organism act, §§106-65.42 to
  106-65.49.**

FARMS AND FARMERS —Cont'd
Biologics, §§106-707 to 106-715.
Board of agriculture.
See AGRICULTURE BOARD.
Boll weevil eradication, §§106-65.67 to 106-65.78.
Cigarettes and tobacco products generally.
See CIGARETTES AND TOBACCO PRODUCTS.
Commercial feed, §§106-284.30 to 106-284.46.
See FEED.
Commercial fertilizers, §§106-655 to 106-677.
See FERTILIZERS.
Commissioner of agriculture.
See AGRICULTURE COMMISSIONER.
**Commission on agriculture and forestry
  awareness, §§120-150 to 120-154.**
Commodities generally, §§78D-1 to 78D-33.
See COMMODITIES.
Cotton.
Generally.
  See COTTON.
**Cotton grower's association, §§106-65.84 to
  106-65.91.**
See COTTON WAREHOUSES.
County planning and zoning.
Property used for farm purposes.
  Regulations affecting, §153A-340(b), (j).
Crops generally.
See CROPS.
Dairies and dairy products.
Generally.
  See MILK AND MILK PRODUCTS.
Ice cream plants, creameries and cheese factories
  generally, §§106-246 to 106-255.
  See ICE CREAM PLANTS, CREAMERIES AND
    CHEESE FACTORIES.
**Department of agriculture and consumer
  services.**
See AGRICULTURE AND CONSUMER
  SERVICES DEPARTMENT.
**Development act generally, §§106-580 to
  106-587.**
Drainage, §§156-1 to 156-141.
See DRAINAGE.
Drainage districts, §§156-54 to 156-138.4.
See DRAINAGE DISTRICTS.
Eggs, §§106-245.13 to 106-245.28.
Extension service.
Agriculture development generally, §§106-580 to
  106-587.
Farm machinery franchises, §§66-180 to 66-188.
Farm name registration, §§80-33 to 80-39.
**Farm nuisance dispute mediation, §7A-38.3,
  FarmMediation Rules 1 to 10.**
**Farm worker council, §§143B-426.25,
  143B-426.26.**
Feed generally, §§106-284.30 to 106-284.46.
See FEED.
Fees and taxes generally.
See AGRICULTURAL FEES AND TAXES.
Fertilizers.
Generally, §§106-655 to 106-677.
  See FERTILIZERS.
Soil additives act, §§106-50.28 to 106-50.41.
  See SOIL ADDITIVES ACT.
Finance authority, §§122D-1 to 122D-23.
See AGRICULTURAL FINANCE AUTHORITY.
**Food, drug and cosmetic act, §§106-120 to
  106-145.**
See FOOD, DRUG AND COSMETIC ACT.
**Fruit handlers unfair practices, §§106-496 to
  106-501.**

FARMS AND FARMERS —Cont'd
Grain dealers, §§106-601 to 106-615.
  See GRAIN DEALERS.
Grapes.
  Wine and grape growers' council, §143B-437.91.
Hall of fame, §§106-568.13 to 106-568.17.
Ice cream plants, creameries and cheese
    factories, §§106-246 to 106-255.
  See ICE CREAM PLANTS, CREAMERIES AND
    CHEESE FACTORIES.
Limestone, marl and landplaster, §§106-92.1 to
    106-92.17.
  See LIMESTONE, MARL AND LANDPLASTER.
Livestock brands, §§80-45 to 80-66.
  See LIVESTOCK BRANDS.
Livestock dealer licensing, §§106-418.8 to
    106-418.16.
Livestock diseases.
  Brucellosis, §§106-388 to 106-398.
    See BRUCELLOSIS.
  Cattle tick, §§106-351 to 106-363.
    See CATTLE TICK.
  Compensation for killing diseased animals,
    §§106-323 to 106-335.
    See LIVESTOCK DISEASES.
  Equine infectious anemia, §§106-405.15 to
    106-405.20.
  Generally, §§106-304 to 106-307.7, 106-400 to
    106-405.
    See LIVESTOCK DISEASES.
  Hog cholera, §§106-310 to 106-322.3.
    See HOG CHOLERA.
  Tuberculosis, §§106-336 to 106-350.
    See TUBERCULOSIS IN LIVESTOCK.
Livestock generally.
  See LIVESTOCK.
Livestock markets.
  Generally, §§106-406 to 106-418.
    See LIVESTOCK MARKETS.
  Prompt payment, §§106-418.1 to 106-418.7A.
    See LIVESTOCK MARKETS.
Marketing and branding farm products,
    §§106-185 to 106-196.
  See FARM PRODUCTS MARKETING AND
    BRANDING.
Marketing associations generally, §§54-129 to
    54-166.
  See MARKETING ASSOCIATIONS.
Marketing authority, §§106-528 to 106-534.
Meat inspections, §§106-549.15 to 106-549.39.
  See MEAT INSPECTIONS.
Migrant farm workers.
  See MIGRANT FARM WORKERS.
Milk and milk products.
  Generally, §§106-267 to 106-268.1.
    See MILK AND MILK PRODUCTS.
  Ice cream plants, creameries and cheese factories,
    §§106-246 to 106-255.
    See ICE CREAM PLANTS, CREAMERIES AND
      CHEESE FACTORIES.
  Regulation of milk and cream generally.
    See MILK AND MILK PRODUCTS.
North Carolina century farms program.
  Agriculture commissioner and board.
    Joint duties, §106-22.
Nuisance liability of agricultural and forestry
    operations, §§106-700, 106-701.
  Farm nuisance dispute mediation, §7A-38.3,
    FarmMediation Rules 1 to 10.
Pest control.
  Biological organism act, §§106-65.42 to 106-65.49.

FARMS AND FARMERS —Cont'd
Pest control —Cont'd
  Boll weevil eradication, §§106-65.67 to 106-65.78.
  Compact, §§106-65.55 to 106-65.61.
  Plant pests, §§106-419 to 106-423.1.
  Structural pest control, §§106-65.22 to 106-65.41.
Plant protection and conservation, §§106-202.12
    to 106-202.22.
  See PLANT PROTECTION AND
    CONSERVATION.
Poultry generally.
  See POULTRY AND POULTRY PRODUCTS.
Poultry products inspections, §§106-549.49 to
    106-549.69.
  See POULTRY PRODUCTS INSPECTIONS.
Preservation of farmland, §§106-735 to 106-744.
  See FARMLAND PRESERVATION.
Promotion of agricultural products, §§106-550
    to 106-568.
  See AGRICULTURAL PRODUCTS PROMOTION.
Prompt pay law, §§106-418.1 to 106-418.7A.
  See LIVESTOCK MARKETS.
Property taxes.
  Agricultural, horticultural and forestland,
    §§105-277.2 to 105-277.7.
    See PROPERTY TAXES.
Rendering plants and rendering operations,
    §§106-168.1 to 106-168.16.
  See RENDERING PLANTS AND RENDERING
    OPERATIONS.
Research, §§106-568.1 to 106-568.12.
  See AGRICULTURAL RESEARCH.
Seeds, §§106-269 to 106-284.22.
  See SEEDS.
Slaughterhouses generally.
  See SLAUGHTERHOUSES.
Soil additives act, §§106-50.28 to 106-50.41.
  See SOIL ADDITIVES ACT.
Soil and water conservation districts, §§139-1
    to 139-57.
  See SOIL AND WATER CONSERVATION
    DISTRICTS.
State parks.
  Gifts of land for state parks and recreational
    areas.
    Submarginal farmland, §113-34(b).
Structural pest control, §§106-65.22 to 106-65.41.
  See STRUCTURAL PEST CONTROL.
Swine farms, §§106-800 to 106-806.
  See HOGS, PIGS AND SWINE.
Tenant farmers.
  See SHARECROPPING.
Tobacco products generally.
  See CIGARETTES AND TOBACCO PRODUCTS.
Vegetable handlers unfair practices, §§106-496
    to 106-501.
Vegetable plant law, §§106-284.14 to 106-284.22.
  See VEGETABLE PLANT LAW.
Wine and grape growers' council, §143B-437.91.

FARMWORKER COUNCIL, §§143B-426.25,
    143B-426.26.
Administrative services, §143B-426.25(h).
Annual report, §143B-426.26(b).
Appointments, §143B-426.25(d).
Clerical equipment and administrative
    services, §143B-426.25(h).
Composition, §143B-426.25(b).
Creation, §143B-426.25(a).
Duties, §143B-426.26(a).
Established, §143B-426.25(a).

FARMWORKER COUNCIL —Cont'd
Meetings, §143B-426.25(f).
Members, §143B-426.25(b).
Quorum, §143B-426.25(e).
Subsistence and travel allowances,
     §143B-426.25(g).
Vacancies, §143B-426.25(c).

FARO BANKS AND TABLES.
Gaming.
  Opening, establishing, etc., bank or table, §14-294.
Illegal operation.
  Testimony enforced in certain criminal
       investigations.
    Immunity of witness, §8-55.

FAST-FOOD BUSINESSES.
Alcoholic beverage permits, §18B-1001.

FAX.
Appeals.
  Filing by electronic means, AppProc Rule 26(a).
Electronic records and signatures.
  Uniform electronic transactions act, §§66-311 to
       66-330.
    See ELECTRONIC TRANSACTIONS.
Filing of pleadings and papers, §§1A-1 Rule 5(b),
     (e), 7A-49.5.
Interstate family support.
  Admissibility as evidence, §52C-3-315(e).
Involuntary commitment affidavit,
     §122C-261(d).
Military and overseas voters.
  Transmission of ballots and ballot materials to
       covered voters.
    Electronic transmission system, §163-258.9(b).
Municipal subdivision construction or
     development.
  Imposition or increase in fees or charges.
    Communicating notice of meeting, §160A-4.1(a).
Nonprofit corporations.
  Notice communicated by, §55A-1-41(b).
Person with disability.
  Use of signature facsimile, §22A-1.
Sanitary districts.
  New or increased services charges or rates.
    Notice of meeting, §130A-64.1.
Signature facsimile.
  Use by person with disability, §22A-1.
State controller.
  Warrants for payment of money,
       §143B-426.40G(a).
Unsolicited facsimiles, §§75-115 to 75-118.
  Credit insurance on credit card balances.
    Prohibited, §58-57-105(a).
  Definitions, §75-115.
  Enforcement actions, §75-118(a).
    Costs and fees, §75-118(b).
    Federal remedies not affected, §75-118(d).
    Unfair practice, §75-118(e).
    Venue, §75-118(c).
  Exceptions, §75-116(b).
  Identifying information on fax.
    Exceptions, §75-117(b).
    Requirements, §75-117(a).
  Prohibition, §75-116(a).

FAYETTEVILLE, CITY OF.
Private parking lots.
  Removal of unauthorized vehicles, §20-219.2.
Traffic control photographic systems,
     §160A-300.1(d).

FAYETTEVILLE STATE UNIVERSITY.
Constituent institution of University of North
     Carolina, §116-4.
  Generally.
    See UNIVERSITY OF NORTH CAROLINA.
Distinguished professors endowment trust
     fund.
  Focused growth institutions.
    Allocation, §116-41.15(b).
    Contributions, matching, §116-41.16(b).
    Defined, §116-41.13A.

FBI.
Agents authorized to enforce criminal laws,
     §15A-406.
DNA database and databanks.
  FBI defined, §15A-266.2.
  Records provided by SBI, §15A-266.3.
Expungement of criminal records.
  Charges dismissed or person found not guilty or
       not responsible.
    Law enforcement agencies ordered to expunge
         records, §15A-146(b).
      As result of identity theft, §15A-147(c).

FDIC.
Banks.
  Deposit insurance, §53-9.1.
Public contracts.
  Deposit of cash in bank or trust company insured
       by FDIC.
    Proposal not considered or accepted unless
         deposit made, §143-129(b).

FEDERAL AID.
Airports.
  Acceptance, §§63-70, 63-71(a).
  Department of transportation.
    Powers as to, §63-71.
  Municipal airports, §63-54.
    Acceptance, §63-54(a).
    Compliance with federal regulations, §63-54(b),
         (c).
Archives and history.
  Historic preservation program.
    Cooperation with federal government, §121-8(d).
Blind persons.
  Aid to the blind.
    Acceptance of aid, §111-25.
    Authority of department of health and human
         services to receive, §111-28.
    Grants affording maximum aid, §111-29.
    Grants from federal government, §111-24.
    Matching federal funds, §111-6.
    Termination of aid, §111-26.
    Use of aid, §111-25.
  Private contributions for particular facilities.
    Treating contributions as state funds to match
         federal funds, §111-12.2.
  Rehabilitation center for the blind and visually
       impaired.
    Authority to receive federal grants-in-aid,
         §111-6.1.
Child support.
  Conformity with federal requirements,
       §110-140(a).
Community colleges.
  Budgets, §115D-58.1.
  State board of community colleges.
    Authority to accept, receive, use or reallocate
         federal funds or aid, §115D-31(b).

FEDERAL AID —Cont'd
Counties.
Public health or mental health grants.
Recovery of indirect costs on certain grants by
counties, §130A-8(a).
Exception, §130A-8(b).
Drinking water.
Receipt of financial and technical assistance,
§130A-326.
Education.
State board of education.
Power to accept federal funds and aid,
§115C-409(a), (b).
Electric membership corporations.
Acceptance of gifts or grants, §117-18.
Application for grant or loan from governmental
agency, §117-26.
Emergency management.
Acceptance, §166A-9.
Employment security section.
Method of handling funds, §96-27.
Governor.
Highway safety act of 1966.
Contracts with United States government,
§147-12(a).
Health.
Public health or mental health grants.
Counties to recover indirect costs on certain
grants, §130A-8(a).
Exception, §130A-8(b).
Highways, roads and streets.
Historical marker program, §136-42.3.
Scenic beauty of areas along highways.
Availability of federal aid funds, §136-124.
Hospital authorities.
Contracts with federal government, §131E-27.
Hospitals.
Construction and enlargement of local hospitals,
§131E-70(c), (e).
Unallocated federal sums or balances,
§131E-70(g).
Municipal hospitals, §131E-11.
Housing authorities and projects.
Authority to secure federal aid, §157-23.
Contracts.
Agreement to sell as security for obligations,
§157-39.8.
Housing finance agency.
Participation in federally assisted lease program
for housing for persons of lower income.
General power of agency, §122A-5.
Junkyard control.
Availability of federal aid funds, §136-155.
Libraries.
Authority to accept and administer funds from
federal government and other agencies.
Department of cultural resources authorized to
accept and administer, §125-8.
Interstate library districts, §125-15.
Local development.
Economic development commissions.
Acceptance, §158-12.
Metropolitan water districts.
Power to receive and accept, §162A-36(a).
Militia.
Support of militia.
Requisition for federal funds, §127A-137.
Outdoor advertising.
Control act.
Availability of federal aid funds, §136-140.

FEDERAL AID —Cont'd
Parking authorities.
Power to accept, §160A-556.
Personnel system.
Application to local employees, §126-1.
Public officers and employees.
Repayment of money owed to state.
Preservation of federal funds, §143-561.
Public schools.
Powers of local boards of education, §115C-47.
Public works.
Relocation assistance.
Real property furnished to federal government,
§133-16.
Railroads.
Revitalization programs, §§136-44.35 to 136-44.39.
Social services.
Acceptance of grants-in-aid authorized, §108A-71.
Solid waste management.
Receipt and distribution of funds, §130A-297.
State departments and agencies.
Acceptance of federal loans and grants.
Permitted, §143-164.
Receipt from federal government and gift not
affected, §147-83.
State treasurer.
Receipts from federal government and gifts not
affected, §147-83.
Telephone membership corporations.
Grants or loans from federal agencies, §117-32.
Transportation department.
Compliance with federal aid acts.
Powers of department, §136-18.
Unemployment compensation.
Employment security section.
Method of handling funds, §96-27.
University of North Carolina.
Acceptance by board of governors, §116-40.
Veterans' recreation authorities.
Acceptance, §165-37.
Vocational and technical education.
Acceptance of benefits of federal vocational act,
§115C-155.
Division of federal funds, §115C-158.
Vocational rehabilitation services.
Federal funds provided under rehabilitation act of
1973, §143-546.1(b).
Water resources development projects,
§§143-215.38 to 143-215.43.
Waters and watercourses.
Natural and scenic rivers system.
Acceptance of federal grants, §113A-36(b).

FEDERAL BUREAU OF INVESTIGATION.
See FBI.

FEDERAL COURTS.
General provisions.
See UNITED STATES COURTS.

FEDERAL CREDIT UNIONS.
Conversion into state credit union,
§54-109.95(b).
Conversion of state credit union, §54-109.95(a).

**FEDERAL DEPOSIT INSURANCE
CORPORATION.**
Banks.
Deposit insurance, §53-9.1.
Public contracts.
Deposit of cash in bank or trust company insured
by FDIC.
Proposal not considered or accepted unless
deposit made, §143-129(b).

FEDERAL ESTATE TAX.
Apportionment, §§28A-27-1 to 28A-27-9.
Credits, §28A-27-5(b) to (d).
Deductions, §28A-27-5(a).
Computations, §28A-27-5(d).
Definitions, §28A-27-1.
Determining apportionment.
Personal representative to determine,
§28A-27-3(a).
Basis for determining, §28A-27-3(b).
Expenses for apportionment to be
apportioned, §28A-27-3(c).
Distribution before final apportionment.
Personal representative may require bond for
tax liability, §28A-27-7(b).
Effective date of provisions, §28A-27-9.
Exemptions, §28A-27-5(a).
Computations, §28A-27-5(d).
Federal tax law to determine liabilities imposed,
§28A-27-8.
Method of apportionment, §28A-27-2(a).
Choosing method, §28A-27-2(b).
Rights and duties of personal representative,
§28A-27-7(a).
Temporary and remainder interests need not be
apportioned, §28A-27-6.
Uncollected taxes, §28A-27-4.
Wills.
Method described in will, §28A-27-2(b).
Tax referenced in trust or will.
Construction of formula provisions in trusts.
Estates of decedents dying in 2010, §36C-1-113.
Construction of formula provisions in wills.
Estates of decedents dying in 2010, §31-46.1.

FEDERAL GOVERNMENT.
General provisions.
See UNITED STATES.

**FEDERAL GOVERNMENT WORKERS
INCOME TAX CREDIT OR REFUND.**
**Credit or partial refund for tax paid on certain
federal government benefits,** §105-151.20.

FEDERAL HOME LOAN BANK BOARD.
**Investment in obligations of agencies
supervised by,** §53-44.2.
Obligations of agencies supervised by.
Securities for deposit of public funds, §53-43.2.

FEDERAL HOUSING ADMINISTRATION.
**Investments in and loans of securities
approved by.**
Financial institutions, insurance companies,
mortgage and loan correspondents and
fiduciaries, §53-45.

FEDERALIST PAPERS.
Basic education program, §115C-81(g).

FEDERAL LAW ENFORCEMENT OFFICERS.
Assistance in enforcing criminal laws in state.
Authority to assist, §15A-406(b).
Federal tort claims act, applicability, §15A-406(e).
Independent investigation into state law
violations not authorized, §15A-406(f).
List of federal law enforcement officers,
§15A-406(a).
Not considered officer, employee of state or local
agency, §15A-406(d).
Powers when assisting, §15A-406(c).

FEDERAL LIEN REGISTRATION, §§44-68.10 to
44-68.17.
Application of provisions.
Uniformity required, §44-68.16.

FEDERAL LIEN REGISTRATION —Cont'd
Attachment.
Certificate of nonattachment.
Filing officer.
Duties, §44-68.14(b), (c).
August 1, 1990.
Liens filed before, §44-68.17.
Certificates.
August 1, 1990.
Certificates filed before, §44-68.17.
Discharge of lien.
Filing officer.
Duties, §44-68.14(b), (c).
Execution, §44-68.13.
Fees, §44-68.14(d).
Filing and indexing, §44-68.15(a), (b).
Filing officer.
Duties, §44-68.14.
Nonattachment of lien.
Filing officer.
Duties, §44-68.14(b), (c).
Notices.
Revocation of certificate.
Filing officer.
Duties, §44-68.14(a).
Release of lien.
Filing officer.
Duties, §44-68.14(b), (c).
Revocation.
Notice.
Filing officer.
Duties, §44-68.14(a).
Subordination of lien.
Filing officer.
Duties, §44-68.14(b), (c).
Citation of act.
Short title, §44-68.10.
Construction and interpretation.
Scope of article, §44-68.11.
Uniformity of application and construction,
§44-68.16.
Discharge.
Certificates.
Filing officer.
Duties, §44-68.14(b), (c).
Fees.
Billing of officials, §44-68.15(c).
Certificates, §44-68.14(d).
Filing and indexing, §44-68.15(a), (b).
Notices, §44-68.14(d).
Filing and indexing, §44-68.15(a), (b).
Notices.
Execution, §44-68.13.
Fees, §44-68.14(d).
Filing and indexing, §44-68.15(a), (b).
Filing.
August 1, 1990.
Notices filed before, §44-68.17.
Duties of filing officer, §44-68.14.
Fee, §44-68.15(a), (b).
Generally, §44-68.12(a).
Personal property liens, §44-68.12(c).
Real property liens, §44-68.12(a).
Refiling.
August 1, 1990.
Refilings filed before, §44-68.17.
Duties of filing officer, §44-68.14(a), (b).
Revocation of certificate.
Duties of filing officer, §44-68.14(a).
Personal property.
Notice of filing lien, §44-68.12(c).

FEDERAL LIEN REGISTRATION —Cont'd
Real property.
Notice of filing lien, §44-68.12(b).
Releases.
August 1, 1990.
Releases filed before, §44-68.17.
Certificate of release.
Filing officer.
Duties, §44-68.14(b), (c).
Scope of article, §44-68.11.
Subordination.
Certificates.
Filing officer.
Duties, §44-68.14(b), (c).
Title of act.
Short title, §44-68.10.

FEDERAL MANDATES.
Certification of legislation required by federal law, §120-36.8.
Local government fiscal information.
Complying federal mandate report, §120-30.49.

FEDERAL PARENT LOCATOR SERVICE.
Access by department of health and human services, §110-139.1.

FEDERAL PARKS.
Construction of federal parkways and entrance roads to parks.
Powers of department of transportation, §136-19(g).
Property tentatively designated as federal parkway, §136-19(i).
National park system, §§104-31 to 104-33.

FEDERAL POWER COMMISSION.
Environment and natural resources.
Department authorized to receive funds from commission, §113-18.

FEDERAL REMEDY RESTORATION ACT.
State employee suits against state, §143-300.35.

FEDERAL RESERVE SYSTEM.
Banks, §§53-50, 53-61, 54C-177.
Definitions, §53-61(a).
Funds transfers, UCC.
Reserve regulations and operating circulars.
Inconsistent provisions superseded, §25-4A-107.
Membership in federal reserve bank, §53-61(b).
Compliance with reserve requirements required, §53-61(d).
Powers vested by federal act, §53-61(c).
Supervision and examination of bank, §53-61(e).
Reserve requirements.
Compliance, §53-61(d).
Members of system, §53-50(b).
Savings banks.
Authority to join federal reserve bank, §54C-177.

FEDERAL SURPLUS PROPERTY.
Surplus property of state.
State agency, §§143-64.1 to 143-64.5.
See SURPLUS PROPERTY.

FEDERAL WATER RESOURCES DEVELOPMENT PROJECTS, §§143-215.38 to 143-215.43.

FEE-BASED PRACTICING PASTORAL COUNSELORS.
Certification of fee-based practicing pastoral counselors, §§90-380 to 90-395.
See PASTORAL COUNSELORS.

FEE-BASED PRACTICING PASTORAL COUNSELORS —Cont'd
Professional counselors.
General provisions, §§90-329 to 90-345.
See PROFESSIONAL COUNSELORS.

FEED, §§106-284.30 to 106-284.46.
Acts.
Prohibited acts, §106-284.39.
Administration of article.
Commissioner of agriculture to administer, §106-284.32.
Adulteration.
Deemed to be adulterated, §106-284.38.
Analysis.
Deficiencies in commercial feed of any component, §106-284.42(g).
Penalties for multiple deficiencies, §106-284.42(k).
Deviation from guaranteed analysis, §106-284.42(h).
Penalty for deviation, §106-284.42(i).
Penalties.
Collection and assessment of penalties, §106-284.42(l).
Deficiencies in commercial feed or any component, §106-284.42(k).
Deviation from guaranteed analysis, §106-284.42(i).
Permitted analytical variation deviation, §106-284.42(j).
Permitted analytical variation, §106-284.42(h).
Schedule of penalties, §106-284.42(j).
Results of analysis, §106-284.42(f).
Sampling and analysis.
Conduct of, §106-284.42(e).
Appeals.
Judicial review of act, orders or rulings, §106-284.44(e).
Bag weights.
Prescribed standard-weight bags or packages, §106-284.36.
Canned pet food.
Defined, §106-284.33.
Inspection fees, §106-284.40(a).
Commissioner of agriculture.
Enforcement of article, §106-284.32.
Condemnation.
Detained commercial feeds, §106-284.43(b).
Confidentiality.
Information obtained to be confidential, §106-284.44(f).
Customer-formula feed.
Defined, §106-284.33.
Labeling, §106-284.35.
Definitions, §106-284.33.
Detained commercial feed.
Condemnation and confiscation, §106-284.43(b).
Withdrawal from distribution orders, §106-284.43(a).
District attorneys.
Prosecution of violations of article, §106-284.44(c).
Enforcement of article.
Inspections authorized, §106-284.42(a).
Right of entry, §106-284.42(a).
Enforcing official, §106-284.32.
Feed advisory service.
Operated by department of agriculture and consumer services, §106-21.1.
Fees.
Inspection fees, §106-284.40.

FEED —Cont'd
Fees —Cont'd
  Registration fee.
    Delinquent fee, §106-284.34(e).
Injunctions.
  Relief from violations of article, §106-284.44(d).
Inspections.
  Canned pet food.
    Fees for inspection, §106-284.40(a).
  Court order, §106-284.42(d).
  Description of samples obtained, §106-284.42(c).
  Enforcement of article, §106-284.42(a).
  Fees.
    Canned pet food, §106-284.40.
    Liability for payment, §106-284.40(c).
    Rate of inspection fee, §106-284.40(a), (b).
  Liability for payment of inspection fees,
    §106-284.40(c).
  Presentation of appropriate credentials,
    §106-284.42(b).
  Refusing admission of commissioner or agent,
    §106-284.42(d).
  Sampling and analysis.
    Description of samples obtained, §106-284.42(c).
Labels.
  Customer-formula feed, §106-284.35.
  Defined, §106-284.33.
  Information required, §106-284.35.
Liability.
  Inspection fees.
    Payment of fee, §106-284.40(c).
Misbranding.
  Deemed to be misbranded, §106-284.37.
Misdemeanors.
  Violations of article, §106-284.44(a).
Notice.
  Violations of article.
    Warning notice in writing, §106-284.44(b).
Orders.
  Detained commercial feeds.
    Withdrawal from distribution orders,
      §106-284.43(a).
Penalties.
  Sampling and analysis.
    Assessment and collection of penalties,
      §106-284.42(l).
    Deficiencies in commercial feed of any
      component, §106-284.42(k).
    Deviation from guaranteed analysis,
      §106-284.42(i).
    Permitted analytical variation, §106-284.42(j).
    Violations of article, §106-284.44.
Permits.
  Registration procedure, §106-284.34.
Permitted analytical variation, §106-284.42(h).
  Penalties, §106-284.42(j).
Prohibited act, §106-284.39.
Publications.
  Information to be published, §106-284.46.
Purpose of article, §106-284.31.
Raw milk dispensed as animal feed,
  §106-266.35.
Registration.
  Application for permit, §106-284.34(a).
  Application for registration.
    Manner of submission, §106-284.34(c).
  Cancellation of registration, §106-284.34(d).
  Delinquent registration fee, §106-284.34(e).
  Expiration of registration, §106-284.34(c).
  Fees, §106-284.34(c).
    Delinquent registration fee, §106-284.34(e).

FEED —Cont'd
Registration —Cont'd
  Filing requirements, §106-284.34(a).
  Issuance, §106-284.34(c).
  Permits.
    Application for permit, §106-284.34(a).
    Issuance, §106-284.34(b).
    Use of permits, §106-284.34(b).
  Refusal of registration, §106-284.34(d).
Reports.
  Inspection fees and reports, §106-284.40.
Right of entry.
  Purposes of enforcement of article, §106-284.42(a).
Rules and regulations.
  Authority to promulgate, §106-284.41(a).
  Issuance, amendment or repeal of rule or
    regulation, §106-284.41(b).
Sampling and analysis.
  Conduct of sampling and analysis, §106-284.42(e).
  Deficiencies in commercial feed of any component,
    §106-284.42(g).
    Penalties for multiple deficiencies,
      §106-284.42(k).
  Deviation from guaranteed analysis,
    §106-284.42(a).
    Penalty for deviation, §106-284.42(i).
  Inspections.
    Description of samples obtained, §106-284.42(c).
  Penalties.
    Assessment and collection of penalties,
      §106-284.42(l).
    Deficiencies in commercial feed of any
      component, §106-284.42(k).
    Deviation from guaranteed analysis,
      §106-284.42(i).
    Permitted analytical variation deviation,
      §106-284.42(j).
  Permitted analytical variation.
    Penalty schedule, §106-284.42(j).
  Results of analysis, §106-284.42(f).
Short title, §106-284.30.
State departments and agencies.
  Corporation with other entities, §106-284.45.
Statement of purpose, §106-284.31.
Title of article, §106-284.30.
United States.
  Corporation with other entities, §106-284.45.
Unlawful acts, §106-284.39.
Violations of article.
  Injunctive relief, §106-284.44(d).
  Misdemeanor offenses, §106-284.44(a).
  Prosecution of violations, §106-284.44(c).
  Warning notice in writing, §106-284.44(b).
Warnings.
  Notice of violations of article, §106-284.44(b).
Weights and measures.
  Bag weights, §106-284.36.

FEED ADVISORY SERVICE.
Operation by department of agriculture and
  consumer services, §106-21.1.

FEEDING GARBAGE TO SWINE, §§106-405.1 to
  106-405.9.
Application for permit, §106-405.3.
Cooking or other treatment, §106-405.6.
Definitions, §106-405.1.
Enforcement of article, §106-405.8.
Fees.
  Permit for feeding garbage to swine.
    Application for permit, §106-405.3(b), (c).
Inspecting conditions, §106-405.7(a).

FEEDING GARBAGE TO SWINE —Cont'd
Investigating conditions, §106-405.7(a).
Penalties for violation of provisions, §106-405.9.
Permit for feeding garbage to swine.
  Applicability of provisions, §106-405.2(c), (d).
  Application for permit, §106-405.3(a).
    Fees, §106-405.3(b), (c).
  Federal permits.
    Exemption of holders from provisions,
      §106-405.2(d).
  Issuance, §106-405.2(a).
  Prohibiting local regulations, §106-405.2(b).
  Revocation of permits, §106-405.4.
Records to be maintained, §106-405.7(b).
Removal of garbage from premises,
  §106-405.7(c).
Revocation of permits for feeding garbage to
  swine, §106-405.4.
Rules and regulations, §106-405.8.
Sanitary conditions, §106-405.5.
Treatment of garbage fed to swine, §106-405.6.

FEEDING MANAGEMENT SERVICE TO
  ANIMAL PRODUCERS.
Feed advisory service operated by department
  of agriculture and consumer services,
  §106-21.1.

FEEDLOTS.
Animal waste management, §§143-215.10A to
  143-215.10M.
  See ANIMAL WASTE MANAGEMENT.

FEES.
Accountants.
  Board of examiners, §93-12.
Acupuncture, §90-457.
Administration department.
  Use of state-owned office space by self-supporting
    agencies, §143-342.1.
Administrative code, §150B-21.25.
Administrative procedure.
  Contested case filing fees, §150B-23.2.
  Subpoenas.
    Witness fees, §150B-39(c).
Adoption.
  Agency placements.
    Schedule of fees included in statement of
      services, §48-3-203(b).
  Dispositional hearing on petition.
    Disclosure of fees and charges, §48-2-602.
  Lawful payments related to adoption, §48-10-103.
  Payments related to adoption.
    Agency fees and charges, §48-10-103(e).
  Preplacement assessments, §48-3-304.
  Report to court, §48-2-504.
  Unlawful payments related to adoption,
    §48-10-102(a).
Adult care homes.
  License fees, §131D-2.5(a).
  Multiunit assisted housing with services.
    Registered program, §131D-2.5(b).
Advance health care directive registry.
  Fee for filing, §§130A-466, 130A-470.
Agriculture.
  See AGRICULTURAL FEES AND TAXES.
Aircraft labor and storage liens.
  Filing, copying and certifying documents relating
    to, §44A-80.
Air pollution control.
  Title V program.
    Assessment of implementation fees,
      §143-215.106A.

FEES —Cont'd
Alarm systems licensing, §74D-7(e).
  Alarm system education fund.
    Deposited into fund, §74D-30(c).
  Transfer of certain fees, §74D-13.
Alcoholic beverages.
  Permits, §18B-902(d).
    Disposition, §18B-902(g).
  Lost permits.
    Issuance of duplicate, §18B-903(f).
  Name change.
    Issuance of new permit, §18B-903(g).
  Nonrefundable, §18B-902(f).
  Registration of persons holding permits,
    §18B-903(b1).
  Renewal, §18B-903(b).
Anatomical gifts.
  Removal, processing, storage, etc. of body parts.
    Authorization for fee, §130A-412.18(b).
Animal waste management, §143-215.10G(a) to
  (c).
Animal waste management system operators.
  Certification, §90A-47.4(a).
  Renewal fee, §90A-47.4(b).
Apprenticeship, §94-12.
Arbitration.
  Witnesses fees, §1-569.17(f).
Arbitration and award.
  Arbitrators.
    Rules for court-ordered arbitration, Arbitration
      Rule 2.
  Rules for court-ordered arbitration.
    Arbitrators, Arbitration Rule 2.
    Trial de novo.
      Filing fee, Arbitration Rule 5.
  Statewide court-ordered nonbinding arbitration in
    certain civil actions, §7A-37.1(c1).
Architects.
  Board, §83A-4.
Asbestos hazard management.
  Accreditation fees, §130A-448(a), (b).
  Removal permits, §130A-450.
Assisted living administrators.
  Certification, §90-288.15A.
Assisted living home medication aides.
  Certification, §131D-4.5.
Athlete agents.
  Registration, §78C-93.
Athletic fees.
  Schools for the deaf, §143B-216.44.
Attorneys at law.
  Attorneys' fees.
    See ATTORNEYS' FEES.
  Continuing legal education, Bar Rule D.1606.
  Organization of judicial district bars, Bar Rules
    A.0902, A.0903.
Auctions and auctioneers.
  Auctioneer recovery fund.
    Fee to be included in fund, §85B-4.1(a).
  Licenses, §85B-6.
Autopsies.
  Medical examiners, §130A-389(a).
Bail bondsmen and runners.
  Deposit of securities.
    Master trust, §58-71-151.
  Disposition, §58-71-180.
  Licenses, §58-71-55.
    Examinations, §58-71-70.
    Renewal, §58-71-75(d).
    Dual license holding, §58-71-82.

FEES —Cont'd
Banks.
Branch banks.
Interstate banking.
Application fees, §53-224.11(b).
Checks.
Remittance covering checks.
No fees to be charged, §53-70.
Directors.
Acceptance prohibited, §53-86.
Officers.
Acceptance prohibited, §53-86.
Banks and consumer finance licensees.
Operating and maintaining office of commissioner
of banks, §53-122(a), (e), (f).
Barbers.
Examinations, §86A-25.
Payment required, §86A-8.
Generally, §86A-25.
Biologics.
Licenses.
Production licenses, §106-710(d).
Birth certificates.
Amendment, §130A-118(d).
New birth certificates, §130A-118(d).
Boards and commissions.
Rules and regulations.
Agencies establishing fees and charges by rule,
§12-3.1(a), (c).
Definitions, §12-3.1(b).
Boxing licenses and permits, §143-655(a).
Brownfields property reuse.
Credit to Brownfields property reuse act
implementation account, §130A-310.39(b).
Failure to pay fees, §130A-310.39(c).
Schedule of fees to be collected, §130A-310.39(a).
Building code.
Code officials qualification board.
Certificates for code enforcement officials,
§143-151.16.
Disposition, §143-151.21.
Door lock exemptions.
Conditions for permit, §143-143.4(b).
Business corporations.
Expedited filings, §55D-11.
Filing, service and copying fees, §55-1-22.
Capital punishment.
Execution fee, §15-190.
Cemeteries.
Change of control of cemetery company.
Application.
Filing fee, §65-59.
Commission, §65-54.
Licenses.
Cemetery companies.
Application.
Filing fee, §65-55(c).
Sale of preneed grave space, etc., §65-58(c).
Sales organizations, management organizations
and brokers.
Application.
Filing fee, §65-57(c).
Vaults.
Delivery or inspection, §65-66(n).
Charitable solicitations.
Licensing.
Fundraising consultants, §131F-15(c), (f).
Solicitor's license, §131F-16(c).
Charitable solicitation sponsors.
License fees, §131F-8(a) to (d).

FEES —Cont'd
Check-cashing business.
License applications, renewal, §53-278(c), (d).
Service fees, §53-280(a).
Notice of fees charged, posting, §53-280(c).
Checks.
Remittances covering checks.
Banks and trust companies not to charge fees,
§53-70.
Child care facilities.
Licenses, §110-90.
**Childhood vaccine-related injury
compensation.**
Covered vaccines.
Providing, §130A-433.
Children's health insurance program.
Enrollment, §108A-70.21(c).
Chiropractors.
Collection of certain fees prohibited, §90-154.1.
Diagnostic imaging technicians, §90-143.2(b).
Licenses.
Application fee, §90-149.
Renewal, §90-155.
CLE, Bar Rule D.1606.
Clerks of court.
Court of appeals.
Fee bill for services, §7A-20(b).
Limitation of actions for fees, §1-52.
Superior court clerks, NC Const Art IV §21.
Accounting for fees and other receipts, §7A-108.
Audit, §7A-108.
Deposits of money held by clerk, §7A-308.1.
Investment of funds in clerk's hands, §7A-308.1.
Statement rendered by county officer
compensated from fees, §128-13.
Penalty for failure to file statement, §128-13.
Closing-out sales.
License fee, §66-77(b).
Coastal area management.
Permits, §113A-119.1(a), (b).
Applications.
Submitted with application, §113A-119(a).
Collection agencies.
Permit fees, §§58-70-35(a), 58-70-45.
Commercial drivers' licenses.
Applications for commercial drivers' licenses,
§20-37.15(a1).
Issuance, §20-37.16(d).
Commercial feed.
Inspection fees and reports, §106-284.40.
Registration fees, §106-284.34.
Commissioner of motor vehicles.
Service of notice, §20-48(c).
Service upon nonresident drivers and personal
representatives of deceased nonresident
drivers, §1-105.
Verification of equipment to be used on vehicles,
§20-39(f).
Commissioners.
Action in which clerk may allow, §1-408.
Community colleges.
Extension courses.
Schedule of uniform registration fees,
§115D-5(b).
Waiver of registration fees, §115D-5(b).
Community service program participation.
Division of adult correction, §143B-708(b).
Computer equipment manufacturers.
Registration, §130A-309.134(d).
Concealed handgun permit, §14-415.13(a).
Criminal records checks, §14-415.19(a).

FEES —Cont'd
Concealed handgun permit —Cont'd
Fingerprint processing, §14-415.19(b).
Retired sworn law enforcement officer,
§14-415.19(a1).
Schedule of fees, §14-415.19(a).
Consumer finance act.
Commissioner of banks.
Payment for expenses of supervision, §53-167.
Processing fee.
Maximum fee, §§53-173(a1), 53-176(b).
Recording fees, §53-177.
Continuing care retirement communities.
Disclosure statements.
Annual revised disclosure statement.
Filing fee, §58-64-30(b).
Return of entrance fee held in escrow,
§58-64-35(d).
Licenses.
Application fee, §58-64-5(b).
Nursing beds and adult care home beds.
Licensure fees, §131E-138.1.
Continuing legal education, Bar Rule D.1606.
**Cooperative agreements among physicians or
between physician, hospital or other
person.**
Application for certificate of public advantage or
filing of periodic reports, §90-21.34.
Cooperative associations.
Incorporation, §54-115.
Coroners.
Generally, §152-5.
Statement rendered by county officers
compensated from fees, §128-13.
Cosmetic art.
Board of cosmetic art.
Collection by executive director, §88B-6(e).
Licensure, §88B-20.
Costs.
Court costs generally.
See COSTS.
Uniform costs and fees in trial division, §§7A-304
to 7A-318, 7A-320.
Councils.
Rules and regulations.
Agencies establishing fees and charges by rule,
§12-3.1(a), (c).
Definitions, §12-3.1(b).
Counties.
Boards of commissioners.
Commissioners to fix fees, §153A-102.
Electronic notice of new fees and increased fees,
§153A-102.1.
Electronic monitoring of offender, fee to cover
costs of, §7A-313.1.
Inspectors of articles of commerce, §§66-3, 66-7.
Payment, §138-2.
Uniform fees in trial divisions.
Requirement to advance certain fees, §7A-317.
County surveyors.
Statements rendered by county officers
compensated from fees, §128-13.
Court of appeals.
Clerk of court.
Fee bill for services, §7A-20(b).
Judges, NC Const Art IV §21.
Credit unions.
Disposition of moneys collected, §54-109.14(b), (c).
Examination fees, §54-109.14(a).
Organization, §54-109.2(e).
Supervision fees, §54-109.14(a).

FEES —Cont'd
Cremation, §90-210.132.
Dams.
Dam safety law.
Applications for construction.
Application fees, §143-215.28A.
Death certificates.
Amendment, §130A-118(d).
Decedents' estates.
Clerks of court.
Miscellaneous fees in administration of estates,
§7A-307(b1).
Dental hygienists.
Generally, §90-232.
Dentists.
Anesthesia and parenteral sedation.
Standards for general anesthesia and
parenteral sedation.
Board of dental examiners to establish by
regulation, §90-30.1.
Examination and inspection.
Dental offices, §90-30.1.
Intern permits, §90-39.
Licenses, §90-39.
Duplicate licenses, §90-35.
Renewal, §§90-31, 90-39.
Dietitians and nutritionists.
Schedule of fees, §90-364.
District courts.
Civil process.
Uniform civil process fees, §7A-311.
Amount, §7A-311(a).
Collection of fees in advance, §7A-311(b).
Completeness and exclusivity of fees and
commissions, §7A-311(c).
Costs are exclusive, §7A-320.
Discovery procedures.
Filing of verified petition, §7A-305.1.
Judges, NC Const Art IV §21.
Uniform costs and fees in trial divisions, §§7A-304
to 7A-318.
Unincorporated seats of court.
Disposition of fees in counties, §7A-317.1.
Division of motor vehicles.
Acknowledgment of signatures, §20-42(a).
Certified copies, §20-42(b).
Divorce.
Resumption of maiden or premarriage surname,
§50-12(e).
Domestic violence centers.
Marriage license fees, §161-11.2.
Drainage districts.
Collection of assessments and disbursements,
§156-113.
Drinking water.
Public water systems.
Community water system.
Operating permit, §130A-328(b).
Disposition of fees collected, §130A-328(e).
Failure to pay, §130A-328(d).
Review of plans and specifications,
§130A-328(c).
Laboratory certification, §130A-326.
Laboratory costs, recovery, §130A-326.
Water well construction.
Analyzing samples from new water well
construction, §130A-5.
Driver education in public schools,
§115C-216(g).
Drivers' licenses, §20-7(i).
Commercial drivers' licenses.
Application fee, §20-37.15(a1).

FEES —Cont'd
Drivers' licenses —Cont'd
Commercial drivers' licenses —Cont'd
Issuance, §20-37.16(d).
Duplicate licenses, §20-14.
Highway fund, placing in, §20-7(j).
Learners' permits, §20-7(l).
Limited driving privileges.
Processing fee, §20-20.2.
Minors, expanding privileges, §20-11(j).
Records.
Copies.
Furnishing, §20-26(c).
Refund in event of mistake of person
ordering, §20-26(e).
Restoration fee.
Person whose license has been revoked,
§20-7(i1).
Drugs.
Expunction of records, §90-96(f).
Wholesale prescription drug distributors.
License application fees, §106-145.4(b).
Dry-cleaning solvent cleanup.
Petition for certification of facility, assessment
agreement or remediation agreement,
§143-215.104F(a1).
Ecosystem enhancement program.
Fund payments, §143-214.12(b).
Electrical contractors.
Licenses, §87-44.
Use of funds collected, §87-45.
Electric membership corporations.
Agreements of electric suppliers.
Utilities commission, resolution of negotiation
issues.
Filing fee, §160A-331.2(c).
Regulatory fee, §117-3.1.
Electrologists.
Board of electrologist examiners.
Duties to collect, §88A-6.
Deposits, §88A-7.
Salaries, compensation and expenses incurred
paid from, §88A-9(a).
Schedule, §88A-9(b).
Employee assistance professionals.
License application fee, §90-503.
Engineers.
Continuing professional competency activities.
Sponsors' licenses, §89C-10(h).
Engineers' licensure, §89C-14(b), (c).
Corporations and business firms, §89C-24.
Duplicate certificates, §89C-18.
Renewal of certificate, §89C-17.
Return on denial of certificate, §89C-14(d).
Executions.
Execution sales.
Uniform civil process fees, §7A-311(a).
Executors and administrators.
Commissions generally, §28A-23-3.
Expert witnesses.
Indigent defense services.
Fees paid by state, §7A-454.
Uniform fees, §7A-314(d).
Expungement of records.
First offenders not over age twenty-one.
Filing of petition.
Drug offenses, §15A-145.2(e).
First offenders under age eighteen.
Filing of petition, §15A-145(e).
Misdemeanor larceny conviction.
Filing of petition, §15A-145(e).

FEES —Cont'd
Facility authorities.
Powers of authority, §160A-480.4.
Family court programs, §7A-314.1(a).
Reduction, procedure for application for,
§7A-314.1(b).
Farm names.
Registration, §80-37.
Cancellation of registry, §80-39.
Farm nuisance disputes.
Prelitigation mediation.
Mediator fees, FarmMediation Rule 6.
Federal liens.
Billing of officials, §44-68.15(c).
Certificates, §44-68.14(d).
Filing and indexing, §44-68.15(a), (b).
Notices, §44-68.14(d).
Filing and indexing, §44-68.15(a), (b).
Firearm rights.
Restoration.
Court fees, §14-415.4(k).
Fireworks.
Display operator's permit, §58-28A-3(b).
Fishing.
Arrest, §§113-222, 113-303.
Licenses.
Coastal recreational fishing license,
§113-174.2(c).
Blocks of 10-day licenses, §113-174.5(b).
For hire blanket license, §113-174.3(a).
Ocean fishing pier blanket license, §113-174.4.
Collection licenses, §113-272.4(c).
Combination hunting and inland fishing
licenses, §113-270.1C(b).
Disposition of license funds, §113-306.
Fishing guides, §113-270.4.
Hook-and-line licenses in inland and joint
fishing waters, §113-271(d).
Lifetime licenses.
Administrative fee for issuing, §113-272.3(d).
Salt water fishing license, §113-174.2(c).
Special device license, §113-272.2(c).
Special trout license, §113-272(d).
Unified hunting and fishing licenses,
§113-351(c).
Service of process, §§113-222, 113-303.
State forests.
Collection of reasonable fees by department of
agriculture and consumer services,
§106-877(b).
License fees for hunting and fishing on
government-owned property unaffected,
§106-881.
State parks.
Collection of reasonable fees by department of
environment and natural resources,
§113-35(b).
License fees for hunting and fishing on
government-owned property unaffected,
§113-39.
Witnesses, §§113-222, 113-303.
Floodplain mapping.
Registers of deeds, §161-11.4.
Fees remitted to state treasurer credited to,
§161-11.5.
Food establishments, §130A-248(d) to (f).
Foreign legal consultants.
Certificate of registration, §84A-2(c).
Foreign or alien insurance companies.
Retaliatory laws, §58-16-25.

FEES —Cont'd
Foresters.
Registration, §§89B-10(a), 89B-11(a).
Examinations, §89B-12.
Gasoline and oil inspection.
Collection of fees by department of revenue, §119-23.
Payment of fees into state treasury, §119-23.
General assembly.
Witness fees and expenses.
Committee activity, §120-19.3.
General contractors.
Licenses, §87-10(a).
Geologists.
Board.
Establishing and collecting, §89E-5(g).
Examinations, §89E-10(b).
Gift cards.
Maintenance fees, §66-67.5.
Grain dealers.
License fees, §§106-604, 106-607, 106-608.
Grand jury.
Uniform fees for jurors, §7A-312(a).
Waiver, §7A-312(b).
Guardians.
Determination of incompetence.
Payment of fees, §35A-1116(c).
Hazardous waste management.
Inactive hazardous sites.
Implementation of remedial action.
Cost of monitoring and enforcing program, §130A-310.9(a).
Risk based environmental remediation of industrial sites, §130A-310.76(a).
Health.
County boards of health, §130A-39(g).
District boards of health, §130A-39(g).
Industrial hygiene consultation services and occupational consultation services, §130A-5.
Health care facilities.
Certificate of public advantage, §131E-192.11.
Review of application, §131E-192.11(b).
Certificates of need, §131E-182(c).
Certification fee for abortion facilities, §131E-269.
Finance act, §§131A-13, 131A-14.
New facilities.
Initial licensure fees, §131E-272.
Review of construction projects and plans, §131E-267.
Health maintenance organizations, §58-67-160.
Hearing aid dealers and fitters.
Licenses.
Application fee, §93D-5(a).
Issuance of license certificate, §93D-8(b).
Reciprocity, §93D-6.
Reissuance of suspended license, §93D-13(b).
Renewal fees, §93D-11.
Hearing impaired.
Interpreters for hearing impaired.
Licenses, §90D-10(b).
Service fee, §8B-10.
Training and licensing preparation program fee, §8B-10.
Highways, roads and streets.
Controlled access facilities.
Commercial enterprises.
Logo sign installation and maintenance, §136-89.56.
Express permit review program, §136-93.1(e), (f).
Home inspectors.
Deposit of moneys received by board, §143-151.63(b).

FEES —Cont'd
Home inspectors —Cont'd
Licenses, §143-151.57.
Hospice license, §131E-202(b).
Hospital, medical and dental service corporations.
Certificate of authority or license, §58-65-55(b).
Hotels, inns and other transient lodging places, §130A-248(d) to (f).
Housing finance agency.
Mortgage insurance authority.
Application fee prescribed, §122A-5.2(c).
Hunting.
Arrest, §113-303.
Licenses, §113-270.2.
Captivity license, §113-272.5(b).
Collection licenses, §113-272.4(c).
Combination hunting and inland fishing license, §113-270.1C(b).
Controlled hunting preserve hunting license, §113-270.2(c).
Controlled hunting preserve operators, §113-273(g).
Disposition of license funds, §113-306(b).
Fur bearer propagation, §113-273(h).
Fur-dealers, §113-273(f).
Fur-dealer stations, §113-273(f).
Game bird propagation, §113-273(h).
Guides, §113-270.4(b).
Lifetime licenses.
Administrative fee for issuing, §113-272.3(d).
Lifetime resident comprehensive hunting license, §113-270.2(a), (c).
New license to replace lost or destroyed license, §113-275(c1).
Nonresident license fee increase, §113-275(a1).
Nonresident state hunting license, §113-270.2(a), (c), (d).
Resident annual comprehensive hunting license, §113-270.2(a), (c).
Resident county hunting license, §113-270.2(a), (c).
Resident state hunting license, §113-270.2(a), (c).
Special activity licenses, §113-270.3(b).
Sportsmen licenses.
Annual license, §113-270.1D(a).
Disabled resident sportsman license, §113-270.1D(b).
Lifetime license, §113-270.1D(b).
Taxidermy, §113-273(k).
Trapping licenses, §113-270.5(b).
Unified hunting and fishing licenses, §113-351(c).
Service of process, §113-303.
State forests.
Collection of reasonable fees by department of agriculture and consumer services, §106-877(b).
License fees for hunting and fishing on government-owned property unaffected, §106-881.
State parks.
Collection of reasonable fees for privileges by department of environment and natural resources, §113-35(b).
License fees for hunting and fishing on government-owned property unaffected, §113-39.
Witnesses, §113-303.

FEES —Cont'd
Identification cards for nonoperators.
    Issuance and reissuance, §20-37.7(d).
Identity theft protection.
    Security freeze, §75-63(o).
Immunization.
    Administering covered vaccines, §130A-433(b).
Impaired driving.
    Immediate civil license revocation.
        Return of license, §20-16.5(j).
    Substance abuse services, §122C-142.1(f).
Indigent defense services.
    Expert witnesses.
        Fees paid by state, §7A-454.
    Representation of indigent persons, §7A-452(b).
    Supporting services.
        Fees and expenses paid by state, §7A-454.
**Industrial commission mediated settlement
    and neutral evaluation conferences.**
    Payment of mediator's fee, ICMediatedSettlmt
        Rule 4(e).
In forma pauperis appeals.
    Clerks' fees, §1-288.
Insurance commissioner.
    Report and payment monthly by commissioner of
        fees received, §58-6-1.
    Schedule of fees and charges, §58-6-5.
Insurance companies.
    License fees.
        Annual continuation fee, §58-6-7(a).
            Defined, §58-6-15.
            When submitted, §58-6-15.
Insurance premium financing.
    Disposition, §58-35-95.
    Excessive finance charges, §58-35-35.
    Licenses, §58-35-5(d), (e).
    Nonrefundable, §58-35-100.
**Insurer supervision, rehabilitation and
    liquidation.**
    Exemption from filing fees, §58-30-310.
Interpreters for hearing impaired.
    Licenses, §90D-10(b).
**Interstate and international law firm
    registration,** Bar Rule E.0203.
**Interstate compact for adult offender
    supervision.**
    Supervision fee, §148-65.7(b).
    Transfer application fee, §148-65.7(a).
Interstate family support, §52C-3-312.
Irrigation contractors, §89G-10.
Jails.
    Uniform jail fees, §7A-313.
Job development investment grant program.
    Applications, §143B-437.55(b).
    Records of recipient, §143B-437.58(a).
Job listing services.
    Receipt, §95-47.27.
Judgments.
    Foreign judgments.
        Enforcement, §1C-1706.
Judicial department.
    Indigent persons.
        Representation of indigent persons, §7A-452(b).
    Revenues and expenses, NC Const Art IV §20.
    Uniform costs and fees in trial divisions, §§7A-304
        to 7A-318.
Judicial officers, NC Const Art IV §21.
Judicial sales.
    Uniform civil process fees, §7A-311(a).
Junkyard control.
    Permits, §136-149.

FEES —Cont'd
Jury.
    Uniform fees for jurors, §7A-312(a).
        Waiver, §7A-312(b).
Justice department.
    Bureau of investigation.
        Performance of certain background
            investigations, §114-19.1(a).
Landlord and tenant.
    Authorized fees, §42-46.
Landscape architects, §89A-6.
Landscape contractors.
    Certificates of registration.
        Application fee, §89D-5(a).
        Duplicate certificates, §89D-5(c).
        Examination fee, §89D-5(b).
        Renewal fee, §89D-5(c).
    Examinations, §89D-5(b).
Lead-based paint abatement permit,
    §130A-453.09(b).
Lead-based paint renovation activities.
    Certification and accreditation fee schedule,
        §130A-453.27.
Learners' permits, §20-7(l).
License taxes.
    General provisions, §§105-33 to 105-109.
    See LICENSE TAXES.
Life insurance.
    Registration of policies, §58-59-30.
Limestone, marl and landplaster.
    Sale of agricultural liming materials and
        landplaster.
        Registration and tonnage fees, §§106-92.7(a),
            106-92.8.
Limitation of actions.
    Action for fee due officer, §1-52.
Limited driving privileges.
    Processing fee, §20-20.2.
Limited liability companies.
    Filing, service and copying fees, §57C-1-22.
Limited partnerships, revised act.
    Schedule, §59-1106.
Liquefied petroleum gas.
    Tank data plates.
        Replacements, §119-61.
Livestock.
    Brands.
        Registration, §80-62.
Livestock market operation fee, §106-408.1.
Loans.
    Conveyance of property other than collateral in
        consideration for loan, §24-8(c).
    Insurance proceeds to lender, §24-8(e).
    Loan amount $300,000 or less, §24-8(a).
    Loan-related goods, products and services.
        Collection of payment for, §24-8(d).
    Small business investment companies.
        Applicability of provisions, §24-8(f).
Lobbying.
    Delinquent reports, late filing fee, §120C-401(e).
    Lobbyist registration, §120C-201.
    Principals, §120C-207.
Locksmith licensing, §74F-9.
Lotteries.
    State lottery.
        Setoff debt collection.
            Collection assistance fee, §18C-134(d).
Magistrates, NC Const Art IV §21.
    Appeals from.
        Stay of payment, §15A-1431(f1).
    Special fees collected by magistrate, §7A-309.

FEES —Cont'd
Manufactured home manufacturers, dealers, salespersons or set-up contractors.
Licensure, §143-143.11(b).
Continuing education program.
Administering, §143-143.11B(b).
Marketing associations.
Filing fees, §54-144.
Marriage and family therapists.
Disposition of funds, §90-270.59.
Document duplication services, §90-270.57(b).
Licenses, §90-270.57(a).
Reinstatement after expiration, §90-270.58A.
Renewal, §90-270.58.
Massage and bodywork therapy.
Approval of schools, §90-631.2.
Board of massage and bodywork therapy, §§90-627, 90-628.
Mass gatherings.
Additional services, §130A-254(e).
Mattresses and bedding.
Licenses, §106-65.103(c) to (d1), (e), (f).
Deposit of fees, §106-65.104.
Meat inspection.
Bison, §106-549.39(b).
Deer.
Production and sale for commercial purposes, §106-549.98.
Hours of inspection, §106-549.39(a).
Ostriches and other ratites, §106-549.39(b).
Overtime work, §106-549.39(a).
Mediation.
Community mediation centers.
Dispute resolution fee, §7A-38.7(a).
Mediators and other neutrals.
Court ordered conferences in superior court civil actions.
Administrative fee, §7A-38.2(d).
Medical examiners.
Postmortem medicolegal examinations and services, §130A-387.
Autopsies, §130A-389(a).
Cremation or burial at sea certification and duties, §130A-388(b).
Medical records.
Searching, handling, copying and mailing, §90-411.
Medicolegal guidelines for attorney-physician relationship.
Witnesses, MLG Rule 5.
Membership camping.
Registration, §66-236.
Midwives.
Approval, §90-178.4(b).
Report to state treasurer, §90-178.4(d).
Milk and milk products.
Inspection fees, §§106-254, 106-267.1.
Mobile homes and trailer parks.
Registration of house trailers, §20-87.
Money transmitters, §53-208.9.
Mortgage bankers, brokers and servicers.
Nationwide registry.
Processing fee for licensing status changes, §53-244.119(e).
Mortgages and deeds of trust.
Appraisal by financial institution employee.
Fee charge authorized, §24-10(h).
High cost home loans.
Definition of points and fees, §24-1.1E(a).
Financing points, fees, prepayments, etc., §24-1.1E(e).

FEES —Cont'd
Mortgages and deeds of trust —Cont'd
High cost home loans —Cont'd
Modification and deferral fees, §24-1.1E(b).
Sales under power of sale.
Trustee's fees, §45-21.15.
Motor carriers.
Generally, §20-385.
Registration, §20-87.
Utilities commission, §62-300.
Motor clubs and associations.
License fees, §58-69-10.
Disposition, §58-69-40.
Motorcycles.
Registration.
Private motorcycles, §20-87.
Motor vehicle certificates of title.
Permanent registration plate holders.
No fee, §20-85(c).
Schedule of fees, §20-85.
Motor vehicle inspections, §20-183.7(a).
Display of information by inspection stations, §20-183.7(f), (h).
Distribution of fees, §20-183.7(c).
Highway trust fund repayment fee, §20-183.7(d2).
Inspection program account, §20-183.7(d).
Self-inspectors, §20-183.7(b).
Telecommunications account, §20-183.7(d1).
Motor vehicle license plates.
Dealers plates.
Temporary plates or markers, §20-79.1(a).
Disposition of fees collected, §20-85(b).
Permanent license plates, §20-84(a).
Schedule of fees, §20-85(a).
Special plates, §§20-79.4(b), 20-79.7.
Special registration plates, §20-79.7.
Motor vehicle manufacturers.
License fees, §20-289.
Motor vehicle registration.
Additional fees, §20-85(a1).
Additional local taxes, §20-97(e).
Carriers.
Property-hauling vehicles, §20-88.
Records.
Failure, common neglect or refusal to keep, §20-91(c).
Reports.
Failure, common neglect or refusal to make, §20-91(c).
Carrying charge.
Partial payment, §20-94.
Common carriers of passengers, §20-87.
Contract carriers, §20-87.
Copies of registration card, §20-57(b).
Dealers, §20-87.
Destroyed vehicles.
Credit, §20-100.
Disposition of fees collected, §20-85(b).
Driveaway companies, §20-87.
House trailers, §20-87.
International registration plan, §20-86.1(a).
Junked vehicles.
Credit, §20-100.
Limousine vehicles, §20-87.
Manufacturers, §20-87.
Motorcycles.
Private motorcycles, §20-87.
Municipalities.
Taxi tax, §20-97(d).
Vehicle taxes, §20-97(b), (c).
One-day title service, §20-85.1(b).

FEES —Cont'd
Motor vehicle registration —Cont'd
Operation of vehicles without registration plates subject to civil penalty, §20-118.3.
Partial payments, §20-94.
Passenger carrier vehicles.
Except for-hire passenger carrier vehicles, §20-87.
Passenger vehicles, §§20-87, 20-87.1.
Property-hauling vehicles, §20-88.
Prorated fee for license plate issued for other than a year, §20-95(a).
Exceptions to provisions, §20-95(b).
Plate with renewal sticker, §20-95(a1).
Schedule of fees, §20-85(a).
Special mobile equipment, §20-87.
Taxes credited to highway fund, §20-97(a).
Taxicabs, §20-87.
Temporary registration marker, §20-50(b).
U-drive-it vehicles, §20-87.
Motor vehicle titling.
Registration.
Security interest.
Notation of security interest, §20-58(b).
Municipalities.
Imposition or increase in fees or charges.
Subdivisions, construction and development.
Notice, public comment, §160A-4.1.
Solid waste disposal facilities, §160A-314.1.
Uniform fees in trial divisions.
Requirement to advance certain fees, §7A-317.
Wireless telecommunications facilities.
Application, consulting and other fees, §160A-400.52(f).
Mutual burial associations.
Membership, §90-210.81.
Nonprofit associations.
Uniform unincorporated nonprofit association act.
Filing fees, §59B-11(f).
Nonprofit corporations, §55A-1-22.
North Carolina register, §150B-21.25.
Notaries public.
Application for commission, §10B-13.
Authorized fees, §§10B-30 to 10B-32.
Electronic notarial acts, §10B-118.
Issuing certificate of authority, §10B-137(b).
Electronic notary registration, §10B-108.
Structured settlement transfers, §1-543.12.
Nuclear facilities, §166A-6.1(a), (b).
Carried forward amount of fees, §166A-6.1(c).
Nursing board.
Expenses payable from fees collected, §90-171.27(a).
Powers as to.
Generally, §90-171.23(b).
Refunds.
Prohibited, §90-171.27(c).
Schedule of fees, §90-171.27(b).
Nursing home administrators' licenses, §90-280(b).
Application fee, §90-280(a).
Disposition of fees collected, §90-281.
Duplicate license, §90-280(d).
Inactive list, §90-280(e).
Renewal, §90-280(b).
Temporary license, §90-280(f).
Training and continuing education courses, §90-280(g).
Occupational licensing boards.
Payment by members of armed forces, §93B-15.

FEES —Cont'd
Oil and gas conservation.
Notice and payment of fee to department before drilling or abandoning well, §113-395.
Opticians.
Licenses, §90-246.
Collection of fees, §90-245.
Examination, §90-246.
Reinstatement of expired license, §90-244(b).
Optometrists.
Licenses.
Generally, §90-123.
Persons in practice before passage of statute.
Certificate of registration without examination, §90-119.
Renewal, §90-123.
Additional late renewal fee, §90-118.10.
Parks and recreation.
State parks system.
Use of fees, §100-14.
Parole.
Supervision fee.
Condition of parole, §15A-1374(c).
Payment to clerk of county where person convicted, §15A-1374(d).
Partnerships.
Filing of documents, §59-35.2.
Pastoral counselors.
Certification of fee-based practicing pastoral counselors.
Disposition of fees, §90-392.
Duplicate and replacement certificates, §90-394.
Issuance of certificate, §90-387.
Refusal, suspension or revocation of certificate, §90-390.
Renewal of certificate, §90-389.
Pawnbrokers and cash converters, §91A-8.
Licenses.
Municipal or county authority to regulate, §91A-12.
Perfusionists, §90-689.
Pesticides.
Applicators, licenses, §143-453(a), (b).
Board.
Disposition of fees, §143-468(a).
Pesticide environmental trust fund, §143-468(b).
Consultants.
Applications.
Non-refundable annual fee, §143-455(a).
Examinations, §143-455(b).
Dealers and manufacturers.
Licenses.
Applications, §143-448(b).
Non-refundable fee, §143-452(b).
Examinations, §143-449(b).
Inspection fees, §143-452(b).
Registration, §143-442(b).
Worker protection designated trainers.
Examination of persons seeking designation as, §143-440(c).
Pharmacists and pharmacies.
Board of pharmacy.
Fees collectible by board, §90-85.24(a).
Out-of-state pharmacies.
Shipping, mailing or delivering dispensed legend drugs in state.
Registration, §90-85.21A(c).
Physical therapists.
Licenses.
Applications, §§90-270.29, 90-270.33.

FEES —Cont'd
Physical therapists —Cont'd
Licenses —Cont'd
Disposition of fees collected, §90-270.28.
Renewal, §§90-270.32(a), 90-270.33.
Schedule of fees, §90-270.33.
Physicians and surgeons.
Licenses, §90-13.1.
Registration.
Annual registration with board, §90-13.2(b).
Failure to register, §90-13.2(e).
Plumbing, heating and fire sprinkler contractors.
Licenses, §§87-22, 87-22.1.
Payable in advance, §87-27.
Podiatrists.
Licenses.
Examination fee, §§90-202.5(a), 90-202.9.
Reexamination, §90-202.6(c).
Issuance of license, §90-202.9.
Renewal, §90-202.10.
Police information network.
Participation, access, §114-10.1(d).
Pollution control.
Sedimentation pollution control act of 1973.
Erosion control plans.
Review fees, §113A-54.2(a), (b), (d).
Polysomnography.
Listing of polysomnographic technologists.
Annual listing, §90-725(a).
Ports authority.
Establishment or increase of fee.
Report to joint legislative commission on governmental operations, §12-3.1(d).
Post-assessment insurance guaranty association.
Exemption, §58-48-70.
Post-release supervision fee, §15A-1368.4(f).
Precious metal dealers.
Employees.
Certificate of compliance, §66-165(b).
Permits, §66-165(a).
Special occasion permit, §66-165(c).
Prepaid legal services plans.
Registration fee, Bar Rule E.0306.
Prison labor.
Work crew fee.
Community work crews to local governmental units, §148-32.2.
Private personnel services.
Defined, §95-47.1.
Overstated earnings expectations.
Reimbursements from employers due to, §95-47.3A.
Prohibited acts as to, §95-47.6.
Schedule of fees.
License applicant to file with commissioner, §95-47.3(a).
Private protective services.
Licenses, §74C-9(e).
Private protective services education fund.
Charged and deposited in fund, §74C-30(c).
Recovery fund.
Fees to be deposited into fund, §74C-30(c).
Special limited guard and patrol license fee, §74C-9(f).
Privilege taxes.
General provisions, §§105-33 to 105-109.
See LICENSE TAXES.
Probate and registration.
Clerks of court.
Miscellaneous fees in administration of estates, §7A-307(b1).

FEES —Cont'd
Probate and registration —Cont'd
Register of deeds.
Generally, §161-10.
Probation.
Electronic monitoring devices, §15A-1343(e).
Payment by defendant, §15A-1343(e).
Supervision fee, §15A-1343(c1).
Professional corporations.
Filing fees, Bar Rule E.0105.
Registration with licensing board, §55B-10, Bar Rule E.0103.
Renewal of certificate of registration, §55B-11.
Professional counselors.
Professional disclosure statement, §90-343.
Schedule of fees, §90-334(f).
Professional employer organizations, §58-89A-65.
Change of names, §58-89A-80(b).
Professional limited liability company practicing law.
Filing fees, Bar Rule E.0105.
Registration, Bar Rule E.0103.
Proprietary schools.
Licenses.
Authority to establish fees, §115D-92.
Psychologists.
Licenses.
Schedule of fees, §90-270.18.
Temporary licenses, §90-270.5(e).
Public livestock market operation fees, §106-408.1.
Public officers and employees.
County officers.
Statement rendered by officers compensated from fees, §128-13.
Penalty for failure to file, §128-13.
Payment, §138-2.
When to be paid in advance, §138-2.
Rules and regulations.
Agencies establishing fees and charges by rule, §12-3.1(a), (c).
Definitions, §12-3.1(b).
Public records, §132-6.2.
Public schools, §115C-103.
Collection, §115C-103.
Powers of local boards of education, §115C-47.
Student fees, §115C-384(a).
Refund upon transfer of pupils, §115C-384(b).
Textbooks.
Damage fees authorized, §§115C-100, 115C-384(c).
Rental fees prohibited, §§115C-100, 115C-384(c).
Public utilities.
State bureau of investigation.
Criminal history record information, §62-333.
Utilities commission, §62-300(a).
Exemptions from certain fees, §62-300(d).
Payment, §62-300(b).
Into treasury, §62-18(b).
Prerequisites to filings, §62-300(c).
Public vehicular area, registering, §20-219.4(c).
Rabies vaccinations.
Countywide rabies clinics, §130A-187(b).
Tags, §130A-190(b).
Radiation protection.
Department of environment and natural resources, §104E-19(a), (c).
Real estate appraisal management companies.
Registration, §93E-2-6(a).
Reinstatement after expiration, §93E-2-6(b).

FEES —Cont'd
Real estate appraisal management companies
—Cont'd
Registration —Cont'd
Renewal, §93E-2-6(a).
Replacement, §93E-2-6(c).
Real estate appraisers.
License or certificate of registered trainee renewal
fees, §93E-1-7(a).
Late filing fees, §93E-1-7(c).
License or certificate of registered trainee
replacement fees, §93E-1-7(d).
Licenses or certificates for registration as trainee,
§93E-1-6(b).
Schools or course sponsors, §93E-1-8(b), (d).
Temporary licensure or certification for
nonresidents, §93E-1-9(c).
Real estate brokers.
Broker transition courses, §93A-4.3(c).
Continuing education, §93A-4.1(d).
License fees, §93-4.
Postlicensing education program, §93A-4(a2).
Referees.
Reference of claim against deceased person.
Recovery of referee's fees, §6-31.
Refrigeration contractors.
Licenses, §87-64.
Payable in advance, §87-63.
Registers of deeds.
Collection prior to rendition of service, §161-10(c).
Exclusive nature of fees, §161-10(b).
Floodplain mapping, fees for, §161-11.4.
Fee remitted to state treasurer credited to,
§161-11.5.
Marriages.
Licenses.
Portion of fee for children's trust fund,
§161-11.1(a).
Portion of fee for domestic violence centers,
§161-11.2.
Records archival, §161-11.6.
Salary in counties where fees formerly allowed,
§161-4.1.
Schedule of fees, §161-10(a).
Statement rendered by county officers
compensated from fees, §128-13.
Penalty for failure to file statement, §128-13.
Uniform fees, §161-10.
Veterans.
Exemption of armed service discharge
documents and certain other records needed
in support of claims for veterans benefits,
§161-10.1.
Rental referral agencies.
Deposits to be applied toward fees, §66-143(b).
Failure to obtain housing, §66-143(c).
Refunds.
Application for refund, §66-143(d).
Restrictions on, §66-143(a).
Rents.
Late rent payment fees, §42-46(a) to (d), (h).
Residential property disclosure act.
Forms prepared by real estate commission,
§47E-10.
Respiratory care practitioners.
Schedule of license fees, §90-660(b).
Restaurants, §130A-248(d) to (f).
Retail installment sales.
Attorneys' fees.
Provisions includable, §25A-21.

FEES —Cont'd
Retail installment sales —Cont'd
Collateral.
Substitution, §25A-26.
Official fees.
Defined, §25A-10.
Substitution of collateral, §25A-26.
Transfer of equity.
Transfer fee, §25A-16.
Retirement communities.
Certified retirement community program,
§143B-437.100(d).
Salvage vehicle certificate of title, §20-109.1(g).
Savings and loan associations.
Examination and investigation.
Deposit of funds collected, §54B-57(b).
Licenses.
Annual license fees, §54B-74.
Out-of-state branch offices.
Supervisory and examination fees, §54B-273(d).
Statement filed by association, §54B-75.
Supervision and examination fees.
Deposit of funds collected, §54B-57(a), (b).
Taxation.
Credit for supervisory fees, §105-130.43.
Savings banks.
Administrator of savings institution division.
Supervision and examination fees, §54C-55(a).
Use of funds collected, §54C-55(b).
Examinations by commissioner of banks,
§54C-55(a).
Use of funds collected, §54C-55(b).
Interstate branch banks.
Regulatory and supervisory oversight,
§54C-207(d).
Licenses.
Annual license fees, §54C-61.
Statements filed by savings banks.
Filing fee, §54C-62.
Schools for the deaf.
Athletic fees, §143B-216.44.
Scrap tire disposal.
Taxation generally, §§105-187.15 to 105-187.19.
Secretary of state.
Copying and certifying documents, §147-37.
Corporations.
Filing, service and copying fees, collection,
§55-1-22.
Secured transactions.
Filing office fees, §25-9-525.
Information requests.
Response charges, §25-9-210(f).
Securities regulation.
Collection and payment over, §78A-45(c).
"No action" letter, §78A-50(e).
Registration.
Amendment of registration statements,
§78A-28(j).
Dealers and salesmen.
Application fee, §78A-37(b).
Securities.
Filing fee, §78A-28(b).
Sedimentation control.
Credited to general fund, §113A-54.2(b).
Authority of local programs to assess fees not
limited, §113A-54.2(d).
Use of fees, §113A-54.2(b).
Erosion control plans.
Review fees, §113A-54.2(a), (b), (d).
Local plans.
Limited erosion and sedimentation control
program, §113A-60(d).

FEES —Cont'd
Sedimentation control —Cont'd
Review fees.
Establishment of fee schedule, §113A-54.2(a).
Seeds.
Licenses and inspections, §106-277.28.
Service of process.
Uniform civil process fees, §7A-311.
Setoff debt collection.
Assistance fees, §105A-13.
Sex offender monitoring, §14-208.45.
Sex offender registration.
Release of online identifiers to entity,
§14-208.15A(c).
Shellfish.
Cultivation of shellfish.
Leases.
Application, §113-202(d1).
Renewal, §113-202(j).
Sheriffs.
Civil process.
Uniform civil process fees, §7A-311.
License or permit to sell crossbows or pistols.
Services provided, §14-404(e).
Limitation of actions for, §1-52.
Statement rendered by county officers
compensated from fees, §128-13.
Penalty for failure to file statement, §128-13.
Social services.
County boards of social services, §108A-10.
Social workers.
Certification and licensure, §90B-6.2(a), (b).
Soil additives act.
Registration of additives, §106-50.31.
Soil scientists, §89F-25.
Solicitors of contributions.
License, §131F-16(c).
Solid waste management.
Hazardous waste generators, transporters and
facilities, §130A-294.1.
Septage management firms, §130A-291.1(e) to
(e2).
Solid waste disposal, §130A-309.08.
Special proceedings.
Commissioners, §1-408.
Surveyors' fees, §1-408.1.
Uniform civil process fees, §7A-311.
Witness fees.
Not entitled to fees in advance, §6-51.
**Speech and language pathologists and
audiologists.**
Licenses, §90-305.
State departments and agencies.
Statutory construction, §12-3.1.
State institutions.
Rules and regulations.
Agencies establishing fees and charges by rule,
§12-3.1(a), (c).
Definitions, §12-3.1(b).
State lottery.
Setoff debt collection.
Collection assistance fee, §18C-134(d).
State treasurer.
Warrants for payment of money.
Fee for causing overdraft of agency account,
§143B-426.40G(b).
Structural pest control.
Applicants for certified applicator's identification
card or license.
Examinations of applicants, §106-65.27(a), (b).

FEES —Cont'd
Structural pest control —Cont'd
Identification cards.
Certified applicators, §106-65.31(a).
Employees, §106-65.31(b1).
Licenses.
Issuance and renewal, §106-65.31(b).
Substance abuse professionals.
Certification, §90-113.38.
Disposition of funds, §90-113.35.
Superior courts.
Accounting for fees and other receipts, §7A-108.
Civil process.
Uniform civil process fees, §7A-311.
Amount, §7A-311(a).
Collection of fees in advance, §7A-311(b).
Completeness and exclusivity of fees and
costs, §7A-311(c).
Clerks of court, NC Const Art IV §21.
Accounting for fees and other receipts, §7A-108.
Audit, §7A-108.
Deposits of money held by clerk, §7A-308.1.
Investment of funds in clerk's hands, §7A-308.1.
Statement rendered by county officer
compensated from fees, §128-13.
Costs are exclusive, §7A-320.
Deposits of money held by clerk, §7A-308.1.
Discovery procedures.
Filing of verified petition, §7A-305.1.
Investment of funds in clerk's hands, §7A-308.1.
Judges, NC Const Art IV §21.
Uniform costs and fees in trial division, §§7A-304
to 7A-318.
Supreme court.
Clerk of the supreme court, §7A-11.
Justices, NC Const Art IV §21.
Librarian of supreme court.
Copying service fees, §7A-13(f).
Fees for copying service, §7A-13(f).
Surplus lines insurance.
Eligibility, applying for, §58-21-20(c).
Licenses.
Agents and brokers, §58-21-65(b).
Surveyors' fees.
In civil actions involving sale of land, §1-408.1.
Tax advice given taxpayer by secretary,
§105-264(d).
Taxicabs.
Registration, §20-87.
**Tax incentives for new and expanding
business,** §105-129.6(a1).
Teacher licensure, §115C-296(a2).
Telephone membership corporations.
Regulatory fee, §117-3.1.
Telephonic sellers.
Registration, §66-261(a), (c).
Television manufacturers.
Registration, §130A-309.135(a).
Time shares.
Registration of time share projects.
Application fee, §93A-52(a).
Renewal fee, §93A-52(d).
Title insurance.
Licenses.
Companies.
Collateral loan certificate, §58-27-10.
Torrens system registration, §43-5.
Trademarks.
Registration.
Renewal fee, §80-5.

FEES —Cont'd
Trust companies.
Fiduciaries, trust institutions acting as.
Investments.
Temporary investment, fees, §53-163.1(d).
Licensed to do business, §53-160.
Turnpike authority.
Toll collection on turnpike projects.
Open road tolls.
Bill for unpaid toll.
Processing fee in addition to bill,
§136-89.215(b).
Underground storage tanks.
Leaking petroleum cleanup, §143-215.94C.
Uniform civil process fees, §7A-311.
Uniform costs and fees in trial division,
§§7A-304 to 7A-318.
Veterinarians.
Licenses.
Renewal.
Additional late renewal fee, §90-187.5.
Veterinary student interns.
Special registration, §90-186.
Veterinary technicians.
Special registration, §90-186.
Viatical life insurance settlements.
Offer or sale of contract, costs of filing, §78A-17.
Viatical settlement brokers and providers.
Licenses, §58-58-210(b).
Renewal fee, §58-58-210(c).
Vital statistics.
State registrar.
Providing copies or searching vital records,
§§130A-93.1(a), 130A-93(i).
Refund of overpayments, §130A-92(b).
Wastewater systems.
Certification of contractors and inspectors,
§90A-75(c).
Late fee for renewal of expired certificate,
§90A-78(b).
On-site subsurface systems.
Review fee, §130A-343(k).
Wastewater treatment.
Certification of water pollution control system
operator.
Fee schedule, §90A-42(a).
Water and air resources.
Applications.
Disposition of fees, §143-215.3(a).
Use of application and permit fees, §143-215.3A.
Water infrastructure.
Water infrastructure fund.
Fee imposed on loan or grant from wastewater
reserve or drinking water reserve,
§159G-24.
Water treatment facility operators.
Certificates, §90A-27.
Water well construction.
Fees of health department for analysis of water
samples, §130A-5.
Weighmasters.
Licenses, §81A-52.
Weights and measures.
Testing and certifying, §81A-12.
Well contractor certification, §87-98.9(a).
Witnesses.
Action for fees, §6-53.
Advance receipt of fees.
Not entitled to fees in advance, §6-51.
Attendance.
Compulsion to attend more than one day, §6-51.

FEES —Cont'd
Witnesses —Cont'd
Attendance —Cont'd
One fee for day's attendance, §6-60.
Proof of attendance, §6-53.
Commissioner of banks.
Employees of office used as witnesses,
§53-122(c).
Criminal actions.
Payment of witness fees in criminal actions,
§7A-316.
When defendant not liable.
Liability of state for witness fees, §7A-315.
Disbursement of expenses, §7A-301.
Expert witnesses.
Indigent defense services.
Fees paid by state, §7A-454.
Uniform fees, §7A-314(d).
Interpreters.
Uniform fees, §7A-314(f).
Legislative committees.
Expenses and fees of witness, §120-19.3.
Not entitled to fees in advance, §6-51.
Poultry products inspection.
Mileage and fees of witnesses, §106-549.68(b).
Proof of single material fact.
Liability for fees of such witnesses, §6-60.
Reference of claim against deceased person.
Recovery of fees of witnesses, §6-31.
State of North Carolina.
Criminal cases when defendant not liable.
Liability of state for witness fees, §7A-315.
Uniform fees for witnesses, §7A-314(a).
Expert witness, §7A-314(d).
Language interpreters, §7A-314(f).
Limit on number, §7A-314(e).
Mileage rate of reimbursement, §7A-314(c).
Out-of-state witnesses, §7A-314(c).
Reimbursement for travel expenses, §7A-314(b).
Workers' compensation.
Expert witnesses, §97-26.1.
Medical records and reports, §97-26.1.
Medical treatment, fees allowed, §97-26.
Occupational disease.
Medical examinations.
Asbestosis and silicosis.
Schedule of fees for examinations and
reports, §97-73.
Zoological authority.
Establishment of admission fees, §143-177.3(b).

FEE SIMPLE.
Condemnation.
State owned railroad companies, §40A-3(a).
Conversion of fee tail to fee simple, §41-1.
Conveyances.
Presumption of fee though word heirs omitted,
§39-1.
Possibility of reverter, right of entry or
executory interest.
Time limit, §41-32.
Wills.
Devise presumed to be in fee, §31-38.

FEET.
Podiatrists.
See PODIATRISTS.

FEE TAIL.
Conversion into fee simple, §41-1.

FELONIES.
Abortion, §§14-44 to 14-46.
Destruction of unborn child.
Use of drugs or instruments, §14-44.

FELONIES —Cont'd

Accessory before fact punishable as principal felon, §14-5.2.

Administration department.
Bribery.
Purchases and contracts to department.
Acceptance of bribes, §143-63.

Adoption.
Unlawful payments related to adoption.
Subsequent violations, §48-10-102(b).

Adulterated or misbranded food, drugs or cosmetics.
Intent to cause serious injury or death, §14-34.4(a).
Intent to extort, §14-34.4(b).

Adult protection.
Abuse of disabled or elder adults, §14-32.3(a).
Neglect of disabled or elder adult, §14-32.3(b).

Aircraft.
Infliction of serious bodily injury by operation of aircraft while impaired, §63-28.

Alcoholic beverages.
Beer franchise agreements.
Felony conviction affecting goodwill, §18B-1305.
Commission.
Felony conviction as grounds for removal from office, §18B-202.
Direct shipments into state, §18B-102.1(e).
Employee discharge.
Felony conviction as grounds for discharge from employment, §18B-202.
Manufacturers.
Second unlawful manufacturing offense, §18B-307(c).
Permit issuance.
Felony conviction as disqualification for permit, §§18B-900(a), 18B-1003(c).

Alligator propagation and production.
Untagged or undocumented alligator possessed by operator of facility, §106-763.1(c).

Anatomical gifts.
Falsification of document, §130A-412.19.
Sale or purchase of parts, §130A-412.18(a).

Animals.
Interference with animal research, §14-159.2(c).

Animal shelters.
Certificates of registration.
Felony conviction as grounds for denial of certificate, §19A-30.

Appearances.
Failure to appear, §15A-543.

Arrest.
Duty of arresting officer to provide information to state, §15A-501.
Electronic recording of custodial interrogations, §15A-211.
Without warrant, §15A-401.

Arson generally.
See ARSON.

Assault.
Habitual misdemeanor assault, §14-33.2.
Lesser included offense, §15-169.
Secret assault, §14-31.
Serious bodily injury.
Assault inflicting, §14-32.4(a).
Strangulation.
Assault inflicting, §14-32.4(b).
Unborn child.
Assault inflicting serious bodily injury on unborn child, §14-23.5.

FELONIES —Cont'd

Assault with deadly weapon.
Intent to kill or inflicting serious injury, §14-32.

Athlete agents, §78C-99.

Athletic contests generally, §§14-373 to 14-379.

Attempt to commit felony.
Punishment for, §14-2.5.

Bail and recognizance.
Failure to appear, §15A-543(b).

Bail bondsmen and runners.
Conviction of felony.
Grounds for denial, suspension, revocation or refusal to renew license, §58-71-80(a), (b).
Reports.
Knowingly and willfully falsifying, §58-71-165.

Bailments.
Conversion, §14-168.1.

Banks.
Bank examiners.
False reports, §53-124.
Keeping or accepting bribe or gratuity, §53-124.
Deposits.
Insolvent banks.
Receiving deposits, §53-132.
Embezzlement or misapplication of funds, §53-129.
False certification of check, §53-131.
False entries in banking accounts, §53-130.
Misrepresenting assets and liabilities of banks, §53-130.

Barbers.
Conviction.
Disqualifications for certificates or permits, §86A-18.

Battery.
Habitual misdemeanor assault, §14-33.2.

Bigamy.
Constitutes a felony, §14-183.

Bills of lading.
Issuing false bills, §21-42.

Birth of child.
Concealment, §14-46.

Bomb scares, §§14-69.1, 14-69.2.

Breaking and entering.
Building that is place of religious worship, §14-54.1(a).
Generally, §14-54.
Habitual breaking and entering status offense, §§14-7.25 to 14-7.31.
See BREAKING AND ENTERING.
Motor vehicles.
Preparation to commit breaking and entering.
Master key, manipulative key or other lock-picking device or hot wiring device.
Possession, buying, selling, transferring, §14-56.4(d).
Prevention of felonies.
All persons authorized to break open and enter house, §15-43.

Breaking out of dwelling house, §14-53.

Bribery.
Athletic contests, §§14-373 to 14-376.

Buildings.
Breaking or entering buildings.
Generally, §14-54.

Burglary.
Generally, §§14-51 to 14-57.
See BURGLARY.
Habitual breaking and entering status offense, §§14-7.25 to 14-7.31.
See BREAKING AND ENTERING.

FELONIES —Cont'd
Burial.
Unmarked human burial and human skeletal remains protection.
Certain prohibited acts, §70-40(b).
Castration, §§14-28, 14-29.
Cemeteries.
Defacing or desecrating grave sites.
Plowing over or covering up graves, §14-149.
Violations of North Carolina cemetery act, §65-71(a).
Check-cashing businesses, §53-287.
Child abuse or neglect, §14-318.4.
Child care facilities.
Fraudulent misrepresentation, §110-107(b).
Subsequent offenses, §110-103(d).
Unauthorized administration of medicine, §110-102.1A(c).
Violation causing serious injury to a child, §110-103(c).
Willful violations, §110-103(b).
Childhood vaccine-related injury compensation.
Certain vaccine diversions, §130A-431.
Children's health insurance program.
Fraud and misrepresentation, §108A-70.28.
Chop shop activity, §14-72.7(a).
Classification.
Default classification, §15A-1340.17(a).
Sentencing commission, §164-41.
Cockfighting, §14-362.
Coin-operated machines.
Burglary, §§14-56.1, 14-56.2.
Collection agencies.
Doing business without permit, §58-70-1.
Commercial drivers' licenses.
Sex offenders obtaining license with P or S endorsement.
False affidavit or swearing, §20-37.14A(c).
Commodities.
Violations of act, §78D-24(a).
Compensation to persons erroneously convicted of felonies, §§148-82 to 148-84.
Amount of compensation, §148-84(a).
Forms, §148-83.
Hearings, §148-83.
Innocent of charges, charges dismissed.
Provision for compensation, §148-82(b).
Job skills training, §148-84(c).
Pardon of innocence.
Provision of compensation, §148-82(a).
Petitions, §148-83.
Provision for compensation, §148-82.
Innocent of charges, charges dismissed, §148-82(b).
Pardon of innocence, §148-82(a).
Tuition, §148-84(c).
Computer crimes.
Accessing computers, §14-454(a).
Computer trespass, §14-458(b).
Damaging computers and computer resources, §14-455(a), (a1).
Government computers.
Accessing, §14-454.1(a), (b).
Altering, damaging or destroying, §14-455(a1).
Denial of government computer services to an authorized user, §14-456.1(a).
Social networking sites.
Sex offenders banned from using, §14-202.5(e).
Solicitation of child by computer, §14-202.3(c).
Computer trespass, §14-458(b).

FELONIES —Cont'd
Concealing birth of child, §14-46.
Concealment of death, §14-401.22(a).
Conspiracy.
Punishment for conspiracy to commit a felony, §14-2.4(a).
Construction sites.
Felonious larceny, possession or receiving of stolen goods from permitted site, §14-72.6(a).
Contaminating food or drink to render one mentally incapacitated or physically helpless, §14-401.16(c).
Contempt.
Criminal contempt.
Circumstances for final imprisonment, §5A-12.
Continuing criminal enterprise, §14-7.20.
Contracts through department of administration.
False certification that bids were submitted without collusion, §143-54(a).
Controlled substances.
Amphetamines.
Trafficking in amphetamines, §90-95(h).
Conditions of prescribed punishments and degree of offenses, §90-95(e).
Conspiracy to violate provision, §90-98.
Continuing criminal enterprise, §90-95.1(a).
Counterfeit substances.
Prohibited acts as to, §90-95(c).
Heroin.
Trafficking in heroin, §90-95(h).
Manufacture, §90-95(b).
Marijuana.
Trafficking in marijuana, §90-95(h).
MDPV.
Trafficking in, §90-95(h).
Mephedrone.
Trafficking in, §90-95(h).
Methamphetamines.
Precursor products, violations of sale restrictions, §90-113.56.
Trafficking in methamphetamines, §90-95(h).
Methaqualone.
Trafficking in methaqualone, §90-95(h).
Minors.
Delivery of drug paraphernalia to, §90-113.23(c).
Employing or intentionally using minor to commit drug law violations, §90-95.4(a), (b).
Participating in a drug violation by a minor, §90-95.7(c).
Promoting drug sales by a minor, §90-95.6(c).
Opium.
Trafficking in opium, §90-95(h).
Possession, §90-95(d).
Precursor chemicals.
Designation, §90-95(d2).
Prohibited acts as to, §90-95(d1), (d1a).
Prohibited acts.
Violations committed intentionally, §90-108(b).
Sales, §90-95(b).
Wholesale prescription drug distributors, §106-145.6(b).
Conversion.
Bailments, §14-168.1.
Corruption.
Elections, §163-275.
Counterfeiting, §14-13.
Bills of lading, §21-42.
Instruments, §14-119(a), (b).
Possessing tools for counterfeiting, §14-14.

FELONIES —Cont'd

Credit cards and devices.
False or fraudulent use of credit device.
Multiple violations, §14-113.6(a).

Credit repair services, §66-225.

Crime against nature, §14-177.

Criminal justice education and training standards commission.
Felony conviction.
Denial, suspension or revocation of certification, §17C-13(b).

Criminal street gangs.
Enhancement of misdemeanor offense to felony.
Offense committed for benefit of or association with gang, §14-50.22.
Patterns of gang activity.
Prohibited acts, §14-50.16(a).
Soliciting or encouraging participation, §14-50.17(b).
Minors, §14-50.18(b).
Withdrawal from gang.
Threats of retaliation or punishment for withdrawing, §14-50.20(b).
Threats to deter another from assisting, §14-50.19(b).

Crops.
Burning crops in the field.
Criminal trespass, §14-141.

Cruelty to animals.
Animal fights and baiting, §14-362.1(d).
Dog fighting and baiting, §14-362.2(b), (c).

Custodial interrogations.
Electronic recording, §15A-211.

Default classification, §15A-1340.17(a).

Definitions, §14-1.
Habitual felons, §14-7.1.

Delinquent and undisciplined juvenile actions.
First appearance of juvenile for felony cases, §7B-1808.

Dental hygienists.
Conviction as grounds for disciplinary measures, §90-229(a).

Dentists.
Conviction.
Grounds for disciplinary action, §90-41(a).

Desecrating, plowing over or covering up graves, §14-149.

Destroying unborn child.
Use of drugs or instruments, §14-44.

Detention facilities.
Assault on person employed at state or local detention facility, §14-34.7(b).
Assault with firearm upon, in performance of duties, §14-34.5(b).
Infliction of physical injury, punishment, §14-34.7(c).

Disability income plan.
Disability or disabled.
Defined as incapacity not resulting from felonious conduct, §135-101.

Discharge of firearm.
From within enclosure, §14-34.9.
Into occupied property or conveyance while in operation, §14-34.1.

Discount buying clubs.
Bond and trust account requirements.
Violations, §66-135(d).

Discovery.
Criminal procedure.
Omission or misrepresentation of evidence, criminal offense, §15A-903(d).

FELONIES —Cont'd

Discrimination.
Offenses committed because of victim's race, etc., §14-3(c).

DNA samples.
Preservation of biological evidence.
Destruction, alteration, concealment or tampering with evidence, §15A-268(i).
Required upon conviction, §15A-266.4.

Domestic criminal trespass, §14-134.3(b).

Domestic violence.
Protective orders.
Firearms violations, §50B-3.1(j).
Violation of valid protective order, §50B-4.1(d), (f).
Entry into safe house or haven where protected person is residing, §50B-4.1(g1).
Possession of deadly weapon, §50B-4.1(g).

Drivers' licenses.
Commercial drivers' licenses.
Sex offenders obtaining license with P or S endorsement.
False affidavit or swearing, §20-37.14A(c).
Forfeiture of licensing privilege, §15A-1331A.
Limited driving privilege, eligibility, §20-179.3(b).
Sale of reproduction, facsimile or simulation of license, §20-30.
Use of motor vehicle in commission of felony, §20-17(a).
Wrongful issuance, §20-34.1(a).

Drug and alcohol screening tests.
Defrauding test.
Second or subsequent offense, §14-401.20(c).

Drug paraphernalia.
Minors.
Delivery of drug paraphernalia to certain younger persons, §90-113.23(c).

Drugs.
Amphetamines.
Trafficking in, §90-95(h).
Conditions of prescribed punishments and degree of offenses, §90-95(e).
Conspiracy to violate provision, §90-98.
Continuing criminal enterprise, §90-95.1(a).
Counterfeit substances.
Prohibited acts as to, §90-95(c).
Heroin.
Trafficking in, §90-95(h).
Manufacturers, §90-95(b).
Enhanced sentencing in certain cases, §15A-1340.16D.
Marijuana.
Trafficking in, §90-95(h).
MDPV.
Trafficking in, §90-95(h).
Mephedrone.
Trafficking in, §90-95(h).
Methamphetamines.
Trafficking in methamphetamines, §90-95(h).
Methaqualone.
Trafficking in, §90-95(h).
Minors.
Delivery of drug paraphernalia to certain youths, §90-113.23(c).
Employing or intentionally using minor to commit drug law violations, §90-95.4(a), (b).
Participating in a drug violation by a minor, §90-95.7(c).
Promoting drug sales by a minor, §90-95.6(c).

FELONIES —Cont'd
Drugs —Cont'd
Opium.
  Trafficking in, §90-95(h).
  Possession, §90-95(d).
Precursor chemicals.
  Designation, §90-95(d2).
  Prohibited acts as to, §90-95(d1), (d1a).
Prohibited acts.
  Violations committed intentionally, §90-108(b).
Sale, §90-95(b).
Wholesale prescription drug distributors,
  §106-145.6(b).
Dry-cleaning solvent cleanup, §143-215.104Q(b),
  (c).
Economic interest statements.
State government ethics act.
  False information, §138A-27.
Elections.
Absentee ballot violations, §163-226.3(a).
Challenge of voters.
  Answer to challenge as felon not to be used on
    prosecution, §163-90.
  False swearing, §163-90.3.
Contributions and expenditures in political
    campaigns.
  False certification knowing information to be
    untrue, §§163-278.27(a1), 163-278.32.
  Violations by business organizations and labor
    unions, §163-278.27(a2).
Corruption.
  Certain acts declared felonies, §163-275.
Disqualification from voting, §163-55(a), NC Const
  Art VI §2.
Disqualifications from office, NC Const Art VI §8.
Voting systems.
  Vendors.
    Willful violation of duties, §163-165.9A(b).
Electrologists, §88A-4(b).
Electronic commerce in government, §66-58.8.
Electronic monitoring devices.
Interference with, §14-226.3.
**Electronic recording of custodial
  interrogations,** §15A-211.
Electronic surveillance.
Advertisement of surveillance devices,
  §15A-288(a2).
Manufacture, possession, purchase or sale of
  devices, §15A-288(a1).
Willful interception or disclosure of wire, oral or
  electronic communications, §15A-287(a1) to
  (a4).
Embezzlement generally.
See EMBEZZLEMENT.
Emergency medical services personnel.
Assault or affray upon while discharging duties,
  §14-34.6.
Emergency personnel.
Assault causing physical injury, §14-288.9(c).
Assault with dangerous weapon or substance,
  §14-288.9(c).
**Endangering executive, legislative or court
  officers,** §§14-16.6 to 14-16.10.
Escape.
Private correction facilities, §14-256.1.
Ethics.
State government ethics act.
  Statements of economic interest.
    False information, §138A-27.
Ethnic animosity.
Offenses committed because of victim's
  nationality, §14-3(c).

FELONIES —Cont'd
Evasion of tax, §105-236.
Explosives.
Malicious use of explosive or incendiary, §14-49.
  Property occupied by persons, §14-49.1.
Used in burglary, §14-57.
Extortion, §14-118.4.
Failure to appear, §15A-543.
False names.
Identification card for nondrivers presented with
  fake name in commission of felony,
  §20-37.8(b).
False pretenses and cheats generally.
See FALSE PRETENSES AND CHEATS.
**False reports concerning mass violence on
  educational property,** §14-277.5(b).
Fictitious names.
Presenting identification card with fake name in
  commission of felony, §20-37.8(b).
Financial transaction cards, §14-113.17(b).
Firearms and other weapons.
Discharge of firearm.
  From within enclosure, §14-34.9.
  Into occupied property or conveyance while in
    operation, §14-34.1.
Enhanced sentence.
  Use or displayed during commission of felony,
    §15A-1340.16A(c).
  Burden of proof, §15A-1340.16A(e).
  Circumstances in which provisions do not
    apply, §15A-1340.16A(f).
  Indictments or informations,
    §15A-1340.16A(d).
Possession of firearms, etc., by felon prohibited.
  Person charged with felony acquitted by reason
    of insanity, §14-415.3(a), (b).
  Person charged with felony found incompetent
    to stand trial, §14-415.3(a), (b).
  Punishment of persons violating prohibition,
    §14-415.1(a).
Sale of handguns to minors, §14-315(a1).
Serial numbers.
  Alteration, destruction or removal of numbers
    from firearm, §14-160.2(c).
Use or display during commission of felony.
  Enhanced sentence, §15A-1340.16A.
Weapons of mass death and destruction.
  Manufacture, assembly, possession, etc.,
    §14-288.8.
  Nuclear, biological or chemical weapons.
    False report or hoax, §§14-288.23(a),
      14-288.24.
    Manufacture, assembly, possession, etc.,
      §14-288.21.
    Use and delivery of weapons, §14-288.22.
Fishing licenses.
Forfeiture of licensing privilege after conviction of
  felony, §15A-1331A.
Food.
Distribution of harmful substances at Halloween
  and other times, §14-401.11.
Food and nutrition services.
Fraud, §108A-53(a).
Illegal possession or use, §108A-53.1.
Forfeitures.
Licensing privilege after conviction of felony,
  §15A-1331A.
Money or other property or interest acquired,
  §14-2.3(a).
  Action to recover, statute of limitation,
    §14-2.3(b).

FELONIES —Cont'd
Forfeitures —Cont'd
Money or other property or interest acquired
—Cont'd
Property traceable to owner or guardian,
inapplicability of forfeiture, §14-2.3(c).
Forgery generally.
See FORGERY.
Franchise tax.
Limited liability companies.
Controlled companies.
Underpayment, fraud to evade, penalty,
§105-114.1(h).
Fraternal benefit societies.
False statements under oath, §58-24-180(e).
Mergers and consolidation.
Violations of provisions of section,
§58-24-180(d).
Fraud.
Rental vehicles, §20-106.1.
Work first program, §108A-39(b).
General assembly.
Restoring rights of citizenship of convicts.
Local, special and private legislation prohibited,
NC Const Art II §24.
Threats to influence legislator in discharge of
duties, §120-86(e).
Ginseng.
Larceny, §14-79.
Habitual felons, §§14-7.1 to 14-7.12, 15A-1340.10.
Charge of habitual felon, §14-7.3.
Defined, §14-7.1.
Evidence of prior convictions, §14-7.4.
Felony offense defined, §14-7.1.
Indictment, §14-7.2.
Charge of habitual felon, §14-7.3.
Judgment, §14-7.5.
Prior convictions.
Evidence, §14-7.4.
Punishment, §14-7.2.
Sentencing, §§14-7.2, 14-7.6.
Status offender.
Charging as, §14-7.1.
Structured sentencing.
Inapplicability to violent habitual felons,
§15A-1340.10.
Verdict, §14-7.5.
Violent habitual felons.
Charge, §14-7.9.
Convicted defined, §14-7.7(a).
Evidence of prior convictions, §14-7.10.
Persons declared to be, §14-7.7(a).
Punishment, §14-7.8.
Sentencing, §14-7.12.
Verdict and judgment, §14-7.11.
Violent felony, crimes included in term,
§14-7.7(b).
Habitual misdemeanor assault, §14-33.2.
Handguns.
Sale to minors, §14-315.
Hazardous waste management, §130A-26.1.
Class I felonies, §130A-26.1(f).
Class J felonies, §130A-26.1(g).
"Knowingly and willingly" defined, §130A-26.1(d).
Highway inspection reports or test reports.
Falsification, §136-13.2.
Highway patrol.
Crossing median of divided highway.
Apprehension of felon, §20-140.3.
Conditions under which authorized, §136-89.58.

FELONIES —Cont'd
Hired property.
Failure to return, §14-167.
Homicide generally.
See HOMICIDE.
Housing authorities and projects.
Fraudulent misrepresentation in obtaining
housing assistance, §157-29.1(b).
Human remains.
Concealing evidence of death.
Dismembering, destroying, §14-401.22(d).
Death not of natural causes, §14-401.22(e).
Disturbing, vandalizing, desecrating,
§14-401.22(c).
Hunting licenses.
Forfeiture of licensing privilege after conviction of
felony, §15A-1331A.
Identification cards for nondrivers.
False or fictitious names.
Presenting identification card with fake name in
commission of felony, §20-37.8(b).
Identity theft, §§14-113.20(a), 14-113.22(a), (a1).
Trafficking in stolen identities, §14-113.20A(b).
Impeachment.
Causes for impeachment, §123-5.
Impersonation.
Law enforcement or other public officer,
§14-277(d1).
Incest, §14-178(b).
Indecent exposure, §14-190.9(a1).
Indigent persons.
False material statements as to indigency.
Defendant seeking appointment of counsel,
§7A-456(a).
Insolvent or imprisoned debtor.
False swearing, §23-43.
**Insurance agents, broker or limited
representatives.**
Unauthorized insurers.
Soliciting, negotiating or selling insurance for,
§58-33-95(a).
Insurance commissioner, false statements to,
§58-2-180.
Insurance fraud.
False statement to procure or deny benefit of
policy or certificate, §58-2-161(b).
Intimidating or interfering with witness,
§14-225(a).
Investment advisers, §78C-39(a) to (a4).
Juvenile proceedings.
Committed to youth development center for
offense classified as class B1, B2, C, D or E
felony.
Continued jurisdiction of juvenile court,
§7B-1602(b).
Delinquent and undisciplined juvenile actions.
First appearance of juvenile for felony case,
§7B-1808.
Kidnapping and abduction.
Abduction of children, §14-41(a).
Punishment for kidnapping, §14-39(b).
Larceny generally.
See LARCENY.
Laser devices.
Pointing at aircraft, §14-280.2(a).
**Law enforcement agency animals, assistance
animals, search and rescue animals.**
Causing serious harm, §14-163.1(b).
Willfully killing, §14-163.1(a1).
Law enforcement officers.
Assault upon in performance of duties, §§14-34.7,
14-34.7(a).
Infliction of physical injury, §14-34.7(c).

FELONIES —Cont'd
Law enforcement officers —Cont'd
Assault upon in performance of duties —Cont'd
Use of firearm, §14-34.5(a).
Leases.
Motor vehicles.
Sublease and loan assumption arranging,
§20-106.2(d), (e).
Legal expense funds for elected officials.
Statements filed with board.
False certification as true and correct,
§163-278.308(e).
Legislators.
Bribery, §120-86(e).
Extortion, §120-86.
License plates.
Transporter, dealer-transporter plates.
Selling, renting, leasing, §20-79.2(b2).
Licensing privileges.
Forfeiture after conviction of felony.
Automatic forfeiture, §15A-1331A(b)..
Definitions, §15A-1331A(a).
Judge to make findings and judgment,
§15A-1331A(c).
Limited driving privilege, §15A-1331A(d).
Lights.
Displaying false lights on seashore, §14-282.
Limited liability companies.
Franchise tax.
Controlled companies.
Underpayment, fraud to evade, penalty,
§105-114.1(h).
Littering, §14-399.
Livestock.
Cattle tick.
Damaging dipping vats, §106-363.
Poisoning livestock, §14-163.
Pursuing or injuring with intent to steal, §14-85.
Tuberculosis.
Sale of tubercular animal a felony, §106-350.
Looting, §14-288.6.
Machine guns.
Sale, use or possession, §14-409.
Maiming.
Castration, §§14-28, 14-29.
Malicious maiming, §14-30.
Malicious throwing of acid or alkali, §14-30.1.
Malicious castration, §14-28.
Malicious conduct by prisoners, §14-258.4(a).
Manslaughter, §14-18.
Unborn child.
Involuntary manslaughter, §14-23.4.
Voluntary manslaughter, §14-23.3.
Manufactured homes uniform standards.
Health and safety of purchaser threatened,
§143-151(b).
Marriage and family therapists.
Conviction as grounds for disciplinary action,
§90-270.60(a).
Meat inspections, §106-549.35(a).
Medicaid.
Fraud of providers, §108A-63(c), (e).
Property of patients violations, §108A-60(b).
Medical waste.
Depositing in navigable waters, §76-40(a1).
Water and air resources.
Prohibited disposal of waste, §143-214.2A(c).
Merchants.
Larceny from a merchant, §14-72.11.
Militia.
Composition of unauthorized militia.
Convicted felons excepted, §127A-7.

FELONIES —Cont'd
Minors.
Controlled substances.
Delivery of drug paraphernalia to certain
youths, §90-113.23(c).
Employing minor to commit drug law violations,
§90-95.4(a), (b).
Participating in a drug violation by a minor,
§90-95.7(c).
Promoting drug sales by a minor, §90-95.6(c).
Juvenile proceedings. See within this heading,
"Juvenile proceedings."
Prostitution.
Participating in prostitution of a minor,
§14-190.19(c).
Promoting prostitution of a minor,
§14-190.18(c).
Sexual exploitation of a minor.
First degree, §14-190.16(d).
Second degree, §14-190.17(d).
Solicitation of child by computer, §14-202.3(c).
Taking indecent liberties with children, §14-202.1.
Miscarriage or injury to pregnant woman.
Use of drugs or instruments to produce, §14-45.
Monopolies and restraint of trade.
Contracts, combinations and conspiracies, §75-1.
Motor carriers embezzling COD shipments,
§62-273.
Motor vehicle financial responsibility.
False affidavit or knowingly swearing or affirming
falsely, §20-279.31(c1).
Motor vehicle parts.
Felony larceny, §14-72.8.
Motor vehicles.
Accidents.
Leaving scene of accident, §20-166(a), (b).
Injury occurring in accident, §20-166(a1).
Passengers, §20-166.2(a).
Certificates of title.
Altering or forging certificate of title,
registration card or application, §20-71(a).
Reproducing or possessing blank title, §20-71(b).
Secondary metals recyclers and salvage yards.
Purchase of vehicles without certificate for
scrap and parts only.
Violations, §20-62.1(c).
Chop shop activity, §14-72.7(a).
Commercial drivers' licenses.
Forfeiture of driving privilege after conviction of
felony, §15A-1331A.
Dealers.
License applications.
Felony conviction as grounds for denial,
§20-294.
Drivers' licenses.
Forfeiture of licensing privilege after conviction
of felony, §15A-1331A.
Limited driving privilege, eligibility,
§20-179.3(b).
Learners' permits.
Sale of reproduction, facsimile or simulation
of license, §20-30.
Sale of reproduction, facsimile or simulation of
license, §20-30.
Use of motor vehicle in commission of felony,
§20-17(a).
Wrongful issuance, §20-34.1(a).
Engine numbers.
Altering or changing, §20-109(a).
Intent to conceal or misrepresent true
identity of vehicle, §20-109(b).

FELONIES —Cont'd
Motor vehicles —Cont'd
Felony death by vehicle, §20-141.4(a1).
  Aggravated felony death by vehicle,
    §20-141.4(a5).
  Punishment, §20-141.4(b).
  Repeat offenders.
    Second degree murder, §20-141.4(a6).
Felony serious injury by vehicle, §20-141.4(a3).
  Aggravated felony serious injury by vehicle,
    §20-141.4(a4).
  Punishments, §20-141.4(b).
Felony violations punished as class 1 felon,
  §20-177.
Fraud.
  Rental vehicles, §20-106.1.
Impaired driving.
  Habitual impaired driving, §20-138.5(b).
Inspections, §20-183.8(c).
Law enforcement, fire department, or rescue
  squad vehicles.
  Approach by motorists.
    Causing serious injury or death, §20-157(i).
Leases.
  Sublease and loan assumption arranging,
    §20-106.2(d), (e).
Manufacturer's certificate of origin.
  False sworn certification, §20-52.1(d).
Odometers.
  Unlawful change of mileage, §20-350.
Parts.
  Felony larceny, §14-72.8.
Preparation to commit breaking and entering.
  Master key, manipulative key or other
    lock-picking device or hot wiring device.
    Possession, buying, selling, transferring,
      §14-56.4(d).
Registration.
  Altering or forging registration card, §20-71(a).
School buses.
  Passing stopped school bus, §20-217(g).
Secondary metals recyclers and salvage yards.
  Purchase of vehicles without title certificate for
    scrap and parts only.
    Violations, §20-62.1(c).
Security interest, registration.
  False filing, §20-58(b).
Serial numbers.
  Altering or changing, §20-109(a).
    Intent to conceal or misrepresent true
      identity of vehicle, §20-109(b).
Smoke screen violations, §20-136(b).
Special identification card.
  Wrongful issuance, §20-34.1(a).
Stolen vehicles.
  Receiving or transferring stolen vehicles,
    §20-106.
Sublease and loan assumption arranging,
  §20-106.2(d).
Total loss claim vehicle.
  Removal of permanent marker affixed to
    vehicles doorjam, §20-71.4(c).
Transporter, dealer-transporter plates.
  Selling, renting, leasing, §20-79.2(b2).
Use of motor vehicle in commission of felony.
  Mandatory revocation of license, §20-17(a).
Murder, §14-17.
  Unborn child, §14-23.2.
Navigable waters.
  Medical waste, depositing, §76-40(a1).
Neglect of disabled or elder adult, §14-32.3(b).

FELONIES —Cont'd
Notaries public, §10B-60(e), (f).
  Electronic notary public act.
    Electronic signature.
      Wrongfully obtaining coding, file or program
        enabling affixation, §10B-146(b).
    Software or hardware.
      Wrongfully manufacturing, distributing or
        possessing, §10B-146(a).
Nuclear, biological or chemical weapons.
  False report or hoax, §§14-288.23(a), 14-288.24.
  Manufacture, assembly, possession, etc.,
    §14-288.21.
  Use and delivery of weapons, §14-288.22.
Obscenity.
  Dissemination to minors under the age of 16
    years, §14-190.7.
  Sexual exploitation of a minor.
    First degree, §14-190.16(d).
    Second degree, §14-190.17(d).
Obstructing justice generally.
  See OBSTRUCTING JUSTICE.
Obstruction of health care facilities.
  Habitual offenders, §14-277.4(c).
Occupational licenses.
  Forfeiture of licensing privilege after conviction of
    felony, §15A-1331A.
Office of information technology services.
  Procurement of information technology.
    Bribery, §147-33.99.
    False certification that information technology
      bid submitted without collusion,
      §147-33.100.
    Financial interest of officers in sources of
      supply, §147-33.99.
Oil or hazardous substances discharges,
  §143-215.88B(e), (f), (h).
Optometrists.
  Conviction as grounds for disciplinary action,
    §90-121.2(a).
Paper currency machines, §14-56.3.
Parole of felons.
  Automatic parole under certain conditions,
    §15A-1371(g).
Patient abuse, §14-32.2(b).
**Peddlers, itinerant merchants and specialty
  markets.**
  Prohibited sales, §66-254.1.
Pederasty.
  Taking indecent liberties with children, §14-202.1.
**Peeping into room occupied by another
  person,** §14-202.
Perjury generally.
  See PERJURY.
Physical therapists.
  Conviction as grounds for disciplinary action,
    §90-270.36.
Physicians and surgeons.
  Practicing without license, §90-18(a).
Pine needles or pine straw.
  Larceny, §14-79.1.
Poisoning livestock, §14-163.
Police.
  Conviction of felony.
    Removal of unfit officers, §128-16.
Possession of burglary tools, §14-55.
Poultry products inspections, §106-549.59(a).
Pregnant women.
  Using drugs or instruments to injure, §14-45.
Preneed funeral contracts and funds,
  §90-210.70(a).

FELONIES —Cont'd

Prescriptions.

Wholesale prescription drug distributors, §106-145.6(b).

Prevention.

Breaking and entering of a house.

Authorization, §15-43.

Probation or parole officers.

Assault upon in performance of duties, §14-34.7(a).

Infliction of physical injury, §14-34.7(c).

Use of firearm, §14-34.5(a).

Prostitution.

Minors.

Participating in prostitution of a minor, §14-190.19(c).

Promoting prostitution of a minor, §14-190.18(c).

Pseudoephedrine products.

Restrictions on sales, violations of, §90-113.56.

Public officers and employees.

Assault with a deadly weapon, §14-34.2.

Disqualifications from holding office, NC Const Art VI §8.

Misconduct in office, §§14-228 to 14-252.

See MISCONDUCT IN PUBLIC OFFICE.

Public works.

Contractor affidavits.

Perjury in affidavit, §133-31.

Racial minorities.

Offenses committed because of victim's race, §14-3(c).

Railroads.

Injury to property of railroads, §§14-278, 14-279.

Officers.

Misconduct in private office, §14-253.

Shooting or throwing at trains or passengers, §14-280.

Rape, §§14-27.2, 14-27.3.

Rape of a child, §14-27.2A.

Rebellion, §14-8.

Rebirthing technique.

Practicing.

Second or subsequent offense, §14-401.21(b).

Religious discrimination.

Offenses committed because of victim's religion, §14-3(c).

Residential mortgage fraud, §14-118.15.

Restoration of felon's citizenship rights, §§13-1 to 13-4.

Restraint.

Felonious restraint, §14-43.3.

Riots and civil disorders.

Engaging to riot, §14-288.2.

Robbery.

Armed robbery, §14-87(a).

Common law robbery, §14-87.1.

Train robbery, §14-88.

Safecracking, §14-89.1.

School buses.

Passing stopped school bus, §20-217(g).

School personnel.

Sexual acts with victim who is student, §14-27.7(b).

Seashore.

Displaying false lights on seashore, §14-282.

Secondary metals recyclers and salvage yards.

Motor vehicles purchased without title certificate.

Purchases for scrap and parts recovery only.

Violations, §20-62.1(c).

FELONIES —Cont'd

Secretly peeping into room occupied by another person, §14-202.

Secret societies.

Violation of article, §14-12.15.

Securities regulation.

Obstruction of investigation, §78A-58.

Securities regulation violations, §78A-57.

Sentencing.

Commitment to division of adult correction, §15A-1352(b).

Enhanced sentence.

Bullet-proof vests.

Defendant wearing or having in possession during commission of felony, §15A-1340.16C(a).

Burden of proof, §15A-1340.16C(d).

Exceptions, §15A-1340.16C(b1), (e).

Indictments or informations, §15A-1340.16C(c).

Firearm or deadly weapon used or displayed during commission of felony, §15A-1340.16A(c).

Burden of proof, §15A-1340.16A(e).

Circumstances in which provisions do not apply, §15A-1340.16A(f).

Indictments or informations, §15A-1340.16A(d).

Methamphetamine manufacture.

Serious injury inflicted on law or emergency personnel, §15A-1340.16D(a).

Applicability, §15A-1340.16D(d).

Burden of proof, §15A-1340.16D(c).

Indictment allegations, §15A-1340.16D(b).

Forfeiture of licensing privilege after conviction of felony, §15A-1331A.

Habitual felons, §§14-7.2, 14-7.6.

Inapplicability of structured sentencing to violent habitual felons, §15A-1340.10.

Violent habitual felons, §14-7.12.

Licensing privileges.

Forfeiture after conviction.

Automatic forfeiture, §15A-1331A(b).

Definitions, §15A-1331A(a).

Judge to make findings and judgment, §15A-1331A(c).

Limited driving privilege, §15A-1331A(d).

Structured sentencing, §§15A-1340.13 to 15A-1340.17.

Violent habitual felons, §14-7.12.

Sex offenders.

Residential restriction violations, §14-208.16(f).

Sex offender and public protection registration.

Failure to register, subsequent violations, §14-208.11(a).

Sex offender monitoring.

Failure to enroll in program, §14-208.44(a).

Tampering with device, §14-208.44(b).

Sexually violent predator.

Child-involved activities.

Working or volunteering for, §14-208.17(c).

Social networking sites.

Sex offenders banned from using, §14-202.5(e).

Unlawful presence on premises for use, care or supervision of children, §14-208.18(h).

Sexual offenses.

Crime against nature, §14-177.

Generally.

See SEXUAL OFFENSES.

Shellfish.

Polluted shellfish.

Taking or selling at night or with prior convictions, §113-209(d).

FELONIES —Cont'd
Sheriffs.
Conviction of felony.
Removal of unfit officers, §128-16.
Education and training standards commission.
Denial, suspension or revocation of certificate.
Felony conviction, §17E-12(b).
Slot machines, §14-309(a) to (c).
Social networking sites.
Sex offenders banned from using, §14-202.5(e).
Social services.
Food and nutrition services.
Fraudulent misrepresentation, §108A-53(a).
Medical assistance program.
Fraud.
Providers of medical assistance, §108A-63(c), (e).
Recipients, §108A-64(c).
Property of patients.
Certain violations as to, §108A-60(b).
Solicitation to commit felony.
Punishment for, §14-2.6(a).
Solid waste management.
Hazardous waste, §130A-26.1.
Speeding to elude arrest, §20-141.5(b).
Classes of felonies, §20-141.5(b1).
Speedy trial, §15-10.
Stalking, §§14-277.3, 14-277.3A(d).
Statements of economic interest.
State government ethics act.
False information, §138A-27.
Statutory rape, §§14-27.2, 14-27.4.
First-degree sexual offense, §14-27.4.
Sexual offense with child, §14-27.4A.
Strangulation.
Assault inflicting, §14-32.4(b).
Submachine guns.
Sale, use or possession, §14-409.
Subversion.
Punishment for violations, §14-12.
Sweepstakes.
Electronic machines and devices prohibited, §14-306.4(f).
Taking indecent liberties with a student, §14-202.4(a).
Taxation, §105-236.
Tax evasion, §105-236.
Telephone records privacy protection, §14-113.33(a).
Telephone sales recovery services, §14-401.15(c).
Time shares.
Registration.
Violation of requirement, §93A-40(b).
Time share registrar.
Violations as to, §93A-58(b).
Toxic substances.
Disclosure of hazardous substance trade secret, §95-197.
Dumping of toxic substances, §14-284.2.
Trademarks.
Criminal use of counterfeit trademark, §80-11.1(b), (c).
Transportation board.
Conflicts of interest, §136-14(i).
Malfeasance, §136-13(c).
Profiting from proposed project, §136-14(f).
Transportation department.
Highway inspection reports.
Falsifying reports, §136-13.2(a), (b).
Trespass.
Crops.
Burning or destroying crops in the field, §14-141.

FELONIES —Cont'd
Trial.
Speedy trial, §15-10.
Trust companies.
Records violations, §53-355.
Unborn child.
Assault inflicting serious bodily injury on unborn child, §14-23.5.
Involuntary manslaughter, §14-23.4.
Murder, §14-23.2.
Voluntary manslaughter, §14-23.3.
Underground petroleum storage tank leak cleanup, §143-215.94X(b), (c).
Unlawful use of audiovisual recording device in motion picture theater, §14-440.1(b), (c).
Uttering, §14-120.
Bills of lading, §21-42.
Vandalism.
Injuring houses, churches, fences and walls, §14-144.
Viatical life insurance settlements.
Fraudulent viatical settlement act, §58-58-265(a).
Violent habitual felons, §§14-7.7 to 14-7.12.
Charge, §14-7.9.
Convicted defined, §14-7.7(a).
Evidence of prior convictions, §14-7.10.
Persons declared to be, §14-7.7(a).
Punishment, §14-7.8.
Sentencing, §14-7.12.
Verdict in judgment, §14-7.11.
Violent felony, crimes included in term, §14-7.7(b).
Vital statistics, §130A-26A(b).
Water and air resources.
Air pollution control violations, §143-215.114B(a) to (i).
Classifications, standards or limitations.
Knowing and willful violations, §143-215.6B.
Medical waste.
Prohibited disposal, §143-214.2A(c).
Water supply and waterworks.
Contamination of public water system, §14-159.1.
Wholesale prescription drug distributors, §106-145.6(b).
Witnesses.
Intimidating or interfering with witness, §14-225(a).
Workers' compensation.
Insurance or proof of financial ability to pay benefits.
Refusal or neglect to secure compensation, §97-94(c).
Willfully fails to bring employer into compliance, §97-94(d).
Work first program fraud, §108A-39(b).
Worthless checks, §14-107(d).

FELONIOUS ASSAULT WITH DEADLY WEAPON, §14-32.

FELONIOUS RESTRAINT, §14-43.3.

FELONS.
Alcoholic beverage permittee.
Certain employees prohibited, §18B-1003(c).
Compensation to persons erroneously convicted of felonies.
Amount of compensation, §148-84.
Hearings, §148-83.
Provision for compensation, §148-82.
Firearms possession, §14-415.1.
Persons charged with felony acquitted by reason of insanity, §14-415.3(a), (b).

FELONS —Cont'd
Firearms possession —Cont'd
Persons charged with felony found incompetent to stand trial, §14-415.3(a), (b).
Physicians and surgeons.
Automatic revocation of license for felony conviction, §90-14(c).

FELONY DEATH BY VEHICLE, §20-141.4(a1).
Aggravated felony death by vehicle, §20-141.4(a5).
Mandatory revocation of driver's license, §§20-17(a), 20-19(i).
Punishment, §20-141.4(b).
Repeat offenders.
Second degree murder, §20-141.4(a6).

FELONY LARCENY OF MOTOR VEHICLE PARTS, §14-72.8.

FELONY MURDER, §14-17.

FELONY SERIOUS INJURY BY VEHICLE, §20-141.4(a3).
Aggravated felony serious injury by vehicle, §20-141.4(a4).
Punishments, §20-141.4(b).

FENCES.
Cemeteries.
Criminal trespass.
Destruction or removal of fence enclosing cemeteries, §14-148.
Drainage.
Right to owner, §156-6.
Housing authorities and projects.
Electrified fences, spikes or barbed wire prohibited, §157-9(d).
Invisible fences.
Unlawful removal of electronic dog collars, §14-401.17.
Mount Mitchell park.
Powers of department of environment and natural resources, §100-12.
Trespass.
Criminal trespass.
Injuring fences, §§14-144, 14-159.

FENCING OF STOLEN PROPERTY.
Art objects, §14-398.
Possessing stolen property, §14-71.1.
Degree of punishment depending on value of property, §14-72.
Felony without regard to value of property, §14-72(c).
Receiving or possessing goods represented as stolen, §14-71(b).
Receiving stolen property, §14-71(a).
Degree of punishment depending on value of property, §14-72.
Felony without regard to value of property, §14-72(c).
Jurisdiction in superior courts, §14-73.
Organized retail theft, §14-86.6(a).

FERAL ANIMALS.
Person bitten by animal required to be vaccinated for rabies.
Location of owner, reasonable effort, euthanized, owner not located, §130A-196(a).
Quarantine in districts infected with rabies.
Destroying, §130A-195.

FERAL SWINE.
Live feral swine caught in traps.
Unlawful to remove and to transport after removal, §113-291.12.
Penalty, §113-294(s).
Transporting live swine, identification required.
Presumption that swine without identification is feral, §106-798(b).

FERRETS.
Impoundment.
Animals not wearing rabies vaccination tags, §130A-192.
Rabies.
Defined, §130A-184.
Generally, §§130A-184 to 130A-201.
See RABIES.

FERRIES.
Arson.
Burning of ferries, §14-63.
Costs.
Application for establishment, alteration or discontinuance.
Allowance of costs to either party or apportioned in discretion of court, §6-21.
County commissioners.
Authority of county commissioners with regard to ferries, §136-88.
Department of transportation.
Letting contracts to bidders after advertisement, §136-28.1(a) to (k).
Construction, maintenance and repair of ferry deemed highway construction, §136-28.1(c).
Ferry repair facilities.
Contracts with electricity generators, §136-28.1(i).
Transportation system defined, §136-5.1.
Establishment.
Department of transportation to establish, §136-82.
General assembly.
Local, private and special legislation prohibited, NC Const Art II §24.
Guard chains or gates.
Safety measures, §136-89.
Liability.
Owners of ferries not under supervision of department of transportation.
Rights and liabilities of owners, §136-88.
Maintenance.
Department of transportation to maintain, §136-82.
Owners of ferries not under supervision of department of transportation.
Rights and liabilities of owners, §136-88.
Purchase in transportation improvement program.
Board of transportation approval, considerations, §143B-350(f2).
Safety, §136-89.
Transportation department.
Establishment and maintenance of ferries, §136-82.

FERRIS WHEELS.
Amusement device safety generally, §§95-111.1 to 95-111.18.
See AMUSEMENT DEVICE SAFETY.

FERTILIZERS, §§106-655 to 106-677.
Administration of article, §106-658.

FERTILIZERS —Cont'd
Analysis of commercial fertilizers.
Duty of commissioner to make analysis,
§106-662(a).
Methods of analysis, §106-662(c).
Result of official analysis, §106-662(d).
Rules and regulations, §106-662(e).
Anhydrous ammonia.
Installation, §106-660(g).
Appeals.
Assessments of penalties for other final orders or
rulings, §106-670.
Board of agriculture.
Authority to make rules and regulations,
§106-673.
Brand names.
Defined, §106-657.
False or misleading statements, §106-663.
Building codes.
Fertilizer, equipment for storage or handling.
Exemption from provisions, §143-138(b8).
Commercial values, §106-664.
Commissioner of agriculture, §106-658.
Analyzing, inspection, sampling and testing
commercial fertilizers, §106-662(a).
Condemnation of commercial fertilizer,
§106-667.
Declaration of policy, §106-672.
Definitions, §106-657.
Distributors.
Defined, §106-657.
Registration requirements, §106-660(b).
Enforcing official, §106-658.
False or misleading statements, §106-663.
Fees.
Inspection fees, §106-671(a).
Reporting system, §106-671(b).
Registration of brands, §106-660(a).
Fluid fertilizers.
Defined, §106-657.
Method of transfer of custody, §106-660(e).
Grade-tonnage reports, §106-677.
Imports.
Sales or exchanges between imports, §106-676.
Information concerning fertilizers.
Publication of information, §106-675.
Inspections.
Duty of commissioner to inspect, §106-662(a).
Fees, §106-671(a).
Reporting system, §106-671(b).
Labeling.
Accompanying delivery, §106-661(b).
Data required, §106-661(a).
Identical guarantees for each product,
§106-661(d).
Mixed fertilizer sold in bags weighing more than
100 pounds, §106-661(c).
Supplied to purchaser, §106-661(b).
Legislative findings and declarations, §106-672.
Licenses.
Fertilizer manufacturers and distributors to be
licensed, §106-660(d).
Revocation or suspension of license, §§106-663,
106-669, 106-677.
Manufacturers.
Defined, §106-657.
Licensing of fertilizer manufacturers and
distributors, §106-660(d).
Revocation or suspension of licenses, §§106-663,
106-669, 106-677.

FERTILIZERS —Cont'd
Manufacturers —Cont'd
Sales or exchanges between manufacturers,
§106-676.
Minimum plant food requirement, §106-659.
Misleading statements, §106-663.
Misrepresentations, §106-663.
Mixed fertilizers.
Defined, §106-657.
Sale in bags weighing more than 100 pounds.
Labeling requirements, §106-661(c).
Penalties.
Appeals from assessment of penalty, §106-670.
Deficiency in plant food, §106-665(b), (c).
Determination and publication of commercial
values, §106-664.
"Stop sale, use or removal" orders, §106-666(a),
(b).
Violations of article, §106-668.
Plant food.
Deficiency in plant food, §106-665(a).
Assessment of penalties, §106-665(b), (c).
Minimum plant food requirement, §106-659.
Policy declaration, §106-672.
Publications.
Commercial values, §106-664.
Information concerning fertilizers, §106-675.
Purpose of article, §106-656.
Registration of brands.
Application, §106-660(a).
Cancellation of registration, §106-669.
Distributor not required to register, §106-660(b).
Fee, §106-660(a).
Guaranteed analysis changed, §106-660(c).
Material changes, §106-660(c).
Refusal of registration, §106-669.
Sources of materials changed, §106-660(c).
Reporting system.
Inspection fees, §106-671(b).
Reports.
Grade-tonnage reports, §106-677.
Rules and regulations.
Authority of board of agriculture to make,
§106-673.
Sampling analysis, §106-662(e).
Sales and use tax.
Exemption, §105-164.13.
Sampling.
Duty of commissioner to sample, §106-662(a).
Methods of sampling, §106-662(b).
Rules and regulations, §106-662(e).
Seizure of commercial fertilizer, §106-667.
Short title, §106-655.
Short weight, §106-674.
Soil additives act, §§106-50.28 to 106-50.41.
See SOIL ADDITIVES ACT.
Statement of purpose, §106-656.
"Stop sale, use or removal" order.
Appeals from final order or ruling, §106-670.
Issuance and enforcement, §106-666(a), (b).
Testing.
Duty of commissioner to test, §106-662(a).
Title of article, §106-655.
Trademarks.
Misleading or deceptive trademark, §106-663.
Violations of article.
Determination and publication of commercial
values, §106-664.
Plant food deficiencies, §106-665(b), (c).
Punishment for violations, §106-668.
Seizure of commercial fertilizer, §106-667.

FERTILIZERS —Cont'd
Violations of article —Cont'd
"Stop sale, use or removal" orders, §106-666(a), (b).
Weights and measures.
Short weight, §106-674.

FETAL DEATH REGISTRATION.
Information.
Required medical information, §130A-114(b).
Report of death, §130A-114(a).
Preparation and filing of report, §130A-114(c).
Required medical information, §130A-114(b).

FETUS.
Abortion generally.
See ABORTION.
Certificate of birth resulting in stillbirth, §130A-114(d).
Cremation of fetal remains.
Acknowledgment of delivery, §90-210.129(o).
Fetal report of death, §90-210.129(p).
Remains of terminated pregnancies.
Manner of disposition.
Disposal by burial or cremation, §130A-131.10(b).
Liability or additional duty not imposed on medical waste treatment facility, §130A-131.10(d).
Relief from obligation to dispose by burial or cremation.
Sending remains to medical or research laboratory or facility, §130A-131.10(c).
Rules to ensure disposition by burial or cremation, §130A-131.10(a).
Unborn victims of violence act/Ethen's law, §§14-23.1 to 14-23.8.
See CRIMINAL LAW AND PROCEDURE.
Using drugs or instruments to destroy unborn child, §14-44.

FICTITIOUS NAMES.
Boxing under fictitious or assumed name, §143-654(b).
Business names, §§66-68 to 66-71.
See ASSUMED NAMES.
Drivers' licenses.
Presenting license with fake name in commission of felony, §20-30.
Identification cards.
Presenting identification card with fake name in commission of felony, §20-37.8(b).
Professional employer organizations.
Conducting business under, §58-89A-80(a).

FIDELITY AND SURETY INSURANCE, §58-7-15.
Foreign or alien insurance companies.
Deposits required, §58-5-10.
Mandatory or voluntary risk sharing plans, §§58-42-1 to 58-42-50.
See MANDATORY OR VOLUNTARY RISK SHARING PLANS.
Mutual insurance companies.
Organization of companies, §58-7-75.

FIDELITY BONDS.
Bonds generally.
See BONDS, SURETY.

FIDUCIARIES.
Accountants.
Employment and compensation.
Powers which may be incorporated by reference in trust instrument, §32-27.

FIDUCIARIES —Cont'd
Accounts and accounting.
Personal accounts.
Deposit in fiduciary's personal account, §32-10.
Actions.
Claims against estate or trust.
Powers which may be incorporated by reference in trust instrument, §32-27.
Administrators.
See EXECUTORS AND ADMINISTRATORS.
Adult care homes.
Bill of rights.
Transfer of management responsibilities, §131D-22.
Agents generally.
See AGENTS.
Appeals.
Stay of further proceedings in court.
Security limited for fiduciaries, §1-294.
Application of payments, §32-3.
Attorneys at law.
Counsel fees allowed attorney serving as fiduciary, §32-61.
Employment and compensation.
Powers which may be incorporated by reference in trust instrument, §32-27.
Banks.
Deposit in name of fiduciary.
Bank authorized to pay amount of deposit, §32-8.
Merger or consolidation.
Fiduciary powers and liabilities of banks or trust companies merging or transferring assets and liabilities, §53-17.
Stockholders.
Fiduciaries not personally liable, §53-40.
Trusts and trustees.
See BANKS.
Bonds, surety.
Appeal perfected staying further proceedings in court below.
Security limited for fiduciaries, §1-294.
Surety companies.
Expense of fiduciary bond charged to fund, §58-73-35.
Capacity to sue in representative capacity.
Affirmative averment in pleading, §1A-1 Rule 9(a).
Cases not provided for in article, §32-12.
Checks.
Checks drawn payable to third persons, §32-6.
Payable to fiduciary, §32-7.
Compensation of trustees and other fiduciaries, §§32-53 to 32-62.
Attorneys serving as fiduciaries.
Counsel fees allowed, §32-61.
Compensation in amount provided by law.
Instrument providing, §32-60.
Definitions, §32-53.
Effective date of provision, §32-62.
Maximum amount provided by law.
Instrument providing, §32-60.
Other fiduciaries, §32-59.
Reasonable compensation.
Entitlement, §32-59.
Service without compensation.
Instrument providing, §32-60.
Trustees.
Excessive compensation received.
Refund on clerk's determination, §32-57(b).
Expense reimbursement, entitlement, §32-58.

FIDUCIARIES —Cont'd
Compensation of trustees and other fiduciaries
  —Cont'd
  Trustees —Cont'd
    Notice of proposed payment, §32-55(a).
      Alternative notice, §32-55(b).
      Beneficiary under legal disability, §32-55(c).
      Right of beneficiaries to file proceeding for
        review of reasonableness.
        Statement required in notice, §32-55(c1).
      When deemed given, §32-55(d).
    Payment without prior approval of clerk of
      superior court, §32-56.
    Reasonable compensation.
      Entitlement, compensation not specified,
        §32-54(a).
      Factors considered in determining, §32-54(b).
    Refunds.
      Clerk's determination excessive compensation
        received, §32-57(b).
    Review of reasonableness, approval or denial of
      payment, §32-57(a).
Condominium owners' associations.
  Executive board, §47C-3-103(a).
Conservatorship.
  Banks, §§53-148 to 53-158.1.
    See BANKS.
  Credit unions.
    Conservation generally, §54-109.92.
  Securities regulation.
    Appointment of conservator for defendant's
      assets, §78A-47(a).
    Exempt transactions, §78A-17.
Construction and interpretation.
  Uniform fiduciaries act.
    Uniformity of interpretation, §32-13.
Contribution.
  Joint tort-feasors.
    Provisions not to apply to breaches of trust or of
      other fiduciary obligations, §1B-1(g).
Corporations.
  Foreign corporations.
    Restrictions on fiduciary powers.
      Business corporations, §55-15-05(a).
  Oaths, §11-5.
  Participation in reorganizations.
    Powers which may be incorporated by reference
      in trust instrument, §32-27.
Credit unions.
  Power of credit unions generally, §54-109.21.
Custodial trusts and trustees, §§33B-1 to 33B-22.
  See CUSTODIAL TRUSTS.
Debts.
  Transfer of negotiable instruments.
    Security for personal debt.
      Liability of creditor or transferee, §32-5.
Decedents' estates.
  Breach of fiduciary duty.
    Jurisdiction.
      Clerks of superior court jurisdiction in estate
        proceedings.
        Limitation on jurisdiction, §28A-2-4(c).
  Collection of rent, income, etc., §32-27.
  Federal estate tax apportionment.
    Distribution of property before final
      apportionment, §28A-27-7.
  Incorporation by reference of certain powers.
    Restriction on exercise of such powers,
      §32-26(b), (c).
Declaratory judgments.
  Renunciation compatible with fiduciary duties,
    §31B-1.2(b).

FIDUCIARIES —Cont'd
Declaratory judgments —Cont'd
  Who may apply for declaration, §1-255.
Definitions.
  Powers of fiduciaries, §32-25.
  Uniform fiduciary act, §32-2.
Deposits.
  Banking deposits in name of fiduciary, §32-8.
  Personal account of fiduciary, §32-10.
  Principal.
    Deposit in name of principal, §32-9.
  Trustees.
    Deposits in name of two or more trustees,
      §32-11.
Durable power of attorney.
  Attorney-in-fact accountable to court appointed
    fiduciary, §32A-10(a).
  Nomination of fiduciary by durable power of
    attorney for consideration by court,
    §32A-10(b).
Embezzlement.
  Property.
    Receipt of property by virtue of office or
      employment, §14-90.
Executors and administrators.
  See EXECUTORS AND ADMINISTRATORS.
Guardians.
  General provisions.
    See GUARDIAN AND WARD.
  Payments to or for minors or incompetents.
    Powers which may be incorporated by reference
      in trust instrument, §32-27.
Health maintenance organizations.
  Responsibilities of directors, officers and partners,
    §58-67-45.
Housing authorities and projects.
  Bond issues.
    Legal investments, §157-25.
Income tax.
  Individual income tax.
    Filing returns, §105-152(b).
Indorsements.
  Negotiable instruments.
    Transfer, §32-5.
In good faith.
  Thing done in, §32-2(b).
Investments.
  Housing authorities and projects.
    Bond issues of authority, §157-25.
  Powers which may be incorporated by reference in
    trust instrument, §32-27.
  Securities approved by secretary of housing and
    urban development, federal housing
    administration and veterans administration,
    §53-45.
Judgments and decrees.
  Defense after judgment set aside.
    No liability for prior distribution of fund,
      §1-108.
Judicial sales.
  Bond of person holding sale, §1-339.10(b), (c).
Law merchant.
  Applicability, §32-12.
Letters testamentary and of administration.
  Grounds for revocation.
    Violation of fiduciary duty, §28A-9-1.
Limitation of actions.
  Bonds, surety, §1-50(a).
    Action against surety, §1-52.

FIDUCIARIES —Cont'd
Loans.
Insured or guaranteed loans.
Securities approved by secretary of housing and urban development, federal housing administration and veterans administration, §53-45.
Lottery retailers.
Fiduciary duty to preserve and account for proceeds, §18C-143(f).
Marital deduction.
Incorporation by reference of certain powers, §32-26.
Mentally ill.
Payments to or for incompetents, §32-27.
Negotiable instruments.
Breach of fiduciary duty, §25-3-307(b).
Defined, §25-3-307(a).
Transfer, §32-5.
Nursing homes.
Patients' bill of rights.
Transfer of management responsibilities, §131E-118.
Partnerships.
Partner accountable as fiduciary, §59-51(a).
Applicability to representatives of deceased partner, §59-51(b).
Personal property.
Retaining original property.
Powers which may be incorporated by reference in trust instrument, §32-27.
Powers.
Definition, §32-25.
Incorporation by reference of certain powers, §32-26(a).
Restriction on exercise of certain powers, §32-26(b), (c).
Trust powers, §32-27.
Trust instruments.
Powers which may be incorporated by reference, §32-27.
Powers of appointment.
Method of release or limitation of power, §39-33.
Not exclusive, §39-34.
Notice.
Necessity for actual notice of release to bind, §39-36.
Principal and income act.
General provisions, §§37A-1-101 to 37A-6-602.
See PRINCIPAL AND INCOME ACT.
Prudent management of institutional funds, §§36E-1 to 36E-11.
See PRUDENT MANAGEMENT OF INSTITUTIONAL FUNDS.
Prudent person rule.
Transfers to minors.
Care of custodial property, §33A-12(b).
Renunciation of fiduciary powers, §31B-1(a).
Declaratory judgment action.
Right to institute, §31B-1.2(b).
Delivery of instrument to other persons by person renouncing, §31B-2.1.
Effect of renunciation, §31B-3(a).
Exclusiveness of remedy, §31B-5.
Filing and registration of instrument, §31B-2.
Review of renunciation.
Declaratory judgment action.
Right to institute, §31B-1.2(b).
Effect of determination, §31B-1.2(c).
Proceeding or action, §31B-1.2(c).

FIDUCIARIES —Cont'd
Renunciation of fiduciary powers —Cont'd
Review of renunciation —Cont'd
Right of fiduciary to institute proceedings, §31B-1.2(a), (b).
Notice of proceedings, giving, §31B-1.2(a).
Right to renounce, §31B-1.1(a), (b).
Attorney-in-fact for principal acting under right, §31B-1.1(c).
Waiver of bar.
Application for appointment or assumption of duties as fiduciary.
Not deemed to waive or bar right to renounce fiduciary powers, §31B-4(c).
Representation.
Persons representing and binding others, §§36C-3-301 to 36C-3-305.
Rules of law and equity.
Applicability, §32-12.
Savings and loan associations.
Officers and directors to act in fiduciary capacity toward association, §54B-103.
Power of state associations to act in fiduciary capacity, §54B-77.
Savings banks.
Directors and officers to act in fiduciary capacity, §54C-103.
State lottery retailers.
Fiduciary duty to preserve and account for proceeds, §18C-143(f).
Stays.
Security limited, §1-294.
Stock and stockholders.
Investments and reinvestments.
Powers which may be incorporated by reference in trust instrument, §32-27.
Superior courts.
Clerks of court.
Authority of clerk to audit accounts of fiduciaries, §7A-103.
Taxation.
Failure to file fiduciary informational return, §105-236(a).
Incorporation by reference of certain powers.
Depriving trust or estate of tax exemptions, deductions or credits, §32-26.
Property taxes.
Payment of taxes by fiduciaries, §105-383.
Reserves.
Establishing and maintaining.
Powers which may be incorporated by reference in trust instrument, §32-27.
Settlement of fiduciary's account.
Prerequisites, §105-240.
Third persons.
Check drawn payable to third person, §32-6.
Title.
Right or title acquired from fiduciary.
Validity, §32-3.
Transfers of money or property.
Responsibility for proper application by fiduciary, §32-3.
Transfers to minors, §§33A-1 to 33A-24.
See TRANSFERS TO MINORS.
Trust companies.
Acting in fiduciary capacity, §53-159.
Generally, §§53-158.10 to 53-163.2.
See TRUST COMPANIES.
Fiduciary records, §53-357.
License to do business, §53-160.
Revocation, §53-163.

FIDUCIARIES —Cont'd
Trust companies —Cont'd
Powers of state trust company, §53-331(b).
Securities intermediary.
Deposit of securities with, §53-159.1.
Trusts.
North Carolina uniform trust code.
General provisions, §§36C-1-101 to 36C-11-1106.
See TRUSTS AND TRUSTEES.
Uniform fiduciaries act.
Short title, §32-1.
Uniformity of interpretation, §32-13.
Uniform prudent management of institutional funds act, §§36E-1 to 36E-11.
See PRUDENT MANAGEMENT OF INSTITUTIONAL FUNDS.
Wills.
Incorporation by reference of certain powers, §32-26(a).

FIELDS.
Setting fire to fields, §14-137.

FIELD TRIALS.
Beagles.
Hunting license exemption, §113-276(k).
Hunting on Sunday exceptions, §103-2.

FIERI FACIAS.
Executions generally.
See EXECUTIONS.

FIFTH WHEEL TRAILER.
Recreational vehicle, §20-4.01.

FIGHTING.
Alcoholic beverage permittees.
Unlawful conduct on premises, §18B-1005(a).
Animal fighting, §14-362.1.
Cockfighting, §14-362.
Dog fighting, §14-362.2.
Assault and battery, §14-33.
Evidence of threats upon plea of self-defense, §14-33.1.
Cockfighting, §14-362.
Disorderly conduct, §14-288.4.
Dog fighting, §14-362.2.

FILING.
Corporate documents.
Generally.
See CORPORATIONS.
Nonprofit corporations, §§55A-1-20 to 55A-1-22.
See NONPROFIT CORPORATIONS.
Pleadings and other papers, §1A-1 Rule 5.
Electronic filing in courts statewide.
Contract with vendor to provide.
Authority of administrative office of the courts, §7A-49.5(c).
Deposit of funds received from contractor.
Court information technology fund, §7A-49.5(d).
Establishment and operation of systems and services.
Duty of director of administrative office of the courts, §7A-343.
Legislative findings, §7A-49.5(a).
Rules.
Supreme court may adopt, §7A-49.5(b).
Waiver of fees for indigents.
Rules to address, §7A-49.5(b).
Extension of time.
Catastrophic conditions existing in one or more counties.
Authority of chief justice, entry of order, §7A-39(b).

FILING —Cont'd
Pleadings and other papers —Cont'd
Filing with court defined, §1A-1 Rule 5(e).
Papers required to be filed with court, §1A-1 Rule 5(d).
Service generally.
See SERVICE OF NOTICE, PROCESS AND OTHER PAPERS.

FILLING STATIONS.
Leaking petroleum underground storage tank cleanup, §§143-215.94A to 143-215.94Y.
See UNDERGROUND PETROLEUM STORAGE TANKS.
Low-cost selling of motor fuels, §75-82(a).
Repair of motor vehicles, §§20-354 to 20-354.9.
See MOTOR VEHICLE REPAIRS.
Self-service stations.
Price advertisements.
Drawing or pumping fuel by purchaser himself, §14-117.2.
Unauthorized vehicles, §20-219.3.
Notice of violations, §20-219.3(b).
Prohibited acts, §20-219.3(a).
Remedies of owner or operator of station, §20-219.3(c), (d).
Removal, §20-219.3(c).

FILMS.
See MOTION PICTURES.

FINANCE.
Agricultural finance authority, §§122D-1 to 122D-23.
See AGRICULTURAL FINANCE AUTHORITY.
Bond issues.
See BOND ISSUES.
Budgets.
See BUDGETS.
Cash management.
Community colleges, §147-86.13.
Failure of employees to follow policy.
Dismissal, §147-86.11(i).
General court of justice, §147-86.14.
Highway fund, §147-86.15.
Highway trust fund, §147-86.15.
Investments.
Net earnings on invested funds.
Payment to beneficial owners of funds, §147-86.11(d).
Legislative declaration.
Policy of state, §147-86.10.
Plan.
Disbursements, §147-86.11(f).
Earnings on trust funds, §147-86.11(d).
Elements, §147-86.11(e).
Interest, §147-86.11(g).
New technologies and procedures, §147-86.11(h).
Uniform statewide plan, §147-86.11(a).
Policy of state, §147-86.10.
Reports.
State treasurer.
Quarterly report, §147-86.11(c).
School administration units, §147-86.12.
State auditor.
Monitoring agency compliance with provisions, §147-86.11(b).
State treasurer.
Reports.
Quarterly report, §147-86.11(c).
Community colleges and technical institutes.
Cash management for community colleges, §147-86.13.

FINANCE —Cont'd
Constitution of North Carolina, NC Const Art V §§1 to 14.
Funds.
  See PUBLIC FUNDS.
Industrial and pollution control facilities financing.
  Industrial and pollution control facilities financing act, §§159C-1 to 159C-27.
    See INDUSTRIAL AND POLLUTION CONTROL FACILITIES FINANCING.
  North Carolina capital facilities financing act.
    North Carolina industrial and pollution control facilities financing act, §§159D-1 to 159D-27.
      See INDUSTRIAL AND POLLUTION CONTROL FACILITIES FINANCING.
Local government finance, §§159-1 to 159-188.
  See LOCAL GOVERNMENT FINANCE.
Parking authorities, §160A-559.
Pest control.
  Compact.
    Financial assets of insurance fund, §106-65.55.
Private capital facilities finance act.
  Institutions for higher education and elementary and secondary education, §§159D-35 to 159D-57.
    See CAPITAL FACILITIES FINANCE AGENCY.
Public transportation authorities, §160A-583.
  Fiscal accountability, §160A-582.
Registered public obligations, §§159E-1 to 159E-15.
  See REGISTERED PUBLIC OBLIGATIONS.
Schools.
  Cash management for school administration units, §147-86.12.
Social services, §§108A-86 to 108A-93.
  See SOCIAL SERVICES.
Taxation.
  See TAXATION.
Veterans' recreation authorities.
  Exemption from local government and county fiscal control acts, §165-35.

FINANCE CHARGES.
Attorneys' fees and notes, etc., in addition to legal rate of finance charges, §6-21.2.
Contract rates and fees, §24-1.1.
Disclosure requirements for credit cards, §24-11.1(b).
Equity lines of credit.
  Fees for modification, extension, renewal, etc., §24-1.2A(b).
Home loans secured by first mortgage or first deed of trust, §24-1.1A(c).
Insurance premium financing.
  Excessive charges, §58-35-35.
Interest generally.
  See INTEREST.
Late fees, §24-10.1.
Loans secured by real property, maximum fees, §24-10.
Manufactured home loans.
  Unearned finance charge credits.
    Prepayment of mobile home loans, §25A-32.1(a), (b).
Motor vehicle retail installment sales.
  Consumer credit installment sale contracts.
    Finance charge rates for used cars, §25A-15(c).

FINANCE CHARGES —Cont'd
Motor vehicle retail installment sales —Cont'd
  Seller to deliver written statement to buyer, §20-303(b).
  Written instruments, §20-303(a).
Retail installment sales.
  Consolidation and refinancing, §25A-31(c).
  Consumer credit installment sale contracts.
    Division of simple transaction into two or more sales to avoid limitations prohibited, §25A-15(e).
    Rates, §25A-15(a).
      Determination, §25A-15(b).
    Residential manufactured homes.
      Sale secured by first lien, §25A-15(f).
    Security interest.
      Rates chargeable, §25A-15(d).
    Used cars.
      Rate chargeable, §25A-15(c).
  Defined, §25A-8(a).
  Exclusions from definition, §25A-8(b).
  Refinancing, §25A-31(c).
  Remedies and penalties, §25A-44.
  Revolving charge account contracts.
    Default or deferral charges, §25A-14(c).
    Insurance.
      Additional charges for insurance, §25A-17(b).
    Rates, §25A-14(a).
    Security interest.
      Rates, §25A-14(b).
  Security interest.
    Transactions in which seller acquires security interest, §25A-8(c).
  Unearned finance charge credits.
    Prepayment of real property and mobile home loans, §25A-32.1(a), (b).
Revolving credit charges, §24-11.

FINANCE COMPANIES.
Annual tax on privilege of doing business, §105-88(a).
  Applicability of provisions, §105-88(b).
  City or county levying license tax, §105-88(e).
  Loan not collectable unless tax paid, §105-88(d).
  Statement to borrower, §105-88(c).
Consumer finance act, §§53-164 to 53-191.
  See CONSUMER FINANCE ACT.
Housing finance agency, §§122A-1 to 122A-23.
  See HOUSING FINANCE AGENCY.

FINANCE LEASES.
Defined, §25-2A-103.
Delay or nondelivery.
  Notice, §25-2A-405(c).
Effect of acceptance, §25-2A-516(2).
Fitness for particular purpose.
  Implied warranties, §25-2A-213.
Infringement.
  Warranty against, §25-2A-211.
Irrevocable promises, §25-2A-407.
Leases, UCC generally, §§25-2A-101 to 25-2A-532.
  See LEASES, UCC.
Losses.
  Casualty to identified goods, §25-2A-221.
  Risk of loss, §25-2A-219.
Merchantability.
  Implied warranties, §25-2A-212.
Notice.
  Delay or nondelivery, §25-2A-405(c).
Supply contracts.
  Lessee under finance lease as beneficiary, §25-2A-209.

FINANCIAL AID.
Scholarships.
See SCHOLARSHIPS.
Student loans.
Default.
Withholding of personal earnings, §§105B-1 to 105B-5.
Education assistance authority, §§116-201 to 116-209.40.
See EDUCATION ASSISTANCE AUTHORITY.
National Guard members.
Disbursements to pay outstanding loans, §§116-209.55, 127A-195.

FINANCIAL INSTITUTIONS.
Bank examiners generally, §§53-117 to 53-123.
See BANK EXAMINERS.
Bank holding companies generally, §§53-225 to 53-232.
See BANK HOLDING COMPANIES.
Banks.
See BANKS.
Campaign contributions and expenditures.
Loan proceeds from financial institution, §163-278.15(b).
Exceptions to prohibitions, §163-278.19(a2).
Child support enforcement.
Data match systems.
Agreements with financial institutions, §110-139.2.
Commissioner of banks.
Generally, §§53-92 to 53-116.
See BANKS COMMISSIONER.
Commodities.
General provisions, §§78D-1 to 78D-33.
See COMMODITIES.
Credit unions.
See CREDIT UNIONS.
Equity line of credit.
Notice regarding advances, form, §45-82.3(f).
Request to terminate made by.
Notice to borrower, form, §45-82.2(d).
Financial records privacy, §§53B-1 to 53B-10.
See FINANCIAL RECORDS PRIVACY.
Gramm-Leach-Bililey act.
Affiliations between depository institutions and insurers, §58-19-2.
Industrial banks generally, §§53-136 to 53-145.
See INDUSTRIAL BANKS.
International banking, §§53-232.1 to 53-232.17.
See INTERNATIONAL BANKING.
Lead-based paint presence on property or other health-related issues.
Providing financial assistance, §130A-131.9F.
Reciprocal interstate banking, §§53-209 to 53-218.
See RECIPROCAL INTERSTATE BANKING.
Savings and loan associations.
See SAVINGS AND LOAN ASSOCIATIONS.
Savings banks, §§54C-1 to 54C-212.
See SAVINGS BANKS.
Trust companies and interstate trust business, §§53-301 to 53-424.
See TRUST COMPANIES.
Unclaimed property generally, §§116B-51 to 116B-80.
See UNCLAIMED PROPERTY.

FINANCIAL LITERACY COUNCIL, §§114-50 to 114-55.
Duties, §114-53.
Established, §114-50.

FINANCIAL LITERACY COUNCIL —Cont'd
Expenses of members, §114-54.
Members, §114-51(a).
Subsistence and travel expenses, §114-54.
Terms, §114-51(b).
Purpose, §114-50.
Quorum, §114-51(c).
Reports, §114-53.
Staff support, §114-52.
State officers, agencies and departments.
Furnishing data and information to council, §114-55.

FINANCIAL PRIVACY ACT, §§53B-1 to 53B-10.
See FINANCIAL RECORDS PRIVACY.

FINANCIAL RECORDS PRIVACY, §§53B-1 to 53B-10.
Access to financial records.
Authorization of customer, §53B-4.
Customer challenge, §53B-7(a).
Delayed notice, §53B-6.
Disclosure of financial records, §53B-8.
Duty of financial institution to locate and make available, §53B-9(a).
Fees, §53B-9(b).
Generally, §53B-4.
Government authority requesting.
Financial institution's right to challenge, §53B-7(b).
Limitation of liability, §53B-9(c).
Notice, §53B-5.
Delayed notice, §53B-6.
Penalty, §53B-10.
Service on customer certification, §53B-5.
Child support enforcement.
Location of absent parents.
Information to be provided, §110-139(d).
Citation of chapter, §53B-1.
Customer challenge.
Access to financial records, §53B-7(a).
Damages.
Disclosures in violation of article, §53B-10(a).
Definitions, §53B-2.
Disclosure of financial records, §53B-8.
Penalty, §53B-10.
Duty of financial institution, §53B-9.
Government participating or inducing violation.
Liability to customer, §53B-10(b).
Government requesting access to records.
Financial institution's right to challenge, §53B-7(b).
Immunity.
Disclosure of financial records by financial institution, §53B-9(c).
Public policy, §53B-3.
Real estate commission.
Exemption, §93A-6.1(b).
Service on customer certification, §53B-5.
Short title, §53B-1.
State policy, §53B-3.
Violations of article.
Penalties, §53B-10.

FINANCIAL REPORTING.
Insurance companies.
Annual audited financial reports, §§58-10-185 to 58-10-265.
See INSURANCE COMPANIES.

FINANCIAL RESPONSIBILITY.
Alcoholic beverage permittees, §18B-1003(b).

FINANCIAL RESPONSIBILITY —Cont'd
Motor vehicles.
Act of 1957 generally, §§20-309 to 20-319.
  See MOTOR VEHICLE FINANCIAL
    RESPONSIBILITY.
Drivers' licenses.
  Proof required for issuance, forms of proof,
    §20-7(c1).
Generally, §§20-279.1 to 20-284.
  See MOTOR VEHICLE FINANCIAL
    RESPONSIBILITY.
Structural pest control.
Conditions, limitations and requirements,
  §106-65.37(b).
Indemnifying persons, §106-65.37(a).

FINANCIAL TRANSACTION CARDS, §§14-113.8
to 14-113.17.
Credit cards.
Fraud by credit devices.
  See CREDIT DEVICE FRAUD.
General provisions.
  See CREDIT CARDS.
Definitions, §14-113.8.
Evidence.
Forgery of transaction card.
  Prima facie evidence of forgery, §14-113.12(a),
    (b).
Theft of financial transaction card.
  Prima evidence of theft, §14-113.10.
Felonies, §14-113.17(b).
Forgery.
Elements of offense, §14-113.11(a).
Embossing financial transaction card falsely,
  §14-113.11(c).
Encoding financial transaction card falsely,
  §14-113.11(d).
Making financial transaction card falsely,
  §14-113.11(b).
Prima facie evidence of forgery, §14-113.12(a), (b).
Two or more cards, possession.
  Prima facies evidence, §14-113.12(a), (b).
Forgery devices.
Criminal possession, §14-113.14(a).
  Incomplete cards, §14-113.14(b).
  Punishment, §14-113.14(b).
Fraud.
Application for financial transaction card.
  False statements or reports on application,
    §14-113.13(c).
Credit devices.
  See CREDIT DEVICE FRAUD.
Criminal factoring of records, §14-113.15A.
Elements of offense, §14-113.13(a).
Furnisher of money, goods, services, etc.
  Elements of financial transaction card fraud
    offense, §14-113.13(b).
Goods and services.
  Criminal receipt of goods and services
    fraudulently obtained, §14-113.15.
    Presumption of criminal receipt, §14-113.16.
Notice of theft, loss, etc., of card.
  False notice, §14-113.13(d).
Prosecution for violation.
  Occurrence of acts constituting crime,
    §14-113.13(e).
Record of sale.
  Fraudulent record, §14-113.13(c1).
Report of theft, loss, etc., of card.
  False report, §14-113.13(d).

FINANCIAL TRANSACTION CARDS —Cont'd
Fraud —Cont'd
Revocation of financial transaction card.
  Construing revocation, §14-113.13(f).
Goods.
Fraudulently obtained goods.
  Criminal receipt of goods, §14-113.15.
    Presumption of criminal receipt, §14-113.16.
Larceny.
Theft of financial transaction card.
  Conduct defined is larceny, §14-113.9(b).
Misdemeanors, §14-113.17(a).
Notice.
Fraud.
  Theft, loss, disappearance, etc., of card falsely
    noted, §14-113.13(d).
Penalties.
Crime act of punishment and penalties,
  §14-113.17.
Presumptions.
Goods and services fraudulently obtained.
  When criminal receipt presumed, §14-113.16.
Records.
Criminal factoring of records, §14-113.15A.
Reports.
Fraud.
  Theft, loss, disappearance of card falsely
    reported, §14-113.13(d).
Theft.
Elements of offense, §14-113.9(a).
Larcenous conduct, §14-113.9(b).
Prima facie evidence of theft, §14-113.10.

FINANCING AGREEMENTS.
General provisions, §§159-148 to 159-152.
See LOCAL GOVERNMENT FINANCE.

FINANCING CONTRACT INDEBTEDNESS.
State capital facilities finance act.
Special indebtedness generally, §§142-80 to
  142-101.
  See CAPITAL FACILITIES FINANCE ACT.

FINANCING HEALTH CARE FACILITIES,
  §§131A-1 to 131A-25.
See HEALTH CARE FACILITY FINANCING.

FINDINGS BY COURT, §1A-1 Rule 52(a).
Amendment, §1A-1 Rule 52(b).
Review on appeal, §1A-1 Rule 52(c).

FINE PRINT SALES.
Applicability of article, §25C-16.
Art dealers.
Disclosures, §25C-11(b).
Catalogs, §25C-11(a).
Consignments, §25C-12(b).
Definitions, §25C-10.
Disclosure.
Disclaimer of art dealer, §25C-14(d).
Limited additions, §25C-14(c).
Mechanical, photomechanical or photographic
  copies, §25C-14(b).
Requirements, §25C-14(a).
Exemptions from article, §25C-16(a) to (c).
General prohibitions, §25C-11.
Rights and liabilities created by article.
Not inclusive, §25C-15(d).
Sale by artist, §25C-12(a).
Violation of article.
Repayment of purchaser's consideration,
  §25C-15(a).
  Wrongful refusal to repay, §25C-15(b).

FINE PRINT SALES —Cont'd
Violation of article —Cont'd
Willful violation, §25C-15(c).
Warranties.
Evidence, §25C-13(c).
Express warranties, §25C-13(a), (b).
FINES.
Address confidentiality program.
Disclosure of address.
Prohibited acts, §15C-9(f).
Falsifying application information.
Civil penalty, §15C-6.
Administration department.
Bribery.
Purchases and contracts to department,
§143-63.
Adoption.
Unlawful payments related to adoption,
§48-10-102(b).
Adult care homes.
Operation without license, §131D-2.6(b).
Aiding and abetting.
Alcoholic beverages.
Sale to or purchase by underage persons.
Requirements for punishment, §18B-302.1(b),
(c).
Alcoholic beverages.
Aiding and abetting.
Sale to or purchase by underage persons.
Requirements for punishment, §18B-302.1(b),
(c).
Direct shipments into state, §18B-102.1(e).
Imports and exports.
Unauthorized imports and exports, §18B-102(b).
Interference with inspections, §18B-502(b).
Manufacturers.
Unauthorized manufacture, §18B-102(b).
Minors.
Sales to, giving to, §18B-302.1(a).
Open container law, §20-138.7(e).
Unlawful transportation, §18B-401(a).
Possession.
By 19 or 20 year old, §18B-203.
Unauthorized possession, §18B-102(b).
Purchase by 19 or 20 year old, §18B-203.
Sales.
Unauthorized sales, §18B-102(b).
Transportation.
Open container violations, §18B-401(a).
Unauthorized transportation, §18B-102(b).
Aliens, verification of work authorization.
Violations, consequences.
First violation.
Failure to file affidavit, §64-31(b).
Second violation, §64-32.
Third and subsequent violations, §64-33.
All-terrain vehicles.
Penalties for violations, §20-171.21.
Ambulatory surgical facility licensure.
Unlicensed operation, §131E-151.
Amusement device safety.
Death resulting from violation, §95-111.13(i).
Anatomical gifts.
Falsification of document, §130A-412.19.
Sale or purchase of parts, §130A-412.18(a).
Animal auctions.
Public auctions.
Unlicensed operation, §19A-33.
Animal cruelty investigators.
Interference with performance of official duties,
§19A-48.

FINES —Cont'd
Animal dealers.
Acting without license, §19A-34.
Cruelty to animals, §19A-35.
Animal shelters.
Cruelty to animals, §19A-35.
Animal waste management system operators.
Willful violations, §90A-47.5(b).
Apportionment to school administrative units,
§115C-452.
Aquatic weed control, §113A-226(a).
Arrest in civil cases, §1-410.
Arson.
Failure of officers to investigate fires, §14-69.
Failure of property owner to comply with orders of
authorities, §14-68.
Atomic energy, radioactivity and ionizing
radiation.
Confidentiality of information, §104E-29(c).
Auctions and auctioneers.
Civil penalties.
Imposition by commission, §85B-3.1(b).
Authorized fines, §15A-1361.
Banks.
Administrative orders of commissioner.
Violations, §53-107.2.
Commissioner of banks.
Failure to make report to commissioner,
§53-107.
Battleship commission.
Employees with interest, §143B-74.3.
Billboards.
Highways, roads and streets.
Obstructing view at entrance to building on
public highway, §136-102.
Blacklisting employees, §14-355.
Boating safety.
Depositing or discharging medical waste,
§75A-10(e).
Navigation rules violations, §75A-6.1(c).
Skin and scuba divers, §75A-13.1(d).
Vessel agents.
Returned checks or drafts by, §75A-5.2(g).
Bonds, surety.
Mortgage in lieu of bond.
Security of costs or fine in criminal action,
§58-74-5.
Cancellation of mortgage in such proceedings,
§58-74-10.
Bottles and bottling.
Polluting bottles used for beverages, §14-288.
Bribery.
Administration department.
Purchases and contracts to department,
§143-63.
Building codes.
Door lock exemptions.
Penalty for violation of provisions,
§143-143.4(h).
Buying or selling untaxed motor fuel,
§105-449.118.
Cable television franchises.
Theft of services, §14-118.5.
Campaign contributions and expenditures.
Voter-owned elections act, §163-278.99D.
Cell phones.
School bus operators.
Unlawful use while bus in motion, §20-137.4.
Text messaging, electronic mail.
Driving while using mobile phone for,
§20-137.4(c).

FINES —Cont'd
Childhood vaccine-related injury compensation.
Diversion of certain vaccines, §130A-431.
Child placing agencies.
Unlicensed operation, §131D-10.7.
Chiropractors.
Unlicensed practice, §90-147.
Cleaning agents containing phosphorus.
Water and air resources.
Manufacturing, selling or distributing agents, §143-214.4(f).
Coastal area management.
Permit violations, §113A-126(c).
Commercial vehicles.
Out of service fines, §20-17.7.
Commodities.
Violations of chapter.
When allowed, §78D-24(b), (c).
Commodity violations, §78D-24(b).
Community colleges.
Traffic regulations, §115D-21(b), (c).
Condominiums, §47C-3-107.1.
Constitution of North Carolina.
Enumeration of permissible punishments, NC Const Art XI §1.
Constitution of the United States.
Excessive fines, US Const Amd 8.
Contempt.
Criminal contempt, §5A-12(a).
Contracts.
Unauthorized use of public purchase or contract procedures for private benefit, §143-58.1(c).
Controlled substances reporting system.
Penalties for violations, §90-113.75(a).
Counterfeiting.
Issuing substitutes for money without authority, §14-15.
Receiving or passing unauthorized substitutes for money, §14-16.
Counties.
Public officers and employees.
Privacy of employee personnel records, §153A-98(f).
Credit card, charge card or debit card.
Fines, fees and costs owed by offenders.
Acceptance in lieu of cash or check, §7A-321(a).
Contracts with vendors, §7A-343.
Credit insurance.
Enforcement of provisions, §58-57-71(a), (c).
Crime victims financial recovery assistance act.
Escrow account.
Establishment and notice, §15B-33(d).
Satisfaction of judgment from, §15B-33(e).
Unclaimed funds, return of, §15B-33(f).
Failure to give notice, §15B-33(a).
Failure to pay, §15B-33(c).
Notice and opportunity to be heard required, §15B-33(b).
Remittance of proceeds from civil penalty, §15B-33(g).
Criminal offenses.
Authorized fines, §15A-1361.
Dam safety law.
Violations of article, §143-215.36(a).
Default.
Imprisonment.
Show cause orders, §§15A-1362(c), 15A-1364(a).
Defendant's liability in criminal actions.
Confession of judgment.
Bond given to secure fine and cost, §6-47.

FINES —Cont'd
Delinquent juveniles.
Alternative dispositions, imposition, §7B-2506.
Dentists.
Subpoenas of board of medical examiner.
Neglect or refusal to obey, §90-27.
Unauthorized practices, §90-40.
Violations of rules and regulations of board, §90-48.
Dietitians and nutritionists, §90-366.
Disabled persons.
Parking violations, §20-37.6(f).
Disbursement of proceeds.
School administrative units, §115C-452.
Discrimination.
Against military personnel, §127B-15.
Dog wardens.
Animal welfare act violations, §19A-36.
Cruelty to animals, §19A-35.
Drainage.
Jurisdiction of county commissioners.
Refusal to comply with requirements, §156-33.
Refusal to serve on board, §156-32.
Obstructions, §§156-19, 156-24, 156-25.
Drainage districts.
Injuring or damaging bridges, fences, ditches, etc., §156-92.
Droughts.
Enforcement provisions, §143-355.6(a).
Local government failure to implement conservation measures, §143-355.6(c).
Drug paraphernalia.
Advertisement, §90-113.24(b).
Manufacture or deliveries, §90-113.23(c).
Possession, §90-113.22(b).
Drugs.
Controlled substance.
Conspiracy to violate provision, §90-98.
Violations generally, §90-95.
Economic interest statements.
State government ethics act.
Failure to file, §138A-25(b).
Elections, §163-272.1.
Public campaign fund.
Regulator violations, §163-278.70.
Voting systems.
Vendors.
Willful violation of duties, §163-165.9A(b).
Electrologists.
Unlicensed practice, §88A-4(b).
Electronic commerce in government, §66-58.7.
Electronic mail.
Driving while using mobile phone for, §20-137.4A(c).
Elementary and secondary education.
Blind children.
Parents, etc., failing to send, §115C-383(c).
Deaf children.
Parents, etc., failing to enroll, §115C-383.
Employee health certificate, §115C-323(e).
Employees making false reports or records, §115C-317.
Fire prevention duties.
Failure to perform, §115C-525(c).
Insurance of public school property.
Noncompliance with provisions, §115C-534(c).
Local boards of education.
Witness failing to appear, §115C-45(b).
Principals or supervisors making false reports or records, §115C-288(b).

FINES —Cont'd
Elementary and secondary education —Cont'd
State board of education.
Disclosure of confidential records, §115C-13.
Student attendance, §115C-380.
Superintendents making false reports or records,
§115C-276(p).
Teachers making false reports or records,
§115C-307(g).
Elevators, §95-110.11.
Employee assistance professionals.
Failure to be licensed.
Civil penalty, §90-506(a), (c).
Employment security.
Witness intimidation, §96-15.2.
Endangered plant species.
Unlawful acts, §106-202.19(a), (a1).
Executions.
Docketed judgments for fines, §15A-1365.
Payment as authorized condition of parole,
§15A-1374(b).
**Fire-safety standard and firefighter protection
act,** §58-92-30(a) to (d).
Fish and fisheries resources.
Buoys, nets, markers, stakes, etc.
Robbing or injuring, §113-268(d).
Coastal and estuarine commercial fishing licenses.
Fraud or deception as to licenses, permits or
records, §113-170.2(b).
Coastal wetlands.
Orders to control activities, §113-230(d).
Commercial fishing, §113-187(d).
Dredging.
Permit violations.
Violations, §113-229(k).
Refusal to stop in obedience to directions of
inspector or director, §113-136(j).
Robbing or injuring hatcheries and other
aquaculture operations, §113-269(e), (f).
Seafood.
Industrial park authority.
Traffic and parking violations, §113-315.34(c).
Taking fish by illegal means, §113-262(a).
Food, drug and cosmetic act.
Violations of article.
Civil penalties, §106-124.1.
Remission of proceeds, §106-124.1(d).
Forests and forestry.
Open fires provisions, §106-948.
Posted notices.
Destruction, §106-905.
Gaming.
Allowing illegal slot machines or punchboards on
premises, §14-297.
Gas conservation, §§113-380, 113-409.
Gasoline adulteration, §119-35.
Gasoline inspection violations, §119-39.
Prosecution of offenders, §119-38.
Gasoline inspectors.
Conflicts of interest, §119-25.
Gasoline pumps.
Devices calculated to falsify measures, §119-33.
Display of grade rating, §119-27.
Gasoline tax.
Buying or selling non-tax-paid motor fuel,
§105-449.118.
Shipping documents, §105-449.115(f).
Geologists.
Civil penalty for license violations, §89E-19(c).
Civil action to recover, §89E-19(d).

FINES —Cont'd
Habeas corpus.
Disobedience to writ, §17-26.
Judges.
Refusal to grant precept to bring up party
detained, §17-20.
Refusal to grant writ of attachment, §17-17.
Refusal or neglect to make return, §17-26.
Unlawful refusal to grant writ, §17-10.
Hazardous waste management.
Class I felonies, §130A-26.1(f).
Class J felonies, §130A-26.1(g).
Highways, roads and streets.
Billboards.
Obstructing view at entrance to building on
public highway, §136-102.
Controlled-access facilities.
Unlawful use, §136-89.58.
Obstructing highway drains, §136-92.
Obstructing highways and roads, §136-90.
"Pull-over" areas, §136-18.4.
Rights of way.
Gates projecting over rights-of-way, §136-94.
Signs, signals or markers.
Blinding, deceptive or distracting lights,
§136-32.2(a).
Damaging or removing signs, §136-33(b1).
Misleading signs, §136-32.1.
Underpasses or overpasses.
Regulation of safety devices, §136-20(e).
Historical and cultural resources, §121-4.
Hogs, pigs and swine.
Transporting live swine, identification required.
Civil penalties for misuse of identification,
§106-798.2.
Civil penalties for transporting without
identification, §106-798.1.
Home care agency licensure.
Smoking, employees prohibited from.
Administrative penalties, §131E-143(b).
Unlicensed operation, §131E-141.1.
Hospice licensure.
Unauthorized disclosure of inspection information,
§131E-207(b).
Hospital discharged patient.
Discharge from hospital.
Failure or refusal to leave hospital, §131E-90.
Hospital employee personnel files.
Unlawful disclosure, §131E-257.2(g).
Unlawful examination or use, §131E-257.2(h).
Hospital inspections by department.
Disclosure of confidential or privileged
information, §131E-80(d).
Hospital licensure.
Disclosure of information, §131E-80(d).
Unlicensed operation, §131E-81(a).
Willful violations, §131E-81(b).
Household goods carriers.
Carriers operating without certificate.
Criminal enforcement, §62-280.1(b).
Utilities commission imposition of fines to
enforce, §62-280.1(c).
Marking or identification of vehicles.
Fines imposed to enforce, §62-280(b).
Housemovers.
Article or rules violations, §20-371(a).
Hunting and wildlife.
Disabled persons.
Special vehicular access identification card and
permit, §113-294(n).
Hunter orange material, §113-291.8(b).

FINES —Cont'd
Hunting and wildlife —Cont'd
Hunting on Sunday, §103-2.
Limitation upon penalty for offense creating by
rules of wildlife resources commission,
§113-135.1(a), (b).
Poisons and pesticides, §113-300.3(c).
Refusal to stop in obedience to directions of
protector, §113-136(j).
Taking fish by illegal means, §113-262(a).
Trapping.
Violation of provisions, §113-294(i), (j).
Unlawful harassment of persons taking wildlife
resources, §113-295(a).
Unlawfully selling, possessing for sale or buying
wildlife, §113-294(a).
Bald eagle or golden eagle, §113-294(l).
Bear, §113-294(c1).
Beaver, §113-294(f).
Cougar, §113-294(c2).
Deer or wild turkey, §113-294(b).
Unlawfully taking, possessing or transporting
wildlife.
Bald eagle or golden eagle, §113-294(l).
Bear, §113-294(c1).
Beaver, §113-294(f).
Cougar, §113-294(c2).
Deer, §113-294(d), (e).
Fox, §113-294(j).
Migratory game birds, §113-294(m).
Vessel equipped with motor.
Taking from or with use of, §113-294(g).
Wild turkey, §113-294(c).
Impaired driving.
Punishment generally, §20-179(g) to (k).
Infractions, §15A-1361.
Enforcement of sanctions.
Use of fine collection procedures, §15A-1116(a).
Inspections.
Alcoholic beverages.
Interference with inspections, §18B-502(b).
Insurance commissioner, false statements to,
§58-2-180.
Interstate earnings of employee.
Collection out of state to avoid exemption, §95-75.
Irrigation contractors.
Civil penalties, §89G-12.
Kennels.
Boarding kennels, §19A-33.
Kidnapping and abduction.
Corporations, §14-39.
Labor.
Earnings of employees in interstate commerce.
Collection out of state to avoid exemption,
§95-75.
Payments to or for benefit of labor organization,
§95-104.
Larceny.
Horses, mules, swine, cattle or dogs, §14-81.
Library books.
Failure to return, §125-11.
Liens.
Docketed judgments for fines, §15A-1365.
Payments as authorized condition of parole,
§15A-1374(b).
Liquid fuels, lubricating oils, greases, etc.
Violations of article, §119-13.
Littering, §14-399(c), (d), (e).
Livestock diseases.
Quarantine.
Hiding or concealing animal subject to,
§106-405(c).

FINES —Cont'd
Lobbying.
Civil fines for violations, §120C-602(b).
Local government finance.
Fiscal control.
Annual independent audit, §159-34(a).
Long-term care facilities.
Smoking, §§131D-4.4(d), 131E-114.3(c).
Manufactured homes.
Licenses.
Obtaining by false representation, §51-15.
Meat and meat products.
Rendering plants and rendering operations,
§106-168.16.
Medical waste.
Water and air resources.
Prohibited disposal of waste, §143-214.2A(c).
Meetings of public bodies.
Disrupting, §143-318.17.
Mental health, developmental disabilities and
substance abuse.
Area authorities.
Unlawful access or disclosure of personnel
records, §122C-158(g), (h).
Camp Butner and community of Butner,
§122C-406.
Consumer advocacy program.
Confidentiality violations, §122C-17(b).
Operating a licensable facility without a license,
§122C-28.
Quality assurance activities.
Unlawful disclosure of confidential information.
Secretary or designee, §122C-192(b).
Smoking in facilities.
Penalty for violation, §122C-6(c).
Unlawful disclosure of confidential information,
§122C-52(e).
Gathered during inspections, §122C-25.
Midwives, §90-178.7(b).
Migrant farm workers.
Motor carrier violations, §20-215.4.
Military personnel.
Discrimination against, §127B-15.
Military property sales facilities.
Dealer violations, §127B-7.
Milk sanitation.
Administrative penalties, §130A-22(a).
Mines and minerals.
Notice of beginning business of manufacturing
products from mineral resources of state,
§113-25.
Minors.
Alcoholic beverages.
Sales to, giving to, §18B-302.1(a).
Mobile phones.
School bus operators.
Unlawful use while bus in motion, §20-137.4.
Text messaging, electronic mail.
Driving while using mobile phone for,
§20-137.4A(c).
Use by minor while operating motor vehicle,
§20-137.3(b), (e).
Money transmitters, §53-208.24(a).
Mopeds, §20-140.4(c).
Motor carriers.
Household goods carriers.
Carriers operating without certificate.
Criminal enforcement, §62-280.1(b).
Utilities commission imposition of fines to
enforce, §62-280.1(c).
Marking or identification of vehicles, §20-398(d).

FINES —Cont'd

Motor carriers —Cont'd

Migrant farm workers, §20-215.4.

Road tax on carriers using fuel purchased outside state.

Failure to file return, §105-449.45(d).

Safety regulation unit.

Furnishing false information, §§20-396, 20-397.

Refusal to allow inspections, §20-390.

Unlawful motor carrier operations, §20-396.

Willful evasion of regulations, §§20-396, 20-397.

Taxation.

Road tax on carriers using fuel purchased outside state.

Violations of provisions, §105-449.51.

Motorcycles, §20-140.4(c).

Motor vehicle insurance.

Rental vehicle violations of insurance provisions, §20-284.

Motor vehicles.

Accidents.

Failure to stop and give name, §20-166(c), (c1).

Action upon civil fine or penalty.

Limitations period, §1-52.

Certificates of title.

Satisfaction of liens.

Lienor refusal to surrender certificate, §20-59.

Transfer of title or interest.

Failure of new owner to apply for new title, §20-73(c).

False statement in making an application, §20-74.

Commercial drivers' licenses.

Driving without license, §20-37.21(a).

Railroad grade crossing, permitting employees to violate requirements, §20-37.21(d).

Violation of employer responsibilities, §20-37.21(c).

Violations of driver notice requirements, §20-37.21(b).

Commercial vehicles.

Impaired driving, §20-138.2(e).

Operating a commercial vehicle after consuming alcohol, §20-138.2A(c).

Dealers.

License applications.

Violations of licensing provisions, §20-308.

Disabled persons.

Parking violations, §20-37.6(f).

Driver's license.

Driving while license revoked, §20-28(a).

Driver training schools.

Violations of licensing provisions, §20-327.

Felony death by vehicles, §20-141.4(b).

Financial responsibility.

False certification, §20-313.1(a).

False information concerning another's responsibility, §20-313.1(b).

Fire department vehicles.

Motorist approach violation, §20-157(a).

Flat trucks.

Violations of operation restriction, §20-120.

Housemovers.

Article or rules violations, §20-371(a).

Injuring vehicle with intent to steal, §20-107(b).

License plates.

Borrowing or lending, §20-111.

Manufacturer's and dealer's special plates.

Registration violations, §20-79(e).

Lights.

Requirement violations, §20-129(a).

FINES —Cont'd

Motor vehicles —Cont'd

Manufacturer's serial or engine numbers.

Altering or changing numbers, §20-109(a), (b).

Prohibitions as to vehicles without numbers, §20-108(a).

Mechanic's or storage liens.

Failure to report unclaimed vehicles, §20-77(d).

Misdemeanor death by vehicle, §20-141.4(b).

Mobile phones.

School bus operators.

Unlawful use while bus in motion, §20-137.4.

Text messaging, electronic mail.

Driving while using mobile phone for, §20-137.4A(c).

Nuclear fuel.

Transportation of spent nuclear fuel, §20-167.1(d).

Open container law violations, §20-138.7(e).

Private lots.

Unauthorized vehicles, §20-219.2(b).

Railroad grade crossing.

Crossing gate violation, §20-142.1(d).

Moving heavy equipment, §20-142.4(f).

Obstructing traffic and pedestrian walkway, §20-142.5.

Stop sign violation, §20-142.2.

Reckless driving, §20-140(d).

School buses.

Operating after consuming alcohol, §20-138.2B(c).

Seat belt.

Violations of mandatory use provision, §20-135.2A(e).

Special identification card for nonoperators.

Fraud or misrepresentation in application, §20-37.7(e).

Speedometer.

Requirement violations, §20-123.2(b).

Stopping.

Obstructing traffic and pedestrian walkway, §20-142.5.

Tampering with vehicle, §20-107(a).

Tandem trailers and subtrailer.

Load limitation violations, §20-115.1(h), (i).

Text messaging, electronic mail.

Driving while using mobile phone for, §20-137.4A(c).

Weight of vehicles and load.

Excessive size or weight.

Violations of special permit terms and condition, §20-119(d), (d1).

Window tinting.

Medical exception, failure to display sticker, §20-127(f).

Motor vehicles insurance.

Rate evasion fraud, §58-2-164(b).

Municipalities.

Personnel records.

Knowingly, willfully and with malice permitting access to, §160A-168(e).

Removing or copying confidential personnel files, §160A-168(f).

Vehicle used on foreshore, beach strand and barrier dune systems, §160A-308.

Violation of ordinances, §§160A-175(a), 160A-308.

National guard.

Courts-martial.

Disposition of fines, §127A-61.

Negligence.

Reckless driving, §20-140(d).

FINES —Cont'd

Neighborhood crime watch programs.
Harassment of participant, §14-226.2.

Nonpayment.
Arrest for nonpayment, §6-48.
Docketed judgments for fines, §15A-1365.
Imprisonment.
Commitment to division of adult correction or local confinement facility, §15A-1352(c).
Criteria, §15A-1364(b).
Order to defendant to show cause why he should not be imprisoned, §§15A-1362(c), 15A-1364(a).
Release upon payment, §23-24.
Lien.
Docketed judgments for fine, §15A-1365.
Modification of fine or cost, §15A-1364(c).
Order to defendant to show cause why he should not be imprisoned, §§15A-1362(c), 15A-1364(a).

Novelty lighter.
Retail sale prohibited.
Violation, §66-16.1(d).

Nursing home administrators, §90-288.

Nursing home licensure.
Inspection violations, §131E-109(b).
Prohibited acts, §131E-109(d).
Unlicensed operation, §131E-109(a).

Nursing pools.
Unauthorized disclosure of inspection information, §131E-154.8(b).

Obstructing justice.
Violating orders of court, §14-226.1.

Occupational safety and health, §95-130.

Occupational therapists, §90-270.79.

Oil or hazardous substances discharges, §143-215.88B(e), (f), (h).

Oil refining facility permit violations, §143-215.102(b).

Oils.
Conservation, §§113-380, 113-409.
Dispensing devices.
Falsification of measures, §119-33.
Inspection violations.
Generally, §119-39.
Inspectors.
Conflicts of interest, §119-25.
Lubricating oils, §§119-4, 119-13.
Terminal facilities, §143-215.98.

Open container law violations, §20-138.7(e).

Opticians.
Allowing unlicensed person to use certificate or license, §90-251.
Sale of flammable frame, §90-255.1.
Unlicensed practice, §90-252.

Optometrists.
Subpoenas of board of examiner.
Neglect or refusal to obey, §90-117.4.
Unauthorized practices, §90-118.11.
Violations of rules and regulations, §90-124.

Organizations.
Payment of fines, §15A-1364(d).

Parking regulations of ports authority, §136-269(c).

Pawnbrokers and cash converters, §91A-11(a).

Payment.
Determination of method of payment.
Criteria, §15A-1362(a).
Installment or delayed payments, §15A-1362(b).
Nonpayment. See within this heading, "Nonpayment."

FINES —Cont'd

Payment —Cont'd
Organizations, §15A-1364(d).

Perfusionists.
Violations, §90-693(a).

Pet shops.
Cruelty to animals, §19A-35.
Unlicensed shops, §19A-33.

Physical therapists.
Unlicensed practice, §90-270.35.

Physician assistants.
Limited volunteer license to practice.
Violation of practice restriction, §90-12.4A(e).
Physician assistant retired limited volunteer license, §90-12.4B(e).

Physicians and surgeons.
Limited volunteer license to practice.
Violation of practice restriction, §90-12.1A(f).
Physician assistant limited volunteer license, §90-12.4A(e).
Physician assistant retired limited volunteer license, §90-12.4B(e).
Retired limited volunteer license, §90-12.1B(e).
Malpractice awards or settlements.
Insurance reporting requirements, noncompliance, §90-14.13(d).
Medical school faculty.
Unauthorized practice, §90-12.3(b).
Privileges to practice in hospitals.
Noncompliance with reporting requirements, §90-14.13(a).
Special purpose license.
Unauthorized practice, §90-12.2A(b).

Podiatrists.
Unlawful practices, §90-202.3.

Pollution control.
Sedimentation pollution control act of 1973, §113A-64(b).

Poultry products inspections, §106-549.59(a1).

Preneed funeral contracts and funds, §90-210.70(b).
Determining penalty amount, §90-210.69(f).

Private personnel services.
Unlicensed operation, §95-47.9(e).

Privileges to practice in hospitals.
Noncompliance with reporting requirements, §90-14.13(a).

Probate and registration.
Maps and plats, §47-32.2.

Property taxes.
Abstracts.
False affirmation, §105-310.
Attempting to evade or defeat taxes, §105-308.
County assessor.
Disclosure of information, §105-296(h).
Liens.
Advertisement of lien.
Wrongful advertisement, §105-369(g).
Listing of property.
Failure to list, §105-308.
Mobile homes.
Tax permit violations, §105-316.6(a) to (d).
Public utilities.
Reports.
False reports, §105-334(b).

Proprietary schools.
Operating without license or bond, §115D-96.

Pseudoephedrine products, sales of.
Retailer's failure to train or supervise employees, §90-113.56(c).

FINES —Cont'd
Psychologists.
Prohibited acts, §90-270.17.
Public lands.
Piers.
Erection on state lakes, §146-13.
Public officers and employees.
Misconduct in public office.
Failing to file report of fines, §14-244.
Public records.
Cultural resources department.
Disposition of records at end of official's term,
§132-4.
Unauthorized removal or destruction, §132-3.
Unlawful possession, §132-5.
Public schools.
Apportionment to school administrative units,
§115C-452.
Contractors selling personally identifiable student
information.
Criminal penalty, §115C-401.1(c).
Public utilities.
Refusal to permit commission to inspect records,
§62-313.
Public works.
Chapter violations, §133-4.
Quo warranto.
Judgment in actions, §1-527.
Rate bureau, §58-36-4(f).
Real estate brokers and salespersons, §93A-8.
Recreational therapists.
Practicing without license, §90C-36.
Remission or revocation of fine or cost,
§§15A-1363, 15A-1364(c).
Rental vehicles.
Violations of insurance provisions, §20-284.
**Retirement system for counties, cities and
towns,** §§128-28, 128-32.
**Retirement system for teachers and state
employees.**
False statements or falsified records, §135-10.
Salvia divinorum.
Manufacture, sale, delivery, possession,
§14-401.23(c).
School buses.
Mobile phones.
Unlawful use by operator while bus in motion,
§20-137.4.
School employees.
Personnel files.
Inspection.
Confidential information in personnel file,
§115C-321(c), (d).
School of science and mathematics.
Nonattendance, §116-235(b).
Traffic violations, §116-235(e).
Service animals, §168-4.5.
Shellfish.
Cultivation of shellfish.
Polluted shellfish.
Taking or selling at night or with prior
convictions, §113-209(d).
Privately leased, franchised or deeded shellfish
bottom areas.
Taking without permission, §113-208(a).
Smoking.
Local government building, vehicle or public place.
Violation of restriction, §130A-498(c1).
Long-term care facilities, §§131D-4.4(d),
131E-114.3(c).

FINES —Cont'd
Smoking —Cont'd
Restaurants or bars.
Violation of prohibition, §130A-497(b).
Social security numbers.
Public records, restricted use.
Recordation of instruments, §132-1.10(d).
Social workers, §90B-12.
Solid waste management.
Disclosure of information received pursuant to
article, §130A-304(b).
**Speech and language pathologists and
audiologists,** §90-306.
Statements of economic interest.
State government ethics act.
Failure to file, §138A-25(b).
State personnel records.
Unlawful disclosure, §§126-27, 126-28.
State personnel system.
Compensation for assisting person in obtaining
state employment, §126-18.
Political activities of employees, §§126-14,
126-14.1.
State treasurer.
False entries in books, §147-76.
Swine near state institutions.
Keeping, §143-153.
**Taking certain wild plants from land of
another,** §14-129.
Taking sea oats from land of another,
§14-129.2(b).
Taxation.
Attempt to evade or defeat tax, §105-236(a), (c).
Fraud.
Aid or assistance in fraud, §105-236.
Text messaging.
Driving while using mobile phone for,
§20-137.4A(c).
Time shares, §93A-56.
Disciplinary action by real estate commission,
§93A-54(a), (a1).
Toxic substances.
Dumping of toxic substances, §14-284.2.
Tramways.
Operation of passenger tramway without
registration, §95-124.
Transportation board.
Conflicts of interest, §136-14(i).
Malfeasance, §136-13(c).
Trust companies.
Administrative enforcement, §53-369(b).
Turnpike authority.
Toll collection on turnpike projects.
Open road tolls.
Penalty for failure to pay, §136-89.216(a).
Unauthorized insurers.
Transacting business, §58-28-13(g).
**Underground petroleum storage tank leak
cleanup.**
Criminal penalties, §143-215.94X(a) to (c).
Unemployment compensation.
Disclosure or improper use of information,
§96-4(x).
Failure to obey subpoena, §96-4(m).
Witness intimidation, §96-15.2.
Voter-owned elections act, §163-278.99D.
Wage and hour act, §95-25.21(c).
Recordkeeping requirements, §95-25.23A.
Civil penalty collection, §95-25.23B.
Water and air resources.
Air pollution control violations, §143-215.114B(a)
to (i).

FINES —Cont'd
Water and air resources —Cont'd
Classifications, standards or limitations,
    §143-215.6B(f) to (i).
Cleaning agents containing phosphorus.
    Manufacturing, selling or distributing agents,
        §143-214.4(f).
Conservation and use of diverted waters within
    emergency areas, §143-354.
Medical waste.
    Civil penalties.
        Prohibited disposal, §143-214.2A(b).
    Criminal penalties.
        Prohibited disposal, §143-214.2A(c).
    Prohibited disposal of waste, §143-214.2A(c).
Reporting of quality.
    Violations of part, §143-215.69(a).
Violations of part regulating water usage,
    §143-215.17(a).
Waters and watercourses.
Natural and scenic rivers system, §113A-42(b).
Water supply of public institutions.
Injuring, §143-152.
Well drilling, construction, etc., §143-355(i).
Witnesses.
Depositions.
    Default before commissioner, §8-80.
    Failure to appear upon subpoena, §8-79.
Failure to attend until discharged, §8-63.
Workers' compensation.
Insurance carrier violation, §97-100(g).
Receiving fee, other consideration or gratuity on
    account of services rendered, §97-90(b).
Unlawful deduction by employers, §97-21.

FINGERPRINTS.
Alarm system licensing.
Criminal background checks.
    Applicants for license or registration,
        §74D-2.1(a).
Alarm systems licensees' employees, §74D-8(a).
Arrest.
Person arrested, §15A-502(a).
    Exceptions, §15A-502(b), (c).
    Law enforcement agencies.
        Forwarding of fingerprints to, §15A-502(e).
Attorneys at law.
Applicants for admission to practice, §84-24.
Automated fingerprint identification system.
Delinquent or undisciplined juveniles fingerprints
    to be placed in, §7B-2102(c).
Bail.
Pretrial release.
    Collection as condition of pretrial release,
        §15A-534.
Bail bondsmen and runners.
Criminal history records checks.
    License applicants to furnish commissioner,
        §58-71-51(a).
    Renewal in even numbered years,
        §58-71-75(b).
Change of name.
Taking for criminal history record check,
    §101-5(b).
Child care providers.
Criminal history record check, §110-90.2.
Chiropractors, §§90-143.3, 114-19.22.
Concealed handgun permit.
Fees for processing, §14-415.19(b).
New set required, §14-415.16(b).

FINGERPRINTS —Cont'd
Concealed handgun permit —Cont'd
Submitted to state bureau of investigation for
    record check, §14-415.13(b).
Submitted with application, §14-415.13(a).
When not required, §14-415.16(d).
Criminal history record checks generally.
See CRIMINAL HISTORY RECORD CHECKS.
Dental hygienists.
Criminal records checks for license applicants,
    §90-224(c).
Dentists.
Criminal records checks for license applicants,
    §90-30(b).
Disposition of charges.
Report, §15A-1382.
Drivers' licenses.
Criminal record checks of persons manufacturing
    or producing, §114-19.24(c).
Emergency medical services.
Criminal background checks, §114-19.21.
Euthanasia technicians, §19A-24(d).
Funeral service.
Criminal records checks for license applicants,
    §90-210.25(a).
Identify theft generally, §§14-113.20 to 14-113.25.
Information technology services office.
Criminal record checks, §114-19.20.
Insurance adjusters.
Public adjusters.
    Applicants for license to furnish commissioner,
        §58-33A-15(c).
    Business entity, §58-33A-15(d).
**Insurance company incorporators and key
    persons,** §58-7-37.
Interpreters and transliterators.
Criminal records checks for license applicants,
    §90D-7(c).
Justice department.
Checks of employees, volunteers and contractors,
    §114-19.19.
Juvenile actions.
Fingerprinting and photographing delinquent or
    undisciplined juveniles, §7B-2102.
    Nontestimonial identification order procedures,
        §§7B-2103 to 7B-2109.
Transfer of jurisdiction for prosecution as adult,
    §7B-2201(a).
Massage and bodywork therapy.
Submission of fingerprint card, §90-629.
Names.
Change of name.
    Taking for criminal history record check,
        §101-5(b).
Nontestimonial identification, §§15A-271 to
    15A-282.
See IDENTIFICATION.
Nursing home administrators.
Criminal background checks, §90-288.01.
Pharmacists and pharmacies.
Criminal records checks for license applicants,
    §90-85.15(c).
Physicians and surgeons.
Criminal records checks for license applicants,
    §90-11(b).
Precious metals dealers.
Applicants for permits to provide, §66-165(a), (c).
Pretrial release.
Collection as condition of pretrial release,
    §15A-534.

FINGERPRINTS —Cont'd
Private personnel services.
Criminal records checks for license applicants, §95-47.2(d).
Private protective services.
Criminal background check.
New applicant to provide department of justice, §74C-8.1(a).
Professional employer organizations.
Furnished by license applicant, §58-89A-60(d).
Psychologists, background checks, §§90-270.22, 114-19.18.
Real estate brokers.
Criminal records checks for license applicants, §93A-4(b1).
Reports.
Disposition of cases, §15A-1382.
Respiratory care practitioners.
Applicants for license, §90-652(a).
Sex offender and public protection registration.
Fingerprints of offender taken at registration, §14-208.7(b).
State bureau of investigation.
Rules and regulations.
Authority to make, §114-18.

FINGERS.
Workers' compensation.
Loss of fingers.
Computation rate compensation, ICWorkComp Rule 405.

FIRE ALARM SYSTEMS.
Building codes.
Special safety to life requirements applicable to existing high-rise buildings.
Requirements for class I buildings, §143-138(i).
Requirements for class II buildings.
Manual fire alarm, §143-138(i).

FIRE AND RESCUE COMMISSION, §§58-78-1 to 58-78-20.
Compensation of members, §58-78-1(f).
Created, §58-78-1(a).
Duties, §58-78-5(a).
Executive director, §58-78-15(a).
Fiscal affairs, §58-78-20.
Funds.
Appropriation, §58-78-20.
Meetings, §58-78-10(c).
Members, §58-78-1(a) to (f).
Organization, §58-78-10(a).
Powers, §58-78-5(a).
Rules and regulations.
Adoption and promulgation, §58-78-10(b).
Staff, §58-78-15(b).
State agencies to furnish information, §58-78-5(b).
Terms, §58-78-1(b).
Transfer to department of insurance, §143A-79.2.
Vacancies, §58-78-1(c).

FIREARMS AND OTHER WEAPONS.
Acquittal by reason of insanity.
Possession by person acquitted of felony prohibited, §14-415.3(a), (b).
Alcohol or controlled substance in body or blood.
Carrying concealed handgun prohibited, §14-415.11(c2).

FIREARMS AND OTHER WEAPONS —Cont'd
Alcohol sold or consumed.
Carrying concealed handgun while consuming alcohol, §14-415.11(c2).
Carrying weapons into establishments where alcohol sold and consumed, §14-269.3(a).
Applicability of provisions, §14-269.3(b).
Antique firearm.
Defined, §14-409.11.
Permit or license to sell pistols.
Inapplicability of provisions to, §14-402(b).
Unlawful for felons to purchase, possess, etc.
Inapplicability, §14-415.1(a).
Arrest.
Use of deadly weapon to resist arrest, §15A-401(f).
Assault and battery, §14-34.2.
Emergency medical services personnel, §14-34.6.
Firefighters, §14-34.6.
Government officials and employees, §14-34.2.
Electronic surveillance orders, §15A-290(c4).
Habitual misdemeanor assault, §14-33.2.
Handicapped persons, §14-32.1.
Law enforcement, probation or parole officer in performance of duties, §14-34.5(a).
Person employed at state or local detention facility in performance of duties, §14-34.5(b).
Pointing gun at person, §14-34.
Assembly.
Carrying into assemblies, §14-269.3(a), (b).
Athletic facilities, athletic fields, playgrounds, swimming pools.
Permittee carrying concealed handgun.
Local ordinance prohibiting, §14-415.23.
Ballistic knives.
Possession and sale, §14-269.6(a), (b).
Blank cartridge pistols.
Sale, §14-407.1.
Bullets.
Teflon-coated bullets.
Manufacture, sale, purchase or possession prohibited, §14-34.3.
Bureau of investigation.
Surplus weapons.
Sale, trade or disposal, §143-63.1(d).
Burglary.
Preparation to commit burglary or other housebreaking, §14-55.
Campus or educational property.
Possessing or carrying unlawful.
Class 1 felony, §14-269.2(b).
Class 1 misdemeanors, §14-269.2(f).
Deadly weapons, §14-269.2(d).
Minors, aiding in possessing or carrying, §14-269.2(e).
Definitions, §14-269.2(a).
Exceptions, §14-269.2(g), (h).
Explosives, §14-269.2(b1).
Minors.
Aiding in possessing or carrying, §14-269.2(c1).
Firearms, §14-269.2(b), (f).
Minors.
Aiding in possessing or carrying, §14-269.2(c).
Campus police, §74G-7.
Concealed weapons, §74G-6(d).
Carrying concealed weapons, §14-269.
Alcohol or controlled substances remaining in body or blood.
Prohibited, §14-415.11(c2).

FIREARMS AND OTHER WEAPONS —Cont'd
Carrying concealed weapons —Cont'd
Concealed handgun permit generally, §§14-415.10 to 14-415.27.
See CONCEALED HANDGUN PERMIT.
Places authorized, §14-415.11.
While consuming alcohol.
Prohibited, §14-415.11(c2).
Charitable institutions.
Furnishing deadly weapons to inmates, §14-258.1(a).
Civil disorders, teaching or demonstrating use or assembling, §14-288.20.
Civil rights.
Restoration of firearms rights, §14-415.4.
Company police, §74E-7.
Concealed handgun permit, §§14-415.10 to 14-415.27.
See CONCEALED HANDGUN PERMIT.
Confiscation and disposition, §14-269.1.
Confiscation and dispositon.
Constitution of North Carolina.
Right to bear arms, NC Const Art I §30.
Constitution of the United States.
Right to bear arms, US Const Amd 2.
Counties.
Confinement facilities.
Furnishing inmates, §14-258.1.
Pellet gun regulation, §153A-130.
Regulation of firearms, §153A-129.
Statewide uniformity of local regulation, §14-409.40.
Courthouses.
Carrying or possession in, §14-269.4.
Crossbows.
Sale, §§14-402 to 14-408.
See CROSSBOWS.
Deadly force.
Investigations of use of deadly force by law enforcement officers, §147-90.
Dealers.
Defined, §14-409.39.
Door lock exemption permit, §§58-79-22, 143-143.4.
Materially false information provided dealer with intent to deceive as to legality of transfer, §14-409.1(c).
Law enforcement or persons acting for.
Inapplicability, §14-409.1(e).
Materially false information defined, §14-409.1(a).
Persons procuring another accountable as principal, §14-409.1(d).
Soliciting or enticing dealers to transfer firearms or ammunition in violation of law, §14-409.1(b).
Definitions, §14-409.1(a).
Law enforcement officers or persons acting at officers direction.
Inapplicability, §14-409.1(e).
Person procuring another to engage in unlawful conduct.
Accountable as principal, §14-409.1(d).
Definitions, §14-409.39.
Antique firearm, §14-409.11.
Historic edged weapons, §14-409.12.
Department of administration.
Sale to local government, law enforcement agency or state, §143-63.1(b).
Destruction of unsold firearms and weapons, §143-63.1(c).

FIREARMS AND OTHER WEAPONS —Cont'd
Disasters.
Prohibitions and restrictions during state of emergency.
County powers, §14-288.13.
Municipal powers, §14-288.12.
Discharge.
From within enclosure, §14-34.9.
Into conveyance while in operation, §14-34.1(b).
Serious bodily injury resulting, §14-34.1(c).
Into occupied property, §14-34.1(a).
Serious bodily injury resulting, §14-34.1(c).
Display during commission of felony.
Enhanced sentence, §15A-1340.16A.
Disposition of deadly weapons, §14-269.1.
District attorneys, assistant district attorneys, investigators employed by.
Carrying concealed weapons.
Inapplicability of prohibition, exceptions, §14-269(b).
Valid permit to carry concealed handgun.
Listed prohibited areas inapplicable, §14-415.27.
Domestic violence.
Emergency or ex parte orders.
Surrender of firearms required, §50B-3.1(a), (d).
Additional relief, §50B-3.1(l).
Disposal, §50B-3.1(h).
Exemptions for official use, §50B-3.1(k).
Hearings, §50B-3.1(b), (c).
Motions for return of firearms, §50B-3.1(f), (g).
Retrieval of firearms, §50B-3.1(e).
Violations, §50B-3.1(i), (j).
Purchase or possession of firearms prohibited.
Persons subject to domestic violence orders, §14-269.8(a).
Felony, §14-269.8(b).
Required surrender of firearms, §50B-3.1(a) to (l).
Violation of valid protective order as felony.
Possession of deadly weapon, §50B-4.1(g).
Emergencies.
Prohibitions and restrictions during state of emergency.
County powers, §14-288.13.
Municipal powers, §14-288.12.
Emergency medical services personnel.
Assault upon, §14-34.6(c).
Enhanced sentence.
Use or display during commission of felony, §15A-1340.16A(c).
Burden of proof, §15A-1340.16A(e).
Circumstances in which provisions do not apply, §15A-1340.16A(f).
Indictments or informations, §15A-1340.16A(d).
Escape.
Conveying to convicts and other prisoners, §14-258.
Use in assisting prisoner to escape, §14-258.2(b).
Felonious assault with, §14-32.
Felons.
Unlawful to purchase, own, possess, care or control firearms or weapons of mass death and destruction, §14-415.1(a).
Antique firearms, inapplicability, §14-415.1(a).
Antitrust violations.
Inapplicability of convictions for, §14-415.1(e).
Class G felon.
Persons violating provisions punished as, §14-415.1(a).
Conviction defined, §14-415.1(b).

FIREARMS AND OTHER WEAPONS —Cont'd
Felons —Cont'd
Unlawful to purchase, own, possess, care or
control firearms or weapons of mass death
and destruction —Cont'd
Firearm defined, §14-415.1(a).
Indictment, §14-415.1(c).
Prior convictions causing dissentitlement,
§14-415.1(b).
Records of prior convictions.
Admissibility for purpose of proving violation,
§14-415.1(b).
Restoration of firearm rights.
Inapplicability, exception, §14-415.1(d).
Felony murder, §14-17.
Firearms rights.
Restoration, §14-415.4.
Firefighters.
Assault or affray on using deadly weapon or
firearm, §14-34.6.
Forfeitures.
Confiscation generally, §14-269.1.
**Furnishing to inmates of charitable, mental or
penal institutions,** §14-258.1.
**General assembly member or legislative
employee.**
Transportation or storage in closed compartment
of locked vehicle.
Parking vehicle in state-owned parking space
assigned or leased to member or employee,
§120-32.1(c1).
Handguns.
Concealed handgun permit, §§14-415.10 to
14-415.27.
See CONCEALED HANDGUN PERMIT.
Defined, §14-409.39.
Highway patrol.
Active members.
Change of type, §20-187.2(b).
Deceased or retiring members.
Service sidearms, §20-187.2(a).
Furnishing to members, §20-190.
Surplus weapons.
Sale, trade or disposal, §143-63.1(d).
Historic edged weapons.
Defined, §14-409.12.
Hunting.
General provisions.
See HUNTING AND WILDLIFE.
Method of taking wildlife, §113-291.1.
Hunting and fishing reservations.
Openly carrying firearm or concealed carrying of
handgun.
State owned reservations, §14-415.11(c3).
Identification marks or numbers.
Alteration, destruction, etc., §14-160.1.
Incompetent persons.
Possession by incompetent persons charged with
felony, §14-415.3(a), (b).
Indictments.
Enhanced sentence.
Use or display of firearm or deadly weapon
during commission of felony,
§15A-1340.16A(d).
Larceny.
When value of property irrelevant, §14-72.
Law enforcement officers.
Assault upon, §§14-34.2, 14-34.5(a).
Licenses.
Sale of pistols, §§14-402 to 14-408.

FIREARMS AND OTHER WEAPONS —Cont'd
Local regulation.
Statewide uniformity.
County or municipality regulations,
§14-409.40(b).
Legislative declarations, §14-409.40(a), (a1).
Local government employees, §14-409.40(e).
Preemption by state, §14-409.40(a), (g).
Public buildings and areas, §14-409.40(f).
Shows, §14-409.40(d).
Zoning, §14-409.40(c), (d).
Mace spray, §14-401.6.
Machine guns.
Defined, §14-409(a).
Unlawful to sell, give away, use or possess,
exceptions, §14-409(b).
Punishment, §14-409(c).
**Mass death and destruction weapons
generally,** §§14-288.8, 14-288.21 to 14-288.24.
See WEAPONS OF MASS DEATH AND
DESTRUCTION.
Mentally ill.
Bar to possession due to mental commitment.
Restoration process to remove bar, §122C-54.1.
Furnishing to inmates of mental institutions,
§14-258.1(a).
Minors.
Defined, §14-269.7(c).
Exceptions, §14-269.7(b).
Handgun defined, §14-269.7(c).
Handgun sales, §14-315(a1).
Permitting young children to use dangerous
firearms, §14-316(a).
Air rifles, air pistols and BB guns not deemed
dangerous firearms, §14-316(b).
Possession of handgun.
Misdemeanor, §14-269.7(a).
Schools, bringing weapons in.
Action against parent for negligent supervision
of minor, §1-538.3.
Selling or giving weapons to minors, §14-315.
Defense, §14-315(b1).
Storage of firearms to protect minors, §14-315.1.
Close proximity of weapon, §14-315.1(b).
Exemptions, §14-315.1(c).
"Minor" defined, §14-315.1(d).
Posting of warning sign, §14-315.2(b), (c).
Prohibited conduct, §14-315.1(a).
Written notice requirements, §14-315.2(a), (c).
Misdemeanor assaults, batteries or affrays,
§14-33(c).
Habitual misdemeanor assault, §14-33.2.
Warrantless arrest, §15A-401.
Municipalities.
Confinement facilities.
Furnishing to inmates, §14-258.1.
Firearms, regulation, §160A-189.
Pellet guns, regulation, §160A-190.
Regulation of instruments of mass death and
destruction within city, §160A-183.
Statewide uniformity of local regulation,
§14-409.40.
Notice of unclaimed firearms, §15-11.2(b).
Out-of-state purchases by citizens of state,
§14-409.10.
Parade, picket line, funeral procession, etc.
Applicability of provisions, §14-277.2(c).
Possession by participants prohibited,
§14-277.2(a).
Term "dangerous weapon."
Construed, §14-277.2(b).

FIREARMS AND OTHER WEAPONS —Cont'd
Peace officers.
Assault upon, §§14-34.2, 14-34.5(a).
Permits.
Concealed handgun permit, §§14-415.10 to
14-415.27.
See CONCEALED HANDGUN PERMIT.
Sale of crossbows or pistols, §§14-402 to 14-408.
Sale of pistols, §§14-402 to 14-408.
**Permitting young children to use dangerous
firearm,** §14-316.
Persons subject to domestic violence orders.
Purchase or possession of firearms prohibited,
§14-269.8(a), (b).
Pointing gun, §14-34.
Habitual misdemeanor assault, §14-33.2.
Police.
Change of type, §20-187.2(b).
Deceased or retiring members of law-enforcement
agencies.
Service sidearms, §20-187.2(a).
Furnishing to members, §20-190.
**Possessing or carrying on campus or other
educational property,** §14-269.2.
Possession of dangerous weapon in prison,
§14-258.2.
Possession of handgun by minor, §14-269.7.
Prisons and prisoners.
Conveying to convicts and other prisoners,
§14-258.
Furnishing to inmates, §14-258.1(a).
Possession by prisoner, §14-258.2(a).
Use in assisting prisoner to escape, §14-258.2(b).
Private protective services.
Armed licensees or registered employees.
Firearm registration permits, §74C-13.
Firearms registration permits, §74C-13.
Private sellers.
Materially false information provided seller with
intent to deceive as to legality of transfer,
§14-409.1(c).
Law enforcement or persons acting for.
Inapplicability, §14-409.1(e).
Materially false information defined,
§14-409.1(a).
Persons procuring another accountable as
principal, §14-409.1(d).
Soliciting or enticing seller to transfer firearms or
ammunition in violation of law, §14-409.1(b).
Definitions, §14-409.1(a).
Law enforcement officers or persons acting at
officers direction.
Inapplicability, §14-409.1(e).
Person procuring another to engage in unlawful
conduct.
Accountable as principal, §14-409.1(d).
Products liability.
Firearms or ammunition.
Burden of proof, §99B-11(b).
Defect in design, §99B-11(a).
Public buildings and grounds.
Carrying or possession on certain state property
prohibited, exceptions, §14-269.4.
**Purchase of firearm out of state by citizens of
state,** §14-409.10.
Recreational facilities.
Permittee carrying concealed handgun.
Local ordinance prohibiting, §14-415.23.
Reports.
Wounds.
Physicians and hospitals to report, §90-21.20(a),
(b).
Contents of reports, §90-21.20(c).

FIREARMS AND OTHER WEAPONS —Cont'd
Reports —Cont'd
Wounds —Cont'd
Physicians and hospitals to report —Cont'd
Immunity from liability, §90-21.20(d).
Rest areas or rest stops along highways.
Openly carrying firearm or concealed carrying of
handgun.
State owned rest areas or rest stops,
§14-415.11(c3).
Restoration of firearms rights, §14-415.4.
Certified copies of order granting petition to
sheriff, §14-415.4(g).
Court fees, §14-415.4(k).
Crime of felons unlawfully possessing firearms.
Inapplicability to person with restored rights,
§14-415.1(d).
Criminal background check of petitioner,
§114-19.28.
Criteria for granting petition, §14-415.4(d).
Department of justice instant background check
system index, §14-415.4(h).
Disqualifers for denial of petition, §14-415.4(e).
Effect of restoration, §14-415.4(i).
Fees, §14-415.4(k).
Hearing procedure, §14-415.4(f).
National instant background check system index,
§14-415.4(h).
Notice of hearing, §14-415.4(f).
Petition for restoration, §14-415.4(c).
Public policy, §14-415.4(b).
Reconsideration upon petition upon denial,
§14-415.4(g).
Riots and civil disorders.
Certain weapons.
Applicability of provisions, §14-288.20(c).
Definitions, §14-288.20(a).
Felony possession, §14-288.20(b).
Frisking, §14-288.10.
Mass death and destruction weapons, §14-288.8.
Prohibitions and restrictions during state of
emergency.
County powers, §14-288.13.
Transporting weapon or substance during
emergency, §14-288.7(a).
Exceptions, §14-288.7(b).
Penalty for violation of provisions, §14-288.7(c).
Robbery.
Train robbery, §14-88.
Use of firearms or other dangerous weapons in
robbery, §14-87(a).
Safety and training course.
Concealed handgun permits, §14-415.12(a).
Exemptions, §14-415.12A.
Sale of pistols, §§14-402 to 14-408.
Blank cartridge pistols, §14-407.1.
Collection.
Issuance of permit to nonresident, §14-404(a).
Dealer records, requirements, §14-406(a).
Misdemeanor for violating, §14-408.
Definitions, §14-402(c).
License or permit required, §14-402(a).
Collection, issuance to nonresident, §14-404(a).
Expiration date, §14-403.
Fee for sheriffs services, §14-404(e).
Form, §14-403.
Inapplicability, §§14-402(b), 14-404(d).
Informing applicant as to action on issuance,
§14-404(f).
Issuance by sheriff, §14-403.

FIREARMS AND OTHER WEAPONS —Cont'd
Sale of pistols —Cont'd
License or permit required —Cont'd
Mental health denial, eligibility upon restoration of rights, §14-404(g).
Records kept by sheriffs, §14-405.
Refusal to issue, grounds, appeal, §14-404(b), (c).
Mail or other parcel delivery.
Display of permit or license, §14-402(a).
Sales or transfers in violation of law.
Materially false information provided dealer or private seller with intent to deceive as to legality of transfer, §14-409.1(c).
Law enforcement or persons acting for.
Inapplicability, §14-409.1(e).
Materially false information defined, §14-409.1(a).
Persons procuring another accountable as principal, §14-409.1(d).
Soliciting or enticing dealer or private seller to transfer firearms or ammunition in violation of law, §14-409.1(b).
Definitions, §14-409.1(a).
Law enforcement officers or persons acting at officers direction.
Inapplicability, §14-409.1(e).
Person procuring another to engage in unlawful conduct.
Accountable as principal, §14-409.1(d).
Schools.
Discipline of students.
Firearm defined, §115C-390.1(b).
Gun Free Schools Act.
Policies and procedures consistent with, §115C-390.1(c).
Suspension for gun possession, §115C-390.10.
Readmission, request for, §115C-390.12.
Driving eligibility certificate.
Effect of disciplinary action for enumerated student conduct, §20-11(n1).
Minors bringing to school.
Action against parent for negligent supervision of minor, §1-538.3.
Possessing or carrying on campus or educational property, §14-269.2.
Principals to report weapons offenses occurring on school property, §115C-288(g).
Reports of incidents of student possession on educational property.
Principal's duty, §115C-390.10(b).
Secret assault, §14-31.
Seized firearms, disposition, §15-11.1(b1).
Selling or giving weapons to minors, §14-315.
Sentencing.
Enhanced sentence.
Firearm or deadly weapon used or displayed during commission of felony, §15A-1340.16A.
Use or display during commission of felony, §15A-1340.16A.
Serial numbers.
Alteration, destruction, removal of numbers from firearm, §14-160.2(a).
Possession of firearm with removed numbers, §14-160.2(b).
Punishment, §14-160.2(c).
Sport shooting range protection, §§14-409.45 to 14-409.47.
Spring loaded projectile knives.
Possession and sale, §14-269.6(a), (b).

FIREARMS AND OTHER WEAPONS —Cont'd
State legislative office building.
Transportation or storage in closed compartment of locked vehicle, §120-32.1(c1).
State of emergency.
Prohibitions and restrictions during.
County powers, §14-288.13.
Municipal powers, §14-288.12.
State officers, officials and employees.
Unlawful to dispose of, §143-63.1(a).
State property.
Unlawful to possess or carry on certain state property, exceptions, §14-269.4.
Storage of weapon to protect minor, §14-315.1.
Submachine guns.
Defined, §14-409(a).
Unlawful to sell, give away, use or possess, exceptions, §14-409(b).
Punishment, §14-409(c).
Tear gas, §14-401.6.
Teflon-coated bullets.
Manufacture, sale, purchase or possession prohibited, §14-34.3.
Trains or passengers, shooting at, §14-280.
Trial.
Searching persons for weapons, §15A-1034(b).
Unclaimed firearms, disposition, §15-11.2(c) to (e).
Disbursement of proceeds of sale, §15-11.2(f).
Notice, §15-11.2(b).
Unclaimed firearm, defined, §15-11.2(a).
Uniformity of rules and regulations.
County or municipality regulations, §14-409.40(b).
Legislative declarations, §14-409.40(a), (a1).
Local government employees, §14-409.40(e).
Preemption by state, §14-409.40(a), (g).
Public buildings and areas, §14-409.40(f).
Shows, §14-409.40(d).
Zoning, §14-409.40(c), (d).
Universities and colleges.
Possessing or carrying on campus or educational property, §14-269.2.
Use during commission of felony.
Enhanced sentence, §15A-1340.16A.
Warning upon sale or transfer of firearm to protect minor, §14-315.2.
Weapon of mass death and destruction.
Manufacture, assembly, possession, etc., §14-288.8.
Nuclear, biological or chemical weapons, §§14-288.21 to 14-288.24.
See WEAPONS OF MASS DEATH AND DESTRUCTION.
Wounds.
Physicians and hospitals to report, §90-21.20.

FIRECRACKERS.
See FIREWORKS.

FIRE DEPARTMENTS.
See FIREFIGHTERS AND FIRE DEPARTMENTS.

FIRE DRILLS.
Public schools.
Powers and duties of principal, §115C-288(d).

FIRE EXTINGUISHERS.
Misuse or damage of system, §14-286.
Roller skating rinks.
Duties of operator, §99E-11.

FIREFIGHTERS AND FIRE DEPARTMENTS.
All-terrain vehicles.
Use on certain highways, §20-171.23(a) to (f).

FIREFIGHTERS AND FIRE DEPARTMENTS
—Cont'd

Annexation initiated by municipality.
Rural fire departments.
  Assumption of proportionate share of fire
    department debt, §160A-58.58.
  Contract to provide fire protection in annexed
    area, §160A-58.57.

Assault on.
Class F felony.
  Using firearm, §14-34.6(c).
Class H felony.
  Inflicting serious bodily injury, using deadly
    weapon other than firearm, §14-34.6(b).
Class I felony, §14-34.6(a).
Emergency personnel, §14-288.9.
  Aggravating factor in sentencing, §15A-1340.16.
Use of deadly weapon, §14-34.2.

Authority of firemen, §58-82-1.

Bioterrorism.
First responder vaccination program.
  First responders exposed to infectious diseases
    when deployed to disaster locations,
    §130A-485.

Burning of fire house, §14-61.

Camp Butner Reservation.
Public safety authority.
  Police and fire protection, §122C-408.

Child labor.
Training for uncompensated members under 18
  years of age, §95-25.5(n).

Controlled access roads.
Means of emergency access required for fire
  vehicles, §20-158.3.

Criminal history record checks, §114-19.12.
Conditional offer pending check, §114-19.12(f).
Confidentiality of information, §114-19.12(b).
  Releases of information, §114-19.12(c).
Convictions, effect, §114-19.12(d).
Defined terms, §114-19.12(a).
  Local fire chief, §114-19.12(g).
Denial of application, factors, §114-19.12(d).
Denial of application, refusal to consent,
  §114-19.12(e).
EMS personnel, §114-19.21.
Local homeland security directory to provide when
  requested, §114-19.12(b).
Refusal to consent, §114-19.12(e).
Releases of information, §114-19.12(c).

Death benefits, §§143-166.1 to 143-166.7.
See DEATH BENEFITS.

Deceased or retiring county firefighters.
Honoring, awarding helmet, §153A-236.

Department of administration.
Purchases and contracts through, §143-49.1.

Disability retirement.
Local governmental employees' retirement system,
  §128-27(c).

Disasters.
First responder vaccination program.
  First responders exposed to infectious diseases
    when deployed to disaster locations,
    §130A-485.

**Failure of owner of property to comply with
orders of chief, §14-68.**

Firemen as traffic officers, §20-114.1(b).

**Hazardous substance list provided by
employer by fire chiefs, §95-194.**

FIREFIGHTERS AND FIRE DEPARTMENTS
—Cont'd

Health insurance for firefighters.
State health plan for teachers and public
  employees.
  Dependent children.
    Subject to same terms and conditions as other
      dependent children, §135-48.1.
  Effective dates of coverage, §135-48.43(e).
  Enrollment terms and conditions, §135-48.42(b).
  Firefighter defined, §135-48.1.
  Generally, §§135-48.1 to 135-48.61.
    See STATE HEALTH PLAN FOR
      TEACHERS AND STATE EMPLOYEES.
  Opportunity to participate, §135-48.8.
  Premium rates.
    Separate premium rates set, §135-48.58.

Highway use tax.
Exemption, §105-187.6(a).

Immunization.
First responder vaccination program.
  First responders exposed to infectious diseases
    when deployed to disaster locations,
    §130A-485.

**Impersonation of firemen or emergency
medical services personnel, §14-276.1.**

Individual income tax.
Eligible firefighters.
  Deduction from taxable income, §105-134.6(d).

Interference with firemen.
Penalty for willful interference, §58-82-1.

Killed or disabled in line of duty.
Tuition and fee waivers to survivor, spouse or
  child, §§115B-1 to 115B-6.

**Leave options for personnel in disaster or
emergency, §166A-17.**

Light-traffic road weight and load limitations.
Exceptions to firefighting vehicles, §20-118(c).

Motor vehicle license plates.
Permanent license plates for rural fire department
  vehicles, §20-84(b).
Special plates, §20-79.4(b).

**Motor vehicle size, weight and load
restrictions.**
Overweight and oversize government owned and
  operated vehicles responding to fire
  emergency.
  Exemption, §20-118.4.

Municipalities, §§160A-291 to 160A-295.3.
Annexation.
  Loss of rural fire employment.
    Actions of city, §160A-294(a), (b).
Employment of firefighters, §160A-291.
Fire chief.
  Appointment, §160A-291.
  Duties, §160A-292.
  Reports, §160A-292.
Fire protection outside city limits, §160A-293.
Helmet of deceased firefighter awarded to
  surviving relative, §160A-294.1.
Hours of labor.
  Applicability of provisions, §160A-295.3.
  Computing hours, §160A-295.1(c).
  Definitions, §160A-295.
  Department of labor, authority to enforce,
    §160A-295.2.
  Firefighters, §160A-295.1(a).
  Personnel who do not fight fires, §160A-295.1(b).
Overtime pay.
  Applicability of provisions, §160A-295.3.
  Computing overtime, §160A-295.1(d).

FIREFIGHTERS AND FIRE DEPARTMENTS
—Cont'd
Municipalities —Cont'd
Overtime pay —Cont'd
Definitions, §160A-295.
Department of labor, authority to enforce, §160A-295.2.
Firefighters, §160A-295.1(a).
Personnel who do not fight fires, §160A-295.1(b).
Powers of cities as to, §160A-291.
Smallpox vaccination of first responders.
Policies for time off due to adverse reaction, §160A-164.1.
State volunteer fire department.
Acceptance of provisions, §58-80-15.
Dispatching firemen and apparatus from municipalities, §58-80-25.
Municipalities not to be unprotected, §58-80-40.
Local appropriations, §58-80-55.
Withdrawal from participation, §58-80-20.
Mutual aid between fire departments, §58-83-1.
Offenses against firemen.
Aggravating factor in sentencing, §15A-1340.16.
Overweight and oversize government owned and operated vehicles responding to fire emergency.
Exemption from weight and size restriction, §20-118.4.
Parking in front of entrance to fire station, §20-162(a).
Retirement.
Local governmental employees' retirement system.
Disability retirement, §128-27(c).
Firefighter defined, §128-21.
Generally, §§128-21 to 128-38.4.
See LOCAL GOVERNMENTAL EMPLOYEES' RETIREMENT SYSTEM.
Rural fire departments.
Annexation initiated by municipality.
Assumption of proportionate share of fire department debt, §160A-58.58.
Contract to provide fire protection in annexed area, §160A-58.57.
Defined, §58-82-5(a).
Liability.
Limited, §58-82-5(b).
Acts or omissions relating to direction of traffic or enforcement of traffic laws, §20-114.1(b1).
Motor vehicle license plates.
Permanent license plates for department vehicles, §20-84(b).
State volunteer fire department, §§58-80-1 to 58-80-60.
See VOLUNTEER FIRE DEPARTMENTS.
Traffic officers.
Firemen as, §20-114.1(b).
Trucks and vehicles generally.
See FIRE TRUCKS AND VEHICLES.
Tuition and fee waivers.
Survivor, spouse or child of firfighter killed or disabled in line of duty, §§115B-1 to 115B-6.
Vaccinations.
First responder vaccination program.
First responders exposed to infectious diseases when deployed to disaster locations, §130A-485.
Volunteer fire departments.
Generally.
See VOLUNTEER FIRE DEPARTMENTS.

FIREFIGHTERS AND FIRE DEPARTMENTS
—Cont'd
Volunteer fire departments —Cont'd
State volunteer fire department, §§58-80-1 to 58-80-60.
See VOLUNTEER FIRE DEPARTMENTS.

FIREFIGHTERS ASSOCIATION OF STATE.
Members, §58-85-20.
Departments, §58-84-50.
Treasurer.
Payment of fund to treasurer by commissioner, §58-84-25(a).
State appropriation, §58-85-10.
Volunteer firefighters association, §58-85-30.

FIREFIGHTERS' RELIEF FUND, §§58-84-5 to 58-84-55.
Accounts and accounting.
Disbursement of funds by trustees.
Account of moneys received and disbursed to be kept, §58-84-40(a) to (d).
Administration, §58-84-25(d).
Application of fund.
State appropriation, §58-85-1.
Appropriation by state.
Applicability of provisions, §58-85-25.
Application of fund, §58-85-1.
Applied to members of regular fire company, §58-85-25.
Treasurer of state firemen's association, §58-85-10.
Who shall participate, §58-85-15.
Bonds, surety.
Treasurer of state firemen's association.
State appropriation.
Bond to be given by treasurer, §58-85-10.
Trustees.
Treasurer of board of trustees, §58-84-30.
Certificate of eligibility, §58-84-46.
Counties.
Allocation of funds to, §58-84-25(b).
Definitions, §58-84-5.
Disbursement of funds.
Board of trustees to disburse, §58-84-35.
Account of moneys received and disbursed to be kept, §58-84-40(a) to (d).
Discrimination.
No discrimination on account of race, §58-84-55.
Fire companies.
State appropriation.
Applied to members of regular fire company, §58-85-25.
State firemen's association.
Departments to be members of association, §58-84-50.
Fire districts.
Distribution of funds to, §58-84-25(c).
Firemen's and rescue squad workers' pension fund, §§58-86-1 to 58-86-91.
See FIREMEN'S AND RESCUE SQUAD WORKERS' PENSION FUND.
Immunity, §58-84-60.
Insurance commissioner.
Certificate of eligibility, §58-84-46.
Disbursement of funds by commissioner, §58-84-25.
Participation in fund.
State appropriation.
Who shall participate, §58-85-15.
Reports.
Disbursement of funds by trustees.
Report of moneys received and disbursed to be filed, §58-84-40(a) to (d).

FIREFIGHTERS' RELIEF FUND —Cont'd
Reports —Cont'd
Treasurer of state firemen's association.
State appropriation.
Filing of report by treasurer, §58-85-10.
State appropriation.
Applicability of provisions, §58-85-25.
Application of fund, §58-85-1.
Fire companies.
Applied to members of regular fire company, §58-85-25.
Participation in fund.
Who shall participate, §58-85-15.
Treasurer of state firemen's association, §58-85-10.
State firemen's association.
Fire companies.
Departments to be members of association, §58-84-50.
Members, §58-85-20.
Treasurer.
Payment of fund to treasurer by commissioner, §58-84-25(a).
State appropriation.
Bond to be given by treasurer, §58-85-10.
Filing of report by treasurer, §58-85-10.
Volunteer firemen's association.
Payment of fund by treasurer to volunteer firemen's association, §58-85-30.
Treasurer of state firemen's association.
Insurance commissioner.
Payment of fund to treasurer by commissioner, §58-84-25(a).
Trustees, §58-84-30.
Disbursement of funds, §58-84-35.
Account of moneys received and disbursed to be kept, §58-84-40(a) to (d).
Volunteer firemen's association, §58-85-30.

FIRE HOSES.
Driving over prohibited, §20-157(d).
Penalty for violation, §20-157(g).
Property damage, §20-157(h).

FIRE HYDRANTS.
Blocking prohibited, §20-157(b).
Penalty for violation, §20-157(g).
Property damage, §20-157(h).
Parking in front of, §20-162(a).

FIRE INSURANCE.
Authorized, §58-7-15.
Beach area essential property insurance, §§58-45-1 to 58-45-96.
See BEACH AREA ESSENTIAL PROPERTY INSURANCE.
Community college buildings and contents, §115D-58.11(a) to (c).
Contracts.
Devices.
Performance of contracts as to devices not prohibited, §58-43-1.
Indemnity contracts for difference in actual value and cost of replacement, §58-43-5.
Counties, cities, school districts.
Plans for erection of buildings to be used by local government.
Inspection by commissioner of insurance as to fire safety.
Approval by commissioner, §58-31-40(b).
Extended coverage, §58-31-15.
Firefighters' relief fund, §§58-84-5 to 58-84-60.
See FIREFIGHTERS' RELIEF FUND.

FIRE INSURANCE —Cont'd
Foreign or alien insurance companies.
Deposits.
Required, §58-5-5.
Funds.
Firefighters' relief fund, §§58-84-5 to 58-84-60.
See FIREFIGHTERS' RELIEF FUND.
Information to be furnished by insurance companies, §58-79-40(a), (b).
Confidentiality of information, §58-79-40(d).
Immunity from liability, §58-79-40(c).
Testimony by officials as to information, §58-79-40(e).
Limitation of actions.
Claim for loss covered by three-year limitation, §1-52.
Limitation of fire insurance risk, §58-43-25.
Limitation of liability on total lost, §58-43-10.
Mandatory or voluntary risk sharing plans, §§58-42-1 to 58-42-50.
See MANDATORY OR VOLUNTARY RISK SHARING PLANS.
Mediation of emergency or disaster claims.
Property insurance, §§58-44-70 to 58-44-120.
See PROPERTY INSURANCE.
Misdemeanors.
Unauthorized insurers.
Violations of provisions, §58-28-45(h).
Mortgages and deeds of trust.
Policies for benefit of mortgagees, §58-43-15.
Mutual insurance companies.
Surplus.
Requirements, §58-7-75.
Penalties.
Unauthorized insurers, §58-28-45(h).
Policies.
Amount.
Limitation, §58-43-5.
Devices.
Performance of contracts as to devices not prohibited, §58-43-1.
Functional replacement, §58-43-5.
Indemnity contracts for difference in actual value and cost of replacement, §58-43-5.
Mortgagees.
Policies for benefit of, §58-43-15.
Standard policy provisions.
Abandonment, §58-44-16(f).
Added provisions, §58-44-16(f).
Appraisal, §58-44-16(f).
Cancellation of policy, §58-44-16(f).
Company's options, §58-44-16(f).
Conditions suspending or restricting policy, §58-44-16(f).
Designated standard fire insurance policy, §58-44-16(a).
Fraud, concealment, §58-44-16(f).
General provisions, §58-44-16(f).
Head of policy requirements, §58-44-16(c).
Incorporation of provisions into policies, §58-44-16(e).
Mortgage interests and obligations, §58-44-16(f).
Other insurance, §58-44-16(f).
Other perils or subjects, §58-44-16(f).
Perils not included, §58-44-16(f).
Permissible variations, §58-44-20.
Pro rata liability, §58-44-16(f).
Reinsurance exception, §58-44-16(d).
Required, exceptions, §58-44-16(b).
Requirements in case loss occurs, §58-44-16(f).
Subrogation, §58-44-16(f).

FIRE INSURANCE —Cont'd
Policies —Cont'd
Standard policy provisions —Cont'd
Suit or action on policy, §58-44-16(f).
Uninsurable and excepted property,
§58-44-16(f).
Waiver provisions, §58-44-16(f).
When loss payable, §58-44-16(f).
Term.
Limitation, §58-43-5.
Premiums.
Excess over actual cash value of property.
Reimbursement, §58-43-10.
Property insurance.
Mediation of emergency or disaster claims,
§§58-44-70 to 58-44-120.
See PROPERTY INSURANCE.
Policies, §§58-44-1 to 58-44-60.
See PROPERTY INSURANCE.
Reports.
Fire incident reports, §58-79-45(a) to (c).
Risks.
Limitation of fire insurance risks, §58-43-25.
Service of process.
Unauthorized insurers, §58-28-45(e).
Standard policy provisions, §58-44-16.
State property.
Inspection by commissioner of insurance,
§58-31-40(a).
Defects noted.
Notification to agency official in charge of
property, §58-31-40(a).
Reports to governor.
Commissioner of insurance, §58-31-45.
State property fire insurance fund, §§58-31-1 to
58-31-20.
Actual cost of restoration or replacement.
Payment of losses, §58-31-10(a).
Adoption of policy forms, §58-31-12.
Appropriations, §58-31-5.
Commissioner.
Rules and regulations, §58-31-10(b).
Creation, §58-31-1.
Description of property belonging to state.
Officers having custody to inform
commissioner, §58-31-35.
Expenses.
Administrative expenses, §58-31-5.
Extended coverage insurance, §58-31-15.
Officers in charge of state property.
Furnishing information to commissioner,
§58-31-35.
Payment of losses, §58-31-10(a).
Policy forms, adoption, §58-31-12.
Purchase of insurance to protect fund from loss,
§58-31-10(b).
Premiums paid by fund, §58-31-10(b).
Rules and regulations.
Promulgation by commissioner, §58-31-10(b).
Sprinkler leakage insurance, §58-31-10(c).
State treasurer.
Custodian of fund, §58-31-1.
Transfers from fund.
To agencies or institutions suffering loss,
§58-31-10(a).
Transfers to fund.
Insufficient amount in fund to pay losses,
§58-31-10(a).
Unauthorized insurers.
Actions.
Criminal action or conviction not to preclude
civil action, §58-28-45(m).

FIRE INSURANCE —Cont'd
Unauthorized insurers —Cont'd
Actions —Cont'd
Prerequisites to instituting or filing,
§58-28-45(f), (g).
Prohibited acts, §58-28-45(a) to (c).
Exceptions, §58-28-45(d).
Service of process, §58-28-45(e).
Violations of provisions.
Controlling persons, §58-28-45(k).
Penalties, §58-28-45(h), (l).
**Use and occupancy and business interruption
insurance,** §58-31-20.

**FIRE INVESTIGATIONS AND INSPECTION OF
PREMISES,** §§58-79-1 to 58-79-45.
See FIRES AND FIRE PREVENTION.

FIRE LANES.
Parking prohibited, §20-162(b).

**FIREMEN'S AND RESCUE SQUAD WORKERS'
PENSION FUND,** §§58-86-1 to 58-86-91.
Administration of fund.
Appropriations for administrative expenses,
§58-86-20.
Board of trustees to administer, §58-86-1.
Annexation.
Firemen whose residence is annexed by a city.
Monthly pensions upon retirement, §58-86-55.
Appropriations.
Administrative expenses of fund, §58-86-20.
Benefits.
Attachment.
Exemption of pensions from attachment,
§58-86-90.
Deductions for payments to certain employees' or
retirees' associations, §58-86-91.
Disabled members.
Totally and permanently disabled members
entitled to monthly benefit, §58-86-55.
Garnishment.
Exemption of pensions from garnishment,
§58-86-90.
Judgments.
Exemption of pensions from judgments,
§58-86-90.
Lump-sum payments, §58-86-60.
Monthly pensions upon retirement, §58-86-55.
Nonassignable, §58-86-90.
Pro rata reduction of benefits.
When fund insufficient to pay in full, §58-86-65.
Board of trustees.
Administration of fund, §58-86-1.
Compensation, §58-86-5.
Creation, §58-86-5.
Duties, §58-86-10.
Lump-sum payments, §58-86-60.
Membership, §58-86-5.
Powers, §58-86-10.
Rules and regulations, §58-86-1.
Contributions to fund, §58-86-20.
Creditable service.
Determination, §58-86-75.
Information furnished by applicants for
membership, §58-86-75.
Service in more than one department or squad.
Length of service not affected, §58-86-80.
Transfer from one department or squad to
another, §58-86-80.
Custodian of fund.
State treasurer to be custodian, §58-86-20.

**FIREMEN'S AND RESCUE SQUAD WORKERS'
PENSION FUND** —Cont'd
**Deductions for payments to certain employees'
or retirees' associations,** §58-86-91.
Definitions, §58-84-5.
Eligible firemen, §58-86-25.
Eligible rescue squad worker, §58-86-30.
Office created, §58-86-15.
Director.
Office created, §58-86-15.
Disabled members.
Totally and permanently disabled member.
Monthly benefit, §58-86-55.
Eligible firemen, §58-86-25.
Eligible rescue squad worker, §58-86-30.
Establishment of fund, §58-86-1.
Expenditures, §58-86-20.
Investments by state treasurer, §§147-69.7,
147-69.8.
Legislative change.
Provisions subject to future legislative change,
§58-86-70.
Lump-sum payments.
Board of trustees to direct payment and
lump-sums in certain cases, §58-86-60.
Membership.
Additional retroactive membership, §58-86-45(a)
to (b).
Application for membership in fund, §§58-86-35,
58-86-40.
Information furnished by applicants for
membership.
Determination of creditable service, §58-86-75.
Monthly payments by members, §§58-86-35,
58-86-40.
Retroactive membership.
Additional retroactive membership, §58-86-45(a)
to (b).
Termination, §§58-86-35, 58-86-40.
Monthly pensions upon retirement, §58-86-55.
Municipalities.
Council may provide for enrolling city employees,
§160A-163(a).
Firemen whose residence is annexed by a city,
§58-86-55.
Payments by members.
Crediting payments to separate accounts of
members, §§58-86-35, 58-86-40.
Delinquent payments.
Termination not a result, §§58-86-35, 58-86-40.
Monthly payments, §§58-86-35, 58-86-40.
Refunds upon termination of membership,
§§58-86-35, 58-86-40.
Time limit for making monthly payment,
§§58-86-35, 58-86-40.
Pro rata reduction of benefits.
When fund insufficient to pay in full, §58-86-65.
Provisions subject to future legislative change,
§58-86-70.
Retirement.
Monthly pensions upon retirement, §58-86-55.
Rules and regulations.
Board of trustees to make necessary rules and
regulations, §58-86-1.
Secured transactions.
Third parties.
Assignments.
Restrictions on assignments, §§25-9-406(i),
25-9-408(f).
State auditor.
Transfer to department of state auditor,
§143A-27.1.

**FIREMEN'S AND RESCUE SQUAD WORKERS'
PENSION FUND** —Cont'd
State treasurer.
Custodian of fund, §58-86-20.
Volunteer firemen, §58-86-25.

FIRE PATROLS.
Designated during season of drought,
§106-899(a).

FIRE PREVENTION INSPECTORS.
County inspection departments.
Generally, §§153A-350 to 153A-375.
See COUNTY INSPECTION DEPARTMENTS.

FIRE PROTECTION DISTRICTS.
County service districts.
Generally, §§153A-300 to 153A-310.
See COUNTY SERVICE DISTRICTS.
Rural fire protection districts.
Generally, §§69-25.1 to 69-25.17.
See RURAL FIRE PROTECTION DISTRICTS.

FIRE PROTECTION GRANT FUND.
Appropriations, §58-85A-1(c).
Creation, §58-85A-1(a).
Distributions, §58-85A-1(b).

**FIRE-SAFETY STANDARD AND
FIREFIGHTER PROTECTION ACT,**
§§58-92-1 to 58-92-55.
Actions.
Civil actions for violations, §58-92-30(f).
Certification of cigarettes.
Availability to attorney general, §58-92-20(c).
Changes in cigarettes thereafter, §58-92-20(g).
Copies of certifications.
Supplying to distributors and agents,
§58-92-25(f).
Fees, §58-92-20(e), (f).
Generally, §58-92-20(a).
Information to be included, §58-92-20(b).
Recertification, §58-92-20(d).
Citation of act, §58-92-1.
Civil offenses.
Violations as, §58-92-30(i).
Definitions, §58-92-10.
Exceptions to provisions.
Out-of-state sales, §58-92-50.
Federal preemption, §58-92-55.
Findings of legislature, §58-92-5.
Forfeitures.
Noncomplying cigarettes, §58-92-30(e).
Implementation of provisions, §58-92-15(h).
Inspections, §§58-92-35(b), 58-92-40.
Legislative findings, §58-92-5.
Marking of cigarette packaging, §58-92-25(a),
(b).
Approval by commissioner, §58-92-25(d), (d1).
Modification of approved marking, §58-92-25(e).
Notification to commissioner of marking selected,
§58-92-25(c).
Out-of-state sales.
Exceptions to provisions, §58-92-50.
Penalties for violations, §58-92-30(a) to (d).
Disposition, §58-92-45.
Payment to commissioner, §58-92-30(h).
Rulemaking, §58-92-35(a).
Seizures.
Noncomplying cigarettes, §58-92-30(g).
Testing of cigarettes, §58-92-15(a).
Certification, §58-92-20.
Exceptions, §58-92-15(g).

FIRE-SAFETY STANDARD AND
FIREFIGHTER PROTECTION ACT —Cont'd
Testing of cigarettes —Cont'd
Methods, §58-92-15(a1) to (a5), (c), (e).
Performance standard, §58-92-15(b).
Local ordinances changing prohibited,
§58-92-15(i).
Reports.
Copies, §58-92-15(d).
Review of effectiveness, §58-92-15(f).
Title of act, §58-92-1.

FIRE SALES, §§66-76 to 66-83.
See CLOSING-OUT SALES.

FIRES AND FIRE PREVENTION.
Alarms.
False alarm, molesting alarm, §14-286.
Arson, §§14-58 to 14-69.3.
See ARSON.
Brushlands, setting fire to, §§14-136 to 14-140.1.
Building codes.
Generally.
See BUILDING CODES.
Special safety to life requirements applicable to
existing high-rise buildings, §143-138(i).
Child care facilities.
Mandatory standards for licensing, §110-91.
Visitation and inspection of centers, §110-92.
Cigarettes.
Fire-safety standard and firefighter protection act,
§§58-92-1 to 58-92-55.
See FIRE-SAFETY STANDARD AND
FIREFIGHTER PROTECTION ACT.
Colleges and universities.
Fraternities, sororities and residence halls.
Supplemental fire safety protection systems,
§§116-44.6 to 116-44.8.
Commissioner of insurance.
Education.
Duties as to, §58-79-35.
Inspection of premises, §58-79-20.
State property, §58-31-40.
Contempt.
Investigations.
Failure to comply with summons or subpoena,
§58-79-15.
Counties.
Fire fighting and prevention services, §153A-233.
Fire marshal.
Appointment, §153A-234.
Firemen's association.
Membership, §58-58-20.
Investigations.
County officers, §58-79-1.
Regulation of explosive, corrosive, inflammable or
radioactive substances, §153A-128.
Rural fire protection districts, §§69-25.1 to
69-25.17.
Service districts generally, §§153A-300 to
153A-310.
Door lock provision of building code.
Exemption permit, §§58-79-22, 143-143.4.
Dormitory fire safety, §§116-44.6 to 116-44.8.
Education, §58-79-35.
Explosives.
See EXPLOSIVES.
Fire and rescue commission, §§58-78-1 to
58-78-20.
See FIRE AND RESCUE COMMISSION.
Fire departments.
See FIREFIGHTERS AND FIRE
DEPARTMENTS.

FIRES AND FIRE PREVENTION —Cont'd
Fire-detection systems.
Molesting systems, §14-286.
Fire-extinguishing systems.
Molesting systems, §14-286.
Fire hoses.
Driving over, §20-157(d).
Penalty for violation, §20-157(g).
Property damage, §20-157(h).
Fire hydrants.
Blocking prohibited, §20-157(b).
Penalty for violation, §20-157(g).
Property damage, §20-157(h).
Fire lanes.
Parking prohibited, §20-162(b).
Fire-safety standard and firefighter protection
act, §§58-92-1 to 58-92-55.
See FIRE-SAFETY STANDARD AND
FIREFIGHTER PROTECTION ACT.
Fire trucks and vehicles generally.
See FIRE TRUCKS AND VEHICLES.
Fireworks, §§14-410 to 14-415.
Forest fires.
Generally.
See FOREST FIRES.
Fraternities.
Supplemental fire safety protection system,
§§116-44.6 to 116-44.8.
General assembly.
Evacuation of state legislative buildings and
grounds, §120-32.1A.
Grass.
Setting fire to grass, §§14-136 to 14-140.1.
Hotels and other transient lodging places,
§§58-81-5 to 58-81-15.
Building inspectors.
Powers and duties not limited, §58-81-15.
Careless or negligent setting of fires, §58-81-5.
Loss by fire.
Liability, §72-4.
Negligent or careless setting of fires, §58-81-5.
Noncompliance with provisions.
Penalty, §58-81-10.
Powers and duties of fire chiefs and building
inspectors not limited, §58-81-15.
House trailers.
Two door requirement, §66-27.5.
Insurance companies.
Confidentiality of information furnished,
§58-79-40(d).
Investigations, §§58-79-1 to 58-79-45.
Attorney general.
Authorized investigations, §58-79-1.
Forest fires.
Deputy investigators, §58-79-25.
Powers of attorney general, §§58-79-5, 58-79-10.
Right of entry, §58-79-10.
Subpoenas, §58-79-10.
Failure to comply.
Contempt, §58-79-15.
Witnesses.
Powers as to, §58-79-10.
Authorized, §58-79-1.
Combustible materials or flammable conditions,
§58-79-20.
Contempt.
Failure to comply with summons or subpoena,
§58-79-15.
County officers, §58-79-1.
Perjury.
False swearing, §58-79-10.

FIRES AND FIRE PREVENTION —Cont'd
Investigations —Cont'd
Police.
Chiefs of police, §58-79-1.
Preliminary investigation, §58-79-1.
Reports, §58-79-1.
Right of entry.
Attorney general, §58-79-10.
State bureau of investigation.
Attorney general acting through bureau,
§58-79-1.
Subpoenas.
Failure to comply.
Contempt, §58-79-15.
Powers of attorney general, §58-79-10.
Witnesses.
Powers of attorney general as to, §58-79-10.
Landlord and tenant.
Agreements to rebuild.
Construction in case of fire, §42-9.
Willful destruction by tenant, §42-11.
Leases.
Agreements to build.
Construction in case of fire, §42-9.
Lighters.
Novelty lights.
Retail sale prohibited, §66-16.1.
Matches, §§66-12 to 66-16.
Minors.
Exposing children to fire, §14-318.
Municipalities.
Fire limits, §§160A-435 to 160A-438.
Open fires regulation, §§106-940 to 106-950.
See OPEN FIRES.
Perjury.
Investigations.
False swearing to attorney general, §58-79-10.
Police.
Inspection of premises.
Chiefs of police, §58-79-20.
Investigations.
Chiefs of police, §58-79-1.
Reports.
Inspection of premises.
Commissioner of insurance, §58-79-20.
Investigations, §58-79-1.
Right of entry.
Attorney general.
Investigations, §58-79-10.
Inspection of premises, §58-79-20.
Rural fire protection districts, §§69-25.1 to
69-25.17.
See RURAL FIRE PROTECTION DISTRICTS.
Safety professionals, §§90-671 to 90-674.
Sanitary districts.
Establishment of fire department, §130A-55.
Schools.
Course of study on fire prevention, §58-79-35.
Duty of principals, §115C-525(a), (c).
Fire drills, §115C-288(d).
Fire prevention day, §58-79-35.
Inspection of schools, §§115C-288(d), 115C-525(b).
Removal of hazards, §115C-525(b).
Sororities.
Supplemental fire safety protection system,
§§116-44.6 to 116-44.8.
State bureau of investigation.
Investigations.
Attorney general acting through bureau,
§58-79-1.

FIRES AND FIRE PREVENTION —Cont'd
State fire and rescue commission, §§58-78-1 to
58-78-20.
See FIRE AND RESCUE COMMISSION.
State property.
Inspection for fire safety.
Commissioner of insurance, §58-31-40.
State volunteer fire department, §§58-80-1 to
58-80-60.
See VOLUNTEER FIRE DEPARTMENTS.
Subpoenas.
Investigations.
Failure to comply.
Contempt, §58-79-15.
Powers of attorney general, §58-79-10.
Timber, unlawful setting fire to.
Damages, §1-539.1(b).
Trespass.
Burning crops in field, §14-141.
Setting fire to grass, brushlands and woodlands,
§14-136.
Willfully or negligently setting fire to woods and
fields, §14-137.
Volunteer fire department fund, §58-87-1.
Volunteer fire departments.
See VOLUNTEER FIRE DEPARTMENTS.
Watchman, fires guarded by, §14-140.1.
Witnesses.
Investigations.
Powers of attorney general, §58-79-10.
Woodland.
Setting fire to, §§14-136 to 14-140.1.

FIRE SPRINKLER CONTRACTORS.
Generally, §§87-16 to 87-27.1.
See PLUMBING, HEATING AND FIRE
SPRINKLER CONTRACTORS.

FIRE TRUCKS AND VEHICLES.
Approach of fire department vehicle.
Motorist's duties, §20-157(a).
**Duty to drive with due regard for safety of
others,** §20-156(b).
Following too closely, §20-157(b), (c).
Penalty for violation, §20-157(g).
Property damage, §20-157(h).
Serious injury or death, causing, §20-157(i).
Highways.
Crossing median of divided highway.
When permitted, §20-140.3.
Horns and warning devices, §20-125(b).
Siren must be audible within 1,000 feet,
§§20-156(b), 20-157(a).
Siren necessary for right of way, §20-157(a).
Lights.
Electronically modulated headlamps, §20-130(d).
Red lights.
Exception to prohibition, §20-130.1(b).
Move over law.
Approach of fire department vehicle, §20-157(a).
Parked or standing on roadway and giving
warning signal.
Duties of driver approaching, §20-157(f).
**Parked or standing on roadway and giving
warning signal.**
Duties of driver approaching, §20-157(f).
Penalty for violation, §20-157(g).
Property damage, §20-157(h).
Serious injury or death, causing, §20-157(i).
Right of way, §§20-156(b), 20-157(a).
Speed, §20-145.
Duty to drive with due regard for safety of others,
§20-156(b).

FIRE TRUCKS AND VEHICLES —Cont'd
Traffic lights.
  Preempting.
    Local authority to permit, §20-169.

FIREWORKS.
Common carriers.
  Receipt, transportation, delivery in regular course
    of business, §14-410(a2).
Definitions, §14-414.
  Exceptions to definition of pyrotechnics, §14-414.
Delivery site.
  Sale deemed made at site, §14-411.
Evidence.
  Possession prima facie evidence of violation,
    §14-412.
Guidelines, testing and training.
  Individual training requirements, §58-28A-2.
  State fire marshal to adopt, §58-28A-1.
**Manufacture, purchase, sale, deal in,
  transport, possess, receive, advertise, use,
  handle, exhibit, discharge.**
  Definitions, §14-410(c).
  Unlawful.
    Exceptions, §14-410(a1).
Misdemeanor violations, §14-415.
Permissible exhibition, use, discharge,
    §14-410(a1).
  Concert or public exhibition, §14-410(a1).
    Defined, §14-410(c).
    Permits for use at public exhibitions,
      §14-413(a), (a1).
      Indoor use, §14-413(b).
        Cities authorized to grant permits by local
          act, §14-413(c).
      Proof of insurance.
        Display operator to provide, §14-413(d).
  Display operator.
    Defined, §14-410(c).
    Direct supervision and control, §14-410(a1).
    Guidelines, testing and training requirements.
      State fire marshal to adopt, §58-28A-1.
    Permit required, §§14-410(a1), 58-28A-3(a).
      Age requirement, §58-28A-3(b).
      Application fee, §58-28A-3(b).
      Duration, §58-28A-3(a).
      Examination requirement, §58-28A-3(b).
      Reciprocity, §58-82A-3(c).
      Refusal to issue, revocation, grounds,
        §58-82A-3(d).
      Requirements, §58-28A-3(b).
    Proof of insurance.
      Required for issuance of permit, §14-413(d).
    Training.
      Individual training requirements, §58-28A-2.
    Written authority from county or city required,
      §14-410(a1).
  Guidelines, testing and training requirements.
    Definitions, §58-28A-1(b).
    Individual training requirements, §58-28A-2.
    Rules, commissioner to adopt, §58-28A-1(c).
    State fire marshal to adopt, §58-28A-1(a).
  Indoor use.
    Permit for public exhibition, §14-413(b).
      Cities authorized to grant permits by local
        act, §14-413(c).
    Requirements, §14-410(a3).
  Training required, §14-410(a1).
    Individual training requirements, §58-28A-2.
  University of North Carolina, §14-410(a1).

FIREWORKS —Cont'd
Persons under age of 16.
  Sale to prohibited, §14-410(b).
Possession.
  Prima facie evidence of violations, §14-412.
**Public exhibition, licensing display operators
  and event employees, §§58-82A-1 to
    58-82A-55.**
  Administration of article, §58-82A-1.5.
  Applications for licenses, §58-82A-2.1(b).
  Assistant display operator license, §58-82A-15.
    Fees, §58-82A-20(c).
      Examinations, §58-82A-30(a).
      Renewal, §58-82A-35(a), (c).
    Qualifications, §58-82A-15(b).
    Required, §58-82A-15(a).
  Commissioner of insurance to administer,
    §58-82A-1.5(a).
    Writings under seal of commissioner, prima
      facie evidence, §58-82A-1.5(b).
  Definitions, §§58-82A-1.1, 58-82A-1(b).
  Discipline, §58-82A-50.
    Sanction and denial procedures, §58-82A-55.
  Dual license holding, §58-82A-40.
  Event employees.
    Examination fee, §58-82A-30(b).
    Qualifications, §58-82A-25.
  Examinations for licensing, §58-82A-30.
    Cheating, discipline, §58-82A-50.
    Event employees, §58-82A-25.
      Fees, §58-82A-30(b).
  Guidelines, §58-82A-1(a).
  Identification card, §58-82A-2.1(c).
  License fees, §58-82A-20.
    Applications, §58-82A-20.
    Examinations, §58-82A-30.
    Renewal, §58-82A-35(a).
  License required, §58-82A-2.1(a).
  Notice of license suspension, revocation, denial,
    §58-82A-55(b).
  Proximate audience display operator license,
    §58-82A-10.
    Fees, §58-82A-20(b).
      Examinations, §58-82A-30(a).
      Renewal, §58-82A-35(a), (c).
  Pyrotechnics display operator license, §58-82A-3.
    Fees, §58-82A-20(a).
      Examinations, §58-82A-30(a).
      Renewal, §58-82A-35(a), (c).
    Qualifications, §58-82A-3(b).
    Required, §58-82A-3(a).
  Qualifications for event employees, §58-82A-25.
    Examination fee, §58-82A-30(b).
  Reciprocity, §58-82A-45.
  Renewal of license, §58-82A-2.5.
    Fees, §58-82A-35(a), (c).
    Findings, §58-82A-35(b).
  Rule making, §58-82A-1(c).
  State fire marshal to establish safety guidelines,
    §58-82A-1.
  Suspension, revocation or refusal to issue license,
    §§58-82A-50, 58-82A-55.
    Contesting, §58-82A-55(a).
    Notice of suspension, revocation or denial,
      §58-82A-55(b).
  Terms of licenses, §58-82A-2.5.
Sale of pyrotechnics.
  Deemed at site of delivery, §14-411.

FISH AND FISHING —Cont'd
Bridges, fishing from.
Power to prohibit or regulate, §160A-302.1.
Buoys.
Damaging or injuring, §113-267.
Child support enforcement.
Forfeiture of licensing privilege, §50-13.12.
Closing forests and woodlands to fishing.
Authority of governor, §106-908.
Coastal and estuarine commercial fishing licenses, §§113-168 to 113-173.
Advance sale of licenses, §113-168.1(j).
Cancellation, §113-168.1(i).
Definitions, §113-168.
Spotter plane, §113-171.1(a).
Duration of licenses and endorsements, §113-168.1(a).
Exportation of fish and equipment.
Rules governing, §113-170.
False information, §113-168.1(i).
Fees.
Fish dealers license, §113-169.3(e), (f).
Land or sell license for vessel fishing beyond territorial waters, §113-169.5(b).
Menhaden license for nonresidents not eligible for SCFL, §113-169.
Ocean fishing piers, §113-169.4(c).
Payment of full annual license fee, §113-168.1(a).
Recreational commercial gear license, §113-173(e), (f).
Recreational fishing tournament license, §113-168.4(c).
Retired standard commercial fishing license, §113-168.3(b).
Spotter plane license, §113-171.1(b).
Standard commercial fishing licenses, §113-168.2(e).
Fish dealers license, §113-169.3.
Format, §113-168.1(e).
Fraud or deception, §113-170.2(a).
Fines, §113-170.2(b).
Importation of fish and equipment.
Rules governing, §113-170.
Ineligibility, §113-168.1(g).
Inspection.
Availability of licenses and endorsements for, §113-168.1(c).
Issuance, §113-168.1(f).
Land or sell license.
Vessel fishing beyond territorial waters, §113-169.5(a).
Fees, §113-169.5(b).
Licensed agents, §113-172(a).
Compensation.
Surcharge, §113-172(b).
Menhaden endorsements, §113-168.5(c).
Menhaden license for nonresidents, §113-169.
Nonresidents.
Reciprocal agreements, §113-170.1.
Ocean fishing piers.
Fees, §113-169.4(c).
Manager who secures license, §113-169.4(d).
Required, §113-169.4(a), (b).
Permits for gear, equipment and other specialized activities.
Commercial operations not using a vessel or transplanting oysters or clams, §113-169.1(a).
Striped bass, taking from Atlantic Ocean, §113-169.1(b).

FISH AND FISHING —Cont'd
Coastal and estuarine commercial fishing licenses —Cont'd
Possession of fisheries resources.
Rules as to, §113-170.5.
Violations as to, §113-170.5.
Primary situs of vessel in state, §113-168.6(a).
Prohibited acts with respect to, §113-170.5.
Reciprocity, §113-170.1.
Recordkeeping.
Confidentiality of records, §113-170.3(c).
Fraud or deception as to records, §113-170.2.
Refusal or neglect to keep records and accounts, §113-170.3(b).
Requirements, §113-170.3(a).
Recreational commercial gear license, §113-173.
Recreational fishing tournament license, §113-168.4(c).
Registration of vessels with division, §113-168.6.
Renewal, §113-168.1(f).
Replacement, §113-168.1(h).
Required, §113-168.1(b).
Fish dealers license, §113-169.3(c), (d).
Recreational commercial gear license, §113-173(a).
Standard commercial fishing licenses, §113-168.2(a).
Residence.
No dual residency, §113-168.1(d).
Retired standard commercial fishing license, §113-168.3.
Rules as to possession, transportation and disposition, §113-170.4.
Sale of fish.
Nonprofit recreational fishing tournament.
Fish taken in connection with, §113-168.4(c).
Requirements, §113-168.4(a), (b).
Shellfish endorsement, §113-168.5(d).
Shellfish license for North Carolina residents without SCFL, §113-169.2.
Specialized activities.
Permits, §113-169.1.
Spotter planes, §113-171.1.
Standard commercial fishing license, §113-168.2.
Surrender of cancelled license, §113-168.1(i).
Suspension or revocation, §113-171(a), (b).
Administrative review, §113-171(e).
Contested case, §113-171(f).
Convictions which may not be considered, §113-171(h).
Individuals in responsible positions of control.
Disclosure of identity, §113-171(g).
Notice, §113-171(d).
Reissuance, §113-171(c).
Transportation of fisheries resources.
Prohibited acts as to, §113-170.5.
Rules as to, §113-170.5.
Coastal fisheries.
Monitoring water quality, §113-221.3(a), (b).
Promotion of coastal fisheries and seafood industry, §§113-308 to 113-315.9.
See SEAFOOD INDUSTRY AND COASTAL FISHERIES PROMOTION.
Coastal habitat protection plans.
Department of environment and natural resources, §143B-279.8.
Coastal recreational fishing licenses, §§113-174 to 113-174.5.
Assignment or transfer prohibited, §113-174.1(c).
Authorization, §113-174.2(a1).

FISH AND FISHING —Cont'd
Coastal recreational fishing licenses —Cont'd
Biological data and survey programs.
  Compliance required, §113-174.1(g).
Blocks of 10-day licenses.
  Failure of vessel owner to comply with
    provisions, §113-174.5(e).
  Fee, §113-174.5(b).
  Recordkeeping by vessel owner, §113-174.5(c).
  Reporting requirements, §113-174.5(d).
  Terms of license, §113-174.5(a).
  Who may purchase, §113-174.5(a).
Compliance with applicable laws required,
    §113-174.1(a1).
Definitions, §113-174.
Exemptions, §113-174.2(d).
False, fraudulent or misleading statements.
  Cancellation of license, §113-174.1(f).
For hire blanket license, §113-174.3(a), (b).
Fourth of July.
  Free fishing day, §113-174.1(a2).
Free fishing day.
  Fourth of July, §113-174.1(a2).
Lost or destroyed licenses.
  Replacement issued, §113-174.1(h).
Ocean fishing pier blanket license, §113-174.4.
Recreational fishing defined, §113-174.
Required to engage in recreational fishing,
    §113-174.1(a).
Sale of fish caught prohibited, §113-174.1(b).
Types issued, fees, duration, §113-174.2(c).
  For hire blanket license, §113-174.3(a), (b).
  Ocean fishing pier blanket license, §113-174.4.
Coastal reserves, §113A-129.2(a).
Coastal wetlands.
Orders to control activities, §113-230(a), (b).
  Dredging permits.
    Powers and duties of department not repealed
      by section, §113-230(h).
  Eminent domain.
    Taking fee of land order inapplicable to,
      §113-230(g).
  Recording copy, §113-230(c).
  Restraining violations, §113-230(e).
  Unreasonable exercise of police power,
    §113-230(f).
  Violations, §113-230(b).
Commercial fishing.
Boat identification numbers.
  Renewal of number, §75A-5.1.
Coastal and estuarine commercial fishing licenses,
    §§113-168 to 113-173.
Penalties, §113-187.
Promotion of coastal fisheries and seafood
    industry, §§113-308 to 113-315.9.
Recreational commercial gear license, §113-173.
Registration of vessels with division,
    §113-168.6(b).
  Annual fee, §113-168.6(c).
  Expiration, §113-168.6(d).
  Place of registration, §113-168.6(d).
  Replacement, §113-168.6(e).
  Unlawful to use unregistered vessel,
    §113-168.6(b).
  Vessels with primary situs in state,
    §113-168.6(a).
Retired standard commercial fishing license,
    §113-168.3.
  Applicability of SCFL provisions, §113-168.3(a).
  Assignment prohibited, §113-168.3(d).
  Eligibility, §113-168.3(b).

FISH AND FISHING —Cont'd
Commercial fishing —Cont'd
Retired standard commercial fishing license
    —Cont'd
  Fees, §113-168.3(b).
  Transfer, §113-168.3(c).
Sales and use tax.
  Exemption of commercial fisheries, §105-164.13.
Spotter planes, §113-171.1.
Standard commercial fishing license, §113-168.2.
  Assignment, §113-168.2(f).
  Fees, §113-168.2(e).
  Identification as commercial fishermen,
    §113-168.2(h).
  Identification, license to serve as, §113-168.2(h).
  One vessel only to be in use, §113-168.2(a1).
  Recordkeeping by fish dealers, §113-168.2(i).
  Recordkeeping requirements, §113-168.2(i).
  Requirement, §113-168.2(a).
  Transfers, §113-168.2(g).
Confiscation.
Proofs and instrumentalities of offenses in
    question, §113-137(i).
Cooperative agreements.
Department of environment and natural
    resources.
  Authority to enter into, §113-224.
Wildlife resources commission, §113-305.
Costs.
Replacement costs of resources, §113-267.
Councils.
Mid-Atlantic fishery management council.
  North Carolina members, §113-260.
South Atlantic fishery management council.
  North Carolina members, §113-259.
Creel limits.
Authority of commission to regulate, §113-292(a).
Cultivation of shellfish, §§113-201 to 113-210.
See SHELLFISH.
Currituck county game commission.
Authority not repealed or abridged by limitation
    upon local regulations, §113-133.1(d).
Dams.
Inspecting plans and specifications of dams,
    §113-263.
Keeping open fishways in dams, §113-293(c).
Obstructing rivers or creeks.
  Unlawful, §113-293.
Dare county game and wildlife commission.
Authority not repealed or abridged by limitation
    upon local regulations, §113-133.1(d).
Dealer's license, §113-169.3.
Definitions, §§113-127 to 113-130.
Activities of public, §113-130.
Agencies, §113-128.
  Powers, §113-128.
Application of article, §113-127.
Coastal and estuarine commercial fishing licenses,
    §113-168.
  Spotter plane, §113-171.1(a).
Dredging.
  Permits, §113-229(n).
Fishermen's economic development program,
    §113-315.17.
Marine, estuarine and wildlife resources,
    §113-129.
Marine fisheries compact, §113-251.
Promotion of coastal fisheries and seafood
    industry, §113-308.
Public activities, §113-130.
Public trust resources, §113-131(e).

FISH AND FISHING —Cont'd
Definitions —Cont'd
  Resources, §113-129.
Department of environment and natural resources.
  Administrative authority, §113-226(a).
  Adoption of federal regulations, §113-228.
  Cooperative agreements, §113-224.
  Duties.
    Generally, §113-181(a).
    Requirement to carry out duties, §113-181(b).
  Fishery management plans, §113-182.1.
  Powers, §§113-131(b), 113-226(a).
    Generally, §113-181(a).
  Proclamations, §113-221.1.
  Rules and regulations, §113-221.
  Taking fish in manner prohibited.
    Authority, §113-261(c).
Disabled sportsman program, §113-296.
  Motorized all-terrain vehicles.
    Use by persons qualified under program, §20-171.26.
Discharge of oil or hazardous substances.
  Damage to fish, liability, §143-215.90(a) to (c).
Dolphins.
  Protection of porpoises, §113-189(b).
Drainage districts.
  Conservation and replacement of fish and wildlife habitat, §156-69.
Dredging permits, §113-229.
Drugs, taking fish by.
  Permits issued by department and commission authorizing, §113-261(b).
  Prohibited, §113-262(a), (b).
Electricity, taking fish by.
  Permits issued by department and commission authorizing, §113-261(b).
  Prohibited, §113-262(a), (b).
Eminent domain.
  Coastal wetlands, orders to control activities.
    Taking fee of land order inapplicable to, §113-230(g).
Enjoyment of marine and estuarine resources, §113-133.
Equipment, requlation.
  Authority of commission, §113-292(a).
Evidence.
  Possession of illegally killed fish as evidence, §113-262(b).
  Replacement costs of resources, §113-267.
  Unlawful possession of game fish, §113-302(a).
  Warning tickets not to constitute evidence of commission of offense, §113-140(g).
Explosives, taking fish by.
  Permits issued by department and commission authorizing, §113-261(b).
  Prohibited, §113-262(a), (b).
Federal laws and regulations.
  Adoption by wildlife resources commission, §113-307.
  Legislative assent to specific federal acts, §113-307.1.
Fees.
  Arrest, §§113-222, 113-303.
  Licenses. See within this heading, "Licenses."
  Service of process, §§113-222, 113-303.
  State forests.
    Collection of reasonable fees by department of agriculture and consumer services, §106-877(b).
    License fees for hunting and fishing on government-owned property unaffected, §106-881.

FISH AND FISHING —Cont'd
Fees —Cont'd
  State parks.
    Collection of reasonable fees by department of environment and natural resources, §113-35(b).
  Witnesses, §§113-222, 113-303.
Felony convictions.
  Forfeiture of licensing privilege, §15A-1331A.
Fines.
  Coastal and estuarine commercial fishing licenses.
    Fraud or deception as to licenses, permits or records, §113-170.2(b).
  Refusal to stop in obedience to directions of inspector or director, §113-136(j).
Fish-cultural stations.
  U.S. acquisition of land for, §104-1.
Fish dealer's license, §113-169.3.
  Application.
    Replacement license, §113-169.3(h).
  Bait operations, §113-169.3(f1).
  Eligibility, §113-169.3(a).
  Fees, §113-169.3(e), (f).
  Finfish dealer license, §113-169.3(f1).
  Purchase and sale of fish, §113-169.3(i).
  Replacement license, §113-169.3(h).
  Requirement, §113-169.3(c).
    Exceptions, §113-169.3(d).
  Transfer prohibited, §113-169.3(j).
Fishermen's economic development program, §§113-315.15 to 113-315.19.
Fishery management plans.
  Achieving sustainable harvest under plan, §113-182.1(g).
  Advisory council, §113-182.1(c).
  Consultation with regional advisory committees regarding preparation, §113-182.1(c1).
  Generally, §113-182.1(a), (b).
  Limiting participation in fishery, recommending to general assemblies, §113-182.1(g).
  Monitoring of progress, §113-182.1(e).
  Revision, §113-182.1(d).
  Rules to implement, §113-182.1(f).
  Temporary management measures to supplement existing plan, §113-182.1(e1).
Fishery resource grant program.
  Application for grant, §113-200(d).
  Award process, §113-200(f).
  Creation, §113-200(a).
  Grants committee, §113-200(e1).
  Priorities, §113-200(b).
  Reports, §113-200(h), (i).
  Restrictions on grants, §113-200(g).
  Review process, §113-200(e).
  Soliciting proposals, procedure, §113-200(c).
Fishing guide licenses.
  Fees, §113-270.4(b).
  Nonresidents, §113-270.4(a).
  Qualifications and duties, §113-270.4(c).
  Required, §113-270.4(a).
Fishing tournaments.
  Recreational fishing tournament license, §113-168.4(c).
Fish inspectors and protectors.
  Arrest warrants, search warrants, orders for arrest.
    Service by inspectors, §113-136(e).
  Arrest without warrant, §113-136(b).
  Conflicts of interest, §113-225.
  Exhibiting upon request items required to be carried, §113-136(k).

FISH AND FISHING —Cont'd
Fish inspectors and protectors —Cont'd
Jurisdiction, §113-136(b).
Peace officer powers, §113-136(a).
Searches within cartilage or living quarters of
    vessel.
    Unreasonable searches and seizures prohibited,
        §113-136(l).
Search on arrest, §113-137(a).
Seizure of lawfully discovered evidence,
    §113-137(b), (c).
    Leaving in possession of defendant, §113-137(f).
    Return of property to owner, §113-137(h).
    Safeguarding pending trial, §113-137(e).
    Sale of perishable fish prior to trial, §113-137(g).
    Summary disposition of live or perishable fish
        or wildlife, §113-137(d).
Stopping temporarily persons or motor vehicles,
    §113-136(f), (g), (j).
Warning tickets, §113-140.
Warrantless arrests, §113-136(a).
Fish kills.
Discharge of oil or hazardous substances.
    Liability, §143-215.90(a) to (c).
Fish restoration and management projects.
Legislative assent to federal acts, §113-307.1(c).
Fishways.
Keeping open fishways in dams, §113-293(c).
Forests and woodlands.
Governor's authority to close to hunting, fishing
    and trapping, §106-908.
Forfeiture of licensing privilege.
Failure to pay child support, §50-13.12.
Felony conviction, §15A-1331A.
Fraud.
Coastal and estuarine commercial fishing licenses,
    §113-170.2.
Free fishing day.
July fourth, §113-276(m).
Guides.
Licenses, §113-270.4.
Harassment of persons taking wildlife
    resources, §113-295.
Hatchery or other aquaculture operation.
Obstructing or polluting flow of water into
    hatcheries, §113-265(a).
Robbing or injuring.
    Destroying or injuring aquaculture facility,
        §113-269(d).
    Misdemeanors, §113-269(e), (f).
    Notarized written authorization for taking,
        §113-269(h).
    Receiving or possessing fish or aquatic species
        stolen from aquaculture facility,
        §113-269(c).
    Restitution to victim, §113-269(g).
    Shellfish lease defined, §113-269(a).
    Taking fish or aquatic species being cultivated
        or reared by owner, §113-269(b).
Hearings.
Coastal wetlands.
    Orders to control activities, §113-230(b).
Dredging permits, §113-229.
Hook-and-line licenses in inland and joint
    fishing waters, §113-271.
Hull insurance, protection and indemnity
    clubs, §§58-20-1 to 58-20-40.
See HULL INSURANCE, PROTECTION AND
    INDEMNITY CLUBS.
Income tax credit.
Donations of real property for fish and wildlife
    conservation, §105-151.12.

FISH AND FISHING —Cont'd
Indian tribes recognized under chapter 71A.
Inapplicability of license provisions.
    Hunting, trapping and fishing on tribal lands,
        §113-276(11).
Injunctions.
Buoys, nets, markers, stakes, etc.
    Robbing or injuring, §113-268(e).
Encroachment upon, usurpation or otherwise
    violating public trust rights of people,
    §113-131(c).
Interference with taking of wildlife resources,
    §113-295(b).
Inspections.
Licensed or commercial premises, §113-302.1.
Insurance.
Hull insurance, protection and indemnity clubs.
    See HULL INSURANCE, PROTECTION AND
        INDEMNITY CLUBS.
July fourth.
Free fishing day, §113-276(m).
Jurisdiction of marine fisheries commission.
Marine resources in Atlantic Ocean, §113-134.1.
Jurisdiction of marine fisheries inspectors,
    §113-136(b).
Land or sell license.
Vessel fishing beyond territorial waters,
    §113-169.5.
Law enforcement officers.
Jurisdiction of fishing agencies not limitation on
    officers authority, §113-132(f).
Licenses.
Armed forces.
    Exemptions, §113-276(12).
Child support enforcement.
    Forfeiture of privilege, §50-13.12.
    Suspension or revocation of fishing licenses.
        Delinquent obligors or individuals not in
            compliance with orders, §§110-142,
            110-142.2.
Coastal and estuarine commercial fishing licenses,
    §§113-168 to 113-173.
Coastal recreational fishing licenses, §§113-174 to
    113-174.5.
Collection licenses.
    Issuance by wildlife resources commission,
        §113-272.4(a).
    Assistants in taking, utilization by licensees,
        authorization, §113-272.4(e).
    Authority delegated to executive director,
        §113-272.4(b).
    Duration period, §113-272.4(c).
    Fee, §113-272.4(c).
    Restrictions imposed, §113-272.4(d).
Combination hunting and inland fishing licenses,
    §113-270.1C(a), (b).
Duration of validity, §113-270.1B(b).
Exemptions and exceptions, §113-276(c) to (n).
Fees.
    Coastal and estuarine commercial fishing
        licenses.
    Fish dealer's license, §113-169.3(e), (f).
    Land or sell license for vessel fishing beyond
        territorial waters, §113-169.5(b).
    Menhaden license for nonresidents not
        eligible for SCFL, §113-169.
    Ocean fishing piers, §113-169.4(c).
    Payment of full annual license fee,
        §113-168.1(a).
    Recreational commercial gear license,
        §113-173(e), (f).

FISH AND FISHING —Cont'd
Licenses —Cont'd
Fees —Cont'd
Coastal and estuarine commercial fishing
licenses —Cont'd
Recreational fishing tournament license,
§113-168.4(c).
Retired standard commercial fishing license,
§113-168.3(b).
Spotter plane license, §113-171.1(b).
Standard commercial fishing licenses,
§113-168.2(e).
Coastal recreational fishing licenses,
§113-174.2(c).
For hire blanket license, §113-174.3(a).
Ocean fishing pier blanket license, §113-174.4.
Collection licenses, §113-272.4(c).
Combination hunting and inland fishing
licenses, §113-270.1C(b).
Disposition of license funds, §113-306.
Fishing guides, §113-270.4.
Government-owned property.
Collecting fees for licenses for fishing on,
§113-39.
Hook-and-line licenses in inland and joint
fishing waters, §113-271(d).
Lifetime licenses.
Administrative fee for issuing, §113-272.3(d).
Salt water fishing license, §113-174.2(c).
Special device license, §113-272.2(c).
Special trout license, §113-272(d).
Unified hunting and fishing licenses,
§113-351(c).
Felony convictions.
Forfeiture of privilege after conviction,
§15A-1331A.
Fish dealers license, §113-169.3.
Free fishing day.
Fourth day of July, §113-276(m).
Guides, §113-270.4.
Hook-and-line licenses and inland and joint
fishing waters.
Fees, §113-271(d).
Requirements generally, §113-271(a).
Indian tribes recognized under chapter 71A.
Inapplicability of provisions.
Hunting, trapping and fishing on tribal lands,
§113-276(l1).
Inland fishing licenses.
Administrative control over licensees and
permittees.
Applicability of section, §113-276.2(a).
Investigations of person subject to
administrative control, §113-276.2(i).
Notice upon refusing to issue or reissue,
§113-276.2(d).
Orders placing restrictions on licensees or
permittees, §113-276.2(j).
Reapplication after refusal of issuance or
reissuance, §113-276.2(h).
Refusal to issue, §113-276.2(b).
Reissuance review, §113-276.2(c).
Return upon revocation, §113-276.2(g).
Revocation, §113-276.2(e).
Bow nets.
Use by other than licensee, §113-276(g).
Collection licenses, §113-272.4.
Conviction of suspension offense.
Mandatory suspension of license or permit,
§113-276.3.

FISH AND FISHING —Cont'd
Licenses —Cont'd
Inland fishing licenses —Cont'd
Discretionary revocation or suspension of
license or permit by court, §113-277(a), (a1).
Concurrent or consecutive suspension,
§113-277(a2).
Conviction defined, §113-277(a3).
Criminal offenses during period of suspension
or revocation, §113-277(b).
Surrender of license or permit, §113-277(a4).
Exemptions and exceptions, §113-276(c) to (n).
Felony convictions.
Forfeiture of privilege after conviction,
§15A-1331A.
General provisions respecting licenses and
permits issued by wildlife resources
commission, §113-275.
Landing nets, §113-272.3(b).
Special device license not required,
§113-276(f).
Lawfully authorized techniques, §113-272.3(a).
Lifetime licenses, §113-272.3(c), (d).
Mandatory suspension of license or permit.
Conviction of suspension offense,
§113-276.3(a).
Beginning of period of suspension,
§113-276.3(a).
Discretionary court suspension supersedes
section's provisions, §113-276.3(e).
Offenses requiring suspension,
§113-276.3(d).
Period of suspension, §113-276.3(d).
Reporting convictions and suspensions,
§113-276.3(c).
Surrender of licenses and permits,
§113-276.3(b).
Permits.
Suspension or revocation.
Discretionary revocation or suspension by
court, §113-277.
Mandatory suspension for offenses,
§113-276.3.
Regulatory authority of commission as to
requirements and exemptions, §113-276.1.
Revocation or suspension of license or permit.
Discretionary revocation or suspension by
court, §113-277.
Mandatory suspension for conviction of
offense, §113-276.3.
Special device licenses, §113-272.2(a), (c).
Special trout licenses, §113-272(a) to (e).
Trout licenses.
Mountain trouts waters, §113-272(a) to (e).
July fourth.
Free fishing day, §113-276(m).
Land or sell license.
Vessel fishing beyond territorial waters,
§113-169.5.
License agents.
Informational materials prepared by
commission.
Distribution to agents, §113-301.1(a).
Mail, issuance by.
Information on laws and regulations applicable
to type of license.
Furnishing licensee, §113-301.1(b).
Marine fisheries commission.
Authority generally, §113-182(a), (b).
Exemptions for certain organized fishing events,
§143B-289.52(i).

FISH AND FISHING —Cont'd
Licenses —Cont'd
Medicaid, food and nutrition services or work first family recipients.
Resident subsistence unified inland/coastal recreational fishing license waiver, §113-351(d).
Migrant farm workers.
Resident privileges, §113-276(j).
Organized fishing events.
Exemption of individuals participating.
Rules, adoption by commission, §§113-276(n), 143B-289.52(i).
Probation.
Purchase of certain licenses as condition, §15A-1343(b1).
Recreational commercial gear license, §113-173.
Recreational fishing tournament license, §113-168.4(c).
Required, §113-270.1B(a).
Resident subsistence unified inland/coastal recreational fishing license waiver, §113-351(d).
Retired standard commercial fishing license, §113-168.3.
Saltwater fishing license, §§113-174 to 113-174.5.
Assignment or transfer of license.
Prohibition, §113-174.1(c).
Biological sampling and survey programs.
Licensed person to comply, §113-174.1(g).
Blocks of 10-day licenses, §113-174.5.
Cancellation, §113-174.1(f).
Definitions, §113-174.
Fees, types of licenses, §113-174.2(c).
Persons 18 or younger enrolled in school.
Exemption, §113-174.2(d).
Required for recreational fishing in coastal waters, §113-174.1(a).
Recreational fishing defined, §113-174.
Sale of fish caught.
License does not authorize, §113-174.1(b).
Separation of revenues.
Precondition for receiving funds under cooperative program, §113-307.1(d).
Shellfish license for North Carolina residents without SCFL, §113-169.2.
Special device licenses.
Inland fishing licenses, §113-272.2(a), (c).
Suspension, revocation and reissuance.
Conviction of suspension offense, §113-276.3.
Discretionary revocation or suspension by court, §113-277.
Mandatory suspension, §113-276.3.
Trout licenses.
Mountain trout waters, §113-272(a) to (e).
Unified hunting and fishing licenses.
Definitions, §113-351(a).
General provisions governing, §113-351(b).
Resident subsistence unified inland/coastal recreational fishing license waiver, §113-351(d).
Types, fees, duration, §113-351(c).
Waivers, §113-351(b).
Resident subsistence unified inland/coastal recreational fishing license waiver, §113-351(d).
Local coastal laws.
Abolition, §113-133.
Local regulation of wildlife resources.
Abolition of local coastal fishing laws, §113-133.
Limitations upon, §113-133.1(c).

FISH AND FISHING —Cont'd
Local regulation of wildlife resources —Cont'd
Repeal generally.
Of special, local and private acts, §113-133.1(b).
Repeal specifically of local acts, §113-133.1(g).
Retention of specific local acts or portions of local acts, §113-133.1(e).
Review by wildlife resources commission of local acts, §113-133.1(f).
Magistrates.
Powers in cases involving fishing offenses, §7A-273.
Marine and estuarine resources belong to people of state, §113-131(a).
Marine fisheries commission.
Generally, §§143B-289.50 to 143B-289.61.
See MARINE FISHERIES COMMISSION.
Marine fisheries compact, §§113-251 to 113-258.
Marine fisheries endowment fund, §143B-289.58.
Marine resources endowment fund, §§113-175, 113-175.5.
Marine resources fund, §§113-175, 113-175.1.
Menhaden.
Coastal and estuarine commercial fishing licenses.
Menhaden endorsements, §113-168.5(c).
Menhaden license for nonresidents, §113-169.
Mid-Atlantic fishery management council.
North Carolina members.
Number of members from state, §113-260(a).
Principal state official with marine fishery management responsibility, first council member, §113-260(b).
Selection of other members from state, §113-260(c).
Migrant farm workers.
Resident privileges, §113-276(j).
Monitoring water quality of coastal fishing waters, §113-221.3(a), (b).
Motor vehicles.
Temporary stops by inspectors or protectors, §113-136(f), (g), (j).
Nets.
Bow nets.
Use by other than licensee, §113-276(g).
Destroying or damaging, §113-268(b) to (e).
Landing nets.
Special device license not required, §113-276(f).
Obstructing rivers or creeks.
Unlawful, §113-293.
Taking fish from nets to use as bait without owner's permission, §113-268(a), (d), (e).
Nonresidents.
Coastal and estuarine commercial fishing licenses.
Reciprocal agreements, §113-170.1.
Fishing guide licenses, §113-270.4(a).
North Carolina aquariums, §§143B-289.40 to 143B-289.44.
See NORTH CAROLINA AQUARIUMS.
Nuisance zoological or botanical species.
Authority of commission to regulate, §113-292(d).
Nurseries.
Obstructing or polluting flow of water into nurseries, §113-265(a).
Obstructing rivers or creeks, §113-293.
Ocean fishing piers.
Coastal and estuarine commercial fishing licenses, §113-169.4.
Coastal recreational fishing license, §113-174.4.
Fishing near piers, §113-185(a).

FISH AND FISHING —Cont'd
Opening and closing seasons.
Authority of commission to regulate, §113-292(b).
Organized fishing events.
Exemption of individuals participating from
license provisions.
Rules, adoption by commission, §§113-276(n),
143B-289.52(i).
Oysters and clams generally.
See SHELLFISH.
Peace officers.
Inspectors granted powers of, §113-136(a).
Permits.
Administrative control of permittees, §113-276.2.
Dredging, §113-229.
Drugs, electricity, explosives or poisons.
Authorizing fish to be taken by use of,
§113-261(b).
Major and minor developments.
Issuance, §113-229(c1).
Suspension or revocation by courts, §113-277.
Pesticide use, §113-300.1.
Piers.
Fishing near piers, §113-185(a).
Ocean fishing pier.
Coastal and estuarine commercial fishing
licenses, §113-169.4.
Coastal recreational fishing license, §113-174.4.
Poisons and pesticides.
Use, §113-300.1.
Poison, taking fish by.
Permits issued by department and commission
authorizing, §113-261(b).
Prohibited, §113-262(a), (b).
Pollution control.
Hatcheries.
Obstructing or polluting flow of water into
hatcheries, §113-265(a).
Throwing fish offal into waters, §113-265(b).
Porpoises.
Protection of porpoises, §113-189(b).
Posted property.
Trespassing upon posted property, §§14-159.6 to
14-159.10.
See TRESPASS.
Private ponds.
Regulation of fish in connection with.
Authority of commission, §113-292(c).
Property of another.
Hunting and fishing on registered property of
another, §§113-281 to 113-287.
Hunting, fishing or trapping on posted property,
§§14-159.6 to 14-159.10.
Public lands.
Fishing licenses.
Fees.
Collecting fees for licenses for fishing on
government-owned property, §113-39.
Nonresidents of counties in which state lakes
are situated, §146-19.
Public trust resources.
Defined, §113-131(e).
Public trust rights.
No adverse possession, §1-45.1.
Reciprocity.
Agreements generally, §113-223.
Licenses, §113-304.
Coastal and estuarine commercial fishing
licenses, §113-170.1.
Recreational commercial gear license.
Assignment prohibited, §113-173(h).

FISH AND FISHING —Cont'd
Recreational commercial gear license —Cont'd
Authorized commercial gear, §113-173(c).
Availability for inspection, §113-173(g).
Exemptions, §113-173(j).
Fees, §113-173(e), (f).
Purchase, §113-173(d).
Renewal, §113-173(d).
Replacement license, §113-173(e).
Reporting requirements, §113-173(i).
Required, §113-173(a).
Sale of fish prohibited, §113-173(b).
Transfer prohibited, §113-173(h).
Restitution.
Robbing or injuring hatcheries and other
aquaculture operation, §113-269(g).
Restrictions, new rules, adopting.
Notification to public, §113-301.1(c), (d).
Revisions of subchapter.
General statement of purpose and effect,
§113-316.
Rules and regulations.
Adoption, §§113-221(a), 113-228.
Affected persons to keep themselves informed,
§113-221(f).
Copies, §113-221(b).
Effective dates, §113-221(d).
Federal laws and regulations.
Adoption, §113-307.
Legislative assent to specific federal acts,
§113-307.1.
Judicial notice of codification of regulations,
§113-221(g).
Notification to members of general public.
New laws and rules affecting public, §113-301.1.
Penalties for violations, §113-187.
Publication, §113-221(c).
Wildlife resources commission.
Violations as misdemeanors, §113-135(a) to (c).
Sale of fish.
Civil penalties, §113-191(c) to (g).
Criminal penalties, §113-191(a), (b).
Nonprofit recreational fishing tournament.
Fish taken in connection with, §113-168.4(c).
Requirements, §113-168.4(a), (b).
Seized or confiscated property, §113-137(i).
Seized perishable or seasonable fish, §113-137(g).
Unlawful sale of fish, §113-183(a), (b).
Sales and use tax.
Commercial fishermen.
Exemptions, §105-164.13.
Salt water fishing license, §§113-174 to 113-174.5.
Scrap fishing.
Measures for fish scrap and oil, §113-186.
Prohibited, §113-185(b).
Seafood.
Promotion of industry generally, §§113-308 to
113-315.9.
See SEAFOOD INDUSTRY AND COASTAL
FISHERIES PROMOTION.
Shellfish generally.
See SHELLFISH.
Searches and seizures.
Exhibiting upon request by inspector of items
required to be carried, §113-136(k).
Search on arrest by inspector or protector,
§113-137(a).
Seizure of lawfully discovered evidence by
inspectors or protectors, §113-137(b), (c).
Leaving property in possession of defendant,
§113-137(f).

FISH AND FISHING —Cont'd
Searches and seizures —Cont'd
    Seizure of lawfully discovered evidence by
        inspectors or protectors —Cont'd
        Return to owner, §113-137(h).
        Safeguarding pending trial, §113-137(a).
        Sale of perishable or seasonable fish prior to
            trial, §113-137(g).
        Sale of seized property, §113-137(i) to (k).
        Summary disposition of live or perishable fish
            or wildlife, §113-137(d).
    Service of search warrants by inspectors and
        protectors, §113-136(e).
    Temporary stops by inspectors or protectors,
        §113-136(f), (g), (j).
    Unreasonable searches and seizures prohibited,
        §113-136(l).
Seasons.
    Authority of commission to regulate, §113-292(a),
        (b).
Sea turtles.
    Protection of sea turtles, §113-189(a).
Service of process.
    Fees, §§113-222, 113-303.
    Service by inspectors and protectors.
        Arrest warrants, search warrants, orders for
            arrest, etc., §113-136(e).
Shellfish.
    General provisions.
        See SHELLFISH.
**Shellfish license for North Carolina residents
    without SCFL,** §113-169.2.
Size limits.
    Authority of commission to regulate, §113-292(a).
South Atlantic fishery management council.
    North Carolina members.
        Number of members from state, §113-259(a).
        Principal state official with marine fishery
            management responsibility, first council
            member, §113-259(b).
        Selection of other members from state,
            §113-259(c).
Special conservation officers.
    Jurisdiction and powers generally, §113-138(d).
    Law enforcement powers, §113-138(a).
    Limitation on exercise of authority, §113-138(b).
    Specification of particular officers or class of
        officers upon whom powers conferred,
        §113-138(c).
Spotter planes, §113-171.1(b).
    Defined, §113-171.1(a).
    Unlawful activities, §113-171.1(c), (d).
Standard weight and measure, §81A-42.
State auditor.
    Marine fisheries commission.
        Examination of accounts and books by auditor,
            §113-257.
State budget act.
    Atlantic states marine fisheries commission.
        Applicability of provisions, §113-258.
State fish.
    Channel bass, §145-6.
State forests.
    Collection of reasonable fees by department of
        agriculture and consumer services,
        §106-877(b).
    License fees for hunting and fishing on
        government-owned property unaffected,
        §106-881.
State parks.
    Collection of reasonable fees by department of
        environment and natural resources,
        §113-35(b).

FISH AND FISHING —Cont'd
Statutes.
    Repeal of certain public, public-local, special and
        private acts, §113-377.8.
Striped bass.
    Coastal and estuarine commercial fishing licenses.
        Permits for taking striped bass from Atlantic
            Ocean, §113-169.1(b).
    Suspending or extending hook and line season.
        Authority of commission, §113-292(c1).
Subpoenas.
    Service by inspectors or protectors, §113-136(e).
Taking of land without compensation.
    Coastal wetlands, orders to control activities,
        §113-230(f).
Transitional provisions.
    Purpose of effect of revisions, §113-316.
Transportation of fish.
    Unlawful transportation, §113-183(a), (b).
Trash fishing.
    Prohibited, §113-185(b).
Trespass.
    Hunting, fishing or trapping on "posted" property,
        §§14-159.6 to 14-159.10.
Trout licenses.
    Public mountain trout waters, §113-272(a) to (e).
Turtles.
    Protection of sea turtles, §113-189(a).
Unified hunting and fishing licenses, §113-351.
United States agencies.
    Taking fish in manner prohibited.
        Authority, §113-261(c).
Unlawful possession of game fish.
    Prima facies evidence possession for purposes of
        resale, §113-302(a).
**Unlawful possession, transportation and sale
    of fish,** §113-183(a), (b).
U.S. fish and wildlife service officers.
    Authorized to enforce criminal laws, §15A-406.
Venue.
    Buoys, nets, markers, stakes, etc.
        Robbing or injuring.
            Injunctive relief to restrain, §113-268(e).
Violations.
    Commercial fishing violations, §113-187.
    Unlawful possession, transportation and sale of
        fish, §113-183(a), (b).
Warning tickets.
    Accounting for and recording of tickets,
        §113-140(e).
    Conditions for issuance, §113-140(c).
    Evidence of commission of offense.
        Tickets not to constitute, §113-140(g).
    Inappropriate issuance, §113-140(d).
    Issuance by inspectors or protectors, §113-140(a).
    Powers of inspectors, protectors or law
        enforcement officers not restricted,
        §113-140(f).
    Standards for issuance, §113-140(b).
Water quality of coastal fishing waters.
    Monitoring, §113-221.3(a).
    Monitoring water quality, §113-221.3(b).
**Watersheds of navigable streams, protection
    of.**
    Legislative assent to specific federal acts,
        §113-307.1(a).
Weights and measures.
    Fish scrap and oil, §113-186.
Wildlife protectors.
    Enforcement authority generally, §113-136.
    Jurisdiction, §113-136(c).

FISH AND FISHING —Cont'd
Wildlife resources commission.
Administrative authority, §113-306(a).
Authority in regulating inland fishing, §113-292(a)
to (e).
Cooperative agreements, §113-305.
Delegation of powers, §113-306(c).
Federal laws and regulations.
Adoption, §113-307.
Jurisdiction, §113-132.
Notification to public affected by laws and rules,
§113-301.1.
Poisons and pesticides.
Use, §113-300.1.
Powers, §113-131(b).
Reciprocal agreements, §113-304.
Rules and regulations.
Violations as misdemeanors, §113-135(a) to (c).
Taking fish in manner prohibited.
Authority, §113-261(c).
Wildlife restoration projects.
Legislative assent to specific federal acts,
§113-307.1(b).
Witnesses.
Fees, §§113-222, 113-303.

FISH AND GAME.
Fishing generally.
See FISH AND FISHING.
Hunting generally.
See HUNTING AND WILDLIFE.
Trapping generally.
See TRAPPING.

FISHERMEN'S ECONOMIC DEVELOPMENT
PROGRAM, §§113-315.15 to 113-315.19.
Authorization to establish, §113-315.18.
Citation of article, §113-315.15.
Definitions, §113-315.17.
Establishment authorized, §113-315.18.
Legislative findings, §113-315.16.
Personnel needs, §113-315.19.
Purpose of article, §113-315.16.
Short title, §113-315.15.

FISHING GUIDES.
Licenses, §113-270.4.

FISHING LICENSES.
See FISH AND FISHING.

FISHING PIERS.
Fishing near piers, §113-185(a).
Ocean fishing pier.
Coastal and estuarine commercial fishing licenses,
§113-169.4.
Coastal recreational fishing license, §113-174.4.

FISH INSPECTORS AND PROTECTORS,
§§113-136, 113-137.

FISH KILLS.
Discharge of oil or hazardous substances.
Liability, §143-215.90(a) to (c).
Response protocols, §143B-279.7.
Development of protocols, §143B-279.7(a).
Reports, §143B-279.7(c).
Secretary of department of environment and
natural resources to take necessary steps to
carry out provisions, §143B-279.7(b).

FITNESS FOR PARTICULAR PURPOSE.
Drinking water act.
Suppliers not deemed to provide implied
warranty, §130A-315(g).

FITNESS FOR PARTICULAR PURPOSE
—Cont'd
Leases, UCC.
Implied warranties, §25-2A-213.
Exclusion or modification, §25-2A-214(2).
Express warranty not to displace inconsistent
implied warranty of fitness, §25-2A-215(c).
Sale of goods, UCC.
Implied warranty, §25-2-315.

511 TRAVELER INFORMATION SYSTEM.
Operated by department of transportation.
Telephone menu requirements, §143-162.1(d).

FIXING ATHLETIC CONTESTS, §§14-373 to
14-379.

FIXTURES.
Ancillary security instruments.
Automatic release, §45-42.3.
Eminent domain.
Removal by owner of fixtures from property taken.
Determination of just compensation, §40A-64(c).
Removal of fixtures on condemned land, §40A-9.
Larceny.
Abolition of exception to property subject to
larceny, §14-83.1.
Leases, UCC.
Defined, §§25-2A-103(1), 25-2A-309.
Lessor's and lessee's rights when goods become
fixtures, §25-2A-309.
Secured transactions.
Defaults.
Procedure when fixtures involved, §25-9-604(b).
Removal of fixtures, §25-9-604(c).
Injury from removal, §25-9-604(d).
Priority of security interests in, §25-9-334(a).
Consent, disclaimer, or right to remove fixture.
Effect on priority, §25-9-334(f).
Construction mortgage, §25-9-334(h).
Continuation of interest, §25-9-334(g).
Purchase money priority, §25-9-334(d).
Real property, interests in, §25-9-334(e).
Real property law security interests,
§25-9-334(b).
Subordination, §25-9-334(c).
Trade fixtures.
Possessory lien.
Persons entitled to, §44A-2(e).

FLAG DESECRATION, §14-381.

FLAGS.
Boating safety.
Diver's flag, §75A-13.1.
Condominiums.
Display of United States or North Carolina flag,
§47C-3-121.
Honor and Remember Flag.
Armed forces members who have died in the line
of duty, §145-32.
Load of motor vehicle extending beyond rear
or body, §20-117(a).
Commercial motor vehicles of certain weight,
§20-117(b).
Official governmental flags.
Defined, §144-7(c).
Display.
Local governments not to prohibit, §144-7(a).
Restrictions authorized, §144-7(b).
Parks and recreation.
Display of flags, §100-18.
Flagpoles.
Donation, §100-19.

FLAGS —Cont'd
Parks and recreation —Cont'd
Flagpoles —Cont'd
Erection in each state park, §100-17.
Planned communities.
Display of American and state flags, §47F-3-121.
Sale of state flags by department of administration to citizens, §66-58(c).
Salute to the North Carolina flag, official state salute, §144-8.
State flag.
Colors of flag, §144-6.
Conformity of flags to law, §144-5.
Description, §144-1.
Desecration, §14-381.
Display.
Charter schools, §115C-238.29F(f).
Condominiums, §47C-3-121.
County courthouses, §144-4.
North Carolina School of Science and Mathematics, §116-235(i).
Planned communities, §47F-3-121.
Public buildings and institutions, §144-3.
University of North Carolina School of the Arts, §116-69.1.
Generally, §144-1.
Motto.
Appearance on flag, §144-2.
Official "prisoner of war/missing in action" flag.
State capitol.
Department of administration authorized to fly on certain holidays, §143-345.9.
Retirement, §144-9.
Sale by department of administration to citizens, §66-58(c).
Salute to the North Carolina flag, §144-8.
United States flag.
Desecration, §14-381.
Display.
Charter schools, §115C-238.29F(f).
North Carolina School of Science and Mathematics, §116-235(i).
Public school.
Adoption of policies requiring, §115C-47.
University of North Carolina School of the Arts, §116-69.1.

FLANAGAN ACT.
Slot machines, §§14-304 to 14-309.1.
See SLOT MACHINES.

FLANGES.
Tires not to have, §20-122(b).

FLASHING.
Exposing parts of persons to minors, §14-190.13.
Indecent exposure, §14-190.9.

FLASHING RED OR YELLOW LIGHTS.
Traffic lights generally, §20-158.

FLATBED TRUCKS.
Loads of logs, cotton bales, boxes, etc.
Load required to be securely fastened, §20-120.

FLAVORS OR FLAVOR EXTRACTS.
Alcoholic beverages.
Exemption from alcoholic beverage provisions, §18B-103.

FLAXSEED.
Standard weight and measure, §81A-42.

FLEA MARKETS.
County regulation, §153A-125.

FLEA MARKETS —Cont'd
Municipal regulation, §160A-178.

FLEEING OR ATTEMPTING TO ELUDE ARREST OR APPREHENSION.
Police chases, speed limits not applicable, §20-145.
Speeding, §20-141.5.
State parks and forest road system, §143-116.8(b).

FLEXIBLE WORK HOURS.
Work options program for state employees, §§126-74 to 126-79.
See WORK OPTIONS FOR STATE EMPLOYEES.

FLIPPING LOANS.
Consumer home loans, §24-10.2(c).

FLOGGING.
Prisoners, prohibited, §148-20.

FLOOD CONTROL.
Bridge construction guidelines.
Hydraulics for flood waters, §136-44.7D.
Dam safety law, §§143-215.23 to 143-215.37.
See DAMS AND RESERVOIRS.
Floodplain regulation, §§143-215.51 to 143-215.61.
See FLOODPLAIN REGULATION.
Hurricanes.
Flood protection and beach erosion control project revolving fund.
Conditions, §143-215.62(b).
Established, §143-215.62(a).
Procedures, §143-215.62(c).
Municipalities.
Service districts.
Purposes for establishing, §160A-536(a).
Special assessments by counties, §§153A-185 to 153A-210.7.
See SPECIAL ASSESSMENTS BY COUNTIES.

FLOODPLAIN REGULATION, §§143-215.51 to 143-215.61.
Artificial obstructions.
Existing obstructions, §143-215.55.
Other approvals required, §143-215.59.
Violations, §143-215.58(b).
Criminal penalty for violation, §143-215.58(a).
Damages.
Liability, §143-215.60.
Definitions, §143-215.52(a), (b).
Delineation of floodplain hazard area.
Department providing advice and assistance, §143-215.56(b).
Floodplain mapping fund, §143-215.56A.
Methods locality may use, §143-215.56(c).
Technical assistance, locality requesting, §143-215.56(a).
Utilization of reports and data supplied by state and federal governments, §143-215.56(a).
Educational program of floodplain management measures.
Department of environment and natural resources directed to pursue, §143-355(b1).
Enjoining violation, §143-215.58(c).
Existing artificial obstructions, §143-215.55.
Flood hazard areas.
New waste disposal facilities, §143-215.54(c).
Ordinances regulating, §143-215.54(a).
Permissible uses, §143-215.54(b).
Flood hazard prevention ordinances.
Minimum standards, §143-215.54A(a).

FLOODPLAIN REGULATION —Cont'd
Flood hazard prevention ordinances —Cont'd
Variances, criteria, §143-215.54A(b).
Floodplain management, §143-215.61.
Legislative declaration, §143-215.51.
Liability for damages, §143-215.60.
Management, §143-215.61.
Map identifying 100-year floodplain and base flood elevations.
Conditions for department to prepare, §143-215.56(d).
Copies provided locality, §143-215.56(f).
Floodplain mapping fund, §143-215.56A.
Fees for, §§161-11.4, 161-11.5.
Incorporation into local ordinance, §143-215.56(g).
Notification to localities prior to preparing, §143-215.56(e).
Submission to federal emergency management agency, §143-215.56(f).
Obstructions.
Existing artificial obstructions, §143-215.55.
Other approvals required, §143-215.59.
Violations, §143-215.58(b).
Permits.
Issuance, §143-215.57(a), (b).
Other approvals required, §143-215.59(a), (b).
Procedures in issuing, §143-215.57(a).
Rules and regulations, §143-215.57(c).
Standards and requirements, §143-215.57(b).
Purpose of part, §143-215.51.
Remedies for enforcing ordinance, §143-215.58(a1).
Rules and regulations.
Adoption and promulgation, §143-215.57(c).
Violations, §143-215.58(a) to (c).

FLOODS.
Bridge construction guidelines.
Hydraulics for flood waters, §136-44.7D.
Dam safety law, §§143-215.23 to 143-215.37.
See DAMS AND RESERVOIRS.
Floodplain regulation, §§143-215.51 to 143-215.61.
See FLOODPLAIN REGULATION.
Hurricanes.
Flood protection and beach erosion control project revolving fund.
Conditions, §143-215.62(b).
Established, §143-215.62(a).
Procedures, §143-215.62(c).
Municipalities.
Assessments.
Authority to make assessments for flood and hurricane protection works, §160A-238.
Floodway regulations ordinances authorized, §160A-458.1.
Property.
Removal of property deposited by flood, §104B-1.
Property insurance.
Notice of non-coverage for flood, earthquake, mudslide or landslide, §58-44-60(a).
Protection works.
Special assessments by counties, §§153A-185 to 153A-210.7.
See SPECIAL ASSESSMENTS BY COUNTIES.
Secondary roads within watershed improvement district.
Closing roads within watershed improvement district, §136-64.1(a) to (d).

FLOODWAYS.
Municipalities.
Floodway regulations ordinances authorized, §160A-458.1.

FLOODWAYS —Cont'd
Swine farms.
Constructing component of liquid animal waste management system within 100-year floodway, §106-803(a2).

FLORISTS.
Sales and use tax.
Florist wire sales.
Sale sourced to business location, §105-164.4B(d).

FLOWER OF STATE.
Dogwood, §145-1.

FLOWERS.
Promotion of use and sale of agricultural products.
Generally, §§106-550 to 106-568.
See AGRICULTURAL PRODUCTS PROMOTION.

FLU.
Charter school students parents or guardians.
Information provided, §115C-238.29F(a).
Church schools and schools of religious charter.
Information provided parents and guardians of students, §115C-548.
Home schools.
Information provided, §115C-565.
Local boards of education.
Information provided parents and guardians, §115C-47.

FLUME COMPANIES.
Eminent domain.
Flume companies exercising right become common carriers, §62-191.

FLUORESCENT LIGHTS.
Containing mercury.
Demolition of buildings in state.
Removal and recycling by contractors or owners, §130A-310.61.
Disposal in unlined landfills prohibited, §103A-309.10(m).
Criminal penalty for violation, §103A-25(d).
Recycling required by public agencies.
Program for collection and recycling.
Establishment required, §130A-310.60(a).
Political subdivision using state funds, §130A-310.60(c).
Report documenting compliance, §130A-310.60(b).

FLU VACCINATION INFORMATION.
Charter schools.
Information provided, §115C-238.29F(a).
Church schools and schools of religious charter.
Information provided, §115C-548.
Home schools.
Information provided, §115C-565.
Local boards of education.
Information provided parents and guardians, §115C-47.

FLYING UNDER THE INFLUENCE, §63-27.
Infliction of serious bodily injury, §63-28.

F.O.B.
Sale of goods, UCC, §25-2-319.
Form of bill of lading required in overseas shipment, §25-2-323.

FOLKMOOT USA.
State international festival, §145-19.

FOLLOWING TOO CLOSELY, §20-152(a), (b).
Fire apparatus, §20-157(b), (c).
Penalty for violation, §20-157(g).
Property damage, §20-157(h).
Serious injury or death, causing, §20-157(i).
Points.
Schedule of point values, §20-16(c).

FOOD.
Amateur athletic events.
Limited food establishments.
Preparing and serving food in conjunction with.
Permits, issuance, §130A-248(a4).
Sanitation, adoption of rules, §130A-248(a4).
Assistance.
Food and nutrition services program, §§108A-51 to 108A-53.1.
See FOOD AND NUTRITION SERVICES PROGRAM.
Bed and breakfast establishments.
Exemption from certain sanitation requirements, §130A-250.
Child care facilities.
Mandatory standards for licensing, §110-91.
Contaminating food or drink to render one mentally incapacitated or physically helpless.
Exceptions, §14-401.16(d).
Felony, §14-401.16(c).
Prohibited acts, §14-401.16(a), (b).
Contamination.
Plan to protect food supply, §130A-481.
Donated food.
Immunity for, §99B-10.
Embargoes.
Adulterated or misbranded foods, §130A-21(a) to (e).
Fees.
Establishment preparing and selling food, §130A-248(d) to (f).
Food and nutrition services program, §§108A-51 to 108A-53.1.
See FOOD AND NUTRITION SERVICES PROGRAM.
Food, drug and cosmetic act.
See FOOD, DRUG AND COSMETIC ACT.
Fruit.
Unfair practices by handlers, §§106-496 to 106-501.
Halloween.
Distribution of certain food prohibited, §14-401.11(a), (b).
Health.
Adulterated or misbranded foods.
Embargoes, §130A-21(a) to (e).
High-calcium foods and beverages.
Local boards of education.
Preference in purchasing contracts, §115C-264.1(a), (b).
Implied warranty of merchantability.
Sale of goods, UCC, §25-2-314.
Limited food establishments.
Amateur athletic events.
Preparing and serving food in conjunction with.
Permits, issuance, §130A-248(a4).
Sanitation, adoption of rules, §130A-248(a4).
Meat inspections, §§106-549.15 to 106-549.39.
See MEAT INSPECTIONS.

FOOD —Cont'd
Merchantability, implied warranty.
Sale of goods, UCC, §25-2-314.
North Carolina sustainable local food advisory council, §§106-830 to 106-833.
Permits or transitional permits.
Establishment preparing and selling food, §130A-248(b) to (c).
Polystyrene foam products used in conjunction with food.
Recycling, §130A-309.10(d).
Poultry generally.
See POULTRY AND POULTRY PRODUCTS.
Poultry products inspections, §§106-549.49 to 106-549.69.
See POULTRY PRODUCTS INSPECTIONS.
Prepared food.
Sales and use tax.
Defined, §105-164.3.
Subject to tax, exception, §105-164.13B(a).
Products liability.
Donated food.
Immunity, §99B-10(a).
Liability of donee that uses or distributes food, §99B-10(b).
Public schools.
Food services, §§115C-263, 115C-264.
High-calcium food and beverages.
Preference to when purchasing, §115C-264.1(a), (b).
Push carts and mobile food units.
Sanitation, rules governing, §130A-248(c1).
Restaurants.
See RESTAURANTS.
Sale of goods, UCC.
Implied warranty of merchantability, §25-2-314.
Sales and use tax.
Administration of local taxes imposed on food, §105-164.13B(b).
Defined, §105-164.3.
Exempt from tax, items subject to tax, §105-164.13B(a).
Local government sales and use tax.
First one-cent tax.
Administration tax levied on, distribution, allocation, §105-469(a).
Rate of tax.
First one-cent tax, §105-467.
Prepared food.
Defined, §105-164.3.
Prepared food and drink.
Defined, §105-164.3.
Sanitation of food and lodging establishments, §§130A-247 to 130A-250.
Sustainable local food advisory council, §§106-830 to 106-833.
Warranties.
Implied warranty of merchantability, §25-2-314.

FOOD ADDITIVES.
Food, drug and cosmetic act.
Additives deemed unsafe, §106-132.
Foods deemed to be adulterated, §106-129.

FOOD AND LODGING ESTABLISHMENT SANITATION, §§130A-247 to 130A-250.

FOOD AND NUTRITION SERVICES PROGRAM, §§108A-51 to 108A-53.1.
Administration of program, §108A-51.
Appeals, §108A-79(h).
Authorization of program, §108A-51.

FOOD AND NUTRITION SERVICES PROGRAM —Cont'd

Controlled substance felony offense conviction.
Eligibility to participate in program, §108A-25.2.
Creation of program, §108A-25(a).
Eligibility determination, §108A-52.
Financial assistance and in-kind goods or services received not considered in determining amount of assistance, §108A-26.
Fraud, §108A-53.
Garnishment of wages to recoup, §108A-25.3.
Illegal possession or use.
Buying, selling, distributing or possessing in manner contrary to authorization or regulation, §108A-53.1(a).
Using, transferring, acquiring, etc., in manner contrary to authorization, §108A-53.1(b).
Setoff debt collection, §§105A-1 to 105A-16.
See SETOFF DEBT COLLECTION.

FOOD BANK INFORMATION AND REFERRAL SERVICE.
Maintenance of information by department of agriculture and consumer services, §106-21.2.

FOOD DONATIONS.
Food bank information and referral service.
Maintenance of information by department of agriculture and consumer services, §106-21.2.
Inspections of donated food, §106-141.1.

FOOD, DRUG AND COSMETIC ACT, §§106-120 to 106-145.
Acts.
Certain acts prohibited, §106-122.
Additives deemed unsafe.
What constitutes unsafe additives, §106-132.
Adulteration.
Cosmetics deemed adulterated, §106-136.
Detention of product or article suspected of being adulterated, §106-125(a).
Declaration of nuisance, §106-125(d).
Delegation of authority, §106-141(c).
Destruction of article, §106-125(c).
Expenses taxed against claimant of article, §106-125(c).
Order for condemnation of article, §106-125(b).
Drugs deemed to be adulterated, §106-133.
Electronic surveillance orders, §15A-290(c5).
Felonies.
Intent to cause serious injury or death, §14-34.4(a).
Intent to extort, §14-34.4(b).
Foods deemed to be adulterated, §106-129.
Advertising.
Definitions and general consideration, §106-121.
Dissemination of advertisement.
Violations made misdemeanor, §106-124(c).
False advertising, §106-138(a).
Exceptions, §106-138(b).
Board of agriculture.
Regulations of board, §106-139.
Standards of quality.
Establishment of reasonable standards, §106-128.
Certain acts prohibited, §106-122.
Citation of act, §106-120.
Color.
Defined, §106-121.

FOOD, DRUG AND COSMETIC ACT —Cont'd
Color additive.
Defined, §106-121.
Commissioner of agriculture.
Enforcement of article, §106-140.
Reports.
Minor violations of article to be reported, §106-127.
Violations of article.
Report of minor violations in discretion of commissioner, §106-127.
Construction and interpretation.
Supplementary construction of article, §106-143.
Consumer commodity.
Defined, §106-121.
Consumer goods.
Declaration of net quantity of contents, §106-139.1.
Regulations by board of agriculture, §106-139(c).
Exemption from certain labeling requirements, §106-139(b).
Consumer protection.
Dissemination of certain information, §106-142(b).
Contaminated with filth.
Defined, §106-121.
Contamination with microorganisms.
Manufacture of foods.
Permits governing manufacture of foods subject to contamination, §106-131.
Cosmetic.
Defined, §106-121.
Counterfeit drug.
Defined, §106-121.
Decrees.
Publication of reports of judgments, decrees and court orders, §106-142(a).
Definitions, §106-121.
Device.
Defined, §106-121.
District attorneys.
Prosecutions of violations of article, §106-126.
Donated food.
Inspections of food.
Applicability of provisions, §106-141.1(c).
Authorized, §106-141.1(a).
Compliance with provisions, §106-141.1(a).
Injunctive relief restraining violations, §106-141.1(b).
Drug.
Defined, §106-121.
Effective date of article, §106-145.
Enforcement of article.
Commissioner of agriculture.
Further powers of commissioner, §106-140.
Regulations by board of agriculture, §106-139(a).
Entry of establishment.
Power of commissioner, §106-140(a).
Examinations.
Conduct of examinations, §106-141(b).
Samples, §106-140(d).
Exemptions from provisions, §106-144.
False advertising, §106-138(a).
Exceptions, §106-138(b).
Federal act.
Defined, §106-121.
Food.
Defined, §106-121.
Food additive.
Defined, §106-121.
General considerations, §106-121.

FOOD, DRUG AND COSMETIC ACT —Cont'd
Hearings.
Procedures, §106-139(d).
Immediate container.
Defined, §106-121.
Injunctions.
Inspections of donated food.
Restraining violations of article, §106-141.1(b).
Restraining violations of provisions, §106-123.
Inspections.
Additives deemed unsafe, §106-132.
Donated food, §106-141.1.
Manufacture of foods subject to contamination
with microorganisms.
Permits governing manufacture, §106-131(c).
Power of commissioner, §106-140(a) to (c).
Investigations.
Conduct of investigations, §106-141(b).
Judgments.
Publication of reports of judgments, decrees and
court orders, §106-142(a).
Labels.
Declaration of net quantity of contents.
Commercial distribution, §106-139.1(c).
Conformity with requirements, §106-139.1(a).
Distributing in commerce, §106-139.1(c).
Statement of net quantity per serving,
§106-139.1(b).
Defined, §106-121.
Prescription drugs.
Requirements for labeling, §106-134.1(b), (d).
Regulations by board of agriculture.
Exemption of certain consumer commodities,
§106-139(b).
Manufacture of foods.
Contamination with microorganisms.
Permits governing manufacture of foods subject
to contamination, §106-131.
Meat and meat products.
Exemptions from provisions, §106-144.
Misbranding.
Cosmetics deemed misbranded, §106-137.
Detention of product or article suspected of being
misbranded, §106-125(a).
Declaration of nuisance, §106-125(d).
Delegation of authority, §106-141(c).
Destruction of article, §106-125(c).
Expenses taxed against claimant of article,
§106-125(c).
Order for condemnation of article, §106-125(b).
Drugs deemed misbranded, §106-134.
Prescription provisions, §106-134.1(d).
Foods deemed misbranded, §106-130.
Prescriptions.
Drugs deemed misbranded, §106-134.1(d).
Misdemeanors, §106-124.
New drugs.
Defined, §106-121.
Regulations for sale.
Applicability of provisions, §106-135(g).
Application, §106-135(a).
Effectiveness, §106-135(b).
Order refusing to permit effectiveness of
application, §106-135(c).
Revocation of application, §106-135(f).
Effectiveness of application, §106-135(b).
Order refusing to permit, §106-135(c).
Exemptions from provisions, §106-135(d), (g).
Order refusing to permit effectiveness of
application, §106-135(c).
Records required, §106-135(e).

FOOD, DRUG AND COSMETIC ACT —Cont'd
New drugs —Cont'd
Regulations for sale —Cont'd
Reports required, §106-135(e).
Revocation of application, §106-135(f).
Notice.
Civil penalties.
Notice prior to assessment, §106-124.1(b).
Nuisances.
Adulterated or misbranded product or article.
Detention of suspected product or article.
Declaration of nuisance, §106-125(d).
Official compendium.
Defined, §106-121.
Orders.
Publication of reports of judgments, decrees and
court orders, §106-142(a).
Regulations for sale of new drugs.
Refusal to commit effectiveness of application,
§106-135(c).
Package.
Defined, §106-121.
Partitioner.
Defined, §106-121.
Permits.
Manufacture of foods subject to contamination
with microorganisms.
Conditions attached, §106-131(a).
Inspections, §106-131(c).
Suspension of permit, §106-131(b).
Person.
Defined, §106-121.
Pesticide chemical.
Defined, §106-121.
Poisons.
Adulteration.
Foods deemed to be adulterated, §106-129.
Putting poisonous foodstuffs, etc., in certain public
places prohibited, §14-401.
Poultry and poultry products.
Exemptions from provisions, §106-144.
**Prescription medicine wholesalers,
manufacturers or repackagers.**
Registration, §106-140.1(a), (b).
Additional establishment, §106-140.1(c).
Assignment of number, §106-140.1(d).
Definition, §106-140.1(j).
Exemptions from registration requirement,
§106-140.1(f).
Fee, §106-140.1(h).
Inspection of establishments registered,
§106-140.1(g).
Inspection of registration, §106-140.1(e).
Name to include partnership or corporation
name, §106-140.1(i).
Rules to implement registration, adoption,
§106-140.1(h).
Prescriptions.
Applicability of provisions, §106-134.1(e).
Label requirements, §106-134.1(b), (d).
Misbranding.
Drugs deemed misbranded, §106-134.1(d).
Removal of certain drugs from requirements of
section, §106-134.1(b), (c).
Required, §106-134.1(a).
Principal display panel.
Defined, §106-121.
Prohibited acts, §106-122.
Publications.
Reports of judgments, decrees and court orders to
be published, §106-142(a).

FOOD, DRUG AND COSMETIC ACT —Cont'd
Purpose of article, §106-121.
Quality standards.
Board of agriculture.
Establishment of reasonable standards, §106-128.
Raw agricultural commodity.
Defined, §106-121.
Records.
Carriers in commerce.
Access, copying, power of commissioner, §106-140(a).
Regulations for sale of new drugs, §106-135(e).
Registration.
Prescription drug wholesalers, manufacturers or repackagers, §106-140.1.
Reports.
Following inspection, §106-140(b).
Minor violations to be reported, §106-127.
Publication of reports of judgments, decrees and court orders, §106-142(a).
Regulations for sale of new drugs, §106-135(e).
Restraining orders.
Injunctions restraining violations, §106-123.
Inspections of donated food, §106-141.1(b).
Rules and regulations.
Board of agriculture to promulgate regulations, §106-139.
Sale of new drugs, §106-135.
Samples acquired during inspection.
Examination, §106-140(d).
Payment for, §106-140(c).
Short title, §106-120.
Solicitors.
Prosecutions of violations of article, §106-126.
Standards of quality.
Board of agriculture.
Establishment of reasonable standards, §106-128.
Superior courts.
Injunctions restraining violations of provisions, §106-123.
Title of article, §106-120.
Training and management practices.
Violations of article.
Civil penalties.
Mitigating factors, §106-124.1(c).
Violations of article.
Certain acts prohibited, §106-122.
Civil penalties, §106-124.1.
Assessment, §106-124.1(a).
Mitigating factors, §106-124.1(c).
Notice prior to assessment, §106-124.1(b).
Remission of proceeds, §106-124.1(d).
Commissioner of agriculture.
Report of minor violations in discretion of commissioner, §106-127.
Dissemination of advertisement, §106-124(c).
Guaranty or undertaking established, §106-124(b).
Injunctions restraining violations, §106-123.
Misdemeanor offenses, §106-124(a).
Mitigating factors.
Civil penalties, §106-124.1(c).
Notice prior to assessment.
Civil penalties, §106-124.1(b).
Prohibited acts, §106-122.
Prosecutions of violations, §106-126.

FOOD FESTIVAL, §145-27.

FOOD STAMPS.
Food and nutrition services program, §§108A-51 to 108A-53.1.
See FOOD AND NUTRITION SERVICES PROGRAM.

FOOT AND MOUTH DISEASE.
Appropriation to combat disease, §§106-308, 106-309.

FOOTBALL.
Protection of athletic contests.
See ATHLETICS.

FOOTPRINTS.
Nontestimonial identification.
Delinquent or undisciplined juvenile actions, §§7B-2103 to 7B-2109.
Generally, §§15A-271 to 15A-282.
See IDENTIFICATION.

FOOT SPECIALISTS.
Podiatrists, §§90-202.2 to 90-202.14.
See PODIATRISTS.

FORCE.
Detaining intoxicated person.
Use of reasonable force by law enforcement officers, §122C-301(b).
Discipline of public school students.
Reasonable force, §115C-390.3.
Investigations of use of deadly force by law enforcement officers, §147-90.
Justifiable use.
Defense of person.
Deadly force justified, §14-51.3(a).
Force except for deadly force justified, §14-51.3(a).
Immunity, exceptions, §14-51.3(b).
Justification not available, §14-51.4.
Protection of home, workplace, motor vehicle.
Defenses under common law.
Not repealed or limited, §14-51.2(g).
Definitions, §14-51.2(a).
Exceptions to justification and immunity in using force, §14-51.2(e).
Fear of imminent death or personal bodily harm to occupant or another when using defensive force.
Presumption, §14-51.2(b).
Rebuttable, inapplicable, §14-51.2(c).
Home defined, §14-51.2(a).
Intent to commit unlawful act with force or violence.
Presumption.
Unlawful and forceful entry, §14-51.2(d).
Justified in using force, immunity, exceptions, §14-51.2(e).
Motor vehicle defined, §14-51.2(a).
No duty to retreat from intruder, §14-51.2(f).
Workplace defined, §14-51.2(a).
Private correctional facilities and employees.
Federal Bureau of prisons contracts.
Use by employees, §148-37.3(a).
Seizure and impoundment of motor vehicles.
Impaired driving arrest, §20-28.3(c1).
Statistics on use of deadly force by law enforcement officers.
Collection by division of criminal statistics, §114-10.02.

FORCE ACCOUNT QUALIFIED LABOR.
Department of transportation.
Report to general assembly, §136-12.

FORCE ACCOUNT QUALIFIED LABOR
—Cont'd
Public contracts.
Work performed by.
Limitation on application of article, §143-135.
Public enterprise improvements.
Cities or towns, §160A-320.
Counties, §153A-280.
Roads or highways.
Maintenance, repair, construction, reconstruction, widening.
Municipality undertaking work by, §§136-41.3, 160A-309.

FORCED OUT SALES, §§66-76 to 66-83.
See CLOSING-OUT SALES.

FOREBEARANCES.
Contract rates and fees, §24-1.1.
Savings and loan association interest rates, §24-1.4.

FORECLOSURE.
Alcoholic beverage ownership or possession acquired by.
Special one-time permit issued, §18B-1002(a).
Attorneys' fees for services rendered assignee or debt buyer.
Party's obligation to pay.
Material furnished court showing, §6-21.2.
Banks.
Foreclosures and execution of deeds by commissioner, validation, §53-35.
Condominiums.
Lien for assessment, §47C-3-116(a), (a1), (a2).
Lien or encumbrance, §47C-2-118(i), (j).
Special declarant rights, §47C-3-104(c), (d).
Emergency program to reduce home foreclosures, §§45-100 to 45-107.
Executors and administrators.
Validation, §45-5.
Guardian's powers.
Administering incompetent's estate, §35A-1251.
Administering minor ward's estate, §35A-1252.
Home foreclosures.
Emergency program to reduce home foreclosures, §§45-100 to 45-107.
Home foreclosure rescue scams, §§75-120 to 75-122.
Home protection program, §122A-5.14.
Judicial sales.
General provisions.
See JUDICIAL SALES.
Limitation of actions.
Mortgages and deeds of trust, §1-47.
Attacking certain foreclosures.
On ground trustee was agent, etc., of owner of debt, §45-21.39.
Deficiency judgments after foreclosure, §1-54.
Taxation, §1-54.
Mortgage bankers, brokers and servicers.
Commissioner.
Foreclosure suspension, §53-244.117.
Mortgages and deeds of trust.
Attorneys' fees.
Conducting foreclosure.
Prohibited to all except licensed attorneys, §84-6.
Services rendered assignee or debt buyer.
Party's obligation to pay.
Material furnished court showing, §6-21.2.

FORECLOSURE —Cont'd
Mortgages and deeds of trust —Cont'd
Corporate mortgages.
Receivers and trustees of corporate mortgages or grantees, §1-507.4.
Default judgment by clerk, §1A-1 Rule 55(a).
Deficiency judgments, §§45-21.36 to 45-21.38C.
Emergency program to reduce home foreclosures, §§45-100 to 45-107.
Confidentiality of records, §45-106.
Definitions, §45-101.
Determination of loans subject to provisions, §45-105.
Extension of filing dates for appropriate loans, §45-105.
Information not public record, §45-106.
Pre-foreclosure information.
Filing, procedures, §45-103(a).
Optional information to facilitate further review, §45-103(b).
Pre-foreclosure notice for home loans, §45-102.
Certification with foreclosure filing, §45-107(a).
Confirmation by clerk, §45-107(b).
Privacy of information, §45-106.
State home foreclosure prevention project, §45-104(a).
State home foreclosure prevention trust fund.
Administration of funds, agreement, §45-104(e).
Allocation of funds to implement act, §45-104(d).
Established, §45-104(b).
Fee paid to fund by mortgage servicer, §45-104(c).
Title of act, §45-100.
Fee for conducting foreclosure.
Prohibited to all except licensed attorneys, §84-6.
FiduciariesTrust instruments.
Powers incorporated by reference, §32-27.
Guardian's powers.
Administering incompetent's estate, §35A-1251.
Administering minor ward's estate, §35A-1252.
Home foreclosure rescue scams, §§75-120 to 75-122.
Home protection program, §122A-5.14.
In rem or quasi in rem jurisdiction, §1-75.8.
Judicial sales.
Who may hold sale, §1-339.4.
Legal services programs.
Eligible cases, §7A-474.3(b).
Limitation of actions, §1-47.
Attacks on certain foreclosures on grounds trustee was agent, etc., of owner of debt, §45-21.39.
Deficiency judgment following foreclosure, §1-54.
Redemption of mortgage, §1-47.
Sales under power of sale.
Application of statute to serial notes, §45-21.11.
Lis pendens, §1-116.
Military service.
Power of sale barred during, §45-21.12A.
Receivers of corporations.
Powers, §§1-507.2, 1-507.4.
Recording, §45-38.
Resolution of foreclosure of owner-occupied residential property by parties.
Opportunity to be offered, §45-21.16C(a).
Continuation of hearing, §45-21.16C(b).

FORECLOSURE —Cont'd
Mortgages and deeds of trust —Cont'd
Reverse mortgages.
Initiation of foreclosure.
Time for, §53-268.
Sales under power of sale.
Article not applicable to foreclosure by court action, §45-21.2.
Barred when foreclosure barred, §45-21.12.
Contents of notice, §45-21.16(c2).
Military service.
Power of sale barred during periods of, §45-21.12A.
Orders signed on days other than first and third Mondays validated, §45-21.41.
Simultaneous foreclosure of two or more instruments, §45-21.9A.
Superior courts.
Clerks of court authorized to order foreclosure, §1-209.
Suspension of foreclosure proceedings.
Effect on notice requirements, §45-21.16B(c).
Hearing following suspension period, §45-21.16B(b).
Notification from commissioner of banks, §45-21.16B(a).
Tolling of deadlines, §45-21.16B(a).
Trustee officer of owner of debt.
Validation of foreclosure sale, §45-21.47.
Validation.
Foreclosures by representatives validated, §45-5.
Sales where posting and publication not complied with, §§45-21.46(a), 45-21.48.
Foreclosure commenced on or after June 1, 1983 and consummated prior to April 1, 1985, §45-21.46(b).
When trustee is officer of owner of debt, §45-21.47.
Venue, §1-76.
Property taxes.
Foreclosure of tax lien, §§105-374 to 105-376.
Residential property disclosure act.
Applicability of act, §47E-2.
Sale under power of sale.
Article not applicable to foreclosure by court action, §45-21.2.
Barred by statute of limitations.
Power barred, exception, §45-21.12.
Orders signed on days other than first and third Mondays validated, §45-21.41.
Stayed by bankruptcy petition.
Before expiration of 10-day upset bid period, §45-21.22(d).
Judge lifting stay, §45-21.22(c).
Secured transactions.
Default.
Enforcement after default, §25-9-601(a).
Execution sale, security interest foreclosed, §25-9-601(f).
State forests.
County lands acquired through tax foreclosure.
Use as demonstration forests, §106-872.
Subprime mortgages.
Emergency program to reduce home foreclosures, §§45-100 to 45-107.
Sales under power of sale, contents of notice, §45-21.16(c2).
Tax liens.
Limitation of actions, §1-54.
Property taxes, §§105-374 to 105-376.

FORECLOSURE —Cont'd
Torrens system registration.
Method of transfer.
Land conveyed as security.
Sale under lien, §43-36(f).
Transfer of proceedings to superior court.
Exceptions, §1-301.2(g).
Trust instrument.
Powers incorporated by reference in, §32-27.
Venue.
Mortgages, §1-76.

FOREIGN BANKING CORPORATIONS.
International banking generally, §§53-232.1 to 53-232.17.
See INTERNATIONAL BANKING.

FOREIGN BIRTH.
Certificate of identification for individual of foreign birth, §130A-108(a).
Readoption in state, §130A-108(b).

FOREIGN CORPORATIONS.
Attachment.
Grounds for attachment, §1-440.3.
Derivative actions.
Applicability, §55-7-47.
Franchise tax generally, §§105-114 to 105-129.
See FRANCHISE TAX.
Garnishment.
To whom process delivered when garnishee corporations, §1-440.26(b).
Generally, §§55-15-01 to 55-15-33.
See CORPORATIONS.
Mergers.
Nonprofit corporations, §55-11-09.
Nonprofit corporations, §§55A-1-01 to 55A-17-05.
See NONPROFIT CORPORATIONS.
Professional corporations, §55B-16.
Service of process.
Personal jurisdiction, manner of serving, §1A-1 Rule 4(j).
Venue of actions against, §1-80.

FOREIGN COUNTRIES.
Depositions.
Persons before whom taken, §1A-1 Rule 28(b).
Reading deposition on the trial.
When deposition may be read, §8-83.
Evidence.
Laws of foreign countries.
Admission into evidence, §8-3(a).
Exhibiting copy of law from printed volume, §8-3(b).
Judicial notice of laws, §8-4.
Missing persons.
Provisions applicable, §28C-20.
Service of process, §1A-1 Rule 4(j3).
Wills.
Certified copies proved in another country, §28A-2A-15.

FOREIGN CURRENCY.
Commodities generally, §§78D-1 to 78D-33.
See COMMODITIES.

FOREIGN DIPLOMATS.
Holders of driver's license issued by United States department of state.
Notice to department of state.
Violation of state or local traffic law, revocation order, §20-37.20.

FOREIGN GOVERNMENTS.
Agreements between North Carolina and foreign governments.
Filing of copies, §66-280(a), (b).
Definition of "foreign government,"§66-280(c).
Business discrimination.
Persons doing business in state entering into agreement with foreign governments, §§75B-1 to 75B-7.

FOREIGN INSURANCE COMPANIES.
Generally.
See FOREIGN OR ALIEN INSURANCE COMPANIES.

FOREIGN JUDGMENTS.
Enforcement, §§1C-1701 to 1C-1708.
Actions to enforce.
Creditor's judgment.
Article not construed to impair, §1C-1707.
Affidavit that judgment final and unsatisfied.
Filing, §1C-1703(a).
Burden of proof.
Motion for enforcement of judgment, §1C-1705(b).
Citation of act.
Short title, §1C-1701.
Construction and interpretation.
Actions to enforce creditor's judgment.
Article not construed to impair, §1C-1707.
Costs, §1C-1706.
Defenses.
Final judgments subject to same defenses as judgments of state, §1C-1703(c).
Notice of defense.
Filing, §1C-1705(a).
Definitions, §1C-1702.
Docketing, §1C-1703(b).
Eastern band of the Cherokee Indians.
Judgments, decrees, and orders of Tribal Court.
Considered foreign judgments by state, §1E-1(b).
Effect, §1C-1703(c).
Fees, §1C-1706.
Filing in office of clerk of superior court, §1C-1703(a).
Notice of filing.
Content, §1C-1704(b).
Service and proof of service, §1C-1704(a).
Hearings.
Motion for enforcement of foreign judgment, §1C-1705(b).
Indexing, §1C-1703(b).
Judgments against public policy.
Provisions not to apply to, §1C-1708.
Limitation of actions.
Ten-year limitation, §1-47.
Motions.
Enforcement of foreign judgments, §1C-1705(b).
Relief from foreign judgments, §1C-1705(a).
Notice of defense.
Filing notice of defense, §1C-1705(a).
Notice of filing.
Contents, §1C-1704(b).
Service and proof of service of notice, §1C-1704(a).
Optional procedure, §1C-1707.
Public policy.
Judgments against.
Provisions of article not to apply to, §1C-1708.
Relief from foreign judgments.
Motion for, §1C-1705(a).

FOREIGN JUDGMENTS —Cont'd
Enforcement —Cont'd
Service of process.
Notice of filing.
Service and proof of service of notice, §1C-1704(a).
Short title, §1C-1701.
Status.
Same effect and subject to same defenses as judgments of state, §1C-1703(c).
Stays, §1C-1705(a).
Title of act.
Short title, §1C-1701.
Recognition of foreign-country money judgments, §§1C-1850 to 1C-1859.
Action seeking recognition.
Original matter.
Recognition raised by, §1C-1855(a).
Statute of limitation, §1C-1858.
Alimony, support, maintenance, matrimonial or family matters.
Inapplicability, §1C-1852(b).
Appeal of foreign-country judgment pending.
Stay of recognition proceedings, §1C-1857.
Applicability of article, §1C-1852(a), (b).
Burden of establishing, §1C-1852(c).
Complaint, counterclaim, cross-claim, affirmative defense.
Raising issue of recognition by, §1C-1855(b).
Conclusions of law stated separately.
Ruling on recognition, §1C-1853(i).
Conclusive between parties.
Effect of recognition, §1C-1856(a).
Conflict with prior final and conclusive judgment, §1C-1853(d).
Conflict with subsequent final and conclusive judgment, §1C-1853(e).
Construing article.
Uniformity of interpretation among states, §1C-1859.
Definitions, §1C-1851.
Denial of recognition, §1C-1853(c).
Burden of establishing ground for nonrecognition, §1C-1853(f) to (g).
Conflict with subsequent final and conclusive judgment, §1C-1853(e).
Due process of law.
Foreign system's procedures not compatible with.
Nonrecognition of judgment, §1C-1853(b).
Effect of recognition, §1C-1856(a).
Enforcement of recognized judgment, §1C-1856(a), (b).
Fact stated specially.
Ruling on recognition, §1C-1853(i).
Fine or penalty, judgment for.
Inapplicability, §1C-1852(b).
Foreign court without jurisdiction.
Nonrecognition of judgment, §1C-1853(b).
Fraudulent judgment.
Denial of recognition, §1C-1853(c).
Fundamentally unfair proceeding.
Denial of recognition, §1C-1853(c).
Ground for nonrecognition.
Burden of establishing, §1C-1853(f) to (g).
Impartial tribunals not provided by foreign system.
Nonrecognition of judgment, §1C-1853(b).
Inapplicability of article, §1C-1852(b).
Inconvenient forum.
Denial of recognition, §1C-1853(c).

FOREIGN JUDGMENTS —Cont'd
Recognition of foreign-country money judgments —Cont'd
Lack of personal jurisdiction.
Recognition not refused, §1C-1854(a), (b).
Nonrecognized judgments, §1C-1853(b).
Burden of establishing ground for
nonrecognition, §1C-1853(f) to (g).
North Carolina uniform foreign-country money
judgments recognition act.
Article cited as, §1C-1850.
Notice of foreign proceeding insufficient.
Denial of recognition, §1C-1853(c).
Original matter.
Recognition raised by action seeking,
§1C-1855(a).
Personal jurisdiction lacking.
Recognition not refused, §1C-1854(a), (b).
Principles of comity or otherwise.
Recognition under, §1C-1852(d).
Recognized judgments, §1C-1853(a).
Conflict with prior final and conclusive
judgment, §1C-1853(e).
Ruling on recognition.
Facts and conclusions of law, stating,
§1C-1853(i).
Short title.
North Carolina uniform foreign-country money
judgments recognition act, §1C-1850.
Statute of limitation.
Action to recognize, §1C-1858.
Stay of recognition proceedings.
Appeal of foreign-country judgment pending,
§1C-1857.
Tax judgments.
Inapplicability, §1C-1852(b).
Uniformity of interpretation among states,
§1C-1859.

FOREIGN LAW.
Determination of foreign law, §1A-1 Rule 44.1.

FOREIGN LEGAL CONSULTANTS, §§84A-1 to
84A-8, Bar Rules F.0101 to F.0113.
Administrative committee recommendations,
Bar Rule F.0107.
Adoption of rules, §84A-8.
Appeals, Bar Rule F.0108.
Applications, Bar Rule F.0101.
Denial, Bar Rule F.0113.
Fees, Bar Rule F.0111.
Forms, Bar Rule F.0102.
Audits, §84A-5.
Board of law examiners.
Delegation of duties by state bar, §84A-7.
Certificate of registration, §84A-2.
Application, §84A-2(a).
Accompanying documents, §84A-2(d).
Fee, §84A-2(c).
Photograph of applicant, §84A-2(b).
Evidence of applicant's application, qualifications,
etc., §84A-2(e).
Good moral character of applicant, §84A-3(c).
Issuance of certificate, §84A-3(b).
Failure to satisfy all provisions, §84A-3(d).
Review by North Carolina state bar, §84A-3(a).
Committee recommendations, Bar Rule F.0107.
Delegation of duties by state bar, §84A-7.
Duties, §84A-5.
Failure to disclose, Bar Rule F.0105.
Fees.
Certificate of registration, §84A-2(c).

FOREIGN LEGAL CONSULTANTS —Cont'd
Fees —Cont'd
Duties of consultant, §84A-5.
Foreign country.
Defined, §84A-1.
Good moral character of applicant.
Certificate of registration, §84A-3(c).
Hearings, Bar Rule F.0109.
Investigations, Bar Rule F.0106.
Licenses, §84A-1.
Examinations, §84A-1(b).
Issuance, §84A-1(a).
Moral character and general fitness.
Burden of proof, Bar Rule F.0104.
Permanent record, Bar Rule F.0112.
Prohibited activities, §84A-4(b).
Public records, §84A-2(f).
Reciprocity, §84A-2(g).
Requirements for applicants, Bar Rule F.0103.
Review and order of council, Bar Rule F.0110.
Rules and regulations.
Adoption of rules, §84A-8.
Scope of practice, §84A-4.
Service of process, §84A-6.
Written legal advice.
Jurisdiction other than admitted to practice in,
§84A-4(c).

FOREIGN LIMITED LIABILITY COMPANIES.
See LIMITED LIABILITY COMPANIES.

**FOREIGN LIMITED LIABILITY
PARTNERSHIPS,** §§59-90 to 59-94.
See LIMITED LIABILITY PARTNERSHIPS.

FOREIGN LIMITED PARTNERSHIPS.
See LIMITED PARTNERSHIPS.

FOREIGN-MONEY CLAIMS, §§1C-1820 to
1C-1834.
Agreements by parties, §1C-1822(a), (b).
Amount of money.
Distribution proceedings, §1C-1827.
Judgments and awards, §1C-1826(g).
Measurement by exchange rate, §1C-1824(b).
Measurement by specified amounts, §1C-1824(a),
(c).
Applicability of article, §1C-1821(a), (b).
Uniformity of application and construction,
§1C-1833.
Asserting claims, §1C-1825(a).
Citation of article, §1C-1834.
Clerks of court.
Powers and liabilities, §1C-1826(j).
Conflict of laws.
Interest rates, §1C-1828(a).
Scope of article, §1C-1821(b).
Costs.
Assessment of cost in U. S. dollars, §1C-1826(c).
Counterclaims, §1C-1825(c).
Currency revalorization, §1C-1831(a), (b).
Defending claims, §1C-1825(b), (c).
Definitions, §1C-1820.
Determining proper money of claim, §1C-1824.
Agreement by parties, §1C-1823(a).
No agreement by parties, §1C-1823(b).
Question of law, §1C-1825(d).
Distribution proceedings.
Conversions of foreign money, §1C-1827.
Docketing of judgments.
Foreign judgments, §1C-1829.
Dollar value or equivalent.
Ascertaining dollar value, §1C-1830(b).
Affidavit stating market value, §1C-1830(d).

FOREIGN-MONEY CLAIMS —Cont'd
Dollar value or equivalent —Cont'd
Ascertaining dollar value —Cont'd
Bank-offered spot rate, computing from, §1C-1830(c).
Computation of dollar equivalent, §1C-1830(a).
Enforcement of judgment in, §1C-1829(d).
Enforcement of judgments.
Affidavit or certificate stating rate of exchange, §1C-1826(i).
Foreign judgments, §1C-1829.
Seizure or restraint of assets, §1C-1830(a) to (d).
Entry of judgment enforcing, §1C-1829(a).
Filing or docketing foreign judgment, §1C-1829(b).
Form of judgment, §1C-1826(f).
General principles of law.
Supplement to provisions of article, §1C-1832.
Interest.
Increase or decrease, §1C-1828(b).
Rate of interest, §1C-1828(a), (c).
Judgments and awards.
Amendment following substitute of new money, §1C-1831(b).
Amount of money, §1C-1826(g).
Clerk's powers and liabilities, §1C-1826(j).
Cost assessed in U. S. dollars, §1C-1826(c).
Discharge of judgment by payment, §1C-1826(h).
Docketing judgment, §1C-1826(h).
Effect of judgments, §1C-1826(h).
Enforcement of judgments.
Affidavit or certificate stating rate of exchange, §1C-1826(i).
Foreign judgments, §1C-1829.
Seizure or restraint of assets, §1C-1830(a) to (d).
Filing of judgment, §1C-1826(h).
Foreign judgment enforcement, §1C-1829.
Form, §1C-1826(f).
Indexing of judgment, §1C-1826(h).
Interest, §1C-1828(a) to (c).
Netting of certain awards, §1C-1826(e).
Payable in foreign money or equivalent, §1C-1826(b), (d).
Stating in amount of money of claim, §1C-1826(a).
Payment of awards, §1C-1826(b), (d).
Satisfaction or partial payment of judgment.
Credit against amount of foreign money specified in judgment, §1C-1829(c).
Scope of article, §1C-1821(a), (b).
Uniformity of application and construction, §1C-1833.
Seizure or restraint of assets, §1C-1830(a) to (d).
Setoffs, §1C-1825(c).
Short title, §1C-1834.
Substitution of currency, §1C-1831(a), (b).
Supplementary general principals of law, §1C-1832.
Uniformity of application and construction, §1C-1833.
United States dollar value of assets to be seized.
Determining, §1C-1830(a) to (d).
Variation by agreement, §1C-1822(a), (b).

FOREIGN OBJECT LEFT IN BODY.
Medical malpractice actions, time limitation for commencing, §1-15(c).

FOREIGN OR ALIEN INSURANCE COMPANIES.
Admission to do business, §58-16-1.
Deposit requirements, §58-5-15.

FOREIGN OR ALIEN INSURANCE COMPANIES —Cont'd
Admission to do business —Cont'd
Kinds of insurance.
Limitations as to, §58-16-10.
Requirements, §58-16-15.
Alien governments.
Companies owned or controlled by.
Exceptions to provisions, §58-16-20(d).
Licenses.
Issuance prohibited, §58-16-20(b).
Prohibited from doing business, §58-16-20(a).
Violations as crimes, §58-16-20(c).
Amendments to documents, §58-16-55.
Approval as domestic insurer, §58-7-60.
Attorney general.
Actions to enforce compliance with provisions, §58-16-50.
Casualty insurance.
Deposits.
Required, §58-5-10.
Charters.
Amendments to documents, §58-16-55.
Deposit of copy with commissioner, §58-16-5.
Commissioner.
Service of process, §58-16-30.
Appointment of commissioner as attorney for service.
Condition for admission to do business, §58-16-5.
Notification of company of service or acceptance of process, §58-16-45.
Unauthorized insurers process act, §58-16-35(b).
Conditions of licensure, §58-16-5.
Conversion to foreign insurer, §58-7-65.
Credit insurance.
Licenses, suspension, revocation or restriction, §58-57-71(d), (e).
Definitions, §58-1-5.
Deposits.
Alien companies generally, §§58-5-100, 58-5-105.
Approval of commissioner, §58-5-95.
Bond in lieu of deposit, §58-5-110.
Depreciation of securities.
Replacements upon, §58-5-25.
Domestic companies may be required to maintain deposits.
Composition of deposit, §58-5-55(c).
Mutual insurance companies, §58-5-55(b).
Stock insurance companies, §58-5-55(a).
Examination by commissioner, §58-5-95.
Faith of state pledged for securities, §58-5-35.
Increase of deposit.
Authority of commissioner, §58-5-40.
Interest, §58-5-63(a).
Lien of policyholders on deposits, §58-5-70.
Subordination, §58-5-71.
Life insurance companies, §58-5-50.
Companies not chartered in United States, §58-5-105.
Liquidation for liabilities, §58-5-63(b).
Companies subject of supervision or rehabilitation, §58-5-63(c).
Power of attorney as to securities deposited.
Delivery to commissioner by company, §58-5-30.
Registration of bonds deposited in name of treasurer or commissioner, §58-5-110.
Costs, §58-5-120.
Expenses, §58-5-120.
Notation of registration, §58-5-115.
Release from registration, §58-5-115.

FOREIGN OR ALIEN INSURANCE
  COMPANIES —Cont'd
Deposits —Cont'd
  Requirements.
    Alien companies generally, §§58-5-100,
      58-5-105.
    Depreciation of securities.
      Replacements upon depreciation, §58-5-25.
    Fidelity, surety and casualty insurance
      companies, §58-5-10.
    Fire and/or marine insurance companies,
      §58-5-5.
    Increase of deposit.
      Authority of commissioner, §58-5-40.
    Minimum deposit required upon admission,
      §58-5-15.
    Power of attorney as to securities.
      Company to deliver to commissioner,
        §58-5-30.
    Type of deposit, §58-5-20.
  Return of deposits, §58-5-80.
  Substitution of securities paid, §58-5-75.
  Taxation.
    Exemption of securities deposited, §58-5-35.
  Treasurer of state to hold securities, §58-5-35.
  Trusts and trustees.
    Deposits held in trust by commissioner or
      treasurer, §58-5-90(a), (b).
      Action to enforce or terminate trust,
        §58-5-90(c).
  Type of deposits, §58-5-20.
Domestic insurers.
  Approval as, §58-7-60.
  Conversion to foreign insurer, §58-7-65.
  Effect of redomestication, §58-7-70.
Enforcement of provisions.
  Actions to enforce compliance, §58-16-50.
Fees.
  Retaliatory laws, §58-16-25.
Fidelity and surety insurance.
  Deposits.
    Required, §58-5-10.
Fire insurance.
  Deposits.
    Required, §58-5-5.
Licenses.
  Conditions of continuance, §58-16-6.
  Conditions of licensure, §58-16-5.
  Restricting license.
    Prohibiting or limiting kinds or amount of
      insurance, §58-3-100(e).
  Retaliatory laws, §58-16-25.
  Revocation, suspension or refusal to renew.
    Credit insurance, §58-57-71(d), (e).
    Notice to agents in state, writing new business
      prohibited, §58-3-100(d).
Life insurance company deposits, §58-5-50.
Limitations upon kinds of insurance, §58-16-10.
Liquidation of deposits for liabilities,
  §58-5-63(b).
  Companies subject of supervision or
    rehabilitation, §58-5-63(c).
Marine insurance.
  Deposits.
    Required, §58-5-5.
Misdemeanors.
  Alien governments.
    Companies owned or controlled by governments,
      §58-16-20(c).
Reciprocal insurance.
  Attorneys.
    Domicile, §58-15-45.

FOREIGN OR ALIEN INSURANCE
  COMPANIES —Cont'd
Reciprocal insurance —Cont'd
  Certification of foreign and alien reciprocals,
    §58-15-40.
Redomestication.
  Effect of, §58-7-70.
Requirements upon admission, §58-16-15.
Retaliatory laws, §58-16-25.
Risk based capital requirements, §58-12-45.
Security substitution upon payment, §58-5-75.
Service of process.
  Alternative service of process, §58-16-40.
  Appointment of commissioner as attorney for
    service.
    Condition for admission to do business,
      §58-16-5.
  Commissioner of insurance, §58-16-30.
    Notification of company of service or acceptance
      of service of process, §58-16-45.
  Unauthorized insurers process act, §58-16-35(b).
Supervision, rehabilitation and liquidation
  generally, §§58-30-1 to 58-30-310.
  See INSURER SUPERVISION,
    REHABILITATION AND LIQUIDATION.
Unauthorized insurers.
  Generally, §§58-28-1 to 58-28-45.
  See UNAUTHORIZED INSURERS.

FOREIGN PERSONAL REPRESENTATIVES.
Ancillary administration, §§28A-26-1 to 28A-26-9.
  See EXECUTORS AND ADMINISTRATORS.

FOREIGN PERSONS.
Aliens.
  See ALIENS.

FOREIGN TRADE ZONES, §§55C-1 to 55C-4.
Definitions.
  "Public corporation,"§55C-2.
Federal law.
  Corporations establishing foreign trade zone to be
    governed by, §55C-4.
Private corporations.
  Application for privilege for establishing foreign
    trade zone.
    Authorized, §55C-3.
  Federal law.
    Private corporation establishing foreign trade
      zone to be governed by, §55C-4.
Public corporations.
  Application for privilege of establishing foreign
    trade zone.
    Authorized, §55C-1.
  Defined, §55C-2.
  Federal law.
    Public corporation establishing foreign trade
      zone to be governed by, §55C-4.

FOREIGN VEHICLES.
Registration, title, §20-53.

FORENSIC ANALYSIS.
Criminal prosecutions.
  Admissible in evidence without testimony of
    analyst who prepared report.
    Affidavit by analyst, §8-58.20(c).
  Chain of custody of evidence subject to forensic
    analysis.
    Establishing without calling unnecessary
      witnesses, §8-58.20(g).
  Copy of laboratory report and affidavit.
    Service on attorney for defendant, §8-58.20(d).

FORENSIC ANALYSIS —Cont'd
Criminal prosecutions —Cont'd
Admissible in evidence without testimony of
analyst who prepared report —Cont'd
Determination of admissibility.
Objection to report and affidavit timely filed,
§8-58.20(f).
Impaired driving prosecution.
Laboratory results of chemical analysis of
blood or urine, §20-139.1(c1) to (c3).
Indication whether laboratory report and
affidavit offered for evidence, §8-58.20(d).
Objection to use of laboratory report.
Defendant or defendant's attorney to file,
time, §8-58.20(e).
Failure to timely file, §8-58.20(f).
Performed in accordance with adopted rules and
procedures, §8-58.20(b).
Chain of custody of evidence subject to forensic
analysis.
Establishing without calling unnecessary
witnesses, §8-58.20(g).
Determination of admissibility of statement.
Objection timely filed, §8-58.20(g).
Objection to introduction of statement filed by
persons in chain of custody, §8-58.20(g).
Failure to file, §8-58.20(g).
Statement signed by each successive person
in chain of custody, §8-58.20(g).
Impaired driving prosecutions.
Laboratory results of chemical analysis of blood or
urine.
Admissibility without further authentication or
testimony of analyst, §20-139.1(c1).
Chain of custody.
Establishing without calling unnecessary
witnesses, §20-139.1(c3).
Notification to defendant of intent to
introduce report, §20-139.1(c1).
Objection to introduction of report by
defendant required, §20-139.1(c1).
Test performance requirements, §20-139.1(c2).

FORENSIC MEDICAL EXAMINATIONS.
**Assistance program for victims of rape and sex
offenses.**
Free exams, §143B-1200.

FORENSIC SCIENCE ADVISORY BOARD.
Established, §114-16.1(a).
Expenses of members, §114-16.1(d).
Functions, §114-16.1(e).
Meetings, §114-16.1(b).
Members, §114-16.1(a).
**Review of work, reports and conclusions by
laboratory scientists,** §114-16.1(f).
Terms of members, §114-16.1(c).

FOREST DEVELOPMENT ACT, §§106-1010 to
106-1018.
Administration of cost sharing.
Authority of secretary, §106-1014.
Approved forest management plan.
Defined, §106-1012.
Approved practices.
Defined, §106-1012.
Commissioner.
Administration of cost sharing.
Authority of commissioner, §106-1014.
Defined, §106-1012.
Equipment.
Authority to purchase, §106-1013(d).

FOREST DEVELOPMENT ACT —Cont'd
Commissioner —Cont'd
Powers and duties, §106-1013(a).
Staff, §106-1013(c).
Definitions, §106-1012.
Department.
Defined, §106-1012.
Disbursing agency, §106-1013(b).
Eligible landowners.
Defined, §106-1012.
Eligible lands.
Defined, §106-1012.
Equipment.
Authority to purchase, §106-1013(d).
Funds used for purchase.
Limited to appropriations from general fund,
§106-1018(e).
Federal cost sharing programs.
Eligible landowners may not use state funds,
§106-1016(c).
Forest development assessments.
Defined, §106-1012.
Forest development fund.
Created, §106-1018(a).
Defined, §106-1012.
Equipment.
Funds used for purchase, §106-1018(e).
Expenditures.
Limitation, §106-1018(e).
Percentage of funds used for program support,
§106-1018(d).
Intention of act, §106-1011(c).
Legislative purpose, §106-1011(a), (b).
Payments.
Funds from federal cost sharing programs,
§106-1016(c).
Limitation of payments, §106-1016(a).
Maximum amount, §106-1016(b).
Title of act, §106-1010.

FORESTERS, §§89B-1 to 89B-15.
Affidavits.
Consulting foresters.
Affidavit of compliance with provisions,
§89B-14(b).
Board of registration.
Appointment of members, §89B-3(a).
Compensation of members, §89B-4.
Composition, §89B-3(a).
Creation, §89B-3(a).
Expenses of members, §89B-4.
Hearings.
Charges against registrants, §89B-13.
Meetings, §89B-5.
Number of members, §89B-3(a).
Oaths.
Members may administer, §89B-6.
Officers, §89B-3(d).
Qualifications of members, §89B-3(a), (b).
Quorum, §89B-3(d).
Records, §89B-8.
Reports, §89B-8.
Roster of registered foresters, §89B-14(a).
Rules and regulations, §89B-6.
Seal, §89B-6.
Special meetings, §89B-5.
Terms of members, §89B-3(a).
Vacancies, §89B-3(c).
Bonds, surety.
Board of registration.
Secretary, §89B-7.

FORESTERS —Cont'd
Child support enforcement.
Forfeiture of licensing privilege, §50-13.12.
Continuing education.
Registration renewal, §89B-11(b).
Corporations.
Professional corporations generally, §§55B-1 to 55B-16.
See PROFESSIONAL CORPORATIONS.
Registration.
Prohibited, §89B-9(b).
Criminal laws.
Enforcement by United States forest service officers, §15A-406.
Definitions, §89B-2.
Examinations.
Fees, §89B-12.
Registration, §89B-12.
Fees.
Registration, §§89B-10(a), 89B-11(a).
Examinations, §89B-12.
Felony convictions.
Forfeiture of license, §15A-1331A.
Hearings.
Charges against registrants, §89B-13.
Legislative declaration.
Intention of chapter, §89B-1(b).
Misdemeanors.
Violations of provisions, §89B-15.
Oaths.
Board of registration.
Members may administer, §89B-6.
Partnerships.
Registration.
Prohibited, §89B-9(b).
Professional corporations generally, §§55B-1 to 55B-16.
See PROFESSIONAL CORPORATIONS.
Reciprocity.
Registration, §89B-9(d).
Records.
Board of registration, §89B-8.
Registration.
Applications, §89B-10(a).
Board. See within this heading, "Board of registration."
Examinations, §89B-12.
False or forged information.
Providing to board in obtaining certificate of registration, §89B-10(b).
Fees, §§89B-10(a), 89B-11(a).
Examinations, §89B-12.
Forester-in-training certificate, §89B-9(b1).
Individual persons only, §89B-9(b).
Nonresidents, §89B-9(c) to (e).
Qualifications, §89B-9(a).
Reciprocity, §89B-9(d).
Renewal, §89B-11.
Required, §89B-1(a).
Revocation or suspension, §89B-13.
Felony convictions, §15A-1331A.
Reissuance, §89B-13.
Roster of registered foresters, §89B-14(a).
Reports.
Board of registration, §89B-8.
Rules and regulations.
Board of registration, §89B-6.
Seals and sealed instruments.
Board of registration, §89B-6.
Funds.
Receipts and disbursements, §89B-7.

FORESTERS —Cont'd
United States forest service.
Officers authorized to enforce criminal laws, §15A-406.
Violations of provisions.
Misdemeanors, §89B-15.

FOREST FIRES.
Attorney general.
Investigations.
Deputy investigators, §58-79-25.
Cooperation between counties and state.
Forest protection and development, §106-906.
Department of agriculture and consumer services.
Powers, §106-895(a), (b).
Prevention, charge of, §143A-65.1.
Destruction of posted forestry notices.
Misdemeanor, §106-905.
Firefighters on standby duty.
Definitions, §106-955.
Distance from duty station, §106-956(a).
Exceptions, §106-956(b).
Electronic paging devices, §106-956(a).
Generally, §106-956(a).
Fire patrol designated during season of drought, §106-899(a).
Forest rangers.
Powers to prevent and extinguish fires, §106-899(a).
Open fires, regulation, §§106-940 to 106-950.
See OPEN FIRES.
Prescribed burning of forestland, §§106-966 to 106-970.
Setting fire to woodland.
Criminal trespass, §14-136.
Willfully or negligently setting fire to woods, §14-137.
Southeastern interstate forest fire protection compact, §§106-930 to 106-933.
Summoning residents to assist in extinguishing.
Powers of forest rangers, §106-899(a).

FOREST INSECT INFESTATION AND DISEASE PROTECTION, §§106-920 to 106-926.
Actions against insects and diseases, §106-923.
Annulment of control zone, §106-926.
Authority of department, §106-921.
Control zone.
Annulment, §106-926.
Cooperative agreements.
Department authority, §106-925.
Definitions, §106-922.
Department of agriculture and consumer services.
Actions against insects and diseases, §106-923.
Authority, §106-921.
Cooperative agreements, §106-925.
Right of entry onto private land, §106-924.
Intent of article, §106-920(a), (b).
Legislative findings, §106-920(a), (b).
Purpose and intent, §106-920(a), (b).
Right of entry.
Private land within control zones, §106-924.

FOREST LAW-ENFORCEMENT OFFICERS, §106-900.

FOREST OF STATE.
Generally.
See STATE FORESTS.

FOREST PRACTICE GUIDELINES RELATED TO WATER QUALITY, §113A-52.1.

FOREST PRODUCTS ASSESSMENT, §§106-1025 to 106-1032.
Commissioner of department of agriculture and consumer services.
Duties, §106-1029(b).
Definitions, §106-1027.
Forest development fund.
Defined, §106-1027.
Operation of system.
Levy of general assembly, §106-1028(a).
Primary forest product.
Defined, §106-1027.
Processors.
Defined, §106-1027.
Purpose of article, §106-1026(a).
Purposes of assessments levied, §106-1026(b).
Rate of assessment, §§106-1028(b), 106-1030(b).
Standards, §106-1030(a).
Secretary of department of revenue.
Duties, §106-1029(a).
Reimbursement for expenditures, §106-1029(c).
Short title, §106-1025.
Title.
Short title, §106-1025.

FOREST PROTECTION AND DEVELOPMENT CORPORATIONS, §§106-980 to 106-996.
Appeal by corporations to governor, §106-985.
Application of corporate income, §106-995.
Borrowing money.
Power limited, §106-993.
Bounties.
Limitation on bounties to stockholders, §106-988.
Cutting and sale of timber, §106-991.
Consent required, §106-992.
Department of agriculture and consumer services.
Department defined, §106-980(a).
Development plans, commissioner to approve, §106-994.
Powers of commissioner, §106-984.
Supervisory duties of commissioner, §106-983.
Development plans.
Commissioner to approve, §106-994.
Directors, §106-942.
Dissolution of corporations, §106-990.
Dividends.
Earnings above dividend requirements payable to state, §106-989.
Limitations, §106-986.
Formation.
Private limited dividend corporations, §106-980(b).
Income.
Application of corporate income, §106-995.
Injunctions.
Commissioner of agriculture and consumer services department.
Power to apply for injunctions, §106-984.
Interest rates.
Maximum rates allowable, §106-992.
Issuance of securities.
Restricted, §106-987.
Limitations as to dividends, §106-986.
Loans.
Power to borrow money limited, §106-993.
Mandamus.
Commissioner of agriculture and consumer services department.
Power to petition for writ of mandamus, §106-984.

FOREST PROTECTION AND DEVELOPMENT CORPORATIONS —Cont'd
Mortgaging property.
Consent required, §106-992.
Number of directors, §106-942.
Private limited dividend corporations.
Formation, §106-980(b).
Provision for appeal by corporations to governor, §106-985.
Reorganization of corporations, §106-996.
Sale of property, §§106-991, 106-992.
Consent required, §106-992.
Secretary of environment and natural resources.
Director, §106-942.
Stock and stockholders.
Earnings above dividend requirements payable to state, §106-989.
Issuance of securities restricted, §106-987.
Limitation on bounties to stockholders, §106-988.
Limitations as to dividends, §106-986.
Supervisory duties of commissioner, §106-983.

FOREST RANGERS.
Appointment, §106-896.
Citations.
Authority to issue, §106-899(b).
Compensation, §106-902.
Duties.
Generally, §106-898.
Expenses.
Payment by state and counties, §106-898.
Forest fires.
Power to prevent and extinguish fires, §106-899(a).
Instructions on forest preservation and development, §106-907(a), (b).
Open fires.
Control of existing fires, §106-947.
Definitions, §106-941.
Powers.
Forest fires.
Prevention and extinguishing, §106-899(a).
Generally, §106-900.
Warning tickets and citations.
Authority to issue, §106-899(b).
Warning tickets.
Authority to issue, §106-899(b).

FOREST RESERVE.
United States acquisition of land for national forest reserve, §104-5.

FOREST ROAD SYSTEM.
Motor vehicle laws applicable to state parks and forest road system, §143-116.8.

FORESTRY COUNCIL, §§143A-66.1 to 143A-66.3.
Annual meeting, time, §143A-66.3.
Best management practices.
Duty to advise commissioner, §143A-66.1.
Chairperson, §143A-66.2(c).
Clerical and other services.
Supplied by commissioner, §143A-66.2(h).
Conflicts in management of forest.
Forum for resolution, §143A-66.1.
Created in department of agriculture and consumer services, §143A-66.1.
Functions and duties, §143A-66.1.
Long range comprehensive plan.
Duty to provide, §143A-66.1.
Meetings, §143A-66.3.

FORESTRY COUNCIL —Cont'd
Members, §143A-66.2(a).
Appointment, §143A-66.2(a), (b).
Per diem, travel, subsistence expenses.
Receipt by members, §143A-66.2(f).
Quorum, §143A-66.2(g).
Rare and endangered species occurring in
private forests.
Protection, §143A-66.1.
Reforestation.
Duties, §143A-66.1.
Removal of members, §143A-66.2(e).
Special meetings, §143A-66.3.
Terms of office, §143A-66.2(d).
Vacancy.
Resignation, death, disability of member creating.
Term of office of appointee, §143A-66.2(d).

FORESTRY DEVELOPMENT ACT.
Primary forest product assessment act,
§§106-1025 to 106-1032.
See FOREST PRODUCTS ASSESSMENT.

FORESTRY NOTICES.
Penalty to destroy, §106-905.

FORESTRY OPERATION NUISANCE
LIABILITY, §§106-700, 106-701.

FORESTRY SERVICES FOR OWNERS AND
OPERATORS OF FORESTLAND.
Administration of provisions.
Under direction of commissioner, §106-1002(a).
Expenses for services and advice, §106-1002(b),
(c).
Scientific forestry services, §106-1001(a), (b).

FORESTS AND FORESTRY.
Agriculture commissioner and board.
Joint duties, §106-22.
Appeals.
Protection and development corporations,
§106-985.
Arrest.
Forest law-enforcement officers.
Powers, §106-900.
Assessment of primary forest products,
§§106-1025 to 106-1032.
See FOREST PRODUCTS ASSESSMENT.
Burning.
Prescribed burning of forestlands, §§106-966 to
106-970.
Citations.
Forest rangers.
Authority to issue, §106-899(b).
Closing forests and woodlands to hunting,
fishing and trapping, §106-908.
Commission on agriculture and forestry
awareness, §§120-150 to 120-154.
Cooperative agreements.
Department authority, §106-925.
Cooperative associations.
Authorized purposes, §§54-111, 54-124.
Corporations for protection and development
of forest, §§106-980 to 106-996.
See FOREST PROTECTION AND
DEVELOPMENT CORPORATIONS.
Counties.
Cooperation between counties and state, §106-906.
Restriction of certain forestry activities prohibited.
Definitions, §153A-452(a).
Exceptions, §153A-452(c).
Generally, §153A-452(b).

FORESTS AND FORESTRY —Cont'd
Definitions.
Forest fires.
Firefighters on standby duty, §106-955.
Forest laws, §106-897.
Insect infestation and disease, §106-922.
Open fires, §106-941.
Owners and operators of forestland, §106-1001(a).
Primary forest product assessment act, §106-1027.
Protection and development of forests,
§106-980(a).
Department of agriculture and consumer
services.
Cooperation between counties and state, §106-906.
Corporations for protection and development of
forests.
Definitions, §106-980(a).
Division of forest resources.
Designation as emergency response agency,
§166A-18.
Forest fires.
Powers, §106-895(a), (b).
Forest maintenance, forest fire prevention,
reforestation, forest preservation.
Department to have charge of work, §143A-65.1.
Forest rangers.
Appointment, §106-896.
Compensation, §106-902.
Forestry council.
Created in department, §143A-66.1.
Generally, §§143A-66.1 to 143A-66.3.
Owners and operators of forestland.
Forestry service and advice for.
Commissioner defined, §106-1001(a).
Department defined, §106-1001(a).
State forests and state recreation forests.
Charge of, §143A-65.1.
Generally.
See STATE FORESTS.
Donations of property for forestry purposes,
§106-882.
Emergency management.
Division of forest resources.
Designation as emergency response agency,
§166A-18.
Forest development act, §§106-1010 to 106-1018.
See FOREST DEVELOPMENT ACT.
Foresters, §§89B-1 to 89B-15.
See FORESTERS.
Forest fires.
Generally.
See FOREST FIRES.
Forest laws defined, §106-897.
Forest rangers.
Generally.
See FOREST RANGERS.
Forestry council, §§143A-66.1 to 143A-66.3.
Governor.
Authority to close forests and woodlands to
hunting, fishing and trapping, §§106-908,
106-909.
Immunities.
Prescribed burning of forestlands, §106-967(b), (c).
Insect infestation and disease protection,
§§106-920 to 106-926.
See FOREST INSECT INFESTATION AND
DISEASE PROTECTION.
Law enforcement officers, §106-900.
Littering state forests, §14-399.
Loans.
Protection and development corporations.
Power to borrow money limited, §106-993.

FORESTS AND FORESTRY —Cont'd

Marketing associations, §§54-129 to 54-166.
See MARKETING ASSOCIATIONS.

Municipalities.
Restriction of certain forest activities prohibited, §160A-458.5.

North Carolina museum of forestry.
Satellite museum of state museum of natural sciences, §143B-344.23.

Notice.
Destruction of posted forestry notices, §106-905.

Nuisances.
Liability of agricultural and forestry operations, §§106-700, 106-701.
Prescribed burning of forestlands.
Not to constitute public or private nuisance, §106-967(a).

Open fires regulation, §§106-940 to 106-950.
See OPEN FIRES.

Owners and operators of forestland.
Scientific forestry services, §106-1001(a), (b).
Services and advice.
Administration of provisions.
Under direction of commissioner, §106-1002(a).
Expenses, §106-1002(b), (c).

Pollution control.
Forest practice guidelines related to water quality.
Best management practices, §113A-52.1.

Prescribed burning of forestlands, §§106-966 to 106-970.
Conduct, §106-968(b).
Definitions, §106-966.
Division of forest resources.
Rules, §106-969.
Exemptions, §106-970.
Immunities, §106-967(b), (c).
Nuisances.
Not to constitute, §106-967(a).
Open-burning permit, §106-968(c).
Prescription, §106-968(a).
Rules, §106-969.

Primary forest product assessment act, §§106-1025 to 106-1032.
See FOREST PRODUCTS ASSESSMENT.

Prisons and prisoners.
Employment of prisoners, §148-26(c).

Property taxes.
Agricultural, horticultural and forestland, §§105-277.2 to 105-277.7.

Protection and development.
Cooperation between counties and state, §106-906.
Corporations, §§106-980 to 106-996.
See FOREST PROTECTION AND DEVELOPMENT CORPORATIONS.
Instructions on forest preservation and development, §106-907(a), (b).

Scientific forestry services.
Authority to render, §106-1001(a), (b).

Sedimentation pollution control act of 1973.
Forest practice guidelines related to water quality.
Best management practices, §113A-52.1.

Southeastern interstate forest fire protection compact, §§106-930 to 106-933.

State forest.
Generally.
See STATE FORESTS.

FORESTS AND FORESTRY —Cont'd

Taxation.
Property taxes.
Agricultural, horticultural and forestland, §§105-277.2 to 105-277.7.
See PROPERTY TAXES.

Trees and timber.
See TREES AND TIMBER.

United States.
Forest development act.
Federal cost sharing programs.
Eligible landowners may not use state funds if funds from federal program received, §106-1016(c).
Forest reserve in North Carolina.
Acquisition of land for, §104-5.
Authorized, §104-5.

Warning tickets.
Issuance, §106-901(a).
Authority to issue, §106-899(b).
Conditions, §106-901(b).
No right to be issued, §106-901(d).
Previously issued tickets, §106-901(c).

Water and air resources.
Sedimentation pollution control act of 1973.
Forest practice guidelines related to water quality.
Best management practices, §113A-52.1.

Western North Carolina arboretum, §§116-240 to 116-244.

Western North Carolina public lands council, §§143B-324.1 to 143B-324.3.

Wildfires.
See FOREST FIRES.

FORFEITURE OF OFFICE.

Budget of state.
Criminal penalties for violations, §143C-10-1.

Quo warranto action by attorney general, §1-515.

FORFEITURES.

Accident and health insurance.
Final payment of premium.
Notice required before forfeiture, §58-50-35.

Actions to recover.
Repeal of statute not to affect actions, §12-2.

Alcoholic beverages, §18B-504.

Apportionment to school administrative units, §115C-452.

Archaeological resources protection.
Violations of provisions, §70-17.

Bail bond, §§15A-544.1 to 15A-544.8.
See BAIL.

Bail bondsmen and runners, §58-71-35.

Bonds, surety.
Failure of surety companies to pay judgment is forfeiture, §58-73-25.

Cable television.
State franchising of cable television service.
Forfeiture of franchise, §66-354(b).

Child support enforcement.
Licensing privileges, §50-13.12.

Chop shops, §14-72.7(e).

Cigarettes.
Fire-safety standard and firefighter protection act.
Noncomplying cigarettes, §58-92-30(e).

Civil penalty and forfeiture fund, §§115C-457.1 to 115C-457.3.

Commercial drivers' licenses.
Child support enforcement, §50-13.12.

FORFEITURES —Cont'd
Commercial drivers' licenses —Cont'd
Conviction of felony, automatic forfeiture,
§15A-1331A.
Constitution of North Carolina.
Local, private and special legislation prohibited,
NC Const Art II §24.
Continuing criminal enterprise.
Forfeiture of profits, §14-7.20(b).
Contracts for deed.
Conditions for forfeiture, right to cure, §47H-3.
Effect of default and forfeiture, §47H-2(e), (f).
Notice of default and intent to forfeit, §47H-4.
Criminal street gangs.
Seizure and forfeiture of property, §14-50.23.
Disbursement of proceeds.
School administrative units, §115C-452.
Drivers' licenses.
Child support enforcement, §50-13.12.
Conviction of felony, automatic forfeiture,
§15A-1331A.
Limited driving privilege, eligibility,
§20-179.3(b).
Drugs.
Controlled substances, §§90-112, 90-112.1.
Vehicles and other personal property used in
controlled substances offenses, §90-112.
Applicability of article, §90-113.7.
Mitigation or remission of forfeitures, §90-112.1.
Electrologists.
Schools of electrology.
Failure to renew certification, §88A-20.
Electronic surveillance devices, §15A-289.
Felonies.
Licensing privilege after conviction of felony,
§15A-1331A.
Money or other property or interest acquired,
§14-2.3(a).
Action to recover, statute of limitation,
§14-2.3(b).
Property traceable to owner or guardian,
inapplicability of forfeiture, §14-2.3(c).
Firearms and other weapons.
Confiscation of deadly weapons generally,
§14-269.1.
**Fire-safety standard and firefighter protection
act.**
Noncomplying cigarettes, §58-92-30(e).
Fishing licenses.
Child support enforcement, §50-13.12.
Conviction of felony, automatic forfeiture,
§15A-1331A.
General assembly.
Local, private and special legislation prohibited,
NC Const Art II §24.
Health.
Money or property unlawfully acquired, §130A-27.
Hunting licenses.
Child support enforcement, §50-13.12.
Conviction of felony, automatic forfeiture,
§15A-1331A.
Impaired driving offenses, §§20-28.2 to 20-28.9.
Landlord and tenant.
Term forfeited for nonpayment of rent, §42-3.
Larceny, conveyances used in committing,
§14-86.1.
Lewd matter, §19-6.
Licensing privileges.
Child support enforcement, §50-13.12.
Conviction of felony, automatic forfeiture,
§15A-1331A.

FORFEITURES —Cont'd
Limitation of action, §1-54.
Littering.
Vehicles or machines involved in disposal of
certain amount of litter, §14-399(g).
Lubricating oils.
Person violating or allowing employee to violate
article, §119-5.
Metal.
Vehicles used to transport unlawfully obtained
regulated metals property, §66-11.2.
Motor vehicles.
Controlled substances.
Conveyances used in violations of provisions,
§§90-112, 90-112.1.
Forfeitures of personal property used in controlled
substances offenses, §90-112.
Applicability of article, §90-113.7.
Mitigation or remission of forfeiture, §90-112.1.
Impaired driving offenses, §§20-28.2 to 20-28.9.
Habitual impaired driving, §20-138.5(e).
Metal.
Vehicles used to transport unlawfully obtained
regulated metals property, §66-11.2.
Nuisances against public morals, abatement,
§§19-6, 19-6.1.
Occupational licenses.
Child support enforcement, §50-13.12.
Conviction of felony, automatic forfeiture,
§15A-1331A.
**Option to purchase contract executed with
residential lease agreement.**
Default and forfeiture, effect, §47G-2(e), (f).
Notice of default and intent to forfeit, §47G-5.
Right to cure the default, §47G-4.
Organized retail theft, §14-86.6(b).
Pawnbrokers and cash converters.
Pawn transactions, §91A-9.
Personal property.
Controlled substances offenses, §90-112.
Applicability of article, §90-113.7.
Mitigation or remission of forfeiture, §90-112.1.
Plant protection and conservation.
Illegally possessed plants, §106-202.20.
Public schools.
Apportionment to school administrative units,
§115C-452.
**Racketeer influenced and corrupt
organizations.**
Forfeiture of property.
See RACKETEER INFLUENCED AND
CORRUPT ORGANIZATIONS (RICO).
Record and tape piracy.
Infringing articles, implements, devices and
equipment, §14-437(b).
Recreational therapists.
Licenses, §90C-29.
Rents.
Term forfeited for nonpayment of rent, §42-3.
Residential mortgage fraud, §14-118.16(a).
Tax credit for qualified business investments,
§105-163.014.
Usury, §24-2.
Venue.
Action of recovery of penalty or forfeiture, §1-77.
Vessels.
Controlled substances.
Conveyances used in violations of provisions.
Generally, §§90-112, 90-112.1.

FORGERY.
Bank deposits and collections.
Customer's duty to discover and report, §25-4-406.

FORGERY —Cont'd
Banks.
  Notes, checks and other securities, §14-119.
    Connecting genuine parts, §14-125.
Bills of exchange, §14-122.
  Selling of certain forged securities, §14-121.
Bills of lading.
  Felony, §21-42.
Bond issues, §14-122.
  Selling of certain forged securities, §14-121.
Checks, §14-119.
Constitution of the United States, US Const Art
    I §8.
Corporations.
  Certificates of corporate stock forged, §14-124.
Counterfeit money, §§14-13 to 14-16.
  See COUNTERFEITING.
Deeds, §14-122.
Diplomas, §14-122.1.
Drugs.
  Controlled substances.
    Acquiring or obtaining possession by,
        §90-108(a).
Education.
  Diplomas, §14-122.1.
  Documents issued by educational institutions.
    Governmental agency, §14-122.1(b).
    Making or using, §14-122.1(a).
    Misdemeanors, §14-122.1(c).
    Postsecondary educational institution,
        §14-122.1(b).
    Secondary school, §14-122.1(b).
  Transcripts, §14-122.1.
Elections.
  Absentee ballots, §163-237(c).
False pretenses and cheats.
  Obtaining signatures by false pretenses, §14-101.
Financial transaction cards.
  Criminal possession of financial transaction card
      forgery devices, §14-113.14(a), (b).
  Elements of offense, §14-113.11(a).
  Embossing financial transaction card falsely,
      §14-113.11(c).
  Encoding financial transaction card falsely,
      §14-113.11(d).
  Making financial transaction card falsely,
      §14-113.11(b).
  Prima facie evidence of forgery, §14-113.12(a), (b).
Indictments.
  Intent to defraud.
    Sufficiency of allegation, §15-151.
Leases, §14-122.
Letters of credit.
  Basis for dishonor, §25-5-108(d).
  Injunction on honoring, §25-5-109(b).
  Issuer allowed to honor despite, §25-5-109(a).
Military affairs.
  Registration of military discharges.
    Forgery of discharge or certificate, §47-112.
**Motor vehicle certificates of title, registration
    cards or applications,** §20-71(a).
**Motor vehicle electronic inspection
    authorization,** §20-183.8(c).
Negotiable instruments.
  Bank notes, checks and other securities, §14-119.
    Connecting genuine parts, §14-125.
  Uttering instrument containing forged
      endorsement, §14-120.
Notes, §14-119.
  Connecting genuine parts of notes, §14-125.
Petitions, §14-123.

FORGERY —Cont'd
Probate and registration.
  Military discharge registration, §47-112.
Promissory notes, §14-122.
  Selling of certain forged securities, §14-121.
Securities, §14-119.
  Selling of certain forged securities, §14-121.
Stock certificates, §14-124.
Universities and colleges.
  Transcripts and diplomas, §14-122.1.
Uttering.
  Elements of offense, §14-120.
  Petitions forged, §14-123.
Wastewater system contractors and inspectors.
  Certification, §90A-81(d).
Wills, §14-122.

**FORGIVABLE EDUCATION LOANS FOR
    SERVICE PROGRAM,** §116-209.45.

FOR-HIRE VEHICLES.
Motor carriers, §§62-259 to 62-280.1.
  See MOTOR CARRIERS.
Passenger vehicles.
  Window tinting exceptions, §20-127(c).
Rental vehicles.
  See RENTAL VEHICLES.
Taxicabs.
  See TAXICABS.

FORMA PAUPERIS.
See IN FORMA PAUPERIS.

FORMER JEOPARDY, US Const Amd 5.
Appeals.
  Correction of errors by appellate division.
    When charges must be dismissed with
        prejudice, §15A-1447(g).
Death by vehicle.
  Manslaughter.
    Subsequent prosecutions prohibited,
        §20-141.4(c).
Dismissal motions, §15A-954(a).
Manslaughter.
  Death by vehicle.
    Subsequent prosecutions prohibited,
        §20-141.4(c).
Probable cause hearings.
  Findings by judge not to preclude subsequent
      prosecution for same offense, §15A-612(b).
  Subsequent prosecution for same offense not
      barred, §15A-612.

FORMER TESTIMONY.
Hearsay exception, §8C-1 Rule 804(b).

FORMS.
Absentees in military service.
  Transfer of property valued at less than five
      thousand dollars.
    Procedure without receivership, §28B-9(a).
Acknowledgments.
  Corporate officials.
    Deeds and other conveyances by corporations,
        §47-41.01(b), (c).
  Grantor, §47-38.
    Husband's and wife's or other grantor's
        acknowledgment before same officer,
        §47-40.
  Power of attorney.
    Certificate of acknowledgment of instrument
        executed by attorney in fact, §47-43.
  Principal acting in own right or representative
      capacity.
    Notarial certificate, §10B-41(a).

FORMS —Cont'd
Advance instruction for mental health treatment, §122C-77.
Affidavit of lost note, §47-46.3.
Aliens.
Verification of work authorization.
Complaint forms.
Contents, §64-27(b).
Design and promulgation, §64-27(a).
Annexation by petition of property owners, §160A-31(b), (b2), (k).
Answers, §1A-1 Rule 84.
Appeals, AppProc Appx D.
Appointment to public office.
Notice, §143-47.7(c).
Arbitration and award.
Rules for court-ordered arbitration, Arbitration Rule 8.
Attorney disciplinary proceedings.
Form letters, district grievance committees.
Letter of notice to respondent attorney, Bar Rule B.0216.
Letter to complainant acknowledging grievance, Bar Rule B.0213.
Letter to complainant from investigating attorney, Bar Rule B.0215.
Letter to complainant/respondent where district committee recommends finding of no probable cause, Bar Rule B.0210.
Letter to complainant where district committee recommends finding of probable cause, Bar Rule B.0212.
Letter to complainant where local grievance alleges fee dispute and other violations, Bar Rule B.0209.
Letter to complainant where local grievance alleges fee dispute only, Bar Rule B.0208.
Letter to investigating attorney assigning grievance, Bar Rule B.0214.
Letter to respondent where district committee recommends finding of probable cause, Bar Rule B.0211.
Letter transmitting completed file to North Carolina state bar, Bar Rule B.0217.
Bad checks.
Letters of notification and demand, §6-21.3(a1), (a2).
Bonds, surety.
Model payment and performance bonds, §44A-33.
Summary ejectment.
Bond to stay execution.
Form of undertaking, §42-34(d).
Certificate of authority for electronic notarial act, §10B-137(a).
Certificate of officer taking proof of instrument.
By proof of signature of subscribing witness, §47-43.4.
By signature of maker, §47-43.3.
By subscribing witness, §47-43.2.
Child care provider criminal history record check.
Statement furnished to child care provider, §110-90.2(c).
Childhood vaccine-related injury compensation.
Official forms of the industrial commission, ChildhoodVaccin Rule 103.
Civil actions, §1A-1 Rule 84.
Claim and delivery.
Notice of hearing, §1-474.1(c).

FORMS —Cont'd
Claim and delivery —Cont'd
Waiver of hearing, §1-474.1(c).
Clerk's certificate.
Upon probate by magistrate, §47-44.
Upon probate by nonresident official without seal, §47-45.
Commodities.
Adoption or modification.
Approval of administrator required, §78D-27(b).
Publication authority of administrator, §78D-27(c).
Complaints, §1A-1 Rule 84.
Concealed handgun permit.
Application form provided by sheriff, §14-415.13(a).
Contents of form, §14-415.14.
Consent to health care for minor.
Authorization, §32A-34.
Corporations.
Contracts in writing for purchase of personal property, §47-41.02(f).
Probate of deeds and other conveyances.
Acknowledgment by corporate official, §47-41.01(b), (c).
Instruments executed by president, presiding member or trustee and 2 other corporate members, §47-41.02(b).
Instruments executed by president, presiding member or trustee and attested by secretary or assistant secretary, §47-41.02(c), (d).
Credit suspension directive.
Notice to borrower, §45-36.7A(c).
Criminal history record checks.
Child care providers.
Statement furnished to child care provider, §110-90.2(c).
Custodial trusts.
Custodial trustees receipt and acceptance, §33B-4(b).
Declaration of trust under act, §33B-18(a).
Transfer under act, §33B-18(a).
Document of rescission.
Erroneous recorded release, §45-36.6(g).
Erroneous satisfaction, §45-36.6(h).
Domestic violence.
Pro se forms, §50B-2(d).
Drainage districts.
Receipt books, §§156-108, 156-109.
Electronic notarial act.
Certificate of authority, §10B-137(a).
Eminent domain.
Private condemnors.
Commissioners.
Report of assessment of compensation, §40A-27.
Public condemnors.
Commissioners.
Report of assessment of compensation, §40A-48(c).
Equity line of credit.
Equity line security instrument.
Certificate evidencing extension, §45-82.1(d).
Future advances.
Notice regarding, §45-82.3(e).
Attorney, financial institution, title insurance company giving, §45-82.3(f).
Notice to borrower.
Attorney, bank, other financial institution making request to terminate, §45-82.2(d).

FORMS —Cont'd
Equity line of credit —Cont'd
Notice to borrower —Cont'd
Title insurance company making request to
terminate, §45-82.2(c).
Termination request, §45-82.2(b).
Executions, §1-313.
Exemptions.
Setting aside exempt property.
Statement by debtor, §1C-1603(c).
Exempt property from claims of creditors.
Notice, §1C-1603(a).
**Exempt property from enforcement of claims
of creditors.**
Statement of debtor, §1C-1603(c).
Foreign-money claims.
Judgments, §1C-1826(f).
Garnishment.
Notice of levy, §1-440.24.
Summons to garnishee, §1-440.23.
General assembly.
Approval of bills, §120-29.1.
Reconvened sessions.
Request that session not be held, §120-6.1(b).
Health.
Communicable diseases.
Form and content of reports, §130A-141.
Temporary order to report health related
information, §130A-141.1.
Health care powers of attorney.
Statutory form, §32A-25.1.
Indictments.
Defects which do not vitiate, §15-155.
Informality.
Bill or warrant not quashed for informality,
§15-153.
Perjury.
Bill for perjury, §15-145.
Insurance.
Accident and health insurance.
Approval by commissioner, §§58-3-150(b),
58-51-95(a).
Group or blanket accident and health
insurance, §58-51-85.
Policies, §58-51-5(a).
Approval of forms by commissioner, §58-51-1.
Other states, §58-51-5(b).
Approval of policy forms by commissioner of
insurance, §58-3-150(a).
Certificate of insurance defined, §58-3-150(d).
Credit insurance.
Disapproval by commissioner, §58-57-30(b).
Notice, §58-57-30(c).
Filing with commissioner, §58-57-30(a).
Action by commissioner on, §58-57-30(b).
Withdrawal of approval by commissioner,
§58-57-30(d), (e).
Existing policy forms, §58-40-115.
Life insurance.
Group life insurance policies, §58-3-150(b).
Policies, filing and approval, §58-41-50(a).
Proof of lost forms.
Insurance companies to furnish, §58-3-40.
Uniform claim forms for health benefit plans,
§58-3-171.
Joint accounts.
Credit unions.
Statement establishing, §54-109.58(a).
Savings and loan associations.
Statement establishing, §54B-129(a).

FORMS —Cont'd
Joint deposits.
Right of survivorship, §41-2.1(g).
Judgments.
Cancellation, assignment, etc., of judgments.
Docket or record book, §1-239.1.
Landlord and tenant.
Summary ejectment.
Undertaking and order to stay execution of
judgment, §42-34(d).
Law students providing legal services.
Withdrawal of dean's certificate, Bar Rule C.0204.
Leases.
Registration of leases, §47-118.
Libraries.
Interstate library compact.
Articles of compact, §125-12.
Loan broker disclosure statements, §66-107.
**Lost note secured by deed of trust, mortgage,
other instrument.**
Affidavit, §47-46.3.
Marriage.
Licenses, §51-16.
Registration of marriage certificates,
§130A-110(a).
**Membership camping contracts, notice of
cancellations,** §66-240.
**Mental health, developmental disability,
substance abuse.**
Advance instruction for mental health treatment,
§122C-77.
Mortgages and deeds of trust.
Affidavit of lost note, §47-46.3.
Equity line of credit.
Equity line security instrument.
Certificate evidencing extension, §45-82.1(d).
Future advances.
Notice regarding, §45-82.3(e).
Attorney, financial institution, title
insurance company giving, §45-82.3(f).
Notice to borrower.
Attorney, bank, other financial institution
making request to terminate, §45-82.2(d).
Title insurance company making request to
terminate, §45-82.2(c).
Termination request, §45-82.2(b).
Lien maturity extension agreement, §45-36.24(d).
Notice of maturity date.
Extension of lien, §45-36.24(e).
Obligation release, §45-36.23(f).
Partial release, §45-36.22(g).
Sales under power of sale.
Requests for notice, §45-21.17A(a).
Satisfaction.
Certificate of satisfaction, §47-46.2.
Notice of satisfaction, §47-46.1.
Motions, §1A-1 Rule 84.
Motor vehicles.
Commissioner of motor vehicles to provide,
§20-41.
Negligence.
Complaints for negligence, §1A-1 Rule 84.
Notarial certificate.
Acknowledgment of principal acting in own right
or representative capacity, §10B-41(a).
Oath or affirmation taken by notary, §10B-43(a),
(d).
Official forms cured, §10B-41(a).
Verification or proof of signature of principal by
subscribing witness, §10B-42(a).

FORMS —Cont'd

Notice.

Service of process by publication, §1A-1 Rule 4(j).

Notice of appointment to public office,
§143-47.7(c).

Notice of open dumps, §130A-301(f).

Oaths, §11-11.

Notarial certificate, §10B-43(a), (d).

Open dump notice, §130A-301(f).

Payment bond, §44A-33(a).

Payment on death accounts.

Form of statement to be signed and executed,
§53-146.2A(a).

Savings banks, §54C-166.1(a).

Savings and loan associations.

Statement establishing, §54B-130A(a).

Performance bond, §44A-33(a).

Personal agency accounts.

Credit unions.

Statement establishing, §54-109.63(a).

Personal property.

Contracts by corporations for purchase of personal
property, §47-41.02(f).

Physicians dispensing prescription drugs.

Registration forms, §90-85.21(b).

Pleadings, §1A-1 Rule 84.

POD accounts.

Form of statement to be signed and executed,
§53-146.2A(a).

Savings banks, §54C-166.1(a).

Savings and loan associations.

Statement establishing, §54B-130A(a).

Power of attorney.

Certificate of acknowledgment of instrument
executed by attorney in fact, §47-43.

Statutory short form, §§32A-1 to 32A-3.

Prisons and prisoners.

Compensation to persons erroneously convicted of
felonies, §148-83.

Probate and registration.

Acknowledgment by grantor, §47-38.

Husband's and wife's or other grantor's
acknowledgment before same officer,
§47-40.

Acknowledgment of corporate official, §47-41.01(b),
(c).

Acknowledgment of instrument executed by
attorney in fact.

Certificate of acknowledgment, §47-43.

Certificate of officer taking proof of instrument.

By proof of signature of subscribing witness,
§47-43.4.

By signature of maker, §47-43.3.

By subscribing witness, §47-43.2.

Certificate of satisfaction of deed of trust or other
instrument, §47-46.2.

Clerk's certificate upon probate by magistrate,
§47-44.

Corporate contracts in writing for purchase of
personal property, §47-41.02(f).

Corporate deeds and other conveyances.

Acknowledgment of corporate official,
§47-41.01(b), (c).

Instruments executed by president, presiding
member or trustee, §47-41.02(b).

Instruments executed by president, presiding
member or trustee and attested by
secretary, §47-41.02(c), (d).

Husband's and wife's or other grantor's
acknowledgment before same officer, §47-40.

FORMS —Cont'd

Probate and registration —Cont'd

Leases.

Registration of lease, §47-118.

Military officers, §47-2.

Notarial certificate deeded sufficient, §47-37.1(a).

Notice of satisfaction of deed of trust or other
instrument, §47-46.1.

Options.

Memorandum of options, §47-117.

Power of attorney.

Certificate of acknowledgment of instrument
executed by attorney in fact, §47-43.

Probate by nonresident official without seal.

Clerk's certificate, §47-45.

**Professional corporation or professional
limited liability company practicing law,**
Bar Rule E.0106.

Publication.

Notice of service of process by publication, §1A-1
Rule 4(j).

Termination of parental rights proceedings.

Unknown parent, §7B-1105(d).

Real property.

Options to purchase real property, §47-119.

Reconvening of legislature.

Request that session not be held, §120-6.1(b).

Residential property disclosure act.

North Carolina real estate commission to prepare
forms, §47E-10.

Restricted driving judgment, §20-16.1(b1).

Retail installment sales.

Consumer credit installment sale contracts,
§25A-28.

Home-solicitation sale.

Agreement or offer, §25A-40(b).

Rules of civil procedure, §1A-1 Rule 84.

Sale of crossbows or pistols.

License or permit, §14-403.

**Satisfaction of deed of trust, mortgage, other
instruments.**

Certificate of satisfaction, §47-46.2.

Notice, §47-46.1.

Secured transactions.

Defaults.

Disposition of collateral after.

Consumer goods transactions.

Notification, §25-9-614.

Notification, §25-9-613.

Financing statements.

Amendment form, §25-9-521(b).

Initial financing statement form, §25-9-521(a).

Service of process.

Notice of service by publication, §1A-1 Rule 4(j).

Small claim actions, §7A-232.

Specific performance.

Complaint for specific performance, §1A-1 Rule
84.

State treasurer.

Furnished by auditor, §147-84.

Taxation.

Furnished by secretary of revenue, §105-254.

Property taxes.

Department of revenue.

Prescribing forms, §105-318.

Mobile homes.

Tax permit, §105-316.5.

Order of collection, §105-321(b).

Release of lien, §105-242(c), (c1).

Termination of parental rights proceedings.

Publication, unknown parent, §7B-1105(d).

FORMS —Cont'd
Third-party practice.
Motion to bring in third-party defendant, §1A-1
Rule 84.
Third-party complaint, §1A-1 Rule 84.
Torrens system registration.
Attorney general to prescribe, §43-3.
Certificate of title, §43-15.
Method of transfer.
Conveyance as security for debt, §43-36.
Release from registration, §43-25.
Transfers to minors.
Creating custodial property and effecting transfer,
§33A-9(a), (b).
Manner of creating custodial property and
effecting transfer, §33A-9.
Trusts and trustees.
Reliance on power of attorney.
Sample form of affidavit of attorney-in-fact,
§32A-40(c).
**Verification or proof of signature of principal
by subscribing witness.**
Notarial certificate, §10B-42(a).
Viatical settlements.
License application, §58-58-210(d).
Warehouse receipts, §25-7-202(a).
Workers' compensation.
Compromise settlement agreements, ICWorkComp
Forms IIa to IIIb.
Official forms, ICWorkComp Rule 103.
Tort claims rules, ICTortClaim Rule T103.
Third party recovery.
Order directing distribution of, ICWorkComp
Form I.

FORMULAS.
Larceny of secret technical processes, §14-75.1.

FORNICATION, §§14-184, 50B-8.
Domestic violence.
Effect upon prosecution for public morals offenses,
§50B-8.
Elements of offense, §14-184.
Hotels and inns.
Man and woman occupying same bedroom for
immoral purposes, §14-186.
Sex offenses generally.
See SEX OFFENSES.

FORSYTH COUNTY.
Acquisition of property, power, §153A-158.1(a).
Ambulance service.
Attachment or garnishment and lien for,
§§44-51.4 to 44-51.8.
False pretenses and cheats.
Obtaining ambulance services without
intending to pay, §14-111.2.
Board of county commissioners.
Filling vacancies on board, §153A-27.1.
**Condemnation or acquisition of land by local
government unit outside county.**
Consent of board of commissioners necessary,
§153A-15.
Counties generally.
See COUNTIES.
**Cropper or tenant refusing to perform terms
of contract.**
Forfeiture of right of possession to premises,
§42-27.
**Dangerous firearm use by young children,
permitting.**
Air rifles, air pistols and BB guns not dangerous
firearm, §14-316(b).

FORSYTH COUNTY —Cont'd
Motor vehicle emission inspections.
Counties inspections required to be performed in,
§143-215.107A(c).
Private parking lots.
Removal of unauthorized vehicles, §20-219.2.
Real estate mortgage loans.
Interest, commissions and repayment, §45-43.
Registration of deeds.
Tax certification, no delinquent taxes due,
§161-31(b).
**Room occupancy tax levied by county, uniform
provisions,** §153A-155.
School property.
Acquisition and improvement, §153A-158.1.
Sheriff.
Vacancy, performance of duties until vacancy
filled, §162-5.1.
Transportation authorities.
Local government sales and use tax for public
transportation.
Regional authority (Triad), §§105-510,
105-510.1.

FORT FISHER RECREATION AREA.
**Twenty-four hour access from Sept. 15 through
March 15.**
Persons paying fees, §113-35(b1).

**FORTHCOMING BOND FOR PERSONAL
PROPERTY,** §1-318.
Procedure on giving bond, §1-319.
Subsequent levies, §1-319.
Summary remedy, §1-320.

FORTIFIED WINE.
Consumption, §18B-301(d).
Definition of fortified wine, §18B-101.
Possession, §18B-301.

FORTS.
**Acquisition of land by US to be added to
military bases,** §104-7.

FORUM NON CONVENIENS.
Change of venue, §1-83.
**Child abuse, neglect or dependency
proceeding.**
Transferring case to another county.
After adjudication, §7B-900.1(a).
Child custody jurisdiction and enforcement,
§§50A-206(a), 50A-207.
**Stay of proceeding to permit trial in foreign
jurisdiction,** §1-75.12.

FORUM SELECTION.
Contracts to improve real property.
Subject to laws of another state.
Void and against public policy, §22B-2.
Contracts with forum selection provisions.
Invalid and against public policy, §22B-3.
Leases, UCC.
Commercial leases.
Limitation on power of parties to choose
applicable law and judicial forum,
§25-2A-106.

FOSTER CARE.
**Abused, neglected or dependent juvenile
actions.**
Appeal of final order for foster care placement.
Authority of court pending appeal, §7B-1003(e).
Dispositional order placing juvenile, requirements,
§7B-905(c).

FOSTER CARE —Cont'd
Abused, neglected or dependent juvenile actions —Cont'd
Review by court of voluntary foster care placements, §7B-910.
Additional hearings, §7B-910(c).
Authority of court upon making findings, §7B-910(b).
Findings to be made, §7B-910(a).
Notice of hearings, §7B-910(c).
Time for holding hearings, §7B-910(c).
Child placement.
Control over child caring facilities, §§110-45 to 110-48.
Foster care and adoption assistance, §§108A-48 to 108A-50.
Criminal history records checks, §114-19.4.
Annual check, §131D-10.3A(b).
Confidential and privileged information, §131D-10.3A(f), (g).
Department of justice to provide information, §131D-10.3A(d).
Destruction of information, §131D-10.3A(g).
Fee for check, §131D-10.3A(i).
Hearing, request by foster parent, §131D-10.3A(f).
Immunity for action taken in carrying out provision, §131D-10.3A(h).
Mandatory checks, §131D-10.3A(a).
Notice of mandatory checks.
Placement on application, §131D-10.3A(e).
Prohibiting person from providing foster care, §131D-10.3A(c).
Review of information, right of individual, §131D-10.3A(f).
Education of children with disabilities.
Cost of educating children in foster homes, §115C-111.3.
Health insurance.
State health plan for teachers and state employees.
Foster child.
Coverage as dependent child, §135-48.41(a).
Providing foster care.
Regulation generally, §§131D-10.1 to 131D-10.9.
See CHILD PLACING AGENCIES.
Register of applicants.
Division to maintain, §131D-10.6C.
Contents, §131D-10.6C(a).
Regulation of agencies receiving or placing children, §§131D-10.1 to 131D-10.9.
See CHILD PLACING AGENCIES.
Special education.
Education of children with disabilities.
Cost of educating children in foster homes, §115C-111.3.
State health plan for teachers and state employees.
Foster child.
Coverage as dependent child, §135-48.41(a).
Training, §131D-10.6A(a).

FOSTER CARE AND ADOPTION ASSISTANCE, §§108A-48 to 108A-50.
Adoption assistance payments.
Granting, rules, §108A-49(b).
Rate of payments, §108A-49.1(b).
HIV foster care and adoption assistance, §108A-49.1(c).
State and county contributions, §108A-49.1(d).
Benefits for certain adoptive children.
Authorization of program, §108A-50(a).

FOSTER CARE AND ADOPTION ASSISTANCE —Cont'd
Benefits for certain adoptive children —Cont'd
Eligibility, §108A-50(c).
When assistance not to be provided, §108A-50(d).
Purpose of program, §108A-50(b).
Special children adoption fund, §108A-50.2.
Special needs adoption incentive fund, §108A-50.1.
Creation of program, §108A-25(a).
Foster care benefits program.
Authorized, §108A-48(a).
Eligibility, §108A-48(b).
Granting assistance, rules, §108A-49(a).
Purposes, §108A-48(a).
Rate of payments, §108A-49.1(a).
HIV foster care and adoption assistance, §108A-49.1(c).
State and county contributions, §108A-49.1(d).
Use of available federal payments, §108A-49(c).
Special children adoption fund, §108A-50.2.
Special needs adoption incentive fund, §108A-50.1.
Using federal payments, §108A-49(c).

FOUR OAKS, TOWN OF.
Satellite annexation.
Limitation on area of satellite corporate limits, inapplicability, §160A-58.1(b).

FOXES.
Calling devices.
Taking with electronic calling devices, §113-291.4(d).
Closed seasons.
Hunting foxes with dogs harmful to turkey restoration, §113-291.4(h).
Contagious diseases.
Population control measures, §113-291.4(i).
Dogs.
Taking with dogs at night or day on year-round basis, §113-291.4(b).
Firearms.
Taking foxes with, §113-291.4(c).
Hunting and wildlife generally.
See HUNTING AND WILDLIFE.
Open seasons for taking foxes with firearms, §113-291.4A(a), (b).
Rabies emergencies.
Plan to reduce threat of rabies exposure to humans and domestic animals, §130A-201.
Rabies emergency for particular county.
Plan to reduce exposure to humans and domestic animals, §113-291.2(a1).
Regulatory powers of wildlife resources commission.
Applicability to foxes, §113-291.4(a).
Sale of parts prohibited, §113-291.3(b).
Sales.
Foxes lawfully taken in areas of open seasons, §113-291.4(g).
Seasons for taking foxes with weapons and trapping.
Continuance of seasons, §113-291.4(f1).
Studies of fox and fur-bearer populations.
Wildlife resources commission to improve capabilities, §113-291.4(e).
Tagging foxes and fox furs, §113-291.4(g).
Trapping, §113-291.4(f), (f1).
Unlawful trapping with electronic calling device, §113-294(j).

FOX HUNTING.
Equine activity liability, §§99E-1 to 99E-3.

FOX HUNTING PRESERVES.
Controlled hunting preserve operator license,
§113-273(g).

FRAGILE RECORDS.
Inspection of public records, §132-6(f).

FRANCHISE CARRIERS.
Junked or destroyed vehicles, §20-100.
Licenses for less than one year, §20-95.
Partial payments, §20-94.
Taxation.
Compensatory nature, §20-97.

FRANCHISES.
Ambulances.
County ambulance services, §153A-250.
Beer franchises, §§18B-1300 to 18B-1308.
See BEER FRANCHISES.
Business opportunity sales, §§66-94 to 66-100.
See BUSINESS OPPORTUNITY SALES.
Cable television.
State franchising of cable television service,
§§66-350 to 66-360.
See CABLE TELEVISION.
Theft of cable television services, §14-118.5.
Carriers.
See FRANCHISE CARRIERS.
Cooperative associations.
Taxes, §54-118.2.
Counties.
Ambulance services, §153A-250.
Ordinances, §153A-46.
Declaratory judgments.
Attorney general as party to proceedings involving
constitutionality, §1-260.
Municipality as party to proceedings involving
validity, §1-260.
Power of courts to construe, §1-254.
Electric membership corporations.
Municipal franchises, §§117-10.1, 117-10.2.
Farm machinery, §§66-180 to 66-188.
See FARM MACHINERY, VEHICLES AND
IMPLEMENTS OF HUSBANDRY.
Gas and gas companies.
Natural gas.
Local distribution companies, §62-36B.
Landfills.
Obtaining franchise to operate from local
government, §130A-294(b1).
Marketing associations, §54-143.1.
Motor carriers, §§62-111 to 62-113.
Motor vehicle dealers, §§20-305, 20-305.5, 20-307,
20-307.1.
Municipalities.
Ordinances, §160A-76(a).
Public utilities, §160A-319(a).
Taxicabs, §160A-304.
Natural gas.
Local distribution companies, §62-36B.
Obscene articles or publications.
Denial of franchise for refusal to accept,
§14-190.4.
Ordinances.
Grant, renewal, extension or amendment by
ordinance.
Procedure, §160A-76(a).
Public transportation authorities.
Effect of provisions on existing franchises and
operations, §160A-584.

FRANCHISES —Cont'd
Public transportation authorities —Cont'd
Power to grant franchises and enter into franchise
agreements, §160A-579.
Public utilities.
Bus companies.
Application of provisions, §62-112(d).
Certificates of convenience and necessity.
Generating facilities, §§62-82, 62-110.1.
Required, §62-110.
Conditions, §62-113(a).
Defined, §62-3.
Effective date, §62-112(a).
Emergency operating authority, §62-116(b).
Motor carriers, §§62-111 to 62-113.
Partnership franchises, §62-115.
Same or similar names, §62-117.
Suspension or revocation, §62-112(b).
Temporary authority to operate, §62-116(a).
Terms, §62-113(a).
Transfer, §62-111(a).
Motor carriers, §62-111(b), (c), (e).
Obtaining franchise for purpose of transferring
same.
Prohibited, §62-111(d).
Quo warranto.
Several claims to same franchise.
Tried in one action, §1-520.
Usurpation.
Action by attorney general, §1-515.
Shellfish.
Cultivation of shellfish.
Claims based upon perpetual franchise for
shellfish cultivation, §113-206(a1).
Leases.
Perpetual franchises, §113-202.2.
Solid waste management.
Obtaining franchise to operate landfill from local
government, §130A-294(b1).
Taxation, §§105-114 to 105-129.
See FRANCHISE TAX.

FRANCHISE TAX, §§105-114 to 105-129.
Burial.
Mutual burial associations, §105-121.1.
Business and energy tax credits, §§105-129.15 to
105-129.19.
Condition for doing business in state.
Payment, §105-114(a2).
Corporations.
Additional nature of tax, §105-122(f).
Apportionment, §105-122(c1).
Appraised value of tangible property, §105-122(d).
Computing total actual investment in tangible
personal property, §105-122(d).
Credits, §105-122(d1).
Deductible liabilities, §105-122(b).
Defined, §105-114(b).
Determination of tax, §105-122(a).
Dissolved domestic corporations, §105-127(f).
Exemptions, §105-125.
Holding companies, §105-120.2.
Imposition of annual franchise or privilege tax,
§105-122(a).
Indebtedness owed to parent, subsidiary or
affiliate, §105-122(b).
Limited liability companies.
Controlled companies, §105-114.1.
Local taxation prohibited, §105-122(g).
Minimum tax, §105-122(d).
Nature of tax upon, §105-114(a).

FRANCHISE TAX —Cont'd
Corporations —Cont'd
Nonprofit corporations.
Exemptions, §105-125.
Payment of tax, §105-122(d).
Annual payment, §105-127(a).
Pollution abatement equipment.
Deducted reserves, §105-122(d).
Deductible liabilities, §105-122(b).
Privilege of carrying on, doing business and/or
continuance of articles of incorporation,
§105-122(d).
Rate of tax, §105-122(d).
Returns, §105-122(a).
Change of income year, §105-122(e).
Due date, §105-122(a).
Stock, surplus and undivided profits.
Determination of total amount, §105-122(b).
Treasurers.
Duties, §105-127(c).
Credit.
Low-income housing tax credits, §§105-129.40 to
105-129.45.
Recycling facility investment.
Major facility investment, §§105-129.25 to
105-129.28.
Research and development credit, §§105-129.50 to
105-129.56.
Tax incentives for new and expanding businesses
generally, §§105-129.2 to 105-129.13.
See TAX INCENTIVES FOR NEW AND
EXPANDING BUSINESSES.
Definitions, §105-114(b).
Holding companies, §105-120.2(c).
Electric companies.
Additional tax imposed by county or city.
Companies not subject to, §105-116(e1).
Annual tax imposed, §105-116(a).
City not to impose or collect greater tax,
§105-116(e).
County or city imposing additional tax.
Companies not subject to, §105-116(e1).
Distribution to cities, §105-116(d).
City's share, §105-116.1(b).
Definitions, §105-116.1(a).
Hold-back amount for 1995-96 fiscal year,
§105-116.1(c) to (d).
Municipality incorporated on or after January 1,
2000, §105-116.1(e).
Payment, return, report, §105-116(b).
Rate of tax, §105-116(a).
Exemptions, §105-125.
Holding companies, §105-120.2.
Defined, §105-120.2(c).
Local taxation prohibited, §105-120.2(e).
Rate of tax, §105-120.2(b).
Reports, §105-120.2(a).
Investment companies.
Exemption, §105-125(b).
Joint municipal electric power and energy act.
Payments in lieu of taxes, §159B-27(b).
Limited liability companies.
Controlled companies.
Constructive ownership, §105-114.1(c).
Definitions, §105-114.1(a).
Noncorporate limited liability company.
Defined, §105-114.1(a).
Percentage included in tax base, §105-114.1(b).
Exemption, §105-114.1(f).
Owner of capital interests affiliated group of
corporations, §105-114.1(e).

FRANCHISE TAX —Cont'd
Limited liability companies —Cont'd
Controlled companies —Cont'd
Time ownership of capital interests determined,
§105-114.1(g).
Underpayment, fraud to evade, penalty,
§105-114.1(h).
Corporate franchise tax.
Credit for additional annual report fees,
§105-122.1.
Low-income housing tax credits, §§105-129.40 to
105-129.45.
Mutual burial associations, §105-121.1.
Nature of taxes, §105-114(a).
New and expanding businesses.
Tax incentives generally, §§105-129.2 to
105-129.13.
See TAX INCENTIVES FOR NEW AND
EXPANDING BUSINESSES.
No double taxation, §105-114(a4).
Payment.
Condition for doing business in state,
§105-114(a2).
Power of attorney.
Secretary of revenue, §105-128.
Privilege or excise taxes, §105-114(a1).
Real estate investment trust.
Exemption, §105-125(b).
Recycling facility investment.
Tax credit for major facility investment,
§§105-129.25 to 105-129.28.
Regulated investment companies.
Exemption, §105-125(b).
Research and development tax credit,
§§105-129.50 to 105-129.56.
Returns.
Corporations, §105-122(a).
Change of income year, §105-122(e).
Extension of time for filing, §105-129.
Scope of tax, §105-114(a1).
Secretary of revenue.
Extension of time for filing returns, §105-129.
Power of attorney, §105-128.
Sewerage companies.
Annual tax imposed, §105-116(a).
City not to impose or collect greater tax,
§105-116(e).
Distribution to cities, §105-116(d).
Payment, return, report, §105-116(b).
Rate of tax, §105-116(a).
**Tax incentives for new and expanding
businesses generally,** §§105-129.2 to
105-129.13.
See TAX INCENTIVES FOR NEW AND
EXPANDING BUSINESSES.
Tax year, §105-114(a3).
Telephone companies.
Distribution of gross receipts taxes to cities,
§105-116.1.
Definitions, §105-116.1(a).
Water companies.
Annual tax imposed, §105-116(a).
City not to impose or collect greater tax,
§105-116(e).
Distribution to cities, §105-116(d).
Payment, return, report, §105-116(b).
Rate of tax, §105-116(a).

FRANCIS X. MARTIN.
Evidence.
Collection of Martin's private acts, §8-2.

FRANKLIN COUNTY.
Acquisition of property, §153A-158.1(a).
Ambulance service.
Attachment or garnishment and lien for, §§44-51.4 to 44-51.8.
Condemnation or acquisition of land by local government unit outside county.
Consent of board of commissioners necessary, §153A-15.
Counties generally.
See COUNTIES.
Cropper or tenant refusing to perform terms of contract.
Forfeiture of right of possession to premises, §42-27.
Housing authority commissioners.
Tenant as commissioner, exemption from provision of law allowing, §157-5.
Maps in special proceedings, recording of photographic copies, §§47-32, 47-32.2.
Oil, gas or mineral claims.
Certain ancient claims extinguished, preservation, procedure, §1-42.1(a) to (d).
School property.
Acquisition and improvement, §153A-158.1.
Special school tax, election to abolish.
Petition required, §115C-505.
Tax elections for industrial development purposes, §§158-16 to 158-24.
Wild plants, taking of certain plants from land of another.
Inapplicability of provisions, §14-129.

FRANKLIN, TOWN OF.
All-terrain vehicles.
Use by employees on certain highways, §20-171.24.
Room occupancy tax.
Uniform provisions.
Authorized to levy, §160A-215(g).
Generally, §160A-215.

FRATERNAL BENEFIT SOCIETIES, §§58-24-1 to 58-24-190.
Administrative procedure act.
Commissioner.
Review of decisions and findings, §58-24-175.
Affidavits.
Consolidations and mergers.
Evidence of furnishing notice or document, §58-24-65(d).
Agents, §58-24-160(a).
Alcoholic beverage permits.
Special one-time permits, §18B-1002(a).
Amendments to laws of society.
Approval by commissioner, §58-24-50(b).
Benefit contracts, §58-24-90(b).
Evidence of adoption.
Printed copies, §58-24-50(e).
Filing with commissioner, §58-24-50(d).
Furnishing to members, §58-24-50(c).
Meetings, §58-24-50(a).
Referendums, §58-24-50(a).
Annual statements, §58-24-30(c).
Applicability of article.
Exemption of certain societies, §58-24-185(a) to (f).
Articles of incorporation.
Filing, §58-24-45(b).
Attachment.
Benefits.
Not subject to attachment, §58-24-85.
Beneficiaries, §58-24-80(a).

FRATERNAL BENEFIT SOCIETIES —Cont'd
Benefits.
Attachment.
Not subject to attachment, §58-24-85.
Cash surrender values, certificate loans and other options.
Calculation of amount by date of issuance, §58-24-95(a), (b).
Certificates.
Valuation.
By date of issuance, §58-24-120(a), (b).
Commissioner's discretion, §58-24-120(c).
Excess reserves, §58-24-120(d).
Filing of annual valuation, §58-24-125(b).
Standard of valuation, §58-24-120.
Contract, §58-24-90(a) to (h).
Issuance on variable basis, §58-24-105(c).
Death benefits.
Payment to personal representative, §58-24-80(c).
Eligibility for benefits, §58-24-75(b).
Funeral benefits.
Payment, §58-24-80(b).
Garnishment.
Not subject to garnishment, §58-24-85.
Minors.
Life insurance, §58-24-75(b).
Nonforfeiture benefits.
Calculation of amount by date of issuance, §58-24-95(a), (b).
Types of benefits, §58-24-75(a).
Bonds, surety.
Filing with articles of incorporation, §58-24-45(b).
Cemeteries.
Exemptions from North Carolina cemetery act, §65-47(b).
Commissioner, §58-24-175.
Communications to members, §58-24-30(b).
Consolidations and mergers.
Affidavits.
Evidence of furnishing notice or document, §58-24-65(d).
Approval by commissioner, §58-24-65(b).
Evidence of furnishing notice or document, §58-24-65(d).
Felonies.
Violation of provisions of section, §58-24-180(d).
Filing with commissioner, §58-24-65(a).
Insurance.
Reinsurance upon consolidation or merger, §58-24-60(b).
Procedure generally, §58-24-65(a) to (e).
Vesting, §58-24-65(c).
Construction and interpretation.
Severability of provisions of article, §58-24-190.
Contracts.
Benefit contract.
Amendments to laws of society, §58-24-90(b).
Assignment by society of terms and conditions, §58-24-90(h).
Attaining age of majority, §58-24-90(c).
Certificate of benefits, §58-24-90(a).
Certified copies.
Evidence of terms and conditions, §58-24-90(e).
Evidence of terms and conditions.
Certified copies, §58-24-90(e).
Filing and approval by commissioner, §58-24-90(f).
Impairment of certificates, §58-24-90(d).
Issuance on variable basis, §58-24-105(c).

FRATERNAL BENEFIT SOCIETIES —Cont'd
Contracts —Cont'd
Benefit contract —Cont'd
Transfer of control of ownership, §58-24-90(g).
Conveyances.
Effect as to conveyances by trustees, §59B-15(a).
Prior deeds validated, §59B-15(b).
Deeds.
Prior deeds validated, §59B-15(b).
Deficiencies, §58-24-145(a).
Action not recognized unless brought by attorney
general, §58-24-145(e).
Commencement of action to enjoin, §58-24-145(b).
Correction, time period, §58-24-145(a).
Enjoining society, §58-24-145(c).
Liquidating society, §58-24-145(d).
Notice by commissioner, §58-24-145(a).
Receiver appointed, commissioner appointed as
receiver, §58-24-145(e).
Voluntary discontinuance of business, applicability
of provisions, §58-24-145(f).
Definitions, §§58-24-1 to 58-24-15.
Directors.
Powers of society to purchase and maintain
insurance for, §58-24-35(c).
Embezzlement.
Treasurers of benevolent organizations, §14-93.
Employees.
Powers of society to purchase and maintain
insurance, §58-24-35(c).
Examinations, §58-24-135(a).
Agents, §58-24-160(a).
Exemption from examination requirement,
§58-24-160(b).
Exemptions from article.
Benefit certificates for death or disability benefits,
§58-24-185(b).
Compensation for procuring new members,
§58-24-185(c).
Death or disability solely from accident,
§58-24-185(d).
General insurance laws of state, also exempt
from, §§58-24-110, 58-24-185(f).
Generally, §58-24-185(a).
Information to commissioner to determine
exemption, §58-24-185(e).
Other provisions of insurance law, §§58-24-110,
58-24-185(f).
Fees.
Financial statements.
Filing annual statements, §58-24-125(a).
Felonies.
Consolidations and mergers.
Violation of provisions of section, §58-24-180(d).
False statements under oath, §58-24-180(e).
Mergers and consolidation.
Violations of provisions of section,
§58-24-180(d).
Financial statements.
Annual statements.
Filing, §58-24-125.
Filing annual statements, §58-24-125(a).
Penalties, §58-24-125(c).
Fines.
Filing annual statements, §58-24-125(c).
Not specified violations, §58-24-180(c).
Solicitation or procurement of membership.
Unauthorized, §58-24-180(b).
Foreign or alien societies, §58-24-140.
Continuation of authorized contracts,
§58-24-150(b).

FRATERNAL BENEFIT SOCIETIES —Cont'd
Foreign or alien societies —Cont'd
Licenses.
Continuation of authorized contracts,
§58-24-150(b).
Refusal to issue, §58-24-150(a).
Required, §58-24-140.
Suspension or revocation, §58-24-150(a).
Formation.
Structure of organization, §58-24-45(a).
Funds.
Establishment, §58-24-105(b).
Generally, §58-24-105(a).
Investments, §58-24-100.
Separate accounts, §58-24-105(c).
Garnishment.
Benefits.
Not subject to garnishment, §58-24-85.
Grievance or complaint procedures,
§58-24-30(d).
Immunities.
Officers.
Civil liability for monetary damages,
§58-24-35(d).
Indemnification.
Officers, directors, employees or agents,
§58-24-35(b).
Injunctions.
Application or petition for.
Attorney general upon request of commissioner,
§58-24-155.
Institutions, §58-24-55.
Insurance.
Directors, officers, employees or agents.
Powers of society to purchase and maintain
insurance, §58-24-35(c).
Exemptions from general insurance laws,
§58-24-110.
Mutual life insurance companies.
Conversion of society into company, §58-24-70.
Reinsurance, §58-24-60(a).
Consolidation or merger, §58-24-60(b).
Investments.
Funds, §58-24-100.
Laws of society.
Amendments.
Approval by commissioner, §58-24-50(b).
Benefit contracts, §58-24-90(b).
Evidence of adoption.
Printed copies, §58-24-50(e).
Filing with commissioner, §58-24-50(d).
Furnishing to members, §58-24-50(c).
Meetings, §58-24-50(a).
Referendums, §58-24-50(a).
Liability.
Officers and members.
Not personally liable for benefits provided by
society, §58-24-35(a).
Licenses, §58-24-45(e).
Agents, §58-24-160(a).
Annual license continuation fee, §58-24-130.
Copy or duplicate.
Prima facie evidence, §58-24-130.
Exemption from licensing requirement,
§58-24-160(b).
Foreign or alien societies.
Continuation of authorized contracts,
§58-24-150(b).
Refusal to issue, §58-24-150(a).
Required, §58-24-140.
Suspension or revocation, §58-24-150(a).

FRATERNAL BENEFIT SOCIETIES —Cont'd
Licenses —Cont'd
Perpetual licensing, §58-24-130.
Preliminary licenses, §58-24-45(c), (d).
Lodge system.
Defined, §58-24-5(a).
Minors.
Organization and operation of lodges for
children, §58-24-5(b).
Long-term care insurance, §§58-55-1 to 58-55-50.
See LONG-TERM CARE INSURANCE.
Long-term care partnerships, §§58-55-55 to
58-55-80.
Meetings.
Generally, §58-24-30(a).
Members.
Liability.
Not personally liable for benefits provided by
society, §58-24-35(a).
Qualifications for membership, §58-24-25(a).
Rights of membership not assignable,
§58-24-25(c).
Social members, §58-24-25(b).
Mergers and consolidations.
Affidavits.
Evidence of furnishing notice or document,
§58-24-65(d).
Approval by commissioner, §58-24-65(b).
Evidence of furnishing notice or document,
§58-24-65(d).
Felonies.
Violations of provisions of section,
§58-24-180(d).
Filing with commissioner, §58-24-65(a).
Procedure generally, §58-24-65(a) to (e).
Reinsurance upon consolidation or merger,
§58-24-60(b).
Vesting, §58-24-65(c).
Minors.
Life insurance, §58-24-75(b).
Lodge systems.
Organization and operation of lodges for
children, §58-24-5(b).
Misdemeanors.
False or fraudulent statements, §58-24-180(a).
Not specified violations, §58-24-180(c).
Solicitation or procurement of membership.
Unauthorized, §58-24-180(b).
Mutual life insurance companies.
Conversion of society into company, §58-24-70.
Officers.
Immunities.
Civil liability for monetary damages,
§58-24-35(d).
Indemnification, §58-24-35(b).
Insurance.
Power of society to purchase and maintain
insurance, §58-24-35(c).
Liability.
Not personally liable for benefits provided by
society, §58-24-35(a).
Offices.
Location of principal office, §58-24-30(a).
Organization, §58-24-45(a) to (f).
Bonds, surety.
Filing with articles of incorporation,
§58-24-45(b).
Filing articles of incorporation, §58-24-45(b).
Licenses, §58-24-45(e).
Preliminary licenses, §58-24-45(c), (d).
Reincorporation, §58-24-45(f).

FRATERNAL BENEFIT SOCIETIES —Cont'd
Organization —Cont'd
Structure, §58-24-45(a).
Penalties.
False or fraudulent statements, §58-24-180(a).
Under oath, §58-24-180(e).
Felonies.
False statements under oath, §58-24-180(e).
Mergers and consolidation.
Violations of provisions of section,
§58-24-180(d).
Filing financial statements, §58-24-125(c).
Mergers and consolidations.
Felonies.
Violations of provisions of section,
§58-24-180(d).
Not specified violations, §58-24-180(c).
Solicitation or procurement of membership.
Unauthorized, §58-24-180(b).
Violation of article, §58-24-180.
Powers.
Generally, §58-24-20(b).
Purposes, §58-24-20(a).
Real property.
Conveyances.
Effect as to conveyances by trustees, §59B-15(a).
Prior deeds validated, §59B-15(b).
Referendums.
Amendments to laws of society, §58-24-50(a).
Reincorporation, §58-24-45(f).
Reinsurance, §58-24-60(a).
Consolidation or merger, §58-24-60(b).
Reports.
Annual reports required, §58-24-125(a).
Filing financial statements, §58-24-125(a).
Penalties, §58-24-125(c).
Valuation, §58-24-125(b).
Representative form of government.
Defined, §58-24-10.
Reserves.
Excess reserves.
Establishment and maintenance, §58-24-120(d).
Impairment.
Apportionment of deficiency among owners,
§58-24-90.
Secret societies and activities, §§14-12.2 to
14-12.15.
See SECRET SOCIETIES.
Securities regulation.
Exempt securities, §78A-16.
Service of process.
Appointment of commissioner, §58-24-170(a).
Procedure, §58-24-170(b).
Severability of provisions of article, §58-24-190.
Taxation.
Exemptions, §58-24-115.
Unfair and deceptive acts and practices,
§58-24-165.
Waiver.
Laws of society.
Not authorized, §58-24-40.

FRATERNAL ORDERS, §§58-25-1 to 58-25-70.
Admission to state.
Conditions precedent to doing business, §58-25-25.
Agents.
Collector or receiver of assessments and dues,
§58-25-15.
Licenses, §58-25-25.
Applicability of article.
Certain lodge systems exempt, §58-25-30.

FRATERNAL ORDERS —Cont'd
Assessments.
Collection, §58-25-15.
Funds derived from, §58-25-10.
Badges.
Unauthorized wearing, §58-25-70.
Conditions precedent to doing business,
§58-25-25.
Conveyances.
Effect as to conveyances by trustees, §59B-15(a).
Prior deeds validated, §59B-15(b).
Criminal law and procedure.
Securing attendance of organizations as
defendants, §15A-773.
Deeds.
Prior deeds validated, §59B-15(b).
Defined, §58-25-5.
Dues.
Collection, §58-25-15.
Funds derived from, §58-25-10.
Exemptions from article, §58-25-30.
Financial statements.
Annual report, §58-25-50.
Funds.
Assessments and dues, §58-25-10.
Payments to expense or general fund, §58-25-55.
Separation of funds.
Annual financial statement, §58-25-50.
General insurance law not applicable, §58-25-1.
Hazing, §§14-35, 14-38.
Licenses.
Agents, §58-25-25.
Meetings.
Governing body, §58-25-20.
Minors.
Insurance, §58-25-35.
Certificates and contributions, §58-25-40.
Continuation of certificate, §58-25-60.
Exchange of certificate, §58-25-45.
Medical examination, §58-25-40.
Reserve fund, §58-25-45.
Offices.
Principal office, §58-25-20.
Payments to expense or general fund,
§58-25-55.
Penalties.
Badges.
Unauthorized wearing, §58-25-70.
Real property.
Conveyances.
Effect as to conveyances by trustees, §59B-15(a).
Prior deeds validated, §59B-15(b).
Reports.
Annual financial statement.
Separation of funds, §58-25-45.
Secret societies and activities, §§14-12.2 to
14-12.15.
Trusts and trustees.
Appointment of trustees to hold property,
§58-25-65.
Conveyances.
Effect as to conveyance by trustees, §59B-15(a).

FRATERNITIES.
Hazing, §§14-35, 14-38.
Supplemental fire safety protection system,
§§116-44.6 to 116-44.8.

FRAUD.
Academic credit.
Assisting, etc., in obtaining credit by fraudulent
means, §14-118.2(a).
Penalty for violations of provisions, §14-118.2(b).

FRAUD —Cont'd
Accounts and accounting.
Accrual of action for relief on ground of, §1-52.
Court process in connection with collection of
account.
Simulation of court process, §14-118.1.
Adoption proceedings.
Waiver of notice, §48-2-406(c).
Advertising.
Deceptive and fraudulent advertising, §14-117.
Gasoline price advertisements.
Purchaser himself drawing or pumping fuel,
§14-117.2.
Affirmative defense, pleading, §1A-1 Rule 8(c).
Alarm systems licensing.
Conviction of crime involving fraud.
Grounds for denial of license, §74D-6.
Alcoholic beverage purchases by minors.
Use of fraudulent identification, §18B-302(e).
Allowing use of identification, §18B-302(f).
Arrest in civil cases.
Cases in which arrest allowed, §1-410.
Arson.
Dwelling houses fraudulently set fire to, §14-65.
Assignments for benefit of creditors.
Judgment of fraud by opposing creditor, §23-17.
Superior or district court to try issue, §23-39.
Attorneys at law.
Client engaging in fraudulent conduct, remedial
measures, ProfCond Rule 3.3.
Defined, ProfCond Rule 1.0.
Lawyer not to counsel client to engage in
fraudulent conduct, ProfCond Rule 1.2.
Liability for fraudulent practice.
Double damages, §84-13.
Bail bondsmen and runners.
Grounds for denial, suspension, revocation or
refusal to renew license, §58-71-80(a).
Bailments.
Hired property, §14-168.
Barbers.
Prohibited acts, §86A-20.
Blackmail.
Elements of offense, §14-118.
Blind persons.
Aid to the blind.
Misrepresentation or fraud in obtaining
assistance, §111-23.
Boating safety.
Fraudulent safety certification card, §75A-16.1(f).
Campgrounds.
Defrauding campground owner, §14-110.
Child care facilities.
Fraudulent misrepresentation, §110-107(a), (b).
Children's health insurance program,
§108A-70.28.
Child support.
Relief from order based on nonpaternity.
Finding that initial order of support based on
fraud, duress, etc, §50-13.13(h).
Chiropractors.
Grounds for disciplinary action, §90-154(b).
Collection agencies.
Court process in connection with collection of
claim.
Simulation of court process, §14-118.1.
Deceptive representation.
Prohibited acts, §58-70-110.
Commodities.
Fraudulent conduct, §78D-6.

FRAUD —Cont'd
Complaints.
Form, §1A-1 Rule 84.
Concealed handgun permit.
Revocation or suspension of permit for fraud in
    obtaining permit, §14-415.18(a).
Consumer finance act.
False or misleading statements.
    Prohibited acts, §53-183.
Contractors.
Improvements to real property.
    Furnishing false statements.
        Misdemeanor, §44A-24.
Custodial trusts.
Limitation of actions against custodial trustee,
    §33B-16(b).
Debts and claims.
Court process in connection with collection of
    claim.
    Simulation of court process, §14-118.1.
Decedents' estates.
Clerks of superior court jurisdiction in estate
    proceedings.
    Limitation on jurisdiction, §28A-2-4(c).
Demands.
Court process in connection with collection of
    demand.
    Simulation of court process, §14-118.1.
Dental hygienists.
Grounds for disciplinary measures, §90-229(a).
Dentists.
Grounds for disciplinary action, §90-41(a).
Licenses.
    License obtained through fraud void, §90-30(a).
Diamonds.
Unfair trade practices in diamond industry.
    What constitutes unfair trade practice, §66-74.
Drug and alcohol screening tests.
Defrauding test, §14-401.20.
Drugs.
Controlled substances.
    Prohibited acts, §90-108(a).
Education.
Academic credit by fraudulent means.
    Assisting, etc., in obtaining credit, §14-118.2(a).
        Penalty for violation of provisions,
            §14-118.2(b).
Elections.
Absentee ballots.
    Misdemeanors, §163-237(c).
Felonies, §163-275.
Registration of voters.
    Felonies, §163-275.
State bureau of investigation.
    Authority to make investigations, §114-15(a).
Electrologists.
Grounds for disciplinary actions, §88A-21(a).
Executors and administrators.
Referral of disputed claims.
    Evidence in action for fraud, §28A-19-15.
Sales of real property.
    Conveyance by deceased in fraud of creditors.
        Property subject to sale, §28A-17-5.
Transfers or conveyances by decedent to defraud
    creditors.
    Action by personal representative to recover,
        §28A-15-10.
False claims act.
False or fraudulent claims against state, §§1-605
    to 1-631.
    See FALSE CLAIMS ACT.

FRAUD —Cont'd
False pretenses and cheats, §§14-100 to 14-113.
See FALSE PRETENSES AND CHEATS.
Financial transaction cards.
Application for financial transaction card.
    False statements or reports on application,
        §14-113.13(c).
Elements of offense, §14-113.13(a).
Furnisher of money, goods, services, etc.
    Elements of financial transaction card fraud
        offense, §14-113.13(b).
Goods and services.
    Criminal receipt of goods and services
        fraudulently obtained, §14-113.15.
    Presumption of criminal receipt, §14-113.16.
Notice of theft, loss, etc., of card.
    False notice, §14-113.13(d).
Prosecution for violation.
    Occurrence of acts constituting crime,
        §14-113.13(e).
Report of theft, loss, etc., of card.
    False report, §14-113.13(d).
Revocation of financial transaction card.
    Construing revocation, §14-113.13(f).
Fish and fishing.
Coastal and estuarine commercial fishing licenses,
    §113-170.2.
Food and nutrition services, §108A-53.
Foreclosure.
Home foreclosure rescue scams, §§75-120 to
    75-122.
Gasoline.
Price advertisements.
    Purchaser himself drawing or pumping fuel,
        §14-117.2.
Home foreclosure rescue scams, §§75-120 to
    75-122.
Hospitals.
Information obtained from patients.
    Acquisition and use of information for
        fraudulent purposes, §14-118.3.
Housemovers.
Licenses.
    Obtaining license or permit by fraud, §20-367.
Housing authorities and projects.
Misrepresentation.
    Fraudulent misrepresentation in obtaining
        housing assistance, §157-29.1.
Husband and wife.
Conveyances.
    Certain conveyances not affected by fraud,
        §39-11.
Identification.
Alcoholic beverage purchases by minors,
    §18B-302(e).
Allowing use of identification, §18B-302(f).
False or fraudulent, §14-100.1.
Financial identity theft.
    Expungement of criminal records.
        Dismissal or finding of not guilty.
            Crime committed by another using
                defendant's identifying information,
                §15A-147.
Identity theft, §§14-113.20 to 14-113.25.
See IDENTITY THEFT.
Expungement of criminal records.
    Dismissal or finding of not guilty.
        Crime committed by another using
            defendant's identifying information,
            §15A-147.
Imprisonment for debt, NC Const Art I §28.

FRAUD —Cont'd
Indictments.
Intent to defraud.
Sufficiency of allegation, §15-151.
Injunctions.
Removal or disposition of property with intent to defraud plaintiff.
Issuance of preliminary injunction when threatened, §1-485.
Insurance.
Arson, §14-65.
Burning of personal property, §14-66.
Dwelling house fraudulently set fire to, §14-65.
False statement to procure or deny benefit of policy or certificate, §58-2-161.
Immunity from liability for reporting fraud, §58-2-160(a), (b).
Life insurance.
Creditors deprived of benefits of policies except in cases of fraud, §58-58-115.
Misrepresentation of policies prohibited, §58-58-40.
Motor vehicle insurance.
Rate evasion fraud, §58-2-164.
Personal property set fire to, §14-66.
Reinsurance.
Reporting and investigation of, §58-2-160(a), (b).
Statements, releases, etc., obtained from persons in shock or under the influence of drugs.
Presumption of fraud, §8-45.5.
"Twisting,"§58-3-115.
Interpreters and transliterators.
Licenses.
Revocation, suspension or denials of licenses, §90D-12.
Judgments.
Relief from judgment or order, §1A-1 Rule 60(b).
Leases, UCC.
Effect on rights and remedies, §25-2A-505(4).
Letters of credit.
Basis for dishonor, §25-5-108(d).
Injunction on honoring, §25-5-109(b).
Issuer allowed to honor despite, §25-5-109(a).
Liens.
Real property.
Furnishing false statements in connection with improvements, §44A-24.
Limitation of actions, §1-52.
Local governmental employees' retirement system.
Protection of records against fraud, §128-32.
Marriage and family therapists.
Grounds for disciplinary action, §90-270.60(a).
Marriage licenses.
Minors procuring license by, §51-2(c).
Obtaining license by false representation, §51-15.
Procuring license by fraud or misrepresentation, §51-2(c).
Massage and bodywork therapy.
Disciplinary action.
Grounds, §90-633.
Medicaid.
Medical assistance provider false claims act, §§108A-70.10 to 108A-70.16.
See MEDICAID.
Providers, §108A-63.
Subpoena to produce documents, §108A-63.1.
Recipients, §108A-64.
Report by Medicaid fraud control unit, §114-2.5A.
Misdemeanors.
Offenses committed with deceit and intent to defraud, §14-3(b).

FRAUD —Cont'd
Misdemeanors —Cont'd
Security interest on personal property.
Fraudulent disposal of property, §14-114(a).
Money transmitters.
Criminal penalty, §53-208.26(b).
Delegates.
False statements by delegate, §53-208.20(a).
Mortgage bankers, brokers and servicers.
Misrepresent or conceal materials or false promises.
Prohibited acts, §53-244.111.
Mortgages and deeds of trust.
Disposal of property.
Intent to commit crime, §14-114(b).
Refusal to turn over property without judgment or order, §14-114(a).
Home foreclosure rescue scams, §§75-120 to 75-122.
Residential mortgage fraud, §§14-118.10 to 14-118.17.
Reverse mortgages.
Prohibited acts by lenders, §53-270.
Motor vehicle insurance.
Rate evasion fraud, §58-2-164.
Motor vehicle repairs.
Altering estimate, bill, etc., §20-354.8.
Remedies for violation, §20-354.9.
Deceptive statements, etc., §20-354.8.
Remedies for violation, §20-354.9.
Motor vehicles.
Rental of motor vehicles, §20-106.1.
Mutual burial associations.
False entries on books of association, §90-210.90.
False or fraudulent statement or representation, §90-210.97.
Inducing change in membership, §90-210.89.
Negotiable instruments.
Alteration of instrument, §25-3-407(a) to (c).
Indorsements.
Responsibility of employer for fraudulent indorsement by employee, §25-3-405(a) to (c).
Nurses.
Prohibited acts, §90-171.44.
Oil and gas conservation.
Drilling wells.
Applications, §113-409.
Optometrists.
Grounds for disciplinary action, §90-121.2(a).
License obtained through fraud void, §90-118(d).
Paralegals.
Fraudulently holding out as paralegal.
Actions by private persons damaged by unauthorized practice, §84-10.1.
Partition.
Report of commissioners.
Impeachment of report for fraud, §46-19(a).
Paternity.
Setting aside orders of paternity, §49-4(h).
Penalties.
Academic credit by fraudulent means.
Assisting, etc., in obtaining credit, §14-118.2(b).
Plaintiff may reply fraud to plea of release, §1-59.
Personal property.
Refusal to turn over without judgment or order, §14-114(a).
Security interests.
Fraudulent disposal of property, §14-114.

FRAUD —Cont'd

Personnel system.

Application for state employment.

Fraudulent disclosure and willful nondisclosure, §126-30(a).

Rules and regulations, §126-30(c).

Verification of accuracy of statements, §126-30(b).

Physical therapists.

Grounds for disciplinary action, §90-270.36.

Preneed funeral contracts and funds, §90-210.70(a), (c).

Refusal to issue or renew, suspension or revocation of licenses, §90-210.69(c).

Presumptions.

Security interest on personal property.

Fraudulent disposal of property, §14-114(b).

Prisons and prisoners.

Debtor and creditor.

Discharge of insolvent prisoners.

Absent suggestion of fraud, discharge granted, §23-34.

Imprisonment of if fraud found, §23-37.

Suggestion of fraud, §23-28.

Trial required where fraud in issue, §23-36.

Who may suggest fraud, §23-33.

Private personnel services.

Contracts, §95-47.4(d).

Prohibited acts, §95-47.6.

Professional counselors.

Disciplinary action against licensee.

Grounds, §90-340(a).

Violation punishable as crime, §90-341.

Public assistance program payments.

Garnishment of wages to recoup fraudulent payments, §108A-25.3.

Real estate brokers.

Grounds for revocation or suspension of licenses, §93A-6(a).

Residential mortgage fraud, §§14-118.10 to 14-118.17.

Respiratory care practitioners.

License application, §90-659.

Retirement system for teachers and state employees.

Protection against fraud, §135-10.

Sale of goods, UCC.

Misrepresentation of buyer's solvency.

Seller's remedies, §25-2-702.

Remedies for fraud, §25-2-721.

Rights of seller's creditors against sold goods, §25-2-402.

Transfer of title obtained by fraud, §25-2-403(1).

Securities regulation, §§78A-8 to 78A-10.

Security interest.

Fraudulent disposal of personal property.

Intent, §14-114(b).

Refusal to turn over property without judgment or order, §14-114(a).

Small business contractors.

False statements, §143B-472.112.

Social security.

Bureau of investigation, investigations by, §114-15(a).

Special matters, pleading, §1A-1 Rule 9(b).

Speech and language pathologists and audiologists.

Grounds for suspension or revocation of license, §90-301.

Obtaining fee by fraud or misrepresentation.

Unethical acts and practices, §90-301A.

FRAUD —Cont'd

State treasurer.

False entries in books, §147-76.

Tax penalties, §105-236.

Trademarks.

Counterfeit trademarks, §§80-11, 80-11.1.

Deceptive or unfair trade practices, §80-12.

Fraudulent registration, §80-10.

Timber marks.

Fraudulent use, §80-20.

Transfers.

Fraudulent transfers, §§39-23.1 to 39-23.12.

See FRAUDULENT TRANSFERS.

Trusts.

Creation induced by fraud, §36C-4-406.

Unemployment compensation benefits.

False statements, §96-18.

Universities and colleges.

Academic credit by fraudulent means.

Assisting, etc., in obtaining credit, §14-118.2(a).

Penalty for violation of provisions, §14-118.2(b).

Viatical life insurance settlements.

Felony offense for fraudulent viatical settlement act, §58-58-265(a).

Investigations of fraudulent acts, §58-58-240.

Workers' compensation.

False statements or representations, §97-88.2(a).

Health care providers, §97-88.3(a).

Hospital liability.

Reliance on written order of physician, §97-88.3(f).

Reporting information relating to possible violations, §97-88.3(e).

Insurance carriers, §97-100(g).

Investigation, §97-88.2(b).

Report to general assembly, §97-88.2(e).

Person convicted benefiting from unlawful conduct.

Order by commission preventing, authority, §97-88.2(a1).

Referral of suspected fraud cases, §97-88.2(b).

Liability of commission, §97-88.2(d).

Work first program, §108A-39.

FRAUDS, STATUTE OF.

See STATUTE OF FRAUDS.

FRAUDULENT TRANSFERS, §§39-23.1 to 39-23.12.

Applicability of provisions.

Uniformity of application, §39-23.11.

Assignments for benefit of creditors.

Trustee to recover property conveyed fraudulently, §23-3.

Child support.

Enforcement of support.

Minor child creditor within meaning of chapter, §50-13.4(f).

Citation of article, §39-23.12.

Construction and interpretation.

Uniformity, §39-23.11.

Definitions, §39-23.1.

Good faith taker for reasonably equivalent value.

Entitlement notwithstanding voidablity of transfer, §39-23.8(d).

Transfer not voidable as to, §39-23.8(a).

Insider giving new value.

Transfers not voidable, §39-23.8(f).

Insolvent.

Assets, §39-23.2(d).

FRAUDULENT TRANSFERS —Cont'd
Insolvent —Cont'd
  Debts, §39-23.2(e).
  Elements, §39-23.2(a).
  Partnerships, §39-23.2(c).
  Presumption, §39-23.2(b).
Intent, §39-23.4(b).
Joinder of remedies, §1A-1 Rule 18(b).
Judgments.
  Execution, §39-23.7(b).
  For value of asset transfer.
    Recovery by creditor where transfer voidable,
      §39-23.8(b), (c).
Leases.
  Termination upon default.
    Transfers not voidable, §39-23.8(e).
Leases, UCC.
  Special rights of creditors, §25-2A-308.
Levy of execution, §39-23.7(b).
Limitation of actions, §39-23.9.
Ordinary course of business.
  Transfers not voidable, §39-23.8(f).
Present and future creditors, §§39-23.4(a),
  39-23.5(a).
  Voidable transfers, §39-23.5(b).
Provisions supplementary, §39-23.10.
Rehabilitation of debtor.
  Transfers not voidable, §39-23.8(f).
Remedies of creditors, §39-23.7(a).
Secured transactions.
  Enforcement of security interest in compliance
    with UCC secured transactions article.
    Transfers not voidable, §39-23.8(e).
Statute of limitations, §39-23.9.
Supplementary provisions, §39-23.10.
Time.
  When transfer made, §39-23.6.
Title of article, §39-23.12.
Transfer not voidable, §39-23.8(e), (f).
**Trustee in deed of trust neither necessary or
  proper party,** §45-45.3(c).
Value, §39-23.3(a).
  Present value, §§39-23.2(c), 39-23.3(c).
  Reasonably equivalent value, §39-23.3(b).
When transfer made or obligation incurred,
  §39-23.6.

FREAK SHOWS.
**Exhibition of mentally ill, retarded or
  deformed children prohibited,** §110-20.1.

FREEDOM OF INFORMATION, §§132-1 to
  132-10.
Access to records, §132-9.
Action to compel disclosure, §132-9.
Attorneys' fees.
  Action to compel disclosure, §132-9(b) to (e).
Bank compliance review documents.
  Unavailability, §53-99.1(b).
Certified copies of records, §132-7.
Compelling disclosure or copying.
  Application for order, §132-9(a).
  Attorneys' fees.
    Action filed in bad faith, frivolous actions,
      §132-9(d).
    Allowing party successfully compelling
      disclosure, §132-9(c).
    Public hospitals.
      When assessment against not allowed,
        §132-9(e).
  Records relating to proposed expansion or location
    of business.
    Burden on custodian, §132-9(b).

FREEDOM OF INFORMATION —Cont'd
Confidential communications.
  Enumeration, §132-1.2.
  Legal counsel's advice to public board or agency,
    §132-1.1.
**Cooperative agreements among physicians or
  between physician, hospital or other
  person.**
  Files of department of health and human services
    public record, §90-21.30.
  Work product of attorney general in suit to cancel
    agreement not public record, §90-21.33(d).
**Criminal investigation or intelligence records
  or information,** §132-1.4.
Cultural resources department.
  Assistance by and to, §132-8.
  Records management program, §132-8.1.
  Selection and preservation of records considered
    essential, §132-8.2.
Custodian designated, §132-2.
Demanding custody, §132-5.
Denial of access.
  Action to compel disclosure, §132-9.
Destruction of records.
  Employment security division records, §132-3(c).
  Prohibition, §132-3(a).
  Revenue records after copies made, §132-3(b).
Discharge papers.
  Restricting access to military discharge
    documents.
    Public records with restricted access, §47-113.2.
Disposition of records at end of official's term,
  §132-4.
**DNA records and DNA samples submitted to
  SBI.**
  Not public records, §15A-266.12(c).
Electronic mail lists of individual subscribers.
  Unit of local government maintaining.
    Public inspection.
      Availability, copy, providing not required,
        §132-1.13(a).
    Use of list by local government, §132-1.13(b).
Expansion or location of business or industry.
  Action to compel disclosure of records relating to.
    Burden on custodian, §132-9(b).
Financial records privacy, §§53B-1 to 53B-10.
  See FINANCIAL RECORDS PRIVACY.
Foster parents.
  Register of applicants.
  Exemption for FOIA, §131D-10.6C(b).
**Industrial commission managed care
  organizations,** ICManagedCare Rule VII.
Inspection and examination of records, §132-6.
Keeping records in safe places, §132-7.
Mediation of public records disputes,
  §7A-38.3E.
**Minors participating in local parks and
  recreation programs.**
  Identifying information in program records.
    County, municipality and zip code of
      participating minor public record,
      §132-1.12(b).
    Information not considered public record,
      §132-1.12(a).
    Not confidential information, §132-1.12(c).
Motor vehicle accident reports.
  Reports by persons not law enforcement officers or
    medical examiners not public records,
    §20-166.1(i).
Municipal employees' personnel files,
  §160A-168.

FREEDOM OF INFORMATION —Cont'd
Personnel records of state employees.
Right to inspect and examine, §126-23(c).
Prisoners, access prohibited, §126-23(d).
Privacy of financial records, §§53B-1 to 53B-10.
See FINANCIAL RECORDS PRIVACY.
Public records.
Definitions, §132-1.
911 database not public record, §132-1.5.
Public security information, §132-1.7(a) to (c).
Regaining custody, §132-5.1.
Civil remedies, §132-5.1.
Savings and loan associations.
Compliance review documents, §54B-63.1(b).
Seal of design professional.
Record revealing confidential, §132-1.2.
Tax information secrecy, §105-259.
University of North Carolina's small business and technology development centers.
Document submitted by individuals seeking
assistance not public records, §116-43.16.
Water and sewer authorities.
Employee personnel files, §162-6.1.

FREE ENTERPRISE SYSTEM.
Basic education program, §115C-81(c).

FREE FISHING DAY.
July fourth, §113-276(m).

FREE FORENSIC MEDICAL EXAMINATIONS.
Assistance program for victims of rape and sex offenses, §143B-1200.

FREE INSURANCE.
Inducement to purchase goods or services, §§66-380 to 66-382.
Definitions, §66-380.
Prohibited, §66-381.
Unfair trade practice, §66-382.

FREESTYLE BICYCLING.
Assumption of inherent risk, §99E-24(a).
Governmental entities.
Limitation of liability, §99E-25(b).
Duty of care not created, §99E-25(d).
Exceptions, §99E-25(c).
Independent concessionaires or other persons or organizations.
Liability not limited by section, §99E-25(e).
Insurance carried by entity.
Not waiver of liability limits, §99E-25(f).
Sovereign immunity not waived, §99E-25(d).
Specifically designated areas for activities.
Required to participate on property owner or controlled by entity, §99E-25(a).
Responsibilities of participants, §99E-24(b).

FREE TRADER AGREEMENTS, §52-10.

FREE TRANSPORTATION OFFERED BY COMMON CARRIERS, §62-144.

FREEZERS.
Chlorofluorocarbon refrigerants, §§130A-309.80 to 130A-309.87.
Energy star qualified products.
Sales and use tax holiday, §105-164.13D(a).

FREIGHT.
Bills of lading.
Issuance, §62-203(a).
Careful handling required, §62-202.
Carriers, §§62-200 to 62-204.
Unclaimed freight, §62-209.

FREIGHT —Cont'd
Emergency operating authority granted to owner of duly licensed vehicles to transport, §62-265.
Line company gross earnings tax.
See FREIGHT LINE COMPANY GROSS EARNINGS TAX.
Lost or damaged goods and property.
Additional nature of provisions, §62-203(g).
Causes of action may be united, §62-203(f).
Claims.
Notice, §62-204.
Time for adjustment and payment, §62-203(b).
Penalty for failure to adjust and pay claim during time, §62-203(c).
Liability for, §62-203(a), (c).
Limitation of actions, §62-204.
Motor carriers.
Exemptions from provisions, §62-203(h).
Rates.
Charges to be at legal rates, §62-201.
Damages for failure or refusal to comply with provisions, §62-201.
Reasonable time for transportation, §62-200(a), (b).
Motor carriers of passengers.
Provisions not applicable, §62-200(d).
Violations of provisions.
Forfeiture, §62-200(b).
Taxation.
Freight line company gross earnings tax.
See FREIGHT LINE COMPANY GROSS EARNINGS TAX.
Unclaimed freight.
Sale, §62-209.
Motor carriers of passengers.
Exemption from provisions, §62-209(d).
Notice, §62-209(a).
Record, §62-209(c).

FREIGHT LINE COMPANY GROSS EARNINGS TAX.
Effective date of provisions, §105-228.2(j).
Enforcement of payment of taxes, §105-228.2(i).
Failure to pay tax, §105-228.2(i).
"Gross earning received from all sources by such freight line companies within state.."
Defined, §105-228.2(e).
In lieu of ad valorem taxes, §§105-228.1, 105-228.2(a).
Purpose of provisions, §105-228.1.
Rate of tax, §105-228.2(d).
Reports, §105-228.2(f) to (h).
Situs of cars in state, §105-228.2(c).
What constitutes freight line company, §105-228.2(b).

FREON, §§130A-309.80 to 130A-309.87.

FRESH PURSUIT.
Campus police officers, §15A-402(f).
Company police, §74E-6.
County and city officers, §15A-402(d).
Officers from other states, §15A-403.

FRIED FOODS.
Child care centers frying foods.
Use of commercial hoods, §110-91.

FRINGE TREE.
Trespass.
Taking, etc., of certain wild plants from land of another, §14-129.

FRISKING.
Persons present on premises or in vehicle to be searched, §15A-255.
Riots and civil disorders.
Curfew violators, §14-288.10(b).
Grounds for frisk of persons during violent disorders, §14-288.10(a).

FRIVOLOUS ACTIONS.
Aliens.
Verification of work authorization.
Complaints.
False and frivolous complaints, §64-28(b).
Attorneys' fees.
Cases involving principals or teachers, §6-21.4.
Child custody or support, §50-13.6.
Interference with civil rights, §99D-1(b).
Nonjustifiable cases, §6-21.5.
Punitive damages, §1D-45.
Retaliatory employment discrimination, §95-243(c).
Defendant unreasonable defending after notice of no personal claim to pay costs, §6-23.
Inmates presenting frivolous complaints.
Court determination, dismissal, §1-110(b).
Limited liability company derivative actions by members.
Actions brought by without reasonable cause, §57C-8-01(f).
Mortgages and deeds of trust.
Consumer home loans.
Attorneys' fees for prevailing party, §24-10.2(f).
Punitive damages.
Attorneys' fees, §1D-45.
Sales representatives.
Action against principal for commission, §66-192(b).
State ethics commission.
Complaints.
Grounds for dismissal after preliminary inquiry, §138A-12(f).

FRIVOLOUS APPEALS, AppProc Rule 34.
Juvenile matters.
No-merit briefs, AppProc Rule 3.1(d).

FRIVOLOUS CLAIMS AND CONTENTIONS.
Aliens.
Verification of work authorization.
Complaints.
False and frivolous complaints, §64-28(b).
Attorneys at law, ProfCond Rule 3.1.

FRIVOLOUS DISCOVERY.
Attorneys at law, ProfCond Rule 3.4.

FRIVOLOUS PLEADINGS, §1A-1 Rule 11(a).

FRIVOLOUS PROSECUTION.
Imprisonment of prosecuting witness for willful nonpayment of costs, §6-50.
Prosecuting witness liable for costs, §6-49.

FROZEN FOOD.
Ice cream plants, creameries and cheese factories.
Inspections generally, §§106-246 to 106-255.
See ICE CREAM PLANTS, CREAMERIES AND CHEESE FACTORIES.
Trade names.
Regulating trade or brand names of frozen or semifrozen desserts, §106-253.

FRUIT.
Damage to agricultural commodities or production systems.
Definitions, §1-539.2B(c).
Double damage liability, §1-539.2B(a).
Valuation, §1-539.2B(b).
Definition of handler, §106-496.
Food, drug and cosmetic act.
Condemnation or destruction of articles found to be unsound, filthy, etc., §106-125(d).
Larceny.
Ungathered crops, §14-78.
Liens.
Effective period for liens on fruit, §44-69.2.
Promotion of use and sale of agricultural products.
Generally, §§106-550 to 106-568.
See AGRICULTURAL PRODUCTS PROMOTION.
State fruit, §145-18(a).
Unfair practices by handlers, §§106-496 to 106-501.
See FRUIT HANDLERS UNFAIR PRACTICES.
Weights and measures.
Standard weights and measures, §81A-42.

FRUIT HANDLERS UNFAIR PRACTICES, §§106-496 to 106-501.
Bond required, §106-498.
Commissioner of agriculture.
Contracts between handlers and producers.
Approval of commissioner, §106-499.
Enforcement of article, §106-500.
Powers of commissioner, §106-500.
Contracts between handlers and producers, §106-499.
Definition of handler, §106-496.
Enforcement of article.
Commissioner of agriculture to enforce, §106-500.
Penalties, §106-501.
Permits required, §106-497.
Protection against unfair trade practices, §106-496.

FRUIT OF THE POISONOUS TREE DOCTRINE, §15A-974.

FRYING PAN LIGHTSHIP MARINE MUSEUM COMMISSION.
Department of cultural resources.
Transfer of commission to department, §143B-51.

FUEL.
Building codes.
Equipment for storage or handling fuel.
Exemption from provisions, §143-138(b8).
Commodities.
General provisions, §§78D-1 to 78D-33.
See COMMODITIES.
Liquid fuels, §§119-7 to 119-13.
Motor fuel.
Alternative fuel generally, §§105-449.130 to 105-449.139.
See ALTERNATIVE FUEL.
Biodiesel.
Biodiesel provider.
Defined, §105-449.60.
Business and energy tax credits.
Biodiesel producers, §105-129.16F.
Renewable fuel facility construction tax credit, §105-129.16D.
Dyed diesel.
See DYED DIESEL FUEL.

FUEL —Cont'd
Motor fuel —Cont'd
Gasoline and oil inspection.
See GASOLINE AND OIL INSPECTION.
Gasoline tax, §§105-449.60 to 105-449.126.
See GASOLINE TAX.
Marketing, §§75-80 to 75-90.
Sales and use tax exemption, §105-164.13.
Privilege tax on fuel to operate industry or plant, §105-187.51A.
Road tax on carriers using fuel purchased outside state, §§105-449.37 to 105-449.57.
See MOTOR CARRIERS.

FUEL ALCOHOL.
Distilleries.
Permits, §18B-1105(b).
Gasoline tax.
Defined, §105-449.60.

FUEL CELL ELECTRIC VEHICLES.
High occupancy vehicle lanes.
Lane restrictions inapplicable, §20-146.2(a).

FUELS TAX.
Administrative provisions.
Applicability of general provisions, §105-269.3.
Alternative fuel, §§105-449.130 to 105-449.139.
See ALTERNATIVE FUEL.
Gasoline tax, §§105-449.60 to 105-449.126.
See GASOLINE TAX.
Manufacturing fuel.
Privilege tax on fuel to operate industry or plant, §105-187.51A.
Road tax on carriers using fuel purchased outside state, §§105-449.37 to 105-449.57.
See MOTOR CARRIERS.

FUEL TANKS ON VEHICLES.
Tank not to project beyond sides of vehicle, §20-117.1(b).

FUGITIVE HUSBANDS.
Interstate family support, §§52C-1-100 to 52C-9-902.
See INTERSTATE FAMILY SUPPORT.

FUGITIVES.
Concealed handgun permit.
Grounds for denial of permit, §14-415.12(b).
Escape.
See ESCAPE.
Extradition.
Fugitives from other states.
See EXTRADITION.
Harboring or aiding escaped prisoners, §14-259.
Rewards.
Governor may offer rewards, §15-53.
Information leading to arrest and conviction, §15-53.1.
Officer entitled to reward, §15-54.
State institutions.
Harboring fugitives, §§14-267, 14-268.

FULL FAITH AND CREDIT, US Const Art IV §1.
Child support.
Past due child support judgment, §50-13.10(b).
Paternity determination by another state, §110-132.1.
Eastern Band of Cherokee Indians.
Judgments, decrees, and orders, §1E-1.
Subject to certain provisions, §1E-1(b).
Tribal Court.
Subject to full faith and credit of Tribal Court, §1E-1(a).

FULL FAITH AND CREDIT —Cont'd
Limited liability companies.
Intent of general assembly, §57C-10-07.
Paternity determination by another state, §110-132.1.
Public records.
Certified and authenticated, §8-35.

FULLY HALOGENATED CHLOROFLUOROCARBONS (CFC).
Containers manufactured with, restrictions, §130A-309.10(b).

FUNDRAISING.
Alcoholic beverage permits issued to nonprofit organization.
Special one-time permit, §18B-1002(a).
Charitable solicitation generally, §§131F-1 to 131F-33.
See CHARITABLE SOLICITATION.
Winery special event permit authorization, §18B-1114.1.

FUNDS TRANSFERS, §§25-4A-101 to 25-4A-507.
Applicability of article, §25-4A-102.
Exclusion of consumer transactions governed by federal law, §25-4A-108.
Attachment and garnishment.
Creditor process served on receiving bank, §25-4A-502(a) to (d).
Attorneys' fees.
Improper execution or failure to execute payment order, §25-4A-305(e).
Beneficiary.
Defined, §25-4A-103.
Misdescription in payment order, §25-4A-207(a) to (d).
Beneficiary's bank.
Defined, §25-4A-103.
Misdescription in payment order, §25-4A-208(a), (b).
Payment orders.
Obligation to pay and give notice to beneficiary, §25-4A-404(a) to (c).
Payment to beneficiary, §25-4A-405(a) to (e).
Set-off by, §25-4A-502(c).
Choice of law, §25-4A-507(a) to (e).
Citation of title, §25-4A-101.
Commercial code general provisions, §§25-1-101 to 25-1-310.
See COMMERCIAL CODE.
Conflict of laws.
Exclusion of consumer transactions governed by federal law, §25-4A-108.
Federal reserve regulations and operating circulars, §25-4A-107.
Consumer transactions governed by federal law.
Exclusion, §25-4A-108.
Creditor process served on receiving bank, §25-4A-502(a) to (d).
Damages.
Improper execution or failure to execute payment order, §25-4A-305(c).
Obligation of beneficiary's bank to pay and give notice to beneficiary.
Refusal to pay after demand and receipt of notice, §25-4A-404(a).
Definitions.
Authorized account, §25-4A-105(a).
Bank, §25-4A-105(a).
Beneficiary, §25-4A-103.

FUNDS TRANSFERS —Cont'd
Definitions —Cont'd
Beneficiary's bank, §25-4A-103.
Creditor process, §25-4A-502(a).
Customer, §25-4A-105(a).
Executed, §25-4A-301.
Execution date, §25-4A-301.
Funds-transfer business day, §25-4A-105(a).
Funds-transfer system, §25-4A-105(a).
Funds-transfer system rule, §25-4A-501(b).
Good faith, §25-4A-105(a).
Intermediary bank, §25-4A-104.
Originator, §25-4A-104.
Originator's bank, §25-4A-104.
Other applicable definitions, §25-4A-105(b) to (d).
Payment date, §25-4A-401.
Payment order, §25-4A-103.
Prove, §25-4A-105(a).
Receiving bank, §25-4A-103.
Security procedure, §25-4A-201.
Sender, §25-4A-103.
Authorized and verified payment orders, §25-4A-202(d).
Federal reserve regulations and operating circulars, §25-4A-107.
Funds-transfer system rule.
Defined, §25-4A-501(b).
Effect of, §25-4A-501(b).
Injunctive relief, §25-4A-503.
Interest.
Rate of interest, §25-4A-506(a), (b).
Intermediary bank.
Defined, §25-4A-104.
Misdescription in payment order, §25-4A-208(a), (b).
Limitation of actions.
Objection to debit of customer's account, §25-4A-505.
Notice.
Cancellation and amendment of payment orders, §25-4A-211(a), (b).
Payment orders.
Obligation of beneficiary's bank to give notice to beneficiary, §25-4A-404(b).
Rejection, §25-4A-210(a).
Payment orders.
Acceptance, §25-4A-209(a) to (d).
Authorized payment orders, §25-4A-202(a), (e), (f).
Cancellation and amendment, §25-4A-211(a) to (g).
Cut-off time, §25-4A-106(a).
Defined, §25-4A-103.
Discharge of underlying obligation, §25-4A-406(b) to (d).
Erroneous payment orders, §25-4A-205(a) to (c).
Execution by receiving bank.
Erroneous execution, §25-4A-303(a) to (c).
Duty of sender to report, §25-4A-304.
"Executed" defined, §25-4A-301.
"Execution date" defined, §25-4A-301.
Failure to execute.
Liability for, §25-4A-305(a) to (f).
Improper execution.
Liability for, §25-4A-305(a) to (f).
Late execution.
Liability for, §25-4A-305(a) to (f).
Obligations of receiving bank, §25-4A-302(a) to (d).
Misdescription.
Beneficiary, §25-4A-207(a) to (d).
Beneficiary's bank, §25-4A-208.

FUNDS TRANSFERS —Cont'd
Payment orders —Cont'd
Misdescription —Cont'd
Intermediary bank, §25-4A-208.
Objection to debit of customer's account.
Preclusion of objection, §25-2A-505.
Obligation of beneficiary's bank, §25-2A-404.
Obligation of sender to pay receiving bank, §§25-2A-402, 25-4A-402(a) to (f).
Order in which payment orders may be charged to account, §25-2A-504.
Order of withdrawals from account, §25-2A-504.
Payment by beneficiary's bank to beneficiary, §§25-2A-405, 25-4A-405(a) to (e).
Payment by originator to beneficiary, §25-4A-406(a).
Payment by sender to receiving bank, §25-4A-403(a) to (d).
Payment date.
Defined, §25-4A-401.
Preclusion of objection to debit of customer's account, §25-4A-505.
Rejection, §25-4A-210(a) to (d).
Liability and duty of receiving bank regarding unaccepted payment order, §25-4A-212.
Security procedure.
Commercial reasonableness, §25-4A-202(c).
Defined, §25-4A-201.
Time of acceptance, §25-4A-209(b).
Time received, §25-4A-106(a), (b).
Transmission through funds-transfer or other communication system, §25-4A-206(a), (b).
Unauthorized payment orders.
Duty of customer to report, §25-4A-204(a), (b).
Refund of payment, §25-4A-204(a), (b).
Verified payment orders, §25-4A-202(b), (e), (f).
Unenforceability of, §25-4A-203(a), (b).
Refunds.
Beneficiary's bank making payment that is provisional under system rule, §25-4A-405(b).
Payment of unauthorized payment orders, §25-4A-204.
Sender paying payment order and not obligated to pay, §25-4A-402.
Scope of article, §25-4A-102.
Exclusion of consumer transactions governed by federal law, §25-4A-108.
Service of process.
Creditor process on receiving bank, §25-4A-502(d).
Setoff by beneficiary's bank, §25-4A-502(a).
Short title, §25-4A-101.
Statute of limitations.
Objection to debit of customer's account, §25-4A-505.
Title of article, §25-4A-101.
Variation by agreement.
Rights and obligations of party, §25-4A-501(a).

FUNERAL CONTRACTS AND FUNDS.
Preneed contracts and funds generally, §§90-210.60 to 90-210.73.
See PRENEED FUNERAL CONTRACTS AND FUNDS.

FUNERAL DIRECTORS.
See FUNERAL SERVICES PROVIDERS.

FUNERAL PROCESSIONS.
Defined, §20-157.1(a).
Firearms and other weapons.
Possession, §14-277.2.

FUNERAL PROCESSIONS —Cont'd
Following vehicles.
Close but safe distance, §20-157.1(d).
Non-compliance with traffic control signals,
§20-157.1(c).
Headlights to be illuminated, §20-157.1(b).
Lead vehicle.
Compliance with traffic-control signals,
§20-157.1(c).
Local authorities.
Regulating use of highways by processions,
§20-169.
Mingling into procession, §20-157.1(i).
Moving violations.
Violations of provisions do not constitute,
§20-157.1(m).
Negligence per se.
Violations of provisions do not constitute,
§20-157.1(k).
Opposite direction vehicles.
Yielding to procession, §20-157.1(g).
Ordinances conflicting with provisions,
§20-157.1(l).
Passing procession, §20-157.1(h).
Police escort, §20-157.1(j).
Regulation by local authorities, §20-169.
Right side of roadway operation, §20-157.1(d).
Same direction vehicles.
Mingling into procession, §20-157.1(i).
Yielding to procession, §20-157.1(h).
Speed, §20-157.1(f).
Yielding to law enforcement, emergency, etc.,
vehicles, §20-157.1(e).

FUNERAL SERVICES PROVIDERS.
Advertisements.
Defined, §90-210.20(a).
Affidavits.
Good moral character of license applicant,
§90-210.26.
Age.
Qualifications for licenses, §90-210.25(a).
Board.
Created, §90-210.18A(b).
Definition of "board," §90-210.20(b).
Expenses of members, §90-210.23(c).
Inspection and regulation of funeral
establishments, §90-210.23(e).
Inspectors.
Appointment, §90-210.24(a).
Identification cards, §90-210.24(c).
Inspection form, §90-210.24(d).
Powers, §90-210.24(b).
Legal counsel, clerical and technical assistance,
employment, §90-210.23(h2).
Meetings, §90-210.22.
Members, §90-210.18A(b).
Mutual burial associations.
Generally, §§90-210.80 to 90-210.107.
See MUTUAL BURIAL ASSOCIATIONS.
Oath of office of members, §90-210.19.
Officers, §90-210.23(b).
Powers generally, §90-210.23(i).
Quorum, §90-210.22.
Real property, powers, §90-210.23(h1).
Removal, §90-210.18A(d).
Resident trainees.
Furnishing information to board, §90-210.23(d).
Powers as to programs for, §90-210.23(f).
Rules and regulations, §90-210.23(a).
Seal, §90-210.23(h).

FUNERAL SERVICES PROVIDERS —Cont'd
Board —Cont'd
Vacancies, §90-210.18A(c).
Burial.
Defined, §90-210.20(c).
Child support enforcement.
Forfeiture of licensing privilege, §50-13.12.
Cremation.
General provisions, §§90-210.120 to 90-210.135.
See CREMATION.
Criminal law and procedure.
Unlawful practices, §90-210.25(f).
Dead human bodies.
Defined, §90-210.20(c1).
Death certificates.
Entitlement of funeral director or funeral service
licensee to certified copy upon request,
§130A-93(c1).
Decedents' estates.
Claims against decedent's estate.
Funeral expenses, second class claim,
limitation, §28A-19-6.
Funeral expenses deemed obligation of estate,
§28A-19-8(a), (b).
Definitions, §90-210.20.
Dissection.
Schools for teaching mortuary science.
Privileges as to use of bodies for dissection,
§90-210.23(g).
Embalmers.
Defined, §90-210.20(d).
Embalming outside establishment.
Registration of facility, §90-210.25(d1).
Licenses.
Qualifications, §90-210.25(a).
Revocation or suspension.
Felony convictions, §15A-1331A.
Embalming.
Defined, §90-210.20(e).
Evidence.
Funeral charges at issue, §8-58.1.
Examination scores not public records,
§90-210.29B.
Executors and administrators.
Carrying out funeral arrangements prior to
appointment, §28A-13-1.
Wrongful death.
Damages recoverable by personal
representative, §28A-18-2(b).
Fees.
Establishment permits, §90-210.28.
Licenses, §90-210.28.
Schedule of fees, §90-210.28.
Felony convictions.
Forfeiture of licenses, §15A-1331A.
Funeral chapels.
Defined, §90-210.20(e1).
Registration.
Fee, §90-210.28.
Required, §90-210.27A(g).
Funeral contracts and funds.
Preneed funeral contracts and funds generally,
§§90-210.60 to 90-210.73.
See PRENEED FUNERAL CONTRACTS AND
FUNDS.
Funeral directing.
Defined, §90-210.20(f).
Practice of funeral directing.
Requirements to engage in, §90-210.25(a2).
Funeral directors.
Defined, §90-210.20(g).

FUNERAL SERVICES PROVIDERS —Cont'd

Funeral directors —Cont'd

Identification of bodies before burial or cremation, §90-210.29A.

Licenses, §§90-210.25, 90-210.26.

Criminal records checks for license applicants, §90-210.25(a).

Revocation or suspension.

Felony convictions, §15A-1331A.

Funeral establishments.

Defined, §90-210.20(h).

Funeral chapels.

Defined, §90-210.20(e1).

Registration.

Fees, §90-210.28.

Required, §90-210.27A(g).

Inspection, §90-210.23(e).

Licenses.

Owners, §90-210.27A(e).

Person under whose name funeral establishment does business, §90-210.27A(f).

Misleading or unregistered name.

Use prohibited, §90-210.27A(i).

Ownerships.

Restrictions, §90-210.27A(e).

Permits, §90-210.25(d).

Fees, §90-210.28.

Preparation room.

Persons allowed in, §90-210.27A(b).

Requirements as to, §90-210.27A(a).

Public health laws and rules.

Applicability, §90-210.27A(h).

Registered name, use required, §90-210.27A(j).

Reposing room.

Requirements as to, §90-210.27A(c).

Identification of bodies before burial or cremation, §90-210.29A.

Injunctions.

Power of board to seek injunction, §90-210.25(g).

Inspectors, §90-210.24.

Legislative declaration, §90-210.18A(a).

Liberal construction of article, §90-210.18A(a).

Licenses.

Criminal records checks for license applicants, §90-210.25(a).

Embalmers.

Qualifications, §90-210.25(a).

Examination scores not public records, §90-210.29B.

Fees, §90-210.28.

Funeral establishments.

Owners, §90-210.27A(e).

Person under whose name funeral establishment does business, §90-210.27A(f).

"Funeral service licensee" defined, §90-210.20(i).

Inactive licenses.

Application, renewal, activities authorized, §90-210.25(a1).

Qualifications, §90-210.25(a).

Good moral character.

Affidavits as to, §90-210.26.

Reciprocity, §90-210.25(b).

Registration, §90-210.25(c).

Revocation or suspension, §90-210.25(e).

Felony convictions, §15A-1331A.

Penalty in compromise, §90-210.25(e).

Statewide license for privilege of practicing.

Firm or corporation.

Not issued in name of, §105-41(e).

FUNERAL SERVICES PROVIDERS —Cont'd

Licenses —Cont'd

Statewide license for privilege of practicing —Cont'd

License not authorization to practice, §105-41(i).

Not transferable, §105-41(a).

Personal privilege licenses, §105-41(e).

Required, §105-41(a).

Tax for each license, §105-41(a).

Counties and cities levying, prohibition, §105-41(h).

Exemptions, §105-41(b).

Unlicensed practice.

Penalty, §90-210.25(f).

License tax.

Statewide license for privilege of practicing, §105-41.

Life insurance information regarding deceased person.

Applicability of section, §58-58-97(e).

Authority to request, §58-58-97(a).

Duty of insurer upon receipt of request, §58-58-97(a).

Failure to receive timely response, §58-58-97(b).

Fraud or mismanagement in practice of funeral service.

Acts constituting, §58-58-97(d).

Location of beneficiaries, §58-58-97(c).

No duty to spend on funeral of deceased.

Notice to beneficiaries, §58-58-97(c).

Misdemeanors.

Unlawful practice, §90-210.25(f).

Oaths.

Board members.

Oath of office of members, §90-210.19.

Penalties.

Revocation or suspension of license.

Payment of penalty in compromise, §90-210.25(e).

Permits.

Funeral establishments, §90-210.25(d).

Fees, §90-210.28.

Student permits, §90-210.29(b).

Practice of funeral directing or funeral service.

Requirements to engage in, §90-210.25(a2).

Practice of funeral service.

Defined, §90-210.20(k).

Unlawful practice, §90-210.25(f).

Preneed funeral contracts and funds generally, §§90-210.60 to 90-210.73.

See PRENEED FUNERAL CONTRACTS AND FUNDS.

Presumptions.

Funeral charges at issue.

Reasonableness, rebuttable presumption, §8-58.1(b).

Services reasonable and necessary.

Permissive presumption, §8-58.1(c).

Reciprocity.

Licenses, §90-210.25(b).

Recovery of human tissue at funeral establishment, §90-210.25(e1).

Reports.

Resident trainees, §90-210.25(a).

Resident trainees.

Certificate of resident traineeship, §90-210.25(a).

Fees, §90-210.28.

Defined, §90-210.20(l).

Information.

Furnishing to board, §90-210.23(d).

FUNERAL SERVICES PROVIDERS —Cont'd
Resident trainees —Cont'd
Powers of board, §90-210.23(f).
Qualifications, §90-210.25(a).
Reports, §90-210.25(a).
Seals and sealed instruments.
Board, §90-210.23(h).
Students.
Authorized practices, §90-210.29(a).
Permits, §90-210.29(b).
Taking of human tissue at funeral establishment, §90-210.25(e1).
Venue.
Injunctions.
Actions by board to enjoin violations, §90-210.25(f).
Witnesses.
Funeral charges at issue.
Injured party or guardian, administrator or executor.
Competency to give evidence regarding amount of charges, §8-58.1.

FUNGIBLE GOODS.
Duplicate receipt or bill.
Rights conferred, §25-7-402.
Warehouses.
Duty to keep goods separate, §25-7-207(a).
Liability for commingling goods, §25-7-207(b).

FUNGICIDES.
Pesticide applicators, §§143-452 to 143-459.
See PESTICIDE APPLICATORS.
Pesticide board generally.
See PESTICIDE BOARD.
Pesticide consultants, §§143-455, 143-456.
Pesticide dealers and manufacturers licenses, §§143-448 to 143-451.
Pesticide registration.
See PESTICIDE REGISTRATION.
Pesticides generally, §§143-434 to 143-470.1.
See PESTICIDES.

FUQUAY-VARINA.
Accessory building of bona fide farm.
Building code exemption.
Zoning ordinance, §160A-360(k).
Satellite annexation.
Limitation on area of satellite corporate limits, inapplicability, §160A-58.1(b).

FURBEARER PROPAGATION.
Licenses, §113-273(i).

FUR-DEALER LICENSES, §113-273(f).

FURNITURE.
Child care facilities.
Mandatory standards for licensing, §110-91.
Creditor obtaining possession of debtor's household furnishings.
Requirements, §1C-1601(g).
Exemption from creditors' claims.
Household furnishings, §1C-1601(a).
Liens.
Possessory liens on personal property.
Persons entitled to lien, §44A-2(e).
Loans.
Household and kitchen furniture.
Usurious loans on furniture, §14-391.
Property taxes.
Exclusion of non-business property.
Household furnishings, §105-275.

FURNITURE —Cont'd
Purchases through department of administration.
Furniture requirements contracts, §143-57.1.
Sales and use.
Tax holiday, inapplicability, §105-164.13C(b).

FUTURE ADVANCEMENTS, §§29-23 to 29-29.

FUTURE ADVANCES.
Secured transactions.
Priority of security interests.
Buyers of goods, ordinary course of business, §25-9-323(d).
Commitment, advances pursuant to, §25-9-323(e).
Buyers of receivables holding interest, §25-9-323(c).
Lessees of goods, §25-9-323(f).
Commitment, advances pursuant to, §25-9-323(g).
Lien creditors, §25-9-323(b).
Time of advance basis, §25-9-323(a).
Security interest in, §25-9-204(c).

FUTURE INTERESTS.
Conveyances.
Inter vivos and testamentary conveyances of future interests permitted, §39-6.3(a) to (c).
Revocation of conveyances to persons not in esse, §§39-6, 39-6.1.
Validation of deed, §39-6.1.
Killing decedent.
Contingent remainders and executory interests, §31A-8.
Mortgages and deeds of trust.
Advances and future obligations, §§45-67 to 45-74.
Property passed by will, §31-40.
Remainders, reversions and executory interests generally.
See REMAINDERS, REVERSIONS AND EXECUTORY INTERESTS.
Renunciation.
Effect, §31B-3(a).
Succession, §31B-1.
Wills.
What property passes by will, §31-40.

FUTURES CONTRACTS.
Commodities as which contracts void, §16-3.
Evidence.
Prosecutions under provisions, §16-6.
Misdemeanors.
Entering into or aiding futures contract, §16-4.
Opening office for sales of futures, §16-5.
Voidability, §16-3.
Witnesses.
Prosecutions under provisions, §16-6.

FUTURES TRADING.
Commodities.
General provisions, §§78D-1 to 78D-33.
See COMMODITIES.

G

GAG ORDERS.
Open court proceedings or reports of public records, §7A-276.1.

GAIN FROM FELONY.
Forfeiture, §14-2.3.

GALLERIES.
Destruction of property of gallery, §14-398.

GALLSTONES.
Food, drug and cosmetic act.
Drug or device, false advertising, §106-138(b).

GAMBLING, §§14-289 to 14-309.15.
Alcoholic beverage permittees.
Conduct unlawful on premises, §18B-1005(a).
Bureau of investigation.
Investigation of gaming law violations, §114-15(a).
Contracts.
Futures contracts, §§16-3 to 16-6.
Void, §16-1.
Witnesses.
Players and betters competent witnesses, §16-2.
Definitions.
Punchboards, §14-296.
Slot machines, §§14-296, 14-306(a).
Sweepstakes, §14-306.4(a).
Destruction of gaming devices.
Opposing, §14-300.
Elections.
Betting or wagering on, §163-274(a).
Elements of offense, §14-292.
False coins or tokens.
Using to obtain property or services from slot
machines, vending machines, etc, §14-108.
Faro banks and tables.
Opening, establishing, etc., bank or table, §14-294.
Futures contracts, §§16-3 to 16-6.
Gaming tables.
Allowing on premises, §14-297.
Destruction by police officers.
Opposing, §14-300.
Faro tables, §14-294.
Keeping, §14-295.
Greyhound racing, §14-309.20.
Houses of public entertainment, §14-293.
Indians.
Authorization, federally recognized tribes, §71A-8.
Individual income tax.
Imposition of tax on nonresidents deriving income
from.
Purposes of part, §105-134.
Lotteries.
Acting as agent for lotteries, §14-291.
Advertising lotteries, §14-289.
Dealing in lotteries, §14-290.
"Numbers" tickets, §14-291.1.
Selling lottery tickets, §14-291.
State lottery, §§18C-101 to 18C-173.
See STATE LOTTERY.
Nuisances.
Offenses against public morals.
Abatement generally, §§19-1 to 19-8.3.
See NUISANCES.
Police.
Destruction of gaming devices.
Opposing destruction, §14-300.
Public entertainment, §14-293.
Punchboards.
Allowing on premises, §14-297.
Definition, §14-296.
Keeping, §14-295.
Operation, §§14-302, 14-303.
Racing greyhounds, §14-309.20.
Raffles.
Defined, §14-309.15(b).
Maximum cash prizes, §14-309.15(d).

GAMBLING —Cont'd
Raffles —Cont'd
Nonprofit organization or association.
Conduct authorized, §14-309.15(a).
Number per year, §14-309.15(c).
Not conducted in conjunction with bingo,
§14-309.15(e).
Proceeds, disposition, §14-309.15(f).
Real property.
Offering as prize, appraised value,
§14-308.15(g).
**Seizure of property exhibited by gamblers and
illegal gaming items,** §§14-298, 14-299.
Disposition, §14-299.
Opposing, §14-300.
Server-based electronic game promotion.
Defined, §14-306.3(c).
Indian tribes, exceptions, §14-306.3(e).
Possession of game terminal, §14-306.3(b).
Prohibited, §14-306.3(a).
Revocation of permits and contracts, §14-306.3(d).
Slot machines.
See SLOT MACHINES.
State lottery, §§18C-101 to 18C-173.
See STATE LOTTERY.
Sweepstakes.
Electronic machines and devices prohibited,
§14-306.4.
Criminal penalties, §14-306.4(f).
Definitions, §14-306.4(a).
Entertaining display, §14-306.4(b).
Indian lands, §14-306.4(d).
Legislative intent, §14-306.4(c).
Separate offense each violation, §14-306.4(e).
Video gaming machines.
ABC law violations, §14-306.2.
Ban on machines, §14-306.1A(a).
Ban on warehousing, §14-306.1A(d).
Criminal offense to make unlawful payout,
§14-306(d).
Definitions, §14-306.1A(b).
Devices not considered slot machines, §14-306(b).
Exemptions from ban, §14-306.1A(c), (e), (f).
Paying more than allowed by law.
Warning sticker or message as to criminal
penalty affixed to machine, §14-306(c).
Pay off in cash.
Exception to slot machine definition
inapplicable, §14-306(d).
Repurchase of prize for cash or reward in cash.
Inapplicability of exception to slot machine
definition, §14-306(d).
Sweepstakes, §14-306.4.
Witnesses.
Testimony enforced in certain criminal
investigations, §8-55.
Immunity of witness, §8-55.

GAME BIRD PROPAGATION.
Licenses, §113-273(h).

GAME LAWS.
Fish and fishing generally.
See FISH AND FISHING.
Hunting and wildlife.
See HUNTING AND WILDLIFE.

GAMING LAW.
Generally, §§14-289 to 14-309.15.
See GAMBLING.

GAMMA HYDROXYBUTYRIC ACID (GHB).
Date rape drug, §90-89.

GAMMA HYDROXYBUTYRIC ACID (GHB)
—Cont'd
Scheduled I controlled substance, §90-89.
Schedule III controlled substance, §90-91(m).
Schedule IV controlled substance, §90-92.

GAMMA RAYS.
Radiation protection act generally, §§104E-1 to
104E-29.
See RADIATION PROTECTION.

GANG RAPE.
Venue, §15A-136.

GANGS, §§14-50.15 to 14-50.30.
Civil actions based on conduct.
Effect of conviction for criminal gang activity,
§14-50.26.
Conditional discharge and dismissal.
First offenders under age of 18, §14-50.29.
Criminal intelligence information.
Dissemination to principals of schools, §14-50.27A.
Deferred prosecution.
Conditional discharge and dismissal.
First offenders under age of 18, §14-50.29.
Definitions, §14-50.16(b) to (d).
Determination of gang activity on conviction
of criminal offense, §14-50.25.
Enhancement of misdemeanor offense to
felony.
Offense committed for benefit of or association
with gang, §14-50.22.
First offenders under age of 18.
Conditional discharge and dismissal.
Effect of discharge and dismissal, §14-50.29(c).
Expungement of records, §14-50.29(d).
Notification to state and local agencies of court's
order, §§14-50.29(e), 15-150.
On completion of probation, §14-50.29(b).
Expungement of records, §15A-145.1.
Affidavit of good behavior, §14-50.30(a).
Affidavits of no previous convictions,
§14-50.30(a).
Discharge and dismissal, §14-50.29(d).
Filing of petition, §14-50.30(a).
Order of court for expungement and restoration
of status, §14-50.30(b).
Supplemental nature of law, §14-50.30(c).
Finding of no previous criminal convictions,
§14-50.29(b).
Placement on probation, §14-50.29(a).
Terms of probation, §14-50.29(b).
Violation of probation, §14-50.29(c).
Judgment of offense indicating gang activity,
§14-50.25.
Juveniles under age of 16, nonapplicability,
§14-50.28.
Local laws not preempted, §14-50.27.
Nuisances, real property used by gang.
Declaration of public nuisance, §14-50.24(a).
Not applicable to innocent owner of property,
§14-50.24(b).
Offenses considered separate, §14-50.21.
Patterns of gang activity.
Defined, §14-50.16(d).
Felony offense, §14-50.16(a).
Prohibited acts, §14-50.16(a).
Principals of schools.
Dissemination of criminal intelligence
information, §14-50.27A.
Probation, conditions, §15A-1343(b1).

GANGS —Cont'd
Seizure and forfeiture of property.
Not applicable to innocent owner of property,
§14-50.23(c).
Property subject to, §14-50.23(a).
Restraining orders, §14-50.23(b).
Separate offenses, §14-50.21.
Soliciting or encouraging participation.
Felony, §14-50.17(b).
Minors.
Culpability for underlying offense committed by
minor, §14-50.18(c).
Felony, §14-50.18(b).
Prohibition, §14-50.18(a).
Offense, §14-50.17(a).
Title of act, §14-50.15.
Withdrawal from gang.
Threats of retaliation or punishment for
withdrawing.
Felony, §14-50.20(b).
Prohibition, §14-50.20(a).
Threats to deter another from assisting.
Felony, §14-50.19(b).
Prohibition, §14-50.19(a).

GARAGES.
Motor vehicle mechanic and storage liens.
Assignment of actions to enforce to magistrates,
§7A-211.1.
Repair of motor vehicles, §§20-354 to 20-354.9.
See MOTOR VEHICLE REPAIRS.

GARBAGE AND TRASH.
Boating safety.
Depositing or discharging litter, §75A-10(c).
Medical waste, §75A-10(d).
Penalty, §75A-10(e).
Computers and televisions.
Recycling, §§130A-309.130 to 130A-309.141.
See RECYCLING.
Counties.
Areas outside corporate limits.
Establishing and operating facilities,
§153A-292(a).
Collection of fees, §153A-293.
Cooperation between department of
transportation and counties, §153A-291.
Costs of providing and operating facility.
Determining for imposition of fees,
§153A-292(b).
County collection and disposal, §153A-292(a) to (f).
Definitions, §§153A-136(c), (d), 153A-294.
Disposal and removal of trash and garbage.
Boards of commissioners to provide for,
§153A-132.1.
Equipment.
Agreement with department of transportation to
make available, §153A-291.
Fees.
Collection, use of facility and availability of
facility.
Authority to impose, determining amount,
§153A-292(b).
Property taxes, billing and collecting in same
manner, §153A-293.
Gate across highway leading to facility.
Erecting, §153A-292(c).
Highway rights-of-way, containers on.
Misdemeanor for placing garbage on
right-of-way, inapplicability, §136-18.3(b).
Permits, issuance by department of
transportation, §136-18.3(a).

GARBAGE AND TRASH —Cont'd
Counties —Cont'd
Highway rights-of-way, containers on —Cont'd
Removal or change of location, order of
department, §136-18.3(d).
Written permission of owner of underlying fee,
required, §136-18.3(c).
Landfills.
Local government landfill liaison, §153A-136(e).
Right of entry, §153A-136(f).
Selection and approval of site, §153A-136(c).
Low-income persons, providing aid to,
§153A-292(f).
Ordinances, §153A-136(b).
Prison and other labor.
Agreement with department of transportation to
make available, §153A-291.
Regulation of disposal facilities, nature of disposal
and method of disposal, §153A-292(a).
Regulation of solid wastes, §153A-136.
Regulation of storage, collection, transportation
and use, §153A-136(a).
Removal and disposal of trash and garbage.
Boards of commissioners to provide for,
§153A-132.1.
Service districts, §§153A-300 to 153A-310.
Site for facility.
Acquiring by purchase or condemnation,
§153A-292(c).
Use of suitable vacant land, §153A-292(c).
Garbage trucks.
Stopping on highways, §20-161(a).
Highway rights-of-way.
Location of collection containers on.
Counties and municipalities, §136-18.3(a) to (d).
Hogs.
Feeding garbage to swine, §§106-405.1 to
106-405.9.
Junkyards generally, §§136-141 to 136-155.
See JUNKYARDS.
Light-traffic road weight and load limitations.
Garbage collection exception, §20-118(c).
Littering.
Generally.
See LITTERING.
**Motor vehicle used for collecting garbage or
recyclable materials.**
Stopping on highways, §20-161(a).
Municipalities.
Accidental spilling during loading of garbage
truck.
Inapplicability of littering statute, §14-399(a2).
Collection and disposal by city.
Fee for collection, imposing, §160A-317(c).
Participation in service provided by city.
Requiring property owner, §160A-317(b).
Placing waste in specific places or receptacles.
Authority to require property owners,
§160A-317(b).
Separation of materials before collection.
Requiring property owner, §160A-317(b).
Extension of corporate limits.
Population of five thousand or more.
Contract with private solid waste collection
firms, §160A-49.3.
Highway rights-of-way, containers on.
Misdemeanor for placing garbage on
right-of-way, inapplicability, §136-18.3(b).
Permits, issuance by department of
transportation, §136-18.3(a).

GARBAGE AND TRASH —Cont'd
Municipalities —Cont'd
Highway rights-of-way, containers on —Cont'd
Removal or change of location, order of
department, §136-18.3(d).
Written permission of owner of underlying fee,
required, §136-18.3(c).
Littering statute, inapplicability.
Accidental spilling during loading of garbage
truck, §14-399(a2).
Recycling program.
Requiring property owner's participation,
§160A-317(b).
Regulation of placing of garbage and trash within
municipal limits, §160A-303.1.
Navigation and pilotage.
Commissioners of navigation to designate place
for, §76-55.
Navigable waters.
Deposit prohibited, §76-40(a).
Public lands.
Dumping rights, §146-11.
Regional solid waste management authorities,
§§153A-421 to 153A-432.
See REGIONAL SOLID WASTE MANAGEMENT
AUTHORITIES.
Sanitary districts.
Collection and disposal.
Corporate powers of sanitary district board,
§130A-55.
**Seat belt use by occupants of truck during
collection rounds.**
Exception to mandatory use requirement,
§20-135.2A(c).
Solid waste management.
General provisions, §§130A-290 to 130A-305.
See SOLID WASTE MANAGEMENT.
Stopping solid waste vehicle on highway,
§20-161(a).
Street and highways.
Litter prevention account, §136-125.1.

GARNER.
Accessory building of bona fide farm.
Building code exemption.
Zoning ordinance, §160A-360(k).
Satellite annexation.
Limitation on area of satellite corporate limits,
inapplicability, §160A-58.1(b).

GARNISHMENT.
Admission by garnishee.
Debt or personal property due defendant payable
at future date.
Denial of allegation by plaintiff, §1-440.28(e).
Indebted to defendant.
Judgment entered by clerk, amount,
§1-440.28(a).
Not in possession of property belonging to
defendant at time of answer, value of property
determined, §1-440.28(c).
Judgment entered by clerk, amount,
§1-440.28(d).
Possession of personal property belonging to
defendant.
Judgment entered by clerk, delivery of property
to sheriff, §1-440.28(b).
Agriculture.
Delinquent fees and taxes.
Collection of delinquent fees and taxes,
§106-9.4(b).

GARNISHMENT —Cont'd

Alimony.
Remedy available, §50-16.7(e).

Ambulances.
County or city ambulance service, §§44-51.4 to 44-51.8.

Ancillary proceeding, §1-440.21(a).

Answer by garnishee.
Admissions in answer, §1-440.28(a) to (g).
Lien or other valid claim asserted, §1-440.28(g).
Setoff, right asserted, §1-440.28(f).

Attachment.
General provisions.
See ATTACHMENT.

Blind persons.
Aid to the blind.
Exemption from garnishment, §111-18.

Bonds, surety.
Garnishee retaining possession, §1-440.32(b).

Child support, §110-136.
Income withholding, §§110-136.3 to 110-136.14.
See CHILD SUPPORT.

Corporations.
Summons and process.
Delivery of garnishment process to corporate garnishee, §1-440.26.

Debtors and creditors.
Payment to defendant by garnishee, §1-440.31.

Denials by garnishee, §1-440.29(a).
Jury trial, §§1-440.28(e), 1-440.29(b).

Executions.
Issuance of execution against garnishee, §1-440.32(a).
Bonds, surety.
Garnishee retaining possession, §1-440.32(b).

Exemptions.
Limitation on wage garnishment, §1-362.

Failure of garnishee to appear.
Generally, §1-440.27(a).
Notice requiring appearance, §1-440.27(b).

Family law arbitration, §50-44(c).

Firemen's and rescue squad workers' pension fund.
Exemption of pensions from garnishment, §58-86-90.

Forms.
Notice of levy, §1-440.24.
Summons to garnishee, §1-440.23.

Fraternal benefit societies.
Benefits.
Not subject to garnishment, §58-24-85.

Fraudulent public assistance program payments.
Recoupment of fraudulent payments, §108A-25.3.

Funds transfers, UCC.
Creditor process served on receiving bank, §25-4A-502.

Garnishee defined, §1-440.21(b).

Hospitals.
Debts owed public hospitals, §§131E-48 to 131E-51.

Insurer supervision, rehabilitation and liquidation.
Garnishment prohibited during pendency of liquidation proceeding, §58-30-295.

Jury.
Denials by garnishee.
Jury trial, §§1-440.28(e), 1-440.29(b).
Time of jury trial, §1-440.30.

Legislative retirement system.
Exemption from garnishment, §120-4.29.

GARNISHMENT —Cont'd

Levy.
How made, §1-440.25.
Notice.
Delivery to garnishee, §1-440.25.
Corporate garnishee, §1-440.26.
Form, §1-440.24.

Liens.
County or city ambulance service, §§44-51.4 to 44-51.8.
Garnishee may assert lien, §1-440.28(g).
Levy on defendant's personal property in hands of garnishee, §1-440.33(c).
More than one order served on garnishee.
Determination of questions of priority, §1-440.33(g).

Limitation on wage garnishment, §1-362.

More than one order served on garnishee.
Determination of questions of priority, §1-440.33(g).

Municipalities.
Taxation.
Remedies for collecting taxes, §160A-207.

Nature of garnishment, §1-440.21(a), (b).

Notice.
Failure of garnishee to appear.
Notice requiring appearance, §1-440.27(b).
Levy.
Delivery to garnishee, §§1-440.25, 1-440.26.
Form, §1-440.24.

Purpose, §1-440.21(a).

Retirement system for teachers and state employees.
Exemption from garnishment, §135-9.

Return where garnishee process issued, §1-440.16(b).

Service of process.
Issuance of summons to garnishee, §1-440.22(a), (b).

Setoff.
Garnishee may assert right of setoff, §1-440.28(f).

Sheriff's return.
Where garnishee process issued, §1-440.16(b).

Summons to garnishee.
Delivery to garnishee, §1-440.25.
Corporate garnishee, §1-440.26(a).
Foreign corporation, §1-440.26(b).
Local agent, §1-440.26(a), (c).
Form, §1-440.23.
Issuance, §1-440.22(a), (b).

Supplemental retirement income act.
Exemption from garnishment, §135-95.

Support and maintenance.
Child support, §110-136.

Taxation.
Collection of taxes, §105-242(b).
Compliance of garnishee, §105-242.1(b).
Exempt property, §105-242(e).
Notice, §105-242.1(a).
Electronic notice, §105-242.1(a1).
Release from liability, §105-242.1(c).

Wages.
Fraudulent public assistance program payments, §108A-25.3.
Limitation on wage garnishment, §1-362.

GARVEE BONDS.

Financing federal-aid highway projects.
Issuance of grant anticipation revenue vehicles, §136-18.
Distribution of funds derived, §136-17.2A(i).

GAS AND GAS COMPANIES.
Bills to show reading of meters, §66-9.
Discharges of oil or hazardous substances,
§§143-215.83 to 143-215.94.
See OIL OR HAZARDOUS SUBSTANCES
DISCHARGES.
Franchised natural gas local distribution
companies.
Natural gas planning.
Reports detailing plans for providing gas service
in areas of franchise territory, §62-36A(a),
(d).
Natural gas service agreements.
Interstate or intrastate pipeline companies.
Orders directing distribution companies to
enter into service agreements within
reasonable time, §62-36B.
Leaking petroleum underground storage tank
cleanup, §§143-215.94A to 143-215.94Y.
See UNDERGROUND PETROLEUM STORAGE
TANKS.
Meters.
Bills to show reading of meters, §66-9.
Master electrical and natural gas meters.
Prohibition, §143-151.42(a).
Exception, §143-151.42(b).
Municipalities.
Lease or purchase of natural gas fields, reserves
and supplies.
Authority to operate, §160A-312(c).
Natural gas expansion fund, §62-158.
Commission's duties, §62-158(c), (d).
Construction of facilities, §62-159(a).
Determination of economic feasibility, §62-159(b).
Exclusive franchises, §62-159(c).
Purpose, §62-158(a).
Rules promulgated by commission, §§62-158(d),
62-159(d).
Sources, §62-158(b).
Natural gas planning, §62-36A.
Certificates of public convenience and necessity,
§62-36A(b1).
Reports, §62-36A(a), (d).
Rulemaking to implement provisions, §62-36A(b).
Natural gas service agreements.
Regulation of, §62-36B.
Offshore oil and gas activities, §§143-215.94AA
to 143-215.94JJ.
See OFFSHORE OIL AND GAS ACTIVITIES.
Oil and gas conservation.
General provisions, §§113-378 to 113-424.
See OIL AND GAS CONSERVATION.
Property taxes.
Public service corporations.
Generally, §§105-333 to 105-344.
See PROPERTY TAXES.
Public utilities generally.
See PUBLIC UTILITIES.
Reports.
Franchised natural gas local distribution
companies.
Natural gas planning.
Reports detailing plans for providing natural
gas service in areas of franchise territory,
§62-36A(a), (d).
Rulemaking to implement provisions,
§62-36A(b).
Trespass.
Criminal trespass, §14-152.
Interfering with gas appliances, §14-151.

GAS CONSERVATION, §§113-378 to 113-424.
See OIL AND GAS CONSERVATION.

GAS COST ADJUSTMENT FOR NATURAL GAS
LOCAL DISTRIBUTION COMPANIES,
§62-133.4.

GASOHOL.
Gasoline tax.
Defined, §105-449.60.

GASOLINE.
Advertising.
Price advertisements.
Drawing or pumping fuel by purchaser himself,
§14-117.2(a), (b).
Commodities.
General provisions, §§78D-1 to 78D-33.
See COMMODITIES.
Dispensing equipment standards for ethanol
blends, §143-143.6.
Fraud.
Price advertisements.
Purchaser himself drawing or pumping fuel,
§14-117.2.
Inspection, §§119-14 to 119-47.
See GASOLINE AND OIL INSPECTION.
Larceny of motor fuels, §14-72.5.
Driver's license, second or subsequent conviction.
Limited driving privilege.
Allowed person whose license revoked,
§20-16(e2).
Mandatory revocation of driver's license,
§20-17(a).
Period driver's license revoked, §20-19(g2).
Sulfur content standards, §119-26.2.

GASOLINE AND OIL INSPECTION, §§119-14 to
119-47.
Administration of provisions.
Commissioner of agriculture to administer,
§119-23.
Inspection tax proceeds.
Allotment for administration expenses,
§119-18(b).
Inspectors, clerks and assistants.
Appoint and employ, §119-25.
Adoption of certain laws as part of article,
§119-45.
Adulteration.
Products offered for sale, §119-35.
Analysis of inspected products.
Charges for analysis of samples, §119-46.
Establishment of laboratory for analysis, §119-30.
Evidence.
Certified copies of official tests admissible in
evidence, §119-36.
Assistants.
Appoint and employ, §119-25.
Bill of sale.
Persons engaged in transporting.
Required to have in possession bill of sale,
§119-42.
Bills of lading.
Transporters.
Required to have in possession an invoice, bill of
sale or bill of lading, §119-42.
Board, §119-26.
Rules and regulations.
Availability to interested parties, §119-29.
Transfer to department of agriculture and
consumer services, §143A-62.

GASOLINE AND OIL INSPECTION —Cont'd

Bonds, surety.
Cancellation of license, §119-19.
Inspectors to be bonded, §119-25.

Carriers.
Invoice, bill of sale or bill of lading.
Required to be in possession of transporters, §119-42.

Certain laws adopted as part of article, §119-45.

Charges for analysis of samples, §119-46.

Citation of act, §119-14.

Clerks.
Appointment and employ, §119-25.

Commissioner of agriculture.
Administration of provisions, §119-23.
Delegation of duties.
Oxygen content standards and reformulated gasoline, §119-26.1(d).

Conflicts of interest.
Inspectors, §119-25.

Containers.
Display required on containers used in making deliveries, §119-43.

Definitions, §119-15.
MTBE in motor fuels, §119-26.3(a).

Department of revenue.
Fees.
Collection of fees by department, §119-23.

Enforcement of provisions.
Inspectors, clerks and assistants.
Appoint and employ, §119-25.

Equipment for measuring liquid petroleum products, §119-33.

Ethanol blended gasoline offered for retail sale.
Pumps or other dispensing devices.
Labels on pumps, §119-27.2(a), (b).

Evidence.
Certified copies of official tests admissible in evidence, §119-36.

Fees.
Collection of fees by department of revenue, §119-23.
Payment of fees into state treasury, §119-23.

Fines.
Prosecution of offenders, §119-38.

Gasoline.
Inspection of gasoline, §119-17.
Renaming, etc., of gasoline.
Filing of notice of intention to rename, etc., with board, §119-26.

Grade rating on pumps, etc., §119-27.

Inspectors.
Appointment and employ, §119-25.
Authority of inspectors, §119-32.
Bond to be given, §119-25.
Conflicts of interest, §119-25.
Equipment for measuring liquid petroleum products, §119-33.
Oath of office, §119-25.
Powers, §119-32.
Samples taken for inspection purposes.
Payment for samples, §119-31.

Invoices.
Persons engaged in transporting.
Required to have in possession an invoice, §119-42.

Kerosene.
Certain kerosene sales prohibited, §119-16.3.
Inspection of kerosene, §119-17.

GASOLINE AND OIL INSPECTION —Cont'd

Kerosene —Cont'd
Sales in proximity to gasoline or gasohol, §119-16.3.

Kerosene distributors.
Deferred payment of inspection tax, §119-18(a1).
Defined, §119-15.
License.
Application, §119-15.2.
Bond or letter of credit required for obtaining and keeping, §119-15.3(a).
Adjustment, §119-15.3(b).
Failure to comply, criminal penalty, §119-15.3(c).
Required, §119-15.1(a), (b).

Kerosene suppliers.
Defined, §119-15.
License.
Application, §119-15.2.
Bond or letter of credit required for obtaining and keeping, §119-15.3(a).
Adjustment, §119-15.3(b).
Failure to comply, criminal penalty, §119-15.3(c).
Required, exception, §119-15.1(a), (b).

Kerosene terminal operators.
License.
Application, §119-15.2.
Bond or letter of credit required for obtaining and keeping, §119-15.3(a).
Adjustment, §119-15.3(b).
Failure to comply, criminal penalty, §119-15.3(c).
Required, exception, §119-15.1(a), (b).

Labels.
Display of grade rating on pumps, etc., §119-27.
Ethanol-blended gasoline offered for retail sale.
Pumps and other dispensing devices, §119-27.2(a), (b).

Laboratories.
Analysis of inspected products.
Establishment of laboratory for analysis, §119-30.

Licenses.
Cancellation of license, §119-19.
Persons required to have, §§119-15.1 to 119-15.3.

Liquefied petroleum gases, §§119-54 to 119-62.
See LIQUEFIED PETROLEUM GAS.

Measuring equipment, §119-33.

Misdemeanors, §119-39.

MTBE in motor fuels.
Definitions, §119-26.3(a).
Prohibited, §119-26.3(b).
Exceptions, §119-26.3(b), (c).
Rulemaking, §119-26.3(d).

Offshore oil and gas activities, §§143-215.94AA to 143-215.94JJ.
See OFFSHORE OIL AND GAS ACTIVITIES.

Oxygen content standards, §119-26.1.

Penalties.
Civil penalties, §119-39.1.
Oxygen content standards and reformulated gasoline, §119-26.1(c), (c1).
Prosecution of offenders, §§119-38, 119-39.

Petroleum products.
Inspection of kerosene, gasoline and other petroleum products provided for, §119-17.

Pumps or other dispensing devices, §119-27.
Ethanol blended gasoline offered for retail sale.
Labels on pumps, §119-27.2(a), (b).

GASOLINE AND OIL INSPECTION —Cont'd
Pumps or other dispensing devices —Cont'd
Self-service gasoline pumps.
Display of owner's or operator's name, address and telephone number, §119-27.1(a).
Enforcement of provisions, §119-27.1(b).
Reformulated gasoline, §119-26.1.
Retailers.
Delivery tickets.
Required to keep copies of delivery tickets, §119-37.
Invoices.
Required to keep copies of invoices, §119-37.
Responsibility of retailers for quality of products, §119-34.
Rules and regulations.
Availability of rules and regulations of board to interested parties, §119-29.
Oxygen content standards and reformulated gasoline, §119-26.1(a), (b).
Violations, civil penalties, §119-26.1(c).
Sales.
Adulteration of products offered for sale, §119-35.
Bill of sale.
Persons engaged in transporting required to have in possession bill of sale, §119-42.
Display of grade rating, etc.
Not labeled pumps or devices, §119-27.
Standards indicated on label not met, §119-27.
Substitutes for or motor fuel improvers.
Regulations for sale of substitutes, §119-28.
Samples taken for inspection.
Charges for analysis of samples, §119-46.
Payment for samples, §119-31.
Secretary of revenue.
Failure to report or pay tax.
Determination of tax liability by secretary, §119-21.
Self-service gasoline pumps.
Display of owner's or operator's name, address and telephone number, §119-27.1(a).
Enforcement of provisions, §119-27.1(b).
State of North Carolina.
Fuels used by state to be inspected, §119-47.
State treasurer.
Disposition of moneys by state treasurer, §119-23.
Substitutes for or motor fuel improvers.
Regulations for sale of substitutes, §119-28.
Sulfur content standards for gasoline, §119-26.2(a).
Rules to implement, adoption, §119-26.2(b).
Taxation.
Deferred payment, §119-18(a1).
Failure to report or pay tax.
Cancellation of license, §119-19.
Secretary of revenue to determine tax liability, §119-21.
Local tax prohibited, §119-18(c).
Proceeds of inspection tax, §119-18(b).
Rate of taxation, §119-18(a).
Time of payment, §119-18(a).
Title of article, §119-14.

GASOLINE TAX, §§105-449.60 to 105-449.126.
Accidental mix refund, §105-449.105(c).
Account number on return, §105-449.104.
Administration of chapter, §105-449.61(c).
Alternative fuels generally, §§105-449.130 to 105-449.139.
See ALTERNATIVE FUEL.

GASOLINE TAX —Cont'd
Amount of fuel sold or used in state.
Failure to disclose correct amount, §105-449.120(a).
Assessment of civil penalty.
Review of assessment, §105-449.119.
Audit of records, §105-449.121(b).
Backup tax on certain fuels, §105-449.87(a).
Liability, §105-449.87(b).
Behind-the-rack transfers.
Excise tax, §105-449.81.
Liability, §105-449.84A.
Blended fuel.
Defined, §105-449.60.
Excise tax, §105-449.81.
Motor fuel excise tax liability, §105-449.84.
Blender.
Defined, §105-449.60.
License required, §105-449.65(a).
Motor fuel excise tax liability, §105-449.84(a).
Separate licenses as motor fuel transporter, §105-449.65(b).
Bonds, surety.
Failure to file replacement bond or additional bond, §105-449.120(a).
Required as condition of obtaining and keeping certain licenses, §105-449.72.
Bulk end-user.
Defined, §105-449.60.
License as bonded or occasional importer, exception, §105-449.66.
License as distributor.
Restrictions, §105-449.68.
Removals by out-of-state users, §105-449.89(a).
Bulk plant operator.
Reliance on shipping documents, §105-449.115(c).
Bulk plants.
Defined, §105-449.60.
Return by distributor showing exports from, §105-449.102(a).
Contents, §105-449.102(b).
Cherokee Indians.
Eastern band. See within this heading, "Eastern band of Cherokee Indians."
Civil penalties.
Refusing to allow samples of motor fuel, §105-449.118A.
Unlawful use of dyed diesel fuel, §105-449.117(b).
Unlawful use of non-tax-paid fuel, §105-449.117(b).
Code.
Defined, §105-449.60.
Collection by supplier of tax on out-of-state removals.
Permissive suppliers, §105-449.71.
Corporate officers, managers and members of limited liability companies, partners.
Personal liability.
Unpaid taxes, §105-242.2(b).
Credit card companies.
Bond when company applies for refund, §105-449.72(e).
Credit card or access code enabling person to remove fuel without paying tax.
Buying fuel at retail, §105-449.88A(b).
Cardholder liability, §105-449.88A(c).
Deduction of amount of tax imposed on fuel purchase with exempt card or code, §105-449.97(d).
Deduction for exempt sales, §105-449.93.

GASOLINE TAX —Cont'd
Deductions allowed supplier when filing
   return, §105-449.97.
Defense to violation.
   State exemption not defense, §105-449.117(c).
Deferred payments.
   Refusing to allow, §105-449.120(a).
Definitions, §105-449.60.
Designated to be paid by person consuming
   fuel, §105-449.62.
Destination state.
   Defined, §105-449.60.
Destination state tax collected on exported
   motor fuel.
   Payment by supplier, §105-449.90A.
Diesel fuel.
   Defined, §105-449.60.
   Dyed diesel fuel.
      Accidental mix with tax paid motor fuel.
         Refund, §105-449.105(c).
      Backup tax, liability, §105-449.87.
      Defined, §105-449.60.
      Listed on shipping document.
         Joint and several liability where fuel not dyed
            diesel fuel, §105-449.82(c).
      Motor fuel excise tax.
         Liability, §105-449.86(b).
         Rate, §105-449.86(a).
      Unlawful for highway use, §105-449.117(a) to
         (c).
Discontinuance of business.
   Liability for taxes, §105-449.75.
   License holder required to notify secretary,
      §105-449.75.
Discounts.
   Importers, §105-449.99(b).
   Percentage discounts.
      Monthly calculation per distributors,
         §105-449.105B.
   Refusing to allow, §105-449.120(a).
   Suppliers, allowed when filing return,
      §105-449.97.
Dispensing non-tax-paid motor fuel,
   §105-449.120(b).
Distribution of revenues, §105-449.125.
Distributors.
   Cancellation or reissuance after cancellation of
      license.
      Notice to suppliers, §105-449.92.
   Defined, §105-449.60.
   Exempt sale deduction.
      Percentage discount, §105-449.93(b).
   License required, §105-449.65(a).
   Monthly hold harmless for licensed distributors,
      §105-449.105B.
   Nonpayment of tax due.
      Notice by suppliers to department,
         §105-449.98(c).
   Notice by supplier to distributor of taxable gallons
      received during reporting period,
      §105-449.98(b).
   Persons who may obtain license, §105-449.67.
   Remittance of tax to suppliers, §105-449.91(a).
      Method, §105-449.91(d).
   Restriction on who can get license as, §105-449.68.
   Return showing exports from bulk plant,
      §105-449.102.
   Separate license as importer for motor fuel
      transporter, §105-449.65(b).
Diverted fuel.
   Liability, §105-449.87(c).

GASOLINE TAX —Cont'd
Double tax prohibited, §105-449.61(b).
Dyed motor fuel storage facilities.
   Marking requirements, §105-449.123(a).
      Exception to facility containing fuel used in
         heating, dying crops or manufacturing
         process, §105-449.123(b).
Eastern band of Cherokee Indians.
   Refund of motor fuels or special fuel taxes.
      Definitions applicable, §105-449.114(b).
      Memorandum of understanding or agreement,
         §105-449.114(c).
      Recognition as possessing sovereign legal rights,
         §105-449.114(a).
Election by supplier to collect tax on
   out-of-state removals, §105-449.70.
   Permissive suppliers, §105-449.71.
Elective supplier.
   Defined, §105-449.60.
Electronic funds transfers.
   Payment of taxes by, §105-241(b).
Examination of books and records by
   secretary.
   Refusal to allow, §105-449.120(a).
Excise tax on motor fuel, §105-449.81.
   Blended fuel.
      Liability, §105-449.84.
   Dyed diesel fuel.
      Tax and liability, §105-449.86.
   Exemptions, §105-449.88.
   Imports.
      Liability for tax, §105-449.83.
   Liability for fuel grade ethanol tax, §105-449.83A.
   Liability on removal.
      Refineries, §105-449.82(a).
      Terminal racks, §105-449.82(c).
      Terminal systems, §105-449.82(b).
   Unaccounted for motor fuel losses, §105-449.85.
Exempt card or exempt access code.
   Persons removing fuel without paying tax.
      Buying fuel at retail, §105-449.88A(b).
      Deduction of amount of excise tax imposed on
         fuel purchased with card or code,
         §105-449.97(d).
      Liability of cardholder, §105-449.88A(c).
Exempt fuel refund, §105-449.105(a).
Exemptions from excise tax, §105-449.88.
Exempt sales deduction.
   Percentage discount, §105-449.93(b).
Exported motor fuel, destination state tax.
   Payment by supplier of tax collected on,
      §105-449.90A.
Exporters.
   Application for license, §105-449.69(e).
   Cancellation or reissuance after cancellation of
      license.
      Notice to suppliers, §105-449.92.
   License required, §105-449.65(a).
   Nonpayment of tax due.
      Notice by suppliers to department,
         §105-449.98(c).
   Notice by supplier of taxable gallons received
      during reporting period, §105-449.98(b).
   Remittance of tax to suppliers, §105-449.91(b).
      Method, §105-449.91(d).
   Unlicensed exporters.
      Liability for tax, §105-449.82(c).
Exports.
   Defined, §105-449.60.
Failing to pay.
   Personal liability.
      Responsible persons in business entities,
         §105-242.2(b).

GASOLINE TAX —Cont'd
False statements, §105-449.120(a).
Federal certificate of registry.
Required for applicants for licenses,
§105-449.69(c).
Federal excise tax, §105-449.81.
**Fiduciary duty of supplier on remitting tax to
secretary,** §105-449.98(a).
Fines.
Buying or selling untaxed motor fuel,
§105-449.118.
Credited to the highway fund, §105-449.126.
Shipping documents, §105-449.115(f).
Fuel alcohol.
Defined, §105-449.60.
Fuel alcohol provider.
Defined, §105-449.60.
Fuel grade ethanol.
Liability for tax on, §105-449.83A.
Gasohol.
Defined, §105-449.60.
Gasoline.
Defined, §105-449.60.
Gross gallons.
Defined, §105-449.60.
Highway.
Defined, §105-449.60.
Highway fund.
Part revenues distributed to wildlife resources
fund, §105-449.126.
Receipt of civil penalties collected under this
article, §105-449.126.
Highway vehicle.
Defined, §105-449.60.
Importers.
Application for license, §105-449.69(d).
Blended fuel.
Motor fuel excise tax, §105-449.84(b).
Bonded importer.
Defined, §105-449.60.
Bulk end-users.
License as bonded or occasional importer,
exception, §105-449.66.
Cancellation or reissuance after cancellation of
license.
Notice to suppliers, §105-449.92.
Defined, §105-449.60.
Discounts, §105-449.99(b).
Exempt sale deduction.
Percentage discount, §105-449.93(b).
Licensed as more than one type of importer.
Prohibition, §105-449.66.
License required, §105-449.65(a).
Monthly hold harmless, §105-449.105B.
Occasional importer.
Defined, §105-449.60.
Remittance of tax to suppliers, §105-449.91(c).
Method, §105-449.91(d).
Returns, §105-449.99(a).
Separate licenses distributor, §105-449.65(b).
Tank wagon importer.
Defined, §105-449.60.
Type of license sought.
Indicated on application, §105-449.66.
Types of importers, §105-449.66.
License must indicate category, §105-449.74.
Imports.
Defined, §105-449.60.
Motor fuel excise tax, §105-449.83.
Informational returns.
Distributor showing exports from bulk plant,
§105-449.102.

GASOLINE TAX —Cont'd
Informational returns —Cont'd
Motor fuel transporters showing deliveries of
imported or exported fuel, §105-449.101.
Terminal operators.
Changes in amount of motor fuel at terminal,
§105-449.100.
In-state-only supplier.
Defined, §105-449.60.
Investigations to identify violations.
Power of secretary, §105-449.117(c).
Letters of credit.
Required as condition of obtaining and keeping
certain licenses, §105-449.72.
Liability.
Backup tax on certain fuels, §105-449.87(b).
Diverted fuel, §105-449.87(c).
Personal liability for failure to pay.
Responsible persons in business entities,
§105-242.2(b).
Tax on behind-the-rack transfers, §105-449.84A.
Tax on fuel grade ethanol, §105-449.83A.
Tax on removals from refinery or terminal,
§105-449.82.
Licenses, §§105-449.65 to 105-449.77.
Applications.
Approval, §105-449.74.
Denial, §105-449.73.
Export activity, §105-449.69(e).
Federal certificate, §105-449.69(c).
Generally, §105-449.69(a).
Specific requirements, §105-449.69(b).
Bond of applicant required for license.
Adjustment, §105-449.72(b).
Additional bond, filing, §105-449.72(c).
Credit card companies.
Company applying for refund, §105-449.72(e).
Exemption from requirement, §105-449.72(f).
Initial bond, §105-449.72(a).
Replacement for previously filed bond,
§105-449.72(d).
Bond, surety.
Cancellation of license, §105-449.76.
Cancellation, §105-449.76.
Notice to suppliers, §105-449.92(a).
Effect of notice, §105-449.92(b).
Cancellation or reissuance after cancellation of
license.
Joint and several liability for selling fuel after
notice, §105-449.92(b).
Notice to suppliers, §105-449.92(a).
Credit card companies.
Bond when company applies for refund,
§105-449.72(e).
Denial, §105-449.73.
Discontinuance of business.
Notification to secretary, §105-449.75.
Display required, §105-449.74.
Distributors.
Restrictions, §105-449.68.
Failing to obtain license required,
§105-449.120(a).
Failure to pay tax.
Cancellation of license, §105-449.76.
False statements, §105-449.120(a).
Federal certificate of registry required for
applicant, §105-449.69(c).
Grounds for denial of application, §105-449.73.
Hearings.
Cancellation of license, §105-449.76.
Import activity, §105-449.69(d).

GASOLINE TAX —Cont'd
Licenses —Cont'd
Issuance, §105-449.74.
  Denial, §105-449.73.
Letter of credit required by applicant for license.
  Adjustment, §105-449.72(b).
  Exemption from requirement, §105-449.72(f).
  Initial letter, §105-449.72(a).
  Replacement for previously filed letter,
    §105-449.72(d).
List of persons who must have license,
  §105-449.65(a).
Multiple activities, §105-449.65(b).
Non-transferable, §105-449.74.
Persons who may obtain license, §105-449.67.
Records kept by secretary, §105-449.77(a).
Reissuance of certain licenses.
  Notice to suppliers, §105-449.92(a).
    Effect of notice, §105-449.92(b).
Requirements for applications.
  Specific requirements, §105-449.69(b).
Restrictions.
  Distributors, §105-449.68.
Revocation, §105-449.76.
Separate tax for person engaged in multiple
  activities, §105-449.65(b).
Supplier election to collect tax on out-of-state
  removals, §105-449.70.
  Permissive suppliers, §105-449.71.
Lists.
License holders, §105-449.77(b).
Persons who must have license, §105-449.65(a).
Local taxation prohibited, §105-449.61(a).
Losses of motor fuel at terminal.
Compensating tax on and liability for
  unaccounted, §105-449.85.
Lost fuel refund, §105-449.105(b).
Metered pumps.
Required, §105-449.122(a).
Misdemeanors.
Class 1 misdemeanors, §105-449.120(a).
Class 2 misdemeanors, §105-449.120(b).
Use of dyed diesel fuel on highway,
  §105-449.117(a).
Use of non-tax-paid fuel on highway,
  §105-449.117(a).
Motor fuel.
Defined, §105-449.60.
Motor fuel excise tax, §105-449.81.
Blender fuel.
  Liability, §105-449.84.
Dyed diesel fuel.
  Tax and liability, §105-449.86.
Exemptions, §105-449.88.
Imports.
  Liability for tax, §105-449.83.
Liability for tax.
  Refinery removals, §105-449.82(a).
  Terminal rack removals, §105-449.82(c).
  Terminal system removals, §105-449.82(b).
Unaccounted for motor fuel losses, §105-449.85.
Motor fuel rate.
Defined, §105-449.60.
Motor fuel transporters.
Defined, §105-449.60.
Informational returns showing deliveries of
  imported or exported motor fuel.
  Contents, §105-449.101(b).
  Due date, §105-449.101(c).
  Requirement, §105-449.101(a).
License required, §105-449.65(a).

GASOLINE TAX —Cont'd
Multiple activities for which license required.
Separate license for each activity, exceptions,
  §105-449.65(b).
Name on return, §105-449.104.
Nature of tax, §105-449.62.
Net gallons.
Defined, §105-449.60.
Non-tax-paid fuel.
Dispensing, §105-449.120(b).
Unlawful use, §105-449.117(a) to (c).
Notice.
Distributors or exporters not paying tax due.
  Department notification by supplier,
    §105-449.98.
Taxable gallons received by supplier during
  reporting period.
  Distributors or exporters notice, §105-449.98(b).
Tax rate, §105-449.80(c).
Out-of-state bulk plant.
Motor fuel excise tax liability, §105-449.83(c).
Out-of-state removals.
Bulk end-users, §105-449.89(a).
Election of supplier to collect tax on, §105-449.70.
  Permissive suppliers, §105-449.71.
Out-of-state terminal.
Motor fuel excise tax liability, §105-449.83(b).
Part of cost of fuel, §105-449.62.
Payment of tax.
Application of payments by supplier received from
  distributors or exporters, §105-449.98(d).
Deferred payments.
  Refusing to allow, §105-449.120(a).
Destination state tax collected on exported motor
  fuel, §105-449.90A.
Distributors or exporters not paying tax due.
  Notice by suppliers to department,
    §105-449.98(c).
Failing to pay, §105-449.120(a).
  Personal liability.
    Responsible persons in business entities,
      §105-242.2(b).
Payable when return due, §105-449.90(a).
Permissive suppliers.
Defined, §105-449.60.
Election to collect tax on out-of-state removals,
  §105-449.71.
Person.
Defined, §105-449.60.
Personal liability.
Unpaid taxes.
  Responsible persons in business entities,
    §105-242.2(b).
Position holder.
Defined, §105-449.60.
Rack.
Defined, §105-449.60.
Railroad tank cars.
Shipping documents required, §105-449.115.
Rate of tax, §105-449.80(a).
Rebates, §§105-449.105 to 105-449.110. See within
  this heading, "Refunds or rebates."
Recordkeeping requirements, §105-449.121(a).
Records.
License holders and license applicants,
  §105-449.77(a).
Records, failure to keep, §105-449.120(a).
Records, inspections, §105-449.121(b).
Records kept by secretary, §105-449.77(a).
Refineries.
Excise tax motor fuel, §105-449.81.

GASOLINE TAX —Cont'd
Refineries —Cont'd
Removals.
Motor fuel excise tax liability, §105-449.82.
Refiners.
License required, §105-449.65(a).
Refunds or rebates, §§105-449.105 to 105-449.110.
Accidental mixes, §105-449.105(c).
Amount of refund, §105-449.105(e).
Applications.
Due date, §105-449.108(a).
Requirements, §105-449.108(b).
Review, §105-449.110(a).
Bulk feed vehicles, §105-449.107(b).
Bulk fertilizer vehicles, §105-449.107(b).
Certain vehicles with power attachments, §105-449.107(b).
Sales tax amount, §105-449.107(c).
Commercial vehicle delivering and spreading mulch, soils, composts, etc., §105-449.107(b).
Commercial vehicles using power takeoff to remove septage, §105-449.107(b).
Credit card companies.
Bond when company applies for refund, §105-449.72(e).
Dump trucks.
Farm use, §105-449.107(b).
Exempt fuel, §105-449.105(a).
False statements, §105-449.120(a).
Garbage trucks, §105-449.107(b).
Interest, §105-449.110(b).
Kerosene.
Exempt fuel, §105-449.105A(a).
Liability for overpayment, §105-449.105A(b).
Late application, §105-449.108(d).
Liability for overpayment.
Kerosene, §105-449.105A(b).
Local government entities.
Quarterly refunds, §105-449.106(a).
Lost fuel, §105-449.105(b).
Nonprofit organizations.
Quarterly refunds, §105-449.106(a).
Off-highway use.
Licensed highway vehicles, §105-449.107(a), (c).
Review of applications, §105-449.110(a).
Special mobile equipment operated off-highway, §105-449.106(c).
Sweepers, §105-449.107(b).
Tank wagons, §105-449.107(b).
Taxis.
Quarterly refunds, §105-449.106(b).
Remittance of tax by supplier to secretary.
Fiduciary duty, §105-449.98(a).
Remittance of tax to suppliers, §105-449.91.
Distributors, §105-449.91(a).
Exporters, §105-449.91(b).
Importers, §105-449.91(c).
Method, §105-449.91(d).
Others, §105-449.91(d).
Removal.
Defined, §105-449.60.
Responsible persons in business entities.
Personal liability.
Unpaid taxes, §105-242.2(b).
Restrictions, §105-449.61(a), (b).
Retailer.
Defined, §105-449.60.
Returns.
Annual filers, §105-449.90(b).
Distributor showing exports from bulk plant, §105-449.102.
Claim for refund.
Return serves as, §105-449.102(a).

GASOLINE TAX —Cont'd
Returns —Cont'd
Distributor showing exports from bulk plant —Cont'd
Contents, §105-449.102(b).
Due date, §105-449.102(c).
Requirement, §105-449.102(a).
Failing to file, §105-449.120(a).
False statements, §105-449.120(a).
Filing period, §105-449.90(a).
Importers, §105-449.99(a).
Informational return.
Distributor showing exports from bulk plant, §105-449.102.
Motor fuel transporters, deliveries of imported or exported motor fuel, §105-449.101.
Contents, §105-449.101(b).
Due date, §105-449.101(c).
Requirement, §105-449.101(a).
Terminal operators, changes in amount of motor fuel at terminal, §105-449.100.
Contents, §105-449.100(b).
Due date, §105-449.100(c).
Requirement, §105-449.100(a).
Monthly filers, §105-449.90(d), (e).
Motor fuel transporters.
Informational return showing deliveries of imported or exported fuel, §105-449.101.
Name and account number, §105-449.104.
Suppliers.
Administrative discounts, §105-449.97(b).
Deductions and discounts allowed, §105-449.97.
Information required, §105-449.96.
Percentage discount, §105-449.97(c).
Taxes not remitted by distributors, §105-449.97(a).
Terminal operators.
Informational return.
Changes in amount of motor fuel at terminal, §105-449.100.
Revenues.
Distribution, §105-449.125.
Review of assessment of civil penalty, §105-449.119.
Road tax on carriers using fuel purchased outside state, §§105-449.37 to 105-449.57.
See MOTOR CARRIERS.
Samples of motor fuel, §105-449.121(b).
Refusing to allow, §105-449.118A.
Secretary.
Defined, §105-449.60.
Determination of wholesale price, §105-449.80(b).
Shipping documents.
Contents, §105-449.115(b).
Defense to civil action.
Compliance with conditions set out, §105-449.115(g).
Duties of person receiving shipment, §105-449.115(e).
Duties of transporter, §105-449.115(d).
Failure to show or give documents required, §105-449.120(a).
Issuance, §105-449.115(a).
Reliance on shipping document, §105-449.115(c).
Sanctions, §105-449.115(f).
Intentional issuance of deficient document, §105-449.115(h).
Transporting fuel without document, §105-449.115A(c).
Tank wagon, transporting fuel by, §105-449.115A.

GASOLINE TAX —Cont'd
Shipping documents —Cont'd
Waiver of penalty imposed.
Establishment of defense, §105-449.115(g).
Stopping vehicles for purposes of taking sample, §105-449.121(b).
Suppliers.
Application of payments received from distributors or exporters, §105-449.98(d).
Cancellation or reissuance of license to distributor, exporter or importer.
Notice to suppliers, §105-449.92(a).
Joint and several liability for selling fuel after notice, §105-449.92(b).
Deductions and discounts allowed when filing return, §105-449.97.
Defined, §105-449.60.
Destination state tax collected on exported motor fuel.
Payment by supplier, §105-449.90A.
Distributors or exporters not paying tax due.
Notice to department, §105-449.98.
Duties.
Application of payments, §105-449.98(d).
Election to collect tax on out-of-state removals, §§105-449.70(a), 105-449.71.
Effect of election, §105-449.70(b).
Permissive suppliers, §105-449.71(a).
Effect of election, §105-449.71(b).
Submission to jurisdiction of state for administration of provisions, §105-449.71(c).
Submission to jurisdiction of state for administration of provisions, §105-449.70(c).
Fiduciary duty on remitting tax to secretary, §105-449.98(a).
License required, §105-449.65(a).
Permissive suppliers.
Persons who may obtain license, §105-449.67.
Remittance of tax to, §105-449.91.
Distributors, §105-449.91(a).
Exporters, §105-449.91(b).
Importers, §105-449.91(c).
Method, §105-449.91(d).
Others, §105-449.91(d).
Remittance to secretary by supplier.
Fiduciary duty, §105-449.98(a).
Returns.
Deductions and discounts allowed, §105-449.97.
Information required, §105-449.96.
Separate license for other activity, §105-449.65(b).
Transfer of fuel to marine vessel, §105-449.89(b).
System transfer.
Defined, §105-449.60.
Excise tax motor fuel, §105-449.81.
Motor fuel excise tax liability, §105-449.83(a).
Tank trucks.
Connections between cargo tank and fuel supply tank prohibited, §105-449.122(b).
Tank wagon.
Defined, §105-449.60.
Shipping document required for transporting fuel by.
Duties of transporter to whom document issued, §105-449.115A(b).
Issuance, requirements for, §105-449.115A(a).
Sanctions, transporting without document, §105-449.115A(c).
Taxable gallons received during reporting period.
Notice by supplier to distributor or exporter, §105-449.98(b).

GASOLINE TAX —Cont'd
Terminal operators.
Changes in amount of motor fuel at terminal.
Informational return, §105-449.100.
Defined, §105-449.60.
Informational return showing changes in amount of motor fuel at terminal, §105-449.100.
License required, §105-449.65(a).
Reliance on shipping documents, §105-449.115(c).
Terminal racks.
Behind-the-rack transfers.
Excise tax, §105-449.81.
Liability, §105-449.84A.
Removals.
Motor fuel excise tax liability, §105-449.82(c).
Behind-the-rack transfer, §105-449.84A.
Terminals.
Blended fuel.
Motor fuel excise tax liability, §105-449.84(c).
Defined, §105-449.60.
Excise tax motor fuel, §105-449.81.
Unaccounted for motor fuel losses.
Liability, §105-449.85(b).
Tax, §105-449.85(a).
Terminal transfer systems.
Defined, §105-449.60.
Removals.
Motor fuel excise tax liability, §105-449.82.
Transmix.
Defined, §105-449.60.
Transporter.
Shipping documents, duties, §105-449.115(d).
Transporting fuel by tank wagon, §105-449.115A(b).
Transport trucks.
Defined, §105-449.60.
Shipping documents, §105-449.115.
Trustee.
Defined, §105-449.60.
Two-party exchange.
Defined, §105-449.60.
Understatement of liability, §105-236.
Wholesale price.
Determination, §105-449.80(b).
Wildlife resources fund.
Allocation from part of the highway fund, §105-449.126.

GAS PIPELINE FACILITIES.
Underground damage prevention, §§87-100 to 87-114.
See UNDERGROUND DAMAGE PREVENTION.

GAS PIPELINE SAFETY, §62-50.
Agreements with federal agencies.
Powers of utilities commission, §62-50(b), (c).
Civil penalty, §62-50(d), (e).
Gas operators.
Defined, §62-50(g).
Utilities commission.
Powers, §62-50(a) to (c).

GAS STATIONS.
Gas and oil inspection, §§119-14 to 119-47.
See GASOLINE AND OIL INSPECTION.
Leaking petroleum underground storage tank cleanup, §§143-215.94A to 143-215.94Y.
See UNDERGROUND PETROLEUM STORAGE TANKS.
Low-cost selling of motor fuels, §75-82(a).
Pumps or other dispensing devices, §119-27.
Ethanol blended gasoline offered for retail sale.
Labels on pumps, §119-27.2(a), (b).

GAS STATIONS —Cont'd
Pumps or other dispensing devices —Cont'd
Self-service gasoline pumps.
Display of owner's or operator's name, address and telephone number, §119-27.1(a).
Enforcement of provisions, §119-27.1(b).
Repair of motor vehicles, §§20-354 to 20-354.9.
See MOTOR VEHICLE REPAIRS.
Self-service stations.
Price advertisements.
Drawing or pumping fuel by purchaser himself, §14-117.2.
Unauthorized vehicles, §20-219.3.
Notice of violations, §20-219.3(b).
Prohibited acts, §20-219.3(a).
Remedies of owner or operator of station, §20-219.3(c), (d).
Removal, §20-219.3(c).

GASTON COLLEGE.
North Carolina center for applied textile technology, §§115D-67.1 to 115D-67.4.

GASTON COUNTY.
Agricultural tendencies in certain counties.
Terms of, §42-23.
All-terrain vehicles.
Use by employees on certain highways, §20-171.24.
Ambulances.
Attachment or garnishment and lien for, §§44-51.4 to 44-51.8.
False pretenses and cheats.
Obtaining ambulance services without intending to pay, §14-111.2.
Condemnation or acquisition of land by local government unit outside county.
Consent of board of commissioners necessary, §153A-15.
Counties generally.
See COUNTIES.
Cropper or tenant refusing to perform terms of contract.
Forfeiture of right of possession to premises, §42-27.
Dangerous firearm use by young children, permitting.
Air rifles, air pistols and BB guns not dangerous firearm, §14-316(b).
False pretenses and cheats.
Ambulance services.
Obtaining services without intending to pay, §14-111.2.
Lake Wylie, regulations for lake and shoreline.
Copy of regulations promulgated sent to clerk of superior court of county, §77-37(d).
Motor vehicle emission inspections.
Counties inspections required to be performed in, §143-215.107A(c).
Oil, gas or mineral claims.
Certain ancient claims extinguished, preservation, procedure, §1-42.3(a) to (d).
Private parking lots.
Removal of unauthorized vehicles, §20-219.2.
Real estate mortgage loans.
Interest, commissions and repayment, §45-43.
Registration of deeds.
Tax certification, no delinquent taxes due, §161-31(b).
School property.
Acquisition and improvement, §153A-158.1.

GASTON COUNTY —Cont'd
Sheriff.
Vacancy, performance of duties until vacancy filled, §162-5.1.
Wild plants, taking of certain plants from land of another.
Inapplicability of provisions, §14-129.

GASTONIA.
All-terrain vehicles.
Use by employees on certain highways, §20-171.24.
Room occupancy tax.
Uniform provisions.
Authorized to levy, §160A-215(g).
Generally, §160A-215.
Satellite annexation.
Limitation on area of satellite corporate limits, inapplicability, §160A-58.1(b).

GAS WARS.
Below-cost selling of motor fuels, §75-82(a).

GATES.
Housing authorities and projects.
Electrified gates, spikes or barbed wire prohibited, §157-9(d).
Housing authority commissioners.
Tenant as commissioner, exemption from provision of law allowing, §157-5.
Rights of way.
Projection of gates over rights of way prohibited, §136-94.

GATES COUNTY.
Blank or master forms of mortgages, deeds of trust, etc.
Indexing and recording, inapplicability of provisions, §47-21.
Counties generally.
See COUNTIES.
Cropper or tenant refusing to perform terms of contract.
Forfeiture of right of possession to premises, §42-27.
Game laws, local acts not repealed, §113-133.1(e).
Grants in navigable waters, registration, §113-205(a).
North Carolina's northeast commission, §§158-8.2 to 158-8.8.
Oil, gas or mineral claims.
Certain ancient claims extinguished, preservation, procedure, §1-42.3(a) to (d).
Open fires, high hazard counties.
Applicability of provisions, §106-942(a).
Ground clearing activities, special permit, §106-942(c).
Woodland fires, permit required, §106-942(b).
Registration of deeds.
Tax certification, no delinquent taxes due, §161-31(b).
School property.
Acquisition and improvement, §153A-158.1.
Special school tax, election to abolish.
Petition required, §115C-505.
Wastewater systems.
Innovative septic tank systems.
Ordinance billing fee as property tax, §130A-343.1(c).

GATEWAY TO COLLEGE PROGRAM, §115D-5(t).

GAY MARRIAGES, §51-1.2.

GED.
Community colleges.
Retention of fees, §115D-5(s).
Jail prisoner's participation.
Person having custody to approve, revocation of
approval, §162-59.1.
Reduction in sentence for participation,
§162-60(b).
Escape, forfeiture of reduction, §162-60(c).
Person in custody judge of faithful participation,
§162-60(c).

GEESE.
Hunting and wildlife generally.
See HUNTING AND WILDLIFE.

GEMS AND GEMSTONES.
Commodities.
General provisions, §§78D-1 to 78D-33.
See COMMODITIES.
Diamonds.
Unfair trade practices in diamond industry,
§§66-73 to 66-75.

GEM, STATE.
Emerald, §145-8.

GENDER.
Construction and interpretation of statutes,
§12-3.

GENDER BASED APPOINTMENTS.
Appointing members to statutorily created
decision making or regulatory entities.
Appointments to reflect proportion that gender
represents in population of state,
§143-157.1(a).
Report by appointing authority of number
appointments of each gender, §143-157.1(b).
Local government reporting, §143-157.1(d).
State reporting, §143-157.1(c).

GENDER DISCRIMINATION.
Discrimination generally.
See DISCRIMINATION.
Fair housing, §§41A-1 to 41A-10.
See FAIR HOUSING.

GENEALOGIES.
Hearsay exception, family records, §8C-1 Rule
803.

GENERAL ASSEMBLY.
Acts.
Coded bill drafting, §120-20.1.
Style of the acts, NC Const Art II §21.
When acts take effect, §120-20.
Actuarial note act, §§120-112 to 120-114.
Adult care homes.
Residents' bill of rights.
Legislative intent, §131D-19.
Advisory opinions.
Legislative ethics committee, §120-104.
Alimony.
Local, private and special legislation prohibited,
NC Const Art II §24.
Appeals.
Investigating committees.
Appeal from denial of right to be heard,
§120-18.
Apportionment, §§120-1, 120-2.
Approval of act amending, deleting, adding to,
modifying or repealing plan.
Attorney general to seek, §120-30.9B(b).
Failure to seek, §120-30.9B(b).

GENERAL ASSEMBLY —Cont'd
Apportionment —Cont'd
Challenge to plan.
Action, §§1-81.1, 1-267.1, 120-2.3 to 120-2.5.
Three-judge panel, §1-267.1.
Dividing precincts.
Compliance with federal law, §120-2.2(c).
Prohibited, §120-2.2(a).
Rejection based upon federal law, §120-2.2(a),
(b).
House of representatives, §120-2(a) to (d), NC
Const Art II §5.
Senate, §120-1(a) to (d), NC Const Art II §3.
Severability of apportionment acts, §120-2.1.
Appropriations.
Budget of state.
General provisions, §§143C-1-1 to 143C-10-3.
See STATE BUDGET.
Committees.
Transportation department.
Reports to committees, §136-44.2B.
Legislative research commission.
Payment of expenses from appropriations,
§120-30.18.
Approval of bills, §120-29.1.
Archives and history division.
Retention of books, records, etc.
Ultimate retention or disposition by division,
§120-37(f).
Arrest.
Duty and privilege of members.
Protection from arrest, §120-9.
Arson.
Burning of certain public buildings, §14-59.
Attorney general.
Opinion on questions of law.
Duties of attorney general, §114-2.
Attorneys at law.
Committee activity.
Examination of witnesses, §120-19.1.
Employment of counsel where state interested.
Inapplicability of certain provision, §120-32.6.
Employment of private counsel.
Inapplicability of certain provision, §120-32.6.
Bicycles.
Legislative findings.
Bicycles and bikeway act, §136-71.8.
Bills.
Actions on bills, NC Const Art II §22.
Approval of bills, §120-29.1.
Action by governor, §120-29.1(a).
Calculation of time for approval, §120-29.1(d).
Failure of governor to take action, §120-29.1(b).
Objections of governor, §120-29.1(c).
Budget of state.
Current operations appropriations act,
enactment process, §§143C-5-1 to 143C-5-5.
Fiscal analysis to be submitted with legislative
bills, §143C-2-3.
Calculation of time for approval, §120-29.1(d).
Coded bill drafting.
Effective date of provisions, §120-20.1(d).
Generally, §120-20.1(a) to (b2).
Resolutions.
Included in terms "act" and "law,"§120-20.1(c).
Enrolling clerk.
Deposit of original bills and resolutions enrolled
for application, §120-33(f).
Duties, §120-33.
Presenting true ratified copies, §120-33(d) to
(d2).

GENERAL ASSEMBLY —Cont'd
Bills —Cont'd
Enrolling clerk —Cont'd
Proofreading bills, §120-33(c).
Ratification of enrolled bills, §120-33(a).
Substituting corresponding Arabic numerals for
written words, §120-33(b).
Typewritten bills, §120-33(c).
Governor's approval, §120-29.1(a).
Governor's failure to take action, §120-29.1(b).
Governor's veto, NC Const Art II §22.
Legislative services commission.
Duties of enrolling clerk, §120-33.
Local government fiscal information act,
§§120-30.41 to 120-30.49.
Objections by governor, §120-29.1(c).
Principal clerk.
Retention of bills and resolutions in office for
certain period, §120-37(f).
Reconvening of legislature, NC Const Art II §22,
Art III §5.
Request that session not be held, §120-6.1(a),
(b).
Revenue bills.
Requirements for passage, NC Const Art II §23.
Veto by governor, NC Const Art II §22.
Voting rights act of 1965.
Submission of changes to United States
attorney general, §§120-30.9A to 120-30.9I.
**Board service by members of general
assembly,** §120-123.
Bomb scares.
Evacuation of state legislative buildings and
grounds, §120-32.1A.
Bond issues.
Requirements for passage of revenue bills, NC
Const Art II §23.
Bribery.
Legislative ethics act.
Code of legislative ethics, §120-86(a).
Bridges.
Local, private and special legislation prohibited,
NC Const Art II §24.
Budget of state.
Development of recommended budget.
Legislative branch estimate, §143C-3-1.
Enactment process, §§143C-5-1 to 143C-5-5.
Fiscal analysis to be submitted with legislative
bills, §143C-2-3.
General provisions, §§143C-1-1 to 143C-10-3.
See STATE BUDGET.
House budget overexpenditures, §143C-6-4(e).
Senate budget overexpenditures, §143C-6-4(d).
Transfers between line items other than house
and senate budgets, §143C-6-4(f).
Buildings.
State legislative building.
Official name, §129-12.1.
Bureau of investigation.
Background investigation of person who must be
confirmed by legislative action.
Requests to bureau of investigation, §120-19.4A.
Capital facilities finance agency.
Private capital facilities finance act.
Annual report to, §159D-53.
Cemeteries.
Local, private and special legislation prohibited,
NC Const Art II §24.
CLE exemption, Bar Rule D.1517.
Clerks.
Approval of bills, §120-29.1.

GENERAL ASSEMBLY —Cont'd
Clerks —Cont'd
Journals.
Indexing of journals by clerks, §120-28.
Preparation and filing by clerks, §120-27.
Legislative services commission.
Duties of enrolling clerk, §120-33.
Principal clerk.
Bills and resolutions.
Retention in office for certain periods,
§120-37(f).
Duties.
Assignment of additional duties, §120-37(d).
Election, §120-37(a).
Employing temporary assistance, §120-37(e).
Retention of books, records, etc., §120-37(f).
Salary, §120-37(c).
Staff employees of office.
Additional full-time employees, §120-37(d).
Term, §120-37(a).
Reading clerk.
Election, §120-37(a).
Salary, §120-37(b).
Term, §120-37(a).
Codification of statutes.
Legislative services officer.
Duties assigned general assembly staff,
§120-36.21.
Revisor of statutes, §120-36.22.
Commissions.
Appointments, §120-121.
Consultants.
Contracting for consultant services,
§120-32.02(a) to (c).
Contributions.
Applying for, receiving or accepting,
§120-32.03(a), (b).
Employees.
Contracting for employment, §120-32.02(a) to
(c).
Environmental review commission, §§120-70.41 to
120-70.47.
Grants.
Applying for, receiving or accepting,
§120-32.03(a), (b).
Historical commission.
Recommendations to legislative committees,
§121-12(d).
Joint legislative commission on governmental
operations, §§120-71 to 120-79.
Legislative appointments to boards and
commissions, §§120-121 to 120-123.
Legislative research commission, §§120-30.10 to
120-30.18.
Legislative services commission, §§120-31 to
120-36.21.
Loans.
Applying for, receiving or accepting,
§120-32.03(a), (b).
Meetings.
Official meetings of commissions, committees
and standing subcommittees, §143-318.14A.
Reports for state institutions and departments,
§120-12.
Service by general assembly members, §120-123.
Vacancies, §120-122.
Committees.
Appropriations.
Transportation department.
Reports to committees, §136-44.2B.

GENERAL ASSEMBLY —Cont'd
Committees —Cont'd
Attorneys at law.
Examination of witnesses, §120-19.1(f).
Bureau of investigation.
Background investigation of person who must
be confirmed by legislative action.
Requests to bureau of investigation,
§120-19.4A.
Chairmen.
Oaths.
Who may administer oaths of office,
§11-7.1(a).
Consultants.
Contracting for consultant services,
§120-32.02(a) to (c).
Contempt, §120-19.4.
Contributions.
Applying for, receiving or accepting,
§120-32.03(a), (b).
Education.
Joint legislative education oversight committee,
§§120-70.80 to 120-70.83.
Employees contracting for employment,
§120-32.02(a) to (c).
Ethics.
Legislative ethics committee, §§120-99 to
120-106.
Finance committees, §122A-16.
Grants.
Applying for, receiving or accepting,
§120-32.03(a), (b).
Hearings.
Examination of witnesses, §§120-19.1,
120-19.2(b).
Counsel, §120-19.1(f).
Fees and expenses of witness, §120-19.3.
Members questions directed to chairman or
presiding officer, §120-19.1(c).
Notice of hearing, §120-19.2(d).
Objections to propriety of questions,
§120-19.1(d).
Transcript, §120-19.1(e).
Under oath, §120-19.1(b).
Holding separate or joint hearings, §120-19.1(a).
Oaths.
Examination of witnesses, §120-19.1(b).
Transcript of proceedings, §120-19.1(e).
When hearings and examinations held,
§120-19.2(b).
Highways.
Joint legislative transportation oversight
committee, §§120-70.50 to 120-70.52.
Local acts affecting state highway system.
Consideration by transportation committees,
§120-19.9.
Historical commission.
Recommendations to legislative committees,
§121-12(d).
Interim committee activity.
Applicability of provisions, §120-19.8.
Investigating committees, §§120-14 to 120-19.
Joint legislative committee on local government,
§§120-157.1 to 120-174.
Joint legislative economic development and global
engagement oversight committee,
§§120-70.130 to 120-70.132.
Joint legislative elections oversight committee,
§§120-70.140 to 120-70.143.
Joint legislative oversight committee on health
and human services, §§120-208 to 120-208.4.

GENERAL ASSEMBLY —Cont'd
Committees —Cont'd
Joint legislative oversight committee on
information technology, §§120-230 to 120-235.
Joint legislative oversight committee on justice
and public safety, §§120-70.93 to 120-70.95.
Legislative services officer.
Authority to assign committee staff assistance,
§120-19.5.
Loans.
Applying for, receiving or accepting,
§120-32.03(a), (b).
Lottery oversight committee, §18C-172.
Meetings.
Official meetings of commissions, committees
and standing subcommittees, §143-318.14A.
Municipal incorporations subcommittees.
Joint legislative committee on local government,
§§120-158 to 120-174.
Public officers and employees.
Furnishing data and information to legislative
committees, §120-19.
Retirement system for general assembly.
Committees on pensions and retirement,
§§120-111.1 to 120-111.4.
Revenue laws study committee, §§120-70.105 to
120-70.107.
Staff assistance, §120-19.5.
Applicability of provisions, §120-19.8.
Limitation by resolution of either house,
§120-19.8.
Standing committee.
Staff assistance, §120-19.5.
State departments and agencies.
Furnishing data and information to legislative
committees, §120-19.
State personnel.
House standing committee on state personnel,
§120-111.5.
Subcommittees, §120-19.7.
Subpoenas.
Failure to respond to subpoena punishable as
contempt, §120-19.4(a).
Filing of complaint, §120-19.4(b).
Form of subpoena, §120-19.2(e).
Issuance of subpoena to obtain testimony,
§120-19.2(c).
Return of subpoena, §120-19.2(f).
Witnesses.
Examination of witnesses, §§120-19.1,
120-19.2(b).
Members questions directed to chairman or
presiding officer, §120-19.1(c).
Notice of hearing, §120-19.2(d).
Objections to propriety of questions,
§120-19.1(d).
Under oath, §120-19.1(b).
Failing to attend as witness before committee,
§14-227.
Fees and expenses of witness, §120-19.3.
Invitations to witnesses, §120-19.2(a).
Perjury before committees, §14-211.
Refusal to testify punishable as contempt,
§120-19.4(a).
Filing of complaint, §120-19.4(b).
Compensation and allowances of member, NC
Const Art II §16.
Confidentiality.
Code of legislative ethics.
Disclosure of confidential information,
§120-87(a), (b).

GENERAL ASSEMBLY —Cont'd

Confidentiality —Cont'd

Legislative communications, §§120-129 to 120-134.

Definitions, §120-129.

Documents prepared by legislative employees, §120-131(a).

When dissemination of information or language not prohibited, §120-131(c).

When documents become available to public, §120-131(b).

Drafting requests, §120-130(a).

Not public records, §120-130(d).

Revelation of legislator's identity restricted, §120-130(a).

Supporting documents, §120-130(c).

Evaluation report preparation requests, §120-131.1(a1).

Fiscal note preparation requests, §120-131.1.

Information requests, §120-130(b).

Not public records, §120-130(d).

Supporting documents, §120-130(c).

Penalty, §§120-131.1(c), 120-134.

Redistricting communications, §120-133.

Testimony by legislative employees, §120-132.

Conflicts of interest.

Service by members of general assembly on certain boards and commissions, §120-123.

Consolidated city-county act.

Local government to be provided for by general assembly, NC Const Art VII §1.

Consultants.

Legislative commissions and committees.

Contracting for consultant services, §120-32.02(a) to (c).

Contempt, §120-19.4.

Legislative services commission.

Subpoena and contempt powers, §120-32.4.

Contesting a seat, §§120-10.1 to 120-10.14.

Abatement of judicial proceedings, §120-10.11.

Answering notice of intent, §120-10.4.

Applicability of provisions, §§120-10.1, 120-10.14.

Bad faith.

Costs assessed, §120-10.13.

Committee.

Discovery.

Compelling discovery, §120-10.8(c).

Procedures, §120-10.8(b).

Referral to, §120-10.8(a).

Report, §120-10.8(d).

Conduct or results of election.

Determinations concerning, §120-10.9(b).

Costs.

Bad faith, §120-10.13.

Definitions, §120-10.2.

Discovery.

Committee.

Compelling discovery, §120-10.8(c).

Depositions, §120-10.6(a).

Witnesses, §120-10.6(b).

Eligibility and qualification.

Determination of, §120-10.9(a).

General court of justice.

Determinations not reviewable by, §120-10.12.

Initiating contest, §120-10.3(a), (b).

Judicial proceedings abated, §120-10.11.

Judicial review.

Determinations not reviewable, §120-10.12.

Jurisdiction, §120-10.10.

Notice of intent, §120-10.3(c).

Answering, §120-10.4.

Defined, §120-10.2.

GENERAL ASSEMBLY —Cont'd

Contesting a seat —Cont'd

Notice of intent —Cont'd

Filing, §120-10.5.

Initiating contest by filing of, §120-10.3(a), (b).

Service, §120-10.5.

Petitions.

Affidavits, §120-10.7(b).

Filing, §120-10.7(a).

Primary elections.

Provisions not applicable to, §120-10.14.

Continuances.

Obligation of services member, §1A-1 Rule 40(b).

Continuing legal education exemption, Bar Rule D.1517.

Contracts.

Public building contracts.

Exemption from certain purchasing requirements, §143-129.3.

Convening.

Members to convene at appointed time and place, §120-6.

Reconvened sessions.

Request that session not be held, §120-6.1(a), (b).

Corporations.

Reservation of power.

Business corporations.

Amendment or repeal of provisions, §55-1-02.

Counties.

Governmental consolidation.

Action by assembly after referendum, §153A-405(d).

House of representatives.

Apportionment, §120-2.

Local government to be provided for by general assembly, NC Const Art VII §1.

Senatorial districts.

Established, §120-1.

Number of senators, §120-1.

Courts.

Administration, NC Const Art IV §15.

Cultural resources department.

Retention of books, records, etc.

Ultimate retention or disposition by department, §120-37(f).

Debts.

Indebtedness of state.

Requirements for passage of revenue bills, NC Const Art II §23.

Deeds.

Giving effect to informal deeds.

Local, private and special legislation prohibited, NC Const Art II §24.

Definitions.

Confidentiality of legislative communications, §120-129.

Contesting a seat, §120-10.2.

Joint legislative commission on governmental operations.

Program evaluation, §120-72.

Local government fiscal information act.

Fiscal note, §120-30.44.

Unit of local government, §120-30.42.

Repayment of money owed to state by legislators, §143-558.

Department of transportation disadvantaged minority-owned and women-owned business program.

Joint legislative commission on, §§120-275 to 120-279.

GENERAL ASSEMBLY —Cont'd

Depositions.
Contesting a seat, §120-10.6(a).

Directory.
Published by division of publications, §147-54.1.

Disasters.
State of disaster, declaring, §166A-6.

District attorneys.
Appointment of district attorneys, NC Const Art
IV §18.

District courts.
Organization and establishment of district courts,
NC Const Art IV §10.

Districts.
Representative districts, §120-2(a) to (d), NC
Const Art II §5.
Senatorial districts, §120-1(a) to (d), NC Const Art
II §3.

Dividing precincts in apportionment acts,
§120-2.2.

Division of publications.
Generally, §147-54.1.

Divorce.
Local, private and special legislation prohibited,
NC Const Art II §24.

Economic development.
Joint legislative economic development and global
engagement oversight committee,
§§120-70.130 to 120-70.132.

Education.
Joint legislative education oversight committee,
§§120-70.80 to 120-70.83.

Elections, NC Const Art II §8.
Contests, §§120-10.1 to 120-10.14. See within this
heading, "Contesting a seat."
Corrupt practices in election.
Expulsion for corrupt practices, §120-8.
Date of election, §163-1(a).
Elections by general assembly to be by viva voce,
NC Const Art VI §5.
House of representatives.
Nomination of candidates, §163-108.1.
Joint legislative elections oversight committee,
§§120-70.140 to 120-70.143.
Primaries moved from date provided.
Holding on same day, §163-1(d).

Electronic voting apparatus.
Installation and use of apparatus, §120-11.2.

Emergency management.
State of disaster, declaring, §166A-6.

Employees.
Confidentiality of legislative communications.
Disciplinary actions, §§120-131.1(c), 120-134.
Legislative commissions and committees.
Contracting for employment, §120-32.02(a) to
(c).

Employment of counsel where state interested.
Inapplicability of certain provision, §120-32.6.

Employment of private counsel.
Inapplicability of certain provision, §120-32.6.

**Endangering executive, legislative or court
officers,** §§14-16.6 to 14-16.10.
Electronic surveillance orders, §15A-290(c4).

Environmental review commission, §§120-70.41
to 120-70.47.

Ethics.
Generally, §§120-85.1 to 120-106.
See LEGISLATIVE ETHICS.
Lobbying.
Generally, §§120C-100 to 120C-800.
See LOBBYISTS AND LOBBYING.

GENERAL ASSEMBLY —Cont'd

Evidence.
Printed statutes and certified copies as evidence,
§8-1.

Expenses.
Committee activity.
Witness fees and expenses, §120-19.3.
Joint operation of general assembly.
Payment for expenses, §120-35.
Legislative ethics committee, §120-101.
Legislative research commission.
Payments from appropriations, §120-30.18.
Members, §120-3(a) to (c).
Officers, §120-3(a) to (c).

Extortion.
Legislative ethics act, §120-86(b) to (e).

Fairs.
Land set apart for state fair.
Repossession of land at will of General
Assembly, §106-504.

Federal mandates.
Certification of legislation required by federal law.
Attachment of certification, §120-36.8(c), (d).
Contents, §120-36.8(a).
Duties of research division, §120-36.8(b).
Required, §120-36.8(a).
Local government fiscal information.
Annual report on federal mandates, §120-30.49.

Fees and charges by state agencies, §12-3.1(a).
Consultation with joint legislative commission on
governmental operations, §12-3.1(a), (a1).

Felonies.
Restoring rights of citizenship of convicts.
Local, special and private legislation prohibited,
NC Const Art II §24.
Threats to influence legislator in discharge of
duties, §120-86(e).

Ferries.
Local, private and special legislation prohibited,
NC Const Art II §24.

Fertilizers.
Commercial fertilizers.
Legislative findings and declarations, §106-672.

Firearms.
Transportation or storage in closed compartment
of locked vehicle, §120-32.1(c1).
Parking space assigned or leased by legislator
or legislative employee, §120-32.1(c1).

Fires and fire protection.
Evacuation of state legislative buildings and
grounds, §120-32.1A.

Fiscal information act, §§120-30.41 to 120-30.49.

**Fluorescent lights and thermostats containing
mercury.**
Recycling program.
Establishment required, §130A-310.60(a).
Report documenting compliance required,
§130A-310.60(b).

Forfeitures.
Local, private and special legislation prohibited,
NC Const Art II §24.

Forms.
Approval of bills, §120-29.1.
Reconvened sessions.
Request that session not be held, §120-6.1(b).

Freedom of speech.
Duty and privilege of members, §120-9.

**Fundraising during legislative session,
limitation,** §163-278.13B.

Funds.
Legislative retirement fund.
Repealed, §120-4.2.

GENERAL ASSEMBLY —Cont'd
General statutes.
Codification of statutes.
Legislative services officer.
Duties assigned general assembly staff,
§120-36.21.
Revisor of statutes, §120-36.22.
Governmental operations.
Joint legislative commission on governmental
operations, §§120-71 to 120-79.
Governor.
Approval of bills, §120-29.1.
Books to be produced for general assembly,
§147-14.
Calculation of time for approval of bills,
§120-29.1(d).
Executive officer's report to governor.
Reports transmitted to general assembly,
§147-5.
Failure to take action on bills, §120-29.1(b).
Objections to bills, §120-29.1(c).
Grants.
Legislative commissions and committees.
Applying for, receiving or accepting,
§120-32.03(a), (b).
Hazardous waste management.
Inactive hazardous sites.
Report to general assembly members with site
in member's district, §130A-310.2(b).
Health.
Human tissue donation program.
Legislative findings and purpose, §130A-413(a).
Local, private and special legislation prohibited,
NC Const Art II §24.
Health care facilities.
Certificate of need law.
Legislative findings of fact, §131E-175.
Finance act.
Legislative findings and declarations, §131A-2.
Highways.
Controlled-access facilities.
Legislative findings and declarations,
§136-89.48.
Joint legislative transportation oversight
committee, §§120-70.50 to 120-70.52.
Local acts affecting state highway system.
Consideration by transportation committees,
§120-19.9.
Local, private and special legislation prohibited,
NC Const Art II §24.
Reports to appropriations committees of general
assembly, §136-44.2B.
Scenic beauty of areas along highways.
Legislative findings and declaration of policy,
§136-122.
Historical commission.
Legislative committees.
Furnishing recommendations to committees,
§121-12(d).
Holiday leave.
Temporary employees, §120-32.5.
House of representatives.
Apportionment, §120-2(a) to (d), NC Const Art II
§5.
Dividing precincts restricted, §120-2.2.
Severability of acts, §120-2.1.
Arrest.
Protection from arrest, §120-9.
Budget overexpenditures, §143C-6-4(e).
Districts, §§120-1, 120-2(a), NC Const Art II §5.
Areas not assigned to district, §120-2(d).

GENERAL ASSEMBLY —Cont'd
House of representatives —Cont'd
Districts —Cont'd
Areas not specifically assigned to, §120-2(e).
Voting tabulation districts, tracks, block groups
and blocks.
Change in voting tabulation district
boundaries not change house district
boundaries, §120-2(c).
Names and boundaries, §120-2(b).
Duties.
Penalty for failure to discharge duty, §120-7.
Elections.
Contests, §§120-10.1 to 120-10.14. See within
this heading, "Contesting a seat."
Corrupt practices in election.
Expulsion for corrupt practices, §120-8.
Electronic voting apparatus.
Installation and use of apparatus, §120-11.2.
Expense allowance, §120-3(a) to (c).
Failure to discharge duty.
Penalty for failure, §120-7.
Freedom of speech, §120-9.
House standing committee on state personnel,
§120-111.5.
Impeachment.
Court of impeachment, §§123-1 to 123-5.
Effect of impeachment, §§123-12, 123-13.
Power to bring, NC Const Art IV §4.
Procedure in impeachment, §§123-6 to 123-11.
See IMPEACHMENT.
Journals.
Deposited with secretary of state, §120-29.
Indexed by clerks, §120-28.
Preparation and filing by clerks, §120-27.
Majority leader.
Salary and expenses, §120-3(a), (c).
Meetings.
Convening at appointed time and place, §120-6.
Time of meeting, §120-11.1.
Minority leader.
Salary and expenses, §120-3(a), (c).
Number of representatives, NC Const Art II §4.
Oaths.
Presiding officers may administer oaths, §120-5.
Officers of house, NC Const Art II §15.
Elected officers.
Salary and expenses, §120-37(a) to (c).
Pay of members and officers, §120-3(a) to (c).
Penalties.
Failure to discharge duty, §120-7.
Qualifications for representative, NC Const Art II
§7.
Salaries, §120-3(a) to (c).
Sessions.
Time of meeting, §120-11.1.
Speaker, NC Const Art II §15.
Expense allowance, §120-3(a), (c).
Legislative research commission.
Ex officio member, §120-30.10(a).
Legislative services commission.
Chairman of commission, §120-31(b).
Member of commission, §120-31(a).
License plate.
Special plate, number, §20-79.5.
Oaths.
Administration of oaths for qualification of
officers of house and members, §120-5.
Salary, §120-3(a), (c).
Succession to office of governor, §147-11.1(b).

GENERAL ASSEMBLY —Cont'd
House of representatives —Cont'd
Speaker pro tempore.
Salary, §120-3(a), (c).
State personnel.
House standing committee on state personnel, §120-111.5.
Subsistence and travel allowances, §120-3.1(a).
Payment of allowances, §120-3.1(b).
When general assembly not in session, §120-3.1(c).
Term of office, NC Const Art II §9.
Travel allowances, §120-3.1(a).
Payment of allowances, §120-3.1(b).
When general assembly not in session, §120-3.1(c).
Vacancies, NC Const Art II §10.
Voting.
Electronic voting apparatus.
Amendment providing for installation and use, §120-11.2(b).
Installation and use of apparatus, §120-11.2(a).
Working plans for installation, §120-11.2(c).
Housing finance agency.
Finance committees of general assembly.
Oversight by committees, §122A-16.
Legislative findings and purposes, §122A-2.
Moderate income persons and families.
Legislative findings and determinations, §122A-5.4(a).
Identity theft.
Reports by state agencies on ways to reduce incidence of, §120-270.
Immunity.
Advisory opinion issued by legislative ethics committee.
Acting in reliance on formal opinion, §120-104(c).
Impeachment, §§123-1 to 123-13.
See IMPEACHMENT.
Inactive hazardous site in member's district.
Report to member, §130A-310.2(b).
Indexes.
Journals indexed by clerks, §120-28.
Local legislation.
Published by division of publications, §147-54.1.
Session laws, §120-34(a), (b).
Information technology.
Joint legislative oversight committee, §§120-230 to 120-235.
Interim committee activity.
Authority to meet in interim period, §120-19.6(a).
Limitation of activities, §120-19.6(c).
Creation of interim committees, §120-19.6(a1).
Limitation by resolution of either house, §120-19.8.
Rules, §120-19.6(b).
Interns.
Legislative intern program council.
Plan for use of legislative intern, §120-57.
Investigating committees.
Appeal from denial of right to be heard, §120-18.
Appearance before committee, §120-17.
Appeal from denial of right to be heard, §120-18.
Application, §120-17.
Chairman may administer oaths, §120-15.
Legislative ethics committee.
Investigations by, §120-103.1.

GENERAL ASSEMBLY —Cont'd
Investigating committees —Cont'd
Oaths.
Chairman may administer oaths, §120-15.
Power of committees, §120-14.
Production of papers, §120-14.
Public officers and employees.
Furnishing data and information to legislative committees, §120-19.
State departments and agencies.
Furnishing data and information to legislative committees, §120-19.
Witnesses, §120-14.
Pay of witnesses, §120-16.
Joint legislative commission on department of transportation disadvantaged minority-owned and women-owned business program, §§120-275 to 120-279.
Cochair, §120-279(a).
Duties, §120-277.
Established, §120-275.
Expenses, §120-279(c).
Membership, §120-276(a).
Monitoring, strategies, recommendations.
Duties, §120-277.
Quorum, §120-279(b).
Report by department, §120-278.
Terms, §120-276(b).
Vacancies, §120-276(c).
Joint legislative commission on governmental operations.
Access to papers and documents, §120-77.
Appointment of members, §120-74.
Co-chairman, §120-75.
Compelling attendance before commission, §120-77.
Compensation of commission members, §120-78.
Composition, §120-74.
Definition.
Program evaluation, §120-72.
DNA databank and database.
Annual report by SBI, §15A-266.5(c).
Duties.
Enumerated, §120-76.
Studies to be conducted, §120-73.
Established, §120-73.
Expenses of commission members, §120-78.
Fees or charges by state agencies.
Establishing or increasing.
Consultation with commission, §12-3.1(a), (a1).
Inactive hazardous sites.
Annual report to by secretary, §130A-310.10(a).
New licensing boards.
Subcommittee to evaluate need, §120-76.
North Carolina utilities commission.
Evaluation, §120-76.
Organization of commission, §120-75.
Powers, §120-76.
Additional powers, §120-77.
Prior consultation with commission required.
Agencies, boards and commission.
Report of action required, consultation requirement satisfied, §120-76.1(b).
Establishment or increase of fees and charges.
Consultation not required, §120-76.1(c).
Governor.
Action without prior consultation, §120-76.1(a).
Program evaluation.
Defined, §120-72.

GENERAL ASSEMBLY —Cont'd
Joint legislative commission on governmental operations —Cont'd
Purpose, §120-71.
Removal from membership, §120-74.
Resignation or removal from membership, §120-74.
Salaries.
  Employees of commission, §120-79(b).
Seafood and aquaculture industries.
  Powers and duties, §120-76.
Staff.
  Assignment and direction of activities of employees, §120-79(a).
  Availability of funds, §120-79(d).
  Salaries, §120-79(b).
  Subsistence and travel allowances, §120-79(b).
  Use of other employees, §120-79(c).
Studies to be conducted, §120-73.
Subsistence and travel expenses, §120-78.
  Staff of commission, §120-79(b).
Taxpayer services.
  Reporting by department of revenue, §105-256(a).
Terms of office, §120-74.
Travel expenses, §120-78.
Vacancies.
  Filling of vacancy, §120-74.
Joint legislative committee on local government, §§120-157.1 to 120-174.
Access to papers or documents, §120-157.4.
Capital projects.
  Purpose to review and monitor, §120-157.2(a).
  Reports to general assembly, §120-157.2(b).
Cochairs, designation, §120-157.3(a).
Compelling attendance of officials, powers, §120-157.4.
Consultants, hiring staff, §120-157.3(c).
Established, §120-157.1(a).
Meetings, §120-157.3(a).
Membership, §120-157.1(a).
Municipal incorporations subcommittee, §§120-158 to 120-174.
  Chair, §120-159(a).
  Created, §120-158(a).
  Meetings, §120-159(b).
  Membership, §120-158(b).
  Petition seeking incorporation.
    Ability to provide service at reasonable tax rate.
      Positive recommendation, §120-170.
    Area unincorporated.
      Positive recommendation, §120-169.
    Contents, information required, §120-163(c).
    Deadline for making recommendations, §120-174.
    Deletion of areas from petition, §120-173.
    Description of proposed municipality.
      Required if not barred from positive recommendation, §120-171(b).
    Determination if requirements met, §120-165(a), (b).
    Development.
      Positive recommendation, §120-168.
    Diversion of local taxes and state shared revenue.
      Impact indicated by subcommittee, §120-169.1(c).
    Filing with subcommittee, §120-163(a).
    Modification, §120-173.

GENERAL ASSEMBLY —Cont'd
Joint legislative committee on local government —Cont'd
Municipal incorporations subcommittee —Cont'd
  Petition seeking incorporation —Cont'd
    Negative recommendation.
      Report to general assembly, §120-171.
    Notice petition received, publication, §120-165(a).
    Notification by petitioners before submitting petition, §120-164(a).
    Publication, §120-164(b).
    Plan for municipal services.
      Positive recommendation, §120-169.1(b).
    Population.
      Positive recommendation, §120-167.
    Positive recommendation.
      Ability to provide service at reasonable tax rate, §120-170.
      Area unincorporated, §120-169.
      Development, §120-168.
      Plan for municipal services, §120-169.1(b).
      Population, §120-167.
      Proximity to another municipality, §120-166(a), (b).
      Report to general assembly, §120-171(c).
    Presentation to subcommittee, §120-163(d).
    Time, §120-163(e).
    Proximity to another municipality.
      Positive recommendation, §120-166(a), (b).
    Referendum on act passed by general assembly, §120-172.
    Report to general assembly, §120-171(a), (c), (d).
    Verification by county board of elections, §120-163(b).
  Terms, §120-159(a).
Purpose, §120-157.2(a).
Quorum, §120-157.3(b).
Subsistence and travel allowances, §120-157.3(c).
Terms, §120-157.1(b).
Vacancy, §120-157.1(c).
Joint legislative economic development and global engagement oversight committee, §§120-70.130 to 120-70.132.
Assistance, §120-70.132(c).
Co-chairs, §120-70.132(a).
Creation, §120-70.130.
Members, §120-70.130.
  Expenses, §120-70.132(d).
Powers, §120-70.131(a).
Quorum, §120-70.132(b).
Reports, §120-70.131(b).
Joint legislative education oversight committee.
Additional powers, §120-70.83.
Appointment, §120-70.80.
Co-chairs, §120-70.82(a).
Creation, §120-70.80.
Expenses.
  Subsistence and travel expenses, §120-70.82(c).
Meetings, §120-70.82(a).
Membership, §120-70.80.
Powers generally, §120-70.81(a).
  Additional powers, §120-70.83.
Quorum, §120-70.82(b).
Reports to general assembly, §120-70.81(b).
Resignation or removal of members, §120-70.80.
Terms of members, §120-70.80.
Vacancies, §120-70.80.

GENERAL ASSEMBLY —Cont'd
Joint legislative elections oversight committee,
    §§120-70.140 to 120-70.143.
  Access to information, §120-70.143.
  Co-chairs, §120-70.142(a).
  Compelling attendance of officials, §120-70.143.
  Creation, §120-70.140.
  Expense reimbursement, §120-70.142(c).
  Interim reports, §120-70.141(b).
  Members, §120-70.140.
  Powers, §120-70.141(a).
  Purpose, §120-70.141(a).
  Quorum, §120-70.142(b).
**Joint legislative oversight committee on health
    and human services,** §§120-208 to 120-208.4.
  Access to papers and documents, §120-208.3.
  Cochairs, designation, §120-208.2(a).
  Compelling officials attendance, §120-208.3.
  Division reports to committee, §120-208.4.
  Duties, §120-208.1(a).
  Established, §120-208(a).
  Meetings, §120-208.2(a).
  Membership, §120-208(a).
  Quorum, §120-208.2(b).
  Recommendations to general assembly,
    §120-208.1(a).
  Reports, §120-208.1(b).
  Staff, §120-208.2(c).
  Subcommittees, establishment, §120-208.2(d).
  Subsistence and travel expenses, §120-208.2(c).
  Terms, §120-208(b).
  Vacancy, §120-208(c).
**Joint legislative oversight committee on
    information technology,** §§120-230 to
    120-235.
  Assistance to committee, §120-233(a).
  Authority to obtain information and data,
    §120-234.
  Co-chair, §120-232(e).
  Consultation with information resource
    management commission, §120-231(b).
  Duties, §120-231(a).
  Established, §120-230.
  Goals and objectives, §120-230.
  Meetings, §120-232(d).
  Membership, §120-232(a).
  Per diem, subsistence and travel allowances,
    §120-233(b).
  Proceeding, provision applicable, §120-234.
  Reimbursement of costs in providing information
    to committee, §120-234.
  Report, §120-231(c).
  Service until successor appointed, §120-232(f).
  Subcommittees, §120-235.
  Terms, §120-232(b).
    Elected members completing term of service,
      §120-232(c).
**Joint legislative oversight committee on
    justice and public safety.**
  Co-chairs, §120-70.95(a).
  Creation, §120-70.93.
  DNA databank and database.
    Annual report by SBI, §15A-266.5(c).
  Expenses, §120-70.95(c).
  Membership, §120-70.93.
  Organization, §120-70.95.
  Powers, §120-70.94(a).
  Purpose, §120-70.94.
  Quorum, §120-70.95(b).
  Reports, §120-70.94(b).
  Staff, §120-70.95(c).

GENERAL ASSEMBLY —Cont'd
**Joint legislative transportation oversight
    committee,** §§120-70.50 to 120-70.52.
  Co-chairpersons, §120-70.52(a).
  Composition, §120-70.50.
  Employment of personnel, §120-70.52(c).
  Established, §120-70.50.
  Expenses.
    Subsistence and travel expenses, §120-70.52(c).
  Funding, §120-70.52(c).
  Meetings, §120-70.52(a).
  Powers generally, §120-70.51(a).
  Quorum, §120-70.52(b).
  Railroads and railroad infrastructure.
    Powers and duties, §120-70.51(a).
  Reports to general assembly, §120-70.51(b).
  Resignation or removal of members, §120-70.50.
  Terms of members, §120-70.50.
  Vacancies.
    Filling, §120-70.50.
Journals, NC Const Art II §17.
  Clerks.
    Indexing of journals by clerks, §120-28.
  Deposited with secretary of state, §120-29.
  Disposition of damaged and unsaleable
    publications, §147-49.
  Filing by clerks of houses, §120-27.
  Preparation and filing by clerks of houses,
    §120-27.
  Printing of session laws.
    Legislative services commission, §120-34.
  Record votes, NC Const Art II §19.
  Sale, §147-48.
Judges.
  Removal, NC Const Art IV §17.
Junkyard control.
  Legislative findings and declarations, §136-142.
Jury.
  Pay of jurors.
    Local, private and special legislation prohibited,
      NC Const Art II §24.
**Justice department, legislative assistance
    from,** §114-8.4.
Labor.
  Local, private and special legislation prohibited,
    NC Const Art II §24.
Land protection and conservation.
  Legislative findings, §106-202.13.
Legislative actuarial note act, §§120-112 to
    120-114.
**Legislative appointments to boards and
    commissions,** §120-121(d).
  Bill enactment required, §120-121(a).
  Conflicts of interest.
    Service by members of general assembly on
      certain boards and commissions, §120-123.
  Contents of bills, §120-121(c).
  Multiple appointments, §120-121(b).
  Service by members of general assembly on
    certain boards and commissions, §120-123.
  Vacancies in appointments, §120-122.
Legislative building.
  Burning of certain public buildings, §14-59.
**Legislative commission of methamphetamine
    abuse.**
  Co-chairs, §120-226(e).
  Establishment, §120-226(a).
  Funding, §120-226(l).
  Meetings, §120-226(h).
  Members, §120-226(c).
    Compensation, §120-226(g).

GENERAL ASSEMBLY —Cont'd

Legislative commission of methamphetamine abuse —Cont'd

Members —Cont'd

Terms, §120-226(d).

Purpose, §120-226(b).

Quorum, §120-226(i).

Reports, §120-226(k).

Staff, §120-226(j).

Vacancies, §120-226(f).

Legislative intern program council.

Plan for use of legislative interns, §120-57.

Legislative power, NC Const Art II §1.

Legislative research commission, §§120-30.10 to 120-30.18.

See LEGISLATIVE RESEARCH COMMISSION.

Legislative retirement fund.

Repealed, §120-4.2(a).

Continuation of authority and duties for administration of certain benefits, §120-4.2(c).

Entitlement to further benefits, §120-4.2(b).

Transfer of membership and benefits from retirement fund to legislative retirement system, §120-4.13(a).

Legislative retirement system.

General provisions, §§120-4.8 to 120-4.34.

See LEGISLATIVE RETIREMENT SYSTEM.

Legislative services commission, §§120-31 to 120-36.22.

See LEGISLATIVE SERVICES COMMISSION.

Legislative services officer.

Appointment, §120-36(a).

Codification of statutes.

Duties assigned to staff of general assembly, §120-36.21.

Committee staff assistance.

Authority to assign, §120-19.5.

Compensation, §120-36(a).

Duties, §120-36(b).

Legitimation.

Local, private and special legislation prohibited, NC Const Art II §24.

License plates.

Special plates, §20-79.4(b).

Lieutenant governor.

President of the senate, NC Const Art II §13.

Limestone, marl and landplaster.

Sale of agricultural liming materials and landplaster.

Legislative findings and declarations, §106-92.15.

Limitation on fundraising during legislative session.

Definitions, §163-278.13B(a).

Exceptions, §163-278.13B(d).

Misdemeanor for violating provisions, §163-278.13B(e).

Prohibited contributions by limited contributor, §163-278.13B(c).

Prohibited solicitations by limited contributee, §163-278.13B(b).

Limited liability companies.

Reservation of power to amend or repeal, §57C-1-02.

Loans.

Legislative commissions and committees.

Applying for, receiving or accepting, §120-32.03(a), (b).

Lobbying.

Generally, §§120C-100 to 120C-800.

See LOBBYISTS AND LOBBYING.

GENERAL ASSEMBLY —Cont'd

Local government.

Provision for local government by general assembly, NC Const Art VII §1.

Local governmental employees' retirement system.

Reservation of power to change, §128-38.

Local government fiscal information.

Administrative rules.

Fiscal impact, §120-30.48.

Citation of act, §120-30.41.

Definitions.

Fiscal note, §120-30.44.

Unit of local government, §120-30.42.

Evaluation reports.

Confidentiality of requests for assistance in preparation, §120-131.1(a1).

Federal mandate report.

Assistance in preparation of report, §120-30.49(b).

Contents, §120-30.49(a).

Copies provided, §120-30.49(c).

Fiscal note.

Attachment to bill, §120-30.45(a), (c), (d).

Confidentiality of requests for assistance in preparation, §120-131.1(a).

Contents, §120-30.45(a).

Copies to be furnished, §120-30.45(f).

Defined, §120-30.44.

Introduction of legislation by request, §120-30.47.

Preparation of note, §120-30.45(e).

Research division duties, §120-30.45(b).

Introduction of legislation by request, §120-30.47.

Legislation introduced by request, §120-30.47.

Purposes of article, §120-30.43.

Short title, §120-30.41.

State appropriations.

Fiscal information related to requests, §120-30.46.

Unit of local government.

Defined, §120-30.42.

Local, private and special legislation.

Limitations, NC Const Art II §24.

Prohibited subjects, NC Const Art II §24.

Lottery oversight committee, §18C-172.

Manual.

Published by division of publications, §147-54.1.

Manufacturing.

Local, private and special legislation prohibited, NC Const Art II §24.

Mass gatherings.

Exceptions to provisions, §143-318.18.

Legislative intent and purpose, §130A-251.

Legislative research commission, §120-30.14.

Members to convene at appointed time and place, §120-6.

Official meetings of commissions, committees and standing subcommittees.

Code sections.

Applicable to meetings of, §143-318.14A(e).

Enumerated, §143-318.14A(a).

Final action only in open meeting, §143-318.14A(c).

Notice, §143-318.14A(b).

Open sessions, §143-318.14A(a).

Violation of section.

Punishable as prescribed by rules of house or senate, §143-318.14A(d).

Public bodies, §§143-318.9 to 143-318.18.

Time of meeting, §120-11.1.

GENERAL ASSEMBLY —Cont'd

Mental health, developmental disabilities and substance abuse.
State facilities.
Ex officio visitors of facilities, §122C-186.

Mercury.
Fluorescent lights and thermostats containing.
Recycling program.
Establishment required, §130A-310.60(a).
Report documenting compliance, §130A-310.60(b).

Methamphetamine.
Legislative commission of methamphetamine abuse, §120-226.

Mines and minerals.
Local, private and special legislation prohibited, NC Const Art II §24.

Municipal incorporations subcommittee.
Joint legislative committee on local government, §§120-158 to 120-174.

Municipalities.
Joint municipal electric power and energy act.
Legislative findings and purposes, §159B-2.
Local government to be provided for by general assembly, NC Const Art VII §1.
Local, private and special legislation prohibited, NC Const Art II §24.

Names.
Altering name of person.
Local, private and special legislation prohibited, NC Const Art II §24.

Notice.
Committee activity.
Examination of witnesses, §120-19.2(d).
Contesting a seat.
Notice of intent. See within this heading, "Contesting a seat."
Meetings of commissions, committees and standing subcommittees.
Official meetings, §143-318.14A(b).
Repayment of money owed to state by legislators.
Legislative ethics committee to be notified, §143-559.

Nuisances.
Abatement of nuisances.
Local, private and special legislation prohibited, NC Const Art II §24.

Oaths, NC Const Art II §12.
Chairman of committees.
Who may administer oaths of office, §11-7.1(a).
Committee activity.
Examination of witnesses, §120-19.1(b).
Investigating committees.
Chairman may administer oaths, §120-15.
Police.
General assembly special police, §120-32.3.
Presiding officers may administer oaths, §120-5.
Supporting constitutions, §11-7, NC Const Art II §12.

Obstructing justice.
Witnesses before legislative committees.
Failing to attend as witness, §14-227.

Officers.
Elected officers, §120-37.
Expense allowances, §120-3.
Legislative ethics committee.
Article applicable to presiding officers, §120-106.
Salaries, §120-3.

Parking.
State legislative building.
Authority to regulate parking, §120-32.1(c).

GENERAL ASSEMBLY —Cont'd

Penalties.
Confidentiality of legislative communications.
Disciplinary actions, §§120-131.1(c), 120-134.
Duty and privilege of members.
Failure to discharge duty, §120-7.
Local, private and special legislation prohibited, NC Const Art II §24.

Pensions.
Committees on pensions and retirement, §§120-111.1 to 120-111.4.

Perjury before legislative committees, §14-211.

Personnel system.
Exemption of officers and employees, §126-5(c1).

Police.
General assembly special police, §§120-32.2, 120-32.3.
State legislative building special police.
Evacuation of buildings and grounds during emergencies, §120-32.1A.

Post-war reserve fund.
Direction of use of fund, §143-193.
Reports, §143-194.

Powers of general assembly, NC Const Art II §20.

Presidential elections.
Appointment of electors, §163-213(a).

Printing of session laws.
Delivery to secretary of state, §120-34(c).
Index references, §120-34(b).
Number of volumes printed, §120-34(c).
Requirements, §120-34(a).

Protests, NC Const Art II §18.

Public buildings and grounds.
Legislative services commission.
Use and maintenance of buildings and grounds, §120-32.1.

Public officers and employees.
Communications with members of the general assembly, §126-90.
Legislative committees and commissions.
Furnishing data and information to, §120-19.
Legislative research commission.
Cooperation with commission, §120-30.16.

Public schools.
Attendance of member's child at local unit's schools, §115C-366(c).

Railroads.
Revitalization programs, §§136-44.35 to 136-44.39.

Reconvening of legislature, NC Const Art II §22, Art III §5.
Request that session not be held, §120-6.1(a), (b).

Record votes.
Keeping in journal, NC Const Art II §19.

Recycling program for products containing mercury.
Fluorescent lights and thermostats containing mercury.
Establishment required, §130A-310.60(a).
Recycling program.
Report documenting compliance, §130A-310.60(b).

Regional public transportation authority.
Authority recommendation of additional revenue sources, §160A-624.
Approval by legislature required, §160A-624.
Reports to general assembly, §160A-625.

Repayment of money owed to state by legislators.
Applicability of statute of limitations, §143-562.
Confidentiality exemption, §143-560.

GENERAL ASSEMBLY —Cont'd
**Repayment of money owed to state by
legislators** —Cont'd
Definition of employing entity, §143-558.
Investigations, §143-559.
Notice.
Legislative ethics committee to be notified of
delinquent legislators, §143-559.
Preservation of federal funds, §143-561.
Repeals.
Local, private and special legislation.
Partial repeal not to affect local, private or
special act, NC Const Art II §24.
Reports.
Executive officer's reports to governor.
Transmitted to general assembly by governor,
§147-5.
State agency reports to general assembly.
Copies, who receives, electronic copy available,
informing members, §120-29.5.
**Research division of legislative services
commission,** §§120-36.1 to 120-36.7.
See LEGISLATIVE SERVICES COMMISSION.
Resolutions.
Actions on resolutions, NC Const Art II §22.
Binding original statutes, resolutions and
documents, §147-42.
Disposition of damaged and unsaleable
publications, §147-49.
Secretary of state to be custodian, §147-39.
Retaliatory actions.
Personnel-related actions, §120-86.1.
Retirement fund.
Legislative retirement fund.
Repealed, §120-4.2.
Retirement system for general assembly.
Actuarial note act, §§120-112 to 120-114.
See RETIREMENT SYSTEM FOR GENERAL
ASSEMBLY.
Committees on pensions and retirement,
§§120-111.1 to 120-111.4.
See RETIREMENT SYSTEM FOR GENERAL
ASSEMBLY.
Legislative retirement system, §§120-4.8 to
120-4.34.
See LEGISLATIVE RETIREMENT SYSTEM.
**Retirement system for teachers and state
employees.**
Creditable service.
Including service rendered as member or officer,
§135-4(j).
Purchase of creditable service, §135-4(j1).
Legislative retirement fund.
Transfer to department of state treasurer,
§143A-37.
Reservation of power to change, §135-18.4.
Revenue bills.
Requirements for passage, NC Const Art II §23.
Revenue laws study committee, §§120-70.105 to
120-70.107.
Co-chairs, §120-70.107(a).
Creation, §120-70.105.
Expenses, §120-70.107(c).
Funding, §120-70.107(c).
Members, §120-70.105(a).
Organization, §120-70.107.
Powers, §§120-70.106(a), 120-70.107(b).
Quorum, §120-70.107(b).
Reports, §120-70.106(b), (c).
Staff, §120-70.107(c).
Terms of office, §120-70.105(b).

GENERAL ASSEMBLY —Cont'd
Revisor of statutes, §120-36.22.
Rules and regulations.
Legislative services commission.
Adoption of rules, §120-31(d).
Use and maintenance of building, §120-32.1(a).
Posting and filing rules adopted, violation,
criminal penalty, waiver, §120-32.1(b).
Salaries.
Clerks.
Principal clerk, §120-37(c).
Reading clerk, §120-37(b).
Elected officers, §120-37.
Joint legislative commission on governmental
operations.
Staff of commission, §120-79(b).
Members, §120-3(a) to (c).
Officers, §120-3(a) to (c).
Research division.
Director of fiscal research, §120-36.2(c).
Professional and clerical employees,
§120-36.2(c).
Sergeant-at-arms, §120-37(b).
Sanitation.
Local, private and special legislation prohibited,
NC Const Art II §24.
School districts.
Local, private and special legislation prohibited,
NC Const Art II §24.
Secretary of state.
Attendance at sessions of legislature, §147-36.
Binding original statutes, resolutions and
documents, §147-42.
Custodian of statutes, resolutions, etc., §147-39.
Journals.
Deposited with secretary of state, §120-29.
Disposition of damaged and unsaleable
publications, §147-49.
Sale, §147-48.
Legislative services commission.
Printing of session laws, §120-34.
Printing of session laws.
Delivery to secretary for distribution,
§120-34(c).
Senate.
Apportionment, §120-1(a) to (d), NC Const Art II
§3.
Dividing precincts restricted, §120-2.2.
Severability of acts, §120-2.1.
Arrest.
Protection from arrest, §120-9.
Budget overexpenditures, §143C-6-4(d).
Deputy president pro tempore.
Salary, §120-3(a), (c).
Districts, §120-1(a) to (d), NC Const Art II.
Area not specifically assigned to district,
§120-1(d).
Boundaries.
Change, §120-1(e).
Establishment of senatorial districts, §120-1(a).
Voting tabulation districts, tracts, block groups
and blocks.
Names and boundaries, §120-1(b).
Voting tabulation district change not to
change district boundaries, §120-1(c).
Duties.
Penalty for failure to discharge duty, §120-7.
Elections.
Contests, §§120-10.1 to 120-10.14. See within
this heading, "Contesting a seat."

GENERAL ASSEMBLY —Cont'd
Senate —Cont'd
Elections —Cont'd
Corrupt practices in election.
Expulsion for corrupt practices, §120-8.
Electronic voting apparatus.
Installation and use of apparatus, §120-11.2.
Expense allowance, §120-3(a), (c).
Failure to discharge duty.
Penalty for failure, §120-7.
Freedom of speech, §120-9.
Impeachment, §§123-1 to 123-13.
See IMPEACHMENT.
Journals.
Deposited with secretary of state, §120-29.
Indexed by clerks, §120-28.
Preparation and filing by clerk, §120-27.
Majority leader, §120-3(a), (c).
Meetings.
Convening at appointed time and place, §120-6.
Time of meeting, §120-11.1.
Minority leader, §120-3(a), (c).
Number of senators, NC Const Art II §2.
Oaths.
Presiding officers may administer oaths, §120-5.
Officers, NC Const Art II §14.
Elected officers, §120-37.
Pay of members and officers, §120-3(a) to (c).
Penalties.
Failure to discharge duty, §120-7.
President.
Lieutenant governor to preside, NC Const Art II
§13.
Oaths.
Administration of oaths for qualification of
senators and officers of senate, §120-5.
Succession to office of governor, §147-11.1(b).
President pro tempore.
Expense allowance, §120-3(a), (c).
Legislative research commission.
Ex officio member, §120-30.10(a).
Legislative services commission.
Chairman of commission, §120-31(b).
Member of commission, §120-31(a).
License plate.
Special plate, number, §20-79.5.
Salary, §120-3(a), (c).
Succession to presidency, NC Const Art II §14.
Temporary succession, NC Const Art II §14.
Qualifications for senator, NC Const Art II §6.
Salaries, §120-3(a) to (c).
Seal or coat of arms of Senate, use of likenesses,
§120-271.
Criminal offense, §120-271(a).
Injunctive relief, §120-271(b).
Sessions.
Time of meeting, §120-11.1.
Subsistence and travel allowances, §120-3.1(a).
Payment of allowances, §120-3.1(b).
When general assembly not in session,
§120-3.1(c).
Terms of office, NC Const Art II §9.
Travel allowances, §120-3.1(a).
Payment of allowances, §120-3.1(b).
When general assembly not in session,
§120-3.1(c).
Vacancies, NC Const Art II §10.
Voting.
Electronic voting apparatus.
Amendment providing for installation and
use, §120-11.2(b).

GENERAL ASSEMBLY —Cont'd
Senate —Cont'd
Voting —Cont'd
Electronic voting apparatus —Cont'd
Installation and use of apparatus,
§120-11.2(a).
Working plans for installation, §120-11.2(c).
Sergeant-at-arms.
Election, §120-37(a).
Employing temporary assistance, §120-37(e).
Salary, §120-37(b).
Term, §120-37(a).
Session laws.
Printing of session laws.
Legislative services commission, §120-34.
Sessions.
Extra sessions on legislative call, NC Const Art II
§11.
Reconvened sessions.
Request that session not be held, §120-6.1(a),
(b).
Regular sessions, NC Const Art II §11.
Time of meeting, §120-11.1.
Severability of apportionment acts, §120-2.1.
Sick leave.
Temporary employees, §120-32.5.
Smoking in public places.
Nonsmoking areas.
General assembly occupying building,
§143-597(a1).
Southern growth policies agreement, §§143-490
to 143-506.
See SOUTHERN GROWTH POLICIES
AGREEMENT.
Special police.
Areas of jurisdiction, §120-32.2(a).
Arrests, §120-32.2(b).
Oath, §120-32.3.
Parking rules.
Enforcement, §120-32.2(c).
State legislative building.
Evacuation of legislative buildings and grounds
during emergencies, §120-32.1A.
State departments and agencies.
Legislative committees and commissions.
Furnishing data and information to, §120-19.
Legislative research commission.
Cooperation with commission, §120-30.16.
Reports.
Certain institutions to report to general
assembly, §143-156.
Report from chief officer to general assembly,
§120-12.
State agency reports to general assembly.
Copies, who receives, electronic copy
available, informing members, §120-29.5.
Vacancies in offices of some departments,
§120-12.1.
State forests.
Acquisition and control.
General assembly authority for payment of
money, §106-879.
State institutions.
Legislative research commission.
Cooperation with commission, §120-30.16.
Reports from state institutions and departments,
§120-12.
State legislative building.
Defined, §120-32.1(d).
Designation, §129-12.1.
Evacuation in emergencies, §120-32.1A.

GENERAL ASSEMBLY —Cont'd
State legislative building —Cont'd
Firearms.
Transportation or storage in closed
compartment of locked vehicle.
Parking space assigned or leased by legislator
or legislative employee, §120-32.1(c1).
Rules not to prohibit, §120-32.1(c1).
Legislative research commission.
Availability of facilities to the commission,
§120-30.18.
Official name, §129-12.1.
Parking regulations, §120-32.1(c).
Research division.
Office space and equipment in state legislative
building, §120-36.5.
Rules and regulations.
Use and maintenance of buildings, §120-32.1(a).
Posting and filing, violation, criminal penalty,
waiver, §120-32.1(b).
Special police.
Evacuation of buildings and grounds during
emergencies, §120-32.1A.
Use and maintenance of building, §120-32.1(a).
Rules and regulations, §120-32.1(a).
Posting, filing, notice of rules, §120-32.1(b).
Violation, criminal penalty, §120-32.1(b).
Waiver of rules adopted, §120-32.1(b).
State literary fund.
Report by state board of education on operation,
§115C-414.
State of disaster, declaring, §166A-6.
State personnel system.
Exemption.
Officers and employees of general assembly,
§126-5(c1).
State treasurer.
Legislative retirement fund.
Transfer to department of state treasurer,
§143A-37.
Structural pest control.
Legislative findings, §106-65.22.
Subpoenas.
Committee activity.
Failure to respond to subpoena punishable as
contempt, §120-19.4.
Form of subpoena, §120-19.2(e).
Issuance of subpoena to obtain testimony,
§120-19.2(c).
Return of subpoena, §120-19.2(f).
Legislative services commission.
Subpoena and contempt powers, §120-32.4.
Subsistence and travel allowances.
Joint legislative commission on governmental
operations, §120-78.
Staff of commission, §120-79(b).
Legislative ethics committee, §120-101.
Legislative research commission, §120-30.18.
Legislative services commission.
Reimbursement for allowance, §120-31(e).
Members of general assembly, §120-3.1.
Subsistence expenses.
Members also members of state board or
commission, §138-5(f).
Supreme court.
Claims against the state.
Original jurisdiction of the supreme court,
§7A-25.
Taxation.
Amendment or repeal of subchapter.
Power of general assembly, §105-1.1.

GENERAL ASSEMBLY —Cont'd
Taxation —Cont'd
Local, private and special legislation prohibited,
NC Const Art II §24.
Power of taxation vested in general assembly,
§105-1.1.
Requirements for passage of revenue bills, NC
Const Art II §23.
Temporary employees.
Leave for temporary employees, §120-32.5.
Terms of office, NC Const Art II §9.
Testimony by legislative employees.
Judicially compelled disclosures, §120-132(c).
Otherwise publicly accessible information,
§120-132(b).
Prohibited disclosures, §120-132(a).
Threats.
Code of legislative ethics.
Intent to influence legislator in discharge of
duties, §120-86(b) to (e).
Personnel-related actions, §120-86.1.
Intent to influence legislator in discharge of
duties.
Compelling threatened person to attempt to
influence legislator, §120-86(b1).
Legislator to threaten other legislator,
§120-86(c).
Penalties, §120-86(e).
Threats to legislator by partner, client, customer
or employer, §120-86(b).
Towns.
Local government to be provided by general
assembly, NC Const Art VII §1.
Townships.
Local, private and special legislation prohibited,
NC Const Art II §24.
Trade.
Local, private and special legislation prohibited,
NC Const Art II §24.
Transportation department.
Data report to general assembly, §136-12(a).
Reports to appropriations committees of general
assembly, §136-44.2B.
Travel allowances.
Joint legislative commission on governmental
operations, §120-78.
Staff of commission, §120-79(b).
Legislative ethics committee, §120-101.
Legislative research commission, §120-30.18.
Legislative services commission.
Reimbursement for subsistence in travel
allowance, §120-31(e).
Members of general assembly, §120-3.1.
Travel expenses.
Members also members of state board or
commission, §138-5(f).
Underground storage tanks.
Leaking petroleum cleanup.
Implementation of provisions of part.
Part not construed to obligate to make
appropriation, §143-215.94J(b).
Vacancies.
Appointment by governor to fill, §163-11(a).
County executive committee of political party of
vacating member.
Recommendation, §163-11(b), (c).
House or senate district committee.
Recommendation, §163-11(d).
Eligibility, voting status determining, §163-11(e).
Filling vacancies, NC Const Art II §10.
Legislative appointments, §120-122.

GENERAL ASSEMBLY —Cont'd
Vacation leave.
Temporary employees, §120-32.5.
Veto by governor, NC Const Art II §22, Art III §5.
Voting.
Electronic voting apparatus.
Installation and use of apparatus, §120-11.2.
Wage and hour act.
Pages in general assembly.
Exemptions, §95-25.14(a).
Waters and watercourses.
Nonnavigable streams.
Local, private and special legislation prohibited,
NC Const Art II §24.
Wills.
Giving effect to informal wills.
Local, private and special legislation prohibited,
NC Const Art II §24.
Witnesses.
Committee activity.
Examination of witnesses, §§120-19.1,
120-19.2(b).
Notice of hearing, §120-19.2(d).
Failing to attend as witness before committees,
§14-227.
Fees and expenses of witness, §120-19.3.
Invitations to witnesses, §120-19.2(a).
Perjury, §14-211.
Refusal to testify punishable as contempt,
§120-19.4.
Investigating committees, §120-14.
Pay of witnesses, §120-16.
Legislative research commission.
Powers and duties, §120-30.17.
Testimony by legislative employees, §120-132.

GENERAL CONTRACTORS, §§87-1 to 87-15.4.
Accredited builder.
Designation of builders, §87-15.4.
Accredited master builder.
Designation of builders, §87-15.4.
Bidding.
Copy of provisions to be included in specifications,
§87-15.
Licenses.
Bid not considered unless contractor licensed,
§87-15.
Board.
Appointment of members, §87-2.
Composition, §87-2.
Creation, §87-2.
Designation of builders, §87-15.4.
Employees, §87-4.
Equipment and supplies, authority to purchase,
§87-9.1(b).
Funds.
Disposition, §87-7.
Liability insurance, authority to purchase,
§87-9.1(b).
Meetings, §87-6.
First meeting, §87-4.
Notice, §87-6.
Number of members, §87-2.
Oath of office of members, §87-3.
Officers, §87-4.
Public awareness program, §87-15.2.
Purchasing authority.
Equipment and supplies, §87-9.1(b).
Real property, §87-9.1(a).
Qualifications of members, §87-2.
Quorum, §87-6.

GENERAL CONTRACTORS —Cont'd
Board —Cont'd
Real property, authority to acquire and own,
§87-9.1(a).
Records, §§87-7, 87-8.
Complaints against licensees, §87-11(c).
Removal of members, §87-2.
Reports.
Annual report to governor, §87-8.
Seal, §87-5.
Terms of members, §87-2.
Vacancies, §87-2.
Building permits.
Requirements for issuance, §87-14(a).
Certified accredited builder.
Designation of builders, §87-15.4.
Certified accredited master builder.
Designation of builders, §87-15.4.
Child support enforcement.
Forfeiture of licensing privilege, §50-13.12.
Complaints against licensees, §87-11(a1).
Confidentiality of complaining party, §87-15.3.
Confidentiality of complaining party.
Complaints against licensees or unlicensed
contractors, §87-15.3.
Defined, §87-1(a).
Exceptions, §87-1(b).
Designation of builders.
Certification of licensees, §87-15.4(a).
Enforcement of provisions, §87-15.4(c).
Equivalent education, designation according to,
§87-15.4(b).
Evidence.
Licenses.
Certificate evidence of license, §87-12.
Federal highway act.
Compliance by department of transportation not
prevented, §87-9.
Fees.
Licenses, §87-10(a).
Fire service mains, §87-10(b1).
Highways.
Federal requirements.
Compliance not prevented, §87-9.
Homeowners recovery fund.
Administration, §87-15.6(a).
Definitions, §87-15.5.
Establishment, §87-15.6(a).
Fees.
Building permits.
Collection, §87-15.6(b).
Purposes, §87-15.6(a).
Reimbursements.
Application, §87-15.8(a).
Investigation, §87-15.8(a).
Determination of procedures, §87-15.7(a).
Eligibility, §87-15.8(a).
Payment, §87-15.8(b).
Subrogation, §87-15.9.
Rules and regulations.
Adoption, §87-15.6(c).
Subrogation.
Reimbursements, §87-15.9.
Use of funds, §87-15.7(b).
Impersonating contractor, §87-13.
Injunctions.
Power of board to seek, §87-13.1.
Insurance.
Board.
Liability insurance, authority to purchase,
§87-9.1(b).

GENERAL CONTRACTORS —Cont'd
Investigations and prosecutions of violations.
Administrative costs, recovery by board, §87-11(e).
Licenses.
Applications, §87-10(a).
Bidding.
Bid not considered unless contractor licensed, §87-15.
Certificates, §87-10(e).
Evidence of license, §87-12.
False certificate, §87-13.
Lost or destroyed certificates.
Replacement, §87-11(d).
Complaints against licensees, §87-11(a1).
Designation of builders, §87-15.4.
Examinations, §87-10(b), (c).
Exception.
Department of transportation contractors, §87-1.2.
Public building project owner, bidding and contracting with, §87-1.1.
Fees, §87-10(a).
Investigations and prosecutions of violations.
Administrative costs, recovery by board, §87-11(e).
Nonresidents.
Certificate of authority required.
Corporations or limited liability companies, §87-10.1(b).
Definitions, §87-10.1(a).
Delinquents, §87-10.1(d).
Information to be provided, §87-10.1(c).
Prerequisites to issuance of certificate of license, §87-10.1(d).
Reciprocity, §87-15.1.
Reexaminations, §87-10(d).
Renewal, §87-10(e).
Revocation.
Felony conviction, §15A-1331(a).
Grounds, §87-11(a).
Reissuance, §87-11(d).
Rules and regulations governing, §87-11(b).
Misdemeanors.
Building permits.
Issuance violations, §87-14(b).
Prohibited acts, §87-13.
Nonresidents.
Licenses, §87-10.1.
Penalties, §87-13.
Building permits.
Issuance violations, §87-14(b).
Prohibited acts, §87-13.
Public awareness program, §87-15.2.
Public building project owners.
Bidding and contracting directly with.
License exception, §87-1.1.
Public utilities contractors.
Water service or sewer lines.
Line terminations and fire service mains, §87-10(b1).
Reciprocity.
Licenses, §87-15.1.
Records.
Board, §§87-7, 87-8.
Complaints against licensees, §87-11(c).
Roster of licensed contractors, §87-8.
Subcontractors.
Payments to subcontractors.
Inapplicability of provisions of chapter to residential contractors, §22C-6.
Unauthorized practice of contracting, §87-13.

GENERAL CONTRACTORS —Cont'd
Water or wastewater systems.
Contracts, §87-9.
Public utilities contractors.
Line terminations and fire service mains, §87-10(b1).

GENERAL COURT OF JUSTICE.
Administration, §7A-2.
Unified judicial system for purposes of administration, §7A-4.
Advance sheets.
Furnishing advance sheets without charge, §7A-6(c).
Age limit for service as justice or judge, §7A-4.20.
Appeals.
Cost on appeal, §6-33.
Appellate division, §§7A-5 to 7A-7, NC Const Art IV §5.
Court of appeals.
See COURT OF APPEALS.
Organization, §7A-5.
Utilities commission.
Parties on appeal, §62-92.
Relief pending review on appeal, §62-95.
Right of appeals from utilities commission, §62-90(d).
Cancellation of court sessions.
Adverse weather, other emergency situations including catastrophic conditions, §7A-39(a).
In chambers jurisdiction not affected, §7A-39(c).
Cash management, §147-86.14.
Catastrophic conditions.
Cancellation of court sessions, closing court offices, §7A-39(a).
In chambers jurisdiction not affected, §7A-39(c).
Clerks of court.
Practice of law.
Prohibited, §84-2.
Closing court offices.
Adverse weather, other emergency situations including catastrophic conditions, §7A-39(a).
In chambers jurisdiction not affected, §7A-39(c).
Costs.
Civil actions, §7A-305(a).
Filings containing certain motions, §7A-305(f).
Criminal actions.
Assessment and collection of costs, §§7A-2, 7A-304(a).
Recovery of cost on appeal, §6-33.
Court of appeals.
See COURT OF APPEALS.
Court reporters.
Appellate division of general court of justice, §7A-6(a).
District courts.
See DISTRICT COURTS.
Divisions.
Enumeration, NC Const Art IV §2.
Emergency situations.
Cancellation of court sessions, closing court offices, §7A-39(a).
In chambers jurisdiction not affected, §7A-39(c).
Financial support of judicial department, §7A-2.
Fluorescent lights and thermostats containing mercury.
Recycling program.
Establishment required, §130A-310.60(a).
Report documenting compliance required, §130A-310.60(b).

GENERAL COURT OF JUSTICE —Cont'd
Inclement weather.
Cancellation of court sessions, closing court offices, §7A-39(a).
In chambers jurisdiction not affected, §7A-39(c).
Judicial conduct.
Authority of supreme court to prescribe standards, §7A-10.1.
Judicial department.
See JUDICIAL DEPARTMENT.
Judicial power, §7A-3.
Vesting, NC Const Art IV §1.
Jurisdiction.
Divisions, §7A-2.
Enforcement of judgments, §7A-3.
Unified judicial system for purposes of jurisdiction, §7A-4.
Meetings of public bodies.
Exception to provisions, §143-318.18.
Mercury.
Fluorescent lights and thermostats containing.
Recycling program.
Establishment required, §130A-310.60(a).
Report documenting compliance, §130A-310.60(b).
Motor vehicle captive finance sources.
Suits against, §20-308.20.
Oaths.
Form of oath, §11-11.
Who may administer oaths of office, §11-7.1(a).
Obstructing justice.
Picketing or parading within certain distance of court, §14-225.1.
Operation.
Unified judicial system for purposes of operation, §7A-4.
Organization of divisions, §§7A-2, 7A-4.
Picketing or parading within certain distance of court.
Obstructing justice, §14-225.1.
Pleadings.
Verification.
Judges or clerks competent to take affidavits, §1-148.
Powers.
Judicial power, §7A-3.
Vesting, NC Const Art IV §1.
Public utilities commission.
Parties on appeal, §62-92.
Relief pending review on appeal, §62-95.
Right of appeal, §62-90(d).
Purposes of chapter, §7A-2.
Retirement.
Age limit for service as justice or judge, §7A-4.20.
Consolidated judicial retirement act, §§135-50 to 135-75.
See RETIREMENT SYSTEM FOR TEACHERS AND STATE EMPLOYEES.
Small claim actions in district courts, §§7A-210 to 7A-232.
See SMALL CLAIMS.
Superior courts.
See SUPERIOR COURTS.
Support of court.
Administration of estates.
Facilities fee as part of costs in administration of estates, §7A-307(a), (b).
Costs in civil actions, §7A-305(a).
Filings containing certain motions, §7A-305(f).
Costs in criminal actions, §7A-304(a).

GENERAL COURT OF JUSTICE —Cont'd
Supreme court.
See SUPREME COURT OF NORTH CAROLINA.
Transfer of civil causes.
Motion to transfer.
Consent of parties required, §7A-258(a).
Contents, §7A-258(d).
Effectiveness when order of transfer filed, §7A-258(h).
Filing of motion, §7A-258(b).
Parties other than plaintiff, §7A-258(c).
In writing requirement, §7A-258(d).
Notice required, §7A-258(e).
Sole method for seeking transfer, §7A-258(g).
Stay of proceedings, §7A-258(f).
Venue determination, §7A-258(f).
Waiver of objection to jurisdiction where motion filed, §7A-258(f).
When second transfer not authorized, §7A-258(i).
Retention and docketing of causes in originally designated trial division until transferred, §7A-256.
Review of transfer matters, §7A-260.
Waiver of proper division, §7A-257.
Exceptions, §7A-257.
Transition provisions, §7A-3.
Vesting of judicial power, NC Const Art IV §1.

GENERAL EDUCATION DEVELOPMENT DEGREE.
Community colleges.
Retention of fees, §115D-5(s).
Jail prisoner's participation.
Person having custody to approve, revocation of approval, §162-59.1.
Reduction in sentence for participation, §162-60(b).
Escape, forfeiture of reduction, §162-60(c).
Person in custody judge of faithful participation, §162-60(c).

GENERAL STATUTES.
Adoption.
Replacement volume 1A, §164-11.9(a).
Replacement volume 1B, §164-11.9(b).
Replacement volumes 1C and 1D, §164-11.8(a), (d).
Replacement volume 2A, §164-11.8(b), (d).
Replacement volume 2B, §164-11.6(a), (c).
Replacement volumes 2B, 2C and 2D, §164-11.7(a), (c).
Replacement volume 2C, §164-11.5(a), (c).
Replacement volume 3A, §§164-11.6(b), (c), 164-11.8(c), (d).
Replacement volume 3B, §164-11.5(b), (c).
Replacement volumes 3B, 3C and 3D, §164-11.7(b), (c).
Volumes 1A, 1B and 1C, §164-11.4.
Volumes 2A, 2B and 2C, §164-11.2.
Volumes 3A, 3B and 3C, §164-11.3.
Citation of revision, §164-1.
Codification of statutes.
Legislative services officer.
Duties assigned general assembly staff, §120-36.21.
Commission.
General statutes commission, §§164-12 to 164-19.
See GENERAL STATUTES COMMISSION.
Definitions, NC Const Art XIV §3.
Effect.
Repeal of other statutes, §164-2.
Offenses, penalties and liabilities not affected, §164-4.

GENERAL STATUTES —Cont'd
Effect —Cont'd
Repeal of other statutes —Cont'd
Pending actions and proceedings not affected, §164-5.
Persons holding office, §164-6.
Rights accrued or suits commenced not affected, §164-3.
Statutes not repealed, §164-7.
When acts take effect, §120-20.
Effective date, §164-8.
When acts take effect, §120-20.
Evidence.
Supplements.
Prima facie evidence of laws, §164-11(a).
Cumulative supplements, §164-11.1.
General assembly staff.
Codification of statutes.
Duties assigned to, §120-36.21.
Legislative services officer.
Codification of statutes.
Duties assigned general assembly staff, §120-36.21.
Completion of general statutes by, §164-9.
Powers in preparing general and permanent laws, §164-10.
Supplements to general statutes, §164-10.
Penalties.
Repeals not to affect, §164-4.
Repeal of other statutes, §164-2.
Offenses, penalties and liabilities not affected, §164-4.
Pending actions and proceedings not affected, §164-5.
Persons holding office.
Effect of repeal on, §164-6.
Rights accrued or suits commenced not affected, §164-3.
Statutes not repealed, §164-7.
Revisor of statutes, §120-36.22.
Supplements, §164-10.
Citation, §164-11(b).
Cumulative supplements.
Prima facie evidence of laws, §164-11.1.
Interim supplements, §164-10.
Prima facie statement of laws, §164-11(a).
Cumulative supplements, §164-11.1.
Title of revision, §164-1.

GENERAL STATUTES COMMISSION, §§164-12 to 164-19.
Appointment of members, §164-14(a).
Reported to secretary of commission, §164-14(e).
Committees, §164-17.
Compensation of members, §164-19.
Composition, §164-14(a).
Creation, §164-12(a).
Duties, §164-13(a).
Funds.
Use of funds, §164-13(b).
Located within general assembly for administrative purposes, §164-12(b).
Meetings, §164-15.
Name, §164-12(a).
Number of members, §164-14(a).
Officers, §164-16.
Election, §164-16.
Terms of office, §164-16.
Policies and guidelines, adoption, §164-17.
Quorum, §164-15.
Recommendations, §164-18.

GENERAL STATUTES COMMISSION —Cont'd
Reports, §164-18.
Secretary.
Revisor of statutes as ex officio secretary, §164-16.
Special meetings, §164-15.
Terms of members, §164-14(b), (c), (f).
Travel allowances of members, §164-19.
Vacancies.
Filling, §164-14(d).

GENERATING FACILITIES.
Certificates for construction.
Analysis for needs for expansion of facilities, §62-110.1(c).
Appeal from award order, §62-82(b).
Application.
Factors in action, §62-110.1(d).
Hearing, §62-82(a).
Notice, §62-82(a).
Electric membership corporations.
Inclusion in definition "public utility,"§62-110.1(b).
Estimate of construction costs.
Condition for receiving certificate, §62-110.1(e).
Nuclear facilities.
Project development cost review, §62-110.7.
Out-of-state electric generating facilities.
Rate recovery of construction costs.
Applicable provisions, §62-110.6(d).
Cancellation of construction, §62-110.6(e).
Petition, §62-110.6(a), (b).
Public hearing, §62-110.6(c).
Progress report by utility, §62-110.1(f).
Rate recovery of construction costs, §62-110.1(f1) to (f3).
Nuclear facilities.
Project development cost review, §62-110.7.
Out-of-state electric generating facilities, §62-110.6.
Required, §62-110.1(a).
Exceptions, §62-110.1(g).
Review by commission, §62-110.1(e1).

GENERATION-SKIPPING TRANSFER TAX.
Amount, §105-32.7(b).
Correct amount of tax payable, return reflecting.
Federal determination changing amount payable, §105-32.8.
Due date, §105-32.7(c).
Federal tax referenced in instrument.
Construction of formula provisions in trusts.
Estates of decedents dying in 2010, §36C-1-113.
Construction of formula provisions in wills.
Estates of decedents dying in 2010, §31-46.1.
Imposition of tax, §105-32.7(a).
Net value of property located in state, §105-32.7(b).
Payment, §105-32.7(c).
Return, §105-32.7(c).
State percentage of tax, §105-32.7(b).

GENERATORS.
Mechanical breakdown service agreement, §66-374.

GENERIC DRUGS.
Drug product selection.
Definitions, §90-85.27.
Equivalent drug product.
Defined, §90-85.27.
Price.
Limitation on selected drugs, §90-85.28(c).

GENERIC DRUGS —Cont'd
Drug product selection —Cont'd
  Equivalent drug product —Cont'd
    Selection by pharmacist, §90-85.28(a).
      Liability of prescriber and pharmacist not
        extended, §90-85.31.
      Prescriber may permit or prohibit,
        §90-85.28(b).
    Liability of prescriber and pharmacist not
      extended, §90-85.31.
    Prescriptions.
      Label, §90-85.29.
      Record, §90-85.30.

GENETIC IDENTIFICATION, §§15A-266 to
  15A-270.
See DNA.

GENETIC INFORMATION.
Employment discrimination based on,
  §95-28.1A.
Health insurance, §58-3-215.

GENETIC MARKERS.
Paternity, actions to establish, §49-14(d).
  Competency of tests, §8-50.1.

GENETIC TESTING.
Child support.
  Orders.
    Relief from order based on nonpaternity,
      §50-13.13(d).
Employment discrimination based on,
  §95-28.1A.
Genetic identification.
  DNA analysis, §§15A-266 to 15A-270.
    See DNA.
Paternity.
  Expedited procedures to establish paternity in
    IV-D cases, §110-132.2.
  Genetic markers, §49-14(d).
    Competency of tests, §8-50.1.
  Setting aside orders of paternity, §49-4(h).

GENOCIDE.
Sudan (Darfur) divestment act, §§147-86.41 to
  147-86.49.

GENTIANS.
Trespass.
  Taking, etc., of certain wild plants from land of
    another, §14-129.

GEOGRAPHICAL LOCATION.
Deceptive representation in telephone
  directory, print advertisement or Internet.
  Exceptions to provisions, §75-42(c).
  Immunity, §75-42(d).
  Prohibited acts, §75-42(a), (b).
  Violations as unfair trade practices, §75-42(e).

GEOGRAPHIC INFORMATION
  COORDINATING COUNCIL, §§143-725 to
  143-727.
Center for geographic information and
  analysis.
  Role, §143-725(b).
Compensation of members, §143-727.
Established, §143-725(a).
Expenses of members, §143-727.
Meetings, §143-726(e).
Members, §143-726(a), (d).
  Compensation, §143-727.
  General assembly appointments, §143-726(c).
  Governor appointments, §143-726(b).

GEOGRAPHIC INFORMATION
  COORDINATING COUNCIL —Cont'd
Offensive geographic place-names.
  Abrogation, §147-54.7.
Reports, §143-726(g).
Scope of responsibility, §143-725(a).
Secretary, §143-726(f).
Staff support, §143-726(f).
Standing committees, §143-726(h).
Workgroups, §143-726(h).

GEOLOGISTS, §§89E-1 to 89E-24.
Appeals.
  Judicial review of final agency decision,
    §89E-20(c).
Applicability of chapter, §89E-6.
  Exemptions, §§89E-6, 89E-7(b).
Attorney general.
  Legal advisor to board, §89E-24.
Board for licensing of geologists.
  Administration of chapter, §§89E-4(a), 89E-5(a).
  Appointment of members, §89E-4(b).
  Attorney general.
    Legal advisor of board, §89E-24.
  Compensation, §89E-4(g).
  Composition, §89E-4(d).
  Contracts for supplies, materials, printing,
    equipment, contractual services.
    Audit of contractor's records.
      Standard clause, §89E-5(e).
    Cost plus percentage of cost agreement
      contracts prohibited, §89E-5(e).
    Submission to attorney general for review,
      §89E-5(e).
  Deposit of funds received.
    Duty of board treasurer, §89E-5(e).
    Interest on funds, §89E-5(e).
  Enforcement of chapter, §89E-5(a).
  Expenditures.
    Authorization, §89E-5(e).
    Payment, §89E-5(e).
  Expenses.
    Reimbursement, §89E-4(g).
  Fees.
    Establishment and collection, §89E-5(g).
  Governor.
    Appointment of members, §89E-4(b).
    Removal of members, §89E-4(b).
  Meetings, §89E-5(f).
  Number of members, §89E-4(b).
  Officers, §89E-5(b).
  Personnel.
    Authority to hire, §89E-4(h).
  Powers and duties.
    Generally, §89E-5(h).
  Purchase and contract division.
    Authorized to utilize services, §89E-5(e).
  Qualifications of members, §89E-4(c).
  Quorum, §89E-5(b).
  Records.
    Maintaining, §89E-14(a).
  Register of applications for licensing.
    Contents, §89E-14(b).
    Maintenance, §89E-14(a).
  Removal of members, §89E-4(b).
  Rules and regulations.
    Adoption, §89E-5(b).
  Seal.
    Adoption, §89E-5(d).
  State geologist.
    Ex officio member, §89E-4(b).

GEOLOGISTS —Cont'd
Board for licensing of geologists —Cont'd
Terms of office, §89E-4(e).
Expiration, §89E-4(f).
Child support enforcement.
Forfeiture of licensing privilege, §50-13.12.
Citation of chapter, §89E-1.
Code of professional conduct.
Adoption, §89E-16.
Comity.
Licenses, §89E-11.
Complaints, §89E-17(a).
Confidentiality.
Examination test scores, applications, etc.,
§89E-14(c).
Corporations, §89E-7(a).
Definitions, §89E-3.
Disciplinary procedures, §89E-19.
Civil penalty for violations, §89E-19(c).
Civil action to recover, §89E-19(d).
Grounds, §89E-19(a).
Hearings, §89E-20.
Professional incompetence, §89E-19(b).
Education.
Licenses.
Minimum qualifications, §89E-9.
Examinations.
Conducted by board, §89E-10(a).
Fees, §89E-10(b).
Professional competence, §89E-19(b).
Qualifications for license, §89E-9.
Results.
Confidential, §89E-14(c).
Fees.
Board.
Establishing and collecting, §89E-5(g).
Examinations, §89E-10(b).
Felony convictions.
Forfeiture of license, §15A-1331A.
Fines.
Civil penalty for license violations, §89E-19(c).
Civil action to recover, §89E-19(d).
Governor.
Board for licensing of geologists.
Appointment and removal of members,
§89E-4(b).
Grounds for discipline, §89E-19(a).
Hearings.
Code of professional conduct.
Revision and amendment to code, §89E-16.
Disciplinary procedures, §89E-20(a).
Incompetence, §89E-19(b).
Injunctions.
Violation of chapter, §89E-23.
Investigations, §89E-17(b).
Confidentiality of proceedings, §89E-17(c).
Licenses.
Applications.
Contents, §89E-8.
Fees, §89E-8.
Register of applications, §89E-14(b).
Comity, §89E-11.
Education.
Minimum qualifications, §89E-9.
Examination.
Qualifications of applicants, §89E-9.
Experience requirements, §89E-9.
Expiration, §89E-12(b).
Issuance, §89E-12(a).
Board, §89E-5(c).

GEOLOGISTS —Cont'd
Licenses —Cont'd
Lost, destroyed or mutilated.
Issuance and replacement of license, §89E-12(c).
Qualifications of applicant.
Board to examine and pass on, §89E-5(c).
Minimum qualifications, §89E-9.
Reciprocity, §89E-11.
Renewal, §89E-12(b).
Standards for licensing and renewal.
Establishment by board, §89E-5(i).
Suspension or revocation.
Disciplinary procedures, §89E-19.
Felony convictions, §15A-1331A.
Reissuance, §89E-21.
Limitation of actions.
Real property improvements.
Recovery of damages for defective or unsafe
conditions.
Six-year limitation, §1-50(a).
Partnerships, §89E-7(a).
Penalties.
Violation of chapter, §89E-22.
Petitions.
Hearings, §89E-20(b).
Professional associations, §89E-7(a).
Professional corporations, §55B-14(b).
Prohibited acts, §89E-18.
Public policy, §89E-2.
Purpose of chapter, §89E-2.
Reciprocity.
Licenses, §89E-11.
Roster of licensed geologists, §89E-15.
Seals.
Board for licensing of geologists.
Adoption of seal, §89E-5(b).
Design, §89E-13.
Required, §89E-13.
Use, §89E-13.
Short title of chapter, §89E-1.
State geologist.
Board for licensing of geologists.
Ex officio member, §89E-4(b).
Unlawful acts, §89E-18.
Violation of chapter.
Injunctions, §89E-23.
Penalties, §89E-22.

GEORGIA HOME BOY.
Gamma hydroxybutyric acid (GHB).
Date rape drug, §90-89.

GERRYMANDERING.
Action challenging plans apportioning state
legislature and congressional districts,
§§120-2.3 to 120-2.5.
Three-judge panel, §1-267.1.

GETAWAY CARS.
Seizure and forfeiture of conveyances used in
committing larceny and similar crimes,
§14-86.1.

GHOST IN THE ATTIC STATUTE, §39-50.

GIFT CARDS.
Maintenance fees.
Definitions, §66-67.5(c).
Disclosure requirement, §66-67.5(a).
Violations as unfair trade practices, §66-67.5(b).
Exception to provisions, §66-67.5(d).

GIFT CERTIFICATES.
Unclaimed property generally, §§116B-51 to
116B-80.
See UNCLAIMED PROPERTY.

GIFTED STUDENTS.
Education of academically and intellectually
    gifted students.
    Components, §115C-150.7(b).
    Guideline development, §115C-150.6.
    Legislative intent, §115C-150.5.
    Local plans.
        Amendment, §115C-150.7(d).
        Development, §115C-150.7(a).
        Disagreement review, §115C-150.8.
        Effective term, §115C-150.7(d).
        Submission to the state board of education,
            §115C-150.7(c).
    Technical assistance, §115C-150.6.
Special education generally.
    See SPECIAL EDUCATION.

GIFTS.
Agriculture.
    Hall of fame.
        Acceptance of gifts, §106-568.17.
Anatomical gifts, §§130A-412.3 to 130A-412.33.
    See ANATOMICAL GIFTS.
Art.
    Promotion of arts.
        Acceptance of gifts by cultural resources
            department, §143-407.
Bees and honey.
    Authority of board to accept, §106-637.
Charitable gift annuities, §58-3-6.
Charitable solicitations, §§131F-1 to 131F-33.
    See CHARITABLE SOLICITATION.
Constitution of the United States.
    Foreign presents to United States officials, US
        Const Art I §9.
Cultural resources department.
    Promotion of arts.
        Acceptance of gifts by department, §143-407.
Deeds.
    Registration required, §47-26.
Donated food.
    Inspections by department of agriculture and
        consumer services, §106-141.1.
Education.
    Charitable gift annuities, §58-3-6.
    State board of education.
        Power to accept gifts, §115C-410.
Electrologists.
    Acceptance by board of electrologist examiners,
        §88A-8.
Employment security section.
    Acceptance and use of donations, §96-25.
Excise stamp tax on conveyances.
    Exempted transfers, §105-228.29.
Exemptions.
    Continuation of exemption of property,
        §1C-1604(b).
Fairs.
    State fair.
        Constructing and financing facilities and
            improvements, §106-503.1(c).
Foreign presents to United States officials, US
    Const Art I §9.
Gift cards.
    Maintenance fees, §66-67.5.
Governor.
    Executive Mansion.
        Department of cultural resources, §143-411.
Guardians.
    Declaring revocable trust irrevocable and making
        gift of incompetent's life interest.
        Approval of judge of superior court.
            Authorized, §35A-1335.

GIFTS —Cont'd
Guardians —Cont'd
    Declaring revocable trust irrevocable and making
        gift of incompetent's life interest —Cont'd
        Approval of judge of superior court —Cont'd
            Fact that incompetent had not previously
                made similar gifts, §35A-1337.
            Prerequisites to approval, §§35A-1336,
                35A-1336.1.
Hospitals.
    Donation of surplus medical equipment,
        §131E-250(a), (b).
Housing finance agency.
    Receipt, administration and compliance with
        conditions and requirements of gift.
        General power of agency, §122A-5.
Inter vivos.
    Presumed absolute gift and not advancement,
        §29-24.
Intestate succession.
    Advancements.
        Gift inter vivos presumed absolute gift, §29-24.
Libraries.
    Acceptance of gifts, devises and endowments.
        Powers and duties of department of cultural
            resources, §125-2.
Lobbyists and lobbyist principals.
    Prohibition, §120C-303.
Local government finance.
    Regulation, NC Const Art V §4.
Mentally ill.
    Declaring trust irrevocable and making gift of life
        interest.
        Approval of judge of superior court, §35A-1350.
        Prerequisites, §35A-1351.
    Authorization of declaration and gift,
        §35A-1350.
    Minors.
        Notice to minors, §35A-1353.
    Objections to proposed declaration and gift,
        §35A-1354.
    Prerequisites to approval of gift, §35A-1351.
    Previously made gifts, §35A-1354.
    State departments and agencies, §35A-1350.
    Validity of declaration and gift, §§35A-1338,
        35A-1355.
    Who deemed specific and residuary devisees of
        incompetent, §35A-1352.
    From income for certain purposes.
        Approval of judge of superior court, §35A-1335.
            Fact that incompetent had not previously
                made similar gifts, §35A-1337.
            Prerequisites to approval, §§35A-1336,
                35A-1336.1.
        State departments and agencies.
            Gifts from income of incompetent to
                departments and agencies, §35A-1335.
        Validity of gift, §35A-1338.
    From principal for certain purposes.
        Approval of judge of superior court.
            Fact that incompetent had previously made
                similar gifts, §35A-1344.
            Prerequisites to approval, §§35A-1341,
                35A-1341.1.
        Legatees and devisees.
            Fact that incompetent had previously made
                similar gifts, §35A-1337.
            Notice to minors and incompetents,
                §35A-1343.
            Objections to proposed gift, §35A-1344.

GIFTS —Cont'd
Mentally ill —Cont'd
From principal for certain purposes —Cont'd
Legatees and devisees —Cont'd
Who deemed specific and residuary legatees
and devisees of incompetent, §35A-1342.
Validity of gift, §35A-1345.
Minors.
Transfers to minors.
General provisions, §§33A-1 to 33A-24.
See TRANSFERS TO MINORS.
Misuse of public office, §138A-32.
Monuments and memorials.
Acceptance of commemorative funds for useful
work, §100-8.
Mosquito control districts.
Acceptance of gifts or endowments.
Corporate powers of board of commissioners,
§130A-355.
Municipalities.
Cemetery trustees.
Acceptance, §160A-349.12.
Nonprofit corporations.
Acceptance after mergers, §55A-11-07.
North Carolina museum of art.
Exemption from taxation, §140-5.16(b).
Special fund, §140-5.16(a).
North Carolina symphony society.
Counties and municipalities authorized to make
contributions, §140-10.
Nurses.
Board of nursing.
Acceptance, §90-171.26.
Nutbush conservation area.
Authorization, §143-289.
Opticians.
Prohibited acts, §90-255.
Parks and recreation.
Acceptance of land for state parks, etc.,
§113-34(b).
Donation of property for park purposes, §113-40.
Pesticides.
Board.
Acceptance of gifts, §143-437.
Powers of attorney.
Authority of attorney-in-fact to make gifts,
§32A-14.1.
Court order authorizing gift, §32A-14.10.
Appeal, §32A-14.11.
Costs and fees, §32A-14.12.
Statutory short form.
Powers conferred by, §32A-2.
Presumption of abandonment, time,
§116B-53(c).
Prisons and prisoners.
Acquisition of property, §148-3(b).
Probate and registration.
Deeds of gift.
Registration required, §47-26.
Public lands.
Allocated state lands, §146-26.
Administration department, §146-27(a).
Public officers and employees.
Benefiting from public contracts, §14-234(a).
Misuse of public office, §138A-32.
Public works.
Contractors.
Regulation of gifts and favors, §133-32(a) to
(d).
Public schools.
Endowment funds, §115C-492.

GIFTS —Cont'd
Riparian buffer protection program.
Acceptance of donated property, §143-214.22.
Roanoke Island historical association.
Authorization to accept, §143-202.
Sanitary districts.
Acceptance of gifts for nonprofit cemetery.
Corporate powers of sanitary district board,
§130A-55.
Secretary of state.
International relations, authority to accept,
§147-54.6(b).
Southern growth policies agreement.
Board.
Acceptance of gifts, §143-496(h).
State debt.
Regulation, NC Const Art V §3.
State departments and agencies.
Mentally ill.
Declaring revocable trust irrevocable and
making of incompetent's life interest,
§35A-1350.
Gifts from income of incompetents, §35A-1335.
Receipts from federal government and gifts not
affected, §147-83.
State parks.
Donation of property for park purposes, §113-40.
State treasurer.
Receipts from federal government and gifts not
affected, §147-83.
State veterans home, §165-49(b).
Tobacco trust fund commission.
Authority to accept, §143-718.
Transfers to minors.
General provisions, §§33A-1 to 33A-24.
See TRANSFERS TO MINORS.
Tryon's Palace.
Restoration.
Acceptance and administration of gifts for
restoration, §121-14.
Unclaimed property generally, §§116B-51 to
116B-80.
See UNCLAIMED PROPERTY.
Unemployment compensation.
Employment security section.
Acceptance and use of donations, §96-25.
Uniform transfers to minors act, §§33A-1 to
33A-24.
See TRANSFERS TO MINORS.
United States.
Foreign presents to United States officials, US
Const Art I §9.
University of North Carolina.
Board of governors.
Acceptance, §116-40.
Unsolicited merchandise.
When deemed gift to recipient, §75-27.
Utilities commission.
Members, commission employees or public staff.
Receiving or accepting, §62-327.
Western North Carolina arboretum.
Acceptance, §116-242.
Wildlife resources commission.
Commission may accept, §143-247.1.
Wills.
General gifts by will.
Execution of power of appointment, §31-43.
Zoological authority.
Cities and counties, §143-177.2.
Right to receive, §143-177.
Tax exemption, §143-177.1.

GIFTS TO MINORS.
General provisions, §§33A-1 to 33A-24.
See TRANSFERS TO MINORS.

GINHOUSES.
Arson, §14-64.

GINSENG.
Larceny, §14-79.

GINSENG DEALERS.
Permits, §106-202.21.
Applications, §106-202.21(b).
Expiration, §106-202.21(b).
Issuance, §106-202.21(e).
Notice of change of address, §106-202.21(d).
Renewal, §106-202.21(c).
Requirement of permit, §106-202.21(a).

GLANDERS.
Compensation for killing diseased animals.
Appraisal of animals affected with glanders,
§106-325.
Control of livestock diseases.
Animals affected with glanders to be killed,
§106-404.

GLASS.
Highway pavement markings.
Arsenic content in glass beads contained in paint
used to mark highways, §136-30.2.
Houses.
Amusement device safety generally, §§95-111.1 to
95-111.18.
See AMUSEMENT DEVICE SAFETY.
Insurance, §58-7-15.
**Placing glass, etc., or injurious obstructions in
road,** §136-91.
Repair of motor vehicles, §§20-354 to 20-354.9.
See MOTOR VEHICLE REPAIRS.
Scrap, salvage or surplus dealers.
Failure to keep purchase records, §66-10(b).

GLASSES.
Eyeglasses.
See EYEGLASSES.

GLASSHOUSES.
Amusement device safety generally, §§95-111.1
to 95-111.18.
See AMUSEMENT DEVICE SAFETY.

GLASS INSURANCE.
Authorized, §58-7-15.
Mandatory or voluntary risk sharing plans,
§§58-42-1 to 58-42-50.
See MANDATORY OR VOLUNTARY RISK
SHARING PLANS.

GLEANING.
Agriculture.
Exemption from civil liability for farmers
permitting, §106-706.

GLOBAL POSITIONING SYSTEM.
**Portable consumer electronic devices
insurance.**
Claims handling, adjuster licenses, §58-33-27.
Generally, §§58-44A-1 to 58-44A-25.
See PORTABLE CONSUMER ELECTRONIC
DEVICES INSURANCE.
Satellite-based monitoring.
Interference with electronic monitoring devices,
§14-226.3.
Probation, post-release supervision, parole.
See SATELLITE-BASED MONITORING.

GLOBAL POSITIONING SYSTEM —Cont'd
Satellite-based monitoring —Cont'd
Sex offender monitoring generally, §§14-208.40 to
14-208.45.
See SEX OFFENDER MONITORING.

GLOBAL TRANSPARK AUTHORITY, §§63A-1 to
63A-25.
Applicability of general laws, §63A-24.
Board of directors.
Appointment, §63A-3(b).
Bylaws, §63A-3(h).
Classification of board to stagger terms,
§63A-3(d1).
Compensation, §63A-3(i).
Composition, §63A-3(b).
Dissolution of authority, §63A-25.
Office, §63A-3(l).
Officers, §63A-3(e).
Ordinances.
Adoption, §63A-7(a).
Organization, §63A-3(h).
Quorum, §63A-3(h).
Removal of members, §63A-3(g).
Terms of office, §63A-3(d), (d1).
Treasurer, §63A-3(j).
Vacancies, §63A-3(f).
Bond issues.
Conditions, §63A-9(b).
Financing agreements, §63A-13.
Hearings.
Conduct, §63A-12.
Interest, §63A-9(a).
Interim receipts or temporary bonds, §63A-9(i).
Investments.
Authorized investments, §63A-9(o).
Issuance, §63A-9(a).
Approval.
Certification, §63A-9(g).
Local government commission, §63A-9(f).
Resolution, §63A-9(k).
Maturity, §63A-9(c).
Officers.
Immunity, §63A-20.
Pledge of faith in credit of state.
Not to constitute debt secured by, §63A-9(m).
Pledges to holders of bonds, §63A-9(n).
Proceeds.
Investment, §63A-9(k).
Use, §63A-9(h).
Refunding bonds or notes, §63A-10.
Registration, §63A-9(e).
Rights of holders, §63A-16.
Security, §63A-9(j).
Security documents, §63A-14.
Signatures, §63A-9(d).
Special user projects, §63A-11.
Taxation, §63A-9(l).
Uniform commercial code.
Status under, §63A-17.
Commercial code.
Bond issues.
Status under code, §63A-17.
Conflicts of interest.
Members, officers or employees, §63A-21.
**Contested case provisions of administrative
procedure.**
Exemption, §150B-1(e).
**Contracts for supplies, materials, printing,
equipment.**
Audit of contractors records.
Standard provision, §63A-24.

GLOBAL TRANSPARK AUTHORITY —Cont'd
Contracts for supplies, materials, printing, equipment —Cont'd
Cost plus percentage of cost agreement or contract.
Prohibited, §63A-24.
Submission of certain contract to attorney for review, §63A-24.
Counties.
Agreements to make payments to authority, §63A-15.
Creation, §63A-3(a).
Definitions, §63A-2.
Disabled persons.
Goals for participation by, §63A-19.
Dissolution, §63A-25.
Eminent domain.
Powers, §63A-6(b).
Enforcement of chapter.
Rights of bondholders, §63A-16.
Exceptions to applicability of general laws, §63A-24.
Executive director, §63A-3(k).
Funds.
Deposits, §63A-8.
Expenditures, §63A-8.
General laws.
Applicability to authority, §63A-24.
Hearings.
Bond issues, §63A-12.
Immunity.
Officers.
Issuance of bonds and notes, §63A-20.
Intent of chapter, §63A-1.
Interest.
Bond issues, §63A-9(a).
Officers.
Conflicts of interest, §63A-21.
Immunity.
Issuance of bonds and notes, §63A-20.
Ordinances.
Adoption, §63A-7(a).
Personnel system.
Exemption of employees, §126-5(c1).
Police.
Special police officers.
Designation, §63A-7(b).
Policies.
Determination, §63A-4(b).
Powers.
General provisions, §63A-4(a).
Police powers, §63A-7.
Racial minorities.
Goals for participation by, §63A-19.
Real property.
Acquisition.
Approval, §63A-6(a).
Eminent domain, §63A-6(b).
Eminent domain, §63A-6(b).
Exchange, §63A-6(c).
Site selection, §63A-6(b).
Refunding bonds or notes, §63A-10.
Reports.
Annual report, §63A-23.
Rulemaking procedures.
Exemption, §150B-1(d).
Sale of merchandise by governmental units.
Exception to provisions, §66-58(b).
Short title of chapter, §63A-1.
Site selection, §63A-6(b).

GLOBAL TRANSPARK AUTHORITY —Cont'd
Special user projects.
Bond issues.
Financing agreements, §63A-13.
Security documents, §63A-14.
Bonds or notes, §63A-11.
Authorized, §63A-11(a).
Contracts with private parties, §63A-11(d).
Security for payment, §63A-11(c).
Where payable from, §63A-11(b).
Defined, §63A-2.
Financing agreements, §63A-13.
Security documents, §63A-14.
State departments and agencies.
Cooperation by, §63A-22.
State personnel system.
Exempt employees, §125-5(c1).
Tax exemptions, §§63A-5, 63A-9(l).
Women.
Goals for participation by, §63A-19.
Zoning.
Powers of authority, §63A-18.

GLOVE COMPARTMENT OF MOTOR VEHICLE.
Open container law.
Passenger area of motor vehicle defined as including, §20-138.7(f).

GLUE SNIFFING.
Toxic vapors generally, §§90-113.8A to 90-113.14.

GOATS.
Compensation for killing diseased animals generally, §§106-323 to 106-335.
See LIVESTOCK DISEASES.
Control of livestock diseases generally, §§106-400 to 106-405.
See LIVESTOCK DISEASES.
Dealer licensing generally, §§106-418.8 to 106-418.16.
See LIVESTOCK DEALER LICENSING.
Diseases generally.
See LIVESTOCK DISEASES.
Dogs killing goats.
Any person may kill, §67-14.
Meat inspections.
Generally, §§106-549.15 to 106-549.39.
See MEAT INSPECTIONS.
Pursuing or injuring with intent to steal, §14-85.
Quarantine of diseased animals generally.
See LIVESTOCK DISEASES.

GODWIN.
Satellite annexation.
Limitation on area of satellite corporate limits, inapplicability, §160A-58.1(b).

GOING OUT OF BUSINESS SALES.
Closing-out sales, §§66-76 to 66-83.
See CLOSING-OUT SALES.

GOLD.
Brands and marks, §80-40.
Articles of gold plate, §80-42.
Violations of provisions.
Misdemeanors, §80-44.
Leases for digging gold required to be in writing, §22-2.
Official state mineral, §145-35.
Precious metal dealers.
General provisions, §§66-163 to 66-173.
See PRECIOUS METAL DEALERS.

GOLDEN EAGLES.
Unlawfully taking, possessing, etc., §113-294(l).

GOLDSBORO.
Room occupancy tax.
  Uniform provisions.
    Authorized to levy, §160A-215(g).
    Generally, §160A-215.

GOLF CARTS.
County regulation of use on streets, roads and
    highways, §153A-245.
Defined, §20-4.01.
Division refusal of registration or issuance of
    certificate title, §20-54.
Municipal regulation of use on streets, roads
    and highways, §160A-300.6.
Sales and use tax.
  Electric golf cart and battery charger.
    Considered single article, §105-164.12A.

GOLF COURSES.
Alcoholic beverage permits.
  Residential sports club permit, §18B-1006(k).
  Sports club defined to include, §18B-1000.
University of North Carolina and constituent
    institutions.
  Beer and wine sales.
    Course open to public, §18B-1006(a).
  Information supplied legislative commission on
      government operations.
    Prior to issuing debt or executing contract,
        §66-58(h).

GONORRHEA.
Sexually transmitted diseases.
  See VENEREAL DISEASES.

GOOD BEHAVIOR.
Expunction of criminal records.
  First offenders not over age twenty-one.
    Drug offenses.
      Affidavit filed by applicant, §15A-145.2(a).
    Toxic vapors offenses.
      Affidavit filed with application, §15A-145.3(a).
  First offenders under age 18.
    Affidavit filed with petition, §15A-145(a).
      Gang offenses, §15A-145.1(a).
  Misdemeanor larceny conviction.
    Affidavit filed with petition, §15A-145(d1).
Prisoners.
  Earned time credit, §§15A-1355(c), 148-13(e).
    Inapplicable to persons sentenced to special
        probation, §148-13(f).
  Impaired drivers.
    Deductions in sentence, regulations, adoption,
        §148-13(b).

GOOD CAUSE.
Continuance granting, §1A-1 Rule 40(b).

GOOD CHARACTER, PROOF.
Change of name.
  Filing with application, §101-4.
Expunction of criminal records.
  First offenders not over age twenty-one.
    Drug offenses.
      Affidavit filed with application, §15A-145.2(a).
    Toxic vapors offenses.
      Affidavit filed with application, §15A-145.3(a).
  First offenders under age 18.
    Affidavit filed with petition, §15A-145(a).
      Gang offenses, §15A-145.1(a).
  Misdemeanor larceny conviction.
    Affidavit filed with petition, §15A-145(d1).

GOOD FAITH.
Commercial code.
  Obligation of good faith, §25-1-304.
Discharge papers.
  Restricting access to military discharge
      documents.
    Good faith immunity, §47-113.2(k).
Documents of title.
  Storage.
    Public sale to prevent decline in value,
        §25-7-206(b).
Durable power of attorney.
  Incapacity or incompetence of principal.
    Protection of person dealing in good faith with
        attorney-in-fact, §32A-9(c).
Fiduciaries.
  Thing done in good faith, §32-2(b).
Nonprofit corporations.
  Directors, discharging duties, §55A-8-30(a).
  Officers, §55A-8-42(a).
Physicians and surgeons.
  Fitness to practice reported or investigated.
    Good faith immunity, §90-14(f).
Principal and income act.
  Conversion to unitrust.
    Good faith immunity, §37A-1-104.8.
Sale of goods, UCC.
  Definition of good faith, §25-2-103(1).
  Purchase of goods, §25-2-103.
Securities regulation.
  Effect, §78A-49(f).

GOOD FRIDAY.
Public holiday, §103-4(a).

GOOD FUNDS SETTLEMENT ACT.
Applicability of chapter, §45A-2.
Citation of chapter, §45A-1.
Damages.
  Violation of chapter, §45A-7.
Deeds.
  Validity, §45A-6.
Definitions, §45A-3.
Dispersement of settlement proceeds, §45A-4.
Lender.
  Duties, §45A-5(a).
Loan documents.
  Validity, §45A-6.
Mortgage broker originating loan.
  Duties of settlement agent to note, §45A-4(b).
  Name included in loan closing instructions,
      §45A-5(b).
Purchaser.
  Duties, §45A-5(a).
Scope of chapter, §45A-2.
Seller.
  Duties, §45A-5(a).
Settlement agents.
  Closing funds received by.
    Accounting, §45A-8(b).
    Embezzlement, §45A-8(c).
    Interest on trust or escrow account paid to
        North Carolina State Bar, §45A-9(a).
    Rules for collection and disbursement adopted
        by bar, §45A-9(b).
    Status, §45A-8(a).
  Duties, §45A-4(a).
Short title, §45A-1.
Violations.
  Penalties, §45A-7.

GOOD NEIGHBOR COUNCIL ACT, §§7A-761,
    143B-392.

GOOD SAMARITAN STATUTES.
First aid or emergency treatment.
Nonliability, §90-21.14(a), (b).
Conflict of laws, §90-21.14(c).
Motor vehicle accidents, §20-166(d).
Non-profit community health centers,
§90-21.14(a), (b).
Volunteer health care providers, §90-21.16.
Oil pollution and hazardous substances
control.
Removal of oil discharges.
Limitation on liability of persons engaged in,
§143-215.93A(a).
Volunteer immunity, §§1-539.10, 1-539.11.

GOOD TIME CREDITS.
Prisons and prisoners.
Allowance of time and privileges, §148-13.

GOODWILL INDUSTRIES.
Property taxes.
Exclusion, §105-275.

GOOSEBERRIES.
Standard weight and measure, §81A-42.

GOVERNMENTAL ACCOUNTABILITY.
State governmental accountability and
internal control act, §§143D-1 to 143D-12.
See STATE GOVERNMENTAL
ACCOUNTABILITY AND INTERNAL
CONTROL ACT.

GOVERNMENTAL IMMUNITY.
Generally.
See SOVEREIGN IMMUNITY.
Tort claims against state.
Generally, §§143-291 to 143-300.1A.
See CLAIMS AGAINST THE STATE.

GOVERNMENT EMPLOYEES INTERCHANGE
PROGRAM, §§126-51 to 126-58.
See PERSONNEL SYSTEM.

GOVERNOR.
Absence from state.
Acting governor, §147-11.1(a), (c).
Acting governor, §147-11.1(a), (b).
Actions against government.
Employment of counsel in cases where state is
interested, §147-17(a).
Allocation of authority between counsel and
state client, §147-17(d).
Final decision making authority.
Designating counsel with, §147-17(d).
Payment of counsel, §147-17(c).
Alcoholic beverages.
State of emergency.
Powers of governor, §18B-110.
Archives and history.
Historical publications.
Editing and publishing of official messages and
other papers of governor, §121-6(b).
Security of historic properties.
Designated employees commissioned special
peace officers by governor, §121-10(a).
Attorneys at law.
Impracticability of representing state entity.
Advice to governor to employ outside counsel,
§147-17.
Balanced growth policy act.
Citizen participation.
Governor to establish process, §143-506.11.
Designation of growth centers, §143-506.10.

GOVERNOR —Cont'd
Banks.
Holidays.
Power to proclaim banking holidays, §53-77.
Bond issues.
Council of state.
Duties performed by other officers, §142-9.
Books and papers.
General assembly.
Production before, §147-14.
Bounty hunters.
Authorized to employ, §15-53.
Budget of state.
Adjustments to budget.
Transfers within Governor's office, §143C-6-4(h).
Change in gubernatorial administration.
Duties of outgoing governor, §143C-3-5(g).
Director of the budget, §143C-2-1(a).
Generally, §§143C-1-1 to 143C-10-3.
See STATE BUDGET.
Capital facilities finance agency.
Private capital facilities finance act.
Annual report to, §159D-53.
CLE exemption, Bar Rule D.1517.
Closing forests and woodlands to fishing,
hunting and trapping.
Authority of governor, §106-908.
Commander in chief, NC Const Art XII §1.
Commissioner of banks.
Appointment, §53-92.
Compensation.
Salary and expense allowance, §147-11(a) to (c).
Surviving spouses of governors, §147-32.
Composer-laureate for state.
Appointment, §143-407.1(a).
Consolidation of state agencies.
Authority to direct agencies to consolidate,
§147-13.1(c).
Studies as to consolidation of agencies.
Authority to conduct, expenditure of funds,
§147-13.1(a), (b).
Continuing legal education exemption, Bar
Rule D.1517.
Contractors.
Plumbing, heating and fire sprinkler contractors.
Board of examiners.
Appointment of members, §87-16.
Contracts to obtain consultant services.
Approval required, §143-64.20(b).
Findings to be made by governor, §143-64.21.
Council of state.
General provisions.
See COUNCIL OF STATE.
Crime commission, §143A-244.
Delinquent and undisciplined juveniles.
Transferring juvenile from jail or penal facility to
residential facility, §7B-2517.
Depositions.
Reading deposition on trial.
When deposition may be read on the trial,
§8-83.
Detainers.
Designation of central administrator, §15A-766.
Disasters.
State of disaster.
Declaring, powers, §166A-6.
State of disaster assistance funds, §166A-6.01.
District court judges.
Vacancy in office.
Appointment from nominations submitted from
district bar, §7A-142.

GOVERNOR —Cont'd
Duties.
Generally, §147-12(a).
Elections, NC Const Art III §2.
Date of election, §163-1(a).
Governor-elect and lieutenant governor-elect.
Office space and expenses, §147-31.1.
Summary of duties.
Counting votes, canvassing, abstracts and
protests, §163-182.17(f).
Vacancy in office.
Election to fill, §163-8.
Emergencies.
Energy crisis administration, §§113B-20 to
113B-24.
Evacuation of public buildings.
Power of governor to order evacuation,
§14-288.19(a).
Penalty for willful refusal to leave building,
§14-288.19(b).
State of emergency.
Alcoholic beverages.
Powers of governor, §18B-110.
Succession to office of governor, §147-11.1(a) to (f).
Emergency management.
Mutual aid agreements.
Power to establish, §166A-10(a), (a1).
Powers, §166A-5.
State of disaster.
Declaring, powers, §166A-6.
State of disaster assistance funds, §166A-6.01.
Emergency war powers.
Citation of article, §147-33.1.
Construction of article, §147-33.6.
Description of powers, §147-33.2.
Federal action controlling, §147-33.5.
Immunities granted, §147-33.4.
Orders, §147-33.3.
Powers.
Description, §147-33.2.
Rules and regulations, §147-33.3.
Short title, §147-33.1.
**Endangering executive, legislative or court
officers,** §§14-16.6 to 14-16.10.
Electronic surveillance orders, §15A-290(c4).
Energy crisis administration, §§113B-20 to
113B-24.
Execution sales.
Notification of governor, §1-339.55.
Executive Mansion.
Department of cultural resources.
Authority of department of administration not
affected, §143-415.
Powers, §143-411.
Purposes, §143-410.
Generally, §147-10.
Western governor's mansion, §143-345.7.
Executive mansion fine arts committee.
Appointments, §143B-80.
Compensation of members, §143B-80.
Creation, §143B-79.
Meetings.
Regular and special meetings, §143B-80.1.
Members, §143B-80.
Powers and duties, §143B-79.
Quorum, §143B-80.
Regular and special meetings, §143B-80.1.
Selection of members, §143B-80.
Executive orders.
Orders creating boards, committees, councils or
commissions.
Expiration of order, §147-16.2(a).

GOVERNOR —Cont'd
Executive orders —Cont'd
Publication, §147-16.1.
Executive organization act of 1971.
See STATE DEPARTMENTS AND AGENCIES.
Executive organization act of 1973.
See STATE DEPARTMENTS AND AGENCIES.
Expenses.
Allowance, §147-11(a).
Lieutenant governor, §147-33.
Governor-elect and lieutenant governor-elect,
§147-31.1.
Representation of governor's office.
Allowance to designated person, §147-11(c).
Extradition.
Duty, §15A-742.
Fugitives from other states.
Duty as to, §15A-722.
Investigation.
Governor may cause investigation to be made,
§15A-724.
Generally, §§15A-721 to 15A-750.
See EXTRADITION.
Federal aid.
Highway safety act of 1966.
Contracts with United States government,
§147-12(a).
Forests and forestry.
Authority to close forests and woodlands to
hunting, fishing and trapping, §106-909.
Forests and woodlands.
Authority to close to hunting, fishing and
trapping, §106-908.
General assembly.
Approval of bills, §120-29.1(a).
Calculation of time for approval, §120-29.1(d).
Failure to take action, §120-29.1(b).
Objections of governor, §120-29.1(c).
Books to be produced for general assembly,
§147-14.
Executive officer's report to governor.
Reports transmitted to general assembly,
§147-5.
Reconvening of legislature, NC Const Art II §22,
Art III §5.
Request that session not be held, §120-6.1(a),
(b).
Veto, NC Const Art II §22.
Geologists.
Board for licensing of geologists.
Appointment and removal of members,
§89E-4(b).
Gifts.
Executive Mansion.
Department of cultural resources, §143-411.
**Governor's administrative rules review
commission.**
Executive organization act of 1973.
Administrative services to commissions.
Provisions inapplicable to governor's
administrative rules review commission,
§143B-14.
Review of rules, §143B-2.
Governor's management council, §§143B-426.22,
143B-426.23.
Highway patrol.
Appointment of commanding officer, §20-185(a).
Patrolmen assigned to governor's office, §20-189.
Housing authorities and projects.
Indian housing authority.
Powers of governor, §157-67.

GOVERNOR —Cont'd
Housing coordination and policy council,
§§122A-5.10 to 122A-5.12.
Impeachment, NC Const Art III §3.
Chief justice.
Presiding officer, §123-2.
Inaugural ceremonies committee, §§143-532 to
143-539.
Indians.
Designation of Indian day, §147-18.
Institute of medicine.
Appointment of members, §90-470.
Internal improvements.
Control of internal improvements, §124-1.
Investigation of corporations.
Power of investigation, §124-7.
Proxies.
Appointment of proxies, etc., §124-6(a).
**Interstate compact for adult offender
supervision.**
Appointment of compact administrator,
§148-65.6(a1).
Execution of compact, §148-65.5.
Executive orders for implementation, §148-65.6(f).
**Interstate compact on the placement of
children.**
Appointment of compact administrator, §7B-3806.
**Joint legislative commission on governmental
operations.**
Prior consultation with commission required.
Action without prior consultation, §120-76.1(a).
License plate.
Special plate, number, §20-79.5.
Management council, §§143B-426.22,
143B-426.23.
Mentally ill.
Succession to office of governor, §147-11.1(c).
Military affairs.
Commander in chief, NC Const Art III §5, Art XII
§1.
Militia.
Commander in chief of militia, §127A-16(a).
Regulations prescribed, §127A-17.
Personal staff of governor, §127A-18.
State active duty status.
Power to place in, §127A-16(b).
State defense militia.
Authority to organize and maintain state
defense militia, §127A-80.
Cadre, §127A-81.
Motor vehicles.
Furnished with driver, §147-10.
Municipalities.
Council.
Filling vacancies on council, §160A-63.
National guard.
Distinguished service medal by governor,
§127A-42.
Natural History Museum.
Advisory commission.
Appointment of members, §143B-344.18.
Nomination of officers.
Timely nominations required where legislative
body must confirm, §147-16.3.
Notaries, §143A-23.
Office.
Space and expenses for governor-elect and
lieutenant governor-elect, §147-31.1.
Office of the information technology services.
General provisions, §§147-33.75 to 147-33.104A.
See INFORMATION TECHNOLOGY
SERVICES.

GOVERNOR —Cont'd
Official correspondence.
Preservation, §147-14.
**Oil pollution and hazardous substances
control.**
Offshore oil and gas activities, §143-215.94II.
Pardons.
Application made to governor in writing, §147-21.
Conditional pardon, §147-23.
Duties of governor when conditions of pardon
violated, §147-24.
Duties, NC Const Art III §5.
Return to governor's office, §147-25.
Pensions.
Surviving spouses, §147-32.
Personnel.
Appointment, §147-12(a).
Competitive service.
Determination of competitive service by
governor, §126-12.
Personnel system.
Exemption of employees of office of governor,
§126-5(c1).
Exempt policymaking positions, §126-5(d).
Pest control.
Compact.
Executive head means governor, §106-65.61.
Pesticides.
Appointment of board, §143-436(b).
Portraits.
Acquisition of portrait of governor during term of
office, §121-13.
Presidential elections.
Appointment of electors, §163-213(b), (c).
Prisons and prisoners.
Transfer of convicted foreign citizens under treaty.
Consent by governor, §148-122.
Transfer of property.
Governor to have final authority, §148-3(a).
Private secretary.
Appointment, §147-14.
Salary, §147-15.
Probate and registration.
Sister state probates without governor's
authentication, §47-80.
Publication of executive orders, §147-16.1.
Public lands.
Conveyances.
Approval, §146-74.
Deeds.
Signing of deeds, §146-75.
Employment of personnel, §146-67.
United States.
Acquisitions for and conveyances to federal
government, §146-36.
Public officers and employees.
Appointments, §147-12(a).
Public utilities.
Utilities commission.
Executive director, §62-15(a).
Reconvening of legislature, NC Const Art II §22,
Art III §5.
Request that session not be held, §120-6.1(a), (b).
Records, §147-16(a).
Official government records.
Preservation, §147-14.
Reports.
State departments and agencies.
Certain institutions to report to governor,
§143-156.

GOVERNOR —Cont'd

Residence, §147-10.
Western residence of the governor.
Repair and reconstruction, §143-345.7.
Retirement system for appellate division.
Emergency justices or judges.
Application to the governor, §7A-39.6.
Rewards.
Fugitives from justice.
Power to offer rewards, §§15-53, 15-53.1.
Richard Caswell memorial commission.
Department of cultural resources.
Transfer of commission to department,
§143B-51.
Riots and civil disorders.
Evacuation of public buildings.
Penalty for willful refusal to leave building,
§14-288.19(b).
Power of governor to order evacuation,
§14-288.19(a).
Rules and regulations.
Emergency war powers, §147-33.3.
Salary, §147-11(a) to (c).
Administrative officers.
Governor to set salaries, §138-4.
Exceptions, §138-4.
Longevity pay, §138-4.
Lieutenant governor, §147-33.
Private secretary, §147-15.
School buses.
Use by state guard or national guard.
Request by governor, §115C-254.
Seals.
Affixing great seal, §147-27.
Courts.
Procuring seals for departments and courts,
§147-28.
Custody of great seal of state, §147-12(a).
Description.
Great seal, §147-26.
Great seal.
Affixing great seal, §147-27.
Dates appearing upon seal, §147-26.
Description, §147-26.
Destruction of old seal, §147-30.
Procuring great seal of state, §147-26.
New seals when necessary, §147-30.
Old seals.
Destruction, §147-30.
Procuring great seal of state, §147-26.
Secretary of state.
Seal of department of state.
Description, §147-29.
Secretary of state.
Duties.
Transfer of duties to department of secretary of
state, §143A-23.
Powers.
Transfer to department of secretary of state,
§143A-23.
Receiving documents from governor, §147-36.
Staff.
Appointment, §147-12(a).
State banking commission.
Appointment of members, §53-92.
State board of education.
Appointment of members, §115C-10.
State boundaries.
Establishment of boundaries, §141-1.
Jurisdiction over territory within state, §141-6(c).
Protection of boundaries, §141-1.

GOVERNOR —Cont'd

State debt.
Duties performed by other officers, §142-9.
Emergencies.
Borrowing on notes in emergencies, §142-16.
Signing certificates and bonds, §142-9.
State departments and agencies.
Bond issues.
Approval by governor, §143-165.
Consolidation of state agencies.
Powers of governor, §147-13.1(a) to (c).
Executive organization act of 1973.
Continuation of powers and duties, §143B-5.
Policy-making authority and administrative
powers of governor, §143B-4.
Powers and duties, §§143B-4, 143B-5.
Investigations.
Authority to direct, §143-159.
Conduct, §143-160.
Reports.
Certain institutions to report to governor,
§143-156.
State of disaster.
Declaring, powers, §166A-6.
State of disaster assistance funds, §166A-6.01.
State personnel system.
Exempt employees of office of governor,
§126-5(c1).
State treasurer.
Additional clerical assistance authorized, §147-86.
Succession to office, §147-11.1, NC Const Art III
§3.
Acting governor generally, §147-11.1(c) to (f).
Lieutenant governor, §147-11.1(a).
President of senate, speaker of house or other
officers, §147-11.1(b).
Surviving spouse of governors.
Compensation, §147-32.
Term of office, §163-1(a).
Thanksgiving day.
Designation, §147-19.
United States.
Highway safety act of 1966.
Contracts with United States government,
§147-12(a).
University of North Carolina.
Board of governors.
Member emeritus, serving on board after
serving as governor, §116-6(g).
Vacancy in office.
Filling, §163-8.
Veto, NC Const Art II §22.
War powers act, §§147-33.1 to 147-33.6.
Work first program.
Duty to sign state plan and submit to federal
officials, §108A-27.10(c).

GOVERNOR MOREHEAD SCHOOL,
§§143B-164.10 to 143B-164.18.
ABC's program.
Annual performance goals, §143B-146.3.
Defined, §143B-146.1(b).
Participation, §143B-146.2.
Admission of pupils, §143B-164.13.
Nonresidents, §143B-164.14.
Age.
Compulsory attendance, §115C-383(a).
Board of directors.
Chairman, §143B-164.12(b).
Clerical and other assistants provided by
secretary of department, §143B-164.12(e).

GOVERNOR MOREHEAD SCHOOL —Cont'd
Board of directors —Cont'd
Created, §143B-164.11(a).
Expense reimbursement, §143B-164.12(d).
Meetings, §143B-164.12(c).
Membership, §143B-164.12(a).
Powers and duties, §143B-164.11(a).
Private nonprofit corporations to support
institution.
Encouragement, §143B-164.11(c).
Quorum, §143B-164.12(c).
Rulemaking, §143B-164.11(a), (b).
Vice-chairman, §143B-164.12(b).
Calendars, §143B-146.11.
Clothing or traveling expenses.
Counties paying for, §143B-164.17.
Compulsory attendance, §115C-383(a).
Criminal history checks of personnel,
§143B-146.16.
Diplomas or marks of achievement.
Conferring upon graduates, §143B-164.15.
Dispute resolution, §143B-146.15.
Education programs in residential schools.
Generally, §§143B-146.1 to 143B-146.21.
See EDUCATION.
Incorporation, §143B-164.10.
Low-performing residential schools,
§§143B-146.5 to 143B-146.9.
Dismissal of administrators and teachers at
residential schools identified as
low-performing, §115C-325(p1).
Managed by department of health and human
services and director of school,
§143B-164.10.
Minimum attendance, §115C-383(a).
Mission, §143B-146.1.
Name, §143B-164.10.
Nonresidents.
Admission of pupils from other states,
§143B-164.14.
Parent, guardian or custodian.
Failure to enroll child, §115C-383(b).
Failure to send child to school, §115C-383(c).
Private nonprofit corporations to support
institution.
Encouragement by board of directors,
§143B-164.11(c).
Establishment, §143B-164.18.
Reports on blind children.
Local school superintendents, §115C-383(d).
School technology plans, §143B-146.13.
Treasurer of institution.
State treasurer ex officio treasurer, §143B-164.16.

GOVERNOR RICHARD CASWELL MEMORIAL
COMMISSION.
Department of cultural resources.
Transfer of commission to department, §143B-51.

GOVERNOR'S ADVISORY COUNCIL ON
AGING, §§143B-180, 143B-181.

GOVERNOR'S CRIME COMMISSION,
§§143B-1100 to 143B-1102.
Adjunct committees, §143B-1102(a).
Actions and recommendations.
Subjection final approval of commission,
§143B-1102(e).
Composition, §143B-1102(b).
Powers and duties, §143B-1102(c).
Removal of members, §143B-1102(d).
Terms, §143B-1102(b).

GOVERNOR'S CRIME COMMISSION —Cont'd
Appointed members, §143B-1100(b).
Chairman, vice-chairman, §143B-1100(b).
Comprehensive statewide plan.
Improvement of criminal justice, duties,
§143B-1101(a).
Corrections planning committee, §143B-1102(a).
Powers and duties, §143B-1102(c).
Created, §143B-1100(a).
Directives of commission.
Administration, §143B-1101(b).
Gang activities, gang prevention.
Powers and duties, §143B-1101(a).
Judicial planning committee, §143B-1102(a).
Powers and duties, §143B-1102(c).
Juvenile code revision committee,
§143B-1102(a).
Powers and duties, §143B-1102(c).
Juvenile justice planning committee,
§143B-1102(a).
Powers and duties, §143B-1102(c).
Law enforcement planning committee,
§143B-1102(a).
Powers and duties, §143B-1102(c).
Meetings, §143B-1100(e).
Members, §143B-1100(a).
Nonvoting members, §143B-1100(a).
Powers and duties, §143B-1101(a).
Quorum, §143B-1100(e).
Removal of members, §143B-1100(d).
Selection of members, §143B-1100(b).
State ethics act.
Treatment as board for purposes of, §143B-1100(f).
Terms of members, §143B-1100(c).
Transfer to department of public safety,
§143A-244.
Voting members, §143B-1100(a).

GOVERNOR'S MANAGEMENT COUNCIL,
§§143B-426.22, 143B-426.23.

GOVERNOR'S SCHOOL OF NORTH
CAROLINA.
Tuition for attending, §115C-12.

GPS.
Portable consumer electronic devices
insurance.
Claims handling, adjuster licenses, §58-33-27.
Generally, §§58-44A-1 to 58-44A-25.
See PORTABLE CONSUMER ELECTRONIC
DEVICES INSURANCE.
Satellite-based monitoring.
Interference with electronic monitoring devices,
§14-226.3.
Probation, post-release supervision, parole.
See SATELLITE-BASED MONITORING.
Sex offender monitoring generally, §§14-208.40 to
14-208.45.
See SEX OFFENDER MONITORING.

GRADE CROSSINGS.
Controlled-access facilities.
Elimination of grade crossings, §136-89.53.
Elimination or safeguarding of crossings,
§136-20.
Railroad grade crossings.
Motor vehicle traffic regulation generally,
§§20-142.1 to 20-142.5.
See RAILROAD GRADE CROSSINGS.

GRADES AND GRADING.
Eggs, §§106-245.14 to 106-245.16.

GRADES AND GRADING —Cont'd
Farm products marketing and branding.
Aggregate state service credit for graders, §106-190.1.
Authorized graders, §106-190.
Certificate of grade.
Prima facie evidence, §106-192.
Establishment and maintenance of standard grades, §§106-185(a), 106-188.
Milk, §§106-267, 106-268, 106-268.1.
Poultry and poultry products, §106-546.

GRAFFITI.
Damage to property generally.
See VANDALISM.

GRAHAM COUNTY.
Ambulances.
Attachment or garnishment and lien for, §§44-51.4 to 44-51.8.
Obtaining ambulance services without intending to pay, §14-111.2.
Requesting ambulances falsely, §14-111.3.
Board of county commissioners.
Filling vacancies on board, §153A-27.1.
Condemnation or acquisition of land by local government unit outside county.
Consent of board of commissioners necessary, §153A-15.
Coroner elected as nominee of political party.
Filling vacancy in office, §152-1.
Counties generally.
See COUNTIES.
County boards of education elected on partisan basis.
Vacancies in office, §115C-37.1.
Dog collars.
Unlawful removal of electronic dog collars, §14-401.17.
Foxes, open seasons for taking.
Wildlife resources commission authorized to continue from year to year, §113-291.4(f1).
Oil, gas or mineral claims.
Certain ancient claims extinguished, preservation, procedure, §1-42.3(a) to (d).
Registration of deeds.
Tax certification, no delinquent taxes due, §161-31(b).
School property.
Acquisition and improvement, §153A-158.1.
Sheriff.
Vacancy, performance of duties until vacancy filled, §162-5.1.
Western North Carolina Development Association, Inc.
Appropriation of funds to, §153A-447(a), (b).
Western North Carolina regional economic development commission, §§158-8.1 to 158-8.8.

GRAIN.
Adulteration, §§106-621 to 106-628.
See GRAIN ADULTERATION.
Commodities.
General provisions, §§78D-1 to 78D-33.
See COMMODITIES.
Larceny.
Ungathered crops, §14-78.
Liens.
Effective period, §44-69.1.

GRAIN ADULTERATION.
Applicability of article, §106-628.

GRAIN ADULTERATION —Cont'd
Commissioner.
Defined, §106-621.
Sign furnished by commissioner, §106-624.
Defenses.
Nonposting not a defense, §106-626.
Definitions, §106-621.
Determination of adulteration, §106-627.
Sampling and analysis, §106-627.
Penalties, §106-623.
Posting of sign, §106-625.
Nonposting not a defense, §106-626.
Prohibited acts, §106-622.
Sampling and analysis.
Determination of adulteration, §106-627.
Signs.
Furnished by commissioner, §106-624.
Nonposting not a defense, §106-626.
Posting of sign, §106-625.
Terms of article, §106-628.
Unlawful acts, §106-622.

GRAIN ALCOHOL.
Use for compounding, mixing or preserving medicines or medical preparations.
Exemptions from alcoholic beverage control regulations, §18B-103.

GRAIN DEALERS, §§106-601 to 106-615.
Bond.
Application for license, §106-604.
Action on bond, §106-605(b).
Execution of bond, §106-605(a).
Exemption, §106-604.
Form of bond, §106-605(a).
Terms of bond, §106-605(a).
Commissioner.
Authority to investigate, §106-612.
Defined, §106-601(b).
Decal on truck or tractor-trailer unit, §106-606.
Definitions.
Cash buyer, §106-601(a).
Commissioner, §106-601(b).
Department, §106-601(c).
Grain, §106-601(d).
Grain dealer, §106-601(e).
Person, §106-601(f).
Producer, §106-601(g).
Injunction for violations of article, §106-615.
Investigations.
Authority to investigate, §106-612.
Licenses.
Application for license, §106-603.
Bond required, §106-604.
Action on bond, §106-605(b).
Execution, terms and form of bond, §106-605(a).
Exemption, §106-604.
Fee, §106-604.
Bond required, §106-604.
Action on bond, §106-605(b).
Execution, terms and form of bond, §106-605(a).
Exemption, §106-604.
Decal on truck or tractor-trailer unit, §106-606.
Denial.
Procedure, §106-611(a).
Fees, §106-604.
Disposition of fees, §106-608.
Renewal of license, §106-607.
Grounds for refusal, suspension or revocation of license, §106-610.

GRAIN DEALERS —Cont'd
Licenses —Cont'd
Operation without license unlawful, §106-615.
  Injunction for violation, §106-615.
Posting of license, §106-606.
Refusal of license.
  Grounds for refusal, §106-610.
Renewal of license, §§106-603, 106-607.
  Fees, §106-607.
    Disposition of fees, §106-608.
Required, §106-602.
Revocation of license.
  Grounds for revocation, §106-610.
  Obtaining another license, time period,
    §106-611(b).
  Procedure, §106-611(a).
Suspension of license.
  Grounds for suspension, §106-610.
  Procedure, §106-611(a).
  Time limit, §106-611(b).
Misdemeanors, §106-614.
Recorders to be kept by dealers, §106-609.
Rules and regulations.
Adoption, §106-613.
Uniform scale ticket.
Board may prescribe form, §106-609.
Injunction, §106-615.

GRAIN MILLS.
Mills generally, §§73-1 to 73-28.
See MILLS.

GRAMM-LEACH-BLILEY ACT.
**Affiliations between depository institutions
  and insurers,** §58-19-2.

GRANARIES.
Arson, §14-62.

GRANDCHILDREN.
Adoption, §50-13.2A.
Biological grandparent, §50-13.2A.
Child custody and visitation.
Grandparents visitation rights, §§50-13.2(b1),
  50-13.5(j).
Incest, §14-178.

GRAND JURY.
Challenges to panel.
Provisions governing, §15A-622(a).
Confidentiality of information.
Bill of indictment, §15A-623(f).
Disclosure of information.
  Contempt, §15A-623(g).
Secrecy of proceedings, §15A-623(e).
Constitution of the United States, US Const
  Amd 5.
Contempt.
Confidentiality of information.
  Unauthorized disclosures, §15A-623(g).
Continuing criminal enterprise.
Examination of witnesses by prosecutor,
  §15A-623(h).
Petition for convening of grand jury, §15A-622.
Defined, §15A-621.
Deliberations, secret listening, §§14-227.2,
  14-227.3.
Discharge of grand jurors, §15A-622(c).
Drugs.
Controlled substances.
  Examination of witnesses by prosecutor,
    §15A-623(h).
  Petition for convening of grand jury, §15A-622.

GRAND JURY —Cont'd
Duties, §15A-628(a).
Evidence, rules of.
Inapplicability, §8C-1 Rule 1101(b).
Excusing grand juror from service, §15A-622(d).
Facts.
Exclusive judge of fact, §15A-624(a).
Fees.
Uniform fees for jurors, §7A-312(a).
  Waiver, §7A-312(b).
Foreman.
Appointment, §15A-622(e).
Duties, §15A-623(b), (c).
Oaths.
  Form of oath, §11-11.
Signature.
  Indictments.
    Signature attesting concurrence of twelve or
      more grand jurors, §15A-644(a).
  Presentments.
    Signature of foreman attesting concurrence of
      twelve or more grand jurors, §15A-644(c).
Impaneling, §15A-622(b).
Provisions governing, §15A-622(a).
Second grand jury, §15A-622(b).
Indictments.
Confidentiality of information.
  Bill of indictment, §15A-623(f).
Foreman.
  Signature, §15A-644(a).
Notice.
  True bill of indictment.
    Notice to defendant, §15A-630.
Number of members required to concur,
  §15A-623(a).
Return of bill of indictment, §15A-628(a), (c).
  Not true bill, §15A-628(a).
    Institution of new charge, §15A-629(b).
    Procedure upon finding of not true bill,
      §15A-629(a).
  True bill, §15A-628(a).
    Notice to defendant, §15A-630.
Submission of bill of indictment by prosecutor,
  §15A-627(a).
  Offenses within original jurisdiction of superior
    court, §15A-627(b).
True bill.
  Return as not true bill, §15A-628(a).
    Institution of new charge, §15A-629(b).
    Procedure upon, §15A-629(a).
  Return as true bill, §15A-628(a).
    Notice to defendant, §15A-630.
Validity inquiry.
  Testimony of jurors, §8C-1 Rule 606.
Instructions to grand jurors, §15A-622(f).
Interpreters.
Permitted in grand jury room during proceedings,
  §15A-623(d).
Investigations.
Powers, §15A-628(a).
Journalist's qualified privilege, §8-53.11.
Judges.
Presiding or convening judge as legal advisor,
  §15A-624(b).
Judicial department.
Superior court division.
  Sessions of court in cities other than county
    seats, §7A-42(e).
Meetings.
Meetings of public bodies.
  Exceptions to provisions, §143-318.18.

GRAND JURY —Cont'd
Notice.
Indictments.
Notice to defendant of true bill of indictment, §15A-630.
Number of grand jurors, §15A-621.
Actions or decisions.
Number required to concur, §15A-623(a).
Oaths.
Foreman and other grand jurors, §15A-622(f).
Form of oath, §11-11.
Persons permitted in grand jury room.
Oath of secrecy, §15A-623(d).
Officers.
Oaths.
Form of oath, §11-11.
Persons permitted in grand jury room during proceedings, §15A-623(d).
Powers, §15A-628(a), (b).
Reconvening, §15A-622(g).
Records.
Matters returned by grand jury to judge.
Clerk to keep, §15A-628(d).
Rules of evidence.
Inapplicability, §8C-1 Rule 1101(b).
Secrecy, §15A-623.
Selection of grand jurors, §15A-622(b).
Provisions governing, §15A-622(a).
Shortening term of grand jury, §15A-622(b).
Subpoenas.
Witnesses, §15A-626(e).
Superior court division of judicial department.
Sessions of court in cities other than county seats, §7A-42(e).
Venue.
Indictment or presentment, §15A-631.
War.
Presentment as dispensable in certain cases, US Const Amd 4.
Witnesses, §15A-626.
Deposing before grand jury.
Form of oath of witness, §11-11.
Immunity, §15A-1053.
Members of grand jury, §15A-626(c).
Prosecution witnesses, §15A-626(b).
Right to call witness or appear as witness, §15A-626(a), (d).
Subpoenas, §15A-626(e).

GRAND LARCENY.
Larceny generally, §§14-70 to 14-86.1.
See LARCENY.

GRAND LODGE OF ANCIENT, FREE AND ACCEPTED MASONS OF NORTH CAROLINA.
Property tax exclusion, §105-275.

GRANDPARENTS.
Abortion.
Parental consent to abortion.
Consent of grandparent when minor living with required, §90-21.7(a).
Adoption.
Action by biological grandparents, §50-13.2A.
Visitation rights of biological grandparents of adoptee, §48-1-106(f).
Child custody and visitation.
Adoption proceedings, §50-13.2A.
Grandparent defined, §50-13.5(j).
Visitation rights, §§50-13.2(b1), 50-13.5(j).
Incest, §14-178.

GRANDPARENTS' VISITATION RIGHTS,
§§50-13.2(b1), 50-13.5(j).
Adoption proceedings, §50-13.2A.
Grandparent defined, §50-13.5(j).

GRANITE.
State rock, §145-10.

GRANTS.
Abandoned manufactured homes.
Identification, deconstruction, recycling, disposal.
Reimbursement to local governments, §130A-309.115.
Alcoholism.
Research authority.
Applications for grants, §122C-433.
Archives and history.
Department of cultural resources, §121-12.1.
Responsibility for administering appropriations for grants-in-aid, §121-12.1.
Expending appropriations for grants-in-aid, §121-12.2.
Bees and honey.
Authority of board to accept, §106-637.
Blind persons.
Aid to the blind.
Affording maximum federal aid, §111-29.
Federal aid, §111-24.
Rehabilitation center for the blind and visually impaired.
Authority to receive federal grants-in-aid, §111-6.1.
Block grants.
Department of administration duties and powers, §143-341.
Budget of state.
Federal block grants, §143C-7-2.
Grant funds administration, §143C-6-23.
Burke county.
Copies of grant.
Admission into evidence, §8-10.
Children's health insurance program.
Outreach efforts, §108A-70.26(b).
Coastal area management.
Planning grants, §113A-112.
Community colleges.
Federal contracts and grants, §115D-58.1.
Financial assistance for students, §115D-40.1.
Community development block grants,
§143B-437.04.
Counties.
Contracts.
Acceptance of grants and loans from other governments, §153A-14.
Public health or mental health grants from federal government.
Recovery of indirect costs on certain grants by counties, §130A-8(a).
Exception, §130A-8(b).
Criminal justice education and training standards.
Authority to accept, §17C-12.
Domestic violence.
Domestic violence center fund, §50B-9.
Dropout prevention grants, §§115C-64.7 to 115C-64.9.
Duke medical school, grants to students,
§116-21.6.
Economic and community development department.
Block grants, §143B-437.04.
Main street solutions fund, §143B-472.35.

GRANTS —Cont'd
Economic and community development department —Cont'd
Power to apply for and accept, §143B-431(d).
Education.
State board of education.
Power to accept grants, §115C-410.
Education access rewards North Carolina scholars fund, §116-209.26.
Electric membership corporations.
Application for grant or loan from governmental agency, §117-26.
Electrologists.
Acceptance by board of electrologist examiners, §88A-8.
Employment and training grant program.
Workforce development, §143B-438.13.
Energy.
Policy act of 1975.
Council.
Authority to apply and utilize, §113B-11(c).
Evidence.
See EVIDENCE.
Facility authorities.
Powers of authority, §160A-480.4.
Family preservation.
Awarding to local agencies, §143B-150.6(d).
Financing family preservation services, §143B-150.5(c).
Fishery resource grant program, §113-200.
General assembly.
Legislative commissions and committees.
Applying for, receiving or accepting, §120-32.03(a), (b).
Health.
Federal public health or mental health grants.
Counties to recover indirect costs, §130A-8(a).
Applicability of section, §130A-8(b).
Grants-in-aid, §130A-7.
Public health or mental health grants from federal government.
Counties to recover indirect costs on certain grants, §130A-8(a).
Health and human services department.
Requests for grants by head of department, §143B-139.2.
Hospital authorities.
Contracts with federal government, §131E-27.
Hospitals.
Construction and enlargement of local hospitals, §131E-70(c), (e).
Housing finance agency.
Receipt, administration and compliance with conditions and requirements of grant.
General power of agency, §122A-5.
Job development investment grant program, §§143B-437.50 to 143B-437.63.
Justice department.
Justice academy, §17D-3.
Local government finance.
Anticipation notes, §§159-171, 159-172.
Defined, §159-13.2(a).
Ordinances, §§159-13.2, 159-17.
Mental health, developmental disability, substance abuse.
Area authorities.
Appropriations.
Allocation of funds, §122C-147.1(d).
Moore county.
Copies of grants.
Admission into evidence, §8-11.

GRANTS —Cont'd
Mosquito control districts.
Receipt of federal and state grants.
Corporate powers of board of commissioners, §130A-355.
Municipalities.
Energy improvements.
Program to finance purchase and installation, §160A-459.1.
Joint municipal electric power and energy act.
Government grants, §159B-32.
Urban development action grants, §160A-457.1.
North Carolina's eastern region.
Authority to apply for, §158-39.
Nutbush conservation area.
Authorized, §143-289.
Onslow county.
Copies of grants.
Admission into evidence, §8-12.
Pollution control.
Sedimentation pollution control act of 1973.
Commission authorized to receive financial and other assistance, §113A-63.
Public lands.
See PUBLIC LANDS.
Roanoke Island historical association.
Authorization to accept, §143-202.
Secretary of state.
Certified copies.
Admission into evidence of copies certified by secretary, §8-6.
Validation of copies of grants certified by clerk, §8-9.
Shellfish.
Cultivation of shellfish.
Leases, §§113-202, 113-206.
Registration of grants in navigable waters, §113-205(a).
Sheriffs' education and training standards commission, §17E-10(b) to (d).
Site development, §143B-437.02.
Solid waste management.
Used oil.
Grants to local governments, §130A-309.22(a) to (d).
Telephone membership corporations.
Loans or grants from federal agencies, §117-32.
Urban redevelopment.
Action grants, §160A-457.1.
Wake Forest medical school, grants to students, §116-21.6.
Water infrastructure.
Loans and grants, §§159G-20 to 159G-67.
See WATER INFRASTRUCTURE.
White goods management account.
Grants to local government, use of account for, §130A-309.83(b) to (d).
Workforce development.
Employment and training grant program, §143B-438.13.
Zoological authority.
Cities and counties, §143-177.2.
Right to receive, §143-177.
Taxation.
Exemption, §143-177.1.

GRANVILLE COUNTY.
Ambulance service.
Attachment or garnishment and lien for, §§44-51.4 to 44-51.8.

GRANVILLE COUNTY —Cont'd
Blank or master forms of mortgages, deeds of trust, etc.
Indexing and recording, inapplicability of provisions, §47-21.
Condemnation or acquisition of land by local government unit outside county.
Consent of board of commissioners necessary, §153A-15.
Game laws, local acts not repealed, §113-133.1(e).
Maps in special proceedings, recording of photographic copies, §§47-32, 47-32.2.
Multi-county water conservation and infrastructure district.
Generally, §158-15.1.
Nutbush conservation area.
Annual contributions to department of environment and natural resources, §143-289.
On-premises unfortified wine licenses.
Discretion to decline to issue, §105-113.71(b).
Probates and registration orders before clerks of inferior courts validated, §47-59.
Registration of deeds.
Tax certification, no delinquent taxes due, §161-31(b).
Room occupancy tax levied by county, uniform provision, §153A-155.
Water and sewer system within Camp Butner reservation, §122C-407(b).
Wild plants, taking of certain plants from land of another.
Inapplicability of provisions, §14-129.

GRAPES.
Weights and measures.
Standard weights and measures, §81A-42.

GRAPHIC ART.
Artwork on consignment, §§25C-1 to 25C-5.
Sale of prints, §§25C-10 to 25C-16.

GRASS.
Criminal trespass.
Setting fire to grass, §14-136.
Fire.
Setting grass on fire, §§14-136 to 14-140.1.
Criminal trespass, §14-136.
Marijuana.
See MARIJUANA.
Seed.
Weights and measures, §81A-42.
Setting fire to grass, brushlands and woodlands, §§14-136 to 14-140.1.

GRASSROOTS ARTS PROGRAM, §§143B-121 to 143B-125.
Adoption of procedures and rules, §143B-123.
Agents, §143B-124.
Counties.
Distribution of funds for counties without organizations meeting department standards, §143B-125.
Distribution of funds, §§143B-122, 143B-125.
Establishment, §143B-121.
Funds.
Designation of organization as official distributing agent, §143B-124.
Disposition of funds for counties without organizations meeting department standards, §143B-125.
Distribution, §143B-122.
Standards for qualification, §143B-123.

GRASSROOTS ARTS PROGRAM —Cont'd
Procedures.
Adoption, §143B-123.
Standards for qualification for funds, §143B-123.

GRASS SEED.
Weights and measures.
Standard weights and measures, §81A-42.

GRATUITIES.
Minimum wage earnings, §95-25.3(f).
Tips defined, §95-25.2.

GRAVESTONES.
Decedents' estates.
Authorized expense of estate, §28A-19-9(a).
Inscription charging crime, §14-401.3.

GRAVEYARDS.
Cemeteries generally.
See CEMETERIES.
Monuments and memorials, §§100-2 to 100-19.
See MONUMENTS AND MEMORIALS.

GRAYWATER.
Policies on reuse of water, §143-355.5.
Rules regulating, §130A-335(b).

GREASES.
Brands and marks.
Juggling mark prohibited, §119-10.
Mixing different brands for sale under standard trade name prohibited, §119-11.
Lubricating oils.
See LUBRICATING OILS.
Penalties.
Aiding and assisting in violation of article, §119-12.
Misdemeanor offenses, §119-13.
Sales.
Advertised name.
Prohibited sale of lubricants different from advertised name, §119-8.
Brands for sale.
Mixing different brands for sale under standard trade name prohibited, §119-11.
Deceptive sale of lubricants as to quality, etc., prohibited, §119-7.
Trademarks.
Juggling trademarks prohibited, §119-10.
Trade names.
Juggling trade names prohibited, §119-10.
Mixing different brands for sale under standard trade name prohibited, §119-11.

GREAT SMOKY MOUNTAINS NATIONAL PARK.
Western North Carolina public lands council, §§143B-324.1 to 143B-324.3.

GREEK INDEPENDENCE DAY.
Public holiday, §103-4(a).

GREENBELT LAW.
Agricultural, horticultural and forestland, §§105-277.2 to 105-277.7.
See PROPERTY TAXES.

GREEN BUSINESS FUND, §§143B-437.4 to 143B-437.8.
Administration, §143B-437.4(a).
Program guidelines, §143B-437.7.
Advisory committee, §143B-437.5.
Agreements required, §143B-437.6.
Cap on grants, §143B-437.4(c).

GREEN BUSINESS FUND —Cont'd
Disbursals from fund.
  Agreements required, §143B-437.6.
Established, §143B-437.4(a).
Matching funds, §143B-437.4(c).
Program guidelines, §143B-437.7.
Purposes, §143B-437.4(b).
Reports, §143B-437.8.

GREENE COUNTY.
Agricultural tendencies in certain counties.
  Terms of, §42-23.
Ambulances.
  Attachment or garnishment and lien for,
    §§44-51.4 to 44-51.8.
  False pretenses and cheats.
    Requesting ambulance falsely, §14-111.3.
**Condemnation or acquisition of land by local
    government unit outside county.**
  Consent of board of commissioners necessary,
    §153A-15.
**Cropper or tenant refusing to perform terms
    of contract.**
  Forfeiture of right of possession to premises,
    §42-27.
Game laws, local acts not repealed,
    §113-133.1(e).
Low-income housing tax credits.
  Qualified building eligible for credit,
    §105-129.41(c).
**Maps in special proceedings, recording of
    photographic copies,** §§47-32, 47-32.2.
North Carolina's eastern region, §§158-30 to
    158-42.
  See NORTH CAROLINA'S EASTERN REGION.
On-premises unfortified wine licenses.
  Discretion to decline to issue, §105-113.71(b).
**Probates and registration orders before clerks
    of inferior courts validated,** §47-59.
Registration of deeds.
  Tax certification, no delinquent taxes due,
    §161-31(b).
School property.
  Acquisition and improvement, §153A-158.1.
Special school tax, election to abolish.
  Petition required, §115C-505.

GREEN LEVEL.
Satellite annexation.
  Limitation on area of satellite corporate limits,
    inapplicability, §160A-58.1(b).

GREENSBORO.
Room occupancy tax.
  Uniform provisions.
    Authorized to levy, §160A-215(g).
    Generally, §160A-215.
Traffic control photographic systems,
    §160A-300.1(d).

GREENVILLE.
Satellite annexation.
  Limitation on area of satellite corporate limits,
    inapplicability, §160A-58.1(b).
Traffic control photographic systems,
    §160A-300.1(d).

GRENADES.
Civil disorders.
  Certain weapons at civil disorders, §14-288.20.
Explosives generally.
  See EXPLOSIVES.
Mass death and destruction weapons.
  Manufacture, assembly, etc., §14-288.8.

GRENADES —Cont'd
Weapons generally.
  See FIREARMS AND OTHER WEAPONS.

GREYHOUND RACING, §14-309.20.
Conducting in state prohibited, §14-309.20(a).
**Interstate or intrastate simulcasting
    prohibited,** §14-309.20(b).
Penalty, §14-309.20(c).

**GRIEVANCE PROCEDURES FOR HEALTH
    INSURERS,** §58-50-62.

GRIEVANCES OF ATTORNEYS.
Attorneys at law.
  Disciplinary rules of state bar generally, Bar
    Rules B.0101 to B.0217.
  See ATTORNEYS AT LAW.

GRIEVANCES OF PRISONERS.
Procedure generally, §§148-118.1 to 148-118.9.
  See PRISONER'S GRIEVANCE PROCEDURE.

GRIFTON SHAD FESTIVAL.
Official state shad festival, §145-33.

GRILLS.
Alcoholic beverage permits, §18B-1000.
Restaurants generally.
  See RESTAURANTS.

GRIMESLAND, TOWN OF.
Satellite annexation.
  Limitation on area of satellite corporate limits,
    inapplicability, §160A-58.1(b).

GRIPS.
Secret societies.
  Use of grips for illegal purposes, §14-12.4.

GRIST MILLS.
Generally, §§73-1 to 73-28.
  See MILLS.

GROCERY STORES.
Alcoholic beverage permits, §18B-1001.
Plastic bag management.
  Retailers.
    Counties containing barrier islands,
      §§130A-309.120 to 130A-309.125.

GROSS RECEIPTS TAX.
**Amusement or entertainment not otherwise
    taxed,** §105-37.1.
**Heavy equipment gross receipts tax in lieu of
    property tax,** §§153A-156.1, 160A-215.2.
Live entertainment for which fee charged,
    §105-37.1.
**Performance, show or exhibition not otherwise
    taxed,** §105-37.1.
Regional transit authority vehicle rental tax,
    §§105-550 to 105-555.
  See REGIONAL TRANSIT AUTHORITY
    VEHICLE RENTAL TAX.
Room occupancy taxes.
  Cities, §160A-215.
Short-term leases and rentals of vehicles.
  Cities levying, §160A-215.1.

GROUND CEDAR.
Trespass.
  Taking, etc., of certain wild plants from land of
    another, §14-129.

GROUND PINE.
Trespass.
  Taking, etc., of certain wild plants from land of
    another, §14-129.

GROUNDWATER.
Construction of water wells, §§87-83 to 87-98.
See WATER WELL CONSTRUCTION.
Drinking water.
See DRINKING WATER.
Underground storage tanks.
Leaking petroleum cleanup.
Groundwater protection loan fund,
§143-215.94P.
Use of water resources.
Regulation generally, §§143-215.11 to
143-215.22B.
See WATER RESOURCE USE REGULATION.

GROUP HOMES FOR THE HANDICAPPED,
§§168-20 to 168-23.
Defined terms, §168-21.
Private agreements, §168-23.
Public policy, §168-20.
Zoning, §168-22.

GROVER.
Room occupancy tax.
Uniform provisions.
Authorized to levy, §160A-215(g).
Generally, §160A-215.

GROWERS AND PRODUCERS ASSOCIATIONS.
Cotton grower's organization, §§106-65.84 to
106-65.91.
Promotion of use and sale of agricultural
products.
Generally, §§106-550 to 106-568.
See AGRICULTURAL PRODUCTS
PROMOTION.

GROWING BUSINESSES TAX CREDITS,
§§105-129.80 to 105-129.89.
Advisory rulings, §105-129.83(k).
Business property investments, §105-129.88.
Double credit, §105-129.88(g).
Eligible investment amount, §105-129.88(b).
Expiration, §105-129.88(d).
General credit, §105-129.88(a).
Threshold, §105-129.88(c).
Transferred property, §105-129.88(e).
Wage standard, §105-129.88(f).
Calculation, §105-129.87(c).
Cap on tax credit, §105-129.84(c).
Carryforward period, §105-129.84(c).
Change in ownership of business, §105-129.83(j).
Company headquarters eligibility,
§105-129.83(b).
Definitions, §105-129.81.
Department reports, §105-129.85(b).
Documentation.
Substantiation, §105-129.86(b).
Double credit, §105-129.87(g).
Eligible business, §105-129.83(a).
Environmental impact, §105-129.83(e).
Equity study, §105-129.82(b).
Expiration, §105-129.83(h).
Filing fee, §105-129.85(a).
Forfeiture, §105-129.83(i).
Health insurance coverage, §105-129.83(d).
Impact study, §105-129.82(b).
Installments, §105-129.87(d).
Legislative reporting, §105-129.82(c).
Overdue tax debts, §105-129.83(g).
Planned expansion, §105-129.83(l).
Public policy, §105-129.80.
Qualified capital intensive corporations,
eligibility, §105-129.83(m).

GROWING BUSINESSES TAX CREDITS
—Cont'd
Qualifying credit, §105-129.87(a).
Real property investments, §105-129.89.
Double credit, §105-129.89(e).
Expiration, §105-129.89(d).
Mixed use property, §105-129.89(c).
Qualifying credit, §105-129.89(a).
Secretary of commerce determination,
§105-129.89(b).
Records.
Substantiation, §105-129.86(a).
Safety and health programs, §105-129.83(f).
Statute of limitations, §105-129.84(d).
Sunset provision, §105-129.82(a).
Tax election, §105-129.84(a).
Tax payment.
Credit treated as, §105-129.84(e).
Threshold, §105-129.87(b).
Transferred jobs, §105-129.87(e).
Wage standard, §§105-129.83(c), 105-129.87.

GROWTH HORMONES.
Biological residues in animals, §§106-549.81 to
106-549.89.
See BIOLOGICAL RESIDUES IN ANIMALS.

GUANACOS.
Llamas classified as livestock.
Definition of llama as including, §106-22.4.

**GUARANTEED ARREST BOND
CERTIFICATES.**
Issuance by motor clubs.
Acceptance in lieu of cash bail or other bond,
§58-69-55(a).
Forfeiture and enforcement, applicable provisions,
§58-69-55(b).
Surety company becoming surety with respect to.
Filing undertaking, amount, §58-69-50(a).
Form of undertaking, §58-69-50(b).

**GUARANTEED ENERGY SAVINGS
CONTRACTS,** §§143-64.17 to 143-64.17M,
143-129.4.
Bonds, surety, §143-64.17B(c), (d).
Continuance of contract, §143-64.17D.
Definitions, §143-64.17.
Duration of contract, §143-64.17D.
Evaluation of sealed proposals, §143-64.17A(b).
Evaluation of use by state agencies,
§143-64.17F(a).
Rule for evaluation, adoption, §143-64.17F(b).
Exclusive nature of provisions, §143-129.4.
Installment and lease purchase contracts,
§143-64.17I.
Interpretation and construction.
Provisions not to limit certain powers of local
governmental units, §143-64.17A(e).
Investment grade audit.
Qualified provider to conduct, §143-64.17B(f).
Maintenance contracts or other maintenance
agreements from qualified provider.
Contract may not require local governmental unit
to purchase, §143-64.17B(e).
Notice.
Entry into contract, §143-64.17B(b).
Requests for proposals, §143-64.17A(a).
Opening of sealed proposals, §143-64.17A(c), (c1).
Payments under contract, §143-64.17E.
Recommendations as to savings.
State energy office, §143-64.17F(c).

**GUARANTEED ENERGY SAVINGS
CONTRACTS** —Cont'd
Reconciliation statement.
Provided annually by qualified provider,
§143-64.17B(g).
Reports, §§143-64.17G, 143-64.17H.
Requests for proposals, §143-64.17A(a).
Requirements, §143-64.17B(a).
Selection of qualified provider.
Factors, §143-64.17A(d).
Shortfalls in savings.
Provider to pay, §143-64.17B(g).
Solicitation, §143-64.17A.
**State appropriations not to be reduced as
result of savings,** §143-64.17E.
State governmental units.
Financing by, §143-64.17J.
Inspection and compliance certification for,
§143-64.17K.
University of North Carolina constituent
institutions, §143-64.17L.
Energy savings analyses required, §143-64.17M.
Termination project.
Investment grade audit.
Results not within guaranteed savings,
§143-64.17B(f).
**University of North Carolina constituent
institutions.**
Authority of board of governors, §143-64.17L(a).
Conditions for authorization, §143-64.17L(a).
Continuing applicability of provisions to contracts,
§143-64.17L(d).
Energy savings analyses required.
Post-implementation, §143-64.17M(b).
Prior to implementation, §143-64.17M(a).
Shortfalls, §143-64.17M(b).
Multiple conservation measures as part of single
project, §143-64.17L(c).
North Carolina State University.
Implementation of measures without contract,
§143-64.17L(e).
Scope of authority, §143-64.17L(b).
Use when feasible.
State agencies, §143-64.17F(a).

GUARANTORS.
Joinder of debtor by surety.
Surety defined to include, §26-12(a).
Notice to creditors to take action, §26-7.
Failure of creditor to take action, §26-9.
How given, prima facie evidence, §26-8.
Surety's recovery on obligation paid.
Surety defined to include, §26-3.1(b).

GUARANTY ASSOCIATION ACT.
**Life and health insurance guaranty
association generally,** §§58-62-2 to 58-62-95.
See LIFE AND HEALTH INSURANCE
GUARANTY ASSOCIATION.

GUARDIAN AD LITEM, §1A-1 Rule 17(b).
Abortion.
Parental consent to abortion.
Petition by guardian ad litem on behalf of
pregnant minor for waiver of parental
consent requirement.
Assistance of court in preparing and filing
petitions, §90-21.8(b).
Proceedings for waiver of parental consent
requirement.
Participation by guardian ad litem on minor's
behalf, §90-21.8(c).

GUARDIAN AD LITEM —Cont'd
Absentees in military service.
Appointment of guardian ad litem by court,
§28B-3(c).
Petition for transfer of property valued at more
than five thousand dollars, §28B-10(d).
**Abused, neglected or dependent juvenile
actions,** §§7B-1200 to 7B-1204.
Advisory committee, §7B-1201(b).
Appointment, duties, §7B-601.
Information, records, reports.
Disclosure, sharing, §7B-700(f).
Local programs.
Administration and establishment, §7B-1201(a).
Alternative plans, §7B-1203.
Conflicts of interest, appointment, §7B-1202.
Office of guardian ad litem services, §7B-1200.
Parent's right.
Appointment, communications, confidentiality
and privilege, practices assisting parent,
§7B-602(b) to (e).
Payment, §7B-603(a) to (c).
Periodic review hearings, placement of juvenile.
Termination of parental rights, §7B-908(b).
Petition alleging abuse, neglect or dependency.
Copy of petition to be provided to guardian ad
litem office, §7B-408.
Volunteers.
Civil liability, §7B-1204.
Administrative office of the courts.
Guardian ad litem program.
Providing services to abused, neglected or
dependent juveniles, §§7B-1200 to 7B-1204.
Adoption.
Adoption of incompetent adults.
Investigation and report to court, §48-5-103(c).
Consent execution for incompetent parents,
§48-3-602.
Representation of adoptee, §48-2-201(b).
Appointment procedure, §1A-1 Rule 17(d).
Discharge and appointment, §35A-1107(a), (b).
**Childhood vaccine-related injury
compensation.**
Filing of claims on behalf of minors or
incompetent persons, §130A-429(a).
Child support.
Relief from order based on nonpaternity.
Guardian ad litem to protect interest of child,
§50-13.13(c).
**Confidentiality and privilege of
communications.**
Abused, neglected or dependent juvenile actions.
Communications between parent, guardian ad
litem and parent's counsel, §7B-602(d).
Termination of parental rights proceedings.
Communications between parent, guardian ad
litem and parent's counsel, §7B-1101.1(d).
**Corporations, trusts or other entities not in
existence,** §1A-1 Rule 17(b), (d).
Costs.
Responsibility of guardian for costs against infant
plaintiff, §6-30.
Decedents' estates.
Unknown heirs and devisees.
Appointment of guardian ad litem, §28A-22-3.
Sale of real property, §28A-17-4.
**Default judgment against infant or
incompetent.**
Appointment required for entry of judgment
against, §1A-1 Rule 55(b).

GUARDIAN AD LITEM —Cont'd
Determination of incompetence.
Attorney as guardian ad litem, §35A-1107(b).
Discharge and appointment, §35A-1107(a), (c).
Domestic relations actions.
When guardian ad litem not required, §1A-1 Rule 17(b).
Duties, §1A-1 Rule 17(e).
Eminent domain.
Public condemnors.
Appointment for infants and incompetents, §40A-50.
Fees, responsibility for payment, §7A-450.1.
Determination of persons responsible, §§7A-450.2, 7A-450.3.
Generally, §1A-1 Rule 17(b).
General or testamentary guardian.
Appointment of guardian ad litem notwithstanding, §1A-1 Rule 17(b).
Incompetence, determination.
Fees, payments, §35A-1116(c1).
Right to an appointment of court-appointed guardian ad litem, §35A-1107(a), (b).
Incompetence, restoration.
Appointment, §35A-1130(c).
Incompetent persons, §§1A-1 Rule 17(b), 35A-1217.
Appointment for incompetent ward.
Guardian not adequately representing ward's interests, §35A-1217.
Appointment procedure, §1A-1 Rule 17(c).
Indigent persons.
Marriage proceedings.
Guardian ad litem for underage parties, §§7A-451(f), 51-2.1.
Interstate compact on juvenile.
Return of escapees or absconders.
Appointment for juvenile, §7B-2805(c).
Judgments and decrees.
Effect where party represented by guardian ad litem, §1A-1 Rule 17(e).
Legitimation of illegitimate children.
Appointment in legitimation proceeding where mother married, §49-12.1(a).
Marriage proceedings.
Guardian ad litem for underage parties, §§7A-451(f), 51-2.1.
Mentally ill, §1A-1 Rule 17(b).
Appointment procedure, §1A-1 Rule 17(c).
Highway projects.
Condemnation proceedings.
Appointment of guardian ad litem, §136-110.
Minors.
Abused, neglected or dependent juvenile actions. See within this heading, "Abused, neglected or dependent juvenile actions."
Appointment of guardian, §1A-1 Rule 17(b), (c), SuperCt Rule 7.1.
Standby guardians for minor children, §35A-1379.
Termination of parental rights proceedings. See within this heading, "Termination of parental rights proceedings."
Missing persons.
Action for receiver.
Filing of answer on behalf of absentee, §28C-2(c).
Office of guardian ad litem services.
Services to abused, neglected or dependent juveniles, §§7B-1200 to 7B-1204.
Searches and seizures.
Unknown or absent defendants, §15-11.1(b).

GUARDIAN AD LITEM —Cont'd
Service of process.
Appointment of unborn persons, §1A-1 Rule 17(b).
Manner of service on minor to exercise personal jurisdiction.
No parent, guardian or other person having care and control of child, §1A-1 Rule 4(j).
Standby guardians for minor children.
Appointment of guardian ad litem, §35A-1379(a).
Duties of guardian ad litem, §35A-1379(b).
Investigation of fitness of intended standby guardian, §35A-1379(c).
Substitution of parties.
Insanity or incompetency, §1A-1 Rule 25(b).
Talent contracts entered into by minors.
Proceeding for court approval, §48A-12(d).
Termination of parental rights proceedings.
Adoption proceedings.
Selection of adoptive parents, §7B-1112.1.
Answer denying allegations, appointment, §7B-908(b), (d).
Appointment.
Answer denying allegations of petition, §7B-1108(b), (d).
Discretion of court, assistance in determining best interests of juvenile, §7B-1108(c).
Attorney appointed to assist nonattorney guardian ad litem, §7B-1108(b).
Copy of all pleadings and papers.
Service on, §7B-1106(a1).
Copy of order.
Service on guardian ad litem for juvenile, §7B-1110(d).
Discretion of court to appoint, assistance in determining best interests, §7B-1108(c).
Parent's right.
Appointment, communications, confidential, privilege, assistance, practice permitted, §7B-1101.1(b) to (e).
Persons who may file petition or motion, intervention, right, §7B-1103(a), (b).
Placement review hearing, §7B-908(b).
Reinstatement of parental rights.
Appointment of guardian ad litem, §7B-1114(c).
Reports from social services department and guardian ad litem, §7B-1114(f).
Search for unknown parent, appointment, §7B-1105(b).
Service of copy of all pleadings and papers, §7B-1106(a1).
Torrens system registration.
Representation of persons under disability, §43-9.
Unborn persons, §1A-1 Rule 17(b).
Appointment procedure, §1A-1 Rule 17(d).
Workers' compensation.
Contested cases, ICWorkComp Rule 604.

GUARDIAN AD LITEM ADVISORY COMMITTEE.
Guardian ad litem program to provide services to abused, neglected or dependent juveniles, §7B-1201(b).

GUARDIAN AND WARD.
Abandoned incompetent spouse's estate.
Sale of spouse's separate property by guardian, §35A-1306.
Abortion.
Parental consent to abortion.
Consent by legal guardian or legal custodian required, §90-21.7(a).

GUARDIAN AND WARD —Cont'd
Absentees in military service.
Appointment of guardian ad litem, §28B-3(c).
Abused, neglected or dependent juvenile actions.
Appointment, authority, §7B-600(a).
Court's inquiry into person's qualifications to act as guardian, §7B-600(c).
Periodic review hearings, placement of juvenile.
Court's inquiry into person's qualifications to act as guardian, §7B-906(g).
Custody removed from parent, appointment after findings, §7B-906(d).
Termination of guardianship, criteria, §7B-600(b).
Accounts and accounting.
Annual accounts.
Approval, §35A-1264.
Compelling accounting, §35A-1265(a).
Contempt, §35A-1265(a).
Corporation as guardian, §35A-1265(b).
Costs of proceedings, §35A-1265(a).
Required, §35A-1264.
Applicability of article, §35A-1260.
Commissions, §35A-1269.
Exhibition of investments and bank statements, §35A-1268.
Expenses and disbursements.
Chargeable in annual account, §35A-1267.
Final account and discharge of guardian, §35A-1266.
Responsibility of guardian for accounting until discharged, §35A-1295(b).
Restoration to competence, §35A-1130(e).
Inventory or account required within three months, §35A-1261.
Compelling inventory or account, §35A-1262(a).
Contempt, §35A-1262(a).
Costs of proceedings.
Personal liability of guardian, §35A-1262(b).
Supplemental inventory, §35A-1263.1.
Removal or resignation of guardian or guardian stopped serving, §35A-1294(a).
Restoration to competence.
Final accounts, §35A-1130(e).
Standby guardians for minor children, §35A-1380.
Ad litem.
See GUARDIAN AD LITEM.
Adoption.
Appointment for minor child.
Consent not required from parent, §48-3-603(a).
Execution of consent, time, §48-3-604(c).
Incompetent adults.
Consent, §48-5-103(a), (b).
Adult care homes.
Bill of rights.
Transfer of management responsibilities, §131D-22.
Advancements.
Guardian party to proceeding, §35A-1324.
Alimony.
Incompetent spouses.
General guardian may commence, defend or maintain actions, §50-22.
Anatomical gifts.
Who may make gift of body or body part of decedent, §130A-412.11(a).
Who may make prior to donor's death, §130A-412.6.
Ancillary guardians.
Appointment for nonresident ward with property in state, §35A-1280(a).
Certified or exemplified copy, evidence of, §35A-1280(c).

GUARDIAN AND WARD —Cont'd
Ancillary guardians —Cont'd
Appointment for nonresident ward with property in state —Cont'd
Notice to appropriate court of ward's residence, §35A-1280(d).
Venue, §35A-1204(c).
Powers, duties and responsibilities with respect to nonresident ward's property, §35A-1280(b).
Annulment of marriage.
Incompetent spouses.
General guardian may commence, defend or maintain actions, §50-22.
Appeals.
Determination of incompetence.
Order of clerk, §35A-1115.
Appointment.
Ancillary guardians.
Nonresident ward having property in state, §35A-1280.
Clerks of superior court.
Jurisdiction.
Standby guardians for minor children, §35A-1371.
Determination of incompetence, §35A-1120.
Interim guardians, §35A-1114.
Incompetent person, guardian for, §§35A-1210 to 35A-1216.
Jurisdiction.
Clerks of superior courts, §35A-1203(a), (e).
Standby guardians for minor children, §35A-1371.
Letters of appointment, §35A-1206.
Minors, guardian for, §§35A-1220 to 35A-1228.
Standby guardians for minor children.
Jurisdiction, §35A-1371.
Petition, §35A-1373.
Written designation, §35A-1374.
Successor guardians, §35A-1293.
Resignation of guardian, §35A-1292.
Venue, §35A-1204.
Transfer to different county, §35A-1205.
Attorneys at law.
Determination of incompetence.
Right to counsel, §35A-1107(a), (b).
Attorneys' fees.
Procedure to compel accounting, §35A-1265(a).
Banks.
Deposit of ward's money held by applicant for letters, §35A-1232(b) to (d).
Stockholders.
Personal liability of guardians, §53-40.
Bond of guardian.
Action on bond.
Persons injured by breach of condition, §35A-1234.
Relief of endangered guardians, §35A-1237.
Several wards with estate in common, §35A-1235.
Adjusting guardians bond.
Authority of clerks of superior court, §35A-1203(c).
Approval, §35A-1230.
Breach of condition.
Action on bond by person issued by, §35A-1234.
Clerk.
Approval, §35A-1230.
Liability.
Taking insufficient bond, §35A-1238(a).
Willfully or negligently does prohibited act, §35A-1238(b).

GUARDIAN AND WARD —Cont'd
Bond of guardian —Cont'd
Clerk —Cont'd
Recording, §35A-1231(a).
Reduced penalty, §35A-1233.
Renewal of bond.
Duties of clerk upon failure to renew, §35A-1236.
Common wards for one guardian, §35A-1235.
Conditions of bond, §35A-1231(a).
Deposited or invested money, ward's estate including.
Excluded from computation of amount of bond, §35A-1232.
Disinterested public agents.
Health and human services bond, §35A-1239.
Health and human services bond, §35A-1239.
Increase on sale of realty or personal property, §35A-1231(b).
Insufficient bond.
Liability of clerk, §35A-1238(a).
Judicial sale, holding, §1-339.10(b), (c).
Limitation of action against surety, §1-52.
Nonresident guardian, §35A-1230.
Penalty.
Reduction by clerk, §35A-1233.
Public guardian, §35A-1271.
Real property.
Increase on sale of realty, §35A-1231(b).
Recording, §35A-1231(a).
Renewal, §35A-1236.
Failure to renew, §35A-1236.
Required, §35A-1230.
Standby guardians for minor children, §35A-1380.
Sureties.
Relief of endangered sureties, §35A-1237.
Terms of bond, §35A-1231(a).
Care, comfort and maintenance.
Guardian of person, duty to provide, §35A-1241(a).
Childhood vaccine-related injury compensation.
Filing of claims on behalf of minors or incompetent persons, §130A-429(a).
Clerk of superior court.
Authority of clerk.
Standby guardians for minor children, §35A-1371.
Bond of guardian.
Approval, §35A-1230.
Liability.
Taking insufficient bond, §35A-1238(a).
Willfully or negligently does prohibited act, §35A-1238(b).
Recording in clerk's office, §35A-1231.
Reduction of penalty, §35A-1233.
Renewal of bond.
Duties of clerk upon failure to renew, §35A-1236.
Interlocutory order on revocation, §35A-1291.
Jurisdiction and authority.
Adjusting guardians bond, §35A-1203(c).
Appointment of guardian, §35A-1203(e).
Original jurisdiction, §35A-1203(a).
Disputes between guardians, determining, §35A-1203(c).
Original jurisdiction to appoint, §35A-1203(a).
Petition to exercise clerk's authority, §35A-1203(d).
Retention of jurisdiction following appointment, §35A-1203(b).

GUARDIAN AND WARD —Cont'd
Clerk of superior court —Cont'd
Jurisdiction and authority —Cont'd
Standby guardians for minor children, §35A-1371.
Receiver for ward's estates.
Acting as or appointing, estate without guardian, §35A-1294(b).
Removal of guardian.
Causes for removal, §35A-1290(b), (c).
Emergency removal without hearing, §35A-1291.
Power and authority, §35A-1290(a).
Transfer of matter to different county, §35A-1205.
Clothing, furniture, vehicles and other personal effects.
Guardian of person, duty to take care of, §35A-1241(a).
Commissions.
Allowable, §35A-1269.
Community third party or pooled trusts.
Acceptance of appointment of guardianship, §36D-4(g).
Compensation of trustees and other fiduciaries, §§32-53 to 32-62.
See FIDUCIARIES.
Compound interest.
Obligation due guardians, §24-4.
Confidentiality.
Status report for incompetent wards.
Restrictions on person with access to information, §35A-1242(c).
Consent.
Guardian of the person.
Power to give for ward, §35A-1241(a).
Construction and interpretation.
Accounts and accounting.
Applicability of article, §35A-1260.
Powers and duties of guardian of the estate, §35A-1250(b).
Powers and duties of guardian of the person.
Applicability of article, §35A-1240.
Contempt.
Accounts and accounting.
Annual accounts.
Compelling accounting, §35A-1265(a).
Inventory or account required within three months.
Compelling inventory or account, §35A-1262(a).
Corporations.
Accounting, procedure to compel.
Persons proceeded against, §35A-1265(a).
Appointment as guardian for incompetent.
Priorities for appointment, §35A-1214.
Incompetent persons.
Appointment as guardian for, §35A-1213(c).
Status reports for incompetent guardians.
Procedure to compel, §35A-1244.
Costs.
Accounts and accounting.
Annual accounts.
Compelling accounting, §35A-1265(a).
Inventory or account required within three months.
Compelling inventory or account.
Personal liability of guardian for costs of proceedings, §35A-1262(b).
Determination of incompetence.
Taxing of costs, §35A-1116(a).

GUARDIAN AND WARD —Cont'd
Costs —Cont'd
Responsibility of guardian for costs against infant plaintiff, §6-30.
Criminal law and procedure.
Victims' rights.
Exercise of incompetent victims rights by guardian, §15A-841.
Curative acts.
Deeds.
Guardians omitting seal, prior to January 1, 1944, validated, §35A-1360.
Validation of certain private sales, §35A-1361(a).
Custody of the person.
Guardian of person entitled to, §35A-1241(a).
Damages.
Guardian of the person.
When not liable for damages, §35A-1241(c).
Death.
Appointment of successor guardian, §35A-1293.
Mortgages.
Powers passed to succeeding guardian, §45-19.
Decedents' estates.
Distribution to guardian of minor, §28A-22-7.
Unborn heirs.
Appointment of guardian ad litem, §28A-22-3.
Declaratory judgments.
Who may apply for declaration, §1-255.
Deeds.
Validation.
Deeds by guardians omitting seal, prior to January 1, 1944, §35A-1360.
Definitions, §35A-1202.
Determination of incompetence, §35A-1101.
Standby guardians for minor children, §35A-1370.
Delinquent and undisciplined juvenile actions.
Appointment, authority, §7B-2001.
Deposit of ward's money by applicant for letters, §35A-1232(b).
Account in an insured savings and loan association.
Money defined, §35A-1232(d).
Account with a financial institution.
Defined, §35A-1232(c).
Exclusion of money in computing amount of bond, §35A-1232(a).
Determination of incompetence.
Adjudication order, §35A-1112.
Appeals.
Orders of clerk, §35A-1115.
Appointment, §35A-1120.
Interim guardians, §35A-1114.
Attorneys at law.
Right to counsel, §35A-1107(a).
Clerk of superior court.
Multidisciplinary evaluation.
Order of clerk, §35A-1111.
Order of clerk, §35A-1112(d).
Appeal from clerk's order, §35A-1115.
Multidisciplinary evaluation, §35A-1111.
Restoration to competency.
Proceedings before clerk, §35A-1130.
Costs.
Taxing of costs, §35A-1116(a).
Definitions, §35A-1101.
Exclusive procedure, §35A-1102.
Guardian ad litem.
Attorney as guardian ad litem, §35A-1107(a), (b).
Hearings.
Appointment of interim guardian, §35A-1114(c).

GUARDIAN AND WARD —Cont'd
Determination of incompetence —Cont'd
Hearings —Cont'd
Generally, §35A-1112.
Incompetence determined in another state, §35A-1113.
Multidisciplinary evaluation.
Extension of time for hearing, §35A-1108(b).
Notice, §35A-1108(a).
Service, §35A-1109.
Interim guardians.
Appointment.
Motion for appointment.
Contents, §35A-1114(b).
Filing, §35A-1114(a).
Hearing, §35A-1114(c).
When petition may be dismissed, §35A-1114(f).
Orders, §35A-1114(d).
Contents, §35A-1114(e).
Defined, §35A-1101.
Jurisdiction, §35A-1103.
Jury.
Right to jury, §35A-1110.
Minors, §35A-1225(b).
Multidisciplinary evaluation.
Defined, §35A-1101.
Designated agency, §35A-1111.
Order of clerk, §35A-1111.
Notice.
Hearing, §35A-1108(a).
Orders.
Adjudication orders, §35A-1112.
Petitions.
Contents, §35A-1106.
Filing, §35A-1105.
Service, §35A-1109.
Who may file, §35A-1105.
Procedure exclusive, §35A-1102.
Restoration to competency.
Proceedings before clerk, §35A-1130.
Service of process.
Notice and petition, §35A-1109.
Venue, §35A-1103.
Change of venue, §35A-1104.
Discharge of guardian.
Final account and discharge of guardian, §35A-1266.
Responsibility of guardian for accounting until discharged, §35A-1295(b).
Restoration to competence, §35A-1130(e).
Disinterested public agent.
Appointment as guardian for incompetent.
Priority for appointments, §35A-1214.
Rule-making power of secretary, §35A-1216.
Defined, §35A-1202.
Status reports for incompetent wards.
Procedure to compel, §35A-1244.
Disputes between guardians.
Authority of clerks of superior court to determine, §35A-1203(c).
Divorce.
Incompetent spouses.
Actions on behalf of.
General guardian may commence, defend or maintain, §50-22.
Domicile.
Establishing ward's place of abode within or without state.
Power of guardian of the person, §35A-1241(a).

GUARDIAN AND WARD —Cont'd
Durable power of attorney.
Attorney-in-fact accountable to court appointed guardian, §32A-10(a).
Nomination of guardian by durable power of attorney for consideration by court, §32A-10(b).
Embezzlement.
Property.
Receipt of property by virtue of office or employment, §14-90.
Eminent domain.
Private condemnors.
Acquisition of title of infants, incompetents, inebriates or trustees without power of sale.
Power of court to appoint guardian, §40A-30.
Evidence.
Ancillary guardian appointed for nonresident ward with property in state.
Certified or exemplified copy of appointment, §35A-1280(c).
Medical, hospital or other charges at issue.
Competency to give evidence regarding amount, §8-58.1(a).
Reasonableness, rebuttable presumption.
Testimony establishing, §8-58.1(b).
Services reasonable and necessary.
Permissive presumption, §8-58.1(c).
Exercising authority of clerk of superior court.
Petitions, §35A-1203(d).
Ex parte order, entry by clerk, §35A-1207(d).
Expenses.
Reimbursement of reasonable and proper expenditures.
Guardian of the person, §35A-1241(b).
Fiduciaries.
General provisions.
See FIDUCIARIES.
Payments to or for minors or incompetents.
Powers which may be incorporated by reference in trust instrument, §32-27.
Findings of general assembly, §35A-1201(a).
Gifts.
From income for certain purposes.
Approval of judge of superior court.
Authorized, §35A-1335.
Fact that incompetent had not previously made similar gifts, §35A-1337.
Prerequisites to approval, §§35A-1336, 35A-1336.1.
Validity of gift, §35A-1338.
Health care powers of attorney.
Appointment of guardian.
Effect on power of attorney, §32A-22(a).
Nomination of guardian by health care power of attorney, §32A-22(b).
Suspension of authority of health care agent.
Authority to petition counrt for, §35A-1208(a).
Hearings.
Appointment of guardians.
Incompetent persons, §35A-1212.
Minors, §35A-1223.
Determination of incompetence.
Appointment of interim guardian, §35A-1114(c).
Generally, §35A-1112.
Incompetence determined in another state, §35A-1113.
Notice, §35A-1108(a).
Service of notice, §35A-1109.
Husband and wife.
Abandoned incompetent spouse's estate.
Sale of spouse's separate property by guardian, §35A-1306.

GUARDIAN AND WARD —Cont'd
Husband and wife —Cont'd
Mortgage or sale of estates held by the entireties, §§35A-1310 to 35A-1314.
See HUSBAND AND WIFE.
Sale of ward's estate.
Spouse entitled to special proceedings for sale of real property, §35A-1307.
Immunities.
Guardian of the person.
Acting within limits imposed by powers and duties or order of appointment, §35A-1241(c).
Incompetent persons.
Abandoned incompetent spouse's estate.
Sale of spouse's separate property by guardian, §35A-1306.
Appointment, §35A-1213(a).
Application, §35A-1210.
Contents, §35A-1210.
Service, §35A-1211(a).
Application for appointment joined with petition for adjudication of incompetence, §35A-1211(b).
Corporations, §35A-1213(c).
Designated agency, clerk naming, §35A-1212(d).
Disinterested public agent, §35A-1213(d).
Disinterested public agents.
When may be appointed, §35A-1214.
Employee of treatment facility.
Restriction, §35A-1213(e).
Evidence, receipt by clerk, §35A-1212(a).
Inquiry by clerk, §35A-1212(a).
Legal rights and privileges retained by ward.
Clerk ordering, §35A-1215(b).
Letters of appointment.
Issuance, §35A-1215(c).
Motions.
Service, §35A-1211(a).
Multidisciplinary evaluation.
Order for, §35A-1212(b).
Nonresidents, §35A-1213(b).
Notice.
Service, §35A-1211(a).
Orders of clerk.
Contents, §35A-1215(a).
Entering of order, §35A-1215(a).
Priorities for appointment, §35A-1214.
Rules and regulations.
Issuance, §35A-1216.
Suitability of prospective guardian.
Report to evaluate, §35A-1212(c).
Venue, §35A-1204(a).
Corporations.
Appointment, §35A-1213(c).
Determination of incompetence, §§35A-1101 to 35A-1116.
Disinterested public agent.
Appointment, §35A-1213(d).
Employee of treatment facility.
Appointment.
Restriction, §35A-1213(e).
Guardian ad litem for incompetent ward.
Appointment.
Ward's interests not adequately represented, §35A-1217.
Guardian of the estate.
Powers in administering estate, §35A-1251.
Hearings before clerk.
Appointment, §35A-1212.

GUARDIAN AND WARD —Cont'd
Incompetent persons —Cont'd
Insurance proceeds received as beneficiary on
death of insured.
Payment to and receipt by public guardian,
§7A-111(b), (d).
Interested person.
Disqualification to testify against guardian of
incompetent, §8C-1 Rule 601(c).
Legal rights and privileges retained by ward.
Clerk ordering, §35A-1215(b).
Modification of guardianship, program or plan.
Petition by designated agency requesting,
§35A-1243(b) to (d).
Money belonging to incapacitated adult without
guardian.
Payment to and receipt by public guardian,
§7A-111(b), (d).
Nonresidents.
Appointment, §35A-1213(b).
Performance of duties imposed on guardian.
Petition by designated agency requiring
guardian to perform, §35A-1243(b) to (d).
Petitions.
Designated agency requesting certain actions
against guardian of incompetent,
§35A-1243(b) to (d).
Removal of guardian.
Petition by designated agency requesting,
§35A-1243(b) to (d).
Restoration to competency.
Petition by designated agency requesting,
§35A-1243(b) to (d).
Sale, lease or exchange of ward's estate,
§35A-1251.
Status reports.
Filing by guardian of the person, §35A-1242.
Compelling, procedure, §35A-1244.
Duties of designated agency after receipt,
§35A-1243.
Sterilization of mentally ill or retarded ward.
Consent or approval of guardian of person,
prohibition to give, §35A-1241(a).
Termination of guardianship.
Adjudication of restoration to competency,
§35A-1295(a).
Venue.
Appointment, §35A-1204(a).
Inebriates.
Guardian of the estate.
Powers in administering estate, §35A-1251.
Interest.
Compound interest.
Obligations due guardians to bear compound
interest, §24-4.
Interim guardian.
Incompetence, determination of.
Appointments, §35A-1114.
Inventories.
Accounts and accounting.
Inventory or account required within three
months, §§35A-1261 to 35A-1263.1.
Procedure to compel inventory, §35A-1262.
Supplemental inventory, §35A-1263.1.
Judicial sales.
Authority of guardian to hold sale, §1-339.4.
Bond of person holding sale, §1-339.10(b), (c).
Juries.
Determination of incompetence.
Right to jury, §35A-1110.

GUARDIAN AND WARD —Cont'd
Jurisdiction.
Clerk of superior court.
Standby guardians for minor children,
§35A-1371.
Determination of incompetence, §35A-1103.
Standby guardians for minor children, §35A-1371.
Larceny.
Concealment of merchandise in mercantile
establishments.
Detention of minors by merchants.
Notice to guardian during period of detention,
§§14-72.1(c), 14-72(d).
Leases.
Power to lease real estate.
Administration of incompetent ward's estate,
§35A-1251.
Administration of minor ward's estate,
§35A-1252.
Special proceedings to sell, exchange, mortgage or
lease ward's real estate, §35A-1301.
Letters of guardianship.
Public guardians, §35A-1273.
Revocation.
Interlocutory orders upon revocation,
§35A-1291.
Liability.
Public guardians, §35A-1272.
Medical, hospital or other charges at issue.
Reasonableness, rebuttable presumption.
Testimony establishing, §8-58.1(b).
Services reasonable and necessary.
Permissive presumption, §8-58.1(c).
**Medical, legal, psychological and other
professional care.**
Consent or approval, power of guardian of person,
§35A-1241(a).
Medical malpractice.
Persons who may consent for another,
§90-21.13(c).
**Mental health, developmental disabilities and
substance abuse.**
Abandoned incompetent spouse's estate.
Sale of spouse's separate property by guardian,
§35A-1306.
Adults adjudicated incompetents.
Mental health officials and employees as public
guardians, §122C-122.
Appointment for incompetent, §§35A-1210 to
35A-1216.
Venue, §35A-1204(a).
Appointment for mentally ill, §1A-1 Rule 17(b).
Guardianship of incompetent adults.
Guardian of the estate.
Powers in administering estate, §35A-1251.
Mental health officials and employees as public
guardians, §122C-122.
Modification of terms of guardianship of
incompetent.
Petition by designated agency requesting,
§35A-1243(b) to (d).
Mortgage or sale of estates held by the entireties,
§§35A-1310 to 35A-1314.
Performance of guardian's duties.
Petition by designated agency requiring,
§35A-1243(b) to (d).
Petition by designated agency requesting certain
actions, §35A-1243(b) to (d).
Remainders, reversions and executory interests.
Sale, lease or mortgages in case of remainders.
Appointment of guardian ad litem, §41-11.

GUARDIAN AND WARD —Cont'd
Mental health, developmental disabilities and substance abuse —Cont'd
Removal of guardian of incompetent.
Petition by designated agency requesting, §35A-1243(b) to (d).
Restoration to competency.
Petition by designated agency requesting, §35A-1243(b) to (d).
Status reports.
Filing by guardian of the person, §35A-1242.
Sterilization of mentally ill or retarded ward.
Consent or approval of guardian of person, prohibition to give, §35A-1241(a).
Medical necessity, procedure to permit, §35A-1245.
Torrens system registration.
Persons under disability may sue by guardian, §43-8.
Venue.
Appointment of guardian for incompetent, §35A-1204(a).
Military affairs.
Children of servicemen.
Temporary guardian to receive and disburse allotments and allowances, §35A-1228.
Veterans' guardianship act, §§34-1 to 34-18.
See VETERANS' GUARDIANSHIP ACT.
Minors, §1A-1 Rule 17(b).
Abused, neglected or dependent juvenile actions.
Appointment, §7B-600(a) to (c).
Court's inquiry into person's qualifications to act as guardian, §7B-600(c).
Periodic review hearings, placement of juvenile, §7B-906(d).
Court's inquiry into person's qualifications to act as guardian, §7B-906(g).
Appointment, §§35A-1220 to 35A-1228.
Absence of natural guardian.
County social services director to be guardian, §35A-1220.
Application for appointment.
Contents, §35A-1221.
Service, §35A-1222.
Who may make, §35A-1221.
Corporations, §35A-1224(c).
Employee of treatment facilities, §35A-1224(e).
Guardian of the estate, §35A-1224(a).
Guardian of the person or general guardian only for minor who has no natural guardian, §35A-1224(a).
Hearings, §35A-1223.
Notice.
Service, §35A-1222.
Incompetent minors.
Petition for adjudication of incompetence and appointment of guardian, §35A-1225.
Letters of appointment.
Issuance, §35A-1226.
Orders of clerk, §35A-1226.
Qualifications, §35A-1224(b), (c).
Social services director of county.
To be guardian in absence of natural guardian, §35A-1220.
Testamentary recommendations of parents.
Effect, §§35A-1224(d), 35A-1225.
Presumptions, §35A-1225(a).
Venue, §35A-1204(b).
Delinquent and undisciplined juvenile actions.
Appointment, authority, §7B-2001.

GUARDIAN AND WARD —Cont'd
Minors —Cont'd
Devise or legacy of personal property.
Distribution, §35A-1227(b).
Funds owed to minors.
Disposition, §35A-1227(a).
Guardian of the estate.
Powers in administering estate, §35A-1252.
Insurance proceeds owed to minors.
Disposition, §35A-1227(a).
Insurance proceeds received by minors on death of insured.
Payment over to and receipt by public guardian, §7A-111(a), (c).
Military service.
Children of servicemen.
Allotments and allowances, §35A-1228.
Money for minor for whom there is no guardian.
Payment over to public guardian, §7A-111(a), (c).
Property due minor.
Disposition, §35A-1227(c).
Remainders, reversions and executory interests.
Sale, lease or mortgage in case of remainders.
Appointment of guardian ad litem, §41-11.
Sale, lease or exchange of ward's estate, §35A-1252.
Standby guardians, §§35A-1370 to 35A-1382. See within this heading, "Standby guardians for minor children."
Termination of guardianship.
Ward ceasing to be minor, §35A-1295(a).
Testamentary recommendation by parent, §§35A-1224(d), 35A-1225.
Guardian for incompetent minor, §35A-1225.
Torrens system registration.
Infants may sue by guardian, §43-8.
Transfers to minors.
Disposition, §35A-1227(d).
Irrevocable transfer for benefit of minor.
Authority to make as custodian, §33A-6(b), (c).
Venue.
Appointment, §35A-1204(b).
Will making testamentary recommendation for appointment of guardian for minor, §§35A-1224(d), 35A-1225.
Incompetent minor, §35A-1225.
Mortgages and deeds of trust.
Sales under power of sale.
Powers passed to succeeding guardian upon death, §45-19.
Special proceedings to sell, exchange, mortgage or lease ward's real estate, §35A-1301.
Substitution of trustees.
Powers pass to succeeding guardian, §45-19.
Motions in the cause.
All requests treated as motions in the cause, §35A-1207(b).
Ex parte order, entry by clerk, §35A-1207(d).
Filing, place for, §35A-1207(a).
Hearing, time, date and place, movant to obtain, §35A-1207(c).
Service or motion and notice of hearing, §35A-1207(c).
Multidisciplinary evaluations.
Appointment of guardians.
Incompetent persons, §35A-1212(b).
Natural death, right to.
Declaration.
Guardian without authority to revoke, §35A-1208(b).

GUARDIAN AND WARD —Cont'd

Nonresidents.

Ancillary guardian for nonresident ward having property in state, §35A-1280.

Venue for appointment, §35A-1204(c).

Removal of nonresident ward's personalty from state.

Banking institution guardian.

Removal without finding as to sureties, §35A-1281(c).

Copy of appointment, guardian to show court, §35A-1281(c).

Party defendant, persons who may be made, §35A-1281(c).

Personal estate defined, §35A-1281(a).

Petition for removal, §35A-1281(b).

Venue for filing petition, §35A-1281(b).

Notice.

Ancillary guardian appointed for nonresident ward with property in state, §35A-1280(d).

Appointment of guardian.

Minors.

Service, §35A-1222.

Determination of incompetence.

Hearings, §35A-1108(a).

Service of notice, §35A-1109.

Motions in the cause.

Service of motion and notice of hearing, §35A-1207(c).

Sale of ward's estate.

Abandoned incompetent spouse's separate property.

Service of notice on abandoning spouse, §35A-1306(b).

Standby guardians.

Appointment by written designation.

Service of petition and notice of hearing, §35A-1374(g).

Nursing homes.

Patients' bill of rights.

Transfer of management responsibilities, §131E-118.

Oaths.

Public guardians, §35A-1270.

Status report for incompetent wards.

Filed under guardians oath or affirmation, §35A-1242(b).

Orders.

Letters of guardianship.

Interlocutory orders upon revocation, §35A-1291.

Special proceedings involving infants.

Approval of clerk's order by judge, §1-402.

Parties, §1A-1 Rule 17(a).

Persons under legal disability.

Torrens system registration.

Guardians may sue, §43-8.

Petitions.

Designated agency requesting certain actions against guardian of incompetent, §35A-1243(b) to (d).

Determination of incompetence.

Contents, §35A-1106.

Filing, §35A-1105.

Service, §35A-1109.

Who may file, §35A-1105.

Exercising authority of clerk of superior court, §35A-1203(d).

Mentally ill.

Gifts from income of incompetents, §35A-1335.

GUARDIAN AND WARD —Cont'd

Petitions —Cont'd

Removal of nonresident ward's personalty from state, §35A-1281(b).

Sale of ward's estate.

Special proceedings to sell, exchange, mortgage or lease real estate, §35A-1301(b), (d).

Standby guardians for minor children.

Appointment by petition, §35A-1373.

Appointment by written designation, §35A-1374.

Place of abode.

Establishing ward's place of abode within or without state.

Power of guardian of the person, §35A-1241(a).

Powers and duties.

Ancillary guardian for nonresident ward with property in state, §35A-1280(b).

Fiduciaries generally, §§32-25 to 32-27.

Guardian of the estate.

Administration of incompetent ward's estate, §35A-1251.

Administration of minor ward's estate, §35A-1252.

Applicability of article, construction, §35A-1250(a), (b).

Specific duties of guardian of the estate, §35A-1253.

Guardian of the person.

Applicability of article, §35A-1240.

Generally, §35A-1241(a).

Status reports for incompetent wards, §35A-1242.

Compelling status reports.

Procedure, §35A-1244.

Public guardians, §35A-1272.

Standby guardians for minor children, §35A-1377.

Presumptions.

Medical, hospital or other charges at issue.

Reasonableness, rebuttable presumption.

Testimony establishing, §8-58.1(b).

Services reasonable and necessary.

Permissive presumption, §8-58.1(c).

Public guardians.

Appointment, §35A-1270.

Bond, §35A-1271.

Compensation, §35A-1272.

Letters of guardianship.

Issuance, §35A-1273.

Liability, §35A-1272.

Oaths, §35A-1270.

Powers and duties, §35A-1272.

Terms of office, §35A-1270.

Purpose of provisions, §35A-1201(b).

Real estate brokers.

Exemption of guardian from provisions, §93A-2(c).

Receiver for estate without guardian.

Accounts, return, audit and settlement, §35A-1294(b).

Clerk acting as or appointing, §35A-1294(b).

Compensation for, §35A-1294(b).

Continuation until other guardian appointed, §35A-1294(b).

Payment over to newly appointed guardian, §35A-1294(c).

Remedy of ward upon emancipation, §35A-1294(c).

Remainders, reversions and executory interests.

Sale, lease or mortgage in case of remainders.

Appointment of guardian ad litem for minors and persons under disability, §41-11.

GUARDIAN AND WARD —Cont'd
Removal of guardian.
Appointment of successor guardian, §35A-1293.
Bond of guardian.
Failure to renew bond, §35A-1236.
Causes for removal.
Clerk removing, §35A-1290(b), (c).
Clerk of superior court.
Causes for removal, §35A-1290(b), (c).
Emergency removal without hearing,
§35A-1291.
Interlocutory orders on revocation, §35A-1291.
Power and authority, §35A-1290(a).
Guardian for incompetent.
Petition by designated agency, §35A-1243(b) to
(d).
Receiver appointed.
Estate without guardian, §35A-1294.
Removal of nonresident ward's personalty
from state, §35A-1281.
Renunciation.
Right of duly appointed guardian, §31B-1(a).
Reports.
Status reports.
Compelling status reports.
Procedure to compel, §35A-1244.
Filing by guardian of the person, §35A-1242.
Duties of designated agency after receipt,
§35A-1243.
Representation.
Persons representing and binding others,
§§36C-3-301 to 36C-3-305.
Resignation of guardian.
Application in writing, §35A-1292(a).
Appointment of successor, §35A-1293.
Liability after discharge, §35A-1292(a).
Partial resignation, §35A-1292(b).
Partial resignation as guardian of estate.
Remaining guardian of the person,
§35A-1292(b).
Receiver appointed.
Estate without guardian, §35A-1294.
Right to natural death.
Declaration.
Guardian without authority to revoke,
§35A-1208(b).
Rules and regulations.
Appointment of guardians.
Incompetent persons, §35A-1216.
Sale of ward's estate.
Abandoned incompetent spouse's separate
property.
Bar to abandoning spouse in property,
§35A-1306(c).
Initiation of special proceeding requesting,
§35A-1306(a).
Issuance of order, required findings,
§35A-1306(c).
Service of notice on ward's spouse,
§35A-1306(b).
Authority of guardian to hold sale, §1-339.4.
Conversion and reconversion, §35A-1303.
Curative acts and statutes.
Certain private sales validated, §35A-1361.
Estate in another county.
Procedure when property lies in county in
which guardian does not reside, §35A-1302.
Funds from sale.
Character of estate sold and subject to same
trust, §35A-1303.

GUARDIAN AND WARD —Cont'd
Sale of ward's estate —Cont'd
Husband and wife.
Incompetent spouses.
Mortgage or sale of estates held by the
entireties, §§35A-1310 to 35A-1314.
Spouse entitled to special proceedings for sale of
real property, §35A-1307.
Incompetent wards, §35A-1251.
Minor wards, §35A-1252.
Petitions.
Special proceedings to sell, exchange, mortgage
or lease real estate, §35A-1301(b), (d).
Procedure for sale.
Property lying in county in which guardian does
not reside, §35A-1302.
Special proceedings to sell, exchange, mortgage or
lease real estate.
Construction of word "guardian,"§35A-1301(a).
Minor ward.
Special requirements, §35A-1301(c).
Order by clerk, §35A-1301(b).
Petition, §35A-1301(b).
Filing, §35A-1301(d).
Private sales.
Courts not divested of power to order,
§35A-1301(f).
Procedure for sale, §35A-1301(e).
Validity of sales, §35A-1301(g).
Timber.
When timber may be sold, §35A-1305.
Savings and loan associations.
Deposit of ward's money held by applicant for
letters, §35A-1232(b) to (d).
Seals and sealed instruments.
Deeds by guardians omitting seal, prior to
January 1, 1944, validated, §35A-1360.
Securities regulation.
Exempt transactions, §78A-17.
Service of process.
Appointment of guardian.
Incompetent persons.
Service of application, motions and notices,
§35A-1211.
Minors.
Service of application and notices, §35A-1222.
Determination of incompetence.
Service of notice and petition, §35A-1109.
Motions in the cause.
Motion and notice of hearing, §35A-1207(c).
Natural persons under disabilities, §1A-1 Rule
4(j).
Sale of ward's estate.
Abandoned incompetent spouse's separate
property, §35A-1306(b).
Standby guardians for minor children.
Appointment by written designation.
Service of petition and notice of hearing,
§35A-1374(g).
Petition of appointment, §35A-1373(c), (d).
Shoplifting.
Concealment of merchandise in mercantile
establishments.
Detention of minors by merchants.
Notice to guardian during period of detention,
§§14-72.1(c), 14-72(d).
Social services.
County directors of social services.
Director and assistant directors as public
guardians, §108A-15.

GUARDIAN AND WARD —Cont'd
Special proceedings.
Order of clerk.
Approval of judge required, §1-402.
Standby guardians for minor children,
§§35A-1370 to 35A-1382.
Accounting by guardian, §35A-1382.
Applicability of provisions, §35A-1372.
Appointment.
Jurisdiction, §35A-1371.
Petition, §35A-1373.
Written designation, §35A-1374.
Authority concurrent to parental rights,
§35A-1377.
Bond of guardian, §35A-1380.
Definitions, §35A-1370.
Designation.
Appointment by written designation.
Alternate standby guardian.
Commencement of proceeding for
appointment, §35A-1374(d).
Commencement of authority of standby
guardian, §35A-1374(c).
Contents of designation, §35A-1374(b).
Custody of minor child.
Claim by parent, §35A-1374(h).
Generally, §35A-1374(a).
Hearing, §35A-1373(i).
Petition by standby guardian to be appointed,
§35A-1374(d) to (g).
Revocation of standby guardianship,
§35A-1374(j).
Complaint for custody, stay of proceedings,
§35A-1374(h).
Defined, §35A-1370.
Hearing and order for appointment,
§35A-1374(i).
Service of petition, §35A-1374(g).
Time for filing petition, §35A-1374(e).
Determination of debilitation, §35A-1375(a), (b).
Commencement of standby guardian's authority
as result of.
Informing petitioner or designator,
§35A-1375(d).
Copy to be supplied to standby guardian,
§35A-1375(c).
Defined, §35A-1370.
Determination of incapacity, §35A-1375(a), (b).
Commencement of standby guardian's authority
as result of.
Informing petitioner or designator,
§35A-1375(d).
Copy to be supplied to standby guardian,
§35A-1375(c).
Defined, §35A-1370.
Guardian ad litem.
Appointment, §35A-1379(a).
Duties, §35A-1379(b).
Investigation of fitness of intended standby
guardian, §35A-1379(c).
Jurisdiction, §35A-1371.
Parental rights.
Authority concurrent to, §35A-1377.
Petition for appointment.
Commencement of standby guardian,
§35A-1373(i) to (l).
Contents, §35A-1373(b).
Filing, §35A-1373(a).
Hearing on, §35A-1373(e), (f), (h).
Letters of appointment, §35A-1373(g).
Renunciation of appointment, §35A-1373(n).

GUARDIAN AND WARD —Cont'd
Standby guardians for minor children —Cont'd
Petition for appointment —Cont'd
Revocation of standby guardianship,
§35A-1373(m).
Service, §35A-1373(c), (d).
Powers and duties, §35A-1378.
Restoration of capacity or ability.
Suspension of guardianship, §35A-1376.
Revocation of standby guardianship.
Appointment by petition, §35A-1373(m).
Appointment by written designation,
§35A-1374(j).
Termination of standby guardianship generally,
§35A-1382.
Suspension of guardianship.
Restoration of capacity or ability, §35A-1376.
Termination of standby guardianship, §35A-1382.
Unwillingness or inability of standby guardian to
serve, §35A-1372.
State departments and agencies.
Gifts from income of incompetents, §35A-1335.
Status reports for incompetent wards.
Designated agencies.
Actions agency may take after receipt,
§35A-1243(b).
Certification that report reviewed, mailing copy
to guardian, §35A-1243(a).
Petitions requesting certain actions,
§35A-1243(b) to (d).
Filing by guardian of the person.
Compelling, procedure, §35A-1244.
Guardian of the person.
Confidentiality, access by persons or agencies,
§35A-1242(c).
Duty to file, §35A-1242(a).
Oath or affirmation, filed under, §35A-1242(b).
Second report, filing, time, §35A-1242(a).
Time for filing after appointment, §35A-1242(a).
Sterilization of mentally ill or retarded ward.
Consent or approval of guardian, §35A-1241(a).
Duty to obtain order permitting guardian to
consent, §90-275.
Medical necessity.
Procedure to permit, §35A-1245.
Mental necessity, procedure to permit, §35A-1245.
Appeal of clerk's order, §35A-1245(f).
Consent requirements, §35A-1245(a).
Court petition for consent, §35A-1245(b).
Entry order, §35A-1245(e).
Hearing on petition, §35A-1245(d).
Service of petition, §35A-1245(c).
Successor guardian.
Accounting by predecessor.
Compelling, §35A-1294(a).
Appointment by clerk.
Resignation of guardian, §35A-1292.
Surplus income and advancements.
Parties to proceeding for advancements,
§35A-1324.
Taxation.
Property taxes.
Payment of taxes by fiduciaries, §105-383.
Termination of guardianship, §35A-1295(a).
Termination of parental rights proceedings.
Persons who may file petition or motion,
intervention, right, §7B-1103(a), (b).
**Testamentary recommendation by parent for
appointment of guardian of minor,**
§§35A-1224(d), 35A-1225.
Guardian for incompetent minor, §35A-1225.

GUARDIAN AND WARD —Cont'd
Torrens system registration.
Infants and persons under disability may sue by guardian, §43-8.
Training, education, employment, rehabilitation or habitation.
Guardian of person, duty to arrange for, §35A-1241(a).
Transfer to minors.
Irrevocable transfer for benefit of minor.
Authority to make as custodian, §33A-6(b), (c).
Trees and timber.
Sale of ward's estate.
When timber may be sold, §35A-1305.
Trust companies.
Acting as guardian authorized, §53-159.
Trusts and trustees.
Revocable trusts.
Guardian exercising powers of settlor, §36C-6-602.1(b).
Uniform fiduciaries act, §§32-1 to 32-13.
See FIDUCIARIES.
Validation.
Deeds by guardians omitting seal, prior to January 1, 1944, §35A-1360.
Sales.
Certain private sales validated, §35A-1361.
Venue.
Appointment, §35A-1204.
Determination of incompetence, §35A-1103.
Change of venue, §35A-1103.
Transfer to different county, §35A-1205.
Veterans' guardianship act, §§34-1 to 34-18.
See VETERANS' GUARDIANSHIP ACT.
Waste.
For and against whom action lies, §1-534.
Witnesses.
Interested person.
Disqualification to testify against guardian of incompetent, §8C-1 Rule 601(c).
Medical, hospital or other charges at issue.
Competency to give evidence regarding amount, §8-58.1(a).
Reasonableness, rebuttable presumption.
Testimony establishing, §8-58.1(b).
Services reasonable and necessary.
Permissive presumption, §8-58.1(c).
Year's allowance for child.
Application, §30-20.
Superior court, §30-27.

GUARDRAILS.
Reports as to damage, §20-166(c1).

GUARDS.
Private protective services, §§74C-1 to 74C-30.
See PRIVATE PROTECTIVE SERVICES.
Sanitary districts.
Corporate powers of sanitary district board, §130A-55.

GUIDANCE COUNSELORS.
Communication between counselors and students, §§8-53.4, 115C-401.

GUIDE DOGS, §§168-4.2 to 168-4.6.
Assaulting assistance animals, §14-163.1.
Blind pedestrians' rights and privileges without guide dog, §20-175.3.
Common carrier fares for blind person accompanied by, §62-144(b).
Donation of service animal for training, §168-4.6.

GUIDE DOGS —Cont'd
Pedestrian's rights and privileges without guide dog, §20-175.3.
Registration of service animal, §168-4.3.
Responsibility for service animals, §168-4.4.
Right of way at crossings, intersections and traffic control signal points.
Guide dog to serve as signal for the blind, §20-175.2.
Right to be accompanied by service animal, §168-4.2.
Penalty for depriving of right, §168-4.5.
Signal for blind persons crossing street, §20-175.2.
Tags, §168-4.2(a).
Training of service animal, §168-4.3.
Donation, §168-4.6.

GUIDES.
Hunting or fishing guides.
License, §113-270.4.

GUILFORD COUNTY.
Ambulances.
Attachment or garnishment and lien for, §§44-51.4 to 44-51.8.
False pretenses and cheats.
Obtaining ambulance services without intending to pay, §14-111.2.
Bicentennial commission.
Department of cultural resources.
Transfer of commission to department, §143B-51.
Blank or master forms of mortgages, deeds of trust, etc.
Indexing and recording, inapplicability of provisions, §47-21.
Board of county commissioners.
Filling vacancies on board, §153A-27.1.
Condemnation or acquisition of land by local government unit outside county.
Consent of board of commissioners necessary, §153A-15.
Coroner elected as nominee of political party.
Filling vacancy in office, §152-1.
Counties generally.
See COUNTIES.
Cropper or tenant refusing to perform terms of contract.
Forfeiture of right of possession to premises, §42-27.
Department of cultural resources.
Bicentennial commission.
Transfer of commission to department, §143B-51.
Dogs used in hunting.
Regulation by wildlife resources commission, §113-291.5(a).
False pretenses and cheats.
Ambulance services.
Obtaining services without intending to pay, §14-111.2.
Motor vehicle emission inspections.
Counties inspections required to be performed in, §143-215.107A(c).
Oil, gas or mineral claims.
Certain ancient claims extinguished, preservation, procedure, §1-42.1(a) to (d).
Private parking lots.
Removal of unauthorized vehicles, §20-219.2.
School property.
Acquisition and improvement, §153A-158.1.

GUILFORD COUNTY —Cont'd
Sheriff.
Vacancy, performance of duties until vacancy
filled, §162-5.1.
Transportation authorities.
Local government sales and use tax for public
transportation.
Regional authority (Triad), §§105-510,
105-510.1.

GUILTY PLEAS, §15A-1011(a).
Acceptance.
District courts, §7A-272(c), (d).
Prerequisites, §15A-1022(a) to (c).
Aggravating factors, §15A-1022.1(a) to (e).
Aggravating factors in felonies.
Procedure in accepting admissions, §15A-1022.1(a)
to (e).
Capital offenses.
Death penalty or life imprisonment, §15A-2001.
Determinations by judge.
Required determination, §15A-1022(a) to (c).
Aggravating factors, §15A-1022.1(a), (c).
Factual basis for plea.
Judge must determine, §15A-1022(c).
Aggravating factors, §15A-1022.1(c).
Felony cases transferred to district court.
Appeals, §15A-1029.1(b).
Consent of parties, §15A-1029.1(a).
Filing of information, §15A-644.1.
First degree murder.
Death penalty or life imprisonment, §15A-2001.
Impaired driving charge.
Acceptance by prosecutor, explanation, §20-138.4.
**Improper pressure on defendant to plead
guilty.**
Determination by judge, §15A-1022(b).
Prohibited, §15A-1021(b).
Inadmissible in evidence, §8C-1 Rule 410.
**Information, filing when plea of guilty or no
contest in district court,** §15A-644.1.
Information to be given defendant,
§15A-1022(a).
Aggravating factors, §15A-1022.1(b).
Informed choice.
Judge must determine, §15A-1022(b).
Other crimes with which defendant charged,
§15A-1011(c).
Probable cause hearings.
Acceptance of guilty plea, §15A-613.
Record of proceedings, §§7A-191.1, 15A-1026.
Withdrawal.
Sentence not in accord with plea arrangement,
§15A-1024.

GUNS.
Generally.
See FIREARMS AND OTHER WEAPONS.

GUNSHOT WOUNDS.
Reports.
Physicians and hospitals to report, §90-21.20.

GUTTERS.
Special assessments by counties, §§153A-185 to
153A-210.7.
See SPECIAL ASSESSMENTS BY COUNTIES.

**GYNECOLOGISTS, DIRECT INSURANCE
ACCESS,** §58-51-38(a).

GYNECOLOGY.
Primary care physicians, medical education,
§143-613.

H

HABEAS CORPUS, §§17-1 to 17-46.
Absentees.
Party ill or infirm.
Cause determined in his absence, §17-37.
Ad prosequendum, §15-10.3.
Alternative in formal procedure, §15A-711.
Mentally ill prisoners, §15-10.4.
Ad testificandum, §§17-41 to 17-46.
Application for writ.
Contents, §17-7.
Denial, §17-4.
Habeas corpus ad testificandum.
Bond of applicant, §17-44.
Contents of application, §17-42.
Expenses, §17-44.
Verification, §17-42.
Issuance of writ without application, §17-8.
Judges to whom directed, §17-6.
Parties.
By whom application made, §17-5.
Signature of applicant, §17-6.
Statements required in applications, §17-7.
Verification by oath of applicant, §17-7.
Who may apply, §17-3.
Written application, §17-6.
Arrest in civil cases.
Party held in execution not to be discharged,
§17-36.
Attachment.
County may be called on to aid execution, §17-22.
Failure to obey writ, §17-16.
Refusal of attachment.
Liability of judge refusing attachment, §17-17.
Sheriffs.
Attachment against sheriff to be directed to
coroner, §17-18.
Order of discharge.
Compelling obedience, §17-23.
Bail.
Right of habeas corpus not abridged, §15A-547.
When party bailed or remanded, §17-35.
Capital punishment.
Procedure when considering application, SuperCt
Rule 25.
Concealing party entitled to writ, §17-28.
Constitution of North Carolina.
Inquiry into restraints on liberty, NC Const Art I
§21.
Remedy without delay for restraint of liberty,
§17-1.
Suspension of habeas corpus, §17-2.
Constitution of the United States.
Habeas corpus not to be suspended, US Const Art
I §9.
Contempt.
Remand of party in custody for contempt, §17-34.
Coroners.
Hearings by coroner, §152-10.
Costs.
Allowance of costs to either party or apportioned
in discretion of court, §6-21.
Court of appeals.
Issuance of remedial writs, §7A-32(a).
Damages.
Order of discharge.
Failure to comply, §17-23.
Defects of form immaterial, §17-11.
Denial of writ, §17-4.

HABEAS CORPUS —Cont'd
Discharge of party.
Bail.
When party bailed or remanded, §17-35.
Executions.
Party held in execution not to be discharged, §17-36.
Grounds, §17-33.
Judgment or order of discharge.
Enforcement, §17-23.
No civil liability for obedience, §17-24.
Jurisdiction of court or officer exceeded, §17-33.
Recommittal after discharge, §17-25.
Remand, §§17-34, 17-35.
Second committal after discharge, §17-38.
When discharged, §17-33.
Executions.
Party held in execution not to be discharged, §17-36.
Extradition.
Fugitives from other states.
Application for writ, §15A-730.
Form of writ.
Defects of form immaterial, §17-11.
Habeas corpus ad testificandum, §§17-41 to 17-46.
Hearings.
Summary hearing of issues, §17-32.
Illness or infirmity of party.
Cause determined in his absence, §17-37.
Industrial commission.
Issuance of writs, §97-101.1.
Issuance of writ.
Grant of writ without delay, §17-9.
Penalty for refusal to grant, §17-10.
Without application, §17-8.
Judges.
Attachment for failure to obey writ, §§17-16, 17-17.
Granting of writ without delay, §17-9.
Penalty for refusal to grant, §17-10.
Impeachment.
Attachment for failure to obey writ.
Judge refusing attachment, §17-17.
Insufficient return.
Liability of judge conniving at, §17-21.
Precept to bring up party detained.
Judge refusing precept, §17-20.
Insufficient return.
Liability of judge conniving at, §17-21.
Precept to bring up party detained, §17-19.
Liability of judge refusing precept, §17-20.
Jurisdiction of court or officer exceeded.
Discharge of party, §17-33.
Laches.
Willful neglect to apply for writ.
Grounds for denial of application, §17-4.
Mental health, developmental disabilities and substance abuse.
Involuntary inpatient commitment.
Availability of relief to respondent, §122C-268.1(j).
Misdemeanors.
Concealing party entitled to writ, §17-28.
False returns, §17-27.
Recommittal after discharge, §17-25.
Motion for appropriate relief.
Availability not a bar to habeas corpus, §15A-1411(c).
Generally, §§15A-1411 to 15A-1422.
See MOTION FOR APPROPRIATE RELIEF.

HABEAS CORPUS —Cont'd
Notice.
District attorney, §17-30.
Interested parties, §17-29.
Oaths and affirmations.
Application for writ.
Verification by oath of applicant, §17-7.
Return of writ.
Verification by oath, §17-14.
Obedience to order of discharge.
No civil liability, §17-24.
Parties.
Application for writ.
By whom application made, §17-5.
Penalties.
Attachment for failure to obey writ.
Liability of judge refusing attachment, §17-17.
Disobedience to writ, §17-26.
Insufficient return.
Liability of judge conniving at, §17-21.
Order of discharge.
Failure to comply, §17-23.
Precept to bring up party detained.
Refusal of precept.
Liability of judge refusing, §17-20.
Refusal to grant writ, §17-10.
Return.
Refusal or neglect to make return, §17-26.
Second committal after discharge, §17-38.
Post-conviction hearing act.
Motion for appropriate relief, §§15A-1411 to 15A-1422.
See MOTION FOR APPROPRIATE RELIEF.
Precept to bring up party detained, §17-19.
County may be called on to aid execution, §17-22.
Refusal of precept.
Liability of judge refusing precept, §17-20.
Production of body if required, §17-15.
Precept to bring up party detained, §17-19.
Refusal of precept.
Liability of judge refusing, §17-20.
Time for, §17-13.
Recommittal after discharge, §17-25.
Remand of party.
Executions.
Party held in execution not to be discharged, §17-36.
When party remanded, §§17-34, 17-35.
Return of writ.
Contents of return, §17-14.
False return, §17-27.
Insufficient return.
Judge conniving at, §17-21.
Proceedings on return, §17-32.
Production of body if required, §17-15.
Time for, §17-13.
Refusal or neglect to make return, §17-26.
Time for, §17-13.
Verification by oath, §17-14.
Written return, §17-14.
Right to remedy, §17-1.
Granting of writ without delay, §17-9.
Penalty for refusal to grant, §17-10.
Who may prosecute writ, §17-3.
Service of writ, §17-12.
County may be called on to aid service, §17-22.
Habeas corpus ad testificandum, §17-43.
Applicant to pay expenses and give bond to return, §17-44.
Duty of officer to whom writ delivered or on whom served, §17-45.

HABEAS CORPUS —Cont'd
Subpoenas.
Witnesses in habeas corpus proceedings, §17-31.
Sufficiency of writ, §17-11.
Supreme court.
Issuance of remedial writs, §7A-32(a).
Suspension.
Prohibited, §17-2, US Const Art I §9.
United States courts.
Persons committed or detained by.
When application denied, §17-4.
Remand of party.
When party remanded, §17-34.
Verification.
Application for habeas corpus ad testificandum, §17-42.
Return of writ.
Verification by oath, §17-14.
Witnesses.
Habeas corpus ad testificandum, §§17-41 to 17-46.
Subpoenas in habeas corpus proceedings, §17-31.

HABEAS CORPUS AD TESTIFICANDUM, §§17-41 to 17-46.
Application for writ.
Bond of applicant, §17-44.
Contents of application, §17-42.
Expenses.
Applicant to pay, §17-44.
Verification, §17-42.
Bond of applicant, §17-44.
Clerks of superior court.
Power to issue writ, §17-41.
Courts of record.
Power to issue writ, §17-41.
Issuance of writ.
Authority to issue, §17-41.
Magistrates.
Power to issue writs, §17-41.
Remand of party, §17-46.
Service of writ, §17-43.
Applicant to pay expenses and give bond to return, §17-44.
Duty of officer to whom writ delivered or on whom served, §17-45.

HABITS.
Relevancy to prove conduct of person, §8C-1
Rule 406.

HABITUAL BREAKING AND ENTERING STATUS OFFENSE, §§14-7.25 to 14-7.31.
See BREAKING AND ENTERING.

HABITUAL FELONS, §§14-7.1 to 14-7.12.
Breaking and entering.
Habitual breaking and entering status offense, §§14-7.25 to 14-7.31.
See BREAKING AND ENTERING.
Charge of habitual felon, §14-7.3.
Class C felony.
Not sentenced to class higher than, §14-7.6.
Commencement of sentence, §14-7.6.
Consecutively.
Sentences to run, §14-7.6.
Defined, §14-7.1.
Evidence of prior convictions, §14-7.4.
Felonies committed before person 16 years of age.
Treatment, §14-7.1.
Felony class level.
Sentencing, §14-7.6.
Felony offense defined, §14-7.1.

HABITUAL FELONS —Cont'd
Indictment, §14-7.2.
Charge of habitual felon, §14-7.3.
Judgment, §14-7.5.
Pardon.
Felonies committed before person 16 years of age.
Treatment of felony for which person pardoned, §14-7.1.
Prior convictions.
Evidence, §14-7.4.
Prior record level, determining, §14-7.6.
Punishment, §14-7.2.
Sentencing, §§14-7.2, 14-7.6.
Structured sentencing.
Inapplicability to violent habitual felons, §15A-1340.10.
Status offender.
Charging as, §14-7.1.
Verdict, §14-7.5.
Violent habitual felons.
Charge, §14-7.9.
Convicted defined, §14-7.7(a).
Evidence of prior convictions, §14-7.10.
Persons declared to be, §14-7.7(a).
Punishment, §14-7.8.
Sentencing, §14-7.12.
Verdict and judgment, §14-7.11.
Violent felony, crimes included in term, §14-7.7(b).

HABITUAL IMPAIRED DRIVING, §20-138.5.

HACKING.
Computer crimes generally, §§14-453 to 14-458.
See COMPUTER CRIMES.

HAGUE CONVENTION.
Child custody jurisdiction and enforcement, §50A-302.
Prosecutor or public official, role of, §50A-315.

HAIL INSURANCE.
Beach area essential property insurance, §58-45-35(e).
Generally, §§58-45-1 to 58-45-96.
See BEACH AREA ESSENTIAL PROPERTY INSURANCE.
Property insurance generally.
See PROPERTY INSURANCE.

HAIR DYE.
Food, drug and cosmetic act.
Cautionary statement required, §106-136.

HAIR REMOVAL.
Laser hair practitioners.
Electrologists generally, §§88A-1 to 88A-23.
See ELECTROLOGISTS.

HAIR SAMPLES.
Nontestimonial identification.
Delinquent or undisciplined juvenile actions, §§7B-2103 to 7B-2109.
Generally, §§15A-271 to 15A-282.
See IDENTIFICATION.

HALF-WAY HOUSES.
Post-release supervision, §§15A-1368 to 15A-1368.6.
See POST-RELEASE SUPERVISION.

HALIFAX COUNTY.
Ambulance service.
Attachment or garnishment and lien for, §§44-51.4 to 44-51.8.
Obtaining ambulance services without intending to pay, §14-111.2.

HALIFAX COUNTY —Cont'd
Ambulance service —Cont'd
Requesting ambulance falsely, §14-111.3.
Blank or master forms of mortgages, deeds of trust, etc.
Indexing and recording, inapplicability of provisions, §47-21.
Condemnation or acquisition of land by local government unit outside county.
Consent of board of commissioners necessary, §153A-15.
Cropper or tenant refusing to perform terms of contract.
Forfeiture of right of possession to premises, §42-27.
Game laws, local acts not repealed, §113-133.1(e).
Grants in navigable waters, registration, §113-205(a).
Housing authority commissioners.
Tenant as commissioner, exemption from provision of law allowing, §157-5.
Low-income housing tax credits.
Qualified building eligible for credit, §105-129.41(c).
Multi-county water conservation and infrastructure district.
Generally, §158-15.1.
North Carolina's northeast commission, §§158-8.2 to 158-8.8.
Officers compensated from fees.
Statement to be rendered, §128-13.
Oil, gas or mineral claims.
Certain ancient claims extinguished, preservation, procedure, §1-42.3(a) to (d).
Probates and registration orders before clerks of inferior courts validated, §47-59.
Registration of deeds.
Tax certification, no delinquent taxes due, §161-31(b).
School property.
Acquisition and improvement, §153A-158.1.
Tax sales, notices by publication validated.
Inapplicability of provisions, §47-108.24.

HALIFAX DAY.
Public holiday, §103-4(a).

HALIWA-SAPONI TRIBE.
Rights, privileges, immunities, obligations and duties, §71A-5.

HALLOWEEN.
Distribution of certain food at Halloween and all other times prohibited, §14-401.11(a), (b).

HALLS OF FAME.
Agriculture, §§106-568.13 to 106-568.17.
See AGRICULTURAL HALL OF FAME.

HALLUCINOGENIC SUBSTANCES.
Schedule I controlled substances, §90-89.
Schedule II controlled substances, §90-90.
Unauthorized substances taxes, §§105-113.105 to 105-113.113.
See UNAUTHORIZED SUBSTANCES TAXES.

HAMLET.
All-terrain vehicles.
Use by employees on certain highways, §20-171.24.

HAMMOCKS BEACH STATE PARK.
Removal from state nature and historic preserve, §143-260.10D.

HAM RADIO OPERATORS.
Interception of radio communications not unlawful, §15A-287(b).

HAND AND ARM SIGNALS.
Operators of motor vehicles, §20-154(b).

HANDGUNS.
Concealed handgun permit, §§14-415.10 to 14-415.27.
See CONCEALED HANDGUN PERMIT.
Generally.
See FIREARMS AND OTHER WEAPONS.

HANDICAPPED PARKING.
Generally, §§20-37.5 to 20-37.6A.

HANDICAPPED PERSONS.
Abused, neglected or exploited disabled adults, §§108A-99 to 108A-111.
See ABUSED, NEGLECTED OR EXPLOITED DISABLED ADULTS.
Alcoholic beverages.
Refusal to sell not to be discriminatory, §18B-305(c).
Animals.
Service animals, §§168-4.2 to 168-4.6.
Blind persons generally, §§111-4 to 111-47.
See BLIND AND VISUALLY IMPAIRED.
Commission for the blind, §§143B-157 to 143B-160.
Consumer and advocacy advisory committee for the blind, §§143B-163, 143B-164.
Professional advisory committee, §§143B-161, 143B-162.
Commission to study the care of the aged and handicapped, §§143-279 to 143-283.
Community third party or pooled trusts.
Persons with severe chronic disabilities, §§36D-1 to 36D-12.
See COMMUNITY THIRD PARTY OR POOLED TRUSTS.
Consumer and advocacy advisory committee for the blind, §§143B-163, 143B-164.
Council on developmental disabilities, §§143B-177 to 143B-179.
Developmental disabilities generally.
See MENTAL HEALTH, DEVELOPMENTAL DISABILITY, SUBSTANCE ABUSE.
Disabled persons generally.
See DISABLED PERSONS.
Education of children with disabilities.
Generally, §§115C-106.1 to 115C-112.1.
See SPECIAL EDUCATION.
Fair housing generally, §§41A-1 to 41A-10.
See FAIR HOUSING.
Generally.
See DISABLED PERSONS.
Governor's council on employment of the handicapped, §§143-283.1 to 143-283.8.
Hearing impaired generally.
See DEAF AND HEARING IMPAIRED.
Human service and volunteer transportation, §§62-289.1 to 62-289.7.
See HUMAN SERVICE AND VOLUNTEER TRANSPORTATION.
Hunting and fishing.
Disabled sportsman program, §113-296.
Special vehicular access identification card and permit.
Violation of rules restricting access to holders, §113-294(n).

HANDICAPPED PERSONS —Cont'd
Indictments.
  Essentials of bill.
    Victim physically helpless, §15-144.2(c).
Interagency coordinating council for children
  with disabilities from birth to five years of
  age, §§143B-179.5, 143B-179.6.
Mentally ill generally.
  See MENTAL HEALTH, DEVELOPMENTAL
    DISABILITY, SUBSTANCE ABUSE.
Parking, §§20-37.6, 20-37.6(a).
  Definitions, §20-37.5.
  Public vehicular areas.
    Signs differing from uniform signs, §136-30(c).
Representatives.
  Persons representing and binding others,
    §§36C-3-301 to 36C-3-305.
Service animals, §§168-4.2 to 168-4.6.
Special education.
  Education of children with disabilities.
    Generally, §§115C-106.1 to 115C-112.1.
    See SPECIAL EDUCATION.

HANDLERS OF FRUIT OR VEGETABLES.
Unfair practices by handlers, §§106-496 to
  106-501.
  Bond required, §106-498.
  Contracts between handlers and producers,
    §106-499.
  Definition of handler, §106-496.
  Enforcement of article.
    Commissioner of agriculture to enforce,
      §106-500.
  Permits required, §106-497.
  Powers of commissioner, §106-500.
  Protection against unfair trade practices,
    §106-496.
  Violations of article or rules made misdemeanor,
    §106-501.

HANDS.
Workers' compensation.
  Loss of hands.
    Permanent total disability.
      Qualification for, lifetime compensation,
        §97-29(d).
    Rates of compensation, ICWorkComp Rule 405.

HANDSHAKES.
Secret societies' use of grips for illegal
  purposes, §14-12.4.

HANDWRITING.
Acknowledgments.
  Proof of handwriting of maker refusing to
    acknowledge, §47-57.
Attested instruments.
  Proof for registration, §47-12.1(a), (b).
Authentication and identification of evidence,
  §8C-1 Rule 901(b).
Holographic wills, §31-3.4.
Nontestimonial identification.
  Delinquent and undisciplined juveniles, §§7B-2103
    to 7B-2109.
  Generally, §§15A-271 to 15A-282.
    See IDENTIFICATION.
Probates on proof of handwriting of maker
  refusing to acknowledge, §47-57.
Proof of unattested instruments, §47-13.

HARASSMENT.
Assaulting law enforcement agency animal,
  assistance animals, search and rescue
  animals, §14-163.1(d).

HARASSMENT —Cont'd
Civil rights, interference with, §99D-1.
Collection agencies.
  Prohibited practices, §58-70-100.
Debt collectors.
  Prohibited acts, §75-52.
Domestic violence.
  Orders for relief, §50B-3(a).
Fish and fisheries resources.
  Unlawful harassment of persons taking wildlife
    resources, §113-295.
Hunting and wildlife.
  Unlawful harassment of persons taking wildlife
    resources, §113-295.
Jury.
  Definition of "juror,"§14-225.2(b).
  Elements of offense, §14-225.2(a).
  Penalties, §14-225.2(c).
Public schools.
  Bullying and harassing behavior, §115C-407.15.
    Construction of provisions, §115C-407.18.
    Policies to be adopted, §115C-407.16.
    Promotion of environments free of,
      §115C-407.17.
  Conflict resolution and mediation models,
    §115C-81(a4).
Sexual harassment.
  Equal employment practices, §§143-422.1 to
    143-422.3.
  Rental of residential property.
    Definitions, §14-395.1(b).
    Offense, §14-395.1(a).
  School employees, §115C-335.5.
Stalking.
  See STALKING.
Telephones, §14-196.
Threats.
  See THREATS.
Workplace violence prevention.
  Civil no-contact orders, §§95-260 to 95-271.
    See WORKPLACE VIOLENCE PREVENTION.

HARBORING OR AIDING ESCAPEE, §14-259.
State institution, §14-267.

HARBOR MASTERS.
How appointed, §76-53.
  No board of navigation, §76-56.

HARBORS.
Municipalities.
  Property taxes.
    Authorized purposes, §160A-209(c).
United States acquisition of land for harbor
  improvements, §104-6.

HARD OF HEARING.
See DEAF AND HEARING IMPAIRED.

HARMFUL MATERIALS.
Displaying, dissemination, sales to minors.
  See OBSCENITY AND PORNOGRAPHY.

HARMLESS ERROR, §1A-1 Rule 61.

HARNETT COUNTY.
Acquisition of property, power, §153A-158.1(a).
Ambulance service.
  Attachment or garnishment and lien for,
    §§44-51.4 to 44-51.8.
Condemnation or acquisition of land by local
  government unit outside county.
  Consent of board of commissioners necessary,
    §153A-15.

HARNETT COUNTY —Cont'd

Cropper or tenant refusing to perform terms of contract.

Forfeiture of right of possession to premises, §42-27.

Dangerous firearm use by young children, permitting.

Air rifles, air pistols and BB guns not dangerous firearm, §14-316(b).

Maps in special proceedings, recording of photographic copies, §47-32.

Violation as misdemeanor, inapplicability of provisions, §47-32.2.

Officers compensated from fees.

Statement to be rendered, §128-13.

Registration of deeds.

Tax certification, no delinquent taxes due, §161-31(b).

School property.

Acquisition and improvement, §153A-158.1.

Tax elections for industrial development purposes, §§158-16 to 158-24.

Tax sales, notices by publication validated.

Inapplicability of provisions, §47-108.24.

HARRISBURG.

Land-use development incentives.

Reduction of energy consumption, §160A-383.4.

HARVEST-YOUR-OWN ACTIVITIES.

Agritourism activity liability, §§99E-30 to 99E-32.

HATCH ACT.

Political activities by public officers and employees.

See POLITICAL ACTIVITIES.

HATCHBACKS.

Open container law.

Definition of passenger area of motor vehicle, §20-138.7(f).

HATCHERIES.

Fish.

Obstructing or polluting flow of water into hatcheries, §113-265(a).

Robbing or injuring, §113-269.

Poultry.

Compulsory testing for disease, §106-548.

Defined, §106-541.

Fines, §106-549.01.

Grade of chicks.

Posting of notice describing grade, §106-546.

License needed to operate, §106-542.

Misdemeanor offenses, §106-549.

Penalties.

Civil penalties, §106-549.01.

Quarantine on premises, §106-548.

Records to be kept, §106-547.

Rules and regulations, §106-540.

Shipments from out of state, §106-544.

HATE CRIMES.

Ethnic intimidation, §14-401.14(a), (b).

Punishment, §14-3(c).

Secret societies and activities generally, §§14-12.2 to 14-12.15.

See SECRET SOCIETIES.

HAULERS.

Vehicle combinations used in connection with motorsports competitions.

Length, §20-116(n).

HAUNTED HOUSES.

Amusement device safety generally, §§95-111.1 to 95-111.18.

See AMUSEMENT DEVICE SAFETY.

Real estate sales disclosures, §39-50.

HAYWOOD COUNTY.

Acquisition of property, power, §153A-158.1(a).

Ambulance service.

Attachment or garnishment and lien for, §§44-51.4 to 44-51.8.

Obtaining ambulance services without intending to pay, §§14-111.1, 14-111.2.

Requesting ambulance falsely, §14-111.3.

Board of county commissioners.

Filling vacancies on board, §153A-27.1.

Condemnation or acquisition of land by local government unit outside county.

Consent of board of commissioners necessary, §153A-15.

Coroner elected as nominee of political party.

Filling vacancy in office, §152-1.

Counties generally.

See COUNTIES.

Dangerous firearm use by young children, permitting.

Air rifles, air pistols and BB guns not dangerous firearm, §14-316(b).

Dog collars.

Unlawful removal of electronic dog collars, §14-401.17.

Game laws, local acts not repealed, §113-133.1(e).

Housing authority commissioners.

Tenant as commissioner, exemption from provision of law allowing, §157-5.

Officers compensated from fees.

Statement to be rendered, §128-13.

Oil, gas or mineral claims.

Certain ancient claims extinguished, preservation, procedure, §1-42.2(a) to (d).

On-premises unfortified wine licenses.

Discretion to decline to issue, §105-113.71(b).

Registration of deeds.

Tax certification, no delinquent taxes due, §161-31(b).

Room occupancy tax levied by county, uniform provision, §153A-155.

School property.

Acquisition and improvement, §153A-158.1.

Sheriff.

Vacancy, performance of duties until vacancy filled, §162-5.1.

Tax deeds in Haywood.

Recitals in tax deeds, §8-22.

Tax elections for industrial development purposes, §§158-16 to 158-24.

Western North Carolina Development Association, Inc.

Appropriation of funds to, §153A-447(a), (b).

Western North Carolina regional economic development commission, §§158-8.1 to 158-8.8.

HAZARDOUS CHEMICALS RIGHT TO KNOW ACT, §§95-173 to 95-218.

See TOXIC MATERIALS AND SUBSTANCES.

HAZARDOUS MATERIALS EMERGENCY RESPONSE, §§166A-20 to 166A-28.

Action for recovery of costs.

Release causing activation of one or more state response teams, §166A-27(b).

HAZARDOUS MATERIALS EMERGENCY RESPONSE —Cont'd

Action for recovery of costs —Cont'd

Release causing activation of regional response team, §166A-27(a).

Contracts with local governments, §166A-23(a).

Coordination with state emergency planning, §166A-22(a).

Costs for clean-up activities.

Reimbursement not provided by secretary, §166A-23(b).

Costs for responses, recovery, §166A-24.

Action for recovery of costs against person who caused release, §§130A-20.01, 166A-27.

Definitions, §166A-21.

Equipment loans, §166A-23(a).

Fund, §166A-28.

Guidelines.

Rules to include, §166A-22(a).

Hazmat teams.

Duties, §166A-22(a).

Required number, §166A-22(a).

Immunity from liability.

Regional response team personnel, §166A-24.

Local response not requiring technical-level entry capabilities.

Reimbursement not provided by secretary, §166A-23(b).

Program established, §166A-22.

Purpose of act, §166A-20(b).

Regional response team advisory committee, §166A-26.

Consultation with.

Developing program, adopting rules, §166A-22(b).

Created, §166A-26(a).

Duties, §166A-26(d).

Meetings, §166A-26(b).

Membership, §166A-26(a).

Reimbursement for expenses, §166A-26(c).

Regional response team personnel.

Immunity from liability, §166A-24.

Regional response teams not state employees, §166A-23(c).

Reimbursement by secretary, §166A-23(a), (b).

Right of entry.

Emergency response team personnel, §166A-25.

Rules establishing, adoption, §166A-22(a).

Standards.

Rules to include, §166A-22(a).

Standby time.

Reimbursement not provided by secretary, §166A-23(b).

State hazmat vehicles.

Use by regional response teams, §166A-23(d).

Title of act, §166A-20(a).

HAZARDOUS MATERIALS, SUBSTANCES AND WASTE.

Brownfields property reuse act of 1997, §§130A-310.30 to 130A-310.40.

See BROWNFIELDS PROPERTY REUSE.

Chlorofluorocarbons refrigerants.

Management of discarded white goods, §§130A-309.80 to 130A-309.87.

See WHITE GOODS.

Contamination at site.

Deed or other instrument of conveyance, contaminated property statement, §143B-279.10(e).

HAZARDOUS MATERIALS, SUBSTANCES AND WASTE —Cont'd

Contamination at site —Cont'd

Land use restrictions imposed by secretary of environment and natural resources.

Reduction of danger to public health, §143B-279.9.

Notice of contamination, survey plat identifying designated area submitted by owner of site, §143B-279.10(a).

Cancellation after contamination eliminated, owner's request, §143B-279.10(f).

Filing copy in register of deeds office, §143B-279.10(b).

Recording copy, §143B-279.10(c).

Secretary may prepare and file, owner's failure, §143B-279.10(d).

Control generally, §§143-215.75 to 143-215.82.

See OIL POLLUTION AND HAZARDOUS SUBSTANCES CONTROL.

Discharges, §§143-215.83 to 143-215.94.

See OIL OR HAZARDOUS SUBSTANCES DISCHARGES.

Dry-cleaning solvent cleanup, §§143-215.104A to 143-215.104U.

See DRY-CLEANING SOLVENT CLEANUP.

Dumping, §14-284.2.

Hazardous materials emergency response, §§166A-20 to 166A-28.

Highway patrol.

Oversized and hazardous shipment escort fee, §20-196.4.

Identification of toxic or hazardous substances, §§95-173 to 95-218.

See TOXIC MATERIALS AND SUBSTANCES.

Land-use restrictions at contaminated site.

Imposed by secretary of environment and natural resources.

Reduction of danger to public health, §143B-279.9.

Lead-based paint hazard management program, §§130A-453.01 to 130A-453.11.

See LEAD-BASED PAINT.

Lead-based paint renovation activities.

Certification and accreditation, §§130A-453.22 to 130A-453.31.

See LEAD-BASED PAINT.

Littering, §14-399(e).

Notice of contamination, survey plat submitted by owner of site, §143B-279.10.

Offshore oil and gas activities, §§143-215.94AA to 143-215.94JJ.

See OFFSHORE OIL AND GAS ACTIVITIES.

Pesticide applicators, §§143-452 to 143-459.

See PESTICIDE APPLICATORS.

Pesticide board generally.

See PESTICIDE BOARD.

Pesticide consultants, §§143-455, 143-456.

Pesticide dealers and manufacturers licenses, §§143-448 to 143-451.

Pesticide registration.

See PESTICIDE REGISTRATION.

Poisons.

See POISONS.

Toxic substances.

See TOXIC MATERIALS AND SUBSTANCES.

Underground petroleum storage tanks.

Leak cleanup, §§143-215.94A to 143-215.94Y.

See UNDERGROUND PETROLEUM STORAGE TANKS.

HAZARDOUS MATERIALS, SUBSTANCES AND WASTE —Cont'd
Underground petroleum storage tanks —Cont'd
Operator training, §§143-215.94NN to 143-215.94UU.
See UNDERGROUND PETROLEUM STORAGE TANKS.
Waste management, §§130A-291 to 130A-310.23.
See HAZARDOUS WASTE MANAGEMENT.
White goods.
Management of discarded white goods, §§130A-309.80 to 130A-309.87.
See WHITE GOODS.

HAZARDOUS RECREATION ACTIVITIES, §§99E-21 to 99E-25.
Assumption of inherent risks, §99E-24(a).
Definitions, §99E-22.
Governmental entities.
Limitation of liability, §99E-25(b).
Duty of care not created, §99E-25(d).
Exceptions, §99E-25(c).
Independent concessionaires or other persons or organizations.
Liability not limited by section, §99E-25(e).
Insurance carried by entity.
Not waiver of liability limits, §99E-25(f).
Sovereign immunity not waived, §99E-25(d).
Operating unsupervised skateboard park.
Wearing of helmet, elbow pads and kneepads.
Satisfaction of requirement, §99E-23(b).
Specifically designated areas for activities.
Required to participate on property owner or controlled by entity, §99E-25(a).
Helmet, elbow pads and kneepads.
Wearing, requirement, §99E-23(a), (b).
Inherent risk.
Assumption, §99E-24(a).
Negligence.
Responsibilities of participants.
Failure to comply, §99E-24(c).
Observers.
Assumption of inherent risks, §99E-24(a).
Participants.
Assumption of inherent risks, §99E-24(a).
Purpose of article, §99E-21.
Responsibilities of participants, §99E-24(b).
Negligence, failure to comply, §99E-24(c).

HAZARDOUS WASTE MANAGEMENT, §§130A-291 to 130A-310.23.
Abandoned, idle or unused property.
Brownfields property reuse act of 1997, §§130A-310.30 to 130A-310.40.
See BROWNFIELDS PROPERTY REUSE.
Appeals.
Hazardous waste facilities.
Preempting local ordinance, §130A-293(e).
Bond issues.
Solid waste management loans and local government special obligation bonds.
Generally, §§159I-1 to 159I-30.
See SOLID WASTE MANAGEMENT LOANS AND SPECIAL OBLIGATION BONDS.
Brownfields property reuse act of 1997.
Generally, §§130A-310.30 to 130A-310.40.
See BROWNFIELDS PROPERTY REUSE.
Chemical storage facilities.
New facilities in flood hazard areas, §143-215.54(c).
Chlorofluorocarbons refrigerants.
Management of discarded white goods, §§130A-309.80 to 130A-309.87.
See WHITE GOODS.

HAZARDOUS WASTE MANAGEMENT —Cont'd
Combustion products landfills.
Construction, requirements for authorization, §130A-295.4(b).
Definitions, §130A-295.4(a).
Response plan required, §130A-295.4(c).
Commission.
Personnel system.
Exemption of employees, §126-5(c1).
Comprehensive waste treatment facility.
Defined, §130A-290.
Containers.
Placement in, §130A-295.03(a), (b).
Contamination at site.
Deed or other instrument of conveyance, contaminated property statement, §143B-279.10(e).
Exceptions to recordation provisions, §143B-279.10(g).
Industrial sites.
Risk based environmental remediation, §§130A-310.65 to 130A-310.77.
Land use restrictions imposed by secretary of environment and natural resources.
Reduction of danger to public health, §143B-279.9.
Notice of contamination, survey plat identifying designated area submitted by owner of site, §143B-279.10(a).
Cancellation after contamination eliminated, owner's request, §143B-279.10(f).
Filing copy in register of deeds office, §143B-279.10(b).
Recording copy, §143B-279.10(c).
Secretary may prepare and file, owner's failure, §143B-279.10(d).
Conveyances.
Hazardous waste landfill facility.
Land used for facility conveyed to state, §130A-292.
Counties.
Local ordinances prohibiting facilities invalid, §130A-293.
Defenses.
Felonies, §130A-26.1(e), (i).
Definitions, §130A-290.
Hazardous waste treatment facility, §130A-290.
Inactive hazardous sites, §130A-310.
Long-term retrievable storage, §130A-290.
Superfund program, §130A-310.20.
Emergency response fund, §130A-306.
Eminent hazard.
Elimination of hazard, §130A-303(b).
Existence of eminent hazard, §130A-303(a).
Environmental review commission.
Powers and duties, §120-70.43(c).
Evidence.
Circumstantial evidence of defendant's possession of actual knowledge, §130A-26.1(c).
Facilities.
Commercial hazardous waste treatment facilities.
Annual report on changes in sensitive land use and population density, §130A-295.01(f).
Definitions, §130A-295.01(a).
Duration of permit issued, §130A-295.01(c).
Inspectors.
Resident inspectors, §130A-295.02.
Notification to residents within certain distance of application filed, §130A-295.01(e).
Record keeping requirements of owner/operators, §130A-295.01(d).

HAZARDOUS WASTE MANAGEMENT —Cont'd
Facilities —Cont'd
Commercial hazardous waste treatment facilities
—Cont'd
Requirements for permits, §130A-295.01(b).
Resident inspectors, §130A-295.02.
Security and surveillance system required,
§130A-295.01(g).
Wind monitor required, §130A-295.01(h).
Containers.
Placement of wastes in, §130A-295.03(a), (b).
Contingency plan.
Information required to be submitted prior to
permit application, §130A-295(d).
Response of local government and emergency
response agencies, §130A-295(e).
Verification data to be included in application
for permit, §130A-295(f).
Continuing releases at permitted facilities.
Corrective actions beyond facility boundary,
§130A-309.
Conveyance of land used for facility to state.
Consideration for conveyance, §130A-292(a).
Liability of lessee, §130A-292(b).
Termination of lease, §130A-292(c), (d).
Criteria and standards to be considered in
location, §130A-294(g).
Defined, §130A-290.
Disposal of solid waste in or upon water,
§130A-294(l).
Fees, §130A-294.1(k), (l).
Permit for facility, §130A-294.1(m), (n).
Resident inspectors at commercial hazardous
waste facilities.
Costs of employment and assignment,
§130A-295.02(h).
Financial assurance requirements, §130A-295(b).
Form of assets used to meet requirements,
§130A-295.04(f).
Guarantors of payment for closure, maintenance
and monitoring, corrective action, and
liability arising from accidents,
§130A-295.04(c).
Maintenance of financial responsibility,
§130A-295.04(h).
Methods of establishing, §130A-295.04(b).
Required to establish, §130A-295.04(a).
Review of filings by state treasurer,
§130A-295.04(g).
Satisfaction of these requirements before permit
review, §130A-295.04(i).
State treasurer.
Review of filings and written opinion on
adequacy, §130A-295.04(g).
Trust fund.
Owners and operators of sanitary landfills
establishing, §130A-295.04(j).
Hearings.
Permit for facility, §130A-294(f).
Inspectors.
Resident inspectors at commercial hazardous
waste facilities, §130A-295.02.
License tax.
Counties, §153A-152.1(a) to (c).
Rates applied by localities to.
Review upon appeal, §130A-294(r).
Local ordinances prohibiting facilities invalid,
§130A-293(a).
Petition to preempt local ordinance,
§130A-293(b) to (f).

HAZARDOUS WASTE MANAGEMENT —Cont'd
Facilities —Cont'd
Monitoring and regulating generators,
§130A-294(i).
Permit for facility.
Application.
Information required to be provided prior to
submitting, §130A-295(d).
Verification data received from local
government and emergency response
agencies, §130A-295(e).
Submitted with permit application,
§130A-295(f).
Commercial hazardous waste treatment
facilities.
Additional requirements for facilities,
§130A-295.01(b).
Duration of permit issued, §130A-295.01(c).
Notification to residents within certain
distance of application filed,
§130A-295.01(e).
Conduct of public hearing, §130A-294(f).
Criteria and standards to be considered,
§130A-294(g).
Fees, §130A-294.1(m), (n).
Financial assurance requirements for applicants
and permit-holders, §130A-295.04.
Need for facility, §130A-295(c).
Requirements.
Additional requirements for facilities,
§130A-295(a).
Commercial hazardous waste treatment
facilities, §130A-295.01(b).
Public education and involvement in
decision-making process, §130A-294(o).
Releases.
Continuing releases at permitted facilities.
Corrective actions beyond facility boundary,
§130A-309.
Corrective action.
Request for determination that corrective
action completed, §130A-308(b).
Required, §130A-308(a).
Requirements.
Additional requirements for facility,
§130A-295(a).
Resident inspectors at commercial hazardous
waste facilities.
Access to operation areas, §130A-295.02(d).
Affiliates adjacent or contiguous to facility.
Subject to inspection, §130A-295.02(k), (l).
Costs of employment and assignment,
§130A-295.02(h).
Duration of assignment, §130A-295.02(i).
Employment, §130A-295.02(a).
Facilities, §130A-295.02(b), (c).
Maintenance or repair.
Presence of inspector required,
§130A-295.02(e).
Peace officers.
Commissioning inspectors as special peace
officers, §130A-295.02(g).
Powers, §130A-295.02(a).
Purpose of provisions, §130A-295.02(f).
Qualifications.
Division to establish requirements,
§130A-295.02(b).
Report on implementation, §130A-295.02(m).
Special purpose commercial hazardous waste
facilities, §130A-295.02(j).

HAZARDOUS WASTE MANAGEMENT —Cont'd
Facilities —Cont'd
Resident inspectors at commercial hazardous
waste facilities —Cont'd
Testing or calibration.
Presence of inspector required,
§130A-295.02(e).
Right of entry by department, §130A-294(s).
Rules and regulations, §130A-294(b), (h).
Transfer facilities.
Compliance with applicable laws and rules,
§130A-295.05(c).
Identification numbers.
Obtaining, §130A-295.05(a).
Required for operation, §130A-295.05(b).
Owner/operators to notify department of all
transporters who use facilities,
§130A-295.05(e).
Record keeping requirements.
Owner/operator, §130A-295.05(c).
Transporters, §130A-295.05(c).
Registration of facilities, §130A-295.05(a).
Transporters to notify department of all
facilities used, §130A-295.05(d).
Volume and quantity or toxicity of waste.
Description of program to minimize or reduce,
§130A-294(k).
False reports.
Penalty, §130A-26.2.
Fees.
Hazardous waste generators, transporters and
facilities.
Deposit of fees collected, §130A-294.1(d).
Facilities, §130A-294.1(k), (l).
Permits, §130A-294.1(m), (n).
Generators of hazardous waste, §130A-294.1(e)
to (i).
Legislative intent, §130A-294.1(a), (c).
Reports by department.
Cost of program, §130A-294.1(p).
Transporters of hazardous waste,
§130A-294.1(j).
Use of funds collected, §130A-294.1(b).
When fees due, §130A-294.1(o).
Risk based environmental remediation of
industrial sites, §130A-310.76(a).
Felonies.
Classification, §130A-26.1(f), (g), (i).
Defenses, §130A-26.1(e), (i).
Definition of "person,"§130A-26.1(a).
Federal violation based on same set of facts.
Conviction as bar to proceedings, §130A-26.1(b).
"Knowingly and willingly.."
Circumstantial evidence of defendant's
possession of actual knowledge,
§130A-26.1(c).
Meaning of term, §130A-26.1(h).
Restrictions on findings concerning defendant's
state of mind, §130A-26.1(d).
Second or subsequent conviction, §130A-26.1(i), (j).
Flood hazard areas.
New facilities in, §143-215.54(c).
Funds.
Emergency response fund, §130A-306.
Establishment of hazardous waste fund,
§130A-298.
Hazardous waste fund, §130A-298.
Inactive hazardous sites cleanup fund.
Established, §130A-310.11(a).
Solid waste disposal tax.
Distribution, §105-187.63.

HAZARDOUS WASTE MANAGEMENT —Cont'd
Funds —Cont'd
Inactive hazardous sites cleanup fund —Cont'd
Use of proceeds, §130A-310.11(b).
Superfund program, §§130A-310.20 to
130A-310.23.
Governor's award of excellence, §130A-294(p).
Hazardous waste long-term storage facility,
§130A-290.
Hearings.
Hazardous waste facilities.
Conduct of public hearing.
Prior to issuance of permit, §130A-294(f).
Petition to preempt local ordinance,
§130A-293(c).
Impoundments.
Locating, cataloging and monitoring, §130A-294(i).
Inactive hazardous sites, §§130A-310 to
130A-310.13.
Access to site, right of secretary, §130A-310.1(i).
Administrative procedure.
Applicability to provisions, §130A-310.12(a).
Administrative search and inspection warrant.
Refusal to grant access to site, §130A-310.1(i).
Citation of part, §130A-310.13.
Cleanup fund.
Established, §130A-310.11(a).
Solid waste disposal tax.
Distribution, §105-187.63.
Use of proceeds, §130A-310.11(b).
Costs.
Actions taken by secretary, §130A-310.1(e).
Declaration that site endangers public health or
environment, §130A-310.3(a).
Definitions, §130A-310.
Determination that site remediated to current
standards, request, §130A-310.7(c).
Furnishing information, documents or records to
secretary, §130A-310.1(f).
General assembly members with site in member's
district.
Reports to, §130A-310.2(b).
Groundwater flow.
Migrating waste to property.
Waiver of recordation of notice of sites,
§130A-310.8(h).
Imminent hazard.
Action taken by secretary, §130A-310.5(a).
Cost, §130A-310.5(c).
Orders by secretary, §130A-310.5(a).
Injunctions, §130A-310.5(b).
Implementation of remedial action.
Fee by party participating for cost of monitoring
and enforcing program, §130A-310.9(a).
Limitation on liability, §130A-310.9(a).
Voluntary remedial action program,
§130A-310.9(b), (c).
Injunctions.
Failure to submit data or comply with orders,
§130A-310.1(d).
Imminent hazard orders, §130A-310.5(b).
Inspection and copying information, documents
and records, §130A-310.1(g).
Inventory, §130A-310.1(a).
Land-use restrictions imposed by owner, operator,
etc., §130A-310.3(f).
Limitation of liability for implementing remedial
action program, §130A-310.9(a).
List.
Priority list, §130A-310.2(a).

HAZARDOUS WASTE MANAGEMENT —Cont'd
Inactive hazardous sites —Cont'd
Notice.
  Copies of proposed plan.
    Availability for inspection and copying,
      §130A-310.4(b).
  Imminent hazard.
    Orders, §130A-310.5(a).
  Local health director.
    Involvement in development of plan,
      §130A-310.4(a).
  Orders.
    Monitoring, testing, analysis and reporting,
      §130A-310.1(c).
    Remedial action, §130A-310.3(c).
  Recordation of sites generally, §§47-29.1(b),
    130A-310.8.
  Remedial action.
    Form and content of notices, §130A-310.4(g).
    Orders, §130A-310.3(c).
    Proposed plan, §130A-310.4(c).
      Hearing on, §130A-310.4(f).
Operator.
  Data to be submitted by, §130A-310.1(b).
    Failure to submit data.
      Injunction, §130A-310.1(d).
  Defined, §130A-310.
Orders.
  Imminent hazard, §130A-310.5(a), (b).
  Monitoring, testing, analysis and reporting,
    §130A-310.1(c).
  Injunction, §130A-310.1(d).
  Remedial action, §130A-310.3(c).
Owner.
  Data to be submitted by, §130A-310.1(b).
    Failure to submit data, §130A-310.1(b).
  Defined, §130A-310.
Pre-1983 landfills.
  Additional actions by department authorized,
    §130A-310.6(g).
  Assessment and development of remedial action
    plan, §130A-310.6(c).
  Priority, §130A-310.6(e).
  Voluntary assessment and remediation by
    local government, reimbursement,
    §130A-310.6(f).
  Cost recovery.
    Local government requesting from
      department, §130A-310.6(f).
    Secretary seeking from local government,
      §130A-310.6(d).
Priority list, §130A-310.2(a).
Recordation of notice of sites, §47-29.1(b).
  Applicability of provisions, §130A-310.8(g).
  Cancellation when hazards eliminated,
    §130A-310.8(f).
  Filing, §130A-310.8(b) to (d).
  Groundwater migrating waste to property.
    Waiver of recordation, §130A-310.8(h).
  Sale, lease, conveyance or transfer of site,
    §130A-310.8(e).
  Submission to department, §130A-310.8(a).
  Waiver of recordation.
    Residential real property contaminated by
      waste migration, §130A-310.8(h).
  Remedial action.
    Defined, §130A-310.
    Federal approval of programs, §130A-310.3(d).
    Notice, §§130A-310.3(c), 130A-310.4(c), (f), (g).
    Orders, §130A-310.3(c).
    Permits, §130A-310.3(e).

HAZARDOUS WASTE MANAGEMENT —Cont'd
Inactive hazardous sites —Cont'd
Remedial action —Cont'd
  Powers and duties of secretary, §130A-310.3(a)
    to (c).
  Proposed plan.
    Copies, §130A-310.4(b).
    Hearings on, §130A-310.4(e), (f).
    Notice, §130A-310.4(c).
    Public meeting to explain, §130A-310.4(d).
  Restrictions on current or future use of real
    property, §130A-310.3(f).
  Voluntary remedial action program,
    §130A-310.9(b), (c).
Reports.
  Annual report by secretary, §130A-310.10(a).
  General assembly members with site in
    member's district.
    Reports to, §130A-310.2(b).
Requests for determination that site remediated
  to current standards, §130A-310.7(c).
Responsible party.
  Default of responsible party, §130A-310.6(a).
  Defined, §130A-310.
  Generally, §130A-310.7(a).
  Inability to locate responsible party,
    §130A-310.6(b).
  Liability, §130A-310.7(a).
    Exceptions, §130A-310.7(b).
Restrictions on current or future use of real
  property comprising.
  Owner, operator or other responsible party
    authorized to impose, §130A-310.3(f).
Risk based environmental remediation at
  contaminated industrial sites, §§130A-310.65
  to 130A-310.77.
Rules and regulations, §130A-310.12(b).
Short title of part, §130A-310.13.
Subpoenas by secretary to collect information,
  §130A-310.1(h).
Voluntary remedial action program.
  Agreement with owner, operator or other
    responsible party for implementation,
    §130A-310.9(b).
  Approving private environmental consulting
    engineering firm to implement,
    §130A-310.9(c).
Industrial sites.
Risk based environmental remediation,
  §§130A-310.65 to 130A-310.77.
Information on handling and disposing,
  §130A-294(n).
Interstate agreements.
Assistance with negotiation by secretary,
  §130A-294(q).
Land-use restrictions at contaminated site.
Imposed by secretary of environment and natural
  resources.
  Reduction of danger to public health,
    §143B-279.9.
License tax on facilities.
Counties, §153A-152.1(a) to (c).
Littering, §14-399(e).
Loans.
Solid waste management loans and local
  government special obligation bonds.
  Generally, §§159I-1 to 159I-30.
    See SOLID WASTE MANAGEMENT LOANS
      AND SPECIAL OBLIGATION BONDS.
Municipalities.
Local ordinances prohibited facilities invalid,
  §130A-293.

HAZARDOUS WASTE MANAGEMENT —Cont'd
Navigable waters.
Deposit prohibited, §76-40(a1).
Notice of contamination, survey plat by owner of contaminated site, §143B-279.10.
Oil.
Used oil.
See USED OIL.
Ordinances.
Hazardous waste facilities.
Local ordinances prohibited facilities invalid, §130A-293.
Permits.
Facilities. See within this heading, "Facilities."
Petitions.
Hazardous waste facilities.
Preempting local ordinance, §130A-293(b) to (f).
Privilege license tax on facilities.
Counties, §153A-152.1(a) to (c).
Recordation.
Commercial hazardous waste treatment facilities.
Record keeping requirements of owner/operators, §130A-295.01(d).
Recordation of environmental notices.
Contaminated site, notice of, §47-29.1(f).
Dry-cleaning solvent remediation.
Notice, §47-29.1(e).
Inactive hazardous substance or waste disposal site, §47-29.1(b).
Oil or hazardous substance discharge site, §47-29.1(d).
Residual petroleum, §47-29.1(g).
Waste disposal permit, §47-29.1(a).
Releases at facilities.
Corrective action.
Request for determination that corrective action completed, §130A-308(b).
Required, §130A-308(a).
Research and development on handling and disposing, §130A-294(n).
Right of entry by department, §130A-294(s).
Risk based environmental remediation of industrial sites, §§130A-310.65 to 130A-310.77.
Air quality standards.
Site specific remediation standards, §130A-310.68(b).
Applicability of part, §130A-310.67(a).
Effective date of part, §130A-310.67(c).
Inapplicability, §130A-310.67(b).
Background standard.
Defined, §130A-310.65.
Remediation standards, §130A-310.68(a).
Brownfields property reuse act.
Compliance with other laws, §130A-310.74.
Carcinogens.
Site specific remediation standards, §130A-310.68(b).
Compliance with other laws, §130A-310.74.
Construction of part, §130A-310.77.
Contaminated industrial site.
Defined, §130A-310.65.
Contamination.
Defined, §130A-310.65.
Current uses.
Remedial action plan, §130A-310.69(b).
Definitions, §130A-310.65.
Effective date of part, §130A-310.67(c).
Estimate of probable costs.
Remedial action plan, §130A-310.69(b).

HAZARDOUS WASTE MANAGEMENT —Cont'd
Risk based environmental remediation of industrial sites —Cont'd
Federal authority.
Part not construed to conflict with, §130A-310.77.
Fee paid by person undertaking remediation, §130A-310.76(a).
Use of funds, §130A-310.76(b).
Financial assurance requirement, §130A-310.72.
Funds to implement and maintain actions and controls.
Financial assurance requirement, §130A-310.72.
Future uses.
Remedial action plan, §130A-310.69(b).
Groundwater.
Site specific remediation standards, §130A-310.68(b).
Human exposure to contamination.
Protection against.
Site specific remediation standards, §130A-310.68(b).
Inapplicability of part, §130A-310.67(b).
Land use restrictions.
Remedial action plan, §130A-310.69(b).
Migration of contamination to adjacent property.
Reasonable assurance that contamination will not migrate, §130A-310.71(b).
No further remediation required.
Determination, §130A-310.73(c).
Notice of intent to remediate, §130A-310.70.
Oversight for assessment and remediation.
Use of registered environmental consultants, §130A-310.75.
Purposes of part, §130A-310.66.
Registered environmental consultants.
Defined, §130A-310.65.
Use to provide oversight, §130A-310.75.
Remedial action plan, §130A-310.69(b), (c).
Defined, §130A-310.65.
Disapproval, review, §130A-310.71(d).
Failure to take timely action on plan.
Plan treated as approved, §130A-310.71(d).
Final report.
Plan fully implemented, §130A-310.73(a).
Fully implemented.
Burden of demonstrating, §130A-310.73(b).
Final report, §130A-310.73(a).
No further remediation required.
Determination, §130A-310.73(c), (d).
Reasonable assurance that contamination will not migrate.
Burden of demonstrating, §130A-310.71(b).
Review and approval, §130A-310.71(a).
Additional information, §130A-310.71(c).
Determination on, §130A-310.71(d).
Supplemental submissions, §§130A-310.69(d), 130A-310.71(c).
Time limit on approving or disapproving, §130A-310.71(d).
Remedial investigation report.
Submitted by person proposing remediation, §130A-310.69(a).
Remediation defined, §130A-310.65.
Remediation standards, §130A-310.68(a).
Attainment of compliance, §130A-310.73(a).
Site specific remediation standards, §130A-310.68(a).
Development requirements, §130A-310.68(b).
Remedial action plan, §130A-310.69(b).
Remediation based on, purposes, §130A-310.66.

HAZARDOUS WASTE MANAGEMENT —Cont'd
Risk based environmental remediation of industrial sites —Cont'd
Soil.
Site specific remediation standards, §130A-310.68(b).
Systemic toxicants.
Defined, §130A-310.65.
Site specific remediation standards, §130A-310.68(b).
Unrestricted use standards.
Defined, §130A-310.65.
Remediation standards, §130A-310.68(a).
Water quality standards.
Site specific remediation standards, §130A-310.68(b).
Rules concerning management of waste, §130A-294(c).
State of North Carolina.
Conveyance of land used for hazardous waste landfill facility, §130A-292.
Superfund program, §§130A-310.20 to 130A-310.23.
Administration, §130A-310.21.
Appropriations.
Not obligated, §130A-310.22(c).
Assurances required by federal law, §130A-310.22(b).
Contracts.
Authorized, §130A-310.22(a).
Definitions, §130A-310.20.
Notices of superfund liens.
Filing, §130A-310.23.
Program administration, §130A-310.21.
Transfer facilities.
Compliance with applicable laws and rules, §130A-295.05(c).
Identification numbers.
Obtaining, §130A-295.05(a).
Required for operation, §130A-295.05(b).
Owner/operators to notify department of all transporters who use facilities, §130A-295.05(e).
Record keeping requirements.
Owner/operators, §130A-295.05(e).
Transporters, §130A-295.05(c).
Registration of facilities, §130A-295.05(a).
Transporters to notify department of all facilities used, §130A-295.05(d).
Used oil.
Regulation of used oil as hazardous waste, §130A-309.18.
White goods.
Management of discarded white goods, §§130A-309.80 to 130A-309.87.
See WHITE GOODS.

HAZING.
Definitions, §14-35.
Punishment for hazing, §14-35.
Self-incrimination.
No indictment to be founded on self-incriminating testimony, §14-38.
Trials for offense of hazing, §14-38.

HAZMAT TEAMS.
General provisions, §§166A-20 to 166A-28.
See HAZARDOUS MATERIALS EMERGENCY RESPONSE.

HEAD BONES AND JOINTS.
Insurance discrimination, §§58-3-121, 58-3-121(a) to (c).

HEADLIGHTS.
All-terrain vehicles, §20-171.19(g).
Bicycles, §20-129(e).
Motorcycles, §20-129(c).
Motor vehicles, §20-129(b).
Requirements, §20-131.

HEAD SHOP ACT.
North Carolina Drug Paraphernalia Act, §§90-113.20 to 90-113.24.

HEALTH.
Abatement of nuisances.
Imminent hazards, §130A-20.
Public health nuisances, §130A-19.
Actions.
Forfeiture of money or property unlawfully acquired, §130A-28.
Recovery of money or property, §130A-27.
Administration of chapter, §130A-4(a).
Administrative penalties, §130A-22.
Asbestos hazard management violations, §130A-22(b1), (b2).
Civil actions to recover penalty, §130A-22(g).
Civil penalty and forfeiture fund.
Remittance of clear proceeds to, §130A-22(i).
Continuing violations, §130A-22(g).
Drinking water, §130A-22(b).
Factors considered in determining amount of penalty, §130A-22(d).
Investigation, inspection, or monitoring costs, §130A-22(j).
Lead-based paint hazard management violations, §130A-22(b3).
Milk sanitation, §130A-22(a), (a1).
Persons contesting penalty.
Administrative hearing and judicial review, §130A-22(e).
Rules and regulations, §130A-22(f).
Sanitary sewage systems, §130A-22(c), (h).
Administrative search and inspection warrant.
Consent to right of entry not given, §130A-17(a).
Adult health.
Commission for public health.
Adoption of rules, §130A-223(b).
Department of health and human services.
Establishment and administration of program, §130A-223(a).
Advance instruction for mental health treatment, §§122C-71 to 122C-77.
See MENTAL HEALTH, DEVELOPMENTAL DISABILITY, SUBSTANCE ABUSE.
Ambulatory surgical facilities.
Licenses, §§131E-145 to 131E-152.
See AMBULATORY SURGICAL FACILITIES.
Anatomical gifts, §§130A-412.3 to 130A-412.33.
See ANATOMICAL GIFTS.
Appeals, §130A-24.
Applicability of provisions to actions taken by department of environment and natural resources, §130A-24(e).
Decisions of local boards of health, §130A-24(c), (d).
Interpretation and enforcement of rules.
Adopted by commission, §130A-24(a).
Adopted by local board of health, §130A-24(b).
Petition for contested case, §130A-24(a1).
Arthritis program, §130A-222(a).
Rules and regulations.
Implementation of program, §130A-222(b).
Asbestos hazard management, §§130A-444 to 130A-451.
See ASBESTOS HAZARD MANAGEMENT.

HEALTH —Cont'd

Assignment to state of rights to third party benefits.

Applying for financial eligibility for medical payment program, §130A-13(a).

Attorneys retained by recipient, compensation, §130A-13(a).

Liability for reimbursement, determining, §130A-13(d).

Rules, adoption, §130A-13(c).

Applying for financial eligiblity for medical payment program.

Shares in recovery, federal and state government, §130A-13(a).

Third party resources collection unit.

Department to establish, §130A-13(b).

Attorneys at law.

District boards of health.

Contracting for services of attorney, §130A-37(b).

Authorities.

Public health authorities, §§130A-45 to 130A-45.13.

See PUBLIC HEALTH AUTHORITIES.

Autopsies.

General provisions, §§130A-398 to 130A-401.

See AUTOPSIES.

Bail.

Detention to protect public health, §15A-534.5.

Bedding.

General provisions, §§106-65.95 to 106-65.107.

Blood banks, §§90-220.12 to 90-220.14.

See BLOOD BANKS.

Brain injury advisory council, §§143B-216.65, 143B-216.66.

Cancer.

Control program.

Duties of department of health and human services, §130A-214.

General provisions, §§130A-205 to 130A-216.

See CANCER.

Secretary of health and human services.

Reports by secretary, §130A-215.

Cardiac rehabilitation certification program, §§131E-165 to 131E-170.

Center for health statistics, §§130A-371 to 130A-374.

Certificates of need.

General provisions, §§131E-175 to 130E-191.1.

See HEALTH CARE FACILITIES.

Child care facilities.

Immunization.

Certificate of immunization, §130A-155(b).

Report of communicable diseases, §130A-136.

Standards for licensing, §110-91.

Childhood vaccine-related injury compensation, §§130A-422 to 130A-434.

See CHILDHOOD VACCINE-RELATED INJURY COMPENSATION.

Chiropractors, §§90-139 to 90-157.3.

See CHIROPRACTORS.

Chronic disease.

Cancer, §§130A-205 to 130A-216.

See CANCER.

Chronic renal disease.

Establishment of program, §130A-220(a), (b).

Church schools and schools of religious charter.

Sanitation, §§130A-235 to 130A-237.

Coastal fishing waters.

Monitoring water quality, §113-221.3(a), (b).

HEALTH —Cont'd

Committees.

Advisory committees, §130A-10.

Communicable diseases generally, §§130A-134 to 130A-148.

See COMMUNICABLE DISEASES.

Constitution of North Carolina.

Local, private and special legislation prohibited, NC Const Art II §24.

Counties.

Boards of health, §130A-35.

Powers and duties, §130A-39.

Consolidated human services agencies, boards and directors.

See CONSOLIDATED HUMAN SERVICES AGENCY.

Health services, §§153A-247 to 153A-250.

Nuisances.

Abatement of public health nuisances, §153A-140.

Public health or mental health grants from federal government.

Recovery of indirect costs on certain grants by counties, §130A-8(a).

Exception, §130A-8(b).

Crustacea.

Adulterated or misbranded crustacea.

Embargoes, §113-221.4.

Sanitation of scallops, shellfish and crustacea, §113-221.2.

Definitions, §130A-2.

Essential public health services, §130A-1.1(b).

State center for health statistics, §130A-372.

Delegation of authority, §130A-6.

Dental health program.

Adoption by commission for public health, §130A-366(b).

Department of health and human services.

Establishment and administration of program, §130A-366(a).

Problem access areas.

Dental providers for, §130A-367.

Dental hygienists.

General provisions, §§90-221 to 90-233.1.

See DENTAL HYGIENISTS.

Dentists.

General provisions.

See DENTISTS AND DENTISTRY.

Department of environment and natural resources.

Abatement of imminent hazard, §130A-20(b).

Abatement of public health nuisance, §130A-19(b).

Actions to recover money, §130A-27.

Administrative penalties, §130A-22.

Appeals procedure.

Applicability of provisions to department, §130A-24(e).

Secretary.

Abatement of imminent hazard, §130A-20(b).

Abatement of public health nuisance, §130A-19(b).

Administrative penalties, §130A-22.

Embargo, §130A-21.

Injunctive relief.

Powers to seek, §130A-18(b).

Provisions administered and enforced by secretary, §130A-4(c).

Right of entry.

Powers to enforce provisions, §130A-17(b).

Suspension and revocation of permits and program participation, §130A-23(e).

HEALTH —Cont'd
**Department of environment and natural
    resources** —Cont'd
  Suspension and revocation of permits and
      program participation, §130A-23(e).
Department of health and human services.
  Abatement of imminent hazard, §130A-20(a).
  Abatement of public health nuisance, §130A-19(a).
  Adult health.
    Establishment of program, §130A-223(a).
  Cancer control program.
    Duties of department, §130A-214.
    General provisions, §§130A-205 to 130A-216.
  Chronic renal disease.
    Establishment of program, §130A-220(a), (b).
  Dental health.
    Establishment and administration of program,
        §130A-366(a).
  Dentists.
    Residency program in public health field
        established, §130A-11.
  Diabetes.
    Establishment of program, §130A-221.
  Duties of department, §130A-214.
  Nutrition program, §130A-361(a).
  Examinations.
    Postmortem medicolegal examinations and
        services, §§130A-377 to 130A-395.
    See MEDICAL EXAMINERS.
  Glaucoma.
    Establishment of program, §130A-221(a).
  Immunization.
    Enforcement of rules concerning
        implementation of program, §130A-152(c).
  Injury prevention program.
    Establishment, §130A-224.
  Medical examiners.
    Postmortem medicolegal examinations and
        services, §§130A-377 to 130A-395.
    See MEDICAL EXAMINERS.
  Mosquito control districts, §§130A-352 to
      130A-358.
  Nutrition program, §130A-361(a).
  Patient health records.
    Confidentiality, §130A-12.
  Postmortem medicolegal examinations and
      services, §§130A-377 to 130A-395.
    See MEDICAL EXAMINERS.
  Private nonprofit foundations.
    Department may assist, §130A-14(a).
      Annual audit of accounts required,
          §130A-14(b).
  Right of entry.
    Power of secretary to enforce provisions,
        §130A-17.
  Sanitation.
    Schools.
      Inspections and reports by department,
          §130A-236.
  Secretary.
    Abatement of imminent hazard, §130A-20(a).
    Abatement of public health nuisance,
        §130A-19(a).
    Administration of chapter, §130A-4(a).
    Appointment of state health director, §130A-3.
    Arthritis program.
      Administration of program, §130A-222(a).
    Cancer control program.
      Reports by secretary, §130A-215.
    Injunctive relief.
      Powers to seek, §130A-18(a).

HEALTH —Cont'd
Department of health and human services
    —Cont'd
  Secretary —Cont'd
    Powers and duties, §130A-5.
    Rights of entry, §130A-17.
    Vital statistics, §§130A-90 to 130A-121.
      See VITAL STATISTICS.
  Solid waste management.
    General provisions, §§130A-290 to 130A-305.
      See SOLID WASTE MANAGEMENT.
  State center for health statistics.
    Established within department, §130A-371.
  Vital statistics, §§130A-90 to 130A-121.
    See VITAL STATISTICS.
Diabetes.
  Establishment of program, §130A-221(a), (b).
  Rules and regulations, §130A-221.
Dietitians and nutritionists.
  Dietetics/nutrition practice act, §§90-350 to
      90-370.
    See DIETITIANS AND NUTRITIONISTS.
Disposition of decedent's body or body parts,
    §130A-420.
District boards of health, §130A-37.
  Powers and duties, §130A-39.
District health departments, §§130A-36 to
    130A-38.
Drinking water.
  Regulation of public water systems supplying
      drinking water, §§130A-311 to 130A-329.
    See WATER SUPPLY AND WATERWORKS.
Embargoes, §130A-21.
Emergency medical services.
  Regulation of emergency medical services,
      §§131E-155 to 131E-161.
    See EMERGENCY MEDICAL SERVICES.
Employee safety and health programs, §§95-250
    to 95-256.
  See EMPLOYEE SAFETY AND HEALTH
      PROGRAMS.
Employment security.
  Medical condition.
    Eligibility conditions, §96-14.
Environmental health specialists.
  General provisions, §§90A-50 to 90A-67.
    See ENVIRONMENTAL HEALTH
        SPECIALISTS.
Essential public health services.
  Defined, §130A-1.1(b).
  List of services not to limit or restrict powers and
      duties of department, §130A-1.1(d).
  Nonessential services, §130A-1.1(c).
Examinations.
  Postmortem medicolegal examinations and
      services, §§130A-377 to 130A-395.
    See MEDICAL EXAMINERS.
  State laboratory of public health to make
      examinations, §130A-88(a).
Federal public health or mental health grants.
  Counties to recover indirect costs on certain
      grants, §130A-8(a).
    Exception, §130A-8(b).
Fees.
  Analyzing samples from new water well
      construction, §130A-5.
  County and district boards of health, §130A-39(g).
  Industrial hygiene consultation services and
      occupational consultation services, §130A-5.
Food.
  Protection from intentional contamination,
      §130A-481.

HEALTH —Cont'd
Forfeitures.
Money or property unlawfully acquired, §130A-27.
General assembly.
Establishment of program, §130A-221(a), (b).
Human tissue donation program.
Legislative findings and purpose, §130A-413(a).
Implementation of provisions, §130A-221(b).
Joint legislative oversight committee on health
and human services, §§120-208 to 120-208.4.
Local, private and special legislation prohibited,
NC Const Art II §24.
Rules and regulations, §130A-221(b).
Grants.
Federal public health or mental health grants.
Counties to recover indirect costs, §130A-8(a).
Applicability of section, §130A-8(b).
Grants-in-aid, §130A-7.
Liberal construction of chapter, §130A-7.
Health care associated infections, §130A-150.
Health care facilities.
Certificates of need, §§131E-175 to 130E-191.1.
See HEALTH CARE FACILITIES.
General provisions.
See HEALTH CARE FACILITIES.
Health care powers of attorney.
Advance instruction for mental health treatment,
§§122C-71 to 122C-77.
See MENTAL HEALTH, DEVELOPMENTAL
DISABILITY, SUBSTANCE ABUSE.
Generally, §§32A-15 to 32A-26.
See HEALTH CARE POWERS OF ATTORNEY.
**Health care providers, self-referrals, §§90-405 to
90-408.**
Health promotion services.
Appropriations, §130A-4.2.
Health systems agencies.
Certificates of need generally, §§131E-175 to
130E-191.1.
See HEALTH CARE FACILITIES.
Hearings.
Suspension or revocation of permits and program
participation, §130A-23(c), (d).
Heart disease and stroke.
Justus-Warren heart disease and stroke
prevention task force, §143B-216.60.
Home care agencies.
Home care agencies licensing, §§131E-135 to
131E-143.
See HEALTH CARE FACILITIES.
**Home care clients' bill of rights, §§131E-144.1 to
131E-144.7.**
Hospitals.
Certificates of need, §§131E-175 to 130E-191.1.
See HEALTH CARE FACILITIES.
Communicable diseases.
Emergency departments, reports to state health
director, §130A-480(a), (b).
Medical facilities may report, §130A-137.
Emergency departments, reports to state health
director of public health threats,
§130A-480(a), (b).
Generally.
See HOSPITALS.
Sanitation, §130A-235.
**Hotels, inns and other transient lodging
places.**
Sanitation of food and lodging establishments,
§§130A-247 to 130A-250.
Human tissue donation program, §130A-413.

HEALTH —Cont'd
Imminent hazards.
Abatement.
Secretary of environment and natural resources
or local health directors, §130A-20(b).
Secretary of health and human services or local
health directors, §130A-20(a).
Suspension or revocation of permits and program
participation, §130A-23(d).
Immunity from liability.
Communicable disease investigations.
Immunity of persons who report, §130A-142.
Persons permitting access to medical records,
§130A-144(c).
Confidential records, access to when public health
concern necessitates.
Permitting examination, review, or copying of
records, immunity from liability for,
§130A-15(c).
Local health departments, §90-21.16(a), (b).
Non-profit community health centers,
§90-21.16(a), (b).
Nonprofit community health referral services,
§90-21.16(d), (e).
Immunization, §§130A-152 to 130A-158.
See IMMUNIZATION.
Infants.
Perinatal health care, §130A-127.
Injunctions.
Secretary of environment and natural resources or
local health directors, §130A-18(b).
Secretary of health and human services or local
health directors, §130A-18(a).
Injury prevention.
Establishment and administration of program,
§130A-224.
Institute of medicine, §90-470.
Insurance.
District health departments.
Board of health.
Authority to provide liability insurance,
§130A-37(k).
Generally.
See HEALTH INSURANCE.
Jails.
Commitment to another jail when county jail
unhealthy, §15-126.
Supervision by department of health and human
services, §148-10.
**Joint legislative oversight committee on health
and human services, §§120-208 to 120-208.4.**
Kindergartens.
Health assessments for kindergarten children in
public schools, §§130A-440 to 130A-443.
Labor.
Occupational safety and health, §§95-126 to
95-155.
See OCCUPATIONAL SAFETY AND HEALTH.
Landlord and tenant.
Good faith complaints.
Health or safety law violations, §42-37.1.
**Lead-based paint hazard management
program, §§130A-453.01 to 130A-453.11.**
See LEAD-BASED PAINT.
Lead-based paint renovation activities.
Certification and accreditation, §§130A-453.22 to
130A-453.31.
See LEAD-BASED PAINT.
**Lead poisoning in children, §§130A-131.5 to
130A-131.9H.**
See LEAD POISONING IN CHILDREN.

HEALTH —Cont'd
Local boards of health.
Powers and duties, §130A-39.
Local governmental employees' retirement system.
District health departments.
Membership of employees, §128-37.
Public health authorities.
Membership of employees, §128-37.
Local health departments, §§130A-34 to 130A-42.
See LOCAL HEALTH DEPARTMENTS.
Maintenance organizations, §§58-67-1 to 58-67-185.
See HEALTH MAINTENANCE ORGANIZATIONS.
Managed care patient assistance program, §143-730.
Mass gatherings.
Commission for public health.
Rules and regulations of commission, §130A-257.
Maternal and child health services, §130A-124(a) to (c).
County appropriations.
Local health departments not to reduce, §130A-4.1(a).
Income earned by local health departments.
Departments required to budget and expend, §130A-4.1(b).
Mattresses and bedding.
General provisions, §§106-65.95 to 106-65.107.
Medical education in primary care, §143-613.
Medical payments programs administered under chapter 130A.
Assignment to state of rights to third party benefits, §130A-13(a).
Attorneys retained by recipient, compensation, §130A-13(a).
Liability for reimbursement, determining, §130A-13(d).
Rules, adoption, §130A-13(c).
Shares in recovery, federal and state government, §130A-13(a).
Third party resources collection unit.
Department to establish, §130A-13(b).
Medical records.
See MEDICAL RECORDS.
Mental health, developmental disability, substance abuse.
See MENTAL HEALTH, DEVELOPMENTAL DISABILITY, SUBSTANCE ABUSE.
Metabolic and other hereditary and congenital disorders.
Birth/three-year-old early intervention program, §130A-126.
Screening of newborns, §130A-125.
Metropolitan water districts.
Commission for public health.
Authorized to create, §130A-29(d).
Milk and milk products.
Embargoes, §106-266.36.
Sanitation, §§106-266.30 to 106-266.35.
Minority health advisory council, §§130A-33.43, 130A-33.44.
Misdemeanors.
Violations of chapter or rules, §130A-25(a).
Imprisonment for certain violations, §130A-25(b).
Discharge, §130A-25(c).
Mosquito control districts.
Commission for public health.
Authorized to create mosquito control districts, §130A-29(d).

HEALTH —Cont'd
Mosquito control districts —Cont'd
General provisions, §§130A-352 to 130A-358.
Municipalities.
Abatement of public health nuisances, §160A-193.
North Carolina brain injury advisory council, §§143B-216.65, 143B-216.66.
Notice.
Suspension and revocation of permits and program participation, §130A-23(c), (d).
Nuisances.
Abatement of imminent hazard, §130A-20.
Abatement of public health nuisances.
Secretary of environment and natural resources and local health directors, §130A-19(b).
Secretary of health and human services and local health directors, §130A-19(a).
Nurses.
General provisions, §§90-171.19 to 90-171.48.
See NURSES.
Nursing home administrators.
General provisions, §§90-275.1 to 90-288.01.
See NURSING HOME ADMINISTRATORS.
Nursing homes.
General provisions.
See NURSING HOMES.
Patients' bill of rights, §§131E-115 to 131E-131.
See NURSING HOMES.
Nutritionists.
Dietetics/nutrition practice act, §§90-350 to 90-370.
See DIETITIANS AND NUTRITIONISTS.
Nutrition program.
Department of health and human services.
Establishment of program, §130A-361(a), (b).
Powers and duties relative to nutrition program, §130A-361(a).
Powers and duties relative to nutrition program, §130A-361(a).
Rules and regulations, §130A-361(b).
Violations, §130A-22(c1).
Occupational safety and health, §§95-126 to 95-155.
See OCCUPATIONAL SAFETY AND HEALTH.
Office of women's health, §130A-131.25.
Optometrists, §§90-114 to 90-127.3.
See OPTOMETRISTS.
Osteopaths.
See OSTEOPATHS.
Patient medical records.
Confidentiality, §130A-12.
Perinatal health care, §130A-127.
Establishment of program, §130A-127(a).
Rules and regulations.
Adoption, §130A-127(b).
Permits.
Suspension or revocation of permit issued under chapter, §130A-23(a), (c), (d).
Findings, §130A-23(a).
Imminent hazard, §130A-23(d).
Notice, §130A-23(c), (d).
Powers of secretary of environment and natural resources, §130A-23(e).
Personnel.
District health departments.
Personnel records, §130A-42.
Pharmacists and pharmacies, §§90-85.2 to 90-85.44.
See PHARMACISTS AND PHARMACIES.
Physical therapists, §§90-270.24 to 90-270.39.
See PHYSICAL THERAPISTS.

HEALTH —Cont'd

Physicians and surgeons.
See PHYSICIANS AND SURGEONS.
Podiatrists, §§90-202.2 to 90-202.14.
See PODIATRISTS.
Postmortem medicolegal examinations and services, §§130A-377 to 130A-395.
See MEDICAL EXAMINERS.
Principals of schools.
Reports of communicable diseases, §130A-136.
Prisons and prisoners.
Health services generally, §148-19(a) to (d).
Sanitary and health conditions of prisoners.
Department of health and human services to supervise, §148-10.
Self-inflicted injuries.
Treatment of injuries upon prisoners, §148-46.2.
Procedure when consent is refused by prisoner, §148-46.2.
Surgical operations on inmates of state institutions.
Procedure when surgical operations necessary, §148-22.2.
Private nonprofit foundations.
Department may assist, §130A-14(a).
Annual audit of accounts required, §130A-14(b).
Programs administered under chapter.
Suspension of participation for violations, §130A-23(b).
Psychologists, §§90-270.1 to 90-270.22.
See PSYCHOLOGISTS.
Public health authorities, §§130A-45 to 130A-45.13.
See PUBLIC HEALTH AUTHORITIES.
Public health law of North Carolina.
Mission of public health system, §130A-1.1(a).
Title of chapter, §130A-1.
Public health services.
County health departments.
Provision of public health services, §130A-34(a).
Public officers and employees.
Delegation of authority, §130A-6.
Public schools.
Employee health certificate, §115C-323.
Form, §115C-323(d).
Nonresident physicians, §115C-323(c).
Requirements, §115C-323(a).
Who may prepare, §115C-323(b).
Kindergartens.
Health assessments for kindergarten children in public schools, §§130A-440 to 130A-443.
Sanitation, §§130A-235 to 130A-237.
Race and ethnicity data.
Patient self-reported data.
Medical providers required to collect, document and report to division of public health, §130A-16.
Recovery of property.
Wrongfully paid or transferred to person under program, §130A-27.
Renal disease.
Chronic renal disease.
Department of health and human services.
Establishment of program, §130A-220(a), (b).
Respiratory care practitioners.
General provisions, §§90-646 to 90-666.
See RESPIRATORY CARE PRACTITIONERS.
Restaurants.
Sanitation of food and lodging establishments, §§130A-247 to 130A-250.

HEALTH —Cont'd

Restitution.
Recovery of money or property wrongfully disbursed, §130A-27.
Right of entry to enforce provisions.
Administrative search and inspection warrant.
Obtaining if consent not given, §130A-17(a).
Imminent hazard existing.
No warrant required for entry, §130A-17(a).
Powers of secretary and local health directors, §130A-17(a).
Powers of secretary of department of environment and natural resources and local health directors, §130A-17(b).
Rules and regulations.
Appeals procedure.
Interpretation and enforcement of rules.
Adopted by commission, §130A-24(a).
Adopted by local boards of health, §130A-24(b).
Petition for contested case, §130A-24.
Sanitary districts.
Commission for public health.
Authorized to create sanitary districts, §130A-29(d).
General provisions, §§130A-47 to 130A-85.
See SANITARY DISTRICTS.
Sanitation.
Church schools and schools of religious charter, §§130A-235 to 130A-237.
Crustacea, §113-221.2.
Definitions, §130A-227(b).
Establishment of program, §130A-227(a).
Hospitals, §130A-235.
Mass gatherings generally, §§130A-251 to 130A-258.
Milk and milk products, §§106-266.30 to 106-266.35.
Private schools, §§130A-235 to 130A-237.
Public schools, §§130A-235 to 130A-237.
Sanitation of food and lodging establishments, §§130A-247 to 130A-250.
Shellfish, §113-221.2.
Scallops.
Sanitation of scallops, shellfish and crustacea, §113-221.2.
Schools, sanitation, §§130A-235 to 130A-237.
Searches and seizures.
Administrative search and inspection warrants, §130A-17.
Self-referrals by health care providers, §§90-405 to 90-408.
Shellfish.
Sanitation of scallops, shellfish and crustacea, §113-221.2.
Sickle cell program, §130A-129.
Sickle cell trait.
See SICKLE CELL TRAIT.
Solid waste management.
General provisions, §§130A-290 to 130A-305.
See SOLID WASTE MANAGEMENT.
Standards.
Commission authorized to establish, §130A-9.
State health standards, §130A-5.1.
State center for health statistics, §§130A-371 to 130A-374.
State health director, §130A-3.
Terrorist incident using nuclear, biological or chemical agents.
Powers and duties, §§130A-475 to 130A-477.

HEALTH —Cont'd

State health planning and development agency.
Department of health and human services designated state agency, §131E-177.

State health standards, §130A-5.1.
Adoption, §130A-5.1(a).
Assistance of other entities, §130A-5.1(b).

State institutions.
Surgical operations on inmates of state institutions.
Procedure when surgical operations necessary, §148-22.2.

State laboratory of public health.
Established, §130A-88(a).
Rules and regulations, §130A-88(b).

Sterilization, §§90-271 to 90-275.
Mentally ill or mentally retarded wards.
Medical necessity cases, §35A-1245.

Substance abuse professionals, §§90-113.30 to 90-113.46A.
See SUBSTANCE ABUSE PROFESSIONALS.

Teen pregnancy prevention.
Establishment of program, §130A-131.15A.

Third party resources collection unit.
Department to establish, §130A-13(b).

Title of chapter.
Public health law of North Carolina, §130A-1.

Tourist camps and homes.
Sanitation of food and lodging establishments, §§130A-247 to 130A-250.

Toxic vapors.
General provisions, §§90-113.8A to 90-113.14.
See TOXIC VAPORS.

Unemployment compensation.
Medical condition.
Eligibility conditions, §96-14.

Veterinarians.
General provisions, §§90-179 to 90-187.15.
See VETERINARIANS.

Vital statistics.
General provisions, §§130A-90 to 130A-121.
See VITAL STATISTICS.

Wastewater systems, §§130A-333 to 130A-343.1.
See WASTEWATER SYSTEMS.

Water and air resources, §§143-211 to 143-215.9C.
See WATER AND AIR RESOURCES.

Women's health, office of, §130A-131.25.

HEALTH AIDS.

Exemption from creditors' claims, §1C-1601(a).

HEALTH AND HUMAN SERVICES DEPARTMENT, §§143B-136.1 to 143B-216.70.

Abortion.
Statistical summary reports concerning medical and demographic characteristics of abortions, §14-45.1(c).

Abuse, neglect or dependency of juveniles, child fatalities.
Central registry.
Report by director of social services where maltreatment involved, §7B-307(c).
Central registry and responsible individuals list, §7B-311.
Report by director of social services to department.
Finding evidence of abuse or neglect in child care facility, §7B-307(b), (c).

Adult care homes.
Division consultants and county DDS adult care home specialists and providers.
Joint training, §143B-139.5B.

HEALTH AND HUMAN SERVICES DEPARTMENT —Cont'd

Adult care homes —Cont'd
Share of costs with counties, §143B-139.5.
Training.
Joint training.
Division consultants and county DDS adult care home specialists and providers, §143B-139.5B.

Adult day care programs, §131D-6.

Advisory committee on cancer coordination and control, §§130A-33.50, 130A-33.51.

Alcohol screening tests.
Devices.
Approval, manner and use by law enforcement, rules, adoption, §20-16.3(b).
Operating a commercial vehicle after consuming alcohol.
Approval of devices used, §20-138.2A(b2).
Operating a school bus, school activity bus, or child care vehicle after consuming alcohol.
Approval of devices used, §20-138.2B(b2).

Ambulatory surgical facilities.
Licenses, §§131E-145 to 131E-152.
See AMBULATORY SURGICAL FACILITIES.

Appeals of right, court of appeals, §7A-29(a).

Arthritis.
Administration of arthritis program, §130A-222(a).
Rules and regulations.
Implementation of program, §130A-222(b).

Audits.
Office of internal auditor, §§143B-216.50, 143B-216.51.

Blind persons.
Aid to the blind, §§111-13 to 111-35.
See BLIND AND VISUALLY IMPAIRED.
Blind or visually handicapped employees.
Enrollment in retirement system for teachers and state employees, §135-16.1(a) to (c).
General provisions, §§111-4 to 111-12.6.
See BLIND AND VISUALLY IMPAIRED.
Operation of highway vending facilities, §§111-48 to 111-52.
See BLIND AND VISUALLY IMPAIRED.
Operation of vending facilities on state property, §§111-41 to 111-47.
See BLIND AND VISUALLY IMPAIRED.

Brain injury advisory council, §§143B-216.65, 143B-216.66.

Budget of state.
Medicaid special fund, §143C-9-1.

Central registry and responsible individuals list.
Abuse, neglect and dependency cases and child fatalities, §7B-311.

Certificates of need.
Health care facilities generally, §§131E-175 to 130E-191.1.
See HEALTH CARE FACILITIES.

Child care commission, §§143B-168.3 to 143B-168.5.

Child care facilities.
Generally, §§110-85 to 110-107.
See CHILD CARE FACILITIES.

Child care services for employees.
Payroll deductions for, §143B-139.6B.

Child fatality review team, §143B-150.20.

Childhood vaccine-related injury compensation, §§130A-422 to 130A-434.
See CHILDHOOD VACCINE-RELATED INJURY COMPENSATION.

HEALTH AND HUMAN SERVICES
  DEPARTMENT —Cont'd
Child support enforcement.
  Generally, §§110-128 to 110-142.2.
    See CHILD SUPPORT.
  State directory of new hires, §110-129.2.
Child welfare services delivery.
  Action by secretary to ensure delivery.
    Cooperation with county board of
      commissioners, county board of social
      services, etc., §108A-74(g).
    County funding of services to continue,
      §108A-74(f).
    Definitions, §108A-74(a).
    Directive plan of action to be developed and
      implemented, §108A-74(e).
    Divestiture of county director of social services
      upon assumption of service by secretary,
      §108A-74(d).
    Intervention in particular service or services
      provided by county department of social
      services, §108A-74(b).
    Withholding funding for services provided by
      county boards of social services,
      §108A-74(c).
**Commission for mental health, developmental
  disabilities and substance abuse services,**
  §§143B-147 to 143B-150.
Commission for public health, §§130A-29 to
  130A-33.
  Abatement of nuisances.
    Offenses against public morals.
      Right of entry, §19-8.2.
  Adult care homes.
    Immunization of employees and residents.
      Rules, adoption, §131D-9(f).
  Adult health.
    Adoption of rules, §130A-223(b).
  Alcohol screening tests.
    Open container law violations.
      Commission approval before use, §20-138.7(d).
  Appointments, §130A-30(a), (b).
    Officers, §130A-31.
  Arthritis.
    Adoption of rules, §130A-222(b).
  Asbestos NESHAP for demolition and renovation.
    Local air pollution programs authorization to
      enforce.
      Rules, adoption, §130A-452(b).
  Birth-three-year old early intervention program.
    Rulemaking authority, §130A-126.
  Child care centers.
    Medical care and sanitation.
      Rules and regulations, adoption, §110-91.
  Child fatality prevention system.
    Access to records, rules, adoption, §7B-1413(f).
  Child immunization programs.
    Medical contraindications, rules, adoption,
      §130A-156.
    Rules, adoption, §130A-152(c1).
  Chronic renal disease.
    Adoption of rules, §130A-220(b).
  Commercial vehicles.
    Operating after consuming alcohol.
      Devises used to conduct screening tests.
        Commission approval before use,
          §20-136.2A(b2).
  Communicable diseases.
    Establishing lists of communicable diseases and
      conditions to be reported, §130A-134.
    Rules of commission, §130A-147.

HEALTH AND HUMAN SERVICES
  DEPARTMENT —Cont'd
Commission for public health —Cont'd
  Compensation, §130A-30(e).
  Creation, §130A-29(a).
  Crustacea.
    Sanitation of scallops, shellfish and crustacea.
      Rules relating to sanitation, §113-221.2.
  Defined, §130A-2.
  Dental health program.
    Adoption of rules by commission, §130A-366(b).
  Diabetes.
    Adoption of rules, §130A-221(b).
  Drinking water testing rules.
    Adoption, §87-97(h), (i).
  Drivers' licenses.
    Denial because of physical or mental disability
      of applicant.
      Review by reviewing board designated by
        chairman of commission, §20-9(g).
    Limited driving privilege alcohol violations.
      Devices used in conducting screening tests.
        Commission approval before use,
          §20-179.3(j).
  Duties, §130A-29(a) to (d).
  Educational institutions.
    Regulation of sanitation by commission,
      §§130A-235, 130A-236.
  Election meetings, §130A-32.
  Glaucoma.
    Adoption of rules, §130A-221(b).
  Governor's emergency war powers.
    Public health laws, suspension or modification.
      Submission to commission, §147-33.2.
  Health assessments for kindergarten children in
    public schools.
    Rules, adoption, §130A-443.
  Hospitals.
    Regulation of sanitation by commission,
      §130A-235.
  Immunization.
    Promulgation of rules concerning
      implementation of program, §130A-152(c).
  Local confinement facilities.
    Sanitation and food, rules, adoption, inspection
      score sheet, adoption, §152A-226.
  Marine toilets.
    Rules sewage treatment devices and holding
      tanks, adoption, §75A-6(o).
  Mass gatherings.
    Rules and regulations of commission,
      §130A-257.
  Meetings.
    Election meetings, §130A-32.
    Regular and special meetings, §130A-33.
  Members, §130A-30(a).
  Metropolitan water districts.
    Commission authorized to create, §130A-29(d).
  Migrant housing.
    Water quality and water sanitation standards.
      Rules, adoption, §95-225(c).
  Mosquito control districts.
    Commission authorized to create, §130A-29(d).
  Newborn screening program.
    Newborn hearing screening included, rules and
      regulation, adoption, §130A-125(b1).
  Nursing homes.
    Immunization of employees and residents.
      Rules, adoption, §131E-113(f).
  Nutrition program to promote public health.
    Rules, adoption, §130A-361(b).

HEALTH AND HUMAN SERVICES
DEPARTMENT —Cont'd
Commission for public health —Cont'd
Officers, §130A-31.
Powers, §130A-29(a) to (d).
Private educational institutions.
　Regulation of sanitation by commission,
　　§§130A-235, 130A-236.
Private hospitals.
　Regulation of sanitation by commission,
　　§130A-235.
Public health services categories.
　Determination of specific services provided,
　　§130A-1.1(b).
Quorum, §130A-30(d).
Radiation protection.
　Rules and regulation not inconsistent with
　　radiation protection commission rules and
　　regulation.
　　Effect, §104E-7(a).
Radiation protection commission.
　Ex officio member, §104E-8(c).
Remains of terminated pregnancies.
　Disposition, rules, adoption, §130A-131.10(a).
Removal of members, §130A-30(c).
Rules and regulations, §130A-29(a) to (e).
　Mass gatherings, §130A-257.
Sanitary districts.
　Commission authorized to create, §130A-29(d).
　Merger.
　　Change of name, notice, §130A-80.3(e).
　　Copies of resolutions filed with commission,
　　　§130A-80.3(a).
　Rules and regulations not to conflict with
　　commission rules and regulation, §130A-55.
Sanitation.
　Regulation of sanitation by commission,
　　§§130A-235, 130A-236.
Scallops.
　Rules relating to sanitation, §113-221.2.
Schools.
　Regulation of sanitation by commission,
　　§§130A-235, 130A-236.
　Sanitary privies provided according to
　　commission specification.
　School not connected to water carried sewage
　　facilities, §115C-522.
Shellfish.
　Rules relating to sanitation, §113-221.2.
Solid waste management loan program.
　Assignment of priorities.
　　Rules, adoption, §159I-11(a).
　Rules, adoption, §159I-28(a).
Special meetings, §130A-33.
Standards.
　Establishment by commission authorized,
　　§130A-9.
Wastewater systems.
　Regulated under rules adopted by commission,
　　§143-215.1(a4).
Water or sewage disposal systems or facilities.
　Metropolitan water districts.
　　Creation.
　　　Notice to and action by commission,
　　　　§162A-33.
　　Inclusion of additional political subdivisions
　　　or unincorporated areas.
　　　Action by commission, §162A-35.
　Revenue bond projects.
　　Approval of commission required, §159-95.

HEALTH AND HUMAN SERVICES
DEPARTMENT —Cont'd
Commission for public health —Cont'd
Well construction act.
　Commission rules to prevail over article,
　　§87-96(b).
Commission for the blind, §§143B-157 to
　143B-160.
Commission of anatomy, §§130A-33.30 to
　130A-33.32.
**Confidentiality of privileged patient medical
　records,** §143B-139.6.
Consolidated county human services.
Adoption of rules, §143B-139.7(a), (b).
Allocation of funds, §143B-139.7(a).
Definitions, §143B-139.7(c).
**Consumer and advocacy advisory committee
　for the blind,** §§143B-163, 143B-164.
**Contested case provisions of administrative
　procedure.**
Exemption, §150B-1(e).
Contracts.
Authority of department to contract with other
　entities, §143B-139.3(a), (b).
Recovery of county funded financial assistance
　program expenditures.
　Contracts and intermediary status authorized
　　between federal agency and county,
　　§143B-139.3(b).
Controlled-drinking programs, §20-139.1(g).
**Costs paid by persons admitted to institutions
　of department,** §§143-117 to 143-127.1.
Action to accrue for costs in favor of state,
　§143-121(a).
Actual cost of care to be paid.
　Secretary to determine and fix, §143-118(a).
Attorney general to prosecute suits at request of
　institution, §143-124.
Compromise of accounts, §143-118(e).
Death of person admitted leaving costs unpaid.
　Lien on decedent's property, §143-126(a).
　　Cancellation of lien upon payment of unpaid
　　　balance, §143-126(e).
　　Filing verified statement of account,
　　　§143-126(b).
　　Limitation of actions, §143-126(d).
　　Notice, §143-126(c).
Definitions, §143-117.1.
Discharge from institution of person refusing to
　pay, §143-119(e).
Financial ability to pay, secretary to ascertain,
　§143-118(d).
General rate of charge, authority of secretary to
　fix, §143-118(a).
Included institutions, §143-117.
Indigent persons.
　Authority to provide care not limited,
　　§143-123(a).
　Collection of costs of indigent succeeding to
　　inheritance or acquiring property,
　　§143-123(b).
Judgment not barred by statute of limitations,
　§143-125.
Lien on property for unpaid balance due
　institution, §143-126.1(a).
Admission of person after judgment or
　settlement of claim, §143-126.1(g).
Applicability to both real and personal property,
　§143-126.1(b).
Cancellation upon payment of unpaid balance,
　§143-126.1(f).

HEALTH AND HUMAN SERVICES
 DEPARTMENT —Cont'd
Costs paid by persons admitted to institutions
 of department —Cont'd
 Lien on property for unpaid balance due
  institution —Cont'd
  Death of person admitted leaving costs unpaid,
   §143-126.
  Filing of verified statement of account,
   §143-126.1(c).
  Limitation of action to enforce, §143-126.1(e).
  Notice, §143-126.1(d).
  Priority, §143-126.1(e).
 List of unpaid accounts for audit, §143-119(d).
 Long-term patients.
  Defined, §143-127.1(c).
  Parental liability, §143-127.1(a), (b).
 No statute of limitation on action for costs,
  §143-122.
 Notification of amount due, §143-119(b).
 Payment into state treasury, §143-127.
 Payment of portion of costs, §143-119(c).
 Payments by person admitted or person legally
  responsible for payments, §143-119(a).
 Prima facie evidence in action for costs,
  §143-121(c).
 Provisions directory and not mandatory,
  §143-121(d).
 Ratification of past acts, §143-121.1.
 Reduction of rates for persons admitted to facility
  for mentally ill research purposes,
  §143-118(f).
 Statute of limitations not to bar judgment,
  §143-125.
 Venue for action for costs, §143-121(b).
 Venue of action to collect costs.
  Right of institution to select, §143-124.
Council for the deaf and the hard of hearing,
 §§143B-216.30 to 143B-216.34.
Council on developmental disabilities,
 §§143B-177 to 143B-179.
Created, §143B-136.1.
Criminal history record checks of employees
 and applicants for employment.
 Conditional offer of employment pending results
  of record checks, §114-19.6(f).
 Conviction revealed by verified criminal history
  record check.
  Just cause for not selecting person or dismissing
   person, §114-19.6(d).
 Definitions, §114-19.6(a).
 Department of justice to provide information,
  §114-19.6(b).
 Just cause for not selecting person for
  employment or dismissing person.
  Record check revealing conviction, §114-19.6(d).
 National criminal record checks, §114-19.6(b).
 Privileged information, §114-19.6(c).
 Refusal to consent to record check.
  Denial of employment or dismissal, §114-19.6(e).
Crisis intervention program.
 Assistance for vulnerable populations,
  §108A-25.4(a).
 Submission of plan, §108A-25.4(b).
Damage of personal property by clients.
 Repair or replacement, §143-127.2.
Deportment of persons in buildings and
 grounds of institutions under jurisdiction
 of department.
 Adoption of rules governing, §143-116.6(a).
 Misdemeanor for violation, §143-116.6(b).

HEALTH AND HUMAN SERVICES
 DEPARTMENT —Cont'd
Directory of new hires, §110-129.2.
Division of adult correction.
 Detailing department employees to division.
  Supervision and furnishing health services to
   division, compensation, §148-19(b).
Division of aging, §143B-181.1(a) to (c).
Division of health service regulation.
 Adult day care homes for aged and disabled.
  Disasters or emergencies.
   Waiver of rules, §131D-7(a).
  Division complaint hotline number.
   Posting required, §131D-2.
  Inspection, §131D-2.
  Multiunit assisted housing with services
   programs.
   Registration with division, disclosure
    statement, §131D-2.
  Training county departments of social services
   specialists, §131D-2.
 Anatomic pathology services billing.
  Communication of requirements to licensed
   practitioners and facilities, §90-701(k).
 Consultants.
  Training offered by department, §143B-139.5B.
 Emergency medical services advisory council.
  Clerical and other services supplied by,
   §143-510(e).
 Health care facilities certificate of need.
  Administrative and judicial review.
   Notice of appeal filed with division,
    §131E-188(b).
 Health care facilities providing temporary shelter
  or services during disaster or emergency.
  Waiver of rules, §131E-112(a).
 Home care agencies.
  Division compliant hotline.
   Client provided notice of, §131E-141(c).
 Hospital bed capacity.
  Temporary increase over licensed capacity.
   Notification to and approval by division,
    §131E-83.
 Medical care data.
  Division defined, §131E-214.1.
  Generally, §§131E-214.1 to 131E-214.4.
 NC NOVA program.
  Special licensure document.
   Issuance, §131E-154.14(e), (f).
   Return, failure to meet criteria,
    §131E-154.14(g).
 Nursing home advisory committees.
  Names of members, term expiration date.
   Copy supplied division, §131E-128(f).
 Plan for serving older adults, inventory of date.
  Cooperation with division of aging,
   §143B-181.1A.
 Residential treatment facilities for mentally ill,
  developmentally disabled and substance
  abusers.
  Division complaint hotline number.
   Facilities required to post, §122C-25(d).
  Licensure of new facilities.
   Letter of support, submission to division,
    §122C-23.1.
 State building code.
  Amendments.
   Notification of non-state owned I-institutional
    buildings, §143-138(b).
  Life safety test results for I-institutional.
   Filing with construction section, §143-138(f).

HEALTH AND HUMAN SERVICES
DEPARTMENT —Cont'd
Division of health service regulation —Cont'd
State building code —Cont'd
Plans and specifications for i-institutional
buildings.
Submission to construction section,
§143-138(e).
Tanning equipment operators.
Training program, development, §104E-9(b).
Traumatic brain injury advisory council.
Membership, §143B-216.66.
University of North Carolina health care system.
Construction documents.
Submission for review and approval, §116-37.
Division of services for the deaf and hard of
hearing, §§143B-216.30 to 143B-216.34.
Drug treatment by nonprofessional
organizations.
Responsibility for issuing license, §90-109.
Duties, §§143B-137.1, 143B-138.1(a) to (e).
Early childhood initiatives, §§143B-168.10 to
143B-168.16.
See EARLY CHILDHOOD INITIATIVES.
Early intervention services.
Responsibilities of secretary regarding
availability, §143B-139.6A.
Eastern North Carolina hospital.
Control of certain hospitals transferred to
department of health and human services,
§131E-67.
Power of secretary to regulate, §131E-67.
Education.
Children with disabilities.
Generally, §§115C-106.1 to 115C-112.1.
See SPECIAL EDUCATION.
Residential schools under control of secretary.
Education programs in, §§143B-146.1 to
143B-146.21.
See EDUCATION.
Emergency medical services, §§143-507 to
143-519.
See EMERGENCY MEDICAL SERVICES.
Emergency rules.
When agency may adopt, §150B-21.1A(a).
Established, §143B-136.1.
Expenses, priorities, §143B-137.1.
Family preservation act, §§143B-150.5,
143B-150.6.
First responders.
Vaccination program, §130A-485.
Food and nutrition services.
Generally, §§108A-51 to 108A-53.1.
Food defense.
Protection from intentional contamination,
§130A-481.
Fraudulent public assistance program
payments.
Garnishment of wages to recoup, §108A-25.3.
Functions, powers, duties and obligations
generally, §143B-138.1(a) to (e).
Governor Morehead school, §§143B-164.10 to
143B-164.18.
See GOVERNOR MOREHEAD SCHOOL.
Governor's advisory council on aging,
§§143B-180, 143B-181.
Grants-in-aid for programs of public
assistance.
Acceptance, §108A-25(c).
Grants-in-aid from non-state agencies.
Requests submitted through secretary,
§143B-139.2.

HEALTH AND HUMAN SERVICES
DEPARTMENT —Cont'd
Head of department, §143B-139.
Health.
Powers generally.
See HEALTH.
Hospitals.
Construction and enlargement of local hospitals,
§131E-70.
Eastern North Carolina hospital.
Control of certain hospitals transferred to
department of health and human services,
§131E-67.
Power of secretary to regulate, §131E-67.
Program of hospital care, §131E-70.
Specialty hospitals.
Control of certain hospitals transferred to
department of health and human services,
§131E-67.
Power of secretary to regulate, §131E-67.
Impaired driving, implied consent offenses.
Access to chemical analysis room.
Written policies, establishment, §20-38.5(a).
Alcohol screening test devices.
Approval, manner and use by law enforcement,
rules, adoption, §20-16.3(b).
Indian child welfare.
Division of social services.
Collaboration with commission of Indian affairs,
§143B-139.5A.
Injury prevention program.
Establishment, §130A-224.
Insect sting reactions.
Training individuals to administer life-saving
treatment to persons suffering, §143-509.
Interagency coordinating council for children
with disabilities from birth to five years of
age, §§143B-179.5, 143B-179.6.
Internal auditor, §§143B-216.50, 143B-216.51.
Internet data warehouse for providers records,
§143B-139.5C(a).
Annual review of updates to policy,
§143B-139.5C(b).
Joint legislative oversight committee on health
and human services.
Division reports to committee, §120-208.4.
Local health and human services agencies.
Adoption of rules by secretary, §143B-139.1.
Long-term care ombudsman program,
§§143B-181.15 to 143B-181.25.
See LONG-TERM CARE OMBUDSMAN.
Lost, destruction or damage.
Property of resident of department institution.
Direct payment or replacement by institution,
§143-295.1.
Low-income energy assistance program.
Focus of payments on elderly population and
disabled persons, §108A-25.4(a).
Submission of plan, §108A-25.4(b).
Medicaid special fund.
Budget of state, §143C-9-1.
Medical assistance program generally,
§§108A-54 to 108A-70.5.
See MEDICAID.
Medical care commission, §§143B-165 to
143B-168.
Medical records.
See MEDICAL RECORDS.
Medication aide registry, §§131E-114.2,
131E-270.

HEALTH AND HUMAN SERVICES DEPARTMENT —Cont'd

Mental health, developmental disabilities and substance abuse.
Administration and enforcement of chapter, §122C-111.
Application of funds belonging to facilities, §122C-185.
Cooperation with other agencies, §122C-113(a) to (b1), (c).
Facility licensing, §122C-27.
Powers and duties of secretary, §122C-112.1(a), (b).
State plan, §122C-102.
Minority health advisory council, §§130A-33.43, 130A-33.44.
Motor vehicle operation on grounds of institutions operated by department.
Adoption of rules by secretary, §143-116.7(b).
Civil penalty for violations, §143-116.7(e).
General fund budget code of institution.
Deposit of fees or civil penalties, §143-116.7(h).
General laws relating to use of highways of state and operation of vehicles applicable, §143-116.7(a).
Infractions, §143-116.7(g).
Parking, §143-116.7(c), (d).
Removal of illegally parked vehicle, §143-116.7(f).
Negligent lost, destruction or damage of property.
Property of resident of department institution.
Direct payment or replacement by institution, §143-295.1.
North Carolina brain injury advisory council, §§143B-216.65, 143B-216.66.
Nursing homes.
Medication error quality initiative.
Development and implementation, §131E-128.5(a).
Office of internal auditor.
Access to records, data or other information of department, §143B-216.50(e).
Appointment by secretary, §143B-216.50(c).
Auditing duties and responsibilities, §143B-216.51(b).
Auditing standards, §143B-216.51(c).
Duties and responsibilities of internal auditor, §143B-216.50(b).
Established, §143B-216.50(a).
Final reports submitted to secretary, §143B-216.51(e).
Implementation of department's response to audit.
Internal auditor to monitor, §143B-216.51(g).
Independent reviews and analyses of various functions and programs, §143B-216.50(a).
Long-term and annual audit plans, development, §143B-216.51(h).
Official designated by secretary, report to, §143B-216.50(d).
Political affiliation not considered in appointing, §143B-216.50(c).
Qualifications, §143B-216.51(a).
Reports.
Final report to secretary, §143B-216.51(e).
Retention of audit report information, §143B-216.51(d).
Retention of file of audit reports and information, §143B-216.51(d).
State auditor considering work of internal auditor, §143B-216.51(f).

HEALTH AND HUMAN SERVICES DEPARTMENT —Cont'd

Office of policy and planning.
Authority of director, §143B-216.70(b).
Establishment, §143B-216.70(a).
Responsibilities, §143B-216.70(a).
Office of rural health and community care.
In-kind watch to nonprofit organizations establishing health programs.
Assignment of office employees, §143B-139.4(c).
Mental health and substance abuse services.
Cooperation with other organization for expansion, §143B-139.4A.
Office of women's health, §130A-131.25.
Parking of vehicles on grounds of institutions under department's jurisdiction.
Providing for registration and parking of vehicles, fee, §143-116.7(d).
Regulating parking and establishing parking areas, §143-116.7(c).
Removal of illegally parked vehicles, §143-116.7(f).
Paternity, establishing.
Additional powers and duties of department, §110-129.1(a).
Patient medical records.
Confidentiality of privileged records, §143B-139.6.
Perinatal health care, §130A-127.
Personal property damaged or stolen by clients.
Repair or replacement, §143-127.2.
Powers and duties generally, §143B-138.1(a) to (e).
Preventative measures, emphasis, §143B-137.1.
Priorities, expenses, §143B-137.1.
Private nonprofit organizations working with department services or programs.
Documentation of assistance and contributions received, §143B-139.4(b).
Employees allowed to provide services to organizations, §143B-139.4(a).
Office of rural health and resources development employees.
Assignment to serve as in-kind watch to organization establishing health programs, §143B-139.4(c).
Radiation protection act.
Generally, §§104E-1 to 104E-29.
See RADIATION PROTECTION.
Powers and functions, §104E-9(a).
Renal disease.
Chronic renal disease.
Department to establish program, §130A-220(a), (b).
Residential schools under control of secretary.
Education programs in, §§143B-146.1 to 143B-146.21.
See EDUCATION.
Retirement system for teachers and state employees.
Blind or visually handicapped employees, §135-16.1(a) to (c).
Rulemaking procedure.
Emergency rules.
When agency may adopt, §150B-21.1A(a).
Sale of merchandise by governmental units.
Exception to prohibition, §66-58(b).
Sanitation program, §130A-227.
Schools.
Criminal record checks of personnel, §114-19.2(c1).
Residential schools under control of secretary.
Education programs in, §§143B-146.1 to 143B-146.21.
See EDUCATION.

HEALTH AND HUMAN SERVICES DEPARTMENT —Cont'd
Secretary.
Early intervention services.
Responsibilities regarding availability, §143B-139.6A.
Grants-in-aid from non-state agencies.
Requests through secretary, §143B-139.2.
Head of department, §143B-139.
Hospitals.
Power of secretary to regulate certain hospitals, §131E-67.
License plate.
Special plate, number, §20-79.5.
Rulemaking authority.
Rules applicable to local health and human services agencies, §143B-139.1.
Vaccines.
Contracts for purchase of covered vaccines.
Authority of secretary of health and human services, §130A-433(a).
Senior Tar Heel legislature, §143B-181.55.
Setoff debt collection, §§105A-1 to 105A-16.
See SETOFF DEBT COLLECTION.
Small claims against institutions of department.
Settlement.
Direct payment or replacement by institution, §143-295.1.
Social services commission, §§143B-153 to 143B-156.
Special education.
Children with disabilities.
Generally, §§115C-106.1 to 115C-112.1.
See SPECIAL EDUCATION.
State child fatality review team, §143B-150.20.
State-county special assistance, §§108A-40 to 108A-47.1.
See SOCIAL SERVICES.
State directory of new hires, §110-129.2.
Subrogation.
Vocational rehabilitation services.
Rights of department, §143-547.
Suppression of nuisances and disorders in buildings and grounds of institutions under department's jurisdiction.
Adoption of rules governing, §143-116.6(a).
Misdemeanor for violating, §143-116.6(b).
Tanning equipment operators.
Division of health service regulation.
Training program, development, §104E-9(b).
Theft of personal property by clients.
Repair or replacement, §143-127.2.
Towing of illegally parked vehicles on grounds of institutions under department's jurisdiction, §143-116.7(f).
Traffic regulation on grounds of buildings under department's jurisdiction.
Adoption of rules by secretary, §143-116.7(b).
Applicability of general laws relating to use of highways and operation of vehicles, §143-116.7(a).
Civil penalty for violations, §143-116.7(e).
General fund budget code of institution.
Deposit of fees or civil penalties collected, §143-116.7(h).
Infractions, §143-116.7(g).
Parking.
Fee for registration and parking of vehicles, §143-116.7(d).

HEALTH AND HUMAN SERVICES DEPARTMENT —Cont'd
Traffic regulation on grounds of buildings under department's jurisdiction —Cont'd
Parking —Cont'd
Regulating parking and establishing parking area, §143-116.7(c).
Removal of illegally parked vehicles, §143-116.7(f).
Transfer of functions, powers, duties, etc., by type I transfer, §143B-138.1(a), (c).
Transfer of functions, powers, duties, etc., by type II transfer, §143B-138.1(b), (d).
Umbilical cord stem cells and umbilical cord blood banking.
Free educational information on web site.
Definitions, §130A-128.1(a).
Health care professionals encouraged to provide publications, §130A-128.1(d).
Immunity for informing women about publications, §130A-128.1(e).
Link to federally sponsored web site.
Satisfaction of obligation, §130A-128.1(c).
Vaccination program.
First responders, §130A-485.
Vocational rehabilitation services.
Duties of secretary, §143-546.1(a).
Services provided by department, §143-545.1(b).
Subrogation, §143-547.
Wastewater systems, §§130A-333 to 130A-343.1.
See WASTEWATER SYSTEMS.
Women's health, office of, §130A-131.25.
Work first program, §§108A-27 to 108A-39.
See WORK FIRST PROGRAM.

HEALTH ASSESSMENTS.
Child care facilities, §110-91.

HEALTH AUTHORITIES.
Public health authorities generally, §§130A-45 to 130A-45.13.
See PUBLIC HEALTH AUTHORITIES.

HEALTH BENEFIT PLANS.
Contracts between plans and health care providers, §§58-50-270 to 58-50-290.
See HEALTH INSURANCE.
External review, §§58-50-75 to 58-50-95.
See HEALTH INSURANCE.
Generally, §§58-3-167 to 58-3-178, 58-3-190 to 58-3-265.
See HEALTH INSURANCE.
Managed care patient assistance program, §143-730.

HEALTH BOARDS, DISTRICT, §130A-37.
Powers and duties, §130A-39.

HEALTH CARE BENEFITS PROVIDERS.
Contracts between plans and health care providers, §§58-50-270 to 58-50-290.
See HEALTH INSURANCE.
Health benefit plans.
External review, §§58-50-75 to 58-50-95.
Generally, §§58-3-167 to 58-3-178, 58-3-190 to 58-3-265.
See HEALTH INSURANCE.
Managed care patient assistance program, §143-730.
Health care sharing organizations.
Exceptions to jurisdiction over providers, §58-49-12.
Hearing aids.
Deductibles, coinsurance and other limitations, §58-3-285(b).

HEALTH CARE BENEFITS PROVIDERS
—Cont'd
Hearing aids —Cont'd
Medical necessity determination, utilization
review, §58-3-285(c).
Required coverage, §58-3-285(a).
Insurance companies generally.
See INSURANCE COMPANIES.
Jurisdiction over providers, §§58-49-1 to
58-49-25.
Authority of commissioner, §58-49-5.
Commissioner, §58-49-5.
Examination by, §58-49-15.
Conflict of laws, §58-49-20.
Disclosure, §58-49-25(a), (b).
Establishment, §58-49-10.
Examination by commissioner, §58-49-15.
Exceptions to jurisdiction, §58-49-12.
Health care sharing organizations.
Exceptions to jurisdiction, §58-49-12.
How to show jurisdiction, §58-49-10.
Purpose of article, §58-49-1.
Stop-loss insurance.
Disclosure of amount, §58-49-25(b).
Subject to state laws, §58-49-20.
Locum tenens contracts, §58-3-231.
Accepting and payment for claims, §58-3-231(b).
Defined terms, §58-3-231(a).
Medical groups or hospitals, §58-3-231(c).
Placement and administrative services,
§58-3-231(e).
Statements of supervision waived, §58-3-231(d).
Medicaid, §§108A-54 to 108A-70.5.
See MEDICAID.
Multiple employer welfare arrangements,
§§58-49-30 to 58-49-65.
Acknowledgment of claims, §58-3-100(c).
Failure to acknowledge after receiving notice.
Civil penalty, §58-3-100(c).
Actuarial certification, §58-49-60(c).
Applicability of other provisions of law,
§58-49-55(a).
Claims.
Acknowledgment of claims, §58-3-100(c).
Failure to acknowledge after receiving notice.
Civil penalty, §58-3-100(c).
Contracts.
Between health benefit plans and health care
providers, §§58-50-270 to 58-50-290.
See HEALTH INSURANCE.
Filing with commissioner, §58-49-40(f).
Defined, §58-49-30(a).
Examinations, §58-49-55(b).
Excess insurance.
Maintenance, §58-49-40(c).
Exemptions, §58-49-35(b).
Financial statements, §58-49-60(d).
Health insurance risk pool.
Notice relating to.
Insurers to provide applicants, §58-3-276.
Impairment or insolvency.
Corrective action plan, §58-49-65(c).
Information provided commissioner, §58-49-30(c).
Licenses.
Application, §58-49-50.
Denial, suspension or revocation.
Grounds, §§58-49-40(e), (g), 58-49-65(a), (b).
Qualifications of applicant, §58-49-40(a).
Required, §58-49-35(a).
Loss reserves, §58-49-40(d).

HEALTH CARE BENEFITS PROVIDERS
—Cont'd
Multiple employer welfare arrangements
—Cont'd
Lymphedema.
Coverage for diagnosis and treatment,
§58-3-280.
Names.
Certain words prohibited in name, §58-49-45.
North Carolina health insurance risk pool.
Notice relating to.
Insurers to provide applicants, §58-3-276.
Policies.
Insurance policies and contracts generally.
See INSURANCE POLICIES OR
CONTRACTS.
Issuance, §58-49-40(b).
Reports.
Additional information required by
commissioner, §58-49-60(b).
Annual reports, §58-49-60(a).
Failure to file, §58-49-60(e).
Suspension of authority to enroll new insured,
§58-49-65(d).
Trustees, managers or administrators.
Qualifications, §58-49-40(e).

**HEALTH CARE DURABLE POWER OF
ATTORNEY.**
General provisions, §§32A-15 to 32A-26.
See HEALTH CARE POWERS OF ATTORNEY.

HEALTH CARE FACILITIES.
**Abused juveniles brought for medial diagnosis
or treatment.**
Obtaining judicial authority to retain physical
custody of juvenile when abuse suspected,
§7B-308.
Abuse of patients, §14-32.2.
Ambulatory surgical facilities.
Licenses, §§131E-145 to 131E-152.
See AMBULATORY SURGICAL FACILITIES.
Bomb scares, §§14-69.1, 14-69.2.
Bond issues.
Authority to finance by bond, NC Const Art V §8.
Cardiac rehabilitation certification program,
§§131E-165 to 131E-170.
See CARDIAC REHABILITATION
CERTIFICATION PROGRAM.
Certificate of public advantage, §§131E-192.1 to
131E-192.13.
Actions on decision to issue or remain in effect,
§131E-192.10(a) to (d).
Applications, §§131E-192.3, 131E-192.11(a).
Review of applications, §131E-192.11(b).
Definitions, §131E-192.2.
Effects of certificate, §131E-192.13(a) to (c).
Fees, §131E-192.11(a).
Applications.
Review of application, §131E-192.11(b).
Findings of general assembly, §131E-192.1.
Issuance, §131E-192.5.
Review after issuance, §131E-192.8.
Judicial review.
Decision to allow certificate to remain in effect
or make changes, §131E-192.10(b).
Attorney general action, §131E-192.10(c).
Decision to issue or not issue, §131E-192.10(a).
Work product of department, attorney general.
Not discoverable or admissible,
§131E-192.10(d).
Objection by attorney general, §131E-192.6.

HEALTH CARE FACILITIES —Cont'd
Certificate of public advantage —Cont'd
Procedure for review, §131E-192.4(a).
Records, §131E-192.7.
Report of activities pursuant to cooperative
  agreement.
  Attorney general, copy submitted to,
    §131E-192.9(a).
  Content requirements, §131E-192.9(a).
  Failure to file or give information.
    Revocation of certificate, §131E-192.9(b).
  Filed every 2 years, §131E-192.9(a).
  Notice of receipt, North Carolina register,
    §131E-192.9(a).
  Public comment after notice of receipt, time,
    §131E-192.9(a).
  Review by department, §131E-192.9(c).
Required, §131E-192.3(a).
Rules and regulations.
  Authority of department and attorney general,
    §131E-192.12.
Standards for review, §131E-192.4(b).
Certificates of need, §§131E-175 to 130E-191.1.
Activities requiring certificates, §131E-178.
  Capital expenditure obligations, §131E-178(c) to
    (e).
  Predevelopment activities, §131E-178(e).
Administrative review, §131E-188(a), (a1).
  Affected persons.
    Defined, §131E-188(c).
Appeals.
  Affected persons.
    Defined, §131E-188(c).
  Bond, surety, §131E-188(b1).
  Frivolous appeals or appeal filed to delay
    applicant, §131E-188(b1).
  Rights of appeal, §131E-188(b).
Application for certificate.
  Capital expenditure amount.
    Adjustment, §131E-181(c).
  Compliance with representations in application.
    Enforcement, §131E-190(i).
    Required, §131E-181(b).
  Decision on application, §131E-186(a).
    Notice, §131E-186(b).
  Fees, §131E-182(c).
  Forms, §131E-182(b).
  Information to be contained, §131E-182(b).
  Review criteria, §131E-183(a).
    Complete for review, §131E-185(c).
    Expedited review, §131E-185(a2).
    Extension of review period, §131E-185(c).
    Particular types of applications, §131E-183(b).
    Process for review, §131E-185(a1).
    Time limit for review of project,
      §131E-185(a1).
  Schedules for submission and review of
    applications, §131E-182(a).
Approval of certificate.
  Required approvals, §131E-184(a), (b).
  Exemptions, §131E-184(c).
Assignability, §131E-181(a).
Capital expenditure.
  Activities requiring certificates, §131E-178(c) to
    (e).
  Defined, §131E-176.
  Exemption from review expenditures exceeding
    2 million dollars, §131E-184(e).
  Required approvals, §131E-184(a).
Certified cost estimates.
  Defined, §131E-176.

HEALTH CARE FACILITIES —Cont'd
Certificates of need —Cont'd
Charges of facility, §131E-179(b).
Chemical dependency or substance abuse facilities
  in correctional institutions.
  Exemption, §131E-184(d).
Civil penalties, §131E-190(f).
  Violations of article, §131E-190(f).
Completion of project, §131E-181.
Conditional issuance.
  Withdrawal of issuance, §131E-189(b).
Contested case hearing.
  Administrative review, §131E-188(a).
    Bond filed, §131E-188(a1).
Definitions, §131E-176.
  Affected persons, §131E-188(c).
Department.
  Defined, §131E-176.
Exemption for substance abuse contractors in
  correctional facilities, §131E-184(d).
Fees, §131E-182(c).
Findings of fact, §131E-175.
Health care facilities.
  Charges of facility, §131E-179(b).
  Defined, §131E-176.
Health maintenance organizations.
  Defined, §131E-176.
Injunctions.
  Noncompliance with representations in
    application for certificate, §131E-190(i).
  Violations of article generally, §131E-190(h).
Issuance.
  Conditional issuance.
    Withdrawal of certificate, §131E-189(b).
  Time line requirements, §131E-187(c).
Judicial review, §131E-188(b).
  Affected persons defined, §131E-188(c).
Legislative findings of fact, §131E-175.
Nature of certificate, §131E-181(a).
New institutional health services.
  Activities requiring certificates, §131E-178(a).
    Acquisition of service, §131E-178(b).
  Defined, §131E-176.
  Development, §131E-190(a).
    Financing, construction or acquisition
      commitments, §131E-190(b).
  No formal commitments made until certificate
    granted, §131E-190(b).
  Offering, §131E-190(a).
    Financing, construction or acquisition
      commitments, §131E-190(b).
  Penalties for violation of provisions,
    §131E-190(d), (e).
Nursing care, §131E-176.
Offering or developing services without certificate,
  §131E-190(d), (e).
  Research activities, §131E-179(c).
    Not requiring certificate, §131E-179(a).
Penalties.
  Civil penalty, §131E-190(f).
  Injunctive relief, §131E-190(h).
  Offering or developing services without
    certificate, §131E-190(d), (e).
Petition for contested case.
  Administrative review.
    Filing, time, §131E-188(a).
Powers and duties of department, §131E-177.
Required approvals, §131E-184(a), (b).
  Exemptions, §131E-184(c).
Research activities, §131E-179(c).
  Not requiring certificate, §131E-179(a).

HEALTH CARE FACILITIES —Cont'd
Certificates of need —Cont'd
Revocation of certificate.
Reasons, §131E-189.
Rights of appeal, §131E-188(b).
State departments and agencies.
Prohibition on assisting entities in violation of
article, §131E-190(g).
State health planning and development agency.
Designation, §131E-177.
Time line requirements.
Issuance, §131E-187(c).
Timetable to be followed.
Withdrawal of certificate, §131E-189(a).
Transferability, §131E-181(a).
Withdrawal of certificate, §131E-189(c).
Withdrawal of certificate, §131E-189.
Confidentiality of information.
Competitive health care information, §131E-97.3.
Elected officials, access to, §131E-97.3(c).
Request for disclosure, §131E-97.3(b).
What is public record, §131E-97.3(a).
Credentialing information, §131E-97.2.
Health care contracts, §131E-99.
Hospices, §131E-207(a) to (c).
Patient information, §131E-97(a), (b).
Personnel files, §131E-97.1(a).
Construction projects and plans.
Review by department of health and human
services.
Fees charged, §131E-267(a).
Adult day care home construction projects,
§131E-267(f).
Ambulatory surgical care construction
projects, §131E-267(d).
Charged on one-time per-project basis,
§131E-267(a).
Disposition, §131E-267(a).
Hospital construction projects, §131E-267(b).
Maximum amount, §131E-267(a).
Nursing home construction projects,
§131E-267(c).
Psychiatric hospital construction projects,
§131E-267(e).
Residential construction projects,
§131E-267(g).
Cooperative agreements.
Certificate of public advantage, §§131E-192.1 to
131E-192.13.
Applications, §131E-192.3(b).
Procedure for review, §131E-192.4(a).
Definitions, §131E-192.2.
Effects of certificate, §131E-192.13(a) to (c).
Findings of general assembly, §131E-192.1.
Issuance, §131E-192.5.
Review after issuance, §131E-192.8.
Judicial review, §131E-192.10(a) to (d).
Objection by attorney general, §131E-192.6.
Records, §131E-192.7.
Report of activities while certificate in effect,
§131E-192.9(a) to (c).
Required, §131E-192.3(a).
Rules and regulations.
Authority of department and attorney
general, §131E-192.12.
Standards for review, §131E-192.4(b).
Criminal record checks of personnel, §114-19.3.
Definitions, §131E-1.
Cardiac rehabilitation certification program,
§131E-166.
Certificate of public advantage, §131E-192.2.

HEALTH CARE FACILITIES —Cont'd
Definitions —Cont'd
Certificates of need, §131E-176.
Finance act, §131A-3.
Home care agencies, §131E-136.
Licenses, §131E-136.
Hospices, §131E-201.
Demonstration at health care facility.
Dangerous weapons, §14-277.2.
Demonstration at private health care facilities.
Possession of weapon, §14-277.2.
**Designation of state health planning and
development agency,** §131E-177.
**Donation of medical equipment no longer
needed.**
Public or state hospital, §131E-250(a), (b).
Emergencies.
Temporary shelter or temporary services during
disaster or emergency.
Waiver of rules for facilities that provide,
§131E-112(a).
Definition of "emergency management
agency,"§131E-112(b).
Emergency medical services.
Regulation of emergency medical services,
§§131E-155 to 131E-161.
See EMERGENCY MEDICAL SERVICES.
Employee personnel files.
Confidentiality, §131E-97.1(a).
Fees.
Certificate of public advantage, §131E-192.11.
Review of application, §131E-192.11(b).
Certification fee for abortion facilities, §131E-269.
Initial licensure fees for new facilities, §131E-272.
Review of construction projects and plans,
§131E-267.
Financing, §§131A-1 to 131A-25.
See HEALTH CARE FACILITY FINANCING.
**Firearm at demonstration at health care
facility,** §14-277.2.
Health and human services department.
Abortion facilities.
Department certification fee authorized,
§131E-269.
Construction projects and plans.
Fee for department review, §131E-267.
Health care associated infections.
Statewide surveillance and reporting system.
Establishment, §130A-150(a).
Hospitals responsible for, §130A-150(c).
Release of data to public, §130A-150(d).
Rules to implement, adoption, §130A-150(b).
Health care personnel registry.
Administrative hearings, §131E-256(d).
Contents, §131E-256(a).
Contest of placement of certain information.
Procedure, §131E-256(d1), (d2).
Disputed entries, statement in registry,
§131E-256(a1).
Establishment, §131E-256.
"Health care facility" defined, §131E-256(b).
"Health care personnel" defined, §131E-256(c).
Immunity, §131E-256(f).
Information furnished to employer, §131E-256(e).
Removal from registry in certain cases of neglect,
§131E-256(i).
Contesting decision to deny removal of single
finding of neglect, §131E-256(i1).
One time with respect to any person,
§131E-256(j).
Reports of disciplinary actions, §131E-256(g).

HEALTH CARE FACILITIES —Cont'd
Health care personnel registry —Cont'd
Rules, §131E-256(h).
Single finding of neglect.
Removal from registry, §131E-256(i).
Contesting denial of removal, §131E-256(i1).
Hiring nurses.
Verification of licensure status, §90-171.43A(a),
(b).
Home care agencies licensing, §§131E-135 to
131E-143.
Adverse action on licenses, §131E-139(a), (b).
Definitions, §131E-136.
Enforcement of rules, §131E-140(b).
Establishment of licensing requirements.
Purpose of part, §131E-135(b).
Injunctions, §131E-142(a) to (c).
Inspections, §131E-141(a), (b).
Penalties.
Violation of provisions, §131E-141.1.
Purpose of act, §131E-135(b).
Requirements, §131E-138(a) to (g).
Rules and regulations, §131E-140(a), (a1).
Services provided in all counties, §131E-137(a),
(c).
Title of part.
Home health agency licensing act, §131E-135(a).
Violation of provisions.
Penalties, §131E-141.1.
Hospices.
Care to be available at all times, §131E-203(c).
Certificates of need.
Definitions, §131E-176.
Citation of article, §131E-200.
Confidentiality of information, §131E-207(a) to (c).
Definitions, §131E-201.
Injunctions.
Violations of article, §131E-206(a) to (c).
Inspections, §131E-204.
Confidentiality of information, §131E-207(a) to
(c).
Licenses, §§131E-200 to 131E-207.
Applications.
Department to provide, §131E-202(b).
Display, §131E-202(b).
Exemptions, §131E-203(b).
Fee, §131E-202(b).
Issuance, §131E-202(b).
Nontransferable, §131E-202(b).
Purpose of article, §131E-200.
Renewal, §131E-202(c).
Required, §131E-203(a).
Rules and regulations.
Adoption by commission, §131E-202(a).
Suspension or revocation.
Grounds, §131E-205(a).
Procedure, §131E-205(b).
Title of article, §131E-200.
Hospital authorities, §§131E-15 to 131E-33.
See HOSPITAL AUTHORITIES.
Hospitals.
See HOSPITALS.
Independent contractors.
Confidential information, information public
record, §131E-97.1(c).
Infections.
Health care associated infections.
Statewide surveillance and reporting system,
§130A-150.
Licensure fees for new facilities, §131E-272.

HEALTH CARE FACILITIES —Cont'd
Malpractice actions generally, §§90-21.11 to
90-21.19B.
See MEDICAL MALPRACTICE.
Managed care patient assistance program,
§143-730.
Medical care commission, §§143B-165 to
143B-168.
Medication aide registry, §§131E-114.2,
131E-270.
Municipal hospitals, §§131E-5 to 131E-14.2.
See MUNICIPAL HOSPITALS.
New facilities.
Initial licensure fees, §131E-272.
Nurses, hiring.
Verification of licensure status, §90-171.43A(a),
(b).
Nursing homes.
Licenses, §§131E-100 to 131E-110.
See NURSING HOMES.
Patients' bill of rights, §§131E-115 to 131E-131.
See NURSING HOMES.
Nursing pools.
General provisions, §§131E-154.1 to 131E-154.8.
See NURSES.
Obstruction of health care facility, §14-277.4.
Patient information.
Confidentiality.
Financial records, §131E-97(b).
Medical records, §131E-97(a).
Personnel files.
Confidentiality, §131E-97.1(a).
Planning and development agency, §§131E-140,
131E-177.
Provider sponsored organizations.
General provisions, §§131E-275 to 131E-314.
See PROVIDER SPONSORED
ORGANIZATIONS.
Sales and use tax.
Refunds.
Certain nonprofit organizations, §105-164.14(b).
Specialty hospitals.
Other programs controlled by department,
§131E-67.
Alcohol detoxification program, §131E-65.
Surplus medical equipment.
Donation by public or state hospital,
§131E-250(a), (b).
**Suspension, cancellation or amendment of
license,** §131E-256.1(a), (b).
Trauma.
Statewide trauma system, §131E-162.

HEALTH CARE FACILITY FINANCING,
§§131A-1 to 131A-25.
**Additional and alternative method for doing
authorized things,** §131A-23.
Applicability of provisions.
Inconsistent laws inapplicable, §131A-25.
Audit of books and accounts, §131A-19.
Bonds and notes.
Application requesting approval of issuance,
§131A-11.
Authentication, §131A-11.
Authorized, §§131A-11, 131A-18.
Defined, §131A-3.
Eligibility for investment, §131A-17.
Exemption from taxation, §131A-21.
Interest, §131A-11.
Interim receipts, §131A-11.
Investment securities, §131A-16.

HEALTH CARE FACILITY FINANCING
—Cont'd
Bonds and notes —Cont'd
Issuance, §131A-11.
Application requesting approval, §131A-11.
Liability of officers, §131A-20.
Limiting or altering rights of holders of bonds or notes, §131A-13(d).
Maturity, §131A-11.
Mutilated, destroyed or lost bonds or notes, §131A-11.
Officers not liable, §131A-20.
Principal and interest, §131A-11.
Redemption, §131A-11.
Refunding bonds or notes, §131A-18.
Remedies of holders of bonds or notes, §131A-15.
Replacement of mutilated, destroyed or lost bonds or notes, §131A-11.
Sale of bonds or notes, §131A-11.
Proceeds of sale, §131A-11.
Supplemental and additional conferred powers, §131A-23.
Tax exemption, §131A-21.
Temporary bonds, §131A-11.
Trust agreement or resolution, §131A-12.
Citation, §131A-1.
Commission.
Defined, §131A-3.
Powers.
Additional powers, §131A-4.
Conflicts of interest, §131A-22.
Construction contracts, §131A-9.
Construction of chapter.
Liberal construction, §131A-24.
Contracts.
Construction contracts, §131A-9.
Conveyance of interest in health care facilities, §131A-8.
Credit of state not pledged, §131A-10.
Criteria and requirements, §131A-5.
Procedural requirements, §131A-7.
Definitions, §131A-3.
Fees.
Fixing and collecting fees, §131A-13(a).
Providing fund sufficient, §131A-13(b).
Trust funds, §131A-14.
Inconsistent laws inapplicable, §131A-25.
Investments.
Bonds and notes, §131A-16.
Eligibility for investment, §131A-17.
Lease agreements, §131A-8.
Legislative findings and declarations, §131A-2.
Loan agreements, §131A-8.
Repayments of loan, §131A-13(a).
Trust funds, §131A-14.
Operation of health care facilities, §131A-8.
Pledges of revenues, §131A-13(c).
Powers.
Additional powers of commission, §131A-4.
Additional powers of public agencies, §131A-6.
Supplemental and additional conferred powers, §131A-23.
Procedural requirements of chapter, §131A-7.
Public agencies.
Defined, §131A-3.
Powers.
Additional powers, §131A-6.
Purchase price payments.
Fixing and collecting, §131A-13(a).
Providing fund sufficient, §131A-13(b).
Trust funds, §131A-14.

HEALTH CARE FACILITY FINANCING
—Cont'd
Purpose of act, §131A-2.
Remedies.
Holders of bonds or notes, §131A-15.
Rents and charges.
Fixing and collecting, §131A-13(a).
Providing fund sufficient, §131A-13(b).
Trust funds, §131A-14.
Reports.
Annual report, §131A-19.
Requirements of chapter, §131A-5.
Procedural requirements, §131A-7.
Revenues.
Pledges of revenues, §131A-13(c).
Sales.
Agreements of sale, §131A-8.
Short title, §131A-1.
Trust agreement or resolution.
Security for bonds or notes, §131A-12.
Trust funds, §131A-14.

HEALTH CARE FOR MINORS, CONSENT TO, §§32A-28 to 32A-34.
Authorization.
Duration, §32A-32.
Form, §32A-34.
Good faith reliance on, §32A-33.
Reliance on authorization, §32A-33.
Revocation, §32A-32.
Statutory form, §32A-34.
Who may make an authorization, §32A-30.
Custodial parents.
Authority, §32A-30.
Definitions, §32A-29.
Extent and limitations of authority, §32A-31.
Public policy, §32A-28(a).
Purpose of article, §32A-28(b).
Treatment by physician.
Consent of minor sufficient, §90-21.5(a).
Consent of parent or guardian.
When not required, §90-21.1.
Who may make an authorization to consent, §32A-30.

HEALTH CARE LIABILITY, §§90-21.50 to 90-21.56.
Admissibility of evidence, §90-21.55(b).
Corporate practice of medicine defense, §90-21.51(e).
Covered benefits, §90-21.51(g).
Damages.
Actions for recovery of, §90-21.51(c), (e).
Contribution and indemnity, §90-21.52(c).
Hold harmless contracts, §90-21.51(f).
Joint liability, §90-21.51(f).
Liability for damages, §90-21.51(b).
Limitation on recovery of damages, §90-21.56(b).
Recovery of damages, §90-21.56(a).
Waiver of right to recovery, §90-21.56(c).
Defense to actions, §90-21.51(c), (e).
Definitions, §90-21.50.
Employer liability, §90-21.52(a).
Exhaustion of administrative remedies and appeals, §90-21.54.
External review decisions, §90-21.55(a), (b).
Indemnification or hold harmless contracts, §90-21.51(h).
Ordinary care, duty to exercise, §90-21.51(a).
Proof of agency, §90-21.51(d).
Separate trial and discovery on claims, §90-21.53.

HEALTH CARE PERSONNEL REGISTRY.
Administrative hearings, §131E-256(d).
Contents, §131E-256(a).
Contesting placement of certain information.
  Procedure, §131E-256(d1), (d2).
Disputed entries, statement in registry,
  §131E-256(a1).
Establishment, §131E-256.
"Health care facility" defined, §131E-256(b).
"Health care personnel" defined, §131E-256(c).
Immunity, §131E-256(f).
Information furnished to employer,
  §131E-256(e).
Removal from registry in certain cases of
  neglect, §131E-256(i).
  Contesting decision to deny removal for single
    finding of neglect, §131E-256(i1).
  One time with respect to any person,
    §131E-256(j).
Reports of disciplinary actions, §131E-256(g).
Rules, §131E-256(h).
Single finding of neglect.
  Removal from registry, §131E-256(i).
    Contesting decision to deny, §131E-256(i1).

HEALTH CARE POWERS OF ATTORNEY,
  §§32A-15 to 32A-26.
Advance directive.
  Combined with or incorporated into, §32A-26.
Advance health care directive registry,
  §§130A-465 to 130A-471.
Attorney-in-fact.
  Combination with general power of attorney,
    §32A-22(d).
  Eligibility to act as, §32A-18.
  General power of attorney.
    Effect of health care power of attorney,
      §32A-22(c).
  Who may act as, §32A-18.
Burial places and gravestones.
  Agent's authority to provide, §28A-19-9(a), (b).
  Reimbursement of agent from estate,
    §28A-19-9(a).
Children.
  Consent to health care for minors.
    Parent authorizing agent to consent, §§32A-28
      to 32A-34.
Death of principal.
  Effective following, §32A-20(a).
  Revocation by, §32A-20(b).
Definitions, §32A-16.
Determination that principal lacks
  understanding and capacity.
  Power effective upon, §32A-20(a).
Disposition of decedent's body or body parts,
  §130A-420(a).
Divorce or separation of principal and spouse
  health care agent.
  Revocation of health care agent's authority,
    §32A-20(c).
Durable power.
  Chapter 32A, Article 2 not applicable, §32A-23.
Effective following death of principal,
  §32A-20(a).
Effective upon determination principal lacks
  sufficient understanding and capacity,
  §32A-20(a).
Eligibility to make health care power of
  attorney, §32A-17.
Execution outside of state, validity, §32A-27.

HEALTH CARE POWERS OF ATTORNEY
  —Cont'd
Execution prior to effective date of act.
  Effect of act, §32A-19(f).
Form.
  Statutory form, §32A-25.1.
Guardians.
  Appointment.
    Effect, §32A-22(a).
  Nomination by health care power of attorney,
    §32A-22(b).
  Suspension of health care agent's authority.
    Petition to court for, §35A-1208(a).
Health care agents.
  Applicability of defenses, §32A-24(d).
  Appointment, §32A-21(a).
  Authority.
    Extent, §32A-19(a), (c).
    Limitations, §32A-19(d), (e).
    Spouse of principal.
      Revocation upon divorce or separation,
        §32A-20(c).
  Decisions, §32A-24(b).
  Defenses, §32A-24(c).
  Defined, §32A-16.
  Medical malpractice.
    Persons who may consent for another,
      §90-21.13(c).
  Reliance on authority, §32A-24(a).
  Removal, §32A-21(a).
  Resignation, §32A-21(a).
  Revoked power of attorney, acting on, §32A-24(d).
  Substitution, §32A-21(a).
  Suspension of authority, §32A-22(a).
    Petition by guardian, §35A-1208(a).
Intent and construction of article, §32A-15(c),
  (d).
Involuntary commitment to mental health
  facility.
  Effect of advance instruction, §32A-19(a1).
Mental health advance instructions.
  Generally, §§122C-71 to 122C-77.
    See MENTAL HEALTH, DEVELOPMENTAL
      DISABILITY, SUBSTANCE ABUSE.
  Incorporation into health care power of attorney,
    §32A-19(b).
  Involuntary commitment to mental health facility.
    Effect of advance instruction, §32A-19(a1).
Minors.
  Consent to health care for minors.
    Parent authorizing agent to consent, §§32A-28
      to 32A-34.
Physicians.
  Determinations by, §32A-20(a).
  Health care agents' reliance on, §32A-24(a).
Principal.
  Grant of authority, §32A-19(a).
Public policy, statement, §32A-15(a).
Purpose of article, §32A-15(b).
Revocation.
  Generally, §32A-20(b).
  Health care agents.
    Death, §32A-21.
    Failure or refusal to act, §32A-21(b).
    Spouse of principal.
      Revoked by divorce or separation, §32A-20(c).
Statutory form, §32A-25.1.
Suicide.
  Actions under not considered suicide, §32A-24.
Validity of power executed in other
  jurisdiction, §32A-27.

HEALTH CARE POWERS OF ATTORNEY
　—Cont'd
Who may make, §32A-17.
Withholding or discontinuing life sustaining procedures.
　Specific authority given, no declaration as to present condition executed, §32A-15(c).

HEALTH CARE PROVIDER REFERRAL FEES AND PAYMENTS FOR SOLICITATIONS, §§90-400 to 90-402.
Health care provider defined, §90-400.
Prohibited, §90-401.
Sanctions, §90-402.

HEALTH CARE PROVIDERS' IMMUNITY.
Nonprofit medical or health care facilities, §90-21.16.

HEALTH CARE PROVIDERS' SELF-REFERRALS, §§90-405 to 90-408.
Claim for payment, §90-406(b), (c).
Cross-referral arrangements, §90-406(d).
　Penalties, §90-407(c), (d).
Definitions, §90-405.
Disciplinary actions.
　Grounds, §90-407(a).
Exceptions for underserved areas.
　Disclosure of investment interests by provider, §90-408(c).
　Generally, §90-408(a).
　Regulations governing applications for exemptions, §90-408(b).
General prohibition, §90-406(a).
Invoices, §90-406(b), (c).
Penalties for designated misconduct, §90-407(b), (d).
Underserved areas.
　Exceptions, §90-408.

HEALTH CARE RECORDS.
See MEDICAL RECORDS.

HEALTH CARE RESEARCH FACILITIES.
Financing health care facility generally, §§131A-1 to 131A-25.
　See HEALTH CARE FACILITY FINANCING.

HEALTH CARE SHARING ORGANIZATIONS.
Health care benefits providers.
　Jurisdiction over providers.
　　Exceptions to jurisdiction, §58-49-12.

HEALTH CHOICE FOR CHILDREN.
Child health insurance fund, §108A-70.20A.
Health insurance program for children.
　Act of 1998, §§108A-70.18 to 108A-70.29.
　　See CHILDREN'S HEALTH INSURANCE PROGRAM.
Provider requirements, §§108C-1 to 108C-12.
　Appeal of adverse determinations.
　　Burden of proof, §108C-12(d).
　　Final decision, §108C-12(c).
　　Law governing, §108C-12(a).
　　Request for hearing considered as contested case, §108C-12(b).
　Applicability of provisions, §108C-1.
　Audits, inspections or investigations.
　　Additional documentation, time for providing, §108C-5(p).
　　Cooperation of provider, §108C-11(a).
　　Correction of errors prior to final determination, §108C-5(o).
　　Department not to interfere with clinical activities, §108C-11(b).

HEALTH CHOICE FOR CHILDREN —Cont'd
Provider requirements —Cont'd
　Audits, inspections or investigations —Cont'd
　　Extrapolation of results, audit resulting in.
　　　Challenge of results, §108C-5(n).
　　　Credentialed auditors, §108C-5(j).
　　　Department notice of intention to use, §108C-5(r).
　　　Duration of time provider subject to being audited, §108C-5(q).
　　　Further audits, §108C-5(l).
　　　Identification of matters to be reviewed, §108C-5(k).
　　　Information to provider, §108C-5(i).
　　Federal requirements for submission of documentation, §108C-11(c).
　　Self-audits, voluntary, §108C-5(m).
　　Unannounced or targeted audits, §108C-5(s).
　Change of ownership.
　　Assigned participation or enrollment agreement, §108C-10(c).
　　Provider not required to accept, §108C-10(d).
　　Notice, §108C-10(b).
　　Occurrences constituting, §108C-10(a).
　Criminal background checks.
　　Conviction of person with certain ownership interest in provider.
　　　Denial or termination of enrollment, §108C-4(b).
　　Department to conduct, §108C-4(a).
　　Offenses as grounds for denial or termination of enrollment, §108C-4(c).
　Definitions, §108C-2.
　Denial or termination of enrollment.
　　Conviction of person with certain ownership interest in provider, §108C-4(b).
　　Offenses as grounds for, §108C-4(c).
　Enrollment criteria.
　　Attestation and training, §108C-9(a).
　　False or misleading statements in application or attestation, §108C-9(d).
　　Statement that organization has met certain business requirements, §108C-9(b).
　　Training to be attended, §108C-9(c).
　High categorical risk designations, §108C-3(g).
　　Effect on screening requirements, §108C-3(h).
　Limited categorical risk designations, §108C-3(c).
　　Effect on screening requirements, §108C-3(d).
　Moderate categorical risk designations, §108C-3(e).
　　Effect on screening requirements, §108C-3(f).
　Overpayments, threshold for recovery, §108C-8.
　Prepayment claims review.
　　Clean claims, processing, §108C-7(d).
　　Clean claims rate, standard for, §108C-7(e).
　　Contested case status, review not to have, §108C-7(f).
　　Deficient documentation, §108C-7(d).
　　Grounds for requiring, §108C-7(a).
　　Notice to provider, §108C-7(b).
　　Prior authorization, medical necessity not subject of review, §108C-7(c).
　　Stay of payment pending, §108C-7(b).
　Registry of third-parties submitting claims on behalf of providers, §108C-6.
　Screening of providers.
　　Enrollment screening, §108C-3(b).
　　High categorical risk designations, §108C-3(g).
　　　Effect on screening requirements, §108C-3(h).
　　Limited categorical risk designations, §108C-3(c).
　　　Effect on screening requirements, §108C-3(d).

HEALTH CHOICE FOR CHILDREN —Cont'd
Provider requirements —Cont'd
Screening of providers —Cont'd
Moderate categorical risk designations,
§108C-3(e).
Effect on screening requirements, §108C-3(f).
Out-of-state providers, §108C-3(j).
Reliance on results from Medicaid contractors,
§108C-3(i).
Required, §108C-3(a).
Suspension of payments.
Application of payments to delinquent
assessment or fine, §108C-5(h).
Audits, extrapolation of results.
Information to provider, §108C-5(i).
Collection of debts owed to state, §108C-5(e).
Delinquent assessment or fine, time when
suspension begins, §108C-5(c).
Exhaustion of appeals prior to becoming final,
§108C-5(b).
Grounds, §108C-5(b).
Payment plan for delinquent assessment or fine,
§108C-5(g).
Program participation suspended, §108C-5(d).
Providers sharing same employee identification
number or corporate parent, §108C-5(f).

HEALTH CLUBS.
Prepaid entertainment contracts.
General provisions, §§66-118 to 66-125.
See PREPAID ENTERTAINMENT
CONTRACTS.

HEALTH COORDINATING COUNCIL.
Defined, §131E-176.
Lobbyists prohibited from serving on,
§131E-191.1.

**HEALTH COVERAGE FOR WORKERS WITH
DISABILITIES ACT.**
Medicaid buy-in for workers with disabilities,
§108A-54.1.

HEALTH DEPARTMENTS, LOCAL, §§130A-34 to
130A-42.
See LOCAL HEALTH DEPARTMENTS.

HEALTH DIRECTOR OF STATE, §138-3.

HEALTH EDUCATION.
Public schools.
Basic education program, §115C-81(e1), (e2).

HEALTH EMERGENCY.
Nuclear, biological or chemical agents.
Terrorist incident using, §§130A-475 to 130A-479.
See TERRORIST INCIDENT USING
NUCLEAR, BIOLOGICAL OR CHEMICAL
AGENTS.

HEALTH INFORMATION EXCHANGE.
Applicability of provisions, §90-413.7(b).
Business associate contracts, §90-413.4(a).
Participating covered entities, §90-413.5(a).
Disclosure of or access to information by
associates, §90-413.5(b).
Citation of act, §90-413.1.
Construction of statutory provisions.
Applicability of provisions, §90-413.7(b).
Rights not impaired by statutes, §90-413.7(a).
**Corporate powers of exchange not otherwise
limited,** §90-413.4(b).
Definitions, §90-413.3.
Legislative intent, §90-413.2.

HEALTH INFORMATION EXCHANGE —Cont'd
Medical records generally.
See MEDICAL RECORDS.
Opting out.
Affect of decision on disclosures, §90-413.6(b).
Denial of treatment or benefits, prohibition,
§90-413.6(c).
Enforcement of decision to opt out or rescind,
§90-413.6(b).
Individual right to opt out or to rescind opt out
decision, §90-413.6(a).
Nondisclosure of information for person exercising
opt out rights, §90-413.6(d).
Exception for emergency medical treatment,
§90-413.6(e).
Notice of rights, required, §90-413.4(a).
Participating covered entities.
Business associate contracts, §90-413.5(a).
Disclosure of information to other covered entities,
§90-413.5(c).
Disclosure of or access to information by
associates, §90-413.5(b).
Good faith reliance on information provided
through exchange, §90-413.5(d).
**Participation agreements with covered
entities,** §90-413.4(a).
Penalties for violations, §90-413.8.
Purpose of act, §90-413.2.
Requirements generally, §90-413.4(a).
Rights not impaired by statutes, §90-413.7(a).
Title of act, §90-413.1.
Unlawful disclosures, penalties, §90-413.8.
Written participation agreement.
Participating covered entities, §90-413.5(a).

HEALTH INSURANCE.
Actions for negligent decisions.
Health care liability, §§90-21.50 to 90-21.56.
See HEALTH CARE LIABILITY.
Adopted children.
Definitions, §58-51-125(a).
Policies to cover, §§58-51-30(a) to (f), 58-51-125(a)
to (c).
Preexisting conditions, §58-51-125(c).
Advance practice registered nurse.
Payment or reimbursement, §58-50-30(d).
Right to choose services, §58-50-30(a1) to (a3), (g),
(h).
**Applicability of acts of general assembly to
health benefit plans.**
Health benefit plan defined, §58-3-167(a).
Law enacted by general assembly, definition
applicable, §58-3-167(b).
Insurer defined, §58-3-167(a).
Renewal of health benefit plan.
Date of renewal when law enacted by general
assembly applies to health benefit plans,
§58-3-167(c).
Authorized, §58-7-15.
Blanket insurance.
Benefits.
To whom payable, §58-51-75(b).
Defined, §58-51-75(a).
Legal liability of policyholders not affected,
§58-51-75(c).
Policies, §58-51-75(a).
Approval of forms, §58-51-85.
Breast cancer.
Mammograms.
Coverage, §58-51-57.

HEALTH INSURANCE —Cont'd
Cancer treatment.
Cervical cancer screening.
  Coverage, §58-51-57.
Colorectal cancer examinations, laboratory tests
  and screening.
  Coverage required of all health benefit plans,
    §58-3-179(a).
  Limitations applicable to services, §58-3-179(b).
  Small employer group health plans,
    §58-50-155(a).
Coverage of certain prescribed drugs.
  Applicability of provisions, §58-51-59(c).
  Generally, §58-51-59(a), (b).
Mammograms.
  Coverage, §58-51-57.
Ovarian cancer.
  Surveillance tests for women at risk, coverage,
    §§58-3-270, 58-50-155(a).
Cervical cancer.
Screening for early detection.
  Coverage requirements, §58-51-57(a), (e).
  Defined, §58-51-57(a1).
Chemical dependency treatment coverage.
Chemical dependency defined, §58-51-50(a).
Durational limits, dollar limits, deductibles,
  coinsurance.
  Applicability, §58-51-50(b).
Group policies or contracts.
  Benefit payments for providers, §58-51-50(d).
  Coverage not required, §58-51-55(c).
  Discrimination against chemically dependent
    individuals, §58-51-55(b).
    Applicability, §58-51-55(d).
    Definitions, §58-51-55(a).
Minimum benefits, §58-51-50(c).
Paul Wellstone and Pete Domenici mental
  health parity and addiction equity act.
  Compliance required of certain plans,
    §58-51-50(f), (g).
Rejection of coverage.
  Inapplicability of provisions, §58-51-50(e).
Hospital and medical service plans, §58-65-75.
Insurers required to offer, §58-51-50(b).
Childbirth.
Maternity coverage, §58-3-170.
Children.
Dependent children.
  Continuation of coverage after terminating date.
    Mentally retarded or physically handicapped
      children, §58-51-25(a).
    Student on medically necessary leave of
      absence from postsecondary educational
      institution, §58-51-25(b).
Health choice for children.
  Provider requirements, §§108C-1 to 108C-12.
Health insurance program for children.
  Act of 1998, §§108A-70.18 to 108A-70.29.
    See CHILDREN'S HEALTH INSURANCE
      PROGRAM.
Nondependent child coverage, §58-3-290.
  Coverage issued regardless of health status,
    §58-3-290(b).
  Defined terms, §58-3-290(a).
  Open enrollment, requirements, §58-3-290(b).
  Premiums, adjustment, §58-3-290(d).
  Rules and regulations, authority to promulgate,
    §58-3-290(c).
**Child support, medical support orders and
  agreements,** §50-13.11.

HEALTH INSURANCE —Cont'd
Chiropractors.
Right to choose services, §58-50-30(a1) to (a3), (g),
  (h).
Choice of service providers, §58-50-30(a1) to
  (a3).
Locum tenens contracts, §58-3-231.
Pediatrician for minors, §58-3-240.
Provider directories, §58-3-245.
Specialist selected as primary care provider,
  §58-3-235.
Uniform provider credentialing, §58-3-230.
Claims.
Notice.
  Claim denial, §58-3-172(a).
    Health benefit plans defined, §58-3-172(b).
  Required policy provisions, §58-51-15(a).
Payment.
  Prompt claim payments under health benefit
    plans, §58-3-225.
  Required policy provisions, §58-51-15(a).
Prompt payments under health benefit plans,
  §58-3-225.
Submission and reimbursement policies of
  insurers.
  Disclosure to contracted providers, §58-3-227(d).
    Availability of information.
      Notifying providers, §58-3-227(e).
    Changes to information.
      Advance notification, §58-3-227(f).
    Definitions, §58-3-227(a).
    Inapplicability of provisions, §58-3-227(i).
    Purpose of provisions, §58-3-227(b).
    Reference information.
      Instructions provided, §58-3-227(g).
Uniform claim forms, §58-3-171(a).
  Health benefit plans defined, §58-3-171(c).
  Workers' compensation insurance policies as
    health benefit plans, §58-3-171(b).
Clinical social workers.
Defined, §58-50-30(c).
Right to choose services, §58-50-30(a1) to (a3), (g),
  (h).
Clinical trials, coverage, §58-3-255(b).
Costs not required to be covered, §58-3-255(d).
Covered clinical trials defined, §58-3-255(a).
Definitions, §58-3-255(a).
Medical necessary costs covered, §58-3-255(c).
**Closed formularies or restricted access to
  prescription drugs,** §58-3-221.
**Colorectal cancer examinations, laboratory
  tests and screening.**
Coverage required of every health benefit plan,
  §58-3-179(a).
Limitations applicable to services, §58-3-179(b).
Small employer group health plans, §58-50-155(a).
Commissioner.
Hearings.
  Withdrawal of approval of forms, §58-51-95(e).
Premiums.
  Approval of rates, §58-51-95(f).
    Revised rates, §58-51-95(f).
  Loss ratio standards, §58-51-95(h).
**Confidentiality of consumer and customer
  information.**
Generally, §§58-39-1 to 58-39-165.
  See INSURANCE CONSUMER AND
    CUSTOMER INFORMATION PRIVACY.
Continuation of coverage.
Dependent children.
  Mentally retarded or physically handicapped
    child, §58-51-25(a).

HEALTH INSURANCE —Cont'd
Continuation of coverage —Cont'd
Dependent children —Cont'd
Student on medically necessary leave of absence
from postsecondary educational institution,
§58-51-25(b).
Group insurance, §§58-53-1 to 58-53-41. See
within this heading, "Group insurance."
**Continuing care retirement community
residents,** §58-3-200(f).
**Contraceptive drugs or devices and outpatient
contraceptive services.**
Coverage by insurer providing health benefit plan,
§58-3-178(a), (b).
Definitions, §58-3-178(c).
Prohibited acts, §58-3-178(d).
Religious employer requesting exclusion of
coverage, §58-3-178(e).
**Contracts between health benefit plans and
health care providers,** §§58-50-270 to
58-50-290.
Amendments.
Defined, §58-50-270.
Mutual consent.
Negotiating terms providing for,
§58-50-280(d).
Proposed amendments.
Labeling requirements, §58-50-280(a).
Objections by provider, time, §58-50-280(b).
Sent to notice contact, §58-50-280(a).
Termination of contract on objection by
provider.
Right of plan or provider, time,
§58-50-280(c).
Definitions, §58-50-270.
Dental services, §58-50-290.
No limitation on fees for noncovered services,
§58-50-290(a), (b).
Notice contact provisions.
Business days, calculation, §58-50-275(b).
Commercial courier service, §58-50-275(b).
Designation of notice contact.
Required, §58-50-275(a).
Electronic medium, §58-50-275(b).
Mail notice, §58-50-275(b).
Methods for sending notices, §58-50-275(b).
Person to whom all correspondence provided,
§58-50-275(a).
Required of all contracts, §58-50-275(a).
Policies and procedures of plan.
Conflicting with or overriding contract.
Prohibition, §58-50-285(b).
Copy given provider prior to execution,
§58-50-285(a).
Termination of contract.
Objection to proposed amendment by provider.
Right of plan or provider, time, §58-50-280(c).
Conversion privileges.
Generally. See within this heading, "Group
insurance."
Credentialing providers.
Effective date of practitioner's participation.
Joining practice under contract with insurer,
§58-3-230(a).
Health benefit plan and insurer defined,
§58-3-230(c).
Process requirements, §58-3-230(a).
Temporary credential, §58-3-230(a).
Time limit on processing applications,
§58-3-230(a).

HEALTH INSURANCE —Cont'd
Credentialing providers —Cont'd
Uniform provider credentialing application form.
Commissioner to adopt by rule, §58-3-230(b).
Credit insurance.
Defined, §58-51-100.
Generally, §§58-57-1 to 58-57-115.
See CREDIT INSURANCE.
Definitions.
Blanket accident and health insurance,
§58-51-75(a).
Credit accident and health insurance, §58-51-100.
Franchise accident and health insurance,
§58-51-90.
Group accident and health insurance,
§58-51-80(a).
Hospitalization insurance, §58-51-105.
Industrial sick benefit insurance, §58-51-65.
Joint action to insure elderly, §58-52-1.
Pharmacy of choice, §58-51-37(b).
Prompt claim payments under health benefit
plans, §58-3-225(a).
Denial of claim, notice, §58-3-172.
**Dental procedures performed in hospital or
ambulatory surgical facility.**
Children under age nine, persons with serious
mental and physical condition and persons
with significant behavior problems.
Definitions, §58-3-122(b).
Health benefit plans to provide coverage for
payment of anesthesia and facility charges,
§58-3-122(a).
Dentists.
Contracts between health benefit plans and health
care providers.
Dental services, §58-50-290.
No limitation on fees for noncovered services,
§58-50-290(a), (b).
Right to choose services, §58-50-30(a1) to (a3), (g),
(h).
Determinations as to coverage, §58-3-200(c).
Diabetes.
Coverage for certain treatment, §58-51-61(a).
Definition of "physician," §58-51-61(b).
Directories of providers, §58-3-245.
Direct payment to government agencies,
§58-3-175.
Disability income insurance, policy standards,
§58-51-130.
Applicability of provisions, §58-51-130(b).
Definitions, §58-51-130(a).
Disclosure standards, §58-51-130(c).
Exceptions, §58-51-130(e).
Other income sources, §58-51-130(h).
Other provisions applicable, §58-51-130(g).
Preexisting conditions, when denial of claim
prohibited, §58-51-130(d).
Required provisions, §58-51-130(f).
Disasters.
Prescription drugs.
Extra prescriptions during state of emergency
or disaster, §58-3-228.
**Disclosure requirements for health benefit
plans,** §58-3-191(b).
Disclosures to contracted providers.
Fee schedules, claim and reimbursement policies
of insurers, §58-3-227(c).
Availability of information.
Notifying providers, §58-3-227(e).
Changes to information.
Advance notification, §58-3-227(f).

HEALTH INSURANCE —Cont'd
Disclosures to contracted providers —Cont'd
Fee schedules, claim and reimbursement policies
　of insurers —Cont'd
　Definitions, §58-3-227(a).
　During contract negotiations, §58-3-227(h).
　Inapplicability of provisions, §58-3-227(i).
　Purpose of provisions, §58-3-227(b).
　Reference information.
　　Instructions provided, §58-3-227(g).
Discrimination.
　Children of insured, §58-51-120(a).
　Mentally ill and chemically dependent, §58-51-55.
Drive-thru deliveries, §58-3-169.
Electronic or on-line system for up-to-date
　network information.
　Plan to provide, §58-3-245(a).
Emergency care.
　Coverage required, §58-3-190.
Emergency, state of.
　Prescription drugs.
　　Extra prescriptions during state of emergency
　　　or disaster, §58-3-228.
Employer distinguishing between employees
　based on use or nonuse of lawful products,
　§95-28.2(d).
Evidence of coverage.
　Notice, expenses may exceed covered amount,
　　§58-3-250(b).
　Payment obligations, explanation by insurer,
　　§58-3-250(a).
Exemptions from provisions, §58-50-65.
External review, §§58-50-75 to 58-50-95.
　Applicability of part, §58-50-75(b).
　Approval of independent review organization.
　　Accreditation program, §58-50-85(c).
　　Application for approving, §58-50-85(a), (b).
　　Commission to approve, §58-50-85(a).
　　Duration of approval, §58-50-85(d).
　　Termination, §58-50-85(e).
　Assigned organization.
　　Approval of independent review organization,
　　　§58-50-85.
　　Expedited review, request.
　　　Decision of organization, time for,
　　　　§58-50-82(e).
　　　Notice of decision or written conformation,
　　　　§58-50-82(f).
　　　Review of documents, considerations in
　　　　reaching decision, §58-50-82(c), (d).
　　Hold harmless provision, §58-50-89.
　　Minimum qualifications for independent
　　　organization, §58-50-87.
　　Notice of decision, time period, included in,
　　　§58-50-80(j), (k).
　　Records review organization, §58-50-90(a), (d),
　　　(e).
　　Report by review organization, §58-50-90(b), (c).
　　Review of information and documents,
　　　considerations in reaching decision,
　　　§58-50-80(i).
　　Selection of review organization, §58-50-94.
　Binding nature of decision.
　　Covered person, binding on, §58-50-84(b).
　　Insurer, binding on, §58-50-84(a).
　Clinical peer reviewers assigned by organization.
　　Hold harmless provision, §58-50-89.
　　Minimum qualifications, §58-50-87(b).
　Conflicts of interest.
　　Independent review organization, §58-50-87(d),
　　　(e).

HEALTH INSURANCE —Cont'd
External review —Cont'd
　Definitions, §58-50-75(c).
　Description of procedures.
　　Insurer to provide, §58-50-93(a).
　　Release of medical records.
　　　Statement informing covered person,
　　　　§58-50-93(c).
　　Statement of right to file request, §58-50-93(b).
　Exhaustion of internal appeal and grievance
　　procedure.
　　Noncertification involving retrospective review
　　　determination, §58-50-79(c).
　　Request for external review may be made before
　　　exhaustion, §58-50-79(d).
　　Required, §58-50-79(a).
　　When person considered to exhaust internal
　　　procedure, §58-50-79(b).
　Expedited review, request, §58-50-77(c).
　　Assigned organization.
　　　Decision of organization, time for,
　　　　§58-50-82(e).
　　　Notice of decision or written conformation,
　　　　§58-50-82(f).
　　　Review of documents, considerations in
　　　　reaching decision, §58-50-82(c), (d).
　　Commission's duties after reviewing request,
　　　time period, §58-50-82(b).
　　Decisions subject to, §58-50-82(a).
　　Retrospective noncertification, inapplicability,
　　　§58-50-82(g).
　　Reversal of noncertification appeal or grievance
　　　review, §58-50-82(f).
　Fees charged by review organization.
　　Reimbursement by insurer, §58-50-92.
　Funding, §58-50-92.
　Hold harmless provision.
　　Commissioner, medical professionals, and
　　　review organizations, §58-50-89.
　Immunity of commissioner, medical professionals,
　　and review organizations, §58-50-89.
　Independent review organization.
　　Approval, §58-50-85.
　　Hold harmless provision, §58-50-89.
　　Minimum qualifications for independent
　　　organization, §58-50-87.
　　Records review organization, §58-50-90(a), (d),
　　　(e).
　　Report by review organization, §58-50-90(b), (c).
　　Selection, §58-50-94.
　Medical professionals.
　　Hold harmless provision, §58-50-89.
　Minimum qualifications for independent
　　organization, §58-50-87(a).
　　Clinical peer reviewers assigned by
　　　organization, §58-50-87(b).
　　Conflicts of interest, §58-50-87(d), (e).
　　Health benefit plan owning or controlling,
　　　prohibition, §58-50-87(c).
　Notice of right, §58-50-77(a).
　　Appeal decision, §58-50-77(c).
　　Copy of procedure included, §58-50-77(e).
　　Final second level grievance review,
　　　§58-50-77(d).
　　Noncertified decision, §58-50-77(b).
　Purposes of part, §58-50-75(a).
　Records of requests, §58-50-90(a), (d), (e).
　Reimbursement by insurer.
　　Fees charged by review organization, §58-50-92.
　Release of medical records.
　　Disclosure by insurer, §58-50-93(c).

HEALTH INSURANCE —Cont'd
External review —Cont'd
Report by commissioner, §58-50-95.
Report by review organization, §58-50-90(b), (c).
Request for review.
  Assigned review committee.
    Information to consider, §58-50-80(i).
  Commission's duties on receiving request, time
    period, §58-50-80(b).
  Making before exhaustion of internal
    procedures, §58-50-79(d).
  Not complete request, additional information to
    be furnished, §58-50-80(c) to (f).
  Notice that request not accepted, §58-50-80(d).
  Reconsideration.
    Additional information supplied commission,
      §58-50-80(g), (h).
  Records of requests, §58-50-90(a), (d), (e).
  Statement of right to file request.
    Included in insurer's disclosure of procedures,
      §58-50-93(b).
  Subsequent request prohibited, §58-50-84(c).
  Time for filing after receipt of notice,
    §58-50-80(a).
Reversal of noncertification appeal or grievance
  review.
  Assigned review committee.
    Notice of decision, §58-50-80(j), (k).
  Expedited review, request, §58-50-82(f).
  Insurer's duty on receipt of notice of
    organization decision, §58-50-80(l).
  Notice, presumption when received,
    §58-50-80(m).
Selection of independent review organization.
  Modifying or withdrawing proposals,
    §58-50-94(c).
  Request for proposals by commissioner,
    §58-50-94(a).
  Review of proposals after public opening,
    selection, §58-50-94(b).
Subsequent request for review.
  Covered person may not file, §58-50-84(c).
Fee based pastoral counselor.
Defined, §58-50-30(c1).
Right to choose services, §58-50-30(a1) to (a3), (g),
  (h).
Fee schedules of insurers.
Disclosure to contracted providers, §58-3-227(c).
  Availability of information.
    Notifying providers, §58-3-227(e).
  Changes to information.
    Advance notification, §58-3-227(f).
  Definitions, §58-3-227(a).
  During contract negotiations, §58-3-227(h).
  Inapplicability of provisions, §58-3-227(i).
  Purpose of provisions, §58-3-227(b).
  Reference information.
    Instructions provided, §58-3-227(g).
**Financial incentives to delay, deny or reduce
  coverage.**
Plan prohibited from offering provider, §58-3-265.
Forms.
Approval by commissioner, §58-51-95(a) to (f).
  Group or blanket accident and health insurance,
    §58-51-85.
Policies, §58-51-5(a).
  Approval of forms by commissioner, §58-51-1.
  Other states, §58-51-5(b).
Franchise accident and health insurance.
Defined, §58-51-90.

HEALTH INSURANCE —Cont'd
Fraternal benefit societies.
Exemptions from provisions, §58-50-65(c).
Genetic information in health insurance.
Definitions, §58-3-215(a).
Genetic information nondiscrimination act of
  2008.
  Compliance required, §58-3-215(d).
Measurements and tests not considered genetic
  tests, §58-3-215(b).
Prohibited acts by insurers, §58-3-215(c).
**Genetic information nondiscrimination act of
  2008.**
Compliance required, §58-3-215(d).
Government agencies, direct payments to.
Generally, §58-3-175(b).
Health benefit plan defined, §58-3-175(a).
Inapplicability of provisions, §58-3-175(c).
When direct payment not required, §58-3-175(d).
Grace period, §58-51-15(a).
Grievance procedures for insurers.
Availability of process, §58-50-62(b).
Discrimination based on actions taken by
  provider.
  Prohibited, §58-50-62(j).
External review of decision, §§58-50-75 to
  58-50-95.
First-level grievance review, §58-50-62(e).
Generally, §58-50-62(c).
Informal consideration of grievances,
  §58-50-62(b1).
Propose of provisions, §58-50-62(a).
Records maintenance, §58-50-62(d).
Second-level grievance review, §58-50-62(f) to (i).
Violations of provisions.
  Effect on insurer, §58-50-62(k).
Group insurance.
Alternative plans, insurer's option to offer,
  §58-53-105.
Basic coverage plans, §58-53-105.
Eligible persons, §58-53-110(c).
Notice, §58-53-110(e).
Provision of group coverage in lieu of issuance
  of individual policy, §58-53-110(d).
Retirement plan offering continuation of
  coverage.
  Applicability of conversion rights,
    §58-53-110(a).
Benefits.
  To whom payable, §58-51-80(e), (f).
  Children of insured, §58-51-120(d).
Chemical dependency treatment, §§58-51-50,
  58-51-55.
  Paul Wellstone and Pete Domenici mental
    health parity and addiction equity act
    compliance, §58-51-50(f), (g).
Continuation of coverage.
  Benefits not included, §58-53-20.
  Dates for termination of continuation privileges,
    §58-53-35(a).
  Exceptions, §58-53-35(b).
  Election by assistance eligible individuals,
    §58-53-41(b), (d).
    Assistance eligible individual defined,
      §58-53-41(a).
    Commencement of elected coverage,
      §58-53-41(c).
    Definitions, §58-53-41(a).
  Notice.
    Form of notice to employee, §58-53-25.

HEALTH INSURANCE —Cont'd
Group insurance —Cont'd
Continuation of coverage —Cont'd
Notice —Cont'd
Inclusion in individual certifications of coverage, §58-53-40.
Premiums.
Payments, §58-53-30.
Requirements for eligibility, §58-53-25.
Self-insurance.
Inapplicability of provisions, §58-53-115.
Termination of continuation privileges.
Dates of termination, §58-53-35.
Termination of employment or membership.
Group hospital, surgical and major medical coverage continued, §58-53-5.
Conversion privileges.
Alternative plans, §58-53-100.
Applicability of provisions, §58-53-115.
Basic coverage plans, §58-53-90(a).
Alternative plans, §58-53-100.
Maximum amounts, §58-53-90(b).
Benefits.
Excess benefits, §58-53-80.
Coverage.
Alternative plans, §58-53-100.
Basic coverage plans, §58-53-90(a).
Individual policy, §58-53-65.
Major medical plans, §58-53-95.
Preexisting conditions covered under group policy, §58-53-85.
Definitions, §58-53-1.
Delivery outside state, §58-53-110(f).
Excess benefits, §58-53-80.
Exclusions from conversion privilege, §58-53-70.
Extent of coverage, §58-53-65.
Grounds for excluding persons from coverage, §58-53-70.
Grounds for not converting policy, §58-53-50.
Information requested from policyholders, §58-53-75.
Limitation on exercising privilege to convert, §58-53-55.
Major medical plans, §58-53-95.
Alternative plans, §58-53-100.
Maximum amounts of basic coverage plans, §58-53-90(b).
Notice of by insurance fiduciary, §58-50-40(g).
Option of insurer to offer alternative plans in addition to those required by part, §58-53-105.
Permissible provisions in individual policy.
Information provisions, §58-53-75.
Premium for individual policy.
Authorized increase in premiums, §58-53-60(b).
Determination, §58-53-60(a).
Rates and adjustments to be filed with commissioner of insurance, §58-53-60(c).
Rate existing conditions covered by group policy to be covered by converted policy, §58-53-85.
Restrictions, §58-53-50.
Right to obtain individual policy.
Termination of group coverage, §58-53-45.
Self-insurance of employer.
Inapplicability of provisions, §58-53-115.
Termination of group coverage.
Right to obtain individual policy, §58-53-45.
Time limitation, §58-53-55.

HEALTH INSURANCE —Cont'd
Group insurance —Cont'd
Definitions, §58-53-1.
"Agents,"§58-51-80(d).
Continuation of conversion privileges, §58-53-1.
"Employees,"§58-51-80(c).
Generally, §58-51-80(a).
Discrimination.
Mentally ill and chemically dependent.
Applicability, §58-51-55(d).
Coverage, §58-51-55(b1), (c).
Definitions, §58-51-55(a).
Prohibited acts, §58-51-55(b), (c).
Sex changes.
Coverage of treatment or studies not required, §58-51-55(e).
Eligibility, §58-53-10.
Children of insured, §58-51-120(b).
Exceptions to eligibility, §58-53-15.
Exceptions to provisions, §58-51-80(h).
Excluded benefits, §58-53-20.
Insurance fiduciary.
Causing cancellation or nonrenewal by willfully failing to pay premiums, §58-50-40(b).
Cessation of individual contributions, inapplicability, §58-50-40(j).
Conversion policies.
Notice of, §58-50-40(g).
Defined, §58-50-40(a).
Exhibiting books and papers to commissioner, §58-50-40(f).
Felony for conviction under provisions, §58-50-40(c).
Restitution, §58-50-40(e).
Insolvency of fiduciary, §58-50-40(h).
Notice of obligations by insurer, §58-50-45(a).
Form, §58-50-45(b).
Portability and accountability.
Notice of, §58-50-40(g).
Restitution.
Felony for conviction under provisions, §58-50-40(e).
Willfully failing to deliver notice of intention to stop payment of premiums, §58-50-40(b), (h).
Mental illness benefits.
Definitions, §58-3-220(h).
Durational limits, §58-3-220(c).
Minimum benefits, §58-3-220(b).
Exceeding authorized, §58-3-220(d).
Paul Wellstone and Pete Domenici mental health parity and addiction equity act of 2008.
Compliance required, §58-3-220(i).
Applicable to plans covering large employers, §58-3-220(j).
Required, §58-3-220(a).
Sex changes or modifications.
Exceptions as to, §58-3-220(e).
Utilization review criteria.
Application authorized, §58-3-220(g).
Weighted average, §58-3-220(f).
Paul Wellstone and Pete Domenici mental health parity and addiction equity act of 2008.
Compliance required by plans providing medical, surgical and mental health benefits, §58-3-220(i).
Applicable to plans covering large employers, §58-3-220(j).
Policies, §58-51-80(a), (b).
Approval of forms, §58-51-85.

HEALTH INSURANCE —Cont'd
Group insurance —Cont'd
Policies —Cont'd
Renewal, §58-51-110(a).
Replacement, §58-51-110(b).
Portability and accountability.
Notice of by insurance fiduciary, §58-50-40(g).
Premiums.
Adjustment of rate, §58-51-80.
Conversion privileges.
Authorized increase in premiums, §58-53-60(b).
Determination of premium for individual policy, §58-53-60(a).
Rates and adjustments to be filed with commissioner of insurance, §58-53-60(c).
Payment of premiums.
Continuation privileges, §58-53-30.
Public schools.
Coverage of students, §58-51-81(a), (b).
Renewal of insurance, §58-51-110(a).
Replacement of contracts, §58-51-110(b).
Retirement plans.
Choosing conversion rights in lieu of continuation upon retirement, §58-53-110(a).
Eligibility of spouses and children for retirement benefits, §58-53-110(c).
Provision of group coverage in lieu of issuance of individual policy, §58-53-110(d).
Reduction or termination of coverage when Medicare eligible, §58-53-110(b).
Termination.
Acts of insurance fiduciary causing, §58-50-40(b) to (h).
Notice by insurer, §58-50-40(i).
Of continuation, §58-53-35(a).
Exceptions, §58-53-35(b).
Gynecologist, direct access to, §58-51-38(a).
Information on to be provided, §58-51-38(b).
Handicapped children.
Insurers to afford coverage to, §58-51-35(a).
Applicability of provisions, §58-51-35(c).
Revocation of license for noncompliance, §58-51-35(b).
Health benefit plan provisions generally, §§58-3-168 to 58-3-178, 58-3-190 to 58-3-265.
Health insurance portability and accountability, §§58-68-25 to 58-68-75.
See HEALTH INSURANCE PORTABILITY AND ACCOUNTABILITY.
Health insurance risk pool.
Generally, §§58-50-175 to 58-50-255.
See HEALTH INSURANCE RISK POOL.
Notice relating to.
Insurers to provide applicants, §58-3-276.
Health insurance risk pool fund.
Distribution of part of premium tax proceeds, §105-228.5B.
Health maintenance organizations, §§58-67-1 to 58-67-185.
See HEALTH MAINTENANCE ORGANIZATIONS.
Hearing aids.
Deductibles, coinsurance and other limitations, §58-3-285(b).
Medical necessity determination, utilization review, §58-3-285(c).
Required coverage, §58-3-285(a).
High-risk populations.
Nondiscrimination against, §58-3-200(e).

HEALTH INSURANCE —Cont'd
Hospitalization insurance.
Defined, §58-51-105.
Hospital, medical and dental service corporations, §§58-65-1 to 58-66-40.
See HOSPITAL, MEDICAL AND DENTAL SERVICE CORPORATIONS.
Hospital, surgical and major medical coverage.
Continued coverage.
Date of termination, §58-53-35.
Eligibility, §58-53-10.
Termination of employment or membership, group coverage, §58-53-5.
Eligibility requirements, §58-53-25.
Form of notice to employee, §58-53-25.
Notice included in individual certificates, §58-53-40.
Premium payments, §58-53-30.
Self-insurance, inapplicability, §58-53-115.
Incentives to delay, deny or reduce coverage.
Plan prohibited from offering provider, §58-3-265.
Incontestability, §58-51-15(a).
Industrial sick benefit insurance.
Defined, §58-51-65.
Policy provisions, §58-51-70.
Insurance identification card.
Design, §58-3-247(b).
Generally, §58-3-247(a).
Insurers to afford coverage to.
Applicability of provisions, §58-51-35(c).
Intoxicants and narcotics, §58-51-16(a) to (c).
Job development investment grant program.
Health insurance requirements, §143B-437.53(c).
Joint action to insure elderly, §§58-52-1 to 58-52-25.
Associations.
Articles of association, §58-52-20.
Authorized, §58-52-5.
Defined, §58-52-1.
Mutual insurers may participate, §58-52-20.
Powers, §58-52-20.
Statements.
Annual statements, §58-52-20.
Authorized, §58-52-5.
Regional plans, §58-52-10.
Definitions, §58-52-1.
Licenses.
No additional licensing required, §58-52-25.
Policies, §58-52-5.
Approval of forms by commissioner, §58-52-15.
Premiums.
Approval of rates by commissioner, §58-52-15.
Regional plans.
Authorized, §58-52-10.
Jurisdiction over providers of health care benefits.
Determination of generally, §§58-49-1 to 58-49-25.
See HEALTH CARE BENEFITS PROVIDERS.
Law enforcement officers.
Separate insurance benefits plan for state and local officers, §143-166.60(a) to (h).
Life and health insurance guaranty association, §§58-62-2 to 58-62-95.
See LIFE AND HEALTH INSURANCE GUARANTY ASSOCIATION.
Local government risk pools, §58-23-5(c).
Locum tenens contracts, §58-3-231.
Accepting and payment for claims, §58-3-231(b).
Defined terms, §58-3-231(a).
Medical groups or hospitals, §58-3-231(c).

HEALTH INSURANCE —Cont'd
Locum tenens contracts —Cont'd
Placement and administrative services,
  §58-3-231(e).
Statements of supervision waived, §58-3-231(d).
Long-term care insurance, §§58-55-1 to 58-55-50.
See LONG-TERM CARE INSURANCE.
Long-term care partnerships, §§58-55-55 to
  58-55-80.
Lymphedema.
Coverage for diagnosis and treatment.
  Deductibles, coinsurance, other limitations.
    Applicability, §58-3-280(b).
  Gradient compression garments, §58-3-280(c).
  Required coverage, §58-3-280(a).
Mammograms.
Low-dose screening mammography.
  Coverage requirement, §58-51-57(a), (c).
  Deductibles, coinsurance and other limitations,
    applicability, §58-51-57(a).
  Defined, §58-51-57(b).
  Reimbursement, §58-51-57(d).
Marriage and family therapists.
Defined, §58-50-30(c4).
Right to choose services, §58-50-30(a1) to (a3).
Mastectomy.
Coverage for reconstructive breast surgery
    resulting from, §58-51-62(a).
  Definitions, §58-51-62(b).
  Prohibited acts, §58-51-62(c).
  Written notice of available coverage,
    §58-51-62(d).
Postmastectomy inpatient care coverage,
  §58-3-168.
Maternity coverage requirement, §58-3-170(a).
Health benefit plans defined, §58-3-170(b).
Minimum hospital stay following birth, §58-3-169.
  Definitions, §58-3-169(a).
  Effect on mother, §58-3-169(g).
  Exceptions, §58-3-169(c).
  Generally, §58-3-169(b).
  Postdelivery follow-up care, §58-3-169(d).
  Prohibited acts, §58-3-169(e), (f).
  Reimbursements, level and type, §58-3-169(h).
  Timely care, §58-3-169(e).
Medicaid.
Additional coverage under health benefit plan.
  Eligible individuals.
    Definitions, §108A-55.4(a).
    Information to be provided to department by
      insurers, §108A-55.4(b) to (b2).
    Non-liability of insurer for compliance with
      department, §108A-55.4(c).
      Contractual obligation as condition,
        §108A-55.4(d).
    Right of recovery of department,
      §108A-55.4(b3) to (b5).
  Coordination, §58-51-115(b).
  Definitions, §58-51-115(a).
Employer-provided family health benefit plans.
  Required coverage of children, §108A-69.
Medical necessity.
Requirements for health benefit plans that limit
    coverage to medically necessary services and
    supplies, §58-3-200(b).
**Medical support orders and agreements for
  children,** §50-13.11.
Medicare supplement insurance, §§58-54-1 to
  58-54-50.
See MEDICARE SUPPLEMENT INSURANCE.

HEALTH INSURANCE —Cont'd
Mental health area authorities.
Life or health insurance for officers and
  employees, §122C-156(b), (c).
Mental illness benefits coverage.
Group health benefit plans, §58-3-220.
Mentally retarded children.
Continuation of coverage, §58-51-25(a).
Insurers to afford coverage to, §58-51-35(a).
  Revocation of license for noncompliance,
    §58-51-35(b).
Multiple employer welfare arrangements.
Regulation generally, §§58-49-30 to 58-49-65.
  See HEALTH CARE BENEFITS PROVIDERS.
Mutual insurance companies.
Surplus, §58-7-75.
Narcotics and intoxicants, §58-51-16(a) to (c).
Negligent decisions by plan providers.
Health care liability, §§90-21.50 to 90-21.56.
  See HEALTH CARE LIABILITY.
Newborns.
Newborn hearing screening.
  Coverage required, §58-3-260(b).
    Health benefit plan and insurer defined,
      §58-3-260(a).
Policies to cover, §58-51-30(a) to (f).
**Non-stock accident and health insurance
  companies.**
Capital and/or surplus.
  Amount required, §58-7-75.
North Carolina health insurance risk pool.
Generally, §§58-50-175 to 58-50-255.
  See HEALTH INSURANCE RISK POOL.
Notice relating to.
  Insurers to provide applicants, §58-3-276.
Notice.
Acknowledgment by insurer of receipt of notice
    under policy.
  No waiver of rights of insurer, §58-50-1.
Claims.
  Denied, §58-3-172.
  Required policy provisions as to notice of claims,
    §58-51-15(a).
Nonpayment of premium.
  Notice required before forfeiture, §58-50-35.
Renewability of individual and blanket
    hospitalization and accident and health
    insurance policies, §58-51-20(a).
Right to return policy and have premium
    refunded, §58-51-10.
Utilization review.
  Noncertification, §58-50-61(h).
Nurses' services, §58-50-25(a).
Direct payments to nurse, §58-50-25(b).
Obstetricians, direct access to, §58-51-38(a).
Information to be provided, §58-51-38(b).
Offset or reversal of payment, §58-50-57(a).
Contract with provider not to contain provision
    authorizing, §58-50-57(b).
Optometrists.
Right to choose services, §58-50-30(a1) to (a3), (g),
  (h).
Osteoporosis or low bone mass.
Bone mass measurement for diagnosis and
    evaluation.
  Health benefit plan to provide coverage,
    §58-3-174(a).
  Definitions, §58-3-174(d).
  Frequency of coverage, §58-3-174(b).
  Screening for nonqualified individuals not
    covered, §58-3-174(c).

HEALTH INSURANCE —Cont'd
Ovarian cancer.
Surveillance tests for women at risk for ovarian
cancer.
Coverage requirement, §§58-3-270(a),
58-50-155(a).
Deductibles, coinsurance and other limitations,
§58-3-270(b).
Definitions, §58-3-270(a).
Parent and child.
Employer-provided family health benefit plan.
Parent required to provide coverage for child.
Employer obligations, §108A-69(b).
Definitions, §108A-69(a).
Recoupment of amount spent on medical care.
Health benefit plan coverage required to be
provided for child, §108A-70(a).
Payment obligations for covered services.
Explanation by insurer, §58-3-250(a).
Notice that actual expenses may exceed covered
amount, §58-3-250(b).
Payment to government agencies.
Direct payment, §58-3-175.
Pediatrician.
Direct access for minors, §58-3-240.
Pharmacist.
Payment or reimbursement, §58-50-30(e).
Right to choose services, §58-50-30(a1) to (a3), (g),
(h).
Pharmacy of choice.
Applicability of provisions, §58-51-37(a).
Definitions, §58-51-37(b).
Generally, §58-51-37(c) to (e).
Rebates or marketing incentives.
Offering on equal basis, §58-51-37(f).
Violations of provisions.
Sanctions and effect, §58-51-37(g) to (k).
Physician assistant.
Denial of reimbursement to agency, institution or
physician, §58-50-26.
Payment or reimbursement, §58-50-30(f).
Right to choose services, §58-50-30(a1) to (a3), (g),
(h).
Plan summaries.
Notice, expenses may exceed covered amount,
§58-3-250(b).
Payment obligations, explanation by insurer,
§58-3-250(a).
Podiatrists.
Right to choose services, §58-50-30(a1) to (a3), (g),
(h).
Policies.
Adopted children.
Policies to cover, §§58-51-30(a) to (f),
58-51-125(a) to (c).
Preexisting conditions, §58-51-125(c).
Age limits, §58-50-20.
All policies issued or delivered in state.
Applicability of provisions, §58-51-15(i).
Applications for, §58-50-5(a).
Alteration, §58-50-5(b).
False statements.
Effect, §58-50-5(c).
Blanket accident and health insurance,
§58-51-75(a).
Approval of forms, §58-51-85.
Closure of a block of business, §58-3-275(a) to (d).
Dependent students on medically necessary leave
of absence from postsecondary educational
institution.
Policy coverage to continue as to, §58-51-25(b).

HEALTH INSURANCE —Cont'd
Policies —Cont'd
Disability income insurance.
Standards for policies, §58-51-130.
Exemption of certain policies from provisions,
§58-50-65.
Filing.
Rules and regulations as to, §58-51-15(g).
Forfeiture.
Notice of nonpayment of premium required
before forfeiture, §58-50-35.
Forms, §58-51-5(a).
Approval by commissioner, §58-51-1.
Other states, §58-51-5(b).
Generally.
See INSURANCE POLICIES OR CONTRACTS.
Group accident and health insurance,
§58-51-80(a), (b).
Approval of forms, §58-51-85.
Renewal, §58-51-110(a).
Replacement, §58-51-110(b).
Industrial sick benefit insurance.
Provisions, §58-51-70.
Intoxicants and narcotics, §58-51-16(a) to (c).
Mentally retarded or physically handicapped
children.
Policy coverage to continue as to, §58-51-25(a).
Narcotics and intoxicants, §58-51-16(a) to (c).
Newborn infants.
Policies to cover, §58-51-30(a) to (f).
Nonconforming policies, §58-50-15(b).
Preexisting condition exclusion.
Adopted children, §58-51-125(c).
Clarification, §58-51-15(h).
"Preexisting conditions.."
Meaning of term, §58-51-60.
Provisions.
Generally, §58-51-15(a), (b).
Inapplicable or inconsistent provisions,
§58-51-15(c).
Industrial benefit insurance, §58-51-70.
Order of certain policy provisions, §58-51-15(d).
Other policy provisions.
Effect, §58-50-15(a).
Requirements of other jurisdictions,
§58-51-15(f).
Renewability.
Applicability of provisions, §58-51-20(d).
Notice, §58-51-20(a).
Policies issued during grace period construed to
be continuation of first policy, §58-51-20(c).
Unilateral acts by insurers prohibited,
§58-51-20(b).
Required provisions, §58-51-15(a).
Requirements, §58-51-5(a).
Other states, §58-51-5(b).
Return of policy.
Notice of right to return policy, §58-51-10.
Third-party ownership not precluded,
§58-51-15(e).
Trust or association outside state issued policy
covering persons in state.
Applicability of provisions, §58-51-15(i).
Policies and procedures of health benefit plan.
Conflicts with contracts between plan and health
care providers.
Prohibition, §58-50-285(b).
Copy provided health care provider prior to
execution of contract with plan, §58-50-285(a).
Portability and accountability, §§58-51-17,
58-68-25 to 58-68-75.
See HEALTH INSURANCE PORTABILITY AND
ACCOUNTABILITY.

HEALTH INSURANCE —Cont'd
Preexisting conditions.
Adopted children, §58-51-125(c).
Disability income insurance, §58-51-130(d).
Preferred providers.
Advertising restrictions, §58-50-56(k).
Contract provisions, §58-50-56(d) to (f).
Contracts or arrangements, §58-50-56(b).
Coverage from nonparticipating provider,
    §58-50-56(i).
Definitions, §58-50-56(a).
Disclosures by insurers, §58-50-56(h).
List of participating providers, §58-50-56(j).
Proposals for participation, §58-50-56(c).
Rules, §58-50-56(g).
Premiums.
Approval of rates by commissioner, §§58-51-1,
    58-51-95(f).
Filing of rates.
    Group or blanket accident and health insurance,
        §58-51-85.
Group accident and health insurance.
    Continuation privileges, §58-53-30.
    Conversion privileges, §58-53-60.
Health-status related factors.
    Increase on renewal, prohibition, §58-51-95(g).
Joint action to insure elderly.
    Approval of rates by commissioner, §58-52-15.
Long-term care policies, §58-51-95(h), (i).
Loss ratio standards, §58-51-95(h).
Nonpayment.
    Notice of nonpayment required before forfeiture,
        §58-50-35.
Refund.
    Notice of right to return policy and have
        premium refunded, §58-51-10.
Prescription drug identification cards.
Plan issuing prescription drug cards to issue
    uniform identification cards, §58-3-177(a).
Definitions, §58-3-177(e).
Electronic verification of claim, §58-3-177(d).
Exceptions, §58-3-177(f).
Information contained in card, §58-3-177(a), (b).
Issued annually if change in coverage,
    §58-3-177(c).
Prescription drugs.
Closed formularies or restricted access to
    perspiration drugs or devices.
Definitions, §58-3-221(c).
Medically necessary nonformulary or restricted
    access drug or device prescribed.
    Voiding or refusing to renew contract
        prohibited, §58-3-221(b).
Payment for drugs or devices specifically
    excluded from coverage not required,
    §58-3-221(d).
Requirements of insurers maintaining,
    §58-3-221(a).
Contraceptive drugs or devices.
    Coverage by insurer providing health benefit
        plan, §58-3-178.
Extra prescriptions during state of emergency or
    disaster.
    Authorization of payment to pharmacies,
        §58-3-228(b).
    Construction of provisions, §58-3-228(d) to (g).
    Required coverage, §58-3-228(a).
Waiver of prescription refills.
    Time period for, §58-3-228(c).

HEALTH INSURANCE —Cont'd
Primary care provider, specialist selected.
Insured diagnosed with serious or chronic
    degenerative, disabling or life threatening
    disease, §58-3-235(a).
    Care authorized by specialist, §58-3-235(b).
    Denial of access by insurer, §58-3-235(a).
    Treatment plan approved by insurer, selection
        under, §58-3-235(b).
Professional counselor.
Defined, §58-50-30(c3).
Right to choose services, §58-50-30(a1) to (a3), (g),
    (h).
Professional employer organizations.
Examination of self-funded plans, §58-89A-107.
Fully insured by, §58-89A-105(a), (e).
Licensee offering plan not fully insured by
    authorized insurer, §58-89A-105(d).
Requirements, §58-89A-106.
**Prompt claim payments under health benefit
    plans.**
Claim status report, §58-3-225(g).
Definitions, §58-3-225(a).
Denial of claim.
    Additional information required by insurer,
        §58-3-225(c), (d).
    Notice, §58-3-225(b), (c).
Duties of insurer, §58-3-225(b).
Interest, §58-3-225(e).
Overpayments.
    Recovery by insurer, §58-3-225(h).
Patient's liability not limited or impaired,
    §58-3-225(m).
Records of insurers, §58-3-225(i).
Submission of claims.
    Time for, §58-3-225(f).
Violations by insurers, §58-3-225(j).
    Exceptions, §58-3-225(k).
Proof of loss.
Required policy provisions, §58-51-15(a).
Prostate-specific antigen (PSA) tests.
Coverage, §58-51-58(a), (c).
Defined, §58-51-58(b).
Provider contracts.
Contracts between health benefit plans and health
    care providers, §§58-50-270 to 58-50-290.
Provider credentialing.
Effective date of practitioner's participation.
    Joining practice under contract with insurer,
        §58-3-230(a).
Health benefit plan and insurer defined,
    §58-3-230(c).
Process requirements, §58-3-230(a).
Temporary credential, §58-3-230(a).
Time limit on processing applications,
    §58-3-230(a).
Uniform provider credentialing application form.
    Commissioner to adopt by rule, §58-3-230(b).
Provider directories.
Allied health professionals, listing, §58-3-245(c).
Information included in directory listing,
    §58-3-245(b).
Plan required to provide, §58-3-245(a).
Provider networks.
Services outside, §58-3-200(d).
Psychologists.
Defined, §58-50-30(b).
Right to choose services, §58-50-30(a1) to (a3), (g),
    (h).

HEALTH INSURANCE —Cont'd

Public school employees, §115C-340(a), (b).
State health plan for teachers and state
employees, §§135-48.1 to 135-48.61.
See STATE HEALTH PLAN FOR TEACHERS
AND STATE EMPLOYEES.

Railroad ticket policies.
Exemptions from certain provisions, §58-50-65(d).

Rates.
Exceptions to applicability of rating provisions,
§58-40-15.

Reinsurance.
Life and health insurance reinsurance
agreements, §58-7-31.

Renewal of health benefit plan.
Date of renewal when law enacted by general
assembly applies to health benefit plans,
§58-3-167(c).

Reports.
External review.
Report by commissioner, §58-50-95.
Report by review organization, §58-50-90(b), (c).
Health benefit plan reporting requirements,
§58-3-191(a).
Access to reports, §58-3-191(b1).

Risk based capital requirements.
Insurance companies, §§58-12-2 to 58-12-70.
See INSURANCE COMPANIES.

Risk pool, §§58-50-175 to 58-50-255.
See HEALTH INSURANCE RISK POOL.

School employees, §115C-340(a), (b).

Secured transactions.
Health-care-insurance receivables.
Third party assignments.
Claims and defenses against assignee, taking
subject to.
Inapplicability of provisions, §25-9-404(e).
Modification of assigned contract,
§25-9-405(d).
Restrictions on assignments, §§25-9-406(i),
25-9-408.

Senior citizens.
Seniors' health insurance information program,
§58-2-31.

Sickle cell trait or hemoglobin C trait.
Policies to be issued to person possessing,
§58-51-45.

Site development grants.
Health insurance for employees.
Required for project eligibility, §143B-437.02(e).

Specialist care referral.
In-plan specialists.
Definitions, §58-3-223(b).
Duties of insurer providing health benefit plan,
§58-3-223(a).

Specialist selected as primary care provider.
Insured diagnosed with serious or chronic
degenerative, disabling or life threatening
disease, §58-3-235(a).
Care authorized by specialist, §58-3-235(b).
Denial of access by insurer, §58-3-235(a).
Treatment plan approved by insurer, selection
under, §58-3-235(b).

**Stock accident and health insurance
companies.**
Capital and/or surplus.
Amount required, §58-7-75.

**Students attending postsecondary educational
institutions.**
Dependent children.
Medically necessary leave of absence.
Continuation of coverage, §58-51-25(b).

HEALTH INSURANCE —Cont'd

Substance abuse professional.
Defined, §58-50-30(c2).
Right to choose services, §58-50-30(a1) to (a3), (g),
(h).

Supplemental contract.
Exemptions from provisions, §58-50-65(b).

Tax-supported institutions.
Coverage for active medical treatment in.
Insurers to afford, §58-51-40(a), (b).
Applicability of provisions, §58-51-40(c).

Teachers and state employees.
State health plan for teachers and state
employees, §§135-48.1 to 135-48.61.
See STATE HEALTH PLAN FOR TEACHERS
AND STATE EMPLOYEES.

**Telephone system for up-to-date network
information.**
Plan to provide, §58-3-245(a).

Third-party administrators, §§58-56-2 to
58-56-66.
See THIRD-PARTY ADMINISTRATORS.

Transplants.
Request for determination of coverage.
Required response time, §58-3-102(a), (b).

Treatment discussions.
Limiting prohibited, §58-3-176(a).
Construction of provisions, §58-3-176(b).
Definitions, §58-3-176(c).

**Uniform prescription drug identification
cards,** §58-3-177.

Uniform provider credentialing, §58-3-230.

Utilization review.
Definitions, §58-50-61(a).
Disclosures requirements, §58-50-61(m).
External review, §§58-50-75 to 58-50-95.
Insurer oversight, §58-50-61(b).
Insurer responsibility, §58-50-61(e).
Noncertification.
Appeals, §58-50-61(j) to (l).
Notice, §58-50-61(h).
Program.
Operations, §58-50-61(d).
Scope and content, §58-50-61(c).
Prospective and concurrent reviews, §58-50-61(f).
Reconsideration.
Requests for, §58-50-61(i).
Records maintenance, §58-50-61(n).
Retrospective reviews, §58-50-61(g).
Violations.
Effect on insurer, §58-50-61(o).

Waiver by insurer.
Acts which do not constitute, §58-50-1.

Workers' compensation insurance.
Exemption from provisions, §58-50-65(a).

Workers' compensation proceedings.
Insurers not party in interest to proceedings,
§97-90.1.
Reimbursement from employer, §97-90.1.

**HEALTH INSURANCE PORTABILITY AND
ACCOUNTABILITY,** §§58-51-17, 58-68-25 to
58-68-75.

Applicability of provisions, §58-51-17(a).
All plans delivered or issued in state,
§58-51-17(d).

Certification of coverage, §58-51-17(c).

Crediting previous coverage, §58-51-17(a).
Alternative method.
Election, §58-68-30(c).
Determination of creditable coverage, §58-68-30(c).

HEALTH INSURANCE PORTABILITY AND ACCOUNTABILITY —Cont'd

Crediting previous coverage —Cont'd
Establishment of period of creditable coverage, §58-68-30(c).
Exceptions, §58-51-17(b).
Method, §58-68-30(c).
Standard method, §58-68-30(c).
Definitions, §58-68-25(a), (b).
Creditable coverage, §58-51-17(a).
Guaranteed availability of individual coverage to certain individuals with prior group coverage, §58-68-60(b), (h).
Preexisting condition exclusion, §58-68-30(b).
Creditable coverage, §58-68-30(c).
Group market reforms, §§58-68-25 to 58-68-55.
Disclosure of information by health insurers, §58-68-50(a).
Description of information, §58-68-50(b).
Discrimination against individual participants and beneficiaries based on health status.
Eligibility to enroll, §58-68-35(a).
Premium contributions, §58-68-35(b).
Excepted benefits.
Conditions, §58-68-55(b).
Exclusion of certain plans.
Excepted benefits, §58-68-55(a).
Preexisting condition exclusions.
Increase portability through limitation on, §58-68-30.
Renewability coverage.
Guaranteed renewability for employers in group market.
Associations.
Application to coverage offered only through, §58-68-45(e).
Exceptions, §58-68-45(b).
Uniform modification of coverage, §58-68-45(d).
Generally, §58-68-45(a).
Termination of coverage.
Requirements for uniform termination, §58-68-45(c).
Size of employer.
Application of certain rules in determining, §58-68-25(c).
Small group market.
Guaranteed availability of coverage for employers in.
Exceptions, §58-68-40(d), (e).
Financial capacity limits.
Applications, §58-68-40(c).
Issuance of coverage, §58-68-40(a).
Network plans.
Special rules for, §58-68-40(b).
Health maintenance organizations.
Preexisting condition exclusion.
Use of affiliation period as alternative to exclusion, §58-68-30(g).
Individual market reforms, §§58-68-60 to 58-68-75.
Excepted benefits, §58-68-75(a).
Certain conditions met, §58-68-75(b).
Guaranteed availability of individual coverage to certain individuals with prior group coverage, §58-68-60.
Guaranteed renewability of individual coverage.
Associations.
Application to coverage offered only through, §58-68-65(e).
Exceptions, §58-68-65(b), (d).

HEALTH INSURANCE PORTABILITY AND ACCOUNTABILITY —Cont'd

Individual market reforms —Cont'd
Guaranteed renewability of individual coverage —Cont'd
Generally, §58-68-65(a).
Termination of coverage.
Requirements for uniform termination, §58-68-65(c).
Preexisting condition exclusions.
Certification of coverage, §58-68-70.
Prior group coverage.
Guaranteed availability of individual coverage to certain individuals with, §58-68-60.
Renewability of individual coverage.
Guaranteed renewability, §58-68-65.
Medicaid or children's health insurance program.
Enrollment rules in case of, §58-68-30(f).
Preexisting condition exclusions.
Alternative method of crediting coverage.
Election, §58-68-30(c).
Breaks in coverage.
Period of creditable coverage not counted, §58-68-30(c).
Time spent on short term limited duration insurance not treated as, §58-68-30(c).
Waiting period not treated as, §58-68-30(c).
Certifications and disclosure of coverage, §58-68-30(e).
Crediting previous coverage, §58-68-30(a), (c).
Definitions, §58-68-30(b).
Determination of creditable coverage, §58-68-30(c).
Establishing periods of creditable coverage, §58-68-30(c).
Exceptions, §58-68-30(d).
Health maintenance organizations.
Use of affiliation period as alternative to exclusion, §58-68-30(g).
Individual market reforms.
Certification of coverage, §58-68-70.
Limitation on exclusion period, §58-68-30(a).
Special enrollment periods, §58-68-30(f).
Standard method of crediting coverage, §58-68-30(c).
Prior group coverage.
Guaranteed availability of individual coverage to certain individuals with.
Alternative coverage permitted, §58-68-60(c).
Construction and interpretation, §58-68-60(g).
Definitions, §58-68-60(b), (h).
Financial capacity limits.
Application, §58-68-60(e).
Generally, §58-68-60(a).
Market requirements, §58-68-60(f).
Network plans.
Special rules for, §58-68-60(d).
Replacement coverage upon termination, §58-68-60(i).
Waiting periods, §58-68-60(j).
Special enrollment periods.
Dependent beneficiaries, §58-68-30(f).
Individuals losing other coverage, §58-68-30(f).
Medicaid or children's health insurance program, §58-68-30(f).
Special enrollees, §58-68-30(f).
Trust or association outside of state issued policy covering persons in state.
Applicability of provisions, §58-51-17(d).

HEALTH INSURANCE PROGRAM FOR CHILDREN.
Act of 1998, §§108A-70.18 to 108A-70.29.
  See CHILDREN'S HEALTH INSURANCE
    PROGRAM.
Health Choice for children.
  Child health insurance fund, §108A-70.20A.
  Provider requirements, §§108C-1 to 108C-12.

HEALTH INSURANCE RISK POOL, §§58-50-175
  to 58-50-255.
Administrator.
  Compensation, §58-50-185(f).
  Functions, §58-50-185(c), (e).
  Reports, §58-50-185(d).
  Selection, §58-50-185(a).
  Term, §58-50-185(b).
Audits, §58-50-235.
Benefits.
  Minimum benefits, §58-50-205(a).
  Nonduplication, §58-50-215(a).
  Recovery.
    Cause of action, §58-50-215(b).
  Rules regarding, §58-50-205(b).
Board of directors, §58-50-180(b), (c).
  Immunity of members, §58-50-180(h).
  Public servants.
    Members as, §58-50-180(i).
  Reports, §58-50-255(b).
  Rulemaking, §58-50-245.
Complaint procedures, §58-50-230.
Cost containment measures and requirements.
  Powers, §58-50-180(e).
Definitions, §58-50-175.
Eligibility for coverage, §58-50-195(a).
  Cessation of, §58-50-195(d), (e).
  Ineligible individuals, §58-50-195(c).
  List of medical or health conditions, §58-50-195(b).
Established, §58-50-180(a).
Executive director.
  Administrator.
    Selection, §58-50-185(a).
  Incentive programs, §58-50-190(c).
  Operation of pool, §58-50-180(f).
  Reports, §58-50-180(g).
Financing, §58-50-255(a).
Fund, §58-50-225(a).
  Disbursements, §58-50-225(b).
  Surcharges, §58-50-225(c).
Immunity.
  Board and employees, §58-50-180(h).
  Collective action, §58-50-250.
**Insurers to provide notice of pool's existence
  to applicants,** §58-3-276(a).
  Definitions, §58-3-276(d).
  Insurer defined, §58-3-276(d).
  Rules to implement requirement, adoption,
    §58-3-276(c).
  Single notice to multiple applicants, §58-3-276(b).
  Time for providing, §58-3-276(b).
Plan of operations, §58-50-180(d).
Policy forms.
  Submittal of, §58-50-190(f).
Powers, §58-50-180(e).
Preexisting conditions, §58-50-210(a).
  Reduction of exclusion period, §58-50-210(c).
Premium subsidies.
  Authority to provide, §58-50-180(e).
Rates, §58-50-190(a), (b).
  Powers, §58-50-180(e).
  Provider reimbursement rates, §58-50-190(d).

HEALTH INSURANCE RISK POOL —Cont'd
Rates —Cont'd
  Submittal of rates and rate schedules,
    §58-50-190(e).
Reinsuring risks of participating insurers.
  Powers, §58-50-180(e).
Reports.
  Administrator, §58-50-185(d).
  Board of directors, §58-50-255(b).
  Executive director, §58-50-180(g).
Rulemaking, §58-50-245.
Tax exemption, §58-50-240.
Unfair referral to pool, §58-50-200.

HEALTH MAINTENANCE ORGANIZATIONS,
  §§58-67-1 to 58-67-185.
Abortion.
  Lawful abortions.
    Requiring health care institution to perform
      abortion, §14-45.1(f).
Acknowledgment of claims, §58-3-100(c).
  Failure to acknowledge after receiving notice.
    Civil penalty, §58-3-100(c).
Action for negligent decisions.
  Health care liability, §§90-21.50 to 90-21.56.
    See HEALTH CARE LIABILITY.
**Administrative penalty in addition to or in
  lieu of suspension or revocation of
  certificate of authority,** §58-67-165(a).
Administrative procedures, §58-67-155.
Advance practice registered nurse.
  Payment or reimbursement, §58-50-30(d).
  Right to choose services, §58-50-30(a1) to (a3), (g),
    (h).
Advertising.
  False or misleading advertising, §58-67-65(a).
  Solicitation of enrollees.
    Not deemed validation of law relating to
      advertising by health professionals,
      §58-67-170(b).
Agents.
  Licensing, §58-67-90.
Applicability of other laws, §58-67-171.
Articles of incorporation.
  Modifications, §58-67-10(d).
Breast cancer.
  Mammograms, coverage, §58-67-76.
Cancer treatment.
  Cervical cancer screening, coverage, §58-67-76.
  Colorectal cancer examinations, laboratory tests
    and screening.
  Coverage required of all health benefit plans,
    §58-3-179(a).
  Limitations applicable to services, §58-3-179(b).
  Coverage of certain prescribed drugs for,
    §58-67-78(a).
  Exceptions, §58-67-78(b), (c).
  Mammograms, coverage, §58-67-76.
Carrier defined, §58-67-5(n).
Cease and desist orders, §58-67-165(c), (d).
Certificates of need.
  Definition of health maintenance organization,
    §131E-176.
  General provisions, §§131E-175 to 130E-191.1.
    See HEALTH CARE FACILITIES.
Cervical cancer.
  Screening for early detection.
    Coverage requirements, §58-67-76(a), (e).
    Defined, §58-67-76(a1).
Chemical dependency.
  Coverage not required, §58-67-75(c).

HEALTH MAINTENANCE ORGANIZATIONS
—Cont'd
Chemical dependency —Cont'd
Defined, §§58-67-70(a), 58-67-75(a).
Discrimination.
Applicability of section, §58-67-75(d).
Prohibited acts, §58-67-75(b).
Sex changes.
Coverage for treatment or studies not
required, §58-67-75(e).
Group plans.
Chemical dependency defined, §58-67-70(a).
Minimum benefits, §58-67-70(c).
Paul Wellstone and Pete Domenici mental
health parity and addiction equity act
compliance, §58-67-70(g), (h).
Provider payments, §58-67-70(d).
Qualified organizations.
Coverage provided under federal act,
§58-67-70(f).
Rejected coverage by group, inapplicability,
§58-67-70(e).
Required to offer coverage, §58-67-70(b).
Children.
Nondependent child coverage, §58-3-290.
Chiropractors.
Right to choose services, §58-50-30(a1) to (a3), (g),
(h).
Choice of service providers, §58-50-30(a1) to
(a3).
Locum tenens contracts, §58-3-231.
Pediatrician for minors, §58-3-240.
Provider directories, §58-3-245.
Specialist selected as primary care provider,
§58-3-235.
Uniform provider credentialing, §58-3-230.
Citation of act.
Short title, §58-67-1.
Claims.
Acknowledgment of claims, §58-3-100(c).
Failure to acknowledge after receiving notice.
Civil penalty, §58-3-100(c).
Incurred by not reported claims, §58-67-135(a).
Computation of liabilities, §58-67-135(b).
Notice of claim denied, §58-3-172(a).
Health benefit plan defined, §58-3-172(b).
Uniform claim forms, §58-3-171(a).
Health benefit plan defined, §58-3-171(c).
Workers' compensation as health benefit plan,
§58-3-171(b).
Clinical social workers.
Defined, §58-50-30(c).
Right to choose services, §58-50-30(a1) to (a3), (g),
(h).
Clinical trials, coverage, §58-3-255(b).
Costs not required to be covered, §58-3-255(d).
Covered clinical trials defined, §58-3-255(a).
Definitions, §58-3-255(a).
Medical necessary costs covered, §58-3-255(c).
**Closed formularies or restricted access to
prescription drugs,** §58-3-221.
Closure of a block of business, §58-3-275(a) to
(d).
Collaboration with local health departments,
§58-67-66.
**Colorectal cancer examinations, laboratory
tests and screening.**
Coverage required of every health benefit plan,
§58-3-179(a).
Limitations applicable to services, §58-3-179(b).

HEALTH MAINTENANCE ORGANIZATIONS
—Cont'd
Commissioner of insurance.
Administrative procedures, §58-67-155.
Cease and desist orders, §58-67-165(c), (d).
Definition of "commissioner,"§58-67-5(a).
Deposits.
Administration, §58-67-25(c).
Minimum required.
Full service organizations, §58-67-25(a).
Single service organizations, §58-67-25(b).
Examinations, §58-67-100.
Hazardous financial condition.
Authority as to, §58-67-105.
Rules and regulations.
Authority as to, §58-67-105(b).
Steps reasonably necessary to rectify situation.
Enumerated, §58-67-105(a).
Insolvency.
Protection against insolvency.
Adequacy of plan, §58-67-110(e).
Commissioner to require deposit,
§58-67-110(a).
Rehabilitation, liquidation or conservation of
health maintenance organizations,
§58-67-145.
Reports.
Annual reports to commissioner, §58-67-55.
Rules and regulations, §58-67-150.
Filing requirement exemptions, §58-67-10(d).
Confidentiality of information, §58-67-180.
Construction and interpretation, §58-67-170.
Continuation of benefits, §58-67-120(a).
Plan for, §58-67-120(a).
**Continuing care retirement community
residents,** §58-3-200(f).
Continuity of care.
Conditions of coverage, §58-67-88(h).
Construction of provision, §58-67-88(i).
Definitions, §58-67-88(a).
Disclosure of right to transition, §58-67-88(j).
Length of transitional period, §58-67-88(d).
Pregnancy, §58-67-88(f).
Scheduled inpatient treatment, §58-67-88(e).
Terminal illness, §58-67-88(g).
Newly covered insured, transition coverage,
§58-67-88(c).
Termination of contract.
Election to continue, §58-67-88(b).
**Contraceptive drugs or devices and outpatient
contraceptive services.**
Coverage by insurer providing health benefit plan,
§58-3-178(a), (b).
Definitions, §58-3-178(c).
Prohibited acts, §58-3-178(d).
Religious employer requesting exclusion of
coverage, §58-3-178(e).
Contracts.
Between health benefit plans and health care
providers, §§58-50-270 to 58-50-290.
See HEALTH INSURANCE.
Certain words prohibited, §58-67-65(d).
Chemical dependency.
Contracts to cover treatment, §58-67-70(a) to (f).
Custodial agreements.
Exclusivity prohibited, §58-67-30(a).
Grounds for disapproval, §58-67-30(b).
Insurers and hospital and medical service
corporations.
Contracts with health maintenance
organizations, §58-67-95(b).

HEALTH MAINTENANCE ORGANIZATIONS
—Cont'd
Contracts —Cont'd
Management agreements.
Exclusivity prohibited, §58-67-30(a).
Grounds for disapproval, §58-67-30(b).
Master group contracts, §58-67-85.
Powers of organizations generally, §58-67-35(a).
Costs and utilization information.
Providing to group subscribers when requested,
§58-67-50(e).
Credentialing providers.
Effective date of practitioner's participation.
Joining practice under contract with insurer,
§58-3-230(a).
Health benefit plan and insurer defined,
§58-3-230(c).
Process requirements, §58-3-230(a).
Temporary credential, §58-3-230(a).
Time limit on processing applications,
§58-3-230(a).
Uniform provider credentialing application form.
Commissioner to adopt by rule, §58-3-230(b).
Definitions, §58-67-5(a) to (p).
Accident, accidental injury and accidental means,
§58-67-80(b).
Applicability of definitions, §58-67-80(a).
Certificate of need law, §131E-176.
Mastectomy.
Coverage for reconstructive breast surgery
following, §58-67-79(b).
Mental illness and chemical dependency,
§58-67-75(a).
**Dental procedures performed in hospital or
ambulatory surgical facility.**
Children under age nine, persons with serious
mental and physical condition and persons
with significant behavior problems.
Definitions, §58-3-122(b).
Health benefit plans to provide coverage for
payment of anesthesia and facility charges,
§58-3-122(a).
Dentists.
Right to choose services, §58-50-30(a1) to (a3), (g),
(h).
Deposits.
Administration, §58-67-25(c).
Minimum required.
Full service organizations, §58-67-25(a).
Single service organizations, §58-67-25(b).
Determinations as to coverage, §58-3-200(c).
Diabetes.
Coverage for certain treatment, §58-67-74(a).
Definition of "physician," §58-67-74.
Directories of providers, §58-3-245.
Direct payment to government agency,
§58-3-175(b).
Health benefit plan defined, §58-3-175(a).
Inapplicability of provisions, §58-3-175(c).
When not required, §58-3-175(d).
**Disclosure requirements for health benefit
plans,** §58-3-191(b).
Discontinuance defined, §58-67-5(o).
Discrimination.
Mentally ill and chemically dependent.
Applicability of section, §58-67-75(d).
Coverage, §58-67-75(b1), (c).
Prohibited acts, §58-67-75(b).
Sex changes.
Coverage for treatment or studies not
required, §58-67-75(e).

HEALTH MAINTENANCE ORGANIZATIONS
—Cont'd
Discrimination —Cont'd
Prohibited acts, §58-67-65(f).
Drive-thru deliveries, §58-3-169.
**Electronic or on-line system for up-to-date
network information.**
Plan to provide, §58-3-245(a).
Emergency care.
Coverage required, §58-3-190.
Enrollees.
Defined, §58-67-5(b).
Deterioration of health.
Cancellation or nonrenewal because of,
§58-67-65(c).
Evidence of coverage.
Enrollees entitled to, §58-67-50(a).
Unable to arrange adequate services.
Refusal to enroll, §58-67-65(e).
Enrollment period, §58-67-125(a).
Group contracts, §58-67-125(b).
Nongroup enrollees, §58-67-125(c).
Evidence of coverage.
Content, §58-67-50(a).
Costs and utilization information.
Provision to group subscribers when requested,
§58-67-50(e).
Defined, §58-67-5(c).
Enrollees entitled to, §58-67-50(a).
Forms.
Approval by commissioner, §58-67-50(c).
Copies to be filed with commissioner,
§58-67-50(a).
Disapproval by commissioner.
Notice, §58-67-50(c).
Information needed for determination by
commissioner.
Power to require, §58-67-50(d).
Notice, expenses may exceed covered amount,
§58-3-250(b).
Payment obligations, explanation by insurer,
§58-3-250(a).
Examinations.
Powers of commissioner, §58-67-100(a).
Report in lieu of, §58-67-100(d).
Exemptions from provisions, §58-67-10(b).
External review of health benefit plan,
§§58-50-75 to 58-50-95.
See HEALTH INSURANCE.
Fee based pastoral counselor.
Defined, §58-50-30(c1).
Right to choose services, §58-50-30(a1) to (a3), (g),
(h).
Fees.
License application and annual continuation fees,
§58-67-160.
Fiduciaries.
Responsibilities of directors, officers and partners,
§58-67-45.
**Financial incentives to delay, deny or reduce
coverage.**
Plan prohibited from offering provider, §58-3-265.
Foreign corporations.
Qualifications to do business in state,
§58-67-10(a).
Genetic information in health insurance,
§58-3-215.
Grandfather clause, §58-67-10(b).
Grievance procedures for insurers, §58-50-62.
External review of decision, §§58-50-75 to
58-50-95.

HEALTH MAINTENANCE ORGANIZATIONS
—Cont'd
Hazardous financial condition.
Authority of commissioner, §58-67-105.
Rules and regulations, §58-67-105(b).
Steps reasonably necessary to rectify situation,
§58-67-105(a).
Health benefit plans generally, §§58-3-167 to
58-3-178.
See HEALTH INSURANCE.
Health care plans.
Defined, §58-67-5(d).
Health care services.
Defined, §58-67-5(e).
**Health insurance portability and
accountability.**
Preexisting condition exclusion.
Use of affiliation period as alternative to
exclusion, §58-68-30(g).
Transition of care after provider contract
terminated, §58-67-88.
Health insurance risk pool.
Notice relating to.
Insurers to provide applicants, §58-3-276.
Hearing aids.
Deductibles, coinsurance and other limitations,
§58-3-285(b).
Medical necessity determination, utilization
review, §58-3-285(c).
Required coverage, §58-3-285(a).
High-risk populations.
Nondiscrimination against, §58-3-200(e).
HMO defined, §58-67-5(f).
Hold harmless agreements, §58-67-115(a).
Special deposit in lieu of, §58-67-115(b).
**Hospital, medical and dental service
corporations.**
Contracts with health maintenance organizations,
§58-67-95(b).
Power to organize and operate health
maintenance organization, §58-67-95(a).
Provisions not applicable to health maintenance
organizations, §58-67-170(a).
Incentives to delay, deny or reduce coverage.
Plan prohibited from offering provider, §58-3-265.
Injunctions, §58-67-165(e).
Insolvency.
Defined, §58-67-5(m).
Hold harmless agreements, §58-67-115(a).
Insolvent defined, §58-67-5(m).
Protection against insolvency.
Adequacy of plan, §58-67-110(e).
Deposit, §58-67-110(a).
Minimum net worth, §58-67-110(b).
Insurance companies.
Contracts with health maintenance organizations,
§58-67-95(b).
General provisions.
See INSURANCE COMPANIES.
Power to organize and operate health
maintenance organizations, §58-67-95(a).
Provisions not applicable to health maintenance
organizations, §58-67-170(a).
Investments, §58-67-60.
Licenses.
Agents, §58-67-90.
Application, §58-67-10(c).
Additional information, §58-67-11(a).
Changes, notification, §58-67-11(b).
Denial, §58-67-20(c).

HEALTH MAINTENANCE ORGANIZATIONS
—Cont'd
Licenses —Cont'd
Fees.
Application and annual continuation fees,
§58-67-160.
Issuance.
Determinations required, §58-67-20(a).
Factors which may be considered,
§58-67-20(b).
Monetary penalty for violations, §58-2-70(a), (c),
(d), (g).
Required, §58-67-10(a).
Restitution for violations, §58-2-70(e) to (g).
Surrender, §58-2-65.
Suspension or revocation.
Administrative penalty in addition to or in lieu
of, §58-67-165(a).
Applicable provisions, §58-2-70(h).
Criminal convictions, §58-2-60(b).
Grounds, §58-67-140(a).
Hearings.
Action following, §58-67-155(b).
Notice, §58-67-155(a).
Notice and hearing, §58-2-70(b).
Procedure, §§58-67-140(b) to (d), 58-67-155.
Liquidation, §58-67-145.
Local health departments.
Collaboration with, §58-67-66.
Locum tenens contracts, §58-3-231.
Accepting and payment for claims, §58-3-231(b).
Defined terms, §58-3-231(a).
Medical groups or hospitals, §58-3-231(c).
Placement and administrative services,
§58-3-231(e).
Statements of supervision waived, §58-3-231(d).
Long-term care insurance, §§58-55-1 to 58-55-50.
See LONG-TERM CARE INSURANCE.
Long-term care partnerships, §§58-55-55 to
58-55-80.
Lymphedema.
Coverage for diagnosis and treatment, §58-3-280.
Malpractice actions generally, §§90-21.11 to
90-21.19B.
See MEDICAL MALPRACTICE.
Mammograms.
Coverage requirements, §58-67-76(a), (c).
Low dose mammography defined, §58-67-76(b).
Reimbursement, §58-67-76(d).
Managed care patient assistance program,
§143-730.
Marriage and family therapists.
Defined, §58-50-30(c4).
Right to choose services, §58-50-30(a1) to (a3).
Mastectomy.
Coverage for reconstructive breast surgery
following, §58-67-79(a).
Definitions, §58-67-79(b).
Notice of available coverage, §58-67-79(d).
Prohibited act, §58-67-79(c).
Master group contracts.
Adding employees to coverage.
Time for, §58-67-85(d).
Authorized, §58-67-85(a).
Employee eligibility, §58-67-85(d1).
Successor corporations.
Liability, §58-67-85(e).
Maternity coverage requirements, §58-3-170(a).
Health benefit plans defined, §58-3-170(b).
Minimum hospital stay following birth, §58-3-169.

HEALTH MAINTENANCE ORGANIZATIONS
—Cont'd
Medical necessity.
Requirements for health benefit plans that limit coverage to medically necessary services and supplies, §58-3-200(b).
Mental health area facilities.
Contracts with health maintenance organizations, §122C-141(c).
Misdemeanors, §58-67-165(b).
Modifications of operations.
Notice to commissioner, §58-67-10(d).
Names.
Prohibited words, §58-67-65(d).
Negligent decisions of plan providers.
Health care liability, §§90-21.50 to 90-21.56.
See HEALTH CARE LIABILITY.
Net worth.
Defined, §58-67-5(i).
Risk based capital requirement, §58-12-70.
Newborn hearing screening.
Coverage required, §58-3-260(b).
Health benefit plan and insurer defined, §58-3-260(a).
North Carolina health insurance risk pool.
Notice relating to.
Insurers to provide applicants, §58-3-276.
Notice.
Claim denied, §58-3-172(a).
Health benefit plan defined, §58-3-172(b).
Exercise of powers, §58-67-35(b).
Modification of operations, §58-67-10(d).
Obstruction of health care facility, §14-277.4.
Offset or reversal of payment, §58-50-57(a).
Contract with provider not to contain provision authorizing, §58-50-57(b).
Optometrists.
Right to choose services, §58-50-30(a1) to (a3), (g), (h).
Osteoporosis or low bone mass.
Bone mass measurement for diagnosis and evaluation.
Health benefit plan to provide coverage, §58-3-174(a).
Definitions, §58-3-174(d).
Frequency of coverage, §58-3-174(b).
Screening for nonqualified individuals not covered, §58-3-174(c).
Participating provider defined, §58-67-5(l).
Payment obligations for covered services.
Explanation by insurer, §58-3-250(a).
Notice that actual expenses may exceed covered amount, §58-3-250(b).
Payment to government agency.
Direct payment, §58-3-175.
Pediatrician.
Direct access for minors, §58-3-240.
Pharmacist.
Payment or reimbursement, §58-50-30(e).
Right to choose services, §58-50-30(a1) to (a3), (g), (h).
Physician assistant.
Payment or reimbursement, §58-50-30(f).
Right to choose services, §58-50-30(a1) to (a3), (g), (h).
Plan summaries.
Notice, expenses may exceed covered amount, §58-3-250(b).
Payment obligations, explanation by insurer, §58-3-250(a).

HEALTH MAINTENANCE ORGANIZATIONS
—Cont'd
Podiatrists.
Right to choose services, §58-50-30(a1) to (a3), (g), (h).
Policies and contracts.
Insurance policies and contracts generally.
See INSURANCE POLICIES OR CONTRACTS.
Powers, §58-67-35(a).
Notice of exercise of powers, §58-67-35(b).
Practice of medicine or dentistry.
Health maintenance organizations not deemed to be practicing medicine or dentistry, §58-67-170(c).
Premiums.
Schedule.
Approval by commissioner, §58-67-50(c).
Disapproval by commissioner.
Notice, §58-67-50(c).
Establishment of premiums, §58-67-50(b).
Filing of copy with commissioner, §58-67-50(b).
Information needed for determination by commissioner.
Power to require, §58-67-50(d).
Prescription drug identification cards.
Plan issuing prescription drug cards to issue uniform identification cards, §58-3-177(a).
Definitions, §58-3-177(e).
Electronic verification of claim, §58-3-177(d).
Exceptions, §58-3-177(f).
Information contained in card, §58-3-177(a), (b).
Issued annually if change in coverage, §58-3-177(c).
Prescription drugs.
Closed formularies or restricted access to perspiration drugs or devices.
Definitions, §58-3-221(c).
Medically necessary nonformulary or restricted access drug or device prescribed.
Voiding or refusing to renew contract prohibited, §58-3-221(b).
Payment for drugs or devices specifically excluded from coverage not required, §58-3-221(d).
Requirements of insurers maintaining, §58-3-221(a).
Contraceptive drugs or devices.
Coverage by insurer providing health benefit plan, §58-3-178.
Primary care provider, specialist selected.
Insured diagnosed with serious or chronic degenerative, disabling or life threatening disease, §58-3-235(a).
Care authorized by specialist, §58-3-235(b).
Denial of access by insurer, §58-3-235(a).
Treatment plan approved by insurer, selection under, §58-3-235(b).
Privileged communications.
Confidentiality of medical information, §58-67-180.
Professional counselor.
Defined, §58-50-30(c3).
Right to choose services, §58-50-30(a1) to (a3), (g), (h).
Prohibited practices, §58-67-65(a) to (f).
Prostate-specific antigen (PSA) tests.
Coverage, §58-67-77(a), (c).
Defined, §58-67-77(b).
Provider contracts.
Contracts between health benefit plans and health care providers, §§58-50-270 to 58-50-290.
See HEALTH INSURANCE.

HEALTH MAINTENANCE ORGANIZATIONS
—Cont'd
Provider credentialing.
Effective date of practitioner's participation.
Joining practice under contract with insurer,
§58-3-230(a).
Health benefit plan and insurer defined,
§58-3-230(c).
Process requirements, §58-3-230(a).
Temporary credential, §58-3-230(a).
Time limit on processing applications,
§58-3-230(a).
Uniform provider credentialing application form.
Commissioner to adopt by rule, §58-3-230(b).
Provider defined, §58-67-5(h).
Provider directories.
Allied health professionals, listing, §58-3-245(c).
Information included in directory listing,
§58-3-245(b).
Plan required to provide, §58-3-245(a).
Provider networks.
Services outside networks, §58-3-200(d).
Psychologists.
Defined, §58-50-30(b).
Right to choose services, §58-50-30(a1) to (a3), (g),
(h).
Public documents.
Filings and reports as, §58-67-175.
Racial minorities.
Discrimination, §58-67-65(f).
Reciprocity.
Organizations of bordering states may be
admitted to do business, §58-67-15.
Reconstructive breast surgery.
Coverage following mastectomy, §58-67-79.
Rehabilitation, liquidation or conservation,
§58-67-145.
Replacement coverage, §58-67-130(a).
Exceptions, §58-67-130(b).
Reports.
Examinations.
Report in lieu of examination, §58-67-100(d).
Health benefit plan reporting requirements,
§58-3-191(a).
Access to reports, §58-3-191(b1).
Public documents, §58-67-175.
Risk based capital requirements.
Insurance companies, §§58-12-2 to 58-12-70.
See INSURANCE COMPANIES.
Rules and regulations, §58-67-150.
Filing requirement exemptions, §58-67-10(d).
Hazardous financial condition, §58-67-105.
Severability of provisions, §58-67-185.
Specialist care referral.
In-plan specialists.
Definitions, §58-3-223(b).
Duties of insurer providing health benefit plan,
§58-3-223(a).
Specialist selected as primary care provider.
Insured diagnosed with serious or chronic
degenerative, disabling or life threatening
disease, §58-3-235(a).
Care authorized by specialist, §58-3-235(b).
Denial of access by insurer, §58-3-235(a).
Treatment plan approved by insurer, selection
under, §58-3-235(b).
Subscriber defined, §58-67-5(k).
Substance abuse professional.
Defined, §58-50-30(c2).
Right to choose services, §58-50-30(a1) to (a3), (g),
(h).

HEALTH MAINTENANCE ORGANIZATIONS
—Cont'd
Telephone system for up-to-date network
information.
Plan to provide, §58-3-245(a).
Title of act.
Short title, §58-67-1.
Transition of care after provider contract
terminated, §58-67-88.
Treatment discussions.
Limiting prohibited, §58-3-176.
Uncovered expenditures defined, §58-67-5(p).
Unfair trade practices, applicable provisions,
§58-67-65(b).
Uniform claim forms, §58-3-171.
Uniform prescription drug identification
cards, §58-3-177.
Uniform provider credentialing, §58-3-230.
Utilization review.
External review, §§58-50-75 to 58-50-95.
Generally, §58-50-61(a) to (o).
Violations of provisions generally, §58-67-165(b).
Working capital.
Defined, §58-67-5(j).

HEALTH ORGANIZATIONS.
Provider sponsored organizations, §§131E-275
to 131E-314.
See PROVIDER SPONSORED ORGANIZATIONS.
Solicitation of contributions, §§131F-1 to
131F-33.
See CHARITABLE SOLICITATION.

HEALTH RECORDS.
Generally.
See MEDICAL RECORDS.

HEALTH SPAS.
Child care facilities.
Drop-in or short-term child care offered.
Not included in term child care, §110-86.
Prepaid entertainment contracts generally,
§§66-118 to 66-125.
See PREPAID ENTERTAINMENT CONTRACTS.

HEALTH STATISTICS, STATE CENTER,
§§130A-371 to 130A-374.
Analysis and indexing, §130A-373(e).
Authority and duties, §130A-373.
Collection, maintenance and analyses of health
data.
Authority and duties, §130A-373(a) to (c).
Confidentiality.
Security of health data, §130A-374(a), (b).
Coordination of health data activities within
state, §130A-373(f).
Definitions, §130A-372.
Department of health and human services.
Center established within department, §130A-371.
Duties, §130A-373.
Established within department, §130A-371.
Governmental organizations.
Collecting data on behalf of, §130A-373(b).
Health data.
Defined, §130A-372.
Mandatory reporting of health data,
§130A-373(c).
Medical records.
Defined, §130A-372.
Nonprofit organizations.
Collecting data on behalf of, §130A-373(b).
Powers and duties, §130A-373.

HEALTH STATISTICS, STATE CENTER

—Cont'd

Publishing, availability and dissemination of statistics, §130A-373(e).

Quality, timely and comprehensive statistics, §130A-373(e).

Security of health data, §130A-374(a), (b).

Sharing health data with other entities, §130A-373(d).

Voluntary basis for collecting data, §130A-373(c).

HEARING AID DEALERS AND FITTERS, §§93D-1 to 93D-16.

Age.

Qualifications for license, §93D-5(a).

Apprenticeship registration.

Applications, §93D-9(a).

Fee, §93D-9(b).

Display of apprenticeship registration, §93D-12.

Holding apprenticeship license for one year as prerequisite to issuance of license, §93D-5(c).

Issuance, §93D-9(b).

Renewal, §93D-9(d), (e).

Fees, §93D-9(e).

Supervision and training by registered sponsor. Prerequisite to issuance, §93D-9(c).

Audiology assistants.

Subject to provisions, §93D-14(c).

Audiology students.

Exemptions from provisions, §93D-14(d).

Board.

Appointment of members, §93D-3(a).

Composition, §93D-3(a).

Creation, §93D-3(a).

Defined, §93D-1.

Disciplinary action, §93D-13.

Duties, §93D-3(c).

Executive secretary, §93D-3(b).

Expenses of members, §93D-3(d).

Injunctions.

Actions for, §93D-4.

Meetings, §93D-3(b).

Number of members, §93D-3(a).

Officers, §93D-3(b).

Qualifications of members, §93D-3(a).

Quorum, §93D-3(b).

Records, §93D-3(b).

Reports.

Annual report to governor, §93D-3(d).

Secretary-treasurer, §93D-3(d).

Bond, surety, §93D-3(d).

Terms of members, §93D-3(a).

Vacancies.

Filling, §93D-3(a).

Certified technicians.

Subject to provisions, §93D-14(c).

Child support enforcement.

Forfeiture of licensing privilege, §50-13.12.

Definitions, §93D-1.

Disciplinary proceedings, §93D-13.

Diseases.

Freedom from contagious or infectious diseases. Prerequisite to issuance of license, §93D-5(a).

Doctoral degree in audiology, certain holders of.

Exemptions from provisions, §93D-14(b).

Education.

Occupational instruction courses, §93D-11.

Qualifications for licenses, §93D-5(a).

HEARING AID DEALERS AND FITTERS

—Cont'd

Examinations.

Licenses, §93D-8(a).

Successfully passing examination required, §93D-5(b).

Exemptions from provisions, §93D-14.

Fees.

Licenses.

Application fee, §93D-5(a).

Issuance of license certificate, §93D-8(b).

Reciprocity, §93D-6.

Reissuance of suspended license, §93D-13(b).

Renewal fees, §93D-11.

Felony convictions.

Forfeiture of license, §15A-1331A.

Fitting and selling hearing aids.

Defined, §93D-1.

License required, §§93D-2, 93D-5(a).

Statements of sale, §93D-7.

Injunctions, §93D-4.

Licenses.

Applications, §93D-5(a).

Apprenticeship licenses.

Holding for one year as prerequisite to issuance of license, §93D-5(c).

Display, §93D-12.

Duties of board as to, §93D-3(c).

Examinations, §93D-8(a).

Scope, §93D-8(a).

Successfully passing examination required, §93D-5(b).

Fees.

Application fee, §93D-5(a).

Issuance of license certificate, §93D-8(b).

Reciprocity, §93D-6.

Reissuance of suspended license, §93D-13(b).

Renewal fees, §93D-11.

Issuance, §93D-8(b).

Qualifications, §93D-5(a).

Reciprocity, §93D-6.

Renewal, §93D-11.

Required, §§93D-2, 93D-5(a).

Revocation or suspension.

Confidentiality of records, §93D-13(c).

Felony convictions, §15A-1331A.

Grounds, §93D-13(a).

Procedure, §93D-13(b).

Reissuance of suspended license, §93D-13(b).

Misdemeanors.

Violations of provisions, §93D-15.

Notice.

Mailing of notices to licensees, §93D-10.

Physicians and surgeons.

Exemption of physicians and surgeons from provisions, §93D-14(a).

Reciprocity.

Licenses, §93D-6.

Registered sponsors.

Apprenticeship registration.

Supervision and training by registered sponsor, §93D-9(c).

Registration, §93D-10.

Rules regarding registration, §93D-9(g).

Registration.

Apprentices, §§93D-9, 93D-10.

Licensees, §93D-10.

Reports.

Board.

Annual report to governor, §93D-3(d).

HEARING AID DEALERS AND FITTERS
—Cont'd
Rules and regulations.
Board, §93D-3(c).
Sales and use tax.
Exemption, §105-164.13.
Severability of provisions, §93D-16.
Speech and language pathologists and
audiologists.
Exemption of practice of fitting and selling
hearing aids, §90-294(e).
Statements of sale, §93D-7.
Subpoenas.
Powers of board, §93D-3(c).
Venue.
Injunctions.
Actions by board to enjoin illegal practices,
§93D-4.
Violations of provisions.
Penalties, §93D-15.

HEARING AIDS.
Health insurance.
Deductibles, coinsurance and other limitations,
§58-3-285(b).
Medical necessity determination, utilization
review, §58-3-285(c).
Required coverage, §58-3-285(a).
State health plan for teachers and state
employees.
Coverage for, §135-48.51.

HEARING LOSS.
Children's health insurance program.
Hearing tests, §108A-70.21(b).
Deaf persons generally.
See DEAF AND HEARING IMPAIRED.
Newborn hearing screening.
Health benefit plan coverage, §58-3-260.
Rules to include in newborn screening program,
§130A-125(b), (b1).
Occupational diseases.
Hearing loss caused by harmful noise in
employment, §97-53.
Workers' compensation, §97-31.

HEARINGS.
Abandoned manufactured homes.
Identification, deconstruction, recycling, disposal.
Disposal of abandoned home required,
§130A-309.114(a).
ABC boards.
Budget hearing, §18B-702(f).
Notice, §18B-702(e).
Removal hearing, §18B-704.
Abortion.
Parental or judicial consent to abortion.
Waiver of parental consent requirement
proceedings, §90-21.8(b).
Absentees in military service.
Action to appoint receiver, §28B-3.
Transfer of property valued at more than five
thousand dollars, §28B-10(c).
Abused, neglected or dependent juvenile
actions.
Adjudicatory hearing, §§7B-801 to 7B-808.
Dispositional hearing, §7B-901.
Interference or obstruction of assessment of
report, §7B-303(c).
Judicial review of responsible individuals list,
§7B-323(b), (c).
Nonsecure custody, §7B-506.

HEARINGS —Cont'd
Abused, neglected or dependent juvenile
actions —Cont'd
Periodic review hearings as to placement.
Custody removed from parent, §7B-906.
Surrender of child for adoption, agency plan for
placement, §7B-909.
Termination of parental rights, §7B-908.
Voluntary foster care placement, §7B-910.
Permanency planning hearing, custody removed
from parent, §7B-907(a).
Administrative procedure, §§150B-22 to 150B-42.
See ADMINISTRATIVE PROCEDURE.
Adoption.
Confidentiality of hearings, §48-2-203.
Dispositional hearing on uncontested petition,
§48-2-601.
Petition for adoption.
Continuance of hearing on court's motion,
§48-2-603(c).
Procedure generally, §48-2-603.
Sanctions for violations of chapter, §48-2-603(b).
Standard of proof, §48-2-603(a).
Petition to adopt adult.
Appearance of parties, §48-2-605(a).
Burden of proof, §48-2-605(b).
Procedure generally, §48-2-605(b).
Adult care homes.
Contesting penalty, §131D-34(e).
Agriculture.
Assessment of fees and taxes.
Procedure for assessment, §106-9.3(c).
Aid to the blind.
Denial of application for aid, §111-16.
Air pollution control.
Local air pollution control programs.
Situations under which commission may hold,
§143-215.112(e).
Alarm systems licensing.
Board, §74D-5(b).
Alcoholic beverage permits.
Local government official designated to make
recommendations.
Testimony at hearing, §18B-904(f).
Location, §18B-906(b).
Annexation.
City property not contiguous to corporate limits.
Public hearing on resolution, §160A-58.7(a).
Municipalities initiating annexation.
Conduct of public hearing, §160A-58.55(g).
Date for public hearing, §160A-58.55(c).
Notice of public hearing, §160A-58.55(d).
Arbitration.
See ARBITRATION.
Attorney disability proceedings, Bar Rule
B.0118.
Attorney discipline.
Formal hearings, Bar Rule B.0114.
Attorneys CLE hearings, Bar Rules D.1001 to
D.1011.
Attorney specialization.
Denial of certification or continued certification,
Bar Rules D.1801 to D.1806.
Auctions and auctioneers.
Commission, §85B-8(e).
Bail.
Source of money or property offered, §15A-539(b).
Bail bondsmen and runners.
Denial, suspension, revocation or refusal to renew
license, §58-71-85(b).

HEARINGS —Cont'd

Boundaries.
Special proceeding to establish boundaries, §38-3(a).

Building code enforcement agencies.
Questions under building code, §143-140.

Bus companies discontinuing or reducing service.
Permission granted with or without public hearing, §62-262.2(b).

Check-cashing businesses.
Licensing.
Denial of license, §53-279(b).

Child custody.
Action or proceeding for custody or visitation.
Heard without jury by judge, §50-13.5(h).

Child support.
Action for support of minor child.
Heard by judge without jury, §50-13.5(h).
Amount of support payments.
Request of party, §50-13.4(c).
Expedited process.
Appeal from orders of child support hearing officer.
De novo hearing, §50-38(a).
Procedure to insure payment.
Cases heard for enforcement.
Informing district court judge, §50-13.9(f).
Delinquency in non-IV-D cases.
Enforcement order, §50-13.9(d).

City councils.
Conduct of public hearings, §160A-81.

City-owned or joint agency communications providers.
Public hearings, §160A-340.3.

Claim and delivery, §1-474.1(a).

Coastal area management.
Areas of environmental concern, §113A-115.
Land-use plans, §113A-110.

Coastal wetland activities.
Orders to control activities, §113-230(b).

Collection agencies.
Denial of permit, §58-70-30.

Commercial drivers' licenses.
Sex offenders prohibited from obtaining license with P or S endorsement.
Denial of license, §20-37.14A(b).

Commodities.
Commencement of administrative proceedings, §78D-30.
Investigations, §78D-21.

Community service program.
Division of adult correction.
Willful failure to comply, §143B-708(f).

Consolidated city-county act.
Urban service districts.
Abolition of districts, §160B-10.
Consolidation of district, §160B-8(c).
Establishment of district, §160B-6(c).
Extension of district, §160B-7(d).

Consumer finance act.
License applications, §53-168(b).

Contempt.
Civil contempt.
Proceedings for civil contempt, §5A-23.
Criminal contempt.
Plenary proceedings for contempt.
Show cause hearings, §5A-15.

Cooperative agreements among physicians or between physician, hospital or other person.
Public hearing on issuance of certificate of public advantage, §90-21.27(a).

HEARINGS —Cont'd

Coroners.
Preliminary hearings.
Duties of coroners, §152-7.
Hearings by coroner in lieu of other preliminary hearing, §152-10.

County boards of adjustment, §153A-345(b).

County boards of commissioners.
Conduct, §153A-52.

County inspection departments, §153A-361.

County planning and zoning.
Public hearing.
Adoption, amendment or repeal of ordinance, §153A-323(a).

County research and production service districts.
Abolition, §153A-316.
Establishment, §153A-312(b).
Extension, §153A-314(c).
Removal of territory.
Public hearing, §153A-314.1(c).

County service districts.
Abolition, §153A-306.
Annexation of territory, §153A-303(e).
Before adopting resolution, §153A-302(c).
Consolidation or extensions, §§153A-303(c), (e), 153A-304(c).
Establishments, §153A-302(c).

County special assessments.
Preliminary assessment roll, §153A-195.
Preliminary resolutions, §153A-192.

County water and sewer districts.
Abolition of districts, §162A-87.2(a).
Creation of district, §162A-86(b), (c).
Extension of districts, §162A-87.1(e).

Credit unions.
Removal of officers, §54-109.19(b).
Suspension and conservation.
Reply to order, §54-109.92(d).

Crematory licensees, §90-210.123(i).

Criminal procedure.
See CRIMINAL LAW AND PROCEDURE.

Dangerous dog determination, §67-4.1(c).

Declaratory judgments.
Hearing before judge where no issues of fact raised or jury trial waived, §1-262.

Default judgments.
Taking account, determining damages, establishing truth of averment, §1A-1 Rule 55(b).

Delinquent and undisciplined juvenile actions.
Adjudicatory hearing.
Conduct generally, §7B-2405.
Due process rights protected, §7B-2405.
Quantum of proof, §7B-2409.
Time and place for holding, §7B-2403.
Admissions by juveniles, when accepted by court, §7B-2407.
Closure of hearings for good cause, §7B-2402.
Continuances, §7B-2406.
Dispositional hearing, §7B-2501.
Medical, surgical, psychiatric, psychological or other evaluation or treatment, determination by court, §7B-2502(b).
Open hearing, §7B-2402.
Post-release supervision, progress review, violation of terms, §7B-2516(a).
Prosecutor to represent state at hearings, §7B-2404.
Record of proceedings, §7B-2411.
Restraint in courtroom at hearing, §7B-2402.1.

HEARINGS —Cont'd
Delinquent and undisciplined juvenile actions —Cont'd
Rules of evidence, §7B-2408.
Secure or nonsecure custody hearings, §7B-1906.
Transfer of jurisdiction of juvenile to superior court.
Probable cause hearing, §7B-2202.
Transfer hearing, §7B-2203.
Dental hygienists.
Disciplinary proceedings, §90-231.
Dentists.
Disciplinary proceedings, §90-41.1.
Disability of attorney, Bar Rule B.0118.
Discipline of attorneys.
Formal hearings, Bar Rule B.0114.
Discipline of public school students.
Long-term suspension, §115C-390.8.
Discovery motions, §15A-902(c).
District attorneys, removal from office, §7A-66.
District courts.
Conduct of hearings, §7A-191.
Dogs.
Dangerous dog determination, §67-4.1(c).
Domestic violence.
Emergency relief, §50B-2(b).
Firearms.
Inquiry as to defendants' access to firearms, §50B-3.1(b).
Drainage districts.
See DRAINAGE DISTRICTS.
Drainage petitions.
Agreement for construction, §156-26(c).
Drivers' licenses.
Revocation or suspension, §20-16(d).
Economic development and training districts.
Annexation of territory to district.
Public hearing, §153A-317.14(c).
Establishment by county.
Public hearing, §153A-317.12(d).
Education of children with disabilities.
Impartial due process hearing, §115C-109.6.
Elections.
Challenge of voters.
Challenge on day of primary or election, §163-88.
Challenge other than on day of primary or election, §163-86.
Challenge to absentee ballots, §163-89(e).
Protest filed with county board, §163-182.10.
Electrologists.
Reports of violations of chapter.
Notice of administrative hearing, §88A-23.
Emancipation of juvenile, §7B-3503.
Employee assistance professionals.
Enforcement or disciplinary actions, §90-507.
Excise stamp tax on conveyances.
Refund of overpayment, §105-228.37(b).
Executors and administrators.
Contested appointments, §28A-6-4.
Letters testamentary and of administration.
Revocation, §28A-9-1.
Resignation.
Hearing on petition, §28A-10-4.
Expedited evictions.
Procedure for expedited hearing, §42-68.
Extradition.
Fugitives from other states.
Writ of habeas corpus, §15A-730.
Family law arbitration, §50-47.
Attorneys at law, §50-48.

HEARINGS —Cont'd
Farm name registration applications, §80-36.
Firearms rights, restoration.
Hearing procedure, §14-415.4(f).
Food, drug and cosmetic act.
Procedures, §106-139(d).
Foreign judgments.
Motion for enforcement of foreign judgment, §1C-1705(b).
Foresters.
Charges against registrants, §89B-13.
Gasoline and oil inspection.
Cancellation of license, §119-19.
Gasoline tax.
Licenses.
Cancellation of license, §105-449.76.
General assembly.
Committees.
Examination of witnesses, §§120-19.1, 120-19.2.
Fees and expenses of witness, §120-19.3.
Geologists.
Code of professional conduct.
Revision and amendment to code, §89E-16.
Disciplinary procedures, §89E-20(a).
Global TransPark authority.
Bond issues, §63A-12.
Grade crossings.
Elimination or safeguarding of crossings, §136-20(b).
Guardians.
Appointment of guardians.
Incompetent persons, §35A-1212.
Minors, §35A-1223.
Motions in the cause, §35A-1207(c).
Sterilization of mentally ill or retarded ward.
Mental necessity, petition for consent, §35A-1245(d).
Habeas corpus.
Summary hearing of issues, §17-32.
Hazardous waste facilities.
Conduct of public hearing prior to issuance of permit, §130A-294(f).
Petition to preempt local ordinance, §130A-293(c).
Health care facilities.
Certificates of need.
Contested case hearing, §131E-188(a).
Health permits and program participation.
Suspension or revocation, §130A-23(c), (d).
Highways, roads and streets.
County public roads incorporated into state highway system.
Filing of complaints, §136-64.
Hospital districts.
Petition for formation of hospital district, §131E-42.
Hospitals.
Administrative procedure.
Contested case hearing petition time limit, §131E-2.
Licenses, §131E-78(b1).
Rate schedules, §58-65-45.
Housemovers.
Revocation of license for unsafe practices, §20-374(b).
Housing authorities and projects.
Creation of authority, §157-4.
Counties, §157-33.
Regional housing authority.
Creation of authority, §157-39.4.
Decreasing area of operation, §157-39.3.
Increasing area of operation, §157-39.2.

HEARINGS —Cont'd
Impaired driving.
Chemical analysis of impairing substances in blood.
Refusal to submit to test.
Hearing before division, §20-16.2(d).
Hearing on record in superior court, §20-16.2(e).
Sentencing hearing, §20-179.
Income tax refunds.
Anticipation loans, §53-248(d).
Incompetence, determination of.
Incompetence determined in another state, §35A-1113.
Interim guardian, appointment, §35A-1114(c), (d).
Place of hearing, §35A-1112(a).
Rights of petitioner and respondents, §35A-1112(b).
Time for holding, §35A-1108(a).
Multidisciplinary evaluation ordered, extension of time, §35A-1108(b).
Incompetence, restoration, §35A-1130(b), (c).
Infractions.
Procedure for hearing and disposition, §§15A-1111 to 15A-1118.
See INFRACTIONS.
Injunctions, §§1-494, 1-495.
Extension, modification or vacation.
Applications, §1-498.
Temporary restraining order, §1A-1 Rule 65(b).
Innocence claim inquiry.
Judicial review by three-judge panel, §15A-1469.
Proceedings before full commission.
Public hearings, §15A-1468(a).
Closure to public and victim, §15A-1468(b).
Insurance adjusters.
Public adjusters.
Denial of license application or refusal to renew license, §58-33A-45(b).
Insurance commissioner, §58-2-20.
Accident and health insurance.
Withdrawal of approval of forms, §58-51-95(e).
Appeals.
Rules for hearing of, §58-2-52(a), (c).
Filing of approvals and disapprovals.
Agency decision for certain purposes, §58-2-53.
Hearing officers, designating, §58-2-55.
Rates, §58-40-105(a).
Applicable procedural provisions, §58-2-52(b).
Imposition of penalties or suspension of licenses, §58-40-110(c).
Unfair trade practices, §58-63-25.
Insurance companies.
Annual audited financial reports.
Annual audit by certified public accountant.
CPA qualified, §58-10-210(f).
Exemption from part.
Request denied, §58-10-260(a).
Refusal to approve formation or initial license, §58-7-37(d).
Risk based capital requirements.
Confidential hearing on commissioner's determination, §58-12-30.
Insurance information privacy violations, §58-39-80(b).
Insurance rates, §58-40-105(a).
Rate bureau.
Disapproval of rates, §58-36-20(a).
Violations of provisions.
Imposition of penalty or suspension of license, §58-40-110(c).

HEARINGS —Cont'd
Insurance supervision, rehabilitation and liquidation.
Claims denial, §58-30-205(b).
Confidentiality of hearings, §58-30-70.
Seizure order by court.
Hearing and review, §58-30-65(e), (f).
Insurance unfair trade practices, §58-63-25(b), (c).
Commissioner's powers and duties as to, §58-63-25(d).
Immunity from prosecution, §58-63-60.
Notice, §58-63-25(a).
Service, §58-63-25(e).
Powers and duties of commissioner as to, §58-63-25(d).
Undefined practices, §58-63-40(a).
Witnesses.
Immunity from prosecution, §58-63-60.
Powers of commissioner as to, §58-63-25(d).
International commercial arbitration and conciliation.
Closing at conclusion of evidence, §1-567.54(f).
Confidentiality of matters, §1-567.54(d).
Experts.
Participation in, §1-567.56(b).
Held at appropriate stage of proceedings, §1-567.54(a).
In camera, held in, §1-567.54(d).
Notice for purposes of inspection of property or documents, §1-567.54(b).
Record or transcript, agreement on, §1-567.54(e).
Service of statements, documents or other information, §1-567.54(c).
Tribunal to decide whether to hold, §1-567.54(a).
Interpreters.
Hearing impaired.
Appointment authorized, §8B-2.
Interrogatories to discover assets of judgment debtors.
Hearing before court or judge to answer oral questions concerning property, §1-352.1.
Investment advisers.
Public hearing, §78C-30(g).
Judicial standards commission.
Disciplinary hearing.
Burden of proof, rights of respondent, JudStdsComm Rule 18.
Ordering, time for holding, notice, conduct, JudStdsComm Rule 17.
Rules of evidence, JudStdsComm Rule 20.
Witnesses, JudStdsComm Rule 19.
Disciplinary hearings.
Due process protections, §7A-377(a).
Not confidential, §7A-377(a5).
Juvenile hearings.
See JUVENILE HEARINGS.
Lake lure marine commission.
Public hearing on creation, §77-81.
Regulations applicable to lake and shoreline area.
Public hearing required, §77-87(a).
Land policy act.
Council, §113A-153(d).
Legislative ethics committee.
Investigation of legislators, §120-103.1(i).
Liens.
Possessory liens on personal property.
Enforcement by sale.
Motor vehicles, §44A-4(b).
Limited driving privileges, §20-179.3(d).
Livestock dealer licensing, §106-418.12.

HEARINGS —Cont'd
Livestock market permits, §106-406.
Local ABC boards.
  Budget hearing, §18B-702(f).
    Notice, §18B-702(e).
  Removal hearing, §18B-704.
Local government finance.
  Bond issues.
    Application to commission for approval,
      §159-52(b).
  Bond order, §159-57.
  Budget hearings, §159-12(b).
Magistrates.
  Suspension of magistrate, §7A-173(c).
Medicaid.
  Contested cases.
    Appeals by recipients.
      Request for hearing, §108A-70.9A(d).
    Simplified procedure, §108A-70.9B(b).
Medical and dental service corporations.
  Rate schedule.
    Revision of existing schedule or establishment
      of new schedule, §58-65-45.
Mental health, developmental disability,
  substance abuse.
  Involuntary commitment.
    See MENTAL HEALTH, DEVELOPMENTAL
      DISABILITY, SUBSTANCE ABUSE.
  Suspension of new admissions to licensed facility.
    Contesting, §122C-23(g).
Metropolitan sewerage districts.
  Creation of district, §162A-66.
  Inclusion of additional political subdivision or
    unincorporated area, §162A-68(b).
Metropolitan water districts.
  Creation of district, §162A-33.
  Inclusion of additional political subdivision or
    unincorporated area, §162A-35.
Milk and milk products.
  Testing dairy products.
    Revocation of license, §106-267.3.
Mine safety and health.
  Accident investigations, §74-24.7(c).
  Modification of safety and health standards,
    §74-24.5.
Missing persons.
  Action for appointment of permanent receiver,
    §28C-6.
Mortgages and deeds of trust.
  Foreclosure sales.
    Validation where hearing not provided,
      §45-21.45.
Motion for appropriate relief, §15A-1420(c).
Motor clubs and associations.
  Denial of license.
    Notice of right to hearing, §58-69-15.
    Right to hearing, §58-69-25.
Motor vehicle captive finance sources.
  Hearings on violations, §20-308.16(b), (c).
Motor vehicle dealer licensing.
  Denial, §§20-295, 20-296.
  Notice, §20-305.3.
  Powers of commissioner, §20-301(c).
  Suspension or revocation, §20-296.
Motor vehicle manufacturer licensing.
  Denial, §§20-295, 20-296.
  Notice, §20-305.3.
  Powers of commissioner, §20-301(c).
  Suspension or revocation, §20-296.
Moving companies.
  Revocation of license for unsafe practices,
    §20-374(b).

HEARINGS —Cont'd
Municipal assessments.
  Preliminary assessment rule, §§160A-227,
    160A-228.
  Preliminary resolution, §§160A-224, 160A-225.
Municipal building inspection.
  Periodic inspection of target areas and housing.
    Public hearing, §160A-424(b).
Municipal charter amendment, §160A-102.
Municipal personnel board, §160A-165.
Municipal service district.
  Abolition of district, §160A-541.
  Consolidation of districts, §160A-539(c).
  Establishment, §160A-537(c).
  Extension of district, §160A-538(d).
  Reduction of district, §160A-538.1(a).
Municipal zoning.
  Procedure for adopting or amending ordinance,
    §160A-364(a).
Mutual burial associations.
  Dispute over liability for benefits, §90-210.102.
Nonprofit corporations.
  Receiver appointment in judicial dissolution,
    §55A-14-32(a).
North Carolina's eastern region.
  Public hearing on creation of region, §158-33(b).
Nursing homes.
  Contesting penalty, §131E-129(e).
Oil and gas conservation.
  See OIL AND GAS CONSERVATION.
Optometrists.
  Disciplinary proceedings, §90-121.3.
Ordinances.
  Public hearing by council.
    Amendment of charter by ordinance, §160A-102.
  Sunday-closing ordinances.
    Limitations on enactment, §160A-191.
Parental authority over juvenile.
  Order directing juvenile to appear before court,
    §7B-3404.
Parking authorities.
  Creation of authority, §160A-552.
Parole.
  See PAROLE.
Personnel system.
  Grievances and disciplinary action, §126-37(a).
  Records.
    Privacy of state employee personnel records.
      Access to material in file for agency hearing,
        §126-29.
Pesticide board.
  Public hearings, §143-461.
Physicians and surgeons.
  Evidence, §90-14.6(a) to (d).
  Licenses.
    Administrative law judges, §90-14.5(a1).
    Decision of committee, §90-14.5(c).
    Denial of license, §90-14.1.
    Depositions, §90-14.5(b).
    Failure to appear for hearing.
      Procedure upon, §90-14.7.
    Hearing committee designation, §90-14.5(a).
    Hearing officers, §90-14.5(d).
    Revocation or suspension of license, §90-14.2(a).
  Record of proceeding required to be made,
    §90-14.6(a).
  Standard of proof.
    Preponderance of evidence, §90-14.6(e).
Police.
  Removal of unfit officers.
    Suspension pending hearing, §128-19.

HEARINGS —Cont'd
Post-release supervision, §15A-1368.6.
Preneed funeral contracts and funds,
§90-210.69(e).
Prisons and prisoners.
Compensation to persons erroneously convicted of
felonies.
Nature of hearing, §148-83.
Private personnel services.
Complaints, §95-47.9(c).
Probation, §15A-1345.
Property taxes.
Public utilities.
Review of appraisal and apportionment,
§105-342(a) to (d).
Public schools.
Education of children with disabilities.
Impartial due process hearing, §115C-109.6.
Reassignment of students, §115C-369.
School budget.
Public hearing by board of education,
§115C-428(b).
Teachers.
Career teachers.
Dismissal or demotion, §115C-325.
Public utilities.
Bus companies.
Discontinuance or reduction in service,
§62-262.2(b).
Rates.
Change of rates, §62-134(b), (c).
Price flexibility or detariffing of services,
§62-134(i).
Scope of rate hearings, §62-137.
Rate bureau.
Disapproval of rates, §58-36-20(a).
Real estate appraisal management companies.
Summary suspension or postponement of
registration, §93E-2-8(b).
Real estate brokers.
Real estate education and recovery fund.
Applications for payment from, §93A-18.
Regional transportation authorities.
Resolution creating.
Public hearing required, notice, publication,
§160A-633(a).
**Remote testimony in civil cases or special
proceedings.**
Developmentally disabled or mentally retarded.
Determining whether to allow, §8C-1 Rule
616(c).
Retailers and wholesale merchants.
Certificates of registration.
Sales and use tax.
Revocations of certificates, §105-164.29(d).
Revenue department.
Secretary of revenue.
Proposed rulemaking, §105-262(b).
Rural fire protection districts.
Changes in area of district, §69-25.11.
Sales and use tax.
Certificates of registration.
Wholesale merchants and retailers.
Revocations of certificates, §105-164.29(d).
Sanitary districts.
Dissolution of certain sanitary districts.
No outstanding indebtedness districts,
§130A-72.
Extension of district.
Procedure for extension, §130A-69.

HEARINGS —Cont'd
Savings and loan associations.
Applicable law, §54B-6.
Incorporation, §54B-13(b), (d).
Notice, §54B-13(c).
Supervisory control by commissioner.
Time for, procedure, §54B-68(a).
Savings banks.
Conduct of hearings.
Applicable law, §54C-6.
Removal of directors, officers and employees,
§54C-82(a).
Supervisory control, §54C-81(a).
Securities regulation.
Cease and desist orders, §78A-47(b).
Public hearings, §78A-49(g).
Seeds.
Notice of violations of article, §106-277.23.
Revocation or refusal of license for cause,
§106-277.19.
Sentence and punishment.
Impaired driving.
Sentencing hearing, §20-179.
Proceedings at sentencing hearing, §15A-1334(b).
Sentence hearing in other district, §15A-1334(c).
Time of sentencing hearing, §15A-1334(a).
Setoff debt collection.
Appeals from, §105A-9.
Contest by debtor of setoff by local agency,
§105A-5(c), (d).
Contested claim of state agency, §105A-8(b), (c).
Sheriffs.
Removal of unfit officers.
Suspension pending hearing, §128-19.
Social security.
Coverage of governmental employees under Title
II of social security act.
Plans for coverage of employees of political
subdivisions, §135-23(b).
Soil and water conservation districts.
Adoption of land-use regulations, §139-9.
Creation of districts, §139-5(c).
Discontinuance of districts, §139-13.
Payment of expenses, §139-5(b).
Solid waste management.
Application for permit, public hearing,
§130A-294(b1).
Special education.
Education of children with disabilities.
Impartial due process hearing, §115C-109.6.
**State department and agency personnel file
access.**
Access to material in file for agency hearing,
§126-29.
Sunday-closing ordinances.
Limitations on enactment, §160A-191.
Temporary restraining order, §1A-1 Rule 65(b).
Termination of parental rights proceedings.
Adjudicatory hearing, §7B-1109.
Permanent placement review, §7B-908.
Pretrial hearing, §7B-1108.1.
Special hearing to determine issues raised by
petition and answer, §7B-1106(b).
Torrens system registration.
Certificate.
Hearing by clerk of superior court, §43-17.4.
Referral of petition in answer to examiner,
§43-11(a).
Removal of land from system, §43-56.
Tramways.
Passenger tramways.
Commissioner of labor, §95-120.

HEARINGS —Cont'd
Transfer of juvenile to superior court for prosecution as adult.
Probable cause hearing, §7B-2202.
Transfer hearing, §7B-2203.
Unemployment compensation.
Employment security division.
Hearing to determine status, rights and liabilities of employers and employing units, §96-4(q).
Appeal of board decisions, §96-4(q), (r).
Claims procedures not limited by provisions, §96-4(v).
Force and effect of determination by division, §96-4(s).
Notices of hearings, §96-4(u).
Rules for conduct of hearings, §96-4(t).
Urban redevelopment.
Powers of redevelopment commissions generally, §160A-512.
Project financing.
Development financing plan.
Public hearing on adoption, §160A-515.1(g).
Redevelopment plans.
Commission, §160A-513(e).
Governing body, §160A-513(h).
Veterans' guardianship act.
Accounts, §34-10.
Water and air resources, §§143-215.4, 143-215.5.
Civil penalties.
Assessment by local government, §143-215.6A(k).
Proposed adoption and assignment of classifications, §143-214.1.
Revision to water quality standards, §143-214.3(a).
Water and sewer authorities.
Rates, fee, charges.
Public hearing, §162A-9(a).
Water resource use.
Capacity use areas, §143-215.15.
Waters and watercourses.
Withdrawing, diverting or obtaining water.
Surface water transfers.
Draft determination on certificate issuance, §143-215.22L(j).
Well construction.
Appeals, §87-92.
Wholesale merchants and retailers.
Certificates of registration.
Sales and use tax.
Revocations of certificates, §105-164.29(d).
Wine distribution agreements.
Amendment, termination, cancellation or nonrenewal.
Good cause, §18B-1205(c), (d).
Workers' compensation.
See WORKERS' COMPENSATION.
Work first program.
Mismanagement of assistance, appointment of personal representative, §108A-37(b).

HEARSAY.
Attacking creditability of declarant, §8C-1 Rule 806.
Civil no-contact orders.
Prior sexual activity of victim inadmissible.
Hearsay exception, §50C-4.
Definitions, §8C-1 Rule 801(a) to (c).
Exceptions.
Admissions by party-opponent, §8C-1 Rule 801(d).

HEARSAY —Cont'd
Exceptions —Cont'd
Availability of declarant immaterial, §8C-1 Rule 803.
Declarant unavailable, §8C-1 Rule 804.
Hearsay within hearsay, §8C-1 Rule 805.
Probable cause hearings, §15A-611(b).
Rule generally, §8C-1 Rule 802.
Supporting creditability of declarant, §8C-1 Rule 806.

HEART DISEASE.
Automated external defibrillator (AED), §90-21.15.
Food, drug and cosmetic act.
Drug or device, false advertising, §106-138(b).
Jail prisoner unconscious or semiconscious.
Duty of custodial personnel.
Reasonable effort to determine if prisoner wearing emergency alert symbol, §153A-225.1(a) to (c).
Justus-Warren heart disease and stroke prevention task force, §143B-216.60.

HEATERS.
Public assistance.
Weatherization assistance program, §108A-70.30.

HEATING CONTRACTORS.
Generally, §§87-16 to 87-27.1.
See PLUMBING, HEATING AND FIRE SPRINKLER CONTRACTORS.

HEATING INSPECTORS.
County inspection departments, §§153A-350 to 153A-375.
See COUNTY INSPECTION DEPARTMENTS.

HEATING OIL.
Leaking petroleum underground storage tank cleanup, §§143-215.94A to 143-215.94Y.
See UNDERGROUND PETROLEUM STORAGE TANKS.
Light-traffic road weight and load limitations.
Exceptions to vehicles transporting for on-premises use, §20-118(c).

HEATING SYSTEMS.
Dwelling unit leased as rental property.
City or county requirements, §160A-443.1.

HEAT PUMPS.
Energy star qualified products.
Sales and use tax holiday, §105-164.13D(a).

HEDGING TRANSACTION.
Insurance companies.
Authority to enter into, §58-7-205(d).

HEIMLICH MANEUVER.
Basic education program, §115C-81(c).

HEIRS.
Agreements with heirs to recover share of decedents' estates.
Provisions governing, §28A-22-11.
Ascertainment of heirs or devisees.
Jurisdiction.
Clerks of superior court jurisdiction in estate proceedings, §28A-2-4(a).
Construed to be "children" in certain limitations, §41-6.
Declaratory judgments, §1-255.
Defined, §§28A-1-1(3), 29-2.
Guardian ad litem.
Appointment for unknown heir, §28A-22-3.

HEIRS —Cont'd
Limitations on failure of issue, §41-4.
Renunciation of succession, right to renounce, §31B-1.
Sale, lease or mortgage of real property, §28A-17-12.
Service of process, §28A-13-3.
Unknown heirs.
Special proceedings prior to distribution, §28A-22-3.
Waste.
Action by heirs, §1-537.
Wills generally.
See WILLS.

HELMET LAW.
All-terrain vehicles, §20-171.19(a).
Electric service employee engaged in power line inspection, §20-171.19(a2).
Minors, §20-171.19(a1).
Child bicycle safety act, §§20-171.6 to 20-171.9.
Motorcycles and mopeds.
Operators and passengers, §20-140.4(a).
Skateboard parks.
Wearing required, §99E-23.

H.E. MCCULLOCH GRANTS.
Evidence.
Title under grants, §8-16.

HEMLOCK.
Taking, etc., of certain wild plants from land of another, §14-129.

HEMLOCK BLUFFS STATE NATURAL AREA.
Removal of land from state nature and historic preserve, §143-260.10C.

HEMODIALYSIS UNITS.
Certificates of need generally, §§131E-175 to 130E-191.1.
See HEALTH CARE FACILITIES.

HEMOGLOBIN C TRAIT.
Employment discrimination against persons possessing hemoglobin C trait, §95-28.1.
Life insurance policies not to be denied solely on grounds of, §58-58-25.

HEMP SEED.
Standard weight and measure, §81A-42.

HENDERSON COUNTY.
Ambulances.
Obtaining ambulance services without intending to pay, §14-111.2.
Ambulance service.
Attachment or garnishment and lien for, §§44-51.4 to 44-51.8.
Board of county commissioners.
Filling vacancies on board, §153A-27.1.
Condemnation or acquisition of land by local government unit outside county.
Consent of board of commissioners necessary, §153A-15.
Coroner elected as nominee of political party.
Filling vacancy in office, §152-1.
Counties generally.
See COUNTIES.
Dog collars.
Unlawful removal of electronic dog collars, §14-401.17.
Foxes, open seasons for taking.
Wildlife resources commission authorized to continue from year to year, §113-291.4(f1).

HENDERSON COUNTY —Cont'd
Game laws, local acts not repealed, §113-133.1(e).
Housing authority commissioners.
Tenant as commissioner, exemption from provision of law allowing, §157-5.
Oil, gas or mineral claims.
Certain ancient claims extinguished, preservation, procedure, §1-42.3(a) to (d).
Real estate mortgage loans.
Interest, commissions and repayment, §45-43.
Registration of deeds.
Tax certification, no delinquent taxes due, §161-31(b).
School property.
Acquisition and improvement, §153A-158.1.
Sheriff.
Vacancy, performance of duties until vacancy filled, §162-5.1.
Small city mixed beverage elections.
Inapplicability of provisions to, §18B-600(e1).
Special school tax, election to abolish.
Petition required, §115C-505.
Tax deeds in Henderson.
Recitals in tax deeds, §8-22.
Tax sales, notices by publication validated.
Inapplicability of provisions, §47-108.24.
Western North Carolina Development Association, Inc.
Appropriation of funds to, §153A-447(a), (b).
Western North Carolina regional economic development commission, §§158-8.1 to 158-8.8.

HENRY MCCULLOCH.
Evidence.
Title under grants.
Conveyances, §8-17.

HEPATICA.
Taking, etc., of certain wild plants from land of another, §14-129.

HEPATITIS.
Adult care home.
Infection prevention requirements, §131D-4.4A.
Arrest.
Detention of defendant for testing, §15A-534.3.
Blood banks.
Selection of donors.
Risk of transmission of agents that may cause hepatitis to be minimized, §90-220.13.
Defendant accused of offense involving sexual intercourse.
Testing on victim's request, §15A-615(a).
Defendant in custody of division of adult correction, §15A-615(c).
Order requiring, §15A-615(b).
Handling of dead body of person infected with hepatitis B.
Notification to persons handling, §130A-395(a), (c).

HERBERT C. BONNER BRIDGE.
Accelerated construction project.
Contract for accelerated construction, §136-89.183B(a).
Report by department, §136-89.183B(c).
Termini location, §136-89.183B(b).

HEROIN.
Controlled substances generally, §§90-86 to 90-113.8.
See DRUGS AND CONTROLLED SUBSTANCES.

HEROIN —Cont'd

Food, drug and cosmetic act.
Drugs deemed misbranded, §106-134.
Schedule I controlled substance, §90-89.
Trafficking in, §90-95(h), (i).

HERRING FESTIVAL.

Town of Jamesville herring festival.
Official state festival, §145-34.

HERTFORD COUNTY.

Ambulance service.
Attachment or garnishment and lien for, §§44-51.4 to 44-51.8.
Cropper or tenant refusing to perform terms of contract.
Forfeiture of right of possession to premises, §42-27.
Game laws, local acts not repealed, §113-133.1(e).
Grants in navigable waters, registration, §113-205(a).
Housing authority commissioners.
Tenant as commissioner, exemption from provision of law allowing, §157-5.
Low-income housing tax credits.
Qualified building eligible for credit, §105-129.41(c).
Maps in special proceedings, recording of photographic copies, §47-32.
Violation as misdemeanor, inapplicability of provisions, §47-32.2.
North Carolina's northeast commission, §§158-8.2 to 158-8.8.
Officers compensated from fees.
Statement to be rendered, §128-13.
Probates and registration orders before clerks of inferior courts validated, §47-59.
Registration of deeds.
Tax certification, no delinquent taxes due, §161-31(b).
Tax elections for industrial development purposes, §§158-16 to 158-24.
Tax sales, notices by publication validated.
Inapplicability of provisions, §47-108.24.
Wastewater systems.
Innovative septic tank systems.
Ordinance billing fee as property tax, §130A-343.1(c).
Watermelon festival.
Adoption as official Northeastern North Carolina watermelon festival, §145-16(a).
Wild plants, taking of certain plants from land of another.
Inapplicability of provisions, §14-129.

HETEROLOGOUS.

Artificial insemination.
Status of child born, §49A-1.

HICKORY.

Room occupancy tax.
Uniform provisions.
Authorized to levy, §160A-215(g).
Generally, §160A-215.
Satellite annexation.
Limitation on area of satellite corporate limits, inapplicability, §160A-58.1(b).

HICKORY NUTS.

Standard weight and measure, §81A-42.

HIGH BLOOD PRESSURE.

Food, drug and cosmetic act.
Drug or device, false advertising, §106-138(b).

HIGH COST HOME LOANS, §24-1.1E.

HIGHER EDUCATION.

Bonds, §§116D-1 to 116D-49.
Capital facilities finance.
Private capital facilities finance act.
Institutions for higher education and elementary and secondary education, §§159D-35 to 159D-57.
See CAPITAL FACILITIES FINANCE AGENCY.
Community colleges.
See COMMUNITY COLLEGES.
Education cabinet, §116C-1.
Education commission, §§143-261 to 143-266.
See EDUCATION COMMISSION.
General provisions.
See COLLEGES AND UNIVERSITIES.
Private capital facilities finance act.
Institutions for higher education and elementary and secondary education, §§159D-35 to 159D-57.
See CAPITAL FACILITIES FINANCE AGENCY.
University of North Carolina.
See UNIVERSITY OF NORTH CAROLINA.
University of North Carolina School of the Arts, §§116-63 to 116-69.1.
See UNIVERSITY OF NORTH CAROLINA SCHOOL OF THE ARTS.

HIGHER EDUCATION BONDS, §§116D-1 to 116D-49.

Community colleges facilities finance, §§116D-41 to 116D-49.
Authorization, §116D-43.
Definitions, §116D-42.
Designation of capital facilities, §116D-44.
Faith and credit, §116D-45.
Issuance, §116D-46.
Application of proceeds, §116D-46(d).
Community college bonds fund, §116D-46(g).
Manner of sale, §116D-46(c).
Refunding bonds and notes, §116D-46(f).
Repayment of notes, §116D-46(e).
Signatures, §116D-46(b).
Terms and conditions, §116D-46(a).
Other agreements, §116D-48.
Procurement of capital facilities, §116D-49.
Short title, §116D-41.
Variable rate demand bonds and notes, §116D-47.
Amount, §116D-47(b).
Generally, §116D-47(a).
Definitions, §116D-1.
Financing capital facilities, §§116D-6 to 116D-13.
Authorization of bonds and notes, §116D-8.
Definitions, §116D-7.
Designation of facilities, §116D-9.
Faith and credit, §116D-10.
Issuance, §116D-11.
Application of proceeds, §116D-11(d).
Expenses, §116D-11(c).
Form and denomination, §116D-11(b).
Manner of sale, §116D-11(c).
Notes, §116D-11(e).
Refunding bonds and notes, §116D-11(f).
Registration, §116D-11(b).
Repayment, §116D-11(e).
Signatures, §116D-11(b).
Terms and conditions, §116D-11(a).
University improvement bonds fund, §116D-11(g).

HIGHER EDUCATION BONDS —Cont'd
Financing capital facilities —Cont'd
Other agreements, §116D-13.
Short title, §116D-6.
Variable rate bonds and notes, §116D-12(a), (b).
General provisions, §116D-2.
Improvements to facilities, §§116D-21 to
116D-31.
Additional and alternative method of doing things
authorized, §116D-31.
Board of governors, §116D-24.
Consultation with joint legislative commission on
governmental operations, §116D-25.
Credit and taxing power of state, §116D-23.
Definitions, §116D-22.
Issuance, §116D-26.
Approval, §116D-26(b).
Authority, §116D-26(a).
Generally, §116D-26(f).
Proceeds, §116D-26(d).
Temporary bonds, §116D-26(e).
Term, §116D-26(c).
Obligated resources, §§116D-28.
State pledge, §116D-28(b).
Sufficient resources, §116D-28(a).
Powers of board of governors, §116D-24.
Purpose, §116D-21.
Refunding bonds, §116D-30.
Trust agreement, §116D-27.
Insurance, §116D-27(c).
Remedies, §116D-27(d).
Securing bonds, §116D-27(a).
Trust funds, §116D-27(b).
Vesting powers in committee, §116D-29.
Inconsistent laws.
Inapplicability to chapter, §116D-2(d).
Investment eligibility, §116D-2(c).
**Minority and historically underutilized
businesses,** §116D-4.
Compliance, §116D-4(a).
Contracting opportunities, §116D-4(b).
Reports, §116D-3.
Board of governors, §116D-3(a).
Community colleges, §116D-3(c).
Treasurer, §116D-3(b).
Signatures, §116D-2(a).
Financing capital facilities.
Issuance of bonds, §116D-11(b).
Tax exemption, §116D-2(b).

HIGHER EDUCATION, STATE BOARD OF,
§116-158.

HIGHLAND SCHOOL IN MACON COUNTY.
Sale of merchandise by governmental units.
Exceptions to provisions, §66-58(b).

HIGH OCCUPANCY VEHICLE LANES,
§20-146.2.

HIGH POINT.
Room occupancy tax.
Uniform provisions.
Authorized to levy, §160A-215(g).
Generally, §160A-215.
Traffic control photographic systems,
§160A-300.1(d).

HIGH-RISE BUILDINGS.
Special safety to life requirements applicable,
§143-138(i).

HIGH ROCK LAKE.
Marine commission, §§77-50 to 77-58.

HIGH ROCK LAKE —Cont'd
Uwharrie regional resources act, §§153C-1 to
153C-4.

HIGH ROCK LAKE MARINE COMMISSION,
§§77-50 to 77-58.
Administrative provisions, powers and duties,
§77-55(a) to (f).
Budgetary and accounting procedures, §77-53.
Commissioners.
Appointment, §77-52.
Compensation, §77-53.
Election of officers, §77-54.
Terms, §77-52.
Creation, §77-51.
Criminal prosecutions.
Venue, §77-58(b).
Definitions, §77-50.
Law enforcement officers.
Authority, §77-58(a).
Extraterritorial jurisdiction, §77-58(c), (d).
Meetings, §77-54.
Officers.
Election by commissioners, §77-54.
Ordinances.
Creation of commission, §77-51.
Effective date, §77-56(b).
Evidence.
Admissibility in court, §77-56(b).
Filing requirements, §77-56(a).
Rules and regulations, §77-57.
Shoreline areas.
Rules and regulations, §77-57.

**HIGH SCHOOL APPRENTICESHIP
ENROLLEES.**
Number of hours of work per week, §95-25.5(c).

HIGH SCHOOL ATHLETIC ASSOCIATION.
**Tort claims against state departments and
agencies,** §§143-291 to 143-300.1A.
See CLAIMS AGAINST THE STATE.

HIGH SCHOOLS.
See SCHOOLS AND EDUCATION.

HIGH SCHOOL TO WORK PARTNERSHIPS.
Duty of local boards of education to facilitate,
§115C-47.

HIGH-SPEED INTERNET ACCESS.
Cities providing communications services,
§§160A-340 to 160A-340.6.
See MUNICIPAL UTILITIES.

HIGH-SPEED RAIL TRANSPORTATION.
**Virginia-North Carolina interstate high-speed
rail compact,** §§136-220 to 136-222.

HIGH WATER MARK.
**Seaward boundary of private property
adjoining ocean,** §77-20(a) to (e).

HIGHWAY PATROL, §§20-184 to 20-196.4.
Added positions.
Filling, §20-185(i).
Aircraft.
Use of aircraft to discover certain motor vehicle
violations, §20-196.2.
Appointment of members, §20-185(a).
Arrest powers, §§20-49, 20-188.
Assault with deadly weapon.
Law enforcement officer assaulted with deadly
weapon, §14-34.2.
Awards.
Certificates of award, §20-187.1(c).

HIGHWAY PATROL —Cont'd
Awards —Cont'd
Committee.
Appointment of members, §20-187.1(a).
Composition, §20-187.1(a).
Duties, §20-187.1(d).
Meetings, §20-187.1(a).
Recommendations, §20-187.1(d).
Term of members, §20-187.1(a).
Qualifications, §20-187.1(b).
Recommendations, §20-187.1(d), (e).
Rules and regulations, §20-187.1(f).
Badges and service sidearms of deceased members, §20-187.2(a).
Commanding officer.
Appointment by governor, §20-185(a).
Awards.
Committee.
Appointment of members, §20-187.1(a).
Rules and regulations, §20-187.1(f).
Composition, §20-185(a).
Death benefits act, §§143-166.1 to 143-166.7.
See DEATH BENEFITS.
Defense of members and other state law enforcement officers in civil action, §20-194(b).
Department of public safety.
Arms.
Furnishing, §20-190.
Expenses of highway patrol.
Providing for, §20-190.
Highway patrol section.
Establishment in department, §20-184.
Motor vehicles.
Furnishing, §20-190.
Transfer to department, §143A-242.
Uniforms.
Adoption and furnishing, §20-190.
Duties, §20-188.
Election abstracts.
Delivery to state board of elections, §163-182.6(a).
Escort fee.
Oversized and hazardous shipment, §20-196.4.
Excess coverage over commercial liability insurance up to limit of tort claims act, §20-194(c).
Expenses.
Department of public safety to provide for, §20-190.
Firearms.
Assault with firearm upon law enforcement officer, §14-34.2.
Change of type of firearm by active member, §20-187.2(b).
Deceased or retiring members entitled to service sidearms, §20-187.2(a).
Department of public safety to furnish, §20-190.
Firearms and other weapons.
Active members.
Change of type, §20-187.2(b).
Deceased or retiring members.
Service sidearms, §20-187.2(a).
Furnishing to members, §20-190.
Surplus weapons.
Sale, trade or disposal, §143-63.1(d).
Governor.
Appointment of commanding officer, §20-185(a).
Patrolmen assigned to governor's office, §20-189.
Highways.
Powers and duties as to patrolling of highways, §20-188.

HIGHWAY PATROL —Cont'd
Judgments rendered as result of civil action against member.
Payment as expense of administration up to limit provided in tort claims act, §20-194(b).
Litter enforcement, prevention, removal efforts.
Detailed information delivered to governor, time, §147-12(b).
Local officers.
Cooperation, §20-195.
Motor carrier enforcement officers.
Supplemental authority, §20-49.2.
Motor vehicle accidents.
Notice of reportable accident to highway patrol.
Accident occurring outside city or town, §20-166.1(a).
Motor vehicle license plates.
Retired highway patrol.
Special plates, §20-79.4(b).
Special license plates, §20-79.4(b).
Motor vehicles.
Assignment of new highway patrol cars, §20-190.3.
Color, §20-190.
Furnishing to members, §20-190.
Horns and warning devices, §20-125(b).
New highway patrol cars.
Assignment, §20-190.3.
Percentage of marked vehicles, §20-190.
Signs showing highways patrolled by, §20-190.2.
Red lights, §20-130.1(b).
Sirens, §20-190.1.
Oath of office of members, §20-186.
Offenses against.
Aggravating factor in sentencing, §15A-1340.16.
Office space.
Use, §20-191.
Overall performance.
Pay and promotions based on, §20-187.3(a).
Oversized and hazardous shipment escort fee, §20-196.4(a) to (c).
Escort fee account, §20-196.4(d).
Police authority of members, §20-49.
Powers, §20-188.
Radio system, §20-196.
Retirement.
Badges and service sidearms of retiring members, §20-187.2(a).
General provisions.
See LAW-ENFORCEMENT OFFICERS' RETIREMENT SYSTEM.
Motor vehicle license plates.
Retired highway patrol.
Special plates, §20-79.4(b).
Special license plates, §20-79.4(b).
Rules and regulations.
Awards, §20-187.1(f).
Secretary of public safety, §20-187.
Salaries, §20-185(a).
Overall performance.
Pay and promotions based on, §20-187.3(a).
Salary classes, ranges and longevity pay, subject to, §20-187.3(a).
Salary increases, §20-187.3(a).
Step in salary range.
Assigning members so that members not in lower range as members of same rank, §20-187.3(b).
Salary continuation plan, §§143-166.13 to 143-166.20.
See LAW ENFORCEMENT OFFICERS.

HIGHWAY PATROL —Cont'd
Sale of merchandise by governmental units.
Inapplicability of prohibition, §66-58(b).
Secretary of public safety.
Cooperation between patrol and local officers.
Encouraging, §20-195.
Orders, §20-187.
Rules and regulations, §20-187.
Supervision, direction and control of highway
patrol, §20-184.
Shifting of patrolmen from one district to
another, §20-192.
Sick leave.
Replacement of officer on final sick leave,
§126-8.2.
State bureau of investigation.
Cooperation of local enforcement officers, §114-17.
Supervisory personnel.
Percentage of total, §20-185(a).
Telephone line use in emergencies, §20-196.
Who may hold supervisory positions over sworn
members of patrol, §20-196.3.
Traffic citations.
Quotas prohibited, §20-187.3(a).
Transfer of personnel, §20-192.
Transfer to department of public safety,
§143A-242.
Uniforms, §20-190.
Unmarked highway patrol vehicles.
Percentage of marked vehicles, §20-190.
Sign showing highways patrolled by, §20-190.2.
Use of facilities, §20-191.
Workers' compensation.
Total incapacity.
Weekly compensation, §97-29(h).
Wrecker services.
Rotation wrecker list.
Charges for work performed, billing
requirements.
Agreement by wrecker services to be included
on list, §20-188.

HIGHWAY SIGNS.
AMBER alert system.
Overhead permanent changeable message boards,
§143B-1021(d).
Billboards.
Blue Ridge parkway.
Control of outdoor advertising, §§113A-165 to
113A-170.
See BLUE RIDGE PARKWAY.
Outdoor advertising control act, §§136-126 to
136-140.
See OUTDOOR ADVERTISING.
Blue Star memorial highway, §136-102.1.
Commercial signs prohibited, §136-32(a).
Controlled access facilities.
Fees for logo sign installation and maintenance,
§136-89.56.
Damaging or removing signs, §136-33(a).
Enforcement of section, §136-33(d).
Penalty for violation of provisions, §136-33(b1).
Possession of highway sign, §136-33(b).
Rewards, §136-33(c).
Installation and maintenance.
Contractor licensing requirements, §136-28.14.
Manufacture by division of adult corrections.
Exception to prohibition of sale of merchandise by
governmental units, §66-58(c).
Misleading signs prohibited, §136-32.1.

HIGHWAY SIGNS —Cont'd
Motorist services directional signs.
Removal of certain directional signs, displays and
devices.
Declaration of policy, §136-140.6.
Deferment procedures, §136-140.8.
Definitions, §136-140.7.
Exemption procedures, §136-140.8.
Policy declaration, §136-140.6.
Political signs in right-of-way.
Authority to place, §136-32(b).
Definition, §136-32(c).
Municipal regulation, §136-32(f).
Placement, location and permission, §136-32(d).
Unlawful removal, §136-32(e).
Protection of cattle, §136-33.1.
Removing signs, §136-33(a).
Enforcement of section, §136-33(d).
Penalty for violation of provisions, §136-33(b1).
Possession of highway sign, §136-33(b).
Rewards, §136-33(c).
Silver alert system.
Overhead permanent changeable message boards.
Making information available to motorists,
§143B-1022(d).
Speed zones.
Marking beginning of reduced speed zones,
§136-33.2A.
Necessary for enforcement of local ordinances,
§20-141.
Stop signs, §20-158.
Tourist-oriented directional sign program,
§§136-140.15 to 136-140.19.
Traffic signs.
See TRAFFIC SIGNS.
Uniform signs and other traffic control
devices, §136-30(a) to (e).
Warning signs.
Closing of state highways during construction.
Injury to barriers, warning signs, etc., §136-26.
Misleading signs prohibited, §136-32.1.
"Yield right-of-way" signs.
General provisions, §20-158.1.

HIGHWAYS, ROADS AND STREETS.
Abandonment.
Cartways, tramways or railways.
Manner of altering or abandoning, §136-70.
Controlled-access facilities.
Authority to abandon, §136-89.50.
Dedication of road or street.
Deemed abandoned if not used within fifteen
years, §136-96.
Road in secondary system.
Municipality, keeping open and assuming
responsibility.
Roads within one mile of corporate limits,
§136-63(b).
Request by board of county commissioners,
§136-63(a).
Segment of road and removal from state highway
system.
For maintenance.
Notice, §136-55.1(a).
Municipalities.
Authority to keep open and assume
maintenance.
Roads within one mile of corporate limits,
§136-55.1(b).

HIGHWAYS, ROADS AND STREETS —Cont'd
Actions.
County public roads incorporated into state
  highway system.
No court action against board of transportation,
  §136-59.
Administration department.
Test drilling or boring.
  Filing record of results with secretary of
    administration, §136-102.3.
Adopt-a-highway program, §136-140.1.
Adverse possession.
No title by possession of public ways, §1-45.
Turnpike companies.
  No title by possession of right of way, §1-44.
Advertising.
Blue Ridge parkway.
  Control of outdoor advertising, §§113A-165 to
    113A-170.
    See BLUE RIDGE PARKWAY.
Outdoor advertising control act, §§136-126 to
  136-140.
  See OUTDOOR ADVERTISING.
Airports.
Connection of state airports with public highway
  system.
  Powers of department of transportation,
    §136-18.
**Alcoholic beverages consumed on public road,
street, highway or sidewalk,** §18B-301(f).
All-terrain vehicles.
County and municipal employees.
  Use on certain highways, §20-171.24(a) to (e).
    Applicable counties and municipalities,
      §20-171.24(f).
Law enforcement officers and fire, rescue and
  emergency medical services.
  Use on certain highways, §20-171.23(a) to (f).
Operation on interstates and limited-access
  highways, §20-171.19(f).
Operation on public streets and highways,
  §20-171.19(e).
AMBER alert system.
Overhead permanent changeable message boards,
  §143B-1021(d).
American ex-prisoners of war highway,
  §136-102.1.
Appeals.
Cartways, church roads or mill roads.
  Special proceeding for establishment, alteration
    or discontinuance.
    Procedure for appeal, §136-68.
Condemnation proceedings.
  Right of appeal, §136-119.
County public roads incorporated into state
  highway system.
  Filing of complaints, §136-64.
Drainage of highway.
  Judgment of commissioners, §136-23.
Appropriations.
Highway appropriations, §143C-6-11.
Primary, secondary and urban road systems,
  §136-44.2.
Reports to appropriations committees of general
  assembly, §136-44.2B.
Archaeology.
Objects on highway right-of-way, §136-42.1.
Assessments.
Basis, §153A-206(b).
Municipalities, §160A-217.
Street light assessments, §153A-206.

HIGHWAYS, ROADS AND STREETS —Cont'd
Attorneys at law.
Condemnation proceedings.
  Employment of outside counsel by attorney
    general, §136-103.1.
Barriers.
Closing of state highways during construction.
  Injury to barriers, warning signs, etc., §136-26.
Beauty, §§136-122 to 136-125.
Litter prevention account, §136-125.1.
Bicycle and bikeways, §§136-71.6 to 136-71.12.
See BICYCLE AND BIKEWAY ACT.
Bids.
Electronic means, accepting bids by, §136-28.1(k).
Letting of contracts to bidders after
  advertisement, §136-28.1(a) to (k).
Small project bidding, §136-28.10(a) to (c).
Billboards.
Obstructing view at entrance to school, church or
  public institution, §136-102(a).
Penalty for violation of provisions, §136-102(b).
Outdoor advertising control act, §§136-126 to
  136-140.
  See OUTDOOR ADVERTISING.
Blind persons.
Operation of highway vending facilities, §§111-48
  to 111-52.
See BLIND AND VISUALLY IMPAIRED.
Blue Ridge Parkway.
Control of outdoor advertising, §§113A-165 to
  113A-170.
Blue Star memorial highway.
Designation, §136-102.1.
Erection of signs, §136-102.1.
Board of transportation, §§136-17.2 to 136-44.
See TRANSPORTATION BOARD.
Bond issues.
GARVEE bonds.
  Issuance of grant anticipation revenue vehicles
    to finance federal-aid highway projects,
    §136-18.
    Distribution of funds derived from,
      §136-17.2A(i).
Local road bonds prohibited, §136-98(b).
Boundaries.
Transportation engineering divisions.
  Designation of boundary, §136-14.1.
Bridges.
See BRIDGES.
Budget.
Highway appropriations, §143C-6-11.
State primary, secondary and urban road systems,
  §136-44.2.
Camp Butner hospital.
Application of state highway and motor vehicle
  laws to roads, etc., at reservation, §122C-402.
Cartways, tramways, etc.
Abandonment or discontinuance, §§136-68,
  136-70.
Alteration, §§136-68, 136-70.
Establishments, alteration or discontinuance,
  §§136-68, 136-70.
  Costs, §6-21.
  Manner of altering or abandoning, §136-70.
  Special proceeding, §136-68.
Laying out, §136-69(a) to (c).
Procedure for laying out, §136-69(a) to (c).
Cattle.
Signs for protection of cattle, §136-33.1.
Cement.
Production in United States.
  Contract requirements relating to construction
    materials, §136-28.7(a) to (d).

HIGHWAYS, ROADS AND STREETS —Cont'd
Census.
Traffic census established, §136-18.
Center lines.
Arsenic content in glass beads contained in paint
used to mark highways, §136-30.2.
Marking with center lines, §136-30.1(a).
Required, §136-30.1(b).
Churches.
Billboard obstructing view at entrance to church
on public highway, §136-102.
Church roads.
Establishment, alteration or discontinuance.
Special proceeding, §136-68.
Petition, §136-71.
Claims.
Adjustment and resolution of contract claims,
§136-29(a) to (d).
Closing of municipal streets.
Permanently, §160A-299.
Powers of cities generally, §160A-296.
Watershed improvement districts, §160A-299.1.
Closing of secondary road.
Within watershed improvement districts.
Temporary inundation by floodwaters,
§136-64.1(a) to (d).
Closing of state highways.
Construction or maintenance, §136-26.
Injury to barriers, warning signs, etc., §136-26.
Coin-operated machines.
Blind persons.
Operation of highway vending facilities,
§§111-48 to 111-52.
Commercial enterprises.
Controlled-access facilities, §136-89.56.
Fees for logo sign installation and maintenance,
§136-89.56.
Commissioners.
Condemnation proceedings.
Appointment of commissioners, §136-109.
Drainage of highway.
Appointment of commissioners, §136-21.
Judgment of commissioners, §136-22.
Right to appeal, §136-23.
View by commissioners, §136-22.
Community colleges.
Applicable provisions, §115D-21(a).
Condemnation, §§136-103 to 136-121.1.
Agreements for entry, §136-118.
Answer to complaint.
Filing of answer, §136-106(a).
Time for filing answer, §136-107.
Information to be contained, §136-106(a).
Plat to be filed, §136-106(c).
Reply and plat, §136-106(c).
Service of process, §136-106(b).
Time for filing answer, §136-107.
Appeals.
Right of appeal, §136-119.
Attorneys at law.
Employment of outside counsel by attorney
general, §136-103.1.
Commissioners.
Appointment of commissioners, §136-109(a).
Powers of commissioners, §136-109(b).
Report of commissioners, §136-109(c).
Mailing of copy to parties, §136-109(d).
Compensation.
Interest as part of just compensation, §136-113.
Payment of compensation, §136-117.

HIGHWAYS, ROADS AND STREETS —Cont'd
Condemnation —Cont'd
Complaint.
Answer to complaint.
Filing, §§136-106(a), 136-107.
Information to be contained, §136-106(a).
Plat to be filed, §136-106(c).
Reply and plat, §136-106(c).
Service of process, §136-106(b).
Time for filing answer, §136-107.
Disbursement of deposit, §136-105.
Serving copy of disbursing order, §136-105.
Filing, §136-103(a), (c).
Deposit to accompany complaint, §136-103(d).
Memorandum of action.
Recording memorandum, §136-111.
Continuances, §136-110.
Cost, §136-119.
Damages.
Determination of issue of damages, §136-109(d).
Interest as part of just compensation, §136-113.
Measure of damages, §136-112.
Declaration of taking, §136-103(a), (b).
Deposit accompanying declaration, §136-103(d).
Disbursement of deposit, §136-105.
Serving copy of disbursing order, §136-105.
Remedy where no declaration of taking filed,
§136-111.
Definitions, §136-115.
Deposits.
Disbursement of deposit, §136-105.
Refund of deposit, §136-121.
Determination of issues other than damages,
§136-108.
Disability.
Appointment of guardian ad litem, §136-110.
Final judgments, §136-116.
Generally, §§136-103 to 136-121.1.
Guardian ad litem.
Appointment of guardians for certain parties,
§136-110.
Incompetence.
Appointment of guardian ad litem, §136-110.
Institution of action, §136-103(a) to (d).
Interest.
Part of just compensation, §136-113.
Issues.
Damages issue, §136-109(d).
Determination of issues other than damages,
§136-108.
Judgments.
Final judgments, §136-116.
Measure of damages, §136-112.
Memorandum of action.
Recording memorandum, §§136-104, 136-111.
Supplemental memorandum of action, §136-104.
Mentally ill.
Appointment of guardian ad litem, §136-110.
Minors.
Appointment of guardian ad litem, §136-110.
Orders, §136-110.
Owner of condemned property.
Reimbursement of taxes paid on property,
§136-121.1(a), (b).
Parties.
Guardians ad litem.
Appointment of guardians for certain parties,
§136-110.
Unknown parties, §136-110.
Payment of compensation, §136-117.

HIGHWAYS, ROADS AND STREETS —Cont'd
Condemnation —Cont'd
Plat.
Answer to complaint, §136-106(c).
Refund of deposit, §136-121.
Reimbursement of owner for taxes paid on
condemned property, §136-121.1(a), (b).
Relocation assistance, §§133-5 to 133-18.
See RELOCATION ASSISTANCE.
Remedies.
Where no declaration of taking filed, §136-111.
Reports.
Commissioners to file report, §136-109.
Right of entry.
Agreements for entry, §136-118.
Surveys, borings, etc., §136-120.
Right of possession, §136-104.
Rules.
Additional rules, §136-114.
Service of process.
Answer to complaint, §136-106(b).
Disbursement of deposit.
Serving copy of disbursing order, §136-105.
Superior courts.
Determination of issue of damages, §136-109(d).
Supplemental memorandum of action.
Recording memorandum, §136-104.
Surveys.
Entry for surveys, §136-120.
Taxation.
Condemnation proceedings.
Reimbursement of owner for taxes paid,
§136-121.1(a), (b).
Title.
Vesting of title, §136-104.
Conduits.
Connection of highways with improved streets,
§136-27.
Cost, §136-27.
**Congestion relief and intermodal
transportation 21st century fund,** §§136-250
to 136-256.
Appropriations to fund.
Funds remain available until expended,
§136-256.
Legislative appropriation required, §136-255.
Commuter rail service grants, §136-253(b).
Establishment, §136-250.
Grants to local governments and transportation
authorities, §136-252.
Approval of grants, §136-253(c).
Cap on grant amount, §136-252(d).
Criteria for approval of grants, §136-252(b).
Eligible entities, §136-252(a).
Matching requirement, §136-252(d).
Multiyear allotments, §136-252(c).
Grants to other units, §136-253.
Approval of grants, §136-253(c).
Commuter rail service grants, §136-253(b).
Eligible entities, §136-253(a).
Lawful purposes, §136-253(a).
Legislative findings, §136-251.
Public policy, §136-251.
**Connection of highways with improved
streets,** §136-27.
Pipelines and conduits, §136-27.
Cost, §136-27.
Consolidated city-county.
Arrangements in consolidated city-county,
§136-66.6.

HIGHWAYS, ROADS AND STREETS —Cont'd
Construction.
Applicability of provisions to drivers of
government vehicles engaged in construction
work, §20-168(b).
Appropriations.
Special appropriations for state construction,
§136-44.2C.
Cement.
Produced in United States, §136-28.7(a) to (d).
Closing of state highways during construction,
§136-26.
Injury to barriers, warning signs, etc., §136-26.
Construction indemnity agreements invalid,
§22B-1.
Contractor licensing requirements for certain
projects, §136-28.14.
Controlled-access facilities.
Authority to construct, §136-89.50.
Disadvantaged minority-owned and women-owned
businesses.
Participation in transportation contracts,
§136-28.4.
Division of parks and recreation.
Roads in areas administered by division,
§136-44.12.
Hurricane evacuation standard for construction
projects, §136-102.7.
Indemnity agreements invalid, §22B-1.
Local authorities, §136-98(b).
Agreement with department of transportation,
§136-98(c).
Permit issued by department of environment and
natural resources.
Department of transportation construction
project.
Modification or cancellation, restrictions,
§136-44.7B.
Recycled materials used in construction,
§136-28.8.
Secondary road systems.
Annual work program, §136-44.7(a).
Submission of construction programs to boards
of county commissioners, §136-44.8(a) to (f).
State highway system.
Powers of department of transportation,
§136-18.
State primary and urban systems.
Annual construction program, §136-44.4.
Steel.
Production in United States, §136-28.7(a) to (d).
Contractor licensing requirements.
Certain projects, §136-28.14.
Contracts.
Adjustment and resolution of completed contract
claims.
Allowance, denial or compromise.
Authority of state highway administrator,
§136-29(a).
Appearance before state highway administrator,
§136-29(a).
Contested case on claim, time.
Dissatisfaction with administrator's decision,
§136-29(b).
Investigation of submitted claim, time.
State highway administrator, §136-29(a).
Provisions part of every contract, §136-29(d).
Submission of claim for amount due, time,
§136-29(a).
Bid analyses.
Confidential information, §136-28.5(b).

HIGHWAYS, ROADS AND STREETS —Cont'd
Contracts —Cont'd
Construction diaries.
When considered public records, §136-28.5(a).
Construction indemnity agreements invalid,
§22B-1.
Construction materials.
Cement and steel, requirements, §136-28.7(a) to
(d).
Construction of roads by local authorities.
Agreement with department of transportation,
§136-98(c).
Existing contracts, §136-98(b).
Design-build contracts, §136-28.11.
Disadvantaged minority-owned and women-owned
businesses.
Comprehensive antidiscrimination enforcement
policy, §136-28.4(b1).
Definitions, §136-28.4(c).
Expiration of section, §136-28.4(e).
Goals for participation.
Annual aspirational goals, §136-28.4(b1).
Policy of state, §136-28.4(a).
Program to remedy discrimination, §136-28.4(b),
(b1).
Reports, §136-28.4(d).
Studies, §136-28.4(b).
Letting to bidders after advertisement,
§136-28.1(a), (b).
Eight hundred thousand dollars, less than,
§136-28.1(b).
Eight hundred thousand dollars or more,
§136-28.1(a).
Electronic means, accepting bids by,
§136-28.1(k).
Emergency, exception to bid requirements,
§136-28.1(e).
Federal aid projects, contract provision,
§136-28.1(a).
Ferryboats, marine floating equipment and
docks.
Construction and repair deemed highway
construction, §136-28.1(c).
Ferry repair facilities, generators of electricity,
contracts with, §136-28.1(i).
Litter removal from state right-of-way,
§136-28.1(l).
Misdemeanors, §143-58.1(c).
Professional services, §136-28.1(f).
Prohibited, §143-58.1(a).
Real-time traveler information at rest areas,
§136-28.1(m).
Research and development contracts,
§136-28.1(g), (h).
Rest areas, weigh stations and welcome centers.
Construction and repair deemed highway
construction, §136-28.1(d).
Right to reject all bids reserved, §136-28.1(a).
Litter removal from rights-of-way.
Coordination with mowing highway
rights-of-way, §136-28.12.
Mowing highway rights-of-way.
Coordination of litter and debris removal,
§136-28.12.
Partnerships with private developers.
Authorized, §136-28.6A(a).
Department to establish policies and
promulgate rules, §136-28.6A(b).
Reports by secretary, §136-28.6A(d).
Restrictions on projects funded or constructed,
§136-28.6A(c).

HIGHWAYS, ROADS AND STREETS —Cont'd
Contracts —Cont'd
Private contract participation by department of
transportation.
Authorized, §136-28.6(a).
County and municipal participation,
§136-28.6(i).
Eligibility of projects, §136-28.6(b), (c).
Plans.
Requirements as to, §136-28.6(f), (g).
Reports by secretary, §136-28.6(h).
Restrictions, §136-28.6(d), (e).
Relocated transportation infrastructure.
Contracts let by others, §136-28.2.
Retainage.
Construction contracts, §136-28.9.
Small project bidding, §136-28.10(a) to (c).
State highway fund.
Contracts for maintenance, etc., of streets,
§136-41.3.
Urban areas.
Improvements in streets to reduce traffic
congestion, §136-66.5(b).
Controlled-access facilities, §§136-89.48 to
136-89.59A.
Abandonment, §136-89.50.
Acquisition of property and property rights,
§136-89.52.
Authority to establish, §136-89.50.
Commercial enterprises, §136-89.56.
Fees.
For logo sign installation and maintenance,
§136-89.56.
Construction, §136-89.50.
Counties.
Authority of local units to consent, §136-89.54.
Declaration of policy, §136-89.48.
Definitions, §136-89.49.
Designation, §136-89.50.
New and existing facilities, §136-89.53.
Design of facility, §136-89.51.
Division and separation into separate roadways,
§136-89.51.
Emergency service vehicles.
Means of immediate access required, §20-158.3.
Establishment of facilities, §136-89.50.
Frontage road.
Defined, §136-89.49.
Local service roads, §136-89.55.
Fuel, gas, food, lodging and camping.
Access to service or frontage roads, §136-89.56.
Signs owned, controlled and erected by
department.
Indication of location on, §136-89.56.
Grade crossings.
Elimination of grade crossings, §136-89.53.
Improvements, §136-89.50.
Legislative findings and declarations, §136-89.48.
Local service roads, §136-89.55.
Local units.
Authority of units to consent, §136-89.54.
Maintenance, §136-89.50.
Maximum speed on, §20-141(d).
Municipalities.
Authority of local units to consent, §136-89.54.
National system of interstate and defense
highways.
Unlawful use of system and other
controlled-access facilities, §136-89.58.
New and existing facilities.
Designation, §136-89.53.

HIGHWAYS, ROADS AND STREETS —Cont'd

Controlled-access facilities —Cont'd

Policy declaration, §136-89.48.

Property.

Acquisition of property and property rights, §136-89.52.

Regulation, §136-89.50.

Removal of wrecked, abandoned, disabled or unattended vehicle, §20-161(f).

Rest area refreshments, §136-89.59.

Separation into separate roadway, §136-89.51.

Unlawful use, §20-140.3.

Vending machines at rest areas.

Placing, department to regulate, §136-89.56.

Conversion.

Funds and property converted to state highway fund, §136-16.

Coordinated street system, §136-66.2.

Corporations.

Dedication of road or street.

Deemed abandoned if not used within fifteen years, §136-96.

Costs.

Application for establishment, alteration or discontinuance, §6-21.

Condemnation proceedings, §136-119.

Connection of highways with improved streets.

Pipelines and conduits, §136-27.

Public roads.

Application for establishment, etc., §6-21.

Counties.

Abandonment or change of road in secondary system.

Request by board of county commissioners, §136-63(a).

Appropriation to municipalities, §136-41.1(a).

Allocation of funds, §136-41.1(a) to (c).

Contracts for maintenance, etc., of streets, §136-41.3.

Eligible municipalities, §§136-41.1(b), 136-41.2(a) to (c).

Incorporated before January 1, 1945, §136-41.2A(a), (b).

Incorporated since January 1, 1945, §136-41.2(d).

Excess accumulation of funds, §136-41.3.

Nature of funds distributed, §136-41.1(d).

Records and annual statement, §136-41.3.

Use of funds, §136-41.3.

Assigning street numbers in unincorporated areas, §153A-239.1(a).

Bond issues.

Prohibition of local road bonds, §136-98(b).

Closing public roads or easements, §153A-241.

Commissioners.

Responsibility of counties for upkeep, etc., terminated, §136-97(a).

Secondary roads construction programs.

Filing of annual statement, §136-44.9.

Submission of programs to boards of county commissioners, §136-44.8(a) to (f).

Construction of roads by local authorities, §136-98(b).

Agreement with department of transportation, §136-98(c).

Controlled-access facilities.

Authority of local units to consent, §136-89.54.

Coordinated street system.

Additions to or removal from state highway system, §136-66.2(e).

HIGHWAYS, ROADS AND STREETS —Cont'd

Counties —Cont'd

Coordinated street system —Cont'd

Comprehensive plan.

Adoption, §136-66.2(b).

Changes in plan, §136-66.2(d).

Designated streets and highways in plan, §136-66.2(c).

Continuation of prior system, §136-66.2(f).

Development of system, §136-66.2(a).

Fishing from bridges.

Regulation or prohibition, §153A-242.

Golf carts, regulation of use, §153A-245.

Improvements to state highway system, §136-66.3.

Incorporation of roads into state highway system.

Action.

No court action against board of transportation, §136-59.

Appeals.

Filing of complaints, §136-64.

Board of transportation.

No court action against board, §136-59.

Change or abandonment of roads.

Power to make changes, §136-54.

Complaints, §136-64.

Court action.

No action against board of transportation, §136-59.

Hearings.

Filing of complaints, §136-64.

Maintenance program.

Vested in department of transportation, §136-51.

Petitions.

Right of petition, §136-62.

Power to make changes, §136-54.

Transportation department.

Filing of complaints, §136-64.

Naming roads and assigning street numbers in unincorporated areas, §153A-239.1(a).

Public roads.

Defined, §153A-238(a).

Responsibility for streets inside municipalities, §136-66.1.

Responsibility of counties for upkeep, etc., terminated, §136-97(a).

Rights of way.

Dedication of rights of way under local ordinances, §§136-66.10, 136-66.11.

Improvements to state highway system, §136-66.3.

Rules and regulations.

Authority of municipalities, §136-66.4.

Secondary road construction programs by department of transportation.

Adoption of annual construction program for each county.

Board of transportation, §136-44.8(e).

Department of transportation to follow, §136-44.8(f).

Map showing tentative road paving projects.

Posting in county courthouse, §136-44.8(a).

Notice of public meeting of board of county commissioners.

Deviations or priority of paving projects, §136-44.8(d).

Presentation by department of annual program for county, §136-44.8(b).

Public meeting on annual construction program for county, §136-44.8(c).

Notice, §136-44.8(b).

HIGHWAYS, ROADS AND STREETS —Cont'd
Counties —Cont'd
  Secondary road construction programs by
      department of transportation —Cont'd
    Public meeting on deviations or priority of
        paving projects, §136-44.8(d).
    Review of changes to which commissioners do
        not consent.
      Petition by board, §136-44.8(f).
  Special assessments.
    Critical infrastructure needs.
      Projects for which capital costs to be financed,
          §153A-210.2(a).
    Subdivision and residential streets, §153A-205.
  State highway system, §136-66.1.
  Taxation.
    Prohibition of local road taxes, §136-98(b).
Crossings.
  Controlled-access facilities.
    Elimination of crossings, §§136-20, 136-89.53.
  Elimination or safeguarding of crossings, §136-20.
  Railroad grade crossings generally, §§20-142.1 to
      20-142.5.
Curb ramps or curb cuts.
  Free copies of article, §136-44.14(d).
  Guidelines to implement article, §136-44.14(c).
  Minimum requirements, §136-44.14(a), (b).
  Municipalities, §160A-307.
Curves.
  Provision and marking of "pull-off" areas,
      §136-18.4.
Dale Earnhardt highway, §136-18.5B.
Damages.
  Condemnation proceedings, §136-109(d).
    Interest as part of just compensation, §136-113.
    Measure of damages, §136-112.
Dedication.
  Abandonment of road or street for fifteen years,
      §136-96.
  Partition, §46-17.1.
  Special proceeding to declare right of way for
      public use.
    Compliance with standards, §136-96.1(c).
    Inapplicability, §136-96.1(d).
    Order from clerk of court, §136-96.1(b).
    Prerequisites, §136-96.1(a).
  Withdrawal of public use dedication by property
      owners association.
    Approval by board of county commissioners,
        §136-96.2(b).
    Effect of withdrawal, §136-96.2(c).
    Filing of declaration, conditions, §136-96.2(a).
    Improvements required, §136-96.2(b).
    Public rights-of-way still to exist after
        withdrawal, §136-96.2(c).
    Qualifying subdivisions, §136-96.2(a).
    Restrictions, §136-96.2(b).
    Signature of clerk, §136-96.2(b).
Definitions.
  Condemnation proceedings, §136-115.
  Controlled-access facilities, §136-89.49.
  Highway trust fund, §136-175.
  Neighborhood public roads, §136-67.
  Obstructing highways and roads.
    Placing glass, etc., or injurious obstructions in
        road, §136-91(b).
  Public roads, §153A-238(a).
  Signs.
    Motorist services directional signs, §136-140.

HIGHWAYS, ROADS AND STREETS —Cont'd
**Department of environment and natural
  resources.**
  Permits issued for highway construction projects.
    Modification or cancellation, restrictions,
        §136-44.7B.
Department of transportation.
  Powers and duties, §§136-17.2 to 136-44.
    See TRANSPORTATION DEPARTMENT.
Design-build contracts.
  Authorized, §136-28.11(a).
  Award, §136-28.11(b) to (d).
  Disadvantaged business participation goals,
      §136-28.11(c).
  Reporting requirements, §136-28.11(e).
Detours.
  Repair of road detour, §136-25.
Development.
  Subdivision streets.
    Minimum standards of board of transportation,
        §136-102.6.
**Diesel vehicles purchased by department of
  transportation.**
  Warranty requirement, §136-28.15.
Disabled persons.
  Curb ramps or curb cuts.
    Free copies of article, §136-44.14(d).
    Guidelines to implement article, §136-44.14(c).
    Minimum requirements, §136-44.14(a), (b).
  Right of access to and use of public places, §168-2.
**Disadvantaged minority-owned and
  women-owned businesses.**
  Comprehensive antidiscrimination enforcement
      policy, §136-28.4(b1).
  Definitions, §136-28.4(c).
  Expiration of section, §136-28.4(e).
  Goals for participation.
    Annual aspirational goals, §136-28.4(b1).
  Policy of state, §136-28.4(a).
  Program to remedy discrimination, §136-28.4(b),
      (b1).
  Reports, §136-28.4(d).
  Studies, §136-28.4(b).
Ditches.
  Diverting water from public road by ditch or
      drain, §136-95.
Division of highways.
  Subdivision streets.
    Compliance with minimum standards of board
        of transportation, §136-102.6(d).
Division of parks and recreation.
  Construction of roads, §136-44.12.
Drainage.
  Application to court, §136-21.
  Appointment of commissioners, §136-21.
  Judgment of commissioners, §136-22.
    Right to appeal, §136-23.
  Maintenance and repair of drainage systems.
    Contractor licensing requirements, §136-28.14.
  Obstructing highway drains misdemeanor,
      §136-92.
  Special proceedings.
    Rights of parties, §136-24.
  Summons and process, §136-21.
  View by commissioners, §136-22.
  Water must be diverted from public road by ditch
      or drain, §136-95.
Drainage districts.
  Drainage across public or private ways, §156-88.
Drilling.
  Test drilling or boring.
    Filing record of results, §136-102.3.

HIGHWAYS, ROADS AND STREETS —Cont'd
Drilling —Cont'd
Test drilling or boring —Cont'd
Penalty for violations of provisions, §136-102.4.
Easements.
Municipal powers, §160A-296.
Neighborhood roads, cartways, church roads, etc.
General provisions, §§136-67 to 136-71.
Public utility lines laid out on petition, §136-71.
Scenic beauty of areas along highways.
Regulation of scenic easements, §136-125.
Edge lines.
Arsenic content in glass beads contained in paint
used to mark highways, §136-30.2.
Marking with edge lines, §136-30.1(a).
Required, §136-30.1(b).
Electric companies.
Eminent domain.
Use or occupancy of public highways, §62-181.
Electric, telegraph or telephone lines.
Right to construct, maintain and operate along
public highway, §62-180.
Eminent domain.
Cartways, church roads or mill roads.
Special proceeding for establishment, alteration
or discontinuance, §136-68.
Condemnation generally, §§136-103 to 136-121.1.
See within this heading, "Condemnation."
Engineers.
Right-of-way acquisitions.
Preliminary engineering annual report,
§136-44.11(a).
Enhancement of scenic beauty, §§136-122 to
136-125.
Litter prevention account, §136-125.1.
**Environmental policies or guidelines affecting
transportation projects.**
Analysis of policies or guidelines adopted by
department, §136-44.7C(a).
Report to board of transportation prior to
approval, time, §136-44.7C(b).
Environment, health and natural resources.
Test drilling or boring upon public land.
Filing record of results with secretary,
§136-102.3.
Express permit review program, §136-93.1.
**Falsification of inspection reports or test
reports required by department,** §136-13.2.
Federal aid.
Historical marker program, §136-42.3.
Scenic beauty of areas along highways.
Availability of federal aid funds, §136-124.
Federal aid highway projects.
GARVEE bonds.
Issuance of grant anticipation revenue vehicles
to finance federal-aid highway projects,
§136-18.
Distribution of funds derived from,
§136-17.2A(i).
Federal funds.
Intrastate system projects and urban loops,
§136-177.1.
Federal parks.
Construction of federal parkways and entrance
roads to parks.
Powers of department of transportation,
§136-19(g).
Property tentatively designated as federal
parkway, §136-19(i).
Fees.
Commercial enterprises.
Logo sign installation and maintenance,
§136-89.56.

HIGHWAYS, ROADS AND STREETS —Cont'd
Ferries.
See FERRIES.
Fire protection.
Pavement of driveways from state-maintained
roads to rural fire district firehouses.
Powers of department of transportation,
§136-18.
Flooding.
Secondary road system.
Closing of secondary roads within watershed
improvement districts.
Temporary inundation by floodwaters,
§136-64.1(a) to (d).
Force account qualified labor.
Cities or towns.
Maintenance and repair work, construction,
reconstruction, §§136-41.3, 160A-309.
Department of transportation.
Report to general assembly, §136-12.
Funds.
Highway trust fund, §§136-175 to 136-185. See
within this heading, "Highway trust fund."
Mobility fund, §§136-187 to 136-189.
State highway fund, §§136-41.1 to 136-41.4.
Allocation of funds, §136-41.1.
Appropriation to municipalities, §136-41.1.
Use of funds, §136-41.3.
Cash management, §147-86.15.
Conversion of funds and property, §136-16.
Eligibility for funds, §136-41.2.
Ineligibility for funds, municipalities,
§136-41.2B.
Motor vehicle registration, plates and certificate
of title fees.
Disposition of fees collected, §20-85(b).
Garbage collection containers.
Location on rights-of-way.
Counties and municipalities, §136-18.3(a) to (d).
GARVEE bonds.
Issuance of grant anticipation revenue vehicles to
finance federal-aid highway projects, §136-18.
Distribution of funds derived from,
§136-17.2A(i).
Gates.
Projecting over rights-of-way forbidden, §136-94.
**Gathering, picketing or protesting on roads or
highways.**
Local ordinance regulating time, place and
manner.
Authorization, §20-174.2(a).
General assembly.
Controlled-access facilities.
Legislative findings and declarations,
§136-89.48.
Joint legislative transportation oversight
committee, §§120-70.50 to 120-70.52.
See GENERAL ASSEMBLY.
Local acts affecting state highway system.
Consideration by transportation committees,
§120-19.9.
Local, private and special legislation prohibited,
NC Const Art II §24.
Reports to appropriations committees of general
assembly, §136-44.2B.
Scenic beauty of areas along highways.
Legislative findings and declaration of policy,
§136-122.
Glass.
Placing glass, etc., or injurious obstructions in
road, §136-91.

HIGHWAYS, ROADS AND STREETS —Cont'd
Golf carts.
Regulation of use by counties, §153A-245.
Regulation of use by municipalities, §160A-300.6.
Grade crossings.
Controlled-access facilities.
Elimination of grade crossings, §§136-20, 136-89.53.
Railroad grade crossings generally, §§20-142.1 to 20-142.5.
Guardians.
Condemnation proceedings.
Appointment of guardian ad litem, §136-110.
Hearings.
County public roads incorporated into state highway system.
Filing of complaints, §136-64.
Highway patrol.
Powers and duties as to patrolling of highways, §20-188.
Highway signs.
See HIGHWAY SIGNS.
Highway trust fund, §§136-175 to 136-185.
Allocation of funds, §136-176(b).
Limitation, §136-177.
Supplement for city streets, §136-181.
Appropriation to municipalities, §136-41.1(a).
Bonds, appropriations for payment, §136-176(b2).
Budget of state.
Crediting interest to highway fund and highway trust fund, §143C-1-4(b).
Cash management, §147-86.15.
Certification of use of cash balances, §136-176(a5).
Contracts.
Anticipation of revenues, §136-176(d).
Creation, §136-176(a).
Debt service and revenue bonds, payment, §136-176(b2).
Definitions, §136-175.
Intrastate system.
Projects funded from trust fund, §136-179.
Use of federal funds, §136-177.1.
Limitations on fund obligated from fund, §136-177.
Maintenance reserve, §136-185.
Matching funds, §136-176(c).
Motor vehicle registration, plates and certificate of title fees.
Disposition of fees collected, §20-85(b).
One-day title service fee, §20-85.1(b).
Project selection and expenditure of funds, §136-176(a4).
Purposes for which fund used, §136-176(a1), (a3).
Reports.
Annual report, §136-184(a).
Intended use of funds, §136-176(a5).
Quarterly reports, §136-184(b).
Reserve accounts, §136-185.
Secondary road construction.
Supplement for, §136-182.
Supplement for city streets.
Allocation, §136-181.
Transfer of allocated funds, §136-176(b1).
Urban loops.
Funds allocated from trust fund, §136-180(a).
Vehicle emissions and maintenance program implementation.
Highway trust fund repayment fee, §20-183.7(d2).
Historical markers.
Cooperation with department of cultural resources, §136-42.2.

HIGHWAYS, ROADS AND STREETS —Cont'd
Historical markers —Cont'd
Correction of historical markers.
Procedure for correction, §136-43.1.
Establishment of program, §136-42.3.
Federal highway fund expenditures, §136-42.3.
Procedure for correction and relocation of markers, §136-43.1.
Purchase by department of transportation, §136-42.3.
Relocation of historical markers.
Procedure for relocation, §136-43.1.
Hurricane evacuation standard for construction projects, §136-102.7.
Hydraulic power companies use.
Eminent domain.
Use or occupancy of public highways, §62-181.
Improvements.
Connection of highways with improved streets, §136-27.
Pipelines and conduits, §136-27.
Local government participation in improvements to state highway system.
Acquisition of right-of-way.
Department authority to pay full costs, §136-66.3(h).
Agreements with local government units to expedite projects.
Authorized, §136-66.8(a).
Form of agreements, §136-66.8(b).
Reports, §136-66.8(c).
Authorized, §136-66.3(a).
Development related improvements, §136-66.3(d).
Project additions, §136-66.3(e).
Types of the participation, §136-66.3(c).
Changes in participation agreement, §136-66.3(i).
Development related improvements, §136-66.3(d).
Limitations on agreements, §136-66.3(c3).
Pedestrian safety improvements, §136-66.3(c4).
Project additions, §136-66.3(e).
Reimbursement of department of transportation for costs, §136-66.3(e1).
Report on agreements, §136-66.3(f).
Rights of way, §136-66.3(g) to (j).
State funds, distribution, §136-66.3(c2).
TIP projects, effect, §136-66.3(c1), (c3).
Agreements with local government units to expedite projects, §136-66.8.
Urban areas.
Reduction in traffic congestion, §136-66.5.
Indemnity agreements.
Construction indemnity agreements invalid, §22B-1.
Infractions.
Obstructing highway drains, §136-92.
Inspections.
Falsifying highway inspection reports, §136-13.2(a).
Interest.
Condemnation proceedings.
Part of just compensation, §136-113.
Intrastate system.
Access to route, determination, §136-178(a).
Addition of routs to system.
Authority of department of transportation, §136-178(a).
Distribution formula for funds expended, §136-17.2A(a).
Adjustment of target amounts, §136-17.2A(h).

HIGHWAYS, ROADS AND STREETS —Cont'd
Intrastate system —Cont'd
Distribution formula for funds expended —Cont'd
Amount expended in distribution region, §136-17.2A(d).
Calculation of tentative percentage share, §136-17.2A(b), (c).
Consideration in developing schedules of improvements, §136-17.2A(f).
Most recent population estimate used, §136-17.2A(e).
Report to general assembly on allocations, obligations and actual expenditures, §136-17.2A(g).
List of route segments or corridors.
Use of funds allocated from trust fund, §136-178(a).
Number of travel lanes, §136-178(a).
Priority projects not completed.
Report to legislature, §136-178(b).
Purposes for establishing, §136-178(a).
Use of funds allocated from trust fund, §136-178(a).
Vertical separation or interchanges at crossings, §136-178(a).
Invalid agreements.
Construction indemnity agreements, §22B-1.
Joint tenants and tenants in common.
Dedication of road or street.
Deemed abandoned if not used within fifteen years, §136-96.
Judgments.
Condemnation proceedings.
Final judgments, §136-116.
Drainage of highway.
Right to appeal, §136-23.
View by commissioners, §136-22.
Judicial sales.
Dedication to public of real property subdivided for sale, §1-339.9(b).
Junkyard control, §§136-141 to 136-155.
See JUNKYARDS.
Leaving vehicle on highway, §20-161.
Letting contracts to bidders after advertisement, §136-28.1(a) to (k).
Lights.
Blinding, deceptive or distracting lights.
Applicability of provisions, §136-32.2(c).
Continuing violation deemed separate offense, §136-32.2(b).
Enforcement of section, §136-32.2(d).
Placing of unlawful, §136-32.2(a).
Stop lights, §20-158.
Streetlight assessments, §153A-206.
Light-traffic roads.
Weight and load limitations for vehicles, §20-118.
Limitation of actions.
Plank roads right of way.
No title by possession of right-of-way, §1-44.
Public ways of any kind.
No title by possession of public ways, §1-45.
Litter enforcement signs, §136-32.3.
Placement along interstate highways, §136-32.3.
Littering, §14-399.
Litter prevention account, §136-125.1.
Litter removal from rights-of-way.
Coordination with mowing highway rights-of-way, §§136-28.1(l), 136-28.12.
Local, private and special legislation prohibited, NC Const Art II §24.

HIGHWAYS, ROADS AND STREETS —Cont'd
Maintenance.
Contractor licensing requirements, §136-28.14.
Controlled-access facilities, §136-89.50.
County public roads incorporated into state highway system, §136-51.
Division of parks and recreation.
Roads in areas administered by division, §136-44.12.
Restriction of right to use highways.
When authorities may restrict, §20-121.
Secondary road systems.
Annual work program, §136-44.7(a).
Priority of paving work, §136-44.7(b).
State highway system, §136-45.
Responsibility for streets inside municipalities, §136-66.1.
Survey of conditions of state highway system and report on findings, §136-44.3.
Maintenance program.
Secondary road systems.
Negotiation of right-of-way, §136-44.7(c).
Maps and plats.
Condemnation proceedings.
Reply and plat with answer to complaint, §136-106(c).
Subdivision streets.
Compliance with minimum standards of board of transportation, §136-102.6(a), (b).
Transportation corridor official maps.
Adoption or amendment, §136-44.50(a).
Requirements, §136-44.50(a1).
What constitutes "amendment,"§136-44.50(e).
Appraisal of right-of-way within corridor.
Criteria, §136-44.54.
Bikeways or greenways.
Not included in term "transportation corridor,"§136-44.50(f).
Building permits.
Contents of submittals, §136-44.51(b).
Effect on applications for, §136-44.51(a).
Restrictions on delay, §136-44.51(b).
Inapplicability of provisions, §136-44.51(c).
Submittal to local jurisdiction not to be construed as permit application, §136-44.51(c).
Distribution, §136-44.50(b).
Environmental impact statement, §136-44.50(d).
Filing, §136-44.50(a).
Effect, §136-44.51(a).
Notice.
Adoption or amendment of map, §136-44.50(a1).
Hearings on variances, §136-44.52(b).
Petitions.
Variances, §136-44.52(a) to (c1).
Registering and indexing, time, §161-14(c).
Right-of-way within corridor.
Advance acquisition within roadway corridor.
Authorized, §136-44.53(a), (d).
Prerequisites, §136-44.53(b).
Reimbursement of city, §136-44.53(c).
Appraisal criteria, §136-44.54.
Variances.
Grant of variance, §136-44.52(d).
Petitions, §136-44.52(a) to (c1).
Procedures for, §136-44.52(a) to (c1).
Requirements for granting, §136-44.52(b).
Markings.
Arsenic content in glass beads contained in paint used to mark highways, §136-30.2.

HIGHWAYS, ROADS AND STREETS —Cont'd
Markings —Cont'd
Center line and pavement edge line markings,
§136-30.1.
Misleading signs prohibited, §136-32.1.
Pavement edge line markings, §136-30.1.
Signs generally.
See HIGHWAY SIGNS.
Masks and hoods.
Wearing of masks, hoods, etc., on public ways,
§14-12.7.
Median strips.
Property acquisitions, §§136-89.52, 136-89.53.
State patrol crossing, §136-89.58.
Metropolitan sewerage districts.
Rights of way and easements in, §162A-74.
Metropolitan water districts.
Rights of way and easements, §162A-54.
Mill roads.
Establishment, alteration or discontinuance,
§136-68.
Misdemeanors.
Obstructing highways and roads, §136-90.
Missing persons.
AMBER alert system.
Overhead permanent changeable message
boards, §143B-1021(d).
Silver alert system.
Overhead permanent changeable message
boards.
Making information available to motorists,
§143B-1022(d).
Mobility fund, §§136-187 to 136-189.
Creation, §136-187(a).
Eligible projects, §136-188(a).
Initial project funded, §136-188(b).
Reporting by department, §136-189.
Use of funds deposited, §136-187(b).
Eligible projects, §136-188(a).
Motorcycle operation, §20-146.1.
Mount Mitchell park.
Powers of department of environment and natural
resources, §100-12.
Mowing highway rights-of-way.
Coordination of litter and debris removal,
§136-28.12.
Municipalities.
Abandonment of segment of road and removal
from state highway system.
Authority to keep open and assume
maintenance.
Roads within one mile of corporate limits,
§136-55.1(b).
Abandonment or change of road in secondary
system.
Authority to keep open and assume
responsibility.
Roads within one mile of corporate limits,
§136-63(b).
Appropriation to municipalities, §§136-41.1 to
136-41.4.
Assessments, §160A-217.
Board of transportation authority, §160A-297.
Bond issues, §136-98(b).
Building setback lines, §160A-306.
Closing streets.
Permanent closings, §160A-299.
Powers of cities generally, §160A-296.
Watershed improvement districts, §160A-299.1.
Construction, §136-98(b).
Controlled-access facilities, §136-89.54.

HIGHWAYS, ROADS AND STREETS —Cont'd
Municipalities —Cont'd
Coordinated street system, §136-66.2.
Curb cut regulations, §160A-307.
Designation of certain locations on official map
books, §160A-77(b).
Driveways.
Curb cut regulations, §160A-307.
Easements in street rights-of-way.
Power to grant, §160A-296.
Golf carts.
Regulation of use on streets, roads and
highways, §160A-300.6.
Improvements to state highway system, §136-66.3.
Inclusion of street in state highway system
right-of-way, §136-66.7(a), (b).
National highway safety act.
Agreements with state and federal government
under, §160A-305.
Powers as to streets, §160A-296.
Public utility closing of streets permanently,
§160A-299(f).
Railroad crossings.
Conflict of laws, §160A-298(f).
Costs, §160A-298(b), (c), (e).
Powers of cities as to, §160A-298(a), (c), (d).
Safety devices, §160A-298(c).
Reduction in traffic congestion, §136-66.5.
Responsibility for streets inside municipalities,
§136-66.1.
Rights-of-way, §§136-66.10, 136-66.11.
Rules and regulations, §136-66.4.
Signs and traffic control devices.
Uniform manual, conformity to, approval by
department, §136-30(b).
State highway system.
Improvements, §136-66.3.
Inclusion of municipal street system in,
§136-66.7(a), (b).
Maintenance of system by municipalities,
§136-66.1.
Responsibility of streets inside municipalities,
§136-66.1.
Taxation.
Local road taxes, §136-98(b).
Property taxes, §160A-209(c).
Traffic congestion reduction, §136-66.5.
Names.
Dale Earnhardt highway, §136-18.5B.
Purple heart memorial highway, §136-18.5A.
State highway system, §136-18.
Wesley D. Webster highway, §136-18.5.
Narrow roads.
Widening.
Use of resurfacing program funds, §136-44.16.
**National system of interstate and defense
highways.**
Unlawful use of system and other
controlled-access facilities, §136-89.58.
Natural gas lines.
Relocation of natural gas line located on
department of transportation right-of-way,
§136-27.2.
Neighborhood public roads, §136-67.
North Carolina mobility fund, §§136-187 to
136-189.
North Carolina turnpike authority,
§§136-89.180 to 136-89.218.
See TURNPIKE AUTHORITY.
Notice.
Abandonment of segment of road and removal
from state highway system.
For maintenance, §136-55.1(a).

HIGHWAYS, ROADS AND STREETS —Cont'd

Notice —Cont'd

Roadway corridor official maps.

Hearing on adoption or amendment, §136-44.50(a1).

Hearing on variances, §136-44.52(b).

No title by possession of public ways, §1-45.

Obstructing highways and roads.

Definitions, §136-91(b).

Drain obstruction a misdemeanor, §136-92.

Infractions, §136-92.

Misdemeanor offenses, §136-90.

Placing glass, etc., or injurious objects in road, §136-91(a).

Definition, §136-91(b).

Penalty for violation of provisions, §136-91(c).

One-way traffic, §20-165.1.

State parks and forest road system, §143-116.8(b).

Openings.

Issuance of permits, §136-93(a).

Operation of vehicles and rules of the road, §§20-138.1 to 20-171.

See TRAFFIC REGULATIONS.

Orders.

Condemnation proceedings, §136-110.

Outdoor advertising.

Blue Ridge Parkway.

Control of outdoor advertising, §§113A-165 to 113A-170.

See BLUE RIDGE PARKWAY.

Control act, §§136-126 to 136-140.

See OUTDOOR ADVERTISING.

Overpasses.

Elimination or safeguarding of inadequate overpasses, §136-20.

Parking.

Generally, §§20-138.1 to 20-171.

See PARKING.

Parking authorities, §§160A-550 to 160A-565.

See PARKING AUTHORITIES.

Parks and recreation.

Park roads part of park system, §136-44.2.

Roads in areas administered by division of parks and recreation.

Construction and maintenance of roads, §136-44.12.

Toll roads.

Private operation in public parks prohibited, §100-16.

Parties.

Condemnation proceedings.

Rights of unknown parties, §136-110.

Drainage of highway.

Rights of parties, §136-24.

Partitions.

Dedication of streets, §46-17.1.

Penalties.

Billboards.

Obstructing view at entrance to school, church or public institution, §136-102(b).

Blinding, deceptive or distracting lights, §136-32.2.

Damaging or removing signs, §136-33(b1).

Obstructing highways and roads.

Placing glass, etc., or injurious obstructions in road, §136-91(c).

Subdivision streets.

Compliance with minimum standards of board of transportation, §136-102.6(j).

Test drilling or boring upon public land or right of way.

Violations of provisions, §136-102.4.

HIGHWAYS, ROADS AND STREETS —Cont'd

Permits.

Department of transportation construction project.

Department of environment and natural resources issuing.

Modification or cancellation, restrictions, §136-44.7B.

Express permit review program.

Establishment of program in each division, §136-93.1(a).

Fees, §136-93.1(e), (f).

Opting out of program, §136-93.1(b).

Staffing or contracting to implement, §136-93.1(d).

Steps for review process, §136-93.1(c).

Openings, structures, pipes or trees.

Issuance of permits, §136-93(a).

Petitions.

Cartways, church roads or mill roads.

Special proceeding for establishment, alteration or discontinuance, §136-68.

Church roads.

Laid out on petition, §136-71.

County public roads incorporated into state highway system.

Right of petition, §136-62.

Drainage of highway, §136-21.

Easements of public utility lines laid out on petition, §136-71.

Pipelines, §136-93(a).

Roadway corridor official maps.

Variances, §136-44.52(a) to (c1).

Pipelines.

Connection of highways with improved streets, §136-27.

Permits.

Issuance of permits, §136-93(a).

Water and sewer lines.

Relocation costs, §136-27.1.

Plank roads.

Limitation of actions.

No title by possession of right-of-way, §1-44.

Poisons.

Putting poisonous foodstuffs, etc., in certain public places prohibited, §14-401.

Powell act.

Appropriations to local governments, §§136-41.1 to 136-41.4.

See POWELL ACT.

Powers of municipalities as to, §160A-296.

Preservation of scenic beauty, §§136-122 to 136-125.

Litter prevention account, §136-125.1.

Primary road systems.

Appropriations, §136-44.2.

Budget and appropriations, §136-44.2.

Construction.

Annual construction program, §136-44.4.

Profanity.

Using profane or indecent language on public highways, §14-197.

Exempt counties, §14-197.

Property.

Controlled-access facilities.

Acquisition of property and property rights, §136-89.52.

Public road defined, §153A-238(a).

Public utilities.

Easements of public utility lines laid out on petition, §136-71.

HIGHWAYS, ROADS AND STREETS —Cont'd
Public utilities —Cont'd
Eminent domain.
Use of highways generally, §§62-180, 62-181.
Petition.
Easements of public utility lines laid out on
petition, §136-71.
Subdivision streets.
Compliance with minimum standards of board
of transportation, §136-102.6(e).
Water and sewer lines.
Relocation costs, §136-27.1.
Public works.
Relocation assistance.
Acquisition of right-of-way for state highway
project, §133-13(c).
"Pull-off" areas.
Provision and marking, §136-18.4.
Purple heart memorial highway, §136-18.5A.
Racing.
Motor vehicles, §20-141.3.
Railroad grade crossings, §§20-142.1 to 20-142.5.
See RAILROAD GRADE CROSSINGS.
Railroads.
Alteration or abandonment of railways.
Manner of altering or abandoning, §136-70.
Intersection with highways, §136-191.
Powers of railroad corporations, §136-190.
Obstructing highways.
Additional nature of provisions, §136-192(d).
Notice, §136-192(a), (b).
Failure to repair after notice, §136-192(c).
Recording.
Condemnation proceedings.
Memorandum of action, §136-111.
To be recorded, §136-104.
Records.
Authorization required for test drilling or boring
upon right-of-way.
Filing of record of results, §136-102.2.
State highway fund.
Appropriation to municipalities.
Annual statement and records, §136-41.3.
Test drilling or boring.
Filing record of results, §136-102.3.
Recycled materials used in construction.
Alternative ways to use recycled materials.
Declaration of public interest, §136-28.8(b).
Applicable to all procurements, §136-28.8(i).
Cooperation with department in carrying out
provisions, §136-28.8(f).
Intent of general assembly, §136-28.8(a).
Minimum content standards, determining,
§136-28.8(h).
Report as to amounts and types of recycled
materials used, §136-28.8(g).
Research by department including demonstration
projects, §136-28.8(c).
Review and revision of existing bid procedures
and specifications, §136-28.8(d), (e).
Rules to implement provisions, adoption,
§136-28.8(j).
Reduction in urban traffic congestion,
§136-66.5.
Refreshments.
Highway rest area refreshments.
Controlled-access facilities, §136-89.59.
Register of deeds.
Condemnation proceedings.
Recording of memorandum of action, §136-104.

HIGHWAYS, ROADS AND STREETS —Cont'd
Relocated transportation infrastructure.
Contracts let by others, §136-28.2.
Relocation assistance, §§133-5 to 133-18.
See RELOCATION ASSISTANCE.
Remedies.
Condemnation proceedings.
Where no declaration of taking filed, §136-111.
Repairs.
Contractor licensing requirements, §136-28.14.
Road detour, §136-25.
Reports.
Appropriations committees of general assembly,
§136-44.2B.
Condemnation proceedings.
Commissioners to file report, §136-109.
Design-build contracts, §136-28.11(e).
Drainage of highway.
View by commissioners, §136-22.
Intrastate system.
Priority projects not completed.
Report to legislature, §136-178(b).
Mobility fund, §136-189.
Preliminary engineering annual report.
Right-of-way acquisitions, §136-44.11(a).
Rest areas.
Contracts for construction, maintenance and
repair.
Department of transportation, §136-28.1(d).
Controlled-access facilities.
Highway rest area refreshments, §136-89.59.
Firearms.
Open carrying or carrying concealed handgun,
§14-415.11(c3).
Promotion of North Carolina farm products,
§136-89.59A.
Real-time traveler information, §136-28.1(m).
Restoration of scenic beauty, §§136-122 to
136-125.
Restriction of right to use highways.
When authorities may restrict, §20-121.
Resurfacing program funds.
Use to widen existing narrow roads, §136-44.16.
Rewards.
Damaging or removing signs, §136-33(c).
Right of entry.
Condemnation proceedings.
Agreements for entry, §136-118.
Surveys, borings, etc., §136-120.
Rights of way.
Acquisition.
County participation in improvements to state
highway system, §136-66.3(g) to (j).
Municipal participation in improvements to
state highway system, §136-66.3(g) to (j).
Archaeological objects on highway right-of-way,
§136-42.1.
Bridges.
Privately owned bridges, construction and
maintenance.
Permitting use and encroachment, §136-18.
Dedication of rights of way under local
ordinances.
Density credit, §136-66.10(b).
Generally, §136-66.10(a).
Severable development rights, §136-66.11(a).
Powers of city or county as to, §136-66.11(b).
Regulations as to, §136-66.11(e).
Status.
Interest in real property, §136-66.11(f).
Transfer, §136-66.11(c), (d).

HIGHWAYS, ROADS AND STREETS —Cont'd

Rights of way —Cont'd

Dedication, special proceeding to declare right of way for public use, §136-96.1.

    Withdrawal of public use dedication by property owners association, §136-96.2.

Gates projecting over rights-of-way forbidden, §136-94.

Limitation of actions.

    No title by possession of right-of-way, §1-44.

Location and acquisition for new roads.

    Powers of department of transportation, §136-18.

Natural gas lines.

    Relocation of natural gas line located on department of transportation right-of-way, §136-27.2.

Neighborhood roads, cartways, church roads, etc.

    General provisions, §§136-67 to 136-71.

Preliminary engineering annual report.

    Right-of-way acquisitions, §136-44.11(a).

        Request for allocation of funds, §136-44.11(b).

Registration of right-of-way plans for all department of transportation projects, §136-19.4(a).

    Certified copy of alteration or amendment, §136-19.4(d).

    Copy of plans certified, §136-19.4(b).

    Electronic transmittal of plans, §136-19.4(b1).

    Recording, register of deeds, §136-19.4(c).

        Fee, §136-19.4(e).

Removal of motor vehicles left on, §20-137.9.

Special proceeding to declare right of way for public use, §136-96.1.

Test drilling or boring upon right-of-way, §136-102.2.

    Penalty for violation of provisions, §136-102.4.

Transportation corridor official maps.

    Advance acquisition of right of way within roadway corridor, §136-44.53.

Utility right-of-way agreements, §136-19.5.

Withdrawal of public use dedication by property owners association, §136-96.2.

Rules and regulations.

Authority of municipalities, §136-66.4.

Condemnation proceedings, §136-114.

Rules of the road, §§20-138.1 to 20-171.

See TRAFFIC REGULATIONS.

Safety devices.

Elimination or safeguarding of grade crossings and inadequate underpasses or overpasses, §136-20.

Sanitary districts.

Corporate powers of sanitary district board, §130A-55.

Scenic beauty restoration, preservation and enhancement, §§136-122 to 136-125.

Acquisition of real property, §136-123(a).

Authorized, §136-123(a).

Declaration of policy, §136-122.

Easements.

    Regulation of scenic easements, §136-125.

Federal aid.

    Availability of funds, §136-124.

Funds.

    Availability of federal aid, §136-124.

Legislative findings, §136-122.

Litter prevention account, §136-125.1.

Oyster shells used as ground cover, prohibition, §136-123(b).

Policy declaration, §136-122.

HIGHWAYS, ROADS AND STREETS —Cont'd

Scenic beauty restoration, preservation and enhancement —Cont'd

Regulation of scenic easements, §136-125.

Scenic highways.

Outdoor advertising adjacent to park.

    Limitations, §136-129.2(a) to (c).

School buses.

Receiving or discharging upon divided highway, §20-217.

Schools.

Billboard obstructing view at entrance to school on public highway, §136-102.

State-maintained public roads.

    Power of department of transportation to maintain and repair, §136-18.

Secondary road system.

Abandonment or change of road in secondary system.

    Municipality, keeping open and assuming responsibility.

        Roads within one mile of corporate limits, §136-63(b).

        Request by board of county commissioners, §136-63(a).

Additions to system, §136-44.10.

Appropriations, §136-44.2.

Closing of secondary roads.

    Within watershed improvement districts.

        Temporary inundation by floodwaters, §136-64.1(a) to (d).

Construction.

    Adoption of annual construction program for each county.

        Board of transportation, §136-44.8(e).

        Department of transportation to follow, §136-44.8(f).

    Allocation from highway trust fund, §136-44.2A.

    Annual work program, §136-44.7(a).

    Federal guidelines for transportation projects, compliance, §136-44.7E.

    Map showing tentative road paving projects.

        Posting in county courthouse, §136-44.8(a).

    Notice of public meeting of board of county commissioners.

        Deviations or priority of paving projects, §136-44.8(d).

        Presentation by department of annual program for county, §136-44.8(b).

    Public meeting on annual construction program for county, §136-44.8(c).

        Notice, §136-44.8(b).

    Public meeting on deviations or priority of paving projects, §136-44.8(d).

    Review of changes to which commissioners do not consent.

        Petition by board, §136-44.8(f).

    Submission of construction programs to boards of county commissioners, §136-44.8(a) to (f).

Federal guidelines for transportation projects, compliance, §136-44.7E.

Flooding.

    Closing of secondary roads within watershed improvement districts.

        Temporary inundation by floodwaters, §136-64.1(a) to (d).

Highway fund.

    Allocation for secondary road improvement program, §136-44.2A.

Highway trust fund.

    Allocation for secondary road construction, §136-44.2A.

HIGHWAYS, ROADS AND STREETS —Cont'd

Secondary road system —Cont'd

Highway trust fund —Cont'd

Construction of secondary roads.

Supplement for secondary road construction, §136-182.

Improvements.

Allocation from highway fund for secondary road improvement program, §136-44.2A.

Maintenance.

Federal guidelines for transportation projects, compliance, §136-44.7E.

Negotiation of right-of-way, §136-44.7(c).

Maintenance funds.

Uniformly applicable formula for allocation, §136-44.6.

Maintenance program.

Annual work program, §136-44.7(a).

Priority of paving of roads, §136-44.7(b).

Mileage study by department of transportation.

Unpaved state-maintained roads in counties eligible for paving, §136-44.5(a).

Allocation of funds to counties for paving, §136-44.5(b), (c).

Copies of study, availability to newspapers, §136-44.5(d).

State agency lands.

Paving of unpaved roads, §136-44.7A.

Statements.

Filing of annual statement, §136-44.9.

Unpaved roads.

Paving of unpaved road crossing state agency land, §136-44.7A.

State maintained roads eligible for paving.

Allocation of funds to counties for paving, §136-44.5(b), (c).

Mileage study by department of transportation, §136-44.5(a).

Copies of study, availability to newspapers, §136-44.5(d).

Supplement for secondary road construction, §136-182.

Watershed improvement districts.

Closing of secondary roads within.

Temporary inundation by floodwaters, §136-64.1(a) to (d).

Work program.

Annual work program, §136-44.7(a).

Secret societies.

Burning or flaming crosses.

Placing cross on public street or highway, §14-12.12(b).

Masks and hoods.

Wearing of masks, hoods, etc., on public ways, §14-12.7.

Selective vegetation removal permit.

Fee, §136-18.7.

Service of process.

Condemnation proceedings.

Answer to complaint, §136-106(b).

Disbursement of deposit order, §136-105.

Setback lines, building by municipalities, §160A-306.

Signs.

See HIGHWAY SIGNS.

Silver alert system.

Overhead permanent changeable message boards.

Making information available to motorists, §143B-1022(d).

Small businesses.

Small project bidding, §136-28.10(a) to (c).

HIGHWAYS, ROADS AND STREETS —Cont'd

Special proceedings.

Cartways, church roads or mill roads.

Establishment, alteration or discontinuance, §136-68.

Drainage of highway.

Right of appeal, §136-23.

Rights of parties, §136-24.

Special registration plate account.

Use of funds, §20-79.7(c).

Speed zones.

Signs marking beginning of reduced speed zones, §136-33.2A.

State highway administrator, §136-4.

Claims by contractors on completed contracts.

Decision by administrator, §136-29(a).

State highway fund.

Appropriation to municipalities, §136-41.1(a).

Allocation of funds, §136-41.1(a) to (c).

Contracts for maintenance, etc., of streets, §136-41.3.

Conversion of funds and property, §136-16.

Eligible municipalities, §§136-41.1(b), 136-41.2(a) to (c).

Incorporated before January 1, 1945, §136-41.2A(a), (b).

Incorporated since January 1, 1945, §136-41.2(d).

Excess accumulation of funds, §136-41.3.

Ineligibility for funds, §136-41.2B.

Nature of funds distributed, §136-41.1(d).

Records and annual statement, §136-41.3.

Small municipalities, accumulation of allocations, §136-41.3.

Use of funds, §136-41.3.

Election regarding allocated funds, use of funds, §136-41.4.

Cash management, §147-86.15.

Conversion of funds and property, §136-16.

Motor vehicle registration, plates and certificate of title fees.

Disposition of fees collected, §20-85(b).

State highway system.

Abandonment of segment of road and removal from state highway system.

Municipalities.

Authority to keep open and assume maintenance.

Roads within one mile of corporate limits, §136-55.1(b).

Notice, §136-55.1(a).

Airports.

Connection of state airports with public highway system, §136-18.

Construction.

Powers of department of transportation, §136-18.

Controlled-access facilities, §§136-89.48 to 136-89.59A. See within this heading, "Controlled-access facilities."

Control, repair and maintenance of highways, §136-45.

County public roads incorporated into state highway system, §§136-51 to 136-64.1. See within this heading, "Counties."

Development of coordinated system.

Additions to or removal from state highway system, §136-66.2(e).

General purpose of law, §136-45.

Maintenance program.

Biennial survey and report as to condition of highways, §136-44.3.

HIGHWAYS, ROADS AND STREETS —Cont'd
State highway system —Cont'd
Maintenance program —Cont'd
Control, repair and maintenance of highways, §136-45.
Powers of department of transportation, §136-18.
Responsibility for streets inside municipalities, §136-66.1.
Municipalities.
Maintenance of system by municipalities, §136-66.1.
Names of state highways, §136-18.
Purpose of law, §136-45.
Signs and traffic control devices.
Uniform manual, conformity to, power of department, §136-30(a).
Statewide annual maintenance program, §136-44.3.
State-maintained subdivision streets.
Traffic calming devices.
Criteria for installation, §136-102.8.
Statewide transportation system, §136-44.1.
Steel.
Production in United States.
Contract requirements relating to construction materials, §136-28.7(a) to (d).
Steep uphill grades.
Provision and marking of "pull-off" areas, §136-18.4.
Stop lights, §20-158.
Stopping.
Restrictions on stopping on highways, §20-161.
Street light assessments, §153A-206.
Administration, §153A-206(e).
Amount, §153A-206(c).
Authorization, §153A-206(a).
Basis, §153A-206(b).
Collection, §153A-206(e).
Procedure, §153A-206(d).
Structures.
Issuance of permits, §136-93(a).
Moved by owners over or along public roads or streets.
Interruption of utility service, §62-52.
Subdivision development.
Applicability of provisions, §136-102.6(g), (h).
Disclosure statement, §136-102.6(f).
Map or plat to be recorded, §136-102.6(a).
Delineation of changes, §136-102.6(b).
Minimum standards of board of transportation, §136-102.6(c).
Compliance with standards required of developers, §136-102.6.
Penalty for violation of provisions, §136-102.6(k).
Plans to be submitted to division of highways, §136-102.6(d).
Purposes of section, §136-102.6(i).
Traffic calming devices.
State-maintained subdivision streets, §136-102.8.
Utilities.
Policies and procedures for accommodating utilities, §136-102.6(e).
Summons and process.
Drainage of highway, §136-21.
Superior courts.
Condemnation proceedings.
Determination of issue of damages, §136-109(d).
Institution of action, §136-103(a).

HIGHWAYS, ROADS AND STREETS —Cont'd
Superior courts —Cont'd
Drainage of highway.
Application to court, §136-21.
Surveys and surveyors.
Condemnation proceedings.
Entry for surveys, §136-120.
Taxation.
Condemnation proceedings.
Reimbursement of owner for taxes paid on condemned property, §136-121.1(a), (b).
Local road taxes prohibited, §136-98(b).
Property taxes.
Authorized purposes, §160A-209.
Test.
Drilling or boring upon public land.
Filing record of results of test, §136-102.3.
Rights-of-way.
Authorization required for test drilling or boring upon right-of-way, §136-102.2.
Title.
Condemnation proceedings.
Vesting of title, §136-104.
Toll roads.
Conversion of free highways into toll facilities.
Prohibited, §136-89.187.
Public toll roads and bridges.
Turnpike authority, §§136-89.180 to 136-89.218.
See TURNPIKE AUTHORITY.
Turnpike system.
Control devices to collect tolls, §20-158.2.
Tourist-oriented directional sign program, §§136-140.15 to 136-140.19.
Traffic calming devices.
Subdivision streets.
Criteria for installation, §136-102.8.
Traffic congestion.
Urban areas.
Improvements in streets to reduce congestion, §136-66.5.
Traffic lights, §20-158.
Traffic regulations generally, §§20-138.1 to 20-171.
See TRAFFIC REGULATIONS.
Traffic signs and traffic control devices.
Generally.
See TRAFFIC SIGNS.
Uniform traffic control devices, §136-30(a) to (e).
Trailers.
Disabled trailers on highways.
Warning signals, §20-161(c).
Tramways.
Alteration or abandonment of tramways.
Manner of altering or abandoning, §136-70.
Laying out, §136-69(a) to (c).
Transportation board.
County public roads incorporated into state highway system.
No court action against board, §136-59.
Secondary road systems.
Additions to system, §136-44.10.
Statewide transportation system.
Formulation of policies, §136-44.1.
Subdivision streets.
Compliance with standards required of developers, §136-102.6.
Transportation corridor official maps, §§136-44.50 to 136-44.54.
Property taxes on property inside certain roadway corridors, §105-277.9.
Registering and indexing, time, §161-14(c).

HIGHWAYS, ROADS AND STREETS —Cont'd
Transportation department.
County public roads incorporated into state highway system.
Filing of complaints with system, §136-64.
Maintenance of county public roads vested in department, §136-51.
Organization of department, §§136-4 to 136-16.
See TRANSPORTATION DEPARTMENT.
Powers and duties, §§136-17.2 to 136-44.
See TRANSPORTATION DEPARTMENT.
Transportation engineering division.
Designation of boundaries, §136-14.1.
Trees and timber.
Cutting down trees.
Restrictions, §136-18.6.
Permits for planting, cutting or removal of vegetation, §136-93(b).
Monetary value of trees removed, §136-93.2.
Outdoor advertising, vegetation cut or removal limits, §136-93(c).
Site located within municipal limits, §136-93(d).
Truck routes, §20-141(i).
Trucks.
Disabled trucks on highways.
Warning signals, §20-161(c).
Tryon's Palace.
Restoration of Tryon's Palace.
Closing streets and including area in restoration project, §121-18.
Turnpike authority, §§136-89.180 to 136-89.218.
See TURNPIKE AUTHORITY.
Turnpikes.
Control devices to collect tolls, §20-158.2.
Limitation of actions.
No title by possession of rights-of-way, §1-44.
Unattended motor vehicles, §20-163.
Underpasses.
Elimination or safeguarding of inadequate underpasses, §136-20.
Universities and colleges.
Design, construction, etc., of roads and streets on campus, §136-18.
Urban areas.
Reduction in traffic congestion, §136-66.5.
Urban loops.
Acceptance of new interstate or freeway as revised termini of, §136-180(b).
Federal funds, §136-177.1.
Funds allocated from trust fund, §136-180(a).
Urban road systems.
Appropriations, §136-44.2.
Budget and appropriations, §136-44.2.
Construction.
Annual construction program, §136-44.4.
U.S. Marine Corps Highway: Home of Carolina-Based Marines since 1941.
Designation, §136-18.5C.
Vegetation removal permits.
Monetary value of trees removed, §136-93.2.
Outdoor advertising, vegetation cut or removal limits, §136-93(c).
Requirement, §136-93(b).
Site located within municipal limits, §136-93(d).
Waters and watercourses.
Diverting water from public road by ditch or drain, §136-95.
Watershed improvement districts.
Closing of secondary roads within.
Temporary inundation by floodwaters, §136-64.1(a) to (d).

HIGHWAYS, ROADS AND STREETS —Cont'd
Weigh stations, §§20-183.9, 20-183.10.
Contracts for construction, maintenance and repair.
Department of transportation, §136-28.1(d).
Welcome centers.
Contracts for construction, maintenance and repair.
Department of transportation, §136-28.1(d).
Real-time traveler information, §136-28.1(m).
Wesley D. Webster highway, §136-18.5.
Widening narrow roads.
Use of resurfacing program funds, §136-44.16.
Work programs.
Secondary road systems, §136-44.7(a).
Priority of paving of roads, §136-44.7(b).

HIGHWAY TRUST FUND, §§136-175 to 136-185.
See HIGHWAYS, ROADS AND STREETS.

HIGHWAY USE TAX, §§105-187.1 to 105-187.10.
Additional to all other taxes and fees, §105-187.2.
Amount.
Maximum tax, §105-187.3(a).
Appeals, §105-187.10(c).
Credits.
Tax paid in another state, §105-187.7(a).
Vehicle previously registered in another state, §105-187.7(b).
Definitions, §105-187.1.
Exemptions.
Full exemption, §105-187.6(a).
Out-of-state vehicles, §105-187.6(c).
Partial exemption, §105-187.6(b).
General fund.
Credit of taxes collected to, §105-187.9(a).
Highway trust fund.
Credit of taxes collected to, §105-187.9(a).
Transfer of taxes deposited.
General fund, §105-187.9(b).
Mobility fund, §105-187.9(c).
Imposition, §105-187.2.
Levy, §105-187.2.
Maximum tax, §105-187.3(a).
Mobility fund.
Credit of taxes collected to, §105-187.9(c).
Motor vehicles.
Renting or leasing.
Alternate tax, §105-187.5.
Retail value, §105-187.3(b).
Department of defense vehicles transferred to state agency, §105-187.3(b).
Return of purchased vehicle.
Refund of tax, §105-187.8.
Payment.
Methods, §105-187.4(a).
Sale by retailer, §105-187.4(b).
Penalties, §105-187.10(a).
Refunds.
Return of purchased motor vehicle, §105-187.8.
Renting or leasing of motor vehicles.
Alternate tax.
Election, §105-187.5(a).
Methods, §105-187.5(c).
Rate, §105-187.5(b).
Reporting, §105-187.5(d).
Retail value.
Motor vehicles, §105-187.3(b).
Department of defense vehicles transferred to state agency, §105-187.3(b).

HIGHWAY USE TAX —Cont'd
Return of purchased motor vehicle.
  Refund of tax, §105-187.8.
Schedules, §105-187.3(c).
Tax paid in another state.
  Credits, §105-187.7(a).
Unpaid taxes, §105-187.10(b).
Vehicle previously registered in another state.
  Credit, §105-187.7(b).

HIGHWAY WORK ZONES.
Speed limit, §20-141(j2).

HILLSBOROUGH.
Room occupancy tax.
  Uniform provisions.
    Authorized to levy, §160A-215(g).
    Generally, §160A-215.

HILLSBOROUGH HISTORICAL COMMISSION,
  §§143B-103 to 143B-106.
Appointments, §143B-106.
Compensation of members, §143B-106.
Creation, §143B-103.
Department of cultural resources.
  Transfer of commission to department, §143B-51.
Duties, §143B-103.
Exemption from provisions, §143B-104.
Members, §143B-106.
Powers and duties, §143B-103.
Quorum, §143B-106.
Reports.
  Submission of annual report, §143B-105.
Selection of members, §143B-106.
Status, §143B-104.

HINNIES.
Equine activity liability, §§99E-1 to 99E-3.

HIRED GUN.
Sentencing.
  Aggravating factor, §15A-1340.16.

HIRED PROPERTY.
Conversion.
  Bailees, lessees, tenants and attorneys in fact,
    §14-168.1.
  Evidence of intent to convert property.
    Prima facie evidence of intent, §14-168.3.
  Prima facie evidence of intent to convert.
    Property other than motor vehicle, §14-168.3.
    Trucks, automobile or other motor vehicles,
      §14-168.5(a).
  Trucks, automobile or other motor vehicles.
    Demand for return, §14-168.5(b).
    Prima facie evidence of intent to convert,
      §14-168.5(a).
Definitions, §14-168.2.
Failure to return hired property, §14-167.
Fraud.
  Hiring with intent to defraud, §14-168.
**Malicious or willful injury to hired personal
  property,** §14-165.
Protection of bailor against acts of bailee.
  Violations made misdemeanors, §14-169.
Subletting hired property, §14-166.
**Vehicles and draft animals, protection of
  bailor against bailee's act,** §§14-165 to
  14-169.
  Borrowing with intent to default, §14-168.
  Conversion by bailees, lessees, tenants or
    attorneys-in-fact, §14-168.1.
    Prima facie evidence of intent to convert,
      §14-168.3.
      Property other than motor vehicle, §14-168.3.

HIRED PROPERTY —Cont'd
**Vehicles and draft animals, protection of
  bailor against bailee's act** —Cont'd
  Conversion by bailees, lessees, tenants or
    attorneys-in-fact —Cont'd
    Prima facie evidence of intent to convert
      —Cont'd
      Truck, automobile or other motor vehicle,
        §14-168.5(a).
    Truck, automobile or other motor vehicle.
      Demand for return, §14-168.5(b).
      Prima facie evidence of intent to convert,
        §14-168.5(a).
  Definitions, §14-168.2.
  Failure to return hired property, §14-167.
    Reports of failure to return hired motor vehicle,
      §20-102.2.
  Malicious or willful injury to hired personal
    property, §14-165.
  Options to purchase.
    Failure to return rented property on which
      there is purchase option, §14-168.4.
  Subletting hired property, §14-166.
  Violations made misdemeanor, §14-169.

HISTORICAL ACTIVITIES.
Agritourism activity liability, §§99E-30 to
  99E-32.

HISTORICAL ASSOCIATIONS.
Counties.
  Assistance to, §153A-437(a) to (c).
Property taxes.
  Exemption of real and personal property,
    §105-278.7.
Roanoke Island historical association,
  §§143-199 to 143-202.
  See ROANOKE ISLAND HISTORICAL
    ASSOCIATION.

HISTORICAL COMMISSION.
Appointments, §143B-63.
  Officers, §143B-64.
Approval before acceptance by state, §100-2.
  Bridges and other structures, §100-3.
  Disqualification to vote, §100-6.
  Works of art, §100-2.
    Disqualification to vote, §100-6.
    Governor to accept works of art approved by
      commission, §100-4.
Archaeological resources protection.
  Rules and regulations, §70-14.
Budget.
  Allotment and expenditure of funds, §143B-53.1.
Compensation of members, §143B-63.
Creation, §143B-62.
Defined, §121-2.
Department of cultural resources.
  Transfer of commission functions to department,
    §143B-51.
Duties, §143B-62.
Executive mansion fine arts committee,
  §143B-79.
  Action approval, §143B-79.
Historical museums.
  State aid.
    Criteria for state aid to historical museums,
      §121-12(c1).
Historic properties.
  Criteria for state aid to historic properties,
    §121-12(c).
  Criteria for state historic properties, §121-12(b).

HISTORICAL COMMISSION —Cont'd
Historic structure rehabilitation tax credit.
 Certification process.
  Fees, adoption of schedule, §105-129.36A(b).
  Rules, adoption, §105-129.36A(a).
Legislative committees.
 Furnishing recommendations to committees,
  §121-12(d).
Meetings.
 Regular and special meetings, §143B-65.
Members, §143B-63.
National register.
 Protection of properties on register, §121-12(a).
North Carolina register of historic places.
 Criteria for inclusion, establishment, §121-4.1(b).
 Time for owners to concur or object to property
  inclusion.
  Rules and regulations to include, §121-4.1(c).
Officers, §143B-64.
Powers and duties, §143B-62.
Protection of properties on national register,
  §121-12(a).
Public buildings.
 Duties as to buildings erected or remodeled by
  state, §100-5.
Quorum, §143B-63.
Recommendations to legislative committees,
  §121-12(d).
Regulation of existing memorials, §100-2.
Reports.
 Expenditure of funds, §143B-53.1.
Selection of members, §143B-63.
Special meetings, §143B-65.
State aid.
 Historical museums.
  Criteria for state aid to historical museums,
   §121-12(c1).
 Historic properties.
  Criteria for state aid to historic properties,
   §121-12(c).
Works of art.
 Approval before acceptance by state, §100-2.
 Disqualification to vote, §100-6.
 Governor to accept works of art approved by
  commission, §100-4.

HISTORICAL DRAMAS.
Outdoor historical dramas.
 Allotments to outdoor historical dramas,
  §143-204.8.
 Amusement tax exemption, §105-40.
 Wage and hour act exemptions, §95-25.14(a).
 Youth employment, §95-25.5(h).

HISTORICAL MARKERS.
**Cooperation with department of cultural
  resources,** §136-42.2.
Correction of historical markers.
 Procedure for correction, §136-43.1.
Establishment of program, §136-42.3.
 Federal highway fund expenditures, §136-42.3.
**Procedure for correction and relocation of
  markers,** §136-43.1.
Purchase by department of transportation,
  §136-42.3.
Relocation of historical markers.
 Procedure for relocation, §136-43.1.

HISTORICAL PRESERVES.
**Dedication of state conservation and historical
  preserves,** §§143-260.6 to 143-260.10F.

HISTORICAL PRESERVES —Cont'd
Registry of natural heritage areas, §§113A-164.1
  to 113A-164.11.

HISTORICAL PUBLICATIONS.
Alkaline (acid-free) paper.
 Printing state publications of historical value on,
  §§125-11.13(a) to (c), 143-170.5.
Colonial North Carolina records, §121-6(c).
**Editing and publishing of official messages and
  other papers of governor,** §121-6(b).
Generally, §121-6(a).

**HISTORIC AND NATURE PRESERVE
  DEDICATIONS,** §§143-260.6 to 143-260.10F.
See NATURE AND HISTORIC PRESERVES.

HISTORIC DISTRICTS AND LANDMARKS,
  §§160A-400.1 to 160A-400.14.
Advertising.
 Outdoor advertising adjacent to districts.
  Limitations, §136-129.2(a) to (c).
Appropriations, §160A-400.12.
Buildings.
 Demolition of buildings and landmarks.
  Delay, §160A-400.14.
Certificate of appropriateness.
 Required for changes in historic properties,
  §160A-400.9.
Changes in historic properties.
 Certain changes not prohibited, §160A-400.13.
 Certificate of appropriateness required,
  §160A-400.9.
Conflict of laws, §160A-400.10.
Counties.
 Exercise of same powers as cities, §160A-400.2.
**Demolition of buildings and landmarks within
  district.**
 Delay, §160A-400.14.
Districts.
 Character of historic district, §160A-400.3.
 Designation.
  Applicability of provisions, §160A-400.4(d).
  Authority to designate, §160A-400.4(a).
  Local preservation commission
   recommendations, §160A-400.4(c).
  Prerequisites, §160A-400.4(b).
 Establishment.
  Criteria, §160A-400.3.
 Zoning ordinance, §160A-400.4.
Eminent domain.
 Powers of local public condemnors, §40A-3(b).
Findings of legislature, §160A-400.1.
Historic preservation commission.
 Appropriations, §160A-400.12.
 Duties, §160A-400.8.
 Establishment, §160A-400.7.
 Joint commission, §160A-400.7.
 Number of members, §160A-400.7.
 Powers and duties, §160A-400.8.
 Qualifications of members, §160A-400.7.
 Terms of members, §160A-400.7.
Injunctions.
 Violations of part, §160A-400.11.
Landmark designation.
 Authority, §160A-400.5.
 Criteria, §160A-400.5.
 Inventory of significant properties, §160A-400.6.
 Ordinance, §160A-400.5.
 Procedures, §160A-400.6.
Legislative findings, §160A-400.1.

HISTORIC DISTRICTS AND LANDMARKS
   —Cont'd
North Carolina register of historic places.
   Criteria for inclusion in register.
      North Carolina historical commission to
         establish, §121-4.1(b).
   Department of cultural resources.
      Power to establish, expand and maintain,
         §121-4.1(a).
   Objection by owner of property for inclusion,
      §121-4.1(c).
   Owners given time to concur or object to inclusion,
      §121-4.1(c).
Outdoor advertising adjacent to districts.
   Limitations, §136-129.2(a) to (c).
Swine houses, lagoons and land areas.
   Siting near historic places, §106-803(a), (b).
Violations of part.
   Remedies, §160A-400.11.
Wireless telecommunications facilities.
   Section not to be construed to limit requirements
      of regulation, §160A-400.52(i).

HISTORIC PRESERVATION.
Abandoned cemeteries, §121-8(g).
Advisory council.
   Department of cultural resources.
      Transfer of council to department, §143B-51.
Agreements, §§121-34 to 121-42.
Continuing programs, §121-8(f).
Cooperation with federal government,
   §121-8(d).
Cooperation with local governments, §121-8(e).
Defined, §121-2.
Designation of historic preservation agency,
   §121-8(a).
State historic sites special fund, §121-7.7.
Statewide historic preservation plan, §121-8(c).
Surveys of historic properties, §121-8(b).
**Tax credit for rehabilitation expenditures for
   historic structures,** §§105-129.35 to
   105-129.39.

**HISTORIC PRESERVATION AND
   CONSERVATION AGREEMENTS,** §§121-34
   to 121-42.
Acquisition of agreements, §§121-37, 121-38(b).
Applicability of article, §121-36(a).
Approval of agreements, §121-37.
**Assessment of land or improvements subject to
   agreement,** §121-40.
Citation of act, §§121-34, 121-42.
Construction and interpretation, §121-36(b), (c).
Definitions, §121-35.
Duration of agreements, §121-38(c).
Effectiveness of agreements, §121-38(c).
Enforceability of agreements, §121-38(a).
   Right of entry, §121-39(b).
   Who may enforce, §121-39(a).
**Future conveyance of property, provision
   requiring payment of fee,** §121-38(e).
Holders.
   Defined, §121-35.
   Enforceability of agreements, §121-39(a).
Public recording of agreements, §121-41.
Register of deeds.
   Public recording of agreements, §121-41(a).
Releases or terminations of agreements,
   §121-41(b).
Right of entry.
   Enforceability of agreements, §121-39(b).
Short title, §121-34.

**HISTORIC PRESERVATION AND
   CONSERVATION AGREEMENTS** —Cont'd
Taxation.
   Assessment of land or improvements subject to
      agreement, §121-40.
Validity of agreements, §121-38.
   Imposition of continuing obligations, §121-38(d).

HISTORIC PROPERTIES.
Acquisition of historic properties, §121-9(b).
   Administration of properties acquired by state,
      §121-9(a).
   Capitol of the state, §121-9(h).
   Emergency acquisition where funds not
      immediately available, §121-9(f).
   Interests which may be acquired, §121-9(c).
   Power to acquire property by condemnation,
      §121-9(g).
   Procedures where assistance extended to cities,
      counties and other agencies or individuals,
      §121-11.
   Reports, §121-9(b1).
   Use of properties so acquired, §121-9(e).
**Administration of properties acquired by
   state,** §121-9(a).
Allotment and expenditure of funds,
   §143B-53.1.
Capitol of the state, §121-9(h).
Condemnation.
   Power to acquire property by condemnation,
      §121-9(g).
**Conveyance of property for preservation
   purposes,** §121-9(d).
Counties.
   Acquisition, maintenance, etc., of property.
      Procedures where assistance extended, §121-11.
Defined, §121-2.
Development of historic properties.
   Procedures where assistance extended to cities,
      counties and other agencies or individuals,
      §121-11.
**Emergency acquisition where funds not
   immediately available,** §121-9(f).
Historical commission.
   Criteria for state aid, §121-12(c).
   Criteria for state historical properties, §121-12(b).
Interests which may be acquired, §121-8(c).
Maintenance of historical properties.
   Procedures where assistance extended to cities,
      counties and other agencies or individuals,
      §121-11.
North Carolina register of historic places.
   Criteria for inclusion in register.
      North Carolina historical commission to
         establish, §121-4.1(b).
   Department of cultural resources.
      Power to establish, expand and maintain,
         §121-4.1(a).
   Objection by owner of property for inclusion,
      §121-4.1(c).
   Owners given time to concur or object to inclusion,
      §121-4.1(c).
Power to acquire property by condemnation,
   §121-9(g).
**Procedures where assistance extended to
   cities, counties and other agencies or
   individuals,** §121-11.
Special peace officers.
   Arrest powers, §121-10(b).
   Bond, §121-10(c).

HISTORIC PROPERTIES —Cont'd
Special peace officers —Cont'd
Designated employees commissioned special peace
officers by governor, §121-10(a).
Oaths, §121-10(d).
State acquired properties.
Administration, §121-9(a).
State aid.
Criteria for state aid to historic properties,
§121-12(c).
State historic sites special fund, §121-7.7.
Surveys of historic properties.
Historic preservation program, §121-8(b).
Swine houses, lagoons and land areas.
Siting near historic places, §106-803(a), (b).
Tax credit for rehabilitation expenditures for
historic structures, §§105-129.35 to
105-129.39.
Use of property so acquired, §121-9(e).

HISTORIC PUBLICATIONS, §121-6.

HISTORIC ROANOKE ISLAND FUND (EFF
7/1/2012), §143B-131.8A.

HISTORIC STRUCTURE REHABILITATION
TAX CREDIT, §§105-129.35 to 105-129.39.
Allocation of credit among owners,
§105-129.35(b).
Amount of credit, §105-129.35(a).
Carryforward, §105-129.37(b).
Certification process.
Fees, adoption of schedule, §105-129.36A(b).
Rules needed to administer, adoption,
§105-129.36A(a).
Death of owner, exemption from forfeiture,
§105-129.37(e).
Definitions, §105-129.35(c).
Expiration of provisions, §105-129.39.
Forfeiture, §105-129.37(c), (d).
Exemptions, §105-129.37(e).
Liability, §105-129.37(f).
Income tax credited, §105-129.37(a).
Installment payments, taking credit in,
§105-129.37(b).
Nonincome producing structure.
Amount of credit, §105-129.36(a).
Definitions, §105-129.36(b).
Reports by department.
Requirements, time for publishing, §105-129.38.
Sunset of provisions, §105-129.39.

HISTORIC VEHICLES.
Exception to inspection requirements,
§20-183.2(a1).

HISTORY.
See ARCHIVES AND HISTORY.

HIT AND RUN, §20-166.
Commercial vehicles.
Disqualification from driving, §20-17.4(a).
Special information in judgment for conviction,
§20-24(e).
Mandatory revocation of driver's license.
Failure to stop and render aid, §20-17(a).
Motor vehicle accidents generally.
See MOTOR VEHICLE ACCIDENTS.
Points.
Schedule of point values, §20-16(c).
Special information in judgment in conviction,
§20-24(e).

HITCHHIKING.
Prohibited, §20-175(a).

HITMEN.
Sentencing.
Aggravating factor, §15A-1340.16.

HIV.
See AIDS AND HIV.

HIVES.
Bees and honey generally, §§106-634 to 106-644.
See BEES AND HONEY.

H.M.O., §§58-67-1 to 58-67-185.
See HEALTH MAINTENANCE ORGANIZATIONS.

HOAXES.
False bomb or other device, §14-69.2(a).
Minors causing bomb scares or threats.
Parental liability for disruption, §1-538.3.
Nuclear, biological or chemical weapons,
§14-288.24.
Perpetrating hoax by use of bomb or device,
§14-69.2.
Public buildings, §14-69.2(c).
Restitution, costs and consequential damages,
ordering, §14-69.2(d).

HOBOS.
Train surfing.
Riding on train unlawfully, §§14-460, 62-319.

HOG CHOLERA, §§106-310 to 106-322.3.
Burial.
Hogs and other livestock dying in transit,
§106-319.
Hogs dying natural death, §106-310.
Compensation for killing diseased animals
generally, §§106-323 to 106-335.
See LIVESTOCK DISEASES.
Confinement of hogs affected with cholera,
§106-311.
Control of livestock diseases generally,
§§106-400 to 106-405.
See LIVESTOCK DISEASES.
Cooperative agreements between state and
federal government, §106-322.1.
Counties.
Authorized to purchase and supply serums,
§106-316.
Destruction of swine affected with or exposed
to hog cholera, §106-322.2.
Indemnity payments, §106-322.2.
When indemnity payments not to be made,
§106-322.3.
Effect of sections, §106-322.
Eradication areas.
Establishment of areas, §106-322.1.
Health certificates.
Issuance for swine and livestock, §106-318.
Importation of hogs and other livestock into
state.
Regulation of transportation or importation,
§106-317.
Indemnity.
Destruction of swine affected with or exposed to
hog cholera, §106-322.2.
When indemnity payments not to be made,
§106-322.3.
Inspections required, §106-318.
Livestock diseases generally, §§106-304 to
106-307.7.
See LIVESTOCK DISEASES.
Manufacture and use of serum and virus
restricted, §106-314.

HOG CHOLERA —Cont'd
Natural death.
Burial of hogs dying natural death required, §106-310.
Penalties for violation of provisions,
§§106-316.4, 106-321.
Prevention of spread of hog cholera.
Purpose of article, §106-316.1.
Price of serum to be fixed, §106-313.
Purpose of article.
Prevention of spread of hog cholera, §106-316.1.
Regulation of transportation or importation of
hogs and other livestock into state,
§106-317.
Segregation of hogs affected with cholera,
§106-311.
Serum.
Counties authorized to purchase and supply serum, §106-316.
Manufacture and use of serum restricted, §106-314.
Price of serum to be fixed, §106-313.
Shipping hogs from cholera-infected territory,
§106-312.
State-federal hog-cholera cooperative
agreements, §106-322.1.
Transportation or importation of hogs and
other livestock into state.
Burial of hogs and other livestock dying in transit, §106-319.
Regulation of transportation or importation, §106-317.
United States.
State-federal hog-cholera cooperative agreements, §106-322.1.
Veterinarian.
Sale, use or distribution of hog-cholera virus or organisms.
Written permission from state veterinarian, §106-315.
Violation of provisions.
Penalties, §§106-316.4, 106-321.
Virus.
Definition of virulent hog-cholera virus, §106-316.2.
Importing hogs inoculated with virulent virus, §106-316.3.
Manufacture and use of serum restricted, §106-314.
Modified live virus vaccines, §106-316.2.
Use of virulent hog-cholera virus prohibited without permit, §106-316.2.

HOGSHEADS.
Truck on which leaf tobacco in hogsheads.
Load to be securely fastened, §20-120.

HOGS, PIGS AND SWINE.
Allowance to officers for keeping and
maintaining hogs taken into custody under
legal process, §1-322.
Animal waste management, §§143-215.10A to
143-215.10M.
See ANIMAL WASTE MANAGEMENT.
Certificate of registration obtained by false
representation, §14-103.
Compensation for killing diseased animals,
§§106-323 to 106-335.
See LIVESTOCK DISEASES.
Control of livestock diseases generally,
§§106-400 to 106-405.
See LIVESTOCK DISEASES.

HOGS, PIGS AND SWINE —Cont'd
County planning and zoning.
Swine farms served by animal waste management systems, §153A-340(b).
Dealer licensing generally, §§106-418.8 to
106-418.16.
See LIVESTOCK DEALER LICENSING.
Diseases generally, §§106-304 to 106-307.7.
See LIVESTOCK DISEASES.
Dogs killing hogs.
Any person may kill, §67-14.
Feeding garbage to swine, §§106-405.1 to
106-405.9.
Application for permit, §106-405.3.
Cooking or other treatment, §106-405.6.
Definitions, §106-405.1.
Enforcement of article, §106-405.8.
Fees.
Permit for feeding garbage to swine.
Application for permit, §106-405.3(b), (c).
Inspecting conditions, §106-405.7(a).
Investigating conditions, §106-405.7(a).
Penalties for violation of provisions, §106-405.9.
Permit for feeding garbage to swine.
Applicability of provisions, §106-405.2(c), (d).
Application for permit, §106-405.3(a).
Fees, §106-405.3(b), (c).
Federal permits.
Exemption of holders from provisions, §106-405.2(d).
Issuance, §106-405.2(a).
Prohibiting local regulations, §106-405.2(b).
Revocation of permits, §106-405.4.
Records to be maintained, §106-405.7(b).
Removal of garbage from premises, §106-405.7(c).
Revocation of permits for feeding garbage to swine, §106-405.4.
Rules and regulations, §106-405.8.
Sanitary conditions, §106-405.5.
Treatment of garbage fed to swine, §106-405.6.
Feral swine.
Identification required to transport.
Presumption that swine without identification feral, §106-798(b).
Live feral swine caught in traps.
Unlawful to remove and to transport after removal, §113-291.12.
Penalty, §113-294(s).
Hog cholera, §§106-310 to 106-322.3.
See HOG CHOLERA.
Larceny, §14-81.
Livestock markets.
Removal of swine from market for slaughter and nonslaughter purposes, §106-410.
Regulation of use of swine removed from market, §106-411.
Meat inspections.
Generally, §§106-549.15 to 106-549.39.
See MEAT INSPECTIONS.
Poisoning of livestock, §14-163.
Pork promotion assessments, §§106-790 to
106-796.
Pursuing or injuring with intent to steal,
§14-85.
Quarantine of diseased animals generally.
See LIVESTOCK DISEASES.
State institutions.
Keeping swine near state institutions, §143-153.
Swine farm siting, §§106-800 to 106-806.
Awarding costs, §106-804(c).
Definitions, §106-802.

HOGS, PIGS AND SWINE —Cont'd
Swine farm siting —Cont'd
Floodway.
Constructing liquid animal waste management
system component within 100-year
floodway, §106-803(a2).
Houses, construction or renovation at preexisting
swine farms.
Conditions, §106-806(b).
Definitions, §106-806(a).
Floodplains, prohibition, §106-806(b).
Inapplicability of provisions, §106-806(d).
Proximity to residence, school, hospital, church
or property boundary, §106-806(c).
Location requirements for swine house or lagoon,
§106-803(a).
Notice.
Written notice, §106-805.
Outdoor perimeter, location requirements,
§106-803(a1).
Permission to locate swine house or lagoon closer
to residence, school, etc., §106-803(b).
Persons directly affected by siting requirements,
§106-804(b).
Purpose, §106-801.
Restriction of other rights persons have,
§106-804(d).
Title of act, §106-800.
Transporting feral swine caught in traps.
Unlawful to remove and to transport after
removal, §113-291.12.
Penalty, §113-294(s).
**Transporting live swine, identification
required.**
Civil penalties for misuse of identification,
§106-798.2.
Civil penalties for transporting without
identification, §§106-798.1, 106-798(b).
Exceptions, §106-798(c).
Fee for identification, §106-798(d).
Presumption that swine feral, §106-798(b).
Requirement generally, §106-798(a).
**Violation points system applicable to permits
for animal waste management systems for
swine farms, §143-215.6E.**

HOKE COUNTY.
Agricultural tendencies in certain counties.
Terms of, §42-23.
Ambulances.
Attachment or garnishment and lien for
ambulance service, §§44-51.4 to 44-51.8.
Obtaining ambulance services without intending
to pay, §14-111.2.
Requesting ambulance falsely, §14-111.3.
**Condemnation or acquisition of land by local
government unit outside county.**
Consent of board of commissioners necessary,
§153A-15.
**Cropper or tenant refusing to perform terms
of contract.**
Forfeiture of right of possession to premises,
§42-27.
**Game laws, local acts not repealed,
§113-133.1(e).**
Housing authority commissioners.
Tenant as commissioner, exemption from provision
of law allowing, §157-5.
**Maps in special proceedings, recording of
photographic copies, §47-32.**
Violation as misdemeanor, inapplicability of
provisions, §47-32.2.

HOKE COUNTY —Cont'd
Oil, gas or mineral claims.
Certain ancient claims extinguished, preservation,
procedure, §1-42.1(a) to (d).
School property.
Acquisition and improvement, §153A-158.1.
**Southeastern North Carolina regional
economic development commission,
§§158-8.3 to 158-8.8.**
Special school tax, election to abolish.
Petition required, §115C-505.

HOLDEN BEACH.
Eminent domain.
Exercise of power, purposes, modified provisions,
§40A-3(b1).
Vesting of title and right to possession,
§40A-42(a).
**Ordinances to regulate and control swimming,
personal watercraft operation, surfing and
littering in Atlantic Ocean, §160A-176.2.**

HOLDER IN DUE COURSE.
Holder defined, §25-1-201(b).
Negotiable instruments.
Value.
When bank gives value for purposes of holder in
due course, §25-4-209.

**HOLD HARMLESS PROMISES OR
AGREEMENTS.**
**Construction indemnity agreements invalid,
§22B-1.**
Farm machinery franchises.
Supplier to hold harmless and indemnify dealer
against judgment, §66-187(b).
Leases, UCC.
Lessees furnishing specifications to lessor or
supplier, §25-2A-211(3).

HOLDING COMPANIES.
Bank holding companies.
Generally, §§53-225 to 53-232.
See BANK HOLDING COMPANIES.
Reciprocal interstate banking act generally,
§§53-209 to 53-218.
See RECIPROCAL INTERSTATE BANKING.
Franchise tax, §105-120.2.
Defined, §105-120.2(c).
Local taxation prohibited, §105-120.2(e).
Rate of tax, §105-120.2(b).
Reports, §105-120.2(a).
**Insurance holding companies, §§58-19-1 to
58-19-70.**
See INSURANCE HOLDING COMPANIES.
**Savings and loan holding companies,
§§54B-261, 54B-262.**
Savings banks, §§54C-178, 54C-195, 54C-196.

HOLDING OVER.
Landlord and tenant.
Summary ejectment, §§42-26 to 42-36.2.
Tenant holding over may be dispossessed in
certain cases, §42-26(a).

HOLIDAY FESTIVALS.
**Winery special event permit authorization,
§18B-1114.1.**

HOLIDAYS AND OBSERVANCES.
Act to be done falls on holiday, §103-5(a), (b).
American family day, §103-7.
**America's four hundredth anniversary
committee.**
Compensation of members, §143B-86.

HOLIDAYS AND OBSERVANCES —Cont'd
America's four hundredth anniversary committee —Cont'd
Creation, §143B-85.
Members, §143B-86.
Powers and duties, §143B-85.
Quorum, §143B-86.
Selection of members, §143B-86.
Arbor week, §103-6.
Banks.
Emergency suspension of business.
Legal holiday for certain purposes, §53-77.3(c).
Governor empowered to proclaim banking holidays, §53-77.
Opening for transactions on holidays not required, §53-54.
Savings banks, §54C-175.
Civil no-contact orders.
Workplace violence prevention.
Orders expiring on, extension, §95-267(d).
Computation of time, §§1-593, 1A-1 Rule 6(a).
County officers and employees, §153A-94(b).
Disability history and awareness month, §103-11.
Enumeration of legal holidays, §103-4(a).
Halloween.
Food distribution.
Certain foods prohibited at Halloween and all other times, §14-401.11.
Indian day.
Designation, §147-18.
Indian solidarity week, §103-8.
National Employ the Physically Handicapped Week.
Celebration, §143-283.3.
Pearl Harbor remembrance day, §103-10.
Prisoners of war recognition day, §103-9.
Public schools.
Number during school calendar, §115C-84.2(a).
Savings and loan associations, §54B-110.
Sundays.
General provisions.
See SUNDAYS.
Public holiday falling on Sunday.
Monday following to be public holiday, §103-4(b).
Thanksgiving day, §103-4(a).
Veterans.
Pearl Harbor remembrance day, §103-10.
Prisoner of war recognition day, §103-9.
Workplace violence prevention.
Civil no-contact orders.
Orders expiring on, extension, §95-267(d).

HOLLY RIDGE.
Satellite annexation.
Limitation on area of satellite corporate limits, inapplicability, §160A-58.1(b).

HOLLY SPRINGS.
Accessory building of bona fide farm.
Building code exemption.
Zoning ordinance, §160A-360(k).
Satellite annexation.
Limitation on area of satellite corporate limits, inapplicability, §160A-58.1(b).

HOLOCAUST.
North Carolina council on the Holocaust, §143A-48.1.
Appointment of members, §143A-48.1(b).
Assistance, §143A-48.1(d).

HOLOCAUST —Cont'd
North Carolina council on the Holocaust —Cont'd
Clerical or other assistance, §143A-48.1(d).
Composition, §143A-48.1(b).
Creation, §143A-48.1(a).
Expenses of members.
Reimbursement, §143A-48.1(c).
Purpose, §143A-48.1(a).
Quorum, §143A-48.1(b).
Terms of members, §143A-48.1(b).

HOLOGRAPHIC WILLS, §31-3.4(a), (b).
Beneficiaries.
Competency as witness, §31-10(b).
Personal property and real property may be devised by, §31-3.2(a).
Probate, §28A-2A-9.
Wills generally.
See WILLS.

HOME APPLIANCE SERVICE AGREEMENT COMPANIES.
Applicability of provisions, §§66-371(a), 66-372(a).
Authority restricted, §66-371(a).
Cancellation of agreement, §66-372(e).
Contents of agreement.
Prohibited contents, §66-372(d).
Required contents, §66-372(e).
Definitions, §§66-371(b), 66-372(b).
Disclosures.
Required disclosures, §66-372(c).
Financial statements, §66-371(a).
Fronting company, §66-372(h).
Funds, §66-372(i).
Insurance.
Requirements, §66-373.
Name, §66-372(l).
Records, §66-372(f).
Registration.
Required, §66-372(j).
Transacting business, §66-371(a).

HOME CARE AGENCY LICENSING.
Adverse action on licenses, §131E-139(a), (b).
Application for license, §131E-138(c).
Criminal history record checks of applicants for employment.
Conditional employment, §131E-265(f).
Confidentiality, §131E-265(a).
Contract agency offering employment, §131E-265(a1).
Factors in determining whether to hire applicant.
Record check revealing one or more convictions of relevant offense, §131E-265(b).
Immunity, §131E-265(c), (g).
Penalty for furnishing false information, §131E-265(e).
Refusal to consent to check, §131E-265(a).
Relevant offense defined, §131E-265(d).
Requirement as condition of employment, §131E-265(a).
Contract agency offering employment, §131E-265(a1).
Submission of request to department of justice, §131E-265(a).
Criminal record checks of providers of treatment for or services to children, elderly, mental health patients, etc., §114-19.3.
Definitions, §131E-136.

HOME CARE AGENCY LICENSING —Cont'd
Enforcement of rules, §131E-140(b).
Establishment of licensing requirements.
  Purpose of part, §131E-135(b).
Home care services, 131E-136.
Injunctions.
  Hindering secretary's performance of duties,
    §131E-142(b).
  Operation without license, §131E-142(a).
  Procedure, §131E-142(c).
Inspections, §131E-141(a), (b).
License required to operate, §131E-138(a).
NC NOVA special licensure designation,
    §§131E-154.12 to 131E-154.14.
  Change in ownership, §131E-154.14(g).
  Confidentiality of information submitted by
    applicants, §131E-154.14(c).
  Definitions, §131E-154.13.
  Duration of designation, §131E-154.14(g).
  Establishment of program, §131E-154.14(a).
  Purpose of provisions, §131E-154.12(b).
  Reapplication intervals, §131E-154.14(d).
  Rules to implement, §131E-154.14(b).
  Title of provisions, §131E-154.12(a).
Posting in conspicuous place, §131E-138(f).
Purpose of act, §131E-135(b).
Renewal of license, §131E-138(d).
Rules, adoption, §131E-138(g).
Rules and regulations, §131E-140(a), (a1).
Services provided in all counties, §131E-137(a),
  (c).
Smoking, employees prohibited from,
    §131E-143(a).
  Administrative penalties, §131E-143(b).
Title of part.
  Home health agency licensure act, §131E-135(a).
Transfer or assignment, restriction,
    §131E-138(e).
Violation of provisions, §131E-141.1.

HOME CARE CLIENTS' BILL OF RIGHTS,
    §§131E-144.1 to 131E-144.7.
Acceptance or refusal of care, §131E-144.3.
Agency's initial evaluation visit.
  Notice to client, §131E-144.4(a).
Complaint process, §131E-144.6(a1).
  Confidentiality of persons registering complaints,
    §131E-144.7(b).
Confidentiality of personal and medical
    information, §§131E-144.3, 131E-144.7(a).
Definitions, §131E-144.2.
Enforcement of rights, §131E-144.6(a).
Enumeration of rights, §131E-144.3.
Free from abuse, neglect and exploitation,
    §131E-144.3.
Grievance about care, right to voice,
    §131E-144.3.
Implementation of provisions, §131E-144.5.
Investigation of violations of rights,
    §131E-144.6(b).
Listing of rights, §131E-144.3.
Notice to client, §131E-144.4.
Plan of care.
  Right to be informed and participate in,
    §131E-144.3.
Public policy, §131E-144.1.
Receipt of declaration of rights, §131E-144.4(b).
Supervisory accessibility and availability,
    §131E-144.3.
Treated with respect, §131E-144.3.

HOME CARE CLIENTS' BILL OF RIGHTS
  —Cont'd
Written statement of fees and charges,
    §131E-144.3.

HOME CARE SERVICES.
Continuing care retirement communities.
  Application to administer continuing care services
    without lodging, §58-64-7(a).
  Binding written service agreements, §58-64-7(b).
  Financial accounting requirements, §58-64-7(c).

HOME FOR AGED AND INFIRM.
Domiciliary homes.
  General provisions.
    See DOMICILIARY HOMES.
Nursing homes.
  General provisions.
    See NURSING HOMES.
Nursing pools.
  General provisions, §§131E-154.1 to 131E-154.8.
    See NURSES.

HOME FORECLOSURE RESCUE SCAMS,
    §§75-120 to 75-122.
Contracts in which transferee pays at least
    50% of fair market value.
  Requirements, §75-121(b).
Definitions, §75-120.
Foreclosure rescue transaction.
  Defined, §75-120.
  Prohibited transactions, §75-121(a).
  Remedies, §75-122.
Prohibited transactions, §75-121(a).
  Remedies, §75-122.
Remedies, §75-122.
Unfair trade practice, §75-122.

HOME FORECLOSURES.
Emergency program to reduce home
    foreclosures, §§45-100 to 45-107.
Foreclosure of mortgages or deeds of trust
    generally.
  See FORECLOSURE.
Home protection program, §122A-5.14.
Rescue scams, §§75-120 to 75-122.

HOME HEALTH AGENCY LICENSING.
Criminal history records checks of employees,
    §114-19.10.

HOME HEALTH AGENCY OFFICES.
Certificates of need, §§131E-175 to 130E-191.1.
  See HEALTH CARE FACILITIES.

HOME IMPROVEMENTS.
High cost home loans, use of proceeds,
    §24-1.1E(c).

HOME INSPECTORS, §§143-151.43 to 143-151.64.
Applicability of provisions.
  Exceptions, §143-151.62.
Associate home inspectors.
  Defined, §143-151.45.
Bond required, §143-151.58(b).
Citation of act.
  Short title, §143-151.43.
Continuing education for licensees,
    §143-151.64(a).
  Credit for unapproved course, §143-151.64(c).
  Extension of time to comply, §143-151.64(d).
  Fees, §143-151.64(b).
  Rules, §143-151.64(e).
Definitions, §143-151.45.

HOME INSPECTORS —Cont'd
Division of engineering and building code.
Duties, §143-151.63(a).
Exceptions to provisions, §143-151.62.
Fees.
Deposit of moneys received by board,
§143-151.63(b).
Licenses, §143-151.57.
Injunctions, §143-151.60.
Legislative declaration, §143-151.44.
Licenses.
Applications.
Contents, §143-151.51(a).
Notification of applicant following evaluation of
application, §143-151.53.
Bond in lieu of insurance, §143-151.51(b).
Change of address by license holder.
Report to board, §143-151.54.
Continuing education, §143-151.64.
Criminal convictions.
Reporting to board, §143-151.54(b).
Denial.
Grounds, §143-151.56(a).
Hearing, §143-151.56(b).
Disciplinary actions.
Reporting to board, §143-151.54(b).
Display of license, §143-151.54(a).
Eligibility for licensure, §143-151.51(a).
Errors and omissions insurance, §143-151.51(b).
Examinations.
Failure of examination.
Subsequent application.
Additional application fee not required,
§143-151.57(b).
Knowledge gained through experience to be
emphasized, §143-151.49(b).
Fees.
Maximum fees, §143-151.57(a).
General liability insurance, §143-151.51(b).
Inactive licenses, §143-151.55(c).
Individuals only to be licensed, §143-151.50(b).
Lapsed license, §143-151.55(d).
Notification of applicant following evaluation of
application, §143-151.53.
Probationary conditions.
Grounds, §143-151.56(a).
Hearing, §143-151.56(b).
Property of board, §143-151.54(a).
License as, §143-151.54.
Renewal, §143-151.55(a).
Late renewal, §143-151.55(b).
Refusal to renew.
Grounds, §143-151.56(a).
Hearing, §143-151.56(b).
Required, §143-151.50(a).
Revocation or suspension.
Grounds, §143-151.56(a).
Hearing, §143-151.56(b).
Reinstatement of revoked license.
Application for, §143-151.56(b).
Surrender of license to board, §143-151.54.
Licensure board.
Books and records.
Oversight of state auditor, §143-151.63(c).
Compensation of members, §143-151.47.
Definition of "board,"§143-151.45.
Deposit of moneys received by board,
§143-151.63(b).
Meetings, §143-151.48(b).
Members, §143-151.46(a).
Officers, §143-151.48(a).

HOME INSPECTORS —Cont'd
Licensure board —Cont'd
Powers, §143-151.49(a).
Terms of members, §143-151.46(b).
Vacancies, §143-151.46(c).
Misdemeanors, §143-151.59.
Purpose of act, §143-151.44.
Records, §143-151.58(d).
Licensure board.
Books and records subject to oversight of state
auditor, §143-151.63(c).
**Report to person for whom inspection
perform, §143-151.58(a).**
**Supervision of licensed associate,
§143-151.58(c).**
Title of act.
Short title, §143-151.43.

HOMELESS PERSONS.
Housing finance authority.
Powers, §122A-5.
Public schools.
Enrollment of homeless children and youth,
§115C-366(a2).
**Special identification cards for nonoperators
of motor vehicles.**
Obtaining without paying fee, §20-37.7(d).

HOME LOANS.
Consumer home loans, §24-10.2.
**Contract rates on loans secured by first
mortgages or first deeds of trust, §24-1.1A.**
Defined.
Contract rates on home loan secured by first
mortgage or first deed of trust, §24-1.1A(e).
Emergency program to reduce home foreclosures,
§45-101.
Mortgage debt collection and servicing, §45-90.
Foreclosure.
Emergency program to reduce home foreclosures,
§§45-100 to 45-107.
Home foreclosure rescue scams, §§75-120 to
75-122.
Mortgages and deeds of trust generally.
See FORECLOSURE.
Generally.
See MORTGAGES AND DEEDS OF TRUST.
High cost home loans, §24-1.1E.
**Home foreclosure rescue scams, §§75-120 to
75-122.**
Late payment charges, §24-10.1.
Rate spread home loans, §24-1.1F.

HOMEMAKERS.
**Displaced homemakers, §§143B-394.4 to
143B-394.10.**
See DISPLACED HOMEMAKERS.

HOMEOPATHIC DRUGS.
Food, drug and cosmetic act.
Drugs deemed adulterated, §106-133.
Drugs deemed misbranded, §106-134.

HOMEOWNERS' INSURANCE.
Beach area essential property insurance.
Generally, §§58-45-1 to 58-45-96.
See BEACH AREA ESSENTIAL PROPERTY
INSURANCE.
Issuance of policy, §58-45-35(b1).
Claim closed without payment.
Termination or refusal to issue or renew
residential real property insurance.
Prohibition, §58-36-115.

HOMEOWNERS' INSURANCE —Cont'd
Inquiry as to policy provisions not resulting in claim.
Termination or refusal to issue or renew residential real property insurance.
Prohibition, §58-36-115.
Notice of residential property insurance rate increase.
North Carolina rate bureau, §58-36-120.
Rate bureau.
Generally, §§58-36-1 to 58-36-115.
See RATE BUREAU.

HOMEOWNERS' OR PROPERTY OWNERS' ASSOCIATIONS.
Alcoholic beverage permits.
Special one-time permits, §18B-1002(a).
Franchise tax.
Exemption, §105-125(a).

HOMEOWNERS RECOVERY FUND, §§87-15.5 to 87-15.9.
Administration, §87-15.6(a).
Building permit fees.
Collection, §87-15.6(b).
Definitions, §87-15.5.
Establishment, §87-15.6(a).
Purposes, §87-15.6(a).
Reimbursements.
Application, §87-15.8(a).
Determination of procedures, §87-15.7(a).
Eligibility, §87-15.8(a).
Payment, §87-15.8(b).
Subrogation, §87-15.9.
Rules and regulations.
Adoption, §87-15.6(c).
Subrogation.
Reimbursements, §87-15.9.
Use of funds, §87-15.7(b).

HOME PROTECTION PROGRAM.
Loss of home due to foreclosure, §122A-5.14.

HOME SCHOOLING.
Courses sold to home schools, private schools, etc, by state board of education.
Exception to prohibition on sale of merchandise by governmental units, §66-58(c).
Definitions, §115C-563(a), (b).
Driving eligibility certificates.
Adoption of procedures to meet requirements, §115C-566(a).
Flu and meningitis and vaccines.
Information provided, §115C-565.
Qualifications, §115C-564.
Requirements.
Exclusivity, §115C-565.
Generally, §115C-564.

HOME-SOLICITATION SALES.
Cancellation.
Buyer's right to cancel, §25A-39(a).
Limitation, §25A-39(e).
Delay of seller, §25A-39(f).
No compensation for services of seller prior to cancellation, §25A-42(c).
Notice of cancellation, §25A-39(b), (c).
Form, §25A-39(d).
Restoration of down payment, §25A-41(a).
Goods as down payment, §25A-41(b).
Return and care of goods, §25A-42(a).
Care of goods by buyer, §25A-42(b).
Defined, §25A-38.

HOME-SOLICITATION SALES —Cont'd
Failure to give right to cancel in off premises sales, §14-401.13.
Form of agreement or offer, §25A-40(b).
Negotiation or transfer of note, contract or other evidence of indebtedness.
Compensation, §25A-42(d).
Time limitation, §25A-42(d).
Statement of buyer's rights, §25A-40(a).

HOMESTEAD CIRCUIT BREAKER.
Property tax.
Affect on attachment of lien, §105-277.1B(m).
Applicability of definitions, §105-277.1B(b).
Applicability of income eligibility limit, §105-277.1B(c).
Apportionment of taxes due and taxes deferred among taxing units, §105-277.1B(f).
Ceasing to use property as permanent residence.
Disqualifying event, §105-277.1B(i).
Classification of residence, §105-277.1B(a).
Creditor limitations, §105-277.1B(l).
Death of owner.
Disqualifying event, exception, §105-277.1B(i).
Deferral of portion of tax, §105-277.1B(f).
Disqualifying events, §105-277.1B(i).
Filing of application, §105-277.1B(n).
Husband and wife owning and occupying residence as tenants by the entirety, §105-277.1B(e).
Interruption of qualification, §105-277.1B(j).
Lien for deferred taxes, §105-277.1B(h).
Multiple owners, §105-277.1B(e).
Payment of deferred taxes.
Uniform provisions, §105-277.1F.
Qualifying owner, §105-277.1B(d).
Tax imitation, §105-277.1B(f).
Temporary absence from residence, §105-277.1B(g).
Transfer of residence.
Disqualifying event, exception, §105-277.1B(i).

HOMESTEAD EXEMPTIONS, §1C-1601.
Acts barring rights of spouse.
Rights lost, §31A-1(b).
Alternative exemptions, §1C-1602.
Amount of personal and real property, §1C-1601.
Appraisal costs.
Laying off homestead and exemption, §6-28.
Reassessment of homestead, §6-29.
Bankruptcy code exemptions.
Inapplicable to residents of state, §1C-1601(f).
Children.
Exemption for benefit of children, NC Const Art X §2.
Conveyance of homestead, NC Const Art X §2.
Costs.
Appraising costs and expenses, §6-28.
Laying off homestead and exemption, §6-28.
Reallotment of homestead for increase in value.
Allowance of costs to either party or apportioned in discretion of court, §6-21.
Reassessment of homestead, §6-29.
Definitions, §1C-1601(b).
Disabled persons.
Property tax exclusion, §105-277.1.
Notice on abstract, §105-309(f).
Effect of exemptions, §1C-1604(a).
Exceptions, §1C-1601(e).
Execution sales, NC Const Art X §2.
Exemption from sale, NC Const Art X §2.

HOMESTEAD EXEMPTIONS —Cont'd
Execution sales —Cont'd
Mechanics' and materialmen's liens.
Inapplicability of exemption, NC Const Art X §3.
Judgment enforcing lien upon homestead.
Limitation as to execution and not to apply, §1-306.
Laborers' liens.
Inapplicability of exemption, NC Const Art X §3.
Mechanics' and materialmen's liens.
Inapplicability of exemption, NC Const Art X §3.
Minors.
Exemption for benefit of children, NC Const Art X §2.
Property tax exclusion.
Elderly and disabled, §105-277.1.
Notice on abstract, §105-309(f).
Recent purchases not exempt, exception, §1C-1601(d).
Senior citizens.
Property tax exclusion, §105-277.1.
Notice on abstract, §105-309(f).
Setting aside exempt property.
Modification, §1C-1603(g).
Motion, §1C-1603(a).
Contents, §1C-1603(b).
Notation of order on judgment docket, §1C-1603(f).
Notice to persons affected, §1C-1603(d).
Petition, §1C-1603(a).
Contents, §1C-1603(b).
Procedure, §1C-1603(e).
Statement by debtor, §1C-1603(c).
Surviving spouse.
Exemption for benefit of surviving spouse, NC Const Art X §2.
Waiver, §1C-1601(c).

HOMESTEAD TAX RELIEF.
Property taxes.
Homestead circuit breaker, §105-277.1B.
Uniform provision for payment of deferred taxes, §105-277.1F.
Homestead exclusion, §105-277.1.
Disabled veterans, §105-277.1C.

HOMICIDE.
Attorney general.
Domestic violence-related homicides.
Reporting and database system, §114-2.7.
Autopsies, §15-7.
Capital punishment.
Crimes punishable by death, NC Const Art XI §2.
Generally.
See DEATH PENALTY.
Death by vehicle, §20-141.4.
Felony death by vehicles, §20-141.4(a1).
Aggravated felony death by vehicle, §20-141.4(a5).
Repeat offenders.
Second degree murder, §20-141.4(a6).
Mandatory revocation of license, §20-17(a).
Permanent revocation, §20-19(i).
Misdemeanor death by vehicles, §20-141.4(a2).
Punishments, §20-141.4(b).
Decedents' estates.
Slayer act, §31A-6.
Definitions, §14-17.
Electronic recording of custodial interrogations, §15A-211.

HOMICIDE —Cont'd
Felony death by vehicles, §20-141.4(a1).
Aggravated felony death by vehicle, §20-141.4(a5).
Punishment, §20-141.4(b).
Repeat offenders.
Second degree murder, §20-141.4(a6).
First degree murder, §14-17.
Guilty plea.
Death penalty or life imprisonment, §15A-2001.
Impaired driving.
Special information if conviction of homicide involves, §20-24(e).
Indictments.
Essentials of bill for homicide, §15-144.
Indigent persons.
Representation of indigent persons.
Appointment of assistant counsel, §7A-450(b1).
Juveniles under 17 years of age.
First degree murder, §14-17.
Killing decedent, §§31A-3 to 31A-15.
See SLAYER ACT.
Malice aforethought.
Allegation required in indictment, §15-144.
Manslaughter.
DNA sample for DNA analysis.
Obtaining upon arrest for, §15A-266.3A.
Double jeopardy.
Death by vehicle.
Subsequent prosecutions prohibited, §20-141.4(c).
Indictments.
Essentials of bill, §15-144.
Motor vehicles.
Revocation or suspension of license.
Mandatory revocation, §20-17(a).
Permanent revocation, §20-19(i).
Punishment for manslaughter, §14-18.
Unborn child.
Involuntary manslaughter, §14-23.4.
Voluntary manslaughter, §14-23.3.
Unborn child.
Involuntary manslaughter, §14-23.4.
Voluntary manslaughter, §14-23.3.
Misdemeanor death by vehicles, §20-141.4(a2).
Punishment, §20-141.4(b).
Murder.
Definitions.
Murder in first and second degree, §14-17.
Degrees, §14-17.
Verdict for murder in first or second degree, §15-172.
DNA sample for DNA analysis.
Obtaining upon arrest for, §15A-266.3A.
First degree.
Juveniles under 17 years of age, §14-17.
Indictments.
Essentials of bill, §15-144.
Indigent persons.
Representation of indigent persons.
Appointment of assistant counsel, §7A-450(b1).
Juvenile committed for placement in youth development center for offense of first degree if committed by adult.
Continued jurisdiction of juvenile court, §7B-1602(a).
Malice aforethought.
Allegation required in indictment, §15-144.
Punishment, §14-17.
Unborn child, §14-23.2.

HOMICIDE —Cont'd
Murder —Cont'd
Verdict.
First or second degree, §15-172.
Postmortem examinations, §15-7.
Second degree murder, §14-17.
Simultaneous death.
Victim survival of slayer, presumption, §28A-24-5.
Slayer act.
Decedents' estates, §31A-6.
Killing decedent generally, §§31A-3 to 31A-15.
See SLAYER ACT.
Suicide.
Crime of suicide abolished, §14-17.1.
Unborn child.
Involuntary manslaughter, §14-23.4.
Murder, §14-23.2.
Voluntary manslaughter, §14-23.3.
Vehicular homicide.
Death by vehicle, §20-141.4.
Mandatory revocation of driver's license, §20-17(a).
Permanent revocation, §20-19(i).
Venue.
Assault in one county, death in another, §15-130.
Assault in this state, death in another, §15-131.
County where death occurs, §15-133.
Verdict.
Murder.
First or second degree, §15-172.
Wills.
Lapse.
Property passes according to lapse statute, §31A-10(a).
Workers' compensation.
Injury or death caused by willful intention of employee to injure or kill another.
No compensation payable, §97-12.

HOMINY.
Standard weight, §81A-42.

HOMOSEXUAL MARRIAGES, §51-1.2.

HONEY.
Generally, §§106-634 to 106-644.
See BEES AND HONEY.

HONEYBEE.
Generally, §§106-634 to 106-644.
See BEES AND HONEY.
State insect, §145-7.

HONOR AND REMEMBER FLAG.
Armed forces members who have died in the line of duty, §145-32.

HOOF AND MOUTH DISEASE.
Livestock diseases.
Emergency measures when threat imminent.
Warrantless inspection, §106-399.5.
Generally, §§106-400 to 106-405.

HORIZONTAL PROPERTY.
Condominiums, §§47C-1-101 to 47C-4-120.
See CONDOMINIUMS.
Unit ownership, §§47A-1 to 47A-28.
See UNIT OWNERSHIP.

HORMONES.
Biological residues in animals, §§106-549.81 to 106-549.89.
See BIOLOGICAL RESIDUES IN ANIMALS.

HORNS AND WARNING DEVICES ON MOTOR VEHICLES.
Ambulances, §§20-156(b), 20-157(a).

HORNS AND WARNING DEVICES ON MOTOR VEHICLES —Cont'd
Disabled trucks and trailers, §20-161(c).
Fire department vehicles.
Siren must be audible within 1,000 feet, §20-157(a).
Siren necessary for right of way, §20-156(b).
Overtaking and passing.
Duty of driver of overtaking vehicle to give audible warning, §20-149(b).
Pedestrians.
Signal to pedestrian by horn or warning device, §20-154(a).
Police department vehicles.
Siren must be audible within 1,000 feet, §20-157(a).
Siren necessary for right of way, §20-156(b).
Requirements generally, §20-125(a).
Safety inspections.
Scope of inspection, §20-183.3(a).
Siren must be audible within 1,000 feet, §§20-156(b), 20-157(a).
Siren necessary for right of way, §20-157(a).
Special horns on vehicles, §20-125(b).
Turning, §20-154.

HORSEBACK RIDING.
Equine activity liability, §§99E-1 to 99E-3.

HORSE INDUSTRY PROMOTION, §§106-820 to 106-825.
Assessment, §§106-823 to 106-825.
Definitions, §106-822.
Purpose, §106-821.
Short title, §106-820.

HORSEPASTURE RIVER.
Natural and scenic rivers system.
Additional component of system, §113A-35.2.

HORSERADISH.
Standard weight and measure, §81A-42.

HORSES.
Allowance to officers for keeping and maintaining horses taken into custody under legal process, §1-322.
Bailments.
Vehicles and draft animals, protection of bailor against bailee's act, §§14-165 to 14-169.
See BAILMENTS.
Bribery of horse show judges or officials, §14-380.1.
Attempts at bribery to be reported, §14-380.2.
Definition of "bribe," §14-380.3.
Printing provisions of article in horse show schedules, §14-380.4.
Carcasses.
Slaughter, sale and transportation of carcasses, §106-549.25.
Cattle tick, §§106-351 to 106-363.
See CATTLE TICK.
Certificate of registration obtained by false representation, §14-103.
Colonial Spanish mustang.
State horse, §145-31.
Compensation for killing diseased animals, §§106-323 to 106-335.
See LIVESTOCK DISEASES.
Control of livestock diseases generally, §§106-400 to 106-405.
See LIVESTOCK DISEASES.
Dealer licensing generally, §§106-418.8 to 106-418.16.
See LIVESTOCK DEALER LICENSING.

HORSES —Cont'd
Diseases generally, §§106-304 to 106-307.7.
  See LIVESTOCK DISEASES.
Equine activity liability, §§99E-1 to 99E-3.
Equine infectious anemia, §§106-405.15 to
  106-405.20.
  Civil penalties, §106-405.20.
  Control and eradication program.
    Implementation of program, §106-405.18.
  Defined, §106-405.15.
  Fine, §106-405.20.
  Implementation of control and eradication
    program, §106-405.18.
  Quarantine of infected or exposed animals,
    §106-405.16.
  Rules and regulations.
    Authority to promulgate and enforce,
      §106-405.17.
  Violation made misdemeanor, §106-405.19.
Larceny.
  Felony, §14-81(a).
  Probation, conditions required, §14-81(b).
  Sentencing to active sentence.
    Judge's authority not limited, §14-81(b).
  Taking horses for temporary purposes, §14-82.
Livestock brands generally, §§80-45 to 80-66.
  See LIVESTOCK BRANDS.
Meat inspection.
  Equine carcasses.
    Slaughter, sale and transportation of carcasses,
      §106-549.25.
Motor vehicles.
  Passing horses or other draft animals.
    Reasonable care, §20-216.
Poisoning of horses, §14-163.
Ponies.
  Outer Banks, §§68-42 to 68-46.
    Colonial Spanish mustang.
      State horse, §145-31.
  Removal or confinement of ponies on Ocracoke
    Island and Shackleford Banks, §68-43.
  Running at large.
    Exceptions to prohibition, §68-42.
Promotion of horse industry.
  Assessment.
    Amount required on referendum ballot,
      §106-823(c).
    Applicability, §106-824(a).
    Approval by majority, §106-824(a).
    Council determinations required, §106-823(b).
    Notice and eligibility for voting, §106-823(d).
    Referendum request, §106-823(a).
    Refund, §106-825(b).
    Unpaid assessment collection, §106-824(b).
    Use of funds collected, §106-825(a).
  Definitions, §106-822.
  Legislative purpose, §106-821.
  Short title of article, §106-820.
Protection of horse shows.
  Bribery of horse show judges or officials,
    §14-380.1.
  Attempts at bribery to be reported, §14-380.2.
  Definition of "bribe," §14-380.3.
  Printing provisions of article in horse show
    schedules, §14-380.4.
Pursuing or injuring with intent to steal,
  §14-85.
Quarantine of diseased animals generally.
  See LIVESTOCK DISEASES.
Sales and use tax.
  Exemption, §105-164.13.

HORSES —Cont'd
Stables.
  Arson, §14-62.
State horse, §145-31.
Traffic laws apply to riding animals, §20-171.

HORSE SHOWS.
Alcoholic beverages.
  Sports club.
    Defined, §18B-1000.
    Residential sports club permit, §18B-1006(k).
Bribery of judges or officials, §§14-380.1 to
  14-380.4.
Equine activity liability, §§99E-1 to 99E-3.

HORSE TRAILERS.
Weigh stations in state.
  Trailers not required to stop at, §20-118.1.

HOSPICES, §§131E-200 to 131E-207.
Assisted living residence.
  Providing care in, §131D-2.2(c).
Care to be available at all times, §131E-203(c).
Certificates of need.
  Definitions, §131E-176.
  Generally, §§131E-175 to 130E-191.1.
    See HEALTH CARE FACILITIES.
Citation of article, §131E-200.
Confidentiality of information, §131E-207(a) to
  (c).
Criminal record checks of providers of
    treatment for or services to children,
    elderly, mental health patients, etc.,
    §114-19.3.
Definitions, §131E-201.
Health care personnel registry, §131E-256.
Home care clients' bill of rights, §§131E-144.1 to
  131E-144.7.
Injunctions.
  Hindering department's performance of duties,
    §131E-206(c).
  Operation without license, §131E-206(a).
  Substantial noncompliance, §131E-206(b).
Inspections, §131E-204.
  Confidentiality of information, §131E-207(a) to (c).
Licenses.
  Applications.
    Department to provide, §131E-202(b).
  Display, §131E-202(b).
  Exemptions, §131E-203(b).
  Fee, §131E-202(b).
    New facilities.
      Initial licensure fees, §131E-272.
  Issuance, §131E-202(b).
  New facilities.
    Initial licensure fees, §131E-272.
  Nontransferable, §131E-202(b).
  Renewal, §131E-202(c).
  Required, §131E-203(a).
  Rules and regulations.
    Adoption by commission, §131E-202(a).
  Suspension or revocation.
    Grounds, §131E-205(a).
    Procedure, §131E-205(b).
Purpose of article, §131E-200.
Title of article, §131E-200.

HOSPITAL AUTHORITIES, §§131E-15 to
  131E-33.
Agents.
  Powers of authority.
    Corporate agents, §131E-23(b).
    Exercise of powers through agents, §131E-23(b).

HOSPITAL AUTHORITIES —Cont'd
Applicability of provisions.
Controlling provisions, §131E-33.
Appropriations, §131E-30.
Audits and auditing.
Reports to be filed, §131E-29.
Bond issues.
Definition of bonds, §131E-16.
Exemption from taxation, §131E-28(c).
Local government finance, §§159-1 to 159-188.
See LOCAL GOVERNMENT FINANCE.
Revenue bonds and notes, §131E-26(a), (b).
Borrowing money.
Contracts with federal government, §131E-27.
Boundaries.
Creation of authority, §131E-20(a), (b).
Buildings.
Subject to building laws, ordinances and
regulations, §131E-25.
Certificate of incorporation.
Admissibility in evidence of copy of certificate,
§131E-19.
Creation of authority, §131E-19.
Change of name, §131E-19(c).
Charges against commissioners.
Removal of commissioners, §131E-22(a) to (d).
Charitable or religious corporation.
Merger into.
Articles of merger must include, §55A-11-10(d).
Authorized, §55A-11-10(a), (b).
Certificates of merger, §55A-11-10(f).
Effective date, §55A-11-10(e).
Effective merger to include, §55A-11-10(g).
Plan must include, §55A-11-10(c).
Sale or conveyance of hospital facility, not
deemed to be, §55A-11-10(h).
Citation of act, §131E-5(a).
Commissioners.
Appointment, §§131E-17(b), 131E-18(a), (b).
After resolution creating authority, §131E-17(b).
Certificate of appointment or reappointment,
§131E-18(e).
Counties with population less than 75,000,
§131E-18(g).
Right to name commissioners, §131E-31(b).
Chairman, §131E-18(c).
Charges against.
Removal, §131E-22(a) to (d).
Compensation, §131E-18(f).
Conflicts of interest, §131E-21.
Counties with population less than 75,000.
Appointment of members, §131E-18(g).
Defined, §131E-16.
Expenses, §131E-18(f).
Number of commissioners, §131E-18(a).
Quorum, §131E-18(h).
Removal.
Authority willfully violated law or contract,
§131E-22(b).
Grounds, §131E-22(a).
Mailing charges to commissioner's home,
§131E-22(c).
Notice and opportunity for hearing,
§131E-22(a).
Preparation for hearing, time for, §131E-22(a).
Record of proceedings, filing, §131E-22(d).
Right to name commissioners, §131E-31(b).
Terms of office, §131E-18(a).
Vacancies filled, §131E-18(b), (d).
Vice-chairman, §131E-18(c).

HOSPITAL AUTHORITIES —Cont'd
Commissioners —Cont'd
Willful violation of law or contract by authority.
Removal of commissioner, §131E-22(b).
Conflicts of interest, §131E-21.
Construction and interpretation.
Controlling provisions, §131E-33.
Contracts.
Federal government contracts, §131E-27.
Controlling provisions, §131E-33.
**Conveyance or transfers of property to
authority,** §131E-31(a), (b).
Counties.
Appropriations by city, town or county, §131E-30.
Creation, §131E-19.
By resolution, §131E-17(a).
Definitions, §131E-16.
Eminent domain, §131E-10.
Power of eminent domain, §§40A-3(c), 131E-24(a).
Certificate of public convenience and necessity.
Prerequisite to exercise of power, §131E-24(c).
Restrictions, §131E-24(b).
Evidence.
Certificate of incorporation.
Copy of certificate admissible in evidence,
§131E-19.
Exemption from taxes and fees, §131E-28(a).
Bonds, notes, debentures, §131E-28(c).
Property of authority, §131E-28(b).
Federal aid.
Contracts with federal government, §131E-27.
Finance.
Local government finance, §§159-1 to 159-188.
See LOCAL GOVERNMENT FINANCE.
Financial interests in facilities.
Disclosures, §131E-21(c).
Exemptions from provision, §131E-21(d), (e).
Restrictions, §131E-21(a).
Stock ownership, effect, §131E-21(b).
Void contracts due to, §131E-21(f).
Grants.
Contracts with federal government, §131E-27.
Incorporation, §131E-19.
Applications for incorporation, §131E-19(a).
Examination by secretary of state, §131E-19(b).
Change of name, §131E-19(c).
Copy of certificate of incorporation, §131E-19(d).
Lease of property to authority, §131E-31(a), (b).
Lease, sale or conveyance of hospital facility,
§131E-13(a).
Bonds outstanding at time of lease, §131E-13(c).
Bonds outstanding at time of sale or conveyance,
§131E-13(b).
Development, construction and operation of
medical office buildings, §131E-13(e).
Inapplicability of other provisions, §131E-13(g).
Length of lease, determination, §131E-13(c).
Nonprofit corporations.
Lease of facilities to, §131E-14.
Pledge of hospital land or leasehold estate,
§131E-13(f).
Procedures before leasing, selling or conveying,
§131E-13(d).
Sublease or assignment of lease, §131E-13(c).
Mortgages and deeds of trust.
Purchase money security interests, §131E-32(a) to
(e).
Municipalities.
Appropriations by city, town or county, §131E-30.
Planning laws, ordinances and regulations,
§131E-25.

HOSPITAL AUTHORITIES —Cont'd
Powers.
Agents.
Corporate agents, §131E-23(b).
Exercise of powers through agents, §131E-23(b).
Applicability of provisions, §131E-23(d).
Certain provisions not applicable to authority, §131E-23(d).
Corporate agents, §131E-23(b).
Eminent domain, §131E-10.
Enumeration, §131E-23(a) to (d).
Exercise of powers through agents, §131E-23(b).
Generally, §131E-23(a) to (d).
Property exempt from taxes, §131E-28(b).
Purchase money security interests.
Contract in amount less than $750,000.
Power without local government commission approval, §131E-32(b).
Contract in amount more than $750,000.
Local government commission approval, §131E-32(b) to (d).
Power to purchase real or personal property under, §131E-32(a).
Purpose, §131E-15(b).
Removal of commissioners, §131E-22(a) to (d).
Reports.
Audit report to be filed, §131E-29.
Sale of hospital facilities to certain nonprofit corporations, §131E-14.
Sanitation.
Subject to sanitary laws, ordinances and regulations, §131E-25.
Short title, §131E-5(a).
United States.
Contracts with federal government, §131E-27.
Willful violation of laws or contract.
Removal of commissioner acquiescing in, §131E-22(b).
Zoning.
Subject to zoning laws, ordinances and regulations, §131E-25.

HOSPITAL DISTRICTS, §§131E-40 to 131E-47.
Additional and alternative methods, §131E-40(c).
Board of county commissioners.
Alternative procedures for creation of district, §131E-41(b).
Creation of district.
Alternative procedures, §131E-41(b).
Governing body of district, §131E-47.
Citation of part.
Hospital district act, §131E-40.
Construction and interpretation.
Liberal construction, §131E-40(d).
Creation of district.
Adoption of resolution, §131E-42(c).
Alternative procedures, §131E-41(b).
Designation, §131E-42(d).
Limitation of actions, §131E-43.
Methods of creation, §131E-41(a), (b).
Notice of creation, §131E-42(e).
Resolutions.
Adoption, §131E-42(c).
Creation by resolution, §131E-41(b).
Elections.
Referendum on repeal of tax levy, §131E-46(a) to (d).
Equipment.
Tax levy for equipment, §131E-45.
Referendum on repeal of tax levy, §131E-46(a) to (d).

HOSPITAL DISTRICTS —Cont'd
Fiscal impact of bills, resolution or rules.
Local government fiscal information, §§120-30.41 to 120-30.49.
General powers, §131E-44(a), (b).
Health care facilities finance act.
Additional powers of public agencies, §131A-6.
Hearings.
Petition for formation of hospital district, §131E-42(a), (b).
Result of hearing, §131E-42(c).
Liberal construction of part, §131E-40(d).
Limitation of actions.
Creation of district, §131E-43.
Maintenance of district.
Tax levy for maintenance, §131E-45.
Referendum on repeal of tax levy, §131E-46(a) to (d).
Municipal hospital facilities act.
Applicability of provisions, §131E-47.
Municipalities.
Body corporate and politic, §131E-44(a).
Name of district, §131E-42(d).
Notice.
Creation of district, §131E-42(e).
Operation of district.
Tax levy for operation, §131E-45.
Referendum on repeal of tax levy, §131E-46(a) to (d).
Petitions.
Formation of hospital district, §131E-41(a).
Hearing on petition, §131E-42(a), (b).
Powers, §131E-44(a), (b).
Purpose of part, §131E-40(b).
Referendum on repeal of tax levy, §131E-46(a) to (d).
Tax levy for operation, equipment and maintenance, §131E-45.
Referendum on repeal of tax levy, §131E-46(a) to (d).
Title.
Hospital district act, §131E-40(a).

HOSPITAL EXPENSES.
Offer to pay, admissibility, §8C-1 Rule 409.

HOSPITAL, MEDICAL AND DENTAL SERVICE CORPORATIONS, §§58-65-1 to 58-66-40.
Acknowledgment of claims, §58-3-100(c).
Failure to acknowledge after receiving notice.
Civil penalty, §58-3-100(c).
Action for negligent decisions.
Health care liability, §§90-21.50 to 90-21.56.
See HEALTH CARE LIABILITY.
Advance practice registered nurse.
Payment or reimbursement, §58-50-30(d).
Right to choose services, §58-50-30(a1) to (a3), (g), (h).
Agents licensing, §58-65-115.
Associations to transact business through licensed agents only, §58-65-120.
Required, §58-65-120.
Amendments to charter, §58-65-130.
Conversion of corporation, §58-65-131(d).
Applicability of other laws, §58-65-2.
Applicability of provisions.
Preexisting hospital service corporations, §58-65-145.
Single employer plans, §58-65-150.
Boards of directors.
Amendments to charter, §58-65-130.
Composition, §58-65-20(b).

HOSPITAL, MEDICAL AND DENTAL SERVICE CORPORATIONS —Cont'd
Boards of directors —Cont'd
Defined, §58-65-20(a).
Breast cancer.
Mammograms.
Coverage, §58-65-92.
Cancer treatment.
Breast cancer.
Mammograms.
Coverage, §58-65-92.
Cervical cancer screening.
Coverage, §58-65-92.
Colorectal cancer examinations, laboratory tests
and screening.
Coverage required of all health benefit plans,
§58-3-179(a).
Limitations applicable to services, §58-3-179(b).
Coverage of certain prescribed drugs for.
Exceptions, §58-65-94(b), (c).
Generally, §58-65-94(a).
Mammograms.
Coverage, §58-65-92.
Certificate of authority or license.
Applications, §58-65-50.
Fees, §58-65-55(a).
Fees, §58-65-55(b).
Issuance, §58-65-55(a).
Monetary penalty for violations, §58-2-70(a), (c),
(d), (g).
Restitution for violations, §58-2-70(e) to (g).
Revocation.
Notice and hearing, §58-2-70(b).
Surrender, §58-2-65.
Suspension.
Applicable provisions, §58-2-70(h).
Criminal convictions, §58-2-60(b).
Notice and hearing, §58-2-70(b).
Cervical cancer.
Screening for early detection.
Coverage requirements, §58-65-92(a), (e).
Defined, §58-65-92(a1).
Chemical dependency treatment.
Chemical dependency defined, §58-65-75(a).
Minimum benefits offered, §58-65-75(c).
Paul Wellstone and Pete Domenici mental health
parity and addiction equity act compliance,
§58-65-75(f), (g).
Provider payments, §58-65-75(d).
Rejected coverage, inapplicability, §58-65-75(e).
Requirement to offer insureds, §58-65-75(b).
Chiropractors.
Right to choose services, §58-50-30(a1) to (a3), (g),
(h).
Choice of providers, §58-65-1(a).
Choice of service providers, §58-50-30(a1) to
(a3).
Locum tenens contracts, §58-3-231.
Pediatrician for minors, §58-3-240.
Provider directories, §58-3-245.
Specialist selected as primary care provider,
§58-3-235.
Uniform provider credentialing, §58-3-230.
Claim denial, notice, §58-3-172(a).
Health benefit plans defined, §58-3-172(b).
Claim forms.
Uniform claim forms, §58-3-171(a).
Health benefit plans defined, §58-3-171(c).
Workers' compensation included in health
benefit plan, §58-3-171(b).

HOSPITAL, MEDICAL AND DENTAL SERVICE CORPORATIONS —Cont'd
Claims.
Acknowledgment of claims, §58-3-100(c).
Failure to acknowledge after receiving notice.
Civil penalty, §58-3-100(c).
Clinical social workers.
Defined, §58-50-30(c).
Right to choose services, §58-50-30(a1) to (a3), (g),
(h).
Clinical trials, coverage, §58-3-255(b).
Costs not required to be covered, §58-3-255(d).
Covered clinical trials defined, §58-3-255(a).
Definitions, §58-3-255(a).
Medical necessary costs covered, §58-3-255(c).
**Closed formularies or restricted access to
prescription drugs,** §58-3-221.
**Colorectal cancer examinations, laboratory
tests and screening.**
Coverage required of every health benefit plan,
§58-3-179(a).
Limitations applicable to services, §58-3-179(b).
Commissioner of insurance.
Examinations by, §58-65-105.
Exemptions from provisions.
Determination, §58-65-165.
Expenses in connection with solicitation of
subscribers.
Subject to inspection by commissioner,
§58-65-110.
Merger or consolidation.
Approval, §58-65-155.
Readable insurance certificates act.
Filing of certificates with commissioner,
§58-66-30(a).
Applicability of provisions, §58-66-35(a).
Approval by commissioner, §58-66-30(a).
Disapproval by commissioner, §58-66-30(a).
Grounds, §58-66-30(b).
Reports filed with, §58-65-100.
Visitations, §58-65-105.
Consolidation, §58-65-155.
**Continuing care retirement community
residents,** §58-3-200(f).
**Contraceptive drugs or devices and outpatient
contraceptive services.**
Coverage by insurer providing health benefit plan,
§58-3-178(a), (b).
Definitions, §58-3-178(c).
Prohibited acts, §58-3-178(d).
Religious employer requesting exclusion of
coverage, §58-3-178(e).
Contracts.
Between health benefit plans and health care
providers, §§58-50-270 to 58-50-290.
See HEALTH INSURANCE.
Chemical dependency treatment.
Contracts to cover, §58-65-75(a) to (e).
Dentists' services, §58-65-30.
Generally, §58-65-25(a).
Hemoglobin seed trait.
Contracts to cover persons possessing,
§58-65-70.
Merged or consolidated corporations, §58-65-155.
Required provisions, §58-65-25(b).
Sickle cell trait.
Contracts to cover persons possessing,
§58-65-70.
Subscribers' contracts.
Dependents, §58-65-60(b).
Employee eligibility, §58-65-60(e3).

HOSPITAL, MEDICAL AND DENTAL SERVICE CORPORATIONS —Cont'd
Contracts —Cont'd
Subscribers' contracts —Cont'd
Forms, §58-65-40.
Group contracts, §58-65-60(c).
Master group contracts, §58-65-60(e) to (e2).
Rate schedule.
Filing as prerequisite, §58-65-40.
Revision hearing, §58-65-45.
Renewal, §58-65-60(a), (f).
Term, §58-65-60(a).
Written contracts, §58-65-60(c), (d).
Tax-supported institutions.
Coverage for active medical treatment in, §58-65-65(a) to (c).
Conversion.
Attorney general.
Enforcement authority, §58-65-132(d).
Foundation to receive fair market value of corporation.
Approval of determination of fair market value, §58-65-133(h).
Certificate of authority.
Issuance, §58-65-132(a).
Effect, §58-65-132(b).
Charter amendment for conversion, §58-65-131(d).
Compliance with provisions required, §58-65-131(c).
Definitions, §58-65-131(b).
Foundation to receive fair market value of corporation.
Advisory committee, §58-65-133(d).
Attorney general.
Approval of determination relating to fair market value, §58-65-133(h).
Board of directors, §58-65-133(c).
Costs, §58-65-133(g).
Creation, §58-65-133(a).
Independent of corporation, §58-65-133(e).
Purpose, §58-65-133(b).
Voting and stock registration agreement, §58-65-133(f).
Legislative declaration, §58-65-131(a).
Plan.
Approval, §58-65-132(a).
Filing, §58-65-131(e).
Legal action on validity of plan, §58-65-132(d).
Public comment on, §58-65-131(g).
Public record, §58-65-131(h).
Requirements, §58-65-131(f).
Review.
Approval, §58-65-132(a).
Costs, §58-65-131(e).
Final decision and order by commissioner, §58-65-132(c).
Public records.
Applications, reports, plans, and other documents, §58-65-131(h).
Cost plus plans, §58-65-135.
Coverage, §58-65-93(a), (c).
Credentialing providers.
Effective date of practitioner's participation.
Joining practice under contract with insurer, §58-3-230(a).
Health benefit plan and insurer defined, §58-3-230(c).
Process requirements, §58-3-230(a).
Temporary credential, §58-3-230(a).
Time limit on processing applications, §58-3-230(a).

HOSPITAL, MEDICAL AND DENTAL SERVICE CORPORATIONS —Cont'd
Credentialing providers —Cont'd
Uniform provider credentialing application form.
Commissioner to adopt by rule, §58-3-230(b).
Definitions, §58-65-1(a).
Accident, accidental injury, and accidental means, §58-65-80(a), (b).
Indemnification of directors, officers, employees, etc, §58-65-166(b).
Mentally ill and chemically dependent, §58-65-90(a).
Readable insurance certificates act, §58-66-15.
Dental procedures performed in hospital or ambulatory surgical facility.
Children under age nine, persons with serious mental and physical condition and persons with significant behavior problems.
Definitions, §58-3-122(b).
Health benefit plans to provide coverage for payment of anesthesia and facility charges, §58-3-122(a).
Dentists.
Right to choose services, §58-50-30(a1) to (a3), (g), (h).
Determinations as to coverage, §58-3-200(c).
Diabetes.
Coverage for certain treatment, §58-65-91(a).
Definition of "physician,"§58-65-91(b).
Directories of providers, §58-3-245.
Direct payment to government agency, §58-3-175(b).
Health benefit plan defined, §58-3-175(a).
Inapplicability of provisions, §58-3-175(c).
When direct payment not required, §58-3-175(d).
Disclosure requirements for health benefit plans, §58-3-191(b).
Discrimination.
Mentally ill and chemically dependent.
Applicability of section, §58-65-90(d).
Coverage, §58-65-90(b1), (c).
Definitions, §58-65-90(a).
Prohibited acts, §58-65-90(b).
Exceptions, §58-65-90(c).
Sex changes.
Coverage for treatment or studies not required, §58-65-90(e).
Prohibited practices, §58-65-85.
Drive-thru deliveries, §58-3-169.
Electronic or on-line system for up-to-date network information.
Plan to provide, §58-3-245(a).
Emergency care.
Coverage required, §58-3-190.
Entitlement to payment or reimbursement, list of providers, §58-65-1(a).
Evidence of coverage.
Notice, expenses may exceed covered amount, §58-3-250(b).
Payment obligations, explanation by insurer, §58-3-250(a).
Exemptions from provisions.
Determination by commissioner of insurance, §58-65-165.
Single employer plans, §58-65-150.
Expenses.
Solicitation of subscribers.
Subject to inspection by commissioner of insurance, §58-65-110.
External review of health benefit plan, §§58-50-75 to 58-50-95.
See HEALTH INSURANCE.

HOSPITAL, MEDICAL AND DENTAL SERVICE CORPORATIONS —Cont'd
Fee based pastoral counselor.
Defined, §58-50-30(c1).
Right to choose services, §58-50-30(a1) to (a3), (g), (h).
Fees.
Certificate of authority or license, §58-65-55(b).
Financial incentives to delay, deny or reduce coverage.
Plan prohibited from offering provider, §58-3-265.
Foreign or alien corporation not authorized to do business, §58-65-1(d).
Genetic information in health insurance, §58-3-215.
Grandfather clause.
Preexisting hospital service corporations, §58-65-145.
Grievance procedures for insurers, §58-50-62.
External review of decision, §§58-50-75 to 58-50-95.
Health benefit plans generally, §§58-3-167 to 58-3-178, 58-3-190 to 58-3-265.
See HEALTH INSURANCE.
Health insurance risk pool.
Notice relating to.
Insurers to provide applicants, §58-3-276.
Health maintenance organizations.
Contracts with health maintenance organizations, §58-67-95(b).
Power to organization and operate health maintenance organization, §58-67-95(a).
Provisions not applicable to health maintenance organizations, §58-67-170(a).
Hearing aids.
Deductibles, coinsurance and other limitations, §58-3-285(b).
Medical necessity determination, utilization review, §58-3-285(c).
Required coverage, §58-3-285(a).
Hearings.
Rate schedule.
Revision of existing schedule or establishment of new schedule, §58-65-45.
High-risk populations.
Nondiscrimination against, §58-3-200(e).
Incentives to delay, deny or reduce coverage.
Plan prohibited from offering provider, §58-3-265.
Indemnification of directors, officers, employees, etc.
Additional indemnification, §58-65-173(a), (b).
Advance for expenses, §58-65-169.
Applicability of part, §58-65-174(a) to (c).
Articles of incorporation.
Mandatory indemnification not limited by, §58-65-168.
Unless articles provide otherwise, §58-65-172.
Authority, §58-65-167(a) to (f).
Court-ordered indemnification, §58-65-170.
Determination and authorization of indemnification, §58-65-171(a) to (c).
Unless articles of incorporation provide otherwise, §58-65-172.
Court-ordered indemnification, §58-65-170.
Definitions, §58-65-166(b).
Determination of indemnification, §58-65-171(a) to (c).
Expenses.
Advance for, §58-65-169.
Insurance, §58-65-173(c).
Mandatory indemnification, §58-65-168.

HOSPITAL, MEDICAL AND DENTAL SERVICE CORPORATIONS —Cont'd
Indemnification of directors, officers, employees, etc —Cont'd
Policy statement, §58-65-166(a).
Prohibited matters, §58-65-167(c).
Scope of part, §58-65-174(a) to (c).
Insurance companies generally.
See INSURANCE COMPANIES.
Investments in securities, §58-65-95(a).
Laws governing, §58-65-1(a).
License.
Revocation and suspension.
Grounds, §58-65-125(a).
Natural persons, made applicable to, §58-65-125(b).
Locum tenens contracts, §58-3-231.
Accepting and payment for claims, §58-3-231(b).
Defined terms, §58-3-231(a).
Medical groups or hospitals, §58-3-231(c).
Placement and administrative services, §58-3-231(e).
Statements of supervision waived, §58-3-231(d).
Long-term care insurance, §§58-55-1 to 58-55-50.
See LONG-TERM CARE INSURANCE.
Long-term care partnerships, §§58-55-55 to 58-55-80.
Lymphedema.
Coverage for diagnosis and treatment, §58-3-280.
Mammograms.
Coverage requirements, §58-65-92(a), (c).
Low dose screening mammography defined, §58-65-92(b).
Reimbursement, §58-65-92(d).
Marriage and family therapists.
Defined, §58-50-30(c4).
Right to choose services, §58-50-30(a1) to (a3).
Mastectomy.
Coverage for reconstructive breast surgery following, §58-65-96(a).
Definitions, §58-65-96(b).
Notice of available coverage, §58-65-96(d).
Prohibited acts, §58-65-96(c).
Maternity coverage requirements, §58-3-170(a).
Health benefit plans defined, §58-3-170(b).
Minimum hospital stay following birth, §58-3-169.
Medical necessity.
Requirements when health benefit plans that limit coverage to medically necessary services and supplies, §58-3-200(b).
Merger, §58-65-155.
Negligent decisions of plan providers.
Health care liability, §§90-21.50 to 90-21.56.
See HEALTH CARE LIABILITY.
Newborn hearing screening.
Coverage required, §58-3-260(b).
Health benefit plan and insurer defined, §58-3-260(a).
North Carolina health insurance risk pool.
Notice relating to.
Insurers to provide applicants, §58-3-276.
Notice.
Amendments to charter, §58-65-130.
Claim denial, §58-3-172.
Conversion.
Public comment on plan of conversion, §58-65-131(g).
Merger or consolidation, §58-65-155.
Rate schedule.
Hearing on revision of existing schedule or establishment of new schedule, §58-65-45.

HOSPITAL, MEDICAL AND DENTAL SERVICE CORPORATIONS —Cont'd

Readable insurance certificates act —Cont'd
Flesch scale analysis readable score.
Definitions of "text,"§58-66-25(e).
Procedure generally, §58-66-25(c), (d).
Required, §58-66-25(a).
Samples which must be analyzed, §58-66-25(b).
Format requirements, §58-66-20(a).
Factors used in determining compliance, §58-66-20(b).
Index of major provisions of certificate.
Required, §58-66-20(a).
Language on which actions may be based, §58-66-40(c).
Non-English language certificate, §58-66-10(d).
Other laws.
Insurers not relieved from provisions, §58-66-40(a).
Purpose of act, §58-66-5.
Title of act.
Short title, §58-66-1.

Reconstructive breast surgery.
Coverage following mastectomy, §58-65-96.
Definitions, §58-65-96(b).
Notice of availability, §58-65-96(d).
Prohibitions, §58-65-96(c).
Scope of required coverage, §58-65-96(a).

Records.
Conversion.
Public access to records, §58-65-131(h).

Reports.
Annual report to commissioner of insurance, §58-65-100.
Health benefit plan reporting requirements, §58-3-191(a).
Access to reports, §58-3-191(b1).

Reserve requirements, §58-65-95(b) to (d).

Risk based capital requirements.
Insurance companies, §§58-12-2 to 58-12-70.
See INSURANCE COMPANIES.

Sickle cell anemia.
Contracts to cover persons possessing sickle cell trait, §58-65-70.

Single employer plan.
Exemptions as to, §58-65-150.

Specialist care referral.
In-plan specialists.
Definitions, §58-3-223(b).
Duties of insurer providing health benefit plan, §58-3-223(a).

Specialist selected as primary care provider.
Insured diagnosed with serious or chronic degenerative, disabling or life threatening disease, §58-3-235(a).
Care authorized by specialist, §58-3-235(b).
Denial of access by insurer, §58-3-235(a).
Treatment plan approved by insurer, selection under, §58-3-235(b).

Substance abuse professional.
Defined, §58-50-30(c2).
Right to choose services, §58-50-30(a1) to (a3), (g), (h).

Telephone system for up-to-date network information.
Plan to provide, §58-3-245(a).

Treatment discussions.
Limiting prohibited, §58-3-176.

Unfair trade practices, laws applicable, §58-65-125(c).

Uniform claim forms, §58-3-171.

HOSPITAL, MEDICAL AND DENTAL SERVICE CORPORATIONS —Cont'd

Uniform prescription drug identification cards, §58-3-177.

Uniform provider credentialing, §58-3-230.

Utilization review.
External review, §§58-50-75 to 58-50-95.
Generally, §§58-50-61, 58-50-61(a) to (o).

HOSPITALS.

Abortion.
Lawful abortions.
Requiring hospital to perform abortion, §14-45.1(f).

Abused juveniles brought for medial diagnosis or treatment.
Obtaining judicial authority to retain physical custody of juvenile when abuse suspected, §7B-308.

Abuse of patients, §14-32.2.

Administrative procedure.
Contested case hearings.
Petition time limit, §131E-2.
Licenses.
Adverse action on licenses, §131E-78(a) to (c1).
Denial or revocation of license, §131E-78(a).

Alcohol detoxification programs.
Specialty hospitals, §131E-65.

Alcoholic beverage control.
Exemption from provisions, §18B-103.

Ambulatory surgical facilities.
Licenses, §§131E-145 to 131E-152.
See AMBULATORY SURGICAL FACILITIES.

Anatomical gifts.
Federally designated organ procurement organizations and tissue banks.
Access to patient's medical records, §130A-412.32(b).
Hold harmless provision.
Hospital made party to action arising out of failure of federally designated organ procurement organization, §130A-412.33(f).
Medical records.
Access by federally designated organ procurement organization and tissue bank.
Deceased patient's medical records, §130A-412.32(d).
Organ procurement organizations.
Coordination agreements with hospitals, §130A-412.17.
Rights and duties, §130A-412.16.
Protocols for organ procurement, §130A-412.32(a).
Immunity of hospitals and hospital personnel in good faith compliance, §130A-412.32(g).
Requirements not to exceed protocol provisions of Title XI of social security act, §130A-412.32(f).
Recipients of gift, §130A-412.13(a).
Signed statement with federally designated organ procurement organization, §130A-412.32(a).

Anatomic pathology services.
Billing patients for services.
Disclosure required, §90-701(b).

Authorities.
General provisions, §§131E-15 to 131E-33.
See HOSPITAL AUTHORITIES.

Automated external defibrillator (AED), §90-21.15.

Bed capacity, temporary increase, §131E-83.

Bills.
Itemized charges.
Discharged patient's bill, §131E-91.

HOSPITALS —Cont'd

Bomb scares, §§14-69.1, 14-69.2.

Bond issues.
Authority to finance by bond issue, NC Const Art V §8.

Branch facilities.
County hospitals, §131E-14.1.

Cancer.
Cancer clinics, §130A-207.

Capacity, temporary increase, §131E-83.

Cardiac rehabilitation certification program, §§131E-165 to 131E-170.

Certificate of public advantage, §§131E-192.1 to 131E-192.13.
See HEALTH CARE FACILITIES.

Certificates of need.
General provisions, §§131E-175 to 130E-191.1.
See HEALTH CARE FACILITIES.

Charitable hospital purposes.
Property tax exemption, §105-278.8.

Commission for health services.
Regulation of sanitation by commission, §130A-235.
Disasters or emergencies, temporary waiver of rules of commission, §131E-84(a).

Committees.
Medical review committee, §131E-95(b), (c).

Communicable diseases.
Emergency departments, surveillance by state health director, reporting requirements, §130A-480(a), (b).
Medical facilities may report, §130A-137.

Confidentiality.
Emergency response plans, §132-1.6.
Employee personnel files, §131E-257.2.
Health care contracts, §131E-99.

Construction and enlargement of local hospitals, §131E-70.
Federal aid, §131E-70(c), (e).
Unallocated federal sums or balances, §131E-70(g).
Grants-in-aid to acquire real estate and construct facilities, §131E-70(f).
Review of construction projects and plans.
Fee charged by department of health and human services, §131E-267(b).
Rules and regulations, §131E-70(d).
State agency for setting up and administering statewide plan, §131E-70(b).
Surveys conducted by department of health and human services, §131E-70(a).

Cooperative agreements.
Between physician, hospital or other person, §§90-21.24 to 90-21.26.
Certificate of public advantage, §§131E-192.1 to 131E-192.13.
See HEALTH CARE FACILITIES.

County health services, §153A-249.

County hospitals.
Branch facilities, §131E-14.1.

Criminal record checks of personnel, §114-19.3.

Definitions, §131E-1.
Certificate of need law, §131E-176.
Garnishment for debts owed public hospitals, §131E-48.
Licenses, §131E-76.
Municipal hospitals, §131E-6.

Department of health and human services.
Inspections, §131E-80(a) to (e).
Licenses.
Enforcement of article and rules, §131E-79(b).

HOSPITALS —Cont'd

Department of health and human services —Cont'd
Program of hospital care, §131E-70.
Review of construction projects and plans.
Fee charged, §131E-267(b).
Specialty hospitals.
Control of certain hospitals transferred to department of health and human services, §131E-67.

Designated development agency, §131E-177.

Disasters or emergencies, temporary waiver of rules of commission, §131E-84(a).

Discharge from hospital.
Authority of administrator or superintendent, §131E-90.
Itemized charges, §131E-91.
Refusal to leave after discharge, §131E-90.

Districts.
See HOSPITAL DISTRICTS.

Donation of medical equipment no longer needed.
Public or state hospitals, §131E-250(a), (b).

Eastern North Carolina hospital.
Control of certain hospitals transferred to department of health and human services, §131E-67.

Emergency medical services.
Generally, §§143-507 to 143-519.
See EMERGENCY MEDICAL SERVICES.
Regulation of emergency medical services, §§131E-155 to 131E-161.
See EMERGENCY MEDICAL SERVICES.

Eminent domain.
Municipal hospitals, §131E-10.
Powers of local public condemnors, §40A-3(b).

Employees.
Criminal record checks, §114-19.3.
Garnishment for debts owed public hospitals.
Discharge or disciplinary action because employee subject to garnishment, §131E-50.
Public hospital personnel, §§131E-257 to 131E-257.2.
Benefit plans for employees.
Payment of cost of, §131E-257.1(b).
Confidentiality of information in employee's personnel file, §131E-257.2(c).
Employee's personnel file defined, §131E-257.2(a).
Inapplicability of certain provisions, §131E-257(c).
Incentive compensation plans.
Public hospital may establish, §131E-257.1(a).
Information that need not be disclosed to employee or to other persons, §131E-257.2(d).
Information with respect to employee matter of public record, §131E-257.2(b).
Investment of escrowed or trusteed retirement and deferred compensation fund, §131E-257.1(c).
Pay expense allowances and other compensation.
Public hospital to determine, §131E-257.1(a).
Personnel policies and procedures.
Hospital may adopt, §131E-257.1(b).
Physician classification and pay plans.
Public hospital may establish, §131E-257.1(a).
Provisions controlling over other inconsistent laws, §131E-257(d).
Public hospital defined, §131E-257(e).

HOSPITALS —Cont'd
Employees —Cont'd
Public hospital personnel —Cont'd
Public hospital personnel act.
Provisions known and cited as, §131E-257(a).
Purposes of provisions, §131E-257(b).
Removal of inaccurate or misleading
information from employee's personnel file,
§131E-257.2(f).
Severance payments and other severance
benefits.
Hospital may pay and provide,
§131E-257.1(b).
Training, research or academic institutions.
Access to selected files permitted,
§131E-257.2(e).
Unlawful access or use of employee's personnel
file, §131E-257.2(h).
Unlawful disclosure of information in
employee's personnel file, §131E-257.2(g).
Work hours, work days and holidays.
Hospital may determine, §131E-257.1(b).
Establishment of hospital.
License required, §131E-77(a).
Federal aid.
Construction and enlargement of local hospitals,
§131E-70(c), (e).
Unallocated federal sums or balances,
§131E-70(g).
Municipal hospitals, §131E-11.
Financing health care facilities generally,
§§131A-1 to 131A-25.
See HEALTH CARE FACILITY FINANCING.
Fraud.
Information obtained from patients.
Acquisition and use of information for
fraudulent purposes, §14-118.3.
Garnishment for debts owed public hospitals.
Definitions, §131E-48.
Discharge or disciplinary action because employee
subject to garnishment, §131E-50.
Exclusive nature of provisions, §131E-51.
Notice.
Motion for garnishment, §131E-49(b).
Order of court.
Duty of garnishee upon receipt, §131E-49(g).
Entry of order, §131E-49(b).
Restrictions, §131E-49(c), (d).
Prerequisites for motion, §131E-49(a).
Review, §131E-49(f).
Processing fee, §131E-49(e).
Satisfaction of judgment, §131E-51.
Grants.
Construction and enlargement of local hospitals,
§131E-70(f).
Health care personnel registry, §131E-256.
Health education facilities.
AHEC program.
Conveyance of hospital facilities to,
§131E-8.1(c).
Sale or lease.
Applicability of section, §131E-8.1(a).
Continued access to identical or equivalent
facilities, §131E-8.1(c).
Effect of provisions on operating contracts,
§131E-8.1(d).
Notice of intent, §131E-8.1(b).
Heath care associated infections.
Statewide surveillance and reporting system.
Establishment, §130A-150(a).

HOSPITALS —Cont'd
Heath care associated infections —Cont'd
Statewide surveillance and reporting system
—Cont'd
Hospitals responsible for surveillance and
reporting, §130A-150(c).
Release of information to public, §130A-150(d).
Rules to implement, adoption, §130A-150(b).
Hiring nurses.
Verification of licensure status, §90-171.43A(a),
(b).
Home care agencies.
Licenses, §§131E-135 to 131E-143.
See HEALTH CARE FACILITIES.
Hospital districts.
See HOSPITAL DISTRICTS.
Immunities.
Directors, trustees or officers of public hospitals.
Limited liability, §131E-47.1(a), (b).
Medical review committee, §131E-95(a).
Infections.
Heath care associated infections.
Statewide surveillance and reporting system,
§130A-150.
Infirmaries.
Licenses.
Definition of infirmary, §131E-76.
Not required to obtain license, §131E-77.
Inspections by department, §131E-80(a).
All locations, §131E-80(a).
At all times subject to, §131E-80(a).
Confidential or privileged information.
Disclosure, restriction, §131E-80(d).
Delegation of authority, §131E-80(b).
Disclosure of information, §131E-80(d), (e).
Examination of records, §131E-80(d).
Immunity for disclosing information.
Persons interviewed, §131E-80(d).
Names of persons furnishing information.
Disclosure, prohibition, §131E-80(d).
Review of writing or other record, §131E-80(d).
Right of proper entry, §131E-80(c).
Licenses.
Administrative procedure.
Adverse action on licenses, §131E-78(a) to (c1).
Denial or revocation of license, §131E-78(a).
Adverse action on licenses, §131E-78(a) to (c1).
Appeals.
Adverse action on licenses, §131E-78(c1).
Application for license, §131E-77(c).
Disclosure of information, §131E-80(e).
Definitions, §131E-76.
Denial of license, §131E-78(a).
Judicial review, §131E-78(c1).
Department of health and human services.
Enforcement of article and rules, §131E-79(b).
Disclosure of information, §131E-80(e).
Enforcement of article and rules, §131E-79(b).
Hearings, §131E-78(a), (b1), (c1).
Hospital.
Defined, §131E-76.
Immunity from liability.
Reports of disciplinary action, §131E-87.
Infirmaries.
Definition of infirmary, §131E-76.
Not required to obtain license, §131E-77.
Information to be disclosed, §131E-80(e).
Injunctive relief, §131E-82(a) to (c).
Inspections and consultations, §131E-80(a) to (e).
Issuance of license, §131E-77(d), (e).
Legislative purpose, §131E-75(b).

HOSPITALS —Cont'd
Licenses —Cont'd
New facilities.
Initial licensure fees, §131E-272.
Nursing homes, §§131E-100 to 131E-110.
See NURSING HOMES.
Penalties for violations of licensing act,
§131E-81(a), (b).
Posting of license, §131E-77(f).
Purpose of article, §131E-75(b).
Renewal of license, §131E-77(d).
Reports.
Disciplinary actions, §131E-87.
Required, §131E-77(a).
Revocation of license, §131E-78(a).
Anatomic pathology services billing violations,
§90-701(j).
Judicial review, §131E-78(c1).
Risk management.
Requirement for issuance or renewal of license,
§131E-96(b).
Rules and regulations, §131E-79(a), (b).
Submission of plans and specifications,
§131E-77(b).
Title of article.
Hospital licensure act, §131E-75(a).
Violations of licensing act.
Penalties, §131E-81(a), (b).
Lien for services rendered injured persons,
§44-49.
Accounting for disbursements, §44-50.1(a) to (c).
Attorneys' fees, §44-50.
Charges, §44-50.
Evidence, §44-50.
Funds for purposes stated.
Duty of receiving person, §44-50.
Limit on recovery, §44-50.
Settlement.
Disputed claims to be settled before payment,
§44-51.
Local government finance.
Application of article to public hospitals,
§159-39(b).
Assets.
Authority of local government commission,
§159-39(e).
Audit.
Public hospitals, §159-39(f).
Bond issues.
Public hospitals, §159-39(k).
Budgets.
Public hospitals to operate under balanced
budget, §159-39(c).
Deposits, §159-39(h), (i).
Electronic payments, §159-39(i), (i1).
Finance officers of public hospitals.
Powers and duties, §159-39(d).
Investments.
Public hospitals, §159-39(g).
Public hospitals defined, §159-39(a).
Regulations.
Special regulations pertaining to public
hospitals, §159-39(e).
Reports.
Public hospitals, §159-39(j).
Revenue bonds.
Anticipation notes.
Nonprofit corporation or association operating
or leasing public hospital, §159-170(d).
Maintenance of hospital.
License required, §131E-77(a).

HOSPITALS —Cont'd
Malpractice actions generally, §§90-21.11 to
90-21.19B.
See MEDICAL MALPRACTICE.
Medicaid, hospital provider assessments,
§§108A-120 to 108A-127.
See MEDICAID.
Medical care commission.
Appointments, §143B-166.
Officers, §143B-168.
Bond issues, §131A-18.
Chairman, §143B-168.
Compensation, §143B-166.
Creation, §143B-165.
Definition, §§131A-3, 131E-76.
Duties, §143B-165.
Licenses.
Promulgation of rules, §131E-79(a).
Meetings, §143B-167.
Members, §143B-166.
Officers.
Appointment, §143B-168.
Powers, §§131A-4, 143B-165.
Quorum, §143B-166.
Refunding bonds, §131A-18.
Selection of members, §143B-166.
Special meetings, §143B-67.
Vice-chairman, §143B-168.
Medical records.
See MEDICAL RECORDS.
Medical review committee.
Definitions, §131E-76.
Immunity of members, §131E-95(a).
Introduction of records into evidence, §131E-95(b),
(c).
Limited liability of members, §131E-90.
Testimony of members of committees, §131E-95(b),
(c).
**Mental health, developmental disabilities and
substance abuse.**
General provisions.
See MENTAL HEALTH, DEVELOPMENTAL
DISABILITY, SUBSTANCE ABUSE.
Motor vehicle accidents.
Notification to medical examiner of death within
hospital from accident, §20-166.1(f).
Municipal hospitals, §§131E-5 to 131E-14.2.
See MUNICIPAL HOSPITALS.
Nurses.
General provisions.
See NURSES.
Nurses, hiring.
Verification of licensure status, §90-171.43A(a),
(b).
Nursing homes.
Licenses, §§131E-100 to 131E-110.
See NURSING HOMES.
Obstruction of health care facility, §14-277.4.
Occupational diseases.
Reports, §130A-457.
Organ procurement organizations.
Coordination agreements with hospitals,
§130A-412.17.
Rights and duties, §130A-412.16.
Outpatient department.
Classified as business occupancy.
Not included in definition of hospital, §131E-76.
Classified as health care occupancy or ambulatory
care occupancy.
Plans for construction or renovation.
Review and approval by department,
§131E-76.

HOSPITALS —Cont'd
Patients.
Abuse, §14-32.2.
Discharge from hospital, §§131E-90, 131E-91.
Fraudulently obtained information.
Acquisition and use of information for
fraudulent purposes, §14-118.3.
Statements obtained from persons in shock or
under influence of drugs.
Presumption of fraud, §8-45.5.
Personnel files of employees.
Privacy, §131E-257.2.
Physical abuse of patients, §14-32.2.
Planning and development agency, §131E-177.
Prescriptions.
Patient counseling, §131E-79.1(a).
Prisons and prisoners.
Inmate's medical records provided division,
§131E-98.
Surgical operations on inmates of state
institutions.
Procedure when surgical operations necessary,
§148-22.2.
Private hospitals.
Regulation of sanitation by commission for public
health, §130A-235.
Privileges to practice in hospitals.
Compliance with bylaws, rules and regulations,
§131E-85(d).
Granting or denial of privileges, §131E-85(a).
Immunity from liability.
Reports of disciplinary action, §131E-87.
Limited privileges, §131E-86(a), (b).
Procedures for considering applicants for hospital
privileges, §131E-85(b), (e).
Reports of disciplinary action, §§90-14.13(a),
131E-87.
Confidentiality and immunity for reporting,
§§90-14.13(e), 131E-87.
Suspension, revocation or modification of
privileges, §131E-85(c).
Reports, §90-14.13(a).
Professional counselors.
Person performing counseling as employee of a
hospital.
Exemption from licensure, §90-332.1(a).
Program of hospital care.
Department of health and human services,
§131E-70.
Property tax exemption.
Property used for charitable hospital purposes,
§105-278.8.
Provider sponsored organizations.
General provisions, §§131E-275 to 131E-314.
See PROVIDER SPONSORED
ORGANIZATIONS.
Records.
Documentary evidence.
Copies of medical records, §8-44.1.
Medical review committee.
Introduction of records into evidence,
§131E-95(b), (c).
Personal data concerning persons admitted or
confined.
Persons required to keep records, §130A-117(a),
(d).
Retention of records, §130A-117(d).
Subpoena commanding production.
Delivery of records by custodian, §1A-1 Rule
45(c).

HOSPITALS —Cont'd
Remains of terminated pregnancies.
Manner of disposal, §130A-131.10.
Reports.
Certain wounds, injuries and illnesses, §90-21.20.
Emergency departments, reports to state health
director.
Public health threats, detection of,
§130A-480(a), (b).
Heath care associated infections.
Statewide surveillance and reporting system,
§130A-150.
Licensing.
Reports of disciplinary actions, §131E-87.
Privileges of physician, actions regarding,
§90-14.13(a).
Confidentiality and immunity for reporting,
§90-14.13(e).
Public hospitals.
Deposits and investments, §159-39(j).
Right of proper entry.
Authority of department, §131E-80(c).
Risk management.
Program required, §131E-96(a), (b).
Sales and use tax.
Refunds.
Nonprofit hospitals, §105-164.14(b).
Sanitation.
Regulation of sanitation by commission,
§130A-235.
Adoption of rules, §130A-235(a).
License or approval revocation for violation of
rules, §130A-235(c).
Water supply wells.
Setback requirements applicable to certain
wells, §130A-235(b).
Smoking in public places.
No smoking in hospital, §143-599.
Specialty hospitals.
Alcohol detoxification programs, §131E-65.
Control of certain hospitals transferred to
department of health and human services,
§131E-67.
Other programs controlled by department,
§131E-67.
State aid.
Municipal hospitals, §131E-11.
Surplus medical equipment.
Donation by public or state hospital,
§131E-250(a), (b).
Swine houses, lagoons and land areas.
Siting requirements near, §106-803(a), (b).
Telephone service.
Shared use and or resale of service, §62-110(d).
**Terrorist incident using nuclear, biological or
chemical agents.**
Emergency departments, surveillance by state
health director, reporting requirements,
§130A-480(a), (b).
Trespass.
Obstruction of health care facility, §14-277.4(a).
Patient discharged from hospital, §131E-90.
**University of North Carolina hospital at
Chapel Hill.**
Bond issues, §116-187.
Employment of attorney for hospital, §114-4.2B.
Funds, §116-37.2.
Liability insurance or self-insurance generally,
§§116-219 to 116-224.
See UNIVERSITY OF NORTH CAROLINA.
Sales and use tax refunds, §105-164.14(c).

HOSPITALS —Cont'd
University of North Carolina hospital at
Chapel Hill —Cont'd
Setoff debt collection.
Generally, §§105A-1 to 105A-16.
See SETOFF DEBT COLLECTION.
Workers' compensation.
Reimbursement allowed, §97-26(b).

HOSTAGES.
Electronic surveillance orders for taking of
hostage, §15A-290(b).
Foreign countries.
Missing persons.
Applicability of provisions, §28C-20.
Seizing building or facility.
Disorderly conduct, §14-288.4.
Taking of hostage by prisoner, §14-258.3.

HOSTILE WITNESSES.
Examination, §1A-1 Rule 43(b).
Leading questions, §8C-1 Rule 611(c).

HOTCHPOT.
Advancements generally, §§29-23 to 29-29.
See INTESTATE SUCCESSION.

HOTELS AND OTHER LODGING PLACES.
Alcoholic beverages.
Brown-bagging permit.
Kind of permit that may be issued, §18B-1001.
Culinary ABC permit.
Kind of permit that may be issued, §18B-1001.
Guest room cabinet ABC permit.
Kind of permit that may be issued, §18B-1001.
Mixed beverage ABC permit.
Kind of permit that may be issued, §18B-1001.
National historic landmark district,
§18B-1006(n).
Mixed beverages catering ABC permit.
Kind of permit that may be issued, §18B-1001.
Off-premises malt beverage ABC permit.
Kind of permit that may be issued, §18B-1001.
On-premises fortified wine ABC permit.
Kind of permit that may be issued, §18B-1001.
On-premises malt beverage ABC permit.
Kind of permit that may be issued to,
§18B-1001.
On-premises unfortified wine ABC permit.
Kind of permit that may be issued, §18B-1001.
Permits, §§18B-1000, 18B-1001.
Possession by resident in hotel room, §18B-300(a).
Possession for special occasions, §18B-301(c).
Special occasion ABC permit.
Kind of permit that may be issued, §18B-1001.
Animals.
Admitting to rooms, §72-7.1.
Assumed names.
Registration of guests to be in true name, §72-30.
Baggage.
Liability for loss of baggage, §72-2.
Bed and breakfast inn.
Defined, §130A-247.
Child care facilities.
Drop-in or short-term child care not included in
term child care, §110-86.
Contracts.
Written statement of time period guest may
occupy room, §72-1(b).
Copies of provisions.
Posting, §72-6.
Definitions.
Sanitation of food and lodging establishments,
§130A-247.

HOTELS AND OTHER LODGING PLACES
—Cont'd
Defrauding innkeeper, §14-110.
Disabled persons.
Right to use of public accommodations, §168-3.
Duties of innkeepers.
Safekeeping of valuables, §72-3.
Suitable lodging accommodations, §72-1(a).
Fees, §130A-248(d) to (f).
Fire prevention, §§58-81-5 to 58-81-15.
Building inspectors.
Powers and duties not limited, §58-81-15.
Careless or negligent setting of fires, §58-81-5.
Fire chiefs.
Powers and duties not limited, §58-81-15.
Loss by fire.
Liability, §72-4.
Negligent or careless setting of fires, §58-81-5.
Noncompliance with provisions, §58-81-10.
Game fish, unlawful possession for resale.
Prima facie evidence, §113-302(a).
Guests' negligence, §72-5.
Husband and wife.
Falsely registering as husband and wife, §14-186.
Immoral purposes.
Opposite sexes occupying same bedroom for
immoral purposes, §14-186.
Inspections.
Sanitation of food and lodging establishments,
§130A-249.
Jewelry and other valuables.
Safekeeping, maximum amount, §72-3.
Liability of innkeepers.
Loss by fire, §72-4.
Loss of baggage, §72-2.
Negligence of guest may be shown, §72-5.
Safekeeping of valuables.
No liability for loss or damage to money or
jewels not deposited, §72-3.
Liens.
Possessory liens on personal property.
Persons entitled to lien, §44A-2(b).
Motor vehicles owned or operated by.
Exemption from provisions, §62-260(a).
Negligence of guests, §72-5.
Parks in which department of environment
and natural resources has jurisdiction.
Department not to construct, maintain, operate or
lease, §66-58(b).
Permits or transitional permits, §130A-248(b) to
(c).
Pets.
Permitting in room, §72-7.1.
Posting of copies of provisions, §72-6.
Railroad corporations.
Establishment of hotel, §136-190.
Registration of guests.
Falsely registering as husband and wife, §14-186.
Tourist camps and homes.
See TOURIST CAMPS AND HOMES.
Removal of property by innkeeper after
expiration of time period on written
statement, §72-1(b).
Restraining lodger from entering room after
expiration of time period on written
statement, §72-1(b).
Room occupancy taxes.
Uniform provisions.
Cities, §160A-215.
Counties, §153A-155.
Safekeeping of valuables generally, §72-3.

HOTELS AND OTHER LODGING PLACES
—Cont'd
Sales and use tax.
Tax at general rate levied on gross receipts,
§105-164.4(a).
Sanitation of food and lodging establishments,
§§130A-247 to 130A-250.
Bed and breakfast establishments.
Exemption, §130A-250.
Definitions, §130A-247.
Establishments providing food or lodging to
regular boarders or permanent house guest
only.
Exemption, §130A-250.
Exemptions from provisions, §130A-250.
Grade cards, §130A-249.
Inspections, §130A-249.
Occasional fundraising events.
Exemption, §130A-250.
Permanent house guests.
Defined, §130A-247.
Private clubs.
Defined, §130A-247.
Exempted from provisions, §130A-250.
Regular boarder.
Defined, §130A-247.
Rules, adoption, §130A-248(a1), (a3).
Variance, §130A-248(a5).
Sexual offenses.
Husband and wife.
Falsely registering as husband and wife,
§14-186.
Opposite sexes occupying same bedroom for
immoral purposes, §14-186.
Smoking guest room in lodging establishment.
Local government's authority to regulate smoking.
Exception, §130A-498(b1).
Smoking prohibited in restaurants and bars.
Exception, §130A-496(b).
Tourist camps and homes.
General provisions.
See TOURIST CAMPS AND HOMES.
University of North Carolina and constituent
institutions.
Information supplied legislative commission on
governmental operations.
Prior to issuing debt or executing contract on
transient lodging facility, §66-58(h).

HOT PURSUIT.
Arrest.
Campus police officers.
Immediate and continuous flight, §15A-402(f).
Company police.
Power to make arrest, §74E-6.
County and city officers.
Immediate and continuous flight, §15A-402(d).
Officers from other states, §15A-403.
Police chases, speed limits not applicable,
§20-145.

HOT WATER HEATERS.
Baffles, heat traps, etc., testing requirements,
§66-27.2.
Boilers generally.
See BOILERS.
Safety.
Baffles, heat traps, etc., testing requirements,
§66-27.2.
Local regulation, §66-27.4.
Relief valves.
Approved relief valves required, §66-27.1(a).

HOT WATER HEATERS —Cont'd
Safety —Cont'd
Relief valves —Cont'd
Installation or sale of unapproved relief valves.
Prohibited, §66-27.1(b).
Thermostat settings.
Presetting, §66-27.1A(a).
Resetting by occupant, §66-27.1A(b).
Warning tags or stickers, §66-27.1A(c).
Violations, §66-27.3.

HOT WIRING DEVICES.
Motor vehicles.
Preparation to commit breaking and entering.
Possession, buying, selling, transferring,
§14-56.4.

HOURS OF LABOR.
Wage and hour act.
General provisions.
See WAGE AND HOUR ACT.

HOUSE ARREST, §15A-1343(b1).
Delinquent juveniles, ordering to submit to,
§7B-2506.
Electronic monitoring devices, §15A-1343(b1).
Counties.
Fee to cover costs of monitoring, §7A-313.1.
House arrest with electronic monitoring, defined,
§15A-1340.11.
Interference with, §14-226.3.
Impaired driving.
Parole.
Electronic monitoring.
Conditions, §15A-1374(a1).
Parole.
Electronic monitoring.
Conditions, §15A-1374(b).
Impaired driving, §15A-1374(a1).
Impaired driving.
Electronic monitoring.
Conditions, §15A-1374(a1).
Pretrial release.
Conditions imposed, §15A-534(a).

HOUSEBREAKING.
Burglary, §§14-51 to 14-57.
See BURGLARY.

HOUSE CARS.
Defined, §20-4.01.
Safety inspections, subject to, §20-183.2(b).

HOUSEHOLD CLEANERS, §§66-85 to 66-88.
Containing phosphorus.
Manufacture, storage or sale.
Prohibition, exceptions, penalties, §143-214.4(a)
to (g).
Labeling cleaners containing volatile
substances capable of producing toxic
effects.
Applicability of provisions after enactment of
federal legislation, §66-88.
Definition, §66-85.
Injunctions.
Sales in violation of provisions, §66-87.
Required, §66-85.
Sales in violation of provisions.
Injunction, §66-87.
Misdemeanor, §66-86.

HOUSEHOLD FURNISHINGS.
Decedents' estates.
Sale or lease, §28A-16-3.

HOUSEHOLD FURNISHINGS —Cont'd
Intestate succession.
Payment of debts from estate of deceased, §29-30(g).
Possessory liens on personal property.
Persons entitled to lien, §44A-2(e).
Usurious loans on furniture, §14-391.

HOUSEHOLD GOODS.
Creditor obtaining possession of debtor's household goods.
Requirements, §1C-1601(g).
Exemption from creditors' claims, §1C-1601(a).
Solicitation for resale by use of collection receptacle.
Collection receptacle defined, §131F-2.
Disclosure sign or label required.
Charitable organization or sponsor soliciting, §131F-9(d).
Organization not charitable organization or sponsor soliciting, §131F-10.

HOUSEHOLD GOODS CARRIERS.
Moving companies generally.
See MOVING COMPANIES.

HOUSEMOVERS, §§20-356 to 20-374.
Beams and dollies.
Requirements, §20-360(b).
Bond or other surety.
In addition to insurance coverages required, §20-359.1(d).
Compliance with municipal regulations, §20-368.
Definitions, §20-356.
Escort vehicle.
Required to furnish, operation, §20-360(d).
Hauling units.
Requirements, §20-360(b).
Individuals moving own building.
License not required, permit required, §20-360(c).
Injunctions, §20-371(b).
Insurance.
Bond or other surety.
In addition to coverages required, §20-359.1(d).
Cancellation, nonrenewal or change.
Notice by insurance company, §20-359.1(c).
Continuous coverage during period of license, §20-359.1(b).
General liability insurance.
Required amount, §20-359.1(a).
Motor vehicle insurance for bodily injury or death.
Required amount, §20-359.1(a).
Workers' compensation insurance.
Requirement, §20-359.1(a).
Invalid sections, §20-372.
Liability, §20-362.
Licenses.
Certificates of insurance providing for continuous coverage, §20-359.1(b).
Duration, §20-359.
Insurance requirements, §20-359.1(a).
Obtaining by fraud, §20-367.
Out-of-state housemovers, §20-369.
Qualifications, §20-358.
Required, §20-357.
Revocation for unsafe practices, §20-374.
Obstructions, §20-363.
Permits.
Applications, §20-361.
Obtaining by fraud, §20-367.
Out-of-state housemovers, §20-369.

HOUSEMOVERS —Cont'd
Permits —Cont'd
Required of licensed movers, §20-360(a).
Qualifications, §20-358.
Right-of-way, §20-365.
Routes, §§20-361, 20-364.
Rules and regulations.
Municipal regulations.
Compliance with, §20-368.
Severability of provisions, §20-372.
Speed limits, §20-370.
Unsafe practices.
Revocation of license, §20-374(a).
Hearing, §20-374(b).
Violations constitute misdemeanor, §20-371(a).
Weather.
Effect of weather, §20-366.

HOUSE OF REPRESENTATIVES.
State house of representatives.
See GENERAL ASSEMBLY.
United States house of representatives.
See CONGRESS.

HOUSES OF MIRRORS.
Amusement device safety generally, §§95-111.1 to 95-111.18.
See AMUSEMENT DEVICE SAFETY.

HOUSE TRAILERS.
Brake requirement, §20-124(f).
Lighting equipment, §20-129.2.
Two door requirement, §66-27.5.
Window tinting exceptions, §20-127(c).

HOUSING.
Cooperative associations.
Authorized purposes, §§54-111, 54-124.
Defensive force used to protect home, §14-51.2.
Disabled persons.
Right to housing, §168-9.
Disclosures.
Death, serious illness or certain criminal convictions of previous occupant.
Deemed not a material fact in real property transactions, §42-14.2.
Discrimination.
Disabled persons.
Right to housing, §168-9.
Fair housing, §§41A-1 to 41A-10.
See FAIR HOUSING.
Domestic violence.
Orders for relief, §50B-3(a).
Fair housing act.
Administration by human relations commission, §7A-761.
General provisions, §§41A-1 to 41A-10.
See FAIR HOUSING.
Heating and air.
Weatherization assistance program, §108A-70.30.
Housing assistance information.
Economic and community development department.
Toll-free telephone number to provide information, §143B-431.1.
Legal services programs.
Safe and sanitary housing, eligible cases, §7A-474.3(b).
Local governments, §§160A-441 to 160A-450.
See LOCAL GOVERNMENTS.
Low-income housing property taxation.
Property taxes.
Designated special class of property, §105-277.16.

HOUSING —Cont'd

Low-income housing property taxation —Cont'd
Property taxes —Cont'd
Property held for charitable purposes as future
site for low or moderate income housing.
Exemption, §105-278.6(e).

Low-income housing tax credits, §§105-129.40 to
105-129.45.

Migrant farm workers.
Standards for housing, §§95-222 to 95-229.1.
See MIGRANT FARM WORKERS.

Minimum housing standards proceedings.
Filing of lis pendens by cities or counties,
§1-120.2.

Municipalities.
Fair housing ordinance.
Amendment, §160A-499.2(b).
Authority to adopt, §160A-499.2(a).
Complaints and results of inspections not
subject to inspection, §160A-499.2(e).
Creation of committee to enforce ordinance,
§160A-499.2(d).
Exemption from coverage, §160A-499.2(c).
Meetings of committee, §160A-499.2(f).
Lease of land for housing, §160A-278.

Public assistance.
Weatherization assistance program, §108A-70.30.

Relocation assistance, §§133-5 to 133-18.
See RELOCATION ASSISTANCE.

Rents.
Control of rents, §42-14.1.
Death, serious illness or certain criminal
convictions of previous occupant.
Deemed not a material fact in real property
transactions, §42-14.2.

Targeted picketing of residence, §14-277.4A.

Trespass.
Injuring houses, §14-144.
Taking possession of house without consent,
§14-159.

Veterans.
Property tax exemption.
Housing of disabled veterans, §105-275.

Weatherization assistance program,
§108A-70.30.

HOUSING AUTHORITIES AND PROJECTS,
§§157-1 to 157-70.

Abolition of authority, §157-4.1(b).

Accounts and accounting.
System as part of city or county accounting
system, §157-4.2.

Actions.
Remedies of obligee, §§157-18 to 157-22.

Alternative organization for authorities,
§157-4.1(a).

Appeals.
Eminent domain.
Issuance of certificate of public convenience and
necessity, §157-28.

Area of operation.
Authority to operate in municipality.
Findings required, §157-39.6.
City authorities, §157-39.1(a), (b).
County authorities, §157-39.1(a).
Indian housing authority, §157-69.
Regional housing authority.
Decreasing area of operation, §157-39.3.
Hearings.
Increasing or decreasing area of operation,
§157-39.4.

HOUSING AUTHORITIES AND PROJECTS
—Cont'd

Area of operation —Cont'd
Regional housing authority —Cont'd
Increasing area of operation, §157-39.2.
Rural housing authorities, §157-39.1(a).

Barbed wire, fences and gates.
Prohibition, §157-9(d).

Bond issues.
Covenants.
Authority to covenant, §157-16.
Cumulative nature of obligee's remedies, §157-20.
Definitions, §157-3.
Form of bonds, §157-15.
Legal investments, §157-25.
Liability of commissioners, §157-14.
National defense housing projects.
Obligations made legal investments, §157-57.
Validation of previous issues, §157-58.
Negotiability, §§157-15, 157-25.
Power to purchase own bonds, §157-15.
Provisions, §157-16.
Refunding bonds.
Authority to issue, §157-14.
Remedies of obligee, §§157-18 to 157-22.
Sales, §157-15.
Types of bonds to be issued, §157-14.
Validation.
Proceedings for issuance, §§157-32, 157-32.3.

Boundaries.
Area of operation, §157-39.1(a) to (c).

Budgets.
Local government finance.
Special provisions pertaining to public housing
authorities, §159-42(c).
System as part of city or county budget system,
§157-4.2.

Building regulations.
Applicability of building regulations, §157-13.

Cancellation of certificate of incorporation,
§157-4.

Citation of article, §157-1.

Commissioners.
Appointment, §157-5(a).
City authority operating beyond 10 mile limit,
§157-39.1(c).
Compensation, §157-5(d).
Conflicts of interest, §157-7.
County authorities, §157-34.
Defined, §157-3.
Indian housing authority, §157-68.
Meetings.
Location, §157-39.7.
Qualifications, §157-5(a), (b).
Regional housing authority, §157-36(a) to (k).
Removal.
Grounds, §157-8.
Residence requirements, §157-39.7.
Tenure, §157-5(d).
Vacancies in office, §157-5(d).
Violation of law.
Removal, §157-8.

Community facilities.
Defined, §157-3.

Compliance with provisions.
Duty of authority, §157-6.

Composition of authority, §157-5(a), (c).

Conflicts of interest.
Commissioners or employees, §157-7.

Consolidated housing authorities.
Establishment, §157-39.5.

HOUSING AUTHORITIES AND PROJECTS
—Cont'd

Contracts.
Federal aid, §157-39.8.
Power to contract with federal government,
§157-23.
Validation, §§157-31, 157-32.2, 157-32.4.
Cooperation of authorities, §157-10.
Council.
Abolition of authority, §157-4.1(b).
Exercise of powers of authority, §157-4.1(a).
Counties.
Area of operation, §157-39.1(a) to (c).
Commissioners, §157-34.
Creation of authority, §157-33.
Low- and moderate-income housing programs.
Authority to establish and develop, §153A-378.
Powers of authority, §157-34.
**Counties of 250 square miles or less and
population of more than 100,000,**
§157-9.2(e).
Bonds or debt, issuing or incurring, §157-9.2(d).
Definitions, §157-9.2(b).
Findings and purpose, §157-9.2(a).
Powers generally, §157-9.2(c).
Proposed financing, notice of, §157-9.2(f).
Creation of authority.
Procedure, §157-4.
Validation, §157-30.
Declaration of necessity, §157-2(a), (b).
Definitions, §157-3.
Eminent domain.
Housing project, §157-49.
Fraudulent misrepresentation in obtaining
housing assistance.
Person, §157-29.1(c).
Municipal cooperation and aid, §157-41.
National defense housing projects, §157-53.
Deposits.
National defense housing projects.
Security for public deposits, §157-57.
Security for funds deposited, §157-24.
Development zone project tax credit,
§105-129.13(b).
Donations.
Advances and donations by city and municipality,
§157-43.
Duties of authority, §157-6.
Electrified fences and gates.
Prohibition, §157-9(d).
Eminent domain, §§157-48 to 157-50.
Certificate of convenience and necessity.
Required, §157-28.
Declaration of necessity, §157-48.
Exercise of right, §157-50.
Finding and declaration of necessity, §157-48.
Housing project.
Defined, §157-49.
Municipal cooperation and aid.
Restrictions on exercise of right, §157-45.
Power of eminent domain, §§40A-3(c), 157-11,
157-50.
Restrictions on right, §157-28.
Employees.
Conflicts of interest, §157-7.
Establishment of authority.
Procedure, §157-4.
Validation, §157-30.
Eviction of tenants, §157-29(c).
Exemptions.
Executions.
Property of authority, §157-21.

HOUSING AUTHORITIES AND PROJECTS
—Cont'd

Exemptions —Cont'd
Real estate licensure requirements, §157-26.1.
Taxation, §157-26.
Farmers of low income.
Defined, §157-3.
Housing applications by farmers, §157-39.
Rural housing projects, §157-38.
Federal aid.
Authority to secure federal aid, §157-23.
Contracts, §157-39.8.
Fences.
Electrified fences, spikes or barbed wire
prohibited, §157-9(d).
Fiduciaries.
Bond issues.
Legal investments, §157-25.
Finding of necessity, §157-2(a), (b).
Foreclosure sale.
Title subject to agreement with government,
§157-22.
**Fraudulent misrepresentation in obtaining
housing assistance.**
Felony, §157-29.1(b).
Misdemeanor, §157-29.1(a).
Person defined, §157-29.1(c).
Gates.
Electrified gates, spikes or barbed wire prohibited,
§157-9(d).
Housing finance agency, §§122A-5.8, 122A-5.9.
Indian housing authority, §§157-66 to 157-70.
Applicability of chapter, §157-67.
Appointment, §157-68.
Area of operation, §157-69.
Commission of Indian affairs.
Authority, §157-67.
Composition, §157-68.
Creation, §157-66.
Governor.
Powers, §157-67.
Powers, §157-67.
Rentals.
Applicability of section 157-29, §157-70.
Tenants.
Selection.
Application of section 157-29, §157-70.
Vacancy, §157-68.
Local government finance.
Special provisions pertaining to public housing
authorities, §159-42.
Local government risk pools, §§58-23-1 to
58-23-45.
See LOCAL GOVERNMENT RISK POOLS.
Low and moderate income, §157-9.1(a).
Applicability of provisions, §157-9.1(b) to (e).
County authority to establish and develop
projects, §153A-378.
Mixed income projects.
Operating expenses of project.
Payment, §157-9.3.
Mortgages and deeds of trust.
Approval of mortgages.
Local government commission, §157-17.1(a).
Consideration of commission, §157-17.1(b).
Rules and regulations, §157-17.1(c).
Defined, §157-3.
Foreclosure sale.
Limitation on remedies of obligee, §157-21.
Title subject to agreement with government,
§157-22.

HOUSING AUTHORITIES AND PROJECTS
—Cont'd
Mortgages and deeds of trust —Cont'd
Power to mortgage.
Project financed with governmental aid,
§157-17.
Remedies conferrable by mortgage, §157-19.
Multi-family rental housing projects.
Persons of low income.
Setting aside of units, §157-9.4(a), (b).
Municipal cooperation and aid, §§157-40 to
157-47.
Actions to be by resolution, §157-44.
Advances.
Advances and donations by city and
municipality, §157-43.
Agreement in aid of housing project, §157-42.
Conveyances in aid of housing projects, §157-42.
Declaration of necessity, §157-40.
Definitions, §157-41.
Donations.
Advances and donations by city and
municipality, §157-43.
Eminent domain.
Restrictions on exercise of right, §157-45.
Findings, §157-40.
Intent of article, §157-46.
Investigation of projects, §157-45.
Leases.
Aid of housing project, §157-42.
Purpose of article, §157-46.
Resolutions.
Actions to be by resolution, §157-44.
Supplemental nature of article, §157-47.
Utilities commission.
Duties, §157-45.
National defense housing projects, §§157-52 to
157-60.
Administration.
Defined, §157-53(a).
Bond issues.
Validation of previous issues, §157-58.
Cooperation with federal government, §157-55.
Definitions, §157-53.
Deposits.
Security for public deposits, §157-57.
Development.
Defined, §157-53(b).
Federal government.
Cooperation with federal government, §157-55.
Defined, §157-53(c).
Sale of projects to federal government, §157-55.
Housing authority.
Cooperation with federal government, §157-55.
Defined, §157-53(d).
Further declaration of powers, §157-59.
Powers conferred supplemental, §157-60.
Rights and powers relative to projects, §157-54.
Initiated.
Defined, §157-53(e).
Investments.
Obligations made legal investments, §157-57.
Persons engaged in national defense activities.
Defined, §157-53(f).
Persons of low income.
Defined, §157-53(g).
Powers conferred supplemental, §157-60.
Purpose of article, §157-52.
Sale of projects to federal government, §157-55.
Security for public deposits, §157-57.

HOUSING AUTHORITIES AND PROJECTS
—Cont'd
National defense housing projects —Cont'd
State public body.
Cooperation in developing projects, §157-56.
Defined, §157-53(h).
Obligee of the authority, remedies.
Additional remedies conferrable by mortgage or
trust indenture, §157-19.
Cumulative remedies, §157-20.
Defined, §157-3.
Foreclosure sale.
Title subject to agreement with government,
§157-22.
General provisions, §157-18.
Limitation on remedies, §157-21.
Officers of authority, §157-5(e).
Operation of authority in municipality.
Findings required, §157-39.6.
Ownership and operation.
Expenses of operating.
Mixed income projects, §157-9.3.
Housing finance agency, §122A-5.9.
Persons of low income.
Defined, §157-3.
Persons of moderate income.
Defined, §157-3.
Planning.
Applicability of planning regulations, §157-13.
Powers of authority.
Counties of 250 square miles or less and
population of more than 100,000, §157-9.2(a)
to (f).
Eminent domain, §157-11.
General provisions, §157-9(a), (b).
Guest and visitors to properties.
Rules governing lawful entry, §157-9(c).
Property.
Acquisition for government, §157-12.
Redevelopment commissions.
Designation as housing authority, §157-4.1(a), (c),
(d).
Regional housing authority.
Area of operation, §157-39.1(a) to (c).
Decreasing area of operation.
Hearings, §157-39.4.
Procedure, §157-39.3.
Increasing area of operation.
Hearings, §157-39.4.
Procedure, §157-39.2.
Commissioners.
Appointment, §157-36(a) to (g).
Certificate of appointment, §157-36(e).
Removal, §157-36(i).
Terms of office, §157-36(h).
Composition, §157-36(j).
Consolidated housing authority, §157-39.5.
Creation.
Hearings, §157-39.4.
Procedure, §157-35.
When authorized, §157-35.
Officers, §157-36(k).
Powers, §157-37.
Rentals.
Distressed rental housing projects.
Housing finance authority, §122A-5.8.
Establishment, §157-29(a), (b).
Indian housing authority.
Applicability of section 157-29, §157-70.
Termination of rental agreement, §157-29(c).

HOUSING AUTHORITIES AND PROJECTS —Cont'd

Rentals —Cont'd
Waiver of default or failure.
Acceptance or receipt not to constitute, §157-29(d).

Reports.
Annual report of authority, §157-27.

Rural housing projects.
Farmers of low income, §157-38.
Housing applications, §157-39.

Security for funds deposited, §157-24.

Spikes, fences and gates.
Prohibition, §157-9(d).

Taxation.
Exemptions from taxation, §157-26.

Tenants.
Eviction, §157-29(c).
Selection.
Indian housing authority.
Applicability of section 157-29, §157-70.
Procedure, §157-29(a), (b).
Summary ejectments, §157-29(e).

Title of article, §157-1.

Utilities commission.
Municipal cooperation and aid.
Duties of commission, §157-45.
Powers of commission, §157-28.

Validation.
Bond issues.
Proceedings for issuance, §§157-32, 157-32.3.
Contracts, agreements, etc., §§157-31, 157-32.2, 157-32.4.
Creation and establishment validated, §§157-30, 157-32.1.
National defense housing projects.
Previous bonds, notes, etc., §157-58.

Violation of law.
Removal of commissioners, §157-8.

Zoning.
Applicability of zoning regulations, §157-13.

HOUSING COORDINATION AND POLICY COUNCIL, §§122A-5.10 to 122A-5.12.
Abrogation of responsibilities, §122A-5.10(b).
Appointment, §122A-5.11(b), (c).
Creation, §122A-5.10(a).
Duties, §122A-5.10(a).
Expenses, §122A-5.11(d).
Meetings, §122A-5.12(a).
Membership, §122A-5.11(a).
Quorum, §122A-5.11(e).
Reports, §122A-5.12(b).
Support services, §122A-5.11(f).

HOUSING DEVELOPMENTS.
Environmental impact statements.
Ordinances requiring for major development projects, §113A-8(a) to (c).

HOUSING FINANCE AGENCY, §§122A-1 to 122A-23.
Actions.
General power of agency to sue and be sued, plead and be impleaded, §122A-5.
Adult care home, group home, and nursing home fire protection fund.
Authorized, §122A-5.13(a).
Rules for management and use, §122A-5.13(b).
Applicability of provisions.
Inconsistent laws inapplicable, §122A-23.

HOUSING FINANCE AGENCY —Cont'd
Appropriations.
Authorization to accept appropriated moneys, §122A-18.
Receipt, administration and compliance with conditions and requirements of appropriation.
General power of agency, §122A-5.

Board of directors.
Appointment, §122A-4(c), (d).
Composition, §122A-4(b).
Executive committee, §122A-4(f).
Oath of office, §122A-4(e).
Officers, §122A-4(f).
Quorum, §122A-4(f).
Reappointments, §122A-4(e).
Removal from office, §122A-4(d).
Secretary, §122A-4.
Terms, §122A-4(d).
Vacancies in office, §122A-4(d).

Bond issues.
Authentication, §122A-8.
Collection and payment of reasonable fees and charges in making, purchasing and servicing bonds.
General power of agency, §122A-5.
Consultants and attorneys to assist with issuance, employment of, §122A-5.
Defined, §122A-3.
Denominations, §122A-8.
Execution, §122A-8.
Exemption from taxation, §122A-19.
Form, §122A-8.
Interest, §122A-8.
Interim receipts or temporary bonds, §122A-8.
Investments.
Obligations eligible for investment, §122A-14.
Issuance, §122A-8.
Liability of officers of agency, §122A-17.
Maturity, §122A-8.
Maximum amount, §122A-8.
Negotiable instruments, §122A-13.
Payment, §122A-8.
Proceeds.
Investment, §122A-11.
Trust funds, §122A-11.
Use of proceeds, §122A-8.
Redemption, §122A-8.
Refunding obligations, §122A-15.
Remedies of bondholders and trustees, §122A-12.
Replacement of lost or mutilated bonds, §122A-8.
Sale, §122A-8.
Security.
Trust agreement or resolution, §122A-9.
Tax exemption, §122A-19.
Temporary bonds, §122A-8.
Trust agreement or resolution.
Security for agency obligations, §122A-9.
Trust funds, §122A-11.
Validity of any pledge, §122A-10.

Borrowing money.
General power of agency, §122A-5.

Bylaws.
Adoption of bylaws.
General power of agency, §122A-5.

Citation of act, §122A-1.
Compensation, §122A-4.
Conflicts of interest, §122A-20.
Construction and interpretation.
Liberal construction of chapter, §122A-22.
Coordination and policy council, §§122A-5.10 to 122A-5.12.
See HOUSING COORDINATION AND POLICY COUNCIL.

HOUSING FINANCE AGENCY —Cont'd
Corporations to receive and administer federal funds.
Power to form, §122A-5.
Counseling services.
General power of agency to provide counseling service, §122A-5.
Creation, §122A-4(a).
Credit of state.
Not pledged, §122A-6.
Satisfying liabilities under energy conservation loan guarantees, §122A-6.1.
Definitions, §122A-3.
Distressed rental housing projects.
Adjustment of income requirements, §122A-5.8(c) to (e).
Powers of board of directors, §122A-5.8(c), (d).
Defined, §122A-5.8(b).
Legislative declaration, §122A-5.8(a).
Energy conservation loan authority.
Authorized expenditures, §122A-5.3(b).
Credit of state.
Not pledged to satisfy liabilities under energy conservation loan guarantees, §122A-6.1.
Expenditures authorized, §122A-5.3(b).
Guaranteeing payment or collection of energy conservation loans, §122A-5.3(a).
Liabilities under energy conservation loan guarantees.
Credit of state not pledged to satisfy, §122A-6.1.
Outstanding loan guarantees.
Limitations on amounts remaining unspent, §122A-5.3(b).
Rules and regulations.
Adoption, modification or repeal, §122A-5.3(c).
Executive director, §122A-4(f).
Federal aid.
Participation in federally assisted lease program for housing for persons of lower income, §122A-5.
Federally insured securities.
Purchase, §122A-5.
Purchase, approval, commitments by lender, §122A-5.1(c).
Fees.
Mortgage insurance authority.
Application fee prescribed, §122A-5.2(c).
Fire protection fund proceeds.
Use to provide staff support for loan processing, §122A-5.13(c).
Funds.
Adult care home, group home, and nursing home fire protection fund, §122A-5.13.
Authorization to accept appropriated moneys, §122A-18.
Bonds and notes.
Trust funds, §122A-11.
Corporations to receive and administer federal funds.
Power to form, §122A-5.
Home ownership assistance fund, §122A-5.7.
Housing trust fund.
General provisions, §§122E-1 to 122E-9.
See HOUSING TRUST FUND.
Mortgage insurance authority.
Payments into housing mortgage insurance fund, §122A-5.2(h).
General assembly.
Finance committees of general assembly.
Oversight by committees, §122A-16.
Legislative findings and purposes, §122A-2.

HOUSING FINANCE AGENCY —Cont'd
General assembly —Cont'd
Moderate income persons and families.
Legislative findings and determinations, §122A-5.4(a).
Gifts.
Receipt, administration and compliance with conditions and requirements of gift, §122A-5.
Grants.
Receipt, administration and compliance with conditions and requirements of grant, §122A-5.
Home foreclosures.
Emergency program to reduce, §§45-100 to 45-107.
State home foreclosure prevention project.
Administration of project, §45-104(a).
Home ownership assistance fund, §122A-5.7.
Home protection program.
Duration of home protection period, §122A-5.14(b).
Established, §122A-5.14(a).
Fund, §122A-5.14(a).
Powers and duties of agency, §122A-5.14(a).
Reports, §122A-5.14(d).
Rules and regulations, §122A-5.14(c).
Housing projects.
Distressed rental housing projects, §122A-5.8.
Ownership and operation.
Authorized, §122A-5.9(a).
Certain statutory provisions not applicable, §122A-5.9(c).
Subsidiary corporations to own and operate.
Authorized, §122A-5.9(b).
Housing trust fund.
General provisions, §§122E-1 to 122E-9.
See HOUSING TRUST FUND.
Inconsistent laws inapplicable, §122A-23.
Insurance.
Mortgage insurance authority, §122A-5.2.
Procuring insurance against losses, §122A-5.
Interest.
Bonds and notes, §122A-8.
Loans.
To and by mortgage lenders, §122A-5.6(b).
Modification of terms of interest.
General power of agency, §122A-5.
Rules and regulations governing agency activity, §122A-5.1(b).
Investments, §122A-11.
Bonds and notes, §122A-14.
Legislative findings, §122A-2.
Loans.
Collection and payment of reasonable fees and charges in connection with making, purchasing and servicing loans, §122A-5.
Energy conservation loan authority, §122A-5.3.
Rehabilitation loan authority, §122A-5.5.
To and by mortgage lenders, §122A-5.
Terms and conditions of loans, §122A-5.6(a) to (e).
Collateral security, §122A-5.6(d).
General obligations, §122A-5.6(d).
Interest, §122A-5.6(b).
Objectives of chapter, §122A-5.6(a).
Origination of new mortgage loans, §122A-5.6(c).
Representations and warranties, §122A-5.6(e).
Rules and regulations, §122A-5.6(a).
Moderate income persons and families.
Definitions, §122A-5.4(b), (c).
Legislative findings, §122A-5.4(a).

HOUSING FINANCE AGENCY —Cont'd
Mortgage insurance authority.
Applications for mortgage insurance, §122A-5.2(a),
(c).
Fee, §122A-5.2(c).
Claims for benefit of insurance, §122A-5.2(g).
Defaults by mortgagor, §122A-5.2(e).
Eligibility of mortgage payments for insurance,
§122A-5.2(b).
Fund.
Payments into housing mortgage insurance
fund, §122A-5.2(h).
Premiums for insurance of mortgage payments,
§122A-5.2(d).
Release of mortgagor from liability, §122A-5.2(f).
Mortgages and deeds of trust.
Insurance.
Mortgage insurance authority, §122A-5.2.
Loans to and by mortgage lenders, §122A-5.6.
Making of mortgage loans to sponsors of
residential housing.
General power of agency, §122A-5.
Mortgage insurance authority, §122A-5.2.
Public or private sale.
General power of agency, §122A-5.
Purchase, approval, commitments by lender,
§122A-5.1(c).
Rehabilitation loan authority, §122A-5.5(a), (b).
Notes.
Anticipation notes authorized, §122A-8.
Authentication, §122A-8.
Collection and payment of reasonable fees and
charges in connection with making,
purchasing and servicing notes.
General power of agency, §122A-5.
Defined, §122A-3.
Denominations, §122A-8.
Execution, §122A-8.
Exemption from taxation, §122A-19.
Form, §122A-8.
Interest, §122A-8.
Investments.
Obligations eligible for investment, §122A-14.
Issuance, §122A-8.
Liability of officers of agency, §122A-17.
Maturity, §122A-8.
Maximum amount, §122A-8.
Negotiable instruments, §122A-13.
Payment, §122A-8.
Proceeds.
Trust funds, §122A-11.
Use of proceeds, §122A-8.
Redemption, §122A-8.
Refunding obligations, §122A-15.
Remedies of bondholders and trustees, §122A-12.
Sale, §122A-8.
Security.
Trust agreement or resolution, §122A-9.
Tax exemption, §122A-19.
Trust agreement or resolution.
Security for agency obligation, §122A-9.
Trust funds, §122A-11.
Validity of any pledge, §122A-10.
Oaths.
Board of directors, §122A-4(e).
Officers.
Bonds and notes.
Liability of officers, §122A-17.
Conflicts of interest, §122A-20.
Offices.
Establishment and maintenance of office, §122A-5.

HOUSING FINANCE AGENCY —Cont'd
Offices —Cont'd
Maintenance of office.
General power of agency, §122A-5.
Personnel.
Conflicts of interest, §122A-20.
Employment of fiscal consultants, engineers, etc.
General power of agency, §122A-5.
Subject to state personnel act, §122A-4(f).
Persons and families of moderate income.
Definitions, §122A-5.4(b), (c).
Legislative findings, §122A-5.4(a).
Pledges.
Bonds and notes.
Validity of any pledge, §122A-10.
Powers, §122A-5.
Supplemental and additional powers, §122A-21.
Purposes of chapter, §122A-2.
Real property.
Powers regarding, §122A-5.
Refunding obligations, §122A-15.
Rehabilitation.
Defined, §122A-3.
Purchase of mortgage loans for rehabilitation of
existing residential housing, §122A-5.5(a).
Rules and regulations, §122A-5.5(b).
Releases.
Mortgage insurance authority.
Release of mortgagor from authority,
§122A-5.2(f).
Reports.
Annual report of activities, §122A-16.
Budget expenditures, §122A-16.
Home protection program, §122A-5.14(d).
Rules and regulations.
Adoption, modification or repeal of rules and
regulations, §122A-5.1(a).
Conditional purchases, §122A-5.1(b).
Effectuation of general purposes of chapter,
§122A-5.1(a).
Energy conservation loan authority.
Adoption, modification or repeal of rules and
regulations, §122A-5.3(c).
Governing agency activity, §122A-5.1.
Homeownership assistance fund.
Adoption of rules, §122A-5.7.
Home protection program, §122A-5.14(c).
Interest rates, §122A-5.1(b).
Making and publishing of rules and regulations.
General power of agency, §122A-5.
Rehabilitation loan authority, §122A-5.5(b).
Specific objectives effectuated, §122A-5.1(a).
Seals and sealed instruments.
Adoption of official seal.
General power of agency, §122A-5.
Duties of secretary of agency, §122A-4(f).
Short title, §122A-1.

HOUSING INSPECTORS.
County inspection departments.
Generally, §§153A-350 to 153A-375.
See COUNTY INSPECTION DEPARTMENTS.

HOUSING TRUST FUND.
Accounts and accounting.
Separate accounts, §122E-5(c).
Allocation of funds, §122E-8(a).
Applications for funds.
Eligible applicants, §122E-7.
Priorities, §122E-8(c), (d).
Rules and regulations, §122E-8(b).
Beneficiaries, §122E-6(a).

HOUSING TRUST FUND —Cont'd
Citation of act.
  Short title, §122E-1.
Composition, §122E-3(b).
Conflicts of interest.
  North Carolina housing partnership, §122E-4(i).
Definitions, §122E-2.
Displacement, §122E-9.
Established, §122E-3(a).
Housing finance agency.
  Administration of provisions, §122E-5(a).
  Definition of "agency,"§122E-2.
  Reports, §122E-5(d).
  Responsibilities, §122E-5(b).
Investments, §122E-3(c).
North Carolina housing partnership.
  Chairman, §122E-4(b).
  Compensation of members, §122E-4(e).
  Composition, §122E-4(b).
  Conflicts of interest, §122E-4(i).
  Creation, §122E-4(a).
  Duties, §122E-4(f).
  Executive director, §122E-4(g).
  Meetings, §122E-4(h).
  Powers, §122E-4(f).
  Purposes, §122E-4(a).
  Quorum, §122E-4(b).
  Terms of members, §122E-4(c).
  Vacancies, §122E-4(d).
  Voting on issues, §122E-4(b).
Projects.
  Eligible projects, §122E-6(b).
Reports.
  Housing finance agency, §122E-5(d).
Rules and regulations.
  Applications for funds, §122E-8(b).
  Displacement, §122E-9.
  Equitable distribution of funds, §122E-7.
State treasurer.
  Trustee of fund, §122E-3(c).
Title of act.
  Short title, §122E-1.
Use of funds, §122E-6.
  Eligible uses, §122E-6(c), (d).

HOV LANES, §20-146.2.

HULL INSURANCE, PROTECTION AND INDEMNITY CLUBS, §§58-20-1 to 58-20-40.
Audit, §58-20-20.
Board of trustees.
  Duties, §§58-20-15, 58-20-15(a).
  Immunity, §58-20-40.
  Operation of clubs, §58-20-15.
  Prohibited actions, §58-20-15(b).
Citation of article, §58-20-1.
Definitions, §58-20-5.
Evaluation of clubs, §58-20-30.
Financial monitoring of clubs, §58-20-30.
Immunity.
  Administrators and boards of trustees, §58-20-40.
Indemnification.
  Mutual agreement, §58-20-20.
    Optional provisions, §58-20-20(b).
    Required provisions, §58-20-20(a).
Insolvency or impairment of club, §58-20-35.
  Assessment of members, §58-20-35(b).
  Procedure once revealed, §58-20-35(a).
Loss and loss adjustment expenses, actuarial evaluation, §58-20-20.
Membership termination, §58-20-25.

HULL INSURANCE, PROTECTION AND INDEMNITY CLUBS —Cont'd
Mutual agreement for indemnification.
  Optional provisions, §58-20-20(b).
  Required provisions, §58-20-20(a).
Organization.
  Authorized, §58-20-10.
  Notice of intent to organize, §58-20-10.
Purposes, §58-20-10.
Short title of article, §58-20-1.
Termination of membership, §58-20-25.

HUMAN BURIAL AND HUMAN SKELETAL REMAINS.
Unmarked human burial and human skeletal remains protection, §§70-26 to 70-40.
  See UNMARKED HUMAN BURIAL AND SKELETAL REMAINS PROTECTION.

HUMANE ORGANIZATIONS.
Solicitation of contributions, §§131F-1 to 131F-33.
  See CHARITABLE SOLICITATION.

HUMAN IMMUNODEFICIENCY VIRUS.
See AIDS AND HIV.

HUMAN PEDIGREE.
Hearsay exception.
  Records of religious organizations, §8C-1 Rule 803.
  Statement of personal or family history, §8C-1 Rule 804(b).

HUMAN RELATIONS COMMISSION.
Civil rights, interference with.
  Action on behalf of person subject to violation, §99D-1(b1).
Clerical and support services, §143B-392(d).
Creation, §7A-761.
Duties, §7A-761.
Equal employment practices.
  Citation of article, §143-422.1.
  Conciliations, §143-422.3.
  Investigations, §143-422.3.
  Legislative declaration, §143-422.2.
  Purpose of article, §143-422.2.
  Receipt of charges, §143-422.3.
  Short title, §143-422.1.
Expense reimbursement, §143B-392(b).
Fair housing act.
  Administration by commission, §7A-761.
Members, §143B-392(a).
Powers and duties, §7A-761.
Quorum, §143B-392(c).
Terms, §143B-392(a).
Vacancies, §143B-392(a).

HUMAN REMAINS.
Concealing evidence of death.
  Dismembering, destroying.
    Criminal penalty, §14-401.22(d).
      Death not of natural causes, §14-401.22(e).
Defined, §14-401.22(f).
Disturbing, vandalizing, desecrating.
  Criminal penalty, exceptions, §14-401.22(c).

HUMAN SERVICE AND VOLUNTEER TRANSPORTATION, §§62-289.1 to 62-289.7.
Carriers.
  Inapplicability of laws and regulations, §62-289.5.
Classification of transportation, §62-289.4.
Commercial transportation.
  Inapplicability of laws and regulations, §62-289.5.

HUMAN SERVICE AND VOLUNTEER TRANSPORTATION —Cont'd

Common carriers.
Inapplicability of laws and regulations, §62-289.5.

Counties.
Local licenses and taxes prohibited, §62-289.7.

Definitions, §62-289.3.

Human service agency.
Defined, §62-289.3.

Human service transportation.
Classification, §62-289.4.
Defined, §62-289.3.

Inapplicability of certain laws and regulations, §62-289.5.

Insurance.
Classification of transportation, §62-289.4.
Volunteer transportation, §62-289.6.

Intention of general assembly, §62-289.2.

Licenses.
Municipal licenses and taxes.
Prohibited, §62-289.7.

Motor carriers.
Inapplicability of laws and regulations, §62-289.5.

Municipalities.
Local licenses and taxes prohibited, §62-289.7.

Nonprofit.
Defined, §62-289.3.

Person.
Defined, §62-289.3.

Purpose of act, §62-289.2.

Short title of act, §62-289.1.

Taxation.
Municipal licenses and taxes.
Prohibited, §62-289.7.

Volunteer transportation.
Classification, §62-289.4.
Defined, §62-289.3.
Insurance, §62-289.6.

HUMAN SKELETAL REMAINS AND UNMARKED HUMAN BURIAL PROTECTION ACT, §§70-26 to 70-40.
See UNMARKED HUMAN BURIAL AND SKELETAL REMAINS PROTECTION.

HUMAN TISSUE.

Anatomical gifts, §§130A-412.3 to 130A-412.33.
See ANATOMICAL GIFTS.

Donation cards.
Availability at division of motors offices, §20-7.3.

Donation program, §130A-413.

Medical examiners.
Discovery of anatomical matter.
Report to medical examiner, §130A-383(b).

Organ donor registry Internet site.
Division of motor vehicles.
Required to establish, §20-43.2(a).
Federally designated organ procurement organizations and eye banks.
Accessing and using information.
Compliance with Part 3A of Article 16 of Chapter 130A required, §20-43.2(b).
Purpose, §20-43.2(a).
Limitation on data available, §20-43.2(a).
Other persons not prohibited from creating registry, §20-43.2(d).
Personally identifiable information.
Use or disclosure, consent required, §20-43.2(c).
Purpose, §20-43.2(a).

Red lights used on organ procurement organization vehicles, §20-130.1(b).

HUMAN TISSUE DONATION PROGRAM.

Cooperation between state departments and agencies, §130A-413(c).

Coordinated program, §130A-413(b).
Cooperation between state departments and agencies and law-enforcement agencies, §130A-413(c).

Establishment, §130A-413(a).

Law-enforcement agencies.
Cooperation in coordinated program, §130A-413(c).

Legislative findings and purpose, §130A-413(a).

Purposes of program, §130A-413(a).

State departments and agencies.
Cooperation in coordinated program, §130A-413(c).
Coordinated program established, §130A-413(b).

HUMAN TRAFFICKING, §§14-43.10 to 14-43.13.

Address confidentiality program, §§15C-1 to 15C-13.
See ADDRESS CONFIDENTIALITY PROGRAM.

Definitions, §14-43.10(a).

DNA sample for DNA analysis.
Obtaining upon arrest for certain offenses, §15A-266.3A.

Elements of offense, §14-43.11(a).
Involuntary servitude, §14-43.12(a).
Sexual servitude, §14-43.13(a).

Felonies, §14-43.11(b).
Involuntary servitude, §14-43.12(b).
Sexual servitude, §14-43.13(b).

Involuntary servitude.
Defined, §14-43.10(a).
Elements of offense, §14-43.12(a).
Felony, §14-43.12(b).
Labor contracts.
Reporting violations arising from, §14-43.12(e).
Parent and child relationship not affected, §14-43.12(d).
Separate offense.
Each violation to constitute, §14-43.12(c).

Public benefits or services.
Eligibility of victims, §14-43.11(d).

Separate offense.
Each violation to constitute, §14-43.11(c).
Involuntary servitude, §14-43.12(c).
Sexual servitude, §14-43.13(c).

Sexual servitude.
Defined, §14-43.10(a).
Elements of offense, §14-43.13(a).
Felony, §14-43.13(b).
Separate offense.
Each violation to constitute, §14-43.13(c).

Victims.
Notifications to be given by district attorney's office, §15A-832(h).

HUNG JURY, §15A-1235.
Grounds for mistrial, §15A-1063.

HUNTER SAFETY COURSE, §113-270.1A.

HUNTERSVILLE.
Traffic control photographic systems, §160A-300.1(d).

HUNTING AND WILDLIFE.
Accounts and accounting.
Wildlife conservation account, §143-247.2.

Acquiring or disposing of wildlife.
Dead wildlife, §113-291.3(b) to (d).
Live wildlife, §113-291.3(a).

HUNTING AND WILDLIFE —Cont'd

Adverse possession of property subject to public trust rights.
No adverse possession, §1-45.1.

All-terrain vehicles, §20-171.22(b).

Animal fights and baiting.
Exception as lawful taking or training of animals, §14-362.1(e).

Applicability of provisions, §143-252.

Arrest.
Fees, §113-303.
Protectors.
Arrest without warrant, §113-136(d).
Search on arrest, §113-137(a).
Service of arrest warrants, §113-136(e).

Article subject to chapter 113, §143-252.

Attorney general.
Attorney for agency, §113-131(d).

Bag limits, §113-291.2(a) to (e).
Foxes.
Open seasons for taking foxes with firearms, §113-291.4A.

Bald eagles.
Unlawfully taking, possessing, etc., §113-294(l).

Beagles.
Field trials for beagles.
Hunting license exemption, §113-276(k).

Bear, §113-291.7.
Nonresident bear hunting license, §113-270.3(b).
Sale of parts prohibited, §113-291.3(b).
Unlawfully taking, possessing or transporting, selling, etc., §113-294(c1).

Beaver, §113-291.9.
Damage control program, §113-291.10.
Trapping.
Use of trap number 330 of connibear type, §113-291.6(d).
Unlawfully selling, possessing for sale or buying, §113-294(f).

Beaver damage control advisory board, §113-291.10.

Big game animals.
Handguns and handgun ammunition, §113-291.1(g1).
Kill reports, §113-270.3(c).
Retrieval and/or dispatching of wounded or dead big game animal, §113-291.1(k).

Bird sanctuaries.
Municipalities, §160A-188.

Black-tailed deer.
Unlawfully transporting or possessing, §113-294(p).

Boats.
Taking wild animals or birds from vessels equipped with motors, §113-294(g).

Bobcats.
Sale of parts, §113-291.3(b).

Bow and arrow.
Method of taking wildlife, §113-291.1(a).
Nongame fish.
Taking in inland and joint fishing waters, §113-275(k).

Captivity license, §113-272.5.

Captivity permits, §113-274(c).

Child support enforcement.
Forfeiture of licensing privilege, §50-13.12.
Suspension or revocation of hunting licenses, §§110-142, 110-142.2.

Closing forests and woodlands to hunting, fishing and trapping, §106-908.

HUNTING AND WILDLIFE —Cont'd

Clothing.
Hunter orange material, §113-291.8(a) to (c).

Coastal reserves, §113A-129.2(a).

Computer assisted remote hunting.
Criminal penalty, §113-294(q).
Defined, §113-291.1A(b).
Prohibited, §113-291.1A(a).

Confiscation.
Fruits and instrumentalities of offenses in question, §113-137(i).

Controlled hunting preserve operator licenses, §113-273(g).

Cooperative agreements, §113-305.

Cougars.
Unlawfully taking, possessing, transporting, etc., §113-294(c2).

Coyotes.
Hunting preserves, §113-273(g).
Traps or snares used under depredation permit, §113-291.6(h).
Unlawfully transporting or breeding, §113-294(o).

Criminal law enforcement authority of wildlife protectors, §113-136(d1).

Criminal negligence.
Enforcement of article, §113-290.1(e).
Impaired at time of violation.
Aggravating factor, §113-290.1(b).
Penalties, §113-290.1(a).
Resulting in death of another person.
Involuntary manslaughter, §113-290.1(f).
Suspension of hunting privileges, §113-290.1(c).
Hunting while license suspended, §113-290.1(d).
Unlawful use of firearms, §113-290.

Currituck county game commission.
Authority not repealed or abridged by limitation upon local regulation, §113-133.1(d).

Dangerous animals.
Possessing or harboring in city, §160A-187.
Possessing or harboring in county, §153A-131.

Dare county game and wildlife commission.
Authority not repealed or abridged by limitation upon local regulations, §113-133.1(d).

Dealer licenses, §113-273.

Deer.
Deer swimming or in water above knees.
Unlawful to take, §113-291.1(j).
Dogs hunting deer.
Muzzle loading firearms season.
Dogs not used for hunting, §113-291.2(a).
Regulation of use, limitations, §113-291.5(a) to (f).
Muzzle loading firearms season.
Dogs not used for hunting, §113-291.2(a).
Taking one antlerless deer, §113-291.2(a).
Night hunting with artificial lights, §113-294(e).
Special antlerless deer tags, §113-291.2(e).
Spotlighting.
Prima facie evidence, §113-302(b).
Sweeping area with lights at night, §113-291.1(e1), (e2).
Unlawfully selling, possessing for sale or buying, §113-294(b).
Unlawfully taking, possessing or transporting, §113-294(d).

Definitions.
Dealer, §113-273(a).
Dealing in furs, §113-273(f).
Endangered and threatened wildlife and species of special concern, §113-331.

HUNTING AND WILDLIFE —Cont'd
Definitions —Cont'd
  Hunting and fishing on registered property of
      another, §113-281.
  Public trust resources, §113-131(e).
**Department of environment and natural
    resources.**
  Powers, §113-131(b).
  Scientific investigations, §113-261(a).
  Taking wildlife in generally prohibited manner.
    Authority, §113-261(c).
Depredation permits, §113-274(c).
Disabled persons.
  Crossbow or other specially equipped bow.
    Permission to use, §113-297(b).
  Method exemptions for, §113-297(a).
  Motorized all-terrain vehicles.
    Use by person qualified under disabled
        sportsmen program, §20-171.26.
  Special vehicular access identification card and
      permit.
    Violation of rules restricting access to holders,
        §113-294(n).
  Unlawful use of facilities provided for disabled
      sportsman, §113-298.
Disabled sportsman program.
  Application, §113-296(c).
  Eligibility for participation, §113-296(b).
  Established, administration, §113-296(a).
  Fee, §113-296(c).
  Motorized all-terrain vehicles.
    Use by person qualified under program,
        §20-171.26(a).
    Lights and horn, requirement, §20-171.26(c).
    Membership and hunting license.
      Evidence of carried with person,
          §20-171.26(e).
    Operation, laws governing, §20-171.26(b).
    Speed restrictions, §20-171.26(d).
  Number of special activities per year, §113-296(f).
  Publicizing activities, §113-296(e).
  Requirements in establishing, §113-296(d).
Dogs.
  Dangerous dogs.
    Dogs used in lawful hunt.
      Inapplicability of provisions of article to,
          §67-4.1(b).
  Field trials with dogs, §113-291.1(d).
  Fighting and baiting.
    Exception as lawful taking of animals,
        §14-362.2(d).
  Foxes, §113-291.4(b).
  Muzzle loading firearm deer season.
    Using dogs to hunt deer prohibited,
        §113-291.2(a).
  Raccoon and opossum hunting at night,
      §113-291.1(e).
  Regulation of dogs used in hunting, §113-291.5(a),
      (b).
    Closed deer season.
      Chasing deer, prohibition, §113-291.5(e).
    Game land, wildlife refuges and public hunting
        grounds, §113-291.5(c).
    Leashing or confining of pet dogs.
      Section not intended to require, §113-291.5(f).
    Number of dogs or breed of dogs.
      Regulations on prohibited, §113-291.5(d).
  Training during closed season, §113-291.1(d1).
  Use in taking wildlife, §113-291.1(a).
  Use to retrieve wounded or dead big game
      animals, §113-291.1(k).

HUNTING AND WILDLIFE —Cont'd
Drainage districts.
  Conservation and replacement, §156-69.
Drugs, taking by using.
  Permits issued by department and commission
      authorizing, §113-261(b).
  Prohibited, §113-262(a), (b).
Eagles.
  Unlawfully taking, possessing, etc., §113-294(l).
Eddie Bridges fund, §143-250.1(a) to (h).
Electricity, taking by using.
  Permits issued by department and commission
      authorizing, §113-261(b).
  Prohibited, §113-262(a), (b).
**Endangered and threatened wildlife and
    species of special concern,** §§113-331 to
    113-337.
  Declaration of policy, §113-332.
  Definitions, §113-331.
  Nongame wildlife advisory committee, §113-335.
    Powers and duties, §113-336.
  Placement of animals on protected animal list,
      §113-334.
  Policy of state, §113-332.
  Unlawful acts, §113-337(a).
    Misdemeanors, §113-337(b).
  Wildlife resources commission.
    Bat exclusion and eviction curriculum,
        §113-333(d).
    Conservation plan, §113-333(b), (c).
    Powers and duties, §113-333(a).
**Enjoyment of wildlife resources belongs to
    people of state,** §113-133.1(a).
Evidence.
  Possession of illegally killed fish as evidence,
      §113-262(b).
  Spotlighting deer.
    Prima facie evidence, §113-302(b).
  Warning tickets not to constitute evidence of
      commission of offense, §113-140(g).
Exotic species.
  Releasing for hunting or trapping, §113-292(e).
Explosives.
  Taking by using explosives.
    Permits issued by department and commission
        authorizing, §113-261(b).
    Prohibited, §113-262(a), (b).
Exportation or importation permits,
    §113-274(c).
Falconry.
  Method of taking wildlife, §113-291.1(a).
Federal laws and regulations.
  Adoption by wildlife resources commission,
      §113-307.
  Legislative assent to specific federal acts,
      §113-307.1.
Fees.
  Arrest, §113-303.
  Licenses, §113-270.2.
    Captivity license, §113-272.5(b).
    Collection licenses, §113-272.4(c).
    Combination fishing and inland hunting
        licenses, §113-270.1C(b).
    Controlled hunting preserve hunting license,
        §113-270.2(c).
    Controlled hunting preserve operators,
        §113-273(g).
    Disposition of license funds, §113-306(b).
    Fur bearer propagation, §113-273(i).
    Fur-dealers, §113-273(f).
    Fur-dealer stations, §113-273(f).

HUNTING AND WILDLIFE —Cont'd
Fees —Cont'd
Licenses —Cont'd
Game bird propagation, §113-273(h).
Guides, §113-270.4(b).
Lifetime resident comprehensive hunting
license, §113-270.2(a), (c).
New license to replace lost or destroyed license,
§113-275(c1).
Nonresident license fee increase, §113-275(a1).
Nonresident state hunting license,
§113-270.2(a), (c), (d).
Resident annual comprehensive hunting license,
§113-270.2(a), (c).
Resident county hunting license, §113-270.2(a),
(c).
Resident state hunting license, §113-270.2(a),
(c).
Special activity licenses, §113-270.3(b).
Sportsmen licenses.
Annual license, §113-270.1D(a).
Disabled resident sportsman license,
§113-270.1D(b).
Lifetime license, §113-270.1D(b).
Taxidermy, §113-273(k).
Trapping licenses, §113-270.5(b).
Unified hunting and fishing licenses,
§113-351(c).
Service of process, §113-303.
State forests.
Collection of reasonable fees for privileges,
§106-877(b).
License fees for hunting and fishing on
government-owned property unaffected,
§106-881.
State parks.
Collection of reasonable fees for privileges,
§113-35(b).
License fees for hunting and fishing on
government-owned property unaffected,
§113-39.
Witnesses, §113-303.
Felony convictions.
Forfeiture of license privilege after conviction,
§15A-1331A.
Field trials with dogs, §113-291.1(d).
Beagles, hunting license exemption, §113-276(k).
Fines.
Limitation upon penalty for offense created by
rules of wildlife resources commission,
§113-135.1(a), (b).
Refusal to stop in obedience to directions of
protector, §113-136(j).
Firearms.
Beaver.
Open season with firearm, §113-291.9(a).
Big game animals.
Handguns and handgun ammunition,
§113-291.1(g1).
Foxes, §113-291.4(c).
Method of taking wildlife, §113-291.1(a).
Misdemeanor for using certain firearms,
§113-291.1(c).
Pistol, use in taking rabbits, squirrels, etc.,
§113-291.1(g).
Pistol, use to dispatch wounded big game animal,
§113-291.1(k).
Unlawful use of firearms.
Criminal negligence, §113-290.
Fires.
Use in taking wild animals or birds, §113-291.1(b).

HUNTING AND WILDLIFE —Cont'd
Food servers.
Preparation of edible wildlife, §113-276(i).
Forests.
Collection of reasonable fees for privileges in state
forests, §106-877(b).
License fees for hunting and fishing on
government-owned property unaffected,
§106-881.
**Forfeiture of licensing privilege for failure to
pay child support,** §50-13.12.
Foxes.
Hunting preserves, §113-273(g).
Open seasons for taking foxes with firearms,
§113-291.4A(a), (b).
Regulation of foxes, §113-291.4.
Sale of parts prohibited, §113-291.3(b).
Study of fox and fur-bearer populations,
§113-291.4.
Trapping unlawfully, §113-294(j).
Fur bearer propagation.
Licenses, §113-273(i).
Fur-dealer licenses, §113-273(f).
Fur-dealer station licenses, §113-273(f).
Game bird propagation.
Licenses, §113-273(h).
Golden eagles.
Unlawfully taking, possessing, etc., §113-294(l).
Governor.
Closing forests and woodlands to hunting and
trapping.
Authority, §106-908.
Guides.
Licenses, §113-270.4.
Handguns.
Big game animals, §113-291.1(g1).
Pistol used to dispatch wounded big game
animal, §113-291.1(k).
Rabbits, squirrels, etc.
Use of pistol, §113-291.1(g).
Harassment.
Persons taking wildlife resources, §113-295.
**Heads, antlers, horns, hides, skins, plumes,
feet and claws.**
Sale, §113-291.3(b).
Hiring hunter or trapper to take game.
Person hiring deemed buyer, hunter or trapper
deemed seller, §113-291.3(d).
Hours for hunting, §113-291.1(a).
Hunter orange material.
Display required, §113-291.8(a) to (c).
Hunter safety course.
Required to procure license or hunt in state,
§113-270.1A(a), (a1).
Wildlife resources commission.
Duties, §113-270.1A(b).
Lifetime licenses.
Sale not prohibited, §113-270.1A(d).
Prohibited acts, §113-270.1A(c).
**Hunting and fishing on registered property of
another.**
Affirmative duty of sportsman to determine if
property is registered and posted, §113-284.
Definitions, §113-281.
Entry permits.
Forms to be furnished, §113-283(a).
Issuance and dating, §113-283(b).
Not substitute for hunting or fishing licenses,
§113-287(d).
Request that individual produce valid entry
permit, §113-287(b).

HUNTING AND WILDLIFE —Cont'd
Hunting and fishing on registered property of another —Cont'd
Entry permits —Cont'd
Required, §113-285(a), (b).
Violations of provisions as misdemeanors, §113-285(c).
Evidence.
Registration of property, §113-287(a).
Law enforcement officers.
Duties, §113-287(c).
Loss of rights by registrant, §113-282(e), (f).
Removal, destruction or mutilation of posted notices, §113-286.
Posting of property, §113-282(d).
Affirmative duty of sportsman to determine if property is registered and posted, §113-284.
Club granted written permission, §14-159.6(a).
Consent from owner or agent required, §14-159.8.
Enforcement by peace officers, §14-159.10.
Entrance on navigable waters not prohibited for purpose of fishing, hunting or trapping, §14-159.9.
Failure to keep registered property posted.
Notification of registrant, §113-282(g).
Methods, §14-159.7.
Misdemeanor offense when written consent not obtained, §14-159.6(a).
Mutilation, etc., of posted signs, §14-159.8.
Posting signs without consent, §14-159.8.
Regulations as to posting, §14-159.7.
Removal, destruction or mutilation of posted notices, §113-286.
Removal of signs after receipt of notice that tract has been deleted from registration.
Failure to remove, §113-282(h).
Written permission required, display upon request of officer, §14-159.6(a).
Registration of property.
Application, §113-282(a), (b).
Action on, §113-282(c).
Fee, §113-282(b).
Evidence, §113-287(a).
Hunting guide licenses.
Fees, §113-270.4(b).
Nonresidents, §113-270.4(a).
Qualifications and duties, §113-270.4(c).
Required, §113-270.4(a).
Hunting preserves.
Controlled preserve operator licenses, §113-273(g).
Hunting stands.
Use in taking wild animals or wild birds, §113-291.1(b).
Income tax credit.
Donations of real property for fish and wildlife conservation, §105-151.12.
Indian tribes recognized under chapter 71A.
Inapplicability of license provisions.
Hunting, trapping and fishing on tribal lands, §113-276(l1).
Injunctions.
Authority of commission to institute action for, §113-306(e).
Encroachment upon usurpation or otherwise violating public trust rights of people, §113-131(c).
Interference with taking of wildlife resources, §113-295(b).
Inspection of licensed or commercial premises, §113-302.1.

HUNTING AND WILDLIFE —Cont'd
Interference with taking of wildlife resources, §113-295.
Interstate wildlife violator compact, §§113-300.5 to 113-300.8.
Administrator of compact.
Appointment, §113-300.7(a).
Amendment proposals, §113-300.7(d).
Contents, §113-300.6.
Definitions, §113-300.6.
Governor to execute, §113-300.6.
Reciprocal disciplinary action, §113-300.7(b).
Rulemaking, §113-300.7(c).
Title of act, §113-300.5.
Violations, §113-300.8.
Jurisdiction.
Wildlife protectors, §113-136(c).
License agents.
Authority of commission to provide for, §113-270.1(a).
Check or draft of agent return by banking facility for lack of funds.
Penalty, §113-270.1(b4).
Contested case provision of administrative procedure act.
Exemption when determining whether to authorize or terminate authority, §113-270.1(b3).
Fee deducted from amount collected, §113-270.1(b).
Informational materials prepared by commission.
Distribution to agents, §113-301.1(a).
Issuance of commission licenses and permits through, §113-270.1A(a), (a1).
Prohibited acts, criminal penalty, §113-270.1(d).
Rules for issuing licenses or permits by agents, §113-270.1(b1).
Rules for taking actions related to agents, §113-270.1(b2).
Licenses.
Administrative control of licensees.
Applicability of section, §113-276.2(a).
Investigations, §113-276.2(i).
Notice of refusal to issue or reissue, §113-276.2(d).
Orders limiting licensees, §113-276.2(j).
Prohibited acts as misdemeanors, §113-276.2(g), (i).
Reapplication after refusal of issuance or reissuance, §113-276.2(h).
Refusal to issuance, §113-276.2(b).
Reissuance review, §113-276.2(c).
Return upon revocation, §113-276.2(g).
Revocation, §113-276.2(e).
Armed forces.
Exemptions, §113-276(12).
Beagles.
Field trials for, hunting license exemption, §113-276(k).
Bear, nonresident hunting license, §113-270.3(b).
Big game hunting licenses, §113-270.3(b).
Bonus antlerless deer license, §113-270.3(b).
Bow and arrow.
Nongame fish.
Taking in inland and joint fishing waters, §113-275(k).
Captivity license, §113-272.5(a).
Black bears, applicability to, §113-272.5(f).
Caging and care, standards, §113-272.5(c).
Cougar, issuing for, §113-272.5(e).

HUNTING AND WILDLIFE —Cont'd
Licenses —Cont'd
Captivity license —Cont'd
  Deviation from requirements, possession
    unlawful, §113-272.5(d).
  Duration, §113-272.5(b).
  Fee, §113-272.5(b).
Certificate of competency.
  Required to procure license, §113-270.1A(a),
    (a1).
Child support enforcement.
  Forfeiture of licensing privilege, §50-13.12.
  Suspension or revocation of license, §§110-142,
    110-142.2.
Collection licenses.
  Issuance by wildlife resources commission,
    §113-272.4(a).
    Assistants in taking, utilization by licensees,
      authorization, §113-272.4(e).
    Authority delegated to executive director,
      §113-272.4(b).
    Duration period, §113-272.4(c).
    Fee, §113-272.4(c).
    Restrictions imposed, §113-272.4(d).
Combination hunting and inland fishing licenses,
  §113-270.1C(a), (b).
Controlled hunting preserve operators,
  §113-273(g).
Conviction of suspension offense.
  Mandatory suspension, §113-276.3.
Dealers, §113-273.
  Controlled hunting preserve operators,
    §113-273(g).
  Dealer defined, §113-273(a).
  Fur bearer propagation license, §113-273(i).
  Fur-dealers, §113-273(f).
  Game bird propagation, §113-273(h).
  Required, §113-273(b).
  Rules governing, §113-273(b).
  Taxidermy, §113-273(k).
Disclosure of information by license applicant,
  §113-275(d).
Duration of validity, §113-270.1B(b).
Effective dates of license issued, §113-275(b).
Enumeration of licenses issued by wildlife
  resources commission, §113-270.2(c).
Exemptions and exceptions, §113-276(c) to (n).
Exhibit or display.
  Refusal, §113-275(h).
Failure to comply with provisions of article or
  rules and regulation, §113-275(i).
Falconry, §113-270.3(b).
False or misleading statements to secure,
  §113-294(h).
Fees, §113-270.2.
  Captivity license, §113-272.5(b).
  Collection licenses, §113-272.4(c).
  Combination fishing and inland hunting
    licenses, §113-270.1C(b).
  Controlled hunting preserve hunting license,
    §113-270.2(c).
  Controlled hunting preserve operators,
    §113-273(g).
  Disposition of license funds, §113-306(b).
  Fur bearer propagation, §113-273(i).
  Fur-dealers, §113-273(f).
  Fur-dealer stations, §113-273(f).
  Game bird propagation, §113-273(h).
  Guides, §113-270.4(b).
  Lifetime resident comprehensive hunting
    license, §113-270.2(a), (c).

HUNTING AND WILDLIFE —Cont'd
Licenses —Cont'd
Fees —Cont'd
  New license to replace lost or destroyed license,
    §113-275(c1).
  Nonresident license fee increase, §113-275(a1).
  Nonresident state hunting license,
    §113-270.2(a), (c), (d).
  Resident annual comprehensive hunting license,
    §113-270.2(a), (c).
  Resident county hunting license, §113-270.2(a),
    (c).
  Resident state hunting license, §113-270.2(a),
    (c).
  Special activity licenses, §113-270.3(b).
  Sportsmen licenses.
    Annual license, §113-270.1D(a).
    Disabled resident sportsman license,
      §113-270.1D(b).
    Lifetime license, §113-270.1D(b).
  Taxidermy, §113-273(k).
  Trapping licenses, §113-270.5(b).
  Unified hunting and fishing licenses,
    §113-351(c).
Felony convictions.
  Forfeiture of privilege after conviction,
    §15A-1331A.
Field trials for beagles.
  Hunting license exemption, §113-276(k).
Fur bearer propagation, §113-273(i).
Fur-dealers, §113-273(f).
Fur-dealer stations, §113-273(f).
Game bird propagation, §113-273(h).
General provisions respecting licenses issued by
  wildlife resources commission, §113-275.
Guides, §113-270.4.
Hunter safety course, §113-270.1A.
Individual license required, §113-275(f).
Issuance by differing methods in different
  localities, §113-270.1(a1).
Kept about person, §113-275(f).
Landholders, exemption from license requirement,
  §113-276(c).
License agents, §113-270.1.
Lost or destroyed licenses, §113-275(c1).
Mail, issuance by.
  Information on laws and rules applicable to
    type of license.
    Furnishing licensee, §113-301.1(b).
Mandatory suspension.
  Conviction of suspension offense, §113-276.3.
Migratory waterfowl, §113-270.3(b).
Minors.
  Persons under 16 years of age, license
    exemption, §113-276(d).
Misdemeanors, §113-275(j).
New license to replace lost or destroyed license,
  §113-275(c1).
Nonresident bear hunting license, §113-270.3(b).
Nonresident license fee increase, §113-275(a).
Probation.
  Purchase of certain licenses required,
    §15A-1343(b1).
Reciprocal agreements, §§113-275(a), 113-304.
Regulatory authority of commission, §113-276.1.
Removal of residence of licensee to another state.
  Continued validity, §113-275(b1).
Required, §113-270.1B(a).
Revocation or suspension.
  Discretionary revocation or suspension by court,
    §113-277.

HUNTING AND WILDLIFE —Cont'd

Licenses —Cont'd

Revocation or suspension —Cont'd

Mandatory suspension.

Conviction of suspension offense, §113-276.3.

Selling.

License agents, §113-270.1.

Separation of revenues.

Precondition for receiving funds under
cooperative program, §113-307.1(d).

Sold for full amount prescribed, §113-275(c), (e).

Special activity licenses, §113-270.3(a), (b).

Sportsmen combination licenses, §113-270.3(d).

Sportsmen licenses, §§113-270.1D, 113-270.3(d),
(e).

Taxidermy, §113-273(k).

Transfers, §113-275(f).

Trapping, §113-270.5(a).

Duration of validity of license, §113-270.1B(b).

Fees, §113-270.5(b).

Requirement of license, §113-270.1B(a).

Unified hunting and fishing licenses.

Definitions, §113-351(a).

General provisions governing, §113-351(b).

Types, fees, duration, §113-351(c).

Waivers, §113-351(b).

Unlawful acts, §113-275(g) to (j).

Voluntary contributions to hunters safety
education program.

Authorized, §113-270.2A(a).

Collection, §113-270.2A(b).

**Lights used to retrieve wounded or dead big
game animals,** §113-291.1(k).

Lights used to take wild animals or birds,
§113-291.1(b).

Live wildlife.

Taking, possessing, buying, selling, §113-291.3(a).

Local regulation of wildlife resources.

Limitation upon local regulations, §113-133.1(d).

Repeal generally of special, local and private acts,
§113-133.1(b).

Repeal specifically of local acts, §113-133.1(g).

Retention of specific local acts or portions of local
acts, §113-133.1(e).

Review of local acts by wildlife resources
commission, §113-133.1(f).

**Magistrates' powers in cases involving hunting
offenses,** §7A-273.

Managed hunts.

Waterfowl.

Screening applicants, fee, §113-291.2(a).

Wildlife resources commission game lands,
§113-264(d).

Manner of taking wild animals and wild birds,
§113-291.1.

Methods for taking wildlife, §113-291.1(a).

Migratory game birds.

Managed hunts, §113-291.2(a).

Methods of taking.

Expansion to conform with federal law,
§113-291.1(f), (f1).

Shooting hours, bag limits and seasons.

Federal law observed, §113-291.2(a).

Unlawfully taking, possessing or transporting,
§113-294(m).

Misdemeanors.

Computer assisted remote hunting, §113-294(q).

Endangered and threatened wildlife and species of
special concern.

Unlawful acts, §113-337(b).

HUNTING AND WILDLIFE —Cont'd

Misdemeanors —Cont'd

Seized property left with defendant.

Failure or inexcusable neglect of defendant to
keep property, §113-137(f).

Specific violations, §113-294.

Violations of rules adopted by wildlife resources
commission, §113-135(a) to (c).

Limitation upon penalty for offense created by
rules, §113-135.1(a), (b).

Motor vehicles.

Taking wild animals or birds from or with use of
vehicle, §113-291.1(b).

Temporary stops by protectors, §113-136(f), (g), (j).

Mule deer.

Unlawfully transporting or possessing,
§113-294(p).

Negligence.

Criminally negligent hunting, §113-290.1.

Nesting or breeding areas.

Intentional destruction of impairment,
§113-291.1(i).

Nests and nest eggs.

Taking, possessing, buying, selling, §113-291.3(a).

**Nets, traps, snares used in taking wild animals
or birds,** §113-291.1(b).

Night hunting deer with artificial light,
§113-294(e).

Prohibiting intentional sweeping of area with
lights, §113-291.1(e1), (e2).

Night hunting for raccoons and opossums,
§113-291.1(e).

Nuisance species.

Authority of commission to introduce, §113-292(d).

Open season.

Bears, §113-291.7.

Foxes.

Taking foxes with firearms, §113-291.4A(a), (b).

Opossums.

Night hunting with dogs, §113-291.1(e).

Sale of parts, §113-291.3(b).

Orange hat, cap or other garmet.

Display of hunter orange required, §113-291.8(a)
to (c).

Otter.

Trapping.

Use of trap number 330 of connibear type,
§113-291.6(d).

**Packages, crates or containers used for
shipping wildlife.**

Marking, adoption of regulations, §113-291.3(c).

Parks.

Collection of reasonable fees for privileges in state
parks, §113-35(b).

Penalties.

Taking fish by illegal means, §113-262(a), (b).

Permits.

Administrative control of permittees, §113-276.2.

Captivity permit, §113-274(c).

Defined, §113-274(a).

Depredation permit, §113-274(c).

Drugs, electricity, explosives or poisons.

Authorizing wildlife to be taken by use of,
§113-261(b).

Exemptions and exceptions, §113-276(c) to (n).

Exportation or importation permit, §113-274(c).

General provisions respecting licenses and
permits issued by wildlife resources
commission, §113-275.

Possession permit, §113-274(c).

Required, §113-274(b).

HUNTING AND WILDLIFE —Cont'd

Permits —Cont'd

Revocation or suspension.

Discretionary revocation or suspension by court, §113-277.

Mandatory suspension.

Conviction of suspension offense, §113-276.3.

Transportation permit, §113-274(c).

Trophy wildlife sale permit, §113-274(c).

Pesticides.

Unlawful use in taking animals or birds.

Criminal penalties, §113-300.3(b), (c).

Separate offense, §113-300.3(a).

Wild animal or bird declared pest.

Use in taking, §113-300.2.

Pests, wild animal or bird declared.

Action by commission after notification, §113-300.2(c).

Agencies that may declare animal or bird pests, §113-300.2(a).

Concurrence of commission required, §113-300.2(b), (e), (f).

Criminal penalty.

Neglect to observe restrictions, §113-300.3(c).

Notice to commission of action taken, §113-300.2(b).

Poisons or pesticides, animal or bird taken with, §113-300.2(d).

Poisons.

Permits issued by department and commission authorizing.

Taking wildlife by poison, §113-261(b).

Prohibited taking, §113-262(a), (b).

Unlawful use in taking animals or birds.

Criminal penalties, §113-300.3(b), (c).

Separate offense, §113-300.3(a).

Use, §113-300.1.

Wild animal or bird declared pest, §113-300.2.

Possession and transportation of taken animals, §113-291.2(c).

Carcasses known or suspected to carry infectious or contagious diseases, §113-291.2(c1).

Closed seasons, §113-291.2(d).

Possession permits, §113-274(c).

Posted property.

Affirmative duty of sportsman to determine if registered and posted, §113-284.

Consent from owner or agent required, §14-159.8.

Definitions, §113-281.

Entrance on navigable waters for purposes of fishing, hunting or trapping, §14-159.9.

Entry permits, §§113-283, 113-285, 113-287.

Failure to keep registered property posted.

Notification of registrant, §113-282(g).

Identifying purple paint marks on trees.

Posting property by, §14-156.7.

Methods of posting, §14-159.7.

Misdemeanor offense when written consent not obtained, §14-159.6(a).

Mutilation, etc., of posted signs, §14-159.8.

Notices, signs or posters.

Posting by placing on property, §14-156.7.

Peace officers to enforce, §14-159.10.

Posting of property generally, §113-282(b).

Posting signs without consent, §14-159.8.

Registration of property, §113-282.

Regulations as to posting, §14-159.7.

Removal, destruction or mutilation of posted notices, §113-286.

Removal of signs after receipt of notice that track deleted from registration.

Failure to remove, §113-282(h).

HUNTING AND WILDLIFE —Cont'd

Posted property —Cont'd

Written permission required, display upon request of officer, §14-159.6(a).

Club granted permission, §14-159.6(a).

Property of another.

Hunting and fishing on registered property of another, §§113-281 to 113-287.

Posted property, §§14-159.6 to 14-159.10.

Protectors.

Arrest powers, §113-136.

Arrest warrants, search warrants, etc.

Service by protectors, §113-136(e).

Criminal laws, enforcement, §113-136(d1).

Exhibiting upon request items required to be carried by law or rule, §113-136(k).

Jurisdiction, §113-136(c).

Peace officer powers, §113-136(a).

Search on arrest, §113-137(a).

Seizure of lawfully discovered property.

Evidence of crime, §113-137(b), (c).

Leaving property with defendant, §113-137(f).

Return to owner, §113-137(h).

Safeguarding pending trial, §113-137(e).

Sale of perishable wildlife pending trial, §113-137(g).

Summary disposition of live or perishable wildlife, §113-137(d).

Stopping temporarily persons or motor vehicles, §113-136(f), (g), (j).

Warning tickets, §113-140.

Public lands.

Hunting licenses.

Collecting fees for hunting on government-owned property, §113-39.

Public hunting grounds.

Coordination with private landowners in establishing, §113-264(c).

Regulatory power over property belonging to commission, §113-264(a).

Public trust resources.

Defined, §113-131(e).

Public trust rights, no adverse possession, §1-45.1.

Rabbits.

Sale of edible parts, §113-291.3(b).

Rabies emergency for particular county.

Plan to reduce exposure by foxes, raccoons, skunks and bobcats, §113-291.2(a1).

Raccoons.

Night hunting with dogs, §113-291.1(e).

Sale of parts, §113-291.3(b).

Reciprocity.

Licenses, §113-304.

Recorded animal or bird calls.

Use in taking wild animals or birds, §113-291.1(b).

Refuges and sanctuaries.

Municipalities, §160A-188.

Reports.

Big game kill reports, §113-270.3(c).

Restrictions generally, §113-291.

Restrictions, new rules, adopting.

Notification to public, §113-301.1(c), (d).

Revisions of subchapter.

General statement of purpose and effect, §113-316.

Revocation or suspension of license or permit.

Discretionary revocation or suspension by court, §113-277(a), (a1).

Concurrent or consecutive, §113-277(a2).

Conviction defined, §113-277(a3).

HUNTING AND WILDLIFE —Cont'd
Revocation or suspension of license or permit
—Cont'd
Discretionary revocation or suspension by court
—Cont'd
Criminal offenses during period of suspension,
§113-277(b).
Surrender, §113-277(a4).
Mandatory suspension of license or permit.
Conviction of suspension offense, §113-276.3(a).
Beginning of period of suspension,
§113-276.3(a).
Discretionary court suspension supersedes
section's provisions, §113-276.3(e).
Offenses requiring suspension, §113-276.3(d).
Period of suspension, §113-276.3(d).
Reporting convictions and suspensions,
§113-276.3(c).
Surrender of licenses and permits,
§113-276.3(b).
Rules and regulations.
Federal laws and regulations.
Adoption, §113-307.
Legislative assent to specific federal acts,
§113-307.1.
Notification to members of general public.
New laws and rules affecting public, §113-301.1.
Wildlife resources commission, §113-134.
Violations as misdemeanors, §113-135(a) to (c).
Limitation upon penalty for offense created by
rules, §113-135.1(a), (b).
Sales.
Seized or confiscated property, §113-137(i).
Trophy wildlife sale permit, §113-274(c).
Unlawfully selling, possessing for sale or buying
wildlife, §113-294(a).
Bear, §113-294(c1).
Beaver, §113-294(f).
Cougars, §113-294(c2).
Deer or wild turkey, §113-294(b).
Searches and seizures.
Exhibiting upon request of protector items
required to be carried by law or rule,
§113-136(k).
Game birds.
Disposition of seized, confiscated or unclaimed
property.
Provisions not to apply to game birds, §15-17.
Issuance of search warrants by wildlife protectors,
§113-136(e).
Search on arrest by protector, §113-137(a).
Seizure of lawfully discovered evidence by
protectors, §113-137(b), (c).
Leaving property in possession of defendant,
§113-137(f).
Return to owner, §113-137(h).
Safeguarding pending trial, §113-137(a).
Sale of seized property, §113-137(i), (j), (k).
Summary disposition of live or perishable
wildlife, §113-137(d).
Temporary stops by protectors, §113-136(f), (g), (j).
Unreasonable searches and seizures prohibited,
§113-136(l).
Seasons.
Bears, §113-291.7.
Foxes.
Continuance of open seasons, §113-291.4(f1).
Training dogs during closed season,
§113-291.1(d1).
Seasons and bag limits.
Authority of commission to fix, §113-291.2(a).

HUNTING AND WILDLIFE —Cont'd
Seasons and bag limits —Cont'd
Closed seasons.
Authority to fix included, §113-291.2(a).
Deer.
Special antlerless deer tags, §113-291.2(e).
Different seasons and bag limits.
Setting in different areas, §113-291.2(a).
Dog use in hunting deer prohibited, §113-291.2(a).
Foxes.
Open seasons for taking foxes with firearms,
§113-291.4A(a), (b).
Migratory game birds.
Federal seasons and bag limits observed,
§113-291.2(a).
Muzzle-loading firearms season for deer.
One antlerless deer taken, §113-291.2(a).
Possession and transportation of taken animals,
§113-291.2(c).
Carcasses known or suspected to carry
infectious or contagious diseases,
§113-291.2(c1).
Closed seasons, §113-291.2(d).
Proclamations by commission, §113-291.2(f).
Setting of season and possession limits.
Authority to fix bag limits includes,
§113-291.2(a).
Special antlerless deer tags, §113-291.2(e).
Special or extended seasons, §113-291.2(a).
Transportation of taken animals, §113-291.2(c).
Carcasses known or suspected to carry
infectious or contagious diseases,
§113-291.2(c1).
Closed seasons, §113-291.2(d).
Wounded or disabled animals.
Reasonable effort to capture and kill,
§113-291.2(b).
**Selling, buying, possessing, importing,
exporting.**
Dead wildlife, §113-291.3(b) to (d).
Live wildlife, §113-291.3(a).
Service of process.
Fees, §113-303.
Service by protectors.
Arrest warrants, search warrants, orders for
arrest, etc., §113-136(e).
Shooting preserves.
Manner of taking wild animals or birds.
Relaxing requirements on controlled shooting
preserves, §113-291.1(h).
Shotguns.
Method of taking wildlife, §113-291.1(a).
Special activity licenses, §113-270.3(a), (b).
Special conservation officers.
Conference of law enforcement powers,
§113-138(a).
Jurisdiction and powers generally, §113-138(d).
Limitation on exercise of authority to confer
powers, §113-138(d).
Specification of particular officers or classes of
officers, §113-138(c).
Sportsmen licenses, §§113-270.1D, 113-270.3(d),
(e).
Spotlighting deer.
Prima facie evidence, §113-302(b).
Squirrels.
Sale of edible parts, §113-291.3(b).
State forests.
Collection of reasonable fees for privileges,
§106-877(b).
License fees for hunting and fishing on
government-owned property unaffected,
§106-881.

HUNTING AND WILDLIFE —Cont'd
State parks.
Collection of reasonable fees for privileges, §113-35(b).
Statutes.
Repeal of certain public, public-local, special and private acts, §113-377.8.
Subpoenas.
Service by protectors, §113-136(e).
Sunday hunting, §103-2.
Taxidermist.
Possessing wildlife authorized to handle, §113-291.3(b).
Taxidermy licenses, §113-273(k).
Transitional provisions.
Purpose and effect of revisions of subchapter, §113-316.
Transportation.
Permits, §113-274(c).
Transportation of taken animals, §113-291.2(c).
Carcasses known or suspected to carry infectious or contagious diseases, §113-291.2(c1).
Closed seasons, §113-291.2(d).
Transporting lawfully taken wildlife, §§113-291.2(c), (d), 113-291.3(b) to (d).
Transporting live wildlife, nests and nest eggs, §113-291.3(a).
Trapping.
Beaver.
Snares used, §113-291.9(d).
Trapping pursuant to beaver damage control program, §113-291.10(d).
Feral swine caught in traps.
Unlawful to remove and to transport after removal, §113-291.12.
Penalty, §113-294(s).
Foxes, §113-291.4(f), (f1).
Hiring hunter or trapper to take game.
Person hiring deemed buyer, hunter or trapper deemed seller, §113-291.3(d).
Indian tribes recognized under chapter 71A.
Inapplicability of license provisions.
Hunting, trapping and fishing on tribal lands, §113-276(l1).
Licenses, §113-270.5(a).
Duration of validity of license, §113-270.1B(b).
Fees, §113-270.5(b).
Required, §113-270.1B(a).
Methods of taking wildlife, §113-291.1(a).
Regulation, §113-291.6.
Restrictions, new rules, adopting.
Notification to public, §113-301.1(c), (d).
Violations generally, §113-294(i), (j).
Trespass.
Hunting, fishing or trapping on "posted" property, §§14-159.6 to 14-159.10.
Registered property, §§113-281 to 113-287.
Land under option by federal government, §14-131.
Trophy wildlife sale permits, §113-274(c).
Unified hunting and fishing licenses, §113-351.
United States agencies.
Scientific investigations, §113-261(a).
Taking wildlife in generally prohibited manner.
Authority, §113-261(c).
Unlawfully selling, possessing for sale or buying, §113-294.
Unlawfully taking, possessing, transporting, §113-294.
Venue.
Interference with taking of wildlife resources.
Injunctive relief, §113-295(b).

HUNTING AND WILDLIFE —Cont'd
Vessels.
Taking wild animals or birds from vessels equipped with motors, §113-294(g).
Violations generally.
Specific violations, §113-294.
Voluntary migratory waterfowl conservation print.
Exclusive production rights, §113-270.2B(a).
Ownership rights, §113-270.2B(a).
Proceeds, §113-270.2B(b).
Warning tickets.
Accounting for and recording of issuance, §113-140(e).
Conditions for issuance, §113-140(c).
Evidence of commission of offense.
Issuance not to constitute, §113-140(g).
Inappropriate issuance, §113-140(d).
Issuance generally, §113-140(a).
Powers of protectors or law enforcement officers not restricted, §113-140(f).
Standards for issuance, §113-140(b).
Watersheds of navigable streams, protection of.
Legislative assent to specific federal acts, §113-307.1(a).
Wildlife endowment fund.
Appropriations and agency receipts.
Fund not to take the place of, §143-250.1(g).
Assets, §143-250.1(c).
Board of trustees.
Accumulation of investment income, §143-250.1(e).
Created, §143-250.1(b).
Officers, §143-250.1(b).
Powers and duties, §143-250.1(b).
Created, §143-250.1(a).
Declared special trust, §143-250.1(d).
Dissolution of wildlife resources commission.
Assumption of trusteeship of fund, §143-250.1(h).
Eddie Bridges fund.
Fund to be known as, §143-250.1.
Expenditures of income, §143-250.1(f).
Supplemental to other income and appropriations, §143-250.1(g).
Use of income and principal, §143-250.1(a).
Wildlife management areas.
Dogs.
Killing or injuring deer or bear.
Dog may be killed without liability, §67-14.1(a).
Running at large.
Unmuzzled dogs running at large.
Impoundment, §67-14.1(b) to (e).
Wildlife management plan.
Development, §113-306(d).
Wildlife resources belong to people of state, §113-131(a).
Wildlife resources commission.
Notification to public affected by laws and rules, §113-301.1.
Scientific investigations, §113-261(a).
Taking wildlife in generally prohibited manner.
Authority, §113-261(c).
Wildlife restoration projects.
Legislative assent to specific federal acts, §113-307.1(b).
Wild turkey.
Sale of parts prohibited, §113-291.3(b).

HUNTING AND WILDLIFE —Cont'd
Wild turkey —Cont'd
Unlawfully selling, possessing for sale or buying, §113-294(b).
Unlawfully taking, possessing or transporting, §113-294(c).
Witnesses.
Fees, §113-303.
Wounded or disabled animals.
Reasonable effort to capture and kill, §113-291.2(b).

HUNTING GUIDES.
Licenses, §113-270.4.

HUNTING PRESERVES.
Controlled preserve operator's license, §113-273(g).

HURRICANE EVACUATION STANDARD.
Bridge or highway construction projects, §136-102.7.

HURRICANE PROTECTION WORKS.
Municipalities.
Service districts.
Purposes for establishing, §160A-536(a).

HURRICANE RELIEF AND ASSISTANCE.
Adjustments to federal taxable income.
Amounts paid taxpayer from disaster relief reserve fund, §105-130.5(b).

HURRICANES.
Beach area essential property insurance.
Generally, §§58-45-1 to 58-45-96.
See BEACH AREA ESSENTIAL PROPERTY INSURANCE.
Flood and hurricane protection works.
Appropriations, §153A-438.
Flood protection and beach erosion control project revolving fund, §143-215.62.
Removal of property deposited by hurricane, §104B-1.
Special assessments by counties generally, §§153A-185 to 153A-210.7.
See SPECIAL ASSESSMENTS BY COUNTIES.

HUSBAND AND WIFE.
Abandonment.
Acts barring rights of spouse, §31A-1(a).
Guardian's sale of abandoned incompetent spouse's estate, §35A-1306.
Willful abandonment, §14-322.
Absentees in military service.
Appointment as receiver, §28B-4(b).
Transfer of property valued at less than $5,000.
Application to superior court, §28B-9(a).
Abuse or neglect of children.
Waiver of husband-wife privilege in child abuse cases, §8-57.1.
Acknowledgments.
Absence of wife does not affect deed as to husband, §39-9.
Before different officers, §39-8.
Before same officer.
Form, §47-40.
Certain conveyances not affected by fraud, §39-11.
Different times and places, §39-8.
Order immaterial, §39-8.
Powers of attorney.
Acknowledgment of spouse of grantor unnecessary, §39-12.
Actions.
Quieting title, §41-10.

HUSBAND AND WIFE —Cont'd
Actions —Cont'd
Torts.
Acts arising outside state, §52-5.1.
Torts between husband and wife, §52-5.
Acts barring property rights of spouse, §31A-1(a).
Acts specified barring rights, §31A-1(a).
Pleading in bar, §31A-1(c).
Rights lost, §31A-1(b).
Sale or conveyance of property without joining spouse at fault, §31A-1(d).
Adoption.
Death of joint petitioner pending final decree, §48-2-204.
Prohibition on adoption, §48-1-103.
Spouse of petitioner must join in petition, §48-2-301(b).
Alimony.
See DIVORCE.
Anatomical gifts.
Who may make gift of body or body part of decedent, §130A-412.11(a).
Annulment of marriage.
General provisions.
See ANNULMENT OF MARRIAGE.
Antenuptial contracts.
Generally, §§52B-1 to 52B-11.
See PREMARITAL AGREEMENTS.
Liability of married persons for debts, contracts or damages incurred before marriage, §52-11.
Bail.
Crimes of domestic violence, §15A-534.1(a).
Retention of defendant in custody without action, time limitation, §15A-534.1(b).
Capacity of married persons to contract, §52-2.
Child custody.
General provisions.
See CHILD CUSTODY.
Child support.
General provisions.
See CHILD SUPPORT.
Community property, divorce.
Equitable distribution of marital property generally, §§50-11, 50-20 to 50-22.
Cross-actions, jurisdiction, §7A-244.
Mediated settlement conferences, district courts, §7A-38.4A.
Community property rights.
Disposition at death, §§31C-1 to 31C-12.
See COMMUNITY PROPERTY.
Constitution of North Carolina.
Women.
Property of married women secured to them, NC Const Art X §4.
Contracts.
Antenuptial contracts.
Generally, §§52B-1 to 52B-11.
See PREMARITAL AGREEMENTS.
Liability of married persons for debts, contracts or damages incurred before marriage, §52-11.
Between husband and wife.
Judgment of superior or other court.
Inapplicability to, §52-10(c).
Not inconsistent with public policy, §52-10(a).
Required to be in writing and acknowledged, §52-10(a).
Certifying officer, §52-10(b).
Statute of fraud.
Required to be in writing and acknowledged, §52-10(a).

HUSBAND AND WIFE —Cont'd
Contracts —Cont'd
Capacity to contract, §52-2.
Distribution of marital property agreements,
§50-20(d).
Examinations.
Validation of contracts where wife is not
privately examined, §52-8.
Joint execution by husband and wife.
Married persons under 18 made competent as to
certain transactions, §39-13.2(a), (b).
Notaries public.
Validation of certificates as to contracts between
husband and wife, §52-7.
Recovery by person suing alone, §52-4.
Separation agreements, §52-10.1.
Validation.
Contracts failing to comply with provisions of
former section 52-6, §52-8.
Validation of contract executed by married women
without private examination.
Contracts executed prior to Feb. 7, 1945,
§39-13.1(b).
Contracts executed since Nov. 7, 1944,
§39-13.1(a).
Conveyances.
Acknowledgments.
Absence of wife's acknowledgment does not
affect deed as to husband, §39-9.
Different times and places, §39-8.
Acts barring property rights.
Conveyance of property by spouse not at fault,
§31A-1(d).
Conveyance by spouse to both spouses.
Tenants by the entirety, interest vested as,
§39-13.3(b).
Conveyance by spouse to other spouse.
Interest vested in grantee spouse, §39-13.3(a).
Tenants by the entirety, dissolution of interest
held as, §39-13.3(c).
Deed of separation.
Conveyance by husband or wife under deed,
§39-13.4.
G.S. 52-10 or 52-10.1.
Applicability of provisions to conveyances by
spouses to spouses, §39-13.3(e).
Instruments affecting married woman's title.
Validation of instruments not executed by
husband, §39-7.1.
Joinder of spouse, §39-7(b).
Grantor's spouse, §39-13.3(d).
Married persons under 18 made competent as to
certain transactions, §39-13.2(a), (b).
Notaries.
Validation of certificates as to conveyances
between husband and wife, §52-7.
Party to convey without joinder, §39-7(b).
Purchase-money mortgages.
Spouse need not join, §39-13.
Validation of conveyance executed by married
women without private examination.
Conveyances executed prior to Feb. 7, 1945,
§39-13.1(b).
Conveyances executed since Nov. 7, 1944,
§39-13.1(a).
Validation of instruments not executed by
husband, §39-7.1.
Waiver of elective life estate.
Execution of conveyance, §39-7(a), (c).
**Corporate stock and investment securities,
joint ownership,** §41-2.2(a).
Death of joint tenant, §41-2.2(c).

HUSBAND AND WIFE —Cont'd
**Corporate stock and investment securities,
joint ownership** —Cont'd
Inheritance laws unaffected, §41-2.2(d).
When joint tenancy and shares if corporate stock
or investment securities exist, §41-2.2(b).
Costs.
Judgments against married persons for costs.
Levy and collection out of separate estate,
§1-223.
Credit.
Equal availability of credit for women, §25B-1(a).
Criminal law and procedure.
Postnuptial crimes, §52-12.
Curtesy.
Abolished, §§29-4, 41-4.
Renunciation by married person under 21 years,
§39-13.2(c).
Damages.
Judgments against married persons for damages.
Levy and collection out of separate estate,
§1-223.
Recovery by person suing alone, §52-4.
Tort actions arising out of acts occurring outside
state, §52-5.1.
Torts between husband and wife, §52-5.
Deeds.
Acknowledgments.
Absence of wife's acknowledgment not to affect
deed as to husband, §39-9.
Different times and places, §39-8.
Certain conveyances not affected by fraud if
acknowledgment or privy examination
regular, §39-11.
Conveyances under deed of separation, §39-13.4.
Married persons under 18 made competent as to
certain transactions, §39-13.2(a), (b).
Power to convey property without joinder,
§39-7(b).
Probates.
Different officers of deeds, §47-87.
Validation of deed executed by married women
without private examination.
Deeds executed prior to Feb. 7, 1945,
§39-13.1(b).
Deeds executed since Nov. 7, 1944, §39-13.1(a).
Validation of instruments not executed by
husband, §39-7.1.
Definitions.
Abandonment and failure to support spouse and
children, §14-322(a).
Dependent spouse.
Duty of supporting spouse, §14-322.
Divorce.
See DIVORCE.
Domestic violence, §§50B-1 to 50B-9.
See DOMESTIC VIOLENCE.
Dower.
Abolished, §29-4.
Renunciation by married person under age of 21
years, §39-13.2(c).
Duress.
Certain conveyances not affected by fraud or
duress, §39-11.
Earnings and damages.
Recovery by person suing alone, §52-4.
Elective life estate, §29-30(a) to (h).
Waiver, §39-7(a), (c).
Executions.
Married women.
Levy and collection from separate property,
§1-304.

HUSBAND AND WIFE —Cont'd
Exemptions.
Property of married women secured to them, NC Const Art X §4.
Property passing by devise, intestate succession or gift to dependent spouse.
Continuation of exemption, §1C-1604(b).
Falsely registering as husband and wife, §14-186.
Forms.
Husband's and wife's acknowledgment before same officer, §47-40.
Fraudulent conveyances.
Certain conveyances not affected by fraud, §39-11.
Free trader agreements, §52-10.
Guardian ad litem for minor in domestic relations actions.
When not required, §1A-1 Rule 17(b).
Guardians.
Abandoned incompetent spouse's estate.
Sale of spouse's separate property by guardian, §35A-1306.
Sale of ward's estate.
Spouse entitled to special proceeding for sale of real property, §35A-1307.
Homesteads.
Acts barring rights of spouse, §31A-1(b).
Hotels.
Falsely registering as husband and wife, §14-186.
Immunities.
Inter-spousal immunity.
Abolished, §52-5.1.
Actions arising out of acts occurring outside state, §52-5.1.
Income tax.
Individual income tax.
Joint returns, §105-152(e).
Payment of tax, §105-157(a).
Insurance.
Life insurance.
Rights of beneficiaries, §58-58-95.
Married person may insure spouse's life, §52-3.
Property insurance.
Policy issued to husband or wife on joint property, §58-44-45.
Inter-spousal immunity.
Abolished, §52-5.1.
Actions arising out of acts occurring outside state, §52-5.1.
Intestate succession.
Acts barring rights of spouse, §31A-1(b).
Joint bank accounts.
Right of survivorship, §41-2.1.
Joint ownership of corporate stock and investments securities, §41-2.2(a).
Death of joint tenant, §41-2.2(c).
Inheritance tax laws unaffected, §41-2.2(d).
When joint tenancy exists, §41-2.2(b).
Judgments against married persons.
Levy and collection out of separate estate or property, §1-223.
Judgments construed to be contract or release between spouses.
Inapplicability of provisions concerning contracts and releases, §52-10(c).
Jurisdiction.
Personal jurisdiction.
Marital relationship, §1-75.4.
Leases.
Power to lease without joinder of spouse, §39-7(b).

HUSBAND AND WIFE —Cont'd
Leases —Cont'd
Validation of leasehold executed by married women without private examination.
Leasehold executed prior to Feb. 7, 1945, §39-13.1(b).
Leaseholds executed since Nov. 7, 1944, §39-13.1(a).
Life estates.
Elective life estate, §29-30.
Waiver, §39-7(a), (c).
Waiver of elective life estate.
Execution of instruments affecting estate, §39-7(a), (c).
Life insurance.
Rights of beneficiaries, §58-58-95.
Magistrates.
Contracts.
Power of magistrate to take acknowledgment of written contract, §7A-292.
Separation agreements.
Power of magistrate to take acknowledgment of agreement, §7A-292.
Marriage.
See MARRIAGE.
Missing persons.
Property owned as tenants by the entirety.
Power of receiver to partition, §28C-8.
Mobile homes.
Tenancy by the entirety in mobile home, §41-2.5(a), (b), (d).
Definition of "mobile home,"§41-2.5(c).
Mortgage or sale of estates held by the entireties, §§35A-1310 to 35A-1314.
Approval by judge, §35A-1311.
Authorized, §35A-1310.
Clerk of court.
Powers, §35A-1310.
Funds.
Clerk may direct application, §35A-1313.
General law applicable, §35A-1311.
Petition.
Authority to file, §35A-1310.
Contents, §35A-1310.
Prior sales and mortgages validated, §35A-1314.
Purchasers and mortgagees protected, §35A-1313.
Title.
Acquisition of title unaffected by provisions, §35A-1313.
Proceeding valid in passing title, §35A-1312.
Validation of prior sales and mortgages, §35A-1314.
Mortgages and deeds of trust.
Joint execution.
Married persons under 18 made competent as to certain transactions, §39-13.2(a), (b).
Power to mortgage without joinder of spouse, §39-7(b).
Purchase-money mortgages.
Spouse need not join in, §39-13.
Spouse of mortgagor has right to redeem, §45-45.
Nonsupport.
Duty of supporting spouse, §14-322.
Notaries public.
Contracts or conveyances between husband and wife.
Validation of certificates of notaries, §52-7.
Opposite sexes occupying same bedroom for immoral purposes, §14-186.
Partition.
Creation of tenancy by entirety in partition of real property, §39-13.5.

HUSBAND AND WIFE —Cont'd
Paternity proceedings, §8-57.2.
Personal property.
Acts barring property rights.
Acts specified, rights lost, §31A-1.
Property of married persons secured, §52-1.
Pleading.
Acts barring rights of spouse, §31A-1(c).
Postnuptial crimes and torts, §52-12.
Powers of attorney.
Authorized to execute, §39-12.
Validation of instruments not executed by
husband, §39-7.1.
Premarital agreements generally, §§52B-1 to
52B-11.
See PREMARITAL AGREEMENTS.
Privilege.
Abused, neglected or dependent juvenile actions.
Inapplicable when guardian ad litem demands
information, §7B-601.
Abuse or neglect of children.
Husband-wife privilege not grounds for
excluding evidence of abuse or neglect,
§8-57.1.
Child support actions instituted by designated
representatives of county commissioners,
§110-130.
Civil actions, §8-56.
Criminal actions, §8-57(a) to (c).
Paternity proceedings, §8-57.2.
Proof or acknowledgment of instrument.
Before different officers, §47-68.
Before same officer.
Form, §47-40.
Free trader.
No examination of husband's assent where wife
free trader, §47-69.
Probate by different officers of deeds by husband
and wife, §47-87.
Wrong order, §47-67.
Property, §52-1, NC Const Art X §4.
Acts barring rights of spouse, §31A-1(b).
Property insurance.
Policy issued to husband or wife on joint property,
§58-44-45.
Property rights barred.
Acts specified, rights lost, §31A-1.
Purchase-money mortgages.
Spouse need not join in, §39-13.
Real property.
Acts barring property rights.
Acts specified, rights lost, §31A-1.
Registration.
Absence of wife's acknowledgment.
Registration of instrument, §39-9.
Release and quick claim of rights.
Judgment of superior or other court.
Inapplicability to, §52-10(c).
Not inconsistent with public policy, §52-10(a).
Required to be in writing and acknowledged,
§52-10(a).
Certifying officer, §52-10(b).
Statute of fraud.
Required to be in writing and acknowledged,
§52-10(a).
Residential property disclosure act.
Transfers resulting from divorce.
Applicability of act, §47E-2.
Resumption of marital relations, §52-10.2.
Sale of personal or real property.
Acts barring property rights.
Sale without joining spouse at fault, §31A-1(d).

HUSBAND AND WIFE —Cont'd
Securities.
Joint ownership of investment securities,
§41-2.2(a).
Death of joint tenant, §41-2.2(c).
Inheritance tax laws unaffected, §41-2.2(d).
When joint tenancy in investment securities
exist, §41-2.2(b).
Separation agreements.
Authorization and requisites, §52-10.1.
Distribution of marital property agreements,
§50-20(d).
Sexual offenses.
Bail, §15A-534.4.
Victim is spouse of person committing act.
Defense that victim is spouse, §14-27.8.
Stock, joint ownership, §41-2.2.
Death of joint tenant, §41-2.2(c).
Inheritance tax laws unaffected, §41-2.2(d).
When joint tenancy and shares of corporate stock
exist, §41-2.2(b).
Support and maintenance.
Child support.
General provisions.
See CHILD SUPPORT.
Failure to support dependent spouse, §14-322.
Generally.
See SUPPORT AND MAINTENANCE.
Interstate family support, §§52C-1-100 to
52C-9-902.
See INTERSTATE FAMILY SUPPORT.
Surviving spouses.
See SURVIVING SPOUSES.
Taxation.
Combined returns, §105-152(e).
Excess funds, §28A-15-9.
Federal income tax refunds.
Death of spouses, §28A-15-6.
Federal marital deduction on distribution of
estates, §28A-22-6.
Joint returns.
Federal income tax refunds, §28A-15-6.
When not authorized, §105-152(e).
Separate returns.
Federal income tax refunds, §28A-15-7.
State income tax returns.
Death of spouse, §28A-15-8.
Tenancy by the entireties.
Absentees in military service.
Partition of property, §28B-6.
Control of real property held in tenancy by the
entirety.
Applicability of section, §39-13.6(c).
Equal rights to control, §39-13.6(a).
Vesting of title, §39-13.6(b).
Conveyance by spouse to other spouse.
Dissolution of interest held as, §39-13.3(c).
Conveyance spouse to both spouses.
Interest created, §39-13.3(b).
Creation in partition of real property, §39-13.5.
Killing decedents.
Disposition of property, §31A-5.
Mobile homes, §41-2.5(a), (b), (d).
Definition of "mobile home,"§41-2.5(c).
Mortgage or sale of estates held by the entireties,
§§35A-1310 to 35A-1314.
Renunciation by surviving tenant, §31B-1.
Title.
Mortgage or sale of estates held by the entireties.
Incompetent spouses.
Proceeding valid in passing title, §35A-1312.

HUSBAND AND WIFE —Cont'd
Title —Cont'd
Quieting title, §41-10.
Torts.
Actions arising out of acts occurring outside state, §52-5.1.
Antenuptial torts, §52-11.
Between husband and wife, §52-5.
Earnings and damages.
Recovery by person suing alone, §52-4.
Postnuptial torts, §52-12.
Uniform interstate family support act,
§§52C-1-100 to 52C-9-902.
See INTERSTATE FAMILY SUPPORT.
Waiver, release or renunciation of interest.
Married persons under 18 made competent as to certain transactions, §39-13.2(a).
Wills.
Acknowledgments.
Different officers, §39-8.
Different times and places, §39-8.
Not revoked by marriage, §31-5.3.
Witnesses.
Child abuse cases.
Waiver of husband-wife privilege, §8-57.1.
Child support actions instituted by designated representative of county commissioners.
Inapplicability of husband-wife privilege, §110-130.
Civil actions, §8-56.
Criminal actions, §8-57(a) to (c).
Wrongful death.
Acts occurring outside state, §52-5.1.

HUSBAND-WIFE PRIVILEGE.
Abused, neglected or dependent juvenile actions.
Inapplicable when guardian ad litem demands information, §7B-601.
Child abuse or neglect.
Waiver, §8-57.1.
Child custody jurisdiction and enforcement,
§50A-310(d).
Child support actions instituted by designated representative of county commissioners.
Inapplicability, §110-130.
Civil actions, §8-56.
Criminal actions, §8-57(a) to (c).
Interstate family support, §52C-3-315(h), (i).
Paternity proceedings, §8-57.2.
Termination of parental rights proceedings.
Inapplicability, §7B-1109(f).

HYBRID ELECTRIC VEHICLES.
Energy credit and banking act.
Participation by state departments, institutions and agencies.
Purchase, §143-58.4.

HYBRID SEEDS, §106-277.17.

HYDE COUNTY.
Ambulances.
Obtaining ambulance services without intending to pay, §14-111.2.
Board of county commissioners.
Filling vacancies on board, §153A-27.1.
Cropper or tenant refusing to perform terms of contract.
Forfeiture of right of possession to premises, §42-27.
Dog collars.
Unlawful removal of electronic dog collars, §14-401.17.

HYDE COUNTY —Cont'd
Foxes, open seasons for taking.
Wildlife resources commission authorized to continue from year to year, §113-291.4(f1).
Game laws, local acts not repealed,
§113-133.1(e).
Grants in navigable waters, registration,
§113-205(a).
Housing authority commissioners.
Tenant as commissioner, exemption from provision of law allowing, §157-5.
Maps in special proceedings, recording of photographic copies, §47-32.
Violation as misdemeanor, inapplicability of provisions, §47-32.2.
North Carolina's northeast commission,
§§158-8.2 to 158-8.8.
Open fires, high hazard counties.
Applicability of provisions, §106-942(a).
Ground clearing activities, special permit, §106-942(c).
Woodland fires, permit required, §106-942(b).
Registration of deeds.
Tax certification that no delinquent taxes due, §161-31(b).
School property.
Acquisition and improvement, §153A-158.1.
Sheriff.
Vacancy, performance of duties until vacancy filled, §162-5.1.
Special school tax, election to abolish.
Petition required, §115C-505.
Swimming, surfing and littering in Atlantic Ocean.
City ordinances effective, §160A-176.1.
Tax sales, notices by publication validated.
Inapplicability of provisions, §47-108.24.

HYDRAULIC BRAKE FLUIDS.
Types and brands approved by commissioner of motor vehicles, §20-124(h).

HYDRAULIC POWER CORPORATIONS.
Eminent domain.
Use or occupancy of public highway, §62-181.

HYDROELECTRIC GENERATORS.
Business and energy tax credits, §§105-129.15 to 105-129.19.

HYDROPHOBIA.
Generally, §§130A-184 to 130A-201.
See RABIES.

HYPODERMICS AND SOPORIFICS.
Controlled substances generally, §§90-86 to 90-113.8.
See DRUGS AND CONTROLLED SUBSTANCES.

HYPOTHETICAL CLAIMS OR DEFENSES,
§1A-1 Rule 8(e).

I

ICE.
Insurance.
Farm owners' and other property policies.
Damage from ice, snow or sleet, §58-44-55.
Tire chains, permissible use, §20-122(b).

ICEBOXES.
Discarding or abandoning iceboxes, §14-318.1.

ICE CREAM PLANTS, CREAMERIES AND CHEESE FACTORIES, §§106-246 to 106-255.
Animals.
Prohibited, §106-246.
Board of agriculture.
Test by board, §106-250.
Butterfat, §106-250.
Certificate to district attorney.
Closure of plants for violation of article, §106-252.
Cleanliness.
Receivers of products to clean utensils before return, §106-249.
Required, §106-246.
Vessels and utensils, §106-247.
Closure of plants.
Certificate to district attorney, §106-252.
Violations of article, §106-252.
Compliance with standards, §106-248.
Desserts.
Frozen or semifrozen desserts.
Regulating trade or brand names, §106-253.
District attorney.
Closure of plants for violation of article.
Certificate to district attorney, §106-252.
Enforcement of provisions.
Department of agriculture and consumer services, §106-251.
Fees.
Inspection fees, §§106-254, 106-267.1.
Frozen or semifrozen desserts.
Regulating trade or brand names, §106-253.
Inspections.
Board of agriculture, §106-251.
Fees, §§106-254, 106-267.1.
Living and sleeping rooms, §106-246.
Misdemeanors.
Violations of article, §106-255.
Purity of products, §106-248.
Standards of purity and sanitation, §106-253.
Receivers of products.
Cleaning utensils before return, §106-249.
Right of entry to make inspections, §106-251.
Sanitation.
Required, §106-246.
Standards of purity and sanitation, §106-253.
Semifrozen desserts.
Regulating trade or brand names, §106-253.
Sleeping rooms, §106-246.
Sterilization.
Vessels and utensils, §106-247.
Test of butterfat, §106-250.
Toilets, §106-246.
Trade or brand names.
Frozen or semifrozen desserts, §106-253.
Utensils.
Cleaning and sterilization of utensils, §106-247.
Receivers of products to clean utensils before return, §106-249.
Vessels.
Cleaning and sterilization of vessels, §106-247.
Violations of article.
Closure of plants, §106-252.
Misdemeanor offenses, §106-255.
Washrooms and toilets, §106-246.

ICE SKATING RINKS.
Amusement device safety.
Amusement device defined as not including, §95-111.3(a).

IDENTIFICATION.
Alcoholic beverage sales to or purchases by underage persons.
Fake identification, §18B-302(d) to (f).

IDENTIFICATION —Cont'd
Appeals.
Protection of identity of persons under age of 18.
Appeal information statement, AppProc Rule 41(b).
Briefs, AppProc Rule 28(a).
Form, AppProc Appx D.
Juvenile matters, AppProc Rules 3.1(b), 3(b).
Juvenile victims of sexual offenses, AppProc Rule 4(e).
Motions in appellate courts, AppProc Rule 37(c).
Oral argument, AppProc Rule 30(a).
Record on appeal.
Notice in filing involving juveniles, AppProc Rule 9(a).
Cigarettes and tobacco products.
Proof of age.
Fake identification offered by minor for purchase of tobacco product, §14-313(c).
Concealed handgun permits.
Identification required to be carried, §14-415.11(a).
Dead bodies before burial or cremation, §90-210.29A.
Delinquent or undisciplined juvenile actions.
Fingerprinting and photographing juveniles, §7B-2102.
Nontestimonial identification order procedures generally, §§7B-2103 to 7B-2109.
DNA analysis, §§15A-266 to 15A-270.
See DNA.
Eyewitness identification reform, §§15A-284.50 to 15A-284.53.
False or fraudulent, §14-100.1.
Foreign birth.
Certificate of identification, §130A-108.
Health care practitioners, §90-640.
Applicability, §90-640(a).
Contents, §90-640(b).
Disciplinary action, §90-640(e).
Display required, §90-640(b).
Exception, §90-640(c).
Practitioner's office, exception, §90-640(c).
Rules for exemptions, §90-640(d).
Violation, §90-640(e).
Identification cards for nonoperators of motor vehicles, §§20-37.7 to 20-37.9.
Leases, UCC.
Identification of goods, §25-2A-217.
Casualty to identified goods, §25-2A-221.
Insurable interest in existing goods.
Vesting in lessee, §25-2A-218.
Lessor's right to identify goods upon lessee's default, §25-2A-524.
Livestock.
Brucellosis.
Sale of diseased animals.
Removal of identification marks, §106-390.
Public livestock markets.
Cattle removed from market for slaughter and nonslaughter purposes, §106-409.
Removal of identification.
Disease control purposes, §106-414.
Swine removed from market for slaughter and nonslaughter purposes, §106-410.
Machines and apparatus, identification marks.
Removing, defacing, etc., §14-401.4.
Motor vehicle engine numbers.
Altering or changing.
Prohibited acts, §20-109(a).
Intent to conceal or misrepresent true identity of vehicle, §20-109(b).

IDENTIFICATION —Cont'd
Motor vehicle engine numbers —Cont'd
New engine.
Division to be notified on installation, §20-70(a).
When required, §20-70(c).
Surrender of certificate of title and registration card on installation, §20-70(b).
Vehicles without manufacturer's numbers.
Prohibitions as to, §20-108(a) to (j).
Nontestimonial identification, §§15A-271 to 15A-282.
Attorneys at law.
Copy of results.
Providing to person involved or his attorney, §15A-282.
Right to counsel, §15A-279(d).
Bodily fluids.
Extraction.
Who may extract, §15A-279(a).
Contempt.
Failure to obey order to appear, §15A-276.
Punishment, §5A-12(a).
Resistance to compliance with procedures, §15A-279(e).
Copy of results.
Providing to person involved, §15A-282.
Defined, §15A-271.
Delinquent or undisciplined juvenile actions, §§7B-2103 to 7B-2109.
Destruction of products.
Motion by suspect, §15A-280.
Detention.
Length of detention, §15A-279(c).
Failure to appear, §15A-276.
Criminal contempt, punishment, §5A-12(a).
Force.
Unreasonable or unnecessary force not to be used, §15A-279(b).
Investigations.
Additional investigative procedures not precluded, §15A-272.
Modification of order, §15A-275.
Order must state that person may request, §15A-278.
Order.
Application for.
Time for, §15A-272.
Contents, §15A-278.
Failure to obey, §15A-276.
Criminal contempt, punishment, §5A-12(a).
Grounds for issuance, §15A-273.
Implementation, §15A-279.
Issuance, §15A-274.
Authority to issue, §15A-271.
Grounds, §15A-273.
Modification, §15A-275.
Order must state that person may request, §15A-278.
Previous orders.
Effect, §15A-279(f).
Request of defendant, §15A-281.
Return, §15A-280.
Service, §15A-277.
Time for, §15A-274.
Request by defendant for order, §15A-281.
Resistance.
Contempt, §15A-279(e).
Evidentiary effect, §15A-279(g).
Return, §15A-280.
Service of order, §15A-277.
Time for, §15A-274.

IDENTIFICATION —Cont'd
Nontestimonial identification —Cont'd
Time limit on procedure, §15A-279.
Personal property.
Trespasses to personal property.
Alteration, destruction or removal of permanent identification marks, §14-160.1.
Precious metals dealers.
Seller to furnish photographic identification to, §66-169(a).
Proof of age of minors.
Alcoholic beverage sales to or purchases by underage persons, §18B-302(d) to (f).
Cigarettes and tobacco products, sales or distribution to, §14-313(b).
Pseudoephedrine products.
Restrictions on sales, §90-113.52(c).
Sale of goods, UCC.
Identification of goods, §25-2-501(1).
Casualty to identified goods, §25-2-613.
Manner of identification, §25-2-501(1).
Seller's right to identify notwithstanding breach, §25-2-704.
Searches and seizures.
Item subject to seizure under search warrant, §15A-242.
State departments and agencies.
Cards for field agents or deputies, §128-14.
Termination of parental rights.
Unknown parent, preliminary hearing to ascertain identity, §7B-1105.
Vital statistics.
Birth certificate where parentage cannot be established.
Certificate of identification in lieu of birth certificate, §130A-107.
Foreign birth.
Certificate of identification for person of foreign birth, §130A-108.

IDENTIFICATION CARDS.
Alcoholic beverage sales to or purchases by underage persons.
Allowing use of identification, §18B-302(f).
Fraudulent use of identification, §18B-302(e).
Production of identification card showing age to be at least required age for purchase, defense, §18B-302(d).
Bail bondsmen and runners, §58-71-40(d).
Cigarette and tobacco product purchases by minors, §14-313(c).
Criminal record checks of persons manufacturing or producing.
Confidentiality, §114-19.24(d).
Department of justice, §114-19.24(a).
Fee to offset costs, §114-19.24(e).
Fingerprints, §114-19.24(c).
Information provided to department, §114-19.24(b).
False or fictitious names.
Possession or manufacture of cards, §14-100.1.
Presenting identification card with fake name in commission of felony, §20-37.8(b).
Identify theft generally, §§14-113.20 to 14-113.25.
Insurance identification card.
Design, §58-3-247(b).
Generally, §58-3-247(a).
Judicial department employees, §7A-343.
Locksmith licensing.
Photo identification card, §74F-11.

IDENTIFICATION CARDS —Cont'd
Manufacturers or producers of cards.
Criminal record checks, §114-19.24.
Medicaid cards.
Medicaid recipient fraud.
Misuse of card, §108A-64(b1).
Prescription drug identification cards.
Uniform identification cards issued by health
benefit plan, §58-3-177.
Pyrotechnics licenses, §58-82A-2.1(c).
**Special identification cards for nonoperators
of motor vehicles,** §§20-37.7 to 20-37.9.
Applications, §§20-7(b), 20-37.7(b).
Change of address.
Notice, §20-37.9(a).
Change of name, §20-37.9(b).
Color photocopies or color reproductions.
Prohibition, §20-30.
Confidentiality of photographic image or
signature, §20-43(a).
Counterfeiting, §20-30.
Electronic system to verify information, §20-37.02.
Eligibility, §20-37.7(a).
Expiration, §20-37.7(d).
Fees, §§20-37.7(d), 20-37.9(c).
Fictitious information, §20-30.
Form, §20-37.7(c).
Fraud or misrepresentation in application.
Misdemeanor, §20-37.7(e).
Fraudulent use, §20-30.
Misdemeanor, §20-37.8(a).
Prohibited, §20-37.8(a).
Homeless persons.
Obtaining without paying fee, §20-37.7(d).
Informing residents of provisions, §20-37.7(h).
National sex offender public registry.
Search.
Applicants residing in state less than 12
months, §20-37.7(b1).
Nonliability of state, §20-37.7(g).
Notification of change of address, §20-37.9(a).
Organ, eye and tissue donor cards.
Availability at division offices issuing cards,
§20-7.3.
Prohibited acts, §20-30.
Record of all recipients of special identification
card, §20-37.7(f).
Residency of state.
Proof required for issuance, documents
evidencing, §20-7(b2), (b3), (b4).
Revoked card, refusal to surrender, §20-30.
Sex offenders.
Ineligibility for issuance.
Registered sex offenders, §20-37.7(b1).
National sex offender public registry search.
Applicants residing in state less than 12
months, §20-37.7(b1).
Social security number or tax payer identification
number.
Providing required for issuance of license,
§20-7(b1).
Wrongful issuance, §20-34.1.
Structural pest control.
Certified applicators.
Issuance, fee, renewal, reissuance, new card,
§106-65.31(a).
Employees.
Issuance, renewal, fees, §106-65.31(b1).
Issuance licensees and certified applicators,
§106-65.25(h).
Rules, committee may provide for, §106-65.31(c).

IDENTIFICATION CARDS —Cont'd
Voter registration cards, §163-82.8.
**IDENTIFICATION CERTIFICATE FOR
INDIVIDUAL OF FOREIGN BIRTH,**
§130A-108(a).
Readoption in state, §130A-108(b).
IDENTIFICATION NUMBERS.
Commercial fishing boats.
False information, §75A-5.1(d).
Renewal of number, §75A-5.1(a), (c).
Motor vehicle engine numbers.
Altering or changing.
Prohibited acts, §20-109(a).
Intent to conceal or misrepresent true
identity of vehicle, §20-109(b).
New engine.
Division to be notified on installation, §20-70(a).
When required, §20-70(c).
Surrender of certificate of title and registration
card on installation, §20-70(b).
Vehicles without manufacturer's numbers.
Prohibitions as to, §20-108(a) to (j).
**IDENTIFICATION OF TOXIC OR HAZARDOUS
SUBSTANCES,** §§95-173 to 95-218.
See TOXIC MATERIALS AND SUBSTANCES.
IDENTITY THEFT, §§14-113.20 to 14-113.25,
75-60 to 75-66.
Additional crimes.
Court records to reflect, §14-113.22(c).
Applicability of provisions, §14-100.1(c).
Attorney General.
Investigation of complaints, §14-113.23.
**Cash registers and other receipt printing
machines.**
Sale of, §14-113.25(a), (b).
Citation of act, §75-60.
**Credit, charge, or debit card numbers on
receipts.**
Printing more than 5 digits prohibited,
§14-113.24(b).
Penalty, §14-113.24(c).
Person defined, §14-113.24(a).
Damages, §§1-539.2C(a), 14-113.22.
Additional nature of rights and remedies,
§1-539.2C(d).
Deceased person.
Recovery by estate, §1-539.2C(b).
Publication of personal information, §75-66(e).
Venue of action for, §1-539.2C(c).
Definitions, §75-61.
Identifying information, §14-113.20(b).
Publication of personal information, §75-66(b), (c).
Destruction of personal information records.
Contracts for, §75-64(c).
Exceptions to provisions, §75-64(e).
Reasonable measures by businesses, §75-64(a), (b),
(d).
Violations, §75-64(f).
Exceptions, §14-113.20(c).
Expungement of criminal records.
Dismissal or finding of not guilty.
Crime committed by another using defendant's
identifying information, §15A-147.
Felonies, §§14-113.20(a), 14-113.22(a), (a1).
Trafficking in stolen identities, §14-113.20A(b).
Identification defined, §14-100.1(d).
Investigation of offenses.
Attorney General, §14-113.23.

IDENTITY THEFT —Cont'd
Investigation of offenses —Cont'd
Local law enforcement agencies, §14-113.21A(a).
Allocation of resources, §14-113.21A(b).
Open case statistics.
Complaint filed not required to be counted for, §14-113.21A(b).
Obtaining credit information lawfully.
Not violation, §14-113.20(c).
Obtaining identification using false or fictitious information, §14-100.1(b).
Penalties, §14-100.1(e).
Possession or manufacture of false or fraudulent identification, §14-100.1(a).
Publication of personal information.
Damages, §75-66(e).
Definitions, §75-66(b), (c).
Exceptions to provisions, §75-66(d).
Prohibited acts, §75-66(a).
Reports by state agencies to general assembly on ways to reduce incidence of, §120-270.
Restitution, §14-113.22(a2).
Security breaches.
Assignment of causes of action prohibited, §75-65(j).
Compliance, what deemed to constitute, §75-65(h).
Consumer protection division of attorney general's office.
Providing notice to, §75-65(e1).
Notice, §75-65(a), (b), (f).
Consumer protection division of attorney general's office.
Providing notice to, §75-65(e1).
Contents, §75-65(d).
Delay, §75-65(c).
Methods, §75-65(e).
Violations, §75-65(i).
Waiver of provisions void and unenforceable, §75-65(g).
Security freeze on consumer's credit report, §75-63(a), (b).
Confirmation by consumer reporting agency, §75-63(c).
Change of information in credit report, §75-63(m).
Duration, §75-63(j).
Exceptions to provisions, §75-63(l), (n).
Fees authorized, §75-63(o).
Freeze only placed with consumer reporting agency to which request directed.
Notice when freeze request directed to national consumer reporting agency, §75-63(a1).
Identification to be required by consumer reporting agency, §75-63(k).
Lifting freeze for specific time or specific party, §75-63(d) to (g).
Methods of placing freeze, §75-63(a).
Notice of rights, §75-63(p).
Personal identification number or password.
Consumer provided with, §75-63(c).
Processes to be disclosed by consumer reporting agency, §75-63(i).
Release of information prohibited, §75-63(a).
Removal, §75-63(j).
Request to consumer reporting agency, §75-63(a).
Temporary lifting of, §75-63(d) to (g), (i).
Third party advised that freeze in effect, §75-63(a).
Third party request for access, §75-63(h).
Time requirements.
Time for placing after receiving request, §75-63(b).

IDENTITY THEFT —Cont'd
Security freeze on consumer's credit report —Cont'd
Time requirements —Cont'd
When consumer reporting agency not required to meet, §75-63(g1).
Violations, §75-63(q).
Security interest or offset, good faith exercise.
Not violation, §14-113.20(c).
Social security numbers.
Cooperation by businesses in implementation of requirements, §75-62(c).
Prohibited acts by businesses, §75-62(a), (d).
Exceptions, §75-62(b).
Title of act, §75-60.
Trafficking in stolen identities, §14-113.20A(a).
Felony, §14-113.20A(b).
Venue.
Criminal proceedings, §14-113.21.
Warrant or court order, good faith compliance with.
Not violation, §14-113.20(c).

IGNITION INTERLOCK SYSTEM.
Impaired driving conviction.
Restoration of license conditioned on use of interlock.
Duration of condition, §20-17.8(c).
Habitual impaired driving, applicability, §20-17.8(a1).
Limited driving privilege, effect, §20-17.8(d).
Medical exception to requirement.
Requesting, requirements for issuing, §20-17.8(l).
Notice of requirement, §20-17.8(e).
Scope, §20-17.8(a).
Violation as driving while license revoked, §20-17.8(f), (g).
Commencement of revocation, §20-17.8(h).
Hearings, §20-17.8(j).
Notification of revocation, §20-17.8(i).
Restoration after revocation for, §20-17.8(k).
When required, §20-17.8(b).
Vehicles subject to requirement, §20-17.8(c1).
Limited driving privileges.
When required as condition, §20-179.3(g5).
Tampering with system, §20-17.8A.
Vehicle registration or certificate of title.
Refusal to register because registration suspended or revoked.
Exception in cases to abide by installation requirements, §20-54.
Revocation of registration because of impaired driving conviction.
Exception in cases to abide by installation requirements, §20-54.1(a).

ILLEGITIMATE CHILDREN.
Paternity proceedings generally.
See PATERNITY.
Support, legitimation, civil actions regarding, §§49-1 to 49-17.
See CHILDREN BORN OUT OF WEDLOCK.

ILLITERACY.
Executors and administrators.
Persons disqualified to serve, §28A-4-2.

IMITATION FOODS.
Food, drug and cosmetic act.
Foods deemed misbranded, §106-130.

IMMEDIATE CIVIL LICENSE REVOCATION,
§20-16.5.
Implied consent violations.
Civil actions, §20-16.5(o).
Costs, §20-16.5(j).
Definitions, §20-16.5(a).
Effect of revocation, §20-16.5(i).
Exceptions, §20-16.5(n).
Hearing, contesting validity, §20-16.5(g).
Limited driving privilege, §20-16.5(p).
Modification of order, §20-16.5(m).
Persons charged with violations, §20-16.5(b).
Precharge test results basis for revocation,
§20-16.5(b1).
Refusal to submit to chemical analysis,
§20-16.5(b).
Report to division, §20-16.5(k).
Report to judicial officials.
Duty of charging officers, §20-16.5(c).
Judicial officer with whom report filed,
§20-16.5(d).
Person not present, procedure for filing,
§20-16.5(f).
Person present, procedure for filing, §20-16.5(e).
Restoration fee, person with no license,
§20-16.5(l).
Return of license, §20-16.5(h).
Fee as costs for action, §20-16.5(j).

IMMIGRATION.
Aliens generally.
See ALIENS.
Constitution of the United States, US Const Art
I §9.
**E-verify program to verify work authorization
of new employees.**
Counties.
Duty to register and participate, §153A-99.1.
Definition of E-Verify, §64-25.
Employers to use, §64-26(a).
Seasonal temporary employee exception to
requirement, §64-26(c).
Violations, consequences, §§64-31 to 64-33.
Municipalities.
Duty to register and participate, §160A-169.1.
State departments, agencies, etc.
Verification of legal status after hiring new
employees, §126-7.1(f).
Work authorization verification generally, §§64-25
to 64-38.
See ALIENS.
Fair housing, §§41A-1 to 41A-10.
See FAIR HOUSING.
Notaries public.
Advertising claiming expertise on immigration
matters.
Prohibition, §10B-20(j).
Prohibition on claiming power to counsel on
immigration matters, §10B-20(n).
Parole.
Early conditional release to ICE, §148-64.1.

**IMMIGRATION AND NATURALIZATION
SERVICE.**
Officers authorized to enforce criminal laws,
§15A-406.

IMMUNITY.
**Abandoned and junked vehicles removed or
disposed of.**
Municipal ordinance authority, §§160A-303.2(a4),
160A-303(f).

IMMUNITY —Cont'd
Abandonment of child.
Temporary custody of infant without court order.
Immunity from civil and criminal liability,
§7B-500(e).
ABC board members.
Limited immunity, §18B-700(j).
Accident-trauma victim identification.
Personal effects search.
Immunity for good faith compliance, §90-602(d),
(e).
Accountants.
Insurance companies.
Annual audited financial reports.
Adverse financial condition reports by CPA,
§58-10-225(b).
Address confidentiality program, §15C-11.
Adult care homes.
Criminal history record checks of employees,
§131D-40(g).
Persons interviewed during inspection,
§131D-2.14.
Quality assurance, medical, or peer review
committees, §131D-21.2(a).
Advance health care directive registry,
§130A-471.
Agricultural finance authority, §122D-23.
Agritourism activity liability, §§99E-30 to
99E-32.
Alcoholic beverage control board members.
Limited immunity, §18B-700(j).
**Alcoholic beverage permittees, agents or
employees.**
Failure to show proper identification.
Refusal to sell, §18B-129(a).
Holding customer's ID while attempting to
determine age, §18B-129(b).
Anatomical gifts.
Generally, §130A-412.20(a) to (c).
Arbitration.
Arbitrators, immunity of, §1-569.14(a).
State court-ordered nonbinding arbitration in
certain civil actions.
Arbitrators.
Immunity as judges from civil liability for
official conduct, §7A-37.1(e).
Architects.
Volunteers during an emergency or disaster.
Qualified immunity, §83A-13.1.
Athletic trainers.
Good faith reports of misconduct or incapacity,
§90-539.
Attorneys at law.
Disciplinary proceedings.
Persons immune from suit, §84-28.2.
Automated external defibrillator (AED).
First-aid or emergency medical personnel,
§90-21.15(c), (d).
Baby drop off.
Temporary custody of infant without court order.
Immunity from civil and criminal liability,
§7B-500(e).
Campus police.
Attorney general and employees thereof, §74G-11.
Cancer.
Reports.
Persons who report cancer, §130A-211.
Certified public accountants.
Insurance companies.
Annual audited financial reports.
Adverse financial condition reports by CPA,
§58-10-225(b).

IMMUNITY —Cont'd
Charities.
Defense of charitable immunity abolished,
§1-539.9.
Child abuse, neglect or dependency.
Persons making report and cooperating in
assessment of report, §7B-309.
Volunteers participating in local guardian ad
litem program, §7B-1204.
**Child care provider criminal history record
check,** §110-90.2(f).
Child custody.
Parenting coordinator, §50-100.
Child passenger safety technicians,
§20-137.5(b).
Exceptions, §20-137.5(c).
Child pornography.
Film or computer images of minor engaging in
sexual activity.
Report by film and photographic processor or
computer technician, §66-67.4(d).
**Child support actions instituted by designated
representative of county commissioners.**
Parent required to answer, §110-130.
Chiropractors.
Criminal history record checks.
Persons performing, §90-143.3(d).
Communicable diseases.
Investigations.
Persons permitting access to medical records,
§130A-144(c).
Reports.
Immunity of persons who report, §130A-142.
Compromise and settlement.
Mediated settlement conferences in superior court
civil actions.
Judicial immunity of mediators, etc.,
§7A-38.1(j).
Concealed handgun permit.
Law enforcement officers.
Qualified retired law enforcement officers.
Certification, §14-415.26(c).
Consent to health care for minors.
Reliance and authorization, §32A-33(b).
Constitution of the United States, US Const Art
IV §2.
Controlled substances reporting system,
§90-113.75(c).
Corporations.
Nonprofit corporations.
Acceptance or rejection of member's vote.
Corporate action in good faith, §55A-7-27(d).
Directors and officers, §55A-8-60.
Director's compliance with standards of
conduct, §55A-8-30(d).
Officers, discharging duties, §55A-8-42(d), (e).
Cruelty to animals.
Veterinarians.
Reporting animal cruelty, §14-360.1.
Defensive force.
Defense of home, workplace, motor vehicle
protection.
Justified in using force, immunity, exceptions,
§14-51.2(e).
Defense of person.
Justified in using, immunity, exceptions,
§14-51.3(b).
Dentists.
Peer review committees.
Members, §90-48.8.
Witnesses, §90-48.9.

IMMUNITY —Cont'd
DNA samples.
Persons authorized to draw blood, §15A-266.6(b).
Domestic violence shelters, §§1-620, 1-621.
Donated food, §99B-10.
Drug paraphernalia.
Control of potential drug paraphernalia products.
Sale of glass tubes or splitters.
Retailers and employees, §90-113.84.
Dry-cleaning solvent cleanup.
State, agencies, officers, employees and agents,
§143-215.104T(b).
Education.
Local boards of education, §115C-42.
Electrologists.
Reports of violations of chapter, §88A-23.
Emergency management, §§166A-14, 166A-15.
Emergency war powers of governor, §147-33.4.
Employee assistance professionals.
Good faith report of violations, §90-510.
**Employer disclosing information about
employee's job history or performance,**
§1-539.12(a) to (d).
Engineers.
Volunteer engineers during emergency or disaster,
§89C-19.1.
Environmental health specialists.
Disciplinary action.
Immunity of board, §90A-64(d).
Equine activity liability, §99E-2(a).
Expedited evictions.
Civil liability, §42-76.
Extradition.
No immunity from other criminal prosecution
while in this state, §15A-748.
Financial records privacy.
Disclosure of financial records by financial
institution, §53B-9(c).
Firefighters' relief fund, §58-84-60.
Fish and fisheries resources.
Hull insurance and protection and indemnity
clubs.
Administrators and boards of trustees,
§58-20-40.
Forestlands, prescribed burning, §106-967(b).
Fraternal benefit societies.
Officers.
Civil liability for monetary damages,
§58-24-35(d).
Gambling contracts.
Confessions of witnesses, §16-2.
General assembly.
Advisory opinion issued by legislative ethics
committee.
Acting in reliance on formal opinion,
§120-104(c).
Geographical location.
Deceptive representation in telephone directory,
print advertisement or Internet, §75-42(d).
Governmental immunity.
Generally.
See SOVEREIGN IMMUNITY.
Tort claims against state.
Generally, §§143-291 to 143-300.1A.
See CLAIMS AGAINST THE STATE.
**Guardian ad litem program providing services
to abused, neglected or dependent
juveniles.**
Volunteers participating in local program,
§7B-1204.

IMMUNITY —Cont'd

Guardians.

Guardian of the person.

Acting within limits imposed by powers and duties or order of appointment, §35A-1241(c).

Hazardous materials emergency response.

Regional response team personnel, §166A-24.

Health care powers of attorney.

Reliance on health care power of attorney, §32A-24(c).

Health information exchange.

Participating covered entities.

Good faith reliance on information provided through exchange, §90-413.5(d).

Hospitals.

Directors, trustees or officers of public hospitals.

Limited liability, §131E-47.1(a).

Exception, §131E-47.1(b).

Medical review committee, §131E-95(a).

Privileges to practice in hospital.

Reports of disciplinary actions, §90-14.13(e).

Husband and wife.

Inter-spousal immunity.

Abolished, §52-5.1.

Actions arising out of acts occurring outside state, §52-5.1.

Impaired driving.

Blood or urine tests of person charged.

Person obtaining, §20-139.1(c), (d3).

Person compelled to provide blood or urine sample, §20-139.1(d2).

Insurance.

Fraud.

Immunity from liability for reporting fraud, §58-2-160(a), (b).

Health insurance risk pool.

Board and employees, §58-50-180(h).

Collective action, §58-50-250.

Interstate insurance product regulation compact.

Commission, §58-91-25(e).

Market assistance program.

Good faith immunity for operation of, §58-40-135.

Property and casualty actuarial opinions.

Qualified immunity of appointed actuary, §58-10-170.

Insurance commissioner.

Examinations, §58-2-133(d).

Insurance consumer and customer information privacy.

Disclosure in accordance with article, §58-39-110.

International commercial arbitration and conciliation.

Conciliators and parties, §1-567.87.

Inter-spousal immunity.

Abolished, §52-5.

Actions arising out of acts occurring outside state, §52-5.1.

Investment advisers.

Rule, form or order.

Good faith act or omission in conformity with, §78C-30(f).

Judicial standards commission.

Conduct in course of official duties, §7A-375(e).

Law enforcement officers.

Assistance to individuals intoxicated in public.

Use of reasonable measures, §122C-301(b).

Liquefied petroleum gas dealers.

Installation, alteration, modification or repair of gas equipment and appliances.

Liability limitations, §119-62.

IMMUNITY —Cont'd

Lobbying.

Advisory opinions by state ethics commission.

Reliance upon requested written opinion, §120C-102(a).

Local ABC board members.

Limited immunity, §18B-700(j).

Local governmental employees' retirement system.

Management of funds, §128-29(f).

Long-term care ombudsman program.

Good faith performance of official duties, §143B-181.24.

Manufactured housing board.

Denial of licenses.

Information based on criminal history record check of license applicants, §143-143.10A(d).

Marriage and family therapists.

Criminal history record checks of license applicants, §90-270.63(d).

Massage and bodywork therapy.

Criminal history record check.

Immunity of board for good faith compliance, §90-629.1(d).

Mediated settlement conferences in superior court civil actions.

Judicial immunity of mediators, etc., §7A-38.1(j).

Mediated settlement conferences or other settlement procedures in district court.

Actions involving equitable distribution, alimony or support.

Mediators and neutrals acting pursuant to provisions, §7A-38.4A(h).

Immunity of mediator, §7A-38.3D(h).

Mediation ordered by clerks of superior courts.

Mediators, §7A-38.3B(e).

Medical assistance provider false claims.

Persons furnishing information to officials, §108A-70.15(a).

Medical board members and staff, §90-14(e).

Medical board review panel, §90-3(a).

Medical records.

Access to confidential records when public health concern necessitates.

Immunity from liability for permitting examination, review, or copying of records, §130A-15(c).

Health information exchange.

Participating covered entities.

Good faith reliance on information provided through exchange, §90-413.5(d).

Mental health, developmental disability, substance abuse.

Advance instruction for mental health treatment.

Providing treatment in reliance on instruction, §122C-75(b).

Area authorities.

Waiver of immunity as to torts of agents, employees and board members, §122C-152(a) to (f).

Consumer advocacy program, §122C-19.

Disclosure of confidential or privileged information during inspection, §122C-192(b).

Facilities, staff, physicians, etc., §122C-210.1.

Methamphetamine watch program.

Immunity from civil and criminal liability.

Good faith actions, §114-43.

Minors.

Motor vehicles.

Parent-child immunity.

Abolition in motor vehicle cases, §1-539.21.

IMMUNITY —Cont'd

Monopolies and restraint of trade.
Examinations by attorney general.
Person examined exempt from prosecution, §75-11.

Motor vehicles.
Parent-child immunity.
Abolished in motor vehicle cases, §1-539.21.
Rendering first aid or emergency assistance at accident scene, §20-166(b).

Motor vehicles insurance.
Rate evasion fraud.
Prevention programs, §58-2-164(d), (e).

Municipalities.
Exercise in conformity with charter and general laws, §160A-11.
Exercise of corporate powers, §160A-12.
Tort liability.
Waiver of immunity by resolution, large cities, §160A-485.5.
Waiver of immunity through insurance purchase, §160A-485.

National guard or state defense militia members, §127A-150(a) to (c).

911 system, §62A-53.
Prepaid wireless, §62A-55.

Nonprofit associations.
Uniform unincorporated nonprofit association act.
General immunity of members from liability, §59B-7(b).

Nonprofit corporations.
Acceptance or rejection of member's vote.
Corporate action in good faith, §55A-7-27(d).
Directors and officers, §55A-8-60.
Director's compliance with standards of conduct, §55A-8-30(d).
Officers, discharging duties, §55A-8-42(d), (e).

Nurses.
Nurse licensure compact.
Officers, employees or agents of state licensing boards, §90-171.90.
Reports of violations.
Immunity from suit, §90-171.47.

Nursing homes.
Medically necessary actions.
Action taken pursuant to physician's order, §131E-124(d).

Occupational diseases.
Reportable diseases, illnesses and injuries.
Immunity of persons who report, §130A-459.

Oil pollution and hazardous substances control.
Removal of oil discharges.
Limitation on liability of persons engaged in, §143-215.93A(a).
Exceptions, §143-215.93A(b).

Parent and child.
Motor vehicles.
Abolition of parent-child immunity in motor vehicle cases, §1-539.21.

Parking in fire lane.
Law enforcement officers carrying out or enforcing provisions, §20-162(b).

Perfusion advisory committee, §90-684(h).

Pharmacists and pharmacies.
Drug, supplies, and medical device repository program, §90-85.44(h).
Impaired pharmacist peer review organizations, §90-85.41(f).
Pharmacy quality assurance programs, §90-85.47(c).

IMMUNITY —Cont'd

Physicians and surgeons.
Advance instruction for mental health treatment.
Providing treatment in reliance on instruction, §122C-75(b).
Aircraft pilot's disability or infirmity.
Report or testimony as to mental or physical disability or infirmity, §90-21.20A.
Malpractice.
Reports of awards or settlements, §90-14.13(e).
Peer review agreements.
Peer review activities conducted in good faith, §90-21.22(f).
Privileges to practice in hospital.
Reports of disciplinary actions, §90-14.13(e).
Reporting or investigating alleged misconduct.
Good faith immunity, §90-14(f).

Principal and income act.
Conversion to unitrust.
Good faith immunity, §37A-1-104.8.

Professional counselors.
Criminal history record checks of license applicants, §90-345(d).

Pseudoephedrine products.
Sales by retailers, §90-113.57.

Psychologists.
Criminal background checks of license applicants.
Immunity of board, §90-270.22(c).

Public health authorities.
Medical review committee, §130A-45.7(a).

Railroad passenger injured while in prohibited place.
Nonliability of railroad, §136-196.

Real estate appraisal board.
Criminal history record checks.
Real estate appraisal management companies, §93E-2-11(d).

Recreational therapists.
Reports of violations, §90C-35.

Recreational trespass.
Limitation of liability, §38A-4.

Renunciation of property or interest.
Distributing or disposing of property in reliance upon terms, §31B-4(b).

Rescue squads.
Volunteer rescue squad members.
Civil liability, §§58-82-5(c), 90-21.14(a), (b).

Residential mortgage fraud.
Reporting, §14-118.17.

Residential school personnel.
Low-performing schools.
Negligence in carrying out provisions relating to personnel, §143B-146.8(e).

Safe haven for infants.
Temporary custody of infant without court order.
Immunity from civil and criminal liability, §7B-500(e).

School buses.
Waiver of immunity as to certain acts of bus drivers, §115C-255.

School employee personnel evaluations.
Persons carrying out provisions, §§115C-333(e), 115C-333.1(g).

Schools.
Asthma medication.
Possession and self-administration by students with asthma or students subject to anaphylactic reactions, §115C-375.2(g).
Criminal record checks of school personnel, §115C-332(g).

IMMUNITY —Cont'd
Secured transactions.
Limitation on liability of secured party, §25-9-628.
Self-defense.
Justifiable use of force.
Defense of home, workplace, motor vehicle
protection.
Justified in using force, immunity, exceptions,
§14-51.2(e).
Defense of person.
Justified in using, immunity, exceptions,
§14-51.3(b).
**Sex offender and public protection
registration.**
Internet.
Release of online identifiers to entity,
§14-208.15A(f).
**Skateboarding, inline skating and freestyle
bicycling.**
Activities on governmental entity's property.
Limitation of liability, §99E-25.
Assumption of inherent risks, limitation on
liability, §§99E-21 to 99E-25.
Social services.
Adult protection.
Certain persons immune from civil or criminal
liability, §108A-102(c).
Emergency services.
Petitioners, §108A-106(g).
Sovereign immunity.
Generally.
See SOVEREIGN IMMUNITY.
Tort claims against state.
Generally, §§143-291 to 143-300.1A.
See CLAIMS AGAINST THE STATE.
Sport shooting range protection.
Persons owning, operating or using sport shooting
ranges, §14-409.46(a), (b).
Substance abuse professionals.
Criminal history record checks.
Immunity of board from civil liability,
§90-113.46A(c).
Support of illegitimate children proceeding.
Mother testifying, §49-6.
Telecommunications companies.
Discontinuation of telecommunications services
used for unlawful purposes, §15A-299(e).
**Terrorist incident using nuclear, biological or
chemical agents.**
Reports.
Immunity of persons making, §§130A-476(d),
130A-480(c).
Trespasser responsibility act.
Possessor of land not liable for injury to
trespasser, exceptions.
Trespasser responsibility act, §§38B-1 to 38B-4.
**Umbilical cord stem cells and umbilical cord
blood banking.**
Providing women with information,
§130A-128.1(e).
**Uniform unincorporated nonprofit association
act.**
General immunity of members from liability,
§59B-7(b).
**Unlawful use of audiovisual recording device
in motion picture theater.**
Detention of person suspected of violation.
Theater owner or lessee, §14-440.1(d).
Veterinarians.
Cruelty to animals.
Reporting, §14-360.1.

IMMUNITY —Cont'd
Volunteer fire department members.
Civil liability, §58-82-5(c).
Volunteer health care providers, §90-21.16.
Volunteers.
Civil liability, §§58-82-5(c), 90-21.14(a), (b).
**Volunteers performing services for charity or
providing emergency services, §1-539.10(a).**
Definitions, §1-539.11.
Liability insurance.
Waiver of qualified immunity, §1-539.10(b).
Persons rendering professional services.
Standard of care and liability not altered,
§1-539.10(c).
Wastewater system contractors and inspectors.
Certification.
Board.
Injunction of violations, immunity regarding,
§90A-81(c).
Witnesses.
Alcoholic beverages.
Illicit sale.
Testimony enforced in certain criminal
investigations, §8-55.
Argument to jury as to impact of immunity,
§15A-1055(b).
Arrest in civil cases, §8-64.
Child support actions instituted by designated
representatives of county commissioners,
§110-130.
Contempt.
Criminal contempt.
Refusal to testify or produce information,
§5A-11(a).
Evidence of grant of immunity may be fully
developed, §15A-1055(a).
Gaming.
Testimony enforced in certain criminal
investigations, §8-55.
Jury.
Argument to jury as to impact of immunity,
§15A-1055(b).
Monopolies and restraints of trade.
Persons compelled to testify, §75-11.
Mother in support of illegitimate child proceeding,
§49-6.
Order to testify of produce other information,
§15A-1051(a).
Application for.
Court proceedings, §15A-1052(a), (b).
Grand jury proceedings, §15A-1053(a), (b).
Court proceedings, §15A-1052(a).
Definition of "other information,"§15A-1051(c).
Grand jury proceedings, §15A-1053(a).
Application, §15A-1053(a), (b).
Jury trial.
Judge to inform jury of grant of immunity,
§15A-1052(c).
When effective, §15A-1051(b).
Self-incrimination, §15A-1051(a).
Sentence concessions, §15A-1054(a).
Evidence of testimonial arrangement may be
fully developed, §15A-1055(a).
Jury.
Argument to jury as to impact of agreement,
§15A-1055(b).
Notice of agreement, §15A-1054(c).
Recommendations, §15A-1054(b).
Supplemental proceedings.
Incriminating answers not used in criminal
proceedings, §1-357.

IMMUNITY OF WITNESSES.
Alcoholic beverage illicit sales.
Testimony enforced in certain criminal investigations, §8-55.
Argument to jury as to impact of immunity, §15A-1055(b).
Arrest in civil cases, §8-64.
Child support actions instituted by designated representatives of county commissioners, §110-130.
Criminal contempt.
Refusal to testify or produce information, §5A-11(a).
Evidence of grant of immunity may be fully developed, §15A-1055(a).
Gaming investigations.
Testimony enforced, §8-55.
Monopolies and restraint of trade.
Persons compelled to testify, §75-11.
Mother in support of illegitimate child proceeding, §49-6.
Order to testify or produce other information.
Application for.
Court proceedings, §15A-1052(a), (b).
Grand jury proceedings, §15A-1053(a), (b).
Court proceedings, §15A-1052(a).
Definition of "other information,"§15A-1051(c).
Grand jury proceedings, §15A-1053(a).
Application, §15A-1053(a), (b).
Jury trial.
Judge to inform jury of grant of immunity, §15A-1052(c).
When effective, §15A-1051(b).
Self-incrimination, §15A-1051(a).
Sentence concessions, §15A-1054(a).
Evidence of testimonial arrangement may be fully developed, §15A-1055(a).
Jury.
Argument to jury as to impact of agreement, §15A-1055(b).
Notice of agreement, §15A-1054(c).
Recommendations, §15A-1054(b).
Supplemental proceedings.
Incriminating answers not used in criminal proceedings, §1-357.

IMMUNIZATION, §§130A-152 to 130A-158.
Adult care homes.
Residents and employees, §131D-9.
Certificate of immunization, §130A-154.
Adults attending school, §130A-155(d).
Child-care facilities.
Maintenance of record, §130A-155(b).
Report to be filed, §130A-155(c).
Submission of certificate to facility, §130A-155(a).
Information to be contained, §130A-154(a).
Maintenance of record, §130A-155(b).
School authorities.
Report to be filed, §130A-155(c).
Submission of certificate to authorities, §130A-155(a).
State other than North Carolina, §130A-154(b).
Submission of certificate to child-care facility, preschool and school authorities, §130A-155(a).
Universities and colleges.
Applicability of provisions, §130A-155.1(e).
Records to be maintained, §130A-155.1(b).
Reports.
Filing of immunization report with department, §130A-155.1(c).

IMMUNIZATION —Cont'd
Certificate of immunization —Cont'd
Universities and colleges —Cont'd
Submission of certificate to, §130A-155.1(a).
Charge for obtaining immunization, §130A-153(a).
Child-care facilities.
Certificate of immunization.
Maintenance of record, §130A-155(b).
Report to be filed, §130A-155(c).
Submission of certificate to facility, §130A-155(a).
Childhood vaccine-related injury compensation, §§130A-422 to 130A-434.
See CHILDHOOD VACCINE-RELATED INJURY COMPENSATION.
Commission for public health.
Promulgation of rules concerning implementation of program, §130A-152(c).
Contracts for purchase of covered vaccines.
Authority of secretary of health and human services, §130A-433(a).
Department of health and human services.
Enforcement of rules concerning implementation of program, §130A-152(c).
Distribution of covered vaccines.
Local health departments' responsibility, §130A-433(a).
Exemption.
Medical exemption, §130A-156.
Religious exemption, §130A-157.
Fees.
Administering covered vaccines, §130A-433(b).
Adoption of rules establishing, §130A-152(c1).
First responders, smallpox vaccination.
Sick leave and salary policy, time off due to adverse reaction, §160A-164.1.
Flu vaccination information.
Charter school students parents or guardians.
Information provided, §115C-238.29F(a).
Church schools and schools of religious charter.
Information provided parents and guardians of students, §115C-548.
Home schools.
Information provided, §115C-565.
Local boards of education.
Information provided parents and guardians, §115C-47.
Health insurance coverage.
State health plan for teachers and state employees, §135-48.50.
Implementation of program.
Promulgation and enforcement of rules concerning implementation, §130A-152(c).
Medical exemption, §130A-156.
Meningococcal disease vaccination information.
Charter school students parents or guardians.
Information provided, §115C-238.29F(a).
Church schools and schools of religious charter.
Information provided parents and guardians of students, §115C-548.
Home schools.
Information provided, §115C-565.
Local boards of education.
Information provided parents and guardians, §115C-47.
Universities and colleges.
Providing students information, §116-260.
Minors, §130A-153(d).

IMMUNIZATION —Cont'd

Negligence.
Restitution.
Vaccine spoiled due to provider negligence, §130A-158.

Nursing homes.
Residents and employees, §131E-113.

Obtaining immunization, §130A-153(a).
Charge, §130A-153(a).

Poultry.
Quarantine of inoculated poultry, §106-307.4.

Records.
Access to records, §130A-153(c).
Certificate of immunization.
Maintenance of record.
By child-care facility and school authorities, §130A-155(b).
By college or university, §130A-155.1(b).

Religious exemption, §130A-157.

Reports, §130A-153(b).
Certificate of immunization.
Filing of report.
By child-care facility and school authorities, §130A-155(c).
By college or university, §130A-155.1(c).

Required, §130A-152(a).
Additional immunization, §130A-152(e).

Requirements that can be placed on child or parent.
Adoption of rules, §130A-152(c1).

Restitution.
Vaccine spoiled due to provider negligence, §130A-158.

Rules and regulations, §130A-152(c).

School authorities.
Certificate of immunization.
Maintenance of record, §130A-155(b).
Report to be filed, §130A-155(c).
Submission of certificate to authorities, §130A-155(a).

Smallpox.
Claims arising from vaccinations of state employees.
Employment vaccination pursuant to homeland security act, §143-300.1A.
County employees.
Vaccination incident to homeland security act.
Adverse reaction, sick leave policy, counties to enact, §153A-94.1.
First responders, smallpox vaccination.
Sick leave and salary policy, time off due to adverse reaction, §160A-164.1.
Public officers and employees.
Sick leave for adverse reaction to vaccination, §126-8.4(a) to (c).
Workers' compensation.
Occupation diseases.
Infection or adverse medical reaction.
Employment vaccination incident to homeland security act, §97-53.

Spoiled vaccine.
Restitution.
Vaccine spoiled due to provider negligence, §130A-158.

Standards of vaccine preparations used, §130A-152(d).

State health plan for teachers and state employees.
Coverage mandates, §135-48.50.

Uninsured or underinsured families below poverty level.
No charge, §130A-153(a).

IMMUNIZATION —Cont'd

Universities and colleges.
Certificate of immunization.
Applicability of provisions, §130A-155.1(e).
Records.
Maintaining immunization records, §130A-155.1(b).
Reports.
Filing of immunization report with department, §130A-155.1(c).
Submission of certificate, §130A-155.1(a).

Vaccine preparations, §130A-152(d).

IMPAIRED DRIVING, §20-138.1(a).

Affidavit by law enforcement officer.
Chemical analysis of impairing substances in blood.
Refusal to submit to analysis, §20-16.2(c1).

Aggravating factors.
Sentencing hearing, determining existence, §20-179.

Aiders and abettors.
Punishment, §20-179(f1).

Alcohol and drug education traffic (ADET) school.
Limited driving privilege, §20-179.3(g2).
Persons authorized to provide instruction, §122C-142.1(d1).
Restoration of license after conviction.
Condition of probation, §20-179(g) to (k).
Obtaining certificate of completion, §20-17.6(c).

Alcohol concentration level, §20-138.1(a).
Expert testimony, §8C-1 Rule 702(a1).
Impaired driving of commercial vehicles, §20-138.2(a).
Mandatory revocation of driver's license.
Alcohol concentration .06 or higher, tests conclusive, §20-17(a).

Alcohol monitoring system.
Condition of probation.
Defendants subject to level one or two punishments, §20-179(h1), (h3).

Alcohol screening tests.
Approval of devices for on-the scene tests.
Department of health and human services, §20-16.3(b).
Tests conducted with approved devices, requirement, §20-16.3(c).
Checking stations or roadblocks.
Requesting driver to submit to, §20-16.3A(b).
Evidence.
Positive or negative results, §20-16.3(d).
Manner of use of devices.
Regulations, adoption by department of health and human services, §20-16.3(b).
Not arrest, §20-16.3(a).
When officer may require, §20-16.3(a).

All-terrain vehicles, §20-171.19(c).

Appeals to superior court.
Aggravating factors, jury trial, §20-179(a1), (a2).
Motion to dismiss or suppress evidence.
Denial.
Appeal by defendant, §20-38.7(b).
Granting.
State appeal of preliminary determination, §20-38.7(a).
New sentencing hearing.
Remanding back to district court, §20-38.7(c).
Right to appeal to superior court following hearing, §20-38.7(d).

IMPAIRED DRIVING —Cont'd
Appeals to superior court —Cont'd
Remanding back to district court, §20-38.7(c).
Right to appeal to superior court following
district hearing, §20-38.7(d).
Vacation of sentence.
Upon notice of appeal, §20-38.7(c).
Appearance of person charged.
Initial appearance before magistrate, §20-38.4.
Applicability.
Implied consent procedures article, §20-38.1.
Arrest, §15A-534.2.
Authority of officers investigating implied consent
offense, §20-38.2.
Processing duties.
Arrest of person for implied consent offense,
§20-38.3.
Territorial jurisdiction of officers to make arrest.
Authority of officers investigating implied
consent offenses, §20-38.2.
Bail and pretrial release.
Order to abstain from alcohol consumption,
§15A-534(i).
Boating under the influence, §75A-10(b), (b1).
Burden of proof.
Sentencing hearing.
Aggravating or mitigating factors, existence,
§20-179(a).
Evidentiary standards, §20-179(o).
Checking stations or roadblocks.
Alcohol screening test.
Requesting driver to submit to, §20-16.3A(b).
Authority to conduct to determine compliance
with chapter, §20-16.3A(a).
Constitutions, operated in accordance with.
Requirement, §20-16.3A(c).
Detention of driver for further investigation,
§20-16.3A(b).
Pattern for stopping vehicles, §20-16.3A(a).
Not to be based on vehicle type, §20-16.3A(a1).
Random or statistically indicated placement,
§20-16.3A(d).
Repeated placement in same location.
To be avoided, §20-16.3A(d).
Requirements for conducting, §20-16.3A(a).
Written policy requirements, §20-16.3A(a).
**Chemical analysis of impairing substances in
blood.**
Access by family and friends or qualified person to
person arrested.
Obtaining blood or urine from person unable to
obtain pretrial release, §20-38.5(a).
Additional analysis.
Right to obtain, §20-139.1(d).
Affidavit by law enforcement officer.
Refusal to submit to analysis, §20-16.2(c1).
Affidavit of chemical analyst.
Use in district court without further
authentication or testimony of analyst,
§20-139.1(e1).
Requirements, §20-139.1(e2).
Alcohol concentration.
Defined, §20-4.01.
Grams of alcohol per 100 milliliters of blood or
200 liters of breath.
Expressed in, §20-4.01.
Results reported in hundredths, §20-4.01.
Alcohol screening tests, §20-16.3.
Checking stations or roadblocks.
Requesting driver to submit to, §20-16.3A(b).

IMPAIRED DRIVING —Cont'd
**Chemical analysis of impairing substances in
blood** —Cont'd
Arrest.
Test as condition of release, §15A-534.2.
Availability of records, §20-27(b).
Basis for officer to require analysis, §20-16.2(a).
Blood or urine tests specified by officer.
Admissibility.
Laboratory test results without further
authentication or testimony of analyst,
§20-139.1(c1).
Chain of custody, establishing without
calling unnecessary witnesses,
§20-139.1(c3).
Notification to defendant of intention to
introduce report, §20-139.1(c1).
Objection by defendant to introducing
report required, §20-139.1(c1).
Test performance requirements,
§20-139.1(c2).
Compelling person to provide blood or urine
sample, §20-139.1(d1), (d2).
Confirmation of officer's request, §20-139.1(c).
Person compelled to provide blood or urine
sample, §20-139.1(d2).
Immunity of person obtaining sample,
§20-139.1(c), (d3).
Person compelled to provide blood or urine
sample, §20-139.1(d2).
Persons who may obtain sample, §20-139.1(c).
Person compelled to provide blood or urine
sample, §20-139.1(d2).
Refusal by person requested to perform tests,
§20-139.1(c), (d2).
Refusal to submit to test.
Compelling person to provide blood or urine
sample, §20-139.1(d1), (d2).
Breath analysis.
Admissibility of results, §20-139.1(b3).
Copy of analysis results.
Failure to provide prior to trial.
Ground for continuance only, §20-139.1(e).
Requesting prior to trial, §20-139.1(e).
Permit to perform, §20-139.1(b), (b1).
Preventive maintenance on breath testing
instruments, §20-139.1(b2).
Refusal to give second or subsequent sample,
§20-139.1(b3).
Results inadmissible if preventive maintenance
not performed, §§20-138.1(b1), 20-139.1(b2).
Impaired driving in commercial vehicle,
§20-138.2(b1).
Sequential breath tests required, §20-139.1(b3).
Chemical analysis room.
Access.
Attorneys and witnesses.
Written procedures, establishment,
§20-38.5(a).
Signs explaining procedure, posting,
§20-38.5(b), (c).
Location of notice of rights in room.
Approval, §20-38.5(a).
Commercial drivers' licenses.
Refusal to submit to chemical test.
Disqualification.
Effect, §20-17.5(c).
Commercial vehicles.
Impaired driving in commercial motor vehicle.
Applicability to offense, §20-138.2(g).

IMPAIRED DRIVING —Cont'd
Chemical analysis of impairing substances in blood —Cont'd
Commercial vehicles —Cont'd
  Impaired driving in commercial motor vehicle
    —Cont'd
    Rebuttal evidence as to results.
      Use, §20-138.2(a1).
Compelling person to provide blood or urine
  sample, §20-139.1(d1), (d2).
Copy of analysis results.
  Breath analysis.
    Failure to provide prior to trial.
      Ground for continuance only, §20-139.1(e).
      Requesting prior to trial, §20-139.1(e).
Death or critical injury involved.
  Refusal to submit to analysis.
    Consequences, §20-16.2(d1).
Duty of law enforcement officer, §20-16.5(c).
Evidence.
  Admissibility, §20-139.1(a).
    Blood or urine samples.
      Laboratory results, requirements for
        admissibility, §20-139.1(c1) to (c4).
    Breath analysis, §20-139.1(b3).
    Refusal to submit to analysis, §20-139.1(f).
    Requirements to be admissible, §20-139.1(b).
  Affidavit of chemical analyst.
    Admissibility without further authentication
      or testimony of analyst, §20-139.1(e1).
    Requirements, §20-139.1(e2).
  Alcohol screening test results.
    Positive or negative results, §20-16.3(d).
  Blood and urine test results.
    Admissibility.
      Lab results, requirements for admissibility,
        §20-139.1(c1) to (c4).
    Laboratory results.
      Admissibility without further
        authentication or testimony of analyst,
        §20-139.1(c1) to (c3).
  Inadmissibility.
    Preventive maintenance on breath testing
      devices not performed, §§20-138.1(b1),
      20-139.1(b2).
    Impaired driving in commercial vehicle,
      §20-138.2(b1).
  Rebuttal evidence as to alcohol concentration
    level.
    Use of results, §20-138.1(a1).
      Impaired driving in commercial vehicle,
        §20-138.2(a1).
  Refusal to submit to analysis.
    Admissibility of evidence of refusal,
      §20-139.1(f).
    Breath analysis.
      Second or subsequent sample,
        §20-139.1(b3).
Habitual impaired driving.
  Applicability of provisions to offense,
    §20-138.5(c).
Hearing before division.
  Refusal to submit to test, §20-16.2(d).
Hearing on record in superior court.
  Refusal to submit to analysis, §20-16.2(e).
Immunity.
  Blood or urine tests, person obtaining,
    §20-139.1(c), (d3).
  Person compelled to provide blood or urine
    sample, §20-139.1(d2).

IMPAIRED DRIVING —Cont'd
Chemical analysis of impairing substances in blood —Cont'd
Impairing substance.
  Defined, §20-4.01.
Implied consent, §20-16.2(a).
  Commercial vehicles.
    Impaired driving in commercial vehicles.
      Implied consent offense, §20-138.2(d).
  Habitual impaired driving as implied consent of
    offense, §20-138.5(c).
  Unconscious or otherwise incapable of refusal,
    §20-16.2(b).
Implied consent offense.
  Defined, §20-16.2(a1).
Judicial notice.
  Permit to conduct breath test or chemical
    analysis.
    Person possesses permit, §20-139.1(b6).
Laboratory results on blood and urine tests.
  Admissibility without further authentication or
    testimony of analyst, §20-139.1(c1) to (c3).
Limited driving privilege.
  License revoked for refusal to submit to test,
    §20-16.2(e1).
Mandatory revocation.
  Refusal to submit to test.
    Designation of proceedings, §20-16.5(o).
    Effect of revocation, §20-16.5(i).
    Exception for license already revoked,
      §20-16.5(n).
    Immediate civil revocation, §20-16.5.
    Limited driving privilege.
      Person's license indefinitely revoked,
        §20-16.5(p).
    Modification of revocation order, §20-16.5(m).
    Report to division, §20-16.5(k).
    Restoration fee for unlicensed persons,
      §20-16.5(l).
    Return of license, §20-16.5(h).
    Revocation report, §20-16.5(c) to (f).
Notification of rights, §20-16.2(a).
Request for chemical analysis before arrest or
  charge, §20-16.2(i).
On-the scene tests by officers.
  Alcohol screening tests, §20-16.3.
Permit to conduct breath test or chemical
  analysis.
  Any person possessing permit may perform
    analysis, §20-139.1(b1).
  Judicial notice, person possesses permit,
    §20-139.1(b6).
  List of persons with permit, posting,
    §20-139.1(b6).
  Requirement, §20-139.1(b).
Preventive maintenance on testing devices,
  §20-139.1(b2).
  Defense.
    Procedures not performed, §20-138.1(b1).
      Impaired driving in commercial vehicle,
        §20-138.2(b1).
Records.
  Availability, §20-27(b).
Refusal to submit to analysis, §20-16.2(c).
  Affidavit by law enforcement officer,
    §20-16.2(c1).
  Breath analysis.
    Second or subsequent sample, §20-139.1(b3).
  Compelling person to provide blood or urine
    sample, §20-139.1(d1), (d2).

IMPAIRED DRIVING —Cont'd
Chemical analysis of impairing substances in blood —Cont'd
Refusal to submit to analysis —Cont'd
Consequences, §20-16.2(d).
Death or critical injury involved, §20-16.2(d1).
Hearing before division, §20-16.2(d).
Hearing on record in superior court, §20-16.2(e).
Limited driving privilege.
Application after revocation of license, conditions for issuing, hearing, §20-16.2(e1).
Reporting refusals, §20-16.2(c1).
Revocation of driver's license, §20-16.2(d).
Death or critical injury involved, §20-16.2(d1).
Limited driving privilege.
Application after revocation of license, conditions for issuing, hearing, §20-16.2(e1).
Mandatory revocation, §20-16.5.
Notice to person charged, §20-16.2(d).
Reporting results, §20-16.2(c1).
Request to submit to analysis, §20-16.2(c).
Right of drivers to request, §20-16.2(i).
Right to chemical analysis before arrest or charge, §20-16.2(i).
Subsequent test allowed, §20-139.1(b5).
Taking person arrested to any place in state for.
Duty of officers, §20-38.3.
Unconscious person may be tested, §20-16.2(b).
Chemical analysis room.
Access.
Attorneys and witnesses.
Written procedures, establishment, §20-38.5(a).
Signs explaining procedure, posting, §20-38.5(b), (c).
Clerks of superior courts.
Records of case disposition.
Duty to maintain, retention, time period, destruction, duties prior to, §7A-109.4.
Information included in electronic records, §7A-109.2(b).
Commercial vehicles, §20-138.2(a).
Alcohol concentration level, §20-138.2(a).
Mandatory revocation of license.
Alcohol concentration level .06 or higher, tests conclusive, §20-17(a).
Chemical analysis of impairing substances in blood.
Applicability, §20-138.2(g).
Rebuttal evidence as to results.
Use, §20-138.2(a1).
Defenses.
Legally entitled to use alcohol or drug.
Defense precluded, §20-138.2(b).
Preventive maintenance on testing devices not performed.
Defense allowed, §20-138.2(b1).
Disqualification from driving, §20-17.4(a), (b), (b1).
Drivers' licenses.
Mandatory revocation of license.
Alcohol concentration level .06 or higher, tests conclusive, §20-17(a).
Effect when impaired driving offense also charged, §20-138.2(e).
Gross vehicle weight rating.
Proving, §20-138.2(a2).
Implied consent offense, §20-138.2(d).
Misdemeanor, §20-138.2(e).
Offense defined, §20-138.2(a).

IMPAIRED DRIVING —Cont'd
Commercial vehicles —Cont'd
Pleading.
Sufficiency, §20-138.2(c).
Restoration of license after conviction, §20-17.6.
Special information inquired in judgment for conviction, §20-24(e).
Community service.
Time limits for performing, §20-179(n).
Concealed handgun permit.
Conviction is grounds for denial of permit, §14-415.12(b).
Consolidation of charges.
Limit on, §20-179(f2).
Continuous alcohol monitoring system.
Condition of probation.
Defendants subject to level one or two punishments, §20-179(h1), (h3).
Order to abstain from alcohol consumption.
Condition of pretrial release, §15A-534(i).
Regulations for continuous alcohol monitoring systems.
Division of adult correction, §15A-1343.3.
Controlled-drinking programs, §20-139.1(g).
Credit for good behavior, §15A-1355(c).
Death or critical injury involved.
Felony death by vehicle, §20-141.4(a1).
Aggravated felony death by vehicle, §20-141.4(a5).
Repeat offender.
Second degree murder, §20-141.4(a6).
Felony serious injury by vehicle, §20-141.4(a3).
Aggravated felony serious injury by vehicle, §20-141.4(a4).
Misdemeanor death by vehicle, §20-141.4(a2).
No double prosecution for manslaughter, §20-141.4(c).
Punishments, §20-141.4(b).
Refusal to submit to test.
Consequences, §20-16.2(d1).
Defenses.
Commercial vehicles.
Legal entitlement to use alcohol or drug.
Defense precluded, §20-138.2(b).
Preclusion of certain defense, §20-138.1(b).
Preventive maintenance on testing devices not performed, §20-138.1(b1).
Definitions.
Offenses involving impaired driving, §20-4.01.
Detention of impaired drivers at time of initial appearance.
Defendant no longer impaired.
Alcohol concentration less than 0.05, §15A-534.2(d).
Findings required by judicial official conducting initial appearance, §15A-534.2(b).
Periodic tests to determine alcohol concentration.
Request that defendant submit to, §15A-534.2(d).
Pretrial release.
Right of defendant subject to detention, §15A-534.2(c).
Results of periodic tests to determine alcohol concentration.
Inadmissibility, §15A-534.2(d).
Dismissal of charge.
Discovery of facts not previously known during trial.
Motion.
When made, §20-38.6(a).

IMPAIRED DRIVING —Cont'd
Dismissal of charge —Cont'd
Insufficient evidence.
Motion.
When made, §20-38.6(a).
Motion.
Appeal of preliminary determinations,
§20-38.7(a), (b).
State granted reasonable time to defend,
§20-38.6(b).
When made, §20-38.6(a).
Prosecutor to explain, §20-138.4.
Drivers' licenses.
Driving after notification or failure to appear,
§20-28(a2).
Conditional restoration, §20-28(c3) to (c5).
Issuance to habitual drunkard.
Prohibited, §20-9(c).
Limited driving privilege.
License revoked for refusal to submit to test,
§20-16.2(e1).
Privilege restrictions, high-risk drivers,
§20-179.3(c1).
Provisional licensees.
Revocation or suspension, §20-13.2(b), (c).
Refusal to submit to test.
Revocation, §20-16.2(d).
Death or critical injury involved, §20-16.2(d1).
Limited driving privilege.
Application after revocation of license,
conditions for issuing, hearing,
§20-16.2(e1).
Mandatory revocation, §20-16.5.
Notice to person charged, §20-16.2(d).
Restoration after conviction, §20-17.6.
Condition of probation, §20-179.1(g) to (k).
Ignition interlock as condition.
Duration of condition, §20-17.8(c).
Habitual impaired driving, applicability,
§20-17.8(a1).
Limited driving privilege, effect, §20-17.8(d).
Medical exception to requirement.
Requesting, requirements for issuing,
§20-17.8(l).
Notice of requirement, §20-17.8(e).
Scope, §20-17.8(a).
Tampering with system, §20-17.8A.
Violation as driving while license revoked,
§20-17.8(f), (g).
Commencement of revocation, §20-17.8(h).
Hearings, §20-17.8(j).
Notification of revocation, §20-17.8(i).
Restoration after revocation for, §20-17.8(k).
When required, §20-17.8(b).
Revocation.
Conditional restoration, §20-28(c3).
After ten years, §20-19(e4).
After three years, §20-19(e1).
After two years, §20-19(e2).
Cancellation, imposition of remaining
revocation, §20-28(c5).
Conditions or restrictions, §20-19(e3).
Substance abuse assessment, §20-28(c4).
Driving after notification or failure to appear,
§20-28(a2).
Mandatory revocation, §20-17(a).
Period of suspension or revocation, §20-19(c1)
to (e).
Permanent revocation, §20-19(e).
Habitual impaired driving, §20-138.5(d).

IMPAIRED DRIVING —Cont'd
Drivers' licenses —Cont'd
Revocation —Cont'd
Refusal to submit to test, §20-16.2(d).
Death or critical injury involved, §20-16.2(d1).
Limited driving privilege.
Application after revocation of license,
conditions for issuing, hearing,
§20-16.2(e1).
Mandatory revocation, §20-16.5.
Notice to person charged, §20-16.2(d).
Driving after notification or failure to appear.
Driver's license revoked, §20-28(a2).
**Driving by person less than 21 years old after
consuming alcohol or drugs.**
Impaired driving offense also charged,
§20-138.3(c).
**Driving on license revoked for prior impaired
driving offense.**
Seizure, impoundment and forfeiture of vehicle,
§§20-28.2 to 20-28.9.
Electronic monitoring.
Parole.
Conditions, §15A-1374(a1).
Electronic records on disposition of cases.
Administrative office of the courts database.
Information complied maintained in, §7A-346.3.
Information included by clerk, §7A-109.2(b).
**Evaluation to determined extent of
impairment.**
Taking person arrested to any place in state for.
Duty of officers, §20-38.3.
Evidence.
Alcohol screening test results.
Positive or negative results, §20-16.3(d).
Chemical analysis of impairing substances in
blood.
Admissibility.
Blood and urine tests.
Laboratory results, requirements for
admissibility, §20-139.1(c1) to (c4).
Breath analysis, §20-139.1(b3).
Refusal to submit to analysis, §20-139.1(f).
Requirements to be admissible, §20-139.1(b).
Affidavit of chemical analyst.
Admissibility without further authentication
or testimony of analyst, §20-139.1(e1).
Requirements, §20-139.1(e1).
Alcohol screening tests.
Positive or negative results, §20-16.3(d).
Blood and urine test results.
Laboratory results.
Admissibility without further
authentication or testimony of analyst,
§20-139.1(c1) to (c3).
Inadmissibility of results.
Preventive maintenance on breath testing
devices not performed, §§20-138.1(b1),
20-139.1(b2).
Impaired driving in commercial vehicle,
§20-138.2(b1).
Rebuttal evidence as to alcohol concentration
level.
Use of results, §20-138.1(a1).
Impaired driving in commercial vehicle,
§20-138.2(a1).
Refusal to submit to analysis.
Admissibility, §20-139.1(f).
Breath analysis.
Second or subsequent sample,
§20-139.1(b3).

IMPAIRED DRIVING —Cont'd
Evidence —Cont'd
Expert testimony.
Impairment, alcohol concentration level,
impairing substances, §8C-1 Rule 702(a1).
Gross vehicle weight rating.
Impaired driving in commercial vehicle,
§20-138.2(a2).
Motion to suppress, §20-38.6.
Appeal of preliminary determinations,
§20-38.7(a), (b).
Records of division of motor vehicles.
Admissibility of records as prima facie evidence
of convictions, §8-35.1.
Sentencing hearing.
Aggravating or mitigating factors, existence.
Evidentiary standards, §20-179(o).
Prior conviction, §20-179(o).
Expert testimony.
Impairment, alcohol concentration level, impairing
substances, §8C-1 Rule 702(a1).
Felonies.
Habitual impaired driving, §20-138.5(b).
Forfeiture of motor vehicle.
Accidents.
Motor vehicles involved in, §20-28.2(c1).
Affidavit of impoundment.
Presented to magistrate by seizing officer,
§20-28.3(c).
Appearance by county board of education,
§20-28.3(k).
Bond, pretrial release of vehicle, §20-28.3(e).
Civil judgment for cots docketed against
defendant, §20-28.3(l).
Continuance of trial involving forfeiture,
§20-28.3(m).
Costs of towing, storage and sale, §20-28.3(l).
Payment of towing and storage costs on release
of vehicle, §20-28.3(n).
County board of education, constructive
possession, §20-28.3(d).
Custody of vehicle, §20-28.3(d).
Definitions, §20-28.2(a), (a1).
Department of public instruction.
Contracts to tow, store, process, maintain, and
sell seized vehicles.
Authorized, §20-28.9(a).
Fees, §20-28.9(b), (c).
Department of public instruction, constructive
possession, §20-28.3(d).
Determination vehicle subject to forfeiture,
§20-28.2(b), (b1).
Division of motor vehicles.
Reports to division, §20-28.8.
Responsibility, §20-28.7.
Driver not convicted.
Release of vehicle to driver, §20-28.4(a).
Duty of charging officer to seize and impound
vehicle, §20-28.3(b).
Effecting order of seizure, §20-28.3(c1).
Facsimile notification of impoundment to
lienholder, §20-28.3(b2).
Force used to seize vehicle, §20-28.3(c1).
Hearing, §20-28.2(d).
Hearing on pretrial release of vehicle.
Defendant owner, §20-28.3(e2).
Impounded vehicles.
Appeal of order, §20-28.5(e).
Proceeds of sale, §20-28.5(b).
Retention of vehicle, §20-28.5(c).
Sale, §20-28.5(a).

IMPAIRED DRIVING —Cont'd
Forfeiture of motor vehicle —Cont'd
Innocent parties.
Duty of prosecutor to notify, §20-28.2(c).
Insurance proceeds accruing to defendant.
Payment into court, §20-28.3(h).
Magistrate review of seizure and impoundment,
§20-28.3(c).
Mechanic's lien on seized vehicle, §20-28.4(b).
No license and no insurance.
Determination vehicle subject to forfeiture,
§20-28.2(b1).
Vehicle subject to seizure, §20-28.3(a).
Notice of hearing on pretrial release of vehicle,
§20-28.3(e2).
Notice to county board of education of proceeding,
§20-28.3(k).
Notification of impoundment, §20-28.3(b1), (b2).
Order of seizure, §20-28.3(c), (c1).
Participation by county board of education,
§20-28.3(k).
Personal property not affixed to vehicle, retrieval
by owners, §20-28.3(j).
Petition for pretrial release of vehicle.
Defendant owner, §20-28.3(e2).
Lienholder, §20-28.3(e3).
Nondefendant owner, §20-28.3(e1).
Pretrial release of vehicle.
Defendant owner, §20-28.3(e2).
Lienholder, §20-28.3(e3).
Nondefendant owner, §20-28.3(e), (e1).
Payment of towing and storage costs,
§20-28.3(n).
Priority of trial of offenses involving forfeiture,
§20-28.3(m).
Probable cause to seize and impound, §20-28.3(b).
Release of vehicle pending trial.
Defendant owner, §20-28.3(e2).
Lienholder, §20-28.3(e3).
Nondefendant owner, §20-28.3(e), (e1).
Payment of towing and storage costs,
§20-28.3(n).
Release of vehicle to innocent owner, §20-28.2(e).
Release of vehicle to insurance company.
Vehicle declared total loss, §20-28.3(h).
Release of vehicle to lienholder, §20-28.2(f).
Release of vehicle upon conclusion of trial,
§20-28.4(a).
Rental vehicles.
Charging officer not seize or impound,
§20-28.3(b).
Reports to division of motor vehicles, §20-28.8.
Responsibility of division of motor vehicles,
§20-28.7.
Restitution.
Costs of towing, storage and sale, §20-28.3(l).
Sale of vehicle by county board of education.
Expedited sale to avoid towing and storage
costs, §20-28.3(i).
Search warrant for purposes of seizing concealed
vehicle, §20-28.3(c1).
Stolen vehicles.
Charging officer not to seize or impound,
§20-28.3(b).
Towing and storage charges, payment.
Order authorizing release vehicle to require,
§20-28.2(h).
Towing of seized vehicle, §20-28.3(d).
Vehicle subject to seizure, §20-28.3(a).
When vehicle becomes property subject to
forfeiture, §20-28.2(b).

IMPAIRED DRIVING —Cont'd

Good behavior, meritorious conduct, work or study, rehabilitation program participation.

Deductions in sentence, regulations, adoption, §148-13(b).

Habitual impaired driving, §20-138.5(a).

Chemical analysis of impairing substances in blood.

Applicability of provisions to offense, §20-138.5(c).

Forfeiture of vehicle, §20-138.5(e).

Implied consent offense, §20-138.5(c).

Restoration of license after conviction.

Ignition interlock, required use.

Applicability of provisions, §20-17.8(a1).

Revocation of license.

Permanent revocation, §20-138.5(d).

Sentence and punishment, §20-138.5(b).

What constitutes, §20-138.5(a).

Hearings.

Chemical analysis of impairing substances in blood.

Refusal to submit to test.

Hearing before division, §20-16.2(d).

Hearing on record in superior court, §20-16.2(e).

Homicide.

Special information if conviction of homicide involves, §20-24(e).

Horses.

Definition of vehicle does not include, §20-138.1(e).

Identification of person arrested.

Taking person arrested to some other place for.

Duty of officers, §20-38.3.

Ignition interlock system.

Impaired driving conviction.

Restoration of license conditioned on use of interlock.

Duration of condition, §20-17.8(c).

Habitual impaired driving, applicability, §20-17.8(a1).

Limited driving privilege, effect, §20-17.8(d).

Medical exception to requirement.

Requesting, requirements for issuing, §20-17.8(l).

Notice of requirement, §20-17.8(e).

Scope, §20-17.8(a).

Violation as driving while license revoked, §20-17.8(f), (g).

Commencement of revocation, §20-17.8(h).

Hearings, §20-17.8(j).

Notification of revocation, §20-17.8(i).

Restoration after revocation for, §20-17.8(k).

When required, §20-17.8(b).

Limited driving privilege.

Ignition interlock allowed, §20-179.3(g3).

Tampering with system, §20-17.8A.

Vehicle registration or certificate of title.

Refusal to register because registration suspended or revoked.

Exception in cases to abide by installation requirements, §20-54.

Revocation of registration because of impaired driving conviction.

Exception in cases to abide by installation requirements, §20-54.1(a).

Vehicles subject to requirement, §20-17.8(c1).

Immediate civil license revocation.

Civil actions, §20-16.5(o).

IMPAIRED DRIVING —Cont'd

Immediate civil license revocation —Cont'd

Costs, §20-16.5(j).

Definitions, §20-16.5(a).

Effect of revocation, §20-16.5(i).

Exceptions, §20-16.5(n).

Hearing, contesting validity, §20-16.5(g).

Limited driving privilege, §20-16.5(p).

Modification of order, §20-16.5(m).

Persons charged with violations, §20-16.5(b).

Precharge test results basis for revocation, §20-16.5(b1).

Refusal to submit to chemical analysis, §20-16.5(b).

Report to division, §20-16.5(k).

Report to judicial officials.

Duty of charging officers, §20-16.5(c).

Judicial officer with whom report filed, §20-16.5(d).

Person not present, procedure for filing, §20-16.5(f).

Person present, procedure for filing, §20-16.5(e).

Restoration fee, person with no license, §20-16.5(l).

Return of license, §20-16.5(h).

Fee as cost for action, §20-16.5(j).

Immunity.

Blood or urine tests.

Person obtaining, §20-139.1(c), (d3).

Person compelled to provide blood or urine sample, §20-139.1(d2).

Impaired driving integrated data system.

Duty of clerk to maintain records, time period, destruction, duties prior to, §7A-109.4.

Electronic records prepared by clerk.

Administrative office of the courts database.

Information complied maintained in, §7A-346.3.

Information included, §7A-109.2(b).

Impairing substances.

Defined, §20-4.01.

Implied consent offenses, §20-16.2.

Driving by person less than 21 years old after consuming alcohol or drugs.

Offense subject to implied consent law, §20-138.3(b).

Impaired driving in commercial vehicles, §20-138.2(d).

Open container law offense subject to implied consent law, §20-138.7(b).

Impoundment of vehicles.

Forfeiture of vehicles, §§20-28.2 to 20-28.9.

Informing person of charges or cause for arrest.

Duty of officer making arrest, §20-38.3.

Initial appearance of defendant.

Detention of impaired drivers, §15A-534.2(b) to (d).

Duty of officer to take person arrested, §20-38.3.

Implied consent offenses.

Finding probable cause, §20-38.4(a).

Forms, adoption, administrative office of the courts, §20-38.4(b).

Place for holding, §20-38.4(a).

Probable cause determination, §20-38.4(a).

Procedures followed, §20-38.4(a).

Procedure, §15A-534.2(a).

Inpatient treatment.

Sentence credit, §20-179(k1).

Investigation of implied consent offense by officers.

Authority, §20-38.2.

IMPAIRED DRIVING —Cont'd
Judicial notice.
  Permit to conduct breath test or chemical
    analysis.
    Person possesses permit, §20-139.1(b6).
Jury trial on aggravating factors.
  Sentencing.
    Appeals to superior court, §20-179(a1), (a2).
Legal entitlement to use alcohol or drug.
  Defense precluded, §20-138.1(b).
    Impaired driving in commercial vehicle,
      §20-138.2(b).
Level five punishment, §20-179(k).
Level four punishment, §20-179(j).
Level one punishment, §20-179(g).
  Aggravated level one punishment, §20-179(f3).
Level three punishment, §20-179(i).
Level two punishment, §20-179(h).
Limited driving privilege.
  Eligibility of persons convicted of offense of
    impaired driving, §20-179.3(b).
  Indefinite revocation for refusal to submit to
    chemical analysis, §20-16.5(p).
  License revoked for refusal to submit to test,
    §20-16.2(e1).
  Privilege restrictions, high-risk drivers,
    §20-179.3(c1).
  Restoration of license after conviction.
    Persons subject to section not eligible for
      limited driving privilege, §20-17.6(a).
Magistrates.
  Initial appearance.
    Implied consent offenses, §20-38.4.
Misdemeanor, §20-138.1(d).
  Impaired driving in commercial vehicle,
    §20-138.2(e).
Mitigating factors.
  Sentencing hearing, determining existence,
    §20-179.
Monitoring electronically.
  Parole.
    Conditions, §15A-1374(a1).
Motions to dismiss or suppress evidence,
  §20-38.6.
  Appeal of preliminary determinations, §20-38.7(a),
    (b).
Motor vehicle registration.
  Revocation of registration.
    Impaired driving while license revoked as result
      of prior impaired driving license revocation,
      §20-54.1.
Nonresidents.
  Revocation of privilege to drive.
    Information by division to state of person's
      residence, §20-16.2(f).
Offenses involving.
  Defined, §20-4.01.
Officers making arrest.
  Processing duties, §20-38.3.
On-the scene tests by officers.
  Alcohol screening tests, §20-16.3.
    Checking stations or roadblocks.
      Requesting driver to submit to, §20-16.3A(b).
Open container law violations.
  Impaired driving offense also charged,
    §20-138.7(e).
Parole, §20-179(p).
  Applicability of article 85, §15A-1370.1.
  Community service parole, §15A-1371(h) to (j).
  Conditions, §15A-1374(a1).

IMPAIRED DRIVING —Cont'd
Parole —Cont'd
  Electronic monitoring.
    Conditions, §15A-1374(a1).
  Eligibility, §15A-1371(a).
  Habitual impaired driving, §20-138.5(b).
  Impaired driving offender confined in local
    confinement facilities.
  Copy of commitment order forwarded to
    post-release supervision and parole
    commission, §148-32.1(c), (e).
  Release on parole, §15A-1371(g).
Photographing and fingerprinting person
  arrested.
  Duty of officers, §20-38.3.
Pleading.
  Sufficiency, §20-138.1(c).
    Commercial vehicles, §20-138.2(c).
Presentence investigation of person convicted,
  §20-179.1.
Prior conviction.
  Sentencing hearing.
    Proof accepted, §20-179(o).
Probation.
  Conditions, §20-179(g) to (k).
  Continuous alcohol monitoring system.
    Condition of probation.
      Defendants subject to level one or two
        punishments, §20-179(h1), (h3).
  Supervised or unsupervised probation, §20-179(r).
Prosecutor.
  Reduction or dismissal of charge.
    Prosecutor to explain, §20-138.4.
Provisional licensee.
  Restoration of license after conviction, §20-17.6.
Punishment.
  Aggravated level one punishment, §20-179(f3).
  Aiders and abettors, §20-179(f1).
  Level five punishment, §20-179(k).
  Level four punishment, §20-179(j).
  Level one punishment, §20-179(g).
    Aggravated level one punishment, §20-179(f3).
  Level three punishment, §20-179(i).
  Level two punishment, §20-179(h).
Punitive damages.
  Exemption from cap, §1D-26.
Railroads.
  Operating trains or streetcars while intoxicated,
    §14-281.
Records of case disposition.
  Duty of clerk to maintain, time period,
    destruction, duties prior to, §7A-109.4.
  Electronic records prepared by clerk.
    Administrative office of the courts data base.
      Information complied maintained in,
        §7A-346.3.
Reduction of charge.
  Prosecutor to explain, §20-138.4.
Restoration of driver's license after conviction,
  §20-17.6.
  Certificate of completion.
    Required for restoring license, §20-17.6(b).
    Requirements for obtaining certificate,
      §20-17.6(c).
  Limited driving privileges.
    Persons subject to section not eligible,
      §20-17.6(e).
  Notice of requirement of section, §20-17.6(d).
  Requirements for restoring license, §20-17.6(b).
  Scope of section, §20-17.6(a).
Roadblocks, §20-16.3A.

IMPAIRED DRIVING —Cont'd
Seizure of vehicles.
Forfeiture of vehicles, §§20-28.2 to 20-28.9.
Sentencing, §20-138.1(d).
Aggravated level one punishment, §20-179(f3).
Aggravating or mitigating factors affecting
sentence.
Aggravating factors, §20-179(d).
Appeals to superior court.
Jury trial on aggravating factors, §20-179(a1),
(a2).
Grossly aggravating factors, §20-179(c).
Hearing to determine, §20-179(a).
Mitigating factors, §20-179(e).
Aiders and abettors, §20-179(f1).
Amelioration of punishment.
Limitation on, §20-179(p).
Appeal to superior court.
Jury trial on aggravating factors, §20-179(a1),
(a2).
Vacation of sentence upon giving notice of
appeal, §20-38.7(c).
Community service.
Time limits for performing, §20-179(n).
Consolidation of charges.
Limit on, §20-179(f2).
Credit for good behavior, §15A-1355(c).
Credit for inpatient treatment, §20-179(k1).
Good behavior, meritorious conduct, work or
study, rehabilitation program participation.
Deductions in sentence, regulations, adoption,
§148-13(b).
Habitual impaired driving, §20-138.5(b).
Jury trial on aggravating factors.
Appeals to superior court, §20-179(a1), (a2).
Level five punishment, §20-179(k).
Level four punishment, §20-179(j).
Level one punishment, §20-179(g).
Aggravated level one punishment, §20-179(f3).
Level three punishment, §20-179(i).
Level two punishment, §20-179(h).
Method of serving, §20-179(s).
Supervised or unsupervised probation, §20-179(r).
Vacation of sentence.
Appeal to superior court by defendant,
§20-38.7(c).
Weekend service, §20-179(s).
Sentencing hearing.
Aggravating or mitigating factors affecting
sentence.
Aggravating factors, §20-179(d).
Appeals to superior court.
Jury trial on aggravating factors, §20-179(a1),
(a2).
Evidentiary standards, §20-179(o).
Grossly aggravating factors.
Determining existence, §20-179(c).
Hearing to determine, §20-179(a).
Mitigating factors, §20-179(e).
Weighing factors, §20-179(f).
Written findings by court, §20-179(c1).
Appeals to superior court.
Jury trial on aggravating factors, §20-179(a1),
(a2).
Burden of proof.
Aggravating or mitigating factors, existence,
§20-179(a).
Evidentiary standards, §20-179(o).

IMPAIRED DRIVING —Cont'd
Sentencing hearing —Cont'd
New sentencing hearing.
Appeal to superior court by defendant.
Case remanded back to district court,
§20-38.7(c).
Right to appeal to superior court following
hearing, §20-38.7(d).
Prior conviction.
Proof accepted, §20-179(o).
Required, §20-179(a).
Serious injury by vehicle.
Felony serious injury by vehicle, §20-141.4(a3).
Aggravated felony serious injury by vehicle,
§20-141.4(a4).
Streetcars.
Operating trains or streetcars while intoxicated,
§14-281.
Substance abuse services.
Assessments, §122C-142.1(b).
Certificate of completion, §122C-142.1(e).
Compliance with rules, §122C-142.1(d).
Curriculum compliance, §122C-142.1(d).
Fees, §122C-142.1(f).
Multiple offenses for which certificate of
completion required, §122C-142.1(f1).
Multiple offenses for which certificate of
completion required, §122C-142.1(f1).
Outcomes evaluation study, §122C-142.1(j).
Out-of-state services, §122C-142.1(g).
Persons authorized to provide instruction,
§122C-142.1(d1).
Private providers.
Authorization to provide services,
§122C-142.1(a1).
Providing services, §122C-142.1(a).
Reports, §122C-142.1(i).
Restoration of license after conviction.
Condition of probation, §20-179(g) to (k).
Obtaining certificate of completion, §20-17.6(c).
Rulemaking authority, §122C-142.1(h).
Compliance with rules, §122C-142.1(d).
School or treatment, §122C-142.1(c).
Persons authorized to provide instruction,
§122C-142.1(d1).
Standards, §122C-142.1(d).
Supervising driver or approved instructor.
Serving as while under influence of impairing
substances or after consuming alcohol,
§20-12.1(a), (b).
Suppression of evidence.
Motion.
Appeal of preliminary determinations,
§20-38.7(a), (b).
Determination after hearing and finding facts,
§20-38.6(e).
Final judgment when motion granted.
Time for entering, §20-38.6(f).
Findings of fact and conclusion of law,
§20-38.6(f).
State granted reasonable time to defend,
§20-38.6(b).
Summarily denying, §20-38.6(d).
Summarily granting, §20-38.6(c).
When made, §20-38.6(a).
Treatment of persons convicted, §20-179.1.
Vacation of sentence.
Appeal to superior court by defendant, §20-38.7(c).
Weekend service of sentence, §20-179(s).
When driving impaired, §20-138.1(a).

IMPAIRED DRIVING —Cont'd
Witnesses.
 Expert testimony.
  Impairment, alcohol concentration level,
   impairing substances, §8C-1 Rule 702(a1).

**IMPAIRED PHARMACIST PEER REVIEW
 ORGANIZATIONS,** §90-85.41.

IMPEACHMENT, §§123-1 to 123-13.
Articles of impeachment preferred.
 Procedure in impeachment, §123-6.
Attorneys at law.
 Accused entitled to counsel, §123-9.
Budget of state.
 Criminal penalties for violations, §143C-10-1.
 Suspension or impeachment for noncompliance,
  §143C-10-3.
Causes for impeachment, §123-5.
Chief justice.
 Governor.
  Presiding officer in impeachment of governor,
   §123-2.
Constitution of the United States, US Const Art
  I §§2, 3, Art II §4, Art III §2.
Court of impeachment.
 Chief justice presides in impeachment of governor,
  §123-2.
 Quorum, §123-1.
 Senate is court of impeachment, §123-1, NC Const
  Art IV §4.
  Power of presiding officer, §123-4.
  Power of senate as a court, §123-3.
  Quorum, §123-1.
 Vesting of judicial power, NC Const Art IV §1.
Effect of impeachment, §123-13.
 Suspension of accused during trial, §123-12.
Felonies.
 Causes for impeachment, §123-5.
General assembly.
 House of representatives.
  Power to impeach, NC Const Art IV §4.
 Senate.
  Trial of impeachments, NC Const Art IV §4.
Governor, NC Const Art III §3.
 Chief justice.
  Presiding officer in impeachment of governor,
   §123-2.
Hearing time fixed, §123-10.
House of representatives.
 Power to impeach, NC Const Art IV §4.
Indictments.
 Effect of impeachment, §123-13.
Industrial commission, §97-78.1.
Judges.
 Habeas corpus.
  Refusal to grant precepts to bring up party
   detained, §17-20.
  Refusal to make attachment for failure to obey
   writ, §17-17.
Judgments.
 Effect of impeachment, §123-13.
Misdemeanors.
 Causes for impeachment, §123-5.
Modes of prosecution, NC Const Art I §22.
Notice.
 Procedure in impeachment.
  Accused to be given notice, §123-8.
Oaths.
 Procedure in impeachment.
  Administering oath to members, §123-11.

IMPEACHMENT —Cont'd
President of senate.
 Power, §123-4.
 When president of senate impeached, §123-7.
President of the United States, US Const Art II
  §4.
Procedure in impeachment.
 Articles of impeachment preferred, §123-6.
 Counsel.
  Accused entitled to counsel, §123-9.
 Notice given to the accused, §123-8.
 Oath administered to members, §123-11.
 Time of hearing fixed, §123-10.
Quorum.
 Court of impeachment, §123-1.
Senate.
 Court of impeachment, §123-1, NC Const Art IV
  §4.
  Power of presiding officer, §123-4.
  Power of the senate as a court, §123-3.
  Quorum, §123-1.
 President of senate.
  Power, §123-4.
  When president of senate impeached, §123-7.
Suspension of accused during trial.
 Effect of impeachment, §123-12.
Time of hearing fixed, §123-10.
Vice-president, US Const Art II §4.
Witnesses.
 See IMPEACHMENT OF WITNESSES.

IMPEACHMENT OF JURY VERDICT.
Criminal cases, §15A-1240.

IMPEACHMENT OF WITNESSES.
Character and conduct of witness, §8C-1 Rule
  608.
Conviction of crime, §8C-1 Rule 609.
Hearsay declarant, §8C-1 Rule 806.
Hostile witnesses, §1A-1 Rule 43(b).
Religious beliefs or opinions, §8C-1 Rule 610.
Use of depositions, §1A-1 Rule 32(a).
Utilities commission proceedings, §62-65(a).
Who may impeach, §8C-1 Rule 607.

IMPERSONATION.
Bail bondsmen and runners.
 Personation of law-enforcement officer, §58-71-95.
Emergency medical services personnel,
  §14-276.1.
Firemen, §14-276.1.
Law enforcement and other officers.
 Elements of offense, §14-277(a), (b).
 Exceptions to provisions, §14-277(c).
 Punishment, §14-277(d1), (e).
Public officers and employees, §14-277(e).
Public weighmasters.
 Prohibited, §81A-55(b).
Soil scientists, §89F-22.
Wastewater system contractors and inspectors.
 Certified contractors and inspectors, §90A-81(d).

IMPLEMENTS OF HUSBANDRY.
See FARM MACHINERY, VEHICLES AND
  IMPLEMENTS OF HUSBANDRY.

IMPLIED CONSENT LAW.
See IMPAIRED DRIVING.

IMPLIED CONSENT OFFENSES.
**Chemical analysis of impairing substances in
  blood,** §20-16.2.
Commercial vehicles.
 Impaired driving in commercial vehicles,
  §20-138.2(d).

IMPLIED CONSENT OFFENSES —Cont'd
Commercial vehicles —Cont'd
Operating a commercial vehicle after consuming alcohol, §20-138.2A(b).
Driving by person less than 21 years old after consuming alcohol or drugs, §20-138.3(b).
Habitual impaired driving, §20-138.5(c).
Impaired driving generally.
See IMPAIRED DRIVING.
Open container law, §20-138.7(b).
Procedures for implied consent offenses.
Generally, §§20-38.1 to 20-38.7.
See IMPAIRED DRIVING.
School buses.
Operating a school bus, school activity bus, or child care vehicle after consuming alcohol, §20-138.2B(b).

IMPLIED WARRANTIES.
Condominiums.
Implied warranty of quality.
Exclusion or modification.
Agreement or expression, §47C-4-115(a).
Purchaser of unit used for residential purposes, restrictions, §47C-4-115(b).
Drinking water act.
Suppliers deemed not to provide, §130A-315(g).
Leases, UCC.
Exclusion or modification, §25-2A-214(2), (3).
Express warranties displace inconsistent implied warranties, §25-2A-215(c).
Fitness for particular purpose, §25-2A-213.
Merchantability, §25-2A-212.
Third-party beneficiaries, §25-2A-216.
Products liability.
Action directly against manufacturer for breach of implied warranty, §99B-2(b).
Privity requirements, §99B-2(b).
Sale of goods, UCC.
Course of dealing, §25-2-314(3).
Exclusion or modification by course of dealing, §25-2-316(3).
Cumulation and conflict, §25-2-317.
Fitness for a particular purpose, §25-2-315.
Merchantability, §25-2-314.
Third party beneficiaries, §25-2-318.
Usage of trade, §25-2-314(3).
Exclusion or modification, §25-2-316(3).

IMPORTS.
See EXPORTS AND IMPORTS.

IMPOSSIBILITY OF PERFORMANCE.
Sale of goods, UCC.
Excuse by failure of presupposed condition, §25-2-615.
Procedure on notice claiming excuse, §25-2-616.
Substituted performance, §25-2-614.

IMPOTENCE.
Food, drug and cosmetic act.
Drug or device, false advertising, §106-138(b).
Void marriages, §51-3.

IMPOUNDED WATER.
Navigable waters.
Impoundment not included in definition of navigable waters, §76-40(d).
Right of withdrawal.
Applicability of provisions, §143-215.50.
Assignment of right of withdrawal, §143-215.45.
Community water supplies.
Right of withdrawal for use, §143-215.49.

IMPOUNDED WATER —Cont'd
Right of withdrawal —Cont'd
Definitions, §143-215.44(b) to (d).
Determining streamflows.
Authority to make determinations, §143-215.48(b).
Minimum average flow, §143-215.48(a).
Discharges of water.
Effect of right of withdrawal, §143-215.47.
Exercise of right of withdrawal, §143-215.46.
Generally, §143-215.44(a).
Interpretation with other statutes, §143-215.50.
Transfer of right of withdrawal, §143-215.45.
Use in community water supplies, §143-215.49.

IMPOUNDMENT.
Cats, §130A-192.
Dogs, §130A-192.
Wildlife management areas.
Unmuzzled dogs running at large, §67-14.1(b) to (e).
Livestock.
Any person may impound livestock at large, §68-17.
Costs and damages.
Demand upon owner, §68-18.
Determination by selected landowners or by referee, §68-19.
Right of impounder to recover, §68-17.
Feeding and watering impounded livestock.
Any person may feed and water, §68-23.
Owner liable, §68-23.
Failure to feed and water.
Misdemeanor, §68-21.
Illegally releasing or receiving impounded livestock.
Misdemeanor, §68-21.
Notice.
Actual notice when owner known, §68-19.
Sale where owner fails to redeem or is unknown, §68-20.
When owner not known, §68-18.1.
Outer Banks.
Stock running at large.
Applicability of general provisions, §68-45.
Sale where owner fails to redeem or is unknown, §68-20.
Violations of provisions, §68-24.
Motor vehicles.
Impaired driving offenses, §§20-28.2 to 20-28.9.
Property impounded for evidence, §15-11.1.
Rabies.
Animals not wearing vaccination tags, §130A-192.
Person bitten by animal required to be vaccinated.
Confinement of animal, §130A-196(b).

IMPRISONMENT.
Jails.
See JAILS.
Prisons and prisoners.
See PRISONS AND PRISONERS.

IMPROPER BACKING.
Movement not safe or interfering with traffic, §20-154.

IMPROPER GOVERNMENT ACTIVITIES.
Communications with members of the general assembly, §126-90.
Limitation of actions, §1-54.
Reporting.
Attorneys' fees, §126-87.

IMPROPER GOVERNMENT ACTIVITIES

—Cont'd

Reporting —Cont'd

Civil actions for injunctive relief or other
remedies, §126-86.

Costs, §126-87.

Injunctive relief, §126-86.

Notice of employee protections and obligations.
Posting by employer, §126-88.

Policy of state, §126-84.

Protection from retaliation, §126-85.
Posting notice of employer protection, §126-88.

Remedies, §§126-86, 126-87.

Retaliation.

Employees retaliating against other employees.
Illegal activities, §126-85(a1).
Refusal to carry out directive, §126-85(b),
(b1).

Head of department or agency.
Illegal activities, §126-85(a).
Refusal to carry out directive, §126-85(b).

Notice of employee protection, posted by
employer, §126-88.

Scope, §126-85(c).

State auditor's duties, §147-64.6B.

Statement of policy, §126-84.

IMPROPER VENUE.

Defense by pretrial motion, §1A-1 Rule 12(b).

IMPROVEMENT OF COUNTY LAND RECORDS PROGRAM, §102-15.

IMPROVEMENTS.

Betterments, §§1-340 to 1-351.
See BETTERMENTS.

Bond issues.
State debt, §§142-1 to 142-29.7.
See STATE DEBT.

Budget of state.
Capital improvement projects, §§143C-8-1 to
143C-8-12.
See STATE BUDGET.

Contracts to improve real property.
Provisions making contract subject to laws of
another state.
Void and against public policy, §22B-2.

Counties.
Ordinances.
Submission of statement concerning
improvements, §153A-325.
Public enterprise improvements, §153A-280.
Special assessments.
Street light assessments, §153A-206.
Subdivision and residential streets, §153A-205.

Drainage districts.
Assessments.
Renovation, enlargement and extension of
canals, structures and boundaries,
§156-93.5.
Bonds.
Increase to extinguish debt, §156-122.
Proceedings as for original bond issue,
§156-123.
Redress to dissatisfied landowners, §156-121.
Renovation, enlargement and extension of
canals, structures and boundaries,
§156-93.5.
Canals, structures and boundaries.
Renovation, enlargement and extension.
Procedures generally, §§156-93.2, 156-93.3.

IMPROVEMENTS —Cont'd

Drainage districts —Cont'd

Construction.

Commissioners.
Control and repairs by commissioners,
§156-92.

Contracts, §§156-84 to 156-86.

Improvement, renovation, enlargement and
extension of canals, structures and
boundaries, §§156-93.2 to 156-93.7.

Lateral drains, §156-93.

Payments, §156-85.

Public or private ways.
Maintenance of drainage across, §156-88.

Railroads, §§156-89 to 156-91.

Right of entry, §156-87.

Superintendent of construction, §156-83.
Estimates.
Monthly estimates for work and payments
thereon, §156-85.

Removal, §156-136.

Trees and timber.
Removal of timber, §156-87.

Easements.
Renovation, enlargement and extension of
canals, structures and boundaries,
§156-93.6.

Fairs.
State fair.
Board authorized to construct and finance
facilities and improvements, §106-503.1.

False statements as to improvements.
Misdemeanor for furnishing, §44A-24.

Highways.
Connection of highways with improved streets,
§136-27.

Local government participation in improvements
to state highway system, §136-66.3.

Agreements with local government units to
expedite projects, §136-66.8.

Urban areas.
Reduction in traffic congestion, §136-66.5.

Limitation of actions.
Injuries arising from defective or unsafe condition,
§1-50(a).

Local improvement districts.
Bankruptcy and insolvency.
Authority to avail of provisions of bankruptcy
law, §23-48.

Municipalities.
Urban areas.
Reduction in traffic congestion, §136-66.5.

Public schools.
School building improvement reports.
Administrative units, §115C-47.
State board of education.
Development of system of reports, §115C-12.

Real property.
Contracts to improve real property.
Subject to laws of another state, §22B-2.
Defective or unsafe condition.
Limitation of actions, §1-50(a).
Subcontractors, payments to, §§22C-1 to 22C-6.

State debt, §§142-1 to 142-29.7.
See STATE DEBT.

IMPUTED NEGLIGENCE.

Dogs.
Dangerous dogs causing injury or property
damage, §67-4.4.
Injuring livestock or fowl, §67-1.

IMPUTED NEGLIGENCE —Cont'd
Dogs —Cont'd
Running at large at night, §67-12.
Motorboat and vessel operation.
Family purpose doctrine applicable, §75A-10.1.
Motor vehicle owned or operated by parent or child.
Abolition of parent-child immunity in motor vehicle cases, §1-539.21.

INACTIVE ACCOUNTS.
Unclaimed property.
Escheat, §§116B-1 to 116B-4.
Generally, §§116B-51 to 116B-80.
See UNCLAIMED PROPERTY.

INACTIVE HAZARDOUS SITES.
Cleanup, §§130A-310 to 130A-310.13.
Risk based environmental remediation at contaminated industrial sites, §§130A-310.65 to 130A-310.77.

INAUGURAL CEREMONIES COMMITTEE.
Allowances of members, §143-539.
Appointments, §143-533.
Time of appointments, §143-534.
Appropriations.
Payments from appropriations, §143-539.
Chairman.
Election, §143-536.
Created, §143-533.
Definitions, §143-532.
Duties.
Generally, §143-538.
Expenses, §143-539.
Filling vacancies, §143-535.
Inaugural period.
Defined, §143-532.
Inaugural planning period.
Defined, §143-532.
Meetings, §143-537.
Members, §143-533.
Mileage.
Per diem and allowances of members, §143-539.
Offices, §143-539.
Powers.
Generally, §143-538.
Qualifications of members, §143-533.
Quorum, §143-536.
Rules and regulations.
Procedural rules, §143-536.
Terms of office, §143-534.
Time of appointments, §143-534.
Vacancies.
Filling, §143-535.

IN-CAMERA HEARINGS.
Rape shield law.
Relevance of victim's past behavior, §8C-1 Rule 412.
Trade secrets, actions for misappropriations, §66-156.

INCAPACITATED PERSONS.
Custodial trusts.
Incapacity of beneficiary.
Determination, §33B-10.
Generally, §§33B-1 to 33B-22.
See CUSTODIAL TRUSTS.
Durable power of attorney.
Incapacity of principal generally, §§32A-8 to 32A-14.
See DURABLE POWER OF ATTORNEY.

INCAPACITATED PERSONS —Cont'd
Incapacity of defendant to proceed, §§15A-1001 to 15A-1009.
See INCAPACITY OF DEFENDANT TO PROCEED.
Incompetency generally.
See INCOMPETENCY.

INCAPACITY OF BENEFICIARY.
Custodial trusts.
Determination, §33B-10.
Generally, §§33B-1 to 33B-22.
See CUSTODIAL TRUSTS.

INCAPACITY OF DEFENDANT TO PROCEED, §§15A-1001 to 15A-1009.
Capacity regained by defendant, §15A-1006.
Commitment.
Civil commitment, §15A-1003(a), (b).
Evidence admissible at proceedings, §15A-1003(c).
Institution of proceedings, §15A-1002(b).
Observation and treatment, §15A-1002(b).
Confidentiality of information.
Reports to court, §15A-1002(d).
Determination of incapacity, §15A-1002(b).
Dismissal of charges, §15A-1008.
Supplemental hearing, §15A-1007(c).
Dismissal with leave.
Charges dismissed.
Court's power not limited by section, §15A-1009(f).
Dismissal with leave no longer in effect, §15A-1009(e).
Effect, §15A-1009(b).
Methods of entering, §15A-1009(c).
Prosecutor authorized to enter, §15A-1009(a).
Reinstatement of proceeding.
Defendant becoming capable of proceeding, §15A-1009(d).
Hearings.
Supplemental hearings, §15A-1007(a).
Court's own determination, §15A-1007(b).
Dismissal of charges, §15A-1007(c).
Motion, §15A-1002(a).
No proceedings when defendant mentally incapacitated, §15A-1001(a).
Exception as to motions which can be handled by counsel without assistance of defendant, §15A-1001(b).
Orders for safeguarding defendant, §15A-1004(a) to (c).
Amendment or supplementation, §15A-1004(f).
Reports to court, §15A-1004(d).
Return of defendant to stand trial, §15A-1004(e).
Reinstatement of proceeding.
Dismissal with leave.
Defendant becoming capable of proceeding, §15A-1009(d).
Reports to court, §§15A-1002(b), (b1), (d), 15A-1005.
Hospital or institution with custody of defendant, §15A-1002(d).
Return of defendant for trial upon gaining capacity, §§15A-1004(e), 15A-1006.
Temporary confinement of defendant, §15A-1002(c).

INCAPACITY OF PRINCIPAL.
Durable power of attorney.
Generally, §§32A-8 to 32A-14.
See DURABLE POWER OF ATTORNEY.

INCENDIARIES.
Drivers' licenses.
Revocation or suspension of license.
Minors, §20-13.2(c2).
Explosives generally.
See EXPLOSIVES.

INCEST, §14-178.
Bail, §15A-534.4.
Child abuse, §14-318.4.
Defenses.
Child under age of sixteen, when other person at
least four years older, §14-178(c).
Elements of offense, §14-178(a).
Intercourse and sexual offenses with certain
victims, §14-27.7(a).
Marriage, prohibited degrees of kinship, §51-4.
Punishment, §14-178(b).
Rehabilitative treatment.
Defendant may pay cost as condition of probation,
§15A-1343(b1).
Venue, §15A-136.

IN CHAMBERS.
District court proceedings, hearings and acts
conducted by judge, §7A-191.
Interlocutory orders, §7A-192.
Injunctions.
Judges having jurisdiction, §1-493.
Jurisdiction of emergency superior court
judges, §7A-48.

INCINERATION.
Disposal of certain wastes by, §130A-309.10(f1),
(f2), (i), (j).

INCITEMENT TO RIOT, §14-288.2.
Riots and civil disorders.
Generally.
See RIOTS AND CIVIL DISORDERS.

INCLEMENT WEATHER.
Cancellation of court sessions, closing court
offices, §7A-39(a).
In chambers jurisdiction not affected, §7A-39(c).
School calendar.
Make up days, §115C-84.2(a).

INCLINED OR VERTICAL WHEELCHAIR
LIFT.
Elevator safety act generally, §§95-110.1 to
95-110.15.
See ELEVATORS.

INCLINED STAIRWAY CHAIRLIFT.
Elevator safety act generally, §§95-110.1 to
95-110.15.
See ELEVATORS.

INCOME.
Loss of income.
Mortality tables as evidence, §8-47.
Principal and income act.
General provisions, §§37A-1-101 to 37A-6-602.
See PRINCIPAL AND INCOME ACT.

INCOME TAX.
Adoption expenses, credit.
Amount, §105-151.32(a).
Reduction of amount, §105-151.32(b).
Repeal of provision, §105-151.32(c).
Bank holding companies.
Dividends.
Adjustment to expenses related to,
§105-130.6A(c), (e), (f), (h).

INCOME TAX —Cont'd
Banks.
Refund anticipation loans, §§53-245 to 53-254.
Bond issues.
Exemption from federal income taxation.
Registered public obligations act.
Generally, §§159E-1 to 159E-15.
See REGISTERED PUBLIC
OBLIGATIONS.
Purpose of act, §159E-3(a), (b).
Federal tax reform allocation committee.
Duties, §143-433.8.
Formulas for allocation, §143-433.9.
Generally, §143-433.7.
Legislative findings, §143-433.6(a) to (d).
Port authority bonds.
Gain from transfer not exempt from taxation,
§136-265(g).
Refunding obligations issued by state.
Gain from transfer not exempt from taxation,
§142-29.6(f).
State bonds, act authorizing not addressing
exemption from taxation.
Not exempt from income taxes on gain from
transfer, §142-12.
Business and energy tax credits, §§105-129.15 to
105-129.19.
Business investments.
Tax credit for qualified business investments,
§§105-163.010 to 105-163.015.
Checkoffs.
Refund contributions.
Wildlife conservation account, §105-269.5.
Child tax credit, §105-151.24(a), (b).
Child with disability requiring special
education and related services.
Education expenses credit, §105-151.33.
Cigarettes manufactured for exportation,
credit, §105-130.45.
Amount of credit allowed, §105-130.45(b).
Cap, §105-130.45(c).
Definitions, §105-130.45(a).
Increasing employment and utilizing state ports.
Allocation, §105-130.46(f).
Allowance of credit, amount, §105-130.46(d).
Carryforward, §105-130.46(h).
Ceiling, §105-130.46(g).
Definitions, §105-130.46(b).
Documentation, §105-130.46(i).
Employment level, eligibility for full credit,
§105-130.46(c).
No double credit, §105-130.46(j).
Partial credit, §105-130.46(e).
Purpose, §105-130.46(a).
Reports, §105-130.46(k).
Information required by corporation attaining
credit, §105-130.45(d).
Clergymen.
Withholding of income taxes from wages.
Ordained or licensed clergymen may elect to be
self-employed, §105-163.1A.
Cogenerating power plants.
Credit for constructing in state.
Corporation or partnership not public utility,
§105-130.25(a).
Application for credit, §105-130.25(d).
Ceiling on credit, §105-130.25(e).
Cogenerating power plant defined,
§105-130.25(b).
Cost paid during earlier year, alternative
method, §105-130.25(c).

INCOME TAX —Cont'd
Collection of taxes.
Assignments, §105-269.13(c).
Debts not collectible, §105-269.13(a).
Retailer debts, §105-269.13(b).
Conservation tillage equipment.
Corporations, §105-130.36.
Individual income tax.
Credit for installation, §105-151.13.
Constitution of North Carolina.
Limitations and restrictions, NC Const Art V §2.
Constitution of the United States, US Const Amd 16.
Corporations.
Accelerated depreciation.
Determining state net income, §105-130.5(a), (b).
Additional nature of tax, §105-130.1.
Additions to federal taxable income in determining state net income, §105-130.5(a).
Adjustments to federal taxable income in determining state net income, §105-130.5(a) to (e).
Adjustments to state net income.
Intercompany transactions lacking economic substance or fair market value, §105-130.5A.
Affiliated corporations.
Intercompany transactions lacking economic substance or fair market value.
Adjustment of net income, combined returns, §105-130.5A.
Air and water transportation corporations.
Allocation and apportionment of income.
Revenue ton mile, §105-130.4(s).
Air-cleaning devices.
Amortization, §105-130.10.
Allocation and apportionment of income, §105-130.4(b).
Air and water transportation corporations, §105-130.4(s).
Alternative apportionment method, §105-130.4(t1).
Apportionable income, §105-130.4(i).
Defined, §105-130.4(a).
Excluded corporations, §105-130.4(r).
Motor carrier of passengers, §105-130.4(p).
Motor carriers of property, §105-130.4(o).
Payroll factor, §105-130.4(k).
Property factor, §105-130.4(j).
Railroad companies, §105-130.4(m).
Sales factor, §105-130.4(l).
Telegraph companies, §105-130.4(q).
Telephone companies, §105-130.4(n).
Definitions, §105-130.4(a).
Intercompany transaction lacking economic substance and not at fair market value, §105-130.5A(h).
Interest and net dividends, §105-130.4(f).
Nonapportionable income, §105-130.4(c) to (h).
Defined, §105-130.4(a).
Intangible property.
Royalties or similar income received from use of, §105-130.4(g).
Sale or other disposition of real property, §105-130.4(e).
Qualified capital intensive corporations, §105-130.4(s1).
Rents and royalties, §105-130.4(c), (d).
Sale or other disposition of real property, §105-130.4(e).

INCOME TAX —Cont'd
Corporations —Cont'd
Amortization.
Air-cleaning devices, §105-130.10.
Equipment mandated by OSHA.
Defined, §105-130.10A(b).
Generally, §105-130.10A(a).
Recycling facilities, §105-130.10.
Waste treatment facilities, §105-130.10.
Bank holding companies.
Dividends.
Adjustment to expenses related to, §105-130.6A(c), (e), (f), (h).
Building and loan associations.
Exemption, §105-130.11(a).
Chambers of commerce.
Exemption, §105-130.11(a), (b).
Change of income year, §105-130.15(b).
Charities.
Contributions.
Deductions, §105-130.9.
Exemption of charitable corporations, §105-130.11(a), (b).
Cigarettes manufactured for exportation, credit, §105-130.45.
Amount of credit allowed, §105-130.45(b).
Cap, §105-130.45(c).
Definitions, §105-130.45(a).
Increasing employment and utilizing state ports, §105-130.46.
Information required by corporation attaining credit, §105-130.45(d).
Citation of act.
Short title, §105-130.
Civic leagues.
Exemption, §105-130.11(a), (b).
Cogenerating power plants.
Credit for construction, §105-130.25.
Computation of net income, §105-130.15(a).
Condominium associations.
Exemption, §105-130.11(a).
Contributions.
Deductions, §105-130.9.
Cooperative associations.
Exemption, §105-130.11(a), (b).
Credits.
Cigarettes manufactured for exportation, §105-130.45.
Amount of credit allowed, §105-130.45(b).
Cap, §105-130.45(c).
Definitions, §105-130.45(a).
Increasing employment and utilizing state ports, §105-130.46.
Information required by corporation attaining credit, §105-130.45(d).
Cogenerating power plants, §105-130.25.
Conservation tillage equipment.
Definition of "conservation tillage equipment,"§105-130.36(b).
Generally, §105-130.36(a).
Disabled persons.
Construction of dwelling units for, §105-130.22.
Gleaned crop.
Definitions, §105-130.37(b).
Generally, §105-130.37(a).
Ports authority wharfage, handling and throughput charges, §105-130.41.
Real property donations, §105-130.34.
S corporation shareholders, §105-131.8.

INCOME TAX —Cont'd
Corporations —Cont'd
Credits —Cont'd
Telephones.
Providing service to low-income residential
consumers at reduced rates, §105-130.39.
Deductions.
Adjustments to federal taxable income to
determine state net income, §105-130.5(b).
Amortization of equipment, §§105-130.10,
105-130.10A.
Contributions, §105-130.9.
Net economic loss, §105-130.8.
Allowance as deduction, §105-130.8(a).
Limitations, §105-130.8(a).
Records to determine and verify amount,
maintaining, inspection, §105-130.8(b).
Redetermination of item closed by statute of
limitations, §105-130.8(b).
Definitions, §§105-130.2, 105-130.4(a).
Estimated tax, §105-163.38.
Depreciation.
Recapture of depreciation required under
internal revenue code.
Inclusion in state net income, §105-130.5(e).
Disabled persons.
Dwelling units for.
Credit for construction of, §105-130.22.
Dividends.
Adjustment for expenses related to.
Bank holding companies, §105-130.6A(c).
Cap, §105-130.6A(e).
Credits, §105-130.6A(f), (h).
Definitions, §105-130.6A(a).
Electric power holding companies,
§105-130.6A(d).
Credits, §105-130.6A(g), (h).
General rule.
Corporations other than bank holding
companies and electric power holding
companies, §105-130.6A(b).
Allocation and apportionment of income.
Interest and net dividends, §105-130.4(f).
Information filed with secretary of revenue.
Persons receiving dividends, §105-130.21(b).
Information to be filed with secretary of
revenue, §105-130.21(b).
S corporations.
Distributions to shareholders, §105-131.6.
Donation of harvested crops to nonprofit
organization.
Credit for gleaned crops, §105-130.37.
Donation of interest in real property, credit,
§105-130.34(a).
Amount, §105-130.34(b).
Carry forward of unused portion, §105-130.34(c).
Not eligible for deduction as charitable
contribution, §105-130.34(d).
Electric power holding companies.
Dividends.
Adjustment for expenses related to,
§105-130.6A(d), (g), (h).
Estimated tax.
Declaration.
Amendment, §105-163.39(c).
Time for filing, §105-163.40(b).
Contents, §105-163.39(b).
Filing.
Amendments to declaration, §105-163.40(b).
Short taxable year, §105-163.40(c).
Time for, §105-163.40(a).

INCOME TAX —Cont'd
Corporations —Cont'd
Estimated tax —Cont'd
Declaration —Cont'd
Required, §105-163.39(a).
Definitions, §105-163.38.
Electronic funds transfer, payment by,
§105-163.40(d).
Interest.
Underpayment, §105-163.41.
Overpayment.
Refund, §105-163.43.
Payment.
Electronic funds transfer, §105-241(b).
Payment of tax.
Electronic funds transfer, §105-163.40(d).
Overpayment.
Refund, §105-163.43.
Underpayment, §105-163.41.
Refund of overpayment, §105-163.43.
Underpayment.
Interest, §105-163.41(a).
When not imposed, §105-163.41(d).
Period of underpayment, §105-163.41(c).
What constitutes, §105-163.41(b).
Exemptions.
Organizations exempt, §105-130.11(a).
Conditional exemptions, §105-130.11(b).
Failure to report state net income.
Intercompany transactions lacking economic
substance or fair market value.
Advice from secretary, requesting,
§105-130A.5A(l).
Affiliated group defined, §105-130A.5A(i).
Appeal of final determination,
§105-130A.5A(o).
Combined return required, §105-130.5A(c),
(e).
Apportionment of net income,
§105-130.5A(h).
Determining transactions not at fair market
value, §105-130.5A(g).
Economic substance defined, §105-130.5A(f).
Extension of time limit, §105-130A.5A(m).
Notice to provide information, §105-130.5A(a).
Other tax adjustments, §105-130A.5A(n).
Penalties, §105-130A.5A(k).
Proposed assessment or refund.
Issuance upon making determination,
§105-130A.5A(j).
Redetermination of state net income,
§105-130.5A(b).
Voluntary redetermination,
§105-130.5A(b1).
Written statement of findings, §105-130.5A(d).
Federal taxable income.
Adjustments in determining state net income,
§105-130.5(a) to (e).
Change, §105-130.20.
Deductions in determining state net income,
§105-130.5(b).
Fiscal year.
Defined, §105-130.2.
Foreign corporations.
Defined, §105-130.2.
Installment method of reporting income.
Prerequisites for use, §105-130.15(c).
Fraternal beneficiary societies.
Exemption, §105-130.11(a), (b).
Gleaned crops, credit, §105-130.37(a).
Definitions, §105-130.37(b).

INCOME TAX —Cont'd
Corporations —Cont'd
Homeowner association income, §105-130.11(c).
Hurricane Floyd reserve fund payments.
Deductions to taxable income, §105-130.5(b).
Income year.
Change of income year, §105-130.15(b).
Defined, §105-130.2.
Information filed with secretary, §105-130.21(a).
Dividend payments, §105-130.21(b).
Insurance companies.
Exemption, §105-130.11(a).
Intangible property.
Royalties or similar income received from use
of.
Allocation and apportionment of income,
§105-130.4(g).
Intercompany transactions lacking economic
substance or fair market value.
Adjustment, redetermination of net income,
§105-130.5A(b).
Voluntary redetermination, §105-130.5A(b1).
Advice from secretary, requesting,
§105-130A.5A(l).
Affiliated group defined, §105-130A.5A(i).
Appeal of final determination, §105-130A.5A(o).
Combined return required, §105-130.5A(c), (e).
Apportionment of net income, §105-130.5A(h).
Not timely filed.
Penalties, §105-130A.5A(k).
Determining transactions not at fair market
value, §105-130.5A(g).
Economic substance defined, §105-130.5A(f).
Extension of time limit, §105-130A.5A(m).
Notice to provide information, §105-130A.5A(a).
Other tax adjustments, §105-130A.5A(n).
Penalties, §105-130A.5A(k).
Proposed assessment or refund.
Issuance upon making determination,
§105-130A.5A(j).
Written statement of findings, §105-130.5A(d).
Interest.
Allocation and apportionment of income.
Interest and net dividends, §105-130.4(f).
International banking facilities.
Deductions in determining state net income,
§105-130.5(b).
Levy, §105-130.3.
Merger or consolidation.
Corporation using installment method of
reporting income, §105-130.15(d).
Motor carriers.
Allocation and apportionment of income.
Business income of motor carriers,
§105-130.4(o), (p).
Net economic loss, §105-130.8.
Net income.
Adjustment, redetermination.
Intercompany transactions lacking economic
substance or fair market value,
§105-130.5A.
Computation, §105-130.15(a).
Federal taxable income.
Adjustments in determining state net income,
§105-130.5(a) to (e).
Recapture of depreciation required under
internal revenue code.
Inclusion in state net income, §105-130.5(e).
Officers.
Personal liability for unpaid taxes,
§105-242.2(b).

INCOME TAX —Cont'd
Corporations —Cont'd
Payment of tax.
Estimated tax.
Overpayment, §105-163.43.
Underpayment, §105-163.41.
Generally, §105-130.19(a).
Personal liability.
Unpaid taxes, §105-242.2(b).
Ports authority.
Credit for ports authority wharfage, handling
and throughput charges, §105-130.41.
Poultry composting facility.
Credit limitations, §105-130.44.
Purpose of provisions, §105-130.1.
Qualified capital intensive corporations.
Allocation and apportionment of income,
§105-130.4(s1).
Railroads.
Application and apportionment of income.
Business income of railroad companies,
§105-130.4(m).
Rate of tax, §105-130.3.
Real estate investment trust, §105-130.12.
Real estate mortgage investment conduits.
Exemption, §105-130.11(d).
Real property donations, credit, §105-130.34(a).
Amount, §105-130.34(b).
Carry forward of unused portion, §105-130.34(c).
Not eligible for deduction as charitable
contribution, §105-130.34(d).
Recapture of depreciation.
Inclusion in state net income, §105-130.5(e).
Recycling facilities.
Amortization, §105-130.10.
Redetermination of state net income.
Intercompany transactions lacking economic
substance or fair market value,
§105-130.5A.
Rents and royalties.
Allocation and apportionment of income,
§105-130.4(c), (d).
Returns, §105-130.16.
Affirmation verifying return, person signing,
§105-130.16.
Consolidated or combined returns, §105-130.14.
Amount of tax shown as due not deficiency,
§105-236(a).
Intercompany transactions lacking economic
substance or fair market value.
Combined return required, §105-130.5A.
Dissolution or withdrawal from state, time for
filing, §105-130.17(e).
Exempt organizations, filing, §105-130.17(d1).
Extension of time to file, §105-130.17(d).
Filing, §105-130.17(a).
Time for filing, §105-130.17(b) to (g).
Intercompany transactions lacking economic
substance or fair market value.
Combined return required, §105-130.5A.
Marketing associations, §105-130.17(c).
Mutual associations to conduct agricultural
business, §105-130.17(c).
S corporations, §105-131.7.
Short period.
Change of income year, §105-130.15(b).
Time for, §105-130.17(b) to (g).
Royalty payments for use of trademarks.
Optional methods for reporting income,
§105-130.7A(a).
Definitions, §105-130.7A(b).

INCOME TAX —Cont'd
Corporations —Cont'd
Royalty payments for use of trademarks —Cont'd
Optional methods for reporting income —Cont'd
Election, §105-130.7A(c).
Indirect transactions, same effect,
§105-130.7A(d).
Savings and loan associations.
Exemption, §105-130.11(a).
Supervisory fees.
Credit limitations, §105-130.43.
S corporations.
Adjustment of basis, §105-131.3.
Adjustment of income, §105-131.2(a).
Adjustment to taxable income.
Shareholders pro rata share of corporations
income, §105-134.6(a).
Citation of division, §105-131(a).
Corporation exempt from corporate income tax,
§105-131.1(a).
Credits, §105-131.8.
Definitions, §105-131(b).
Distribution, §105-131.6.
Interpretation of division, §105-131(c).
Net income.
Characterization of income, §105-131.2(c).
Shareholders.
Pro rata share of net income, §105-131.1(b).
Returns, §105-131.7.
Shareholders.
Basis, §105-131.3.
Credits, §105-131.8.
Part-year resident shareholder, §105-131.5.
Pro rata share of net income, §105-131.1(b).
Shareholders pro rata share of corporations
income.
Adjustment to taxable income, §105-134.6(a).
Shareholder's pro rata share of corporation's
income, §105-134.5(d).
Short title, §105-131(a).
Shame transactions.
Intercompany transactions lacking economic
substance or fair market value,
§105-130.5A.
Surtax.
Expiration, §105-130.3B(b).
Imposition, §105-130.3B(a).
Taxable year.
Defined, §105-130.2.
Telegraph companies.
Allocation and apportionment of income.
Business income of telegraph companies,
§105-130.4(q).
Telephone companies.
Allocation and apportionment of income.
Business income of telephone companies,
§105-130.4(n).
Credits for providing service to low-income
residential consumers at reduced rates,
§105-130.39.
Title of act.
Short title, §105-130.
Unpaid taxes.
Personal liability, §105-242.2(b).
Waste treatment facilities.
Amortization, §105-130.10.
Withdrawal from state.
Corporation using installment method of
reporting income, §105-130.15(d).
Counties.
Levy prohibited, §105-247.

INCOME TAX —Cont'd
Credits.
Adoption expenses, §105-151.32.
Business and energy tax credits, §§105-129.15 to
105-129.19.
See BUSINESS AND ENERGY TAX CREDITS.
Corporations. See within this heading,
"Corporations."
Earned income tax credit, §105-151.31.
Education expenses credit.
Child with disability requiring special education
and related services, §105-151.33.
Estates and trusts, §105-160.3.
Income taxes paid to other states, §105-160.4(a)
to (e).
Historic structure rehabilitation tax credit,
§§105-129.35 to 105-129.39.
Individual income tax. See within this heading,
"Individual income tax."
Long-term care insurance, §105-151.28.
Low-income housing tax credits, §§105-129.40 to
105-129.45.
Oyster shells recycling, §105-130.48.
Partnerships, §105-269.15.
Ports authority.
Wharfage, handling and throughput charges,
§105-130.41.
Poultry composting facility.
Construction, §105-151.25(a).
Property owned by the entirety,
§105-151.25(b).
Production companies.
Qualifying expenses, §§105-130.47, 105-151.29.
Qualified business investments, §§105-163.010 to
105-163.015.
Recycling facilities.
Tax credit for major recycling facility
investment, §§105-129.25 to 105-129.28.
Renewable energy investment tax credit,
§105-129.16A.
Renewable energy property.
Donation to nonprofit organization or
government unit to acquire, §105-129.16H.
Facilities, §105-129.16I.
Research and development tax credit,
§§105-129.50 to 105-129.56.
S corporation shareholders, §105-131.8.
Small business unemployment insurance
refundable tax credit, §105-129.16J.
Tax incentives for new and expanding businesses
generally, §§105-129.2 to 105-129.13.
See TAX INCENTIVES FOR NEW AND
EXPANDING BUSINESSES.
Telephone service to low-income residents at
reduced rates.
Credit to corporation providing, §105-130.39(a),
(b).
Work opportunity tax credit, §105-129.16G.
Crops.
Gleaned crops.
Individual income tax.
Credits, §105-151.14(a), (b).
Decedents' estates.
Excess funds, §28A-15-9.
State income tax returns, §28A-15-8.
Deductions.
Corporations.
Adjustments to federal taxable income in
determining state net income,
§105-130.5(b).

INCOME TAX —Cont'd
Deductions —Cont'd
Corporations —Cont'd
Amortization of equipment, §§105-130.10, 105-130.10A.
Contributions, §105-130.9.
Net economic loss, §105-130.8.
Individual income tax, §105-134.6(b).
Definitions.
Corporations, §§105-130.2, 105-130.4(a).
Conservation tillage equipment, §105-130.36(b).
Estimated tax, §105-163.38.
Gleaned crop, §105-130.37(b).
Renewable biomass resources, §105-129.15.
S corporations, §105-131(b).
Estates and trusts, §105-160.1.
Individual income tax, §105-134.1.
Conservation tillage equipment, §105-151.13(b).
Gleaned crops, §105-151.14(b).
Taxable income, §105-134.5.
Refund anticipation loans, §53-246.
Tax credit for qualified business investments, §105-163.010.
Withholding of income taxes from wages, §105-163.1.
Disabled persons.
Individual income tax.
Credits.
Construction of dwelling units for, §105-151.1.
Credit for the disabled, §105-151.18.
Definitions, §105-151.18(c).
Disabled dependent, §105-151.18(b).
Disabled taxpayer, §105-151.18(a).
Limitations, §105-151.18(d).
Dividends.
Corporations.
Adjustment to expenses related to, §105-130.6A.
Information filed with secretary of revenue.
Persons receiving dividends, §105-130.21(b).
S corporations.
Distributions to shareholders, §105-131.6.
Earned income tax credit.
Amount, §105-151.31(a).
Nonresident or part-time resident.
Reduction, §105-151.31(a).
Refundable excess, §105-151.31(b).
Sunset, §105-151.31(c).
Education expenses credit.
Child with disability requiring special education and related services, §105-151.33(a).
Amount, §105-151.33(b).
Reduction, §105-151.33(e).
Carryforward, §105-151.33(f).
Definitions, §105-151.33(i).
Disqualification, §105-151.33(d).
Eligible dependent defined, §105-151.33(a).
Enrollment in school for semester, §105-151.33(c).
Information required to claim deduction, §105-151.33(f).
Initial eligibility, §105-151.33(a).
Related services defined, §105-151.33(i).
Special education defined, §105-151.33(i).
Time enrolled in public school.
Reduction of amount, §105-151.33(e).
Transfer to fund for special education and related services, §105-151.33(h).
Two semesters during taxable year, §105-151.33(c).
Unused portion of credit.
Carryforward, §105-151.33(f).

INCOME TAX —Cont'd
Electric power holding companies.
Dividends.
Adjustment for expenses related to, §105-130.6A(d), (g), (h).
Estates and trusts, §§105-160 to 105-160.8.
Amount of tax, §105-160.2.
Changes, §105-160.8.
Corrections, §105-160.8.
Credits, §105-160.3(a).
Credits not allowed, §105-160.3(b).
Income taxes paid to other states, §105-160.4(a) to (e).
Definitions, §105-160.1.
Imposition of tax, §105-160.2.
Payment.
Place of payment, §105-160.7(a).
Returns, §105-160.5.
Place of filing, §105-160.6.
Time of filing, §105-160.6.
Short title, §105-160.
Taxable income, §105-160.2.
Title of provisions, §105-160.
Estimated tax.
Corporations.
Declaration, §105-163.39.
Filing, §105-163.40.
Definitions, §105-163.38.
Refund of overpayment, §105-163.43.
Underpayment, §105-163.41.
Individuals.
Definition of "tax,"§105-163.15(g).
Liberal construction of provisions, §105-163.24.
Overpayment.
Refund, §105-163.16.
Required installments, §105-163.15(c).
Amount, §105-163.15(d), (e).
Underpayment, §105-163.15(a), (f), (h).
Amount of underpayment, §105-163.15(b).
Exemptions.
Organizations exempt, §105-130.11.
Port authority bond issues.
Gain from transfer not exempt, §136-265(g).
Refunding obligations issued by state.
Gain from transfer not exempt from taxation, §142-29.6(f).
State bonds, act authorizing issue not addressing exemption.
Not exempt from income taxes on gain from transfer, §142-12.
Withholding of income taxes from wages.
Allowable exemptions, §105-163.5(a).
Certificates, §105-163.5(b), (c), (e).
New withholding exemption certificate, §105-163.5(d).
Farm machinery.
Credit for property taxes paid, §105-151.21.
Federal government workers.
Credit or partial refund for tax paid on certain federal retirement benefits, §105-151.20.
Fiduciaries.
Individual income tax.
Filing returns, §105-152(b).
Guardian of estate, specific duties, §35A-1253.
Historic structure rehabilitation tax credit, §§105-129.35 to 105-129.39.
Hurricane Floyd reserve fund payments.
Deductions to taxable income, §105-130.5(b).
Hurricane relief and assistance.
Adjustment to federal taxable income.
Amount paid to taxpayer from disaster relief reserve fund, §105-130.5.

INCOME TAX —Cont'd
Husband and wife.
Excess funds, §28A-15-9.
Individual income tax.
Joint returns, §105-152(e).
Payment of tax, §105-157(a).
State income tax returns.
Death of spouse, §28A-15-8.
Income tax credit for property taxes.
Farm machinery, §105-151.21(a).
Adjustments, §105-151.21(c).
Definitions, §105-151.21(b).
Income tax credit for qualified business investments.
Definitions, §105-163.010.
Individual income tax.
Accelerated depreciation.
Deductions to taxable income, §105-134.6(b).
Adjusted gross income, §105-134.1.
Modifications, §105-134.6.
Adjustments to taxable income, §105-134.6.
Charitable contribution credit by nonitemizers, §105-151.26.
Applicability of provisions, §105-163.15(j), (k).
Charitable contribution tax by nonitemizers, §105-151.26.
Child care.
Credit for certain employment-related expenses, §105-151.11(a).
Applicable percentage, §105-151.11(a1).
Limitations, §105-151.11(b), (c).
Children.
Credits, §105-151.24(a), (b).
Citation of act.
Short title, §105-133.
Conservation tillage equipment.
Credit for installation.
Definition of "conservation tillage equipment,"§105-151.13(b).
Generally, §105-151.13(a).
Tenants by the entireties, §105-151.13(c).
Credits.
Charitable contributions by nonitemizers, §105-151.26.
Child care.
Employment-related expenses, §105-151.11.
Children, §105-151.24(a), (b).
Conservation tillage equipment, §105-151.13.
Disabled persons, §105-151.18.
Construction of dwelling units for, §105-151.1.
Definitions, §105-151.18(c).
Dependents, §105-151.18(b).
Limitations, §105-151.18(d).
Taxpayers, §105-151.18(a).
Donation of certain real property, §105-151.12.
Gleaned crops.
Generally, §105-151.14.
Government retirement benefits, §105-151.20.
Income taxes paid other states, §105-151(a).
Refund, §105-151(b).
Long-term care insurance.
Premiums paid, §105-151.28.
Ports authority wharfage, handling and throughput charges, §105-151.22(a).
Definitions, §105-151.22(c).
Limitations, §105-151.22(b).
Sunset, §105-151.22(d).
Poultry composting facility, §105-151.25.
Qualified business investments, §§105-163.010 to 105-163.015.
Real property donations, §105-151.12.

INCOME TAX —Cont'd
Individual income tax —Cont'd
Credits —Cont'd
Withheld amounts, §105-163.10.
Deductions, §105-134.6(b).
Personal exemption, §105-134.6(a1).
Standard deduction amount, §105-134.6(a2).
Deficiency.
Large deficiency, penalty, §105-236(a).
Definitions, §105-134.1.
Conservation tillage equipment, §105-151.13(b).
Gleaned crops, §105-151.14(b).
Taxable income, §105-134.5.
Depreciation.
Deductions to taxable income, §105-134.6(b).
Disabled persons.
Credits, §105-151.18.
Construction of dwelling units for, §105-151.1.
Definitions, §105-151.18(c).
Disabled dependent, §105-151.18(b).
Disabled taxpayer, §105-151.18(a).
Limitations, §105-151.18(d).
Donations of interest in real property, credit, §105-151.12(a).
Amounts, §105-151.12(b).
Carry over of unused portion, §105-151.12(b).
Marshland, §105-151.12(e).
Partners of partnership qualifying for credit.
Maximum dollar limit, §105-151.12.
Erroneous conviction and imprisonment compensation.
Deduction from taxable income, §105-134.6(b).
Estimated tax.
Adjustments to taxable income, §105-134.6(d).
Construction and interpretation.
Liberal construction of provisions, §105-163.24.
Definition of "tax,"§105-163.15(g).
Overpayment.
Refund, §105-163.16.
Required installments, §105-163.15(c).
Amount, §105-163.15(d), (e).
Underpayment, §105-163.15(a), (f), (h).
Amount of underpayment, §105-163.15(b).
Federal government workers.
Credit or partial refund for tax paid on certain federal government benefits.
Credit, §105-151.20(b).
Deceased taxpayers, §105-151.20(d).
Definitions, §105-151.20(a).
Establishment of claims, §105-151.20(d).
Federal retiree accounts, §105-151.20(e).
Purposes, §105-151.20(a).
Refund alternatives, §105-151.20(c).
Fiduciaries.
Returns.
Filing by, §105-152(b).
Firefighters.
Deduction from taxable income, §105-134.6(d).
Gambling.
Imposition of tax on nonresidents deriving income from.
Purposes of part, §105-134.
Gleaned crops.
Credits.
Definitions, §105-151.14(b).
Generally, §105-151.14(a).
Government retirement benefits.
Credits, §105-151.20.
Heads of households.
Defined, §105-134.1.

INCOME TAX —Cont'd

Individual income tax —Cont'd

Heads of households —Cont'd

Rate of tax, §105-134.2(a).

Husband and wife.

Payment of tax, §105-157(a).

Returns.

Joint returns, §105-152(e).

Imposition of tax, §105-134.2(a).

Alternative tax, §105-134.2(b).

Surtax, §105-134.2A(a).

Information at source returns, §105-154.

Interest upon obligations.

Deductions from taxable income, §105-134.6(b).

Inventories, §105-134.8.

Investments.

Tax credits for qualified business investments, §§105-163.010 to 105-163.015.

Long-term care insurance.

Credit for premiums paid, §105-151.28.

Married individual defined, §105-134.1.

Married individuals filing joint returns.

Rate of tax, §105-134.2(a).

Retirement benefits, deduction, §105-134.6(b).

Married individuals not filing jointly.

Rate, §105-134.2(a).

Military affairs.

Abatement of income taxes of certain members of armed forces upon death, §105-158.

Modifications to adjusted gross income, §105-134.6.

Net operating loss deduction, §105-134.6(d).

Nonresidents, §105-134.5(b).

Nonresident individual defined, §105-134.1.

North Carolina taxable income, §105-134.5(b).

North Carolina taxable income, §105-134.5.

Other adjustments to taxable income, §105-134.6(d).

Parental savings trust fund.

Deduction, amounts contributed, §105-134.6(d).

Partnerships.

Member's distributive share of business's income, §105-134.5(d).

Part-year residents.

North Carolina taxable income, §105-134.5(c).

Payment of tax.

Additional tax, §105-159.

Estimated tax.

Overpayment, §105-163.16.

Underpayment, §105-163.15.

Time for payment, §105-157(a).

Year for which paid, §105-134.3.

Personal exemption, §105-134.6(a1).

Persons affected, §105-134.

Political contributions.

Designation of tax by individual to political party, §105-159.1(a).

Paid preparer of tax returns, §105-159.1(e).

Remission of funds by secretary, §105-159.1(b).

Return to indicate contribution neither increases or decreases tax liability, §105-159.1(d).

Ports authority.

Credit for wharfage, handling and throughput charges, §105-151.22(a).

Definitions, §105-151.22(c).

Limitations, §105-151.22(b).

Sunset, §105-151.22(d).

Poultry composting facility.

Credit, §105-151.25.

INCOME TAX —Cont'd

Individual income tax —Cont'd

Public campaign fund.

Allocation to fund by individual, §105-159.2(a).

Instructions for individual to designate allocation, §105-159.2(c).

Returns to give individual opportunity to designate allocation, §105-159.2(b).

Purpose of provisions, §105-134.

Qualified business investments.

Tax credits, §§105-163.010 to 105-163.015.

Rate of tax, §105-134.2(a).

Alternative tax, §105-134.2(b).

Surtax, §105-134.2A(a).

Real property donations, credit, §105-151.12(a).

Amount, §105-151.12(b).

Marshlands, §105-151.12(e).

Partners of partnership qualifying for credit.

Maximum dollar limit, §105-151.12.

Refunds.

Contribution to wildlife conservation account, §105-269.5.

Deduction of tax refunds included in taxpayer's gross income, §105-134.6(b).

Retired federal government workers.

Partial refund or alternative, §105-151.20(c).

Required installments.

Farmer or fisherman, §105-163.15(i).

Rescue squad workers.

Deduction from taxable income, §105-134.6(d).

Residents.

Defined, §105-134.1.

North Carolina taxable income, §105-134.5(a).

Part-year residents.

North Carolina taxable income, §105-134.5(c).

Retired federal government workers.

Credit or partial refund for tax paid on certain federal retirement benefits, §105-151.20.

Retirement benefits.

Defined, §105-134.1.

Retirement plans.

Deduction of amount received from taxable income, §105-134.6(b).

Returns.

Agent filing, §105-152(b).

Corrections and changes, §105-159.

Deceased persons, §105-152(b).

Executors and administrators.

Filing for deceased persons, §105-152(b).

Forms, §105-155(d).

Guardians.

Filing by, §105-152(b).

Husband and wife.

Joint returns, §105-152(e).

Information at the source returns, §105-154.

Time for filing, §105-155(a).

Information required with return, §105-152(c).

Secretary may require additional information, §105-152(d).

Joint returns.

Husband and wife, §105-152(e).

Place of filing, §105-155(a).

Time for filing, §105-155(a).

Extension, §105-155(a).

Who required to file, §105-152(a).

S corporations.

Adjustments to taxable income.

Shareholder's pro rata share or corporate income, §105-134.6(a).

Defined, §105-134.1.

INCOME TAX —Cont'd
Individual income tax —Cont'd
　S corporations —Cont'd
　　Shareholder's pro rata share of corporation's
　　　income, §105-134.5(d).
　　Shareholder's pro rata share or corporate
　　　income.
　　　Adjustments to taxable income, §105-134.6(a).
　Severance wages.
　　Deduction from taxable income, §105-134.6(b).
　Standard deduction amount, §105-134.6(a2).
　Surtax.
　　Expiration, §105-134.2A(b).
　　Impositions, §105-134.2A(a).
　Taxable income.
　　Additions to taxable income, §105-134.6(c).
　　Adjustments to taxable income, §105-134.6.
　　　Transitional adjustments, §105-134.7.
　　Deduction, §105-134.6(b).
　　Inventories, §105-134.8.
　　North Carolina taxable income, §105-134.5.
　　Other adjustments to taxable income,
　　　§105-134.6(d).
　　Personal exemption, §105-134.6(a1).
　　Standard deduction amount, §105-134.6(a2).
　　Transitional adjustments, §105-134.7.
　Taxable year.
　　Computation of state taxable income basis of,
　　　§105-134.5(e).
　Title of act.
　　Short title, §105-133.
　Trusts and estates.
　　Provisions not to apply to, §105-163.15(k).
　Underestimation of taxable income.
　　Penalty for large individual income tax
　　　deficiency, §105-236(a).
　Unmarried individuals.
　　Rate of tax, §105-134.2(a).
　Withholding of income taxes from wages,
　　§§105-163.1 to 105-163.24. See within this
　　heading, "Withholding of income taxes from
　　wages."
　Year of assessment, §105-134.3.
Information at source returns, §105-154.
International banking facility.
　Deductions in determining state net income,
　　§105-130.5(b).
Limited liability companies, §57C-10-06.
　Personal liability for unpaid taxes, §105-242.2(b).
Loans.
　Refund anticipation loans, §§53-245 to 53-254.
Long-term care insurance.
　Credit for premiums paid, §105-151.28(a).
　Double benefit prohibited, §105-151.28(b).
　Qualified long-term care insurance defined,
　　§105-151.28(c).
　Sunset provisions, §105-151.28(d).
Lottery winnings.
　State lottery prizes subject to state income tax,
　　§18C-132(l).
　Withholding taxes from state lottery winnings,
　　§105-163.2B.
Low-income housing tax credits, §§105-129.40 to
　105-129.45.
Marital deduction.
　Fiduciaries.
　　Incorporation by reference of certain powers,
　　　§32-26.
Military affairs.
　Individual income tax.
　　Abatement of income taxes of certain members
　　　of armed forces upon death, §105-158.

INCOME TAX —Cont'd
Municipalities.
　Levy prohibited, §105-247.
Natural and scenic rivers system.
　Contribution or donation of scenic easement.
　　Deemed contribution to state of North Carolina,
　　　§113A-39.
New and expanding businesses.
　Tax incentives generally, §§105-129.2 to
　　105-129.13.
　　See TAX INCENTIVES FOR NEW AND
　　　EXPANDING BUSINESSES.
Nonresident owner or partner.
　Payment of tax on behalf of, §105-154(d).
Oyster shells.
　Credits.
　　Recycling oyster shells, §105-130.48.
Partnerships.
　Credits.
　　Allowance, §105-269.15(b).
　　Distributive share, determination,
　　　§105-269.15(c).
　　Qualification, §105-269.15(a).
　Member's distributive share of business's income,
　　§105-134.5(d).
　Payment of tax on behalf of nonresident partner,
　　§105-154(d).
　Personal liability for unpaid taxes, §105-242.2(b).
　Returns.
　　Information at the source returns, §105-154(c).
　　Publicly traded partnerships, §105-154(e).
　Subject to taxation according to classification,
　　§59-84.1(b).
Pension payments, withholding, §105-163.2A.
Personal liability.
　Unpaid taxes.
　　Responsible persons in business entities,
　　　§105-242.2(b).
Political parties.
　Designation of tax by individual to political party
　　financing fund, §105-159.1.
Ports authority.
　Bond issues.
　　Gain from transfer not exempt from taxation,
　　　§136-265(g).
　Credits.
　　Wharfage, handling and throughput charges,
　　　§§105-130.41(a), 105-151.22(a).
　　Definitions, §§105-130.41(c), 105-151.22(c).
　　Limitation, §§105-130.41(b), 105-151.22(b).
　　Report, §§105-130.41(c1), 105-151.22(c1).
　　Sunset, §§105-130.41(d), 105-151.22(d).
Poultry composting facility.
　Credit for construction, §105-151.25(a).
　Property owned by the entirety, §105-151.25(b).
Principal and income act.
　Allocation of disbursements during administration
　　of trust, §37A-5-505.
Production companies.
　Credit for qualifying expenses, §§105-130.47(b),
　　105-151.29(b).
　　Acknowledgment in production credits.
　　　Required, §105-151.29(j).
　　Alternative credit, §§105-130.47(b1),
　　　105-151.29(b1).
　　Amount, §105-151.29(b).
　　　Limitation, §§105-130.47(f), 105-151.29(f).
　　Burden of proving eligibility, §105-130.47(g).
　　Computation, §105-151.29(b).
　　Definitions, §§105-130.47(a), 105-151.29(a).

INCOME TAX —Cont'd
Production companies —Cont'd
Credit for qualifying expenses —Cont'd
Episodic TV series.
Computation, §105-151.29(b).
Limitations, §§105-130.47(f), 105-151.29(f).
News program or live sporting event, TV
production.
No credit allowed, §§105-130.47(f),
105-151.29(f).
Notice of intent to claim, §105-151.29(j).
Obscene material.
No credit allowed, §§105-130.47(f),
105-151.29(f).
Pass-through entities, §§105-130.47(c),
105-151.29(c).
Political advertising.
No credit allowed, §§105-130.47(f),
105-151.29(f).
Qualifying expenses defined, §§105-130.47(a),
105-151.29(a).
Radio production.
No credit allowed, §§105-130.47(f),
105-151.29(f).
Records required, inspection, §§105-130.47(g),
105-151.29(g).
Refund of excess tax imposed.
Credit exceeding amount of tax imposed,
§§105-130.47(e), 105-151.29(e).
Report, §§105-130.47(h), 105-151.29(h).
Return, claiming credit on, §§105-130.47(d),
105-151.29(d).
Sunset, §§105-130.47(k), 105-151.29(k).
Public campaign fund.
Allocation to fund by individual, §105-159.2(a).
Instructions for individual to designate
allocation, §105-159.2(c).
Returns to give individual opportunity to
designate allocation, §105-159.2(b).
Public works.
Relocation assistance.
Payments not to be considered as income,
§133-15.
Qualified business investment tax credit,
§§105-163.010 to 105-163.015.
Amount of credit allowed, limitation,
§105-163.012(a), (b).
Application for credit, §105-163.011(c).
Brokered investments, no credit, §105-163.011(a).
Carry-over, §105-163.012(a).
Definitions, §105-163.010.
False application, §105-163.014(b).
Forfeiture.
Effect, §105-163.014(e).
False application, §105-163.014(b).
Participation in business, §105-163.014(a).
Transfer or redemption of investment,
§105-163.014(d).
Individuals, §105-163.011(b).
Pass-through entities, §105-163.011(b1).
Penalties, §105-163.011(d).
Qualified business defined, §105-163.010.
Qualified business ventures, §105-163.012(b).
Defined, §105-163.010.
Registration, §105-163.013(b).
Qualified grantee businesses.
Defined, §105-163.010.
Registration, §105-163.013(c).
Qualified licensee business.
Defined, §105-163.010.
Registration, §105-163.013(b1).

INCOME TAX —Cont'd
Qualified business investment tax credit
—Cont'd
Redemption of investment, §105-163.014(d).
Reduction of credit, §105-163.012(c), (d).
Registration.
Application, §105-163.013(d).
Fees, §105-163.013(d).
Qualified business ventures, §105-163.013(b).
Qualified grantee businesses, §105-163.013(c).
Qualified licensee business, §105-163.013(b1).
Report, §105-163.013(g).
Revocation, §105-163.013(e).
Transfer, §105-163.013(f).
Repeal, §105-163.015.
Transfer of investment, §105-163.014(d).
Rate of tax.
Limitation, NC Const Art V §2.
Real estate investment trusts, §105-130.12.
Reciprocity.
Withholding of income taxes from wages,
§105-163.22.
Recycling facilities.
Tax credit for major recycling facility investment,
§§105-129.25 to 105-129.28.
Refunds.
Action taken by department, time limitations,
§105-241.7(c).
Anticipation loans.
Appeals.
Decision of commissioner, §53-252.
Cease and desist orders, §53-251(a).
Commissioner.
Appeal of decisions, §53-252.
Definitions, §53-246.
Disclosures, §53-249(d).
Enforcement of article, §53-253.
Exemptions from article, §53-254.
Facilitator of loans.
Prohibited activities, §53-250.
Fees.
Filing of fee schedule, §53-249(a).
Notice of unconscionable fee, §53-249(b).
Posting of schedule, §53-249(c).
Informal hearings, §53-248(d).
Penalties.
Civil penalty, §53-251(c).
Failure to register, §53-247(b).
Prohibited activities, §53-250.
Registration.
Display of certificate, §53-248(c).
Exemptions, §53-247(c).
Failure to register.
Penalties, §53-247(b).
Initial registration, §53-248(a).
Renewal, §53-248(b).
Required, §53-247(a).
Revocation, §53-251(b).
Rules and regulations.
Promulgation, §53-253.
Scope of article, §53-245(b).
Title of article, §53-245(a).
Circumstances requiring initiation by department,
§105-241.7(a).
Effect of denial, §105-241.7(f).
Individual income tax.
Contribution to wildlife conservation account,
§105-269.5.
Deduction of tax refunds included in taxpayer's
gross income, §105-134.6(b).
Initiation by department, §105-241.7(a).

INCOME TAX —Cont'd
Refunds —Cont'd
  Initiation by taxpayer, §105-241.7(b).
  Notice of denial, §105-241.7(d).
  Restoration of item of income.
    Included in taxpayer's gross income for earlier
      taxable year, §105-266.2.
  Restrictions on granting, §105-241.7(e).
  Statute of limitations for obtaining.
    Actions taken by department upon request,
      §105-241.7(c).
    Exceptions, §105-241.6(b).
    Time period, §105-241.6(a).
Renewable energy.
  Renewable energy investment tax credit,
    §105-129.16A.
  Renewable energy property.
    Donation to nonprofit organization or
      government unit to acquire, §105-129.16H.
  Renewable energy property facilities,
    §105-129.16I.
Research and development tax credit,
  §§105-129.50 to 105-129.56.
Responsible persons in business entities.
  Personal liability.
    Unpaid taxes, §105-242.2(b).
Restrictions and limitations, NC Const Art V §2.
Retired federal government workers.
  Individual income tax.
    Credit or partial refund for tax paid on certain
      federal retirement benefits, §105-151.20.
Returns.
  Corporations, §105-130.16.
    Consolidated or combined returns, §105-130.14.
      Amount of tax shown as due not deficiency,
        §105-236(a).
      Intercompany transactions lacking economic
        substance or fair market value.
        Combined return required, §105-130.5A.
    Dissolution or withdrawal from state, time for
      filing, §105-130.17(e).
    Exempt organizations, filing, §105-130.17(d1).
    Extension of time to file, §105-130.17(d).
    Filing, §105-130.17(a).
      Time for filing, §105-130.17(b) to (g).
    Intercompany transactions lacking economic
      substance or fair market value.
      Combined return required, §105-130.5A.
    Marketing associations, §105-130.17(c).
    Mutual associations to conduct agricultural
      business, §105-130.17(c).
    S corporations, §105-131.7.
    Short period.
      Change of income year, §105-130.15(b).
    Time for filing, §105-130.17(b) to (g).
  Failure to file tax return, penalty, §105-236(a).
  Frivolous return, filing, penalty, §105-236(a).
  Individuals.
    Agent filing, §105-152(b).
    Corrections and changes, §105-159.
    Deceased persons, §105-152(b).
    Executors and administrators.
      Filing for deceased persons, §105-152(b).
    Forms, §105-155(d).
    Guardians.
      Filing by, §105-152(b).
    Husband and wife.
      Joint returns, §105-152(e).
    Information at the source returns, §105-154.
    Information required with return, §105-152(c).
      Secretary may require additional information,
        §105-152(d).

INCOME TAX —Cont'd
Returns —Cont'd
  Individuals —Cont'd
    Joint returns.
      Husband and wife, §105-152(e).
    Place of filing, §105-155(a).
    Time for, §105-155(a).
    Who required to file, §105-152(a).
  Information at the source returns.
    Foreign corporation filing.
      Not evidence of doing business in state,
        §105-154(b).
    Information required.
      Persons required to file, §105-154(b).
      Return to contain, §105-154(b).
    Nonresident owner or partner.
      Payment of tax on behalf of, §105-154(d).
    Partnerships, §105-154(c).
      Publicly traded partnerships, §105-154(e).
  Partnerships.
    Information at the source returns, §105-154(c).
    Publicly traded partnerships, §105-154(e).
Royalty payments for use of trademarks.
  Corporations.
    Optional methods for reporting income,
      §105-130.7A.
S corporations.
  Adjustment of basis, §105-131.3.
  Adjustment of income, §105-131.2(a).
  Adjustment to taxable income.
    Shareholder's pro rata share of corporation's
      income, §105-134.6(a).
  Carrybacks.
    Restrictions, §105-131.4(a).
  Carryforwards.
    Restrictions, §105-131.4(a).
  Citation of division, §105-131(a).
  Corporation exempt from corporate income tax,
    §105-131.1(a).
  Credits, §105-131.8.
  Definitions, §§105-131(b), 105-134.1.
  Distribution, §105-131.6.
  Dividends.
    Distributions to shareholders, §105-131.6.
  Interpretation of division, §105-131(c).
  Losses and reduction.
    Restrictions amount, §105-131.4(b) to (d).
  Net income.
    Characterization of income, §105-131.2(c).
    Shareholders.
      Pro rate share of net income, §105-131.1(b).
  Payments.
    Agreements by nonresident shareholders to file
      return and pay tax, §105-131.7(c) to (e).
    Composite payments, §105-131.7(b).
  Returns, §105-131.7(a).
    Agreements by nonresident shareholders to file
      return and pay tax, §105-131.7(c) to (e).
    Composite returns, §105-131.7(b).
  Shareholders.
    Agreements by nonresidents to file return and
      pay tax, §105-131.7(c) to (e).
    Basis, §§105-131.3, 105-131.3(a).
    Acquisition received by gift, time,
      §105-131.3(g).
    Adjustment, §105-131.3(b).
      Nonresident, §105-131.3(d).
    Nonresident, §105-131.3(c).
      Adjustment, §105-131.3(d).
    Reduction, §105-131.3(e), (f).

INCOME TAX —Cont'd
S corporations —Cont'd
Shareholders —Cont'd
Credits, §§105-131.8, 105-131.8(b).
Taxes paid to other states, §105-131.8(a).
Distributions to shareholders.
Accumulated adjustments account,
§105-131.6(c).
Adjusted basis of stock defined, §105-131.6(c).
Taxable distributions, §105-131.6(a), (b).
Dividends.
Distributions to shareholders, §105-131.6.
Part-year resident shareholder, §105-131.5.
Pro rate share of net income, §105-131.1(b).
Shareholder's pro rata share of corporation's
income, §105-134.5(d).
Adjustments to, §105-134.6(a).
Short title, §105-131(a).
Small business unemployment insurance
refundable tax credit.
Amount of credit, §105-129.16J(a).
Applicability, §105-129.16J(c).
Refundable amount, §105-129.16J(b).
Special education and related services.
Education expenses credit, §105-151.33.
State bonds, act authorizing issuance not
addressing exemption from taxation.
Not exempt on gain from transfer of instrument,
§142-12.
State lottery winnings.
Prizes subject to state income tax, §18C-132(l).
Withholding taxes from state lottery winnings,
§105-163.2B.
State refunding obligations.
Gain from transfer not exempt from taxation,
§142-29.6(f).
Surtax.
Corporations.
Expiration, §105-130.3B(b).
Imposition, §105-130.3B(a).
Tax incentives for new and expanding
businesses generally, §§105-129.2 to
105-129.13.
See TAX INCENTIVES FOR NEW AND
EXPANDING BUSINESSES.
Telephone service to low-income residents at
reduced rates.
Credits.
Credit to corporation providing, §105-130.39(a),
(b).
Tenants by the entireties.
Husband and wife.
Control of real property held in tenancy by the
entirety, §39-13.6(c).
Trusts and trustees.
Estates and trusts generally, §§105-160 to
105-160.8. See within this heading, "Estates
and trusts."
Individual income tax.
Estimated tax.
Provisions not to apply to estates or trusts,
§105-163.15(k).
Unemployment compensation.
Small business unemployment insurance
refundable tax credit, §105-129.16J.
Withholding of income tax from unemployment
compensation, §96-12(g).
United States.
Withholding from federal employees, §105-163.23.
Wildlife.
Individual income tax refund.
Contribution to wildlife conservation account,
§105-269.5.

INCOME TAX —Cont'd
Withholding of income taxes from state lottery
winnings, §105-163.2B.
Withholding of income taxes from wages,
§§105-163.1 to 105-163.24.
Amount withheld, §105-163.2(a).
Calculating employee's anticipated income tax
liability, §105-163.2(a).
Clergymen.
Ordained or licensed clergymen may elect to be
an employee, §105-163.1A.
Construction and interpretation.
Liberal construction of provisions, §105-163.24.
Crediting of amounts withheld to individual for
calendar year, §105-163.10.
Definitions, §105-163.1.
Employer required to deduct and to withhold,
§105-163.2(a).
Estimated withholding, §105-163.2(d).
Exemptions.
Allowable exemptions, §105-163.5(a).
Certificates, §105-163.5(b), (c), (e).
New withholding exemption certificate,
§105-163.5(d).
Federal corrections, §105-163.6A.
Federal employees, §105-163.23.
Information to secretary.
Required, §105-163.7(b).
Liability of withholding agents and others.
Others, §105-163.8.
Withholding agents, §105-163.8.
Miscellaneous payroll period, §105-163.2(c).
Nonresident withholding agent's act in compliance
with provisions.
Not evidence that nonresident doing business in
state, §105-163.4.
Other persons withholding.
Liability, §105-163.8.
Overpayment.
Refund, §§105-163.9, 105-163.16.
Payment of amounts withheld, §105-163.6(a).
Categories, §105-163.6(e).
Monthly, §105-163.6(c).
Quarterly payments, §105-163.6(b).
Refund of overpayment, §§105-163.9,
105-163.16.
Payors paying contractors' certain amount
required to withhold, §105-163.3(a).
Annual statement, report to secretary,
§105-163.3(d).
Exemptions, §105-163.3(b).
Records, §105-163.3(e).
Repaying amounts withheld improperly,
§105-163.3(f).
Returns, filing, §105-163.3(c).
Penalty for improper withholding, §105-163.5(f).
Pension payers must withhold taxes,
§105-163.2A(b).
Amount withheld, §105-163.2A(c).
Definitions, §105-163.2A(a).
Election by recipient not to have taxes withheld,
§105-163.2A(d).
Exempted pension payments, §105-163.2A(e).
Liability for withholding and payment of taxes,
§105-163.2A(b).
More than one arrangement for making
payments.
Separate treatment for each arrangement,
§105-163.2A(b).
Nonperiodic distribution, amount withheld,
§105-163.2A(c).

INCOME TAX —Cont'd
Withholding of income taxes from wages —Cont'd
Pension payers must withhold taxes —Cont'd
Notice to recipient of right to elect not to withhold, §105-163.2A(d).
Periodic payment, amount withheld, §105-163.2A(c).
Residents of state, applicability of provisions, §105-163.2A(b).
Reciprocity, §105-163.22.
Refund to employer, §105-163.9.
Returns.
Federal corrections, §105-163.6A.
When employer must file return, §105-163.6(a).
Categories, §105-163.6(e).
Monthly, §105-163.6(c).
Quarterly, §105-163.6(b).
Semiweekly, §105-163.6(d).
Statement to employees.
Required, §105-163.7(a), (b).
Tables and rules adopted by secretary, §105-163.2(b).
Alternatives to tables, §105-163.2(b).
Alternative tables, §105-163.2(e).
Withholding agents.
Liability, §105-163.8.
Withholding of income tax from unemployment compensation, §96-12(g).
Work opportunity tax credit, §105-129.16G.

INCOME TAX CHECKOFFS.
Refund contributions.
Wildlife conservation account, §105-269.5.

INCOME TAX RETURN PREPARERS.
Defined, §105-228.90(b).
Designation of tax by individual to political party.
Preparer not to designate, §105-159.1(e).
Fraudulently evading tax on return.
Aiding or assisting, penalty, §105-236(a).
Unauthorized disclosure of tax information, §75-28.

INCOME WITHHOLDING.
Alimony.
Limitation on amount withheld, §110-136.6(b1).
Child support.
Assignment of wages, §110-136.1.
Employer reporting to directory of new hires.
Notice to employer to withhold, §110-129.2(f).
Garnishment.
Continuing wage garnishment proceedings, §110-136.6(b), (b1).
Wage garnishment order, §110-136.
Generally, §§110-136.3 to 110-136.14.
See CHILD SUPPORT.
Interstate family support act, §§52C-5-501 to 52C-5-507.
See INTERSTATE FAMILY SUPPORT.
National medical support notice, §§110-136.11 to 110-136.14.
Unemployment compensation benefits, §110-136.2(f).
Garnishment.
Child support.
Continuing wage garnishment proceedings, §110-136.6(b), (b1).
Wage garnishment order, §110-136.
Withholding of income generally, §§110-136.3 to 110-136.14.
See CHILD SUPPORT.

INCOME WITHHOLDING —Cont'd
Garnishment —Cont'd
Wages.
Limitation on wage garnishment, §1-362.
Income tax.
Withholding of income taxes from wages, §§105-163.1 to 105-163.24.
See INCOME TAX.
Withholding of income tax from unemployment compensation, §96-12(g).
Interstate family support act, §§52C-5-501 to 52C-5-507.
See INTERSTATE FAMILY SUPPORT.
Postseparation support.
Limitation on amount withheld, §110-136.6(b1).
Public officers and employees.
Annuity contracts.
Salary deductions, §147-9.3.
Insurance.
Payroll deduction.
Competitive selection of products, §58-31-60(c).
Repayment of money owed to state, §§143-552 to 143-562.
See PUBLIC OFFICERS AND EMPLOYEES.
Public schools.
Employees.
Repayment of money owed state, §§143-552 to 143-554.
Retirement system for teachers and state employees.
Consolidated judicial retirement act.
Contributions by members, §135-68(a), (b).
Social security.
Coverage under Title II of social security act.
Contributions by state employees, §135-22.
Supplemental retirement income act.
Contributions, §135-93.

INCOMPETENCY.
Administration of estates, costs.
Additional costs assessed before clerk, §7A-307(d).
Assessment of costs, §7A-307(a).
Completeness and exclusivity of costs, §7A-307(c).
Courtroom and related judicial facilities.
Amount of facilities fee, §7A-307(b).
Use of facilities, §7A-307(a).
General court of justice.
Support of court, §7A-307(a).
Liability of parties for costs, §7A-307(e).
Custodial trusts.
Determination on incapacity of beneficiary, §33B-10.
Generally, §§33B-1 to 33B-22.
See CUSTODIAL TRUSTS.
Default judgment against incompetent person.
Appointment of guardian ad litem.
Required for entry of judgment against, §1A-1 Rule 55(b).
Determination of incompetence, §§35A-1101 to 35A-1116.
Adjudication orders, §35A-1112(d).
Affidavit.
Proving mailing of notice and petition, §35A-1109.
Appeal from order adjudicating incompetence, §35A-1115.
Appointment of guardian, §35A-1120.
Appointment of guardian following adjudication, §35A-1112(e).
Appointment of interim guardian, §35A-1114.

INCOMPETENCY —Cont'd
Determination of incompetence —Cont'd
Attorney general to represent petitioner on appeal
    by respondent.
  Court of appeals may request, §35A-1115.
Attorneys' fees, §35A-1116(a).
  Court-appointed counsel, §35A-1116(c).
Autism defined, §35A-1101.
Cerebral palsy defined, §35A-1101.
Certificate of acceptance.
  Proving mailing of notice and petition,
    §35A-1109.
Certified copy of adjudication sent to clerk in
    county of ward's legal residence, §35A-1112(f).
Change of venue, §35A-1104.
Clerk of superior court.
  Original jurisdiction over proceedings,
    §35A-1103(a).
    Clerk having interest in proceedings,
      jurisdiction vested in superior court
      judge, §35A-1103(d).
  Transfer of proceedings, exceptions, §1-301.2(g).
Continuance of hearing.
  Multidisciplinary evaluation ordered,
    §35A-1108(b).
Costs.
  Applicability to all parties to any proceeding
    under chapter, §35A-1116(d).
  Assessment in taxing, §35A-1116(a).
  Multidisciplinary evaluation, §35A-1116(b).
  Witness fees and fees of court-appointed counsel
    or guardian ad litem, §35A-1116(c).
Definitions, §35A-1101.
Dismissal of proceedings.
  Finder of fact not finding respondent
    incompetent, §35A-1112(c).
  Voluntary dismissal, §35A-1112(g).
  Appointment of interim guardian,
    §35A-1114(f).
Epilepsy defined, §35A-1101.
Exclusive procedure for adjudicating person to be
    incompetent adult or incompetent child,
    §35A-1102.
Guardian ad litem.
  Attorney as guardian ad litem, §35A-1107(a),
    (b).
  Fees of court-appointed guardian ad litem,
    §35A-1116(c1).
Hearing.
  Appointment of interim guardian, §35A-1114(c),
    (d).
  Dismissal if finder of fact does not find
    respondent incompetent, §35A-1112(c).
  Incompetence determined in another state,
    §35A-1113.
  Open to public unless respondent requests
    otherwise, §35A-1112(a).
  Place of hearing, §35A-1112(a).
  Rights of petitioner and respondent,
    §35A-1112(b).
  Time for holding, §35A-1108(a).
    Extension if multidisciplinary evaluation
      ordered, §35A-1108(b).
Incompetence determined in another state.
  Hearing, §35A-1113.
Incompetent adult defined, §35A-1101.
Incompetent child defined, §35A-1101.
Indigent defined, §35A-1101.
Inebriety defined, §35A-1101.
Interim guardian, appointment.
  Bond, posting, §35A-1114(e).

INCOMPETENCY —Cont'd
Determination of incompetence —Cont'd
Interim guardian, appointment —Cont'd
  Hearing, §35A-1114(c), (d).
  Notice of hearing, §35A-1114(c).
  Order appointing, §35A-1114(d), (e).
  Termination of guardianship, §35A-1114(e).
  Verified motion, filing, §35A-1114(a).
    Contents, §35A-1114(b).
  Voluntary dismissal of petition of adjudication
    of incompetence, §35A-1114(f).
Jurisdiction over proceedings under subchapter.
  Clerk of superior court has original jurisdiction,
    §35A-1103(a).
Jury trial, right to, §35A-1110.
Mailing notice and petition to respondent,
    §35A-1109.
Mediator.
  Fees, §35A-1116(c2).
Mental illness defined, §35A-1101.
Mental retardation defined, §35A-1101.
Multidisciplinary evaluation.
  Clerk may order respondent to attend,
    §35A-1111(d).
  Consideration at hearing for adjudication of
    incompetence, §35A-1111(e).
  Costs, §35A-1116(b).
  Defined, §35A-1101.
  Designated agency to prepare or assemble,
    §35A-1111(b).
  Evaluation not containing medical,
    psychological or social work evaluations,
    filing, §35A-1111(c).
  Evaluation not to be public record,
    §35A-1111(b).
  Extension of time for hearing upon ordering,
    §35A-1108(b).
  Requesting and ordering evaluations,
    §35A-1111(a).
  Time for filing with clerk, §35A-1111(b).
Notice of hearing.
  Appointment of interim guardian, §35A-1114(c).
  Service, §35A-1109.
  Time clerk to file, §35A-1108(a).
Notices, service of subsequent notices,
    §35A-1108(c).
Order adjudicating respondent incompetent,
    §35A-1112(d).
Petition, verification, §35A-1105.
  Contents, §35A-1106.
  Service, §35A-1109.
Restoration to competency, §35A-1130.
Right to counsel, §35A-1107(a).
Right to jury, §35A-1110.
Service of application for appointment of guardian
    when joined with petition for adjudication of
    incompetence, §35A-1211(b).
Service of notice of hearing in petition, §35A-1109.
Service of subsequent notices to parties,
    §35A-1108.
Sheriff to serve notice and petition without
    demanding fees in advance, §35A-1109.
Stay of appointment of guardian.
  Appeal of order adjudicating incompetence,
    §35A-1115.
Superior court judges jurisdiction.
  Clerk having interest in proceedings,
    §35A-1103(d).
Transfer of proceeding for appointment of
    guardian, §35A-1112(e).

INCOMPETENCY —Cont'd
Determination of incompetence —Cont'd
Venue for proceedings, §35A-1103(b).
Change of venue, §35A-1104.
Proceedings involving same respondent brought in more than one county, §35A-1103(c).
Voluntary dismissal, §35A-1112(g).
Interim appointment of guardian, §35A-1114(f).
Witness fees, §35A-1116(c).
Durable power of attorney.
Incapacity or incompetence of principal.
Generally, §§32A-8 to 32A-14.
See DURABLE POWER OF ATTORNEY.
Guardians.
Generally.
See GUARDIAN AND WARD.
Insurance proceeds or money belonging to incapacitated adult.
Payment to and receipt by clerks of superior courts or public guardians, §7A-111(b), (d).
Judicial sales.
Confirmation of public sale of real property, §1-339.28(b).
Mental health, developmental disability, substance abuse.
See MENTAL HEALTH, DEVELOPMENTAL DISABILITY, SUBSTANCE ABUSE.
Restoration to competency.
Accounts from guardian, filing an approval, §35A-1130(e).
Appeal from clerks order denying petition, §35A-1130(f).
Discharge of guardian, §35A-1130(e).
Guardian ad litem.
Appointment, §35A-1130(c).
Hearing, §35A-1130(c).
Setting for hearing, §35A-1130(b).
Jury trial, §35A-1130(c).
Motion, §35A-1130(a).
Multidisciplinary evaluation, §35A-1130(c).
Order adjudicating restoration to competency, §35A-1130(d).
Order denying petition, §35A-1130(f).
Right to representation by counsel or guardian ad litem, §35A-1130(c).
Service of notice and motion on guardian and ward, §35A-1130(b).

INCOMPETENCY ADJUDICATION, §§35A-1101 to 35A-1116.
See INCOMPETENCY.

INCONVENIENT FORUM.
Change of venue, §1-83.
Child abuse, neglect or dependency proceeding.
Transferring case to another county.
After adjudication, §7B-900.1(a).
Stay of proceeding to permit trial in foreign jurisdiction, §1-75.12.

INCORPORATION.
Business corporations.
Formation generally.
See CORPORATIONS.
Commercial banks, §§53-2 to 53-17.2.
See BANKS.
Municipalities.
General assembly to provide for local government, NC Const Art VII §1.
Joint legislative committee on local government.
Municipal incorporations subcommittee, §§120-158 to 120-174.

INCORPORATION —Cont'd
Nonprofit corporations.
Formation generally.
See NONPROFIT CORPORATIONS.

INCORPOREAL HEREDITAMENTS.
Limitation of actions.
Injury to, §1-50(a).

INCRIMINATION.
Self-incrimination generally.
See SELF-INCRIMINATION.

INDECENCY.
Obscenity.
General provisions, §§14-190.1 to 14-190.20.
See OBSCENITY AND PORNOGRAPHY.

INDECENT EXPOSURE, §14-190.9.
Breastfeeding excluded from definition, §14-190.9(b).
Elements of offense, §14-190.9(a), (a1).
Local government regulation, §14-190.9(c).
Sex offenses generally.
See SEX OFFENSES.

INDECENT LIBERTIES BETWEEN CHILDREN.
Elements of offense, §14-202.2(a).
Misdemeanor offense, §14-202.2(b).

INDECENT LIBERTIES WITH A MINOR.
Bail, §15A-534.4.
Electronic surveillance orders, §15A-290(c1).
Elements of offense, §14-202.1(a).
Felony offense, §14-202.1(b).

INDEMNIFICATION.
Abandoned and junked vehicle removal and disposal.
Abandoned junked vehicle.
Municipalities, §160A-303.2(a2).
Private property.
Municipalities, §160A-303(c).
Business corporations.
Additional indemnification, §55-8-57(a), (b).
Agents, §55-8-56.
Articles of incorporation.
Restrictions on indemnification, §55-8-58(a).
Conflicts of interest.
Court-ordered indemnification, §55-8-54.
Expenses.
Certain powers of corporation not limited, §55-8-58(b).
Evaluation as to reasonableness, §55-8-55(c).
Expenses in defending proceedings.
Advance for expenses, §55-8-53.
Indemnification not void or voidable on grounds of, §55-8-51(f).
Mandatory indemnification, §55-8-52.
Restrictions on indemnification, §55-8-51(d), (e).
Court-ordered indemnification.
Directors, §55-8-54.
Directors.
Advance for expenses, §55-8-53.
Authority to indemnify, §55-8-51(a) to (c).
Determinations required, §55-8-55(a), (b).
Manner of authorization, §55-8-55(c).
Effective date of article.
Restriction on applicability of provisions, §55-8-58(c).
Employees, §55-8-56.
Insurance.
Purchase and maintenance, §55-8-57(c).

INDEMNIFICATION —Cont'd
Business corporations —Cont'd
Mandatory indemnification.
Directors, §55-8-52.
Officers, employees and agents, §55-8-56.
Officers, §55-8-56.
Community third party or pooled trusts.
Board members, §36D-4(b).
Construction indemnity agreements, §22B-1.
Contribution.
Joint tort-feasors.
Right of indemnity not impaired, §1B-1(f).
Electric membership corporations.
Directors, officers, employees and agents, §117-46.
Executors and administrators.
Rights of surety in danger of loss, §28A-8-5.
Farm machinery franchises.
Supplier to indemnify dealer against judgment for
damages or settlement, §66-187(b).
Fraternal benefit societies.
Officers, directors, employees or agents,
§58-24-35(b).
**Improvement to real property defective or
unsafe.**
Limitation of action for indemnification, §1-50(a).
Insurance agents.
Credit information or credit scores of insurer
used.
Action, error or omission from use, §58-36-90(e).
**Interstate insurance product regulation
compact.**
Commission, §58-91-25(e).
**Limited liability company managers, directors,
executives and members, §57C-3-31.**
Permissive indemnification, §57C-3-32(a).
Livestock.
Diseased animals.
Compensation for killing.
Owner's claim for indemnity supported by
reports, §106-334.
Hog cholera.
Destruction of swine affected with or exposed to
hog cholera, §106-322.2.
When indemnity payments not to be made,
§106-322.3.
**Local boards of education members or
employees.**
Paying judgment against member or employee,
§115C-43(b), (c).
Motor vehicle dealers.
Dealer management computer systems.
Request for information from dealer,
§20-305.7(g2).
Nonprofit corporations.
Additional indemnification and insurance,
§55A-8-57.
Advance for expenses, §55A-8-53.
Agents, §55A-8-56.
Applicability of part, §55A-8-58.
Authority to indemnify, §55A-8-51.
Authorization of indemnification and evaluation to
reasonableness of expenses, §55A-8-55.
Court-ordered indemnification, §55A-8-54.
Definitions, §55A-8-50(b).
Determination, §55A-8-55.
Directors.
Notice to members, §55A-16-21.
Employees, §55A-8-56.
Expenses.
Advance for expenses, §55A-8-53.
Insurance, §55A-8-57.

INDEMNIFICATION —Cont'd
Nonprofit corporations —Cont'd
Mandatory indemnification, §55A-8-52.
Officers, §55A-8-56.
Policy statement, §55A-8-50(a).
Powers generally, §55A-8-51.
Oil and gas conservation.
Landowner protection.
Indemnification of surface owner for damage to
adjacent property, §113-422.
Partnerships.
When partnership must indemnify partner,
§59-48.
Public policy.
Construction indemnity agreements invalid,
§22B-1.
Savings and loan associations.
Blanket indemnity bond, §54B-109(a).
Fines and penalties.
Indemnification of persons fined or penalized.
Prohibited, §54B-72.
Rules and regulations, §54B-109(f).
Unauthorized investments.
Indemnity bond, §54B-109(c), (d).
Withdrawable accounts.
New account books.
Loss that might result from issuance,
§54B-134.
Savings banks.
Fines or penalties.
Reimbursement or indemnification prohibited,
§54C-85.
Structural pest control.
Financial responsibility, §106-65.37(a).
Telephone membership corporations.
Directors, officers, employees and agents, §117-46.
Trust companies.
Directors.
Surety and indemnity bond, §53-358(a), (b).

INDEPENDENCE DAY.
Public holiday, §103-4(a).

INDEXES.
Clerks of superior courts.
Immediate indexing.
Documents received for docketing, §7A-109(c).
Minimum criteria, §7A-109(b).
Record-keeping requirements generally,
§7A-109(a) to (e).
General assembly.
Journals indexed by clerks, §120-28.
Local legislation.
Published by division of publications, §147-54.1.
Session laws, §120-34(b).
Judgments, §1-233.
Motor vehicles.
Registration records, §20-56(a).
Stolen vehicles.
Index of seized, stolen or recovered vehicles.
Examination of receipt of application for
registration, §20-55.
Public lands.
Grants.
Index system for grants, §146-44.
Record of surveys, §§146-40 to 146-42.
Registers of deeds.
Indexing procedures, §161-14.2.
Board of county commissioners may require
transcribing and indexing of books, §161-18.
General index, §161-21.

INDEXES —Cont'd
Registers of deeds —Cont'd
Indexing procedures —Cont'd
Index and cross-index of immediate prior
owners of land, §161-22.1.
Index of registered instrument, §161-22.
Land records management.
Minimum standards for, §161-22.3.
Parcel identifier number indexes, §161-22.2.
Public lands.
Entries.
Record of surveys, §§146-40 to 146-42.
Registered instruments, §161-22.
Standards.
Land records management, §161-22.3.
Secretary of state.
Public lands.
Index system for grants, §146-44.
Torrens system registration.
Cross-indexing of lands by register of deeds,
§43-14.

INDEXING JUDGMENTS, §1-233.

INDIAN BEACH.
All-terrain vehicles.
Use by employees on certain highways,
§20-171.24.
Eminent domain.
Exercise of power, purposes, modified provisions,
§40A-3(b1).
Vesting of title and right to possession,
§40A-42(a).

INDIAN DAY.
Designation, §147-18.

INDIAN HOUSING AUTHORITY, §§157-66 to
157-70.
Applicability of chapter, §157-67.
Appointment, §157-68.
Area of operation, §157-69.
Commission of Indian affairs.
Authority, §157-67.
Composition, §157-68.
Creation, §157-66.
Governor.
Powers, §157-67.
Powers.
General provisions, §157-67.
Rentals.
Applicability of section, §§157-29, 157-70.
Tenants.
Selection, §§157-29, 157-70.
Vacancy, §157-68.

INDIANS.
See NATIVE AMERICANS.

INDIAN SOLIDARITY WEEK.
Designation, §103-8.

INDICTMENTS.
Accomplices and accessories.
Before the fact accessories.
Accessory before fact punishable as principal
felon, §14-5.2.
Attorneys at law.
Unauthorized practice of law.
Duty of district attorney to indict persons upon
receipt of information of violation, §84-7.
Breaking and entering.
Habitual breaking and entering status offense.
Requirements, §14-7.28(b).

INDICTMENTS —Cont'd
Breaking and entering —Cont'd
Habitual breaking and entering status offense
—Cont'd
Separate indictments, §14-7.28(a).
Bribery of officials.
Public officers and employees, §14-217(b).
Bullet-proof vests.
Defendant wearing or having in possession during
commission of felony.
Allegations, §15A-1340.16C(c).
Capital punishment.
Waiver.
Indictment may not be waived in capital case,
§15A-642(b).
Child support.
District attorneys.
Reports to district attorneys of aid to dependent
children and illegitimate births.
Criminal offenses, §15-155.2(b).
Consolidation of charges, §15A-643.
Constitution of North Carolina.
Modes of prosecution, NC Const Art I §22.
Right of accused to be informed of accusation, NC
Const Art I §23.
Constitution of the United States, US Const
Amd 5.
Contents, §15A-644(a).
Corporations.
Securing attendance of organizations as
defendants, §15A-773.
Defective indictments.
Limitation on subsequent prosecution for same
offense, §15-1.
Definitions.
Defects which do not vitiate, §15-155.
Generally, §15A-641(a).
Dismissal.
Motion to dismiss.
Grounds, §15A-955.
Domestic violence.
Violation of valid protective order as felony,
§50B-4.1(e).
Embezzlement.
Description in bill for embezzlement of money,
§15-150.
Enhanced sentence.
Bullet-proof vests.
Defendant wearing or having in possession
during commission of felony.
Allegations, §15A-1340.16C(c).
Firearm or deadly weapon.
Use or display during commission of felony.
Allegations, §15A-1340.16A(d).
Methamphetamine manufacture.
Serious injury inflicted on law enforcement or
emergency personnel.
Allegations, §15A-1340.16D(b).
False pretenses and cheats.
Sufficiency, §14-100(a).
Firearms.
Unlawful possession by felon, §14-415.1(c).
Use or display during commission of felony.
Enhanced sentence.
Allegations, §15A-1340.16A(d).
Forgery.
Intent to defraud.
Sufficiency of allegation, §15-151.
Forms.
Defects which do not vitiate, §15-155.

INDICTMENTS —Cont'd
Forms —Cont'd
Informality.
Bill or warrant not quashed for informality,
§15-153.
Perjury.
Bill for perjury, §15-145.
Fraud.
Intent to defraud.
Sufficiency of allegation, §15-151.
Grand jury.
Confidentiality of information.
Bill of indictment, §15A-623(f).
Foreman.
Signature, §15A-644(a).
Notice.
True bill of indictment.
Notice to defendant, §15A-630.
Number of members required to concur,
§15A-623(a).
Return of bill of indictment, §15A-628(a), (c).
Not true bill, §15A-628(a).
Institution of new charge, §15A-629(b).
Procedure upon finding of not true bill,
§15A-629(a).
True bill, §15A-628(a).
Notice to defendant, §15A-630.
Submission of bill of indictment by prosecutor,
§15A-627(a).
Offenses within original jurisdiction of superior
court, §15A-627(b).
True bill.
Return as not true bill, §15A-628(a).
Institution of new charge, §15A-629(b).
Procedure upon, §15A-629(a).
Return as true bill, §15A-628(a).
Notice to defendant, §15A-630.
Validity inquiry.
Testimony of jurors, §8C-1 Rule 606.
Venue to present or indict, §15A-631.
Habitual felons, §§14-7.2, 14-7.3.
Violent habitual felons, §14-7.9.
Hazing.
Self-incriminating testimony.
No indictment to be founded on
self-incriminating testimony, §14-38.
Homicide.
Essentials of bill for homicide, §15-144.
Impeachment.
Effect of impeachment, §123-13.
Informality.
Bill or warrant not quashed for informality,
§15-153.
Joinder.
Offenses and defendants, §15A-643.
Joint tenants and tenants in common.
Manner of alleging joint ownership of property,
§15-148.
Jury.
Reading of indictment to prospective jurors or to
jury.
Prohibited, §15A-1221(b).
Larceny.
Description in bill for larceny of money, §15-149.
Separate offenses.
Charging in same indictment, §15-151.
Life imprisonment without parole.
Second or subsequent conviction of class B1
felony, §15A-1340.16B(d).
Manslaughter.
Essentials of bill, §15-144.

INDICTMENTS —Cont'd
Methamphetamine manufacture.
Serious injury inflicted on law enforcement or
emergency personnel.
Enhanced sentence.
Allegations, §15A-1340.16D(b).
Money.
Description of money.
Bill for embezzlement, §15-150.
Bill for larceny, §15-149.
Murder.
Essentials of bill, §15-144.
Necessity, US Const Amd 5.
Organizations or groups, §15A-773.
Partnerships.
Securing attendance of organizations as
defendants, §15A-773.
Perjury.
Form of bill for perjury, §15-145.
Subornation of perjury.
Sufficiency of bill, §15-146.
**Pleadings in felony cases and misdemeanor
cases initiated in supreme court division.**
Amendment.
No amendment of indictment, §15A-923(e).
Form of indictment, §15A-923(b).
Prosecution on indictment, §15A-923(a).
Waiver of indictment, §15A-923(c).
Plea of guilty or no contest in district court,
§15A-644.1.
Previous convictions.
Allegations, §15A-645.
Property.
Joint ownership of property.
Manner of alleging, §15-148.
Quashing.
Defects which do not vitiate, §15-155.
Informality.
Bill or warrant not quashed for informality,
§15-153.
Rape.
Essentials of bill, §15-144.1(a).
Age.
Victim female child under age of 13,
§15-144.1(b).
Mentally ill.
Victim mentally defective or incapacitated,
§15-144.1(c).
Minors.
Victim female child under 13, §15-144.1(b).
Physically helpless victim, §15-144.1(c).
Sexual offenses.
Essentials of bill, §15-144.2(a).
Age.
Victim 13 years of age or less, §15-144.2(b).
Mentally ill.
Victim mentally defective or incapacitated,
§15-144.2(c).
Minors.
Victim age 13 or less, §15-144.2(b).
Physically helpless victim, §15-144.2(c).
Signatures.
Required signatures, §15A-644(a).
Stolen goods.
Receiving stolen goods.
Charging with separate offenses in same
indictment, §15-151.
Subornation of perjury.
Sufficiency of bill, §15-146.
Superior court.
Prosecutions originating in superior court to be
upon indictment or information, §15A-642(a).

INDICTMENTS —Cont'd

Superseding indictments, §15A-646.

Time.

Defects which do not vitiate, §15-155.

Venue.

Grand jury.

Venue to present or indict, §15A-631.

Violent habitual felons, §14-7.9.

Waiver, §15A-642(b), (c).

INDIGENT DEFENSE SERVICES.

Abused, neglected or dependent juvenile proceedings.

Payment of appointed counsel.

Office responsible for providing counsel, §7B-603(b).

Administrative support to office.

Director of administrative office of the courts to provide, §7A-498.2(c).

Appellate counsel.

Appointment, compensation eligibility.

Capital cases, IDS Rules 2B.1 to 2B.4.

Standards for, IDS Appxs 2B.1 to 2B.3.

Non-capital criminal and non-criminal cases, IDS Rules 3.1 to 3.7.

Trial division file and documentary exhibits.

Furnishing upon request, §7A-452(e).

Appellate defender, §7A-498.8.

Appointment by commission, §7A-498.8(a).

Appointment fee in criminal cases.

Added to amount court determines to be owned, §7A-455.1(b).

Assessed once for each attorney appointed, §7A-455.1(e).

Contempt.

Failure to pay grounds for, §7A-455.1(d).

Denial of appointment.

Failure to pay grounds for, §7A-455.1(d).

Each person for whom counsel appointed to pay, §7A-455.1(a).

Failure or refusal to pay, §7A-455.1(d).

Indigent persons attorney fee fund.

Fee credited to, §7A-455.1(f).

Rules and forms, office to develop, §7A-455.1(g).

Withdrawal of counsel.

Failure to pay grounds for, §7A-455.1(d).

Appropriated funds.

Allocation and disbursement by office, §7A-498.3(d).

Use, commission approval, §7A-498.2(e).

Budget of office, §7A-498.2(d).

Reduction or modification.

Approval of commission required, §7A-498.2(e).

Capital cases.

Appellate defender.

Additional conditions of appointment, setting, IDS Rule 2B.4.

Appeal to IDS commission.

Determination that lawyer not qualified, IDS Appx 2B.2.

Appointment and representation, IDS Rule 2B.2.

Conflict of interest, IDS Rule 2B.2.

Application for appointment, IDS Appx 2B.2.

Appointment of appellate counsel, IDS Rule 2B.2.

Capital appeals roster.

Creation, IDS Appx 2B.2.

Removal from, IDS Appx 2B.3.

Certiorari.

When appointed counsel required to file writ, IDS Rule 2B.4.

INDIGENT DEFENSE SERVICES —Cont'd

Capital cases —Cont'd

Compensation, IDS Rule 2B.3.

Conditions of appointment, IDS Rule 2B.4.

Conflict of interest in appellate defender, IDS Rule 2B.2.

Contract services.

Recoupment of services, IDS Rule 2B.3.

Coverage of part, IDS Rule 2B.1.

Experts, appointment and compensation, other expenses.

Appointment of experts.

Application to court, IDS Rule 2D.4.

Confidentiality of applications, IDS Rule 2D.2.

Notice of disapproval of application, IDS Rule 2D.3.

Disapproval of application, IDS Rule 2D.3.

Notice of disapproval, IDS Rule 2D.3.

Other programs, plans or contracts.

Authority to implement, IDS Rule 2D.5.

Payment.

Application to IDS, IDS Rule 2D.1.

Retention of expert.

Application to IDS, IDS Rule 2D.1.

Knowledge and experience.

Standards and qualifications, IDS Appx 2B.1.

On-going training.

Required to retain eligibility for appointment, IDS Appx 2B.3.

Other appellate counsel.

Assignment to defendant, IDS Rule 2B.2.

Other programs, plans and contracts.

Authority to implement, IDS Rule 2B.1.

Post conviction counsel.

Application for appointment, IDS Appx 2C.2.

Appointment of counsel, IDS Rule 2C.2.

Compensation, IDS Rule 2C.3.

Conditions of appointment, requirements, IDS Rule 2C.4.

Contract services.

Recoupment, IDS Rule 2C.3.

Coverage of part, IDS Rule 2C.1.

Experience and knowledge.

Standards for, IDS Appx 2C.1.

List of eligible lawyers, IDS Rule 2C.2.

On-going training.

Required to remain eligible, IDS Appx 2C.3.

Other programs, plans and contracts.

Authority to implement, IDS Rule 2C.1.

Post-conviction roster.

Creation, IDS Appx 2C.2.

Removal from, IDS Appx 2C.3.

Recoupment of fees, IDS Rule 2C.3.

Replacement of counsel.

Appointment of substitute, IDS Rule 2A.5.

Standards for, IDS Appx 2C.

Submissions with application for appointment, IDS Appx 2C.2.

Substitution of counsel.

Replacement of counsel, IDS Rule 2A.5.

Third party contributing non-counsel funds.

Funds placed in trust, accounting, IDS Rule 2C.3.

Training session.

Required to remain eligible, IDS Appx 2C.3.

Two lawyers appointed, IDS Rule 2C.2.

Waiver of experience and knowledge standards, IDS Appx 2C.1.

Recoupment of fees, IDS Rule 2B.3.

Replacement of counsel, substitute appointed, IDS Rule 2B.4.

INDIGENT DEFENSE SERVICES —Cont'd
Capital cases —Cont'd
Standards and qualifications, IDS Appx 2B.
Submissions with application for appointment,
  IDS Appx 2B.2.
Substitution of counsel.
Replacement of counsel, IDS Rule 2B.4.
Third party contributing non-counsel funds.
Funds placed in trust, accounting, IDS Rule
  2B.3.
Training session.
Required to retain eligibility for appointment,
  IDS Appx 2B.3.
Trial counsel.
Appeal to IDS commission.
  Review of determination that attorney not
    qualified, IDS Appx 2A.2.
Appointment of trial counsel, IDS Rule 2A.2.
  Application for appointment as lead or
    associate counsel, IDS Appx 2A.2.
Capital defendant defined, IDS Rule 2A.1.
Capital offense defined, IDS Rule 2A.1.
Capital trial roster.
  Creation, IDS Appx 2A.2.
  Removal for, IDS Appx 2A.3.
Compensation, IDS Rule 2A.4.
Conditions of appointment, requirements, IDS
  Rule 2A.5.
Contract services.
  Recoupment, IDS Rule 2A.4.
Coverage of subpart, IDS Rule 2A.1.
First lawyer appointed, IDS Rule 2A.2.
Lead and associate counsel, appointment, IDS
  Rule 2A.2.
  Standards for, IDS Appx 2A.
List of lawyers eligible for appointment, IDS
  Rule 2A.2.
Local counsel, provisional appointment, IDS
  Rule 2A.2.
Non-capital charges joined with capital charges,
  applicability to, IDS Rule 2A.1.
Notification by court of need to appoint counsel,
  IDS Rule 2A.2.
On-going training to remain eligible for
  appointment, IDS Appx 2A.3.
Other programs, plans and contracts.
  Implementation authorized, IDS Rule 2A.1.
Provisional appointment, local counsel, IDS
  Rule 2A.2.
Qualifications and experience.
  Standards for lead and associate counsel, IDS
    Appx 2A.1.
Recoupment of compensation, IDS Rule 2A.4.
Replacement of counsel with new counsel, IDS
  Rule 2A.5.
Second trial counsel appointed, IDS Rule 2A.2.
Standby counsel.
  Waiver of counsel by defendant, IDS Rule
    2A.3.
Submissions with application for appointment,
  IDS Appx 2A.2.
Substitution of counsel.
  Replacement of counsel with new counsel,
    IDS Rule 2A.5.
Third party contributing non-counsel funds.
  Funds placed in trust, accounting, IDS Rule
    2A.4.
Training session.
  Required to remain eligible for appointment,
    IDS Appx 2A.3.
Waiver of counsel, IDS Rule 2A.3.

INDIGENT DEFENSE SERVICES —Cont'd
Capital cases —Cont'd
Trial counsel —Cont'd
  Waiver of qualifications and experience
    standards.
    Standards for lead and associate counsel, IDS
      Appx 2A.1.
  Withdrawal of retained counsel.
    Ineligibility to be appointed to represent
      defendant, IDS Rule 2A.2.
  Waiver of knowledge and experience
    requirements.
    Standards and qualifications, IDS Appx 2B.1.
Class action unpaid residuals.
  Payment to indigent person's attorney fund,
    §1-267.10(b).
Commission on indigent defense services.
  Approval of office budget, §7A-498.5(g).
  Chair, §7A-498.4(h).
  Compensation, §7A-498.4(j).
  Compositions, §7A-498.4(b).
  Conflicts of interest, §7A-498.4(d).
  Delivery of service methods, §7A-498.5(d).
    Consultation with district bar, §7A-498.5(e).
  Development of standards, §7A-498.5(c).
  Direction to attend meetings, §7A-498.4(i).
  Director of office.
    Appointment, §§7A-498.5(b), 7A-498.6(a).
  Establishment, §7A-498.4(a).
  Expert witnesses, rate of compensation,
    §7A-498.5(f).
  Inaugural meeting, §7A-498.4(k).
  Powers and duties, §7A-498.5.
  Procedures for distribution of appropriated funds,
    §7A-498.5(f).
  Purpose, §7A-498.5(a).
  Quorum, §7A-498.4(g).
  Rulemaking authority, §7A-498.5(h).
  Term of office, §7A-498.4(c).
  Vacancies, §7A-498.4(f).
  Voting, §7A-498.4(e).
Copies, fee for preparation.
  Not chargeable to attorney appointed to represent
    indigent person at state expense, §7A-308(b1).
**Counties not served by office of indigent
  defense services.**
  Superior court clerk informed if person without
    counsel for 48 hours, §7A-453(b).
**Defendant states indigency and desire for
  counsel.**
  Custodial authority's duty to inform superior
    court clerks or office of indigent defense
    services, §7A-453(c).
Defender districts, §7A-498.7(a).
Determination of indigency.
  Policies and procedures, office to develop and
    implement, §7A-498.3(b).
  Preliminary determination by office of indigent
    defense services, §7A-453(a).
Director of office.
  Acceptance of gifts, donations or devises,
    §7A-498.6(b).
  Administration of office, §7A-498.6(b).
  Appointment, §§7A-498.5(b), 7A-498.6(a).
  Assistance to commission, §7A-498.6(b).
  Budget submission, §7A-498.6(b).
  Conduct of training programs, §7A-498.6(b).
  Duties as assigned, §7A-498.6(b).
  Financial recordkeeping, §7A-498.6(b).
  Hiring professional staff, §7A-498.6(b).
  Intergovernmental cooperation, §7A-498.6(b).

INDIGENT DEFENSE SERVICES —Cont'd
Director of office —Cont'd
Longevity pay, §7A-498.6(c).
Powers and duties, §7A-498.6(b).
Retirement.
Consolidated judicial retirement act, §§135-50
to 135-75.
See RETIREMENT SYSTEM FOR
TEACHERS AND STATE EMPLOYEES.
Salary, §7A-498.6(a).
Longevity pay, §7A-498.6(c).
District or regional public defender offices.
Establishing, §7A-498.7(a).
**Establishment of office within judicial
department,** §7A-498.2(a).
Experts.
Capital cases.
Appointment and compensation, other expenses,
IDS Rules 2D.1 to 2D.5.
Fees paid by state, §7A-454.
**Independent of administrative office of the
courts,** §7A-498.2(b).
Indigent services act of 2000.
Article cited as, §7A-498.
Interstate compact on juvenile.
Return of escapees or absconders.
Appointment of counsel in accordance with
rules of, §7B-2805(c).
Liens.
Counsel services for indigents.
Petitions for value of legal services,
§7A-455(b1).
Money value of services rendered by counsel.
Counsel services for indigents.
Judgment lien on amount.
Petitions for value of legal services,
§7A-455(b1).
Non-capital criminal and non-criminal cases.
Appellate counsel.
Abuse, neglect, dependency, termination of
parental rights.
Litigation of motions challenging final orders
pending direct appeal, IDS Rule 3.2.
Appellate roster.
Creation, IDS Rule 3.4.
Removal from, IDS Rule 3.6.
Appointment of appellate defender, IDS Rule
3.2.
Assignment to private counsel or public
defender, IDS Rule 3.2.
Compensation, IDS Rule 3.3.
Conditions of appointment, requirements, IDS
Rule 3.4.
Conflicts of interest.
Appellate defender, IDS Rule 3.2.
Contract services.
Recoupment, IDS Rule 3.3.
Coverage of part, IDS Rule 3.1.
Experience and knowledge requirement, IDS
Rule 3.4.
Fee application.
Private assigned counsel, IDS Rule 3.3.
Indigent determination prior to appointment.
In trial court, IDS Rule 3.2.
Judgment or decree and appellate entries and
rulings.
Forwarding to appointed counsel, IDS Rule
3.2.
Notice of assignment, IDS Rule 3.2.
Other programs, plans and contracts.
Authority to implement, IDS Rule 3.7.

INDIGENT DEFENSE SERVICES —Cont'd
Non-capital criminal and non-criminal cases
—Cont'd
Appellate counsel —Cont'd
Recoupment of fees, IDS Rule 3.3.
Replacement of counsel.
Substitute, IDS Rule 3.5.
Review of appellate defender decision.
Attorney not eligible for appointment, IDS
Rule 3.4.
Roster of attorneys, IDS Rule 3.4.
Setting fee.
Private assigned counsel, IDS Rule 3.3.
Standards, IDS Rule 3.4.
Submissions with application for appointment,
IDS Rule 3.4.
Substitution of counsel, IDS Rule 3.5.
Third party contributing non-counsel funds.
Funds placed in trust, accounting, IDS Rule
3.3.
Training session to remain eligible, IDS Rule
3.4.
Trial level.
Affidavit of Indigency.
Required, IDS Rule 1.4.
Appellate case, defined, inapplicability of part,
IDS Rule 1.1.
Appointment procedure, IDS Rule 1.5.
Capital case, defined, inapplicability of part,
IDS Rule 1.1.
Clerk of superior court.
Responsibilities as to in-custody defendants,
IDS Rule 1.3.
Compensation of appointed counsel, IDS Rule
1.9.
Continued representation, obligation of
appointed counsel, IDS Rule 1.7.
Contract with IDS, IDS Rule 1.8.
Compensation of contract counsel, IDS Rule
1.9.
Recoupment for services of contract counsel,
IDS Rule 1.11.
Withdrawal of contract counsel, IDS Rule 1.7.
Coverage of rule, IDS Rule 1.1.
Delegation to another attorney.
Material responsibilities, IDS Rule 1.5.
Determining Indigency.
Procedure, IDS Rule 1.4.
District bar.
Plan for appointment, district without public
defender, IDS Rule 1.5.
Experts, fees for, IDS Rule 1.10.
Fee schedules, IDS Rule 1.9.
Fees for support services, IDS Rule 1.10.
In-custody defendants.
Responsibilities of public defenders and
clerks, IDS Rule 1.3.
Indigency defined, IDS Rule 1.4.
Indigency, determining, IDS Rule 1.4.
Investigators, fees for, IDS Rule 1.10.
Non-criminal cases defined, IDS Rule 1.1.
Obligation of appointed counsel, IDS Rule 1.7.
Outside compensation prohibited, IDS Rule 1.9.
Payment of appointed counsel, IDS Rule 1.9.
Plan for appointment, IDS Rule 1.5.
Procedure for determining indigency, IDS Rule
1.4.
Public defenders.
Appointment procedure in districts with, IDS
Rule 1.5.

INDIGENT DEFENSE SERVICES —Cont'd
Non-capital criminal and non-criminal cases
—Cont'd
Trial level —Cont'd
Public defenders —Cont'd
Responsibilities as to in-custody defendants,
IDS Rule 1.3.
Record keeping.
Plans for assignment of counsel, IDS Rule 1.5.
Recoupment of fees, IDS Rule 1.11.
Special counsel office.
Procedure for appointment, districts with,
IDS Rule 1.5.
Standard of indigency, IDS Rule 1.4.
Standby counsel in criminal case.
Waiver of counsel by defendant, IDS Rule 1.6.
Substitute attorney.
Delegation of material responsibilities to, IDS
Rule 1.5.
Support services. fees for, IDS Rule 1.10.
Third party contributing non-counsel funds.
Funds placed in trust, accounting, IDS Rule
1.9.
Trail level defined, IDS Rule 1.1.
Waiver of counsel, IDS Rule 1.6.
Withdrawal of appointed counsel, IDS Rule 1.7.
Office of indigent defense services.
Legislative reporting.
Local government services contracts,
§7A-346.2(a).
Offices of public defenders.
Counties in which established, §7A-498.7(a).
Partial indigency.
Liens.
Amount of money value of counsel services.
Petitions for value of legal services,
§7A-455(b1).
Petitions.
Money value of services rendered by counsel.
Judgment lien on amount.
Petitions for value of legal services,
§7A-455(b1).
Post-conviction counsel.
Appointment, compensation, eligibility.
Capital cases, IDS Rules 2C.1 to 2C.4.
Standards for, IDS Appxs 2C.1 to 2C.3.
Powers, §7A-498.2(b).
Public defenders.
Appointment, duties, §7A-498.7(b) to (k).
Purpose of article, §7A-498.1.
Reports.
Office of indigent defense services.
Legislative reporting on local government
services contracts, §7A-346.2(a).
Rules and procedures adopted by office,
§7A-498.3(c).
Supporting services.
Fees and expenses paid by state, §7A-454.
System for providing legal representation.
Responsibility of office to establish, §7A-498.3(a).
Termination of parental rights.
Parent's right to counsel and appointment of
counsel, §7B-1101.1(a).
Trial counsel.
Appointment, eligibility, compensation.
Capital cases, IDS Rules 2A.1 to 2A.5.
Standards for, IDS Appxs 2A.1 to 2A.3.
Non-capital criminal and non-criminal cases,
IDS Rules 1.1 to 1.11.

INDIGENT PERSONS.
Abused, neglected or dependent juvenile
actions.
Appointment of counsel for parent, §7B-602.
Payment of court-appointed counsel, §7B-603(a)
to (c).
Access to civil justice act, §§7A-474.1 to
7A-474.5.
See LEGAL SERVICES PROGRAMS.
Affidavit as to inability to advance court costs.
Required to sue as indigent, §1-110(a).
Appeals in forma pauperis, §1-288.
Appearances.
First appearance before district court judge.
Determination whether defendant has been
assigned counsel.
Duty of judge, §15A-603(a).
Proceedings when defendant asserts indigence
and desires counsel, §15A-603(c).
Right to be furnished counsel.
Defendant to be informed by judge,
§15A-603(b).
Arbitration and award.
Hearings.
Proceedings in forma pauperis, Arbitration Rule
3.
Arrest in civil cases.
Order for arrest.
Information to be included in order, §1-413.
Attorneys at law.
Class action unpaid residuals.
Payment to indigent person's attorney fund and
state bar for services for indigents,
§1-267.10(b).
Fees for preparation of copies.
Not chargeable to attorney appointed to
represent indigent at state expense,
§7A-308(b1).
Geographically based field programs.
Access to civil justice act.
See LEGAL SERVICES PROGRAMS.
Indigent defense services act, §§7A-498 to
7A-498.8.
See INDIGENT DEFENSE SERVICES.
Legal services provided by law students.
Rules governing, Bar Rules C.0201 to C.0207.
Nonprofit corporations rendering legal services to
indigents, §84-5.1.
Representation of indigent persons. See within
this heading, "Representation of indigent
persons."
Authority to sue as indigent.
Court authorized to allow, §1-110(a).
Blind persons.
Aid to the blind, §§111-13 to 111-35.
See BLIND AND VISUALLY IMPAIRED.
Cancer.
Financial aid for diagnosis and treatment,
§130A-206.
Capital punishment.
Representation of indigent persons.
Appointment of counsel in capital cases,
§7A-451(b) to (e), IndigCounsel Model Plan
Art VII, IndigCounsel Model Plan Art VIII
§8.2.
Indigent defense services act, §§7A-498 to
7A-498.8.
See INDIGENT DEFENSE SERVICES.
Class action unpaid residuals.
Payment to indigent person's attorney fund and
state bar for services for indigents,
§1-267.10(b).

INDIGENT PERSONS —Cont'd
Commitment.
Involuntary outpatient commitment, §7A-451.1.
Costs.
Payment of costs, §6-24.
Criteria for suing as indigent, §1-110(a).
Delinquent and undisciplined juvenile actions.
Appointment of counsel for juvenile, §7B-2000(a).
Payment, §7B-2002.
Presumption of indigence, §7B-2000(b).
Secure or nonsecure custody hearings.
Appointment of counsel for juvenile, §7B-1906(c).
Summons to notify parent of right to counsel and appointment of counsel, §7B-1805(b).
Department of health and human services.
Costs of care paid by persons admitted to institutions of department.
Power to admit indigent persons, §143-123.
District courts.
Small claims actions.
Appeals, §7A-228(b).
Energy assistance, §§143B-472.121 to 143B-472.123.
Established legal services programs.
Access to civil justice act, §§7A-474.1 to 7A-474.5.
Executions.
Execution against the person.
Appointment of counsel, §1-311.
Contents of execution, §1-313.
Fees.
Representation of indigents, §7A-452(b).
Frivolous complaint.
Prisoners filing pro se motions to proceed as indigent.
Determination by court, dismissal, §1-110(b).
Geographically based field programs.
Access to civil justice act.
See LEGAL SERVICES PROGRAMS.
Guilty pleas.
Waiver of right to counsel, §7A-457(b).
Incompetence, restoration.
Guardian ad litem appointed, §35A-1130(c).
In forma pauperis.
See IN FORMA PAUPERIS.
Innocence claim inquiry.
Formal inquiry.
Advice of counsel, indigency, appointment, §15A-1467(b).
Judicial review by three-judge panel.
Appointment of counsel, relief from costs, §15A-1469(e).
Involuntary outpatient commitment, §7A-451.1.
Judicial department.
Appointment of assistant counsel for representation, §7A-450(b1).
Landlord and tenant.
Summary ejectment.
Stay of judgment.
Indigent defendant appellant, §42-34(c1).
Law students providing legal services.
Rules governing, Bar Rules C.0201 to C.0207.
Legal services programs.
Access to civil justice act, §§7A-474.1 to 7A-474.5.
Marriage proceedings.
Guardian ad litem for underage parties, §7A-451(f).
Mental health, developmental disability, substance abuse.
Attorneys at law.
Appointment, §122C-270.

INDIGENT PERSONS —Cont'd
Mental health, developmental disability, substance abuse —Cont'd
Involuntary commitment.
Appointment of counsel.
Substance abuser's commitment hearing, §122C-286(d).
Duty of assigned counsel.
Substance abusers, §122C-289.
Outpatient commitment.
Representation.
Counsel fees, §7A-451.1.
Motion for appropriate relief, §15A-1421.
Appointment of counsel for indigent defendant, §15A-1421.
Nonprofit corporations rendering legal services to indigents.
Authorized, certain corporations, §84-5.1(a).
Conditioning services upon purchase of product, good or service.
Prohibition, §84-5.1(b).
Parolees.
Entitlement to counsel, §148-62.1.
Post conviction DNA testing.
Defendant's motion.
Appointment of counsel, §15A-269(c).
Appeal of denial of motion, §15A-270.1.
Prisoners.
Frivolous complaint.
Determination by court, dismissal, §1-110(b).
Pre se motions to proceed as indigent, §1-110(b).
Public assistance.
Generally.
See SOCIAL SERVICES.
Public schools.
Compulsory attendance law.
Investigation of indigency, §115C-382.
Representation of indigent persons, §§7A-450 to 7A-458.
Abused, neglected or dependent juvenile actions.
Appointment of counsel for parent, §7B-602.
Payment of court-appointed counsel, §7B-603(a) to (c).
Notice in summons of right to counsel and appointment information, §7B-406(b).
Access to civil justice act, §§7A-474.1 to 7A-474.5.
See LEGAL SERVICES PROGRAMS.
Acquittals.
Applicability of partial payments and liens provisions when indigent not finally convicted, §7A-455(c).
Appellate counsel appointed.
Trial division file and documentary exhibits.
Furnishing upon request, §7A-452(e).
Appointment of counsel, §7A-452(c).
Appellate appointments, IndigCounsel Model Plan Art VIII §8.1.
Capital cases, IndigCounsel Model Plan Art VIII §8.2.
Capital cases, IndigCounsel Model Plan Art VII §7.2.
Appellate appointments, §7A-451(b) to (e), IndigCounsel Model Plan Art VIII §8.2.
Applicability of provisions, IndigCounsel Model Plan Art VII §7.1.
Qualifications of appointed attorneys, IndigCounsel Model Plan Art VII §7.3.
Clerks of court.
Appointment by, IndigCounsel Model Plan Art VI §6.7.

INDIGENT PERSONS —Cont'd
Representation of indigent persons —Cont'd
Appointment of counsel —Cont'd
Clerks of court —Cont'd
Record of attorney subject to appointment.
Maintenance, IndigCounsel Model Plan Art
VI §6.2.
Committee on indigent appointments.
Authority, IndigCounsel Model Plan Art IV
§4.6.
Chairman, IndigCounsel Model Plan Art IV
§4.4.
Deletion of attorneys from lists, IndigCounsel
Model Plan Art V §§5.6, 5.7.
Established, IndigCounsel Model Plan Art IV
§4.1.
Lists of attorneys.
Development, IndigCounsel Model Plan Art
III §3.5.
Review, IndigCounsel Model Plan Art III
§3.7.
Meetings, IndigCounsel Model Plan Art IV
§§4.5, 4.7, 4.8.
Members, IndigCounsel Model Plan Art IV
§§4.2, 4.3.
Quorum, IndigCounsel Model Plan Art IV
§4.7.
Requests for placement on lists.
Review, IndigCounsel Model Plan Art V
§§5.2, 5.4, 5.5.
Discretion of court, IndigCounsel Model Plan
Art VI §6.3.
Inherent discretionary power, IndigCounsel
Model Plan Art X §10.2.
Generally, Bar Rule D.0404.
General provisions, §§7A-450 to 7A-458.
See INDIGENT DEFENSE SERVICES.
Lists of attorneys, IndigCounsel Model Plan
Arts III, V.
Appointment in accordance with,
IndigCounsel Model Plan Art VI §6.1.
Defendant's attorneys on list may be
appointed to represent, IndigCounsel
Model Plan Art III §§3.2 to 3.4.
Deletion from, IndigCounsel Model Plan Art V
§§5.6, 5.7.
Development by committee on indigent
appointments, IndigCounsel Model Plan
Art III §3.5.
Placement on, IndigCounsel Model Plan Art
III §3.1.
Requests for, IndigCounsel Model Plan Art
V §§5.1 to 5.8.
Public defender.
Consultation of lists, IndigCounsel Model
Plan Art VI §6.6.
Requirements for inclusion, IndigCounsel
Model Plan Art III §3.6.
Review by committee on indigent
appointments, IndigCounsel Model Plan
Art III §3.7.
Supplying to clerks, IndigCounsel Model Plan
Art VI §6.1.
Model plan, IndigCounsel Model Plan Arts I to
X.
Administrator, IndigCounsel Model Plan Art
IX §§9.1 to 9.3.
Applicability, IndigCounsel Model Plan Art II.
Authority for issuance, IndigCounsel Model
Plan Art X §10.1.

INDIGENT PERSONS —Cont'd
Representation of indigent persons —Cont'd
Appointment of counsel —Cont'd
Model plan —Cont'd
Clerks of superior court.
Duties, IndigCounsel Model Plan Art IX
§§9.4, 9.5.
Construction of regulations.
Liberal construction, IndigCounsel Model
Plan Art X §10.3.
Effective date of regulations, IndigCounsel
Model Plan Art X §10.4.
Generally, IndigCounsel Model Plan Arts I to
X.
Inherent discretionary power of court,
IndigCounsel Model Plan Art X §10.2.
Purpose, IndigCounsel Model Plan Art I.
Multiple defendants.
Appointment to represent in single case,
IndigCounsel Model Plan Art VI §6.5.
Notice of appointment, IndigCounsel Model
Plan Art VI §6.4.
Record of attorney subject to appointment.
Clerks to maintain, IndigCounsel Model Plan
Art VI §6.2.
Assignment of counsel, §7A-452(a).
Authority for rules and regulations of state bar
relating to, Bar Rule D.0401.
Authority to issue rules and regulations,
IndigCounsel §1.1.
Capital cases.
Appellate level, §7A-451(b) to (e), IndigCounsel
§4.10.
Assistant counsel, IndigCounsel §4.8.
Postconviction counsel, §7A-451(b) to (e).
Qualifications, IndigCounsel §4.9.
Change of status, §7A-450(d).
Commitment.
Counsel fees, §7A-451.1.
Committee on indigent appointments. See within
this subheading, "Appointment of counsel."
Compensation of counsel, §7A-452(d).
Appellate level, IndigCounsel §6.2.
Copies of orders, IndigCounsel §6.4.
Entry of orders, IndigCounsel §6.3.
Judgment against defendant, IndigCounsel §6.1.
Judgment for payment, IndigCounsel §6.5.
Orders, IndigCounsel §6.1.
Outside compensation, IndigCounsel §6.6.
Procedure for payment, Bar Rule D.0406.
Continuation of entitlement to services of counsel,
§7A-451(b).
Counsel fees for outpatient involuntary
commitment proceedings, §7A-451.1.
Custodian of possibly indigent person, duties.
In addition to duties imposed upon arresting
officers, §7A-453(d).
In counties designated by office of indigent
defense services, §7A-453(a).
In counties not designated by office of indigent
defense services, §7A-453(b).
Statement that defendant desires counsel,
§7A-453(c).
Definition of indigent person, §7A-450(a).
Delinquent and undisciplined juvenile actions.
Appointment of counsel and payment of fees,
§§7B-2000, 7B-2002.
Secure or nonsecure custody hearings,
§7B-1906(c).
Summons to notify parent of right to counsel
and appointment of counsel, §7B-1805(b).

INDIGENT PERSONS —Cont'd
Representation of indigent persons —Cont'd
Determination of fiduciaries at indigency
  determination, §7A-450.2.
Determination of indigency, Bar Rule D.0402,
  IndigCounsel §2.4.
  Affidavit, IndigCounsel §§2.1, 2.3.
  Authority to make determinations, §7A-452(c).
  Bases for determination, IndigCounsel §2.4.
  Examination of defendants, IndigCounsel §2.2.
  Preliminary determination by office of indigent
    defense services, §7A-453(a).
Duty of custodian of possibly indigent person,
  §7A-453(a) to (d).
Eligible counsels.
  Maintenance of records, IndigCounsel §4.6.
Entitlement to counsel, §§7A-450(b), 7A-452(c).
  Actions and proceedings where indigent entitled
    to services of counsel, §7A-451(a).
  Beginning of entitlement to services of counsel,
    §7A-451(b).
  Capital cases.
    Postconviction counsel, §7A-451(b) to (e).
  Continuation of entitlement through critical
    stages of action or proceeding, §7A-451(b).
  Counsel fees for outpatient involuntary
    commitment proceedings, §7A-451.1.
  Responsibility for payment by certain
    fiduciaries, §7A-450.1.
    Determination of fiduciaries, §7A-450.2.
    Determination of responsibility at hearing,
      §7A-450.3.
    Exemptions, §7A-450.4.
  Scope of entitlement, §7A-451(a).
  When entitlement begins, §7A-451(b).
Established legal services programs.
  Access to civil justice act, §§7A-474.1 to
    7A-474.5.
False material statements as to Indigency.
  Felony, §7A-456(a).
  Notice to person of penalty, §7A-456(b).
Fees of counsel, §7A-452(d).
  Fixing of counsel fees, §7A-458.
  Liability for payment of fees, §7A-452(b).
  Preparation compensable, §7A-458.
Generally, IndigCounsel §4.1.
Geographically based field programs.
  Access to civil justice act.
    See LEGAL SERVICES PROGRAMS.
Guilty pleas.
  Waiver of right to counsel, §7A-457(b).
Hearing impaired.
  Interpreters, §7A-450(a).
Indigent defense services.
  See INDIGENT DEFENSE SERVICES.
Interstate compact on juvenile.
  Return of escapees or absconders, §7B-2805(c).
Law students, legal services provided by, Bar
  Rules C.0201 to C.0207.
Liens.
  Counsel services for indigent.
    Judgment lien on amount, §7A-455(b).
Lists of attorneys. See within this subheading,
  "Appointment of counsel."
Marriage proceedings.
  Guardian ad litem for underage parties,
    §7A-451(f).
Mental health, developmental disability,
  substance abuse.
  Involuntary commitment.
    Substance abuser's commitment hearing,
      §122C-286(d).

INDIGENT PERSONS —Cont'd
Representation of indigent persons —Cont'd
Model plan.
  Adoption, IndigCounsel §4.1.
  Certification, IndigCounsel §4.2.
  Compliance, IndigCounsel §4.2.
  Filing, IndigCounsel §4.5.
Model plan of the state bar, Bar Rules D.0501 to
  D.0510.
  Administrator of regulations, Bar Rule D.0509.
  Appellate appointments, Bar Rule D.0508.
  Applicability of regulations, Bar Rule D.0502.
  Appointment in capital cases, Bar Rule D.0507.
  Appointment in noncapital cases, Bar Rule
    D.0506.
  Appointment of members to committee on
    indigent, Bar Rule D.0504.
  Construction of regulations, Bar Rule D.0510.
  Discretion of court to decline appointment, Bar
    Rule D.0510.
  Effective date of regulations, Bar Rule D.0510.
  List of attorneys, Bar Rules D.0503, D.0505.
  Purposes of regulations, Bar Rule D.0501.
Money value of services rendered by counsel.
  Judgment lien on amount, §7A-455(b).
Murder.
  Appointment of assistant counsel, §7A-450(b1).
Orders for appointment of council, IndigCounsel
  §4.7.
Out-of-court proceedings.
  Waiver of right to counsel, §7A-457(c).
Partial indigency, §7A-455(a).
  Applicability of provisions when indigent not
    finally convicted, §7A-455(c).
  Liens.
    Amount of money value of counsel services,
      §7A-455(b).
Pleas of guilty.
  Waiver of counsel, §7A-457(b).
Professional relationship of counsel to indigent
  person, §7A-450(b).
Public defender appointments, IndigCounsel
  §§4.11, 4.12.
Redetermination of indigency, §7A-450(c).
Residency requirement, IndigCounsel §4.3.
Responsibility for payment by certain fiduciaries,
  §7A-450.1.
  Determination of fiduciaries, §7A-450.2.
  Determination of responsibility at hearing,
    §7A-450.3.
  Exemptions, §7A-450.4.
Selection by defendant prohibited, IndigCounsel
  §4.4.
Social security.
  Obtaining number when judgment to be
    entered, §7A-455(d).
Source of counsel, §7A-452(a).
Specialized programs, IndigCounsel §4.13.
State bar council.
  Implementing regulations by council.
    Capital cases.
      Appointment and compensation of
        postconviction counsel to comply with
        rules and regulations, §7A-451(d).
Termination of parental rights proceedings.
  Adjudicatory hearing, appointment for parents,
    §7B-1109(b).
  Parent's right to counsel and appointment of
    counsel, §7B-1101.1(a).
Waiver of right to counsel, §7A-457(a), Bar Rule
  D.0403.
  Acceptance, IndigCounsel §3.3.

INDIGENT PERSONS —Cont'd
Representation of indigent persons —Cont'd
Waiver of right to counsel —Cont'd
Form, IndigCounsel §3.1.
Matters to be considered in determining
acceptance of waiver, §7A-457(a).
Out-of-court proceedings, §7A-457(c).
Personal inquiry by judge, IndigCounsel §3.2.
Pleas of guilty, §7A-457(b).
Refusal to execute, IndigCounsel §3.1.
Withdrawal by counsel, Bar Rule D.0405,
IndigCounsel §5.1.
Appellate level, IndigCounsel §5.2.
Good cause, IndigCounsel §5.3.
Permission to withdraw, IndigCounsel §5.1.
Small claims actions.
Appeals, §7A-228(b1).
Social services.
See SOCIAL SERVICES.
Suits by indigent.
Payment of costs, §6-24.
Temporary assistance for needy families.
Work first program.
Generally, §§108A-27 to 108A-39.
See WORK FIRST PROGRAM.
Termination of parental rights.
Indigent defense services act, §§7A-498 to
7A-498.8.
See INDIGENT DEFENSE SERVICES.
Termination of parental rights proceedings.
Adjudicatory hearing, appointment of counsel for
indigent parents, §7B-1109(b).
Parent's right to counsel and appointment of
counsel, §7B-1101.1(a).
Welfare policy of state, NC Const Art XI §4.
Work first program.
Temporary assistance for needy families.
Generally, §§108A-27 to 108A-39.
See WORK FIRST PROGRAM.

INDIRECT CRIMINAL CONTEMPT, §5A-13(b).

**INDIVIDUAL RETIREMENT ACCOUNTS OR
ANNUITIES.**
Exemption from creditors' claims, §1C-1601(a).
Renunciation of succession, §31B-1.

INDIVIDUALS WITH DISABILITY.
See DISABLED PERSONS.

INDOOR CLEAN AIR ACT.
**Smoking in public buildings or places of
employment,** §§130A-491 to 130A-498.
See SMOKING.
Smoking in public places, §§143-595 to 143-601.
See SMOKING.

INDORSEMENTS.
See ENDORSEMENTS.

INDUCEMENTS.
Wine distribution agreements.
Prohibited, §18B-1202.

INDUSTRIAL ACCIDENTS.
Occupational safety and health, §§95-126 to
95-155.
See OCCUPATIONAL SAFETY AND HEALTH.
Workers' compensation, §§97-1 to 97-101.1.
See WORKERS' COMPENSATION.

**INDUSTRIAL AND POLLUTION CONTROL
FACILITIES FINANCING,** §§159C-1 to
159C-27.
Applicability of article.
Additional methods, §159C-24.

**INDUSTRIAL AND POLLUTION CONTROL
FACILITIES FINANCING** —Cont'd
Applicability of article —Cont'd
Inconsistent laws inapplicable, §159C-26.
Liberal construction, §159C-25.
Authorities.
Annual reports, §159C-22.
Commissioners.
Appointment, §159C-4(a).
Compensation, §159C-4(e).
Officers, §159C-4(c).
Qualifications, §159C-4(b).
Quorum, §159C-4(d).
Removal from office, §159C-4(b).
Term of office, §159C-4(a).
Conflict of interest of officials, §159C-16.
Consultants and employees.
Powers as to, §159C-5.
Creation.
Authorized, §159C-4(a).
Ratification, §159C-27.
Dissolution of authorities, §159C-21.
Notification of department of commerce of
formation, §159C-4(f).
Powers, §159C-5.
Ratification of creation, §159C-27.
Bond issues.
Approval bonds by local government commission.
Application for approval, filing, §159C-8(a).
Factors considered on determining whether to
approve, §159C-8(b).
Obligor's ability to perform, evaluation,
§159C-8(d).
Refunding bonds, §159C-19(a1).
Required for issuance, §159C-8(a).
Special purpose project, public hearing, required
for approval, §159C-8(c).
Capital facilities finance agency, §§159D-1 to
159D-27.
Credit of state not pledged, §159C-17.
Eligibility for investment, §159C-18.
Financing agreements, §159C-11.
Immunity of commissioners.
No personal liability for executing or issuing,
§159C-23.
Interest.
Exemption from taxation, §159C-14.
Issuance.
Approval, §159C-4(d).
Authority.
Refunding bonds, §159C-19(a).
Purposes.
Refunding bonds, §159C-19.
Refunding bonds, §159C-19(a).
Proceeds.
Exemption from taxation, §159C-14.
Trust funds, §159C-13.
Public or private sale of bonds, §159C-9.
Refunding bonds.
Approval of local government commission,
§159C-19(a1).
Issuance, resolution, purposes, §159C-19(a).
Sale or exchange, §159C-19(c).
Sale of bonds, §159C-9.
Refunding bonds, §159C-19(b).
Security documents, §159C-12.
Taxation.
Exemption from taxation, §159C-14.
Trust agreements.
Security by agreements, §159C-12.

INDUSTRIAL AND POLLUTION CONTROL
    FACILITIES FINANCING —Cont'd
Bonds.
  Approval of project before issued, §159C-7.
  Authorization to issue, §159C-6(a).
  Consent of state, political subdivision, etc., not
      required, §159C-6(g).
  Interim receipts or temporary bonds, issuance,
      §159C-6(f).
  Loans to obligor, §159C-6(e).
  Preliminary expenditures, reimbursement from
      proceeds, §159C-6(d).
  Proceeds, use, §159C-6(b).
  Recovery zone facility bonds, §159C-6(a1).
  Refinancing costs, proceeds not used for,
      §159C-6(c).
  Terms and conditions, §159C-6(a).
Capital facilities finance agency, §§159D-1 to
    159D-27.
  Bonds.
    Approval by local government commission prior
        to issuance.
      Application for approval, filing, §159D-8(a).
      Factors considered, §159D-8(b).
      Financial date and information, submittal,
          §159D-8(c).
      Required, §159D-8(a).
    Approval of project by secretary of commerce
        prior to issuance.
      Certificate approval, §159D-7(h), (i).
      Certification of department of environment
          and natural resources, §159D-7(e).
      Findings required, §159D-7(b).
      Forms and rules, data and information about
          project, §159D-7(g).
      Initial operator, identified in application,
          §159D-7(c).
      Public hearing required by county,
          §159D-7(d).
      Required, §159D-7(a).
      Wage requirement, waiver, §159D-7(f).
    Authority to issues, §159D-6(a).
    Banks and trust companies acting as depository
        of proceeds, §159D-12(b).
    Board of directors not personally liable,
        §159D-24.
    Consent of state or political subdivision.
      Issuing without obtaining, §159D-6(e).
    Consent to location by board of commissioners
        required, §159D-10.
    Credit of state not pledged, §159D-17.
    Financing agreements, §159D-11.
    Legal to invest in bonds, §159D-18.
    Payment from revenues and other funds,
        statement, §159D-17.
    Preliminary expenditures, reimbursement from
        proceeds, §159D-6(d).
    Proceeds, use, §159D-6(b).
    Refinancing cost of project, use of proceeds,
        §159D-6(c).
    Refunding bonds.
      Approvals required, §159D-19(a1).
      Authorization to issue, §159D-19(a).
      Purposes, §159D-19(a).
      Sale or exchange, §159D-19(b).
      Terms and conditions, provisions governing,
          §159D-19(a1).
    Sale, §159D-9.
    Security documents securing, §159D-12(a).
    Sinking fund, §159D-12(a).
    Tax exemption, interest on bonds, §159D-14.

INDUSTRIAL AND POLLUTION CONTROL
    FACILITIES FINANCING —Cont'd
Capital facilities finance agency —Cont'd
  Bonds —Cont'd
    Terms and conditions, §159D-6(a).
    Trust funds, proceeds, §159D-13.
  Conflict of interest, disclosure, §159D-16.
  Consent to location by board of commissioners.
    Required prior to issuance of bonds, §159D-10.
  Construction contracts.
    Agreement that contract solicited, negotiated,
        awarded and executed by operator,
        §159D-15.
  Definitions, §159D-3.
  Exemption from taxes, §159D-14.
  Financing agreements.
    Additional provision if necessary, §159D-11(g).
    Assignment of agency rights, §159D-11(f).
    Interest of agency in project under agreement,
        §159D-11(e).
    Nature of agreement, §159D-11(b).
    Provision required, §159D-11(a).
    Purchase of project by obligor, requirement,
        lease agreement, §159D-11(c).
    Rights and remedies of agency in event of
        default, §159D-11(d).
  General powers, §159D-5.
  Inconsistent laws inapplicable, §159D-27.
  Interest directly or indirectly in contract,
      disclosure, §159D-16.
  Investing in bonds, §159D-18.
  Jurisdiction, §159D-4.1.
  Legislative findings and purpose, §159D-2(a), (b).
  Liberal construction of article, §159D-26.
  Location of projects, §159D-10.
  North Carolina industrial and pollution control
      facilities financing act.
    Short title, §159D-1.
  Project approval by secretary of commerce.
    Required prior to issuance of bonds, §159D-7.
  Public hearing on project by county.
    Required for approval by secretary of commerce,
        §159D-7(d).
  Refunding bonds, §159D-19.
  Security documents securing bonds, §159D-12(a).
  Supplemental and additional method, §159D-25.
  Tax exemption, §159D-14.
  Transfer of duties, powers, jurisdiction and
      responsibilities to agency, §159D-4.1.
  Trust funds, money received, §159D-13.
Citation.
  Short title, §159C-1.
Conflict of laws.
  Inconsistent laws applicable, §159C-26.
Conflicts of interest.
  Public officers, §159C-16.
Construction contracts, §159C-15.
Construction of article.
  Inconsistent laws applicable, §159C-26.
  Liberal construction, §159C-25.
Contracts.
  Construction contracts, §159C-15.
Credit of state not pledged, §159C-17.
Definitions, §159C-3.
Dissolution of authorities, §159C-21.
Eminent domain.
  No power of eminent domain, §159C-20.
Exemptions from taxation, §159C-14.
Financing agreements.
  Assignment of authority's interest, §159C-11(c).

INDUSTRIAL AND POLLUTION CONTROL FACILITIES FINANCING —Cont'd

Financing agreements —Cont'd

Authority's interest in project under agreement, §159C-11(c).

In the nature of lease, purchase by obligor on expiration or termination, §159C-11(b).

Provisions required, §159C-11(a).

Interstate environmental compact.

Citation of article, §113A-21.

Compact provisions, §113A-23.

Legislative findings, §113A-22.

Provisions generally, §113A-23.

Purpose, §113A-22.

Short title, §113A-21.

Investments.

Bonds eligible for investment, §159C-18.

Legislative findings and purposes, §159C-2(a) to (c).

Location of projects, §159C-10.

Municipalities.

Emission of pollutants.

Prohibited, §160A-185.

Nonpoint source pollution control program.

Committee.

Composition, §106-852.

Duties, §106-852.

Creation of program, §106-850(a).

Participation in program, §106-851.

Requirements of program, §106-850(b).

Review of program, §106-850(c).

Committee, §106-852.

State funds for program to remain available until expended for the program, §106-850(d).

Voluntary participation, §106-851.

Plastic yokes or ring type holding devices.

Containers, §14-399.2.

Policy of state, NC Const Art XIV §5.

Pollution prevention pays programs.

Department of environment and natural resources, §113-8.01.

Projects.

Approval by secretary of commerce.

Certificate of approval, §159C-7(g).

Department of environment and natural resources.

Certificate of, §159C-7(d).

Findings, §159C-7(b).

Initial operator, findings as to, §159C-7(b1).

Public hearings, §159C-7(c).

Required, §159C-7(a).

Rules, §159C-7(f).

Wage requirement, §159C-7(b).

Waiver, §159C-7(e).

Location, §159C-10.

Public hearings.

Special purpose project.

Required for approval of bond issuance, §159C-8(c).

Public officers.

Conflicts of interest, §159C-16.

Refunding bonds, §159C-19.

Reports.

Annual reports of authorities, §159C-22.

Revenues.

Trust funds, §159C-13.

Special purpose project.

Public hearing.

Required for approval of bond issuance, §159C-8(c).

INDUSTRIAL AND POLLUTION CONTROL FACILITIES FINANCING —Cont'd

State.

Credit of state not pledged, §159C-17.

Taxation.

Exemptions from taxation, §159C-14.

Title.

Short title, §159C-1.

Trust agreements.

Security for bonds, §159C-12.

Trust funds.

Revenues and proceeds of bonds constitutes trust funds, §159C-13.

Water and air resources, §§143-211 to 143-215.9C.

See WATER AND AIR RESOURCES.

INDUSTRIAL BANKS, §§53-136 to 53-145.

Applicability of general provisions, §53-143.

Powers generally, §53-141.

Branch banks.

Power to establish, §53-141.

Capital stock.

Amount authorized, §53-139.

Certificate of incorporation to set forth, §53-137.

Sale, §53-140.

Commissioner of banks.

Supervision by, §53-144.

Consumer finance act.

Exemption, §53-191.

Defined, §53-136.

Depositories.

Designation, §53-142.

Incorporation, §53-137.

Minors.

Deposit account.

Operating in name of minor, §53-43.5(a).

Safe deposit boxes.

Leasing or renting to minors, §53-43.5(b), (c).

Names.

Certificate of incorporation to set forth, §53-137.

Corporate title, §53-138.

Powers, §53-141.

Rules and regulations.

State banking commission, §53-144.

Supervision.

Applicability of general law, §53-145.

Commissioner of banks, §53-134.

INDUSTRIAL CLEANERS.

Containing phosphorus.

Manufacture, storage or sale.

Prohibition, exceptions, penalties, §143-214.4(a) to (g).

INDUSTRIAL COMMISSION.

Administrative procedure act.

Full exemption, §150B-1(c).

Administrator, §97-78(b).

Longevity pay in lieu of merit and other raises, §97-78(b4).

Salary, §97-78(b1).

Appeals.

Administrative decisions appealed, ICWorkComp Rule 703.

Appeal to court of appeals, ICWorkComp Rule 702.

Awards of commission, §97-86.

Payment of award pending appeal in certain cases, §97-86.1.

Commission appeals, ICWorkComp Rule 701.

INDUSTRIAL COMMISSION —Cont'd
Appeals —Cont'd
Court of appeals.
Review of final orders, §7A-250(b).
Insurers.
Expenses of appeals brought by insurers,
§97-88.
Right of appeal from industrial commission to
court of appeals, §7A-29(a).
Appointment of members, §97-77(a), (a1).
Confirmation by general assembly, §97-77(a1).
Award, findings of fact, other matters.
Filing with record of proceedings, time, §97-84.
Awards, §§97-85 to 97-87.
Blank forms and literature.
Providing, §97-81(a).
Business transacted by commission,
ICWorkComp Rule 102.
Chairman, §97-77(b).
**Chief judicial officer and chief executive
officer.**
Chairman, §97-77(b).
Child vaccine-related injury compensation,
§§130A-422 to 130A-434.
See CHILDHOOD VACCINE-RELATED INJURY
COMPENSATION.
Clerical assistance, §97-78(b).
Code of judicial conduct.
Applicability to commissioners and deputy
commissioners, §97-78.1.
Commissioner.
Contested cases.
Disqualification, ICWorkComp Rule 615.
**Compliance with payment and termination of
claims provisions.**
Strategic plan for tracking, §97-78(f).
Demonstration of success in implementing,
§97-78(g).
Composition, §97-77(a).
Compromise and settlement.
Approval of settlements, §97-17.
Contempt, §97-80(g), (h).
**Contested case provisions of administrative
procedure.**
Exemption, §150B-1(e).
Court of appeals.
Remedial writs.
Power of court to issue, §7A-32(c).
Review of final orders, §7A-250(b).
Right of appeal from industrial commission to
court of appeals, §7A-29(a).
Creation, §97-77(a).
Death benefits act.
Rules, ICDeathBenefits Rules I to V.
See DEATH BENEFITS.
Definition of "commission," §97-2.
Depositions, §97-80(d).
Deputy commissioners.
Appointment, §97-79(b).
Chief deputy commissioner.
Designation by chairman, salary, §97-78(b2).
Longevity pay in lieu of merit and other raises,
§97-78(b4).
Determination of disputes by, §97-84.
Disqualification in contested cases, ICWorkComp
Rule 615.
Powers, §97-79(b).
Salaries, §97-78(b3).
Chief deputy, §97-78(b2).
Determination of disputes, §97-84.

INDUSTRIAL COMMISSION —Cont'd
Disciplinary procedures for judges.
Applicability to commissioners and deputy
commissioners, §97-78.1.
Discovery.
Power to limit, §97-80(f).
Disputes.
Appeals, §97-86.
Payment of award pending appeal in certain
cases, §97-86.1.
Award.
Authority of clerk to enter judgments, §1-209.
Conclusive as to facts, §97-86.
Hearings.
Interest on awards after hearing, §97-86.2.
Payment of award pending appeal in certain
cases.
Generally, §97-86.1(a), (b).
Not admission of liability or estoppel to deny
liability, §97-86.1(c).
Repayment, §97-86.1(d).
Review, §97-85.
Certified questions of law, §97-86.
Commission to determine all questions, §97-91.
Hearings, §§97-83, 97-84.
Facilities, §97-83.1.
Security, §97-83.1.
Review of award, §97-85.
Employers report of injury, ICWorkComp Rule
104.
Executive secretary, §97-78(b).
Longevity pay in lieu of merit and other raises,
§97-78(b4).
Salary, §97-78(b1).
Expenses of members, §97-78(c), (d).
Forms.
Official forms, ICWorkComp Rule 103.
Habeas corpus.
Issuance of writs, §97-101.1.
Hearings.
Attorneys' fees, §97-88.1.
Agreements for fees.
Approval, §97-90(c).
Approval by commission, §97-90(a), (b).
Conduct of hearings, §97-79(d).
Disputes, §§97-83, 97-84.
Facilities, §97-83.1.
Security, §97-83.1.
Hours of business, ICWorkComp Rule 101.
Tort claims rules, ICTortClaim Rule T101.
Impeachment as provided for judges.
Applicability to commissioners and deputy
commissioners, §97-78.1.
**Information to commissioner of labor upon
request,** §97-81(e).
Insurance.
Proof of insurance coverage, ICWorkComp Rule
301.
Interrogatories.
Power to limit, §97-80(f).
Liability.
Referral of suspected fraud case, §97-88.2(d).
**Longevity pay in lieu of merit and other
raises.**
Administrator, executive secretary, chief deputy
commissioner, §97-78(b4).
Managed care organizations.
Application of provisions.
Waiver, ICManagedCare Rule X.
Construction of provisions.
Purpose of rules, ICManagedCare Rule I.

INDUSTRIAL COMMISSION —Cont'd
Managed care organizations —Cont'd
Contract provisions, ICManagedCare Rule VI.
Definitions, ICManagedCare Rule II.
Department of insurance.
Qualification, ICManagedCare Rule III.
Employee information, ICManagedCare Rule VII.
Employer.
Defined, ICManagedCare Rule II.
Employer network.
Defined, ICManagedCare Rule II.
Health care provider.
Defined, ICManagedCare Rule II.
Inclusive provider panels, ICManagedCare Rule VIII.
Information for employee/patient, ICManagedCare Rule VII.
Lists of physicians, ICManagedCare Rule VIII.
Managed care organization (MCO).
Defined, ICManagedCare Rule II.
Notice to commission, ICManagedCare Rule V.
Patient information, ICManagedCare Rule VII.
Purpose, ICManagedCare Rule I.
Qualification.
Department of insurance, ICManagedCare Rule III.
Generally, ICManagedCare Rule IV.
Qualified physicians, ICManagedCare Rule VIII.
Quality assurance, ICManagedCare Rule IX.
Required contract provisions, ICManagedCare Rule VI.
Revocation, ICManagedCare Rule IV.
Utilization review, ICManagedCare Rule IX.
Waiver, ICManagedCare Rule X.
Mediated settlement and neutral evaluation conferences.
Agreement of parties.
Compensation of mediator, ICMediatedSettlmt Rule 7(a).
Order for, ICMediatedSettlmt Rule 1(a).
Selection of mediator, ICMediatedSettlmt Rule 2(a).
Appeals.
Motions, ICMediatedSettlmt Rule 10.
Application of provisions.
Waiver of rules, ICMediatedSettlmt Rule 9.
Appointment from lists, ICMediatedSettlmt Rule 8(c).
Appointment of mediator, ICMediatedSettlmt Rule 8(b).
Attendance, ICMediatedSettlmt Rule 4(a).
Waiver of attendance requirement, ICMediatedSettlmt Rule 4(b).
Attorneys' fees.
Sanctions for failure to attend, ICMediatedSettlmt Rule 5.
Authority of mediators, ICMediatedSettlmt Rule 6(a).
Commission, appointment of mediator, ICMediatedSettlmt Rule 2(b).
Commission, order of, ICMediatedSettlmt Rule 1(c).
Compensation of mediator, ICMediatedSettlmt Rule 7(b).
Commission, waiver of rules, ICMediatedSettlmt Rule 9.
Completion.
Request to extend date, ICMediatedSettlmt Rule 3(c).
Content of order, ICMediatedSettlmt Rule 1(f).

INDUSTRIAL COMMISSION —Cont'd
Mediated settlement and neutral evaluation conferences —Cont'd
Costs.
Sanctions for failure to attend, ICMediatedSettlmt Rule 5.
Delay of other proceedings, ICMediatedSettlmt Rule 3(e).
Duties of mediators, ICMediatedSettlmt Rule 6(b).
Duties of parties, representatives and attorneys, ICMediatedSettlmt Rule 4.
Exemptions, ICMediatedSettlmt Rule 1(r).
Fees.
Payment of mediator's, ICMediatedSettlmt Rule 4(e).
Sanctions for failure to attend, ICMediatedSettlmt Rule 5.
Finalizing agreement, ICMediatedSettlmt Rule 4(d).
Neutral evaluation procedures, ICMediatedSettlmt Rule 9(I).
Generally, ICMediatedSettlmt Rule 3.
Lists of mediators, ICMediatedSettlmt Rule 8(c).
Mediation coordinator.
Motions, ICMediatedSettlmt Rule 10.
Mediators.
Appointments from lists, ICMediatedSettlmt Rule 8(b).
Authority, ICMediatedSettlmt Rule 6(a).
Certification and decertification, ICMediatedSettlmt Rule 8.
Compensation, ICMediatedSettlmt Rule 7.
Duties, ICMediatedSettlmt Rule 6(b).
Failure to appear at conference, ICMediatedSettlmt Rule 8(d).
Fees.
Payment, ICMediatedSettlmt Rule 4(c), (e).
Sanctions for failure to attend, ICMediatedSettlmt Rule 5.
Payment of fees, ICMediatedSettlmt Rule 4(c), (e).
Selection by mutual consent, ICMediatedSettlmt Rules 2, 8(a).
Motions, ICMediatedSettlmt Rule 11.
Authorization of use of neutral evaluation procedures, ICMediatedSettlmt Rule 1(i).
Dispense with or defer conference, ICMediatedSettlmt Rule 1(g).
Neutral evaluation.
Applicability of mediation rules and duties, ICMediatedSettlmt Rule 9(j).
Authority of evaluator to assist negotiations, ICMediatedSettlmt Rule 9(h).
Duties of evaluator, ICMediatedSettlmt Rule 9(g).
Ex parte communications.
Prohibited, ICMediatedSettlmt Rule 9(k).
Finalizing agreement, ICMediatedSettlmt Rule 9(i).
Motion to authorize use of procedures, ICMediatedSettlmt Rule 1(i).
Nature of neutral evaluation, ICMediatedSettlmt Rule 9(a).
Pre-conference submissions, ICMediatedSettlmt Rule 9(c).
Replies to, ICMediatedSettlmt Rule 9(d).
Procedure for conference, ICMediatedSettlmt Rule 9(e).
Modification, ICMediatedSettlmt Rule 9(d).
Standards of conduct for neutrals.
Adherence to, ICMediatedSettlmt Rule 9(l).

INDUSTRIAL COMMISSION —Cont'd
**Mediated settlement and neutral evaluation
    conferences** —Cont'd
Neutral evaluation —Cont'd
When conference held, ICMediatedSettlmt Rule
    9(b).
Notice of mediation order, ICMediatedSettlmt
    Rule 4(c).
Order for, ICMediatedSettlmt Rule 1.
Payment of mediator by parties,
    ICMediatedSettlmt Rule 7(c).
Pro se representation.
Cases involving plaintiffs not represented by
    counsel, ICMediatedSettlmt Rule 1(j).
̄̇ cesses, ICMediatedSettlmt Rule 3(d).
̇ ferral upon receipt of form 33 request for
    hearing, ICMediatedSettlmt Rule 1(b).
̇ ports.
̇ Duties of mediators, ICMediatedSettlmt Rule
    6(b).
Request of a party.
Order for, ICMediatedSettlmt Rule 1(d).
Sanctions, ICMediatedSettlmt Rule 5.
Saturdays, Sundays and legal holidays.
References to number of days to include,
    ICMediatedSettlmt Rule 12.
Scheduling of conference.
Duties of mediators, ICMediatedSettlmt Rule
    6(b).
Time conference held, ICMediatedSettlmt Rule
    3(b).
Timing of order, ICMediatedSettlmt Rule 1(e).
Waiver of rules, ICMediatedSettlmt Rule 10.
When conference held, ICMediatedSettlmt Rule
    3(b).
Where held, ICMediatedSettlmt Rule 3(a).
Mediation to order, §97-80(c).
Medical examinations.
Qualified physician to make examinations.
Appointment, §97-89.
Fees, §97-89.
Approval by commission, §97-90(a), (b).
Recovery from third-party tort-feasor is not
    prevented, §97-90(d).
Modification of award, §97-47.
Notice.
Employment covered by act, ICWorkComp Rule
    201.
Number of members, §97-77(a).
Offices, §97-79(a).
Location, ICWorkComp Rule 101.
Tort claims rules, ICTortClaim Rule T101.
Ombudsman program, §97-79(f).
Parties to proceedings.
Power to make additional parties plaintiff or
    defendant, §97-79(e).
Penalties.
Collection of fines and penalties.
Actions, §97-101.
Powers, §97-80(b).
**Public school employee injured during episode
    of violence.**
Entitlement to salary and other benefits.
Appeal of board of education decision,
    §115C-338(c).
Questions arising under provisions.
Determination by commission, §97-91.
Records.
Not open to public, §97-92(b).
Rehabilitation professionals, ICRehabProf Rules
    I to IX.
Application of rules, ICRehabProf Rule I.

INDUSTRIAL COMMISSION —Cont'd
Rehabilitation professionals —Cont'd
Cases rules applicable to, ICRehabProf Rule I.
Communication, ICRehabProf Rule VI.
Definitions, ICRehabProf Rule III.
Enumeration of qualifications, ICRehabProf Rule
    IV.
Goals of rehabilitation, ICRehabProf Rule III.
Interaction with physicians, ICRehabProf Rule
    VII.
Interpretation of rules, ICRehabProf Rule II.
Medical rehabilitation, ICRehabProf Rule III.
Medical rehabilitation goals, ICRehabProf Rule
    III.
Motions.
Change of rehabilitation professional,
    ICRehabProf Rule IX.
Notice, ICRehabProf Rule VII.
Parties.
Defined, ICRehabProf Rule III.
Physician.
Defined, ICRehabProf Rule III.
Professional responsibility, ICRehabProf Rule V.
Purpose of rules, ICRehabProf Rule II.
Qualifications, ICRehabProf Rule IV.
Records, ICRehabProf Rule VII.
Reports, ICRehabProf Rule VII.
Return to work, ICRehabProf Rule VIII.
Responsibility of professionals, ICRehabProf Rule
    V.
Return to employment.
Goals of rehabilitation, ICRehabProf Rule III.
Return to work, ICRehabProf Rule VIII.
Defined, ICRehabProf Rule III.
Second opinions, ICRehabProf Rule VII.
Suitable employment.
Defined, ICRehabProf Rule III.
Vocational rehabilitation.
Defined, ICRehabProf Rule III.
Work restrictions.
Return to work, ICRehabProf Rule VIII.
Reports.
Annual report of administration of article,
    §97-78(e).
Tabulation of accident reports, §97-81(b).
Resolving requests for medical compensation.
Strategic plan, §97-78(f).
Demonstration of success in implementing plan,
    §97-78(g).
Rules and regulations, §97-80(a).
Procedure for rulemaking, ICWorkComp Rule 803.
Waiver, ICWorkComp Rule 801.
Rules of civil procedure.
Court actions before commission.
When rules to govern, §1A-1 Rule 1.
Salaries, §97-78(a), (d).
Administrator, §97-78(b1).
Deputy commissioners, §97-78(b3).
Chief deputy, §97-78(b2).
Executive secretary, §97-78(b1).
Longevity pay.
Administrator, executive secretary, chief deputy
    commissioner, §97-78(b4).
**School employee injured during episode of
    violence.**
Entitlement to salary and other benefits.
Appeal of board of education decision,
    §115C-338(c).
Sessions.
Place for, §97-79(c).
Studies and investigations, §97-81(c), (d).

INDUSTRIAL COMMISSION —Cont'd
Subpoenas, §97-80(e).
Superior courts.
Authority of clerk to enter judgments, §1-209.
Terms of members, §97-77(a).
Tort claims against state departments and agencies.
Tort claim rules, ICTortClaim Rules T101 to T502. See CLAIMS AGAINST THE STATE.
Transaction of business, ICWorkComp Rule 102.
Utilization of rehabilitation professionals, ICRehabProf Rule I to X. See within this heading, "Rehabilitation professionals."
Vacancy, §97-77(a1).
Vice-chairman, §97-77(b).
Witnesses.
Powers as to, §97-80.

INDUSTRIAL DEVELOPMENT, §§158-16 to 158-24.
Applicability of article.
Counties to which article applies, §158-24.
Commission, §158-21.
Board of county commissioners.
May function and carry out duties of commission, §158-23.
Bureau.
Annual audit, §158-22.
Counties to which article applies, §158-24.
Environmental impact statements.
Ordinances requiring for major development projects, §113A-8(a) to (c).
Taxation.
Authorized activities, §158-7.1(b).
Elections.
Announcing results, §158-19.
Calling for tax election, §158-16.
Canvassing of results, §158-19.
Counting of ballots, §158-19.
Designation of ballot box, §158-18.
Form of ballot, §158-18.
Registration of voters, §158-17.
Supervision of county board of elections, §158-17.
When ballot supplied, §158-18.
Levy, §158-20.
Rate, §§158-16, 158-20.

INDUSTRIAL DEVELOPMENT FINANCING.
Authority.
Bond issues.
Capital projects for industry.
County may create authorities to issue bonds, NC Const Art V §9.
Capital projects for industry.
Authorities may issue bonds, NC Const Art V §9.
Local government finance.
General provisions, §§159-1 to 159-188. See LOCAL GOVERNMENT FINANCE.
Bond issues.
Authority.
Capital projects for industry.
Authorities may issue bonds, NC Const Art V §9.
Constitution of North Carolina.
Capital projects for industry.
Bond issues to finance.
County may create authorities to issue bonds, NC Const Art V §9.

INDUSTRIAL DEVELOPMENT FINANCING —Cont'd
Industrial and pollution control facilities financing.
Industrial and pollution control facilities financing act, §§159C-1 to 159C-27. See INDUSTRIAL AND POLLUTION CONTROL FACILITIES FINANCING.
North Carolina capital facilities financing act.
North Carolina industrial and pollution control facilities financing act, §§159D-1 to 159D-27. See INDUSTRIAL AND POLLUTION CONTROL FACILITIES FINANCING.

INDUSTRIAL DEVELOPMENT FUND, §143B-437.01.
Job development investment grant program.
Transfer of funds upon disbursement of grant, §143B-437.61.

INDUSTRIAL ESPIONAGE.
Larceny of secret technical processes, §14-75.1.

INDUSTRIAL HYGIENE.
Safety professionals, §§90-671 to 90-674.

INDUSTRIAL HYGIENISTS.
Definitions, §90-515.
Engineers.
Engaging in practice of, §90-516(f).
Injunctions.
Illegal practices, §90-516(d).
Issues of title, §90-516(a) to (c).
Venue.
Actions brought under article, §90-516(e).

INDUSTRIAL MACHINERY REFURBISHING COMPANIES.
Privilege tax imposed on, §105-187.51B.

INDUSTRIAL PARKS.
Commerce department.
Development tiers, exceptions.
Eco-industrial parks, §143B-437.08(j).
Multijurisdictional industrial parks, §143B-437.08(h).
Seafood industrial parks, §143B-437.08(i).
Two-county industrial parks, §143B-437.08(g).
Seafood industrial park authorities, §§113-315.25 to 113-315.39. See SEAFOOD INDUSTRIAL PARK AUTHORITY.

INDUSTRIAL SICK BENEFIT INSURANCE.
Accident and health insurance generally.
See HEALTH INSURANCE.
Defined, §58-51-65.
Policy provisions, §58-51-70.

INDUSTRIAL SITES.
Risk based remediation of contaminated industrial sites, §§130A-310.65 to 130A-310.77. See HAZARDOUS WASTE MANAGEMENT.

INEFFECTIVE ASSISTANCE OF COUNSEL.
Motion for appropriate relief.
Waiver of attorney-client privilege, §15A-1415(e).

INFANTILE PARALYSIS.
Food, drug and cosmetic act.
Drug or device, false advertising, §106-138(b).

INFANTS.
Abandonment of child, §§14-318.2, 14-318.4.

INFANTS —Cont'd
Abused, neglected or dependent juveniles.
Generally, §§7B-100 to 7B-1414.
See CHILD ABUSE, NEGLECT OR
DEPENDENCY.
Adoption.
General provisions.
See ADOPTION.
Baby drop off, §§14-318.2, 14-318.4.
Bastardy.
Illegitimate children, support, legitimation, civil
actions, §§49-1 to 49-17.
See CHILDREN BORN OUT OF WEDLOCK.
ternity.
Proceedings to establish generally.
See PATERNITY.
d care facilities.
e CHILD CARE FACILITIES.
d placement.
See CHILD PLACEMENT.
Children and minors generally.
See CHILDREN AND MINORS.
Consent to health care for minors, §§32A-28 to
32A-34.
Cremation of fetal remains.
Acknowledgment of delivery, §90-210.129(o).
Fetal report of death, §90-210.129(p).
Custody.
See CHILD CUSTODY.
Family preservation act, §§143B-150.5,
143B-150.6.
General provisions.
See CHILDREN AND MINORS.
Health care for minors, consent to, §§32A-28 to
32A-34.
Illegitimate children.
Paternity.
Proceedings to establish generally.
See PATERNITY.
Support, legitimation, civil actions regarding,
§§49-1 to 49-17.
See CHILDREN BORN OUT OF WEDLOCK.
Juvenile code.
Abused, neglected or dependent juveniles.
Generally, §§7B-100 to 7B-1414.
See CHILD ABUSE, NEGLECT OR
DEPENDENCY.
Generally.
See JUVENILE CODE.
Juvenile services.
See YOUTH SERVICES.
Minors generally.
See CHILDREN AND MINORS.
Parent and child.
See PARENT AND CHILD.
Safe haven for infants, §§14-318.2, 14-318.4.
Youth services.
See YOUTH SERVICES.

INFECTIONS.
Adult care homes.
Medication aides.
Infection control training, §131D-4.5B.
Prevention requirements, §131D-4.4.
Reporting communicable disease outbreaks.
Guidelines, §131D-4.4B.
Supervisors.
Infection control training, §131D-4.5C.
Health care associated infections.
Statewide surveillance and reporting system,
§130A-150.

INFECTIOUS DISEASES.
Communicable diseases generally.
See COMMUNICABLE DISEASES.
Nuclear, biological or chemical agents.
Terrorist incident using, §§130A-475 to 130A-479.
See TERRORIST INCIDENT USING
NUCLEAR, BIOLOGICAL OR CHEMICAL
AGENTS.

INFERENCES.
Presumptions generally.
See PRESUMPTIONS.
Sexual exploitation of minor.
Depiction of minor, §§14-190.16(b), 14-190.17A(b),
14-190.17(b).

**INFLUENCING EMPLOYEES IN VIOLATING
DUTIES OWED EMPLOYERS,** §§14-353,
14-354.

INFORMANTS.
**Criminal investigation and intelligence
records.**
Law enforcement not required to disclose,
§132-1.4(h).
Criminal procedure.
Identity to be disclosed, §15A-978(b).

IN FORMA PAUPERIS.
Appeals, §1-288.
Appeal bond, AppProc Rule 17(d).
Dismissal of actions.
Rules of civil procedure, §1A-1 Rule 41(d).

INFORMATIONS.
Consolidation of charges, §15A-643.
Contents, §15A-644(b).
Defined, §15A-641(b).
Informality.
Bill or warrant not quashed for informality,
§15-153.
Joinder.
Offenses and defendants, §15A-643.
**Pleadings in felony cases and misdemeanor
cases initiated in supreme court division.**
Amendment, §15A-923(d).
Form, §15A-923(b).
Prosecution on information, §15A-923(a).
Plea of guilty or no contest in district court,
§15A-644.1.
Previous convictions.
Allegations, §15A-645.
Superior court.
Prosecutions originating in superior court to be
upon indictment or information, §15A-642(a).
Superseding informations, §15A-646.

INFORMATION TECHNOLOGY SERVICES.
Biennial state information technology plan,
§147-33.72B.
**Business and disaster plan with respect to
information technology.**
State agencies to develop and review,
§147-33.89(a).
Cost-sharing basis.
Office providing services on, §147-33.83(c).
Disaster recovery plan.
State agencies to establish, §147-33.89(a).
State agencies to submit to office annually,
§147-33.89(b).
Disaster recovery planning team.
State agencies to establish, §147-33.89(a).
Dispute resolution panel, §147-33.93.

INFORMATION TECHNOLOGY SERVICES
—Cont'd
Disputes between CIO and agencies.
Resolution, procedure, §147-33.72D.
Information resource management commission.
Administrative procedure.
Special provisions, §§150B-38 to 150B-42.
School computer purchases.
Guidelines for useful life of computers purchased, §115C-529.
Information technology fund, §147-33.72H.
Joint legislative oversight committee on information technology, §§120-230 to 120-235.
Legacy information technology systems assessment.
Analysis for needs, costs and time frame, §147-33.90(a) to (c).
Local governmental entities.
Procurement of information technology, §147-33.96(b).
Telecommunications services for, §147-33.92(a), (b).
Use of services, programs and contracts, §147-33.82(b).
Office of information technology services, §§147-33.75 to 147-33.104A.
Applicability of provisions.
Exempt agencies, §147-33.80.
Budgets, §147-33.88(a).
Confidentiality, §147-33.83(b).
Cost-sharing basis.
Office providing services on, §147-33.83(c).
Criminal record checks.
Fee, §114-19.20(b).
Provision generally, §114-19.20(a).
Definitions, §147-33.81.
Local governmental entities, §147-33.82(b).
Duties, §§147-33.82(a), 147-33.83(a).
Procurement of information technology, §147-33.95(b).
Electronic procurement.
Application service provider, §143-48.3(c).
Authority to use, §147-33.95(e).
Exempt agencies, §147-33.80.
Fee disputes, resolution, §147-86.2.
Governor.
Authority over office, §147-33.75(b).
Transferred to office of Governor, §147-33.75(a).
Powers, §147-33.83(a).
Procurement of information technology, §147-33.95(b).
Reports, §§147-33.87, 147-33.88(b).
Procurement of information technology, §147-33.97(b), (c).
Webportal system.
Development and implementation, §66-58.20(b).
Procurement of information technology, §§147-33.95 to 147-33.104A.
Aggregation of purchases.
Cost savings, §147-33.72F.
Attorney general.
Assistance by, §147-33.103(a).
Board of awards.
Review, §147-33.101(a).
Bribery, §147-33.99.
Certain purchases prohibited, §147-33.104A.
Applicability of exemptions, §147-33.104A(a).
List of manufacturers, §147-33.104A(c).

INFORMATION TECHNOLOGY SERVICES
—Cont'd
Procurement of information technology
—Cont'd
Certain purchases prohibited —Cont'd
Manufacturer compliance required, §147-33.104A(b).
Certification that information technology bids submitted without collusion, §147-33.100.
Cost savings, §147-33.72F.
Director of the budget.
Review and approval, §147-33.101(b).
Disclosures by vendor submitting bid, §147-33.97(a1).
Retention of statements, §147-33.97(a2).
Electronic bidding, §147-33.95(d).
Electronic procurement system, authority to use, §147-33.95(e).
Financial interest of officers in sources of supply, §147-33.99.
Generally, §147-33.95(a).
Liability for violations, §147-33.102.
Local governments, §147-33.96(b).
Policy of state, §147-33.97(a).
Powers and duties, §147-33.95(b).
Reporting, §147-33.97(b), (c).
Reverse auctions, §147-33.95(c).
Rules.
Authority to adopt, §147-33.95(f).
State agency contractual authority restricted, §147-33.96(a).
Unauthorized use of public purchase or contract procedures for private benefit, §147-33.98(a).
Criminal penalty, §147-33.98(c).
Exceptions to prohibition, §147-33.98(b).
Public contracts, §143-129.8.
Revenue department.
Deviations authorized for department.
Generally, §147-33.84(a).
Plans, policies and rules to be adopted by, §147-33.84(b), (c).
Review, §147-33.84(d).
Security for information technology services.
Approval of technology purchased or use by state agency, §147-33.111(a).
Assessment of agency compliance with standards, §147-33.112.
Assessments of network vulnerability, §147-33.111(a1).
State auditor, assessment of security practices not affected, §147-33.111(d).
Contracts for assessment of network vulnerability.
Approval by CIO, §147-33.111(c).
Cooperation by heads of state agencies, §147-33.113(a), (b).
State entities establishing own security standards, §147-33.111(b).
Statewide standards.
CIO to establish, §147-33.110.
State chief information officer.
Agency information technology projects.
Review and approval, §147-33.72C(a).
Suspension of approval, §147-33.72C(c).
Appointment, §147-33.76(a).
Approval of technology purchased or use by state agency, §§147-33.82(d), 147-33.111(a).
Assessment of agency compliance.
Security standards, §147-33.112.
Assessments of network vulnerability, §147-33.111(a1).
State auditor, assessment of security practices not affected, §147-33.111(d).

INFORMATION TECHNOLOGY SERVICES
—Cont'd

State chief information officer —Cont'd
Background investigations, authority to require, §147-33.77(g).
Biennial state information technology plan.
Development, §147-33.72B(a).
Budget requests, §147-33.77(e).
Contracts for assessment of network vulnerability.
Approval, §147-33.111(c).
Custody of books and records of office, §147-33.77(d).
utes between officer and agencies.
solution, procedure, §147-33.72D.
l of office, §147-33.76(a).
-range plan.
sponsible for developing and administering, §147-33.76(b1).
ers, §147-33.77(a) to (c), (f), (g).
ect management assistant.
esignation, duties, §147-33.72E(b).
ary, §147-33.76(c).
Statewide security standards.
CIO to establish, §147-33.110.
State information technology management.
Agency information technology projects.
Contracts between agency and private party.
Vendor performance review and accountability, §147-33.72C(e).
Implementation, §147-33.72C(b).
Performance contracting.
Vendor performance review and accountability, §147-33.72C(e).
Quality assurance.
Projects not subject to review and approval, §147-33.72C(d).
Review and approval, §147-33.72C(a).
Suspension of approval, §147-33.72C(c).
Agency responsibilities, §147-33.72E(a).
Biennial state information technology plan.
Agency plan developed by executive agencies, §147-33.72B(c).
Development by chief information officer, §147-33.72B(a).
Elements, §147-33.72B(b).
Cost savings, procurement procedures, §147-33.72F.
Disputes between CIO and agencies.
Agency request for review, §147-33.72D(a).
Review process, §147-33.72D(b).
Purposes, §147-33.72A.
State chief information officer responsibilities, §147-33.72E(b).
State treasurer.
Fee disputes, resolution, §147-86.2.
Telecommunications services.
Local governmental units and other entities, §147-33.92(a), (b).
State agencies, §147-33.91.

INFORMED CONSENT.
See CONSENT.

INFRACTIONS.
All-terrain vehicles, §20-171.21.
Appeals.
Review of disposition by superior court, §15A-1115.
Appeal of district court decision, §15A-1115(a).
Review of infractions originally disposed of in superior court, §15A-1115(b).

INFRACTIONS —Cont'd
Appearances.
Appearance bonds, §15A-1113(c).
Failure to appear to answer charge.
No order for arrest, §15A-1116(b).
Arrest.
Detention of person charged, §15A-1113(b).
Territorial jurisdiction, §15A-1113(d).
Failure to appear to answer charge.
No order for arrest, §15A-1116(b).
Bonds, surety.
Appearance bonds, §15A-1113(c).
Burden of proof, §15A-1114(f).
Child bicycle safety act, §20-171.9(d).
Cigarettes and tobacco products.
Fake identification offered by minor for purchase of tobacco product, §14-313(c).
Purchased by minors, §14-313(c).
Cleaning agents containing phosphorus.
Water and air resources.
Using agents, §143-214.4(g).
Concealed handgun permit, §14-415.21(a).
Contempt.
Enforcement of sanctions.
Use of contempt procedures, §15A-1116(a).
Costs, §15A-1118.
Defined, §14-3.1(a).
Disabled persons.
Motor vehicles.
Parking violations, §20-37.6(f).
District attorneys.
Hearing procedure.
Duties, §15A-1114(e).
Preparation of trial dockets, §7A-61.
District courts.
Costs in criminal actions.
Applicability of section to infractions disposed of in district courts, §7A-304(e).
Hearings conducted in open court, §7A-191.
Jurisdiction for adjudication and disposition, §7A-253.
No right to trial by jury in adjudicatory hearings, §7A-196(c).
Reporting not provided in hearings to adjudicate, §7A-198(e).
Education.
Motor vehicles.
Powers of local boards of education to regulate parking.
Violations of regulations of local boards of education, §115C-46(a).
Enforcement of sanctions.
Order of arrest.
Not to be used, §15A-1116.
Fines.
Enforcement of sanctions.
Use of fine collection procedures, §15A-1116(a).
Highways, roads and streets.
Obstructing highway drains, §136-92.
Hunting and wildlife.
Hunter orange material.
Violations of requirements, §113-291.8(b).
Identity theft.
Cash registers and other receipt printing machines.
Sale of, §14-113.25(b).
Credit, charge, or debit card numbers on receipts, §14-113.24(c).
Jurisdiction.
Adjudication and disposition, §15A-1114(a).

INFRACTIONS —Cont'd

Jurisdiction —Cont'd

Detention of person charged.

Territorial jurisdiction, §15A-1113(d).

District courts, §7A-253.

Jury.

District court adjudicatory hearings for infractions.

No right to trial by jury, §7A-196(c).

No trial by jury, §15A-1114(b).

Landlord and tenant.

Smoke detectors, §42-44(a1), (a2).

Lasers.

Criminal use of laser device, §14-34.8(c).

Magistrates.

Powers in infraction actions, §7A-273.

Mobile phones.

Use by minor while operating motor vehicle, §20-137.3(b), (e).

Mopeds, §20-140.4(c).

Motor carrier safety regulation unit.

Safety inspection of vehicles.

Failure to conduct inspection, §20-384.

Motorcycles, §20-140.4(c).

Motor vehicle license plates.

Covering or making illegible plate or renewal sticker, §20-63(g).

Transporter, dealer-transporter plates, §20-79.2(b2).

Motor vehicles.

Commercial drivers' licenses, §20-37.21(b), (c).

Driving without license, §20-37.21(a).

Violations of driver notice requirements, §20-37.21(b).

Disabled persons.

Parking violations, §20-37.6(f).

Fire department vehicles.

Motorist approach violation, §20-157(a).

Inspections, §20-183.8(a).

Lights.

Requirement violations, §20-129(a).

Passing vehicles.

Driver of overtaken vehicle not giving way to right in favor of overtaking vehicle, §20-149(b).

Penalty not specified, §20-176.

Public schools.

Powers of local boards of education to regulate parking.

Violations of regulations of local board of education, §115C-46(a).

Railroad grade crossings.

Crossing gate violation, §20-142.1(d).

Heavy equipment.

Moving at railroad grade crossing.

Violations of requirements, §20-142.4(f).

Stop sign violation, §20-142.2.

Vehicles required to stop, §20-142.3(c).

Seat belt.

Violations of mandatory use provision, §20-135.2A(e).

Speedometer.

Requirement violations, §20-123.2(b).

Stopping.

Traffic obstructed, §20-142.5.

Tandem trailers and subtrailer.

Load limitation violations, §20-115.1(h).

Transporting children under 12 years of age in open bed or open cargo area of vehicle, §20-135.2B(c).

INFRACTIONS —Cont'd

Municipalities.

Violation of ordinance is misdemeanor or infraction, §160A-175(b).

Novelty lighter.

Retail sale prohibited.

Violation, §66-16.1(d).

Parking in private parking space.

Removal of unauthorized vehicles.

Violations of provisions, §20-219.2(b).

Parking on community college campuses, §115D-21(b).

Parking on public school grounds, §115C-46(a).

Penalties, §14-3.1(a).

Authorized penalties, §15A-1361.

Pleas, §15A-1114(d).

Procedure for hearing and disposition.

Appeals.

Review of disposition by superior court, §15A-1115.

Appeal of district court decision, §15A-1115(a).

Review of infractions originally disposed of in superior court, §15A-1115(b).

Appearance bonds, §15A-1113(c).

Arrest.

Failure to appear to answer charge.

No order for arrest, §15A-1116(b).

Burden of proof, §15A-1114(f).

Contempt.

Enforcement of sanctions.

Use, §15A-1116(a).

Costs, §15A-1118.

Detention of person charged, §15A-1113(b).

Territorial jurisdiction, §15A-1113(d).

Disposition, §14-3.1(b).

General procedure, §15A-1111.

Review by superior court, §15A-1115.

District attorneys.

Duties, §15A-1114(e).

Enforcement of sanctions, §15A-1116.

Fines.

Enforcement of sanctions.

Use of fine collection procedures, §15A-1116(a).

General procedure for disposition, §15A-1111.

Hearing procedure, §15A-1114.

Burden of proof, §15A-1114(f).

Civil or criminal sessions, §15A-1114(c).

District attorneys.

Duties, §15A-1114(e).

Jurisdiction, §15A-1114(a).

Jury trial.

No trial by jury, §15A-1114(b).

Pleas, §15A-1114(d).

Recording not necessary, §15A-1114(g).

Jurisdiction, §15A-1114(a).

Jury trial.

No trial by jury, §15A-1114(b).

Pleas, §15A-1114(d).

Prehearing procedure, §15A-1113.

Appearance bonds, §15A-1113(c).

Detention of person charged, §15A-1113(b).

Territorial jurisdiction, §15A-1113(d).

Process, §15A-1113(a).

Use of same process for two offenses, §15A-1113(e).

Recordings.

Not necessary, §15A-1114(g).

Sanctions.

Enforcement, §15A-1116.

INFRACTIONS —Cont'd
Procedure for hearing and disposition —Cont'd
Summons and process, §15A-1113(a).
Use of same process for two offenses,
§15A-1113(e).
Superior courts.
Review of disposition, §15A-1115.
Appeal of district court decision, §15A-1115(a).
Review of infractions originally disposed of in
superior court, §15A-1115(b).
Venue, §15A-1112.
Public schools.
Motor vehicles.
Powers of local board of education to regulate
parking.
Violations of regulations of local board of
education, §115C-46(a).
Records.
Hearing procedure.
Recording not necessary, §15A-1114(g).
Smoke detectors.
Landlord and tenant, §42-44(a1), (a2).
Smoking in local government building, vehicle
or public place.
Violation of restriction, §130A-498(c1).
Smoking in restaurants or bars.
Violation of prohibition, §130A-497(b).
Social security numbers.
Public records, restricted use.
Recordation of instruments, §132-1.10(d).
Summons and process, §15A-1113(a).
Use of same process for two offenses,
§15A-1113(e).
Superior court jurisdictions, §7A-271(d).
Superior courts.
Costs in criminal actions.
Applicability of section to infractions appealed
to superior court, §7A-304(e).
Review of disposition, §15A-1115.
Appeal of district court decision, §15A-1115(a).
Review of infractions originally disposed of in
superior court, §15A-1115(b).
Venue.
Hearing and disposition of infractions, §15A-1112.
Water and air resources.
Cleaning agents containing phosphorus.
Using agents, §143-214.4(g).

INFRINGEMENT.
Leases, UCC.
Warranty against, §25-2A-211.
Exclusion or modification, §25-2A-214(4).
Sale of goods, UCC.
Buyer's obligation against infringement,
§25-2-312(3).
Notice of claim or litigation to person answerable
over, §25-2-607.
Warranty against infringement, §25-2-312(3).
Trademarks.
Counterfeit trademarks, §§80-11, 80-11.1.
Criminal use of counterfeit trademark, §80-11.1.
Deceptive or unfair trade practices, §80-12.

INHALANTS.
Toxic vapors generally.
See TOXIC VAPORS.

INHERENT RISKS.
Equine activity liability, §§99E-1 to 99E-3.
Roller skating rink safety and liability,
§§99E-10 to 99E-14.

INHERITANCE.
Decedents' estates.
General provisions.
See DECEDENTS' ESTATES.
Executors and administrators.
General provisions.
See EXECUTORS AND ADMINISTRATORS.
Inheritance tax.
See INHERITANCE TAX.
Intestate succession.
General provisions.
See INTESTATE SUCCESSION.
Simultaneous death, revised act, §§28A-24-1 to
28A-24-8.
See SIMULTANEOUS DEATH.
Small estates, §§28A-25-1 to 28A-25-6.
See SMALL ESTATES.
Surviving spouses.
General provisions.
See SURVIVING SPOUSES.
Wills.
General provisions.
See WILLS.

INHERITANCE TAX.
Bond issues.
Port authority bonds.
Gain from transfer not exempt, §136-265(g).
Refunding obligations issued by state.
Gain from transfer not exempt from taxation,
§142-29.6(f).
State bonds, act authorizing not addressing
exemption from taxation.
Not exempt from tax on gain from transfer,
§142-12.
Corporations.
Joint ownership of corporate stock and investment
securities.
Inheritance tax laws unaffected, §41-2.2(d).
Estate tax.
Apportionment of federal estate tax, §§28A-27-1 to
28A-27-9.
See FEDERAL ESTATE TAX.
Exemptions.
Port authority bond issues.
Gain from transfer not exempt, §136-265(g).
Refunding obligations issued by state.
Gain from transfer not exempt from taxation,
§142-29.6(f).
State bonds, act authorizing not addressing
exemption from taxation.
Not exempt on gain from transfer, §142-12.
Individual income tax.
Adjustments to taxable income, §105-134.6(d).
Intestate succession.
Descent and distribution, §29-13(a).
Determination of 120-hour survivorship
requirement, §29-13(b).
Investments.
Joint ownership of corporate stock and investment
securities.
Inheritance tax laws unaffected, §41-2.2(d).
Joint tenants and tenants in common.
Joint ownership of corporate stock and investment
securities.
Inheritance tax laws unaffected, §41-2.2(d).
Port authority bond issues.
Gain from transfer not exempt from taxation,
§136-265(g).
Probate and registration.
Inheritance and estate tax waiver.
Registration, §47-18.2.

INHERITANCE TAX —Cont'd
Registration.
Inheritance and estate tax waiver, §47-18.2.
Renunciation of property and fiduciary
powers, §31B-1(b).
Savings banks.
Joint accounts.
Provisions not to repeal or modify estate tax
law, §54C-165(b).
Securities.
Joint ownership of investment securities.
Inheritance tax laws unaffected, §41-2.2(d).
State bonds, act authorizing not addressing
exemption from taxation.
Not exempt from tax on gain from transfer,
§142-12.
State refunding obligations.
Gain from transfer not exempt from taxation,
§142-29.6(f).
Waiver.
Registration, §47-18.2.

INITIATIVE.
Referenda.
See REFERENDUM.

INJUNCTIONS.
Abortion.
Obstruction of abortion clinic, §14-277.4(d).
Woman's right to know act.
Civil remedies, §90-21.88(b).
Adoption.
Prohibited placement activities, §48-10-101(d).
Unlawful payments related to adoption,
§48-10-102(c).
Adult care homes.
Operation without license.
Action by department, §131D-2.6(a).
Affidavits.
Preliminary injunction.
Issuance, §1-485.
Air pollution control.
Enforcement procedures, §143-215.114C.
Airports.
Zoning.
Violations of provisions, §63-35.
Alarm systems licensing.
Violations of provisions, §74D-11(a).
Alcoholic beverages.
Beer franchises.
Wrongful termination of agreement,
§18B-1306(a).
Alimony.
Remedy available, §50-16.7(f).
Ambulatory surgical facilities.
Licensing of facilities, §131E-152(a) to (c).
Antifreeze.
Violations of article.
Applying for and granting preliminary or
permanent injunction, §106-579.12(d).
Appeals.
Pending appeal, §1A-1 Rule 62(c).
Restraining orders and injunctions in effect
pending appeals, §1-500.
Aquatic weed control.
Violation of article, §113A-226(b).
Arbitration.
Motion to compel arbitration, §1-569.7(a).
Architects.
Violations of provisions, §83A-17.
Athletic trainers.
Illegal practices, §90-537.

INJUNCTIONS —Cont'd
Atomic energy.
Radiation protection.
Violations of provisions, §104E-23(b).
Attachment.
Transfer of certificate of stock, §1-440.19(c).
Warehouse receipts.
Transfer of negotiable warehouse receipts,
§1-440.20(b).
Attorneys at law.
State bar.
Discipline.
Practice of law by attorney, §84-28(f).
Unauthorized practice, §84-37(b).
District attorneys to bring injunction
proceedings upon application, §84-7.
Auctions and auctioneers.
Violations of provisions, §85B-9(b).
Automobile dealers associations, §20-308.1(d).
Bankruptcy and insolvency.
Trespass on land.
Insolvency of defendant.
When allegation of insolvency unnecessary,
§1-486.
Banks.
Dissolution and liquidation.
Taking possession by commissioner, §53-20(f).
Unlawful use of "banks," "banking," "banker" or
"trust company" in nonbanking entity name,
§53-127(e).
Barbers.
Illegal practice, §86A-20.1.
Bills of lading.
Enjoining negotiation of document, §25-7-602.
Biologics.
Violations of provisions, §106-714(b).
Blue Ridge parkway.
Control of outdoor advertising.
Violations, §113A-170.
Boilers.
Commissioner of labor.
Uniform boiler and pressure vessel act.
Power to enjoin violations, §95-69.11.
Bonds, surety, §1A-1 Rule 65(c).
Appeals.
Restraining orders and injunctions in effect
pending appeals, §1-500.
Boxing, §143-658(c).
Breach of trust, §36C-10-1001.
Building code.
Code officials qualification board.
Certificates for code enforcement officials.
Violations, §143-151.18.
Business combinations, §75E-4.
Business corporations.
Judicial dissolution.
Powers of court, §55-14-31(c).
Business opportunity sales.
Violations of provisions, §66-100(c).
Cable television systems.
Theft of services, §14-118.5.
Campus police.
Prevention of violations, §74G-13(b).
Cease and desist orders.
See CEASE AND DESIST ORDERS.
Cemeteries.
Commission.
Power to bring action for, §65-53.
Certified public accountants.
Power of board of examiners to apply to courts for
injunctive relief, §93-12.

INJUNCTIONS —Cont'd
Charitable solicitation.
Power of attorney general to seek, §131F-24(a).
Power of department to seek, §131F-23(c).
Child care facilities, §110-104.
Child custody.
Enforcement of custody orders.
Power of court having jurisdiction, §50-13.3(b).
Simultaneous proceedings, §50A-206(c).
Child placing agencies.
Interference department carrying out duties, §131D-10.8(b).
Operating without license, §131D-10.8(a).
Child support.
Enforcement of support, §50-13.4(f).
Chiropractors.
Unlicensed practice, §90-147.
Civil investigative demand.
False claims act.
Failure to comply, §1-614(g).
Civil no-contact orders.
Workplace violence prevention, §§95-260 to 95-271.
See WORKPLACE VIOLENCE PREVENTION.
Civil rights, interference with, §99D-1(b), (b1).
Claim and delivery.
Notice containing order enjoining defendant from disposing of property, §1-474.1(a).
Closing-out sales.
Violations of provisions, §66-83.
Coastal area management.
Permits.
Violations, §113A-126(a).
Collection agencies.
Violations of provisions.
Restraining orders, §58-70-40(a).
Commercial code.
Enjoining negotiation of document, §25-7-602.
Commercial feed.
Relief from violations of article, §106-284.44(d).
Commodities.
Enforcement of act, §78D-22(b).
Remedies under chapter, §78D-23.
Company police act.
Violation of chapter or rule, §74E-13(b).
Consumer finance act.
Powers of commissioner of banks, §53-187.
Contents, §1A-1 Rule 65(d).
Contractors.
Electrical contractors.
Violations of provisions, §87-48(b).
General contractors.
Violations of provisions, §87-13.1.
Plumbing, heating and fire sprinkler contractors.
Violations of provisions, §87-25.1.
Refrigeration contractors.
Violations of provisions, §87-61.1(a).
Control share acquisitions, §75E-4.
Cooperative associations.
Unauthorized use of term "mutual" in name.
Violators may be enjoined from doing business, §54-112.
Corporations.
Nonprofit corporations.
Corporate power to act.
Ultra vires, §55A-3-04.
Cosmetic art, §88B-28.
Cotton gins.
Operation without registration, §§106-451.44.
Cotton merchants.
Operation without registration, §106-451.44.

INJUNCTIONS —Cont'd
Cotton warehouses.
Operation without registration, §106-451.44.
Counties.
Inspection departments.
Equitable enforcement of article, §153A-372.
Ordinances.
Enforcement, §153A-123(d).
Subdivisions.
Transferring lots in unapproved subdivisions, §153A-334(a).
Credit.
Women.
Right of action to enforce article, §25B-3(b).
Credit device fraud.
Telecommunication services, §14-113.6(c).
Credit repair services.
Violation of provisions, §66-225.
Cruelty to animals.
Civil remedies generally, §§19A-1 to 19A-4.
New animals.
Enjoining defendant from acquiring, §19A-4(b).
Permanent injunction, §19A-4(a).
Preliminary injunction, §19A-3.
Dams.
Dam safety law.
Violations, §143-215.36(c).
Debt adjusting, §14-425.
Dentists.
Unauthorized practice, §90-40.1.
Dietitians and nutritionists.
Violation of provisions, §90-367.
Disabled persons.
Protection act.
Relief available, §168A-11(b).
Discrimination.
Discrimination in business.
Enforcement of provisions, §75B-4.
Dissolution.
Damages on, §1A-1 Rule 65(e).
District courts.
Enforcement or invalidation of statutes.
Injunctive and declaratory relief to enforce or invalidate.
Grounds for transfer, §7A-245(b).
Extension, modification or vacation.
Applications.
Before whom heard, §1-498.
Jurisdiction of judge, §1-493.
Return, §1-494.
Divorce.
Distribution by court of marital and divisible property.
Equitable distribution, §50-20(i).
Order for custody of minor child.
Enforcement, §50-13.3(b).
Documents of title.
Enjoining negotiations of document, §25-7-602.
Dry-cleaning solvent cleanup, §143-215.104R.
Eggs.
Granting temporary or permanent injunction for violations, §106-245.24(b).
Elections.
Contributions and expenditures in political campaigns.
Violations of provisions, §163-278.28(a).
Military and overseas voters.
Injunction or other equitable relief, §163-258.18.
Electrologists.
Violations of chapter, §88A-22(a).

INJUNCTIONS —Cont'd

Electronic commerce in government.
Jurisdiction over transactions, §66-58.6(b).

Eminent domain.
Private condemnors.
Provisions not to preclude injunctive relief, §40A-28(g).
Public condemnors.
Remedy not precluded by provisions, §40A-42(f).

Employee assistance professionals.
Enforcement of article, §90-506(a).

Employment security.
Contributions.
Injunction to restrain collection.
Not to be issued, §96-10(f).
Operation by employer in violation of provisions, §96-10(g).

Energy.
Crisis administration.
Enforcement of act by injunction, §113B-24(c).

Enforcement or invalidation of statute, ordinance or regulation.
Superior court jurisdiction, §7A-245(a).

Engineers and land surveyors.
Violations of provisions, §89C-10(c).

Environmental health specialists.
Violations, §90A-66.

Ethics.
State government ethics act, §138A-45(g).

Execution sales.
Dissolution of order restraining or enjoining sale.
Procedure upon, §1-339.59(a), (b).

Expedited evictions.
Preliminary injunction against illegal activity pending completion of discovery, §42-70(e).
Preliminary injunction in emergency situation, §42-74.

Facsimile solicitation.
Unsolicited facsimiles, §75-118(a).

Fair housing.
Appropriateness of relief, §41A-7(j).

False claims act.
Civil investigative demand.
Failure to comply, §1-614(g).

Family law arbitration, §50-44(c).

Findings of fact and conclusions of law on preliminary injunction, §1A-1 Rule 52(a).

Fish and fisheries resources.
Buoys, nets, markers, stakes, etc.
Robbing or injuring, §113-268(e).
Encroachment upon, usurpation or otherwise violating public trust rights of people, §113-131(c).
Interference with taking of wildlife resources, §113-295(b).

Floodplain regulations.
Restraining violations of ordinances, §143-215.58(c).

Flour, corn meal and grain.
Grain dealers.
Violations of article, §106-615.

Food, drugs and cosmetics.
Inspections of donated food.
Restraining violations of article, §106-141.1(b).
Restraining violations of provisions, §106-123.

Fraternal benefit societies.
Application or petition for.
Attorney general upon request of commissioner, §58-24-155.

INJUNCTIONS —Cont'd

Fraud.
Removal or disposition of property with intent to defraud plaintiff.
Issuance of preliminary injunction when threatened, §1-485.

Funds transfers, UCC, §25-4A-503.

Funeral service.
Violations of provisions.
Power of board to seek injunction, §90-210.25(f).

General assembly.
Seal or coat of arms of Senate.
Use of likenesses, §120-271(b).

Geologists.
Violation of chapter, §89E-23.

Harmful materials sales to minors.
Disobedience.
Contempt, §19-20(a).
Permanent injunction, §19-18(b).
Preliminary injunction, §19-19(c), (d).
Notice of issuance, §19-19(d).
Temporary restraining order, §19-19(a), (b).

Hazardous waste management.
Inactive hazardous sites.
Failure to submit data or comply with orders, §130A-310.1(d).
Imminent hazard.
Violation of orders, §130A-310.5(b).

Health.
Secretary of environment and natural resources or local health directors, §130A-18(b).
Secretary of health and human services or local health directors, §130A-18(a).

Health care facilities.
Certificates of need.
Noncompliance with representations in application for certificate, §131E-190(i).
Home care agencies, §131E-142(a) to (c).
Hospices.
Violation of article, §131E-206(a) to (c).

Health maintenance organizations.
Violations of provisions, §58-67-165(e).

Hearing aid dealers and fitters.
Board.
Actions for, §93D-4.

Hearings.
Extension, modification or vacation.
Applications.
Before whom heard, §1-498.
Judges.
Before what judge returnable, §1-494.
Stipulation as to judge to hear, §1-495.
Return, §1-494.
Stipulation as to judge to hear, §1-495.

Historic districts and landmarks.
Violations of part, §160A-400.11.

Home care agencies, §131E-142(a) to (c).

Home inspectors.
Violations of provisions, §143-151.60.

Hospices.
Violation of article, §131E-206(a) to (c).

Hospitals.
Certificate of need law.
Enforcement and sanctions of article, §131E-190(h).
Licensing act, §131E-82(a), (b), (c).

Household cleaners.
Labeling cleaners containing volatile substances capable of producing toxic effects.
Sales in violation of provisions, §66-87.

Housemovers, §20-371(b).

INJUNCTIONS —Cont'd

Hunting and wildlife.

Authority of commission to institute action for, §113-306(e).

Encroachment upon usurpation or otherwise violating public trust rights of people, §113-131(c).

Interference with taking of wildlife resources, §113-295(b).

Industrial hygienists.

Illegal practices, §90-516(d).

Insurance.

Accident and health insurance.

Pharmacy of choice.

Violations of provisions, §58-51-37(h).

Holding companies.

Mandatory injunction directing commissioner to act, §58-19-70(b).

Violations of provisions, §58-19-45(a).

Supervision, rehabilitation and liquidation of insurers, §58-30-20.

Supervision proceedings.

Enforcement of supervision order, §58-30-60(i).

Unauthorized insurers.

Powers of commissioner, §58-28-20.

Unfair trade practices.

Undefined practices, §§58-63-40(b) to (d), 58-63-45.

Violations of provisions.

Restraining orders, §58-2-60(a).

Interpreters and transliterators.

Violations of license provisions, §90D-13.

Investment advisers.

Violation of chapter, §78C-28(a).

Irrigation contractors, §89G-13(a).

Issuance.

Judges.

Preliminary injunction.

When issued, §1-485.

What judges have jurisdiction, §1-493.

Judges.

Extension, modification or vacation.

Applications.

Before whom heard, §1-498.

Hearings.

Before what judge returnable, §1-494.

Stipulation as to judge to hear, §1-495.

Issuance.

Preliminary injunction.

When issued, §1-485.

What judges have jurisdiction, §1-493.

Return.

Before what judge returnable, §1-494.

Jurisdiction.

What judges have jurisdiction, §1-493.

Labor.

Retaliatory employment discrimination.

Relief granted in civil actions, §95-243(c).

Landscape architects, §89A-8(b).

Landscape contractors.

Violations of provisions, §89D-10.

Letters of credit.

Fraud or forgery.

Injunction on honoring, §25-5-109(b).

Limitation of actions.

Time of stay by injunction.

Not considered part of time limited for commencement of action, §1-23.

Limited liability companies.

Foreign limited liability companies.

Actions by attorney general, §57C-7-13.

INJUNCTIONS —Cont'd

Liquefied petroleum gases.

Violations of provisions, §119-59(b).

Littering.

Violations of section, §14-399(f).

Loan brokers.

Violations of provisions, §66-111(b).

Local government finance.

Offending officers, §159-182.

Local governments.

Housing.

Petition for injunction restraining public officer from carrying out order or decision, §160A-446(f).

Locksmith licensing, §74F-17.

Manufactured homes.

Enforcement of provisions, §143-151.1.

Marketing associations.

Breach of marketing contract, §54-152(c).

Marriage and family therapists.

Violations of provisions, §90-270.62.

Massage and bodywork therapy.

Violations of provisions, §90-634(c).

Medical assistance provider false claims, §108A-70.14(j).

Membership camping contracts violations, §66-247(c).

Mental health, mental retardation and substance abuse.

Facilities.

Licenses.

Enjoining violations of provisions, §122C-29(a), (b).

Mines and minerals.

Safety and health.

Powers of commissioner of labor, §74-24.12.

Uranium.

Exploration for uranium.

Violations of provisions, §74-87(b).

Money transmitters, §53-208.25(a).

Monopolies and restraint of trade.

Action to obtain mandatory order, §75-14.

Lender requiring borrower to deal with particular insurer, §75-19.

Mortgages and deeds of trust.

Enjoining or restraining sale.

Equitable grounds, §45-21.34.

Sales under power of sale.

Procedure upon dissolution of order restraining or enjoining, §45-21.22.

Motion pictures.

Fair competition.

Enforcement of provisions, §75C-5.

Motor carriers.

Insurance verification by for-hire carriers.

Failure to comply.

Civil penalty, restraining collection, §20-382.2(c).

Unlawful operation, §62-279.

Motor fuel marketing violations, §75-86.

Motor vehicle captive finance sources, §20-308.16(d).

Motor vehicle repairs.

Remedies for violation of article, §20-354.9.

Motor vehicles.

New motor vehicles warranties act, §20-351.8.

Odometers.

Violations of provisions, §20-349.

Municipalities.

Enforcement of ordinances.

Real property violations, §160A-175(e).

INJUNCTIONS —Cont'd
Municipalities —Cont'd
Zoning.
Appeals, certiorari to superior court,
§160A-393(m).
Remedies for violations, §160A-389.
Nonprofit corporations.
Attorney general.
Exercise of corporate franchises not granted,
§55A-3-05.
Corporate power to act.
Ultra vires, §55A-3-04.
Judicial dissolution, §55A-14-31(c).
Notaries public.
Violations of chapter, §10B-60(i).
Notice.
Preliminary injunction, §1A-1 Rule 65(a).
Temporary restraining order, §1A-1 Rule 65(b).
Nuisances.
Abatement of offenses against public morals,
§§19-1 to 19-8.3.
See NUISANCES.
Nurses.
Nursing pools, §131E-154.7.
Violations of provisions, §90-171.46.
Nursing pools, §131E-154.7.
Nursing homes.
Patients' bill of rights.
Civil action for injunctive relief to enforce
provision of article, §131E-123.
Restraining or preventing establishment, conduct,
management or operation of nursing home
without license, §131E-110(a) to (c).
Obstructing justice.
Violating orders of court, §14-226.1.
Obstruction of health care facilities,
§14-277.4(d).
Occupational safety and health.
Imminent danger, §95-140(b).
Occupational therapists.
Violation of article, §90-270.80.
Oil and gas conservation.
Violations of laws and regulations, §113-408.
Oil pollution and hazardous substances
control.
Offshore oil and gas activities.
Violations of part, §143-215.94FF(a).
Opticians.
Violations of provisions, §90-254.
Optometrists.
Illegal practices, §90-121.1.
Ordinances.
Real property.
Enforcement of violation of real property,
§160A-175(e).
Pastoral counselors.
Certification of fee-based practicing pastoral
counselors.
Injunctive relief against violations, §90-393.
Perfusionists, §90-692.
Pharmacists and pharmacies.
Board of pharmacy.
Authority, §90-85.39.
Physical therapists.
Violations of provisions.
Actions for injunctive relief, §90-270.37(a).
Venue, §90-270.37(b).
Physicians and surgeons.
Violations of provisions, §90-14.12.
Pipelines.
Safety standards for gas pipeline facilities.
Violations of provisions, §62-50(f).

INJUNCTIONS —Cont'd
Plant protection and conservation.
Violations of article, §106-202.19(c).
Podiatrists, §90-202.13.
Pollution control.
Sedimentation pollution control act of 1973.
Violations of programs, §113A-65.
Power of sale, sales under.
Dissolution of order restraining or enjoining sale.
Judge ordering sale, §45-21.22(a), (b).
Preliminary injunctions.
Extension.
Application.
Before whom heard, §1-498.
Findings of fact and conclusions of law necessary,
§1A-1 Rule 52(a).
Issuance.
Grounds, §1-485.
Modification.
Application.
Before whom heard, §1-498.
Notice required, §1A-1 Rule 65(a).
Vacation.
Application.
Before whom heard, §1-498.
When issued, §1-485.
Preneed funeral contracts and funds.
Violations of article, §90-210.70(e).
Private personnel services.
Violations of provisions, §95-47.10.
Private protective services.
Violations of provisions.
Powers of board, §74C-17(a).
Professional counselors.
Board not required to post bond, §90-342.
Professional employer organizations,
§58-89A-165(a), (e).
Psychologists.
Violations of provisions, §90-270.19.
Public officers and employees.
Improper government activities.
Reporting.
Civil actions for injunctive relief, §126-86.
Public utilities.
Violations of provisions applicable to water or
sewer utilities service, §62-310(b).
Quo warranto.
Possession of office not enjoined pending trial,
§1-524(a).
Applicability of provisions, §1-524(b).
Racketeer influenced and corrupt
organizations.
Prohibited activities, §75D-8.
Real estate appraisal management companies.
Violations, §93E-2-10(b).
Real estate brokers.
Violations of provisions, §93A-6(c).
Records.
Public records.
Regaining custody of public records, §132-5.1.
Recreational therapists, §90C-37.
Rerefined or reprocessed oil.
Injunctions following multiple offenses, §119-13.3.
Respiratory care practitioners.
Regulatory violations, §90-663.
Retaliatory employment discrimination.
Relief granted in civil actions, §95-243(c).
Return.
Judges.
Before what judge returnable, §1-494.

INJUNCTIONS —Cont'd
Safety professionals.
Unlawful representation, §90-672(a).
Sale of merchandise by governmental units.
Actions for injunctive relief, §66-58(m).
Savings and loan associations.
Interstate branches, §54B-274(c).
Violations of provisions, §54B-8(d).
Commissioner may request attorney general to
institute action for, §54B-65(c).
Savings banks.
Dissolution.
Involuntary liquidation.
Continued operation of savings bank,
§54C-83(l).
Interstate branch banks, §54C-208.
Unlawful operation as savings bank, §54C-8(c).
Unlawful use of "banks," "banking," "banker" or
"trust company" in nonbanking entity name,
§53-127(e).
Scope, §1A-1 Rule 65(d).
Secured transactions.
Remedies for noncompliance with article,
§25-9-625(a).
Limitation of liability, §25-9-628.
Securities regulation.
Violations of provisions, §78A-47(a).
Security, §1A-1 Rule 65(c).
Sewers.
Violations of public utilities provisions applicable
to sewers, §62-310(b).
**Sheriffs' education and training standard
commission.**
Violation of chapter by justice officer, §17E-9(c).
Social workers, certification and licensure.
Violations of provisions, §90B-13.
Soil additives act, §106-50.38.
Soil scientists.
Power of board to seek injunction, §89F-23.
**Speech and language pathologists and
audiologists.**
Violations of provisions.
Power of board to bring action, §90-304(a).
State of emergency.
Public or private educational institutions,
§14-288.18(a), (b).
Stays.
Exceptions to automatic stay, §1A-1 Rule 62(a).
Substance abuse professionals.
Illegal practices, §90-113.45.
Superior courts.
Enforcement or invalidation of statutes.
Injunctive and declaratory relief to enforce or
invalidate, §7A-245.
Extension, modification or vacation.
Applications.
Before whom heard, §1-498.
Jurisdiction of judge, §1-493.
Return, §1-494.
Swine farms.
Relief generally, §106-804(a).
Targeted picketing of residence, §14-277.4A(d).
Taxation.
Property taxes.
Restrictions on use of injunction, §105-379(a).
Telephone solicitations.
Action by subscriber seeking, §75-105(b).
Temporary restraining orders.
Duration, §1A-1 Rule 65(b).
Extension.
Application.
Before whom heard, §1-498.

INJUNCTIONS —Cont'd
Temporary restraining orders —Cont'd
Hearing, §1A-1 Rule 65(b).
Modification.
Application.
Before whom heard, §1-498.
Notice, §1A-1 Rule 65(b).
Vacation.
Application.
Before whom heard, §1-498.
Time shares.
Violations of provisions, §93A-54(c).
Trade secrets.
Misappropriation, §66-154(a).
Tramways.
Passenger tramways.
Restraining operation of tramways or
compelling compliance with commissioner's
orders, §95-123.
Trees and timber.
Title to timberlands.
Trial of title, §1-487.
When timber may be cut, §1-488.
Trespass.
Trial of title to timberlands, §1-487.
When timber may be cut, §1-488.
When solvent defendant restrained, §1-486.
Trespass.
Insolvency of defendant.
When allegation of insolvency unnecessary,
§1-486.
Trees and timber.
Solvent defendant.
When restrained, §1-486.
Trial of title to timberlands, §1-487.
When timber may be cut, §1-488.
Trust companies.
Seizure by commissioner.
Objection and response to seizure, §53-382(a).
Unlawful use of "banks," "banking," "banker" or
"trust company" in nonbanking entity name,
§53-127(e).
Trusts and trustees.
Breach of trust, §36C-10-1001.
Unauthorized disclosure of information,
§48-10-105(c).
Unemployment compensation.
Contributions.
Injunction to restrain collection.
Not to be issued, §96-10(f).
Operation by employer in violation of provisions,
§96-10(g).
Unit ownership.
Relief for noncompliance with regulations and
covenants, §47A-10.
Unsolicited facsimiles, §75-118(a).
Uranium.
Exploration for uranium.
Violations of provisions, §74-87(b).
Veterinarians.
Violations of provisions, §90-187.13.
Viatical settlements, §58-58-290(a).
Violating orders of court, §14-226.1.
Wage and hour act.
Violations of provisions, §95-25.24.
Warehouse receipts.
Enjoining negotiation of document, §25-7-602.
Wastewater system contractors and inspectors.
Certification, §90A-81(c).
Water and air resources.
Enforcement procedures, §143-215.6C.

INJUNCTIONS —Cont'd
Water and air resources —Cont'd
Water and air quality reporting, §143-215.69(c).
Waters and watercourses.
Natural and scenic rivers system.
Violations of provisions, §113A-42(a).
Use of water resources.
Capacity use areas.
Enforcement procedures, §143-215.17(c).
Water supply and waterworks.
Violations of public utilities provisions applicable
to water service, §62-310(b).
Weights and measures.
Violations of provisions, §81A-30.
Well contractors, §87-98.13.
Wells.
Construction.
Violations of provisions, §87-95.
Wildlife resources commission.
Prevention of irreparable injury to wildlife,
§113-306(e).
Wine distribution agreements, §18B-1207.
Women.
Credit rights.
Actions to enforce article, §25B-3(b).
Workplace violence prevention.
Civil no-contact orders, §§95-260 to 95-271.
See WORKPLACE VIOLENCE PREVENTION.

INJURED IN LINE OF DUTY.
**Law enforcement officers, firefighters, rescur
squad workers.**
Tuition and fee waivers to spouse or child,
§§115B-1 to 115B-6.

INJURING MOTOR VEHICLE, §20-107.

INJURY TO PROPERTY.
Vandalism.
See VANDALISM.

IN KIND DISTRIBUTIONS.
**Powers of fiduciaries incorporated by
reference,** §32-27.

INKJETS.
**Agreement prohibiting reusing,
remanufacturing or refilling.**
Void and unenforceable, §75-36.

INLAND FISHING LICENSES.
Generally.
See FISH AND FISHING.

INLAND WATERWAYS.
Acquisition of land for, §§104-12, 104-19, 104-25.
Bridges over waterways, §§104-17, 104-23.
Condemnation of land, §§104-13, 104-20.
Expenses and awards.
Method of payment, §§104-15, 104-22.
Public purpose.
Use declared paramount public purpose,
§§104-14, 104-21.
Jurisdiction.
Concurrent jurisdiction over waterways, §§104-18,
104-24.
Public purpose.
Use declared paramount public purpose, §§104-14,
104-21.
Right of entry.
Private lands.
Utilities commission to secure, §§104-13,
104-20.
State and United States may enter upon lands,
§104-16.

INLAND WATERWAYS —Cont'd
**Steam vessels not having United States
licensed pilots subject to pilot laws,** §76-44.
Surveys and surveyors.
State and United States may enter upon lands for
survey, §104-16.
Vessels exempt from pilot laws, §76-44.

INLINE SKATING.
Assumption of inherent risk, §99E-24(a).
Governmental entities.
Limitation of liability, §99E-25(b).
Duty of care not created, §99E-25(d).
Exceptions, §99E-25(c).
Independent concessionaires or other persons or
organizations.
Liability not limited by section, §99E-25(e).
Insurance carried by entity.
Not waiver of liability limits, §99E-25(f).
Sovereign immunity not waived, §99E-25(d).
Specifically designated areas for activities.
Requirement to participate on property owner
or controlled by entity, §99E-25(a).
Responsibilities of participants, §99E-24(b).

INMATE GRIEVANCE PROCEDURE,
§§148-118.1 to 148-118.9.
See PRISONER'S GRIEVANCE PROCEDURE.

INMATE LABOR, §§148-26 to 148-49.
See PRISON LABOR.

INMATES OF STATE INSTITUTIONS.
**Mental health, developmental disabilities and
substance abuse generally.**
See MENTAL HEALTH, DEVELOPMENTAL
DISABILITY, SUBSTANCE ABUSE.
Prisons and prisoners.
See PRISONS AND PRISONERS.

INNOCENCE CLAIM INQUIRY, §§15A-1460 to
15A-1475.
Claim of factual innocence defined, §15A-1460.
**Compensation under article 8 of chapter 148 of
general statutes.**
Eligibility, person determined innocent of all
charges, §15A-1469(i).
Death of convicted person.
Claim not considered, §15A-1467(a).
Definitions, §15A-1460.
Discretion of commission.
Determining whether to grant formal inquiry,
§15A-1467(a).
Evidence favorable to convicted person.
Disclosure to convicted person, §15A-1468(d).
Evidence of wrongdoing.
Referred to appropriate authority, §15A-1468(d).
**Extraordinary procedure to investigate and
determine claims.**
Purposes of article, §15A-1461.
Formal inquiry.
Discontinuance.
Convicted person uncooperative, §15A-1467(g).
Discovery and disclosure, §15A-1467(f).
Discretion of commission to grant, §15A-1467(a).
Indigency status, appointment of counsel,
§15A-1467(b).
Measures to obtain information, §15A-1467(d).
Notice to victim.
Inquiry granted, §15A-1467(c).
Process to compel attendance of witnesses and
production of documents.
Authority to issue, §15A-1467(d).

INNOCENCE CLAIM INQUIRY —Cont'd
Formal inquiry —Cont'd
Right to advice of counsel, §15A-1467(b).
Waiver of convicted persons procedure safeguards and privileges.
Statement from convicted person required, §15A-1467(b).
Full commission proceedings.
Closure of proceedings to public and victim, §15A-1468(b).
Confidentiality, records of proceedings, §15A-1468(e).
Notice to victim, §15A-1468(b).
Conclusion in case, §15A-1468(c).
Public hearings after completion of formal inquiry, §15A-1468(a).
Recording, transcription, §15A-1468(e).
Referral of case for judicial review, §15A-1468(c).
Vote to establish further case disposition, §15A-1468(c).
Witnesses.
Compelling testimony, §15A-1468(a1).
Further review of decision of commission or three-judge panel.
No right to, §15A-1470(a).
Innocence inquiry commission.
Administrative support.
Administrative office of court to provide, §15A-1462(b).
Budget or appropriated funds.
Reduction or modification of budget, use of funds.
Approval of commission required, §15A-1462(b).
Chair, §15A-1463(c).
Director.
Employment, qualifications, duties, §15A-1465(a).
Subpoenas.
Power of director to serve, §15A-1467(e).
Duties, §15A-1466.
Established, §15A-1462(a).
Independent commission under judicial department, §15A-1462(a).
Majority vote, §15A-1463(c).
Meetings, §15A-1463(c).
Places for holding, §15A-1465(c).
Notice of meetings, §15A-1463(c).
Powers, §15A-1466.
Quorum, §15A-1463(c).
Records not considered public records, §132-1.4(a).
Report, §15A-1475.
Services to assist in performance of duties.
Contract for, authority of director, §15A-1465(b).
Staff.
Employment by director, §15A-1465(b).
Voting members, number, appointment, §15A-1463(a).
Alternate members, §15A-1463(b).
Removal, §15A-1464(a).
Subsistence and travel expenses, §15A-1464(b).
Terms, §15A-1464(a).
Vacancies, §15A-1464(a).
Judicial review.
Three-judge panel.
Appointment, §15A-1469(a).
Compensation under article 8 of chapter 148 of general statutes.
Eligibility, person determined innocent of all charges, §15A-1469(i).

INNOCENCE CLAIM INQUIRY —Cont'd
Judicial review —Cont'd
Three-judge panel —Cont'd
Conference of attorneys before senior judge, §15A-1469(g).
District attorney of district of conviction.
Representation of state, §15A-1469(c).
Entry of order setting case for hearing, §15A-1469(b).
Evidentiary hearing, rights of convicted person, §15A-1469(d).
Indigency status.
Appointment of counsel, relief from costs, §15A-1469(e).
Notice to victim of case related hearings, §15A-1469(f).
Presiding judge, §15A-1469(a).
Prosecutorial misconduct alleged.
Special prosecutor to represent state, appointment, §15A-1469(a1).
Response to commission's decision.
Filing by state time, §15A-1469(b).
Ruling on convicted person's innocence, §15A-1469(h).
Special prosecutor to represent state.
Appointment, allegation of prosecutorial misconduct, §15A-1469(a1).
Time for appointing panel, §15A-1469(a).
Motion for appropriate relief.
Claim not motion, §15A-1411(d).
Referral of claim to innocence inquiry commission.
Relief available, §15A-1417(a).
Post conviction relief by convicted person.
Retention of rights, §15A-1470(b).
Post-trial motion, §15A-1401.
Prosecutorial misconduct allegations.
Special prosecutor, right to request, §7A-64(a1).
Purposes of article, §15A-1461.
Referral of claim to commission, §15A-1467(a).
Subpoenas.
Power of director to serve, §15A-1467(e).
Summary screening and dismissal of claim.
Power of commission, §15A-1467(a).
Waiver of convicted persons procedure safeguards and privileges.
Statement from convicted person required for formal inquiry, §15A-1467(b).

INNOCENCE INQUIRY COMMISSION.
Generally, §§15A-1460 to 15A-1475.
See INNOCENCE CLAIM INQUIRY.

INNS.
Generally.
See HOTELS AND OTHER LODGING PLACES.

INOCULATIONS.
Immunization generally, §§130A-152 to 130A-158.
See IMMUNIZATION.
Rabies.
Vaccinations.
See RABIES.

INORGANIC SALTS.
Antifreeze solutions compounded with, manufacture or sale prohibited, §66-66.

INQUESTS.
Compensation of jurors at inquest, §152-9.
Duties of coroners, §152-7.
Medical examiners to be notified of certain deaths.
Holding of inquests by coroner, §130A-394.

IN REM JURISDICTION.
Grounds, §1-75.8.
Interlocutory orders for protection of rem,
§1-75.9.
Manner of exercising, §1-75.9.
Proof of jurisdiction.
Judgment against nonappearing defendant,
§1-75.11.
Quasi in rem jurisdiction.
Grounds, §1-75.8.
Interlocutory orders for protection of rem, §1-75.9.
Manner of exercising, §1-75.9.
Proof of jurisdiction.
Judgment against nonappearing defendant,
§1-75.11.
Requirements, §1-75.3(c).
Requirements, §1-75.3(c).
Service of process.
Manner of service to exercise, §1A-1 Rule 4(k).

IN REM PROCEEDINGS.
Torrens system registration, §§43-1 to 43-64.
See TORRENS SYSTEM REGISTRATION.

INS.
Officers authorized to enforce criminal laws,
§15A-406.

INSANITY.
Generally.
See MENTAL HEALTH, DEVELOPMENTAL
DISABILITY, SUBSTANCE ABUSE.

INSANITY DEFENSE.
Civil commitment of defendant found not
guilty by reason of insanity.
Crime alleged involving serious physical injury or
death, §15A-1321(b).
Crime alleged not involving serious physical
injury or death, §15A-1321(a).
DNA sample required for certain crimes,
§15A-266.4.
Temporary restraint, §15A-1322.
Verdicts to so state, §15A-1237(c).
Incapacity of defendant to proceed, §§15A-1001
to 15A-1009.
Notice of intent to raise, §15A-959.
Pretrial determination of insanity, §15A-959.

INSECTICIDES.
Pesticide applicators, §§143-452 to 143-459.
See PESTICIDE APPLICATORS.
Pesticide board generally.
See PESTICIDE BOARD.
Pesticide consultants, §§143-455, 143-456.
Pesticide dealers and manufacturers licenses,
§§143-448 to 143-451.
Pesticide registration.
See PESTICIDE REGISTRATION.
Pesticides generally.
See PESTICIDES.

INSECTS.
Boll weevil eradication, §§106-65.67 to 106-65.78.
Mosquito control districts, §§130A-352 to
130A-358.
Pest control.
See PEST CONTROL.
State insect.
Honeybee, §145-7.
Structural pest control.
See STRUCTURAL PEST CONTROL.

INSECT STINGS.
Life-saving treatment to persons suffering
severe adverse reaction.
Department of health and human services to
promote means of training individuals to
administer, §143-509.

INSIDER INFORMATION.
Public officers and employees.
Misuse of confidential information, §14-234.1.

INSIGNIAS.
Insurance companies, §58-3-50.
Motor vehicles.
Operation of vehicles resembling law enforcement
vehicles prohibited, §20-137.2(a).
Misdemeanor, §20-137.2(b).

INSOLVENCY.
Bankruptcy and insolvency.
See BANKRUPTCY AND INSOLVENCY.
Banks.
See BANKS.
Prisoners.
Generally.
See DISCHARGE OF INSOLVENT
PRISONERS.

INSPECTION OF MOTOR VEHICLES.
Generally, §§20-183.2 to 20-183.8G.
See MOTOR VEHICLE INSPECTIONS.

INSPECTIONS.
Administrative search and inspection
warrants.
Authorized, §15-27.2(a).
Construction and interpretation.
Not to be regarded as search warrants for
certain purposes, §15-27.2(g).
Evidence.
Use of facts obtained, §15-27.2(f).
General search warrant provisions not to apply,
§15A-259.
Health purposes, §130A-17.
Issuance.
Conditions, §15-27.2(c).
Requirements, §15-27.2(d).
Who may issue, §15-27.2(b).
Period of validity, §15-27.2(e).
Adult care homes, §§131D-2.11, 131E-105.
Refusal to allow inspection, §131D-34(d).
Agriculture.
Marketing and branding farm products.
Authorized inspections, §106-194.
Authorized inspectors, §106-190.
Farm product inspection account, §106-194.1.
Alcoholic beverages.
Authority to inspect licensed premises,
§18B-502(a).
Disposition of seized beverages, §18B-503.
Interference with inspections, §18B-502(b).
State warehouse.
Private warehouses, §18B-204(b).
Ambulatory surgical facilities.
Licensing of facilities, §131E-150(a), (b).
Animal waste management, §143-215.10F.
Arson.
Failure of property owner to comply with public
authorities, §14-68.
Barbers, §86A-15(b).
Bees and honey.
Conduct of inspections and other activities,
§106-643.

INSPECTIONS —Cont'd
Bees and honey —Cont'd
Moveable frame hives.
Inspection for disease or disorder, §106-641.
Penalties for preventing inspection, §106-644(a),
(b).
Boilers.
Certificates.
Defined, §95-69.9(e).
Refusal to issue or renew, §95-69.17(b), (c).
Inspectors, §95-69.15.
Misrepresentation as inspector, §95-69.20(a).
Powers and duties of commissioner, §95-69.11.
Required, §95-69.16.
Boll weevil eradication.
Entry of premises, §106-65.71.
Building codes.
Local inspection departments.
Code officials qualification board.
Defined, §143-151.8(a).
Building inspections.
County inspection departments, §§153A-350 to
153A-375.
See COUNTY INSPECTION DEPARTMENTS.
Buildings.
Municipal building inspection, §§160A-411 to
160A-439.
See MUNICIPAL BUILDING INSPECTION.
Cardiac rehabilitation certification program,
§131E-170(a), (b).
Cash converters.
Law enforcement officers.
Cash purchases, §91A-7.1(b).
Child safety seat inspections.
Child passenger safety technicians, §20-137.5.
Commercial feed.
Description of samples obtained, §106-284.42.
Presentation of appropriate credentials,
§106-284.42(b).
Purpose of enforcement of article, §106-284.42(a).
Refusing admission of commissioner or agent,
§106-284.42(d).
Reports and inspection fees, §106-284.40.
Cosmetic art, §88B-27.
Shops and schools, §88B-4(b).
Operation of shop while board inspects for
compliance, §88B-14(c).
County inspection departments, §§153A-350 to
153A-375.
See COUNTY INSPECTION DEPARTMENTS.
County inspectors of articles of commerce,
§§66-1 to 66-7.
Dams.
Dam safety law, §143-215.32.
Plans and specifications of dams, §113-263.
Right of entry, §143-215.37.
Donated food.
By department of agriculture and consumer
services, §106-141.1.
Drugs.
Controlled substances, §90-107.
**Economic and community development
department.**
Main street solutions fund, §143B-472.35(j).
Emergency medical services.
Equipment sanitation, supply and design.
Inspection of ambulance for compliance,
§131E-157(b).
Fertilizers.
Commercial fertilizers.
Duty of commissioner to inspect, §106-662(a).

INSPECTIONS —Cont'd
Fertilizers —Cont'd
Commercial fertilizers —Cont'd
Fees for inspection, §106-671(a), (b).
**Fire investigations and inspections of
premises,** §§58-79-1 to 58-79-45.
**Fire-safety standard and firefighter protection
act,** §§58-92-35(b), 58-92-40.
Fires and fire protection, §58-79-20.
Fish and fishing.
Inspectors, §113-136.
Conflicts of interest, §113-225.
Seizure of lawfully discovered evidence,
§113-137.
Warning tickets, §113-140.
Jurisdiction of fisheries agencies generally.
Seafood industrial park authority, §113-315.34.
Food, drug and cosmetic act.
Additives deemed unsafe, §106-132.
Donated food to be inspected, §106-141.1.
Manufacture of foods subject to contamination
with microorganisms.
Permits governing manufacture, §106-131(c).
Power of commissioner, §106-140(a) to (c).
Gasoline and oil inspection, §§119-14 to 119-47.
See GASOLINE AND OIL INSPECTION.
Health care facilities.
Cardiac rehabilitation certification program,
§131E-170(a), (b).
Home care agencies, §131E-141.
Hospices, §131E-204.
Confidentiality of information, §131E-207(a) to
(c).
Highway inspection reports.
Falsification, §136-13.2.
Hogs.
Feeding garbage to swine, §106-405.7(a).
Home inspectors.
General provisions, §§143-151.43 to 143-151.64.
See HOME INSPECTORS.
Hospitals.
Licenses, §131E-80(a) to (e).
**Hotels, inns and other transient lodging
places.**
Sanitation of food and lodging establishments,
§130A-249.
**Ice cream plants, creameries and cheese
factories generally,** §§106-246 to 106-255.
**Interstate insurance product regulation
compact.**
Records, §58-91-40(a).
Jails.
Local confinement facilities, §§153A-221.1,
153A-222.
Labor.
Commissioner of labor.
Powers generally, §95-4.
Department of labor.
Inspection service fees, §§95-107, 95-108.
Law enforcement agents.
Inspection of licensed premises, §18B-502.
Limestone, marl and landplaster.
Sale of agricultural liming materials and
landplaster, §106-92.10.
Livestock.
Cattle tick.
Local state inspectors, §106-354.
Control of livestock diseases, §106-401.1.
Diseases.
Examination before slaughter, §106-549.17.
Hog cholera, §106-318.

INSPECTIONS —Cont'd
Livestock —Cont'd
Threat of disease imminent.
Warrantless inspection of vehicles, §106-399.5.
Local ABC officers.
Inspection of licensed premises, §18B-502.
Lubricating oils.
Commissioner of agriculture.
Duties of inspection devolve upon commissioner, §119-6.
Massage and bodywork therapy.
Approval of schools.
Fees for additional inspections, §90-631.2(d).
Renewal inspections, §90-631.2(c).
Mattresses and bedding.
Examination of records of bedding, §106-65.105(d).
Opening seams of bedding to examine filling, §106-65.105(d).
Meat generally, §§106-549.15 to 106-549.39.
See MEAT INSPECTIONS.
Medicaid and Health Choice provider requirements.
Provider requirements, §108C-11.
Mental health, developmental disabilities and substance abuse.
Facilities.
Licenses, §§122C-21, 122C-25.
Migrant farm workers.
Preoccupancy inspection.
Housing standards.
Application for inspection, §95-226.
Heating equipment.
When not required, §95-225(e).
Milk and milk products.
Definitions, §106-268.
Enforcement, §106-268.
Promulgation of rules and regulations for inspection, §106-267.
Records and reports of milk distributors and processors.
Commissioner of agriculture authorized to inspect, §106-264.
Mines.
Reclamation, §74-56(a).
Safety and health, §74-24.7(a).
Authorized representative of miners to be allowed to accompany commissioner, §74-24.7(g).
Request for inspection.
Notice to commissioner or director, §74-24.7(f).
Right of entry, §74-24.7(b).
Mosquito control districts.
Corporate powers of board of commissioners, §130A-355.
Motor carrier safety regulation unit.
Penalty for failure to conduct safety inspection, §20-384.
Motor vehicles generally, §§20-183.2 to 20-183.8G.
See MOTOR VEHICLE INSPECTIONS.
Nurses.
Nursing pools, §131E-154.5.
Nursing homes, §131E-105(a) to (c).
Food service inspection.
Frequency, §130A-235(a1).
In accordance with rules adopted by commission, §131E-105(a).
Refusal to allow, civil penalty, §131E-129(d).
Review of records, §131E-105(b).
Right of entry, §131E-105(c).

INSPECTIONS —Cont'd
Occupational safety and health.
Assaulting or killing person engaged in inspection functions.
Criminal liability, §95-139(f).
Commissioner of labor.
Right of entry, §95-136(a).
Subpoenas, §95-136(b).
Director.
Powers as to, §95-133(b).
Right of entry, §95-136(a).
Employer and employee representatives.
Right to accompany and consult with commissioner or director, §95-136(c).
Information obtained.
Powers of commissioner as to, §95-136(e).
Notice, §95-136(f).
Unauthorized advance notice.
Penalty, §95-139(d).
Reinspection.
Willful serious violation found, §95-136(a).
Request for inspection, §95-136(d).
Rules and regulations as to, §95-136(g).
Special emphasis inspection program, §95-136.1.
Oil pollution and hazardous substances control, §143-215.79.
Confidential information, §143-215.80.
Personnel system.
Records of each employee.
Files not subject to inspection, §126-22(a).
Exception, former state employees, §126-22(c), (d).
Right to inspect, examine copy, §126-23(a).
Pesticides.
Board may provide inspections, §143-466(c), (d).
Plant pests.
Agents of board, §106-422.
Narcissus inspection, §106-423.
Nursery inspection, §106-423.
Pollution control.
Sedimentation pollution control act of 1973.
Land-disturbing activities.
Periodic inspections, §113A-61.1(a), (b).
Poultry products, §§106-549.49 to 106-549.69.
See POULTRY PRODUCTS INSPECTIONS.
Private schools.
Sanitation, §130A-237.
Proprietary schools, §115D-89.
Public building contracts.
Safety officers, §143-135.7.
Public records, §132-6.
Public schools.
Fire hazards.
Inspection of schools for fire hazards, §115C-525(b).
Sanitation, §130A-237.
Right of entry generally.
See RIGHT OF ENTRY.
Riots.
Motor vehicles in or approaching riots area, §14-288.11.
Sale of goods, UCC.
Buyer's right to inspect goods, §25-2-513.
Disputed goods.
Preserving evidence of goods in dispute, §25-2-515.
Sales.
Disposition of seized alcoholic beverages.
Procedure, §18B-503(e).
Proceeds of sale, §18B-503(f).

INSPECTIONS —Cont'd
Schools.
Sanitation standards.
Principal to make inspection, §130A-237.
Sedimentation control commission.
Erosion control plans.
Inspection of area for compliance with plan,
§113A-54.1(e).
Seeds.
Agricultural and vegetable seeds to be inspected,
§106-277.21.
Right of entry for purpose of inspection,
§106-277.20.
Social services.
Local confinement facilities, §131D-11.
Soil additives act.
Sampling and inspection of additives, §106-50.36.
Solid waste management.
Projects for which loans made, §159I-27(a), (b).
Structural pest control.
Violations of article, §106-65.30(a), (c).
Toxic substances.
Identification.
Fire chief, §95-194(c).
Tramways.
Passenger tramways.
Commissioner of labor, §95-121.
Transportation department.
Highway inspection reports.
Falsifying reports, §136-13.2.
Vegetables, §106-284.19.
Veterinarians.
Power of board, §90-186.
Wage and hour act.
Commissioner of labor, §95-25.15(a).
Warrants.
Administrative search and inspection warrants,
§15-27.2.
Wastewater systems.
Required before systems covered or placed into
use, §130A-337(a).
Water infrastructure.
Inspection of projects, §159G-43.
Waters and watercourses.
Use of water resources.
Capacity use areas, §143-215.19(a) to (e).
Weights and measures.
Duties of commissioner, §81A-15.
Wildlife protectors.
Entry and inspection of licensed or commercial
premises, §113-302.1.

INSPECTION SERVICE FEES BY
DEPARTMENT OF LABOR.
Assessment and collections, §95-107.
Certificates of safe operation, §95-107.
Disposition of fees, §95-108.

INSTALLATION CHARGES.
Sales and use tax.
Exemption, §105-164.13.

INSTALLMENT CONTRACTS.
Land contracts.
Contracts for deed, §§47H-1 to 47H-8.
See CONTRACTS FOR DEED.
Leases, UCC.
Default.
Defined, §25-2A-103(1).
Lessee's rights and remedies, §25-2A-508.
Rejection and default, §25-2A-510.
Sale of goods, UCC, §25-2-612.

INSTALLMENT LAND CONTRACTS.
Contracts for deed, §§47H-1 to 47H-8.
See CONTRACTS FOR DEED.

INSTALLMENT LAND SALES DISCLOSURES,
§§47E-1 to 47E-10.
See RESIDENTIAL PROPERTY DISCLOSURE
ACT.

INSTALLMENT LOANS.
Corporations, §53-176(f).
Due date of first payment, §53-176(e).
Election to make loan under, §53-176(d).
Loan processing fee, §53-176(b).

INSTALLMENT PURCHASE CONTRACTS.
Department of administration.
Purchasing buildings , utilities and structures,
§143-341.
Public school equipment, §115C-528.

INSTALLMENT SALES.
See RETAIL INSTALLMENT SALES.

INSTITUTE OF MEDICINE, §90-470.

INSTITUTIONAL FUNDS.
Prudent management of institutional funds,
§§36E-1 to 36E-11.
See PRUDENT MANAGEMENT OF
INSTITUTIONAL FUNDS.

INSTRUCTIONS TO JURY.
See JURY AND JURY TRIAL.

INSUFFICIENCY OF PROCESS OR SERVICE.
Defense by pretrial motion, §1A-1 Rule 12(b).

INSUFFICIENCY OF THE EVIDENCE.
New trial.
Grounds for motion, §1A-1 Rule 59(a).

INSUFFICIENT FUNDS.
Bad checks.
See BAD CHECKS.

INSULIN.
Food, drug and cosmetic act.
Drugs deemed misbranded, §106-134.
Sales and use tax exemption, §105-164.13.
State health plan for teachers and state
employees.
Coverage mandates, §135-48.50.

INSURABLE INTEREST.
Artworks on consignment, §25C-5.
Life insurance, §§58-58-70 to 58-58-86.
See LIFE INSURANCE.

INSURANCE.
Accident and health insurance.
Generally.
See HEALTH INSURANCE.
Health insurance portability and accountability,
§§58-68-25 to 58-68-75.
See HEALTH INSURANCE PORTABILITY
AND ACCOUNTABILITY.
Hospital, medical and dental service corporations,
§§58-65-1 to 58-66-40.
See HOSPITAL, MEDICAL AND DENTAL
SERVICE CORPORATIONS.
Jurisdiction over providers of health care benefits.
Determination generally, §§58-49-1 to 58-49-25.
See HEALTH CARE BENEFITS
PROVIDERS.
Life and health insurance guaranty association,
§§58-62-2 to 58-62-95.
See LIFE AND HEALTH INSURANCE
GUARANTY ASSOCIATION.

INSURANCE —Cont'd

Accident and health insurance —Cont'd

Long-term care insurance, §§58-55-1 to 58-55-50.
See LONG-TERM CARE INSURANCE.

Long-term care partnerships, §§58-55-55 to 58-55-80.

Medicare supplement insurance, §§58-54-1 to 58-54-50.
See MEDICARE SUPPLEMENT INSURANCE.

Multiple employer welfare arrangements.
Regulation generally, §§58-49-30 to 58-49-65.
See HEALTH CARE BENEFITS PROVIDERS.

Risk pool, §§58-50-175 to 58-50-255.
See HEALTH INSURANCE RISK POOL.

Small employer group health coverage, §§58-50-100 to 58-50-156.
See SMALL EMPLOYER GROUP HEALTH COVERAGE.

Third-party administrators, §§58-56-2 to 58-56-66.
See THIRD-PARTY ADMINISTRATORS.

Actions.

Health care liability.
Negligent decision of health benefit plan providers, §§90-21.50 to 90-21.56.

Actuaries.

See ACTUARIES.

Adjusters.

Generally.
See INSURANCE ADJUSTERS.

Public adjusters, §§58-33A-1 to 58-33A-95.
See INSURANCE ADJUSTERS.

Administrative procedure.

Hearings.
Department of insurance and commissioner of insurance.
Special provisions, §§150B-38 to 150B-42.

Agencies.

Examination.
Commissioner of other authorized employee, §58-2-195(e).

Records.
Commissioner may require, §58-2-195(a).
Employee responsible for keeping.
Required, §58-2-195(b).
Enforcement of provisions, §58-2-195(d).
Violations of provisions, §58-2-195(c).

Reports.
Commissioner may require, §58-2-195(a).
Employee responsible for making.
Required, §58-2-195(b).
Violations of provisions, §58-2-195(c), (d).

Agents.

See INSURANCE AGENTS.

Agricultural finance authority.

Agricultural loans, §122D-9.

Alarm systems licensing.

Liability insurance.
Cancellation of policy, §74D-9(e).
Certificate of insurance to be maintained on file, §74D-9(f).
Requirements, §74D-9(d).

Alcoholic beverages.

County alcoholic beverage control board.
Defense of employees and officers.
Insurer provides defense, §160A-167.

Alien insurance companies.

Generally.
See FOREIGN OR ALIEN INSURANCE COMPANIES.

INSURANCE —Cont'd

Amusement device safety.

Liability insurance, §95-111.12.

Annual audited financial reports, §§58-10-185 to 58-10-265.
See INSURANCE COMPANIES.

Annuities.

See ANNUITIES.

Artwork on consignment.

Provisions as to insurable interest.
Not affected, §25C-5.

Assessment companies.

See ASSESSMENT COMPANIES.

Attorneys' fees.

Allowance of counsel fees as part of costs.
Basis for and amount of fees, §6-21.1(a).
Order of judge, findings of fact required, §6-21.1(b).

Authorized kinds of insurance, §58-7-15.

Banks.

Deposit insurance.
Requirements, §53-9.1.

Beach area essential property insurance.

Generally, §§58-45-1 to 58-45-96.
See BEACH AREA ESSENTIAL PROPERTY INSURANCE.

Underwriting associations, §§58-45-10 to 58-45-80.
See BEACH AREA ESSENTIAL PROPERTY INSURANCE.

Brokers.

See INSURANCE BROKERS.

Building code council.

Department of insurance.
Transfer to department, §143A-78.

Burial insurance.

Mutual burial associations, §§90-210.80 to 90-210.107.
See MUTUAL BURIAL ASSOCIATIONS.

Campus police.

Liability insurance policy or certificate of self-insurance, §74G-3.

Cancellation of insurance.

See INSURANCE POLICIES OR CONTRACTS.

Ceding insurer.

Generally.
See REINSURANCE.

Certificates of insurance.

Criteria for preparing, §58-3-150(f).
Defined, §58-3-150(d).
Policies distinguished, §58-3-150(e).
Rights conferred, §58-3-150(e).

Childbirth.

Maternity coverage, §§58-3-169, 58-3-170.

Child support.

Medical insurance, §50-13.11.

Citation of law.

Short title, §58-1-1.

Claims.

Secured transactions.
Inapplicability of article 9.
Transfers of policy interest or assignment of claim, §25-9-109(d).

Supervision, rehabilitation and liquidation of insurers, §§58-30-185 to 58-30-235.
See INSURER SUPERVISION, REHABILITATION AND LIQUIDATION.

Collision insurance.

Authorized, §58-7-15.

Commissioner, §§58-2-1 to 58-2-250.
See INSURANCE COMMISSIONER.

INSURANCE —Cont'd

Community colleges.
Annuity contracts, §115D-25.
Fire and casualty insurance on institutional
  buildings and contents.
    Funding, §115D-58.11(b).
    Purchase authorized, §115D-58.11(c).
    Purchase required, §115D-58.11(a).
Health insurance for employees, §115C-340(a), (b).
Liability insurance, §115D-58.12(a) to (e).
State funds to pay premiums, §115D-31.1.

Companies.
Generally.
    See INSURANCE COMPANIES.

Company police, §74E-3.

Compromise and settlement.
Advance or partial payments.
    Effect, §1-540.3(a).
Motor vehicles.
    Property damage claims arising from motor
      vehicle collisions or accidents.
        Settlement not to constitute admission of
          liability nor bar party seeking damages
          for bodily injury or death, §1-540.2.

Condominiums.
Property and liability insurance, §47C-3-113.
    Assessment to pay costs, §47C-3-115(c).

Confidentiality.
Consumer and customer information.
    Generally, §§58-39-1 to 58-39-165.
        See INSURANCE CONSUMER AND
          CUSTOMER INFORMATION PRIVACY.
Property and casualty actuarial opinions,
    §58-10-175(b), (c).

Consumer protection.
Free insurance as inducement to purchase goods
    or services, §§66-380 to 66-382.

Continuing care retirement communities.
General provisions, §§58-64-1 to 58-64-85.
    See CONTINUING CARE RETIREMENT
      COMMUNITIES.

Continuing education program for licensees,
§§58-33-130, 58-33-135.

Contribution.
Joint tort-feasors.
    Rights of liability insurer, §1B-1(e).

Cotton.
Warehouses, §106-451.11(b).

Counties.
Defense of employees and officers.
    Civil and criminal actions.
        Insurer provides defense, §160A-167.
Liability insurance, §153A-435(a), (b).
Public officers and employees, §153A-92.
Rail transportation liability.
    Contracts allocating financial responsibility.
        Insurance required, §153A-279(c).

Credit cards.
Credit card guaranty or collateral.
    Prohibited, §58-3-147.
Solicitation, negotiation or payment of premiums
    through credit card or debit card services,
    §58-3-145.

Credit insurance, §§58-57-1 to 58-57-115.
    See CREDIT INSURANCE.

Credit scoring.
Motor vehicle or property insurance, §58-36-90.

Credit unions.
Members.
    Cooperative marketing arrangements to
      facilitate members' purchase of,
      §54-109.75(b).

INSURANCE —Cont'd

Credit unions —Cont'd
Members —Cont'd
    Purchase of insurance for, §54-109.75(a).
    Source of insurance, §54-109.75(c).
Officers.
    Liability insurance for, §54-109.76.
Share and deposit insurance, §54-109.78(a).
    Prerequisite to granting of charter,
      §54-109.78(b).

Customer information safeguards act.
Generally, §§58-39-130 to 58-39-165.
    See INSURANCE CONSUMER AND
      CUSTOMER INFORMATION PRIVACY.

Debit cards.
Solicitation, negotiation or payment of premiums
    through credit card or debit card services,
    §58-3-145.

Decedents' estates.
Killing decedents.
    Proceeds payable to slayer, §31A-11(a).

Deceptive trade practices.
Generally, §§58-63-1 to 58-63-75.
    See INSURANCE UNFAIR TRADE
      PRACTICES.

Definitions, §58-1-5.
Accident, accidental injury and accidental means,
    §58-3-30(b).
Applicability of definitions, §58-3-30(a).
Accident and health insurance.
    Blanket accident and health insurance,
      §58-51-75(a).
    Credit accident and health insurance,
      §58-51-100.
    Franchise accident and health insurance,
      §58-51-90.
    Group accident and health insurance,
      §58-51-80(a).
    Hospitalization insurance, §58-51-105.
    Industrial sick benefit insurance, §58-51-65.
    Joint action to insure elderly, §58-52-1.
    Pharmacy of choice, §58-51-37(b).
Beach area property essential property insurance,
    §§58-45-5, 58-45-6.
Credit insurance, §58-57-5.
Credit property insurance.
    Dual credit property, §58-57-90(a).
    Personal household property, §58-57-90(a).
    Single interest credit property, §58-57-90(a).
"Equity security," §58-7-145(f).
Health insurance portability and accountability,
    §58-68-25(a), (b).
    Guaranteed availability of individual coverage
      to certain individuals with prior group
      coverage, §58-68-60(b), (h).
    Preexisting condition exclusion, §58-68-30(b).
        Creditable coverage, §58-68-30(c).
Holding companies, §58-19-5.
Insurance premium financing, §58-35-1.
Life and health insurance guaranty association,
    §58-62-16.
Life insurance.
    Credit life insurance, §58-58-10.
    Domestic insurance companies, §58-7-15.
    Employee life insurance, §58-58-150.
    Industrial life insurance, §58-58-5.
    Policies.
        Interest rates on life insurance policy loans,
          §58-61-5.
    Prearrangement insurance policy provisions,
      §58-60-35(a).

INSURANCE —Cont'd

Definitions —Cont'd

Life insurance —Cont'd

Requisites of contract, §58-58-1.

Solicitation, §58-60-10.

Long-term care insurance, §58-55-20.

Facilities, services and conditions, §58-55-35.

Medicare supplement insurance, §58-54-1.

Motor vehicle reinsurance facility, §58-37-1.

Post-assessment insurance guaranty association, §58-48-20.

Preferred providers, §58-50-56(a).

Rates, §§58-40-5, 58-40-10.

Readable policies, §58-38-15.

"Text,"§58-38-25(e).

Reciprocal insurance, §58-15-5.

Reinsurance intermediary, §58-9-2(a).

Risk retention groups, §58-22-10.

Small employer group health coverage, §58-50-110.

Supervision, rehabilitation and liquidation of insurers, §58-30-10.

Surplus lines, §58-21-10.

Third party administrators, §58-56-2.

Unauthorized insurers false advertising process act, §58-29-5.

Unfair trade practices, §58-63-5.

Utilization review, §58-50-61(a).

Department.

See INSURANCE DEPARTMENT.

Deposits.

Banks.

Requirements as to deposit insurance, §53-9.1.

Disability income insurance.

Standards for policies, §58-51-130.

Disability insurance.

Accident and health insurance generally.

See HEALTH INSURANCE.

Disabled persons.

Discrimination.

Prohibited, §168-10.

Disaster.

Stay of requirement for proof of loss, §58-2-46.

Discovery.

Scope of discovery.

Insurance agreements, §1A-1 Rule 26(b).

Discrimination by insurance companies.

Prohibited acts, §58-3-120.

Domestic reciprocals, §§58-15-100 to 58-15-150.

See RECIPROCAL INSURANCE.

Drive-thru deliveries, §58-3-169.

Duress.

Statements, releases, etc., obtained from persons in shock or under the influence of drugs.

Presumption of fraud, §8-45.5.

Education.

Continuing education program for licensees, §§58-33-130, 58-33-135.

Local boards of education.

Liability insurance, §115C-42.

Elderly.

Joint action to insure, §§58-52-1 to 58-52-25.

See HEALTH INSURANCE.

Electrical materials, devices, appliances and equipment sales.

Acceptable listings as to safety of goods, §66-25.

Legal responsibility for proper insulation unaffected, §66-26.

Liability.

Effect of provisions, §66-26.

INSURANCE —Cont'd

Elevator insurance.

Authorized, §58-7-15.

Embezzlement.

Agents, brokers or administrators embezzling money or substitutes for money, §58-2-162.

Reports, §58-2-163.

Emblems.

Companies, §58-3-50.

Emergency care.

Coverage required, §58-3-190.

Employer discrimination against lawful use of lawful products during nonworking hours.

Health, disability or life insurance policies distinguishing between employees, §95-28.2(b).

Employment security.

General provisions, §§96-1 to 96-29.

See UNEMPLOYMENT COMPENSATION.

Evidence.

Documents executed by commissioner.

Certificate as evidence of authority to do business, §58-2-115.

Originals and certified copies, §58-2-110.

Liability insurance.

Existence inadmissible, §8C-1 Rule 411.

Mental health area authorities, §122C-152(f).

Tort action against community college trustees, §115D-58.12(d).

Examinations by commissioner.

Generally.

See INSURANCE COMMISSIONER.

Exemptions from general insurance laws, §58-24-110.

Fair access to insurance requirements, §§58-46-1 to 58-46-60.

See PROPERTY INSURANCE.

False statement to procure or deny benefit, §58-2-161.

Family leave credit insurance, §58-57-115.

Fidelity and surety insurance, §58-7-15.

Foreign or alien insurance companies.

Deposits.

Required, §58-5-10.

Fiduciaries, §32-27.

Financial reporting.

Annual audited financial reports, §§58-10-185 to 58-10-265.

See INSURANCE COMPANIES.

Financial responsibility.

Motor vehicles generally, §§20-279.1 to 20-284.

See MOTOR VEHICLE FINANCIAL RESPONSIBILITY.

Fire department.

Volunteer fire department.

Defense of employees and officers.

Insurer provides defense, §160A-167.

Fire insurance.

See FIRE INSURANCE.

Fish and fisheries resources.

Hull insurance, protection and indemnity clubs, §§58-20-1 to 58-20-40.

See HULL INSURANCE, PROTECTION AND INDEMNITY CLUBS.

Foreign or alien insurance companies.

See FOREIGN OR ALIEN INSURANCE COMPANIES.

Fraternal benefit societies.

Directors, officers, employees or agents.

Powers of society to purchase and maintain insurance, §58-24-25(c).

INSURANCE —Cont'd
Fraternal orders.
  General provisions, §§58-25-1 to 58-25-70.
    See FRATERNAL ORDERS.
Fraud.
  Arson, §14-65.
  Burning of personal property, §14-66.
  Motor vehicle insurance.
    Rate evasion fraud, §58-2-164.
  Statements, releases, etc., obtained from persons
    in shock or under the influence of drugs.
    Presumption of fraud, §8-45.5.
Free insurance as inducement to purchase
  goods or services, §§66-380 to 66-382.
General contractor's board.
  Liability insurance, authority to purchase,
    §87-9.1(b).
Group insurance.
  Accident and health insurance.
    Generally.
      See HEALTH INSURANCE.
  Annuities.
    Group annuity contracts, §58-58-145(a).
    Assignment of interest in, §58-58-155.
    Certificates.
      Contents, §58-58-145(b).
      Issuance, §58-58-145(b).
      Non-applicability of provisions,
        §58-58-145(d).
      Provision in contract regarding,
        §58-58-145(c).
  Commissioner.
    Approval of master plan and certificates,
      §58-3-20.
  Life insurance generally.
    See LIFE INSURANCE.
  Restrictions on group plans, §58-3-20.
  Small employer group health coverage,
    §§58-50-100 to 58-50-156.
    See SMALL EMPLOYER GROUP HEALTH
      COVERAGE.
Guardian's powers in administering
  incompetent's estate, §35A-1251.
Health benefit plan external review, §§58-50-75
  to 58-50-95.
  See HEALTH INSURANCE.
Health benefit plans.
  Generally, §§58-3-167 to 58-3-178, 58-3-190 to
    58-3-265.
  See HEALTH INSURANCE.
Health care benefits providers.
  Determination of jurisdiction over, §§58-49-1 to
    58-49-25.
  See HEALTH CARE BENEFITS PROVIDERS.
  Regulation of multiple employer welfare
    arrangements, §§58-49-30 to 58-49-65.
  See HEALTH CARE BENEFITS PROVIDERS.
Health care liability.
  Negligent decision of health benefit plan
    providers, §§90-21.50 to 90-21.56.
Health departments.
  District health departments.
    District boards of health.
      Authority to provide liability insurance,
        §130A-37(k).
Health insurance.
  Accident and health insurance generally.
    See HEALTH INSURANCE.
  Credit insurance generally, §§58-57-1 to
    58-57-115.
    See CREDIT INSURANCE.

INSURANCE —Cont'd
Health insurance —Cont'd
  Group insurance.
    Student coverage, §58-51-81(a).
  Risk pool, §§58-50-175 to 58-50-255.
    See HEALTH INSURANCE RISK POOL.
Health insurance portability and
  accountability, §§58-68-25 to 58-68-75.
  See HEALTH INSURANCE PORTABILITY AND
    ACCOUNTABILITY.
Health maintenance organizations, §§58-67-1 to
  58-67-185.
  See HEALTH MAINTENANCE
    ORGANIZATIONS.
Holding companies, §§58-19-1 to 58-19-70.
  See INSURANCE HOLDING COMPANIES.
Home appliance service agreement companies.
  See HOME APPLIANCE SERVICE AGREEMENT
    COMPANIES.
Homicide.
  Killing decedents.
    Additional liability for insurance company,
      §31A-11(c).
    Decedent beneficiary, §31A-11(b).
    Proceeds payable to slayer, §31A-11(a).
Hospital, medical and dental service
  corporations, §§58-65-1 to 58-66-40.
  See HOSPITAL, MEDICAL AND DENTAL
    SERVICE CORPORATIONS.
Housing finance agency.
  Mortgage insurance authority, §122A-5.2.
  Procuring insurance against losses.
    General power of agency, §122A-5.
Hull insurance, protection and indemnity
  clubs, §§58-20-1 to 58-20-40.
  See HULL INSURANCE, PROTECTION AND
    INDEMNITY CLUBS.
Human service and volunteer transportation.
  Classification of transportation, §62-289.4.
  Volunteer transportation, §62-289.6.
Incapacitated persons.
  Proceeds belonging to incapacitated adult as
    beneficiary on death of insured.
    Payment to and receipt by clerk of superior
      court or public guardian, §7A-111(b), (d).
Incident affecting operations of department.
  Stay of deadlines, §58-2-47.
Information privacy protection.
  Consumer and customer information.
    Generally, §§58-39-1 to 58-39-165.
    See INSURANCE CONSUMER AND
      CUSTOMER INFORMATION PRIVACY.
Information to be furnished to commissioner,
  §58-6-20.
Insurance information and privacy act.
  Generally, §§58-39-1 to 58-39-76.
    See INSURANCE CONSUMER AND
      CUSTOMER INFORMATION PRIVACY.
Insurance regulatory information system.
  Test data.
    Not public records, §58-2-220.
Insurance scores.
  Motor vehicle or property insurance, §58-36-90.
Interstate insurance product regulation
  compact, §§58-91-1 to 58-91-80.
  See INTERSTATE INSURANCE PRODUCT
    REGULATION COMPACT.
Jurisdiction.
  Personal jurisdiction.
    Grounds, §1-75.4.
Kinds of insurance authorized, §58-7-15.

INSURANCE —Cont'd
Labor.
Discrimination against lawful use of lawful
products during nonworking hours prohibited.
Health, disability or life insurance policies
distinguishing between employees,
§95-28.2(b).
Landlord and tenant.
Lien on crops, §42-15.1.
Law-enforcement officers.
Separate insurance benefits plan for
law-enforcement officers, §143-166.60(a) to
(h).
Leases, UCC.
Leased goods, §25-2A-218.
Lending institutions.
Not to require insurance as condition of loan,
§58-3-135.
Liability insurance.
Counties.
Purchase, waiver of governmental immunity,
§153A-435(a), (b).
District health departments.
District boards of health.
Authority to provide insurance, §130A-37(k).
General contractor's board.
Authority to purchase, §87-9.1(b).
Mental health, developmental disabilities and
substance abuse.
Area authorities.
Agents, employees and board members to
secure insurance, §122C-152(a) to (f).
Motor vehicle insurance generally.
See MOTOR VEHICLE INSURANCE.
Occupational licensing boards, §93B-16(a), (b), (c).
Personal watercraft rental businesses,
§75A-13.3(c1).
Risk retention groups generally, §§58-22-1 to
58-22-70.
See RISK RETENTION GROUPS.
Structural pest control.
Financial responsibility of licensee or certified
applicator or other applicants,
§106-65.37(a).
Volunteer immunity.
Volunteers performing services for charitable
organizations or providing emergency
services.
Waiver of immunity if covered by liability
insurance, §1-539.10(b).
Liability insurance commission, §§58-32-1 to
58-32-30.
See LIABILITY INSURANCE COMMISSION.
**Life and health insurance guaranty
association,** §§58-62-2 to 58-62-95.
See LIFE AND HEALTH INSURANCE
GUARANTY ASSOCIATION.
Life insurance.
Credit life insurance generally, §§58-57-1 to
58-57-115.
See CREDIT INSURANCE.
Generally, §§58-58-1 to 58-61-15.
See LIFE INSURANCE.
Life and health insurance guaranty association,
§§58-62-2 to 58-62-95.
See LIFE AND HEALTH INSURANCE
GUARANTY ASSOCIATION.
Third-party administrators, §§58-56-2 to 58-56-66.
See THIRD-PARTY ADMINISTRATORS.
Viatical settlements, §§58-58-200 to 58-58-310.
See VIATICAL SETTLEMENTS.

INSURANCE —Cont'd
Limited liability companies.
Purchase on behalf of managers, directors,
executives, employees or agents of company,
§57C-3-32(c).
Limited representatives.
See INSURANCE LIMITED
REPRESENTATIVES.
Liquefied petroleum gas.
Dealers.
Liability insurance or substitute required,
§119-56.
"Lloyds" insurance association, §58-17-1.
Loans.
Interest rates on life insurance policy loans,
§§58-61-1 to 58-61-15.
Lender requiring borrower to deal with particular
insurer, §§75-17 to 75-19.
Local government risk pools, §§58-23-1 to
58-23-45.
See LOCAL GOVERNMENT RISK POOLS.
Long-term care insurance, §§58-55-1 to 58-55-50.
See LONG-TERM CARE INSURANCE.
Long-term care partnerships, §§58-55-55 to
58-55-80.
Managing general agents, §§58-34-2 to 58-34-15.
See MANAGING GENERAL INSURANCE
AGENTS.
Mandatory or voluntary risk sharing plans,
§§58-42-1 to 58-42-50.
See MANDATORY OR VOLUNTARY RISK
SHARING PLANS.
Marine insurance.
Foreign or alien insurance companies.
Deposits.
Required, §58-5-5.
Limitation of risk.
Exception as to, §58-3-105.
Mutual insurance companies.
Surplus.
Requirements, §58-7-75.
Market assistance program.
Good faith immunity from operation of programs,
§58-40-135.
Marriage.
Married may insure spouse's life, §52-3.
Mass gatherings.
Provisional permit.
Liability insurance, §130A-255(c).
Maternity coverage, §§58-3-169, 58-3-170.
Mediation.
Prelitigation mediation of insurance claims,
§7A-38.3A.
Medicaid.
ERISA plans may not require Medicaid to pay
first, §58-51-116.
Medical service corporations.
Hospital, medical and dental service corporations,
§§58-65-1 to 58-66-40.
See HOSPITAL, MEDICAL AND DENTAL
SERVICE CORPORATIONS.
Medicare supplement insurance, §§58-54-1 to
58-54-50.
See MEDICARE SUPPLEMENT INSURANCE.
**Mental health, developmental disabilities and
substance abuse.**
Area authorities.
Agents, employees and board members to secure
liability insurance, §122C-152(a) to (f).
Military personnel.
Life insurance.
Dishonest and predatory sales to military
personnel, §§58-58-320 to 58-58-350.

INSURANCE —Cont'd
Minors.
Administration of insurance proceeds to which minor entitled, §35A-1227(a).
Proceeds belonging to minor as beneficiary on death of insured.
Payment to and receipt by clerk of superior court or public guardian, §7A-111(a), (c).
Missing persons.
Absentee insurance fund, §28C-19(a), (b).
Determination that absentee not dead, §28C-18(d).
Failure of insurer to pay, §28C-18(b).
Payment of insurance policies, §28C-18(a).
Required survivor of beneficiary.
Failure to establish, §28C-18(c).
Monopolies and restraint of trade.
Lender requiring borrower to deal with particular insurer.
Contempt.
Disregard of injunction or other court order, §75-19.
Injunction, §75-19.
Nondiscriminatory approval of insurer.
Lender may require, §75-18.
Penalty, §75-19.
Prohibited, §75-17.
Mortality tables, §§8-46, 8-47.
Mortgage guaranty insurance, §§58-10-120 to 58-10-145.
Report of policyholder's position, §58-10-140.
Mortgage insurance authority, §122A-5.2.
Mortgage insurance consolidations.
Commissioner authorized to adopt rules, §58-2-210.
Motor carriers.
Liability insurance, §62-268.
Verification by for-hire carriers, §20-382(c).
Failure to comply.
Civil penalty, §20-382.2(a) to (d).
Motor clubs and associations, §§58-69-2 to 58-69-60.
See MOTOR CLUBS AND ASSOCIATIONS.
Motor vehicle insurance.
Financial responsibility generally, §§20-279.1 to 20-284.
See MOTOR VEHICLE FINANCIAL RESPONSIBILITY.
Generally.
See MOTOR VEHICLE INSURANCE.
Reinsurance facility generally, §§58-37-1 to 58-37-65.
See MOTOR VEHICLE INSURANCE.
Motor vehicle service agreement companies.
See MOTOR VEHICLE SERVICE AGREEMENT COMPANIES.
Multiple employer welfare arrangements.
Regulation generally, §§58-49-30 to 58-49-65.
See HEALTH CARE BENEFITS PROVIDERS.
Municipalities.
Defense of employees and officers.
Civil and criminal actions.
Insurer provides defense, §160A-167.
Employees.
Council may purchase life, health and other forms of insurance, §160A-162(b).
Health insurance for employees, §160A-163(e).
Railroads.
Contracts allocating financial responsibility.
Insurance required, §160A-326(c).

INSURANCE —Cont'd
Municipalities —Cont'd
Tort liability.
Waiver of immunity through insurance purchase, §160A-485.
Mutual burial associations, §§90-210.80 to 90-210.107.
See MUTUAL BURIAL ASSOCIATIONS.
Mutual insurance companies, §§58-8-1 to 58-8-60.
See MUTUAL INSURANCE COMPANIES.
Mutual life insurance companies.
Conversion of society into company, §58-24-70.
NAIC filing requirements.
Applicability of article, §58-4-1.
Filing requirements, §58-4-5(a), (b).
Immunity of members of NAIC, §58-4-10.
Revocation or suspension of certificate of authority, §58-4-15.
Scope of article, §58-4-1.
Test ratios, data or information generated.
Dissemination, §58-4-25.
Negligent decision of health benefit plan providers.
Health care liability, §§90-21.50 to 90-21.56.
Nonprofit corporations.
Purchase on behalf of directors, officers or employees, §55A-8-57(b).
North Carolina health insurance risk pool, §§58-50-175 to 58-50-255.
See HEALTH INSURANCE RISK POOL.
North Carolina rate bureau, §§58-36-1 to 58-36-120.
See RATE BUREAU.
Occupational licensing boards.
Commercial liability insurance, §93B-16(a), (b), (c).
Pest control.
Insurance fund.
Articles of compact, §106-65.55.
Cooperation of state agencies with fund, §106-65.56.
Request for assistance.
Pest control compact, §106-65.59.
Physicians and surgeons.
Report of medical malpractice award or settlement.
Confidentiality and immunity for reporting, §90-14.13(e).
Insurance company reports, §90-14.13(c).
Noncompliance, §90-14.13(d).
Physicians without professional liability insurance, §90-14.13(b).
Planned community act.
Common elements, §47F-3-113.
Policies.
See INSURANCE POLICIES OR CONTRACTS.
Portable consumer electronic devices.
Claims handling, adjuster licenses, §58-33-27.
Generally, §§58-44A-1 to 58-44A-25.
See PORTABLE CONSUMER ELECTRONIC DEVICES INSURANCE.
Post assessment insurance guaranty association, §§58-48-1 to 58-48-130.
See POST ASSESSMENT INSURANCE GUARANTY ASSOCIATION.
Powers of attorney.
Powers conferred by statutory short form, §32A-2.
Premium financing, §§58-35-1 to 58-35-100.
See INSURANCE PREMIUM FINANCING.

INSURANCE —Cont'd
Premiums.
  See INSURANCE PREMIUMS.
Premium tax, §§105-228.5 to 105-228.10.
Preneed funeral contracts and funds.
  Sales of insurance policies not regulated by
    article, §90-210.71.
Privacy protection.
  Consumer and customer information.
    Generally, §§58-39-1 to 58-39-165.
      See INSURANCE CONSUMER AND
        CUSTOMER INFORMATION PRIVACY.
Private protective services.
  Adjusters.
    Exemption from act, §74C-3(b).
  Certificate of liability insurance.
    Cancellation by insurance carriers, §74C-10(f).
    Employees not required to obtain, §74C-10(g).
    Required, §74C-10(e), (h).
  Trainee permit.
    Holder not required to obtain, §74C-10(g).
Products liability.
  Risk retention groups.
    Generally, §§58-22-1 to 58-22-70.
      See RISK RETENTION GROUPS.
Professional liability insurance.
  Statements.
    Annual statements by professional liability
      insurers, §58-2-170.
  State officials and employees, §58-31-25.
Property insurance.
  Beach area essential property insurance,
    §§58-45-1 to 58-45-96.
      See BEACH AREA ESSENTIAL PROPERTY
        INSURANCE.
  Credit property insurance, §58-57-90.
  Fair access to insurance requirements, §§58-46-1
    to 58-46-60.
      See PROPERTY INSURANCE.
  Fire insurance.
    Generally.
      See FIRE INSURANCE.
  Mediation of emergency or disaster claims,
    §§58-44-70 to 58-44-120.
      See PROPERTY INSURANCE.
  Policies, §§58-44-1 to 58-44-60.
    See PROPERTY INSURANCE.
  Residential real property insurance.
    Claim closed without payment.
      Termination or refusal to issue or renew.
        Prohibition, §58-36-115.
    Inquiry as to policy provisions not resulting in
      claim.
      Termination or refusal to issue or renew.
        Prohibition, §58-36-115.
Protected cell companies, §§58-10-75 to
  58-10-110.
  See INSURANCE COMPANIES.
Public adjusters, §§58-33A-1 to 58-33A-95.
  See INSURANCE ADJUSTERS.
Public officers and employees.
  Defense of state employees.
    Coverage afforded excess coverage over any
      commercial liability insurance,
      §143-300.6(c).
  Employee insurance committee, §58-31-60(b).
  Selection of insurance product proposals.
    Procedure, §58-31-60(c1).
  Payroll deductions, §58-31-60(c).
Public school property.
  State insurance, §§115C-533 to 115C-543.
    See SCHOOL BUILDINGS AND PROPERTY.

INSURANCE —Cont'd
Public schools.
  Health insurance.
    School employees, §115C-340(a), (b).
  Liability insurance.
    Powers of local boards to secure, §115C-47.
  Proceeds of claims, §115C-449.
  School buses.
    Liability insurance, §§115C-255, 115C-262.
Public works.
  Design and construction insurance.
    Purchase, §58-31-65(a).
  Owner controlled or wrap-up insurance program,
    §58-31-65(a).
    Definitions, §58-31-65(b).
  Self-insurance.
    Providing, §58-31-65(a).
Rate bureau, §§58-36-1 to 58-36-120.
  See RATE BUREAU.
Rates, §§58-40-1 to 58-40-140.
  See INSURANCE RATES.
Readable policies generally, §§58-38-1 to
  58-38-40.
  See INSURANCE POLICIES OR CONTRACTS.
Real property.
  Warranties.
    Real property warranty as contract of
      insurance, §58-1-20(a).
Rebates.
  Prohibited.
    Premiums on credit insurance, §58-57-95.
  Unfair trade practices.
    Prohibited acts, §58-63-15.
Reciprocal insurance, §§58-15-1 to 58-15-150.
Regional public transportation authority.
  Contracts allocating financial responsibility.
    Insurance required, §160A-626(c).
  Liability insurance, §160A-627.
Registers of deeds, §161-4.2.
Reinsurance.
  See REINSURANCE.
Reinsurance intermediaries, §§58-9-2 to 58-9-26.
  See REINSURANCE INTERMEDIARIES.
Rental car companies.
  Limited license to sell insurance, §58-33-17.
Renunciation.
  Beneficiaries of life insurance policies.
    Right to renounce succession, §31B-1(a).
Rescue squads.
  Defense of employees and officers.
    Civil and criminal actions.
      Insurer provides defense, §160A-167.
Retail installment sales.
  Certificates of insurance, §25A-36(a).
  Consumer credit installment sales contracts.
    Additional charges for insurance, §25A-17(c).
  Premium included in contract.
    Crediting to unpaid balance of the contract,
      §25A-36(b).
  Revolving charge account contracts.
    Additional charges for insurance, §25A-17(a).
Risk based capital requirements.
  Insurance companies, §§58-12-2 to 58-12-70.
    See INSURANCE COMPANIES.
Risk retention groups, §§58-22-1 to 58-22-70.
  See RISK RETENTION GROUPS.
Sale of goods, UCC.
  C.I.F. and C. & F. terms, §25-2-320.
    Form of bill of lading required in overseas
      shipment, §25-2-323.
    Net landed weight, §25-2-321.

INSURANCE —Cont'd
Sale of goods, UCC —Cont'd
C.I.F. and C. & F. terms —Cont'd
Payment on arrival, §25-2-321.
Warranty of condition on arrival, §25-2-321.
Insurable interest in goods, §25-2-501.
Salvage vehicles.
Surrender of title to vehicle deemed salvage
vehicle, §20-109.1.
Savings and loan associations.
Accounts.
Requirements, §54B-17.
Loans.
Insured or guaranteed loans, §54B-158.
Savings banks.
Accounts.
Required insurance, §54C-17.
School buildings and property.
State insurance of public school property,
§§115C-533 to 115C-543.
See SCHOOL BUILDINGS AND PROPERTY.
School buses.
Liability insurance, §§115C-255, 115C-262.
Secured transactions.
Inapplicability of article 9.
Transfers of policy interest or assignment of
claim, §25-9-109(d).
Self-service storage companies.
Rental insurance.
Limited license, §58-33-18.
Senior citizens.
Joint action to insure elderly, §§58-52-1 to
58-52-25.
See HEALTH INSURANCE.
Service agreement companies.
Applicability of requirements, §66-373(e).
Filing of forms with commissioner, §66-373(b).
Policy requirements, §66-373(c).
Requirement for insurance, §66-373(a).
Rulemaking to implement provisions, §66-373(d).
Small employer group health coverage,
§§58-50-100 to 58-50-156.
See SMALL EMPLOYER GROUP HEALTH
COVERAGE.
State fire and rescue commission, §§58-78-1 to
58-78-20.
See FIRE AND RESCUE COMMISSION.
State properties, officials and employees.
Description of property belonging to state.
Officers having custody to inform commissioner,
§58-31-35.
Extended coverage insurance on state property,
§58-31-15.
Professional liability insurance for state officials
and employees, §58-31-25.
Report to governor.
Commissioner of insurance, §58-31-45.
State property fire insurance fund, §§58-31-1 to
58-31-20.
Use and occupancy and business interruption
insurance on state property, §58-31-15.
State property fire insurance fund, §§58-31-1 to
58-31-20.
See FIRE INSURANCE.
Structural pest control.
Liability insurance.
Financial responsibility of licensee or certified
applicator or other applicants,
§106-65.37(a).

INSURANCE —Cont'd
**Supervision, rehabilitation and liquidation of
insurers.**
Generally, §§58-30-1 to 58-30-310.
See INSURER SUPERVISION,
REHABILITATION AND LIQUIDATION.
Surplus lines, §§58-21-1 to 58-21-105.
See SURPLUS LINES INSURANCE.
Third-party administrators.
Generally, §§58-56-2 to 58-56-66.
See THIRD-PARTY ADMINISTRATORS.
Title insurance.
Generally, §§58-26-1 to 58-27-15.
See TITLE INSURANCE.
Title of law.
Short title, §58-1-1.
Town or county mutual insurance companies,
§58-7-75.
Transfers to minors.
Investments and premiums on life insurance or
endowment policy, §33A-12.
Transportation department.
Vessels operated by department.
Authority to insure vessels, §136-82.1.
Twisting with respect to insurance policies.
Insurance producers, prohibition, §58-33-75.
Unauthorized insurers.
Generally, §§58-28-1 to 58-28-45.
See UNAUTHORIZED INSURERS.
**Unauthorized insurers false advertising
process act.**
Generally, §§58-29-1 to 58-29-25.
See UNAUTHORIZED INSURERS.
Unclaimed property generally, §§116B-51 to
116B-80.
See UNCLAIMED PROPERTY.
Underground storage tanks.
Leaking petroleum cleanup.
Pools authorized, §143-215.94I.
Underinsured motorists, §20-279.21(b).
Underwriting association.
Beach area essential property, §§58-45-10 to
58-45-80.
See BEACH AREA ESSENTIAL PROPERTY
INSURANCE.
Undue influence.
Statements, releases, etc., obtained from persons
in shock or under the influence of drugs.
Presumption of fraud, §8-45.5.
Unemployment compensation.
General provisions, §§96-1 to 96-29.
See UNEMPLOYMENT COMPENSATION.
Unfair trade practices.
Generally, §§58-63-1 to 58-63-75.
See INSURANCE UNFAIR TRADE
PRACTICES.
Uninsured motorists, §20-279.21(b).
Unit ownership, §47A-24.
University of North Carolina.
Appropriated funds.
Used only as provided, §116-224.
Board of governors.
Further action authorized, §116-223.
Power to secure insurance or provide
self-insurance, §116-219.
Confidentiality of records, §116-222.
Defense of actions against covered persons,
§116-220(d).
Liability insurance trust fund council, §116-220(c).
Nuclear reactors.
Purchase of insurance in connection with
construction and operation, §116-40.2.

INSURANCE —Cont'd
University of North Carolina —Cont'd
Self-insurance, §§116-220 to 116-220.2.
Sovereign immunity.
Provisions not deemed to waive sovereign
immunity of state, §116-221.
Vessels.
Department of transportation.
Authority to insure vessels operated by
department, §136-82.1.
Viatical settlements, §§58-58-200 to 58-58-310.
See VIATICAL SETTLEMENTS.
Violations of provisions.
Civil penalties or restitution, §58-2-70.
Volunteer fire department.
Department of insurance.
Transfer to department, §143A-79.
Warehouses.
Public warehousemen.
When insurance required, §66-38.
Western residence of the governor, §143-345.7.
Wills.
Renunciation.
Beneficiaries of life insurance policies.
Right to renounce succession, §31B-1(a).
Mailing copy to insurance company, §31B-2(c).
Workers' compensation insurance.
Generally.
See WORKERS' COMPENSATION
INSURANCE.
Self-insurance, §§58-47-60 to 58-47-205.
See WORKERS' COMPENSATION.
Self-insurance security association, §§97-130 to
97-143.
See SELF-INSURANCE SECURITY
ASSOCIATION.

INSURANCE ADJUSTERS.
Agent or limited representative.
Acting as adjuster, §58-33-70(b).
Assumed name, operating under, §58-33-83.
Authorized companies.
Acting for, §58-33-115.
Bankruptcy, insolvency or receivership.
Commissioner to be notified, §58-33-46(c).
Continuing education program for licensees,
§58-33-130(a).
Advisory committees, §58-33-135.
Compliance with provisions.
What constitutes, §58-33-130(h).
Course provider fees, §58-33-133(a) to (b1).
Crediting of fees collected, §58-33-130(c).
Courses of study.
Approval by commissioner, §58-33-130(i).
Hour requirements, §58-33-130(d).
Powers and duties of commissioner generally,
§§58-33-130, 58-33-135.
Renewal of license.
Requirements for, §58-33-130(c).
Criminal history record check.
Applicant for license, §58-33-48.
Discrimination.
Prohibited, §58-33-80.
Emergency insurance adjustments.
Permitted without license, §58-33-70(e).
Learner's permit, §58-33-70(c).
Licenses.
Acting without license, §§58-30-130, 58-33-120.
Agent's license.
Agent's and adjuster's licenses not to be held
simultaneously, §58-33-26(p).

INSURANCE ADJUSTERS —Cont'd
Licenses —Cont'd
Applicability of article, §58-33-1.
Application, §58-33-31(a).
Documents necessary to verify information,
requiring, §58-33-31(c).
Required, §58-33-30(a).
Continuing education program for licensees,
§§58-33-130, 58-33-135.
Criminal history record check of applicants,
§58-33-48(a).
Costs paid by applicant, §58-33-48(a).
Fingerprints furnished commissioner,
§58-33-48(a).
Inapplicability of provisions, §58-33-48(c).
Privileged and confidential information,
§58-33-48(b).
Definitions, §58-33-10.
Denial, §58-33-30(g).
Duplicate licenses.
Lost, stolen or destroyed license, §58-33-50(d).
Education and training, §58-33-30(d).
Examination, §58-33-30(e).
Exceptions to requirement, §58-33-26(n).
Insurers, §58-33-26(o).
Fees, §58-33-125(a) to (h).
General requirements, §58-33-26(a).
Interstate reciprocity.
Administrative action against licensee,
reporting, §58-33-32(k).
Application requirements, waiver, §58-33-32(i).
Conditions for receiving nonresident license,
§58-33-32(c).
Continuing education requirements,
satisfaction, §58-33-32(j).
Criminal prosecutions, reporting, §58-33-32(l).
Examination, when not required, §58-33-32(g).
Greater fee not to be assessed, §58-33-32(h).
Purposes of section, §58-33-32(a).
Nonresident, §58-33-30(h).
Interstate reciprocity, §58-33-32.
Reciprocity, §58-33-30(j).
Retaliatory provisions, §58-33-30(i).
Notice.
Suspension, revocation or nonrenewal,
§58-33-50(a), (b).
Portable consumer electronic devices insurance.
Claims handling, §58-33-27.
Public adjusters generally, §§58-33A-1 to
58-33A-95.
Reciprocity.
Interstate reciprocity, §58-33-32.
Required, §§58-33-5, 58-33-26(b).
Portable consumer electronic devices insurance,
§58-33-27(c).
Exception, §58-33-27(b).
Surrender.
Termination of residency, §58-33-50(c).
Suspension, revocation, refusal to renew, placing
licensee on probation.
Authority of commissioner, §58-33-46(a).
Grounds, §58-33-46(a).
Issuance of another license, requirements,
§58-33-46(d).
Notice, §58-33-50(a), (b).
Other provisions, applicability, §58-33-46(b).
Temporary licensing.
Authority of commissioner to issue,
§58-33-66(a).
Grounds for issuing, §58-33-66(a).

INSURANCE ADJUSTERS —Cont'd
Licenses —Cont'd
Temporary licensing —Cont'd
Limiting authority of temporary licensee,
§58-33-66(b).
Revoking, §58-33-66(b).
Sponsor, requiring temporary licensee to have,
§58-33-66(b).
Termination on transfer of business,
§58-33-66(b).
Violations of insurance laws.
License not to be issued, §58-33-46(e).
Violations of licensing laws.
Impositions of penalties or remedies,
§58-33-46(f).
Misdemeanors, §58-3-130.
Penalties.
Violations of insurance law generally, §58-3-130.
Practice of law.
Engaging in prohibited, §58-33-70(a).
Public adjusters, §§58-33A-1 to 58-33A-95.
Administrative action taken in another
jurisdiction or by other governmental agency.
Report, time, §58-33A-90(a).
Appointment by insurer to act on insurer's behalf
for specific claim or purpose.
Required, §58-33A-10(b).
Article 63 of chapter 58.
Licensed adjuster subject to, §58-33A-40(d).
Bond or irrevocable letter of credit.
Amount, §58-33A-50(a).
Asking for evidence of financial responsibility.
Commissioner's authority, §58-33A-50(c).
Required to secure financial responsibility,
§58-33A-50(a).
Requirements, §58-33A-50(a).
Termination.
Authority to act as public adjuster
terminates, §58-33A-50(d).
Commissioner notified, §58-33A-50(b).
Business entity acting as public adjuster.
Criminal history record check.
Applicant for license, §58-33A-15(d).
Defined, §58-33A-5.
Fingerprints.
Applicants for license to furnish
commissioner, §58-33A-15(d).
License.
Application, §58-33A-10(c).
Criminal history record check, §58-33A-15(d).
Fingerprints.
Applicants for license to furnish
commissioner, §58-33A-15(d).
Required, §58-33A-10(c).
Suspension, revocation, refusal, §58-33A-45(c).
Castrophic incident.
Defined, §58-33A-5.
Catastrophic incident.
Catastrophic fees, limits, §58-33A-60(d).
Change in licensee's address, legal name.
Commissioner informed, §58-33A-40(c).
Charging specific claimant fee when appointed by
insurer.
Prohibition, §58-33A-10(b).
Civil penalty, §58-33A-45(d).
Grounds for imposing, §58-33A-45(a).
Claims process disclosure, §58-33A-65(f).
Commissions, service fees, other valuable
consideration.
Catastrophic fees, limits on, §58-33A-60(d).

INSURANCE ADJUSTERS —Cont'd
Public adjusters —Cont'd
Commissions, service fees, other valuable
consideration —Cont'd
Compensation from construction, salvage,
building appraisal, motor vehicle repair
firm.
Disclosure, §58-33A-80(g).
Compensation from insured's specific loss.
Disclosure, §58-33A-80(h).
Contract provisions regarding compensation,
§58-33A-65(b).
Insurer paying insured policy limits,
§58-33A-65(c).
Persons not investigating or settling claims.
Paying, §58-33A-60(c).
Unlicensed adjusters.
Prohibited from accepting, §58-33A-60(b).
Prohibited from paying to, §58-33A-60(a).
Continuing education.
Approved courses used to satisfy requirement,
§58-33A-55(c).
Completion in conjunction with license renewal
cycle.
Requirement, §58-33A-55(a).
Exemptions, §58-33A-55(b).
Minimum hours, §58-33A-55(a).
Contract between adjuster and insured.
Claims process disclosure, §58-33A-65(f).
Compensation provisions, §58-33A-65(b).
Co-payee on insured's claim.
Specifying, §58-33A-65(b).
Execution, §58-33A-65(g).
Prohibited provisions, §58-33A-65(e).
Provisions required and permitted,
§58-33A-65(b).
Requirements, §58-33A-65(a).
Right to rescind, §58-33A-65(i).
Return of anything of value given by insured
upon rescission, §58-33A-65(j).
Written contract required, §58-33A-65(a).
Co-payee on insured's claim.
Contract specifying, §58-33A-65(b).
Criminal history record check.
Applicants for license, §58-33A-15(c).
Business entity, §58-33A-15(d).
Confidentiality of information, §58-33A-15(e).
Criminal prosecution of adjuster.
Report, time, §58-33A-90(b).
Definitions, §58-33A-5.
Disclosure.
Claims process, §58-33A-65(f).
Compensation from construction, salvage,
building appraisal, motor vehicle repair
firm, §58-33A-80(g).
Compensation from insured's specific loss,
§58-33A-80(h).
Financial interest with other party involved in
claim, §58-33A-65(d).
Enforcement of chapter.
Commissioner's authority, §58-33A-45(e).
Escrow or trust accounts.
Deposit of funds held on behalf of insured,
§58-33A-70.
Ethical requirements, §58-33A-80(i).
Financial interest in claim.
Restrictions, §58-33A-80(d).
Financial interest with other party involved in
claim.
Disclosure, §58-33A-65(d).

INSURANCE ADJUSTERS —Cont'd
Public adjusters —Cont'd
Financial responsibility.
  Securing, §58-33A-50.
Fingerprints.
  Applicants for license to furnish commissioner,
    §58-33A-15(c).
  Business entity applicants, §58-33A-15(d).
Good faith rendering of service.
  Duty, §58-33A-80(a).
Grounds for discipline, §58-33A-45(a).
Hearing.
  Denial of license application or refusal to renew
    license, §58-33A-45(b).
Hours for soliciting clients.
  Restrictions, §58-33A-80(k).
Insurer paying insured policy limits,
  §58-33A-65(c).
License.
  Application, §58-33A-15(a).
    Business entity acting as public adjuster,
      §58-33A-10(c).
    Change in information.
      Commissioner informed, §58-33A-40(c).
    Declaration as to truth, correctness of
      statements made, §58-33A-15(b).
    Denial.
      Notice, hearing, §58-33A-45(b).
    Verification of information, §58-33A-20(c).
  Article 63 of chapter 58.
    Licensed adjuster subject to, §58-33A-40(d).
  Contents, §58-33A-40(h).
  Continuing education.
    Renewal, §58-33A-55.
  Criminal history record check.
    Applicants for license, §58-33A-15(c).
      Business entity, §58-33A-15(d).
    Confidentiality of information, §58-33A-15(e).
  Criteria for issuance.
    Nonresident license, §58-33A-35(a).
    Resident license, §58-33A-20(a).
  Duration, §58-33A-40(b).
  Examination, §58-33A-25(a).
    Administering and collecting fees.
      Arrangements, §58-33A-25(b).
    Exemptions.
      Previously licensed in another state based
        on examination, §58-33A-30(a).
      Previously licensed in state, §58-33A-30(c).
    Failure to appear or pass.
      Reapplication, §58-33A-25(d).
    Fee remitted with application, §58-33A-25(c).
    Waiver of procedures.
      Military service, long-term medical
        disability, §58-33A-40(g).
  Exemptions from requirement of license,
    §58-33A-10(d).
  Fingerprints.
    Applicant to furnish commissioner,
      §58-33A-15(c).
    Business entity, §58-33A-15(d).
  Issuance, §58-33A-40(a).
  Lapse.
    Renewal, §58-33A-40(e).
  Lapse license fee, §58-33A-40(e), (f).
  Long-term medical disability.
    Waiver of renewal procedures, §58-33A-40(g).
  Military service.
    Waiver of renewal procedures, §58-33A-40(g).
  Ministerial duties relating to.
    Contract with nongovernmental entities to
      perform, §58-33A-40(i).

INSURANCE ADJUSTERS —Cont'd
Public adjusters —Cont'd
License —Cont'd
  National criminal history record check.
    Applicants for license, §58-33A-15(c).
  Nonresident license.
    Criteria for issuance, §58-33A-35(a).
    Maintenance of license in home state.
      Condition of continuation of license issued
        in state, §58-33A-35(c).
    Termination of state license.
      Home state license terminated,
        §58-33A-35(c).
    Verification of information, §58-33A-35(b).
  Previously licensed in another state based on
    examination.
    Application for resident license after moving
      to state, §58-33A-30(b).
    Exemption from examination, §58-33A-30(a).
  Previously licensed in state.
    Exemption from examination, §58-33A-30(c).
  Qualifications.
    Resident license, §58-33A-20(b).
  Reinstatement of license, §58-33A-40(f).
  Renewal, §58-33A-40(b).
    Continuing education, §58-33A-55.
    Failure to apply before expiration,
      §58-33A-40(f).
    Lapse, §58-33A-40(e).
    Waiver of procedures.
      Military service, long-term medical
        disability, §58-33A-40(g).
  Required, §58-33A-10(a).
    Business entity acting as public adjuster,
      §58-33A-10(c).
    Exemptions, §58-33A-10(d).
  Resident license.
    Criteria for issuance, §58-33A-20(a).
    Qualifications, §58-33A-20(b).
    Verification of information, §58-33A-20(c).
  Suspension, revocation, refusal to issue or
    renew.
    Business entity's license, §58-33A-45(c).
    Denial of application or renewal.
      Notice, hearing, §58-33A-45(b).
    Grounds, §58-33A-45(a).
Long-term medical disability.
  Waiver of license renewal procedures,
    §58-33A-40(g).
Loss settlement.
  Agreeing to without insured's knowledge and
    consent, §58-33A-80(j).
Military service.
  Waiver of license renewal procedures,
    §58-33A-40(g).
Misrepresenting status as public adjuster,
  §58-33A-10(b).
National criminal history record check.
  Applicants for license, §58-33A-15(c).
    Business entity, §58-33A-15(d).
  Confidentiality of information, §58-33A-15(e).
Needed repairs or services in connection with loss.
  Referring or directing insured to get,
    §58-33A-80(f).
Nonresidents.
  License reciprocity, §58-33A-35.
Notice.
  Denial of license application or refusal to renew
    license, §58-33A-45(b).
Notification letter signed by insured.
  Provided insurer, §58-33A-65(h).

INSURANCE ADJUSTERS —Cont'd

Public adjusters —Cont'd

Objectivity and loyalty.

Duty to serve client, §58-33A-80(a).

Probation.

Placing licensee on.

Grounds, §58-33A-45(a).

Purpose of article, §58-33A-1.

Rules to carry out, adoption, §58-33A-95.

Reciprocity.

Nonresident license, §58-33A-35.

Records.

Proprietary information confidential, §58-33A-75(c).

Required records, §58-33A-75(a).

Retention, time period, §58-33A-75(b).

Reports.

Actions taken against adjuster, §58-33A-90.

Rules, adoption, §58-33A-95.

Salvage interest in property.

Acquiring, restrictions, §58-33A-80(e).

Scope of article, §58-33A-1.

Soliciting insured during loss-producing occurrence.

Prohibition, §58-33A-80(b).

Termination of authority to act as adjuster.

Termination of evidence of financial responsibility, §58-33A-50(d).

Unlicensed adjusters.

Accepting commission, service fee.

Prohibition, §58-33A-60(b).

Paying commission, service fee.

Prohibition, §58-33A-60(a).

Unlicensed employees or representatives.

Allowing to conduct business, §58-33A-80(c).

Referral of business to repair source.

Gratuity accepted for referral, prohibition, §58-33-76(b).

Prohibition, §58-33-76(a).

Violations, §58-33-76(c).

Violation of insurance laws, §58-33-120.

INSURANCE AGENTS.

Actions.

Soliciting agent represents the company, §58-58-30.

Adverse underwriting decisions.

Reasons for making, obligation to give, §§58-39-55 to 58-39-65.

Agreements restricting agent's commission.

Prohibited, §58-43-30.

Applications for insurance.

False statement, §58-33-105.

Appointment as agent for insurer.

Appointment fee, insurer to remit, §58-33-40(d).

Authority upon being appointed, §58-33-40(b).

Duration of appointment, §58-33-40(e).

Agents with license in effect prior to statute's enactment, §58-33-40(g).

Malice in reporting, failure to report as required, §58-33-56(l).

Notification of termination.

Additional information discovered, §58-33-56(c).

Authority of commissioner as to materials received, §58-33-56(i).

Comments concerning substance of notification, filing, §58-33-56(e).

Confidentiality of materials obtained by commissioner, §58-33-56(h).

No waiver of privilege or claim of confidentiality, §58-33-56(j).

INSURANCE AGENTS —Cont'd

Appointment as agent for insurer —Cont'd

Notification of termination —Cont'd

Copy of notification mailed to producer, §58-33-56(d).

Grounds for suspension or revocation of license reason for termination, §58-33-56(a).

Immunity for statements or information provided, §58-33-56(f), (g).

Other grounds as reason for termination, §58-33-56(b).

Releasing information on final adjudicated actions, §58-33-56(k).

Renewal appointment fee, insurer to remit, §58-33-40(f).

Required to act as agent for insurer, §58-33-40(a).

Required to place insurance, §58-33-26(i).

Revocation.

Suspension, revocation or refusal to renew license, §58-33-46(d).

Temporary license because of death or disability of agent.

Representation of insurers that had appointed agent, §58-33-66(c).

Termination.

Notification to commissioner, §58-33-56.

Who may be appointed, §58-33-40(b).

Assumed name, operating under, §58-33-83.

Bankruptcy, insolvency or receivership.

Commissioner to be notified, §58-33-46(c).

Charges in excess of premium prohibited, §58-33-85(b).

Statewide multiline limited assessable mutual insurance companies, exception, §58-8-36.

Commissions.

Agreements restricting, §58-43-30.

Commissions, brokerage, service fee or other valuable consideration.

Assigning or directing payment, §58-33-82(e).

License required to accept, §58-33-82(d).

Renewal or other deferred commissions, §58-33-82(c).

Unlicensed person, paying to or accepting, §58-33-82(a), (b).

Companies not licensed to do business in state.

Soliciting for prohibited, §58-33-26(h).

Confidentiality.

Consumer and customer information.

Generally, §§58-39-1 to 58-39-165.

See INSURANCE CONSUMER AND CUSTOMER INFORMATION PRIVACY.

Consumer reports.

Investigative consumer reports, §58-39-40.

Continuing education program for licensees, §58-33-130(b).

Advisory committees.

Appointment, §58-33-135(a).

Composition, §58-33-135(b), (c).

Commissioner.

Powers and duties of commissioner generally, §§58-33-130, 58-33-135.

Compliance with provisions.

What constitutes, §58-33-130(h).

Course provider fees, §58-33-130(a) to (b1).

Crediting of fees collected, §58-33-130(c).

Courses of study.

Approval by commissioner, §58-33-130(i).

Hour requirements, §58-33-130(d).

Renewal of license.

Requirement for, §58-33-130(c).

Countersignatures, §58-33-60.

INSURANCE AGENTS —Cont'd
Credit information or credit scores of insurer used.
Indemnification.
Action, error or omission from use, §58-36-90(e).
Criminal history record check.
Applicant for license, §58-33-48.
Customer information safeguards act,
§§58-39-130 to 58-39-165.
See INSURANCE CONSUMER AND CUSTOMER INFORMATION PRIVACY.
Discrimination.
Prohibited, §58-33-80.
Electronic filing.
Licensees or applicants for licenses.
Commissioner of insurance.
Rules requiring, §58-2-250.
Embezzlement by insurance agents, §58-2-162.
Report to commissioner, §58-2-163.
Examination.
Commissioner or other authorized facility, §58-2-195(e).
Indemnification.
Credit information or credit scores of insurer used.
Action, error or omission from use, §58-36-90(e).
Information practices.
Notice, §§58-39-25 to 58-39-28.
Information privacy protection.
Consumer and customer information.
Generally, §§58-39-1 to 58-39-165.
See INSURANCE CONSUMER AND CUSTOMER INFORMATION PRIVACY.
Information security program, §§58-39-130 to 58-39-165.
Licenses.
Acting without license, §§58-3-130, 58-33-120.
Adjuster's license.
Agent's and adjuster's licenses not to be held simultaneously, §58-33-26(p).
Portable consumer electronic devices insurance.
Claims handling, §58-33-27.
Agent for United States military personnel in foreign countries, §58-33-15.
Applicability of article, §58-33-1.
Application, §58-33-31(a).
Business entities, §58-33-31(b).
Documents necessary to verify information, requiring, §58-33-31(c).
Required, §58-33-30(a).
Business entities, §58-33-26(j).
Criminal history record check of applicants, §58-33-48(a).
Costs paid by applicant, §58-33-48(a).
Fingerprints furnished commissioner, §58-33-48(a).
Inapplicability of provisions, §58-33-48(c).
Privileged and confidential information, §58-33-48(b).
Definitions, §58-33-10.
Denial, §58-33-30(g).
Duplicate licenses.
Lost, stolen or destroyed license, §58-33-50(d).
Education and training, §58-33-30(d).
Electronic filing.
Commissioner of insurance.
Rules requiring, §58-2-250.
Examination, §58-33-30(e).
Exceptions to requirement, §58-33-26(n).
Insurers, §58-33-26(o).
Fees, §58-33-120.

INSURANCE AGENTS —Cont'd
Licenses —Cont'd
General requirements, §58-33-26(a).
Interstate reciprocity.
Administrative action against licensee, reporting, §58-33-32(k).
Application requirements, waiver, §58-33-32(i).
Conditions for receiving nonresident license, §58-33-32(c).
Continuing education requirements, satisfaction, §58-33-32(j).
Criminal prosecutions, reporting, §58-33-32(l).
Examination, when not required, §58-33-32(g).
Greater fee not to be assessed, §58-33-32(h).
Purposes of section, §58-33-32(a).
Surplus lines license, §58-33-32(d).
Viatical settlement broker or provider, §58-33-32(e).
Kinds of insurance agent may be licensed for, §58-33-26(c), (c1).
Life and health insurance license.
Medicare supplements and long-term care insurance, authorized to sell, §58-33-26(f).
Required to sell accident and health insurance, §58-33-26(d).
Variable contracts, authorized to sell, §58-33-26(e).
Name, social security number or other identifying number, §58-33-26(k).
Nonresident, §58-33-30(h).
Interstate reciprocity, §58-33-32.
Reciprocity, §58-33-30(j).
Retaliatory provisions, §58-33-30(i).
Notice.
Suspension, revocation or nonrenewal, §58-33-50(a), (b).
Property and liability licensee.
Selling accident and health insurance prohibited, §58-33-26(d).
Reciprocal insurance, §58-15-55.
Reciprocity.
Interstate reciprocity, §58-33-32.
Renewal, §58-33-26(m).
Rental car companies.
Limited license to sell insurance, §58-33-17.
Required, §§58-33-5, 58-33-26(b).
Restricted license for overseas military agents, §58-33-15.
Self service storage renter's insurance.
Limited license.
Issuance to self service storage company, §58-33-18.
Surplus lines insurance, §58-21-65.
Surrender.
Termination of residency, §58-33-50(c).
Suspension, revocation, refusal to renew, placing licensee on probation.
Authority of commissioner, §58-33-46(a).
Grounds, §58-33-46(a).
Issuance of another license, requirements, §58-33-46(d).
Notice, §58-33-50(a), (b).
Other provisions, applicability, §58-33-46(b).
Return to commissioner, §58-33-26(l).
Revocation of appointment, §58-33-46(d).
Temporary licensing.
Authority of commissioner to issue, §58-33-66(a).
Death or disability of agent.
Representation of insurers that had appointed agent at time of death or disability, §58-33-66(c).

INSURANCE AGENTS —Cont'd
Licenses —Cont'd
Temporary licensing —Cont'd
Grounds for issuing, §58-33-66(a).
Limiting authority of temporary licensee,
§58-33-66(b).
Revoking, §58-33-66(b).
Sponsor, requiring temporary licensee to have,
§58-33-66(b).
Termination on transfer of business,
§58-33-66(b).
Title insurance company agents.
Annual license, §58-26-10.
Violations of insurance laws.
License not to be issued, §58-33-46(e).
Violations of licensing laws.
Impositions of penalties or remedies,
§58-33-46(f).
Life insurance solicitation.
Information to be given prospective purchasers,
§58-60-20(b).
Misleading titles prohibited, §58-60-20(c).
Regulation of solicitation generally, §§58-60-1 to
58-60-35.
See LIFE INSURANCE.
Limited representatives generally.
See INSURANCE LIMITED
REPRESENTATIVES.
Liquidation of insurers.
Duties of agents.
Failure to provide information to liquidator,
§58-30-127(c).
Generally, §58-30-127(a).
Policy issued through an agent, determination
of, §58-30-127(b).
Provisions of section are additional to other
duties, §58-30-127(d).
Managing general agents, §§58-34-2 to 58-34-15.
Misdemeanors.
Acting without license, §58-3-130.
Premiums.
Obtaining by fraud, §58-33-100(b).
Notice.
Closure of a block of business by insurer,
§58-3-275(a).
Information practices, §§58-39-25 to 58-39-28.
Penalties, §58-3-130.
Policies.
Signing certain blank policies, §58-33-110.
**Portable consumer electronic devices
insurance.**
Claims handling, §58-33-27.
Premiums.
Obtaining by fraud, §58-33-100(b).
Payment to agent valid, §58-33-100(a).
Privacy protection.
Consumer and customer information.
Generally, §§58-39-1 to 58-39-165.
See INSURANCE CONSUMER AND
CUSTOMER INFORMATION PRIVACY.
Rebates.
Credit life and credit accident and health
insurance, §58-33-90.
Rebates or discounts prohibited, §58-33-85(a).
Reciprocal insurance.
Licenses, §58-15-55.
Records.
Commissioner may require, §58-2-195(a).
Enforcement of provisions, §58-2-195(d).
Violations of provisions, §58-2-195(c).

INSURANCE AGENTS —Cont'd
Referral of business to repair source.
Gratuity accepted for referral, prohibition,
§58-33-76(b).
Prohibition, §58-33-76(a).
Violations, §58-33-76(c).
Rental car companies.
Limited license to sell insurance, §58-33-17.
Repair source, referral of business to,
§58-33-76.
Reports.
Commissioner may require, §58-2-195(a).
Enforcement of provisions, §58-2-195(d).
Mortgage guaranty insurance.
Policyholder's position, §58-10-140.
Violations of provisions, §58-2-195(c).
Representations.
Controversies between insured and insurer,
§58-33-20.
Retention of funds by agent.
Credit life and credit accident and health
insurance, §58-33-90.
Security program.
Information security program, §§58-39-130 to
58-39-165.
Self service storage renter's insurance.
Limited license.
Issuance to self service storage company,
§58-33-18.
**Supervision, rehabilitation and liquidation of
insurers.**
Duties of agents.
Failure to provide information to liquidator,
§58-30-127(c).
Generally, §58-30-127(a).
Policy issued through an agent, determination
of, §58-30-127(b).
Provisions of section are additional to other
duties, §58-30-127(d).
Surplus lines insurance.
Licenses, §58-21-65.
Title insurance company agents.
Annual license, §58-26-10.
Twisting.
Prohibited, §§58-3-115, 58-33-75.
Unauthorized insurers.
Soliciting, negotiating or selling insurance for.
Civil action or license revocation proceeding,
§58-33-95(b).
Criminal penalty, §58-33-95(a).
Strict liability for losses or unpaid claims,
§58-33-95(a).
Terms defined, §58-33-95(c), (d).
Violation of insurance laws, §58-33-120.

INSURANCE BROKERS.
Assumed name, operating under, §58-33-83.
Bankruptcy, insolvency or receivership.
Commissioner to be notified, §58-33-46(c).
Charges in excess of premium prohibited,
§58-33-85(b).
Statewide multiline limited assessable mutual
insurance companies, exception, §58-8-36.
**Closure of a block of business by insurer,
notice,** §58-3-275(a).
**Commissions, brokerage, service fee or other
valuable consideration.**
Assigning or directing payment, §58-33-82(e).
License required to accept, §58-33-82(d).
Renewal or other deferred commissions,
§58-33-82(c).

INSURANCE BROKERS —Cont'd

Commissions, brokerage, service fee or other valuable consideration —Cont'd

Unlicensed person, paying to or accepting, §58-33-82(a), (b).

Companies not licensed to do business in state.

Soliciting for prohibited, §58-33-26(h).

Continuing education program for licensees, §58-33-130(b).

Advisory committees.

Appointments, §58-33-135(a).

Composition, §58-33-135(b), (c).

Compliance with provisions.

What constitutes, §58-33-130(h).

Course provider fees, §58-33-130(a) to (b1).

Crediting of fees collected, §58-33-130(c).

Courses of study.

Approval by commissioner, §58-33-130(i).

Hour requirements, §58-33-130(d).

Powers and duties of commissioner generally, §§58-33-130, 58-33-135.

Renewal of license.

Requirement for, §58-33-130(c).

Countersignatures, §58-33-60.

Criminal history record check.

Applicant for license, §58-33-48.

Discrimination.

Prohibited, §58-33-80.

Embezzlement by insurance brokers, §58-2-162.

Report to commissioner, §58-2-163.

Insurer-controlled brokers.

Definitions, §58-3-155(a).

Determination of control, §58-3-155(b).

Disclosures by broker, §58-3-155(c).

Policyholders, claimants, etc.

Section not to affect rights of, §58-3-155(d).

Licenses.

Acting without license, §§58-3-130, 58-33-120.

Applicability of article, §58-33-1.

Application, §58-33-31(a).

Business entities, §58-33-31(b).

Documents necessary to verify information, requiring, §58-33-31(c).

Required, §58-33-30(a).

Bond and other requirements, §58-33-30(f).

Business entities, §58-33-26(j).

Continuing education program for licensees, §§58-33-130, 58-33-135.

Criminal history record check of applicants, §58-33-48(a).

Costs paid by applicant, §58-33-48(a).

Fingerprints furnished commissioner, §58-33-48(a).

Inapplicability of provisions, §58-33-48(c).

Privileged and confidential information, §58-33-48(b).

Definitions, §58-33-10.

Denial, §58-33-30(g).

Duplicate licenses.

Lost, stolen or destroyed license, §58-33-50(d).

Education and training, §58-33-30(d).

Examination, §58-33-30(e).

Exceptions to requirement, §58-33-26(n).

Insurers, §58-33-26(o).

Fees, §58-33-125(a) to (h).

General requirements, §58-33-26(a).

Interstate reciprocity.

Administrative action against licensee, reporting, §58-33-32(k).

Application requirements, waiver, §58-33-32(i).

INSURANCE BROKERS —Cont'd

Licenses —Cont'd

Interstate reciprocity —Cont'd

Conditions for receiving nonresident license, §58-33-32(c).

Continuing education requirements, satisfaction, §58-33-32(j).

Criminal prosecutions, reporting, §58-33-32(l).

Examination, when not required, §58-33-32(g).

Greater fee not to be assessed, §58-33-32(h).

Purposes of section, §58-33-32(a).

Surplus lines license, §58-33-32(d).

Kinds of insurance, §58-33-26(c), (c1).

Name, social security number or other identifying number, §58-33-26(k).

Nonresident, §58-33-30(h).

Interstate reciprocity, §58-33-32.

Reciprocity, §58-33-30(j).

Retaliatory provisions, §58-33-30(i).

Notice.

Suspension, revocation or nonrenewal, §58-33-50(a), (b).

Reciprocity.

Interstate reciprocity, §58-33-32.

Renewal, §58-33-26(m).

Required, §§58-33-5, 58-33-26(b).

Portable consumer electronic devices insurance, claims handling, §58-33-27(c).

Exception, §58-33-27(b).

Surplus lines insurance, §58-21-65.

Surrender.

Termination of residency, §58-33-50(c).

Suspension, revocation, refusal to renew, placing licensee on probation.

Authority of commissioner, §58-33-46(a).

Grounds, §58-33-46(a).

Issuance of another license, requirements, §58-33-46(d).

Notice, §58-33-50(a), (b).

Other provisions, applicability, §58-33-46(b).

Temporary licensing.

Authority of commissioner to issue, §58-33-66(a).

Grounds for issuing, §58-33-66(a).

Limiting authority of temporary licensee, §58-33-66(b).

Revoking, §58-33-66(b).

Sponsor, requiring temporary licensee to have, §58-33-66(b).

Termination on transfer of business, §58-33-66(b).

Violations of insurance laws.

License not to be issued, §58-33-46(e).

Violations of licensing laws.

Impositions of penalties or remedies, §58-33-46(f).

Limited representatives generally.

See INSURANCE LIMITED REPRESENTATIVES.

Misdemeanors, §58-3-130.

Premiums.

Obtaining by fraud, §58-33-100(b).

Penalties, §58-3-130.

Premiums.

Obtaining by fraud, §58-33-100(b).

Payment to broker valid, §58-33-100(a).

Rebates or discounts prohibited, §58-33-85(a).

Representation.

Controversies between insured and insurer, §58-33-20.

INSURANCE BROKERS —Cont'd
Surplus lines insurance.
Licenses, §58-21-65.
Twisting.
Prohibited, §58-33-75.
Unauthorized insurers.
Soliciting, negotiating or selling insurance for.
Civil action or license revocation proceeding,
§58-33-95(b).
Criminal penalty, §58-33-95(a).
Strict liability for losses or unpaid claims,
§58-33-95(a).
Terms defined, §58-33-95(c), (d).
Violation of insurance laws, §58-33-120.

INSURANCE COMMISSIONER, §§58-2-1 to
58-2-250.
Accident and health insurance.
Credit insurance generally, §§58-57-1 to
58-57-115.
See CREDIT INSURANCE.
Forms.
Approval, §§58-51-85, 58-51-95(a).
Group accident and health insurance.
Conversion privileges.
Premium rates and adjustments to be filed
with commissioner, §58-53-60(c).
Hearings.
Withdrawal of approval of forms, §58-51-95(e).
Premiums.
Approval of rates, §58-51-95(f).
Revised rates, §58-51-95(f).
Loss ratio standards, §58-51-95(h).
Actuaries, §58-2-25(a).
Chief actuary, §58-2-20.
Qualifications of, §58-2-171.
Adjusters.
Generally.
See INSURANCE ADJUSTERS.
Public adjusters, §§58-33A-1 to 58-22A-95.
See INSURANCE ADJUSTERS.
Agents.
Generally.
See INSURANCE AGENTS.
Annuities.
Generally.
See ANNUITIES.
Assessment companies, §§58-11-1 to 58-11-35.
See ASSESSMENT COMPANIES.
Bail bondsmen and runners.
See BAIL BONDSMEN AND RUNNERS.
Beach area essential property insurance,
§§58-45-1 to 58-45-96.
See BEACH AREA ESSENTIAL PROPERTY
INSURANCE.
Cease and desist orders.
Unauthorized insurers, §§58-28-20 to 58-28-35.
Chief actuary, §58-2-20.
Chief deputy commissioner, §58-2-15.
Chief officer of department, §58-2-5.
Committees.
Appointment, §58-2-30.
Companies.
Authority over all insurance companies,
§58-2-125.
Generally.
See INSURANCE COMPANIES.
**Confidentiality of market conduct analysis,
financial analysis, and related documents,**
§58-2-240(a).

INSURANCE COMMISSIONER —Cont'd
Consultants.
Contracts for consultants, §58-2-25(a).
Continuing care retirement communities.
Registration, disclosure, contract, etc.,
requirements, §§58-64-1 to 58-64-85.
See CONTINUING CARE RETIREMENT
COMMUNITIES.
Continuing education program for licensees.
Instructor qualifications, §58-33-132.
Powers and duties of commissioner generally,
§§58-33-130, 58-33-135.
Contracts.
Consulting contracts, §58-2-25(a).
Councils.
Appointment, §58-2-30.
Counties, municipalities, school districts.
Plans for erection of building to be used by.
Approval as to fire safety, §58-31-40(b).
Credit insurance.
Generally, §§58-57-1 to 58-57-115.
See CREDIT INSURANCE.
Defined, §58-1-5.
Deposits.
Selection of bank or trust company, §58-5-1.
Deputies, §58-2-25(a).
Chief deputy commissioner, §58-2-15.
Dissolution of insurers, §58-7-73.
Documents executed by commissioner.
Evidence.
Certificate as evidence of authority to do
business, §58-2-115.
Original and certified copies, §58-2-110.
Duties.
Investigation of charges, §58-2-155.
Election, §58-2-5.
**Electronic filings by licensees or applicants for
licenses.**
Administrative fee, authority to charge,
§58-2-250(c).
Definitions, §58-2-250(a).
Provisions not to supersede other provision of law
requiring, §58-2-250(d).
Rules requiring, adoption, §58-2-250(b).
Examinations, §58-2-50.
Beach area essential property insurance.
Insurance underwriting association, §58-45-70.
Conduct, §58-2-131(c) to (e).
Conflicts of interest, §58-2-133(a).
Contempt of court, §58-2-131(j).
Definitions, §58-2-131(b).
Dispensing with further examination,
§58-2-131(g).
Fees, §58-6-5.
Foreign or alien insurers.
Report by domiciliary insurance regulator
accepted in lieu of, §58-2-131(f).
Frequency, §58-2-131(d).
Holding companies, §58-19-35(a), (b), (d).
Confidentiality of information, §58-19-40.
Immunity, §58-2-133(d).
Insurance underwriting association.
Beach area essential property insurance,
§58-45-70.
Life and health insurance guaranty association,
§58-62-66.
Impaired insurers, §58-62-56(e).
Notice, §58-2-131(h).
Post assessment insurance guaranty association,
§58-48-65.
Insolvent insurers, §58-48-60(b).
Report, §58-48-60(c).

INSURANCE COMMISSIONER —Cont'd

Examinations —Cont'd

Powers in connection with, §58-2-131(i) to (m).

Public reports.

Hearings before information made public, §58-2-131(l).

Purposes, §58-2-131(a).

Rates.

Commissioner to examine organizations, §58-40-90.

Refusal to submit to examination, §58-2-133(c).

Reimbursement by insurer, §58-2-134(a).

Limited on amount paid by insurer, §58-2-134(b).

Reinsurance intermediaries, §58-9-21(f).

Report, §58-2-132.

Confidential information, §58-2-132(e), (f), (h), (i).

Contents, §58-2-132(a).

Definitions, §58-2-132(j).

Filing, §58-2-132(b).

Review, §58-2-132(c), (d), (g).

Retention of professionals and specialists, §§58-2-131(k), 58-2-133(b).

Scheduling.

Criteria for determining, §58-2-131(d).

Scope.

Criteria for determining, §58-2-131(d).

Subpoena power, §58-2-131(j).

Termination or suspension, §58-2-131(m).

Unfair trade practices.

Power of commissioner, §58-63-20.

Workers' compensation self-insurance.

Employer groups, §58-47-100.

Third-party administrators and service companies, §58-47-195.

Fair access to insurance requirements.

Appeals, §58-46-30.

Immunity of commissioner from liability, §58-46-35.

Plan.

Action on, §58-46-20(b).

Fees and charges.

Schedule, §58-6-5.

Financial analysis.

Confidentiality of records, §58-2-240(a).

Definitions, §58-2-240(b), (c).

Financial analyst and examiners.

Education requirements, §58-2-25(b).

Employment, §58-2-25(a).

Financial reporting.

Annual audited financial reports.

Generally, §§58-10-185 to 58-10-265.

See INSURANCE COMPANIES.

Firefighters' relief fund.

Certificate of eligibility, §58-84-46.

Disbursement of funds by commissioner, §58-84-25.

Fire insurance.

Generally.

See FIRE INSURANCE.

Fire safety inspections.

State property, §58-51-40(a).

Plans for erection of building to be used by local governments.

Approval as to fire safety, §58-51-40(b).

Foreign or alien insurance companies.

Generally, §§58-16-1 to 58-16-55.

See FOREIGN OR ALIEN INSURANCE COMPANIES.

INSURANCE COMMISSIONER —Cont'd

Forms.

Approval, §58-3-150(a).

Fraternal benefit societies.

Directors, officers, employees or agents.

Powers of society to purchase and maintain insurance, §58-24-35(c).

Exemptions from general insurance laws, §58-24-110.

Mutual life insurance companies.

Conversion of society into company, §58-24-70.

Reinsurance, §58-24-60(a).

Consolidation or merger, §58-24-60(b).

Fraud.

Immunity from liability for reporting, §58-2-160(a), (b).

Request for and release of information, §58-2-160(c).

Group insurance.

Approval of master plan and certificates, §58-3-20.

Hazardous conditions in state owned building.

Use limited or prohibited until hazard abated.

Commissioner to advise proper agency, §58-31-13.

Health benefit plan external review, §§58-50-75 to 58-50-95.

See HEALTH INSURANCE.

Health care benefits providers.

Determination of jurisdiction over, §§58-49-1 to 58-49-25.

See HEALTH CARE BENEFITS PROVIDERS.

Multiple employer welfare arrangements.

Regulation generally, §§58-49-30 to 58-49-65.

See HEALTH CARE BENEFITS PROVIDERS.

Health insurance.

Credit insurance generally, §§58-57-1 to 58-57-115.

See CREDIT INSURANCE.

Generally.

See HEALTH INSURANCE.

Health maintenance organizations, §§58-67-1 to 58-67-185.

See HEALTH MAINTENANCE ORGANIZATIONS.

Hearing officers.

Designating, §58-2-55.

Hearings, §58-2-50.

Accident and health insurance.

Withdrawal of approval of forms, §58-51-95(e).

Appeals.

Rules for hearing of, §58-2-52(a), (c).

Applicable procedural provisions, §58-2-52(b).

Filing of approvals and disapprovals.

Agency decision for certain purposes, §58-2-53.

Rates, §58-40-105(a).

Imposition of penalties or suspension of licenses, §58-40-110(c).

Unfair trade practices, §58-63-25.

Holding companies generally, §§58-19-1 to 58-19-70.

See INSURANCE HOLDING COMPANIES.

Hospital, medical and dental service corporations, §§58-65-1 to 58-66-40.

See HOSPITAL, MEDICAL AND DENTAL SERVICE CORPORATIONS.

Hull insurance, protection and indemnity clubs, §§58-20-1 to 58-20-40.

See HULL INSURANCE, PROTECTION AND INDEMNITY CLUBS.

INSURANCE COMMISSIONER —Cont'd

Immunity.
Examinations, §58-2-133(d).
Fraud.
Immunity from liability for reporting, §58-2-160(a), (b).
Information furnished to commissioner, §58-6-20.
Insurance policies or contracts.
Generally.
See INSURANCE POLICIES OR CONTRACTS.
Interagency consultation.
Authority of commissioner, §58-2-128(b).
Definitions, §58-2-128(d).
Privileged information, §58-2-128(c).
Purpose of provisions, §58-2-128(a).
Interstate insurance product regulation compact, §§58-91-1 to 58-91-80.
See INTERSTATE INSURANCE PRODUCT REGULATION COMPACT.
Investigations, §58-2-50.
Complaints of violations, §58-2-155.
License plate.
Special plate, number, §20-79.5.
Life and health insurance guaranty association.
Generally, §§58-62-2 to 58-62-95.
See LIFE AND HEALTH INSURANCE GUARANTY ASSOCIATION.
Life insurance.
Generally, §§58-58-1 to 58-61-15.
See LIFE INSURANCE.
Limited representatives generally.
See INSURANCE LIMITED REPRESENTATIVES.
Local investigators of fire and fire prevention inspectors.
Supervision, §58-2-95.
Longevity pay, §58-2-10.
Long-term care insurance.
Generally, §§58-55-1 to 58-55-50.
See LONG-TERM CARE INSURANCE.
Long-term care partnerships, §§58-55-55 to 58-55-80.
Managing general agents.
Generally.
See MANAGING GENERAL INSURANCE AGENTS.
Market conduct analysis.
Confidentiality of records, §58-2-240(a).
Definitions, §58-2-240(b), (c).
Public access to certain information not limited, §58-2-240(d).
Master trusts.
Use, §58-5-1.
Mortgage guaranty insurance, §§58-10-120 to 58-10-145.
Mortgage insurance consolidations.
Commissioner authorized to adopt rules, §58-2-210.
Motor vehicle insurance.
Generally.
See MOTOR VEHICLE INSURANCE.
Motor vehicle safety program, §58-31-52(a) to (e).
Multiple employer welfare arrangements.
Regulation generally, §§58-49-30 to 58-49-65.
See HEALTH CARE BENEFITS PROVIDERS.
Mutual insurance companies.
Generally, §§58-8-1 to 58-8-60.
See MUTUAL INSURANCE COMPANIES.

INSURANCE COMMISSIONER —Cont'd

Notice of changes to president or chief executive officer of insurer, §58-7-46.
Office of commissioner to be a public office, §58-2-100.
Orders.
Judicial review, §58-2-75.
Appeals from supreme court, §58-2-75(d).
Credit insurance, §58-57-75.
Jurisdiction of trial judge, §58-2-75(c).
Motor vehicle reinsurance facility, §58-37-65(f).
Orders as to plan of operation, §58-37-40(d).
Petition, §58-2-75(a).
Place of hearing.
Change, §58-2-75(b).
Post-assessment insurance guaranty association, §58-48-45(c).
Premiums.
Rate, §§58-2-80 to 58-2-90.
Presumption of correctness and propriety, §58-2-75(b).
Rates, §58-40-105(b).
Stay.
Commencement of proceedings not to operate as stay of commissioner order, §58-2-75(e).
Transcript of hearing.
Commissioner to provide, §58-2-75(b).
Unauthorized insurers.
Domestic companies, §58-14-15.
Signing, §58-2-45.
Writing.
Required, §58-2-45.
Post assessment insurance guaranty association.
Generally, §§58-48-1 to 58-48-130.
See POST ASSESSMENT INSURANCE GUARANTY ASSOCIATION.
Powers, §§58-2-40, 58-2-95, 143A-74.
Transfer to department of insurance, §143A-75.
Professional employer organizations generally, §§58-89A-1 to 58-89A-180.
See PROFESSIONAL EMPLOYER ORGANIZATIONS.
Property insurance generally.
See PROPERTY INSURANCE.
Protected cell companies, §§58-10-75 to 58-10-110.
See INSURANCE COMPANIES.
Public adjusters, §§58-33A-1 to 58-33A-95.
See INSURANCE ADJUSTERS.
Pyrotechnics licenses.
Administration of article, §58-82A-1.5(a).
Writings under seal of commissioner, prima facie evidence, §58-82A-1.5(b).
Generally, §§58-82A-1 to 58-82A-55.
Rate bureau.
Generally, §§58-36-1 to 58-36-120.
See RATE BUREAU.
Rates.
Regulation generally, §§58-40-1 to 58-40-140.
See INSURANCE RATES.
Readable insurance policies generally, §§58-38-1 to 58-38-40.
See INSURANCE POLICIES OR CONTRACTS.
Reciprocal insurance.
Generally, §§58-15-1 to 58-15-150.
See RECIPROCAL INSURANCE.
Records.
Inspection.
Subject to, §58-2-100.

INSURANCE COMMISSIONER —Cont'd

Reinsurance.
  Fraud.
    Reporting and investigation, §58-2-160(a), (b).
    Request for and release of information,
      §58-2-160(c).
  Generally.
    See REINSURANCE.
Reinsurance intermediaries.
  Generally, §§58-9-2 to 58-9-26.
    See REINSURANCE INTERMEDIARIES.
Reports.
  Fees and taxes received, §58-6-1.
  Reports to governor and general assembly,
    §58-2-120.
  Special reports, §58-2-190.
Risk retention groups.
  Generally, §§58-22-1 to 58-22-70.
    See RISK RETENTION GROUPS.
Rules and regulations, §58-2-40.
Salary, §58-2-10.
Schedule of fees and charges, §58-6-5.
Seal, §58-2-35.
Senior citizens.
  Joint action to insure elderly, §§58-52-1 to
    58-52-25.
    See HEALTH INSURANCE.
**Seniors' health insurance information
  program, §58-2-31.**
Service of process.
  Fire insurance.
    Unauthorized insurers, §58-28-45(e).
  Reciprocal insurance, §58-15-85.
  Unauthorized insurers false advertising process
    act.
    Acts appointing commissioner as attorney for
      service, §58-29-20(a).
    Manner of service on commissioner,
      §58-29-20(b), (c).
Small employer group health coverage.
  Generally, §§58-50-100 to 58-50-156.
    See SMALL EMPLOYER GROUP HEALTH
      COVERAGE.
State fire marshal, §58-80-1.
  Fireworks.
    Permissible exhibition, use, discharge.
      Guidelines, testing and training
        requirements, adoption, §58-28A-1(a).
    Public exhibition, licensing display operators
      and event employees.
      Safety guidelines, adoption, §58-82A-1.
  State volunteer fire department.
    Chief of department, §58-80-10.
Statements.
  Duties as to, §58-2-40.
  False statements, §58-2-180.
  Professional liability insurers.
    Filing with commissioner, §58-2-170(a), (b).
State property.
  Inspection for protection from fire, §58-31-40(a).
**Supervision, rehabilitation and liquidation of
  insurers.**
  Generally, §§58-30-1 to 58-30-310.
    See INSURER SUPERVISION,
      REHABILITATION AND LIQUIDATION.
Surplus lines insurance.
  Generally, §§58-21-1 to 58-21-105.
    See SURPLUS LINES INSURANCE.
Taxes relating to insurance.
  Collection of certain taxes and administration,
    §105-228.9.

INSURANCE COMMISSIONER —Cont'd

**Taxpayer identification numbers in public
  documents.**
  Redaction not required, §58-2-245.
Term of office, §§58-2-5, 163-1(a).
Third-party administrators.
  Generally, §§58-56-2 to 58-56-66.
    See THIRD-PARTY ADMINISTRATORS.
Title insurance.
  Generally, §§58-26-1 to 58-27-15.
    See TITLE INSURANCE.
**Transfer of powers to department of
  insurance, §143A-75.**
Unauthorized insurers.
  Domestic companies.
    Cease and desist orders, §58-14-15.
  Generally, §§58-28-1 to 58-28-45.
    See UNAUTHORIZED INSURERS.
**Unauthorized insurers false advertising
  process act.**
  Action by commissioner under unfair trade
    practices act, §58-29-15.
  Attorney for service of process.
    Act constituting appointment as, §58-29-20(a).
    Manner of service on, §58-29-20(b).
  Generally, §§58-29-1 to 58-29-25.
    See UNAUTHORIZED INSURERS.
  Notice of unlawful advertising, §58-29-10.
**Underground petroleum storage tank leak
  cleanup.**
  Insurance pools by owners and operators of
    underground storage tanks, §143-215.94I.
Unfair trade practices.
  Generally, §§58-63-1 to 58-63-75.
    See INSURANCE UNFAIR TRADE
      PRACTICES.

INSURANCE COMPANIES.
Accident and health insurance.
  Credit insurance generally, §§58-57-1 to
    58-57-115.
    See CREDIT INSURANCE.
  Generally.
    See HEALTH INSURANCE.
  Small employer group health coverage,
    §§58-50-100 to 58-50-156.
    See SMALL EMPLOYER GROUP HEALTH
      COVERAGE.
Actions for negligent decision.
  Health care liability, §§90-21.50 to 90-21.56.
Adjusters.
  Generally.
    See INSURANCE ADJUSTERS.
  Public adjusters, §§58-33A-1 to 58-33A-95.
    See INSURANCE ADJUSTERS.
Adverse underwriting decisions.
  Defined, §58-39-15.
  Reasons for making, obligation to give, §§58-39-55
    to 58-39-65.
**Affidavit of company president or other chief
  officer.**
  Compliance with insurance law.
    Required to do business, §58-2-150.
Agents generally.
  See INSURANCE AGENTS.
Alien insurance companies.
  Generally.
    See FOREIGN OR ALIEN INSURANCE
      COMPANIES.

INSURANCE COMPANIES —Cont'd
Annual audited financial reports, §§58-10-185 to 58-10-265.
Annual audit by certified public accountant.
Coercion, manipulation, misleading, fraudulently influencing CPA.
Prohibited acts by directors or officers, §58-10-250(b), (c).
Consolidated or combined financial statements.
Group of insurers utilizing pooling or reinsurance agreement, §58-10-215.
Cooling off period.
Former officers or employees of insurer seeking qualification as CPA, §58-10-210(l).
Disagreements with former CPA.
Letter submitted to commissioner, §58-10-205(c).
Dismissal or resignation of CPA for immediately preceding report, §58-10-205(c).
Grounds for not recognizing CPA or report prepared by, §58-10-210(e).
Nonaudit services provided insurer, §58-10-210(g).
Hearing as to whether CPA qualified, §58-10-210(f).
Independence of services, §58-10-210(g).
Exemption from requirements, request, §58-10-210(h).
Lead audit partner rotation required, §58-10-210(d).
Effective date of requirements, §58-10-260(d).
Letter from CPA.
Filing with commissioner, §58-10-205(b).
Letter of accountant's qualifications.
Furnished insurer, contents, §58-10-235.
Mediation or arbitration of disputes, §58-10-210(c).
Nonaudit services provided insurer, §58-10-210(g), (i).
Preapproval, §58-10-210(j), (k).
Preapproval of services provided insurer, §58-10-210(j), (k).
Qualifications of CPA, §58-10-210(a).
Recognition of CPA as qualified, §58-10-210(b).
Registration of CPA or firm retained to conduct audit, §58-10-205(a).
Required of all insurers, §58-10-195(a).
Scope of audit and report of CPA, §58-10-220.
Work papers of CPA.
Availability for review by commissioner, §58-10-240(b).
Contents, §58-10-240(a).
Copies made and retained by commissioner, §58-10-240(c).
Defined, §58-10-240(a).
Retention, §58-10-240(b).
Audit committees.
Board of directors members, §58-10-245(c).
Consulting, advisory, other compensatory fees.
Acceptance, §58-10-245(d).
Controlling person designating members, §58-10-245(f).
Defined, §58-10-190.
Designation, §58-10-195(d).
Disputes between management and CPA.
Resolution, §58-10-245(b).
Effective date of requirements, §58-10-260(e).
Hardship.
Waiver from requirements, §58-10-245(i).
Inapplicability of provisions, §58-10-245(a).

INSURANCE COMPANIES —Cont'd
Annual audited financial reports —Cont'd
Audit committees —Cont'd
Independence requirements, §58-10-245(d).
Member ceases to be independent, §58-10-245(e).
Proportion of independent members, §58-10-245(h).
Reports from CPA performing audit, §58-10-245(g).
Responsibility, §58-10-245(b).
Services provided by qualified CPA.
Preapproval, §58-10-210(j), (k).
Waiver from requirements.
Hardship, §58-10-245(i).
British insurers.
Letter of accountant, §58-10-265(b).
Statement of total business, §58-10-265(a).
Canadian insurers.
Annual statement of total business, §58-10-265(a).
Exemption.
Submission of accounts' reports, §58-10-185(c).
Letter of accountant, §58-10-265(b).
Capital and surplus requirements not met by insurer.
Report by CPA to insurer, §58-10-225(a).
Facts affecting report, obligation of CPA, §58-10-225(c).
Immunity for statements made in report, §58-10-225(b).
Coercion, manipulation, misleading, fraudulently influencing CPA.
Prohibited acts by directors or officers, §58-10-250(b), (c).
Communication as to unremediated weaknesses in internal control over financial reporting, §58-10-230(a).
Contents, §58-10-230(a).
Remedial actions taken, description, §58-10-230(a).
Time for preparing, §58-10-230(a).
Compliance with part.
Effective date.
Domestic insurers, §58-10-260(b).
Foreign insurers, §58-10-260(c).
Consolidated or combined financial statements.
Group of insurers utilizing pooling or reinsurance agreement, §58-10-215.
Contents, §58-10-200(b).
Definitions, §58-10-190.
Early filing required by commissioner.
Advance notice, §58-10-195(a).
Effective dates.
Audit committee requirements, §58-10-260(e).
Compliance with part, §58-10-260(b), (c).
Lead audit partner rotation requirement, §58-10-260(d).
Management's report on internal control over financial reporting requirements, §58-10-260(f).
Examinations by commissioner.
Part not to limit commissioner's authority, §58-10-185(e).
Exemption from part, §58-10-185(b).
Application for, §58-10-260(a).
Foreign or alien insurers filing substantially similar reports in another state, §58-10-185(c), (d).
Hearing on request after denial, §58-10-260(a).

INSURANCE COMPANIES —Cont'd
Annual audited financial reports —Cont'd
Extension of filing deadline, §58-10-195(b).
Management's report on internal control over
financial reporting, §58-10-195(c).
False or misleading statements.
Prohibited acts by directors or officers,
§58-10-250(a).
Filing required, §58-10-195(a).
Financial position of insurer reported,
§58-10-200(a).
Financial statements included in report.
Preparation, requirements, contents,
§58-10-200(a).
Foreign or alien insurers.
Filing management's report of internal control
over financial reporting.
Exemption, §58-10-185(d).
Filing substantially similar reports in another
state.
Exemption, §58-10-185(c).
Insurers subject to part, §58-10-185(b).
Management's report on internal control over
financial reporting.
Basis upon which assertions made.
Documentation, available on examination,
§58-10-255(e).
Contents, §58-10-255(d).
Effective date of requirements, §58-10-260(f).
Extension of filing deadline, §58-10-195(c).
Insurers required to file, §58-10-255(a).
Internal control over financial reporting defined,
§58-10-190.
Risk-based capital event.
Requiring insurer in to file, §58-10-255(b).
Section 404 report filed in satisfaction of
requirement, §58-10-255(c).
Time for filing, §58-10-255(a).
Extension of filing deadline, §58-10-195(c).
Material misstatement of financial condition.
Report by CPA to insurer, §58-10-225(a).
Facts affecting report, obligation of CPA,
§58-10-225(c).
Immunity of CPA for statements made,
§58-10-225(b).
Omission of facts.
Prohibited acts by directors or officers,
§58-10-250(a).
Prohibited acts by directors or officers, §58-10-250.
Purpose of part, §58-10-185(a).
Time for filing, §58-10-195(a).
Extension, §58-10-195(b).
Management's report on internal control over
financial reporting, §58-10-195(c).
Annual report, §55-16-22(a1).
Annuities.
See ANNUITIES.
Applicability of provisions, §58-7-1.
Approval of formation or initial license.
Refusal to approve, §58-7-37(c), (d).
Assessment companies, §§58-11-1 to 58-11-35.
See ASSESSMENT COMPANIES.
Assets.
Acceptance of assets subject to lien in favor of
claimants, §58-13-25(c).
Acquisition.
Securities or investments.
Purchasing above market value, §58-7-167(b).
Violation of law.
Disallowing of amounts of assets, §58-7-160.
Admitted assets, §58-7-162.

INSURANCE COMPANIES —Cont'd
Assets —Cont'd
Alien insurers, §58-7-198.
Allowable assets, §58-7-162.
Cash, §58-7-172.
Deposit, §58-7-172.
Disposal.
Ineligible property.
Effect of failure to dispose, §58-7-188(a).
Time limit, §58-7-188(a).
Unqualified investments, §58-7-167(c).
Foreign or alien insurers, §58-7-198.
Free and unencumbered assets, percentage
required, §58-13-25(a).
Investments.
Disposal of ineligible property.
Effect of failure to dispose, §58-7-188(b).
Time limit, §58-7-188(a).
Disposal of unqualified investments,
§58-7-167(c).
Permitted investments, §58-7-173.
Real estate, §58-7-187(a) to (d).
Special consent investments, §58-7-183(a) to (c).
Valuation.
Real property, §58-7-193(c), (d).
Maintenance of assets in state, §58-7-50(b).
Exceptions to provisions, §58-7-50(d), (e).
Not allowed, §58-7-163.
Prior and preferential claim of claimants,
§58-13-25(d).
Protected cell companies, §§58-10-75 to 58-10-110.
Protection.
Applicability of article, §58-13-10.
Citation of article, §58-13-1.
Definitions, §58-13-15.
Examination by commissioner, §58-13-20(b).
Exceptions, §58-13-20(a).
Hypothecation, prohibition, §58-13-25.
Pledge of assets restricted, §58-13-25.
Purposes of article, §58-13-5.
Qualified United States financial institution,
defined, §58-13-20(c).
Reasons, §58-13-5.
Scope of article, §58-13-10.
Short title of article, §58-13-1.
Publication, §58-3-60.
Removal from state, §58-7-50(c).
Replacing of certain assets, §58-7-197(a) to (e).
Statement filed by insurer, §58-13-25(b).
Audits.
Annual audited financial reports, §§58-10-185 to
58-10-265. See within this heading, "Annual
audited financial reports."
Authorization upon submission of fees,
§58-6-15.
Authorized kinds of insurance, §58-7-15.
**Background check of applicants for new
license,** §58-7-37.
Banks.
Disclosure of regulatory rating prepared by bank
commissioner, §53-99(d).
Beach area essential property insurance,
§§58-45-1 to 58-45-96.
See BEACH AREA ESSENTIAL PROPERTY
INSURANCE.
Boards of directors.
Classes of directors, §58-7-45(a).
Election, §58-7-45(a).
First meeting, §58-7-40.
Investments in or loans to, §58-7-200(c) to (e).

INSURANCE COMPANIES —Cont'd
Boards of directors —Cont'd
Vacancies.
Filling, §58-7-45(a).
Bylaws.
Adoption, §§58-7-40, 58-7-45(a).
Amendments.
Filing, §58-7-45(b).
Cancellation of insurance.
Generally.
See INSURANCE POLICIES OR CONTRACTS.
Capital.
Amount required, §58-7-75.
Casualty, fidelity and surety companies.
Loss and expense reserves, §58-3-81.
Premium deficiency reserves, §58-3-72.
Cease and desist orders.
Producer-controlled property or casualty insurers.
Lack of material compliance with section,
§58-3-165(l).
Ceding insurer.
Generally.
See REINSURANCE.
Certificates of authority.
Required before issuing policies, §58-7-10.
Cessation of business.
Statements or communications made in good
faith.
No liability for, §58-41-40(a).
Change of residential or e-mail address.
Licensee to notify commission, §58-2-69(b).
Charters.
Extension of existing charters, §58-7-5.
Chattel mortgages.
Investments, §58-7-180(a) to (d).
Child support.
Lien on insurance settlements, §§58-3-135,
58-3-185(a), (b).
Settlement payments, receiving person's duty to
retain funds, §44-50.
Claims.
Acknowledgment of claim, §58-3-100(c).
Civil penalty for failure to acknowledge,
§58-3-100(c).
Failure to acknowledge after receiving notice.
Civil penalty, §58-3-100(c).
Closure of a block of business.
Applicability, §58-3-275(d).
Definitions, §58-3-275(c).
Procedure, §58-3-275(a).
Rulemaking to implement, §58-3-275(b).
Commissioner.
Authority over all insurance companies,
§58-2-125.
Taxes relating to insurance.
Collection and administration, §105-228.9.
Compliance with law required, §58-2-150.
Confidentiality.
Consumer and customer information.
Generally, §§58-39-1 to 58-39-165.
See INSURANCE CONSUMER AND
CUSTOMER INFORMATION PRIVACY.
Market conduct analysis, financial analysis, and
related documents, §58-2-240(a).
Definitions, §58-2-240(b), (c).
Public access to certain information not limited,
§58-2-240(c).
Risk based capital requirements.
Hearings on commissioner's determinations,
§58-12-30.

INSURANCE COMPANIES —Cont'd
Confidentiality —Cont'd
Risk based capital requirements —Cont'd
Information filed with commissioner,
§58-12-35(a).
Taxpayer identification numbers in public
documents.
Redaction not required, §58-2-245.
Consolidation, §58-7-150.
Authorized, §58-7-150(a).
Conditions, §58-7-150(a).
Reinsurance by other insurer deemed
consolidation, §58-7-150(b).
Consumer reports.
Investigative consumer reports, §58-39-40.
Controlling shareholders.
Investments in or loans to, §58-7-200(c) to (e).
**Conversion of domestic mutual to stock
insurer,** §58-10-10(a).
Approval of plan, §58-10-10(b).
Insurer with guaranty capital, §58-10-10(c).
Distribution of assets, surplus or capital.
Director, officers or employees not to receive,
§58-10-10(g).
Experts for reviewing plan, retention by
commissioner at insurer's expense,
§58-10-10(e).
Fee, commission, compensation, etc.
Director, officers or employees not to receive,
§58-10-10(g).
Plan of conversion.
Acquisition of beneficial interest, §58-10-12(e).
Application for approval of plan and charter
amendment, §58-10-12(c).
Definitions, §58-10-12(a).
Distributing consideration to members.
Delaying or restricting, time period,
§58-10-12(d).
Requirements, §58-10-12(b).
Sale or transfer of stock.
Delaying or restricting, time period,
§58-10-12(d).
Public hearing, scheduling, §58-10-10(d).
Rules, adoption by commissioner, §58-10-10(h).
Transfer of assets, rights, franchises, etc., to stock
company, §58-10-10(f).
**Conversion of stock corporations into mutual
corporations,** §§58-10-1, 58-10-5.
Corporation law.
Applicability of general corporation law, §58-7-1.
Credit insurance.
Generally, §§58-57-1 to 58-57-115.
See CREDIT INSURANCE.
**Criminal history record search of applicants
for new license,** §58-7-37.
Customer information safeguards act,
§§58-39-130 to 58-39-165.
See INSURANCE CONSUMER AND CUSTOMER
INFORMATION PRIVACY.
**Death benefits paid in services or
merchandise.**
Issuing contracts prohibited, §58-3-55.
Deceptive trade practices.
Generally, §§58-63-1 to 58-63-75.
See INSURANCE UNFAIR TRADE
PRACTICES.
Definitions.
Generally, §§58-1-5, 58-12-2.
Department of insurance generally.
See INSURANCE DEPARTMENT.

INSURANCE COMPANIES —Cont'd
Depository institutions.
Affiliations with.
Gramm-Leach-Bliley act.
Compliance with provision required,
§58-19-2(b).
Depository institution defined, §58-19-2(a).
Deposits.
Foreign or alien insurance companies, §§58-5-5 to
58-5-40.
See FOREIGN OR ALIEN INSURANCE
COMPANIES.
Derivative transactions.
Investments, §58-7-205.
Discrimination.
Between individuals of same class, prohibition,
§58-3-120(b).
In favor of any person, prohibition, §58-3-120(a).
Dissolution of insurers, §58-7-73.
Dividends or other distributions.
Conversion of stock corporations into mutual
corporations.
Repayment of dividends to corporation for
beneficiaries, §58-10-5.
Impairment of capital.
Dividends not payable when capital impaired,
§58-7-125.
Liability of stockholders for unlawful
stockholders, §58-7-125.
Liability of stockholders not restricted,
§58-7-130(d).
Other requirements and limitations, §58-7-130(e).
Rate bureau.
Payment of dividends not prohibited or
regulated by rate bureau division,
§58-36-60.
Restricted by commissioner, grounds, §58-7-130(a).
Transfer out of paid-in and contributed surplus,
§58-7-130(c).
Unassigned surplus, declared from, §58-7-130(b).
Domestic reciprocals, §§58-15-100 to 58-15-150.
See RECIPROCAL INSURANCE.
Electronic filing.
Licensees, applicants for licenses, §58-2-250.
E-mail address.
Information provided commissioner, §58-2-69(b).
Emblems, §58-3-50.
Examinations.
Generally.
See INSURANCE COMMISSIONER.
Reimbursement of costs by insurers, §58-2-134(a).
Limit on amount paid, §58-2-134(b).
Fair access to insurance requirements,
§§58-46-1 to 58-46-60.
See PROPERTY INSURANCE.
Fees.
License fees.
Annual continuation fee, §58-6-7(a).
Defined, §58-6-15.
When submitted, §58-6-15.
Financial disclosure, §§58-3-65, 58-40-130(a) to
(e).
Designation of statistical organizations,
§58-40-130(b).
Publication of financial information, §58-3-65.
Rate regulation, §58-40-130(a), (d).
Financial statements, §58-2-165(a).
Annual audited financial reports, §§58-10-185 to
58-10-265. See within this heading, "Annual
audited financial reports."
Format, to, §58-2-165(b).

INSURANCE COMPANIES —Cont'd
Financial statements —Cont'd
Preparation, §58-2-165(c).
Town or county mutual, §58-2-165(a1).
Fire insurance.
Generally.
See FIRE INSURANCE.
Foreign or alien insurance companies.
Generally.
See FOREIGN OR ALIEN INSURANCE
COMPANIES.
Franchise tax.
Exemption, §105-125(a).
Group insurance.
Accident and health insurance generally.
See HEALTH INSURANCE.
Life insurance generally.
See LIFE INSURANCE.
Health care liability, §§90-21.50 to 90-21.56.
Health insurance.
Credit insurance generally, §§58-57-1 to
58-57-115.
See CREDIT INSURANCE.
Generally.
See HEALTH INSURANCE.
Health maintenance organizations, §§58-67-1 to
58-67-185.
See HEALTH MAINTENANCE
ORGANIZATIONS.
Hearings.
Annual audited financial reports.
Annual audit by certified public accountant.
CPA qualified, §58-10-210(f).
Exemption from part.
Request denied, §58-10-260(a).
Refusal to approve formation or initial license,
§58-7-37(d).
Risk based capital requirements.
Confidential hearing on commissioner's
determination, §58-12-30.
Hedging transaction.
Authority to enter into, §58-7-205(d).
Holding companies.
Generally, §§58-19-1 to 58-19-70.
See INSURANCE HOLDING COMPANIES.
Hospital, medical and dental service
corporations, §§58-65-1 to 58-66-40.
See HOSPITAL, MEDICAL AND DENTAL
SERVICE CORPORATIONS.
Hull insurance, protection and indemnity
clubs, §§58-20-1 to 58-20-40.
See HULL INSURANCE, PROTECTION AND
INDEMNITY CLUBS.
Impairment.
Contributing to impairment.
Acts resulting in, §58-30-12(c).
Penalties, §58-30-12(c).
Duty to report, §58-30-12(b).
Definitions, §58-30-12(a).
Income generation transaction, §58-7-205(e).
Incorporation.
Background check of applicants for new license,
§58-7-37.
Capital and/or surplus.
Amount required, §58-7-75.
Certificate of incorporation, §58-7-35.
First meeting, §58-7-40.
Procedure, §58-7-35.
Refusal to approve formation.
Grounds, §58-7-37(c).
Notice, hearing, §58-7-37(d).

INSURANCE COMPANIES —Cont'd
Information practices.
Notice, §§58-39-25 to 58-39-28.
Information privacy protection.
Consumer and customer information.
Generally, §§58-39-1 to 58-39-165.
See INSURANCE CONSUMER AND
CUSTOMER INFORMATION PRIVACY.
Information security program, §§58-39-130 to
58-39-165.
Insignias, §58-3-50.
Insurance regulatory fund.
Created, use of proceeds, §58-6-25(d).
Investments.
Acquisition.
General qualifications, §58-7-167(a) to (c).
Purchasing above market value, §58-7-167(b).
Authorization, §58-7-168.
Derivative transactions.
Conditions, §58-7-205(b).
Counterparty exposure amount, §58-7-205(f).
Definitions, §58-7-205(a).
Documentation and records required,
§58-7-205(i).
Guidelines and internal procedures,
§58-7-205(h).
Hedging transaction, §58-7-205(d).
Income generation transaction, §58-7-205(e).
Other transactions, approval, §58-7-205(g).
Requirements for derivative instruments,
§58-7-205(j).
Rules, adoption by commissioner, §58-7-205(c).
Directors, officers, controlling stockholders or
other persons.
Investments in limited, §58-7-200(c) to (e).
Disposal of ineligible property.
Effect of failure to dispose, §58-7-188(b).
Time limit, §58-7-188(a).
Diversification.
Amount of investments required to be
maintained, §58-7-170(a).
Deposits with financial institutions, limiting,
§58-7-170(j).
Limitations on eligible investments,
§58-7-170(b).
Medium or low quality obligations, limitation,
§58-7-170(d).
Documentation that limit not exceeded,
§58-7-170(f).
Failure to obtain approval for investment in
excess of limitation, §58-7-170(i).
Medium or low quality obligations defined,
§58-7-170(e).
Mortgages, limitation on percentage of
investments in, §58-7-170(c).
Provision supersede inconsistent provisions,
§58-7-170(k).
Eligible investments, §58-7-165.
Foreign or territorial investment.
Canadian securities inapplicability of provision,
§58-7-178(c).
Insurers authorized to transact business in
foreign country or territory, §58-7-178(a).
Insurers not authorized to transact business in
foreign country or territory, §58-7-178(b).
Hedging transaction, §58-7-205(d).
Income generation transaction, §58-7-205(e).
Medium or low quality obligations, §58-7-170(d) to
(f).
Mortgages, §58-7-179(a) to (e).
Chattel mortgages, §58-7-180(a) to (d).

INSURANCE COMPANIES —Cont'd
Investments —Cont'd
Mortgages —Cont'd
Limitation, §58-7-170(c).
Permitted insurer investments, §58-7-173.
Prohibited investments, §58-7-185(a).
Securities or property of other persons,
§58-7-185(b).
Real estate, §58-7-187(a) to (d).
Valuation, §58-7-193(c), (d).
Replacing of certain assets, §58-7-197(a) to (e).
Securities approved by secretary of housing and
urban development, federal housing
administration and veterans administration,
§53-45.
Special consent investments, §58-7-183(a) to (c).
Title insurers, §58-7-182.
Transactions allowed or prohibited, §58-7-200(a).
Derivative transactions allowed, §§58-7-200(b),
58-7-205(b).
Directors, officers, controlling stockholders or
other persons.
Investments in prohibited, §58-7-200(c) to (e).
Unlawful acquisition.
Disallowance of amounts of assets, §58-7-160.
Valuation, §58-7-192(d).
Kinds of insurance authorized, §58-7-15.
Legal expense funds for elected officials.
Limitations on donations, §163-278.316(d).
Prohibited donations, §163-278.316(e).
Liabilities.
Publication, §58-3-60.
Reporting certain liabilities, §58-7-197(b).
Licenses.
Background of incorporators and key personnel.
Criminal history search of applicants for new
license, §58-7-37(a).
Fingerprints and photograph of applicants for
new license.
Submission to commissioner required,
§58-7-37(a).
Key person defined, §58-7-37(b).
Power of commissioner, §58-7-37(e).
Rules for obtaining background information,
adoption, §58-7-37(f).
Electronic filing.
Applicants for licenses, §58-2-250.
E-mail address.
Applicant to provide commissioner, §58-2-69(b).
Fees.
Annual continuation fee, §58-6-7(a).
Rating bureau exempt from, §58-6-7(d).
When submitted, §58-6-15.
Foreign companies.
Conditions of licensure, §58-16-5.
Restricting license.
Prohibiting or limiting kinds or amount of
insurance, §58-3-100(e).
Revocation, suspension or refusal to renew.
Notice to agents in state, writing new
business prohibited, §58-3-100(d).
Issuance.
New company, §58-7-40.
Misdemeanors.
Failure to secure license, §58-3-85.
Notification by license applicants to insurance
commissioner.
Criminal convictions, §58-2-69(c).
Definitions, §58-2-69(a).
Online services, §58-2-69(f).
Contracts for, §58-2-69(g).

INSURANCE COMPANIES —Cont'd
Licenses —Cont'd
Notification by license applicants to insurance
commissioner —Cont'd
Residential address, §58-2-69(b).
Service of notice, §58-2-69(d), (e).
Oath required, §58-2-150.
Perpetual license, §58-6-7(a).
Refusal to approve initial license.
Grounds, §58-7-37(c).
Notice, hearing, §58-7-37(d).
Renewal, §58-6-15.
Required to do business, §§58-3-85, 58-6-7(a).
Residential address.
Applicant to inform commissioner, §58-2-69(b).
Restricting license.
Prohibiting or limiting kinds or amount of
insurance, §58-3-100(e).
Revocation, suspension or refusal to renew.
Authority of commissioner, §58-3-100(a).
Foreign insurance companies.
Notice to agents in state, writing insurance
prohibited, §58-3-100(d).
Grounds, §58-3-100(a).
Holding companies.
Violations of provisions, §58-19-65.
Individuals, making applicable to, §58-3-100(b).
"Twisting,"§58-3-115.
Sale or major reorganization of company.
License to be restricted, §58-3-160.
Self-service storage companies.
Rental insurance.
Limited license, §58-33-18.
Term, §58-6-15.
Lien for services rendered injured persons.
Accounting for disbursements, §44-50.1(a) to (c).
Liens.
Child support obligors.
Lien on insurance settlements, §§58-3-135,
58-3-185(a), (b).
**Life and health insurance guaranty
association,** §§58-62-2 to 58-62-95.
See LIFE AND HEALTH INSURANCE
GUARANTY ASSOCIATION.
Life insurance.
Generally, §§58-58-1 to 58-61-15.
See LIFE INSURANCE.
Reinsurance, §58-58-65.
Reserve fund.
Calculation of reserve fund of domestic
companies, §58-58-45.
Limitation of risk.
Exceptions, §§58-3-105, 58-3-110.
Fidelity or surety business.
Limitations on exposure, §58-3-110(a).
Limitations on guarantees of any single
institution, §58-3-110(c).
Transportation or warehousing bonds,
§58-3-110(b).
Generally, §§58-3-105, 58-3-110.
Liquidation generally, §§58-30-1 to 58-30-310.
See INSURER SUPERVISION,
REHABILITATION AND LIQUIDATION.
Loans.
Authorization, §58-7-168.
Eligible investments, §58-7-165.
Mortgage loans, §58-7-179(a) to (e).
Policy loans, §58-7-175.
Securities approved by secretary of housing and
urban development, federal housing
administration and veterans administration,
§53-45.

INSURANCE COMPANIES —Cont'd
Loans —Cont'd
To directors, officers, controlling shareholders or
others, §58-7-200(c) to (e).
Long-term care insurance.
Generally, §§58-55-1 to 58-55-50.
See LONG-TERM CARE INSURANCE.
Long-term care partnerships, §§58-55-55 to
58-55-80.
Loss and expense reserves.
Casualty insurance or surety company, §58-3-81.
Managing general agents, §§58-34-2 to 58-34-15.
See MANAGING GENERAL INSURANCE
AGENTS.
Mortgage guaranty insurance, §§58-10-120 to
58-10-145.
Contingency reserve.
Annual contribution, factors to determine,
§58-10-135(a).
Calculations to develop, sequence,
§58-10-135(g).
Larger reserve maintained under laws or
regulations of another jurisdiction,
§58-10-135(h).
Liability, reported as, §58-10-135(c).
Withdrawals, §58-10-135(d) to (f).
Definitions, §58-10-120.
Kinds of insurance authorized, §58-7-15.
Minimum policyholder position, §58-10-125(a).
Capital and surplus requirements,
§58-10-125(c).
Cessation of new business.
Company not having minimum position,
§58-10-125(b).
Waiver of requirement, §58-10-125(i).
Factors considered, §58-10-125(j).
Period of waiver, §58-10-125(l).
Review of request, §58-10-125(k).
Monoline requirement for insurers, §58-10-145.
Unearned premium reserve.
Computation, §58-10-130(a).
Loss reserve, case basis method used to
determine, §58-10-130(c).
Mortgage loans.
Investments, §§58-7-170(c), 58-7-179(a) to (e).
Motor vehicle declared total loss.
Total loss claim.
Marking registration card and title certificate,
§20-71.3(a1).
Motor vehicle insurance.
Generally.
See MOTOR VEHICLE INSURANCE.
Mutual insurance companies, §§58-8-1 to
58-8-60.
See MUTUAL INSURANCE COMPANIES.
Names, §58-7-35.
Companies must do business in own names,
§58-3-50.
Words which must be included, §58-7-35.
Negligent decisions.
Health care liability, §§90-21.50 to 90-21.56.
Nonrenewal of business.
Entire book of business, §58-41-45(a).
Loss of reinsurance, §58-41-30.
Notice, §58-41-20(a) to (c).
Timing of notice to insured, §58-41-40(b).
Penalties, §58-41-55.
Statements or communications made in good
faith.
No liability for, §§58-41-40, 58-41-40(a).

INSURANCE COMPANIES —Cont'd
North Carolina rate bureau, §§58-36-1 to
   58-36-120.
   See RATE BUREAU.
Notice.
   First meeting, §58-7-40.
   Information practices, §§58-39-25 to 58-39-28.
   Refusal to approve formation or initial license,
      §58-7-37(d).
Oath as to compliance with insurance law.
   Required to do business, §58-2-150.
Officers, §58-7-140.
   Changes to president or chief executive officer.
      Notice, §58-7-46.
   Investments in or loans to, §58-7-200(c) to (e).
Penalties.
   Failure to acknowledge claim after receiving
      notice.
      Civil penalty, §58-3-100(c).
   Publication of assets and liabilities.
      Violations of provisions, §58-3-60.
   Violations of article.
      Misdemeanors, §58-21-105(a).
Policies or contracts generally.
   See INSURANCE POLICIES OR CONTRACTS.
Pool of assets and liabilities.
   Protected cell companies, §§58-10-75 to 58-10-110.
**Post assessment insurance guaranty
   association,** §§58-48-1 to 58-48-130.
   See POST ASSESSMENT INSURANCE
      GUARANTY ASSOCIATION.
Premium deficiency reserves.
   Acquisition costs and premium taxes previously
      incurred not considered, §58-3-72(c).
   Anticipates investment income, reduction not
      taken, §58-3-72(d).
   Calculation for recorded unearned premium
      reserves, §58-3-72(b).
   Date of determination, §58-3-72(a).
   Financial statement or report to include in
      liabilities, §58-3-72(a).
   Grouping policies for determining if deficiency
      exists, §58-3-72(e).
   Other basis use to produce adequate or reasonable
      reserves, §58-3-72(f).
Premiums.
   Generally.
      See INSURANCE PREMIUMS.
Premium tax, §§105-228.5 to 105-228.10.
Privacy protection.
   Consumer and customer information.
      Generally, §§58-39-1 to 58-39-165.
         See INSURANCE CONSUMER AND
            CUSTOMER INFORMATION PRIVACY.
**Producer-controlled property or casualty
   insurers.**
   Business transacted with, §58-3-165(a) to (n).
   Cease and desist orders.
      Lack of material compliance with section,
         §58-3-165(l).
   Definitions, §58-3-165.
Professional liability insurance.
   Reports to commissioner, §58-2-170(c).
Property insurance.
   Beach area essential property insurance,
      §§58-45-1 to 58-45-96.
      See BEACH AREA ESSENTIAL PROPERTY
         INSURANCE.
   Fair access to insurance requirements, §§58-46-1
      to 58-46-60.
      See PROPERTY INSURANCE.

INSURANCE COMPANIES —Cont'd
Property insurance —Cont'd
   Fire insurance generally.
      See FIRE INSURANCE.
   Generally.
      See PROPERTY INSURANCE.
Protected cell companies.
   Administrative and accounting procedures,
      §58-10-85(e).
   Assessment by guaranty fund or association,
      prohibited, §58-10-95(d).
   Assets owned by company, §58-10-85(c).
   Attribution of assets and liabilities, §58-10-85(b).
   Availability of assets to creditors, §58-10-95(a).
   Charging assets with liabilities of other business,
      §58-10-90(a).
   Closing out protected cell account.
      Cessation of business, §58-10-90(g).
   Conservation, rehabilitation or liquidation,
      §58-10-100(a).
      Amount recoverable, §58-10-100(b).
   Contributions to guaranty fund or association,
      prohibited, §58-10-95(d).
   Definitions, §58-10-80.
   Duties of directors, §58-10-85(e).
   Establishment, §58-10-85(a).
   Fraudulent purpose or fraudulent conveyance.
      Establishment of cell does not constitute,
         §58-10-95(e).
   Income, gains and losses, §58-10-90(b).
   Insurance securitization, §58-10-90(d).
      Contracts or other documentation,
         requirements, §58-10-90(e).
   Issuing insurance or reinsurance.
      Directly to policyholders or reinsureds,
         prohibition, §58-10-90(f).
   Legal person separate from company.
      Creation of protected cell does not create,
         §58-10-85(c).
   Name, §58-10-85(a).
   Obligations, creditor's recourse, §58-10-95(b), (c).
   Plan of operation, §58-10-85(a).
   Protected cell accounts.
      Holding assets in accounts, requirement,
         §58-10-85(a).
      Transfer of assets to, §58-10-85(a).
   Protection from creditors, §58-10-95(a).
   Purpose and legislative intent, §58-10-75.
   Rules, adoption by commissioner, §58-10-110.
   Satisfaction of protected cell liabilities.
      Only protected cell assets available,
         §58-10-90(a).
   Security interest attaching to protected cell
      assets, §58-10-85(c).
   Third party managing protected cell assets or
      protected cell, §58-10-85(d).
   Transaction of insurance business.
      Not deemed, §58-10-105.
   Trustee of protected cell assets, §58-10-85(c).
   Value of protected cell assets, §58-10-85(f).
      Fair market value, §58-10-90(c).
Protection.
   Hypothecation.
      Restrictions, §58-13-25.
Public adjusters, §§58-33A-1 to 58-33A-95.
   See INSURANCE ADJUSTERS.
Rate bureau, §§58-36-1 to 58-36-120.
   See RATE BUREAU.
Rate regulation generally, §§58-40-1 to
   58-40-140.
   See INSURANCE RATES.

INSURANCE COMPANIES —Cont'd
Readable insurance policies generally,
  §§58-38-1 to 58-38-40.
  See INSURANCE POLICIES OR CONTRACTS.
Real property.
  Investments, §58-7-187(a) to (d).
  Authorized by section, §58-7-187(a).
  Conditions, §58-7-187(c).
  Limitation on amount of property, §58-7-187(d).
  Types of property, §58-7-187(b).
  Valuation, §58-7-193(c), (d).
Rebates.
  Prohibited.
  Premiums on credit insurance, §58-57-95.
Reciprocal insurance.
  Generally, §§58-15-1 to 58-15-150.
  See RECIPROCAL INSURANCE.
Records.
  Agencies, agents, brokers and producers of record,
    §58-2-195.
  Exhibiting books and papers to commissioner.
    Required, §58-2-200.
  Inspection by commissioner, §58-2-185.
  Maintenance in state.
    Exceptions, §58-7-55.
  Maintenance of records, §58-7-50(a).
    Exceptions to provisions, §58-7-50(d), (e).
  Removal from state, §58-7-50(c).
    Exceptions, §58-7-55.
  Requirements, §58-2-185.
Refusal to approve formation, §58-7-37(c), (d).
Regulatory charge.
  Computation, §58-6-25(a).
  Definitions, §58-6-25(e).
  Insurance regulatory fund.
    Created, use of proceeds, §58-6-25(d).
  Levy, §58-6-25(a).
  Payment, §58-6-25(c).
  Rate, §58-6-25(b).
  Returns, §58-6-25(c).
Rehabilitation generally, §§58-30-1 to 58-30-310.
  See INSURER SUPERVISION,
    REHABILITATION AND LIQUIDATION.
Reinsurance.
  See REINSURANCE.
Reinsurance intermediaries, §§58-9-2 to 58-9-26.
  See REINSURANCE INTERMEDIARIES.
Reorganization.
  License.
    Restricted, §58-3-160.
Reports.
  Agencies, agents, brokers and producers of record,
    §58-2-195.
  Annual audited financial reports, §§58-10-185 to
    58-10-265. See within this heading, "Annual
    audited financial reports."
  Annual report, §55-16-22(a1).
  Financial data, §58-40-130(a), (d), (e).
  Financial statements, §58-2-165.
  Liabilities.
    Reporting certain liabilities, §58-7-197(b).
  Special reports.
    Commissioner may require, §58-2-190.
Reserves.
  Contingency reserve.
    Mortgage guaranty insurers, §58-10-135.
  Fire and marine insurance companies.
    Loss reserves, §58-3-75.
  Loss and expense reserves.
    Casualty insurance or surety company.
      Date of determination, §58-3-81(a).

INSURANCE COMPANIES —Cont'd
Reserves —Cont'd
  Loss and expense reserves —Cont'd
    Casualty insurance or surety company —Cont'd
      Diminished by allowance or credit for
        reinsurance covenable, §58-3-81(a).
      Financial statement or report to include in
        liabilities, §58-3-81(a).
      Other basis for adequate or reasonable
        reserves, §58-3-81(e).
      Outstanding losses and loss expenses,
        §58-3-81(b).
      Record of losses and claims notices to be kept,
        §58-3-81(f).
      Workers' compensation insurance, minimum
        loss and loss expense, §58-3-81(c).
    Fire and marine insurance companies, §58-3-75.
  Mortgage guaranty insurers.
    Contingency reserve, §58-10-135.
    Unearned premium reserve, §58-10-130.
  Premium deficiency reserves.
    Acquisition costs and premium taxes previously
      incurred not considered, §58-3-72(c).
    Anticipates investment income, reduction not
      taken, §58-3-72(d).
    Calculation for recorded unearned premium
      reserves, §58-3-72(b).
    Date of determination, §58-3-72(a).
    Financial statement or report to include in
      liabilities, §58-3-72(a).
    Grouping policies for determining if deficiency
      exists, §58-3-72(e).
    Other basis use to produce adequate or
      reasonable reserves, §58-3-72(f).
  Reciprocal insurance, §58-15-75.
  Unearned premium reserves.
    Computation, §58-3-71(b) to (f).
      Rules, §58-3-71(g).
    Mortgage guaranty insurance, §58-10-130.
    Required, §58-3-71(a).
    Requirements.
      Reciprocal insurance, §58-15-75.
Residential address.
  Information provided commissioner, §58-2-69(b).
Retaliatory premium taxes, §105-228.8.
Risk based capital requirements, §§58-12-2 to
  58-12-70.
  Additional capital endorsed by General Assembly,
    §58-12-4.
  Announcements as to risk based capital levels
    prohibited, §58-12-35(b).
  Authorized control level event.
    Actions taken by commission, §58-12-21(b).
    Defined, §58-12-21(a).
  Company action level event.
    Defined, §58-12-11(a).
    Financial plan in event of, §58-12-11(b).
      Copies submitted to other state, §58-12-11(f).
      Time for submitting, §58-12-11(c).
      Unsatisfactory, commissioner determining,
        §58-12-11(d), (e).
  Confidential hearing on commissioner's
    determination, §58-12-30.
  Confidentiality of information filed with
    commissioner, §58-12-35(a).
  Definitions, §58-12-2.
  Exemptions from provisions, §58-12-40(c), (d).
  Foreign insurers.
    Mandatory control level event, §58-12-45(c).
    Risk based capital plan.
      When commissioner may require,
        §58-12-45(b).

INSURANCE COMPANIES —Cont'd
Risk based capital requirements —Cont'd
Foreign insurers —Cont'd
Submission of report.
Request of commissioner, §58-12-45(a).
Health organization's risk based capital.
Determining, §58-12-6(d).
HMO net worth requirement, §58-12-70.
Legislative findings, §58-12-4.
Life or health insurer's risk based capital.
Determination, §58-12-6(b).
Mandatory control level event.
Defined, §58-12-25(a).
Foreign insurers, §58-12-45(c).
Life and health insurers, §58-12-25(b).
Property and casualty insurers, §58-12-25(c).
Notices resulting in regulatory action.
Effective date, §58-12-50.
Phase in provision, §58-12-55.
Health organization, §58-12-65.
Property or casualty, §58-12-60.
Property or casualty insurer's risk based capital.
Determining, §58-12-6(d).
Rate making.
Information not used by commissioner for,
§58-12-40(b).
Regulatory action level event.
Actuaries and investment experts, retaining,
§58-12-16(d).
Corrective actions, determining, §58-12-16(c).
Defined, §58-12-16(a).
Risk based capital plan.
Submission, §58-12-16(b).
Report of risk based capital levels.
Adjustment by commission, report inaccurate,
§58-12-6(c).
Filing, filing date, §58-12-6(a).
Risk based capital plan.
Company action level event, §58-12-11(b) to (f).
Regulatory action level event, §58-12-16(b).
Supplemental nature of provisions, §58-12-40(a).
Risk retention groups.
Generally, §§58-22-1 to 58-22-70.
See RISK RETENTION GROUPS.
Sale of company.
License.
Restrictions, §58-3-160.
Salvage vehicles.
Surrender of title to vehicles deemed salvage
vehicle, §20-109.1.
Secretary of state.
Incorporation.
Certificate of secretary of state, §58-7-35.
Securities or property of other persons.
Underwriting or participating in offering,
prohibition, §58-7-185(b).
Security program.
Information security program, §§58-39-130 to
58-39-165.
**Segregated and insulated pool of assets and
liabilities.**
Protected cell companies, §§58-10-75 to 58-10-110.
Self-service storage companies.
Rental insurance.
Limited license, §58-33-18.
Senior citizens.
Joint action to insure elderly, §§58-52-1 to
58-52-25.
See HEALTH INSURANCE.
Service of process.
Unauthorized insurers false advertising process
act, §§58-29-1 to 58-29-25.
See UNAUTHORIZED INSURERS.

INSURANCE COMPANIES —Cont'd
Shares and shareholders.
Amount of capital required, §58-7-75.
Assessment of stock, §58-7-110.
Controlling shareholders.
Investments in or loans to, §58-7-200(c) to (e).
Conversion of stock corporations into mutual
corporations, §§58-10-1, 58-10-5.
Dividends or other distributions.
Liability not restricted, §58-7-130(d).
Other requirements and limitations,
§58-7-130(e).
Restricted by commissioner, grounds,
§58-7-130(a).
Transfer out of paid-in and contributed surplus,
§58-7-130(c).
Equity securities.
Defined, §58-7-145(f).
Exemptions from provisions, §58-7-145(g).
Rules and regulations, §58-7-145(h).
Sale.
Arbitrage transactions, §58-7-145(e).
Dealers, §58-7-145(d).
Delivery of security sold, §58-7-145(c).
Equity securities held less than six months,
§58-7-145(b).
Severability of provisions, §58-7-145(i).
Statement of ownership, §58-7-145(a).
Impairment of capital, §58-7-75.
Assessment of shares, §58-7-110.
Dividends not payable when capital impaired.
Liability of stockholders for unlawful
dividends, §58-7-125.
Reduction of capital stock, §§58-7-105, 58-7-120.
Increase of capital stock, §§58-7-105, 58-7-115.
Certificate of authority to transact new
business, §§58-7-105, 58-7-115.
Payment in cash for capital stock, §58-7-80.
Reduction of capital stock, §§58-7-105, 58-7-120.
Certificate of authority to conduct new business,
§§58-7-105, 58-7-120.
Small employer group health coverage.
Generally, §§58-50-100 to 58-50-156.
See SMALL EMPLOYER GROUP HEALTH
COVERAGE.
Special act.
Domestic companies incorporated by special acts.
Extension of charters, §58-7-5.
Statements.
Professional liability insurers, §58-2-170.
Publication of financial information, §58-3-65.
Statistical organizations.
Status as insurance company, §§58-36-4(g),
58-40-50(i).
Supervision generally, §§58-30-1 to 58-30-310.
See INSURER SUPERVISION,
REHABILITATION AND LIQUIDATION.
Surplus.
Amount required, §58-7-75.
Impairment of surplus, §58-7-75.
Surplus lines insurance.
Generally, §§58-21-1 to 58-21-105.
See SURPLUS LINES INSURANCE.
Taxation.
Commissioner of insurance.
Election of certain taxes relating to insurance,
§105-228.9.
Counties.
No additional local taxes, §105-228.10.
Credits.
Gross premiums tax.
Assessments paid to insurance guaranty
associations, §105-228.5A.

INSURANCE COMPANIES —Cont'd
Taxation —Cont'd
Definitions, §105-228.3.
Gross premiums tax, §§105-228.5, 105-228.6.
Information to be furnished to commissioner,
§58-6-20.
Local taxes.
No additional local taxes, §105-228.10.
Municipalities.
No additional local taxes, §105-228.10.
Persons procuring insurance directly with
unlicensed insurer.
Collection of tax by commissioner of insurance,
§105-228.9.
Premiums tax.
Additional local fire and lightning rate,
§105-228.5(d).
Measurement of additional tax imposed,
§105-228.5(b).
Additional statewide fire and lightning rate,
§105-228.5(d).
Article 65 corporations.
Measurement of tax imposed, §105-228.5(b).
Rate of tax, §105-228.5(d).
Calculation of tax base, §105-228.5(b1).
Credits.
Assessments paid to insurance guaranty
associations, §105-228.5A.
Exclusions, §105-228.5(c).
Exemptions, §105-228.5(g).
Health insurance risk pool fund.
Distribution of part of proceeds, §105-228.5B.
Installment payments, §105-228.5(f).
Levy, §105-228.5(a).
Payment, §105-228.5(e).
Rate of taxes, §105-228.5(d).
Reports, §105-228.5(e).
Retaliatory taxes, §105-228.8.
Computing taxes that another state imposes
upon state companies, §105-228.8(d).
Definitions, §105-228.8(b).
Imposition of premium tax upon companies
chartered in another state, §105-228.8(a).
Inapplicability to special purpose obligations
or assessments, §105-228.8(e).
Retaliation on basis other than aggregate
basis, §105-228.8(f).
Taxes deemed imposed directly upon state,
§105-228.8(c).
When companies subject to tax to report and
pay, §105-228.8(a).
Self-insurers.
Measurement of tax imposed, §105-228.5(b).
Tax base, §105-228.5(b).
Calculation, §105-228.5(b1).
Withdrawal from state.
Taxes in case of, §105-228.6.
Workers' compensation.
Rate of tax, §105-228.5(d).
Retaliatory premium taxes, §105-228.8.
Risk retention groups.
Collection of tax by commissioner of insurance,
§105-228.9.
Surplus lines.
Collection by commissioner of insurance,
§105-228.9.
Third-party administrators.
Generally, §§58-56-2 to 58-56-66.
See THIRD-PARTY ADMINISTRATORS.
Title insurance.
Generally, §§58-26-1 to 58-27-15.
See TITLE INSURANCE.

INSURANCE COMPANIES —Cont'd
Total loss claim.
Motor vehicle declared total loss.
Marking registration card and title certificate,
§20-71.3(a1).
Types of business entitled to do.
Upon payment of license fees and taxes,
§58-6-7(c).
Unauthorized insurers.
Generally, §§58-28-1 to 58-28-45.
See UNAUTHORIZED INSURERS.
**Unauthorized insurers false advertising
process act.**
Generally, §§58-29-1 to 58-29-25.
See UNAUTHORIZED INSURERS.
Unclaimed property generally, §§116B-51 to
116B-80.
See UNCLAIMED PROPERTY.
Unfair claims settlement practices, §58-63-15.
Applicability to risk retention groups, §58-22-20.
Unfair trade practices.
Generally, §§58-63-1 to 58-63-75.
See INSURANCE UNFAIR TRADE
PRACTICES.
Valuation of securities and investments,
§58-7-192(d).

**INSURANCE CONSUMER AND CUSTOMER
INFORMATION PRIVACY,** §§58-39-1 to
58-39-165.
**Access to individual's personal recorded
information.**
Request by individual, §58-39-45.
Account numbers.
General prohibition on disclosure, §59-39-76(a).
Definitions, §59-39-76(b).
Exceptions, §59-39-76(c).
Action by individual for violations.
Costs and attorney's fees, §58-39-105(c).
Damages, §58-39-105(b).
Equitable relief, §58-39-105(a).
Exclusive remedy, §58-39-105(e).
Statute of limitations, §58-39-105(d).
Adverse underwriting decisions.
Defined, §58-39-15.
Notice of reasons, §58-39-55(a).
Orally giving reasons and summary of rights,
§58-39-55(d).
Other agent or institution satisfying obligations,
§58-39-55(c).
Previous decisions.
Basing decision on, §58-39-65.
Seeking information concerning, prohibition,
§58-39-60.
Rights of applicant or policyholder or individual
upon request, §58-39-55(b).
Summary of rights, providing, §58-39-55(a).
Appeal of right.
Final order of commissioner, §58-39-100.
Authorization for disclosure, §59-39-75.
Cease and desist orders, §58-39-90.
Penalty for violating, §58-39-95(b).
Civil penalties, §58-39-95(a).
Civil penalty and forfeiture fund.
Proceeds of civil penalty remitted to, §58-39-95(c).
Conditions for disclosure, §59-39-75.
Consumer reports.
Defined, §58-39-15.
Investigative consumer reports, §58-39-40.
**Correction, amendment or deletion of
individual's recorded information.**
Request by individual, §58-39-50.

INSURANCE CONSUMER AND CUSTOMER INFORMATION PRIVACY —Cont'd

Credit insurance, applicability to, §58-39-10(e).

Criminal activity, fraud or misrepresentation suspected.
Pretext interview, use to obtain information, §58-39-20.

Customer information safeguards act, §§58-39-130 to 58-39-165.
Definitions, §58-39-140.
Purpose, §58-39-130.
Scope, §58-39-135.
Short title, §58-39-1.

Definitions.
Account numbers, disclosure, §58-39-76.
Customer information safeguards act, §58-39-140.
Insurance information and privacy act, §58-39-15.

Disclosure authorization forms.
Personal or privileged information disclosure, requirements, §58-39-35.

Disclosure limitations and conditions, §59-39-75.

Effective date of rights granted, §58-39-120.

Examinations and investigations by commissioner.
Affairs of insurance institution or agent, §58-39-125(a).
Affairs of insurance-support organization, §58-39-125(b).

False pretenses.
Obtaining information under, criminal penalty, §58-39-115.

Governmental authority records, information gathered from.
Inapplicability of act, §58-39-10(d).

Hearing on violations, §58-39-80(b).

Immunity.
Disclosure in accordance with article, §58-39-110.

Individual remedies, §58-39-105.

Information security program, §58-39-145.
Effective date, §58-39-165.
Objects, §58-39-150.
Rules, §58-39-155.
Violations, §58-39-160.

Institution, agents or insurance-support organizations.
Applicability of act to, §58-39-10(a).

Insurance information and privacy protection act, §§58-39-1 to 58-39-76.
Definitions, §58-39-15.
Purpose of article, §58-39-5.
Short title, §58-39-1.
Standards for collection, use and disclosure of information.
Purpose of article, §58-39-5.

Investigative consumer reports.
Defined, §58-39-15.
Personal interview, §58-39-40(b), (c).
Requirements before making, §58-39-40(a).

Limitations on disclosure, §59-39-75.

Market and research survey information.
Specification of questions designed to obtain, §58-39-30.

Medical-record information.
Access to individual's personal recorded information, §58-39-45(c).

Mortgage guaranty insurance company.
Notice of insurance information practices, §58-39-28(b).

Notice of hearings on violations, §58-39-80(a).

INSURANCE CONSUMER AND CUSTOMER INFORMATION PRIVACY —Cont'd

Notice of insurance information practices.
Abbreviated notice in lieu of notice, §58-39-25(c).
Blanket or group insurance plan, §58-39-27(g).
Combined or separate notices, §58-39-27(c).
Exceptions to required notice, §58-39-27(d) to (f).
Federal privacy disclosure, §58-39-26(a).
Information included, §58-39-26(b).
When provided, §58-39-26(c).
Joint notice provided by institution or agent, §58-39-27(a).
Mortgage guaranty insurance company, §58-39-28(b).
Other institution or agent satisfying obligation, §58-39-25(d).
Provided applicants and policyholders, §58-39-25(a).
Requirements, §58-39-25(b).
Single notice to two or more policyholders or applicants, §58-39-27(b).
Title insurance company, §58-39-28(a).
When provided, §58-39-25(a).
Written notice required, contents, §58-39-25(b).

Penalties, §58-39-95.

Personal information.
Access to individual's recorded information.
Request by individual, §58-39-45.
Correction, amendment or deletion of individual's recorded information.
Request by individual, §58-39-50.
Disclosure authorization forms, requirements, §58-39-35.
Disclosure limitations and conditions, §59-39-75.

Persons rights extended to, §58-39-10(b).

Powers of commissioner, §58-39-125.

Pretext interview.
Defined, §58-39-15.
Use to obtain information, §58-39-20.

Reasons permitting disclosure, §59-39-75.

Request by individual.
Access to individual's personal recorded information.
Consumer reporting agency.
Not included in term insurance-support organization, §58-39-45(g).
Duties owed individual requesting, §58-39-45(a).
Fee to cover costs, charging, §58-39-45(d).
Identification of source of information, §58-39-45(b).
Medical-record information, §58-39-45(c).
Natural persons, extension of rights to, §58-39-45(f).
Other institution or agent satisfying obligation, §58-39-45(e).
Rights of individual requesting, §58-39-45(a).
Correction, amendment or deletion of recorded information.
Consumer reporting agency.
Not included in term insurance-support organization, §58-39-50(f).
Duties and rights owed individual, §58-39-50(a).
Natural persons, extension of rights to, §58-39-50(e).
Notice to individual, furnishing information, §58-39-50(b).
Refusal, disagreement with, §58-39-50(c), (d).

Resident of state, when considered, §58-39-10(c).

Security program, §58-39-145.
Effective date, §58-39-165.

INSURANCE CONSUMER AND CUSTOMER INFORMATION PRIVACY —Cont'd

Security program —Cont'd
Objects, §58-39-150.
Rules, §58-39-155.
Violations, §58-39-160.
Service of process on support organization.
Organization outside state, §58-39-85.
Statement of charges.
Violations, service, §58-39-80(a).
Title insurance company.
Notice of insurance information practices, §58-39-28(a).
Violations.
Cease and desist orders, §58-39-90.
Hearing and procedures, §58-39-80.
Individual remedies, §58-39-105.
Information security program, §58-39-160.
Penalties, §58-39-95.

INSURANCE CONSUMER PROTECTION FUND.
Appropriations, §58-2-215(c).
Creation, §58-2-215(a).
Uses, §58-2-215(b).

INSURANCE DEPARTMENT.
Accident and health insurance.
Credit insurance generally, §§58-57-1 to 58-57-115.
See CREDIT INSURANCE.
Generally.
See HEALTH INSURANCE.
Adjusters.
Generally.
See INSURANCE ADJUSTERS.
Public adjusters, §§58-33A-1 to 58-33A-95.
See INSURANCE ADJUSTERS.
Agents.
Generally.
See INSURANCE AGENTS.
Annuities.
Generally.
See ANNUITIES.
Assessment companies, §§58-11-1 to 58-11-35.
See ASSESSMENT COMPANIES.
Beach area essential property insurance, §§58-45-1 to 58-45-96.
See BEACH AREA ESSENTIAL PROPERTY INSURANCE.
Brokers.
Generally.
See INSURANCE BROKERS.
Building code council.
Transfer to department, §143A-78.
Commissioner generally, §§58-2-1 to 58-2-250.
See INSURANCE COMMISSIONER.
Companies generally.
See INSURANCE COMPANIES.
Consumer protection fund.
Appropriations, §58-2-215(c).
Creation, §58-2-215(a).
Uses, §58-2-215(b).
Continuing care retirement communities.
Generally, §§58-64-1 to 58-64-85.
See CONTINUING CARE RETIREMENT COMMUNITIES.
Creation, §§58-2-1, 143A-73.
Credit insurance.
Generally, §§58-57-1 to 58-57-115.
See CREDIT INSURANCE.
Defined, §58-1-5.

INSURANCE DEPARTMENT —Cont'd
Duties, §58-2-1.
Established, §58-2-1.
Fair access to insurance requirements, §§58-46-1 to 58-46-60.
See PROPERTY INSURANCE.
Fire insurance.
Generally.
See FIRE INSURANCE.
Foreign or alien insurance companies.
Generally.
See FOREIGN OR ALIEN INSURANCE COMPANIES.
Fraternal benefit societies.
Directors, officers, employees or agents.
Powers of society to purchase and maintain insurance, §58-24-35(c).
Exemptions from general insurance laws, §58-24-110.
Generally.
See FRATERNAL BENEFIT SOCIETIES.
Mutual life insurance companies.
Conversion of society into company, §58-24-70.
Reinsurance, §58-24-60(a).
Consolidation or merger, §58-24-60(b).
Health care benefits providers.
Determination of jurisdiction over generally, §§58-49-1 to 58-49-25.
See HEALTH CARE BENEFITS PROVIDERS.
Regulation of multiple employer welfare arrangements generally, §§58-49-30 to 58-49-65.
See HEALTH CARE BENEFITS PROVIDERS.
Health insurance.
Credit insurance generally, §§58-57-1 to 58-57-115.
See CREDIT INSURANCE.
Generally.
See HEALTH INSURANCE.
Health maintenance organizations, §§58-67-1 to 58-67-185.
See HEALTH MAINTENANCE ORGANIZATIONS.
Holding companies generally, §§58-19-1 to 58-19-70.
See INSURANCE HOLDING COMPANIES.
Hospital, medical and dental service corporations, §§58-65-1 to 58-66-40.
See HOSPITAL, MEDICAL AND DENTAL SERVICE CORPORATIONS.
Hull insurance, protection and indemnity clubs, §§58-20-1 to 58-20-40.
See HULL INSURANCE, PROTECTION AND INDEMNITY CLUBS.
Incident affecting operations of department.
Stay of deadlines, §58-2-47.
Insurance policies or contracts.
Generally.
See INSURANCE POLICIES OR CONTRACTS.
Liability insurance commission.
Generally, §§58-32-1 to 58-32-30.
See LIABILITY INSURANCE COMMISSION.
Transfer to department, §143A-79.1.
Life and health insurance guaranty association, §§58-62-2 to 58-62-95.
See LIFE AND HEALTH INSURANCE GUARANTY ASSOCIATION.
Life insurance.
Generally, §§58-58-1 to 58-61-15.
See LIFE INSURANCE.

INSURANCE DEPARTMENT —Cont'd
Limited representatives generally.
See INSURANCE LIMITED
REPRESENTATIVES.
Long-term care insurance.
Generally, §§58-55-1 to 58-55-50.
See LONG-TERM CARE INSURANCE.
Long-term care partnerships, §§58-55-55 to
58-55-80.
Managing general agents.
Generally.
See MANAGING GENERAL INSURANCE
AGENTS.
Motor vehicle insurance.
Generally.
See MOTOR VEHICLE INSURANCE.
Mutual insurance companies.
Generally, §§58-8-1 to 58-8-60.
See MUTUAL INSURANCE COMPANIES.
Personnel.
Powers of commissioner, §58-2-25(a).
Placing of insurance for state agencies by,
§58-31-55.
Post assessment insurance guaranty
association, §§58-48-1 to 58-48-130.
See POST ASSESSMENT INSURANCE
GUARANTY ASSOCIATION.
Powers of insurance commissioner.
Transfer to department, §143A-75.
Property insurance generally.
See PROPERTY INSURANCE.
Public adjusters, §§58-33A-1 to 58-33A-95.
See INSURANCE ADJUSTERS.
Rate bureau.
Generally, §§58-36-1 to 58-36-120.
See RATE BUREAU.
Rate regulation generally, §§58-40-1 to
58-40-140.
See INSURANCE RATES.
Readable insurance policies generally,
§§58-38-1 to 58-38-40.
See INSURANCE POLICIES OR CONTRACTS.
Reciprocal insurance.
Generally, §§58-15-1 to 58-15-150.
See RECIPROCAL INSURANCE.
Reinsurance.
Generally.
See REINSURANCE.
Reinsurance intermediaries, §§58-9-2 to 58-9-26.
See REINSURANCE INTERMEDIARIES.
Risk retention groups.
Generally, §§58-22-1 to 58-22-70.
See RISK RETENTION GROUPS.
Seal, §58-2-35.
Senior citizens.
Joint action to insure elderly, §§58-52-1 to
58-52-25.
See HEALTH INSURANCE.
Small employer group health coverage.
Generally, §§58-50-100 to 58-50-156.
See SMALL EMPLOYER GROUP HEALTH
COVERAGE.
State agencies.
Placing of insurance for state agencies by,
§58-31-55.
State fire and rescue commission.
Transfer to department, §143A-79.2.
State fire protection grant fund.
Created in department, §58-85A-1(a).
Method for distributing, development,
implementation, §58-85A-1(b).

INSURANCE DEPARTMENT —Cont'd
Supervision, rehabilitation and liquidation of
insurers.
Generally, §§58-30-1 to 58-30-310.
See INSURER SUPERVISION,
REHABILITATION AND LIQUIDATION.
Surplus lines insurance.
Generally, §§58-21-1 to 58-21-105.
See SURPLUS LINES INSURANCE.
Third-party administrators.
Generally, §§58-56-2 to 58-56-66.
See THIRD-PARTY ADMINISTRATORS.
Title insurance.
Generally, §§58-26-1 to 58-27-15.
See TITLE INSURANCE.
Transfer of powers of insurance commissioner
to department, §143A-75.
Unauthorized insurers.
Generally, §§58-28-1 to 58-28-45.
See UNAUTHORIZED INSURERS.
Unauthorized insurers false advertising
process act.
Generally, §§58-29-1 to 58-29-25.
See UNAUTHORIZED INSURERS.
Unfair trade practices.
Generally, §§58-63-1 to 58-63-75.
See INSURANCE UNFAIR TRADE
PRACTICES.
Volunteer fire department.
Transfer to department, §143A-79.

INSURANCE DISCRIMINATION.
Accident and health insurance.
Coverage of bones and joints, §§58-3-121,
58-3-121(a) to (c).
Group accident and health insurance.
Mentally ill and chemically dependent.
Applicability, §58-51-55(d).
Coverage, §58-51-55(b1), (c).
Definitions, §58-51-55(a).
Prohibited acts, §58-51-55(b), (c).
Sex changes , coverage of treatment or
studies not required, §58-51-55(e).
Bones, coverage of, §58-3-121(a) to (c).
Disabled persons.
Prohibited, §168-10.
Employer discrimination against lawful use of
lawful products during nonworking hours.
Health, disability or life insurance policies
distinguishing between employees,
§95-28.2(b).
Joints, coverage of, §58-3-121(a) to (c).
Life insurance.
Prohibited acts, §58-58-35.
Motor vehicles.
Prohibited practices, §58-3-25.
Race, color or national or ethnic origin.
Prohibited acts, §58-3-25(c).
Rates not to be unfairly discriminatory,
§58-40-20(a), (e).
Method of rate making, §58-36-10.
Unfair trade practices.
Prohibited acts, §58-63-15.

INSURANCE FRAUD.
Burning dwelling, §14-65.
Burning personal property, §14-66.
False statement to procure or deny benefit of
policy or certificate, §58-2-161(b).
Action, §58-2-161(b).
Criminal penalties, §58-2-161(b).
Insurer defined, §58-2-161(a).

INSURANCE FRAUD —Cont'd
False statement to procure or deny benefit of policy or certificate —Cont'd
Statement defined, §58-2-161(a).
Immunity from liability for reporting, §58-2-160(a), (b).
Life insurance.
Creditors deprived of benefits of policies except in cases of fraud, §58-15-115.
Misrepresentation of policies prohibited, §58-58-40.
Reinsurance.
Reporting and investigation, §58-2-160(a), (b).
Request for and release of information, §58-2-160(c).
Twisting, §58-3-115.

INSURANCE HOLDING COMPANIES, §§58-19-1 to 58-19-70.
Acquisition of control of or merger with domestic insurer.
Approval by commissioner, §58-19-15(d), (f).
Exceptions to provisions, §58-19-15(h).
Foreign or alien insurer.
Report of change of control, §58-19-17(b).
Definitions, §58-19-17(a).
Hearing, §58-19-15(e).
Jurisdiction of courts, §58-19-15(j).
Mailing of notices and other materials.
Expenses, §58-19-15(g).
Prohibited acts, §58-19-15(i).
Restrictions, §58-19-15(a).
Statement to be filed, §58-19-15(a) to (c).
Contents of statement, §58-19-15(b).
Oath or affirmation, §58-19-15(b).
Violations of provisions, §58-19-15(i).
Appeals.
Orders of commissioner, §58-19-70(a).
Cease and desist orders.
Violations of provisions, §58-19-50(c).
Commissioner.
Acquisition of control of or merger with domestic insurer.
Approval by commissioner, §58-19-15(d), (f).
Appeals from order of commissioner, §58-19-70(a).
Examinations, §§58-19-35, 58-19-40.
Mandatory injunction or writ of mandamus directing commissioner to act, §58-19-70(b).
Confidentiality of information.
Information obtained by commissioner, §58-19-40.
Definitions, §58-19-5.
Dividends.
Extraordinary dividends, §58-19-30(c).
Reporting of dividends by registered insurers, §58-19-25(d).
Examinations, §58-19-35(a), (b), (d).
Confidentiality of information, §58-19-40.
Felonies.
False statements or reports, §58-19-50(e).
Findings of legislature, §58-19-1(a).
Gramm-Leach-Bliley act.
Affiliations with depository institutions, §58-19-2.
Injunctions.
Mandatory injunction directing commissioner to act, §58-19-70(b).
Violations of provisions, §58-19-45(a).
Investments, §58-19-10(b), (d).
Disposal of investments if insurer ceases to control subsidiary, §58-19-10(e).
Exemption from certain provisions, §58-19-10(c).

INSURANCE HOLDING COMPANIES —Cont'd
Liquidation or rehabilitation of domestic insurer.
Recovery.
Generally, §58-19-60(a).
Liability, §58-19-60(c), (e).
Maximum amount recoverable, §58-19-60(d).
Restrictions, §58-19-60(b).
Mandamus.
Writ of mandamus directing commissioner to act, §58-19-70(b).
Penalties.
Criminal penalties for violations, §58-19-50(d).
Registration statement.
Failure to file, §58-19-50(a).
Transactions or investments in violation of provisions.
Director of officer, §58-19-50(b).
Policy of state, §58-19-1(b).
Purposes of provisions, §58-19-1(b).
Registration of insurers.
Affiliated insurers.
Disclaimer of affiliation with authorized insurer, §58-19-25(j).
Registration on behalf of, §58-19-25(h).
Disclaimer of affiliation with authorized insurer, §58-19-25(j).
Dividends and distributions.
Reporting to commissioner by registered insurers, §58-19-25(d).
Exemption from provisions of section, §58-19-25(i).
Information necessary to comply with provisions.
Persons required to provide to insurers, §58-19-25(e).
Required, §58-19-25(a).
Statements, §58-19-25(a) to (c).
Consolidated registration statement, §58-19-25(g).
Contents, §58-19-25(b).
Failure to file, §58-19-25(k).
Penalty, §58-19-50(a).
Termination of registration, §58-19-25(f).
Subsidiaries, §58-19-10.
Cessation of control of subsidiary.
Disposal of investments therein, §58-19-10(e).
Defined, §58-19-5.
Organization or acquisition, §58-19-10(a).
Surplus.
Determination of reasonableness, §58-19-30(d).
Transactions.
Standards, §58-19-30(a), (b).
Violations of provisions.
Cease and desist orders, §58-19-50(c).
Injunctions, §58-19-45(a).
Receivership, §58-19-55.
Revocation or suspension, §58-19-65.
Voting securities.
Prohibitions against voting, §58-19-45(b).
Sequestration, §58-19-45(c).

INSURANCE INFORMATION AND PRIVACY PROTECTION ACT, §§58-39-1 to 58-39-76.
See INSURANCE CONSUMER AND CUSTOMER INFORMATION PRIVACY.

INSURANCE INSTRUCTOR LICENSES, §58-33-132(a).
Summary suspension, §58-33-132(b).

INSURANCE LIMITED REPRESENTATIVES.
Assumed name, operating under, §58-33-83.

INSURANCE LIMITED REPRESENTATIVES
  —Cont'd
Unauthorized insurers —Cont'd
  Soliciting, negotiating or selling insurance for
      —Cont'd
    Terms defined, §58-33-95(c), (d).
Violation of insurance laws, §58-33-120.

INSURANCE POINTS.
Motor vehicle insurance.
  At-fault accidents and certain moving violations,
      §58-36-75(a) to (g).
  Classifications and safe driver incentive plan,
      §58-36-65(a) to (m).

INSURANCE POLICIES OR CONTRACTS.
Accident and health insurance.
  Adopted children.
    Policies to cover, §§58-51-30(a) to (f),
        58-51-125(a) to (c).
  Age limits, §58-50-20.
  Applicability to all policies issued or delivered in
      state, §58-51-15(i).
  Applications for, §58-50-5(a).
    Alteration, §58-50-5(b).
    False statements.
      Effect, §58-50-5(c).
  Blanket accident and health insurance,
      §58-51-75(a).
    Approval of forms, §58-51-85.
  Dependent students on medically necessary leave
      of absence from postsecondary educational
      institution.
    Policy coverage to continue as to, §58-51-25(b).
  Disability income insurance.
    Standards for policies, §58-51-130.
  Exemption of certain policies from provisions,
      §58-50-65.
  Filing.
    Rules and regulations as to, §58-51-15(g).
  Foreign or alien insurers, §58-51-15(f).
  Forfeiture.
    Notice of nonpayment of premium required
        before forfeiture, §58-50-35.
  Forms, §58-51-5(a).
    Approval by commissioner, §58-51-1.
    Other states, §58-51-5(b).
  Group accident and health insurance,
      §58-51-80(a), (b).
    Approval of forms, §58-51-85.
    Renewal, §58-51-110(a).
    Replacement, §58-51-110(b).
  Inapplicable or inconsistent provisions,
      §58-51-15(c).
  Industrial sick benefit insurance.
    Provisions, §58-51-70.
  Intoxicants and narcotics, §58-51-16(a) to (c).
  Mentally retarded or physically handicapped
      children.
    Policy coverage to continue as to, §58-51-25(a).
  Narcotics and intoxicants, §58-51-16(a) to (c).
  Newborn infants.
    Policies to cover, §58-51-30(a) to (f).
  Nonconforming policies, §58-50-15(b).
  Order in which provisions printed, §58-51-15(d).
  Other jurisdictions, §58-51-15(f).
  Other policy provisions, §58-51-15(b).
  Preexisting condition exclusion.
    Clarification, §58-51-15(h).
  "Preexisting conditions.."
    Meaning of term, §58-51-60.

INSURANCE POLICIES OR CONTRACTS
  —Cont'd
Accident and health insurance —Cont'd
  Provisions.
    Generally, §58-51-15(a), (b).
    Inapplicable or inconsistent provisions,
        §58-51-15(c).
    Industrial benefit insurance, §58-51-70.
    Order of certain policy provisions, §58-51-15(d).
    Other policy provisions.
      Effect, §58-50-15(a).
    Requirements of other jurisdictions,
        §58-51-15(f).
  Renewability.
    Applicability of provisions, §58-51-20(d).
    Notice, §58-51-20(a).
    Policies issued during grace period construed to
        be continuation of first policy, §58-51-15(c).
    Unilateral acts by insurers prohibited,
        §58-51-15(b).
  Required policy provisions, §58-51-15(a).
  Requirements, §§58-51-5, 58-51-5(a).
    Other states, §58-51-5(b).
  Return of policy.
    Notice of right to return policy, §58-51-10.
  Third-party ownership not precluded,
      §58-51-15(e).
  Trust or association outside state.
    Applicability to policies covering persons in
        state, §58-51-15(i).
Actions or suit on policies or contracts.
  Conditions or stipulations.
    Court or jurisdiction for bringing action or suit.
      Prohibited, §58-3-35(a).
    Prohibited conditions or stipulations void,
        §58-3-35(c).
    Time for bringing action or suit.
      Less than period prescribed by law,
          prohibited, §58-3-35(b).
Additional insurance clauses.
  Prohibited, §58-3-15.
Annuities.
  Standard nonforfeiture law for individual deferred
      annuities, §58-58-61.
  Standard provisions, §58-58-23.
Assessment companies.
  "Assessment plan" to be printed on, §58-11-10.
  Revocation for noncompliance, §58-11-15.
  Conformance with charter and bylaws required,
      §58-11-5.
Binders.
  Lenders engaged in mortgage or deed of trust
      loans.
    Acceptance or denial of temporary insurance
        contracts, §58-3-140.
Cancellation.
  Applicability of article, §58-41-10(a).
  Certificates of insurance.
    Notice of cancellation, nonrenewal or material
        change to policy, §58-3-150(g).
  Citation of article, §58-41-1.
  Commercial general liability insurance.
    Extended reporting periods, §58-40-140.
  Grounds, §58-41-15(a).
  Intent of legislature, §58-41-5(a), (b).
  In-term cancellation of entire book of business,
      §58-41-45(b).
  Legislative findings, §58-41-5(a), (b).
  Loss of reinsurance, §58-41-30.
  Nonpayment of premium, §58-41-15(d).

INSURANCE POLICIES OR CONTRACTS
—Cont'd
Cancellation —Cont'd
  Notice.
    Copies sent to agent or broker, §58-41-15(e).
    Required, §58-41-15(b).
    Timing of notice to insured, §58-41-40(b).
  Penalties, §58-41-55.
  Policy in effect for less than sixty days,
    §58-41-15(c).
  Provisions not exclusive, §58-41-10(b).
  Short title, §58-41-1.
  Statements or communications made in good
    faith.
    No liability for, §§58-41-40, 58-41-40(a).
  Workers' compensation insurance.
    Before expiration of policy, §58-36-105.
Certificates of authority.
  Prerequisite to issuance of policies, §58-7-10.
Certificates of insurance.
  Criteria for preparing, §58-3-150(f).
  Defined, §58-3-150(d).
  False or misleading information, §58-3-150(f).
  Notice of cancellation, nonrenewal or material
    change to policy, §58-3-150(g).
  Policies distinguished, §58-3-150(e).
  Rights conferred, §58-3-150(e).
Charitable gift annuities, §58-3-6.
Choice of law provisions.
  Court or jurisdiction in which action or suit may
    be brought.
    Condition or stipulation in policy prohibited,
     §58-3-35(a).
Closure of a block of business, §58-3-275(a) to
  (d).
Coinsurance clauses, §58-3-15.
Commercial general liability insurance.
  Extended reporting periods, §58-40-140(a).
  Health care provider professional liability
    insurance, §58-40-140(b), (c).
Commercial mortgages.
  Defined, §58-3-150(d).
Conditions.
  Court or jurisdiction action may be brought.
    Prohibited, §58-3-35(a).
  Forbidden conditions or stipulations void,
    §58-3-35(c).
  Time within which suit or action may be
    commenced.
    Less than period prescribed by law, prohibited,
     §58-3-35(b).
Construction, §58-1-10.
Credit insurance.
  Amounts authorized, §58-57-15.
  Contents, §58-57-25(b).
  Credit unemployment insurance.
    Provisions, §58-57-110(a) to (c).
  Insurance to be evidenced by individual policy,
    §58-57-25(a).
  Issuance, §58-57-55.
  Kinds of policies authorized, §58-57-10.
  Notification when policy not delivered to debtor,
    §58-57-25(e).
  Prohibited provisions, §58-57-25(d).
  Required provisions, §58-57-25(c).
**Death benefits paid in services or
  merchandise.**
  Issuance of contract providing prohibited,
    §58-3-55.
Deductibles.
  Requirements for additional insurance or
    coinsurance clauses, §58-3-15.

INSURANCE POLICIES OR CONTRACTS
—Cont'd
Deemer provisions.
  Law has deemed filing or contract to be approved,
    §58-3-151.
Disability income insurance.
  Standards for policies, §58-51-130.
Discrimination by insurance companies.
  Prohibited acts, §58-3-120.
Documents submitted to department.
  Paper size, stapling or binding, §58-3-150(c).
Excess liability policies.
  Uninsured and underinsured motorist coverages,
    §58-3-152.
Exclusive nature of provisions, §58-3-5.
False statement to procure or deny benefit,
  §58-2-161.
Family leave credit insurance, §58-57-115.
Farmowners' and other policies.
  Ice, snow or sleet damage, §58-44-55.
Fire insurance.
  Amount.
    Limitation, §58-43-5.
  Devices.
    Performance of contracts as to devices not
     prohibited, §58-43-1.
  Functional replacement, §58-43-5.
  Indemnity contracts for difference in actual value
    and cost of replacement, §58-43-5.
  Mortgagees.
    Policies for benefit of, §58-43-15.
  Standard policy provisions, §58-44-16.
    Permissible variations, §58-44-20.
  Term.
    Limitation, §58-43-5.
Forms.
  Approval, §58-41-50(a).
    Commissioner of insurance, §58-3-150(a).
  Certificate of insurance defined, §58-3-150(d).
  Existing policy forms, §58-40-115.
  Group and blanket accident and health insurance
    and group life insurance policies,
    §58-3-150(b).
  Lost forms.
    Proof furnished, §58-3-40.
Information as to policies.
  Furnishing to commissioner, §58-6-20.
**Information concerning policy limits or
  coverage.**
  Motor vehicle insurance.
    Insurer providing person claiming injury or
     damage subject to policy, §58-3-33.
Interest rates on life insurance policies loans.
  Purpose of provisions, §58-61-1.
**Law has deemed filing or contract to be
  approved.**
  Deemer provisions, §58-3-151.
**Life and health insurance guaranty
  association.**
  Powers and duties of association generally,
    §58-62-36(a) to (t).
Life insurance.
  Forfeiture.
    Notice of nonpayment of premium required,
     §58-58-120.
  Group insurance.
    Authorized policies, §58-58-135.
    Standard provisions, §58-58-140.
  Interest rates on life insurance policy loans,
    §§58-61-1 to 58-61-15.
  Renunciation, §58-58-100.

INSURANCE POLICIES OR CONTRACTS
—Cont'd
Life insurance —Cont'd
Standard nonforfeiture law, §58-58-55(a) to (i).
Standard provisions, §58-58-22.
Annuity and pure endowment contracts, §58-58-23.
Standard valuation law, §58-58-50(a) to (l).
Statements required, §58-58-1.
Survivorship fund in life insurance contract.
Prohibited, §58-58-15.
Viatical life insurance settlements, §§58-58-200 to 58-58-310.
See VIATICAL SETTLEMENTS.

Limitation of action.
Condition or stipulation in policy or contract.
Prohibition, less time than that prescribed by law, §58-3-35(b).

Long-term care insurance.
Generally, §§58-55-1 to 58-55-50.
See LONG-TERM CARE INSURANCE.
Long-term care partnerships, §§58-55-55 to 58-55-80.

Medicare supplement insurance.
Generally, §§58-54-1 to 58-54-50.
See MEDICARE SUPPLEMENT INSURANCE.

Misdemeanors.
Willful violations of provisions, §58-50-70.

Missing persons.
Payment on policies, §28C-18.

Mortgage or deed of trust loans.
Commercial mortgages.
Defined, §58-3-150(d).
Temporary contracts.
Acceptance or denial binders by lenders, §58-3-140.

Motor vehicle insurance.
Information to be contained in policies, §20-279.21(d).
Liability policies, §20-279.21.
Cancellation or nonrenewal.
Notice, §20-279.22.
Surrender of license, §20-279.30.
Other policies not affected, §20-279.23(a), (b).
Termination.
Notice, §20-279.22.
Surrender of license, §20-279.30.
Multiple policies, §20-279.21(j).
Operator policies, §20-279.21(c).
Other than auto liability, §20-279.23(a), (b).
Owner's policies, §20-279.21(b).
Policy limits or coverage.
Insurer providing person claiming injury or damage subject to policy, §58-3-33.
Taxicab operators, §20-279.21(c).

Mutual insurance companies.
Assignment, §58-8-45.
Contingent liability printed on policy, §58-8-35.
Nonassessable policies.
Foreign or alien companies, §58-8-40.
Prerequisites to issuance, §58-8-1.

Nature of insurance contracts, §58-1-10.

Paper size, stapling or binding.
Documents submitted to department, §58-3-150(c).

Policy limits or coverage.
Motor vehicle insurance.
Insurer providing person claiming injury or damage subject to policy, §58-3-33.

Principal and income act.
Allocation of receipts not normally apportioned during administration of trust, §37A-4-407(a) to (c).

INSURANCE POLICIES OR CONTRACTS
—Cont'd
Proof of lost forms.
Furnishing, §58-3-40.

Property insurance.
Conditions of insurance to be stated, §58-44-1.
Encumbrances.
Notice of encumbrance.
Effect of failure to give, §58-44-40.
Fire insurance policies.
Standard policy, §58-44-16.
Permissible variations, §58-44-20.
Husband and wife.
Policy issued to husband or wife on point property, §58-44-45.
Items to be stated in policies, §58-44-5.
Standard policy.
Fire insurance policies, §58-44-16.
Permissible variations, §58-44-20.
Increase of hazard, unoccupancy and other insurance.
Notice by insured or agent as, §58-44-30.
Nuclear reaction, nuclear radiation or radioactive contamination.
Optional provisions as to loss or damage from, §58-44-25.
Permissible variations, §58-44-20.
Umpire.
Judge to select, §58-44-35.

Punishment for violations, §58-50-70.

Rate regulation generally, §§58-40-1 to 58-40-140.
See INSURANCE RATES.

Readable policies, §§58-38-1 to 58-38-40.
Actions arising from policies approved pursuant to provisions.
Language on which actions may be based, §58-38-40(c).
Applicability of provisions, §58-38-10(a).
Exceptions, §58-38-10(b).
Filing requirements, §58-38-35(a).
Citation of act.
Short title, §58-38-1.
Construction and interpretation, §58-38-40(a), (b).
Definitions, §58-38-15.
"Text,"§58-38-25(e).
Disapproval of policy by commissioner.
Grounds, §58-38-30(b).
Exclusive nature of provisions, §58-38-10(c).
Exemptions from provisions, §58-38-10(b).
Filing policies with commissioner, §58-38-30(a).
Applicability of requirements, §58-38-35(a).
Flesch scale analysis readability score.
Defined, §58-38-15.
Procedures, §58-38-25(a) to (d).
Format requirements, §58-38-20(a).
Determination of whether policy in compliance.
Factors to be considered, §58-38-20(b).
Hospital, medical and dental service corporations.
Readable insurance certificates act, §§58-66-1 to 58-66-40.
See HOSPITAL, MEDICAL AND DENTAL SERVICE CORPORATIONS.
Legislative declaration.
Purpose of act, §58-38-5.
Non-English language policies.
When deemed in compliance, §58-38-10(d).
Purpose of act, §58-38-5.
Scope of application, §58-38-10.
Title of act.
Short title, §58-38-1.

INSURANCE POLICIES OR CONTRACTS
—Cont'd
Real property warranties, §58-1-20(a).
Reciprocal insurance, §58-15-50.
Additional nature of authority to enter into
reciprocal insurance contracts, §58-15-20(b).
Assessable policies.
Subscribers contingent assessment liability,
§58-15-60.
Eligible contracting persons, §58-15-20(a).
Nonassessable policies.
Certificate authorizing, §58-15-65(a), (b).
Revocation upon impairment of surplus,
§58-15-65(c).
Surplus requirement, §58-15-65(d).
Reinsurance.
Assumption reinsurance.
Notice, §58-10-30(a) to (h).
Policyholder rights, §58-10-35(a) to (d).
Renewal.
Notice, §58-41-25.
Policies with premium or coverage changes,
§58-41-25(a) to (e).
Timing of notice to insured, §58-41-40(b).
Secured transactions.
Inapplicability of article 9.
Transfers of policy interest or assignment of
claim, §25-9-109(d).
Service of process.
Violations as to.
Penalty, §58-43-35.
State law governs, §58-3-1.
Exclusive nature of law, §58-3-5.
Statute of limitations.
Condition or stipulation as to time for bringing
action.
Prohibited, period less than prescribed by law,
§58-3-35(b).
Stipulations.
Court or jurisdiction action may be brought.
Prohibited, §58-3-35(a).
Forbidden conditions or stipulations void,
§58-3-35(c).
Time within which suit or action may be
commenced.
Less than period prescribed by law, prohibited,
§58-3-35(b).
**Supervision, rehabilitation and liquidation of
insurers.**
Liquidation.
Continuance of coverage, §58-30-110.
Surplus lines.
Valid and enforceable, §58-21-55.
Temporary contracts.
Lenders engaged in mortgage or deed of trust
loans.
Acceptance or denial binders, §58-3-140.
Twisting.
Insurance producers, prohibition, §58-33-75.
Venue for bringing action or suit.
Condition or stipulation prohibited, §58-3-35(a).
Viatical life insurance settlements, §§58-58-200
to 58-58-310.
See VIATICAL SETTLEMENTS.
Warranties.
Manufacturers, distributors or sellers of goods or
services, §58-1-15.
Statements in policies not warranties, §58-3-10.

INSURANCE PREMIUM FINANCING, §§58-35-1
to 58-35-100.
Administrative action taken against company.
Report to commissioner, §58-35-22(b).

INSURANCE PREMIUM FINANCING —Cont'd
Agents.
Exemptions from license requirement,
§58-35-10(c).
Banks.
Exemption from license requirement, §58-35-10(a).
Bonds, surety.
Licensees, §58-35-15(a).
Brokers.
Exemptions from license requirements,
§58-35-10(c).
**Cancellation of insurance contract upon
default.**
Procedure, §58-35-85.
Cash surrender value.
Cancellation of insurance contract upon default.
Collection of cash surrender value, §58-35-85.
Commissioner of insurance, §58-35-25.
Confession of judgment.
Provisions in agreements giving power of attorney
to confess judgment in state.
Prohibited, §58-35-60.
Conviction of proprietor, officer or partner.
Crimes involving dishonesty or breach of trust.
Commissioner notified, time, §58-35-22(a).
Copies of agreements, §58-35-65.
Credit unions.
Exception to license requirement, §58-35-10(a).
Definitions, §58-35-1.
Fees.
Disposition, §58-35-95.
Excessive finance charges, §58-35-35.
Licenses, §58-35-5(d), (e).
Nonrefundable, §58-35-100.
Forms.
Filing with and approval by commissioner,
§58-35-45(a).
Insurance premium finance agreements,
§58-35-50(a).
Blanks.
Filling out before signing, §58-35-50(d).
Hearings.
Power of commissioner of insurance, §58-35-25.
Insurance companies.
Exemption from license requirement, §58-35-10(b).
Insurance premium financing agreements.
Assignment, §58-35-40(b), (c).
Filing on notice not necessary to validity,
§58-35-40(b).
Payments by insured without notice of
assignment, §58-35-70.
Contents, §58-35-50(b), (c).
Copies.
Delivery of copy to insurer, §58-35-65.
Defined, §58-35-1.
Delinquency and collection charge on installments
in default.
Agreements may provide for, §58-35-55(f).
False information.
Penalty, §58-35-90.
Forms, §58-35-50(a).
Blanks.
Filling out before signing, §58-35-50(d).
Prohibited provisions, §58-35-60.
Investigations.
Power of commissioner of insurance, §58-35-25.
Licenses.
Applications, §58-35-5(b), (c).
Bond, surety, §58-35-15(a).
Branch office licenses, §58-35-5(e).

INSURANCE PREMIUM FINANCING —Cont'd
Licenses —Cont'd
Change of office location.
  Notice to commissioner by licensee, §58-35-15(f).
Display, §58-35-15(e).
Engaging in business without license.
  Penalty, §58-35-90.
Fees, §58-35-5(d), (e).
Issuance, §58-35-15(a).
One office per license, §58-35-15(d).
Refusal, §58-35-15(a).
  Grounds, §58-35-20(a).
  Notice to applicant, §58-35-15(b).
Renewal, §58-35-15(c).
  Refusal to renew.
    Grounds, §58-35-20(a).
Required, §58-35-5(a).
  Exceptions, §58-35-10.
Surrender of license, §58-35-20(b).
Suspension or revocation, §58-35-20.
  Grounds, §58-35-20(a).
Term, §58-35-15(c).
Transfer or assignment prohibited, §58-35-15(e).
Types, §58-35-5(e).
Misdemeanors.
Records.
  Prohibited acts as to, §58-35-30(b).
Violations of provisions, §58-35-90.
Notice.
Cancellation of insurance contract upon default,
  §58-35-85.
Payments by insured.
Assignment of agreement.
  Payments without notice of assignment,
    §58-35-70.
Credit upon anticipation of payment.
  Amount, §58-35-80(b).
  Authorized, §58-35-80(a).
Default.
  Cancellation of insurance contract upon default.
    Procedure, §58-35-85.
Release on payment in full, §58-35-75(b).
Statement of account, §58-35-75(a).
Penalties.
Excessive finance charges, §58-35-35.
Violations of provisions, §58-35-90.
Rebates.
Prohibited, §58-35-40(a), (c).
Records.
False statements.
  Misdemeanor, §58-35-30(b).
Licensees, §58-35-30(a).
Refusal to exhibit to commissioner.
  Misdemeanor, §58-35-30(b).
Reports.
Criminal or administrative actions, §58-35-22.
Licensees, §58-35-30(a).
Savings and loan associations.
Exemption from license requirement, §58-35-10(a).
Service charges.
Authorized, §58-35-55(b), (d).
Computation, §58-35-55(c), (d).
Limitations on, §58-35-55(a).
  Multiple agreements for obtaining excessive
    charges prohibited, §58-35-55(e).
Rate plan.
  Filing with commissioner, §58-35-45(b).

INSURANCE PREMIUMS.
Absentees in military service.
Receivers' power to pay, §28B-6.

INSURANCE PREMIUMS —Cont'd
Accident and health insurance.
Approval of rates by commissioner, §§58-51-1,
  58-51-95(f).
  Revised rates, §58-51-95(f).
Benefits reasonable in relation, §58-51-95(h).
Filing of rates.
  Group or blanket accident and health insurance,
    §58-51-85.
Group accident and health insurance.
  Adjustment of rate, §58-51-80(g).
  Continuation privileges.
    Payment of premiums, §58-53-30.
  Conversion privileges, §58-53-60.
Joint action to insure elderly.
  Approval of rates by commissioner, §58-52-15.
Long-term care policies, §58-51-95(h), (i).
Loss ratio standards, §58-51-95(h).
Nonpayment.
  Notice required before forfeiture, §58-50-35.
Refund.
  Notice of right to return policy and have
    premium refunded, §58-51-10.
Renewal.
  Increase due to health status-related factors
    prohibited, §58-51-95(g).
Credit cards.
Solicitation, negotiation or payment of premiums
  through credit card or debit card services,
  §58-3-145.
Credit insurance.
Credit property insurance, §58-57-90(b).
Credits, §58-57-50(e).
Rate standards, §§58-57-35 to 58-57-45.
Refunds.
  Calculations, §58-57-50(b), (c).
  Generally, §58-57-50(a) to (e).
  Minimum amount, §58-57-50(d).
Debit cards.
Solicitation, negotiation or payment of premiums
  through credit card or debit card services,
  §58-3-145.
Financing, §§58-35-1 to 58-35-100.
See INSURANCE PREMIUM FINANCING.
Fire insurance.
Excess over actual cash value of property.
  Reimbursement, §58-43-10.
Information as to.
Furnishing to commissioner, §58-6-20.
Life insurance.
Assessment life insurance companies.
  Minimum premium rates, §58-58-125.
Default.
  Notice of nonpayment.
    Required before forfeiture, §58-58-120.
Employee life insurance.
  Payment, §58-58-150.
Missing persons.
Receivers.
  Authorization to pay, §28C-8.
North Carolina rate bureau, §§58-36-1 to
  58-36-120.
See RATE BUREAU.
Rate regulation generally, §§58-40-1 to
  58-40-140.
See INSURANCE RATES.
**Supervision, rehabilitation and liquidation of
  insurers.**
Recovery of premiums owed, §58-30-175(a).
  Obligation of insurer to pay unpaid premiums,
    §58-30-175(b).

INSURANCE PREMIUMS —Cont'd
Surplus lines.
Effect of payment of licensee, §58-21-60.

INSURANCE PRODUCERS.
Insurance adjusters.
See INSURANCE ADJUSTERS.
Insurance agents.
See INSURANCE AGENTS.
Insurance brokers.
See INSURANCE BROKERS.
Insurance limited representatives.
See INSURANCE LIMITED
REPRESENTATIVES.
Motor vehicle damage appraisers.
See MOTOR VEHICLE DAMAGE APPRAISERS.
Public adjusters, §§58-33A-1 to 58-33A-95.
See INSURANCE ADJUSTERS.

INSURANCE RATES, §§58-40-1 to 58-40-140.
Accident and health insurance.
Exceptions to applicability of rating provisions,
§58-40-15.
Group accident and health insurance.
Conversion privileges.
Premium rates and adjustments, §58-53-60.
Acting in concert.
Insurers authorized to act in concert, §§58-40-65,
58-40-70.
Agreements among insurers.
Adherence agreements.
Prohibited, §58-40-75.
Apportionment agreement, §58-40-95.
Annuities.
Exemption from applicability of rating provisions,
§58-40-15.
Appeal of commissioner's orders and decisions,
§58-40-105(b).
Compelling action withheld or delayed by
commissioner, §58-2-40.
Extent of review, §58-2-90(a), (b).
Generally, §58-2-80.
Ground for relief limited to those set forth in,
§58-2-90(c).
Notice of appeal.
Time for, §58-2-85.
Prejudicial error, due account taken, §58-2-90(c).
Presumption of correctness and propriety,
§58-2-80.
Prima facie correct, §§58-2-40, 58-2-90(e).
Procedure, §58-2-85.
Stay of commissioner's order or decision.
Appeal to operate as, §58-2-85.
Title of cause on appeal, §58-2-85.
Withheld or delayed actions, §58-2-90(d).
Applicability of provisions, §58-40-15.
Apportionment agreements among insurers,
§58-40-95.
Beach and coastal areas.
Mitigation and construction features.
Schedule of credits to policyholders based on,
§58-36-15(d1).
Territorial boundaries.
Revision, monitoring, review by bureau,
§58-36-10.
Beach area essential property insurance.
Rates, rating plans, rating rules, §58-45-45.
Change in coverage or rates.
Notice, §58-41-20(d) to (f).
Timing of notice to insured, §58-41-40(b).
Commissioner.
Disapproval of rates, §58-40-45(a).

INSURANCE RATES —Cont'd
Commissioner —Cont'd
Examination of organizations, §58-40-90.
Hearings, §58-40-105(a).
Imposition of penalties or suspension of
licenses, §58-40-110(c).
Notice, §58-40-105(a).
Joint underwriting and joint reinsurance
organizations.
Unfair or unreasonable practices.
Cease and desist orders, §58-40-60(c).
Judicial review of orders and decisions,
§58-40-105(b).
Willfully withholding or furnishing false or
misleading information, §58-40-45(c).
Construction and interpretation, §§58-40-120,
58-40-125.
Credit insurance.
Premium rates, §§58-57-35 to 58-57-45,
58-57-90(b).
Credit property insurance, §58-57-90.
**Criteria for determining compliance with
standards, §58-40-25.**
Definitions, §§58-40-5, 58-40-10.
Discrimination.
Rates not to be unfairly discriminatory,
§58-40-20(a), (e).
Dividends.
Payment of dividends not affected, §58-40-120.
Examinations.
Commissioner to examine organizations,
§58-40-90.
Excessive rates, §58-40-20(a).
Method of rate making, §58-36-10.
Existing rates, §58-40-115.
Fair access to insurance requirements.
Rates, rating plans, rating rules, forms, §58-46-55.
Filing, §§58-40-30(a) to (d), 58-41-50(a) to (g).
Charging unfiled rates, §58-41-50(f).
Construction of provisions, §58-40-30(d).
Exceeding filing, §58-40-30(c).
Inspection, §58-40-35.
Prior to effective date, §58-40-30(a).
Rates prepared by statistical organization,
§58-40-40(b).
Statistical and rating information required,
§58-41-50(c) to (e).
Supporting data, §58-40-30(b).
Inspection, §58-40-35.
Health insurance risk pool, §58-50-190.
Powers, §58-50-180(e).
Hearings.
Commissioner, §58-40-105(a).
Rate bureau.
Disapproval of rates, §58-36-20(a).
Violations of provisions.
Imposition of penalty or suspension of license,
§58-40-110(c).
Inadequate rates, §58-40-20(a), (d).
Method of rate making, §58-36-10.
Insurers authorized to act in concert,
§§58-40-65, 58-40-70.
**Joint underwriting and joint reinsurance
organizations.**
Examination by commissioner, §58-40-90.
Filings required, §58-40-60(a).
Changes or amendments to documents,
§58-40-60(b).
Unfair or unreasonable activities.
Cease and desist orders, §58-40-60(c).

INSURANCE RATES —Cont'd
Legislative declaration.
Purposes of provisions, §58-40-1.
Life insurance.
Exceptions to applicability of rating provisions,
§58-40-15.
Lists.
Commissioner to compel and make available to
public, §58-2-40.
Loss and expense experience, §58-40-85.
Method of rate making, §58-36-10.
Modification.
Financial disclosure of companies, §58-40-130(a)
to (e).
Review and modification by commissioner,
§58-40-130(c).
Upon financial disclosure of companies,
§58-40-130.
North Carolina rate bureau, §§58-36-1 to
58-36-120.
See RATE BUREAU.
Notice.
Coverage or rate change, §§58-36-45, 58-41-20(d)
to (f).
Timing of notice to insured, §58-41-40(b).
Hearings.
Commissioner, §58-40-105(a).
Imposition of penalties or suspension of
licenses, §58-40-110(c).
Residential property insurance rate increase.
Public notice, §58-36-120.
Penalties.
Violations of provisions.
Notice and hearing required for imposition of
penalty, §58-40-110(c).
Policy forms.
Existing policy forms, §58-40-115.
Reinsurance.
Exception to applicability of rating provisions,
§58-40-15.
Reports.
Loss and expense experience, §58-40-85.
**Request for review of rate, rating plan, rating
system or underwriting rule,** §58-40-100(a).
Rejection of request.
Complaint to commissioner, §58-40-100(a).
Residential property insurance rate increase.
Public notice, §58-36-120.
Standards.
Applicable standards in making and using rates,
§58-36-10.
Determination of compliance.
Criteria, §58-40-25.
Generally, §58-40-20.
Noncomplying rates.
Interim use, §58-40-45(b).
Orders of commissioner as to, §58-40-45(a).
Statistical organizations.
Consultation with other rating organizations and
insurers, §58-40-80.
Defined, §58-40-5.
Examination by commissioner, §58-40-90.
Exchange of information or experience data,
§58-40-80.
Filing requirements.
Rates prepared by organizations, §58-40-40(b).
Financial disclosure.
Compilation of experience and data,
§58-40-130(b).
Insurance company, status as, §58-40-50(i).

INSURANCE RATES —Cont'd
Statistical organizations —Cont'd
Licenses.
Applications.
Action on, §58-40-50(d).
Amendments, §58-40-50(e).
Supporting information, §58-40-50(c).
Required, §58-40-50(a).
Statistical plan, §58-40-50(g).
Suspension, §58-40-110(b), (c).
Refusal to supply services.
Prohibited, §58-40-50(b).
Statistical plan, §58-40-50(g).
Unfair and unreasonable practices prohibited,
§58-40-50(h).
Use of rates prepared by.
Authorized, §58-40-40(a).
Uniqueness of risk.
Use of individual form or rate, §58-41-50(g).
Violations of provisions.
Hearings.
Required, §58-40-110(c).
Suspension of licenses, §58-40-110(b).

INSURANCE REGULATORY CHARGE, §58-6-25.

**INSURANCE REGULATORY INFORMATION
SYSTEM.**
Test data not public records, §58-2-220.

INSURANCE SCORES.
Motor vehicle or property insurance, §58-36-90.

INSURANCE-SUPPORT ORGANIZATIONS.
Defined, §58-39-15.
Information privacy protection.
Consumer and customer information generally,
§§58-39-1 to 58-39-165.
See INSURANCE CONSUMER AND
CUSTOMER INFORMATION PRIVACY.

INSURANCE UNDERWRITING ASSOCIATION.
Beach and coastal areas.
Geographic territories established for rating
purposes, §58-36-10.
Beach area essential property, §§58-45-10 to
58-45-80.
See BEACH AREA ESSENTIAL PROPERTY
INSURANCE.

INSURANCE UNFAIR TRADE PRACTICES,
§§58-63-1 to 58-63-75.
Acts prohibited, §58-63-10.
Additional nature of provisions, §58-63-55.
Advertising.
False advertising.
Prohibited acts, §58-63-15.
Appeals.
Cease and desist orders.
Judicial review, §58-63-35.
Undefined practices.
Judicial review by intervenor, §58-63-45.
Boycotts.
Prohibited acts, §58-63-15.
Cease and desist orders.
Effect.
No person absolved from liability under other
law, §58-63-35(d).
Finality.
When order becomes final, §58-63-35(c).
Issuance, §58-63-32(a).
Judicial review, §58-63-35.
Additional evidence, §58-63-35(b).

INSURANCE UNFAIR TRADE PRACTICES
  —Cont'd
Cease and desist orders —Cont'd
  Judicial review —Cont'd
    Order of court, §58-63-35(b).
      Effect, §58-63-35(d).
      Petition, §58-63-35(a).
    Modification or setting aside, §58-63-32(b), (c).
  Violations.
    Penalty, §58-63-50.
Coercion.
  Prohibited acts, §58-63-15.
Commissioner.
  Additional nature of powers, §58-63-55.
  Powers.
    Examination and investigation, §58-63-20.
    Rule-making authority, §58-63-65.
Confidentiality of information.
  Misuse of borrowers' confidential information,
    §58-63-15.
Defamation.
  Prohibited acts, §58-63-15.
Definitions, §58-63-5.
Discrimination.
  Prohibited acts, §58-63-15.
Enumerated, §58-63-15.
Examinations.
  Power of commissioner, §58-63-20.
Fraud.
  Prohibited acts, §58-63-15.
**Health care service discount practices by
  insurers and service corporations,**
    §58-63-70(a).
  Substantial assistance in accomplishing,
    §58-63-70(b).
Health insurance risk pool.
  Unfair referral to pool, §58-50-200.
Hearings, §58-63-25(b), (c).
  Immunity from prosecution, §58-63-60.
  Notice, §58-63-25(a).
    Service, §58-63-25(e).
  Powers and duties of commissioner as to,
    §58-63-25(d).
  Undefined practices, §58-63-40(a).
  Witnesses.
    Immunity from prosecution, §58-63-60.
    Powers of commissioner as to, §58-63-25(d).
Injunctions.
  Undefined practices, §§58-63-40(b) to (d),
    58-63-45.
Intimidation, §58-63-15.
Investigations.
  Power of commissioner, §58-63-20.
Legislative declaration.
  Purpose of provisions, §58-63-1.
Life insurance.
  Solicitation.
    Failure to comply with requirements, §58-60-30.
Prohibited, §58-63-10.
Purpose of provisions, §58-63-1.
Rebates.
  Prohibited acts, §58-63-15.
Rules and regulations, §58-63-65.
**Senior specific certifications and professional
  designations.**
  Life insurance or annuity products.
    Use of fraudulent marketing practice in
      solicitation.
      Rules to protect consumers, §58-63-75.
Settlements.
  Unfair claim settlement practices, §58-63-15.

INSURANCE UNFAIR TRADE PRACTICES
  —Cont'd
Statements.
  False financial statements.
    Prohibited acts, §58-63-15.
**Unauthorized insurers false advertising
  process act.**
  Action by commissioner under unfair trade
    practices act, §58-29-15.
Undefined practices.
  Hearing, §58-63-40(a).
    Notice, §58-63-40(a).
  Injunctions.
    Judicial review by intervenor, §58-63-45.
    Petition by commissioner for, §58-63-40(b).
      Action by court on, §58-63-40(c), (d).
  Judicial review by intervenor, §58-63-45.
  Report by commissioner, §58-63-40(a).
Viatical life insurance settlement, §58-58-295.
Witnesses.
  Immunity from prosecution, §58-63-60.
Workers' compensation self-insurance.
  Third-party administrators and service companies.
    Applicability of provisions to, §58-47-200.

**INSURER SUPERVISION, REHABILITATION
  AND LIQUIDATION,** §§58-30-1 to 58-30-310.
Actions.
  Liquidation.
    Actions by and against liquidator, §58-30-130.
  Rehabilitation.
    Actions by and against rehabilitator, §58-30-90.
Administrative supervision.
  Administrative supervisor, §58-30-62(g).
  Applicability of section, §58-30-62(b).
  Compliance with requirements of commissioner.
    Time limitation, §58-30-62(e).
  Confidentiality, §58-30-62(f).
  Contesting action of commissioner, §58-30-62(h).
  Exceeding powers, §58-30-62(a).
  Liability of commissioner, §58-30-62(k).
  Meetings between commissioner and supervisor,
    §58-30-62(j).
  Notice to insurer, §58-30-62(d).
  Section not to limit powers granted to
    commissioner, §58-30-62(i).
  When subject to administrative supervision,
    §58-30-62(c).
Agents.
  Liquidation.
    Failure to provide information to liquidator,
      §58-30-127(c).
    Generally, §58-30-127(a).
    Policy issued through an agent, determination
      of, §58-30-127(b).
    Provisions of section are additional to other
      duties, §58-30-127(d).
Applicability of provisions.
  Persons covered, §58-30-5.
Attachment.
  Prohibited during pendency of liquidation
    proceeding, §58-30-295.
Audits.
  Books or records.
    Person defined, §58-30-22(a).
    Powers of commissioner and receiver,
      §§58-30-22, 58-30-22(b).
  External audit of receiver's books, §58-30-255.
Bonds, surety.
  Claims of surety, §58-30-210.

INSURER SUPERVISION, REHABILITATION AND LIQUIDATION —Cont'd

Bonds, surety —Cont'd

Commissioner and deputies.

Responsibility on official bonds, §58-30-30.

Claims, §§58-30-185 to 58-30-235.

Contingent claims, §58-30-195(a), (b).

Denial of claim.

Notice, §58-30-205(a).

Objections, §58-30-205(a).

Hearing, §58-30-205(b).

Employment contracts, §58-30-195(e).

Filing, §58-30-185(a).

Foreign or alien insurers.

Domiciliary liquidators in other states.

Filing of claims with, §58-30-270(c).

Interstate priorities generally, §58-30-300.

Resident's claims against insurers domiciled in reciprocal states, §58-30-290.

Subordination of claims for noncooperation, §58-30-305.

Guaranty associations.

Claims of, §58-30-190(e).

Late filings, §58-30-185(c).

Interest on claims, §58-30-230(b).

Interstate priorities.

Generally, §58-30-300(a).

Secured claims, §58-30-300(c).

Special deposit claims, §58-30-300(b).

Late filings, §58-30-185(b) to (d).

Guaranty associations, §58-30-185(c).

Other claimants not previously considered, §58-30-185(d).

Sharing in distributions, §58-30-185(b).

Nonresident's claims against insurers domiciled in this state.

Filing, §58-30-285(a).

Proof of claims, §58-30-285(b).

Periodic payment of judgments, §58-30-195(d).

Priority of distribution, §58-30-220.

Proof of claim.

Contents of statement, §58-30-190(a).

Form, §58-30-190(b).

Incomplete claims, §58-30-190(b).

Judgment or order against insured, §58-30-190(d).

Other information and documents, §58-30-190(b).

Requests for information or evidence, §58-30-190(c).

Recommendations of liquidator to court.

Action by court on, §58-30-225(b).

Generally, §58-30-225(a).

Third party claims, §58-30-200(c).

Resident's claims against insurers domiciled in reciprocal states.

Allowance of claim.

Effect of final allowance by court, §58-30-290(c).

Filing, §58-30-290(a).

Proof of claims, §58-30-290(b).

Secured claimants, §58-30-195(c).

Secured creditors.

Determination of claim by court, §58-30-215(a).

Surrender of security.

Effect, §58-30-215(b).

Structured settlements, §58-30-195(d).

Sureties, §58-30-210.

Third party claims, §58-30-200(a), (b).

Guaranty associations.

Exception of claims covered by, §58-30-200(d).

INSURER SUPERVISION, REHABILITATION AND LIQUIDATION —Cont'd

Claims —Cont'd

Third party claims —Cont'd

Recommendations to court by liquidator, §58-30-200(c).

Unclaimed funds, §58-30-235(a).

Commissioner.

Bond, surety.

Responsibility on official bond, §58-30-30.

Cooperation of officers, owners and employees, §58-30-25(a), (c).

Failure to cooperate, §58-30-25(d).

Fees.

Exemptions, §58-30-310.

Obstruction or interference with commissioner, §58-30-25(b).

Powers of commissioner not limited by provisions, §58-30-1(a).

Confidentiality of information.

Hearings, §58-30-70.

Construction and interpretation, §58-30-1(a), (b).

Continuances.

Delinquency proceedings, §58-30-50.

Contracts.

Executory contracts and unexpired leases.

Acceptance or rejection by receiver.

Authority of receiver, subject to court approval, §58-30-35(a).

Breach of contract or lease, §58-30-35(g).

Defaults in contracts or leases, requirements to assume, §58-30-35(b).

Lessee's rights and options, §58-30-35(h).

Prohibitions on assignment or assumption, §58-30-35(c).

Termination or modification, §58-30-35(e).

Time period, §58-30-35(d).

Assignment, §58-30-35(f), (k).

Breach of contract.

When rejection constitutes, §58-30-35(g).

Defaults in contracts or leases.

Requirements for receiver to assume, §58-30-35(b).

Lessee's rights and options after rejection by receiver, §58-30-35(h).

Prohibitions on assignment or assumption by receiver, §58-30-35(c).

Termination or modification, §58-30-35(i), (j).

Restrictions, §58-30-35(e).

Custodian.

Turnover of property by.

Definition of "custodian,"§58-30-40(a).

Generally, §58-30-40(b), (c).

Powers and duties of court, §58-30-40(d), (e).

Definitions, §58-30-10.

Delinquency proceedings.

Condition on release from delinquency proceedings, §58-30-55.

Continuation, §58-30-50.

Release from delinquency proceedings.

Condition on, §58-30-55.

Dissolution of insurer, §58-30-115.

Duty to report impairment, §58-30-12.

Execution.

Levy of execution.

Prohibited during pendency of liquidation proceeding, §58-30-295.

Fees.

Commissioner.

Exemption from filing fees, §58-30-310.

INSURER SUPERVISION, REHABILITATION AND LIQUIDATION —Cont'd
Foreign or alien insurers.
Ancillary formal proceedings, §58-30-275.
  Order appointing ancillary receiver,
    §58-30-275(b).
  Petition for appointment of ancillary receiver,
    §58-30-275(a).
  Powers of ancillary receiver, §58-30-275(c), (d).
Ancillary summary proceedings, §58-30-280.
Claims.
  Domiciliary liquidators in other states.
    Filing of claims with, §58-30-270(c).
  Interstate priorities generally, §58-30-300.
  Resident's claims against insurers domiciled in
    reciprocal states, §58-30-290.
  Subordination of claims for noncooperation,
    §58-30-305.
Conservation of property found in state.
  Liquidation of assets.
    Petition for order, §58-30-260(d).
  Order, §58-30-260(a) to (c).
  Termination of conservation.
    Petition for order, §58-30-260(e).
Interstate priorities generally, §58-30-300.
Liquidation of property found in state.
  Claims of residents of state.
    Payment, §58-30-265(f).
  Federal courts.
    Appointment as receivers, §58-30-265(e).
  Liquidator as ancillary receiver, §58-30-265(d).
  Orders of court, §58-30-265(a) to (c).
Liquidation of property in other states.
  Domiciliary liquidators in other states,
    §58-30-270(a), (b).
  Claims to be filed with, §58-30-270(c).
Summary proceedings.
  Ancillary summary proceedings, §58-30-280.
Garnishment.
Prohibited during pendency of liquidation
  proceeding, §58-30-295.
Grounds for liquidation, §58-30-100.
Grounds for rehabilitation, §58-30-75.
Hearings.
Claims.
  Denial.
    Objections, §58-30-205(b).
Confidentiality of hearings, §58-30-70.
Seizure order by court.
  Hearing and review, §58-30-65(e), (f).
**Immunity and indemnification of receiver and
  employees.**
Administrative expenses of insurer.
  Indemnification, §58-30-71(e).
Applicability of provisions, §58-30-71(k), (m).
Attorneys' fees.
  Payment, §58-30-71(d).
Generally, §58-30-71(b), (c), (l).
Other rights not affected, §58-30-71(j).
Persons entitled to protection, §58-30-71(a).
Segregation of funds for, §58-30-71(f), (g).
Settlements.
  Payment of settlement amount, §58-30-71(h), (i).
Injunctions, §58-30-20(a).
Out-of-state courts, §58-30-20(b).
Supervision proceedings.
  Enforcement of supervision order, §58-30-60(i).
Jurisdiction, §58-30-15(a) to (c), (e).
Voidable preferences and liens, §58-30-150(g).
Liens.
Voidable preferences and liens, §§58-30-150,
  58-30-155.

INSURER SUPERVISION, REHABILITATION AND LIQUIDATION —Cont'd
Limitation of actions.
Rehabilitation.
  Actions by and against rehabilitator,
    §58-30-90(b).
Liquidation.
Accounting by liquidator.
  Declaration of insolvency, §58-30-105(d).
  Orders to require, §58-30-105(e).
Actions by and against liquidator.
  Generally, §58-30-130(a), (b).
  Guaranty associations.
    Standing to appear, §58-30-130(c).
Agents.
  Failure to provide information to liquidator,
    §58-30-127(c).
  Generally, §58-30-127(a).
  Policy issued through an agent, determination
    of, §58-30-127(b).
  Provisions of section are additional to other
    duties, §58-30-127(d).
Assessments.
  Court order adjudging liability, §58-30-165(e).
  Failure to pay assessment.
    Court order adjudging liability, §58-30-165(e).
    Proceedings upon, §58-30-165(c) to (f).
  Levy of assessment, §58-30-165(b).
  Report by liquidator to court, §58-30-165(a).
  Show cause orders.
    Court order adjudging liability, §58-30-165(e).
    Failure to pay assessment, §58-30-165(c) to
      (f).
    Notice, §58-30-165(d).
Assets.
  Distribution, §58-30-230(a).
    Claims generally, §§58-30-185 to 58-30-235.
      See within this heading, "Claims."
  Priority, §58-30-220.
  Proposal by domiciliary liquidator to
    distribute assets, §58-30-180.
  Reciprocal insurance, §58-15-145.
  Unclaimed funds, §58-30-235(a).
  Withheld funds, §58-30-235(b).
  List of assets, §58-30-135(a), (c).
  Reduction to liquidity, §58-30-135(b).
Claims.
  Generally, §§58-30-185 to 58-30-235. See within
    this heading, "Claims."
Continuation of coverage, §58-30-110(a), (b).
  Life or health insurance or annuities,
    §58-30-110(c), (d).
Dissolution of insurer, §58-30-115.
Distribution.
  Guaranty associations.
    Proposal by domiciliary liquidator to
      distribute assets, §58-30-180(d).
  Proposal by domiciliary liquidator to distribute
    assets.
    Amount relative to claim payments,
      §58-30-180(c).
    Contents, §58-30-180(b).
    Guaranty associations, §58-30-180(d).
    Notice, §58-30-180(e).
    Time for, §58-30-180(a).
Fraudulent transfers after petition.
  Generally, §58-30-145(a), (b).
  Negotiability of instruments not affected,
    §58-30-145(c).
Fraudulent transfers prior to petition.
  Generally, §58-30-140(a), (b).

INSURER SUPERVISION, REHABILITATION AND LIQUIDATION —Cont'd

Liquidation —Cont'd

Fraudulent transfers prior to petition —Cont'd
Liability of persons receiving, §58-30-140(d).
Reinsurer.
Transactions with, §58-30-140(c).
Grounds, §58-30-100.
Guaranty associations.
Proposal by domiciliary liquidator to distribute assets, §58-30-180(d).
Notice, §58-30-125(a).
Effect, §58-30-125(c).
Potential claimants, §58-30-125(b).
Orders, §58-30-105(a).
Effect, §58-30-105(b), (c), (e).
Petition for liquidation.
Rehabilitator, §58-30-95(a).
Powers of liquidator, §58-30-120(a).
Enumeration not exclusive, §58-30-120(b).
Premiums.
Recovery of premiums owed, §58-30-175.
Proposal by domiciliary liquidator to distribute assets.
Amount relative to claim payments, §58-30-180(c).
Contents, §58-30-180(b) to (d).
Guaranty associations, §58-30-180(d).
Notice, §58-30-180(e).
Time for, §58-30-180(a).
Reciprocal insurance.
Domestic reciprocals, §§58-15-145, 58-15-150.
Records.
Disposition during and after termination of liquidation, §58-30-250.
Reinsurers.
Liability, §58-30-170.
Reopening liquidation, §58-30-245.
Termination of proceedings.
Application, §58-30-240(b).
Liquidator, §58-30-240(a).
Records.
Disposition during and after termination of liquidation, §58-30-250.
Reopening liquidation, §58-30-245.
Voidable preferences and liens.
Generally, §§58-30-150, 58-30-155.

Notice.

Assessments.
Show cause order, §58-30-165(d).
Liquidation, §58-30-125.
Proposal by domiciliary liquidator to distribute assets, §58-30-180(e).

Orders, §58-30-20(a).

Dissolution of insurer, §58-30-115.
Liquidation orders, §58-30-105.
Out-of-state courts, §58-30-20(b).
Rehabilitation orders, §58-30-80.
Seizure order by court.
Generally, §58-30-65(b) to (d).
Hearing and review, §58-30-65(e), (f).
Petition for, §58-30-65(a).
Supervision proceedings.
Summary orders generally, §58-30-60.

Policies.

Liquidation.
Continuance of coverage, §58-30-110.

Premiums.

Recovery of premiums owed, §58-30-175(a).
Obligation of insurer to pay unpaid premiums, §58-30-175(b).

INSURER SUPERVISION, REHABILITATION AND LIQUIDATION —Cont'd

Purpose of provisions, §58-30-1(c).

Reciprocal insurance.

Liquidation of domestic reciprocals, §§58-15-145, 58-15-150.

Records.

Audits.
Person defined, §58-30-22(a).
Powers of commissioner and receiver, §58-30-22(b).

Rehabilitation.

Accounting by rehabilitator, §58-30-80(b).
Actions by and against rehabilitator.
Generally, §58-30-90(a).
Guaranty associations.
Standing to appear, §58-30-90(c).
Limitation of actions, §58-30-90(b).
Fraudulent transfers.
Power of rehabilitator to avoid, §58-30-85(f).
Grounds, §58-30-75.
Orders, §58-30-80(a), (b).
Anticipatory breach of contract.
Order not to constitute, §58-30-80(c).
Powers and duties of rehabilitator.
Enumerated, §58-30-85(a).
List not limiting, §58-30-85(b).
Fraudulent transfer, avoidance of, §58-30-85(f).
Legal remedies, authority to pursue, §58-30-85(d).
Life insurers, powers relative to, §58-30-85(e).
Necessary and appropriate actions, §58-30-85(c).
Termination of rehabilitation.
Petition, §58-30-95(b).

Reinsurers.

Liquidation.
Liability of reinsurer, §58-30-170.

Scope of provisions.

Persons covered, §58-30-5.

Setoffs.

Accounting statements, §58-30-160(d).
Exceptions, §58-30-160(b).
Generally, §58-30-160(a).
Local agents.
Setoffs permitted to, §58-30-160(c).
Reinsurance, §58-30-160(e).

Supervision proceedings, §58-30-60(b), (c).

Compliance with requirements of commissioner.
Time for, §58-30-60(d).
Hearings, §58-30-60(e).
Notice of hearing, §58-30-60(e).
Request for administrative hearing, §58-30-60(f).
Injunctions.
Enforcement of supervision order, §58-30-60(i).
Review of action of supervisor.
Request for commissioner to review, §58-30-60(g).
Summary orders, §58-30-60(a).
Violation of orders, §58-30-60(h), (j).
Penalty, §58-30-60(h).

Utility service.

Alteration, refusal or discontinuance, §58-30-45(b).
Restriction, §58-30-45(a).

Venue, §58-30-15(d), (e).

Voidable preferences and liens.

Attorneys at law.
Payments or transfers to for services rendered, §58-30-150(j).
Bonds, surety.
Discharge of liability of surety under releasing bond, §58-30-150(h).

INSURER SUPERVISION, REHABILITATION AND LIQUIDATION —Cont'd
Voidable preferences and liens —Cont'd
Bonds, surety —Cont'd
Lien dissolved by furnishing of bond, §58-30-150(e).
Claims of holders of void or voidable rights, §58-30-155(a).
Late filing, §58-30-155(b).
Further credit extended to insure in good faith, §58-30-150(i).
Generally, §58-30-150(a) to (f).
Jurisdiction.
Summary jurisdiction of court, §58-30-150(g).
Liability, §58-30-150(h), (k).
Lien defined, §58-30-150(c).
Preference defined, §58-30-150(a).
Transfer defined, §58-30-150(b).
New and contemporaneous consideration, §58-30-150(d).

INSURRECTION OR REBELLION.
Constitution of the United States, US Const Art I §8.
Militia.
Unorganized militia.
Ordered out for service, §127A-87.
Rebellion against state, §14-8.
Riots and civil disorders, §§14-288.1 to 14-288.20.
See RIOTS AND CIVIL DISORDERS.
Secret political and military organizations, §14-10.
Subversive activities, §§14-11 to 14-12.1.

INTAKE SERVICES.
Delinquent and undisciplined juveniles, §7B-1700.

INTANGIBLE PERSONAL PROPERTY.
Applicability of provisions, §105-276.
Collection of taxes.
Subject to attachment or garnishment, §105-242(b).
Exempt property, §105-242(e).
Defined, §105-273.
Listing of property.
Place for listing, §105-305.
Applicability of provisions, §105-305(a).

INTELLECTUAL PROPERTY.
Constitutional protection, US Const Art I §8.
Corporate income tax.
Allocation and apportionment of income, §105-130.4.
International commercial arbitrations.
Arbitration deemed commercial, §1-567.31(e).
Invention development.
Employee's rights, §66-57.1.
Employer's rights, §66-57.2.
Services contracts, §§66-209 to 66-216.
Bond or other financial requirements, §66-214.
Contracting requirements, §66-212.
Cover sheet, notice, §66-211.
Definitions, §66-209.
Disclosure prior to contract, §66-210.
Enforcement, §66-216.
Mandatory terms, §66-213.
Remedies, §66-215.
Recorded musical performances.
Common law right restrict or collect royalties on commercial use abrogated, §66-28.

INTELLECTUAL PROPERTY —Cont'd
Trademark registration, §§80-1 to 80-14.
See TRADEMARKS.
Trade secrets, §§66-152 to 66-157.
See TRADE SECRETS.

INTENT.
Special matters, pleading, §1A-1 Rule 9(b).

INTERCEPTION OF COMMUNICATIONS.
Electronic surveillance generally, §§15A-286 to 15A-298.
See ELECTRONIC SURVEILLANCE.

INTERCHANGE OF GOVERNMENT EMPLOYEES, §§126-51 to 126-58.
See PERSONNEL SYSTEM.

INTEREST.
Accident and health insurance.
Prompt claim payments under health benefit plans, §58-3-225(e).
Accounts and accounting.
Default judgments.
Clerk to ascertain interest upon default judgment on account, §24-6.
Accrual.
Time from which interest runs, §24-3.
Agriculture.
Assessment of fees and taxes.
Procedure for assessment, §106-9.3(h).
Bills of exchange.
Default judgments.
Clerk to ascertain interest upon default judgment on bill of exchange, §24-6.
Bond issues.
Corporate bonds may be sold below par, §24-2.
Refunding bonds.
State debt, §§142-29.6(a), 142-29.7.
Bonds, surety.
Default judgments.
Clerk to ascertain interest, §24-6.
Penal bonds.
Exceptions to contract rate, §24-5(a).
Legal rate from date of entry of judgment, §24-5(a1).
Brownfields property reuse.
Unpaid fees, §130A-310.39(c).
Budget of state.
Crediting interest to general fund, §143C-1-4(a).
Crediting interest to highway fund and highway trust fund, §143C-1-4(b).
Charge cards.
Disclosure requirements.
Generally, §24-11.2.
Community colleges.
Deposits.
Investment of idle cash, §115D-58.6.
Compound interest.
Guardians.
Obligations due guardians to bear compound interest, §24-4.
Condominium common expenses.
Past due assessment, §47C-3-115(b).
Construction loans.
Definition, §24-10(c).
Maximum fees on loans secured by real property, §24-10(a).
Less than three hundred thousand dollars, §24-10(d).
Prepayment, §24-10(b).
Consumer finance act.
Computation of charges, §53-173(b).

INTEREST —Cont'd

Consumer finance act —Cont'd

Insurance.

   Credit life and credit accident and health insurance.

      Premiums not deemed interest or charges, §53-189(b).

Judgments.

   Limitation on interest after judgment, §53-173(c).

Maturity of loans.

   Limitation of interest after, §53-173(d).

   Optional maturities, §53-176.

Maximum rate, §53-173(a).

   Further charges prohibited, §53-178.

Optional rates, §53-176(a).

Schedule of charges, §53-181(b).

Contractors.

Subcontractors.

   Payments to subcontractors.

      Late payments, §22C-5.

Contract rates and fees, §24-1.1(a).

Computed monthly and collected 31 days or less in advance.

   Interest not deemed in excess of rates, §24-1.1(b).

Home loans secured by first mortgages or first deeds of trust, §24-1.1A.

Loans in excess of $300,000.

   Section not limit on fees, §24-1.1(f).

Maximum rate of interest.

   Commissioner to publish, computing, §24-1.1(c).

Modification, renewal, extension or amendment fee, §24-1.1(d).

Origination fee, §24-1.1(e).

Contracts.

Bearing of interest, §24-5(a).

   Penal bonds.

      Exception as to, §24-5(a).

Maximum fees on loans secured by real property, §24-10(a).

Rates, §24-1.

Real property.

   Maximum fees on loans secured by real property.

      Construction loans construed, §24-10(c).

   Prepayment, §24-10(b).

Corporations.

Appraisal rights.

   Payment for shares, §55-13-25(a).

Sale below par permitted, §24-2.

Costs.

Attorneys' fees in notes, conditional sale contracts, etc., in addition to interest, §6-21.2.

Interest from verdict to judgment added as costs, §24-7.

County energy improvements revolving loan program.

Interest rate, §153A-455(b).

Covenants.

Default judgments.

   Clerk to ascertain interest upon default judgment on covenant to pay money, §24-6.

Credit cards.

Disclosure requirements.

   Generally, §24-11.1.

Loans exempt from interest rate and fee limitations, §24-9(d).

Credit unions.

Defined, §54-109.65.

Rate, §54-109.65.

INTEREST —Cont'd

Default judgments.

Clerk to ascertain upon default judgment on bond, bill, note or signed account, §24-6.

Definitions.

Construction loans, §24-10(c).

Drainage districts.

Assessment anticipation notes, §156-97.1.

Bond issues, §§156-95, 156-97.

   Payment.

      Duty of treasurer, §156-112.

Economic development loans.

Certain fees or other funds paid by borrowers.

   Not subject to claim or defense of usury, §24-9.3.

Eminent domain.

Public condemnors.

   Compensation.

      Interest as part of just compensation, §40A-53.

Employment security.

Contributions.

   Past-due contributions, §96-10(a).

Energy conservation finance act.

Certificates of participation, §142-67(b).

Financing contract.

   Calculation of interest component of installment payments under, §142-65(f).

Equity lines of credit.

Loans exempt from interest rate and fee limitations, §24-9(c).

Rates of interest, §24-1.2A.

Excise stamp tax on conveyances.

Overpayment of tax, §105-228.37(f).

Exemption of loans from rate and fee limitations.

Credit card plans, §24-9(c).

Definitions, §24-9(a).

Equity lines of credit, §24-9(c).

Usury prohibited as defense, §24-9(b).

Family law arbitration, §50-51(c).

Fiduciaries.

Reduction of interest rates.

   Powers which may be incorporated by reference in trust instrument, §32-27.

Finance.

Cash management plan, maximization, §147-86.11(g).

Foreign-money claims.

Increase or decrease, §1C-1828(b).

Rate of interest, §1C-1828(a), (c).

Forest protection and development corporations.

Maximum rates allowable, §106-992.

Funds transfers, UCC.

Rate of interest, §25-4A-506.

Global TransPark authority.

Bond issues, §63A-9(a).

Guardians.

Compound interest.

   Obligations due guardians to bear compound interest, §24-4.

Health care facilities.

Finance act.

   Bonds and notes, §131A-11.

Highways, roads and streets.

Condemnation proceedings.

   Part of just compensation, §136-113.

Housing finance agency.

Bonds and notes, §122A-8.

INTEREST —Cont'd
Housing finance agency —Cont'd
Loans.
To and by mortgage lenders, §122A-5.6(b).
Modification of terms of interest.
General power of agency, §122A-5.
Rules and regulations governing agency activity,
§122A-5.1(b).
Insurance.
Foreign or alien insurance company deposits,
§58-5-63(a).
Life insurance policy loans, §§58-61-1 to 58-61-15.
See LIFE INSURANCE.
International commercial arbitration and
conciliation.
Authority to award, §1-567.61(f).
Judgments, §24-5(a).
Clerk to ascertain interest upon default judgment
on bond, covenant, bill, note or signed
account, §24-6.
Interest from verdict to judgment added as costs,
§24-7.
Legal rate, §24-1.
Limitation on interest after judgment, §53-173(c).
Prejudgment interest, §24-5(b).
Late payment charges.
Authorized, §24-10.1(a).
Home loans, §24-10.1(c).
Restrictions, §24-10.1(b).
Legal rate, §24-1.
Letters of credit.
Damages for wrongful dishonor or breach,
§25-5-111(d).
Life insurance.
Interest on death benefits, §58-58-110.
Interest rates on life insurance loans, §§58-61-1 to
58-61-15.
See LIFE INSURANCE.
Loan-related goods, products and services.
Collection of payment for, §24-8(d).
Insurance proceeds to lender, §24-8(e).
Items included, §24-8(d).
Loans exempt from rate and fee limitations.
Credit card plans, §24-9(c).
Definitions, §24-9(a).
Equity lines of credit, §24-9(c).
Usury prohibited as defense, §24-9(b).
Loans generally.
See LOANS.
Local governmental employees' retirement
system.
Management of funds.
Annual allowance of regular interest,
§128-29(b).
Maximum rates.
Contract rates, §24-1.1.
Conveyance of property other than collateral in
consideration for loan, §24-8(c).
Forfeitures for usury, §24-2.
Guardians.
Obligations due guardians to bear compound
interest, §24-4.
Insurance proceeds to lender, §24-8(e).
Late fees, §24-10.1.
Legal rate, §24-1.
Loan amount $300,000 or less, §24-8(a).
Loan-related goods, products and services.
Collection of payment for, §24-8(d).
Mortgages and deeds of trust.
First mortgages and deeds of trust, §24-1.1A.
Secondary or junior mortgages, §24-14.

INTEREST —Cont'd
Maximum rates —Cont'd
Mortgages and deeds of trust —Cont'd
Second or junior lien on real property, §24-10(g).
Penalty for usury, §24-2.
Real property.
Maximum fees on loans secured by real
property, §24-10(a).
Revolving credit charges, §24-11.
Small business investment companies.
Applicability of provisions, §24-8(f).
Mortgage bankers, brokers and servicers.
Lenders.
When bankers and brokers considered lenders,
§24-2.5.
Mortgages and deeds of trust.
First mortgages and deeds of trust, §24-1.1A(a).
Additional charges allowed.
Certain lenders, §24-1.1A(c2).
Small loans, certain lenders, §24-1.1A(c1).
Compensation to mortgage banker, broker, etc.,
for services rendered, §24-1.1A(i).
Deferred payments of interest, §24-1.1A(g).
Exemption of certain investments, §24-1.1A(d).
Fee chargeable, §§24-1.1A(c), 24-10.
Graduation of periodic payments, §24-1.1A(h).
"Home loan" construed, §24-1.1A(e).
Maximum fees on loans secured by real
property, §24-10.
Natural person applying for loan, §24-1.1A(a1).
Prepayment fees, §24-1.1A(b).
Saving clauses, §24-1.1A(f).
High cost home loans, §24-1.1E.
Increased interest rate.
Limitations on loans, §24-1.1E(b).
Reverse mortgages.
Shared appreciation.
Defined, §53-257.
Total annual percentage rate.
Defined, §53-257.
Secondary or junior mortgages, §24-10(g).
Limitations, §24-14.
Motor vehicles.
Civil penalties for violations.
Overdue payment, §20-178.1(d).
Retail installment sales.
Credit installment sale contracts.
Finance charge.
Used cars, §25A-15(c).
Municipalities.
Assessments.
Delinquent assessments, §160A-233(a).
Energy improvements.
Program to finance purchase and installation.
Loans under program, §160A-459.1(b).
Joint municipal electric power and energy act.
Bond issues.
Rate, §159B-15(a).
Variable rates, §159B-15(a).
Negotiable instruments, §25-3-112.
Notes.
Default judgments.
Clerk to ascertain interest upon default
judgment on note, §24-6.
Occupational licensing boards.
State treasurer's investment program.
Use of interest earned by occupational licensing
boards under program, §93B-11.
Partition.
Owelty, §46-11.

INTEREST —Cont'd
Pawnbrokers and cash converters.
Municipal or county authority to regulate, §91A-12.
Rates of interest, §91A-8.
Payment.
Time from which interest runs, §24-3.
Penal bonds, §24-5(a), (a1).
Penalties.
Usury, §24-2.
Prejudgment interest, §24-5(b).
Prepayment of loan.
No prepayment terms or prepayment terms not in accordance with law, §24-2.4.
Principal and income act.
Interest, dividends, payments made in lieu of. Allocation, §37A-4-409.
Public utilities.
Certain repayments to consumers not subject to claim or defense of usury, §24-9.1.
Refunds to customers for over collections or advancements, §62-130.
Railroads.
Internal improvements, §124-5.1(b).
Rates of interest.
Contract rates, §24-1.1.
Conveyance of property other than collateral in consideration for loan, §24-8(c).
Equity lines of credit, §24-1.2A.
Extension of credit by banks and savings and loan associations, §24-2.2.
Forfeitures for usury, §24-2.
Funds transfers, UCC, §25-4A-506.
Guardians.
Obligations due guardians to bear compound interest, §24-4.
Insurance proceeds to lender, §24-8(e).
Late fees, §24-10.1.
Legal rate, §24-1.
Loan amount $300,000 or less, §24-8(a).
Loan-related goods, products and services. Collection of payment for, §24-8(d).
Mortgages and deeds of trust.
First mortgages and deeds of trust, §24-1.1A.
Secondary or junior mortgages, §24-14.
Second or junior lien on real property, §24-10(g).
Penalty for usury, §24-2.
Real property.
Maximum fees on loans secured by real property, §24-10(a).
Revolving credit charges, §24-11.
Savings and loan associations, §24-1.4(b).
Associations domiciled in North Carolina, §24-1.4(a).
Extensions of credit, §24-2.2.
Small business investment companies. Applicability of provisions, §24-8(f).
Real property.
Maximum fees on loans secured by real property, §24-10(a).
Construction loan construed, §24-10(c).
Less than three hundred thousand dollars, §24-10(d).
Prepayment, §24-10(b).
Second or junior lien on real property, §24-10(g).
Retail installment sales finance charges.
Consolidation and refinancing, §25A-31(c).
Consumer credit installment sale contracts.
Division of simple transaction into two or more sales to avoid limitations prohibited, §25A-15(e).

INTEREST —Cont'd
Retail installment sales finance charges —Cont'd
Consumer credit installment sale contracts —Cont'd
Rates, §25A-15(a).
Determination, §25A-15(b).
Residential manufactured homes.
Sale secured by first lien, §25A-15(f).
Security interest.
Rates chargeable, §25A-15(d).
Used cars.
Rate chargeable, §25A-15(c).
Defined, §25A-8(a).
Exclusions from definition, §25A-8(b).
Refinancing, §25A-31(c).
Remedies and penalties, §25A-44.
Revolving charge account contracts.
Default or deferral charges, §25A-14(c).
Insurance.
Additional charges for insurance, §25A-17(b).
Rates, §25A-14(a).
Security interest.
Rates, §25A-14(b).
Security interest.
Transactions in which seller acquires security interest, §25A-8(c).
Unearned finance charge credits.
Prepayment of real property and mobile home loans, §25A-32.1.
Retirement system for teachers and state employees.
Consolidated judicial retirement act.
Assets of retirement system.
Regular interest allowance, §135-67(e).
Definition of regular interest, §135-1.
Consolidated judicial retirement act, §135-53.
Management of funds.
Regular interest allowance, §135-7(b).
Revolving credit charges, §24-11.
Savings and loan associations.
Effect of loan provisions, §54B-167.
Rates, §24-1.4(b).
Associations domiciled in North Carolina, §24-1.4(a).
Extensions of credit, §24-2.2.
Savings banks.
Forced retirement of deposit accounts, §54C-179(b), (c).
Loans.
Maximum rates.
Applicable law, §54C-125(c).
Securities regulation.
Exemptions, §78A-63(i).
Security interests.
Revolving credit charges, §24-11.
Small business investment companies.
Applicability of provisions, §24-8(f).
State debt.
Attachment of interest coupons, §142-1.
Bond issues.
Reimbursement of treasurer for interest, §142-15.
Coupons.
Attachment, §142-1.
Registration as to principal and interest, §142-6.
Refunding bonds, §142-29.7.
Registration.
Conversion and reconversion, §142-6(b).
Reimbursement of treasurer for interest, §142-15.

INTEREST —Cont'd
State debt —Cont'd
State treasurer.
  Reimbursement of treasurer for interest,
    §142-15.
Taxation.
  Exemption from taxation, §142-12.
    Continuation of state tax exemption,
      §142-12.1(c), (d).
    Federal taxation of interest income on state
      or local bonds, effect, §142-12.1(a), (b).
State employees.
Retirement system for teachers and state
  employees.
  Definition of regular interest, §135-1.
State funds.
Investments of general fund and highway funds,
  §147-69.1(d).
State literary fund.
Terms of loans, §115C-459.
State treasurer.
Depositories.
  Contracts as to payment interest, §147-81.
Statewide accounts receivable program,
§147-86.23.
Subcontractors, payments to.
Late payments, §22C-5.
Taxation.
Exemption from taxation.
  Interest on state or local bonds, §142-12.
Generally, §105-241.21.
Property taxes.
  Nonpayment of taxes, §105-360(a).
  Overpayments, §105-360(d).
Teachers.
Retirement system for teachers and state
  employees. See within this heading,
  "Retirement system for teachers and state
  employees."
Time from which interest runs, §24-3.
Time shares.
Independent escrow agent.
  Escrow account.
    Interest-bearing account, §93A-42(d).
Traffic violation.
Civil penalties imposed.
  Overdue payment, §20-178.1(d).
Trust companies.
Seizure by commissioner.
  Dividends to shareholders and creditors.
    Unclaimed dividends, §53-392.
Unclaimed property generally, §§116B-51 to
116B-80.
  See UNCLAIMED PROPERTY.
Underground storage tanks.
Leaking petroleum cleanup.
  Groundwater protection loan fund,
    §143-215.94P(a).
Unemployment compensation.
Contributions.
  Past-due contributions, §96-10(a).
Usury.
Affirmative defense, pleading, §1A-1 Rule 8(c).
Bond issues.
  Corporate bonds sold below par, §24-2.
Consumer credit installment sale contract.
  Finance charge rates, §25A-15.
Contract rates, §24-1.1.
Corporations.
  Bonds may be sold below par, §24-2.

INTEREST —Cont'd
Usury —Cont'd
Cost to be recovered by parties seeking recovery
  on usurious contracts, §6-25.
Economic development loans.
  Certain fees or other funds paid by borrowers.
    Not subject to claim or defense of usury,
      §24-9.3.
Forfeitures of usurious interest, §24-2.
Household and kitchen furniture loans.
  Usurious late loans on furniture, §14-391.
Judgments.
  Legal rate of interest, §24-1.
Jurisdiction of courts of state, §24-2.1.
Late fees, §24-10.1.
Legal rate, §§24-1, 24-1.1.
Loans exempt from rate and fee limitations.
  Credit card plans, §24-9(c).
  Definitions, §24-9(a).
  Equity lines of credit, §24-9(c).
  Usury prohibited as defense, §24-9(b).
Mortgages and deeds of trust.
  First mortgages and deeds of trust, §24-1.1A.
  Late payment charges, §24-10.1(c).
  Maximum fees on loans secured by real
    property, §24-10.
  Rate spread home loans.
    Violations, §24-1.1F(d).
  Secondary or junior mortgages, §24-14.
Penalty, §24-2.
Public utilities.
  Certain repayments to consumers not subject to
    claim or defense of usury, §24-9.1.
Rate spread home loans.
  Violations, §24-1.1F(d).
Real property.
  Maximum fees on loans secured by real
    property, §24-10.
Retail installment sales finance charge.
  Consumer credit installment sale contract rate,
    §25A-15.
Revolving credit charges, §24-11.
State opt-out from federal preemption, §24-2.3(a),
  (b).
Transactions governed by chapter.
  Acquisition of right to receive payments under
    loan.
    Jurisdiction of courts of state, consent to,
      §24-2.1(e).
  Extensions of credit deemed made in state,
    §24-2.1(a).
  Public policy, §24-2.1(g).
  Severability of provisions, §24-2.1(f).
  Solicitation or communication to borrow from
    outside of state.
    Considered acceptance or offer to borrow,
      §24-2.1(c), (d).
  Solicitation or communication to lend from
    outside of state.
    Considered offer or agreement to lend in
      state, §24-2.1(b), (d).
Wage assignments.
  Usurious loans on assignment of wages,
    §14-391.
Workers' compensation.
Rates of compensation.
  Commuted values.
    Discount table to be used, ICWorkComp Rule
      406.

INTERESTED PARTIES.
Habeas corpus.
Notice, §17-29.

INTERESTED PARTIES —Cont'd
Letters testamentary and of administration.
Grounds for revocation, §28A-9-1.
Missing persons.
Notice of action for receiver, §28C-4.
Probate of wills.
Clerk of superior court.
Conflicts of interest, §28A-2-3.
Public officers or employees benefiting from public contracts, §14-234.

INTERESTED WITNESSES.
Competency of witnesses, §§8-49, 8-57.2.
Disqualification, §8C-1 Rule 601(c).
Not excluded by interest or crime, §8-49.
Paternity cases.
Presumed father or mother as witness, §8-57.2.

INTEREST ON LAWYER'S TRUST ACCOUNTS.
Rules governing administration of plan, Bar
Rules D.1301 to D.1316.
See ATTORNEYS AT LAW.

INTEREST RATE SWAP AGREEMENTS FOR GOVERNMENTAL UNITS, §§159-193 to
159-200.
See SWAP AGREEMENTS.

INTERFERENCE WITH CIVIL RIGHTS, §99D-1.
Civil action.
Compensatory and punitive damages, §99D-1(b),
(b1).
Costs and attorney's fees, §99D-1(b), (b1).
Government unit or government official.
Restriction on bringing against, §99D-1(c).
Human relations commission bringing,
§99D-1(b1).
Personal action, §99D-1(b).
Conduct constituting, §99D-1(a).
Future acts.
Restraining and enjoining, §99D-1(b), (b1).

INTERFERING WITH EMERGENCY COMMUNICATIONS, §14-286.2.

INTERIOR DESIGN SERVICES.
Sales and use tax exemption.
Services provided with taxes purchase,
§105-164.13.

INTERLOCAL COOPERATION.
Appropriations.
Joint agencies, §160A-462(b).
Authorized, §160A-461.
Contracts or agreements.
Authorized, §160A-461.
Provisions, §160A-464.
Regional councils of governments.
Power to contract, §160A-475.
Revenue and expenses for joint undertakings,
§160A-466.
Definitions, §160A-460.
Economic development, interlocal agreements,
§158-7.4.
Expenses for joint undertakings, §160A-466.
Industrial or commercial parks or sites.
Interlocal agreements concerning economic
development, §158-7.4(a).
Binding effect, action to specifically enforce,
§158-7.4(c).
Length of undertaking, §158-7.4(b).
Joint agencies, §160A-462(a).
Appropriations for, §160A-462(b).
Personnel, §160A-463(a).

INTERLOCAL COOPERATION —Cont'd
One officer exercising function for all participating units, §160A-463(b).
Personnel.
Joint agencies, §160A-463(a).
One officer exercising function for all participating
units, §160A-463(b).
Regional councils of governments.
Power to employ personnel, §160A-475.
Project development financing debt instruments.
Interlocal agreement for purposes of issuing.
Private development project benefited,
§159-103(c).
Regional councils of governments.
Charter, §160A-470.
Contents, §160A-472.
Contracts or agreements.
Power to contract, §160A-475.
Creation, §160A-470(a).
Eminent domain, §160A-475.
Fiscal affairs, §160A-476.
Meetings, §160A-473.
Membership, §160A-471.
Officers.
Election, §160A-473.
Personnel.
Power to employ personnel, §160A-475.
Pledge of property to as security for indebtedness,
§160A-475.
Powers, §160A-475.
Supplementary nature of powers, §160A-478.
Reports, §160A-477.
Sales and use tax refunds, §105-164.14(c).
Units of local government.
Appropriations to council, §160A-476.
Creation of councils, §160A-470(a).
Defined, §160A-470(b).
Membership in council, §160A-471.
Withdrawal from council, §160A-474.
Withdrawal from council, §160A-474.
Reports.
Regional councils of governments, §160A-477.
Revenue for joint undertakings, §160A-466.

INTERLOCUTORY DECREES.
Appeals.
Court of appeals.
Appeals of right from the courts of the trial
divisions, §7A-27(d).
District courts.
Appeals of right from district courts to court of
appeals, §7A-27(d).
Review on appeal from judgment, §1-278.
Superior courts.
Appeals of right from superior courts to court of
appeals, §7A-27(d).
District courts.
Appeals of right from district courts to courts of
appeals, §7A-27(d).
Exercise of power to issue interlocutory orders,
§7A-192.
Letters testamentary and of administration.
Revocation of letters, §28A-9-5.

INTERLOCUTORY ORDERS.
Discretionary review on certification by supreme court.
Interlocutory orders by court of appeals, AppProc
Rule 15(h).
Jurisdiction in rem or quasi in rem.
Protection of res while action pending, §1-75.9.

INTERLOCUTORY SUMMARY JUDGMENTS,
§1A-1 Rule 56(c).

INTERMEDIATE CARE FACILITIES.
**Capital expenditure used for renovating or
replacing.**
Exemption from certificate of need review,
§131E-184(e).
Certificates of need, §§131E-175 to 130E-191.1.
See HEALTH CARE FACILITIES.
**Financing health care facilities generally,
§§131A-1 to 131A-25.**
See HEALTH CARE FACILITY FINANCING.
**Long-term care ombudsman program,
§§143B-181.15 to 143B-181.25.**
See LONG-TERM CARE OMBUDSMAN.

INTERMENT.
Cemeteries.
General provisions, §§65-4 to 65-113.
See CEMETERIES.
Cremation.
General provisions, §§90-210.120 to 90-210.135.
See CREMATION.

INTERNAL IMPROVEMENTS.
Appropriations.
State deemed shareholder in corporation accepting
appropriation, §124-2.
Council of state.
Control of internal improvements, §124-1.
Investigation of corporations.
Power of investigation, §124-7.
Encumbrances.
Approval of encumbrance on state's interest in
corporations, §124-5(a).
Governor.
Control of internal improvements, §124-1.
Investigation of corporations.
Power of investigation, §124-7.
Proxies.
Appointment of proxies, etc., §124-6(a).
Investigations.
Power of investigation of corporations, §124-7.
Proxies.
Appointment of proxies, etc., §124-6(a).
Railroad companies.
Appointment of directors, §124-6(b).
Report by railroad, canal or other public work.
Additional information provided by state owned
railroad.
Request of governor or general assembly,
§124-3(b), (c).
Attorney-client privilege not waived.
State owned railroad providing information,
§124-3(b).
Confidential information.
State owned railroad providing information,
§124-3(c).
Contents, §124-3(a).
President or chief officer to make, §124-3(a).
Shareholders.
Proxies.
Appointment of proxies, etc., §124-6(a).
State deemed shareholder and corporation
accepting appropriation, §124-2.

INTERNAL MEDICINE.
Primary care physicians, medical education,
§143-613.

INTERNAL REVENUE SERVICE.
Agents authorized to enforce criminal laws,
§15A-406.

INTERNATIONAL BANKING, §§53-232.1 to
53-232.17.
Agencies.
Authority to establish and operate, §53-232.3(c),
(d).
Restrictions, §53-232.8(d), (e).
Defined, §53-232.2(a).
Termination of operation, §53-232.13(b).
Appeals.
Commissioner's decisions, §53-232.17.
**Applicability of North Carolina business
corporation act, §53-232.5.**
Applicability of provisions, §53-232.4(a).
Exceptions, §53-232.4(b).
Branches.
Authority to establish and operate, §53-232.3(c),
(d).
Restrictions, §53-232.8(d), (e).
Defined, §53-232.2(a).
Termination of operation, §53-232.13(b).
Business corporation act.
Applicability, §53-232.5.
Cease and desist orders, §53-232.16.
Citation of act.
Short title, §53-232.1(a).
Commissioner of banks.
Appeal of commissioner's decisions, §53-232.17.
Cease and desist orders, §53-232.16.
Definition of "commissioner,"§53-232.2(a).
International representative offices.
Review of operations, §53-232.14(c).
Corporate income tax.
Deductions in determining state income,
§105-130.5(b).
Corporations, §§53-232.10(d), 53-232.12.
Actions against.
International banking corporation or
nonresident of state, §53-232.7(b), (c).
Resident of state, §53-232.7(a).
Defined, §53-232.2(a).
Dissolution, §53-232.13(a), (c).
Financial certification, §53-232.11(a).
Home state, §53-232.3(e).
Investments.
Restrictions, §53-232.11(b).
Licenses.
Applications.
Approval or disapproval by commissioner,
§53-232.8(c).
Contents, §53-232.8(a).
Documents to accompany, §53-232.8(b).
Effect of issuance, §53-232.9(a), (e), (f).
Issuance by commissioner, §53-232.6(b).
Renewal, §53-232.9(b).
Surrender of license on refusal to renew,
§53-232.9(d).
Requirement for carrying on banking business,
§53-232.6(a).
Revocation, §53-232.9(c).
Surrender of license, §53-232.9(d).
Loans.
Restrictions, §53-232.11(b).
Powers, §53-232.3(a) to (e).
Reports, §53-232.12(a).
Exemption from certain requirements,
§53-232.12(b).
Securities held in state, §53-232.10(d).
Securities to be held in state.
Generally, §53-232.10(a).
Powers of commissioner, §53-232.10(c).
Reports, §53-232.10(d).

INTERNATIONAL BANKING —Cont'd
Corporations —Cont'd
Securities to be held in state —Cont'd
Valuation of securities, §53-232.10(b).
Transacting business in state.
Requirements, §53-232.6(a).
Definitions, §53-232.2(a).
Federal international bank institutions.
Authority to establish and operate, §53-232.3(a),
(b).
Defined, §53-232.2(a).
International bank agencies.
Authority to establish and operate, §53-232.3(c),
(d).
Restrictions, §53-232.8(d), (e).
Defined, §53-232.2(a).
Termination of operation, §53-232.13(b).
International bank branches.
Authority to establish and operate, §53-232.3(c),
(d).
Restrictions, §53-232.8(d), (e).
Defined, §53-232.2(a).
Termination of operation, §53-232.13(b).
International banking corporations,
§§53-232.10(d), 53-232.12.
Actions against.
International banking corporation or
nonresident of state, §53-232.7(b), (c).
Resident of state, §53-232.7(a).
Defined, §53-232.2(a).
Dissolution, §53-232.13(a), (c).
Financial certification, §53-232.11(a).
Home state, §53-232.3(e).
Investments.
Restrictions, §53-232.11(b).
Licenses.
Applications.
Approval or disapproval by commissioner,
§53-232.8(c).
Contents, §53-232.8(a).
Documents to accompany, §53-232.8(b).
Effect of issuance, §53-232.9(a), (e), (f).
Issuance by commissioner, §53-232.6(b).
Renewal, §53-232.9(b).
Surrender of license on refusal to renew,
§53-232.9(d).
Requirement for carrying on banking business,
§53-232.6(a).
Revocation, §53-232.9(c).
Surrender of license, §53-232.9(d).
Loans.
Restrictions, §53-232.11(b).
Powers, §53-232.3(a) to (e).
Reports, §53-232.12(a).
Exemption from certain requirements,
§53-232.12(b).
Securities held in state, §53-232.10(d).
Securities to be held in state.
Generally, §53-232.10(a).
Powers of commissioner, §53-232.10(c).
Reports, §53-232.10(d).
Valuation of securities, §53-232.10(b).
Transacting business in state.
Requirements, §53-232.6(a).
International representative offices.
Authority to establish and operate, §53-232.3(c),
(d).
Conversion to international branch bank or
international bank agency, §53-232.14(d).
Defined, §53-232.2(a).
Generally, §53-232.14(a).

INTERNATIONAL BANKING —Cont'd
International representative offices —Cont'd
Powers, §53-232.14(e).
Registration, §53-232.14(b).
Review of operations by commissioner,
§53-232.14(c).
Termination of operation, §53-232.13(b).
Investments.
Restrictions on international banking
corporations, §53-232.11(b).
Legal and financial terms used in article.
Reference to equivalent terms used in foreign
country, §53-232.2(b).
Legislative declaration.
Intent of provisions, §53-232.1(b).
Licenses.
International banking corporations, §§53-232.8,
53-232.9.
Reports.
International banking corporations,
§§53-232.10(d), 53-232.12.
Representative offices.
Authority to establish and operate, §53-232.3(c),
(d).
Conversion to international branch bank or
international bank agency, §53-232.14(d).
Defined, §53-232.2(a).
Generally, §53-232.14(a).
Powers, §53-232.14(e).
Registration, §53-232.14(b).
Review of operation by commissioner,
§53-232.14(c).
Termination of operation, §53-232.13(b).
Rules and regulations.
Banking commission, §53-232.15.
State banking commission.
Rules and regulations, §53-232.15.
Title of act.
Short title, §53-232.1(a).

**INTERNATIONAL COMMERCIAL
ARBITRATION AND CONCILIATION,**
§§1-567.30 to 1-567.87.
**Agreements expressly excluding applicability
of article,** §1-567.31(g).
Amiable compositeur (amicable compounder).
Tribunal deciding on, §1-567.58(c).
Appeals, §1-567.67(a), (b).
Applicability of article, §1-567.31(a).
Arbitral tribunal.
Conducting arbitration in manner deemed
appropriate.
No agreement on procedure, §1-567.49(b).
Decisions made by majority, §1-567.59.
Interim measures.
Power to order, §1-567.47.
Jurisdiction.
Competence to rule on, §§1-567.46(a), 1-567.47.
Place of meetings for consultation, §1-567.50(b).
Arbitration agreement.
Defined, §1-567.37(a).
Valid, enforceable and irrevocable, §1-567.37(c).
Written agreement, §1-567.37(b).
Arbitration institution.
Appointing to conduct arbitration, §1-567.41(g).
Arbitrators.
Agreement on appointment, §1-567.41(b), (c).
Appointment, §1-567.41(b) to (g).
Substitute or replacement arbitrator.
Termination of mandate, §1-567.45(a) to (c).
Arbitration institution, appointing, §1-567.41(g).

**INTERNATIONAL COMMERCIAL
  ARBITRATION AND CONCILIATION**
  —Cont'd
Arbitrators —Cont'd
  Challenges to, §1-567.42(d), (e).
    Agreement on procedure, §1-567.43(a).
    Arbitral tribunal to decide issue, §1-567.43(b).
    Rejection of challenge, request to superior court
        to decide, §1-567.43(c).
    Written statement of reasons for challenge,
        §1-567.43(b).
  Compensation, §1-567.41(h).
  Disclosure required.
    Information causing impartiality to be
        questioned, §1-567.42(a).
    Continuing duty, §1-567.42(c).
    Mandatory and not waived, §1-567.42(b).
  Failure to act.
    Termination of mandate, §1-567.44(a) to (c).
  Nationality, §1-567.41(a).
  Number, §1-567.40.
  Procedure for appointment, §1-567.41(b) to (g).
  Substitute or replacement arbitrator.
    Termination of mandate, §1-567.45(a).
    Previously held hearing, repeal, §1-567.45(b).
    Validity of ruling of tribunal not effected,
        §1-567.45(c).
  Superior court appointing.
    Failure to agree, §1-567.41(d) to (f).
  Termination of mandate.
    Substitute or replacement arbitrator,
        §1-567.45(a) to (c).
    Termination of proceedings, §1-567.62(c).
    Unable to perform or failure to act,
        §1-567.44(a).
    Arbitrator withdraws or agrees to
        termination, effect, §1-567.44(c).
    Decision by superior court, request for,
        §1-567.44(b).
  Unable to perform.
    Termination of mandate, §1-567.44(a) to (c).
Attorneys at law.
  Representation by attorney, §1-567.48(b).
    Conciliation proceedings, §1-567.79.
Attorneys' fees.
  Awarding, order of costs, §1-567.61(h).
Award.
  Additional award.
    Extension of period for making, §1-567.63(d).
    Forma and content requirements, §1-567.63(e).
    Request, time, §1-567.63(c).
  Confirmation, §1-567.65.
  Copies delivered to parties, §1-567.61(d).
  Correction or interpretation.
    Extension of time, §1-567.63(d).
    Forma and content requirements, §1-567.63(e).
    Request, time for, §1-567.63(a).
    Tribunal correcting on own initiative, time,
        §1-567.63(b).
  Costs, awarding, §1-567.61(h).
  Date and place of arbitration, stating required,
        §1-567.61(c).
  Enforcement, §1-567.65.
  Foreign currency, denominated in, §1-567.61(e).
  Interest, authority to award, §1-567.61(f).
  Modification, §1-567.64.
  Reasons upon which based not stated,
        §1-567.61(b).
  Settlement.
    Agreed terms, status and effect, §1-567.60(c).
  Signature of arbitrators required, §1-567.61(a).

**INTERNATIONAL COMMERCIAL
  ARBITRATION AND CONCILIATION**
  —Cont'd
Award —Cont'd
  Specific performance, awarding, §1-567.61(g).
  Vacating of award, §1-567.64.
  Writing required, §1-567.61(a).
Burden of proof.
  Tribunal conducting proceeding, §1-567.49(b).
**Challenge to arbitrators appointed or
  designated,** §§1-567.42, 1-567.43.
Claims.
  Stating, requirements, §1-567.53(a).
    Amending or supplementing, §1-567.53(b).
    More than two parties to arbitration,
        §1-567.53(c).
Commencement of proceedings, §1-567.51.
**Commercial arbitration or conciliation
  considered,** §1-567.31(e).
**Compelling arbitration, stay of judicial
  proceedings.**
  Application to superior court for order,
        §1-567.38(a).
  Beginning or continuing arbitration while
        application pending, §1-567.38(b).
Conciliators.
  Conduct of proceedings, §1-567.78(c).
  Draft conciliation agreement.
    Preparation, §1-567.80(a).
  Duties, §1-567.78(b).
  Immunities, §1-567.87(b).
  Selection, §1-567.78(a).
  Service of process.
    Not subject to service or matters related to
        conciliation, §1-567.87(a).
  Settlements.
    Acceptance by parties, §1-567.80(b).
Conflict of laws.
  Application of law as determined by conflict rules.
    Failure of parties to designate applicable law,
        §1-567.58(b).
  Dispute decided on rules of law as chosen by
        parties, §1-567.58(a).
  Substantive law, designation construed to refer to,
        §1-567.58(a).
Consolidation of arbitration agreements,
        §1-567.57(b).
Construction and interpretation.
  Severability of provisions, §1-567.33A.
Contracts.
  Severability of arbitration laws, §1-567.46(a).
Cost of arbitration.
  Awarding, §1-567.61(h).
Cost of conciliation.
  Borne equally by parties, §1-567.85(b).
  Expenses of party borne by party, §1-567.85(b).
  Giving notice of costs, §1-567.85(a).
  Included in costs, §1-567.85(a).
  Setting costs on termination, §1-567.85(a).
Counterclaims.
  Provisions referring to claims apply to
        counterclaims, §1-567.32(d).
  Stating, requirements, §1-567.53(a).
    Amending or supplementing, §1-567.53(b).
    More than two parties to arbitration,
        §1-567.53(c).
Courts.
  Applications to superior court, §1-567.66.
  Extent of intervention, §1-567.35.
Default of party, §1-567.55.

INTERNATIONAL COMMERCIAL ARBITRATION AND CONCILIATION
—Cont'd

Defenses.
Stating, requirements, §1-567.53(a).
Amending or supplementing, §1-567.53(b).
More than two parties to arbitration, §1-567.53(c).
Definitions, §1-567.32(a).
Arbitration agreement, §1-567.37(a).
Designation of law or legal system, §1-567.58(a), (b).
Discovery.
Assistance of superior court in obtaining, request, §1-567.57(a).
Tribunal conducting proceeding, §1-567.49(b).
Draft conciliation agreement.
Acceptance of settlement, §1-567.80(b).
Preparation, §1-567.80(a).
Enforceability of decree, §1-567.84.
Equal treatment of parties, §1-567.48(a).
Evidence.
Admission made in course of conciliation.
Admissibility, §1-567.81(a).
Documentary evidence, translation, tribunal ordering, §1-567.52(b).
Documents prepared, §1-567.81(c).
Offering in violation of provisions, §1-567.81(b).
Tribunal conducting proceeding.
Not limited to rules of evidence, §1-567.49(b).
Ex aequo et bono (on the basis of fundamental fairness).
Tribunal deciding on, §1-567.58(c).
Expenses of party to conciliation.
Borne by party, §1-567.85(b).
Experts.
Appointment by tribunal, §1-567.56(a).
Hearings.
Participation in, §1-567.56(b).
Relevant information or property.
Parties providing access to, §1-567.56(a).
Freedom to determination issue.
Right of parties to authorize third parties to make determination, §1-567.32(b).
Hearings.
Closing at conclusion of evidence, §1-567.54(f).
Confidentiality of matters, §1-567.54(d).
Experts.
Participation in, §1-567.56(b).
Held at appropriate stage of proceedings, §1-567.54(a).
In camera, held in, §1-567.54(d).
Notice for purposes of inspection property or documents, §1-567.54(b).
Record or transcript, agreement on, §1-567.54(e).
Service of statements, documents or other information, §1-567.54(c).
Tribunal to decide whether to hold, §1-567.54(a).
Immunities.
Conciliators and parties, §1-567.87.
Interim relief.
Arbitral tribunal.
Power to order, §1-567.47.
Interim relief directly from superior court.
Arbitrator not available or not appointed, §1-567.39(a).
Relief granted, §1-567.39(c).
Finding of fact of arbitral tribunal.
Preclusive effect given, §1-567.39(d), (e).
Limiting availability by written agreement, §1-567.39(f).

INTERNATIONAL COMMERCIAL ARBITRATION AND CONCILIATION
—Cont'd

Interim relief directly from superior court
—Cont'd
Other cases, §1-567.39(b).
International agreements.
Article subject, §1-567.31(a).
International arbitration or conciliation considered, §1-567.31(c), (d).
Jurisdiction, §1-567.36(a), (b).
Arbitral tribunal.
Competence to rule on its jurisdiction, §§1-567.46(a), 1-567.47.
Ruling on jurisdiction as preliminary question.
Appeal of ruling to superior court, §1-567.46(c).
Ruling on jurisdiction in award on the merits, §1-567.46(c).
Time for raising plea of lack of jurisdiction, §1-567.46(b).
Effect of consenting to conciliation, §1-567.86.
Language or languages to be used.
Agreement by parties, §1-567.52(a).
Documentary evidence, translation, tribunal may order, §1-567.52(b).
Translators, employing, §1-567.52(c).
Tribunal determining.
No agreement by parties, §1-567.52(a).
Limitation of actions.
Tolling on beginning of conciliation proceedings, §1-567.82(b).
Mediation, conciliation or other procedures.
Settlement of dispute, §1-567.60(a).
Number of arbitrators, §1-567.40.
Objection to noncompliance.
Waiver of right to object, §1-567.34.
Other dispute resolution laws.
Not affected, §1-567.31(f).
Parties.
Default, §1-567.55.
Equal treatment, §1-567.48(a).
Place of arbitration, §1-567.50(a).
Place of arbitration in state.
Required for provisions to apply, §1-567.31(b).
Policy of state, §1-567.30.
Purpose of article, §1-567.30.
Rules of interpretation, §1-567.32(b) to (d).
Rules of procedure.
Agreement of parties on, §1-567.49(a).
Decisions on, §1-567.59.
Tribunal conducting arbitration in manner deemed appropriate.
No agreement on procedure, §1-567.49(b).
Rules referred to in agreement.
Agreement of parties includes, §1-567.32(c).
Setoffs.
Stating, requirements, §1-567.53(a).
Amending or supplementing, §1-567.53(b).
More than two parties to arbitration, §1-567.53(c).
Settlement.
Award.
Agreed terms, status and effect, §1-567.60(c).
Mediation, conciliation, use to settle, §1-567.60(a).
Termination of proceedings, §1-567.60(b).
Tribunal may encourage, §1-567.60(a).
Severability of provisions, §1-567.33A.
Short title of article, §1-567.30.
Site of arbitration, §1-567.50(a).
Specific performance, awarding, §1-567.61(g).

INTERNATIONAL COMMERCIAL
    ARBITRATION AND CONCILIATION
    —Cont'd
Statute of limitations.
    Tolling at beginning of conciliation proceedings,
        §1-567.82(b).
Stay of arbitration.
    Submitting dispute to conciliation, §1-567.82(a).
Stay of judicial proceeding and compel
    arbitration.
    Application to superior court for order,
        §1-567.38(a).
        Beginning or continuing arbitration while
            application pending, §1-567.38(b).
Termination of arbitrators mandate.
    Substitute or replacement arbitrator, §1-567.45(a)
        to (c).
    Termination of proceedings, §1-567.62(c).
    Unable to perform or failure to act, §1-567.44(a) to
        (c).
Termination of conciliation.
    All parties, §1-567.83(a).
    Particular party or parties, §1-567.83(b).
Termination of proceedings, §1-567.62(a).
    Mandate of tribunal terminates, §1-567.62(c).
    Order of termination, §1-567.62(b).
    Settlement, §1-567.60(b).
Terms of contract.
    Deciding in accordance with, §1-567.58(d).
Translators, employing, §1-567.52(c).
Tribunal exceeding scope of authority.
    Time for raising of plea, §1-567.46(b).
Usage of trade, taking into consideration,
    §1-567.58(d).
Venue, §1-567.36(a), (b).
Waiver.
    Right to object, §1-567.34.
When proceeding starts, §1-567.51.
Written agreement.
    Effect, §1-567.84.
Written communications or submissions.
    Court, administrative or special proceedings,
        §1-567.33(c).
    Receipt, §1-567.33(a).
        Last known place of business, domicile or
            mailing address, §1-567.33(b).

INTERNATIONAL FESTIVAL OF STATE.
Folkmoot USA, §145-19.

INTERNATIONAL LAW.
Congress.
    Power to punish offenses against, US Const Art I
        §8.

INTERNATIONAL RELATIONS.
Secretary of state, powers and duties,
    §147-54.6.

INTERNET.
Abortion.
    Woman's right to know act.
        Internet web site to be maintained by
            department, §§90-21.83, 90-21.84.
Advance health care directive registry.
    Access to registry, §130A-469.
Agency rulemaking procedure.
    Notice of proposed rules.
        Information posted on web site when notice
            submitted, §150B-19.1(c).
Appeals.
    Filing by electronic means, AppProc Rule 26(a).

INTERNET —Cont'd
Cities providing communications services,
    §§160A-340 to 160A-340.6.
    See MUNICIPAL UTILITIES.
Computer crimes.
    See COMPUTER CRIMES.
Consumer protection.
    Geographical location.
        Deceptive representation in telephone directory,
            print advertisement or Internet, §75-42.
Cyber-bullying.
    Use with intent to intimidate or torment minor,
        §14-458.1.
Cyberstalking, §14-196.3.
Department of commerce.
    Economic development grants.
        Reports posted online, §143B-437.07(b).
Department of health and human services.
    Internet data warehouse for provider records,
        §143B-139.5C.
Economic development grant.
    Reports posted online.
        Duty of department of commerce,
            §143B-437.07(b).
Electronic auction service.
    State surplus property.
        Sale or disposal using, §143-64.03(d).
Geographical location.
    Deceptive representation in telephone directory,
        print advertisement or Internet, §75-42.
Health benefit plans.
    Electronic or on-line system for up-to-date
        information, §58-3-245(a).
Interactive digital media.
    Research and development tax credit,
        §105-129.56.
Military and overseas voters.
    Confirmation of receipt of application and voted
        ballot.
        Electronic free access system, §163-258.14.
Money transmitters licenses.
    Engaged in the business of money transmission.
        Website available to in-state citizens,
            §53-208.3(c).
Motor vehicle registration plates, registration
    certificates and certificates of title.
    Online motor vehicle registration vendor,
        §20-63(j), (k).
Municipal subdivision construction or
    development.
    Fees and charges, imposition, increase.
        Web site maintained by city or county.
            Communicating notice of meeting,
                §160A-4.1(a), (a1).
North Carolina administrative code.
    Code made available on, §150B-21.24(b).
North Carolina register.
    Register made available on, §150B-21.24(a).
Notaries public.
    Electronic notary public act, §§10B-100 to
        10B-146.
    See NOTARIES PUBLIC.
Open meetings act.
    Notice of official meetings.
        Posting notice of all regular and special
            meetings, §143-318.12(e).
        Schedule of regular meetings on web site,
            §143-318.12(d).
Optometrists.
    Report of judgments, awards, payments or
        settlements to board.
        Publication of information collected,
            §90-121.6(c).

INTERNET —Cont'd

Organ donor registry Internet site.
Division of motor vehicles, §20-43.2.

Property tax information contained on web site.
Amount of taxes due.
Person relying on information, §105-361(e).
Understatement of taxes and special assessment.
Liability of tax collector, §105-361(e).

Records of superior courts in clerks offices.
Electronic access to records.
Contracts to provide access to public, §7A-109(d), (e).

Sex offenders.
Access to list of online identifiers in central registry, §14-208.14(a).
Change of online identifier, §14-208.9(e).
Failure to notify sheriff, §14-208.11(a).
Release of online identifiers, §14-208.15A.
Social networking sites.
Banned from use of, §14-202.5.
Liability of sites in compliance, §14-202.5A.

Sexual offenses.
Solicitation of child by computer, §14-202.3(a).

Social networking sites.
Sex offenders.
Banned from use of, §14-202.5.
Liability of sites in compliance, §14-202.5A.

Social security numbers or driver's license numbers.
Removal from public records posted on web site.
Registers of deeds and clerks of court, §132-1.10(f1).

State auditor.
Improper government activities, reports of.
Auditor to provide web site for receipt of reports, §147-64.6B(a).

Tickets sold in excess of printed price.
Internet resale, §14-344.1.
Software to interfere with operations of ticket seller, §14-344.2.

Turnpike authority.
Internet report of funds expended, §136-89.195.

Unlawful transfer of recording over Internet by third parties.
Internet provider not deemed in violation of provisions, §14-433(c).

INTERNSHIP COUNCIL.
Applications.
Committees for screening applications, §143B-419.
Members, §143B-418.
Powers and duties, §143B-417.

INTERPLEADER AND INTERVENTION.
Administrative procedure.
Appeals.
Motion to intervene, §150B-46.
Hearings.
Motion to intervene, §§150B-23(d), 150B-38(f).
Attachment.
Third persons claiming attached property, §1-440.43.
Bills of lading.
Determination of conflicting claims, §25-7-603.
Child support.
Action for support of minor child, §50-13.5(e).
Complaint for interpleader and declaratory relief.
Form, §1A-1 Rule 84.
Delivery of property to intervener, §1-483.

INTERPLEADER AND INTERVENTION —Cont'd

Documents of title, §25-7-603.
Determination of conflicting claims, §25-7-603.
Funds subject to competing claims.
Deposit of funds in interest bearing accounts, §1A-1 Rule 22(b).
Interpleader generally, §1A-1 Rule 22.
Intervention of right, §1A-1 Rule 24(a).
Permissive intervention, §1A-1 Rule 24(b).
Plaintiff exposed to double or multiple liability.
Persons having claims against plaintiff joined as defendants and required to interplead, §1A-1 Rule 22(a).
Procedure for intervention, §1A-1 Rule 24(c).
Property claimed by third person, §1-482.
Public utilities.
Attorney general.
Intervention in commission proceedings, §62-20.
Right to intervene, §1A-1 Rule 24(a).
Sale of goods, UCC.
Documents of title.
Determination of conflicting claims, §25-7-603.
Notice of claim or litigation to person answerable over, §25-2-607(5).
Utilities commission proceedings, §62-73.
Warehouse receipts.
Determination of conflicting claims, §25-7-603.

INTERPRETATION OF REVENUE LAWS.
Secretary of revenue.
Change in interpretation.
Authority of secretary to make, effective date, §105-264(c).
Duty of secretary, §105-264(a).
Local taxes based on state taxes, §105-264.1.

INTERPRETATION OF STATUTES.
Generally, §§12-2 to 12-4.

INTERPRETERS.
Education of children with disabilities.
Interpreters and transliterators for hearing impaired.
Job-related training requirement, §115C-110.2.
Foreign language interpreter appointed by court.
Payment of reasonable fees, §7A-314(f).
Fraud.
Licenses.
Revocation, suspension or denials of licenses, §90D-12.
Grand jury.
Permitted in grand jury room during proceedings, §15A-623(d).
Hearing impaired, interpreters for.
Administrative office of the courts.
Policies and procedures for appointment and payment, §7A-343.
Administrative proceedings.
Appointment if deaf person party or witness before, §8B-2(c).
Appointment.
Compensation, §8B-8.
Waiver of appointed interpreter, §8B-3(a), (b).
Arrest of deaf person.
Arresting officer to procure, §8B-2(d).
Civil, criminal or juvenile proceedings.
Appointment if deaf person party or witness, §8B-2(a).

INTERPRETERS —Cont'd
Hearing impaired, interpreters for —Cont'd
Compensation, fees and expenses.
  Administrative agencies.
    Payment for services before, §8B-8(e).
  City or county administrative proceedings.
    Payment for services, §8B-8(f).
  Civil cases and special proceedings.
    Payment for services, §8B-8(c).
  Criminal and juvenile proceedings.
    Payment for services, §8B-8(b).
  Fixed by appointing authority, §8B-8(a).
  Legislative bodies.
    Payment for services before, §8B-8(d).
  Reasonable fee for services, entitlement,
    included in, §8B-8(a).
  Travel and subsistence expenses, §8B-8(a).
Competence.
  Determination, §8B-1.
Confidentiality.
  Privileged communications, §8B-5.
Coordination of interpreter services, §8B-6.
Definitions, §8B-1.
  Licensure act, §90D-3.
Determination of competence, §8B-1.
Fees.
  Licenses, §90D-10(b).
  Training and licensing preparation program fee,
    §8B-10.
Funds.
  Responsibility for payment to implement
    chapter, §8B-9.
Legislative committees.
  Appointment if deaf person witness before,
    §8B-2(b).
Licensure of interpreters and transliterators
  generally, §§90D-1 to 90D-14.
Lists of interpreters, §8B-6.
Notice.
  Need for interpreter, §8B-4.
Oath, §8B-7.
Parent of juvenile brought before court deaf.
  Appointment for parent, §8B-2(e).
Preliminary determination for appointment,
  §8B-2(f).
Privileged communications, §8B-5.
Proof of deafness, §8B-4.
Removal, §8B-2(g).
Responsibility for payment of funds to implement
  chapter, §8B-9.
Right to interpreter, §8B-1.
Training and licensing preparation program fee,
  §8B-10.
Waiver of appointed interpreter, §8B-3(a), (b).
Injunctions.
Violations of license provisions, §90D-13.
Licenses, §§90D-1 to 90D-14.
Applicability of provisions, §90D-4(b).
Board, §90D-5.
  Civil penalties.
    Schedule of penalties, establishment by board,
      §90D-14(c).
  Compensation, §90D-5(f).
  Costs assessed for disciplinary actions,
    §90D-14(c).
  Creation, §90D-5(a).
  Duties, §90D-6.
  Fees and expenses, §90D-10(a), (b).
  Meetings, §90D-5(h).
  Members, §90D-5(b), (c), (d), (e).
  Officers, §90D-5(g).

INTERPRETERS —Cont'd
Licenses —Cont'd
Board —Cont'd
  Powers, §90D-6.
Civil penalties, §90D-14(a).
  Factors considered, §90D-14(b).
  Schedule of penalties, establishment by board,
    §90D-14(c).
Continuing education.
  Provisional licenses, §90D-8(a).
  Renewals, §90D-11.
Costs assessed for disciplinary actions, §90D-14(c).
Criminal records checks for license applicants,
  §90D-7(c).
Definitions, §90D-3.
Disciplinary actions, §90D-12.
  Costs assessed for disciplinary actions,
    §90D-14(c).
Exemptions, §90D-4(b).
Fees, §90D-10(b).
Injunctions, §90D-13.
Legislative intent, §90D-2.
Nonresidents.
  Reciprocity, §90D-9(a), (b).
Provisional licenses, §90D-8(a), (a1), (b), (c).
Purpose of act, §90D-2.
Qualifications, §90D-7(a), (b).
  Provisional licenses, §90D-8(a), (a1), (c).
Reciprocity, §90D-9(a), (b).
Renewals, §90D-11.
  Provisional licenses, §90D-8(b).
Required, §90D-4(a).
Revocation, suspension or denials of licenses,
  §90D-12.
Short title, §90D-1.
Titles, use of, §90D-4(a).
Violations of provisions, §90D-12.
  Civil penalties, §90D-14(a).
    Factors considered, §90D-14(b).
    Schedule of penalties, establishment by board,
      §90D-14(c).
  Costs assessed for disciplinary actions,
    §90D-14(c).
  Injunctions, §90D-13.
Reciprocity.
Licenses, §90D-9(a), (b).
Special education.
Education of children with disabilities.
  Interpreters and transliterators for hearing
    impaired.
    Job-related training requirement,
      §115C-110.2.
Witnesses.
Deaf and hearing-impaired interpreters.
  Policies and procedures for appointment and
    payment, §7A-343.
Foreign language interpreters.
  Policies and procedures for appointment and
    payment, §§7A-314(f), 7A-343.
Subject to provisions relating to qualifications as
  expert, §8C-1 Rule 604.

INTERRACIAL MARRIAGES.
Validated, §51-3.1.

INTERROGATION OF DELINQUENT OR
  UNDISCIPLINED JUVENILE.
Procedures generally, §7B-2101.

INTERROGATION OF WITNESSES.
Interrogation by court, §8C-1 Rule 614.
Leading questions, §8C-1 Rule 611(c).

INTERROGATION OF WITNESSES —Cont'd
Procedure, §8C-1 Rule 611(a).
Scope of cross-examination, §8C-1 Rule 611.

INTERROGATORIES.
Answers, §1A-1 Rule 33(a).
Availability, §1A-1 Rule 33(a).
Limited liability companies.
Interrogatories by secretary of state, §§57C-1-31 to 57C-1-33.
Assets of judgment debtor, discovery, §1-352.1.
Business records.
Option to produce, §1A-1 Rule 33(c).
Civil investigative demand.
Medical assistance provider false claim, §108A-70.14.
Corporations.
Business corporations.
Secretary of state, §§55-1-31 to 55-1-33.
Depositions.
See DEPOSITIONS.
Discovery.
See DISCOVERY.
Discovery methods, §1A-1 Rule 26(a).
Discovery of assets of judgment debtor, §1-352.1.
Executions.
Discovery of assets of judgment debtor, §1-352.1.
Expedited evictions.
Time for response, §42-70(d).
Failure to serve answers to interrogatories, §1A-1 Rule 37(d).
Larceny.
Mutilation, larceny or destruction of public records and papers, §14-76.
Limited liability companies.
Interrogatories by secretary of state, §§57C-1-31 to 57C-1-33.
Medical assistance provider false claim.
Civil investigative demand, §108A-70.14.
Medical malpractice.
Arbitration of negligent health claims, §90-21.63(c).
Nonprofit corporations.
Failure to answer, §55A-1-32.
Information disclosed by.
Confidentiality, §55A-1-33.
Secretary of state, §55A-1-31.
Procedure, §1A-1 Rule 33(a).
Scope, §1A-1 Rule 33(b).
Secretary of state.
Interrogatories to limited liability companies, §§57C-1-31 to 57C-1-33.
Nonprofit corporations, §55A-1-31.
Summary judgment.
Affidavit supplemented or opposed by answers to, §1A-1 Rule 56(e).
Supplemental proceedings.
Discovery of assets of judgment debtor, §1-352.1.
Use at trial, §1A-1 Rule 33(b).
Workers' compensation.
Industrial commission.
Power to limit, §97-80(f).

INTERSECTIONS.
Authority of local officials to regulate turning, §20-153(c).
Blind pedestrians, §20-175.1.
Defined, §§20-4.01, 20-150(c).
Failure to stop and yield right of way, §20-158(b).

INTERSECTIONS —Cont'd
Lanes.
Keeping to right in crossing intersections or railroads, §20-147.
Left turns, §§20-153(b), 20-155.
Modification of method of turning, §20-153(c).
Motorcycles.
Failure to stop and yield at traffic light.
Defense, §20-158(e).
Overtaking and passing.
Limitations on privilege, §20-150(c).
Parking near, §20-162(a).
Pedestrians.
Right of way, failure to yield, §20-158(b).
Power outage or other malfunction.
Traffic signal not illuminated due to.
Rules for proceeding through intersection, §20-158(b).
Railroad intersections.
Automatic signals at railroad intersections.
Commission may require, §136-20.1(b).
Grade crossings generally.
See RAILROAD GRADE CROSSINGS.
Highways.
Intersection with, §136-191.
Powers of railroad corporations, §136-190.
Powers of railroad corporations, §136-190.
Red lights, §20-158(b).
Right of way, §20-155(a).
Stop signs and traffic lights, §20-158(b).
Yield signs, §20-158.1.
Right side of highway.
Vehicle crossing intersection to keep to, §20-147.
Right turns, §20-153(a).
Modification of method of turning, §20-153(c).
Right turn on red, §20-158(b).
Stop lights, §20-158.
Stopping.
Certain highways, §20-158.
Traffic obstructed, §20-142.5.
Stop signs and traffic lights.
Right of way, §20-158(a), (b).
Walk or don't walk traffic-control signals or devices, §20-172(a), (b).

INTER-SPOUSAL IMMUNITY.
Abolished, §52-5.1.
Tort action arising out of acts occurring outside state, §52-5.1.

INTERSTATE AGREEMENT ON DETAINERS, §§15A-761 to 15A-767.
Appropriate court.
Defined, §15A-762.
Cooperation in enforcement, §15A-763.
Designation of enforcement officers, §15A-766.
Distribution of copies of provisions, §15A-767.
Escape from temporary custody, §15A-764.
Text of agreement, §15A-761.
Warden's, etc., duties, §15A-765.

INTERSTATE AGREEMENT ON QUALIFICATIONS OF EDUCATIONAL PERSONNEL, §§115C-349 to 115C-358.
See SCHOOL EMPLOYEES.

INTERSTATE BRANCH BANKING.
Generally, §§53-224.9 to 53-224.31.
See BRANCH BANKS.
Savings and loan associations.
Out-of-state branch offices, §§54B-265 to 54B-278.
See SAVINGS AND LOAN ASSOCIATIONS.

INTERSTATE BRANCH BANKING —Cont'd
Savings banks.
  Out-of-state branch banks, §§54C-199 to 54C-212.
    See SAVINGS BANKS.

INTERSTATE COMMERCE.
Congress, US Const Art I §§8, 9.
Constitution of the United States, US Const Art
  I §§8, 9.
Earnings of employees in interstate commerce.
  Collections out of state to avoid exemptions.
    Abetting.
      Resident not to abet collection out of state,
        §95-74.
    Actions.
      Institution of foreign suit as evidence of
        intent to violate, §95-76.
    Construction and interpretation, §95-77.
    Evidence of intent to violate provisions, §95-76.
    Penalties for violations, §95-75.
    Prohibited, §95-73.
    Remedies for violations, §95-75.
    Resident not to abet collection out of state,
      §95-74.
Limited liability companies.
  Applicability of provisions to, §57C-10-02.
Occupational safety and health.
  Standards not to unduly burden interstate
    commerce, §95-131(e).
Public utilities.
  Separation or allocation of revenue and costs of.
    Commission may require, §62-35(b).
Sales and use tax.
  Refunds, §105-164.14(a).
    Economic incentive refunds, §105-164.14A(a).

INTERSTATE COMPACT FOR ADULT
  OFFENDER SUPERVISION, §§148-65.4 to
  148-65.9.
Citation, §148-65.4.
Compact administrator.
  Appointment, §148-65.6(a1).
Form, §148-65.5.
Governor.
  Appointment of compact administrator,
    §148-65.6(a1).
  Execution of compact, §148-65.5.
  Executive orders for implementation, §148-65.6(f).
Hearings on interstate parole and probation,
    §148-65.8(a), (b).
  Alleged parole or probation violations,
    §148-65.8(d).
  Records, §148-65.8(c1).
  Rights of offender, §148-65.8(c).
Interstate compact fund, §148-65.7(a).
Sentences.
  North Carolina sentence to be served in other
    jurisdiction, §148-65.9.
Short title, §148-65.4.
State council for interstate adult offender
  supervision.
  Established, §148-65.6(a).
  Meetings, §148-65.6(b).
  Members, §148-65.6(a), (d).
  Powers and duties, §148-65.6(c), (e).
Supervision fee, §148-65.7(b).
Text, §148-65.5.
Transfer application fee, §148-65.7(a).

INTERSTATE COMPACT FOR JUVENILES,
    §§7B-4000 to 7B-4002.
Article cited as, §7B-4000.

INTERSTATE COMPACT FOR JUVENILES
  —Cont'd
Citation of article, §7B-4000.
Dispute resolution, §7B-4001.
Dissolution, §7B-4001.
Execution.
  Governor authorized and directed, §7B-4001.
Implementation.
  Governor to provide for by executive order,
    §7B-4002(f).
Interstate commission for juveniles, §7B-4001.
North Carolina state council for interstate
  juvenile supervision, §7B-4002(a) to (e).
Purpose and policy of compacting states,
    §7B-4001.
Withdrawal, default, termination, judicial
  enforcement, §7B-4001.

INTERSTATE COMPACT ON EDUCATIONAL
  OPPORTUNITY FOR MILITARY
  CHILDREN, §§115C-407.5 to 115C-407.8.

INTERSTATE COMPACT ON JUVENILES,
    §§7B-2800 to 7B-2827.
Absconders.
  Out-of-state confinement amendment, §7B-2827.
  Return, §7B-2805.
    Voluntary return procedure, §7B-2806.
Administrators.
  Authority to enter into supplementary agreement,
    §7B-2817.
  Designation by governor, §§7B-2812, 7B-2816.
  Discharging financial obligations imposed,
    §7B-2818.
  Hearings before, §7B-2823.
Amendment to compact concerning interstate
  rendition of juveniles alleged to be
  delinquent.
  Additional remedies and binding between party
    states, §7B-2826(a).
  Construction of provisions, §7B-2826(b).
  Petition, §7B-2826(b).
  Requisition, §7B-2826(b).
Binding upon executing state until renounced,
    §7B-2814.
Confinement of probationers or parolees,
  escapees or absconders.
  Out-of-state confinement amendment, §7B-2827.
Cooperative care, treatment and rehabilitation
  of delinquents.
  Supplementary agreement, §7B-2810.
Cost, payment of, §7B-2808(a).
  Asserting right against person, agency or other
    entity, §7B-2808(b).
Court defined, §7B-2803.
Definitions, §7B-2803.
  Juvenile.
    Return of runaways, §7B-2804(c).
  Sending state.
    Out-of-state confinement amendment, §7B-2827.
Delinquent juvenile defined, §7B-2803.
Detention practices, §7B-2809.
Donations, gifts and grants, acceptance by
  party state, §7B-2811.
Due process at parole or probation violation
  hearing, §7B-2824.
Effectuation of purposes and intent,
  enforcement generally, §7B-2819.
Enforcement of compact, §7B-2819.
Escapees.
  Out-of-state confinement amendment, §7B-2827.
  Return, §7B-2805.

INTERSTATE COMPACT ON JUVENILES
—Cont'd
Execution of compact on behalf of state.
Governor authorized and directed to execute,
§7B-2800.
Federal and other aid, acceptance, §7B-2811.
Financial obligations imposed, discharging,
§7B-2818.
Findings, §7B-2801.
Full force and effect of law within state,
§7B-2813.
**Governor authorized and directed to execute
compact,** §7B-2800.
**Governors of party states to designate
administrators,** §§7B-2812, 7B-2816.
Hearing officers, §7B-2823.
Hearing on return of runaways, §7B-2821.
**Hearing procedures for parolees or
probationers,** §7B-2822.
**Interstate rendition of juveniles alleged to be
delinquent.**
Amendment of compact binding on party states,
§7B-2826(a).
Construction of provisions and procedures,
petition, requisition, §7B-2826(b).
Jails, juvenile not to be placed or detained in,
§7B-2809.
**Lockups, juvenile not to be placed or detained
in,** §7B-2809.
Notice of renunciation, §7B-2814.
Operative immediately upon execution,
§7B-2813.
Out-of-state confinement amendment,
§7B-2827(a), (b).
Confinement or ordering confinement of
delinquent juvenile in compact institution,
§7B-2827.
**Parental rights and responsibilities, compact
not in derogation of,** §7B-2802.
Parole and probation hearing procedures,
§7B-2822.
Parole or probation violation hearings.
Due process rights, §7B-2824.
Effect of hearing outside state, §7B-2825.
Payment of cost, responsibility, §7B-2808(a).
Asserting right against person, agency or other
entity, §7B-2808(b).
**Petition appropriate court in demanding state
for issuance of requisition.**
Return of runaways, §7B-2804(a).
Policy of states party to compact, §7B-2801.
Prisons.
Juvenile not to be placed or detained in,
§7B-2809.
**Probationer or parolee residing in receiving
state,** §7B-2807(a), (b).
Officers of sending state entering receiving state
and apprehending and retaking juvenile,
§7B-2807(c).
Transporting juvenile to sending state, payment of
cost, §7B-2807(d).
Visitation and supervision duties.
Exercise by receiving state, §7B-2807(a), (b).
Probationers or parolees, confinement.
Out-of-state confinement amendment, §7B-2827.
Probation or parole defined, §7B-2803.
Provisions severable, §7B-2815.
Purposes, §7B-2801.
**Reasonable and liberal construction of
compact,** §7B-2801.

INTERSTATE COMPACT ON JUVENILES
—Cont'd
**Remedies and procedures in addition to and
not in substitution for other rights,
remedies and procedures,** §7B-2802.
Renunciation of compact, §7B-2814.
Requisition.
Return of runaways, §7B-2804(a).
Residence defined, §7B-2803.
Return of escapees or absconders.
Counsel or guardian ad litem, appointment,
§7B-2805(c).
Detention order, §7B-2805(a).
Requisition for return, §7B-2805(a).
Taking juvenile into custody without requisition,
§7B-2804(a).
Transportation cost, responsibility for payment,
§7B-2805(b).
Voluntary return procedure, §7B-2806.
Return of runaways.
Additional procedures not precluded, §7B-2820.
Detention order, §7B-2804(a).
Hearing on petition, §7B-2804(a).
Hearing to determine whether petitioner entitled
to legal custody, §7B-2821.
Juvenile defined, §7B-2804(c).
Period of time for holding juvenile in custody,
§7B-2821.
Petitioning appropriate court in demanding state
for requisition, §7B-2804(a).
Procedures for return, §7B-2821.
Requisition, §7B-2804(a).
Taking juvenile into custody without requisition,
§7B-2804(a).
Testing legality of proceedings, §7B-2821.
Transportation cost, responsibility for payment,
§7B-2804(b).
Runaways.
Return, §7B-2804.
Additional procedures not precluded, §7B-2820.
Proceedings for return, §7B-2821.
Severability of provisions, §7B-2815.
State defined, §7B-2803.
Supplementary agreement, §7B-2810.
Authority of compact administrator, §7B-2817.
Time for sending notice of renunciation,
§7B-2814.
Voluntary return procedure, §7B-2806.

**INTERSTATE COMPACT ON THE
PLACEMENT OF CHILDREN,** §§7B-3800 to
7B-3806.
See CHILD PLACEMENT.

INTERSTATE COMPACTS.
Adoption.
Interstate compact on adoption and medical
assistance, §§7B-3900 to 7B-3906.
See ADOPTION.
**Atlantic States Marine Fisheries Compact and
Commission,** §§113-251 to 113-258.
Child placement.
Interstate compact on the placement of children,
§§7B-3800 to 7B-3806.
Constitution of the United States.
Between state and foreign power, US Const Art I
§10.
Between the states, US Const Art I §10.
Corrections compact, §§148-119 to 148-121.
Detainers.
Interstate agreement on detainers, §§15A-761 to
15A-767.
See INTERSTATE AGREEMENT ON
DETAINERS.

INTERSTATE COMPACTS —Cont'd

Driver's license compact, §§20-4.21 to 20-4.30.
See DRIVER'S LICENSE COMPACT.

Education.
Interstate compact on education, §115C-104.
Interstate compact on educational opportunity for military children, §§115C-407.5 to 115C-407.8.

Educational personnel.
Interstate agreement on qualifications, §§115C-349 to 115C-358.
See SCHOOL EMPLOYEES.

Emergency management assistance compact, §§166A-40 to 166A-53.

Environmental compact, §§113A-21 to 113A-23.

Forest fire protection.
Southeastern interstate forest fire protection compact, §§106-930 to 106-933.

High-speed rail transportation.
Virginia-North Carolina interstate high-speed rail compact, §§136-220 to 136-222.

Hunting and wildlife.
Interstate wildlife violator compact, §§113-300.5 to 113-300.8.

Insurance product regulation, §§58-91-1 to 58-91-80.
See INTERSTATE INSURANCE PRODUCT REGULATION COMPACT.

Juveniles.
Interstate compact for juveniles, §§7B-4000 to 7B-4002.
Interstate compact on juveniles, §§7B-2800 to 7B-2827.
See INTERSTATE COMPACT ON JUVENILES.

Libraries.
Interstate library compact, §§125-12 to 125-17.

Marine fisheries compact, §§113-251 to 113-258.

Mental health.
Interstate compact on mental health, §§122C-361 to 122C-366.

Mines and minerals.
Interstate mining compact, §§74-37, 74-38.

Motor vehicles.
Driver's license compact, §§20-4.21 to 20-4.30.
See DRIVER'S LICENSE COMPACT.
Vehicle equipment safety compact, §§20-183.13 to 20-183.21.
See MOTOR VEHICLE EQUIPMENT.

National crime prevention and privacy compact, §114-19.50.

National guard.
Mutual assistance compact, §§127A-175 to 127A-184.
See NATIONAL GUARD.

Nurse licensure compact, §§90-171.80 to 90-171.94.
See NURSE LICENSURE COMPACT.

Parole.
Interstate compact for adult offender supervision, §§148-65.4 to 148-65.9.
See INTERSTATE COMPACT FOR ADULT OFFENDER SUPERVISION.

Pest control compact, §§106-65.55 to 106-65.61.

Placement of children.
Interstate compact, §§7B-3800 to 7B-3806.

Probation.
Interstate compact for adult offender supervision, §§148-65.4 to 148-65.9.
See INTERSTATE COMPACT FOR ADULT OFFENDER SUPERVISION.

Southeastern interstate forest fire protection compact, §§106-930 to 106-933.

INTERSTATE COMPACTS —Cont'd

Southern dairy compact, §§106-810, 106-811.

Southern growth policies agreement, §§143-490 to 143-506.
See SOUTHERN GROWTH POLICIES AGREEMENT.

Southern states energy compact, §§104D-1 to 104D-5.

Vehicle equipment safety compact, §§20-183.13 to 20-183.21.
See MOTOR VEHICLE EQUIPMENT.

INTERSTATE DEPOSITIONS AND DISCOVERY, §§1F-1 to 1F-7.
See DEPOSITIONS.

INTERSTATE FAMILY SUPPORT, §§52C-1-100 to 52C-9-902.

Actions.
Minor parent, §52C-3-302.

Act or similar law not enacted by responding state.
State tribunal may make findings required by law of responding state, §52C-3-304(b).

Additional nature of remedies, §52C-1-103.

Application of provisions, §§52C-3-301(a), 52C-9-901.
Law of this state, §52C-3-303.
Severability, §52C-9-902.

Attorney-client relationship.
Support enforcement agency, §52C-3-307(c).

Attorneys' fees, §52C-3-312(b).

Bases for jurisdiction over nonresident, §52C-2-201.

Child.
Defined, §52C-1-101.

Child support orders generally. See within this heading, "Support orders."

Child support payments.
Certified copies.
Admissibility as evidence, §52C-3-315(c).

Choice of law, §52C-6-604.

Commencement of proceedings, §52C-3-301(c).

Communications between tribunals, §52C-3-316.

Confidentiality, §52C-3-311.

Confirmed orders, §52C-6-608.

Conflict of laws.
Act or similar law not enacted by responding state.
State tribunal may make findings required by law of responding state, §52C-3-304(b).

Contesting validity of orders, §52C-6-606.

Continuing, exclusive jurisdiction, §52C-2-205(f).
Enforcement powers, §52C-2-205(c).
Exercise of jurisdiction, §52C-2-205(a).
Initiating tribunal, §52C-2-206(a).
Modification of child support order of another state, §§52C-2-205(f), 52C-6-611(d).
No continuing, exclusive jurisdiction, §52C-2-206(c).
No exercise of jurisdiction, §52C-2-205(b).
Recognizing jurisdiction of another state, §52C-2-205(d).
Responding tribunal, §52C-2-206(b).
Spousal support orders, §52C-2-205.
Temporary support orders, §52C-2-205(e).

Controlling order.
Two or more orders issued, §52C-2-207.

Costs, §52C-3-312.
Prevailing party, §52C-3-312(b).

INTERSTATE FAMILY SUPPORT —Cont'd
Credit for payments, §52C-2-209.
Cumulative nature of remedies, §52C-1-103.
Defenses.
  Nonparentage, §52C-3-314.
Definitions, §52C-1-101.
Delay tactics.
  Costs and fees imposed, §52C-3-312(c).
Disbursement of payments, §52C-3-318.
Discovery.
  Tribunal requesting assistance with, §52C-3-317.
District attorney.
  Representation of obligee, §52C-3-308.
District court jurisdiction, §52C-1-102.
Due process.
  Issuance of support orders, §52C-4-401.
Duty of support.
  Defined, §52C-1-101.
Enumeration of proceedings, §52C-3-301(b).
Evidence.
  Special rules of evidence and procedure,
    §52C-3-315.
Exclusive jurisdiction, §52C-2-205.
Exemptions.
  Limited immunity of petitioner, §52C-3-313(c).
Extradition.
  Conditions of rendition, §52C-8-802.
  Grounds for rendition, §52C-8-801.
Fax.
  Admissibility as evidence, §52C-3-315(e).
Fees, §52C-3-312.
Filing fee, §52C-3-312(a).
Governor.
  Defined, §52C-8-801(a).
Health care bills.
  Admissibility as evidence, §52C-3-315(d).
Home state.
  Defined, §52C-1-101.
Husband-wife privilege, §52C-3-315(h), (i).
Immunity, §52C-3-315(i).
Inappropriate tribunal, §52C-3-306.
Income.
  Defined, §52C-1-101.
Income-withholding orders of another state.
  Administrative enforcement.
    Sending documents to be registered to state
      support enforcement agency, §52C-5-507(a).
    Enforcement of order by agency,
      §52C-5-507(b).
  Compliance with law of obligor's principal place of
    employment.
    Duty of employer, §52C-5-502(d).
  Compliance with terms of order.
    Employer to withhold and distribute funds,
      §52C-5-502(c).
  Contest of validity or enforcement by obligor,
    §52C-5-506(a).
    Notice of contest, obligor to give, §52C-5-506(b).
  Copy of order supplied obligor.
    Duty of employer on receiving order,
      §52C-5-502(a).
  Defined, §52C-1-101.
  Effect of registration for enforcement, §52C-6-603.
  Employment security division.
    Sending order to, obligor receiving
      unemployment compensation,
      §52C-5-501(a).
  Immunity of employer complying with order,
    §52C-5-504.
  Multiple orders, compliance with, §52C-5-503.
  Notice of registration of order, §52C-6-605.

INTERSTATE FAMILY SUPPORT —Cont'd
Income-withholding orders of another state
    —Cont'd
  Penalties for noncompliance, §52C-5-505.
  Procedure to register for enforcement, §52C-6-602.
  Registration for enforcement, §52C-6-601.
  Sending to obligor's employer.
    Filing petition, pleading or registering not
      required, §52C-5-501(a).
  Treating order as if issued by court of this state.
    Duty of employer receiving order, §52C-5-502(b).
Inference affect.
  Refusal to answer on grounds of
    self-incrimination, §52C-3-315(g).
Initiating state.
  Defined, §52C-1-101.
Initiating tribunal.
  Act or similar law not enacted by responding
    state.
    Issuance of certificate and findings required by
      law of responding state, §52C-3-304(b).
  Authority to act as, §52C-2-203.
  Defined, §52C-1-101.
  Enforcement and modification of support order,
    §52C-2-206(a).
  Forwarding copies of petition and other
    documents.
    Duty, §52C-3-304(a).
  Proceeding to determine parentage, §52C-7-701(a).
  Responding tribunal.
    Proceeding to determine parentage,
      §52C-7-701(a), (b).
Interstate rendition, §§52C-8-801, 52C-8-802.
Issuing state.
  Defined, §52C-1-101.
  Governing law, §52C-6-604(a).
Issuing tribunal.
  Defined, §52C-1-101.
Jurisdiction.
  Extended personal jurisdiction, §52C-2-201.
  Generally, §52C-1-102.
  Limited immunity of petitioner, §52C-3-313(a).
  Simultaneous proceedings in another state,
    §52C-2-204(a).
    No jurisdiction exercised, §52C-2-204(b).
Law.
  Defined, §52C-1-101.
Limitation of actions.
  Proceeding for arrears, §52C-6-604(b).
Mail.
  Duties and powers of responding tribunal,
    §52C-3-305(a), (e).
  Inappropriate tribunal, §52C-3-306.
  Registered orders.
    Contesting validity or enforcement,
      §52C-6-606(c).
Minor parents.
  Actions by, §52C-3-302.
Modification of orders, §52C-6-609.
  Effect of registration for modification, §52C-6-610.
  Orders of another state.
    Continuing, exclusive jurisdiction,
      §§52C-2-205(f), 52C-6-611(d).
    Filing of certified copy, §52C-6-611(e).
    Non-modifiable orders, §52C-6-611(c).
    Notice to issuing tribunal, §52C-6-614.
    Recognition of order modified in another state,
      §52C-6-612.
    Requirements, procedures and defenses,
      §52C-6-611(b).
    Responding tribunal, §52C-6-611(a).

INTERSTATE FAMILY SUPPORT —Cont'd
Modification of support orders.
Orders of another state.
Jurisdiction of state tribunal, parties residing in state, §52C-6-613(a).
Provision of act, procedure and substantive law of state, applicability, §52C-6-613(b).
Multiple child support orders.
Two or more obligees, §52C-2-208.
Nondisclosure of information, §52C-3-311.
Nonparentage.
Defenses, §52C-3-314.
Nonresidents.
Bases for jurisdiction over, §52C-2-201.
Procedure when exercising jurisdiction over, §52C-2-202.
Notice.
Income-withholding order from another state.
Contest by obligor, §52C-5-506(b).
Issuance of support orders, §52C-4-401(c).
Modification of orders of another state.
Notice to issuing tribunal, §52C-6-614.
Order issued in another state, §52C-6-605(a).
Contents of notice, §52C-6-605(b).
Registration of order, §52C-6-605(c).
Obligee.
Defined, §52C-1-101.
Obligor.
Defined, §52C-1-101.
Parentage bills.
Admissibility as evidence, §52C-3-315(d).
Parentage proceedings, §52C-7-701.
Parent and child defense of immunity,
§52C-3-315(i).
Paternity.
Choice of law, §52C-7-701(b).
Initiating or responding tribunal, §52C-7-701(a).
Nonparentage as defense, §52C-3-314.
Proceeding to determine parentage, §52C-7-701.
Payments.
Credit for payments, §52C-2-209.
Receipt and disbursement, §52C-3-318.
Petitions.
Copies forwarded by state tribunal, §52C-3-304(a).
Establishing support order, §52C-4-401.
Registration, §52C-6-602(c).
Requirements, §52C-3-310(b).
Verification, §52C-3-310(a).
Admissibility as evidence, §52C-3-315(b).
Photocopies.
Admissibility as evidence, §52C-3-315(e).
Physical presence of petitioner.
Special rules of evidence and procedure, §52C-3-315(a).
Pleadings and accompanying documents,
§52C-3-310.
Privileged communications.
Husband and wife, §52C-3-315(h).
Procedure.
Special rules of evidence and procedure, §52C-3-315.
Procedure to register.
Orders of another state.
Modification of orders, §52C-6-609.
Procedure when exercising jurisdiction over
nonresident, §52C-2-202.
Proceedings under this chapter.
Commencement of proceedings, §52C-3-301(c).
Enumeration, §52C-3-301(b).
Receipt and disbursements of payments,
§52C-3-318.

INTERSTATE FAMILY SUPPORT —Cont'd
Recognition of order modified in another state,
§52C-6-612.
Recognition of support orders.
Continuing, exclusive jurisdiction, tribunal with, §52C-2-207(d).
Only one tribunal issuing order, §52C-2-207(a).
Two or more orders issued.
Determining which order to recognize.
Basis for determination stated in order, §52C-2-207(e).
Certified copy of order, filing by party obtaining, §52C-2-207(f).
Rules, §52C-2-207(b).
Request by resident obligee for state tribunal to determine, §52C-2-207(c).
Register.
Defined, §52C-1-101.
Registering tribunal.
Defined, §52C-1-101.
Registration of orders, §52C-6-601.
Confirmed order, §52C-6-608.
Contesting validity or enforcement, §52C-6-606.
Burden of proof, §52C-6-607(a).
Confirmation of order, §52C-6-607(c).
Defenses, §52C-6-607(b).
Failure to contest in timely manner, §52C-6-606(b).
Hearing, §52C-6-606(a), (c).
Effect of registration for enforcement, §52C-6-603.
Effect of registration for modification, §52C-6-610.
Generally, §52C-6-601.
Issued in another state, §52C-6-603(a).
Enforceability of order, §52C-6-603(b).
Modification, §52C-6-603(c).
Notice of registration order, §52C-6-605.
Petition to establish, §52C-4-401.
Procedure to register for enforcement, §52C-6-602.
Recognition of order modified in another state, §52C-6-612.
Registration of order of another state for modification, §52C-6-609.
Rendition.
Child support proceedings, §52C-8-802(a), (b).
Decline to honor demand, §52C-8-802(c).
Delay of proceedings, §52C-8-802(b).
Demand by governor, §52C-8-801(b).
Applicability of demand, §52C-8-801(c).
Demand of governor.
Decline to honor demand, §52C-8-802(c).
Governor.
Defined, §52C-8-801(a).
Representation of obligee, §52C-3-308.
Responding state.
Defined, §52C-1-101.
Responding tribunal.
Application of law of this state, §52C-3-303.
Authority to act as, §52C-2-203.
Calculations on which support order is based, §52C-3-305(c).
Conditioning payment of support order, §52C-3-305(d).
Defined, §52C-1-101.
Enforcement and modification of support order, §52C-2-206(b).
Filing of papers, §52C-3-305(a).
Forwarding of papers from inappropriate tribunal, §52C-3-306.
Issuance of support order, §52C-4-401(a).
Mailing of copies of order, §52C-3-305(e).

INTERSTATE FAMILY SUPPORT —Cont'd
Responding tribunal —Cont'd
Modification of child support order of another
state, §52C-6-611(a).
Powers and duties, §52C-3-305(b).
Self-incrimination.
Refusal to answer on grounds of, §52C-3-315(g).
Service of process.
Limited immunity of petitioner, §52C-3-313(b).
Severability, §52C-9-902.
Short title, §52C-1-100.
Simultaneous proceedings in another state,
§52C-2-204.
Spousal-support order.
Defined, §52C-1-101.
State.
Defined, §52C-1-101.
State information agency.
Department of health and human services.
Division of social services, §52C-3-309(a).
Powers and duties, §52C-3-309(b).
Statute of limitations.
Proceeding for arrears, §52C-6-604(b).
Support enforcement agency.
Defined, §52C-1-101.
Fiduciary relationships, §52C-3-307(c).
Provision of services, §52C-3-307(a).
Enumeration of services, §52C-3-307(b).
Support orders.
Defined, §52C-1-101.
Registration.
Filing of documents, §52C-6-602(b).
Pleadings and petitions, §52C-6-602(c).
Procedure to register, §52C-6-602(a).
Telephone conversation.
Testimony or deposition by telephone,
§52C-3-315(f).
Transmission of documentary evidence,
§52C-3-315(e).
Temporary child support order, §52C-4-401(b).
Title of provisions, §52C-1-100.
Transmitted documents from another state.
Admissibility as evidence, §52C-3-315(e).
Tribunal.
Communications between, §52C-3-316.
Defined, §52C-1-101.
Two or more obligees.
Multiple child support orders, §52C-2-208.
Two or more orders issued.
Controlling order, identifying, §52C-2-207.
Uniformity of application and construction,
§52C-9-901.
Verification of petition, §§52C-3-310(a),
52C-3-315(b).
Videotape.
Testimony or deposition of witness, §52C-3-315(f).

INTERSTATE HIGHWAYS.
Litter enforcement signs.
Placement, §136-32.3.
Maximum speed vehicle to be operated,
§20-141(d).
Minimum speed vehicle to be operated,
§20-141(c).
Tandem trailers and semitrailers.
Operated on, §20-115.1.
Tolling.
General power of turnpike authority,
§136-89.198(a).
Severability of provision, §136-89.198(c).
Toll location, §136-89.198(b).

INTERSTATE HIGHWAYS —Cont'd
Tolling —Cont'd
Use of revenue collected, §136-89.198(a).
**Unlawful use of national system of interstate
and defense highways,** §20-140.3.

**INTERSTATE INSURANCE PRODUCT
REGULATION COMPACT,** §§58-91-1 to
58-91-80.
Amendments, §58-91-65(c).
Binding effect, §58-91-80(b).
Commission, §58-91-15(b).
Advisory committees, §58-91-25(c).
Bylaws prescribed, §58-91-25(a).
Defense of members, §58-91-25(e).
Dispute resolution, §58-91-45.
Establishment, §58-91-15(a).
Finance, §58-91-60(a) to (g).
Immunity, §58-91-25(e).
Indemnification, §58-91-25(e).
Interpretation of actions, advisory opinions,
§58-91-80(b).
Legislative committee, §58-91-25(c).
Liabilities, §58-91-15(c).
Management committee, §58-91-25(b).
Powers and duties, §58-91-25(b1).
Meetings, §58-91-30(a), (c).
Membership, §58-91-25(a).
Powers, §58-91-20.
Records, §§58-91-25(d), 58-91-40(a), (b).
Rulemaking.
Authority, §§58-91-20, 58-91-35(a).
Records, §58-91-40(a).
Review of product approval decisions,
§58-91-55.
Date effective, §58-91-35(c).
Procedure, §58-91-35(b).
Product filing and approval, §58-91-50(b).
Venue for actions involving, §58-91-15(d).
Voting, §§58-91-25(a), 58-91-30(b).
Compacting states, generally, §58-91-65(a).
Compliance, §58-91-40(c).
Constitutional violations, effect of provisions,
§58-91-80(b).
Construction and interpretation.
Liberal construction, §58-91-75(b).
Severability, §58-91-75(a).
Date effective, §58-91-65(b).
Default, §58-91-70(b).
Definitions, §58-91-10.
Opt out, §58-91-35(c).
Dispute resolution, §58-91-45.
Dissolution, §58-91-70(c).
Effect on enforcement of other laws,
§58-91-80(a).
Enforcement, §58-91-40(d).
Finance.
Accounts, §58-91-60(f).
Budget, §58-91-60(c).
Credit pledge, §58-91-60(e).
Establishment and organization of committee,
§58-91-60(a).
Filing fees, §58-91-60(b).
Property interests, §58-91-60(g).
Taxation, §58-91-60(d).
**Judicial review of rules or operating
procedures,** §58-91-35(g).
Legislative intent, §58-91-1.
Product filing and approval, §58-91-50(a).
Continuing supervision after approval,
§58-91-55(b).

INTERSTATE INSURANCE PRODUCT REGULATION COMPACT —Cont'd
Product filing and approval —Cont'd
Effect of approval, §58-91-50(c).
Fees, §58-91-60(b).
Review of disapproval, §58-91-55(a).
Purposes, §58-91-5.
Reinstatement, §58-91-70(a), (b).
Termination, §58-91-70(b).
Uniform standards.
Opt out, §58-91-35(c).
Effect, §58-91-35(e).
Procedure, §58-91-35(d).
Stay, §58-91-35(f).
Withdrawal, §58-91-70(a).

INTERSTATE LAW FIRMS.
Interstate and international law firm registration, Bar Rules E.0201 to E.0206.
Registration, Bar Rules E.0201 to E.0206.

INTERSTATE RECIPROCITY IN INSURANCE PRODUCER LICENSING, §58-33-32.

INTERSTATE SAVINGS AND LOAN BRANCH ASSOCIATIONS.
Out-of-state branch offices, §§54B-265 to 54B-278.
See SAVINGS AND LOAN ASSOCIATIONS.

INTERSTATE SAVINGS BRANCH BANKS.
Out-of-state branch offices, §§54C-199 to 54C-212.
See SAVINGS BANKS.

INTERSTATE WILDLIFE VIOLATOR COMPACT, §§113-300.5 to 113-300.8.

INTERVAL OWNERSHIP.
Time shares, §§93A-39 to 93A-59.
See TIME SHARES.

INTERVENTION.
As of right, §1A-1 Rule 24(a).
Attachment.
Third persons claiming attached property, §1-440.43.
Delivery of property to intervener, §1-483.
Municipal planning and regulation of development.
Zoning appeals, certiorari to superior court, §160A-393(h).
Of right, §1A-1 Rule 24(a).
Property claimed by third person, §1-482.
Termination of parental rights proceedings.
Who may intervene, §7B-1103(b).
Utilities commission proceedings.
Persons authorized to file complaint, §62-73.

INTER VIVOS GIFTS.
Intestate succession.
Presumed.
Absolute gift and not advancement, §29-24.

INTER VIVOS TRUSTS.
Community property rights at death.
Defection of title of surviving spouse, §31C-4.
Renunciation of succession by beneficiary, §31B-1.

INTESTATE SUCCESSION.
Adopted children.
Adoptive parents and heirs of adoptive parents.
Succession from adopted children, §29-17(c).
Natural parents and heirs of natural parents, §29-17(b).
Succession from adopted children, §29-17(d).

INTESTATE SUCCESSION —Cont'd
Adopted children —Cont'd
Succession by, through and from adopted children, §29-17(a).
When adopted child considered child of natural parents for purposes of intestate succession, §29-17(e).
Adoption.
Inheritance rights of child subject to adoption.
Consequences of consent by parent to adoption, §48-3-607(c).
Advancements.
Death of advancee before intestate donor, §29-27.
Defined, §29-2.
Effect, §29-25.
Generally, §29-23.
Gift inter vivos.
Presumption of gift, §29-24.
Inventory.
Failure to give inventory, §29-28.
Release by advancee, §29-29.
Taking into account and computation of estate, §29-23.
Valuation.
Determination, §29-26.
Aliens, §29-11.
Ancestral property.
Distinctions between ancestral and nonancestral property.
Abolished, §29-3.
Brothers and sisters.
Distribution among classes, §29-16(b).
Certain distinctions as to intestate succession abolished, §29-3.
Claims against the estate.
Descent and distribution subject to payment, §29-13(a).
Determination of 120-hour survivorship requirement, §29-13(b).
Collateral succession.
Limitation, §29-7.
Computation of next of kin, §§29-5, 104A-1.
Costs of administration.
Descent and distribution subject to payment, §29-13(a).
Curtesy.
Abolished, §29-4.
Definitions, §29-2.
Descent and distribution, §29-13.
Distinctions between real and personal property abolished, §29-3.
Distribution among classes.
Brothers and sisters and their lineal descendants, §29-16(b).
Lineal descendants, §29-16(a).
Uncles and aunts and their lineal descendants, §29-16(c).
Dower abolished, §29-4.
Elective share of surviving spouse, §§30-3.1 to 30-3.6, 31-5.3.
Elective shares, §§29-14, 29-15.
Escheats, §29-12.
Estate.
Defined, §29-2.
Estate proceedings.
Controversies concerning intestate succession.
Determination as estate proceeding, §29-12.1.
Estate taxes.
Descent and distribution subject to payment, §29-13(a).
Determination of 120-hour survivorship requirement, §29-13(b).

INTESTATE SUCCESSION —Cont'd

Excise stamp tax on conveyances.
Exempted transfers, §105-228.29.

Exemptions.
Continuation of exemption of property,
§1C-1604(b).

Gifts.
Advancements.
Gift inter vivos presumed absolute gift, §29-24.

Heirs.
Defined, §29-2.

Homicide.
Killing decedents.
Slayer barred from intestate succession, §31A-4.

Household furnishings.
Payment of debts from estate of deceased,
§29-30(g).

Husband and wife.
Acts barring rights of spouse, §31A-1(b).

Illegitimate children.
Descent and distribution upon intestacy, §29-20.
Legitimated children.
Succession by, through and from, §29-18.
Person's illegitimate child entitled to take by,
through and from, §29-19(b).
Shares of others than surviving spouse, §29-22.
Succession by, through and from, §29-19(a) to (d).
Surviving spouses.
Share of surviving spouse of illegitimate
intestate, §29-21.
Shares of others than surviving spouse, §29-22.

Inheritance taxes.
Descent and distribution subject to payment,
§29-13(a).
Determination of 120-hour survivorship
requirement, §29-13(b).

Inventories.
Advancements.
Failure of donor to give inventory on oath,
§29-28.

Jury.
Election of surviving spouse to take life interest.
Appointment of jury, §29-30(d).
Final report of jury, §29-30(e).

Kinship.
Degrees of kinship.
Computation, §§29-5, 104A-1.

Legitimated children.
Succession by, through and from, §29-18.

Legitimation, effect, §49-11.
Mother married, legitimation when, §49-12.1.
Subsequent marriage, legitimation by, §49-12.

Lineal descendants.
Defined, §29-2.
Determination of share, §29-16(a).
Unlimited, §29-6.

Motor vehicles.
Transfer of title or interest, §20-77(b).

Net estate.
Defined, §29-2.

Next of kin, §41-6.1.
Defined, §41-6.1.

Notice.
Election of surviving, §29-30(c).

Parent and child.
Acts barring rights of parents, §31A-2.

Partial intestacy, §29-8.

**Partition procedure applicable to elective life
estate,** §29-30(f).

Personal property.
Distinctions between real and personal property
abolished, §29-3.

INTESTATE SUCCESSION —Cont'd

Petition for election of life estate, §29-30(c1),
(c2).

Presumptions.
Gift inter vivos presumed gift and not
advancement, §29-24.

Pretermitted children, §29-9.

Real property.
Distinctions between real and personal property
abolished, §29-3.

Relations of the whole blood.
Distinctions between relations of the whole blood
and those of the half blood.
Abolished, §29-3.

Renunciation, §29-10.
Acceptance of property, interest or benefit.
Effect on right of renunciation, §31B-4(e).
Applicability of chapter, §31B-1(b).
Bar, §31B-4(a).
Disposition of property in reliance on invalid
renunciation.
Immunity from liability, §31B-4(d).
Effect of renunciation, §31B-3(a).
Exclusiveness of remedy, §31B-5.
Instruments.
Contents, §31B-1(c).
Copies, §31B-2(c).
Delivery to other persons by person renouncing,
§31B-2.1.
Filing, §31B-2(c).
Effect of failure to file, §31B-2(e).
Indexing, §31B-2(c).
Registration, §31B-2(d), (e).
Effect of failure to register, §31B-2(e).
When filed, §31B-2(a).
Where filed, §31B-2(c).
Parent of minor, §31B-1(d).
Record of renunciation.
Contents, §31B-2(c).
Right to renounce succession, §31B-1(a).
Short title, §31B-7.
Spouse's interest, §31B-2(b).
Tax consequences, §31B-1(b).
Waiver, §31B-4(a).
Binding on certain persons, §31B-4(b).
Disposition of property in reliance on invalid
renunciation.
Immunity from liability, §31B-4(d).

Shares.
Defined, §29-2.

Shares of others than surviving spouse, §29-15.

Short title of act, §29-1.

Simultaneous death, revised act, §§28A-24-1 to
28A-24-8.
See SIMULTANEOUS DEATH.

Small estates, §§28A-25-1 to 28A-25-6.
See SMALL ESTATES.

Surviving spouses.
Determination of 120-hour survivorship
requirement, §29-13(b).
Illegitimate children.
Share of surviving spouse, §29-21.
Shares of others than surviving spouse, §29-22.
Life interest.
Election to take life interest in lieu of intestate
share, §29-30(a) to (h).
Petition for election of life estate, §29-30(c1), (c2).
Share of surviving spouse.
Equitable distributions of property, §29-14(c).
Personal property, §29-14(b).
Real property, §29-14(a).

INTESTATE SUCCESSION —Cont'd
Surviving spouses —Cont'd
Shares of others than surviving spouse, §29-15.
Time.
Election of surviving spouse to take life interest.
Filing of notice, §29-30(c).
Title of act, §29-1.
Unborn infants, §29-9.
Uncles and aunts.
Distribution among classes, §29-16(c).
Unlimited lineal succession, §29-6.
Waiver.
Renunciation, §31B-4.
Surviving spouses.
Election to life interest in lieu of intestate
share, §29-30(h).
Waste.
Heirs.
Action by heirs, §1-537.

INTIMIDATION.
Elections.
Officers of election.
Felony, §163-275.
Voters.
Intimidation by officers, §163-271.
Misdemeanor, §163-274(a).
Ethnic intimidation, §14-401.14(a), (b).
Insurance.
Unfair trade practices.
Prohibited acts, §58-63-15.
Obstructing health care facilities, §14-277.4.
Real estate appraisers.
By real estate appraisal management companies,
§93E-2-7(a).
Secret societies.
Placing exhibit with intention of intimidating,
§14-12.13.
Wearing of disguise, §14-12.14.
Witnesses, §14-226(a).
Electronic surveillance orders, §15A-290(c3).

INTOXICATING LIQUORS.
See ALCOHOLIC BEVERAGES.

INTOXICATION, §§14-443 to 14-447.
Acquittal of defendant because of alcoholism.
Disposition of defendant, §14-446.
Aircraft operation while impaired, §§63-27,
63-28.
Alcohol detoxification programs.
Specialty hospitals, §131E-65.
**Alcoholic beverage sales to intoxicated
persons prohibited,** §18B-305(a).
Alcoholism.
Defined, §14-443.
Barbers.
Disqualifications for certificates or permits,
§86A-18.
Boating safety.
Operation of boat or manipulation of water skis
while intoxicated, §75A-10(b), (b1).
Carriers.
Ejection of intoxicated person, §62-151.
Ticket may be refused intoxicated person, §62-150.
Carrier ticket agent.
Refusing ticket to intoxicated person, §62-150.
**Chemical analysis of impairing substances in
blood generally.**
See IMPAIRED DRIVING.
Chiropractors.
Addiction or severe dependency upon alcohol.
Grounds for disciplinary action, §90-154(b).

INTOXICATION —Cont'd
Chiropractors —Cont'd
Grounds for disciplinary action, §90-154(b).
Criminal procedure.
Notice to state of defenses, §15A-905(c), (d).
Defense of alcoholism, §14-445(a).
Disposition of defendant acquitted because of
alcoholism, §14-446.
Request for additional information, §14-445(b).
Dental hygienists.
Grounds for disciplinary measures, §90-229(a).
Drivers' licenses.
Issuance to habitual drunkard.
Prohibited, §20-9(c).
Revocation of license of habitual users of alcohol
and narcotics, §20-17.1.
Impaired driving generally.
See IMPAIRED DRIVING.
Incompetence, determination of, §§35A-1101 to
35A-1116.
See INCOMPETENCY.
Law enforcement officers.
Assistance to individual intoxicated in public.
Actions permitted to be taken, §122C-301(a).
Immunity for reasonable measures taken,
§122C-301(b).
Reasonable force to restrain individual,
§122C-301(b).
Removal of unfit officers, §128-16.
Nursing home administrators.
Grounds for denial, revocation or suspension of
license, §90-285.1.
Physical therapists.
Grounds for disciplinary action, §90-270.36.
Physicians and surgeons.
Ground for denial, revocation or suspension of
license, §90-14(a).
Public conveyances.
Driver of public conveyance preventing intoxicated
person from entering, §62-150.
Driver of public conveyance putting intoxicated
person off of conveyance, §62-151.
Public intoxication.
Assistance to individual intoxicated in public.
Detention by facility to which officer takes
individual.
Time limits on detention, §122C-301(c).
Employment of officers to assist.
Cities and counties, §122C-302.
Involuntary commitment.
Person assisted to facility substance abuser,
§122C-301(d).
Jails, use for care of, §122C-303.
Law enforcement officers.
Actions permitted to be taken, §122C-301(a).
Immunity for reasonable measures taken,
§122C-301(b).
Reasonable force to restrain individual,
§122C-301(b).
Cities.
Employment of officers to assist individual
intoxicated in public, §122C-302.
Counties.
Employment of officers to assist individual
intoxicated in public, §122C-302.
Definitions.
Alcoholism, §14-443.
Intoxication, §14-443.
Public intoxication, §14-443.
Public place, §14-443.
Entering plea to charge, §14-445(c).

INTOXICATION —Cont'd
Public intoxication —Cont'd
Home of individual intoxicated in public.
Transportation by officer to, §122C-301(a).
Hospital of physician's office.
Transportation by officer to, §122C-301(a).
Detention of individual, time limits,
§122C-301(c).
Involuntary commitment.
Assistance to individual intoxicated in public.
Officer detaining individual, §122C-301(a).
Person assisted to facility substance abuser,
§122C-301(d).
Jails.
Use for care of intoxicated individuals,
§122C-303.
No prosecution for public intoxication, §14-447(a).
Officers to assist individuals intoxicated in public.
Cities and counties, §122C-302.
Penalties.
Ways of being intoxicated and disruptive in
public, §14-444(b).
Prehearing review of drinking history, §14-445(d).
Public place.
Defined, §14-443.
Residence of another willing to accept intoxicated
person.
Transportation by officer to, §122C-301(a).
Shelter facility.
Transportation by officer to, §122C-301(a).
Detention of individual, time limits,
§122C-301(c).
Shelter or health-care facility.
Transport and release of person to appropriate
facility, §14-447(b).
Ways of being intoxicated and disruptive in public,
§14-444(b).
Penalty for violation of provisions, §14-444(b).
Railroads.
Ejection of passenger who becomes intoxicated,
§136-198.
Ticket may be refused intoxicated person,
§136-197.
Specialty hospitals.
Alcohol detoxification programs, §131E-65.
Workers' compensation.
Injury or death caused by intoxication of
employee.
No compensation payable, §97-12.
Use of intoxicant or controlled substance, §97-12.

INTRAGOVERNMENTAL SERVICE FUNDS.
Financial plans.
Generally, §§159-11(d), 159-13.1.

**INTRASTATE SYSTEM AND
TRANSPORTATION IMPROVEMENT
PROGRAM.**
Distribution formula for funds expended,
§136-17.2A.

INVALID AGREEMENTS.
Construction indemnity agreements, §22B-1.
Contract provisions waiving jury trial, §22B-10.
Contracts to improve real property.
Provisions making contract subject to laws of
another state, §22B-2.
Contracts with forum selection provisions,
§22B-3.

INVASION OF PRIVACY.
Confidentiality.
See CONFIDENTIALITY OF INFORMATION.

INVASION OF PRIVACY —Cont'd
Freedom of information, §§132-1 to 132-10.
**Insurance consumer and customer information
privacy.**
Immunity from suit.
Disclosure in accordance with article,
§58-39-110.
Privacy of state employer personnel records,
§§126-22 to 126-29.
Searches and seizures generally.
See SEARCHES AND SEIZURES.

INVASIONS.
Constitution of the United States, US Const Art
I §§8 to 10, Art IV §4.
Unorganized militia.
Ordered out for service, §127A-87.

INVENTION DEVELOPMENT.
Definitions.
Invention development services, §66-209.
Employers and employees.
Inventions developed by employees, §§66-57.1,
66-57.2.
Employment agreements.
Certain agreements void, §66-57.1.
Reporting inventions to employer.
Employer may require, §66-57.2.
Right of employees to certain inventions,
§66-57.1.
Rights of employers, §66-57.2.
Larceny of secret technical processes, §14-75.1.
Patents.
Constitutional provisions, US Const Art I §8.
Services.
Contracts.
Contents, §66-213.
Cover notice, §66-211.
Disclosures made prior to contract, §66-210.
Financial requirements, §66-214.
Requirements for contracting, §66-212.
Standard provisions for cover notice, §66-211.
Voidable contracts, §66-215.
Damages.
Violations of provisions, §66-215.
Definitions, §66-209.
Disclosures made prior to contract, §66-210.
Enforcement of article, §66-216.
Financial requirements, §66-214.
Violations of provisions.
Civil penalties, §66-216.
Damages, §66-215.

INVENTIONS.
Larceny of secret technical processes, §14-75.1.

INVENTORIES.
Absentees in military service.
Final inventory upon termination of receivership,
§28B-8(c).
Receiver to file, §28B-5(b).
Assignments for benefit of creditors.
Trustee of deed of trust to file with clerk of
superior court, §23-2.
Budget of state.
Capital improvement projects.
Inventory of facilities, §143C-8-2.
Cigarettes and tobacco products.
Cigarette tax.
Tax with respect to inventory on effective date
of tax increase, §105-113.4D.
Tobacco products tax.
Recordkeeping requirements, §105-113.40.

INVENTORIES —Cont'd
Closing-out sales.
Required of applicants for licenses, §66-77(a).
Coal and petroleum suppliers.
Reporting petroleum fuel capacity, §§143-345.13, 143-345.14.
Conservation easements, §113A-235(c).
Decedents' estates.
Appraisers, §28A-20-4.
Compelling inventory, §28A-20-2(a).
Failure to file.
Liability for costs, §28A-20-2(b).
Removal of representative, §28A-20-2(a).
Required within three months, §28A-20-1.
Supplemental inventory.
Enforcement, §28A-20-3(b).
Erroneous or misleading inventory, §28A-20-3(a).
Durable power of attorney.
Incapacity or incompetency of principal.
Filing inventory of principal's property with clerk, §32A-11(b).
Guardians.
Accounts and accounting.
Inventory or account required within three months, §35A-1261.
Procedure to compel inventory, §35A-1262.
Supplemental inventory, §35A-1263.1.
Intestate succession.
Advancements, §29-28.
Missing persons.
Filing by temporary receiver, §28C-3.
Permanent receivers, §28C-7.
Power of attorney.
Durable power of attorney.
Incapacity or incompetency of principal.
Filing inventory of principal's property with clerk, §32A-11(b).
Receivers.
Corporate receivers, §1-507.3.
Searches and seizures.
List of items seized pursuant to search warrant, §15A-254.
Trust companies.
Seizure by commissioner.
Inventory of assets and liabilities, §53-385.
Trustees of deeds of trust.
Assignment for benefit of creditors, §23-2.
Trusts and trustees.
Class in esse.
Sale of property held by, §41-11.1(l).

INVENTORY SHORTAGES.
Deductions from employees' wages.
When withholding authorized, §95-25.8(c), (e).

INVERSE CONDEMNATION, §40A-51.

INVESTIGATIONS.
Abandonment.
Welfare recipients, §15-155.2.
Abused, neglected or dependent juveniles.
Criminal investigation upon director finding evidence of abuse, §7B-307.
Physician or medical facility receiving judicial authority to retain custody of abused juvenile.
Notice to director of social services, treatment as report of suspected abuse, §7B-308(b).
Adult care homes.
Death of resident within seven days of use of physical restraint, §131D-34.1(c).
Residents' bill of rights, §131D-26(a1), (b).

INVESTIGATIONS —Cont'd
Agriculture.
Marketing and branding farm products.
Board of agriculture to investigate marketing of farm products, §106-187.
Air pollution control.
Permits, §143-215.108(d).
Alarm systems licensing.
Powers of board, §74D-5(a).
Alcoholic beverages.
Expenses.
Restitution, §18B-505.
Law enforcement agents, §18B-500.
Local ABC officers, §18B-501.
Permits.
Prior to issuance, §18B-902(b).
Restitution.
Expenses, §18B-505.
Arson.
Public officers and employees.
Failure of officers to investigate incendiary fires, §14-69.
Auctions and auctioneers.
Commission, §85B-8(e).
Banks.
Commissioner of banks.
Confidentiality of official records, §53-99.
Insolvent banks.
General or special investigations, §53-100.
Official communications relating to, §53-109.
Insolvent banks.
General or special investigations, §53-100.
Blind persons.
Aid to the blind.
Determining eligibility of applicant, §111-14.
Cemeteries.
Commission.
Powers and duties, §65-53.
Check-cashing businesses.
Licensing, §53-278(b).
Child placing agencies.
Death of resident of facility within seven days of use of physical restraint, §131D-10.6B(c).
Children.
Abandoned or neglected.
Welfare recipients, §15-155.2.
Child support.
District attorneys.
Reports to district attorneys of aid to dependent children and illegitimate births.
Action on, §15-155.2(a).
Commodities, §78D-21.
Continuing care retirement communities, §58-64-50(a).
Powers of commissioner, §58-64-50(b), (c).
Deadly force.
Investigations of use of deadly force by law enforcement officers, §147-90.
Disability income plan.
Medical board, §135-102(d).
Elections.
County boards of elections, §163-33.
State board of elections, §163-22(d).
Electrologists.
Board of electrologist examiners.
Powers, §88A-6.
Elevators.
Accidents, §95-110.9(b).
Employee assistance professionals.
Violations of provisions, §90-510.

INVESTIGATIONS —Cont'd

Engineers and land surveyors.
Duties of board, §89C-10(f).

Ethics.
State ethics commission.
Investigation by commission on own motion, §138A-12(b1).

Extradition.
Fugitives from other states.
Governor may cause investigation to be made, §15A-724.

Fair housing complaints, §§41A-7(e), 41A-8.

Fire investigations and inspection of premises, §§58-79-1 to 58-79-45.
See FIRES AND FIRE PREVENTION.

Flour, corn meal and grain.
Grain dealers.
Authority to investigate, §106-612.

Food, drugs and cosmetics.
Conduct of investigations, §106-141(b).

Geologists, §89E-17(b).
Confidentiality of proceedings, §89E-17(c).

Grand jury.
Powers, §15A-628(a).

Health.
Communicable diseases, §130A-144(a) to (c).

Hogs.
Feeding garbage to swine, §106-405.7(a).

Housing authorities and projects.
Municipal cooperation and aid.
Investigation of projects, §157-45.

Identity theft, §§14-113.21A, 14-113.23.

Illegitimacy.
Child support.
Reports to district attorneys of aid to dependent children and illegitimate births.
Action on, §15-155.2(a).

Insurance commissioners, §58-2-50.
Complaints of violations, §58-2-155.

Insurance premium financing.
Power of commissioner of insurance, §58-35-25.

Insurance unfair trade practices.
Power of commissioner, §58-63-20.

Internal improvements.
Power of investigation of corporations, §124-7.

Judicial standards commission.
Confidentiality, JudStdsComm Rule 6.
Formal investigation.
Investigative panel ordering, JudStdsComm Rule 9.
Initial review upon receipt of complaint or information, JudStdsComm Rule 9.

Labor.
Retaliatory employment discrimination, §95-242(a).

Lead poisoning hazard, §130A-131.9A.

Legislative ethics committee, §120-103.1.

Lobbying.
Complaints of violations of chapter, §120C-601(a).

Local governmental employees' retirement system.
Board of trustees.
Duties of actuary, §128-28(n), (o).

Meat and meat products.
Biological residues in animals.
Discovering violations of article, §106-549.86.

Medicaid and Health Choice provider requirements.
Provider requirements, §108C-11.

Medical board proceedings, §§90-5.3, 90-14(h) to (n), 90-16.

INVESTIGATIONS —Cont'd

Mental health, developmental disability, substance abuse.
Death of client, §122C-31.
Reports of abuse or exploitation.
Investigation required, §122C-66(f).

Milk and milk products.
Records and reports of milk distributors and processors.
Commissioner of agriculture authorized to investigate, §106-264.

Mine safety and health, §74-24.7.
Modification of safety and health standards, §74-24.5.

Monopolies and restraint of trade.
Attorney general, §75-9.
Power to compel examination, §75-10.
False swearing by persons examined.
Perjury, §75-12.
Immunity of person examined from prosecution, §75-11.
Refusal to furnish information, §75-12.
False swearing by persons examined.
Perjury, §75-12.

Mortgage bankers, brokers and servicers.
Commissioner.
Investigation and examination authority, §53-244.115(a).

Motor clubs and associations.
Powers of commissioner of insurance, §58-69-20.

Motor vehicle accidents.
Appropriate law enforcement officers, §20-166.1(e).

Motor vehicle dealers.
Franchise-related form agreements, §20-297.1(f).

Motor vehicles.
Impaired driving.
Presentence investigation of persons convicted, §20-179.1.
Police authority of division, §20-49.

Nonresidential buildings that fail to meet minimum standards, §160A-439(b).

Nurses.
Nurse licensure compact.
Change of residence.
Pending investigations, completion, §90-171.85(b).
Current significance investigative information, §90-171.86.
Practices violating provisions, §90-171.37.

Nursing homes.
Patients' bill of rights, §131E-124(a1), (b).

Occupational safety and health.
Assaulting or killing person engaged in investigation functions.
Criminal liability, §95-139(f).
Director.
Powers, §95-133(b).

Parole.
Investigators and investigations of cases of prisoners, §148-53.

Personnel system.
Political hirings.
Violations, §126-14.4.

Physical therapists.
Board of examiners, §90-270.26.

Post-assessment insurance guaranty association.
Duty to investigate claims, §58-48-35(a).

Preneed funeral contracts and funds.
Violations, §90-210.70.

INVESTIGATIONS —Cont'd
Presentence investigations.
Criminal law and procedure, §15A-1332.
Prisons and prisoners.
Administrative remedy procedure.
Grievance resolution board.
Powers of board, §148-118.9.
Private personnel services.
Overstated earnings expectations from employers, §95-47.3A(b).
Private protective services.
Powers of attorney general, §74C-7.
Powers of board, §74C-5.
Proprietary schools, §115D-89(c).
Real estate brokers and salespersons.
Private real estate schools.
Commission, §93A-33.
Retirement system for teachers and state employees.
Actuary to make investigations, §135-6(m), (n).
Savings and loan associations.
Examination and investigation.
See SAVINGS AND LOAN ASSOCIATIONS.
Interstate branches.
Regulatory and supervisory oversight, §54B-273.
Savings banks.
Interstate branch banks.
Regulatory and supervisory oversight, §54C-207(c).
Securities regulation.
Obstruction of investigation, §78A-58.
Seeds.
Complaints by buyers, §106-277.30(a).
Damages recoverable, §106-277.34(b).
Evidence introduced in action, §106-277.34(a).
Referral of investigation to seed board, §106-277.30(c).
Requesting investigation, §106-277.30(b).
Social services.
County directors of social services, §108A-14(a).
State auditor.
Improper government activities, reports of.
Investigation by auditor, §147-64.6B(b).
State departments and agencies.
Conduct, §143-160.
Governor given authority to direct, §143-159.
Special investigations, §143-158.
Conduct, §143-160.
Stenographic record of proceedings, §143-161.
Subjects, §143-159.
State ethics commission.
Investigation by commission on own motion, §138A-12(b1).
State government ethics act.
Inquiries generally, §138A-12.
Powers generally, §138A-10(a).
State lottery.
Potential contractors, §18C-152.
Structural pest control.
Licensees or identification card holders.
Denial, revocation or suspension of license or identification card, §106-65.28(e).
Superintendents of schools.
Failure to perform duties, §115C-274(b).
Trust companies.
Merger or consolidation.
Articles of merger, §53-360(a).
Investigation of proposed transaction, §53-361(b).

INVESTIGATIONS —Cont'd
Trust companies —Cont'd
Seizure by commissioner.
Claims against company, §53-387.
Urban redevelopment.
Powers of redevelopment commissions, §160A-512.
Utilities commission.
Accidents involving public utilities, §62-41.
Duty to investigate books and papers of utilities, §62-34(a).
Initiation of investigations, §62-13(d).
Powers, §62-37(a).
Report of findings, §62-37(b).
Veterinarians.
Powers of board, §90-185.
Viatical settlements.
Fraudulent acts, §58-58-240.
License applicants, §58-58-210(f).
Weights and measures.
Duties of commissioner, §81A-15.

INVESTIGATIVE DEMAND.
Medicaid.
False claims by providers.
Civil investigative demand, §108A-70.14.

INVESTIGATORIAL ASSISTANTS.
District attorneys' offices, §7A-69.

INVESTING IN BUSINESS PROPERTY TAX CREDIT.
Business and energy tax credits, §§105-129.15 to 105-129.19.

INVESTING IN MACHINERY AND EQUIPMENT TAX CREDIT.
Tax incentives for new and expanding businesses, §105-129.9.

INVESTMENT ADVISERS.
Actions.
Civil liabilities for violations, §78C-38.
Administration of chapter, §78C-26(a).
Advisory activities.
Prohibited activities, §78C-8(a).
Exemptions, §78C-8(f).
Appeals.
Judicial review of orders, §78C-29(a), (b).
Bonds, surety, §78C-17(e).
Burden of proof.
Civil or administrative proceedings, §78C-40.
Child support enforcement.
Forfeiture of licensing privilege, §50-13.12.
Citation of chapter, §78C-1.
Civil liabilities.
Contract violations.
Suit not based on contract, §78C-38(e).
Controlling persons, §78C-38(b).
Generally, §78C-38(a).
Limitation of action, §78C-38(d).
Survival of action, §78C-38(c).
Confidentiality of information, §78C-26(b).
Construction and interpretation.
Severability of provisions, §78C-48.
Statutory policy, §78C-47.
Contempt.
Violation of order of court, §78C-27(c).
Contracts.
Contents, §78C-8(c).
Exemptions, §78C-8(d).
Crimes at common law or by statute.
Punishment for, §78C-39(c).
Criminal penalties, §78C-39(a) to (a4).

INVESTMENT ADVISERS —Cont'd
Criminal prosecution.
Referral of evidence to prosecutors, §78C-39(b).
Custody of security or funds.
Violation of rule or order of administrator, §78C-8(e).
Definitions, §78C-2.
False or misleading filings, §78C-9.
Fees.
Disposition, §78C-26(c).
Felony convictions.
Forfeiture of license, §15A-1331A.
Filing of documents, §78C-31(a), (c1) to (c3).
Financial statements.
Form.
Rule or order prescribing, audit, §78C-30(c).
Hearings.
Public hearing, §78C-30(g).
Immunity.
Rule, form or order.
Good faith act or omission in conformity with, §78C-30(f).
Information furnished to clients, §78C-18(b).
Injunctions.
Violation of chapter, §78C-28(a).
Interpretive opinions by administrator, §78C-31(e).
Investigations, §78C-27(a), (b).
Files and records relating to criminal investigations, §78C-31(c1).
Investment advisor representatives.
Registration.
Required, §78C-16(a1), (b) to (b2).
Misleading filings, §78C-9.
Misrepresentations, §78C-8(b).
Penalties for violations.
Civil penalties, §78C-28(c).
Policy of state, §78C-47.
Prospectus, pamphlet, circular, form letter, advertisement.
Filing.
Rule or order requiring, §78C-30(d).
Records, §78C-18(a).
Amendment, §78C-18(d).
Examination, §78C-18(e).
Financial records.
Amendment, §78C-18(d).
Public records.
Administrator may make available, §78C-31(d).
Registration.
Application, §78C-17(a).
Consent appointing administrator as attorney to receive service of process, §78C-46(b).
Filing, §78C-20(a).
Information may be made available to public, §78C-31(c).
Register of applications, §78C-31(b).
Bar or censure of registrant, §78C-19(a), (b).
Notice, §78C-19(f).
Bonds, surety, §78C-17(e).
Cancellation, §78C-19(d).
Notice, §78C-19(f).
Denial, §78C-19(a), (b).
Notice, §78C-19(f).
Documentation, filing required, §78C-17(a1).
Exercise of authority of administrator not prevented, §78C-20(c).
Expiration, §78C-16(c).
Federal law.
Compliance with state requirements, §78C-16(d).

INVESTMENT ADVISERS —Cont'd
Registration —Cont'd
Fees, §78C-17(b) to (b2).
Fraudulent representations, §78C-10.
Investment advisor representatives.
Required, §78C-16(a1), (b) to (b2).
Minimum net capital requirement, §78C-17(d).
Required, §78C-16(a).
Revocation, §78C-19(a), (b).
Notice, §78C-19(f).
Successor, §78C-17(c).
Felony convictions, §15A-1331A.
Suspension, §78C-19(a), (b).
Notice, §78C-19(f).
Summary postponement or suspension of registration, §78C-19(c).
Unlawful representations, §78C-10.
Withdrawal from registration, §78C-19(e).
Reports.
Financial reports, §78C-18(c).
Rights and remedies in addition to other rights and remedies, §78C-38(g).
Rules forms, orders.
Adoption, amendment, etc, §78C-30(a) to (g).
Scope of provisions, §78C-46(a).
Service of process.
Administrator as attorney to receive service of process, §78C-46(b) to (d).
Severability of provisions, §78C-48.
Short title of chapter, §78C-1.
Subpoenas.
Enforcement, §78C-27(d).
Violation of chapter.
Cease and desist orders, §78C-28(b).
Civil penalties, §78C-28(c).
Criminal penalties, §78C-39(a) to (a4).
Injunction, §78C-28(a).
Referral of evidence to prosecutors, §78C-39(b).
Waiver of compliance with provisions.
Void, §78C-38(f).

INVESTMENT COMPANIES.
Franchise tax on domestic and foreign corporations.
Exempt corporations.
Regulated investment companies, §105-125(b).

INVESTMENTS.
ABC boards, §18B-702(t).
Absentees in military service.
Receivers.
Power to invest property or income, §28B-6.
Agricultural finance authority.
Bond issues.
Legal investments, §122D-17.
Moneys of authority.
Authorized investments, §122D-16(b).
Banks.
See BANKS.
Capital facilities finance act.
Special indebtedness, §142-93.
Cemeteries.
Abandoned and neglected cemeteries.
Money for maintenance and preservation, §65-94.
Corporate trustees, §65-60.1(e).
Community college investment of idle cash, §§115D-58.6 to 115D-58.10.
Credit unions.
Authorized investments, §54-109.82.
Crime victims compensation.
Crime victims compensation fund.
Investments by state treasurer, §15B-23.

INVESTMENTS —Cont'd

Decedents' estates.

Powers of personal representative or fiduciary, §28A-13-3(a).

Disability income plan.

Trust fund.

Assets of fund, §135-110(d).

Drainage districts.

Surplus funds, §156-135.1.

Education.

State board of education.

Authority to invest school funds, §115C-411.

Education assistance authority.

Bond issues.

Eligibility for investment, §116-209.10.

Energy conservation finance act.

Financing contracts and certificates of participation.

Investment eligibility, §142-70.

Facility authorities.

Bonds eligible for investment, §160A-480.13.

Fiduciaries.

Securities approved by secretary of housing and urban development, federal housing administration and veterans administration, §53-45.

Fraternal benefit societies.

Funds, §58-24-100.

Health care facilities.

Finance act.

Bonds or notes eligible for investment, §131A-17.

Refunding bonds or notes, §131A-18.

Health maintenance organizations, §58-67-60.

Hospital, medical and dental service corporations.

Investments and reserves, §58-65-95(a) to (d).

Housing authorities and projects.

Local government finance.

Special provisions pertaining to public housing authorities, §159-42(i).

National defense housing projects.

Obligations made legal investments, §157-57.

Housing finance agency, §122A-11.

Bonds and notes.

Obligations eligible for investment, §122A-14.

Housing trust fund, §122E-3(c).

Husband and wife.

Joint ownership of corporate stock and investment securities, §41-2.2(a).

Death of joint tenant, §41-2.2(c).

Inheritance tax laws unaffected, §41-2.2(d).

When joint tenancy exist, §41-2.2(b).

Income tax.

Tax credits for qualified business investments, §§105-163.010 to 105-163.015.

Inheritance taxes.

Joint ownership of corporate stock and investment securities.

Inheritance tax laws unaffected, §41-2.2(d).

Institutional funds.

Prudent management of institutional funds.

General provisions, §§36E-1 to 36E-11.

See PRUDENT MANAGEMENT OF INSTITUTIONAL FUNDS.

Insurance companies.

See INSURANCE COMPANIES.

Local ABC boards, §18B-702(t).

Local governmental employees' retirement system.

Common and preferred stocks.

Authority to invest in certain stocks, §128-29.1.

INVESTMENTS —Cont'd

Local government finance.

Bond issues.

Bonds or notes eligible for investment, §159-140.

Capital reserve funds, §159-21.

Fiscal control.

Idle funds, §159-30.

Public hospitals, §159-39(g).

Reports.

Semiannual report on status, §159-33.

Missing persons.

Receivers.

Power to invest or reinvest property or income, §28C-8.

Municipalities.

Joint municipal electric power and energy act.

Bonds eligible for investment, §159B-21.

Mutual burial associations.

Funds of association, §90-210.86.

North Carolina enterprise corporations.

Primary investments, §53A-43.

Prohibited investments, §53A-44.

Parking authorities.

Bonds legal investments for public officers and fiduciaries, §160A-560.

Pollution control.

Industrial and pollution control facilities financing act.

Bonds eligible for investment, §159C-18.

Post-war reserve fund, §143-192.

Principal and income act.

General provisions, §§37A-1-101 to 37A-6-602.

See PRINCIPAL AND INCOME ACT.

Private protective services recovery fund, §74C-30(d).

Prudent investor rule.

Trusts and trustees, §§36C-9-901 to 36C-9-907.

Charitable remainder trusts, effect on, §36C-9-906.

Compliance, §§36C-9-901(a), 36C-9-905.

Default rule, §36C-9-901(b).

Definition of terms, §36C-9-901(c).

Diversification, §36C-9-903.

Duties at inception of trusteeship;, §36C-9-904.

Inapplicability of act, §36C-9-901(d).

Kinds of property or types of investments, §36C-9-902(e).

Portfolio strategy, §36C-9-902(b).

Reasonable effect to verify facts, §36C-9-902(d).

Relevant factors, §36C-9-902(c).

Reviewing compliance, §36C-9-905.

Short title, §36C-9-907.

Standard of care, §36C-9-902(a).

Trustee's duty of prudent administration, §36C-8-804.

Prudent management of institutional funds.

General provisions, §§36E-1 to 36E-11.

See PRUDENT MANAGEMENT OF INSTITUTIONAL FUNDS.

Public schools.

Endowment funds, §115C-491.

Idle cash, §115C-443.

Public school building capital fund, §115C-546.1(b).

Reports on status, §115C-446.

State board of education.

Authority to invest school funds, §115C-411.

Qualified business investments tax credits, §§105-163.010 to 105-163.015.

INVESTMENTS —Cont'd
Real estate education and recovery fund,
§93A-16(c).
Retirement system for teachers and state
employees.
Consolidated judicial retirement act.
State treasurer to invest assets of system,
§135-66.
Savings and loan associations, §§54B-180 to
54B-197.
See SAVINGS AND LOAN ASSOCIATIONS.
Savings banks, §§54C-129 to 54C-142.
See SAVINGS BANKS.
Holding companies, §54C-195(d).
State funds.
Administration of state treasurer's programs,
§147-69.3.
General fund, §147-69.1.
State psychiatric hospital financing act.
Special indebtedness, §142-112.
State treasurer.
Administration of state treasurer's investment
programs, §147-69.3.
General fund.
Authorized investments, §147-69.1.
Highway fund.
Authorized investment, §147-69.1.
Highway trust fund.
Authorized investments, §147-69.1.
Special funds held by state treasurer, §147-69.2.
Superior courts.
Clerks of court.
Funds in clerk's hands which may be invested,
§7A-112.
Fees, §7A-308.1.
Tax credits for qualified business investments,
§§105-163.010 to 105-163.015.
Title insurance.
Companies, §§58-7-182, 58-26-15.
Torrens system registration.
Assurance fund, §43-49.
Transfers to minors, §33A-12.
Trust companies.
Bonds.
Purchase for own account, §53-342(e).
Fiduciary capacity, trust institutions acting in.
Depository institution, funds held by.
Terms and conditions for investment,
§53-163.1(b).
Fees for temporary investment, §53-163.1(d).
Permissible investments, §53-163.1(c).
Securities, investment in, §53-163.2.
Time frame in which investment required,
§53-163.1(a).
Securities, §53-342.
State trust company facilities, §53-340(a).
Types not specified, §53-342(f).
Trusts and trustees.
Authority to acquire all investments, §32-71(b).
Conflict between trustee's fiduciary and personal
interest, §36C-8-802(f).
Exclusion of fiduciary from direction on
investment.
Immunity from liability, §32-72(d).
Prudent investor rule, §§36C-9-901 to 36C-9-907.
Charitable remainder trusts, effect on,
§36C-9-906.
Compliance, §§36C-9-901(a), 36C-9-905.
Default rule, §36C-9-901(b).
Definition of terms, §36C-9-901(c).
Diversification, §36C-9-903.

INVESTMENTS —Cont'd
Trusts and trustees —Cont'd
Prudent investor rule —Cont'd
Duties at inception of trusteeship;, §36C-9-904.
Inapplicability of act, §36C-9-901(d).
Kinds of property or types of investments,
§36C-9-902(e).
Portfolio strategy, §36C-9-902(b).
Reasonable effect to verify facts, §36C-9-902(d).
Relevant factors, §36C-9-902(c).
Reviewing compliance, §36C-9-905.
Short title, §36C-9-907.
Standard of care, §36C-9-902(a).
Trustee's duty of prudent administration,
§36C-8-804.
United States government obligations, §32-72(c).
Whole property of two or more trusts.
Records maintained clearly indicating respective
interests, §36C-8-810(d).
University of North Carolina.
Distinguished professors endowment trust fund,
§116-41.14.
Trust funds, §116-36.1(h).
Urban redevelopment.
Powers of redevelopment commissions, §160A-512.
Workers' compensation.
Self-insurance.
Employer groups, §58-47-80.
INVESTMENT SECURITIES, §§25-8-101 to
25-8-511.
Acquisition of security, asset or interest
therein, §25-8-104.
Generally, §25-8-104(a).
Satisfying requirement of transfer or delivery,
§25-8-104(d).
Security entitlement, §25-8-104(b), (c).
Applicability of provisions, §25-8-110.
Assurance that indorsement or instruction is
effective.
Additional assurance, §25-8-402(b).
Allowed required assurance, §25-8-402(a).
Appropriate evidence of appointment or
incumbency, defined, §25-8-402(c).
Guarantee of the signature, defined, §25-8-402(c).
Authenticating trustee, transfer agent and
registrar, §25-8-407.
Bona fide purchasers.
Enforcement of completed or altered instrument,
§25-8-206.
Characterization of person, business or
transaction, §25-8-102(d).
Choice of law, §25-8-110.
Citation of chapter, §25-8-101.
Clearing corporation rules, §25-8-111.
Completion of instrument.
Contains all necessary signatures, §25-8-206(a).
Enforceable only to its original terms,
§25-8-206(b).
Control, §25-8-106.
Bearer form certificated securities, §25-8-106(a).
Registered form certificated securities,
§25-8-106(b).
Required, §25-8-106(g).
Security entitlements, §25-8-106(d), (e).
Substitutions or changes, §25-8-106(f).
Uncertificated securities, §25-8-106(c).
Creditor's legal process, §25-8-112.
Certificated securities, §25-8-112(a).
Creditor whose debtor is owner of, §25-8-112(e).
In possession of another, §25-8-112(d).

INVESTMENT SECURITIES —Cont'd
Creditor's legal process —Cont'd
Security entitlements, §25-8-112(c).
Uncertificated securities, §25-8-112(b).
Defenses.
Issue and issuer, §§25-8-202, 25-8-203.
Additional issuer's defenses, §25-8-202(d).
Entitlement holders, §25-8-202(f).
Issuer asserts security is not valid, §25-8-202(b).
Lack of genuineness of certificated security, §25-8-202(c).
Material change, §25-8-202(e).
Purchaser for value without notice, §25-8-202(a).
Definitions, §25-8-102(a).
Investment company security, §25-8-103.
Issuer's jurisdiction, §25-8-110.
Other applicable definitions, §25-8-102(b), (c).
Demand that issuer not register transfer.
Liability, §25-8-403(d), (e).
Notice, §25-8-403(a).
Withholding registration of transfer, §25-8-403(b).
Time period for withholding, §25-8-403(c).
Determination of security or financial asset, §25-8-103.
Application of provisions, §25-8-103(d).
Clearinghouse corporations, §25-8-103(e).
Commodity contract, §25-8-103(f).
Financial asset, when, §25-8-103(g).
Investment company security, defined, §25-8-103(b).
Issued by corporation or similar entity, §25-8-103(a).
Partnership or limited liability company, §25-8-103(c).
Duty of issuer to register transfer.
Generally, §25-8-401(a).
Liability, §25-8-401(b).
Evidentiary rules concerning certificated securities, §25-8-114.
Husband and wife.
Joint ownership, §41-2.2.
Indorsement, §25-8-304.
Effectiveness of endorsement, instruction or entitlement.
Appropriate person, defined, §25-8-107(a).
Change of capacity, §25-8-107(d).
Change of circumstances, §25-8-107(e).
Conditions for effectiveness, §25-8-107(b).
Additional conditions, §25-8-107(c).
Intermediary as purchaser for value, §25-8-116.
Issuer, §25-8-201.
Assurance that indorsement or instruction is effective, §25-8-402.
Demand that issuer not register transfer, §25-8-403.
Duty of issuer to register transfer, §25-8-401.
Effect of unauthorized signature, §25-8-205.
Generally, §25-8-201(a).
Guarantors, §25-8-201(b).
Jurisdiction, §25-8-110(a).
Defined, §25-8-110(d).
Lien, §25-8-209.
Liability to adverse claimant, §25-8-115.
Registered owners.
Rights of issuer with respect to registered owners, §25-8-207(a).
Interpretation of provisions, §25-8-207(b).
Signature.
Effect of signature authenticating trustee, registrar or transfer agent, §25-8-208.

INVESTMENT SECURITIES —Cont'd
Issuer —Cont'd
Transfer, §25-8-201(c).
Effect of issuer's restrictions on transfer, §25-8-204.
Effect of signature authenticating trustee, registrar or transfer agent, §25-8-208.
Warranties.
Effect of signature authenticating trustee, registrar or transfer agent, §25-8-208.
Joint ownership, §41-2.2.
Lost, destroyed or wrongfully taken security certificates, §25-8-405.
Issuance of new certificate, §25-8-405(a).
Obligation to notify issuer, §25-8-406.
Registration, §25-8-405(b).
Notice of adverse claim, §25-8-105.
Events which do constitute notice, §25-8-105(d).
Events which do not constitute notice, §25-8-105(c).
Filing of a financial statement, §25-8-105(e).
Generally, §25-8-105(a).
Transfer of financial asset or interest therein, §25-8-105(b).
Overissue, §25-8-210.
Application of provisions, §25-8-210(b).
Compelling purchase, §25-8-210(c).
Generally, §25-8-210(a).
Recovery of price, §25-8-210(d).
Registration.
Demand that issuer not register transfer, §25-8-403.
Duty of issuer to register transfer, §25-8-401.
Effect of signature authenticating trustee, registrar or transfer agent, §25-8-208.
Indorsement or instruction effective, §25-8-402.
Wrongful registration, §25-8-404.
Secured transactions.
Priority of security interests, §25-9-331.
Provisions concerning investment property.
See SECURED TRANSACTIONS.
Securities intermediary's jurisdiction, §25-8-110(b), (e), (f).
Security entitlements.
Assertion of adverse claim against entitlement holder, §25-8-502.
Priority among security interests and entitlement holders.
Asset held by securities intermediary, §25-8-511(b).
Clearing corporations, §25-8-511(c).
Generally, §25-8-511(a).
Rights of purchaser from entitlement holder, §25-8-510.
Assertion of adverse claims, §25-8-510(b).
Cases not covered by priority rules, §25-8-510(c).
Notice of adverse claims, §25-8-510(a).
Priority of securities intermediary as purchaser over conflicting purchaser, §25-8-510(d).
Securities account, defined, §25-8-501.
Securities intermediary.
Acquisition of security entitlement from.
Generally, §25-8-501(b).
Holding of financial asset, §25-8-501(c), (d).
Issuance of security, §25-8-501(e).
Securities account, defined, §25-8-501(a).
Duty to change holder's position to other form of holding, §25-8-508.
Duty to comply with entitlement order.
Generally, §25-8-507(a).

INVESTMENT SECURITIES —Cont'd
Security entitlements —Cont'd
Securities intermediary —Cont'd
Duty to comply with entitlement order —Cont'd
Transfer pursuant to ineffective order,
§25-8-507(b).
Duty to exercise rights as directed by
entitlement holder, §25-8-506.
Duty to maintain financial asset.
Clearing corporations, §25-8-504(d).
Generally, §25-8-504(a).
Granting of security interests in, §25-8-504(b).
Satisfying duty, §25-8-504(c).
Duty with respect to payments and
distributions.
Generally, §25-8-505(a).
Obligation to entitlement holder, §25-8-505(b).
Property interest of entitlement holder in
financial asset held by.
Actions, §25-8-503(e).
Creditors' claims, §25-8-503(a).
Enforcement, §25-8-503(c), (d).
Pro rata interest, §25-8-503(b).
Specification of duties by other statute or
regulation, §25-8-509.
Short title of chapter, §25-8-101.
Signatures.
Effect of signature authenticating trustee,
registrar or transfer agent, §25-8-208.
Effect of unauthorized signature, §25-8-205.
Statute of frauds, §25-8-113.
Transfer.
Delivery, §25-8-301.
Certificated security, §25-8-301(a).
Uncertificated security, §25-8-301(b).
Effect of guaranteeing signature, indorsement or
instruction, §25-8-306.
Effect of signature authenticating trustee,
registrar or transfer agent, §25-8-208.
Indorsement, §25-8-304.
Assumption of obligations, §25-8-304(f).
Bearer form, §25-8-304(e).
Blank or special, §25-8-304(a).
Effect of guaranteeing, §25-8-306.
Interpretation of provisions, §25-8-304(c).
Missing necessary indorsement, §25-8-304(d).
Separately transferable units, §25-8-304(b).
Instruction, §25-8-305.
Effect of guaranteeing, §25-8-306.
Generally, §25-8-305(a).
Obligations assumed, §25-8-305(b).
Protected purchaser, §25-8-303.
Defined, §25-8-303(a).
Free of adverse claims, §25-8-303(b).
Rights of purchaser, §25-8-302.
Extent of rights acquired, §25-8-302(b).
Generally, §25-8-302(a).
Registration of transfer, §25-8-307.
Taking from protected purchaser, §25-8-302(c).
Signature.
Effect of guaranteeing, §25-8-306.
Warranties.
Additional assumptions of liability, §25-8-208(b).
Direct holding, §25-8-108.
Agents, §25-8-108(g).
Brokers, §25-8-108(i).
Certificated securities, §25-8-108(f).
Generally, §25-8-108(a).
Indorsements.
Security certificates, §25-8-108(d).

INVESTMENT SECURITIES —Cont'd
Warranties —Cont'd
Direct holding —Cont'd
Person who originates registration of transfer,
§25-8-108(b).
Redelivery, §25-8-108(h).
Uncertificated securities, §25-8-108(c), (e).
Effect of signature authenticating trustee,
registrar or transfer agent, §25-8-208.
Indirect holding, §25-8-109.
Delivering security certificate, §25-8-109(b).
Entitlement holders, §25-8-109(c).
Generally, §25-8-109(a).
Uncertificated security credited to securities
account, §25-8-109(b).
Person signing security as authenticator,
§25-8-208(a).
Where security certificate located, §25-8-110(c).
Wrongful registration.
Liability, §25-8-404(a).
Effective indorsement or instruction,
§25-8-404(c).
Restitution, §25-8-404(b).

**INVESTOR PROTECTION AND EDUCATION
TRUST FUND,** §147-54.5(a) to (f).

INVISIBLE FENCES.
Electronic dog collars.
Unlawful removal, §14-401.17.

INVOICES.
**Alcoholic beverages transported by motor
carriers,** §18B-1115(d).
Eggs, §106-245.19.
Motor vehicle repairs.
Contents, §20-354.6.
Providing upon completed repair, §20-354.6.
Paternity, civil action to establish.
Admissibility of invoices for services rendered,
§49-14(g).
Simulation.
Prohibited, §75-35.

INVOLUNTARY COMMITMENT.
**Mental health, developmental disabilities and
substance abuse.**
See MENTAL HEALTH, DEVELOPMENTAL
DISABILITY, SUBSTANCE ABUSE.

INVOLUNTARY DISMISSAL OF ACTION, §1A-1
Rule 41(b).

INVOLUNTARY MANSLAUGHTER.
Death by vehicle.
Double jeopardy.
Subsequent prosecution prohibited, §20-141.4(c).
Mandatory revocation of driver's license.
Permanent revocation, §20-19(i).
Indictments.
Essentials of bill, §15-144.
Motor vehicles.
Death by vehicle, §20-141.4.
Revocation or suspension of license, §20-17(a).
Permanent revocation, §20-19(i).
Punishment, §14-18.
Unborn child, §14-23.4.
Unborn child, §14-23.4(a).
Class F felony, §14-23.4(b).

INVOLUNTARY SERVITUDE.
Constitution of North Carolina.
Prohibited, NC Const Art I §17.
Constitution of the United States, US Const
Amds 13, 15.

INVOLUNTARY SERVITUDE —Cont'd
Defined, §14-43.10(a).
Elements of offense, §14-43.12(a).
Felony, §14-43.12(b).
Kidnapping and abduction, §14-39.
Labor contracts.
Reporting violations arising from, §14-43.12(e).
Marriage.
Validation of marriage between slaves, §51-5.
Parent and child relationship not affected, §14-43.12(d).
Separate offense.
Each violation to constitute, §14-43.12(c).

IOLTA, ProfCond Rule 1.15-4.
Rules governing administration of plan, Bar Rules D.1301 to D.1316.

IONIZING RADIATION.
Radiation protection act generally, §§104E-1 to 104E-29.
See RADIATION PROTECTION.

IRA'S.
Exemption from creditors' claims, §1C-1601(a).
Renunciation.
Right to renounce by beneficiary, §31B-1(a).

IREDELL COUNTY.
Acquisition of property, power, §153A-158.1(a).
Ambulances.
Attachment or garnishment and lien for, §§44-51.4 to 44-51.8.
Obtaining ambulance services without intending to pay, §14-111.2.
Blank or master forms of mortgages, deeds of trusts, etc.
Indexing and recording, inapplicability of provisions, §47-21.
Condemnation or acquisition of land by local government unit outside county.
Consent of board of commissioners necessary, §153A-15.
Counties generally.
See COUNTIES.
Game laws, local acts not repealed, §113-133.1(e).
Oil, gas or mineral claims.
Certain ancient claims extinguished, preservation, procedure, §1-42.2(a) to (d).
Probates and registration orders before clerks of inferior courts validated, §47-59.
Registration of deeds.
Tax certification, no delinquent taxes due, §161-31(b).
School property.
Acquisition and improvement, §153A-158.1.
Special school tax, election to abolish.
Petition required, §115C-505.
Tax sales, notices by publication validated.
Inapplicability of provisions, §47-108.24.

IRREVOCABLE TRUSTS.
See TRUSTS AND TRUSTEES.

IRRIGATION.
Condominiums.
Irrigation of landscaping, §47C-3-122.
Cooperative associations.
Authorized purposes, §§54-111, 54-124.
Drainage, §§156-1 to 156-141.
See DRAINAGE.
Planned community act.
Irrigation of landscaping, §47F-3-122.

IRRIGATION CONTRACTORS, §§89G-1 to 89G-13.
Advertising or other use of designation, §89G-2.
Board.
Duties, §89G-5.
Legal representation, §89G-4(g).
Members, §89G-4(a).
Officers, §89G-4(e).
Powers, §89G-5.
Qualifications, §89G-4(b).
Quorum for meetings, §89G-4(e).
Reimbursement and per diem, §89G-4(f).
Removal of members, §89G-4(d).
Vacancies in office, §89G-4(c).
Civil penalties.
Adoption of schedule, §89G-12(c).
Amount and remittance of proceeds, §89G-12(a).
Considerations in fixing amount, §89G-12(b).
Complaints against licensees, §89G-13(b).
Continuing education requirements, §89G-9(b).
Definitions, §89G-1.
Disciplinary action against licensee, §89G-11.
Exemptions from provisions, §89G-3.
Fees, §89G-10(a).
Review of fees, §89G-10(c).
Injunction of violations, §89G-13(a).
Licenses.
Application, §89G-6(a).
Bond, §89G-6(a).
Continuing education requirements, §89G-9(b).
Disciplinary action, §89G-11.
Display, §89G-7(b).
Examination, §89G-6(b).
Cost of examination services, §89G-10(b).
Expiration, §89G-9(a).
Fees, §89G-10(a).
Review of fees, §89G-10(c).
Issuance, §89G-6(c).
Licensing board, §89G-4.
Qualifications, §89G-6(a).
Reciprocal issuance, §89G-8.
Renewal, §89G-9(a).
Required, §89G-2.
Seal of licensee, §89G-7(a).
Notice of complaints against licensees, §89G-13(b).
Seal of licensee, §89G-7(a).
Violations.
Civil penalties, §89G-12.
Complaints against licensees, §89G-13(b).
Disciplinary action against licensee, §89G-11.
Injunction, §89G-13(a).

IRS.
Agents authorized to enforce criminal laws, §15A-406.

ISLANDS.
Public lands.
Title to lands formed by acts of nature, §146-6(d).

ISRAEL.
University of North Carolina.
North Carolina-Israel visiting scholar program, §116-230.

ITINERANT MERCHANTS.
Generally, §§66-250 to 66-258.
See PEDDLERS, ITINERANT MERCHANTS AND SPECIALTY MARKETS.
Regulation of itinerant merchants, §153A-125.
Municipalities, §160A-178.